For
reference

Not to be taken
from the room.

W9-BNZ-366

WITHDRAWN

The Who, What, and Where of America: Understanding the Census Results

The Who, What, and Where of America: Understanding the Census Results

Editors
Martha Farnsworth Riche
Deirdre A. Gaquin

BERNAN PRESS
Lanham, MD

©2003 Bernan Press, an imprint of Bernan Associates, a division of
The Kraus Organization Limited.

No part of this publication may be reproduced, stored in a retrieval system, or transmitted, in any form or by any means, electronic, mechanical, photocopying, recording, or otherwise, without the prior written permission of the copyright holder. Bernan does not claim copyright in U.S. government information.

ISBN: 0-89059-763-4

Cover photos: Comstock.com

Composed and printed by Automated Graphic Systems, Inc., White Plains, MD, on acid-free paper that meets the American National Standards Institute Z39-48 standard.

2004 2003   4 3 2 1

BERNAN PRESS

4611-F Assembly Drive

Lanham, MD 20706

800-274-4447

email: info@bernan.com

www.bernan.com

ACC Library Services
Austin, Texas

This title is part of the *County and City Extra* series.
The ISSN for this series is 1059-9096.

Contents

Contents

ABOUT THE EDITORS

Martha Farnsworth Riche, Ph.D., served as Director of the U.S. Census Bureau between 1994 and 1998. She is currently a consultant on demographic changes and their effects on policies, programs, and products. Dr. Riche began her career as an economist with the U.S. Bureau of Labor Statistics, and then moved to the private sector where she was a founding editor of *American Demographics*, the nation's first magazine devoted to interpreting demographic and economic information for policy-makers. In 1991, Dr. Riche became Director of Policy Studies for the Population Reference Bureau, a nonprofit organization devoted to educating the public about the demographic component of policy issues. A fellow of the American Statistical Association, she is the author of numerous articles, papers, and publications in academic and business journals, and a frequent speaker before university, business, and policy audiences.

Deirdre A. Gaquin has been a data use consultant to private organizations, government agencies, and universities for over 20 years. Prior to that, she was Director of Data Access Services at Data Use & Access Laboratories, a pioneer in private sector distribution of federal statistical data. A former President of the Association of Public Data Users, Ms. Gaquin has served on numerous boards, panels, and task forces concerned with federal statistical data and has worked on four decennial censuses. She holds a Master of Urban Planning (MUP) degree from Hunter College. Ms. Gaquin is also an editor of Bernan Press' *County and City Extra: Annual Metro, City, and County Data Book*; *Places, Towns and Townships*; and *Education Statistics of the United States*.

Katherine A. DeBrandt is a senior data analyst with Bernan Press. She received her B.A. in political science from Colgate University. She is also a co-editor of *County and City Extra: Annual Metro, City, and County Data Book*; *State Profiles, The Population and Economy of Each U.S. State*; and *A Statistical Portrait of the United States: Social Conditions & Trends,* all published by Bernan Press.

Mary Meghan Ryan, a data analyst with Bernan Press, is a former economist with the American Economics Group. Additionally, she has worked as a research assistant for FRANDATA. Ms. Ryan received her bachelor's degree in economics from the University of Maryland. Ms. Ryan also co-edits Bernan Press' *Business Statistics of the United States* and the *Handbook of U.S. Labor Statistics*.

ACKNOWLEDGMENTS

The Who, What, and Where of America: Understanding the Census Results is part of Bernan Press' *County and City Extra* series. The editors of *The Who, What, and Where of America* extend their appreciation to Courtenay Slater and the late George Hall, the originators of *County and City Extra*. Their initial contributions continue to enrich the *County and City Extra* series.

We are extremely grateful to Kara Gottschlich, Bernan Press' production team leader, for managing the production aspects of this volume as well as for preparing the graphics and cover design. Production coordinator Christopher Jorgenson capably assisted Kara in coordinating this project. We also appreciate the assistance of staff editor Jacalyn Houston, who copy edited this volume. With support from Director of Publishing Tamera Wells-Lee; Automated Graphics Systems; and International Mapping Associates, Kara, Chris, and Jacalyn assisted the editors tremendously with finalizing this special edition.

As always, we are especially grateful to the many federal agency personnel who assisted us in obtaining the data, provided excellent resources on their Web sites, and patiently answered our questions.

INTRODUCTION

The Who, What, and Where of America: Understanding the Census Results is a special edition that complements Bernan's *County and City Extra*, an annual publication providing the most up-to-date statistical information for every state, county, and metropolitan area and for all cities in the United States with a population of 25,000 or more.

Every 10 years, the United States conducts its Census of Population and Housing, resulting in a wealth of information about every geographic entity in the United States. *The Who, What, and Where of America: Understanding the Census Results* includes detailed information gathered from the census long form filled out by a sample of the population—as well as basic information from the short form that most housing units received. Data are included for every state, county, and metropolitan area, and for every city with a population of 25,000 or more.

Subjects Covered and Volume Organization

Immediately following this introduction is a layout of the column headings to be found in the main data tables, followed by rankings of states, counties, cities, and metropolitan areas on a number of key demographic and housing characteristics. An introductory article then lays out the basic findings of the census.

The main body of the volume includes three sections. Part A presents detailed information about age, race, Hispanic origin, household structures, ancestry, and languages spoken at home. Part B provides information about education, labor force status, work and family patterns, income, and poverty. Part C addresses migration patterns, housing, and transportation to work.

Each section begins with a discussion that focuses your attention on trends and issues that affect communities nationwide. The goal is to help you understand your own community and see how it relates to other communities and to the nation as a whole. The text is accompanied by tables that illustrate where these trends are particularly advanced, or not important at all. A color map portfolio enhances this focus, enabling readers to identify the county-by-county nature of key information. Each section also includes detailed tables for all states, counties, and metropolitan areas, and cities with populations of 25,000 or more.

The Appendices include definitions of geographic concepts (Appendix A); a listing of source tables from the Census Bureau and definitions of the data items (Appendix F); listings of metropolitan areas with their component counties delineated as of June 30, 1999 listed alphabetically (Appendix B) and within each state (Appendix C); a list of cities by county (Appendix E); and maps showing counties, metropolitan areas, and selected places within each state (Appendix D).

Symbols and Terms

The following symbols are used in this volume:

...   Indicates that data are not available

X   Indicates that data are not applicable or meaningful

Figures that are less than half of the unit of measure shown appear in this volume as zero.

Sources

All data in this volume have been compiled from the Census Bureau's files of decennial census data. All data are subject to errors arising from factors such as reporting errors, incomplete coverage, nonresponse, imputations, sampling error, and processing error.

Responsibility of the editors and publisher of this volume is limited to reasonable care in the reproduction and presentation of data obtained from sources believed to be reliable.

COLUMN HEADINGS FOR PART A

Table A-2. States — **Age, Ethnicity, and Household Structure**

FIPS CODE	STATE	Total population												
				Children under 18 years (percent)				Adults 18 years and over (percent)						
		Number	Median age	Under 18 years	Under 5 years	5 to 14 years	15 to 17 years	18 years and over	18 to 24 years	25 to 44 years	45 to 64 years	65 to 84 years	85 years and over	+/− U.S. percent under 18 years	+/− U.S. percent 65 years and over
		1	2	3	4	5	6	7	8	9	10	11	12	13	14

Table A-2. States — **Age, Ethnicity, and Household Structure**

STATE	Male population													
			Male children under 18 years (percent)				Male adults 18 years and over (percent)							
	Number	Male median age	Under 18 years	Under 5 years	5 to 14 years	15 to 17 years	18 years and over	18 to 24 years	25 to 44 years	45 to 64 years	65 to 84 years	85 years and over	+/− U.S. percent under 18 years	+/− U.S. percent 65 years and over
	15	16	17	18	19	20	21	22	23	24	25	26	27	28

Table A-2. States — **Age, Ethnicity, and Household Structure**

STATE	Female population													
			Female children under 18 years (percent)				Female adults 18 years and over (percent)							
	Number	Female median age	Under 18 years	Under 5 years	5 to 14 years	15 to 17 years	18 years and over	18 to 24 years	25 to 44 years	45 to 64 years	65 to 84 years	85 years and over	+/− U.S. percent under 18 years	+/− U.S. percent 65 years and over
	29	30	31	32	33	34	35	36	37	38	39	40	41	42

Table A-2. States — **Age, Ethnicity, and Household Structure**

STATE	Non-Hispanic White population													
			Non-Hispanic White children under 18 years (percent)				Non-Hispanic White adults 18 years and over (percent)							
	Number	Non-Hispanic White median age	Under 18 years	Under 5 years	5 to 14 years	15 to 17 years	18 years and over	18 to 24 years	25 to 44 years	45 to 64 years	65 to 84 years	85 years and over	+/− U.S. percent under 18 years	+/− U.S. percent 65 years and over
	43	44	45	46	47	48	49	50	51	52	53	54	55	56

Table A-2. States — **Age, Ethnicity, and Household Structure**

STATE		Black or African American population												
			Black or African American children under 18 years (percent)				Black or African American adults 18 years and over (percent)							
	Number	Black or African American median age	Under 18 years	Under 5 years	5 to 14 years	15 to 17 years	18 years and over	18 to 24 years	25 to 44 years	45 to 64 years	65 to 84 years	85 years and over	+/− U.S. percent under 18 years	+/− U.S. percent 65 years and over
	57	58	59	60	61	62	63	64	65	66	67	68	69	70

Table A-2. States — **Age, Ethnicity, and Household Structure**

STATE		American Indian and Alaska Native population												
			American Indian and Alaska Native children under 18 years (percent)				American Indian and Alaska Native adults 18 years and over (percent)							
	Number	American Indian and Alaska Native median age	Under 18 years	Under 5 years	5 to 14 years	15 to 17 years	18 years and over	18 to 24 years	25 to 44 years	45 to 64 years	65 to 84 years	85 years and over	+/− U.S. percent under 18 years	+/− U.S. percent 65 years and over
	71	72	73	74	75	76	77	78	79	80	81	82	83	84

Table A-2. States — **Age, Ethnicity, and Household Structure**

STATE			Asian, Hawaiian, and Pacific Islander population												
				Asian, Hawaiian, and Pacific Islander children under 18 years (percent)				Asian, Hawaiian, and Pacific Islander adults 18 years and over (percent)							
	Number	Asian median age	Native Hawaiian and Other Pacific Islander median age	Under 18 years	Under 5 years	5 to 14 years	15 to 17 years	18 years and over	18 to 24 years	25 to 44 years	45 to 64 years	65 to 84 years	85 years and over	+/− U.S. percent under 18 years	+/− U.S. percent 65 years and over
	85	86	87	88	89	90	91	92	93	94	95	96	97	98	99

Table A-2. States — **Age, Ethnicity, and Household Structure**

STATE		Hispanic or Latino[1] population												
			Hispanic or Latino children under 18 years (percent)				Hispanic or Latino adults 18 years and over (percent)							
	Number	Hispanic or Latino median age	Under 18 years	Under 5 years	5 to 14 years	15 to 17 years	18 years and over	18 to 24 years	25 to 44 years	45 to 64 years	65 to 84 years	85 years and over	+/− U.S. percent under 18 years	+/− U.S. percent 65 years and over
	100	101	102	103	104	105	106	107	108	109	110	111	112	113

[1] Hispanic or Latino persons may be of any race.

COLUMN HEADINGS FOR PART A

Table A-2. States — **Age, Ethnicity, and Household Structure**

STATE		Some other race population												
			Some other race children under 18 years (percent)				Some other race adults 18 years and over (percent)							
	Number	Some other race median age	Under 18 years	Under 5 years	5 to 14 years	15 to 17 years	18 years and over	18 to 24 years	25 to 44 years	45 to 64 years	65 to 84 years	85 years and over	+/− U.S. percent under 18 years	+/− U.S. percent 65 years and over
	114	115	116	117	118	119	120	121	122	123	124	125	126	127

Table A-2. States — **Age, Ethnicity, and Household Structure**

STATE		Two or more races population												
			Two or more races children under 18 years (percent)				Two or more races adults 18 years and over (percent)							
	Number	Two or more races median age	Under 18 years	Under 5 years	5 to 14 years	15 to 17 years	18 years and over	18 to 24 years	25 to 44 years	45 to 64 years	65 to 84 years	85 years and over	+/− U.S. percent under 18 years	+/− U.S. percent 65 years and over
	128	129	130	131	132	133	134	135	136	137	138	139	140	141

Table A-2. States — **Age, Ethnicity, and Household Structure**

STATE		Households											
			Family households (percent)								Nonfamily households (percent)		
				Married-couple family households		Female family householder		Male family householder					
	Number	Average household size	Total family households	Total	With own children under 18 years	Total	With own children under 18 years	Total	With own children under 18 years	Total nonfamily households	Two or more adults	Female living alone	Male living alone
	142	143	144	145	146	147	148	149	150	151	152	153	154

Table A-2. States — **Age, Ethnicity, and Household Structure**

STATE	Households										Population 30 years and over by care of grandchildren		
	Cohabiting couples (percent)												
	Total cohabiting couples	Two males	Two females	One male/ one female	+/− U.S. percent family households	+/− U.S. percent married- couple family households	+/− U.S. percent female headed family households	+/− U.S. percent cohabiting couples	+/− U.S. percent same-sex couples	+/− U.S. percent one-person households	Total population 30 years and over	Percent living with grand- children	Percent responsible for care of grand- children
	155	156	157	158	159	160	161	162	163	164	165	166	167

COLUMN HEADINGS FOR PART A

Table A-2. States — **Age, Ethnicity, and Household Structure**

| STATE | Households | | | | | | | | | | | |
| | | Householder under 65 years (percent) | | | | Householder 65 years and over (percent) | | | | | | |
	Householder all ages	Under 65 years	15 to 24 years	25 to 44 years	45 to 64 years	65 years and over	65 to 84 years	85 years and over	+/− U.S. percent householder 15 to 24 years	+/− U.S. percent householder 25 to 44 years	+/− U.S. percent householder 65 years and over
	168	169	170	171	172	173	174	175	176	177	178

Table A-2. States — **Age, Ethnicity, and Household Structure**

| STATE | Family households | | | | | | | | | | | |
| | | Householder under 65 years (percent) | | | | Householder 65 years and over (percent) | | | | | | |
	Householder all ages	Under 65 years	15 to 24 years	25 to 44 years	45 to 64 years	65 years and over	65 to 84 years	85 years and over	+/− U.S. percent householder 15 to 24 years	+/− U.S. percent householder 25 to 44 years	+/− U.S. percent householder 65 years and over
	179	180	181	182	183	184	185	186	187	188	189

Table A-2. States — **Age, Ethnicity, and Household Structure**

| STATE | Married-couple family households | | | | | | | | | |
| | | Householder under 65 years (percent) | | | | | | | | |
	Householder all ages	Under 65 years	15 to 24 years	25 to 44 years	45 to 64 years	65 years and over (percent)	+/− U.S. percent householder 15 to 24 years	+/− U.S. percent householder 25 to 44 years	+/− U.S. percent householder 65 years and over
	190	191	192	193	194	195	196	197	198

Table A-2. States — **Age, Ethnicity, and Household Structure**

| STATE | Family households, male householder, no wife present | | | | | | | | | |
| | | Householder under 65 years (percent) | | | | | | | | |
	Householder all ages	Under 65 years	15 to 24 years	25 to 44 years	45 to 64 years	65 years and over (percent)	+/− U.S. percent householder 15 to 24 years	+/− U.S. percent householder 25 to 44 years	+/− U.S. percent householder 65 years and over
	199	200	201	202	203	204	205	206	207

COLUMN HEADINGS FOR PART A

Table A-2. States — **Age, Ethnicity, and Household Structure**

STATE	Family households, female householder, no husband present								
		Householder under 65 years (percent)							
	Householder all ages	Under 65 years	15 to 24 years	25 to 44 years	45 to 64 years	65 years and over (percent)	+/– U.S. percent householder 15 to 24 years	+/– U.S. percent householder 25 to 44 years	+/– U.S. percent householder 65 years and over
	208	209	210	211	212	213	214	215	216

Table A-2. States — **Age, Ethnicity, and Household Structure**

STATE	Nonfamily households											Householders 65 years and over	
		Householder under 65 years (percent)				Householder 65 years and over (percent)							
	Householder all ages	Under 65 years	15 to 24 years	25 to 44 years	45 to 64 years	65 years and over	65 to 84 years	85 years and over	+/– U.S. percent householder 15 to 24 years	+/– U.S. percent householder 25 to 44 years	+/– U.S. percent householder 65 years and over	Total households	Percent living alone
	217	218	219	220	221	222	223	224	225	226	227	228	229

Table A-2. States — **Age, Ethnicity, and Household Structure**

STATE	Non-Hispanic White households												
		Family households (percent)						Nonfamily households (percent)				
			Married couple family households		Female family householder		Male family householder						
	Number	Total family households	Total	With own children under 18 years	Total	With own children under 18 years	Total	With own children under 18 years	Total nonfamily households	Two or more adults	Living alone	+/– U.S. percent family households	+/– U.S. percent one-person households
	230	231	232	233	234	235	236	237	238	239	240	241	242

Table A-2. States — **Age, Ethnicity, and Household Structure**

STATE	Black or African American households												
		Family households (percent)						Nonfamily households (percent)				
			Married-couple family households		Female family householder		Male family householder						
	Number	Total family households	Total	With own children under 18 years	Total	With own children under 18 years	Total	With own children under 18 years	Total nonfamily households	Two or more adults	Living alone	+/– U.S. percent family households	+/– U.S. percent one-person households
	243	244	245	246	247	248	249	250	251	252	253	254	255

COLUMN HEADINGS FOR PART A

Table A-2. States — **Age, Ethnicity, and Household Structure**

	American Indian and Alaska Native households												
STATE		Family households (percent)						Nonfamily households (percent)				
			Married-couple family households		Female family householder		Male family householder						
	Number	Total family households	Total	With own children under 18 years	Total	With own children under 18 years	Total	With own children under 18 years	Total nonfamily households	Two or more adults	Living alone	+/− U.S. percent family households	+/− U.S. percent one-person households
	256	257	258	259	260	261	262	263	264	265	266	267	268

Table A-2. States — **Age, Ethnicity, and Household Structure**

	Asian, Hawaiian, and Pacific Islander households												
STATE		Family households (percent)						Nonfamily households (percent)				
			Married-couple family households		Female family householder		Male family householder						
	Number	Total family households	Total	With own children under 18 years	Total	With own children under 18 years	Total	With own children under 18 years	Total nonfamily households	Two or more adults	Living alone	+/− U.S. percent family households	+/− U.S. percent one-person households
	269	270	271	272	273	274	275	276	277	278	279	280	281

Table A-2. States — **Age, Ethnicity, and Household Structure**

	Hispanic or Latino[1] households												
STATE		Family households (percent)						Nonfamily households (percent)				
			Married-couple family households		Female family householder		Male family householder						
	Number	Total family households	Total	With own children under 18 years	Total	With own children under 18 years	Total	With own children under 18 years	Total nonfamily households	Two or more adults	Living alone	+/− U.S. percent family households	+/− U.S. percent one-person households
	282	283	284	285	286	287	288	289	290	291	292	293	294

[1] Hispanic or Latino persons may be of any race.

Table A-2. States — **Age, Ethnicity, and Household Structure**

	Place of birth for foreign-born population														
STATE									Latin America (percent)					
											Central America			
	Total population	Foreign-born population	Percent foreign-born	+/− U.S. percent foreign-born	Percent from Europe	Percent from Asia	Percent from Africa	Percent from Oceania	Total	Caribbean	Total from Central America	Mexico	Other Central America	South America	Percent from Northern America
	295	296	297	298	299	300	301	302	303	304	305	306	307	308	309

COLUMN HEADINGS FOR PART A

Table A-2. States — Age, Ethnicity, and Household Structure

STATE	Languages spoken at home (percent, except where noted)											
	Population 5 years and over						Population 5 years and over in households				Children 5 to 17 years who live in linguistically isolated households	Population 65 years and over who live in linguistically isolated households
								Households where all members speak only English	Households where some members speak a non-English language			
	Number	Speak only English	Speak Spanish	Speak another Indo-European language	Speak an Asian or Pacific Island language	Speak other languages	Number		Not linguistically isolated	Linguistically isolated		
	310	311	312	313	314	315	316	317	318	319	320	321

Table A-3. States and Counties — Age, Ethnicity, and Household Structure

STATE/ County code	MSA/PMSA/ NECMA code[1]	STATE County	Population by age (percent)										Non-Hispanic White		
														Age (percent)	
			Total population	Under 5 years	5 to 17 years	18 to 24 years	25 to 44 years	45 to 64 years	65 years and over	Median age	+/− U.S. percent under 18 years	+/− U.S. percent 65 years and over	Total population	Under 18 years	65 years and over
			1	2	3	4	5	6	7	8	9	10	11	12	13

[1]MSA = Metropolitan Statistical Area. PMSA = Primary MSA. NECMA = New England County Metropolitan Area. See the Appendix A for explanation of these concepts. See Appendix B for list of metropolitan areas identified by type, with component counties.

Table A-3. States and Counties — Age, Ethnicity, and Household Structure

STATE County	Black or African American			American Indian and Alaska Native			Asian, Hawaiian, and Pacific Islander			Hispanic or Latino[1]			Two or more races		
		Age (percent)			Age (percent)			Age (percent)			Age (percent)			Age (percent)	
	Total population	Under 18 years	65 years and over	Total population	Under 18 years	65 years and over	Total population	Under 18 years	65 years and over	Total population	Under 18 years	65 years and over	Total population	Under 18 years	65 years and over
	14	15	16	17	18	19	20	21	22	23	24	25	26	27	28

[1]Hispanic or Latino persons may be of any race.

Table A-3. States and Counties — Age, Ethnicity, and Household Structure

STATE County	Family households (percent)						Nonfamily households (percent)						Percent of householders 65 years and over who live alone	Grandparents who are responsible for the care of their grandchildren
	Married-couple family households			Other family households			Two or more unrelated persons		Male living alone		Female living alone			
	Total households	Total	With children	Householder 65 years or over	Total	With children	Householder 65 years or over	Total	Householder 65 years or over	Total	Householder 65 years or over	Total	Householder 65 years or over		
	29	30	31	32	33	34	35	36	37	38	39	40	41	42	43

COLUMN HEADINGS FOR PART A

Table A-3. States and Counties — Age, Ethnicity, and Household Structure

STATE County	Households with Non-Hispanic White householder		Households with Black or African American householder		Households with American Indian and Alaska Native householder		Households with Asian, Hawaiian, and Pacific Islander householder		Households with Hispanic or Latino[1] householder		Foreign-born population					Percent in non-English speaking households	
												Place of birth (percent)				
	Number of households	Percent that are family house-holds	Number of households	Percent that are family house-holds	Number of households	Percent that are family house-holds	Number of households	Percent that are family house-holds	Number of households	Percent that are family house-holds	Percent of total population that is foreign-born	Europe	Asia	Latin America	Linguis-tically isolated	Not linguis-tically isolated
	44	45	46	47	48	49	50	51	52	53	54	55	56	57	58	59

[1] Hispanic or Latino persons may be of any race.

Table A-4. Metropolitan Areas — Age, Ethnicity, and Household Structure

CMSA/MSA/ PMSA/NECMA code[1]	Area name	Population by age (percent)										Non-Hispanic White		
													Age (percent)	
		Total population	Under 5 years	5 to 17 years	18 to 24 years	25 to 44 years	45 to 64 years	65 years and over	Median age	+/− U.S. percent under 18 years	+/− U.S. percent 65 years and over	Total population	Under 18 years	65 years and over
		1	2	3	4	5	6	7	8	9	10	11	12	13

[1] MSA = Metropolitan Statistical Area. PMSA = Primary MSA. NECMA = New England County Metropolitan Area. See the Appendix A for explanation of these concepts. See Appendix B for list of metropolitan areas identified by type, with component counties.

Table A-4. Metropolitan Areas — Age, Ethnicity, and Household Structure

Area name	Black or African American			American Indian and Alaska Native			Asian, Hawaiian, and Pacific Islander			Hispanic or Latino[1]			Two or more races		
		Age (percent)			Age (percent)			Age (percent)			Age (percent)			Age (percent)	
	Total population	Under 18 years	65 years and over	Total population	Under 18 years	65 years and over	Total population	Under 18 years	65 years and over	Total population	Under 18 years	65 years and over	Total population	Under 18 years	65 years and over
	14	15	16	17	18	19	20	21	22	23	24	25	26	27	28

[1] Hispanic or Latino persons may be of any race.

Table A-4. Metropolitan Areas — Age, Ethnicity, and Household Structure

Area name	Family households (percent)						Nonfamily households (percent)								Percent of householders 65 years and over who live alone	Grandparents who are responsible for the care of their grandchildren
	Married-couple family households			Other family households			Two or more unrelated persons		Male living alone		Female living alone					
	Total households	Total	With children	House-holder 65 years or over	Total	With children	House-holder 65 years or over	Total	House-holder 65 years or over	Total	House-holder 65 years or over	Total	House-holder 65 years or over			
	29	30	31	32	33	34	35	36	37	38	39	40	41		42	43

xx

COLUMN HEADINGS FOR PART A

Table A-4. Metropolitan Areas — **Age, Ethnicity, and Household Structure**

Area name	Households with Non-Hispanic White householder		Households with Black or African American householder		Households with American Indian and Alaska Native householder		Households with Asian, Hawaiian, and Pacific Islander householder		Households with Hispanic or Latino[1] householder		Foreign-born population	Place of birth (percent)			Percent in non-English speaking households	
	Number of households	Percent that are family households	Number of households	Percent that are family households	Number of households	Percent that are family households	Number of households	Percent that are family households	Number of households	Percent that are family households	Percent of total population that is foreign-born	Europe	Asia	Latin America	Linguistically isolated	Not linguistically isolated
	44	45	46	47	48	49	50	51	52	53	54	55	56	57	58	59

[1]Hispanic or Latino persons may be of any race.

Table A-5. Cities — **Age, Ethnicity, and Household Structure**

STATE Place code	City	Population by age (percent)							Median age	+/– U.S. percent under 18 years	+/– U.S. percent 65 years and over	Non-Hispanic White	Age (percent)	
		Total population	Under 5 years	5 to 17 years	18 to 24 years	25 to 44 years	45 to 64 years	65 years and over				Total population	Under 18 years	65 years and over
		1	2	3	4	5	6	7	8	9	10	11	12	13

Table A-5. Cities — **Age, Ethnicity, and Household Structure**

City	Black or African American	Age (percent)		American Indian and Alaska Native	Age (percent)		Asian, Hawaiian, and Pacific Islander	Age (percent)		Hispanic or Latino[1]	Age (percent)		Two or more races	Age (percent)	
	Total population	Under 18 years	65 years and over	Total population	Under 18 years	65 years and over	Total population	Under 18 years	65 years and over	Total population	Under 18 years	65 years and over	Total population	Under 18 years	65 years and over
	14	15	16	17	18	19	20	21	22	23	24	25	26	27	28

[1]Hispanic or Latino persons may be of any race.

Table A-5. Cities — **Age, Ethnicity, and Household Structure**

City	Family households (percent)						Nonfamily households (percent)						Percent of householders 65 years and over who live alone	Grandparents who are responsible for the care of their grandchildren
	Married-couple family households			Other family households			Two or more unrelated persons		Male living alone		Female living alone			
	Total households	Total	With children	Householder 65 years or over	Total	With children	Householder 65 years or over	Total	Householder 65 years or over	Total	Householder 65 years or over	Total	Householder 65 years or over	
	29	30	31	32	33	34	35	36	37	38	39	40	41	42	43

COLUMN HEADINGS FOR PART A

Table A-5. Cities — **Age, Ethnicity, and Household Structure**

City	Households with Non-Hispanic White householder		Households with Black or African American householder		Households with American Indian and Alaska Native householder		Households with Asian, Hawaiian, and Pacific Islander householder		Households with Hispanic or Latino[1] householder		Foreign-born population				Percent in non-English speaking households	
											Percent of total population that is foreign-born	Place of birth (percent)				
	Number of households	Percent that are family households	Number of households	Percent that are family households	Number of households	Percent that are family households	Number of households	Percent that are family households	Number of households	Percent that are family households		Europe	Asia	Latin America	Linguistically isolated	Not linguistically isolated
	44	45	46	47	48	49	50	51	52	53	54	55	56	57	58	59

[1] Hispanic or Latino persons may be of any race.

COLUMN HEADINGS FOR PART B

Table B-2. States — **Education, Labor Force, and Income**

FIPS CODE	STATE	Total population 25 years and over	Percent with a high school diploma or less	Percent with a high school diploma or more (25 years and over)								
				Total	+/− U.S.	Male	Female	Non-Hispanic White	Black or African American	American Indian and Alaska Native	Asian, Hawaiian, and Pacific Islander	Hispanic or Latino[1]
		1	2	3	4	5	6	7	8	9	10	11

[1] Hispanic or Latino persons may be of any race.

Table B-2. States — **Education, Labor Force, and Income**

STATE	Percent with a high school diploma by age				Percent with bachelor's degree or more (25 years and over)								
	18 to 24 years	25 to 44 years	45 to 64 years	65 years and over	Total	+/− U.S.	Male	Female	Non-Hispanic White	Black or African American	American Indian and Alaska Native	Asian, Hawaiian, and Pacific Islander	Hispanic or Latino[1]
	12	13	14	15	16	17	18	19	20	21	22	23	24

[1] Hispanic or Latino persons may be of any race.

Table B-2. States — **Education, Labor Force, and Income**

STATE	Percent with a bachelor's degree or more by age and sex											
	18 to 24 years			25 to 44 years			45 to 64 years			65 years and over		
	Total	Male	Female	Total	Male	Female	Total	Male	Female	Total	Male	Female
	25	26	27	28	29	30	31	32	33	34	35	36

COLUMN HEADINGS FOR PART B

Table B-2. States — **Education, Labor Force, and Income**

STATE	Total population 3 years and over		Enrolled in nursery school		Enrolled in kindergarten through 12th grade (percent, except where noted)						
	Number enrolled	Percent enrolled in public schools	Number enrolled	Percent enrolled in public schools	Number enrolled	Enrolled in public schools	Non-Hispanic White enrolled in public schools	Black or African American enrolled in public schools	American Indian and Alaska Native enrolled in public schools	Asian, Hawaiian, and Pacific Islander enrolled in public schools	Hispanic or Latino[1] enrolled in public schools
	37	38	39	40	41	42	43	44	45	46	47

[1]Hispanic or Latino persons may be of any race.

Table B-2. States — **Education, Labor Force, and Income**

STATE	Enrolled in college or graduate school (percent, except where noted)							Adult school enrollment					
								18 to 24 years			25 years and over		
	Number enrolled	Enrolled in public schools	Non-Hispanic White enrolled in public schools	Black or African American enrolled in public schools	American Indian and Alaska Native enrolled in public schools	Asian, Hawaiian, and Pacific Islander enrolled in public schools	Hispanic or Latino[1] enrolled in public schools	Total population	Percent enrolled in all school levels	Percent enrolled in college or graduate school	Total population	Percent enrolled in all school levels	Percent enrolled in college or graduate school
	48	49	50	51	52	53	54	55	56	57	58	59	60

[1]Hispanic or Latino persons may be of any race.

Table B-2. States — **Education, Labor Force, and Income**

STATE	School enrollment and high school completion for population 16 to 19 years												
	Total Population			Non-Hispanic White		Black or African American		American Indian and Alaska Native		Asian, Hawaiian, and Pacific Islander		Hispanic or Latino[1]	
	Number	Percent not enrolled in school/ not high school graduate	Percent not enrolled in school/not high school graduate/not employed	Number	Percent not enrolled in school/ not high school graduate	Number	Percent not enrolled in school/ not high school graduate	Number	Percent not enrolled in school/ not high school graduate	Number	Percent not enrolled in school/ not high school graduate	Number	Percent not enrolled in school/ not high school graduate
	61	62	63	64	65	66	67	68	69	70	71	72	73

[1]Hispanic or Latino persons may be of any race.

Table B-2. States — **Education, Labor Force, and Income**

STATE	Work status in 1999 by sex, race, and Hispanic origin											
	Total population 16 years and over						Male population 16 years and over					
		Worked full-time (percent)		Worked part-time (percent)				Worked full-time (percent)		Worked part-time (percent)		
	Number	Total	Full-year	Total	Full-year	Did not work in 1999 (percent)	Number	Total	Full-year	Total	Full-year	Did not work in 1999 (percent)
	74	75	76	77	78	79	80	81	82	83	84	85

COLUMN HEADINGS FOR PART B

Table B-2. States — **Education, Labor Force, and Income**

STATE	Work status in 1999 by sex, race, and Hispanic origin											
	Female population 16 years and over						Non-Hispanic White population 16 years and over					
		Worked full-time (percent)		Worked part-time (percent)				Worked full-time (percent)		Worked part-time (percent)		
	Number	Total	Full-year	Total	Full-year	Did not work in 1999 (percent)	Number	Total	Full-year	Total	Full-year	Did not work in 1999 (percent)
	86	87	88	89	90	91	92	93	94	95	96	97

Table B-2. States — **Education, Labor Force, and Income**

STATE	Work status in 1999 by sex, race, and Hispanic origin											
	Black or African American population 16 years and over						American Indian and Alaska Native population 16 years and over					
		Worked full-time (percent)		Worked part-time (percent)				Worked full-time (percent)		Worked part-time (percent)		
	Number	Total	Full-year	Total	Full-year	Did not work in 1999 (percent)	Number	Total	Full-year	Total	Full-year	Did not work in 1999 (percent)
	98	99	100	101	102	103	104	105	106	107	108	109

Table B-2. States — **Education, Labor Force, and Income**

STATE	Work status in 1999 by sex, race, and Hispanic origin											
	Asian, Hawaiian, and Pacific Islander population 16 years and over						Hispanic or Latino[1] population 16 years and over					
		Worked full-time (percent)		Worked part-time (percent)				Worked full-time (percent)		Worked part-time (percent)		
	Number	Total	Full-year	Total	Full-year	Did not work in 1999 (percent)	Number	Total	Full-year	Total	Full-year	Did not work in 1999 (percent)
	110	111	112	113	114	115	116	117	118	119	120	121

[1] Hispanic or Latino persons may be of any race.

Table B-2. States — **Education, Labor Force, and Income**

STATE	Employment status by sex and age, 2000											
	Total population 16 years and over			Male population 16 years and over			Female population 16 years and over			Total population 16 to 24 years		
	Number	Labor force participation rate	Unemployment rate	Number	Labor force participation rate	Unemployment rate	Number	Labor force participation rate	Unemployment rate	Number	Labor force participation rate	Unemployment rate
	122	123	124	125	126	127	128	129	130	131	132	133

COLUMN HEADINGS FOR PART B

Table B-2. States — **Education, Labor Force, and Income**

STATE	Employment status by sex and age, 2000								
	Total population 25 to 44 years			Total population 45 to 64 years			Total population 65 years and over		
	Number	Labor force participation rate	Unemployment rate	Number	Labor force participation rate	Unemployment rate	Number	Labor force participation rate	Unemployment rate
	134	135	136	137	138	139	140	141	142

Table B-2. States — **Education, Labor Force, and Income**

STATE	Family status of children under 18 years, by employment status of parents and age of children											
	Children under 18 years in families				Children under 6 years in families				Children 6 to 7 years in families			
	Number	Percent living with two parents, both in the labor force	Percent living with two parents, father only in the labor force	Percent living with one parent, who is in the labor force	Number	Percent living with two parents, both in the labor force	Percent living with two parents, father only in the labor force	Percent living with one parent, who is in the labor force	Number	Percent living with two parents, both in the labor force	Percent living with two parents, father only in the labor force	Percent living with one parent, who is in the labor force
	143	144	145	146	147	148	149	150	151	152	153	154

Table B-2. States — **Education, Labor Force, and Income**

STATE	Employment status of family householders						Women 16 years and over by presence of children and employment status		
	Total families	Total married-couple families	Percent of married-couple families with both in the labor force	+/− U.S. percent of couples with both employed	Total other families	Percent of other family householders in labor force	Total women 16 years and over	Percent with children under 18 years	Percent with children under 18 years and in the labor force
	155	156	157	158	159	160	161	162	163

Table B-2. States — **Education, Labor Force, and Income**

STATE	Class of worker for employed civilians 16 years and over						
	Total employed civilian population 16 years and over	Percent private wage and salary workers	Percent government workers	Percent self-employed workers, including incorporated business owners	Percent unpaid family workers	Percent who worked at home	+/− U.S. percent worked at home
	164	165	166	167	168	169	170

COLUMN HEADINGS FOR PART B

Table B-2. States — **Education, Labor Force, and Income**

STATE	Occupation for employed population 16 years and over						
	Employed civilian population 16 years and over	Percent management, professional, and related occupations	Percent service occupations	Percent sales and office occupations	Percent farming, fishing, and forestry occupations	Percent construction, extraction, and maintenance occupations	Percent production, transportation, and material moving occupations
	171	172	173	174	175	176	177

Table B-2. States — **Education, Labor Force, and Income**

STATE	Industry for employed population 16 years and over (percent, except where noted)													
	Number of employed civilian population 16 years and over	Agriculture, forestry, fishing and hunting, mining	Construction	Manufacturing	Wholesale trade	Retail trade	Transportation and warehousing, and utilities	Information	Finance, insurance, real estate, rental and leasing	Professional, scientific, management, administrative, and waste management services	Educational, health, and social services	Arts, entertainment, recreation, accommodation, and food services	Other services (except public administration)	Public administration
	178	179	180	181	182	183	184	185	186	187	188	189	190	191

Table B-2. States — **Education, Labor Force, and Income**

STATE		Veteran status				Median household income	+/− U.S. median income
	Percent of the population 5 years and over with a disability	Total population 18 years and over	Veterans 18 years and over (percent)	Veterans 18 to 64 years (percent)	Veterans 65 years and over (percent)	Median household income	+/− U.S. median income
	192	193	194	195	196	197	198

Table B-2. States — **Education, Labor Force, and Income**

STATE	Median household income by age of householder							Median family income by family type					
	Under 25 years	25 to 34 years	35 to 44 years	45 to 54 years	55 to 64 years	65 to 74 years	75 years and over	All families	Married-couple families with children	Married-couple families without children	Male family householder with children	Male family householder without children	Female family householder with children	Female family householder without children
	199	200	201	202	203	204	205	206	207	208	209	210	211	212

Table B-2. States — Education, Labor Force, and Income

STATE	Median nonfamily household income by household type							Median income for population 15 years and over with income				
	All nonfamily households	Male householder not living alone	Male householder living alone	Male householder living alone, 65 years or over	Female householder not living alone	Female householder living alone	Female householder living alone, 65 years or over	Males 15 years and over	Males 15 years and over who worked full-year, full-time	Females 15 years and over	Females 15 years and over who worked full-year, full-time	Per capita income
	213	214	215	216	217	218	219	220	221	222	223	224

Table B-2. States — Education, Labor Force, and Income

STATE	Sources of income for households									
	Total households	Percent with earnings	Percent with wage or salary income	Percent with self-employment income	Percent with interest, dividends, or net rental income	Percent with Social Security income	Percent with Supplemental Security income	Percent with public assistance	Percent with retirement income	Percent with other types of income
	225	226	227	228	229	230	231	232	233	234

Table B-2. States — Education, Labor Force, and Income

STATE			Households with income over $100,000 by age of householder (percent)				
	Percent of all households with income over $100,000	+/− U.S. for income >$100,000	Householder under 25 years	Householder 25 to 44 years	Householder 45 to 64 years	Householder 65 to 74 years	Householder 75 years or over
	235	236	237	238	239	240	241

Table B-2. States — Education, Labor Force, and Income

STATE	Total households with income below poverty as a percent of all households in group									
	Percent of all households with income below poverty	Married-couple family households	Male householder family households	Female householder family households	Male householder nonfamily households	Female householder nonfamily households	Householder under 25 years	Householder 25 to 44 years	Householder 45 to 54 years	Householder 65 years and over
	242	243	244	245	246	247	248	249	250	251

COLUMN HEADINGS FOR PART B

Table B-2. States — **Education, Labor Force, and Income**

STATE	Total families with income below poverty as a percent of all families in group						
	Total families	Total families	Non-Hispanic White	Black or African American	American Indian and Alaska Native	Asian, Hawaiian, and Pacific Islander	Hispanic or Latino[1]
	252	253	254	255	256	257	258

[1] Hispanic or Latino persons may be of any race.

Table B-3. States and Counties — **Education, Labor Force, and Income**

STATE/ County code	MSA/PMSA/ NECMA code[1]	STATE County	High school graduates			College graduates		College graduates (percent)				
			Total population 25 years and over	Percent with a high school diploma or less	Percent with a high school diploma or more	Percent with a bachelor's degree or more	+/- U.S. percent with bachelor's degree or more	Non-Hispanic White	Black or African American	American Indian and Alaska Native	Asian, Hawaiian, and Pacific Islander	Hispanic or Latino[2]
			1	2	3	4	5	6	7	8	9	10

[1] MSA = Metropolitan Statistical Area. PMSA = Primary MSA. NECMA = New England County Metropolitan Area. See the Appendix A for explanation of these concepts. See Appendix B for list of metropolitan areas identified by type, with component counties.
[2] Hispanic or Latino persons may be of any race.

Table B-3. States and Counties — **Education, Labor Force, and Income**

STATE County	School enrollment			Population 16 to 19 years				Employment status, 2000			Work status in 1999 of the population 16 years and over (percent)		
											Worked in 1999		
	Grades kindergarten through 12	College or graduate school	Percent private	Number	Percent in armed forces	Percent high school graduates	Percent not enrolled, not grads, not in armed forces, not employed	Total population 16 years and over	Percent in labor force	Unemploy- ment rate	Full-time	Part-time	Did not work in 1999
	11	12	13	14	15	16	17	18	19	20	21	22	23

Table B-3. States and Counties — **Education, Labor Force, and Income**

STATE County	Full-year full-time employed (percent)								Children under 18 years in families						Total employed by class of worker (percent)			
										With two parents (percent)								
	Total	Men	Women	Non-Hispanic White	Black or African American	American Indian and Alaska Native	Asian, Hawaiian, and Pacific Islander	Hispanic or Latino[1]	Number	Both in labor force	Father only in labor force	With one parent who is in labor force (percent)	+/- U.S. percent of children with no stay-at-home parent (percent)	+/- U.S. percent two-income couples	Private	Govern-ment	Self-employed	Unpaid family worker
	24	25	26	27	28	29	30	31	32	33	34	35	36	37	38	39	40	41

[1] Hispanic or Latino persons may be of any race.

COLUMN HEADINGS FOR PART B

Table B-3. States and Counties — **Education, Labor Force, and Income**

STATE County	Percent who worked at home	Percent of the population 5 years and over with a disability	Veterans as a percent of the population 18 years and over	Occupation for employed population 16 years and over (percent)						Industry for employed population 16 years and over (percent)					
				Management, professional, and related occupations	Service occupations	Sales and office occupations	Farming, fishing, and forestry occupations	Construction, extraction, and maintenance occupations	Production, transportation, and material moving occupations	Agriculture, forestry, fishing, and mining	Construction and manufacturing	Wholesale and retail trade	Transportation and warehousing, and utilities	Service industries	Public administration
	42	43	44	45	46	47	48	49	50	51	52	53	54	55	56

Table B-3. States and Counties — **Education, Labor Force, and Income**

STATE County	Median family income					Median income for full-year, full-time workers				Households by source of income (percent)								
	Median household income	All families	Families with children			Median nonfamily household income	Men	Women	Per capita income	With earnings	With interest, dividend, or rental income	With Social Security income	With public assistance income	With retirement income	Households with income over $100,000 (percent)	+/– U.S. percent for income over $100,000	Households with income below poverty (percent)	Families with children with income below poverty (percent)
			Married couple	Male householder	Female householder													
	57	58	59	60	61	62	63	64	65	66	67	68	69	70	71	72	73	74

Table B-4. Metropolitan Areas — **Education, Labor Force, and Income**

CMSA/MSA/PMSA/NECMA code[1]	Area name	High school graduates			College graduates		College graduates (percent)				
		Total population 25 years and over	Percent with a high school diploma or less	Percent with a high school diploma or more	Percent with a bachelor's degree or more	+/– U.S. percent with bachelor's degree or more	Non-Hispanic White	Black or African American	American Indian and Alaska Native	Asian, Hawaiian, and Pacific Islander	Hispanic or Latino[2]
		1	2	3	4	5	6	7	8	9	10

[1]MSA = Metropolitan Statistical Area. PMSA = Primary MSA. NECMA = New England County Metropolitan Area. See the Appendix A for explanation of these concepts. See Appendix B for list of metropolitan areas identified by type, with component counties.
[2]Hispanic or Latino persons may be of any race.

Table B-4. Metropolitan Areas — **Education, Labor Force, and Income**

Area name	School enrollment			Population 16 to 19 years				Employment status, 2000			Work status in 1999 of the population 16 years and over (percent)		
											Worked in 1999		
	Grades kindergarten through 12	College or graduate school	Percent private	Number	Percent in armed forces	Percent high school graduates	Percent not enrolled, not grads, not in armed forces, not employed	Total population 16 years and over	Percent in labor force	Unemployment rate	Full-time	Part-time	Did not work in 1999
	11	12	13	14	15	16	17	18	19	20	21	22	23

COLUMN HEADINGS FOR PART B

Table B-4. Metropolitan Areas — Education, Labor Force, and Income

Area name	Full-year full-time employed (percent)								Children under 18 years in families (percent, except where noted)						Total employed by class of worker (percent)			
												With two parents							
														With one parent who is in labor force	+/− U.S. percent of children with no stay-at-home parent	+/− U.S. percent two-income couples				Unpaid family worker
	Total	Men	Women	Non-Hispanic White	Black or African American	American Indian and Alaska Native	Asian, Hawaiian, and Pacific Islander	Hispanic or Latino[1]	Number	Both in labor force	Father only in labor force					Private	Government	Self-employed	
	24	25	26	27	28	29	30	31	32	33	34	35	36	37	38	39	40	41

[1] Hispanic or Latino persons may be of any race.

Table B-4. Metropolitan Areas — Education, Labor Force, and Income

Area name				Occupation for employed population 16 years and over (percent)						Industry for employed population 16 years and over (percent)					
	Percent who worked at home	Percent of the population 5 years and over with a disability	Veterans as a percent of the population 18 years and over	Management, professional, and related occupations	Service occupations	Sales and office occupations	Farming, fishing, and forestry occupations	Construction, extraction, and maintenance occupations	Production, transportation and material moving occupations	Agriculture, forestry, fishing, and mining	Construction and manufacturing	Wholesale and retail trade	Transportation and warehousing, and utilities	Service industries	Public administration
	42	43	44	45	46	47	48	49	50	51	52	53	54	55	56

Table B-4. Metropolitan Areas — Education, Labor Force, and Income

Area name	Median family income					Median nonfamily household income	Median income for full-year, full-time workers		Per capita income	Households by source of income (percent)								
				Families with children														
	Median household income	All families	Married couple	Male householder	Female householder		Men	Women		With earnings	With interest, dividend, or rental income	With Social Security income	With public assistance income	With retirement income	Households with income over $100,000 (percent)	+/− U.S. percent for income over $100,000	Households with income below poverty (percent)	Families with children with income below poverty (percent)
	57	58	59	60	61	62	63	64	65	66	67	68	69	70	71	72	73	74

Table B-5. Cities — Education, Labor Force, and Income

STATE Place code	City	High school graduates			College graduates		College graduates (percent)					
		Total population 25 years and over	Percent with a high school diploma or less	Percent with a high school diploma or more	Percent with a bachelor's degree or more	+/− U.S. percent with bachelor's degree or more	Non-Hispanic White	Black or African American	American Indian and Alaska Native	Asian, Hawaiian, and Pacific Islander	Hispanic or Latino[1]
		1	2	3	4	5	6	7	8	9	10

[1] Hispanic or Latino persons may be of any race.

COLUMN HEADINGS FOR PART B

Table B-5. Cities — **Education, Labor Force, and Income**

City	School enrollment			Population 16 to 19 years				Employment status, 2000			Work status in 1999 of the population 16 years and over		
											Worked in 1999		
	Grades kindergarten through 12	College or graduate school	Percent private	Number	Percent in armed forces	Percent high school graduates	Percent not enrolled, not grads, not in armed forces, not employed	Total population 16 years and over	Percent in labor force	Unemployment rate	Full-time	Part-time	Did not work in 1999
	11	12	13	14	15	16	17	18	19	20	21	22	23

Table B-5. Cities — **Education, Labor Force, and Income**

City	Full-year full-time employed (percent)								Children under 18 years in families (percent, except where noted)						Total employed by class of worker (percent)			
										With two parents								
	Total	Men	Women	Non-Hispanic White	Black or African American	American Indian and Alaska Native	Asian, Hawaiian, and Pacific Islander	Hispanic or Latino[1]	Number	Both in labor force	Father only in labor force	With one parent who is in labor force	+/− U.S. percent of children with no stay-at-home parent	+/− U.S. percent two-income couples	Private	Government	Self-employed	Unpaid family worker
	24	25	26	27	28	29	30	31	32	33	34	35	36	37	38	39	40	41

[1]Hispanic or Latino persons may be of any race.

Table B-5. Cities — **Education, Labor Force, and Income**

City	Percent who worked at home	Percent of the population 5 years and over with a disability	Veterans as a percent of the population 18 years and over	Occupation for employed population 16 years and over (percent)						Industry for employed population 16 years and over (percent)					
				Management, professional, and related occupations	Service occupations	Sales and office occupations	Farming, fishing, and forestry occupations	Construction, extraction, and maintenance occupations	Production, transportation and material moving occupations	Agriculture, forestry, fishing, and mining	Construction and manufacturing	Wholesale and retail trade	Transportation and warehousing, and utilities	Service industries	Public administration
	42	43	44	45	46	47	48	49	50	51	52	53	54	55	56

Table B-5. Cities — **Education, Labor Force, and Income**

City	Median household income	Median family income				Median nonfamily household income	Median income for full-year, full-time workers		Per capita income	Households by source of income (percent)								
		All families	Families with children															
			Married couple	Male householder	Female householder		Men	Women		With earnings	With interest, dividend, or rental income	With Social Security income	With public assistance income	With retirement income	Households with income over $100,000 (percent)	+/− U.S. percent for income over $100,000	Households with income below poverty (percent)	Families with children with income below poverty (percent)
	57	58	59	60	61	62	63	64	65	66	67	68	69	70	71	72	73	74

COLUMN HEADINGS FOR PART C

Table C-2. States — Migration, Housing, and Transportation

FIPS CODE	STATE	Total population 5 years and over	Residence in 1995 (percent)							
			Same house	Same county, different house	Same state, different county	Different state				Outside the United States
						Northeast states	Midwest states	Southern states	Western states	
		1	2	3	4	5	6	7	8	9

Table C-2. States — Migration, Housing, and Transportation

STATE	Residence in 1995, non-Hispanic White population (percent)									Residence in 1995, Black or African American population (percent)								
	Non-Hispanic White population 5 years and over	Same house	Same county, different house	Same state, different county	Different state				Outside the United States	Black or African American population 5 years and over	Same house	Same county, different house	Same state, different county	Different state				Outside the United States
					Northeast states	Midwest states	Southern states	Western states						Northeast states	Midwest states	Southern states	Western states	
	10	11	12	13	14	15	16	17	18	19	20	21	22	23	24	25	26	27

Table C-2. States — Migration, Housing, and Transportation

STATE	Residence in 1995, American Indian and Alaska Native population (percent)									Residence in 1995, Asian, Hawaiian, and Pacific Islander population (percent)								
	American Indian and Alaska Native population 5 years and over	Same house	Same county, different house	Same state, different county	Different state				Outside the United States	Asian, Hawaiian, and Pacific Islander population 5 years and over	Same house	Same county, different house	Same state, different county	Different state				Outside the United States
					Northeast states	Midwest states	Southern states	Western states						Northeast states	Midwest states	Southern states	Western states	
	28	29	30	31	32	33	34	35	36	37	38	39	40	41	42	43	44	45

Table C-2. States — Migration, Housing, and Transportation

STATE	Residence in 1995, Hispanic or Latino[1] population (percent)									Total occupied housing units			
	Hispanic or Latino[1] population 5 years and over	Same house	Same county, different house	Same state, different county	Different state				Outside the United States	Total occupied housing units	Owner-occupied	Renter-occupied	Percent owner-occupied
					Northeast states	Midwest states	Southern states	Western states					
	46	47	48	49	50	51	52	53	54	55	56	57	58

[1] Hispanic or Latino persons may be of any race.

COLUMN HEADINGS FOR PART C

Table C-2. States — **Migration, Housing, and Transportation**

	Homeownership by age of householder											
	15 to 24 years		25 to 44 years		45 to 64 years		65 to 74 years		75 to 84 years		85 years and over	
STATE	Number of householders	Percent owners	Number of householders	Percent owners	Number of householders	Percent owners	Number of householders	Percent owners	Number of householders	Percent owners	Number of householders	Percent owners
	59	60	61	62	63	64	65	66	67	68	69	70

Table C-2. States — **Migration, Housing, and Transportation**

	Homeownership by race and Hispanic origin of householder									
	Non-Hispanic White		Black or African American		American Indian and Alaska Native		Asian, Hawaiian, and Pacific Islander		Hispanic or Latino[1]	
STATE	Number of householders	Percent owners	Number of householders	Percent owners	Number of householders	Percent owners	Number of householders	Percent owners	Number of householders	Percent owners
	71	72	73	74	75	76	77	78	79	80

[1] Hispanic or Latino persons may be of any race.

Table C-2. States — **Migration, Housing, and Transportation**

	Homeownership by household type																	
	Family households								Nonfamily households									
			Married-couple families				Other family						Two or more adults		Male living alone		Female living alone	
			Total		With children		Total		With children									
STATE	Number of house-holders	Per-cent owners	Number of house-holders	Per-cent owners	Number of house-holders	Per-cent owners	Number of house-holders	Per-cent owners	Number of house-holders	Per-cent owners	Number of house-holders	Per-cent owners	Number of house-holders	Per-cent owners	Number of house-holders	Per-cent owners	Number of house-holders	Per-cent owners
	81	82	83	84	85	86	87	88	89	90	91	92	93	94	95	96	97	98

Table C-2. States — **Migration, Housing, and Transportation**

	Homeownership by household size				Average household size		Median household income		
	One-person households		Two or more person households						
STATE	Number of householders	Percent owners	Number of householders	Percent owners	Owner-occupied households	Renter-occupied households	All households	Owner-occupied households	Renter-occupied households
	99	100	101	102	103	104	105	106	107

COLUMN HEADINGS FOR PART C

Table C-2. States — **Migration, Housing, and Transportation**

STATE	Mean household income by tenure and age of householder									Median monthly owner costs as a percent of income				
		Owner-occupied units				Renter-occupied units								
	Total occupied housing units	Total	15 to 34 years	35 to 64 years	65 years and over	Total	15 to 34 years	35 to 64 years	65 years and over	Median housing value (owner estimated)	With a mortgage	Without a mortgage	Median gross rent	Median gross rent as a percent of income
	108	109	110	111	112	113	114	115	116	117	118	119	120	121

Table C-2. States — **Migration, Housing, and Transportation**

STATE	Households who pay 35 percent or more of income for housing expenses, by tenure, age of householder, and household income (percent)													
	Owner-occupied households							Renter-occupied households						
	Total	15 to 24 years	25 to 44 years	45 to 64 years	65 years and over	Households with income under $50,000	Households with income over $100,000	Total	15 to 24 years	25 to 44 years	45 to 64 years	65 years and over	Households with income under $50,000	Households with income over $100,000
	122	123	124	125	126	127	128	129	130	131	132	133	134	135

Table C-2. States — **Migration, Housing, and Transportation**

STATE	Means of transportation to work (percent, except where noted)								Mean travel time to work (minutes)			Vehicles available					
		Car, truck, or van															
	Total number of workers 16 years and over	Drove alone	Carpooled	Public transportation	Motorcycle or bicycle	Walked	Other means	Worked at home	Time for all workers who did not work at home	Time on public transportation	Time by all other means	Total households	No vehicles	One vehicle	Two vehicles	Three or more vehicles	Average vehicles available
	136	137	138	139	140	141	142	143	144	145	146	147	148	149	150	151	152

Table C-3. States and Counties — **Migration, Housing, and Transportation**

STATE/ County code	MSA/PMSA/ NECMA code[1]	STATE County		Residence in 1995 (percent)						Occupied housing units		Householders 65 years and over	
			Total population 5 years and over	Same house	Same county, different house	Same state, different county	Different state	Outside the United States		Number	Percent owner-occupied	Number	Percent owner-occupied
			1	2	3	4	5	6		7	8	9	10

[1]MSA = Metropolitan Statistical Area. PMSA = Primary MSA. NECMA = New England County Metropolitan Area. See the Appendix A for explanation of these concepts. See Appendix B for list of metropolitan areas identified by type, with component counties.

COLUMN HEADINGS FOR PART C

Table C-3. States and Counties — **Migration, Housing, and Transportation**

STATE County	Owner-occupied by household type (percent)								Median household income			Median housing value (owner estimated)	Median monthly owner costs as a percent of income	
	Family households					Nonfamily households								
		Married-couple		Other family										
	Total family households	Total	With own children under 18 years	Total	With own children under 18 years	Total nonfamily households	Two or more adults	Living alone	All households	Owner-occupied households	Renter-occupied households		With a mortgage	Without a mortgage
	11	12	13	14	15	16	17	18	19	20	21	22	23	24

Table C-3. States and Counties — **Migration, Housing, and Transportation**

STATE County		Percent who pay 35 percent or more of income for housing expenses		Means of transportation to work (percent except where noted)						Vehicles available (percent of households)		
					Car, truck, or van							
	Median gross rent	Owners	Renters	Number of workers 16 years and over	Drove alone	Carpooled	Public transportation	Other means	Walked	No vehicles	One vehicle	Two or more vehicles
	25	26	27	28	29	30	31	32	33	34	35	36

Table C-4. Metropolitan Areas — **Migration, Housing, and Transportation**

CMSA/MSA/ PMSA/NECMA code[1]	Area name		Residence in 1995 (percent)						Occupied housing units		Householders 65 years and over	
		Total population 5 years and over	Same house	Same county, different house	Same state, different county	Different state	Outside the United States	Number	Percent owner occupied	Number	Percent owner occupied
			1	2	3	4	5	6	7	8	9	10

[1]MSA = Metropolitan Statistical Area. PMSA = Primary MSA. NECMA = New England County Metropolitan Area. See the Appendix A for explanation of these concepts. See Appendix B for list of metropolitan areas identified by type, with component counties.

Table C-4. Metropolitan Areas — **Migration, Housing, and Transportation**

Area name	Owner-occupied by household type (percent)								Median household income			Median housing value (owner estimated)	Median monthly owner costs as a percent of income	
	Family households					Nonfamily households								
		Married-couple		Other family										
	Total family households	Total	With own children under 18 years	Total	With own children under 18 years	Total nonfamily households	Two or more adults	Living alone	All households	Owner-occupied households	Renter-occupied households		With a mortgage	Without a mortgage
	11	12	13	14	15	16	17	18	19	20	21	22	23	24

COLUMN HEADINGS FOR PART C

Table C-4. Metropolitan Areas — **Migration, Housing, and Transportation**

Area name	Percent who pay 35 percent or more of income for housing expenses		Means of transportation to work (percent except where noted)							Vehicles available (percent of households)		
				Car, truck, or van							
	Median gross rent	Owners	Renters	Number of workers 16 years and over	Drove alone	Carpooled	Public transportation	Other means	Walked	No vehicles	One vehicle	Two or more vehicles
	25	26	27	28	29	30	31	32	33	34	35	36

Table C-5. Cities — **Migration, Housing, and Transportation**

STATE Place code	City		Residence in 1995 (percent)						Occupied housing units		Householders 65 years and over	
		Total population 5 years and over	Same house	Same county, different house	Same state, different county	Different state	Outside the United States	Number	Percent owner occupied	Number	Percent owner occupied
		1	2	3	4	5	6	7	8	9	10

Table C-5. Cities — **Migration, Housing, and Transportation**

City	Owner-occupied by household type (percent)								Median household income			Median monthly owner costs as a percent of income	
	Family households				Nonfamily households								
		Married-couple		Other family									
	Total family households	Total	With own children under 18 years	Total	With own children under 18 years	Total nonfamily households	Two or more adults	Living alone	All households	Owner-occupied households	Renter-occupied households	Median housing value (owner estimated)	With a mortgage	Without a mortgage
	11	12	13	14	15	16	17	18	19	20	21	22	23	24

Table C-5. Cities — **Migration, Housing, and Transportation**

City	Percent who pay 35 percent or more of income for housing expenses		Means of transportation to work (percent except where noted)							Vehicles available (percent of households)		
				Car, truck, or van							
	Median gross rent	Owners	Renters	Number of workers 16 years and over	Drove alone	Carpooled	Public transportation	Other means	Walked	No vehicles	One vehicle	Two or more vehicles
	25	26	27	28	29	30	31	32	33	34	35	36

Highlights

Highlights

Most people who use this book will be updating their knowledge about the places they care about. But it would be a mistake to think of the census results as simply timely snapshots, and to compare them with earlier pictures to see how things have changed. Instead, these snapshots offer an important foundation for thinking about the future, including the way their population trends position counties or cities within the changing national context.

In short, the American population is changing in fundamental ways, and Census 2000 provides a good opportunity to transform our "mental model" of how Americans really look and function. In years to come, decisions made on the basis of the old model will be an increasingly uncomfortable fit with the people they are designed for. So users should keep the following new framework in mind as they extract the numbers they need.

From Pyramids to Pillars

The most fundamental demographic change that is re-shaping the U.S. population is its longer life expectancy.

Census 2000 shows that Americans are well on the way to something no population has ever known: with fewer people dying before old age, each age group, except the very oldest, is converging on roughly the same size.

The demographer's basic tool is called an age pyramid because until now, the picture of a population by age has reflected the large numbers of each generation that died before reaching each successive life-stage. So traditionally the picture has shown a relatively small group of older people at the top, a moderate amount of middle-aged people in the middle, with the bulk of the population—young adults, teenagers, and children at the bottom.

As recently as 1970, the pyramid was a good representation of the U.S. population. (See chart.) (The Depression cinched that pyramid around the middle, and the post-war Baby Boom widened it just above the bottom.) However, the health improvements of the twentieth century have increased the numbers of each generation who survive to the next life-stage, so the

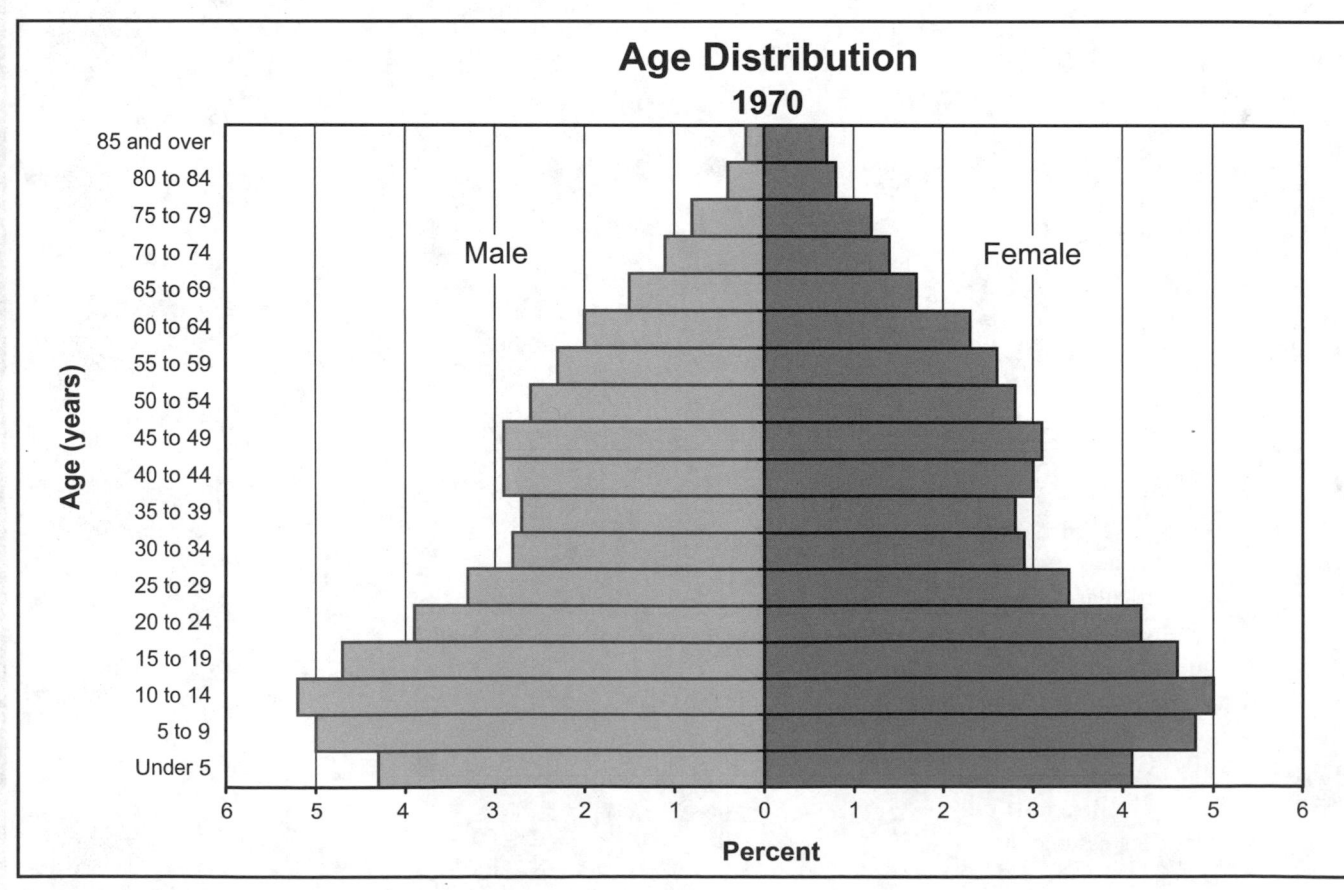

Source: U.S. Census Bureau, 1970 Census of Population and Housing.

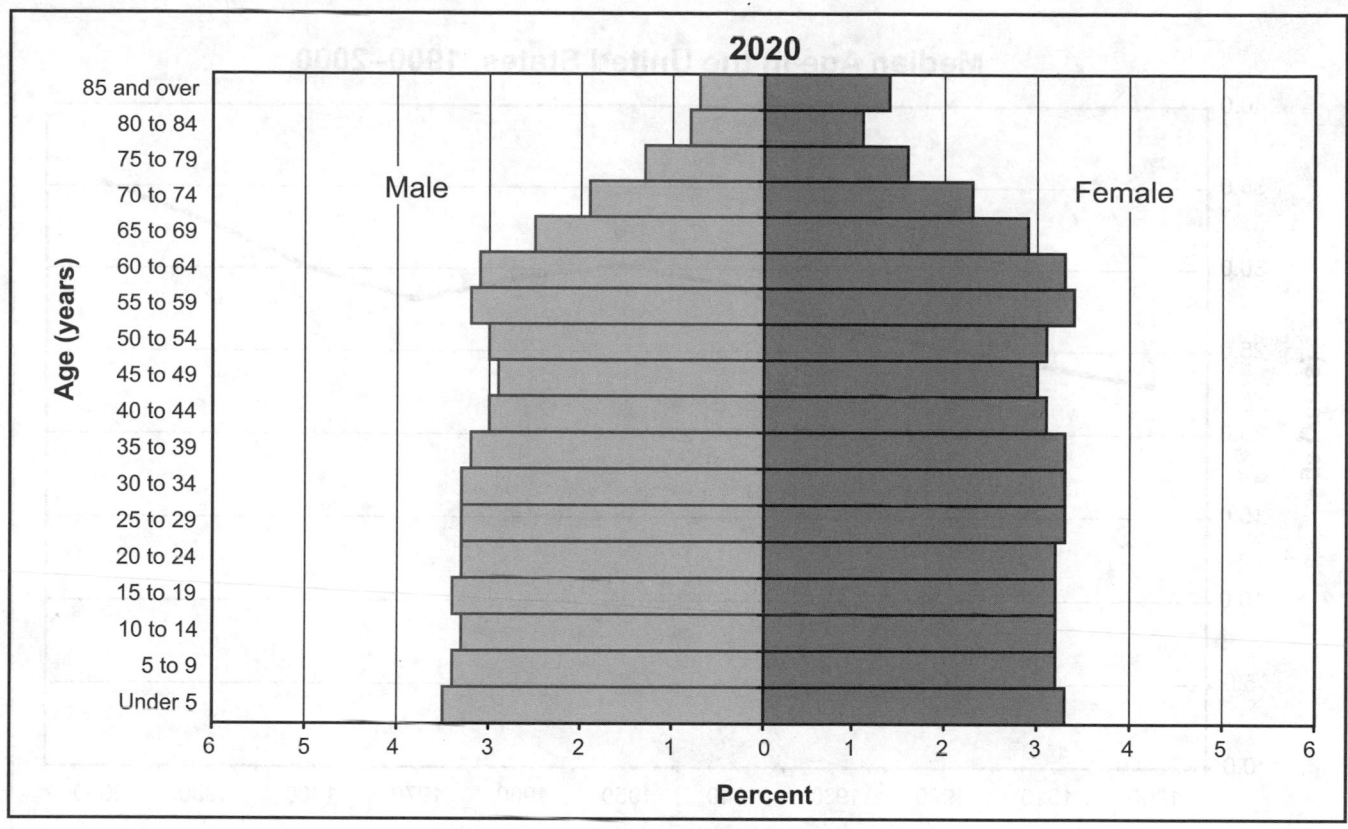

2020

Male

Female

Age (years)

85 and over
80 to 84
75 to 79
70 to 74
65 to 69
60 to 64
55 to 59
50 to 54
45 to 49
40 to 44
35 to 39
30 to 34
25 to 29
20 to 24
15 to 19
10 to 14
5 to 9
Under 5

6 5 4 3 2 1 0 1 2 3 4 5 6

Percent

Source: U.S. Census Bureau. "Projections of the Total Population." (Middle Series) January, 2000.

pyramid is turning into a pillar. Thus, across the country there are more older people, and more middle-aged people relative to young people than ever before.

The change in the median age of the population provides a quick insight into the magnitude of this transformation. (See chart.) Census 2000 found that the median age of the American population is 36 years—the "oldest" it has ever been, but "younger" than it is projected to be ever again. In 1900, the median age was 23 in 2100, according to current Census Bureau projections, it will be 40.

Depending on a variety of factors, this trend is very pronounced in some places, but barely visible in others. Throughout this volume, there are measures to identify the degree to which this new dynamic is reshaping the population in a particular county or city. Across the board, longer lives are growing the American population. In fact, over the twentieth century, mortality improvements grew the American population almost twice as much as immigration did—yet immigration achieved far more attention.

Some Americans assume that the population is aging because Americans are having fewer children, but Census 2000 shows that Americans continue to have an average of two children. Thanks to a larger population, the census reported more children than the 1990 census did. In fact, in every year since 1990, Americans had more children than they did the year before. So the population is aging because of improvements in Americans' mortality.

Demographers estimate that about half the Americans counted in Census 2000 would not have been alive if mortality rates had stayed the same as they were in 1900. So the growth in life expectancy, combined with Americans' longstanding preference for the two-child family, has produced a population with more older people and about the same number of young people. How this dynamic plays out from place to place is a key factor in understanding the population demands on local government, resources for local businesses, and challenges for local communities.

The New "Traditional" Family

The transformation in Americans' age picture is also changing the way the nation looks when it's "at home." Census 2000 found that the nation's households are smaller than they used to be, and that a smaller proportion of them are families. (See chart.) With more middle-aged and older people, traditional families (married couples with children) automatically become relatively less numerous, as

3

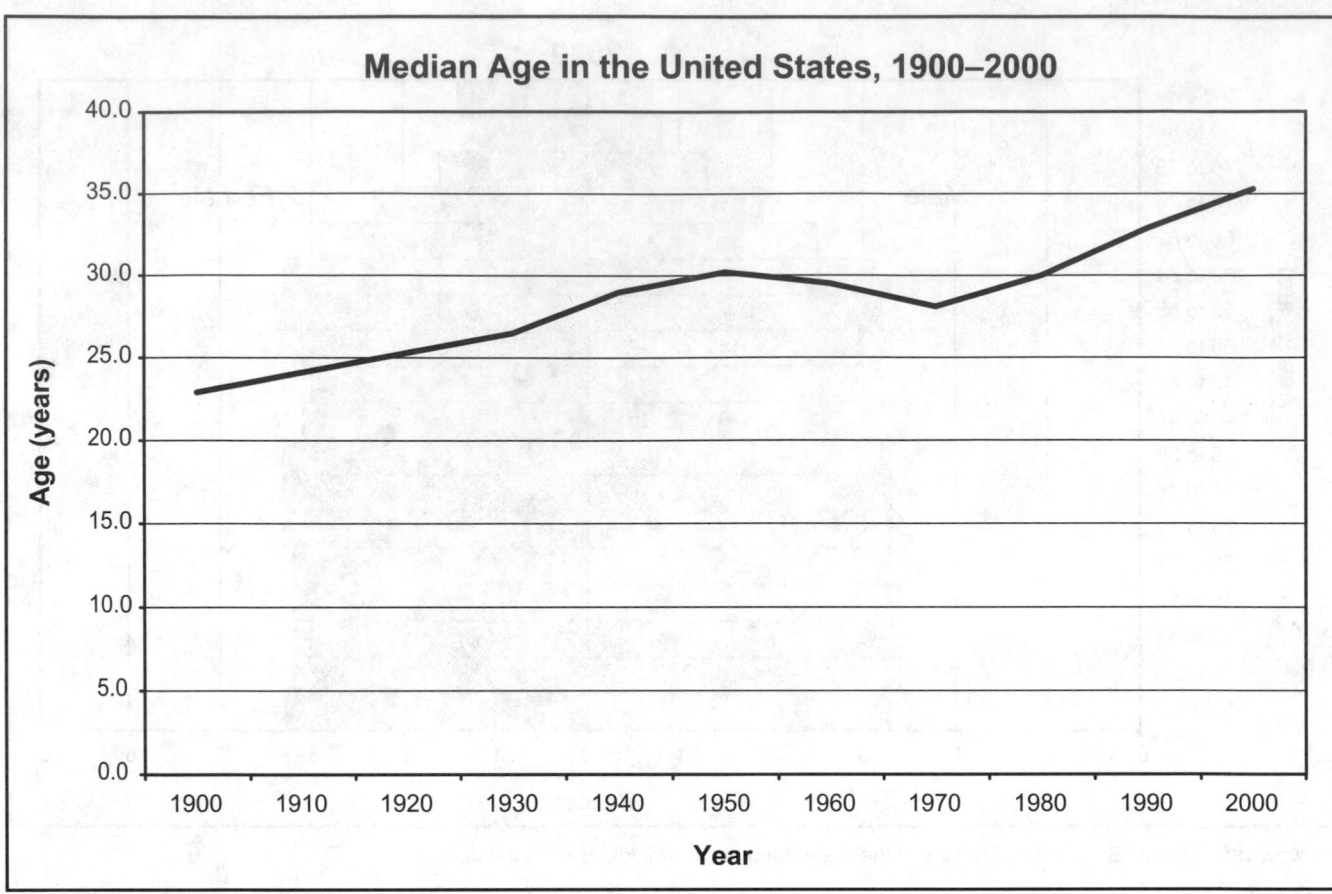

Median Age in the United States, 1900–2000

Source: U.S. Census Bureau.

Americans' longer lives are growing the number of years after the children have grown. In fact, the average American is spending just over a third of the time in between 20 and 70 raising children.

Not so long ago, the traditional family was the most common living arrangement. However, the combination of longer life expectancy and the two-child family has made married couples without children the nation's new "traditional" family—couples simply have more time together after their children have reached age 18. Census 2000 found that the old "traditional" family now accounts for little more than a third of all families and less than a fourth of all households.

Households that do not contain a family (persons related by blood or marriage) make up the rest of the nation's households. These "nonfamily" households are growing rapidly, and the majority of them consist of people living alone. Single-person households are the nation's second most numerous household type, also outnumbering the "traditional" family, and Census 2000 found that they account for over 25 percent of all households.

This is not surprising, considering that people ages 65 and older are the largest share of single-person households. Until recent decades, a widowed parent, most often a mother, would move into a child's household. Since 1960, older people's increasing financial independence has been accompanied by increasing residential independence. However, Census 2000 reported that single-person households are common in every age group—one in 10 Americans ages 25 to 44, the most common ages for marriage, lives alone.

Obviously, the decline of the "traditional" family and the rise of childless households is a statistical artifact: for census purposes, children are no longer "children" once they reach 18. Many of the childless households Census 2000 found actually have children in them aged 18 and older. In fact, sharp-eyed readers will notice that Americans aged 18 to 24 are less "adult" than they used to be, in the sense that they have become financially or residentially independent. Census 2000 reported that three out of five Americans this age live with their parents or other relatives. And researchers into the census database will find that these young adults are making an

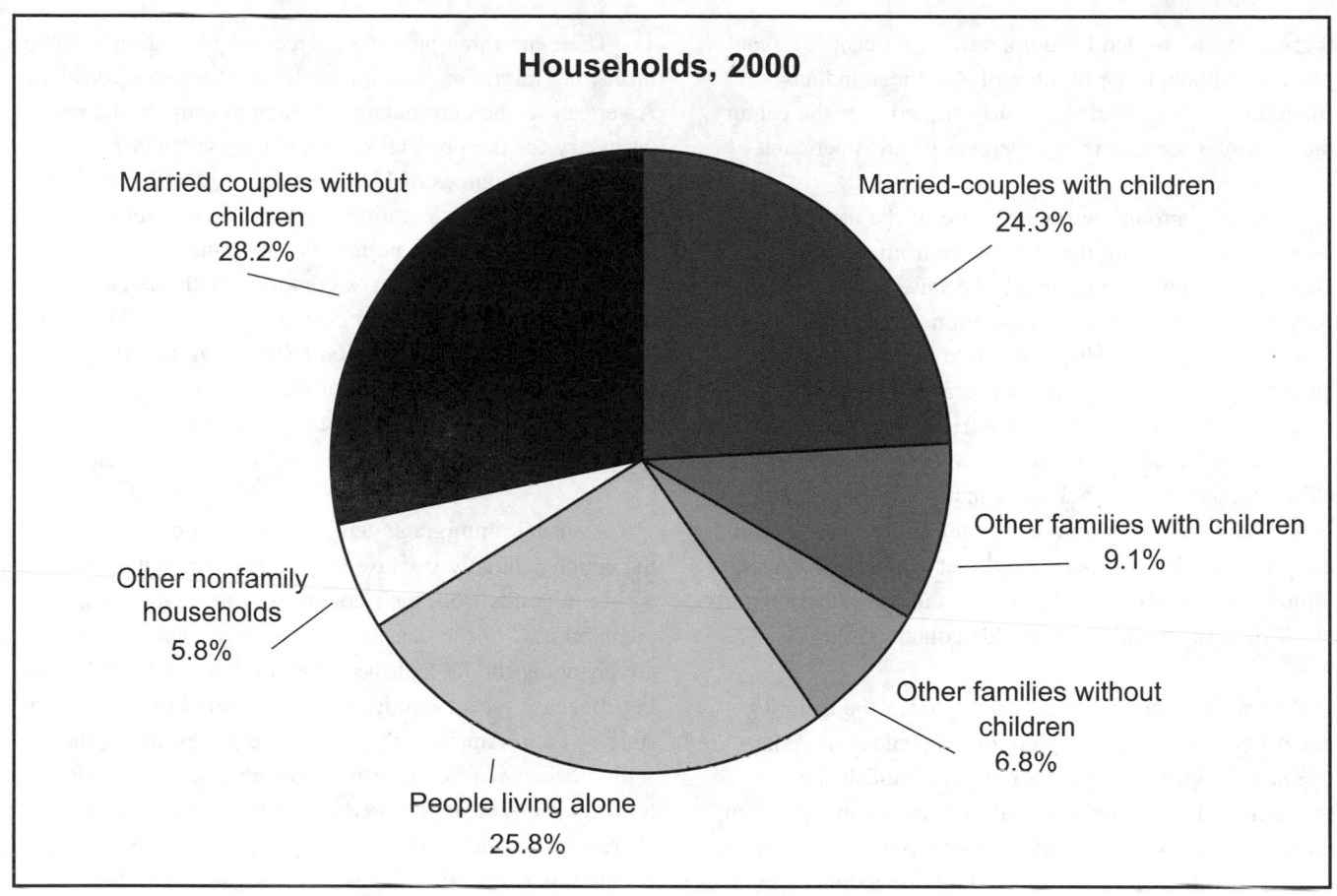

Households, 2000

- Married couples without children 28.2%
- Married-couples with children 24.3%
- Other families with children 9.1%
- Other families without children 6.8%
- People living alone 25.8%
- Other nonfamily households 5.8%

Source. Census 2000 Summary File 3—United States, U.S. Census Bureau. Table P10.

increasingly complex transition to adulthood, as they are spending their post-adolescence, pre-adult years mixing school, work, both, or neither in a variety of ways.

In short, while Americans are living longer healthier lives, they are also taking longer to become independent, just as older people are much less dependent. This book uses the official definitions of independent adulthood— ages 18 to 65—as a quick guide to the population structure of states, counties, cities, and metropolitan areas. But the reality is that dependency lasts longer for young people than it used to and starts later for more of the 65-plus. A good mental model for decision-makers to adopt would put adult independence around age 25 and adult dependency at 70 or beyond.

Really Multiracial Now

Perhaps the greatest curiosity about the census results has centered on the nation's changing racial make-up, partly because immigration has been swelling the nation's minority populations, partly because for the first time the census allowed people to choose more than one category to describe their racial origins. Judging by the results, the new

"mental model" of Americans is an increasingly multiracial model, as larger shares of the population are nonwhite. This is especially characteristic of its younger members, that is current and future parents.

Some of the shift toward a "majority minority" population is simply because the census design has shifted to be more representative of the nonwhite population. That is, the U.S. population has always been multiracial in one form or another, but early censuses focused largely on the white population, while subsequent censuses went to extremes to force people into black and white categories. For instance, even though the nation inherited a large Hispanic population with territorial acquisitions in the South and Southwest, this population was not counted separately until 1970.

Census 2000 reported that non-Hispanic whites account for less than 70 percent of the population—a smaller share than ever before—and that the minority population is more diverse as well as more numerous. For the first time, Hispanics slightly outnumber non-Hispanic blacks; together, they account for about 25 percent of the population. Asian and Pacific Islanders, another population that has been swelled by immigration, account for about 4 percent. Although the number of American Indians (including Alaska Natives) nearly tripled over the century, they account for less than 1 percent of all Americans.

Minority groups' growing share of the nation's population is slowing the shift away from the traditional child-rearing household, largely because minorities are younger than the majority population. Census 2000 found that the average non-Hispanic white is 38 years old, a decade or more older than the average Hispanic or American Indian. The average African American and Asian and Pacific Islander is younger, too, in their early 30s. Other things equal, populations that tend to have more young adults in them tend to contain more families with children. So Census 2000 found that a minority of white family households have children in them, while a majority of all minority family households contain children.

Minority households also differ from the majority pattern because large numbers of Hispanics and Asians are recent immigrants who have not yet established or reconstituted their families, and because minorities often have slightly different types of households. For example, nuclear families are often more fluid and extended families more prominent, especially for child rearing or caring for elders. Thus, readers will find that single-parent and "sub-families" (a nuclear family or portions of a nuclear family living in the household of another, related family) are relatively more common, while husband-wife families are less common in these population groups.

Still Growing, but Where?

As these pages show, parts of the old "mental model" are still valid. America's population continues to grow at a steady clip, and many Americans continue to be born in some other country.

Population growth has shaped America since its beginnings, and Census 2000 found the U.S. population growing at a rate of about 1 percent a year. At this rate, the United States is adding twice as many people to the population each decade as it was a century ago. Between the 1990 census and Census 2000, the U.S. population grew by over 25 million people—more than in any decade but one in the nation's history. As the population base becomes larger, demographers are looking for the growth rate to slow to 0.7 percent a year. At that rate the population will more than double over the twenty-first century.

There are three possible sources of population growth: births, net migration, and longer lives ("delayed" deaths). American women are having children at roughly the rate necessary for the population to replace itself, but not to grow. So the sources of U.S. population growth now are longer lives and immigration. The former is a subtle change, the latter more noticeable, as immigrants are coming from different places compared with the past, bringing new languages and customs. Census 2000 found that net migration (immigration minus emigration) contributed about 30 percent of the increase in the population since the 1990 census. That's about the same proportion as in the first decade of the twentieth century.

As usual, immigrants tend to cluster in certain parts of the country, largely because they follow the paths taken by earlier migrants from their countries. One of the most common uses of the census is to identify where immigrants are changing the face of the population, and where they are not. Because recent immigrants have tended to come from Asia or Latin America, they make the places where they settle distinctly different from other places, particularly in terms of racial diversity. Perhaps more than any other characteristic, race and ethnic origin differentiate communities, counties, states, and regions from one another. There are few, if any places that mirror the national portrait along this dimension.

Still Moving On

Another common use of the census is to track trends that grow population more in some places than in others. Census 2000 is the first to report that more than half of Americans live in suburbs, not central cities or rural areas. So the new "mental model" of Americans is now a suburban model, with a relatively small share of the population living in the small towns and rural areas that formed the national identity not so long ago.

Unlike recent censuses, Census 2000 did not report large regional population shifts. Americans are still mobile, but they are choosing a wider array of destinations than in the past. Partly, this reflects the changes discussed earlier; for example, couples moving to a retirement home choose different places from young adults moving to start a career. Partly, it reflects the recent evolution of the economy, in which new technologies allow some employers to move to underemployed work forces, rather than the other way around. It also reflects the way new modes of communications permit more people to live and do business where they like, even in sparsely populated attractive places.

Instead, concerns focus on those communities that are stagnating or losing population. As always, there are communities that movers find unattractive, or that businesses abandon. The people who are left behind have fewer opportunities, especially if they are less well equipped than those who moved on.

Census 2000 documents other effects of prior population movements. Young adults always constitute the bulk of interstate movers, and states and regions that lost large numbers of movers during the 1970s and the 1980s also lost their eventual children. Consequently, states in the South and West tend to have a much larger share of the nation's children now, compared with the Northeastern states that young adults left.

But Still Moving Up?

Sociologists will scrutinize Census 2000 for evidence that the American Dream is still intact and Americans are still socially and economically mobile. Education is clearly the key to full economic participation, and Census 2000 reported a record share of adult Americans with a college diploma: fully a quarter of all adults ages 25 and older. It also found that far more Americans have completed college than failed to finish high school. Indeed, the new "mental model" of Americans features a high-school graduate with some higher education, as the generations with large numbers of high school dropouts are now past working age. To be sure, the tables that follow locate pockets of Americans whose educational preparation is little better than the average American of a century ago.

Census 2000 also reported record gains in the work place for women and minority populations. Much of this is the result of vigorous efforts to end discrimination in employment, along with gains in educational attainment that have eroded and even erased the traditional advantage held by white men. Moreover, the increasing share of adult life spent outside parenting means that women now have few or no gender role responsibilities during a considerable portion of their working-age years. For all these reasons, the work force is more diverse than it has ever been.

The shift to larger numbers of older people means that Census 2000 found almost as many working-age women over 45 as under it. So the new "mental model" of the work place features large numbers of women whose children are grown and for whom "family-work" issues are no longer pressing. One consequence is an increased number of women business-owners.

The new "mental model" also includes a shift in Americans' occupations. Overall, Census 2000 reported a record low proportion of Americans in farming-related jobs—about 2 percent. Instead, it reported a record high share of Americans in white-collar jobs, with nearly 60 percent of the work force engaged in managerial, professional, and sales and office occupations.

The breadth of these gains puts a spotlight on what Census 2000 says about trends in wealth and poverty. In constant as well as current dollars, it reported an increase over 1990 and all previous censuses for household income, particularly for households that contain two or more well-educated working people. However, persistent evidence of poverty will encourage researchers to comb the detailed data that only a census provides for answers as to why some people were left behind in the best of all economic times. Census data will allow researchers to filter out the effects of demographic characteristics, such as the pronounced age difference between the majority and minority populations, or the economic disadvantage of having only one earner in a household. Then they will concentrate on the role of variables that policies can address, like education, economic development, or home ownership.

For aside from its constitutional mandate of apportioning political representation, the census serves to guide public policy. When policy makers have adopted the new mental model that Census 2000 outlines, they may well shift their attention to:

- the economic well-being of the elderly women the census counted who outlived their husbands and/or didn't accumulate retirement income of their own;
- the stress on the young parents the census found who are paying for their education and establishing a home with entry level salaries while they juggle work and family;
- the future of the "working poor" whom the census shows are following the rules without the human capital needed to profit from them; and
- the implications of the literally unpredictable choices Americans made among 63 different categories of race and Hispanic origin.

Meanwhile, look to the 2010 census for lessons about how a greater share of older to younger people changes the shape of households and families, work and other life stages, and the way communities are laid out and organized.

Where Undercounts and Overcounts Matter

After analyzing the data collected from a large sample survey, the Census Bureau determined that net of all errors, Census 2000 overcounted the household population by 0.5 percent, and is the most accurate census in history. Thus, all tabulations in this book are based on the official census results, unadjusted for undercounts and overcounts.

However, the Census Bureau views accuracy in "net" terms. That is, the 2000 census was the most accurate in history because in working so hard to count everyone, it double counted more people than usual. However, the people who are double counted are different from the people who are missed—and they live in different places. For these places, data users need to be aware of the potential for error.

Retirement communities and college towns are most likely to be overcounted, and people who use data for these places need to take that into account. College students will dutifully fill out a census form, while their parents record them on the form at home. (People are only supposed to be counted once—at the place where they live more than six months out of the year.) People with two homes may correctly fill out a form at the home they live at for most of the year, but the census taker at their other address has no way of knowing that. (The census is based on an address list of housing units, not a name list of residents.) If the neighbors report that the house is occupied, without stating that it's only occupied for a few months of the year, the census will count these residents twice.

Children with more than one home were both overcounted and undercounted, again in different places. The Census Bureau says it overcounted children of divorced parents, largely in the suburbs. It also undercounted children whose households are fractured in other ways (by desertion, never-married mothers, etc.), largely in central cities. The children who were overcounted tend to be from wealthier families, while the children who were undercounted tend to be from poorer families.

The impact of undercount continues to affect the black male population disproportionately— the net undercount of black males was the largest, about 5 percent. So data users need to be aware that counts of black men, particularly young men in central cities, are going to fall a bit short of reality.

Area Rankings

Area Rankings

Area Rankings

Area Rankings

Area Rankings

Area Rankings

Area Rankings

TABLE 1—States and the District of Columbia
Selected Rankings

Population, 2000			Percent Under 18 Years, 2000				Percent 18 to 24 Years, 2000			
Population Rank	State	[A-2. col 1] Population	Population Rank	Under 18 Years Rank	State	[A-2. col 4, 5 and 6] Percent Under 18 Years	Population Rank	18 to 24 Years Rank	State	[A-2. col 8] Percent 18 to 24 Years
X	United States	281 421 906	X	X	United States	25.6	X	X	United States	9.6
1	California	33 871 648	34	1	Utah	32.1	34	1	Utah	14.3
2	Texas	20 851 820	48	2	Alaska	30.4	50	2	District of Columbia	12.8
3	New York	18 976 457	39	3	Idaho	28.5	47	3	North Dakota	11.3
4	Florida	15 982 378	2	4	Texas	28.2	31	4	Mississippi	11.0
5	Illinois	12 419 293	36	5	New Mexico	27.9	39	5	Idaho	10.7
6	Pennsylvania	12 281 054	22	6	Louisiana	27.3	22	6	Louisiana	10.6
7	Ohio	11 353 140	1	7	California	27.2	2	7	Texas	10.5
8	Michigan	9 938 444	31	7	Mississippi	27.2	27	8	Oklahoma	10.4
9	New Jersey	8 414 350	46	9	South Dakota	26.9	32	9	Kansas	10.3
10	Georgia	8 186 453	20	10	Arizona	26.6	46	9	South Dakota	10.3
11	North Carolina	8 049 313	10	11	Georgia	26.5	10	11	Georgia	10.2
12	Virginia	7 078 515	32	11	Kansas	26.5	30	11	Iowa	10.2
13	Massachusetts	6 349 097	38	13	Nebraska	26.3	38	11	Nebraska	10.2
14	Indiana	6 080 485	21	14	Minnesota	26.2	14	14	Indiana	10.1
15	Washington	5 894 121	5	15	Illinois	26.1	43	14	Rhode Island	10.1
16	Tennessee	5 689 283	8	15	Michigan	26.1	26	14	South Carolina	10.1
17	Missouri	5 595 211	14	17	Indiana	25.9	51	14	Wyoming	10.1
18	Wisconsin	5 363 675	51	17	Wyoming	25.9	20	18	Arizona	10.0
19	Maryland	5 296 486	27	19	Oklahoma	25.8	11	18	North Carolina	10.0
20	Arizona	5 130 632	19	20	Maryland	25.6	1	20	California	9.9
21	Minnesota	4 919 479	15	20	Washington	25.6	24	20	Colorado	9.9
22	Louisiana	4 468 976	24	22	Colorado	25.5	25	20	Kentucky	9.9
23	Alabama	4 447 100	17	22	Missouri	25.5	23	23	Alabama	9.8
24	Colorado	4 301 261	44	22	Montana	25.5	33	23	Arkansas	9.8
25	Kentucky	4 041 769	35	22	Nevada	25.5	5	25	Illinois	9.7
26	South Carolina	4 012 012	18	22	Wisconsin	25.5	36	25	New Mexico	9.7
27	Oklahoma	3 450 654	33	27	Arkansas	25.4	18	25	Wisconsin	9.7
28	Oregon	3 421 399	7	27	Ohio	25.4	45	28	Delaware	9.6
29	Connecticut	3 405 565	23	29	Alabama	25.2	16	28	Tennessee	9.6
30	Iowa	2 926 324	26	29	South Carolina	25.2	12	28	Virginia	9.6
31	Mississippi	2 844 658	47	31	North Dakota	25.1	37	28	West Virginia	9.6
32	Kansas	2 688 418	30	32	Iowa	25.0	42	32	Hawaii	9.5
33	Arkansas	2 673 400	41	32	New Hampshire	25.0	21	32	Minnesota	9.5
34	Utah	2 233 169	45	34	Delaware	24.8	17	32	Missouri	9.5
35	Nevada	1 998 257	29	35	Connecticut	24.7	44	32	Montana	9.5
36	New Mexico	1 819 046	9	35	New Jersey	24.7	28	32	Oregon	9.5
37	West Virginia	1 808 344	28	35	Oregon	24.7	8	37	Michigan	9.4
38	Nebraska	1 711 263	25	38	Kentucky	24.6	49	37	Vermont	9.4
39	Idaho	1 293 953	3	38	New York	24.6	15	37	Washington	9.4
40	Maine	1 274 923	16	38	Tennessee	24.6	3	40	New York	9.3
41	New Hampshire	1 235 786	12	41	Virginia	24.5	7	40	Ohio	9.3
42	Hawaii	1 211 537	11	42	North Carolina	24.4	48	42	Alaska	9.1
43	Rhode Island	1 048 319	42	43	Hawaii	24.3	13	42	Massachusetts	9.1
44	Montana	902 195	49	44	Vermont	24.2	35	44	Nevada	8.9
45	Delaware	783 600	6	45	Pennsylvania	23.8	6	44	Pennsylvania	8.9
46	South Dakota	754 844	40	46	Maine	23.6	19	46	Maryland	8.4
47	North Dakota	642 200	13	46	Massachusetts	23.6	4	47	Florida	8.3
48	Alaska	626 932	43	46	Rhode Island	23.6	41	47	New Hampshire	8.3
49	Vermont	608 827	4	49	Florida	22.7	40	49	Maine	8.2
50	District of Columbia	572 059	37	50	West Virginia	22.2	9	50	New Jersey	8.0
51	Wyoming	493 782	50	51	District of Columbia	20.0	29	51	Connecticut	7.9

TABLE 1—States and the District of Columbia
Selected Rankings

Percent 25 to 44 Years, 2000				Percent 45 to 64 Years, 2000				Percent 65 Years and Over, 2000			
Popu-lation Rank	25 to 44 Years Rank	State	[A-2. col 9] Percent 25 to 44 Years	Popu-lation Rank	45 to 64 Years Rank	State	[A-2. col 10] Percent 45 to 64 Years	Popu-lation Rank	65 Years and Over Rank	State	[A-2. col 11] Percent 65 Years and Over
X	X	United States	30.4	X	X	United States	21.9	X	X	United States	12.4
50	1	District of Columbia	33.2	37	1	West Virginia	25.2	4	1	Florida	17.6
24	2	Colorado	32.8	40	2	Maine	24.8	6	2	Pennsylvania	15.6
48	3	Alaska	32.7	49	3	Vermont	24.7	37	3	West Virginia	15.3
10	4	Georgia	32.6	44	4	Montana	24.4	30	4	Iowa	14.9
1	5	California	31.9	51	5	Wyoming	24.1	47	5	North Dakota	14.7
12	6	Virginia	31.8	41	6	New Hampshire	23.8	43	6	Rhode Island	14.6
35	7	Nevada	31.7	28	7	Oregon	23.7	40	7	Maine	14.4
19	8	Maryland	31.6	16	8	Tennessee	23.2	46	8	South Dakota	14.3
13	9	Massachusetts	31.4	29	9	Connecticut	23.1	33	9	Arkansas	14.0
9	9	New Jersey	31.4	19	9	Maryland	23.1	29	10	Connecticut	13.8
2	9	Texas	31.4	25	11	Kentucky	23.0	38	11	Nebraska	13.6
11	12	North Carolina	31.2	6	11	Pennsylvania	23.0	13	12	Massachusetts	13.5
15	13	Washington	31.0	12	11	Virginia	23.0	17	12	Missouri	13.5
41	14	New Hampshire	30.9	42	14	Hawaii	22.9	44	14	Montana	13.4
3	14	New York	30.9	35	14	Nevada	22.9	42	15	Hawaii	13.3
5	16	Illinois	30.7	26	14	South Carolina	22.9	7	15	Ohio	13.3
29	17	Connecticut	30.5	23	17	Alabama	22.8	32	17	Kansas	13.2
21	17	Minnesota	30.5	9	18	New Jersey	22.7	9	17	New Jersey	13.2
45	19	Delaware	30.3	15	18	Washington	22.7	27	17	Oklahoma	13.2
16	19	Tennessee	30.3	33	20	Arkansas	22.6	18	20	Wisconsin	13.1
42	21	Hawaii	30.1	4	20	Florida	22.6	23	21	Alabama	13.0
25	22	Kentucky	30.0	7	20	Ohio	22.6	20	21	Arizona	13.0
8	23	Michigan	29.9	45	23	Delaware	22.4	45	21	Delaware	13.0
20	24	Arizona	29.7	8	23	Michigan	22.4	3	24	New York	12.9
43	24	Rhode Island	29.7	11	23	North Carolina	22.4	28	25	Oregon	12.8
26	24	South Carolina	29.7	48	26	Alaska	22.3	49	26	Vermont	12.7
18	27	Wisconsin	29.6	13	26	Massachusetts	22.3	25	27	Kentucky	12.5
14	28	Indiana	29.5	17	26	Missouri	22.3	14	28	Indiana	12.4
7	29	Ohio	29.4	3	26	New York	22.3	16	28	Tennessee	12.4
28	30	Oregon	29.3	30	30	Iowa	22.2	50	30	District of Columbia	12.3
17	31	Missouri	29.2	27	30	Oklahoma	22.2	8	30	Michigan	12.3
23	32	Alabama	29.1	18	30	Wisconsin	22.2	5	32	Illinois	12.1
22	33	Louisiana	29.0	24	33	Colorado	22.1	21	32	Minnesota	12.1
40	33	Maine	29.0	14	33	Indiana	22.1	31	32	Mississippi	12.1
49	33	Vermont	29.0	36	33	New Mexico	22.1	26	32	South Carolina	12.1
4	36	Florida	28.8	43	36	Rhode Island	22.0	41	36	New Hampshire	12.0
32	37	Kansas	28.7	50	37	District of Columbia	21.8	11	36	North Carolina	12.0
36	38	New Mexico	28.6	21	38	Minnesota	21.7	36	38	New Mexico	11.7
6	38	Pennsylvania	28.6	47	39	North Dakota	21.6	22	39	Louisiana	11.6
31	40	Mississippi	28.5	22	40	Louisiana	21.5	51	39	Wyoming	11.6
38	40	Nebraska	28.5	39	41	Idaho	21.4	39	41	Idaho	11.3
27	42	Oklahoma	28.4	5	41	Illinois	21.4	19	41	Maryland	11.3
39	43	Idaho	28.2	38	41	Nebraska	21.4	12	43	Virginia	11.2
34	43	Utah	28.2	32	44	Kansas	21.3	15	43	Washington	11.2
51	43	Wyoming	28.2	31	45	Mississippi	21.2	35	45	Nevada	10.9
33	46	Arkansas	28.1	10	46	Georgia	21.1	1	46	California	10.6
30	47	Iowa	27.7	46	46	South Dakota	21.1	2	47	Texas	9.9
37	47	West Virginia	27.7	20	48	Arizona	20.8	24	48	Colorado	9.7
46	49	South Dakota	27.4	1	49	California	20.4	10	49	Georgia	9.6
44	50	Montana	27.3	2	50	Texas	20.1	34	50	Utah	8.5
47	50	North Dakota	27.3	34	51	Utah	16.9	48	51	Alaska	5.6

16

TABLE 1—States and the District of Columbia
Selected Rankings

Percent Non-Hispanic White, 2000				Percent Black or African American, 2000				Percent American Indian and Alaska Native, 2000			
Population Rank	Non-Hispanic White Rank	State	[A-2. col 43] Percent Non-Hispanic White	Population Rank	Black or African American Rank	State	[A-2. col 57] Percent Black or African American	Population Rank	American Indian and Alaska Native Rank	State	[A-2. col 71] Percent American Indian and Alaska Native
X	X	United States	69.1	X	X	United States	12.2	X	X	United States	0.9
40	1	Maine	96.5	50	1	District of Columbia	60.0	48	1	Alaska	15.5
49	2	Vermont	96.1	31	2	Mississippi	36.3	36	2	New Mexico	9.5
41	3	New Hampshire	95.1	22	3	Louisiana	32.3	46	3	South Dakota	8.2
37	4	West Virginia	94.5	26	4	South Carolina	29.5	27	4	Oklahoma	7.7
30	5	Iowa	92.7	10	5	Georgia	28.6	44	5	Montana	6.1
47	6	North Dakota	91.8	19	6	Maryland	27.7	20	6	Arizona	4.9
44	7	Montana	89.5	23	7	Alabama	25.9	47	6	North Dakota	4.9
25	8	Kentucky	89.3	11	8	North Carolina	21.5	51	8	Wyoming	2.3
51	9	Wyoming	88.8	12	9	Virginia	19.6	15	9	Washington	1.5
21	10	Minnesota	88.2	45	10	Delaware	19.0	39	10	Idaho	1.4
46	11	South Dakota	88.1	16	11	Tennessee	16.3	35	11	Nevada	1.3
39	12	Idaho	88.0	3	12	New York	15.7	11	11	North Carolina	1.3
38	13	Nebraska	87.4	33	13	Arkansas	15.6	28	11	Oregon	1.3
18	13	Wisconsin	87.4	5	14	Illinois	15.0	34	11	Utah	1.3
14	15	Indiana	85.9	4	15	Florida	14.5	21	15	Minnesota	1.1
34	16	Utah	85.3	8	16	Michigan	14.1	24	16	Colorado	1.0
6	17	Pennsylvania	84.1	9	17	New Jersey	13.4	1	17	California	0.9
7	18	Ohio	84.0	2	18	Texas	11.4	32	17	Kansas	0.9
17	19	Missouri	83.8	7	19	Ohio	11.3	38	17	Nebraska	0.9
28	20	Oregon	83.5	17	20	Missouri	11.1	18	17	Wisconsin	0.9
32	21	Kansas	83.1	6	21	Pennsylvania	9.9	33	21	Arkansas	0.7
13	22	Massachusetts	81.9	29	22	Connecticut	9.0	22	22	Louisiana	0.6
43	22	Rhode Island	81.9	14	23	Indiana	8.3	40	22	Maine	0.6
16	24	Tennessee	79.2	27	24	Oklahoma	7.5	8	22	Michigan	0.6
15	25	Washington	78.9	25	25	Kentucky	7.3	23	25	Alabama	0.5
33	26	Arkansas	78.6	1	26	California	6.0	17	25	Missouri	0.5
8	27	Michigan	78.5	35	26	Nevada	6.6	43	25	Rhode Island	0.5
29	28	Connecticut	77.4	32	28	Kansas	5.6	2	25	Texas	0.5
24	29	Colorado	74.4	18	28	Wisconsin	5.6	45	29	Delaware	0.4
27	30	Oklahoma	74.1	13	30	Massachusetts	5.3	50	29	District of Columbia	0.4
45	31	Delaware	72.5	43	31	Rhode Island	4.3	31	29	Mississippi	0.4
23	32	Alabama	70.3	38	32	Nebraska	3.9	3	29	New York	0.4
11	33	North Carolina	70.2	24	33	Colorado	3.7	26	29	South Carolina	0.4
12	34	Virginia	70.1	48	34	Alaska	3.5	49	29	Vermont	0.4
5	35	Illinois	67.8	21	35	Minnesota	3.4	29	35	Connecticut	0.3
48	36	Alaska	67.6	15	36	Washington	3.1	4	35	Florida	0.3
26	37	South Carolina	66.2	37	36	West Virginia	3.1	10	35	Georgia	0.3
9	38	New Jersey	66.0	20	38	Arizona	3.0	42	35	Hawaii	0.3
4	39	Florida	65.4	30	39	Iowa	2.0	14	35	Indiana	0.3
35	40	Nevada	65.1	36	40	New Mexico	1.8	30	35	Iowa	0.3
20	41	Arizona	63.8	42	41	Hawaii	1.7	19	35	Maryland	0.3
10	42	Georgia	62.7	28	42	Oregon	1.6	16	35	Tennessee	0.3
22	43	Louisiana	62.5	41	43	New Hampshire	0.7	12	35	Virginia	0.3
19	44	Maryland	62.1	34	43	Utah	0.7	5	44	Illinois	0.2
3	45	New York	62.0	47	45	North Dakota	0.6	25	44	Kentucky	0.2
31	46	Mississippi	60.8	46	45	South Dakota	0.6	13	44	Massachusetts	0.2
2	47	Texas	52.4	51	45	Wyoming	0.6	41	44	New Hampshire	0.2
1	48	California	46.6	40	48	Maine	0.5	9	44	New Jersey	0.2
36	49	New Mexico	44.7	49	48	Vermont	0.5	7	44	Ohio	0.2
50	50	District of Columbia	27.7	39	50	Idaho	0.4	6	44	Pennsylvania	0.2
42	51	Hawaii	22.8	44	51	Montana	0.3	37	44	West Virginia	0.2

TABLE 1—States and the District of Columbia
Selected Rankings

Percent Asian, Hawaiian, and Pacific Islander, 2000				Percent Hispanic or Latino[1], 2000				Percent Two or More Races, 2000			
Population Rank	Asian, Hawaiian, and Pacific Islander Rank	State	[A-2. col 85] Percent Asian, Hawaiian, and Pacific Islander	Population Rank	Hispanic or Latino Rank	State	[A-2. col 100] Percent Hispanic or Latino	Population Rank	Two or More Races Rank	State	[A-2. col 128] Percent Two or More Races
X	X	United States	3.7	X	X	United States	12.5	X	X	United States	2.6
42	1	Hawaii	50.9	36	1	New Mexico	42.1	42	1	Hawaii	21.8
1	2	California	11.2	1	2	California	32.4	48	2	Alaska	5.6
9	3	New Jersey	5.8	2	3	Texas	32.0	1	3	California	5.0
15	3	Washington	5.8	20	4	Arizona	25.2	27	4	Oklahoma	4.9
3	5	New York	5.5	35	5	Nevada	19.7	35	5	Nevada	4.1
35	6	Nevada	4.9	24	6	Colorado	17.1	36	6	New Mexico	3.9
48	7	Alaska	4.6	4	7	Florida	16.8	15	6	Washington	3.9
19	8	Maryland	4.0	3	8	New York	15.1	28	8	Oregon	3.3
13	9	Massachusetts	3.8	9	9	New Jersey	13.3	3	9	New York	3.2
12	10	Virginia	3.7	5	10	Illinois	12.3	20	10	Arizona	3.1
5	11	Illinois	3.4	29	11	Connecticut	9.4	24	10	Colorado	3.1
28	12	Oregon	3.1	34	12	Utah	9.0	43	12	Rhode Island	2.8
21	13	Minnesota	2.9	43	13	Rhode Island	8.6	9	13	New Jersey	2.7
2	14	Texas	2.7	28	14	Oregon	8.0	50	14	District of Columbia	2.6
50	15	District of Columbia	2.6	50	15	District of Columbia	7.9	4	14	Florida	2.6
29	16	Connecticut	2.5	39	15	Idaho	7.9	2	16	Texas	2.5
24	17	Colorado	2.3	15	17	Washington	7.5	32	17	Kansas	2.4
43	17	Rhode Island	2.3	42	18	Hawaii	7.2	13	17	Massachusetts	2.4
34	17	Utah	2.3	32	19	Kansas	6.9	29	19	Connecticut	2.3
45	20	Delaware	2.1	13	20	Massachusetts	6.7	34	19	Utah	2.3
10	20	Georgia	2.1	51	21	Wyoming	6.4	12	21	Virginia	2.2
20	22	Arizona	1.9	38	22	Nebraska	5.5	39	22	Idaho	2.1
8	23	Michigan	1.8	10	23	Georgia	5.3	19	22	Maryland	2.1
6	23	Pennsylvania	1.8	27	24	Oklahoma	5.2	8	22	Michigan	2.1
4	25	Florida	1.7	45	25	Delaware	4.8	5	25	Illinois	2.0
32	25	Kansas	1.7	11	26	North Carolina	4.6	44	26	Montana	1.9
18	27	Wisconsin	1.6	12	26	Virginia	4.6	51	26	Wyoming	1.9
11	28	North Carolina	1.4	19	28	Maryland	4.3	45	28	Delaware	1.8
27	28	Oklahoma	1.4	48	29	Alaska	4.1	21	28	Minnesota	1.8
22	30	Louisiana	1.3	18	30	Wisconsin	3.6	17	30	Missouri	1.6
38	30	Nebraska	1.3	14	31	Indiana	3.5	10	31	Georgia	1.5
41	30	New Hampshire	1.3	33	32	Arkansas	3.2	38	31	Nebraska	1.5
30	33	Iowa	1.2	8	32	Michigan	3.2	7	31	Ohio	1.5
7	33	Ohio	1.2	6	32	Pennsylvania	3.2	33	34	Arkansas	1.4
17	35	Missouri	1.1	21	35	Minnesota	2.9	14	34	Indiana	1.4
36	35	New Mexico	1.1	30	36	Iowa	2.8	11	34	North Carolina	1.4
39	37	Idaho	1.0	22	37	Louisiana	2.4	46	34	South Dakota	1.4
14	37	Indiana	1.0	26	38	South Carolina	2.3	6	38	Pennsylvania	1.3
16	37	Tennessee	1.0	17	39	Missouri	2.1	49	38	Vermont	1.3
26	40	South Carolina	0.9	16	39	Tennessee	2.1	18	38	Wisconsin	1.3
33	41	Arkansas	0.8	44	41	Montana	2.0	25	41	Kentucky	1.2
49	41	Vermont	0.8	7	42	Ohio	1.9	22	41	Louisiana	1.2
23	43	Alabama	0.7	23	43	Alabama	1.6	41	41	New Hampshire	1.2
25	43	Kentucky	0.7	41	43	New Hampshire	1.6	47	41	North Dakota	1.2
40	43	Maine	0.7	25	45	Kentucky	1.4	16	41	Tennessee	1.2
46	43	South Dakota	0.7	46	45	South Dakota	1.4	23	46	Alabama	1.1
31	47	Mississippi	0.6	31	47	Mississippi	1.3	30	46	Iowa	1.1
51	47	Wyoming	0.6	47	48	North Dakota	1.2	40	46	Maine	1.1
44	49	Montana	0.5	49	49	Vermont	0.9	26	49	South Carolina	1.0
47	49	North Dakota	0.5	40	50	Maine	0.7	37	49	West Virginia	1.0
37	49	West Virginia	0.5	37	51	West Virginia	0.7	31	51	Mississippi	0.8

[1] Hispanic or Latino persons may be of any race.

TABLE 1—States and the District of Columbia
Selected Rankings

Population Rank	Family Households Rank	State	[A-2. col 144] Percent Family Households	Population Rank	Married-Couple Families With Own Children Under 18 Years Rank	State	[A-2. col 146] Percent Married-Couple Families With Own Children Under 18 Years	Population Rank	Female Householders With Own Children Under 18 Years Rank	State	[A-2. col 148] Percent Female Householders With Own Children Under 18 Years
		Percent Family Households, 2000				**Percent Married-Couple Families with Own Children Under 18 Years, 2000**				**Percent Female Family Householders with Own Children Under 18 Years, 2000**	
X	X	United States	68.5	X	X	United States	24.3	X	X	United States	7.0
34	1	Utah	76.9	34	1	Utah	36.1	50	1	District of Columbia	10.1
39	2	Idaho	71.9	48	2	Alaska	29.3	31	1	Mississippi	10.1
31	3	Mississippi	71.8	39	3	Idaho	28.9	22	3	Louisiana	9.7
42	4	Hawaii	71.6	2	4	Texas	28.0	10	4	Georgia	8.3
2	5	Texas	71.4	1	5	California	26.9	26	4	South Carolina	8.3
10	6	Georgia	70.7	9	6	New Jersey	26.2	36	6	New Mexico	8.1
9	6	New Jersey	70.7	41	7	New Hampshire	26.1	23	7	Alabama	8.0
33	8	Arkansas	70.6	21	8	Minnesota	26.0	3	7	New York	8.0
23	9	Alabama	70.4	32	9	Kansas	25.9	19	9	Maryland	7.9
26	10	South Carolina	70.3	38	10	Nebraska	25.5	48	10	Alaska	7.6
22	11	Louisiana	70.2	24	11	Colorado	25.4	45	11	Delaware	7.5
25	12	Kentucky	69.8	10	12	Georgia	25.2	43	11	Rhode Island	7.5
16	13	Tennessee	69.7	5	13	Illinois	25.1	2	13	Texas	7.4
1	14	California	69.4	46	13	South Dakota	25.1	8	14	Michigan	7.3
11	14	North Carolina	69.4	51	13	Wyoming	25.1	16	14	Tennessee	7.3
48	16	Alaska	69.3	42	16	Hawaii	24.8	33	16	Arkansas	7.1
36	17	New Mexico	69.2	47	17	North Dakota	24.7	11	16	North Carolina	7.1
19	18	Maryland	69.1	15	17	Washington	24.7	7	16	Ohio	7.1
27	18	Oklahoma	69.1	14	19	Indiana	24.6	1	19	California	7.0
45	20	Delaware	68.9	30	19	Iowa	24.6	17	19	Missouri	7.0
14	20	Indiana	68.9	12	19	Virginia	24.6	25	21	Kentucky	6.9
12	20	Virginia	68.9	18	22	Wisconsin	24.4	29	22	Connecticut	6.8
37	23	West Virginia	68.8	29	23	Connecticut	24.3	27	22	Oklahoma	6.8
41	24	New Hampshire	68.6	25	24	Kentucky	24.2	4	24	Florida	6.7
8	25	Michigan	68.4	19	25	Maryland	24.1	5	24	Illinois	6.7
20	26	Arizona	68.2	36	25	New Mexico	24.1	12	24	Virginia	6.7
29	27	Connecticut	68.0	27	27	Oklahoma	24.0	14	27	Indiana	6.6
5	27	Illinois	68.0	49	28	Vermont	23.9	35	27	Nevada	6.6
32	27	Kansas	68.0	8	29	Michigan	23.8	20	29	Arizona	6.5
51	30	Wyoming	67.8	20	30	Arizona	23.5	13	29	Massachusetts	6.5
17	31	Missouri	67.7	33	31	Arkansas	23.4	15	31	Washington	6.3
7	32	Ohio	67.6	44	31	Montana	23.4	9	32	New Jersey	6.2
6	33	Pennsylvania	67.5	22	33	Louisiana	23.3	6	33	Pennsylvania	6.1
30	34	Iowa	67.3	17	33	Missouri	23.3	40	34	Maine	6.0
46	34	South Dakota	67.3	11	33	North Carolina	23.3	28	34	Oregon	6.0
38	36	Nebraska	66.9	23	36	Alabama	23.2	49	34	Vermont	6.0
18	36	Wisconsin	66.9	13	36	Massachusetts	23.2	24	37	Colorado	5.9
4	38	Florida	66.8	28	36	Oregon	23.2	46	37	South Dakota	5.9
35	38	Nevada	66.8	31	39	Mississippi	23.1	18	37	Wisconsin	5.9
21	40	Minnesota	66.6	7	39	Ohio	23.1	32	40	Kansas	5.8
44	41	Montana	66.5	16	39	Tennessee	23.1	44	40	Montana	5.8
15	42	Washington	66.4	35	42	Nevada	23.0	38	40	Nebraska	5.8
28	43	Oregon	66.3	45	43	Delaware	22.8	51	40	Wyoming	5.8
3	44	New York	66.2	26	44	South Carolina	22.6	21	44	Minnesota	5.7
40	45	Maine	66.1	40	45	Maine	22.5	42	45	Hawaii	5.6
49	46	Vermont	65.9	6	45	Pennsylvania	22.5	39	45	Idaho	5.6
24	47	Colorado	65.8	3	47	New York	22.4	41	47	New Hampshire	5.5
43	48	Rhode Island	65.3	37	48	West Virginia	21.9	34	47	Utah	5.5
13	49	Massachusetts	64.9	43	49	Rhode Island	21.8	37	47	West Virginia	5.5
47	49	North Dakota	64.9	4	50	Florida	19.9	30	50	Iowa	5.3
50	51	District of Columbia	46.6	50	51	District of Columbia	8.7	47	51	North Dakota	5.1

TABLE 1—States and the District of Columbia
Selected Rankings

Percent Nonfamily Households, 2000				Percent Women Living Alone, 2000				Percent Men Living Alone, 2000			
Population Rank	Nonfamily Households Rank	State	[A-2. col 151] Percent Nonfamily Households	Population Rank	Women Living Alone Rank	State	[A-2. col 153] Percent Women Living Alone	Population Rank	Men Living Alone Rank	State	[A-2. col 154] Percent Men Living Alone
X	X	United States	31.5	X	X	United States	14.8	X	X	United States	11.0
50	1	District of Columbia	53.4	50	1	District of Columbia	24.5	50	1	District of Columbia	19.2
13	2	Massachusetts	35.1	43	2	Rhode Island	17.0	48	2	Alaska	13.4
47	2	North Dakota	35.1	13	3	Massachusetts	16.8	47	3	North Dakota	13.1
43	4	Rhode Island	34.7	3	4	New York	16.7	35	4	Nevada	13.0
24	5	Colorado	34.2	6	5	Pennsylvania	16.5	51	5	Wyoming	12.6
49	6	Vermont	34.1	37	6	West Virginia	16.3	44	6	Montana	12.5
40	7	Maine	33.9	47	7	North Dakota	16.2	24	7	Colorado	12.1
3	8	New York	33.8	30	8	Iowa	16.0	46	7	South Dakota	12.1
28	9	Oregon	33.7	40	8	Maine	16.0	38	9	Nebraska	11.8
15	10	Washington	33.6	7	10	Ohio	15.9	15	9	Washington	11.8
44	11	Montana	33.5	29	11	Connecticut	15.8	21	11	Minnesota	11.7
21	12	Minnesota	33.4	17	11	Missouri	15.8	36	11	New Mexico	11.7
4	13	Florida	33.2	38	13	Nebraska	15.7	32	13	Kansas	11.5
35	13	Nevada	33.2	4	14	Florida	15.5	43	13	Rhode Island	11.5
38	15	Nebraska	33.1	5	14	Illinois	15.5	18	13	Wisconsin	11.5
18	15	Wisconsin	33.1	32	16	Kansas	15.4	8	16	Michigan	11.4
30	17	Iowa	32.7	46	16	South Dakota	15.4	17	16	Missouri	11.4
46	17	South Dakota	32.7	23	18	Alabama	15.3	3	16	New York	11.4
6	19	Pennsylvania	32.5	27	18	Oklahoma	15.3	7	16	Ohio	11.4
7	20	Ohio	32.4	25	20	Kentucky	15.2	5	20	Illinois	11.3
17	21	Missouri	32.3	18	20	Wisconsin	15.2	27	20	Oklahoma	11.3
51	22	Wyoming	32.2	21	22	Minnesota	15.1	13	22	Massachusetts	11.2
29	23	Connecticut	32.0	49	22	Vermont	15.1	28	22	Oregon	11.2
5	23	Illinois	32.0	16	24	Tennessee	15.0	20	24	Arizona	11.1
32	23	Kansas	32.0	33	25	Arkansas	14.9	4	24	Florida	11.1
20	26	Arizona	31.8	14	25	Indiana	14.9	30	24	Iowa	11.1
8	27	Michigan	31.6	19	25	Maryland	14.9	6	24	Pennsylvania	11.1
41	28	New Hampshire	31.4	44	25	Montana	14.9	49	24	Vermont	11.1
37	29	West Virginia	31.2	8	29	Michigan	14.8	14	29	Indiana	11.0
45	30	Delaware	31.1	9	29	New Jersey	14.8	22	29	Louisiana	11.0
14	30	Indiana	31.1	11	29	North Carolina	14.8	40	29	Maine	11.0
12	30	Virginia	31.1	28	29	Oregon	14.8	41	32	New Hampshire	10.9
19	33	Maryland	30.9	45	33	Delaware	14.7	23	33	Alabama	10.8
27	33	Oklahoma	30.9	12	34	Virginia	14.5	25	33	Kentucky	10.8
36	35	New Mexico	30.8	26	35	South Carolina	14.4	16	33	Tennessee	10.8
48	36	Alaska	30.7	22	36	Louisiana	14.3	42	36	Hawaii	10.7
1	37	California	30.6	15	36	Washington	14.3	37	36	West Virginia	10.7
11	37	North Carolina	30.6	24	38	Colorado	14.1	33	38	Arkansas	10.6
16	39	Tennessee	30.3	31	38	Mississippi	14.1	29	38	Connecticut	10.6
25	40	Kentucky	30.2	20	40	Arizona	13.7	11	38	North Carolina	10.6
22	41	Louisiana	29.8	10	40	Georgia	13.7	26	38	South Carolina	10.6
26	42	South Carolina	29.7	36	40	New Mexico	13.7	2	38	Texas	10.6
23	43	Alabama	29.6	51	40	Wyoming	13.7	12	43	Virginia	10.5
33	44	Arkansas	29.4	41	44	New Hampshire	13.5	1	44	California	10.4
10	45	Georgia	29.3	1	45	California	13.1	31	44	Mississippi	10.4
9	45	New Jersey	29.3	2	46	Texas	13.0	45	46	Delaware	10.2
2	47	Texas	28.6	39	47	Idaho	12.3	19	47	Maryland	10.1
42	48	Hawaii	28.4	35	48	Nevada	11.9	39	48	Idaho	10.0
31	49	Mississippi	28.2	42	49	Hawaii	11.1	10	49	Georgia	9.9
39	50	Idaho	28.1	48	50	Alaska	10.0	9	50	New Jersey	9.7
34	51	Utah	23.1	34	50	Utah	10.0	34	51	Utah	7.7

TABLE 1—States and the District of Columbia
Selected Rankings

Percent Cohabitating Couples Households, 2000				Percent Foreign-Born Population, 2000				Percent of Population Over 25 Years with High School Diploma or Less, 2000			
Population Rank	Cohabitating Couples Households Rank	State	[A-2. col 155] Percent Cohabitating Couples Households	Population Rank	Foreign-born Population Rank	State	[A-2. col 297] Percent Foreign-born Population	Population Rank	High School Diploma or Less Rank	State	[B-2. col 2] Percent High School Diploma or Less
X	X	United States	5.0	X	X	United States	11.1	X	X	United States	48.2
49	1	Vermont	7.3	1	1	California	26.2	37	1	West Virginia	64.2
48	2	Alaska	7.2	3	2	New York	20.4	25	2	Kentucky	59.4
35	3	Nevada	7.0	42	3	Hawaii	17.5	33	3	Arkansas	58.8
40	4	Maine	6.9	9	3	New Jersey	17.5	22	4	Louisiana	57.6
41	5	New Hampshire	6.6	4	5	Florida	16.7	31	5	Mississippi	56.5
36	6	New Mexico	6.2	35	6	Nevada	15.8	6	6	Pennsylvania	56.2
20	7	Arizona	6.1	2	7	Texas	13.9	16	7	Tennessee	55.7
28	8	Oregon	6.0	50	8	District of Columbia	12.9	23	8	Alabama	55.1
15	8	Washington	6.0	20	9	Arizona	12.8	14	8	Indiana	55.1
45	10	Delaware	5.9	5	10	Illinois	12.3	26	10	South Carolina	53.6
1	11	California	5.8	13	11	Massachusetts	12.2	7	11	Ohio	53.1
50	11	District of Columbia	5.8	43	12	Rhode Island	11.4	17	12	Missouri	51.4
4	13	Florida	5.6	29	13	Connecticut	10.9	27	13	Oklahoma	50.9
42	13	Hawaii	5.6	15	14	Washington	10.4	40	14	Maine	50.8
43	13	Rhode Island	5.6	19	15	Maryland	9.8	11	15	North Carolina	50.3
24	16	Colorado	5.4	24	16	Colorado	8.6	10	16	Georgia	50.1
18	16	Wisconsin	5.4	28	17	Oregon	8.5	30	17	Iowa	50.0
19	18	Maryland	5.3	36	18	New Mexico	8.2	43	18	Rhode Island	49.8
13	19	Massachusetts	5.2	12	19	Virginia	8.1	18	19	Wisconsin	49.5
51	19	Wyoming	5.2	10	20	Georgia	7.1	2	20	Texas	49.2
29	21	Connecticut	5.1	34	20	Utah	7.1	4	21	Florida	48.9
14	21	Indiana	5.1	48	22	Alaska	5.9	45	22	Delaware	48.8
8	21	Michigan	5.1	45	23	Delaware	5.7	35	23	Nevada	48.7
21	21	Minnesota	5.1	8	24	Michigan	5.3	3	23	New York	48.7
3	21	New York	5.1	21	24	Minnesota	5.3	46	25	South Dakota	48.3
44	26	Montana	4.0	11	24	North Carolina	5.3	8	26	Michigan	47.9
7	26	Ohio	4.9	39	27	Idaho	5.0	36	27	New Mexico	47.7
22	28	Louisiana	4.8	32	27	Kansas	5.0	9	28	New Jersey	47.3
17	28	Missouri	4.8	38	29	Nebraska	4.4	5	29	Illinois	46.0
30	30	Iowa	4.7	41	29	New Hampshire	4.4	49	30	Vermont	45.9
9	30	New Jersey	4.7	6	31	Pennsylvania	4.1	38	31	Nebraska	44.7
6	30	Pennsylvania	4.7	27	32	Oklahoma	3.8	12	32	Connecticut	44.5
46	30	South Dakota	4.7	49	32	Vermont	3.8	32	32	Virginia	44.5
5	34	Illinois	4.6	18	34	Wisconsin	3.6	44	34	Montana	44.1
10	35	Georgia	4.5	14	35	Indiana	3.1	47	35	North Dakota	44.0
39	35	Idaho	4.5	30	35	Iowa	3.1	42	36	Hawaii	43.9
12	35	Virginia	4.5	7	37	Ohio	3.0	39	37	Idaho	43.8
11	38	North Carolina	4.4	40	38	Maine	2.9	32	37	Kansas	43.8
26	38	South Carolina	4.4	26	38	South Carolina	2.9	20	39	Arizona	43.3
47	40	North Dakota	4.3	33	40	Arkansas	2.8	1	39	California	43.3
37	40	West Virginia	4.3	16	40	Tennessee	2.8	51	41	Wyoming	43.1
25	42	Kentucky	4.2	17	42	Missouri	2.7	19	42	Maryland	42.9
38	42	Nebraska	4.2	22	43	Louisiana	2.6	50	43	District of Columbia	42.8
2	42	Texas	4.2	51	44	Wyoming	2.3	41	44	New Hampshire	42.7
31	45	Mississippi	4.1	23	45	Alabama	2.0	13	45	Massachusetts	42.5
16	46	Tennessee	3.9	25	45	Kentucky	2.0	28	46	Oregon	41.1
32	47	Kansas	3.8	47	47	North Dakota	1.9	21	47	Minnesota	40.9
27	48	Oklahoma	3.7	44	48	Montana	1.8	48	48	Alaska	39.5
33	49	Arkansas	3.6	46	48	South Dakota	1.8	15	49	Washington	37.8
34	50	Utah	3.3	31	50	Mississippi	1.4	34	50	Utah	36.9
23	51	Alabama	3.1	37	51	West Virginia	1.1	24	51	Colorado	36.3

TABLE 1—States and the District of Columbia
Selected Rankings

Percent of Population Over 25 Years with Bachelor's Degree or More, 2000				Percent of Population 16 to 19 Years Not Enrolled in School and Not High School Graduate, 2000				Labor Force Participation Rate, 2000			
Popu-lation Rank	Bachelor's Dregree or More Rank	State	[B-2. col 18] Percent Bachelor's Degree or More	Popu-lation Rank	At-Risk Youth Rank	State	[B-2. col 62] Percent At-Risk Youth	Popu-lation Rank	Labor Force Partic-ipation Rate Rank	State	[B-2. col 123] Percent Labor Force Participation Rate
X	X	United States	24.4	X	X	United States	9.8	X	X	United States	63.9
50	1	District of Columbia	39.1	35	1	Nevada	16.0	48	1	Alaska	71.3
13	2	Massachusetts	33.2	20	2	Arizona	14.8	21	2	Minnesota	71.2
24	3	Colorado	32.7	10	3	Georgia	13.5	41	3	New Hampshire	70.5
29	4	Connecticut	31.4	11	4	North Carolina	12.5	24	4	Colorado	70.1
19	4	Maryland	31.4	2	4	Texas	12.5	38	5	Nebraska	69.7
9	6	New Jersey	29.8	31	6	Mississippi	12.2	49	6	Vermont	69.3
12	7	Virginia	29.5	24	7	Colorado	12.1	18	7	Wisconsin	69.1
49	8	Vermont	29.4	36	7	New Mexico	12.1	34	8	Utah	69.0
41	9	New Hampshire	28.7	23	9	Alabama	12.0	46	9	South Dakota	68.4
15	10	Washington	27.7	4	10	Florida	11.9	30	10	Iowa	68.2
21	11	Minnesota	27.4	22	11	Louisiana	11.7	19	11	Maryland	67.8
3	11	New York	27.4	25	12	Kentucky	11.5	32	12	Kansas	67.5
1	13	California	26.6	26	13	South Carolina	11.1	47	12	North Dakota	67.5
42	14	Hawaii	26.2	28	14	Oregon	10.4	51	12	Wyoming	67.5
5	15	Illinois	26.1	45	15	Delaware	10.3	12	15	Virginia	66.8
34	15	Utah	26.1	17	16	Missouri	10.2	29	16	Connecticut	66.6
32	17	Kansas	25.8	1	17	California	10.1	14	16	Indiana	66.6
43	18	Rhode Island	25.6	50	17	District of Columbia	10.1	15	18	Washington	66.5
28	19	Oregon	25.1	5	19	Illinois	9.9	13	19	Massachusetts	66.2
45	20	Delaware	25.0	27	19	Oklahoma	9.9	10	20	Georgia	66.1
48	21	Alaska	24.7	14	21	Indiana	9.8	39	20	Idaho	66.1
44	22	Montana	24.4	16	21	Tennessee	9.8	45	22	Delaware	65.7
10	23	Georgia	24.3	33	23	Arkansas	9.5	11	22	North Carolina	65.7
38	24	Nebraska	23.7	37	24	West Virginia	9.0	5	24	Illinois	65.4
20	25	Arizona	23.5	48	25	Alaska	8.7	44	24	Montana	65.4
36	25	New Mexico	23.5	8	25	Michigan	8.7	40	26	Maine	65.3
2	27	Texas	23.2	3	25	New York	8.7	17	27	Missouri	65.2
40	28	Maine	22.9	34	25	Utah	8.7	35	27	Nevada	65.2
11	29	North Carolina	22.5	15	25	Washington	8.7	28	27	Oregon	65.2
6	30	Pennsylvania	22.4	19	30	Maryland	8.4	7	30	Ohio	64.8
18	30	Wisconsin	22.4	7	31	Ohio	8.3	8	31	Michigan	64.6
4	32	Florida	22.3	39	32	Idaho	8.2	43	31	Rhode Island	64.6
47	33	North Dakota	22.0	43	32	Rhode Island	8.2	42	33	Hawaii	64.5
51	34	Wyoming	21.9	32	34	Kansas	8.0	9	34	New Jersey	64.2
8	35	Michigan	21.8	44	35	Montana	7.9	50	35	District of Columbia	63.6
39	36	Idaho	21.7	46	35	South Dakota	7.9	2	35	Texas	63.6
17	37	Missouri	21.6	12	37	Virginia	7.7	16	37	Tennessee	63.5
46	38	South Dakota	21.5	51	38	Wyoming	7.5	26	38	South Carolina	63.4
30	39	Iowa	21.2	29	39	Connecticut	7.4	1	39	California	62.4
7	40	Ohio	21.1	41	40	New Hampshire	7.3	27	40	Oklahoma	62.1
26	41	South Carolina	20.4	9	41	New Jersey	7.2	6	41	Pennsylvania	61.9
27	42	Oklahoma	20.3	6	42	Pennsylvania	7.1	20	42	Arizona	61.1
16	43	Tennessee	19.6	38	43	Nebraska	7.0	3	42	New York	61.1
14	44	Indiana	19.4	13	44	Massachusetts	6.6	36	44	New Mexico	61.0
23	45	Alabama	19.0	18	45	Wisconsin	6.4	25	45	Kentucky	60.9
22	46	Louisiana	18.7	40	46	Maine	6.2	33	46	Arkansas	60.6
35	47	Nevada	18.2	21	47	Minnesota	5.9	23	47	Alabama	59.7
25	48	Kentucky	17.1	49	47	Vermont	5.9	22	48	Louisiana	59.4
31	49	Mississippi	16.9	42	49	Hawaii	5.8	31	48	Mississippi	59.4
33	50	Arkansas	16.7	30	49	Iowa	5.8	4	50	Florida	58.6
37	51	West Virginia	14.8	47	51	North Dakota	4.8	37	51	West Virginia	54.5

TABLE 1—States and the District of Columbia
Selected Rankings

Unemployment Rate, 2000				Percent Veterans Over 18 Years, 2000				Median Family Household Income, 2000			
Population Rank	Unemployment Rate Rank	State	[B-2. col 124] Unemployment Rate	Population Rank	Veterans Rank	State	[B-2. col 194] Percent Veterans	Population Rank	Median Family Household Income Rank	State	[B-2. col 206] Median Family Household Income (Dollars)
X	X	United States	5.8	X	X	United States	12.6	X	X	United States	50 046
50	1	District of Columbia	10.8	48	1	Alaska	16.4	29	1	Connecticut	65 521
48	2	Alaska	9.0	44	2	Montana	16.1	9	2	New Jersey	65 370
31	3	Mississippi	7.4	35	3	Nevada	16.0	19	3	Maryland	61 876
22	4	Louisiana	7.3	40	4	Maine	15.9	13	4	Massachusetts	61 664
36	4	New Mexico	7.3	51	5	Wyoming	15.8	48	5	Alaska	59 036
37	4	West Virginia	7.3	15	6	Washington	15.3	41	6	New Hampshire	57 575
3	7	New York	7.1	4	7	Florida	15.2	42	7	Hawaii	56 961
1	8	California	7.0	28	8	Oregon	15.1	21	8	Minnesota	56 874
28	9	Oregon	6.5	41	9	New Hampshire	15.0	24	9	Colorado	55 883
42	10	Hawaii	6.3	20	10	Arizona	14.9	5	10	Illinois	55 545
44	10	Montana	6.3	39	11	Idaho	14.8	45	11	Delaware	55 257
23	12	Alabama	6.2	27	12	Oklahoma	14.7	12	12	Virginia	54 169
35	12	Nevada	6.2	12	12	Virginia	14.7	15	13	Washington	53 760
15	12	Washington	6.2	36	14	New Mexico	14.5	8	14	Michigan	53 457
33	15	Arkansas	6.1	46	15	South Dakota	14.4	1	15	California	53 025
2	15	Texas	6.1	45	16	Delaware	14.3	18	16	Wisconsin	52 911
5	17	Illinois	6.0	37	16	West Virginia	14.3	43	17	Rhode Island	52 781
26	18	South Carolina	5.9	17	18	Missouri	14.2	3	18	New York	51 691
39	19	Idaho	5.8	33	19	Arkansas	14.1	34	19	Utah	51 022
8	19	Michigan	5.8	26	20	South Carolina	14.0	35	20	Nevada	50 849
9	19	New Jersey	5.8	24	21	Colorado	13.9	14	21	Indiana	50 261
25	22	Kentucky	5.7	38	22	Nebraska	13.7	7	22	Ohio	50 037
6	22	Pennsylvania	5.7	6	22	Pennsylvania	13.7	32	23	Kansas	49 624
20	24	Arizona	5.6	49	24	Vermont	13.6	10	24	Georgia	49 280
4	24	Florida	5.6	23	25	Alabama	13.5	6	25	Pennsylvania	49 184
43	24	Rhode Island	5.6	32	25	Kansas	13.5	28	26	Oregon	48 680
10	27	Georgia	5.5	7	25	Ohio	13.5	49	27	Vermont	48 625
16	27	Tennessee	5.5	30	28	Iowa	13.3	38	28	Nebraska	48 032
29	29	Connecticut	5.3	19	28	Maryland	13.3	30	29	Iowa	48 005
17	29	Missouri	5.3	42	30	Hawaii	13.1	20	30	Arizona	46 723
11	29	North Carolina	5.3	14	30	Indiana	13.1	11	31	North Carolina	46 335
27	29	Oklahoma	5.3	16	30	Tennessee	13.1	50	32	District of Columbia	46 283
51	29	Wyoming	5.3	11	33	North Carolina	13.0	17	33	Missouri	46 044
45	34	Delaware	5.2	18	34	Wisconsin	12.9	2	34	Texas	45 861
7	35	Ohio	5.0	10	35	Georgia	12.8	51	35	Wyoming	45 685
34	35	Utah	5.0	21	35	Minnesota	12.8	4	36	Florida	45 625
14	37	Indiana	4.9	43	35	Rhode Island	12.8	40	37	Maine	45 179
40	38	Maine	4.8	47	38	North Dakota	12.7	26	38	South Carolina	44 227
19	39	Maryland	4.7	25	39	Kentucky	12.5	47	39	North Dakota	43 654
18	39	Wisconsin	4.7	8	40	Michigan	12.4	16	40	Tennessee	43 517
13	41	Massachusetts	4.6	29	41	Connecticut	12.1	39	41	Idaho	43 490
47	41	North Dakota	4.6	22	41	Louisiana	12.1	46	42	South Dakota	43 237
46	43	South Dakota	4.4	31	43	Mississippi	12.0	23	43	Alabama	41 657
24	44	Colorado	4.3	2	44	Texas	11.7	25	44	Kentucky	40 939
30	45	Iowa	4.2	13	45	Massachusetts	11.5	27	45	Oklahoma	40 709
32	45	Kansas	4.2	5	46	Illinois	10.9	44	46	Montana	40 487
49	45	Vermont	4.2	9	47	New Jersey	10.6	22	47	Louisiana	39 774
12	45	Virginia	4.2	34	47	Utah	10.6	36	48	New Mexico	39 425
21	49	Minnesota	4.1	1	49	California	10.4	33	49	Arkansas	38 663
41	50	New Hampshire	3.8	50	50	District of Columbia	9.7	31	50	Mississippi	37 406
38	51	Nebraska	3.5	3	51	New York	9.5	37	51	West Virginia	36 484

TABLE 1—States and the District of Columbia
Selected Rankings

	Median Nonfamily Household Income, 2000				Percent of all Households with Income Over $100,000, 2000				Percent of all Households with Income Below Poverty, 2000		
Population Rank	Median Non-family House-hold Income Rank	State	[B-2. col 213] Median Nonfamily Household Income (Dollars)	Population Rank	With Income Over $100,000 Rank	State	[B-2. col 235] Percent With Income Over $100,000	Population Rank	With Income Below Poverty Rank	State	[B-2. col 242] Percent With Income Below Poverty
X	X	United States	25 705	X	X	United States	12.3	X	X	United States	11.8
50	1	District of Columbia	34 130	9	1	New Jersey	21.3	31	1	Mississippi	19.7
48	2	Alaska	33 796	29	2	Connecticut	20.2	22	2	Louisiana	19.1
19	3	Maryland	32 654	19	3	Maryland	18.1	37	3	West Virginia	18.0
1	4	California	32 024	13	4	Massachusetts	17.7	50	4	District of Columbia	17.1
9	5	New Jersey	31 298	1	5	California	17.3	36	5	New Mexico	16.8
29	6	Connecticut	30 873	42	6	Hawaii	16.6	23	6	Alabama	16.7
24	7	Colorado	30 728	50	7	District of Columbia	16.4	25	7	Kentucky	16.2
42	8	Hawaii	30 272	48	8	Alaska	16.1	33	8	Arkansas	15.8
35	9	Nevada	30 088	3	9	New York	15.3	27	9	Oklahoma	14.6
45	10	Delaware	29 891	12	10	Virginia	15.1	44	10	Montana	14.1
13	11	Massachusetts	29 774	5	11	Illinois	14.4	26	10	South Carolina	14.1
12	12	Virginia	29 642	24	12	Colorado	14.2	16	12	Tennessee	14.0
15	13	Washington	29 394	45	13	Delaware	14.0	2	12	Texas	14.0
41	14	New Hampshire	28 945	41	14	New Hampshire	13.8	3	14	New York	13.9
5	15	Illinois	28 368	8	15	Michigan	12.7	10	15	Georgia	12.6
21	16	Minnesota	27 913	21	16	Minnesota	12.6	47	16	North Dakota	12.5
3	17	New York	27 073	15	16	Washington	12.6	46	16	South Dakota	12.5
20	18	Arizona	26 828	10	18	Georgia	12.3	11	18	North Carolina	12.4
10	19	Georgia	26 509	43	19	Rhode Island	11.5	43	18	Rhode Island	12.4
34	20	Utah	26 405	2	19	Texas	11.5	20	20	Arizona	11.8
8	21	Michigan	26 194	35	21	Nevada	11.3	1	20	California	11.8
18	22	Wisconsin	25 837	34	22	Utah	11.2	17	20	Missouri	11.8
28	23	Oregon	25 761	20	23	Arizona	10.8	4	23	Florida	11.7
2	24	Texas	25 623	4	24	Florida	10.4	40	24	Maine	11.5
4	25	Florida	24 799	6	25	Pennsylvania	10.3	39	25	Idaho	11.2
49	26	Vermont	24 557	28	26	Oregon	10.0	51	25	Wyoming	11.2
7	27	Ohio	24 005	7	27	Ohio	9.8	6	27	Pennsylvania	11.0
14	28	Indiana	23 689	11	28	North Carolina	9.4	28	28	Oregon	10.8
43	29	Rhode Island	23 561	18	28	Wisconsin	9.4	7	29	Ohio	10.7
11	30	North Carolina	23 240	32	30	Kansas	9.3	42	30	Hawaii	10.5
32	31	Kansas	23 002	14	31	Indiana	9.2	5	31	Illinois	10.1
38	32	Nebraska	22 985	17	32	Missouri	8.8	32	31	Kansas	10.1
30	33	Iowa	22 454	49	33	Vermont	8.7	8	31	Michigan	10.1
17	34	Missouri	22 293	16	34	Tennessee	8.3	13	34	Massachusetts	9.8
6	35	Pennsylvania	22 205	38	35	Nebraska	8.1	15	34	Washington	9.8
39	36	Idaho	21 861	26	35	South Carolina	8.1	38	36	Nebraska	9.7
36	37	New Mexico	21 791	23	37	Alabama	7.6	49	36	Vermont	9.7
40	38	Maine	21 715	36	37	New Mexico	7.6	12	38	Virginia	9.6
51	39	Wyoming	21 689	22	39	Louisiana	7.4	14	39	Indiana	9.5
26	40	South Carolina	21 508	39	40	Idaho	7.3	35	40	Nevada	9.4
16	41	Tennessee	21 032	30	40	Iowa	7.3	30	41	Iowa	9.3
46	42	South Dakota	20 672	25	42	Kentucky	7.2	34	42	Utah	8.9
47	43	North Dakota	20 296	40	43	Maine	7.1	24	43	Colorado	8.8
44	44	Montana	19 484	51	44	Wyoming	6.7	45	43	Delaware	8.8
27	45	Oklahoma	19 331	27	45	Oklahoma	6.6	18	45	Wisconsin	8.4
25	46	Kentucky	18 972	33	46	Arkansas	6.0	48	46	Alaska	8.3
22	47	Louisiana	18 393	31	46	Mississippi	6.0	19	46	Maryland	8.3
33	48	Arkansas	17 999	46	48	South Dakota	5.9	9	46	New Jersey	8.3
23	49	Alabama	17 866	47	49	North Dakota	5.7	29	49	Connecticut	8.0
31	50	Mississippi	16 616	44	50	Montana	5.6	21	50	Minnesota	7.9
37	51	West Virginia	16 007	37	51	West Virginia	5.0	41	51	New Hampshire	6.9

TABLE 1—States and the District of Columbia
Selected Rankings

Percent of Population that Resides in the Same House in 1995 and 2000

Population Rank	Same Residence Rank	State	[C-2. col 1] Percent Same Residence
X	X	United States	54.1
6	1	Pennsylvania	63.5
37	2	West Virginia	63.3
3	3	New York	61.8
9	4	New Jersey	59.8
40	5	Maine	59.6
49	6	Vermont	59.1
22	7	Louisiana	59.0
13	8	Massachusetts	58.5
31	8	Mississippi	58.5
29	10	Connecticut	58.2
43	11	Rhode Island	58.1
7	12	Ohio	57.5
23	13	Alabama	57.4
8	14	Michigan	57.3
21	15	Minnesota	57.0
30	16	Iowa	56.9
42	17	Hawaii	56.8
5	17	Illinois	56.8
47	17	North Dakota	56.8
18	20	Wisconsin	56.5
45	21	Delaware	56.0
25	22	Kentucky	55.9
26	22	South Carolina	55.9
19	24	Maryland	55.7
46	24	South Dakota	55.7
41	26	New Hampshire	55.4
14	27	Indiana	55.0
38	28	Nebraska	54.7
36	29	New Mexico	54.4
16	30	Tennessee	53.9
17	31	Missouri	53.6
44	31	Montana	53.6
33	33	Arkansas	53.3
11	34	North Carolina	53.0
32	35	Kansas	52.4
12	30	Virginia	52.2
27	37	Oklahoma	51.3
51	37	Wyoming	51.3
1	39	California	50.2
50	40	District of Columbia	49.9
39	41	Idaho	49.6
2	41	Texas	49.6
34	43	Utah	49.3
10	44	Georgia	49.2
4	45	Florida	48.9
15	46	Washington	48.6
28	47	Oregon	46.8
48	48	Alaska	46.2
20	49	Arizona	44.3
24	50	Colorado	44.1
35	51	Nevada	37.4

Percent Owner-Occupied Housing Units, 2000

Population Rank	Owner-Occupied Rank	State	[C-2. col 57] Percent Owner-Occupied
X	X	United States	66.2
37	1	West Virginia	75.2
21	2	Minnesota	74.5
8	3	Michigan	73.8
23	4	Alabama	72.5
39	5	Idaho	72.4
31	5	Mississippi	72.4
45	7	Delaware	72.3
30	7	Iowa	72.3
26	9	South Carolina	72.2
40	10	Maine	71.6
34	11	Utah	71.5
14	12	Indiana	71.4
6	13	Pennsylvania	71.3
25	14	Kentucky	70.7
49	15	Vermont	70.6
17	16	Missouri	70.3
4	17	Florida	70.1
36	18	New Mexico	70.0
51	18	Wyoming	70.0
16	20	Tennessee	69.9
41	21	New Hampshire	69.7
33	22	Arkansas	69.4
11	22	North Carolina	69.4
32	24	Kansas	69.3
44	25	Montana	69.1
7	25	Ohio	69.1
27	27	Oklahoma	68.4
18	27	Wisconsin	68.4
46	29	South Dakota	68.2
12	30	Virginia	68.1
20	31	Arizona	68.0
22	32	Louisiana	67.9
19	33	Maryland	67.7
10	34	Georgia	67.5
38	35	Nebraska	67.4
24	36	Colorado	67.3
5	36	Illinois	67.3
29	38	Connecticut	66.8
47	39	North Dakota	66.6
9	40	New Jersey	65.6
15	41	Washington	64.6
28	42	Oregon	64.2
2	43	Texas	63.8
48	44	Alaska	62.5
13	45	Massachusetts	61.7
35	46	Nevada	60.9
43	47	Rhode Island	60.0
1	48	California	56.9
42	49	Hawaii	56.5
3	50	New York	53.0
50	51	District of Columbia	40.8

Median Housing Value (Owner Estimated), 2000

Population Rank	Median Housing Value Rank	State	[C-2. col 116] Median Housing Value (Dollars)
X	X	United States	111 800
42	1	Hawaii	249 300
1	2	California	198 900
13	3	Massachusetts	182 800
9	4	New Jersey	167 900
29	5	Connecticut	160 600
24	6	Colorado	160 100
15	7	Washington	158 800
50	8	District of Columbia	153 500
3	9	New York	147 600
28	10	Oregon	145 800
19	11	Maryland	143 300
34	12	Utah	142 600
48	13	Alaska	137 400
35	14	Nevada	132 500
43	15	Rhode Island	130 500
5	16	Illinois	127 800
41	17	New Hampshire	127 500
45	18	Delaware	122 000
12	19	Virginia	118 800
21	20	Minnesota	118 100
49	21	Vermont	111 200
8	22	Michigan	110 300
18	23	Wisconsin	109 900
20	24	Arizona	109 400
39	25	Idaho	102 100
10	26	Georgia	100 600
7	27	Ohio	100 500
44	28	Montana	95 800
11	28	North Carolina	95 800
6	30	Pennsylvania	94 800
36	31	New Mexico	94 600
40	32	Maine	94 300
4	33	Florida	93 200
14	34	Indiana	92 500
51	35	Wyoming	91 500
16	36	Tennessee	88 300
17	37	Missouri	86 900
38	37	Nebraska	86 900
26	39	South Carolina	83 100
30	40	Iowa	82 100
32	41	Kansas	81 000
25	42	Kentucky	79 600
2	43	Texas	77 800
22	44	Louisiana	77 500
23	45	Alabama	76 700
46	46	South Dakota	74 300
47	47	North Dakota	68 300
27	48	Oklahoma	67 700
33	49	Arkansas	67 400
37	50	West Virginia	66 000
31	51	Mississippi	64 700

TABLE 1—States and the District of Columbia
Selected Rankings

Median Gross Rent, 2000				Percent Drove Alone to Work, 2000				Mean Travel Time to Work for all Workers, 2000			
Population Rank	Median Gross Rent Rank	State	[C-2. col 119] Median Gross Rent (Dollars)	Population Rank	Drove Alone Rank	State	[C-2. col 136] Percent Drove Alone	Population Rank	Mean Travel Time Rank	State	[C-2. col 143] Mean Travel Time (Minutes)
X	X	United States	602	X	X	United States	75.7	X	X	United States	25.5
42	1	Hawaii	779	8	1	Michigan	83.2	3	1	New York	31.7
9	2	New Jersey	751	23	2	Alabama	83.0	19	2	Maryland	31.2
1	3	California	747	7	3	Ohio	82.8	9	3	New Jersey	30.0
48	4	Alaska	720	14	4	Indiana	81.8	50	4	District of Columbia	29.7
35	5	Nevada	699	41	4	New Hampshire	81.8	5	5	Illinois	28.0
19	6	Maryland	689	16	6	Tennessee	81.7	1	6	California	27.7
13	7	Massachusetts	684	32	7	Kansas	81.5	10	6	Georgia	27.7
29	8	Connecticut	681	17	8	Missouri	80.5	13	8	Massachusetts	27.0
3	9	New York	672	37	9	West Virginia	80.3	12	8	Virginia	27.0
24	10	Colorado	671	25	10	Kentucky	80.2	4	10	Florida	26.2
15	11	Washington	663	43	11	Rhode Island	80.1	37	10	West Virginia	26.2
12	12	Virginia	650	29	12	Connecticut	80.0	42	12	Hawaii	26.1
41	13	New Hampshire	646	38	12	Nebraska	80.0	22	13	Louisiana	25.7
4	14	Florida	641	27	12	Oklahoma	80.0	15	14	Washington	25.5
45	15	Delaware	639	33	15	Arkansas	79.9	2	15	Texas	25.4
28	16	Oregon	620	18	16	Wisconsin	79.5	41	16	New Hampshire	25.3
20	17	Arizona	619	31	17	Mississippi	79.4	6	17	Pennsylvania	25.2
50	18	District of Columbia	618	11	17	North Carolina	79.4	20	18	Arizona	24.9
10	19	Georgia	613	26	17	South Carolina	79.4	23	19	Alabama	24.8
5	20	Illinois	605	45	20	Delaware	79.2	31	20	Mississippi	24.6
34	21	Utah	597	4	21	Florida	78.8	16	21	Tennessee	24.5
2	22	Texas	574	30	22	Iowa	78.6	29	22	Connecticut	24.4
21	23	Minnesota	566	40	22	Maine	78.6	24	23	Colorado	24.3
43	24	Rhode Island	553	22	24	Louisiana	78.1	26	23	South Carolina	24.3
49	24	Vermont	553	47	25	North Dakota	77.7	8	25	Michigan	24.1
11	26	North Carolina	548	2	25	Texas	77.7	45	26	Delaware	24.0
8	27	Michigan	546	21	27	Minnesota	77.6	11	26	North Carolina	24.0
18	28	Wisconsin	540	10	28	Georgia	77.5	17	28	Missouri	23.8
6	29	Pennsylvania	531	46	29	South Dakota	77.3	25	29	Kentucky	23.5
14	30	Indiana	521	12	30	Virginia	77.1	35	30	Nevada	23.3
39	31	Idaho	515	39	31	Idaho	77.0	7	31	Ohio	22.9
7	31	Ohio	515	6	32	Pennsylvania	76.5	40	32	Maine	22.7
26	33	South Carolina	510	36	33	New Mexico	75.8	14	33	Indiana	22.6
16	34	Tennessee	505	34	34	Utah	75.5	43	34	Rhode Island	22.5
36	35	New Mexico	503	51	35	Wyoming	75.4	28	35	Oregon	22.2
32	36	Kansas	498	49	36	Vermont	75.2	33	36	Arkansas	21.9
40	37	Maine	497	24	37	Colorado	75.1	21	36	Minnesota	21.9
38	38	Nebraska	491	35	38	Nevada	74.5	36	36	New Mexico	21.9
17	39	Missouri	484	20	39	Arizona	74.1	27	39	Oklahoma	21.7
30	40	Iowa	470	44	40	Montana	73.9	49	40	Vermont	21.6
22	41	Louisiana	466	13	41	Massachusetts	73.8	34	41	Utah	21.3
27	42	Oklahoma	456	19	42	Maryland	73.7	18	42	Wisconsin	20.8
33	43	Arkansas	453	15	43	Washington	73.3	39	43	Idaho	20.0
23	44	Alabama	447	5	44	Illinois	73.2	48	44	Alaska	19.6
44	44	Montana	447	28	44	Oregon	73.2	32	45	Kansas	19.0
25	46	Kentucky	445	9	46	New Jersey	73.0	30	46	Iowa	18.5
31	47	Mississippi	439	1	47	California	71.8	38	47	Nebraska	18.0
51	48	Wyoming	437	48	48	Alaska	66.5	51	48	Wyoming	17.8
46	49	South Dakota	426	42	49	Hawaii	63.9	44	49	Montana	17.7
47	50	North Dakota	412	3	50	New York	56.3	46	50	South Dakota	16.6
37	51	West Virginia	401	50	51	District of Columbia	38.4	47	51	North Dakota	15.8

TABLE 2—75 Largest Counties by 2000 Population
Selected Rankings

Population, 2000			Percent Under 18 Years, 2000				Percent 18 to 24 Years, 2000			
Population Rank	County	[A-3. col 1] Population	Population Rank	Under 18 Years Rank	County	[A-3. col 2 and 3] Percent Under 18 Years	Population Rank	18 to 24 Years Rank	County	[A-3. col 4] Percent 18 to 24 Years
1	Los Angeles County, CA	9 519 338	13	1	San Bernardino County, CA	32.2	74	1	Suffolk County, MA	15.2
2	Cook County, IL	5 376 741	58	2	Fresno County, CA	32.0	56	2	Travis County, TX	14.6
3	Harris County, TX	3 400 578	75	3	El Paso County, TX	31.9	43	3	Salt Lake County, UT	13.0
4	Maricopa County, AZ	3 072 149	43	4	Salt Lake County, UT	30.3	33	4	Franklin County, OH	11.7
5	Orange County, CA	2 846 289	16	5	Riverside County, CA	30.2	6	5	San Diego County, CA	11.4
6	San Diego County, CA	2 813 833	27	6	Bronx County, NY	29.7	18	6	Philadelphia County, PA	11.1
7	Kings County, NY	2 465 326	3	7	Harris County, TX	28.9	58	7	Fresno County, CA	11.0
8	Miami-Dade County, FL	2 253 362	24	8	Bexar County, TX	28.4	55	8	Fulton County, GA	10.9
9	Queens County, NY	2 229 379	64	8	Ventura County, CA	28.4	45	9	Orange County, FL	10.8
10	Dallas County, TX	2 218 899	44	10	Shelby County, TN	28.2	24	10	Bexar County, TX	10.7
11	Wayne County, MI	2 061 162	20	11	Tarrant County, TX	28.0	27	10	Bronx County, NY	10.7
12	King County, WA	1 737 034	11	11	Wayne County, MI	28.0	53	10	Pima County, AZ	10.7
13	San Bernardino County, CA	1 709 434	1	13	Los Angeles County, CA	27.9	10	13	Dallas County, TX	10.6
14	Santa Clara County, CA	1 682 585	10	14	Dallas County, TX	27.8	75	14	El Paso County, TX	10.5
15	Broward County, FL	1 623 018	29	15	Sacramento County, CA	27.5	39	15	Milwaukee County, WI	10.4
16	Riverside County, CA	1 545 387	71	16	Pierce County, WA	27.1	57	15	Prince George's County, MD	10.4
17	New York County, NY	1 537 195	5	17	Orange County, CA	27.0	17	17	Harris County, TX	10.3
18	Philadelphia County, PA	1 517 550	4	18	Maricopa County, AZ	26.9	7	17	Kings County, NY	10.3
19	Middlesex County, MA	1 465 396	57	19	Prince George's County, MD	26.8	1	17	Los Angeles County, CA	10.3
20	Tarrant County, TX	1 446 219	42	20	Du Page County, IL	26.7	4	20	Maricopa County, AZ	10.2
21	Alameda County, CA	1 443 741	7	20	Kings County, NY	26.7	13	20	San Bernardino County, CA	10.2
22	Suffolk County, NY	1 419 369	38	22	Contra Costa County, CA	26.5	48	22	Honolulu County, HI	10.1
23	Cuyahoga County, OH	1 393 978	61	23	Duval County, FL	26.3	17	22	New York County, NY	10.1
24	Bexar County, TX	1 392 931	39	23	Milwaukee County, WI	26.3	50	24	Marion County, IN	10.0
25	Clark County, NV	1 375 765	59	25	Essex County, NJ	26.0	2	25	Cook County, IL	9.8
26	Nassau County, NY	1 334 544	22	25	Suffolk County, NY	26.0	20	25	Tarrant County, TX	9.8
27	Bronx County, NY	1 332 650	2	27	Cook County, IL	25.9	32	27	Hennepin County, MN	9.7
28	Allegheny County, PA	1 281 666	52	28	Hamilton County, OH	25.8	71	27	Pierce County, WA	9.7
29	Sacramento County, CA	1 223 499	50	29	Marion County, IN	25.7	61	29	Duval County, FL	9.6
30	Oakland County, MI	1 194 156	68	30	Monroe County, NY	25.6	52	29	Hamilton County, OH	9.6
31	Palm Beach County, FL	1 131 184	6	30	San Diego County, CA	25.6	72	29	Mecklenburg County, NC	9.6
32	Hennepin County, MN	1 116 200	65	30	Worcester County, MA	25.6	66	29	Middlesex County, NJ	9.6
33	Franklin County, OH	1 068 978	25	30	Clark County, NV	25.5	44	29	Shelby County, TN	9.6
34	St. Louis County, MO	1 016 315	47	33	Fairfield County, CT	25.5	21	34	Alameda County, CA	9.5
35	Hillsborough County, FL	998 948	36	35	Fairfax County, VA	25.3	68	34	Monroe County, NY	9.5
36	Fairfax County, VA	969 749	49	35	Montgomery County, MD	25.3	9	34	Queens County, NY	9.5
37	Erie County, NY	950 265	35	37	Hillsborough County, FL	25.2	29	37	Sacramento County, CA	9.4
38	Contra Costa County, CA	948 816	45	37	Orange County, FL	25.2	59	38	Essex County, NJ	9.3
39	Milwaukee County, WI	940 164	18	37	Philadelphia County, PA	25.2	35	38	Hillsborough County, FL	9.3
40	Westchester County, NY	923 459	34	37	St. Louis County, MO	25.2	5	38	Orange County, CA	9.3
41	Pinellas County, FL	921 482	69	41	Essex County, MA	25.1	12	41	King County, WA	9.2
42	Du Page County, IL	904 161	33	41	Franklin County, OH	25.1	16	41	Riverside County, CA	9.2
43	Salt Lake County, UT	898 387	30	41	Oakland County, MI	25.1	14	41	Santa Clara County, CA	9.2
44	Shelby County, TN	897 472	23	44	Cuyahoga County, OH	24.9	25	44	Clark County, NV	9.1
45	Orange County, FL	896 344	72	44	Mecklenburg County, NC	24.9	8	44	Miami-Dade County, FL	9.1
46	Bergen County, NJ	884 118	40	44	Westchester County, NY	24.9	64	46	Ventura County, CA	9.0
47	Fairfield County, CT	882 567	8	47	Miami-Dade County, FL	24.7	19	47	Middlesex County, MA	8.9
48	Honolulu County, HI	876 156	14	47	Santa Clara County, CA	24.7	62	47	San Francisco County, CA	8.9
49	Montgomery County, MD	873 341	26	49	Nassau County, NY	24.6	73	49	Jefferson County, KY	8.8
50	Marion County, IN	860 454	21	50	Alameda County, CA	24.5	37	50	Erie County, NY	8.7
51	Hartford County, CT	857 183	51	50	Hartford County, CT	24.5	11	50	Wayne County, MI	8.7
52	Hamilton County, OH	845 303	53	50	Pima County, AZ	24.5	28	52	Allegheny County, PA	8.6
53	Pima County, AZ	843 746	55	53	Fulton County, GA	24.4	63	52	Baltimore County, MD	8.6
54	New Haven County, CT	824 008	54	53	New Haven County, CT	24.4	54	52	New Haven County, CT	8.6
55	Fulton County, GA	816 006	73	55	Jefferson County, KY	24.3	65	55	Worcester County, MA	8.4
56	Travis County, TX	812 280	37	56	Erie County, NY	24.2	42	56	Du Page County, IL	8.2
57	Prince George's County, MD	801 515	60	57	Macomb County, MI	24.1	34	56	St. Louis County, MO	8.2
58	Fresno County, CA	799 407	67	57	Montgomery County, PA	24.1	60	58	Macomb County, MI	8.0
59	Essex County, NJ	793 633	32	59	Hennepin County, MN	23.9	23	59	Cuyahoga County, OH	7.9
60	Macomb County, MI	788 149	48	60	Honolulu County, HI	23.7	51	60	Hartford County, CT	7.8
61	Duval County, FL	778 879	56	60	Travis County, TX	23.7	70	60	San Mateo County, CA	7.8
62	San Francisco County, CA	776 733	63	62	Baltimore County, MD	23.6	38	62	Contra Costa County, CA	7.6
63	Baltimore County, MD	754 292	66	62	Middlesex County, NJ	23.6	69	62	Essex County, MA	7.6
64	Ventura County, CA	753 197	15	64	Broward County, FL	23.5	22	62	Suffolk County, NY	7.6
65	Worcester County, MA	750 963	46	65	Bergen County, NJ	22.9	36	65	Fairfax County, VA	7.3
66	Middlesex County, NJ	750 162	9	66	Queens County, NY	22.8	26	65	Nassau County, NY	7.3
67	Montgomery County, PA	750 097	70	66	San Mateo County, CA	22.8	67	67	Montgomery County, PA	7.2
68	Monroe County, NY	735 343	12	68	King County, WA	22.4	30	67	Oakland County, MI	7.2
69	Essex County, MA	723 419	19	68	Middlesex County, MA	22.4	15	69	Broward County, FL	7.1
70	San Mateo County, CA	707 161	28	70	Allegheny County, PA	21.9	40	70	Westchester County, NY	7.0
71	Pierce County, WA	700 820	31	71	Palm Beach County, FL	21.2	47	71	Fairfield County, CT	6.9
72	Mecklenburg County, NC	695 454	74	72	Suffolk County, MA	20.1	49	72	Montgomery County, MD	6.7
73	Jefferson County, KY	693 604	41	73	Pinellas County, FL	19.2	46	73	Bergen County, NJ	6.6
74	Suffolk County, MA	689 807	17	74	New York County, NY	16.6	31	74	Palm Beach County, FL	6.5
75	El Paso County, TX	679 622	62	75	San Francisco County, CA	14.4	41	75	Pinellas County, FL	6.3

TABLE 2—75 Largest Counties by 2000 Population
Selected Rankings

Percent 25 to 44 Years, 2000				Percent 45 to 64 Years, 2000				Percent 65 Years and Over, 2000			
Population Rank	25 to 44 Years Rank	County	[A-3. col 5] Percent 25 to 44 Years	Population Rank	45 to 64 Years Rank	County	[A-3. col 6] Percent 45 to 64 Years	Population Rank	65 Years and Over Rank	County	[A-3. col 7] Percent 65 Years and Over
62	1	San Francisco County, CA	41.0	36	1	Fairfax County, VA	25.3	31	1	Palm Beach County, FL	23.2
17	2	New York County, NY	38.6	46	2	Bergen County, NJ	24.4	41	2	Pinellas County, FL	22.6
56	3	Travis County, TX	36.9	41	2	Pinellas County, FL	24.4	28	3	Allegheny County, PA	17.8
72	4	Mecklenburg County, NC	36.5	49	4	Montgomery County, MD	24.1	15	4	Broward County, FL	16.0
14	5	Santa Clara County, CA	35.8	26	5	Nassau County, NY	24.0	37	4	Erie County, NY	16.0
55	6	Fulton County, GA	35.7	30	6	Oakland County, MI	23.9	23	6	Cuyahoga County, OH	15.6
74	7	Suffolk County, MA	35.5	38	7	Contra Costa County, CA	23.8	46	7	Bergen County, NJ	15.2
12	8	King County, WA	35.0	34	8	St. Louis County, MO	23.4	26	8	Nassau County, NY	15.0
10	9	Dallas County, TX	34.8	40	8	Westchester County, NY	23.4	67	9	Montgomery County, PA	14.9
21	10	Alameda County, CA	34.2	28	10	Allegheny County, PA	23.3	63	10	Baltimore County, MD	14.6
36	10	Fairfax County, VA	34.2	63	10	Baltimore County, MD	23.3	51	10	Hartford County, CT	14.6
45	12	Orange County, FL	34.1	70	10	San Mateo County, CA	23.3	54	12	New Haven County, CT	14.5
32	13	Hennepin County, MN	33.9	47	13	Fairfield County, CT	23.2	53	13	Pima County, AZ	14.2
20	14	Tarrant County, TX	33.8	67	13	Montgomery County, PA	23.2	18	14	Philadelphia County, PA	14.1
3	15	Harris County, TX	33.7	22	13	Suffolk County, NY	23.2	34	14	St. Louis County, MO	14.1
19	16	Middlesex County, MA	33.6	69	16	Essex County, MA	23.1	40	16	Westchester County, NY	14.0
70	16	San Mateo County, CA	33.6	51	16	Hartford County, CT	23.1	69	17	Essex County, MA	13.9
33	18	Franklin County, OH	33.5	12	18	King County, WA	23.0	62	18	San Francisco County, CA	13.8
5	19	Orange County, CA	33.4	42	19	Du Page County, IL	22.8	60	19	Macomb County, MI	13.6
9	20	Queens County, NY	33.3	73	19	Jefferson County, KY	22.8	52	20	Hamilton County, OH	13.5
50	21	Marion County, IN	33.1	60	19	Macomb County, MI	22.8	48	20	Honolulu County, HI	13.5
57	21	Prince George's County, MD	33.1	37	22	Erie County, NY	22.7	73	20	Jefferson County, KY	13.5
66	23	Middlesex County, NJ	32.9	68	23	Monroe County, NY	22.6	47	23	Fairfield County, CT	13.3
1	24	Los Angeles County, CA	32.8	17	24	New York County, NY	22.5	8	23	Miami-Dade County, FL	13.3
49	25	Montgomery County, MD	32.7	54	25	New Haven County, CT	22.4	68	25	Monroe County, NY	13.0
25	26	Clark County, NV	32.6	19	26	Middlesex County, MA	22.3	65	25	Worcester County, MA	13.0
42	26	Du Page County, IL	32.6	25	27	Clark County, NV	22.2	39	27	Milwaukee County, WI	12.9
61	28	Duval County, FL	32.5	23	28	Cuyahoga County, OH	22.1	19	28	Middlesex County, MA	12.8
30	28	Oakland County, MI	32.5	48	29	Honolulu County, HI	22.0	9	29	Queens County, NY	12.7
6	30	San Diego County, CA	32.3	31	29	Palm Beach County, FL	22.0	16	30	Riverside County, CA	12.6
2	31	Cook County, IL	31.9	57	29	Prince George's County, MD	22.0	70	31	San Mateo County, CA	12.5
35	31	Hillsborough County, FL	31.9	62	29	San Francisco County, CA	22.0	66	32	Middlesex County, NJ	12.3
15	33	Broward County, FL	31.8	53	33	Pima County, AZ	21.8	17	33	New York County, NY	12.1
4	34	Maricopa County, AZ	31.6	65	33	Worcester County, MA	21.8	11	33	Wayne County, MI	12.1
71	34	Pierce County, WA	31.6	9	35	Queens County, NY	21.7	35	35	Hillsborough County, FL	12.0
60	36	Macomb County, MI	31.5	64	35	Ventura County, CA	21.7	59	36	Essex County, NJ	11.9
29	37	Sacramento County, CA	31.4	21	37	Alameda County, CA	21.6	22	37	Suffolk County, NY	11.8
22	37	Suffolk County, NY	31.4	15	37	Broward County, FL	21.6	2	38	Cook County, IL	11.7
59	39	Essex County, NJ	31.3	35	37	Hillsborough County, FL	21.6	4	38	Maricopa County, AZ	11.7
44	39	Shelby County, TN	31.3	8	37	Miami-Dade County, FL	21.6	7	40	Kings County, NY	11.5
8	41	Miami-Dade County, FL	31.2	66	37	Middlesex County, NJ	21.6	38	41	Contra Costa County, CA	11.3
65	41	Worcester County, MA	31.2	59	42	Essex County, NJ	21.5	30	41	Oakland County, MI	11.3
47	43	Fairfield County, CT	31.1	32	42	Hennepin County, MN	21.5	49	43	Montgomery County, MD	11.2
46	44	Bergen County, NJ	30.9	52	44	Hamilton County, OH	21.4	50	44	Marion County, IN	11.1
38	44	Contra Costa County, CA	30.9	71	44	Pierce County, WA	21.4	29	44	Sacramento County, CA	11.1
7	44	Kings County, NY	30.9	61	46	Duval County, FL	21.2	6	44	San Diego County, CA	11.1
64	44	Ventura County, CA	30.9	44	47	Shelby County, TN	21.0	74	44	Suffolk County, MA	11.1
24	48	Bexar County, TX	30.8	14	48	Santa Clara County, CA	20.9	32	48	Hennepin County, MN	10.9
27	49	Bronx County, NY	30.7	11	49	Wayne County, MI	20.8	25	49	Clark County, NV	10.7
48	49	Honolulu County, HI	30.7	29	50	Sacramento County, CA	20.7	12	50	King County, WA	10.5
43	49	Salt Lake County, UT	30.7	2	51	Cook County, IL	20.6	24	51	Bexar County, TX	10.4
40	49	Westchester County, NY	30.7	7	51	Kings County, NY	20.6	61	51	Duval County, FL	10.4
73	53	Jefferson County, KY	30.6	5	53	Orange County, CA	20.5	21	53	Alameda County, CA	10.2
67	53	Montgomery County, PA	30.6	55	54	Fulton County, GA	20.4	71	53	Pierce County, WA	10.2
13	55	San Bernardino County, CA	30.5	72	54	Mecklenburg County, NC	20.4	27	55	Bronx County, NY	10.1
69	56	Essex County, MA	30.4	50	56	Marion County, IN	20.1	45	56	Orange County, FL	10.0
39	56	Milwaukee County, WI	30.4	18	56	Philadelphia County, PA	20.1	44	56	Shelby County, TN	10.0
11	56	Wayne County, MI	30.4	20	56	Tarrant County, TX	20.1	64	56	Ventura County, CA	10.0
54	59	New Haven County, CT	30.1	33	59	Franklin County, OH	20.0	58	59	Fresno County, CA	9.9
51	60	Hartford County, CT	30.0	39	60	Milwaukee County, WI	19.9	75	60	El Paso County, TX	9.8
63	61	Baltimore County, MD	29.9	45	60	Orange County, FL	19.9	33	60	Franklin County, OH	9.8
52	62	Hamilton County, OH	29.7	24	62	Bexar County, TX	19.8	5	60	Orange County, CA	9.8
23	63	Cuyahoga County, OH	29.5	3	63	Harris County, TX	19.7	42	63	Du Page County, IL	9.7
75	63	El Paso County, TX	29.5	4	63	Maricopa County, AZ	19.7	1	63	Los Angeles County, CA	9.7
68	65	Monroe County, NY	29.4	6	65	San Diego County, CA	19.6	14	65	Santa Clara County, CA	9.5
18	65	Philadelphia County, PA	29.4	1	66	Los Angeles County, CA	19.2	55	66	Fulton County, GA	8.5
16	67	Riverside County, CA	29.1	27	67	Bronx County, NY	18.8	72	66	Mecklenburg County, NC	8.5
34	67	St. Louis County, MO	29.1	10	67	Dallas County, TX	18.8	13	66	San Bernardino County, CA	8.5
26	69	Nassau County, NY	29.0	16	67	Riverside County, CA	18.8	20	69	Tarrant County, TX	8.3
58	70	Fresno County, CA	28.8	13	70	San Bernardino County, CA	18.5	43	70	Salt Lake County, UT	8.1
53	70	Pima County, AZ	28.8	75	71	El Paso County, TX	18.4	10	71	Dallas County, TX	8.0
37	72	Erie County, NY	28.5	58	72	Fresno County, CA	18.3	36	72	Fairfax County, VA	7.8
28	73	Allegheny County, PA	28.4	56	73	Travis County, TX	18.2	57	73	Prince George's County, MD	7.7
41	74	Pinellas County, FL	27.5	74	74	Suffolk County, MA	18.1	3	74	Harris County, TX	7.4
31	75	Palm Beach County, FL	27.1	43	75	Salt Lake County, UT	17.9	56	75	Travis County, TX	6.7

TABLE 2—75 Largest Counties by 2000 Population
Selected Rankings

Percent Non-Hispanic White, 2000				Percent Black or African American, 2000				Percent American Indian and Alaska Native, 2000			
Population Rank	Non-Hispanic White Rank	County	[A-3. col 11] Percent Non-Hispanic White	Population Rank	Black or African American Rank	County	[A-3. col 14] Percent Black or African American	Population Rank	American Indian and Alaska Native Rank	County	[A-3. col 17] Percent American Indian and Alaska Native
60	1	Macomb County, MI	91.4	57	1	Prince George's County, MD	62.6	53	1	Pima County, AZ	3.3
65	2	Worcester County, MA	86.4	44	2	Shelby County, TN	48.4	4	2	Maricopa County, AZ	1.8
67	3	Montgomery County, PA	85.4	55	3	Fulton County, GA	44.4	58	3	Fresno County, CA	1.6
28	4	Allegheny County, PA	83.8	18	4	Philadelphia County, PA	43.1	34	4	St. Louis County, MO	1.4
19	5	Middlesex County, MA	83.6	11	5	Wayne County, MI	42.0	16	5	Riverside County, CA	1.2
69	6	Essex County, MA	83.1	59	6	Essex County, NJ	41.0	29	6	Sacramento County, CA	1.1
41	7	Pinellas County, FL	82.8	7	7	Kings County, NY	36.2	13	6	San Bernardino County, CA	1.1
30	8	Oakland County, MI	81.4	27	8	Bronx County, NY	35.5	32	8	Hennepin County, MN	1.0
37	9	Erie County, NY	80.9	61	9	Duval County, FL	27.8	12	9	King County, WA	0.9
43	9	Salt Lake County, UT	80.9	72	10	Mecklenburg County, NC	27.7	39	9	Milwaukee County, WI	0.9
32	11	Hennepin County, MN	79.0	23	11	Cuyahoga County, OH	27.3	27	11	Bronx County, NY	0.8
42	12	Du Page County, IL	78.7	2	12	Cook County, IL	26.0	25	11	Clark County, NV	0.8
22	12	Suffolk County, NY	78.7	39	13	Milwaukee County, WI	24.4	37	11	Erie County, NY	0.8
68	14	Monroe County, NY	77.0	50	14	Marion County, IN	24.1	6	11	San Diego County, CA	0.8
73	15	Jefferson County, KY	76.5	52	15	Hamilton County, OH	23.4	64	11	Ventura County, CA	0.8
71	16	Pierce County, WA	76.0	74	16	Suffolk County, MA	21.9	24	16	Bexar County, TX	0.7
34	16	St. Louis County, MO	76.0	15	17	Broward County, FL	20.3	75	16	El Paso County, TX	0.7
54	18	New Haven County, CT	74.8	10	18	Dallas County, TX	20.2	1	16	Los Angeles County, CA	0.7
33	19	Franklin County, OH	74.4	8	19	Miami-Dade County, FL	20.1	14	16	Santa Clara County, CA	0.7
26	20	Nassau County, NY	73.9	63	20	Baltimore County, MD	19.9	21	20	Alameda County, CA	0.6
63	21	Baltimore County, MD	73.5	9	21	Queens County, NY	19.8	38	20	Contra Costa County, CA	0.6
12	22	King County, WA	73.3	71	22	Pierce County, WA	18.9	5	20	Orange County, CA	0.6
47	23	Fairfield County, CT	73.0	73	23	Jefferson County, KY	18.8	43	20	Salt Lake County, UT	0.6
51	23	Hartford County, CT	73.0	3	24	Harris County, TX	18.4	20	20	Tarrant County, TX	0.6
52	25	Hamilton County, OH	72.4	45	25	Orange County, FL	18.0	56	20	Travis County, TX	0.6
46	26	Bergen County, NJ	72.1	33	26	Franklin County, OH	17.6	10	26	Dallas County, TX	0.5
31	27	Palm Beach County, FL	70.6	17	27	New York County, NY	17.3	72	26	Mecklenburg County, NC	0.5
50	28	Marion County, IN	68.9	49	28	Montgomery County, MD	15.0	62	26	San Francisco County, CA	0.5
4	29	Maricopa County, AZ	66.2	35	29	Hillsborough County, FL	14.8	61	29	Duval County, FL	0.4
23	30	Cuyahoga County, OH	66.0	21	30	Alameda County, CA	14.7	3	29	Harris County, TX	0.4
36	31	Fairfax County, VA	64.3	40	31	Westchester County, NY	14.0	35	29	Hillsborough County, FL	0.4
40	32	Westchester County, NY	64.1	31	32	Palm Beach County, FL	13.8	60	29	Macomb County, MI	0.4
61	33	Duval County, FL	63.6	68	33	Monroe County, NY	13.5	17	29	New York County, NY	0.4
35	34	Hillsborough County, FL	63.3	43	34	Salt Lake County, UT	12.9	9	29	Queens County, NY	0.4
39	35	Milwaukee County, WI	62.2	20	35	Tarrant County, TX	12.6	70	29	San Mateo County, CA	0.4
20	36	Tarrant County, TX	61.9	28	36	Allegheny County, PA	12.3	74	29	Suffolk County, MA	0.4
66	37	Middlesex County, NJ	61.8	51	37	Hartford County, CT	11.5	11	29	Wayne County, MI	0.4
53	38	Pima County, AZ	61.4	54	38	New Haven County, CT	11.2	63	38	Baltimore County, MD	0.3
72	39	Mecklenburg County, NC	61.2	47	39	Fairfield County, CT	10.0	2	38	Cook County, IL	0.3
25	40	Clark County, NV	60.1	26	39	Nassau County, NY	10.0	42	38	Du Page County, IL	0.3
49	41	Montgomery County, MD	59.4	30	39	Oakland County, MI	10.0	33	38	Franklin County, OH	0.3
15	42	Broward County, FL	58.0	29	42	Sacramento County, CA	9.8	7	38	Kings County, NY	0.3
38	43	Contra Costa County, CA	57.7	1	43	Los Angeles County, CA	9.6	50	38	Marion County, IN	0.3
29	43	Sacramento County, CA	57.7	38	44	Contra Costa County, CA	9.2	68	38	Monroe County, NY	0.3
45	45	Orange County, FL	57.6	56	45	Travis County, TX	9.1	49	38	Montgomery County, MD	0.3
64	46	Ventura County, CA	56.6	66	46	Middlesex County, NJ	9.0	54	38	New Haven County, CT	0.3
56	47	Travis County, TX	56.4	25	47	Clark County, NV	8.9	30	38	Oakland County, MI	0.3
6	48	San Diego County, CA	54.9	41	47	Pinellas County, FL	8.9	45	38	Orange County, FL	0.3
74	49	Suffolk County, MA	52.0	13	47	San Bernardino County, CA	8.9	18	38	Philadelphia County, PA	0.3
5	50	Orange County, CA	51.1	32	50	Hennepin County, MN	8.8	41	38	Pinellas County, FL	0.3
16	51	Riverside County, CA	50.9	36	51	Fairfax County, VA	8.4	57	38	Prince George's County, MD	0.3
11	52	Wayne County, MI	49.9	62	52	San Francisco County, CA	7.6	40	38	Westchester County, NY	0.3
70	53	San Mateo County, CA	49.7	67	53	Montgomery County, PA	7.4	15	53	Broward County, FL	0.2
2	54	Cook County, IL	47.6	24	54	Bexar County, TX	7.0	23	53	Cuyahoga County, OH	0.2
44	55	Shelby County, TN	46.3	34	54	St. Louis County, MO	7.0	69	53	Essex County, MA	0.2
17	56	New York County, NY	45.8	42	56	Du Page County, IL	6.8	59	53	Essex County, NJ	0.2
55	57	Fulton County, GA	45.3	16	57	Riverside County, CA	6.2	36	53	Fairfax County, VA	0.2
10	58	Dallas County, TX	44.3	6	58	San Diego County, CA	5.6	47	53	Fairfield County, CT	0.2
14	59	Santa Clara County, CA	44.0	12	59	King County, WA	5.3	55	53	Fulton County, GA	0.2
13	60	San Bernardino County, CA	43.8	46	60	Bergen County, NJ	5.2	52	53	Hamilton County, OH	0.2
62	61	San Francisco County, CA	43.6	58	61	Fresno County, CA	5.1	51	53	Hartford County, CT	0.2
18	62	Philadelphia County, PA	42.6	4	62	Maricopa County, AZ	3.6	48	53	Honolulu County, HI	0.2
3	63	Harris County, TX	42.0	70	63	San Mateo County, CA	3.4	73	53	Jefferson County, KY	0.2
21	64	Alameda County, CA	40.8	19	64	Middlesex County, MA	3.3	8	53	Miami-Dade County, FL	0.2
58	65	Fresno County, CA	39.6	75	65	El Paso County, TX	3.0	19	53	Middlesex County, MA	0.2
59	66	Essex County, NJ	37.6	22	65	Suffolk County, NY	3.0	66	53	Middlesex County, NJ	0.2
24	67	Bexar County, TX	35.6	53	67	Pima County, AZ	2.9	31	53	Palm Beach County, FL	0.2
7	68	Kings County, NY	34.7	14	68	Santa Clara County, CA	2.7	71	53	Pierce County, WA	0.2
9	69	Queens County, NY	32.9	65	68	Worcester County, MA	2.7	44	53	Shelby County, TN	0.2
1	70	Los Angeles County, CA	30.9	60	70	Macomb County, MI	2.6	22	53	Suffolk County, NY	0.2
57	71	Prince George's County, MD	24.4	69	71	Essex County, MA	2.5	65	53	Worcester County, MA	0.2
8	72	Miami-Dade County, FL	20.7	48	72	Honolulu County, HI	2.2	28	72	Allegheny County, PA	0.1
48	73	Honolulu County, HI	20.0	64	73	Ventura County, CA	1.9	46	72	Bergen County, NJ	0.1
75	74	El Paso County, TX	17.0	5	74	Orange County, CA	1.6	67	72	Montgomery County, PA	0.1
27	75	Bronx County, NY	14.6	37	75	Erie County, NY	1.0	26	72	Nassau County, NY	0.1

TABLE 2—75 Largest Counties by 2000 Population
Selected Rankings

\[Asian\] Percent Asian, Hawaiian, and Pacific Islander, 2000				Percent Hispanic or Latino[1], 2000				Percent Two or More Races, 2000			
Population Rank	Asian, Hawaiian, and Pacific Islander Rank	County	[A-3. col 20] Percent Asian, Hawaiian, and Pacific Islander	Population Rank	Hispanic or Latino Rank	County	[A-3. col 23] Percent Hispanic or Latino	Population Rank	Two or More Races Rank	County	[A-3. col 26] Percent Two or More Races
48	1	Honolulu County, HI	55.0	75	1	El Paso County, TX	78.3	48	1	Honolulu County, HI	20.1
62	2	San Francisco County, CA	31.4	8	2	Miami-Dade County, FL	57.3	29	2	Sacramento County, CA	6.3
14	3	Santa Clara County, CA	25.9	24	3	Bexar County, TX	54.3	9	3	Queens County, NY	6.2
70	4	San Mateo County, CA	21.3	27	4	Bronx County, NY	48.4	21	4	Alameda County, CA	6.0
21	5	Alameda County, CA	21.0	1	5	Los Angeles County, CA	44.6	27	5	Bronx County, NY	5.9
9	6	Queens County, NY	17.7	58	6	Fresno County, CA	44.1	71	6	Pierce County, WA	5.6
66	7	Middlesex County, NJ	13.9	13	7	San Bernardino County, CA	39.2	38	7	Contra Costa County, CA	5.5
5	7	Orange County, CA	13.9	16	8	Riverside County, CA	36.2	13	7	San Bernardino County, CA	5.5
36	9	Fairfax County, VA	12.8	64	9	Ventura County, CA	33.5	70	9	San Mateo County, CA	5.4
1	10	Los Angeles County, CA	12.2	3	10	Harris County, TX	33.0	58	10	Fresno County, CA	5.1
29	11	Sacramento County, CA	11.5	5	11	Orange County, CA	30.8	1	10	Los Angeles County, CA	5.1
12	12	King County, WA	11.3	10	12	Dallas County, TX	29.9	6	12	San Diego County, CA	5.0
49	12	Montgomery County, MD	11.3	53	13	Pima County, AZ	29.4	14	12	Santa Clara County, CA	5.0
38	14	Contra Costa County, CA	11.2	56	14	Travis County, TX	28.2	16	14	Riverside County, CA	4.7
46	15	Bergen County, NJ	10.7	17	15	New York County, NY	27.2	74	14	Suffolk County, MA	4.7
17	16	New York County, NY	9.4	6	16	San Diego County, CA	26.7	62	16	San Francisco County, CA	4.5
6	17	San Diego County, CA	9.3	9	17	Queens County, NY	25.0	25	17	Clark County, NV	4.4
58	18	Fresno County, CA	8.1	4	18	Maricopa County, AZ	24.8	12	17	King County, WA	4.4
22	19	Suffolk County, NY	7.9	14	19	Santa Clara County, CA	24.0	7	17	Kings County, NY	4.4
7	20	Kings County, NY	7.6	25	20	Clark County, NV	21.9	5	20	Orange County, CA	4.3
74	21	Suffolk County, MA	7.0	70	21	San Mateo County, CA	21.8	36	21	Fairfax County, VA	4.1
19	22	Middlesex County, MA	6.3	2	22	Cook County, IL	19.9	8	21	Miami-Dade County, FL	4.1
34	23	St. Louis County, MO	5.7	7	23	Kings County, NY	19.8	17	21	New York County, NY	4.1
25	24	Clark County, NV	5.6	20	24	Tarrant County, TX	19.7	64	24	Ventura County, CA	4.0
64	25	Ventura County, CA	5.4	21	25	Alameda County, CA	19.0	24	24	Bexar County, TX	3.9
3	26	Harris County, TX	5.1	45	26	Orange County, FL	18.8	45	26	Orange County, FL	3.8
2	27	Cook County, IL	4.9	35	27	Hillsborough County, FL	18.0	59	27	Essex County, NJ	3.7
13	27	San Bernardino County, CA	4.9	38	28	Contra Costa County, CA	17.7	49	27	Montgomery County, MD	3.7
32	29	Hennepin County, MN	4.8	15	29	Broward County, FL	16.7	15	29	Broward County, FL	3.6
26	30	Nassau County, NY	4.7	29	30	Sacramento County, CA	16.0	53	30	Pima County, AZ	3.5
56	31	Travis County, TX	4.5	40	31	Westchester County, NY	15.7	40	31	Westchester County, NY	3.2
40	31	Westchester County, NY	4.5	74	32	Suffolk County, MA	15.6	75	32	El Paso County, TX	3.1
18	33	Philadelphia County, PA	4.3	59	33	Essex County, NJ	15.5	4	34	Maricopa County, AZ	3.1
30	34	Oakland County, MI	4.1	62	34	San Francisco County, CA	14.1	3	34	Harris County, TX	3.0
10	35	Dallas County, TX	4.0	66	35	Middlesex County, NJ	13.6	56	36	Travis County, TX	3.0
67	35	Montgomery County, PA	4.0	31	36	Palm Beach County, FL	12.4	10	36	Dallas County, TX	2.8
59	37	Essex County, NJ	3.8	37	37	Erie County, NY	11.8	32	36	Hennepin County, MN	2.8
57	37	Prince George's County, MD	3.8	47	37	Fairfield County, CT	11.8	35	36	Hillsborough County, FL	2.8
16	37	Riverside County, CA	3.8	51	39	Hartford County, CT	11.5	66	36	Middlesex County, NJ	2.8
37	40	Erie County, NY	3.7	49	39	Montgomery County, MD	11.5	57	36	Prince George's County, MD	2.8
20	40	Tarrant County, TX	3.7	69	41	Essex County, MA	11.0	43	36	Salt Lake County, UT	2.8
47	42	Fairfield County, CT	3.3	36	41	Fairfax County, VA	11.0	20	42	Tarrant County, TX	2.7
45	42	Orange County, FL	3.3	42	43	Du Page County, IL	10.5	47	43	Fairfield County, CT	2.6
63	44	Baltimore County, MD	3.2	46	44	Bergen County, NJ	10.3	11	43	Wayne County, MI	2.6
33	45	Franklin County, OH	3.1	26	45	Nassau County, NY	10.0	46	43	Bergen County, NJ	2.5
72	45	Mecklenburg County, NC	3.1	54	45	New Haven County, CT	10.0	33	46	Franklin County, OH	2.5
27	47	Bronx County, NY	3.0	22	47	Suffolk County, NY	9.0	51	46	Hartford County, CT	2.5
55	47	Fulton County, GA	3.0	39	48	Milwaukee County, WI	8.8	18	46	Philadelphia County, PA	2.5
61	49	Duval County, FL	2.7	18	49	Philadelphia County, PA	8.5	39	50	Milwaukee County, WI	2.4
51	50	Hartford County, CT	2.5	57	50	Prince George's County, MD	7.1	31	50	Palm Beach County, FL	2.4
65	50	Worcester County, MA	2.5	65	51	Worcester County, MA	6.8	69	52	Essex County, MA	2.3
42	52	Du Page County, IL	2.4	48	52	Honolulu County, HI	6.7	19	52	Middlesex County, MA	2.3
69	52	Essex County, MA	2.4	72	53	Mecklenburg County, NC	6.5	68	52	Monroe County, NY	2.3
39	52	Milwaukee County, WI	2.4	55	54	Fulton County, GA	5.8	26	52	Nassau County, NY	2.3
68	52	Monroe County, NY	2.4	12	55	King County, WA	5.5	54	56	New Haven County, CT	2.2
54	52	New Haven County, CT	2.4	34	55	St. Louis County, MO	5.5	22	56	Suffolk County, NY	2.2
15	57	Broward County, FL	2.3	68	57	Monroe County, NY	5.2	61	58	Duval County, FL	2.0
4	57	Maricopa County, AZ	2.3	41	58	Pinellas County, FL	4.6	60	58	Macomb County, MI	2.0
35	59	Hillsborough County, FL	2.2	19	59	Middlesex County, MA	4.5	30	58	Oakland County, MI	2.0
60	59	Macomb County, MI	2.2	61	60	Duval County, FL	4.1	65	58	Worcester County, MA	2.0
71	59	Pierce County, WA	2.2	32	60	Hennepin County, MN	4.1	42	62	Du Page County, IL	1.8
53	62	Pima County, AZ	2.1	11	62	Wayne County, MI	3.8	50	62	Marion County, IN	1.8
41	62	Pinellas County, FL	2.1	50	63	Marion County, IN	3.7	41	62	Pinellas County, FL	1.8
23	64	Cuyahoga County, OH	1.9	23	64	Cuyahoga County, OH	3.3	63	65	Baltimore County, MD	1.7
28	65	Allegheny County, PA	1.7	43	65	Salt Lake County, UT	3.2	23	65	Cuyahoga County, OH	1.7
24	65	Bexar County, TX	1.7	30	66	Oakland County, MI	2.5	73	65	Jefferson County, KY	1.7
44	65	Shelby County, TN	1.7	44	66	Shelby County, TN	2.5	72	65	Mecklenburg County, NC	1.7
11	65	Wayne County, MI	1.7	33	68	Franklin County, OH	2.3	55	69	Fulton County, GA	1.6
52	69	Hamilton County, OH	1.5	67	69	Montgomery County, PA	2.1	37	70	Erie County, NY	1.4
31	69	Palm Beach County, FL	1.5	63	70	Baltimore County, MD	1.8	52	70	Hamilton County, OH	1.4
50	71	Marion County, IN	1.4	73	71	Jefferson County, KY	1.7	34	70	St. Louis County, MO	1.4
8	71	Miami-Dade County, FL	1.4	60	72	Macomb County, MI	1.6	67	73	Montgomery County, PA	1.3
43	71	Salt Lake County, UT	1.4	71	73	Pierce County, WA	1.4	28	74	Allegheny County, PA	1.2
73	74	Jefferson County, KY	1.3	52	74	Hamilton County, OH	1.1	44	74	Shelby County, TN	1.2
75	75	El Paso County, TX	1.1	28	75	Allegheny County, PA	0.9				

[1] Hispanic or Latino persons may be of any race.

TABLE 2—75 Largest Counties by 2000 Population
Selected Rankings

Percent Married-Couple Families, 2000				Percent Married-Couple Families with Own Children Under 18 Years, 2000				Percent Single-Parent Households with Children Under 18 Years, 2000			
Population Rank	Married-Couple Families Rank	County	[A-3. col 30] Percent Married-Couple Families	Population Rank	Married-Couple Families With Own Children Under 18 Years Rank	County	[A-3. col 31] Percent Married-Couple Families With Own Children Under 18 Years	Population Rank	Single-Parent Households Rank	County	[A-3. col 34] Percent Single-Parent Households
26	1	Nassau County, NY	64.2	75	1	El Paso County, TX	33.3	27	1	Bronx County, NY	22.1
22	2	Suffolk County, NY	63.2	43	2	Salt Lake County, UT	32.8	18	2	Philadelphia County, PA	14.3
42	3	Du Page County, IL	62.0	42	3	Du Page County, IL	32.4	44	2	Shelby County, TN	14.3
36	4	Fairfax County, VA	60.2	13	4	San Bernardino County, CA	32.0	7	4	Kings County, NY	14.0
64	4	Ventura County, CA	60.2	64	5	Ventura County, CA	31.8	57	4	Prince George's County, MD	14.0
43	6	Salt Lake County, UT	58.9	22	6	Suffolk County, NY	31.3	11	6	Wayne County, MI	13.9
46	7	Bergen County, NJ	58.7	36	7	Fairfax County, VA	31.1	59	7	Essex County, NJ	13.2
66	8	Middlesex County, NJ	58.2	26	8	Nassau County, NY	30.8	58	8	Fresno County, CA	12.7
67	9	Montgomery County, PA	58.1	5	9	Orange County, CA	30.0	13	9	San Bernardino County, CA	12.6
75	10	El Paso County, TX	57.9	16	10	Riverside County, CA	29.8	75	10	El Paso County, TX	12.2
16	11	Riverside County, CA	57.5	58	11	Fresno County, CA	29.3	39	10	Milwaukee County, WI	12.2
5	12	Orange County, CA	57.0	14	12	Santa Clara County, CA	28.7	61	12	Duval County, FL	11.6
13	13	San Bernardino County, CA	56.8	66	13	Middlesex County, NJ	28.5	50	12	Marion County, IN	11.6
47	14	Fairfield County, CT	56.2	49	14	Montgomery County, MD	28.4	55	14	Fulton County, GA	11.2
49	15	Montgomery County, MD	56.1	3	15	Harris County, TX	28.2	8	14	Miami-Dade County, FL	11.2
14	15	Santa Clara County, CA	56.1	20	16	Tarrant County, TX	28.1	29	14	Sacramento County, CA	11.2
38	17	Contra Costa County, CA	55.8	46	17	Bergen County, NJ	27.8	24	17	Bexar County, TX	11.1
48	18	Honolulu County, HI	55.4	38	17	Contra Costa County, CA	27.8	1	18	Los Angeles County, CA	10.8
60	19	Macomb County, MI	55.0	47	17	Fairfield County, CT	27.8	74	18	Suffolk County, MA	10.8
30	20	Oakland County, MI	54.9	40	20	Westchester County, NY	27.5	71	20	Pierce County, WA	10.7
40	20	Westchester County, NY	54.9	67	21	Montgomery County, PA	27.1	52	21	Hamilton County, OH	10.6
70	22	San Mateo County, CA	54.1	1	22	Los Angeles County, CA	26.8	73	21	Jefferson County, KY	10.6
58	23	Fresno County, CA	53.8	30	23	Oakland County, MI	26.3	45	21	Orange County, FL	10.6
71	24	Pierce County, WA	53.7	24	24	Bexar County, TX	26.1	23	24	Cuyahoga County, OH	10.5
20	25	Tarrant County, TX	53.6	71	25	Pierce County, WA	26.0	10	24	Dallas County, TX	10.5
65	26	Worcester County, MA	53.2	70	26	San Mateo County, CA	25.6	33	26	Franklin County, OH	10.4
4	27	Maricopa County, AZ	52.7	65	26	Worcester County, MA	25.6	3	27	Harris County, TX	10.3
19	28	Middlesex County, MA	52.3	6	28	San Diego County, CA	25.5	35	28	Hillsborough County, FL	10.2
69	29	Essex County, MA	51.9	10	29	Dallas County, TX	25.3	68	28	Monroe County, NY	10.2
34	30	St. Louis County, MO	51.7	48	29	Honolulu County, HI	25.3	25	30	Clark County, NV	10.0
24	31	Bexar County, TX	51.6	60	31	Macomb County, MI	25.2	16	30	Riverside County, CA	10.0
3	31	Harris County, TX	51.6	19	32	Middlesex County, MA	25.0	51	32	Hartford County, CT	9.9
31	33	Palm Beach County, FL	51.4	69	33	Essex County, MA	24.0	2	33	Cook County, IL	9.6
6	34	San Diego County, CA	51.3	4	33	Maricopa County, AZ	24.6	20	33	Tarrant County, TX	9.6
63	35	Baltimore County, MD	50.5	21	35	Alameda County, CA	24.4	37	35	Erie County, NY	9.4
54	36	New Haven County, CT	49.8	72	36	Mecklenburg County, NC	23.5	54	36	New Haven County, CT	9.3
25	37	Clark County, NV	49.6	8	37	Miami-Dade County, FL	23.4	15	37	Broward County, FL	9.2
51	37	Hartford County, CT	49.6	9	38	Queens County, NY	23.3	53	37	Pima County, AZ	9.2
72	39	Mecklenburg County, NC	48.7	29	38	Sacramento County, CA	23.3	6	37	San Diego County, CA	9.2
8	39	Miami-Dade County, FL	48.7	34	38	St. Louis County, MO	23.3	4	40	Maricopa County, AZ	9.1
53	39	Pima County, AZ	48.7	45	41	Orange County, FL	22.8	72	41	Mecklenburg County, NC	9.0
1	42	Los Angeles County, CA	48.5	25	42	Clark County, NV	22.5	63	42	Baltimore County, MD	8.9
35	43	Hillsborough County, FL	48.3	54	43	New Haven County, CT	22.4	9	42	Queens County, NY	8.9
68	44	Monroe County, NY	48.2	61	44	Duval County, FL	22.3	21	44	Alameda County, CA	8.8
9	45	Queens County, NY	48.1	68	45	Monroe County, NY	22.2	34	44	St. Louis County, MO	8.8
10	46	Dallas County, TX	47.9	12	46	King County, WA	22.1	65	44	Worcester County, MA	8.8
45	46	Orange County, FL	47.9	57	46	Prince George's County, MD	22.1	69	47	Essex County, MA	8.7
21	48	Alameda County, CA	47.8	63	48	Baltimore County, MD	22.0	64	48	Ventura County, CA	8.6
61	49	Duval County, FL	47.5	2	49	Cook County, IL	21.9	38	49	Contra Costa County, CA	8.2
37	49	Erie County, NY	47.5	51	49	Hartford County, CT	21.9	43	50	Salt Lake County, UT	8.1
29	51	Sacramento County, CA	47.4	35	49	Hillsborough County, FL	21.9	56	51	Travis County, TX	8.0
12	52	King County, WA	47.2	56	49	Travis County, TX	21.9	28	52	Allegheny County, PA	7.8
15	53	Broward County, FL	46.8	32	53	Hennepin County, MN	21.7	32	52	Hennepin County, MN	7.8
28	54	Allegheny County, PA	46.6	59	54	Essex County, NJ	21.4	5	52	Orange County, CA	7.8
32	55	Hennepin County, MN	46.0	53	55	Pima County, AZ	20.8	17	55	New York County, NY	7.5
73	56	Jefferson County, KY	45.6	15	56	Broward County, FL	20.7	41	55	Pinellas County, FL	7.5
41	57	Pinellas County, FL	45.4	37	56	Erie County, NY	20.7	40	55	Westchester County, NY	7.5
2	58	Cook County, IL	45.0	44	56	Shelby County, TN	20.7	47	58	Fairfield County, CT	7.3
57	59	Prince George's County, MD	44.9	33	59	Franklin County, OH	20.5	49	59	Montgomery County, MD	7.2
52	60	Hamilton County, OH	44.1	52	60	Hamilton County, OH	20.1	31	59	Palm Beach County, FL	7.2
44	61	Shelby County, TN	43.6	7	61	Kings County, NY	20.0	48	61	Honolulu County, HI	7.0
33	62	Franklin County, OH	43.5	73	62	Jefferson County, KY	19.5	12	61	King County, WA	7.0
56	62	Travis County, TX	43.5	11	62	Wayne County, MI	19.5	14	63	Santa Clara County, CA	6.9
59	64	Essex County, NJ	43.4	50	64	Marion County, IN	19.2	66	64	Middlesex County, NJ	6.5
23	65	Cuyahoga County, OH	43.1	28	65	Allegheny County, PA	19.0	30	65	Oakland County, MI	6.4
50	66	Marion County, IN	42.1	23	66	Cuyahoga County, OH	18.5	22	65	Suffolk County, NY	6.4
11	67	Wayne County, MI	41.7	31	67	Palm Beach County, FL	18.4	60	67	Macomb County, MI	6.3
39	68	Milwaukee County, WI	39.9	55	68	Fulton County, GA	18.3	70	67	San Mateo County, CA	6.3
7	69	Kings County, NY	39.7	39	69	Milwaukee County, WI	17.8	36	69	Fairfax County, VA	6.0
55	70	Fulton County, GA	38.1	27	70	Bronx County, NY	16.8	19	70	Middlesex County, MA	5.8
18	71	Philadelphia County, PA	32.7	41	71	Pinellas County, FL	15.1	67	71	Montgomery County, PA	5.5
62	71	San Francisco County, CA	32.7	18	72	Philadelphia County, PA	14.0	42	72	DuPage County, IL	5.3
27	73	Bronx County, NY	32.2	74	73	Suffolk County, MA	13.3	26	73	Nassau County, NY	5.1
74	74	Suffolk County, MA	30.2	62	74	San Francisco County, CA	13.0	46	74	Bergen County, NJ	4.7
17	75	New York County, NY	25.8	17	75	New York County, NY	10.2	62	75	San Francisco County, CA	4.2

TABLE 2—75 Largest Counties by 2000 Population
Selected Rankings

Percent Men Living Alone, 2000				Percent Women Living Alone, 2000				Percent Foreign-Born Population, 2000			
Population Rank	Men Living Alone Rank	County	[A-3. col 38] Percent Men Living Alone	Population Rank	Women Living Alone Rank	County	[A-3. col 40] Percent Women Living Alone	Population Rank	Foreign-born Population Rank	County	[A-3. col 54] Percent Foreign-born Population
17	1	New York County, NY	20.6	17	1	New York County, NY	27.3	8	1	Miami-Dade County, FL	50.9
62	2	San Francisco County, CA	19.1	41	2	Pinellas County, FL	20.6	9	2	Queens County, NY	46.1
74	3	Suffolk County, MA	16.2	74	3	Suffolk County, MA	20.1	7	3	Kings County, NY	37.8
56	4	Travis County, TX	15.2	28	4	Allegheny County, PA	20.0	62	4	San Francisco County, CA	36.8
55	5	Fulton County, GA	14.4	18	5	Philadelphia County, PA	19.9	1	5	Los Angeles County, CA	36.2
12	6	King County, WA	14.1	62	6	San Francisco County, CA	19.5	14	6	Santa Clara County, CA	34.1
39	6	Milwaukee County, WI	14.1	23	7	Cuyahoga County, OH	19.4	70	7	San Mateo County, CA	32.3
18	8	Philadelphia County, PA	13.9	52	8	Hamilton County, OH	19.1	5	8	Orange County, CA	29.9
52	9	Hamilton County, OH	13.8	39	9	Milwaukee County, WI	18.8	17	9	New York County, NY	29.4
32	9	Hennepin County, MN	13.8	37	10	Erie County, NY	18.4	27	10	Bronx County, NY	29.0
50	11	Marion County, IN	13.7	32	11	Hennepin County, MN	18.0	75	11	El Paso County, TX	27.4
33	12	Franklin County, OH	13.6	50	11	Marion County, IN	18.0	21	12	Alameda County, CA	27.2
23	13	Cuyahoga County, OH	13.4	31	11	Palm Beach County, FL	18.0	49	13	Montgomery County, MD	26.7
41	13	Pinellas County, FL	13.4	55	14	Fulton County, GA	17.8	74	14	Suffolk County, MA	25.5
25	15	Clark County, NV	12.8	73	14	Jefferson County, KY	17.8	15	15	Broward County, FL	25.3
28	16	Allegheny County, PA	12.7	15	16	Broward County, FL	17.3	46	16	Bergen County, NJ	25.1
73	16	Jefferson County, KY	12.7	33	17	Franklin County, OH	17.2	36	17	Fairfax County, VA	24.5
53	16	Pima County, AZ	12.7	34	18	St. Louis County, MO	17.1	66	18	Middlesex County, NJ	24.2
11	19	Wayne County, MI	12.5	63	19	Baltimore County, MD	16.9	3	19	Harris County, TX	22.2
2	20	Cook County, IL	12.4	2	19	Cook County, IL	16.9	40	19	Westchester County, NY	22.2
15	21	Broward County, FL	12.3	7	19	Kings County, NY	16.9	6	21	San Diego County, CA	21.5
10	21	Dallas County, TX	12.3	54	19	New Haven County, CT	16.9	59	22	Essex County, NJ	21.2
37	23	Erie County, NY	12.1	69	23	Essex County, MA	16.8	58	23	Fresno County, CA	21.1
72	23	Mecklenburg County, NC	12.1	51	24	Hartford County, CT	16.7	10	24	Dallas County, TX	20.9
3	25	Harris County, TX	12.0	68	24	Monroe County, NY	16.7	64	25	Ventura County, CA	20.7
68	26	Monroe County, NY	11.9	27	26	Bronx County, NY	16.4	2	26	Cook County, IL	19.8
61	27	Duval County, FL	11.8	12	26	King County, WA	16.4	48	27	Honolulu County, HI	19.2
30	27	Oakland County, MI	11.8	19	26	Middlesex County, MA	16.4	38	28	Contra Costa County, CA	19.0
20	27	Tarrant County, TX	11.8	40	29	Westchester County, NY	16.3	16	28	Riverside County, CA	19.0
35	30	Hillsborough County, FL	11.7	59	30	Essex County, NJ	16.1	13	30	San Bernardino County, CA	18.6
44	31	Shelby County, TN	11.6	53	31	Pima County, AZ	15.8	25	31	Clark County, NV	18.0
21	32	Alameda County, CA	11.5	11	31	Wayne County, MI	15.8	26	32	Nassau County, NY	17.9
60	33	Macomb County, MI	11.4	67	33	Montgomery County, PA	15.7	31	33	Palm Beach County, FL	17.4
1	34	Los Angeles County, CA	11.3	30	34	Oakland County, MI	15.6	47	34	Fairfield County, CT	16.9
54	34	New Haven County, CT	11.3	60	35	Macomb County, MI	15.5	29	35	Sacramento County, CA	16.1
45	34	Orange County, FL	11.3	72	35	Mecklenburg County, NC	15.5	12	36	King County, WA	15.4
71	34	Pierce County, WA	11.3	49	35	Montgomery County, MD	15.5	42	37	Du Page County, IL	15.3
29	34	Sacramento County, CA	11.3	46	38	Bergen County, NJ	15.4	19	38	Middlesex County, MA	15.2
51	39	Hartford County, CT	11.1	9	38	Queens County, NY	15.4	56	39	Travis County, TX	15.1
31	39	Palm Beach County, FL	11.1	29	40	Sacramento County, CA	15.3	4	40	Maricopa County, AZ	14.4
27	41	Bronx County, NY	11.0	44	40	Shelby County, TN	15.3	45	40	Orange County, FL	14.4
65	41	Worcester County, MA	11.0	35	42	Hillsborough County, FL	15.2	57	42	Prince George's County, MD	13.8
7	43	Kings County, NY	10.9	65	42	Worcester County, MA	15.2	20	43	Tarrant County, TX	12.7
4	43	Maricopa County, AZ	10.9	10	44	Dallas County, TX	14.9	53	44	Pima County, AZ	11.9
6	43	San Diego County, CA	10.9	56	44	Travis County, TX	14.9	51	45	Hartford County, CT	11.7
34	46	St. Louis County, MO	10.8	61	46	Duval County, FL	14.7	35	46	Hillsborough County, FL	11.5
59	47	Essex County, NJ	10.7	47	46	Fairfield County, CT	14.7	69	47	Essex County, MA	11.3
19	47	Middlesex County, MA	10.7	21	48	Alameda County, CA	14.5	22	48	Suffolk County, NY	11.2
48	49	Honolulu County, HI	10.6	70	49	San Mateo County, CA	14.4	24	49	Bexar County, TX	10.9
24	50	Bexar County, TX	10.5	57	50	Prince George's County, MD	14.1	43	50	Salt Lake County, UT	10.4
8	50	Miami-Dade County, FL	10.5	38	51	Contra Costa County, CA	13.8	30	51	Oakland County, MI	10.0
63	52	Baltimore County, MD	10.3	4	52	Maricopa County, AZ	13.6	32	52	Hennepin County, MN	9.9
14	52	Santa Clara County, CA	10.3	24	53	Bexar County, TX	13.4	72	53	Mecklenburg County, NC	9.8
69	54	Essex County, MA	10.2	66	53	Middlesex County, NJ	13.4	55	54	Fulton County, GA	9.6
70	54	San Mateo County, CA	10.2	1	55	Los Angeles County, CA	13.3	41	55	Pinellas County, FL	9.5
9	56	Queens County, NY	10.1	6	55	San Diego County, CA	13.2	54	56	New Haven County, CT	9.0
57	57	Prince George's County, MD	9.9	42	57	Du Page County, IL	13.1	18	56	Philadelphia County, PA	9.0
67	58	Montgomery County, PA	9.8	20	57	Tarrant County, TX	13.1	60	58	Macomb County, MI	8.8
42	59	Du Page County, IL	9.7	3	59	Harris County, TX	13.0	71	59	Pierce County, WA	8.1
46	60	Bergen County, NJ	9.3	71	59	Pierce County, WA	13.0	65	60	Worcester County, MA	7.9
43	60	Salt Lake County, UT	9.3	45	61	Orange County, FL	12.9	68	61	Monroe County, NY	7.3
40	60	Westchester County, NY	9.3	8	62	Miami-Dade County, FL	12.8	63	62	Baltimore County, MD	7.1
47	63	Fairfield County, CT	9.2	36	63	Fairfax County, VA	12.5	67	63	Montgomery County, PA	7.0
38	64	Contra Costa County, CA	9.0	26	64	Nassau County, NY	12.3	39	64	Milwaukee County, WI	6.8
66	65	Middlesex County, NJ	8.9	5	64	Orange County, CA	12.3	11	65	Wayne County, MI	6.7
49	65	Montgomery County, MD	8.9	58	66	Fresno County, CA	12.1	23	66	Cuyahoga County, OH	6.4
36	67	Fairfax County, VA	8.8	16	67	Riverside County, CA	12.0	33	67	Franklin County, OH	6.0
5	67	Orange County, CA	8.8	25	68	Clark County, NV	11.6	61	68	Duval County, FL	5.9
16	69	Riverside County, CA	8.6	43	69	Salt Lake County, UT	11.5	50	69	Marion County, IN	4.6
58	70	Fresno County, CA	8.5	14	70	Santa Clara County, CA	11.1	37	70	Erie County, NY	4.5
13	71	San Bernardino County, CA	8.2	48	71	Honolulu County, HI	11.0	34	71	St. Louis County, MO	4.2
64	72	Ventura County, CA	7.9	22	71	Suffolk County, NY	11.0	28	72	Allegheny County, PA	3.8
75	73	El Paso County, TX	7.5	64	71	Ventura County, CA	11.0	44	72	Shelby County, TN	3.8
22	74	Suffolk County, NY	7.3	75	74	El Paso County, TX	10.2	52	74	Hamilton County, OH	3.4
26	75	Nassau County, NY	6.5	13	74	San Bernardino County, CA	10.2	73	74	Jefferson County, KY	3.4

TABLE 2—75 Largest Counties by 2000 Population
Selected Rankings

Percent of Population Over 25 Years with High School Diploma or Less, 2000

Population Rank	High School Diploma or Less Rank	County	[B-3. col 2] Percent High School Diploma or Less
27	1	Bronx County, NY	63.5
18	2	Philadelphia County, PA	62.1
7	3	Kings County, NY	57.9
75	4	El Paso County, TX	56.8
8	5	Miami-Dade County, FL	54.5
11	6	Wayne County, MI	53.7
58	7	Fresno County, CA	53.6
9	8	Queens County, NY	53.4
59	9	Essex County, NJ	51.6
13	10	San Bernardino County, CA	50.8
25	11	Clark County, NV	50.4
60	12	Macomb County, MI	49.8
16	13	Riverside County, CA	49.7
39	14	Milwaukee County, WI	49.2
1	15	Los Angeles County, CA	48.9
23	16	Cuyahoga County, OH	48.4
50	17	Marion County, IN	48.0
54	18	New Haven County, CT	47.8
74	19	Suffolk County, MA	47.6
28	20	Allegheny County, PA	47.5
24	21	Bexar County, TX	47.4
73	22	Jefferson County, KY	47.2
37	23	Erie County, NY	47.0
3	23	Harris County, TX	47.0
10	25	Dallas County, TX	46.7
65	25	Worcester County, MA	46.7
2	27	Cook County, IL	46.5
15	28	Broward County, FL	46.4
61	29	Duval County, FL	46.3
51	29	Hartford County, CT	46.3
35	31	Hillsborough County, FL	45.9
41	32	Pinellas County, FL	45.6
44	33	Shelby County, TN	45.4
22	34	Suffolk County, NY	45.1
52	35	Hamilton County, OH	45.0
66	36	Middlesex County, NJ	44.7
45	37	Orange County, FL	44.0
69	38	Essex County, MA	43.5
31	39	Palm Beach County, FL	43.3
63	40	Baltimore County, MD	43.2
48	41	Honolulu County, HI	43.0
71	42	Pierce County, WA	42.9
57	43	Prince George's County, MD	42.4
20	44	Tarrant County, TX	42.2
33	45	Franklin County, OH	41.4
68	46	Monroe County, NY	41.3
4	47	Maricopa County, AZ	40.6
26	48	Nassau County, NY	40.1
53	49	Pima County, AZ	39.9
46	50	Bergen County, NJ	39.6
29	50	Sacramento County, CA	39.6
64	50	Ventura County, CA	39.6
47	53	Fairfield County, CT	39.2
67	54	Montgomery County, PA	38.8
40	55	Westchester County, NY	38.5
5	56	Orange County, CA	38.0
6	57	San Diego County, CA	37.3
43	58	Salt Lake County, UT	37.2
21	59	Alameda County, CA	36.7
34	60	St. Louis County, MO	36.0
55	61	Fulton County, GA	35.4
19	62	Middlesex County, MA	34.9
17	63	New York County, NY	34.8
72	64	Mecklenburg County, NC	33.7
38	65	Contra Costa County, CA	32.9
30	66	Oakland County, MI	32.8
62	67	San Francisco County, CA	32.7
56	67	Travis County, TX	32.7
14	69	Santa Clara County, CA	32.5
70	70	San Mateo County, CA	32.2
42	71	Du Page County, IL	30.6
32	72	Hennepin County, MN	30.5
12	73	King County, WA	28.9
49	74	Montgomery County, MD	24.2
36	75	Fairfax County, VA	23.1

Percent of Population Over 25 Years with Bachelor's Degree or More, 2000

Population Rank	Bachelor's Degree or More Rank	County	[B-3. col 4] Percent Bachelor's Degree or More
36	1	Fairfax County, VA	54.8
49	2	Montgomery County, MD	54.6
17	3	New York County, NY	49.4
62	4	San Francisco County, CA	45.0
19	5	Middlesex County, MA	43.6
42	6	Du Page County, IL	41.7
55	7	Fulton County, GA	41.4
40	8	Westchester County, NY	40.9
56	9	Travis County, TX	40.6
14	10	Santa Clara County, CA	40.5
12	11	King County, WA	40.0
47	12	Fairfield County, CT	39.9
32	13	Hennepin County, MN	39.1
70	14	San Mateo County, CA	39.0
67	15	Montgomery County, PA	38.7
46	16	Bergen County, NJ	38.2
30	16	Oakland County, MI	38.2
72	18	Mecklenburg County, NC	37.1
26	19	Nassau County, NY	35.4
34	19	St. Louis County, MO	35.4
38	21	Contra Costa County, CA	35.0
21	22	Alameda County, CA	34.9
66	23	Middlesex County, NJ	33.0
74	24	Suffolk County, MA	32.5
33	25	Franklin County, OH	31.8
69	26	Essex County, MA	31.3
68	27	Monroe County, NY	31.2
5	28	Orange County, CA	30.8
63	29	Baltimore County, MD	30.6
51	30	Hartford County, CT	29.6
6	31	San Diego County, CA	29.5
52	32	Hamilton County, OH	29.2
28	33	Allegheny County, PA	28.3
2	34	Cook County, IL	28.0
48	35	Honolulu County, HI	27.9
31	36	Palm Beach County, FL	27.7
54	37	New Haven County, CT	27.6
59	38	Essex County, NJ	27.5
22	38	Suffolk County, NY	27.5
43	40	Salt Lake County, UT	27.4
57	41	Prince George's County, MD	27.2
10	42	Dallas County, TX	27.0
3	43	Harris County, TX	26.9
64	43	Ventura County, CA	26.9
65	43	Worcester County, MA	26.9
53	46	Pima County, AZ	26.7
20	47	Tarrant County, TX	26.6
45	48	Orange County, FL	26.1
4	49	Maricopa County, AZ	25.9
50	50	Marion County, IN	25.4
44	51	Shelby County, TN	25.3
23	52	Cuyahoga County, OH	25.1
35	52	Hillsborough County, FL	25.1
1	54	Los Angeles County, CA	24.9
73	55	Jefferson County, KY	24.8
29	55	Sacramento County, CA	24.8
15	57	Broward County, FL	24.5
37	57	Erie County, NY	24.5
9	59	Queens County, NY	24.3
39	60	Milwaukee County, WI	23.6
41	61	Pinellas County, FL	22.9
24	62	Bexar County, TX	22.7
61	63	Duval County, FL	21.9
7	64	Kings County, NY	21.8
8	65	Miami-Dade County, FL	21.7
71	66	Pierce County, WA	20.6
18	67	Philadelphia County, PA	17.9
60	68	Macomb County, MI	17.6
58	69	Fresno County, CA	17.5
25	70	Clark County, NV	17.3
11	71	Wayne County, MI	17.2
75	72	El Paso County, TX	16.6
16	72	Riverside County, CA	16.6
13	74	San Bernardino County, CA	15.9
27	75	Bronx County, NY	14.6

Percent of Population 16 to 19 Years Not Enrolled in School, Not High School Graduate, Not in Armed Forces, or Employed, 2000

Population Rank	At-Risk Rank	County	[B-3. col 17] Percent At-Risk Youth
27	1	Bronx County, NY	11.1
10	2	Dallas County, TX	9.6
25	3	Clark County, NV	9.5
3	4	Harris County, TX	8.4
4	4	Maricopa County, AZ	8.4
55	6	Fulton County, GA	8.0
7	6	Kings County, NY	8.0
50	6	Marion County, IN	8.0
11	9	Wayne County, MI	7.6
35	10	Hillsborough County, FL	7.5
2	11	Cook County, IL	7.4
18	11	Philadelphia County, PA	7.4
1	13	Los Angeles County, CA	7.1
44	13	Shelby County, TN	7.1
17	15	New York County, NY	7.0
59	16	Essex County, NJ	6.9
58	16	Fresno County, CA	6.9
31	16	Palm Beach County, FL	6.9
20	16	Tarrant County, TX	6.9
24	20	Bexar County, TX	6.8
8	20	Miami-Dade County, FL	6.8
53	20	Pima County, AZ	6.8
73	23	Jefferson County, KY	6.7
39	23	Milwaukee County, WI	6.7
13	23	San Bernardino County, CA	6.7
75	26	El Paso County, TX	6.6
61	27	Duval County, FL	6.5
56	27	Travis County, TX	6.5
45	29	Orange County, FL	6.2
9	29	Queens County, NY	6.2
52	31	Hamilton County, OH	6.0
16	31	Riverside County, CA	6.0
23	33	Cuyahoga County, OH	5.9
41	33	Pinellas County, FL	5.9
72	35	Mecklenburg County, NC	5.7
29	36	Sacramento County, CA	5.6
51	37	Hartford County, CT	5.5
15	38	Broward County, FL	5.4
54	38	New Haven County, CT	5.4
71	40	Pierce County, WA	5.2
21	41	Alameda County, CA	5.1
5	42	Orange County, CA	4.9
74	42	Suffolk County, MA	4.9
40	42	Westchester County, NY	4.9
33	45	Franklin County, OH	4.6
43	45	Salt Lake County, UT	4.6
6	45	San Diego County, CA	4.6
64	45	Ventura County, CA	4.6
14	49	Santa Clara County, CA	4.5
37	50	Erie County, NY	4.4
70	50	San Mateo County, CA	4.4
62	52	San Francisco County, CA	4.2
65	52	Worcester County, MA	4.2
57	54	Prince George's County, MD	4.1
63	55	Baltimore County, MD	3.9
38	55	Contra Costa County, CA	3.9
68	57	Monroe County, NY	3.8
32	58	Hennepin County, MN	3.7
47	59	Fairfield County, CT	3.6
66	59	Middlesex County, NJ	3.6
60	61	Macomb County, MI	3.5
69	62	Essex County, MA	3.4
36	63	Fairfax County, VA	3.3
49	63	Montgomery County, MD	3.3
22	63	Suffolk County, NY	3.3
48	66	Honolulu County, HI	3.2
12	66	King County, WA	3.2
34	66	St. Louis County, MO	3.2
28	69	Allegheny County, PA	3.1
42	70	Du Page County, IL	2.8
30	71	Oakland County, MI	2.6
19	72	Middlesex County, MA	2.5
26	73	Nassau County, NY	2.3
46	74	Bergen County, NJ	1.7
67	74	Montgomery County, PA	1.7

TABLE 2—75 Largest Counties by 2000 Population
Selected Rankings

Unemployment Rate, 2000

Population Rank	Unemployment Rate Rank	County	[B-3. col 20] Unemployment Rate
27	1	Bronx County, NY	14.3
58	2	Fresno County, CA	11.8
18	3	Philadelphia County, PA	10.9
7	4	Kings County, NY	10.7
59	5	Essex County, NJ	9.3
75	6	El Paso County, TX	9.2
55	7	Fulton County, GA	8.9
8	8	Miami-Dade County, FL	8.7
17	9	New York County, NY	8.5
11	9	Wayne County, MI	8.5
1	11	Los Angeles County, CA	8.2
13	12	San Bernardino County, CA	8.1
9	13	Queens County, NY	7.7
2	14	Cook County, IL	7.5
16	14	Riverside County, CA	7.5
37	16	Erie County, NY	7.3
74	17	Suffolk County, MA	7.0
39	18	Milwaukee County, WI	6.9
44	19	Shelby County, TN	6.8
29	20	Sacramento County, CA	6.6
25	21	Clark County, NV	6.5
3	22	Harris County, TX	6.4
23	23	Cuyahoga County, OH	6.2
51	23	Hartford County, CT	6.2
28	25	Allegheny County, PA	6.1
71	25	Pierce County, WA	6.1
68	27	Monroe County, NY	6.0
54	28	New Haven County, CT	5.9
57	29	Prince George's County, MD	5.8
48	30	Honolulu County, HI	5.7
24	31	Bexar County, TX	5.6
10	31	Dallas County, TX	5.6
35	31	Hillsborough County, FL	5.6
6	31	San Diego County, CA	5.6
21	35	Alameda County, CA	5.5
50	36	Marion County, IN	5.4
15	37	Broward County, FL	5.3
53	37	Pima County, AZ	5.3
72	39	Mecklenburg County, NC	5.2
66	39	Middlesex County, NJ	5.2
64	41	Ventura County, CA	5.1
52	42	Hamilton County, OH	5.0
73	42	Jefferson County, KY	5.0
5	42	Orange County, CA	5.0
45	42	Orange County, FL	5.0
31	42	Palm Beach County, FL	5.0
38	47	Contra Costa County, CA	4.8
61	47	Duval County, FL	4.8
47	47	Fairfield County, CT	4.8
4	50	Maricopa County, AZ	4.7
69	51	Essex County, MA	4.6
62	51	San Francisco County, CA	4.6
34	51	St. Louis County, MO	4.6
12	54	King County, WA	4.5
67	54	Montgomery County, PA	4.5
43	54	Salt Lake County, UT	4.5
20	54	Tarrant County, TX	4.5
40	58	Westchester County, NY	4.4
41	59	Pinellas County, FL	4.3
65	59	Worcester County, MA	4.3
63	61	Baltimore County, MD	4.2
33	61	Franklin County, OH	4.2
46	63	Bergen County, NJ	4.1
60	63	Macomb County, MI	4.1
56	63	Travis County, TX	4.1
14	66	Santa Clara County, CA	3.9
22	66	Suffolk County, NY	3.9
32	68	Hennepin County, MN	3.8
26	69	Nassau County, NY	3.7
30	69	Oakland County, MI	3.7
19	71	Middlesex County, MA	3.4
42	72	Du Page County, IL	3.3
70	72	San Mateo County, CA	3.3
49	74	Montgomery County, MD	3.1
36	75	Fairfax County, VA	2.5

Percent Veterans Over 18 Years, 2000

Population Rank	Veterans Rank	County	[B-3. col 44] Percent Veterans
71	1	Pierce County, WA	18.9
41	2	Pinellas County, FL	17.8
61	3	Duval County, FL	17.3
53	4	Pima County, AZ	16.0
25	5	Clark County, NV	15.5
24	6	Bexar County, TX	15.4
31	7	Palm Beach County, FL	15.1
28	8	Allegheny County, PA	14.3
35	8	Hillsborough County, FL	14.3
6	10	San Diego County, CA	14.0
73	11	Jefferson County, KY	13.7
4	11	Maricopa County, AZ	13.7
29	13	Sacramento County, CA	13.6
34	13	St. Louis County, MO	13.6
63	15	Baltimore County, MD	13.4
37	15	Erie County, NY	13.4
16	15	Riverside County, CA	13.4
36	18	Fairfax County, VA	13.3
57	18	Prince George's County, MD	13.3
48	20	Honolulu County, HI	13.2
50	21	Marion County, IN	12.7
45	21	Orange County, FL	12.7
65	21	Worcester County, MA	12.7
60	24	Macomb County, MI	12.6
23	25	Cuyahoga County, OH	12.5
52	26	Hamilton County, OH	12.3
67	26	Montgomery County, PA	12.3
20	26	Tarrant County, TX	12.3
12	29	King County, WA	12.2
13	30	San Bernardino County, CA	12.1
44	30	Shelby County, TN	12.1
69	32	Essex County, MA	12.0
51	33	Hartford County, CT	11.9
54	33	New Haven County, CT	11.9
33	35	Franklin County, OH	11.8
64	35	Ventura County, CA	11.8
39	37	Milwaukee County, WI	11.7
38	38	Contra Costa County, CA	11.6
11	38	Wayne County, MI	11.6
15	40	Broward County, FL	11.5
68	40	Monroe County, NY	11.5
75	42	El Paso County, TX	11.4
22	42	Suffolk County, NY	11.4
32	44	Hennepin County, MN	11.3
72	45	Mecklenburg County, NC	11.0
18	46	Philadelphia County, PA	10.9
30	47	Oakland County, MI	10.7
26	48	Nassau County, NY	10.6
47	49	Fairfield County, CT	10.3
58	50	Fresno County, CA	10.2
43	50	Salt Lake County, UT	10.2
55	52	Fulton County, GA	10.0
19	52	Middlesex County, MA	10.0
49	54	Montgomery County, MD	9.9
56	54	Travis County, TX	9.9
46	56	Bergen County, NJ	9.8
66	57	Middlesex County, NJ	9.7
42	58	Du Page County, IL	9.5
10	59	Dallas County, TX	9.4
5	60	Orange County, CA	9.3
21	61	Alameda County, CA	9.2
70	61	San Mateo County, CA	9.2
40	61	Westchester County, NY	9.2
3	64	Harris County, TX	9.1
2	65	Cook County, IL	8.9
14	66	Santa Clara County, CA	8.4
59	67	Essex County, NJ	8.1
1	68	Los Angeles County, CA	7.4
62	69	San Francisco County, CA	7.0
74	69	Suffolk County, MA	7.0
9	71	Queens County, NY	5.9
27	72	Bronx County, NY	5.8
8	73	Miami-Dade County, FL	5.4
17	73	New York County, NY	5.4
7	75	Kings County, NY	5.0

Median Household Income, 2000

Population Rank	Median Household Income Rank	County	[B-3. col 57] Median Household Income (Dollars)
36	1	Fairfax County, VA	81 050
14	2	Santa Clara County, CA	74 335
26	3	Nassau County, NY	72 030
49	4	Montgomery County, MD	71 551
70	5	San Mateo County, CA	70 819
42	6	Du Page County, IL	67 887
22	7	Suffolk County, NY	65 288
47	8	Fairfield County, CT	65 249
46	9	Bergen County, NJ	65 241
38	10	Contra Costa County, CA	63 675
40	11	Westchester County, NY	63 582
30	12	Oakland County, MI	61 907
66	13	Middlesex County, NJ	61 446
67	14	Montgomery County, PA	60 829
19	15	Middlesex County, MA	60 821
64	16	Ventura County, CA	59 666
5	17	Orange County, CA	58 820
21	18	Alameda County, CA	55 946
57	19	Prince George's County, MD	55 256
62	20	San Francisco County, CA	55 221
12	21	King County, WA	53 157
60	22	Macomb County, MI	52 102
48	23	Honolulu County, HI	51 914
32	24	Hennepin County, MN	51 711
69	25	Essex County, MA	51 576
51	26	Hartford County, CT	50 756
63	27	Baltimore County, MD	50 667
72	28	Mecklenburg County, NC	50 579
34	29	St. Louis County, MO	50 532
54	30	New Haven County, CT	48 834
43	31	Salt Lake County, UT	48 373
65	32	Worcester County, MA	47 874
55	33	Fulton County, GA	47 321
6	34	San Diego County, CA	47 067
17	35	New York County, NY	47 030
56	36	Travis County, TX	46 761
20	37	Tarrant County, TX	46 179
2	38	Cook County, IL	45 922
4	39	Maricopa County, AZ	45 358
71	40	Pierce County, WA	45 204
31	41	Palm Beach County, FL	45 062
59	42	Essex County, NJ	44 944
68	43	Monroe County, NY	44 891
25	44	Clark County, NV	44 616
29	45	Sacramento County, CA	43 816
10	46	Dallas County, TX	43 324
16	47	Riverside County, CA	42 887
33	48	Franklin County, OH	42 734
3	49	Harris County, TX	42 598
9	50	Queens County, NY	42 439
1	51	Los Angeles County, CA	42 189
13	52	San Bernardino County, CA	42 066
15	53	Broward County, FL	41 691
45	54	Orange County, FL	41 311
52	55	Hamilton County, OH	40 964
11	56	Wayne County, MI	40 776
61	57	Duval County, FL	40 703
35	58	Hillsborough County, FL	40 663
50	59	Marion County, IN	40 421
44	60	Shelby County, TN	39 593
73	61	Jefferson County, KY	39 457
74	62	Suffolk County, MA	39 355
23	63	Cuyahoga County, OH	39 168
37	64	Erie County, NY	38 567
28	65	Allegheny County, PA	38 329
24	66	Bexar County, TX	38 328
39	67	Milwaukee County, WI	38 100
41	68	Pinellas County, FL	37 111
53	69	Pima County, AZ	36 758
8	70	Miami-Dade County, FL	35 966
58	71	Fresno County, CA	34 725
7	72	Kings County, NY	32 135
75	73	El Paso County, TX	31 051
18	74	Philadelphia County, PA	30 746
27	75	Bronx County, NY	27 611

TABLE 2—75 Largest Counties by 2000 Population
Selected Rankings

Percent of all Households with Income Over $100,000, 2000				Percent of all Households with Income Below Poverty, 2000				Percent of Population that Resides in the Same House in 1995 and 2000			
Population Rank	With Income Over $100,000 Rank	County	[B-3. col 71] Percent with Income Over $100,000	Population Rank	With Income Below Poverty Rank	County	[B-3. col 73] Percent With Income Below Poverty	Population Rank	Same Residence Rank	County	[C-3. col 2] Percent Same Residence
36	1	Fairfax County, VA	37.6	27	1	Bronx County, NY	29.0	26	1	Nassau County, NY	69.9
14	2	Santa Clara County, CA	34.6	7	2	Kings County, NY	24.0	22	2	Suffolk County, NY	64.7
49	3	Montgomery County, MD	32.4	18	3	Philadelphia County, PA	21.8	28	3	Allegheny County, PA	64.6
26	4	Nassau County, NY	32.3	75	4	El Paso County, TX	21.6	37	4	Erie County, NY	62.9
70	4	San Mateo County, CA	32.3	74	5	Suffolk County, MA	18.4	7	4	Kings County, NY	62.9
47	6	Fairfield County, CT	31.0	58	6	Fresno County, CA	18.2	46	6	Bergen County, NJ	62.8
40	6	Westchester County, NY	31.0	8	7	Miami-Dade County, FL	18.1	18	7	Philadelphia County, PA	61.9
46	8	Bergen County, NJ	28.6	17	8	New York County, NY	16.6	9	8	Queens County, NY	61.8
42	9	Du Page County, IL	27.5	59	9	Essex County, NJ	15.4	67	9	Montgomery County, PA	61.2
38	10	Contra Costa County, CA	26.7	1	10	Los Angeles County, CA	15.1	40	9	Westchester County, NY	61.2
22	11	Suffolk County, NY	25.5	44	11	Shelby County, TN	14.9	27	11	Bronx County, NY	60.5
30	12	Oakland County, MI	25.3	11	11	Wayne County, MI	14.9	11	12	Wayne County, MI	60.0
19	13	Middlesex County, MA	24.9	24	13	Bexar County, TX	14.3	23	13	Cuyahoga County, OH	59.6
62	14	San Francisco County, CA	24.7	9	14	Queens County, NY	14.1	34	14	St. Louis County, MO	59.2
17	15	New York County, NY	23.9	55	15	Fulton County, GA	13.9	65	15	Worcester County, MA	59.0
67	16	Montgomery County, PA	23.5	13	16	San Bernardino County, CA	13.5	69	16	Essex County, MA	58.7
5	16	Orange County, CA	23.5	53	17	Pima County, AZ	13.3	54	17	New Haven County, CT	58.5
66	18	Middlesex County, NJ	22.9	39	18	Milwaukee County, WI	13.2	60	18	Macomb County, MI	58.3
64	19	Ventura County, CA	22.8	3	19	Harris County, TX	13.1	63	19	Baltimore County, MD	58.1
21	20	Alameda County, CA	22.2	23	20	Cuyahoga County, OH	12.7	51	20	Hartford County, CT	58.0
55	21	Fulton County, GA	21.5	37	21	Erie County, NY	12.3	59	21	Essex County, NJ	57.9
69	22	Essex County, MA	19.0	2	22	Cook County, IL	12.2	19	21	Middlesex County, MA	57.9
12	23	King County, WA	18.7	73	22	Jefferson County, KY	12.2	66	23	Middlesex County, NJ	57.5
59	24	Essex County, NJ	18.5	52	24	Hamilton County, OH	12.0	68	24	Monroe County, NY	57.4
48	25	Honolulu County, HI	18.2	16	24	Riverside County, CA	12.0	42	25	Du Page County, IL	57.3
32	26	Hennepin County, MN	17.9	61	26	Duval County, FL	11.6	47	25	Fairfield County, CT	57.3
34	27	St. Louis County, MO	17.5	28	27	Allegheny County, PA	11.5	2	27	Cook County, IL	57.0
72	28	Mecklenburg County, NC	17.2	35	27	Hillsborough County, FL	11.5	17	28	New York County, NY	56.9
51	29	Hartford County, CT	17.1	29	27	Sacramento County, CA	11.5	70	29	San Mateo County, CA	56.6
57	30	Prince George's County, MD	17.0	10	30	Dallas County, TX	11.3	48	30	Honolulu County, HI	56.3
31	31	Palm Beach County, FL	16.2	33	30	Franklin County, OH	11.3	30	31	Oakland County, MI	55.8
56	32	Travis County, TX	16.1	56	30	Travis County, TX	11.3	52	32	Hamilton County, OH	55.4
54	33	New Haven County, CT	15.8	45	33	Orange County, CA	10.9	75	33	El Paso County, TX	55.2
6	34	San Diego County, CA	15.7	15	34	Broward County, FL	10.8	62	34	San Francisco County, CA	54.2
63	35	Baltimore County, MD	15.3	68	34	Monroe County, NY	10.8	73	35	Jefferson County, KY	53.6
60	35	Macomb County, MI	15.3	50	36	Marion County, IN	10.6	38	36	Contra Costa County, CA	53.2
2	37	Cook County, IL	15.1	6	37	San Diego County, CA	10.3	49	37	Montgomery County, MD	52.7
1	37	Los Angeles County, CA	15.1	62	38	San Francisco County, CA	10.2	57	37	Prince George's County, MD	52.7
65	39	Worcester County, MA	14.8	21	39	Alameda County, CA	9.8	39	39	Milwaukee County, WI	52.3
3	40	Harris County, TX	14.4	48	40	Honolulu County, HI	9.7	1	40	Los Angeles County, CA	52.0
20	41	Tarrant County, TX	13.9	4	40	Maricopa County, AZ	9.7	32	41	Hennepin County, MN	51.8
10	42	Dallas County, TX	13.7	54	40	New Haven County, CT	9.7	64	42	Ventura County, CA	51.7
4	43	Maricopa County, AZ	13.3	71	43	Pierce County, WA	9.6	24	43	Bexar County, TX	51.2
68	44	Monroe County, NY	13.1	20	43	Tarrant County, TX	9.6	14	43	Santa Clara County, CA	51.2
43	45	Salt Lake County, UT	13.0	65	43	Worcester County, MA	9.6	44	43	Shelby County, TN	51.2
15	46	Broward County, FL	12.8	25	46	Clark County, NV	9.5	58	46	Fresno County, CA	51.0
52	46	Hamilton County, OH	12.8	69	46	Essex County, MA	9.5	21	47	Alameda County, CA	50.8
74	48	Suffolk County, MA	12.4	41	46	Pinellas County, FL	9.5	41	48	Pinellas County, FL	50.4
29	49	Sacramento County, CA	12.3	51	49	Hartford County, CT	9.1	8	49	Miami-Dade County, FL	50.2
9	50	Queens County, NY	12.2	31	50	Palm Beach County, FL	9.0	43	50	Salt Lake County, UT	50.0
16	50	Riverside County, CA	12.2	40	51	Westchester County, NY	8.5	31	51	Palm Beach County, FL	49.5
44	52	Shelby County, TN	11.6	72	52	Mecklenburg County, NC	8.2	74	52	Suffolk County, MA	49.3
25	53	Clark County, NV	11.5	12	53	King County, WA	7.8	36	53	Fairfax County, VA	49.2
33	53	Franklin County, OH	11.5	5	54	Orange County, CA	7.7	61	54	Duval County, FL	48.9
11	53	Wayne County, MI	11.5	43	54	Salt Lake County, UT	7.7	13	55	San Bernardino County, CA	48.2
35	56	Hillsborough County, FL	11.3	32	56	Hennepin County, MN	7.4	5	56	Orange County, CA	48.0
13	57	San Bernardino County, CA	11.0	64	57	Ventura County, CA	7.2	3	57	Harris County, TX	47.8
8	58	Miami-Dade County, FL	10.8	19	58	Middlesex County, MA	7.0	12	58	King County, WA	47.6
23	59	Cuyahoga County, OH	10.7	57	58	Prince George's County, MD	7.0	29	59	Sacramento County, CA	47.5
73	59	Jefferson County, KY	10.7	47	60	Fairfield County, CT	6.9	50	60	Marion County, IN	47.2
45	59	Orange County, FL	10.7	34	61	St. Louis County, MO	6.7	15	61	Broward County, FL	47.1
28	62	Allegheny County, PA	10.5	38	62	Contra Costa County, CA	6.6	71	62	Pierce County, WA	46.9
71	63	Pierce County, WA	10.4	63	63	Baltimore County, MD	6.4	16	63	Riverside County, CA	46.7
24	64	Bexar County, TX	9.9	66	64	Middlesex County, NJ	6.1	33	64	Franklin County, OH	46.4
50	64	Marion County, IN	9.9	14	64	Santa Clara County, CA	6.1	53	65	Pima County, AZ	46.2
61	66	Duval County, FL	9.7	60	66	Macomb County, MI	5.9	35	66	Hillsborough County, FL	46.0
41	67	Pinellas County, FL	9.5	22	67	Suffolk County, NY	5.6	10	67	Dallas County, TX	45.3
37	68	Erie County, NY	9.4	30	68	Oakland County, MI	5.4	6	68	San Diego County, CA	45.1
7	68	Kings County, NY	9.4	46	69	Bergen County, NJ	5.3	20	69	Tarrant County, TX	44.9
53	70	Pima County, AZ	9.0	26	69	Nassau County, NY	5.3	72	70	Mecklenburg County, NC	43.6
58	71	Fresno County, CA	8.6	49	71	Montgomery County, MD	4.9	55	71	Fulton County, GA	42.8
39	72	Milwaukee County, WI	7.9	70	71	San Mateo County, CA	4.9	45	72	Orange County, FL	42.3
75	73	El Paso County, TX	6.3	67	73	Montgomery County, PA	4.7	4	73	Maricopa County, AZ	41.6
18	73	Philadelphia County, PA	6.3	36	74	Fairfax County, VA	3.6	56	74	Travis County, TX	37.6
27	75	Bronx County, NY	6.1	42	75	Du Page County, IL	3.5	25	75	Clark County, NV	34.5

TABLE 2—75 Largest Counties by 2000 Population
Selected Rankings

Percent Owner-Occupied Housing Units, 2000				Median Housing Value (Owner Estimated), 2000				Median Gross Rent, 2000			
Population Rank	Owner-Occupied Rank	County	[C-3. col 8] Percent Owner-Occupied	Population Rank	Median Housing Value Rank	County	[C-3. col 22] Median Housing Value (Dollars)	Population Rank	Median Gross Rent Rank	County	[C-3. col 25] Median Gross Rent (Dollars)
26	1	Nassau County, NY	80.3	70	1	San Mateo County, CA	449 900	14	1	Santa Clara County, CA	1 185
22	2	Suffolk County, NY	79.8	62	2	San Francisco County, CA	422 700	70	2	San Mateo County, CA	1 144
60	3	Macomb County, MI	78.9	14	3	Santa Clara County, CA	422 600	36	3	Fairfax County, VA	998
42	4	Du Page County, IL	76.4	17	4	New York County, NY	361 100	26	4	Nassau County, NY	964
30	5	Oakland County, MI	74.8	21	5	Alameda County, CA	291 900	22	5	Suffolk County, NY	945
31	6	Palm Beach County, FL	74.7	40	6	Westchester County, NY	285 800	62	6	San Francisco County, CA	928
34	7	St. Louis County, MO	74.1	48	7	Honolulu County, HI	274 600	5	7	Orange County, CA	923
67	8	Montgomery County, PA	73.5	47	8	Fairfield County, CT	265 100	49	8	Montgomery County, MD	914
36	9	Fairfax County, VA	71.0	38	9	Contra Costa County, CA	253 800	38	9	Contra Costa County, CA	898
41	10	Pinellas County, FL	70.8	5	10	Orange County, CA	253 000	64	10	Ventura County, CA	892
15	11	Broward County, FL	69.5	19	11	Middlesex County, MA	244 400	46	11	Bergen County, NJ	872
38	12	Contra Costa County, CA	69.3	46	12	Bergen County, NJ	240 800	21	12	Alameda County, CA	852
47	13	Fairfield County, CT	69.2	26	13	Nassau County, NY	240 200	66	13	Middlesex County, NJ	845
43	14	Salt Lake County, UT	69.0	64	14	Ventura County, CA	238 800	40	14	Westchester County, NY	839
16	15	Riverside County, CA	68.8	7	15	Kings County, NY	229 200	47	15	Fairfield County, CT	838
49	16	Montgomery County, MD	68.7	12	16	King County, WA	226 400	42	16	Du Page County, IL	837
63	17	Baltimore County, MD	67.6	36	17	Fairfax County, VA	222 400	19	17	Middlesex County, MA	835
64	17	Ventura County, CA	67.6	6	18	San Diego County, CA	212 000	48	18	Honolulu County, HI	802
4	19	Maricopa County, AZ	67.5	49	19	Montgomery County, MD	210 600	17	19	New York County, NY	796
46	20	Bergen County, NJ	67.2	69	20	Essex County, MA	206 800	74	20	Suffolk County, MA	791
28	21	Allegheny County, PA	67.0	9	21	Queens County, NY	206 200	9	21	Queens County, NY	775
66	22	Middlesex County, NJ	66.7	1	22	Los Angeles County, CA	201 400	6	22	San Diego County, CA	761
11	23	Wayne County, MI	66.6	74	23	Suffolk County, MA	201 300	12	23	King County, WA	758
32	24	Hennepin County, MN	66.2	59	24	Essex County, NJ	188 400	15	24	Broward County, FL	757
37	25	Erie County, NY	65.3	42	25	Du Page County, IL	187 600	67	24	Montgomery County, PA	757
68	26	Monroe County, NY	65.1	27	26	Bronx County, NY	183 800	31	26	Palm Beach County, FL	739
73	27	Jefferson County, KY	64.9	22	27	Suffolk County, NY	183 500	57	27	Prince George's County, MD	737
13	28	San Bernardino County, CA	64.5	55	28	Fulton County, GA	175 800	56	28	Travis County, TX	727
53	29	Pima County, AZ	64.3	30	29	Oakland County, MI	173 800	25	29	Clark County, NV	716
51	30	Hartford County, CT	64.2	66	30	Middlesex County, NJ	164 400	55	30	Fulton County, GA	709
35	31	Hillsborough County, FL	64.1	67	31	Montgomery County, PA	158 900	30	31	Oakland County, MI	707
65	31	Worcester County, MA	64.1	2	32	Cook County, IL	154 300	1	32	Los Angeles County, CA	704
75	33	El Paso County, TX	63.6	43	33	Salt Lake County, UT	153 500	45	33	Orange County, FL	699
69	34	Essex County, MA	63.5	54	34	New Haven County, CT	145 500	72	34	Mecklenburg County, NC	693
71	34	Pierce County, WA	63.5	71	35	Pierce County, WA	144 400	59	35	Essex County, NJ	675
23	36	Cuyahoga County, OH	63.2	57	36	Prince George's County, MD	143 700	7	36	Kings County, NY	672
61	37	Duval County, FL	63.1	65	37	Worcester County, MA	142 600	63	37	Baltimore County, MD	670
54	37	New Haven County, CT	63.1	51	38	Hartford County, CT	142 500	4	38	Maricopa County, AZ	666
44	37	Shelby County, TN	63.1	32	39	Hennepin County, MN	141 100	54	38	New Haven County, CT	666
72	40	Mecklenburg County, NC	62.3	29	39	Sacramento County, CA	141 100	69	40	Essex County, MA	665
19	41	Middlesex County, MA	61.8	72	41	Mecklenburg County, NC	139 000	16	41	Riverside County, CA	660
57	41	Prince George's County, MD	61.8	16	42	Riverside County, CA	135 000	29	42	Sacramento County, CA	659
70	43	San Mateo County, CA	61.5	60	43	Macomb County, MI	134 900	32	43	Hennepin County, MN	654
5	44	Orange County, CA	61.4	25	44	Clark County, NV	132 200	2	44	Cook County, IL	648
24	45	Bexar County, TX	61.2	56	45	Travis County, TX	127 600	13	44	San Bernardino County, CA	648
20	46	Tarrant County, TX	60.8	63	46	Baltimore County, MD	125 700	10	46	Dallas County, TX	647
45	47	Orange County, FL	60.7	13	47	San Bernardino County, CA	124 900	8	46	Miami-Dade County, FL	647
40	48	Westchester County, NY	60.1	4	48	Maricopa County, AZ	122 000	51	48	Hartford County, CT	645
52	49	Hamilton County, OH	59.8	31	49	Palm Beach County, FL	115 000	43	49	Salt Lake County, UT	638
12	49	King County, WA	59.8	34	50	St. Louis County, MO	114 800	71	50	Pierce County, WA	624
14	49	Santa Clara County, CA	59.8	33	51	Franklin County, OH	113 700	35	51	Hillsborough County, FL	623
50	52	Marion County, IN	59.3	8	52	Miami-Dade County, FL	113 200	27	52	Bronx County, NY	620
18	52	Philadelphia County, PA	59.3	23	53	Cuyahoga County, OH	110 100	41	53	Pinellas County, FL	616
25	54	Clark County, NV	59.1	52	54	Hamilton County, OH	109 000	68	54	Monroe County, NY	612
29	55	Sacramento County, CA	58.2	15	55	Broward County, FL	102 800	20	54	Tarrant County, TX	612
2	56	Cook County, IL	57.9	58	56	Fresno County, CA	102 600	61	56	Duval County, FL	604
8	57	Miami-Dade County, FL	57.8	53	56	Pima County, AZ	102 600	60	57	Macomb County, MI	603
33	58	Franklin County, OH	56.9	73	58	Jefferson County, KY	100 800	34	58	St. Louis County, MO	601
58	59	Fresno County, CA	56.5	39	59	Milwaukee County, WI	100 500	33	59	Franklin County, OH	595
6	60	San Diego County, CA	55.4	45	60	Orange County, FL	100 300	3	60	Harris County, TX	590
3	61	Harris County, TX	55.3	68	61	Monroe County, NY	98 200	65	61	Worcester County, MA	580
21	62	Alameda County, CA	54.7	50	62	Marion County, IN	97 200	18	62	Philadelphia County, PA	569
48	63	Honolulu County, HI	54.5	11	63	Wayne County, MI	96 200	50	63	Marion County, IN	567
10	64	Dallas County, TX	52.6	35	64	Hillsborough County, FL	91 800	44	64	Shelby County, TN	566
39	64	Milwaukee County, WI	52.6	10	65	Dallas County, TX	90 800	24	65	Bexar County, TX	556
55	66	Fulton County, GA	52.0	44	65	Shelby County, TN	90 800	39	66	Milwaukee County, WI	555
56	67	Travis County, TX	51.5	20	67	Tarrant County, TX	88 600	53	67	Pima County, AZ	544
1	68	Los Angeles County, CA	47.9	37	68	Erie County, NY	88 200	23	68	Cuyahoga County, OH	541
59	69	Essex County, NJ	45.6	61	69	Duval County, FL	86 100	58	69	Fresno County, CA	534
9	70	Queens County, NY	42.8	41	70	Pinellas County, FL	85 600	11	70	Wayne County, MI	530
62	71	San Francisco County, CA	35.0	3	71	Harris County, TX	84 200	28	71	Allegheny County, PA	516
74	72	Suffolk County, MA	33.9	28	72	Allegheny County, PA	83 500	37	71	Erie County, NY	516
7	73	Kings County, NY	27.1	24	73	Bexar County, TX	71 800	73	73	Jefferson County, KY	494
17	74	New York County, NY	20.1	75	74	El Paso County, TX	67 100	52	74	Hamilton County, OH	485
27	75	Bronx County, NY	19.5	18	75	Philadelphia County, PA	61 000	75	75	El Paso County, TX	468

TABLE 3—All Counties
Selected Rankings

Population, 2000			Percent Under 18 Years, 2000				Percent 18 to 24 Years, 2000			
Population Rank	County	[A-3. col 1] Population	Population Rank	Under 18 Years Rank	County	[A-3. col 2 and 3] Percent Under 18 Years	Population Rank	18 to 24 Years Rank	County	[A-3. col 4] Percent 18 to 24 Years
1	Los Angeles County, CA	9 519 338	2 681	1	Wade Hampton Census Area, AK	46.6	2 294	1	Williamsburg city, VA	45.4
2	Cook County, IL	5 376 741	2 268	2	Shannon County, SD	45.0	2 028	2	Radford city, VA	44.5
3	Harris County, TX	3 400 578	2 526	3	Todd County, SD	44.0	1 104	3	Harrisonburg city, VA	41.7
4	Maricopa County, AZ	3 072 149	3 063	4	Buffalo County, SD	41.7	2 701	4	Lexington city, VA	41.6
5	Orange County, CA	2 846 289	2 666	5	Northwest Arctic Borough, AK	41.4	1 469	5	Madison County, ID	39.9
6	San Diego County, CA	2 813 833	2 917	6	Sioux County, ND	40.7	774	6	Riley County, KS	34.5
7	Kings County, NY	2 465 326	3 025	7	Ziebach County, SD	40.5	997	7	Charlottesville city, VA	34.1
8	Miami-Dade County, FL	2 253 362	2 021	8	Bethel Census Area, AK	39.9	1 091	8	Whitman County, WA	32.7
9	Queens County, NY	2 229 379	2 129	9	San Juan County, UT	39.3	350	9	Brazos County, TX	32.2
10	Dallas County, TX	2 218 899	2 874	10	Menominee County, WI	39.0	2 192	10	Clay County, SD	31.4
11	Wayne County, MI	2 061 162	2 786	11	Dewey County, SD	38.9	621	11	Montgomery County, VA	31.2
12	King County, WA	1 737 034	714	12	Apache County, AZ	38.5	782	12	Athens County, OH	31.0
13	San Bernardino County, CA	1 709 434	2 854	12	Dillingham Census Area, AK	38.5	520	12	Clarke County, GA	31.0
14	Santa Clara County, CA	1 682 585	2 588	12	Juab County, UT	38.5	765	14	Isabella County, MI	29.6
15	Broward County, FL	1 623 018	2 649	15	North Slope Borough, AK	38.2	1 040	15	Oktibbeha County, MS	29.4
16	Riverside County, CA	1 545 387	667	16	McKinley County, NM	38.0	1 345	16	Albany County, WY	28.5
17	New York County, NY	1 537 195	3 078	17	Lake and Peninsula Borough, AK	37.9	2 100	17	Chattahoochee County, GA	28.4
18	Philadelphia County, PA	1 517 550	871	18	Starr County, TX	37.4	642	18	Story County, IA	28.3
19	Middlesex County, MA	1 465 396	2 271	19	Millard County, UT	37.3	1 322	19	McDonough County, IL	27.8
20	Tarrant County, TX	1 446 219	2 348	20	Franklin County, ID	37.2	450	19	Monroe County, IN	27.8
21	Alameda County, CA	1 443 741	961	21	Maverick County, TX	37.0	1 044	21	Watauga County, NC	27.7
22	Suffolk County, NY	1 419 369	2 514	21	Nome Census Area, AK	37.0	1 560	22	Adair County, MO	27.5
23	Cuyahoga County, OH	1 393 978	2 670	21	Thurston County, NE	37.0	1 146	23	Lafayette County, MS	27.2
24	Bexar County, TX	1 392 931	2 676	24	Morgan County, UT	36.9	397	24	Centre County, PA	27.0
25	Clark County, NV	1 375 765	2 135	25	Duchesne County, UT	36.8	1 444	25	Brookings County, SD	26.7
26	Nassau County, NY	1 334 544	2 899	26	Corson County, SD	36.7	525	26	Douglas County, KS	26.4
27	Bronx County, NY	1 332 650	2 186	27	Rolette County, ND	36.5	2 461	26	Wayne County, NE	26.4
28	Allegheny County, PA	1 281 666	2 689	28	Benson County, ND	36.3	843	28	Bulloch County, GA	26.3
29	Sacramento County, CA	1 223 499	2 946	28	Franklin County, NE	36.3	806	29	Jackson County, IL	26.0
30	Oakland County, MI	1 194 156	2 997	30	Jackson County, SD	36.2	1 046	30	Lincoln Parish, LA	25.9
31	Palm Beach County, FL	1 131 184	1 839	30	Jefferson County, ID	36.2	722	30	Payne County, OK	25.9
32	Hennepin County, MN	1 116 200	284	30	Webb County, TX	36.2	535	30	Tompkins County, NY	25.9
33	Franklin County, OH	1 068 978	1 042	33	Box Elder County, UT	36.0	362	33	Tippecanoe County, IN	25.5
34	St. Louis County, MO	1 016 315	2 249	34	Big Horn County, MT	35.9	1 696	34	Nodaway County, MO	25.2
35	Hillsborough County, FL	998 948	1 142	35	Holmes County, OH	35.7	1 829	35	Fredericksburg city, VA	24.2
36	Fairfax County, VA	969 749	532	36	Navajo County, AZ	35.5	1 251	36	Latah County, ID	23.9
37	Erie County, NY	950 265	2 376	37	Emery County, UT	35.4	358	37	Onslow County, NC	23.7
38	Contra Costa County, CA	948 816	96	38	Hidalgo County, TX	35.3	1 008	38	Prince Edward County, VA	23.5
39	Milwaukee County, WI	940 164	3 060	38	Mellette County, SD	35.3	2 524	39	Dawes County, NE	23.4
40	Westchester County, NY	923 459	2 209	40	Glacier County, MT	35.2	1 688	39	Rowan County, KY	23.4
41	Pinellas County, FL	921 482	241	41	Davis County, UT	35.1	2 302	41	Claiborne County, MS	23.3
42	DuPage County, IL	904 161	3 052	41	Oldham County, TX	35.1	881	41	Coles County, IL	23.3
43	Salt Lake County, UT	898 387	1 092	41	Tooele County, UT	35.1	488	41	Johnson County, IA	23.3
44	Shelby County, TN	897 472	2 734	41	Yukon-Koyukuk Census Area, AK	35.1	634	41	Monongalia County, WV	23.3
45	Orange County, FL	896 344	1 061	45	Bingham County, ID	35.0	259	45	Alachua County, FL	23.2
46	Bergen County, NJ	884 118	3 110	46	Clark County, ID	34.8	308	46	Champaign County, IL	23.0
47	Fairfield County, CT	882 567	3 067	46	Rich County, UT	34.8	786	47	Walker County, TX	22.9
48	Honolulu County, HI	876 156	2 125	48	Gaines County, TX	34.7	469	48	Lee County, AL	22.7
49	Montgomery County, MD	873 341	2 389	49	Roosevelt County, MT	34.6	562	49	Cache County, UT	22.2
50	Marion County, IN	860 454	1 557	49	Uintah County, UT	34.6	844	50	Blue Earth County, MN	22.1
51	Hartford County, CT	857 183	926	51	Franklin County, WA	34.5	585	51	DeKalb County, IL	21.8
52	Hamilton County, OH	845 303	1 850	51	Sevier County, UT	34.5	1 302	52	Kittitas County, WA	21.6
53	Pima County, AZ	843 746	2 876	53	Kearny County, KS	34.4	240	53	Leon County, FL	21.3
54	New Haven County, CT	824 008	264	53	Merced County, CA	34.4	2 164	54	Gunnison County, CO	21.1
55	Fulton County, GA	816 006	1 995	55	Adams County, WA	34.3	457	55	Orange County, NC	20.9
56	Travis County, TX	812 280	1 103	55	Finney County, KS	34.3	159	55	Utah County, UT	20.9
57	Prince George's County, MD	801 515	2 970	57	Reagan County, TX	34.2	2 439	57	Stevens County, MN	20.8
58	Fresno County, CA	799 407	2 074	57	Wasatch County, UT	34.2	531	58	Hays County, TX	20.6
59	Essex County, NJ	793 633	3 097	59	Glasscock County, TX	34.1	1 288	59	Iron County, UT	20.5
60	Macomb County, MI	788 149	2 969	59	Hudspeth County, TX	34.1	651	60	Benton County, OR	20.1
61	Duval County, FL	778 879	2 863	59	Martin County, TX	34.1	812	60	Nacogdoches County, TX	20.1
62	San Francisco County, CA	776 733	1 717	62	Cassia County, ID	34.0	1 101	62	Mecosta County, MI	20.0
63	Baltimore County, MD	754 292	159	63	Utah County, UT	33.9	1 614	63	Clark County, AR	19.9
64	Ventura County, CA	753 197	2 640	64	Power County, ID	33.8	1 115	63	Dunn County, WI	19.9
65	Worcester County, MA	750 963	160	64	Tulare County, CA	33.8	943	65	Johnson County, MO	19.8
66	Middlesex County, NJ	750 162	2 324	64	Zavala County, TX	33.8	398	66	Boone County, MO	19.7
67	Montgomery County, PA	750 097	174	67	Cameron County, TX	33.7	1 276	66	Calloway County, KY	19.7
68	Monroe County, NY	735 343	1 252	68	LaGrange County, IN	33.6	740	66	Grand Forks County, ND	19.7
69	Essex County, MA	723 419	1 785	68	Moore County, TX	33.6	352	69	Hampshire County, MA	19.3
70	San Mateo County, CA	707 161	2 499	68	Rosebud County, MT	33.6	1 217	70	Houghton County, MI	19.1
71	Pierce County, WA	700 820	1 154	68	Santa Cruz County, AZ	33.6	915	71	Winona County, MN	18.8
72	Mecklenburg County, NC	695 454	2 778	72	Beaver County, UT	33.4	700	72	Madison County, KY	18.7
73	Jefferson County, KY	693 604	1 868	72	Deaf Smith County, TX	33.4	1 466	73	Ellis County, KS	18.6
74	Suffolk County, MA	689 807	3 139	72	King County, TX	33.4	357	73	McLean County, IL	18.6
75	El Paso County, TX	679 622	1 658	75	Sanpete County, UT	33.2	723	75	Gallatin County, MT	18.5
			1 806	75	Uinta County, WY	33.2				

TABLE 3—All Counties
Selected Rankings

Population Rank	25 to 44 Years Rank	County	Percent 25 to 44 Years [A-3. col 5]	Population Rank	45 to 64 Years Rank	County	Percent 45 to 64 Years [A-3. col 6]	Population Rank	65 Years and Over Rank	County	Percent 65 Years and Over [A-3. col 7]
		Percent 25 to 44 Years, 2000				Percent 45 to 64 Years, 2000				Percent 65 Years and Over, 2000	
2 819	1	Aleutians West Census Area, AK...	50.9	3 134	1	San Juan County, CO	40.9	3 140	1	Kalawao County, HI	49.7
3 014	2	Aleutians East Borough, AK	46.0	3 141	2	Loving County, TX	40.3	387	2	Charlotte County, FL	34.7
1 613	3	Summit County, CO	44.5	3 140	3	Kalawao County, HI	40.1	2 964	3	McIntosh County, ND	34.2
421	4	Alexandria city, VA	44.1	2 963	4	Storey County, NV	36.8	600	4	Highlands County, FL	33.1
2 728	5	Bailey County, TX	42.9	2 951	5	Catron County, NM	36.2	458	5	Citrus County, FL	32.3
291	6	Arlington County, VA	42.8	2 156	6	San Juan County, WA	35.4	177	6	Sarasota County, FL	31.4
1 064	7	Eagle County, CO	42.5	2 953	7	Custer County, CO	34.5	409	7	Hernando County, FL	30.9
62	8	San Francisco County, CA	41.0	3 113	8	Esmeralda County, NV	34.1	1 950	8	Llano County, TX	30.6
2 083	9	West Feliciana Parish, LA	40.7	2 937	9	Ouray County, CO	34.0	3 042	9	Divide County, ND	29.4
2 417	10	Manassas Park city, VA	40.5	3 125	10	Hinsdale County, CO	33.9	3 123	9	Harding County, NM	29.4
2 197	11	Union County, FL	39.9	2 955	11	Adams County, ID	32.9	2 998	11	McPherson County, SD	29.3
2 488	12	Nantucket County, MA	39.8	3 121	12	Mineral County, CO	32.7	476	12	Indian River County, FL	29.2
320	13	Loudoun County, VA	39.0	1 518	13	Jefferson County, WA	32.4	918	13	Flagler County, FL	28.6
2 328	14	Greensville County, VA	38.9	3 104	13	Prairie County, MT	32.4	2 326	13	Lancaster County, VA	28.6
2 816	15	Crowley County, CO	38.8	2 633	13	Valley County, ID	32.4	425	15	Martin County, FL	28.3
2 101	16	Pitkin County, CO	38.7	2 503	16	Clear Creek County, CO	32.2	2 205	16	Sierra County, NM	27.9
17	17	New York County, NY	38.6	2 230	17	Trinity County, CA	32.1	2 875	17	Smith County, KS	27.6
636	17	Paulding County, GA	38.6	2 423	18	Kiowa County, OK	32.0	876	17	Sumter County, FL	27.6
113	19	Collin County, TX	38.4	1 100	19	Calaveras County, CA	31.7	2 941	19	Nelson County, ND	27.5
2 921	19	Concho County, TX	38.4	3 116	19	Roberts County, TX	31.7	3 037	20	Logan County, ND	27.1
311	21	Douglas County, CO	38.3	3 023	21	Highland County, VA	31.5	2 986	20	Pawnee County, NE	27.1
1 883	22	Teton County, WY	38.0	2 687	21	Rappahannock County, VA	31.5	1 728	22	Curry County, OR	26.9
856	23	Anderson County, TX	37.7	3 092	21	Wheeler County, OR	31.5	1 153	23	Baxter County, AR	26.8
2 691	23	Brown County, IL	37.7	1 188	24	Camden County, MO	31.3	170	23	Pasco County, FL	26.8
92	23	Gwinnett County, GA	37.7	2 317	25	Alcona County, MI	31.0	3 084	23	Sheridan County, ND	26.8
2 862	26	Gilpin County, CO	37.5	644	25	Monroe County, FL	31.0	3 126	26	Hooker County, NE	26.7
2 717	26	Pershing County, NV	37.5	2 839	27	Cook County, MN	30.9	2 981	27	Cheyenne County, KS	26.6
577	28	Scott County, MN	37.4	2 657	28	Custer County, SD	30.8	2 905	28	Traverse County, MN	26.5
139	29	Denton County, TX	37.2	2 822	28	Hamilton County, NY	30.8	265	29	Lake County, FL	26.4
529	29	Forsyth County, GA	37.2	2 101	30	Pitkin County, CO	30.7	3 048	30	De Baca County, NM	26.3
76	31	DeKalb County, GA	37.0	3 031	31	Haines Borough, AK	30.6	2 956	30	Decatur County, KS	26.3
3 074	31	Denali Borough, AK	37.0	2 949	32	Sierra County, CA	30.5	2 281	30	Northumberland County, VA	26.3
1 286	33	Lassen County, CA	36.9	3 004	33	Granite County, MT	30.4	2 600	33	Hutchinson County, SD	26.2
56	33	Travis County, TX	36.9	1 950	33	Llano County, TX	30.4	2 799	33	Republic County, KS	26.2
89	35	Cobb County, GA	36.7	1 745	33	Plumas County, CA	30.4	1 810	35	La Paz County, AZ	26.1
2 325	36	DeKalb County, MO	36.6	2 456	36	Archuleta County, CO	30.2	2 531	36	Hickory County, MO	26.0
85	36	Wake County, NC	36.6	2 927	36	Wahkiakum County, WA	30.2	2 928	36	Jewell County, KS	26.0
665	38	Coryell County, TX	36.5	2 663	36	Wallowa County, OR	30.2	2 994	36	Rawlins County, KS	26.0
101	38	Denver County, CO	36.5	3 103	39	Alpine County, CA	30.1	2 843	36	Wells County, ND	26.0
1 423	38	Elmore County, ID	36.5	1 822	39	Lincoln County, NM	30.1	2 504	40	Towns County, GA	25.9
72	38	Mecklenburg County, NC	36.5	2 512	39	Mathews County, VA	30.1	2 885	41	Osborne County, KS	25.8
2 684	42	Liberty County, FL	36.4	2 622	39	Ontonagon County, MI	30.1	3 066	42	Comanche County, KS	25.7
1 812	42	Routt County, CO	36.4	2 121	39	Park County, CO	30.1	3 072	43	Cottle County, TX	25.6
2 814	42	Scott County, IL	36.4	2 720	44	Boise County, ID	30.0	2 976	43	Elk County, KS	25.6
232	45	Williamson County, TX	35.9	1 877	44	Los Alamos County, NM	30.0	2 894	43	Emmons County, ND	25.6
385	46	Cherokee County, GA	35.8	2 705	44	Madison County, MT	30.0	3 009	43	Griggs County, ND	25.6
245	46	Clayton County, GA	35.8	2 453	47	Middlesex County, VA	29.9	2 771	47	Haskell County, TX	25.5
88	46	Hudson County, NJ	35.8	1 942	48	Benton County, MO	29.8	3 039	47	Jerauld County, SD	25.5
1 244	46	Manassas city, VA	35.8	2 547	48	Clay County, NC	29.8	2 950	47	Rush County, KS	25.5
14	46	Santa Clara County, CA	35.8	2 010	48	Faribault County, MN	29.8	136	50	Lee County, FL	25.4
1 338	51	Bee County, TX	35.7	3 038	48	Keweenaw County, MI	29.8	1 747	51	Gillespie County, TX	25.3
2 100	51	Chattahoochee County, GA	35.7	1 851	48	Lincoln County, MT	29.8	3 012	51	Hettinger County, ND	25.3
55	51	Fulton County, GA	35.7	2 126	48	Nelson County, VA	29.8	3 119	51	Kent County, TX	25.3
200	54	Prince William County, VA	35.5	3 050	54	Jeff Davis County, TX	29.7	3 015	51	Potter County, SD	25.3
74	54	Suffolk County, MA	35.5	2 440	54	Jefferson County, MT	29.7	2 218	55	Iron County, MI	25.1
414	56	Kings County, CA	35.4	1 757	54	Teller County, CO	29.7	2 740	56	Washington County, KS	25.0
980	57	Barrow County, GA	35.2	2 094	57	Brown County, IN	29.6	2 909	57	Baylor County, TX	24.9
254	58	Durham County, NC	35.1	3 090	57	Jackson County, CO	29.6	3 073	57	Garfield County, NE	24.9
12	59	King County, WA	35.0	235	57	Marin County, CA	29.6	209	57	Manatee County, FL	24.9
300	60	Hamilton County, IN	34.9	2 862	60	Gilpin County, CO	29.5	2 400	57	Sabine County, TX	24.9
455	60	Henry County, GA	34.9	2 880	60	Musselshell County, MT	29.5	3 047	60	Burke County, ND	24.8
2 056	60	Karnes County, TX	34.9	3 062	60	Oliver County, ND	29.5	2 860	61	Gregory County, SD	24.8
1 679	60	Tattnall County, GA	34.9	1 431	60	Stone County, MO	29.5	2 929	61	Woodson County, KS	24.8
10	64	Dallas County, TX	34.8	3 074	64	Denali Borough, AK	29.4	3 008	61	Eddy County, ND	24.7
3 102	65	Bristol Bay Borough, AK	34.7	2 658	64	Ferry County, WA	29.4	2 965	64	Kinney County, TX	24.7
234	65	Howard County, MD	34.7	2 531	64	Hickory County, MO	29.4	1 025	64	Kerr County, TX	24.6
1 675	65	Powhatan County, VA	34.7	2 924	64	Mineral County, MT	29.4	2 775	66	Thayer County, NE	24.6
707	68	Carver County, MN	34.6	2 960	64	Roger Mills County, OK	29.4	2 317	66	Alcona County, MI	24.5
141	68	Virginia Beach city, VA	34.6	1 193	69	Bonner County, ID	29.3	3 002	68	Grant County, ND	24.5
400	70	Montgomery County, TN	34.5	685	69	Brunswick County, NC	29.3	217	68	Marion County, FL	24.5
2 264	70	Sussex County, VA	34.5	1 728	69	Curry County, OR	29.3	2 848	68	Nuckolls County, NE	24.5
165	72	Dakota County, MN	34.4	2 893	69	Custer County, ID	29.3	2 891	72	Chautauqua County, KS	24.4
1 293	72	Hoke County, NC	34.4	3 064	69	Daniels County, MT	29.3	228	72	Collier County, FL	24.4
2 243	72	Mono County, CA	34.4	2 625	69	Lemhi County, ID	29.3	2 938	72	Hand County, SD	24.4
2 780	72	Teton County, ID	34.4	555	69	Nevada County, CA	29.3	2 803	75	Kingsbury County, SD	24.3
				2 314	69	Pend Oreille County, WA	29.3	2 747	75	Lincoln County, MN	24.3
				1 542	69	Roscommon County, MI	29.3	3 096	75	Motley County, TX	24.3
								2 649	75	Russell County, KS	24.3
								2 970	75	Trego County, KS	24.3
								2 915	75	Webster County, NE	24.3

TABLE 3—All Counties
Selected Rankings

Percent Non-Hispanic White, 2000				Percent Black or African American, 2000				Percent American Indian and Alaska Native, 2000			
Population Rank	Non-Hispanic White Rank	County	[A-3. col 11] Percent Non-Hispanic White	Population Rank	Black or African American Rank	County	[A-3. col 14] Percent Black or African American	Population Rank	American Indian and Alaska Native Rank	County	[A-3. col 17] Percent American Indian and Alaska Native
3 128	1	Slope County, ND	100.0	2 467	1	Jefferson County, MS	86.1	2 268	1	Shannon County, SD	93.7
2 375	2	Mitchell County, IA	99.8	1 590	2	Macon County, AL	84.7	2 681	2	Wade Hampton Census Area, AK	91.7
3 115	3	Billings County, ND	99.7	2 302	3	Claiborne County, MS	84.3	2 526	3	Todd County, SD	82.6
3 133	3	Blaine County, NE	99.7	2 449	4	Greene County, AL	80.8	2 666	4	Northwest Arctic Borough, AK	82.0
3 039	5	Jerauld County, SD	99.5	1 713	5	Holmes County, MS	78.8	2 021	5	Bethel Census Area, AK	81.4
2 715	6	Elliott County, KY	99.4	1 289	6	Petersburg city, VA	78.3	2 874	6	Menominee County, WI	81.1
3 009	6	Griggs County, ND	99.4	2 438	7	Hancock County, GA	77.3	2 917	7	Sioux County, ND	80.1
2 201	6	Magoffin County, KY	99.4	2 195	8	Lowndes County, AL	73.5	3 063	8	Buffalo County, SD	79.1
2 998	6	McPherson County, SD	99.4	2 103	9	Sumter County, AL	73.3	714	9	Apache County, AZ	76.9
3 101	10	Garfield County, MT	99.3	2 213	10	Wilcox County, AL	72.2	667	10	McKinley County, NM	74.5
2 983	10	Hanson County, SD	99.3	2 318	11	Bullock County, AL	72.1	2 514	11	Nome Census Area, AK	74.4
3 023	10	Highland County, VA	99.3	2 356	12	Humphreys County, MS	71.6	3 078	12	Lake and Peninsula Borough, AK	73.1
2 453	10	Howard County, IA	99.3	2 510	13	Tunica County, MS	70.7	2 786	13	Dewey County, SD	72.0
2 049	10	Lawrence County, KY	99.3	2 355	14	Allendale County, SC	70.6	3 025	14	Ziebach County, SD	71.5
2 934	10	Mercer County, MO	99.3	1 268	15	Sunflower County, MS	70.1	2 186	15	Rolette County, ND	71.0
2 469	10	Webster County, WV	99.3	2 730	16	Sharkey County, MS	70.0	2 734	16	Yukon-Koyukuk Census Area, AK	70.6
2 679	10	Wolfe County, KY	99.3	1 384	17	Coahoma County, MS	69.5	2 854	17	Dillingham Census Area, AK	69.6
2 888	18	Edmunds County, SD	99.2	2 260	18	Noxubee County, MS	69.0	2 649	18	North Slope Borough, AK	68.5
2 845	18	Florence County, WI	99.2	2 435	19	Quitman County, MS	68.6	2 899	19	Corson County, SD	60.0
2 435	18	Jasper County, IL	99.2	1 167	20	Leflore County, MS	68.2	2 249	20	Big Horn County, MT	59.7
3 054	18	Liberty County, MT	99.2	2 414	20	Wilkinson County, MS	68.2	2 209	21	Glacier County, MT	59.3
2 312	18	Lyon County, IA	99.2	2 493	22	East Carroll Parish, LA	67.9	2 129	22	San Juan County, UT	56.6
2 814	18	Scott County, IL	99.2	2 301	22	Perry County, AL	67.9	2 389	23	Roosevelt County, MT	55.0
2 971	18	Trego County, KS	99.2	117	24	Orleans Parish, LA	67.1	2 946	24	Bennett County, SD	51.8
3 080	25	Campbell County, SD	99.1	1 185	25	Williamsburg County, SC	66.4	3 060	24	Mellette County, SD	51.8
2 747	25	Lincoln County, MN	99.1	1 096	26	Bolivar County, MS	65.6	2 670	26	Thurston County, NE	50.2
2 986	25	Pawnee County, NE	99.1	771	27	Washington County, MS	64.5	532	27	Navajo County, AZ	47.9
2 882	28	Adams County, IA	99.0	82	28	Baltimore city, MD	64.1	2 689	28	Benson County, ND	47.5
2 977	28	Bowman County, ND	99.0	3 043	29	Issaquena County, MS	63.5	2 997	29	Jackson County, SD	45.8
3 027	28	Boyd County, NE	99.0	975	30	Dallas County, AL	63.4	2 685	30	Blaine County, MT	44.9
2 784	28	Cameron County, PA	99.0	1 787	31	Lee County, SC	62.6	3 102	31	Bristol Bay Borough, AK	43.5
2 894	28	Emmons County, ND	99.0	57	31	Prince George's County, MD	62.6	1 733	32	Adair County, OK	42.9
2 070	28	Estill County, KY	99.0	1 803	33	Bertie County, NC	62.5	1 532	33	Cibola County, NM	40.1
1 401	28	Garrett County, MD	99.0	1 979	34	Bamberg County, SC	62.3	2 768	34	Prince of Wales-Outer Ketchikan Cons, AK	39.8
2 938	28	Hand County, SD	99.0	2 264	34	Sussex County, VA	62.3	3 124	35	Yakutat City and Borough, AK	39.7
2 014	28	Lafayette County, WI	99.0	2 835	36	Stewart County, GA	62.0	3 014	36	Aleutians East Borough, AK	37.7
2 554	28	Pocahontas County, IA	99.0	2 739	37	Talbot County, GA	61.4	473	37	San Juan County, NM	37.0
2 624	28	Van Buren County, IA	99.0	2 179	38	Madison Parish, LA	61.1	437	38	Robeson County, NC	36.8
2 071	39	Butler County, IA	98.9	559	38	Orangeburg County, SC	61.1	2 960	39	Skagway-Hoonah-Angoon Census Area, AK	34.1
1 982	39	Fentress County, TN	98.9	229	40	Hinds County, MS	61.0	2 923	40	Lyman County, SD	32.1
2 350	39	Grant County, WV	98.9	2 755	41	Calhoun County, GA	60.7	1 045	41	Cherokee County, OK	31.8
3 013	39	Greeley County, NE	98.9	2 369	42	Terrell County, GA	60.4	2 499	42	Rosebud County, MT	31.4
3 012	39	Hettinger County, ND	98.9	539	43	Dougherty County, GA	60.3	2 723	43	Mountrail County, ND	30.0
1 773	39	Jackson County, IA	98.9	2 328	44	Greensville County, VA	60.2	2 444	44	Roberts County, SD	29.4
2 867	39	LaMoure County, ND	98.9	1 666	44	Hertford County, NC	60.2	2 502	45	Charles Mix County, SD	28.7
1 687	39	Lincoln County, WV	98.9	2 626	44	Randolph County, GA	60.2	463	46	Coconino County, AZ	28.2
2 407	39	Martin County, IN	98.9	94	47	District of Columbia	60.0	2 235	47	Swain County, NC	27.0
2 259	39	Martin County, KY	98.9	2 967	48	Clay County, GA	59.9	2 837	48	Mahnomen County, MN	26.6
2 354	39	Pope County, MN	98.9	1 619	48	Fairfield County, SC	59.7	1 391	49	Caddo County, OK	23.7
3 005	39	Sheridan County, KS	98.9	3 061	50	Taliaferro County, GA	59.7	1 502	50	Lake County, MT	23.1
3 084	39	Sheridan County, ND	98.9	2 098	51	Tallahatchie County, MS	59.6	2 819	51	Aleutians West Census Area, AK	21.9
2 540	39	Turner County, SD	98.9	1 689	52	Northampton County, NC	59.4	1 187	52	Delaware County, OK	21.2
2 707	53	Audubon County, NE	98.8	1 941	53	Hale County, AL	59.1	1 139	53	Sequoyah County, OK	20.3
2 858	53	Cavalier County, ND	98.8	2 157	53	Macon County, GA	58.9	1 122	54	Beltrami County, MN	19.4
2 478	53	Cedar County, NE	98.8	2 753	55	Warren County, GA	58.9	1 225	55	Fremont County, WY	19.3
2 603	53	Daviess County, MO	98.8	1 505	56	Phillips County, AR	58.8	2 808	56	McKenzie County, ND	19.1
2 497	53	Hamilton County, NE	98.8	2 401	57	Kemper County, MS	58.0	1 155	57	Mayes County, OK	18.9
2 329	53	Holt County, NE	98.8	849	58	Edgecombe County, NC	57.8	3 103	58	Alpine County, CA	18.7
1 451	53	Jackson County, WV	98.8	996	59	Gadsden County, FL	57.5	2 385	58	Latimer County, OK	18.7
1 957	53	Lewis County, WV	98.8	2 163	59	Jefferson Davis County, MS	57.0	2 541	60	Sitka City and Borough, AK	18.6
2 857	53	Owsley County, KY	98.8	280	61	Richmond city, VA	57.0	2 304	61	Okfuskee County, OK	18.3
2 811	53	Polk County, NE	98.8	1 935	62	Jefferson County, GA	56.7	2 658	62	Ferry County, WA	17.8
3 015	53	Potter County, SD	98.8	1 235	63	Marion County, SC	56.5	2 777	63	Coal County, OK	16.9
1 649	53	Shelby County, IL	98.8	1 872	64	Brunswick County, VA	56.4	1 977	63	Hill County, MT	16.9
2 796	53	Wirt County, WV	98.8	1 719	65	Hampton County, SC	56.2	2 392	63	Nowata County, OK	16.9
2 587	66	Adair County, IA	98.7	1 694	66	Clay County, MS	56.1	1 561	63	Seminole County, OK	16.9
2 644	66	Antelope County, NE	98.7	2 258	67	Lee County, AR	55.7	2 095	67	Craig County, OK	16.6
1 552	66	Benton County, IA	98.7	2 694	67	Charles City County, VA	55.4	575	68	Sandoval County, NM	16.5
1 488	66	Carter County, KY	98.7	2 810	69	Emporia city, VA	55.4	1 309	69	Ottawa County, OK	16.0
2 116	66	Clay County, IL	98.7	2 725	70	Tensas Parish, LA	54.4	2 719	69	Wrangell-Petersburg Census Area, AK	16.0
2 844	66	Craig County, VA	98.7	2 153	70	Chicot County, AR	54.2	2 150	71	Hughes County, OK	15.8
2 380	66	Crawford County, IN	98.7	2 450	70	McCormick County, SC	54.2	1 243	72	Pontotoc County, OK	15.6
2 946	66	Franklin County, NE	98.7	1 794	73	Warren County, NC	54.2	2 007	73	Sawyer County, WI	15.4
2 702	66	Gentry County, MO	98.7	76	74	DeKalb County, GA	54.1	2 066	74	Choctaw County, OK	15.3
3 109	66	Golden Valley County, MT	98.7	1 446	75	Yazoo County, MS	53.6	1 845	74	Jefferson County, OR	15.3
1 785	66	Hancock County, IL	98.7					1 819	74	McIntosh County, OK	15.3
2 194	66	Jackson County, KY	98.7								
2 601	66	Lac qui Parle County, MN	98.7								
2 964	66	McIntosh County, ND	98.7								
2 479	66	Tyler County, WV	98.7								
1 450	66	Vernon County, WI	98.7								
1 020	66	Warren County, PA	98.7								
1 917	66	Wetzel County, WV	98.7								

TABLE 3—All Counties
Selected Rankings

Percent Asian, Hawaiian, and Pacific Islander, 2000				Percent Hispanic or Latino[1], 2000				Percent Two or More Races, 2000			
Population Rank	Asian, Hawaiian, and Pacific Islander Rank	County	[A-3. col 20] Percent Asian, Hawaiian, and Pacific Islander	Population Rank	Hispanic or Latino Rank	County	[A-3. col 23] Percent Hispanic or Latino	Population Rank	Two or More Races Rank	County	[A-3. col 26] Percent Two or More Races
3 140	1	Kalawao County, HI	80.3	872	1	Starr County, TX	98.1	363	1	Hawaii County, HI	29.3
48	2	Honolulu County, HI	55.0	961	2	Maverick County, TX	95.3	818	2	Kauai County, HI	24.0
818	3	Kauai County, HI	44.9	284	3	Webb County, TX	94.4	422	3	Maui County, HI	23.0
422	4	Maui County, HI	41.0	2 608	4	Brooks County, TX	92.0	48	4	Honolulu County, HI	20.1
363	5	Hawaii County, HI	37.6	2 324	5	Zavala County, TX	91.4	2 095	5	Craig County, OK	11.2
62	6	San Francisco County, CA	31.4	2 832	6	Jim Hogg County, TX	90.6	1 139	6	Sequoyah County, OK	9.2
3 014	7	Aleutians East Borough, AK	26.7	96	7	Hidalgo County, TX	88.4	2 837	7	Mahnomen County, MN	8.7
14	8	Santa Clara County, CA	25.9	2 220	8	Duval County, TX	88.2	1 045	8	Cherokee County, OK	8.4
2 819	9	Aleutians West Census Area, AK	25.3	1 790	9	Willacy County, TX	86.1	2 719	8	Wrangell-Petersburg Census Area, AK	8.4
70	10	San Mateo County, CA	21.3	3 138	10	Kenedy County, TX	86.0	2 392	10	Nowata County, OK	8.1
21	11	Alameda County, CA	21.0	2 422	11	Dimmit County, TX	85.3	1 820	11	McIntosh County, OK	8.0
2 167	12	Kodiak Island Borough, AK	18.0	2 285	12	Zapata County, TX	84.9	1 155	12	Mayes County, OK	7.7
9	13	Queens County, NY	17.7	2 655	13	Presidio County, TX	84.8	3 124	12	Yakutat City and Borough, AK	7.7
66	14	Middlesex County, NJ	13.9	174	14	Cameron County, TX	84.5	1 733	14	Adair County, OK	7.4
5	14	Orange County, CA	13.9	2 838	15	Mora County, NM	81.8	2 854	14	Dillingham Census Area, AK	7.4
150	16	Solano County, CA	13.5	2 868	16	Guadalupe County, NM	81.0	703	14	Rogers County, OK	7.4
36	17	Fairfax County, VA	12.8	1 154	17	Santa Cruz County, AZ	80.9	1 119	17	Okmulgee County, OK	7.3
1	18	Los Angeles County, CA	12.2	75	18	El Paso County, TX	78.3	1 187	18	Delaware County, OK	7.1
1 715	19	Fairfax city, VA	12.0	1 392	19	San Miguel County, NM	77.9	1 309	18	Ottawa County, OK	7.1
97	20	San Joaquin County, CA	11.9	2 797	20	La Salle County, TX	77.3	3 078	20	Lake and Peninsula Borough, AK	7.0
29	21	Sacramento County, CA	11.5	1 128	21	Jim Wells County, TX	75.9	150	20	Solano County, CA	7.0
649	22	Sutter County, CA	11.4	1 002	22	Val Verde County, TX	75.7	1 380	22	Juneau City and Borough, AK	6.8
12	23	King County, WA	11.3	2 969	23	Hudspeth County, TX	75.4	712	22	Muskogee County, OK	6.8
49	23	Montgomery County, MD	11.3	2 004	24	Frio County, TX	73.9	1 009	22	Osage County, OK	6.8
38	25	Contra Costa County, CA	11.2	2 219	25	Reeves County, TX	73.6	2 768	22	Prince of Wales-Outer Ketchikan Cens, AK	6.8
166	26	Fort Bend County, TX	11.0	1 074	26	Rio Arriba County, NM	73.0	933	26	Washington County, OK	6.5
46	27	Bergen County, NJ	10.7	384	27	Imperial County, CA	72.4	212	27	Anchorage Municipality, AK	6.3
321	28	Yolo County, CA	9.8	2 993	28	Culberson County, TX	72.3	2 168	27	Atoka County, OK	6.3
88	29	Hudson County, NJ	9.5	2 942	29	Costilla County, CO	67.4	2 158	27	Ketchikan Gateway Borough, AK	6.3
17	30	New York County, NY	9.4	1 520	30	Uvalde County, TX	66.1	29	27	Sacramento County, CA	6.3
6	31	San Diego County, CA	9.3	1 360	31	Kleberg County, TX	65.6	2 385	31	Latimer County, OK	6.2
108	32	Ramsey County, MN	8.7	313	32	Dona Ana County, NM	63.4	264	31	Merced County, CA	6.2
190	33	Somerset County, NJ	8.5	1 967	33	Pecos County, TX	61.1	2 649	31	North Slope Borough, AK	6.2
291	34	Arlington County, VA	8.4	2 573	34	Conejos County, CO	59.1	9	31	Queens County, NY	6.2
58	35	Fresno County, CA	8.1	1 147	35	Atascosa County, TX	58.7	97	31	San Joaquin County, CA	6.2
42	36	DuPage County, IL	7.9	1 397	36	Taos County, NM	58.0	2 541	36	Sitka City and Borough, AK	6.1
803	37	Yuba County, CA	7.8	1 559	37	Luna County, NM	57.9	21	37	Alameda County, CA	6.0
234	38	Howard County, MD	7.6	1 868	38	Deaf Smith County, TX	57.7	2 946	37	Bennett County, SD	6.0
7	38	Kings County, NY	7.6	8	39	Miami-Dade County, FL	57.3	3 113	37	Esmeralda County, NV	6.0
535	40	Tompkins County, NY	7.4	2 790	40	Hidalgo County, NM	56.3	2 150	37	Hughes County, OK	6.0
92	41	Gwinnett County, GA	7.1	182	41	Nueces County, TX	55.7	132	37	Stanislaus County, CA	6.0
264	41	Merced County, CA	7.1	2 908	42	Crockett County, TX	55.1	2 429	37	Valdez-Cordova Census Area, AK	6.0
74	43	Suffolk County, MA	7.0	739	43	Valencia County, NM	55.0	27	43	Bronx County, NY	5.9
133	43	Washington County, OR	7.0	24	44	Bexar County, TX	54.3	2 777	43	Coal County, OK	5.9
113	45	Collin County, TX	6.9	1 338	45	Bee County, TX	54.0	88	43	Hudson County, NJ	5.9
2 649	46	North Slope Borough, AK	6.8	2 582	46	Castro County, TX	51.8	2 066	46	Choctaw County, OK	5.8
308	47	Champaign County, IL	6.5	2 911	47	Sutton County, TX	51.7	727	46	Creek County, OK	5.8
2 406	47	Falls Church city, VA	6.5	3 106	48	Terrell County, TX	51.3	2 308	46	Haskell County, OK	5.8
147	47	Monterey County, CA	6.5	160	49	Tulare County, CA	50.8	1 453	49	Geary County, KS	5.7
123	50	Morris County, NJ	6.4	333	50	Yuma County, AZ	50.5	1 267	49	McCurtain County, OK	5.7
212	51	Anchorage Municipality, AK	6.3	2 965	51	Kinney County, TX	50.1	2 211	51	Marshall County, OK	5.6
19	51	Middlesex County, MA	6.3	2 444	52	Parmer County, TX	49.8	71	51	Pierce County, WA	5.6
2 541	53	Sitka City and Borough, AK	6.2	2 970	53	Reagan County, TX	49.7	321	51	Yolo County, CA	5.6
179	53	Washtenaw County, MI	6.2	732	54	San Patricio County, TX	49.4	803	51	Yuba County, CA	5.6
90	55	Snohomish County, WA	6.1	417	55	Santa Fe County, NM	49.1	38	55	Contra Costa County, CA	5.5
79	56	Multnomah County, OR	6.0	1 378	56	Grant County, NM	48.9	2 167	55	Kodiak Island Borough, AK	5.5
1 091	57	Whitman County, WA	5.8	2 678	57	Crosby County, TX	48.8	1 243	55	Pontotoc County, OK	5.5
71	58	Pierce County, WA	5.7	1 895	58	Socorro County, NM	48.6	2 320	55	Pushmataha County, OK	5.5
195	58	Rockland County, NY	5.7	27	59	Bronx County, NY	48.4	13	55	San Bernardino County, CA	5.5
25	60	Clark County, NV	5.6	2 092	60	Dawson County, TX	48.1	2 254	60	Murray County, OK	5.4
2 158	60	Ketchikan Gateway Borough, AK	5.6	880	60	San Benito County, CA	48.1	880	60	San Benito County, CA	5.4
83	60	Norfolk County, MA	5.6	1 199	62	Hale County, TX	48.0	70	60	San Mateo County, CA	5.4
134	60	Richmond County, NY	5.6	2 728	63	Bailey County, TX	47.7	1 561	60	Seminole County, OK	5.4
421	64	Alexandria city, VA	5.5	2 056	63	Karnes County, TX	47.7	830	60	Wagoner County, OK	5.4
64	65	Ventura County, CA	5.4	2 148	65	Colfax County, NM	47.5	2 942	65	Costilla County, CO	5.3
320	66	Loudoun County, VA	5.3	1 785	66	Moore County, TX	47.4	2 397	65	Johnston County, OK	5.3
223	67	Atlantic County, NJ	5.2	1 995	67	Adams County, WA	47.2	649	65	Sutter County, CA	5.3
249	67	Kitsap County, WA	5.2	1 855	68	Colusa County, CA	47.0	627	68	Fairbanks North Star Borough, AK	5.2
3	69	Harris County, TX	5.1	926	69	Franklin County, WA	46.9	414	68	Kings County, CA	5.2
1 380	69	Juneau City and Borough, AK	5.1	147	69	Monterey County, CA	46.9	249	68	Kitsap County, WA	5.2
268	69	Thurston County, WA	5.1	2 628	71	Floyd County, TX	46.0	947	68	Le Flore County, OK	5.2
167	72	Mercer County, NJ	5.0	2 653	72	Yoakum County, TX	45.9	440	68	Madera County, CA	5.2
997	73	Charlottesville city, VA	4.9	3 123	73	Harding County, NM	45.7	2 514	68	Nome Census Area, AK	5.2
2	73	Cook County, IL	4.9	3 053	74	Edwards County, TX	45.6	1 017	68	Pittsburg County, OK	5.2
13	73	San Bernardino County, CA	4.9	2 792	74	Saguache County, CO	45.6	2 960	68	Skagway-Hoonah-Angoon Census Area, AK	5.2

[1] Hispanic or Latino persons may be of any race.

TABLE 3—All Counties
Selected Rankings

Percent Married-Couple Families, 2000				Percent Married-Couple Families with Own Children Under 18 Years, 2000				Percent Single-Parent Households With Children Under 18 Years, 2000			
Population Rank	Married-Couple Families Rank	County	[A-3. col 30] Percent Married-Couple Families	Population Rank	Married-Couple Families With Own Children Under 18 Years Rank	County	[A-3. col 31] Percent Married-Couple Families with Own Children Under 18 Years	Population Rank	Single-Parent Households Rank	County	[A-3. col 34] Percent Single-Parent Households
3 139	1	King County, TX	85.6	2 100	1	Chattahoochee County, GA	54.7	2 526	1	Todd County, SD	30.1
2 676	2	Morgan County, UT	79.7	2 676	2	Morgan County, UT	45.1	2 268	2	Shannon County, SD	28.9
2 100	3	Chattahoochee County, GA	75.8	159	3	Utah County, UT	43.6	3 063	3	Buffalo County, SD	27.9
1 798	3	Elbert County, CO	75.8	2 348	4	Franklin County, ID	43.3	2 918	4	Sioux County, ND	27.5
311	5	Douglas County, CO	74.9	872	5	Starr County, TX	43.2	3 025	5	Ziebach County, SD	23.8
2 348	6	Franklin County, ID	74.5	241	6	Davis County, UT	42.6	2 874	6	Menominee County, WI	23.0
3 067	7	Rich County, UT	73.8	311	6	Douglas County, CO	42.6	2 666	7	Northwest Arctic Borough, AK	22.8
1 839	8	Jefferson County, ID	73.6	961	8	Maverick County, TX	42.4	2 681	8	Wade Hampton Census Area, AK	22.2
564	9	Fayette County, GA	72.9	3 139	9	King County, TX	42.3	27	9	Bronx County, NY	22.1
3 135	10	McPherson County, NE	72.8	1 839	10	Jefferson County, ID	42.2	2 356	10	Humphreys County, MS	20.7
1 035	10	Rockwall County, TX	72.8	284	11	Webb County, TX	42.0	2 318	11	Bullock County, AL	20.6
3 122	12	Banner County, NE	72.7	2 970	12	Reagan County, TX	41.7	1 713	11	Holmes County, MS	20.6
529	13	Forsyth County, GA	72.6	2 074	13	Wasatch County, UT	41.6	2 786	13	Dewey County, SD	20.4
2 983	14	Hanson County, SD	72.3	166	14	Fort Bend County, TX	41.5	1 167	13	Leflore County, MS	20.4
1 042	15	Box Elder County, UT	72.1	1 042	15	Box Elder County, UT	41.1	1 384	15	Coahoma County, MS	20.2
978	16	Oldham County, KY	72.0	2 588	16	Juab County, UT	40.6	2 186	16	Rolette County, ND	19.7
1 142	17	Holmes County, OH	71.8	2 271	17	Millard County, UT	40.5	2 467	17	Jefferson County, MS	19.5
2 074	18	Wasatch County, UT	71.6	1 092	18	Tooele County, UT	40.4	1 446	18	Yazoo County, MS	19.4
241	19	Davis County, UT	71.5	96	19	Hidalgo County, TX	39.6	2 494	19	East Carroll Parish, LA	19.3
2 376	19	Emery County, UT	71.5	1 142	19	Holmes County, OH	39.6	2 649	20	North Slope Borough, AK	19.0
3 116	21	Roberts County, TX	71.2	552	21	Stafford County, VA	39.4	1 268	20	Sunflower County, MS	19.0
2 271	22	Millard County, UT	71.1	2 895	22	Haskell County, KS	39.1	1 505	22	Phillips County, AR	18.8
159	22	Utah County, UT	71.1	707	22	Carver County, MN	38.9	2 514	23	Nome Census Area, AK	18.7
1 850	24	Sevier County, UT	71.0	636	23	Paulding County, GA	38.9	2 389	23	Roosevelt County, MT	18.7
2 303	25	Fremont County, ID	70.7	1 035	25	Rockwall County, TX	38.8	1 096	25	Bolivar County, MS	18.5
3 052	26	Oldham County, TX	70.6	562	26	Cache County, UT	38.7	2 213	25	Wilcox County, AL	18.5
3 056	27	Armstrong County, TX	70.5	300	26	Hamilton County, IN	38.7	2 195	27	Lowndes County, AL	18.4
2 814	27	Hartley County, TX	70.5	3 067	28	Rich County, UT	38.6	771	28	Washington County, MS	18.0
2 895	27	Haskell County, KS	70.5	2 376	29	Emery County, UT	38.4	2 301	29	Perry County, AL	17.8
3 062	30	Oliver County, ND	70.4	2 135	30	Duchesne County, UT	38.2	2 510	30	Tunica County, MS	17.7
2 327	31	Poquoson city, VA	70.3	577	30	Scott County, MN	38.2	2 179	31	Madison Parish, LA	17.4
427	31	Williamson County, TN	70.3	1 565	32	Lee County, GA	38.1	667	31	McKinley County, NM	17.4
862	33	Kendall County, IL	70.2	213	33	McHenry County, IL	38.0	2 438	33	Hancock County, GA	17.1
2 444	34	Parmer County, TX	70.1	2 125	34	Gaines County, TX	37.9	2 436	33	Quitman County, MS	17.1
1 675	34	Powhatan County, VA	70.1	2 167	34	Kodiak Island Borough, AK	37.9	3 014	35	Aleutians East Borough, AK	17.0
2 906	36	Oneida County, ID	69.9	880	34	San Benito County, CA	37.9	975	36	Dallas County, AL	16.9
1 357	37	Sioux County, IA	69.8	427	34	Williamson County, TN	37.9	1 289	37	Petersburg city, VA	16.8
2 311	37	Spencer County, KY	69.8	3 110	38	Clark County, ID	37.8	2 730	37	Sharkey County, MS	16.8
636	39	Paulding County, GA	69.5	756	39	Sherburne County, MN	37.7	2 449	39	Greene County, AL	16.7
1 508	40	Oconee County, GA	69.4	1 798	40	Elbert County, CO	37.6	2 734	40	Yukon-Koyukuk Census Area, AK	16.5
2 970	40	Reagan County, TX	69.4	789	40	Liberty County, GA	37.6	3 060	41	Mellette County, SD	16.4
2 653	40	Yoakum County, TX	69.4	978	40	Oldham County, KY	37.6	117	42	Orleans Parish, LA	16.3
1 385	43	Botetourt County, VA	69.3	1 658	40	Sanpete County, UT	37.6	2 967	43	Clay County, GA	16.2
3 097	43	Glasscock County, TX	69.3	564	44	Fayette County, GA	37.5	245	43	Clayton County, GA	16.2
2 655	45	Caribou County, ID	69.2	1 850	45	Sevier County, UT	37.5	2 689	45	Benson County, ND	16.1
166	45	Fort Bend County, TX	69.2	2 444	46	Parmer County, TX	37.4	1 693	45	Crisp County, GA	16.1
568	47	Geauga County, OH	69.1	665	47	Coryell County, TX	37.3	1 590	45	Macon County, AL	16.1
3 129	47	Grant County, NE	69.1	529	48	Forsyth County, GA	37.2	2 302	48	Claiborne County, MS	16.0
2 588	47	Juab County, UT	69.1	2 793	49	Gray County, KS	37.1	2 369	48	Terrell County, GA	16.0
552	47	Stafford County, VA	69.1	2 969	49	Hudspeth County, TX	37.1	2 258	50	Lee County, AR	15.9
3 057	51	Gosper County, NE	68.7	2 876	49	Kearny County, KS	37.1	2 260	50	Noxubee County, MS	15.9
300	51	Hamilton County, IN	68.7	862	49	Kendall County, IL	37.1	2 098	52	Tallahatchie County, MS	15.8
339	51	Livingston County, MI	68.7	3 135	49	McPherson County, NE	37.1	1 684	53	Burke County, GA	15.7
2 135	54	Duchesne County, UT	68.6	2 681	49	Wade Hampton Census Area, AK	37.1	1 694	53	Clay County, MS	15.7
572	54	Washington County, UT	68.6	320	55	Loudoun County, VA	36.9	539	53	Dougherty County, GA	15.7
840	56	York County, VA	68.5	1 508	55	Oconee County, GA	36.9	2 103	53	Sumter County, AL	15.7
579	57	Columbia County, GA	68.4	579	57	Columbia County, GA	36.8	2 609	57	Clay County, TN	15.6
494	57	Delaware County, OH	68.4	1 061	58	Bingham County, ID	36.6	1 676	57	Hopewell city, VA	15.6
1 092	57	Tooele County, UT	68.4	232	58	Williamson County, TX	36.6	1 595	57	Mitchell County, GA	15.6
385	60	Cherokee County, GA	68.3	1 024	60	Camden County, GA	36.5	2 355	60	Allendale County, SC	15.5
2 125	60	Gaines County, TX	68.3	1 103	60	Finney County, KS	36.5	912	60	Crittenden County, AR	15.5
1 252	60	LaGrange County, IN	68.3	3 097	62	Glasscock County, TX	36.4	1 790	60	Fluvanna County, VA	15.5
1 658	60	Sanpete County, UT	68.3	111	63	Will County, IL	36.3	82	63	Baltimore city, MD	15.4
2 742	60	Stanton County, NE	68.3	1 717	64	Cassia County, ID	36.1	2 021	63	Bethel Census Area, AK	15.4
3 026	60	Wayne County, UT	68.3	2 129	64	San Juan County, UT	36.1	229	63	Hinds County, MS	15.4
1 234	60	Woodford County, IN	68.3	2 021	66	Bethel Census Area, AK	35.9	2 560	63	Jenkins County, GA	15.4
2 497	67	Hamilton County, NE	68.1	1 406	66	Summit County, UT	35.9	1 420	67	St. Francis County, AR	15.3
851	67	Hancock County, IN	68.1	1 002	66	Val Verde County, TX	35.9	2 414	67	Wilkinson County, MS	15.3
213	69	McHenry County, IL	68.0	2 653	66	Yoakum County, TX	35.9	437	69	Robeson County, NC	15.2
577	69	Scott County, MN	68.0	84	70	Lake County, IL	35.8	714	70	Apache County, AZ	15.0
961	71	Maverick County, TX	67.9	1 154	71	Santa Cruz County, AZ	35.6	1 935	70	Jefferson County, GA	15.0
356	72	Carroll County, MD	67.8	1 557	71	Uintah County, UT	35.6	1 308	70	Sumter County, GA	15.0
2 793	72	Gray County, KS	67.8	2 303	73	Fremont County, ID	35.5	3 124	70	Yakutat City and Borough, AK	15.0
2 440	72	Jefferson County, MT	67.8	455	73	Henry County, GA	35.5	2 157	74	Macon County, GA	14.9
1 061	75	Bingham County, ID	67.7	1 288	73	Iron County, UT	35.5	1 235	74	Marion County, SC	14.9
508	75	Hendricks County, IN	67.7	840	73	York County, VA	35.5				
455	75	Henry County, GA	67.7								
1 565	75	Lee County, GA	67.7								

TABLE 3—All Counties
Selected Rankings

Population Rank	Men Living Alone Rank	County	[A-3. col 38] Percent Men Living Alone	Population Rank	Women Living Alone Rank	County	[A-3. col 40] Percent Women Living Alone	Population Rank	Foreign-born Population Rank	County	[A-3. col 54] Percent Foreign-born Population
2 101	1	Kalawao County, HI	56.1	3 140	1	Kalawao County, HI	33.3	8	1	Miami-Dade County, FL	50.9
2 677	2	Denali Borough, AK	27.0	17	2	New York County, NY	27.3	9	2	Queens County, NY	46.1
160	3	Esmeralda County, NV	24.9	2 701	3	Lexington city, VA	26.3	88	3	Hudson County, NJ	38.5
2 349	4	Aleutians West Census Area, AK	23.8	421	4	Alexandria city, VA	24.8	7	4	Kings County, NY	37.8
873	5	Aleutians East Borough, AK	21.9	1 932	5	Bristol city, VA	24.7	961	4	Maverick County, TX	37.8
242	5	Harding County, NM	21.9	94	6	District of Columbia	24.5	1 154	6	Santa Cruz County, AZ	37.7
312	7	Yukon-Koyukuk Census Area, AK	21.7	2 922	7	Norton city, VA	23.5	872	7	Starr County, TX	36.9
962	8	Yakutat City and Borough, AK	21.4	2 810	8	Emporia city, VA	23.3	62	8	San Francisco County, CA	36.8
3 140	9	Bristol Bay Borough, AK	20.9	3 141	8	Loving County, TX	23.3	1	9	Los Angeles County, CA	36.2
1 840	10	San Juan County, CO	20.8	1 829	10	Fredericksburg city, VA	22.9	2 655	10	Presidio County, TX	35.8
285	11	New York County, NY	20.6	3 126	11	Hooker County, NE	22.8	14	11	Santa Clara County, CA	34.1
2 971	12	Petroleum County, MT	20.1	2 294	11	Williamsburg city, VA	22.8	2 969	12	Hudspeth County, TX	33.2
2 075	13	Loving County, TX	20.0	2 897	13	Clifton Forge city, VA	22.7	70	13	San Mateo County, CA	32.3
167	14	Jones County, SD	19.9	1 597	14	Staunton city, VA	22.5	384	14	Imperial County, CA	32.2
1 043	14	Skagway-Hoonah-Angoon Census Area, AK	19.9	291	15	Arlington County, VA	22.5	5	15	Orange County, CA	29.9
2 589	16	San Miguel County, CO	19.7	3 073	16	Garfield County, NE	22.2	96	16	Hidalgo County, TX	29.5
2 272	17	McMullen County, TX	19.3	168	17	St. Louis city, MO	22.1	17	17	New York County, NY	29.4
94	18	District of Columbia	19.2	2 058	18	Martinsville city, VA	22.0	27	18	Bronx County, NY	29.0
1 093	19	San Francisco County, CA	19.1	280	18	Richmond city, VA	22.0	147	18	Monterey County, CA	29.0
97	20	Pitkin County, CO	18.7	3 045	18	Wheatland County, MT	22.0	284	18	Webb County, TX	29.0
1 143	21	Alexandria city, VA	18.6	2 706	21	Galax city, VA	21.9	3 110	21	Clark County, ID	28.2
553	21	Prince of Wales-Outer Ketchikan Cens, AK	18.6	3 066	22	Comanche County, KS	21.6	291	22	Arlington County, VA	27.8
2 896	21	Slope County, ND	18.6	2 756	23	Covington city, VA	21.5	1 855	23	Colusa County, CA	27.6
708	24	Arlington County, VA	18.5	3 088	23	Foard County, TX	21.5	75	24	El Paso County, TX	27.4
637	25	Denver County, CO	18.4	542	23	Roanoke city, VA	21.5	1 670	24	Seward County, KS	27.4
1 036	26	St. Louis city, MO	18.1	2 931	26	Hall County, TX	21.4	21	26	Alameda County, CA	27.2
563	27	Valdez-Cordova Census Area, AK	17.8	3 072	27	Cottle County, TX	21.3	49	27	Montgomery County, MD	26.7
301	28	Lake and Peninsula Borough, AK	17.4	942	27	Danville city, VA	21.3	115	28	Passaic County, NJ	26.6
3 068	29	Eureka County, NV	17.2	959	27	Ohio County, WV	21.3	174	29	Cameron County, TX	25.6
2 377	30	Alpine County, CA	17.1	3 021	30	Adams County, ND	21.1	74	30	Suffolk County, MA	25.4
2 136	30	Hinsdale County, CO	17.1	2 629	30	Fulton County, KY	21.1	421	31	Alexandria city, VA	25.4
578	30	Monroe County, FL	17.1	2 861	30	Stafford County, KS	21.1	1 715	31	Stafford County, KS	25.4
1 566	33	Catron County, NM	17.0	2 757	33	Bedford city, VA	20.9	15	33	Broward County, FL	25.3
214	33	Keweenaw County, MI	17.0	101	33	Denver County, CO	20.9	926	34	Franklin County, WA	25.2
2 126	33	Sierra County, NM	17.0	2 774	35	Greer County, OK	20.8	46	35	Bergen County, NJ	25.1
2 168	36	Billings County, ND	16.9	2 907	35	Sheridan County, MT	20.8	106	35	Union County, NJ	25.1
881	36	Fall River County, SD	16.9	3 042	37	Divide County, ND	20.6	264	37	Merced County, CA	24.8
428	38	Steele County, ND	16.8	2 941	37	Nelson County, ND	20.6	36	38	Fairfax County, VA	24.5
3 111	39	Granite County, MT	16.7	41	37	Pinellas County, FL	20.6	66	39	Middlesex County, NJ	24.2
757	39	Mineral County, NV	16.7	2 909	40	Baylor County, TX	20.5	2 285	40	Zapata County, TX	24.1
1 799	39	Sierra County, CA	16.7	2 751	40	Buena Vista city, VA	20.5	1 208	41	Hendry County, FL	24.0
790	42	Gunnison County, CO	16.6	2 577	40	Franklin city, VA	20.5	333	41	Yuma County, AZ	24.0
979	42	Lake County, MI	16.6	2 938	40	Hand County, SD	20.5	1 002	43	Val Verde County, TX	23.4
1 659	42	Prairie County, MT	16.6	2 610	40	Lake County, TN	20.5	1 995	44	Adams County, WA	22.9
565	42	Sherman County, OR	16.6	2 028	40	Radford city, VA	20.5	1 103	45	Finney County, KS	22.7
1 851	46	Cook County, MN	16.5	2 626	40	Randolph County, GA	20.5	160	46	Tulare County, CA	22.6
2 445	46	Miner County, SD	16.5	2 916	40	Webster County, NE	20.5	1 334	47	Ford County, KS	22.5
666	46	Towner County, ND	16.5	3 008	48	Eddy County, ND	20.4	3	48	Harris County, TX	22.2
530	49	Fredericksburg city, VA	16.4	2 939	48	Mason County, TX	20.4	40	48	Westchester County, NY	22.2
2 794	49	Huerfano County, CO	16.4	2 487	48	Richardson County, NE	20.4	2 819	50	Aleutians West Census Area, AK	21.5
2 970	51	Harding County, SD	16.3	3 130	48	Thomas County, NE	20.4	6	50	San Diego County, CA	21.5
2 877	52	Albany County, WY	16.2	82	52	Baltimore city, MD	20.3	59	52	Essex County, NJ	21.2
863	52	Jackson County, IL	16.2	747	53	Lynchburg city, VA	20.2	149	52	Santa Barbara County, CA	21.2
3 136	52	Perkins County, SD	16.2	1 493	54	Saline County, IL	20.1	58	54	Fresno County, CA	21.1
2 682	52	Suffolk County, MA	16.2	74	54	Suffolk County, MA	20.1	10	55	Dallas County, TX	20.9
321	56	Harlan County, NE	16.0	1 609	54	Winchester city, VA	20.1	1 785	55	Moore County, TX	20.9
1 509	56	Lake County, CO	16.0	2 522	54	Woods County, OK	20.1	64	57	Ventura County, CA	20.7
580	56	Ness County, KS	16.0	28	58	Allegheny County, PA	20.0	3 140	58	Kalawao County, HI	20.4
1 062	59	North Slope Borough, AK	15.9	997	58	Charlottesville city, VA	20.0	321	59	Yolo County, CA	20.3
233	60	Brown County, IL	15.8	2 630	58	Childress County, TX	20.0	440	60	Madera County, CA	20.1
1 025	60	Clear Creek County, CO	15.8	3 070	58	Golden Valley County, ND	20.0	2 444	60	Parmer County, TX	20.1
1 104	60	Deuel County, NE	15.8	177	58	Sarasota County, FL	20.0	2	62	Cook County, IL	19.8
3 098	60	Gogebic County, MI	15.8	2 882	63	Adams County, IA	19.9	1 559	63	Luna County, NM	19.5
112	60	Nelson County, ND	15.8	2 926	63	Donley County, TX	19.9	97	63	San Joaquin County, CA	19.5
1 718	60	Ontonagon County, MI	15.8	18	63	Philadelphia County, PA	19.9	649	65	Sutter County, CA	19.3
2 130	66	Daggett County, UT	15.7	1 697	63	Stutsman County, ND	19.9	48	66	Honolulu County, HI	19.2
2 022	66	Haines Borough, AK	15.7	3 040	67	Garden County, NE	19.8	195	67	Rockland County, NY	19.1
1 407	66	Madison County, MT	15.7	2 866	67	Hardeman County, TX	19.8	38	68	Contra Costa County, CA	19.0
1 003	69	Inyo County, CA	15.6	2 788	67	Norton County, KS	19.8	16	68	Riverside County, CA	19.0
2 654	69	Lake of the Woods County, MN	15.6	2 650	67	Russell County, KS	19.8	2 125	70	Gaines County, TX	18.9
84	69	Mineral County, MT	15.6	2 357	71	Calhoun County, IA	19.7	880	71	San Benito County, CA	18.8
1 155	69	Trinity County, CA	15.6	1 590	71	Macon County, AL	19.7	1 341	72	DeSoto County, FL	18.7
1 558	73	Mono County, CA	15.5	1 322	71	McDonough County, IL	19.7	313	72	Dona Ana County, NM	18.7
2 304	73	Richmond city, VA	15.5	2 799	71	Republic County, KS	19.7	13	74	San Bernardino County, CA	18.6
456	73	Wibaux County, MT	15.5	1 566	71	Salem city, VA	19.7	3 014	75	Aleutians East Borough, AK	18.3
				2 971	71	Trego County, KS	19.7	228	75	Collier County, FL	18.3
								166	75	Fort Bend County, TX	18.3
								132	75	Stanislaus County, CA	18.3

TABLE 3—All Counties
Selected Rankings

Percent of Population Over 25 Years with High School Diploma or Less, 2000				Percent of Population Over 25 Years with Bachelor's Degree or More, 2000				Percent of Population 16 to 19 Years Not Enrolled in School, Not High School Graduate, Not in Armed Forces, or Employed, 2000			
Population Rank	High School Diploma or Less Rank	County	[B-3. col 2] Percent High School Diploma or Less	Population Rank	Bachelor's Degree or More Rank	County	[B-3. col 4] Percent Bachelor's Degree or More	Population Rank	At-Risk Youth Rank	County	[B-3. col 17] Percent At-Risk Youth
872	1	Starr County, TX	79.6	2 406	1	Falls Church city, VA	63.7	2 763	1	San Saba County, TX	28.1
2 681	2	Wade Hampton Census Area, AK	77.1	1 877	2	Los Alamos County, NM	60.5	2 268	2	Shannon County, SD	27.6
1 142	3	Holmes County, OH	76.9	291	3	Arlington County, VA	60.2	944	3	Greene County, NY	27.3
3 014	4	Aleutians East Borough, AK	75.9	2 101	4	Pitkin County, CO	57.1	2 562	4	Johnson County, GA	25.2
2 732	5	Menifee County, KY	75.8	36	5	Fairfax County, VA	54.8	1 493	5	Saline County, IL	24.6
2 635	6	Atkinson County, GA	75.5	49	6	Montgomery County, MD	54.6	1 749	6	Jones County, TX	23.9
2 194	7	Jackson County, KY	75.0	421	7	Alexandria city, VA	54.3	3 025	7	Ziebach County, SD	23.4
2 210	8	Powell County, KY	74.9	234	8	Howard County, MD	52.9	2 347	8	Lake County, MI	23.1
1 572	9	Clay County, KY	74.2	194	9	Boulder County, CO	52.4	2 925	9	Coke County, TX	21.7
2 201	10	Magoffin County, KY	72.8	311	10	Douglas County, CO	51.9	2 666	10	Northwest Arctic Borough, AK	20.4
1 909	11	Union County, TN	72.7	457	11	Orange County, NC	51.5	2 610	11	Lake County, TN	20.3
2 412	12	Clay County, WV	72.3	235	12	Marin County, CA	51.3	2 179	11	Madison Parish, LA	20.3
2 935	13	Echols County, GA	72.0	17	13	New York County, NY	49.4	2 544	11	Taylor County, GA	20.3
2 817	13	Van Buren County, TN	72.0	300	14	Hamilton County, IN	48.9	1 949	14	McCreary County, KY	20.2
2 232	15	Butler County, KY	71.9	2 728	15	San Miguel County, CO	48.3	941	15	Granville County, NC	20.1
1 208	16	Hendry County, FL	71.5	1 613	16	Summit County, CO	48.3	2 498	16	Crittenden County, KY	20.0
2 969	16	Hudspeth County, TX	71.5	179	17	Washtenaw County, MI	48.1	2 732	16	Menifee County, KY	20.0
2 613	16	Lee County, KY	71.5	646	18	Albemarle County, VA	47.7	2 704	18	Treutlen County, GA	19.8
2 138	19	Grundy County, TN	71.4	131	18	Johnson County, KS	47.7	1 142	19	Holmes County, OH	19.7
1 687	19	Lincoln County, WV	71.4	488	20	Johnson County, IA	47.6	1 473	19	McDowell County, WV	19.7
961	21	Maverick County, TX	71.3	535	21	Tompkins County, NY	47.5	2 679	21	Wolfe County, KY	19.6
2 219	22	Reeves County, TX	71.2	651	22	Benton County, OR	47.4	2 470	22	Mitchell County, TX	19.4
1 949	23	McCreary County, KY	71.1	113	23	Collin County, TX	47.3	2 044	23	Lee County, TX	19.0
1 624	24	Assumption Parish, LA	70.7	320	24	Loudoun County, VA	47.2	2 393	24	Caldwell Parish, LA	18.8
1 984	24	Rockcastle County, KY	70.7	190	25	Somerset County, NJ	46.5	2 142	24	La Salle Parish, LA	18.8
2 666	26	Northwest Arctic Borough, AK	70.6	1 883	26	Teton County, WY	45.8	2 857	24	Owsley County, KY	18.8
2 272	27	Leslie County, KY	70.5	1 715	27	Fairfax city, VA	45.7	1 038	24	Vance County, NC	18.8
1 769	27	Macon County, TN	70.5	1 406	28	Summit County, UT	45.5	1 067	28	Avoyelles Parish, LA	18.3
3 063	29	Buffalo County, SD	70.4	62	29	San Francisco County, CA	45.0	3 061	28	Taliaferro County, GA	18.3
2 684	29	Liberty County, FL	70.4	2 294	29	Williamsburg city, VA	45.0	2 630	30	Childress County, TX	18.2
2 259	29	Martin County, KY	70.4	642	31	Story County, IA	44.5	2 921	31	Concho County, TX	18.1
2 441	29	Metcalfe County, KY	70.4	427	32	Williamson County, TN	44.4	1 268	31	Sunflower County, MS	18.1
1 796	29	Wayne County, KY	70.4	1 345	33	Albany County, WY	44.1	2 886	33	Pope County, IL	17.8
2 616	34	Gallatin County, KY	70.3	123	33	Morris County, NJ	44.1	2 204	34	Greene County, MS	17.7
1 350	34	Knox County, KY	70.3	1 091	35	Whitman County, WA	44.0	582	35	Richmond County, VA	17.5
1 473	34	McDowell County, WV	70.3	85	36	Wake County, NC	43.9	2 545	35	Burke County, NC	17.4
2 857	34	Owsley County, KY	70.3	3 134	37	San Juan County, CO	43.7	2 801	36	Hyde County, NC	17.4
1 982	38	Fentress County, TN	70.2	2 164	38	Gunnison County, CO	43.6	2 635	38	Atkinson County, GA	16.9
1 202	38	Murray County, GA	70.2	19	38	Middlesex County, MA	43.6	2 449	38	Greene County, AL	16.9
2 055	40	Casey County, KY	70.1	1 846	40	Blaine County, ID	43.1	2 797	38	La Salle County, TX	16.9
1 790	40	Willacy County, TX	70.1	83	41	Norfolk County, MA	42.9	2 046	38	Union County, KY	16.9
2 070	42	Estill County, KY	70.0	525	42	Douglas County, KS	42.7	1 572	42	Clay County, KY	16.8
2 154	42	Lewis County, KY	70.0	1 064	43	Eagle County, CO	42.6	2 730	42	Sharkey County, MS	16.8
2 419	44	Charlton County, GA	69.8	2 701	43	Lexington city, VA	42.6	2 764	42	Wheeler County, GA	16.8
2 324	44	Zavala County, TX	69.8	138	45	Chester County, PA	42.5	2 691	45	Brown County, IL	16.7
2 679	46	Wolfe County, KY	69.7	1 812	45	Routt County, CO	42.5	2 682	45	Luce County, MI	16.7
2 322	47	Edmonson County, KY	69.6	445	47	Hunterdon County, NJ	41.8	2 372	47	Catahoula Parish, LA	16.6
2 165	47	Morgan County, KY	69.6	398	48	Boone County, MO	41.7	1 223	48	Habersham County, GA	16.5
2 021	49	Bethel Census Area, AK	69.4	42	48	DuPage County, IL	41.7	1 350	48	Knox County, KY	16.5
2 715	49	Elliott County, KY	69.4	240	48	Leon County, FL	41.7	3 100	50	Harding County, SD	16.4
2 610	49	Lake County, TN	69.4	948	51	James City County, VA	41.5	2 652	51	Pulaski County, IL	16.3
2 111	52	Brantley County, GA	69.3	55	52	Fulton County, GA	41.4	2 608	52	Brooks County, TX	16.2
1 754	52	Grainger County, TN	69.3	371	53	Chittenden County, VT	41.2	2 234	52	Summers County, WV	16.2
2 328	52	Greensville County, VA	69.3	494	54	Delaware County, OH	41.0	2 753	52	Warren County, GA	16.2
1 729	52	Scott County, TN	69.3	723	54	Gallatin County, MT	41.0	2 197	55	Union County, FL	16.1
2 469	52	Webster County, WV	69.3	1 251	54	Latah County, ID	41.0	2 194	56	Jackson County, KY	16.0
1 806	57	Morgan County, TN	69.2	40	57	Westchester County, NY	40.9	2 613	56	Lee County, KY	16.0
1 252	58	LaGrange County, IN	68.9	997	58	Charlottesville city, VA	40.8	2 670	58	Thurston County, NE	15.7
2 285	59	Zapata County, TX	68.7	140	59	Dane County, WI	40.6	623	58	Whitfield County, GA	15.7
2 655	60	Presidio County, TX	68.6	56	59	Travis County, TX	40.6	1 307	60	Harlan County, KY	15.5
1 486	61	Hardee County, FL	68.5	774	61	Riley County, KS	40.5	2 683	60	Lafayette County, FL	15.5
938	62	St. Martin Parish, LA	68.4	14	61	Santa Clara County, CA	40.5	1 679	60	Tattnall County, GA	15.5
2 608	63	Clay County, TN	68.3	2 156	63	San Juan County, WA	40.2	819	63	Spalding County, GA	15.4
1 298	63	Cocke County, TN	68.3	254	64	Durham County, NC	40.1	2 628	64	Floyd County, TX	15.3
2 246	65	Vinton County, OH	68.2	12	65	King County, WA	40.0	1 873	65	Jackson County, AR	15.2
2 083	65	West Feliciana Parish, LA	68.2	47	66	Fairfield County, CT	39.9	2 259	65	Martin County, KY	15.2
1 478	67	Lauderdale County, TN	68.1	520	67	Clarke County, GA	39.8	1 161	65	Polk County, GA	15.2
1 527	67	Wyoming County, WV	68.1	89	67	Cobb County, GA	39.8	474	65	Potter County, TX	15.2
2 437	69	Bacon County, GA	68.0	1 508	67	Oconee County, GA	39.8	2 946	69	Bennett County, SD	15.1
2 293	69	Bollinger County, MO	68.0	450	70	Monroe County, IN	39.6	1 693	69	Crisp County, GA	15.1
2 276	71	Bledsoe County, TN	67.9	227	71	Larimer County, CO	39.5	2 125	71	Gaines County, TX	15.0
1 652	72	Juniata County, PA	67.7	94	72	District of Columbia	39.1	2 662	71	Pawnee County, KS	15.0
1 625	72	Lincoln County, KY	67.7	32	72	Hennepin County, MN	39.1	2 000	71	Scurry County, TX	15.0
2 446	74	Cameron Parish, LA	67.6	70	74	San Mateo County, CA	39.0	2 835	74	Stewart County, GA	14.9
2 364	74	Heard County, GA	67.6	2 503	75	Clear Creek County, CO	38.8	2 398	75	Evans County, GA	14.8
2 368	74	Jackson County, TN	67.6					3 054	75	Liberty County, MT	14.8
1 965	74	Wayne County, TN	67.6					2 514	75	Nome Census Area, AK	14.8
								2 109	75	Wilbarger County, TX	14.8

TABLE 3—All Counties

Selected Rankings

Unemployment Rate, 2000[1]

Population Rank	Unemployment Rate Rank	County	[B-3. col 20] Unemployment Rate
3 014	1	Aleutians East Borough, AK	41.4
2 294	1	Williamsburg city, VA	41.4
2 268	3	Shannon County, SD	33.0
2 681	4	Wade Hampton Census Area, AK	23.9
2 917	5	Sioux County, ND	23.3
714	6	Apache County, AZ	21.8
3 063	7	Buffalo County, SD	21.6
872	8	Starr County, TX	20.9
2 734	9	Yukon-Koyukuk Census Area, AK	19.9
2 658	10	Ferry County, WA	18.8
2 526	11	Todd County, SD	18.4
2 302	12	Claiborne County, MS	18.0
961	13	Maverick County, TX	17.6
3 025	14	Ziebach County, SD	17.4
1 713	15	Holmes County, MS	17.3
667	16	McKinley County, NM	17.2
1 559	17	Luna County, NM	17.1
2 324	18	Zavala County, TX	16.7
2 874	19	Menominee County, WI	16.5
2 765	20	Southeast Fairbanks Census Area, AK	16.4
2 514	21	Nome Census Area, AK	16.2
1 167	22	Leflore County, MS	15.9
2 997	23	Jackson County, SD	15.7
2 389	23	Roosevelt County, MT	15.7
1 919	25	Knott County, KY	15.6
2 960	25	Skagway-Hoonah-Angoon Census Area, AK	15.6
2 666	27	Northwest Arctic Borough, AK	15.5
2 209	28	Glacier County, MT	15.4
2 213	29	Wilcox County, AL	15.2
1 096	30	Bolivar County, MS	15.1
2 129	30	San Juan County, UT	15.1
2 493	32	East Carroll Parish, LA	15.0
2 768	32	Prince of Wales-Outer Ketchikan Cens, AK	15.0
2 671	34	Gilmer County, WV	14.9
2 649	34	North Slope Borough, AK	14.9
2 298	36	Mackinac County, MI	14.7
2 301	36	Perry County, AL	14.7
2 021	38	Bethel Census Area, AK	14.5
2 730	38	Sharkey County, MS	14.5
2 469	38	Webster County, WV	14.5
1 473	41	McDowell County, WV	14.4
27	42	Bronx County, NY	14.3
2 786	42	Dewey County, SD	14.3
3 078	42	Lake and Peninsula Borough, AK	14.3
2 186	42	Rolette County, ND	14.3
1 504	46	Cheboygan County, MI	14.2
2 422	46	Dimmit County, TX	14.2
2 467	46	Jefferson County, MS	14.2
1 947	49	Mariposa County, CA	14.1
2 516	50	Benewah County, ID	13.9
2 249	50	Big Horn County, MT	13.9
2 230	50	Trinity County, CA	13.9
1 851	53	Lincoln County, MT	13.8
1 326	53	Waller County, TX	13.8
1 790	53	Willacy County, TX	13.8
3 031	56	Haines Borough, AK	13.7
2 438	56	Hancock County, GA	13.7
3 043	58	Issaquena County, MS	13.5
1 046	59	Lincoln Parish, LA	13.3
1 808	59	Prince Edward County, VA	13.3
2 757	61	Bedford city, VA	13.2
2 899	61	Corson County, SD	13.2
2 942	61	Costilla County, CO	13.2
1 307	61	Harlan County, KY	13.2
2 258	61	Lee County, AR	13.2
440	61	Madera County, CA	13.2
2 449	67	Greene County, AL	13.1
264	67	Merced County, CA	13.1
2 838	67	Mora County, NM	13.1
2 655	70	Presidio County, TX	13.0
2 689	71	Benson County, ND	12.9
2 163	71	Jefferson Davis County, MS	12.9
2 847	71	Mineral County, NV	12.9
1 603	71	Peach County, GA	12.9
2 201	75	Magoffin County, KY	12.8
2 259	75	Martin County, KY	12.8
788	75	Otsego County, NY	12.8
1 268	75	Sunflower County, MS	12.8
2 046	75	Union County, KY	12.8

Percent Veterans Over 18 Years, 2000

Population Rank	Veterans Rank	County	[B-3. col 44] Percent Veterans
1 423	1	Elmore County, ID	33.2
2 643	2	Fall River County, SD	25.8
374	3	Hampton city, VA	25.5
317	4	Okaloosa County, FL	25.0
458	5	Citrus County, FL	24.3
2 205	6	Sierra County, NM	24.1
2 847	7	Mineral County, NV	23.6
3 113	8	Esmeralda County, NV	23.2
409	9	Hernando County, FL	23.1
1 810	9	La Paz County, AZ	23.1
1 594	11	Churchill County, NV	23.0
1 728	11	Curry County, OR	23.0
1 914	11	Lampasas County, TX	23.0
1 333	11	Nye County, NV	23.0
387	15	Charlotte County, FL	22.8
918	16	Flagler County, FL	22.6
1 942	17	Benton County, MO	22.4
2 531	18	Hickory County, MO	22.3
249	18	Kitsap County, WA	22.3
2 317	20	Alcona County, MI	22.2
2 963	21	Storey County, NV	22.1
690	22	Island County, WA	22.0
1 950	22	Llano County, TX	22.0
389	24	Clay County, FL	21.9
459	24	Cochise County, AZ	21.9
1 453	24	Geary County, KS	21.9
925	24	Mason County, WA	21.9
2 953	28	Custer County, CO	21.8
2 423	28	Sanders County, MT	21.8
2 657	30	Custer County, SD	21.7
2 314	30	Pend Oreille County, WA	21.7
3 068	30	Sherman County, OR	21.7
876	30	Sumter County, FL	21.7
3 092	30	Wheeler County, OR	21.7
2 622	35	Ontonagon County, MI	21.5
1 471	36	Iosco County, MI	21.4
2 924	36	Mineral County, MT	21.4
344	36	Mohave County, AZ	21.4
120	39	Brevard County, FL	21.3
979	39	Fremont County, CO	21.3
600	39	Highlands County, FL	21.3
3 038	39	Keweenaw County, MI	21.3
637	39	Laramie County, WY	21.3
217	39	Marion County, FL	21.3
1 736	39	Pacific County, WA	21.3
2 851	46	Forest County, PA	21.2
265	46	Lake County, FL	21.2
2 951	48	Catron County, NM	21.1
192	48	Escambia County, FL	21.1
1 518	48	Jefferson County, WA	21.1
2 965	48	Kinney County, TX	21.1
1 100	52	Calaveras County, CA	21.0
2 013	52	Marion County, AR	21.0
753	54	Clallam County, WA	20.9
460	54	Santa Rosa County, FL	20.9
1 920	56	Bandera County, TX	20.8
1 153	56	Baxter County, AR	20.8
2 668	56	Powell County, MT	20.8
2 274	56	Stewart County, TN	20.8
809	60	Carteret County, NC	20.7
2 658	60	Ferry County, WA	20.7
489	60	Houston County, GA	20.7
1 671	63	Aransas County, TX	20.6
1 947	63	Mariposa County, CA	20.6
781	63	Otero County, NM	20.6
1 734	63	Vilas County, WI	20.6
244	67	Bell County, TX	20.5
476	67	Indian River County, FL	20.5
662	67	Josephine County, OR	20.5
718	67	Leavenworth County, KS	20.5
2 230	67	Trinity County, CA	20.5
322	72	Yavapai County, AZ	20.4
2 072	73	Aitkin County, MN	20.3
1 264	73	Lyon County, NV	20.3
400	73	Montgomery County, TN	20.3

Median Household Income, 2000

Population Rank	Median Household Income Rank	County	[B-3. col 57] Median Household Income (Dollars)
311	1	Douglas County, CO	82 929
36	2	Fairfax County, VA	81 050
320	3	Loudoun County, VA	80 648
445	4	Hunterdon County, NJ	79 888
1 877	5	Los Alamos County, NM	78 993
123	6	Morris County, NJ	77 340
190	7	Somerset County, NJ	76 933
2 406	8	Falls Church city, VA	74 924
14	9	Santa Clara County, CA	74 335
234	10	Howard County, MD	74 167
541	11	Putnam County, NY	72 279
26	12	Nassau County, NY	72 030
49	13	Montgomery County, MD	71 551
235	14	Marin County, CA	71 306
564	15	Fayette County, GA	71 227
300	16	Hamilton County, IN	71 026
113	17	Collin County, TX	70 835
70	18	San Mateo County, CA	70 819
427	19	Williamson County, TN	69 104
529	20	Forsyth County, GA	68 890
195	21	Rockland County, NY	67 971
42	22	DuPage County, IL	67 887
1 715	23	Fairfax city, VA	67 642
339	24	Livingston County, MI	67 400
494	25	Delaware County, OH	67 258
84	26	Lake County, IL	66 973
552	27	Stafford County, VA	66 809
577	28	Scott County, MN	66 612
272	29	Washington County, MN	66 305
200	30	Prince William County, VA	65 960
671	31	Calvert County, MD	65 945
707	32	Carver County, MN	65 540
138	33	Chester County, PA	65 295
22	34	Suffolk County, NY	65 288
379	35	Sussex County, NJ	65 266
47	36	Fairfield County, CT	65 249
46	37	Bergen County, NJ	65 241
1 035	38	Rockwall County, TX	65 164
1 406	39	Summit County, UT	64 962
213	40	McHenry County, IL	64 826
862	41	Kendall County, IL	64 625
87	42	Monmouth County, NJ	64 271
166	43	Fort Bend County, TX	63 831
38	44	Contra Costa County, CA	63 675
40	45	Westchester County, NY	63 582
83	46	Norfolk County, MA	63 432
978	47	Oldham County, KY	63 229
2 649	48	North Slope Borough, AK	63 173
291	49	Arlington County, VA	63 001
164	50	Waukesha County, WI	62 839
629	51	Ozaukee County, WI	62 745
1 064	52	Eagle County, CO	62 682
1 798	53	Elbert County, CO	62 480
111	54	Will County, IL	62 238
451	55	Charles County, MD	62 199
1 380	56	Juneau City and Borough, AK	62 034
855	57	Fauquier County, VA	61 999
30	58	Oakland County, MI	61 907
165	59	Dakota County, MN	61 863
114	60	Anne Arundel County, MD	61 768
131	61	Johnson County, KS	61 455
66	62	Middlesex County, NJ	61 446
2 819	63	Aleutians West Census Area, AK	61 406
2 327	64	Poquoson city, VA	60 920
385	65	Cherokee County, GA	60 896
67	66	Montgomery County, PA	60 829
19	67	Middlesex County, MA	60 821
2 417	68	Manassas Park city, VA	60 794
232	69	Williamson County, TX	60 642
92	70	Gwinnett County, GA	60 537
1 244	71	Manassas city, VA	60 409
283	72	Frederick County, MD	60 276
568	73	Geauga County, OH	60 200
356	74	Carroll County, MD	60 021
91	75	Bucks County, PA	59 727

[1]The Census Bureau is aware that there may be a problem in the employment status data in some areas where colleges are located, overstating the unemployment rate. The exact cause is unknown but the Census Bureau is researching the problem.

TABLE 3—All Counties
Selected Rankings

Percent of All Households with Income Over $100,000, 2000

Population Rank	With Income over $100,000 Rank	County	[B-3. col 71] Percent With Income over $100,000
36	1	Fairfax County, VA	37.6
445	2	Hunterdon County, NJ	37.0
311	3	Douglas County, CO	36.7
2 406	4	Falls Church city, VA	35.9
190	4	Somerset County, NJ	35.9
123	6	Morris County, NJ	35.8
320	7	Loudoun County, VA	35.3
235	8	Marin County, CA	35.1
14	9	Santa Clara County, CA	34.6
1 877	10	Los Alamos County, NM	34.1
49	11	Montgomery County, MD	32.4
26	12	Nassau County, NY	32.3
70	12	San Mateo County, CA	32.3
234	14	Howard County, MD	31.9
541	15	Putnam County, NY	31.4
47	16	Fairfield County, CT	31.0
40	16	Westchester County, NY	31.0
195	18	Rockland County, NY	30.8
113	19	Collin County, TX	30.4
427	20	Williamson County, TN	30.2
84	21	Lake County, IL	29.1
564	22	Fayette County, GA	28.8
300	22	Hamilton County, IN	28.8
1 406	24	Summit County, UT	28.7
46	25	Bergen County, NJ	28.6
97	26	Monmouth County, NJ	27.9
42	27	DuPage County, IL	27.5
138	28	Chester County, PA	27.4
494	28	Delaware County, OH	27.4
529	30	Forsyth County, GA	27.2
291	31	Arlington County, VA	26.7
38	31	Contra Costa County, CA	26.7
1 715	33	Fairfax city, VA	26.5
83	34	Norfolk County, MA	26.3
166	35	Fort Bend County, TX	25.5
339	35	Livingston County, MI	25.5
22	35	Suffolk County, NY	25.5
30	38	Oakland County, MI	25.3
1 035	39	Rockwall County, TX	25.1
19	40	Middlesex County, MA	24.9
62	41	San Francisco County, CA	24.7
707	42	Carver County, MN	24.1
17	43	New York County, NY	23.9
629	43	Ozaukee County, WI	23.9
855	45	Fauquier County, VA	23.8
1 064	46	Eagle County, CO	23.7
200	47	Prince William County, VA	23.6
67	48	Montgomery County, PA	23.5
978	48	Oldham County, KY	23.5
5	48	Orange County, CA	23.5
379	48	Sussex County, NJ	23.5
2 101	52	Pitkin County, CO	23.1
272	52	Washington County, MN	23.1
167	54	Mercer County, NJ	23.0
66	55	Middlesex County, NJ	22.9
1 963	56	Goochland County, VA	22.8
64	56	Ventura County, CA	22.8
568	58	Geauga County, OH	22.7
131	58	Johnson County, KS	22.7
2 488	60	Nantucket County, MA	22.6
2 649	60	North Slope Borough, AK	22.6
21	62	Alameda County, CA	22.2
106	63	Union County, NJ	22.1
421	64	Alexandria city, VA	22.0
671	64	Calvert County, MD	22.0
220	66	Santa Cruz County, CA	21.9
114	67	Anne Arundel County, MD	21.8
213	67	McHenry County, IL	21.8
194	69	Boulder County, CO	21.7
139	69	Denton County, TX	21.7
91	71	Bucks County, PA	21.6
55	72	Fulton County, GA	21.5
164	72	Waukesha County, WI	21.5
89	74	Cobb County, GA	21.3
577	75	Scott County, MN	21.2

Percent of All Households with Income Below Poverty, 2000

Population Rank	With Income Below Poverty Rank	County	[B-3. col 73] Percent With Income Below Poverty
3 063	1	Buffalo County, SD	56.2
872	2	Starr County, TX	48.5
2 268	3	Shannon County, SD	45.5
3 025	4	Ziebach County, SD	45.1
3 140	5	Kalawao County, HI	44.7
2 857	6	Owsley County, KY	43.9
2 526	7	Todd County, SD	42.7
2 324	8	Zavala County, TX	41.5
1 713	9	Holmes County, MS	40.6
2 213	10	Wilcox County, AL	40.5
1 572	11	Clay County, KY	39.5
2 103	12	Sumter County, AL	38.2
2 608	13	Brooks County, TX	37.7
714	14	Apache County, AZ	36.7
2 259	15	Martin County, KY	36.3
2 414	16	Wilkinson County, MS	36.2
2 493	17	East Carroll Parish, LA	36.0
2 467	18	Jefferson County, MS	35.9
1 473	18	McDowell County, WV	35.9
2 201	20	Magoffin County, KY	35.7
2 356	21	Humphreys County, MS	35.6
961	22	Maverick County, TX	35.4
1 350	23	Knox County, KY	35.1
2 655	24	Presidio County, TX	35.0
2 917	25	Sioux County, ND	34.7
2 449	26	Greene County, AL	34.6
2 899	27	Corson County, SD	34.5
2 679	28	Wolfe County, KY	34.3
2 016	29	Breathitt County, KY	34.2
1 237	30	Evangeline Parish, LA	33.9
2 272	31	Leslie County, KY	33.8
3 060	32	Mellette County, SD	33.7
2 725	32	Tensas Parish, LA	33.7
2 355	34	Allendale County, SC	33.6
2 318	34	Bullock County, AL	33.6
2 301	36	Perry County, AL	33.4
2 435	37	Quitman County, MS	33.3
2 195	38	Lowndes County, AL	33.2
667	39	McKinley County, NM	33.1
2 969	40	Hudspeth County, TX	32.9
1 790	40	Willacy County, TX	32.9
2 967	42	Clay County, GA	32.8
2 730	43	Sharkey County, MS	32.7
1 384	44	Coahoma County, MS	32.6
2 422	44	Dimmit County, TX	32.6
1 949	44	McCreary County, KY	32.6
1 394	47	Bell County, KY	32.1
1 590	48	Macon County, AL	32.0
2 179	48	Madison Parish, LA	32.0
2 302	50	Claiborne County, MS	31.9
1 307	50	Harlan County, KY	31.9
96	50	Hidalgo County, TX	31.9
3 043	50	Issaquena County, MS	31.9
2 260	50	Noxubee County, MS	31.9
1 167	55	Leflore County, MS	31.7
1 096	56	Bolivar County, MS	31.5
2 786	56	Dewey County, SD	31.5
2 713	58	Hancock County, TN	31.2
975	59	Dallas County, AL	31.0
1 919	59	Knott County, KY	31.0
2 510	59	Tunica County, MS	31.0
2 613	62	Lee County, KY	30.8
2 098	62	Tallahatchie County, MS	30.8
1 047	64	Floyd County, KY	30.7
2 258	64	Lee County, AR	30.7
1 505	64	Phillips County, AR	30.7
2 028	67	Radford city, VA	30.6
2 469	67	Webster County, WV	30.6
2 194	69	Jackson County, KY	30.5
2 797	70	La Salle County, TX	30.2
2 186	71	Rolette County, ND	30.1
1 796	72	Wayne County, KY	30.0
2 997	73	Jackson County, SD	29.9
1 440	74	Mingo County, WV	29.8
2 942	75	Costilla County, CO	29.7

Percent of Population that Resides in the Same House in 1995 and 2000

Population Rank	Same Residence Rank	County	[C-3. col 2] Percent Same Residence
3 140	1	Kalawao County, HI	90.5
3 084	2	Sheridan County, ND	80.6
3 080	3	Campbell County, SD	80.0
1 724	4	St. James Parish, LA	78.8
3 012	5	Hettinger County, ND	77.3
3 117	5	Wheeler County, NE	77.3
3 128	7	Slope County, ND	77.1
3 062	8	Oliver County, ND	76.9
2 858	9	Cavalier County, ND	76.8
1 484	10	Buchanan County, VA	76.4
3 037	10	Logan County, ND	76.4
3 112	12	Keya Paha County, NE	76.2
3 023	13	Highland County, VA	76.0
2 195	14	Lowndes County, AL	75.7
1 473	14	McDowell County, WV	75.7
3 010	16	Kidder County, ND	75.3
3 047	17	Burke County, ND	75.2
3 002	17	Grant County, ND	75.2
1 527	17	Wyoming County, WV	75.2
2 272	20	Leslie County, KY	75.1
3 027	21	Boyd County, NE	75.0
3 039	21	Jerauld County, SD	75.0
2 681	21	Wade Hampton Census Area, AK	75.0
2 802	24	Big Stone County, MN	74.9
1 185	24	Williamsburg County, SC	74.9
3 009	26	Griggs County, ND	74.6
1 893	27	Washington County, AL	74.5
2 190	28	Amite County, MS	74.4
1 246	28	Elk County, PA	74.4
3 133	30	Blaine County, NE	74.3
2 694	30	Charles City County, VA	74.3
2 966	30	Perkins County, SD	74.3
3 054	33	Liberty County, MT	74.2
2 395	34	St. Helena Parish, LA	74.1
3 018	35	Faulk County, SD	73.9
3 042	36	Carter County, MT	73.8
2 555	37	Divide County, ND	73.6
2 654	37	Mercer County, ND	73.6
3 078	37	Tucker County, WV	73.6
3 078	40	Lake and Peninsula Borough, AK	73.4
2 873	41	Marshall County, SD	73.3
2 306	41	Telfair County, GA	73.3
3 013	43	Greeley County, NE	73.2
2 998	43	McPherson County, SD	73.2
2 957	45	Douglas County, SD	73.1
2 938	45	Hand County, SD	73.1
3 123	47	Harding County, NM	73.0
3 115	48	Billings County, ND	72.9
2 983	49	Hanson County, SD	72.8
1 890	49	Jasper County, MS	72.8
3 138	49	Kenedy County, TX	72.8
3 132	49	Loup County, NE	72.8
3 061	49	Taliaferro County, GA	72.8
2 478	54	Cedar County, NE	72.7
1 554	55	Letcher County, KY	72.6
3 065	55	McCone County, MT	72.6
3 005	55	Sheridan County, KS	72.6
2 907	55	Sheridan County, MT	72.6
1 998	59	Dickenson County, VA	72.5
2 601	60	Lac qui Parle County, MN	72.4
2 517	60	Murray County, MN	72.4
872	60	Starr County, TX	72.4
2 830	63	Kittson County, MN	72.3
1 658	63	Pointe Coupee Parish, LA	72.3
2 355	65	Allendale County, SC	72.2
2 987	65	Gove County, KS	72.2
1 417	65	Perry County, KY	72.2
2 401	68	Kemper County, MS	72.1
1 440	68	Mingo County, WV	72.1
1 624	70	Assumption Parish, LA	72.0
3 008	70	Eddy County, ND	72.0
2 867	70	LaMoure County, ND	72.0
2 608	73	Brooks County, TX	71.9
1 919	73	Knott County, KY	71.9
3 097	75	Glasscock County, TX	71.8
2 201	75	Magoffin County, KY	71.8
2 431	75	Marshall County, MN	71.8
1 260	75	Putnam County, OH	71.8
2 739	75	Talbot County, GA	71.8

TABLE 3—All Counties
Selected Rankings

Percent Owner-Occupied Housing Units, 2000

Population Rank	Owner-Occupied Rank	County	[C-3. col 8] Percent Owner-Occupied
2 317	1	Alcona County, MI	89.5
1 798	2	Elbert County, CO	89.4
3 038	3	Keweenaw County, MI	89.3
1 675	4	Powhatan County, VA	88.9
2 196	5	New Kent County, VA	88.8
2 676	6	Morgan County, UT	88.3
1 893	7	Washington County, AL	88.2
529	8	Forsyth County, GA	88.1
339	8	Livingston County, MI	88.1
311	10	Douglas County, CO	87.9
1 683	10	San Jacinto County, TX	87.9
2 121	12	Park County, CO	87.8
1 385	13	Botetourt County, VA	87.7
2 281	14	Northumberland County, VA	87.4
568	15	Geauga County, OH	87.3
3 095	16	Piute County, UT	87.2
3 128	16	Slope County, ND	87.2
1 078	18	Chisago County, MN	87.0
2 009	18	Smith County, MS	87.0
2 111	20	Brantley County, GA	86.9
2 204	20	Greene County, MS	86.9
1 890	22	Jasper County, MS	86.8
978	22	Oldham County, KY	86.8
636	22	Paulding County, GA	86.8
1 963	25	Goochland County, VA	86.7
801	26	Bedford County, VA	86.6
564	26	Fayette County, GA	86.6
577	26	Scott County, MN	86.6
2 171	29	Dixie County, FL	86.5
409	29	Hernando County, FL	86.5
876	31	Sumter County, FL	86.4
2 025	32	Choctaw County, AL	86.3
1 840	33	George County, MS	86.2
2 127	33	Gilchrist County, FL	86.2
2 400	33	Sabine County, TX	86.2
2 700	36	Bland County, VA	86.1
2 568	36	Franklin County, MS	86.1
1 602	36	Harris County, GA	86.1
2 413	36	Montmorency County, MI	86.1
1 477	40	Cass County, MN	86.0
2 190	41	Amite County, MS	85.9
834	41	Barry County, MI	85.9
2 024	43	Benzie County, MI	85.8
1 605	43	Jones County, MS	85.8
2 634	43	Perry County, TN	85.8
1 542	43	Roscommon County, MI	85.8
272	43	Washington County, MN	85.8
458	48	Citrus County, FL	85.6
2 322	48	Edmonson County, KY	85.6
2 845	48	Florence County, WI	85.6
1 516	48	Gladwin County, MI	85.6
3 062	48	Oliver County, ND	85.6
1 724	48	St. James Parish, LA	85.6
2 817	48	Van Buren County, TN	85.6
2 130	55	Presque Isle County, MI	85.5
1 864	56	Adams County, WI	85.4
1 986	56	Kalkaska County, MI	85.4
2 877	56	Lake of the Woods County, MN	85.4
3 037	56	Logan County, ND	85.4
2 072	60	Aitkin County, MN	85.3
2 920	60	Crane County, TX	85.3
1 791	60	Fluvanna County, VA	85.3
455	60	Henry County, GA	85.3
2 495	60	Oscoda County, MI	85.3
671	65	Calvert County, MD	85.2
2 446	65	Cameron Parish, LA	85.2
750	65	Clinton County, MI	85.2
1 367	65	Isanti County, MN	85.2
2 464	65	Livingston County, KY	85.2
2 504	65	Towns County, GA	85.2
2 802	71	Big Stone County, MN	85.1
1 871	71	Jefferson County, KS	85.1
2 216	71	King William County, VA	85.1
1 637	74	Antrim County, MI	85.0
2 094	74	Brown County, IN	85.0
595	74	Lapeer County, MI	85.0
1 711	74	Ogemaw County, MI	85.0
2 395	74	St. Helena Parish, LA	85.0
1 336	74	Wilson County, TX	85.0

Median Housing Value (Owner Estimated), 2000

Population Rank	Median Housing Value Rank	County	[C-3. col 22] Median Housing Value (Dollars)
2 488	1	Nantucket County, MA	583 500
2 101	2	Pitkin County, CO	497 000
235	3	Marin County, CA	493 300
70	4	San Mateo County, CA	449 900
62	5	San Francisco County, CA	422 700
14	6	Santa Clara County, CA	422 600
17	7	New York County, NY	361 100
220	8	Santa Cruz County, CA	353 300
1 883	9	Teton County, WY	344 500
2 091	10	Dukes County, MA	315 500
1 064	11	Eagle County, CO	300 900
2 728	12	San Miguel County, CO	297 900
21	13	Alameda County, CA	291 900
2 156	14	San Juan County, WA	286 400
40	15	Westchester County, NY	285 800
880	16	San Benito County, CA	283 900
1 406	17	Summit County, UT	281 600
48	18	Honolulu County, HI	274 600
1 613	19	Summit County, CO	268 800
1 846	20	Blaine County, ID	266 500
125	21	Sonoma County, CA	265 200
47	22	Fairfield County, CT	265 100
149	23	Santa Barbara County, CA	264 100
2 406	24	Falls Church city, VA	262 400
147	25	Monterey County, CA	254 800
38	26	Contra Costa County, CA	253 800
5	27	Orange County, CA	253 000
123	28	Morris County, NJ	250 400
445	29	Hunterdon County, NJ	246 700
1 812	30	Routt County, CO	246 200
19	31	Middlesex County, MA	244 400
433	32	Napa County, CA	242 200
422	33	Maui County, HI	241 900
46	34	Bergen County, NJ	240 800
26	35	Nassau County, NY	240 200
64	36	Ventura County, CA	238 800
2 937	37	Ouray County, CO	238 600
311	38	Douglas County, CO	237 600
1 798	39	Elbert County, CO	235 400
195	40	Rockland County, NY	234 300
291	41	Arlington County, VA	233 700
194	42	Boulder County, CO	231 000
7	43	Kings County, NY	229 200
83	44	Norfolk County, MA	226 700
12	45	King County, WA	226 400
36	46	Fairfax County, VA	222 400
190	46	Somerset County, NJ	222 400
236	48	San Luis Obispo County, CA	218 600
3 125	49	Hinsdale County, CO	218 100
134	50	Richmond County, NY	216 600
818	51	Kauai County, HI	214 600
1 877	52	Los Alamos County, NM	213 000
6	53	San Diego County, CA	212 000
49	54	Montgomery County, MD	210 600
233	55	Placer County, CA	208 800
69	56	Essex County, MA	206 800
9	57	Queens County, NY	206 200
541	58	Putnam County, NY	205 500
427	59	Williamson County, TN	204 700
421	60	Alexandria city, VA	202 400
320	61	Loudoun County, VA	202 300
1	62	Los Angeles County, CA	201 400
74	63	Suffolk County, MA	201 300
555	64	Nevada County, CA	199 300
234	65	Howard County, MD	198 600
2 269	66	Grand County, CO	196 900
87	67	Monmouth County, NJ	195 800
644	68	Monroe County, FL	195 700
173	69	Clackamas County, OR	193 700
2 503	70	Clear Creek County, CO	193 500
84	71	Lake County, IL	191 600
342	72	El Dorado County, CA	191 500
2 243	73	Mono County, CA	189 500
90	74	Snohomish County, WA	188 600
59	75	Essex County, NJ	188 400

Median Gross Rent, 2000

Population Rank	Median Gross Rent Rank	County	[C-3. col 25] Median Gross Rent (Dollars)
14	1	Santa Clara County, CA	1 185
235	2	Marin County, CA	1 162
70	3	San Mateo County, CA	1 144
311	4	Douglas County, CO	1 053
2 488	5	Nantucket County, MA	1 016
1 064	6	Eagle County, CO	1 007
36	7	Fairfax County, VA	998
2 406	8	Falls Church city, VA	965
26	9	Nassau County, NY	964
320	10	Loudoun County, VA	954
2 101	11	Pitkin County, CO	947
1 715	12	Fairfax city, VA	945
22	12	Suffolk County, NY	945
2 417	14	Manassas Park city, VA	930
62	15	San Francisco County, CA	928
220	16	Santa Cruz County, CA	924
5	17	Orange County, CA	923
49	18	Montgomery County, MD	914
541	19	Putnam County, NY	913
1 406	20	Summit County, UT	909
2 649	21	North Slope Borough, AK	902
38	22	Contra Costa County, CA	898
190	22	Somerset County, NJ	898
291	24	Arlington County, VA	897
2 819	25	Aleutians West Census Area, AK	892
64	25	Ventura County, CA	892
564	27	Fayette County, GA	890
195	28	Rockland County, NY	884
123	29	Morris County, NJ	883
234	30	Howard County, MD	879
1 613	31	Summit County, CO	874
46	32	Bergen County, NJ	872
445	33	Hunterdon County, NJ	867
125	34	Sonoma County, CA	864
1 380	35	Juneau City and Borough, AK	863
200	36	Prince William County, VA	862
421	37	Alexandria city, VA	861
451	38	Charles County, MD	858
83	39	Norfolk County, MA	853
21	40	Alameda County, CA	852
66	41	Middlesex County, NJ	845
2 862	42	Gilpin County, CO	842
2 666	42	Northwest Arctic Borough, AK	842
552	42	Stafford County, VA	842
40	45	Westchester County, NY	839
47	46	Fairfield County, CT	838
671	47	Calvert County, MD	837
42	47	DuPage County, IL	837
19	49	Middlesex County, MA	835
149	50	Santa Barbara County, CA	830
194	51	Boulder County, CO	825
92	52	Gwinnett County, GA	824
644	53	Monroe County, FL	820
109	54	Ocean County, NJ	819
433	55	Napa County, CA	818
2 021	56	Bethel Census Area, AK	814
2 728	57	San Miguel County, CO	811
89	58	Cobb County, GA	806
2 121	58	Park County, CO	806
570	60	Spotsylvania County, VA	805
48	61	Honolulu County, HI	802
1 244	62	Manassas city, VA	801
114	63	Anne Arundel County, MD	798
113	63	Collin County, TX	798
150	65	Solano County, CA	797
17	66	New York County, NY	796
2 167	67	Kodiak Island Borough, AK	791
74	67	Suffolk County, MA	791
379	69	Sussex County, NJ	790
422	70	Maui County, HI	788
232	71	Williamson County, TX	787
1 072	72	Douglas County, NV	780
233	72	Placer County, CA	780
3 102	74	Bristol Bay Borough, AK	778
147	75	Monterey County, CA	776

TABLE 4—75 Largest Metropolitan Areas by 2000 Population
Selected Rankings

Population, 2000			Percent Under 18 Years, 2000			
Population Rank	Metropolitan Area	[A-4. col 1] Population	Population Rank	Under 18 Years Rank	Metropolitan Area	[A-4. col 2 and 3] Percent Under 18 Years
1	Los Angeles-Long Beach, CA	9 519 338	66	1	Fresno, CA	31.6
2	New York, NY	9 314 235	11	2	Riverside-San Bernardino, CA	31.3
3	Chicago, IL	8 272 768	46	2	Salt Lake City-Ogden, UT	31.3
4	Boston-Worcester-Lawrence-Lowell-Brockton, MA-NH	6 057 826	8	4	Houston, TX	29.1
5	Philadelphia, PA-NJ	5 100 931	72	5	Ventura, CA	28.4
6	Washington, DC-MD-VA-WV	4 923 153	59	6	Grand Rapids-Muskegon-Holland, MI	28.3
7	Detroit, MI	4 441 551	54	6	Memphis, TN-AR-MS	28.3
8	Houston, TX	4 177 646	38	6	San Antonio, TX	28.3
9	Atlanta, GA	4 112 198	31	9	Fort Worth-Arlington, TX	28.0
10	Dallas, TX	3 519 176	10	10	Dallas, TX	27.9
11	Riverside-San Bernardino, CA	3 254 821	1	10	Los Angeles-Long Beach, CA	27.9
12	Phoenix-Mesa, AZ	3 251 876	74	12	Omaha, NE-IA	27.2
13	Minneapolis-St. Paul, MN-WI	2 968 806	35	12	Sacramento, CA	27.2
14	Orange County, CA	2 846 289	14	14	Orange County, CA	27.0
15	San Diego, CA	2 813 833	3	15	Chicago, IL	26.9
16	Nassau-Suffolk, NY	2 753 913	12	16	Phoenix-Mesa, AZ	26.8
17	St. Louis, MO-IL	2 603 607	13	17	Minneapolis-St. Paul, MN-WI	26.7
18	Baltimore, MD	2 552 994	45	17	New Orleans, LA	26.7
19	Seattle-Bellevue-Everett, WA	2 414 616	9	19	Atlanta, GA	26.6
20	Tampa-St. Petersburg-Clearwater, FL	2 395 997	33	19	Cincinnati, OH-KY-IN	26.6
21	Oakland, CA	2 392 557	37	19	Indianapolis, IN	26.6
22	Pittsburgh, PA	2 358 695	71	19	Tulsa, OK	26.6
23	Miami, FL	2 253 362	7	23	Detroit, MI	26.5
24	Cleveland-Lorain-Elyria, OH	2 250 871	28	23	Kansas City, MO-KS	26.5
25	Denver, CO	2 109 282	42	25	Milwaukee-Waukesha, WI	26.4
26	Newark, NJ	2 032 989	39	26	Norfolk-Virginia Beach-Newport News, VA-NC	26.3
27	Portland-Vancouver, OR-WA	1 918 009	17	26	St. Louis, MO-IL	26.3
28	Kansas City, MO-KS	1 776 062	75	28	Albuquerque, NM	26.2
29	San Francisco, CA	1 731 183	57	29	Jacksonville, FL	26.0
30	New Haven-Bridgeport-Stamford-Danbury-Waterbury, CT	1 706 575	73	30	Syracuse, NY	25.8
31	Fort Worth-Arlington, TX	1 702 625	25	31	Denver, CO	25.7
32	San Jose, CA	1 682 585	58	32	Rochester, NY	25.6
33	Cincinnati, OH-KY-IN	1 646 395	15	32	San Diego, CA	25.6
34	Orlando, FL	1 644 561	41	34	Columbus, OH	25.5
35	Sacramento, CA	1 628 197	26	34	Newark, NJ	25.5
36	Fort Lauderdale, FL	1 623 018	60	34	Oklahoma City, OK	25.5
37	Indianapolis, IN	1 607 486	24	37	Cleveland-Lorain-Elyria, OH	25.4
38	San Antonio, TX	1 592 383	27	37	Portland-Vancouver, OR-WA	25.4
39	Norfolk-Virginia Beach-Newport News, VA-NC	1 569 541	48	39	Austin-San Marcos, TX	25.3
40	Las Vegas, NV-AZ	1 563 282	18	39	Baltimore, MD	25.3
41	Columbus, OH	1 540 157	43	39	Charlotte-Gastonia-Rock Hill, NC-SC	25.3
42	Milwaukee-Waukesha, WI	1 500 741	16	39	Nassau-Suffolk, NY	25.3
43	Charlotte-Gastonia-Rock Hill, NC-SC	1 499 293	21	39	Oakland, CA	25.3
44	Bergen-Passaic, NJ	1 373 167	5	39	Philadelphia, PA-NJ	25.3
45	New Orleans, LA	1 337 726	40	45	Las Vegas, NV-AZ	25.2
46	Salt Lake City-Ogden, UT	1 333 914	62	45	Richmond-Petersburg, VA	25.2
47	Greensboro-Winston-Salem-High Point, NC	1 251 509	6	45	Washington, DC-MD-VA-WV	25.2
48	Austin-San Marcos, TX	1 249 763	67	48	Birmingham, AL	25.1
49	Nashville, TN	1 231 311	30	49	New Haven-Bridgeport-Stamford-Danbury-Waterbury, CT	25.0
50	Raleigh-Durham-Chapel Hill, NC	1 187 941	61	50	Louisville, KY-IN	24.8
51	Buffalo-Niagara Falls, NY	1 170 111	56	50	Monmouth-Ocean, NJ	24.8
52	Middlesex-Somerset-Hunterdon, NJ	1 169 641	49	50	Nashville, TN	24.8
53	Hartford, CT	1 148 618	65	53	Dayton-Springfield, OH	24.7
54	Memphis, TN-AR-MS	1 135 614	23	53	Miami, FL	24.7
55	West Palm Beach-Boca Raton, FL	1 131 184	34	53	Orlando, FL	24.7
56	Monmouth-Ocean, NJ	1 126 217	32	53	San Jose, CA	24.7
57	Jacksonville, FL	1 100 491	64	57	Greenville-Spartanburg-Anderson, SC	24.5
58	Rochester, NY	1 098 201	70	57	Tucson, AZ	24.5
59	Grand Rapids-Muskegon-Holland, MI	1 088 514	51	59	Buffalo-Niagara Falls, NY	24.3
60	Oklahoma City, OK	1 083 346	52	59	Middlesex-Somerset-Hunterdon, NJ	24.3
61	Louisville, KY-IN	1 025 598	2	59	New York, NY	24.3
62	Richmond-Petersburg, VA	996 512	53	62	Hartford, CT	24.2
63	Providence-Warwick-Pawtucket, RI	962 886	50	62	Raleigh-Durham-Chapel Hill, NC	24.2
64	Greenville-Spartanburg-Anderson, SC	962 441	44	64	Bergen-Passaic, NJ	24.0
65	Dayton-Springfield, OH	950 558	47	64	Greensboro-Winston-Salem-High Point, NC	24.0
66	Fresno, CA	922 516	4	66	Boston-Worcester-Lawrence-Lowell-Brockton, MA-NH	23.9
67	Birmingham, AL	921 106	69	67	Albany-Schenectady-Troy, NY	23.8
68	Honolulu, HI	876 156	68	68	Honolulu, HI	23.7
69	Albany-Schenectady-Troy, NY	875 583	63	68	Providence-Warwick-Pawtucket, RI	23.7
70	Tucson, AZ	843 746	19	68	Seattle-Bellevue-Everett, WA	23.7
71	Tulsa, OK	803 235	36	71	Fort Lauderdale, FL	23.5
72	Ventura, CA	753 197	22	72	Pittsburgh, PA	22.2
73	Syracuse, NY	732 117	20	73	Tampa-St. Petersburg-Clearwater, FL	21.8
74	Omaha, NE-IA	716 998	55	74	West Palm Beach-Boca Raton, FL	21.2
75	Albuquerque, NM	712 738	29	75	San Francisco, CA	18.7

TABLE 4—75 Largest Metropolitan Areas by 2000 Population
Selected Rankings

Percent 18 to 24 Years, 2000				Percent 25 to 44 Years, 2000			
Popu-lation Rank	18 to 24 Years Rank	Metropolitan Area	[A-4. col 4] Percent 18 to 24 Years	Popu-lation Rank	25 to 44 Years Rank	Metropolitan Area	[A-4. col 5] Percent 25 to 44 Years
48	1	Austin-San Marcos, TX	13.2	29	1	San Francisco, CA	36.6
46	2	Salt Lake City-Ogden, UT	12.8	32	2	San Jose, CA	35.8
50	3	Raleigh-Durham-Chapel Hill, NC	11.6	9	3	Atlanta, GA	35.7
15	4	San Diego, CA	11.4	48	4	Austin-San Marcos, TX	35.5
60	5	Oklahoma City, OK	11.3	50	5	Raleigh-Durham-Chapel Hill, NC	35.1
39	6	Norfolk-Virginia Beach-Newport News, VA-NC	11.1	10	6	Dallas, TX	34.9
66	7	Fresno, CA	10.9	25	7	Denver, CO	34.4
41	8	Columbus, OH	10.7	19	8	Seattle-Bellevue-Everett, WA	34.3
70	8	Tucson, AZ	10.7	6	9	Washington, DC-MD-VA-WV	34.1
1	10	Los Angeles-Long Beach, CA	10.3	43	10	Charlotte-Gastonia-Rock Hill, NC-SC	33.8
63	10	Providence-Warwick-Pawtucket, RI	10.3	14	11	Orange County, CA	33.4
38	10	San Antonio, TX	10.3	8	12	Houston, TX	33.3
59	13	Grand Rapids-Muskegon-Holland, MI	10.2	13	12	Minneapolis-St. Paul, MN-WI	33.3
49	13	Nashville, TN	10.2	31	14	Fort Worth-Arlington, TX	33.1
64	15	Greenville-Spartanburg-Anderson, SC	10.1	52	15	Middlesex-Somerset-Hunterdon, NJ	33.0
68	15	Honolulu, HI	10.1	49	15	Nashville, TN	33.0
12	15	Phoenix-Mesa, AZ	10.1	21	17	Oakland, CA	32.9
10	18	Dallas, TX	10.0	1	18	Los Angeles-Long Beach, CA	32.8
65	18	Dayton-Springfield, OH	10.0	41	19	Columbus, OH	32.7
8	18	Houston, TX	10.0	2	20	New York, NY	32.6
75	21	Albuquerque, NM	9.8	4	21	Boston-Worcester-Lawrence-Lowell-Brockton, MA-NH	32.3
74	21	Omaha, NE-IA	9.8	37	21	Indianapolis, IN	32.3
73	21	Syracuse, NY	9.8	27	21	Portland-Vancouver, OR-WA	32.3
45	24	New Orleans, LA	9.7	15	21	San Diego, CA	32.3
11	24	Riverside-San Bernardino, CA	9.7	34	25	Orlando, FL	32.2
2	26	New York, NY	9.6	3	26	Chicago, IL	32.1
31	27	Fort Worth-Arlington, TX	9.5	39	27	Norfolk-Virginia Beach-Newport News, VA-NC	31.9
69	28	Albany-Schenectady-Troy, NY	9.4	36	28	Fort Lauderdale, FL	31.8
9	28	Atlanta, GA	9.4	62	29	Richmond-Petersburg, VA	31.7
3	28	Chicago, IL	9.4	28	30	Kansas City, MO-KS	31.6
47	28	Greensboro-Winston-Salem-High Point, NC	9.4	26	30	Newark, NJ	31.6
54	28	Memphis, TN-AR-MS	9.4	57	32	Jacksonville, FL	31.5
34	28	Orlando, FL	9.4	40	32	Las Vegas, NV-AZ	31.5
14	34	Orange County, CA	9.3	12	34	Phoenix-Mesa, AZ	31.4
71	34	Tulsa, OK	9.3	47	35	Greensboro-Winston-Salem-High Point, NC	31.2
67	36	Birmingham, AL	9.2	54	35	Memphis, TN-AR-MS	31.2
13	36	Minneapolis-St. Paul, MN-WI	9.2	23	35	Miami, FL	31.2
27	36	Portland-Vancouver, OR-WA	9.2	74	35	Omaha, NE-IA	31.2
58	36	Rochester, NY	9.2	44	40	Bergen-Passaic, NJ	31.1
32	36	San Jose, CA	9.2	7	40	Detroit, MI	31.1
23	41	Miami, FL	9.1	33	42	Cincinnati, OH-KY-IN	30.9
42	41	Milwaukee-Waukesha, WI	9.1	72	42	Ventura, CA	30.9
43	43	Charlotte-Gastonia-Rock Hill, NC-SC	9.0	61	44	Louisville, KY-IN	30.8
33	43	Cincinnati, OH-KY-IN	9.0	68	45	Honolulu, HI	30.7
57	43	Jacksonville, FL	9.0	35	45	Sacramento, CA	30.7
19	43	Seattle-Bellevue-Everett, WA	9.0	30	47	New Haven-Bridgeport-Stamford-Danbury-Waterbury, CT	30.6
72	43	Ventura, CA	9.0	38	47	San Antonio, TX	30.6
4	48	Boston-Worcester-Lawrence-Lowell-Brockton, MA-NH	8.9	75	49	Albuquerque, NM	30.5
25	48	Denver, CO	8.9	67	49	Birmingham, AL	30.5
62	48	Richmond-Petersburg, VA	8.9	59	51	Grand Rapids-Muskegon-Holland, MI	30.4
5	51	Philadelphia, PA-NJ	8.8	53	52	Hartford, CT	30.2
37	52	Indianapolis, IN	8.7	42	52	Milwaukee-Waukesha, WI	30.2
40	52	Las Vegas, NV-AZ	8.7	16	52	Nassau-Suffolk, NY	30.2
61	52	Louisville, KY-IN	8.7	64	55	Greenville-Spartanburg-Anderson, SC	30.1
21	52	Oakland, CA	8.7	60	55	Oklahoma City, OK	30.1
35	52	Sacramento, CA	8.7	5	55	Philadelphia, PA-NJ	30.1
17	52	St. Louis, MO-IL	8.7	17	55	St. Louis, MO-IL	30.1
51	58	Buffalo-Niagara Falls, NY	8.6	45	59	New Orleans, LA	29.9
6	58	Washington, DC-MD-VA-WV	8.6	11	59	Riverside-San Bernardino, CA	29.9
18	60	Baltimore, MD	8.5	46	59	Salt Lake City-Ogden, UT	29.9
28	60	Kansas City, MO-KS	8.5	71	62	Tulsa, OK	29.8
53	62	Hartford, CT	8.3	63	63	Providence-Warwick-Pawtucket, RI	29.6
52	63	Middlesex-Somerset-Hunterdon, NJ	8.2	24	64	Cleveland-Lorain-Elyria, OH	29.4
7	64	Detroit, MI	8.1	58	64	Rochester, NY	29.4
22	64	Pittsburgh, PA	8.1	69	66	Albany-Schenectady-Troy, NY	29.3
29	66	San Francisco, CA	8.0	66	67	Fresno, CA	28.9
26	67	Newark, NJ	7.9	73	67	Syracuse, NY	28.9
24	68	Cleveland-Lorain-Elyria, OH	7.8	70	69	Tucson, AZ	28.8
30	69	New Haven-Bridgeport-Stamford-Danbury-Waterbury, CT	7.7	51	70	Buffalo-Niagara Falls, NY	28.5
44	70	Bergen-Passaic, NJ	7.6	56	70	Monmouth-Ocean, NJ	28.5
16	71	Nassau-Suffolk, NY	7.5	20	70	Tampa-St. Petersburg-Clearwater, FL	28.5
20	71	Tampa-St. Petersburg-Clearwater, FL	7.5	65	73	Dayton-Springfield, OH	28.4
36	73	Fort Lauderdale, FL	7.1	22	74	Pittsburgh, PA	28.1
56	74	Monmouth-Ocean, NJ	6.7	55	75	West Palm Beach-Boca Raton, FL	27.1
55	75	West Palm Beach-Boca Raton, FL	6.5				

TABLE 4—75 Largest Metropolitan Areas by 2000 Population
Selected Rankings

Percent 45 to 64 Years, 2000				Percent 65 Years and Over, 2000			
Population Rank	45 to 64 Years Rank	Metropolitan Area	[A-4. col 6] Percent 45 to 64 Years	Population Rank	65 Years and Over Rank	Metropolitan Area	[A-4. col 7] Percent 65 Years and Over
22	1	Pittsburgh, PA	23.9	55	1	West Palm Beach-Boca Raton, FL	23.2
16	2	Nassau-Suffolk, NY	23.6	20	2	Tampa-St. Petersburg-Clearwater, FL	19.2
29	2	San Francisco, CA	23.6	22	3	Pittsburgh, PA	17.7
65	4	Dayton-Springfield, OH	23.3	56	4	Monmouth-Ocean, NJ	16.9
53	4	Hartford, CT	23.3	36	5	Fort Lauderdale, FL	16.0
69	6	Albany-Schenectady-Troy, NY	23.2	51	6	Buffalo-Niagara Falls, NY	15.9
44	6	Bergen-Passaic, NJ	23.2	63	7	Providence-Warwick-Pawtucket, RI	14.6
61	6	Louisville, KY-IN	23.2	24	8	Cleveland-Lorain-Elyria, OH	14.5
18	9	Baltimore, MD	23.0	69	9	Albany-Schenectady-Troy, NY	14.3
64	9	Greenville-Spartanburg-Anderson, SC	23.0	70	10	Tucson, AZ	14.2
56	9	Monmouth-Ocean, NJ	23.0	44	11	Bergen-Passaic, NJ	14.1
20	9	Tampa-St. Petersburg-Clearwater, FL	23.0	53	12	Hartford, CT	13.9
6	9	Washington, DC-MD-VA-WV	23.0	30	13	New Haven-Bridgeport-Stamford-Danbury-Waterbury, CT	13.8
24	14	Cleveland-Lorain-Elyria, OH	22.9	5	14	Philadelphia, PA-NJ	13.6
62	14	Richmond-Petersburg, VA	22.9	65	15	Dayton-Springfield, OH	13.5
47	16	Greensboro-Winston-Salem-High Point, NC	22.8	68	15	Honolulu, HI	13.5
40	16	Las Vegas, NV-AZ	22.8	16	17	Nassau-Suffolk, NY	13.4
30	16	New Haven-Bridgeport-Stamford-Danbury-Waterbury, CT	22.8	73	17	Syracuse, NY	13.4
26	16	Newark, NJ	22.8	23	19	Miami, FL	13.3
58	16	Rochester, NY	22.8	29	20	San Francisco, CA	13.2
51	21	Buffalo-Niagara Falls, NY	22.7	58	21	Rochester, NY	12.9
52	21	Middlesex-Somerset-Hunterdon, NJ	22.7	17	21	St. Louis, MO-IL	12.9
27	21	Portland-Vancouver, OR-WA	22.7	67	23	Birmingham, AL	12.7
19	21	Seattle-Bellevue-Everett, WA	22.7	4	23	Boston-Worcester-Lawrence-Lowell-Brockton, MA-NH	12.7
67	25	Birmingham, AL	22.6	42	25	Milwaukee-Waukesha, WI	12.6
21	26	Oakland, CA	22.5	47	26	Greensboro-Winston-Salem-High Point, NC	12.5
57	27	Jacksonville, FL	22.4	61	26	Louisville, KY-IN	12.5
71	27	Tulsa, OK	22.4	34	28	Orlando, FL	12.4
45	29	New Orleans, LA	22.3	64	29	Greenville-Spartanburg-Anderson, SC	12.3
75	30	Albuquerque, NM	22.2	26	30	Newark, NJ	12.2
4	30	Boston-Worcester-Lawrence-Lowell-Brockton, MA-NH	22.2	7	31	Detroit, MI	12.1
7	30	Detroit, MI	22.2	18	32	Baltimore, MD	12.0
5	30	Philadelphia, PA-NJ	22.2	33	33	Cincinnati, OH-KY-IN	11.9
17	34	St. Louis, MO-IL	22.1	2	33	New York, NY	11.9
73	34	Syracuse, NY	22.1	12	33	Phoenix-Mesa, AZ	11.9
68	36	Honolulu, HI	22.0	40	36	Las Vegas, NV-AZ	11.8
28	36	Kansas City, MO-KS	22.0	52	36	Middlesex-Somerset-Hunterdon, NJ	11.8
55	36	West Palm Beach-Boca Raton, FL	22.0	71	36	Tulsa, OK	11.8
25	39	Denver, CO	21.9	35	39	Sacramento, CA	11.5
40	39	Nashville, TN	21.9	28	40	Kansas City, MO-KS	11.4
63	41	Providence-Warwick-Pawtucket, RI	21.8	45	40	New Orleans, LA	11.4
35	41	Sacramento, CA	21.8	60	40	Oklahoma City, OK	11.4
70	41	Tucson, AZ	21.8	75	43	Albuquerque, NM	11.3
33	44	Cincinnati, OH-KY-IN	21.7	62	43	Richmond-Petersburg, VA	11.3
42	44	Milwaukee-Waukesha, WI	21.7	57	45	Jacksonville, FL	11.1
60	44	Oklahoma City, OK	21.7	15	45	San Diego, CA	11.1
72	44	Ventura, CA	21.7	37	47	Indianapolis, IN	10.9
43	48	Charlotte-Gastonia-Rock Hill, NC-SC	21.6	59	48	Grand Rapids-Muskegon-Holland, MI	10.8
36	48	Fort Lauderdale, FL	21.6	3	49	Chicago, IL	10.7
23	48	Miami, FL	21.6	21	50	Oakland, CA	10.6
2	51	New York, NY	21.5	74	50	Omaha, NE-IA	10.6
37	52	Indianapolis, IN	21.4	38	50	San Antonio, TX	10.6
34	53	Orlando, FL	21.3	11	53	Riverside-San Bernardino, CA	10.5
54	54	Memphis, TN-AR-MS	21.2	27	54	Portland-Vancouver, OR-WA	10.4
13	54	Minneapolis-St. Paul, MN-WI	21.2	39	55	Norfolk-Virginia Beach-Newport News, VA-NC	10.3
74	54	Omaha, NE-IA	21.2	43	56	Charlotte-Gastonia-Rock Hill, NC-SC	10.2
41	57	Columbus, OH	21.1	19	56	Seattle-Bellevue-Everett, WA	10.2
3	58	Chicago, IL	20.9	41	58	Columbus, OH	10.0
32	58	San Jose, CA	20.9	66	58	Fresno, CA	10.0
9	60	Atlanta, GA	20.7	49	58	Nashville, TN	10.0
31	61	Fort Worth-Arlington, TX	20.6	72	58	Ventura, CA	10.0
50	61	Raleigh-Durham-Chapel Hill, NC	20.6	54	62	Memphis, TN-AR-MS	9.9
14	63	Orange County, CA	20.5	14	63	Orange County, CA	9.8
39	64	Norfolk-Virginia Beach-Newport News, VA-NC	20.4	1	64	Los Angeles-Long Beach, CA	9.7
59	65	Grand Rapids-Muskegon-Holland, MI	20.3	13	65	Minneapolis-St. Paul, MN-WI	9.6
8	66	Houston, TX	20.2	32	66	San Jose, CA	9.5
38	66	San Antonio, TX	20.2	25	67	Denver, CO	9.0
12	68	Phoenix-Mesa, AZ	19.8	6	67	Washington, DC-MD-VA-WV	9.0
15	69	San Diego, CA	19.6	31	69	Fort Worth-Arlington, TX	8.8
10	70	Dallas, TX	19.5	50	70	Raleigh-Durham-Chapel Hill, NC	8.6
1	71	Los Angeles-Long Beach, CA	19.2	46	71	Salt Lake City-Ogden, UT	8.3
48	72	Austin-San Marcos, TX	18.7	10	72	Dallas, TX	7.7
66	73	Fresno, CA	18.6	9	73	Atlanta, GA	7.6
11	73	Riverside-San Bernardino, CA	18.6	8	74	Houston, TX	7.4
46	75	Salt Lake City-Ogden, UT	17.8	48	75	Austin-San Marcos, TX	7.2

TABLE 4—75 Largest Metropolitan Areas by 2000 Population
Selected Rankings

		Percent Non-Hispanic White, 2000				Percent Black or African American, 2000	
Population Rank	Non-Hispanic White Rank	Metropolitan Area	[A-4. col 11] Percent Non-Hispanic White	Population Rank	Black or African American Rank	Metropolitan Area	[A-4. col 14] Percent Black or African American
22	1	Pittsburgh, PA	89.1	54	1	Memphis, TN-AR-MS	43.2
69	2	Albany-Schenectady-Troy, NY	88.1	45	2	New Orleans, LA	37.4
73	3	Syracuse, NY	87.9	39	3	Norfolk-Virginia Beach-Newport News, VA-NC	30.8
13	4	Minneapolis-St. Paul, MN-WI	84.8	67	4	Birmingham, AL	30.0
56	4	Monmouth-Ocean, NJ	84.8	62	4	Richmond-Petersburg, VA	30.0
33	6	Cincinnati, OH-KY-IN	83.5	9	6	Atlanta, GA	28.8
59	7	Grand Rapids-Muskegon-Holland, MI	83.0	18	7	Baltimore, MD	27.2
4	8	Boston-Worcester-Lawrence-Lowell-Brockton, MA-NH	82.9	6	8	Washington, DC-MD-VA-WV	25.9
74	9	Omaha, NE-IA	82.8	2	9	New York, NY	24.4
46	9	Salt Lake City-Ogden, UT	82.8	7	10	Detroit, MI	22.8
51	11	Buffalo-Niagara Falls, NY	82.5	50	11	Raleigh-Durham-Chapel Hill, NC	22.6
58	12	Rochester, NY	82.3	26	12	Newark, NJ	22.1
61	13	Louisville, KY-IN	82.0	57	13	Jacksonville, FL	21.6
65	14	Dayton-Springfield, OH	81.6	43	14	Charlotte-Gastonia-Rock Hill, NC-SC	20.5
27	15	Portland-Vancouver, OR-WA	81.5	36	15	Fort Lauderdale, FL	20.3
63	16	Providence-Warwick-Pawtucket, RI	81.2	47	16	Greensboro-Winston-Salem-High Point, NC	20.1
37	17	Indianapolis, IN	80.8	23	16	Miami, FL	20.1
41	18	Columbus, OH	80.4	5	18	Philadelphia, PA-NJ	20.0
28	19	Kansas City, MO-KS	78.4	3	19	Chicago, IL	18.8
49	20	Nashville, TN	78.0	24	20	Cleveland-Lorain-Elyria, OH	18.3
64	21	Greenville-Spartanburg-Anderson, SC	77.7	17	21	St. Louis, MO-IL	18.2
53	22	Hartford, CT	77.4	64	22	Greenville-Spartanburg-Anderson, SC	17.5
17	22	St. Louis, MO-IL	77.4	8	23	Houston, TX	17.4
16	24	Nassau-Suffolk, NY	76.4	49	24	Nashville, TN	15.6
19	25	Seattle-Bellevue-Everett, WA	76.2	42	25	Milwaukee-Waukesha, WI	15.5
20	26	Tampa-St. Petersburg-Clearwater, FL	76.0	10	26	Dallas, TX	14.9
24	27	Cleveland-Lorain-Elyria, OH	75.4	65	27	Dayton-Springfield, OH	14.2
42	28	Milwaukee-Waukesha, WI	74.5	37	28	Indianapolis, IN	13.9
30	29	New Haven-Bridgeport-Stamford-Danbury-Waterbury, CT	73.9	61	29	Louisville, KY-IN	13.8
71	29	Tulsa, OK	73.9	55	29	West Palm Beach-Boca Raton, FL	13.8
60	31	Oklahoma City, OK	72.9	34	31	Orlando, FL	13.7
47	32	Greensboro-Winston-Salem-High Point, NC	72.3	41	32	Columbus, OH	13.2
43	33	Charlotte-Gastonia-Rock Hill, NC-SC	71.3	33	33	Cincinnati, OH-KY-IN	12.9
55	34	West Palm Beach-Boca Raton, FL	70.6	28	34	Kansas City, MO-KS	12.5
57	35	Jacksonville, FL	70.4	21	34	Oakland, CA	12.5
25	36	Denver, CO	70.3	51	36	Buffalo-Niagara Falls, NY	11.7
5	36	Philadelphia, PA-NJ	70.3	31	37	Fort Worth-Arlington, TX	11.0
7	38	Detroit, MI	69.7	30	38	New Haven-Bridgeport-Stamford-Danbury-Waterbury, CT	10.6
52	39	Middlesex-Somerset-Hunterdon, NJ	68.1	60	39	Oklahoma City, OK	10.4
50	40	Raleigh-Durham-Chapel Hill, NC	66.8	20	40	Tampa-St. Petersburg-Clearwater, FL	10.1
67	41	Birmingham, AL	66.5	58	41	Rochester, NY	10.0
18	42	Baltimore, MD	66.3	1	42	Los Angeles-Long Beach, CA	9.6
12	43	Phoenix-Mesa, AZ	65.8	53	43	Hartford, CT	9.4
31	44	Fort Worth-Arlington, TX	65.6	71	44	Tulsa, OK	8.8
34	45	Orlando, FL	65.1	16	45	Nassau-Suffolk, NY	8.4
44	46	Bergen-Passaic, NJ	64.8	74	46	Omaha, NE-IA	8.1
35	47	Sacramento, CA	64.2	44	47	Bergen-Passaic, NJ	8.0
62	48	Richmond-Petersburg, VA	64.0	22	47	Pittsburgh, PA	8.0
40	49	Las Vegas, NV-AZ	63.0	40	49	Las Vegas, NV-AZ	7.9
70	50	Tucson, AZ	61.4	52	49	Middlesex-Somerset-Hunterdon, NJ	7.9
39	51	Norfolk-Virginia Beach-Newport News, VA-NC	61.1	48	51	Austin-San Marcos, TX	7.8
48	52	Austin-San Marcos, TX	60.7	11	52	Riverside-San Bernardino, CA	7.6
9	53	Atlanta, GA	59.9	35	53	Sacramento, CA	7.5
26	54	Newark, NJ	58.9	59	54	Grand Rapids-Muskegon-Holland, MI	7.3
3	55	Chicago, IL	58.0	38	55	San Antonio, TX	6.5
36	55	Fort Lauderdale, FL	58.0	73	56	Syracuse, NY	6.4
72	57	Ventura, CA	56.6	69	57	Albany-Schenectady-Troy, NY	5.9
10	58	Dallas, TX	56.2	56	58	Monmouth-Ocean, NJ	5.7
6	59	Washington, DC-MD-VA-WV	56.1	15	59	San Diego, CA	5.6
15	60	San Diego, CA	54.9	25	60	Denver, CO	5.4
45	61	New Orleans, LA	54.7	13	61	Minneapolis-St. Paul, MN-WI	5.2
54	62	Memphis, TN-AR-MS	51.9	29	61	San Francisco, CA	5.2
14	63	Orange County, CA	51.1	66	63	Fresno, CA	5.0
29	63	San Francisco, CA	51.1	4	64	Boston-Worcester-Lawrence-Lowell-Brockton, MA-NH	4.9
75	65	Albuquerque, NM	47.8	63	65	Providence-Warwick-Pawtucket, RI	4.3
21	66	Oakland, CA	47.5	19	65	Seattle-Bellevue-Everett, WA	4.3
11	67	Riverside-San Bernardino, CA	47.2	12	67	Phoenix-Mesa, AZ	3.6
8	68	Houston, TX	46.0	70	68	Tucson, AZ	2.9
32	69	San Jose, CA	44.0	32	69	San Jose, CA	2.7
66	70	Fresno, CA	40.6	27	70	Portland-Vancouver, OR-WA	2.5
2	71	New York, NY	39.6	75	71	Albuquerque, NM	2.4
38	72	San Antonio, TX	39.3	68	72	Honolulu, HI	2.2
1	73	Los Angeles-Long Beach, CA	30.9	72	73	Ventura, CA	1.9
23	74	Miami, FL	20.7	14	74	Orange County, CA	1.6
68	75	Honolulu, HI	20.0	46	75	Salt Lake City-Ogden, UT	1.0

TABLE 4—75 Largest Metropolitan Areas by 2000 Population
Selected Rankings

Percent American Indian and Alaska Native, 2000				Percent Asian, Hawaiian, and Pacific Islander, 2000			
Population Rank	American Indian and Alaska Native Rank	Metropolitan Area	[A-4. col 17] Percent American Indian and Alaska Native	Population Rank	Asian, Hawaiian, and Pacific Islander Rank	Metropolitan Area	[A-4. col 20] Percent Asian, Hawaiian, and Pacific Islander
71	1	Tulsa, OK	6.7	68	1	Honolulu, HI	55.0
75	2	Albuquerque, NM	5.6	32	2	San Jose, CA	25.9
60	3	Oklahoma City, OK	4.0	29	3	San Francisco, CA	23.4
70	4	Tucson, AZ	3.3	21	4	Oakland, CA	17.1
12	5	Phoenix-Mesa, AZ	2.1	14	5	Orange County, CA	13.9
66	6	Fresno, CA	1.7	1	6	Los Angeles-Long Beach, CA	12.2
11	7	Riverside-San Bernardino, CA	1.1	52	7	Middlesex-Somerset-Hunterdon, NJ	11.3
40	8	Las Vegas, NV-AZ	1.0	19	8	Seattle-Bellevue-Everett, WA	9.8
35	8	Sacramento, CA	1.0	35	9	Sacramento, CA	9.3
19	8	Seattle-Bellevue-Everett, WA	1.0	15	9	San Diego, CA	9.3
25	11	Denver, CO	0.9	2	11	New York, NY	9.2
27	11	Portland-Vancouver, OR-WA	0.9	44	12	Bergen-Passaic, NJ	8.2
46	13	Salt Lake City-Ogden, UT	0.8	66	13	Fresno, CA	7.2
15	13	San Diego, CA	0.8	6	14	Washington, DC-MD-VA-WV	6.6
72	13	Ventura, CA	0.8	72	15	Ventura, CA	5.4
51	16	Buffalo-Niagara Falls, NY	0.7	8	16	Houston, TX	5.2
1	16	Los Angeles-Long Beach, CA	0.7	40	17	Las Vegas, NV-AZ	5.0
42	16	Milwaukee-Waukesha, WI	0.7	27	18	Portland-Vancouver, OR-WA	4.8
13	16	Minneapolis-St. Paul, MN-WI	0.7	3	19	Chicago, IL	4.7
38	16	San Antonio, TX	0.7	11	20	Riverside-San Bernardino, CA	4.4
32	16	San Jose, CA	0.7	13	21	Minneapolis-St. Paul, MN-WI	4.1
73	16	Syracuse, NY	0.7	26	21	Newark, NJ	4.1
10	23	Dallas, TX	0.6	10	23	Dallas, TX	4.0
31	23	Fort Worth-Arlington, TX	0.6	4	24	Boston-Worcester-Lawrence-Lowell-Brockton, MA-NH	3.9
21	23	Oakland, CA	0.6	48	25	Austin-San Marcos, TX	3.6
74	23	Omaha, NE-IA	0.6	16	26	Nassau-Suffolk, NY	3.5
14	23	Orange County, CA	0.6	5	27	Philadelphia, PA-NJ	3.4
48	28	Austin-San Marcos, TX	0.5	9	28	Atlanta, GA	3.3
43	28	Charlotte-Gastonia-Rock Hill, NC-SC	0.5	31	29	Fort Worth-Arlington, TX	3.2
59	28	Grand Rapids-Muskegon-Holland, MI	0.5	25	30	Denver, CO	3.0
28	28	Kansas City, MO-KS	0.5	46	30	Salt Lake City-Ogden, UT	3.0
63	28	Providence-Warwick-Pawtucket, RI	0.5	50	32	Raleigh-Durham-Chapel Hill, NC	2.9
7	33	Detroit, MI	0.4	56	33	Monmouth-Ocean, NJ	2.8
47	33	Greensboro-Winston-Salem-High Point, NC	0.4	30	33	New Haven-Bridgeport-Stamford-Danbury-Waterbury, CT	2.8
8	33	Houston, TX	0.4	39	33	Norfolk-Virginia Beach-Newport News, VA-NC	2.8
45	33	New Orleans, LA	0.4	18	36	Baltimore, MD	2.7
2	33	New York, NY	0.4	34	36	Orlando, FL	2.7
39	33	Norfolk-Virginia Beach-Newport News, VA-NC	0.4	60	38	Oklahoma City, OK	2.5
50	33	Raleigh-Durham-Chapel Hill, NC	0.4	41	39	Columbus, OH	2.4
62	33	Richmond-Petersburg, VA	0.4	63	39	Providence-Warwick-Pawtucket, RI	2.4
29	33	San Francisco, CA	0.4	7	41	Detroit, MI	2.3
20	33	Tampa-St. Petersburg-Clearwater, FL	0.4	36	41	Fort Lauderdale, FL	2.3
9	43	Atlanta, GA	0.3	53	41	Hartford, CT	2.3
18	43	Baltimore, MD	0.3	57	41	Jacksonville, FL	2.3
67	43	Birmingham, AL	0.3	12	45	Phoenix-Mesa, AZ	2.2
41	43	Columbus, OH	0.3	45	46	New Orleans, LA	2.1
37	43	Indianapolis, IN	0.3	62	46	Richmond-Petersburg, VA	2.1
57	43	Jacksonville, FL	0.3	70	46	Tucson, AZ	2.1
61	43	Louisville, KY-IN	0.3	42	49	Milwaukee-Waukesha, WI	1.9
49	43	Nashville, TN	0.3	20	49	Tampa-St. Petersburg-Clearwater, FL	1.9
34	43	Orlando, FL	0.3	69	51	Albany-Schenectady-Troy, NY	1.8
58	43	Rochester, NY	0.3	43	51	Charlotte-Gastonia-Rock Hill, NC-SC	1.8
17	43	St. Louis, MO-IL	0.3	58	51	Rochester, NY	1.8
6	43	Washington, DC-MD-VA-WV	0.3	28	54	Kansas City, MO-KS	1.7
69	55	Albany-Schenectady-Troy, NY	0.2	75	55	Albuquerque, NM	1.6
44	55	Bergen-Passaic, NJ	0.2	59	55	Grand Rapids-Muskegon-Holland, MI	1.6
4	55	Boston-Worcester-Lawrence-Lowell-Brockton, MA-NH	0.2	38	55	San Antonio, TX	1.6
3	55	Chicago, IL	0.2	54	58	Memphis, TN-AR-MS	1.5
33	55	Cincinnati, OH-KY-IN	0.2	49	58	Nashville, TN	1.5
24	55	Cleveland-Lorain-Elyria, OH	0.2	74	58	Omaha, NE-IA	1.5
65	55	Dayton-Springfield, OH	0.2	73	58	Syracuse, NY	1.5
36	55	Fort Lauderdale, FL	0.2	55	58	West Palm Beach-Boca Raton, FL	1.5
64	55	Greenville-Spartanburg-Anderson, SC	0.2	24	63	Cleveland-Lorain-Elyria, OH	1.4
53	55	Hartford, CT	0.2	23	63	Miami, FL	1.4
68	55	Honolulu, HI	0.2	17	63	St. Louis, MO-IL	1.4
54	55	Memphis, TN-AR-MS	0.2	65	66	Dayton-Springfield, OH	1.3
23	55	Miami, FL	0.2	47	66	Greensboro-Winston-Salem-High Point, NC	1.3
52	55	Middlesex-Somerset-Hunterdon, NJ	0.2	51	68	Buffalo-Niagara Falls, NY	1.2
16	55	Nassau-Suffolk, NY	0.2	33	68	Cincinnati, OH-KY-IN	1.2
30	55	New Haven-Bridgeport-Stamford-Danbury-Waterbury, CT	0.2	64	68	Greenville-Spartanburg-Anderson, SC	1.2
26	55	Newark, NJ	0.2	37	68	Indianapolis, IN	1.2
5	55	Philadelphia, PA-NJ	0.2	71	68	Tulsa, OK	1.2
55	55	West Palm Beach-Boca Raton, FL	0.2	22	73	Pittsburgh, PA	1.1
56	74	Monmouth-Ocean, NJ	0.1	61	74	Louisville, KY-IN	1.0
22	74	Pittsburgh, PA	0.1	67	75	Birmingham, AL	0.8

TABLE 4—75 Largest Metropolitan Areas by 2000 Population
Selected Rankings

Percent Hispanic or Latino[1], 2000				Percent Two or More Races, 2000			
Population Rank	Hispanic or Latino Rank	Metropolitan Area	[A-4. col 23] Percent Hispanic or Latino	Population Rank	Two or More Races Rank	Metropolitan Area	[A-4. col 26] Percent Two or More Races
23	1	Miami, FL	57.3	68	1	Honolulu, HI	20.1
38	2	San Antonio, TX	51.2	21	2	Oakland, CA	5.8
1	3	Los Angeles-Long Beach, CA	44.6	35	3	Sacramento, CA	5.5
66	4	Fresno, CA	44.1	71	4	Tulsa, OK	5.2
75	5	Albuquerque, NM	41.6	66	5	Fresno, CA	5.1
11	6	Riverside-San Bernardino, CA	37.8	1	5	Los Angeles-Long Beach, CA	5.1
72	7	Ventura, CA	33.5	11	5	Riverside-San Bernardino, CA	5.1
14	8	Orange County, CA	30.8	15	8	San Diego, CA	5.0
8	9	Houston, TX	29.9	32	8	San Jose, CA	5.0
70	10	Tucson, AZ	29.4	29	10	San Francisco, CA	4.8
15	11	San Diego, CA	26.7	2	11	New York, NY	4.7
48	12	Austin-San Marcos, TX	26.2	75	12	Albuquerque, NM	4.5
2	13	New York, NY	25.1	60	13	Oklahoma City, OK	4.4
12	13	Phoenix-Mesa, AZ	25.1	14	14	Orange County, CA	4.3
32	15	San Jose, CA	24.0	40	15	Las Vegas, NV-AZ	4.2
10	16	Dallas, TX	23.0	19	15	Seattle-Bellevue-Everett, WA	4.2
40	17	Las Vegas, NV-AZ	20.6	23	17	Miami, FL	4.1
25	18	Denver, CO	18.8	72	18	Ventura, CA	4.0
21	19	Oakland, CA	18.5	38	19	San Antonio, TX	3.7
31	20	Fort Worth-Arlington, TX	18.2	36	20	Fort Lauderdale, FL	3.6
44	21	Bergen-Passaic, NJ	17.3	27	20	Portland-Vancouver, OR-WA	3.6
3	22	Chicago, IL	17.1	70	22	Tucson, AZ	3.5
29	23	San Francisco, CA	16.8	25	23	Denver, CO	3.3
36	24	Fort Lauderdale, FL	16.7	34	24	Orlando, FL	3.2
34	25	Orlando, FL	16.5	6	24	Washington, DC-MD-VA-WV	3.2
35	26	Sacramento, CA	14.4	12	26	Phoenix-Mesa, AZ	3.1
26	27	Newark, NJ	13.3	44	27	Bergen-Passaic, NJ	3.0
55	28	West Palm Beach-Boca Raton, FL	12.4	8	28	Houston, TX	2.9
52	29	Middlesex-Somerset-Hunterdon, NJ	11.2	26	28	Newark, NJ	2.9
30	30	New Haven-Bridgeport-Stamford-Danbury-Waterbury, CT	11.0	63	28	Providence-Warwick-Pawtucket, RI	2.9
46	31	Salt Lake City-Ogden, UT	10.8	48	31	Austin-San Marcos, TX	2.8
20	32	Tampa-St. Petersburg-Clearwater, FL	10.4	46	32	Salt Lake City-Ogden, UT	2.6
16	33	Nassau-Suffolk, NY	10.3	10	33	Dallas, TX	2.5
53	34	Hartford, CT	9.3	31	33	Fort Worth-Arlington, TX	2.5
63	35	Providence-Warwick-Pawtucket, RI	9.2	3	35	Chicago, IL	2.4
6	36	Washington, DC-MD-VA-WV	8.7	52	35	Middlesex-Somerset-Hunterdon, NJ	2.4
27	37	Portland-Vancouver, OR-WA	7.4	30	35	New Haven-Bridgeport-Stamford-Danbury-Waterbury, CT	2.4
68	38	Honolulu, HI	6.7	39	35	Norfolk-Virginia Beach-Newport News, VA-NC	2.4
60	38	Oklahoma City, OK	6.7	55	35	West Palm Beach-Boca Raton, FL	2.4
9	40	Atlanta, GA	6.5	4	40	Boston-Worcester-Lawrence-Lowell-Brockton, MA-NH	2.3
59	41	Grand Rapids-Muskegon-Holland, MI	6.4	53	40	Hartford, CT	2.3
42	42	Milwaukee-Waukesha, WI	6.3	13	40	Minneapolis-St. Paul, MN-WI	2.3
50	43	Raleigh-Durham-Chapel Hill, NC	6.1	7	43	Detroit, MI	2.2
4	44	Boston-Worcester-Lawrence-Lowell-Brockton, MA-NH	6.0	28	43	Kansas City, MO-KS	2.2
56	45	Monmouth-Ocean, NJ	5.6	16	43	Nassau-Suffolk, NY	2.2
74	46	Omaha, NE-IA	5.5	41	46	Columbus, OH	2.1
28	47	Kansas City, MO-KS	5.2	20	46	Tampa-St. Petersburg-Clearwater, FL	2.1
19	47	Seattle-Bellevue-Everett, WA	5.2	59	48	Grand Rapids-Muskegon-Holland, MI	2.0
43	49	Charlotte-Gastonia-Rock Hill, NC-SC	5.1	58	48	Rochester, NY	2.0
47	50	Greensboro-Winston-Salem-High Point, NC	5.0	57	50	Jacksonville, FL	1.9
5	50	Philadelphia, PA-NJ	5.0	9	51	Atlanta, GA	1.8
71	52	Tulsa, OK	4.8	42	51	Milwaukee-Waukesha, WI	1.8
45	53	New Orleans, LA	4.4	74	51	Omaha, NE-IA	1.8
58	54	Rochester, NY	4.3	5	51	Philadelphia, PA-NJ	1.8
57	55	Jacksonville, FL	3.9	73	51	Syracuse, NY	1.8
24	56	Cleveland-Lorain-Elyria, OH	3.3	18	56	Baltimore, MD	1.7
13	56	Minneapolis-St. Paul, MN-WI	3.3	24	56	Cleveland-Lorain-Elyria, OH	1.7
49	58	Nashville, TN	3.2	50	56	Raleigh-Durham-Chapel Hill, NC	1.7
39	59	Norfolk-Virginia Beach-Newport News, VA-NC	3.1	69	59	Albany-Schenectady-Troy, NY	1.6
51	60	Buffalo-Niagara Falls, NY	2.9	65	59	Dayton-Springfield, OH	1.6
7	60	Detroit, MI	2.9	56	59	Monmouth-Ocean, NJ	1.6
69	62	Albany-Schenectady-Troy, NY	2.7	49	59	Nashville, TN	1.6
64	63	Greenville-Spartanburg-Anderson, SC	2.6	45	59	New Orleans, LA	1.6
37	63	Indianapolis, IN	2.6	37	64	Indianapolis, IN	1.5
54	65	Memphis, TN-AR-MS	2.3	61	64	Louisville, KY-IN	1.5
62	65	Richmond-Petersburg, VA	2.3	62	64	Richmond-Petersburg, VA	1.5
18	67	Baltimore, MD	2.0	51	67	Buffalo-Niagara Falls, NY	1.4
73	67	Syracuse, NY	2.0	17	67	St. Louis, MO-IL	1.4
67	69	Birmingham, AL	1.8	43	69	Charlotte-Gastonia-Rock Hill, NC-SC	1.3
41	69	Columbus, OH	1.8	47	69	Greensboro-Winston-Salem-High Point, NC	1.3
61	71	Louisville, KY-IN	1.5	33	71	Cincinnati, OH-KY-IN	1.1
17	71	St. Louis, MO-IL	1.5	54	71	Memphis, TN-AR-MS	1.1
65	73	Dayton-Springfield, OH	1.1	64	73	Greenville-Spartanburg-Anderson, SC	1.0
33	74	Cincinnati, OH-KY-IN	1.0	22	73	Pittsburgh, PA	1.0
22	75	Pittsburgh, PA	0.7	67	75	Birmingham, AL	0.9

[1] Hispanic or Latino persons may be of any race.

TABLE 4—75 Largest Metropolitan Areas by 2000 Population
Selected Rankings

	Percent Married-Couple Families, 2000				Percent Married-Couple Families with Own Children Under 18 Years, 2000		
Population Rank	Married-Couple Families Households Rank	Metropolitan Area	[A-4. col 30] Percent Married-Couple Families Households	Population Rank	Married-Couple Families With Own Children Under 18 Years Households Rank	Metropolitan Area	[A-4. col 31] Percent Married-Couple Families With Own Children Under 18 Years Households
16	1	Nassau-Suffolk, NY	63.6	46	1	Salt Lake City-Ogden, UT	34.3
46	2	Salt Lake City-Ogden, UT	61.4	75	2	Albuquerque, NM	22.9
72	3	Ventura, CA	60.2	74	3	Omaha, NE-IA	25.5
52	4	Middlesex-Somerset-Hunterdon, NJ	59.9	73	4	Syracuse, NY	23.2
56	5	Monmouth-Ocean, NJ	58.1	72	5	Ventura, CA	31.8
11	6	Riverside-San Bernardino, CA	57.2	71	6	Tulsa, OK	24.6
14	7	Orange County, CA	57.0	70	7	Tucson, AZ	20.8
44	8	Bergen-Passaic, NJ	56.7	69	8	Albany-Schenectady-Troy, NY	22.0
59	9	Grand Rapids-Muskegon-Holland, MI	56.4	68	9	Honolulu, HI	25.3
32	10	San Jose, CA	56.1	67	10	Birmingham, AL	23.3
31	11	Fort Worth-Arlington, TX	55.4	66	11	Fresno, CA	29.5
68	11	Honolulu, HI	55.4	65	12	Dayton-Springfield, OH	21.5
66	13	Fresno, CA	55.0	64	13	Greenville-Spartanburg-Anderson, SC	23.5
8	14	Houston, TX	54.2	63	14	Providence-Warwick-Pawtucket, RI	21.8
64	15	Greenville-Spartanburg-Anderson, SC	54.1	62	15	Richmond-Petersburg, VA	23.2
43	16	Charlotte-Gastonia-Rock Hill, NC-SC	54.0	61	16	Louisville, KY-IN	21.9
71	17	Tulsa, OK	53.8	60	17	Oklahoma City, OK	23.3
13	18	Minneapolis-St. Paul, MN-WI	53.2	59	18	Grand Rapids-Muskegon-Holland, MI	28.0
38	18	San Antonio, TX	53.2	58	19	Rochester, NY	23.2
26	20	Newark, NJ	53.1	57	20	Jacksonville, FL	23.6
10	21	Dallas, TX	53.0	56	21	Monmouth-Ocean, NJ	26.8
30	21	New Haven-Bridgeport-Stamford-Danbury-Waterbury, CT	53.0	55	22	West Palm Beach-Boca Raton, FL	18.4
12	21	Phoenix-Mesa, AZ	53.0	54	23	Memphis, TN-AR-MS	22.1
47	24	Greensboro-Winston-Salem-High Point, NC	52.9	53	24	Hartford, CT	22.9
9	25	Atlanta, GA	52.4	52	25	Middlesex-Somerset-Hunterdon, NJ	29.9
28	25	Kansas City, MO-KS	52.4	51	26	Buffalo-Niagara Falls, NY	21.0
74	27	Omaha, NE-IA	52.3	50	27	Raleigh-Durham-Chapel Hill, NC	24.8
34	28	Orlando, FL	52.1	49	28	Nashville, TN	24.0
49	29	Nashville, TN	52.0	48	29	Austin-San Marcos, TX	25.4
39	29	Norfolk-Virginia Beach-Newport News, VA-NC	52.0	47	30	Greensboro-Winston-Salem-High Point, NC	22.8
27	29	Portland-Vancouver, OR-WA	52.0	45	31	New Orleans, LA	21.1
67	32	Birmingham, AL	51.6	44	32	Bergen-Passaic, NJ	27.2
37	33	Indianapolis, IN	51.5	43	33	Charlotte-Gastonia-Rock Hill, NC-SC	25.1
57	33	Jacksonville, FL	51.5	42	34	Milwaukee-Waukesha, WI	22.5
55	35	West Palm Beach-Boca Raton, FL	51.4	41	35	Columbus, OH	23.0
53	36	Hartford, CT	51.3	40	36	Las Vegas, NV-AZ	21.9
60	36	Oklahoma City, OK	51.3	39	37	Norfolk-Virginia Beach-Newport News, VA-NC	24.9
15	36	San Diego, CA	51.3	38	38	San Antonio, TX	26.4
3	39	Chicago, IL	51.2	37	39	Indianapolis, IN	24.3
33	39	Cincinnati, OH-KY-IN	51.2	36	40	Fort Lauderdale, FL	20.7
22	39	Pittsburgh, PA	51.2	35	41	Sacramento, CA	24.4
50	39	Raleigh-Durham-Chapel Hill, NC	51.2	34	42	Orlando, FL	23.1
4	43	Boston-Worcester-Lawrence-Lowell-Brockton, MA-NH	51.1	33	43	Cincinnati, OH-KY-IN	24.4
65	43	Dayton-Springfield, OH	51.1	32	44	San Jose, CA	28.7
21	45	Oakland, CA	51.0	31	45	Fort Worth-Arlington, TX	28.5
35	46	Sacramento, CA	50.8	30	46	New Haven-Bridgeport-Stamford-Danbury-Waterbury, CT	25.1
17	46	St. Louis, MO-IL	50.8	29	47	San Francisco, CA	19.0
58	48	Rochester, NY	50.6	28	48	Kansas City, MO-KS	24.5
25	49	Denver, CO	50.5	27	49	Portland-Vancouver, OR-WA	24.9
40	49	Las Vegas, NV-AZ	50.5	26	50	Newark, NJ	26.2
6	49	Washington, DC-MD-VA-WV	50.5	25	51	Denver, CO	24.9
73	52	Syracuse, NY	50.1	24	52	Cleveland-Lorain-Elyria, OH	21.4
62	53	Richmond-Petersburg, VA	50.0	23	53	Miami, FL	23.4
61	54	Louisville, KY-IN	49.9	22	54	Pittsburgh, PA	20.8
19	54	Seattle-Bellevue-Everett, WA	49.9	21	55	Oakland, CA	25.7
5	56	Philadelphia, PA-NJ	49.7	20	56	Tampa-St. Petersburg-Clearwater, FL	18.1
7	57	Detroit, MI	49.5	19	57	Seattle-Bellevue-Everett, WA	23.9
69	58	Albany-Schenectady-Troy, NY	49.4	18	58	Baltimore, MD	22.5
48	59	Austin-San Marcos, TX	49.3	17	59	St. Louis, MO-IL	23.6
18	60	Baltimore, MD	49.0	16	60	Nassau-Suffolk, NY	31.1
42	60	Milwaukee-Waukesha, WI	49.0	15	61	San Diego, CA	25.5
63	60	Providence-Warwick-Pawtucket, RI	49.0	14	62	Orange County, CA	30.0
24	63	Cleveland-Lorain-Elyria, OH	48.9	13	63	Minneapolis-St. Paul, MN-WI	26.7
41	63	Columbus, OH	48.9	12	64	Phoenix-Mesa, AZ	24.3
75	65	Albuquerque, NM	48.8	11	65	Riverside-San Bernardino, CA	30.9
20	65	Tampa-St. Petersburg-Clearwater, FL	48.8	10	66	Dallas, TX	28.0
23	67	Miami, FL	48.7	9	67	Atlanta, GA	26.7
70	67	Tucson, AZ	48.7	8	68	Houston, TX	29.7
1	69	Los Angeles-Long Beach, CA	48.5	7	69	Detroit, MI	23.2
51	70	Buffalo-Niagara Falls, NY	48.2	6	70	Washington, DC-MD-VA-WV	25.1
36	71	Fort Lauderdale, FL	46.8	5	71	Philadelphia, PA-NJ	23.2
54	72	Memphis, TN-AR-MS	46.6	4	72	Boston-Worcester-Lawrence-Lowell-Brockton, MA-NH	24.4
45	73	New Orleans, LA	45.5	3	73	Chicago, IL	26.1
29	74	San Francisco, CA	43.1	2	74	New York, NY	19.8
2	75	New York, NY	40.8	1	75	Los Angeles-Long Beach, CA	26.8

TABLE 4—75 Largest Metropolitan Areas by 2000 Population
Selected Rankings

Percent Single-Parent Households with Children Under 18 Years, 2000				Percent Men Living Along, 2000			
Population Rank	Single-Parent Households Rank	Metropolitan Area	[A-4. col 34] Percent Single-Parent Households	Population Rank	Men Living Alone Rank	Metropolitan Area	[A-4. col 38] Percent Men Living Alone
54	1	Memphis, TN-AR-MS	13.6	29	1	San Francisco, CA	14.7
45	2	New Orleans, LA	12.5	48	2	Austin-San Marcos, TX	13.1
66	3	Fresno, CA	12.4	19	2	Seattle-Bellevue-Everett, WA	13.1
2	4	New York, NY	11.4	25	4	Denver, CO	12.9
39	4	Norfolk-Virginia Beach-Newport News, VA-NC	11.4	40	5	Las Vegas, NV-AZ	12.7
11	6	Riverside-San Bernardino, CA	11.3	70	5	Tucson, AZ	12.7
23	7	Miami, FL	11.2	2	7	New York, NY	12.4
1	8	Los Angeles-Long Beach, CA	10.8	36	8	Fort Lauderdale, FL	12.3
75	9	Albuquerque, NM	10.7	69	9	Albany-Schenectady-Troy, NY	12.2
38	9	San Antonio, TX	10.7	75	9	Albuquerque, NM	12.2
57	11	Jacksonville, FL	10.5	41	9	Columbus, OH	12.2
35	12	Sacramento, CA	10.4	51	12	Buffalo-Niagara Falls, NY	12.1
18	13	Baltimore, MD	10.1	42	12	Milwaukee-Waukesha, WI	12.1
61	13	Louisville, KY-IN	10.1	45	12	New Orleans, LA	12.1
62	13	Richmond-Petersburg, VA	10.1	33	15	Cincinnati, OH-KY-IN	12.0
8	16	Houston, TX	10.0	24	15	Cleveland-Lorain-Elyria, OH	12.0
73	16	Syracuse, NY	10.0	60	15	Oklahoma City, OK	12.0
7	18	Detroit, MI	9.9	20	15	Tampa-St. Petersburg-Clearwater, FL	12.0
58	18	Rochester, NY	9.9	7	19	Detroit, MI	11.9
17	18	St. Louis, MO-IL	9.9	74	20	Omaha, NE-IA	11.7
42	21	Milwaukee-Waukesha, WI	9.8	27	20	Portland-Vancouver, OR-WA	11.7
9	22	Atlanta, GA	9.7	71	20	Tulsa, OK	11.7
65	22	Dayton-Springfield, OH	9.7	65	23	Dayton-Springfield, OH	11.6
37	22	Indianapolis, IN	9.7	61	23	Louisville, KY-IN	11.6
40	22	Las Vegas, NV-AZ	9.7	13	23	Minneapolis-St. Paul, MN-WI	11.6
41	26	Columbus, OH	9.6	22	23	Pittsburgh, PA	11.6
60	26	Oklahoma City, OK	9.6	37	27	Indianapolis, IN	11.5
33	28	Cincinnati, OH-KY-IN	9.5	28	27	Kansas City, MO-KS	11.5
24	28	Cleveland-Lorain-Elyria, OH	9.5	17	27	St. Louis, MO-IL	11.5
34	28	Orlando, FL	9.5	10	30	Dallas, TX	11.4
63	28	Providence-Warwick-Pawtucket, RI	9.5	63	30	Providence-Warwick-Pawtucket, RI	11.4
67	32	Birmingham, AL	9.4	50	30	Raleigh-Durham-Chapel Hill, NC	11.4
51	32	Buffalo-Niagara Falls, NY	9.4	73	30	Syracuse, NY	11.4
10	34	Dallas, TX	9.3	3	34	Chicago, IL	11.3
31	34	Fort Worth-Arlington, TX	9.3	1	34	Los Angeles-Long Beach, CA	11.3
28	34	Kansas City, MO-KS	9.3	58	34	Rochester, NY	11.3
5	34	Philadelphia, PA-NJ	9.3	31	37	Fort Worth-Arlington, TX	11.2
36	38	Fort Lauderdale, FL	9.2	8	37	Houston, TX	11.2
59	38	Grand Rapids-Muskegon-Holland, MI	9.2	49	37	Nashville, TN	11.2
15	38	San Diego, CA	9.2	6	37	Washington, DC-MD-VA-WV	11.2
70	38	Tucson, AZ	9.2	4	41	Boston-Worcester-Lawrence-Lowell-Brockton, MA-NH	11.1
71	38	Tulsa, OK	9.2	55	41	West Palm Beach-Boca Raton, FL	11.1
47	43	Greensboro-Winston-Salem-High Point, NC	9.1	53	43	Hartford, CT	11.0
26	43	Newark, NJ	9.1	54	43	Memphis, TN-AR-MS	11.0
74	43	Omaha, NE-IA	9.1	57	45	Jacksonville, FL	10.9
12	43	Phoenix-Mesa, AZ	9.1	5	45	Philadelphia, PA-NJ	10.9
49	47	Nashville, TN	9.0	15	45	San Diego, CA	10.9
64	48	Greenville-Spartanburg-Anderson, SC	8.9	18	48	Baltimore, MD	10.8
53	48	Hartford, CT	8.9	12	48	Phoenix-Mesa, AZ	10.8
69	50	Albany-Schenectady-Troy, NY	8.8	67	50	Birmingham, AL	10.7
43	50	Charlotte-Gastonia-Rock Hill, NC-SC	8.8	47	50	Greensboro-Winston-Salem-High Point, NC	10.7
6	50	Washington, DC-MD-VA-WV	8.8	62	50	Richmond-Petersburg, VA	10.7
3	53	Chicago, IL	8.6	35	50	Sacramento, CA	10.7
21	53	Oakland, CA	8.6	43	54	Charlotte-Gastonia-Rock Hill, NC-SC	10.6
72	53	Ventura, CA	8.6	64	54	Greenville-Spartanburg-Anderson, SC	10.6
25	56	Denver, CO	8.3	68	54	Honolulu, HI	10.6
30	56	New Haven-Bridgeport-Stamford-Danbury-Waterbury, CT	8.3	23	57	Miami, FL	10.5
50	56	Raleigh-Durham-Chapel Hill, NC	8.3	21	57	Oakland, CA	10.5
20	56	Tampa-St. Petersburg-Clearwater, FL	8.3	34	59	Orlando, FL	10.4
27	60	Portland-Vancouver, OR-WA	8.1	30	60	New Haven-Bridgeport-Stamford-Danbury-Waterbury, CT	10.3
46	60	Salt Lake City-Ogden, UT	8.1	32	60	San Jose, CA	10.3
48	62	Austin-San Marcos, TX	8.0	59	62	Grand Rapids-Muskegon-Holland, MI	10.2
13	63	Minneapolis-St. Paul, MN-WI	7.9	39	62	Norfolk-Virginia Beach-Newport News, VA-NC	10.2
14	64	Orange County, CA	7.8	38	62	San Antonio, TX	10.2
4	65	Boston-Worcester-Lawrence-Lowell-Brockton, MA-NH	7.7	9	65	Atlanta, GA	10.1
19	66	Seattle-Bellevue-Everett, WA	7.4	26	66	Newark, NJ	9.6
22	67	Pittsburgh, PA	7.2	44	67	Bergen-Passaic, NJ	9.1
55	67	West Palm Beach-Boca Raton, FL	7.2	56	67	Monmouth-Ocean, NJ	9.1
68	69	Honolulu, HI	7.0	52	69	Middlesex-Somerset-Hunterdon, NJ	8.8
32	70	San Jose, CA	6.9	14	69	Orange County, CA	8.8
44	71	Bergen-Passaic, NJ	6.6	46	71	Salt Lake City-Ogden, UT	8.7
52	72	Middlesex-Somerset-Hunterdon, NJ	5.9	11	72	Riverside-San Bernardino, CA	8.4
16	73	Nassau-Suffolk, NY	5.8	66	73	Fresno, CA	8.3
56	74	Monmouth-Ocean, NJ	5.6	72	74	Ventura, CA	7.9
29	75	San Francisco, CA	5.4	16	75	Nassau-Suffolk, NY	6.9
62		San Francisco County, CA	4.2				

TABLE 4—75 Largest Metropolitan Areas by 2000 Population
Selected Rankings

Percent Women Living Alone, 2000

Population Rank	Women Living Alone Rank	Metropolitan Area	[A-4. col 40] Percent Women Living Alone
22	1	Pittsburgh, PA	18.4
2	2	New York, NY	18.3
51	3	Buffalo-Niagara Falls, NY	18.1
55	4	West Palm Beach-Boca Raton, FL	18.0
20	5	Tampa-St. Petersburg-Clearwater, FL	17.7
29	6	San Francisco, CA	17.5
36	7	Fort Lauderdale, FL	17.3
24	8	Cleveland-Lorain-Elyria, OH	17.2
69	9	Albany-Schenectady-Troy, NY	17.1
63	10	Providence-Warwick-Pawtucket, RI	17.0
42	11	Milwaukee-Waukesha, WI	16.5
73	12	Syracuse, NY	16.4
65	13	Dayton-Springfield, OH	16.3
53	13	Hartford, CT	16.3
33	15	Cincinnati, OH-KY-IN	16.2
61	15	Louisville, KY-IN	16.2
56	15	Monmouth-Ocean, NJ	16.2
5	15	Philadelphia, PA-NJ	16.2
4	19	Boston-Worcester-Lawrence-Lowell-Brockton, MA-NH	16.1
67	20	Birmingham, AL	16.0
41	21	Columbus, OH	15.9
17	21	St. Louis, MO-IL	15.9
30	23	New Haven-Bridgeport-Stamford-Danbury-Waterbury, CT	15.8
58	23	Rochester, NY	15.8
70	23	Tucson, AZ	15.8
62	26	Richmond-Petersburg, VA	15.7
18	27	Baltimore, MD	15.6
47	27	Greensboro-Winston-Salem High Point, NC	15.6
28	27	Kansas City, MO-KS	15.6
37	30	Indianapolis, IN	15.5
60	31	Oklahoma City, OK	15.4
7	32	Detroit, MI	15.3
19	32	Seattle-Bellevue-Everett, WA	15.3
74	34	Omaha, NE-IA	15.2
71	34	Tulsa, OK	15.2
6	34	Washington, DC-MD-VA-WV	15.2
3	37	Chicago, IL	15.1
25	37	Denver, CO	15.1
13	39	Minneapolis-St. Paul, MN-WI	15.0
49	39	Nashville, TN	15.0
45	39	New Orleans, LA	15.0
50	42	Raleigh-Durham-Chapel Hill, NC	14.9
64	43	Greenville-Spartanburg-Anderson, SC	14.8
44	44	Bergen-Passaic, NJ	14.7
27	45	Portland-Vancouver, OR-WA	14.6
75	46	Albuquerque, NM	14.5
54	47	Memphis, TN-AR-MS	14.4
26	47	Newark, NJ	14.4
35	47	Sacramento, CA	14.4
21	50	Oakland, CA	14.2
43	51	Charlotte-Gastonia-Rock Hill, NC-SC	13.9
57	51	Jacksonville, FL	13.9
10	53	Dallas, TX	13.6
59	53	Grand Rapids-Muskegon-Holland, MI	13.6
12	55	Phoenix-Mesa, AZ	13.5
48	56	Austin-San Marcos, TX	13.4
52	56	Middlesex-Somerset-Hunterdon, NJ	13.4
1	58	Los Angeles-Long Beach, CA	13.3
9	59	Atlanta, GA	13.2
15	59	San Diego, CA	13.2
39	61	Norfolk-Virginia Beach-Newport News, VA-NC	13.1
34	61	Orlando, FL	13.1
38	61	San Antonio, TX	13.1
23	64	Miami, FL	12.8
31	65	Fort Worth-Arlington, TX	12.7
8	66	Houston, TX	12.3
14	66	Orange County, CA	12.3
66	68	Fresno, CA	11.8
40	69	Las Vegas, NV-AZ	11.7
16	70	Nassau-Suffolk, NY	11.6
11	71	Riverside-San Bernardino, CA	11.1
32	71	San Jose, CA	11.1
68	73	Honolulu, HI	11.0
72	73	Ventura, CA	11.0
46	75	Salt Lake City-Ogden, UT	10.7

Percent Foreign-Born Population, 2000

Population Rank	Foreign-born Population Rank	Metropolitan Area	[A-4. col 54] Percent Foreign-born Population
23	1	Miami, FL	50.9
1	2	Los Angeles-Long Beach, CA	36.2
32	3	San Jose, CA	34.1
2	4	New York, NY	33.7
29	5	San Francisco, CA	32.0
14	6	Orange County, CA	29.9
44	7	Bergen-Passaic, NJ	25.7
36	8	Fort Lauderdale, FL	25.3
21	9	Oakland, CA	24.0
15	10	San Diego, CA	21.5
66	11	Fresno, CA	21.0
52	12	Middlesex-Somerset-Hunterdon, NJ	20.8
72	13	Ventura, CA	20.7
8	14	Houston, TX	20.5
68	15	Honolulu, HI	19.2
26	16	Newark, NJ	19.0
11	17	Riverside-San Bernardino, CA	18.8
55	18	West Palm Beach-Boca Raton, FL	17.4
3	19	Chicago, IL	17.2
6	20	Washington, DC-MD-VA-WV	16.9
10	21	Dallas, TX	16.8
40	22	Las Vegas, NV-AZ	16.5
16	23	Nassau-Suffolk, NY	14.4
12	24	Phoenix-Mesa, AZ	14.1
35	25	Sacramento, CA	13.9
19	26	Seattle-Bellevue-Everett, WA	13.7
30	27	New Haven-Bridgeport-Stamford-Danbury-Waterbury, CT	13.1
4	28	Boston-Worcester-Lawrence-Lowell-Brockton, MA-NH	12.4
48	29	Austin-San Marcos, TX	12.2
34	30	Orlando, FL	12.0
63	31	Providence-Warwick-Pawtucket, RI	11.9
70	31	Tucson, AZ	11.9
31	33	Fort Worth-Arlington, TX	11.4
25	34	Denver, CO	11.1
27	35	Portland-Vancouver, OR-WA	10.8
9	36	Atlanta, GA	10.3
53	36	Hartford, CT	10.3
38	38	San Antonio, TX	10.2
20	39	Tampa-St. Petersburg-Clearwater, FL	9.8
50	40	Raleigh-Durham-Chapel Hill, NC	9.2
56	41	Monmouth-Ocean, NJ	8.6
46	41	Salt Lake City-Ogden, UT	8.6
75	43	Albuquerque, NM	7.9
7	44	Detroit, MI	7.5
13	45	Minneapolis-St. Paul, MN-WI	7.1
5	46	Philadelphia, PA-NJ	7.0
43	47	Charlotte-Gastonia-Rock Hill, NC-SC	6.7
18	48	Baltimore, MD	5.7
47	48	Greensboro-Winston-Salem-High Point, NC	5.7
60	48	Oklahoma City, OK	5.7
58	48	Rochester, NY	5.7
57	52	Jacksonville, FL	5.4
42	52	Milwaukee-Waukesha, WI	5.4
59	54	Grand Rapids-Muskegon-Holland, MI	5.2
24	55	Cleveland-Lorain-Elyria, OH	5.1
45	56	New Orleans, LA	4.8
74	56	Omaha, NE-IA	4.8
69	58	Albany-Schenectady-Troy, NY	4.7
49	58	Nashville, TN	4.7
41	60	Columbus, OH	4.6
28	61	Kansas City, MO-KS	4.5
39	61	Norfolk-Virginia Beach-Newport News, VA-NC	4.5
62	61	Richmond-Petersburg, VA	4.5
51	64	Buffalo-Niagara Falls, NY	4.4
73	65	Syracuse, NY	4.3
71	66	Tulsa, OK	4.1
64	67	Greenville-Spartanburg-Anderson, SC	3.6
37	68	Indianapolis, IN	3.4
54	69	Memphis, TN-AR-MS	3.3
17	70	St. Louis, MO-IL	3.1
61	71	Louisville, KY-IN	2.7
33	72	Cincinnati, OH-KY-IN	2.6
22	72	Pittsburgh, PA	2.6
67	74	Birmingham, AL	2.3
65	74	Dayton-Springfield, OH	2.3

TABLE 4—75 Largest Metropolitan Areas by 2000 Population
Selected Rankings

	Percent of Population Over 25 Years with High School Diploma or Less, 2000				Percent of Population Over 25 Years with Bachelor's Degree or More, 2000		
Population Rank	High School Diploma or Less Rank	Metropolitan Area	[B-4. col 2] Percent High School Diploma or Less	Population Rank	Bachelor's Degree or More Rank	Metropolitan Area	[B-4. col 4] Percent Bachelor's Degree or More
66	1	Fresno, CA	54.5	29	1	San Francisco, CA	43.6
23	1	Miami, FL	54.5	6	2	Washington, DC-MD-VA-WV	41.8
64	3	Greenville-Spartanburg-Anderson, SC	54.0	32	3	San Jose, CA	40.5
22	4	Pittsburgh, PA	52.6	50	4	Raleigh-Durham-Chapel Hill, NC	38.9
40	5	Las Vegas, NV-AZ	51.4	52	5	Middlesex-Somerset-Hunterdon, NJ	37.4
63	6	Providence-Warwick-Pawtucket, RI	51.1	48	6	Austin-San Marcos, TX	36.7
47	7	Greensboro-Winston-Salem-High Point, NC	50.9	19	7	Seattle-Bellevue-Everett, WA	35.9
45	8	New Orleans, LA	50.7	21	8	Oakland, CA	35.0
11	9	Riverside-San Bernardino, CA	50.3	25	9	Denver, CO	34.2
2	10	New York, NY	50.2	30	10	New Haven-Bridgeport-Stamford-Danbury-Waterbury, CT	34.0
61	11	Louisville, KY-IN	50.0	4	11	Boston-Worcester-Lawrence-Lowell-Brockton, MA-NH	33.8
24	12	Cleveland-Lorain-Elyria, OH	49.5	13	12	Minneapolis-St. Paul, MN-WI	33.3
5	13	Philadelphia, PA-NJ	49.4	44	13	Bergen-Passaic, NJ	32.5
33	14	Cincinnati, OH-KY-IN	48.9	9	14	Atlanta, GA	32.0
65	14	Dayton-Springfield, OH	48.9	26	15	Newark, NJ	31.5
1	14	Los Angeles-Long Beach, CA	48.9	16	16	Nassau-Suffolk, NY	31.3
20	17	Tampa-St. Petersburg-Clearwater, FL	48.6	14	17	Orange County, CA	30.8
73	18	Syracuse, NY	48.4	53	18	Hartford, CT	30.5
51	19	Buffalo-Niagara Falls, NY	48.1	3	19	Chicago, IL	30.1
54	20	Memphis, TN-AR-MS	48.1	10	20	Dallas, TX	30.0
37	21	Indianapolis, IN	48.0	15	21	San Diego, CA	29.5
38	22	San Antonio, TX	47.8	18	22	Baltimore, MD	29.2
67	23	Birmingham, AL	47.5	2	22	New York, NY	29.2
7	24	Detroit, MI	47.2	62	22	Richmond-Petersburg, VA	29.2
49	25	Nashville, TN	46.7	41	25	Columbus, OH	29.1
59	26	Grand Rapids-Muskegon-Holland, MI	46.6	27	26	Portland-Vancouver, OR-WA	28.8
56	26	Monmouth-Ocean, NJ	46.6	28	27	Kansas City, MO-KS	28.5
36	28	Fort Lauderdale, FL	46.4	75	28	Albuquerque, NM	28.4
8	28	Houston, TX	46.4	69	29	Albany-Schenectady-Troy, NY	28.2
26	30	Newark, NJ	46.3	74	30	Omaha, NE-IA	28.0
44	31	Bergen-Passaic, NJ	45.8	68	31	Honolulu, HI	27.9
71	32	Tulsa, OK	45.7	5	32	Philadelphia, PA-NJ	27.7
57	33	Jacksonville, FL	45.5	55	32	West Palm Beach-Boca Raton, FL	27.7
17	34	St. Louis, MO-IL	45.3	56	34	Monmouth-Ocean, NJ	27.6
18	35	Baltimore, MD	45.2	8	35	Houston, TX	27.2
43	36	Charlotte-Gastonia-Rock Hill, NC-SC	45.1	58	36	Rochester, NY	27.1
58	37	Rochester, NY	44.8	42	37	Milwaukee-Waukesha, WI	27.0
34	38	Orlando, FL	44.7	49	38	Nashville, TN	26.9
69	39	Albany-Schenectady-Troy, NY	44.6	72	38	Ventura, CA	26.9
53	39	Hartford, CT	44.6	70	40	Tucson, AZ	26.7
42	39	Milwaukee-Waukesha, WI	44.6	43	41	Charlotte-Gastonia-Rock Hill, NC-SC	26.5
41	42	Columbus, OH	44.3	46	41	Salt Lake City-Ogden, UT	26.5
60	43	Oklahoma City, OK	44.1	35	43	Sacramento, CA	25.9
31	44	Fort Worth-Arlington, TX	43.7	37	44	Indianapolis, IN	25.8
62	45	Richmond-Petersburg, VA	43.6	33	45	Cincinnati, OH-KY-IN	25.3
30	46	New Haven-Bridgeport-Stamford-Danbury-Waterbury, CT	43.3	17	45	St. Louis, MO-IL	25.3
55	46	West Palm Beach-Boca Raton, FL	43.3	31	47	Fort Worth-Arlington, TX	25.1
3	48	Chicago, IL	43.2	12	47	Phoenix-Mesa, AZ	25.1
39	49	Norfolk-Virginia Beach-Newport News, VA-NC	43.1	1	49	Los Angeles-Long Beach, CA	24.9
68	50	Honolulu, HI	43.0	34	50	Orlando, FL	24.8
16	51	Nassau-Suffolk, NY	42.6	67	51	Birmingham, AL	24.7
10	52	Dallas, TX	42.2	36	52	Fort Lauderdale, FL	24.5
75	53	Albuquerque, NM	42.0	60	53	Oklahoma City, OK	24.4
4	54	Boston-Worcester-Lawrence-Lowell-Brockton, MA-NH	41.7	63	53	Providence-Warwick-Pawtucket, RI	24.4
28	54	Kansas City, MO-KS	41.7	73	55	Syracuse, NY	24.1
12	56	Phoenix-Mesa, AZ	41.6	39	56	Norfolk-Virginia Beach-Newport News, VA-NC	23.8
9	57	Atlanta, GA	40.4	22	56	Pittsburgh, PA	23.8
52	58	Middlesex-Somerset-Hunterdon, NJ	40.3	24	58	Cleveland-Lorain-Elyria, OH	23.3
74	59	Omaha, NE-IA	40.2	51	59	Buffalo-Niagara Falls, NY	23.2
70	60	Tucson, AZ	39.9	71	59	Tulsa, OK	23.2
72	61	Ventura, CA	39.6	59	61	Grand Rapids-Muskegon-Holland, MI	22.9
14	62	Orange County, CA	38.0	47	61	Greensboro-Winston-Salem-High Point, NC	22.9
35	63	Sacramento, CA	37.5	57	61	Jacksonville, FL	22.9
15	64	San Diego, CA	37.3	7	64	Detroit, MI	22.8
46	65	Salt Lake City-Ogden, UT	37.0	54	65	Memphis, TN-AR-MS	22.7
27	66	Portland-Vancouver, OR-WA	36.6	45	66	New Orleans, LA	22.6
25	67	Denver, CO	35.6	38	67	San Antonio, TX	22.4
21	68	Oakland, CA	35.2	61	68	Louisville, KY-IN	22.2
48	69	Austin-San Marcos, TX	35.1	65	69	Dayton-Springfield, OH	22.1
50	70	Raleigh-Durham-Chapel Hill, NC	35.0	23	70	Miami, FL	21.7
13	71	Minneapolis-St. Paul, MN-WI	34.8	20	70	Tampa-St. Petersburg-Clearwater, FL	21.7
6	72	Washington, DC-MD-VA-WV	34.0	64	72	Greenville-Spartanburg-Anderson, SC	20.7
32	73	San Jose, CA	32.5	66	73	Fresno, CA	16.8
19	74	Seattle-Bellevue-Everett, WA	30.9	40	74	Las Vegas, NV-AZ	16.4
29	75	San Francisco, CA	30.8	11	75	Riverside-San Bernardino, CA	16.3

TABLE 4—75 Largest Metropolitan Areas by 2000 Population
Selected Rankings

Percent of Population 16 to 19 Years Not Enrolled in School, Not High School Graduate, Not in Armed Forces, or Employed, 2000

Population Rank	At-Risk Youth Rank	Metropolitan Area	[B-4. col 17] Percent At-Risk Youth
40	1	Las Vegas, NV-AZ	9.6
12	2	Phoenix-Mesa, AZ	8.8
8	3	Houston, TX	7.8
10	4	Dallas, TX	7.6
2	5	New York, NY	7.3
75	6	Albuquerque, NM	7.2
66	6	Fresno, CA	7.2
54	6	Memphis, TN-AR-MS	7.2
1	9	Los Angeles-Long Beach, CA	7.1
25	10	Denver, CO	7.0
45	10	New Orleans, LA	7.0
55	12	West Palm Beach-Boca Raton, FL	6.9
31	13	Fort Worth-Arlington, TX	6.8
23	13	Miami, FL	6.8
70	13	Tucson, AZ	6.8
20	16	Tampa-St. Petersburg-Clearwater, FL	6.7
9	17	Atlanta, GA	6.6
64	18	Greenville-Spartanburg-Anderson, SC	6.5
38	18	San Antonio, TX	6.5
11	20	Riverside-San Bernardino, CA	6.4
67	21	Birmingham, AL	6.3
3	22	Chicago, IL	6.2
43	23	Charlotte-Gastonia-Rock Hill, NC-SC	6.1
37	23	Indianapolis, IN	6.1
61	23	Louisville, KY-IN	6.1
10	26	Baltimore, MD	5.8
57	26	Jacksonville, FL	5.8
34	26	Orlando, FL	5.8
48	29	Austin-San Marcos, TX	5.7
30	30	Cincinnati, OH-KY-IN	5.6
47	30	Greensboro-Winston-Salem-High Point, NC	5.6
71	30	Tulsa, OK	5.6
36	33	Fort Lauderdale, FL	5.4
27	33	Portland-Vancouver, OR-WA	5.4
7	35	Detroit, MI	5.3
60	35	Oklahoma City, OK	5.3
24	37	Cleveland-Lorain-Elyria, OH	5.2
65	37	Dayton-Springfield, OH	5.2
28	39	Kansas City, MO-KS	5.1
14	40	Orange County, CA	4.9
17	40	St. Louis, MO-IL	4.9
42	42	Milwaukee-Waukesha, WI	4.8
35	42	Sacramento, CA	4.8
49	44	Nashville, TN	4.7
53	45	Hartford, CT	4.6
21	45	Oakland, CA	4.6
5	45	Philadelphia, PA-NJ	4.6
63	45	Providence-Warwick-Pawtucket, RI	4.6
50	45	Raleigh-Durham-Chapel Hill, NC	4.6
15	45	San Diego, CA	4.6
73	45	Syracuse, NY	4.6
72	45	Ventura, CA	4.6
41	53	Columbus, OH	4.5
30	53	New Haven-Bridgeport-Stamford-Danbury-Waterbury, CT	4.5
26	53	Newark, NJ	4.5
74	53	Omaha, NE-IA	4.5
32	53	San Jose, CA	4.5
59	58	Grand Rapids-Muskegon-Holland, MI	4.4
46	58	Salt Lake City-Ogden, UT	4.4
51	60	Buffalo-Niagara Falls, NY	4.3
39	60	Norfolk-Virginia Beach-Newport News, VA-NC	4.3
29	62	San Francisco, CA	4.2
62	63	Richmond-Petersburg, VA	4.1
58	63	Rochester, NY	4.1
6	65	Washington, DC-MD-VA-WV	4.0
44	66	Bergen-Passaic, NJ	3.9
69	67	Albany-Schenectady-Troy, NY	3.8
4	68	Boston-Worcester-Lawrence-Lowell-Brockton, MA-NH	3.4
19	68	Seattle-Bellevue-Everett, WA	3.4
68	70	Honolulu, HI	3.2
52	71	Middlesex-Somerset-Hunterdon, NJ	3.1
13	71	Minneapolis-St. Paul, MN-WI	3.1
22	71	Pittsburgh, PA	3.1
16	74	Nassau-Suffolk, NY	2.8
56	75	Monmouth-Ocean, NJ	2.7

Unemployment Rate, 2000

Population Rank	Unemployment Rate Rank	Metropolitan Area	[B-4. col 20] Unemployment Rate
66	1	Fresno, CA	12.0
23	2	Miami, FL	8.7
2	2	New York, NY	8.7
1	4	Los Angeles-Long Beach, CA	8.2
11	5	Riverside-San Bernardino, CA	7.8
51	6	Buffalo-Niagara Falls, NY	7.0
45	7	New Orleans, LA	6.8
40	8	Las Vegas, NV-AZ	6.5
54	9	Memphis, TN-AR-MS	6.4
3	10	Chicago, IL	6.2
8	10	Houston, TX	6.2
26	10	Newark, NJ	6.2
5	10	Philadelphia, PA-NJ	6.2
73	10	Syracuse, NY	6.2
35	15	Sacramento, CA	6.1
7	16	Detroit, MI	5.9
75	17	Albuquerque, NM	5.8
22	17	Pittsburgh, PA	5.8
53	19	Hartford, CT	5.7
68	19	Honolulu, HI	5.7
58	19	Rochester, NY	5.7
69	22	Albany-Schenectady-Troy, NY	5.6
27	22	Portland-Vancouver, OR-WA	5.6
63	22	Providence-Warwick-Pawtucket, RI	5.6
15	22	San Diego, CA	5.6
67	26	Birmingham, AL	5.5
38	26	San Antonio, TX	5.5
17	26	St. Louis, MO-IL	5.5
24	29	Cleveland-Lorain-Elyria, OH	5.3
36	29	Fort Lauderdale, FL	5.3
30	29	New Haven-Bridgeport-Stamford-Danbury-Waterbury, CT	5.3
70	29	Tucson, AZ	5.3
43	33	Charlotte-Gastonia-Rock Hill, NC-SC	5.2
42	33	Milwaukee-Waukesha, WI	5.2
21	33	Oakland, CA	5.2
44	36	Bergen-Passaic, NJ	5.1
65	36	Dayton-Springfield, OH	5.1
72	36	Ventura, CA	5.1
9	39	Atlanta, GA	5.0
64	39	Greenville-Spartanburg-Anderson, SC	5.0
39	39	Norfolk-Virginia Beach-Newport News, VA-NC	5.0
14	39	Orange County, CA	5.0
55	39	West Palm Beach-Boca Raton, FL	5.0
18	44	Baltimore, MD	4.9
10	44	Dallas, TX	4.9
12	44	Phoenix-Mesa, AZ	4.9
20	44	Tampa-St. Petersburg-Clearwater, FL	4.9
56	48	Monmouth-Ocean, NJ	4.8
60	48	Oklahoma City, OK	4.8
47	50	Greensboro-Winston-Salem-High Point, NC	4.7
46	50	Salt Lake City-Ogden, UT	4.7
57	52	Jacksonville, FL	4.6
61	52	Louisville, KY-IN	4.6
34	52	Orlando, FL	4.6
19	52	Seattle-Bellevue-Everett, WA	4.6
71	52	Tulsa, OK	4.6
31	57	Fort Worth-Arlington, TX	4.5
49	57	Nashville, TN	4.5
59	59	Grand Rapids-Muskegon-Holland, MI	4.4
37	59	Indianapolis, IN	4.4
52	59	Middlesex-Somerset-Hunterdon, NJ	4.4
4	62	Boston-Worcester-Lawrence-Lowell-Brockton, MA-NH	4.3
33	62	Cincinnati, OH-KY-IN	4.3
28	62	Kansas City, MO-KS	4.3
6	65	Washington, DC-MD-VA-WV	4.2
50	66	Raleigh-Durham-Chapel Hill, NC	4.1
62	66	Richmond-Petersburg, VA	4.1
48	68	Austin-San Marcos, TX	4.0
41	68	Columbus, OH	4.0
25	70	Denver, CO	3.9
32	70	San Jose, CA	3.9
16	72	Nassau-Suffolk, NY	3.8
29	72	San Francisco, CA	3.8
74	74	Omaha, NE-IA	3.7
13	75	Minneapolis-St. Paul, MN-WI	3.5

TABLE 4—75 Largest Metropolitan Areas by 2000 Population
Selected Rankings

Percent Veterans Over 18 Years, 2000

Population Rank	Veterans Rank	Metropolitan Area	[B-4. col 44] Percent Veterans
39	1	Norfolk-Virginia Beach-Newport News, VA-NC	18.9
57	2	Jacksonville, FL	18.0
20	3	Tampa-St. Petersburg-Clearwater, FL	17.1
40	4	Las Vegas, NV-AZ	16.3
70	5	Tucson, AZ	16.0
38	6	San Antonio, TX	15.7
75	7	Albuquerque, NM	15.3
65	8	Dayton-Springfield, OH	15.2
55	9	West Palm Beach-Boca Raton, FL	15.1
22	10	Pittsburgh, PA	14.7
60	11	Oklahoma City, OK	14.6
74	11	Omaha, NE-IA	14.6
71	13	Tulsa, OK	14.4
34	14	Orlando, FL	14.3
35	15	Sacramento, CA	14.2
15	16	San Diego, CA	14.0
17	16	St. Louis, MO-IL	14.0
28	18	Kansas City, MO-KS	13.9
56	18	Monmouth-Ocean, NJ	13.9
12	18	Phoenix-Mesa, AZ	13.9
61	21	Louisville, KY-IN	13.8
62	22	Richmond-Petersburg, VA	13.7
18	23	Baltimore, MD	13.6
51	23	Buffalo-Niagara Falls, NY	13.6
27	23	Portland-Vancouver, OR-WA	13.6
69	26	Albany-Schenectady-Troy, NY	13.2
24	26	Cleveland-Lorain-Elyria, OH	13.2
68	26	Honolulu, HI	13.2
19	29	Seattle-Bellevue-Everett, WA	13.1
25	30	Denver, CO	13.0
64	30	Greenville-Spartanburg-Anderson, SC	13.0
37	30	Indianapolis, IN	13.0
73	30	Syracuse, NY	13.0
33	34	Cincinnati, OH-KY-IN	12.8
6	34	Washington, DC-MD-VA-WV	12.8
67	36	Birmingham, AL	12.7
31	36	Fort Worth-Arlington, TX	12.7
11	36	Riverside-San Bernardino, CA	12.7
41	39	Columbus, OH	12.6
63	40	Providence-Warwick-Pawtucket, RI	12.5
54	41	Memphis, TN-AR-MS	12.4
47	42	Greensboro-Winston-Salem-High Point, NC	12.3
43	43	Charlotte-Gastonia-Rock Hill, NC-SC	12.2
53	43	Hartford, CT	12.2
5	43	Philadelphia, PA-NJ	12.2
58	46	Rochester, NY	12.1
49	47	Nashville, TN	12.0
45	47	New Orleans, LA	12.0
42	49	Milwaukee-Waukesha, WI	11.9
13	49	Minneapolis-St. Paul, MN-WI	11.9
9	51	Atlanta, GA	11.8
72	51	Ventura, CA	11.8
7	53	Detroit, MI	11.7
59	54	Grand Rapids-Muskegon-Holland, MI	11.6
36	55	Fort Lauderdale, FL	11.5
4	56	Boston-Worcester-Lawrence-Lowell-Brockton, MA-NH	11.4
46	57	Salt Lake City-Ogden, UT	11.1
48	58	Austin-San Marcos, TX	11.0
16	58	Nassau-Suffolk, NY	11.0
30	58	New Haven-Bridgeport-Stamford-Danbury-Waterbury, CT	11.0
50	61	Raleigh-Durham-Chapel Hill, NC	10.7
66	62	Fresno, CA	10.4
10	63	Dallas, TX	10.2
21	64	Oakland, CA	10.1
52	65	Middlesex-Somerset-Hunterdon, NJ	9.8
8	66	Houston, TX	9.5
26	66	Newark, NJ	9.5
3	68	Chicago, IL	9.4
14	69	Orange County, CA	9.3
44	70	Bergen-Passaic, NJ	9.2
29	71	San Francisco, CA	8.4
32	71	San Jose, CA	8.4
1	73	Los Angeles-Long Beach, CA	7.4
2	74	New York, NY	6.2
23	75	Miami, FL	5.4

Median Household Income, 2000

Population Rank	Median Household Income Rank	Metropolitan Area	[B-4. col 57] Median Household Income (Dollars)
32	1	San Jose, CA	74 335
16	2	Nassau-Suffolk, NY	68 351
52	3	Middlesex-Somerset-Hunterdon, NJ	66 731
29	4	San Francisco, CA	63 297
6	5	Washington, DC-MD-VA-WV	62 216
72	6	Ventura, CA	59 666
44	7	Bergen-Passaic, NJ	59 405
21	8	Oakland, CA	59 365
14	9	Orange County, CA	58 820
26	10	Newark, NJ	56 957
30	11	New Haven-Bridgeport-Stamford-Danbury-Waterbury, CT	56 054
56	12	Monmouth-Ocean, NJ	54 865
13	13	Minneapolis-St. Paul, MN-WI	54 304
19	14	Seattle-Bellevue-Everett, WA	52 804
53	15	Hartford, CT	52 603
4	16	Boston-Worcester-Lawrence-Lowell-Brockton, MA-NH	52 306
9	17	Atlanta, GA	51 948
68	18	Honolulu, HI	51 914
3	19	Chicago, IL	51 680
25	20	Denver, CO	51 191
18	21	Baltimore, MD	49 938
7	22	Detroit, MI	49 175
48	23	Austin-San Marcos, TX	48 950
50	24	Raleigh-Durham-Chapel Hill, NC	48 845
46	25	Salt Lake City-Ogden, UT	48 594
10	26	Dallas, TX	48 364
5	27	Philadelphia, PA-NJ	47 536
27	28	Portland-Vancouver, OR-WA	47 077
15	29	San Diego, CA	47 067
62	30	Richmond-Petersburg, VA	46 800
35	31	Sacramento, CA	46 602
28	32	Kansas City, MO-KS	46 193
43	33	Charlotte-Gastonia-Rock Hill, NC-SC	46 119
59	34	Grand Rapids-Muskegon-Holland, MI	46 116
31	35	Fort Worth-Arlington, TX	45 962
42	36	Milwaukee-Waukesha, WI	45 901
37	37	Indianapolis, IN	45 548
55	38	West Palm Beach-Boca Raton, FL	45 062
74	39	Omaha, NE-IA	44 981
41	40	Columbus, OH	44 782
12	41	Phoenix-Mesa, AZ	44 752
8	42	Houston, TX	44 655
17	43	St. Louis, MO-IL	44 437
33	44	Cincinnati, OH-KY-IN	44 248
49	45	Nashville, TN	44 223
58	46	Rochester, NY	43 955
69	47	Albany-Schenectady-Troy, NY	43 250
40	48	Las Vegas, NV-AZ	42 468
39	49	Norfolk-Virginia Beach-Newport News, VA-NC	42 448
57	50	Jacksonville, FL	42 439
11	51	Riverside-San Bernardino, CA	42 404
1	52	Los Angeles-Long Beach, CA	42 189
24	53	Cleveland-Lorain-Elyria, OH	42 089
34	54	Orlando, FL	41 871
36	55	Fort Lauderdale, FL	41 691
65	56	Dayton-Springfield, OH	41 550
63	57	Providence-Warwick-Pawtucket, RI	41 462
2	58	New York, NY	41 053
47	59	Greensboro-Winston-Salem-High Point, NC	40 913
61	60	Louisville, KY-IN	40 821
54	61	Memphis, TN-AR-MS	40 201
73	62	Syracuse, NY	39 750
67	63	Birmingham, AL	39 278
38	64	San Antonio, TX	39 140
75	65	Albuquerque, NM	39 088
51	66	Buffalo-Niagara Falls, NY	38 488
64	67	Greenville-Spartanburg-Anderson, SC	38 458
71	68	Tulsa, OK	38 261
22	69	Pittsburgh, PA	37 467
20	70	Tampa-St. Petersburg-Clearwater, FL	37 406
60	71	Oklahoma City, OK	36 797
70	72	Tucson, AZ	36 758
23	73	Miami, FL	35 966
45	74	New Orleans, LA	35 317
66	75	Fresno, CA	34 960

TABLE 4—75 Largest Metropolitan Areas by 2000 Population
Selected Rankings

Percent of all Households with Income Over $100,000, 2000				Percent of all Households with Income Below Poverty, 2000			
Population Rank	With Income over $100,000 Rank	Metropolitan Area	[B-4. col 71] Percent with Income over $100,000	Population Rank	With Income Below Poverty Rank	Metropolitan Area	[B-4. col 73] Percent with Income Below Poverty
32	1	San Jose, CA	34.6	23	1	Miami, FL	18.1
29	2	San Francisco, CA	29.0	2	1	New York, NY	18.1
16	3	Nassau-Suffolk, NY	28.8	66	3	Fresno, CA	18.0
52	4	Middlesex-Somerset-Hunterdon, NJ	27.8	45	4	New Orleans, LA	17.4
6	5	Washington, DC-MD-VA-WV	25.1	1	5	Los Angeles-Long Beach, CA	15.1
44	6	Bergen-Passaic, NJ	24.9	54	6	Memphis, TN-AR-MS	14.5
21	7	Oakland, CA	24.0	38	7	San Antonio, TX	13.7
26	8	Newark, NJ	23.8	67	8	Birmingham, AL	13.3
30	9	New Haven-Bridgeport-Stamford-Danbury-Waterbury, CT	23.5	70	8	Tucson, AZ	13.3
14	9	Orange County, CA	23.5	60	10	Oklahoma City, OK	13.1
72	11	Ventura, CA	22.8	63	11	Providence-Warwick-Pawtucket, RI	12.8
56	12	Monmouth-Ocean, NJ	20.9	11	11	Riverside-San Bernardino, CA	12.8
4	13	Boston-Worcester-Lawrence-Lowell-Brockton, MA-NH	18.9	75	13	Albuquerque, NM	12.6
3	14	Chicago, IL	18.2	64	14	Greensboro-Spartanburg-Anderson, SC	12.3
68	14	Honolulu, HI	18.2	8	14	Houston, TX	12.3
53	16	Hartford, CT	17.9	51	16	Buffalo-Niagara Falls, NY	12.1
9	17	Atlanta, GA	17.5	73	16	Syracuse, NY	12.1
19	18	Seattle-Bellevue-Everett, WA	17.4	22	18	Pittsburgh, PA	11.3
13	19	Minneapolis-St. Paul, MN-WI	16.9	71	18	Tulsa, OK	11.3
10	20	Dallas, TX	16.8	61	20	Louisville, KY-IN	11.0
25	21	Denver, CO	16.5	5	20	Philadelphia, PA-NJ	11.0
55	22	West Palm Beach-Boca Raton, FL	16.2	36	22	Fort Lauderdale, FL	10.8
7	23	Detroit, MI	16.1	24	23	Cleveland-Lorain-Elyria, OH	10.6
2	24	New York, NY	16.0	47	24	Greensboro-Winston-Salem-High Point, NC	10.5
18	25	Baltimore, MD	15.9	57	25	Jacksonville, FL	10.4
5	25	Philadelphia, PA-NJ	15.9	39	25	Norfolk-Virginia Beach-Newport News, VA-NC	10.4
50	25	Raleigh-Durham-Chapel Hill, NC	15.9	20	25	Tampa-St. Petersburg-Clearwater, FL	10.4
48	28	Austin-San Marcos, TX	15.8	48	28	Austin-San Marcos, TX	10.3
15	29	San Diego, CA	15.7	65	28	Dayton-Springfield, OH	10.3
8	30	Houston, TX	15.4	15	28	San Diego, CA	10.3
1	31	Los Angeles-Long Beach, CA	15.1	35	31	Sacramento, CA	10.2
35	32	Sacramento, CA	14.1	33	32	Cincinnati, OH-KY-IN	10.1
31	33	Fort Worth-Arlington, TX	13.3	41	32	Columbus, OH	10.1
62	33	Richmond-Petersburg, VA	13.3	49	32	Nashville, TN	10.1
43	35	Charlotte-Gastonia-Rock Hill, NC-SC	13.1	7	35	Detroit, MI	10.0
27	35	Portland-Vancouver, OR-WA	13.1	50	35	Raleigh-Durham-Chapel Hill, NC	10.0
12	37	Phoenix-Mesa, AZ	12.9	58	35	Rochester, NY	10.0
36	38	Fort Lauderdale, FL	12.8	12	38	Phoenix-Mesa, AZ	9.9
33	39	Cincinnati, OH-KY-IN	12.6	40	39	Las Vegas, NV-AZ	9.8
37	39	Indianapolis, IN	12.6	34	39	Orlando, Fl	9.8
46	39	Salt Lake City-Ogden, UT	12.6	18	41	Baltimore, MD	9.7
28	42	Kansas City, MO-KS	12.5	3	41	Chicago, IL	9.7
42	43	Milwaukee-Waukesha, WI	12.4	10	41	Dallas, TX	9.7
41	44	Columbus, OH	12.3	68	41	Honolulu, HI	9.7
17	45	St. Louis, MO-IL	12.2	17	41	St. Louis, MO-IL	9.7
49	46	Nashville, TN	12.0	42	46	Milwaukee-Waukesha, WI	9.6
11	47	Riverside-San Bernardino, CA	11.5	26	46	Newark, NJ	9.6
58	48	Rochester, NY	11.4	69	48	Albany-Schenectady-Troy, NY	9.5
69	49	Albany-Schenectady-Troy, NY	11.3	31	48	Fort Worth-Arlington, TX	9.5
24	50	Cleveland-Lorain-Elyria, OH	11.2	62	50	Richmond-Petersburg, VA	9.2
74	50	Omaha, NE-IA	11.2	4	51	Boston-Worcester-Lawrence-Lowell-Brockton, MA-NH	9.1
63	52	Providence-Warwick-Pawtucket, RI	11.1	43	52	Charlotte-Gastonia-Rock Hill, NC-SC	9.0
67	53	Birmingham, AL	11.0	55	52	West Palm Beach-Boca Raton, FL	9.0
57	53	Jacksonville, FL	11.0	9	54	Atlanta, GA	8.7
34	55	Orlando, FL	10.9	27	55	Portland-Vancouver, OR-WA	8.6
54	56	Memphis, TN-AR-MS	10.8	21	56	Oakland, CA	8.5
23	56	Miami, FL	10.8	37	57	Indianapolis, IN	8.4
59	58	Grand Rapids-Muskegon-Holland, MI	10.7	28	57	Kansas City, MO-KS	8.4
40	59	Las Vegas, NV-AZ	10.6	30	59	New Haven-Bridgeport-Stamford-Danbury-Waterbury, CT	8.3
61	60	Louisville, KY-IN	10.5	53	60	Hartford, CT	8.2
65	61	Dayton-Springfield, OH	10.0	74	60	Omaha, NE-IA	8.2
38	62	San Antonio, TX	9.9	59	62	Grand Rapids-Muskegon-Holland, MI	8.1
47	63	Greensboro-Winston-Salem-High Point, NC	9.8	14	63	Orange County, CA	7.7
75	64	Albuquerque, NM	9.7	29	64	San Francisco, CA	7.6
39	64	Norfolk-Virginia Beach-Newport News, VA-NC	9.7	46	65	Salt Lake City-Ogden, UT	7.5
73	66	Syracuse, NY	9.5	19	65	Seattle-Bellevue-Everett, WA	7.5
20	67	Tampa-St. Petersburg-Clearwater, FL	9.4	25	67	Denver, CO	7.4
45	68	New Orleans, LA	9.3	44	68	Bergen-Passaic, NJ	7.2
22	69	Pittsburgh, PA	9.2	72	68	Ventura, CA	7.2
51	70	Buffalo-Niagara Falls, NY	9.1	6	70	Washington, DC-MD-VA-WV	6.8
70	71	Tucson, AZ	9.0	56	71	Monmouth-Ocean, NJ	6.4
71	72	Tulsa, OK	8.9	13	72	Minneapolis-St. Paul, MN-WI	6.3
64	73	Greenville-Spartanburg-Anderson, SC	8.8	32	73	San Jose, CA	6.1
66	74	Fresno, CA	8.5	16	74	Nassau-Suffolk, NY	5.5
60	75	Oklahoma City, OK	8.1	52	75	Middlesex-Somerset-Hunterdon, NJ	5.1

Percent of Population that Resides in the Same House in 1995 and 2000				Percent Owner-Occupied Housing Units, 2000			
Population Rank	Same Residence Rank	Metropolitan Area	[C-4. col 2] Percent Same Residence	Population Rank	Owner-Occupied Rank	Metropolitan Area	[C-4. col 8] Percent Owner-Occupied
16	1	Nassau-Suffolk, NY	67.2	16	1	Nassau-Suffolk, NY	80.0
22	2	Pittsburgh, PA	66.4	56	2	Monmouth-Ocean, NJ	78.7
51	3	Buffalo-Niagara Falls, NY	63.5	59	3	Grand Rapids-Muskegon-Holland, MI	74.9
5	4	Philadelphia, PA-NJ	62.1	55	4	West Palm Beach-Boca Raton, FL	74.7
44	5	Bergen-Passaic, NJ	61.6	7	5	Detroit, MI	72.4
2	6	New York, NY	61.2	13	5	Minneapolis-St. Paul, MN-WI	72.4
56	7	Monmouth-Ocean, NJ	60.8	64	7	Greenville-Spartanburg-Anderson, SC	71.5
24	8	Cleveland-Lorain-Elyria, OH	60.3	17	8	St. Louis, MO-IL	71.4
26	9	Newark, NJ	59.9	22	9	Pittsburgh, PA	71.3
69	10	Albany-Schenectady-Troy, NY	59.6	46	9	Salt Lake City-Ogden, UT	71.3
45	10	New Orleans, LA	59.6	52	11	Middlesex-Somerset-Hunterdon, NJ	71.2
73	12	Syracuse, NY	59.3	20	12	Tampa-St. Petersburg-Clearwater, FL	70.8
58	13	Rochester, NY	58.8	67	13	Birmingham, AL	70.7
7	14	Detroit, MI	58.5	5	14	Philadelphia, PA-NJ	69.9
53	15	Hartford, CT	58.3	36	15	Fort Lauderdale, FL	69.5
63	15	Providence-Warwick-Pawtucket, RI	58.3	47	16	Greensboro-Winston-Salem-High Point, NC	68.7
4	17	Boston-Worcester-Lawrence-Lowell-Brockton, MA-NH	58.0	61	17	Louisville, KY-IN	68.6
30	18	New Haven-Bridgeport-Stamford-Danbury-Waterbury, CT	57.9	43	18	Charlotte-Gastonia-Rock Hill, NC-SC	68.4
52	19	Middlesex-Somerset-Hunterdon, NJ	57.4	24	19	Cleveland-Lorain-Elyria, OH	68.3
18	20	Baltimore, MD	57.0	58	20	Rochester, NY	68.2
17	21	St. Louis, MO-IL	56.7	12	21	Phoenix-Mesa, AZ	68.0
68	22	Honolulu, HI	56.3	28	22	Kansas City, MO-KS	67.9
3	23	Chicago, IL	56.2	37	23	Indianapolis, IN	67.8
67	24	Birmingham, AL	55.8	62	24	Richmond-Petersburg, VA	67.7
29	25	San Francisco, CA	55.2	75	25	Albuquerque, NM	67.6
65	26	Dayton-Springfield, OH	54.8	73	25	Syracuse, NY	67.6
42	26	Milwaukee-Waukesha, WI	54.8	72	25	Ventura, CA	67.6
33	28	Cincinnati, OH-KY-IN	54.7	57	28	Jacksonville, FL	67.3
64	28	Greenville-Spartanburg-Anderson, SC	54.7	65	29	Dayton-Springfield, OH	67.2
61	28	Louisville, KY-IN	54.7	18	30	Baltimore, MD	66.9
59	31	Grand Rapids-Muskegon-Holland, MI	54.5	71	30	Tulsa, OK	66.9
13	32	Minneapolis-St. Paul, MN-WI	54.3	11	32	Riverside-San Bernardino, CA	66.6
47	33	Greensboro-Winston-Salem-High Point, NC	54.2	25	33	Denver, CO	66.5
62	34	Richmond-Petersburg, VA	53.0	9	34	Atlanta, GA	66.4
74	35	Omaha, NE-IA	52.3	53	35	Hartford, CT	66.3
1	36	Los Angeles-Long Beach, CA	52.0	34	35	Orlando, FL	66.3
21	37	Oakland, CA	51.7	51	37	Buffalo-Niagara Falls, NY	66.2
72	37	Ventura, CA	51.7	33	37	Cincinnati, OH-KY-IN	66.2
28	39	Kansas City, MO-KS	51.4	30	37	New Haven-Bridgeport-Stamford-Danbury-Waterbury, CT	66.2
54	39	Memphis, TN-AR-MS	51.4	49	40	Nashville, TN	66.0
66	41	Fresno, CA	51.3	74	40	Omaha, NE-IA	66.0
38	41	San Antonio, TX	51.3	54	42	Memphis, TN-AR-MS	65.4
32	43	San Jose, CA	51.2	60	43	Oklahoma City, OK	64.7
75	44	Albuquerque, NM	50.6	69	44	Albany-Schenectady-Troy, NY	64.6
46	44	Salt Lake City-Ogden, UT	50.6	3	44	Chicago, IL	64.6
37	46	Indianapolis, IN	50.3	50	46	Raleigh-Durham-Chapel Hill, NC	64.5
23	47	Miami, FL	50.2	70	47	Tucson, AZ	64.3
6	47	Washington, DC-MD-VA-WV	50.2	6	48	Washington, DC-MD-VA-WV	64.0
43	49	Charlotte-Gastonia-Rock Hill, NC-SC	49.9	31	49	Fort Worth-Arlington, TX	63.6
71	50	Tulsa, OK	49.7	44	50	Bergen-Passaic, NJ	63.4
55	51	West Palm Beach-Boca Raton, FL	49.5	38	50	San Antonio, TX	63.4
20	52	Tampa-St. Petersburg-Clearwater, FL	49.1	39	52	Norfolk-Virginia Beach-Newport News, VA-NC	63.0
57	53	Jacksonville, FL	49.0	27	53	Portland-Vancouver, OR-WA	62.9
41	54	Columbus, OH	48.8	41	54	Columbus, OH	62.3
60	55	Oklahoma City, OK	48.6	35	55	Sacramento, CA	62.1
8	56	Houston, TX	48.3	19	56	Seattle-Bellevue-Everett, WA	62.0
49	57	Nashville, TN	48.1	45	57	New Orleans, LA	61.8
39	58	Norfolk-Virginia Beach-Newport News, VA-NC	48.0	4	58	Boston-Worcester-Lawrence-Lowell-Brockton, MA-NH	61.6
14	58	Orange County, CA	48.0	14	59	Orange County, CA	61.4
35	58	Sacramento, CA	48.0	40	60	Las Vegas, NV-AZ	61.1
11	61	Riverside-San Bernardino, CA	47.5	42	60	Milwaukee-Waukesha, WI	61.1
19	62	Seattle-Bellevue-Everett, WA	47.4	26	62	Newark, NJ	60.8
36	63	Fort Lauderdale, FL	47.1	21	63	Oakland, CA	60.5
70	64	Tucson, AZ	46.2	63	64	Providence-Warwick-Pawtucket, RI	59.9
31	65	Fort Worth-Arlington, TX	45.7	32	65	San Jose, CA	59.8
27	66	Portland-Vancouver, OR-WA	45.5	8	66	Houston, TX	59.6
15	67	San Diego, CA	45.1	10	67	Dallas, TX	58.9
9	68	Atlanta, GA	44.6	48	68	Austin-San Marcos, TX	58.3
25	68	Denver, CO	44.6	23	69	Miami, FL	57.8
50	68	Raleigh-Durham-Chapel Hill, NC	44.6	66	70	Fresno, CA	57.7
10	71	Dallas, TX	44.1	15	71	San Diego, CA	55.4
34	72	Orlando, FL	44.0	68	72	Honolulu, HI	54.5
12	73	Phoenix-Mesa, AZ	41.9	29	73	San Francisco, CA	49.0
48	74	Austin-San Marcos, TX	39.4	1	74	Los Angeles-Long Beach, CA	47.9
40	75	Las Vegas, NV-AZ	35.8	2	75	New York, NY	34.7

TABLE 4—75 Largest Metropolitan Areas by 2000 Population
Selected Rankings

Median Housing Value (Owner Estimated), 2000				Median Gross Rent, 2000			
Population Rank	Median Housing Value Rank	Metropolitan Area	[C-4. col 22] Median Housing Value (Dollars)	Population Rank	Median Gross Rent Rank	Metropolitan Area	[C-4. col 25] Median Gross Rent (Dollars)
29	1	San Francisco, CA	449 400	32	1	San Jose, CA	1 185
32	2	San Jose, CA	422 600	29	2	San Francisco, CA	1 023
21	3	Oakland, CA	277 400	16	3	Nassau-Suffolk, NY	954
68	4	Honolulu, HI	274 600	14	4	Orange County, CA	923
14	5	Orange County, CA	253 000	72	5	Ventura, CA	892
72	6	Ventura, CA	238 800	21	6	Oakland, CA	868
2	7	New York, NY	230 400	52	7	Middlesex-Somerset-Hunterdon, NJ	858
44	8	Bergen-Passaic, NJ	222 700	44	8	Bergen-Passaic, NJ	822
16	9	Nassau-Suffolk, NY	212 600	6	9	Washington, DC-MD-VA-WV	811
15	10	San Diego, CA	212 000	68	10	Honolulu, HI	802
19	11	Seattle-Bellevue-Everett, WA	211 700	56	11	Monmouth-Ocean, NJ	780
1	12	Los Angeles-Long Beach, CA	201 400	15	12	San Diego, CA	761
26	13	Newark, NJ	196 200	19	13	Seattle-Bellevue-Everett, WA	758
30	14	New Haven-Bridgeport-Stamford-Danbury-Waterbury, CT	189 000	36	14	Fort Lauderdale, FL	757
4	15	Boston-Worcester-Lawrence-Lowell-Brockton, MA-NH	186 000	9	15	Atlanta, GA	746
52	16	Middlesex-Somerset-Hunterdon, NJ	180 600	55	16	West Palm Beach-Boca Raton, FL	739
6	17	Washington, DC-MD-VA-WV	172 900	26	17	Newark, NJ	729
25	18	Denver, CO	170 900	30	18	New Haven-Bridgeport-Stamford-Danbury-Waterbury, CT	726
27	19	Portland-Vancouver, OR-WA	167 100	48	19	Austin-San Marcos, TX	721
3	20	Chicago, IL	161 700	2	20	New York, NY	715
56	21	Monmouth-Ocean, NJ	156 200	4	21	Boston-Worcester-Lawrence-Lowell-Brockton, MA-NH	707
35	22	Sacramento, CA	155 600	1	22	Los Angeles-Long Beach, CA	704
46	23	Salt Lake City-Ogden, UT	148 300	40	23	Las Vegas, NV-AZ	703
53	24	Hartford, CT	146 300	25	24	Denver, CO	700
13	25	Minneapolis-St. Paul, MN-WI	139 200	34	25	Orlando, FL	698
50	26	Raleigh-Durham-Chapel Hill, NC	138 500	50	26	Raleigh-Durham-Chapel Hill, NC	686
9	27	Atlanta, GA	132 600	27	27	Portland-Vancouver, OR-WA	672
18	28	Baltimore, MD	132 400	35	27	Sacramento, CA	672
42	29	Milwaukee-Waukesha, WI	130 800	3	29	Chicago, IL	669
11	30	Riverside-San Bernardino, CA	129 700	10	30	Dallas, TX	667
7	31	Detroit, MI	127 800	12	31	Phoenix-Mesa, AZ	661
63	32	Providence-Warwick-Pawtucket, RI	127 600	53	32	Hartford, CT	653
40	33	Las Vegas, NV-AZ	125 700	11	32	Riverside-San Bernardino, CA	653
48	34	Austin-San Marcos, TX	121 300	5	34	Philadelphia, PA-NJ	648
49	35	Nashville, TN	120 800	23	35	Miami, FL	647
12	36	Phoenix-Mesa, AZ	119 600	13	36	Minneapolis-St. Paul, MN-WI	641
5	37	Philadelphia, PA-NJ	119 400	43	37	Charlotte-Gastonia-Rock Hill, NC-SC	627
41	38	Columbus, OH	118 700	18	38	Baltimore, MD	626
75	39	Albuquerque, NM	118 500	46	39	Salt Lake City-Ogden, UT	625
24	40	Cleveland-Lorain-Elyria, OH	116 600	57	40	Jacksonville, FL	616
43	41	Charlotte-Gastonia-Rock Hill, NC-SC	116 200	39	41	Norfolk-Virginia Beach-Newport News, VA-NC	615
62	42	Richmond-Petersburg, VA	115 000	62	42	Richmond-Petersburg, VA	613
55	42	West Palm Beach-Boca Raton, FL	115 000	49	43	Nashville, TN	610
23	44	Miami, FL	113 200	20	44	Tampa-St. Petersburg-Clearwater, FL	608
33	45	Cincinnati, OH-KY-IN	111 600	31	45	Fort Worth-Arlington, TX	607
59	46	Grand Rapids-Muskegon-Holland, MI	111 000	58	46	Rochester, NY	594
37	47	Indianapolis, IN	109 200	8	47	Houston, TX	592
39	48	Norfolk-Virginia Beach-Newport News, VA-NC	107 100	69	48	Albany-Schenectady-Troy, NY	586
66	49	Fresno, CA	105 000	41	48	Columbus, OH	586
28	50	Kansas City, MO-KS	104 400	7	50	Detroit, MI	583
36	51	Fort Lauderdale, FL	102 800	42	51	Milwaukee-Waukesha, WI	580
70	52	Tucson, AZ	102 600	28	52	Kansas City, MO-KS	575
69	53	Albany-Schenectady-Troy, NY	102 200	37	53	Indianapolis, IN	570
10	54	Dallas, TX	102 100	75	54	Albuquerque, NM	563
74	55	Omaha, NE-IA	100 100	54	54	Memphis, TN-AR-MS	563
61	56	Louisville, KY-IN	99 800	38	56	San Antonio, TX	556
47	57	Greensboro-Winston-Salem-High Point, NC	99 600	74	57	Omaha, NE-IA	548
34	58	Orlando, FL	99 500	24	58	Cleveland-Lorain-Elyria, OH	545
65	59	Dayton-Springfield, OH	98 300	63	58	Providence-Warwick-Pawtucket, RI	545
17	60	St. Louis, MO-IL	96 200	70	60	Tucson, AZ	544
45	61	New Orleans, LA	95 800	59	61	Grand Rapids-Muskegon-Holland, MI	543
67	62	Birmingham, AL	93 500	47	62	Greensboro-Winston-Salem-High Point, NC	538
58	63	Rochester, NY	93 300	66	63	Fresno, CA	536
57	64	Jacksonville, FL	92 500	73	64	Syracuse, NY	535
54	65	Memphis, TN-AR-MS	90 900	65	65	Dayton-Springfield, OH	526
64	66	Greenville-Spartanburg-Anderson, SC	88 700	17	66	St. Louis, MO-IL	525
31	67	Fort Worth-Arlington, TX	87 500	45	67	New Orleans, LA	515
51	68	Buffalo-Niagara Falls, NY	86 900	51	68	Buffalo-Niagara Falls, NY	510
8	69	Houston, TX	86 200	71	69	Tulsa, OK	508
20	70	Tampa-St. Petersburg-Clearwater, FL	84 800	67	70	Birmingham, AL	507
22	71	Pittsburgh, PA	84 300	33	71	Cincinnati, OH-KY-IN	505
71	72	Tulsa, OK	81 900	64	72	Greenville-Spartanburg-Anderson, SC	504
73	73	Syracuse, NY	80 600	61	73	Louisville, KY-IN	496
60	74	Oklahoma City, OK	76 900	60	74	Oklahoma City, OK	487
38	75	San Antonio, TX	74 100	22	75	Pittsburgh, PA	482

TABLE 5—All Metropolitan Areas
Selected Rankings

Population, 2000			Percent Under 18 Years, 2000			
Population Rank	Metropolitan Area	[A-4. col 1] Population	Population Rank	Under 18 Years Rank	Metropolitan Area	[A-4. col 2 and 3] Percent Under 18 Years
1	Los Angeles-Long Beach, CA	9 519 338	205	1	Laredo, TX	36.2
2	New York, NY	9 314 235	94	2	McAllen-Edinburg-Mission, TX	35.2
3	Chicago, IL	8 272 768	195	3	Merced, CA	34.4
4	Boston-Worcester-Lawrence-Lowell-Brockton, MA-NH	6 057 826	135	4	Provo-Orem, UT	34.0
5	Philadelphia, PA-NJ	5 100 931	147	5	Brownsville-Harlingen-San Benito, TX	33.7
6	Washington, DC-MD-VA-WV	4 923 153	136	5	Visalia-Tulare-Porterville, CA	33.7
7	Detroit, MI	4 441 551	80	7	Bakersfield, CA	31.9
8	Houston, TX	4 177 646	79	7	El Paso, TX	31.9
9	Atlanta, GA	4 112 198	189	9	Yakima, WA	31.7
10	Dallas, TX	3 519 176	66	10	Fresno, CA	31.6
11	Riverside-San Bernardino, CA	3 254 821	11	11	Riverside-San Bernardino, CA	31.3
12	Phoenix-Mesa, AZ	3 251 876	46	11	Salt Lake City-Ogden, UT	31.3
13	Minneapolis-St. Paul, MN-WI	2 968 806	115	13	Modesto, CA	31.1
14	Orange County, CA	2 846 289	206	14	Richland-Kennewick-Pasco, WA	30.9
15	San Diego, CA	2 813 833	95	14	Stockton-Lodi, CA	30.9
16	Nassau-Suffolk, NY	2 753 913	182	16	Odessa-Midland, TX	30.3
17	St. Louis, MO-IL	2 603 607	217	17	Las Cruces, NM	29.7
18	Baltimore, MD	2 552 994	255	17	Yuba City, CA	29.7
19	Seattle-Bellevue-Everett, WA	2 414 616	311	19	Victoria, TX	29.2
20	Tampa-St. Petersburg-Clearwater, FL	2 395 997	168	20	Anchorage, AK	29.1
21	Oakland, CA	2 392 557	8	20	Houston, TX	29.1
22	Pittsburgh, PA	2 358 695	132	22	Corpus Christi, TX	28.8
23	Miami, FL	2 253 362	211	22	Elkhart-Goshen, IN	28.8
24	Cleveland-Lorain-Elyria, OH	2 250 871	228	22	Yuma, AZ	28.8
25	Denver, CO	2 109 282	276	25	Flagstaff, AZ-UT	28.7
26	Newark, NJ	2 032 989	128	25	Newburgh, NY-PA	28.7
27	Portland-Vancouver, OR-WA	1 918 009	181	27	Brazoria, TX	28.5
28	Kansas City, MO-KS	1 776 062	129	28	Lafayette, LA	28.4
29	San Francisco, CA	1 731 183	125	28	Salinas, CA	28.4
30	New Haven-Bridgeport-Stamford-Danbury-Waterbury, CT	1 706 575	72	28	Ventura, CA	28.4
31	Fort Worth-Arlington, TX	1 702 625	119	31	Boise City, ID	28.3
32	San Jose, CA	1 682 585	199	31	Clarksville-Hopkinsville, TN-KY	28.3
33	Cincinnati, OH-KY-IN	1 646 395	59	31	Grand Rapids-Muskegon-Holland, MI	28.3
34	Orlando, FL	1 644 561	204	31	Houma, LA	28.3
35	Sacramento, CA	1 628 197	54	31	Memphis, TN-AR-MS	28.3
36	Fort Lauderdale, FL	1 623 018	38	31	San Antonio, TX	28.3
37	Indianapolis, IN	1 607 486	277	37	Albany, GA	28.2
38	San Antonio, TX	1 592 383	213	37	Greeley, CO	28.2
39	Norfolk-Virginia Beach-Newport News, VA-NC	1 569 541	155	37	Killeen-Temple, TX	28.2
40	Las Vegas, NV-AZ	1 563 282	294	40	Sumter, SC	28.1
41	Columbus, OH	1 540 157	31	41	Fort Worth-Arlington, TX	28.0
42	Milwaukee-Waukesha, WI	1 500 741	316	41	Pocatello, ID	28.0
43	Charlotte-Gastonia-Rock Hill, NC-SC	1 499 293	97	41	Wichita, KS	28.0
44	Bergen-Passaic, NJ	1 373 167	10	44	Dallas, TX	27.9
45	New Orleans, LA	1 337 726	157	44	Fayetteville, NC	27.9
46	Salt Lake City-Ogden, UT	1 333 914	1	44	Los Angeles-Long Beach, CA	27.9
47	Greensboro-Winston-Salem-High Point, NC	1 251 509	245	47	Monroe, LA	27.8
48	Austin-San Marcos, TX	1 249 763	275	47	Sioux City, IA-NE	27.8
49	Nashville, TN	1 231 311	102	49	Fort Wayne, IN	27.7
50	Raleigh-Durham-Chapel Hill, NC	1 187 941	101	50	Colorado Springs, CO	27.5
51	Buffalo-Niagara Falls, NY	1 170 111	117	50	Jackson, MS	27.5
52	Middlesex-Somerset-Hunterdon, NJ	1 169 641	284	50	Lawton, OK	27.5
53	Hartford, CT	1 148 618	118	53	Flint, MI	27.4
54	Memphis, TN-AR-MS	1 135 614	209	53	Lake Charles, LA	27.4
55	West Palm Beach-Boca Raton, FL	1 131 184	270	55	Alexandria, LA	27.3
56	Monmouth-Ocean, NJ	1 126 217	100	55	Vallejo-Fairfield-Napa, CA	27.3
57	Jacksonville, FL	1 100 491	88	57	Baton Rouge, LA	27.2
58	Rochester, NY	1 098 201	268	57	Dover, DE	27.2
59	Grand Rapids-Muskegon-Holland, MI	1 088 514	74	57	Omaha, NE-IA	27.2
60	Oklahoma City, OK	1 083 346	35	57	Sacramento, CA	27.2
61	Louisville, KY-IN	1 025 598	152	61	Macon, GA	27.1
62	Richmond-Petersburg, VA	996 512	76	61	Tacoma, WA	27.1
63	Providence-Warwick-Pawtucket, RI	962 886	192	63	Amarillo, TX	27.0
64	Greenville-Spartanburg-Anderson, SC	962 441	107	63	Augusta-Aiken, GA-SC	27.0
65	Dayton-Springfield, OH	950 558	296	63	Kankakee, IL	27.0
66	Fresno, CA	922 516	240	63	Kenosha, WI	27.0
67	Birmingham, AL	921 106	14	63	Orange County, CA	27.0
68	Honolulu, HI	876 156	208	63	Racine, WI	27.0
69	Albany-Schenectady-Troy, NY	875 583	274	63	Rochester, MN	27.0
70	Tucson, AZ	843 746	143	63	Salem, OR	27.0
71	Tulsa, OK	803 235	127	63	Shreveport-Bossier City, LA	27.0
72	Ventura, CA	753 197	3	72	Chicago, IL	26.9
73	Syracuse, NY	732 117	134	72	Rockford, IL	26.9
74	Omaha, NE-IA	716 998	198	74	Fort Smith, AR-OK	26.8
75	Albuquerque, NM	712 738	196	74	Longview-Marshall, TX	26.8
			12	74	Phoenix-Mesa, AZ	26.8

TABLE 5—All Metropolitan Areas
Selected Rankings

	Percent 18 to 24 Years, 2000				Percent 25 to 44 Years, 2000		
Popu-lation Rank	18 to 24 Years Rank	Metropolitan Area	[A-4. col 4] Percent 18 to 24 Years	Popu-lation Rank	25 to 44 Years Rank	Metropolitan Area	[A-4. col 5] Percent 25 to 44 Years
235	1	Bryan-College Station, TX	32.2	29	1	San Francisco, CA	36.6
278	2	Bloomington, IN	27.8	86	2	Jersey City, NJ	35.8
257	3	State College, PA	27.0	32	2	San Jose, CA	35.8
302	4	Lawrence, KS	26.4	9	4	Atlanta, GA	35.7
239	5	Jacksonville, NC	23.7	48	5	Austin-San Marcos, TX	35.5
290	6	Iowa City, IA	23.3	50	6	Raleigh-Durham-Chapel Hill, NC	35.1
191	7	Gainesville, FL	23.2	10	7	Dallas, TX	34.9
233	8	Athens, GA	23.1	25	8	Denver, CO	34.4
214	9	Champaign-Urbana, IL	23.0	19	9	Seattle-Bellevue-Everett, WA	34.3
283	10	Auburn-Opalika, AL	22.7	168	10	Anchorage, AK	34.2
210	11	Lafayette, IN	22.3	6	11	Washington, DC-MD-VA-WV	34.1
135	12	Provo-Orem, UT	20.9	161	12	Boulder-Longmont, CO	34.0
315	13	Corvallis, OR	20.1	43	13	Charlotte-Gastonia-Rock Hill, NC-SC	33.8
258	14	Columbia, MO	19.7	14	14	Orange County, CA	33.4
162	15	Tallahassee, FL	19.4	8	15	Houston, TX	33.3
238	16	Bloomington-Normal, IL	18.6	13	15	Minneapolis-St. Paul, MN-WI	33.3
222	17	Yolo, CA	18.3	199	17	Clarksville-Hopkinsville, TN-KY	33.1
260	18	Greenville, NC	17.4	31	17	Fort Worth-Arlington, TX	33.1
281	19	Muncie, IN	16.9	155	17	Killeen-Temple, TX	33.1
303	20	Grand Forks, ND-MN	16.5	52	20	Middlesex-Somerset-Hunterdon, NJ	33.0
225	20	Tuscaloosa, AL	16.5	49	20	Nashville, TN	33.0
218	22	Fargo-Moorhead, ND-MN	16.3	21	22	Oakland, CA	32.9
180	23	Lubbock, TX	16.2	181	23	Brazoria, TX	32.8
289	24	Hattiesburg, MS	15.8	157	23	Fayetteville, NC	32.8
266	25	Waterloo-Cedar Falls, IA	15.7	1	23	Los Angeles-Long Beach, CA	32.8
176	26	Lincoln, NE	15.5	41	26	Columbus, OH	32.7
304	27	Missoula, MT	15.3	101	27	Colorado Springs, CO	32.6
223	27	St. Cloud, MN	15.3	120	27	Madison, WI	32.6
316	29	Pocatello, ID	14.7	2	27	New York, NY	32.6
229	30	Charlottesville, VA	14.6	4	30	Boston-Worcester-Lawrence-Lowell-Brockton, MA-NH	32.3
114	30	Lansing-East Lansing, MI	14.6	37	30	Indianapolis, IN	32.3
155	32	Killeen-Temple, TX	14.5	27	30	Portland-Vancouver, OR-WA	32.3
194	33	Waco, TX	14.4	274	30	Rochester, MN	32.3
224	34	Bellingham, WA	14.3	15	30	San Diego, CA	32.3
276	34	Flagstaff, AZ-UT	14.3	34	35	Orlando, FL	32.2
120	34	Madison, WI	14.3	3	36	Chicago, IL	32.1
174	37	Fort Collins-Loveland, CO	14.2	219	36	Sioux Falls, SD	32.1
267	38	La Crosse, WI-MN	14.1	112	38	Des Moines, IA	32.0
312	39	Jonesboro, AR	14.0	187	38	Green Bay, WI	32.0
284	39	Lawton, OK	14.0	106	38	Lexington, KY	32.0
178	39	San Luis Obispo-Atascadero-Paso Robles, CA	14.0	39	41	Norfolk-Virginia Beach-Newport News, VA-NC	31.9
269	42	Abilene, TX	13.8	202	42	Burlington, VT	31.8
157	42	Fayetteville, NC	13.8	36	42	Fort Lauderdale, FL	31.8
200	44	Chico-Paradise, CA	13.7	144	42	Huntsville, AL	31.8
199	44	Clarksville-Hopkinsville, TN-KY	13.7	99	45	Columbia, SC	31.7
242	44	Eau Claire, WI	13.7	62	45	Richmond-Petersburg, VA	31.7
106	44	Lexington, KY	13.7	125	45	Salinas, CA	31.7
126	48	Santa Barbara-Santa Maria-Lompoc, CA	13.5	93	48	Ann Arbor, MI	31.6
161	49	Boulder-Longmont, CO	13.3	28	48	Kansas City, MO-KS	31.6
253	49	Wichita Falls, TX	13.3	26	48	Newark, NJ	31.6
48	51	Austin-San Marcos, TX	13.2	76	48	Tacoma, WA	31.6
213	52	Greeley, CO	13.1	91	48	Wilmington-Newark, DE-MD	31.6
217	52	Las Cruces, NM	13.1	57	53	Jacksonville, FL	31.5
295	54	San Angelo, TX	13.0	40	53	Las Vegas, NV-AZ	31.5
93	55	Ann Arbor, MI	12.8	246	53	Vineland-Millville-Bridgeton, NJ	31.5
88	55	Baton Rouge, LA	12.8	139	56	Appleton-Oshkosh-Neenah, WI	31.4
46	55	Salt Lake City-Ogden, UT	12.8	119	56	Boise City, ID	31.4
241	58	Terre Haute, IN	12.5	220	56	Fort Walton Beach, FL	31.4
150	59	Springfield, MO	12.3	262	56	Hagerstown, MD	31.4
245	60	Monroe, LA	12.1	12	56	Phoenix-Mesa, AZ	31.4
151	61	Eugene-Springfield, OR	12.0	240	61	Kenosha, WI	31.3
156	61	Fayetteville-Springdale-Rogers, AR	12.0	169	61	New London-Norwich, CT	31.3
113	61	Kalamazoo-Battle Creek, MI	12.0	166	61	Portland, ME	31.3
165	64	Columbus, GA-AL	11.8	18	64	Baltimore, MD	31.2
149	64	Hamilton-Middletown, OH	11.8	47	64	Greensboro-Winston-Salem-High Point, NC	31.2
171	64	Santa Cruz-Watsonville, CA	11.8	54	64	Memphis, TN-AR-MS	31.2
167	67	South Bend, IN	11.7	23	64	Miami, FL	31.2
87	67	Springfield, MA	11.7	74	64	Omaha, NE-IA	31.2
202	69	Burlington, VT	11.6	146	64	Reno, NV	31.2
99	69	Columbia, SC	11.6	44	70	Bergen-Passaic, NJ	31.1
50	69	Raleigh-Durham-Chapel Hill, NC	11.6	7	70	Detroit, MI	31.1
293	72	Jackson, TN	11.5	284	70	Lawton, OK	31.1
205	73	Laredo, TX	11.4	171	70	Santa Cruz-Watsonville, CA	31.1
15	73	San Diego, CA	11.4	96	74	Charleston-North Charleston, SC	31.0
277	75	Albany, GA	11.3	33	75	Cincinnati, OH-KY-IN	30.9
248	75	Bangor, ME	11.3	174	75	Fort Collins-Loveland, CO	30.9
94	75	McAllen-Edinburg-Mission, TX	11.3	72	75	Ventura, CA	30.9
60	75	Oklahoma City, OK	11.3				

TABLE 5—All Metropolitan Areas
Selected Rankings

Percent 45 to 64 Years, 2000				Percent 65 Years and Over, 2000			
Population Rank	45 to 64 Years Rank	Metropolitan Area	[A-4. col 6] Percent 45 to 64 Years	Population Rank	65 Years and Over Rank	Metropolitan Area	[A-4. col 7] Percent 65 Years and Over
244	1	Santa Fe, NM	27.7	251	1	Punta Gorda, FL	34.7
251	2	Punta Gorda, FL	26.2	90	2	Sarasota-Bradenton, FL	28.5
190	3	Barnstable-Yarmouth, MA	26.1	116	3	Fort Myers-Cape Coral, FL	25.4
261	4	Steubenville-Weirton, OH-WV	26.0	153	4	Fort Pierce-Port St. Lucie, FL	24.9
173	5	Charleston, WV	25.7	170	5	Ocala, FL	24.5
105	5	Johnson City-Kingsport-Bristol, TN-VA	25.7	175	6	Naples, FL	24.4
184	7	Wilmington, NC	25.6	55	7	West Palm Beach-Boca Raton, FL	23.2
212	8	Medford-Ashland, OR	25.4	190	8	Barnstable-Yarmouth, MA	23.1
237	8	Parkersburg-Marietta, WV-OH	25.4	103	9	Daytona Beach, FL	22.8
226	10	Redding, CA	25.3	108	10	Melbourne-Titusville-Palm Bay,FL	19.9
292	11	Danville, VA	25.1	20	11	Tampa-St. Petersburg-Clearwater, FL	19.2
183	11	Roanoke, VA	25.1	185	12	Johnstown, PA	19.1
234	11	Wheeling, WV-OH	25.1	84	13	Scranton-Wilkes-Barre-Hazleton, PA	18.9
203	14	Myrtle Beach, SC	25.0	261	14	Steubenville-Weirton, OH-WV	18.5
259	15	Pittsfield, MA	24.9	104	15	Lakeland-Winter Haven, FL	18.3
111	15	Santa Rosa, CA	24.9	279	16	Sharon, PA	18.1
188	17	Asheville, NC	24.8	259	17	Pittsfield, MA	18.0
197	17	Olympia, WA	24.8	234	18	Wheeling, WV-OH	17.9
116	19	Fort Myers-Cape Coral, FL	24.7	22	19	Pittsburgh, PA	17.7
154	19	Huntington-Ashland, WV-KY-OH	24.7	265	20	Altoona, PA	17.3
103	21	Daytona Beach, FL	24.6	300	21	Cumberland, MD-WV	17.2
301	21	Kokomo, IN	24.6	56	22	Monmouth-Ocean, NJ	16.9
175	23	Naples, FL	24.5	292	23	Danville, VA	16.6
90	23	Sarasota-Bradenton, FL	24.5	158	23	Utica-Rome, NY	16.6
151	25	Eugene-Springfield, OR	24.4	228	23	Yuma, AZ	16.6
273	25	Glens Falls, NY	24.4	89	26	Youngstown-Warren, OH	16.5
300	27	Cumberland, MD-WV	24.3	81	27	Allentown-Bethlehem-Easton, PA	16.0
193	27	Lynchburg, VA	24.3	36	27	Fort Lauderdale, FL	16.0
108	27	Melbourne-Titusville-Palm Bay,FL	24.3	298	27	Gadsden, AL	16.0
110	30	Chattanooga, TN-GA	24.2	254	27	Jamestown, NY	16.0
179	30	Duluth-Superior, MN-WI	24.2	212	27	Medford-Ashland, OR	16.0
250	30	Florence, AL	24.2	280	27	Williamsport, PA	16.0
185	30	Johnstown, PA	24.2	51	33	Buffalo-Niagara Falls, NY	15.9
78	30	Knoxville, TN	24.2	318	33	Enid, OK	15.9
215	30	Mansfield, OH	24.2	172	35	Binghamton, NY	15.8
89	30	Youngstown-Warren, OH	24.2	179	35	Duluth-Superior, MN-WI	15.8
288	37	Anniston, AL	24.1	183	35	Roanoke, VA	15.8
123	37	Canton-Massillon, OH	24.1	200	38	Chico-Paradise, CA	15.7
298	37	Gadsden, AL	24.1	307	39	Elmira, NY	15.6
145	37	Hickory-Morganton-Lenoir, NC	24.1	140	40	Atlantic-Cape May, NJ	15.5
265	41	Altoona, PA	24.0	173	40	Charleston, WV	15.5
131	41	York, PA	24.0	188	42	Asheville, NC	15.4
248	43	Bangor, ME	23.9	285	43	Decatur, IL	15.3
83	43	Harrisburg-Lebanon-Carlisle, PA	23.9	105	43	Johnson City-Kingsport-Bristol, TN-VA	15.3
22	43	Pittsburgh, PA	23.9	237	43	Parkersburg-Marietta, WV-OH	15.3
285	46	Decatur, IL	23.8	252	43	Pueblo, CO	15.3
282	46	Grand Junction, CO	23.8	250	47	Florence, AL	15.2
170	46	Ocala, FL	23.8	133	47	Reading, PA	15.2
84	46	Scranton-Wilkes-Barre-Hazleton, PA	23.8	226	47	Redding, CA	15.2
186	50	Bremerton, WA	23.7	123	50	Canton-Massillon, OH	15.1
247	50	Decatur, AL	23.7	282	50	Grand Junction, CO	15.1
153	50	Fort Pierce-Port St. Lucie, FL	23.7	291	50	Sherman-Denison, TX	15.1
243	50	Panama City, FL	23.7	154	53	Huntington-Ashland, WV-KY-OH	15.0
146	50	Reno, NV	23.7	203	53	Myrtle Beach, SC	15.0
227	55	Benton Harbor, MI	23.6	299	55	St. Joseph, MO	14.9
317	55	Casper, WY	23.6	308	56	Dubuque, IA	14.8
16	55	Nassau-Suffolk, NY	23.6	83	57	Harrisburg-Lebanon-Carlisle, PA	14.7
166	55	Portland, ME	23.6	273	58	Glens Falls, NY	14.6
124	55	Saginaw-Bay City-Midland, MI	23.6	63	58	Providence-Warwick-Pawtucket, RI	14.6
29	55	San Francisco, CA	23.6	241	58	Terre Haute, IN	14.6
201	55	Springfield, IL	23.6	227	61	Benton Harbor, MI	14.5
221	55	Topeka, KS	23.6	24	61	Cleveland-Lorain-Elyria, OH	14.5
138	63	Davenport-Moline-Rock Island, IA-IL	23.5	193	61	Lynchburg, VA	14.5
272	63	Florence, SC	23.5	142	61	Peoria-Pekin, IL	14.5
171	63	Santa Cruz-Watsonville, CA	23.5	178	61	San Luis Obispo-Atascadero-Paso Robles, CA	14.5
280	63	Williamsport, PA	23.5	297	66	Lewiston-Auburn, ME	14.4
249	67	Rocky Mount, NC	23.4	215	66	Mansfield, OH	14.4
279	67	Sharon, PA	23.4	69	68	Albany-Schenectady-Troy, NY	14.3
140	69	Atlantic-Cape May, NJ	23.3	163	68	Erie, PA	14.3
65	69	Dayton-Springfield, OH	23.3	262	70	Hagerstown, MD	14.2
164	69	Dutchess County, NY	23.3	232	70	Lima, OH	14.2
53	69	Hartford, CT	23.3	70	70	Tucson, AZ	14.2
69	73	Albany-Schenectady-Troy, NY	23.2	288	73	Anniston, AL	14.1
81	73	Allentown-Bethlehem-Easton, PA	23.2	44	73	Bergen-Passaic, NJ	14.1
44	73	Bergen-Passaic, NJ	23.2	314	73	Great Falls, MT	14.1
177	73	Galveston-Texas City, TX	23.2	184	73	Wilmington, NC	14.1
61	73	Louisville, KY-IN	23.2				
142	73	Peoria-Pekin, IL	23.2				

TABLE 5—All Metropolitan Areas
Selected Rankings

Percent Non-Hispanic White, 2000				Percent Black or African American, 2000			
Population Rank	Non-Hispanic White Rank	Metropolitan Area	[A-4. col 11] Percent Non-Hispanic White	Population Rank	Black or African American Rank	Metropolitan Area	[A-4. col 14] Percent Black or African American
265	1	Altoona, PA	97.3	277	1	Albany, GA	51.0
308	2	Dubuque, IA	96.7	310	2	Pine Bluff, AR	49.4
237	2	Parkersburg-Marietta, WV-OH	96.7	294	3	Sumter, SC	46.8
248	4	Bangor, ME	96.3	117	4	Jackson, MS	45.6
297	4	Lewiston-Auburn, ME	96.3	54	5	Memphis, TN-AR-MS	43.2
84	6	Scranton-Wilkes-Barre-Hazleton, PA	96.2	249	5	Rocky Mount, NC	43.2
185	7	Johnstown, PA	95.9	165	7	Columbus, GA-AL	40.0
242	8	Eau Claire, WI	95.7	272	8	Florence, SC	39.3
105	8	Johnson City-Kingsport-Bristol, TN-VA	95.7	148	9	Montgomery, AL	39.0
154	10	Huntington-Ashland, WV-KY-OH	95.6	152	10	Macon, GA	37.4
223	11	St. Cloud, MN	95.5	45	10	New Orleans, LA	37.4
273	12	Glens Falls, NY	95.4	127	12	Shreveport-Bossier City, LA	37.3
166	13	Portland, ME	95.3	157	13	Fayetteville, NC	34.9
305	14	Bismarck, ND	95.1	160	13	Savannah, GA	34.9
234	15	Wheeling, WV-OH	95.0	107	15	Augusta-Aiken, GA-SC	34.2
202	16	Burlington, VT	94.8	260	16	Greenville, NC	33.7
179	17	Duluth-Superior, MN-WI	94.5	245	16	Monroe, LA	33.7
267	17	La Crosse, WI-MN	94.5	162	18	Tallahassee, FL	33.5
259	19	Pittsfield, MA	94.1	286	19	Goldsboro, NC	33.2
261	20	Steubenville-Weirton, OH-WV	94.0	292	20	Danville, VA	32.7
139	21	Appleton-Oshkosh-Neenah, WI	93.8	99	21	Columbia, SC	32.0
271	21	Wausau, WI	93.8	88	22	Baton Rouge, LA	31.6
218	23	Fargo-Moorhead, ND-MN	93.7	39	23	Norfolk-Virginia Beach-Newport News, VA-NC	30.8
280	24	Williamsport, PA	93.6	270	24	Alexandria, LA	30.7
306	25	Owensboro, KY	93.5	96	25	Charleston-North Charleston, SC	30.5
100	26	Barnstable-Yarmouth, MA	93.4	67	26	Birmingham, AL	30.0
150	26	Springfield, MO	93.4	62	26	Richmond-Petersburg, VA	30.0
207	28	Cedar Rapids, IA	93.2	293	28	Jackson, TN	29.2
300	28	Cumberland, MD-WV	93.2	225	29	Tuscaloosa, AL	29.1
304	30	Missoula, MT	92.9	9	30	Atlanta, GA	28.8
219	31	Sioux Falls, SD	92.8	129	31	Lafayette, LA	28.2
279	32	Sharon, PA	92.7	98	32	Mobile, AL	27.4
299	33	St. Joseph, MO	92.2	18	33	Baltimore, MD	27.2
241	33	Terre Haute, IN	92.2	289	34	Hattiesburg, MS	26.3
303	35	Grand Forks, ND-MN	92.0	6	35	Washington, DC-MD-VA-WV	25.9
254	35	Jamestown, NY	92.0	130	36	Beaumont-Port Arthur, TX	24.8
172	37	Binghamton, NY	91.7	2	37	New York, NY	24.4
317	37	Casper, WY	91.7	209	38	Lake Charles, LA	23.7
231	39	Joplin, MO	91.6	256	39	Dothan, AL	23.0
131	39	York, PA	91.6	263	39	Texarkana, TX-Texarkana, AR	23.0
173	41	Charleston, WV	91.5	7	41	Detroit, MI	22.8
159	42	Evansville-Henderson, IN-KY	91.3	50	42	Raleigh-Durham-Chapel Hill, NC	22.6
287	43	Sheboygan, WI	91.1	283	43	Auburn-Opalika, AL	22.4
264	44	Billings, MT	91.0	26	44	Newark, NJ	22.1
257	45	State College, PA	90.8	92	45	Little Rock-North Little Rock, AR	21.9
78	46	Knoxville, TN	90.6	57	46	Jacksonville, FL	21.6
123	47	Canton-Massillon, OH	90.4	144	47	Huntsville, AL	20.8
301	47	Kokomo, IN	90.4	233	48	Athens, GA	20.7
251	47	Punta Gorda, FL	90.4	43	49	Charlotte-Gastonia-Rock Hill, NC-SC	20.5
158	47	Utica-Rome, NY	90.4	199	49	Clarksville-Hopkinsville, TN-KY	20.5
149	51	Hamilton-Middletown, OH	90.3	36	51	Fort Lauderdale, FL	20.3
215	51	Mansfield, OH	90.3	155	51	Killeen-Temple, TX	20.3
281	53	Muncie, IN	90.2	268	53	Dover, DE	20.2
278	54	Bloomington, IN	90.0	246	53	Vineland-Millville-Bridgeton, NJ	20.2
307	55	Elmira, NY	89.9	118	55	Flint, MI	20.1
163	56	Erie, PA	89.8	47	55	Greensboro-Winston-Salem-High Point, NC	20.1
187	57	Green Bay, WI	89.7	23	55	Miami, FL	20.1
121	57	Spokane, WA	89.7	5	58	Philadelphia, PA-NJ	20.0
316	59	Pocatello, ID	89.6	82	59	Gary, IN	19.6
314	60	Great Falls, MT	89.5	196	59	Longview-Marshall, TX	19.6
109	61	Lancaster, PA	89.4	141	59	Trenton, NJ	19.6
262	62	Hagerstown, MD	89.3	284	62	Lawton, OK	19.3
236	62	Janesville-Beloit, WI	89.3	137	63	Biloxi-Gulfport-Pascagoula, MS	19.2
135	62	Provo-Orem, UT	89.3	216	64	Tyler, TX	19.1
274	65	Rochester, MN	89.2	3	65	Chicago, IL	18.8
22	66	Pittsburgh, PA	89.1	191	65	Gainesville, FL	18.8
290	67	Iowa City, IA	89.0	24	67	Cleveland-Lorain-Elyria, OH	18.3
176	68	Lincoln, NE	88.7	288	68	Anniston, AL	18.2
151	69	Eugene-Springfield, OR	88.6	239	68	Jacksonville, NC	18.2
212	69	Medford-Ashland, OR	88.6	17	68	St. Louis, MO-IL	18.2
188	71	Asheville, NC	88.4	193	71	Lynchburg, VA	17.7
312	71	Jonesboro, AR	88.4	91	72	Wilmington-Newark, DE-MD	17.6
69	73	Albany-Schenectady-Troy, NY	88.1	64	73	Greenville-Spartanburg-Anderson, SC	17.5
238	73	Bloomington-Normal, IL	88.1	8	74	Houston, TX	17.4
232	73	Lima, OH	88.1	122	75	Pensacola, FL	16.4

TABLE 5—All Metropolitan Areas
Selected Rankings

Percent American Indian and Alaska Native, 2000

Population Rank	American Indian and Alaska Native Rank	Metropolitan Area	[A-4. col 17] Percent American Indian and Alaska Native
276	1	Flagstaff, AZ-UT	26.9
309	2	Rapid City, SD	7.6
168	3	Anchorage, AK	7.2
71	4	Tulsa, OK	6.7
75	5	Albuquerque, NM	5.6
198	6	Fort Smith, AR-OK	5.2
284	7	Lawton, OK	4.9
189	8	Yakima, WA	4.2
60	9	Oklahoma City, OK	4.0
314	10	Great Falls, MT	3.8
204	11	Houma, LA	3.6
70	12	Tucson, AZ	3.3
264	13	Billings, MT	3.1
316	14	Pocatello, ID	3.0
224	15	Bellingham, WA	2.8
305	15	Bismarck, ND	2.8
244	17	Santa Fe, NM	2.7
226	18	Redding, CA	2.4
318	19	Enid, OK	2.3
187	19	Green Bay, WI	2.3
302	19	Lawrence, KS	2.3
304	19	Missoula, MT	2.3
12	23	Phoenix-Mesa, AZ	2.1
303	24	Grand Forks, ND-MN	2.0
255	24	Yuba City, CA	2.0
200	26	Chico-Paradise, CA	1.9
179	26	Duluth-Superior, MN-WI	1.9
247	28	Decatur, AL	1.8
146	28	Reno, NV	1.8
219	28	Sioux Falls, SD	1.8
66	31	Fresno, CA	1.7
275	31	Sioux City, IA-NE	1.7
228	31	Yuma, AZ	1.7
157	34	Fayetteville, NC	1.6
156	34	Fayetteville-Springdale-Rogers, AR	1.6
231	34	Joplin, MO	1.6
197	37	Olympia, WA	1.5
252	37	Pueblo, CO	1.5
80	39	Bakersfield, CA	1.4
186	39	Bremerton, WA	1.4
217	39	Las Cruces, NM	1.4
143	39	Salem, OR	1.4
121	39	Spokane, WA	1.4
76	39	Tacoma, WA	1.4
317	45	Casper, WY	1.3
218	45	Fargo-Moorhead, ND-MN	1.3
291	45	Sherman-Denison, TX	1.3
136	45	Visalia-Tulare-Porterville, CA	1.3
115	49	Modesto, CA	1.2
221	49	Topeka, KS	1.2
313	51	Cheyenne, WY	1.1
151	51	Eugene-Springfield, OR	1.1
212	51	Medford-Ashland, OR	1.1
11	51	Riverside-San Bernardino, CA	1.1
126	51	Santa Barbara-Santa Maria-Lompoc, CA	1.1
111	51	Santa Rosa, CA	1.1
97	51	Wichita, KS	1.1
282	58	Grand Junction, CO	1.0
40	58	Las Vegas, NV-AZ	1.0
195	58	Merced, CA	1.0
35	58	Sacramento, CA	1.0
125	58	Salinas, CA	1.0
171	58	Santa Cruz-Watsonville, CA	1.0
19	58	Seattle-Bellevue-Everett, WA	1.0
95	58	Stockton-Lodi, CA	1.0
222	58	Yolo, CA	1.0
139	67	Appleton-Oshkosh-Neenah, WI	0.9
248	67	Bangor, ME	0.9
101	67	Colorado Springs, CO	0.9
25	67	Denver, CO	0.9
268	67	Dover, DE	0.9
213	67	Greeley, CO	0.9
169	67	New London-Norwich, CT	0.9
122	67	Pensacola, FL	0.9
27	67	Portland-Vancouver, OR-WA	0.9
246	67	Vineland-Millville-Bridgeton, NJ	0.9

Percent Asian, Hawaiian, and Pacific Islander, 2000

Population Rank	Asian, Hawaiian, and Pacific Islander Rank	Metropolitan Area	[A-4. col 20] Percent Asian, Hawaiian, and Pacific Islander
68	1	Honolulu, HI	55.0
32	2	San Jose, CA	25.9
29	3	San Francisco, CA	23.4
21	4	Oakland, CA	17.1
14	5	Orange County, CA	13.9
1	6	Los Angeles-Long Beach, CA	12.2
95	7	Stockton-Lodi, CA	11.9
52	8	Middlesex-Somerset-Hunterdon, NJ	11.3
100	9	Vallejo-Fairfield-Napa, CA	11.1
255	10	Yuba City, CA	9.9
19	11	Seattle-Bellevue-Everett, WA	9.8
222	11	Yolo, CA	9.8
86	13	Jersey City, NJ	9.5
35	14	Sacramento, CA	9.3
15	14	San Diego, CA	9.3
2	16	New York, NY	9.2
44	17	Bergen-Passaic, NJ	8.2
66	18	Fresno, CA	7.2
195	19	Merced, CA	7.1
6	20	Washington, DC-MD-VA-WV	6.6
214	21	Champaign-Urbana, IL	6.5
125	21	Salinas, CA	6.5
168	23	Anchorage, AK	6.3
76	24	Tacoma, WA	5.7
72	25	Ventura, CA	5.4
186	26	Bremerton, WA	5.2
8	26	Houston, TX	5.2
197	28	Olympia, WA	5.1
40	29	Las Vegas, NV-AZ	5.0
141	29	Trenton, NJ	5.0
27	31	Portland-Vancouver, OR-WA	4.8
3	32	Chicago, IL	4.7
146	32	Reno, NV	4.7
115	34	Modesto, CA	4.5
315	35	Corvallis, OR	4.4
11	35	Riverside-San Bernardino, CA	4.4
274	37	Rochester, MN	4.3
235	38	Bryan-College Station, TX	4.2
13	39	Minneapolis-St. Paul, MN-WI	4.1
26	39	Newark, NJ	4.1
126	39	Santa Barbara-Santa Maria-Lompoc, CA	4.1
271	39	Wausau, WI	4.1
10	43	Dallas, TX	4.0
290	43	Iowa City, IA	4.0
257	43	State College, PA	4.0
140	46	Atlantic-Cape May, NJ	3.9
4	46	Boston-Worcester-Lawrence-Lowell-Brockton, MA-NH	3.9
93	48	Ann Arbor, MI	3.8
210	48	Lafayette, IN	3.8
48	50	Austin-San Marcos, TX	3.6
191	50	Gainesville, FL	3.6
16	52	Nassau-Suffolk, NY	3.5
80	53	Bakersfield, CA	3.4
200	53	Chico-Paradise, CA	3.4
120	53	Madison, WI	3.4
5	53	Philadelphia, PA-NJ	3.4
171	53	Santa Cruz-Watsonville, CA	3.4
136	53	Visalia-Tulare-Porterville, CA	3.4
9	59	Atlanta, GA	3.3
278	59	Bloomington, IN	3.3
302	59	Lawrence, KS	3.3
161	62	Boulder-Longmont, CO	3.2
31	62	Fort Worth-Arlington, TX	3.2
111	62	Santa Rosa, CA	3.2
287	62	Sheboygan, WI	3.2
229	66	Charlottesville, VA	3.0
25	66	Denver, CO	3.0
46	66	Salt Lake City-Ogden, UT	3.0
258	69	Columbia, MO	2.9
155	69	Killeen-Temple, TX	2.9
50	69	Raleigh-Durham-Chapel Hill, NC	2.9
101	72	Colorado Springs, CO	2.8
176	72	Lincoln, NE	2.8
56	72	Monmouth-Ocean, NJ	2.8
30	72	New Haven-Bridgeport-Stamford-Danbury-Waterbury, CT	2.8
39	72	Norfolk-Virginia Beach-Newport News, VA-NC	3.0
178	72	San Luis Obispo-Atascadero-Paso Robles, CA	2.8
97	72	Wichita, KS	2.8

TABLE 5—All Metropolitan Areas
Selected Rankings

		Percent Hispanic or Latino[1], 2000				Percent Two or More Races, 2000	
Population Rank	Hispanic or Latino Rank	Metropolitan Area	[A-4. col 23] Percent Hispanic or Latino	Population Rank	Two or More Races Rank	Metropolitan Area	[A-4. col 26] Percent Two or More Races
205	1	Laredo, TX	94.4	68	1	Honolulu, HI	20.1
94	2	McAllen-Edinburg-Mission, TX	88.4	168	2	Anchorage, AK	6.3
147	3	Brownsville-Harlingen-San Benito, TX	84.5	195	3	Merced, CA	6.2
79	4	El Paso, TX	78.3	95	3	Stockton-Lodi, CA	6.2
217	5	Las Cruces, NM	63.4	100	3	Vallejo-Fairfield-Napa, CA	6.2
23	6	Miami, FL	57.3	115	6	Modesto, CA	6.0
132	7	Corpus Christi, TX	54.6	86	7	Jersey City, NJ	5.9
38	8	San Antonio, TX	51.2	21	8	Oakland, CA	5.8
136	9	Visalia-Tulare-Porterville, CA	50.8	76	9	Tacoma, WA	5.6
228	10	Yuma, AZ	50.5	222	9	Yolo, CA	5.6
125	11	Salinas, CA	46.9	35	11	Sacramento, CA	5.5
195	12	Merced, CA	45.4	255	12	Yuba City, CA	5.4
1	13	Los Angeles-Long Beach, CA	44.6	186	13	Bremerton, WA	5.2
244	14	Santa Fe, NM	44.4	71	13	Tulsa, OK	5.2
66	15	Fresno, CA	44.1	66	15	Fresno, CA	5.1
75	16	Albuquerque, NM	41.6	1	15	Los Angeles-Long Beach, CA	5.1
86	17	Jersey City, NJ	39.8	11	15	Riverside-San Bernardino, CA	5.1
311	18	Victoria, TX	39.2	284	18	Lawton, OK	5.0
80	19	Bakersfield, CA	38.4	15	18	San Diego, CA	5.0
252	20	Pueblo, CO	38.0	32	18	San Jose, CA	5.0
11	21	Riverside-San Bernardino, CA	37.8	125	21	Salinas, CA	4.8
189	22	Yakima, WA	35.9	29	21	San Francisco, CA	4.8
182	23	Odessa-Midland, TX	35.8	2	23	New York, NY	4.7
126	24	Santa Barbara-Santa Maria-Lompoc, CA	34.2	136	24	Visalia-Tulare-Porterville, CA	4.6
72	25	Ventura, CA	33.5	75	25	Albuquerque, NM	4.5
115	26	Modesto, CA	31.8	80	25	Bakersfield, CA	4.5
14	27	Orange County, CA	30.8	60	27	Oklahoma City, OK	4.4
295	28	San Angelo, TX	30.6	126	27	Santa Barbara-Santa Maria-Lompoc, CA	4.4
95	29	Stockton-Lodi, CA	30.5	14	29	Orange County, CA	4.3
8	30	Houston, TX	29.9	200	30	Chico-Paradise, CA	4.2
70	31	Tucson, AZ	29.4	101	30	Colorado Springs, CO	4.2
180	32	Lubbock, TX	27.4	155	30	Killeen-Temple, TX	4.2
213	33	Greeley, CO	27.0	40	30	Las Vegas, NV-AZ	4.2
171	34	Santa Cruz-Watsonville, CA	26.8	226	30	Redding, CA	4.2
15	35	San Diego, CA	26.7	111	30	Santa Rosa, CA	4.2
48	36	Austin-San Marcos, TX	26.2	19	30	Seattle-Bellevue-Everett, WA	4.2
222	37	Yolo, CA	25.9	23	37	Miami, FL	4.1
2	38	New York, NY	25.1	171	37	Santa Cruz-Watsonville, CA	4.1
12	38	Phoenix-Mesa, AZ	25.1	198	39	Fort Smith, AR-OK	4.0
32	40	San Jose, CA	24.0	72	39	Ventura, CA	4.0
10	41	Dallas, TX	23.0	197	41	Olympia, WA	3.9
181	42	Brazoria, TX	22.8	252	41	Pueblo, CO	3.9
206	43	Richland-Kennewick-Pasco, WA	21.5	146	43	Reno, NV	3.8
40	44	Las Vegas, NV-AZ	20.6	178	43	San Luis Obispo-Atascadero-Paso Robles, CA	3.8
255	45	Yuba City, CA	20.0	244	43	Santa Fe, NM	3.8
192	46	Amarillo, TX	19.6	38	46	San Antonio, TX	3.7
175	46	Naples, FL	19.6	151	47	Eugene-Springfield, OR	3.6
100	48	Vallejo-Fairfield-Napa, CA	19.1	36	47	Fort Lauderdale, FL	3.6
246	49	Vineland-Millville-Bridgeton, NJ	18.9	217	47	Las Cruces, NM	3.6
25	50	Denver, CO	18.8	27	47	Portland-Vancouver, OR-WA	3.6
21	51	Oakland, CA	18.5	239	51	Jacksonville, NC	3.5
31	52	Fort Worth-Arlington, TX	18.2	70	51	Tucson, AZ	3.5
177	53	Galveston-Texas City, TX	18.0	189	51	Yakima, WA	3.5
235	54	Bryan-College Station, TX	17.9	220	54	Fort Walton Beach, FL	3.4
194	54	Waco, TX	17.9	143	54	Salem, OR	3.4
269	56	Abilene, TX	17.5	25	56	Denver, CO	3.3
111	57	Santa Rosa, CA	17.4	206	56	Richland-Kennewick-Pasco, WA	3.3
44	58	Bergen-Passaic, NJ	17.3	315	58	Corvallis, OR	3.2
3	59	Chicago, IL	17.1	157	58	Fayetteville, NC	3.2
29	60	San Francisco, CA	16.8	34	58	Orlando, FL	3.2
36	61	Fort Lauderdale, FL	16.7	221	58	Topeka, KS	3.2
146	62	Reno, NV	16.6	6	58	Washington, DC-MD-VA-WV	3.2
34	63	Orlando, FL	16.5	132	63	Corpus Christi, TX	3.1
178	64	San Luis Obispo-Atascadero-Paso Robles, CA	16.3	79	63	El Paso, TX	3.1
155	65	Killeen-Temple, TX	15.7	212	63	Medford-Ashland, OR	3.1
143	65	Salem, OR	15.7	12	63	Phoenix-Mesa, AZ	3.1
35	67	Sacramento, CA	14.4	309	63	Rapid City, SD	3.1
26	68	Newark, NJ	13.3	121	63	Spokane, WA	3.1
55	69	West Palm Beach-Boca Raton, FL	12.4	224	69	Bellingham, WA	3.0
87	70	Springfield, MA	12.2	44	69	Bergen-Passaic, NJ	3.0
253	71	Wichita Falls, TX	11.7	313	69	Cheyenne, WY	3.0
101	72	Colorado Springs, CO	11.3	199	69	Clarksville-Hopkinsville, TN-KY	3.0
52	73	Middlesex-Somerset-Hunterdon, NJ	11.2	302	69	Lawrence, KS	3.0
275	73	Sioux City, IA-NE	11.2	169	69	New London-Norwich, CT	3.0
216	75	Tyler, TX	11.1	246	69	Vineland-Millville-Bridgeton, NJ	3.0
				97	69	Wichita, KS	3.0
				228	69	Yuma, AZ	3.0

[1]Hispanic or Latino persons may be of any race.

TABLE 5—All Metropolitan Areas
Selected Rankings

Percent Married-Couple Families, 2000				Percent Married-Couple Families with Own Children Under 18 Years, 2000			
Population Rank	Married-Couple Families Rank	Metropolitan Area	[A-4. col 30] Percent Married Couple Families	Population Rank	Married-Couple Families with Own Children Under 18 Years Rank	Metropolitan Area	[A-4. col 31] Percent Married-Couple Families with Own Children Under 18 Years
135	1	Provo-Orem, UT	71.1	135	1	Provo-Orem, UT	43.6
94	2	McAllen-Edinburg-Mission, TX	66.0	205	2	Laredo, TX	42.0
205	3	Laredo, TX	65.0	94	3	McAllen-Edinburg-Mission, TX	39.6
16	4	Nassau-Suffolk, NY	63.6	147	4	Brownsville-Harlingen-San Benito, TX	35.0
228	4	Yuma, AZ	63.6	46	5	Salt Lake City-Ogden, UT	34.3
181	6	Brazoria, TX	63.1	195	6	Merced, CA	33.9
147	7	Brownsville-Harlingen-San Benito, TX	61.9	239	7	Jacksonville, NC	33.6
239	7	Jacksonville, NC	61.9	79	8	El Paso, TX	33.3
46	9	Salt Lake City-Ogden, UT	61.4	136	9	Visalia-Tulare-Porterville, CA	32.8
271	10	Wausau, WI	60.6	181	10	Brazoria, TX	32.7
109	11	Lancaster, PA	60.5	72	11	Ventura, CA	31.8
72	12	Ventura, CA	60.2	155	12	Killeen-Temple, TX	31.5
52	13	Middlesex-Somerset-Hunterdon, NJ	59.9	199	13	Clarksville-Hopkinsville, TN-KY	31.2
251	14	Punta Gorda, FL	59.7	16	14	Nassau-Suffolk, NY	31.1
128	15	Newburgh, NY-PA	59.6	11	15	Riverside-San Bernardino, CA	30.9
247	16	Decatur, AL	59.5	115	16	Modesto, CA	30.8
213	17	Greeley, CO	59.4	128	16	Newburgh, NY-PA	30.8
199	18	Clarksville-Hopkinsville, TN-KY	59.2	125	18	Salinas, CA	30.6
136	18	Visalia-Tulare-Porterville, CA	59.2	80	19	Bakersfield, CA	30.4
155	20	Killeen-Temple, TX	59.1	213	20	Greeley, CO	30.2
204	21	Houma, LA	58.8	14	21	Orange County, CA	30.0
287	21	Sheboygan, WI	58.8	52	22	Middlesex-Somerset-Hunterdon, NJ	29.9
195	23	Merced, CA	58.7	8	23	Houston, TX	29.7
206	23	Richland-Kennewick-Pasco, WA	58.7	206	23	Richland-Kennewick-Pasco, WA	29.7
131	23	York, PA	58.7	95	23	Stockton-Lodi, CA	29.7
175	26	Naples, FL	58.5	66	26	Fresno, CA	29.5
211	27	Elkhart-Goshen, IN	58.4	189	26	Yakima, WA	29.5
156	28	Fayetteville-Springdale-Rogers, AR	58.3	119	28	Boise City, ID	29.3
186	29	Bremerton, WA	58.2	182	29	Odessa-Midland, TX	29.2
311	29	Victoria, TX	58.2	204	30	Houma, LA	28.7
149	31	Hamilton-Middletown, OH	58.1	32	30	San Jose, CA	28.7
56	31	Monmouth-Ocean, NJ	58.1	168	32	Anchorage, AK	28.6
139	33	Appleton-Oshkosh-Neenah, WI	57.9	274	32	Rochester, MN	28.6
79	33	El Paso, TX	57.9	101	34	Colorado Springs, CO	28.5
316	33	Pocatello, ID	57.9	31	34	Fort Worth-Arlington, TX	28.5
119	36	Boise City, ID	57.8	284	34	Lawton, OK	28.5
308	37	Dubuque, IA	57.7	223	34	St. Cloud, MN	28.5
274	38	Rochester, MN	57.3	316	38	Pocatello, ID	28.4
115	39	Modesto, CA	57.2	100	38	Vallejo-Fairfield-Napa, CA	28.4
11	39	Riverside-San Bernardino, CA	57.2	255	38	Yuba City, CA	28.4
220	41	Fort Walton Beach, FL	57.1	157	41	Fayetteville, NC	28.1
189	41	Yakima, WA	57.1	10	42	Dallas, TX	28.0
14	43	Orange County, CA	57.0	59	42	Grand Rapids-Muskegon-Holland, MI	28.0
198	44	Fort Smith, AR-OK	56.8	228	42	Yuma, AZ	28.0
182	44	Odessa-Midland, TX	56.8	149	45	Hamilton-Middletown, OH	27.9
125	44	Salinas, CA	56.8	164	46	Dutchess County, NY	27.8
44	47	Bergen-Passaic, NJ	56.7	311	46	Victoria, TX	27.8
105	47	Johnson City-Kingsport-Bristol, TN-VA	56.7	271	46	Wausau, WI	27.8
216	47	Tyler, TX	56.7	139	49	Appleton-Oshkosh-Neenah, WI	27.7
101	50	Colorado Springs, CO	56.6	186	49	Bremerton, WA	27.7
164	50	Dutchess County, NY	56.6	211	49	Elkhart-Goshen, IN	27.7
250	50	Florence, AL	56.6	44	52	Bergen-Passaic, NJ	27.2
145	50	Hickory-Morganton-Lenoir, NC	56.6	109	53	Lancaster, PA	27.1
100	54	Vallejo-Fairfield-Napa, CA	56.5	219	54	Sioux Falls, SD	27.0
255	54	Yuba City, CA	56.5	1	55	Los Angeles-Long Beach, CA	26.8
59	56	Grand Rapids-Muskegon-Holland, MI	56.4	56	55	Monmouth-Ocean, NJ	26.8
223	56	St. Cloud, MN	56.4	9	57	Atlanta, GA	26.7
305	58	Bismarck, ND	56.2	217	57	Las Cruces, NM	26.7
282	58	Grand Junction, CO	56.2	13	57	Minneapolis-St. Paul, MN-WI	26.7
232	58	Lima, OH	56.2	308	60	Dubuque, IA	26.5
170	58	Ocala, FL	56.2	305	61	Bismarck, ND	26.4
133	58	Reading, PA	56.2	132	61	Corpus Christi, TX	26.4
291	58	Sherman-Denison, TX	56.2	247	61	Decatur, AL	26.4
80	64	Bakersfield, CA	56.1	156	61	Fayetteville-Springdale-Rogers, AR	26.4
153	64	Fort Pierce-Port St. Lucie, FL	56.1	38	61	San Antonio, TX	26.4
237	64	Parkersburg-Marietta, WV-OH	56.1	97	61	Wichita, KS	26.4
32	64	San Jose, CA	56.1	187	67	Green Bay, WI	26.3
116	68	Fort Myers-Cape Coral, FL	55.9	93	68	Ann Arbor, MI	26.2
231	68	Joplin, MO	55.9	102	68	Fort Wayne, IN	26.2
318	70	Enid, OK	55.8	26	68	Newark, NJ	26.2
208	70	Racine, WI	55.8	287	68	Sheboygan, WI	26.2
154	72	Huntington-Ashland, WV-KY-OH	55.7	3	72	Chicago, IL	26.1
196	73	Longview-Marshall, TX	55.6	240	72	Kenosha, WI	26.1
134	73	Rockford, IL	55.6	202	74	Burlington, VT	26.0
95	73	Stockton-Lodi, CA	55.6	76	74	Tacoma, WA	26.0

TABLE 5—All Metropolitan Areas
Selected Rankings

Percent Single-Parent Households with Children Under 18 Years, 2000

Population Rank	Single-Parent Households Rank	Metropolitan Area	[A-4. col 34] Percent Single-Parent Households
277	1	Albany, GA	14.7
54	2	Memphis, TN-AR-MS	13.6
117	3	Jackson, MS	13.1
246	3	Vineland-Millville-Bridgeton, NJ	13.1
310	5	Pine Bluff, AR	13.0
118	6	Flint, MI	12.9
136	6	Visalia-Tulare-Porterville, CA	12.9
152	8	Macon, GA	12.8
165	9	Columbus, GA-AL	12.7
294	9	Sumter, SC	12.7
80	11	Bakersfield, CA	12.6
245	11	Monroe, LA	12.6
127	11	Shreveport-Bossier City, LA	12.6
45	14	New Orleans, LA	12.5
66	15	Fresno, CA	12.4
217	15	Las Cruces, NM	12.4
195	15	Merced, CA	12.4
79	18	El Paso, TX	12.2
157	19	Fayetteville, NC	12.1
129	19	Lafayette, LA	12.1
270	21	Alexandria, LA	11.9
107	21	Augusta-Aiken, GA-SC	11.9
189	23	Yakima, WA	11.8
284	24	Lawton, OK	11.6
95	24	Stockton-Lodi, CA	11.6
88	26	Baton Rouge, LA	11.5
268	26	Dover, DE	11.5
148	26	Montgomery, AL	11.5
263	26	Texarkana, TX-Texarkana, AR	11.5
272	30	Florence, SC	11.4
205	30	Laredo, TX	11.4
2	30	New York, NY	11.4
39	30	Norfolk-Virginia Beach-Newport News, VA-NC	11.4
11	34	Riverside-San Bernardino, CA	11.3
168	35	Anchorage, AK	11.2
147	35	Brownsville-Harlingen-San Benito, TX	11.2
132	35	Corpus Christi, TX	11.2
23	35	Miami, FL	11.2
115	39	Modesto, CA	11.1
249	39	Rocky Mount, NC	11.1
160	39	Savannah, GA	11.1
137	42	Biloxi-Gulfport-Pascagoula, MS	11.0
86	42	Jersey City, NJ	11.0
286	44	Goldsboro, NC	10.8
1	44	Los Angeles-Long Beach, CA	10.8
87	44	Springfield, MA	10.8
75	47	Albuquerque, NM	10.7
130	47	Beaumont-Port Arthur, TX	10.7
96	47	Charleston-North Charleston, SC	10.7
289	47	Hattiesburg, MS	10.7
155	47	Killeen-Temple, TX	10.7
209	47	Lake Charles, LA	10.7
98	47	Mobile, AL	10.7
38	47	San Antonio, TX	10.7
76	47	Tacoma, WA	10.7
256	56	Dothan, AL	10.6
94	56	McAllen-Edinburg-Mission, TX	10.6
182	56	Odessa-Midland, TX	10.6
252	56	Pueblo, CO	10.6
309	56	Rapid City, SD	10.6
255	56	Yuba City, CA	10.6
307	62	Elmira, NY	10.5
260	62	Greenville, NC	10.5
293	62	Jackson, TN	10.5
57	62	Jacksonville, FL	10.5
122	62	Pensacola, FL	10.5
99	67	Columbia, SC	10.4
285	67	Decatur, IL	10.4
226	67	Redding, CA	10.4
35	67	Sacramento, CA	10.4
199	71	Clarksville-Hopkinsville, TN-KY	10.3
276	71	Flagstaff, AZ-UT	10.3
204	71	Houma, LA	10.3
85	71	Toledo, OH	10.3
206	75	Richland-Kennewick-Pasco, WA	10.2
162	75	Tallahassee, FL	10.2
311	75	Victoria, TX	10.2

Percent Men Living Alone, 2000

Population Rank	Men Living Alone Rank	Metropolitan Area	[A-4. col 38] Percent Men Living Alone
29	1	San Francisco, CA	14.7
278	2	Bloomington, IN	14.3
214	2	Champaign-Urbana, IL	14.3
290	4	Iowa City, IA	14.1
283	5	Auburn-Opalika, AL	13.7
179	6	Duluth-Superior, MN-WI	13.6
146	6	Reno, NV	13.6
303	8	Grand Forks, ND-MN	13.5
304	8	Missoula, MT	13.5
86	10	Jersey City, NJ	13.4
317	11	Casper, WY	13.3
218	12	Fargo-Moorhead, ND-MN	13.2
191	12	Gainesville, FL	13.2
314	12	Great Falls, MT	13.2
48	15	Austin-San Marcos, TX	13.1
258	15	Columbia, MO	13.1
19	15	Seattle-Bellevue-Everett, WA	13.1
302	18	Lawrence, KS	13.0
162	18	Tallahassee, FL	13.0
25	20	Denver, CO	12.9
210	21	Lafayette, IN	12.8
176	21	Lincoln, NE	12.8
40	23	Las Vegas, NV-AZ	12.7
120	23	Madison, WI	12.7
257	23	State College, PA	12.7
70	23	Tucson, AZ	12.7
97	23	Wichita, KS	12.7
313	28	Cheyenne, WY	12.5
259	28	Pittsfield, MA	12.5
85	28	Toledo, OH	12.5
235	31	Bryan-College Station, TX	12.4
2	31	New York, NY	12.4
168	33	Anchorage, AK	12.3
161	33	Boulder-Longmont, CO	12.3
285	33	Decatur, IL	12.3
36	33	Fort Lauderdale, FL	12.3
244	33	Santa Fe, NM	12.3
201	33	Springfield, IL	12.3
225	33	Tuscaloosa, AL	12.3
69	40	Albany-Schenectady-Troy, NY	12.2
75	40	Albuquerque, NM	12.2
172	40	Binghamton, NY	12.2
41	40	Columbus, OH	12.2
51	44	Buffalo-Niagara Falls, NY	12.1
42	44	Milwaukee-Waukesha, WI	12.1
45	44	New Orleans, LA	12.1
221	44	Topeka, KS	12.1
33	48	Cincinnati, OH-KY-IN	12.0
24	48	Cleveland-Lorain-Elyria, OH	12.0
144	48	Huntsville, AL	12.0
60	48	Oklahoma City, OK	12.0
121	48	Spokane, WA	12.0
20	48	Tampa-St. Petersburg-Clearwater, FL	12.0
224	54	Bellingham, WA	11.9
315	54	Corvallis, OR	11.9
7	54	Detroit, MI	11.9
177	54	Galveston-Texas City, TX	11.9
260	54	Greenville, NC	11.9
207	59	Cedar Rapids, IA	11.8
106	59	Lexington, KY	11.8
169	59	New London-Norwich, CT	11.8
158	59	Utica-Rome, NY	11.8
238	63	Bloomington-Normal, IL	11.7
138	63	Davenport-Moline-Rock Island, IA-IL	11.7
108	63	Melbourne-Titusville-Palm Bay, FL	11.7
74	63	Omaha, NE-IA	11.7
243	63	Panama City, FL	11.7
27	63	Portland-Vancouver, OR-WA	11.7
309	63	Rapid City, SD	11.7
84	63	Scranton-Wilkes-Barre-Hazleton, PA	11.7
71	63	Tulsa, OK	11.7
93	72	Ann Arbor, MI	11.6
264	72	Billings, MT	11.6
65	72	Dayton-Springfield, OH	11.6
308	72	Dubuque, IA	11.6
254	72	Jamestown, NY	11.6
113	72	Kalamazoo-Battle Creek, MI	11.6
61	72	Louisville, KY-IN	11.6
13	72	Minneapolis-St. Paul, MN-WI	11.6
22	72	Pittsburgh, PA	11.6
167	72	South Bend, IN	11.6
253	72	Wichita Falls, TX	11.6

TABLE 5—All Metropolitan Areas
Selected Rankings

Percent Women Living Alone, 2000

Population Rank	Women Living Alone Rank	Metropolitan Area	[A-4. col 40] Percent Women Living Alone
90	1	Sarasota-Bradenton, FL	19.2
259	2	Pittsfield, MA	19.0
190	3	Barnstable-Yarmouth, MA	18.9
84	4	Scranton—Wilkes-Barre—Hazleton, PA	18.8
234	4	Wheeling, WV-OH	18.8
22	6	Pittsburgh, PA	18.4
2	7	New York, NY	18.3
201	8	Springfield, IL	18.2
51	9	Buffalo-Niagara Falls, NY	18.1
183	9	Roanoke, VA	18.1
278	11	Bloomington, IN	18.0
300	11	Cumberland, MD-WV	18.0
185	11	Johnstown, PA	18.0
55	11	West Palm Beach-Boca Raton, FL	18.0
20	15	Tampa-St. Petersburg-Clearwater, FL	17.7
173	16	Charleston, WV	17.6
188	17	Asheville, NC	17.5
29	17	San Francisco, CA	17.5
221	17	Topeka, KS	17.5
166	20	Portland, ME	17.4
265	21	Altoona, PA	17.3
179	21	Duluth-Superior, MN-WI	17.3
36	21	Fort Lauderdale, FL	17.3
158	21	Utica-Rome, NY	17.3
24	25	Cleveland-Lorain-Elyria, OH	17.2
87	25	Springfield, MA	17.2
69	27	Albany-Schenectady-Troy, NY	17.1
172	27	Binghamton, NY	17.1
214	27	Champaign-Urbana, IL	17.1
241	27	Terre Haute, IN	17.1
140	31	Atlantic-Cape May, NJ	17.0
63	31	Providence-Warwick-Pawtucket, RI	17.0
261	31	Steubenville-Weirton, OH-WV	17.0
307	34	Elmira, NY	16.8
297	34	Lewiston-Auburn, ME	16.8
292	36	Danville, VA	16.7
318	36	Enid, OK	16.7
120	36	Madison, WI	16.7
281	36	Muncie, IN	16.7
251	36	Punta Gorda, FL	16.7
285	41	Decatur, IL	16.6
218	41	Fargo-Moorhead, ND-MN	16.6
267	41	La Crosse, WI-MN	16.6
299	41	St. Joseph, MO	16.6
159	45	Evansville-Henderson, IN-KY	16.5
254	45	Jamestown, NY	16.5
42	45	Milwaukee-Waukesha, WI	16.5
244	45	Santa Fe, NM	16.5
266	45	Waterloo-Cedar Falls, IA	16.5
288	50	Anniston, AL	16.4
264	50	Billings, MT	16.4
305	50	Bismarck, ND	16.4
200	50	Chico-Paradise, CA	16.4
138	50	Davenport-Moline-Rock Island, IA-IL	16.4
103	50	Daytona Beach, FL	16.4
112	50	Des Moines, IA	16.4
298	50	Gadsden, AL	16.4
306	50	Owensboro, KY	16.4
73	50	Syracuse, NY	16.4
229	60	Charlottesville, VA	16.3
65	60	Dayton-Springfield, OH	16.3
163	60	Erie, PA	16.3
260	60	Greenville, NC	16.3
53	60	Hartford, CT	16.3
154	60	Huntington-Ashland, WV-KY-OH	16.3
167	60	South Bend, IN	16.3
33	67	Cincinnati, OH-KY-IN	16.2
83	67	Harrisburg-Lebanon-Carlisle, PA	16.2
176	67	Lincoln, NE	16.2
61	67	Louisville, KY-IN	16.2
56	67	Monmouth-Ocean, NJ	16.2
5	67	Philadelphia, PA-NJ	16.2
279	67	Sharon, PA	16.2
85	67	Toledo, OH	16.2
89	67	Youngstown-Warren, OH	16.2

Percent Foreign-Born Population, 2000

Population Rank	Foreign-born Population Rank	Metropolitan Area	[A-4. col 54] Percent Foreign-born Population
23	1	Miami, FL	50.9
86	2	Jersey City, NJ	38.5
1	3	Los Angeles-Long Beach, CA	36.2
32	4	San Jose, CA	34.1
2	5	New York, NY	33.7
29	6	San Francisco, CA	32.0
14	7	Orange County, CA	29.9
94	8	McAllen-Edinburg-Mission, TX	29.5
205	9	Laredo, TX	29.0
125	9	Salinas, CA	29.0
79	11	El Paso, TX	27.4
44	12	Bergen-Passaic, NJ	25.7
147	13	Brownsville-Harlingen-San Benito, TX	25.6
36	14	Fort Lauderdale, FL	25.3
195	15	Merced, CA	24.8
21	16	Oakland, CA	24.0
228	16	Yuma, AZ	24.0
136	18	Visalia-Tulare-Porterville, CA	22.6
15	19	San Diego, CA	21.5
126	20	Santa Barbara-Santa Maria-Lompoc, CA	21.2
66	21	Fresno, CA	21.0
52	22	Middlesex-Somerset-Hunterdon, NJ	20.8
72	23	Ventura, CA	20.7
8	24	Houston, TX	20.5
222	25	Yolo, CA	20.3
95	26	Stockton-Lodi, CA	19.5
68	27	Honolulu, HI	19.2
26	28	Newark, NJ	19.0
11	29	Riverside-San Bernardino, CA	18.8
217	30	Las Cruces, NM	18.7
115	31	Modesto, CA	18.3
175	31	Naples, FL	18.3
171	33	Santa Cruz-Watsonville, CA	18.2
55	34	West Palm Beach-Boca Raton, FL	17.4
3	35	Chicago, IL	17.2
100	35	Vallejo-Fairfield-Napa, CA	17.2
80	37	Bakersfield, CA	16.9
6	37	Washington, DC-MD-VA-WV	16.9
189	37	Yakima, WA	16.9
10	40	Dallas, TX	16.8
255	41	Yuba City, CA	16.6
40	42	Las Vegas, NV-AZ	16.5
16	43	Nassau-Suffolk, NY	14.4
111	44	Santa Rosa, CA	14.3
35	45	Phoenix-Mesa, AZ	14.1
146	45	Reno, NV	14.1
141	47	Sacramento, CA	13.9
47		Trenton, NJ	13.9
19	49	Seattle-Bellevue-Everett, WA	13.7
30	50	New Haven-Bridgeport-Stamford-Danbury-Waterbury, CT	13.1
206	51	Richland-Kennewick-Pasco, WA	12.8
4	52	Boston-Worcester-Lawrence-Lowell-Brockton, MA-NH	12.4
48	53	Austin-San Marcos, TX	12.2
34	54	Orlando, FL	12.0
63	55	Providence-Warwick-Pawtucket, RI	11.9
70	55	Tucson, AZ	11.9
143	57	Salem, OR	11.5
31	58	Fort Worth-Arlington, TX	11.4
25	59	Denver, CO	11.1
27	60	Portland-Vancouver, OR-WA	10.8
9	61	Atlanta, GA	10.3
235	61	Bryan-College Station, TX	10.3
53	61	Hartford, CT	10.3
38	64	San Antonio, TX	10.2
224	65	Bellingham, WA	9.8
20	65	Tampa-St. Petersburg-Clearwater, FL	9.8
244	67	Santa Fe, NM	9.7
153	68	Fort Pierce-Port St. Lucie, FL	9.5
161	69	Boulder-Longmont, CO	9.4
140	70	Atlantic-Cape May, NJ	9.3
213	70	Greeley, CO	9.3
116	72	Fort Myers-Cape Coral, FL	9.2
50	72	Raleigh-Durham-Chapel Hill, NC	9.2
182	74	Odessa-Midland, TX	9.1
178	75	San Luis Obispo-Atascadero-Paso Robles, CA	8.9
90	75	Sarasota-Bradenton, FL	8.9

TABLE 5—All Metropolitan Areas
Selected Rankings

Percent of Population Over 25 Years with High School Diploma or Less, 2000				Percent of Population Over 25 Years with Bachelor's Degree or More, 2000			
Population Rank	High School Diploma or Less Rank	Metropolitan Area	[B-4. col 2] Percent High School Diploma or Less	Population Rank	Bachelor's Degree or More Rank	Metropolitan Area	[B-4. col 4] Percent Bachelor's Degree or More
204	1	Houma, LA	70.1	161	1	Boulder-Longmont, CO	52.4
94	2	McAllen-Edinburg-Mission, TX	69.8	290	2	Iowa City, IA	47.6
185	3	Johnstown, PA	69.2	315	3	Corvallis, OR	47.4
246	4	Vineland-Millville-Bridgeton, NJ	67.8	29	4	San Francisco, CA	43.6
265	5	Altoona, PA	66.2	302	5	Lawrence, KS	42.7
292	6	Danville, VA	65.4	6	6	Washington, DC-MD-VA-WV	41.8
205	7	Laredo, TX	65.0	258	7	Columbia, MO	41.7
147	8	Brownsville-Harlingen-San Benito, TX	64.9	120	8	Madison, WI	40.6
261	9	Steubenville-Weirton, OH-WV	64.6	32	9	San Jose, CA	40.5
215	10	Mansfield, OH	64.5	229	10	Charlottesville, VA	40.1
300	11	Cumberland, MD-WV	63.5	244	11	Santa Fe, NM	39.9
249	12	Rocky Mount, NC	63.3	278	12	Bloomington, IN	39.6
279	13	Sharon, PA	62.2	174	13	Fort Collins-Loveland, CO	39.5
234	14	Wheeling, WV-OH	62.0	50	14	Raleigh-Durham-Chapel Hill, NC	38.9
154	15	Huntington-Ashland, WV-KY-OH	61.7	191	15	Gainesville, FL	38.7
109	16	Lancaster, PA	61.5	214	16	Champaign-Urbana, IL	38.0
211	17	Elkhart-Goshen, IN	61.3	52	17	Middlesex-Somerset-Hunterdon, NJ	37.4
145	17	Hickory-Morganton-Lenoir, NC	61.3	235	18	Bryan-College Station, TX	37.0
133	17	Reading, PA	61.3	93	19	Ann Arbor, MI	36.9
136	17	Visalia-Tulare-Porterville, CA	61.3	48	20	Austin-San Marcos, TX	36.7
280	17	Williamsport, PA	61.3	162	20	Tallahassee, FL	36.7
262	22	Hagerstown, MD	61.1	257	22	State College, PA	36.3
129	22	Lafayette, LA	61.1	238	23	Bloomington-Normal, IL	36.2
89	24	Youngstown-Warren, OH	61.0	19	24	Seattle-Bellevue-Everett, WA	35.9
131	25	York, PA	60.9	21	25	Oakland, CA	35.0
232	26	Lima, OH	60.6	202	26	Burlington, VT	34.8
297	27	Lewiston-Auburn, ME	60.3	274	27	Rochester, MN	34.7
84	27	Scranton-Wilkes-Barre-Hazleton, PA	60.3	25	28	Denver, CO	34.2
195	29	Merced, CA	60.1	166	28	Portland, ME	34.2
310	30	Pine Bluff, AR	60.0	171	28	Santa Cruz-Watsonville, CA	34.2
228	31	Yuma, AZ	59.9	233	31	Athens, GA	34.1
105	32	Johnson City-Kingsport-Bristol, TN-VA	59.6	222	31	Yolo, CA	34.1
270	33	Alexandria, LA	59.1	30	33	New Haven-Bridgeport-Stamford-Danbury-Waterbury, CT	34.0
198	34	Fort Smith, AR-OK	59.0	141	33	Trenton, NJ	34.0
123	35	Canton-Massillon, OH	58.9	4	35	Boston-Worcester-Lawrence-Lowell-Brockton, MA-NH	33.8
104	35	Lakeland-Winter Haven, FL	58.9	190	36	Barnstable-Yarmouth, MA	33.6
250	37	Florence, AL	58.8	13	37	Minneapolis-St. Paul, MN-WI	33.3
247	38	Decatur, AL	58.7	304	38	Missoula, MT	32.8
189	38	Yakima, WA	58.7	176	39	Lincoln, NE	32.6
288	40	Anniston, AL	58.3	44	40	Bergen-Passaic, NJ	32.5
298	41	Gadsden, AL	58.2	9	41	Atlanta, GA	32.0
272	42	Florence, SC	57.8	101	42	Colorado Springs, CO	31.8
170	43	Ocala, FL	57.7	26	43	Newark, NJ	31.5
237	44	Parkersburg-Marietta, WV-OH	57.6	135	43	Provo-Orem, UT	31.5
209	45	Lake Charles, LA	57.5	16	45	Nassau-Suffolk, NY	31.3
163	46	Erie, PA	57.1	144	46	Huntsville, AL	30.9
80	47	Bakersfield, CA	56.9	14	47	Orange County, CA	30.8
306	47	Owensboro, KY	56.9	53	48	Hartford, CT	30.5
79	49	El Paso, TX	56.8	3	49	Chicago, IL	30.1
241	50	Terre Haute, IN	56.7	10	50	Dallas, TX	30.0
263	50	Texarkana, TX-Texarkana, AR	56.7	197	51	Olympia, WA	29.8
299	52	St. Joseph, MO	56.6	276	52	Flagstaff, AZ-UT	29.5
130	53	Beaumont-Port Arthur, TX	56.5	15	52	San Diego, CA	29.5
83	54	Harrisburg-Lebanon-Carlisle, PA	56.3	218	54	Fargo-Moorhead, ND-MN	29.4
86	54	Jersey City, NJ	56.3	126	54	Santa Barbara-Santa Maria-Lompoc, CA	29.4
301	54	Kokomo, IN	56.3	18	56	Baltimore, MD	29.2
81	57	Allentown-Bethlehem-Easton, PA	56.1	99	56	Columbia, SC	29.2
173	58	Charleston, WV	56.0	2	56	New York, NY	29.2
296	58	Kankakee, IL	56.0	62	56	Richmond-Petersburg, VA	29.2
140	60	Atlantic-Cape May, NJ	55.9	41	60	Columbus, OH	29.1
115	61	Modesto, CA	55.7	168	61	Anchorage, AK	28.9
281	62	Muncie, IN	55.6	27	62	Portland-Vancouver, OR-WA	28.8
312	63	Jonesboro, AR	55.5	112	63	Des Moines, IA	28.7
287	63	Sheboygan, WI	55.5	106	63	Lexington, KY	28.7
231	65	Joplin, MO	55.4	28	65	Kansas City, MO-KS	28.5
193	65	Lynchburg, VA	55.4	111	65	Santa Rosa, CA	28.5
294	65	Sumter, SC	55.4	75	67	Albuquerque, NM	28.4
286	68	Goldsboro, NC	55.3	114	67	Lansing-East Lansing, MI	28.4
254	68	Jamestown, NY	55.3	69	69	Albany-Schenectady-Troy, NY	28.2
236	68	Janesville-Beloit, WI	55.3	210	69	Lafayette, IN	28.2
308	71	Dubuque, IA	55.0	117	71	Jackson, MS	28.1
82	71	Gary, IN	55.0	201	71	Springfield, IL	28.1
275	71	Sioux City, IA-NE	55.0	74	73	Omaha, NE-IA	28.0
285	74	Decatur, IL	54.9	283	74	Auburn-Opalika, AL	27.9
273	75	Glens Falls, NY	54.8	68	74	Honolulu, HI	27.9
				175	74.0	Naples, FL	27.9

TABLE 5—All Metropolitan Areas
Selected Rankings

Population Rank	At-Risk Youth Rank	Metropolitan Area (Percent of Population 16 to 19 Years Not Enrolled in School, Not High School Graduate, Not in Armed Forces, or Employed, 2000)	[B-4. col 17] Percent At-Risk Youth	Population Rank	Unemployment Rate Rank	Metropolitan Area (Unemployment Rate, 2000)	[B-4. col 20] Unemployment Rate
94	1	McAllen-Edinburg-Mission, TX	11.1	195	1	Merced, CA	13.1
298	2	Gadsden, AL	10.5	136	2	Visalia-Tulare-Porterville, CA	12.7
205	3	Laredo, TX	10.3	66	3	Fresno, CA	12.0
145	4	Hickory-Morganton-Lenoir, NC	10.1	94	3	McAllen-Edinburg-Mission, TX	12.0
270	5	Alexandria, LA	9.8	80	5	Bakersfield, CA	11.8
40	6	Las Vegas, NV-AZ	9.6	115	6	Modesto, CA	11.6
228	6	Yuma, AZ	9.6	147	7	Brownsville-Harlingen-San Benito, TX	11.4
153	8	Fort Pierce-Port St. Lucie, FL	9.3	228	7	Yuma, AZ	11.4
192	9	Amarillo, TX	8.9	189	9	Yakima, WA	11.1
247	9	Decatur, AL	8.9	255	9	Yuba City, CA	11.1
175	9	Naples, FL	8.9	95	11	Stockton-Lodi, CA	10.3
245	12	Monroe, LA	8.8	246	12	Vineland-Millville-Bridgeton, NJ	9.9
12	12	Phoenix-Mesa, AZ	8.8	200	13	Chico-Paradise, CA	9.3
127	14	Shreveport-Bossier City, LA	8.7	205	13	Laredo, TX	9.3
189	14	Yakima, WA	8.7	79	15	El Paso, TX	9.2
252	16	Pueblo, CO	8.6	217	15	Las Cruces, NM	9.2
129	17	Lafayette, LA	8.4	86	17	Jersey City, NJ	8.7
147	18	Brownsville-Harlingen-San Benito, TX	8.1	23	17	Miami, FL	8.7
104	18	Lakeland-Winter Haven, FL	8.1	2	17	New York, NY	8.7
148	18	Montgomery, AL	8.1	226	17	Redding, CA	8.7
273	21	Glens Falls, NY	8.0	235	21	Bryan-College Station, TX	8.5
262	21	Hagerstown, MD	8.0	125	21	Salinas, CA	8.5
206	21	Richland-Kennewick-Pasco, WA	8.0	277	23	Albany, GA	8.3
211	24	Elkhart-Goshen, IN	7.8	310	23	Pine Bluff, AR	8.3
8	24	Houston, TX	7.8	1	25	Los Angeles-Long Beach, CA	8.2
249	24	Rocky Mount, NC	7.8	245	25	Monroe, LA	8.2
86	27	Jersey City, NJ	7.7	162	25	Tallahassee, FL	8.2
196	27	Longview-Marshall, TX	7.7	300	28	Cumberland, MD-WV	8.0
244	27	Santa Fe, NM	7.7	127	28	Shreveport-Bossier City, LA	8.0
10	30	Dallas, TX	7.6	233	30	Athens, GA	7.9
231	30	Joplin, MO	7.6	272	30	Florence, SC	7.9
203	30	Myrtle Beach, SC	7.6	154	30	Huntington-Ashland, WV-KY-OH	7.9
125	30	Salinas, CA	7.6	121	30	Spokane, WA	7.9
285	34	Decatur, IL	7.5	307	34	Elmira, NY	7.8
170	34	Ocala, FL	7.5	129	34	Lafayette, LA	7.8
143	34	Salem, OR	7.5	11	34	Riverside-San Bernardino, CA	7.8
136	34	Visalia-Tulare-Porterville, CA	7.5	269	37	Abilene, TX	7.7
132	38	Corpus Christi, TX	7.4	140	37	Atlantic-Cape May, NJ	7.7
152	38	Macon, GA	7.4	130	37	Beaumont-Port Arthur, TX	7.7
307	40	Elmira, NY	7.3	185	37	Johnstown, PA	7.7
2	40	New York, NY	7.3	234	37	Wheeling, WV-OH	7.7
75	42	Albuquerque, NM	7.2	194	42	Waco, TX	7.6
288	42	Anniston, AL	7.2	143	43	Salem, OR	7.5
80	42	Bakersfield, CA	7.2	141	43	Trenton, NJ	7.5
116	42	Fort Myers-Cape Coral, FL	7.2	224	45	Bellingham, WA	7.4
66	42	Fresno, CA	7.2	132	46	Corpus Christi, TX	7.3
54	42	Memphis, TN-AR-MS	7.2	212	46	Medford-Ashland, OR	7.3
195	42	Merced, CA	7.2	206	48	Richland-Kennewick-Pasco, WA	7.2
291	42	Sherman-Denison, TX	7.2	285	49	Decatur, IL	7.1
173	50	Charleston, WV	7.1	118	49	Flint, MI	7.1
204	50	Houma, LA	7.1	281	49	Muncie, IN	7.1
117	50	Jackson, MS	7.1	222	49	Yolo, CA	7.1
1	50	Los Angeles-Long Beach, CA	7.1	270	53	Alexandria, LA	7.0
25	54	Denver, CO	7.0	51	53	Buffalo-Niagara Falls, NY	7.0
230	54	Jackson, MI	7.0	191	53	Gainesville, FL	7.0
45	54	New Orleans, LA	7.0	249	53	Rocky Mount, NC	7.0
95	54	Stockton-Lodi, CA	7.0	295	53	San Angelo, TX	7.0
286	58	Goldsboro, NC	6.9	294	53	Sumter, SC	7.0
282	58	Grand Junction, CO	6.9	276	59	Flagstaff, AZ-UT	6.9
98	58	Mobile, AL	6.9	293	59	Jackson, TN	6.9
55	58	West Palm Beach-Boca Raton, FL	6.9	209	59	Lake Charles, LA	6.9
227	62	Benton Harbor, MI	6.8	237	59	Parkersburg-Marietta, WV-OH	6.9
137	62	Biloxi-Gulfport-Pascagoula, MS	6.8	316	59	Pocatello, ID	6.9
118	62	Flint, MI	6.8	263	59	Texarkana, TX-Texarkana, AR	6.9
31	62	Fort Worth-Arlington, TX	6.8	179	65	Duluth-Superior, MN-WI	6.8
23	62	Miami, FL	6.8	260	65	Greenville, NC	6.8
70	62	Tucson, AZ	6.8	196	65	Longview-Marshall, TX	6.8
20	68	Tampa-St. Petersburg-Clearwater, FL	6.6	45	65	New Orleans, LA	6.8
9	69	Atlanta, GA	6.6	292	69	Danville, VA	6.7
79	69	El Paso, TX	6.6	177	69	Galveston-Texas City, TX	6.7
217	69	Las Cruces, NM	6.6	210	69	Lafayette, IN	6.7
146	69	Reno, NV	6.6	98	69	Mobile, AL	6.7
294	69	Sumter, SC	6.6	124	69	Saginaw-Bay City-Midland, MI	6.7
188	74	Asheville, NC	6.5	288	74	Anniston, AL	6.6
276	74	Flagstaff, AZ-UT	6.5	107	74	Augusta-Aiken, GA-SC	6.6
64	74	Greenville-Spartanburg-Anderson, SC	6.5	157	74	Fayetteville, NC	6.6
38	74	San Antonio, TX	6.5	82	74	Gary, IN	6.6
299	74	St. Joseph, MO	6.5	152	74	Macon, GA	6.6
				182	74	Odessa-Midland, TX	6.6
				126	74	Santa Barbara-Santa Maria-Lompoc, CA	6.6
				261	74	Steubenville-Weirton, OH-WV	6.6

TABLE 5—All Metropolitan Areas
Selected Rankings

Percent Veterans Over 18 Years, 2000

Population Rank	Veterans Rank	Metropolitan Area	[B-4. col 44] Percent Veterans
220	1	Fort Walton Beach, FL	25.0
251	2	Punta Gorda, FL	22.8
186	3	Bremerton, WA	22.3
313	4	Cheyenne, WY	21.3
108	4	Melbourne-Titusville-Palm Bay,FL	21.3
170	4	Ocala, FL	21.3
122	7	Pensacola, FL	21.1
243	8	Panama City, FL	20.1
101	9	Colorado Springs, CO	20.0
155	10	Killeen-Temple, TX	19.7
314	11	Great Falls, MT	19.6
157	12	Fayetteville, NC	19.5
284	12	Lawton, OK	19.5
103	14	Daytona Beach, FL	19.2
116	14	Fort Myers-Cape Coral, FL	19.2
90	14	Sarasota-Bradenton, FL	19.2
39	17	Norfolk-Virginia Beach-Newport News, VA-NC	18.9
76	17	Tacoma, WA	18.9
153	19	Fort Pierce-Port St. Lucie, FL	18.8
190	20	Barnstable-Yarmouth, MA	18.4
212	21	Medford-Ashland, OR	18.3
197	21	Olympia, WA	18.3
268	23	Dover, DE	18.0
57	23	Jacksonville, FL	18.0
137	25	Biloxi-Gulfport-Pascagoula, MS	17.9
199	25	Clarksville-Hopkinsville, TN-KY	17.9
175	27	Naples, FL	17.6
309	28	Rapid City, SD	17.5
165	29	Columbus, GA-AL	17.1
282	29	Grand Junction, CO	17.1
20	29	Tampa-St. Petersburg-Clearwater, FL	17.1
104	32	Lakeland-Winter Haven, FL	17.0
226	32	Redding, CA	17.0
239	34	Jacksonville, NC	16.9
96	35	Charleston-North Charleston, SC	16.8
121	35	Spokane, WA	16.8
168	37	Anchorage, AK	16.7
252	37	Pueblo, CO	16.7
256	39	Dothan, AL	16.6
300	40	Cumberland, MD-WV	16.4
288	41	Anniston, AL	16.3
40	41	Las Vegas, NV-AZ	16.3
169	41	New London-Norwich, CT	16.3
203	44	Myrtle Beach, SC	16.2
261	44	Steubenville-Weirton, OH-WV	16.2
107	46	Augusta-Aiken, GA-SC	16.0
286	46	Goldsboro, NC	16.0
294	46	Sumter, SC	16.0
70	46	Tucson, AZ	16.0
184	46	Wilmington, NC	16.0
228	46	Yuma, AZ	16.0
265	52	Altoona, PA	15.9
221	52	Topeka, KS	15.9
297	54	Lewiston-Auburn, ME	15.8
237	54	Parkersburg-Marietta, WV-OH	15.8
146	54	Reno, NV	15.8
152	57	Macon, GA	15.7
38	57	San Antonio, TX	15.7
160	57	Savannah, GA	15.7
307	60	Elmira, NY	15.6
273	60	Glens Falls, NY	15.6
100	62	Vallejo-Fairfield-Napa, CA	15.5
264	63	Billings, MT	15.4
144	63	Huntsville, AL	15.4
291	63	Sherman-Denison, TX	15.4
253	63	Wichita Falls, TX	15.4
75	67	Albuquerque, NM	15.3
318	67	Enid, OK	15.3
234	67	Wheeling, WV-OH	15.3
89	67	Youngstown-Warren, OH	15.3
65	71	Dayton-Springfield, OH	15.2
179	71	Duluth-Superior, MN-WI	15.2
183	71	Roanoke, VA	15.2
84	71	Scranton-Wilkes-Barre-Hazleton, PA	15.2
151	75	Eugene-Springfield, OR	15.1
185	75	Johnstown, PA	15.1
55	75	West Palm Beach-Boca Raton, FL	15.1
280	75	Williamsport, PA	15.1
255	75	Yuba City, CA	15.1

Median Household Income, 2000

Population Rank	Median Household Income Rank	Metropolitan Area	[B-4. col 57] Median Household Income (Dollars)
32	1	San Jose, CA	74 335
16	2	Nassau-Suffolk, NY	68 351
52	3	Middlesex-Somerset-Hunterdon, NJ	66 731
29	4	San Francisco, CA	63 297
6	5	Washington, DC-MD-VA-WV	62 216
72	6	Ventura, CA	59 666
44	7	Bergen-Passaic, NJ	59 405
21	8	Oakland, CA	59 365
14	9	Orange County, CA	58 820
26	10	Newark, NJ	56 957
141	11	Trenton, NJ	56 613
30	12	New Haven-Bridgeport-Stamford-Danbury-Waterbury, CT	56 054
161	13	Boulder-Longmont, CO	55 861
168	14	Anchorage, AK	55 546
93	15	Ann Arbor, MI	55 016
56	16	Monmouth-Ocean, NJ	54 865
13	17	Minneapolis-St. Paul, MN-WI	54 304
171	18	Santa Cruz-Watsonville, CA	53 998
100	19	Vallejo-Fairfield-Napa, CA	53 431
164	20	Dutchess County, NY	53 086
111	21	Santa Rosa, CA	53 076
19	22	Seattle-Bellevue-Everett, WA	52 804
53	23	Hartford, CT	52 603
4	24	Boston-Worcester-Lawrence-Lowell-Brockton, MA-NH	52 306
91	25	Wilmington-Newark, DE-MD	52 121
9	26	Atlanta, GA	51 948
68	27	Honolulu, HI	51 914
3	28	Chicago, IL	51 680
274	29	Rochester, MN	51 316
25	30	Denver, CO	51 191
128	31	Newburgh, NY-PA	51 151
169	32	New London-Norwich, CT	50 646
18	33	Baltimore, MD	49 938
120	34	Madison, WI	49 223
7	35	Detroit, MI	49 175
48	36	Austin-San Marcos, TX	48 950
50	37	Raleigh-Durham-Chapel Hill, NC	48 845
174	38	Fort Collins-Loveland, CO	48 655
181	39	Brazoria, TX	48 632
46	40	Salt Lake City-Ogden, UT	48 594
10	41	Dallas, TX	48 364
125	42	Salinas, CA	48 305
175	43	Naples, FL	48 289
208	44	Racine, WI	48 059
149	45	Hamilton-Middletown, OH	47 885
5	46	Philadelphia, PA-NJ	47 536
139	47	Appleton-Oshkosh-Neenah, WI	47 438
27	48	Portland-Vancouver, OR-WA	47 077
15	49	San Diego, CA	47 067
238	50	Bloomington-Normal, IL	47 021
197	51	Olympia, WA	46 975
240	52	Kenosha, WI	46 970
101	53	Colorado Springs, CO	46 844
186	54	Bremerton, WA	46 840
62	55	Richmond-Petersburg, VA	46 800
126	56	Santa Barbara-Santa Maria-Lompoc, CA	46 677
112	57	Des Moines, IA	46 651
35	58	Sacramento, CA	46 602
187	59	Green Bay, WI	46 447
287	60	Sheboygan, WI	46 237
207	61	Cedar Rapids, IA	46 206
28	62	Kansas City, MO-KS	46 193
43	63	Charlotte-Gastonia-Rock Hill, NC-SC	46 119
59	64	Grand Rapids-Muskegon-Holland, MI	46 116
202	65	Burlington, VT	46 056
31	66	Fort Worth-Arlington, TX	45 962
190	67	Barnstable-Yarmouth, MA	45 933
42	68	Milwaukee-Waukesha, WI	45 901
135	69	Provo-Orem, UT	45 833
244	70	Santa Fe, NM	45 822
146	71	Reno, NV	45 815
37	72	Indianapolis, IN	45 548
236	73	Janesville-Beloit, WI	45 517
109	74	Lancaster, PA	45 507
131	75	York, PA	45 268

TABLE 5—All Metropolitan Areas
Selected Rankings

Percent of all Households with Income Over $100,000, 2000				Percent of all Households with Income Below Poverty, 2000			
Population Rank	Households With Income over $100,000 Rank	Metropolitan Area	[B-4. col 71] Percent With Income over $100,000	Population Rank	Households With Income Below Poverty Rank	Metropolitan Area	[B-4. col 73] Percent With Income Below Poverty
32	1	San Jose, CA	34.6	94	1	McAllen-Edinburg-Mission, TX	31.9
29	2	San Francisco, CA	29.0	147	2	Brownsville-Harlingen-San Benito, TX	29.3
16	3	Nassau-Suffolk, NY	28.8	205	3	Laredo, TX	28.1
52	4	Middlesex-Somerset-Hunterdon, NJ	27.8	235	4	Bryan-College Station, TX	27.7
6	5	Washington, DC-MD-VA-WV	25.1	283	5	Auburn-Opalika, AL	25.2
44	6	Bergen-Passaic, NJ	24.9	191	6	Gainesville, FL	23.2
21	7	Oakland, CA	24.0	217	7	Las Cruces, NM	22.3
26	8	Newark, NJ	23.8	233	8	Athens, GA	21.7
30	9	New Haven-Bridgeport-Stamford-Danbury-Waterbury, CT	23.5	79	9	El Paso, TX	21.6
14	9	Orange County, CA	23.5	129	10	Lafayette, LA	21.1
141	11	Trenton, NJ	23.0	260	11	Greenville, NC	20.8
72	12	Ventura, CA	22.8	277	12	Albany, GA	19.7
171	13	Santa Cruz-Watsonville, CA	21.9	270	13	Alexandria, LA	19.5
161	14	Boulder-Longmont, CO	21.7	245	13	Monroe, LA	19.5
56	15	Monmouth-Ocean, NJ	20.9	310	13	Pine Bluff, AR	19.5
93	16	Ann Arbor, MI	19.6	289	16	Hattiesburg, MS	19.0
4	17	Boston-Worcester-Lawrence-Lowell-Brockton, MA-NH	18.9	136	16	Visalia-Tulare-Porterville, CA	19.0
168	18	Anchorage, AK	18.8	278	18	Bloomington, IN	18.9
3	19	Chicago, IL	18.2	162	19	Tallahassee, FL	18.8
68	19	Honolulu, HI	18.2	225	19	Tuscaloosa, AL	18.8
175	21	Naples, FL	18.1	154	21	Huntington-Ashland, WV-KY-OH	18.6
111	21	Santa Rosa, CA	18.1	180	22	Lubbock, TX	18.1
53	23	Hartford, CT	17.9	23	22	Miami, FL	18.1
9	24	Atlanta, GA	17.5	2	22	New York, NY	18.1
19	25	Seattle-Bellevue-Everett, WA	17.4	66	25	Fresno, CA	18.0
164	26	Dutchess County, NY	17.2	127	25	Shreveport-Bossier City, LA	18.0
100	27	Vallejo-Fairfield-Napa, CA	17.0	195	27	Merced, CA	17.8
13	28	Minneapolis-St. Paul, MN-WI	16.9	80	28	Bakersfield, CA	17.7
10	29	Dallas, TX	16.8	257	28	State College, PA	17.7
91	30	Wilmington-Newark, DE-MD	16.6	200	30	Chico-Paradise, CA	17.6
25	31	Denver, CO	16.5	194	30	Waco, TX	17.6
55	32	West Palm Beach-Boca Raton, FL	16.2	45	32	New Orleans, LA	17.4
7	33	Detroit, MI	16.1	263	32	Texarkana, TX-Texarkana, AR	17.4
2	34	New York, NY	16.0	204	34	Houma, LA	17.2
126	34	Santa Barbara-Santa Maria-Lompoc, CA	16.0	302	35	Lawrence, KS	17.1
18	36	Baltimore, MD	15.9	288	36	Anniston, AL	16.9
5	36	Philadelphia, PA-NJ	15.9	132	37	Corpus Christi, TX	16.8
50	36	Raleigh-Durham-Chapel Hill, NC	15.9	222	37	Yolo, CA	16.8
48	39	Austin-San Marcos, TX	15.8	189	39	Yakima, WA	16.4
15	40	San Diego, CA	15.7	272	40	Florence, SC	16.3
244	41	Santa Fe, NM	15.6	294	40	Sumter, SC	16.3
8	42	Houston, TX	15.4	298	42	Gadsden, AL	16.2
128	43	Newburgh, NY-PA	15.2	98	43	Mobile, AL	16.1
125	43	Salinas, CA	15.2	88	44	Baton Rouge, LA	16.0
1	45	Los Angeles-Long Beach, CA	15.1	214	44	Champaign-Urbana, IL	16.0
274	45	Rochester, MN	15.1	312	44	Jonesboro, AR	16.0
169	47	New London-Norwich, CT	14.5	292	47	Danville, VA	15.9
35	48	Sacramento, CA	14.1	256	47	Dothan, AL	15.9
174	49	Fort Collins-Loveland, CO	13.9	249	47	Rocky Mount, NC	15.9
181	50	Brazoria, TX	13.6	209	50	Lake Charles, LA	15.8
238	51	Bloomington-Normal, IL	13.5	234	50	Wheeling, WV-OH	15.8
31	52	Fort Worth-Arlington, TX	13.3	228	50	Yuma, AZ	15.8
62	52	Richmond-Petersburg, VA	13.3	130	53	Beaumont-Port Arthur, TX	15.7
43	54	Charlotte-Gastonia-Rock Hill, NC-SC	13.1	276	53	Flagstaff, AZ-UT	15.7
27	54	Portland-Vancouver, OR-WA	13.1	255	55	Yuba City, CA	15.6
177	56	Galveston-Texas City, TX	13.0	165	56	Columbus, GA-AL	15.5
120	56	Madison, WI	13.0	250	56	Florence, AL	15.5
222	56	Yolo, CA	13.0	290	56	Iowa City, IA	15.5
149	59	Hamilton-Middletown, OH	12.9	304	56	Missoula, MT	15.5
12	59	Phoenix-Mesa, AZ	12.9	284	60	Lawton, OK	15.4
146	59	Reno, NV	12.9	281	60	Muncie, IN	15.4
229	62	Charlottesville, VA	12.8	86	62	Jersey City, NJ	15.3
36	62	Fort Lauderdale, FL	12.8	105	62	Johnson City-Kingsport-Bristol, TN-VA	15.3
86	62	Jersey City, NJ	12.8	196	62	Longview-Marshall, TX	15.3
33	65	Cincinnati, OH-KY-IN	12.6	182	62	Odessa-Midland, TX	15.3
37	65	Indianapolis, IN	12.6	258	66	Columbia, MO	15.2
46	65	Salt Lake City-Ogden, UT	12.6	300	66	Cumberland, MD-WV	15.2
315	68	Corvallis, OR	12.5	1	68	Los Angeles-Long Beach, CA	15.1
28	68	Kansas City, MO-KS	12.5	152	68	Macon, GA	15.1
190	70	Barnstable-Yarmouth, MA	12.4	117	70	Jackson, MS	15.0
42	70	Milwaukee-Waukesha, WI	12.4	295	71	San Angelo, TX	14.9
41	72	Columbus, OH	12.3	198	72	Fort Smith, AR-OK	14.8
144	72	Huntsville, AL	12.3	315	73	Corvallis, OR	14.6
101	74	Colorado Springs, CO	12.2	54	74	Memphis, TN-AR-MS	14.5
17	74	St. Louis, MO-IL	12.2	252	74	Pueblo, CO	14.5
				95	74	Stockton-Lodi, CA	14.5

TABLE 5—All Metropolitan Areas
Selected Rankings

Percent of Population that Resides in the Same House in 1995 and 2000				Percent Owner-Occupied Housing Units, 2000			
Population Rank	Same Residence Rank	Metropolitan Area	[C-4. col 2] Percent Same Residence	Population Rank	Owner-Occupied Rank	Metropolitan Area	[C-4. col 8] Percent Owner-Occupied
185	1	Johnstown, PA	71.4	251	1	Punta Gorda, FL	83.7
261	2	Steubenville-Weirton, OH-WV	68.8	16	2	Nassau-Suffolk, NY	80.0
84	3	Scranton-Wilkes-Barre-Hazleton, PA	68.3	170	3	Ocala, FL	79.8
16	4	Nassau-Suffolk, NY	67.2	153	4	Fort Pierce-Port St. Lucie, FL	78.8
265	5	Altoona, PA	66.7	56	5	Monmouth-Ocean, NJ	78.7
22	6	Pittsburgh, PA	66.4	190	6	Barnstable-Yarmouth, MA	77.8
234	7	Wheeling, WV-OH	66.2	90	7	Sarasota-Bradenton, FL	76.8
279	8	Sharon, PA	65.3	204	8	Houma, LA	76.7
300	9	Cumberland, MD-WV	65.1	116	9	Fort Myers-Cape Coral, FL	76.5
204	10	Houma, LA	64.5	230	9	Jackson, MI	76.5
158	11	Utica-Rome, NY	64.1	124	11	Saginaw-Bay City-Midland, MI	76.3
89	11	Youngstown-Warren, OH	64.1	103	12	Daytona Beach, FL	76.2
51	13	Buffalo-Niagara Falls, NY	63.5	279	12	Sharon, PA	76.2
292	13	Danville, VA	63.5	131	14	York, PA	76.1
273	15	Glens Falls, NY	62.2	274	15	Rochester, MN	76.0
123	16	Canton-Massillon, OH	62.1	185	16	Johnstown, PA	75.9
173	16	Charleston, WV	62.1	271	17	Wausau, WI	75.7
5	16	Philadelphia, PA-NJ	62.1	175	18	Naples, FL	75.6
124	16	Saginaw-Bay City-Midland, MI	62.1	247	19	Decatur, AL	75.5
271	20	Wausau, WI	61.7	261	20	Steubenville-Weirton, OH-WV	75.4
44	21	Bergen-Passaic, NJ	61.6	59	21	Grand Rapids-Muskegon-Holland, MI	74.9
298	21	Gadsden, AL	61.6	55	22	West Palm Beach-Boca Raton, FL	74.7
154	21	Huntington-Ashland, WV-KY-OH	61.6	108	23	Melbourne-Titusville-Palm Bay, FL	74.6
237	21	Parkersburg-Marietta, WV-OH	61.6	237	23	Parkersburg-Marietta, WV-OH	74.6
259	25	Pittsfield, MA	61.5	298	25	Gadsden, AL	74.4
2	26	New York, NY	61.2	145	26	Hickory-Morganton-Lenoir, NC	74.3
94	27	McAllen-Edinburg Mission, TX	61.1	250	27	Florence, AL	74.2
133	27	Reading, PA	61.1	105	27	Johnson City-Kingsport-Bristol, TN-VA	74.2
81	29	Allentown-Bethlehem-Easton, PA	61.0	179	29	Duluth-Superior, MN-WI	74.1
280	29	Williamsport, PA	61.0	181	30	Brazoria, TX	74.0
179	31	Duluth-Superior, MN-WI	60.9	133	30	Reading, PA	74.0
254	31	Jamestown, NY	60.9	102	32	Fort Wayne, IN	73.9
246	31	Vineland-Millville-Bridgeton, NJ	60.9	193	32	Lynchburg, VA	73.9
250	34	Florence, AL	60.8	89	32	Youngstown-Warren, OH	73.9
56	34	Monmouth-Ocean, NJ	60.8	232	35	Lima, OH	73.8
172	36	Binghamton, NY	60.6	234	36	Wheeling, WV-OH	73.6
82	36	Gary, IN	60.6	308	37	Dubuque, IA	73.5
215	36	Mansfield, OH	60.6	104	38	Lakeland-Winter Haven, FL	73.4
24	39	Cleveland-Lorain-Elyria, OH	60.3	118	39	Flint, MI	73.2
163	40	Erie, PA	60.2	94	40	McAllen-Edinburg-Mission, TX	73.1
109	40	Lancaster, PA	60.2	272	41	Florence, SC	73.0
131	40	York, PA	60.2	154	41	Huntington-Ashland, WV-KY-OH	73.0
308	43	Dubuque, IA	60.0	301	41	Kokomo, IN	73.0
307	43	Elmira, NY	60.0	203	41	Myrtle Beach, SC	73.0
232	43	Lima, OH	60.0	265	45	Altoona, PA	72.9
270	46	Alexandria, LA	59.9	123	45	Canton-Massillon, OH	72.9
26	46	Newark, NJ	59.9	173	45	Charleston, WV	72.9
83	48	Harrisburg-Lebanon-Carlisle, PA	59.7	207	48	Cedar Rapids, IA	72.7
69	49	Albany-Schenectady-Troy, NY	59.6	282	48	Grand Junction, CO	72.7
272	49	Florence, SC	59.6	288	50	Anniston, AL	72.5
105	49	Johnson City-Kingsport-Bristol, TN-VA	59.6	7	51	Detroit, MI	72.4
129	49	Lafayette, LA	59.6	13	51	Minneapolis-St. Paul, MN-WI	72.4
45	49	New Orleans, LA	59.6	142	53	Peoria-Pekin, IL	72.3
164	54	Dutchess County, NY	59.5	223	53	St. Cloud, MN	72.3
287	55	Sheboygan, WI	59.3	227	55	Benton Harbor, MI	72.2
73	55	Syracuse, NY	59.3	300	55	Cumberland, MD-WV	72.2
230	57	Jackson, MI	59.0	211	55	Elkhart-Goshen, IN	72.2
128	57	Newburgh, NY-PA	59.0	228	55	Yuma, AZ	72.2
247	59	Decatur, AL	58.9	273	59	Glens Falls, NY	72.0
145	59	Hickory-Morganton-Lenoir, NC	58.9	215	60	Mansfield, OH	71.8
205	61	Laredo, TX	58.8	285	61	Decatur, IL	71.7
58	61	Rochester, NY	58.8	98	61	Mobile, AL	71.7
140	63	Atlantic-Cape May, NJ	58.7	167	61	South Bend, IN	71.7
193	63	Lynchburg, VA	58.7	81	64	Allentown-Bethlehem-Easton, PA	71.6
147	65	Brownsville-Harlingen-San Benito, TX	58.5	149	64	Hamilton-Middletown, OH	71.6
7	65	Detroit, MI	58.5	134	64	Rockford, IL	71.6
248	67	Bangor, ME	58.4	64	67	Greenville-Spartanburg-Anderson, SC	71.5
130	67	Beaumont-Port Arthur, TX	58.4	209	67	Lake Charles, LA	71.5
53	69	Hartford, CT	58.3	119	69	Boise City, ID	71.4
63	69	Providence-Warwick-Pawtucket, RI	58.3	287	69	Sheboygan, WI	71.4
4	71	Boston-Worcester-Lawrence-Lowell-Brockton, MA-NH	58.0	17	69	St. Louis, MO-IL	71.4
30	72	New Haven-Bridgeport-Stamford-Danbury-Waterbury, CT	57.9	139	72	Appleton-Oshkosh-Neenah, WI	71.3
142	72	Peoria-Pekin, IL	57.9	138	72	Davenport-Moline-Rock Island, IA-IL	71.3
77	74	Akron, OH	57.8	22	72	Pittsburgh, PA	71.3
227	75	Benton Harbor, MI	57.7	46	72	Salt Lake City-Ogden, UT	71.3

TABLE 5—All Metropolitan Areas
Selected Rankings

		Median Housing Value (Owner Estimated), 2000				Median Gross Rent, 2000	
Popu-lation Rank	Median Housing Value Rank	Metropolitan Area	[C-4. col 22] Median Housing Value (Dollars)	Popu-lation Rank	Median Gross Rent Rank	Metropolitan Area	[C-4. col 25] Median Gross Rent (Dollars)
29	1	San Francisco, CA	449 400	32	1	San Jose, CA	1 185
32	2	San Jose, CA	422 600	29	2	San Francisco, CA	1 023
171	3	Santa Cruz-Watsonville, CA	353 300	16	3	Nassau-Suffolk, NY	954
21	4	Oakland, CA	277 400	171	4	Santa Cruz-Watsonville, CA	924
68	5	Honolulu, HI	274 600	14	5	Orange County, CA	923
111	6	Santa Rosa, CA	265 200	72	6	Ventura, CA	892
126	7	Santa Barbara-Santa Maria-Lompoc, CA	264 100	21	7	Oakland, CA	868
125	8	Salinas, CA	254 800	111	8	Santa Rosa, CA	864
14	9	Orange County, CA	253 000	52	9	Middlesex-Somerset-Hunterdon, NJ	858
72	10	Ventura, CA	238 800	126	10	Santa Barbara-Santa Maria-Lompoc, CA	830
161	11	Boulder-Longmont, CO	231 000	161	11	Boulder-Longmont, CO	825
2	12	New York, NY	230 400	44	12	Bergen-Passaic, NJ	822
44	13	Bergen-Passaic, NJ	222 700	6	13	Washington, DC-MD-VA-WV	811
178	14	San Luis Obispo-Atascadero-Paso Robles, CA	218 600	68	14	Honolulu, HI	802
16	15	Nassau-Suffolk, NY	212 600	100	14	Vallejo-Fairfield-Napa, CA	802
15	16	San Diego, CA	212 000	56	16	Monmouth-Ocean, NJ	780
19	17	Seattle-Bellevue-Everett, WA	211 700	125	17	Salinas, CA	776
1	18	Los Angeles-Long Beach, CA	201 400	15	18	San Diego, CA	761
26	19	Newark, NJ	196 200	19	19	Seattle-Bellevue-Everett, WA	758
30	20	New Haven-Bridgeport-Stamford-Danbury-Waterbury, CT	189 000	36	20	Fort Lauderdale, FL	757
100	21	Vallejo-Fairfield-Napa, CA	187 200	175	21	Naples, FL	753
4	22	Boston-Worcester-Lawrence-Lowell-Brockton, MA-NH	186 000	9	22	Atlanta, GA	746
52	23	Middlesex-Somerset-Hunterdon, NJ	180 600	55	23	West Palm Beach-Boca Raton, FL	739
190	24	Barnstable-Yarmouth, MA	178 000	168	24	Anchorage, AK	736
244	25	Santa Fe, NM	174 900	26	25	Newark, NJ	729
6	26	Washington, DC-MD-VA-WV	172 900	141	26	Trenton, NJ	727
25	27	Denver, CO	170 900	30	27	New Haven-Bridgeport-Stamford-Danbury-Waterbury, CT	726
174	28	Fort Collins-Loveland, CO	168 200	190	28	Barnstable-Yarmouth, MA	723
27	29	Portland-Vancouver, OR-WA	167 100	48	29	Austin-San Marcos, TX	721
315	30	Corvallis, OR	166 500	178	30	San Luis Obispo-Atascadero-Paso Robles, CA	719
222	31	Yolo, CA	164 400	2	31	New York, NY	715
93	32	Ann Arbor, MI	163 800	128	32	Newburgh, NY-PA	713
86	33	Jersey City, NJ	162 800	4	33	Boston-Worcester-Lawrence-Lowell-Brockton, MA-NH	707
3	34	Chicago, IL	161 700	164	33	Dutchess County, NY	707
56	35	Monmouth-Ocean, NJ	156 200	1	35	Los Angeles-Long Beach, CA	704
35	36	Sacramento, CA	155 600	86	36	Jersey City, NJ	703
135	37	Provo-Orem, UT	153 600	40	36	Las Vegas, NV-AZ	703
168	38	Anchorage, AK	152 300	25	38	Denver, CO	700
164	39	Dutchess County, NY	150 800	34	39	Orlando, FL	698
224	40	Bellingham, WA	149 500	244	40	Santa Fe, NM	688
146	40	Reno, NV	149 500	222	41	Yolo, CA	687
175	42	Naples, FL	149 000	50	42	Raleigh-Durham-Chapel Hill, NC	686
46	43	Salt Lake City-Ogden, UT	148 300	174	43	Fort Collins-Loveland, CO	678
120	44	Madison, WI	146 600	146	44	Reno, NV	675
53	45	Hartford, CT	146 300	90	45	Sarasota-Bradenton, FL	673
186	46	Bremerton, WA	145 200	27	46	Portland-Vancouver, OR-WA	672
76	47	Tacoma, WA	144 400	35	46	Sacramento, CA	672
101	48	Colorado Springs, CO	143 600	140	48	Atlantic-Cape May, NJ	671
141	48	Trenton, NJ	143 600	3	49	Chicago, IL	669
95	50	Stockton-Lodi, CA	139 800	186	50	Bremerton, WA	667
169	51	New London-Norwich, CT	139 700	10	50	Dallas, TX	667
13	52	Minneapolis-St. Paul, MN-WI	139 200	91	50	Wilmington-Newark, DE-MD	667
197	53	Olympia, WA	138 800	93	53	Ann Arbor, MI	665
50	54	Raleigh-Durham-Chapel Hill, NC	138 500	229	54	Charlottesville, VA	661
128	55	Newburgh, NY-PA	137 800	12	54	Phoenix-Mesa, AZ	661
213	56	Greeley, CO	136 600	101	56	Colorado Springs, CO	657
151	57	Eugene-Springfield, OR	136 000	197	57	Olympia, WA	655
229	58	Charlottesville, VA	135 600	53	58	Hartford, CT	653
9	59	Atlanta, GA	132 600	11	58	Riverside-San Bernardino, CA	653
91	60	Wilmington-Newark, DE-MD	132 500	5	60	Philadelphia, PA-NJ	648
18	61	Baltimore, MD	132 400	23	61	Miami, FL	647
212	62	Medford-Ashland, OR	132 100	116	62	Fort Myers-Cape Coral, FL	646
143	63	Salem, OR	131 600	169	62	New London-Norwich, CT	646
42	64	Milwaukee-Waukesha, WI	130 800	120	64	Madison, WI	641
166	65	Portland, ME	129 800	13	64	Minneapolis-St. Paul, MN-WI	641
11	66	Riverside-San Bernardino, CA	129 700	202	66	Burlington, VT	636
304	67	Missoula, MT	128 700	43	67	Charlotte-Gastonia-Rock Hill, NC-SC	627
202	68	Burlington, VT	128 100	18	68	Baltimore, MD	626
7	69	Detroit, MI	127 800	153	68	Fort Pierce-Port St. Lucie, FL	626
63	70	Providence-Warwick-Pawtucket, RI	127 600	251	68	Punta Gorda, FL	626
40	71	Las Vegas, NV-AZ	125 700	46	71	Salt Lake City-Ogden, UT	625
115	72	Modesto, CA	123 900	276	72	Flagstaff, AZ-UT	624
290	73	Iowa City, IA	123 700	76	72	Tacoma, WA	624
140	74	Atlantic-Cape May, NJ	123 400	224	74	Bellingham, WA	622
276	75	Flagstaff, AZ-UT	122 300	95	75	Stockton-Lodi, CA	617

TABLE 6—75 Largest Cities by 2000 Population
Selected Rankings

Population, 2000			Percent Under 18 Years, 2000				Percent 18 to 24 Years, 2000			
Population Rank	City	[A-5. col 1] Population	Population Rank	Under 18 Years Rank	City	[A-5. col 2 and 3] Percent Under 18 Years	Population Rank	18 to 24 Years Rank	City	[A-5. col 4] Percent 18 to 24 Years
1	New York City, NY	8 008 278	51	1	Santa Ana city, CA	34.1	73	1	Norfolk city, VA	18.3
2	Los Angeles city, CA	3 694 834	37	2	Fresno city, CA	32.8	74	2	Baton Rouge city, LA	17.4
3	Chicago city, IL	2 895 964	69	3	Bakersfield city, CA	32.6	16	3	Austin city, TX	16.4
4	Houston city, TX	1 954 848	71	4	Stockton city, CA	32.2	20	4	Boston city, MA	16.2
5	Philadelphia city, PA	1 517 550	10	5	Detroit city, MI	31.1	61	5	Raleigh city, NC	16.1
6	Phoenix city, AZ	1 320 994	23	6	El Paso city, TX	30.9	52	6	Pittsburgh city, PA	14.7
7	San Diego city, CA	1 223 341	55	7	Anaheim city, CA	30.2	64	7	Lexington-Fayette, KY	14.5
8	Dallas city, TX	1 188 204	67	8	Riverside city, CA	30.0	45	8	Minneapolis city, MN	14.4
9	San Antonio city, TX	1 144 554	65	9	Anchorage city, AK	29.1	15	9	Columbus city, OH	13.9
10	Detroit city, MI	951 270	34	10	Long Beach city, CA	29.0	30	10	Tucson city, AZ	13.7
11	San Jose city, CA	893 889	6	11	Phoenix city, AZ	28.9	39	11	Atlanta city, GA	13.3
12	Indianapolis consolidated city, IN	792 217	19	12	Milwaukee city, WI	28.7	51	12	Santa Ana city, CA	12.9
13	San Francisco city, CA	776 733	33	13	Cleveland city, OH	28.5	54	13	Cincinnati city, OH	12.8
14	Jacksonville, FL	735 503	9	14	San Antonio city, TX	28.4	21	13	Washington city, DC	12.8
15	Columbus city, OH	711 644	53	15	Arlington city, TX	28.2	67	15	Riverside city, CA	12.7
16	Austin city, TX	656 302	27	16	Fort Worth city, TX	28.1	7	16	San Diego city, CA	12.4
17	Baltimore city, MD	651 154	60	17	Corpus Christi city, TX	28.0	59	17	St. Paul city, MN	12.3
18	Memphis city, TN	649 845	18	18	Memphis city, TN	27.8	19	18	Milwaukee city, WI	12.1
19	Milwaukee city, WI	596 956	63	18	Newark city, NJ	27.8	63	18	Newark city, NJ	12.1
20	Boston city, MA	589 141	62	20	Aurora city, CO	27.6	8	20	Dallas city, TX	11.8
21	Washington city, DC	572 059	4	21	Houston city, TX	27.4	37	20	Fresno city, CA	11.8
22	Nashville-Davidson consolidated city, TN	569 891	38	21	Virginia Beach city, VA	27.4	24	20	Seattle city, WA	11.8
23	El Paso city, TX	564 280	42	23	Mesa city, AZ	27.3	22	23	Nashville-Davidson consolidated city, TN	11.5
24	Seattle city, WA	563 375	40	24	Sacramento city, CA	27.2	31	24	New Orleans city, LA	11.3
25	Denver city, CO	554 636	59	25	St. Paul city, MN	27.0	70	25	Birmingham city, AL	11.2
26	Charlotte city, NC	542 131	50	25	Wichita city, KS	27.0	58	25	Buffalo city, NY	11.2
27	Fort Worth city, TX	535 420	14	27	Jacksonville, FL	26.7	3	25	Chicago city, IL	11.2
28	Portland city, OR	529 025	31	27	New Orleans city, LA	26.7	27	25	Fort Worth city, TX	11.2
29	Oklahoma City, OK	505 963	48	29	Colorado Springs city, CO	26.5	4	25	Houston city, TX	11.2
30	Tucson city, AZ	486 591	8	29	Dallas city, TX	26.5	44	30	Omaha city, NE	11.1
31	New Orleans city, LA	484 674	2	29	Los Angeles city, CA	26.5	5	30	Philadelphia city, PA	11.1
32	Las Vegas city, NV	478 868	11	32	San Jose city, CA	26.4	2	32	Los Angeles city, CA	11.0
33	Cleveland city, OH	478 393	58	33	Buffalo city, NY	26.3	42	32	Mesa city, AZ	11.0
34	Long Beach city, CA	461 381	3	34	Chicago city, IL	26.1	56	32	Toledo city, OH	11.0
35	Albuquerque city, NM	448 627	56	34	Toledo city, OH	26.1	43	32	Tulsa city, OK	11.0
36	Kansas City, MO	441 269	12	36	Indianapolis consolidated city, IN	25.7	6	36	Phoenix city, AZ	10.9
37	Fresno city, CA	427 224	32	36	Las Vegas city, NV	25.7	17	37	Baltimore city, MD	10.8
38	Virginia Beach city, VA	425 257	49	36	St. Louis city, MO	25.7	34	37	Long Beach city, CA	10.8
39	Atlanta city, GA	416 629	44	39	Omaha city, NE	25.6	18	37	Memphis city, TN	10.8
40	Sacramento city, CA	407 075	29	40	Oklahoma City, OK	25.5	71	37	Stockton city, CA	10.8
41	Oakland city, CA	399 477	36	41	Kansas City, MO	25.3	53	41	Arlington city, TX	10.7
42	Mesa city, AZ	397 215	5	42	Philadelphia city, PA	25.2	25	41	Denver city, CO	10.7
43	Tulsa city, OK	393 051	70	43	Birmingham city, AL	25.1	9	41	San Antonio city, TX	10.7
44	Omaha city, NE	390 112	41	44	Oakland city, CA	24.9	35	44	Albuquerque city, NM	10.6
45	Minneapolis city, MN	382 452	17	45	Baltimore city, MD	24.7	60	44	Corpus Christi city, TX	10.6
46	Honolulu CDP, HI	371 619	26	45	Charlotte city, NC	24.7	72	44	Jersey City, NJ	10.6
47	Miami city, FL	362 563	72	47	Jersey City, NJ	24.6	29	44	Oklahoma City, OK	10.6
48	Colorado Springs city, CO	360 798	57	47	Tampa city, FL	24.6	49	44	St. Louis city, MO	10.6
49	St. Louis city, MO	348 189	43	47	Tulsa city, OK	24.6	55	49	Anaheim city, CA	10.4
50	Wichita city, KS	343 997	54	50	Cincinnati city, OH	24.5	26	50	Charlotte city, NC	10.3
51	Santa Ana city, CA	337 512	35	51	Albuquerque city, NM	24.4	48	51	Colorado Springs city, CO	10.2
52	Pittsburgh city, PA	334 563	74	51	Baton Rouge city, LA	24.4	66	51	Louisville city, KY	10.2
53	Arlington city, TX	332 695	30	51	Tucson city, AZ	24.4	28	51	Portland city, OR	10.2
54	Cincinnati city, OH	330 662	1	54	New York City, NY	24.2	40	51	Sacramento city, CA	10.2
55	Anaheim city, CA	327 357	15	55	Columbus city, OH	24.1	12	55	Indianapolis consolidated city, IN	10.1
56	Toledo city, OH	313 587	73	56	Norfolk city, VA	24.0	50	55	Wichita city, KS	10.1
57	Tampa city, FL	303 512	7	57	San Diego city, CA	23.9	62	57	Aurora city, CO	10.0
58	Buffalo city, NY	292 648	66	58	Louisville city, KY	23.7	69	57	Bakersfield city, CA	10.0
59	St. Paul city, MN	287 151	75	59	Hialeah city, FL	23.0	1	57	New York City, NY	10.0
60	Corpus Christi city, TX	277 569	16	60	Austin city, TX	22.5	57	60	Tampa city, FL	9.9
61	Raleigh city, NC	276 579	39	61	Atlanta city, GA	22.3	38	60	Virginia Beach city, VA	9.9
62	Aurora city, CO	275 936	22	62	Nashville-Davidson consolidated city, TN	22.2	23	62	El Paso city, TX	9.8
63	Newark city, NJ	273 546	45	63	Minneapolis city, MN	21.9	11	62	San Jose city, CA	9.8
64	Lexington-Fayette, KY	260 512	25	64	Denver city, CO	21.8	14	64	Jacksonville, FL	9.7
65	Anchorage city, AK	260 283	47	65	Miami city, FL	21.7	41	64	Oakland city, CA	9.7
66	Louisville city, KY	256 420	68	66	St. Petersburg city, FL	21.5	10	66	Detroit city, MI	9.6
67	Riverside city, CA	255 093	64	67	Lexington-Fayette, KY	21.3	36	66	Kansas City, MO	9.6
68	St. Petersburg city, FL	247 793	28	68	Portland city, OR	21.0	65	68	Anchorage city, AK	9.5
69	Bakersfield city, CA	247 385	61	69	Raleigh city, NC	20.8	33	68	Cleveland city, OH	9.5
70	Birmingham city, AL	243 072	21	70	Washington city, DC	20.0	46	70	Honolulu CDP, HI	8.9
71	Stockton city, CA	242 714	52	71	Pittsburgh city, PA	19.8	13	70	San Francisco city, CA	8.9
72	Jersey City, NJ	240 055	20	72	Boston city, MA	19.7	32	72	Las Vegas city, NV	8.8
73	Norfolk city, VA	234 403	46	73	Honolulu CDP, HI	19.1	47	73	Miami city, FL	8.6
74	Baton Rouge city, LA	227 920	24	74	Seattle city, WA	15.5	75	74	Hialeah city, FL	8.2
75	Hialeah city, FL	226 411	13	75	San Francisco city, CA	14.4	68	75	St. Petersburg city, FL	7.8

TABLE 6—75 Largest Cities by 2000 Population
Selected Rankings

Percent 25 to 44 Years, 2000				Percent 45 to 64 Years, 2000				Percent 65 Years and Over, 2000			
Population Rank	25 to 44 Years Rank	City	[A-4. col 5] Percent 25 to 44 Years	Population Rank	45 to 64 Years Rank	City	[A-5. col 6] Percent 45 to 64 Years	Population Rank	65 Years and Over Rank	City	[A-5. col 7] Percent 65 Years and Over
13	1	San Francisco city, CA	41.0	46	1	Honolulu CDP, HI	24.1	46	1	Honolulu CDP, HI	18.0
24	2	Seattle city, WA	38.9	68	2	St. Petersburg city, FL	23.1	68	2	St. Petersburg city, FL	17.5
16	3	Austin city, TX	37.5	75	3	Hialeah city, FL	22.9	47	3	Miami city, FL	17.0
45	4	Minneapolis city, MN	36.9	28	4	Portland city, OR	22.3	75	4	Hialeah city, FL	16.5
61	5	Raleigh city, NC	36.6	13	5	San Francisco city, CA	22.0	52	5	Pittsburgh city, PA	16.4
25	6	Denver city, CO	36.5	35	6	Albuquerque city, NM	21.9	66	6	Louisville city, KY	14.6
26	7	Charlotte city, NC	36.4	65	6	Anchorage city, AK	21.9	5	7	Philadelphia city, PA	14.1
53	8	Arlington city, TX	36.1	47	8	Miami city, FL	21.8	13	8	San Francisco city, CA	13.8
20	9	Boston city, MA	35.9	21	8	Washington city, DC	21.8	49	9	St. Louis city, MO	13.7
11	9	San Jose city, CA	35.9	24	10	Seattle city, WA	21.7	70	10	Birmingham city, AL	13.6
8	11	Dallas city, TX	35.6	32	11	Las Vegas city, NV	21.6	58	11	Buffalo city, NY	13.5
39	12	Atlanta city, GA	35.4	29	12	Oklahoma City, OK	21.4	42	12	Mesa city, AZ	13.3
15	12	Columbus city, OH	35.4	43	13	Tulsa city, OK	21.3	17	13	Baltimore city, MD	13.2
72	14	Jersey City, NJ	35.0	1	14	New York City, NY	21.2	56	13	Toledo city, OH	13.2
62	15	Aurora city, CO	34.9	17	15	Baltimore city, MD	21.1	43	15	Tulsa city, OK	12.8
28	15	Portland city, OR	34.9	60	16	Corpus Christi city, TX	21.0	33	16	Cleveland city, OH	12.6
38	17	Virginia Beach city, VA	34.6	14	16	Jacksonville, FL	21.0	57	17	Tampa city, FL	12.5
7	18	San Diego city, CA	34.4	22	16	Nashville-Davidson consolidated city, TN	21.0	54	18	Cincinnati city, OH	12.3
2	19	Los Angeles city, CA	34.3	48	19	Colorado Springs city, CO	20.9	21	18	Washington city, DC	12.3
65	20	Anchorage city, AK	34.2	64	19	Lexington-Fayette, KY	20.9	24	20	Seattle city, WA	12.1
22	20	Nashville-Davidson consolidated city, TN	34.2	31	19	New Orleans city, LA	20.9	30	21	Tucson city, AZ	12.0
41	20	Oakland city, CA	34.2	66	22	Louisville city, KY	20.8	35	22	Albuquerque city, NM	11.9
4	23	Houston city, TX	34.1	41	22	Oakland city, CA	20.8	50	22	Wichita city, KS	11.9
51	24	Santa Ana city, CA	34.0	36	24	Kansas City, MO	20.6	44	24	Omaha city, NE	11.8
55	25	Anaheim city, CA	33.7	44	24	Omaha city, NE	20.6	36	25	Kansas City, MO	11.7
3	26	Chicago city, IL	33.6	57	26	Tampa city, FL	20.5	31	25	New Orleans city, LA	11.7
6	27	Phoenix city, AZ	33.4	52	27	Pittsburgh city, PA	20.4	1	25	New York City, NY	11.7
64	28	Lexington-Fayette, KY	33.3	12	28	Indianapolis consolidated city, IN	20.3	28	28	Portland city, OR	11.6
34	28	Long Beach city, CA	33.3	62	29	Aurora city, CO	20.2	74	29	Baton Rouge city, LA	11.5
21	30	Washington city, DC	33.2	70	30	Birmingham city, AL	20.1	32	29	Las Vegas city, NV	11.5
27	31	Fort Worth city, TX	33.1	5	30	Philadelphia city, PA	20.1	29	29	Oklahoma City, OK	11.5
12	32	Indianapolis consolidated city, IN	33.0	26	32	Charlotte city, NC	20.0	40	32	Sacramento city, CA	11.4
1	32	New York City, NY	33.0	72	32	Jersey City, NJ	20.0	25	33	Denver city, CO	11.2
48	34	Colorado Springs city, CO	32.9	40	32	Sacramento city, CA	20.0	22	33	Nashville-Davidson consolidated city, TN	11.2
36	35	Kansas City, MO	32.8	50	32	Wichita city, KS	20.0	60	35	Corpus Christi city, TX	11.1
59	36	St. Paul city, MN	32.5	25	36	Denver city, CO	19.8	12	35	Indianapolis consolidated city, IN	11.1
14	37	Jacksonville, FL	32.4	11	36	San Jose city, CA	19.8	18	37	Memphis city, TN	10.9
32	37	Las Vegas city, NV	32.4	38	38	Virginia Beach city, VA	19.7	19	37	Milwaukee city, WI	10.9
57	37	Tampa city, FL	32.4	18	39	Memphis city, TN	19.6	73	37	Norfolk city, VA	10.9
63	40	Newark city, NJ	32.1	56	39	Toledo city, OH	19.6	23	40	El Paso city, TX	10.7
54	41	Cincinnati city, OH	31.8	58	41	Buffalo city, NY	19.5	20	41	Boston city, MA	10.5
35	42	Albuquerque city, NM	31.2	74	42	Baton Rouge city, LA	19.3	10	41	Detroit city, MI	10.5
40	42	Sacramento city, CA	31.2	10	43	Detroit city, MI	19.2	41	41	Oakland city, CA	10.5
9	42	San Antonio city, TX	31.2	23	43	El Paso city, TX	19.2	9	44	San Antonio city, TX	10.4
49	42	St. Louis city, MO	31.2	9	43	San Antonio city, TX	19.2	7	44	San Diego city, CA	10.4
44	46	Omaha city, NE	31.0	39	46	Atlanta city, GA	19.1	59	44	St. Paul city, MN	10.4
30	46	Tucson city, AZ	31.0	53	47	Arlington city, TX	19.0	71	44	Stockton city, CA	10.4
50	46	Wichita city, KS	31.0	4	47	Houston city, TX	19.0	3	48	Chicago city, IL	10.3
29	49	Oklahoma City, OK	30.9	30	47	Tucson city, AZ	19.0	14	48	Jacksonville, FL	10.3
18	50	Memphis city, TN	30.8	7	50	San Diego city, CA	18.9	64	50	Lexington-Fayette, KY	10.0
47	50	Miami city, FL	30.8	3	51	Chicago city, IL	18.8	39	51	Atlanta city, GA	9.9
33	52	Cleveland city, OH	30.7	33	51	Cleveland city, OH	18.8	72	52	Jersey City, NJ	9.7
66	52	Louisville city, KY	30.7	49	51	St. Louis city, MO	18.8	2	52	Los Angeles city, CA	9.7
19	54	Milwaukee city, WI	30.4	71	51	Stockton city, CA	18.8	48	54	Colorado Springs city, CO	9.6
67	54	Riverside city, CA	30.4	6	55	Phoenix city, AZ	18.7	27	55	Fort Worth city, TX	9.5
43	56	Tulsa city, OK	30.3	69	56	Bakersfield city, CA	18.6	63	56	Newark city, NJ	9.3
69	57	Bakersfield city, CA	30.1	54	56	Cincinnati city, OH	18.6	37	57	Fresno city, CA	9.1
17	57	Baltimore city, MD	30.1	63	56	Newark city, NJ	18.6	45	57	Minneapolis city, MN	9.1
42	57	Mesa city, AZ	30.1	2	59	Los Angeles city, CA	18.5	34	59	Long Beach city, CA	9.0
68	57	St. Petersburg city, FL	30.1	42	60	Mesa city, AZ	18.4	69	60	Bakersfield city, CA	8.8
56	57	Toledo city, OH	30.1	61	61	Raleigh city, NC	18.2	15	60	Columbus city, OH	8.8
70	62	Birmingham city, AL	30.0	67	62	Riverside city, CA	18.1	67	60	Riverside city, CA	8.8
46	63	Honolulu CDP, HI	29.9	27	63	Fort Worth city, TX	18.0	26	63	Charlotte city, NC	8.7
73	63	Norfolk city, VA	29.9	19	63	Milwaukee city, WI	18.0	8	64	Dallas city, TX	8.6
10	65	Detroit city, MI	29.6	15	65	Columbus city, OH	17.8	4	65	Houston city, TX	8.4
58	66	Buffalo city, NY	29.5	34	65	Long Beach city, CA	17.8	38	65	Virginia Beach city, VA	8.4
31	67	New Orleans city, LA	29.4	59	65	St. Paul city, MN	17.8	61	67	Raleigh city, NC	8.3
5	67	Philadelphia city, PA	29.4	55	65	Anaheim city, CA	17.7	6	68	Phoenix city, AZ	8.1
23	69	El Paso city, TX	29.3	20	68	Boston city, MA	17.7	11	68	San Jose city, CA	8.1
75	69	Hialeah city, FL	29.3	45	68	Minneapolis city, MN	17.7	55	70	Anaheim city, CA	8.0
60	71	Corpus Christi city, TX	29.2	8	71	Dallas city, TX	17.6	62	71	Aurora city, CO	7.4
37	71	Fresno city, CA	29.2	37	72	Fresno city, CA	17.1	16	72	Austin city, TX	6.7
52	73	Pittsburgh city, PA	28.6	16	73	Austin city, TX	17.0	53	73	Arlington city, TX	6.1
71	74	Stockton city, CA	27.8	73	74	Norfolk city, VA	16.9	51	74	Santa Ana city, CA	5.4
74	75	Baton Rouge city, LA	27.4	51	75	Santa Ana city, CA	13.5	65	75	Anchorage city, AK	5.3

TABLE 6—75 Largest Cities by 2000 Population
Selected Rankings

Percent Non-Hispanic White, 2000				Percent Black or African American, 2000				Percent American Indian and Alaska Native, 2000			
Population Rank	Non-Hispanic White Rank	City	[A-5. col 11] Percent Non-Hispanic White	Population Rank	Black or African American Rank	City	[A-5. col 14] Percent Black or African American	Population Rank	American Indian and Alaska Native Rank	City	[A-5. col 17] Percent American Indian and Alaska Native
64	1	Lexington-Fayette, KY	79.2	10	1	Detroit city, MI	81.4	65	1	Anchorage city, AK	7.2
48	2	Colorado Springs city, CO	75.4	70	2	Birmingham city, AL	73.3	43	2	Tulsa city, OK	4.5
28	2	Portland city, OR	75.4	31	3	New Orleans city, LA	67.1	35	3	Albuquerque city, NM	3.9
44	4	Omaha city, NE	75.3	17	4	Baltimore city, MD	64.1	29	4	Oklahoma City, OK	3.3
42	5	Mesa city, AZ	73.0	39	5	Atlanta city, GA	61.2	30	5	Tucson city, AZ	2.3
50	6	Wichita city, KS	71.7	18	5	Memphis city, TN	61.2	45	6	Minneapolis city, MN	2.0
65	7	Anchorage city, AK	69.9	21	7	Washington city, DC	60.0	6	6	Phoenix city, AZ	2.0
38	8	Virginia Beach city, VA	69.4	63	8	Newark city, NJ	53.4	42	8	Mesa city, AZ	1.6
68	9	St. Petersburg city, FL	68.9	49	9	St. Louis city, MO	51.0	37	9	Fresno city, CA	1.5
12	10	Indianapolis consolidated city, IN	67.8	33	10	Cleveland city, OH	50.7	69	10	Bakersfield city, CA	1.3
24	10	Seattle city, WA	67.8	74	11	Baton Rouge city, LA	49.7	25	10	Denver city, CO	1.3
56	10	Toledo city, OH	67.8	73	12	Norfolk city, VA	43.8	40	12	Sacramento city, CA	1.2
43	13	Tulsa city, OK	67.2	5	13	Philadelphia city, PA	43.1	59	12	St. Paul city, MN	1.2
52	14	Pittsburgh city, PA	67.1	54	14	Cincinnati city, OH	42.8	50	12	Wichita city, KS	1.2
15	15	Columbus city, OH	66.9	58	15	Buffalo city, NY	37.2	19	15	Milwaukee city, WI	1.1
22	16	Nashville-Davidson consolidated city, TN	65.3	19	16	Milwaukee city, WI	37.0	67	15	Riverside city, CA	1.1
29	17	Oklahoma City, OK	64.6	3	17	Chicago city, IL	36.6	28	17	Portland city, OR	1.0
59	18	St. Paul city, MN	64.1	41	18	Oakland city, CA	35.4	24	17	Seattle city, WA	1.0
45	19	Minneapolis city, MN	62.7	66	19	Louisville city, KY	32.9	71	17	Stockton city, CA	1.0
14	20	Jacksonville, FL	62.2	26	20	Charlotte city, NC	32.6	48	20	Colorado Springs city, CO	0.9
66	21	Louisville city, KY	61.9	36	21	Kansas City, MO	30.7	51	20	Santa Ana city, CA	0.9
61	22	Raleigh city, NC	60.3	14	22	Jacksonville, FL	29.0	55	22	Anaheim city, CA	0.8
53	23	Arlington city, TX	59.8	72	23	Jersey City, NJ	28.0	62	22	Aurora city, CO	0.8
62	24	Aurora city, CO	59.2	61	24	Raleigh city, NC	27.5	58	22	Buffalo city, NY	0.8
36	25	Kansas City, MO	57.9	52	25	Pittsburgh city, PA	26.8	34	22	Long Beach city, CA	0.8
32	25	Las Vegas city, NV	57.9	1	26	New York City, NY	26.4	44	22	Omaha city, NE	0.8
6	27	Phoenix city, AZ	55.8	22	27	Nashville-Davidson consolidated city, TN	25.9	11	22	San Jose city, CA	0.8
26	28	Charlotte city, NC	55.1	57	27	Tampa city, FL	25.9	23	28	El Paso city, TX	0.7
30	29	Tucson city, AZ	54.1	8	29	Dallas city, TX	25.8	27	28	Fort Worth city, TX	0.7
16	30	Austin city, TX	53.0	4	30	Houston city, TX	25.2	32	28	Las Vegas city, NV	0.7
54	31	Cincinnati city, OH	52.4	12	30	Indianapolis consolidated city, IN	25.2	2	28	Los Angeles city, CA	0.7
58	32	Buffalo city, NY	52.0	20	32	Boston city, MA	24.9	9	28	San Antonio city, TX	0.7
25	33	Denver city, CO	51.9	15	33	Columbus city, OH	24.1	60	33	Corpus Christi city, TX	0.6
57	34	Tampa city, FL	51.0	56	34	Toledo city, OH	23.4	41	33	Oakland city, CA	0.6
69	35	Bakersfield city, CA	50.9	68	35	St. Petersburg city, FL	22.3	7	33	San Diego city, CA	0.6
35	36	Albuquerque city, NM	49.9	47	36	Miami city, FL	21.9	53	36	Arlington city, TX	0.5
20	37	Boston city, MA	49.4	27	37	Fort Worth city, TX	20.1	16	36	Austin city, TX	0.5
7	38	San Diego city, CA	49.3	38	38	Virginia Beach city, VA	18.8	8	36	Dallas city, TX	0.5
73	39	Norfolk city, VA	46.9	45	39	Minneapolis city, MN	17.6	36	36	Kansas City, MO	0.5
27	40	Fort Worth city, TX	45.9	40	40	Sacramento city, CA	15.3	1	30	New York City, NY	0.5
19	41	Milwaukee city, WI	45.7	43	40	Tulsa city, OK	15.3	73	36	Norfolk city, VA	0.5
67	42	Riverside city, CA	45.5	29	42	Oklahoma City, OK	15.1	13	36	San Francisco city, CA	0.5
74	43	Baton Rouge city, LA	44.7	34	43	Long Beach city, CA	14.9	20	43	Boston city, MA	0.4
13	44	San Francisco city, CA	43.6	53	44	Arlington city, TX	13.4	26	43	Charlotte city, NC	0.4
49	45	St. Louis city, MO	43.0	64	44	Lexington-Fayette, KY	13.4	15	43	Columbus city, OH	0.4
5	46	Philadelphia city, PA	42.6	62	46	Aurora city, CO	13.2	4	43	Houston city, TX	0.4
40	47	Sacramento city, CA	40.6	44	47	Omaha city, NE	13.1	14	43	Jacksonville, FL	0.4
33	48	Cleveland city, OH	39.0	59	48	St. Paul city, MN	11.3	61	43	Raleigh city, NC	0.4
60	49	Corpus Christi city, TX	38.5	50	48	Wichita city, KS	11.3	57	43	Tampa city, FL	0.4
37	50	Fresno city, CA	37.0	2	50	Los Angeles city, CA	11.1	56	43	Toledo city, OH	0.4
11	51	San Jose city, CA	35.8	71	51	Stockton city, CA	11.0	38	43	Virginia Beach city, VA	0.4
55	52	Anaheim city, CA	35.7	25	52	Denver city, CO	10.9	21	43	Washington city, DC	0.4
1	53	New York City, NY	35.0	32	53	Las Vegas city, NV	10.2	17	53	Baltimore city, MD	0.3
8	54	Dallas city, TX	34.6	16	54	Austin city, TX	9.9	3	53	Chicago city, IL	0.3
18	55	Memphis city, TN	33.3	69	55	Bakersfield city, CA	9.0	33	53	Cleveland city, OH	0.3
34	56	Long Beach city, CA	33.2	24	56	Seattle city, WA	8.3	10	53	Detroit city, MI	0.3
71	57	Stockton city, CA	32.4	37	57	Fresno city, CA	8.1	12	53	Indianapolis consolidated city, IN	0.3
9	58	San Antonio city, TX	31.8	7	58	San Diego city, CA	7.7	72	53	Jersey City, NJ	0.3
39	59	Atlanta city, GA	31.3	13	59	San Francisco city, CA	7.6	64	53	Lexington-Fayette, KY	0.3
3	59	Chicago city, IL	31.3	67	60	Riverside city, CA	7.1	66	53	Louisville city, KY	0.3
17	61	Baltimore city, MD	31.0	9	61	San Antonio city, TX	6.6	22	53	Nashville-Davidson consolidated city, TN	0.3
4	62	Houston city, TX	30.7	28	62	Portland city, OR	6.4	31	53	New Orleans city, LA	0.3
2	63	Los Angeles city, CA	29.6	48	63	Colorado Springs city, CO	6.3	63	53	Newark city, NJ	0.3
21	64	Washington city, DC	27.7	65	64	Anchorage city, AK	5.8	5	53	Philadelphia city, PA	0.3
31	65	New Orleans city, LA	26.7	6	65	Phoenix city, AZ	4.9	49	53	St. Louis city, MO	0.3
70	66	Birmingham city, AL	23.6	60	66	Corpus Christi city, TX	4.6	68	53	St. Petersburg city, FL	0.3
72	66	Jersey City, NJ	23.6	30	67	Tucson city, AZ	4.2	39	67	Atlanta city, GA	0.2
41	68	Oakland city, CA	23.4	11	68	San Jose city, CA	3.4	74	67	Baton Rouge city, LA	0.2
46	69	Honolulu CDP, HI	18.6	35	69	Albuquerque city, NM	3.1	70	67	Birmingham city, AL	0.2
23	70	El Paso city, TX	18.3	23	69	El Paso city, TX	3.1	54	67	Cincinnati city, OH	0.2
63	71	Newark city, NJ	14.3	55	71	Anaheim city, CA	2.5	75	67	Hialeah city, FL	0.2
51	72	Santa Ana city, CA	12.4	42	72	Mesa city, AZ	2.4	46	67	Honolulu CDP, HI	0.2
47	73	Miami city, FL	11.9	75	73	Hialeah city, FL	2.2	18	67	Memphis city, TN	0.2
10	74	Detroit city, MI	10.6	51	74	Santa Ana city, CA	1.6	47	67	Miami city, FL	0.2
75	75	Hialeah city, FL	8.1	46	75	Honolulu CDP, HI	1.5	52	67	Pittsburgh city, PA	0.2

TABLE 6—75 Largest Cities by 2000 Population
Selected Rankings

Percent Asian, Hawaiian, and Pacific Islander, 2000				Percent Hispanic or Latino[1], 2000				Percent Two or More Races, 2000			
Population Rank	Asian, Hawaiian, and Pacific Islander Rank	City	[A-5. col 20] Percent Asian, Hawaiian, and Pacific Islander	Population Rank	Hispanic or Latino Rank	City	[A-5. col 23] Percent Hispanic or Latino	Population Rank	Two or More Races Rank	City	[A-5. col 26] Percent Two or More Races
46	1	Honolulu CDP, HI	62.9	75	1	Hialeah city, FL	90.5	46	1	Honolulu CDP, HI	15.0
13	2	San Francisco city, CA	31.4	23	2	El Paso city, TX	76.7	71	2	Stockton city, CA	6.8
11	3	San Jose city, CA	27.2	51	3	Santa Ana city, CA	76.1	40	3	Sacramento city, CA	6.7
71	4	Stockton city, CA	20.5	47	4	Miami city, FL	65.8	65	4	Anchorage city, AK	6.3
40	5	Sacramento city, CA	17.5	9	5	San Antonio city, TX	58.6	72	5	Jersey City, NJ	6.2
72	6	Jersey City, NJ	16.3	60	6	Corpus Christi city, TX	54.3	37	6	Fresno city, CA	5.7
41	7	Oakland city, CA	15.7	55	7	Anaheim city, CA	46.8	34	7	Long Beach city, CA	5.5
7	8	San Diego city, CA	14.1	2	8	Los Angeles city, CA	46.5	67	7	Riverside city, CA	5.5
24	9	Seattle city, WA	13.6	35	9	Albuquerque city, NM	39.9	11	9	San Jose city, CA	5.4
34	10	Long Beach city, CA	13.0	37	9	Fresno city, CA	39.9	2	10	Los Angeles city, CA	5.2
55	11	Anaheim city, CA	12.4	67	11	Riverside city, CA	38.2	41	10	Oakland city, CA	5.2
59	11	St. Paul city, MN	12.4	4	12	Houston city, TX	37.4	47	12	Miami city, FL	5.1
37	13	Fresno city, CA	11.4	30	13	Tucson city, AZ	35.8	55	13	Anaheim city, CA	5.0
2	14	Los Angeles city, CA	10.2	34	14	Long Beach city, CA	35.7	69	13	Bakersfield city, CA	5.0
1	15	New York City, NY	9.9	8	15	Dallas city, TX	35.6	1	13	New York City, NY	5.0
51	16	Santa Ana city, CA	9.2	6	16	Phoenix city, AZ	34.1	63	13	Newark city, NJ	5.0
20	17	Boston city, MA	7.6	69	17	Bakersfield city, CA	32.3	7	13	San Diego city, CA	5.0
28	18	Portland city, OR	6.7	71	18	Stockton city, CA	32.2	62	18	Aurora city, CO	4.8
65	19	Anchorage city, AK	6.3	25	19	Denver city, CO	31.7	24	18	Seattle city, WA	4.8
45	19	Minneapolis city, MN	6.3	16	20	Austin city, TX	30.6	43	18	Tulsa city, OK	4.8
67	21	Riverside city, CA	6.0	11	21	San Jose city, CA	30.2	35	21	Albuquerque city, NM	4.7
53	22	Arlington city, TX	5.9	27	22	Fort Worth city, TX	29.7	20	21	Boston city, MA	4.7
4	23	Houston city, TX	5.3	63	23	Newark city, NJ	29.4	45	23	Minneapolis city, MN	4.6
32	24	Las Vegas city, NV	4.9	72	24	Jersey City, NJ	28.3	51	23	Santa Ana city, CA	4.6
16	25	Austin city, TX	4.8	1	25	New York City, NY	27.0	29	25	Oklahoma City, OK	4.5
38	25	Virginia Beach city, VA	4.8	3	26	Chicago city, IL	26.0	28	25	Portland city, OR	4.5
69	27	Bakersfield city, CA	4.4	7	27	San Diego city, CA	25.4	13	25	San Francisco city, CA	4.5
3	27	Chicago city, IL	4.4	32	28	Las Vegas city, NV	23.6	32	28	Las Vegas city, NV	4.4
5	29	Philadelphia city, PA	4.3	41	29	Oakland city, CA	21.9	59	29	St. Paul city, MN	4.3
62	30	Aurora city, CO	4.2	40	30	Sacramento city, CA	21.6	48	30	Colorado Springs city, CO	4.1
50	31	Wichita city, KS	3.8	62	31	Aurora city, CO	19.9	30	31	Tucson city, AZ	4.0
15	32	Columbus city, OH	3.5	42	32	Mesa city, AZ	19.8	9	32	San Antonio city, TX	3.9
29	32	Oklahoma City, OK	3.5	57	33	Tampa city, FL	19.3	25	33	Denver city, CO	3.8
26	34	Charlotte city, NC	3.3	53	34	Arlington city, TX	18.3	75	33	Hialeah city, FL	3.8
61	34	Raleigh city, NC	3.3	20	35	Boston city, MA	14.5	50	35	Wichita city, KS	3.6
48	36	Colorado Springs city, CO	3.1	13	36	San Francisco city, CA	14.1	6	36	Phoenix city, AZ	3.4
73	36	Norfolk city, VA	3.1	48	37	Colorado Springs city, CO	11.9	23	37	El Paso city, TX	3.3
8	38	Dallas city, TX	2.8	19	37	Milwaukee city, WI	11.9	53	38	Arlington city, TX	3.2
25	38	Denver city, CO	2.8	29	39	Oklahoma City, OK	10.0	60	38	Corpus Christi city, TX	3.2
14	38	Jacksonville, FL	2.8	50	40	Wichita city, KS	9.6	57	38	Tampa city, FL	3.2
19	38	Milwaukee city, WI	2.8	5	41	Philadelphia city, PA	8.5	4	41	Houston city, TX	3.1
52	38	Pittsburgh city, PA	2.8	59	42	St. Paul city, MN	7.9	42	41	Mesa city, AZ	3.1
68	38	St. Petersburg city, FL	2.8	21	42	Washington city, DC	7.9	38	41	Virginia Beach city, VA	3.1
27	44	Fort Worth city, TX	2.7	45	44	Minneapolis city, MN	7.6	16	44	Austin city, TX	3.0
74	45	Baton Rouge city, LA	2.6	58	45	Buffalo city, NY	7.4	3	44	Chicago city, IL	3.0
21	45	Washington city, DC	2.6	26	45	Charlotte city, NC	7.4	15	44	Columbus city, OH	3.0
30	47	Tucson city, AZ	2.5	44	45	Omaha city, NE	7.4	19	47	Milwaukee city, WI	2.9
64	48	Lexington-Fayette, KY	2.3	33	48	Cleveland city, OH	7.2	73	47	Norfolk city, VA	2.9
35	49	Albuquerque city, NM	2.2	61	49	Raleigh city, NC	7.1	56	47	Toledo city, OH	2.9
31	49	New Orleans city, LA	2.2	43	49	Tulsa city, OK	7.1	8	50	Dallas city, TX	2.7
57	49	Tampa city, FL	2.2	36	51	Kansas City, MO	6.9	36	50	Kansas City, MO	2.7
22	52	Nashville-Davidson consolidated city, TN	2.1	28	52	Portland city, OR	6.8	27	52	Fort Worth city, TX	2.6
6	52	Phoenix city, AZ	2.1	65	53	Anchorage city, AK	5.7	21	52	Washington city, DC	2.6
49	52	St. Louis city, MO	2.1	56	54	Toledo city, OH	5.5	5	54	Philadelphia city, PA	2.5
39	55	Atlanta city, GA	2.0	24	55	Seattle city, WA	5.3	58	55	Buffalo city, NY	2.4
36	55	Kansas City, MO	2.0	10	56	Detroit city, MI	5.0	10	56	Detroit city, MI	2.3
44	57	Omaha city, NE	1.9	39	57	Atlanta city, GA	4.5	33	57	Cleveland city, OH	2.2
43	58	Tulsa city, OK	1.8	22	57	Nashville-Davidson consolidated city, TN	4.5	22	57	Nashville-Davidson consolidated city, TN	2.2
42	59	Mesa city, AZ	1.7	46	59	Honolulu CDP, HI	4.4	68	57	St. Petersburg city, FL	2.2
17	60	Baltimore city, MD	1.6	38	60	Virginia Beach city, VA	4.2	14	60	Jacksonville, FL	2.1
18	60	Memphis city, TN	1.6	14	61	Jacksonville, FL	4.1	49	60	St. Louis city, MO	2.1
9	60	San Antonio city, TX	1.6	68	62	St. Petersburg city, FL	4.0	66	62	Louisville city, KY	2.0
54	63	Cincinnati city, OH	1.5	12	63	Indianapolis consolidated city, IN	3.8	44	62	Omaha city, NE	2.0
33	63	Cleveland city, OH	1.5	73	64	Norfolk city, VA	3.7	61	62	Raleigh city, NC	2.0
12	65	Indianapolis consolidated city, IN	1.4	64	64	Lexington-Fayette, KY	3.3	26	65	Charlotte city, NC	1.9
58	66	Buffalo city, NY	1.3	31	66	New Orleans city, LA	3.1	52	65	Pittsburgh city, PA	1.9
60	66	Corpus Christi city, TX	1.3	18	67	Memphis city, TN	2.9	12	67	Indianapolis consolidated city, IN	1.8
23	66	El Paso city, TX	1.3	15	68	Columbus city, OH	2.4	64	67	Lexington-Fayette, KY	1.8
66	66	Louisville city, KY	1.3	74	69	Baton Rouge city, LA	1.9	54	69	Cincinnati city, OH	1.7
63	70	Newark city, NJ	1.2	49	69	St. Louis city, MO	1.9	17	70	Baltimore city, MD	1.6
10	71	Detroit city, MI	1.0	66	71	Louisville city, KY	1.8	31	71	New Orleans city, LA	1.4
56	71	Toledo city, OH	1.0	17	72	Baltimore city, MD	1.7	39	72	Atlanta city, GA	1.2
70	73	Birmingham city, AL	0.7	70	73	Birmingham city, AL	1.5	74	72	Baton Rouge city, LA	1.2
47	74	Miami city, FL	0.6	52	74	Pittsburgh city, PA	1.4	18	74	Memphis city, TN	1.1
75	75	Hialeah city, FL	0.3	54	75	Cincinnati city, OH	1.2	70	75	Birmingham city, AL	0.8

[1] Hispanic or Latino persons may be of any race.

TABLE 6—75 Largest Cities by 2000 Population
Selected Rankings

Population Rank	Married-Couple Families Rank	City	[A-5. col 30] Percent Married-Couple Families	Population Rank	Married-Couple Families with Own Children Under 18 Years Rank	City	[A-5. col 31] Percent Married-Couple Families with Own Children Under 18 Years	Population Rank	Single-Parent Households Rank	City	[A-5. col 34] Percent Single-Parent Households
51	1	Santa Ana city, CA	62.3	51	1	Santa Ana city, CA	44.0	10	1	Detroit city, MI	21.5
75	2	Hialeah city, FL	58.1	55	2	Anaheim city, CA	33.9	63	2	Newark city, NJ	19.9
55	3	Anaheim city, CA	57.9	11	3	San Jose city, CA	30.9	33	3	Cleveland city, OH	17.7
11	4	San Jose city, CA	57.4	23	4	El Paso city, TX	30.8	18	4	Memphis city, TN	16.9
38	5	Virginia Beach city, VA	57.0	69	5	Bakersfield city, CA	30.1	58	5	Buffalo city, NY	16.7
23	6	El Paso city, TX	55.8	38	6	Virginia Beach city, VA	29.8	31	6	New Orleans city, LA	16.3
42	7	Mesa city, AZ	54.2	53	7	Arlington city, TX	28.9	19	7	Milwaukee city, WI	16.1
69	8	Bakersfield city, CA	53.9	67	8	Riverside city, CA	28.8	17	8	Baltimore city, MD	15.4
53	9	Arlington city, TX	53.2	65	9	Anchorage city, AK	28.6	70	9	Birmingham city, AL	15.1
48	10	Colorado Springs city, CO	52.5	71	10	Stockton city, CA	27.4	49	10	St. Louis city, MO	14.8
65	11	Anchorage city, AK	52.2	37	11	Fresno city, CA	26.9	37	11	Fresno city, CA	14.7
60	12	Corpus Christi city, TX	51.4	75	12	Hialeah city, FL	26.7	54	12	Cincinnati city, OH	14.4
67	13	Riverside city, CA	50.7	48	13	Colorado Springs city, CO	25.7	5	13	Philadelphia city, PA	14.3
71	14	Stockton city, CA	49.7	6	14	Phoenix city, AZ	25.4	71	14	Stockton city, CA	14.2
32	15	Las Vegas city, NV	49.1	42	15	Mesa city, AZ	25.2	73	15	Norfolk city, VA	14.1
9	15	San Antonio city, TX	49.1	60	16	Corpus Christi city, TX	25.1	72	16	Jersey City, NJ	13.7
50	17	Wichita city, KS	48.3	9	17	San Antonio city, TX	25.0	34	16	Long Beach city, CA	13.7
6	18	Phoenix city, AZ	48.2	62	18	Aurora city, CO	24.9	66	18	Louisville city, KY	13.6
62	19	Aurora city, CO	48.0	27	19	Fort Worth city, TX	24.5	39	19	Atlanta city, GA	13.5
37	20	Fresno city, CA	47.8	2	20	Los Angeles city, CA	23.5	56	20	Toledo city, OH	13.4
14	21	Jacksonville, FL	47.7	4	21	Houston city, TX	23.1	69	21	Bakersfield city, CA	13.2
27	22	Fort Worth city, TX	46.6	50	21	Wichita city, KS	23.1	74	22	Baton Rouge city, LA	12.9
29	23	Oklahoma City, OK	46.4	14	23	Jacksonville, FL	22.5	23	23	El Paso city, TX	12.3
46	24	Honolulu CDP, HI	46.2	7	24	San Diego city, CA	22.4	67	23	Riverside city, CA	12.3
7	25	San Diego city, CA	45.4	32	25	Las Vegas city, NV	22.2	36	25	Kansas City, MO	12.1
26	26	Charlotte city, NC	44.7	34	26	Long Beach city, CA	22.0	41	25	Oakland city, CA	12.1
64	27	Lexington-Fayette, KY	44.6	26	27	Charlotte city, NC	21.4	1	27	New York City, NY	12.0
44	28	Omaha city, NE	44.3	29	28	Oklahoma City, OK	20.8	14	28	Jacksonville consolidated city, FL	11.9
4	29	Houston city, TX	44.2	44	29	Omaha city, NE	20.7	40	28	Sacramento city, CA	11.9
35	30	Albuquerque city, NM	44.1	8	30	Dallas city, TX	20.4	3	30	Chicago city, IL	11.8
43	31	Tulsa city, OK	43.9	35	31	Albuquerque city, NM	20.2	21	30	Washington city, DC	11.8
2	32	Los Angeles city, CA	42.9	64	32	Lexington-Fayette, KY	19.4	12	32	Indianapolis consolidated city, IN	11.7
12	33	Indianapolis consolidated city, IN	41.5	16	33	Austin city, TX	19.3	15	33	Columbus city, OH	11.6
22	34	Nashville-Davidson consolidated city, TN	40.9	59	34	St. Paul city, MN	19.2	47	33	Miami city, FL	11.6
30	35	Tucson city, AZ	40.8	40	35	Sacramento city, CA	19.1	9	33	San Antonio city, TX	11.6
61	36	Raleigh city, NC	40.2	30	36	Tucson city, AZ	19.0	57	33	Tampa city, FL	11.6
8	37	Dallas city, TX	39.8	43	36	Tulsa city, OK	19.0	60	37	Corpus Christi city, TX	11.5
34	38	Long Beach city, CA	39.7	12	38	Indianapolis consolidated city, IN	18.9	65	38	Anchorage city, AK	11.2
40	39	Sacramento city, CA	39.6	61	39	Raleigh city, NC	18.5	51	38	Santa Ana city, CA	11.2
56	40	Toledo city, OH	39.2	1	40	New York City, NY	18.4	62	40	Aurora city, CO	11.1
28	41	Portland city, OR	39.1	46	41	Honolulu CDP, HI	18.2	6	40	Phoenix city, AZ	11.1
68	41	St. Petersburg city, FL	39.1	72	42	Jersey City, NJ	18.1	27	42	Fort Worth city, TX	11.0
16	43	Austin city, TX	39.0	3	43	Chicago city, IL	17.8	20	43	Boston city, MA	10.9
36	44	Kansas City, MO	38.8	22	44	Nashville-Davidson consolidated city, TN	17.3	2	43	Los Angeles city, CA	10.9
1	45	New York City, NY	38.2	41	44	Oakland city, CA	17.3	4	45	Houston city, TX	10.8
47	46	Miami city, FL	37.8	28	46	Portland city, OR	17.2	59	45	St. Paul city, MN	10.8
73	47	Norfolk city, VA	37.7	56	47	Toledo city, OH	17.1	30	45	Tucson city, AZ	10.8
59	48	St. Paul city, MN	37.4	15	48	Columbus city, OH	17.0	35	48	Albuquerque city, NM	10.7
72	49	Jersey City, NJ	37.2	73	48	Norfolk city, VA	17.0	8	49	Dallas city, TX	10.6
57	49	Tampa city, FL	37.2	57	50	Tampa city, FL	16.8	29	50	Oklahoma City, OK	10.5
74	51	Baton Rouge city, LA	37.0	36	51	Kansas City, MO	16.7	55	51	Anaheim city, CA	10.4
15	52	Columbus city, OH	36.4	63	52	Newark city, NJ	16.1	52	51	Pittsburgh city, PA	10.4
3	53	Chicago city, IL	36.3	74	53	Baton Rouge city, LA	16.0	32	53	Las Vegas city, NV	10.3
25	54	Denver city, CO	35.3	25	54	Denver city, CO	15.6	75	54	Hialeah city, FL	10.2
41	55	Oakland city, CA	35.0	18	55	Memphis city, TN	15.4	22	55	Nashville-Davidson consolidated city, TN	10.1
18	56	Memphis city, TN	34.7	47	56	Miami city, FL	15.3	43	55	Tulsa city, OK	10.1
24	57	Seattle city, WA	33.7	19	57	Milwaukee city, WI	15.2	38	55	Virginia Beach city, VA	10.1
19	58	Milwaukee city, WI	33.2	68	58	St. Petersburg city, FL	14.5	44	58	Omaha city, NE	10.0
5	59	Philadelphia city, PA	32.7	5	59	Philadelphia city, PA	14.0	53	59	Arlington city, TX	9.9
13	59	San Francisco city, CA	32.7	31	60	New Orleans city, LA	13.8	26	60	Charlotte city, NC	9.8
63	61	Newark city, NJ	32.4	45	61	Minneapolis city, MN	13.6	45	60	Minneapolis city, MN	9.8
66	62	Louisville city, KY	32.1	24	62	Seattle city, WA	13.4	68	60	St. Petersburg city, FL	9.8
52	62	Pittsburgh city, PA	32.1	70	63	Birmingham city, AL	13.3	50	63	Wichita city, KS	9.6
70	64	Birmingham city, AL	31.7	10	64	Detroit city, MI	13.1	48	64	Colorado Springs city, CO	9.0
31	64	New Orleans city, LA	31.7	13	64	San Francisco city, CA	13.0	61	64	Raleigh city, NC	9.0
45	66	Minneapolis city, MN	29.9	33	66	Cleveland city, OH	12.9	42	66	Mesa city, AZ	8.8
33	67	Cleveland city, OH	29.3	66	66	Louisville city, KY	12.8	7	67	San Diego city, CA	8.6
58	68	Buffalo city, NY	28.5	58	68	Buffalo city, NY	12.5	64	68	Lexington-Fayette, KY	8.4
20	69	Boston city, MA	28.3	20	69	Boston city, MA	12.4	25	69	Denver city, CO	8.3
17	70	Baltimore city, MD	28.0	52	70	Pittsburgh city, PA	11.9	11	69	San Jose city, CA	8.3
10	71	Detroit city, MI	27.8	54	71	Cincinnati city, OH	11.4	16	71	Austin city, TX	8.2
54	72	Cincinnati city, OH	27.1	49	71	St. Louis city, MO	11.4	28	72	Portland city, OR	8.0
49	73	St. Louis city, MO	26.3	17	73	Baltimore city, MD	10.7	46	73	Honolulu CDP, HI	5.9
39	74	Atlanta city, GA	25.1	39	74	Atlanta city, GA	9.9	24	74	Seattle city, WA	5.4
21	75	Washington city, DC	23.4	21	75	Washington city, DC	8.7	13	75	San Francisco city, CA	4.2

TABLE 6—75 Largest Cities by 2000 Population
Selected Rankings

Percent Men Living Alone, 2000				Percent Women Living Alone, 2000				Percent Foreign-Born Population, 2000			
Population Rank	Men Living Alone Rank	City	[A-5. col 38] Percent Men Living Alone	Population Rank	Women Living Alone Rank	City	[A-5. col 40] Percent Women Living Alone	Population Rank	Foreign-born Population Rank	City	[A-5. col 54] Percent Foreign-born Population
45	1	Minneapolis city, MN	19.7	21	1	Washington city, DC	24.5	75	1	Hialeah city, FL	72.1
21	2	Washington city, DC	19.2	54	2	Cincinnati city, OH	23.8	47	2	Miami city, FL	59.5
13	3	San Francisco city, CA	19.1	52	3	Pittsburgh city, PA	22.9	51	3	Santa Ana city, CA	53.3
54	4	Cincinnati city, OH	19.0	49	4	St. Louis city, MO	22.1	2	4	Los Angeles city, CA	40.9
24	5	Seattle city, WA	18.9	24	5	Seattle city, WA	21.8	55	5	Anaheim city, CA	37.9
25	6	Denver city, CO	18.4	66	6	Louisville city, KY	21.5	11	6	San Jose city, CA	36.9
49	7	St. Louis city, MO	18.1	25	7	Denver city, CO	20.9	13	7	San Francisco city, CA	36.8
39	8	Atlanta city, GA	17.8	58	8	Buffalo city, NY	20.7	1	8	New York City, NY	35.9
58	9	Buffalo city, NY	16.9	45	8	Minneapolis city, MN	20.7	72	9	Jersey City, NJ	34.0
20	10	Boston city, MA	16.7	39	10	Atlanta city, GA	20.6	34	10	Long Beach city, CA	28.6
16	11	Austin city, TX	16.5	20	11	Boston city, MA	20.4	41	11	Oakland city, CA	26.6
66	12	Louisville city, KY	16.4	59	11	St. Paul city, MN	20.4	4	12	Houston city, TX	26.4
52	12	Pittsburgh city, PA	16.4	17	13	Baltimore city, MD	20.3	23	13	El Paso city, TX	26.1
33	14	Cleveland city, OH	16.2	68	14	St. Petersburg city, FL	20.2	20	14	Boston city, MA	25.8
28	15	Portland city, OR	15.7	5	15	Philadelphia city, PA	19.9	7	15	San Diego city, CA	25.7
15	16	Columbus city, OH	15.6	70	16	Birmingham city, AL	19.7	46	16	Honolulu CDP, HI	25.3
8	17	Dallas city, TX	15.5	13	17	San Francisco city, CA	19.5	71	17	Stockton city, CA	24.5
59	17	St. Paul city, MN	15.5	22	18	Nashville-Davidson consolidated city, TN	19.3	8	18	Dallas city, TX	24.4
68	17	St. Petersburg city, FL	15.5	33	19	Cleveland city, OH	19.0	63	19	Newark city, NJ	24.1
31	20	New Orleans city, LA	15.4	43	19	Tulsa city, OK	19.0	3	20	Chicago city, IL	21.7
36	21	Kansas City, MO	15.2	36	21	Kansas City, MO	18.8	37	21	Fresno city, CA	20.3
19	21	Milwaukee city, WI	15.2	1	21	New York City, NY	18.8	40	21	Sacramento city, CA	20.3
57	23	Tampa city, FL	15.0	28	21	Portland city, OR	18.8	67	23	Riverside city, CA	19.9
47	24	Miami city, FL	14.9	57	24	Tampa city, FL	18.7	6	24	Phoenix city, AZ	19.5
43	24	Tulsa city, OK	14.9	15	25	Columbus city, OH	18.6	32	25	Las Vegas city, NV	18.9
61	26	Raleigh city, NC	14.8	41	26	Oakland city, CA	18.4	25	26	Denver city, CO	17.4
70	27	Birmingham city, AL	14.7	19	27	Milwaukee city, WI	18.3	24	27	Seattle city, WA	16.9
30	27	Tucson city, AZ	14.7	61	28	Raleigh city, NC	18.2	16	28	Austin city, TX	16.6
50	27	Wichita city, KS	14.7	40	28	Sacramento city, CA	18.2	27	29	Fort Worth city, TX	16.3
17	30	Baltimore city, MD	14.6	56	28	Toledo city, OH	18.2	62	30	Aurora city, CO	16.2
3	31	Chicago city, IL	14.5	12	31	Indianapolis consolidated city, IN	18.1	53	31	Arlington city, TX	15.3
56	31	Toledo city, OH	14.5	44	31	Omaha city, NE	18.1	45	32	Minneapolis city, MN	14.5
34	33	Long Beach city, CA	14.4	3	33	Chicago city, IL	18.0	59	33	St. Paul city, MN	14.3
4	34	Houston city, TX	14.3	64	33	Lexington-Fayette, KY	18.0	30	33	Tucson city, AZ	14.3
74	35	Baton Rouge city, LA	14.2	31	35	New Orleans city, LA	17.7	69	35	Bakersfield city, CA	13.6
41	36	Oakland city, CA	14.1	30	36	Tucson city, AZ	17.5	28	36	Portland city, OR	13.0
22	37	Nashville-Davidson consolidated city, TN	14.0	74	37	Baton Rouge city, LA	17.4	21	37	Washington city, DC	12.9
46	38	Honolulu CDP, HI	13.9	8	37	Dallas city, TX	17.4	57	38	Tampa city, FL	12.2
72	38	Jersey City, NJ	13.9	18	39	Memphis city, TN	17.1	61	39	Raleigh city, NC	11.7
73	38	Norfolk city, VA	13.9	29	40	Oklahoma City, OK	17.0	9	39	San Antonio city, TX	11.7
5	38	Philadelphia city, PA	13.9	35	41	Albuquerque city, NM	16.8	42	41	Mesa city, AZ	11.2
40	38	Sacramento city, CA	13.9	26	42	Charlotte city, NC	16.6	26	42	Charlotte city, NC	11.0
12	43	Indianapolis consolidated city, IN	13.8	50	43	Wichita city, KS	16.4	68	43	St. Petersburg city, FL	9.1
44	43	Omaha city, NE	13.8	73	44	Norfolk city, VA	16.3	5	44	Philadelphia city, PA	9.0
35	45	Albuquerque city, NM	13.7	16	45	Austin city, TX	16.2	35	45	Albuquerque city, NM	8.9
2	45	Los Angeles city, CA	13.7	10	46	Detroit city, MI	16.0	29	46	Oklahoma City, OK	8.5
29	45	Oklahoma City, OK	13.7	46	47	Honolulu CDP, HI	15.8	65	47	Anchorage city, AK	8.2
10	48	Detroit city, MI	13.6	27	48	Fort Worth city, TX	15.5	50	48	Wichita city, KS	8.1
64	48	Lexington-Fayette, KY	13.6	47	48	Miami city, FL	15.5	19	49	Milwaukee city, WI	7.7
18	50	Memphis city, TN	13.4	4	50	Houston city, TX	15.3	48	50	Colorado Springs city, CO	7.0
7	51	San Diego city, CA	13.3	72	50	Jersey City, NJ	15.3	22	51	Nashville-Davidson consolidated city, TN	6.9
27	52	Fort Worth city, TX	13.0	62	52	Aurora city, CO	15.2	15	52	Columbus city, OH	6.7
1	52	New York City, NY	13.0	34	53	Long Beach city, CA	15.1	60	53	Corpus Christi city, TX	6.7
26	54	Charlotte city, NC	12.8	63	54	Newark city, NJ	14.9	39	54	Atlanta city, GA	6.6
53	55	Arlington city, TX	12.5	2	55	Los Angeles city, CA	14.8	44	54	Omaha city, NE	6.6
32	55	Las Vegas city, NV	12.5	48	56	Colorado Springs city, CO	14.6	38	54	Virginia Beach city, VA	6.6
48	57	Colorado Springs city, CO	12.4	14	56	Jacksonville, FL	14.6	43	57	Tulsa city, OK	6.5
65	58	Anchorage city, AK	12.3	7	56	San Diego city, CA	14.6	14	58	Jacksonville, FL	5.9
6	58	Phoenix city, AZ	12.3	9	59	San Antonio city, TX	14.1	64	58	Lexington-Fayette, KY	5.9
62	60	Aurora city, CO	12.1	42	60	Mesa city, AZ	13.9	36	60	Kansas City, MO	5.8
63	61	Newark city, NJ	11.7	71	61	Stockton city, CA	13.6	52	61	Pittsburgh city, PA	5.6
14	62	Jacksonville, FL	11.6	37	62	Fresno city, CA	13.5	49	61	St. Louis city, MO	5.6
9	63	San Antonio city, TX	10.9	6	63	Phoenix city, AZ	13.1	73	63	Norfolk city, VA	5.0
60	64	Corpus Christi city, TX	10.4	60	64	Corpus Christi city, TX	12.8	10	64	Detroit city, MI	4.8
42	65	Mesa city, AZ	10.2	69	65	Bakersfield city, CA	12.7	17	65	Baltimore city, MD	4.6
37	66	Fresno city, CA	9.7	32	66	Las Vegas city, NV	12.5	12	65	Indianapolis consolidated city, IN	4.6
71	67	Stockton city, CA	9.3	53	67	Arlington city, TX	12.3	33	67	Cleveland city, OH	4.5
67	68	Riverside city, CA	9.0	67	67	Riverside city, CA	12.3	74	68	Baton Rouge city, LA	4.4
11	69	San Jose city, CA	8.8	38	69	Virginia Beach city, VA	11.6	58	68	Buffalo city, NY	4.4
69	70	Bakersfield city, CA	8.7	23	70	El Paso city, TX	11.1	31	70	New Orleans city, LA	4.2
38	70	Virginia Beach city, VA	8.7	65	71	Anchorage city, AK	11.0	18	71	Memphis city, TN	4.0
23	72	El Paso city, TX	8.0	55	72	Anaheim city, CA	10.0	54	72	Cincinnati city, OH	3.8
55	73	Anaheim city, CA	7.7	11	73	San Jose city, CA	9.5	66	72	Louisville city, KY	3.8
75	74	Hialeah city, FL	5.6	75	74	Hialeah city, FL	9.1	56	74	Toledo city, OH	3.0
51	75	Santa Ana city, CA	5.2	51	75	Santa Ana city, CA	7.2	70	75	Birmingham city, AL	2.1

TABLE 6—75 Largest Cities by 2000 Population
Selected Rankings

Percent of Population Over 25 Years with High School Diploma or Less, 2000

Population Rank	High School Diploma or Less Rank	City	[B-5. col 2] Percent High School Diploma or Less
75	1	Hialeah city, FL	73.0
51	2	Santa Ana city, CA	72.8
63	3	Newark city, NJ	72.5
47	4	Miami city, FL	67.1
33	5	Cleveland city, OH	64.2
5	6	Philadelphia city, PA	62.1
10	7	Detroit city, MI	60.4
17	8	Baltimore city, MD	59.8
49	9	St. Louis city, MO	56.2
19	10	Milwaukee city, WI	55.3
58	11	Buffalo city, NY	54.5
71	12	Stockton city, CA	54.1
56	13	Toledo city, OH	54.0
23	14	El Paso city, TX	53.9
72	15	Jersey City, NJ	53.0
66	16	Louisville city, KY	52.8
70	17	Birmingham city, AL	52.2
1	17	New York City, NY	52.2
55	19	Anaheim city, CA	52.1
18	20	Memphis city, TN	51.6
52	21	Pittsburgh city, PA	51.5
27	22	Fort Worth city, TX	51.3
3	23	Chicago city, IL	51.2
73	23	Norfolk city, VA	51.2
37	25	Fresno city, CA	51.1
2	26	Los Angeles city, CA	50.8
32	27	Las Vegas city, NV	50.4
4	28	Houston city, TX	50.0
8	29	Dallas, TX	49.3
54	30	Cincinnati city, OH	49.1
9	30	San Antonio city, TX	49.1
60	32	Corpus Christi city, TX	48.9
31	33	New Orleans city, LA	48.8
57	34	Tampa city, FL	48.4
67	35	Riverside city, CA	48.1
12	36	Indianapolis consolidated city, IN	48.0
69	37	Bakersfield city, CA	47.5
14	38	Jacksonville, FL	47.3
34	39	Long Beach city, CA	46.2
6	39	Phoenix city, AZ	46.2
68	41	St. Petersburg city, FL	46.1
39	42	Atlanta city, GA	45.4
36	42	Kansas City, MO	45.4
20	44	Boston city, MA	45.1
29	45	Oklahoma City, OK	44.9
50	46	Wichita city, KS	44.8
40	47	Sacramento city, CA	44.2
41	48	Oakland city, CA	43.7
30	49	Tucson city, AZ	43.6
15	50	Columbus city, OH	43.5
74	51	Baton Rouge city, LA	43.3
22	52	Nashville-Davidson consolidated city, TN	43.1
21	53	Washington city, DC	42.8
46	54	Honolulu CDP, HI	42.6
59	55	St. Paul city, MN	41.9
25	56	Denver city, CO	41.1
44	56	Omaha city, NE	41.1
42	58	Mesa city, AZ	41.0
43	59	Tulsa city, OK	40.9
62	60	Aurora city, CO	39.8
11	60	San Jose city, CA	39.8
35	62	Albuquerque city, NM	38.2
64	63	Lexington-Fayette, KY	36.6
28	63	Portland city, OR	36.6
53	65	Arlington city, TX	36.0
45	66	Minneapolis city, MN	35.8
38	67	Virginia Beach city, VA	35.5
26	68	Charlotte city, NC	35.0
7	69	San Diego city, CA	34.2
65	70	Anchorage city, AK	33.9
16	71	Austin city, TX	33.6
13	72	San Francisco city, CA	32.7
48	73	Colorado Springs city, CO	31.2
61	74	Raleigh city, NC	27.7
24	75	Seattle city, WA	25.8

Percent of Population Over 25 Years with Bachelor's Degree or More, 2000

Population Rank	Bachelor's Degree or More Rank	City	[B-5. col 4] Percent Bachelor's Degree or More
24	1	Seattle city, WA	47.2
13	2	San Francisco city, CA	45.0
61	3	Raleigh city, NC	44.9
16	4	Austin city, TX	40.4
21	5	Washington city, DC	39.1
45	6	Minneapolis city, MN	37.4
26	7	Charlotte city, NC	36.4
20	8	Boston city, MA	35.6
64	8	Lexington-Fayette, KY	35.6
7	10	San Diego city, CA	35.0
39	11	Atlanta city, GA	34.6
25	12	Denver city, CO	34.5
48	13	Colorado Springs city, CO	33.6
28	14	Portland city, OR	32.6
59	15	St. Paul city, MN	32.0
35	16	Albuquerque city, NM	31.8
74	17	Baton Rouge city, LA	31.7
11	18	San Jose city, CA	31.6
46	19	Honolulu CDP, HI	31.1
41	20	Oakland city, CA	30.9
22	21	Nashville-Davidson consolidated city, TN	30.5
53	22	Arlington city, TX	30.4
15	23	Columbus city, OH	29.0
65	24	Anchorage city, AK	28.9
44	25	Omaha city, NE	28.7
43	26	Tulsa city, OK	28.3
38	27	Virginia Beach city, VA	28.1
8	28	Dallas, TX	27.7
72	29	Jersey City, NJ	27.5
1	30	New York City, NY	27.4
4	31	Houston city, TX	27.0
54	32	Cincinnati city, OH	26.6
52	33	Pittsburgh city, PA	26.2
31	34	New Orleans city, LA	25.8
36	35	Kansas City, MO	25.7
3	36	Chicago city, IL	25.5
12	36	Indianapolis consolidated city, IN	25.5
2	36	Los Angeles city, CA	25.5
57	39	Tampa city, FL	25.4
50	40	Wichita city, KS	25.3
62	41	Aurora city, CO	24.6
29	42	Oklahoma City, OK	24.0
34	43	Long Beach city, CA	23.9
40	43	Sacramento city, CA	23.9
30	45	Tucson city, AZ	22.9
68	46	St. Petersburg city, FL	22.8
6	47	Phoenix city, AZ	22.7
27	48	Fort Worth city, TX	22.3
42	49	Mesa city, AZ	21.6
9	49	San Antonio city, TX	21.6
66	51	Louisville city, KY	21.3
14	52	Jacksonville, FL	21.1
18	53	Memphis city, TN	20.9
55	54	Anaheim city, CA	19.6
60	54	Corpus Christi city, TX	19.6
73	54	Norfolk city, VA	19.6
69	57	Bakersfield city, CA	19.3
17	58	Baltimore city, MD	19.1
67	58	Riverside city, CA	19.1
49	58	St. Louis city, MO	19.1
37	61	Fresno city, CA	19.0
70	62	Birmingham city, AL	18.5
58	63	Buffalo city, NY	18.3
23	63	El Paso city, TX	18.3
19	63	Milwaukee city, WI	18.3
32	66	Las Vegas city, NV	18.2
5	67	Philadelphia city, PA	17.9
56	68	Toledo city, OH	16.8
47	69	Miami city, FL	16.2
71	70	Stockton city, CA	15.4
33	71	Cleveland city, OH	11.4
10	72	Detroit city, MI	11.0
75	73	Hialeah city, FL	10.4
51	74	Santa Ana city, CA	9.2
63	75	Newark city, NJ	9.0

Percent of Population 16 to 19 Years Not Enrolled in School, Not High School Graduate, Not in Armed Forces, or Employed, 2000

Population Rank	At-Risk Youth Rank	City	[B-5. col 17] Percent At-Risk Youth
8	1	Dallas city, TX	12.6
25	1	Denver city, CO	12.6
32	3	Las Vegas city, NV	11.9
6	4	Phoenix city, AZ	11.8
33	5	Cleveland city, OH	11.7
17	6	Baltimore city, MD	11.6
63	7	Newark city, NJ	11.4
51	8	Santa Ana city, CA	11.2
54	9	Cincinnati city, OH	10.7
4	9	Houston city, TX	10.7
47	9	Miami city, FL	10.7
10	12	Detroit city, MI	10.5
49	13	St. Louis city, MO	10.3
3	14	Chicago city, IL	10.2
41	15	Oakland city, CA	9.9
39	16	Atlanta city, GA	9.4
27	17	Fort Worth city, TX	9.3
66	17	Louisville city, KY	9.3
58	19	Buffalo city, NY	8.9
70	20	Birmingham city, AL	8.8
2	20	Los Angeles city, CA	8.8
72	22	Jersey City, NJ	8.6
75	23	Hialeah city, FL	8.5
18	23	Memphis city, TN	8.5
19	23	Milwaukee city, WI	8.5
12	26	Indianapolis consolidated city, IN	8.4
34	26	Long Beach city, CA	8.4
57	28	Tampa city, FL	8.2
31	29	New Orleans city, LA	8.0
29	30	Oklahoma City, OK	7.9
56	30	Toledo city, OH	7.9
1	32	New York City, NY	7.8
30	33	Tucson city, AZ	7.7
36	34	Kansas City, MO	7.6
9	34	San Antonio city, TX	7.6
55	36	Anaheim city, CA	7.5
60	36	Corpus Christi city, TX	7.5
37	36	Fresno city, CA	7.5
43	36	Tulsa city, OK	7.5
5	40	Philadelphia city, PA	7.4
62	41	Aurora city, CO	7.1
35	42	Albuquerque city, NM	6.9
16	42	Austin city, TX	6.9
40	42	Sacramento city, CA	6.9
14	45	Jacksonville, FL	6.8
68	45	St. Petersburg city, FL	6.8
71	47	Stockton city, CA	6.7
21	47	Washington city, DC	6.7
50	47	Wichita city, KS	6.7
22	50	Nashville-Davidson consolidated city, TN	6.6
26	51	Charlotte city, NC	6.5
53	52	Arlington city, TX	6.2
74	53	Baton Rouge city, LA	6.1
23	53	El Paso city, TX	6.1
42	55	Mesa city, AZ	6.0
44	55	Omaha city, NE	6.0
45	57	Minneapolis city, MN	5.8
59	58	St. Paul city, MN	5.7
73	59	Norfolk city, VA	5.6
48	60	Colorado Springs city, CO	5.5
15	60	Columbus city, OH	5.5
28	62	Portland city, OR	5.3
11	62	San Jose city, CA	5.3
69	64	Bakersfield city, CA	5.2
67	65	Riverside city, CA	5.1
64	66	Lexington-Fayette, KY	4.9
65	67	Anchorage city, AK	4.7
20	67	Boston city, MA	4.7
52	69	Pittsburgh city, PA	4.4
61	70	Raleigh city, NC	4.3
7	70	San Diego city, CA	4.3
13	72	San Francisco city, CA	4.2
38	73	Virginia Beach city, VA	3.7
46	74	Honolulu CDP, HI	3.2
24	75	Seattle city, WA	2.8

TABLE 6—75 Largest Cities by 2000 Population
Selected Rankings

Unemployment Rate, 2000				Percent Veterans Over 18 Years, 2000				Median Household Income, 2000			
Population Rank	Unemployment Rate Rank	City	[B-5. col 20] Unemployment Rate	Population Rank	Veterans Rank	City	[B-5. col 44] Percent Veterans	Population Rank	Median Household Income Rank	City	[B-5. col 57] Median Household Income (Dollars)
63	1	Newark city, NJ	16.1	38	1	Virginia Beach city, VA	19.5	11	1	San Jose city, CA	70 243
39	2	Atlanta city, GA	14.0	48	2	Colorado Springs city, CO	19.4	65	2	Anchorage city, AK	55 546
10	3	Detroit city, MI	13.8	14	3	Jacksonville, FL	17.2	13	3	San Francisco city, CA	55 221
58	4	Buffalo city, NY	12.5	73	4	Norfolk city, VA	16.9	38	4	Virginia Beach city, VA	48 705
71	5	Stockton city, CA	12.4	65	5	Anchorage city, AK	16.7	53	5	Arlington city, TX	47 622
47	6	Miami city, FL	11.7	68	6	St. Petersburg city, FL	16.4	55	6	Anaheim city, CA	47 122
49	7	St. Louis city, MO	11.3	35	7	Albuquerque city, NM	15.4	26	7	Charlotte city, NC	46 975
33	8	Cleveland city, OH	11.2	32	8	Las Vegas city, NV	15.3	61	8	Raleigh city, NC	46 612
37	8	Fresno city, CA	11.2	62	9	Aurora city, CO	14.9	62	9	Aurora city, CO	46 507
5	10	Philadelphia city, PA	10.9	60	10	Corpus Christi city, TX	14.6	24	10	Seattle city, WA	45 736
70	11	Birmingham city, AL	10.8	42	11	Mesa city, AZ	14.5	7	11	San Diego city, CA	45 733
17	12	Baltimore city, MD	10.7	9	11	San Antonio city, TX	14.5	46	12	Honolulu CDP, HI	45 112
21	12	Washington city, DC	10.7	30	13	Tucson city, AZ	14.0	48	13	Colorado Springs city, CO	45 081
3	14	Chicago city, IL	10.1	29	14	Oklahoma City, OK	13.9	32	14	Las Vegas city, NV	44 069
75	14	Hialeah city, FL	10.1	50	15	Wichita city, KS	13.4	51	15	Santa Ana city, CA	43 412
52	14	Pittsburgh city, PA	10.1	44	16	Omaha city, NE	13.4	42	16	Mesa city, AZ	42 817
72	17	Jersey City, NJ	10.0	43	16	Tulsa city, OK	13.4	16	17	Austin city, TX	42 689
1	18	New York City, NY	9.6	36	18	Kansas City, MO	13.1	67	18	Riverside city, CA	41 646
34	19	Long Beach city, CA	9.4	7	19	San Diego city, CA	12.8	6	19	Phoenix city, AZ	41 207
19	19	Milwaukee city, WI	9.4	57	19	Tampa city, FL	12.8	14	20	Jacksonville, FL	40 316
31	19	New Orleans city, LA	9.4	56	21	Toledo city, OH	12.6	12	21	Indianapolis consolidated city, IN..	40 154
2	22	Los Angeles city, CA	9.3	12	22	Indianapolis consolidated city, IN..	12.5	28	22	Portland city, OR	40 146
23	23	El Paso city, TX	9.0	66	22	Louisville city, KY	12.5	21	23	Washington city, DC	40 127
18	24	Memphis city, TN	8.6	52	22	Pittsburgh city, PA	12.5	41	24	Oakland city, CA	40 055
69	25	Bakersfield city, CA	8.5	23	25	El Paso city, TX	12.4	44	25	Omaha city, NE	40 006
57	25	Tampa city, FL	8.5	46	26	Honolulu CDP, HI	12.3	69	26	Bakersfield city, CA	39 982
74	27	Baton Rouge city, LA	8.3	70	27	Birmingham city, AL	12.1	50	27	Wichita city, KS	39 939
41	27	Oakland city, CA	8.3	28	28	Portland city, OR	11.9	64	28	Lexington-Fayette city, KY	39 813
51	29	Santa Ana city, CA	8.0	40	29	Sacramento city, CA	11.7	22	29	Nashville-Davidson consolidated city, TN	39 797
67	30	Riverside city, CA	7.9	53	30	Arlington city, TX	11.6	20	30	Boston city, MA	39 629
40	30	Sacramento city, CA	7.9	33	30	Cleveland city, OH	11.6	25	31	Denver city, CO	39 500
56	32	Toledo city, OH	7.7	6	30	Phoenix city, AZ	11.6	59	32	St. Paul city, MN	38 774
4	33	Houston city, TX	7.6	49	30	St. Louis city, MO	11.6	3	33	Chicago city, IL	38 625
66	34	Louisville city, KY	7.4	58	34	Buffalo city, NY	11.5	1	34	New York City, NY	38 293
54	35	Cincinnati city, OH	7.3	22	34	Nashville-Davidson consolidated city, TN	11.5	35	35	Albuquerque city, NM	38 272
20	36	Boston city, MA	7.2	64	36	Lexington-Fayette city, KY	11.4	45	36	Minneapolis city, MN	37 974
60	36	Corpus Christi city, TX	7.2	18	37	Memphis city, TN	11.3	15	37	Columbus city, OH	37 897
32	38	Las Vegas city, NV	7.0	69	38	Bakersfield city, CA	11.2	72	38	Jersey City, NJ	37 862
73	38	Norfolk city, VA	7.0	17	38	Baltimore city, MD	11.2	8	39	Dallas city, TX	37 628
8	40	Dallas city, TX	6.7	25	38	Denver city, CO	11.2	34	40	Long Beach city, CA	37 270
28	41	Portland city, OR	6.5	27	41	Fort Worth city, TX	11.1	36	41	Kansas City, MO	37 198
65	42	Anchorage city, AK	6.4	15	42	Columbus city, OH	10.9	27	42	Fort Worth city, TX	37 074
36	43	Kansas City, MO	6.3	5	42	Philadelphia city, PA	10.9	40	43	Sacramento city, CA	37 049
55	44	Anaheim city, CA	6.2	26	44	Charlotte city, NC	10.8	2	44	Los Angeles city, CA	36 687
9	45	San Antonio city, TX	6.1	31	44	New Orleans city, LA	10.8	4	45	Houston city, TX	36 616
27	46	Fort Worth city, TX	6.0	19	46	Milwaukee city, WI	10.7	60	46	Corpus Christi city, TX	36 414
45	47	Minneapolis city, MN	5.8	74	47	Baton Rouge city, LA	10.6	9	47	San Antonio city, TX	36 214
7	47	San Diego city, CA	5.8	54	48	Cincinnati city, OH	10.5	71	48	Stockton city, CA	35 453
30	47	Tucson city, AZ	5.8	67	48	Riverside city, CA	10.5	43	49	Tulsa city, OK	35 316
35	50	Albuquerque city, NM	5.7	59	50	St. Paul city, MN	10.3	29	50	Oklahoma City, OK	34 947
25	50	Denver city, CO	5.7	71	50	Stockton city, CA	10.3	39	51	Atlanta city, GA	34 770
46	50	Honolulu CDP, HI	5.7	10	52	Detroit city, MI	10.2	68	52	St. Petersburg city, FL	34 415
59	50	St. Paul city, MN	5.7	24	52	Seattle city, WA	10.2	57	53	Tampa city, FL	34 415
6	54	Phoenix city, AZ	5.6	37	54	Fresno city, CA	9.9	56	54	Toledo city, OH	32 546
26	55	Charlotte city, NC	5.5	61	55	Raleigh city, NC	9.8	18	55	Memphis city, TN	32 285
12	55	Indianapolis consolidated city, IN..	5.5	21	56	Washington city, DC	9.7	37	56	Fresno city, CA	32 236
64	57	Lexington-Fayette city, KY	5.4	34	57	Long Beach city, CA	9.5	19	57	Milwaukee city, WI	32 216
43	57	Tulsa city, OK	5.4	39	58	Atlanta city, GA	9.2	23	58	El Paso city, TX	32 124
61	59	Raleigh city, NC	5.3	16	58	Austin city, TX	9.2	73	59	Norfolk city, VA	31 815
50	59	Wichita city, KS	5.3	45	60	Minneapolis city, MN	9.1	30	60	Tucson city, AZ	30 981
22	61	Nashville-Davidson consolidated city, TN	5.2	8	61	Dallas city, TX	8.2	5	61	Philadelphia city, PA	30 746
29	61	Oklahoma City, OK	5.2	4	61	Houston city, TX	8.2	74	62	Baton Rouge city, LA	30 368
24	63	Seattle city, WA	5.1	41	63	Oakland city, CA	8.1	17	63	Baltimore city, MD	30 078
68	63	St. Petersburg city, FL	5.1	55	64	Anaheim city, CA	7.9	10	64	Detroit city, MI	29 526
15	65	Columbus city, OH	4.9	11	65	San Jose city, CA	7.7	54	65	Cincinnati city, OH	29 493
14	65	Jacksonville, FL	4.9	3	65	Chicago city, IL	7.3	75	66	Hialeah city, FL	29 492
13	67	San Francisco city, CA	4.6	13	67	San Francisco city, CA	7.0	66	67	Louisville city, KY	28 843
16	68	Austin city, TX	4.4	20	68	Boston city, MA	6.4	52	68	Pittsburgh city, PA	28 588
48	68	Colorado Springs city, CO	4.4	2	68	Los Angeles city, CA	6.4	49	69	St. Louis city, MO	27 156
44	70	Omaha city, NE	4.3	72	70	Jersey City, NJ	5.9	31	70	New Orleans city, LA	27 133
11	70	San Jose city, CA	4.3	63	70	Newark city, NJ	5.9	63	71	Newark city, NJ	26 913
53	72	Arlington city, TX	4.2	1	72	New York City, NY	5.7	70	72	Birmingham city, AL	26 735
42	72	Mesa city, AZ	4.2	47	73	Miami city, FL	4.2	33	73	Cleveland city, OH	25 928
62	74	Aurora city, CO	4.1	51	73	Santa Ana city, CA	4.2	58	74	Buffalo city, NY	24 536
38	75	Virginia Beach city, VA	3.5	75	75	Hialeah city, FL	2.1	47	75	Miami city, FL	23 483

TABLE 6—75 Largest Cities by 2000 Population
Selected Rankings

Percent of all Households with Income Over $100,000, 2000

Population Rank	With Income over $100,000 Rank	City	[B-5. col 71] Percent With Income over $100,000
11	1	San Jose city, CA	30.8
13	2	San Francisco city, CA	24.7
65	3	Anchorage city, AK	18.8
46	4	Honolulu CDP, HI	17.0
21	5	Washington city, DC	16.4
26	6	Charlotte city, NC	15.9
24	6	Seattle city, WA	15.9
7	8	San Diego city, CA	15.6
39	9	Atlanta city, GA	15.1
61	10	Raleigh city, NC	14.6
55	11	Anaheim city, CA	14.5
41	11	Oakland city, CA	14.5
1	13	New York City, NY	13.7
16	14	Austin city, TX	13.6
2	14	Los Angeles city, CA	13.6
53	16	Arlington city, TX	13.0
20	17	Boston city, MA	12.8
8	18	Dallas city, TX	12.4
32	19	Las Vegas city, NV	12.1
38	19	Virginia Beach city, VA	12.1
34	21	Long Beach city, CA	12.0
4	22	Houston city, TX	11.8
67	23	Riverside city, CA	11.7
3	24	Chicago city, IL	11.6
48	24	Colorado Springs city, CO	11.6
25	26	Denver city, CO	11.5
72	26	Jersey City, NJ	11.5
64	26	Lexington-Fayette, KY	11.5
6	26	Phoenix city, AZ	11.5
22	30	Nashville-Davidson consolidated city, TN	10.6
57	31	Tampa city, FL	10.5
45	32	Minneapolis city, MN	10.4
28	33	Portland city, OR	10.2
51	34	Santa Ana city, CA	10.1
69	35	Bakersfield city, CA	10.0
44	35	Omaha city, NE	10.0
12	37	Indianapolis consolidated city, IN	9.8
35	38	Albuquerque city, NM	9.7
62	38	Aurora city, CO	9.7
43	38	Tulsa city, OK	9.7
42	41	Mesa city, AZ	9.6
40	42	Sacramento city, CA	9.4
74	43	Baton Rouge city, LA	9.3
14	43	Jacksonville, FL	9.3
59	43	St. Paul city, MN	9.3
27	46	Fort Worth city, TX	8.9
9	47	San Antonio city, TX	8.6
36	48	Kansas City, MO	8.3
50	48	Wichita city, KS	8.3
71	50	Stockton city, CA	8.2
60	51	Corpus Christi city, TX	8.0
31	52	New Orleans city, LA	7.8
29	52	Oklahoma City, OK	7.8
37	54	Fresno city, CA	7.6
68	54	St. Petersburg city, FL	7.6
54	56	Cincinnati city, OH	7.4
15	56	Columbus city, OH	7.4
18	58	Memphis city, TN	7.3
52	59	Pittsburgh city, PA	7.0
23	60	El Paso city, TX	6.9
47	61	Miami city, FL	6.8
17	62	Baltimore city, MD	6.3
10	62	Detroit city, MI	6.3
73	62	Norfolk city, VA	6.3
5	62	Philadelphia city, PA	6.3
66	66	Louisville city, KY	6.0
63	67	Newark city, NJ	5.3
56	68	Toledo city, OH	5.2
30	69	Tucson city, AZ	5.0
19	70	Milwaukee city, WI	4.7
49	71	St. Louis city, MO	4.6
70	72	Birmingham city, AL	4.5
58	73	Buffalo city, NY	4.1
75	73	Hialeah city, FL	4.1
33	75	Cleveland city, OH	3.4

Percent of all Households with Income Below Poverty, 2000

Population Rank	With Income Below Poverty Rank	City	[B-5. col 73] Percent With Income Below Poverty
47	1	Miami city, FL	29.4
63	2	Newark city, NJ	28.8
31	3	New Orleans city, LA	25.6
58	4	Buffalo city, NY	25.4
33	5	Cleveland city, OH	24.6
10	6	Detroit city, MI	24.3
70	7	Birmingham city, AL	23.3
74	8	Baton Rouge city, LA	22.8
49	9	St. Louis city, MO	22.1
17	10	Baltimore city, MD	21.8
5	10	Philadelphia city, PA	21.8
39	12	Atlanta city, GA	20.7
37	12	Fresno city, CA	20.7
54	14	Cincinnati city, OH	20.5
23	15	El Paso city, TX	20.4
75	16	Hialeah city, FL	20.3
52	16	Pittsburgh city, PA	20.3
66	18	Louisville city, KY	20.1
1	19	New York City, NY	19.7
71	20	Stockton city, CA	19.5
20	21	Boston city, MA	18.7
2	22	Los Angeles city, CA	18.6
18	22	Memphis city, TN	18.6
34	24	Long Beach city, CA	18.2
19	24	Milwaukee city, WI	18.2
73	26	Norfolk city, VA	18.1
72	27	Jersey City, NJ	18.0
3	28	Chicago city, IL	17.4
56	29	Toledo city, OH	17.1
21	29	Washington city, DC	17.1
30	31	Tucson city, AZ	16.9
60	32	Corpus Christi city, TX	16.3
4	32	Houston city, TX	16.3
57	32	Tampa city, FL	16.3
41	35	Oakland city, CA	16.1
40	36	Sacramento city, CA	15.9
9	37	San Antonio city, TX	15.6
69	38	Bakersfield city, CA	15.5
51	39	Santa Ana city, CA	15.4
29	40	Oklahoma City, OK	14.7
8	41	Dallas city, TX	14.4
27	42	Fort Worth city, TX	14.2
67	43	Riverside city, CA	14.1
45	44	Minneapolis city, MN	14.0
15	45	Columbus city, OH	13.8
36	46	Kansas City, MO	13.4
59	47	St. Paul city, MN	13.0
43	47	Tulsa city, OK	13.0
64	49	Lexington-Fayette, KY	12.9
16	50	Austin city, TX	12.8
35	51	Albuquerque city, NM	12.7
6	52	Phoenix city, AZ	12.4
25	53	Denver city, CO	12.1
46	53	Honolulu CDP, HI	12.1
7	53	San Diego city, CA	12.1
68	53	St. Petersburg city, FL	12.1
14	57	Jacksonville, FL	11.9
22	57	Nashville-Davidson consolidated city, TN	11.9
28	57	Portland city, OR	11.9
12	60	Indianapolis consolidated city, IN	10.9
24	61	Seattle city, WA	10.7
50	61	Wichita city, KS	10.7
55	63	Anaheim city, CA	10.5
32	64	Las Vegas city, NV	10.4
44	64	Omaha city, NE	10.4
13	66	San Francisco city, CA	10.2
61	67	Raleigh city, NC	9.9
26	68	Charlotte city, NC	9.3
53	69	Arlington city, TX	8.8
48	70	Colorado Springs city, CO	8.4
42	71	Mesa city, AZ	7.9
62	72	Aurora city, CO	7.6
11	73	San Jose city, CA	7.1
65	74	Anchorage city, AK	6.4
38	75	Virginia Beach city, VA	6.3

Percent of Population that Resides in the Same House in 1995 and 2000

Population Rank	Same Residence Rank	City	[C-5. col 2] Percent Same Residence
5	1	Philadelphia city, PA	61.9
1	2	New York City, NY	61.0
10	3	Detroit city, MI	60.0
17	4	Baltimore city, MD	57.1
31	5	New Orleans city, LA	56.8
52	5	Pittsburgh city, PA	56.8
46	7	Honolulu CDP, HI	56.3
33	8	Cleveland city, OH	55.8
56	9	Toledo city, OH	55.0
70	10	Birmingham city, AL	54.7
3	11	Chicago city, IL	54.4
63	11	Newark city, NJ	54.4
72	13	Jersey City, NJ	54.3
13	14	San Francisco city, CA	54.2
58	15	Buffalo city, NY	54.1
23	15	El Paso city, TX	54.1
44	17	Omaha city, NE	53.2
66	18	Louisville city, KY	51.9
18	18	Memphis city, TN	51.9
60	20	Corpus Christi city, TX	51.8
20	20	San Jose city, CA	51.8
41	22	Oakland city, CA	51.5
9	23	San Antonio city, TX	51.0
49	24	St. Louis city, MO	50.7
21	25	Washington city, DC	49.9
74	26	Baton Rouge city, LA	49.8
36	26	Kansas City, MO	49.8
75	28	Hialeah city, FL	49.7
2	29	Los Angeles city, CA	49.5
68	29	St. Petersburg city, FL	49.5
47	31	Miami city, FL	49.3
59	32	St. Paul city, MN	49.1
19	33	Milwaukee city, WI	48.0
14	34	Jacksonville, FL	48.9
40	35	Sacramento city, CA	48.6
71	36	Stockton city, CA	48.5
20	37	Boston city, MA	47.8
67	38	Riverside city, CA	47.5
12	39	Indianapolis consolidated city, IN	47.4
50	39	Wichita city, KS	47.4
51	41	Santa Ana city, CA	47.2
4	42	Houston city, TX	46.9
29	43	Oklahoma City, OK	46.6
35	44	Albuquerque city, NM	46.4
57	44	Tampa city, FL	46.4
37	46	Fresno city, CA	46.2
54	47	Cincinnati city, OH	46.1
38	48	Virginia Beach city, VA	45.8
22	49	Nashville-Davidson consolidated city, TN	45.5
43	50	Tulsa city, OK	45.4
34	51	Long Beach city, CA	45.2
28	52	Portland city, OR	45.0
27	53	Fort Worth city, TX	44.7
55	54	Anaheim city, CA	44.5
39	55	Atlanta city, GA	44.2
24	56	Seattle city, WA	44.1
26	57	Charlotte city, NC	44.0
69	58	Bakersfield city, CA	43.9
7	59	San Diego city, CA	43.6
6	60	Phoenix city, AZ	43.3
8	61	Dallas city, TX	43.2
30	62	Tucson city, AZ	42.8
25	63	Denver city, CO	42.7
45	63	Minneapolis city, MN	42.7
73	63	Norfolk city, VA	42.7
64	66	Lexington-Fayette, KY	42.5
15	67	Columbus city, OH	41.7
65	68	Anchorage city, AK	41.6
53	69	Arlington city, TX	40.7
42	70	Mesa city, AZ	40.2
62	71	Aurora city, CO	40.1
48	71	Colorado Springs city, CO	40.1
61	73	Raleigh city, NC	37.3
16	74	Austin city, TX	36.0
32	75	Las Vegas city, NV	35.5

TABLE 6—75 Largest Cities by 2000 Population
Selected Rankings

Percent Owner-Occupied Housing Units, 2000				Median Housing Value (Owner Estimated), 2000				Median Gross Rent, 2000			
Population Rank	Owner-Occupied Rank	City	[C-5 col 8] Percent Owner-Occupied	Population Rank	Median Housing Value Rank	City	[C-5 col 22] Median Housing Value (Dollars)	Population Rank	Median Gross Rent Rank	City	[C-5 col 25] Median Gross Rent (Dollars)
42	1	Mesa city, AZ	66.5	13	1	San Francisco city, CA	422 700	11	1	San Jose city, CA	1 123
38	2	Virginia Beach city, VA	65.6	11	2	San Jose city, CA	375 500	13	2	San Francisco city, CA	928
62	3	Aurora city, CO	63.9	46	3	Honolulu CDP, HI	317 300	55	3	Anaheim city, CA	818
68	4	St. Petersburg city, FL	63.6	24	4	Seattle city, WA	252 100	51	4	Santa Ana city, CA	815
14	5	Jacksonville, FL	63.2	41	5	Oakland city, CA	227 300	20	5	Boston city, MA	803
11	6	San Jose city, CA	61.8	1	6	New York City, NY	221 200	7	6	San Diego city, CA	763
50	7	Wichita city, KS	61.6	7	7	San Diego city, CA	220 000	46	7	Honolulu CDP, HI	760
23	8	El Paso city, TX	61.4	2	8	Los Angeles city, CA	215 600	65	8	Anchorage city, AK	736
48	9	Colorado Springs city, CO	60.8	20	9	Boston city, MA	210 100	38	9	Virginia Beach city, VA	734
6	10	Phoenix city, AZ	60.7	55	10	Anaheim city, CA	204 000	16	10	Austin city, TX	724
35	11	Albuquerque city, NM	60.4	34	11	Long Beach city, CA	198 600	24	11	Seattle city, WA	721
69	11	Bakersfield city, CA	60.4	51	12	Santa Ana city, CA	173 300	61	12	Raleigh city, NC	718
65	13	Anchorage city, AK	60.0	25	13	Denver city, CO	160 100	1	13	New York City, NY	705
56	14	Toledo city, OH	59.8	28	14	Portland city, OR	154 700	62	14	Aurora city, CO	700
60	15	Corpus Christi city, TX	59.6	21	15	Washington city, DC	153 500	32	15	Las Vegas city, NV	699
44	15	Omaha city, NE	59.6	61	16	Raleigh city, NC	152 400	41	16	Oakland city, CA	696
29	17	Oklahoma City, OK	59.5	65	17	Anchorage city, AK	152 300	26	17	Charlotte city, NC	684
5	18	Philadelphia city, PA	59.3	3	18	Chicago city, IL	144 300	72	18	Jersey City, NJ	675
32	19	Las Vegas city, NV	59.1	39	19	Atlanta city, GA	144 100	2	19	Los Angeles city, CA	672
12	20	Indianapolis consolidated city, IN	58.8	48	20	Colorado Springs city, CO	143 300	67	20	Riverside city, CA	670
9	21	San Antonio city, TX	58.1	62	21	Aurora city, CO	139 700	42	21	Mesa city, AZ	669
36	22	Kansas City, MO	57.7	72	22	Jersey City, NJ	137 900	48	22	Colorado Springs city, CO	652
26	23	Charlotte city, NC	57.5	67	23	Riverside city, CA	136 000	34	23	Long Beach city, CA	639
67	24	Riverside city, CA	56.7	32	24	Las Vegas city, NV	133 100	53	24	Arlington city, TX	635
27	25	Fort Worth city, TX	55.9	63	25	Newark city, NJ	132 800	25	25	Denver city, CO	631
18	25	Memphis city, TN	55.9	26	26	Charlotte city, NC	131 500	40	26	Sacramento city, CA	625
28	27	Portland city, OR	55.8	40	27	Sacramento city, CA	126 000	8	27	Dallas city, TX	623
43	28	Tulsa city, OK	55.6	35	28	Albuquerque city, NM	123 700	6	28	Phoenix city, AZ	622
64	29	Lexington-Fayette, KY	55.3	38	29	Virginia Beach city, VA	121 500	28	29	Portland city, OR	622
22	29	Nashville-Davidson consolidated city, TN	55.3	16	30	Austin city, TX	120 800	21	30	Washington city, DC	618
57	31	Tampa city, FL	55.1	71	31	Stockton city, CA	117 500	3	31	Chicago city, IL	616
10	32	Detroit city, MI	54.9	47	32	Miami city, FL	116 400	22	32	Nashville-Davidson consolidated city, TN	615
59	33	St. Paul city, MN	54.8	22	33	Nashville-Davidson consolidated city, TN	114 200	75	33	Hialeah city, FL	614
53	34	Arlington city, TX	54.7	45	34	Minneapolis city, MN	113 700	39	34	Atlanta city, GA	606
70	35	Birmingham city, AL	53.5	42	35	Mesa city, AZ	112 100	14	35	Jacksonville, FL	598
30	35	Tucson city, AZ	53.5	64	36	Lexington-Fayette, KY	109 700	15	36	Columbus city, OH	586
25	37	Denver city, CO	52.5	6	37	Phoenix city, AZ	107 000	63	36	Newark city, NJ	586
66	37	Louisville city, KY	52.5	59	38	St. Paul city, MN	105 000	71	38	Stockton city, CA	581
74	39	Baton Rouge city, LA	52.4	69	39	Bakersfield city, CA	103 500	57	39	Tampa city, FL	577
52	40	Pittsburgh city, PA	52.1	75	40	Hialeah city, FL	102 300	4	40	Houston city, TX	575
71	41	Stockton city, CA	51.9	15	41	Columbus city, OH	99 100	45	40	Minneapolis city, MN	575
61	42	Raleigh city, NC	51.6	12	42	Indianapolis consolidated city, IN	96 900	5	42	Philadelphia city, PA	569
45	43	Minneapolis city, MN	51.4	37	43	Fresno city, CA	94 900	12	43	Indianapolis consolidated city, IN	567
75	44	Hialeah city, FL	50.8	53	44	Arlington city, TX	94 800	68	43	St. Petersburg city, FL	567
37	45	Fresno city, CA	50.7	44	45	Omaha city, NE	93 300	59	45	St. Paul city, MN	565
17	46	Baltimore city, MD	50.3	54	46	Cincinnati city, OH	93 200	69	46	Bakersfield city, CA	564
55	47	Anaheim city, CA	50.1	74	47	Baton Rouge city, LA	93 100	35	47	Albuquerque city, NM	560
40	47	Sacramento city, CA	50.1	30	48	Tucson city, AZ	91 200	27	48	Fort Worth city, TX	559
7	49	San Diego city, CA	49.5	73	49	Norfolk city, VA	88 300	60	49	Corpus Christi city, TX	555
51	50	Santa Ana city, CA	49.3	31	50	New Orleans city, LA	88 100	9	50	San Antonio city, TX	549
15	51	Columbus city, OH	49.1	8	51	Dallas city, TX	87 400	36	51	Kansas City, MO	548
33	52	Cleveland city, OH	48.5	14	52	Jacksonville, FL	84 100	18	51	Memphis city, TN	548
24	53	Seattle city, WA	48.4	36	53	Kansas City, MO	83 300	37	53	Fresno city, CA	538
46	54	Honolulu CDP, HI	46.9	66	54	Louisville city, KY	81 900	73	53	Norfolk city, VA	538
49	54	St. Louis city, MO	46.9	43	54	Tulsa city, OK	81 900	44	55	Omaha city, NE	537
31	56	New Orleans city, LA	46.5	57	56	Tampa city, FL	80 700	47	56	Miami city, FL	535
4	57	Houston city, TX	45.8	19	57	Milwaukee city, WI	79 600	64	57	Lexington-Fayette, KY	528
73	58	Norfolk city, VA	45.6	68	58	St. Petersburg city, FL	78 200	19	58	Milwaukee city, WI	527
19	59	Milwaukee city, WI	45.3	29	59	Oklahoma City, OK	78 100	30	59	Tucson city, AZ	516
16	60	Austin city, TX	44.9	4	60	Houston city, TX	77 500	43	60	Tulsa city, OK	511
3	61	Chicago city, IL	43.8	50	61	Wichita city, KS	75 000	50	61	Wichita city, KS	505
39	62	Atlanta city, GA	43.7	56	62	Toledo city, OH	73 700	52	62	Pittsburgh city, PA	500
58	63	Buffalo city, NY	43.5	18	63	Memphis city, TN	72 300	17	63	Baltimore city, MD	498
8	64	Dallas city, TX	43.2	33	64	Cleveland city, OH	71 100	31	64	New Orleans city, LA	488
41	65	Oakland city, CA	41.4	60	65	Corpus Christi city, TX	70 500	10	65	Detroit city, MI	486
34	66	Long Beach city, CA	41.1	17	66	Baltimore city, MD	69 900	74	66	Baton Rouge city, LA	483
21	67	Washington city, DC	40.8	23	66	El Paso city, TX	69 900	29	67	Oklahoma City, OK	481
54	68	Cincinnati city, OH	39.0	27	68	Fort Worth city, TX	69 700	23	68	El Paso city, TX	474
2	69	Los Angeles city, CA	38.6	9	69	San Antonio city, TX	67 500	58	69	Buffalo city, NY	472
13	70	San Francisco city, CA	35.0	49	70	St. Louis city, MO	63 500	56	70	Toledo city, OH	469
47	71	Miami city, FL	34.9	10	71	Detroit city, MI	62 800	33	71	Cleveland city, OH	465
20	72	Boston city, MA	32.2	70	72	Birmingham city, AL	62 200	70	72	Birmingham city, AL	446
1	73	New York City, NY	30.2	5	73	Philadelphia city, PA	61 000	54	73	Cincinnati city, OH	444
72	74	Jersey City, NJ	28.2	52	74	Pittsburgh city, PA	60 700	66	74	Louisville city, KY	443
63	75	Newark city, NJ	23.8	58	75	Buffalo city, NY	58 800	49	75	St. Louis city, MO	442

Age, Ethnicity, and Household Structure

(For explanation of symbols, see page xi.)

Prevalent Race or Hispanic Origin

2000

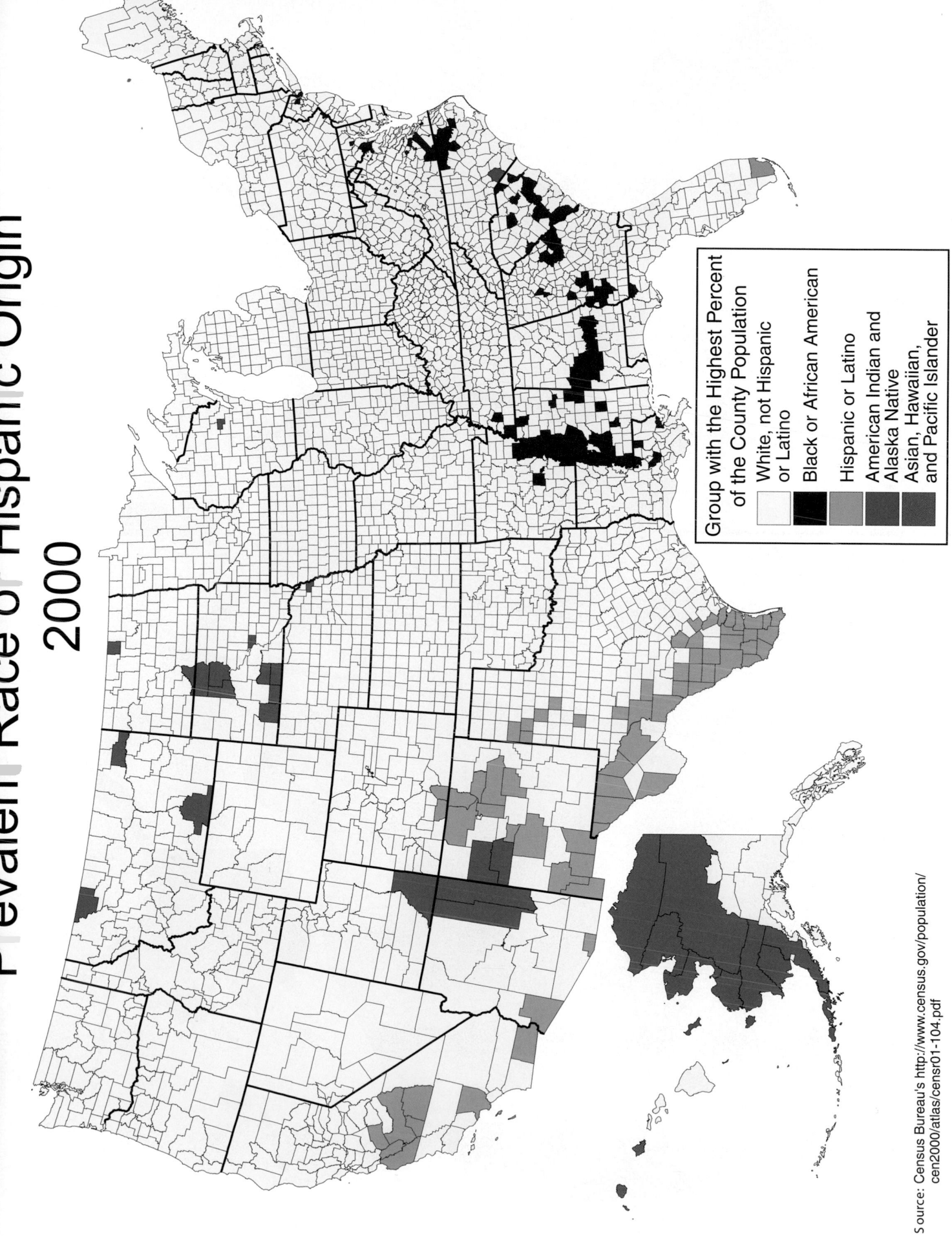

Group with the Highest Percent of the County Population

- White, not Hispanic or Latino
- Black or African American
- Hispanic or Latino
- American Indian and Alaska Native
- Asian, Hawaiian, and Pacific Islander

Source: Census Bureau's http://www.census.gov/population/ cen2000/atlas/censr01-104.pdf

Prevalent Minority Population 2000

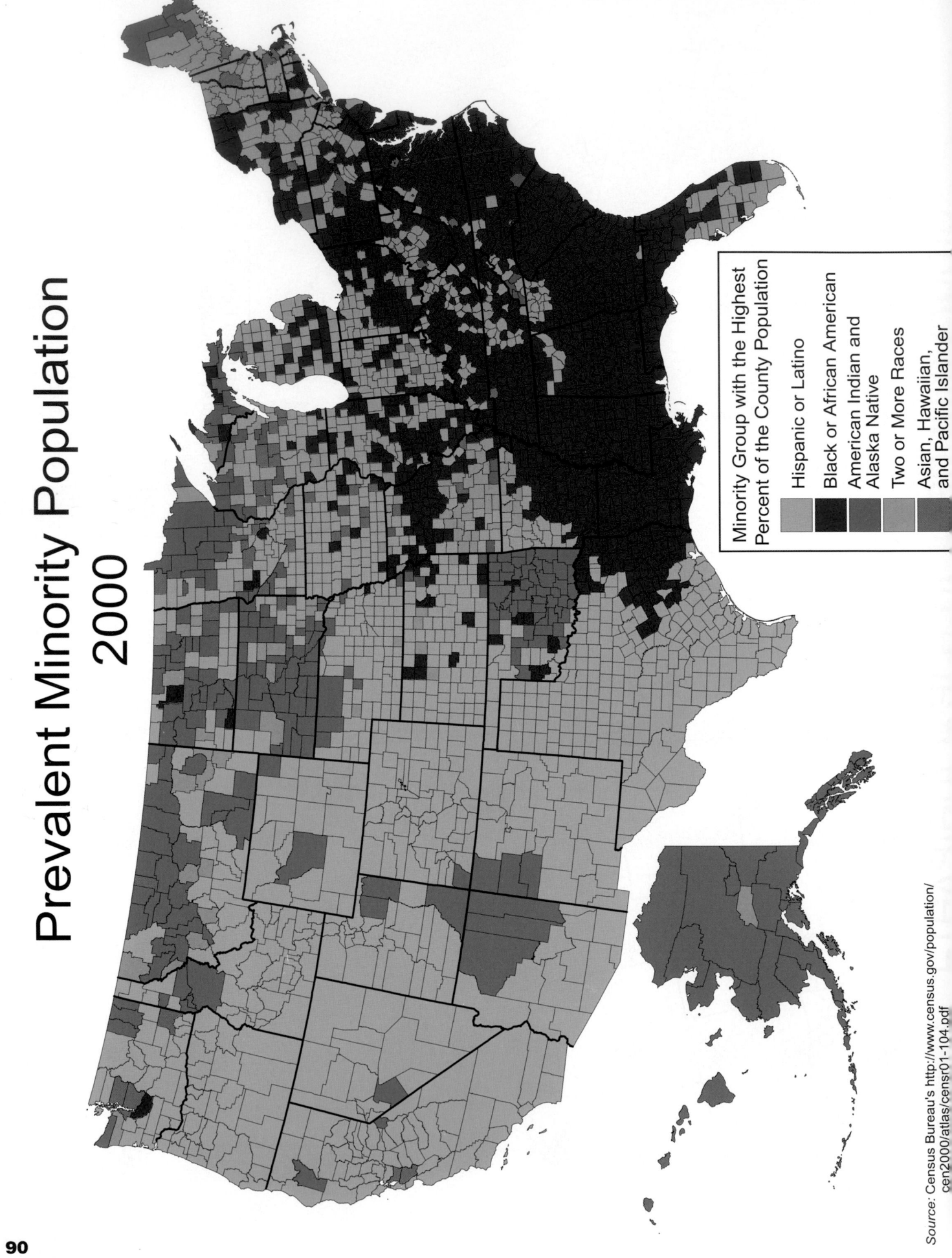

Minority Group with the Highest
Percent of the County Population

- Hispanic or Latino
- Black or African American
- American Indian and Alaska Native
- Two or More Races
- Asian, Hawaiian, and Pacific Islander

Source: Census Bureau's http://www.census.gov/population/cen2000/atlas/censr01-104.pdf

Diversity Index
2000

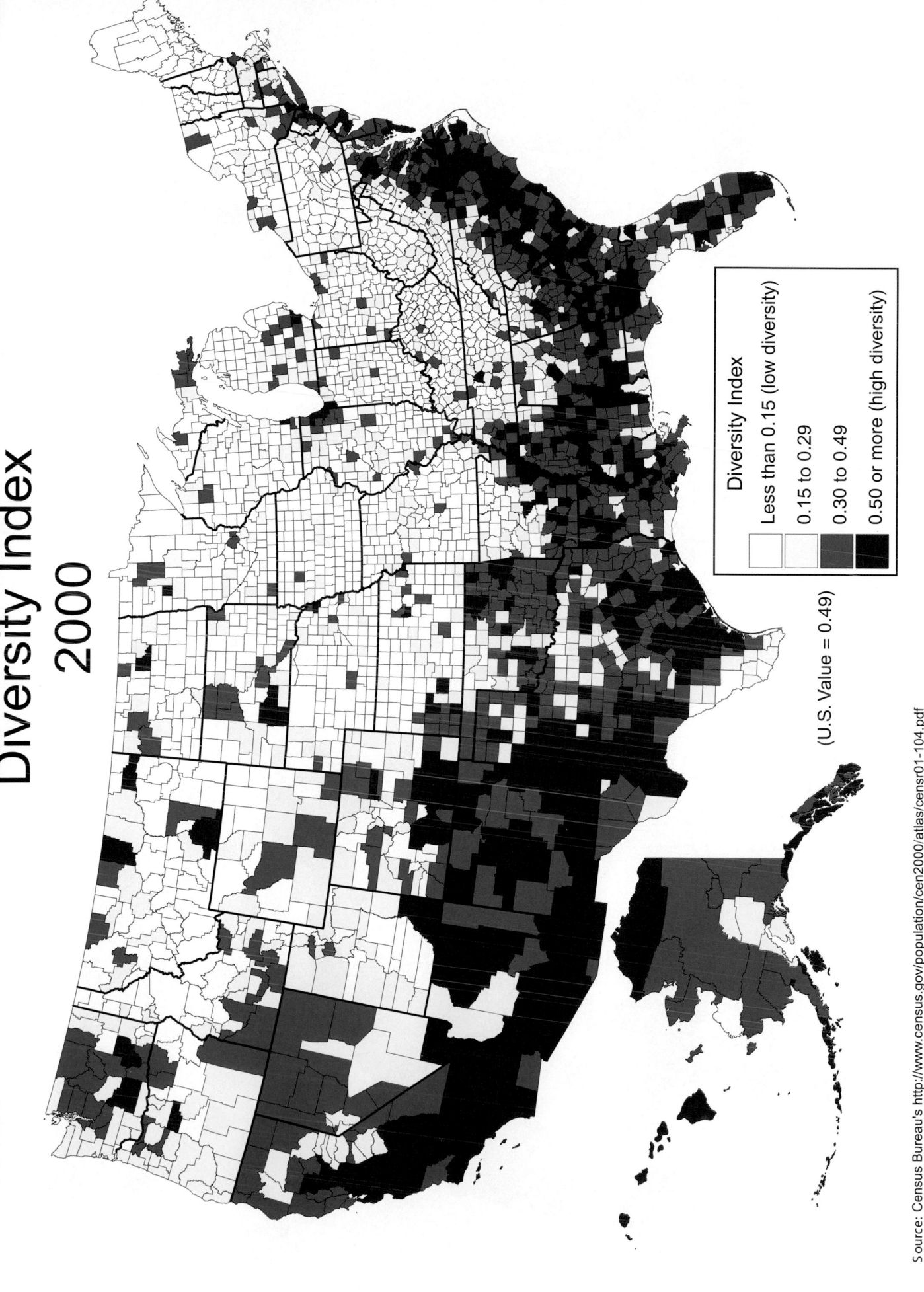

Diversity Index

Less than 0.15 (low diversity)

0.15 to 0.29

0.30 to 0.49

0.50 or more (high diversity)

(U.S. Value = 0.49)

Source: Census Bureau's http://www.census.gov/population/cen2000/atlas/censr01-104.pdf
Note: The Diversity Index measures the likelihood of living near persons of other races or Hispanic origin.

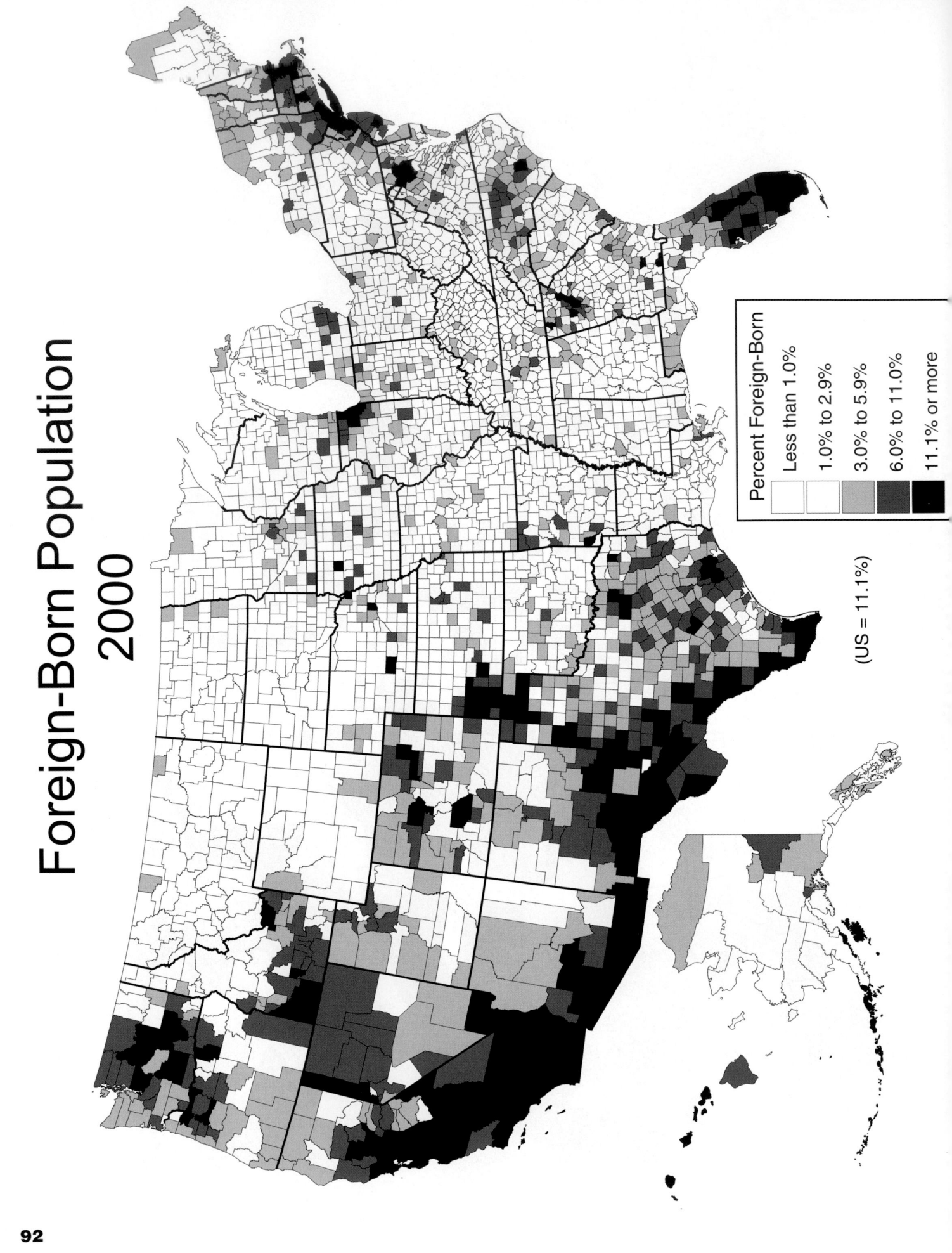

Foreign-Born Population 2000

Percent Foreign-Born

- Less than 1.0%
- 1.0% to 2.9%
- 3.0% to 5.9%
- 6.0% to 11.0%
- 11.1% or more

(US = 11.1%)

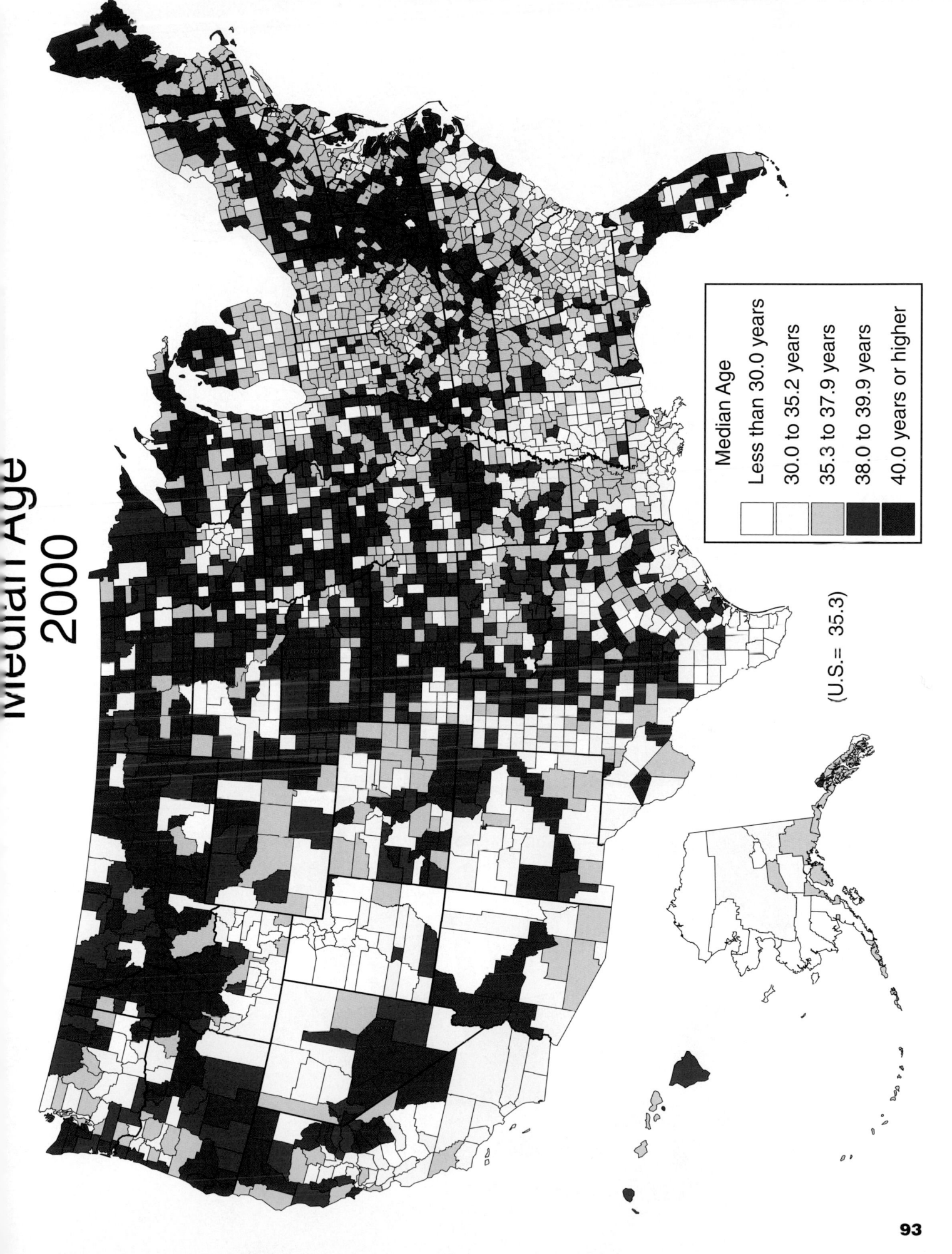

Median Age
2000

Median Age

Less than 30.0 years

30.0 to 35.2 years

35.3 to 37.9 years

38.0 to 39.9 years

40.0 years or higher

(U.S.= 35.3)

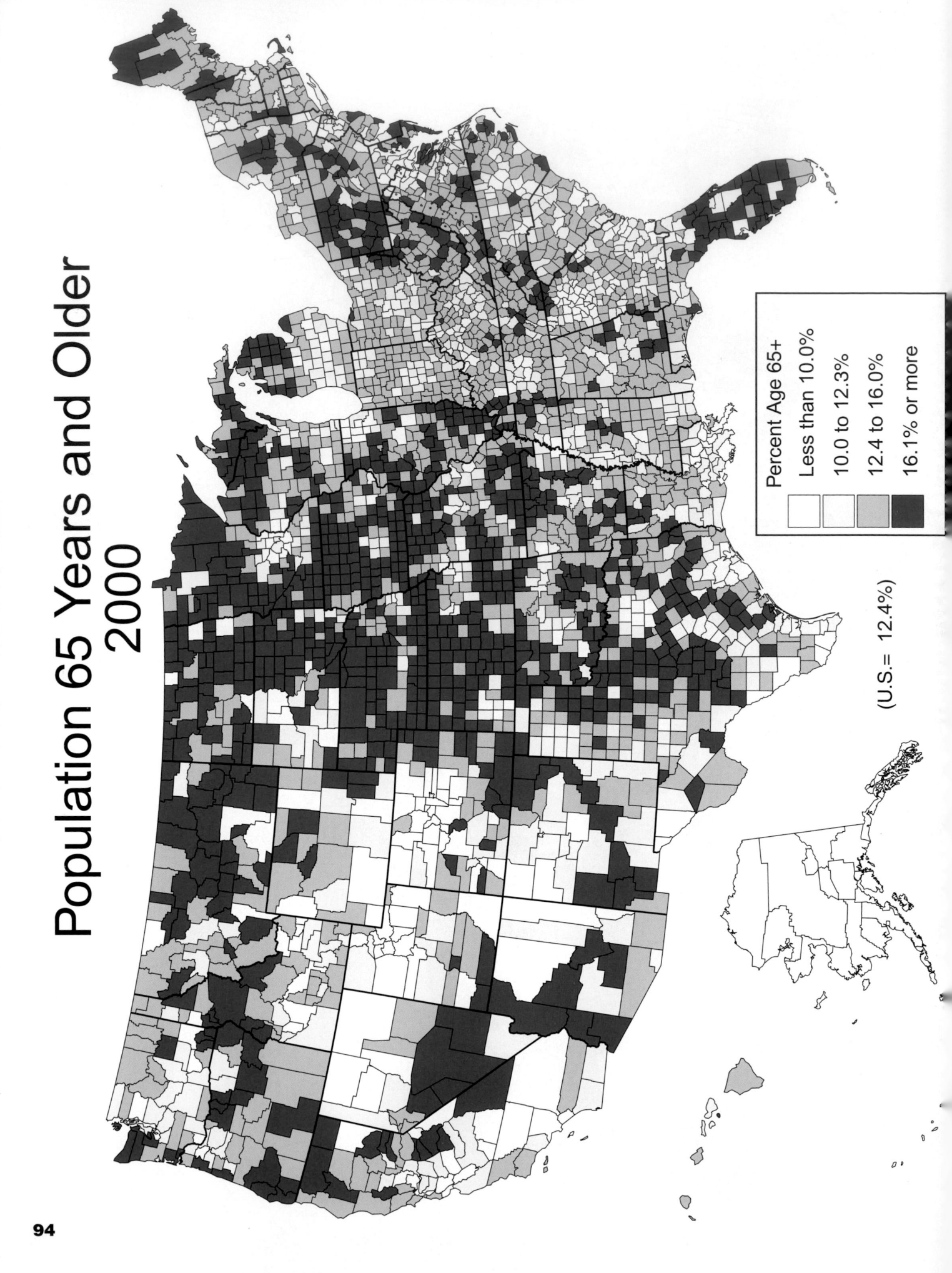

Population 65 Years and Older
2000

Percent Age 65+

Less than 10.0%
10.0 to 12.3%
12.4 to 16.0%
16.1% or more

(U.S.= 12.4%)

94

Population Under 18 Years Old
2000

Persons Under Age 18

	Less than 20.0%
	20.0 to 25.6%
	25.7 to 29.9%
	30.0% or more

25.7%)

96

"Tra

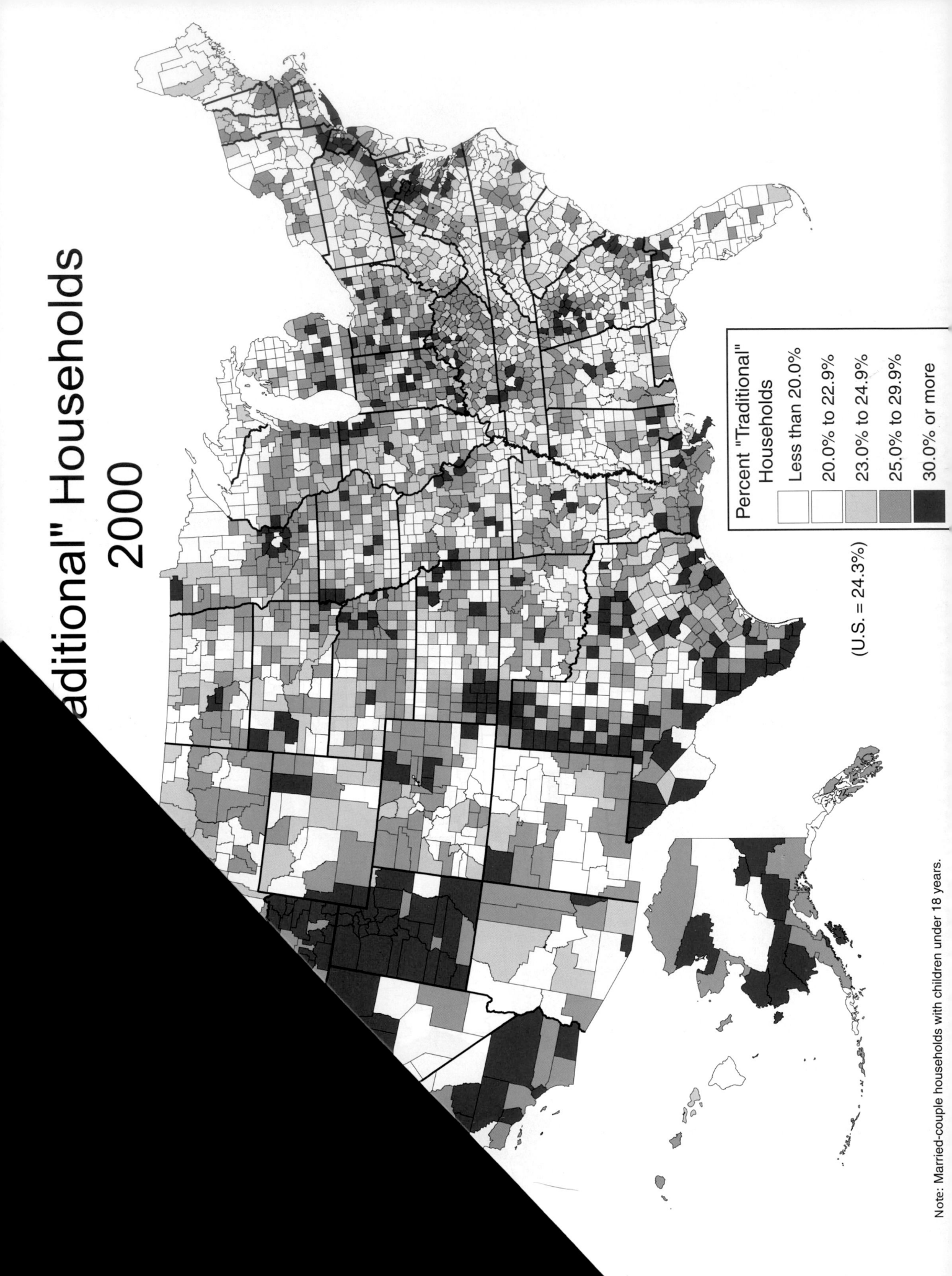

aditional" Households
2000

Percent "Traditional" Households

- Less than 20.0%
- 20.0% to 22.9%
- 23.0% to 24.9%
- 25.0% to 29.9%
- 30.0% or more

(U.S. = 24.3%)

Note: Married-couple households with children under 18 years.

Age, Ethnicity, and Household Structure

Once a decade, the census provides an opportunity to benchmark "what's happening right here" against key national trends. Americans rarely stop to think that the interesting population changes they hear about nationally might not be happening in their city, their county, or even their state. But the trends the news media report are a blend of vastly different situations across the country.

Some places are changing even faster than the national picture; others are lagging or even going in a different direction. Obviously, it's important for local decision-makers to know how their locality fits into the national picture. Maybe they need new policies to remain part of the mainstream; or maybe they need to adjust their thinking to changes they can't do anything about.

Some of the tables that follow measure specific places against the national averages, showing those that are most "different" for important topics. All the tables offer data Americans need to situate their state, county, or city in the national portrait, and make decisions accordingly.

Minority/Majority Geography

Probably the most visible place-based demographic difference is in racial and ethnic composition. Seen from afar, the U.S. population may be a melting pot, but at close range it looks more like a salad that's been tossed unevenly. As Table A-2 shows, almost no place in America resembles the 2000 national averages the census reported.

New Jersey comes the closest to matching the national portrait of race and Hispanic origin, followed by Illinois and Florida, though each state differs along one or more dimension. (Table A-1.1.) All other states diverge widely from the national portrait along one dimension or another. For example, over 95 percent of the population of Vermont, New Hampshire, and Maine is non-Hispanic white, compared with less than half the population of California, Hawaii, and New Mexico. Indeed, an important use of this book is providing a benchmark for counties and cities against nationwide trends.

The maps on pages 89-92 show how America's multiracial society is distributed across the country. Perhaps the most useful way to look at them is to identify counties that are really diverse. (See page 91.) These are largely counties in a band stretching from coast to coast along the southern part of the country, reaching north along the East

Table A-1.1.

Only a few states resemble the national portrait of race and Hispanic origin.

Race and Hispanic Origin, Selected States, 2000

(Percent distribution.)

Race and Hispanic origin	United States	New Jersey	Illinois	Florida
White non-Hispanic	69.1	66.0	67.8	65.4
Hispanic or Latino	12.5	13.3	12.3	16.8
Black or African American	12.2	13.4	15.0	14.5
Asian, Hawaiian, and Pacific Islander	3.7	5.8	3.4	1.7
American Indian and Alaska Native	0.9	0.2	0.2	0.3

Source: Census 2000 Summary File 3—United States, U.S. Census Bureau, 2002. Table 145A-I.
Note: Hispanics and Latinos are included in all races except non-Hispanic White. This table excludes those who reported two or more races, or "other" race.

Coast. Conversely, the northern part of the country contains the least diverse counties, except along the West Coast.

These are two almost mirror images—one representing the United States as it used to think of itself, the other representing its future. Readers from counties located in the lower band need to pay particular attention to racial and ethnic differences in the subjects found in this book. Meanwhile, readers from counties located in the upper band need to situate their relatively homogeneous populations in the context of more diverse counties elsewhere.

Most counties have a population that is majority white non-Hispanic, but many counties have a majority population that is some other race or ethnic group. (See page 89.) Counties in the Southwest that were originally settled by the Spanish have a population that is majority Hispanic. Similarly, many counties in the Southeast have a population that is majority African-American. Several counties in the western part of the central United States, north and south, have a majority population that is American Indian. These counties contain (or are contained in) tribal reservations. And Hawaii contains the only counties that have a majority Asian population.

The map that shows the prevalence of minority population gives a handy insight into the nation's diversity geography. (See page 90.) Counties in states west of the Mississippi are more likely to have significant Hispanic origin populations, while counties east of the Mississippi are more likely to have significant African-American populations.

Counties with a high concentration of Asians are scattered across the country, particularly in the northern states, while American Indians cluster around tribal lands. Meanwhile, counties where a high percentage of the population reported "two or more" races (not Hispanic) in Census 2000 are found in the middle parts of the country. In many cases, they are adjacent to large American Indian populations. So this finding probably reflects the greater likelihood of Indians to marry people of other races, as tends to happen with small populations.

Older Places, Younger Places

Few Americans realize how state-to-state migration has divided states and counties along another demographic dimension: the age structure of communities. (See Table A-1.2.) The introduction (pages 2-3) describes how longer lives are making the nation more diverse with respect to people's ages. Thanks to interstate migrants, who tend to be predominantly young adults, followed by new retirees, this diversity is particularly pronounced geographically. Although Census 2000 found that migration slowed during the 1990s, the effects of heavy migration to the South and the Southwest during the two previous decades are showing up now. Essentially, the formerly 20-something migrants have been having their children in their new locations, leaving their old locations in the Northeast and the Midwest with fewer parents.

The median age is the first way to key in on differences from the national age picture. The median age has risen across the country as a result of Americans' increasing life expectancy, but it is not the same everywhere. This simple check reveals that seven states are two or more years older than the national median age of

Table A-1.2.
Only a few states resemble the national age portrait.
Age, Selected States, 2000

(Percent distribution.)

State	Under 18 years	18 to 24 years	25 to 44 years	45 to 64 years	65 years and over
United States	25.6	9.6	30.4	21.9	12.4
Illinois	26.1	9.7	30.7	21.4	12.1
Indiana	25.9	10.1	29.5	22.1	12.4
Michigan	26.1	9.4	29.9	22.4	12.3

Source: Census 2000 Summary File 3—United States, U.S. Census. Table P8.

Table A-1.3.
Age differences among states are increasingly noticeable.
Median Age, Selected States, 2000

Oldest states	Median age	Youngest states	Median age
West Virginia	38.9	Utah	27.1
Florida	38.7	Texas	32.3
Maine	38.6	Alaska	32.4
Pennsylvania	38.0	Idaho	33.2
Vermont	37.7	California	33.3
Montana	37.5		
Connecticut	37.4		

Source: Census 2000 Summary File 1—United States, U.S. Census Bureau, 2002. Table P13.

35.3, and five states are two or more years younger. (See Table A-1.2 and A-2.)

It's important to make another check—the differences in the percentage of the population that is under age 18 or over 65—because if more than one trend is going on, the median age simply averages them. Among the two "oldest" states, for instance, Florida has large numbers of children due to in-migration of Hispanics and other groups from the Caribbean, as well as large numbers of retirees; while West Virginia is a case of "aging in place," that is, younger people left while older people stayed behind.

As a state equivalent, the District of Columbia is shown in all the state tables that follow. However, it is largely excluded from this analysis because it is really a central city, with its suburbs located in other states. So its demographic statistics are consistently extreme, compared with the states. For instance, it has a lower proportion of children under 18 than any state—because families with children tend to live in the suburbs.

This benchmarking finds that the shift to an older America is particularly pronounced in the Northeast and the Midwest, because these states account for fewer of America's children. Florida is known for its high proportion of retirees—nearly 18 percent of Floridians are age 65 and older. But by and large, states that have been losing young adults to other regions are creating an "elderly" belt anchored by Iowa, where 15 percent of the population is age 65 and older, and running from North Dakota through Ohio, West Virginia, and Pennsylvania to Maine.

Meanwhile, parts of the country that received young migrants a decade or two ago are looking at a large youth population (page 95). A state like Arizona is in a very different position from an aging state like West Virginia. Over 30 percent of Arizona's population is under age 18, compared with just 22 percent in West Virginia. Arizona also benefits from retirees, so its population aged 65 and older is above the national average. The tables that follow

Table A-1.4. Age by Race, Hispanic Origin, and Metropolitan/Central City Residence, United States, 2000

(Number, percent.)

Race, Hispanic origin, sex and metropolitan area status	Total population	Children under 18 years (percent of total population)				Adults 18 years and over (percent of total population)					
		Total	Under 5 years	5 to 14 years	15 to 17 years	Total	18 to 24 years	25 to 44 years	45 to 64 years	65 to 84 years	85 years and over
Total Population	281 421 906	25.6	6.8	14.6	4.2	74.4	9.6	30.4	21.9	11.0	1.5
One race only	274 150 980	25.2	6.6	14.5	4.2	74.8	9.6	30.4	22.1	11.1	1.5
White	211 353 725	23.4	6.1	13.4	4.0	76.6	8.9	29.7	23.6	12.6	1.8
Black or African American	34 361 740	31.3	8.0	18.3	5.0	68.7	10.9	31.0	18.6	7.3	0.9
American Indian and Alaska Native	2 447 989	33.3	8.4	19.3	5.6	66.7	11.5	31.4	18.1	5.2	0.5
Asian	10 171 820	23.9	6.4	13.4	4.1	76.1	10.8	36.6	21.0	7.1	0.6
Native Hawaiian and Other Pacific Islander	378 782	31.8	8.3	18.1	5.5	68.2	13.6	33.2	16.5	4.5	0.4
Some other race	15 436 924	35.8	10.6	19.9	5.3	64.2	14.9	34.6	11.8	2.7	0.2
Two or more races	7 270 926	40.7	13.3	21.9	5.4	59.3	11.8	28.3	14.2	4.6	0.5
Hispanic or Latino [1]	35 238 481	34.8	10.4	19.4	5.0	65.2	13.3	33.4	13.7	4.4	0.4
White alone, not Hispanic or Latino	194 514 140	22.6	5.7	13.0	3.9	77.4	8.6	29.4	24.3	13.2	1.9
Male Population	137 916 186	26.8	7.1	15.3	4.4	73.2	10.0	31.0	21.7	9.6	0.9
One race only	134 281 247	26.4	6.9	15.1	4.4	73.6	10.0	31.0	22.0	9.7	0.9
White	103 677 217	24.6	6.4	14.0	4.2	75.4	9.2	30.5	23.6	11.1	1.0
Black or African American	16 284 366	33.5	8.6	19.7	5.3	66.5	11.3	30.8	17.8	6.0	0.5
American Indian and Alaska Native	1 216 063	34.2	8.6	19.9	5.7	65.8	11.9	31.4	17.6	4.5	0.3
Asian	4 896 515	25.5	6.7	14.4	4.4	74.5	11.2	36.4	20.1	6.2	0.5
Native Hawaiian and Other Pacific Islander	191 966	32.5	8.3	18.4	5.7	67.5	13.8	33.3	16.1	4.0	0.3
Some other race	8 015 120	35.4	10.4	19.6	5.3	64.6	15.7	35.5	11.2	2.2	0.1
Two or more races	3 634 939	41.4	13.6	22.4	5.5	58.6	12.0	28.6	13.8	3.9	0.3
Hispanic or Latino [1]	18 056 347	34.9	10.4	19.4	5.1	65.1	14.2	34.1	12.9	3.7	0.3
White alone, not Hispanic or Latino	95 128 520	23.8	6.0	13.6	4.1	76.2	8.9	30.2	24.4	11.6	1.1
Female Population	143 505 720	24.5	6.5	14.0	4.0	75.5	9.2	29.8	22.1	12.3	2.1
One race only	139 869 733	24.1	6.3	13.8	4.0	75.9	9.2	29.9	22.3	12.5	2.1
White	107 676 508	22.4	5.8	12.8	3.8	77.6	8.5	29.0	23.6	14.1	2.5
Black or African American	18 077 374	29.2	7.5	17.1	4.6	70.8	10.6	31.2	19.2	8.5	1.2
American Indian and Alaska Native	1 231 926	32.3	8.1	18.7	5.5	67.7	11.2	31.4	18.7	5.8	0.6
Asian	5 275 305	22.5	6.1	12.5	3.9	77.5	10.4	36.7	21.8	7.9	0.7
Native Hawaiian and Other Pacific Islander	186 816	31.1	8.2	17.7	5.2	68.9	13.4	33.0	16.9	5.0	0.5
Some other race	7 421 804	36.2	10.7	20.1	5.3	63.8	14.1	33.7	12.4	3.3	0.3
Two or more races	3 635 987	39.9	13.1	21.5	5.3	60.1	11.6	28.0	14.7	5.2	0.6
Hispanic or Latino [1]	17 182 134	34.7	10.4	19.3	4.9	65.3	12.4	32.6	14.5	5.2	0.6
White alone, not Hispanic or Latino	99 385 620	21.5	5.5	12.4	3.7	78.5	8.3	28.8	24.2	14.7	2.6
Total population											
Total population	281 421 906	25.6	6.8	14.6	4.2	74.4	9.6	30.4	21.9	11.0	1.5
Male	137 916 186	26.8	7.1	15.3	4.4	73.2	10.0	31.0	21.7	9.6	0.9
Female	143 505 720	24.5	6.5	14.0	4.0	75.5	9.2	29.8	22.1	12.3	2.1
In Central Cities of Metropolitan Areas											
Total population	85 399 835	25.1	7.1	14.1	3.9	74.9	11.9	31.8	19.7	10.1	1.5
Male	41 453 945	26.4	7.4	14.9	4.1	73.6	12.3	32.8	19.2	8.5	0.8
Female	43 945 890	23.8	6.7	13.4	3.7	76.2	11.6	30.8	20.1	11.6	2.1
In Metropolitan Areas, not in Central Cities											
Total population	140 581 876	26.1	6.8	15.1	4.3	73.9	8.3	30.7	22.8	10.7	1.3
Male	69 000 689	27.4	7.1	15.7	4.5	72.6	8.7	31.0	22.7	9.5	0.8
Female	71 581 187	25.0	6.5	14.4	4.1	75.0	7.9	30.4	22.9	11.9	1.9
Not in Metropolitan Areas											
Total population	55 440 195	25.2	6.3	14.4	4.6	74.8	9.4	27.4	23.2	12.9	1.8
Male	27 461 552	26.2	6.5	14.9	4.8	73.8	10.0	28.1	23.3	11.4	1.1
Female	27 978 643	24.3	6.1	13.9	4.4	75.7	8.9	26.7	23.2	14.3	2.6

Source: Census 2000 Summary File 3—United States, U.S. Census Bureau, 2002. Tables P8 and 145A-I.
[1] Hispanic or Latino persons may be of any race.

measure each state and county against the national average for both the older and the younger population; they also provide numbers for readers to measure the entire age structure of the places they care about.

Working-age populations are of particular interest to economic planners, as they can vary according to economic conditions. That is, these populations can grow at different rates according to differences in job availability. Most people prefer to migrate when they are just starting their work lives, but employment opportunities, or lack of them, can encourage mid-life adults to move. These moves in and out change the age structure of a place's working age population. For instance, Alaska, Colorado, and Georgia now have relatively larger populations at ages 25 to 44; Montana and the Dakotas have relatively smaller ones. Other states that have a noticeably older working-age population are Maine, Vermont, and West Virginia.

Educators, work force planners, and health care providers are all influenced by the age structure of a particular population. The nation's multicultural mosaic adds a further set of differences. Essentially, thanks to differences in migration and fertility, younger populations are more likely to be minority, particularly Hispanic, while older ones are more likely to be white non-Hispanic.

As the chart shows, non-Hispanic whites and Hispanics are almost a mirror image. Over a third of Hispanics are under age 18, and almost half are under age 24. In contrast, nearly 40 percent of non-Hispanic whites are age 45 and older, compared with less than 20 percent of Hispanics. In short, changes in the nation's age and racial makeup interact with migration trends to give counties and communities distinctively different faces.

New "traditional" families, and old ones too

Places that differ from the national age portrait also differ from the nation's household portrait. Put simply, populations that are predominantly middle-aged and/or older have relatively fewer "traditional" families, that is, married couples with children at home. Instead, they are dominated by the "new" traditional family: married couples without children in the home, largely couples whose youngest child is age 18 or older. Meanwhile, populations where younger adults are in the majority look very much like the country as a whole did a half century ago in that traditional families are the norm.

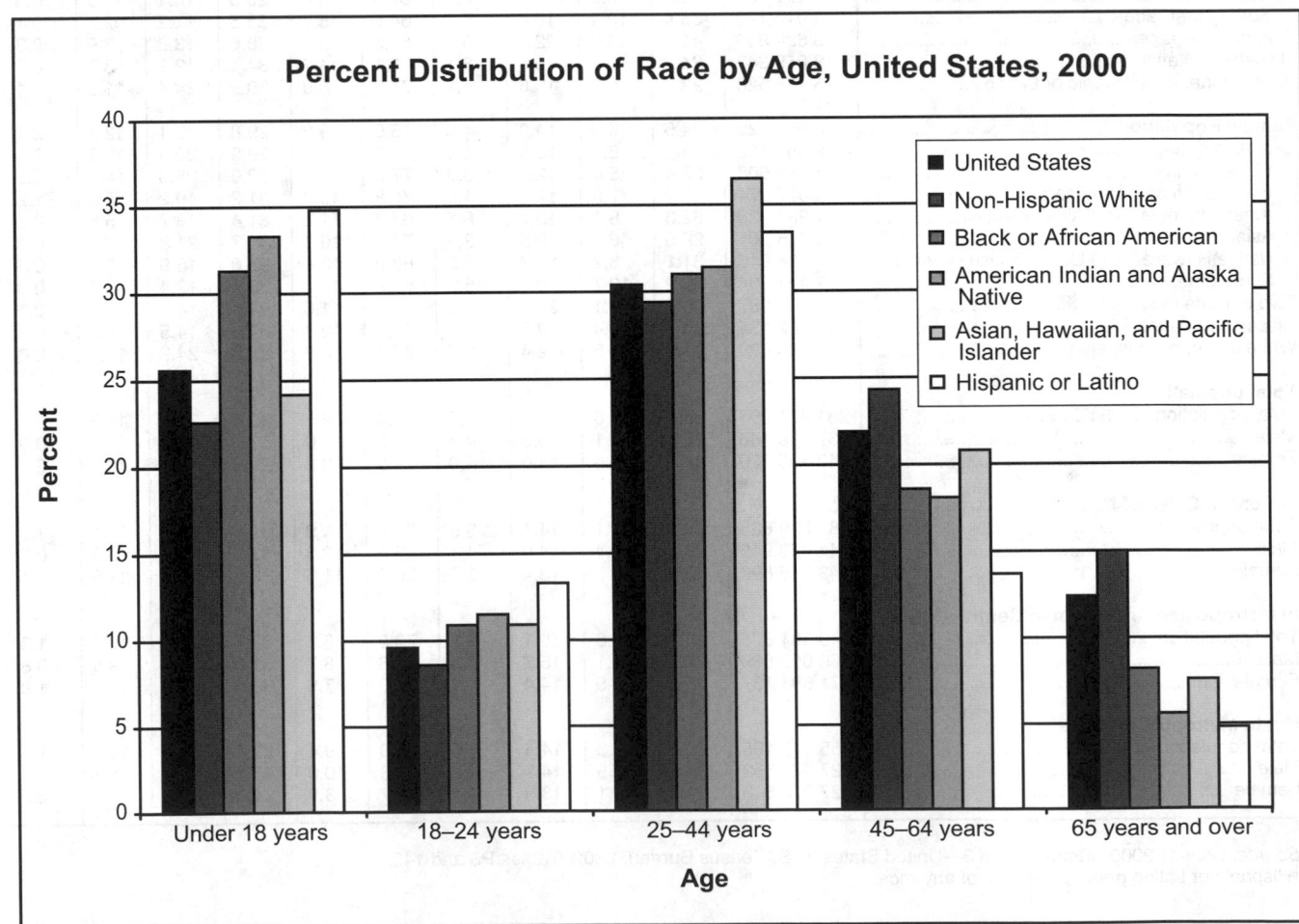

Percent Distribution of Race by Age, United States, 2000

Legend:
- United States
- Non-Hispanic White
- Black or African American
- American Indian and Alaska Native
- Asian, Hawaiian, and Pacific Islander
- Hispanic or Latino

Source: Census 2000 Summary File 3—United States, U.S. Census Bureau. Table P145.

Table A-1.5. Household Type By Age of Householder and Metropolitan/Central City Residence, United States, 2000

(Number, percent.)

Metropolitan area status and household type	Total households	Householder 15 to 64 years				Householder 65 years and over		
		Total households	15 to 24 years	25 to 44 years	45 to 64 years	Total households	65 to 74 years	75 years and over
UNITED STATES	105 539 122	83 263 669	5 435 076	42 414 484	35 414 109	22 275 453	11 617 977	10 657 476
Total Households	100.0	100.0	100.0	100.0	100.0	100.0	100.0	100.0
Family households	68.5	72.4	49.1	74.8	73.0	53.9	62.6	44.4
Married couple families	52.5	55.0	24.2	55.2	59.4	43.5	52.3	34.0
With own children under 18 years	24.3	30.7	. . .	. . .	. . .	0.4	. . .	. . .
Female family householder	11.8	12.8	17.3	14.5	10.1	8.3	8.3	8.3
With own children under 18 years	7.0	8.8	. . .	. . .	. . .	0.0	. . .	. . .
Male family householder	4.1	4.6	7.6	5.2	3.5	2.1	2.1	2.1
With own children under 18 years	2.1	2.6	. . .	. . .	. . .	0.1	. . .	. . .
Nonfamily households	31.5	27.6	50.9	25.2	27.0	46.1	37.4	55.6
Two or more adults	5.8	6.8	. . .	. . .	. . .	1.9	. . .	. . .
Total living alone	25.8	20.8	. . .	. . .	. . .	44.2	. . .	. . .
Female living alone	14.8	9.8	. . .	. . .	. . .	33.5	. . .	. . .
Male living alone	11.0	11.0	. . .	. . .	. . .	10.7	. . .	. . .
IN CENTRAL CITIES OF METROPOLITAN AREAS	32 772 574	26 367 541	2 424 776	13 966 916	9 975 849	6 405 033	3 239 533	3 165 500
Total Households	100.0	100.0	100.0	100.0	100.0	100.0	100.0	100.0
Family households	61.2	64.1	43.2	66.7	65.6	49.4	57.0	41.7
Married couple families	41.4	42.6	17.6	43.3	47.6	36.4	43.2	29.5
With own children under 18 years	19.4	24.0	. . .	. . .	. . .	0.5	. . .	. . .
Female family householder	15.3	16.4	18.5	17.9	13.9	10.5	11.1	9.9
With own children under 18 years	9.2	11.4	. . .	. . .	. . .	0.1	. . .	. . .
Male family householder	4.6	5.1	7.1	5.5	4.0	2.5	2.7	2.3
With own children under 18 years	2.2	2.6	. . .	. . .	. . .	0.1	. . .	. . .
Nonfamily households	38.8	35.9	56.8	33.3	34.4	50.6	43.0	58.3
Two or more adults	7.8	9.2	. . .	. . .	. . .	2.2	. . .	. . .
Total living alone	30.9	26.7	. . .	. . .	. . .	48.3	. . .	. . .
Female living alone	17.4	12.8	. . .	. . .	. . .	36.4	. . .	. . .
Male living alone	13.5	13.9	. . .	. . .	. . .	12.0	. . .	. . .
IN METROPOLITAN AREAS, NOT IN CENTRAL CITIES	51 578 534	41 006 828	1 915 992	20 959 928	18 130 908	10 571 706	5 623 689	4 948 017
Total Households	100.0	100.0	100.0	100.0	100.0	100.0	100.0	100.0
Family households	72.3	76.3	52.8	78.3	76.5	56.7	65.6	46.6
Married couple families	58.2	61.0	28.3	61.2	64.3	47.1	56.2	36.8
With own children under 10 years	27.0	34.0	. . .	. . .	. . .	0.4	. . .	. . .
Female family householder	10.3	11.0	15.9	12.3	8.9	7.6	7.4	7.8
With own children under 18 years	5.9	7.4	. . .	. . .	. . .	0.0	. . .	. . .
Male family householder	3.9	4.3	8.6	4.8	3.3	2.0	2.0	2.0
With own children under 18 years	2.0	2.5	. . .	. . .	. . .	0.1	. . .	. . .
Nonfamily households	27.7	23.7	47.2	21.7	23.5	43.3	34.4	53.4
Two or more adults	5.0	5.8	. . .	. . .	. . .	1.9	. . .	. . .
Total living alone	22.7	17.9	. . .	. . .	. . .	41.4	. . .	. . .
Female living alone	13.2	8.5	. . .	. . .	. . .	31.6	. . .	. . .
Male living alone	9.4	9.3	. . .	. . .	. . .	9.9	. . .	. . .
NOT IN METROPOLITAN AREAS	21 188 014	15 889 300	1 094 308	7 487 640	7 307 352	5 298 714	2 754 755	2 543 959
Total Households	100.0	100.0	100.0	100.0	100.0	100.0	100.0	100.0
Family households	70.4	76.0	55.8	80.4	74.5	53.7	63.3	43.4
Married couple families	56.2	59.9	31.7	60.5	63.5	45.1	55.0	34.3
With own children under 18 years	23.9	31.8	. . .	. . .	. . .	0.4	. . .	. . .
Female family householder	10.4	11.5	17.2	14.3	7.8	6.9	6.6	7.2
With own children under 18 years	6.3	8.3	. . .	. . .	. . .	0.0	. . .	. . .
Male family householder	3.9	4.5	7.0	5.5	3.2	1.8	1.7	1.8
With own children under 18 years	2.2	2.9	. . .	. . .	. . .	0.1	. . .	. . .
Nonfamily households	29.6	24.0	44.2	19.6	25.5	46.3	36.7	56.6
Two or more adults	4.3	5.2	. . .	. . .	. . .	1.5	. . .	. . .
Total living alone	25.3	18.8	. . .	. . .	. . .	44.8	. . .	. . .
Female living alone	14.6	8.2	. . .	. . .	. . .	33.8	. . .	. . .
Male living alone	10.7	10.6	. . .	. . .	. . .	11.0	. . .	. . .

Source: SF3 Tables P12, P13, PCT2, and PCT3. U.S. Census Bureau, Washington, DC.
. . . = Not available.

(Number, percent.)

| Household type | Total households | One race only | | | | | | | Two or more races | Hispanic or Latino | White alone, not Hispanic or Latino |
		Total households	White	Black or African American	American Indian and Alaska Native	Asian	Native Hawaiian and Other Pacific Islander	Some other race			
NUMBER											
Total Households	105 539 122	103 554 859	83 697 584	12 023 966	770 334	3 129 127	100 151	3 833 697	1 984 263	9 272 610	78 983 497
Family Households	72 261 780	70 879 361	56 470 094	8 209 432	563 651	2 350 399	79 254	3 206 531	1 382 419	7 483 038	52 769 534
Married couple families	55 458 451	54 532 895	46 215 581	3 859 545	346 536	1 932 421	56 454	2 122 358	925 556	5 110 849	43 574 658
With householder 65 years or over	9 698 675	9 613 108	8 798 849	508 965	31 957	181 782	4 108	87 447	85 567	402 222	8 506 660
With own children under 18 years	25 674 582	25 127 062	20 195 837	2 005 140	196 460	1 121 946	36 084	1 571 595	547 520	3 446 673	18 564 045
Other Families	16 803 329	16 346 466	10 254 513	4 349 887	217 115	417 978	22 800	1 084 173	456 863	2 372 189	9 194 876
Female family householder	12 500 761	12 176 425	7 342 021	3 664 658	159 486	276 118	15 432	718 710	324 336	1 605 176	6 620 510
With householder 65 years or over	2 308 659	2 271 100	1 655 021	488 687	21 865	46 016	2 257	57 254	37 559	181 929	1 545 518
With own children under 18 years	9 531 656	9 254 921	5 578 870	2 652 453	135 869	170 783	13 371	703 575	276 735	1 454 055	4 977 206
Nonfamily Households	33 277 342	32 675 498	27 227 490	3 814 534	206 683	778 728	20 897	627 166	601 844	1 789 572	26 213 963
Two or more adults	6 073 618	5 921 041	4 913 142	548 143	47 875	196 527	6 534	208 820	152 577	505 272	4 660 242
With householder 65 years or over	418 794	412 618	351 848	47 654	1 792	5 920	192	5 212	6 176	23 445	335 553
Total living alone	27 203 724	26 754 457	22 314 348	3 266 391	158 808	582 201	14 363	418 346	449 267	1 284 300	21 553 721
With householder 65 years or over	10 056 109	9 752 211	8 693 444	849 236	34 131	103 491	2 271	69 638	97 114	321 329	8 463 783
PERCENT											
Total Households	100.0	100.0	100.0	100.0	100.0	100.0	100.0	100.0	100.0	100.0	100.0
Family Households	68.5	68.4	67.5	68.3	73.2	75.1	79.1	83.6	69.7	80.7	66.8
Married couple families	52.5	52.7	55.2	32.1	45.0	61.8	56.4	55.4	46.6	55.1	55.2
With householder 65 years or over	9.2	9.3	10.5	4.2	4.1	5.8	4.1	2.3	4.3	4.3	10.8
With own children under 18 years	24.3	24.3	24.1	16.7	25.5	35.9	36.0	41.0	27.6	37.2	23.5
Other Families	15.9	15.8	12.3	36.2	28.2	13.4	22.8	28.3	23.0	25.6	11.6
Female family householder	11.8	11.8	8.8	30.5	20.7	8.8	15.4	18.7	16.3	17.3	8.4
With householder 65 years or over	2.2	2.2	2.0	4.1	2.8	1.5	2.3	1.5	1.9	2.0	2.0
With own children under 18 years	9.0	8.9	6.7	22.1	17.6	5.5	13.4	18.4	13.9	15.7	6.3
Nonfamily Households	31.5	31.6	32.5	31.7	26.8	24.9	20.9	16.4	30.3	19.3	33.2
Two or more adults	5.8	5.7	5.9	4.6	6.2	6.3	6.5	5.4	7.7	5.4	5.9
With householder 65 years or over	0.4	0.4	0.4	0.4	0.2	0.2	0.2	0.1	0.3	0.3	0.4
Total living alone	25.8	25.8	26.7	27.2	20.6	18.6	14.3	10.9	22.6	13.9	27.3
With householder 65 years or over	9.5	9.4	10.4	7.1	4.4	3.3	2.3	1.8	4.9	3.5	10.7

Source: Census 2000 Summary File 3—United States, U.S. Census Bureau, 2002. Tables P12 and P146A-I.

The map on page 96 shows the geography of the old "traditional" family. Other things equal, metropolitan households (suburbs and central cities) contain the bulk of the nation's "traditional" families because they have so many people in the ages when people tend to have children: 25 to 44. At the same time, they also contain large numbers of young adults, living on their own or sharing with others. Thus, metropolitan households contain more people living alone than "traditional" families. They also contain more than twice as many "new" traditional families as old ones.

Non-metropolitan (small town and rural areas) households contain more people age 45 and older. Thus, the "new" traditional family of married couples without children under age 18 is the dominant household type there as well. Again, because non-metropolitan populations are relatively old and contain large numbers of retirees, there are slightly more single-person households than "traditional" families.

Utah stands out as the state where the old "traditional" family dominates—over a third of Utah's households are married couples with children in the home. The traditional family is still dominant in other relatively "young" states, while "older" states have relatively few traditional families. (See Table A-1.7.)

Census 2000 put a new face into its portrait of the nation's families: Americans who are raising their grandchildren. Historically, grandparents have been important as caregivers—higher adult mortality rates orphaned many children, and extended families were more likely to share homes, especially in rural areas. Now, few children are orphaned but with parents and grandparents

Table A-1.7.
"Young" states have more traditional families.

Married-couple Families with Children Under 18 Years, Selected States, 2000

(Percent.)

State	Most "traditional" families	State	Fewest "traditional" families
Utah	36.1	Florida	19.9
Alaska	29.3	Rhode Island	21.8
Idaho	28.9	West Virginia	21.9
Texas	28.0	New York	22.4
California	26.9	Maine	22.5
		Pennsylvania	22.5

Source: Census 2000 Summary File 3—United States, U.S. Census Bureau, 2002. Table P12.

tending to live in separate households, mothers and fathers are likely to send their children to a grandparent if they are having trouble maintaining a home of their own.

In 2000, nearly 2.5 million grandparents were responsible for grandchildren under age 18. The great majority were householders whose grandchildren lived with them. Another 3.3 million grandparents shared a home with their grandchildren but without responsibility for them. More than half of these grandparents had welcomed the younger generation into their home, while slightly less than half were living in a child's household.

Nearly a third of the nation's households are made up of people living alone, or with other, unrelated adults. Although there are large numbers of single-person households in every age group, women over 65, mostly widows, represent the largest population of live-alones. Thus, in "older" states like Rhode Island, Massachusetts, New York, West Virginia, and Pennsylvania, more than 16 percent of all households are single women. Still, fully 10 percent of households in "young" states like Utah and Alaska are made up of women living alone. With longer life spans, women especially are likely to live alone at some time—whether before they marry and have children, or after the children are grown and the marriage ended by death or divorce.

Single-parent households are a particular concern to state and local policy-makers, as the parent is responsible for both earning and caretaking. The geography of single-parent households is complex, as several factors work together to produce high concentrations. First, the states where single-parent households are particularly numerous are "young" states in the Southeast and Southwest. Children become adults at age 18, legally and therefore statistically. So older populations have proportionately

Table A-1.8. Grandparents' Responsibility for Care of Grandchildren, United States, 2000

(Number, percent.)

	Total	Householder or spouse	Parent or parent-in-law of householder	Other relative or nonrelative of householder
NUMBER				
Total Persons 30 Years and Over	158 881 037	141 130 999	2 892 199	14 857 839
Living with own grandchildren under 18 years	5 771 671	4 405 482	1 287 336	78 853
Grandparent responsible for own grandchildren under 18 years	2 426 730	2 275 665	111 977	39 088
Less than 1 year	555 668	. . .	. . .	. . .
1 to 4 years	937 654	. . .	. . .	. . .
5 years or more	933 408	. . .	. . .	. . .
Grandparent not responsible for own grandchildren under 18 years	3 344 941	2 129 817	1 175 359	39 765
Not living with own grandchildren under 18 years	153 109 366	136 725 517	1 604 863	14 778 986
PERCENT				
Total Persons 30 Years and Over	100.0	100.0	100.0	100.0
Living with own grandchildren under 18 years	3.6	3.1	44.5	0.5
Grandparent responsible for own grandchildren under 18 years	1.5	1.6	3.9	0.3
Less than 1 year	16.6	. . .	. . .	. . .
1 to 4 years	28.0	. . .	. . .	. . .
5 years or more	27.9	. . .	. . .	. . .
Grandparent not responsible for own grandchildren under 18 years	2.1	1.5	40.6	0.3
Not living with own grandchildren under 18 years	96.4	96.9	55.5	99.5

Source: Census 2000 Summary File 3—United States, U.S. Census Bureau, 2002. Tables PCT8 and PCT9.

. . . = Not available.

Table A-1.9.
"Younger" states have many single parents.
Single-parent Family Households, Selected States, 2000

State	Most single parents	State	Fewest single parents
Mississippi	12.2	North Dakota	6.9
Louisiana	11.9	Iowa	7.2
New Mexico	11.3	West Virginia	7.4
Alaska	11.2	Utah	7.5
Georgia	10.3	New Hampshire	7.7
South Carolina	10.3		

Source: Census 2000 Summary File 3—United States, U.S. Census Bureau, 2002. Table P12.

fewer single parents, as well as fewer married couples with children, than younger ones do.

Second, single-parent households are noticeably concentrated in states where (as Part B will show), educational attainment is relatively low. That is, although single-parent households can be found all across the income spectrum, they are particularly numerous among people with low educational attainment. In essence, having children at a young age, whether married or unmarried, tends to replace schooling with parenting.

In contrast, states where single parents are a relatively low proportion of households are "old" states—except for Utah, where Mormon culture encourages young marriages and frowns on divorce and childbearing by single people. This contrast shows the power of the age picture in setting the demographic scene for any given place. West Virginia has relatively low educational attainment, like the states with high numbers of single parents, but West Virginia is the nation's "oldest" state, with a relatively low proportion of its citizens in the childrearing ages. Readers will also remark the racial and ethnic contrast between these two groups of states. That is because the nation's Hispanic, black, and American Indian populations lag considerably in average schooling completed. (See Part B)

Table A-1.10.
Cohabitation is more common in some states than others.
Unmarried Partner Households, Selected States, 2000

State	Most cohabitation	State	Least cohabitation
Vermont	7.3	Alabama	3.1
Alaska	7.2	Utah	3.3
Nevada	7.0	Arkansas	3.6
Maine	6.9	Oklahoma	3.7
New Hampshire	6.6	Kansas	3.8
		Tennessee	3.9

Source: Census 2000 Summary File 3—United States, U.S. Census Bureau, 2002. Table PCT 1.

Cohabiting couples are a relatively new phenomenon, leading the census to try new ways of asking people about their household relationships. By definition, co-habitation has fuzzier boundaries than marriage and divorce. People who cohabit may spend time in other households as well, so the census estimates may well understate the degree of cohabitation. According to these estimates, 5 percent of the nation's households were cohabiting households in 2000. Nearly nine in 10 of these households were male/female households. The remainder, which we call "same-sex" households in this book, was evenly divided between male/male and female/female.

The geography of same-sex households bears out the common observation that coastal states tend to lead the nation in social trends, while states in the interior tend to be more traditional. Vermont has the highest proportion of same-sex households—fully 1 percent—followed closely by California, Arizona, Massachusetts, and Washington. Fewer households in inland states, particularly states that are more rural, reported that they were same-sex households. Still, at least 0.4 percent of households in every state were "same-sex."

Where Immigrants Go

Immigration has consistently altered the nation's cultural, racial, and ethnic background, as the source of new immigrants shifts around the world. The new arrivals of the 1990s were no exception. Census 2000 found that over one in 10 people in the resident population were foreign-born, and over half of them were not U.S. citizens, at least not yet. The great majority of the non-citizens were from Central America, especially Mexico. Overall, Latin America accounts for roughly half of the nation's foreign-born, Asia for roughly a fourth, and Europe for roughly an eighth.

Table A-1.11.
Some states are more popular than others as "entry" states for immigrants.
Foreign-born Populations, 2000

(Percent.)

State	Large foreign-born populations	State	Small foreign-born populations
California	26.2	West Virginia	1.1
New York	20.4	Mississippi	1.4
Hawaii	17.5	Montana	1.8
New Jersey	17.5	South Dakota	1.8
Florida	16.7	North Dakota	1.9

Source: Census 2000 Summary File 3—United States, U.S. Census Bureau, 2002. Table P21.

Table A-1.12. Place of Birth and Citizenship Status of the Foreign-born Population, United States, 2000

(Number, percent.)

Place of birth	Total	Citizen	Not a citizen
NUMBER			
Total Population	281 421 906	262856643	18 565 263
Foreign-born	31 107 889	12 542 626	18 565 263
Europe	4 915 557	2 748 036	2 167 521
Asia	8 226 254	4 179 035	4 047 219
Africa	881 300	318 166	563 134
Oceania	168 046	57 449	110 597
Latin America	16 086 974	4 857 597	11 229 377
Caribbean	2 953 066	1 467 369	1 485 697
Central America	11 203 637	2 639 599	8 564 038
Mexico	9 177 487	2 061 788	7 115 699
Other Central America	2 026 150	577 811	1 448 339
South America	1 930 271	750 629	1 179 642
Northern America	829 442	382 100	447 342
Born at sea	316	243	73
PERCENT			
Total Population	100.0	93.4	6.6
Foreign-born	100.0	40.3	59.7
Europe	100.0	55.9	44.1
Asia	100.0	50.8	49.2
Africa	100.0	36.1	63.9
Oceania	100.0	34.2	65.8
Latin America	100.0	30.2	69.8
Caribbean	100.0	49.7	50.3
Central America	100.0	23.6	76.4
Mexico	100.0	22.5	77.5
Other Central America	100.0	28.5	71.5
South America	100.0	38.9	61.1
Northern America	100.0	46.1	53.9
Born at sea	100.0	76.9	23.1

Source: Census 2000 Summary File 3—United States, U.S. Census Bureau, 2002. Table PCT20.

Contemporary transportation and communications modes have changed the nature of immigration. First, "circular" migration—of people who come here to work or live for a while, and then return home—has become easier, at least until September 11, 2001. Second, people can live here for a long time while keeping their ties back home via electronic communications or relatively inexpensive plane fares. So the large numbers of foreign-born who are not U.S. citizens may well stay that way. Certainly, a college education has become a prime U.S. "product," as the nation's institutions of higher education welcome more and more foreign students, here to learn skills they may take home with them, or decide to use here.

These and other trends create vast differences across the country in terms of the foreign-born population, as the map on page 92 shows. In general, the foreign-born are highly concentrated in relatively few states, leaving the bulk of the country hearing about large numbers of foreign-born but rarely coming into contact with them. As usual, the "entry" states are those that are near points of entry and have relatively plentiful employment opportunities. And those that have few foreign-born tend to be distant inland states, with relatively few employment opportunities. (See Table A-1.12.)

These differences create a problem for some states that other states don't share: a significant population that doesn't speak English at home or even anywhere. Nationwide, roughly 13 percent of the population lives in households in which every member speaks a language other than English. (See Table A-1.13.) Nearly 5 percent are in households that are "linguistically isolated," due to their inadequate grasp of English. These states pose a particular problem for educators, due to the large numbers of children who arrive at school with little or no English ability. (See Table A-1.13.)

Most of the "linguistically isolated" population lives in the South and Southwest where Mexican immigrants predominate along with native-born Hispanics, many of whom descend from the region's original Spanish colonizers. New York and New Jersey also have large numbers of "linguistically isolated," mostly Spanish speaking immigrants from Central and South America. These states are also home to large numbers of Puerto Ricans, who tend to maintain close ties with their easily accessible homeland. Such large Spanish-speaking populations make it possible for many to live completely in their native language.

In contrast, some states with large concentrations of people whose native language is one of many Asian languages—Hawaii, California, Washington, Alaska, and Nevada— have relatively smaller numbers of linguistically isolated households. Still, these states need to pay special attention to the educational needs of linguistically isolated

Table A-1.13. States with Large Linguistically Isolated Populations, Selected States, 2000

(Percentage of the population.)

State	Total population	5 to 17 years
California	11.3	13.5
Texas	8.1	8.9
New York	7.8	7.4
Nevada	6.9	8.4
Arizona	6.7	8.5
New Jersey	6.3	5.9
New Mexico	6.2	6.7
Florida	6.1	5.8

Source: Census 2000 Summary File 3—United States, U.S. Census Bureau, 2002. Table PCT14.

Table A-1.14. Language Spoken at Home, United States, 2000

(Number, percent.)

Language	All ages	5 to 17 years	18 to 64 years	65 years and over
Total Population 5 Years and Over	262 375 152	53 096 003	174 300 177	34 978 972
Speak only English	215 423 557	43 316 237	141 543 188	30 564 132
Speak Spanish	28 101 052	6 830 100	19 594 395	1 676 557
Speak other Indo-European language	10 017 989	1 445 063	6 641 018	1 931 908
Speak Asian/PI language	6 960 065	1 158 936	5 171 548	629 581
Speak other languages	1 872 489	345 667	1 350 028	176 794
Total Population 5 Years and Over in Households	254 620 291	52 826 320	168 794 767	32 999 204
All speak only English	194 490 246	38 188 151	128 313 221	27 988 874
Some speak another language	26 209 365	7 164 181	17 253 676	1 791 508
Not linguistically isolated	25 755 081	6 945 797	17 026 834	1 782 450
Linguistically isolated	454 284	218 384	226 842	9 058
All speak another language	33 920 680	7 473 988	23 227 870	3 218 822
Not linguistically isolated	22 481 392	5 004 769	15 528 175	1 948 448
Linguistically isolated	11 439 288	2 469 219	7 699 695	1 270 374
Total Population 5 Years and Over in Linguistically Isolated Households	11 893 572	2 687 603	7 926 537	1 279 432
Speak only English	156 018	156 018	0	0
Speak Spanish	7 671 481	1 859 994	5 269 793	541 694
Speak other Indo-European language	1 707 111	238 752	1 014 243	454 116
Speak Asian/PI language	2 078 992	380 442	1 455 914	242 636
Speak other languages	279 970	52 397	186 587	40 986
Total Population 5 Years and Over	100.0	100.0	100.0	100.0
Speak only English	82.1	81.6	81.2	87.4
Speak Spanish	10.7	12.9	11.2	4.8
Speak other Indo-European language	3.8	2.7	3.8	5.5
Speak Asian/PI language	2.7	2.2	3.0	1.8
Speak other languages	0.7	0.7	0.8	0.5
Total Population 5 Years and Over in Households	100.0	100.0	100.0	100.0
All speak only English	76.4	72.3	76.0	84.8
Some speak another language	10.3	13.6	10.2	5.4
Not linguistically isolated	10.1	13.1	10.1	5.4
Linguistically isolated	0.2	0.4	0.1	0.0
All speak another language	13.3	14.1	13.8	9.8
Not linguistically isolated	8.8	9.5	9.2	5.9
Linguistically isolated	4.5	4.7	4.6	3.8
Total Population 5 Years and Over in Linguistically Isolated Households	100.0	100.0	100.0	100.0
Speak only English	1.3	5.8	0.0	0.0
Speak Spanish	64.5	69.2	66.5	42.3
Speak other Indo-European language	14.4	8.9	12.8	35.5
Speak Asian/PI language	17.5	14.2	18.4	19.0
Speak other languages	2.4	1.9	2.4	3.2

Source: Census 2000 Summary File 3—United States, U.S. Census Bureau, 2002. Table PCT12, PCT13, and PCT14.

Table A-1.15. Ancestry, United States, 2000

(Number, percent.)

Ancestry	Number	Percent
Total Population	281 421 906	100.0
Arab	1 202 871	0.4
Asian Indian	1 899 599	0.7
Austrian	735 128	0.3
British	1 085 720	0.4
Canadian	647 376	0.2
Chinese (includes Taiwanese)	2 879 636	1.0
Czech (includes Czechoslovakian)	1 703 930	0.6
Cuban	1 241 685	0.4
Danish	1 430 897	0.5
Dominican Republic	764 945	0.3
Dutch	4 542 494	1.6
English	24 515 138	8.7
European	1 968 696	0.7
Filipino	2 364 815	0.8
Finnish	623 573	0.2
French (except Basque; includes Alsatian)	8 325 509	3.0
French Canadian (includes Acadian/Cajun)	2 435 098	0.9
German	42 885 162	15.2
Greek	1 153 307	0.4
Hungarian	1 398 724	0.5
Irish (includes Celtic)	30 594 130	10.9
Italian	15 723 555	5.6
Japanese	1 148 932	0.4
Korean	1 228 427	0.4
Lithuanian	659 992	0.2
Mexican	20 640 711	7.3
Norwegian	4 477 725	1.6
Polish	8 977 444	3.2
Portuguese	1 177 112	0.4
Puerto Rican	3 406 178	1.2
Russian	2 052 214	0.9
Salvadoran	655 165	0.2
Scotch-Irish	4 319 232	1.5
Scottish	4 890 581	1.7
Slovak	797 764	0.3
Spanish (includes Spaniard)	786 139	0.3
Subsaharan African:	1 781 877	0.6
Swedish	3 998 310	1.4
Swiss	911 502	0.3
Ukrainian	892 922	0.3
United States or American	20 625 093	7.3
Vietnamese	1 223 736	0.4
Welsh	1 753 794	0.6
West Indian (excluding Hispanic groups)	1 869 504	0.7

Source: Census 2000 Summary Files 1 and 3—United States, U.S. Census Bureau, 2002. SF3 Table PCT18; SF1 Tables PCT7 and PCT11.

Note: This table blends several census questions in an effort to identify the most often reported ancestries of the American people. The table includes any group that was identified by at least two-tenths of one percent of respondents (about 600,000 people). Most ancestries are from the ancestry question on the long form where persons could specify as many ancestries as they chose. Asian and Hispanic entries were not tabulated as ancestries in SF3. In this table, Asian Indian, Chinese, Filipino, Japanese, Korean, and Vietnamese are from the race question on the short form; Mexican, Cuban, Puerto Rican, and Salvadoran are from the Hispanic origin question on the short form. However, Asian and Hispanic persons who answered the long form may also have specified additional ancestries in the ancestry question.

children, who tend to be concentrated in a few counties or communities. They also need to identify those pockets of elderly people who may need help interfacing with programs designed to aid them.

Many Americans have personal experience with making the transition to a new language as well as a new country. Others can repeat the stories their forbears told. One of the most popular census findings is the tally of the ancestries Americans report on the detailed census form. Despite the many new immigrants from Latin America and Asia, the most common ancestries Census 2000 found were familiar: 15 percent of Americans said they had German ancestry, 11 percent said Irish, and 9 percent said English. (See Table A-1.15.) (Many people report more than one ancestry.) The next largest ancestries reported were Mexican—and American!

Table A-2. States — Age, Ethnicity, and Household Structure

FIPS CODE	STATE	Number	Median age	Under 18 years	Under 5 years	5 to 14 years	15 to 17 years	18 years and over	18 to 24 years	25 to 44 years	45 to 64 years	65 to 84 years	85 years and over	+/– U.S. percent under 18 years	+/– U.S. percent 65 years and over
				Children under 18 years (percent)				Adults 18 years and over (percent)							
		1	2	3	4	5	6	7	8	9	10	11	12	13	14
00	UNITED STATES ...	281 421 906	35.3	25.6	6.8	14.6	4.2	74.4	9.6	30.4	21.9	11.0	1.5	0.0	0.0
01	ALABAMA	4 447 100	35.8	25.2	6.6	14.3	4.3	74.8	9.8	29.1	22.8	11.6	1.5	-0.4	0.6
02	ALASKA	626 932	32.4	30.4	7.5	17.7	5.2	69.6	9.1	32.7	22.3	5.2	0.4	4.8	-6.8
04	ARIZONA	5 130 632	34.2	26.6	7.4	15.1	4.1	73.4	10.0	29.7	20.8	11.7	1.3	1.0	0.6
05	ARKANSAS..............	2 673 400	36.0	25.4	6.8	14.2	4.4	74.6	9.8	28.1	22.6	12.3	1.7	-0.2	1.6
06	CALIFORNIA.............	33 871 648	33.3	27.2	7.2	15.8	4.2	72.8	9.9	31.9	20.4	9.4	1.2	1.6	-1.8
08	COLORADO	4 301 261	34.3	25.5	6.9	14.4	4.2	74.5	9.9	32.8	22.1	8.6	1.1	-0.1	-2.7
09	CONNECTICUT	3 405 565	37.4	24.7	6.5	14.3	3.8	75.3	7.9	30.5	23.1	11.9	1.9	-0.9	1.4
10	DELAWARE	783 600	36.0	24.8	6.5	14.3	4.0	75.2	9.6	30.3	22.4	11.6	1.3	-0.8	0.6
11	DISTRICT OF COLUMBIA	572 059	34.6	20.0	5.7	11.4	2.9	80.0	12.8	33.2	21.8	10.8	1.5	-5.6	-0.1
12	FLORIDA.................	15 982 378	38.7	22.7	5.9	13.1	3.7	77.3	8.3	28.8	22.6	15.5	2.0	-2.9	5.2
13	GEORGIA................	8 186 453	33.4	26.5	7.2	15.0	4.2	73.5	10.2	32.6	21.1	8.6	1.1	0.9	-2.8
15	HAWAII...................	1 211 537	36.2	24.3	6.4	13.9	4.0	75.7	9.5	30.1	22.9	11.9	1.4	-1.3	0.9
16	IDAHO....................	1 293 953	33.2	28.5	7.5	15.9	5.1	71.5	10.7	28.2	21.4	9.9	1.4	2.9	-1.1
17	ILLINOIS.................	12 419 293	34.7	26.1	7.0	14.8	4.2	73.9	9.7	30.7	21.4	10.6	1.5	0.5	-0.3
18	INDIANA.................	6 080 485	35.2	25.9	7.0	14.6	4.3	74.1	10.1	29.5	22.1	10.9	1.5	0.3	0.0
19	IOWA.....................	2 926 324	36.6	25.0	6.4	14.1	4.5	75.0	10.2	27.7	22.2	12.7	2.2	-0.6	2.5
20	KANSAS..................	2 688 418	35.2	26.5	7.0	14.9	4.6	73.5	10.3	28.7	21.3	11.3	1.9	0.9	0.8
21	KENTUCKY	4 041 769	35.9	24.6	6.6	13.8	4.2	75.4	9.9	30.0	23.0	11.1	1.4	-1.0	0.1
22	LOUISIANA	4 468 976	34.0	27.3	7.1	15.4	4.8	72.7	10.6	29.0	21.5	10.3	1.3	1.7	-0.8
23	MAINE	1 274 923	38.6	23.6	5.6	13.8	4.3	76.4	8.2	29.0	24.8	12.6	1.8	-2.0	2.0
24	MARYLAND	5 296 486	36.0	25.6	6.6	14.8	4.1	74.4	8.4	31.6	23.1	10.1	1.2	0.0	-1.1
25	MASSACHUSETTS ...	6 349 097	36.5	23.6	6.2	13.6	3.8	76.4	9.1	31.4	22.3	11.7	1.8	-2.0	1.1
26	MICHIGAN	9 938 444	35.5	26.1	6.7	15.0	4.3	73.9	9.4	29.9	22.4	10.9	1.4	0.5	-0.1
27	MINNESOTA	4 919 479	35.4	26.2	6.7	14.9	4.6	73.8	9.5	30.5	21.7	10.3	1.7	0.6	-0.3
28	MISSISSIPPI	2 844 658	33.8	27.2	7.1	15.4	4.7	72.8	11.0	28.5	21.2	10.6	1.5	1.6	-0.3
29	MISSOURI...............	5 595 211	36.1	25.5	6.6	14.5	4.4	74.5	9.5	29.2	22.3	11.8	1.7	-0.1	1.1
30	MONTANA...............	902 195	37.5	25.5	6.1	14.6	4.8	74.5	9.5	27.3	24.4	11.7	1.7	-0.1	1.0
31	NEBRASKA..............	1 711 263	35.3	26.3	6.8	14.7	4.7	73.7	10.2	28.5	21.4	11.6	2.0	0.7	1.2
32	NEVADA..................	1 998 257	35.0	25.5	7.2	14.5	3.8	74.5	8.9	31.7	22.9	10.1	0.8	-0.1	-1.5
33	NEW HAMPSHIRE	1 235 786	37.1	25.0	6.1	14.7	4.2	75.0	8.3	30.9	23.8	10.5	1.5	-0.6	-0.4
34	NEW JERSEY	8 414 350	36.7	24.7	6.6	14.3	3.8	75.3	8.0	31.4	22.7	11.6	1.6	-0.9	0.8
35	NEW MEXICO...........	1 819 046	34.6	27.9	7.1	16.0	4.8	72.1	9.7	28.6	22.1	10.4	1.3	2.3	-0.7
36	NEW YORK	18 976 457	35.9	24.6	6.5	14.2	4.0	75.4	9.3	30.9	22.3	11.3	1.6	-1.0	0.5
37	NORTH CAROLINA ...	8 049 313	35.3	24.4	6.7	13.9	3.8	75.6	10.0	31.2	22.4	10.8	1.3	-1.2	0.4
38	NORTH DAKOTA.......	642 200	36.2	25.1	6.1	14.1	4.8	74.9	11.3	27.3	21.6	12.4	2.3	-0.5	2.3
39	OHIO.....................	11 353 140	36.2	25.4	6.6	14.5	4.3	74.6	9.3	29.4	22.6	11.8	1.5	-0.2	0.9
40	OKLAHOMA	3 450 654	35.5	25.8	6.8	14.4	4.6	74.2	10.4	28.4	22.2	11.6	1.6	0.2	0.8
41	OREGON	3 421 399	36.3	24.7	6.5	13.9	4.2	75.3	9.5	29.3	23.7	11.1	1.7	-0.9	0.4
42	PENNSYLVANIA.......	12 281 054	38.0	23.8	5.9	13.8	4.1	76.2	8.9	28.6	23.0	13.7	1.9	-1.8	3.2
44	RHODE ISLAND	1 048 319	36.7	23.6	6.0	13.7	3.9	76.4	10.1	29.7	22.0	12.6	2.0	-2.0	2.2
45	SOUTH CAROLINA ...	4 012 012	35.4	25.2	6.6	14.5	4.1	74.8	10.1	29.7	22.9	10.9	1.2	-0.4	-0.3
46	SOUTH DAKOTA.......	754 844	35.6	26.9	6.8	15.1	5.0	73.1	10.3	27.4	21.1	12.3	2.1	1.3	1.9
47	TENNESSEE............	5 689 283	35.9	24.6	6.6	13.9	4.1	75.4	9.6	30.3	23.2	11.0	1.4	-1.0	0.0
48	TEXAS....................	20 851 820	32.3	28.2	7.7	15.8	4.6	71.8	10.5	31.4	20.1	8.8	1.1	2.6	-2.5
49	UTAH.....................	2 233 169	27.1	32.1	9.4	17.2	5.5	67.9	14.3	28.2	16.9	7.6	1.0	6.5	-3.9
50	VERMONT	608 827	37.7	24.2	5.6	14.2	4.4	75.8	9.4	29.0	24.7	11.1	1.6	-1.4	0.3
51	VIRGINIA................	7 078 515	35.7	24.5	6.5	14.1	4.0	75.5	9.6	31.8	23.0	10.0	1.2	-1.1	-1.2
53	WASHINGTON...........	5 894 121	35.3	25.6	6.7	14.6	4.3	74.4	9.4	31.0	22.7	9.8	1.4	0.0	-1.2
54	WEST VIRGINIA	1 808 344	38.9	22.2	5.6	12.6	4.0	77.8	9.6	27.7	25.2	13.6	1.8	-3.4	2.9
55	WISCONSIN..............	5 363 675	36.0	25.5	6.4	14.6	4.5	74.5	9.7	29.6	22.2	11.3	1.8	-0.1	0.7
56	WYOMING	493 782	36.2	25.9	6.3	14.6	5.1	74.1	10.1	28.2	24.1	10.3	1.4	0.3	-0.8

Table A-2. States — Age, Ethnicity, and Household Structure

STATE	Male population												
		Male children under 18 years (percent)				Male adults 18 years and over (percent)							
	Number	Male median age	Under 18 years	Under 5 years	5 to 14 years	15 to 17 years	18 years and over	18 to 24 years	25 to 44 years	45 to 64 years	65 to 84 years	85 years and over	+/− U.S. percent under 18 years	+/− U.S. percent 65 years and over
	15	16	17	18	19	20	21	22	23	24	25	26	27	28
UNITED STATES ...	137 916 186	34.0	26.8	7.1	15.3	4.4	73.2	10.0	31.0	21.7	9.6	0.9	1.2	-2.0
ALABAMA	2 144 463	34.4	26.8	7.0	15.3	4.5	73.2	10.1	29.6	22.7	10.0	0.8	1.2	-1.6
ALASKA	324 282	32.4	30.3	7.5	17.6	5.3	69.7	9.3	32.5	22.8	4.8	0.3	4.7	-7.3
ARIZONA	2 556 483	32.9	27.3	7.6	15.5	4.2	72.7	10.5	30.5	20.1	10.7	0.9	1.7	-0.8
ARKANSAS..............	1 303 332	34.6	26.8	7.1	15.0	4.7	73.2	10.1	28.8	22.4	10.8	1.0	1.2	-0.5
CALIFORNIA............	16 843 062	32.2	28.1	7.5	16.3	4.4	71.9	10.4	32.6	20.0	8.2	0.8	2.5	-3.5
COLORADO..............	2 163 954	33.2	26.0	7.0	14.7	4.3	74.0	10.5	33.5	21.9	7.4	0.6	0.4	-4.3
CONNECTICUT	1 648 523	36.1	26.1	6.9	15.2	4.1	73.9	8.4	30.8	23.1	10.4	1.1	0.5	-0.9
DELAWARE	380 003	34.9	26.1	6.8	15.2	4.2	73.9	9.6	30.8	22.2	10.4	0.8	0.5	-1.2
DISTRICT OF COLUMBIA	268 827	33.7	21.4	6.1	12.2	3.1	78.6	12.4	34.8	21.5	9.0	0.9	-4.2	-2.5
FLORIDA..................	7 787 742	37.3	23.9	6.2	13.8	4.0	76.1	8.7	29.6	22.2	14.2	1.4	-1.7	3.2
GEORGIA.................	4 022 230	32.1	27.6	7.5	15.6	4.5	72.4	10.8	33.2	20.8	7.2	0.5	2.0	-4.7
HAWAII...................	608 269	35.1	24.9	6.5	14.3	4.1	75.1	10.2	30.5	22.6	10.5	1.2	-0.7	-0.6
IDAHO	648 699	32.2	29.3	7.7	16.3	5.3	70.7	10.9	28.5	21.4	8.9	0.9	3.7	-2.5
ILLINOIS	6 074 136	33.3	27.3	7.3	15.5	4.5	72.7	10.2	31.3	21.2	9.0	0.8	1.7	-2.5
INDIANA	2 979 756	33.9	27.1	7.3	15.2	4.6	72.9	10.5	30.2	22.1	9.3	0.8	1.5	-2.2
IOWA......................	1 434 419	35.2	26.1	6.7	14.8	4.7	73.9	10.4	28.4	22.5	11.2	1.2	0.5	0.0
KANSAS..................	1 327 761	33.7	27.6	7.3	15.5	4.8	72.4	10.8	29.3	21.4	9.8	1.1	2.0	-1.5
KENTUCKY..............	1 974 840	34.6	25.9	6.9	14.6	4.4	74.1	10.3	30.5	22.9	9.5	0.8	0.3	-2.1
LOUISIANA	2 159 852	32.6	28.8	7.4	16.2	5.1	71.2	10.9	29.3	21.4	8.9	0.7	3.2	-2.8
MAINE	620 214	37.6	24.9	5.8	14.5	4.6	75.1	8.5	29.2	25.1	11.2	1.0	-0.7	-0.1
MARYLAND	2 554 588	34.9	27.1	7.0	15.7	4.3	72.9	8.8	31.7	22.9	8.8	0.7	1.5	-2.9
MASSACHUSETTS ...	3 058 375	35.4	25.2	6.6	14.5	4.0	74.8	9.3	32.0	22.3	10.2	1.0	-0.4	-1.2
MICHIGAN	4 871 161	34.3	27.3	7.0	15.7	4.5	72.7	9.6	30.3	22.4	9.5	0.8	1.7	-2.1
MINNESOTA	2 434 526	34.4	27.1	6.9	15.5	4.8	72.9	9.8	31.1	21.9	9.1	1.0	1.5	-2.3
MISSISSIPPI	1 373 314	32.2	28.8	7.5	16.3	5.0	71.2	11.5	28.7	21.1	9.1	0.9	3.2	-2.5
MISSOURI	2 718 409	34.8	26.9	6.9	15.3	4.6	73.1	9.9	29.8	22.2	10.4	1.0	1.3	-1.1
MONTANA	449 733	36.6	26.4	6.3	15.0	5.0	73.6	9.9	27.2	24.7	10.7	1.1	0.8	-0.6
NEBRASKA..............	843 112	34.0	27.3	7.1	15.3	4.9	72.7	10.6	29.3	21.5	10.2	1.1	1.7	-1.1
NEVADA..................	1 016 086	34.5	25.8	7.3	14.7	3.8	74.2	9.1	32.5	22.6	9.5	0.6	0.2	-2.4
NEW HAMPSHIRE.....	608 140	36.4	26.1	6.4	15.3	4.5	73.9	8.5	31.1	24.1	9.4	0.8	0.5	-2.2
NEW JERSEY	4 077 993	35.5	26.2	7.0	15.1	4.1	73.8	8.5	31.9	22.4	10.0	0.9	0.6	-1.5
NEW MEXICO...........	891 544	33.4	28.9	7.3	16.7	5.0	71.1	10.1	28.8	21.8	9.6	0.9	3.3	-2.0
NEW YORK...............	9 134 254	34.5	26.3	6.9	15.1	4.2	73.7	9.7	31.4	22.0	9.7	0.9	0.7	-1.7
NORTH CAROLINA ...	3 940 711	33.8	25.5	7.0	14.5	4.0	74.5	10.6	31.9	22.0	9.2	0.7	-0.1	-2.5
NORTH DAKOTA......	320 695	34.8	25.8	6.3	14.6	5.0	74.2	12.0	27.8	21.9	11.0	1.5	0.2	0.0
OHIO......................	5 511 578	34.9	26.8	7.0	15.3	4.5	73.2	9.6	30.0	22.6	10.2	0.8	1.2	-1.4
OKLAHOMA.............	1 695 531	33.9	27.0	7.2	15.1	4.8	73.0	10.9	29.0	22.0	10.1	0.9	1.4	-1.3
OREGON.................	1 695 966	35.1	25.6	6.7	14.4	4.4	74.4	9.8	29.9	23.7	9.9	1.1	0.0	-1.4
PENNSYLVANIA	5 927 076	36.5	25.3	6.3	14.6	4.4	74.7	9.2	29.4	23.1	11.9	1.1	-0.3	0.5
RHODE ISLAND	503 226	35.4	25.4	6.4	14.8	4.2	74.6	10.4	30.0	22.1	10.9	1.1	-0.2	-0.4
SOUTH CAROLINA ...	1 947 380	34.0	26.5	7.0	15.2	4.4	73.5	10.6	30.1	22.6	9.4	0.7	0.9	-2.3
SOUTH DAKOTA......	374 554	34.4	27.8	7.0	15.7	5.2	72.2	10.7	27.9	21.4	11.0	1.2	2.2	-0.2
TENNESSEE............	2 768 101	34.5	25.9	6.9	14.7	4.3	74.1	10.0	30.9	23.1	9.4	0.8	0.3	-2.2
TEXAS....................	10 335 429	31.3	29.1	8.0	16.4	4.8	70.9	10.9	31.9	19.8	7.7	0.6	3.5	-4.1
UTAH......................	1 119 973	26.7	33.1	9.7	17.7	5.7	66.9	14.0	28.8	16.7	6.8	0.6	7.5	-4.9
VERMONT	298 298	36.6	25.4	5.8	14.9	4.7	74.6	9.8	29.0	25.0	9.8	0.9	-0.2	-1.6
VIRGINIA.................	3 469 059	34.5	25.6	6.8	14.7	4.2	74.4	10.1	32.2	22.8	8.6	0.7	0.0	-3.1
WASHINGTON..........	2 930 661	34.4	26.4	6.9	15.1	4.5	73.6	9.7	31.6	22.7	8.7	0.9	0.8	-2.8
WEST VIRGINIA	879 250	37.5	23.5	5.9	13.3	4.3	76.5	10.0	28.2	25.5	11.8	1.0	-2.1	0.4
WISCONSIN.............	2 648 363	35.0	26.5	6.6	15.2	4.7	73.5	10.0	30.2	22.3	10.0	1.0	0.9	-1.4
WYOMING	248 253	35.3	26.5	6.4	14.9	5.3	73.5	10.5	28.3	24.5	9.3	0.9	0.9	-2.2

STATE	Number	Female median age	Under 18 years	Under 5 years	5 to 14 years	15 to 17 years	18 years and over	18 to 24 years	25 to 44 years	45 to 64 years	65 to 84 years	85 years and over	+/− U.S. percent under 18 years	+/− U.S. percent 65 years and over
			Female children under 18 years (percent)				Female adults 18 years and over (percent)							
	29	30	31	32	33	34	35	36	37	38	39	40	41	42
UNITED STATES ...	143 505 720	36.5	24.5	6.5	14.0	4.0	75.5	9.2	29.8	22.1	12.3	2.1	-1.1	2.0
ALABAMA	2 302 637	37.2	23.8	6.3	13.5	4.0	76.2	9.6	28.6	22.8	13.0	2.1	-1.8	2.8
ALASKA	302 650	32.5	30.5	7.6	17.8	5.1	69.5	8.8	32.9	21.7	5.6	0.6	4.9	-6.2
ARIZONA	2 574 149	35.5	25.8	7.2	14.6	4.0	74.2	9.5	28.9	21.4	12.7	1.7	0.2	2.0
ARKANSAS.............	1 370 068	37.4	24.2	6.5	13.5	4.2	75.8	9.5	27.5	22.7	13.7	2.4	-1.4	3.7
CALIFORNIA	17 028 586	34.4	26.3	7.0	15.3	4.0	73.7	9.4	31.2	20.8	10.6	1.7	0.7	-0.2
COLORADO.............	2 137 307	35.4	25.0	6.8	14.1	4.1	75.0	9.4	32.0	22.3	9.7	1.6	-0.6	-1.1
CONNECTICUT	1 757 042	38.6	23.3	6.1	13.6	3.6	76.7	7.5	30.2	23.1	13.3	2.6	-2.3	3.5
DELAWARE	403 597	37.1	23.5	6.3	13.4	3.7	76.5	9.5	29.8	22.6	12.8	1.8	-2.1	2.2
DISTRICT OF COLUMBIA	303 232	35.6	18.7	5.3	10.7	2.7	81.3	13.2	31.7	22.1	12.3	2.0	-6.9	2.0
FLORIDA.................	8 194 636	40.1	21.6	5.6	12.5	3.5	78.4	7.9	28.0	23.0	16.8	2.6	-4.0	7.0
GEORGIA................	4 164 223	34.6	25.4	7.0	14.4	4.0	74.6	9.7	32.0	21.5	9.9	1.6	-0.2	-1.0
HAWAII..................	603 268	37.4	23.7	6.2	13.5	3.9	76.3	8.7	29.7	23.1	13.2	1.7	-1.9	2.4
IDAHO...................	645 254	34.2	27.6	7.3	15.4	4.9	72.4	10.5	27.8	21.4	10.8	1.8	2.0	0.3
ILLINOIS.................	6 345 157	36.0	24.9	6.7	14.1	4.0	75.1	9.2	30.1	21.6	12.0	2.1	-0.7	1.8
INDIANA.................	3 100 729	36.5	24.7	6.6	14.0	4.1	75.3	9.7	28.9	22.1	12.4	2.1	-0.9	2.1
IOWA....................	1 491 905	38.0	23.9	6.2	13.5	4.3	76.1	9.8	26.9	22.0	14.2	3.2	-1.7	5.0
KANSAS.................	1 360 657	36.5	25.4	6.7	14.2	4.4	74.6	9.7	28.2	21.2	12.8	2.6	-0.2	3.1
KENTUCKY	2 066 929	37.1	23.4	6.3	13.1	4.0	76.6	9.5	29.5	23.0	12.6	2.0	-2.2	2.1
LOUISIANA	2 309 124	35.3	25.8	6.7	14.6	4.6	74.2	10.4	28.8	21.6	11.6	1.8	0.2	1.0
MAINE	654 709	39.6	22.4	5.3	13.1	4.0	77.6	7.9	28.9	24.4	13.9	2.5	-3.2	4.0
MARYLAND	2 741 898	37.0	24.1	6.3	14.0	3.8	75.9	8.1	31.6	23.3	11.2	1.7	-1.5	0.5
MASSACHUSETTS ...	3 290 722	37.7	22.1	5.9	12.7	3.5	77.9	9.0	30.9	22.3	13.2	2.5	-3.5	3.4
MICHIGAN	5 067 283	36.6	24.9	6.4	14.3	4.1	75.1	9.1	29.4	22.4	12.2	2.0	-0.7	1.8
MINNESOTA............	2 484 953	36.3	25.2	6.4	14.4	4.4	74.8	9.3	30.0	21.6	11.5	2.5	-0.4	1.6
MISSISSIPPI............	1 471 344	35.3	25.7	6.8	14.6	4.4	74.3	10.5	28.3	21.3	12.0	2.1	0.1	1.7
MISSOURI	2 876 802	37.4	24.2	6.3	13.8	4.1	75.8	9.3	28.6	22.4	13.1	2.5	-1.4	3.2
MONTANA	452 462	38.5	24.6	5.9	14.1	4.6	75.4	9.0	27.3	24.1	12.7	2.3	-1.0	2.6
NEBRASKA.............	868 151	36.6	25.3	6.6	14.2	4.5	74.7	9.8	27.8	21.4	13.0	2.8	-0.3	3.4
NEVADA................	982 171	35.6	25.2	7.1	14.3	3.8	74.8	8.7	31.0	23.2	10.8	1.1	-0.4	-0.5
NEW HAMPSHIRE.....	627 646	37.8	23.9	5.8	14.2	3.9	76.1	8.2	30.7	23.6	11.5	2.2	-1.7	1.3
NEW JERSEY...........	4 336 357	38.0	23.4	6.3	13.5	3.6	76.6	7.6	30.8	22.9	13.2	2.2	-2.2	3.0
NEW MEXICO...........	927 502	35.6	26.9	6.9	15.4	4.6	73.1	9.4	28.4	22.4	11.3	1.6	1.3	0.5
NEW YORK..............	9 842 203	37.2	23.1	6.1	13.3	3.7	76.9	8.9	30.4	22.6	12.8	2.2	-2.5	2.6
NORTH CAROLINA ...	4 108 602	36.7	23.2	6.3	13.3	3.6	76.8	9.4	30.5	22.8	12.3	1.9	-2.4	1.7
NORTH DAKOTA......	321 505	37.5	24.3	5.9	13.7	4.6	75.7	10.6	26.8	21.3	13.9	3.1	-1.3	4.6
OHIO.....................	5 841 562	37.5	24.1	6.3	13.7	4.0	75.9	9.0	28.8	22.7	13.3	2.1	-1.5	3.0
OKLAHOMA............	1 755 123	36.9	24.7	6.5	13.8	4.4	75.3	9.8	27.8	22.4	13.0	2.3	-0.9	2.9
OREGON................	1 725 433	37.5	23.8	6.3	13.5	4.1	76.2	9.0	29.0	23.8	12.3	2.2	-1.8	2.2
PENNSYLVANIA.......	6 353 978	39.4	22.3	5.6	13.0	3.8	77.7	8.6	27.9	22.9	15.5	2.6	-3.3	5.7
RHODE ISLAND	545 093	38.0	22.0	5.6	12.7	3.6	78.0	9.9	29.3	21.9	14.1	2.8	-3.6	4.5
SOUTH CAROLINA ...	2 064 632	36.7	23.9	6.2	13.8	3.9	76.1	9.7	29.3	23.1	12.2	1.8	-1.7	1.6
SOUTH DAKOTA	380 290	36.7	25.9	6.6	14.6	4.7	74.1	9.9	26.8	20.9	13.5	2.9	0.3	4.0
TENNESSEE	2 921 182	37.2	23.3	6.2	13.2	3.8	76.7	9.3	29.8	23.2	12.4	2.0	-2.3	2.0
TEXAS...................	10 516 391	33.4	27.2	7.5	15.3	4.4	72.8	10.0	30.8	20.4	9.9	1.6	1.6	-0.9
UTAH....................	1 113 196	27.7	31.1	9.1	16.7	5.3	68.9	14.5	27.5	17.2	8.3	1.3	5.5	-2.8
VERMONT	310 529	38.7	23.2	5.3	13.6	4.2	76.8	8.9	28.9	24.5	12.3	2.3	-2.4	2.2
VIRGINIA................	3 609 456	36.8	23.5	6.2	13.5	3.8	76.5	9.1	31.3	23.2	11.2	1.7	-2.1	0.6
WASHINGTON..........	2 963 460	36.3	24.8	6.5	14.2	4.2	75.2	9.2	30.5	22.7	11.0	1.9	-0.8	0.4
WEST VIRGINIA	929 094	40.2	21.0	5.4	11.9	3.8	79.0	9.2	27.3	24.8	15.2	2.5	-4.6	5.3
WISCONSIN............	2 715 312	37.1	24.5	6.2	14.0	4.3	75.5	9.4	29.0	22.0	12.6	2.5	-1.1	2.7
WYOMING	245 529	37.1	25.3	6.1	14.3	4.9	74.7	9.8	28.1	23.7	11.3	1.8	-0.3	0.7

Table A-2. States — Age, Ethnicity, and Household Structure

STATE	Non-Hispanic White population													
			Non-Hispanic White children under 18 years (percent)				Non-Hispanic White adults 18 years and over (percent)							
	Number	Non-Hispanic White median age	Under 18 years	Under 5 years	5 to 14 years	15 to 17 years	18 years and over	18 to 24 years	25 to 44 years	45 to 64 years	65 to 84 years	85 years and over	+/− U.S. percent under 18 years	+/− U.S. percent 65 years and over
	43	44	45	46	47	48	49	50	51	52	53	54	55	56
UNITED STATES ...	194 514 140	38.6	22.6	5.7	13.0	3.9	77.4	8.6	29.4	24.3	13.2	1.9	-3.0	2.6
ALABAMA	3 127 039	38.3	22.8	6.0	12.9	3.9	77.2	8.8	29.0	24.7	13.2	1.6	-2.8	2.4
ALASKA	423 660	35.5	26.5	6.3	15.4	4.7	73.5	8.4	33.8	25.3	5.6	0.5	0.9	-6.3
ARIZONA	3 272 065	40.3	20.7	5.4	11.9	3.5	79.3	8.2	28.5	24.8	15.9	1.9	-4.9	5.3
ARKANSAS	2 100 065	38.4	23.1	6.0	13.0	4.1	76.9	9.0	27.8	24.3	13.9	1.9	-2.5	3.3
CALIFORNIA	15 771 163	40.3	20.4	4.9	12.0	3.4	79.6	7.5	30.4	25.8	13.9	2.1	-5.2	3.6
COLORADO	3 201 519	37.2	22.7	5.7	13.1	3.9	77.3	8.9	32.5	24.6	9.9	1.3	-2.9	-1.1
CONNECTICUT	2 637 525	40.2	22.2	5.7	13.0	3.5	77.8	6.8	29.6	25.1	14.0	2.3	-3.4	3.9
DELAWARE	568 356	38.8	22.0	5.6	12.8	3.7	78.0	8.9	29.4	24.2	13.9	1.6	-3.6	3.1
DISTRICT OF COLUMBIA	158 617	35.1	8.5	3.0	4.4	1.1	91.5	17.0	39.6	23.5	9.6	1.8	-17.1	-1.0
FLORIDA	10 456 458	43.1	19.3	4.9	11.2	3.2	80.7	6.8	26.8	24.8	19.6	2.7	-6.3	9.9
GEORGIA	5 129 727	36.7	23.5	6.3	13.3	3.8	76.5	8.8	31.7	24.1	10.7	1.3	-2.1	-0.4
HAWAII	276 191	40.4	16.0	4.4	9.2	2.4	84.0	9.1	33.2	28.8	11.6	1.4	-9.6	0.5
IDAHO	1 138 460	35.1	27.0	6.9	15.1	5.0	73.0	10.3	27.7	22.6	10.8	1.5	1.4	-0.1
ILLINOIS...................	8 423 408	38.3	22.8	5.8	13.1	3.9	77.2	8.5	29.9	23.8	13.0	2.0	-2.8	2.5
INDIANA	5 220 722	36.6	24.6	6.4	14.0	4.2	75.4	9.7	29.3	23.1	11.7	1.6	-1.0	0.9
IOWA	2 713 026	37.9	24.1	6.0	13.7	4.4	75.9	9.9	27.4	23.0	13.4	2.3	-1.5	3.4
KANSAS...................	2 234 488	37.4	24.6	6.2	13.9	4.5	75.4	9.6	28.1	22.8	12.7	2.2	-1.0	2.5
KENTUCKY	3 610 112	36.8	23.8	6.2	13.4	4.1	76.2	9.6	29.8	23.7	11.6	1.5	-1.8	0.7
LOUISIANA	2 794 348	37.1	23.8	6.1	13.4	4.3	76.2	9.7	29.2	23.5	12.3	1.5	-1.8	1.4
MAINE	1 230 645	39.1	23.2	5.4	13.5	4.3	76.8	8.0	29.0	25.1	12.9	1.8	-2.4	2.3
MARYLAND	3 287 071	38.9	23.0	5.8	13.4	3.8	77.0	7.4	30.3	25.2	12.5	1.6	-2.6	1.7
MASSACHUSETTS ...	5 197 124	38.8	21.7	5.6	12.5	3.5	78.3	8.2	30.8	23.9	13.3	2.1	-3.9	3.0
MICHIGAN	7 805 325	37.5	24.1	6.1	13.8	4.2	75.9	8.9	29.6	23.8	12.1	1.6	-1.5	1.3
MINNESOTA	4 340 672	37.2	24.4	6.0	13.9	4.4	75.6	9.1	30.2	23.1	11.3	1.9	-1.2	0.9
MISSISSIPPI	1 728 608	37.7	23.2	6.1	13.1	4.0	76.8	9.7	28.4	24.1	13.0	1.7	-2.4	2.3
MISSOURI................	4 687 837	37.6	24.0	6.1	13.7	4.2	76.0	9.2	28.8	23.3	12.8	1.9	-1.6	2.3
MONTANA	807 588	38.9	23.9	5.6	13.7	4.6	76.1	9.2	27.2	25.3	12.6	1.8	-1.7	2.0
NEBRASKA	1 495 553	37.3	24.7	6.1	14.0	4.6	75.3	9.7	28.0	22.6	12.7	2.2	-0.9	2.5
NEVADA...................	1 301 738	39.7	21.2	5.5	12.3	3.4	78.8	7.3	30.4	26.9	13.1	1.1	-4.4	1.9
NEW HAMPSHIRE.....	1 175 083	37.6	24.6	5.9	14.5	4.1	75.4	8.1	30.7	24.2	10.8	1.6	-1.0	0.0
NEW JERSEY	5 554 478	40.2	22.3	5.8	13.0	3.5	77.7	6.6	29.5	24.9	14.6	2.1	-3.3	4.3
NEW MEXICO...........	813 380	42.0	20.3	4.7	11.9	3.8	79.7	7.7	27.4	27.9	14.8	1.9	-5.3	4.4
NEW YORK...............	11 761 679	39.4	21.8	5.6	12.6	3.6	78.2	8.0	29.3	24.4	14.2	2.2	-3.8	4.0
NORTH CAROLINA ...	5 648 953	38.1	21.8	5.8	12.5	3.5	78.2	8.8	30.7	24.6	12.6	1.5	-3.8	1.7
NORTH DAKOTA......	589 853	37.5	23.7	5.7	13.3	4.7	76.3	11.1	27.2	22.4	13.2	2.5	-1.9	3.3
OHIO	9 537 082	37.6	24.0	6.1	13.7	4.2	76.0	9.0	29.2	23.5	12.6	1.6	-1.6	1.9
OKLAHOMA	2 556 373	38.7	22.6	5.7	12.7	4.2	77.4	9.4	28.0	24.3	13.7	2.0	-3.0	3.2
OREGON	2 857 100	39.0	22.6	5.6	12.9	4.1	77.4	8.7	28.5	25.6	12.6	1.9	-3.0	2.1
PENNSYLVANIA.......	10 327 998	39.7	22.2	5.4	12.9	3.9	77.8	8.4	28.2	24.1	15.0	2.1	-3.4	4.7
RHODE ISLAND	858 665	39.4	21.0	5.2	12.3	3.5	79.0	9.2	29.3	23.8	14.4	2.3	-4.6	4.3
SOUTH CAROLINA ...	2 654 401	38.2	22.1	5.8	12.6	3.6	77.9	9.2	29.5	25.0	12.7	1.4	-3.5	1.7
SOUTH DAKOTA.......	664 810	37.5	24.6	6.0	13.9	4.7	75.4	10.0	27.3	22.3	13.4	2.3	-1.0	3.3
TENNESSEE............	4 508 623	37.8	22.7	5.9	12.9	3.8	77.3	8.9	30.0	24.7	12.2	1.5	-2.9	1.3
TEXAS.....................	10 927 538	38.1	22.9	5.8	13.1	4.0	77.1	8.7	30.2	24.4	12.1	1.6	-2.7	1.4
UTAH.......................	1 905 227	28.1	31.1	8.8	16.8	5.5	68.9	14.0	27.5	17.9	8.4	1.1	5.5	-3.0
VERMONT................	585 217	38.1	23.8	5.4	14.0	4.4	76.2	9.1	29.0	25.0	11.3	1.7	-1.8	0.6
VIRGINIA	4 963 910	38.0	22.4	5.8	12.9	3.7	77.6	8.7	30.9	25.1	11.5	1.4	-3.2	0.5
WASHINGTON..........	4 649 156	37.9	23.2	5.7	13.4	4.1	76.8	8.6	30.4	24.7	11.3	1.7	-2.4	0.6
WEST VIRGINIA	1 709 317	39.3	21.9	5.5	12.4	4.0	78.1	9.4	27.7	25.5	13.8	1.8	-3.7	3.2
WISCONSIN..............	4 687 649	37.9	23.5	5.7	13.5	4.3	76.5	9.2	29.4	23.4	12.4	2.0	-2.1	2.0
WYOMING	438 538	37.6	24.9	5.8	14.1	5.1	75.1	9.7	28.0	25.0	10.9	1.5	-0.7	0.0

STATE	Number	Black or African American median age	Black or African American children under 18 years (percent)				Black or African American adults 18 years and over (percent)						+/− U.S. percent under 18 years	+/− U.S. percent 65 years and over
			Under 18 years	Under 5 years	5 to 14 years	15 to 17 years	18 years and over	18 to 24 years	25 to 44 years	45 to 64 years	65 to 84 years	85 years and over		
	57	58	59	60	61	62	63	64	65	66	67	68	69	70
UNITED STATES ...	34 361 740	30.2	31.3	8.0	18.3	5.0	68.7	10.9	31.0	18.6	7.3	0.9	5.7	−4.2
ALABAMA	1 153 044	29.9	31.0	7.9	18.0	5.2	69.0	12.0	28.9	18.6	8.2	1.3	5.4	−2.9
ALASKA	21 968	27.3	35.1	8.8	20.5	5.8	64.9	11.5	34.8	15.4	2.8	0.4	9.5	−9.2
ARIZONA	154 316	29.0	30.7	8.0	18.2	4.6	69.3	11.5	33.6	17.9	5.6	0.7	5.1	−6.1
ARKANSAS.............	417 881	27.9	33.6	8.8	19.0	5.8	66.4	12.3	28.1	17.1	7.5	1.4	8.0	−3.5
CALIFORNIA............	2 219 190	31.5	30.2	7.3	18.2	4.6	69.8	9.8	32.5	19.4	7.3	0.8	4.6	−4.2
COLORADO.............	159 279	30.3	30.1	7.9	17.6	4.7	69.9	10.3	35.1	18.4	5.7	0.4	4.5	−6.3
CONNECTICUT	305 902	29.9	31.9	8.3	18.8	4.8	68.1	10.7	31.9	18.5	6.4	0.6	6.3	−5.4
DELAWARE	148 823	30.4	30.9	7.9	18.1	4.8	69.1	10.8	31.7	19.1	6.8	0.8	5.3	−4.8
DISTRICT OF COLUMBIA............	343 213	36.1	25.1	6.5	14.8	3.8	74.9	9.9	28.7	22.3	12.6	1.5	−0.5	1.7
FLORIDA.................	2 312 105	28.7	33.1	8.3	19.4	5.4	66.9	11.3	30.6	17.6	6.6	0.7	7.5	−5.0
GEORGIA................	2 342 110	29.3	31.7	8.3	18.4	5.0	68.3	11.4	33.0	17.3	5.8	0.8	6.1	−5.8
HAWAII..................	20 945	27.2	25.0	9.2	13.4	2.4	75.0	17.1	43.5	12.0	2.2	0.3	−0.6	−10.0
IDAHO...................	5 244	24.1	35.8	11.8	18.9	5.2	64.2	13.4	35.4	11.0	4.1	0.3	10.2	−8.0
ILLINOIS................	1 864 619	29.7	32.3	8.3	18.9	5.0	67.7	10.6	29.9	18.8	7.6	0.8	6.7	−4.1
INDIANA.................	504 449	29.3	32.2	8.8	18.4	5.0	67.8	11.1	30.0	18.1	7.7	0.9	6.6	−3.8
IOWA....................	59 758	25.3	34.7	9.7	19.9	5.1	65.3	13.4	30.2	15.4	5.7	0.7	9.1	−4.7
KANSAS.................	150 584	28.6	32.4	8.5	18.8	5.2	67.6	12.1	31.1	16.7	6.7	0.9	6.8	−4.7
KENTUCKY..............	293 915	30.1	30.0	8.1	17.1	4.7	70.0	12.0	31.1	18.2	7.5	1.2	4.4	−3.7
LOUISIANA.............	1 444 566	28.2	33.5	8.6	19.1	5.8	66.5	12.2	28.2	18.0	7.2	1.0	9.5	−4.3
MAINE...................	6 047	23.0	35.1	9.7	20.6	4.9	64.9	17.2	30.5	13.3	3.6	0.3	9.5	−8.5
MARYLAND..............	1 468 243	32.2	29.5	7.5	17.4	4.6	70.5	9.5	33.1	20.5	6.7	0.7	3.9	−5.0
MASSACHUSETTS ...	337 157	29.7	31.4	8.0	18.6	4.9	68.6	11.1	33.0	17.6	6.2	0.6	5.8	−5.6
MICHIGAN	1 401 723	29.9	32.1	8.1	19.3	4.7	67.9	10.2	30.3	18.9	7.7	0.9	6.5	−3.9
MINNESOTA............	167 857	25.2	37.7	10.1	22.3	5.3	62.3	11.9	34.7	12.5	2.9	0.2	12.1	−9.2
MISSISSIPPI	1 033 437	27.5	33.7	8.7	19.1	5.8	66.3	12.0	28.4	16.8	7.1	1.2	8.1	−4.1
MISSOURI...............	622 087	29.6	32.5	8.1	19.2	5.2	67.5	10.7	30.2	18.0	7.7	1.0	6.9	−3.8
MONTANA...............	2 359	23.6	32.6	9.1	19.0	4.5	67.4	19.5	27.8	15.4	3.9	0.8	7.0	−7.7
NEBRASKA..............	67 435	27.0	34.9	9.2	20.2	5.5	65.1	11.6	30.5	16.5	5.6	0.8	9.3	−6.0
NEVADA.................	132 490	30.6	30.8	8.2	18.2	4.4	69.2	9.6	33.5	19.2	6.5	0.4	5.2	−5.5
NEW HAMPSHIRE.....	8 984	28.3	31.3	8.3	18.6	4.4	68.7	11.7	34.8	17.5	4.3	0.4	5.7	−7.7
NEW JERSEY..........	1 127 266	31.6	29.9	7.7	17.5	4.6	70.1	10.0	32.2	19.5	7.7	0.8	4.3	−4.0
NEW MEXICO..........	33 513	29.8	30.4	8.6	17.3	4.5	69.6	12.1	30.3	18.4	7.9	1.0	4.8	−3.5
NEW YORK..............	2 986 242	31.6	29.8	7.6	17.5	4.8	70.2	10.4	31.1	19.9	7.9	0.8	4.2	−3.7
NORTH CAROLINA ...	1 734 154	31.0	29.8	7.6	17.6	4.6	70.2	11.0	31.1	19.1	7.9	1.0	4.2	−3.5
NORTH DAKOTA.......	3 673	22.5	36.5	10.2	22.0	4.3	63.5	23.6	29.7	7.9	1.5	0.8	10.9	−10.1
OHIO	1 288 359	30.5	31.9	8.3	18.8	4.8	68.1	10.2	29.6	18.8	8.5	1.0	6.3	−2.9
OKLAHOMA.............	258 532	28.1	32.4	8.6	18.5	5.3	67.6	12.8	30.5	16.9	6.3	1.0	6.8	−5.1
OREGON	53 032	29.5	31.0	8.5	17.6	4.9	69.0	11.5	32.7	18.2	5.0	0.0	5.4	−5.8
PENNSYLVANIA.......	1 211 669	31.2	30.8	7.7	18.4	4.7	69.2	10.4	29.8	18.8	9.1	1.0	5.2	−2.2
RHODE ISLAND	45 236	26.8	32.8	7.9	20.1	4.8	67.2	13.4	30.7	16.5	6.1	0.5	7.2	−5.8
SOUTH CAROLINA ...	1 182 727	30.5	31.1	7.6	18.3	5.2	68.9	11.2	29.4	19.4	7.8	1.0	5.5	−3.6
SOUTH DAKOTA.......	4 518	24.8	34.8	11.2	16.3	7.3	65.2	14.7	36.6	10.7	2.9	0.3	9.2	−9.2
TENNESSEE............	929 864	29.5	31.8	8.3	18.5	5.0	68.2	11.5	30.7	18.1	7.0	1.0	6.2	−4.5
TEXAS	2 385 554	29.8	31.0	8.0	18.0	5.1	69.0	11.1	32.8	17.8	6.5	0.9	5.4	−5.0
UTAH	16 150	24.8	35.2	10.6	19.4	5.2	64.8	15.3	33.2	12.1	3.9	0.3	9.6	−8.2
VERMONT	2 981	23.4	37.1	9.6	22.3	5.2	62.9	20.1	27.7	12.0	2.9	0.2	11.5	−9.3
VIRGINIA................	1 384 008	32.0	29.2	7.2	17.3	4.7	70.8	10.6	32.1	19.2	7.9	0.9	3.6	−3.5
WASHINGTON..........	185 052	29.7	30.7	7.8	18.0	4.8	69.3	11.2	35.8	16.8	5.0	0.5	5.1	−6.8
WEST VIRGINIA.......	55 999	33.5	25.5	6.6	14.8	4.1	74.5	12.1	28.8	20.8	10.7	2.2	−0.1	0.4
WISCONSIN............	300 355	25.4	37.8	10.0	22.1	5.7	62.2	11.6	30.1	15.3	4.8	0.4	12.2	−7.2
WYOMING	3 126	26.5	25.5	5.5	13.7	6.4	74.5	17.7	31.2	21.9	3.7	0.0	−0.1	−8.7

| STATE | Number | American Indian and Alaska Native median age | American Indian and Alaska Native children under 18 years (percent) | | | | American Indian and Alaska Native adults 18 years and over (percent) | | | | | | +/− U.S. percent under 18 years | +/− U.S. percent 65 years and over |
| | | | Under 18 years | Under 5 years | 5 to 14 years | 15 to 17 years | 18 years and over | 18 to 24 years | 25 to 44 years | 45 to 64 years | 65 to 84 years | 85 years and over | | |
	71	72	73	74	75	76	77	78	79	80	81	82	83	84
UNITED STATES ...	2 447 989	28.0	33.3	8.4	19.3	5.6	66.7	11.5	31.4	18.1	5.2	0.5	7.7	-6.8
ALABAMA	22 897	32.3	28.2	6.0	15.8	6.4	71.8	11.6	32.4	23.3	4.1	0.3	2.6	-8.0
ALASKA	97 012	25.8	38.4	9.1	22.9	6.4	61.6	10.5	29.0	16.2	5.4	0.5	12.8	-6.5
ARIZONA	253 542	24.2	38.8	9.7	22.8	6.3	61.2	11.8	28.9	14.9	5.0	0.6	13.2	-6.8
ARKANSAS	18 492	31.4	30.6	7.7	17.2	5.7	69.4	10.8	31.0	21.7	5.5	0.3	5.0	-6.6
CALIFORNIA	312 215	29.3	30.7	7.6	18.2	4.9	69.3	11.3	33.0	19.3	5.3	0.4	5.1	-6.7
COLORADO	43 101	29.4	28.7	8.0	15.9	4.9	71.3	12.5	36.7	18.2	3.5	0.4	3.1	-8.5
CONNECTICUT	9 419	30.6	27.2	7.1	15.6	4.5	72.8	11.6	32.8	21.0	7.0	0.4	1.6	-5.1
DELAWARE	3 111	35.4	26.3	6.9	15.4	4.0	73.7	10.6	32.5	21.5	8.5	0.6	0.7	-3.3
DISTRICT OF COLUMBIA	2 006	36.0	22.1	7.2	12.0	2.9	77.9	10.5	34.6	23.4	9.3	0.0	-3.5	-3.1
FLORIDA	54 428	33.6	24.0	5.8	13.5	4.6	76.0	11.1	36.2	22.5	5.8	0.4	-1.6	-6.2
GEORGIA	23 688	31.3	24.5	6.0	14.2	4.3	75.5	12.2	36.8	21.7	4.4	0.4	-1.1	-7.6
HAWAII	3 216	32.7	20.8	4.8	11.3	4.8	79.2	15.0	37.2	22.7	4.3	0.0	-4.8	-8.1
IDAHO	17 528	27.6	34.5	9.0	19.8	5.7	65.5	11.4	31.7	17.4	4.6	0.3	8.9	-7.4
ILLINOIS	30 407	28.9	29.2	7.2	16.6	5.4	70.8	12.1	35.2	19.4	3.8	0.3	3.6	-8.3
INDIANA	17 168	31.9	26.7	7.2	15.6	3.9	73.3	10.0	35.9	21.7	5.0	0.7	1.1	-6.7
IOWA	9 263	26.1	35.0	8.9	20.9	5.3	65.0	14.3	33.0	14.5	2.8	0.4	9.4	-9.2
KANSAS	24 723	28.3	30.5	8.2	17.3	5.0	69.5	12.9	32.5	18.8	5.0	0.4	4.9	-7.0
KENTUCKY	9 080	34.3	22.5	5.1	13.1	4.2	77.5	11.1	39.5	21.3	5.4	0.2	-3.1	-6.8
LOUISIANA	25 833	29.3	32.3	7.6	18.7	6.0	67.7	12.6	30.1	18.5	6.0	0.4	6.7	-5.9
MAINE	7 521	29.3	32.0	8.5	18.2	5.3	68.0	9.9	33.3	19.2	5.1	0.5	6.4	-6.8
MARYLAND	15 651	33.8	23.5	4.9	13.8	4.7	76.5	10.2	36.2	23.9	5.7	0.5	-2.1	-6.1
MASSACHUSETTS ...	15 305	30.4	27.9	6.1	17.1	4.8	72.1	11.4	31.8	22.3	6.0	0.5	2.3	-5.8
MICHIGAN	60 842	29.7	31.1	7.9	17.9	5.3	68.9	11.7	32.9	19.0	4.9	0.3	5.5	-7.2
MINNESOTA	54 568	25.5	37.1	9.4	21.1	6.6	62.9	11.2	31.2	16.2	3.9	0.4	11.5	-8.2
MISSISSIPPI	11 836	27.2	34.1	8.7	19.7	5.7	65.9	12.4	30.6	17.0	5.4	0.5	8.5	-6.5
MISSOURI	26 200	33.2	26.6	6.2	15.5	4.9	73.4	11.3	33.9	21.5	6.1	0.6	1.0	-5.7
MONTANA	55 218	24.4	39.1	10.1	22.3	6.8	60.9	11.7	28.1	16.5	4.3	0.3	13.5	-7.8
NEBRASKA	15 421	23.8	38.4	10.2	21.9	6.3	61.6	12.8	29.6	14.4	4.4	0.3	12.8	-7.7
NEVADA	26 485	30.8	29.6	7.8	16.5	5.3	70.4	9.9	34.7	19.6	5.7	0.5	4.0	-6.2
NEW HAMPSHIRE	2 660	33.1	23.9	3.6	14.0	6.2	76.1	14.2	31.4	25.8	3.3	1.4	-1.7	-7.7
NEW JERSEY	17 987	30.9	27.5	7.2	16.3	4.0	72.5	11.3	33.5	21.2	5.8	0.7	1.9	-5.9
NEW MEXICO	172 276	25.6	37.3	9.2	21.9	6.2	62.7	11.9	29.3	15.6	5.3	0.5	11.7	-6.6
NEW YORK	79 314	28.8	31.7	8.3	18.9	4.4	68.3	10.6	32.8	18.2	6.0	0.6	6.1	-5.7
NORTH CAROLINA ...	100 956	29.8	30.1	7.9	17.2	5.0	69.9	11.5	31.4	20.6	5.9	0.5	4.5	-6.0
NORTH DAKOTA	31 308	22.6	41.4	10.7	24.1	6.6	58.6	12.4	28.0	13.8	4.3	0.2	15.8	-7.9
OHIO	26 999	33.4	25.3	6.9	13.5	4.8	74.7	11.7	34.7	23.5	4.3	0.5	-0.3	-7.6
OKLAHOMA	266 801	26.7	35.7	9.2	20.5	6.0	64.3	11.7	28.0	17.7	6.3	0.6	10.1	-5.5
OREGON	43 434	29.2	30.3	7.3	17.2	5.8	69.7	12.5	32.3	20.1	4.5	0.3	4.7	-7.6
PENNSYLVANIA	19 511	32.7	27.3	6.5	15.8	5.0	72.7	11.4	33.0	21.2	6.2	0.9	1.7	-5.2
RHODE ISLAND	5 124	26.3	38.2	10.0	21.3	6.9	61.8	10.2	29.2	15.1	6.6	0.7	12.6	-5.1
SOUTH CAROLINA ...	14 688	31.2	25.8	6.2	14.8	4.7	74.2	10.8	35.4	22.7	5.0	0.4	0.2	-7.0
SOUTH DAKOTA	61 724	20.8	44.6	11.8	25.8	7.0	55.4	11.9	26.3	12.9	3.9	0.3	19.0	-8.2
TENNESSEE	15 541	34.8	24.2	5.5	13.2	5.5	75.8	10.4	36.3	23.9	4.9	0.3	-1.4	-7.2
TEXAS	113 755	29.9	28.6	7.2	16.4	5.0	71.4	11.6	34.4	20.1	4.9	0.4	3.0	-7.1
UTAH	28 646	23.2	37.0	9.5	21.1	6.5	63.0	14.6	32.3	12.5	3.1	0.4	11.4	-8.9
VERMONT	2 602	34.5	26.5	4.5	14.7	7.3	73.5	8.8	34.2	27.6	2.6	0.3	0.9	-9.5
VIRGINIA	22 394	33.5	22.7	5.7	12.9	4.1	77.3	11.7	36.1	23.7	5.3	0.4	-2.9	-6.6
WASHINGTON	91 299	28.6	33.2	8.3	18.9	6.0	66.8	10.9	32.9	18.2	4.4	0.3	7.6	-7.6
WEST VIRGINIA	3 770	37.5	21.8	4.5	12.7	4.6	78.2	11.2	29.4	30.6	6.7	0.3	-3.8	-5.4
WISCONSIN	49 661	27.3	36.3	9.1	20.6	6.5	63.7	10.9	31.9	16.2	4.3	0.4	10.7	-7.7
WYOMING	11 363	26.0	36.7	9.3	21.7	5.6	63.3	11.3	29.5	17.6	4.6	0.3	11.1	-7.6

| STATE | Number | Asian median age | Native Hawaiian and Other Pacific Islander median age | Asian, Hawaiian, and Pacific Islander children under 18 years (percent) | | | | Asian, Hawaiian, and Pacific Islander adults 18 years and over (percent) | | | | | | +/- U.S. percent under 18 years | +/- U.S. percent 65 years and over |
| | | | | Under 18 years | Under 5 years | 5 to 14 years | 15 to 17 years | 18 years and over | 18 to 24 years | 25 to 44 years | 45 to 64 years | 65 to 84 years | 85 years and over | | |
	85	86	87	88	89	90	91	92	93	94	95	96	97	98	99
UNITED STATES ...	10 550 602	32.7	27.5	24.2	6.5	13.6	4.2	75.8	10.9	36.5	20.8	7.0	0.6	-1.4	-4.8
ALABAMA	31 095	30.9	28.4	23.8	7.3	12.5	4.0	76.2	13.1	39.5	19.3	4.2	0.2	-1.8	-8.0
ALASKA	28 618	34.5	22.4	28.1	7.2	16.0	5.0	71.9	9.3	34.4	22.6	5.4	0.2	2.5	-6.9
ARIZONA	97 389	31.9	26.2	23.3	6.9	12.7	3.8	76.7	11.7	39.8	19.3	5.6	0.4	-2.3	-6.5
ARKANSAS	20 615	30.4	23.4	25.1	7.6	12.7	4.8	74.9	13.5	37.6	19.3	4.3	0.2	-0.5	-7.9
CALIFORNIA	3 796 833	34.2	28.2	23.9	5.9	13.7	4.3	76.1	10.3	34.7	21.7	8.6	0.7	-1.7	-3.1
COLORADO	97 604	30.9	28.0	24.5	7.2	13.1	4.2	75.5	11.2	40.1	17.6	6.3	0.2	-1.1	-5.8
CONNECTICUT	83 634	30.7	27.9	26.0	7.9	14.2	3.9	74.0	11.0	40.5	18.4	3.8	0.2	0.4	-8.4
DELAWARE	16 388	32.2	27.2	22.6	7.4	12.3	2.9	77.4	9.8	41.6	21.3	4.4	0.2	-3.0	-7.8
DISTRICT OF COLUMBIA	15 145	30.1	24.6	11.5	4.8	5.3	1.4	88.5	22.3	41.5	18.6	5.2	0.9	-14.1	-6.4
FLORIDA	271 189	33.4	28.9	22.9	6.1	12.5	4.3	77.1	10.2	38.1	22.8	5.7	0.3	-2.7	-6.4
GEORGIA	175 329	30.8	26.3	25.2	6.9	13.9	4.3	74.8	11.4	40.7	18.9	3.7	0.1	-0.4	-8.6
HAWAII	616 511	42.7	28.8	20.4	4.8	11.9	3.8	79.6	8.1	29.2	24.5	15.8	2.0	-5.2	5.4
IDAHO	12 553	31.9	24.2	23.3	6.1	12.4	4.8	76.7	11.3	39.6	18.2	7.4	0.3	-2.3	-4.7
ILLINOIS	427 251	31.7	27.9	23.3	6.7	12.7	3.9	76.7	11.4	37.8	21.4	5.7	0.4	-2.3	-6.3
INDIANA	58 955	29.8	26.7	22.7	7.3	11.8	3.7	77.3	15.4	39.8	18.2	3.7	0.2	-2.9	-8.5
IOWA	35 978	27.6	25.4	27.4	7.9	14.7	4.8	72.6	15.4	38.0	16.0	3.1	0.2	1.8	-9.2
KANSAS	45 980	29.1	26.7	25.3	7.6	13.1	4.5	74.7	14.0	38.2	18.5	3.8	0.3	-0.3	-8.4
KENTUCKY	30 149	30.5	26.7	23.9	7.6	13.1	3.3	76.1	12.0	42.2	18.4	3.2	0.2	-1.7	-8.9
LOUISIANA	56 871	30.0	28.2	27.3	7.3	15.0	5.0	72.7	12.6	35.5	19.7	4.5	0.3	1.7	-7.5
MAINE	8 560	28.8	31.6	31.3	8.6	16.5	6.3	68.7	13.7	31.9	18.0	4.9	0.2	5.7	-7.3
MARYLAND	211 743	33.7	30.7	23.6	6.5	13.1	4.0	76.4	10.2	37.3	22.5	6.2	0.3	-2.0	-5.9
MASSACHUSETTS ...	240 081	29.3	27.8	24.6	7.2	13.6	3.8	75.4	14.5	39.1	16.6	4.8	0.4	-1.0	-7.2
MICHIGAN	177 493	29.4	26.7	26.9	8.1	14.6	4.3	73.1	12.0	39.7	17.5	3.6	0.2	1.3	-8.5
MINNESOTA	140 969	24.5	28.9	37.6	9.6	21.7	6.3	62.4	12.7	33.8	12.4	3.2	0.2	12.0	-9.0
MISSISSIPPI	18 386	30.4	30.0	25.2	6.6	14.1	4.5	74.8	13.5	37.3	18.9	4.6	0.4	-0.4	-7.4
MISSOURI	63 500	30.3	25.9	23.2	7.5	11.8	3.9	76.8	12.5	40.6	19.0	4.5	0.2	-2.4	-7.7
MONTANA	4 810	29.1	29.9	28.1	6.2	17.8	4.2	71.9	13.4	33.2	18.2	6.8	0.3	2.5	-5.4
NEBRASKA	21 799	28.2	20.4	26.3	7.6	13.7	5.0	73.7	14.4	36.8	18.7	3.7	0.1	0.7	-8.6
NEVADA	96 927	35.9	28.6	21.2	5.5	11.9	3.7	78.8	9.9	36.3	24.7	7.6	0.3	-4.4	-4.5
NEW HAMPSHIRE	15 679	30.2	32.5	26.6	8.0	14.5	4.1	73.4	12.0	40.3	16.4	4.4	0.3	1.0	-7.7
NEW JERSEY	484 503	32.7	28.1	25.9	7.6	14.5	3.8	74.1	8.7	39.6	20.7	4.8	0.3	0.3	-7.3
NEW MEXICO	19 534	33.0	29.3	24.2	8.0	12.4	3.8	75.8	10.1	37.7	21.3	6.2	0.4	-1.4	-5.7
NEW YORK	1 052 326	33.0	28.6	22.6	6.2	12.7	3.8	77.4	11.0	38.1	21.4	6.3	0.5	-3.0	-5.6
NORTH CAROLINA ...	114 991	29.5	26.1	27.0	7.9	14.8	4.3	73.0	12.4	39.7	17.2	3.5	0.2	1.4	-8.7
NORTH DAKOTA	3 529	29.8	22.0	26.8	5.6	15.2	6.0	73.2	13.0	39.4	17.3	3.2	0.3	1.2	-8.9
OHIO	134 772	30.7	27.8	23.5	7.4	12.5	3.6	76.5	11.8	40.8	18.9	4.7	0.3	-2.1	-7.4
OKLAHOMA	47 386	29.6	26.2	23.1	6.4	12.3	4.4	76.9	15.6	37.8	19.0	4.2	0.3	-2.5	-7.9
OREGON	106 719	31.1	25.6	24.9	7.1	13.8	4.0	75.1	12.1	37.8	18.7	6.0	0.5	-0.7	-5.9
PENNSYLVANIA	220 352	30.0	29.0	25.3	7.3	13.6	4.5	74.7	13.7	37.0	19.3	4.5	0.2	-0.3	-7.7
RHODE ISLAND	24 266	26.6	26.3	27.9	7.0	15.5	5.4	72.1	18.3	34.6	15.0	4.1	0.2	2.3	-8.1
SOUTH CAROLINA ...	37 889	31.5	27.8	23.8	6.7	12.9	4.2	76.2	12.6	37.5	21.3	4.6	0.3	-1.8	-7.6
SOUTH DAKOTA	4 972	27.9	25.8	30.2	10.3	16.0	3.9	69.8	14.3	37.0	14.4	4.0	0.0	4.6	-8.4
TENNESSEE	56 291	30.5	26.0	24.7	7.5	13.1	4.0	75.3	12.3	41.0	18.3	3.5	0.2	-0.9	-8.7
TEXAS	568 392	31.3	26.7	25.3	7.3	13.7	4.3	74.7	10.9	39.3	20.0	4.3	0.2	-0.3	-7.9
UTAH	51 244	29.6	21.4	29.4	8.9	15.5	5.0	70.6	15.5	34.7	15.3	4.7	0.5	3.8	-7.3
VERMONT	5 005	27.1	29.2	31.9	10.6	16.1	5.2	68.1	17.6	33.3	14.2	2.7	0.3	6.3	-9.4
VIRGINIA	259 972	32.3	28.1	23.3	6.5	12.8	3.9	76.7	10.8	39.1	21.5	5.0	0.3	-2.3	-7.1
WASHINGTON	342 717	32.8	26.0	24.3	6.3	13.7	4.4	75.7	11.2	36.5	20.4	7.0	0.6	-1.3	-4.8
WEST VIRGINIA	9 850	31.1	29.3	22.9	6.6	12.4	3.9	77.1	14.9	35.4	20.9	5.3	0.6	-2.7	-6.5
WISCONSIN	84 654	22.9	25.4	38.7	9.7	22.6	6.3	61.3	13.7	31.7	12.2	3.5	0.2	13.1	-8.7
WYOMING	3 204	32.6	26.4	23.2	6.0	12.8	4.4	76.8	12.5	37.7	18.7	7.8	0.2	-2.4	-4.4

Table A-2. States — Age, Ethnicity, and Household Structure

			Hispanic or Latino[1] population											
			Hispanic or Latino children under 18 years (percent)				Hispanic or Latino adults 18 years and over (percent)							
STATE	Number	Hispanic or Latino median age	Under 18 years	Under 5 years	5 to 14 years	15 to 17 years	18 years and over	18 to 24 years	25 to 44 years	45 to 64 years	65 to 84 years	85 years and over	+/− U.S. percent under 18 years	+/− U.S. percent 65 years and over
	100	101	102	103	104	105	106	107	108	109	110	111	112	113
UNITED STATES ...	35 238 481	25.8	34.8	10.4	19.4	5.0	65.2	13.3	33.4	13.7	4.4	0.4	9.2	−7.6
ALABAMA	72 627	24.9	33.4	11.3	17.3	4.8	66.6	16.4	35.7	11.2	3.0	0.3	7.8	−9.1
ALASKA	25 765	23.8	39.5	12.8	21.1	5.7	60.5	12.9	33.0	12.5	2.0	0.1	13.9	−10.3
ARIZONA	1 295 617	24.1	38.0	11.6	21.1	5.2	62.0	13.7	31.8	12.3	3.9	0.3	12.4	−8.2
ARKANSAS	85 576	23.6	36.8	12.8	18.7	5.3	63.2	16.4	34.3	9.9	2.3	0.2	11.2	−9.9
CALIFORNIA	10 969 132	25.0	36.8	10.7	21.0	5.1	63.2	13.0	33.3	12.6	3.9	0.3	11.2	−8.2
COLORADO	735 099	25.5	34.9	10.8	19.0	5.1	65.1	13.8	32.8	13.8	4.3	0.4	9.3	−7.7
CONNECTICUT	318 947	25.4	35.8	10.2	20.5	5.1	64.2	13.1	34.0	13.7	3.2	0.3	10.2	−9.0
DELAWARE	37 321	24.1	36.1	11.7	19.5	5.0	63.9	14.8	35.5	10.7	2.6	0.2	10.5	−9.6
DISTRICT OF COLUMBIA	45 015	28.3	24.8	8.8	12.5	3.5	75.2	16.5	40.2	14.4	3.6	0.4	−0.8	−8.4
FLORIDA	2 680 314	32.6	25.9	7.1	14.6	4.2	74.1	10.8	34.1	18.8	9.3	1.0	0.3	−2.0
GEORGIA	429 976	24.6	31.0	11.3	15.4	4.4	69.0	19.4	38.8	8.7	1.8	0.2	5.4	−10.4
HAWAII	87 582	23.0	39.3	12.2	21.5	5.7	60.7	13.9	29.6	12.7	4.0	0.4	13.7	−8.0
IDAHO	101 594	21.8	41.8	12.9	22.7	6.2	58.2	14.4	31.1	10.5	2.0	0.2	16.2	−10.2
ILLINOIS	1 529 141	24.6	36.0	11.4	19.5	5.0	64.0	14.7	34.2	12.0	2.9	0.2	10.4	−9.3
INDIANA	210 538	24.1	35.3	12.2	18.2	4.9	64.7	16.6	33.2	11.4	3.2	0.3	9.7	−8.9
IOWA	81 501	22.6	38.9	13.9	20.2	4.7	61.1	14.8	33.0	9.9	2.6	0.2	13.3	−9.6
KANSAS	186 299	23.0	39.0	13.1	20.5	5.4	61.0	14.8	32.6	10.6	2.7	0.3	13.4	−9.4
KENTUCKY	56 414	25.1	31.6	11.8	15.5	4.4	68.4	18.5	35.3	11.0	3.2	0.3	6.0	−8.9
LOUISIANA	107 854	29.8	28.1	8.3	15.4	4.4	71.9	13.1	32.8	18.3	7.0	0.7	2.5	−4.7
MAINE	9 226	23.8	37.3	10.7	20.0	6.6	62.7	13.9	31.4	13.2	3.8	0.4	11.7	−8.2
MARYLAND	227 105	27.2	31.3	10.1	16.8	4.4	68.7	13.9	37.8	13.5	3.2	0.3	5.7	−8.9
MASSACHUSETTS ...	427 340	24.5	36.3	10.1	21.0	5.2	63.7	14.3	33.9	12.5	2.7	0.3	10.7	−9.4
MICHIGAN	322 160	23.8	37.6	11.9	20.3	5.5	62.4	13.9	32.0	12.4	3.8	0.2	12.0	−8.4
MINNESOTA	141 786	23.0	38.7	13.2	20.4	5.2	61.3	15.9	34.3	9.2	1.8	0.2	13.1	−10.5
MISSISSIPPI	37 790	26.2	30.6	9.3	16.4	4.9	69.4	17.1	33.4	14.6	3.9	0.5	5.0	−8.0
MISSOURI	116 373	24.5	36.2	11.8	19.3	5.1	63.8	14.6	32.8	12.4	3.6	0.4	10.6	−8.4
MONTANA	18 490	22.7	41.6	11.9	23.1	6.7	58.4	11.8	29.1	13.3	3.9	0.3	16.0	−8.2
NEBRASKA	93 872	23.1	39.2	13.5	20.2	5.5	60.8	14.7	33.6	9.6	2.7	0.2	13.6	−9.5
NEVADA	393 539	24.7	37.0	12.1	20.4	4.5	63.0	13.4	35.1	11.5	2.8	0.2	11.4	−9.4
NEW HAMPSHIRE	19 910	24.2	36.4	11.4	20.2	4.8	63.6	13.8	32.5	13.9	3.1	0.3	10.8	−9.0
NEW JERSEY	1 116 149	28.7	30.1	8.7	16.9	4.5	69.9	12.7	35.9	16.3	4.7	0.4	4.5	−7.4
NEW MEXICO	765 610	28.4	33.8	9.1	19.1	5.5	66.2	11.3	29.5	17.6	7.2	0.8	8.2	−4.5
NEW YORK	2 865 016	28.6	30.9	8.7	17.6	4.6	69.1	12.3	33.9	17.1	5.3	0.5	5.3	−6.6
NORTH CAROLINA ...	372 964	24.0	31.4	12.0	15.3	4.1	68.6	21.7	37.8	7.6	1.4	0.1	5.8	−10.9
NORTH DAKOTA	7 568	21.5	39.7	11.7	21.9	6.2	60.3	16.6	29.6	10.1	3.7	0.3	14.1	−8.4
OHIO	213 889	24.5	36.6	11.5	19.7	5.4	63.4	13.7	31.9	13.3	4.2	0.2	11.0	−7.9
OKLAHOMA	177 768	22.7	39.0	12.8	20.2	6.0	61.0	16.0	31.7	10.6	2.6	0.2	13.4	−9.6
OREGON	273 938	22.8	39.0	13.4	20.7	4.8	61.0	15.4	33.9	9.7	1.9	0.1	13.4	−10.4
PENNSYLVANIA	392 121	24.2	37.6	10.9	21.2	5.5	62.4	13.7	31.7	13.2	3.5	0.3	12.0	−8.6
RHODE ISLAND	90 452	23.6	38.6	11.2	21.6	5.8	61.4	14.1	31.9	12.1	3.0	0.3	13.0	−9.2
SOUTH CAROLINA ...	92 828	24.9	29.7	10.6	15.0	4.1	70.3	21.3	36.6	9.7	2.6	0.2	4.1	−9.7
SOUTH DAKOTA	10 386	22.2	41.4	12.9	22.4	6.1	58.6	13.9	31.5	9.3	3.2	0.7	15.8	−8.5
TENNESSEE	119 425	24.8	31.2	11.4	15.3	4.5	68.8	18.9	37.5	9.9	2.3	0.3	5.6	−9.8
TEXAS	6 670 122	25.5	35.7	10.6	19.7	5.4	64.3	13.1	32.1	13.9	4.7	0.4	10.1	−7.3
UTAH	200 005	23.0	38.3	13.2	19.8	5.3	61.7	15.9	32.9	10.3	2.5	0.2	12.7	−9.7
VERMONT	5 316	24.5	32.1	8.1	17.7	6.2	67.9	19.6	25.5	17.4	4.8	0.7	6.5	−6.9
VIRGINIA	327 273	26.2	31.0	10.2	16.3	4.5	69.0	15.5	38.9	12.0	2.4	0.2	5.4	−9.8
WASHINGTON	439 841	22.7	39.7	13.2	21.2	5.3	60.3	14.6	33.0	10.3	2.1	0.2	14.1	−10.1
WEST VIRGINIA	11 774	28.1	31.2	8.6	18.3	4.4	68.8	14.4	30.7	16.8	6.1	0.6	5.6	−5.6
WISCONSIN	191 049	22.8	38.7	12.7	20.5	5.6	61.3	15.8	32.5	10.2	2.6	0.2	13.1	−9.6
WYOMING	31 384	24.8	35.1	11.3	18.5	5.2	64.9	14.1	28.9	16.2	5.1	0.5	9.5	−6.8

[1] Hispanic or Latino persons may be of any race.

STATE	Number	Some other race median age	Some other race children under 18 years (percent)				Some other race adults 18 years and over (percent)						+/− U.S. percent under 18 years	+/− U.S. percent 65 years and over
			Under 18 years	Under 5 years	5 to 14 years	15 to 17 years	18 years and over	18 to 24 years	25 to 44 years	45 to 64 years	65 to 84 years	85 years and over		
	114	115	116	117	118	119	120	121	122	123	124	125	126	127
UNITED STATES ...	15 436 924	24.6	35.8	10.6	19.9	5.3	64.2	14.9	34.6	11.8	2.7	0.2	10.2	−9.6
ALABAMA	29 155	23.5	35.4	13.2	17.2	4.9	64.6	19.1	37.7	6.7	1.1	0.1	9.8	−11.4
ALASKA	9 869	27.0	31.9	9.3	17.5	5.1	68.1	12.8	39.9	13.6	1.8	0.0	6.3	−10.7
ARIZONA	597 173	23.7	37.7	11.5	20.9	5.3	62.3	15.1	33.6	10.9	2.5	0.2	12.1	−9.8
ARKANSAS	41 164	22.9	37.2	12.8	18.7	5.7	62.8	18.1	35.0	8.3	1.2	0.1	11.6	−11.1
CALIFORNIA	5 725 844	24.4	37.0	10.6	21.0	5.4	63.0	14.3	34.3	11.5	2.7	0.2	11.4	−9.6
COLORADO	310 552	24.7	35.1	10.6	19.2	5.2	64.9	15.2	34.8	12.0	2.6	0.2	9.5	−9.6
CONNECTICUT	148 809	24.4	36.6	10.0	21.0	5.6	63.4	14.1	35.0	11.8	2.3	0.2	11.0	−10.0
DELAWARE	16 241	23.8	36.2	11.4	19.8	5.0	63.8	15.7	38.3	8.0	1.7	0.0	10.6	−10.8
DISTRICT OF COLUMBIA	21 728	26.3	26.9	10.0	13.0	3.9	73.1	10.1	38.7	12.4	2.7	0.2	1.3	−9.5
FLORIDA	472 333	25.6	32.4	9.2	17.7	5.5	67.6	15.5	35.9	12.9	3.0	0.3	6.8	−9.2
GEORGIA	193 934	23.9	31.6	11.6	15.5	4.6	68.4	21.5	38.7	7.2	0.9	0.1	6.0	−11.5
HAWAII	14 821	27.6	24.0	7.4	13.1	3.5	76.0	17.6	38.2	15.2	4.5	0.6	−1.6	−7.4
IDAHO	55 070	22.1	40.0	12.1	21.7	6.2	60.0	15.2	32.5	10.2	2.0	0.1	14.4	−10.4
ILLINOIS	724 021	24.3	35.8	10.9	19.4	5.4	64.2	15.8	34.7	11.5	2.2	0.1	10.2	−10.2
INDIANA	98 092	23.5	34.9	12.2	18.2	4.5	65.1	18.3	35.2	9.3	2.0	0.2	9.3	−10.3
IOWA	37 964	22.8	37.8	13.7	19.4	4.7	62.2	16.8	35.2	8.7	1.5	0.1	12.2	−10.9
KANSAS	91 189	23.2	37.8	12.0	20.3	5.4	62.2	15.9	34.2	9.8	2.0	0.2	12.2	−10.2
KENTUCKY	22 116	22.9	34.8	13.0	17.3	4.6	65.2	20.2	37.0	6.6	1.1	0.1	9.2	−11.2
LOUISIANA	31 803	26.4	29.7	9.3	16.0	4.4	70.3	15.4	35.7	14.6	4.3	0.3	4.1	−8.0
MAINE	2 637	22.0	36.5	10.4	17.5	8.6	63.5	14.4	36.1	11.9	1.1	0.1	10.9	−11.3
MARYLAND	96 773	25.7	32.2	10.2	17.4	4.5	67.8	15.3	38.9	11.7	1.8	0.2	6.6	−10.5
MASSACHUSETTS ...	236 883	23.9	36.3	9.7	21.2	5.4	63.7	15.4	33.5	11.6	2.9	0.3	10.7	−9.3
MICHIGAN	131 003	23.9	35.7	10.9	19.4	5.4	64.3	15.4	34.4	11.7	2.6	0.2	10.1	−9.7
MINNESOTA	65 184	23.2	36.5	12.6	19.0	4.9	63.5	17.6	36.4	8.2	1.2	0.2	10.9	−11.2
MISSISSIPPI	13 696	24.4	29.0	10.1	14.4	4.4	71.0	22.2	37.8	10.1	0.9	0.0	3.4	−11.6
MISSOURI	45 524	23.5	35.6	11.7	18.7	5.3	64.4	16.7	35.4	9.7	2.3	0.2	10.0	−10.0
MONTANA	5 098	25.7	33.2	8.7	17.9	6.6	66.8	13.3	32.8	17.3	3.0	0.4	7.6	−9.1
NEBRASKA	47 789	23.4	36.9	12.8	18.6	5.6	63.1	16.2	35.8	9.0	2.0	0.1	11.3	−10.4
NEVADA	158 101	24.2	36.6	11.4	20.4	4.8	63.4	14.8	36.2	10.4	1.8	0.1	11.0	−10.6
NEW HAMPSHIRE	7 441	23.5	35.8	10.9	20.4	4.4	64.2	15.9	34.8	11.5	1.9	0.1	10.2	−10.5
NEW JERSEY	456 829	27.0	31.2	8.7	17.4	5.0	68.8	14.3	37.0	14.4	2.9	0.2	5.6	−9.4
NEW MEXICO	308 063	26.5	34.6	9.8	19.0	5.8	65.4	12.6	32.1	15.7	4.5	0.5	9.0	−7.6
NEW YORK	1 352 395	27.2	32.0	8.9	18.2	4.9	68.0	13.6	34.8	15.4	3.8	0.3	6.4	−8.4
NORTH CAROLINA ...	185 138	23.6	31.8	12.1	15.6	4.1	68.2	22.6	38.4	6.4	0.8	0.0	6.2	−11.7
NORTH DAKOTA	2 360	22.2	34.7	8.8	19.6	6.4	65.3	19.2	34.1	8.6	2.6	0.8	9.1	−9.1
OHIO	89 149	23.3	37.2	11.8	19.8	5.5	62.8	14.8	34.0	11.2	2.7	0.2	11.6	−9.6
OKLAHOMA	84 830	23.3	36.9	11.5	19.4	6.0	63.1	17.4	34.2	9.6	1.8	0.2	11.3	−10.5
OREGON	146 837	23.1	36.8	12.7	19.3	4.8	63.2	16.8	36.0	8.9	1.3	0.1	11.2	−11.1
PENNSYLVANIA	188 186	23.2	38.6	11.0	21.9	5.7	61.4	14.6	32.3	11.8	2.6	0.1	13.0	−9.8
RHODE ISLAND	53 339	23.7	37.6	10.3	21.6	5.7	62.4	15.0	32.2	11.7	3.3	0.2	12.0	−9.0
SOUTH CAROLINA ...	38 962	23.0	30.1	11.1	14.8	4.2	69.9	23.9	37.3	7.5	1.1	0.1	4.5	−11.3
SOUTH DAKOTA	3 442	24.9	34.0	11.6	20.0	2.4	66.0	14.9	39.5	9.1	1.9	0.6	8.4	−10.0
TENNESSEE	55 625	23.9	31.1	11.7	14.8	4.5	68.9	21.6	39.0	7.3	0.9	0.1	5.5	−11.5
TEXAS	2 455 972	24.4	36.6	10.9	20.1	5.5	63.4	14.6	33.8	11.7	3.0	0.2	11.0	−9.3
UTAH	94 089	23.5	36.5	12.2	19.2	5.1	63.5	16.4	35.2	10.0	1.7	0.2	10.9	−10.6
VERMONT	1 274	21.9	34.9	7.9	21.7	5.2	65.1	23.5	28.4	10.6	2.7	0.0	9.3	−9.8
VIRGINIA	138 381	25.1	31.2	10.2	16.5	4.5	68.8	17.1	40.8	9.6	1.2	0.1	5.6	−11.2
WASHINGTON	229 131	22.9	39.2	12.4	21.3	5.5	60.8	15.4	33.9	9.8	1.6	0.2	13.6	−10.8
WEST VIRGINIA	3 139	20.3	39.4	10.3	23.5	5.6	60.6	21.5	25.9	10.6	2.6	0.0	13.8	−9.9
WISCONSIN	84 281	23.0	36.7	11.9	19.4	5.5	63.3	17.6	34.2	9.4	1.9	0.2	11.1	−10.5
WYOMING	12 595	25.5	32.1	10.3	15.8	6.0	67.9	15.8	32.8	15.8	3.2	0.4	6.5	−8.9

| STATE | Number | Two or more races median age | Two or more races children under 18 years (percent) | | | | Two or more races adults 18 years and over (percent) | | | | | | +/− U.S. percent under 18 years | +/− U.S. percent 65 years and over |
| | | | Under 18 years | Under 5 years | 5 to 14 years | 15 to 17 years | 18 years and over | 18 to 24 years | 25 to 44 years | 45 to 64 years | 65 to 84 years | 85 years and over | | |
	128	129	130	131	132	133	134	135	136	137	138	139	140	141
UNITED STATES ...	7 270 926	22.7	40.7	13.3	21.9	5.4	59.3	11.8	28.3	14.2	4.6	0.5	15.1	-7.5
ALABAMA	49 238	25.3	36.9	13.2	18.6	5.1	63.1	11.2	27.2	18.3	6.0	0.3	11.3	-6.1
ALASKA	35 240	16.6	52.3	15.8	29.7	6.9	47.7	9.7	24.4	11.2	2.2	0.1	26.7	-10.2
ARIZONA	156 497	20.0	45.7	15.5	24.6	5.6	54.3	12.1	26.3	11.5	3.9	0.4	20.1	-8.1
ARKANSAS	38 082	25.2	38.1	12.6	19.9	5.6	61.9	9.8	25.5	18.7	7.1	0.9	12.5	-4.6
CALIFORNIA	1 694 607	22.9	40.5	12.3	22.7	5.4	59.5	11.7	29.1	13.8	4.5	0.4	14.9	-7.6
COLORADO	132 146	20.5	43.6	14.3	23.5	5.8	56.4	12.7	27.8	12.2	3.4	0.3	18.0	-8.8
CONNECTICUT	80 007	23.3	39.1	13.4	20.8	4.9	60.9	12.0	28.8	14.8	4.8	0.5	13.5	-7.2
DELAWARE	14 353	18.8	47.5	18.2	23.0	6.3	52.5	13.0	24.8	11.6	2.8	0.2	21.9	-9.5
DISTRICT OF COLUMBIA	14 661	30.2	22.3	8.1	11.6	2.6	77.7	14.5	40.1	16.0	6.0	1.1	-3.3	-5.4
FLORIDA	409 021	27.5	33.7	10.7	18.2	4.9	66.3	11.4	31.3	17.1	5.9	0.6	8.1	-6.0
GEORGIA	124 217	23.0	39.4	14.4	20.3	4.7	60.6	12.7	30.4	13.3	3.7	0.3	13.8	-8.4
HAWAII	263 587	22.4	41.9	11.8	23.7	6.4	58.1	11.6	27.1	14.3	4.6	0.4	16.3	-7.5
IDAHO	26 990	19.4	44.7	14.6	23.9	6.2	55.3	11.8	25.2	13.3	4.5	0.5	19.1	-7.5
ILLINOIS	249 431	22.5	41.2	14.8	21.4	5.1	58.8	11.7	28.7	13.4	4.6	0.4	15.6	-7.5
INDIANA	84 487	18.6	46.5	17.5	23.8	5.2	53.5	12.0	23.8	13.0	4.3	0.5	20.9	-7.7
IOWA	33 624	16.2	51.8	19.2	26.6	5.9	48.2	12.5	21.4	10.5	3.3	0.5	26.2	-8.7
KANSAS	63 823	18.2	48.3	16.7	26.1	5.6	51.7	11.6	23.8	12.0	3.8	0.4	22.7	-8.3
KENTUCKY	47 341	20.5	43.8	17.3	21.8	4.7	56.2	11.4	23.9	14.9	5.4	0.6	18.2	-6.6
LOUISIANA	53 939	25.3	36.5	12.0	19.5	5.0	63.5	11.5	26.8	17.6	6.7	0.8	10.9	-5.0
MAINE	13 736	21.6	39.9	11.3	22.9	5.7	60.1	10.4	27.4	16.4	5.2	0.7	14.3	-6.6
MARYLAND	113 055	22.4	42.2	14.7	22.2	5.3	57.8	11.3	28.5	13.9	3.8	0.3	16.6	-8.4
MASSACHUSETTS ...	154 532	24.4	36.4	11.6	19.8	5.0	63.6	13.1	31.2	14.0	4.7	0.5	10.8	-7.2
MICHIGAN	207 041	19.9	44.6	15.4	23.8	5.3	55.4	11.4	25.9	13.6	4.1	0.4	19.0	-8.0
MINNESOTA	88 777	16.6	51.1	17.8	27.2	6.1	48.9	12.2	24.6	9.1	2.5	0.4	25.5	-9.6
MISSISSIPPI	21 950	23.7	38.8	14.0	19.5	5.3	61.2	13.3	23.2	16.7	6.8	1.3	13.2	-4.5
MISSOURI	90 948	21.4	41.9	14.6	22.0	5.4	58.1	11.5	26.1	14.7	5.2	0.6	16.3	-6.7
MONTANA	17 106	20.4	44.0	12.5	24.4	7.1	56.0	11.7	25.1	14.3	4.5	0.5	18.4	-7.5
NEBRASKA	25 032	16.6	51.1	18.5	26.0	6.6	48.9	12.9	23.2	9.4	3.1	0.3	25.5	-9.1
NEVADA	81 171	22.2	42.2	14.3	22.9	4.9	57.8	11.1	28.3	14.0	4.2	0.2	16.6	-8.1
NEW HAMPSHIRE	14 574	22.0	38.4	12.5	19.5	6.4	61.6	12.4	28.5	15.2	5.0	0.6	12.8	-6.9
NEW JERSEY	228 326	27.0	35.7	11.3	19.5	4.9	64.3	10.7	32.7	15.8	4.6	0.5	10.1	-7.4
NEW MEXICO	70 080	22.4	42.3	13.1	23.0	6.3	57.7	10.5	25.1	15.3	6.1	0.6	16.7	-5.8
NEW YORK	615 062	28.1	33.2	10.6	18.0	4.6	66.8	11.4	32.2	17.1	5.5	0.6	7.6	-6.4
NORTH CAROLINA ...	111 909	21.0	42.7	16.5	21.8	4.4	57.3	13.2	28.1	12.4	3.2	0.4	17.1	-8.9
NORTH DAKOTA	7 545	17.2	48.0	15.4	26.3	6.4	52.0	12.5	23.8	11.4	3.9	0.4	22.4	-8.3
OHIO	173 338	18.8	46.2	16.5	24.2	5.5	53.8	11.1	24.5	13.2	4.4	0.5	20.6	-7.5
OKLAHOMA	168 426	23.5	39.7	12.3	21.4	6.0	60.3	11.4	24.8	16.7	6.6	0.8	14.1	-5.1
OREGON	113 867	20.8	42.9	13.5	23.5	6.0	57.1	12.3	25.7	14.5	4.2	0.4	17.3	-7.9
PENNSYLVANIA	155 159	19.9	44.1	15.0	23.6	5.5	55.9	12.5	24.5	13.5	4.8	0.6	18.5	-7.1
RHODE ISLAND	29 588	22.9	39.3	12.7	20.7	5.9	60.7	12.8	26.7	15.0	5.6	0.7	13.7	-6.2
SOUTH CAROLINA ...	42 068	21.3	42.0	15.2	21.6	5.2	58.0	13.7	26.3	13.1	4.3	0.5	16.4	-7.7
SOUTH DAKOTA	10 711	16.2	51.1	16.9	26.6	7.6	48.9	11.5	22.8	10.2	3.9	0.6	25.5	-8.3
TENNESSEE	69 508	22.5	40.7	14.9	21.0	4.9	59.3	11.0	26.4	15.6	5.5	0.7	15.1	-6.3
TEXAS	530 162	23.5	39.9	13.6	20.9	5.4	60.1	11.8	29.0	14.4	4.4	0.5	14.3	-7.6
UTAH	51 480	16.9	50.8	19.9	24.8	6.2	49.2	13.9	23.2	9.5	2.4	0.3	25.2	-9.9
VERMONT	8 129	24.2	38.5	10.5	22.1	6.0	61.5	12.0	26.7	17.2	4.9	0.6	12.9	-7.0
VIRGINIA	156 831	21.6	42.0	14.8	21.8	5.4	58.0	12.8	28.9	12.8	3.1	0.3	16.4	-9.0
WASHINGTON	230 850	18.9	46.2	14.7	25.2	6.3	53.8	12.4	26.0	12.0	3.1	0.3	20.6	-9.1
WEST VIRGINIA	18 104	23.0	39.5	13.9	20.1	5.4	60.5	11.6	21.8	18.6	7.7	0.9	13.9	-3.9
WISCONSIN	71 171	17.1	50.9	17.0	27.0	6.9	49.1	12.2	22.7	10.5	3.4	0.3	25.3	-8.8
WYOMING	9 399	20.6	42.2	14.6	21.3	6.2	57.8	12.0	25.2	15.5	4.6	0.5	16.6	-7.4

STATE	Number	Average household size	Total family households	Married-couple family households		Female family householder		Male family householder		Total nonfamily households	Two or more adults	Female living alone	Male living alone
				Total	With own children under 18 years	Total	With own children under 18 years	Total	With own children under 18 years				
	142	143	144	145	146	147	148	149	150	151	152	153	154
UNITED STATES ...	105 539 122	2.59	68.5	52.5	24.3	11.8	7.0	4.1	2.1	31.5	5.8	14.8	11.0
ALABAMA	1 737 385	2.49	70.4	53.0	23.2	13.9	8.0	3.5	1.7	29.6	3.5	15.3	10.8
ALASKA	221 804	2.74	69.3	53.3	29.3	10.6	7.6	5.3	3.6	30.7	7.3	10.0	13.4
ARIZONA	1 901 625	2.64	68.2	52.9	23.5	10.6	6.5	4.7	2.6	31.8	7.0	13.7	11.1
ARKANSAS..............	1 042 807	2.49	70.6	55.1	23.4	11.8	7.1	3.7	2.0	29.4	3.9	14.9	10.6
CALIFORNIA.............	11 512 020	2.87	69.4	52.1	26.9	12.2	7.0	5.1	2.6	30.6	7.1	13.1	10.4
COLORADO.............	1 659 308	2.53	65.8	52.8	25.4	9.2	5.9	3.9	2.1	34.2	7.9	14.1	12.1
CONNECTICUT	1 302 227	2.53	68.0	52.7	24.3	11.7	6.8	3.6	1.6	32.0	5.6	15.8	10.6
DELAWARE	298 755	2.54	68.9	52.3	22.8	12.6	7.5	4.0	2.1	31.1	6.2	14.7	10.2
DISTRICT OF COLUMBIA.............	248 590	2.16	46.6	23.4	8.7	19.1	10.1	4.2	1.6	53.4	9.7	24.5	19.2
FLORIDA..................	6 341 121	2.46	66.8	51.1	19.9	11.7	6.7	4.1	2.0	33.2	6.6	15.5	11.1
GEORGIA.................	3 007 678	2.65	70.7	52.5	25.2	14.0	8.3	4.1	2.0	29.3	5.7	13.7	9.9
HAWAII....................	403 572	2.92	71.6	54.5	24.8	12.0	5.6	5.0	2.2	28.4	6.6	11.1	10.7
IDAHO.....................	470 133	2.69	71.9	59.6	28.9	8.4	5.6	3.8	2.4	28.1	5.8	12.3	10.0
ILLINOIS..................	4 592 740	2.63	68.0	52.2	25.1	11.9	6.7	4.0	1.9	32.0	5.2	15.5	11.3
INDIANA..................	2 337 229	2.53	68.9	54.5	24.6	10.7	6.6	3.8	2.2	31.1	5.2	14.9	11.0
IOWA......................	1 150 197	2.46	67.3	55.9	24.6	8.2	5.3	3.2	1.9	32.7	5.5	16.0	11.1
KANSAS..................	1 038 940	2.51	68.0	55.7	25.9	8.9	5.8	3.4	2.0	32.0	5.0	15.4	11.5
KENTUCKY..............	1 591 739	2.47	69.8	54.7	24.2	11.5	6.9	3.5	1.9	30.2	4.2	15.2	10.8
LOUISIANA..............	1 657 107	2.62	70.2	49.6	23.3	16.3	9.7	4.3	2.2	29.8	4.5	14.3	11.0
MAINE	518 372	2.39	66.1	53.4	22.5	9.1	6.0	3.5	2.2	33.9	7.0	16.0	11.0
MARYLAND	1 981 795	2.61	69.1	51.2	24.1	13.7	7.9	4.2	2.1	30.9	6.0	14.9	10.1
MASSACHUSETTS ...	2 444 588	2.51	64.9	50.0	23.2	11.5	6.5	3.5	1.5	35.1	7.1	16.8	11.2
MICHIGAN	3 788 780	2.56	68.4	52.3	23.8	12.1	7.3	4.0	2.1	31.6	5.4	14.8	11.4
MINNESOTA	1 896 209	2.52	66.6	54.6	26.0	8.5	5.7	3.5	1.9	33.4	6.6	15.1	11.7
MISSISSIPPI	1 047 555	2.63	71.8	60.6	23.1	17.0	10.1	4.3	2.1	28.2	3.6	14.1	10.4
MISSOURI	2 107 214	2.48	67.7	52.7	23.3	11.3	7.0	3.7	2.1	32.3	5.1	15.8	11.4
MONTANA	359 070	2.45	66.5	54.1	23.4	8.7	5.8	3.7	2.3	33.5	6.1	14.9	12.5
NEBRASKA..............	666 995	2.49	66.9	54.9	25.6	8.8	6.0	3.0	1.8	33.1	5.6	15.7	11.8
NEVADA..................	751 977	2.62	66.8	50.6	23.0	10.7	6.6	5.5	3.0	33.2	8.4	11.9	13.0
NEW HAMPSHIRE.....	474 750	2.53	68.6	56.2	26.1	8.6	5.5	3.8	2.2	31.4	7.0	13.5	10.9
NEW JERSEY...........	3 065 774	2.68	70.7	54.4	26.2	12.2	6.2	4.1	1.7	29.3	4.8	14.8	9.7
NEW MEXICO...........	678 032	2.63	69.2	51.1	24.1	12.9	8.1	5.1	3.2	30.8	5.5	13.7	11.7
NEW YORK...............	7 060 595	2.61	66.2	47.6	22.4	14.3	8.0	4.3	1.9	33.8	5.7	16.7	11.4
NORTH CAROLINA ...	3 133 282	2.49	69.4	53.4	23.3	12.1	7.1	3.8	1.9	30.6	5.3	14.8	10.6
NORTH DAKOTA.......	257 234	2.41	64.9	54.1	24.7	7.6	5.1	3.2	1.8	35.1	5.8	16.2	13.1
OHIO.......................	4 446 621	2.49	67.6	52.2	23.1	11.7	7.1	3.8	2.0	32.4	5.1	15.9	11.4
OKLAHOMA	1 343 506	2.49	69.1	54.3	24.0	10.9	6.8	3.8	2.2	30.9	4.3	15.3	11.3
OREGON	1 335 109	2.51	66.3	53.0	23.2	9.3	6.0	3.9	2.3	33.7	7.7	14.8	11.2
PENNSYLVANIA........	4 779 186	2.48	67.5	52.4	22.5	11.3	6.1	3.8	1.9	32.5	4.9	16.5	11.1
RHODE ISLAND	408 412	2.47	65.3	49.1	21.8	12.3	7.5	3.8	1.8	34.7	6.2	17.0	11.5
SOUTH CAROLINA ...	1 534 334	2.53	70.3	52.0	22.6	14.3	8.3	4.0	2.0	29.7	4.7	14.4	10.6
SOUTH DAKOTA.......	290 336	2.50	67.3	55.0	25.1	8.7	5.9	3.6	2.3	32.7	5.2	15.4	12.1
TENNESSEE.............	2 234 229	2.48	69.7	53.5	23.1	12.5	7.3	3.7	1.8	30.3	4.5	15.0	10.8
TEXAS.....................	7 307 294	2.74	71.4	55.0	28.0	12.2	7.4	4.2	2.1	28.6	4.9	13.0	10.6
UTAH......................	701 933	3.13	76.9	64.2	36.1	8.9	5.5	3.8	2.0	23.1	5.4	10.0	7.7
VERMONT	240 744	2.44	65.9	53.5	23.9	8.8	6.0	3.6	2.3	34.1	7.9	15.1	11.1
VIRGINIA..................	2 700 335	2.54	68.9	53.7	24.6	11.5	6.7	3.7	1.9	31.1	6.1	14.5	10.5
WASHINGTON...........	2 272 261	2.53	66.4	52.9	24.7	9.5	6.3	4.0	2.4	33.6	7.4	14.3	11.8
WEST VIRGINIA........	737 360	2.40	68.8	54.6	21.9	10.4	5.5	3.8	1.9	31.2	4.1	16.3	10.7
WISCONSIN.............	2 086 304	2.50	66.9	54.0	24.4	9.2	5.9	3.6	2.0	33.1	6.4	15.2	11.5
WYOMING	193 959	2.48	67.8	55.7	25.1	8.5	5.8	3.6	2.3	32.2	5.9	13.7	12.6

STATE	Cohabiting couples (percent)				+/− U.S. percent family households	+/− U.S. percent married-couple family households	+/− U.S. percent female headed family households	+/− U.S. percent cohabiting couples	+/− U.S. percent same-sex couples	+/− U.S. percent one-person households	Population 30 years and over by care of grandchildren		
	Total cohabiting couples	Two males	Two females	One male/ one female							Total population 30 years and over	Percent living with grand-children	Percent responsible for care of grand-children
	155	156	157	158	159	160	161	162	163	164	165	166	167
UNITED STATES ...	5.0	0.3	0.3	4.3	0.0	0.0	0.0	0.0	0.0	0.0	158 881 037	3.6	1.5
ALABAMA	3.1	0.3	0.2	2.6	1.9	0.5	2.1	-1.9	-0.1	0.3	2 526 157	4.0	2.2
ALASKA	7.2	0.2	0.3	6.7	0.8	0.8	-1.2	2.2	-0.1	-2.4	326 384	3.2	1.7
ARIZONA	6.1	0.4	0.4	5.3	-0.3	0.4	-1.2	1.1	0.1	-1.0	2 821 947	4.1	1.9
ARKANSAS...............	3.6	0.2	0.2	3.1	2.1	2.6	0.0	-1.4	-0.1	-0.3	1 514 546	3.8	2.2
CALIFORNIA	5.8	0.5	0.4	4.9	0.9	-0.4	0.4	0.8	0.3	-2.3	18 329 469	5.1	1.6
COLORADO..............	5.4	0.3	0.4	4.7	-2.7	0.3	-2.6	0.4	0.1	0.4	2 392 487	2.8	1.2
CONNECTICUT	5.1	0.3	0.3	4.5	-0.5	0.2	-0.1	0.1	0.0	0.6	2 040 482	2.7	0.9
DELAWARE	5.9	0.4	0.3	5.2	0.4	-0.2	0.8	0.9	0.1	-0.8	452 524	3.7	1.6
DISTRICT OF COLUMBIA...........	5.8	1.0	0.4	4.3	-21.9	-29.1	7.3	0.8	0.9	17.9	319 590	5.3	2.6
FLORIDA..................	5.6	0.4	0.3	4.9	-1.7	-1.4	-0.1	0.6	0.1	0.8	9 794 873	3.5	1.5
GEORGIA.................	4.5	0.4	0.3	3.8	2.2	0.0	2.2	-0.5	0.1	-2.2	4 432 868	4.4	2.1
HAWAII....................	5.6	0.3	0.3	4.9	3.1	2.0	0.2	0.6	0.1	-4.0	704 169	7.0	2.0
IDAHO.....................	4.5	0.2	0.3	4.1	3.4	7.1	-3.4	-0.5	-0.1	-3.5	686 268	2.5	1.2
ILLINOIS..................	4.6	0.3	0.3	4.0	-0.5	-0.3	0.1	-0.4	0.0	0.9	6 912 992	3.7	1.5
INDIANA..................	5.1	0.3	0.3	4.6	0.4	2.0	-1.1	0.1	-0.1	0.1	3 400 798	2.8	1.4
IOWA......................	4.7	0.2	0.2	4.4	-1.2	3.4	-3.6	-0.3	-0.2	1.4	1 666 705	1.7	0.8
KANSAS..................	3.8	0.2	0.2	3.4	-0.5	3.2	-2.9	-1.2	-0.2	1.1	1 486 028	2.4	1.2
KENTUCKY..............	4.2	0.2	0.3	3.7	1.3	2.2	-0.3	-0.8	-0.1	0.2	2 308 910	3.0	1.6
LOUISIANA	4.8	0.3	0.3	4.1	1.7	-2.9	4.5	-0.2	0.0	-0.5	2 407 400	5.1	2.8
MAINE	6.9	0.3	0.4	6.2	-2.4	0.9	-2.7	1.9	0.1	1.2	781 580	1.7	0.6
MARYLAND	5.3	0.3	0.4	4.7	0.6	-1.3	1.9	0.3	0.0	-0.8	3 084 714	4.1	1.7
MASSACHUSETTS ...	5.2	0.4	0.4	4.4	-3.6	-2.5	-0.3	0.2	0.2	2.2	3 745 923	2.6	0.7
MICHIGAN	5.1	0.2	0.2	4.6	-0.1	-0.2	0.3	0.1	-0.1	0.4	5 625 377	3.0	1.2
MINNESOTA	5.1	0.3	0.3	4.6	-1.9	2.1	-3.3	0.1	-0.1	1.0	2 770 840	1.6	0.6
MISSISSIPPI	4.1	0.2	0.3	3.6	3.3	-1.9	5.2	-0.9	-0.1	-1.2	1 523 747	5.5	3.2
MISSOURI................	4.8	0.2	0.2	4.3	-0.8	0.2	-0.5	-0.2	-0.1	1.5	3 182 715	2.8	1.4
MONTANA................	4.9	0.2	0.2	4.5	-2.0	1.6	-3.1	-0.1	-0.2	1.6	522 648	2.1	1.2
NEBRASKA..............	4.2	0.2	0.2	3.8	-1.6	2.4	-3.0	-0.8	-0.2	1.7	950 599	1.8	0.9
NEVADA..................	7.0	0.4	0.3	6.3	-1.7	-1.9	-1.1	2.0	0.1	-1.0	1 141 554	4.0	1.6
NEW HAMPSHIRE.....	6.6	0.2	0.4	6.0	0.1	3.7	-3.2	1.6	0.0	-1.4	737 636	2.0	0.6
NEW JERSEY...........	4.7	0.3	0.3	4.1	2.2	1.9	0.4	-0.3	0.0	-1.3	5 003 491	3.7	1.2
NEW MEXICO............	6.2	0.3	0.4	5.5	0.7	-1.4	1.1	1.2	0.1	-0.4	1 001 610	4.6	2.4
NEW YORK...............	5.1	0.4	0.3	4.4	-2.3	-4.9	2.5	0.1	0.1	2.3	10 946 850	3.8	1.3
NORTH CAROLINA ...	4.4	0.3	0.3	3.8	0.9	0.9	0.3	-0.6	0.0	-0.4	4 573 967	3.5	1.7
NORTH DAKOTA......	4.3	0.2	0.2	4.0	-3.6	1.6	-4.2	-0.7	-0.3	3.5	359 314	1.3	0.7
OHIO......................	4.9	0.2	0.2	4.4	-0.9	-0.3	-0.1	-0.1	-0.1	1.5	6 512 056	2.8	1.3
OKLAHOMA..............	3.7	0.2	0.3	3.2	0.6	1.8	-0.9	-1.3	-0.1	0.9	1 915 455	3.5	2.1
OREGON..................	6.0	0.3	0.4	5.3	-2.2	0.5	-2.5	1.0	0.1	0.2	1 973 406	2.6	1.1
PENNSYLVANIA........	4.7	0.3	0.2	4.2	-1.0	-0.1	-0.5	-0.3	-0.1	1.8	7 306 204	2.8	1.1
RHODE ISLAND	5.6	0.3	0.4	4.9	-3.2	-3.4	0.5	0.6	0.1	2.7	615 542	2.8	0.8
SOUTH CAROLINA ...	4.4	0.3	0.3	3.8	1.8	-0.5	2.5	-0.6	0.0	-0.8	2 263 664	4.4	2.3
SOUTH DAKOTA.......	4.7	0.2	0.2	4.3	-1.2	2.5	-3.1	-0.3	-0.2	1.7	416 175	1.9	1.1
TENNESSEE.............	3.9	0.3	0.3	3.4	1.2	1.0	0.7	-1.1	-0.1	0.0	3 263 776	3.7	1.9
TEXAS.....................	4.2	0.3	0.3	3.6	2.9	2.5	0.4	-0.8	0.0	-2.2	10 908 461	5.1	2.4
UTAH......................	3.3	0.3	0.3	2.8	8.4	11.7	-2.9	-1.7	-0.1	-8.1	1 002 254	3.9	1.6
VERMONT	7.3	0.4	0.6	6.4	-2.6	1.0	-3.0	2.3	0.3	0.4	363 640	1.5	0.5
VIRGINIA..................	4.5	0.3	0.3	3.9	0.4	1.2	-0.3	-0.5	0.0	-0.8	4 071 538	3.4	1.5
WASHINGTON...........	6.0	0.4	0.4	5.2	-2.1	0.4	-2.3	1.0	0.2	0.3	3 353 576	2.5	1.1
WEST VIRGINIA	4.3	0.2	0.2	3.9	0.3	2.1	-1.4	-0.7	-0.2	1.3	1 098 093	2.8	1.5
WISCONSIN..............	5.4	0.2	0.2	4.9	-1.6	1.5	-2.6	0.4	-0.2	0.9	3 061 260	1.8	0.8
WYOMING	5.2	0.2	0.2	4.7	-0.7	3.2	-3.3	0.2	-0.2	0.5	278 775	2.2	1.3

Table A-2. States — Age, Ethnicity, and Household Structure

STATE		Households									
		Householder under 65 years (percent)				Householder 65 years and over (percent)					
	Householder all ages	Under 65 years	15 to 24 years	25 to 44 years	45 to 64 years	65 years and over	65 to 84 years	85 years and over	+/− U.S. percent householder 15 to 24 years	+/− U.S. percent householder 25 to 44 years	+/− U.S. percent householder 65 years and over
	168	169	170	171	172	173	174	175	176	177	178
UNITED STATES ...	105 539 122	78.9	5.1	40.2	33.6	21.1	18.8	2.3	0.0	0.0	0.0
ALABAMA	1 737 385	77.8	5.8	38.1	33.8	22.2	20.0	2.3	0.7	-2.1	1.1
ALASKA	221 804	89.9	6.0	46.7	37.2	10.1	9.4	0.7	0.9	6.5	-11.0
ARIZONA	1 901 625	77.9	6.2	39.6	32.0	22.1	19.9	2.2	1.1	-0.6	1.0
ARKANSAS.............	1 042 807	76.4	6.2	37.1	33.2	23.6	21.0	2.6	1.1	-3.1	2.5
CALIFORNIA............	11 512 020	81.1	4.6	43.1	33.5	18.9	16.8	2.1	-0.5	2.9	-2.2
COLORADO.............	1 659 308	83.9	6.3	43.8	33.7	16.1	14.4	1.7	1.2	3.6	-5.0
CONNECTICUT	1 302 227	77.5	3.3	39.5	34.7	22.5	19.8	2.7	-1.8	-0.7	1.4
DELAWARE	298 755	78.3	4.7	39.9	33.7	21.7	19.7	2.0	-0.4	-0.3	0.6
DISTRICT OF COLUMBIA	248 590	80.2	6.7	42.0	31.6	19.8	17.4	2.3	1.6	1.8	-1.3
FLORIDA.................	6 341 121	72.3	4.3	35.8	32.1	27.7	24.6	3.1	-0.8	-4.4	6.6
GEORGIA...............	3 007 678	83.3	5.8	44.4	33.2	16.7	15.1	1.6	0.7	4.2	-4.4
HAWAII..................	403 572	77.4	3.8	37.0	36.6	22.6	20.3	2.3	-1.3	-3.2	1.5
IDAHO...................	470 133	80.1	7.1	39.2	33.7	19.9	17.6	2.4	2.0	-1.0	-1.2
ILLINOIS.................	4 592 740	79.1	4.8	41.1	33.2	20.9	18.5	2.4	-0.3	0.9	-0.2
INDIANA.................	2 337 229	79.1	6.0	39.8	33.2	20.9	18.6	2.3	0.9	-0.4	-0.2
IOWA.....................	1 150 197	75.7	6.4	36.8	32.5	24.3	21.1	3.2	1.3	-3.4	3.2
KANSAS.................	1 038 940	78.0	6.9	38.9	32.2	22.0	19.2	2.8	1.8	-1.3	0.9
KENTUCKY	1 591 739	78.8	5.9	39.0	34.0	21.2	19.0	2.2	0.8	-1.2	0.1
LOUISIANA.............	1 657 107	79.4	6.1	39.4	33.9	20.6	18.6	2.0	1.0	-0.8	-0.5
MAINE...................	518 372	77.1	4.3	37.3	35.5	22.9	20.2	2.6	-0.8	-2.9	1.8
MARYLAND.............	1 981 795	81.1	3.9	41.6	35.5	18.9	17.1	1.8	-1.2	1.4	-2.2
MASSACHUSETTS ...	2 444 588	77.7	3.9	40.3	33.5	22.3	19.6	2.7	-1.2	0.1	1.2
MICHIGAN	3 788 780	78.9	5.0	39.8	34.1	21.1	18.8	2.3	-0.1	-0.4	0.0
MINNESOTA	1 896 209	79.9	5.6	41.7	32.6	20.1	17.4	2.7	0.5	1.5	-1.0
MISSISSIPPI............	1 047 555	78.3	5.7	39.0	33.6	21.7	19.4	2.3	0.6	-1.2	0.6
MISSOURI...............	2 197 214	77.6	5.8	38.9	32.9	22.4	19.8	2.6	0.7	-1.3	1.3
MONTANA...............	359 070	77.8	6.3	35.6	35.8	22.2	19.7	2.5	1.2	-4.6	1.1
NEBRASKA.............	666 995	77.4	6.9	38.8	31.7	22.6	19.6	3.0	1.8	-1.4	1.5
NEVADA.................	751 977	81.8	5.3	41.8	34.7	18.2	17.0	1.2	0.2	1.6	-2.9
NEW HAMPSHIRE.....	474 750	80.6	3.8	41.0	35.7	19.4	17.4	2.1	-1.3	0.8	-1.7
NEW JERSEY...........	3 065 774	77.5	2.6	40.0	34.9	22.5	20.1	2.5	-2.5	-0.2	1.4
NEW MEXICO...........	678 032	79.6	6.0	38.7	34.9	20.4	18.4	2.0	0.9	-1.5	-0.7
NEW YORK..............	7 060 595	78.0	3.7	39.8	34.5	22.0	19.5	2.5	-1.4	-0.4	0.9
NORTH CAROLINA ...	3 133 282	80.0	5.8	41.1	33.1	20.0	18.1	1.8	0.7	0.9	-1.1
NORTH DAKOTA.......	257 234	76.2	8.0	36.6	31.5	23.8	20.6	3.3	2.9	-3.6	2.7
OHIO.....................	4 446 621	78.0	5.4	39.0	33.6	22.0	19.8	2.3	0.3	-1.2	0.9
OKLAHOMA.............	1 343 506	77.8	7.0	37.7	33.1	22.2	19.7	2.5	1.9	-2.5	1.1
OREGON	1 335 109	79.0	6.2	38.0	34.0	21.0	18.4	2.6	1.1	-2.2	-0.1
PENNSYLVANIA........	4 779 186	74.4	4.0	36.6	33.8	25.6	22.9	2.7	-1.1	-3.6	4.5
RHODE ISLAND	408 412	76.1	4.7	38.5	32.9	23.9	21.0	2.9	-0.4	-1.7	2.8
SOUTH CAROLINA ...	1 534 334	79.5	5.4	39.3	34.8	20.5	18.8	1.8	0.3	-0.9	-0.6
SOUTH DAKOTA.......	290 336	76.0	7.2	37.2	31.7	24.0	20.8	3.1	2.1	-3.0	2.9
TENNESSEE............	2 234 229	79.4	5.7	39.6	34.2	20.6	18.5	2.1	0.6	-0.6	-0.5
TEXAS...................	7 397 294	82.3	6.4	43.7	32.2	17.7	15.9	1.8	1.3	3.5	-3.4
UTAH.....................	701 933	82.9	8.9	43.6	30.4	17.1	15.2	1.9	3.8	3.4	-4.0
VERMONT	240 744	79.4	4.8	38.1	36.5	20.6	18.2	2.4	-0.3	-2.1	-0.5
VIRGINIA.................	2 700 335	81.3	5.0	41.6	34.7	18.7	16.9	1.8	-0.1	1.4	-2.4
WASHINGTON..........	2 272 261	81.4	5.7	41.4	34.3	18.6	16.4	2.2	0.6	1.2	-2.5
WEST VIRGINIA	737 360	74.4	5.1	33.6	35.6	25.6	22.8	2.8	0.0	-6.6	4.5
WISCONSIN.............	2 086 304	78.4	5.8	39.6	33.0	21.6	19.0	2.6	0.7	-0.6	0.5
WYOMING	193 959	80.5	7.2	37.2	36.1	19.5	17.3	2.1	2.1	-3.0	-1.6

STATE	Family households										
	Householder all ages	Householder under 65 years (percent)				Householder 65 years and over (percent)			+/− U.S. percent householder 15 to 24 years	+/− U.S. percent householder 25 to 44 years	+/− U.S. percent householder 65 years and over
		Under 65 years	15 to 24 years	25 to 44 years	45 to 64 years	65 years and over	65 to 84 years	85 years and over			
	179	180	181	182	183	184	185	186	187	188	189
UNITED STATES ...	72 261 780	83.4	3.7	43.9	35.8	16.6	15.5	1.1	-1.4	3.7	-4.5
ALABAMA	1 223 185	82.8	4.5	42.7	35.6	17.2	16.1	1.1	-0.6	2.5	-3.9
ALASKA	153 611	91.6	4.7	49.5	37.4	8.4	8.0	0.4	-0.4	9.3	-12.7
ARIZONA	1 296 593	81.1	4.5	43.3	33.3	18.9	17.7	1.2	-0.6	3.1	-2.2
ARKANSAS.............	736 063	81.8	5.2	41.8	34.9	18.2	17.0	1.2	0.1	1.6	-2.9
CALIFORNIA............	7 985 489	84.9	3.4	46.4	35.1	15.1	14.0	1.1	-1.7	6.2	-6.0
COLORADO	1 092 352	86.9	4.1	46.8	36.0	13.1	12.3	0.7	-1.0	6.6	-8.0
CONNECTICUT	885 747	82.6	2.4	42.8	37.4	17.4	16.2	1.2	-2.7	2.6	-3.7
DELAWARE	205 775	82.5	3.3	43.7	35.5	17.5	16.7	0.8	-1.8	3.5	-3.6
DISTRICT OF COLUMBIA..........	115 963	81.3	4.3	41.9	35.0	18.7	17.2	1.5	-0.8	1.7	-2.4
FLORIDA..................	4 238 409	76.7	3.2	39.4	34.1	23.3	21.7	1.6	-1.9	-0.8	2.2
GEORGIA.................	2 126 360	86.9	4.4	47.5	34.9	13.1	12.4	0.8	-0.7	7.3	-8.0
HAWAII....................	289 012	79.2	2.9	38.4	37.9	20.8	19.0	1.7	-2.2	-1.8	-0.3
IDAHO.....................	337 884	84.4	5.3	43.8	35.3	15.6	14.5	1.2	0.2	3.6	-5.5
ILLINOIS..................	3 125 318	83.9	3.3	44.5	36.1	16.1	15.0	1.1	-1.8	4.3	-5.0
INDIANA..................	1 611 045	84.1	4.3	44.3	35.6	15.9	14.9	1.0	-0.8	4.1	-5.2
IOWA......................	774 246	81.3	3.9	41.5	35.9	18.7	17.4	1.3	-1.2	1.3	-2.4
KANSAS..................	706 786	83.2	4.5	43.7	34.9	16.8	15.6	1.2	-0.6	3.5	-4.3
KENTUCKY..............	1 110 426	84.2	4.9	43.7	35.6	15.8	14.9	0.9	-0.2	3.5	-5.3
LOUISIANA.............	1 163 191	84.0	4.8	43.7	35.5	16.0	15.0	1.0	-0.3	3.5	-5.1
MAINE....................	342 431	82.7	2.7	42.1	37.8	17.3	16.2	1.1	-2.4	1.9	-3.8
MARYLAND.............	1 368 647	85.1	2.6	44.6	37.8	14.9	14.1	0.8	-2.5	4.4	-6.2
MASSACHUSETTS ...	1 587 537	82.5	2.2	43.6	36.7	17.5	16.3	1.2	-2.9	3.4	-3.6
MICHIGAN	2 591 312	83.5	3.3	43.6	36.6	16.5	15.5	1.0	-1.8	3.4	-4.6
MINNESOTA	1 262 953	84.4	3.2	45.4	35.9	15.6	14.5	1.1	-1.9	5.2	-5.5
MISSISSIPPI............	752 234	83.6	4.8	43.8	35.0	16.4	15.3	1.2	-0.3	3.6	-4.7
MISSOURI................	1 486 546	82.7	4.1	43.3	35.3	17.3	16.2	1.1	-1.0	3.1	-3.8
MONTANA...............	238 733	82.6	3.9	40.3	38.5	17.4	16.3	1.1	-1.2	0.1	-3.7
NEBRASKA..............	446 551	82.6	4.2	43.4	35.0	17.4	16.2	1.2	-0.9	3.2	-3.7
NEVADA..................	502 508	84.8	4.4	45.3	35.1	15.2	14.6	0.7	-0.7	5.1	-5.9
NEW HAMPSHIRE.....	325 581	85.0	2.1	45.1	37.8	15.0	14.1	0.9	-3.0	4.9	-6.1
NEW JERSEY..........	2 167 577	82.8	2.0	43.2	37.6	17.2	16.1	1.1	-3.1	3.0	-3.9
NEW MEXICO...........	468 899	83.3	4.9	42.9	35.5	16.7	15.6	1.1	-0.2	2.7	-4.4
NEW YORK...............	4 673 485	83.0	2.7	43.0	37.3	17.0	15.8	1.2	-2.4	2.8	-4.1
NORTH CAROLINA ...	2 173 346	84.2	4.4	44.6	35.2	15.8	14.9	0.9	-0.7	4.4	-5.3
NORTH DAKOTA.......	166 963	81.4	4.3	41.4	35.7	18.6	17.1	1.5	-0.8	1.2	-2.5
OHIO.......................	3 007 207	82.9	3.8	43.0	36.1	17.1	16.1	0.9	-1.3	2.8	-4.0
OKLAHOMA	927 703	82.9	5.5	42.6	34.8	17.1	16.0	1.1	0.4	2.4	-4.0
OREGON	884 875	83.1	4.1	41.8	37.1	16.9	15.6	1.3	-1.0	1.6	-4.2
PENNSYLVANIA........	3 225 707	80.1	2.5	40.6	37.0	19.9	18.6	1.3	-2.6	0.4	-1.2
RHODE ISLAND	266 655	82.0	3.0	43.1	35.9	18.0	16.8	1.2	-2.1	2.9	-3.1
SOUTH CAROLINA ...	1 078 736	83.7	4.2	42.9	36.6	16.3	15.4	0.9	-0.9	2.7	-4.8
SOUTH DAKOTA.......	195 455	81.4	4.4	42.1	34.9	18.6	17.3	1.3	-0.7	1.9	-2.5
TENNESSEE.............	1 557 620	84.0	4.6	43.3	36.1	16.0	15.1	1.0	-0.5	3.1	-5.1
TEXAS.....................	5 283 474	85.9	4.8	47.2	33.9	14.1	13.3	0.8	-0.3	7.0	-7.0
UTAH......................	539 728	86.3	7.5	47.1	31.8	13.7	12.8	0.9	2.4	6.9	-7.4
VERMONT	158 684	84.1	2.6	42.2	39.3	15.9	14.8	1.0	-2.5	2.0	-5.2
VIRGINIA..................	1 859 983	85.1	3.4	44.7	37.0	14.9	14.1	0.9	-1.7	4.5	-6.2
WASHINGTON..........	1 509 395	85.1	3.9	44.8	36.4	14.9	13.8	1.0	-1.2	4.6	-6.2
WEST VIRGINIA	507 255	80.8	3.9	38.7	38.1	19.2	17.9	1.3	-1.2	-1.5	-1.9
WISCONSIN.............	1 395 037	83.1	3.3	43.7	36.2	16.9	15.8	1.1	-1.8	3.5	-4.2
WYOMING	131 508	84.9	4.7	41.6	38.6	15.1	14.1	1.0	-0.4	1.4	-6.0

Table A-2. States — Age, Ethnicity, and Household Structure

STATE		Married-couple family households							
		Householder under 65 years (percent)							
	Householder all ages	Under 65 years	15 to 24 years	25 to 44 years	45 to 64 years	65 years and over (percent)	+/– U.S. percent householder 15 to 24 years	+/– U.S. percent householder 25 to 44 years	+/– U.S. percent householder 65 years and over
	190	191	192	193	194	195	196	197	198
UNITED STATES ...	55 458 451	82.5	2.4	42.2	37.9	17.5	-2.7	2.0	-3.6
ALABAMA	921 298	82.5	3.2	41.1	38.1	17.5	-1.9	0.9	-3.6
ALASKA	118 332	91.6	3.5	47.8	40.2	8.4	-1.6	7.6	-12.7
ARIZONA	1 005 901	78.9	3.1	40.8	35.0	21.1	-2.0	0.6	0.0
ARKANSAS	574 619	80.8	3.8	39.5	37.5	19.2	-1.3	-0.7	-1.9
CALIFORNIA	5 995 225	84.1	2.2	45.2	36.7	15.9	-2.9	5.0	-5.2
COLORADO	875 669	86.1	2.9	45.5	37.7	13.9	-2.2	5.3	-7.2
CONNECTICUT	686 713	82.0	1.0	41.3	39.7	18.0	-4.1	1.1	-3.1
DELAWARE	156 351	81.0	1.7	41.4	38.0	19.0	-3.4	1.2	-2.1
DISTRICT OF COLUMBIA............	58 050	79.7	1.6	39.2	38.9	20.3	-3.5	-1.0	-0.8
FLORIDA.................	3 242 027	73.8	1.9	36.3	35.6	26.2	-3.2	-3.9	5.1
GEORGIA................	1 579 407	86.5	2.9	46.1	37.5	13.5	-2.2	5.9	-7.6
HAWAII	220 144	79.7	2.2	38.2	39.3	20.3	-2.9	-2.0	-0.8
IDAHO	280 206	83.2	4.3	41.8	37.1	16.8	-0.8	1.6	-4.3
ILLINOIS.................	2 396 891	83.5	1.9	43.6	38.0	16.5	-3.2	3.4	-4.6
INDIANA..................	1 272 826	83.3	2.7	42.2	38.3	16.7	-2.4	2.0	-4.4
IOWA.....................	643 097	80.1	2.4	39.4	38.2	19.9	-2.7	-0.8	-1.2
KANSAS..................	578 340	82.1	3.2	41.8	37.1	17.9	-1.9	1.6	-3.2
KENTUCKY..............	870 930	83.8	3.6	42.1	38.1	16.2	-1.5	1.9	-4.9
LOUISIANA	822 374	83.4	3.0	41.9	38.4	16.6	-2.1	1.7	-4.5
MAINE	276 856	81.7	1.6	39.4	40.7	18.3	-3.5	-0.8	-2.8
MARYLAND	1 015 033	84.3	1.3	42.7	40.3	15.7	-3.8	2.5	-5.4
MASSACHUSETTS ...	1 221 127	82.1	0.9	42.5	38.7	17.9	-4.2	2.3	-3.2
MICHIGAN	1 980 112	82.7	1.8	41.6	39.3	17.3	-3.3	1.4	-3.8
MINNESOTA	1 035 612	83.3	1.8	43.5	38.0	16.7	-3.3	3.3	-4.4
MISSISSIPPI	529 852	83.0	3.5	41.5	38.1	17.0	-1.6	1.3	-4.1
MISSOURI...............	1 157 550	81.4	2.8	40.8	37.8	18.6	-2.3	0.6	-2.5
MONTANA	194 207	81.4	2.5	37.7	41.1	18.6	-2.6	-2.5	-2.5
NEBRASKA..............	365 981	81.4	2.7	41.4	37.4	18.0	-2.4	1.2	-2.5
NEVADA..................	380 469	83.2	2.9	42.9	37.4	16.8	-2.2	2.7	-4.3
NEW HAMPSHIRE.....	266 624	84.4	1.2	43.4	39.8	15.6	-3.9	3.2	-5.5
NEW JERSEY...........	1 668 616	82.7	0.9	42.7	39.2	17.3	-4.2	2.5	-3.8
NEW MEXICO	346 478	81.9	3.1	40.6	38.1	18.1	-2.0	0.4	-3.0
NEW YORK..............	3 359 150	82.1	1.3	41.3	39.5	17.9	-3.8	1.1	-3.2
NORTH CAROLINA ...	1 672 543	83.7	3.0	43.0	37.7	16.3	-2.1	2.8	-4.8
NORTH DAKOTA.......	139 203	80.1	2.6	39.4	38.1	19.9	-2.5	-0.8	-1.2
OHIO	2 319 012	82.0	2.2	41.0	38.8	18.0	-2.9	0.8	-3.1
OKLAHOMA	729 743	81.8	4.2	40.4	37.2	18.2	-0.9	0.2	-2.9
OREGON	707 602	81.8	2.8	39.5	39.5	18.2	-2.3	0.7	-2.9
PENNSYLVANIA.......	2 504 664	79.6	1.3	39.0	39.3	20.4	-3.8	-1.2	-0.7
RHODE ISLAND	200 729	81.0	1.2	41.0	38.8	19.0	-3.9	0.8	-2.1
SOUTH CAROLINA ...	797 922	83.1	2.8	40.9	39.5	16.9	-2.3	0.7	-4.2
SOUTH DAKOTA......	159 559	79.7	2.8	40.0	36.9	20.3	-2.3	-0.2	-0.8
TENNESSEE............	1 194 205	83.5	3.3	41.4	38.8	16.5	-1.8	1.2	-4.6
TEXAS...................	4 068 697	85.4	3.6	46.0	35.9	14.6	-1.5	5.8	-6.5
UTAH.....................	450 765	85.8	6.8	46.7	32.3	14.2	1.7	6.5	-6.9
VERMONT	128 731	83.3	1.5	39.9	41.9	16.7	-3.6	-0.3	-4.4
VIRGINIA.................	1 449 217	84.7	2.2	43.1	39.4	15.3	-2.9	2.9	-5.8
WASHINGTON..........	1 201 324	83.8	2.6	42.7	38.6	16.2	-2.5	2.5	-4.9
WEST VIRGINIA	402 781	81.0	2.9	37.4	40.7	19.0	-2.2	-2.8	-2.1
WISCONSIN.............	1 127 613	82.0	1.8	41.6	38.6	18.0	-3.3	1.4	-3.1
WYOMING	108 074	83.6	3.5	39.2	41.0	16.4	-1.6	-1.0	-4.7

| | Householder all ages | Family households, male householder, no wife present Householder under 65 years (percent) | | | | 65 years and over (percent) | +/− U.S. percent householder 15 to 24 years | +/− U.S. percent householder 25 to 44 years | +/− U.S. percent householder 65 years and over |
STATE		Under 65 years	15 to 24 years	25 to 44 years	45 to 64 years				
	199	200	201	202	203	204	205	206	207
UNITED STATES ...	4 302 568	89.2	9.6	50.9	28.7	10.8	4.5	10.7	-10.3
ALABAMA	61 129	86.5	9.1	46.9	30.6	13.5	4.0	6.7	-7.6
ALASKA	11 822	92.8	6.9	55.3	30.5	7.2	1.8	15.1	-13.9
ARIZONA	88 917	92.4	13.3	54.1	25.0	7.6	8.2	13.9	-13.5
ARKANSAS...............	38 867	88.5	10.8	49.5	28.1	11.5	5.7	9.3	-9.6
CALIFORNIA	589 186	90.9	9.4	53.2	28.2	9.1	4.3	13.0	-12.0
COLORADO..............	64 545	93.2	11.4	52.4	29.3	6.8	6.3	12.2	-14.3
CONNECTICUT	46 703	85.3	7.5	47.2	30.6	14.7	2.4	7.0	-6.4
DELAWARE	11 854	89.2	9.2	49.4	30.6	10.8	4.1	9.2	-10.3
DISTRICT OF COLUMBIA............	10 355	84.1	7.7	44.4	32.0	15.9	2.6	4.2	-5.2
FLORIDA....................	257 223	89.4	9.6	50.9	28.9	10.6	4.5	10.7	-10.5
GEORGIA..................	124 524	91.0	10.8	52.9	27.4	9.0	5.7	12.7	-12.1
HAWAII.....................	20 325	81.9	6.2	41.5	34.3	18.1	1.1	1.3	-3.0
IDAHO	17 981	93.2	11.5	55.4	26.3	6.8	6.4	15.2	-14.3
ILLINOIS...................	183 729	88.1	10.0	49.5	28.6	11.9	4.9	9.3	-9.2
INDIANA....................	88 995	90.7	11.3	53.3	26.1	9.3	6.2	13.1	-11.8
IOWA........................	37 197	90.6	11.5	52.7	26.3	9.4	6.4	12.5	-11.7
KANSAS....................	35 650	91.5	12.8	53.3	25.4	8.5	7.7	13.1	-12.6
KENTUCKY...............	56 411	88.7	9.5	49.3	29.8	11.3	4.4	9.1	-9.8
LOUISIANA	70 745	86.9	10.1	47.2	29.6	13.1	5.0	7.0	-8.0
MAINE	18 162	89.4	7.6	54.0	27.8	10.6	2.5	13.8	-10.5
MARYLAND	82 569	88.8	7.5	50.2	31.1	11.2	2.4	10.0	-9.9
MASSACHUSETTS ...	86 023	85.1	7.2	46.4	31.5	14.9	2.1	6.2	-6.2
MICHIGAN	151 436	88.5	9.1	50.3	29.0	11.5	4.0	10.1	-9.6
MINNESOTA	65 496	91.8	10.1	53.6	28.0	8.2	5.0	13.4	-12.9
MISSISSIPPI.............	44 565	86.5	8.8	47.4	30.3	13.5	3.7	7.2	-7.6
MISSOURI.................	81 113	89.7	9.8	52.6	27.4	10.3	4.7	12.4	-10.8
MONTANA.................	13 360	90.3	9.9	51.8	28.6	9.7	4.8	11.6	-11.4
NEBRASKA...............	21 808	90.1	12.3	52.5	25.3	9.9	7.2	12.3	-11.2
NEVADA...................	41 220	92.5	11.2	55.1	26.3	7.5	6.1	14.9	-13.6
NEW HAMPSHIRE.....	17 938	90.5	7.0	53.6	29.9	9.5	1.9	13.4	-11.6
NEW JERSEY...........	126 002	85.4	7.5	47.6	30.4	14.6	2.4	7.4	-6.5
NEW MEXICO............	34 797	90.6	12.0	51.1	27.5	9.4	6.9	10.9	-11.7
NEW YORK................	303 252	87.1	7.7	48.1	31.2	12.9	2.6	7.9	-8.2
NORTH CAROLINA ...	120 403	90.0	11.2	51.7	27.1	10.0	6.1	11.5	-11.1
NORTH DAKOTA.......	8 199	89.6	11.7	50.1	27.8	10.4	6.6	9.9	-10.7
OHIO	166 791	88.2	8.9	50.6	28.7	11.8	3.8	10.4	-9.3
OKLAHOMA..............	51 165	90.5	11.7	51.5	27.3	9.5	6.6	11.3	-11.6
OREGON	52 486	91.9	10.5	52.9	28.4	8.1	5.4	12.7	-13.0
PENNSYLVANIA........	181 295	84.9	7.2	47.4	30.3	15.1	2.1	7.2	-6.0
RHODE ISLAND	15 714	85.5	9.3	47.5	28.7	14.5	4.2	7.3	-6.6
SOUTH CAROLINA ...	61 055	88.0	9.4	49.1	29.5	12.0	4.3	8.9	-9.1
SOUTH DAKOTA.......	10 553	91.3	11.6	51.5	28.2	8.7	6.5	11.3	-12.4
TENNESSEE.............	83 308	88.6	9.5	50.0	29.1	11.4	4.4	9.8	-9.7
TEXAS......................	310 908	90.5	11.8	52.1	26.6	9.5	6.7	11.9	-11.6
UTAH........................	26 402	91.0	13.3	50.0	27.7	9.0	8.2	9.8	-12.1
VERMONT.................	8 722	91.5	7.8	53.3	30.5	8.5	2.7	13.1	-12.6
VIRGINIA..................	100 050	88.8	8.6	50.7	29.5	11.2	3.5	10.5	-9.9
WASHINGTON...........	91 088	92.7	10.2	54.2	28.3	7.3	5.1	14.0	-13.8
WEST VIRGINIA	27 911	84.7	9.2	45.2	30.3	15.3	4.1	5.0	-5.8
WISCONSIN..............	75 594	90.4	9.8	52.7	27.9	9.6	4.7	12.5	-11.5
WYOMING	7 025	93.6	9.6	52.4	31.5	6.4	4.5	12.2	-14.7

Table A-2. States — Age, Ethnicity, and Household Structure

	Family households, female householder, no husband present								
STATE	Householder all ages	Householder under 65 years (percent)				65 years and over (percent)	+/− U.S. percent householder 15 to 24 years	+/− U.S. percent householder 25 to 44 years	+/− U.S. percent householder 65 years and over
		Under 65 years	15 to 24 years	25 to 44 years	45 to 64 years				
	208	209	210	211	212	213	214	215	216
UNITED STATES ...	12 500 761	85.3	7.5	49.1	28.6	14.7	2.4	8.9	-6.4
ALABAMA	240 758	83.1	8.4	47.6	27.1	16.9	3.3	7.4	-4.2
ALASKA	23 457	91.1	9.6	55.0	26.4	8.9	4.5	14.8	-12.2
ARIZONA	201 775	87.4	7.8	50.8	28.8	12.6	2.7	10.6	-8.5
ARKANSAS..............	122 577	84.7	10.0	49.8	24.9	15.3	4.9	9.6	-5.8
CALIFORNIA............	1 401 078	85.9	6.1	48.6	31.2	14.1	1.0	8.4	-7.0
COLORADO..............	152 138	89.0	8.2	51.8	29.0	11.0	3.1	11.6	-10.1
CONNECTICUT	152 331	84.6	7.1	48.2	29.3	15.4	2.0	8.0	-5.7
DELAWARE	37 570	86.4	8.1	51.4	26.8	13.6	3.0	11.2	-7.5
DISTRICT OF COLUMBIA..........	47 558	82.5	6.9	44.7	31.0	17.5	1.8	4.5	-3.6
FLORIDA...................	739 159	85.0	6.8	48.9	29.3	15.0	1.7	8.7	-6.1
GEORGIA.................	422 429	86.9	8.0	51.2	27.7	13.1	2.9	11.0	-8.0
HAWAII....................	48 543	76.3	4.9	38.3	33.1	23.7	-0.2	-1.9	2.6
IDAHO	39 697	88.3	9.7	52.2	26.5	11.7	4.6	12.0	-9.4
ILLINOIS..................	544 698	84.6	7.2	47.0	30.4	15.4	2.1	6.8	-5.7
INDIANA	249 224	86.1	9.7	51.3	25.1	13.9	4.6	11.1	-7.2
IOWA.......................	93 952	85.8	11.0	51.4	23.5	14.2	5.9	11.2	-6.9
KANSAS..................	92 796	87.1	9.6	52.2	25.3	12.9	4.5	12.0	-8.2
KENTUCKY..............	183 085	84.4	9.6	49.2	25.5	15.6	4.5	9.0	-5.5
LOUISIANA	270 072	85.0	8.6	48.3	28.1	15.0	3.5	8.1	-6.1
MAINE	47 413	86.2	7.7	53.6	24.9	13.8	2.6	13.4	-7.3
MARYLAND	271 045	86.7	6.0	50.1	30.6	13.3	0.9	9.9	-7.8
MASSACHUSETTS ...	280 387	83.5	6.3	47.3	29.8	16.5	1.2	7.1	-4.6
MICHIGAN	459 764	85.3	7.9	50.1	27.3	14.7	2.8	9.9	-6.4
MINNESOTA	161 845	88.6	9.0	54.0	25.6	11.4	3.9	13.8	-9.7
MISSISSIPPI	177 817	84.5	7.9	49.6	26.9	15.5	2.8	9.4	-5.6
MISSOURI	247 083	86.3	8.6	51.6	26.1	13.7	3.5	11.4	-7.4
MONTANA	31 166	87.2	9.4	51.4	26.4	12.8	4.3	11.2	-8.3
NEBRASKA	58 762	87.4	10.5	52.9	24.0	12.6	5.4	12.7	-8.5
NEVADA..................	80 819	88.1	7.8	51.7	28.7	11.9	2.7	11.5	-9.2
NEW HAMPSHIRE.....	41 019	86.6	6.1	52.7	27.9	13.4	1.0	12.5	-7.7
NEW JERSEY	372 959	82.1	4.9	44.2	33.0	17.9	-0.2	4.0	-3.2
NEW MEXICO...........	87 624	86.0	8.8	49.0	28.3	14.0	3.7	8.8	-7.1
NEW YORK...............	1 011 083	84.8	5.6	47.0	31.9	15.2	0.5	7.1	-5.9
NORTH CAROLINA ...	380 400	84.9	8.3	49.9	26.7	15.1	3.2	9.7	-6.0
NORTH DAKOTA......	19 561	87.1	13.6	51.6	21.9	12.9	8.5	11.4	-8.2
OHIO	521 404	85.2	9.5	49.4	26.3	14.8	4.4	9.2	-6.3
OKLAHOMA.............	146 795	85.9	9.7	50.7	25.5	14.1	4.6	10.5	-7.0
OREGON	124 787	86.9	9.1	50.3	27.4	13.1	4.0	10.1	-8.0
PENNSYLVANIA.......	539 748	80.6	6.6	45.5	28.6	19.4	1.5	5.3	-1.7
RHODE ISLAND	50 212	85.2	8.2	50.1	26.9	14.8	3.1	9.9	-6.3
SOUTH CAROLINA ...	219 759	84.7	7.9	48.8	28.1	15.3	2.8	8.6	-5.8
SOUTH DAKOTA......	25 343	87.5	11.3	51.5	24.8	12.5	6.2	11.3	-8.6
TENNESSEE............	280 107	84.5	8.5	49.0	27.0	15.5	3.4	8.8	-5.6
TEXAS....................	903 869	86.4	7.8	50.7	27.8	13.6	2.7	10.5	-7.5
UTAH......................	62 561	87.5	9.4	48.5	29.5	12.5	4.3	8.3	-8.6
VERMONT	21 231	86.5	7.7	51.8	27.0	13.5	2.6	11.6	-7.6
VIRGINIA.................	310 716	85.4	7.1	50.1	28.2	14.6	2.0	9.9	-6.5
WASHINGTON..........	216 983	88.9	8.5	52.7	27.7	11.1	3.4	12.5	-10.0
WEST VIRGINIA........	76 563	78.2	7.4	43.4	27.3	21.8	2.3	3.2	0.7
WISCONSIN.............	191 830	87.0	9.5	52.5	25.0	13.0	4.4	12.3	-8.1
WYOMING	16 409	89.3	10.5	53.3	25.5	10.7	5.4	13.1	-10.4

STATE	Householder all ages	Nonfamily households										Householders 65 years and over	
		Householder under 65 years (percent)				Householder 65 years and over (percent)			+/– U.S. percent householder 15 to 24 years	+/– U.S. percent householder 25 to 44 years	+/– U.S. percent householder 65 years and over		
		Under 65 years	15 to 24 years	25 to 44 years	45 to 64 years	65 years and over	65 to 84 years	85 years and over				Total households	Percent living alone
	217	218	219	220	221	222	223	224	225	226	227	228	229
UNITED STATES ...	33 277 342	69.1	8.3	32.1	28.7	30.9	25.9	5.0	3.2	-8.1	9.8	22 275 453	44.2
ALABAMA	514 200	65.7	8.8	27.2	29.7	34.3	29.2	5.1	3.7	-13.0	13.2	386 445	44.4
ALASKA	68 193	86.1	9.1	40.2	36.8	13.9	12.6	1.3	4.0	0.0	-7.2	22 421	39.4
ARIZONA	605 032	70.9	9.7	31.9	29.3	29.1	24.8	4.4	4.6	-8.3	8.0	420 828	39.3
ARKANSAS	306 744	63.5	8.5	25.9	29.0	36.5	30.4	6.1	3.4	-14.3	15.4	245 825	44.3
CALIFORNIA	3 526 531	72.6	7.1	35.6	29.8	27.4	23.1	4.3	2.0	-4.6	6.3	2 173 596	41.5
COLORADO	566 956	78.1	10.6	38.2	29.3	21.9	18.4	3.5	5.5	-2.0	0.8	267 101	44.7
CONNECTICUT	416 480	66.6	5.3	32.5	28.9	33.4	27.4	6.0	0.2	-7.7	12.3	293 067	45.6
DELAWARE	92 980	68.9	7.6	31.5	29.8	31.1	26.5	4.6	2.5	-8.7	10.0	64 931	42.4
DISTRICT OF COLUMBIA	132 627	79.3	8.8	42.0	28.6	20.7	17.6	3.0	3.7	1.8	-0.4	49 134	52.2
FLORIDA	2 102 712	63.4	6.7	28.6	28.1	36.6	30.6	6.0	1.6	-11.6	15.5	1 757 202	41.1
GEORGIA	881 318	74.8	9.0	36.8	28.9	25.2	21.6	3.6	3.9	-3.4	4.1	502 011	42.7
HAWAII	114 560	72.7	5.9	33.5	33.3	27.3	23.5	3.7	0.8	-6.7	6.2	91 201	31.8
IDAHO	132 249	69.1	11.8	27.6	29.7	30.9	25.5	5.4	6.7	-12.6	9.8	93 716	42.0
ILLINOIS	1 467 422	68.7	7.9	33.7	27.1	31.3	26.0	5.3	2.8	-6.5	10.2	961 890	46.2
INDIANA	726 184	67.8	9.9	30.0	28.0	32.2	26.9	5.3	4.8	-10.2	11.1	489 525	46.2
IOWA	375 951	64.2	11.6	27.0	25.5	35.8	28.6	7.2	6.5	-13.2	14.7	279 468	47.1
KANSAS	332 154	66.9	12.0	28.7	26.2	33.1	26.7	6.4	6.9	-11.5	12.0	228 643	47.0
KENTUCKY	481 313	66.6	8.2	28.2	30.1	33.4	28.4	5.0	3.1	-12.0	12.3	336 668	46.5
LOUISIANA	493 916	68.6	9.2	29.3	30.1	31.4	26.9	4.5	4.1	-10.9	10.3	341 369	43.9
MAINE	175 941	66.2	7.5	27.8	31.0	33.8	28.1	5.6	2.4	-12.4	12.7	118 536	47.6
MARYLAND	613 148	72.2	6.8	34.9	30.5	27.8	23.8	4.1	1.7	-5.3	6.7	375 132	43.3
MASSACHUSETTS ...	857 051	68.6	6.9	34.2	27.5	31.4	25.8	5.6	1.8	-6.0	10.3	546 231	47.6
MICHIGAN	1 197 468	69.1	8.7	31.5	28.8	30.9	26.0	5.0	3.6	-8.7	9.8	798 099	44.8
MINNESOTA	633 256	70.9	10.5	34.4	26.0	29.1	23.2	5.9	5.4	-5.8	8.0	380 478	46.8
MISSISSIPPI	295 321	64.7	7.8	26.8	30.2	35.3	29.9	5.4	2.7	-13.4	14.2	227 601	44.6
MISSOURI	710 668	66.9	9.2	29.7	27.9	33.1	27.4	5.8	4.1	-10.5	12.0	492 745	46.3
MONTANA	120 337	68.1	11.2	26.4	30.5	31.9	26.5	5.4	6.1	-13.8	10.8	79 850	46.3
NEBRASKA	220 444	66.8	12.4	29.3	25.1	33.2	26.3	6.8	7.3	-10.9	12.1	150 880	47.3
NEVADA	249 469	75.8	7.3	34.6	33.9	24.2	21.8	2.3	2.2	-5.6	3.1	136 812	39.9
NEW HAMPSHIRE	149 169	70.9	7.4	32.2	31.3	29.1	24.5	4.6	2.3	-8.0	8.0	92 214	44.9
NEW JERSEY	898 197	64.7	4.3	32.2	28.2	35.3	29.7	5.6	-0.8	-8.0	14.2	690 495	44.1
NEW MEXICO	209 133	71.2	8.6	29.1	33.5	28.8	24.8	4.0	3.5	-11.1	7.7	138 572	41.4
NEW YORK	2 387 110	68.2	5.8	33.4	29.0	31.8	26.6	5.2	0.7	-6.8	10.7	1 552 789	46.8
NORTH CAROLINA ...	959 936	70.6	9.1	33.0	28.5	29.4	25.4	4.0	4.0	-7.2	8.3	625 273	43.9
NORTH DAKOTA	90 271	66.5	14.9	27.9	23.7	33.5	26.9	6.6	9.8	-12.3	12.4	61 339	48.3
OHIO	1 439 414	67.7	8.7	30.5	28.4	32.3	27.3	5.0	3.6	-9.7	11.2	979 029	46.1
OKLAHOMA	415 803	66.3	10.4	26.8	29.2	33.7	28.1	5.7	5.3	-13.4	12.6	298 823	45.7
OREGON	450 234	71.0	10.2	30.4	30.4	29.0	23.8	5.2	5.1	-9.8	7.9	280 216	44.0
PENNSYLVANIA	1 553 479	62.6	7.0	28.3	27.2	37.4	31.6	5.8	1.9	-11.9	16.3	1 223 077	46.0
RHODE ISLAND	141 757	65.0	8.0	29.7	27.2	35.0	29.0	6.1	2.9	-10.5	13.9	97 601	49.1
SOUTH CAROLINA ...	455 598	69.4	8.4	30.5	30.5	30.6	26.6	4.0	3.3	-9.7	9.5	315 303	42.9
SOUTH DAKOTA	94 881	65.0	12.9	26.9	25.2	35.0	28.0	7.0	7.8	-13.3	13.9	69 616	46.5
TENNESSEE	676 609	69.0	8.2	31.0	29.7	31.0	26.3	4.7	3.1	-9.2	9.9	459 403	44.4
TEXAS	2 113 820	73.4	10.6	34.9	27.9	26.6	22.5	4.1	5.5	-5.3	5.5	1 306 279	41.5
UTAH	162 205	71.8	13.5	32.2	26.1	28.2	23.2	5.1	8.4	-8.0	7.1	119 831	36.9
VERMONT	82 060	70.2	9.1	30.1	31.0	29.8	24.7	5.1	4.0	-10.1	8.7	49 652	46.7
VIRGINIA	840 352	73.1	8.6	34.9	29.5	26.9	23.1	3.8	3.5	-5.3	5.8	504 099	43.3
WASHINGTON	762 866	74.1	9.4	34.7	29.9	25.9	21.4	4.6	4.3	-5.5	4.8	422 695	44.5
WEST VIRGINIA	230 105	60.4	7.8	22.4	30.1	39.6	33.5	6.1	2.7	-17.8	18.5	188 734	46.9
WISCONSIN	691 267	68.7	10.9	31.3	26.5	31.3	25.4	5.8	5.8	-8.9	10.2	451 227	46.4
WYOMING	62 451	71.4	12.4	28.0	31.0	28.6	24.1	4.5	7.3	-12.2	7.5	37 781	45.6

STATE	Number	Total family households	Married-couple family households		Female family householder		Male family householder		Total nonfamily households	Two or more adults	Living alone	+/− U.S. percent family households	+/− U.S. percent one-person households
			Total	With own children under 18 years	Total	With own children under 18 years	Total	With own children under 18 years					
	230	231	232	233	234	235	236	237	238	239	240	241	242
UNITED STATES ...	78 983 497	66.8	55.2	23.5	8.4	4.6	3.3	1.7	33.2	5.9	27.3	-1.7	1.5
ALABAMA	1 273 242	70.5	59.4	24.8	8.2	4.3	2.9	1.4	29.5	3.5	26.0	2.0	0.2
ALASKA	166 838	68.3	56.3	29.3	7.7	5.6	4.3	2.9	31.7	7.6	24.0	-0.2	-1.8
ARIZONA	1 397 040	64.7	53.4	19.7	7.9	4.6	3.4	1.9	35.3	7.4	27.9	-3.8	2.1
ARKANSAS...........	852 927	70.6	59.0	23.9	8.4	4.8	3.2	1.7	29.4	3.8	25.6	2.1	-0.2
CALIFORNIA	6 673 836	62.7	50.4	20.7	8.8	4.6	3.6	1.8	37.3	8.3	29.0	-5.8	3.2
COLORADO............	1 327 444	64.1	53.4	24.0	7.6	4.7	3.1	1.8	35.9	8.3	27.6	-4.4	1.8
CONNECTICUT	1 059 715	67.1	55.8	24.5	8.2	4.1	3.0	1.3	32.9	5.6	27.3	-1.4	1.5
DELAWARE	227 711	68.0	56.3	23.3	8.5	4.6	3.2	1.6	32.0	6.1	25.8	-0.5	0.0
DISTRICT OF COLUMBIA............	83 742	30.8	26.8	9.3	2.8	1.2	1.1	0.4	69.2	16.0	53.2	-37.7	27.4
FLORIDA.................	4 566 541	64.0	53.0	17.7	7.9	4.2	3.1	1.6	36.0	6.8	29.2	-4.5	3.4
GEORGIA...............	2 017 242	70.2	59.2	26.3	8.0	4.2	3.1	1.6	29.8	5.6	24.1	1.7	-1.7
HAWAII....................	122 694	62.7	51.9	22.0	7.4	4.1	3.4	1.8	37.3	10.0	27.3	-5.8	1.5
IDAHO.....................	428 555	71.3	59.8	27.9	8.0	5.2	3.5	2.2	28.7	5.7	23.0	2.8	-2.8
ILLINOIS..................	3 405 787	66.0	55.0	24.4	7.9	4.1	3.1	1.4	34.0	5.4	28.6	-2.5	2.8
INDIANA.................	2 050 401	69.0	56.8	25.1	8.8	5.3	3.4	2.0	31.0	5.1	25.9	0.5	0.1
IOWA.....................	1 088 899	67.2	56.5	24.4	7.6	4.9	3.0	1.8	32.8	5.4	27.5	-1.3	1.7
KANSAS.................	899 972	67.5	57.0	25.3	7.6	4.8	2.9	1.8	32.5	4.9	27.6	-1.0	1.8
KENTUCKY.............	1 439 760	70.2	56.8	24.8	10.1	5.8	3.4	1.8	29.8	4.1	25.7	1.7	-0.1
LOUISIANA	1 105 452	69.4	56.8	25.5	9.0	4.8	3.6	1.9	30.6	4.8	25.8	0.9	0.0
MAINE	505 297	66.1	53.7	22.4	9.0	5.8	3.4	2.1	33.9	6.9	27.0	-2.4	1.2
MARYLAND	1 302 282	68.3	56.9	25.3	8.1	4.2	3.3	1.7	31.7	6.2	25.5	-0.2	-0.3
MASSACHUSETTS ...	2 085 454	64.0	51.6	23.0	9.3	4.7	3.1	1.2	36.0	7.1	28.9	-4.5	3.1
MICHIGAN	3 088 895	68.4	56.1	24.8	8.8	5.0	3.5	1.9	31.6	5.4	26.2	-0.1	0.4
MINNESOTA	1 735 421	66.3	55.8	25.7	7.4	4.7	3.1	1.7	33.7	6.5	27.2	-2.2	1.4
MISSISSIPPI	685 549	71.4	59.6	25.6	8.5	4.5	3.3	1.7	28.6	3.6	25.0	2.0	0.8
MISSOURI..............	1 882 812	67.9	55.9	24.2	8.6	5.2	3.3	2.0	32.1	5.1	27.1	-0.6	1.3
MONTANA..............	331 568	65.9	54.8	23.0	7.6	5.1	3.5	2.1	34.1	6.1	27.9	-2.6	2.1
NEBRASKA.............	603 693	66.6	56.1	25.2	7.6	4.9	2.9	1.6	33.4	5.4	28.0	-1.9	2.2
NEVADA.................	550 056	64.0	50.9	19.8	8.9	5.0	4.3	2.3	36.0	8.7	27.2	-4.5	1.4
NEW HAMPSHIRE.....	456 148	68.5	56.3	26.0	8.5	5.3	3.7	2.2	31.5	6.9	24.5	0.0	-1.3
NEW JERSEY..........	2 182 369	68.8	57.5	25.6	8.3	3.4	3.0	1.1	31.2	4.8	26.4	0.3	0.6
NEW MEXICO..........	362 890	64.0	52.6	20.5	8.2	4.9	3.1	1.8	36.0	5.9	30.0	-4.5	4.2
NEW YORK.............	4 763 779	63.8	51.9	22.6	8.6	4.2	3.3	1.4	36.2	6.1	30.1	-4.7	4.3
NORTH CAROLINA ...	2 321 636	68.9	58.2	23.8	7.8	4.3	3.0	1.6	31.1	5.3	25.8	0.4	0.0
NORTH DAKOTA.......	242 300	64.4	54.9	24.6	6.6	4.3	2.9	1.5	35.6	5.8	29.8	-4.1	4.0
OHIO	3 797 190	68.1	55.5	24.2	9.1	5.2	3.5	1.9	31.9	5.0	26.9	-0.4	1.1
OKLAHOMA	1 056 941	68.5	56.5	23.4	8.8	5.2	3.2	1.8	31.5	4.1	27.4	0.0	1.6
OREGON	1 177 750	65.5	53.3	21.9	8.8	5.5	3.4	2.0	34.5	7.6	26.9	-3.0	1.1
PENNSYLVANIA.......	4 129 114	67.5	55.4	23.2	8.7	4.3	3.4	1.7	32.5	4.8	27.6	-1.0	1.8
RHODE ISLAND	351 002	64.0	50.9	21.2	9.8	5.2	3.3	1.5	36.0	6.2	29.8	-4.5	4.0
SOUTH CAROLINA ...	1 076 317	69.7	58.4	23.9	8.0	4.4	3.2	1.7	30.3	5.0	25.3	1.2	-0.5
SOUTH DAKOTA.......	267 618	66.6	56.5	25.2	7.0	4.7	3.1	1.8	33.4	5.1	28.3	-1.9	2.5
TENNESSEE............	1 828 668	69.8	57.5	24.0	9.0	4.9	3.2	1.6	30.2	4.4	25.8	1.3	0.0
TEXAS....................	4 478 556	67.5	56.7	24.4	7.9	4.5	2.9	1.5	32.5	5.3	27.2	-1.0	1.4
UTAH.....................	620 009	76.6	65.1	35.6	8.3	5.0	3.1	1.7	23.4	5.2	18.2	8.1	-7.6
VERMONT...............	233 583	66.0	53.7	23.9	8.7	5.9	3.6	2.3	34.0	7.8	26.2	-2.5	0.4
VIRGINIA.................	2 004 156	68.0	57.3	24.8	7.8	4.2	3.0	1.6	32.0	6.2	25.8	-0.5	0.0
WASHINGTON..........	1 907 298	65.5	53.5	23.4	8.5	5.5	3.5	2.1	34.5	7.4	27.1	-3.0	1.3
WEST VIRGINIA	701 781	69.1	55.5	22.2	9.9	5.2	3.7	1.9	30.9	4.1	26.8	0.6	1.0
WISCONSIN.............	1 888 577	66.4	55.8	24.5	7.4	4.5	3.3	1.8	33.6	6.4	27.2	-2.1	1.4
WYOMING	176 982	67.7	56.5	25.0	7.9	5.4	3.3	2.1	32.3	5.9	26.5	-0.8	0.7

Table A-2. States — Age, Ethnicity, and Household Structure

STATE	Number	Black or African American households										+/− U.S. percent family households	+/− U.S. percent one-person households
		Family households (percent)							Nonfamily households (percent)				
		Total family households	Married-couple family households		Female family householder		Male family householder		Total nonfamily households	Two or more adults	Living alone		
			Total	With own children under 18 years	Total	With own children under 18 years	Total	With own children under 18 years					
	243	244	245	246	247	248	249	250	251	252	253	254	255
UNITED STATES ...	12 023 966	68.3	32.1	16.7	30.5	19.2	5.7	2.9	31.7	4.6	27.2	-0.2	1.4
ALABAMA	413 673	69.8	33.2	17.1	31.6	19.4	4.9	2.2	30.2	3.1	27.1	1.3	1.3
ALASKA	7 508	71.4	47.4	33.0	19.2	14.7	4.8	4.1	28.6	6.7	21.9	2.9	-3.9
ARIZONA	55 071	64.7	36.5	19.9	21.4	14.6	6.7	4.3	35.3	7.0	28.3	-3.8	2.5
ARKANSAS	145 438	69.5	32.5	17.2	31.6	20.7	5.4	2.7	30.5	3.5	27.0	1.0	1.2
CALIFORNIA	788 392	66.3	32.1	16.7	28.1	17.6	6.0	3.3	33.7	5.5	28.2	-2.2	2.4
COLORADO	59 518	65.2	38.6	21.8	21.3	15.0	5.4	3.3	34.8	5.5	29.2	-3.3	3.4
CONNECTICUT	105 870	68.3	31.0	16.7	31.9	21.6	5.4	3.0	31.7	4.6	27.1	-0.2	1.3
DELAWARE	52 362	69.9	34.2	16.8	29.7	19.4	6.0	3.4	30.1	5.9	24.3	1.4	-1.5
DISTRICT OF COLUMBIA	139 143	55.5	20.0	6.8	30.2	16.2	5.3	2.2	44.5	5.7	38.8	-13.0	13.0
FLORIDA	752 783	71.9	34.8	19.2	30.7	19.8	6.4	3.4	28.1	5.2	22.8	3.4	-3.0
GEORGIA	803 387	70.2	34.3	19.1	30.3	19.1	5.6	2.8	29.8	5.3	24.6	1.7	-1.2
HAWAII	7 327	73.5	61.6	42.3	7.3	5.9	4.6	3.6	26.5	5.0	21.4	5.0	-4.4
IDAHO	1 492	62.5	52.0	34.5	8.1	4.8	2.4	1.3	37.5	10.3	27.1	-6.0	1.3
ILLINOIS	624 639	68.5	29.3	14.2	33.4	20.3	5.8	2.8	31.5	4.1	27.4	0.0	1.6
INDIANA	184 808	66.1	30.3	14.8	30.2	20.4	5.5	3.2	33.9	4.7	29.3	-2.4	3.5
IOWA	20 969	65.0	31.6	17.4	27.5	20.9	5.9	3.6	35.0	6.0	29.0	-3.5	3.2
KANSAS	54 464	67.1	34.2	18.8	27.1	18.8	5.9	3.8	32.9	4.3	28.6	-1.4	2.8
KENTUCKY	111 437	64.7	29.7	14.7	30.1	20.5	4.9	2.6	35.3	4.4	30.8	-3.8	5.0
LOUISIANA	478 950	71.9	32.6	17.1	33.7	21.1	5.6	2.8	28.1	3.6	24.5	3.4	-1.3
MAINE	1 886	63.3	37.1	23.0	19.5	17.7	6.8	5.1	36.7	11.0	25.7	-5.2	-0.1
MARYLAND	525 794	68.7	35.0	17.8	28.1	17.2	5.6	2.9	31.3	5.2	26.1	0.2	0.3
MASSACHUSETTS ...	115 736	66.6	31.2	18.3	29.8	20.2	5.7	3.0	33.4	5.8	27.6	-1.9	1.8
MICHIGAN	491 963	67.1	28.3	13.9	32.8	20.9	6.0	3.0	32.9	4.4	28.5	-1.4	2.7
MINNESOTA	55 913	66.0	29.5	19.8	30.0	24.2	6.5	4.3	34.0	6.3	27.7	-2.5	1.9
MISSISSIPPI	339 157	72.6	32.4	17.7	34.2	21.4	6.1	2.9	27.4	3.3	24.1	4.1	-1.7
MISSOURI	227 340	65.9	27.6	13.9	32.8	21.5	5.6	3.0	34.1	4.2	29.8	-2.6	4.0
MONTANA	858	52.9	35.7	21.3	12.5	9.3	4.8	4.1	47.1	9.7	37.4	-15.6	11.6
NEBRASKA	24 346	65.0	28.6	15.9	30.5	21.9	5.9	3.3	35.0	4.9	30.1	-3.5	4.3
NEVADA	49 184	66.2	34.3	17.0	24.8	17.4	7.1	4.3	33.8	7.0	26.8	-2.3	1.0
NEW HAMPSHIRE	3 151	65.2	44.0	25.0	15.2	11.6	6.0	4.9	34.8	10.0	24.8	-3.3	-1.0
NEW JERSEY	382 711	68.9	33.3	17.1	29.5	17.5	6.2	3.2	31.1	4.4	26.6	0.4	0.8
NEW MEXICO	12 895	64.6	40.8	21.7	17.9	12.3	5.9	4.6	35.4	5.5	29.9	-3.9	4.1
NEW YORK	1 031 866	66.8	28.5	14.9	32.5	19.6	5.8	2.7	33.2	4.3	28.8	-1.7	3.0
NORTH CAROLINA ...	627 854	69.1	35.5	17.8	28.4	17.6	5.2	2.5	30.9	4.4	26.5	0.6	0.7
NORTH DAKOTA	1 153	66.3	44.8	29.5	11.1	11.1	10.3	7.6	33.7	7.1	26.6	-2.2	0.8
OHIO	489 208	64.0	27.7	13.1	31.1	21.2	5.3	2.8	36.0	4.3	31.7	-4.5	5.9
OKLAHOMA	92 704	66.8	32.6	17.7	28.8	20.0	5.4	3.3	33.2	4.2	29.0	-1.7	3.2
OREGON	18 618	63.4	32.9	18.6	24.2	17.5	6.3	3.7	36.6	7.7	28.9	-5.1	3.1
PENNSYLVANIA	434 217	64.9	26.1	12.3	32.6	20.0	6.2	3.2	35.1	4.6	30.5	-3.6	4.7
RHODE ISLAND	15 828	66.2	31.5	18.0	29.0	22.2	5.6	3.6	33.8	5.3	28.5	-2.3	2.7
SOUTH CAROLINA ...	408 372	71.7	34.9	17.8	31.3	18.9	5.5	2.5	28.3	3.5	24.8	3.2	-1.0
SOUTH DAKOTA	1 349	68.3	44.7	28.8	13.2	10.2	10.5	7.3	31.7	10.7	20.9	-0.2	-4.9
TENNESSEE	331 948	69.2	31.2	16.1	32.3	20.7	5.7	2.7	30.8	4.2	26.6	0.7	0.8
TEXAS	842 713	68.6	35.2	19.0	28.1	17.8	5.3	2.8	31.4	4.1	27.3	0.1	1.5
UTAH	5 112	69.5	42.2	26.4	19.6	14.1	7.7	5.7	30.5	6.9	23.6	1.0	-2.2
VERMONT	878	55.5	31.4	20.0	17.2	15.8	6.8	5.0	44.5	14.0	30.5	-13.0	4.7
VIRGINIA	493 797	69.4	37.0	18.8	26.9	16.9	5.5	2.8	30.6	4.9	25.7	0.9	-0.1
WASHINGTON	68 959	64.8	35.9	21.6	22.4	16.0	6.4	4.2	35.2	6.3	28.9	-3.7	3.1
WEST VIRGINIA	21 811	60.1	29.3	13.2	24.7	14.6	6.1	3.2	39.9	4.6	35.3	-8.4	9.5
WISCONSIN	98 260	68.7	25.7	13.7	37.3	27.4	5.7	3.4	31.3	4.9	26.4	0.2	0.6
WYOMING	1 154	64.1	45.0	25.7	11.7	10.1	7.5	5.8	35.9	6.0	29.9	-4.4	4.1

Table A-2. States — Age, Ethnicity, and Household Structure

			American Indian and Alaska Native households										
			Family households (percent)						Nonfamily households (percent)				
			Married-couple family households		Female family householder		Male family householder						
STATE	Number	Total family households	Total	With own children under 18 years	Total	With own children under 18 years	Total	With own children under 18 years	Total nonfamily households	Two or more adults	Living alone	+/− U.S. percent family households	+/− U.S. percent one-person households
	256	257	258	259	260	261	262	263	264	265	266	267	268
UNITED STATES ...	770 334	73.2	45.0	25.5	20.7	13.3	7.5	4.4	26.8	6.2	20.6	4.7	−5.2
ALABAMA	8 368	73.6	54.9	30.1	13.0	8.7	5.6	3.6	26.4	4.1	22.3	5.1	−3.5
ALASKA	26 616	72.3	38.9	25.8	23.3	15.8	10.0	6.2	27.7	5.9	21.8	3.8	−4.0
ARIZONA	67 858	78.7	42.5	26.8	28.1	16.7	8.1	4.6	21.3	4.5	16.8	10.2	−9.0
ARKANSAS	6 468	70.8	53.4	27.8	11.8	7.9	5.6	3.7	29.2	5.4	23.8	2.3	−2.0
CALIFORNIA	96 479	72.7	45.9	26.6	19.1	11.8	7.7	4.3	27.3	8.0	19.2	4.2	−6.6
COLORADO	14 528	70.0	44.8	25.5	18.3	12.5	6.9	3.3	30.0	8.3	21.7	1.5	−4.1
CONNECTICUT	3 278	63.0	37.8	17.8	18.5	11.4	6.7	2.8	37.0	6.7	30.3	−5.5	4.5
DELAWARE	1 175	64.3	41.6	18.6	14.8	9.9	7.9	4.9	35.7	13.4	22.3	−4.2	−3.5
DISTRICT OF COLUMBIA	763	43.6	15.2	7.1	21.9	12.1	6.6	1.7	56.4	11.4	45.0	−24.9	19.2
FLORIDA	19 623	67.7	46.1	22.1	15.5	10.3	6.0	3.1	32.3	8.5	23.9	−0.8	−1.9
GEORGIA	8 251	74.5	55.8	29.8	13.3	8.3	5.4	2.3	25.5	7.2	18.3	6.0	−7.5
HAWAII	1 109	69.8	48.6	24.6	15.1	10.6	6.0	4.8	30.2	11.2	19.0	1.3	−6.8
IDAHO	5 462	76.2	48.6	27.6	19.0	12.3	8.5	5.3	23.8	6.2	17.6	7.7	−8.2
ILLINOIS	10 180	71.1	48.8	31.2	14.7	9.6	7.6	4.5	28.9	6.5	22.3	2.6	−3.5
INDIANA	6 546	69.0	48.4	24.9	13.6	9.1	7.0	5.1	31.0	9.1	21.9	0.5	−3.9
IOWA	2 792	71.0	38.3	25.0	23.9	18.0	8.8	4.9	29.0	8.9	20.1	2.5	−5.7
KANSAS	8 420	71.7	50.1	26.3	16.4	11.4	5.2	3.0	28.3	6.4	21.9	3.2	−3.9
KENTUCKY	3 597	63.2	42.6	21.4	15.0	11.3	5.6	3.5	36.8	9.1	27.7	5.3	1.9
LOUISIANA	8 590	75.6	51.6	28.8	16.8	10.4	7.2	4.6	24.4	4.6	19.8	7.1	−6.0
MAINE	2 727	64.1	38.0	22.6	18.4	15.3	7.8	4.6	35.9	10.0	25.9	−4.4	0.1
MARYLAND	5 812	71.6	47.6	23.7	17.4	10.5	6.5	3.8	28.4	6.5	22.0	3.1	−3.8
MASSACHUSETTS ...	5 538	67.2	38.8	19.6	21.9	14.4	6.5	2.9	32.8	6.5	26.4	−1.3	0.6
MICHIGAN	20 422	70.1	45.0	24.5	18.0	12.1	7.0	4.3	29.9	8.2	21.8	1.6	−4.0
MINNESOTA	16 579	70.7	32.8	19.4	28.2	20.2	9.7	6.5	29.3	7.1	22.2	2.2	−3.6
MISSISSIPPI	3 660	73.5	42.0	24.7	25.0	14.0	6.5	4.2	26.5	5.8	20.7	5.0	−5.1
MISSOURI	10 006	67.9	48.9	25.0	13.8	8.3	5.2	3.9	32.1	7.3	24.9	−0.6	−0.9
MONTANA	15 834	78.9	44.2	27.6	26.7	17.5	8.0	5.4	21.1	4.3	16.8	10.4	−9.0
NEBRASKA	4 189	75.2	37.0	23.3	29.0	21.2	9.3	5.8	24.8	5.6	19.2	6.7	−6.6
NEVADA	9 055	69.4	40.8	21.2	20.1	11.4	8.4	5.0	30.6	7.3	23.3	0.9	−2.5
NEW HAMPSHIRE	947	69.4	53.6	23.2	7.8	5.2	7.9	4.2	30.6	9.5	21.1	0.9	−4.7
NEW JERSEY	5 674	74.4	46.9	26.3	18.8	10.9	8.7	3.9	25.6	6.4	19.2	5.9	−6.6
NEW MEXICO	47 487	79.1	43.2	27.2	26.3	15.5	9.7	6.1	20.9	3.6	17.3	10.6	−8.5
NEW YORK	25 618	69.3	37.3	22.2	24.2	15.6	7.8	4.2	30.7	6.4	24.4	0.8	−1.4
NORTH CAROLINA ...	34 775	75.1	48.8	25.4	19.4	11.9	7.0	4.2	24.9	4.6	20.3	6.6	−5.5
NORTH DAKOTA	8 925	76.7	35.7	22.6	31.8	22.7	9.3	6.7	23.3	5.7	17.6	8.2	−8.2
OHIO	10 348	65.1	41.3	20.7	17.2	11.3	6.7	4.4	34.9	8.2	26.7	−3.4	0.9
OKLAHOMA	85 177	74.4	52.0	27.4	16.8	10.4	5.5	3.1	25.6	4.2	21.4	5.9	−4.4
OREGON	14 746	68.6	42.6	21.7	18.6	12.9	7.4	5.1	31.4	8.0	22.6	0.1	−0.2
PENNSYLVANIA	7 184	66.7	41.9	21.9	17.2	10.9	7.6	4.1	33.3	7.0	26.3	−1.8	0.5
RHODE ISLAND	1 607	64.5	29.9	15.5	29.7	22.2	4.8	2.3	35.5	2.4	33.1	−4.0	7.3
SOUTH CAROLINA ...	5 374	71.5	50.9	25.8	15.6	8.6	5.0	2.4	28.5	5.0	23.5	3.0	−2.3
SOUTH DAKOTA	15 422	78.8	30.5	21.2	36.8	24.9	11.5	7.7	21.2	4.3	16.9	10.3	−8.9
TENNESSEE	6 191	71.3	52.2	28.0	13.7	8.4	5.4	2.3	28.7	7.0	21.7	2.8	−4.1
TEXAS	39 513	72.6	52.0	28.3	14.5	9.6	6.1	3.4	27.4	6.5	20.9	4.1	−4.9
UTAH	7 729	78.0	46.1	31.4	23.1	15.8	8.8	4.9	22.0	6.3	15.7	9.5	−10.1
VERMONT	1 038	63.8	41.0	21.1	16.5	12.0	6.3	4.7	36.2	11.8	24.4	−4.7	−1.4
VIRGINIA	8 274	70.5	51.9	26.6	14.4	8.8	4.2	2.9	29.5	9.2	20.3	2.0	−5.5
WASHINGTON	29 399	71.1	40.2	22.7	22.0	15.6	9.0	5.6	28.9	7.9	20.9	2.6	−4.9
WEST VIRGINIA	1 595	68.0	49.7	24.1	10.6	6.3	7.8	2.6	32.0	6.3	25.6	−0.5	−0.2
WISCONSIN	16 033	71.8	36.7	21.3	26.5	18.9	8.5	5.2	28.2	7.5	20.7	3.3	−5.1
WYOMING	3 353	74.5	42.1	23.6	23.9	15.6	8.5	5.2	25.5	4.6	20.9	6.0	−4.9

			Asian, Hawaiian, and Pacific Islander households										
			Family households (percent)						Nonfamily households (percent)				
			Married-couple family households		Female family householder		Male family householder						
STATE	Number	Total family households	Total	With own children under 18 years	Total	With own children under 18 years	Total	With own children under 18 years	Total nonfamily households	Two or more adults	Living alone	+/− U.S. percent family households	+/− U.S. percent one-person households
	269	270	271	272	273	274	275	276	277	278	279	280	281
UNITED STATES ...	3 229 278	75.2	61.6	35.9	9.0	4.2	4.6	1.5	24.8	6.3	18.5	6.7	−7.3
ALABAMA	9 558	70.0	56.4	33.1	8.8	6.0	4.9	1.6	30.0	8.0	22.0	1.5	−3.8
ALASKA	7 206	77.6	57.9	38.6	12.4	8.4	7.3	4.6	22.4	5.3	17.0	9.1	−8.8
ARIZONA	31 575	69.5	57.0	34.2	7.9	4.5	4.6	1.9	30.5	8.0	22.5	1.0	−3.3
ARKANSAS	6 010	72.1	57.3	37.0	8.5	5.2	6.3	3.2	27.9	6.1	21.8	3.6	−4.0
CALIFORNIA	1 136 310	77.2	61.8	35.3	10.4	4.6	5.0	1.5	22.8	6.2	16.7	8.7	−9.1
COLORADO	31 027	69.8	57.0	34.4	8.5	5.4	4.3	1.7	30.2	7.4	22.8	1.3	−3.0
CONNECTICUT	26 265	72.9	64.1	41.0	5.7	3.2	3.1	1.1	27.1	6.5	20.6	4.4	−5.2
DELAWARE	5 434	78.4	67.2	37.4	7.0	3.5	4.2	2.2	21.6	6.1	15.6	9.9	−10.2
DISTRICT OF COLUMBIA	6 502	40.7	28.3	12.8	8.6	3.5	3.8	0.4	59.3	11.3	48.0	−27.8	22.2
FLORIDA	85 036	74.4	66.5	35.9	9.0	4.9	4.8	1.9	25.6	7.0	18.6	5.9	−7.2
GEORGIA	51 421	78.3	66.6	43.3	7.0	3.7	4.7	1.5	21.7	6.2	15.5	9.8	−10.3
HAWAII	201 643	75.6	57.1	24.3	13.2	4.7	5.3	1.7	24.4	4.2	20.2	7.1	−5.6
IDAHO	3 911	65.5	54.1	29.8	7.1	4.9	4.2	2.5	34.5	7.8	26.7	−3.0	0.9
ILLINOIS	136 187	74.5	63.8	37.0	7.0	3.0	3.7	1.0	25.5	5.6	19.9	6.0	−5.9
INDIANA	20 022	64.8	56.3	32.9	5.6	3.5	2.9	1.1	35.2	9.3	25.9	−3.7	0.1
IOWA	10 693	68.5	55.2	35.5	8.7	5.4	4.6	1.7	31.5	9.0	22.6	0.0	−3.2
KANSAS	14 376	69.9	57.9	36.7	7.1	4.3	5.0	2.0	30.1	8.5	21.6	1.4	−4.2
KENTUCKY	9 739	67.0	58.0	34.8	5.8	3.1	3.2	1.3	33.0	7.5	25.5	−1.5	−0.3
LOUISIANA	16 831	74.5	61.1	39.4	8.3	4.9	5.1	1.7	25.5	7.3	18.2	6.0	−7.6
MAINE	2 168	70.9	50.2	29.2	15.6	9.8	5.2	4.1	29.1	7.2	21.8	2.4	−4.0
MARYLAND	65 010	78.1	67.0	38.4	7.1	3.4	4.0	1.3	21.9	5.3	16.6	9.6	−9.2
MASSACHUSETTS ...	73 735	70.9	58.5	35.6	8.2	4.6	4.2	1.3	29.1	8.6	20.5	2.4	−5.3
MICHIGAN	56 378	72.8	63.9	39.4	5.9	3.0	3.0	1.0	27.2	7.3	19.9	4.3	−5.9
MINNESOTA	35 604	74.8	60.4	43.3	9.7	6.8	4.7	2.3	25.2	6.7	18.5	6.3	−7.3
MISSISSIPPI	5 165	72.7	60.5	37.6	8.2	4.3	3.9	1.3	27.3	8.3	19.1	4.2	−6.7
MISSOURI	21 131	65.7	53.1	30.3	8.4	5.1	4.2	1.8	34.3	8.1	26.1	−2.8	0.3
MONTANA	1 425	58.5	48.1	28.2	9.1	6.2	1.3	0.8	41.5	9.1	32.4	−10.0	6.6
NEBRASKA	6 506	67.7	55.2	32.6	8.0	4.3	4.5	2.1	32.3	9.3	23.0	−0.8	−2.8
NEVADA	30 531	71.9	54.5	29.0	11.7	6.4	5.8	2.3	28.1	8.3	19.8	3.4	−6.0
NEW HAMPSHIRE	4 669	75.1	64.9	42.2	6.7	4.5	3.5	1.2	24.9	6.5	18.4	6.6	−7.4
NEW JERSEY	145 230	83.0	73.2	45.5	6.3	3.0	3.5	1.0	17.0	4.4	12.7	14.5	−13.1
NEW MEXICO	6 284	69.1	55.0	32.9	10.4	6.3	3.7	1.9	30.9	7.2	23.7	0.6	−2.1
NEW YORK	323 779	74.9	61.9	35.7	8.1	3.1	4.9	1.2	25.1	6.3	18.8	6.4	−7.0
NORTH CAROLINA ...	33 599	75.7	63.3	40.6	7.2	4.4	5.1	2.3	24.3	7.2	17.2	7.2	−8.6
NORTH DAKOTA	1 111	73.0	56.7	36.9	12.6	9.5	3.7	1.3	27.0	7.0	20.0	4.5	−5.8
OHIO	46 043	69.1	59.4	34.7	6.0	3.0	3.7	1.2	30.9	7.6	23.2	0.6	−2.6
OKLAHOMA	14 862	67.2	54.2	33.1	8.1	4.3	4.9	1.7	32.8	8.8	24.1	−1.3	−1.7
OREGON	33 763	69.8	56.8	33.9	8.3	4.7	4.7	1.5	30.2	7.8	22.5	1.3	−3.3
PENNSYLVANIA	68 958	72.0	60.7	36.8	7.4	3.9	4.0	1.1	28.0	6.2	21.8	3.5	−4.0
RHODE ISLAND	7 056	69.9	53.8	37.2	10.8	7.7	5.4	2.9	30.1	10.0	20.1	1.4	−5.7
SOUTH CAROLINA ...	11 850	72.1	60.8	38.4	6.7	4.0	4.6	2.7	27.9	7.4	20.5	3.6	−5.3
SOUTH DAKOTA	1 288	61.7	48.3	27.7	9.0	7.2	4.4	3.3	38.3	11.0	27.3	−6.8	1.5
TENNESSEE	17 622	71.5	60.7	36.7	6.9	4.2	3.8	1.6	28.5	7.0	21.5	3.0	−4.3
TEXAS	179 266	74.9	63.4	40.1	7.2	3.8	4.3	1.3	25.1	5.7	19.4	6.4	−6.4
UTAH	13 951	76.6	62.6	40.5	8.4	4.6	5.6	2.2	23.4	8.2	15.3	8.1	−10.5
VERMONT	1 270	70.5	59.4	37.6	9.0	4.7	2.0	0.9	29.5	7.4	22.1	2.0	−3.7
VIRGINIA	78 401	76.7	64.3	37.8	8.2	4.0	4.2	1.1	23.3	6.7	16.6	8.2	−9.2
WASHINGTON	106 931	72.1	57.1	33.5	10.2	5.6	4.8	2.0	27.9	6.3	21.5	3.6	−4.3
WEST VIRGINIA	3 224	64.9	56.7	32.1	6.1	3.1	2.1	0.5	35.1	10.5	24.6	−3.6	−1.2
WISCONSIN	21 877	71.3	59.7	41.4	7.4	5.2	4.2	1.9	28.7	7.7	21.0	2.8	−4.8
WYOMING	845	64.5	52.7	27.3	9.3	6.7	2.5	1.3	35.5	6.3	29.2	−4.0	3.4

STATE	Number	Total family households	Married-couple family households Total	With own children under 18 years	Female family householder Total	With own children under 18 years	Male family householder Total	With own children under 18 years	Total nonfamily households	Two or more adults	Living alone	+/− U.S. percent family households	+/− U.S. percent one-person households
	282	283	284	285	286	287	288	289	290	291	292	293	294
UNITED STATES ...	9 272 610	80.7	55.1	37.2	17.3	11.5	8.3	4.2	19.3	5.4	13.9	12.2	-11.9
ALABAMA	19 798	76.0	55.8	36.5	10.5	7.1	9.8	3.3	24.0	8.4	15.6	7.5	-10.2
ALASKA	6 407	75.5	52.0	35.7	15.3	12.2	8.2	6.2	24.5	8.0	16.5	7.0	-9.3
ARIZONA	331 850	81.7	55.8	38.2	17.0	11.5	9.0	5.2	18.3	5.6	12.7	13.2	-13.1
ARKANSAS.............	21 674	80.6	58.1	42.5	11.2	8.3	11.4	6.3	19.4	7.1	12.3	12.1	-13.5
CALIFORNIA............	2 574 994	84.7	59.3	42.7	16.6	11.0	8.8	4.9	15.3	4.8	10.5	16.2	-15.3
COLORADO.............	208 192	76.7	53.3	34.4	15.3	10.6	8.1	4.2	23.3	6.1	17.2	8.2	-8.6
CONNECTICUT	91 298	78.4	41.1	26.5	29.7	22.8	7.6	4.2	21.6	5.7	15.8	9.9	-10.0
DELAWARE	9 662	79.8	53.5	35.7	17.1	12.2	9.1	6.0	20.2	6.9	13.4	11.3	-12.4
DISTRICT OF COLUMBIA............	14 449	59.6	35.5	22.5	13.8	8.4	10.2	4.3	40.4	10.5	29.9	-8.9	4.1
FLORIDA.................	851 742	77.2	55.2	30.3	15.1	8.6	6.9	3.1	22.8	6.1	16.7	8.7	-9.1
GEORGIA................	102 650	80.5	58.4	42.8	9.4	6.6	12.7	4.3	19.5	9.2	10.2	12.0	-15.6
HAWAII..................	21 490	76.0	48.9	29.5	19.5	13.8	7.5	5.0	24.0	8.1	15.9	7.5	-9.9
IDAHO...................	25 016	83.1	61.7	47.1	12.8	10.2	8.5	4.7	16.9	5.7	11.2	14.6	-14.6
ILLINOIS.................	373 499	84.2	61.4	44.9	13.4	8.9	9.4	4.5	15.8	4.6	11.1	15.7	-14.7
INDIANA.................	56 960	77.1	53.9	36.4	13.0	9.1	10.2	4.9	22.9	7.7	15.2	8.6	-10.6
IOWA....................	20 905	76.3	53.3	38.4	12.9	10.0	10.1	5.8	23.7	8.7	15.0	7.8	-10.8
KANSAS.................	49 451	78.7	58.2	42.3	11.9	9.3	8.6	4.3	21.3	5.8	15.4	10.2	-10.4
KENTUCKY.............	15 340	69.4	49.7	32.1	9.9	7.5	9.7	4.1	30.6	10.3	20.3	0.9	-5.5
LOUISIANA.............	34 051	72.2	51.8	29.0	13.9	8.0	6.4	3.0	27.8	7.1	20.8	3.7	-5.0
MAINE...................	2 308	69.3	47.6	29.4	16.4	11.8	5.3	4.1	30.7	9.2	21.5	0.8	-4.3
MARYLAND	59 669	79.6	56.9	38.5	13.8	9.3	8.9	4.4	20.4	7.1	13.3	11.1	-12.5
MASSACHUSETTS ...	123 443	75.0	36.6	24.6	31.1	24.6	7.3	4.2	25.0	7.1	17.8	6.5	-8.0
MICHIGAN	84 443	75.2	50.5	32.2	16.1	11.8	8.5	4.8	24.8	7.0	17.8	6.7	-8.0
MINNESOTA	35 171	75.4	49.8	35.3	14.8	12.2	10.8	5.5	24.6	9.2	15.5	6.9	-10.3
MISSISSIPPI	9 781	70.8	47.0	29.5	14.6	10.1	9.2	4.0	29.2	10.6	18.6	2.3	-7.2
MISSOURI	32 361	72.2	50.6	32.4	13.0	9.5	8.5	4.7	27.8	8.0	19.9	3.7	-5.9
MONTANA	5 177	70.9	49.3	30.5	16.1	12.9	5.4	4.1	29.1	8.7	20.5	2.4	-5.3
NEBRASKA.............	20 919	70.4	55.0	41.4	10.5	10.5	9.0	5.0	21.0	6.5	13.1	9.9	-12.7
NEVADA.................	99 288	81.3	58.1	42.7	12.7	9.2	10.5	5.9	18.7	6.7	11.9	12.8	-13.9
NEW HAMPSHIRE.....	5 772	71.0	48.6	28.8	16.7	13.8	5.7	2.7	29.0	8.8	20.2	2.5	-5.6
NEW JERSEY..........	315 560	80.3	50.7	31.9	20.4	13.2	9.1	4.7	19.7	5.4	14.4	11.8	-11.4
NEW MEXICO..........	242 878	75.5	50.9	28.8	17.2	11.3	7.3	4.7	24.5	5.0	19.5	7.0	-6.3
NEW YORK.............	840 357	75.9	40.5	25.1	27.7	17.9	7.7	3.5	24.1	5.2	19.0	7.4	-6.8
NORTH CAROLINA ...	93 499	80.3	55.2	39.9	10.1	7.5	15.0	5.7	19.7	9.4	10.2	11.8	-15.6
NORTH DAKOTA.......	2 137	68.7	47.6	31.0	14.6	12.0	6.6	4.6	31.3	8.0	23.2	0.2	-2.6
OHIO....................	62 102	70.9	46.4	28.6	17.4	12.6	7.2	4.0	29.1	7.6	21.5	2.4	-4.3
OKLAHOMA.............	47 397	78.1	56.7	40.6	12.0	9.1	9.4	4.6	21.9	6.6	15.3	9.6	-10.5
OREGON	64 749	79.7	56.9	43.0	12.2	9.7	10.5	5.5	20.3	8.3	12.0	11.2	-13.8
PENNSYLVANIA.......	109 484	75.1	41.6	27.0	25.7	19.5	7.9	4.7	24.9	6.5	18.3	6.6	-7.5
RHODE ISLAND	24 939	82.3	39.2	27.7	33.8	27.6	9.3	5.4	17.7	4.4	13.2	13.8	-12.6
SOUTH CAROLINA ...	24 259	74.3	52.9	35.9	10.8	7.9	10.7	4.1	25.7	12.1	13.6	5.8	-12.2
SOUTH DAKOTA.......	2 658	74.7	52.1	33.4	11.4	10.1	11.2	8.4	25.3	8.4	17.0	6.2	-8.8
TENNESSEE...........	31 613	74.4	51.5	34.3	10.4	7.4	12.5	4.4	25.6	11.0	14.5	5.9	-11.3
TEXAS..................	1 794 271	82.5	59.7	40.2	16.0	10.2	6.8	3.3	17.5	4.2	13.3	14.0	-12.5
UTAH....................	48 190	82.7	59.5	43.2	13.4	9.7	9.8	5.0	17.3	6.0	11.3	14.2	-14.5
VERMONT...............	1 567	61.3	49.0	24.0	9.1	7.1	3.2	1.7	38.7	9.8	28.9	-7.2	3.1
VIRGINIA................	83 553	79.6	57.5	40.5	12.8	8.8	9.4	4.4	20.4	8.2	12.1	11.1	-13.7
WASHINGTON..........	110 036	78.5	55.1	40.3	14.4	11.3	9.0	5.1	21.5	7.9	13.7	10.0	-12.1
WEST VIRGINIA........	3 686	65.5	48.6	25.1	11.9	8.2	4.9	2.9	34.5	7.9	26.6	-3.0	0.8
WISCONSIN............	49 345	77.5	51.1	35.8	16.5	12.8	9.9	5.1	22.5	7.5	15.0	9.0	-10.8
WYOMING	9 570	69.0	48.8	26.8	13.0	9.1	7.2	5.2	31.0	7.2	23.8	0.5	-2.0

[1] Hispanic or Latino persons may be of any race.

STATE	Total population	Foreign-born population	Percent foreign-born	+/− U.S. percent foreign-born	Percent from Europe	Percent from Asia	Percent from Africa	Percent from Oceania	Latin America (percent)						Percent from Northern America
									Total	Caribbean	Central America			South America	
											Total from Central America	Mexico	Other Central America		
	295	296	297	298	299	300	301	302	303	304	305	306	307	308	309
UNITED STATES ...	281 421 906	31 107 889	11.1	0.0	1.7	2.9	0.3	0.1	5.7	1.0	4.0	3.3	0.7	0.7	0.3
ALABAMA	4 447 100	87 772	2.0	−9.1	0.4	0.6	0.1	0.0	0.8	0.1	0.6	0.5	0.1	0.1	0.1
ALASKA	626 932	37 170	5.9	−5.2	1.2	3.0	0.1	0.2	1.1	0.2	0.6	0.4	0.2	0.2	0.5
ARIZONA	5 130 632	656 183	12.8	1.7	1.4	1.5	0.2	0.1	9.1	0.1	8.8	8.5	0.3	0.2	0.5
ARKANSAS	2 673 400	73 690	2.8	−8.3	0.4	0.6	0.1	0.0	1.6	0.0	1.5	1.3	0.3	0.1	0.1
CALIFORNIA	33 871 648	8 864 255	26.2	15.1	2.1	8.6	0.3	0.2	14.5	0.2	13.7	11.6	2.1	0.6	0.4
COLORADO	4 301 261	369 903	8.6	−2.5	1.5	1.7	0.2	0.1	4.8	0.1	4.5	4.2	0.3	0.2	0.3
CONNECTICUT	3 405 565	369 967	10.9	−0.2	4.1	2.1	0.3	0.0	3.8	1.5	0.8	0.4	0.4	1.4	0.6
DELAWARE	783 600	44 898	5.7	−5.4	1.3	1.7	0.3	0.0	2.2	0.6	1.3	1.0	0.3	0.3	0.2
DISTRICT OF COLUMBIA	572 059	73 561	12.9	1.8	2.3	2.2	1.6	0.1	6.5	1.5	4.0	0.3	3.6	1.1	0.2
FLORIDA	15 982 378	2 670 828	16.7	5.6	2.2	1.5	0.2	0.0	12.2	6.9	2.7	1.2	1.5	2.6	0.6
GEORGIA	8 186 453	577 273	7.1	−4.0	0.9	1.8	0.5	0.0	3.7	0.5	2.8	2.3	0.5	0.4	0.2
HAWAII	1 211 537	212 229	17.5	6.4	0.9	14.6	0.1	1.1	0.6	0.1	0.3	0.2	0.1	0.2	0.3
IDAHO	1 293 953	64 080	5.0	−6.1	0.9	0.6	0.0	0.0	3.0	0.0	2.8	2.7	0.1	0.1	0.4
ILLINOIS	12 419 293	1 529 058	12.3	1.2	3.1	2.9	0.2	0.0	5.9	0.2	5.3	5.0	0.3	0.3	0.2
INDIANA	6 080 485	186 534	3.1	−8.0	0.7	0.8	0.1	0.0	1.3	0.1	1.1	1.0	0.1	0.1	0.1
IOWA	2 926 324	91 085	3.1	−8.0	0.7	1.0	0.1	0.0	1.1	0.0	1.0	0.9	0.2	0.1	0.1
KANSAS	2 688 418	134 735	5.0	−6.1	0.6	1.4	0.1	0.0	2.7	0.1	2.6	2.4	0.2	0.1	0.1
KENTUCKY	4 041 769	80 271	2.0	−9.1	0.5	0.7	0.1	0.0	0.6	0.1	0.5	0.4	0.1	0.1	0.1
LOUISIANA	4 468 976	115 885	2.6	−8.5	0.4	1.0	0.1	0.0	1.0	0.2	0.7	0.2	0.5	0.1	0.1
MAINE	1 274 923	36 691	2.9	−8.2	0.9	0.5	0.1	0.0	0.2	0.0	0.1	0.0	0.0	0.1	1.2
MARYLAND	5 296 486	518 315	9.8	−1.3	1.6	3.4	1.2	0.0	3.3	0.9	1.6	0.4	1.2	0.8	0.2
MASSACHUSETTS	6 349 097	772 983	12.2	1.1	3.9	3.2	0.8	0.0	3.7	1.8	0.8	0.1	0.7	1.1	0.6
MICHIGAN	9 938 444	523 589	5.3	−5.8	1.6	2.1	0.2	0.0	0.9	0.1	0.7	0.6	0.1	0.1	0.5
MINNESOTA	4 919 479	260 463	5.3	−5.8	0.9	2.1	0.7	0.0	1.3	0.1	1.0	0.8	0.1	0.2	0.3
MISSISSIPPI	2 844 658	39 908	1.4	−9.7	0.3	0.5	0.0	0.0	0.5	0.1	0.4	0.3	0.1	0.1	0.1
MISSOURI	5 595 211	151 196	2.7	−8.4	0.8	0.9	0.2	0.0	0.7	0.1	0.5	0.5	0.1	0.1	0.1
MONTANA	902 195	16 396	1.8	−9.3	0.7	0.4	0.0	0.0	0.2	0.0	0.1	0.1	0.0	0.0	0.5
NEBRASKA	1 711 263	74 638	4.4	−6.7	0.6	1.1	0.2	0.0	2.3	0.0	2.2	1.8	0.4	0.1	0.1
NEVADA	1 998 257	316 593	15.8	4.7	1.6	3.6	0.2	0.1	9.7	0.5	8.8	7.7	1.1	0.4	0.5
NEW HAMPSHIRE	1 235 786	54 154	4.4	−6.7	1.5	1.1	0.2	0.0	0.6	0.2	0.2	0.1	0.1	0.3	1.0
NEW JERSEY	8 414 350	1 476 327	17.5	6.4	4.2	4.9	0.7	0.0	7.5	2.8	1.9	0.8	1.1	2.8	0.2
NEW MEXICO	1 819 046	149 606	8.2	−2.9	0.8	0.8	0.1	0.0	6.3	0.1	6.1	5.9	0.2	0.1	0.2
NEW YORK	18 976 457	3 868 133	20.4	9.3	4.6	4.8	0.6	0.0	10.0	5.3	1.9	0.8	1.1	2.7	0.3
NORTH CAROLINA	8 049 313	430 000	5.3	−5.8	0.7	1.2	0.3	0.0	3.0	0.2	2.6	2.1	0.5	0.2	0.2
NORTH DAKOTA	642 200	12 114	1.9	−9.2	0.6	0.4	0.1	0.0	0.2	0.0	0.1	0.1	0.0	0.1	0.5
OHIO	11 353 140	339 279	3.0	−8.1	1.2	1.1	0.2	0.0	0.4	0.1	0.2	0.2	0.1	0.1	0.1
OKLAHOMA	3 450 654	131 747	3.8	−7.3	0.5	1.2	0.1	0.0	1.9	0.1	1.8	1.6	0.1	0.1	0.1
OREGON	3 421 399	289 702	8.5	−2.6	1.6	2.3	0.1	0.1	3.8	0.1	3.6	3.3	0.3	0.1	0.5
PENNSYLVANIA	12 281 054	508 291	4.1	−7.0	1.5	1.5	0.2	0.0	0.8	0.3	0.3	0.2	0.1	0.2	0.1
RHODE ISLAND	1 048 319	119 277	11.4	0.3	3.7	1.9	1.2	0.0	4.2	1.9	1.3	0.2	1.1	1.0	0.4
SOUTH CAROLINA	4 012 012	115 978	2.9	−8.2	0.7	0.7	0.1	0.0	1.2	0.1	1.0	0.8	0.2	0.2	0.1
SOUTH DAKOTA	754 844	13 495	1.8	−9.3	0.6	0.5	0.2	0.0	0.3	0.0	0.3	0.2	0.1	0.0	0.1
TENNESSEE	5 689 283	159 004	2.8	−8.3	0.5	0.9	0.2	0.0	1.1	0.1	0.9	0.8	0.2	0.1	0.1
TEXAS	20 851 820	2 899 642	13.9	2.8	0.7	2.2	0.3	0.0	10.4	0.2	9.9	9.0	0.9	0.3	0.2
UTAH	2 233 169	158 664	7.1	−4.0	1.1	1.3	0.1	0.3	3.9	0.0	3.3	3.0	0.3	0.6	0.3
VERMONT	608 827	23 245	3.8	−7.3	1.5	0.7	0.1	0.0	0.2	0.0	0.1	0.0	0.0	0.1	1.3
VIRGINIA	7 078 515	570 279	8.1	−3.0	1.2	3.3	0.6	0.0	2.7	0.3	1.7	0.5	1.2	0.7	0.2
WASHINGTON	5 894 121	614 457	10.4	−0.7	2.1	4.1	0.3	0.1	2.9	0.1	2.7	2.5	0.2	0.2	0.8
WEST VIRGINIA	1 808 344	19 390	1.1	−10.0	0.4	0.5	0.0	0.0	0.1	0.0	0.1	0.1	0.0	0.0	0.1
WISCONSIN	5 363 675	193 751	3.6	−7.5	1.0	1.2	0.1	0.0	1.2	0.1	1.1	1.0	0.1	0.1	0.1
WYOMING	493 782	11 205	2.3	−8.8	0.6	0.4	0.1	0.0	0.9	0.0	0.8	0.8	0.0	0.1	0.2

	Languages spoken at home (percent, except where noted)											
	Population 5 years and over						Population 5 years and over in households					
									Households where some members speak a non-English language			
STATE	Number	Speak only English	Speak Spanish	Speak another Indo-European language	Speak an Asian or Pacific Island language	Speak other languages	Number	Households where all members speak only English	Not linguistically isolated	Linguistically isolated	Children 5 to 17 years who live in linguistically isolated households	Population 65 years and over who live in linguistically isolated households
	310	311	312	313	314	315	316	317	318	319	320	321
UNITED STATES ...	262 375 152	82.1	10.7	3.8	2.7	0.7	254 620 291	76.4	18.9	4.7	5.1	3.9
ALABAMA	4 152 278	96.1	2.2	1.1	0.5	0.2	4 037 963	92.9	6.4	0.7	0.7	0.2
ALASKA	579 740	85.7	2.9	2.2	3.8	5.4	560 669	78.4	19.3	2.3	2.4	4.7
ARIZONA	4 752 724	74.1	19.5	2.1	1.3	2.9	4 643 420	66.2	27.2	6.7	8.5	3.5
ARKANSAS	2 492 205	95.0	3.3	0.9	0.6	0.1	2 418 558	91.7	6.9	1.4	1.6	0.3
CALIFORNIA	31 416 629	60.5	25.8	4.3	8.6	0.8	30 601 299	52.0	36.6	11.3	13.5	8.9
COLORADO	4 006 285	84.9	10.5	2.5	1.6	0.5	3 903 691	78.4	17.5	4.1	4.6	2.9
CONNECTICUT	3 184 514	81.7	8.4	7.9	1.5	0.5	3 076 664	75.5	20.3	4.2	3.9	4.7
DELAWARE	732 378	90.5	4.7	3.1	1.3	0.4	707 783	85.7	12.3	2.1	2.1	1.2
DISTRICT OF COLUMBIA	539 658	83.2	9.2	4.4	1.7	1.5	504 214	77.6	17.7	4.7	4.7	2.4
FLORIDA	15 043 603	76.9	16.5	5.0	1.1	0.5	14 656 157	71.4	22.6	6.1	5.8	6.3
GEORGIA	7 594 476	90.1	5.6	2.2	1.5	0.5	7 361 034	85.6	11.3	3.1	2.9	0.9
HAWAII	1 134 351	73.4	1.7	1.3	23.6	0.3	1 098 936	59.7	34.5	5.8	5.0	10.3
IDAHO	1 196 793	90.7	6.7	1.6	0.7	0.3	1 165 386	85.4	12.3	2.2	2.7	0.9
ILLINOIS	11 547 505	80.8	10.9	5.5	2.2	0.7	11 226 083	75.4	19.2	5.4	5.6	4.0
INDIANA	5 657 818	93.6	3.3	2.2	0.6	0.2	5 479 893	89.7	9.0	1.3	1.2	0.9
IOWA	2 738 499	94.2	2.9	1.8	0.9	0.2	2 634 322	90.4	8.2	1.4	1.5	0.6
KANSAS	2 500 360	91.3	5.5	1.6	1.3	0.3	2 418 376	86.9	10.7	2.4	2.5	1.0
KENTUCKY	3 776 230	96.1	1.9	1.4	0.6	0.2	3 661 392	93.1	6.1	0.8	0.7	0.3
LOUISIANA	4 153 367	90.8	2.5	5.4	1.0	0.2	4 017 572	84.7	14.0	1.3	0.8	3.2
MAINE	1 204 164	92.2	0.8	6.3	0.5	0.2	1 169 385	87.3	11.8	1.0	0.4	2.8
MARYLAND	4 945 043	87.4	4.7	4.0	2.7	1.2	4 811 450	82.0	15.3	2.6	2.4	2.2
MASSACHUSETTS ...	5 954 249	81.3	6.2	8.9	2.9	0.7	5 733 243	75.4	20.0	4.6	4.9	5.0
MICHIGAN	9 268 782	91.6	2.7	3.3	1.1	1.4	9 020 384	87.1	11.3	1.7	1.6	1.9
MINNESOTA	4 591 491	91.5	2.9	2.4	2.3	1.0	4 456 013	87.1	10.8	2.1	2.5	1.4
MISSISSIPPI	2 641 453	96.4	1.9	0.9	0.5	0.3	2 546 199	93.1	6.4	0.6	0.5	0.3
MISSOURI	5 226 022	94.9	2.1	1.9	0.8	0.3	5 063 961	91.3	7.7	1.0	1.0	0.6
MONTANA	847 362	94.8	1.5	2.1	0.4	1.2	822 728	90.2	9.2	0.6	0.6	0.9
NEBRASKA	1 594 700	92.1	4.9	1.7	0.9	0.3	1 544 041	87.9	10.0	2.2	2.4	0.9
NEVADA	1 853 720	76.9	16.2	2.5	3.7	0.7	1 820 133	69.7	23.3	6.9	8.4	2.8
NEW HAMPSHIRE	1 160 340	91.7	1.6	5.5	0.9	0.3	1 124 775	86.3	12.4	1.2	1.1	2.1
NEW JERSEY	7 856 268	74.5	12.3	8.4	3.5	1.3	7 662 551	68.1	25.6	6.3	5.9	5.7
NEW MEXICO	1 689 911	63.5	28.7	1.3	0.7	5.8	1 653 780	51.4	42.5	6.2	6.7	8.7
NEW YORK	17 749 110	72.0	13.6	9.3	3.8	1.2	17 174 354	65.0	27.2	7.8	7.4	8.7
NORTH CAROLINA ...	7 513 165	92.0	5.0	1.6	1.0	0.4	7 259 647	88.1	9.4	2.5	2.5	0.5
NORTH DAKOTA	603 106	93.7	1.4	4.0	0.3	0.6	579 430	89.1	10.0	0.9	0.5	2.4
OHIO	10 599 968	93.9	2.0	2.8	0.8	0.5	10 301 216	89.9	9.0	1.1	1.0	1.5
OKLAHOMA	3 215 719	92.6	4.4	1.1	1.1	0.8	3 103 285	88.4	9.8	1.8	1.8	0.7
OREGON	3 199 323	87.9	6.8	2.6	2.4	0.4	3 122 005	82.9	13.4	3.7	4.8	1.7
PENNSYLVANIA	11 555 538	91.6	3.1	3.7	1.2	0.4	11 123 328	87.3	11.0	1.7	1.8	1.8
RHODE ISLAND	985 184	80.0	8.1	9.3	2.0	0.6	946 340	73.5	21.4	5.1	6.3	5.5
SOUTH CAROLINA ...	3 748 669	94.8	2.9	1.5	0.7	0.2	3 613 748	90.9	7.9	1.2	1.0	0.4
SOUTH DAKOTA	703 820	93.5	1.4	2.8	0.4	1.8	675 435	88.3	10.5	1.2	1.2	1.3
TENNESSEE	5 315 920	95.2	2.5	1.3	0.7	0.3	5 168 025	92.0	6.9	1.1	1.0	0.3
TEXAS	19 241 518	68.8	27.0	1.9	1.9	0.4	18 681 439	61.3	30.6	8.1	8.9	6.6
UTAH	2 023 875	87.5	7.4	2.5	1.9	0.8	1 983 553	79.7	17.4	2.9	2.7	1.6
VERMONT	574 842	94.1	1.0	4.2	0.5	0.2	554 031	89.7	9.6	0.7	0.5	1.4
VIRGINIA	6 619 266	88.9	4.8	3.0	2.6	0.8	6 387 802	84.1	13.4	2.5	2.4	1.3
WASHINGTON	5 501 398	86.0	5.8	3.2	4.4	0.5	5 365 753	80.3	15.8	3.8	4.5	2.8
WEST VIRGINIA	1 706 931	97.3	1.0	1.1	0.4	0.2	1 663 780	94.7	5.1	0.2	0.2	0.2
WISCONSIN	5 022 073	92.7	3.4	2.5	1.2	0.3	4 866 312	88.2	10.3	1.5	1.8	1.4
WYOMING	462 809	93.6	4.0	1.4	0.5	0.5	448 723	88.8	10.4	0.8	0.7	1.2

STATE/County code	MSA/PMSA/NECMA code[1]	STATE County	Total population	Under 5 years	5 to 17 years	18 to 24 years	25 to 44 years	45 to 64 years	65 years and over	Median age	+/− U.S. percent under 18 years	+/− U.S. percent 65 years and over	Total population	Under 18 years	65 years and over
						Population by age (percent)								Non-Hispanic White Age (percent)	
			1	2	3	4	5	6	7	8	9	10	11	12	13
00 000	...	UNITED STATES......	281 421 906	6.8	18.9	9.6	30.4	21.9	12.4	35.3	0.0	0.0	194 514 140	22.6	15.0
01 000	...	ALABAMA	4 447 100	6.6	18.6	9.8	29.1	22.8	13.0	35.8	-0.5	0.6	3 127 039	22.8	14.8
01 001	5240	Autauga County	43 671	7.2	21.4	8.2	30.5	22.5	10.2	35.1	2.9	-2.2	34 760	27.5	10.5
01 003	5160	Baldwin County	140 415	6.1	18.3	7.2	28.1	24.8	15.4	39.0	-1.3	3.0	120 916	23.2	16.6
01 005	...	Barbour County	29 038	6.2	19.2	9.5	29.7	21.9	13.5	35.8	-0.3	1.1	14 788	21.0	16.5
01 007	...	Bibb County	20 826	6.7	18.7	9.6	30.5	22.9	11.6	34.7	-0.3	-0.8	15 867	24.2	12.6
01 009	1000	Blount County	51 024	7.2	18.4	8.3	29.3	24.1	12.7	36.4	-0.1	0.3	47 135	24.6	13.4
01 011	...	Bullock County	11 714	6.1	19.6	9.7	30.6	21.1	12.9	35.0	0.0	0.5	2 795	14.8	20.8
01 013	...	Butler County	21 399	6.5	20.4	8.8	25.2	22.7	16.4	37.7	1.2	4.0	12 421	22.2	19.9
01 015	0450	Calhoun County	112 249	6.2	17.4	10.5	27.7	24.1	14.1	37.2	-2.1	1.7	87 679	21.8	15.5
01 017	...	Chambers County	36 583	6.7	18.0	8.4	27.4	23.5	16.1	37.7	-1.0	3.7	22 112	21.2	19.7
01 019	...	Cherokee County	23 988	6.0	16.1	7.8	27.8	26.3	16.0	40.0	-3.6	3.6	22 229	21.6	16.5
01 021	...	Chilton County	39 593	6.7	19.0	8.9	29.1	23.5	12.8	35.9	0.0	0.4	33 867	24.7	13.5
01 023	...	Choctaw County	15 922	6.7	19.2	7.7	26.8	25.1	14.4	37.9	0.2	2.0	8 698	22.1	16.9
01 025	...	Clarke County	27 867	7.4	20.6	8.4	28.0	22.1	13.4	35.5	2.3	1.0	15 584	24.3	15.8
01 027	...	Clay County	14 254	6.0	17.7	7.7	27.1	24.8	16.7	38.7	-2.0	4.3	11 588	22.6	18.1
01 029	...	Cleburne County	14 123	6.0	18.2	8.3	28.4	25.3	13.8	37.5	-1.5	1.4	13 217	23.9	14.0
01 031	...	Coffee County	43 615	6.2	18.5	9.0	28.1	23.8	14.3	37.2	-1.0	1.9	33 109	22.7	15.9
01 033	2650	Colbert County	54 984	6.1	17.7	8.2	27.7	24.9	15.4	38.7	-1.9	3.0	44 558	22.3	16.3
01 035	...	Conecuh County	14 089	5.9	19.9	8.7	25.3	24.4	15.8	38.0	0.1	3.4	7 772	20.7	19.1
01 037	...	Coosa County	12 202	6.0	17.7	8.6	28.9	24.5	14.2	37.7	-2.0	1.8	7 768	21.7	16.7
01 039	...	Covington County	37 631	5.9	17.7	8.1	26.0	24.5	17.9	39.8	-2.1	5.5	32 198	22.1	18.9
01 041	...	Crenshaw County	13 665	5.9	18.8	7.5	26.2	24.3	17.3	38.8	-1.0	4.9	10 020	23.1	18.1
01 043	...	Cullman County	77 483	6.3	17.9	9.0	28.2	24.0	14.6	37.5	-1.5	2.2	73 763	23.8	15.1
01 045	2180	Dale County	49 129	7.7	18.9	9.4	30.5	21.6	11.7	34.3	0.9	-0.7	35 744	23.3	13.7
01 047	...	Dallas County	46 365	7.3	21.2	9.5	25.9	22.2	13.9	35.3	2.8	1.5	16 376	20.4	19.9
01 049	...	DeKalb County	64 452	6.8	17.9	9.0	29.6	23.0	13.8	36.3	-1.0	1.4	58 485	23.7	14.8
01 051	5240	Elmore County	65 874	6.3	19.2	8.9	32.0	22.7	10.9	35.3	-0.2	-1.5	50 383	25.0	12.3
01 053	...	Escambia County	38 440	6.1	18.0	9.5	29.4	23.6	13.4	36.9	-1.6	1.0	24 538	21.8	15.8
01 055	2880	Etowah County	103 459	6.5	17.4	8.6	27.4	24.1	16.0	38.3	-1.8	3.6	85 000	21.9	17.4
01 057	...	Fayette County	18 495	5.8	18.1	8.1	26.8	25.0	16.2	39.0	-1.8	3.8	16 001	23.1	16.5
01 059	...	Franklin County	31 223	6.2	18.0	9.0	28.5	23.5	14.9	36.7	-1.5	2.5	27 316	23.3	16.0
01 061	...	Geneva County	25 764	5.6	18.4	7.7	26.7	25.3	16.3	39.3	-1.7	3.9	22 203	22.8	17.3
01 063	...	Greene County	9 974	7.5	21.6	8.7	25.7	21.4	15.0	35.9	3.4	2.6	1 853	16.9	24.9
01 065	...	Hale County	17 185	8.1	21.3	9.0	27.0	21.1	13.6	34.4	3.7	1.2	6 796	22.6	17.2
01 067	...	Henry County	16 310	6.6	17.6	8.6	25.1	25.9	16.2	39.3	-1.5	3.8	10 716	20.9	18.6
01 069	2180	Houston County	88 787	6.7	19.1	8.1	29.2	23.3	13.6	36.7	0.1	1.2	64 683	23.2	15.5
01 071	...	Jackson County	53 926	6.3	17.8	8.3	28.8	25.4	13.3	37.6	-1.6	0.9	49 216	23.5	13.8
01 073	1000	Jefferson County	662 047	6.5	18.3	9.6	29.8	22.1	13.7	36.0	-0.9	1.3	379 986	21.0	16.8
01 075	...	Lamar County	15 904	5.7	18.0	8.7	28.1	23.7	15.9	38.2	-2.0	3.5	13 768	22.6	16.6
01 077	2650	Lauderdale County..........	87 966	5.9	17.1	10.0	28.2	23.7	15.1	37.6	-2.7	2.7	77 119	22.1	15.8
01 079	2030	Lawrence County	34 803	6.3	19.4	8.6	30.0	23.7	12.1	35.9	0.0	-0.3	26 899	23.7	13.5
01 081	0580	Lee County	115 092	6.2	17.1	22.7	28.1	17.8	8.1	27.5	-2.4	-4.3	84 196	20.6	8.6
01 083	3440	Limestone County	65 676	6.8	18.0	9.0	32.1	22.9	11.2	35.8	-0.9	-1.2	54 160	24.2	12.0
01 085	...	Lowndes County	13 473	7.5	22.6	9.2	26.8	21.6	12.4	33.9	4.4	0.0	3 476	20.1	18.6
01 087	...	Macon County	24 105	6.4	18.8	16.9	23.0	20.9	14.0	32.0	-0.5	1.6	3 303	18.1	18.2
01 089	3440	Madison County	276 700	6.8	18.8	9.3	31.7	22.7	10.8	35.7	-0.1	-1.6	196 392	23.6	13.0
01 091	...	Marengo County	22 539	7.0	21.5	8.0	26.6	22.2	14.8	36.4	2.8	2.4	10 570	22.5	18.0
01 093	...	Marion County	31 214	5.9	16.5	8.3	28.2	25.2	15.8	38.9	-3.3	3.4	29 444	22.3	16.2
01 095	...	Marshall County	82 231	6.7	18.2	8.3	29.1	23.5	14.3	36.9	-0.8	1.9	75 675	24.0	15.1
01 097	5160	Mobile County	399 843	7.3	20.2	10.0	28.8	21.8	12.0	34.4	1.8	-0.4	249 878	23.7	13.9
01 099	...	Monroe County	24 324	7.4	20.8	8.6	27.0	22.3	13.9	35.4	2.5	1.5	13 926	24.0	16.2
01 101	5240	Montgomery County.......	223 510	6.9	18.9	11.0	30.5	21.0	11.8	33.5	0.1	-0.6	108 028	20.3	16.4
01 103	2030	Morgan County	111 064	6.6	18.8	8.5	30.0	23.7	12.3	36.6	-0.3	-0.1	92 338	23.7	13.5
01 105	...	Perry County	11 861	7.4	22.4	11.4	23.6	20.2	15.1	33.3	4.1	2.7	3 639	18.2	22.2
01 107	...	Pickens County	20 949	6.8	20.5	8.1	26.9	22.5	15.2	36.9	1.6	2.8	11 759	22.3	18.3
01 109	...	Pike County	29 605	6.7	17.5	16.0	26.0	21.3	12.5	32.5	-1.5	0.1	17 812	20.2	14.7
01 111	...	Randolph County	22 380	6.5	18.6	8.9	27.2	23.0	15.8	37.7	-0.6	3.4	16 940	23.0	18.0
01 113	1800	Russell County	49 756	7.2	19.3	9.0	29.0	22.5	13.1	35.4	0.8	0.7	27 689	22.6	15.6
01 115	1000	St. Clair County..............	64 742	6.5	18.9	8.0	30.6	24.3	11.7	36.4	-0.3	-0.7	57 996	25.2	12.1
01 117	1000	Shelby County	143 293	7.5	18.6	8.1	33.9	23.4	8.4	34.9	0.4	-4.0	127 048	25.7	8.9
01 119	...	Sumter County	14 798	7.1	21.9	11.9	25.7	19.4	13.9	32.1	3.3	1.5	3 808	17.2	19.1
01 121	...	Talladega County	80 321	6.3	18.7	8.9	29.0	23.7	13.4	36.6	-0.7	1.0	53 365	22.6	15.6
01 123	...	Tallapoosa County	41 475	6.2	17.9	7.5	27.2	24.7	16.5	39.3	-1.6	4.1	30 388	21.4	18.8
01 125	8600	Tuscaloosa County	164 875	6.3	17.1	16.5	28.1	20.8	11.2	31.9	-2.3	-1.2	111 273	20.4	12.8
01 127	...	Walker County	70 713	6.3	17.2	8.8	27.9	25.1	14.7	38.3	-2.2	2.3	64 690	22.8	15.2

[1]MSA = Metropolitan Statistical Area. PMSA = Primary MSA. NECMA = New England County Metropolitan Area. See the Appendix A for explanation of these concepts. See Appendix B for list of metropolitan areas identified by type, with component counties.

Table A-3. States and Counties — Age, Ethnicity, and Household Structure

STATE County	Black or African American Total population 14	Under 18 years 15	65 years and over 16	American Indian and Alaska Native Total population 17	Under 18 years 18	65 years and over 19	Asian, Hawaiian, and Pacific Islander Total population 20	Under 18 years 21	65 years and over 22	Hispanic or Latino[1] Total population 23	Under 18 years 24	65 years and over 25	Two or more races Total population 26	Under 18 years 27	65 years and over 28
UNITED STATES....	34 361 740	31.3	8.2	2 447 989	33.3	5.6	10 550 602	24.2	7.6	35 238 481	34.8	4.8	7 270 926	40.7	5.0
ALABAMA	1 153 044	31.0	9.5	22 897	28.2	4.4	31 095	23.8	4.4	72 627	33.4	3.3	49 238	36.9	6.4
Autauga County	7 481	32.8	10.0	307	30.0	1.6	265	35.5	0.0	394	33.2	3.3	525	41.1	6.3
Baldwin County	14 233	32.7	9.2	790	22.7	4.1	576	26.0	1.9	2 341	28.3	4.1	1 712	35.5	9.6
Barbour County	13 487	30.8	10.8	101	6.9	0.0	30	33.3	0.0	509	17.7	3.3	219	17.8	10.5
Bibb County	4 632	29.4	8.4	61	14.8	0.0	12	0.0	0.0	181	48.1	3.3	119	27.7	17.6
Blount County	563	33.0	13.3	182	24.2	2.7	127	15.0	2.4	2 629	43.3	0.8	552	22.5	8.3
Bullock County	8 444	30.3	11.0	57	8.8	0.0	10	0.0	0.0	359	8.4	0.0	80	0.0	0.0
Butler County	8 814	33.4	11.6	7	28.6	0.0	54	57.4	0.0	118	10.2	16.1	47	14.9	12.8
Calhoun County	20 458	30.1	9.8	437	16.9	1.1	692	21.8	8.5	1 912	33.1	4.3	1 138	30.5	9.7
Chambers County	14 019	29.9	10.5	80	52.5	0.0	10	0.0	0.0	274	23.7	13.9	147	34.7	13.6
Cherokee County	1 286	23.4	13.5	88	6.8	0.0	34	5.9	0.0	232	47.0	1.7	140	59.3	0.0
Chilton County	4 270	30.9	10.5	125	37.6	6.4	71	8.5	0.0	1 016	35.8	0.4	435	37.5	12.6
Choctaw County	6 941	30.7	11.7	25	16.0	0.0	15	33.3	13.3	144	6.9	2.8	89	37.1	2.2
Clarke County	11 987	32.6	10.6	51	47.1	21.6	114	51.8	0.0	173	21.3	19.1	54	25.9	7.4
Clay County	2 369	30.3	10.9	24	0.0	0.0	4	0.0	0.0	207	22.7	10.1	130	23.1	13.1
Cleburne County	513	26.1	16.0	52	13.5	0.0	0	X	X	160	28.8	0.0	181	34.8	11.0
Coffee County	8 113	30.5	10.2	256	21.1	7.8	386	18.1	3.4	1 131	36.5	3.3	773	39.2	6.5
Colbert County	9 254	30.3	11.7	120	30.8	0.0	175	14.3	18.9	539	30.4	10.2	384	36.2	10.2
Conecuh County	6 177	32.3	12.1	14	0.0	0.0	18	0.0	0.0	66	22.7	0.0	54	37.0	0.0
Coosa County	4 311	27.1	9.7	52	23.1	19.2	0	X	X	44	38.6	0.0	52	28.8	11.5
Covington County.........	4 553	31.4	12.1	206	20.9	6.3	64	25.0	0.0	382	43.2	9.7	257	40.5	11.3
Crenshaw County	3 466	28.2	15.6	18	44.4	0.0	0	X	X	107	40.2	1.9	51	43.1	11.8
Cullman County.............	820	22.6	11.1	313	34.2	2.9	249	10.8	0.0	1 576	34.8	1.6	1 034	38.3	3.0
Dale County	10 150	35.4	7.3	240	23.3	4.6	541	13.5	8.9	1 594	38.5	2.1	1 137	50.7	4.5
Dallas County	29 411	32.9	10.6	130	23.8	10.0	117	26.5	9.4	231	35.9	5.2	224	42.9	10.7
DeKalb County	1 050	29.3	10.4	501	34.9	3.8	138	36.2	11.6	3 449	37.3	0.6	1 169	32.2	2.7
Elmore County	13 671	27.1	6.4	217	13.4	2.8	263	22.4	4.9	745	32.6	7.1	686	34.8	5.2
Escambia County	11 683	27.7	9.2	1 013	29.2	8.9	114	5.3	26.3	405	31.4	4.7	711	38.1	9.6
Etowah County	14 672	31.4	11.1	375	39.7	3.5	430	22.1	4.4	1 651	31.1	4.2	1 462	54.4	5.1
Fayette County	2 225	28.3	15.3	20	30.0	0.0	74	48.6	0.0	96	25.0	2.1	93	43.0	7.5
Franklin County	1 301	29.6	15.8	119	27.7	1.7	73	31.5	0.0	2 238	30.4	1.6	290	27.6	6.2
Geneva County	2 978	31.5	10.5	147	12.9	12.9	30	0.0	0.0	319	43.3	5.0	169	36.1	7.1
Greene County	8 063	31.9	12.9	0	X	X	5	0.0	0.0	56	39.3	14.3	28	32.1	0.0
Hale County	10 160	33.7	11.4	27	29.6	0.0	11	0.0	0.0	127	22.8	24.4	78	44.9	0.0
Henry County	5 190	30.0	12.3	15	0.0	0.0	0	X	X	312	36.2	0.0	130	46.2	10.8
Houston County	21 567	33.1	8.9	406	17.2	2.2	527	27.5	8.0	982	38.5	6.1	766	33.3	8.1
Jackson County............	2 122	32.6	12.3	729	24.7	1.8	105	18.1	5.7	619	33.1	3.2	1 193	29.9	5.3
Jefferson County	259 123	30.1	10.1	1 506	20.9	5.4	5 948	23.6	4.1	10 486	31.0	3.5	6 100	34.8	5.4
Lamar County	1 839	29.1	12.1	43	37.2	11.6	38	42.1	0.0	131	21.4	5.3	91	61.5	0.0
Lauderdale County........	8 775	29.2	10.8	238	26.1	1.7	328	29.0	0.0	819	27.8	6.8	792	35.9	9.1
Lawrence County	4 603	29.9	10.3	1 827	35.5	0.9	71	25.4	0.0	230	37.0	4.8	1 192	34.3	5.0
Lee County	25 753	30.7	7.7	305	37.7	0.0	1 875	19.4	4.3	1 944	28.9	3.3	1 265	44.5	1.5
Limestone County	8 841	25.3	8.7	290	24.8	2.8	314	38.2	0.6	1 452	37.3	2.0	716	31.7	9.2
Lowndes County	9 896	33.4	10.3	2	0.0	100.0	0	X	X	109	50.5	1.8	44	38.6	0.0
Macon County	20 410	26.5	13.5	28	0.0	35.7	150	21.3	5.3	164	32.9	12.2	172	21.5	2.9
Madison County	62 240	29.5	6.0	2 444	32.2	1.4	4 804	23.9	4.6	5 486	36.0	3.3	5 914	39.3	4.2
Marengo County	11 603	33.7	12.1	44	50.0	11.4	10	0.0	0.0	203	22.2	3.4	164	48.2	12.2
Marion County	1 076	20.1	8.6	85	24.7	5.9	132	28.0	12.1	350	43.7	1.4	140	30.7	24.3
Marshall County	974	29.4	10.0	460	23.9	7.0	262	18.7	1.9	4 181	37.7	2.1	916	36.5	7.6
Mobile County	133 662	34.0	9.3	2 698	29.4	4.8	5 384	28.7	3.5	4 414	31.2	6.1	4 802	36.5	7.7
Monroe County..............	9 775	33.4	10.9	219	37.0	14.6	51	25.5	5.9	107	46.7	1.9	232	40.1	13.8
Montgomery County......	108 713	31.1	7.7	666	30.3	3.3	1 859	14.9	5.6	2 477	24.9	2.0	2 201	37.2	5.8
Morgan County..............	12 347	32.8	7.6	794	24.6	5.4	571	42.0	1.6	3 621	35.6	1.7	1 777	37.5	7.0
Perry County	8 048	35.1	11.5	10	0.0	100.0	9	0.0	100.0	149	32.9	19.5	115	23.5	20.9
Pickens County	8 992	33.8	11.3	36	2.8	8.3	26	15.4	15.4	82	26.8	9.8	84	41.7	0.0
Pike County	10 841	30.4	9.3	168	41.1	7.7	191	8.4	9.4	303	37.3	2.0	361	28.3	10.5
Randolph County	4 773	30.7	9.6	32	0.0	68.8	45	40.0	0.0	403	49.4	1.5	276	31.5	0.7
Russell County	20 095	31.0	10.6	300	26.0	1.7	297	16.2	5.1	736	36.8	3.7	689	44.6	4.1
St. Clair County............	5 495	24.6	7.9	141	14.2	18.4	109	22.9	15.6	424	36.1	1.9	591	43.7	3.4
Shelby County	10 758	29.5	5.8	722	31.7	4.3	1 006	23.9	2.9	2 882	28.7	1.1	1 020	33.2	1.7
Sumter County	10 852	33.2	12.0	19	5.3	0.0	20	55.0	0.0	174	38.5	4.0	48	16.7	22.9
Talladega County	25 470	29.6	8.9	225	24.0	16.4	339	38.1	0.9	597	23.1	10.2	451	43.9	10.0
Tallapoosa County	10 582	31.3	10.3	92	39.1	9.8	85	45.9	0.0	162	43.2	1.9	189	24.3	7.9
Tuscaloosa County	47 935	29.6	8.3	648	21.1	5.2	1 561	15.8	3.8	2 062	36.2	3.2	1 602	36.5	6.1
Walker County...............	4 532	29.2	10.6	201	26.4	4.0	161	26.1	5.6	668	37.3	1.5	616	33.0	14.4

[1]Hispanic or Latino persons may be of any race.

STATE County	Total households	Family households (percent)						Nonfamily households (percent)						Percent of householders 65 years and over who live alone	Grandparents who are responsible for the care of their grandchildren
		Married-couple family households			Other family households			Two or more unrelated persons		Male living alone		Female living alone			
		Total	With children	Householder 65 years or over	Total	With children	Householder 65 years or over	Total	Householder 65 years or over	Total	Householder 65 years or over	Total	Householder 65 years or over		
	29	30	31	32	33	34	35	36	37	38	39	40	41	42	43
UNITED STATES....	105 539 122	52.5	24.3	9.2	15.9	9.1	2.2	5.8	0.4	11.0	2.3	14.8	7.1	44.2	2 426 730
ALABAMA	1 737 385	53.0	23.2	9.3	17.4	9.6	2.8	3.5	0.3	10.8	2.2	15.3	7.6	44.4	56 369
Autauga County	15 972	61.6	30.1	8.7	16.2	9.5	2.1	2.3	0.1	8.0	1.5	12.0	5.9	40.5	449
Baldwin County	55 356	60.6	25.2	13.3	12.7	7.2	2.0	3.5	0.3	9.5	2.6	13.8	7.3	38.7	1 291
Barbour County	10 432	48.9	20.8	9.9	22.4	13.0	2.9	2.2	0.3	10.1	2.8	16.4	10.4	50.1	389
Bibb County................	7 383	59.0	25.1	9.3	16.4	8.5	3.7	2.3	0.5	10.3	1.8	12.0	6.3	37.5	325
Blount County.............	19 153	66.6	28.9	10.1	10.7	5.8	2.0	1.8	0.1	8.1	2.3	12.7	7.5	44.4	446
Bullock County	3 993	35.8	13.3	8.4	32.4	20.6	4.9	3.1	0.8	12.0	2.7	16.7	9.2	45.8	227
Butler County	8 386	47.9	20.1	9.5	22.4	13.0	3.9	2.4	0.4	11.1	2.8	16.3	10.6	49.5	431
Calhoun County	45 380	52.9	21.3	9.8	16.4	8.8	2.9	3.9	0.3	10.5	2.0	16.4	8.6	44.9	1 723
Chambers County	14 545	49.0	18.7	10.5	21.7	11.2	3.7	2.3	0.2	10.8	2.5	16.2	9.3	44.9	600
Cherokee County	9 718	62.2	23.1	12.3	12.1	6.0	2.9	1.9	0.0	10.0	2.8	13.8	8.0	41.5	365
Chilton County.............	15 270	61.8	28.0	9.8	12.8	7.3	1.8	2.4	0.2	9.2	2.6	13.7	7.9	47.3	519
Choctaw County...........	6 344	53.1	22.6	8.9	18.6	10.4	3.9	1.6	0.5	10.6	2.8	16.1	9.1	47.4	300
Clarke County	10 638	54.1	25.0	9.1	19.1	11.0	3.3	1.5	0.1	9.4	2.1	15.8	10.3	49.9	530
Clay County.................	5 770	56.6	21.8	12.0	14.2	8.6	2.1	2.4	0.6	10.6	2.5	16.2	9.2	44.2	208
Cleburne County	5 616	62.5	27.5	10.2	11.6	5.7	1.4	3.1	0.6	10.0	2.3	12.8	7.7	45.1	117
Coffee County	17 444	57.2	24.0	11.1	15.1	9.1	2.2	2.9	0.2	9.9	2.0	14.9	8.2	43.1	442
Colbert County	22 488	56.7	23.6	11.5	14.8	7.6	2.5	2.5	0.3	10.0	2.6	16.0	8.7	44.0	677
Conecuh County	5 775	48.4	19.9	10.5	19.7	10.9	4.2	1.9	0.1	13.1	2.7	17.0	10.0	46.1	209
Coosa County	4 694	57.3	21.9	12.0	16.4	8.1	3.2	2.0	0.0	12.0	3.0	12.2	6.3	38.0	303
Covington County..........	15 639	55.3	22.8	12.1	13.8	7.6	2.3	2.4	0.5	10.7	3.2	17.8	11.4	49.4	437
Crenshaw County	5 573	51.2	21.3	10.1	19.0	10.1	4.5	1.7	0.3	11.3	3.6	16.8	10.5	48.6	124
Cullman County............	30 796	61.8	26.6	11.2	11.5	5.9	2.0	2.7	0.2	9.9	2.0	14.1	7.8	42.2	772
Dale County	18 890	55.9	25.8	9.2	16.6	10.8	1.9	3.1	0.3	11.3	2.4	13.1	6.5	43.5	541
Dallas County	17 869	40.7	17.1	7.7	30.0	16.9	5.2	1.6	0.4	11.9	3.5	15.9	9.1	48.7	1 022
DeKalb County	25 147	60.5	26.8	10.1	13.3	7.0	2.5	2.4	0.2	9.2	2.2	14.5	8.2	44.9	568
Elmore County	22 692	62.6	29.0	9.7	14.9	8.7	2.3	2.5	0.2	8.7	1.6	11.3	6.1	38.8	747
Escambia County	14 277	52.5	22.3	9.5	18.3	10.1	3.4	3.0	0.3	10.3	2.7	16.0	8.8	46.4	471
Etowah County	41 634	54.3	21.9	11.0	16.8	8.5	3.4	2.6	0.3	9.9	3.0	16.4	9.8	46.7	1 079
Fayette County	7 479	59.4	25.0	10.1	12.1	5.9	2.4	1.8	0.2	10.7	3.5	16.0	10.6	52.6	184
Franklin County	12 247	59.8	25.0	11.0	13.8	7.9	2.3	2.0	0.2	9.0	2.5	15.5	9.4	46.9	377
Geneva County	10 470	56.6	23.3	11.7	15.4	8.4	2.9	1.8	0.2	10.4	2.6	15.8	9.8	45.5	239
Greene County.............	3 956	36.6	15.7	7.7	31.3	16.7	6.7	1.5	0.2	15.1	4.8	15.4	7.8	46.5	305
Hale County	6 427	46.9	22.5	9.4	25.5	13.8	4.2	1.4	0.2	11.9	2.7	14.4	7.7	43.0	332
Henry County	6 531	54.7	21.5	11.0	18.1	9.3	3.3	1.9	0.2	10.0	2.9	15.2	10.3	47.7	222
Houston County	35 861	53.5	22.9	9.6	17.0	10.4	2.2	3.1	0.3	10.5	2.3	15.8	8.0	46.0	973
Jackson County............	21 611	58.8	23.8	10.0	14.5	7.5	2.8	2.3	0.2	9.6	2.5	14.7	8.6	46.0	834
Jefferson County	263 255	46.8	20.7	8.8	20.5	10.7	3.7	4.0	0.3	11.3	2.1	17.4	7.9	43.9	9 007
Lamar County	6 451	58.3	23.9	12.1	14.5	7.8	2.6	1.5	0.3	10.1	2.4	15.4	10.2	45.6	143
Lauderdale County........	36 128	56.5	23.4	11.2	13.5	7.6	2.2	3.5	0.2	11.3	2.3	15.2	8.5	44.2	607
Lawrence County	13 555	61.8	27.9	8.9	13.9	7.2	2.2	1.8	0.3	9.6	2.4	12.9	7.4	46.1	626
Lee County	45 751	45.1	21.9	5.8	15.3	8.7	1.9	12.0	0.2	13.7	1.2	14.0	4.5	41.9	1 088
Limestone County	24 668	60.2	27.2	9.0	14.2	8.0	2.1	2.1	0.0	10.1	2.2	13.3	7.0	45.1	749
Lowndes County	4 905	42.4	17.5	7.2	30.6	18.4	5.7	2.2	0.7	12.5	3.2	12.4	6.5	42.0	305
Macon County	8 914	33.2	12.3	7.0	28.8	16.1	4.7	5.0	0.4	13.3	3.2	19.7	9.6	51.2	445
Madison County	110 085	54.2	24.6	8.5	14.8	8.9	1.8	3.9	0.2	12.5	1.6	14.7	5.7	41.0	2 731
Marengo County	8 788	49.4	23.0	9.1	22.7	12.4	4.8	1.4	0.1	10.4	3.1	16.1	9.9	48.2	468
Marion County	12 676	58.9	23.1	10.9	12.8	7.1	2.4	1.8	0.2	10.3	2.6	16.2	10.5	49.3	330
Marshall County	32 636	59.5	25.3	10.7	13.7	7.7	2.0	2.3	0.2	9.5	2.4	15.0	8.6	46.2	894
Mobile County	150 255	50.3	23.0	8.5	21.1	12.0	3.3	3.8	0.3	10.6	2.2	14.1	6.8	42.5	6 531
Monroe County.............	9 402	53.6	24.6	9.9	18.9	10.9	3.6	1.8	0.4	12.3	2.5	13.4	8.1	43.2	492
Montgomery County......	86 031	44.8	20.0	7.6	21.5	12.7	2.9	4.2	0.3	11.5	2.1	18.0	7.6	47.4	2 638
Morgan County.............	43 515	58.7	25.9	9.5	13.9	8.1	2.0	2.4	0.1	10.5	1.8	14.3	7.1	43.4	1 000
Perry County	4 336	40.2	17.0	10.2	30.7	17.8	5.1	1.3	0.2	12.8	4.2	15.1	8.6	45.1	352
Pickens County	8 103	51.0	21.5	10.4	21.3	12.3	3.5	1.4	0.2	9.8	2.4	16.4	9.5	45.7	366
Pike County.................	11 929	44.4	19.1	7.6	19.8	11.0	3.1	6.1	0.6	14.1	2.6	15.5	7.6	47.5	514
Randolph County	8 635	55.6	22.7	11.6	16.3	9.4	2.8	2.6	0.3	11.3	2.3	14.2	8.6	42.6	221
Russell County.............	19 728	45.8	20.2	7.7	22.3	12.5	3.6	3.8	0.4	12.4	2.9	15.7	7.6	47.4	557
St. Clair County	24 098	64.1	28.4	10.2	12.6	7.1	1.8	2.5	0.3	9.3	2.1	11.4	6.5	41.4	678
Shelby County	54 601	64.1	31.6	6.9	10.6	5.7	1.4	3.5	0.2	9.2	1.3	12.5	4.0	38.5	931
Sumter County	5 722	35.0	17.1	6.6	29.3	15.7	5.1	4.8	0.6	13.4	2.7	17.5	9.4	49.6	305
Talladega County	30 686	54.1	22.3	9.4	17.6	10.0	2.5	2.4	0.3	9.9	2.7	16.0	8.9	48.8	1 180
Tallapoosa County	16 631	52.9	20.9	10.4	18.2	9.5	3.5	2.3	0.2	10.4	2.9	16.2	9.0	45.9	547
Tuscaloosa County	64 517	47.9	21.0	7.7	17.3	9.8	2.4	6.4	0.2	12.3	1.8	16.0	6.8	45.5	1 929
Walker County..............	28 336	57.0	23.4	10.4	15.4	7.4	2.9	2.3	0.2	9.7	2.1	15.6	9.1	45.2	1 146

Table A-3. States and Counties — Age, Ethnicity, and Household Structure

STATE County	Households with Non-Hispanic White householder		Households with Black or African American householder		Households with American Indian and Alaska Native householder		Households with Asian, Hawaiian, and Pacific Islander householder		Households with Hispanic or Latino[1] householder		Foreign-born population	Place of birth (percent)			Percent in non-English speaking households	
	Number of households	Percent that are family households	Number of households	Percent that are family households	Number of households	Percent that are family households	Number of households	Percent that are family households	Number of households	Percent that are family households	Percent of total population that is foreign-born	Europe	Asia	Latin America	Linguistically isolated	Not linguistically isolated
	44	45	46	47	48	49	50	51	52	53	54	55	56	57	58	59
UNITED STATES....	78 983 497	66.8	12 023 966	68.3	770 334	73.2	3 229 278	75.2	9 272 610	80.7	11.1	1.7	2.9	5.7	4.7	18.9
ALABAMA	1 273 242	70.5	413 673	69.8	8 368	73.6	9 558	70.0	19 798	76.0	2.0	0.4	0.6	0.8	0.7	6.4
Autauga County	13 058	78.2	2 566	74.2	58	87.9	43	79.1	107	89.7	1.2	0.5	0.4	0.3	0.5	5.7
Baldwin County	49 080	73.0	4 650	74.3	330	90.0	140	62.9	605	79.0	2.1	0.7	0.3	0.7	0.5	7.2
Barbour County	5 792	71.9	4 446	70.8	36	100.0	3	0.0	103	65.0	1.5	0.1	0.1	1.3	1.0	4.5
Bibb County.................	5 961	75.7	1 306	74.4	17	82.4	6	100.0	43	88.4	0.4	0.1	0.1	0.3	0.4	4.2
Blount County	18 164	76.9	146	65.8	72	86.1	48	45.8	606	93.1	3.1	0.2	0.2	2.7	1.6	8.1
Bullock County	971	71.7	2 921	67.8	11	100.0	5	100.0	78	29.5	3.1	0.3	0.1	2.6	2.4	7.5
Butler County	5 204	70.8	3 117	69.5	2	100.0	11	81.8	73	71.2	0.4	0.2	0.1	0.1	0.1	5.2
Calhoun County	36 218	70.0	7 731	66.6	213	56.8	228	52.2	597	68.5	1.7	0.4	0.5	0.7	0.5	5.9
Chambers County	9 384	69.5	5 002	73.0	31	100.0	0	X	108	65.7	0.8	0.3	0.1	0.2	0.3	6.0
Cherokee County	9 123	74.5	461	72.2	51	21.6	19	89.5	49	98.0	1.1	0.4	0.2	0.4	0.3	3.9
Chilton County	13 442	74.5	1 450	75.9	59	100.0	13	100.0	239	84.1	1.9	0.2	0.1	1.4	1.1	5.0
Choctaw County...........	3 622	72.1	2 632	70.4	16	100.0	2	100.0	54	90.7	0.6	0.1	0.2	0.3	0.5	4.2
Clarke County	6 288	73.1	4 229	73.5	11	0.0	40	67.5	91	89.0	0.5	0.2	0.3	0.1	0.1	5.3
Clay County.................	4 816	70.7	843	72.4	4	100.0	0	X	76	59.2	0.9	0.2	0.1	0.5	0.5	5.4
Cleburne County	5 241	74.5	230	67.0	31	83.9	0	X	56	69.6	0.9	0.3	0.0	0.6	0.4	4.9
Coffee County	13 801	72.0	2 953	72.5	110	81.8	94	67.0	289	85.1	2.7	1.0	0.8	0.7	0.6	8.8
Colbert County.............	18 584	71.5	3 501	71.6	36	69.4	60	90.0	140	73.6	0.9	0.3	0.2	0.3	0.3	4.6
Conecuh County	3 329	69.3	2 405	66.5	6	100.0	12	50.0	23	60.9	0.4	0.0	0.1	0.1	0.3	4.5
Coosa County	3 203	73.0	1 448	74.9	18	88.9	0	X	8	50.0	0.3	0.2	0.1	0.1	0.2	4.3
Covington County.........	13 647	69.4	1 743	65.4	77	67.5	22	100.0	86	90.7	0.6	0.2	0.2	0.2	0.1	4.1
Crenshaw County	4 199	70.4	1 336	69.7	6	0.0	0	X	16	75.0	0.3	0.1	0.0	0.0	0.0	4.3
Cullman County............	29 633	73.3	329	62.0	117	76.9	62	56.5	446	81.8	1.7	0.3	0.2	1.2	0.9	5.3
Dale County	14 439	71.5	3 586	74.5	107	79.4	118	70.3	421	85.7	3.1	1.2	0.8	0.9	0.8	9.7
Dallas County	7 055	60.7	10 028	72.0	27	77.8	53	88.7	65	67.7	0.7	0.2	0.2	0.2	0.2	5.2
DeKalb County	23 488	73.6	385	71.9	137	75.2	49	100.0	804	82.6	4.1	0.2	0.2	3.6	3.2	5.9
Elmore County	18 719	77.6	3 480	77.6	74	66.2	65	29.2	221	85.5	1.1	0.4	0.3	0.3	0.2	5.4
Escambia County	9 822	71.5	3 699	67.7	415	75.4	34	100.0	111	76.6	0.6	0.2	0.3	0.2	0.2	4.2
Etowah County	35 147	71.6	5 569	65.8	145	86.9	145	77.9	343	87.8	1.6	0.2	0.4	0.9	0.6	5.2
Fayette County	6 597	71.4	812	72.2	10	100.0	15	66.7	21	66.7	0.7	0.1	0.2	0.2	0.2	3.3
Franklin County	10 990	73.3	545	65.5	41	95.1	19	100.0	606	83.2	5.6	0.2	0.2	5.1	4.2	5.6
Geneva County	9 187	72.1	1 111	71.4	52	59.6	18	100.0	67	65.7	0.8	0.2	0.1	0.4	0.3	5.0
Greene County	862	66.9	3 067	68.5	0	X	5	100.0	30	16.7	0.7	0.4	0.0	0.3	0.0	5.6
Hale County	2 772	75.0	3 564	69.9	19	100.0	0	X	64	70.3	0.3	0.1	0.1	0.2	0.1	4.7
Henry County	4 445	72.9	1 965	73.7	7	100.0	0	X	96	61.5	1.1	0.1	0.0	1.1	0.7	5.0
Houston County	26 818	71.3	8 165	67.9	197	45.7	164	73.8	250	78.8	1.6	0.5	0.5	0.5	0.4	5.1
Jackson County............	20 004	70.2	600	60.9	228	75.9	30	90.0	138	89.9	0.7	0.1	0.2	0.4	0.2	3.8
Jefferson County	160 317	66.0	95 906	69.2	592	74.7	1 999	69.1	2 930	77.4	2.3	0.4	0.8	0.9	0.9	6.9
Lamar County	5 624	73.4	726	68.0	19	78.9	4	100.0	56	82.1	0.8	0.1	0.2	0.4	0.1	4.1
Lauderdale County	31 971	70.2	3 397	68.4	126	58.7	84	86.9	310	68.1	1.0	0.2	0.3	0.4	0.4	4.6
Lawrence County	10 797	75.8	1 738	70.5	494	87.0	26	92.3	83	75.9	0.5	0.1	0.1	0.3	0.3	5.5
Lee County	34 307	58.6	9 690	67.3	88	42.0	683	63.5	718	54.6	2.7	0.6	1.3	0.5	0.7	8.1
Limestone County	20 932	74.4	2 960	74.4	84	76.2	73	97.3	391	80.1	1.7	0.2	0.3	1.2	0.9	5.9
Lowndes County	1 474	69.9	3 414	74.4	2	0.0	0	X	13	84.6	0.3	0.1	0.0	0.2	0.0	5.2
Macon County	1 364	68.0	7 402	61.4	20	60.0	45	51.1	30	40.0	1.5	0.1	0.6	0.3	0.6	6.7
Madison County	82 007	69.1	22 580	67.7	814	71.5	1 460	77.0	1 572	74.7	4.0	1.0	1.5	0.9	0.8	8.3
Marengo County	4 407	73.4	4 249	71.4	12	100.0	10	0.0	78	47.4	0.7	0.0	0.0	0.6	0.4	6.0
Marion County	12 176	71.6	337	68.5	26	88.5	26	100.0	61	85.2	0.5	0.0	0.2	0.2	0.2	4.3
Marshall County	30 744	73.1	343	58.0	221	74.2	69	89.9	955	83.8	4.0	0.2	0.3	3.5	2.4	6.3
Mobile County	98 747	70.8	46 581	72.8	1 000	75.0	1 473	73.2	1 309	66.5	2.3	0.5	1.1	0.5	0.7	7.8
Monroe County.............	5 721	73.3	3 489	70.4	72	88.9	12	100.0	41	85.4	0.3	0.1	0.1	0.1	0.1	5.2
Montgomery County......	45 782	64.6	38 122	68.1	242	62.0	596	69.3	728	67.3	2.0	0.6	0.8	0.4	0.5	7.0
Morgan County.............	37 235	72.8	4 419	69.9	304	75.3	142	76.8	999	83.4	2.7	0.3	0.4	1.9	1.8	5.7
Perry County	1 491	69.0	2 798	72.1	6	0.0	0	X	53	88.7	0.5	0.2	0.1	0.1	0.2	2.8
Pickens County	4 848	72.9	3 201	71.5	11	72.7	8	50.0	25	92.0	0.4	0.2	0.1	0.1	0.1	4.0
Pike County	7 418	64.5	4 228	63.6	45	88.9	59	54.2	74	60.8	1.9	0.4	0.8	0.4	0.9	5.5
Randolph County	6 742	71.7	1 684	71.2	21	100.0	11	100.0	93	79.6	1.2	0.3	0.2	0.7	0.8	4.3
Russell County.............	11 611	67.3	7 511	69.6	123	43.1	83	67.5	198	69.2	2.0	0.6	0.6	0.7	0.8	6.2
St. Clair County............	22 133	77.1	1 560	71.3	88	65.9	47	74.5	116	81.9	0.6	0.3	0.1	0.2	0.1	5.0
Shelby County	48 966	75.2	3 924	72.3	265	77.7	378	59.8	773	68.2	2.4	0.5	0.7	1.0	0.6	7.2
Sumter County	1 657	61.1	4 015	65.9	12	0.0	5	100.0	45	91.1	0.5	0.2	0.1	0.2	0.5	4.8
Talladega County	21 676	71.8	8 600	72.2	111	57.7	97	42.3	134	80.6	0.7	0.2	0.2	0.2	0.2	5.8
Tallapoosa County	12 543	70.9	3 904	72.2	38	52.6	19	52.6	53	77.4	0.4	0.3	0.1	0.0	0.1	5.4
Tuscaloosa County	45 342	64.7	17 445	67.1	220	63.6	531	57.1	538	69.0	2.1	0.6	0.8	0.6	0.7	7.2
Walker County.............	26 144	72.9	1 676	66.7	74	77.0	56	71.4	152	78.9	0.7	0.1	0.2	0.4	0.2	5.1

[1]Hispanic or Latino persons may be of any race.

Table A-3. States and Counties — Age, Ethnicity, and Household Structure

STATE/ County code	MSA/PMSA/ NECMA code[1]	STATE County	Population by age (percent) Total population	Under 5 years	5 to 17 years	18 to 24 years	25 to 44 years	45 to 64 years	65 years and over	Median age	+/− U.S. percent under 18 years	+/− U.S. percent 65 years and over	Non-Hispanic White Total population	Age (percent) Under 18 years	65 years and over
			1	2	3	4	5	6	7	8	9	10	11	12	13
		ALABAMA—Cont'd													
01 129	...	Washington County	18 097	7.4	21.4	9.1	26.7	22.7	12.7	34.9	3.1	0.3	11 697	25.6	14.3
01 131	...	Wilcox County	13 183	8.2	22.2	9.1	25.7	21.0	13.8	33.8	4.7	1.4	3 602	19.1	22.3
01 133	...	Winston County	24 843	6.2	17.5	7.5	29.1	25.5	14.2	38.0	-2.0	1.8	24 021	23.5	14.4
02 000	...	ALASKA	626 932	7.5	22.9	9.1	32.7	22.3	5.6	32.4	4.7	-6.8	423 660	26.5	6.1
02 013	...	Aleutians East Borough	2 697	4.1	11.9	9.5	46.0	26.1	2.3	37.0	-9.7	-10.1	518	10.0	0.4
02 016	...	Aleutians West Census Area	5 465	4.5	12.6	5.1	50.9	25.2	1.7	36.1	-8.6	-10.7	2 059	16.4	0.9
02 020	0380	Anchorage Municipality	260 283	7.6	21.5	9.5	34.2	21.9	5.3	32.4	3.4	-7.1	181 919	25.4	6.0
02 050	...	Bethel Census Area	16 006	10.0	29.9	9.9	28.2	16.7	5.3	25.3	14.2	-7.1	1 935	19.3	3.3
02 060	...	Bristol Bay Borough	1 258	7.1	24.2	6.6	34.7	22.4	5.0	36.0	5.6	-7.4	659	23.5	3.9
02 068	...	Denali Borough	1 893	5.2	18.9	6.4	37.0	29.4	3.1	37.6	-1.6	-9.3	1 606	23.2	2.9
02 070	...	Dillingham Census Area	4 922	9.9	28.6	7.6	29.0	19.3	5.6	28.9	12.8	-6.8	1 035	19.7	3.9
02 090	...	Fairbanks North Star Borough	82 840	8.0	22.0	12.1	33.5	19.7	4.7	29.5	4.3	-7.7	63 018	27.6	5.0
02 100	...	Haines Borough	2 392	5.3	20.6	4.7	28.2	30.6	10.7	40.7	0.2	-1.7	1 950	23.7	11.2
02 110	...	Juneau City and Borough	30 711	6.5	21.0	7.6	33.2	25.4	6.2	35.3	1.8	-6.2	22 501	24.0	6.4
02 122	...	Kenai Peninsula Borough	49 691	6.7	23.2	6.9	29.8	26.1	7.3	36.3	4.2	-5.1	42 290	28.7	7.7
02 130	...	Ketchikan Gateway Borough	14 070	6.6	21.6	7.8	31.1	25.4	7.5	36.0	2.5	-4.9	10 250	24.9	7.9
02 150	...	Kodiak Island Borough	13 913	9.7	22.9	8.6	33.8	20.5	4.6	31.6	6.9	-7.8	7 950	29.3	3.9
02 164	...	Lake and Peninsula Borough	1 823	8.1	29.8	8.2	28.5	19.6	5.7	29.2	12.2	-6.7	347	23.6	4.6
02 170	...	Matanuska-Susitna Borough	59 322	7.0	25.2	7.6	31.0	23.4	5.8	34.1	6.5	-6.6	51 135	30.4	6.3
02 180	...	Nome Census Area	9 196	8.7	28.3	9.6	29.4	18.1	6.0	27.6	11.3	-6.4	1 738	19.6	4.2
02 185	...	North Slope Borough	7 385	9.6	28.6	9.2	30.4	18.0	4.2	27.0	12.5	-8.2	1 239	18.5	1.0
02 188	...	Northwest Arctic Borough	7 208	10.6	30.8	10.1	28.1	15.3	5.2	23.9	15.7	-7.2	874	14.3	2.5
02 201	...	Prince of Wales-Outer Ketchikan Cens	6 146	7.2	23.7	7.3	30.2	25.8	5.7	34.7	5.2	-6.7	3 196	24.8	4.9
02 220	...	Sitka City and Borough	8 835	5.9	21.0	9.7	30.2	25.7	7.6	35.2	1.2	-4.8	5 876	23.7	7.6
02 232	...	Skagway-Hoonah-Angoon Census Area	3 436	5.4	21.4	7.0	29.7	29.4	7.1	37.8	1.1	-5.3	1 973	21.3	7.8
02 240	...	Southeast Fairbanks Census Area	6 174	7.0	25.8	7.4	28.0	25.7	6.1	33.7	7.1	-6.3	4 817	31.2	6.4
02 261	...	Valdez-Cordova Census Area	10 195	6.5	23.2	7.1	30.8	26.6	5.7	36.1	4.0	-6.7	7 596	26.4	5.7
02 270	...	Wade Hampton Census Area	7 028	10.5	36.1	9.5	25.9	12.9	5.1	20.0	20.9	-7.3	343	17.5	2.0
02 280	...	Wrangell-Petersburg Census Area	6 684	6.7	23.0	5.1	30.0	25.5	9.7	37.2	4.0	-2.7	4 843	26.3	10.4
02 282	...	Yakutat City and Borough	808	5.9	21.5	7.9	32.2	28.0	4.5	37.2	1.7	-7.9	398	16.1	4.0
02 290	...	Yukon-Koyukuk Census Area	6 551	7.3	27.8	8.3	27.2	22.3	7.2	31.1	9.4	-5.2	1 595	24.7	5.8
04 000	...	ARIZONA	5 130 632	7.4	19.2	10.0	29.7	20.8	13.0	34.2	0.9	0.6	3 272 065	20.7	17.7
04 001	...	Apache County	69 423	9.0	29.5	9.4	25.2	18.6	8.4	27.0	12.8	-4.0	12 126	26.3	12.6
04 003	...	Cochise County	117 755	6.5	19.7	9.4	26.2	23.6	14.6	36.9	0.5	2.2	70 626	20.5	19.0
04 005	2620	Coconino County	116 320	7.3	21.3	14.6	29.3	20.5	6.9	29.6	2.9	-5.5	67 088	20.9	8.0
04 007	...	Gila County	51 335	5.8	19.4	6.4	22.1	26.3	20.0	42.3	-0.5	7.6	35 422	19.9	24.7
04 009	...	Graham County	33 489	7.7	22.4	12.3	27.7	18.2	11.7	30.9	4.4	-0.7	18 470	25.8	15.7
04 011	...	Greenlee County	8 547	8.1	23.7	7.2	28.5	22.6	9.8	33.6	6.1	-2.6	4 558	27.6	9.9
04 012	...	La Paz County	19 715	4.8	16.2	6.1	20.5	26.4	26.1	46.8	-4.7	13.7	12 561	12.0	36.9
04 013	6200	Maricopa County	3 072 149	7.8	19.1	10.2	31.6	19.7	11.7	33.0	1.2	-0.7	2 033 420	21.7	15.9
04 015	4120	Mohave County	155 032	6.0	17.1	6.4	23.5	26.7	20.4	42.9	-2.6	8.0	130 287	20.5	23.0
04 017	...	Navajo County	97 470	8.5	27.0	8.9	25.4	20.4	9.9	30.2	9.8	-2.5	41 120	27.3	14.6
04 019	8520	Pima County	843 746	6.5	18.0	10.7	28.8	21.8	14.2	35.7	-1.2	1.8	517 982	18.3	19.4
04 021	6200	Pinal County	179 727	6.7	18.3	8.7	27.7	22.3	16.3	37.1	-0.7	3.9	105 665	17.9	23.7
04 023	...	Santa Cruz County	38 381	8.3	25.3	7.9	27.0	20.9	10.6	31.8	7.9	-1.8	6 626	16.0	22.5
04 025	...	Yavapai County	167 517	5.1	16.0	7.1	22.6	27.3	21.9	44.5	-4.6	9.5	144 984	18.9	24.2
04 027	9360	Yuma County	160 026	7.8	21.0	10.2	25.5	18.9	16.6	33.9	3.1	4.2	71 130	15.8	31.0
05 000	...	ARKANSAS	2 673 400	6.8	18.7	9.8	28.1	22.6	14.0	36.0	-0.2	1.6	2 100 065	23.1	15.7
05 001	...	Arkansas County	20 749	6.6	18.3	8.1	26.4	24.6	15.9	38.7	-0.8	3.5	15 550	22.1	18.1
05 003	...	Ashley County	24 209	6.7	20.2	8.2	26.9	24.3	13.8	36.2	1.2	1.4	16 631	23.7	15.3
05 005	...	Baxter County	38 386	4.4	14.5	5.9	21.1	27.3	26.8	48.1	-6.8	14.4	37 285	18.8	27.2
05 007	2580	Benton County	153 406	7.5	19.1	8.6	29.5	20.9	14.3	35.3	0.9	1.9	132 967	24.8	16.2
05 009	...	Boone County	33 948	6.3	17.7	8.1	26.8	24.6	16.6	38.9	-1.7	4.2	32 838	23.8	17.0
05 011	...	Bradley County	12 600	5.9	17.6	10.1	26.6	22.0	17.8	38.0	-2.2	5.4	7 865	20.3	22.0
05 013	...	Calhoun County	5 744	5.4	19.4	7.1	27.9	24.4	15.7	39.2	-0.9	3.3	4 232	22.6	17.4
05 015	...	Carroll County	25 357	6.2	17.7	8.2	26.3	25.7	15.8	39.4	-1.8	3.4	22 204	22.1	17.7
05 017	...	Chicot County	14 117	6.9	20.4	8.5	26.3	22.0	15.9	36.2	1.6	3.5	5 994	19.5	20.7
05 019	...	Clark County	23 546	6.0	15.8	19.9	24.2	19.4	14.7	31.8	-3.9	2.3	17 337	19.1	16.1
05 021	...	Clay County	17 609	6.0	17.1	7.8	25.2	24.5	19.4	40.5	-2.6	7.0	17 252	23.0	19.6
05 023	...	Cleburne County	24 046	5.1	16.3	6.6	24.0	26.9	21.1	43.7	-4.3	8.7	23 414	21.1	21.2
05 025	...	Cleveland County	8 571	6.7	19.6	7.8	27.8	24.5	13.7	36.9	0.6	1.3	7 232	24.7	14.4
05 027	...	Columbia County	25 603	6.2	18.9	12.3	25.2	21.4	16.0	35.7	-0.6	3.6	15 758	21.3	18.3

[1]MSA = Metropolitan Statistical Area. PMSA = Primary MSA. NECMA = New England County Metropolitan Area. See the Appendix A for explanation of these concepts. See Appendix B for list of metropolitan areas identified by type, with component counties.

Table A-3. States and Counties — Age, Ethnicity, and Household Structure

STATE County	Black or African American Total population	Age (percent) Under 18 years	65 years and over	American Indian and Alaska Native Total population	Age (percent) Under 18 years	65 years and over	Asian, Hawaiian, and Pacific Islander Total population	Age (percent) Under 18 years	65 years and over	Hispanic or Latino[1] Total population	Age (percent) Under 18 years	65 years and over	Two or more races Total population	Age (percent) Under 18 years	65 years and over
	14	15	16	17	18	19	20	21	22	23	24	25	26	27	28
ALABAMA—Cont'd															
Washington County.......	4 996	34.2	11.1	1 176	36.7	5.6	49	30.6	0.0	88	33.0	10.2	153	35.3	7.2
Wilcox County	9 523	34.8	10.6	23	26.1	8.7	10	0.0	20.0	27	29.6	7.4	10	20.0	0.0
Winston County	88	55.7	11.4	150	36.0	4.7	56	17.9	0.0	378	29.4	5.8	206	19.9	11.2
ALASKA	21 968	35.1	3.2	97 012	38.4	5.9	28 618	28.1	5.5	25 765	39.5	2.1	35 240	52.3	2.3
Aleutians East Borough	34	0.0	0.0	1 018	33.8	5.1	720	1.1	0.8	334	3.6	0.0	84	29.8	2.4
Aleutians West Census Area	122	0.0	0.0	1 199	28.4	5.9	1 383	7.1	0.0	582	15.1	0.0	190	46.8	1.1
Anchorage Municipality .	15 201	34.8	3.3	18 800	34.1	4.5	16 293	30.4	6.0	14 738	39.7	2.2	16 465	53.1	1.7
Bethel Census Area	127	49.6	0.0	13 023	42.1	5.8	199	22.1	3.5	172	40.7	5.8	638	63.9	1.4
Bristol Bay Borough	13	30.8	0.0	547	41.3	6.2	9	0.0	0.0	12	16.7	0.0	18	33.3	16.7
Denali Borough	24	8.3	8.3	87	29.9	5.7	45	15.6	0.0	56	33.9	7.1	91	38.5	2.2
Dillingham Census Area	6	0.0	0.0	3 425	42.9	6.5	35	37.1	0.0	107	43.9	0.0	365	52.1	4.4
Fairbanks North Star Borough	4 940	37.7	2.7	5 413	34.6	5.3	2 270	23.5	5.5	3 486	39.7	2.5	4 311	52.9	2.3
Haines Borough	5	0.0	60.0	298	33.9	9.7	26	7.7	0.0	31	32.3	0.0	80	55.0	5.0
Juneau City and Borough.....................	235	21.3	16.2	3 558	33.7	5.8	1 560	33.1	7.1	972	40.8	1.2	2 099	50.3	4.0
Kenai Peninsula Borough.....................	201	30.8	1.5	3 883	35.4	4.9	522	25.9	8.4	1 051	44.3	4.0	1 881	44.1	3.6
Ketchikan Gateway Borough.....................	60	30.0	0.0	1 915	34.9	9.2	784	35.5	5.7	312	37.2	2.6	884	46.3	1.7
Kodiak Island Borough ..	89	50.6	0.0	1 939	39.9	6.1	2 511	32.6	6.5	849	42.0	0.8	770	46.2	6.0
Lake and Peninsula Borough.....................	0	X	X	1 332	40.5	6.4	10	0.0	0.0	20	70.0	0.0	128	55.5	2.3
Matanuska-Susitna Borough.....................	569	41.5	1.6	2 935	38.2	3.7	429	27.0	6.5	1 476	43.7	0.8	2 884	52.6	3.0
Nome Census Area.......	31	29.4	0.0	6 840	30.0	6.0	62	11.3	0.0	122	55.7	0.0	479	61.0	0.8
North Slope Borough	58	20.7	5.2	5 062	42.1	5.3	504	30.2	3.2	169	47.9	0.0	458	60.9	2.2
Northwest Arctic Borough.....................	22	9.1	4.5	5 914	44.7	5.9	64	37.5	0.0	70	55.7	0.0	297	59.3	0.7
Prince of Wales-Outer Ketchikan Cens	16	18.8	0.0	2 446	35.0	7.4	21	19.0	9.5	115	53.0	0.0	417	53.2	2.9
Sitka City and Borough .	31	0.0	12.9	1 642	29.4	11.9	548	36.9	2.4	289	38.1	6.9	537	45.1	2.8
Skagway-Hoonah-Angoon Census Area.	8	37.5	0.0	1 172	33.8	7.3	13	0.0	0.0	136	50.0	0.0	177	40.7	2.8
Southeast Fairbanks Census Area	125	36.8	2.4	778	33.4	7.1	38	15.8	5.3	179	48.0	1.1	283	54.4	2.1
Valdez-Cordova Census Area	30	20.0	0.0	1 322	37.1	7.6	395	27.8	5.8	283	38.5	1.8	609	52.4	3.4
Wade Hampton Census Area.........................	7	0.0	42.9	6 445	47.8	5.2	9	0.0	0.0	29	51.7	0.0	205	64.4	4.4
Wrangell-Petersburg Census Area	4	100.0	0.0	1 071	31.9	10.6	122	22.1	12.3	106	32.1	0.0	564	55.7	2.8
Yakutat City and Borough.....................	2	0.0	0.0	321	38.0	5.0	23	13.0	13.0	8	0.0	0.0	62	53.2	1.6
Yukon-Koyukuk Census Area.........................	5	0.0	0.0	4 627	38.2	8.0	23	26.1	0.0	63	34.9	0.0	264	47.0	2.3
ARIZONA	154 316	30.7	6.3	253 542	38.8	5.6	97 389	23.3	5.9	1 295 317	38.0	4.2	156 497	45.7	4.4
Apache County.............	144	16.0	4.2	53 376	41.1	7.4	198	29.8	1.0	2 912	38.2	9.4	1 158	58.6	2.8
Cochise County............	5 057	27.7	2.5	1 551	31.1	6.9	2 237	19.4	12.1	36 193	36.3	8.6	4 441	48.7	6.2
Coconino County..........	1 368	32.7	7.5	32 826	40.9	5.7	1 088	22.5	1.0	12 692	36.1	4.7	2 691	51.6	2.1
Gila County	117	8.5	6.0	6 469	41.4	5.6	217	16.1	6.5	8 450	33.6	12.5	1 246	43.9	10.5
Graham County	752	18.9	4.8	4 794	44.2	4.1	214	23.4	0.0	8 990	32.7	8.7	858	40.7	5.8
Greenlee County	49	30.6	6.1	183	42.6	2.2	13	46.2	0.0	3 702	36.0	10.2	308	58.8	7.5
La Paz County	142	32.4	9.9	2 495	35.2	8.6	90	14.4	10.0	4 426	39.1	5.6	485	40.2	12.8
Maricopa County	111 584	31.7	6.0	55 177	34.8	3.0	70 105	24.0	5.8	763 333	38.8	2.8	94 572	46.2	3.6
Mohave County............	770	30.1	9.0	3 719	34.5	7.9	1 014	20.2	6.6	16 999	38.4	5.9	4 111	41.5	7.4
Navajo County.............	908	24.9	10.1	46 723	42.3	6.5	238	22.7	4.6	7 808	39.7	5.9	1 807	50.6	4.5
Pima County................	24 460	28.6	7.9	27 440	34.2	4.9	17 991	21.2	5.7	247 061	36.0	5.9	29 339	43.5	4.7
Pinal County................	4 889	25.6	7.4	13 261	39.9	4.9	1 234	31.0	4.7	53 782	35.3	5.6	6 138	45.2	6.7
Santa Cruz County........	122	18.0	27.0	248	15.7	9.3	319	35.1	0.6	31 041	37.4	8.1	951	34.1	6.6
Yavapai County............	449	32.7	17.8	2 597	36.5	8.2	923	17.7	5.2	16 300	36.2	6.3	3 662	39.2	7.0
Yuma County	3 505	29.7	4.3	2 683	30.2	10.3	1 508	22.1	12.5	80 828	40.3	4.7	4 730	49.1	6.4
ARKANSAS...............	417 881	33.6	8.9	18 492	30.6	5.8	20 615	25.1	4.5	85 576	36.8	2.5	38 082	38.1	7.9
Arkansas County..........	4 915	33.6	9.2	69	15.9	20.3	55	18.2	16.4	75	29.3	5.3	103	37.9	17.5
Ashley County	6 431	33.0	11.5	113	36.3	7.1	78	30.8	10.3	781	38.3	2.7	299	42.1	11.4
Baxter County..............	31	54.8	0.0	201	16.4	10.9	152	8.6	17.1	409	35.7	0.3	349	23.5	14.0
Benton County	778	37.8	1.9	2 934	37.2	4.7	1 688	25.8	3.6	13 214	40.2	1.3	2 754	43.1	3.0
Boone County	33	75.8	0.0	281	23.8	3.9	41	2.4	4.9	430	27.7	7.2	346	32.7	5.2
Bradley County............	3 623	29.5	13.8	0	X	X	15	0.0	33.3	1 026	26.0	1.7	99	28.3	5.1
Calhoun County	1 384	30.6	11.3	6	50.0	0.0	4	0.0	0.0	71	40.8	0.0	26	7.7	30.8
Carroll County	16	31.3	0.0	216	31.5	0.5	34	2.9	20.6	2 623	37.1	2.0	424	46.0	9.4
Chicot County..............	7 649	33.2	12.6	23	56.5	0.0	95	15.8	23.2	395	39.2	4.8	70	50.0	0.0
Clark County................	5 280	29.1	11.9	135	29.6	8.9	109	5.5	0.0	523	36.1	0.0	189	28.8	18.0
Clay County.................	19	52.6	0.0	99	18.2	13.1	27	29.6	0.0	92	35.9	10.9	137	30.7	21.2
Cleburne County	66	74.2	0.0	64	7.8	37.5	42	35.7	14.3	311	36.3	10.3	163	27.0	29.4
Cleveland County	1 126	35.3	11.3	28	28.6	0.0	48	16.7	6.3	115	30.4	1.7	38	47.4	2.6
Columbia County..........	9 353	31.4	12.7	66	10.6	7.6	43	7.0	0.0	231	16.5	7.8	194	41.8	5.7

[1] Hispanic or Latino persons may be of any race.

STATE County	Total households	Family households (percent)						Nonfamily households (percent)						Percent of householders 65 years and over who live alone	Grandparents who are responsible for the care of their grandchildren
		Married-couple family households			Other family households			Two or more unrelated persons		Male living alone		Female living alone			
		Total	With children	Householder 65 years or over	Total	With children	Householder 65 years or over	Total	Householder 65 years or over	Total	Householder 65 years or over	Total	Householder 65 years or over		
	29	30	31	32	33	34	35	36	37	38	39	40	41	42	43
ALABAMA—Cont'd															
Washington County......	6 676	61.0	29.5	10.3	15.0	8.4	2.5	1.2	0.3	9.9	2.7	13.0	8.4	45.9	317
Wilcox County.............	4 791	40.6	18.4	9.3	30.4	18.5	5.0	1.6	0.3	11.3	2.6	16.1	9.4	45.2	289
Winston County............	10 125	60.0	24.7	9.8	13.0	7.2	2.2	1.7	0.4	10.9	2.5	14.4	8.3	46.8	205
ALASKA	221 804	53.3	29.3	4.5	15.9	11.2	1.3	7.3	0.3	13.4	1.4	10.0	2.6	39.4	5 419
Aleutians East Borough	524	44.7	22.3	2.7	21.2	17.0	1.5	6.3	0.0	21.9	3.1	5.9	0.4	45.0	15
Aleutians West Census Area.......	1 274	45.6	28.7	1.3	13.4	7.5	1.4	8.9	0.2	23.8	1.4	8.2	1.0	46.3	32
Anchorage Municipality .	95 080	52.2	28.6	4.0	16.0	11.2	0.9	8.5	0.4	12.3	1.1	11.0	2.6	41.5	1 719
Bethel Census Area......	4 222	49.1	35.9	5.1	26.6	15.4	6.3	4.6	0.1	13.1	1.4	6.6	1.4	19.5	482
Bristol Bay Borough	492	50.8	29.9	4.3	11.0	8.5	0.8	6.7	0.0	20.9	2.0	10.6	2.0	44.4	15
Denali Borough	788	45.7	22.7	3.2	11.9	8.1	0.8	7.4	0.0	27.0	0.5	8.0	0.1	13.9	7
Dillingham Census Area	1 511	49.8	32.0	5.3	22.4	13.8	3.8	4.2	0.1	15.4	2.6	8.3	1.2	29.2	106
Fairbanks North Star Borough..................	29 772	55.7	31.5	3.5	13.7	10.2	1.0	7.1	0.4	14.3	1.4	9.2	2.0	41.5	511
Haines Borough	985	53.1	22.7	8.5	12.8	8.7	0.8	7.6	0.6	15.7	2.8	11.7	4.5	42.4	10
Juneau City and Borough.....................	11 534	52.6	26.3	4.7	14.6	10.3	1.3	8.4	0.2	11.2	1.2	13.2	3.0	40.8	174
Kenai Peninsula Borough.....................	18 412	55.6	27.8	6.3	13.6	9.9	0.8	6.1	0.2	14.6	1.8	10.1	3.3	40.5	289
Ketchikan Gateway Borough.....................	5 399	51.9	26.4	5.1	15.6	10.9	1.9	6.4	0.1	14.8	1.5	11.3	4.0	43.3	55
Kodiak Island Borough..	4 431	60.9	37.9	3.5	13.9	10.5	0.9	5.5	0.2	13.7	1.4	6.1	2.4	45.0	109
Lake and Peninsula Borough.....................	587	49.6	29.3	6.1	21.8	14.7	3.2	4.9	0.0	17.4	2.2	6.3	1.0	25.7	61
Matanuska-Susitna Borough.....................	20 552	59.7	32.5	5.9	14.0	10.6	0.7	6.0	0.3	12.3	1.4	8.0	2.6	37.3	364
Nome Census Area.......	2 686	42.7	28.1	4.2	28.5	18.7	5.6	5.7	0.2	14.8	1.5	8.3	2.3	27.2	256
North Slope Borough	2 116	43.0	29.1	3.7	29.7	19.0	3.9	5.8	0.0	15.9	1.2	5.6	0.6	18.6	164
Northwest Arctic Borough.....................	1 778	47.5	32.7	7.4	31.8	22.8	5.3	4.2	0.1	11.2	0.4	5.2	0.4	6.1	227
Prince of Wales-Outer Ketchikan Cens..........	2 270	52.9	27.0	4.5	15.5	10.7	1.7	5.7	0.1	18.6	3.2	7.3	2.0	45.0	103
Sitka City and Borough .	3 281	54.3	26.8	4.8	14.1	8.8	2.8	7.2	0.0	11.8	0.9	12.6	4.1	39.4	65
Skagway-Hoonah-Angoon Census Area.	1 369	48.2	22.0	4.7	14.9	8.5	2.6	6.7	0.3	19.9	2.8	10.2	2.9	43.4	62
Southeast Fairbanks Census Area	2 071	56.9	30.3	5.4	14.3	9.7	1.5	5.1	0.1	14.9	2.9	8.7	3.1	46.3	36
Valdez-Cordova Census Area	3 884	53.3	28.1	4.1	13.1	9.7	0.9	6.8	0.2	17.8	2.7	9.1	2.4	49.1	82
Wade Hampton Census Area........................	1 610	47.0	37.1	6.3	34.0	22.2	9.4	2.9	0.0	10.6	0.8	5.4	1.2	11.6	263
Wrangell-Petersburg Census Area	2 605	55.6	27.4	7.9	13.2	10.1	0.7	5.0	0.2	15.2	2.7	11.1	5.2	47.6	78
Yakutat City and Borough.....................	266	39.1	18.8	2.6	21.4	15.0	2.3	7.9	0.0	21.4	1.5	10.2	1.9	40.9	4
Yukon-Koyukuk Census Area........................	2 305	38.1	22.9	4.9	26.2	16.5	4.1	5.2	0.3	21.7	3.6	8.7	2.7	40.3	130
ARIZONA	1 901 625	52.9	23.5	11.2	15.3	9.2	1.7	7.0	0.6	11.1	2.4	13.7	6.3	39.3	52 210
Apache County.............	19 932	49.5	28.9	7.7	27.1	15.0	4.1	2.2	0.4	11.9	2.8	9.4	4.1	36.5	2 112
Cochise County...........	43 896	55.8	23.1	12.7	14.9	9.2	2.1	4.1	0.5	12.0	3.7	13.2	6.7	40.3	1 616
Coconino County..........	40 386	50.6	24.8	6.3	16.6	10.6	1.7	10.7	0.3	11.2	1.6	10.8	3.1	36.0	1 670
Gila County	20 165	56.2	18.9	16.9	14.3	8.0	2.6	3.7	0.7	11.0	3.9	14.8	8.4	37.9	1 011
Graham County............	10 120	57.3	28.0	11.2	18.6	11.9	3.0	3.2	0.6	8.3	2.7	12.5	7.8	41.5	635
Greenlee County...........	3 131	59.8	31.4	8.0	12.9	8.8	1.5	2.8	0.3	15.0	2.8	9.5	5.7	46.3	145
La Paz County	8 392	54.9	14.7	22.9	12.2	7.2	1.7	6.3	2.2	14.4	5.3	12.2	7.7	32.6	249
Maricopa County	1 133 048	52.7	24.6	9.8	15.2	9.1	1.5	7.7	0.5	10.9	2.0	13.6	6.1	40.6	25 907
Mohave County	62 796	56.1	17.6	17.5	13.5	8.2	1.8	6.4	1.3	11.4	4.1	12.6	7.4	35.7	1 811
Navajo County..............	30 055	55.6	28.5	10.2	21.4	12.9	2.6	3.0	0.4	9.4	2.5	10.5	5.2	36.8	2 280
Pima County................	332 497	48.7	20.8	10.9	15.6	9.2	1.9	7.3	0.6	12.7	2.6	15.8	7.1	41.8	8 471
Pinal County................	61 413	57.8	20.1	17.4	16.3	10.3	2.2	5.0	1.0	9.7	2.9	11.3	6.0	30.0	2 246
Santa Cruz County.......	11 821	63.2	35.6	10.5	17.9	10.7	2.8	2.4	0.5	6.9	1.9	9.6	5.1	33.6	736
Yavapai County	70 069	56.1	17.7	17.6	10.9	6.5	1.8	6.4	1.0	11.2	3.9	15.4	8.8	38.4	1 405
Yuma County	53 904	63.6	28.0	17.9	14.3	9.1	1.9	3.8	1.0	8.0	3.4	10.4	6.2	31.5	1 916
ARKANSAS..............	1 042 807	55.1	23.4	10.6	15.5	9.1	2.2	3.9	0.3	10.6	2.4	14.9	8.1	44.3	33 618
Arkansas County..........	8 473	53.5	21.0	10.6	17.6	10.8	2.6	2.8	0.0	11.2	2.5	14.9	9.4	47.2	390
Ashley County..............	9 365	57.4	23.9	10.5	16.6	9.5	2.6	2.2	0.3	9.6	2.3	14.3	8.9	45.7	456
Baxter County..............	17 099	59.7	17.1	21.0	9.5	5.0	1.8	3.4	0.6	11.6	4.5	15.8	10.7	39.3	276
Benton County.............	58 242	63.5	28.0	13.7	11.5	7.1	1.3	4.0	0.3	8.6	2.1	12.5	6.6	36.3	1 303
Boone County..............	13 864	59.9	23.7	13.1	12.1	7.1	2.3	2.5	0.4	9.9	2.2	15.6	9.1	41.8	324
Bradley County............	4 834	52.6	19.8	11.9	18.1	10.4	3.8	1.7	0.0	11.5	2.7	16.0	10.4	45.6	247
Calhoun County	2 327	55.4	25.2	10.9	15.3	7.2	3.7	2.2	0.0	12.3	3.9	14.6	10.9	50.1	115
Carroll County.............	10 199	57.1	21.1	13.6	13.0	7.9	1.7	4.6	0.3	10.3	2.0	15.0	8.4	39.8	198
Chicot County..............	5 199	45.1	19.1	10.5	25.1	13.2	5.2	2.8	0.3	10.6	3.0	16.4	9.9	44.7	387
Clark County	8 893	52.1	21.5	11.1	15.1	9.0	2.8	6.1	0.3	10.0	2.8	17.6	10.2	47.7	187
Clay County................	7 368	57.5	22.9	13.6	10.3	5.9	2.0	3.5	0.5	11.1	3.7	17.6	12.3	49.9	125
Cleburne County	10 181	62.7	20.7	18.2	10.2	5.9	2.3	2.8	0.4	9.2	2.3	15.1	9.0	35.3	260
Cleveland County	3 266	64.1	27.3	12.2	12.9	7.6	2.1	1.6	0.2	9.7	2.0	11.6	7.5	39.4	136
Columbia County..........	10 001	49.8	20.7	10.2	18.0	9.7	3.5	3.0	0.3	11.9	3.6	17.3	10.9	50.8	462

STATE County	Households with Non-Hispanic White householder		Households with Black or African American householder		Households with American Indian and Alaska Native householder		Households with Asian, Hawaiian, and Pacific Islander householder		Households with Hispanic or Latino[1] householder		Foreign-born population	Place of birth (percent)			Percent in non-English speaking households	
	Number of households	Percent that are family households	Number of households	Percent that are family households	Number of households	Percent that are family households	Number of households	Percent that are family households	Number of households	Percent that are family households	Percent of total population that is foreign-born	Europe	Asia	Latin America	Linguistically isolated	Not linguistically isolated
	44	45	46	47	48	49	50	51	52	53	54	55	56	57	58	59
ALABAMA—Cont'd																
Washington County	4 493	76.1	1 721	75.2	402	78.1	8	100.0	31	74.2	0.5	0.1	0.2	0.1	0.1	4.6
Wilcox County	1 605	64.2	3 175	74.4	5	100.0	2	0.0	6	50.0	0.3	0.0	0.1	0.1	0.1	7.8
Winston County	9 833	73.3	24	58.3	60	60.0	29	65.5	103	65.0	1.0	0.1	0.2	0.7	0.2	5.2
ALASKA	166 838	68.3	7 508	71.4	26 616	72.3	7 206	77.6	6 407	75.5	5.9	1.2	3.0	1.1	2.3	19.3
Aleutians East Borough	153	56.9	5	0.0	339	70.5	9	66.7	9	66.7	18.3	0.1	14.5	3.2	0.7	10.4
Aleutians West Census Area	716	56.1	5	0.0	388	64.4	103	71.8	29	58.6	21.5	0.8	15.3	4.4	5.0	36.2
Anchorage Municipality	72 584	67.6	5 388	70.7	5 602	65.3	4 647	76.0	3 889	74.9	8.2	1.6	4.0	1.7	2.7	18.0
Bethel Census Area	1 002	58.9	33	87.9	2 969	81.9	68	58.8	60	65.0	1.4	0.4	0.7	0.1	12.2	68.6
Bristol Bay Borough	305	56.1	6	33.3	170	74.7	1	0.0	5	40.0	0.6	0.0	0.4	0.0	0.1	10.5
Denali Borough	672	57.6	11	18.2	37	94.6	24	8.3	25	60.0	2.9	1.1	1.2	0.0	1.0	10.7
Dillingham Census Area	479	61.0	5	80.0	913	77.3	6	83.3	30	86.7	1.0	0.2	0.4	0.2	5.5	49.5
Fairbanks North Star Borough	24 086	69.5	1 558	76.6	1 614	62.4	588	70.4	942	74.4	4.0	1.0	2.0	0.5	0.9	12.9
Haines Borough	830	65.4	5	0.0	115	70.4	8	75.0	3	100.0	4.1	1.7	0.5	0.3	0.0	6.9
Juneau City and Borough	9 186	66.6	116	69.0	1 129	63.9	402	81.1	275	78.9	5.7	0.9	3.1	0.8	1.1	15.6
Kenai Peninsula Borough	16 489	69.4	48	64.6	1 018	70.2	137	64.2	209	74.6	2.7	0.7	1.0	0.5	1.1	10.9
Ketchikan Gateway Borough	4 200	66.8	28	64.3	689	68.9	174	96.6	84	76.2	5.7	0.9	3.9	0.3	1.2	12.2
Kodiak Island Borough	2 919	72.0	17	100.0	593	72.5	495	93.3	172	94.2	16.7	0.5	12.7	2.5	8.2	25.8
Lake and Peninsula Borough	155	66.5	0	X	391	72.9	10	40.0	2	100.0	0.7	0.0	0.3	0.2	1.9	24.4
Matanuska-Susitna Borough	18 769	73.5	159	67.3	562	81.9	62	100.0	342	76.9	2.6	1.2	0.6	0.3	0.5	9.4
Nome Census Area	809	61.2	16	56.3	1 735	77.1	24	95.8	24	62.5	1.5	0.5	0.6	0.2	2.3	45.0
North Slope Borough	577	58.6	29	34.5	1 258	79.3	142	78.2	26	65.4	5.8	0.2	4.3	0.6	5.7	65.9
Northwest Arctic Borough	409	63.1	7	42.9	1 282	84.6	15	86.7	19	89.5	1.1	0.1	0.5	0.2	3.2	62.2
Prince of Wales-Outer Ketchikan Cens	1 340	65.4	6	50.0	814	73.0	6	100.0	15	40.0	1.8	0.2	0.2	0.3	0.4	10.6
Sitka City and Borough	2 393	66.3	6	0.0	546	69.2	119	100.0	74	81.1	5.1	0.5	3.0	0.1	1.1	14.7
Skagway-Hoonah-Angoon Census Area	900	57.5	0	X	387	73.6	8	75.0	26	84.6	2.0	0.3	0.1	0.5	0.2	15.0
Southeast Fairbanks Census Area	1 686	72.5	40	92.5	244	62.7	9	22.2	44	77.3	9.9	8.0	0.8	0.3	5.0	17.2
Valdez-Cordova Census Area	3 107	66.4	11	27.3	456	62.3	101	84.2	65	76.9	5.1	1.0	2.8	0.8	1.6	12.0
Wade Hampton Census Area	171	56.1	5	0.0	1 384	84.6	7	57.1	8	50.0	0.3	0.1	0.1	0.1	4.0	75.4
Wrangell-Petersburg Census Area	2 057	68.7	0	X	369	68.3	26	92.3	18	100.0	2.8	0.9	1.2	0.5	0.7	11.3
Yakutat City and Borough	130	43.1	2	X	110	78.2	10	80.0	0	X	0.6	0.2	0.0	0.0	0.3	23.0
Yukon-Koyukuk Census Area	708	64.7	2	0.0	1 502	65.6	5	20.0	12	66.7	1.0	0.4	0.2	0.1	1.2	28.8
ARIZONA	1 397 040	64.7	55 071	64.7	67 858	78.7	31 575	69.5	331 850	81.7	12.8	1.4	1.5	9.1	6.7	27.2
Apache County	4 729	70.2	29	69.0	14 170	78.6	60	88.3	816	78.7	0.9	0.1	0.1	0.5	11.8	67.2
Cochise County	30 124	67.3	1 763	71.5	439	77.0	555	63.1	10 493	80.4	12.3	1.6	1.4	8.9	4.9	33.0
Coconino County	27 356	61.9	501	66.7	8 238	83.9	364	55.5	3 617	74.1	4.3	0.7	0.7	2.5	4.7	35.3
Gila County	15 500	68.4	33	72.7	1 602	84.6	48	70.8	2 753	74.0	3.6	1.1	0.3	2.0	3.1	24.7
Graham County	6 413	73.5	97	74.2	1 044	88.3	47	83.0	2 400	77.2	2.6	0.3	0.2	2.0	2.9	36.8
Greenlee County	1 906	70.0	22	77.3	30	80.0	4	100.0	1 145	76.6	3.4	0.4	0.0	2.6	3.0	37.1
La Paz County	6 283	64.0	52	65.4	840	71.7	39	84.6	1 137	81.0	9.7	0.5	0.2	8.3	3.7	24.2
Maricopa County	856 511	64.7	40 573	65.0	15 807	74.1	22 730	72.2	186 066	82.4	14.4	1.6	1.9	10.1	7.3	24.3
Mohave County	55 432	68.6	276	66.7	1 229	73.1	341	71.3	4 784	82.7	5.9	1.1	0.5	3.5	2.1	14.4
Navajo County	15 753	73.7	246	66.3	11 640	82.0	65	75.4	2 056	79.4	1.7	0.3	0.2	1.0	8.4	45.3
Pima County	234 832	60.2	9 148	61.1	7 968	75.4	6 250	60.7	71 125	78.1	11.9	1.5	1.7	8.0	5.2	31.0
Pinal County	43 693	71.4	1 147	69.2	3 143	84.2	266	66.9	12 765	81.8	9.0	0.5	0.5	7.5	4.4	29.8
Santa Cruz County	3 171	66.2	47	61.7	100	78.0	67	97.0	8 468	86.7	37.7	0.3	0.5	36.7	21.5	63.6
Yavapai County	63 677	66.1	139	43.2	789	78.6	266	59.0	4 418	81.0	5.9	1.4	0.5	3.4	2.1	12.2
Yuma County	31 660	71.2	998	67.8	819	70.9	473	74.0	19 807	80.9	24.0	0.5	0.6	22.0	13.3	40.4
ARKANSAS	852 927	70.6	145 438	69.5	6 468	70.8	6 010	72.1	21 674	80.6	2.8	0.4	0.6	1.6	1.4	6.9
Arkansas County	6 550	70.7	1 803	72.9	44	65.9	11	100.0	23	95.7	0.4	0.1	0.2	0.1	0.3	5.3
Ashley County	6 702	75.7	2 336	67.7	41	73.2	15	100.0	221	84.2	2.2	0.2	0.1	1.8	1.4	5.5
Baxter County	16 666	69.3	14	57.1	58	56.9	72	38.9	130	91.5	1.6	1.0	0.3	0.3	0.3	5.2
Benton County	52 837	74.3	247	66.4	862	74.1	480	77.5	3 241	86.1	6.4	0.4	0.8	5.0	4.0	10.2
Boone County	13 491	72.1	0	X	114	57.0	17	5.9	118	89.8	1.0	0.3	0.2	0.3	0.1	6.4
Bradley County	3 157	71.6	1 487	67.6	0	X	0	X	145	83.4	4.3	0.4	0.1	3.4	2.2	6.8
Calhoun County	1 793	69.4	495	74.9	0	X	4	100.0	19	73.7	0.9	0.1	0.0	0.8	0.8	4.3
Carroll County	9 480	69.5	4	100.0	65	44.6	4	100.0	554	87.2	7.5	0.7	0.1	6.7	5.6	9.7
Chicot County	2 412	71.8	2 604	69.5	10	100.0	53	54.7	116	64.7	2.3	0.0	0.4	1.7	1.2	7.2
Clark County	6 589	65.9	2 042	68.5	51	56.9	16	0.0	105	87.6	2.0	0.3	0.3	1.2	1.1	6.0
Clay County	7 226	68.0	5	100.0	46	60.9	15	60.0	29	55.2	0.3	0.1	0.2	0.1	0.2	4.0
Cleburne County	9 994	73.1	5	100.0	34	32.4	15	73.3	60	66.7	1.1	0.5	0.1	0.4	0.2	4.8
Cleveland County	2 812	78.5	404	67.3	14	57.1	6	100.0	26	73.1	1.4	0.2	0.1	0.7	0.2	3.9
Columbia County	6 556	67.6	3 300	68.2	37	75.7	6	100.0	74	43.2	0.9	0.2	0.1	0.4	0.2	5.8

[1] Hispanic or Latino persons may be of any race.

STATE/ County code	MSA/PMSA/ NECMA code[1]	STATE County	Population by age (percent)								+/- U.S. percent under 18 years	+/- U.S. percent 65 years and over	Non-Hispanic White		
														Age (percent)	
			Total population	Under 5 years	5 to 17 years	18 to 24 years	25 to 44 years	45 to 64 years	65 years and over	Median age			Total population	Under 18 years	65 years and over
			1	2	3	4	5	6	7	8	9	10	11	12	13
		ARKANSAS—Cont'd													
05 029	...	Conway County.............	20 336	6.3	19.2	8.2	26.7	23.9	15.7	37.9	-0.2	3.3	16 886	23.9	16.9
05 031	3700	Craighead County..........	82 148	6.8	17.4	14.0	28.7	21.3	11.7	33.0	-1.5	-0.7	72 604	22.8	12.7
05 033	2720	Crawford County............	53 247	7.5	20.7	8.4	29.2	22.9	11.3	35.1	2.5	-1.1	48 425	27.2	11.9
05 035	4920	Crittenden County..........	50 866	8.4	22.7	9.4	29.1	20.5	9.9	32.0	5.4	-2.5	25 639	23.8	12.0
05 037	...	Cross County.................	19 526	6.8	20.9	8.7	28.2	21.7	13.7	35.9	2.0	1.3	14 505	24.7	15.1
05 039	...	Dallas County.................	9 210	5.0	21.0	8.9	24.3	23.8	17.0	38.4	0.3	4.6	5 215	21.9	20.4
05 041	...	Desha County.................	15 341	7.4	21.5	8.7	25.6	22.5	14.3	35.5	3.2	1.9	7 634	22.4	17.2
05 043	...	Drew County..................	18 723	6.7	19.0	12.6	27.3	21.2	13.1	34.0	0.0	0.7	13 096	23.2	14.3
05 045	4400	Faulkner County.............	86 014	6.8	18.8	15.3	30.1	19.6	9.5	31.0	-0.1	-2.9	75 068	24.7	10.2
05 047	...	Franklin County..............	17 771	6.5	19.3	8.7	26.6	23.3	15.7	37.6	0.1	3.3	16 749	25.1	16.3
05 049	...	Fulton County.................	11 642	5.6	17.2	6.4	23.8	26.9	20.1	43.0	-2.9	7.7	11 365	22.9	20.3
05 051	...	Garland County.............	88 068	5.5	16.0	7.3	25.0	24.8	21.4	42.5	-4.2	9.0	76 869	19.8	22.9
05 053	...	Grant County.................	16 464	6.5	19.5	8.2	29.5	24.2	12.0	36.6	0.3	-0.4	15 697	26.0	12.2
05 055	...	Greene County...............	37 331	6.7	18.3	9.3	28.6	23.0	14.1	36.2	-0.7	1.7	36 110	24.9	14.1
05 057	...	Hempstead County........	23 587	7.6	19.7	9.7	27.7	21.1	14.2	35.2	1.6	1.8	14 071	22.6	18.0
05 059	...	Hot Spring County	30 353	6.5	18.4	8.3	26.7	24.3	15.7	38.4	-0.8	3.3	26 320	23.8	16.3
05 061	...	Howard County	14 300	6.9	20.0	8.3	28.1	21.5	15.3	36.1	1.2	2.9	10 250	23.9	17.4
05 063	...	Independence County.....	34 233	6.5	18.1	9.1	27.9	23.9	14.5	37.7	-1.1	2.1	32 276	24.1	15.0
05 065	...	Izard County..................	13 249	5.1	15.9	7.1	25.0	25.8	21.1	42.6	-4.7	8.7	12 680	20.7	21.8
05 067	...	Jackson County..............	18 418	5.7	16.6	11.5	25.9	24.2	16.2	38.2	-3.4	3.8	14 753	20.9	18.2
05 069	6240	Jefferson County............	84 278	6.9	19.2	10.9	28.1	22.1	12.8	35.1	0.4	0.4	40 415	20.0	17.1
05 071	...	Johnson County.............	22 781	6.5	18.5	9.5	27.9	22.6	14.9	36.4	-0.7	2.5	20 541	24.3	16.0
05 073	...	Lafayette County............	8 559	6.0	19.3	8.2	24.2	24.6	17.6	39.3	-0.4	5.2	5 257	20.9	20.8
05 075	...	Lawrence County	17 774	6.3	17.6	9.6	25.9	23.2	17.5	38.2	-1.8	5.1	17 274	23.9	17.7
05 077	...	Lee County....................	12 580	6.6	19.6	10.8	28.2	20.7	14.1	34.6	0.5	1.7	5 067	18.0	16.9
05 079	...	Lincoln County...............	14 492	5.6	16.4	12.2	33.1	20.7	12.0	34.7	-3.7	-0.4	9 366	21.0	14.2
05 081	...	Little River County	13 628	7.0	18.1	8.7	25.5	25.7	14.9	38.2	-0.6	2.5	9 993	23.2	16.7
05 083	...	Logan County................	22 486	6.5	19.3	7.4	26.8	24.0	16.0	38.0	0.1	3.6	21 464	25.5	16.5
05 085	4400	Lonoke County..............	52 828	7.0	21.8	7.9	31.3	21.7	10.4	34.7	3.1	-2.0	47 577	28.2	10.5
05 087	...	Madison County..............	14 243	6.5	20.4	7.7	26.8	24.4	14.3	37.7	1.2	1.9	13 433	26.5	14.8
05 089	...	Marion County...............	16 140	5.1	17.1	6.0	23.3	28.4	20.1	44.1	-3.5	7.7	15 623	22.1	20.4
05 091	8360	Miller County	40 443	7.5	18.9	9.8	28.5	22.0	13.3	34.9	0.7	0.9	29 674	23.8	14.5
05 093	...	Mississippi County.........	51 979	8.0	21.5	9.6	28.0	20.3	12.6	33.1	3.8	0.2	33 164	24.2	15.2
05 095	...	Monroe County	10 254	7.0	21.2	7.4	23.9	22.7	17.7	38.3	2.5	5.3	6 017	22.3	20.0
05 097	...	Montgomery County.......	9 245	6.0	17.7	6.4	24.7	26.3	18.9	41.5	-2.0	6.5	8 820	22.8	19.5
05 099	...	Nevada County	9 955	6.5	18.9	8.6	25.3	24.9	15.9	37.7	-0.3	3.5	6 640	23.4	18.0
05 101	...	Newton County	8 608	5.8	19.1	7.5	25.1	27.7	14.8	40.1	-0.8	2.4	8 258	24.7	14.7
05 103	...	Ouachita County	28 790	6.1	19.7	8.2	26.0	22.7	17.2	38.7	0.1	4.8	17 131	22.3	20.0
05 105	...	Perry County	10 209	6.2	19.3	7.3	27.5	24.8	14.9	38.0	-0.2	2.5	9 637	25.2	15.1
05 107	...	Phillips County	26 445	8.5	23.6	9.5	23.5	21.0	13.9	33.0	6.4	1.5	10 226	21.4	18.7
05 109	...	Pike County	11 303	6.3	18.6	7.4	26.1	24.4	17.1	38.9	-0.8	4.7	10 381	24.1	17.9
05 111	...	Poinsett County	25 614	6.8	19.1	8.9	27.1	23.8	14.2	36.6	0.2	1.8	23 078	24.7	14.8
05 113	...	Polk County	20 229	6.6	19.0	7.7	25.2	24.5	17.0	38.6	-0.1	4.6	18 854	24.7	17.7
05 115	...	Pope County	54 469	6.3	19.3	11.5	28.4	21.9	12.7	34.8	-0.1	0.3	50 605	25.0	13.2
05 117	...	Prairie County	9 539	5.9	18.0	7.5	26.7	24.7	17.3	40.1	-1.8	4.9	8 054	21.9	18.3
05 119	4400	Pulaski County	361 474	7.2	18.0	9.5	31.1	22.7	11.5	35.0	-0.5	-0.9	227 495	20.4	14.9
05 121	...	Randolph County............	18 195	6.0	18.5	8.4	25.7	24.3	17.1	38.8	-1.2	4.7	17 553	24.2	17.4
05 123	...	St. Francis County	29 329	7.6	20.2	10.2	29.0	20.8	12.1	33.8	2.1	-0.3	13 216	21.7	15.3
05 125	4400	Saline County	83 529	6.4	19.0	7.8	30.2	24.2	12.4	36.8	-0.3	0.0	78 835	25.0	12.8
05 127	...	Scott County	10 996	7.4	19.2	8.4	26.2	24.1	14.7	37.3	0.9	2.3	9 970	25.8	16.0
05 129	...	Searcy County	8 261	5.4	17.3	7.1	24.2	26.9	19.1	42.3	-3.0	6.7	8 023	22.6	19.5
05 131	2720	Sebastian County...........	115 071	7.4	18.6	9.2	29.6	22.3	12.9	35.5	0.3	0.5	92 077	23.6	15.1
05 133	...	Sevier County	15 757	8.0	20.3	9.4	27.9	21.3	13.2	33.6	2.6	0.8	11 429	23.9	16.6
05 135	...	Sharp County	17 119	5.7	16.1	6.4	22.5	25.7	23.6	44.3	-3.9	11.2	16 499	21.6	24.0
05 137	...	Stone County	11 499	5.6	16.7	7.2	23.3	28.6	18.8	43.1	-3.4	6.4	11 156	21.9	18.7
05 139	...	Union County	45 629	6.1	19.8	8.4	26.9	22.6	16.2	37.7	0.2	3.8	29 933	22.3	19.1
05 141	...	Van Buren County	16 192	5.3	16.3	6.8	22.9	25.3	23.4	44.2	-4.1	11.0	15 492	21.2	24.1
05 143	2580	Washington County.........	157 715	7.5	17.6	15.3	30.4	19.3	9.9	30.8	-0.6	-2.5	133 340	23.3	11.3
05 145	...	White County	67 165	6.3	18.1	12.5	27.4	22.0	13.7	35.1	-1.3	1.3	62 154	23.7	14.3
05 147	...	Woodruff County	8 741	7.0	18.8	8.7	24.5	24.1	16.8	38.4	0.1	4.4	5 932	22.4	17.6
05 149	...	Yell County...................	21 139	6.5	19.4	9.5	27.3	22.4	14.9	36.1	0.2	2.5	17 641	24.1	17.4
06 000	...	CALIFORNIA............	33 871 648	7.2	20.0	9.9	31.9	20.4	10.6	33.3	1.5	-1.8	15 771 163	20.4	16.0
06 001	5775	Alameda County	1 443 741	6.7	17.8	9.5	34.2	21.6	10.2	34.5	-1.2	-2.2	589 243	18.1	14.3
06 003	...	Alpine County.................	1 208	5.0	17.7	11.3	26.0	30.1	9.9	39.3	-3.0	-2.5	870	17.5	11.3
06 005	...	Amador County	35 100	4.0	16.7	6.5	26.4	28.3	18.1	42.7	-5.0	5.7	28 935	19.9	20.7

[1]MSA = Metropolitan Statistical Area. PMSA = Primary MSA. NECMA = New England County Metropolitan Area. See the Appendix A for explanation of these concepts. See Appendix B for list of metropolitan areas identified by type, with component counties.

Table A-3. States and Counties — **Age, Ethnicity, and Household Structure**

STATE / County	Black or African American — Total population (14)	Age (percent) Under 18 years (15)	Age (percent) 65 years and over (16)	American Indian and Alaska Native — Total population (17)	Age (percent) Under 18 years (18)	Age (percent) 65 years and over (19)	Asian, Hawaiian, and Pacific Islander — Total population (20)	Age (percent) Under 18 years (21)	Age (percent) 65 years and over (22)	Hispanic or Latino[1] — Total population (23)	Age (percent) Under 18 years (24)	Age (percent) 65 years and over (25)	Two or more races — Total population (26)	Age (percent) Under 18 years (27)	Age (percent) 65 years and over (28)
ARKANSAS—Cont'd															
Conway County	2 670	31.3	11.9	33	27.3	6.1	46	13.0	4.3	413	38.7	1.9	294	52.0	3.7
Craighead County	6 403	34.8	3.8	311	26.4	4.8	517	36.6	0.8	1 520	35.9	6.1	920	35.0	8.0
Crawford County	404	30.0	19.1	901	34.5	4.4	631	31.5	5.4	1 650	43.5	3.5	1 469	42.3	4.4
Crittenden County	23 692	38.9	8.0	239	35.6	7.1	233	27.5	8.2	825	35.6	1.9	354	39.0	12.7
Cross County	4 567	36.5	10.2	82	22.0	0.0	54	13.0	7.4	290	44.5	3.4	64	42.2	6.3
Dallas County	3 826	31.3	12.7	10	50.0	10.0	0	X	X	163	33.7	12.3	19	0.0	0.0
Desha County	7 085	35.0	11.8	70	57.1	2.9	121	49.6	3.3	350	35.1	2.9	121	32.2	24.0
Drew County	5 007	30.1	11.2	47	10.6	0.0	46	0.0	17.4	413	48.4	1.5	212	61.3	4.2
Faulkner County	7 262	31.2	4.4	431	24.1	1.2	569	17.8	0.0	1 597	36.4	2.1	1 224	34.5	7.8
Franklin County	161	44.7	0.0	126	52.4	2.4	97	30.9	4.1	283	37.5	2.5	408	32.4	9.8
Fulton County	8	100.0	0.0	58	27.6	3.4	18	0.0	55.6	53	18.9	17.0	150	16.0	10.7
Garland County	6 975	32.1	11.4	565	21.1	4.4	303	22.4	10.9	2 082	41.1	7.2	1 476	36.8	13.8
Grant County	382	26.2	11.3	105	22.9	13.3	33	3.0	15.2	140	47.1	2.1	125	26.4	3.2
Greene County	115	18.3	30.4	140	24.3	7.9	34	0.0	14.7	337	32.9	11.3	610	32.1	10.5
Hempstead County	7 036	32.7	11.1	75	22.7	6.7	102	41.2	8.8	1 968	36.4	1.3	440	47.7	4.3
Hot Spring County	2 926	28.5	13.6	163	40.5	3.7	55	25.5	12.7	506	55.9	4.3	420	33.3	15.2
Howard County	3 149	33.6	12.4	48	33.3	4.2	53	34.0	0.0	652	34.4	0.0	259	57.1	4.2
Independence County	752	32.3	8.4	113	25.7	7.1	249	23.3	5.2	371	31.3	4.3	479	37.2	7.7
Izard County	186	3.8	0.0	85	40.0	2.4	18	11.1	0.0	108	51.9	7.4	182	34.1	11.0
Jackson County	3 281	27.7	8.2	86	24.4	17.4	39	41.0	0.0	160	16.3	5.6	125	35.2	5.6
Jefferson County	41 667	31.6	9.1	259	23.9	18.1	443	27.1	5.6	878	36.6	6.4	737	38.0	3.4
Johnson County	293	40.3	5.1	110	23.6	13.6	37	59.5	0.0	1 446	36.6	3.1	524	26.9	4.2
Lafayette County	3 143	32.4	12.5	23	8.7	0.0	26	42.3	7.7	79	34.2	2.5	50	32.0	36.0
Lawrence County	95	11.6	11.6	139	26.6	2.2	46	34.8	0.0	78	21.5	12.8	140	15.7	16.4
Lee County	7 004	32.8	12.6	78	28.2	11.5	3	0.0	0.0	455	19.1	4.6	35	8.6	37.1
Lincoln County	4 720	23.6	8.4	37	24.3	8.1	36	13.9	0.0	273	27.1	2.2	87	32.2	21.8
Little River County	2 786	27.4	11.2	309	40.5	6.5	56	8.9	0.0	259	44.0	2.3	242	49.6	12.0
Logan County	292	27.4	2.4	148	23.6	6.1	72	30.6	0.0	189	29.1	3.7	349	46.4	9.2
Lonoke County	3 483	32.0	11.1	129	20.2	2.3	247	21.9	1.2	791	36.7	2.4	692	47.5	8.4
Madison County	23	56.5	26.1	168	29.2	3.0	55	43.6	12.7	400	33.8	2.8	198	28.3	14.6
Marion County	5	100.0	0.0	161	30.4	9.9	67	9.0	25.4	87	31.0	6.9	180	23.3	13.9
Miller County	9 081	33.7	9.6	183	17.5	10.9	177	23.2	7.3	611	23.1	15.7	734	44.0	11.2
Mississippi County	17 085	39.3	8.2	213	43.2	6.1	90	21.1	0.0	1 096	40.6	3.0	493	36.5	10.8
Monroe County	4 061	36.1	15.1	11	54.5	0.0	2	0.0	0.0	102	44.1	5.9	89	56.2	0.0
Montgomery County	0	X	X	48	22.9	14.6	17	35.3	0.0	267	47.2	1.9	100	36.0	10.0
Nevada County	3 069	28.9	12.0	7	42.9	0.0	0	X	X	163	38.0	0.0	75	40.0	26.7
Newton County	19	15.8	10.5	77	18.2	9.1	11	81.8	0.0	91	57.1	5.5	160	21.9	27.5
Ouachita County	11 098	30.9	13.6	69	24.6	5.8	71	12.7	5.6	286	36.0	4.2	202	51.0	7.4
Perry County	149	30.2	14.1	95	24.2	0.5	65	46.7	0.0	158	31.0	3.2	154	37.0	16.9
Phillips County	15 550	39.0	10.9	23	0.0	56.5	184	29.3	8.2	336	37.5	7.1	221	51.1	6.8
Pike County	435	33.3	13.3	55	36.4	0.0	38	31.6	0.0	357	36.4	2.5	77	20.8	15.6
Poinsett County	1 794	36.6	9.4	81	8.6	16.0	26	0.0	0.0	380	54.5	0.5	259	22.8	16.6
Polk County	14	7.1	0.0	211	37.9	4.7	50	0.0	14.0	679	35.9	4.4	445	33.9	13.7
Pope County	1 275	37.9	3.5	405	22.2	9.9	298	19.8	6.4	1 131	39.5	4.6	855	30.8	13.8
Prairie County	1 217	36.4	12.2	18	44.4	0.0	14	50.0	0.0	190	23.7	14.2	167	15.0	15.6
Pulaski County	115 016	33.8	6.1	1 513	29.9	4.4	4 455	20.7	4.4	8 936	32.5	2.1	5 180	39.2	5.3
Randolph County	102	39.2	9.8	132	22.0	0.0	11	81.8	0.0	118	30.5	0.0	258	39.5	17.4
St. Francis County	14 436	35.6	10.1	18	33.3	0.0	120	9.2	18.3	1 443	7.2	3.7	417	14.4	2.9
Saline County	1 920	31.6	9.1	466	28.8	3.0	459	34.2	3.1	939	36.3	0.3	1 021	30.5	7.4
Scott County	20	40.0	0.0	228	36.4	1.8	71	43.7	0.0	589	37.2	0.5	144	25.7	6.3
Searcy County	3	0.0	66.7	41	4.9	4.9	30	26.7	0.0	49	46.9	6.1	114	24.6	3.5
Sebastian County	7 095	33.4	6.2	2 051	34.0	4.4	3 681	29.4	5.4	7 455	38.1	1.6	3 248	44.1	4.5
Sevier County	817	29.4	11.5	264	49.2	2.7	15	0.0	0.0	3 039	42.7	1.4	263	36.5	12.9
Sharp County	56	28.6	0.0	106	15.1	17.0	28	0.0	0.0	145	41.4	15.9	311	29.9	14.8
Stone County	11	45.5	0.0	66	31.8	6.1	6	0.0	0.0	123	50.4	8.1	152	21.1	37.5
Union County	14 557	33.0	10.7	133	27.8	23.3	185	25.4	9.2	515	31.8	9.9	407	33.4	4.9
Van Buren County	25	48.0	32.0	82	15.9	13.4	48	45.8	4.2	215	41.4	3.7	333	21.6	11.4
Washington County	3 364	29.6	2.4	2 020	27.7	6.3	3 363	25.8	0.7	13 109	38.1	1.0	3 193	41.2	4.5
White County	2 648	30.8	5.7	265	34.3	1.5	217	20.7	4.1	1 168	35.4	2.6	772	41.5	11.1
Woodruff County	2 681	33.2	15.4	5	0.0	60.0	7	14.3	0.0	53	30.2	17.0	77	41.5	5.2
Yell County	181	22.7	13.3	122	36.1	3.3	169	23.1	8.9	2 721	35.5	0.8	385	45.5	4.2
CALIFORNIA	2 219 190	30.2	8.2	312 215	30.7	5.7	3 796 833	23.9	9.3	10 969 132	36.8	4.2	1 694 607	40.5	4.9
Alameda County	212 442	27.6	9.9	9 095	26.8	5.2	302 995	23.9	8.7	273 887	33.4	4.6	87 220	40.1	4.3
Alpine County	0	X	X	226	35.0	7.5	4	0.0	0.0	76	53.9	1.3	61	41.0	0.0
Amador County	1 185	7.3	2.4	598	17.4	8.4	370	23.8	8.9	3 104	29.0	4.2	1 052	43.8	8.2

[1]Hispanic or Latino persons may be of any race.

STATE County	Total households	Family households (percent) Married-couple family households Total	With children	Householder 65 years or over	Other family households Total	With children	Householder 65 years or over	Nonfamily households (percent) Two or more unrelated persons Total	Householder 65 years or over	Male living alone Total	Householder 65 years or over	Female living alone Total	Householder 65 years or over	Percent of householders 65 years and over who live alone	Grandparents who are responsible for the care of their grandchildren
	29	30	31	32	33	34	35	36	37	38	39	40	41	42	43
ARKANSAS—Cont'd															
Conway County	7 981	58.2	23.5	11.8	14.3	8.3	2.4	2.4	0.3	10.8	3.2	14.3	8.8	45.3	285
Craighead County	32 301	53.5	24.3	8.0	15.5	8.6	1.7	5.8	0.3	10.3	1.7	14.9	7.2	47.1	852
Crawford County	19 705	62.9	29.0	9.8	14.1	8.8	1.8	3.0	0.4	8.4	1.8	11.6	6.5	40.9	667
Crittenden County	18 460	47.1	22.1	6.5	25.7	15.5	3.4	3.5	0.6	10.8	1.6	12.8	6.2	42.7	963
Cross County	7 421	56.8	25.4	9.2	17.8	10.7	2.8	2.1	0.4	8.9	2.3	14.4	8.8	47.4	348
Dallas County	3 508	52.8	21.0	11.8	17.0	9.3	3.6	1.8	0.1	14.0	3.4	14.3	9.2	45.0	204
Desha County	5 942	47.4	20.8	8.9	23.8	14.2	3.3	2.1	0.2	11.0	3.1	15.7	8.6	48.7	371
Drew County	7 333	52.1	23.8	9.0	16.7	9.0	2.5	5.0	0.3	11.4	2.8	14.7	7.9	47.5	246
Faulkner County	31 853	57.1	27.8	8.0	14.1	8.7	1.4	6.4	0.3	10.1	1.4	12.3	5.3	40.8	719
Franklin County	6 925	60.6	26.3	11.4	12.0	7.0	1.5	2.9	0.4	8.6	2.7	15.7	10.2	49.1	190
Fulton County	4 819	62.9	22.5	16.1	10.0	5.3	2.7	2.9	0.9	10.4	3.3	13.8	8.4	37.4	199
Garland County	37 796	53.8	18.1	16.2	13.4	7.6	2.3	4.0	0.4	10.9	3.3	17.9	10.3	41.7	986
Grant County	6 213	67.3	30.1	9.9	9.7	5.3	2.3	2.8	0.0	9.6	2.0	10.7	6.4	40.8	203
Greene County	14 689	59.3	24.8	10.4	13.0	7.9	1.8	3.5	0.4	8.3	1.8	15.9	10.2	48.8	386
Hempstead County	8 963	51.9	22.7	10.0	19.5	11.0	3.2	3.2	0.3	11.7	2.7	13.7	8.4	45.4	390
Hot Spring County	11 992	61.3	24.6	12.8	12.8	7.4	2.3	2.4	0.5	10.0	2.5	13.5	8.4	41.2	538
Howard County	5 467	56.2	26.1	11.1	15.6	8.9	2.7	2.6	0.1	10.3	2.5	15.2	9.1	45.4	119
Independence County	13 479	59.8	26.1	10.9	12.1	6.4	1.9	2.6	0.4	10.8	2.6	14.7	8.9	46.8	350
Izard County	5 396	58.9	20.3	16.5	10.6	6.1	1.9	2.8	0.5	11.5	3.7	16.4	11.4	44.4	120
Jackson County	6 981	53.8	20.1	10.9	15.7	8.3	3.2	2.5	0.4	10.6	3.2	17.4	10.8	49.2	275
Jefferson County	30 555	48.9	20.7	8.7	21.9	13.0	3.4	3.1	0.2	11.3	2.6	14.8	8.9	48.3	1 528
Johnson County	8 704	59.1	25.7	11.4	12.7	7.0	2.6	3.6	0.5	10.0	3.0	14.6	8.8	44.9	245
Lafayette County	3 406	51.0	18.7	11.5	18.2	8.5	3.8	2.0	0.2	10.7	2.8	18.1	10.9	47.0	203
Lawrence County	7 144	57.9	23.8	12.8	12.5	7.3	1.7	2.8	0.4	9.5	3.0	17.3	11.6	49.5	172
Lee County	4 208	45.3	15.5	11.1	26.4	15.9	4.3	1.6	0.1	11.5	3.5	15.2	10.0	46.7	441
Lincoln County	4 259	55.2	23.3	11.1	18.3	10.3	3.4	3.1	0.2	9.7	2.0	13.8	8.9	42.9	200
Little River County	5 482	55.4	23.0	9.7	16.2	9.9	2.0	2.1	0.5	11.5	2.7	14.7	9.4	49.9	205
Logan County	8 733	59.8	25.7	12.1	13.2	7.6	2.3	2.7	0.3	9.6	3.5	14.6	9.7	47.2	272
Lonoke County	19 257	64.6	33.0	8.0	13.6	8.2	1.6	2.9	0.3	8.0	1.8	10.9	5.6	43.1	538
Madison County	5 457	63.9	28.8	11.7	11.0	7.1	1.9	2.7	0.2	11.0	3.2	11.4	7.2	43.0	104
Marion County	6 762	62.9	19.8	17.1	9.4	6.0	1.4	2.8	0.3	11.1	3.6	13.8	8.4	38.9	132
Miller County	15 691	52.0	22.4	9.3	19.3	11.6	2.4	3.2	0.4	10.2	2.2	15.4	8.7	47.5	663
Mississippi County	19 309	50.0	23.3	8.9	22.3	12.9	3.0	2.9	0.4	9.7	2.1	15.1	8.2	45.8	1 215
Monroe County	4 106	46.8	18.0	10.3	20.4	10.6	5.1	3.0	0.8	12.0	5.2	17.8	10.3	48.9	209
Montgomery County	3 765	62.2	22.7	16.1	10.7	5.4	1.6	2.6	0.2	11.9	3.1	12.5	8.1	38.2	132
Nevada County	3 905	53.6	21.7	10.4	17.1	9.8	3.3	1.7	0.4	10.4	3.2	17.2	12.8	53.2	269
Newton County	3 517	60.5	25.6	12.1	11.2	6.5	1.8	2.5	0.3	12.2	3.3	13.6	8.0	44.1	117
Ouachita County	11 597	51.4	21.2	11.4	18.2	11.0	3.5	2.4	0.2	10.4	2.7	17.7	11.1	47.8	450
Perry County	3 999	62.5	25.6	11.4	11.4	6.6	2.5	3.0	0.3	10.5	3.1	12.6	7.8	43.5	153
Phillips County	9 701	40.9	16.7	8.3	29.3	18.8	4.5	2.2	0.3	10.5	3.3	17.1	9.7	49.6	590
Pike County	4 489	61.5	25.4	12.8	10.9	6.7	1.9	2.1	0.3	10.6	2.9	14.9	10.2	46.6	84
Poinsett County	9 971	55.7	23.6	9.8	16.5	9.4	2.9	3.0	0.4	9.8	2.9	15.1	9.1	47.9	462
Polk County	8 064	60.9	26.1	13.6	11.5	6.2	3.0	2.6	0.4	9.7	3.1	15.2	9.2	41.9	235
Pope County	20 693	58.8	26.3	9.7	13.8	8.0	1.9	4.4	0.2	10.2	2.5	12.8	7.2	45.2	572
Prairie County	3 869	56.3	23.3	11.5	15.1	7.9	3.1	2.9	0.3	11.2	4.3	14.4	9.4	47.9	173
Pulaski County	148 032	47.1	20.1	7.7	18.0	11.1	2.0	4.9	0.2	12.6	1.7	17.3	6.9	46.5	4 469
Randolph County	7 250	59.2	22.8	13.2	13.9	8.1	1.6	1.9	0.2	10.3	3.0	14.6	9.4	45.3	167
St. Francis County	10 027	45.4	20.5	8.3	26.7	15.3	4.3	2.6	0.5	11.0	2.0	14.2	7.9	43.1	610
Saline County	31 813	64.8	28.1	10.8	12.3	7.4	1.4	3.3	0.3	8.5	1.8	11.1	5.8	37.7	807
Scott County	4 341	60.8	27.0	12.6	11.7	6.3	2.1	2.9	0.3	10.6	1.8	14.1	8.9	41.7	87
Searcy County	3 533	58.1	20.4	14.6	11.9	6.7	2.2	2.0	0.3	12.0	3.3	16.0	11.1	45.7	61
Sebastian County	45 348	52.8	23.8	8.8	15.4	9.5	2.1	4.4	0.2	11.6	2.3	15.8	8.0	48.2	1 225
Sevier County	5 709	60.6	28.2	10.6	13.8	9.2	1.8	3.0	0.2	9.0	2.1	13.7	8.3	45.0	183
Sharp County	7 231	60.0	19.6	18.6	11.6	5.9	2.2	2.8	0.6	9.6	3.9	16.0	11.3	41.4	215
Stone County	4 762	64.0	23.3	16.3	9.1	3.5	1.9	2.1	0.3	11.6	2.5	13.3	7.4	35.0	120
Union County	17 994	51.5	22.1	10.6	19.6	10.8	3.7	2.1	0.2	10.6	2.2	16.2	9.4	44.5	640
Van Buren County	6 790	58.4	19.5	18.2	11.5	6.2	2.3	3.3	0.3	11.0	3.7	15.7	11.4	41.9	196
Washington County	60 183	53.3	24.9	7.9	12.8	7.8	1.3	8.1	0.3	11.7	1.5	14.1	6.0	44.4	1 081
White County	25 158	61.0	26.3	10.8	12.7	7.4	1.8	2.9	0.4	9.5	2.5	13.8	8.3	45.5	731
Woodruff County	3 557	47.7	19.8	9.2	21.6	10.9	4.2	2.7	0.4	11.6	4.5	16.4	10.2	51.7	186
Yell County	7 901	58.1	24.9	11.3	15.9	8.9	1.8	2.6	0.2	8.8	2.6	14.5	9.5	47.6	199
CALIFORNIA	11 512 020	52.1	26.9	8.3	17.3	9.6	2.2	7.1	0.6	10.4	2.1	13.1	5.8	41.5	294 969
Alameda County	523 787	47.8	24.4	6.6	17.5	8.8	2.4	8.7	0.5	11.5	2.0	14.5	5.5	43.7	11 531
Alpine County	492	45.7	16.9	8.3	15.0	8.1	1.2	11.4	0.0	17.1	3.5	10.8	3.9	43.4	23
Amador County	12 741	58.5	18.1	17.3	12.7	8.2	2.1	4.8	0.6	10.0	3.1	14.0	8.1	36.0	170

Table A-3. States and Counties — Age, Ethnicity, and Household Structure

STATE County	Households with Non-Hispanic White householder — Number of households	Percent that are family households	Households with Black or African American householder — Number of households	Percent that are family households	Households with American Indian and Alaska Native householder — Number of households	Percent that are family households	Households with Asian, Hawaiian, and Pacific Islander householder — Number of households	Percent that are family households	Households with Hispanic or Latino[1] householder — Number of households	Percent that are family households	Foreign-born population — Percent of total population that is foreign-born	Place of birth (percent) — Europe	Asia	Latin America	Percent in non-English speaking households — Linguistically isolated	Not linguistically isolated
	44	45	46	47	48	49	50	51	52	53	54	55	56	57	58	59
ARKANSAS—Cont'd																
Conway County	6 816	72.9	968	67.8	9	77.8	20	100.0	107	77.6	1.2	0.1	0.2	1.0	0.5	5.1
Craighead County	29 138	69.3	2 304	64.8	93	69.9	89	76.4	403	81.9	2.0	0.2	0.6	1.0	1.0	5.4
Crawford County	18 379	76.8	137	70.8	300	82.7	140	96.4	362	86.7	2.4	0.3	0.8	1.2	0.9	7.6
Crittenden County	10 381	71.6	7 623	74.4	110	78.2	49	100.0	214	74.3	1.2	0.2	0.4	0.6	0.8	6.4
Cross County	5 801	74.1	1 480	75.7	37	94.6	11	100.0	86	84.9	1.0	0.1	0.1	0.7	0.5	5.3
Dallas County	2 100	72.2	1 360	66.5	3	66.7	0	X	41	65.9	0.9	0.0	0.0	0.8	0.7	7.4
Desha County	3 213	70.6	2 520	71.8	26	73.1	26	84.6	133	76.7	2.1	0.3	0.5	1.2	0.6	5.4
Drew County	5 301	69.8	1 892	65.3	23	65.2	21	71.4	80	87.5	1.5	0.3	0.2	0.8	0.6	6.0
Faulkner County	28 289	71.7	2 505	65.0	190	77.4	152	74.3	432	64.8	1.7	0.3	0.5	0.7	0.7	7.0
Franklin County	6 624	72.8	13	100.0	46	73.9	36	41.7	96	75.0	1.3	0.3	0.4	0.6	0.6	4.8
Fulton County	4 699	72.8	0	X	21	28.6	0	X	14	85.7	0.4	0.1	0.1	0.1	0.0	3.5
Garland County	33 824	67.3	2 550	67.3	232	56.5	93	28.0	596	71.5	2.0	1.3	0.3	0.0	1.2	0.4
Grant County	5 966	77.1	120	66.7	46	82.6	10	50.0	30	80.0	0.6	0.2	0.1	0.3	0.2	4.5
Greene County	14 270	72.2	34	85.3	51	92.2	28	82.1	113	69.0	0.5	0.1	0.1	0.3	0.2	4.5
Hempstead County	5 689	70.8	2 684	70.9	7	100.0	25	52.0	491	81.1	6.4	0.3	0.3	5.8	3.9	9.6
Hot Spring County	10 561	75.2	1 140	62.6	37	70.3	19	47.4	113	79.6	1.2	0.4	0.1	0.7	0.5	4.4
Howard County	4 059	74.1	1 196	63.0	24	91.7	13	100.0	132	83.3	3.5	0.0	0.3	3.2	3.2	7.6
Independence County	12 883	72.0	269	63.9	27	77.8	34	82.4	123	78.0	1.2	0.3	0.6	0.2	0.6	5.0
Izard County	5 280	69.4	1	100.0	28	75.0	7	100.0	24	70.8	0.8	0.4	0.1	0.2	0.3	5.1
Jackson County	5 918	69.9	928	66.2	38	81.6	11	100.0	45	73.3	0.5	0.3	0.1	0.0	0.3	4.7
Jefferson County	16 225	70.9	13 670	70.5	107	79.4	120	92.5	262	78.6	1.1	0.1	0.5	0.3	0.4	7.1
Johnson County	8 040	71.4	98	80.6	38	63.2	7	100.0	383	81.7	4.5	0.2	0.1	4.1	3.8	4.8
Lafayette County	2 235	69.8	1 128	67.7	6	100.0	7	28.6	18	72.2	1.0	0.1	0.2	0.7	0.3	6.4
Lawrence County	6 982	70.6	15	86.7	47	80.9	12	100.0	32	28.1	0.6	0.1	0.2	0.3	0.2	2.7
Lee County	1 932	71.7	2 177	70.9	29	100.0	3	100.0	73	100.0	0.3	0.1	0.0	0.3	0.1	6.8
Lincoln County	3 108	73.6	1 033	72.1	16	93.8	0	X	76	86.8	0.7	0.2	0.0	0.5	0.1	4.0
Little River County	4 155	72.2	1 109	65.9	84	86.9	26	100.0	62	91.9	1.7	0.3	0.3	1.0	0.7	5.7
Logan County	8 433	73.0	85	65.9	44	81.8	24	100.0	49	69.4	0.9	0.3	0.3	0.2	0.3	5.4
Lonoke County	17 506	78.3	1 253	74.2	34	55.9	62	100.0	230	89.9	1.4	0.5	0.4	0.4	0.0	5.0
Madison County	5 188	75.7	8	25.0	44	72.7	23	78.3	121	59.5	1.8	0.2	0.0	1.4	1.0	6.1
Marion County	6 567	72.5	0	X	45	75.6	28	71.4	32	53.1	1.1	0.7	0.1	0.0	0.5	4.4
Miller County	11 805	71.4	3 267	72.0	105	68.6	80	45.0	234	73.9	1.1	0.1	0.4	0.5	0.4	5.7
Mississippi County	13 201	72.2	5 603	72.2	51	94.1	33	51.5	273	78.8	1.2	0.2	0.1	0.8	0.5	6.5
Monroe County	2 601	68.4	1 467	64.8	5	100.0	0	X	21	66.7	0.5	0.2	0.0	0.4	0.4	4.7
Montgomery County	3 635	73.4	0	X	30	66.7	6	66.7	59	62.7	2.0	0.0	0.1	1.6	1.0	6.1
Nevada County	2 674	69.4	1 150	74.0	2	100.0	0	X	41	100.0	1.1	0.2	0.0	0.9	0.9	4.2
Newton County	3 388	72.0	13	15.4	28	75.0	0	X	19	73.7	0.5	0.2	0.1	0.1	0.1	3.6
Ouachita County	7 179	69.6	4 221	70.2	33	51.5	32	56.3	91	54.9	0.7	0.1	0.1	0.3	0.3	5.2
Perry County	3 778	74.0	55	87.3	48	75.0	5	100.0	56	55.4	0.8	0.3	0.2	0.4	0.1	0.0
Phillips County	4 276	68.8	5 238	71.0	12	100.0	59	88.1	94	75.5	1.1	0.3	0.4	0.3	0.3	7.8
Pike County	4 218	72.2	128	77.3	21	90.5	4	50.0	90	93.3	2.2	0.1	0.3	1.8	1.3	5.3
Poinsett County	9 199	72.6	583	62.6	41	63.4	6	100.0	69	73.9	0.9	0.1	0.1	0.7	0.5	4.8
Polk County	7 657	72.3	4	100.0	59	71.2	9	0.0	209	79.4	2.7	0.5	0.2	1.7	1.0	6.6
Pope County	19 376	72.8	486	64.4	147	57.1	80	78.8	314	80.9	1.7	0.4	0.5	0.7	0.6	5.9
Prairie County	3 377	71.8	435	66.7	5	100.0	1	100.0	33	100.0	0.4	0.3	0.1	0.1	0.3	3.9
Pulaski County	100 619	63.5	41 339	68.7	567	61.4	1 452	66.5	2 686	73.6	3.0	0.6	1.1	1.0	1.2	8.5
Randolph County	7 067	73.3	25	28.0	64	67.2	2	100.0	15	100.0	0.9	0.2	0.1	0.5	0.6	3.6
St. Francis County	5 261	70.9	4 577	74.4	6	83.3	31	64.5	93	61.3	0.3	0.0	0.1	0.1	0.3	4.3
Saline County	30 366	77.1	530	72.5	199	88.9	102	81.4	281	77.2	1.3	0.4	0.5	0.4	0.5	6.2
Scott County	4 041	72.4	6	100.0	96	60.4	15	100.0	134	84.3	3.5	0.4	0.2	2.9	1.7	7.3
Searcy County	3 449	69.9	1	100.0	18	38.9	6	100.0	8	100.0	0.6	0.1	0.2	0.1	0.2	3.8
Sebastian County	38 323	67.4	2 576	66.4	710	73.8	1 124	81.3	1 809	79.7	6.9	0.3	2.4	3.9	3.1	10.2
Sevier County	4 556	73.2	319	62.7	62	50.0	0	X	682	91.9	12.7	0.2	0.1	12.2	8.6	12.7
Sharp County	6 977	71.6	18	61.1	39	51.3	15	0.0	57	80.7	0.8	0.3	0.2	0.1	0.1	5.1
Stone County	4 636	73.1	2	100.0	27	63.0	0	X	32	100.0	0.8	0.3	0.1	0.2	0.0	5.4
Union County	12 368	71.4	5 260	70.2	37	54.1	43	72.1	161	78.3	1.2	0.3	0.3	0.5	0.5	4.4
Van Buren County	6 591	69.7	5	100.0	31	80.6	5	60.0	53	86.8	1.4	0.7	0.2	0.3	0.2	4.8
Washington County	53 367	65.5	1 049	52.1	690	66.5	1 000	64.0	3 242	84.2	7.4	0.5	1.3	5.1	4.0	10.4
White County	23 594	73.9	889	71.2	80	77.5	39	100.0	343	70.0	1.5	0.4	0.3	0.6	0.4	5.7
Woodruff County	2 460	69.4	1 057	69.4	2	100.0	4	100.0	16	68.8	0.6	0.1	0.1	0.3	0.2	3.1
Yell County	7 061	73.0	89	42.7	35	94.3	46	87.0	597	90.5	10.2	0.6	0.6	8.9	6.9	9.5
CALIFORNIA	6 673 836	62.7	788 392	66.3	96 479	72.7	1 136 310	77.2	2 574 994	84.7	26.2	2.1	8.6	14.5	11.3	36.6
Alameda County	261 309	58.7	82 246	61.9	3 048	65.5	92 833	76.7	68 102	79.3	27.2	2.4	14.9	8.4	10.2	35.2
Alpine County	382	59.4	0	X	81	71.6	0	X	16	81.3	3.2	1.7	0.2	1.1	1.5	13.4
Amador County	11 817	70.8	26	100.0	171	79.5	76	71.1	457	75.3	3.4	1.0	0.7	1.1	0.8	9.3

[1] Hispanic or Latino persons may be of any race.

Table A-3. States and Counties — **Age, Ethnicity, and Household Structure**

STATE/ County code	MSA/PMSA/ NECMA code¹	STATE County	Population by age (percent) Total population	Under 5 years	5 to 17 years	18 to 24 years	25 to 44 years	45 to 64 years	65 years and over	Median age	+/− U.S. percent under 18 years	+/− U.S. percent 65 years and over	Non-Hispanic White Total population	Age (percent) Under 18 years	65 years and over
			1	2	3	4	5	6	7	8	9	10	11	12	13
		CALIFORNIA—Cont'd													
06 007	1620	Butte County	203 171	5.7	18.2	13.7	25.0	21.6	15.7	35.8	−1.8	3.3	162 142	20.6	18.4
06 009	...	Calaveras County	40 554	4.2	18.4	5.3	22.3	31.7	18.0	44.6	−3.1	5.6	35 528	21.2	19.5
06 011	...	Colusa County	18 804	8.1	23.5	10.4	26.9	20.1	11.0	31.5	5.9	−1.4	8 939	23.6	19.0
06 013	5775	Contra Costa County	948 816	6.9	19.6	7.6	30.9	23.8	11.3	36.4	0.8	−1.1	547 837	21.9	14.9
06 015	...	Del Norte County	27 507	5.4	19.7	7.8	32.9	21.6	12.6	36.4	−0.6	0.2	19 272	23.5	16.2
06 017	6920	El Dorado County	156 299	5.7	20.3	6.8	27.9	26.8	12.5	39.4	0.3	0.1	132 617	24.4	13.7
06 019	2840	Fresno County	799 407	8.4	23.6	11.0	28.8	18.3	9.9	29.9	6.3	−2.5	316 488	21.8	17.1
06 021	...	Glenn County	26 453	7.5	23.0	8.6	26.8	21.2	12.8	33.7	4.8	0.4	16 397	24.1	18.5
06 023	...	Humboldt County	126 518	5.6	17.5	12.5	27.4	24.4	12.6	36.3	−2.6	0.2	103 584	20.8	14.1
06 025	...	Imperial County	142 361	7.6	23.8	9.8	30.9	17.7	10.2	31.0	5.7	−2.2	28 489	19.7	20.0
06 027	...	Inyo County	17 945	5.5	19.0	5.5	23.8	26.9	19.3	42.8	−1.2	6.9	13 300	20.0	23.4
06 029	0680	Kern County	661 645	8.3	23.5	10.2	30.0	18.6	9.4	30.6	6.1	−3.0	326 523	25.0	14.4
06 031	...	Kings County	129 461	7.9	20.9	11.6	35.4	16.7	7.5	30.2	3.1	−4.9	53 689	23.0	12.3
06 033	...	Lake County	58 309	5.2	18.7	6.2	23.2	27.1	19.4	42.7	−1.8	7.0	47 015	21.1	21.8
06 035	...	Lassen County	33 828	4.9	16.8	10.4	36.9	21.9	9.0	34.6	−4.0	−3.4	23 935	23.7	11.6
06 037	4480	Los Angeles County........	9 519 338	7.7	20.3	10.3	32.8	19.2	9.7	32.0	2.3	−2.7	2 946 145	17.8	17.5
06 039	2840	Madera County	123 109	7.6	21.9	9.7	29.4	20.6	10.7	32.7	3.8	−1.7	57 641	21.8	17.9
06 041	7360	Marin County..................	247 289	5.4	14.9	5.5	31.1	29.6	13.5	41.3	−5.4	1.1	194 008	18.7	15.8
06 043	...	Mariposa County	17 130	4.8	17.4	6.6	25.1	29.0	17.0	42.9	−3.5	4.6	14 483	20.3	18.9
06 045	...	Mendocino County	86 265	6.0	19.4	8.6	25.4	27.0	13.6	38.9	−0.3	1.2	64 482	21.3	16.7
06 047	4940	Merced County	210 554	8.7	25.7	10.2	28.4	17.7	9.4	29.0	8.7	−3.0	84 807	24.7	16.3
06 049	...	Modoc County	9 449	5.4	20.2	6.0	22.9	28.2	17.3	41.8	−0.1	4.9	7 608	22.1	19.9
06 051	...	Mono County	12 853	5.9	16.7	10.0	34.4	25.8	7.3	36.0	−3.1	−5.1	9 801	19.5	8.8
06 053	7120	Monterey County	401 762	7.7	20.7	10.9	31.7	19.0	10.0	31.7	2.7	−2.4	161 630	18.8	17.7
06 055	8720	Napa County	124 279	6.0	18.1	8.3	28.0	24.2	15.3	38.3	−1.6	2.9	85 597	19.5	20.3
06 057	...	Nevada County	92 033	4.6	18.3	6.3	24.0	29.3	17.5	43.1	−2.8	5.1	82 925	21.9	18.6
06 059	5945	Orange County...............	2 846 289	7.5	19.4	9.3	33.4	20.5	9.8	33.3	1.2	−2.6	1 455 470	21.0	14.9
06 061	6920	Placer County	248 399	6.3	20.0	6.9	29.1	24.6	13.1	38.0	0.6	0.7	207 124	24.8	14.3
06 063	...	Plumas County	20 824	4.7	18.0	6.3	22.7	30.4	17.9	44.2	−3.0	5.5	18 493	20.9	19.2
06 065	6780	Riverside County	1 545 387	7.7	22.5	9.2	29.1	18.8	12.6	33.1	4.5	0.2	787 318	22.5	20.3
06 067	6920	Sacramento County	1 223 499	7.1	20.3	9.4	31.4	20.7	11.1	33.8	1.7	−1.3	705 922	22.0	14.5
06 069	...	San Benito County	53 234	8.7	23.4	8.9	31.8	19.2	7.9	31.4	6.4	−4.5	24 338	26.5	11.5
06 071	6780	San Bernardino County ..	1 709 434	8.2	24.0	10.2	30.5	18.5	8.5	30.3	6.5	−3.9	749 224	24.4	13.7
06 073	7320	San Diego County...........	2 813 833	7.0	18.6	11.4	32.3	19.6	11.1	33.2	−0.1	−1.3	1 544 484	19.3	15.8
06 075	7360	San Francisco County	776 733	4.0	10.4	8.9	41.0	22.0	13.8	36.5	−11.3	1.4	338 886	7.6	13.9
06 077	8120	San Joaquin County	563 598	7.8	23.1	9.9	29.2	19.5	10.6	31.9	5.2	−1.8	265 960	23.6	15.6
06 079	7460	San Luis Obispo County .	246 681	4.9	16.6	14.0	26.9	23.1	14.5	37.3	−4.2	2.1	187 597	19.2	17.5
06 081	7360	San Mateo County	707 161	6.3	16.5	7.8	33.6	23.3	12.5	36.8	−2.9	0.1	351 542	18.1	17.8
06 083	7480	Santa Barbara County	399 347	6.4	18.4	13.5	29.1	20.1	12.7	33.4	−0.9	0.3	226 841	18.0	18.4
06 085	7400	Santa Clara County	1 682 585	7.0	17.7	9.2	35.8	20.9	9.5	34.0	−1.0	−2.9	741 000	19.1	14.0
06 087	7485	Santa Cruz County	255 602	6.0	17.6	11.8	31.1	23.5	9.9	35.0	−2.1	−2.5	167 347	18.7	12.9
06 089	6690	Shasta County	163 256	5.9	20.2	8.2	25.2	25.3	15.2	38.9	0.4	2.8	141 087	24.1	16.5
06 091	...	Sierra County	3 555	4.1	19.3	5.1	23.6	30.5	17.3	43.7	−2.3	4.9	3 180	21.7	18.6
06 093	...	Siskiyou County	44 301	5.1	18.7	6.9	22.5	28.5	18.2	43.0	−1.9	5.8	37 052	21.4	20.0
06 095	8720	Solano County	394 542	7.2	21.1	9.2	31.6	21.4	9.5	33.9	2.6	−2.9	193 819	23.2	12.9
06 097	7500	Sonoma County	458 614	5.9	18.4	8.9	29.4	24.9	12.5	37.5	−1.4	0.1	340 842	20.9	15.5
06 099	5170	Stanislaus County	446 997	7.9	23.2	9.8	29.3	19.5	10.4	31.7	5.4	−2.0	254 650	24.8	14.8
06 101	9340	Sutter County	78 930	7.2	21.7	9.0	28.6	21.5	12.1	34.1	3.2	−0.3	47 154	24.1	16.7
06 103	...	Tehama County	56 039	6.3	21.1	7.9	25.7	23.1	15.9	37.8	1.7	3.5	43 972	23.6	18.9
06 105	...	Trinity County	13 022	4.1	18.8	4.7	23.6	32.1	16.8	44.6	−2.8	4.4	11 231	21.0	18.8
06 107	8780	Tulare County	368 021	8.9	24.9	10.6	27.8	18.1	9.7	29.2	8.1	−2.7	153 340	23.9	16.9
06 109	...	Tuolumne County	54 501	4.7	16.1	7.8	25.7	27.4	18.5	42.9	−4.9	6.1	46 204	20.1	20.7
06 111	8735	Ventura County	753 197	7.4	20.9	9.0	30.9	21.7	10.0	34.2	2.6	−2.4	426 179	23.5	13.9
06 113	9270	Yolo County	168 660	6.4	18.7	18.3	28.6	18.8	9.2	29.5	−0.6	−3.2	97 551	21.1	12.8
06 115	9340	Yuba County	60 219	8.0	22.9	10.6	28.3	19.9	10.2	31.4	5.2	−2.2	39 426	25.5	13.6
08 000	...	COLORADO................	4 301 261	6.9	18.6	9.9	32.8	22.1	9.7	34.3	−0.2	−2.7	3 201 519	22.7	11.3
08 001	2080	Adams County	363 857	8.3	20.2	10.2	34.3	19.2	7.8	31.4	2.8	−4.6	230 332	24.3	10.1
08 003	...	Alamosa County	14 966	6.6	20.8	15.3	27.7	19.9	9.6	30.6	1.7	−2.8	8 118	22.4	11.4
08 005	2080	Arapahoe County	487 967	6.8	19.9	8.5	33.3	23.0	8.6	34.5	1.0	−3.8	360 187	24.1	10.4
08 007	...	Archuleta County	9 898	5.4	19.8	5.8	26.8	30.2	11.9	40.8	−0.5	−0.5	7 920	22.6	12.8
08 009	...	Baca County	4 517	5.5	19.0	5.8	22.5	25.0	22.3	42.9	−1.2	9.9	4 097	23.3	23.8
08 011	...	Bent County	5 998	5.8	18.0	8.9	29.5	21.8	16.0	37.3	−1.9	3.6	3 746	21.3	19.1
08 013	1125	Boulder County	291 288	6.0	16.8	13.3	34.0	22.1	7.8	33.4	−2.9	−4.6	243 414	21.0	8.8
08 015	...	Chaffee County	16 242	4.3	15.3	7.5	28.8	27.1	16.9	41.8	−6.1	4.5	14 136	19.7	18.4
08 017	...	Cheyenne County	2 231	6.3	22.3	7.3	26.3	21.3	16.5	37.9	2.9	4.1	2 032	26.7	17.8

¹MSA = Metropolitan Statistical Area. PMSA = Primary MSA. NECMA = New England County Metropolitan Area. See the Appendix A for explanation of these concepts. See Appendix B for list of metropolitan areas identified by type, with component counties.

Table A-3. States and Counties — Age, Ethnicity, and Household Structure

STATE County	Black or African American Total population	Under 18 years	65 years and over	American Indian and Alaska Native Total population	Under 18 years	65 years and over	Asian, Hawaiian, and Pacific Islander Total population	Under 18 years	65 years and over	Hispanic or Latino[1] Total population	Under 18 years	65 years and over	Two or more races Total population	Under 18 years	65 years and over
	14	15	16	17	18	19	20	21	22	23	24	25	26	27	28
CALIFORNIA—Cont'd															
Butte County	2 535	32.5	8.2	3 803	33.9	5.6	6 823	39.6	4.9	21 377	37.4	4.3	8 587	42.0	5.5
Calaveras County	161	13.7	26.7	807	32.0	6.3	290	23.8	6.6	2 732	34.8	5.5	1 389	41.9	8.5
Colusa County	86	32.6	11.6	357	39.8	5.0	360	36.4	11.1	8 831	39.7	2.9	848	41.9	4.7
Contra Costa County	87 444	31.9	8.1	5 501	27.7	5.2	106 589	24.7	8.5	168 059	36.1	4.3	52 185	45.3	4.1
Del Norte County	1 176	0.9	0.0	1 571	31.8	11.3	659	43.7	6.4	3 708	26.9	1.9	1 359	51.1	5.4
El Dorado County	991	37.2	7.2	1 506	24.4	7.1	3 259	23.0	8.4	14 418	38.3	3.9	4 728	42.5	7.7
Fresno County	41 110	35.6	7.1	12 587	36.9	5.1	64 547	39.8	7.6	352 205	38.9	4.3	40 431	43.5	5.2
Glenn County	193	34.2	0.0	573	42.1	9.6	894	45.6	3.0	7 785	41.2	2.7	1 082	40.8	7.2
Humboldt County	979	29.3	3.5	7 087	34.0	6.6	1 997	29.9	3.8	7 750	33.4	5.0	6 167	37.6	6.7
Imperial County	5 136	11.5	7.0	2 566	35.2	11.0	2 879	28.1	7.8	103 086	35.7	7.7	5 156	40.3	8.4
Inyo County	17	41.2	23.5	1 706	33.1	11.1	240	36.3	3.8	2 247	40.5	5.7	877	41.6	5.9
Kern County	38 804	33.5	5.9	9 014	31.7	6.0	22 340	28.7	9.1	254 059	40.5	3.7	29 500	44.7	4.9
Kings County	10 517	18.4	3.9	2 135	34.9	6.4	4 038	25.5	8.6	56 487	35.9	3.6	6 706	47.6	3.8
Lake County	1 206	20.9	29.0	1 763	39.0	5.5	640	23.9	8.6	6 474	39.9	5.9	2 076	41.5	9.2
Lassen County	2 952	2.6	0.7	1 235	33.9	4.7	274	16.4	2.9	4 557	20.0	2.3	1 158	33.2	8.7
Los Angeles County	916 907	29.5	9.6	68 471	31.3	5.3	1 161 484	22.0	10.4	4 243 487	36.1	4.3	486 792	35.7	5.7
Madera County	4 813	17.6	8.6	3 167	28.4	3.5	1 840	23.8	9.6	54 483	39.1	3.5	6 444	39.7	6.3
Marin County	7 168	18.8	5.7	800	16.9	4.6	11 320	19.2	8.1	27 441	27.7	4.1	9 056	37.7	4.1
Mariposa County	103	22.3	4.9	539	36.4	8.7	118	20.3	3.4	1 282	35.3	4.8	734	32.2	7.2
Mendocino County	594	23.2	4.9	4 244	39.4	6.0	923	18.0	16.3	14 001	40.2	2.3	3 837	40.7	5.3
Merced County	7 838	35.0	9.7	2 207	29.2	1.7	14 858	45.2	5.9	95 610	41.4	3.9	12 982	43.2	6.1
Modoc County	46	19.6	4.3	458	38.0	9.2	38	21.1	13.2	989	43.5	3.2	334	45.5	5.1
Mono County	36	0.0	0.0	231	30.3	5.2	153	0.0	9.2	2 248	37.3	0.8	358	35.5	8.7
Monterey County	14 998	22.1	7.4	3 928	26.4	4.7	26 044	23.2	14.1	188 388	37.6	3.2	19 298	40.1	4.7
Napa County	1 625	31.6	6.0	1 033	29.3	9.7	4 259	21.6	9.6	29 348	36.6	2.9	4 718	41.0	4.6
Nevada County	197	25.9	6.6	621	27.2	11.6	711	24.1	10.4	5 177	35.1	6.3	3 127	34.5	7.1
Orange County	44 256	29.6	4.0	17 664	29.0	5.1	394 874	24.1	7.5	876 451	37.2	3.1	121 239	40.1	4.1
Placer County	1 940	27.1	10.2	1 700	24.9	6.9	7 606	24.2	10.3	23 796	35.6	6.1	8 553	44.0	6.4
Plumas County	148	52.7	11.5	481	42.6	3.5	116	12.2	11.2	1 000	00.1	0.0	674	34.0	0.3
Riverside County	95 638	34.8	6.6	18 277	33.5	6.3	58 367	25.4	7.2	559 328	40.1	3.9	72 517	46.2	4.1
Sacramento County	119 526	34.4	6.4	13 386	30.0	5.3	141 150	30.2	9.4	195 613	37.4	4.7	76 799	45.6	3.9
San Benito County	388	34.7	0.0	672	38.7	6.8	1 131	25.6	8.3	25 580	37.4	4.9	2 849	43.7	3.6
San Bernardino County	151 879	36.8	4.8	19 054	31.9	5.2	84 122	27.0	6.7	669 902	40.2	3.9	93 662	46.6	4.2
San Diego County	158 371	30.6	6.6	22 613	30.0	5.0	202 195	20.5	9.5	750 951	36.5	4.4	139 772	43.7	4.1
San Francisco County	59 060	21.7	15.0	3 524	14.6	6.8	243 519	17.4	16.2	109 565	22.4	8.8	35 315	27.1	7.7
San Joaquin County	36 829	35.0	6.9	5 679	27.9	5.0	66 850	36.0	9.0	172 027	38.7	4.6	34 867	45.1	4.5
San Luis Obispo County	4 556	12.0	3.1	1 982	19.1	6.8	7 015	16.3	9.3	40 114	32.9	3.8	9 304	37.9	6.3
San Mateo County	24 395	23.4	11.0	2 749	22.7	7.2	150 695	21.0	9.0	154 302	31.0	5.1	30 024	39.0	5.2
Santa Barbara County	9 057	23.8	6.8	4 318	32.4	5.8	16 535	18.9	9.7	136 737	36.2	4.2	17 745	39.5	4.8
Santa Clara County	45 076	24.9	5.1	11 233	28.4	5.0	435 994	24.3	7.2	404 012	33.7	4.5	83 765	40.1	4.8
Santa Cruz County	2 751	27.0	3.8	2 679	24.7	5.9	8 812	16.1	10.5	68 572	35.9	3.2	10 467	33.9	4.2
Shasta County	655	24.0	12.8	3 897	37.1	4.8	3 354	36.0	7.8	8 827	40.8	5.0	6 874	45.6	6.3
Sierra County	9	100.0	0.0	90	41.1	11.1	11	54.5	0.0	216	38.9	5.6	66	18.2	7.6
Siskiyou County	558	24.9	12.7	1 623	35.9	7.6	700	40.9	7.4	3 203	39.2	7.3	1 638	39.9	11.4
Solano County	57 017	31.1	6.5	3 282	26.8	6.8	53 088	25.8	9.3	69 606	37.5	4.0	27 588	48.9	3.6
Sonoma County	6 486	29.2	4.7	5 163	30.4	4.4	14 820	24.5	7.6	79 624	36.1	2.9	19 236	42.4	4.3
Stanislaus County	10 550	36.2	5.6	5 224	28.3	6.8	20 196	34.6	6.7	141 926	41.1	3.8	26 758	41.8	5.3
Sutter County	1 625	27.7	7.8	1 146	30.8	8.5	9 023	29.8	8.2	17 502	39.5	2.8	4 160	41.9	5.5
Tehama County	156	41.7	10.3	1 133	28.8	8.0	520	39.2	8.8	8 876	44.3	3.7	1 970	43.0	7.0
Trinity County	45	6.7	0.0	635	33.5	4.7	83	8.4	0.0	474	34.4	3.6	587	41.2	5.1
Tulare County	6 196	40.2	7.3	4 702	35.0	7.6	12 616	36.0	9.7	186 913	41.6	3.9	17 034	42.8	6.1
Tuolumne County	1 256	3.1	0.4	961	32.0	6.8	509	28.3	11.0	4 412	25.7	6.6	1 614	37.3	8.7
Ventura County	14 048	27.8	5.3	6 283	31.0	6.1	40 851	23.2	9.2	251 965	36.5	4.2	30 410	44.0	3.6
Yolo County	3 262	25.4	7.6	1 714	27.5	5.5	16 507	16.8	3.5	43 747	36.1	4.5	9 506	38.1	3.4
Yuba County	2 006	36.6	6.8	1 622	28.7	3.9	4 689	48.0	4.4	10 370	41.5	2.8	3 352	46.2	3.6
COLORADO	159 279	30.1	6.1	43 101	28.7	3.9	97 604	24.5	6.6	735 099	34.9	4.7	132 146	43.6	3.7
Adams County	10 321	36.1	4.0	3 528	26.0	3.5	11 850	30.1	7.4	102 548	36.0	3.7	13 830	45.8	2.4
Alamosa County	100	18.0	6.0	258	31.8	5.4	155	25.8	0.0	6 222	33.5	8.0	599	40.6	2.7
Arapahoe County	36 313	32.4	3.9	3 250	22.7	2.3	19 247	24.8	6.7	57 759	35.7	2.6	18 021	48.8	2.3
Archuleta County	29	72.4	0.0	135	43.0	12.6	26	19.2	0.0	1 647	34.7	8.3	306	54.9	1.6
Baca County	0	X	X	48	16.7	16.7	11	18.2	18.2	304	39.5	4.9	101	37.6	5.0
Bent County	210	2.4	3.3	71	12.7	5.6	82	11.0	34.1	1 809	31.5	10.1	243	44.0	9.5
Boulder County	2 321	20.1	3.7	1 935	33.9	4.0	9 375	24.1	3.0	30 368	35.1	2.7	6 206	35.1	3.3
Chaffee County	256	0.0	2.3	177	18.6	4.0	66	43.9	0.0	1 351	17.0	8.9	294	38.4	7.5
Cheyenne County	0	X	X	15	33.3	0.0	4	100.0	0.0	180	48.3	3.3	15	73.3	13.3

[1]Hispanic or Latino persons may be of any race.

Table A-3. States and Counties — Age, Ethnicity, and Household Structure

STATE County	Total households	Family households (percent)						Nonfamily households (percent)						Percent of householders 65 years and over who live alone	Grandparents who are responsible for the care of their grandchildren
		Married-couple family households			Other family households			Two or more unrelated persons		Male living alone		Female living alone			
		Total	With children	Householder 65 years or over	Total	With children	Householder 65 years or over	Total	Householder 65 years or over	Total	Householder 65 years or over	Total	Householder 65 years or over		
	29	30	31	32	33	34	35	36	37	38	39	40	41	42	43
CALIFORNIA—Cont'd															
Butte County	79 674	47.8	19.7	11.9	14.7	9.4	1.9	10.4	0.8	10.8	2.6	16.4	8.6	43.5	1 329
Calaveras County	16 449	60.0	20.0	15.3	11.1	6.9	1.7	5.6	0.8	10.0	3.2	13.3	7.1	36.8	397
Colusa County	6 081	59.7	31.9	9.7	15.1	9.1	2.3	3.4	0.4	10.4	2.9	11.3	6.6	43.4	237
Contra Costa County	344 422	55.8	27.8	8.5	15.1	8.2	2.0	6.3	0.5	9.0	2.0	13.8	6.2	42.5	7 482
Del Norte County	9 185	49.0	21.5	10.4	19.8	13.7	2.2	6.0	1.2	12.0	3.3	13.3	6.2	40.8	204
El Dorado County	59 013	61.2	26.6	11.3	12.3	8.0	1.4	6.5	0.6	9.0	2.1	11.1	5.5	36.3	1 189
Fresno County	253 304	53.8	29.3	8.5	20.6	12.7	2.3	5.0	0.4	8.5	2.0	12.1	6.1	41.9	8 771
Glenn County	9 197	57.6	29.0	10.8	15.9	10.5	1.9	4.6	0.5	9.1	2.7	12.9	7.9	44.3	244
Humboldt County	51 235	43.8	18.3	8.4	16.5	10.8	2.0	10.8	0.7	13.1	2.8	15.8	6.6	46.0	1 129
Imperial County	39 433	58.9	34.9	10.1	21.6	12.8	3.7	2.5	0.6	8.2	2.9	8.7	5.2	36.1	1 854
Inyo County	7 673	50.1	19.3	12.6	14.1	9.0	2.1	4.2	0.7	15.6	5.0	16.0	9.2	48.2	153
Kern County	208 786	56.1	30.4	8.4	19.4	12.6	2.2	4.2	0.5	8.9	2.1	11.3	5.6	41.1	8 273
Kings County	34 429	59.2	34.1	7.6	19.6	12.9	2.4	4.2	0.6	7.0	1.7	9.9	5.2	39.1	1 376
Lake County	23 984	47.8	16.5	13.9	16.4	10.6	2.7	6.8	1.4	13.3	4.8	15.8	8.7	42.9	696
Lassen County	9 629	56.9	26.7	10.3	13.7	9.6	1.4	5.0	0.4	11.6	3.1	12.8	6.3	44.0	263
Los Angeles County	3 136 279	48.5	26.8	7.1	20.2	10.8	2.5	6.7	0.5	11.3	2.0	13.3	5.2	41.6	88 511
Madera County	36 207	62.9	30.6	12.1	16.9	10.3	1.9	3.7	0.5	6.8	1.8	9.7	5.9	34.6	1 759
Marin County	100 736	49.2	21.7	9.2	11.7	6.7	1.6	9.3	0.9	11.3	2.4	18.5	7.3	45.3	590
Mariposa County	6 592	54.6	18.0	13.4	13.2	7.1	2.7	5.6	1.5	12.3	4.1	14.3	8.1	41.1	99
Mendocino County	33 331	50.5	21.8	10.0	15.7	10.6	1.4	6.8	0.7	11.6	2.9	15.3	7.7	46.7	869
Merced County	63 933	58.7	33.9	9.1	19.7	12.4	2.2	3.9	0.4	7.4	2.0	10.3	5.4	38.5	2 218
Modoc County	3 766	54.2	20.5	11.8	13.3	8.1	2.4	4.4	1.0	12.4	4.0	15.7	10.3	48.5	76
Mono County	5 163	52.0	22.2	6.8	10.1	7.1	0.4	11.5	0.7	15.5	2.0	10.9	2.3	35.1	30
Monterey County	121 199	56.8	30.6	9.3	16.3	9.3	2.2	5.8	0.7	8.3	2.0	12.9	6.3	40.2	3 327
Napa County	45 395	54.7	24.6	10.9	13.3	7.2	2.0	6.1	0.6	9.3	2.7	16.6	8.9	46.1	758
Nevada County	36 956	57.6	21.3	14.8	13.1	8.1	1.9	6.4	0.6	9.2	2.8	13.6	7.3	36.7	624
Orange County	936 154	57.0	30.0	8.1	15.0	7.8	1.9	7.0	0.5	8.8	1.6	12.3	5.5	40.7	18 792
Placer County	93 510	60.3	28.1	11.3	12.8	7.9	1.6	5.6	0.5	8.9	1.8	12.3	6.1	37.5	1 629
Plumas County	9 006	58.1	20.2	15.1	9.7	6.5	1.3	4.7	0.7	13.6	2.9	13.9	6.8	36.3	116
Riverside County	506 781	57.5	29.8	11.4	16.5	10.0	2.1	5.3	0.9	8.6	2.6	12.0	6.8	39.5	16 863
Sacramento County	453 841	47.4	23.3	8.1	18.6	11.2	2.0	7.3	0.5	11.3	2.1	15.3	6.0	43.2	10 483
San Benito County	15 911	66.3	37.9	8.1	15.5	10.4	2.0	4.1	0.4	6.3	1.2	7.8	4.3	34.4	467
San Bernardino County	528 839	56.8	32.0	7.4	20.2	12.6	2.2	4.6	0.4	8.2	1.8	10.2	4.9	40.0	19 737
San Diego County	995 492	51.3	25.5	8.8	15.9	9.2	2.0	8.6	0.6	10.9	2.1	13.2	5.8	41.1	21 244
San Francisco County	329 850	32.7	13.0	6.8	12.0	4.2	2.6	16.8	0.9	19.1	3.1	19.5	7.0	49.3	5 474
San Joaquin County	181 612	55.6	29.7	8.6	19.0	11.6	2.2	4.8	0.5	8.5	2.1	12.2	6.5	43.2	6 666
San Luis Obispo County	92 732	51.1	21.5	11.7	12.4	7.3	1.7	10.5	0.8	10.8	2.6	15.1	8.1	42.9	1 502
San Mateo County	254 219	54.1	25.6	9.4	13.7	6.3	2.2	7.5	0.6	10.2	2.0	14.4	6.5	41.1	4 993
Santa Barbara County	136 769	52.3	25.8	10.4	13.7	7.5	2.2	9.7	0.9	9.8	2.5	14.4	7.2	41.8	2 693
Santa Clara County	566 485	56.1	28.7	7.5	14.4	6.9	2.0	8.1	0.5	10.3	1.5	11.1	4.5	37.6	11 912
Santa Cruz County	91 244	48.3	23.7	7.3	15.1	9.0	1.9	11.5	0.6	11.0	1.8	14.1	6.1	44.8	1 463
Shasta County	63 497	53.6	21.7	11.8	15.9	10.4	2.1	5.9	0.7	10.6	2.9	14.0	7.1	40.6	1 418
Sierra County	1 523	53.9	20.8	13.5	11.1	8.5	1.1	5.9	0.8	16.7	3.8	12.3	7.2	41.8	33
Siskiyou County	18 573	53.2	19.6	13.7	13.1	9.2	1.6	5.2	1.0	12.4	3.9	16.1	8.7	43.6	350
Solano County	130 440	57.1	29.7	7.8	18.2	10.8	2.2	5.2	0.4	8.4	1.6	11.1	5.0	38.7	4 100
Sonoma County	172 690	51.4	24.1	9.1	14.4	8.5	1.8	8.5	0.7	10.0	2.4	15.7	7.7	46.6	2 451
Stanislaus County	145 253	57.2	30.8	9.0	18.7	11.1	2.3	4.7	0.4	7.8	1.9	11.6	6.1	40.6	4 894
Sutter County	27 098	58.6	29.3	10.5	16.2	9.6	2.1	4.2	0.4	8.9	2.0	12.2	6.1	38.2	800
Tehama County	21 090	55.0	23.3	13.0	15.9	10.0	2.5	5.1	0.9	10.4	3.5	13.6	8.2	41.6	569
Trinity County	5 582	51.8	16.9	13.2	13.4	9.0	1.5	5.2	0.6	15.6	4.5	14.0	7.3	43.6	111
Tulare County	110 356	59.2	32.8	9.2	20.3	12.9	2.5	3.5	0.4	6.7	2.0	10.3	5.8	38.9	4 078
Tuolumne County	20 989	55.3	18.7	16.4	12.8	7.4	2.1	5.9	0.7	11.7	3.6	14.3	8.0	37.7	332
Ventura County	243 503	60.2	31.8	8.7	15.5	8.6	2.0	5.5	0.5	7.9	1.8	11.0	5.6	39.9	5 654
Yolo County	59 358	48.4	25.6	6.9	15.1	9.0	1.9	13.2	0.4	10.1	2.1	13.2	5.6	45.5	1 287
Yuba County	20 552	53.8	27.2	8.5	19.0	12.0	2.2	5.6	0.6	10.4	2.5	11.2	5.8	42.4	676
COLORADO	1 659 308	52.8	25.4	7.3	13.1	8.1	1.3	7.9	0.3	12.1	1.8	14.1	5.4	44.7	28 524
Adams County	128 290	55.3	28.4	6.5	17.0	10.2	1.4	6.5	0.3	10.3	1.4	10.9	4.3	41.1	3 979
Alamosa County	5 475	53.6	25.2	7.6	14.4	11.2	1.2	4.8	0.0	11.1	1.8	16.0	6.7	49.1	118
Arapahoe County	190 961	52.2	26.6	6.3	14.0	8.8	1.1	6.9	0.3	11.8	1.3	15.1	4.7	44.0	2 468
Archuleta County	3 989	59.4	23.0	11.4	12.9	8.5	1.5	5.7	0.5	10.3	1.9	11.7	4.1	30.9	87
Baca County	1 907	56.9	22.5	17.4	10.2	5.9	1.7	2.6	0.4	14.8	3.9	15.5	10.5	42.5	27
Bent County	2 001	54.9	23.9	11.8	14.7	8.9	2.0	3.0	0.4	13.9	4.4	13.4	8.6	47.4	57
Boulder County	114 793	49.8	24.7	5.9	10.8	7.0	0.8	13.2	0.2	12.3	1.2	13.9	4.6	45.7	1 031
Chaffee County	6 612	57.0	19.4	14.3	9.3	6.1	1.4	5.5	0.3	12.2	3.0	16.1	8.8	42.6	125
Cheyenne County	878	60.3	29.0	12.5	9.0	5.8	1.8	1.7	0.0	15.3	4.2	13.8	7.9	45.7	10

Table A-3. States and Counties — Age, Ethnicity, and Household Structure

STATE County	Households with Non-Hispanic White householder — Number of households	Percent that are family households	Households with Black or African American householder — Number of households	Percent that are family households	Households with American Indian and Alaska Native householder — Number of households	Percent that are family households	Households with Asian, Hawaiian, and Pacific Islander householder — Number of households	Percent that are family households	Households with Hispanic or Latino[1] householder — Number of households	Percent that are family households	Foreign-born population — Percent of total population that is foreign-born	Place of birth (percent) Europe	Asia	Latin America	Percent in non-English speaking households — Linguistically isolated	Not linguistically isolated
	44	45	46	47	48	49	50	51	52	53	54	55	56	57	58	59
CALIFORNIA—Cont'd																
Butte County	68 052	61.6	1 020	52.9	1 362	64.8	1 693	68.3	5 627	73.1	7.7	1.0	2.4	3.7	3.3	14.9
Calaveras County..........	14 878	70.4	68	85.3	269	73.6	84	71.4	820	84.9	3.0	1.1	0.4	0.9	0.7	11.0
Colusa County..............	3 761	67.1	15	80.0	138	67.4	83	98.8	1 991	89.0	27.6	0.3	0.7	25.9	15.0	33.9
Contra Costa County	229 189	67.1	30 880	71.2	1 938	69.9	32 390	80.9	41 241	83.1	19.0	2.3	7.8	7.8	6.3	27.3
Del Norte County	7 675	67.5	24	45.8	436	62.4	177	92.1	519	89.8	5.7	1.0	1.3	3.0	3.8	11.7
El Dorado County..........	52 336	72.8	319	70.2	498	73.9	1 043	78.5	3 699	82.9	7.2	1.6	1.3	3.4	2.2	13.4
Fresno County..............	130 516	67.2	13 399	71.8	3 713	76.6	15 112	82.4	86 712	84.8	21.1	0.7	5.2	14.8	11.7	39.4
Glenn County................	6 651	69.1	59	100.0	213	72.3	184	87.5	1 871	87.4	17.8	0.6	2.2	14.8	11.5	23.3
Humboldt County	43 905	59.3	310	64.5	2 367	69.6	603	66.7	2 378	67.2	4.5	1.3	0.9	1.9	1.6	12.0
Imperial County	11 801	67.5	856	68.1	815	76.8	932	75.0	24 902	87.6	32.2	0.3	1.2	30.5	18.5	59.8
Inyo County	6 186	62.3	3	100.0	640	67.0	73	72.6	619	84.0	7.6	1.0	1.0	4.9	4.4	11.5
Kern County	126 726	70.0	10 874	72.4	2 895	78.0	6 121	81.9	58 597	87.9	16.9	0.6	2.4	13.6	9.9	31.7
Kings County	18 606	74.2	1 796	74.5	681	78.3	1 123	78.5	11 644	86.9	16.0	0.8	2.0	13.1	10.1	38.5
Lake County	20 507	63.1	558	46.6	563	82.2	235	68.1	1 611	80.1	6.6	1.7	0.6	3.7	2.5	12.6
Lassen County	8 372	69.9	79	45.6	316	77.5	45	53.3	528	82.6	2.3	0.7	0.3	1.2	0.9	11.3
Los Angeles County......	1 325 885	56.4	345 153	63.2	20 264	73.8	368 564	75.0	1 012 555	85.0	36.2	2.0	10.7	22.5	16.7	45.7
Madera County.............	21 795	74.3	927	74.3	650	87.7	410	83.2	11 937	90.4	20.1	0.9	0.9	17.9	12.5	34.0
Marin County................	86 724	59.2	1 569	67.4	229	57.6	3 848	68.1	6 539	76.8	16.6	4.6	3.8	6.7	5.3	21.5
Mariposa County	5 871	67.7	22	54.5	214	64.5	29	34.5	307	67.4	2.8	1.0	0.4	0.9	0.1	7.0
Mendocino County	27 507	64.0	180	48.9	1 299	74.1	277	67.9	3 204	86.7	10.2	1.4	0.6	7.9	4.1	18.2
Merced County	33 190	72.0	2 837	72.3	719	73.7	2 999	88.4	22 548	88.1	24.8	2.1	4.5	17.9	13.0	42.0
Modoc County	3 296	66.3	2	0.0	139	81.3	9	66.7	207	82.6	5.9	0.7	0.5	3.9	3.0	12.5
Mono County	4 227	62.1	14	100.0	90	53.3	98	31.6	591	72.8	12.4	1.7	0.4	9.1	6.6	16.2
Monterey County	68 367	63.8	4 002	69.7	1 154	77.2	8 211	75.0	37 387	90.3	29.0	1.9	3.9	22.6	15.4	41.5
Napa County	36 414	64.1	293	75.4	302	86.1	1 153	81.4	6 510	86.6	18.1	2.4	2.3	12.8	7.4	24.9
Nevada County	34 185	70.5	73	69.9	211	71.1	307	73.3	1 380	81.7	4.4	1.7	0.3	1.6	0.7	11.1
Orange County.............	603 927	65.4	15 740	69.6	5 002	74.7	111 836	83.0	182 929	87.5	29.9	2.0	10.9	15.8	13.0	36.0
Placer County...............	81 372	72.5	719	68.6	615	75.4	2 409	76.2	6 583	79.8	7.1	1.8	1.8	2.7	2.2	14.7
Plumas County..............	8 231	68.1	41	61.0	143	68.5	33	78.8	366	61.5	2.5	0.8	0.3	1.1	0.8	8.3
Riverside County...........	319 710	68.0	29 821	76.6	5 384	80.0	16 297	79.4	128 145	88.0	19.0	1.4	2.6	14.1	8.5	33.4
Sacramento County	299 256	62.2	42 009	69.2	4 510	66.4	41 087	76.4	54 089	75.9	16.1	3.0	7.3	4.6	7.0	24.5
San Benito County	8 992	77.4	212	83.0	189	72.0	378	85.7	5 817	88.2	18.8	0.8	1.1	16.5	7.6	40.2
San Bernardino County.	287 584	70.9	47 849	77.5	5 460	75.5	23 499	84.1	154 321	87.8	18.6	1.0	3.6	13.4	8.0	36.1
San Diego County........	657 282	61.9	54 826	68.4	7 522	69.8	74 052	77.4	182 122	82.2	21.5	2.0	7.0	11.4	8.1	34.0
San Francisco County...	184 523	31.6	24 273	50.3	1 321	33.8	79 765	67.3	31 874	61.0	36.8	5.1	22.6	7.8	15.0	39.0
San Joaquin County......	104 627	69.3	11 715	75.5	1 841	74.3	17 477	82.6	41 376	84.2	19.5	1.1	7.2	10.6	10.1	32.7
San Luis Obispo County	77 781	62.6	767	50.3	831	59.2	2 190	56.8	9 479	76.2	8.9	1.5	1.7	5.0	3.3	18.1
San Mateo County	150 403	61.5	6 945	60.4	1 010	50.8	45 007	78.3	30 700	83.1	32.3	3.9	14.5	11.9	9.1	41.8
Santa Barbara County ..	93 985	60.5	3 101	65.6	1 350	77.7	5 154	64.9	31 405	84.1	21.2	2.6	2.8	15.0	9.9	31.8
Santa Clara County.......	315 370	63.4	16 087	67.1	3 094	75.6	127 964	80.5	91 466	82.7	34.1	3.4	19.5	9.8	12.2	42.5
Santa Cruz County........	70 128	59.8	907	61.1	829	69.5	2 812	62.6	14 517	83.8	18.2	2.5	2.0	13.0	7.9	27.6
Shasta County	57 117	69.0	259	64.9	1 244	76.9	801	82.4	2 381	73.7	4.0	0.8	1.5	1.1	1.2	10.1
Sierra County	1 395	64.2	0	X	26	84.6	5	0.0	67	73.1	3.0	0.7	0.6	1.5	1.7	8.5
Siskiyou County	16 210	65.3	237	59.9	572	72.9	192	80.7	925	80.1	5.4	1.4	0.8	2.6	2.2	11.5
Solano County..............	75 623	71.2	18 610	75.2	1 075	66.4	14 310	86.5	16 661	85.2	16.9	1.5	8.5	6.2	4.7	30.6
Sonoma County............	143 605	63.5	2 038	67.6	1 559	75.5	4 337	75.6	17 222	83.7	14.3	2.3	2.4	8.8	5.4	21.3
Stanislaus County	97 654	71.2	3 550	71.4	1 673	77.9	5 088	86.3	32 967	88.3	18.3	1.6	3.8	12.0	8.5	32.3
Sutter County	18 952	71.2	603	69.5	439	72.7	2 215	86.7	4 295	85.1	19.3	0.9	7.8	10.3	9.5	26.7
Tehama County	17 870	69.3	73	69.9	393	61.1	147	72.8	2 146	86.6	7.9	0.7	0.4	6.4	4.4	15.3
Trinity County	5 037	65.0	14	14.3	226	69.5	14	100.0	141	73.8	1.6	0.8	0.3	0.2	0.4	7.4
Tulare County	59 303	72.6	1 725	80.2	1 452	77.7	3 038	83.4	43 171	89.0	22.6	0.9	2.3	19.1	13.2	40.6
Tuolumne County..........	19 200	68.1	55	49.1	334	64.7	174	56.9	851	73.8	3.2	1.3	0.6	0.8	0.7	9.4
Ventura County............	167 512	71.5	4 844	73.4	1 912	75.0	11 503	83.0	54 525	88.0	20.7	1.8	4.1	14.0	7.9	34.1
Yolo County	39 508	60.9	1 118	61.0	532	68.4	4 995	48.3	11 454	80.2	20.3	2.8	6.0	10.3	9.2	31.5
Yuba County	15 489	69.6	650	74.8	526	81.2	819	88.6	2 384	85.2	13.2	1.4	4.4	7.0	6.8	22.5
COLORADO..............	1 327 444	64.1	59 518	65.2	14 528	70.0	31 027	69.8	208 192	76.7	8.6	1.5	1.7	4.8	4.1	17.5
Adams County.............	91 723	69.0	3 664	67.8	1 224	69.7	3 192	82.3	27 140	82.6	12.5	1.2	2.2	8.7	7.1	22.0
Alamosa County...........	3 286	66.6	27	66.7	93	59.1	39	38.5	2 035	71.3	4.7	0.3	0.3	4.0	5.3	34.5
Arapahoe County..........	150 687	64.8	14 367	66.8	1 172	69.9	6 067	74.0	15 773	76.4	11.0	2.1	3.2	4.5	4.5	16.8
Archuleta County..........	3 310	72.1	8	100.0	50	62.0	0	X	554	73.1	2.9	1.5	0.1	1.0	2.0	17.2
Baca County................	1 762	66.6	0	X	27	59.3	5	60.0	87	78.2	2.5	0.3	0.3	1.8	0.8	9.5
Bent County	1 430	68.9	8	25.0	20	60.0	13	100.0	505	73.9	4.4	0.6	0.4	3.2	3.0	19.4
Boulder County	101 048	59.3	825	61.3	522	77.0	3 134	65.0	7 979	76.3	9.4	2.1	2.5	4.0	3.5	15.8
Chaffee County	6 118	66.9	8	25.0	50	64.0	19	42.1	347	61.4	2.0	1.0	0.2	0.4	1.1	10.5
Cheyenne County	825	68.8	0	X	2	100.0	0	X	45	84.4	4.1	0.6	0.3	3.2	3.3	7.9

[1] Hispanic or Latino persons may be of any race.

Items 44—59

Table A-3. States and Counties — Age, Ethnicity, and Household Structure

STATE/County code	MSA/PMSA/NECMA code[1]	STATE County	Population by age (percent)							Median age	+/- U.S. percent under 18 years	+/- U.S. percent 65 years and over	Non-Hispanic White		
			Total population	Under 5 years	5 to 17 years	18 to 24 years	25 to 44 years	45 to 64 years	65 years and over				Total population	Age (percent) Under 18 years	65 years and over
			1	2	3	4	5	6	7	8	9	10	11	12	13
		COLORADO—Cont'd													
08 019	...	Clear Creek County	9 322	5.9	16.7	5.5	32.7	32.2	7.0	40.2	-3.1	-5.4	8 795	22.1	7.2
08 021	...	Conejos County	8 400	7.8	24.3	8.6	23.6	20.6	15.1	34.2	6.4	2.7	3 266	30.5	16.9
08 023	...	Costilla County	3 663	5.4	19.7	6.5	23.2	28.5	16.8	42.1	-0.6	4.4	1 027	19.6	18.6
08 025	...	Crowley County	5 518	4.4	14.4	10.6	38.8	20.9	10.9	36.6	-6.9	-1.5	3 674	18.5	13.5
08 027	...	Custer County	3 503	5.3	17.0	4.9	23.2	34.5	15.0	44.9	-3.4	2.6	3 308	21.7	15.1
08 029	...	Delta County	27 834	6.0	17.9	6.7	23.7	26.1	19.7	42.3	-1.8	7.3	23 946	22.6	21.7
08 031	2080	Denver County	554 636	6.7	15.1	10.7	36.5	19.8	11.2	33.1	-3.9	-1.2	287 857	12.4	16.1
08 033	...	Dolores County	1 844	5.1	16.6	6.6	27.1	27.2	17.5	42.4	-4.0	5.1	1 662	20.9	17.8
08 035	2080	Douglas County	175 766	9.7	21.7	4.6	38.3	21.6	4.1	33.7	5.7	-8.3	157 697	30.9	4.3
08 037	...	Eagle County	41 659	6.9	16.5	11.3	42.5	20.0	2.8	31.2	-2.3	-9.6	30 883	20.8	3.4
08 039	...	Elbert County	19 872	6.4	23.6	5.5	32.8	25.6	6.0	37.2	4.3	-6.4	18 543	29.5	6.2
08 041	1720	El Paso County	516 929	7.5	19.9	10.5	32.6	20.7	8.6	33.0	1.7	-3.8	393 713	25.2	10.0
08 043	...	Fremont County	46 145	4.8	15.8	7.4	33.3	24.1	14.5	38.8	-5.1	2.1	37 421	21.8	16.9
08 045	...	Garfield County	43 791	7.6	19.6	9.1	32.8	22.1	8.7	34.2	1.5	-3.7	35 519	24.9	10.4
08 047	...	Gilpin County	4 757	5.7	15.5	5.2	37.5	29.5	6.6	38.3	-4.5	-5.8	4 375	20.4	6.9
08 049	...	Grand County	12 442	5.7	16.0	9.4	34.3	26.7	7.9	36.9	-4.0	-4.5	11 546	21.0	8.3
08 051	...	Gunnison County	13 956	4.7	13.3	21.1	32.8	21.4	6.7	30.4	-7.7	-5.7	12 932	17.4	6.9
08 053	...	Hinsdale County	790	6.1	13.7	5.2	29.6	33.9	11.5	43.9	-5.9	-0.9	756	19.6	11.8
08 055	...	Huerfano County	7 862	4.5	16.3	7.4	28.1	26.6	17.1	41.7	-4.9	4.7	4 534	17.2	20.1
08 057	...	Jackson County	1 577	5.5	19.7	5.1	27.3	29.6	12.7	40.5	-0.5	0.3	1 434	22.8	13.5
08 059	2080	Jefferson County	527 056	6.3	19.0	8.1	32.1	25.0	9.6	36.8	-0.4	-2.8	447 187	23.7	10.6
08 061	...	Kiowa County	1 622	5.9	20.0	7.2	24.5	24.9	17.4	39.7	0.2	5.0	1 521	25.6	18.3
08 063	...	Kit Carson County	8 011	6.1	20.7	7.6	28.2	22.5	14.9	37.4	1.1	2.5	6 671	25.5	17.0
08 065	...	Lake County	7 812	7.8	19.1	12.8	32.9	21.1	6.3	30.5	1.2	-6.1	4 812	20.0	8.8
08 067	...	La Plata County	43 941	5.2	17.4	13.7	29.5	24.8	9.3	35.6	-3.1	-3.1	36 190	21.0	10.0
08 069	2670	Larimer County	251 494	6.0	17.6	14.2	30.9	21.8	9.6	33.2	-2.1	-2.8	220 432	22.4	10.4
08 071	...	Las Animas County	15 207	5.4	18.9	8.2	23.3	25.5	18.8	40.9	-1.4	6.4	8 385	20.6	20.8
08 073	...	Lincoln County	6 087	5.3	18.5	7.0	33.3	21.9	14.1	37.8	-1.9	1.7	5 088	24.5	16.5
08 075	...	Logan County	20 504	6.0	18.6	11.6	28.4	20.9	14.5	36.5	-1.1	2.1	17 384	23.6	16.5
08 077	2995	Mesa County	116 255	6.1	18.8	9.4	26.8	23.8	15.1	38.1	-0.8	2.7	101 015	23.2	16.5
08 079	...	Mineral County	831	4.5	15.5	4.1	26.2	32.7	17.0	45.0	-5.7	4.6	787	19.2	17.4
08 081	...	Moffat County	13 184	6.6	21.7	8.0	30.2	24.2	9.3	35.4	2.6	-3.1	11 645	27.5	10.0
08 083	...	Montezuma County	23 830	7.3	20.3	7.3	25.9	25.2	14.0	38.0	1.9	1.6	18 454	24.5	16.2
08 085	...	Montrose County	33 432	6.6	20.3	7.0	25.8	25.0	15.3	38.8	1.2	2.9	27 464	24.3	17.5
08 087	...	Morgan County	27 171	8.5	21.8	8.3	28.9	19.5	12.9	33.5	4.6	0.5	18 362	25.1	17.5
08 089	...	Otero County	20 311	6.2	20.6	8.3	25.1	23.6	16.1	37.7	1.1	3.7	12 003	21.8	20.8
08 091	...	Ouray County	3 742	4.9	17.6	4.2	26.9	34.0	12.3	43.4	-3.2	-0.1	3 524	22.0	12.5
08 093	...	Park County	14 523	6.0	17.6	5.0	33.8	30.1	7.5	40.0	-2.1	-4.9	13 467	22.9	7.5
08 095	...	Phillips County	4 480	6.9	20.1	6.0	25.3	22.3	19.3	39.8	1.3	6.9	3 872	25.0	21.6
08 097	...	Pitkin County	14 872	4.1	12.4	7.4	38.7	30.7	6.7	38.4	-9.2	-5.7	13 433	15.9	7.4
08 099	...	Prowers County	14 483	8.0	21.9	11.1	26.3	19.9	12.8	32.4	4.2	0.4	9 403	25.5	16.8
08 101	6560	Pueblo County	141 472	6.6	19.0	9.3	27.6	22.2	15.3	36.7	-0.1	2.9	81 404	20.9	19.3
08 103	...	Rio Blanco County	5 986	5.8	20.9	8.9	28.0	25.3	11.2	37.5	1.0	-1.2	5 542	26.2	11.9
08 105	...	Rio Grande County	12 413	6.7	21.5	7.7	25.6	23.7	14.9	37.3	2.5	2.5	6 997	22.9	18.8
08 107	...	Routt County	19 690	5.5	17.0	10.1	36.4	25.9	5.0	35.0	-3.2	-7.4	18 732	22.3	5.2
08 109	...	Saguache County	5 917	6.8	21.6	8.1	25.8	27.2	10.6	36.9	2.7	-1.8	3 042	21.1	14.1
08 111	...	San Juan County	558	4.7	14.9	3.8	28.3	40.9	7.5	43.7	-6.1	-4.9	509	19.1	7.3
08 113	...	San Miguel County	6 594	4.4	13.3	10.1	42.9	25.9	3.4	34.2	-8.0	-9.0	5 979	17.2	3.6
08 115	...	Sedgwick County	2 747	5.6	16.9	7.0	23.3	24.8	22.4	43.2	-3.2	10.0	2 398	20.8	23.4
08 117	...	Summit County	23 548	5.3	12.1	15.5	44.5	19.4	3.2	30.8	-8.3	-9.2	20 276	16.3	3.6
08 119	...	Teller County	20 555	5.6	20.3	4.8	32.3	29.7	7.3	39.4	0.2	-5.1	19 097	25.1	7.7
08 121	...	Washington County	4 926	6.3	20.1	6.3	24.8	24.2	18.3	40.2	0.7	5.9	4 603	25.4	19.0
08 123	3060	Weld County	180 936	7.7	20.5	13.1	29.7	20.0	9.0	30.9	2.5	-3.4	126 484	24.1	11.2
08 125	...	Yuma County	9 841	6.6	21.8	7.2	26.0	22.3	16.0	37.3	2.7	3.6	8 466	25.7	18.6
09 000	...	CONNECTICUT	3 405 565	6.5	18.2	7.9	30.5	23.1	13.8	37.4	-1.0	1.4	2 637 525	22.2	16.3
09 001	5483	Fairfield County	882 567	7.2	18.4	6.9	31.1	23.2	13.3	37.3	-0.1	0.9	644 541	23.4	16.1
09 003	3283	Hartford County	857 183	6.4	18.2	7.8	30.0	23.1	14.6	37.7	-1.1	2.2	625 655	21.0	18.1
09 005	...	Litchfield County	182 193	5.8	18.7	5.6	29.9	25.8	14.3	39.6	-1.2	1.9	172 230	24.0	14.7
09 007	3283	Middlesex County	155 071	6.1	17.1	7.1	31.3	24.9	13.6	38.6	-2.5	1.2	138 950	22.0	14.6
09 009	5483	New Haven County	824 008	6.3	18.1	8.6	30.1	22.4	14.5	37.0	-1.3	2.1	616 338	21.1	17.6
09 011	5523	New London County	259 088	6.2	18.1	8.5	31.3	22.8	13.0	37.0	-1.4	0.6	219 195	22.7	14.5
09 013	3283	Tolland County	136 364	5.9	17.2	13.0	30.8	23.0	10.2	35.7	-2.6	-2.2	124 053	23.1	10.9
09 015	...	Windham County	109 091	6.1	19.0	9.6	30.4	22.6	12.3	36.3	-0.6	-0.1	96 563	23.7	13.5

[1]MSA = Metropolitan Statistical Area. PMSA = Primary MSA. NECMA = New England County Metropolitan Area. See the Appendix A for explanation of these concepts. See Appendix B for list of metropolitan areas identified by type, with component counties.

Table A-3. States and Counties — Age, Ethnicity, and Household Structure

STATE County	Black or African American			American Indian and Alaska Native			Asian, Hawaiian, and Pacific Islander			Hispanic or Latino[1]			Two or more races		
	Total population	Age (percent) Under 18 years	65 years and over	Total population	Age (percent) Under 18 years	65 years and over	Total population	Age (percent) Under 18 years	65 years and over	Total population	Age (percent) Under 18 years	65 years and over	Total population	Age (percent) Under 18 years	65 years and over
	14	15	16	17	18	19	20	21	22	23	24	25	26	27	28
COLORADO—Cont'd															
Clear Creek County	16	12.5	0.0	75	21.3	0.0	48	4.2	27.1	245	31.0	0.0	181	46.4	6.6
Conejos County	19	63.2	0.0	183	40.4	8.7	16	25.0	0.0	4 965	32.7	14.2	292	36.6	11.0
Costilla County	18	16.7	55.6	91	28.6	9.9	56	23.2	23.2	2 469	27.5	15.6	194	23.7	20.1
Crowley County	381	0.3	0.0	151	37.1	2.0	66	3.2	4.5	1 247	24.0	7.9	67	44.8	4.5
Custer County	29	75.9	0.0	58	20.7	17.2	0	X	X	100	31.0	11.0	15	20.0	46.7
Delta County	133	0.0	0.0	191	8.4	11.0	59	0.0	5.1	3 083	35.4	7.8	543	31.7	8.1
Denver County	60 579	29.5	9.8	7 330	28.4	3.4	15 619	19.8	8.5	176 063	33.9	4.6	21 346	36.2	4.8
Dolores County	0	X	X	63	23.8	17.5	7	0.0	0.0	70	27.1	17.1	46	58.7	6.5
Douglas County	1 844	35.6	1.0	771	24.1	1.7	4 402	27.9	4.1	8 438	37.5	1.2	3 518	50.5	1.4
Eagle County	51	3.9	0.0	176	21.6	2.3	365	6.0	2.7	9 714	32.3	1.1	788	28.8	0.0
Elbert County	38	28.9	0.0	162	29.6	4.3	54	22.2	1.9	774	36.2	4.1	402	45.3	4.2
El Paso County	31 940	31.9	4.3	4 812	31.6	3.6	14 445	22.4	6.9	58 419	36.4	3.8	21 841	50.0	2.7
Fremont County	2 495	1.8	0.0	598	13.9	0.8	228	20.2	3.9	4 711	20.1	5.4	1 001	34.8	12.1
Garfield County	90	26.7	0.0	280	30.0	2.1	134	30.6	0.0	7 375	37.5	1.5	830	40.7	3.3
Gilpin County	55	0.0	16.4	28	14.3	0.0	40	25.0	0.0	186	38.7	1.1	119	39.5	0.0
Grand County	14	71.4	0.0	54	7.4	0.0	63	23.8	4.8	607	31.5	3.1	173	34.7	1.2
Gunnison County	76	10.5	0.0	96	16.7	0.0	41	0.0	2.4	641	30.4	5.3	270	28.9	2.2
Hinsdale County	0	X	X	10	60.0	0.0	2	0.0	0.0	9	22.2	0.0	13	0.0	15.4
Huerfano County	204	5.9	4.4	192	32.3	0.0	33	0.0	24.2	2 774	27.2	14.1	394	30.5	7.1
Jackson County	5	60.0	0.0	14	14.3	0.0	2	0.0	0.0	110	58.2	1.8	31	45.2	12.9
Jefferson County	4 103	28.1	2.4	3 827	26.5	3.1	12 189	27.2	6.0	52 511	34.5	3.6	12 760	44.8	2.6
Kiowa County	5	60.0	0.0	20	40.0	0.0	2	100.0	0.0	51	31.4	3.9	18	0.0	11.1
Kit Carson County	147	0.0	0.0	50	8.0	18.0	13	46.2	15.4	1 080	37.7	3.6	52	84.6	11.5
Lake County	0	X	X	32	21.9	18.8	42	40.5	0.0	2 833	38.7	2.0	206	34.5	1.9
La Plata County	118	32.2	3.4	2 321	29.7	4.0	254	9.4	5.5	4 519	32.6	7.4	1 166	38.5	4.9
Larimer County	1 736	29.7	0.6	1 875	28.9	3.4	3 752	24.6	5.0	20 631	33.5	3.2	5 918	41.2	5.2
Las Animas County	32	53.1	0.0	412	30.3	6.6	85	32.9	11.8	6 348	28.6	16.8	618	39.8	8.9
Lincoln County	309	4.2	0.0	63	25.4	0.0	37	16.2	5.4	531	26.2	1.9	107	54.2	2.8
Logan County	330	6.1	0.0	130	3.8	0.0	148	27.7	1.4	2 396	32.8	4.2	368	60.3	3.5
Mesa County	516	29.5	1.2	1 154	33.7	7.3	511	22.7	10.4	11 629	36.8	5.3	2 478	43.4	5.6
Mineral County	0	X	X	6	33.3	33.3	0	X	X	10	20.0	20.0	28	39.3	0.0
Moffat County	40	37.5	0.0	92	10.9	3.3	37	67.6	0.0	1 223	30.7	4.4	247	51.8	3.2
Montezuma County	11	27.3	72.7	2 712	38.1	3.8	27	11.1	11.1	2 233	37.7	9.0	554	45.7	5.1
Montrose County	164	57.3	0.0	380	30.5	11.3	285	54.0	0.0	4 998	39.1	5.1	704	42.6	4.3
Morgan County	55	60.0	7.3	136	36.0	4.4	46	6.5	23.9	8 511	41.8	3.1	528	43.9	8.9
Otero County	118	61.0	0.0	289	42.6	5.9	153	22.2	24.8	7 699	34.2	9.2	575	45.9	7.0
Ouray County	3	0.0	0.0	30	33.3	0.0	13	69.2	0.0	121	28.1	15.7	68	26.5	11.8
Park County	128	46.9	6.3	103	41.7	0.0	51	31.4	0.0	573	38.0	8.0	287	27.9	8.4
Phillips County	14	50.0	0.0	25	8.0	8.0	8	0.0	0.0	531	42.4	3.4	42	31.0	21.4
Pitkin County	64	12.5	3.1	17	0.0	0.0	187	13.4	0.0	934	23.1	0.0	248	28.2	0.0
Prowers County	44	13.6	0.0	151	26.5	9.9	87	24.1	24.1	4 803	38.7	5.2	348	58.6	4.9
Pueblo County	2 430	20.6	10.7	2 176	26.6	6.3	875	20.8	11.9	53 804	32.7	9.8	5 461	43.1	7.6
Rio Blanco County	0	X	X	63	20.6	3.2	28	46.4	14.3	296	32.1	2.0	82	42.7	0.0
Rio Grande County	9	100.0	0.0	98	34.7	0.0	61	4.9	45.9	5 183	35.3	9.6	455	43.3	9.5
Routt County	19	52.6	0.0	71	12.7	8.5	124	23.4	0.0	611	30.6	2.5	200	37.5	1.5
Saguache County	11	63.6	0.0	75	18.7	8.0	34	29.4	0.0	2 607	36.7	7.0	164	39.0	6.1
San Juan County	0	X	X	10	40.0	0.0	8	25.0	0.0	31	19.4	16.1	0	X	X
San Miguel County	22	9.1	0.0	46	17.4	0.0	91	38.5	0.0	391	17.4	0.5	80	16.3	5.0
Sedgwick County	5	0.0	80.0	12	33.3	16.7	17	0.0	82.4	300	38.0	12.3	52	32.7	15.4
Summit County	203	9.9	0.0	79	11.4	0.0	183	20.2	0.0	2 306	24.2	0.9	741	28.1	0.0
Teller County	128	32.8	0.0	193	28.5	4.1	80	42.5	0.0	705	40.6	1.6	527	36.1	4.7
Washington County	2	0.0	0.0	27	18.5	7.4	14	35.7	21.4	281	44.5	6.4	23	34.8	8.7
Weld County	969	32.8	1.8	1 650	34.4	3.6	1 659	22.2	7.5	48 898	38.7	3.9	5 213	42.2	3.1
Yuma County	7	0.0	0.0	24	16.7	0.0	7	100.0	0.0	1 243	43.9	0.2	149	51.7	1.3
CONNECTICUT	305 902	31.9	7.0	9 419	27.2	7.3	83 634	26.0	4.0	318 947	35.8	3.4	80 007	39.1	5.3
Fairfield County	88 226	31.9	7.7	1 628	25.4	6.8	28 813	27.1	4.1	104 210	31.8	3.9	23 215	37.2	5.4
Hartford County	98 294	31.6	6.8	1 708	22.5	9.8	21 416	27.2	4.5	98 469	38.2	3.6	21 741	39.1	5.8
Litchfield County	1 869	28.6	9.4	312	11.2	13.1	2 345	31.6	4.9	3 901	35.5	4.5	1 813	42.5	6.1
Middlesex County	6 609	33.0	5.9	264	19.3	18.9	2 340	22.8	4.2	4 560	37.1	2.5	2 705	44.5	4.8
New Haven County	92 143	33.4	6.9	2 378	30.3	6.1	19 727	22.8	3.5	82 722	38.0	3.1	18 523	39.1	5.2
New London County	13 269	28.3	6.0	2 293	33.8	6.7	5 077	29.7	4.1	13 531	36.2	2.4	7 901	42.5	5.2
Tolland County	3 377	15.4	2.0	339	19.5	1.8	3 212	20.9	3.5	4 114	28.1	1.6	1 852	33.3	3.1
Windham County	2 115	27.6	4.3	497	24.1	3.0	704	21.4	2.4	7 440	39.1	1.8	2 257	41.2	3.5

[1]Hispanic or Latino persons may be of any race.

Table A-3. States and Counties — Age, Ethnicity, and Household Structure

STATE County	Total households	Married-couple family households — Total	With children	Householder 65 years or over	Other family households — Total	With children	Householder 65 years or over	Two or more unrelated persons — Total	Householder 65 years or over	Male living alone — Total	Householder 65 years or over	Female living alone — Total	Householder 65 years or over	Percent of householders 65 years and over who live alone	Grandparents who are responsible for the care of their grandchildren
	29	30	31	32	33	34	35	36	37	38	39	40	41	42	43
COLORADO—Cont'd															
Clear Creek County	4 028	55.4	22.0	5.7	10.1	7.0	0.4	7.4	0.3	15.8	1.4	11.2	2.8	39.6	52
Conejos County............	2 981	56.7	28.0	14.6	17.8	10.7	3.9	2.1	0.6	12.3	3.8	11.1	7.0	36.1	102
Costilla County	1 496	52.7	21.6	11.7	16.2	8.5	4.3	3.1	0.9	14.2	4.7	13.8	7.5	42.1	78
Crowley County	1 362	55.8	26.6	10.1	15.7	9.0	3.2	3.0	0.1	10.8	3.8	14.7	9.5	50.0	50
Custer County	1 490	65.4	21.7	13.0	7.4	5.2	0.5	3.5	0.4	13.0	3.6	10.7	6.2	41.5	27
Delta County	11 062	60.3	22.3	16.4	11.5	6.9	1.8	3.2	0.5	10.0	3.6	14.9	9.2	40.6	173
Denver County	239 415	35.3	15.6	6.0	15.0	8.3	1.8	10.5	0.4	18.4	2.4	20.9	7.1	53.7	4 710
Dolores County	783	55.9	17.5	13.3	12.8	7.4	3.2	4.5	0.0	14.0	2.8	12.8	7.7	38.9	17
Douglas County............	61 029	74.9	42.6	4.2	7.2	5.2	0.2	4.7	0.1	6.5	0.5	6.9	1.5	31.0	434
Eagle County	15 210	50.5	27.4	2.7	9.2	6.1	0.3	19.4	0.2	11.5	0.5	9.4	1.3	36.1	125
Elbert County	6 760	75.8	37.6	6.7	8.7	5.3	0.7	3.3	0.3	5.9	1.1	6.4	2.1	30.6	66
El Paso County	192 599	56.6	28.5	7.0	13.5	8.9	1.3	6.1	0.6	11.1	1.5	12.7	4.8	42.6	3 489
Fremont County	15 254	56.2	21.9	12.9	13.0	8.3	1.8	3.9	0.6	11.3	3.3	15.6	9.6	45.9	303
Garfield County	16 215	57.8	29.7	6.7	12.1	7.8	0.6	7.3	0.2	11.0	2.0	11.8	5.1	48.6	247
Gilpin County	2 057	55.8	23.3	3.1	7.1	5.4	0.3	10.3	0.3	15.4	2.3	11.4	5.3	66.8	16
Grand County	5 060	54.9	23.1	6.7	8.3	5.6	0.5	11.7	0.1	15.2	2.1	9.9	2.4	38.0	41
Gunnison County	5 666	45.8	20.2	5.2	7.6	4.6	0.9	19.6	0.3	16.6	1.7	10.4	2.2	37.9	4
Hinsdale County	357	61.1	16.5	13.7	8.1	5.0	0.8	5.9	0.0	17.1	1.1	7.8	0.8	11.9	0
Huerfano County	3 074	49.3	16.8	13.0	12.7	8.2	2.4	5.0	0.4	16.4	3.7	16.6	10.0	46.6	58
Jackson County	667	57.7	24.9	9.6	9.4	5.4	0.6	4.5	0.0	14.1	3.7	14.2	7.6	52.8	0
Jefferson County	206 256	56.3	26.7	7.5	12.3	7.6	1.1	6.9	0.3	11.1	1.6	13.4	4.9	42.0	2 506
Kiowa County	655	58.2	22.3	12.4	9.9	6.3	0.9	2.0	0.0	13.0	2.9	16.9	12.7	54.0	13
Kit Carson County........	3 000	60.7	28.3	11.7	9.6	5.7	1.9	2.7	0.1	11.2	2.5	15.8	10.2	48.1	36
Lake County	2 971	52.3	26.2	5.6	12.7	8.5	0.8	9.1	0.1	16.0	1.5	9.9	3.6	44.3	48
La Plata County	17 346	50.4	22.4	7.5	12.7	7.6	1.4	12.1	0.3	11.8	1.8	13.0	4.6	41.3	173
Larimer County............	97 128	55.0	25.5	7.8	10.6	6.6	0.8	11.1	0.2	10.3	1.4	13.0	5.3	43.0	978
Las Animas County......	6 155	50.1	19.8	11.7	16.3	9.5	3.3	3.9	0.5	12.8	4.0	17.0	10.4	48.0	197
Lincoln County	2 056	55.9	26.5	12.3	12.2	8.2	1.6	3.6	0.7	12.0	2.7	16.4	10.6	47.7	34
Logan County	7 540	56.9	26.3	11.6	10.1	6.9	1.4	4.6	0.1	12.1	3.5	16.4	10.5	51.7	128
Mesa County	45 840	56.2	23.5	11.8	13.1	8.5	1.6	5.7	0.4	10.2	2.5	14.8	8.1	43.6	863
Mineral County	381	59.3	22.0	14.4	8.4	3.1	1.6	4.7	0.5	13.4	3.7	14.2	4.2	32.3	13
Moffat County	5 003	58.9	29.2	6.6	13.3	9.9	1.3	4.1	0.2	14.6	2.8	9.1	4.6	47.6	106
Montezuma County	9 212	55.8	24.8	10.7	15.2	9.2	2.1	4.5	0.2	10.8	2.8	13.6	6.9	42.6	229
Montrose County	13 008	59.0	25.3	12.1	12.3	7.1	1.6	4.4	0.5	9.5	3.4	14.8	8.0	44.5	256
Morgan County..............	9 511	60.6	29.6	10.8	12.7	8.9	0.9	3.7	0.3	9.3	2.4	13.8	8.3	47.0	307
Otero County................	7 902	53.2	22.2	11.1	16.1	11.0	2.4	3.1	0.1	11.4	3.6	16.2	10.1	50.1	189
Ouray County	1 577	62.7	23.2	11.7	8.8	5.8	1.3	4.5	0.5	12.2	0.8	11.8	3.3	23.1	7
Park County	5 925	63.7	25.7	7.1	8.2	5.8	0.6	7.0	0.0	12.3	1.7	8.8	2.2	33.7	109
Phillips County	1 786	61.0	26.9	14.5	8.9	6.7	1.0	3.1	0.4	9.6	3.4	17.4	11.4	48.0	6
Pitkin County	6 822	39.0	17.6	5.2	8.4	5.1	0.6	16.8	0.6	18.7	1.0	17.0	1.9	31.0	0
Prowers County............	5 325	58.5	30.4	10.0	12.4	7.7	2.0	3.9	0.3	10.2	2.0	14.9	8.8	46.8	163
Pueblo County..............	54 618	51.0	21.6	11.5	17.9	10.6	2.7	4.6	0.5	11.0	3.0	15.5	8.6	44.2	1 980
Rio Blanco County	2 320	60.3	27.0	10.1	11.3	8.2	1.3	3.9	0.2	12.4	1.6	12.2	5.4	37.9	59
Rio Grande County	4 698	60.3	27.3	11.7	12.4	9.4	1.2	3.2	0.4	12.0	3.3	12.1	6.2	41.7	150
Routt County	7 980	51.7	25.6	3.6	9.4	6.6	1.1	14.5	0.1	14.2	1.1	10.2	2.8	44.4	56
Saguache County.........	2 311	52.6	23.8	9.2	14.6	9.1	1.9	5.6	0.3	14.7	2.0	12.5	5.1	38.1	65
San Juan County	269	41.3	11.5	5.9	16.7	12.6	0.7	5.6	0.0	20.8	2.6	15.6	3.7	48.6	7
San Miguel County	3 010	39.0	15.8	2.7	8.8	7.1	0.2	19.5	0.5	19.7	1.2	12.9	1.6	48.8	17
Sedgwick County	1 161	59.9	21.4	18.0	8.5	4.7	1.9	1.8	0.5	15.2	3.5	14.6	9.4	38.8	31
Summit County	9 106	45.1	20.5	2.9	8.2	4.5	0.2	25.1	0.4	14.5	0.7	7.1	0.8	30.0	31
Teller County	7 980	65.8	27.4	6.9	8.6	5.7	0.8	6.0	0.2	9.2	1.5	10.3	2.9	35.7	90
Washington County.......	1 982	60.8	25.4	15.6	10.3	5.3	1.5	2.7	0.2	12.6	3.5	13.5	7.5	38.9	22
Weld County................	63 197	59.4	30.2	8.0	12.7	7.7	1.1	7.0	0.2	9.4	1.7	11.6	5.4	43.6	1 716
Yuma County	3 806	61.1	28.0	13.2	8.9	5.4	1.1	3.0	0.6	10.6	2.3	16.4	10.4	46.2	45
CONNECTICUT	1 302 227	52.7	24.3	9.5	15.3	8.5	2.3	5.6	0.4	10.6	2.5	15.8	7.8	45.6	18 898
Fairfield County	324 403	56.2	27.8	9.7	14.7	7.3	2.6	5.2	0.5	9.2	2.4	14.7	7.1	42.6	4 531
Hartford County............	335 184	49.6	21.9	9.7	17.0	9.9	2.4	5.5	0.4	11.1	2.6	16.7	8.3	46.4	5 429
Litchfield County...........	71 594	58.0	26.5	9.9	11.6	6.0	2.2	5.2	0.5	10.3	2.6	14.9	7.8	45.3	682
Middlesex County..........	61 288	54.5	24.6	9.2	11.7	6.2	1.9	6.5	0.4	10.9	2.3	16.3	7.5	45.9	669
New Haven County	319 309	49.8	22.4	9.4	16.6	9.3	2.4	5.5	0.4	11.3	2.7	16.9	8.5	45.2	5 327
New London County	99 864	53.0	23.8	9.2	14.8	9.0	2.2	5.9	0.4	11.8	2.5	14.5	7.2	45.2	1 274
Tolland County	49 444	59.1	27.4	8.3	10.2	6.1	1.6	7.2	0.3	10.3	1.9	13.1	5.8	43.2	400
Windham County...........	41 141	53.6	24.4	8.3	15.4	9.6	1.8	6.8	0.5	10.1	2.4	14.1	7.3	47.7	586

Table A-3. States and Counties — Age, Ethnicity, and Household Structure

STATE County	Households with Non-Hispanic White householder		Households with Black or African American householder		Households with American Indian and Alaska Native householder		Households with Asian, Hawaiian, and Pacific Islander householder		Households with Hispanic or Latino[1] householder		Foreign-born population				Percent in non-English speaking households	
											Percent of total population that is foreign-born	Place of birth (percent)				
	Number of households	Percent that are family households	Number of households	Percent that are family households	Number of households	Percent that are family households	Number of households	Percent that are family households	Number of households	Percent that are family households		Europe	Asia	Latin America	Linguistically isolated	Not linguistically isolated
	44	45	46	47	48	49	50	51	52	53	54	55	56	57	58	59
COLORADO—Cont'd																
Clear Creek County	3 851	66.0	8	0.0	34	38.2	22	90.9	81	64.2	1.9	1.1	0.2	0.3	0.2	7.6
Conejos County............	1 206	75.6	4	100.0	62	74.2	4	100.0	1 726	73.8	3.0	0.3	0.1	2.5	6.8	54.6
Costilla County	447	66.9	6	100.0	42	78.6	25	100.0	978	68.2	6.9	0.4	0.2	6.0	12.6	57.9
Crowley County............	1 071	69.5	3	0.0	26	96.2	3	66.7	259	80.7	1.1	0.2	0.0	0.8	1.6	21.7
Custer County	1 413	73.6	7	0.0	24	58.3	0	X	40	80.0	1.7	1.1	0.0	0.0	0.2	7.3
Delta County	10 010	71.5	0	X	62	95.2	23	8.7	802	75.4	4.2	0.5	0.2	3.3	2.9	10.9
Denver County	153 669	41.0	24 362	59.4	2 502	63.2	6 049	55.8	49 870	73.9	17.4	1.8	2.3	12.3	9.8	24.1
Dolores County	734	68.5	0	X	15	80.0	5	60.0	13	100.0	0.9	0.2	0.2	0.6	0.5	9.8
Douglas County............	55 846	81.9	653	85.3	282	70.2	1 279	88.7	2 318	84.2	5.2	1.5	1.9	0.7	0.7	12.0
Eagle County................	12 750	55.7	13	61.5	40	55.0	130	46.2	2 128	85.3	18.2	1.9	0.7	14.4	8.0	24.9
Elbert County	6 389	84.4	11	100.0	53	98.1	21	42.9	208	87.5	1.9	0.8	0.2	0.5	0.3	10.8
El Paso County	154 839	69.1	11 586	75.6	1 669	70.2	4 369	72.6	16 964	75.3	6.4	2.1	2.0	1.8	1.7	16.8
Fremont County	13 963	69.0	34	85.3	120	69.2	39	94.9	829	72.5	1.5	0.7	0.2	0.5	0.7	10.5
Garfield County	14 268	68.1	13	92.3	108	77.8	34	64.7	1 712	85.4	10.4	1.0	0.2	8.9	4.4	16.5
Gilpin County	1 932	62.4	32	46.9	10	100.0	10	80.0	58	79.3	3.4	1.7	0.6	0.9	0.1	7.2
Grand County	4 787	63.4	4	100.0	15	80.0	27	25.9	169	66.3	3.4	1.8	0.4	0.8	1.4	10.0
Gunnison County	5 341	53.6	25	60.0	35	11.4	24	33.3	174	60.3	2.9	1.3	0.2	1.0	1.6	9.9
Hinsdale County	350	68.6	0	X	2	100.0	0	X	3	100.0	2.0	1.5	0.3	0.3	1.8	5.7
Huerfano County	1 965	64.1	14	0.0	72	55.6	17	17.6	929	62.1	1.6	0.4	0.1	0.6	2.2	24.9
Jackson County............	631	66.1	2	100.0	10	70.0	0	X	20	90.0	1.9	0.8	0.1	1.0	0.9	5.3
Jefferson County	182 055	68.0	1 572	59.8	1 505	74.5	3 592	75.2	15 608	76.0	5.4	1.7	1.6	1.6	1.8	13.3
Kiowa County	623	68.7	0	X	8	62.5	0	X	13	61.5	1.4	0.1	0.0	1.2	0.6	5.2
Kit Carson County........	2 718	68.7	0	X	8	75.0	5	60.0	252	87.3	5.8	0.2	0.1	5.3	4.6	11.3
Lake County	2 090	56.3	0	X	14	42.9	14	35.7	823	88.0	15.6	0.8	0.4	14.1	13.0	19.3
La Plata County	14 899	63.3	50	58.0	657	65.6	105	39.0	1 424	64.6	2.7	0.8	0.3	1.1	1.3	13.6
Larimer County	87 874	65.3	542	65.3	671	66.5	1 281	62.9	5 839	72.6	4.3	1.0	1.2	1.5	1.5	12.8
Las Animas County......	3 479	67.5	5	100.0	140	57.9	12	50.0	2 530	65.0	2.3	0.4	0.3	1.6	2.7	28.8
Lincoln County	1 948	67.7	10	70.0	13	61.5	4	75.0	60	81.7	1.8	0.3	0.3	1.1	1.5	6.0
Logan County...............	6 857	66.0	25	68.0	4	100.0	43	100.0	584	76.9	3.1	0.7	0.1	2.3	1.6	11.1
Mesa County	41 295	68.6	166	59.6	366	69.7	108	80.6	3 455	77.7	3.0	0.6	0.3	1.7	1.2	12.1
Mineral County	375	68.3	0	X	2	0.0	0	X	2	100.0	0.7	0.5	0.0	0.0	0.0	3.4
Moffat County	4 494	72.1	12	100.0	18	50.0	12	100.0	419	71.8	4.1	0.6	0.1	3.2	2.8	9.4
Montezuma County	7 536	70.4	8	0.0	780	80.4	2	100.0	798	70.7	2.2	0.9	0.1	1.0	1.6	18.5
Montrose County	11 255	70.8	40	100.0	159	84.3	55	69.1	1 381	74.8	5.6	0.5	0.3	4.6	3.7	12.4
Morgan County............	7 288	69.4	13	84.6	41	92.7	13	100.0	2 116	86.9	14.6	0.3	0.2	14.1	10.3	22.5
Otero County................	5 161	66.6	24	91.7	100	72.0	63	60.3	2 535	75.5	4.9	0.4	0.4	4.1	4.7	27.8
Ouray County	1 499	71.6	3	0.0	13	38.5	2	100.0	40	70.0	3.2	1.8	0.3	0.9	0.3	10.6
Park County	5 584	72.1	36	77.8	21	85.7	11	18.2	180	80.6	2.2	1.2	0.3	0.2	0.5	7.7
Phillips County	1 607	68.2	7	14.3	21	81.0	0	X	139	89.9	8.1	0.4	0.2	7.4	5.3	7.9
Pitkin County	6 366	47.1	36	5.6	12	0.0	74	48.6	259	70.3	10.9	3.6	1.0	4.3	2.5	14.9
Prowers County............	3 843	68.4	20	0.0	55	54.5	22	54.5	1 368	80.3	10.6	0.5	0.3	9.7	9.1	24.2
Pueblo County.............	34 513	65.9	920	62.1	865	69.5	286	68.2	17 884	75.0	3.0	0.5	0.4	1.9	2.3	23.4
Rio Blanco County	2 190	71.0	0	X	19	100.0	7	100.0	87	82.8	3.2	0.9	0.4	1.6	1.5	10.2
Rio Grande County	2 882	70.2	0	X	20	100.0	37	56.8	1 735	76.9	6.0	0.3	0.0	5.5	3.6	36.6
Routt County	7 654	61.0	9	22.2	43	65.1	60	60.0	183	68.9	4.1	2.1	0.3	0.8	0.6	10.6
Saguache County	1 378	61.2	0	X	37	48.6	9	100.0	859	76.9	14.5	0.5	0.4	13.3	10.2	34.8
San Juan County	245	57.6	0	X	0	X	3	100.0	21	57.1	2.5	0.7	0.4	0.5	1.5	18.6
San Miguel County	2 806	47.3	9	100.0	23	52.2	23	60.9	131	55.7	7.3	2.0	0.7	4.0	3.3	12.4
Sedgwick County	1 039	67.8	5	20.0	5	60.0	9	88.9	92	76.1	2.7	0.1	0.0	2.5	1.8	10.7
Summit County	8 293	52.1	42	0.0	29	75.9	71	42.3	526	74.7	11.6	3.8	0.4	5.9	4.9	13.4
Teller County	7 637	74.7	44	93.2	42	88.1	13	46.2	135	60.7	1.8	1.1	0.3	0.2	0.0	8.3
Washington County	1 904	70.5	2	100.0	11	100.0	3	0.0	65	87.7	2.5	0.2	0.1	2.1	0.9	7.6
Weld County................	48 932	69.3	234	56.4	464	80.4	534	70.4	12 600	83.4	9.3	0.5	0.4	8.2	5.9	22.1
Yuma County	3 474	68.1	0	X	19	100.0	0	X	303	89.1	7.9	0.5	0.0	7.4	4.6	10.9
CONNECTICUT	1 059 715	67.1	105 870	68.3	3 278	63.0	26 265	72.9	91 298	78.4	10.9	4.1	2.1	3.8	4.2	20.3
Fairfield County	251 711	69.7	29 766	70.6	448	66.7	8 861	77.5	28 864	80.6	16.9	5.5	2.8	7.6	6.1	24.7
Hartford County............	259 445	65.1	35 000	67.7	641	55.9	6 717	74.9	29 534	77.5	11.7	4.9	2.0	3.6	5.1	22.8
Litchfield County	68 606	69.6	685	65.5	164	51.2	569	85.1	1 122	66.7	5.4	2.8	1.1	0.9	1.3	12.7
Middlesex County.........	56 281	66.0	2 361	66.4	104	44.2	644	69.3	1 237	76.2	6.0	3.0	1.2	1.1	1.5	13.1
New Haven County	251 550	65.2	32 550	67.2	907	64.5	6 776	66.1	24 011	77.7	9.0	3.7	2.0	2.5	4.0	19.8
New London County	88 013	67.4	4 416	69.1	790	71.1	1 575	69.5	3 659	78.8	5.4	2.0	1.4	1.3	1.7	13.6
Tolland County	46 592	69.7	572	57.0	132	47.7	885	68.0	781	64.1	5.9	2.1	2.0	0.9	1.1	13.6
Windham County..........	37 517	68.6	520	62.7	92	75.0	238	60.1	2 090	82.4	4.3	1.7	0.6	1.1	2.2	15.1

[1] Hispanic or Latino persons may be of any race.

Table A-3. States and Counties — Age, Ethnicity, and Household Structure

STATE/ County code	MSA/PMSA/ NECMA code[1]	STATE County	Total population	Under 5 years	5 to 17 years	18 to 24 years	25 to 44 years	45 to 64 years	65 years and over	Median age	+/− U.S. percent under 18 years	+/− U.S. percent 65 years and over	Non-Hispanic White Total population	Under 18 years	65 years and over
			1	2	3	4	5	6	7	8	9	10	11	12	13
10 000	...	DELAWARE	783 600	6.5	18.2	9.6	30.3	22.4	13.0	36.0	-1.0	0.6	568 356	22.0	15.5
10 001	2190	Kent County	126 697	7.2	20.0	10.2	29.7	21.3	11.6	34.4	1.5	-0.8	91 515	25.2	13.4
10 003	9160	New Castle County	500 265	6.6	18.2	10.2	31.7	21.7	11.6	35.0	-0.9	-0.8	353 821	22.1	14.0
10 005	...	Sussex County	156 638	5.8	16.7	6.9	26.4	25.6	18.5	41.1	-3.2	6.1	123 020	19.6	21.4
11 000	...	DISTRICT OF COLUMBIA	572 059	5.7	14.3	12.8	33.2	21.8	12.3	34.6	-5.7	-0.1	158 617	8.5	11.4
11 001	8840	District of Columbia	572 059	5.7	14.3	12.8	33.2	21.8	12.3	34.6	-5.7	-0.1	158 617	8.5	11.4
12 000	...	FLORIDA	15 982 378	5.9	16.9	8.3	28.8	22.6	17.6	38.7	-2.9	5.2	10 456 458	19.3	22.3
12 001	2900	Alachua County	217 955	5.1	15.0	23.2	27.8	19.4	9.5	29.0	-5.6	-2.9	151 933	16.9	11.1
12 003	...	Baker County	22 259	7.1	20.3	9.8	30.7	23.0	9.0	34.0	1.7	-3.4	18 310	27.5	10.0
12 005	6015	Bay County	148 217	6.1	18.0	8.6	30.3	23.7	13.3	37.4	-1.6	0.9	122 663	22.3	14.6
12 007	...	Bradford County	26 088	5.4	16.4	9.7	32.6	23.1	12.9	37.2	-3.9	0.5	19 582	21.9	14.9
12 009	4900	Brevard County	476 230	5.2	16.7	6.8	27.2	24.3	19.9	41.4	-3.8	7.5	398 332	20.1	21.9
12 011	2680	Broward County	1 623 018	6.3	17.2	7.1	31.8	21.6	16.0	37.8	-2.2	3.6	940 692	18.2	23.4
12 013	...	Calhoun County	13 017	5.8	17.3	8.7	32.0	22.5	13.8	36.2	-2.6	1.4	10 013	23.7	15.6
12 015	6580	Charlotte County	141 627	3.5	12.2	4.5	18.9	26.2	34.7	54.3	-10.0	22.3	128 021	14.5	36.5
12 017	...	Citrus County	118 085	3.8	13.3	4.5	19.4	26.7	32.3	52.6	-8.6	19.9	109 691	16.3	33.4
12 019	3600	Clay County	140 814	6.5	21.4	7.9	30.4	24.0	9.8	35.9	2.2	-2.6	119 296	26.7	10.7
12 021	5345	Collier County	251 377	5.3	14.5	6.4	24.9	24.5	24.4	44.1	-5.9	12.0	185 063	15.2	31.6
12 023	...	Columbia County	56 513	6.4	18.9	9.4	27.5	23.7	14.0	37.3	-0.4	1.6	44 075	24.0	15.4
12 027	...	DeSoto County	32 209	5.8	16.7	11.6	26.4	20.1	19.4	36.5	-3.2	7.0	19 677	19.1	28.6
12 029	...	Dixie County	13 827	5.4	16.6	8.2	26.6	26.1	17.0	40.7	-3.7	4.6	12 211	21.8	18.3
12 031	3600	Duval County	778 879	7.1	19.1	9.6	32.5	21.2	10.4	34.1	0.5	-2.0	495 011	22.4	12.6
12 033	6080	Escambia County	294 410	6.0	17.5	12.0	29.2	22.0	13.3	35.4	-2.2	0.9	208 348	20.0	15.5
12 035	2020	Flagler County	49 832	4.3	13.7	4.6	20.3	28.6	28.6	50.4	-7.7	16.2	41 625	16.6	29.5
12 037	...	Franklin County	11 057	4.6	13.5	7.8	30.5	27.8	16.0	40.8	-7.6	3.6	8 817	18.4	17.6
12 039	8240	Gadsden County	45 087	6.7	19.8	9.3	28.9	23.0	12.3	35.5	0.8	-0.1	16 178	16.6	18.3
12 041	...	Gilchrist County	14 437	5.7	18.6	14.2	25.2	22.7	13.6	35.4	-1.4	1.2	12 829	24.6	14.7
12 043	...	Glades County	10 576	5.8	16.3	7.9	26.4	24.4	19.2	40.2	-3.6	6.8	7 249	17.4	25.6
12 045	...	Gulf County	13 332	4.6	17.0	7.0	29.3	25.8	16.3	40.3	-4.1	3.9	10 494	21.3	17.9
12 047	...	Hamilton County	13 327	5.7	17.7	10.8	32.4	22.4	11.0	35.1	-2.3	-1.4	7 318	20.9	14.9
12 049	...	Hardee County	26 938	7.7	20.0	11.1	29.0	18.6	13.6	32.7	2.0	1.2	14 841	21.3	22.2
12 051	...	Hendry County	36 210	7.9	22.1	13.2	29.1	17.9	9.8	29.5	4.3	-2.6	16 043	24.4	16.3
12 053	8280	Hernando County	130 802	4.5	14.3	5.4	20.8	24.0	30.9	49.5	-6.9	18.5	116 552	17.4	32.9
12 055	...	Highlands County	87 366	5.2	14.0	6.2	19.4	22.0	33.1	50.0	-6.5	20.7	66 849	14.6	40.5
12 057	8280	Hillsborough County	998 948	6.8	18.5	9.3	31.9	21.6	12.0	35.1	-0.4	-0.4	632 304	21.4	14.6
12 059	...	Holmes County	18 564	5.6	17.5	8.7	29.0	24.5	14.8	37.5	-2.6	2.4	16 615	23.9	15.8
12 061	...	Indian River County	112 947	4.6	14.6	6.0	22.4	23.2	29.2	47.0	-6.5	16.8	94 318	16.5	33.6
12 063	...	Jackson County	46 755	5.4	17.0	9.7	29.6	23.7	14.6	37.6	-3.3	2.2	32 119	21.5	16.2
12 065	...	Jefferson County	12 902	5.1	17.6	8.2	29.0	25.5	14.5	39.4	-3.0	2.1	7 481	20.4	16.3
12 067	...	Lafayette County	7 022	5.7	15.8	10.9	33.8	21.6	12.1	34.8	-4.2	-0.3	5 295	22.3	15.4
12 069	5960	Lake County	210 528	5.2	15.1	5.8	24.0	23.5	26.4	45.1	-5.4	14.0	177 267	17.7	29.8
12 071	2700	Lee County	440 888	5.2	14.3	6.1	24.2	24.7	25.4	45.2	-6.2	13.0	361 259	16.2	29.6
12 073	8240	Leon County	239 452	5.7	15.5	21.3	29.0	20.1	8.3	29.5	-4.5	-4.1	153 618	19.1	10.2
12 075	...	Levy County	34 450	5.7	18.0	6.6	25.5	26.3	17.9	41.1	-2.0	5.5	28 649	21.9	19.6
12 077	...	Liberty County	7 021	5.4	16.5	9.4	36.4	22.0	10.4	35.0	-3.8	-2.0	5 224	23.2	11.8
12 079	...	Madison County	18 733	5.8	19.6	9.2	27.9	23.0	14.6	36.3	-0.3	2.2	10 441	21.7	17.9
12 081	7510	Manatee County	264 002	5.7	14.9	6.4	25.0	23.1	24.9	43.6	-5.1	12.5	212 481	16.9	29.6
12 083	5790	Marion County	258 916	5.1	16.3	6.4	23.9	23.8	24.5	43.8	-4.3	12.1	208 175	18.7	27.8
12 085	2710	Martin County	126 731	4.3	14.2	5.3	23.0	24.8	28.3	47.3	-7.2	15.9	108 599	16.1	31.9
12 086	5000	Miami-Dade County	2 253 362	6.4	18.3	9.1	31.2	21.6	13.3	35.6	-1.0	0.9	465 894	25.2	17.5
12 087	...	Monroe County	79 589	4.1	12.8	6.3	31.3	31.0	14.5	42.6	-8.8	2.1	61 527	14.8	15.8
12 089	3600	Nassau County	57 663	6.1	18.9	7.4	28.9	26.1	12.6	38.3	-0.7	0.2	51 276	24.6	12.8
12 091	2750	Okaloosa County	170 498	6.3	18.2	9.5	31.4	22.4	12.1	36.1	-1.2	-0.3	138 101	23.1	14.0
12 093	...	Okeechobee County	35 910	6.5	18.7	9.7	27.2	21.4	16.5	36.7	-0.5	4.1	25 643	21.9	21.4
12 095	5960	Orange County	896 344	6.8	18.4	10.8	34.1	19.9	10.0	33.3	-0.5	-2.4	516 024	20.5	13.0
12 097	5960	Osceola County	172 493	6.6	20.1	9.1	31.3	21.5	11.3	34.6	1.0	-1.1	103 187	23.1	14.6
12 099	8960	Palm Beach County	1 131 184	5.5	15.7	6.5	27.1	22.0	23.2	41.8	-4.5	10.8	798 753	16.7	30.2
12 101	8280	Pasco County	344 765	5.2	14.9	5.8	24.4	22.9	26.8	44.9	-5.6	14.4	309 809	18.8	28.8
12 103	8280	Pinellas County	921 482	4.9	14.3	6.3	27.5	24.4	22.6	43.0	-6.5	10.2	762 823	16.7	25.7
12 105	3980	Polk County	483 924	6.4	17.9	8.3	26.5	22.6	18.3	38.6	-1.4	5.9	361 079	20.7	22.3
12 107	...	Putnam County	70 423	6.2	18.4	7.6	24.5	24.9	18.5	40.5	-1.1	6.1	53 101	20.9	21.2
12 109	3600	St. Johns County	123 135	5.2	17.8	7.0	27.6	26.5	15.9	40.6	-2.7	3.5	109 546	22.1	16.6
12 111	2710	St. Lucie County	192 695	5.5	16.9	6.7	25.2	23.0	22.7	42.0	-3.3	10.3	142 949	18.5	27.5
12 113	6080	Santa Rosa County	117 743	6.6	19.8	7.2	31.5	24.0	11.0	36.8	0.7	-1.4	105 016	25.9	11.7

[1]MSA = Metropolitan Statistical Area. PMSA = Primary MSA. NECMA = New England County Metropolitan Area. See the Appendix A for explanation of these concepts. See Appendix B for list of metropolitan areas identified by type, with component counties.

Table A-3. States and Counties — Age, Ethnicity, and Household Structure

STATE County	Black or African American — Total population	Age (percent) Under 18 years	Age (percent) 65 years and over	American Indian and Alaska Native — Total population	Age (percent) Under 18 years	Age (percent) 65 years and over	Asian, Hawaiian, and Pacific Islander — Total population	Age (percent) Under 18 years	Age (percent) 65 years and over	Hispanic or Latino[1] — Total population	Age (percent) Under 18 years	Age (percent) 65 years and over	Two or more races — Total population	Age (percent) Under 18 years	Age (percent) 65 years and over
	14	15	16	17	18	19	20	21	22	23	24	25	26	27	28
DELAWARE	148 823	30.9	7.6	3 111	26.3	9.1	16 388	22.6	4.6	37 321	36.1	2.8	14 353	47.5	3.0
Kent County	25 626	31.0	7.6	1 079	26.0	9.0	2 110	20.4	6.6	4 278	38.7	3.8	2 950	51.0	2.8
New Castle County	99 778	30.7	7.1	973	27.6	3.8	13 401	23.1	4.4	26 307	36.2	2.5	9 154	45.4	3.1
Sussex County	23 419	31.8	9.9	1 059	25.3	14.1	877	20.9	3.9	6 736	34.2	3.3	2 249	51.4	2.8
DISTRICT OF COLUMBIA	343 213	25.1	14.1	2 006	22.1	9.3	15 145	11.5	6.0	45 015	24.8	4.0	14 661	22.3	7.1
District of Columbia	343 213	25.1	14.1	2 006	22.1	9.3	15 145	11.5	6.0	45 015	24.8	4.0	14 661	22.3	7.1
FLORIDA	2 312 105	33.1	7.4	54 428	24.0	6.2	271 189	22.9	6.0	2 680 314	25.9	10.4	409 021	33.7	6.5
Alachua County	40 994	32.0	7.3	420	12.9	2.1	7 908	12.9	2.6	12 333	19.2	3.8	5 262	33.7	3.8
Baker County	2 891	25.1	5.5	82	17.1	0.0	56	0.0	0.0	477	31.7	4.2	485	43.7	0.8
Bay County	15 944	32.9	7.6	1 130	22.2	4.8	2 494	21.8	3.7	3 534	30.2	6.9	2 946	44.8	5.9
Bradford County	5 570	21.3	6.9	56	0.0	0.0	100	31.0	11.0	489	6.7	9.0	435	32.9	6.0
Brevard County	38 680	32.9	10.4	2 070	18.7	9.4	7 400	20.0	8.4	21 902	30.0	8.4	10 093	40.2	7.5
Broward County	329 749	34.2	5.4	3 962	28.6	5.5	37 150	24.3	4.9	271 523	27.4	6.7	58 884	31.5	5.8
Calhoun County	2 166	19.5	8.2	79	16.5	2.5	98	16.3	12.2	454	17.6	3.7	224	33.5	9.8
Charlotte County	6 384	27.3	19.5	405	8.9	19.5	889	17.5	20.0	4 585	27.9	11.8	1 804	32.1	21.6
Citrus County	2 674	30.0	16.7	230	16.5	9.1	1 145	18.4	9.8	3 058	26.2	22.7	1 490	37.0	15.4
Clay County	9 165	35.0	4.2	470	17.2	8.3	2 990	22.8	8.3	6 181	36.7	4.1	3 578	44.2	4.0
Collier County	11 673	35.3	6.1	1 067	26.1	5.5	1 397	22.0	6.3	49 252	31.7	3.7	6 131	35.7	4.5
Columbia County	9 725	29.1	9.5	197	16.2	9.6	395	24.8	7.8	1 493	34.9	5.8	873	39.9	7.7
DeSoto County	3 834	29.1	8.1	567	16.0	7.9	172	26.2	5.2	8 078	27.5	2.8	733	37.0	4.6
Dixie County	1 136	22.7	8.4	10	0.0	20.0	52	3.8	0.0	247	26.3	1.2	218	31.7	10.1
Duval County	216 517	33.9	7.3	2 995	26.2	3.5	21 061	23.8	4.9	31 809	30.5	4.6	15 870	42.5	3.4
Escambia County	62 691	33.1	9.0	2 522	26.3	6.5	6 800	23.5	6.5	7 816	26.1	6.0	7 171	39.8	4.8
Flagler County	4 092	21.7	20.7	133	19.5	0.0	629	29.6	10.2	2 552	26.3	19.6	937	34.9	22.9
Franklin County	1 874	16.8	9.5	27	0.0	55.6	48	20.8	25.0	267	10.1	0.0	131	13.0	7.6
Gadsden County	25 913	31.5	9.7	76	25.0	7.0	140	20.4	13.0	2 773	36.6	1.6	247	47.4	2.8
Gilchrist County	975	18.3	2.9	25	28.0	0.0	2	0.0	0.0	354	24.9	4.5	283	30.4	9.2
Glades County	1 060	24.8	6.3	441	40.8	10.2	62	40.3	0.0	1 589	34.9	3.1	306	37.3	3.3
Gulf County	2 181	22.0	11.5	74	28.4	2.7	81	21.0	2.5	282	16.3	3.2	259	28.6	15.8
Hamilton County	4 963	26.6	6.7	90	10.0	0.0	25	0.0	0.0	926	29.7	0.0	227	5.3	17.2
Hardee County	2 168	19.6	6.5	194	30.4	0.0	44	22.7	0.0	9 702	39.1	2.4	435	46.2	4.8
Hendry County	5 189	32.9	8.0	330	21.8	5.8	224	29.0	4.0	14 259	34.8	3.3	1 094	31.5	1.6
Hernando County	5 187	30.5	13.5	367	21.3	10.1	777	27.2	20.5	6 717	30.3	16.9	1 701	38.6	10.9
Highlands County	8 138	37.0	8.6	247	14.2	10.1	964	25.7	7.7	10 462	33.0	9.1	1 397	41.9	9.9
Hillsborough County	147 966	34.5	6.6	4 175	25.9	4.1	22 111	23.2	5.1	179 637	30.5	8.6	27 612	36.2	5.5
Holmes County	1 168	11.7	6.0	165	17.6	0.0	139	36.0	10.1	234	12.4	8.5	255	23.5	3.1
Indian River County	8 945	33.0	9.9	237	16.0	5.1	902	24.4	6.5	7 300	32.4	3.6	1 708	41.5	8.0
Jackson County	12 486	24.2	11.9	348	14.7	10.1	247	24.7	15.0	1 136	16.5	7.7	550	37.3	3.8
Jefferson County	4 975	26.4	12.5	69	11.6	0.0	62	16.1	30.6	242	15.3	2.5	118	33.1	0.0
Lafayette County	1 015	14.3	2.6	36	25.0	5.6	4	0.0	50.0	623	27.9	0.0	83	6.0	7.2
Lake County	16 878	34.5	10.9	810	33.6	1.6	1 466	23.3	7.6	11 836	34.7	4.6	2 934	37.6	10.1
Lee County	28 570	37.3	7.5	1 340	27.8	9.9	3 397	21.0	10.1	41 993	34.0	5.1	7 590	38.4	7.4
Leon County	69 303	25.9	5.5	624	22.8	3.0	4 919	18.5	2.8	8 220	18.2	2.9	3 727	32.0	3.7
Levy County	3 708	32.4	10.4	130	33.8	7.7	119	23.5	9.2	1 406	30.9	10.9	480	36.0	3.1
Liberty County	1 186	18.9	7.3	161	9.9	3.7	28	39.3	0.0	282	17.4	1.1	173	16.2	8.1
Madison County	7 688	30.4	10.5	28	17.9	17.9	36	41.7	0.0	541	29.8	2.6	188	16.5	18.6
Manatee County	21 580	36.0	6.9	741	29.4	3.9	2 352	20.2	10.0	24 501	36.5	3.6	3 862	45.3	6.0
Marion County	29 401	33.3	12.1	1 314	26.5	6.5	2 273	27.9	9.8	15 535	31.9	9.8	3 680	35.9	10.4
Martin County	6 691	30.8	8.7	496	46.8	3.0	864	30.2	7.4	9 490	35.0	4.2	1 483	38.8	5.8
Miami-Dade County	452 333	33.1	7.2	4 841	26.3	7.3	31 297	20.7	7.0	1 291 681	21.4	14.3	91 465	26.1	8.4
Monroe County	3 760	24.8	11.0	262	12.6	0.0	601	16.5	10.0	12 500	23.7	10.8	1 639	26.5	3.4
Nassau County	4 240	26.2	13.9	193	15.5	4.1	427	27.6	4.9	1 047	40.8	4.8	615	40.5	2.4
Okaloosa County	15 116	29.9	3.8	854	20.5	5.7	4 622	19.3	5.8	6 901	31.2	4.3	5 843	46.0	3.0
Okeechobee County	2 633	26.8	6.5	175	31.4	5.1	334	27.8	6.3	6 727	36.0	2.4	859	31.3	9.1
Orange County	161 558	34.0	6.4	2 862	20.9	4.9	29 601	23.2	5.1	168 191	30.4	6.2	34 049	34.6	4.1
Osceola County	12 873	33.3	8.1	493	23.7	8.9	3 745	24.3	4.2	50 742	32.5	6.3	6 506	36.0	5.5
Palm Beach County	156 496	35.6	5.9	2 706	30.7	4.7	17 318	23.6	5.9	140 568	29.0	6.8	27 518	32.0	6.2
Pasco County	6 770	32.0	10.0	1 051	25.2	6.0	3 589	27.3	7.9	19 555	32.0	8.9	5 280	36.6	10.8
Pinellas County	82 384	33.7	8.2	2 903	15.3	6.0	19 009	25.4	6.0	42 128	27.8	8.5	16 536	37.9	6.6
Polk County	63 709	34.6	8.4	2 172	30.2	7.3	5 964	29.3	7.1	45 650	35.9	4.0	8 820	38.5	6.3
Putnam County	11 757	34.3	11.4	378	25.9	18.3	305	17.0	14.1	4 125	43.2	5.1	1 114	39.1	8.3
St. Johns County	7 414	30.4	13.2	170	11.8	2.4	1 258	23.1	2.9	3 596	30.8	7.5	1 340	41.0	5.4
St. Lucie County	28 947	34.7	9.5	492	17.5	11.6	1 914	24.3	8.3	16 004	32.9	7.2	3 739	38.4	8.9
Santa Rosa County	4 777	32.1	5.6	1 006	21.0	2.2	1 719	18.7	5.1	2 821	31.4	7.2	2 587	40.9	1.7

[1] Hispanic or Latino persons may be of any race.

STATE County	Total households	Married-couple family households Total	With children	Householder 65 years or over	Other family households Total	With children	Householder 65 years or over	Two or more unrelated persons Total	Householder 65 years or over	Male living alone Total	Householder 65 years or over	Female living alone Total	Householder 65 years or over	Percent of householders 65 years and over who live alone	Grandparents who are responsible for the care of their grandchildren
	29	30	31	32	33	34	35	36	37	38	39	40	41	42	43
DELAWARE	298 755	52.3	22.8	9.9	16.5	9.6	2.1	6.2	0.5	10.2	2.3	14.7	6.9	42.4	7 204
Kent County	47 199	53.5	24.5	9.0	17.9	11.5	2.1	5.6	0.5	10.1	2.3	12.9	6.3	42.8	1 397
New Castle County	188 974	50.8	23.6	8.4	17.0	9.5	2.2	6.6	0.4	10.4	2.0	15.3	6.5	43.8	4 298
Sussex County	62 582	56.2	19.3	15.2	14.2	8.7	2.1	5.3	0.7	9.7	3.0	14.5	8.6	39.4	1 509
DISTRICT OF COLUMBIA................	248 590	23.4	8.7	4.7	23.3	11.8	4.0	9.7	0.7	19.2	3.0	24.5	7.3	52.2	8 183
District of Columbia	248 590	23.4	8.7	4.7	23.3	11.8	4.0	9.7	0.7	19.2	3.0	24.5	7.3	52.2	8 183
FLORIDA.................	6 341 121	51.1	19.9	13.4	15.7	8.8	2.2	6.6	0.7	11.1	3.0	15.5	8.4	41.1	147 893
Alachua County	87 536	39.7	17.1	6.4	15.2	8.7	1.7	16.0	0.4	13.2	1.5	15.9	4.9	43.0	1 654
Baker County	7 075	62.1	31.3	8.4	18.0	10.9	2.2	2.9	0.2	7.9	1.2	9.1	4.6	35.0	417
Bay County	59 594	53.2	21.7	10.2	15.0	9.1	2.0	5.8	0.5	11.7	2.4	14.3	6.4	41.0	1 532
Bradford County	8 525	56.5	23.4	11.4	16.6	9.2	2.7	4.0	0.5	9.1	2.3	13.7	7.6	40.4	271
Brevard County	198 371	53.7	19.2	15.5	13.6	7.8	2.3	5.9	0.7	11.7	3.3	15.1	8.5	38.9	4 283
Broward County	654 787	46.8	20.7	10.4	16.4	9.2	2.0	7.2	0.8	12.3	3.1	17.3	9.6	49.1	12 996
Calhoun County	4 472	54.6	24.3	9.6	16.5	8.5	4.4	2.5	0.0	11.8	3.1	14.6	9.3	46.8	158
Charlotte County	63 918	59.7	12.9	28.0	9.4	4.9	2.0	4.9	1.1	9.3	5.0	16.7	11.9	35.2	838
Citrus County	52 661	58.8	13.7	25.4	10.3	5.8	2.1	4.8	1.3	10.0	4.8	16.0	11.1	35.5	868
Clay County	50 365	64.6	31.0	8.5	14.3	9.1	1.3	4.3	0.2	7.5	1.4	9.3	4.6	37.9	1 727
Collier County	103 126	58.5	16.7	22.3	11.1	6.4	1.5	5.9	1.0	9.5	3.4	14.9	8.6	32.7	1 346
Columbia County	20 954	53.9	22.6	10.9	17.6	9.8	2.8	4.7	0.6	11.2	3.2	12.7	7.2	41.9	907
DeSoto County	10 784	57.8	18.9	21.0	14.6	8.1	1.7	6.7	1.3	8.9	2.8	12.1	6.9	28.8	346
Dixie County	5 225	55.0	19.1	13.8	15.8	8.7	1.7	5.3	0.8	11.4	6.1	12.5	7.1	44.6	208
Duval County	303 871	47.5	22.3	7.0	19.4	11.6	2.2	6.6	0.4	11.8	1.9	14.7	6.1	45.4	8 960
Escambia County	111 006	47.9	19.2	10.2	19.2	11.2	2.8	6.0	0.4	11.6	2.3	15.2	7.1	41.3	2 674
Flagler County	21 284	64.2	16.6	25.3	9.6	5.2	1.6	4.5	1.1	8.2	3.7	13.5	9.4	31.8	429
Franklin County	4 103	51.3	15.7	12.9	15.2	9.7	2.4	4.9	0.6	14.6	4.8	14.1	6.5	41.5	145
Gadsden County	15 842	46.5	19.5	9.0	26.4	14.0	4.2	3.2	0.4	10.0	2.5	14.0	7.3	42.1	981
Gilchrist County	5 001	59.8	24.9	11.9	14.2	9.0	2.3	4.7	0.3	9.7	2.2	11.5	6.5	37.7	123
Glades County	3 876	59.5	18.2	17.9	12.8	8.1	1.4	5.2	1.1	11.6	5.5	10.9	7.0	38.1	91
Gulf County	4 914	55.7	20.0	14.0	16.5	8.7	3.5	2.2	0.4	11.8	4.0	13.8	7.9	40.1	247
Hamilton County	4 155	50.5	21.1	9.5	22.6	12.7	4.8	2.9	0.0	11.0	3.4	13.0	5.5	38.5	149
Hardee County	8 195	60.6	27.3	15.1	17.3	8.7	3.1	4.1	0.5	7.4	3.5	10.6	6.5	34.9	352
Hendry County	10 854	56.5	28.9	9.6	19.9	12.4	1.6	5.2	0.6	9.7	3.1	8.6	5.0	40.8	450
Hernando County	55 456	61.1	16.3	26.4	11.4	6.2	2.3	4.2	1.0	8.3	4.0	15.0	10.9	33.3	1 143
Highlands County	37 505	58.2	14.2	28.4	11.2	6.6	2.1	4.6	1.1	9.0	4.2	17.1	12.6	34.7	747
Hillsborough County	391 424	48.3	21.9	8.4	17.3	10.2	2.0	7.5	0.5	11.7	2.1	15.2	6.3	43.5	9 643
Holmes County	6 924	57.1	23.7	12.0	14.0	7.7	2.8	2.7	0.3	10.8	3.0	15.4	8.8	43.7	182
Indian River County	49 196	55.1	15.4	23.0	11.8	6.4	2.2	5.0	1.0	10.7	4.6	17.4	11.7	38.3	955
Jackson County	16 586	52.9	20.8	10.8	17.3	10.4	2.9	2.7	0.1	10.2	2.8	16.8	10.8	49.5	548
Jefferson County	4 697	53.0	21.0	11.3	18.1	9.5	4.1	3.8	0.4	10.3	2.2	14.8	7.1	37.1	203
Lafayette County	2 151	58.8	24.5	12.4	16.1	9.0	2.0	3.3	0.7	9.4	3.3	12.5	8.0	43.0	123
Lake County	88 383	59.6	17.3	22.1	11.3	6.4	2.0	4.5	1.0	9.3	3.8	15.2	10.4	36.1	1 729
Lee County	188 755	55.9	15.9	20.9	12.2	6.9	2.0	6.2	0.9	10.5	3.8	15.3	9.3	35.4	3 232
Leon County	96 691	40.4	18.7	5.6	16.3	9.6	1.5	13.7	0.3	13.4	1.5	16.2	4.3	43.7	1 814
Levy County	13 886	54.2	19.2	14.6	15.6	9.4	2.3	5.3	0.7	11.6	4.4	13.4	8.1	41.5	304
Liberty County	2 227	52.3	23.2	8.8	17.2	11.1	1.3	4.6	0.7	12.8	3.6	13.1	7.5	50.7	71
Madison County	6 635	48.0	19.0	11.1	23.4	12.2	3.9	3.1	0.5	10.5	3.1	15.0	9.1	44.0	321
Manatee County	112 456	53.2	16.0	19.1	12.7	7.2	1.9	5.7	0.9	10.4	4.0	18.0	11.7	41.9	2 033
Marion County	106 707	56.2	17.4	20.3	14.0	7.7	2.5	4.8	1.0	9.5	4.0	15.5	9.5	36.2	2 511
Martin County	55 379	56.0	16.2	22.5	9.9	5.7	1.7	5.1	1.0	11.1	4.2	17.8	11.6	38.5	587
Miami-Dade County	777 378	48.7	23.4	9.1	22.4	11.2	3.3	5.6	0.8	10.5	2.4	12.8	6.3	39.9	27 002
Monroe County	35 106	47.8	15.8	10.0	11.1	5.7	1.4	12.4	1.2	17.1	3.0	11.6	4.7	37.9	409
Nassau County	21 952	63.1	26.5	10.9	12.3	7.2	1.8	4.3	0.3	8.7	1.9	11.5	6.1	38.0	719
Okaloosa County	66 373	57.1	25.0	10.3	13.5	8.7	1.5	5.9	0.3	11.2	2.1	12.3	5.7	39.1	1 479
Okeechobee County	12 614	56.8	22.0	15.3	15.8	9.1	2.5	5.9	1.3	11.2	4.3	10.3	6.6	36.5	382
Orange County	336 366	47.9	22.8	7.3	18.3	10.6	1.9	9.6	0.4	11.3	1.6	12.9	4.9	40.4	9 506
Osceola County	60 966	56.6	26.3	9.7	17.8	10.8	1.8	6.6	0.5	8.3	1.9	10.8	5.3	37.6	2 086
Palm Beach County	474 295	51.4	18.4	17.5	13.1	7.2	1.8	6.3	1.0	11.1	3.6	18.0	11.1	42.0	7 761
Pasco County	147 713	55.1	17.0	20.3	12.2	6.6	2.2	5.5	1.0	10.0	4.2	17.3	11.9	40.7	2 556
Pinellas County	415 199	45.4	15.1	13.9	13.6	7.5	2.2	7.0	0.8	13.4	3.9	20.6	11.9	48.5	5 729
Polk County	187 162	55.3	20.3	15.3	15.7	9.0	2.4	4.9	0.7	9.9	3.0	14.2	8.4	38.2	6 077
Putnam County	27 813	54.0	18.7	15.2	15.9	9.4	2.7	4.9	0.8	10.7	4.1	14.4	8.5	40.4	885
St. Johns County	49 621	57.6	23.2	12.9	11.5	6.9	1.5	6.7	0.8	9.6	2.5	14.7	7.3	39.2	936
St. Lucie County	76 903	56.2	18.6	19.3	14.5	8.1	2.2	5.8	1.0	9.4	3.6	14.1	8.9	35.6	1 890
Santa Rosa County	43 845	63.3	28.8	10.2	13.2	8.7	1.4	4.3	0.4	8.7	1.7	10.4	4.9	35.7	1 202

STATE County	Households with Non-Hispanic White householder		Households with Black or African American householder		Households with American Indian and Alaska Native householder		Households with Asian, Hawaiian, and Pacific Islander householder		Households with Hispanic or Latino[1] householder		Foreign-born population	Place of birth (percent)			Percent in non-English speaking households	
	Number of households	Percent that are family households	Number of households	Percent that are family households	Number of households	Percent that are family households	Number of households	Percent that are family households	Number of households	Percent that are family households	Percent of total population that is foreign-born	Europe	Asia	Latin America	Linguistically isolated	Not linguistically isolated
	44	45	46	47	48	49	50	51	52	53	54	55	56	57	58	59
DELAWARE	227 711	68.0	52 362	69.9	1 175	64.3	5 434	78.4	9 662	79.8	5.7	1.3	1.7	2.2	2.1	12.3
Kent County	35 686	70.8	8 892	72.4	380	68.7	582	78.0	1 157	76.1	4.0	1.1	1.3	1.1	1.5	11.5
New Castle County	140 096	66.8	35 301	68.4	409	67.5	4 598	78.2	7 002	78.7	6.6	1.5	2.2	2.2	2.3	13.4
Sussex County	51 929	69.6	8 169	73.4	386	56.7	254	81.9	1 503	87.6	4.5	0.7	0.4	3.2	1.8	9.3
DISTRICT OF COLUMBIA	83 742	30.8	139 143	55.5	763	43.6	6 502	40.7	14 449	59.6	12.9	2.3	2.2	6.5	4.7	17.7
District of Columbia	83 742	30.8	139 143	55.5	763	43.6	6 502	40.7	14 449	59.6	12.9	2.3	2.2	6.5	4.7	17.7
FLORIDA	4 566 541	64.0	752 783	71.9	19 623	67.7	85 036	74.4	851 742	77.2	16.7	2.2	1.5	12.2	6.1	22.6
Alachua County	64 129	53.9	14 220	64.6	191	56.5	3 069	48.3	4 310	46.1	7.3	1.4	2.9	2.2	1.6	15.2
Baker County	6 201	79.5	633	83.1	26	61.5	16	100.0	64	92.2	1.1	0.3	0.1	0.5	0.4	4.2
Bay County	51 055	68.3	5 600	67.9	400	76.3	659	69.5	1 164	65.1	3.6	1.3	1.3	0.6	0.7	9.9
Bradford County	7 173	73.4	1 126	73.4	5	100.0	24	95.8	84	23.8	1.8	0.5	0.4	0.6	0.4	5.9
Brevard County	172 246	66.7	13 792	70.6	903	66.7	2 257	69.0	6 810	75.3	6.5	2.1	1.4	2.2	1.2	12.7
Broward County	437 887	56.6	103 464	76.4	1 409	68.3	11 904	76.2	86 780	78.0	25.3	3.6	1.9	18.1	6.6	29.2
Calhoun County	3 820	71.0	418	75.1	32	100.0	38	63.2	106	57.5	2.2	0.5	0.6	1.1	1.0	8.3
Charlotte County	59 265	68.9	2 101	72.8	231	62.8	259	64.9	1 465	76.7	8.0	2.9	0.7	2.9	1.2	11.5
Citrus County	49 732	69.1	959	66.0	123	81.3	399	81.2	1 090	67.2	4.9	2.5	0.7	0.8	1.1	9.2
Clay County	43 813	78.7	3 165	77.8	231	64.9	771	86.5	1 689	86.6	4.5	1.0	1.7	1.4	0.8	12.5
Collier County	86 494	67.0	3 134	78.4	321	81.3	415	65.3	11 838	86.1	18.3	3.1	0.5	13.6	8.4	21.3
Columbia County	17 015	72.0	3 129	67.4	70	64.3	141	86.5	381	75.9	2.3	0.6	0.6	0.9	0.5	8.3
DeSoto County	8 134	73.9	943	66.9	126	36.5	73	61.6	1 553	71.2	18.7	0.5	0.4	16.9	10.2	16.0
Dixie County	4 878	71.2	239	64.9	3	0.0	10	100.0	43	55.8	2.0	0.4	0.3	1.2	0.3	7.0
Duval County	205 850	65.1	77 200	70.0	1 003	73.6	6 365	76.4	10 379	73.8	5.9	1.5	2.3	1.6	1.7	13.0
Escambia County	83 006	65.9	21 540	70.8	843	64.2	1 835	76.2	2 112	70.5	3.7	0.8	1.6	0.8	0.9	10.0
Flagler County	18 201	73.7	1 753	66.1	75	65.3	184	97.8	839	86.4	9.9	4.5	1.1	3.5	1.7	14.7
Franklin County	3 669	66.5	317	61.2	23	73.9	15	100.0	41	92.7	1.9	0.6	0.3	0.6	0.3	5.3
Gadsden County	6 723	67.5	8 266	76.0	16	62.5	55	70.9	776	87.5	4.1	0.3	0.2	3.5	2.6	7.5
Gilchrist County	4 662	74.1	128	76.6	8	75.0	2	100.0	99	67.7	1.7	0.6	0.0	0.9	0.6	5.6
Glades County	3 008	71.0	255	70.2	167	64.7	22	100.0	375	82.7	7.9	0.2	0.6	6.8	4.3	17.1
Gulf County	4 131	72.3	627	72.1	10	80.0	13	46.2	31	71.0	2.1	0.5	0.3	1.1	0.4	4.6
Hamilton County	2 639	73.4	1 340	71.1	8	100.0	14	100.0	126	88.9	2.3	0.3	0.1	1.9	1.0	6.5
Hardee County	5 591	75.5	525	67.6	67	88.1	8	100.0	1 984	87.3	17.5	0.5	0.2	16.7	10.7	28.1
Hendry County	5 865	71.7	1 531	74.3	111	74.8	52	86.5	3 228	86.3	24.0	0.6	0.5	22.5	14.3	30.4
Hernando County	50 842	72.0	1 854	73.6	143	78.3	227	90.3	2 039	81.5	5.3	2.6	0.5	1.3	1.5	12.8
Highlands County	31 324	68.4	2 666	71.5	101	75.2	283	88.3	2 950	75.7	9.1	1.0	0.9	5.9	4.4	13.0
Hillsborough County	269 439	63.3	51 912	68.0	1 630	60.1	6 738	73.0	57 285	74.2	11.5	1.4	1.9	7.6	4.9	22.3
Holmes County	6 616	71.0	154	64.0	75	77.0	34	100.0	56	71.4	1.7	0.3	0.6	0.7	0.3	6.6
Indian River County	43 700	65.9	3 099	70.1	77	79.2	293	88.4	1 686	81.3	8.1	2.2	0.7	4.3	2.6	12.0
Jackson County	12 271	72.4	3 842	64.0	92	65.2	48	77.1	239	55.6	1.5	0.3	0.3	0.7	0.4	7.0
Jefferson County	2 906	70.5	1 678	71.6	32	68.8	23	100.0	42	71.4	1.2	0.4	0.2	0.7	0.0	5.1
Lafayette County	1 912	74.8	106	74.5	6	16.7	4	50.0	100	89.0	6.6	0.3	0.0	6.2	5.0	8.7
Lake County	78 066	70.0	5 595	74.7	217	89.4	397	84.9	3 283	86.4	5.1	1.3	0.6	2.6	1.6	11.1
Lee County	165 098	66.8	9 245	74.0	471	69.0	1 077	66.9	11 458	80.2	9.2	2.4	0.7	5.0	3.6	14.7
Leon County	64 926	57.1	26 146	56.2	216	59.3	1 800	63.8	2 617	47.5	4.7	1.0	1.6	1.5	1.0	11.4
Levy County	11 997	69.2	1 227	74.5	49	79.6	47	66.0	434	73.3	2.6	0.8	0.3	1.1	1.3	9.1
Liberty County	1 884	70.9	245	64.1	41	65.9	7	100.0	32	56.3	2.1	0.6	0.2	1.3	1.5	5.6
Madison County	4 098	70.5	2 391	72.5	9	44.4	7	100.0	81	91.4	2.0	0.3	0.2	1.3	0.6	6.1
Manatee County	98 163	64.3	6 835	75.3	309	77.3	735	75.1	5 796	79.9	8.4	2.1	0.8	4.5	2.9	13.7
Marion County	90 048	69.3	9 815	72.4	419	76.1	699	86.7	4 990	80.9	5.2	1.3	0.7	2.5	1.7	11.5
Martin County	50 547	65.0	1 945	69.2	77	84.4	248	63.3	2 381	83.7	8.1	2.5	0.5	4.4	3.5	12.2
Miami-Dade County	188 146	55.0	138 054	74.4	1 676	68.7	10 739	73.2	437 427	76.9	50.9	2.0	1.3	47.2	21.0	53.1
Monroe County	29 076	56.6	1 229	64.6	71	60.6	203	61.1	4 128	73.7	14.7	3.5	0.9	9.4	5.2	23.1
Nassau County	19 892	75.7	1 513	73.3	90	85.6	98	75.5	210	73.8	2.7	0.8	0.6	1.0	0.3	7.6
Okaloosa County	56 289	70.6	5 395	69.4	359	75.5	1 132	72.1	1 926	76.2	5.3	1.8	2.1	1.1	0.8	13.2
Okeechobee County	10 283	71.3	583	69.0	20	80.0	91	65.9	1 548	82.9	11.5	0.4	0.6	10.1	6.1	18.4
Orange County	215 590	61.5	52 268	72.3	1 055	68.2	9 231	75.9	52 296	77.1	14.4	1.5	2.6	9.3	5.9	26.4
Osceola County	40 119	69.8	3 783	82.8	154	83.1	1 205	79.9	15 173	84.3	14.0	2.2	1.8	9.1	7.8	32.6
Palm Beach County	373 870	61.2	47 553	76.3	767	64.8	5 681	75.9	41 303	79.3	17.4	3.5	1.5	11.2	6.0	21.4
Pasco County	136 969	66.4	2 341	74.8	402	78.1	1 061	78.8	5 669	82.3	7.0	3.0	0.9	1.8	1.9	13.3
Pinellas County	361 216	57.6	29 067	68.0	1 149	74.5	5 792	78.3	13 991	68.1	9.5	3.8	1.9	2.3	2.7	14.4
Polk County	150 206	70.0	21 043	72.2	771	63.4	1 651	78.4	11 850	81.2	6.9	0.9	0.9	4.6	3.2	13.3
Putnam County	22 415	69.2	3 835	71.7	145	55.9	92	89.1	1 076	79.5	3.4	0.7	0.4	2.0	2.0	9.1
St. Johns County	45 056	69.2	2 645	67.8	93	48.4	388	67.8	1 037	71.0	4.9	2.4	0.9	0.9	0.8	10.5
St. Lucie County	62 188	69.1	9 376	74.6	144	58.3	556	87.6	3 958	82.5	10.5	2.2	0.9	6.7	3.1	15.8
Santa Rosa County	40 311	76.7	1 481	73.4	356	67.4	400	80.8	699	82.7	3.0	1.0	1.2	0.5	0.4	9.3

[1] Hispanic or Latino persons may be of any race.

STATE/ County code	MSA/PMSA/ NECMA code[1]	STATE County	Population by age (percent)										Non-Hispanic White		
														Age (percent)	
			Total population	Under 5 years	5 to 17 years	18 to 24 years	25 to 44 years	45 to 64 years	65 years and over	Median age	+/− U.S. percent under 18 years	+/− U.S. percent 65 years and over	Total population	Under 18 years	65 years and over
			1	2	3	4	5	6	7	8	9	10	11	12	13
		FLORIDA—Cont'd													
12 115	7510	Sarasota County	325 957	3.9	12.3	5.0	21.8	25.6	31.4	50.5	-9.5	19.0	292 123	14.5	34.0
12 117	5960	Seminole County	365 196	6.4	18.9	8.1	32.6	23.5	10.5	36.2	-0.4	-1.9	274 799	23.5	11.8
12 119	...	Sumter County	53 345	4.0	12.2	6.0	22.9	27.3	27.6	49.2	-9.5	15.2	41 768	14.6	33.0
12 121	...	Suwannee County	34 844	5.9	18.1	8.6	25.0	25.5	16.9	39.7	-1.7	4.5	28 204	22.0	18.8
12 123	...	Taylor County	19 256	5.9	18.7	8.3	28.2	25.1	13.8	37.8	-1.1	1.4	14 897	23.7	15.6
12 125	...	Union County	13 442	5.5	16.4	8.5	39.9	22.5	7.3	35.7	-3.8	-5.1	9 636	23.9	8.5
12 127	2020	Volusia County	443 343	4.9	15.3	8.3	25.3	24.2	22.1	42.4	-5.5	9.7	363 298	18.1	24.9
12 129	...	Wakulla County	22 863	6.0	19.7	7.8	31.8	24.5	10.2	36.8	0.0	-2.2	19 410	25.4	10.8
12 131	...	Walton County	40 601	5.3	16.4	7.2	28.6	26.6	15.8	40.5	-4.0	3.4	35 193	20.9	16.9
12 133	...	Washington County	20 973	6.0	17.5	8.1	28.4	24.8	15.2	38.8	-2.2	2.8	16 844	22.7	16.9
13 000	...	GEORGIA	8 186 453	7.2	19.2	10.2	32.6	21.1	9.6	33.4	0.7	-2.8	5 129 727	23.5	12.0
13 001	...	Appling County	17 419	7.5	19.7	9.6	27.8	23.3	12.0	35.4	1.5	-0.4	13 084	24.7	13.2
13 003	...	Atkinson County	7 609	9.5	20.7	10.6	30.1	19.7	9.3	30.7	4.5	-3.1	4 745	26.7	11.9
13 005	...	Bacon County	10 103	7.7	18.0	9.7	29.1	22.5	13.0	34.8	0.0	0.6	8 044	22.7	14.6
13 007	...	Baker County	4 074	7.1	20.3	10.1	26.9	22.0	13.5	35.0	1.7	1.1	1 881	22.1	15.6
13 009	...	Baldwin County	44 700	5.1	16.6	14.7	31.0	22.1	10.6	34.2	-4.0	-1.8	23 995	17.5	14.0
13 011	...	Banks County	14 422	7.6	18.4	8.7	31.0	23.7	10.4	35.2	0.3	-2.0	13 200	25.8	10.7
13 013	0520	Barrow County	46 144	8.1	20.1	8.3	35.2	19.0	9.3	32.5	2.5	-3.1	38 600	27.2	9.6
13 015	0520	Bartow County	76 019	7.7	20.1	8.1	33.3	21.4	9.4	33.7	2.1	-3.0	65 693	27.0	10.0
13 017	...	Ben Hill County	17 484	7.4	20.3	9.5	26.7	23.0	13.1	34.8	2.0	0.7	10 863	23.6	15.7
13 019	...	Berrien County	16 235	7.6	19.5	8.5	28.8	23.2	12.4	35.2	1.4	0.0	13 732	25.4	13.4
13 021	4680	Bibb County	153 887	7.4	19.2	10.1	29.0	21.6	12.7	34.7	0.9	0.3	76 278	20.1	17.6
13 023	...	Bleckley County	11 666	6.1	20.6	11.0	27.3	21.4	13.6	35.1	1.0	1.2	8 456	23.4	16.0
13 025	...	Brantley County	14 629	7.2	21.1	8.3	30.2	23.1	10.1	34.6	2.6	-2.3	13 688	27.9	10.3
13 027	...	Brooks County	16 450	6.4	20.8	9.3	26.1	22.4	15.1	36.3	1.5	2.7	9 377	21.5	18.5
13 029	7520	Bryan County	23 417	7.6	23.5	7.6	32.4	21.6	7.2	33.3	5.4	-5.2	19 140	30.1	7.4
13 031	...	Bulloch County	55 983	5.8	16.6	26.3	24.5	17.4	9.4	26.1	-3.3	-3.0	38 013	20.3	10.7
13 033	...	Burke County	22 243	8.1	23.2	8.7	27.8	21.2	11.0	33.0	5.6	-1.4	10 405	25.2	13.2
13 035	...	Butts County	19 522	6.3	17.8	9.1	33.1	23.8	10.0	35.9	-1.6	-2.4	13 358	23.0	11.5
13 037	...	Calhoun County	6 320	5.6	16.4	10.3	34.2	20.7	12.8	35.6	-3.7	0.4	2 393	18.8	17.6
13 039	...	Camden County	43 664	8.7	23.0	13.2	33.9	16.2	4.9	28.2	6.0	-7.5	31 863	29.7	5.0
13 043	...	Candler County	9 577	7.6	19.2	8.8	26.5	22.7	15.1	35.6	1.1	2.7	6 002	23.7	18.4
13 045	0520	Carroll County	87 268	7.1	18.8	12.8	30.2	21.1	10.0	32.5	0.2	-2.4	69 136	24.5	11.2
13 047	1560	Catoosa County	53 282	6.8	19.0	8.0	30.9	23.4	11.8	35.8	0.1	-0.6	50 883	25.4	12.1
13 049	...	Charlton County	10 282	6.3	21.2	10.2	33.1	19.3	9.9	33.4	1.8	-2.5	7 035	26.6	10.8
13 051	7520	Chatham County	232 048	6.7	18.4	11.2	29.4	21.4	13.0	34.4	-0.6	0.6	125 717	19.3	16.2
13 053	1800	Chattahoochee County ...	14 882	8.4	20.1	28.4	35.7	5.7	1.8	23.2	2.8	-10.6	8 186	24.1	2.1
13 055	...	Chattooga County	25 470	6.4	16.6	10.0	30.0	22.8	14.2	36.5	-2.7	1.8	21 816	23.1	15.5
13 057	0520	Cherokee County	141 903	8.5	19.7	7.6	35.8	21.8	6.6	34.0	2.5	-5.8	127 488	27.7	6.9
13 059	0500	Clarke County	101 489	5.4	12.5	31.0	28.0	15.1	8.0	25.4	-7.8	-4.4	62 893	10.9	9.6
13 061	...	Clay County	3 357	6.8	18.9	8.3	20.9	25.6	19.5	41.9	0.0	7.1	1 287	14.6	27.2
13 063	0520	Clayton County	236 517	8.4	21.5	10.3	35.8	18.2	5.9	30.2	4.2	-6.5	82 842	20.9	13.2
13 065	...	Clinch County	6 878	7.1	20.8	8.4	29.2	22.2	12.2	34.9	2.2	-0.2	4 687	25.0	13.7
13 067	0520	Cobb County	607 751	7.1	18.8	9.0	36.7	21.4	6.9	33.2	0.2	-5.5	417 925	23.6	9.1
13 069	...	Coffee County	37 413	7.7	20.4	10.9	30.5	20.7	9.7	32.1	2.4	-2.7	24 738	25.3	12.4
13 071	...	Colquitt County	42 053	7.5	19.8	10.5	27.5	21.7	13.0	33.7	1.6	0.6	27 329	23.2	16.6
13 073	0600	Columbia County	89 288	6.9	22.6	7.1	31.1	24.2	8.0	35.4	3.8	-4.4	72 608	28.8	8.5
13 075	...	Cook County	15 771	7.9	20.9	8.6	28.5	21.0	13.1	34.3	3.1	0.7	10 485	23.9	15.6
13 077	0520	Coweta County	89 215	8.0	20.7	7.7	33.4	21.7	8.5	33.6	3.0	-3.9	68 913	27.5	9.1
13 079	...	Crawford County	12 495	6.0	21.5	8.1	32.0	23.3	9.1	35.2	1.8	-3.3	9 065	27.4	9.3
13 081	...	Crisp County	21 996	8.0	21.1	8.6	27.4	22.0	12.8	34.4	3.4	0.4	11 798	22.0	17.6
13 083	1560	Dade County	15 154	5.9	17.9	12.0	27.9	24.3	12.0	36.1	-1.9	-0.4	14 699	24.0	12.0
13 085	...	Dawson County	15 999	7.1	18.0	7.6	32.2	25.7	9.3	36.2	-0.6	-3.1	15 523	24.9	9.5
13 087	...	Decatur County	28 240	7.8	20.8	9.0	28.4	20.7	13.3	34.4	2.9	0.9	15 795	23.5	16.5
13 089	0520	DeKalb County	665 865	7.0	17.5	10.9	37.0	19.5	8.1	32.3	-1.2	-4.3	215 308	13.7	17.0
13 091	...	Dodge County	19 171	6.1	19.9	8.8	29.5	22.4	13.3	35.8	0.3	0.9	13 125	22.8	15.7
13 093	...	Dooly County	11 525	6.6	18.9	11.1	29.4	22.6	11.5	35.1	-0.2	-0.9	5 178	19.9	16.7
13 095	0120	Dougherty County	96 065	7.6	20.0	12.0	28.1	20.5	11.8	32.2	1.9	-0.6	35 730	18.5	19.6
13 097	0520	Douglas County	92 174	7.3	20.3	8.7	33.7	22.3	7.6	33.8	1.9	-4.8	69 880	25.4	9.0
13 099	...	Early County	12 354	7.1	21.5	7.7	26.7	20.8	16.2	36.4	2.9	3.8	6 193	21.0	21.4
13 101	...	Echols County	3 754	6.7	23.0	12.5	31.4	17.4	9.0	29.7	4.0	-3.4	2 670	27.3	11.4
13 103	7520	Effingham County	37 535	7.6	22.4	8.4	31.9	21.7	8.0	33.6	4.3	-4.4	31 463	28.8	8.1
13 105	...	Elbert County	20 511	6.2	19.8	7.6	28.0	23.4	15.1	37.2	0.3	2.7	13 487	22.7	18.0
13 107	...	Emanuel County	21 837	6.5	21.4	10.5	26.1	22.3	13.2	34.9	2.2	0.8	13 699	23.7	16.5
13 109	...	Evans County	10 495	6.6	21.3	9.8	28.7	21.3	12.3	34.0	2.2	-0.1	6 318	23.7	14.7

[1]MSA = Metropolitan Statistical Area. PMSA = Primary MSA. NECMA = New England County Metropolitan Area. See the Appendix A for explanation of these concepts. See Appendix B for list of metropolitan areas identified by type, with component counties.

STATE County	Black or African American Total population	Age (percent) Under 18 years	65 years and over	American Indian and Alaska Native Total population	Age (percent) Under 18 years	65 years and over	Asian, Hawaiian, and Pacific Islander Total population	Age (percent) Under 18 years	65 years and over	Hispanic or Latino[1] Total population	Age (percent) Under 18 years	65 years and over	Two or more races Total population	Age (percent) Under 18 years	65 years and over
	14	15	16	17	18	19	20	21	22	23	24	25	26	27	28
FLORIDA—Cont'd															
Sarasota County	13 677	32.9	11.1	812	20.1	9.2	2 659	19.7	7.4	14 373	28.4	8.0	3 359	38.1	8.3
Seminole County	34 106	32.0	7.7	1 434	18.5	4.7	8 798	24.5	5.5	40 656	29.8	6.8	9 335	37.5	3.9
Sumter County	7 480	24.5	8.2	251	15.9	14.7	274	20.4	16.8	3 263	17.4	5.0	827	11.6	12.6
Suwannee County	4 089	33.0	9.5	154	20.1	11.7	102	13.7	28.4	1 812	30.6	5.7	631	41.2	7.0
Taylor County	3 540	28.0	8.6	38	15.8	36.8	76	10.5	6.6	441	36.3	0.0	321	26.5	0.0
Union County	3 005	17.4	3.8	57	3.5	14.0	49	8.2	16.3	446	7.8	4.9	336	28.3	1.5
Volusia County	40 116	30.3	9.6	1 364	11.6	8.9	4 957	20.0	9.6	29 273	30.8	9.5	6 874	36.0	7.6
Wakulla County	2 673	24.6	6.9	60	33.3	13.3	182	35.2	0.0	305	21.6	9.8	278	49.3	1.1
Walton County	2 753	22.6	10.4	488	33.8	6.1	204	16.2	13.7	908	35.0	7.2	1 089	31.0	7.4
Washington County	2 806	25.0	8.8	272	27.6	7.0	163	33.7	8.0	511	31.1	2.9	404	33.2	10.4
GEORGIA	2 342 110	31.7	6.6	23 688	24.5	4.8	175 329	25.2	3.8	429 976	31.0	2.0	124 217	39.4	4.1
Appling County	3 318	33.2	9.6	7	0.0	0.0	115	46.1	0.0	813	39.5	3.1	93	43.0	24.7
Atkinson County	1 500	31.8	9.3	9	0.0	0.0	39	30.8	0.0	1 324	41.2	0.5	39	10.3	7.7
Bacon County	1 672	38.0	7.2	7	0.0	0.0	76	52.6	0.0	243	19.8	9.9	64	42.2	0.0
Baker County	2 020	31.0	12.8	0	X	X	9	0.0	0.0	108	38.9	0.0	61	54.1	0.0
Baldwin County	19 324	26.7	6.8	108	11.1	11.1	527	20.9	2.5	638	26.2	3.6	292	32.5	0.0
Banks County	533	25.5	14.8	53	30.2	0.0	21	19.0	0.0	440	37.0	0.0	164	24.4	6.1
Barrow County	4 727	30.7	7.4	80	18.8	21.3	1 070	40.8	7.1	1 163	26.1	11.3	607	51.2	3.6
Bartow County	6 324	31.4	7.8	293	32.4	1.0	621	41.1	5.5	2 460	34.3	1.1	795	45.5	1.1
Ben Hill County	5 679	34.8	9.4	70	38.6	17.1	36	19.4	44.4	756	29.4	1.9	104	40.4	15.4
Berrien County	1 880	34.7	7.8	85	27.1	5.9	53	15.1	0.0	327	47.1	1.2	191	56.5	8.9
Bibb County	72 921	32.7	8.2	328	30.2	9.1	1 618	32.6	2.0	1 635	36.5	4.2	1 548	43.9	5.6
Bleckley County	2 818	36.0	7.8	0	X	X	47	19.1	0.0	179	20.1	3.9	165	52.7	6.1
Brantley County	471	34.6	10.8	10	70.0	0.0	61	26.2	0.0	170	25.3	2.9	248	46.7	3.2
Brooks County	6 446	34.6	11.1	20	25.0	15.0	59	37.3	0.0	463	30.9	5.2	195	42.1	0.0
Bryan County	3 187	35.3	6.8	82	18.3	26.8	316	21.8	0.0	422	42.2	4.0	313	51.1	8.9
Bulloch County	15 771	27.7	6.9	73	13.7	4.1	603	18.4	0.0	1 110	22.1	1.1	535	26.9	12.0
Burke County	11 498	36.9	9.2	24	0.0	0.0	16	12.5	0.0	291	44.3	2.7	84	21.4	4.8
Butts County	5 694	26.2	7.0	81	6.2	7.4	59	33.9	0.0	175	20.6	2.9	198	38.9	2.5
Calhoun County	3 887	23.9	10.1	0	X	X	1	0.0	0.0	57	22.8	0.0	33	33.3	0.0
Camden County	8 791	37.4	5.9	129	6.2	0.0	461	18.4	6.3	1 768	37.9	0.5	794	51.8	2.0
Candler County	2 614	32.1	11.7	23	0.0	0.0	0	X	X	905	32.6	3.5	100	40.0	7.0
Carroll County	14 077	30.1	5.7	258	21.7	3.9	471	25.9	10.0	2 400	28.0	2.5	1 198	51.3	1.8
Catoosa County	747	34.9	3.5	218	36.2	6.0	432	27.3	2.8	709	39.4	4.5	414	44.2	16.2
Charlton County	2 960	29.1	7.8	39	12.8	7.7	84	45.2	6.0	10	10.0	40.0	154	32.5	9.1
Chatham County	94 398	32.2	9.4	495	18.4	16.4	4 174	23.3	9.0	5 041	29.1	2.8	2 892	39.6	8.0
Chattahoochee County	4 350	32.3	2.1	149	24.2	0.0	281	17.8	0.7	1 576	33.8	0.1	670	52.2	0.0
Chattooga County	2 765	18.3	6.5	31	29.0	0.0	97	29.9	15.5	602	32.2	5.6	199	46.7	5.0
Cherokee County	3 194	33.1	6.8	547	23.0	2.2	1 450	28.7	8.1	7 902	30.8	1.9	1 909	39.9	3.5
Clarke County	27 978	30.3	6.7	240	29.2	6.7	3 298	19.5	1.1	6 170	29.6	1.7	1 321	30.4	1.3
Clay County	2 011	32.7	14.8	7	0.0	0.0	12	50.0	0.0	12	58.3	41.7	30	23.3	0.0
Clayton County	120 825	35.4	1.9	827	24.5	2.3	10 411	26.9	2.7	17 625	32.7	1.3	5 541	43.3	2.4
Clinch County	2 017	33.4	9.7	74	36.5	6.8	30	43.3	0.0	42	45.2	14.3	47	61.7	0.0
Cobb County	113 176	32.0	2.2	1 758	23.1	2.2	18 821	24.2	3.3	46 944	30.4	1.7	12 470	36.5	3.1
Coffee County	9 703	33.8	5.5	36	38.9	0.0	234	25.6	3.4	2 565	33.4	1.2	305	41.3	1.0
Colquitt County	9 930	36.2	7.9	59	1.7	11.9	29	0.0	24.1	4 578	33.4	2.6	486	44.4	3.9
Columbia County	9 933	32.0	6.3	399	31.3	3.3	2 917	26.4	5.7	2 253	36.5	6.3	1 503	51.0	1.2
Cook County	4 613	37.5	8.3	69	34.8	34.8	72	33.3	19.4	417	47.7	1.4	143	49.7	2.1
Coweta County	16 126	34.0	7.5	109	22.0	0.0	586	31.4	3.2	2 682	21.3	1.5	1 038	35.2	5.2
Crawford County	3 215	27.3	8.6	30	3.3	0.0	5	0.0	0.0	107	35.5	0.0	71	42.3	28.2
Crisp County	9 422	37.4	7.5	33	27.3	12.1	207	41.5	8.7	477	35.4	8.4	138	27.5	0.0
Dade County	73	2.7	16.4	55	30.9	0.0	49	0.0	28.6	165	30.3	0.0	118	15.3	21.2
Dawson County	12	0.0	0.0	111	26.1	0.0	49	30.6	0.0	87	23.0	0.0	217	45.6	2.8
Decatur County	11 246	34.9	10.4	84	20.2	8.3	66	27.3	0.0	871	38.5	0.9	307	40.1	7.2
DeKalb County	360 024	31.0	4.0	1 922	21.4	1.6	26 825	21.1	5.0	51 587	24.7	2.4	14 964	32.3	2.9
Dodge County	5 583	32.9	8.4	43	9.3	18.6	99	16.2	15.2	238	30.3	0.0	119	63.9	0.0
Dooly County	5 969	30.2	7.5	34	26.5	0.0	47	12.8	0.0	327	36.7	0.9	20	15.0	45.0
Dougherty County	57 967	33.1	7.2	141	21.3	0.0	715	19.9	3.2	1 079	23.9	3.5	648	50.9	6.9
Douglas County	18 825	33.3	3.1	469	40.3	5.1	917	23.9	3.1	2 628	35.0	2.4	1 817	50.3	2.6
Early County	6 005	36.1	10.8	0	X	X	11	0.0	0.0	176	53.4	10.8	31	25.8	48.4
Echols County	278	35.6	11.5	0	X	X	29	58.6	0.0	769	35.4	0.0	38	52.6	0.0
Effingham County	4 695	34.1	7.8	169	24.3	0.0	345	25.5	1.7	378	37.3	16.9	495	66.7	1.6
Elbert County	6 322	31.1	10.1	7	0.0	0.0	69	39.1	14.5	546	44.5	2.2	100	47.0	0.0
Emanuel County	7 190	35.8	8.4	78	5.1	0.0	51	33.3	0.0	732	23.9	2.9	93	73.1	0.0
Evans County	3 439	33.4	10.4	36	27.8	8.3	67	29.9	0.0	630	38.9	0.5	97	35.1	2.1

[1] Hispanic or Latino persons may be of any race.

STATE County	Total households	Married-couple family households			Other family households			Two or more unrelated persons		Male living alone		Female living alone		Percent of householders 65 years and over who live alone	Grandparents who are responsible for the care of their grandchildren
		Total	With children	Householder 65 years or over	Total	With children	Householder 65 years or over	Total	Householder 65 years or over	Total	Householder 65 years or over	Total	Householder 65 years or over		
	29	30	31	32	33	34	35	36	37	38	39	40	41	42	43
FLORIDA—Cont'd															
Sarasota County	150 166	53.3	13.4	22.9	10.1	5.3	1.9	6.2	1.2	10.4	3.9	20.0	12.9	39.4	1 723
Seminole County	139 631	55.4	26.2	8.2	14.7	8.3	1.8	7.0	0.3	9.7	1.5	13.2	5.3	39.7	2 879
Sumter County	20 736	61.7	13.0	26.6	11.0	6.1	2.2	3.7	1.0	9.6	4.7	14.0	9.8	32.8	503
Suwannee County	13 490	57.4	21.6	13.5	15.1	9.0	2.2	4.2	0.7	9.7	2.8	13.6	8.7	41.2	573
Taylor County	7 161	53.8	21.7	11.3	18.2	11.0	2.7	3.8	0.5	11.0	3.2	13.2	7.3	42.1	313
Union County	3 365	59.8	31.1	8.5	19.1	12.6	1.6	3.0	0.1	8.3	1.7	9.8	4.5	37.9	149
Volusia County	184 721	51.2	16.7	16.5	14.2	7.8	2.4	6.7	0.9	11.2	3.6	16.7	10.2	41.1	3 947
Wakulla County	8 456	55.0	25.6	7.7	19.1	11.8	1.9	4.0	0.6	12.3	2.0	9.7	3.9	36.5	340
Walton County	16 566	54.6	18.9	11.8	13.6	8.0	2.5	4.8	0.4	12.6	3.8	14.4	6.4	41.2	269
Washington County	7 971	56.8	22.1	11.9	15.4	8.6	2.3	2.8	0.3	10.8	3.2	14.2	8.6	44.9	280
GEORGIA	3 007 678	52.5	25.2	7.1	18.2	10.4	2.2	5.7	0.3	9.9	1.6	13.7	5.6	42.7	92 265
Appling County	6 594	57.5	24.9	8.6	17.0	9.3	3.0	2.3	0.3	9.8	2.6	13.4	7.5	45.8	291
Atkinson County	2 729	55.2	28.7	7.3	18.2	10.9	2.2	3.4	0.2	10.8	3.2	12.4	6.9	50.7	174
Bacon County	3 849	57.2	25.3	9.4	18.0	9.5	3.8	1.5	0.0	10.9	1.6	12.4	6.3	37.5	140
Baker County	1 508	50.9	21.5	9.6	21.5	10.9	4.7	2.5	0.5	11.2	2.7	13.9	8.9	44.0	76
Baldwin County	14 782	44.8	19.0	7.5	22.5	13.4	3.0	7.2	0.3	10.9	1.3	14.6	6.6	42.0	486
Banks County	5 322	66.5	29.8	8.5	11.1	5.5	2.1	3.0	0.4	9.2	2.1	10.2	5.6	41.1	167
Barrow County	16 392	61.8	32.1	6.2	15.1	8.5	2.2	4.5	0.3	7.6	1.7	11.0	5.5	45.2	493
Bartow County	27 173	63.4	31.2	7.8	14.1	7.2	2.0	3.7	0.1	7.3	1.1	11.4	5.6	40.5	794
Ben Hill County	6 677	48.4	21.8	7.2	22.1	12.7	4.9	2.9	0.2	10.4	2.5	16.2	9.5	49.5	253
Berrien County	6 263	56.3	25.4	9.5	16.2	10.4	1.8	3.8	0.3	9.4	1.8	14.3	7.8	45.3	207
Bibb County	59 632	43.4	18.6	8.6	23.7	14.1	3.0	4.7	0.4	11.0	1.9	17.1	7.7	44.5	2 305
Bleckley County	4 359	51.3	22.1	10.2	20.0	11.0	2.9	3.1	0.0	10.4	2.3	15.2	8.3	44.8	117
Brantley County	5 441	62.5	29.3	8.2	14.2	9.0	2.2	2.8	0.3	9.8	2.4	10.6	5.2	41.3	230
Brooks County	6 167	49.5	20.0	9.3	22.4	11.5	4.6	2.8	0.4	10.1	3.4	15.3	7.6	43.6	289
Bryan County	8 089	64.6	34.8	6.2	16.6	10.5	1.6	2.5	0.3	7.5	1.5	8.9	3.8	39.5	347
Bulloch County	20 757	45.5	21.3	7.1	14.4	8.7	1.6	15.5	0.3	10.0	1.7	14.6	6.4	47.2	521
Burke County	7 928	46.2	23.1	5.7	27.1	15.7	3.9	3.0	0.2	11.2	2.9	12.6	7.7	51.9	481
Butts County	6 462	56.5	25.5	7.0	18.9	9.4	3.7	3.6	0.4	9.9	1.7	11.1	6.4	42.2	331
Calhoun County	1 964	41.9	18.1	7.9	27.0	13.6	5.6	2.2	0.3	13.0	3.4	15.8	9.4	48.3	120
Camden County	14 722	63.1	36.5	4.4	14.8	11.1	1.1	4.5	0.1	8.5	0.9	9.1	3.2	42.6	359
Candler County	3 386	51.8	23.7	9.5	21.1	12.7	2.9	3.3	0.0	9.2	2.7	14.7	8.4	47.4	172
Carroll County	31 606	56.8	26.6	7.4	16.5	8.9	2.0	5.5	0.3	8.3	1.7	12.8	6.2	45.1	1 030
Catoosa County	20 445	61.8	27.4	9.8	13.6	8.5	1.7	3.4	0.2	8.3	1.5	13.0	6.9	41.8	535
Charlton County	3 327	56.6	25.6	8.6	18.8	13.0	2.6	3.0	0.3	9.3	2.4	12.4	7.1	45.1	117
Chatham County	89 863	46.3	19.3	9.2	20.2	11.6	3.1	6.4	0.3	11.1	2.2	16.0	7.4	43.2	3 139
Chattahoochee County	2 944	75.8	54.7	2.5	14.0	10.9	0.4	1.8	0.2	5.0	1.1	3.4	1.6	46.2	55
Chattooga County	9 590	54.3	22.5	10.5	17.1	9.3	3.3	3.4	0.2	9.9	2.6	15.4	9.8	46.8	292
Cherokee County	49 562	68.3	35.4	5.5	11.2	6.5	1.2	4.5	0.2	7.0	0.8	9.0	3.6	39.5	1 049
Clarke County	39 678	33.3	14.2	5.3	16.7	9.3	1.8	20.2	0.2	13.1	1.5	16.6	4.8	46.7	925
Clay County	1 355	40.3	9.7	11.9	28.6	16.2	4.1	3.2	0.4	13.1	4.8	14.8	10.2	47.8	90
Clayton County	82 272	46.4	25.1	4.6	25.9	16.2	1.6	5.9	0.3	9.7	0.9	12.2	2.6	35.4	2 984
Clinch County	2 518	50.1	24.6	7.6	22.0	10.9	4.3	3.4	0.6	11.6	2.7	13.0	7.3	44.3	161
Cobb County	227 590	55.5	28.5	5.5	13.9	8.0	1.1	7.5	0.2	10.0	0.9	13.2	3.3	37.8	3 489
Coffee County	13 355	54.7	26.8	6.9	18.8	11.0	2.3	3.8	0.4	8.6	1.7	14.0	7.0	47.5	545
Colquitt County	15 500	51.8	24.0	9.4	20.2	11.6	2.5	3.2	0.4	9.3	2.4	15.5	8.9	48.1	713
Columbia County	31 112	68.4	36.8	7.2	13.4	7.8	1.5	2.8	0.2	6.6	1.1	8.9	3.8	35.2	825
Cook County	5 899	53.3	23.7	10.7	19.9	12.0	2.8	3.1	0.3	8.5	1.7	15.2	8.8	43.1	309
Coweta County	31 429	62.7	31.1	6.5	16.1	8.8	2.1	3.6	0.2	8.3	1.4	9.3	4.0	37.8	790
Crawford County	4 466	63.0	28.7	8.4	15.4	8.2	1.7	2.7	0.0	10.2	1.9	8.7	4.5	38.8	292
Crisp County	8 346	46.2	19.2	7.8	24.9	16.1	2.8	2.8	0.3	10.1	3.0	16.0	8.7	51.8	510
Dade County	5 627	63.7	27.5	9.5	12.5	5.2	3.0	2.3	0.2	8.8	2.5	12.8	7.1	42.9	122
Dawson County	6 070	66.3	27.2	9.0	11.1	6.9	1.4	4.3	0.3	8.4	0.7	10.0	3.4	27.6	104
Decatur County	10 409	49.4	22.5	9.1	23.9	13.7	3.6	2.5	0.0	9.5	2.6	14.7	8.4	46.2	473
DeKalb County	249 391	41.4	19.8	5.6	22.0	11.9	1.9	9.7	0.3	11.0	1.1	15.9	4.2	40.2	7 617
Dodge County	7 079	49.1	22.3	9.1	20.8	11.2	3.4	2.3	0.1	12.9	3.0	14.9	8.7	47.9	237
Dooly County	3 897	47.4	20.8	8.2	23.7	12.7	3.5	2.8	0.2	9.9	1.7	16.1	8.8	47.1	203
Dougherty County	35 608	41.5	17.4	7.8	27.1	15.7	3.4	4.6	0.3	10.6	1.9	16.2	7.3	44.4	1 708
Douglas County	32 879	59.9	29.4	6.3	16.3	9.9	1.3	5.5	0.2	8.3	1.0	10.1	3.7	37.6	858
Early County	4 703	45.6	18.6	9.4	24.6	13.7	4.7	2.9	0.6	9.2	3.6	17.7	11.0	49.8	143
Echols County	1 258	56.2	30.0	7.6	18.4	11.5	1.6	6.4	1.5	9.6	2.5	9.4	5.5	42.6	33
Effingham County	13 128	65.6	35.1	6.8	14.3	8.2	1.9	3.1	0.3	7.7	1.5	9.3	5.0	41.6	422
Elbert County	8 028	53.2	22.5	10.4	19.3	10.7	3.9	2.5	0.2	10.0	2.4	15.0	9.1	44.2	267
Emanuel County	8 040	50.4	23.2	9.0	20.9	13.2	2.8	3.7	0.6	9.5	2.0	15.6	8.7	46.4	317
Evans County	3 783	49.2	21.9	9.5	22.6	14.5	3.1	3.3	0.2	10.5	2.0	14.3	6.9	40.8	203

Table A-3. States and Counties — Age, Ethnicity, and Household Structure

STATE County	Households with Non-Hispanic White householder — Number of households	Percent that are family households	Households with Black or African American householder — Number of households	Percent that are family households	Households with American Indian and Alaska Native householder — Number of households	Percent that are family households	Households with Asian, Hawaiian, and Pacific Islander householder — Number of households	Percent that are family households	Households with Hispanic or Latino[1] householder — Number of households	Percent that are family households	Foreign-born population — Percent of total population that is foreign-born	Place of birth (percent) — Europe	Asia	Latin America	Percent in non-English speaking households — Linguistically isolated	Not linguistically isolated
	44	45	46	47	48	49	50	51	52	53	54	55	56	57	58	59
FLORIDA—Cont'd																
Sarasota County	139 172	62.7	4 845	68.7	380	62.9	743	82.2	4 329	75.9	9.3	4.3	0.8	2.9	2.9	12.1
Seminole County	110 257	68.8	11 806	69.2	645	72.4	2 848	80.1	12 547	80.4	9.1	1.9	2.0	4.3	2.5	19.2
Sumter County	18 347	72.4	1 658	73.4	95	49.5	72	79.2	388	87.6	5.5	1.1	0.5	3.3	1.1	7.0
Suwannee County	11 347	71.8	1 435	78.1	48	47.9	32	75.0	524	80.5	4.7	0.5	0.4	3.7	2.5	7.8
Taylor County	5 790	72.5	1 155	66.4	18	22.2	18	100.0	87	100.0	1.7	0.7	0.4	0.3	0.2	6.8
Union County	2 880	80.3	415	73.7	6	33.3	10	100.0	34	20.6	2.1	0.4	0.1	1.4	0.6	5.8
Volusia County	159 121	64.5	13 703	67.5	472	69.3	1 600	65.3	8 318	80.2	6.4	2.2	1.0	2.3	2.1	13.6
Wakulla County	7 481	74.4	776	71.0	11	100.0	30	100.0	86	48.8	1.5	0.4	0.5	0.3	0.0	9.9
Walton County	14 872	68.2	821	68.0	217	68.2	79	34.2	182	79.1	3.2	1.4	0.4	1.0	0.6	7.3
Washington County	6 724	73.3	843	65.0	113	47.8	17	100.0	120	95.8	2.5	1.0	0.7	0.5	1.1	5.7
GEORGIA	2 017 242	70.2	803 387	70.2	8 251	74.5	51 421	78.3	102 650	80.5	7.1	0.9	1.8	3.7	3.1	11.3
Appling County	5 155	74.7	1 174	71.4	7	100.0	29	100.0	208	80.3	3.4	0.3	0.4	2.6	2.2	7.5
Atkinson County	1 889	71.4	514	72.8	4	100.0	9	100.0	318	86.2	12.1	0.1	0.3	11.4	10.8	7.1
Bacon County	3 189	74.7	554	79.6	7	100.0	23	100.0	70	58.6	1.6	0.1	0.3	1.0	0.9	4.4
Baker County	809	66.7	645	78.0	0	X	5	100.0	29	82.8	1.9	0.0	0.2	1.5	1.5	6.6
Baldwin County	8 813	64.5	5 596	71.5	20	85.0	192	63.0	148	78.4	1.9	0.4	1.0	0.5	0.8	8.3
Banks County	4 924	78.2	172	61.0	13	84.6	6	100.0	127	80.3	2.1	0.3	0.1	1.7	1.3	5.2
Barrow County	14 018	76.4	1 615	77.7	21	90.5	270	84.8	341	80.2	3.6	0.6	1.6	1.2	1.8	7.2
Bartow County	23 925	77.8	2 170	73.2	131	86.3	144	88.2	639	84.7	2.5	0.2	0.4	1.9	1.5	8.0
Ben Hill County	4 284	69.5	2 073	70.5	25	100.0	21	38.1	237	84.0	3.4	0.2	0.1	3.0	2.2	5.4
Berrien County	5 398	72.4	698	71.6	24	54.2	8	100.0	84	79.8	1.4	0.2	0.3	0.9	0.5	7.5
Bibb County	32 245	65.2	25 998	69.7	118	71.2	496	65.9	529	66.2	1.9	0.3	0.8	0.5	0.6	7.0
Bleckley County	3 409	70.1	861	74.4	0	X	8	100.0	37	100.0	1.4	0.3	0.2	0.9	1.0	4.4
Brantley County	5 111	76.2	161	79.5	0	X	13	100.0	76	85.5	0.9	0.1	0.2	0.4	0.3	5.5
Brooks County	3 785	71.1	2 178	74.3	10	30.0	24	100.0	142	59.2	1.7	0.4	0.2	1.1	0.7	5.8
Bryan County	6 704	81.0	1 079	84.3	50	72.0	112	70.5	70	71.4	2.5	1.0	1.2	0.3	0.5	8.1
Bulloch County	14 699	60.3	5 377	58.9	44	43.2	224	54.9	276	64.9	3.1	0.6	0.9	1.2	1.1	8.3
Burke County	3 852	76.7	3 965	70.0	15	100.0	4	100.0	78	84.6	0.8	0.3	0.1	0.5	0.3	7.9
Butts County	4 752	75.0	1 579	76.1	27	92.6	16	50.0	39	53.8	0.9	0.1	0.3	0.3	0.2	5.7
Calhoun County	810	69.0	1 120	68.2	0	X	1	0.0	21	100.0	1.9	0.0	1.1	0.7	0.0	6.3
Camden County	11 136	78.0	2 889	75.9	42	88.1	82	76.8	404	85.9	2.3	0.7	0.8	0.5	0.5	11.3
Candler County	2 318	74.5	832	66.9	0	X	0	X	228	77.6	6.1	0.1	0.2	5.9	4.1	8.0
Carroll County	25 991	73.3	4 588	71.6	114	82.5	110	71.8	622	83.3	2.9	0.5	0.5	1.8	1.5	7.0
Catoosa County	19 613	75.4	266	66.2	96	85.4	163	73.6	203	77.3	1.7	0.4	0.5	0.5	0.5	6.7
Charlton County	2 454	76.2	788	73.9	9	100.0	21	100.0	6	0.0	0.9	0.2	0.5	0.1	0.5	5.2
Chatham County	53 832	64.2	32 288	70.0	203	67.5	1 372	67.3	1 498	70.0	4.0	0.9	1.4	1.2	1.4	9.8
Chattahoochee County	1 786	88.1	884	90.5	30	100.0	25	100.0	185	96.8	6.0	1.5	1.2	2.8	1.1	19.0
Chattooga County	8 673	71.6	724	67.7	14	85.7	29	89.7	116	74.1	1.9	0.1	0.3	1.4	1.0	5.1
Cherokee County	45 884	79.5	983	75.6	201	71.1	354	74.6	1 819	83.6	5.8	1.0	0.9	3.6	2.5	10.1
Clarke County	26 589	42.3	10 077	66.5	89	62.9	1 143	57.3	1 541	72.6	8.4	0.8	2.4	4.2	4.3	12.6
Clay County	567	70.2	770	67.4	7	85.7	2	100.0	3	100.0	0.7	0.2	0.4	0.1	0.2	4.5
Clayton County	32 520	70.1	41 878	71.6	279	84.2	2 577	88.7	3 926	85.5	10.9	0.5	3.7	5.6	5.2	15.1
Clinch County	1 845	72.4	628	70.4	13	100.0	7	42.9	15	66.7	1.4	0.3	0.4	0.7	0.1	5.9
Cobb County	165 389	69.2	41 335	66.1	548	71.9	6 018	76.5	11 398	79.9	11.6	1.5	2.8	5.9	4.5	15.7
Coffee County	9 648	72.6	2 907	74.6	9	77.8	103	68.0	660	83.2	5.4	0.2	0.5	4.7	3.1	8.8
Colquitt County	11 125	71.6	3 464	69.6	23	43.5	5	100.0	860	87.2	6.5	0.2	0.1	6.3	5.1	8.0
Columbia County	25 955	81.3	3 269	82.5	128	76.6	801	94.8	676	87.0	4.8	1.4	2.3	0.7	0.9	12.6
Cook County	4 183	72.1	1 556	76.8	9	100.0	22	72.7	99	67.7	2.3	0.2	0.3	1.7	1.4	6.3
Coweta County	25 153	78.8	5 266	79.6	30	50.0	146	95.9	616	78.6	3.7	0.8	0.5	2.1	1.6	8.0
Crawford County	3 312	79.0	1 092	76.5	16	50.0	0	X	22	63.6	0.5	0.2	0.0	0.3	0.2	5.7
Crisp County	4 811	70.0	3 321	71.6	4	100.0	59	62.7	123	78.9	2.1	0.1	0.5	1.4	1.2	6.4
Dade County	5 484	76.9	31	22.6	16	50.0	3	100.0	30	100.0	1.4	0.3	0.3	0.7	0.9	4.5
Dawson County	5 899	77.8	5	40.0	44	56.8	19	100.0	34	35.3	1.4	0.8	0.1	0.4	0.8	6.1
Decatur County	6 339	71.8	3 751	74.4	32	100.0	6	100.0	220	88.2	2.3	0.2	0.2	1.7	1.3	6.7
DeKalb County	102 174	52.1	122 877	71.3	678	62.8	8 345	72.4	12 155	74.8	15.2	1.5	3.7	7.7	7.1	16.0
Dodge County	5 210	69.4	1 760	71.6	22	63.6	20	100.0	58	48.3	1.4	0.2	0.3	0.7	0.5	5.1
Dooly County	2 023	68.8	1 771	74.3	1	100.0	9	33.3	87	62.1	1.5	0.1	0.3	1.1	0.8	7.0
Dougherty County	15 827	65.9	19 064	70.9	61	41.0	191	68.6	400	68.8	1.7	0.2	0.7	0.6	0.4	8.8
Douglas County	25 704	70.7	5 071	72.2	140	77.1	298	70.5	672	82.6	3.9	0.9	0.8	1.7	1.1	10.0
Early County	2 627	73.5	2 026	66.5	0	X	11	0.0	33	57.6	0.7	0.0	0.1	0.6	0.2	6.1
Echols County	986	74.5	96	79.2	0	X	6	100.0	162	69.8	12.6	0.0	0.3	12.3	6.6	22.0
Effingham County	11 375	80.1	1 423	77.3	55	100.0	64	100.0	114	64.0	1.3	0.4	0.7	0.3	0.4	6.4
Elbert County	5 576	71.6	2 254	75.7	0	X	14	100.0	164	66.5	1.9	0.3	0.2	1.3	0.6	5.7
Emanuel County	5 433	70.8	2 379	73.9	43	39.5	15	53.3	156	55.8	4.1	0.5	0.1	2.9	2.1	7.3
Evans County	2 409	72.0	1 128	72.1	10	100.0	20	70.0	201	66.7	4.3	0.1	0.5	3.7	4.1	6.1

[1] Hispanic or Latino persons may be of any race.

STATE/ County code	MSA/PMSA/ NECMA code[1]	STATE County	Population by age (percent)										Non-Hispanic White		
														Age (percent)	
			Total population	Under 5 years	5 to 17 years	18 to 24 years	25 to 44 years	45 to 64 years	65 years and over	Median age	+/- U.S. percent under 18 years	+/- U.S. percent 65 years and over	Total population	Under 18 years	65 years and over
			1	2	3	4	5	6	7	8	9	10	11	12	13
		GEORGIA—Cont'd													
13 111	...	Fannin County	19 798	5.3	15.7	6.8	24.9	28.3	19.0	43.1	-4.7	6.6	19 189	20.7	19.3
13 113	0520	Fayette County	91 263	5.8	23.2	6.3	27.9	27.8	9.0	38.2	3.3	-3.4	74 832	27.9	10.0
13 115	...	Floyd County	90 565	6.7	17.8	10.8	28.8	22.1	13.9	35.7	-1.2	1.5	71 572	22.5	15.8
13 117	0520	Forsyth County	98 407	9.6	18.4	6.0	37.2	21.8	7.1	34.6	2.3	-5.3	90 808	27.7	7.5
13 119	...	Franklin County	20 285	6.3	17.6	9.8	27.2	23.7	15.4	37.6	-1.8	3.0	17 948	23.0	16.0
13 121	0520	Fulton County	816 006	7.0	17.4	10.9	35.7	20.4	8.5	32.7	-1.3	-3.9	370 049	19.5	10.7
13 123	...	Gilmer County	23 456	7.3	16.9	8.8	28.1	25.6	13.2	37.3	-1.5	0.8	21 386	23.7	14.2
13 125	...	Glascock County	2 556	6.5	17.1	7.4	27.6	23.0	18.4	39.6	-2.1	6.0	2 304	23.3	17.9
13 127	...	Glynn County	67 568	6.4	18.9	8.3	27.7	24.0	14.6	37.9	-0.4	2.2	46 621	21.6	17.2
13 129	...	Gordon County	44 104	7.2	18.9	9.3	31.7	22.5	10.4	34.1	0.4	-2.0	38 596	25.5	11.5
13 131	...	Grady County	23 659	6.9	20.3	9.4	27.9	22.3	13.2	35.5	1.5	0.8	14 953	23.3	15.9
13 133	...	Greene County	14 406	6.8	18.3	9.0	24.6	27.0	14.4	39.1	-0.6	2.0	7 510	17.4	19.4
13 135	0520	Gwinnett County	588 448	7.9	20.2	8.5	37.7	20.3	5.3	32.5	2.4	-7.1	394 889	26.6	7.0
13 137	...	Habersham County	35 902	6.1	17.2	11.2	28.6	23.0	13.8	36.4	-2.4	1.4	30 434	22.0	15.8
13 139	...	Hall County	139 277	8.1	18.8	10.8	32.2	20.7	9.4	32.2	1.2	-3.0	98 988	23.9	12.0
13 141	...	Hancock County	10 076	5.7	18.6	10.1	31.7	21.8	12.2	35.8	-1.4	-0.2	2 140	12.1	20.1
13 143	...	Haralson County	25 690	6.9	19.2	8.5	29.1	23.2	13.2	36.1	0.4	0.8	23 799	25.6	13.2
13 145	1800	Harris County	23 695	6.0	19.4	6.1	29.6	26.9	12.0	38.5	-0.3	-0.4	18 370	24.8	11.5
13 147	...	Hart County	22 997	6.0	17.5	7.6	28.1	24.4	16.4	39.2	-2.2	4.0	18 042	21.4	18.9
13 149	...	Heard County	11 012	8.0	20.8	7.5	30.8	21.4	11.6	34.1	3.1	-0.8	9 557	28.4	11.3
13 151	0520	Henry County	119 341	8.1	21.1	7.6	34.9	21.0	7.4	33.4	3.5	-5.0	95 541	28.1	8.1
13 153	4680	Houston County	110 765	7.0	21.1	9.6	32.1	20.9	9.4	34.0	2.4	-3.0	76 337	25.6	11.5
13 155	...	Irwin County	9 931	6.8	22.2	8.6	26.9	21.1	14.4	34.6	3.3	2.0	7 131	25.5	15.7
13 157	...	Jackson County	41 589	7.2	19.6	8.7	31.8	22.3	10.4	34.6	1.1	-2.0	36 474	26.1	10.8
13 159	...	Jasper County	11 426	6.8	20.5	6.8	29.5	24.6	11.8	36.3	1.6	-0.6	7 975	25.3	12.4
13 161	...	Jeff Davis County	12 684	7.6	19.4	9.6	27.8	23.7	11.9	35.0	1.3	-0.5	10 019	25.9	12.7
13 163	...	Jefferson County	17 266	6.9	21.6	9.0	27.5	21.4	13.7	34.9	2.8	1.3	7 255	22.7	18.9
13 165	...	Jenkins County	8 575	7.0	21.7	9.2	25.8	22.5	13.9	35.4	3.0	1.5	4 795	23.6	16.6
13 167	...	Johnson County	8 560	6.8	23.4	9.0	24.1	21.1	15.6	34.9	4.5	3.2	5 319	24.2	19.0
13 169	4680	Jones County	23 639	6.4	20.8	7.8	30.6	24.2	10.3	36.1	1.5	-2.1	17 595	27.1	10.4
13 171	...	Lamar County	15 912	6.2	18.4	11.2	28.4	22.9	12.9	35.7	-1.1	0.5	10 759	22.7	14.4
13 173	...	Lanier County	7 241	7.3	20.1	10.7	30.9	20.6	10.5	33.3	1.7	-1.9	5 100	25.2	12.3
13 175	...	Laurens County	44 874	7.0	19.7	8.9	28.3	22.9	13.2	35.8	1.0	0.8	28 237	23.1	15.6
13 177	0120	Lee County	24 757	7.3	23.3	8.6	32.9	21.5	6.3	32.6	4.9	-6.1	20 204	30.5	6.0
13 179	...	Liberty County	61 610	10.4	21.5	18.1	33.9	12.1	4.0	25.0	6.2	-8.4	27 319	26.4	5.4
13 181	...	Lincoln County	8 348	5.0	19.4	7.3	27.3	26.1	14.9	39.3	-1.3	2.5	5 338	22.1	17.3
13 183	...	Long County	10 304	10.8	21.9	13.6	31.9	16.1	5.6	26.5	7.0	-6.8	6 649	29.6	6.2
13 185	...	Lowndes County	92 115	6.9	19.2	15.0	31.2	18.6	9.1	30.2	0.4	-3.3	55 901	22.3	10.7
13 187	...	Lumpkin County	21 016	6.2	18.0	15.5	28.9	21.5	9.8	32.5	-1.5	-2.6	19 418	23.6	10.1
13 189	0600	McDuffie County	21 231	7.3	20.6	8.8	28.3	22.7	12.4	35.2	2.2	0.0	12 719	23.8	14.6
13 191	...	McIntosh County	10 847	6.4	21.8	7.4	26.9	26.0	11.4	37.0	2.5	-1.0	6 623	24.3	12.3
13 193	...	Macon County	14 074	7.3	20.3	9.5	28.2	21.6	13.0	35.1	1.9	0.6	5 257	23.2	18.2
13 195	0500	Madison County	25 730	6.9	19.4	8.1	30.5	24.2	10.9	35.8	0.6	-1.5	22 624	25.3	11.5
13 197	...	Marion County	7 144	6.5	21.9	9.4	27.8	23.6	10.8	35.2	2.7	-1.6	4 168	25.3	11.1
13 199	...	Meriwether County	22 534	6.7	20.2	9.1	27.4	22.9	13.8	36.4	1.2	1.4	12 537	22.6	17.2
13 201	...	Miller County	6 383	5.9	20.4	6.7	26.6	23.2	17.2	38.2	0.6	4.8	4 442	22.1	20.1
13 205	...	Mitchell County	23 932	7.1	20.4	10.0	29.6	21.2	11.9	34.0	1.8	-0.5	11 720	22.4	15.7
13 207	...	Monroe County	21 757	6.2	20.0	8.6	30.5	24.7	10.0	36.4	0.5	-2.4	15 170	25.5	10.8
13 209	...	Montgomery County	8 270	6.7	18.3	13.3	29.6	21.6	10.5	33.6	-0.7	-1.9	5 744	24.0	12.1
13 211	...	Morgan County	15 457	6.6	20.0	7.9	28.6	24.4	12.5	36.8	0.9	0.1	10 560	24.8	13.7
13 213	...	Murray County	36 506	8.1	19.7	9.7	33.0	21.5	8.0	32.6	2.1	-4.4	33 865	27.2	8.3
13 215	1800	Muscogee County	186 291	7.3	19.5	12.0	29.8	19.7	11.7	32.6	1.1	-0.7	90 547	21.1	16.4
13 217	0520	Newton County	62 001	7.7	19.9	9.2	31.6	21.5	10.0	33.3	1.9	-2.4	46 021	25.5	10.9
13 219	0500	Oconee County	26 225	7.0	23.3	6.9	30.2	24.0	8.5	35.2	4.6	-3.9	23 055	29.6	8.9
13 221	...	Oglethorpe County	12 635	6.7	18.8	7.8	30.8	23.7	12.2	36.8	-0.2	-0.2	9 889	24.5	12.7
13 223	0520	Paulding County	81 678	9.4	21.3	7.6	38.6	17.2	6.0	31.2	5.0	-6.4	73 063	30.0	6.3
13 225	4680	Peach County	23 668	6.5	19.5	14.7	28.0	21.6	9.8	31.8	0.3	-2.6	11 590	24.2	12.6
13 227	0520	Pickens County	22 983	6.4	17.2	7.4	29.9	25.9	13.2	37.9	-2.1	0.8	21 931	23.1	13.4
13 229	...	Pierce County	15 636	6.5	19.8	8.9	27.9	24.6	12.3	36.2	0.6	-0.1	13 458	25.6	12.6
13 231	...	Pike County	13 688	6.9	20.7	7.9	30.8	22.8	11.0	35.7	1.9	-1.4	11 337	27.5	11.1
13 233	...	Polk County	38 127	7.0	18.9	9.3	29.2	22.3	13.2	35.1	0.2	0.8	29 745	24.0	14.9
13 235	...	Pulaski County	9 588	6.5	16.6	9.7	31.4	22.6	13.2	36.7	-2.6	0.8	5 908	20.4	15.8
13 237	...	Putnam County	18 812	6.3	16.9	8.1	26.9	27.5	14.4	39.6	-2.5	2.0	12 515	18.6	18.0
13 239	...	Quitman County	2 598	5.4	18.6	7.8	23.7	24.8	19.8	42.0	-1.7	7.4	1 362	15.9	26.6
13 241	...	Rabun County	15 050	5.6	16.3	7.1	24.9	28.0	18.1	42.0	-3.8	5.7	13 996	21.1	18.8
13 243	...	Randolph County	7 791	7.0	20.3	11.3	24.3	21.7	15.4	36.1	1.6	3.0	3 035	19.5	20.0

[1] MSA = Metropolitan Statistical Area. PMSA = Primary MSA. NECMA = New England County Metropolitan Area. See the Appendix A for explanation of these concepts. See Appendix B for list of metropolitan areas identified by type, with component counties.

STATE County	Black or African American Total population 14	Age (percent) Under 18 years 15	65 years and over 16	American Indian and Alaska Native Total population 17	Age (percent) Under 18 years 18	65 years and over 19	Asian, Hawaiian, and Pacific Islander Total population 20	Age (percent) Under 18 years 21	65 years and over 22	Hispanic or Latino[1] Total population 23	Age (percent) Under 18 years 24	65 years and over 25	Two or more races Total population 26	Age (percent) Under 18 years 27	65 years and over 28
GEORGIA—Cont'd															
Fannin County	10	40.0	0.0	64	12.5	21.9	86	54.7	8.1	161	37.3	0.0	287	26.1	11.8
Fayette County	10 940	34.5	3.9	130	16.9	6.9	2 072	30.0	1.4	2 281	30.6	9.5	1 244	41.9	7.7
Floyd County	11 889	30.8	9.2	234	20.5	2.6	1 290	31.6	4.3	4 965	34.2	1.1	1 161	41.0	5.2
Forsyth County	680	32.1	3.5	439	36.2	0.0	795	21.9	1.3	5 370	31.4	2.3	1 046	34.5	5.9
Franklin County	2 000	32.1	10.6	37	32.4	0.0	46	28.3	6.5	115	16.5	10.4	155	23.9	18.1
Fulton County	361 951	29.1	7.6	1 959	25.1	5.5	24 107	22.5	3.1	47 735	25.8	1.9	13 332	31.8	4.5
Gilmer County	42	23.8	0.0	87	4.6	9.2	135	27.4	0.7	1 713	30.9	3.2	382	40.3	3.4
Glascock County	220	27.3	22.3	8	37.5	0.0	0	X	X	13	23.1	23.1	0	X	X
Glynn County	17 543	33.7	10.1	101	47.5	0.0	562	19.6	2.7	2 053	32.1	2.5	877	46.2	4.6
Gordon County	1 520	27.4	7.1	163	25.2	8.6	210	29.5	3.3	3 283	30.0	0.9	594	45.1	1.7
Grady County	7 178	34.0	9.6	194	26.8	19.1	40	35.0	5.0	1 212	32.4	1.6	141	63.8	3.5
Greene County	6 525	33.4	9.4	16	25.0	0.0	56	8.9	0.0	359	44.8	0.6	64	76.6	7.8
Gwinnett County	77 954	32.5	1.5	1 825	19.5	6.2	41 527	27.8	3.1	63 574	30.9	1.4	14 343	36.5	2.1
Habersham County	1 579	16.3	5.4	136	22.8	0.0	822	34.7	1.6	2 730	37.3	0.8	500	39.0	5.6
Hall County	10 049	30.8	6.8	442	13.8	9.5	1 904	30.7	3.6	27 318	36.0	1.1	2 029	34.8	3.5
Hancock County	7 791	27.2	10.2	24	12.5	0.0	0	X	X	36	8.3	0.0	104	58.7	2.9
Haralson County	1 328	28.6	11.6	12	0.0	0.0	37	16.2	37.8	161	32.3	0.0	352	45.7	20.5
Harris County	4 770	28.1	14.5	51	0.0	0.0	159	20.8	5.7	148	25.0	6.1	213	19.7	6.6
Hart County	4 523	30.1	7.8	27	18.5	0.0	135	41.5	0.0	247	53.4	0.0	102	64.7	6.9
Heard County	1 190	28.3	15.1	31	54.8	22.6	63	14.3	7.9	64	26.6	3.1	94	48.9	0.0
Henry County	17 448	33.1	4.5	342	23.1	2.9	2 186	28.3	6.1	2 611	38.1	3.2	1 486	38.5	3.0
Houston County	27 044	33.5	5.0	415	12.0	2.9	1 947	25.6	4.5	3 553	33.2	3.3	1 942	50.5	1.9
Irwin County	2 500	37.0	12.0	11	36.4	0.0	38	63.2	0.0	222	43.7	0.0	39	38.5	30.8
Jackson County	3 117	23.6	11.2	63	12.7	30.2	314	43.3	1.9	1 231	41.1	0.6	465	59.6	1.7
Jasper County	3 141	31.1	11.3	19	47.4	0.0	95	48.4	0.0	150	38.0	4.7	46	41.3	0.0
Jeff Davis County	1 892	31.3	11.9	6	0.0	0.0	87	28.7	0.0	608	30.6	0.0	93	53.8	9.7
Jefferson County	9 787	32.3	10.1	31	48.4	0.0	20	0.0	0.0	121	60.3	0.0	65	61.5	0.0
Jenkins County	3 463	34.8	10.8	11	0.0	0.0	9	0.0	0.0	258	35.3	16.7	194	59.8	12.9
Johnson County	3 152	40.0	9.9	0	X	X	32	87.5	0.0	65	15.4	6.2	20	15.0	15.0
Jones County	5 511	27.0	10.3	72	44.4	0.0	115	6.1	22.6	200	38.0	6.0	202	33.2	1.0
Lamar County	4 658	28.7	10.0	140	8.6	11.4	33	0.0	0.0	220	37.3	5.5	113	33.6	14.2
Lanier County	1 837	32.3	6.9	80	16.3	0.0	6	0.0	0.0	186	42.5	0.0	82	45.1	7.3
Laurens County	15 498	32.7	9.6	147	27.2	0.7	268	20.9	0.0	507	36.1	8.3	333	51.4	1.8
Lee County	3 696	27.8	8.5	79	41.8	0.0	127	34.6	5.5	518	50.4	4.4	242	40.9	0.0
Liberty County	26 164	35.7	3.3	365	27.1	0.0	1 209	16.1	4.0	5 010	36.8	0.9	2 305	60.6	0.8
Lincoln County	2 874	28.5	10.0	8	0.0	0.0	17	0.0	0.0	83	38.6	9.6	24	41.7	20.8
Long County	2 533	37.0	6.0	67	41.8	4.5	74	9.5	9.5	864	36.9	0.0	210	59.0	4.3
Lowndes County	31 681	32.4	6.9	287	35.2	0.7	869	18.5	3.3	2 567	28.6	3.5	1 295	35.8	5.3
Lumpkin County	251	15.5	17.9	219	25.6	4.6	110	10.9	0.0	675	40.4	0.0	353	36.0	13.6
McDuffie County	8 080	34.2	9.3	131	31.3	0.0	61	77.0	0.0	152	22.4	0.0	125	9.6	13.6
McIntosh County	3 993	34.7	9.8	93	29.0	0.0	31	35.5	0.0	43	51.2	0.0	84	23.8	45.2
Macon County	8 292	30.5	10.4	109	9.2	6.4	37	43.2	0.0	335	33.4	0.0	120	30.8	10.8
Madison County	2 155	30.3	8.4	75	20.0	12.0	155	33.5	1.3	512	40.2	2.7	231	45.9	0.0
Marion County	2 426	32.7	11.8	44	56.8	0.0	18	72.2	0.0	428	32.0	0.0	105	41.9	18.1
Meriwether County	9 561	31.9	9.7	43	46.5	4.7	22	9.1	0.0	124	54.0	6.5	270	40.0	1.5
Miller County	1 902	35.5	10.8	0	X	X	26	57.7	0.0	8	0.0	0.0	5	100.0	0.0
Mitchell County	11 509	31.7	8.5	26	0.0	15.4	51	23.5	0.0	558	45.7	0.9	108	57.4	1.9
Monroe County	6 250	27.8	8.4	67	50.7	0.0	60	13.3	0.0	214	28.0	6.1	49	42.9	0.0
Montgomery County	2 274	26.9	7.6	10	0.0	0.0	44	0.0	0.0	155	36.8	0.0	35	37.1	5.7
Morgan County	4 528	30.0	10.0	23	0.0	0.0	63	42.9	7.9	141	34.0	14.2	165	45.5	4.2
Murray County	335	30.7	9.3	123	48.0	4.1	56	0.0	30.4	2 064	37.4	1.4	312	37.5	1.6
Muscogee County	80 509	32.4	7.7	1 048	24.2	6.1	3 368	26.1	5.2	8 459	30.5	4.4	3 650	43.3	4.7
Newton County	13 939	33.5	7.6	157	21.7	12.7	448	29.2	4.2	1 086	34.0	6.1	518	51.2	1.9
Oconee County	1 567	30.3	10.0	98	28.6	0.0	466	36.7	1.3	937	38.4	1.9	180	68.9	0.0
Oglethorpe County	2 552	29.0	11.1	22	0.0	0.0	11	0.0	27.3	116	28.4	0.0	53	11.3	0.0
Paulding County	5 906	36.6	2.4	224	29.0	0.0	419	30.5	2.6	1 207	37.5	1.4	969	41.0	8.4
Peach County	10 710	27.3	7.8	49	44.9	0.0	136	26.5	1.5	1 023	30.5	2.9	138	26.8	0.0
Pickens County	372	26.3	17.7	47	12.8	0.0	63	36.5	23.8	368	37.0	3.0	204	38.2	5.9
Pierce County	1 721	32.7	11.7	28	0.0	10.7	0	X	X	389	26.2	2.3	80	20.0	28.8
Pike County	2 051	27.1	11.0	24	0.0	0.0	61	59.0	0.0	125	32.8	1.6	88	34.1	22.7
Polk County	5 234	30.8	10.7	67	38.8	0.0	133	48.0	0.0	2 787	34.2	1.1	275	38.2	9.8
Pulaski County	3 236	26.1	10.2	32	34.4	0.0	42	47.6	0.0	335	30.4	1.5	57	31.6	0.0
Putnam County	5 661	32.5	7.2	19	31.6	0.0	47	27.7	0.0	421	25.9	2.1	189	40.7	13.8
Quitman County	1 195	32.7	12.4	12	33.3	33.3	0	X	X	12	0.0	0.0	17	70.6	0.0
Rabun County	153	43.1	17.0	42	16.7	38.1	55	10.9	0.0	684	35.4	2.0	152	33.6	19.7
Randolph County	4 693	32.2	12.7	0	X	X	0	X	X	60	35.0	0.0	3	0.0	0.0

[1] Hispanic or Latino persons may be of any race.

Table A-3. States and Counties — Age, Ethnicity, and Household Structure

STATE County	Total households	Married-couple family households Total	With children	Householder 65 years or over	Other family households Total	With children	Householder 65 years or over	Two or more unrelated persons Total	Householder 65 years or over	Male living alone Total	Householder 65 years or over	Female living alone Total	Householder 65 years or over	Percent of householders 65 years and over who live alone	Grandparents who are responsible for the care of their grandchildren
	29	30	31	32	33	34	35	36	37	38	39	40	41	42	43
GEORGIA—Cont'd															
Fannin County	8 378	60.4	21.6	14.2	11.9	5.5	2.5	2.2	0.3	10.7	3.7	14.8	9.6	43.9	173
Fayette County	31 491	72.9	37.5	9.0	9.8	5.9	1.1	2.4	0.1	5.5	0.9	9.4	4.6	34.8	607
Floyd County	34 030	55.5	24.4	9.8	16.4	8.7	2.6	3.7	0.3	9.0	2.1	15.5	9.1	46.9	1 051
Forsyth County	34 603	72.6	37.2	6.6	9.4	4.6	1.5	3.2	0.2	6.8	0.7	8.0	3.1	31.4	514
Franklin County	7 891	57.7	24.3	11.2	15.1	7.6	3.0	2.4	0.1	10.2	3.1	14.7	9.5	46.7	251
Fulton County	321 266	38.1	18.3	4.8	20.3	11.2	2.3	9.4	0.3	14.4	1.6	17.8	5.3	48.1	8 384
Gilmer County	9 047	61.8	24.5	10.9	12.2	7.0	2.1	3.8	0.6	9.6	2.6	12.6	6.2	39.3	244
Glascock County	1 013	57.8	26.5	10.5	13.5	7.0	3.0	2.3	1.1	8.7	1.7	17.7	11.5	47.7	35
Glynn County	27 248	51.2	20.7	10.8	17.2	10.5	2.5	4.5	0.4	10.5	2.1	16.6	8.0	42.6	1 006
Gordon County	16 151	62.8	28.8	8.2	13.8	7.9	1.7	3.2	0.2	8.1	1.6	12.2	6.4	44.2	653
Grady County	8 817	52.9	23.3	9.1	21.4	11.6	3.5	3.4	0.1	8.0	2.2	14.3	8.2	44.8	369
Greene County	5 492	50.3	16.6	10.7	23.4	13.2	3.5	3.2	0.2	10.0	2.6	13.1	7.7	41.7	257
Gwinnett County	202 567	62.5	35.4	4.3	13.3	7.6	1.0	5.8	0.1	8.0	0.6	10.4	2.6	37.6	3 711
Habersham County	13 316	62.1	25.2	12.4	12.5	7.3	1.8	3.2	0.2	8.7	1.9	13.5	7.8	40.5	300
Hall County	47 391	61.7	29.7	8.2	14.8	7.7	2.3	4.4	0.2	8.0	1.3	11.2	5.6	39.3	1 379
Hancock County	3 246	39.1	14.2	8.0	33.7	17.1	6.9	1.0	0.2	12.5	4.1	13.7	7.8	44.0	147
Haralson County	9 825	57.8	24.9	9.1	16.2	8.5	3.5	3.0	0.2	8.9	1.9	14.1	8.1	43.7	291
Harris County	8 858	64.9	27.2	9.3	14.5	7.0	2.8	2.6	0.1	7.5	1.6	10.5	6.5	40.0	299
Hart County	9 097	57.3	22.0	12.6	15.8	7.6	3.0	2.3	0.3	9.3	1.8	15.2	8.4	39.1	204
Heard County	4 049	59.3	28.9	7.7	16.5	9.7	2.3	2.8	0.6	10.0	2.4	11.3	6.7	46.4	157
Henry County	41 332	67.7	35.5	6.6	13.4	8.1	1.3	3.5	0.2	6.8	1.1	8.6	3.2	34.5	989
Houston County	40 959	56.8	27.4	7.9	17.6	11.4	1.7	3.5	0.2	10.4	1.6	11.7	5.2	41.1	1 322
Irwin County	3 691	56.4	26.2	11.2	18.7	10.8	1.8	2.1	0.1	8.4	2.5	14.4	9.0	46.8	158
Jackson County	15 029	61.7	28.6	7.6	15.1	8.1	2.5	3.4	0.1	9.8	2.2	10.0	5.9	44.2	552
Jasper County	4 176	57.8	25.3	9.8	17.6	9.6	3.3	3.3	0.9	10.1	1.6	11.2	6.3	35.9	122
Jeff Davis County	4 844	56.5	26.4	9.8	19.7	8.4	3.4	1.7	0.3	9.6	1.5	12.4	7.2	39.1	264
Jefferson County	6 302	44.2	19.7	8.0	28.0	15.0	5.5	1.9	0.3	9.6	3.0	16.2	8.6	45.5	358
Jenkins County	3 211	42.5	18.9	6.4	28.5	15.4	3.9	3.3	0.7	10.9	3.9	14.8	8.6	53.0	170
Johnson County	3 117	48.6	20.4	9.9	22.9	12.7	3.4	1.6	0.4	11.7	2.1	15.2	9.9	46.8	210
Jones County	8 649	60.4	28.6	7.6	16.8	9.7	2.7	2.5	0.0	7.6	1.3	12.6	6.1	41.8	217
Lamar County	5 668	55.0	23.8	9.9	19.8	10.1	3.5	3.4	0.1	9.2	2.5	12.5	5.9	38.1	258
Lanier County	2 609	56.9	28.7	7.9	17.8	9.7	2.3	3.8	0.0	10.3	1.6	11.2	7.2	46.6	99
Laurens County	17 098	51.3	21.9	8.7	20.4	12.2	2.9	2.7	0.2	9.8	2.1	15.7	8.6	47.6	608
Lee County	8 219	67.7	38.1	6.2	15.6	10.4	1.8	2.5	0.1	6.8	1.1	7.4	2.9	33.4	297
Liberty County	19 434	60.7	37.6	3.3	18.2	13.5	1.2	4.7	0.1	9.1	1.0	7.3	1.9	39.0	731
Lincoln County	3 247	55.9	23.4	11.8	17.2	7.5	3.7	3.1	0.2	12.5	3.0	11.2	7.0	38.8	126
Long County	3 576	56.3	32.9	4.4	19.0	13.6	1.2	4.8	0.3	11.5	1.1	8.3	3.3	42.6	139
Lowndes County	32 660	48.9	23.7	6.8	19.7	12.1	2.3	7.2	0.4	9.8	1.7	14.4	6.0	44.9	1 054
Lumpkin County	7 532	59.2	27.6	7.5	12.0	6.9	1.9	6.7	0.3	10.5	2.3	11.5	4.9	42.4	142
McDuffie County	7 980	51.5	22.6	7.7	22.4	13.5	3.7	2.8	0.4	9.1	2.4	14.2	7.6	46.1	288
McIntosh County	4 198	54.4	21.6	8.6	18.0	10.0	2.4	4.0	1.1	12.3	2.7	11.8	5.6	40.7	220
Macon County	4 813	44.5	21.2	8.0	28.0	14.9	4.2	2.2	0.3	10.8	4.0	14.6	8.6	50.1	319
Madison County	9 822	60.4	27.4	8.6	14.2	7.5	1.7	4.0	0.3	10.3	1.9	11.1	5.7	41.7	307
Marion County	2 685	52.0	25.1	6.3	20.4	11.5	2.2	3.3	0.2	11.5	3.2	12.9	8.5	57.3	116
Meriwether County	8 289	48.4	20.3	9.6	25.0	12.4	5.6	2.8	0.2	9.6	2.5	14.2	7.9	40.2	420
Miller County	2 481	51.3	21.0	11.2	19.7	10.5	4.1	2.2	0.0	10.9	3.8	15.9	8.2	44.0	110
Mitchell County	8 040	46.4	18.6	9.5	27.8	15.6	4.2	2.6	0.2	9.1	1.2	14.1	6.9	36.7	357
Monroe County	7 723	59.8	27.2	7.2	17.8	8.4	4.0	3.4	0.3	7.8	1.5	11.1	5.9	38.9	341
Montgomery County	2 947	55.4	26.9	8.6	16.5	9.3	1.3	3.0	0.5	11.5	3.3	13.5	7.6	51.0	98
Morgan County	5 579	60.1	26.5	9.2	18.0	9.0	4.0	2.6	0.3	8.2	1.6	11.1	5.9	35.9	299
Murray County	13 305	62.2	30.3	6.6	15.6	9.8	1.5	3.5	0.3	8.2	1.1	10.5	4.4	39.9	520
Muscogee County	69 787	45.5	21.4	7.7	23.1	13.6	3.1	4.7	0.3	10.3	1.9	16.4	7.7	46.2	2 571
Newton County	21 989	59.8	27.9	8.1	18.4	10.5	2.1	3.6	0.2	8.0	1.6	10.2	5.2	39.6	712
Oconee County	9 041	69.4	36.9	7.1	11.9	7.6	0.9	3.3	0.1	5.8	1.7	9.7	4.9	44.7	186
Oglethorpe County	4 885	56.2	25.0	7.8	17.1	10.2	2.4	4.1	0.1	10.3	2.5	12.4	6.9	47.6	194
Paulding County	28 159	69.5	38.9	5.3	12.2	7.6	1.0	3.7	0.2	6.8	0.8	7.8	2.9	36.5	597
Peach County	8 414	47.3	20.1	8.8	24.2	13.5	2.1	5.9	0.1	8.9	1.2	13.7	7.2	43.1	364
Pickens County	8 982	65.2	25.1	11.7	11.6	6.5	1.9	2.8	0.2	8.6	1.3	11.8	6.2	35.2	137
Pierce County	5 945	59.7	26.4	9.9	14.8	8.3	2.6	2.3	0.1	9.5	1.5	13.6	8.6	44.7	189
Pike County	4 756	65.9	30.7	9.2	14.0	6.7	2.5	2.7	0.3	7.4	2.2	10.0	6.0	40.7	141
Polk County	14 031	55.7	24.7	9.1	18.4	9.2	3.5	3.1	0.2	8.7	2.6	14.0	7.9	45.1	587
Pulaski County	3 418	50.4	20.3	8.8	18.3	10.3	3.2	3.6	0.7	9.3	2.1	18.4	10.7	50.1	79
Putnam County	7 385	57.8	19.2	12.9	16.4	8.7	2.5	3.6	0.1	10.3	2.1	11.9	5.8	33.7	179
Quitman County	1 056	50.5	16.0	14.2	21.8	10.1	5.3	2.8	0.0	12.7	3.9	12.2	6.7	35.2	74
Rabun County	6 307	57.7	21.6	13.6	11.9	5.9	2.7	3.8	0.4	10.6	3.0	16.0	8.8	41.2	88
Randolph County	2 916	44.4	17.1	9.3	24.3	13.5	4.3	1.5	0.1	9.3	2.9	20.5	12.2	52.4	208

Table A-3. States and Counties — Age, Ethnicity, and Household Structure

STATE County	Households with Non-Hispanic White householder — Number of households	Percent that are family households	Households with Black or African American householder — Number of households	Percent that are family households	Households with American Indian and Alaska Native householder — Number of households	Percent that are family households	Households with Asian, Hawaiian, and Pacific Islander householder — Number of households	Percent that are family households	Households with Hispanic or Latino[1] householder — Number of households	Percent that are family households	Foreign-born population — Percent of total population that is foreign-born	Place of birth (percent) — Europe	Asia	Latin America	Percent in non-English speaking households — Linguistically isolated	Not linguistically isolated
	44	45	46	47	48	49	50	51	52	53	54	55	56	57	58	59
GEORGIA—Cont'd																
Fannin County	8 180	72.1	0	X	40	75.0	12	100.0	50	68.0	1.1	0.3	0.3	0.4	0.2	4.6
Fayette County	26 850	81.6	3 216	90.1	30	70.0	529	87.0	601	84.5	5.0	1.3	1.7	1.4	1.2	11.0
Floyd County	27 822	71.6	4 309	68.0	79	89.9	354	83.9	1 305	89.3	5.2	0.3	1.2	3.5	3.1	8.5
Forsyth County	32 717	81.9	145	75.2	120	95.8	286	80.8	1 159	85.4	6.0	1.3	0.7	3.3	2.8	10.8
Franklin County	7 180	72.2	656	79.6	5	100.0	5	20.0	17	52.9	1.2	0.4	0.3	0.4	0.1	5.1
Fulton County	165 505	53.1	131 787	63.0	715	64.2	7 549	69.6	12 066	72.2	9.6	1.4	2.5	4.6	4.2	14.3
Gilmer County	8 569	73.8	19	0.0	40	80.0	31	74.2	352	78.4	5.8	0.4	0.2	5.1	4.7	6.5
Glascock County	937	71.0	64	71.9	2	100.0	0	X	4	100.0	0.0	0.0	0.0	0.0	0.0	1.6
Glynn County	20 029	68.0	6 274	68.9	36	63.9	214	69.2	528	74.1	3.3	0.6	0.6	1.7	1.1	9.0
Gordon County	14 562	76.5	603	68.7	56	44.6	62	82.3	776	85.1	6.4	0.3	0.4	5.5	4.0	8.7
Grady County	6 070	74.9	2 382	73.6	69	36.2	8	75.0	290	77.2	3.9	0.2	0.1	3.5	2.5	5.0
Greene County	3 263	72.9	2 142	74.7	7	100.0	18	50.0	80	88.8	2.6	0.6	0.3	1.4	1.3	5.3
Gwinnett County	145 252	75.2	27 416	75.3	640	75.3	11 952	86.8	14 806	87.6	16.9	2.1	5.8	7.7	7.2	19.4
Habersham County	12 164	74.0	290	61.4	35	100.0	202	92.6	585	89.4	7.8	0.5	1.7	5.4	4.8	10.2
Hall County	37 774	75.0	3 397	74.1	202	86.6	396	90.2	5 392	88.6	16.2	0.5	1.2	14.1	10.5	14.0
Hancock County	776	69.1	2 450	74.0	11	27.3	0	X	1	100.0	0.3	0.1	0.1	0.0	0.0	4.1
Haralson County	9 181	74.6	485	69.9	0	X	15	66.7	36	30.6	0.9	0.4	0.2	0.3	0.1	4.5
Harris County	6 974	80.5	1 711	74.4	31	100.0	53	83.0	62	82.3	1.9	0.8	0.4	0.1	0.1	8.2
Hart County	7 517	72.6	1 471	75.5	11	0.0	41	68.3	38	100.0	1.3	0.5	0.3	0.2	0.2	5.0
Heard County	3 570	76.9	412	68.7	7	0.0	23	73.9	12	66.7	0.7	0.2	0.3	0.2	0.2	4.6
Henry County	34 002	81.1	5 643	79.8	119	94.1	479	93.1	745	83.5	3.4	0.6	1.3	1.1	0.5	10.0
Houston County	29 577	74.8	9 492	72.5	204	74.5	517	79.7	957	82.8	3.4	0.7	1.4	1.2	1.0	9.7
Irwin County	2 800	76.3	821	70.3	0	X	9	100.0	49	100.0	1.3	0.0	0.3	0.9	0.7	4.1
Jackson County	13 512	76.7	1 072	75.9	25	76.0	63	96.8	276	76.4	2.5	0.4	0.4	1.6	1.2	8.1
Jasper County	3 008	77.6	1 077	69.5	0	X	34	82.4	44	75.0	2.1	0.3	0.7	1.2	0.7	3.8
Jeff Davis County	3 929	77.1	706	70.4	6	100.0	37	81.1	145	80.7	3.8	0.3	0.6	2.9	0.7	8.4
Jefferson County	2 988	70.4	3 253	73.5	7	100.0	20	70.0	11	100.0	0.5	0.2	0.0	0.2	0.5	4.3
Jenkins County	1 890	74.6	1 201	65.8	11	100.0	0	0.0	92	75.0	0.9	0.0	0.0	0.9	1.2	6.2
Johnson County	2 127	69.2	958	76.5	0	X	4	0.0	23	100.0	0.2	0.1	0.0	0.1	0.0	2.3
Jones County	6 478	77.6	2 007	75.9	26	100.0	33	97.0	46	52.2	1.0	0.1	0.4	0.3	0.6	6.6
Lamar County	3 868	77.7	1 657	66.8	56	100.0	8	100.0	50	74.0	1.0	0.1	0.2	0.6	0.5	4.4
Lanier County	1 925	73.9	588	77.7	31	67.7	0	X	47	85.1	1.1	0.2	0.1	0.6	0.6	5.2
Laurens County	11 457	72.2	5 316	70.8	57	33.3	104	87.5	133	56.4	1.1	0.2	0.4	0.3	0.5	4.8
Lee County	6 956	84.8	1 056	74.4	18	100.0	41	75.6	79	97.5	1.7	0.3	0.7	0.6	0.2	7.2
Liberty County	9 368	77.6	8 182	79.5	121	90.9	363	78.2	1 208	84.8	5.7	1.4	1.3	2.5	1.1	19.1
Lincoln County	2 208	72.1	998	74.7	0	X	8	100.0	16	100.0	0.7	0.5	0.1	0.2	0.1	4.2
Long County	2 453	75.8	863	71.1	17	94.1	16	0.0	208	86.5	5.4	0.4	0.6	4.3	3.5	11.4
Lowndes County	21 435	66.3	10 103	72.2	94	96.8	198	86.4	644	82.9	2.7	0.5	0.6	1.4	0.8	7.6
Lumpkin County	7 066	71.1	82	56.1	102	70.6	61	86.0	125	85.0	2.9	0.0	0.3	1.9	1.2	12.1
McDuffie County	5 012	74.0	2 830	73.7	43	100.0	4	100.0	39	94.9	0.6	0.3	0.1	0.2	0.2	5.2
McIntosh County	2 701	70.7	1 399	73.6	40	70.0	14	64.3	8	100.0	1.0	0.4	0.3	0.2	0.0	8.9
Macon County	1 901	72.7	2 807	71.8	9	100.0	3	100.0	40	100.0	1.8	0.1	0.1	1.5	0.4	9.2
Madison County	8 854	73.8	755	81.7	29	75.9	36	91.7	93	88.2	2.0	0.3	0.5	1.1	1.2	5.4
Marion County	1 624	74.4	908	67.2	17	100.0	4	100.0	109	80.7	5.0	0.5	0.2	4.2	3.6	6.7
Meriwether County	5 143	71.5	3 027	76.6	21	61.9	6	83.3	11	81.8	0.7	0.3	0.0	0.4	0.2	6.4
Miller County	1 787	71.0	684	70.5	0	X	5	100.0	5	100.0	0.4	0.1	0.3	0.0	0.4	3.4
Mitchell County	4 441	73.4	3 466	74.6	19	100.0	11	81.8	98	89.8	1.6	0.2	0.1	1.2	1.5	6.6
Monroe County	5 591	79.3	2 046	73.5	6	100.0	25	56.0	42	100.0	1.0	0.2	0.2	0.5	0.5	6.7
Montgomery County	2 218	71.3	661	71.9	4	100.0	12	83.3	45	100.0	3.9	0.1	0.7	2.0	0.2	7.3
Morgan County	4 083	78.7	1 412	77.8	5	100.0	19	52.6	24	41.7	1.1	0.5	0.3	0.3	0.0	5.6
Murray County	12 591	77.7	78	83.3	23	100.0	6	0.0	559	83.9	3.6	0.2	0.3	3.3	2.6	6.5
Muscogee County	36 848	66.1	28 604	71.2	359	75.5	936	87.0	2 457	71.9	4.7	1.4	1.2	1.8	1.3	11.7
Newton County	17 189	77.3	4 352	80.6	46	93.5	92	95.7	246	82.5	2.5	0.8	0.6	1.0	0.8	6.6
Oconee County	8 140	81.1	543	74.4	39	100.0	100	96.0	210	97.6	4.4	0.9	1.1	2.0	1.2	8.8
Oglethorpe County	3 919	73.2	919	74.0	19	73.7	3	100.0	24	45.8	0.8	0.3	0.1	0.4	0.5	4.8
Paulding County	25 607	81.7	1 817	81.7	52	76.9	89	94.4	299	89.0	2.1	0.5	0.5	0.7	0.3	8.3
Peach County	4 516	75.0	3 561	67.0	15	86.7	31	64.5	260	76.5	3.8	0.2	0.3	3.0	1.7	9.2
Pickens County	8 672	76.9	127	60.6	22	0.0	18	100.0	83	97.6	2.0	0.7	0.2	0.9	0.8	5.8
Pierce County	5 181	75.8	642	67.3	22	50.0	0	X	94	58.5	2.1	0.3	0.0	1.8	1.6	4.5
Pike County	4 008	81.0	656	73.9	4	100.0	9	100.0	40	85.0	1.0	0.2	0.3	0.3	0.3	6.2
Polk County	11 536	73.0	1 788	76.3	29	100.0	17	100.0	642	86.8	6.0	0.2	0.2	5.4	3.9	7.6
Pulaski County	2 299	71.4	1 039	62.5	0	X	13	100.0	67	67.2	2.6	0.3	0.2	1.8	1.5	8.2
Putnam County	5 363	74.5	1 863	73.5	10	0.0	7	100.0	103	77.7	2.5	0.5	0.2	1.8	1.1	8.7
Quitman County	608	72.2	439	72.4	4	100.0	0	X	3	0.0	0.7	0.0	0.0	0.7	0.0	6.9
Rabun County	6 007	70.0	48	50.0	7	71.4	4	0.0	176	76.7	4.1	0.7	0.2	3.1	2.6	7.8
Randolph County	1 293	69.1	1 600	68.0	0	X	0	X	20	100.0	0.7	0.2	0.0	0.5	0.5	7.3

[1] Hispanic or Latino persons may be of any race.

STATE/ County code	MSA/PMSA/ NECMA code[1]	STATE County	Population by age (percent)										Non-Hispanic White		
														Age (percent)	
			Total population	Under 5 years	5 to 17 years	18 to 24 years	25 to 44 years	45 to 64 years	65 years and over	Median age	+/- U.S. percent under 18 years	+/- U.S. percent 65 years and over	Total population	Under 18 years	65 years and over
			1	2	3	4	5	6	7	8	9	10	11	12	13
		GEORGIA—Cont'd													
13 245	0600	Richmond County	199 775	7.2	19.7	11.8	30.4	20.0	10.9	32.3	1.2	-1.5	88 675	19.8	15.9
13 247	0520	Rockdale County............	70 111	6.6	21.0	8.5	30.6	24.0	9.3	35.4	1.9	-3.1	50 852	24.9	11.3
13 249	...	Schley County...............	3 766	8.2	20.9	8.1	27.9	23.6	11.2	34.5	3.4	-1.2	2 469	25.6	12.0
13 251	...	Screven County	15 374	6.6	21.2	9.2	26.8	22.1	14.1	36.2	2.1	1.7	8 158	23.2	17.6
13 253	...	Seminole County	9 369	7.2	18.8	8.7	26.4	23.2	15.7	37.5	0.3	3.3	5 713	19.6	19.4
13 255	0520	Spalding County	58 417	7.3	19.9	9.2	29.7	22.2	11.6	34.6	1.5	-0.8	38 270	23.4	14.3
13 257	...	Stephens County	25 435	6.4	16.9	10.8	26.8	23.5	15.7	37.5	-2.4	3.3	21 628	21.8	16.7
13 259	...	Stewart County	5 252	6.4	18.7	8.4	24.9	23.2	18.4	38.8	-0.6	6.0	1 916	18.6	23.9
13 261	...	Sumter County	33 200	7.9	20.1	11.6	27.9	19.9	12.5	32.6	2.3	0.1	15 655	21.0	17.8
13 263	...	Talbot County................	6 498	6.1	18.0	8.1	26.5	26.9	14.4	39.5	-1.6	2.0	2 345	18.5	18.0
13 265	...	Taliaferro County...........	2 077	6.4	17.9	6.7	27.0	23.4	18.6	40.2	-1.4	6.2	794	18.0	26.3
13 267	...	Tattnall County...............	22 305	5.9	17.1	11.1	34.9	19.7	11.3	33.9	-2.7	-1.1	13 251	21.4	15.4
13 269	...	Taylor County................	8 815	7.1	19.8	9.6	27.6	22.7	13.1	35.7	1.2	0.7	4 833	22.6	15.8
13 271	...	Telfair County................	11 794	6.0	16.5	10.5	30.0	21.9	15.1	36.8	-3.2	2.7	7 007	20.9	19.0
13 273	...	Terrell County................	10 970	7.8	20.9	9.9	25.6	22.6	13.3	35.4	3.0	0.9	4 109	18.6	20.1
13 275	...	Thomas County..............	42 737	6.7	20.4	8.0	28.3	22.5	14.0	36.3	1.4	1.6	24 868	23.1	16.7
13 277	...	Tift County	38 407	7.7	19.7	11.6	28.5	20.9	11.6	33.0	1.7	-0.8	24 161	22.7	14.8
13 279	...	Toombs County	26 067	8.0	20.5	9.3	28.0	22.0	12.2	34.2	2.8	-0.2	17 225	24.1	14.8
13 281	...	Towns County................	9 319	4.5	11.6	9.4	20.4	28.1	25.9	48.6	-9.6	13.5	9 057	15.9	26.5
13 283	...	Treutlen County.............	6 854	7.2	18.5	11.7	27.8	21.3	13.6	33.9	0.0	1.2	4 442	22.9	16.2
13 285	...	Troup County.................	58 779	7.2	20.7	9.5	28.3	21.7	12.6	34.6	2.2	0.2	38 244	24.7	14.8
13 287	...	Turner County	9 504	8.0	21.6	10.4	26.5	20.8	12.8	33.3	3.9	0.4	5 292	23.8	17.8
13 289	4680	Twiggs County	10 590	7.0	20.0	9.7	29.2	22.4	11.7	35.4	1.3	-0.7	5 701	23.4	12.7
13 291	...	Union County	17 289	4.8	14.9	6.7	23.8	28.3	21.6	44.8	-6.0	9.2	16 864	20.0	21.9
13 293	...	Upson County	27 597	6.4	19.2	8.1	28.0	23.5	14.9	37.4	-0.1	2.5	19 299	23.3	17.5
13 295	1560	Walker County	61 053	6.4	18.2	8.5	29.1	23.9	13.8	37.1	-1.1	1.4	57 261	24.4	13.5
13 297	0520	Walton County	60 687	8.1	20.4	8.1	32.4	21.6	9.6	33.9	2.8	-2.8	49 909	27.0	10.3
13 299	...	Ware County	35 483	6.3	18.4	9.4	27.8	22.7	15.5	36.8	-1.0	3.1	24 444	21.9	17.9
13 301	...	Warren County	6 336	7.0	19.4	9.5	24.7	23.3	16.1	37.8	0.7	3.7	2 494	17.4	22.4
13 303	...	Washington County.........	21 176	6.4	20.5	8.8	30.6	21.1	12.7	35.6	1.2	0.3	9 662	22.0	16.1
13 305	...	Wayne County	26 565	6.6	19.0	8.4	31.1	23.5	11.3	35.5	-0.1	-1.1	19 857	24.7	13.1
13 307	...	Webster County	2 390	6.4	18.4	8.7	27.7	24.0	14.7	37.5	-0.9	2.3	1 180	22.3	17.3
13 309	...	Wheeler County	6 179	5.9	16.4	10.6	31.7	22.8	12.6	36.1	-3.4	0.2	3 847	20.8	16.0
13 311	...	White County	19 944	6.2	16.9	9.3	28.2	24.9	14.5	38.3	-2.6	2.1	18 788	22.7	14.9
13 313	...	Whitfield County............	83 525	7.9	19.3	9.9	31.2	21.4	10.4	33.0	1.5	-2.0	60 559	23.9	13.3
13 315	...	Wilcox County	8 577	6.2	16.7	9.9	30.8	22.8	13.6	36.7	-2.8	1.2	5 279	21.2	17.0
13 317	...	Wilkes County	10 687	5.8	18.2	8.0	26.7	23.8	17.5	39.0	-1.7	5.1	5 783	22.0	19.6
13 319	...	Wilkinson County	10 220	7.3	19.8	9.2	28.0	22.4	13.3	35.8	1.4	0.9	5 843	23.1	16.0
13 321	...	Worth County	21 967	7.1	21.6	7.7	27.8	23.7	12.2	35.7	3.0	-0.2	15 050	24.9	13.5
15 000	...	HAWAII	1 211 537	6.4	17.9	9.5	30.1	22.9	13.3	36.2	-1.4	0.9	276 191	16.0	12.9
15 001	...	Hawaii County	148 677	6.0	20.1	8.2	26.6	25.7	13.4	38.6	0.4	1.0	43 845	15.3	15.6
15 003	3320	Honolulu County	876 156	6.4	17.3	10.1	30.7	22.0	13.5	35.7	-2.0	1.1	175 331	16.1	12.6
15 005	...	Kalawao County	147	0.0	0.0	0.0	10.2	40.1	49.7	58.6	-25.7	37.3	14	0.0	0.0
15 007	...	Kauai County	58 463	6.2	20.2	7.1	27.4	25.2	13.9	38.4	0.7	1.5	16 173	16.9	12.9
15 009	...	Maui County..................	128 094	6.6	18.9	7.6	31.0	24.4	11.5	36.8	-0.2	-0.9	40 828	15.8	11.5
16 000	...	IDAHO......................	1 293 953	7.5	20.9	10.7	28.2	21.4	11.3	33.2	2.7	-1.1	1 138 460	27.0	12.3
16 001	1080	Ada County	300 904	7.6	19.5	10.1	32.8	20.8	9.1	32.8	1.4	-3.3	272 487	26.4	9.7
16 003	...	Adams County	3 476	4.2	19.5	5.3	21.8	32.9	16.3	44.4	-2.0	3.9	3 295	23.3	16.9
16 005	6340	Bannock County	75 565	8.1	19.9	14.7	27.2	19.8	10.3	29.8	2.3	-2.1	67 720	27.0	10.7
16 007	...	Bear Lake County	6 411	6.6	26.2	7.3	22.6	21.5	15.8	35.8	7.1	3.4	6 178	32.2	16.3
16 009	...	Benewah County	9 171	6.5	20.3	7.2	25.3	26.3	14.3	39.2	1.1	1.9	8 055	25.1	15.4
16 011	...	Bingham County	41 735	8.8	26.2	9.6	25.7	19.4	10.4	29.7	9.3	-2.0	32 918	32.9	12.0
16 013	...	Blaine County	18 991	6.1	17.9	7.5	32.5	28.4	7.7	37.4	-1.7	-4.7	16 486	22.3	8.7
16 015	...	Boise County	6 670	6.5	20.5	4.9	27.1	30.0	11.1	40.4	1.3	-1.3	6 259	26.6	11.6
16 017	...	Bonner County	36 835	5.7	19.8	6.6	25.5	29.3	13.2	40.8	-0.2	0.8	35 125	24.9	13.6
16 019	...	Bonneville County	82 522	8.2	23.8	9.2	27.5	21.1	10.2	31.8	6.3	-2.2	74 621	31.0	11.0
16 021	...	Boundary County	9 871	7.2	22.0	6.8	24.3	26.3	13.4	38.3	3.5	1.0	9 220	28.5	14.2
16 023	...	Butte County	2 899	6.6	22.4	6.5	23.8	25.9	14.9	38.8	3.3	2.5	2 620	27.1	16.0
16 025	...	Camas County	991	4.5	20.2	7.2	27.7	27.2	13.1	39.7	-1.0	0.7	957	25.3	13.5
16 027	1080	Canyon County	131 441	9.1	21.9	10.7	28.3	19.1	10.9	30.5	5.3	-1.5	102 016	27.8	13.3
16 029	...	Caribou County	7 304	7.5	24.2	8.2	24.6	21.9	13.6	35.0	6.0	1.2	6 952	31.1	14.1
16 031	...	Cassia County...............	21 416	8.2	25.8	9.0	25.4	18.9	12.7	31.1	8.3	0.3	17 029	31.8	14.8
16 033	...	Clark County.................	1 022	8.3	26.5	8.4	30.8	16.7	9.2	30.7	9.1	-3.2	640	30.0	13.9
16 035	...	Clearwater County	8 930	4.8	18.1	5.9	26.4	29.2	15.6	41.7	-2.8	3.2	8 339	22.6	16.1

[1]MSA = Metropolitan Statistical Area. PMSA = Primary MSA. NECMA = New England County Metropolitan Area. See the Appendix A for explanation of these concepts. See Appendix B for list of metropolitan areas identified by type, with component counties.

STATE County	Black or African American Total population	Age (percent) Under 18 years	65 years and over	American Indian and Alaska Native Total population	Age (percent) Under 18 years	65 years and over	Asian, Hawaiian, and Pacific Islander Total population	Age (percent) Under 18 years	65 years and over	Hispanic or Latino[1] Total population	Age (percent) Under 18 years	65 years and over	Two or more races Total population	Age (percent) Under 18 years	65 years and over
	14	15	16	17	18	19	20	21	22	23	24	25	26	27	28
GEORGIA—Cont'd															
Richmond County	98 824	32.2	7.4	596	24.7	7.2	3 235	20.4	3.8	5 637	32.2	3.4	3 912	49.4	3.4
Rockdale County	12 885	36.0	4.7	155	49.0	0.0	1 147	27.3	2.7	4 407	31.6	2.2	905	39.8	3.2
Schley County	1 180	34.5	10.5	3	0.0	33.3	0	X	X	102	55.9	2.0	31	41.9	0.0
Screven County	6 872	32.7	10.2	20	0.0	0.0	43	18.6	0.0	214	33.6	4.7	109	44.0	22.9
Seminole County	3 281	36.7	10.6	9	66.7	0.0	5	0.0	0.0	340	31.5	0.0	26	0.0	38.5
Spalding County	17 996	34.0	6.9	108	8.3	5.6	424	30.9	5.4	968	37.3	3.7	683	47.1	1.2
Stephens County	2 960	28.8	10.1	62	12.9	0.0	141	7.8	19.9	242	34.7	3.7	412	55.3	8.0
Stewart County	3 258	28.7	15.3	10	30.0	0.0	42	16.7	0.0	23	52.2	39.1	17	76.5	0.0
Sumter County	16 277	34.3	8.1	72	40.3	18.1	188	16.5	4.8	853	35.9	0.0	263	50.2	9.9
Talbot County	3 990	27.6	12.3	8	12.5	0.0	0	X	X	35	17.1	54.3	130	13.1	10.8
Taliaferro County	1 241	26.1	14.3	0	X	X	0	X	X	5	0.0	0.0	37	86.5	0.0
Tattnall County	6 901	21.1	6.6	66	42.4	0.0	52	19.2	0.0	1 905	37.0	1.0	361	69.3	1.4
Taylor County	3 830	32.1	10.1	4	50.0	0.0	8	50.0	0.0	86	25.6	0.0	88	40.9	10.2
Telfair County	4 533	25.2	10.0	0	X	X	10	0.0	0.0	230	16.5	0.0	20	15.0	0.0
Terrell County	6 622	35.2	9.2	27	0.0	0.0	87	32.2	11.5	117	15.4	17.1	52	25.0	0.0
Thomas County	16 650	32.8	10.7	117	31.6	11.1	209	34.4	4.8	620	35.5	4.4	353	30.3	3.7
Tift County	10 561	35.3	7.4	76	19.7	5.3	340	38.5	4.7	3 051	35.5	1.6	357	44.3	10.9
Toombs County	6 172	37.5	9.2	113	49.6	0.0	136	21.3	5.1	2 358	37.4	1.8	182	35.2	12.6
Towns County	8	0.0	0.0	2	0.0	0.0	77	45.5	0.0	146	11.6	3.4	29	37.9	13.8
Treutlen County	2 239	31.0	9.2	11	36.4	0.0	58	15.5	6.9	77	23.4	0.0	22	63.6	0.0
Troup County	18 613	33.6	8.9	136	14.0	4.4	445	18.2	1.6	1 029	32.3	3.4	509	60.3	6.9
Turner County	3 902	37.0	6.5	18	16.7	0.0	46	67.4	0.0	255	29.8	7.1	25	0.0	64.0
Twiggs County	4 529	30.4	11.2	8	75.0	0.0	73	20.5	0.0	74	36.5	0.0	256	46.9	2.7
Union County	116	0.0	0.0	42	0.0	35.7	31	0.0	6.5	96	52.0	11.5	140	12.1	5.7
Upson County	7 357	30.1	9.5	172	41.9	0.0	189	29.6	13.8	431	30.4	0.5	203	42.9	3.4
Walker County	2 328	30.5	9.4	151	20.5	4.0	285	20.0	8.8	451	32.2	9.8	668	29.3	23.1
Walton County	8 690	34.8	6.8	155	14.8	4.5	489	33.5	1.0	1 052	41.8	2.2	516	34.7	4.7
Ware County	9 817	30.7	10.3	62	32.3	11.3	115	29.6	14.8	898	30.2	4.6	265	33.6	17.0
Warren County	3 733	31.6	10.0	02	50.0	0.0	7	0.0	0.0	36	72.2	0.0	49	65.3	12.2
Washington County	11 254	30.8	9.9	3	0.0	0.0	22	22.7	13.6	116	38.8	2.6	157	36.3	8.9
Wayne County	5 416	28.3	6.9	102	28.4	0.0	130	26.2	3.8	929	23.7	2.2	312	46.5	7.0
Webster County	1 103	26.2	13.1	0	X	X	0	X	X	105	39.0	0.0	2	0.0	100.0
Wheeler County	2 124	23.4	7.5	2	0.0	0.0	8	0.0	0.0	173	39.3	0.0	42	14.3	2.4
White County	398	23.1	12.3	105	56.2	0.0	90	27.8	0.0	307	35.5	3.9	338	23.4	4.7
Whitfield County	3 158	27.5	8.4	207	31.9	0.0	864	24.7	6.6	18 342	38.0	1.3	1 505	39.1	2.9
Wilcox County	3 180	25.7	8.1	5	40.0	0.0	12	0.0	33.3	91	14.3	2.2	16	81.3	12.5
Wilkes County	4 644	26.0	15.7	25	0.0	0.0	9	44.4	0.0	137	35.8	0.0	101	46.5	0.0
Wilkinson County	4 086	32.6	9.4	30	0.0	93.3	15	0.0	0.0	145	35.9	1.4	164	24.4	1.8
Worth County	6 556	36.5	0.5	10	20.0	0.0	55	14.5	18.2	211	51.2	0.0	103	48.5	4.9
HAWAII	20 945	25.0	2.4	3 216	20.8	4.3	616 511	20.4	17.8	87 582	39.3	4.4	263 587	41.9	5.0
Hawaii County	730	34.2	4.9	619	26.5	2.4	55 935	20.9	19.0	14 055	43.5	4.0	43 578	43.6	4.9
Honolulu County	19 688	24.9	2.2	1 881	16.4	4.5	481 668	19.9	17.7	58 731	38.2	4.2	176 540	41.2	5.2
Kalawao County	0	X	X	15	0.0	100.0	118	0.0	49.2	0	X	X	0	X	X
Kauai County	152	31.6	9.9	236	29.2	5.5	26 243	22.2	19.6	4 920	41.8	8.2	14 055	45.2	4.5
Maui County	375	8.8	6.9	465	27.5	2.2	52 547	23.6	16.2	9 876	38.7	4.6	29 414	42.1	4.2
IDAHO	5 244	35.8	4.4	17 528	34.5	5.0	12 553	23.3	7.7	101 594	41.8	2.2	26 990	44.7	5.0
Ada County	1 835	35.0	5.2	2 324	26.2	3.9	5 151	23.3	4.2	13 498	36.9	1.9	7 136	43.7	3.4
Adams County	2	0.0	0.0	57	24.6	3.5	15	13.3	0.0	61	47.5	4.9	47	36.2	14.9
Bannock County	424	19.6	16.3	2 284	35.6	6.6	936	19.0	9.3	3 560	42.4	3.5	1 342	54.8	3.4
Bear Lake County	5	0.0	0.0	34	52.9	8.8	2	0.0	0.0	187	51.3	1.6	31	67.7	0.0
Benewah County	16	68.8	0.0	857	40.6	6.3	19	0.0	15.8	143	44.8	4.2	139	36.0	10.1
Bingham County	39	35.9	0.0	2 747	38.4	5.1	255	15.7	29.4	5 493	45.5	1.9	826	59.1	8.0
Blaine County	49	10.2	6.1	55	18.2	0.0	273	43.6	0.0	1 998	35.6	0.8	369	36.6	4.9
Boise County	12	100.0	0.0	66	33.3	9.1	14	14.3	14.3	201	35.3	1.5	135	28.1	1.5
Bonner County	53	24.5	0.0	297	36.7	9.4	149	5.4	28.2	694	47.3	3.5	598	41.3	1.7
Bonneville County	510	51.8	0.8	523	36.3	2.7	527	28.3	6.5	5 626	42.0	2.5	1 091	48.2	3.8
Boundary County	4	100.0	0.0	193	27.5	6.2	70	35.7	0.0	278	48.2	0.0	134	37.3	0.0
Butte County	9	55.6	0.0	13	38.5	0.0	8	100.0	0.0	215	48.8	2.8	47	19.1	10.6
Camas County	13	15.4	7.7	2	0.0	0.0	0	X	X	18	11.1	5.6	12	8.3	0.0
Canyon County	337	35.6	4.2	875	36.0	4.6	1 242	23.8	9.3	24 503	42.9	2.0	3 679	47.4	4.8
Caribou County	11	81.8	0.0	23	52.2	0.0	1	0.0	0.0	243	43.2	1.6	110	44.5	4.5
Cassia County	44	70.5	0.0	178	42.1	7.3	109	33.0	38.5	4 007	43.6	3.1	384	40.4	6.8
Clark County	2	0.0	0.0	10	40.0	0.0	0	X	X	364	42.9	1.4	9	77.8	0.0
Clearwater County	7	28.6	0.0	177	23.2	14.1	60	30.0	3.3	158	24.1	1.3	206	32.5	8.7

[1] Hispanic or Latino persons may be of any race.

Table A-3. States and Counties — Age, Ethnicity, and Household Structure

STATE County	Total households	Family households (percent) — Married-couple family households: Total	With children	Householder 65 years or over	Other family households: Total	With children	Householder 65 years or over	Nonfamily households (percent) — Two or more unrelated persons: Total	Householder 65 years or over	Male living alone: Total	Householder 65 years or over	Female living alone: Total	Householder 65 years or over	Percent of householders 65 years and over who live alone	Grandparents who are responsible for the care of their grandchildren
	29	30	31	32	33	34	35	36	37	38	39	40	41	42	43
GEORGIA—Cont'd															
Richmond County	73 939	42.7	19.9	7.1	24.9	14.8	2.9	4.8	0.5	11.1	2.0	16.5	6.6	44.8	3 312
Rockdale County	24 051	63.0	30.5	8.4	16.3	9.5	2.2	3.8	0.4	7.7	1.1	9.2	3.6	29.7	755
Schley County	1 426	50.8	22.4	7.9	22.1	13.5	1.7	2.2	0.9	10.6	1.5	14.4	9.3	50.8	56
Screven County	5 795	50.9	23.5	10.4	20.4	10.5	2.5	2.1	0.1	11.1	3.2	15.5	9.2	48.7	359
Seminole County	3 562	52.2	19.5	10.9	21.1	11.5	4.5	2.4	0.1	9.8	2.6	14.4	9.7	44.3	146
Spalding County	21 523	50.4	21.7	8.1	23.1	12.4	3.1	4.2	0.3	9.3	2.0	13.1	6.8	43.4	904
Stephens County	9 969	57.2	24.2	11.1	13.8	7.7	2.2	3.5	0.6	11.0	2.6	14.5	8.6	44.6	301
Stewart County	2 002	39.2	14.9	9.1	27.9	12.8	4.5	3.2	0.6	13.1	3.6	16.6	9.4	47.7	133
Sumter County	11 990	46.1	20.5	8.0	25.3	15.0	2.5	3.6	0.4	8.8	1.7	16.3	7.3	45.2	447
Talbot County	2 525	47.8	16.2	10.2	24.2	13.3	4.8	2.5	0.4	11.4	3.6	14.1	7.5	41.7	108
Taliaferro County	865	40.0	14.1	10.6	24.3	12.9	4.5	2.8	0.8	13.5	3.2	19.4	12.0	48.9	20
Tattnall County	7 059	51.5	23.9	7.6	17.9	10.3	3.1	3.9	0.0	11.8	3.4	14.9	8.3	52.4	311
Taylor County	3 276	47.0	18.6	9.0	23.1	12.5	3.9	2.5	0.4	11.8	3.1	15.7	8.0	45.5	150
Telfair County	4 151	50.4	22.2	9.6	18.8	9.8	3.6	2.4	0.3	10.8	2.9	17.6	10.0	48.7	194
Terrell County	3 979	43.6	16.8	9.8	29.2	16.0	4.3	2.7	0.3	9.0	1.9	15.6	8.6	42.3	284
Thomas County	16 305	54.1	22.0	9.1	20.7	12.1	3.6	4.1	0.6	9.8	2.3	16.0	9.1	46.2	519
Tift County	13 931	52.7	23.0	8.6	20.2	12.6	2.5	3.8	0.2	9.4	1.6	13.9	7.9	45.5	597
Toombs County	9 870	49.4	22.7	7.4	20.3	12.3	2.7	3.4	0.0	9.9	2.0	17.1	8.7	51.2	473
Towns County	4 005	63.8	17.9	20.9	7.4	3.9	2.0	2.8	0.8	10.6	5.1	15.3	9.1	37.5	57
Treutlen County	2 551	50.0	22.1	9.1	22.0	12.1	4.1	2.7	0.8	9.5	2.4	15.8	9.9	46.6	112
Troup County	21 930	49.2	22.7	8.1	22.3	12.3	3.8	3.6	0.3	9.8	2.0	15.0	7.9	44.7	1 056
Turner County	3 450	50.3	21.9	10.2	24.1	13.8	2.7	2.4	0.1	8.2	2.1	15.0	10.4	49.0	179
Twiggs County	3 802	51.4	22.1	7.9	23.4	11.7	4.6	2.8	0.1	10.2	2.1	12.2	7.3	42.7	207
Union County	7 175	62.4	19.1	19.4	10.2	5.3	1.9	3.3	0.4	9.6	2.5	14.5	9.5	35.4	138
Upson County	10 752	50.9	20.4	9.5	21.6	11.9	3.3	2.4	0.2	9.0	2.7	16.1	9.4	48.3	317
Walker County	23 684	58.7	25.1	10.2	15.8	8.5	2.6	2.8	0.1	7.8	2.2	14.9	8.3	45.1	718
Walton County	21 307	63.7	30.1	8.2	15.9	9.3	2.1	3.8	0.3	7.0	1.1	9.6	5.2	37.7	579
Ware County	13 478	50.6	20.1	10.1	18.6	10.2	3.6	2.8	0.2	10.9	2.7	17.1	9.5	46.9	492
Warren County	2 429	44.5	17.2	10.7	25.2	13.6	3.9	2.8	0.5	12.1	3.4	15.5	7.8	42.7	137
Washington County	7 439	47.3	21.6	8.6	25.3	14.4	4.2	2.6	0.3	9.7	2.0	15.1	8.9	45.4	383
Wayne County	9 348	59.6	27.1	9.3	15.7	8.9	3.0	2.0	0.1	9.8	2.0	12.9	6.6	41.0	328
Webster County	919	51.4	22.4	10.2	22.5	10.2	3.4	2.4	0.2	8.7	3.2	15.0	10.9	50.4	30
Wheeler County	2 022	56.0	23.0	8.5	19.4	10.4	3.1	2.3	0.4	11.1	3.4	16.6	11.7	55.8	130
White County	7 730	64.4	26.1	13.2	10.7	6.3	1.5	3.3	0.4	8.3	1.6	13.4	7.1	36.4	151
Whitfield County	29 362	61.1	29.7	8.1	14.9	7.7	2.2	3.6	0.3	7.7	1.5	12.8	6.7	43.4	858
Wilcox County	2 772	52.2	22.7	9.4	19.0	10.1	4.1	2.2	0.3	11.0	3.1	15.7	9.9	48.7	61
Wilkes County	4 318	48.5	18.8	11.1	20.5	11.8	3.4	2.9	0.0	11.2	4.7	16.9	11.0	52.0	104
Wilkinson County	3 847	50.7	20.2	10.1	22.4	13.2	3.7	2.7	0.5	10.4	2.0	13.7	8.1	41.6	211
Worth County	8 125	56.8	27.1	7.9	19.3	9.9	3.3	2.4	0.6	8.4	2.1	13.1	8.1	46.3	489
HAWAII	403 572	54.5	24.8	11.1	17.1	7.8	3.8	6.6	0.5	10.7	2.3	11.1	4.9	31.8	14 029
Hawaii County	52 945	51.8	22.5	11.3	18.2	10.2	2.7	6.9	0.7	11.6	2.9	11.5	5.2	35.5	1 546
Honolulu County	286 731	55.4	25.3	11.2	16.9	7.0	4.1	6.2	0.5	10.6	2.2	11.0	4.9	30.8	10 302
Kalawao County	132	10.6	0.0	10.6	0.0	0.0	0.0	0.0	0.0	56.1	22.7	33.3	22.0	80.8	0
Kauai County	20 201	55.1	25.2	11.7	17.3	10.0	3.5	6.1	0.7	9.8	1.9	11.6	5.6	32.1	760
Maui County	43 563	52.5	24.0	9.6	16.7	9.2	3.0	8.9	0.5	10.7	2.2	11.2	4.5	33.8	1 421
IDAHO	470 133	59.6	28.9	10.0	12.3	8.0	1.2	5.8	0.3	10.0	2.1	12.3	6.3	42.0	8 110
Ada County	113 577	56.1	28.4	7.2	12.7	8.4	1.0	7.5	0.3	10.6	1.4	13.1	5.6	45.3	1 265
Adams County	1 430	64.3	21.2	15.3	9.3	6.2	1.2	2.9	0.0	13.5	3.6	9.9	5.2	35.0	21
Bannock County	27 214	58.2	28.4	9.2	13.1	8.3	1.5	6.2	0.3	10.4	1.6	12.3	5.8	40.4	421
Bear Lake County	2 269	67.2	32.2	15.2	8.7	5.6	1.5	1.6	0.3	9.9	4.6	12.6	9.6	45.6	28
Benewah County	3 578	59.2	24.7	11.6	12.1	7.2	1.2	4.7	0.7	12.9	4.2	11.1	6.6	44.5	83
Bingham County	13 311	67.7	36.6	11.5	13.6	9.1	1.4	1.6	0.1	7.9	1.9	9.2	5.4	35.8	459
Blaine County	7 757	53.5	25.5	6.7	8.9	5.9	0.4	10.1	0.3	13.4	2.1	14.1	3.0	40.3	16
Boise County	2 608	62.5	23.5	11.3	10.4	7.1	1.0	5.4	0.8	12.7	2.5	9.0	3.8	32.2	66
Bonner County	14 760	58.7	22.9	11.5	11.2	8.2	0.9	6.1	0.6	12.0	2.7	11.9	5.7	39.3	280
Bonneville County	28 742	62.6	33.1	9.8	12.2	8.2	1.1	3.8	0.2	9.3	1.9	12.1	6.0	41.6	315
Boundary County	3 702	62.9	24.9	12.4	12.8	9.0	1.7	4.2	0.5	12.0	2.4	11.1	5.6	35.4	108
Butte County	1 086	63.2	27.3	14.1	11.0	6.5	1.7	2.6	0.6	10.3	2.6	13.0	7.2	37.2	24
Camas County	398	57.3	25.6	14.1	6.3	3.8	1.0	4.5	0.0	12.1	0.8	9.8	8.0	36.8	0
Canyon County	45 065	62.0	31.6	9.8	13.9	9.2	1.4	4.4	0.4	7.8	1.8	11.8	6.7	42.5	1 094
Caribou County	2 547	69.2	34.3	13.3	8.0	5.9	0.6	2.3	0.2	9.4	2.6	11.1	6.8	39.8	52
Cassia County	7 108	66.6	36.1	12.6	11.6	7.9	1.4	2.4	0.2	8.6	2.4	10.7	6.8	39.5	83
Clark County	339	61.9	37.8	9.4	13.9	9.4	0.0	4.4	0.6	9.7	1.5	10.0	6.8	45.2	4
Clearwater County	3 444	61.0	22.1	13.8	11.2	7.3	1.5	3.8	0.6	12.1	2.8	11.9	7.9	40.3	54

Table A-3. States and Counties — Age, Ethnicity, and Household Structure

STATE County	Households with Non-Hispanic White householder — Number of households	Percent that are family households	Households with Black or African American householder — Number of households	Percent that are family households	Households with American Indian and Alaska Native householder — Number of households	Percent that are family households	Households with Asian, Hawaiian, and Pacific Islander householder — Number of households	Percent that are family households	Households with Hispanic or Latino[1] householder — Number of households	Percent that are family households	Foreign-born population — Percent of total population that is foreign-born	Place of birth (percent) Europe	Asia	Latin America	Percent in non-English speaking households — Linguistically isolated	Not linguistically isolated
	44	45	46	47	48	49	50	51	52	53	54	55	56	57	58	59
GEORGIA—Cont'd																
Richmond County.........	37 278	61.7	33 470	73.8	265	56.6	944	72.5	1 514	75.4	3.4	1.0	1.2	0.9	0.7	11.2
Rockdale County..........	18 486	78.1	4 048	83.2	30	100.0	332	90.1	955	81.4	7.6	0.9	1.4	4.9	3.6	11.3
Schley County.............	971	72.2	424	72.9	3	66.7	0	X	21	90.5	1.8	0.8	0.0	1.0	0.6	7.6
Screven County...........	3 396	69.3	2 337	73.7	6	100.0	8	100.0	42	83.3	1.7	0.4	0.6	0.7	0.7	8.0
Seminole County..........	2 430	72.5	1 068	75.8	3	100.0	1	100.0	45	51.1	1.1	0.2	0.0	0.6	0.5	6.4
Spalding County..........	15 042	72.6	5 921	74.6	4	100.0	134	74.6	254	83.9	2.2	0.2	0.8	1.0	1.0	5.6
Stephens County.........	8 555	71.8	1 180	65.0	30	43.3	49	71.4	69	88.4	1.4	0.3	0.3	0.6	0.5	5.6
Stewart County............	792	66.0	1 191	67.4	0	X	15	86.7	0	X	1.6	0.4	0.8	0.4	0.4	5.1
Sumter County	6 259	69.2	5 362	72.6	13	100.0	71	100.0	234	91.9	2.0	0.1	0.5	1.3	1.4	8.0
Talbot County..............	1 002	73.5	1 484	70.8	0	X	0	X	24	29.2	0.7	0.6	0.0	0.1	0.0	5.1
Taliaferro County.........	362	57.5	500	69.0	0	X	0	X	3	100.0	0.5	0.4	0.0	0.1	0.0	3.3
Tattnall County............	5 155	69.1	1 453	69.8	21	61.9	16	43.8	391	75.7	5.8	0.2	0.1	5.3	4.7	9.9
Taylor County..............	1 902	72.0	1 331	67.9	2	100.0	2	100.0	19	57.9	1.0	0.0	0.1	0.7	0.1	6.1
Telfair County.............	2 751	71.5	1 347	64.7	0	X	0	X	57	66.7	1.1	0.3	0.0	0.7	0.4	6.3
Terrell County.............	1 740	69.6	2 173	75.6	27	33.3	10	100.0	25	80.0	1.7	0.4	0.8	0.4	0.4	6.4
Thomas County............	10 168	70.0	5 780	70.1	34	94.1	65	90.8	152	78.3	1.4	0.2	0.4	0.8	1.1	6.1
Tift County..................	9 588	71.6	3 539	74.2	42	76.2	74	100.0	601	83.5	5.5	0.3	0.8	4.4	3.4	8.8
Toombs County............	7 080	69.0	2 194	69.0	25	92.0	29	100.0	507	80.7	5.9	0.2	0.3	5.2	3.3	11.1
Towns County.............	3 927	71.7	0	X	2	0.0	24	70.8	36	38.9	2.7	1.1	0.6	1.0	1.1	6.1
Treutlen County...........	1 771	71.6	740	73.4	0	X	21	47.6	11	100.0	1.9	0.3	0.7	0.9	0.7	7.8
Troup County...............	14 878	72.1	6 532	70.1	64	100.0	101	68.3	271	69.4	2.0	0.3	0.6	0.9	0.8	6.5
Turner County.............	2 175	73.4	1 213	75.1	0	X	2	100.0	59	100.0	2.4	0.6	0.1	1.7	1.8	8.6
Twiggs County	2 197	76.0	1 515	73.6	2	0.0	19	89.5	19	52.6	0.8	0.1	0.5	0.2	0.0	5.6
Union County...............	7 028	73.1	0	X	11	100.0	10	0.0	54	55.6	1.3	0.7	0.2	0.3	0.1	3.6
Upson County..............	7 714	72.8	2 778	70.8	50	100.0	29	100.0	131	80.9	2.0	0.5	0.5	1.0	0.6	6.1
Walker County.............	22 499	74.5	770	79.7	27	77.8	83	67.5	113	63.7	1.0	0.2	0.4	0.3	0.4	6.3
Walton County.............	17 892	79.9	2 881	77.5	56	73.2	86	86.0	292	85.6	2.0	0.5	0.6	0.7	0.6	8.5
Ware County...............	9 035	69.0	3 018	67.4	20	100.0	28	100.0	216	69.9	1.8	0.2	0.2	1.2	1.2	6.1
Warren County	1 089	68.6	1 318	70.8	2	0.0	5	60.0	5	100.0	0.5	0.2	0.1	0.1	0.3	7.1
Washington County.......	3 671	72.9	3 716	72.2	0	X	21	81.0	21	81.0	0.5	0.2	0.2	0.2	0.1	4.4
Wayne County..............	7 487	76.2	1 493	71.8	36	94.4	40	62.5	214	68.2	1.5	0.4	0.3	0.8	1.0	7.2
Webster County...........	480	73.5	418	74.9	0	X	0	X	19	57.9	2.0	0.1	0.0	1.9	0.4	9.9
Wheeler County	1 443	68.6	515	75.5	2	100.0	6	0.0	47	63.8	1.9	0.1	0.1	1.7	1.4	5.0
White County...............	7 382	75.1	121	60.3	34	88.2	28	92.9	52	96.2	2.0	0.9	0.3	0.7	0.9	7.3
Whitfield County	23 507	73.4	1 132	68.0	59	100.0	268	89.9	4 217	91.2	16.6	0.3	1.0	15.1	11.5	14.6
Wilcox County	1 941	72.5	805	67.8	2	100.0	0	X	24	75.0	0.8	0.0	0.2	0.7	0.1	4.0
Wilkes County	2 384	71.9	1 875	65.7	4	100.0	5	100.0	36	27.8	1.3	0.3	0.0	0.8	0.8	4.6
Wilkinson County	2 423	71.8	1 338	74.7	10	100.0	8	100.0	28	89.3	1.4	0.1	0.2	1.1	0.3	5.5
Worth County	5 870	76.6	2 162	74.8	0	X	25	44.0	42	81.0	1.0	0.2	0.2	0.5	0.2	2.9
HAWAII..................	122 694	62.7	7 327	73.5	1 109	69.8	201 643	75.6	21 490	76.0	17.5	0.9	14.6	0.6	5.8	34.5
Hawaii County	20 843	62.0	251	74.5	250	58.8	19 707	74.7	3 431	76.8	10.2	1.0	7.2	0.6	3.5	25.5
Honolulu County	75 887	63.8	6 887	73.9	620	75.6	156 354	75.4	14 303	75.8	19.2	0.8	16.4	0.5	6.4	36.8
Kalawao County	14	0.0	0	X	15	0.0	103	13.6	0	X	20.4	0.0	10.2	0.0	20.4	19.7
Kauai County	7 354	63.0	53	52.8	70	55.7	9 003	78.2	1 208	77.9	13.0	0.7	11.2	0.2	3.4	28.8
Maui County	18 596	59.3	136	61.0	154	77.3	16 476	77.5	2 548	75.0	16.5	1.2	12.6	1.1	5.5	32.0
IDAHO	428 555	71.3	1 492	62.5	5 462	76.2	3 911	65.5	25 016	83.1	5.0	0.9	0.6	3.0	2.2	12.3
Ada County	105 276	68.9	569	50.3	767	75.0	1 759	66.2	3 636	71.1	4.3	1.6	1.2	1.1	1.5	11.2
Adams County.............	1 367	73.8	2	100.0	25	84.0	3	100.0	12	66.7	1.7	0.8	0.1	0.2	0.6	7.4
Bannock County...........	24 792	71.0	194	55.2	693	78.8	282	57.1	999	79.1	2.2	0.5	0.8	0.6	0.7	11.1
Bear Lake County	2 206	76.2	5	0.0	5	100.0	0	X	49	73.5	1.1	0.4	0.0	0.6	0.5	7.5
Benewah County	3 231	70.3	2	100.0	254	80.7	7	85.7	40	85.0	0.6	0.4	0.0	0.1	0.1	7.8
Bingham County...........	10 949	80.6	7	100.0	831	81.9	123	76.4	1 307	88.1	6.1	0.2	0.2	5.4	3.6	16.8
Blaine County..............	7 037	61.7	15	66.7	11	54.5	64	57.8	557	74.7	10.6	2.5	0.9	6.4	3.9	12.7
Boise County...............	2 514	73.1	0	X	25	84.0	3	100.0	33	63.6	2.4	0.8	0.1	1.1	0.6	7.9
Bonner County	14 275	69.8	12	100.0	82	50.0	64	79.7	165	76.4	2.0	0.8	0.3	0.2	0.2	6.8
Bonneville County	26 687	74.5	118	88.1	120	84.2	190	60.0	1 414	80.1	3.9	0.4	0.4	2.8	1.7	11.3
Boundary County	3 518	72.9	0	X	97	71.1	16	100.0	39	46.2	2.9	1.1	0.4	0.4	0.6	10.7
Butte County	1 024	73.4	2	100.0	2	100.0	0	X	51	82.4	3.9	0.6	0.2	2.9	3.1	6.1
Camas County	390	73.1	1	100.0	2	100.0	0	X	4	100.0	1.8	0.3	0.1	1.2	0.0	6.0
Canyon County............	37 993	74.1	114	69.3	240	72.1	367	70.8	5 692	89.4	8.6	0.7	0.6	7.2	4.9	19.0
Caribou County	2 443	77.2	2	100.0	10	100.0	1	100.0	70	74.3	1.8	0.5	0.0	1.3	0.9	9.3
Cassia County	5 879	77.5	0	X	26	100.0	54	44.4	1 098	84.6	7.3	0.5	0.1	6.5	5.7	19.1
Clark County	246	71.5	0	X	4	50.0	0	X	89	88.8	28.2	0.3	0.0	27.7	22.0	21.1
Clearwater County	3 270	71.8	0	X	74	86.5	14	85.7	31	77.4	1.2	0.3	0.4	0.3	0.3	7.1

[1]Hispanic or Latino persons may be of any race.

STATE/ County code	MSA/PMSA/ NECMA code[1]	STATE County	Total population	Population by age (percent)						Median age	+/– U.S. percent under 18 years	+/– U.S. percent 65 years and over	Non-Hispanic White		
				Under 5 years	5 to 17 years	18 to 24 years	25 to 44 years	45 to 64 years	65 years and over				Total population	Under 18 years	65 years and over
			1	2	3	4	5	6	7	8	9	10	11	12	13
		IDAHO—Cont'd													
16 037	...	Custer County	4 342	5.3	20.4	5.0	25.6	29.3	14.4	41.2	0.0	2.0	4 096	24.9	15.1
16 039	...	Elmore County	29 130	8.2	19.6	13.7	36.5	15.0	7.1	29.1	2.1	-5.3	23 273	25.3	8.3
16 041	...	Franklin County	11 329	9.7	27.5	9.2	24.5	17.4	11.7	27.7	11.5	-0.7	10 585	36.7	12.4
16 043	...	Fremont County	11 819	7.6	25.5	9.5	24.9	20.1	12.5	31.9	7.4	0.1	10 275	31.5	13.7
16 045	...	Gem County	15 181	7.0	20.9	8.4	24.4	23.6	15.7	37.5	2.2	3.3	13 676	26.3	16.9
16 047	...	Gooding County	14 155	7.6	22.1	8.4	25.9	20.5	15.5	35.1	4.0	3.1	11 400	27.0	18.5
16 049	...	Idaho County	15 511	5.2	19.7	6.5	23.6	28.3	16.7	42.3	-0.8	4.3	14 492	24.0	17.5
16 051	...	Jefferson County	19 155	8.7	27.5	9.8	25.1	19.6	9.3	28.8	10.5	-3.1	16 932	35.0	10.2
16 053	...	Jerome County	18 342	8.1	23.6	8.7	27.0	20.3	12.3	32.9	6.0	-0.1	14 695	28.8	14.6
16 055	...	Kootenai County	108 685	6.8	20.3	8.6	28.2	23.8	12.3	36.1	1.4	-0.1	102 180	26.4	12.8
16 057	...	Latah County	34 935	5.4	14.8	23.9	27.2	19.2	9.4	27.9	-5.5	-3.0	32 298	19.8	9.9
16 059	...	Lemhi County	7 806	5.1	20.4	5.6	22.8	29.3	16.7	42.7	-0.2	4.3	7 482	25.2	17.3
16 061	...	Lewis County	3 747	4.9	20.2	5.6	23.0	27.9	18.4	42.5	-0.6	6.0	3 414	24.1	19.6
16 063	...	Lincoln County	4 044	7.6	22.9	8.7	25.7	21.8	13.2	34.3	4.8	0.8	3 356	28.8	15.1
16 065	...	Madison County	27 467	7.1	19.0	39.9	15.9	12.0	6.0	20.7	0.4	-6.4	25 939	25.6	6.2
16 067	...	Minidoka County	20 174	8.0	23.6	9.2	25.9	20.2	13.1	33.5	5.9	0.7	14 566	27.7	16.7
16 069	...	Nez Perce County	37 410	6.0	17.7	10.1	26.6	22.8	16.8	38.1	-2.0	4.4	34 026	22.5	17.7
16 071	...	Oneida County	4 125	7.4	24.6	7.6	22.9	21.5	16.0	36.0	6.3	3.6	3 963	31.3	16.7
16 073	...	Owyhee County	10 644	7.7	23.7	8.8	26.6	20.9	12.3	32.9	5.7	-0.1	7 593	27.8	15.5
16 075	...	Payette County	20 578	7.4	22.9	7.7	26.9	21.8	13.3	34.4	4.6	0.9	17 400	28.4	14.9
16 077	...	Power County	7 538	8.2	25.6	8.6	24.9	22.6	10.2	31.6	8.1	-2.2	5 615	29.9	13.1
16 079	...	Shoshone County	13 771	5.6	17.4	6.8	25.7	27.1	17.4	41.8	-2.7	5.0	13 141	22.6	17.8
16 081	...	Teton County	5 999	8.6	23.2	7.9	34.4	18.4	7.4	31.3	6.1	-5.0	5 217	30.1	8.5
16 083	...	Twin Falls County	64 284	7.4	20.5	10.6	26.0	21.4	14.1	34.9	2.2	1.7	56 348	26.2	15.6
16 085	...	Valley County	7 651	4.1	19.5	4.1	25.1	32.4	14.7	43.5	-2.1	2.3	7 345	23.3	15.2
16 087	...	Washington County	9 977	6.9	20.3	7.3	24.2	24.2	17.2	39.2	1.5	4.8	8 236	25.1	20.0
17 000	...	**ILLINOIS**	12 419 293	7.0	19.1	9.7	30.7	21.4	12.1	34.7	0.4	-0.3	8 423 408	22.8	14.9
17 001	...	Adams County	68 277	6.2	18.8	9.0	26.4	22.1	17.6	38.3	-0.7	5.2	64 618	24.2	18.2
17 003	...	Alexander County	9 590	6.3	19.6	7.4	26.1	23.8	16.8	38.0	0.2	4.4	5 961	21.7	21.5
17 005	...	Bond County	17 633	5.6	16.3	11.6	29.7	22.3	14.6	36.8	-3.8	2.2	15 842	22.7	15.7
17 007	6880	Boone County	41 786	7.4	22.4	7.8	29.9	21.8	10.7	34.5	4.1	-1.7	35 564	27.9	12.1
17 009	...	Brown County	6 950	4.0	13.7	12.6	37.7	19.4	12.7	35.2	-8.0	0.3	5 417	22.5	16.2
17 011	...	Bureau County	35 503	5.9	18.9	7.4	26.4	23.7	17.7	39.6	-0.9	5.3	33 171	23.7	18.5
17 013	...	Calhoun County	5 084	5.3	17.7	7.6	26.2	24.0	19.1	40.5	-2.7	6.7	5 002	23.3	19.2
17 015	...	Carroll County	16 674	5.6	18.8	6.6	25.4	24.5	19.2	40.8	-1.3	6.8	16 047	23.6	19.7
17 017	...	Cass County	13 695	6.7	18.6	8.6	28.0	22.5	15.6	37.2	-0.4	3.2	12 326	24.0	17.2
17 019	1400	Champaign County	179 669	5.8	15.3	23.0	28.3	17.8	9.8	28.6	-4.6	-2.6	139 527	19.6	11.5
17 021	...	Christian County	35 372	6.0	18.0	7.5	28.5	22.6	17.3	38.9	-1.7	4.9	33 880	24.3	17.9
17 023	...	Clark County	17 008	5.9	18.9	7.1	26.8	23.2	17.9	39.2	-0.9	5.5	16 774	24.6	18.1
17 025	...	Clay County	14 560	5.9	18.1	8.1	25.8	23.0	19.2	39.7	-1.7	6.8	14 373	23.8	19.4
17 027	7040	Clinton County	35 535	6.0	18.9	9.1	30.5	21.1	14.5	36.6	-0.8	2.1	33 245	25.4	15.1
17 029	...	Coles County	53 196	5.3	14.4	23.3	24.1	19.6	13.3	30.8	-6.0	0.9	50 350	19.4	13.8
17 031	1600	Cook County	5 376 741	7.2	18.7	9.8	31.9	20.6	11.7	33.6	0.2	-0.7	2 557 658	18.8	17.2
17 033	...	Crawford County	20 452	5.5	17.4	8.7	28.8	22.9	16.7	38.6	-2.8	4.3	18 826	23.4	17.8
17 035	...	Cumberland County	11 253	6.4	20.3	8.1	27.5	21.9	15.9	37.2	1.0	3.5	11 087	26.5	16.0
17 037	1600	DeKalb County	88 969	6.3	17.0	21.8	27.8	17.4	9.8	28.4	-2.4	-2.6	75 874	22.7	11.2
17 039	...	De Witt County	16 798	6.1	18.4	7.8	28.2	23.5	15.9	38.5	-1.2	3.5	16 351	24.4	16.1
17 041	...	Douglas County	19 922	6.9	20.2	8.1	26.8	22.0	16.0	37.4	1.4	3.6	18 921	26.5	16.8
17 043	1600	DuPage County	904 161	7.2	19.4	8.2	32.6	22.8	9.7	35.2	0.9	-2.7	711 651	25.2	11.5
17 045	...	Edgar County	19 704	5.8	18.1	8.2	26.8	23.4	17.8	39.3	-1.8	5.4	19 145	24.0	18.1
17 047	...	Edwards County	6 971	5.6	17.5	7.9	26.2	24.4	18.5	40.5	-2.6	6.1	6 846	22.8	18.7
17 049	...	Effingham County	34 264	7.2	21.4	8.3	28.2	21.1	13.9	35.7	2.9	1.5	33 593	28.3	14.1
17 051	...	Fayette County	21 802	6.0	17.7	9.3	29.2	21.9	15.9	37.5	-2.0	3.5	20 398	25.0	16.8
17 053	...	Ford County	14 241	6.6	19.3	7.0	26.2	21.6	19.4	39.4	0.2	7.0	13 862	25.4	19.8
17 055	...	Franklin County	39 018	5.7	17.3	7.8	26.1	24.3	18.6	40.3	-2.7	6.2	38 188	22.8	18.8
17 057	...	Fulton County	38 250	5.6	16.4	8.6	28.1	23.0	18.3	39.2	-3.7	5.9	36 146	22.8	19.2
17 059	...	Gallatin County	6 445	5.3	16.9	8.3	25.3	26.2	18.0	40.7	-3.5	5.6	6 277	22.0	18.4
17 061	...	Greene County	14 761	6.3	19.1	9.0	26.4	21.8	17.5	37.9	-0.3	5.1	14 450	25.5	17.8
17 063	1600	Grundy County	37 535	6.7	20.1	8.5	30.1	22.4	12.2	36.3	1.1	-0.2	35 255	25.8	12.9
17 065	...	Hamilton County	8 621	5.7	18.3	8.0	24.8	24.0	19.2	40.6	-1.7	6.8	8 409	23.5	19.3
17 067	...	Hancock County	20 121	5.6	19.0	7.2	25.5	24.5	18.2	40.3	-1.1	5.8	19 869	24.6	18.3
17 069	...	Hardin County	4 800	5.7	14.8	7.8	26.3	26.8	18.6	42.1	-5.2	6.2	4 532	20.3	19.4
17 071	...	Henderson County	8 213	5.8	17.5	7.5	26.0	26.5	16.7	41.0	-2.4	4.3	8 024	23.0	16.9
17 073	1960	Henry County	51 020	6.0	19.3	7.7	26.4	24.2	16.4	39.1	-0.4	4.0	48 385	24.3	17.0
17 075	...	Iroquois County	31 334	6.2	19.3	7.1	25.6	23.7	18.1	39.6	-0.2	5.7	29 583	24.5	19.0

[1]MSA = Metropolitan Statistical Area. PMSA = Primary MSA. NECMA = New England County Metropolitan Area. See the Appendix A for explanation of these concepts. See Appendix B for list of metropolitan areas identified by type, with component counties.

STATE County	Black or African American			American Indian and Alaska Native			Asian, Hawaiian, and Pacific Islander			Hispanic or Latino[1]			Two or more races		
	Total population	Under 18 years	65 years and over	Total population	Under 18 years	65 years and over	Total population	Under 18 years	65 years and over	Total population	Under 18 years	65 years and over	Total population	Under 18 years	65 years and over
	14	15	16	17	18	19	20	21	22	23	24	25	26	27	28
IDAHO—Cont'd															
Custer County	0	X	X	16	0.0	0.0	0	X	X	195	43.6	0.0	52	38.5	13.5
Elmore County	951	28.4	1.1	236	47.5	0.0	524	19.8	5.9	3 483	41.0	1.8	937	47.0	3.3
Franklin County	1	100.0	0.0	33	24.2	0.0	20	55.0	0.0	590	44.1	1.4	180	55.6	2.2
Fremont County	12	100.0	0.0	63	17.5	0.0	25	0.0	0.0	1 303	46.8	1.8	229	45.9	13.1
Gem County	0	X	X	179	29.1	0.0	95	33.7	7.4	1 070	47.2	3.8	273	56.8	4.8
Gooding County	14	100.0	0.0	44	27.3	15.9	36	11.1	19.4	2 422	41.6	1.2	407	37.8	11.8
Idaho County	0	X	X	478	38.1	3.3	40	17.5	25.0	216	38.4	0.0	269	42.0	11.2
Jefferson County	67	61.2	0.0	139	51.8	3.6	33	45.5	0.0	1 920	45.1	1.2	276	47.1	6.9
Jerome County	80	67.5	0.0	157	41.4	1.3	69	20.3	43.5	3 159	44.3	1.8	418	44.5	6.9
Kootenai County	255	52.2	0.0	1 393	31.4	5.2	624	33.8	8.2	2 485	39.1	2.6	1 986	44.3	1.9
Latah County	127	0.0	9.4	246	14.6	2.4	758	21.8	2.8	778	30.1	1.0	824	36.0	6.1
Lemhi County	3	100.0	0.0	20	04.0	0.0	8	37.5	0.0	160	40.6	5.0	133	18.0	4.5
Lewis County	9	0.0	0.0	144	21.5	11.1	13	46.2	7.7	92	46.7	0.0	85	54.1	2.4
Lincoln County	29	27.6	0.0	46		6.5	25	44.0	8.0	550	41.6	2.5	85	31.8	9.4
Madison County	64	75.0	0.0	102	32.4	0.0	214	7.0	15.0	947	37.1	2.3	240	46.7	0.4
Minidoka County	31	35.5	0.0	113	41.6	0.9	55	10.9	7.3	5 197	42.1	3.3	555	51.0	5.6
Nez Perce County	123	33.3	12.2	1 854	39.8	5.3	321	17.1	5.6	652	38.3	8.7	551	34.7	11.8
Oneida County	5	100.0	0.0	9	0.0	0.0	8	0.0	0.0	130	49.2	0.0	14	71.4	0.0
Owyhee County	16	0.0	0.0	358	34.6	5.6	66	13.6	34.8	2 447	42.0	2.7	299	43.8	9.0
Payette County	5	40.0	0.0	171	30.4	0.0	148	16.2	37.8	2 438	45.0	1.4	636	43.2	7.9
Power County	0	X	X	283	37.5	1.1	7	0.0	42.9	1 607	47.9	1.7	91	29.7	0.0
Shoshone County	13	38.5	0.0	151	23.2	6.0	40	27.5	2.5	183	32.2	14.8	254	38.6	10.6
Teton County	6	0.0	0.0	26	34.6	0.0	20	40.0	0.0	700	44.3	0.0	29	37.9	0.0
Twin Falls County	53	24.5	0.0	473	30.7	7.0	432	23.4	6.9	6 130	41.4	2.1	1 380	41.5	10.7
Valley County	0	X	X	45	15.6	0.0	33	36.4	21.2	124	35.5	3.2	116	36.2	0.0
Washington County	8	0.0	100.0	26	19.2	0.0	108	15.7	8.3	1 369	39.6	2.3	376	45.7	5.3
ILLINOIS	1 864 619	32.3	8.3	30 407	29.2	4.1	427 251	23.3	6.1	1 529 141	36.0	3.1	249 431	41.2	5.0
Adams County	2 012	34.0	8.0	117	29.1	7.7	209	22.5	6.2	617	45.2	1.9	727	47.3	5.2
Alexander County	3 345	33.1	9.0	13	0.0	0.0	44	45.5	13.9	144	22.9	13.9	101	44.6	6.9
Bond County	1 307	10.6	4.1	110	20.9	0.0	16	0.0	18.8	259	26.3	3.1	150	50.0	10.7
Boone County	170	30.6	1.2	90	28.9	0.0	131	23.7	10.7	5 287	40.8	2.0	966	52.8	2.9
Brown County	1 246	0.0	0.0	7	0.0	0.0	10	0.0	0.0	263	2.3	0.0	17	23.5	35.3
Bureau County	65	53.8	9.2	90	21.1	7.8	206	21.4	1.5	1 690	41.4	7.4	428	45.8	7.9
Calhoun County	0	X	X	18	0.0	0.0	9	0.0	0.0	35	8.6	34.3	22	9.1	0.0
Carroll County	88	34.1	17.0	30	46.7	0.0	61	23.0	0.0	297	49.2	6.1	154	48.1	7.1
Cass County	27	40.7	0.0	15	0.0	0.0	51	31.4	3.9	1 207	36.5	1.2	125	31.2	4.0
Champaign County	20 064	32.9	6.3	390	31.8	7.4	11 631	12.5	1.8	4 933	19.3	2.0	3 470	39.9	1.5
Christian County	786	8.1	3.3	68	16.2	11.0	220	33.2	6.8	269	13.4	1.1	157	45.9	5.1
Clark County	20	90.0	0.0	20	10.0	0.0	27	0.0	0.0	31	19.4	12.9	136	47.8	2.2
Clay County	0	X	X	18	50.0	0.0	72	27.8	12.5	76	48.7	0.0	27	29.6	11.1
Clinton County	1 444	11.5	1.8	47	6.4	6.4	100	24.0	14.0	561	25.7	9.3	158	40.5	9.5
Coles County	1 324	25.6	2.9	97	14.4	6.2	389	15.7	7.7	654	20.9	5.0	485	44.9	4.9
Cook County	1 399 451	31.9	9.1	14 419	31.5	4.6	262 592	21.6	7.1	1 071 241	35.5	3.4	142 129	36.2	5.6
Crawford County	924	6.1	0.0	6	0.0	0.0	88	21.6	8.0	416	24.5	1.7	237	41.4	18.1
Cumberland County	23	47.8	21.7	33	60.6	0.0	17	11.8	11.8	65	43.1	0.0	55	32.7	10.9
DeKalb County	3 969	18.3	2.4	140	21.4	3.6	2 238	16.0	0.4	5 652	32.9	1.5	1 781	43.3	2.8
De Witt County	40	0.0	20.0	16	31.3	25.0	44	36.4	0.0	203	29.1	2.5	147	36.7	10.9
Douglas County	30	10.0	0.0	39	23.1	0.0	72	27.8	0.0	746	39.9	1.7	138	29.7	0.0
DuPage County	27 003	32.6	2.6	1 574	29.5	0.8	71 547	27.0	4.5	81 055	34.8	2.2	16 698	44.6	4.2
Edgar County	254	0.8	3.1	53	20.8	13.2	12	16.7	66.7	138	18.8	5.8	114	44.7	20.2
Edwards County	7	0.0	28.6	11	0.0	9.1	40	20.0	0.0	16	62.5	0.0	36	41.7	22.2
Effingham County	53	79.2	0.0	77	36.4	0.0	136	34.6	0.0	313	33.2	3.5	107	48.6	11.2
Fayette County	1 105	0.0	0.0	33	42.4	24.2	19	42.1	0.0	179	25.7	5.0	64	10.9	42.2
Ford County	81	34.6	0.0	2	50.0	0.0	61	26.2	14.8	166	53.6	0.0	96	54.2	5.2
Franklin County	51	5.9	17.6	107	15.0	27.1	40	55.0	7.5	367	49.9	2.7	332	23.5	7.5
Fulton County	1 398	2.2	2.5	51	43.1	3.9	46	21.7	0.0	447	15.2	4.9	235	37.4	7.2
Gallatin County	15	46.7	33.3	52	28.8	0.0	16	37.5	18.8	80	35.0	0.0	26	0.0	7.7
Greene County	111	7.2	0.0	47	8.5	0.0	16	18.8	25.0	70	45.7	0.0	77	39.0	13.0
Grundy County	69	49.3	0.0	71	22.5	0.0	108	14.8	6.5	1 812	44.0	2.1	393	51.4	2.3
Hamilton County	21	71.4	0.0	71	67.6	0.0	19	0.0	31.6	27	25.9	25.9	78	32.1	25.6
Hancock County	22	36.4	0.0	49	38.8	12.2	22	31.8	0.0	63	11.1	19.0	97	20.6	16.5
Hardin County	135	9.6	6.7	0	X	X	31	32.3	6.5	64	48.4	3.1	52	48.1	3.8
Henderson County	44	63.6	0.0	28	28.6	17.9	9	77.8	22.2	46	21.7	8.7	64	31.3	4.7
Henry County	497	32.4	7.8	58	41.4	0.0	117	37.6	3.4	1 386	46.5	3.1	802	51.5	4.5
Iroquois County	290	54.1	9.7	39	48.7	2.6	112	30.4	0.9	1 043	42.7	1.9	332	36.1	2.7

[1]Hispanic or Latino persons may be of any race.

STATE County	Total households	Married-couple family households			Other family households			Two or more unrelated persons		Male living alone		Female living alone		Percent of householders 65 years and over who live alone	Grandparents who are responsible for the care of their grandchildren
		Total	With children	Householder 65 years or over	Total	With children	Householder 65 years or over	Total	Householder 65 years or over	Total	Householder 65 years or over	Total	Householder 65 years or over		
	29	30	31	32	33	34	35	36	37	38	39	40	41	42	43
IDAHO—Cont'd															
Custer County	1 766	59.5	25.8	11.4	8.0	5.9	1.0	4.4	0.2	15.2	5.0	12.9	7.5	49.8	18
Elmore County	9 096	63.0	34.1	7.4	12.3	8.8	0.8	4.1	0.1	11.4	1.7	9.1	3.9	40.7	177
Franklin County	3 487	74.5	43.3	13.4	8.4	4.8	1.6	0.9	0.1	6.4	1.8	9.8	6.6	35.7	57
Fremont County	3 892	70.7	35.5	14.6	7.9	5.3	1.5	2.3	0.3	8.1	2.5	11.0	6.7	36.0	73
Gem County	5 530	64.0	28.2	14.0	11.5	6.3	2.3	3.7	0.4	8.6	3.0	12.2	7.4	38.2	159
Gooding County	5 067	63.2	30.8	14.0	11.1	7.6	1.0	3.9	0.5	8.6	3.4	13.2	8.7	43.8	155
Idaho County	6 089	60.3	23.7	14.4	10.7	6.8	1.5	4.0	0.4	12.0	4.1	13.0	7.4	41.3	153
Jefferson County	5 901	73.6	42.2	11.5	9.2	5.2	1.3	1.8	0.2	6.3	1.6	9.0	6.3	37.6	98
Jerome County	6 299	65.2	32.9	12.1	11.4	7.9	1.1	4.0	0.4	9.1	2.8	10.3	6.7	40.8	149
Kootenai County	41 380	59.1	26.7	10.5	13.4	9.0	1.4	5.7	0.3	9.4	2.0	12.4	6.3	40.7	723
Latah County	13 063	52.0	23.8	7.8	8.3	5.4	0.8	13.4	0.2	12.7	1.9	13.5	4.9	43.8	54
Lemhi County	3 268	58.4	22.2	13.2	8.9	6.3	1.1	5.0	0.6	15.0	4.8	12.7	8.9	47.9	80
Lewis County	1 566	58.0	21.6	13.8	10.0	6.6	1.5	3.8	0.7	13.0	4.3	15.1	10.0	47.3	44
Lincoln County	1 443	61.6	31.6	10.9	11.4	6.2	0.8	4.4	0.8	10.8	3.4	11.8	7.6	47.0	37
Madison County	7 154	59.9	34.0	8.2	8.3	5.2	1.2	19.3	0.1	4.8	1.0	7.7	4.3	35.8	60
Minidoka County	6 994	65.3	32.1	13.2	11.8	6.7	1.9	2.9	0.2	8.4	2.4	11.6	7.2	38.5	188
Nez Perce County	15 285	52.9	20.9	12.4	13.4	8.1	1.6	7.0	0.6	11.5	3.0	15.1	8.1	43.1	253
Oneida County	1 454	69.9	34.8	15.6	7.8	4.7	1.0	0.2	0.0	9.5	2.5	12.5	8.7	40.4	18
Owyhee County	3 736	63.4	31.1	11.5	11.3	7.0	1.1	3.5	0.6	11.4	2.6	10.5	7.1	42.3	83
Payette County	7 383	61.3	29.3	11.7	14.5	9.5	2.5	3.7	0.4	9.0	2.9	11.5	6.1	38.1	245
Power County	2 556	65.5	33.4	9.4	12.0	7.7	1.8	2.3	0.0	8.1	0.5	12.1	8.9	45.7	61
Shoshone County	5 910	52.6	18.3	11.8	12.6	8.8	1.7	5.2	0.3	13.4	3.8	16.1	9.8	49.6	131
Teton County	2 094	60.9	33.0	7.2	10.7	7.1	0.9	7.3	0.3	11.9	1.6	9.1	3.9	39.4	40
Twin Falls County	23 811	57.1	26.3	11.6	14.0	8.7	1.4	5.3	0.5	9.7	2.4	13.9	8.2	44.2	482
Valley County	3 213	63.2	23.2	12.9	8.2	5.4	0.9	4.1	0.6	14.2	2.8	10.3	5.0	35.1	93
Washington County	3 761	61.6	27.7	14.3	11.3	5.8	2.4	3.7	0.6	8.6	3.7	14.8	10.2	44.6	106
ILLINOIS	4 592 740	52.2	25.1	8.6	15.9	8.5	2.3	5.2	0.3	11.3	2.3	15.5	7.4	46.2	103 717
Adams County	26 862	55.7	24.2	11.8	11.9	7.5	1.6	4.0	0.4	11.0	3.1	17.4	10.6	50.0	476
Alexander County	3 827	45.3	17.0	10.4	20.7	12.9	2.7	1.9	0.3	13.2	3.6	18.9	11.9	53.4	225
Bond County	6 147	60.1	25.4	12.3	10.6	7.5	1.2	3.7	0.3	10.9	3.1	14.6	9.9	48.6	142
Boone County	14 631	65.1	32.1	9.1	12.9	8.4	1.3	3.0	0.1	8.3	2.1	10.7	6.2	44.2	273
Brown County	2 107	57.5	23.4	13.3	8.2	6.0	0.6	3.3	0.0	15.8	3.0	15.2	10.8	49.8	46
Bureau County	14 164	59.0	24.4	12.9	11.1	6.3	1.5	2.9	0.5	10.9	3.0	16.1	10.9	48.2	182
Calhoun County	2 054	60.9	25.8	13.9	9.6	4.6	2.3	2.9	0.1	12.4	5.6	14.2	10.5	49.5	33
Carroll County	6 776	58.1	22.6	14.1	11.1	6.8	2.0	3.6	0.5	12.2	3.1	14.9	10.3	44.6	114
Cass County	5 374	56.8	26.0	11.6	12.6	7.3	1.8	4.5	0.2	11.0	2.9	15.1	10.0	48.4	171
Champaign County	70 619	44.6	20.2	7.5	11.7	7.6	1.1	12.3	0.2	14.3	1.6	17.1	6.3	47.4	951
Christian County	13 930	55.7	23.1	12.0	12.7	8.1	2.1	3.2	0.2	11.6	3.6	16.7	11.9	52.1	240
Clark County	6 991	57.2	24.1	12.0	12.4	8.1	1.4	2.2	0.3	11.0	3.6	17.1	11.1	52.0	100
Clay County	5 824	56.3	23.3	12.6	12.6	7.6	2.8	3.1	0.6	10.5	3.1	17.5	11.8	48.2	113
Clinton County	12 795	60.8	29.0	12.9	12.1	7.1	1.4	3.2	0.3	9.2	2.1	14.8	9.3	43.8	209
Coles County	21 049	46.9	19.7	9.4	11.2	6.8	1.3	10.8	0.2	12.2	2.0	18.8	9.3	51.1	291
Cook County	1 974 408	45.0	21.9	7.6	19.8	9.6	3.2	5.9	0.4	12.4	2.4	16.9	7.0	45.9	58 833
Crawford County	7 845	58.0	23.6	12.5	11.7	7.4	1.9	3.4	0.4	10.6	3.3	16.4	11.0	49.1	154
Cumberland County	4 346	58.8	27.0	11.2	12.1	7.0	1.8	3.7	0.4	10.2	3.4	15.2	11.1	52.1	57
DeKalb County	31 669	51.8	25.6	7.8	12.0	7.6	1.6	10.7	0.3	12.0	1.9	13.6	6.2	45.9	289
De Witt County	6 736	57.9	24.5	11.5	11.5	7.0	2.2	3.8	0.2	11.4	2.8	15.5	10.0	47.8	80
Douglas County	7 606	60.9	27.1	12.6	11.5	7.2	1.7	3.0	0.3	8.2	2.0	16.4	10.1	45.5	90
DuPage County	326 011	62.0	32.4	7.5	10.5	5.3	1.3	4.7	0.2	9.7	1.4	13.1	5.5	43.6	3 396
Edgar County	7 859	55.4	22.5	13.3	12.6	7.8	1.6	3.6	0.2	10.6	2.1	17.9	12.5	49.3	115
Edwards County	2 901	60.7	24.5	13.8	9.2	5.4	1.4	2.4	0.2	9.0	2.2	18.8	12.3	48.6	26
Effingham County	13 024	58.4	28.5	10.2	12.3	7.7	2.0	3.2	0.1	10.7	2.8	15.4	9.2	49.2	143
Fayette County	8 159	56.5	23.9	12.1	13.3	7.5	2.0	3.2	0.5	10.8	2.7	16.2	11.3	49.0	238
Ford County	5 640	59.1	24.6	14.2	11.1	7.5	1.2	1.9	0.2	10.0	2.1	17.9	12.6	48.5	96
Franklin County	16 391	53.9	21.4	11.9	13.1	7.3	2.2	3.2	0.3	11.1	3.2	18.6	12.4	51.9	297
Fulton County	14 915	57.8	21.8	14.1	11.6	6.8	1.6	3.2	0.3	10.4	3.7	17.1	11.2	48.4	322
Gallatin County	2 717	56.2	21.0	13.3	11.4	7.3	1.2	3.0	0.3	11.3	4.1	18.1	12.9	53.4	68
Greene County	5 757	57.1	24.8	13.1	14.0	8.0	2.4	3.2	0.2	9.9	3.4	15.8	10.9	47.6	153
Grundy County	14 300	60.3	28.1	9.4	11.8	7.6	1.1	4.4	0.3	11.0	2.3	12.4	7.7	47.8	150
Hamilton County	3 499	61.7	25.5	14.4	9.8	5.6	1.9	1.7	0.2	10.4	3.5	16.4	11.9	48.2	120
Hancock County	8 088	59.6	25.0	12.8	10.0	5.4	2.1	3.5	0.3	10.6	3.5	16.2	10.0	47.0	111
Hardin County	1 965	56.6	21.3	12.3	12.5	8.2	2.4	2.2	0.1	11.7	3.7	16.9	11.9	51.3	12
Henderson County	3 365	60.0	22.7	12.0	11.1	6.4	1.9	3.8	0.2	12.2	3.7	13.0	8.6	46.5	122
Henry County	20 057	60.2	24.7	12.1	11.4	7.0	1.6	3.4	0.3	9.5	2.7	15.5	11.0	49.5	257
Iroquois County	12 212	60.5	25.3	13.7	10.9	6.6	1.9	3.3	0.5	10.0	3.3	15.2	10.2	45.8	189

Table A-3. States and Counties — Age, Ethnicity, and Household Structure

STATE County	Households with Non-Hispanic White householder		Households with Black or African American householder		Households with American Indian and Alaska Native householder		Households with Asian, Hawaiian, and Pacific Islander householder		Households with Hispanic or Latino[1] householder		Foreign-born population	Place of birth (percent)			Percent in non-English speaking households	
	Number of households	Percent that are family households	Number of households	Percent that are family households	Number of households	Percent that are family households	Number of households	Percent that are family households	Number of households	Percent that are family households	Percent of total population that is foreign-born	Europe	Asia	Latin America	Linguistically isolated	Not linguistically isolated
	44	45	46	47	48	49	50	51	52	53	54	55	56	57	58	59
IDAHO—Cont'd																
Custer County	1 694	67.5	0	X	8	75.0	0	X	59	64.4	2.3	0.3	0.0	1.5	1.3	7.8
Elmore County	7 689	74.0	260	80.0	58	72.4	103	73.8	829	88.9	7.7	1.5	1.0	4.7	4.6	16.4
Franklin County	3 340	82.9	0	X	2	100.0	2	100.0	121	86.0	3.4	0.3	0.1	2.8	2.0	12.3
Fremont County	3 574	77.4	0	X	18	66.7	9	0.0	248	97.6	7.3	0.4	0.2	6.5	3.4	12.2
Gem County	5 224	75.2	0	X	46	43.5	24	83.3	196	85.2	4.9	0.7	0.3	3.7	1.6	9.8
Gooding County	4 362	71.4	0	X	22	90.9	12	100.0	607	92.8	11.6	1.1	0.1	10.2	7.1	17.1
Idaho County	5 786	70.8	0	X	154	72.7	5	40.0	44	81.8	1.2	0.5	0.2	0.3	0.1	6.3
Jefferson County	5 418	82.2	9	100.0	32	84.4	3	100.0	408	91.7	5.9	0.2	0.0	5.2	3.1	13.1
Jerome County	5 383	75.3	14	100.0	34	85.3	25	100.0	767	85.8	10.5	1.0	0.1	9.3	7.0	15.2
Kootenai County	39 586	72.2	53	73.6	488	80.7	146	62.3	577	86.3	2.4	0.9	0.4	0.3	0.3	7.4
Latah County	12 344	60.4	20	40.0	110	42.7	186	68.8	190	54.7	4.3	1.0	1.8	0.5	0.6	8.8
Lemhi County	3 166	67.3	0	X	6	100.0	0	X	31	58.1	1.5	0.7	0.2	0.2	0.0	7.8
Lewis County	1 470	68.2	5	100.0	48	70.8	2	100.0	16	43.8	1.1	0.3	0.1	0.3	0.3	5.7
Lincoln County	1 244	70.5	4	100.0	19	68.4	9	77.8	136	98.5	10.1	0.3	0.3	9.2	6.1	12.8
Madison County	6 740	68.7	7	0.0	38	47.4	99	46.5	254	69.3	3.5	0.3	0.3	1.9	0.9	20.8
Minidoka County	5 484	74.6	6	100.0	42	100.0	5	100.0	1 389	86.4	10.9	0.5	0.2	10.0	7.7	20.3
Nez Perce County	14 162	66.5	34	32.4	598	71.4	92	35.9	206	53.4	1.9	0.5	0.7	0.3	0.5	7.1
Oneida County	1 414	77.4	0	X	0	X	4	100.0	36	91.7	2.1	0.4	0.1	1.4	0.8	8.0
Owyhee County	2 923	72.5	6	100.0	114	85.1	26	100.0	622	83.9	11.9	0.3	0.1	11.2	6.9	21.2
Payette County	6 569	74.3	0	X	38	100.0	36	44.4	602	92.5	5.5	0.6	0.3	4.3	2.7	13.8
Power County	2 119	75.2	0	X	79	86.1	3	0.0	346	89.3	10.5	0.2	0.1	10.1	5.2	24.3
Shoshone County	5 709	65.2	3	100.0	63	50.8	9	22.2	45	77.8	2.0	0.7	0.2	0.2	0.4	6.5
Teton County	1 947	70.8	4	0.0	10	100.0	4	0.0	123	87.8	9.9	0.9	0.1	7.9	4.1	11.4
Twin Falls County	21 734	70.6	16	37.5	139	67.6	103	85.4	1 508	80.8	6.4	1.8	0.5	3.8	2.9	13.7
Valley County	3 112	71.8	0	X	17	70.6	13	30.8	28	67.9	1.4	0.6	0.1	0.4	0.7	6.5
Washington County	3 265	72.3	8	0.0	11	81.8	44	47.7	342	80.1	7.1	0.3	0.3	6.2	2.8	16.5
ILLINOIS	3 405 787	66.0	624 639	68.5	10 180	71.1	136 187	74.5	373 499	84.2	12.3	3.1	2.9	5.9	5.4	19.2
Adams County	25 702	67.7	736	62.1	42	85.7	58	39.7	154	72.1	0.8	0.3	0.3	0.2	0.2	5.4
Alexander County	2 601	66.9	1 161	62.8	6	100.0	22	100.0	16	100.0	0.9	0.1	0.3	0.3	0.0	4.9
Bond County	5 882	70.7	154	74.7	34	58.8	3	0.0	44	65.9	0.8	0.2	0.1	0.4	0.2	4.9
Boone County	13 113	76.5	69	84.1	48	100.0	51	80.4	1 225	90.9	7.5	1.0	0.3	6.0	3.4	14.9
Brown County	2 088	65.7	4	0.0	0	X	4	100.0	5	100.0	1.6	0.2	0.1	1.2	0.0	2.9
Bureau County	13 548	69.6	15	60.0	32	93.8	51	90.2	461	70.6	2.6	0.5	0.5	1.5	1.3	8.1
Calhoun County	2 019	70.0	0	X	14	100.0	0	X	19	89.5	1.0	0.4	0.2	0.4	0.4	4.8
Carroll County	6 588	69.2	32	100.0	7	42.9	11	63.6	92	60.9	1.9	0.8	0.3	0.5	0.3	6.8
Cass County	5 041	68.8	14	0.0	7	100.0	7	100.0	274	78.8	7.8	0.2	0.2	7.3	6.0	6.7
Champaign County	56 681	56.9	7 141	60.7	159	52.2	4 092	47.2	1 476	47.3	8.0	1.5	4.7	1.1	2.5	13.0
Christian County	13 751	68.3	39	71.8	18	100.0	44	86.4	29	93.1	1.3	0.3	0.5	0.4	0.6	3.8
Clark County	6 936	69.6	2	100.0	16	87.5	5	0.0	5	100.0	0.6	0.2	0.1	0.0	0.1	4.2
Clay County	5 755	68.8	0	X	0	X	39	66.7	26	96.2	0.7	0.2	0.4	0.1	0.1	3.7
Clinton County	12 520	72.9	121	52.9	17	82.4	5	100.0	103	80.6	1.2	0.3	0.3	0.5	0.3	6.7
Coles County	20 165	58.7	448	35.0	30	33.3	104	57.7	209	51.2	1.6	0.5	0.7	0.4	0.5	6.8
Cook County	1 116 221	58.3	475 495	68.3	4 624	71.9	87 233	71.9	266 374	83.8	19.8	5.4	4.3	9.6	9.0	28.0
Crawford County	7 628	69.6	47	83.0	6	100.0	30	43.3	77	80.5	1.3	0.3	0.2	0.8	0.2	5.7
Cumberland County	4 299	71.2	1	100.0	2	100.0	6	66.7	17	11.8	0.6	0.4	0.1	0.1	0.2	3.9
DeKalb County	28 056	64.4	1 354	49.8	46	65.2	524	45.0	1 377	74.4	5.8	1.2	1.6	2.6	2.1	12.5
De Witt County	6 612	69.2	8	0.0	9	55.6	13	7.7	43	90.7	1.2	0.4	0.3	0.5	0.1	4.3
Douglas County	7 319	71.8	6	0.0	9	100.0	15	100.0	221	86.9	2.5	0.2	0.2	2.0	3.2	14.3
DuPage County	272 478	70.5	9 883	69.9	519	85.2	21 234	86.2	19 138	86.6	15.3	3.9	6.2	4.6	4.8	22.2
Edgar County	7 769	68.0	8	0.0	13	53.8	8	0.0	22	100.0	0.6	0.3	0.0	0.2	0.1	4.0
Edwards County	2 865	69.8	2	0.0	7	85.7	10	100.0	0	X	0.4	0.1	0.2	0.0	0.1	3.7
Effingham County	12 848	70.9	5	100.0	33	78.8	44	68.2	75	48.0	1.0	0.2	0.3	0.5	0.6	5.5
Fayette County	8 068	69.9	7	0.0	17	64.7	2	0.0	19	84.2	0.4	0.3	0.1	0.0	0.1	4.9
Ford County	5 528	70.4	24	50.0	1	100.0	15	66.7	48	56.3	1.1	0.5	0.4	0.1	0.1	5.3
Franklin County	16 126	67.1	5	20.0	60	45.0	4	100.0	73	67.1	0.7	0.4	0.1	0.1	0.2	4.4
Fulton County	14 731	69.3	42	66.7	22	77.3	9	100.0	52	88.5	0.8	0.3	0.1	0.3	0.1	3.6
Gallatin County	2 679	67.3	2	0.0	2	100.0	5	80.0	20	100.0	0.4	0.1	0.1	0.2	0.3	4.5
Greene County	5 696	71.0	0	X	27	88.9	0	X	6	100.0	0.3	0.1	0.0	0.1	0.2	4.0
Grundy County	13 700	71.4	19	57.9	21	81.0	40	70.0	460	93.0	2.7	0.7	0.2	1.6	0.8	8.5
Hamilton County	3 411	72.1	0	X	15	60.0	13	53.8	14	85.7	0.4	0.1	0.2	0.1	0.0	6.6
Hancock County	7 998	69.6	0	X	21	100.0	2	100.0	36	63.9	0.5	0.4	0.1	0.0	0.1	4.4
Hardin County	1 936	69.1	5	60.0	0	X	11	81.8	3	100.0	1.6	1.1	0.5	0.0	0.0	5.4
Henderson County	3 315	71.0	2	100.0	10	50.0	2	100.0	17	88.2	0.4	0.1	0.1	0.2	0.0	5.4
Henry County	19 354	71.3	184	66.8	10	100.0	24	79.2	352	90.9	1.7	0.7	0.3	0.7	0.6	6.7
Iroquois County	11 807	71.1	59	62.7	10	100.0	47	85.1	211	90.0	2.4	0.7	0.3	1.3	1.0	7.8

[1] Hispanic or Latino persons may be of any race.

STATE/ County code	MSA/PMSA/ NECMA code[1]	STATE . County	Population by age (percent)										Non-Hispanic White		
														Age (percent)	
			Total population	Under 5 years	5 to 17 years	18 to 24 years	25 to 44 years	45 to 64 years	65 years and over	Median age	+/− U.S. percent under 18 years	+/− U.S. percent 65 years and over	Total population	Under 18 years	65 years and over
			1	2	3	4	5	6	7	8	9	10	11	12	13
		ILLINOIS—Cont'd													
17 077	...	Jackson County	59 612	5.0	14.2	26.0	26.1	17.7	11.1	27.5	-6.5	-1.3	47 525	17.5	12.8
17 079	...	Jasper County	10 117	5.8	20.1	9.1	26.0	22.5	16.5	38.1	0.2	4.1	10 034	25.9	16.5
17 081	...	Jefferson County	40 045	5.8	18.4	8.7	28.5	23.3	15.3	37.6	-1.5	2.9	35 579	23.4	16.4
17 083	7040	Jersey County	21 668	5.9	19.6	10.0	27.4	22.8	14.4	37.3	-0.2	2.0	21 122	25.2	14.7
17 085	...	Jo Daviess County	22 289	5.6	17.5	6.8	25.3	26.9	17.9	41.6	-2.6	5.5	21 845	23.0	18.1
17 087	...	Johnson County	12 878	4.5	14.0	11.1	34.1	22.8	13.5	36.7	-7.2	1.1	10 679	21.8	16.0
17 089	1600	Kane County	404 119	8.7	21.5	9.0	32.0	20.4	8.3	32.2	4.5	-4.1	273 069	26.3	11.2
17 091	3740	Kankakee County	103 833	6.9	20.1	9.5	28.6	21.7	13.1	35.2	1.3	0.7	80 835	24.0	15.0
17 093	1600	Kendall County	54 544	8.0	21.5	7.5	32.6	22.0	8.4	34.1	3.8	-4.0	48 289	28.1	9.3
17 095	...	Knox County	55 836	5.8	16.2	9.9	26.7	23.9	17.5	39.4	-3.7	5.1	49 269	21.0	19.0
17 097	1600	Lake County	644 356	8.2	21.1	8.8	31.7	21.6	8.5	33.8	3.6	-3.9	472 991	27.1	10.4
17 099	...	La Salle County	111 509	6.2	18.9	8.1	27.9	22.3	16.5	38.1	-0.6	4.1	102 385	24.3	17.6
17 101	...	Lawrence County	15 452	5.6	17.1	7.8	26.0	23.4	20.2	40.8	-3.0	7.8	15 104	22.5	20.4
17 103	...	Lee County	36 062	5.4	18.8	7.7	30.3	23.0	14.7	37.9	-1.5	2.3	32 551	24.7	15.8
17 105	...	Livingston County	39 678	5.8	19.1	8.3	29.5	22.1	15.2	37.3	-0.8	2.8	36 069	25.5	16.5
17 107	...	Logan County	31 183	5.4	16.5	11.7	29.7	21.8	14.9	37.0	-3.8	2.5	28 380	23.1	16.2
17 109	...	McDonough County	32 913	4.2	13.5	27.8	21.3	19.2	14.1	29.0	-8.0	1.7	30 449	17.6	15.0
17 111	1600	McHenry County	260 077	8.1	22.2	6.8	33.8	21.2	8.0	34.2	4.6	-4.4	233 278	29.4	8.6
17 113	1040	McLean County	150 433	6.4	17.0	18.6	29.2	19.0	9.8	30.5	-2.3	-2.6	132 511	22.2	10.7
17 115	2040	Macon County	114 706	6.4	18.2	9.9	26.4	23.8	15.3	38.0	-1.1	2.9	95 202	21.8	17.0
17 117	...	Macoupin County	49 019	5.8	19.0	8.2	26.7	22.9	17.5	38.9	-0.9	5.1	47 855	24.4	17.7
17 119	7040	Madison County	258 941	6.3	18.6	9.3	29.1	22.4	14.3	36.9	-0.8	1.9	230 991	23.5	15.1
17 121	...	Marion County	41 691	6.4	19.1	8.1	26.7	23.1	16.6	38.4	-0.2	4.2	39 118	24.6	17.0
17 123	...	Marshall County	13 180	5.4	17.9	7.3	25.5	25.0	18.8	40.9	-2.4	6.4	12 883	22.8	18.9
17 125	...	Mason County	16 038	5.8	18.5	7.8	26.4	24.3	17.2	39.5	-1.4	4.8	15 733	24.0	17.3
17 127	...	Massac County	15 161	6.2	16.7	8.0	27.3	24.0	17.8	39.6	-2.8	5.4	13 970	22.3	18.2
17 129	7880	Menard County	12 486	5.8	20.8	6.9	28.8	24.4	13.3	38.0	0.9	0.9	12 194	26.4	13.5
17 131	...	Mercer County	16 957	5.6	19.1	7.3	26.7	25.3	16.0	39.5	-1.0	3.6	16 636	24.3	16.2
17 133	7040	Monroe County	27 619	6.6	19.9	7.3	30.9	21.9	13.3	37.5	0.8	0.9	27 222	26.4	13.5
17 135	...	Montgomery County........	30 652	5.7	17.9	8.3	29.3	21.8	16.9	38.1	-2.1	4.5	28 988	24.4	17.8
17 137	...	Morgan County	36 616	5.3	17.4	11.0	27.5	23.1	15.7	37.8	-3.0	3.3	33 639	22.2	16.5
17 139	...	Moultrie County	14 287	6.5	19.1	7.9	25.9	23.0	17.7	38.7	-0.1	5.3	14 034	25.3	17.9
17 141	6880	Ogle County	51 032	6.2	21.2	7.3	28.4	23.5	13.4	37.2	1.7	1.0	47 086	26.4	14.4
17 143	6120	Peoria County	183 433	6.8	18.3	10.3	27.9	22.6	14.1	36.0	-0.6	1.7	143 993	21.2	16.5
17 145	...	Perry County	23 094	5.3	16.6	10.0	29.7	22.3	16.1	37.6	-3.8	3.7	20 616	23.1	17.6
17 147	...	Piatt County	16 365	6.2	19.1	6.8	27.5	25.0	15.4	39.6	-0.4	3.0	15 983	24.6	15.6
17 149	...	Pike County	17 384	5.8	18.3	7.7	25.5	23.5	19.3	39.8	-1.6	6.9	16 885	24.3	19.6
17 151	...	Pope County	4 413	5.0	16.5	10.7	23.9	26.1	17.7	41.1	-4.2	5.3	4 104	21.2	18.8
17 153	...	Pulaski County	7 348	6.4	21.0	8.6	26.0	20.7	17.4	37.7	1.7	5.0	4 840	23.5	19.0
17 155	...	Putnam County	6 086	5.9	19.2	7.0	26.9	25.1	16.0	39.6	-0.6	3.6	5 793	24.2	16.2
17 157	...	Randolph County	33 893	5.5	16.6	9.6	30.3	22.5	15.5	37.6	-3.6	3.1	29 877	23.2	17.3
17 159	...	Richland County	16 149	6.0	18.5	8.4	26.6	22.9	17.6	39.1	-1.2	5.2	15 847	24.4	17.8
17 161	1960	Rock Island County........	149 374	6.4	17.4	10.0	27.4	23.8	15.0	37.8	-1.9	2.6	121 690	20.9	17.3
17 163	7040	St. Clair County	256 082	6.9	20.8	8.8	29.5	21.0	13.1	35.3	2.0	0.7	171 297	23.8	15.6
17 165	...	Saline County.................	26 733	5.8	18.3	8.2	25.2	23.7	18.9	39.9	-1.6	6.5	25 104	22.8	19.6
17 167	7880	Sangamon County	188 951	6.3	18.6	8.1	29.8	23.6	13.7	37.3	-0.8	1.3	164 500	23.1	14.6
17 169	...	Schuyler County	7 189	5.8	17.4	7.0	26.2	24.3	19.3	40.9	-2.5	6.9	7 084	22.9	19.6
17 171	...	Scott County	5 537	6.1	18.8	7.9	27.3	23.4	16.5	38.8	-0.8	4.1	5 492	25.0	16.6
17 173	...	Shelby County	22 893	5.9	19.0	7.6	26.2	23.5	17.7	39.3	-0.8	5.3	22 617	24.8	17.8
17 175	...	Stark County	6 332	6.5	18.6	6.8	25.3	23.7	19.1	39.9	-0.6	6.7	6 177	24.5	19.5
17 177	...	Stephenson County	48 979	6.1	19.2	7.7	27.7	23.1	16.3	38.5	-0.4	3.9	43 413	23.3	17.7
17 179	6120	Tazewell County	128 485	6.3	18.1	8.2	28.6	24.0	14.9	38.1	-1.3	2.5	124 357	24.3	15.2
17 181	...	Union County	18 293	5.2	18.0	7.4	26.9	25.0	17.5	40.3	-2.5	5.1	17 365	22.6	18.2
17 183	...	Vermilion County............	83 919	6.6	18.3	8.6	27.1	23.4	16.0	38.0	-0.8	3.6	70 942	23.1	17.6
17 185	...	Wabash County	12 937	5.8	18.4	9.1	26.3	23.4	17.0	39.0	-1.5	4.6	12 609	24.1	17.8
17 187	...	Warren County	18 735	5.6	17.5	12.1	24.8	23.6	16.4	37.8	-2.6	4.0	17 681	22.4	16.8
17 189	...	Washington County.........	15 148	5.7	19.5	7.6	27.3	23.1	16.7	38.8	-0.5	4.3	14 895	25.0	16.9
17 191	...	Wayne County	17 151	6.0	17.8	7.9	25.8	23.8	18.8	39.9	-1.9	6.4	16 769	23.5	19.0
17 193	...	White County	15 371	4.9	16.5	7.9	25.2	24.6	20.9	42.0	-4.3	8.5	15 076	21.5	21.0
17 195	...	Whiteside County	60 653	6.3	18.9	8.0	27.2	23.6	16.1	38.5	-0.5	3.7	53 728	23.4	17.3
17 197	1600	Will County	502 266	8.3	21.6	8.2	33.1	20.6	8.2	33.3	4.2	-4.2	388 386	28.2	9.5
17 199	...	Williamson County	61 296	6.0	17.0	8.6	27.9	24.1	16.5	38.8	-2.7	4.1	57 910	22.2	17.2
17 201	6880	Winnebago County	278 418	7.0	19.4	8.3	29.9	22.6	12.7	35.9	0.7	0.3	220 718	23.2	14.9
17 203	6120	Woodford County	35 469	6.5	20.2	8.6	26.4	23.5	14.9	37.8	1.0	2.5	34 718	26.4	15.1

[1]MSA = Metropolitan Statistical Area. PMSA = Primary MSA. NECMA = New England County Metropolitan Area. See the Appendix A for explanation of these concepts. See Appendix B for list of metropolitan areas identified by type, with component counties.

STATE County	Black or African American	Age (percent)		American Indian and Alaska Native	Age (percent)		Asian, Hawaiian, and Pacific Islander	Age (percent)		Hispanic or Latino[1]	Age (percent)		Two or more races	Age (percent)	
	Total population	Under 18 years	65 years and over	Total population	Under 18 years	65 years and over	Total population	Under 18 years	65 years and over	Total population	Under 18 years	65 years and over	Total population	Under 18 years	65 years and over
	14	15	16	17	18	19	20	21	22	23	24	25	26	27	28
ILLINOIS—Cont'd															
Jackson County............	7 421	26.5	5.8	193	24.4	2.1	1 964	15.4	2.4	1 360	22.7	1.1	1 250	39.0	1.5
Jasper County..............	0	X	X	2	0.0	0.0	10	0.0	60.0	7	0.0	71.4	57	40.4	7.0
Jefferson County..........	3 236	27.3	5.2	90	27.8	10.0	110	30.0	0.0	585	39.8	6.7	546	54.0	9.0
Jersey County	144	45.1	2.8	76	46.1	5.3	109	23.9	0.0	82	28.0	2.4	135	42.2	1.5
Jo Daviess County	23	17.4	0.0	48	33.3	6.3	14	0.0	57.1	245	23.3	6.1	163	26.4	9.8
Johnson County............	1 789	1.0	0.0	27	22.2	0.0	15	13.3	0.0	280	5.4	0.4	88	20.5	22.7
Kane County................	23 149	38.8	3.5	1 276	24.2	3.1	7 238	30.6	2.9	95 965	38.5	1.9	9 781	47.8	2.7
Kankakee County..........	15 792	36.8	7.8	311	23.2	6.1	749	32.0	7.7	4 949	39.9	1.8	1 551	53.8	2.9
Kendall County.............	618	36.2	1.3	166	25.9	4.8	697	39.6	3.0	4 082	40.2	1.6	1 002	52.2	1.6
Knox County.................	3 499	23.0	7.0	128	31.3	0.0	456	21.9	2.6	1 903	31.9	6.3	747	53.8	1.9
Lake County.................	43 614	33.8	5.5	1 553	27.6	1.7	25 667	28.1	5.2	93 075	37.3	1.9	13 267	47.3	2.8
La Salle County............	1 931	23.8	2.6	190	20.0	10.0	591	25.7	7.4	5 780	38.1	4.5	1 093	43.7	4.5
Lawrence County..........	142	18.3	15.5	6	0.0	0.0	22	0.0	36.4	96	28.1	6.3	76	61.8	11.8
Lee County..................	1 795	9.6	3.2	52	5.8	0.0	266	19.2	6.4	1 128	29.8	7.4	362	51.9	6.4
Livingston County.........	2 045	7.7	0.4	85	28.2	0.0	67	6.0	26.9	1 092	31.8	3.0	456	48.7	5.9
Logan County...............	1 916	5.7	0.6	44	0.0	0.0	196	13.8	9.7	496	19.6	2.2	171	22.2	2.3
McDonough County	1 040	18.8	1.5	38	0.0	0.0	610	15.1	1.1	543	21.9	2.9	297	21.2	2.7
McHenry County...........	1 440	42.5	0.2	405	27.2	4.4	3 425	27.7	3.4	19 585	37.1	1.9	3 038	51.4	2.0
McLean County............	9 055	31.9	2.9	291	12.0	2.4	3 261	18.2	4.4	3 597	34.7	2.1	2 316	57.3	1.5
Macon County..............	15 941	36.0	7.7	133	24.1	0.0	790	25.7	2.7	1 083	35.1	4.9	1 746	60.0	3.4
Macoupin County	325	32.0	22.2	81	25.9	0.0	140	18.6	8.6	387	50.6	0.0	241	35.3	9.5
Madison County............	18 645	36.1	8.1	783	22.2	1.9	1 339	27.5	5.4	4 296	37.5	4.6	3 386	41.6	7.7
Marion County..............	1 632	36.3	13.2	93	41.9	7.5	223	30.9	0.0	380	42.9	16.1	356	50.0	10.1
Marshall County...........	65	58.5	0.0	8	0.0	37.5	35	22.9	45.7	112	46.4	8.9	77	51.9	14.3
Mason County..............	56	55.4	0.0	67	50.7	9.0	28	10.7	0.0	44	25.0	18.2	104	32.7	22.1
Massac County	773	23.5	17.5	12	0.0	0.0	52	28.8	0.0	174	32.8	2.9	197	58.4	4.6
Menard County.............	66	31.8	0.0	32	34.4	18.8	19	26.3	0.0	96	41.7	3.1	102	41.2	5.9
Mercer County..............	61	13.1	9.8	18	61.1	5.6	47	34.0	0.0	124	59.7	0.8	74	47.3	12.2
Monroe County............	17	82.4	0.0	54	31.5	0.0	85	40.0	9.4	148	43.2	0.0	136	41.2	11.0
Montgomery County......	1 147	6.5	1.6	48	4.2	8.3	72	22.2	0.0	340	14.7	4.1	81	34.6	0.0
Morgan County.............	1 945	21.6	5.9	77	2.6	14.3	174	42.5	5.7	456	27.6	6.1	209	50.4	6.2
Moultrie County............	36	44.4	0.0	32	21.9	18.8	29	55.2	0.0	89	27.0	21.3	67	46.3	4.5
Ogle County.................	134	35.1	0.0	255	36.1	2.4	181	30.4	6.6	3 131	40.2	1.4	554	48.2	2.2
Peoria County	29 007	39.5	5.7	324	30.2	7.1	3 205	21.4	5.3	3 801	38.3	3.1	3 363	54.8	4.6
Perry County	1 843	8.2	3.4	57	29.8	5.3	92	4.3	0.0	362	16.6	3.3	173	42.8	5.8
Piatt County.................	64	75.0	0.0	40	67.5	0.0	64	31.3	3.1	120	65.0	6.7	92	19.6	12.0
Pike County..................	241	2.9	0.0	16	25.0	6.3	68	30.9	22.1	106	15.1	16.0	82	26.8	17.1
Pope County	176	17.6	2.3	31	54.8	0.0	2	100.0	0.0	31	38.7	0.0	67	26.9	10.4
Pulaski County	2 234	36.0	15.0	0	0.0	55.0	79	2.5	0.0	108	22.2	6.5	96	53.1	10.4
Putnam County	37	45.9	10.8	15	46.7	13.3	8	62.5	0.0	203	38.4	13.8	40	57.5	0.0
Randolph County..........	3 252	11.3	1.9	19	0.0	0.0	157	33.1	3.8	417	12.7	0.0	207	49.3	7.7
Richland County...........	19	31.6	0.0	3	0.0	66.7	44	22.7	0.0	117	34.2	0.0	91	25.3	23.1
Rock Island County.......	10 541	32.2	7.2	641	37.8	3.7	1 486	27.3	3.0	13 044	38.4	4.0	3 025	53.5	4.0
St. Clair County............	73 292	35.5	8.6	781	34.7	6.9	2 373	19.9	4.3	5 537	37.9	5.1	3 602	50.2	5.1
Saline County...............	1 094	47.8	9.4	75	14.7	8.0	45	17.8	11.1	183	33.9	4.4	215	35.3	6.0
Sangamon County	17 794	37.4	7.1	385	30.1	1.0	2 002	25.1	6.6	1 630	32.8	6.4	2 743	49.2	7.7
Schuyler County...........	12	0.0	0.0	22	0.0	0.0	12	58.3	41.7	48	60.4	0.0	27	59.3	0.0
Scott County.................	3	0.0	0.0	13	38.5	0.0	4	0.0	0.0	12	0.0	33.3	11	9.1	0.0
Shelby County..............	33	60.6	0.0	29	24.1	6.9	74	24.3	13.5	80	33.8	0.0	78	33.3	20.5
Stark County................	5	60.0	40.0	5	0.0	0.0	14	14.3	14.3	76	47.4	2.6	66	63.6	1.5
Stephenson County.......	3 737	36.0	6.7	152	24.3	0.0	184	34.8	0.0	712	44.7	2.4	832	62.1	1.8
Tazewell County...........	1 187	8.9	4.1	285	14.4	4.2	572	24.0	7.5	1 225	33.4	7.9	961	47.2	10.0
Union County	121	24.0	3.3	79	6.3	0.0	86	25.6	0.0	497	45.3	1.0	201	38.8	14.9
Vermilion County..........	8 704	31.9	8.9	127	24.4	6.3	560	35.7	4.1	2 507	38.6	2.0	1 305	53.7	2.0
Wabash County............	34	38.2	0.0	23	0.0	0.0	38	44.7	0.0	97	20.6	9.3	136	35.3	7.4
Warren County.............	265	22.6	8.3	22	0.0	0.0	91	13.2	23.1	527	38.0	7.2	220	50.9	5.0
Washington County.......	25	68.0	0.0	59	11.9	16.9	19	10.5	0.0	64	50.0	1.6	87	47.1	5.7
Wayne County..............	23	56.5	0.0	38	18.4	23.7	117	37.6	6.0	142	43.7	5.6	85	51.8	2.4
White County...............	44	0.0	0.0	47	4.3	25.5	12	33.3	0.0	33	21.2	18.2	162	32.1	22.2
Whiteside County..........	591	44.3	11.5	274	23.4	0.0	225	41.3	2.2	5 405	37.5	7.2	1 091	52.4	4.4
Will County..................	51 890	33.8	4.5	1 017	33.9	1.8	11 443	30.4	4.9	44 138	37.9	2.8	8 547	50.1	3.6
Williamson County	1 595	31.1	4.8	160	11.9	0.0	212	11.3	13.2	943	40.9	4.0	577	52.7	7.3
Winnebago County.......	29 556	37.0	5.8	846	27.7	3.1	4 582	31.0	3.7	19 029	40.5	3.0	5 990	52.1	4.4
Woodford County	127	68.5	6.3	33	24.2	0.0	122	24.6	1.6	319	37.0	2.5	221	45.2	12.2

[1] Hispanic or Latino persons may be of any race.

Table A-3. States and Counties — Age, Ethnicity, and Household Structure

STATE County	Total households	Family households (percent)						Nonfamily households (percent)						Percent of householders 65 years and over who live alone	Grandparents who are responsible for the care of their grandchildren
		Married-couple family households			Other family households			Two or more unrelated persons		Male living alone		Female living alone			
		Total	With children	Householder 65 years or over	Total	With children	Householder 65 years or over	Total	Householder 65 years or over	Total	Householder 65 years or over	Total	Householder 65 years or over		
	29	30	31	32	33	34	35	36	37	38	39	40	41	42	43
ILLINOIS—Cont'd															
Jackson County	24 293	40.4	17.7	7.4	12.4	7.4	1.4	12.3	0.1	16.2	1.8	18.5	7.4	50.5	341
Jasper County	3 929	64.2	27.6	13.9	8.2	6.0	1.1	2.5	0.2	10.0	2.9	14.9	10.1	46.2	27
Jefferson County	15 351	56.3	23.3	10.6	12.5	8.4	1.8	3.5	0.3	11.6	3.8	16.1	10.0	52.0	321
Jersey County	8 092	61.9	29.0	10.9	10.3	6.1	1.7	4.0	0.1	9.6	3.3	14.3	9.1	49.2	158
Jo Daviess County	9 200	58.6	22.1	14.4	9.5	5.4	1.7	4.3	0.5	12.2	3.4	15.4	9.2	43.4	139
Johnson County	4 154	61.9	24.9	13.5	10.8	5.8	2.4	3.2	0.8	11.2	3.5	12.9	8.2	41.3	83
Kane County	133 733	62.1	34.4	7.1	14.1	8.2	1.4	4.2	0.3	8.7	1.5	10.9	5.1	43.0	2 570
Kankakee County	38 209	54.3	25.0	9.9	16.4	9.9	2.3	4.5	0.4	10.1	2.1	14.8	8.2	45.0	1 026
Kendall County	18 789	70.2	37.1	7.4	9.6	5.6	1.0	3.9	0.2	7.3	1.4	9.1	5.1	43.0	235
Knox County	22 056	52.7	20.1	12.0	13.1	8.3	2.0	4.6	0.3	11.4	3.5	18.1	11.2	50.7	345
Lake County	216 484	64.1	35.8	7.4	12.2	7.3	1.3	4.0	0.3	8.7	1.5	11.0	4.6	40.9	3 292
La Salle County	43 346	56.3	24.8	12.0	12.6	7.5	2.1	3.7	0.4	11.6	3.0	15.8	9.7	46.8	742
Lawrence County	6 319	55.5	20.8	13.1	12.5	8.0	2.2	3.1	0.2	10.3	3.4	18.6	11.9	49.8	115
Lee County	13 258	57.0	24.1	11.0	11.9	8.2	1.2	4.5	0.6	11.7	3.1	14.9	9.6	49.6	270
Livingston County	14 400	57.5	25.4	12.1	12.3	8.4	1.3	3.5	0.3	11.0	2.5	15.8	9.4	46.5	344
Logan County	11 107	56.6	24.4	11.1	11.9	7.7	1.6	3.7	0.2	10.0	2.9	17.8	11.4	52.4	218
McDonough County	12 390	47.8	19.0	11.0	9.7	5.8	1.5	10.8	0.3	12.1	2.1	19.7	10.5	49.6	124
McHenry County	89 377	68.0	38.0	7.1	10.1	5.6	1.3	4.1	0.3	8.2	1.3	9.6	4.5	40.1	920
McLean County	56 792	51.3	24.5	7.4	11.5	7.4	1.0	9.6	0.2	11.7	1.6	15.9	6.5	48.6	606
Macon County	46 518	50.9	19.9	10.8	16.0	10.4	2.1	4.3	0.4	12.3	2.4	16.6	9.3	46.7	906
Macoupin County	19 282	59.4	24.7	12.9	11.6	7.2	2.0	3.5	0.3	10.5	3.4	15.0	10.0	46.9	390
Madison County	101 958	53.7	24.0	10.0	15.2	9.1	2.2	4.8	0.3	10.8	2.6	15.5	8.8	47.5	2 026
Marion County	16 616	54.9	22.2	11.5	14.7	9.6	1.9	3.3	0.2	9.8	2.7	17.2	11.5	51.2	510
Marshall County	5 247	62.4	24.8	14.4	9.5	5.6	1.5	3.0	0.2	10.5	3.2	14.6	10.0	45.0	67
Mason County	6 377	60.3	23.3	13.8	12.2	7.3	1.8	2.8	0.3	11.0	2.6	13.8	9.8	44.0	112
Massac County	6 256	55.2	22.7	11.8	13.7	8.7	2.2	2.9	0.6	10.9	2.6	17.2	10.7	47.6	130
Menard County	4 875	61.5	28.7	10.5	11.4	8.1	1.4	3.3	0.5	9.6	2.1	14.2	8.5	46.1	18
Mercer County	6 590	63.9	26.4	12.9	10.5	5.8	2.1	2.8	0.3	9.3	3.0	13.4	8.9	43.7	110
Monroe County	10 260	65.7	32.3	10.4	9.9	5.6	0.9	3.2	0.3	9.1	2.5	12.2	7.4	46.2	98
Montgomery County	11 525	56.1	23.3	12.8	13.0	9.0	1.4	3.2	0.4	9.9	2.5	17.8	11.5	49.2	135
Morgan County	14 021	54.1	22.5	11.3	12.3	7.3	1.9	4.4	0.4	11.7	2.7	17.5	10.2	48.8	221
Moultrie County	5 427	63.3	26.9	13.3	10.0	5.4	1.1	2.9	0.6	10.3	2.2	13.6	9.4	43.8	112
Ogle County	19 229	61.7	28.4	11.1	11.6	7.5	1.5	4.1	0.3	10.9	2.4	11.7	7.1	42.2	300
Peoria County	72 739	49.1	20.1	9.8	15.8	10.4	1.8	5.4	0.4	12.2	2.3	17.4	8.5	47.2	1 488
Perry County	8 485	56.6	23.4	12.7	12.1	7.4	1.8	3.4	0.4	10.4	3.0	17.5	11.2	48.8	152
Piatt County	6 454	62.6	26.8	12.5	10.3	6.3	1.6	3.5	0.2	8.8	2.0	14.8	9.3	44.1	78
Pike County	6 869	59.1	24.7	13.8	11.1	6.2	2.3	2.0	0.2	10.8	3.8	16.9	12.6	50.4	102
Pope County	1 775	57.0	22.3	13.0	12.9	7.9	2.0	2.5	0.8	11.9	3.5	15.6	8.2	42.5	34
Pulaski County	2 872	48.6	20.3	11.7	18.8	10.7	3.3	2.6	0.4	14.1	4.9	15.9	11.1	50.9	129
Putnam County	2 403	62.2	24.8	12.4	10.6	5.9	2.0	2.8	0.5	10.9	3.5	13.5	9.2	45.8	52
Randolph County	12 085	57.8	25.1	11.8	11.4	6.4	2.5	3.7	0.4	10.2	3.3	16.8	11.0	49.3	155
Richland County	6 658	55.2	22.7	12.1	13.0	8.2	1.8	4.0	0.1	9.9	3.4	17.8	11.2	50.9	101
Rock Island County	60 686	49.9	20.1	10.3	15.0	9.1	1.9	4.9	0.4	12.5	2.9	17.7	9.6	49.8	1 270
St. Clair County	96 777	48.7	22.5	8.9	21.2	12.5	3.2	4.1	0.5	11.0	2.6	15.0	7.8	45.5	2 733
Saline County	10 970	53.7	22.0	11.4	12.4	7.2	2.1	2.5	0.3	11.3	3.8	20.1	12.7	54.4	138
Sangamon County	78 781	48.5	21.6	8.7	15.1	9.6	1.7	5.5	0.4	12.4	2.4	18.5	8.5	50.2	1 186
Schuyler County	2 971	61.7	25.4	13.9	7.9	3.9	2.3	3.1	0.2	12.9	2.9	14.4	9.5	42.9	91
Scott County	2 216	59.2	27.2	12.1	11.6	7.0	1.9	2.9	0.4	10.9	2.9	15.4	10.2	47.7	22
Shelby County	9 037	61.4	25.0	13.5	10.9	6.5	1.9	2.4	0.4	10.8	3.8	14.6	10.2	46.8	134
Stark County	2 516	60.1	25.0	13.5	9.8	5.0	1.9	2.8	0.4	10.3	2.8	17.0	12.8	49.7	50
Stephenson County	19 778	56.6	23.3	12.1	11.8	7.9	1.5	4.0	0.3	10.9	2.7	16.7	9.9	47.5	286
Tazewell County	50 374	59.9	25.3	12.1	11.6	7.0	1.6	3.7	0.3	10.0	2.2	14.7	8.4	43.3	880
Union County	7 320	54.9	22.7	12.0	13.6	7.8	1.7	3.2	0.4	9.5	2.8	18.8	12.3	51.9	114
Vermilion County	33 378	51.5	20.2	10.9	15.8	10.1	2.0	3.7	0.4	11.7	3.3	17.3	10.6	51.0	664
Wabash County	5 191	58.9	25.4	11.3	10.2	6.0	2.2	3.9	0.2	11.4	3.1	15.6	10.0	49.1	121
Warren County	7 175	56.3	22.5	11.5	13.6	8.2	2.1	3.5	0.1	9.8	3.0	16.8	10.9	50.6	142
Washington County	5 848	62.9	28.6	13.0	10.7	5.6	2.3	2.3	0.3	9.6	3.4	14.5	10.6	47.3	99
Wayne County	7 151	58.1	23.1	13.6	11.7	7.4	2.0	2.9	0.2	10.3	3.1	17.1	12.5	49.8	123
White County	6 548	57.4	21.7	14.0	9.6	5.6	1.5	3.1	0.2	11.2	3.0	18.6	13.2	50.8	159
Whiteside County	23 744	57.9	23.4	12.7	13.6	8.6	1.7	3.7	0.3	10.6	2.6	14.3	9.5	45.0	521
Will County	167 602	65.9	36.3	7.1	12.7	7.0	1.5	3.7	0.2	7.9	1.3	9.8	4.8	40.9	3 560
Williamson County	25 464	54.6	22.2	11.1	13.0	8.1	1.9	3.7	0.3	10.6	2.8	18.0	10.9	50.8	563
Winnebago County	107 966	53.2	23.9	9.3	15.3	9.8	1.6	5.1	0.4	11.5	2.3	14.8	7.3	46.1	2 523
Woodford County	12 827	68.3	31.0	12.2	8.5	4.8	1.3	2.7	0.3	8.0	2.1	12.5	8.9	44.5	152

Table A-3. States and Counties — Age, Ethnicity, and Household Structure

STATE / County	Households with Non-Hispanic White householder		Households with Black or African American householder		Households with American Indian and Alaska Native householder		Households with Asian, Hawaiian, and Pacific Islander householder		Households with Hispanic or Latino[1] householder		Foreign-born population	Place of birth (percent)			Percent in non-English speaking households	
	Number of households	Percent that are family households	Number of households	Percent that are family households	Number of households	Percent that are family households	Number of households	Percent that are family households	Number of households	Percent that are family households	Percent of total population that is foreign-born	Europe	Asia	Latin America	Linguistically isolated	Not linguistically isolated
	44	45	46	47	48	49	50	51	52	53	54	55	56	57	58	59
ILLINOIS—Cont'd																
Jackson County	19 789	54.1	2 831	51.1	80	61.3	842	39.9	464	37.3	5.2	0.8	3.0	0.8	2.1	9.9
Jasper County	3 898	72.8	0	X	0	X	0	X	7	0.0	0.2	0.0	0.2	0.0	0.1	3.5
Jefferson County	14 246	69.2	811	62.9	37	100.0	38	94.7	96	64.6	0.8	0.2	0.2	0.2	0.3	5.6
Jersey County	7 987	71.9	5	100.0	26	92.3	28	100.0	8	75.0	1.0	0.3	0.3	0.1	0.1	5.9
Jo Daviess County	9 064	68.1	12	50.0	20	90.0	0	X	76	65.8	1.7	0.8	0.1	0.6	0.4	5.2
Johnson County	4 099	72.9	5	0.0	6	100.0	7	0.0	5	60.0	1.5	0.4	0.1	0.8	0.1	3.6
Kane County	102 071	73.4	7 376	74.4	412	76.0	1 909	87.5	21 257	89.2	15.7	1.5	1.3	12.5	9.5	21.6
Kankakee County	31 216	69.8	5 193	71.1	114	48.2	224	82.1	1 186	88.7	3.5	0.6	0.7	2.0	1.5	9.2
Kendall County	17 167	78.9	200	80.0	53	50.9	183	83.1	1 001	92.7	5.3	1.3	0.8	3.0	1.1	13.1
Knox County	20 490	66.0	814	62.3	45	31.1	72	69.4	500	72.4	1.6	0.3	0.4	0.7	0.4	6.8
Lake County	172 992	74.7	13 917	73.3	471	73.5	7 321	85.6	20 036	89.5	14.8	3.4	3.1	7.9	6.1	21.7
La Salle County	41 071	68.2	258	74.0	86	72.1	204	67.6	1 570	86.5	2.7	0.7	0.4	1.5	1.1	8.1
Lawrence County	6 193	68.3	72	43.1	0	X	7	0.0	27	66.7	0.6	0.1	0.1	0.3	0.4	3.9
Lee County	12 705	68.8	129	69.0	10	60.0	107	60.7	243	76.1	1.9	0.8	0.6	0.4	0.5	6.5
Livingston County	13 989	69.6	55	78.2	17	58.8	23	56.5	225	74.7	1.3	0.4	0.2	0.6	0.6	6.0
Logan County	10 827	68.2	71	60.6	23	100.0	62	79.0	55	89.1	1.4	0.3	0.6	0.5	0.1	6.9
McDonough County	11 591	58.4	346	38.2	23	78.3	228	39.5	128	73.4	2.8	0.6	1.6	0.4	0.9	7.7
McHenry County	83 100	77.5	478	71.5	124	87.1	1 006	79.3	4 300	90.0	7.2	2.1	1.0	3.8	2.8	13.3
McLean County	51 105	62.6	3 279	65.0	108	40.7	1 029	60.4	1 020	70.7	3.3	0.6	1.7	0.7	1.1	8.2
Macon County	39 853	67.1	5 887	64.7	53	41.5	254	78.3	264	72.0	1.4	0.4	0.5	0.3	0.3	6.2
Macoupin County	18 958	71.1	103	61.2	14	50.0	49	51.0	84	86.9	0.5	0.2	0.2	0.0	0.1	4.4
Madison County	92 564	68.6	6 478	72.2	345	66.4	387	62.8	1 302	83.9	1.3	0.4	0.4	0.3	0.3	6.7
Marion County	15 707	70.1	592	57.8	38	60.5	80	96.3	127	65.4	0.8	0.3	0.3	0.1	0.2	5.7
Marshall County	5 186	71.9	13	100.0	4	50.0	0	X	29	79.3	1.0	0.6	0.3	0.1	0.2	5.0
Mason County	6 279	72.5	0	X	12	100.0	9	100.0	23	52.2	0.4	0.3	0.1	0.0	0.3	5.1
Massac County	5 777	70.1	375	46.7	2	100.0	31	100.0	39	76.9	0.4	0.1	0.2	0.1	0.0	5.2
Menard County	4 802	72.7	5	100.0	11	100.0	10	30.0	34	94.1	0.7	0.3	0.2	0.1	0.2	5.5
Mercer County	6 544	74.0	3	100.0	4	75.0	11	100.0	18	100.0	0.6	0.3	0.2	0.1	0.0	6.8
Monroe County	10 160	75.6	0	X	17	100.0	19	52.6	37	75.7	0.8	0.4	0.2	0.1	0.3	6.8
Montgomery County	11 380	69.2	28	28.6	20	75.0	20	85.0	63	76.2	0.9	0.4	0.2	0.3	0.1	4.4
Morgan County	13 431	66.1	381	74.5	27	100.0	39	79.5	70	81.4	1.1	0.4	0.3	0.3	0.1	6.1
Moultrie County	5 333	73.3	8	75.0	18	83.3	2	100.0	37	51.4	0.6	0.3	0.1	0.1	1.2	9.3
Ogle County	18 135	73.2	48	87.5	74	43.2	63	52.4	863	78.3	4.3	0.8	0.5	3.0	1.9	9.7
Peoria County	60 011	63.9	9 847	69.0	109	61.5	1 194	72.3	944	83.2	3.2	0.7	1.6	0.6	0.9	9.5
Perry County	8 168	69.2	170	51.2	23	100.0	34	61.8	49	53.1	1.0	0.2	0.3	0.5	0.3	5.0
Piatt County	6 378	72.9	2	0.0	12	100.0	10	100.0	17	41.2	0.6	0.1	0.3	0.0	0.1	5.5
Pike County	6 778	70.3	3	100.0	10	70.0	7	100.0	47	59.6	1.1	0.4	0.4	0.2	0.3	3.8
Pope County	1 729	69.6	12	66.7	4	100.0	0	X	0	X	0.7	0.1	0.0	0.5	0.0	4.4
Pulaski County	1 052	60.0	650	60.0	4	0.0	8	100.0	25	56.0	0.7	0.1	0.2	0.3	0.5	2.8
Putnam County	2 333	72.3	12	100.0	5	60.0	0	X	51	90.2	1.8	0.6	0.2	1.0	0.8	9.3
Randolph County	11 670	69.3	311	69.8	5	0.0	32	65.6	29	31.0	0.8	0.2	0.3	0.3	0.4	4.9
Richland County	6 538	68.9	6	0.0	0	X	14	35.7	48	18.8	0.6	0.3	0.2	0.1	0.1	5.0
Rock Island County	52 197	64.2	3 798	63.5	188	75.5	433	79.7	3 567	76.8	4.6	0.9	0.8	2.8	2.0	10.6
St. Clair County	68 462	68.9	25 150	72.0	198	82.3	619	79.5	1 527	73.7	2.1	0.5	0.8	0.7	0.6	8.2
Saline County	10 512	66.6	292	55.5	47	42.6	6	0.0	38	68.4	0.7	0.3	0.2	0.1	0.2	5.2
Sangamon County	70 286	63.6	6 381	64.9	171	35.1	673	61.8	567	69.3	1.9	0.6	0.8	0.2	0.3	6.6
Schuyler County	2 944	70.0	3	100.0	17	29.4	5	0.0	2	100.0	0.4	0.1	0.2	0.1	0.1	4.2
Scott County	2 204	70.8	3	0.0	0	X	0	X	5	60.0	0.5	0.2	0.1	0.1	0.2	3.6
Shelby County	8 942	72.4	0	X	9	77.8	26	76.9	37	59.5	0.4	0.1	0.2	0.1	0.1	4.3
Stark County	2 482	69.9	2	0.0	0	X	2	0.0	17	88.2	0.4	0.1	0.2	0.2	0.1	5.0
Stephenson County	17 999	68.3	1 321	70.5	81	51.9	41	87.8	189	73.5	1.9	0.8	0.3	0.7	0.7	7.3
Tazewell County	49 453	71.5	77	61.0	86	48.8	137	94.2	355	80.6	1.1	0.4	0.4	0.2	0.2	5.2
Union County	7 109	68.6	11	36.4	48	62.5	31	54.8	76	92.1	1.9	0.3	0.3	1.4	1.1	5.5
Vermilion County	29 547	67.4	2 782	60.8	72	59.7	162	65.4	544	88.1	1.7	0.3	0.4	0.9	0.5	6.9
Wabash County	5 094	69.5	16	0.0	11	54.5	8	100.0	36	52.8	0.7	0.3	0.2	0.2	0.0	6.5
Warren County	6 892	69.7	91	67.0	9	100.0	27	70.4	152	75.7	1.4	0.3	0.5	0.5	0.7	6.8
Washington County	5 783	73.4	4	100.0	23	87.0	3	33.3	21	100.0	0.6	0.3	0.1	0.1	0.4	7.1
Wayne County	7 055	69.6	4	0.0	12	0.0	26	100.0	33	100.0	0.9	0.3	0.4	0.2	0.1	4.0
White County	6 457	67.3	11	0.0	14	100.0	0	X	10	50.0	0.3	0.2	0.1	0.0	0.0	2.1
Whiteside County	21 787	71.1	136	62.5	102	76.5	48	81.3	1 564	77.0	2.8	0.5	0.3	1.9	1.5	9.7
Will County	136 876	77.8	15 754	76.4	339	78.8	3 134	90.4	10 365	89.3	7.1	1.5	1.7	3.5	2.3	15.4
Williamson County	24 577	67.6	471	69.4	51	19.6	49	83.7	220	79.5	1.1	0.3	0.2	0.4	0.2	5.3
Winnebago County	90 332	67.5	10 237	70.9	306	84.0	1 376	76.4	4 928	81.8	6.1	1.5	1.3	3.1	2.6	12.3
Woodford County	12 697	76.8	7	28.6	16	100.0	31	80.6	49	91.8	1.0	0.3	0.3	0.3	0.1	6.2

[1] Hispanic or Latino persons may be of any race.

STATE/ County code	MSA/PMSA/ NECMA code[1]	STATE County	Population by age (percent)							Median age	+/− U.S. percent under 18 years	+/− U.S. percent 65 years and over	Non-Hispanic White	Age (percent)	
			Total population	Under 5 years	5 to 17 years	18 to 24 years	25 to 44 years	45 to 64 years	65 years and over				Total population	Under 18 years	65 years and over
			1	2	3	4	5	6	7	8	9	10	11	12	13
18 000	...	INDIANA....................	6 080 485	7.0	18.9	10.1	29.5	22.1	12.4	35.2	0.2	0.0	5 220 722	24.6	13.3
18 001	2760	Adams County	33 625	8.0	23.2	8.9	26.4	20.0	13.5	32.9	5.5	1.1	32 269	30.8	13.8
18 003	2760	Allen County...............	331 849	7.6	20.0	9.4	30.1	21.4	11.4	34.1	1.9	−1.0	270 235	25.6	12.9
18 005	...	Bartholomew County.......	71 435	7.4	19.0	7.7	29.8	23.9	12.2	36.2	0.7	−0.2	66 379	25.9	12.8
18 007	...	Benton County	9 421	6.3	21.2	7.1	27.9	21.7	15.8	36.7	1.8	3.4	8 978	26.9	16.3
18 009	...	Blackford County...........	14 048	6.4	18.3	7.3	27.8	24.7	15.4	38.5	−1.0	3.0	13 709	24.4	15.7
18 011	3480	Boone County	46 107	7.3	20.9	6.5	30.1	23.3	11.7	36.9	2.5	−0.7	44 899	27.9	12.0
18 013	...	Brown County	14 957	5.3	18.0	6.3	27.9	29.6	12.9	40.8	−2.4	0.5	14 514	23.3	13.2
18 015	...	Carroll County	20 165	6.8	19.6	7.7	28.4	23.6	14.0	37.2	0.7	1.6	19 389	26.1	14.4
18 017	...	Cass County	40 930	7.0	18.8	8.9	28.3	22.6	14.4	36.7	0.1	2.0	37 041	24.9	15.7
18 019	4520	Clark County	96 472	6.8	17.4	9.0	30.7	23.7	12.4	36.5	−1.5	0.0	86 313	23.1	12.9
18 021	8320	Clay County	26 556	6.5	19.7	8.7	27.6	22.4	15.1	37.1	0.5	2.7	26 014	25.9	15.2
18 023	3920	Clinton County	33 866	7.2	20.1	8.5	28.7	20.9	14.6	35.6	1.6	2.2	31 141	26.5	15.7
18 025	...	Crawford County	10 743	6.4	19.2	8.4	28.3	24.9	12.8	37.3	−0.1	0.4	10 606	25.5	12.7
18 027	...	Daviess County	29 820	7.6	21.4	8.4	26.3	21.7	14.6	35.5	3.3	2.2	28 805	28.8	14.9
18 029	1640	Dearborn County	46 109	6.8	20.9	7.9	30.0	23.3	11.1	36.2	2.0	−1.3	45 060	27.4	11.3
18 031	...	Decatur County	24 555	7.5	18.8	8.8	29.2	22.5	13.3	35.8	0.6	0.9	23 904	25.9	13.6
18 033	2760	DeKalb County	40 285	7.6	20.6	8.5	30.2	21.7	11.4	34.7	2.5	−1.0	39 130	27.9	11.6
18 035	5280	Delaware County	118 769	5.9	16.2	16.9	25.7	21.8	13.5	33.8	−3.6	1.1	107 158	21.0	14.0
18 037	...	Dubois County	39 674	7.1	20.3	7.8	29.8	22.1	12.9	36.1	1.7	0.5	38 422	27.1	13.3
18 039	2330	Elkhart County	182 791	8.1	20.8	9.4	29.9	21.0	10.9	33.0	3.2	−1.5	152 389	26.9	12.5
18 041	...	Fayette County.............	25 588	6.5	17.9	8.7	27.0	24.4	15.6	38.0	−1.3	3.2	24 877	24.2	15.5
18 043	4520	Floyd County	70 823	6.4	19.4	8.4	30.0	23.6	12.2	36.8	0.1	−0.2	65 651	24.9	12.7
18 045	...	Fountain County	17 954	6.6	19.7	7.4	27.7	23.1	15.6	37.7	0.6	3.2	17 653	26.4	15.7
18 047	...	Franklin County	22 151	6.9	21.2	7.7	29.2	22.3	12.7	35.9	2.4	0.3	21 819	28.0	12.8
18 049	...	Fulton County	20 511	6.6	19.3	7.8	27.5	23.5	15.3	37.9	0.2	2.9	19 477	25.5	15.8
18 051	...	Gibson County	32 500	6.5	18.4	8.4	28.2	23.0	15.6	38.0	−0.8	3.2	31 201	24.5	15.8
18 053	...	Grant County................	73 403	6.0	17.6	11.8	25.7	23.9	14.9	37.4	−2.1	2.5	64 679	22.1	16.0
18 055	...	Greene County	33 157	6.2	18.5	7.7	28.2	24.1	15.3	38.1	−1.0	2.9	32 510	23.4	15.3
18 057	3480	Hamilton County	182 740	9.2	21.6	5.5	34.9	21.3	7.5	34.1	5.1	−4.9	170 750	30.4	7.8
18 059	3480	Hancock County	55 391	6.7	19.7	6.6	30.0	25.6	11.3	37.4	0.7	−1.1	54 276	26.3	11.3
18 061	4520	Harrison County	34 325	6.4	19.6	8.5	30.3	23.7	11.4	36.6	0.3	−1.0	33 489	25.9	11.5
18 063	3480	Hendricks County...........	104 093	7.3	20.7	7.0	32.2	23.1	9.7	35.6	2.3	−2.7	99 616	27.7	10.0
18 065	...	Henry County	48 508	6.1	18.0	7.4	28.0	24.8	15.7	38.7	−1.6	3.3	47 436	24.0	15.8
18 067	3850	Howard County	84 964	7.1	18.5	8.2	28.4	24.4	13.4	37.1	−0.1	1.0	75 565	24.2	14.2
18 069	2760	Huntington County	38 075	6.7	19.4	9.8	28.2	21.8	14.0	36.2	0.4	1.6	37 012	25.7	14.2
18 071	...	Jackson County	41 335	7.1	18.4	8.8	30.2	22.1	13.3	35.8	−0.2	0.9	39 386	25.4	13.8
18 073	...	Jasper County	30 043	6.9	20.5	10.1	27.6	22.3	12.4	35.0	1.7	0.0	28 788	26.9	12.8
18 075	...	Jay County	21 806	7.4	19.5	7.6	27.5	23.3	14.7	36.7	1.2	2.3	21 091	26.4	14.9
18 077	...	Jefferson County...........	31 705	6.1	18.3	10.6	28.5	23.3	13.1	36.6	−1.3	0.7	30 262	24.3	13.3
18 079	...	Jennings County	27 554	7.5	20.2	8.0	30.6	23.0	10.7	34.6	2.0	−1.7	26 594	27.4	10.7
18 081	3480	Johnson County	115 209	7.5	19.7	8.6	30.9	22.4	11.0	34.9	1.5	−1.4	111 079	27.0	11.2
18 083	...	Knox County	39 256	5.8	17.2	13.7	25.4	22.6	15.3	36.7	−2.7	2.9	37 577	22.8	15.8
18 085	...	Kosciusko County	74 057	7.4	20.3	8.7	29.1	22.5	12.0	35.1	2.0	−0.4	68 780	27.0	12.6
18 087	...	LaGrange County...........	34 909	9.7	23.9	10.4	26.2	19.7	10.0	29.5	7.9	−2.4	33 414	33.7	10.4
18 089	2960	Lake County................	484 564	7.1	19.7	9.2	28.4	22.6	13.0	35.9	1.1	0.6	293 292	22.7	15.6
18 091	...	LaPorte County.............	110 106	6.4	18.1	8.5	29.8	23.6	13.6	37.1	−1.2	1.2	93 445	23.2	15.0
18 093	...	Lawrence County	45 922	6.5	18.1	7.6	28.3	24.9	14.8	38.2	−1.1	2.4	44 594	24.2	15.0
18 095	3480	Madison County	133 358	6.3	17.5	9.1	28.4	23.8	14.9	37.4	−1.9	2.5	118 911	23.1	15.8
18 097	3480	Marion County..............	860 454	7.4	18.3	10.0	33.1	20.1	11.1	33.6	0.0	−1.3	592 627	22.5	12.9
18 099	...	Marshall County	45 128	7.3	20.7	8.7	28.3	21.8	13.2	35.5	2.3	0.8	41 652	27.3	14.2
18 101	...	Martin County	10 369	6.4	18.8	6.7	28.4	25.4	14.3	38.5	−0.5	1.9	10 258	25.3	14.3
18 103	...	Miami County	36 082	6.4	19.5	8.3	29.7	23.2	12.9	36.6	0.2	0.5	33 543	25.9	13.4
18 105	1020	Monroe County	120 563	5.0	12.9	27.8	27.2	17.9	9.1	27.6	−7.8	−3.3	108 470	17.6	9.9
18 107	...	Montgomery County........	37 629	6.5	19.3	9.0	28.5	22.7	13.9	36.6	0.1	1.5	36 261	25.7	14.2
18 109	3480	Morgan County	66 689	7.2	20.0	7.7	30.7	23.8	10.7	36.0	1.5	−1.7	65 311	27.1	10.7
18 111	...	Newton County	14 566	6.2	20.3	7.8	28.5	24.3	13.0	37.3	0.8	0.6	13 904	25.9	13.3
18 113	...	Noble County	46 275	7.9	21.0	9.4	30.1	20.6	11.0	33.3	3.2	−1.4	42 311	27.9	11.8
18 115	1640	Ohio County	5 623	5.9	19.0	7.9	28.5	25.0	13.8	38.4	−0.8	1.4	5 535	25.0	13.7
18 117	...	Orange County	19 306	6.6	19.1	7.9	27.9	23.7	14.8	37.5	0.0	2.4	18 838	25.4	14.8
18 119	...	Owen County	21 786	6.5	20.1	7.3	28.8	24.4	12.8	37.6	0.9	0.4	21 217	26.3	13.0
18 121	...	Parke County	17 241	5.5	18.5	7.0	28.9	25.4	14.7	38.9	−1.7	2.3	16 621	24.3	15.0
18 123	...	Perry County	18 899	5.4	17.6	9.7	29.0	23.4	14.9	38.0	−2.7	2.5	18 409	23.1	15.3
18 125	...	Pike County.................	12 837	6.4	17.6	7.8	28.2	24.7	15.3	38.8	−1.7	2.9	12 582	23.5	15.4
18 127	2960	Porter County	146 798	6.5	19.1	10.0	28.7	24.8	10.9	36.3	−0.1	−1.5	135 274	25.0	11.4
18 129	2440	Posey County	27 061	6.4	20.9	7.4	29.0	23.8	12.4	37.4	1.6	0.0	26 411	27.2	12.6
18 131	...	Pulaski County	13 755	6.3	20.6	7.4	27.6	22.8	15.3	37.8	1.2	2.9	13 215	26.6	15.8

[1]MSA = Metropolitan Statistical Area. PMSA = Primary MSA. NECMA = New England County Metropolitan Area. See the Appendix A for explanation of these concepts. See Appendix B for list of metropolitan areas identified by type, with component counties.

STATE County	Black or African American			American Indian and Alaska Native			Asian, Hawaiian, and Pacific Islander			Hispanic or Latino[1]			Two or more races		
	Total population	Under 18 years	65 years and over	Total population	Under 18 years	65 years and over	Total population	Under 18 years	65 years and over	Total population	Under 18 years	65 years and over	Total population	Under 18 years	65 years and over
	14	15	16	17	18	19	20	21	22	23	24	25	26	27	28
INDIANA	504 449	32.2	8.6	17 168	26.7	5.7	58 955	22.7	3.9	210 538	35.3	3.5	84 487	46.5	4.8
Adams County	40	47.5	0.0	15	0.0	0.0	66	21.2	0.0	1 071	43.2	7.5	257	37.4	6.6
Allen County	37 085	36.4	5.9	1 246	26.2	4.0	4 599	27.4	3.8	13 824	36.8	1.9	5 988	52.8	3.1
Bartholomew County	1 302	30.6	6.9	219	28.8	9.6	1 215	21.6	3.7	1 704	32.3	3.3	620	49.2	4.8
Benton County	17	29.4	0.0	10	0.0	0.0	11	18.2	72.7	280	50.7	2.9	145	31.0	9.0
Blackford County	1	0.0	0.0	45	31.1	4.4	25	28.0	0.0	153	43.8	0.7	134	29.1	11.2
Boone County	97	39.2	0.0	26	0.0	30.8	229	31.0	0.0	466	51.1	1.5	447	36.2	4.5
Brown County	57	0.0	7.0	47	34.0	0.0	41	48.8	0.0	88	31.8	2.3	177	26.6	2.8
Carroll County	37	43.2	0.0	36	16.7	0.0	24	50.0	25.0	677	33.1	1.2	51	41.2	0.0
Cass County	417	32.6	3.6	147	32.0	0.0	284	32.7	7.7	2 838	35.3	1.7	526	35.6	5.3
Clark County	6 096	30.9	10.7	317	16.1	1.9	430	17.7	7.9	1 790	34.1	2.2	1 617	46.8	3.7
Clay County	91	42.9	26.4	91	33.0	0.0	74	52.7	0.0	139	36.7	1.4	142	45.1	2.1
Clinton County	52	13.5	0.0	21	33.3	0.0	39	20.5	0.0	2 448	37.5	2.9	214	36.9	5.1
Crawford County	14	0.0	42.9	40	37.5	0.0	23	69.6	0.0	28	21.4	17.9	32	25.0	37.5
Daviess County	106	13.2	20.8	86	25.6	2.3	94	16.0	12.8	606	38.0	1.2	149	61.1	10.1
Dearborn County	319	33.2	0.0	42	35.7	0.0	110	8.2	35.5	176	51.7	4.0	345	36.8	4.9
Decatur County	17	58.8	0.0	10	0.0	0.0	314	40.8	1.3	135	47.4	6.7	171	41.5	1.8
DeKalb County	75	5.3	4.0	72	30.6	0.0	205	45.4	7.3	512	35.4	3.1	275	46.2	12.0
Delaware County	7 761	31.5	10.3	259	24.7	5.8	766	17.5	1.7	1 546	40.0	5.4	1 461	43.5	7.7
Dubois County	21	0.0	28.6	23	0.0	0.0	33	9.1	12.1	995	37.1	1.0	277	50.9	0.7
Elkhart County	9 354	36.5	5.2	692	34.0	5.9	1 624	29.3	3.0	16 195	37.1	1.3	3 659	53.8	2.4
Fayette County	318	20.4	28.3	22	0.0	0.0	53	43.4	0.0	159	35.8	6.9	165	49.7	8.5
Floyd County	3 226	35.7	7.1	104	0.0	6.7	374	19.0	4.5	685	48.0	1.9	930	55.5	5.9
Fountain County	4	0.0	0.0	65	6.2	9.2	48	27.1	0.0	92	15.2	6.5	97	25.8	14.4
Franklin County	2	50.0	0.0	13	0.0	0.0	63	36.5	0.0	86	30.2	17.4	155	38.1	12.9
Fulton County	173	41.0	9.2	74	17.6	16.2	64	71.9	3.1	465	25.8	1.1	293	28.3	9.6
Gibson County	674	33.4	13.4	31	22.6	0.0	144	16.7	19.4	272	35.3	1.1	156	48.1	17.9
Grant County	5 092	32.5	8.6	364	25.8	3.6	495	20.0	3.2	1 699	40.4	6.1	1 261	54.6	6.2
Greene County	33	33.3	24.2	149	30.2	13.4	38	15.8	2.6	262	32.4	4.2	206	20.1	16.5
Hamilton County	2 365	29.4	3.5	405	21.2	4.2	4 141	31.3	2.8	3 241	40.8	1.9	2 049	48.6	2.4
Hancock County	27	11.1	63.0	105	3.8	25.7	217	26.3	6.0	304	38.5	8.6	478	40.0	1.0
Harrison County	115	24.3	28.7	154	30.5	0.0	91	18.7	8.8	377	37.9	1.9	110	45.5	14.5
Hendricks County	1 050	20.5	1.4	227	25.1	5.3	704	20.7	2.1	1 073	36.4	1.3	1 518	47.6	3.2
Henry County	351	23.9	16.0	95	30.5	0.0	62	0.0	19.4	406	39.9	3.7	173	38.2	9.2
Howard County	5 474	32.7	9.3	322	28.9	1.9	714	25.6	5.3	1 761	43.2	3.6	1 282	56.5	3.7
Huntington County	100	58.0	0.0	136	31.6	0.0	117	38.5	1.7	431	40.1	11.8	335	49.9	5.7
Jackson County	343	30.6	12.2	79	30.4	2.5	321	24.6	0.0	777	14.3	0.3	442	54.5	3.4
Jasper County	50	30.0	0.0	62	40.3	17.7	32	43.8	0.0	836	39.7	2.0	325	44.6	6.5
Jay County	39	46.2	10.3	8	0.0	0.0	98	44.9	12.2	423	45.2	1.4	201	39.3	23.9
Jefferson County	463	23.5	8.0	93	5.4	5.4	113	6.2	10.6	435	36.8	8.0	347	28.5	11.2
Jennings County	191	14.1	27.2	104	26.0	18.3	76	21.1	0.0	249	46.2	0.0	324	40.4	3.4
Johnson County	1 032	30.5	0.0	170	15.3	10.0	979	30.7	4.8	1 156	32.3	1.6	814	43.7	6.0
Knox County	702	16.8	1.9	125	36.8	4.8	238	25.2	5.9	379	36.4	2.9	293	36.2	10.9
Kosciusko County	391	35.8	12.3	184	25.5	12.5	393	24.9	2.8	3 651	38.5	1.9	957	44.2	5.0
LaGrange County	94	41.5	0.0	56	16.1	0.0	140	20.0	0.0	1 063	35.4	0.7	199	51.8	3.0
Lake County	122 279	31.7	10.5	1 236	27.3	4.3	4 170	27.5	5.0	58 798	35.9	6.6	9 656	44.1	6.6
LaPorte County	11 005	29.1	6.4	247	16.6	0.0	400	27.5	6.0	3 158	38.4	2.7	2 232	42.8	4.3
Lawrence County	235	29.4	7.2	123	44.7	0.0	196	39.3	0.0	312	31.7	12.8	467	38.5	4.7
Madison County	10 447	27.9	7.2	390	7.2	23.8	557	33.2	6.1	1 879	34.8	2.8	1 315	40.1	10.3
Marion County	207 357	32.5	8.5	2 873	28.1	5.1	11 816	21.1	5.2	32 188	30.5	1.8	15 634	48.6	2.7
Marshall County	91	39.6	0.0	104	24.0	0.0	141	35.5	5.7	2 668	33.6	0.7	514	54.7	1.4
Martin County	7	0.0	0.0	28	0.0	0.0	2	0.0	0.0	12	0.0	16.7	62	32.3	11.3
Miami County	950	12.8	8.2	301	13.3	7.6	134	40.3	5.2	650	39.5	5.1	634	43.4	2.5
Monroe County	3 611	23.0	2.2	274	17.5	5.5	3 954	9.6	1.2	2 034	15.4	1.2	2 220	38.9	2.9
Montgomery County	316	26.3	11.1	49	32.7	0.0	56	12.5	12.5	595	21.7	4.0	309	50.2	5.8
Morgan County	55	49.1	0.0	171	28.1	17.5	267	13.1	13.1	285	37.5	5.3	553	38.9	6.0
Newton County	26	23.1	23.1	80	26.3	17.5	83	30.1	0.0	420	39.5	4.0	94	54.3	5.3
Noble County	149	45.0	0.0	31	25.8	19.4	270	38.9	8.1	3 220	39.0	1.2	431	46.6	7.9
Ohio County	20	0.0	20.0	0	X	X	0	X	X	36	22.2	0.0	32	12.5	37.5
Orange County	63	38.1	22.2	100	23.0	16.0	7	0.0	85.7	145	38.6	11.7	224	58.9	4.9
Owen County	68	57.4	0.0	83	24.1	1.2	31	16.1	9.7	183	48.1	7.1	210	46.2	2.4
Parke County	313	2.2	1.9	76	19.7	23.7	30	26.7	6.7	99	36.4	8.1	123	25.2	1.6
Perry County	268	1.1	0.0	3	0.0	0.0	8	0.0	0.0	109	43.1	0.0	108	40.7	0.9
Pike County	9	0.0	0.0	14	14.3	0.0	61	52.5	3.3	106	50.0	10.4	70	57.1	8.6
Porter County	1 596	29.9	3.3	292	18.8	13.0	1 096	21.4	2.5	7 053	35.8	4.2	2 364	40.2	5.2
Posey County	266	32.3	0.0	46	10.9	2.2	31	71.0	0.0	146	32.2	4.8	183	38.8	11.5
Pulaski County	183	22.4	5.5	28	17.9	14.3	21	47.6	0.0	167	27.5	3.0	152	58.6	0.0

[1] Hispanic or Latino persons may be of any race.

STATE County	Total households	Family households (percent)						Nonfamily households (percent)						Percent of householders 65 years and over who live alone	Grandparents who are responsible for the care of their grandchildren
		Married-couple family households			Other family households			Two or more unrelated persons		Male living alone		Female living alone			
		Total	With children	Householder 65 years or over	Total	With children	Householder 65 years or over	Total	Householder 65 years or over	Total	Householder 65 years or over	Total	Householder 65 years or over		
	29	30	31	32	33	34	35	36	37	38	39	40	41	42	43
INDIANA	2 337 229	54.5	24.6	9.1	14.5	8.8	1.8	5.2	0.3	11.0	2.2	14.9	7.5	46.2	48 181
Adams County	11 803	62.0	30.3	11.0	11.4	7.3	1.8	2.6	0.2	9.7	2.5	14.3	9.5	48.1	33
Allen County	128 891	52.1	25.1	8.3	15.1	9.7	1.5	5.4	0.3	12.0	2.0	15.4	7.0	47.2	2 373
Bartholomew County	27 958	59.4	26.9	9.0	12.8	7.8	1.7	3.9	0.3	10.8	2.5	13.1	7.1	46.5	566
Benton County	3 584	61.2	28.3	11.4	11.3	6.9	2.0	3.3	0.2	9.4	2.3	14.8	10.8	49.2	99
Blackford County	5 680	57.8	23.8	11.8	13.0	8.4	2.2	3.2	0.3	10.2	2.1	15.9	10.4	46.6	111
Boone County	17 091	63.6	32.4	8.5	10.7	6.3	1.7	4.5	0.4	9.2	2.1	12.0	6.8	45.6	223
Brown County	5 911	65.1	24.5	11.5	9.7	5.5	1.5	4.7	0.6	10.2	1.4	10.4	5.0	32.0	110
Carroll County	7 717	63.3	27.9	11.0	9.9	6.0	1.5	3.8	0.2	10.6	2.5	12.4	8.0	45.3	109
Cass County	15 672	57.3	24.5	10.9	13.0	7.6	1.9	3.9	0.3	10.0	2.6	15.9	9.6	48.1	214
Clark County	38 774	52.9	22.6	8.1	15.8	9.5	2.1	5.0	0.1	11.0	2.0	15.3	7.5	48.0	870
Clay County	10 198	60.4	26.9	11.1	12.5	6.5	2.0	3.3	0.5	8.8	2.3	15.1	10.1	47.5	306
Clinton County	12 550	58.3	26.9	10.6	14.0	8.6	1.2	4.2	0.2	10.8	3.3	12.7	8.3	49.1	250
Crawford County	4 167	58.7	24.6	9.4	14.2	8.4	1.4	4.5	0.9	10.8	2.6	11.8	6.9	45.0	112
Daviess County	10 932	60.9	29.4	11.3	11.6	7.1	1.7	2.7	0.2	9.4	2.6	15.3	9.5	47.7	181
Dearborn County	16 822	63.4	29.9	9.3	13.1	8.3	1.8	3.4	0.3	9.0	2.2	11.1	6.2	42.4	305
Decatur County	9 420	60.6	27.2	10.5	13.0	7.6	1.7	3.6	0.1	9.8	2.1	12.9	7.7	44.2	169
DeKalb County	15 146	60.6	28.8	8.8	12.0	8.3	1.1	4.0	0.2	11.0	1.9	12.5	7.4	48.1	253
Delaware County	47 131	50.3	20.0	9.5	13.3	8.6	1.6	8.4	0.4	11.4	2.4	16.7	8.2	48.0	855
Dubois County	14 764	62.0	31.2	9.8	10.9	6.0	1.6	3.5	0.3	10.0	2.0	13.6	7.7	45.2	147
Elkhart County	66 124	58.4	27.7	9.2	14.3	9.5	1.2	4.8	0.4	9.4	1.7	13.2	6.8	44.5	1 524
Fayette County	10 192	56.4	23.4	11.2	13.8	8.0	2.4	4.0	0.3	9.0	2.2	16.8	10.4	47.8	194
Floyd County	27 532	56.3	25.7	8.8	15.6	9.5	1.6	4.6	0.3	9.6	1.9	13.9	6.7	44.5	450
Fountain County	7 061	59.5	25.0	12.0	12.3	7.7	1.7	3.7	0.4	9.4	2.4	15.1	10.5	47.6	198
Franklin County	7 857	66.5	31.4	11.3	11.5	6.2	1.7	2.8	0.3	9.4	2.3	9.8	6.8	40.5	96
Fulton County	8 077	58.3	25.1	11.1	12.6	7.3	1.7	4.2	0.5	10.6	3.9	14.3	9.3	50.0	196
Gibson County	12 838	59.3	25.5	11.4	11.6	7.1	1.9	3.4	0.5	10.3	2.3	15.4	10.1	47.1	226
Grant County	28 333	54.9	20.5	10.7	14.5	8.7	1.9	3.9	0.4	9.8	2.6	16.9	10.4	50.0	758
Greene County	13 365	60.1	25.7	11.1	10.3	6.4	1.5	3.2	0.5	10.9	2.4	15.5	10.1	48.9	213
Hamilton County	65 992	68.7	38.7	6.1	8.8	5.8	0.7	3.9	0.3	7.5	1.3	11.0	4.3	44.1	479
Hancock County	20 811	68.1	31.1	9.8	10.2	6.0	1.6	3.0	0.2	7.4	2.0	11.2	6.0	40.9	269
Harrison County	12 924	62.8	29.2	8.5	12.6	7.7	1.5	3.9	0.4	9.0	2.7	11.6	6.6	47.3	179
Hendricks County	37 323	67.7	33.2	8.5	10.5	7.0	1.2	3.5	0.5	7.8	1.3	10.4	5.1	38.5	630
Henry County	19 506	59.7	24.3	12.0	12.1	7.0	1.6	3.2	0.3	9.9	2.6	15.0	9.4	46.0	479
Howard County	34 846	53.3	21.9	9.5	14.7	9.1	1.8	3.8	0.2	11.7	2.1	16.4	8.3	47.6	777
Huntington County	14 277	60.7	27.1	11.1	12.1	7.9	1.4	3.9	0.1	10.1	1.8	13.3	7.0	41.3	318
Jackson County	16 085	59.2	26.2	10.2	13.1	7.8	1.8	4.3	0.3	10.1	1.8	13.4	8.6	45.8	474
Jasper County	10 672	66.3	30.7	11.7	10.7	5.9	1.7	3.1	0.3	8.1	1.5	11.8	7.4	39.4	254
Jay County	8 404	59.3	26.3	11.3	12.2	6.8	1.9	3.7	0.3	10.0	2.3	14.8	9.6	46.8	103
Jefferson County	12 172	55.8	23.6	10.1	14.3	8.6	1.9	4.3	0.2	11.2	2.1	14.5	7.9	45.3	295
Jennings County	10 196	62.5	30.5	8.4	12.5	7.7	1.3	4.5	0.5	8.9	2.1	11.5	7.4	48.5	413
Johnson County	42 510	63.1	30.3	8.3	11.6	7.5	1.2	4.2	0.4	8.6	1.5	12.6	6.1	43.3	910
Knox County	15 540	52.5	21.9	9.9	13.0	8.4	1.9	4.9	0.3	12.2	3.4	17.5	10.2	52.8	305
Kosciusko County	27 310	62.2	28.9	10.2	11.5	7.3	1.1	4.4	0.3	9.8	1.8	12.1	6.4	41.5	397
LaGrange County	11 242	68.3	35.3	10.9	11.0	6.5	1.1	2.9	0.3	8.6	1.6	9.3	5.3	35.9	134
Lake County	181 589	49.9	22.5	9.4	20.3	10.9	3.4	4.0	0.4	11.2	2.6	14.6	7.2	42.7	5 804
LaPorte County	41 086	54.8	23.2	10.5	15.4	9.3	2.1	4.6	0.4	10.8	2.4	14.5	8.3	45.2	919
Lawrence County	18 487	57.6	24.5	10.1	12.8	7.3	2.4	4.0	0.3	10.8	2.6	14.8	8.8	47.0	530
Madison County	52 993	53.7	21.1	11.0	15.4	9.5	2.0	3.7	0.4	11.0	2.5	16.1	9.3	47.1	1 310
Marion County	352 261	42.1	19.2	6.8	18.9	11.6	2.1	7.3	0.3	13.7	2.1	18.0	6.8	49.0	8 626
Marshall County	16 503	61.7	28.6	11.1	12.3	7.3	1.8	3.7	0.3	8.9	1.9	13.4	8.0	42.7	293
Martin County	4 196	58.7	26.5	10.4	10.2	5.8	2.0	3.6	0.1	12.8	4.0	14.6	8.9	50.9	65
Miami County	13 679	59.6	25.0	10.7	12.5	8.2	1.5	3.3	0.2	10.5	2.2	14.1	8.2	45.5	175
Monroe County	46 939	42.4	17.8	6.6	10.7	6.9	1.0	14.6	0.3	14.3	1.8	18.0	5.8	49.1	544
Montgomery County	14 595	59.3	26.3	10.2	11.7	7.8	1.1	3.8	0.1	9.6	2.5	15.6	9.9	51.9	233
Morgan County	24 473	64.6	29.3	8.3	13.4	8.2	1.9	3.7	0.3	8.5	1.8	9.9	6.1	42.7	769
Newton County	5 373	64.8	28.9	10.6	10.6	6.1	1.9	3.8	0.3	8.6	2.2	12.2	7.6	43.4	117
Noble County	16 730	61.8	30.6	9.1	12.2	7.6	1.5	4.2	0.3	9.6	1.8	12.2	6.3	42.8	370
Ohio County	2 199	63.8	27.1	11.1	9.3	4.5	2.0	3.7	0.3	9.5	2.0	13.6	7.6	42.0	33
Orange County	7 658	59.0	26.1	10.4	12.0	7.2	1.7	3.0	0.2	10.7	3.2	15.3	9.0	49.8	146
Owen County	8 281	62.5	25.9	10.9	12.4	8.1	1.3	3.7	0.2	10.2	2.5	11.1	5.6	39.6	204
Parke County	6 422	60.4	23.8	11.3	12.3	7.7	2.3	3.1	0.2	10.7	2.7	13.4	8.9	45.7	144
Perry County	7 256	57.6	24.0	11.1	12.4	7.7	1.8	3.4	0.3	10.3	2.6	16.3	9.8	48.4	131
Pike County	5 083	60.8	23.4	12.3	11.4	6.1	1.7	2.7	0.4	10.3	1.9	14.7	9.0	43.1	81
Porter County	54 721	60.3	27.9	8.5	12.6	7.6	1.7	4.9	0.4	10.0	1.9	12.2	6.3	43.7	908
Posey County	10 223	64.7	30.3	10.0	10.6	6.5	1.4	2.8	0.2	9.5	2.7	12.5	8.0	48.1	223
Pulaski County	5 175	59.9	26.3	12.9	13.8	8.8	1.9	2.7	0.3	11.1	2.6	12.4	8.0	41.3	117

Table A-3. States and Counties — Age, Ethnicity, and Household Structure

STATE County	Households with Non-Hispanic White householder		Households with Black or African American householder		Households with American Indian and Alaska Native householder		Households with Asian, Hawaiian, and Pacific Islander householder		Households with Hispanic or Latino[1] householder		Foreign-born population	Place of birth (percent)			Percent in non-English speaking households	
	Number of households	Percent that are family households	Number of households	Percent that are family households	Number of households	Percent that are family households	Number of households	Percent that are family households	Number of households	Percent that are family households	Percent of total population that is foreign-born	Europe	Asia	Latin America	Linguistically isolated	Not linguistically isolated
	44	45	46	47	48	49	50	51	52	53	54	55	56	57	58	59
INDIANA	2 050 401	69.0	184 808	66.1	6 546	69.0	20 022	64.8	56 960	77.1	3.1	0.7	0.8	1.3	1.3	9.0
Adams County	11 445	73.6	4	100.0	6	0.0	23	100.0	283	71.7	1.1	0.3	0.2	0.3	2.8	15.9
Allen County	108 666	66.7	13 285	68.1	517	63.8	1 531	73.7	3 666	78.3	4.0	1.0	1.2	1.5	1.7	10.1
Bartholomew County	26 413	72.3	478	65.7	39	84.6	474	75.5	415	72.8	3.8	0.8	1.3	1.5	1.2	7.7
Benton County	3 463	72.3	10	40.0	5	100.0	6	100.0	56	83.9	0.8	0.4	0.0	0.3	0.1	7.3
Blackford County	5 589	70.8	0	X	5	60.0	0	X	45	100.0	0.1	0.0	0.1	0.0	0.0	4.4
Boone County	16 789	74.5	7	0.0	16	50.0	76	85.5	86	66.3	1.5	0.8	0.5	0.2	0.3	5.2
Brown County	5 777	74.7	29	41.4	14	85.7	7	100.0	11	100.0	1.0	0.4	0.3	0.1	0.0	5.4
Carroll County	7 519	73.1	8	0.0	9	66.7	6	100.0	164	79.9	2.2	0.2	0.1	1.9	0.7	5.8
Cass County	14 760	70.3	101	77.2	41	73.2	69	91.3	604	64.7	4.3	0.5	0.5	3.2	2.1	9.1
Clark County	35 131	68.9	2 319	67.7	169	55.0	180	47.8	531	75.3	1.7	0.4	0.4	0.7	0.7	5.6
Clay County	9 986	73.0	36	33.3	43	65.1	14	100.0	57	77.2	0.6	0.2	0.1	0.1	0.1	4.4
Clinton County	11 837	72.0	34	0.0	11	90.9	22	100.0	581	81.9	4.8	0.2	0.1	4.4	2.6	9.9
Crawford County	4 119	72.8	0	X	15	93.3	0	X	14	85.7	0.3	0.2	0.1	0.0	0.1	3.1
Daviess County	10 678	72.6	50	46.0	24	79.2	19	100.0	141	71.6	1.9	0.3	0.2	1.3	2.5	14.4
Dearborn County	16 468	76.7	107	68.2	17	47.1	35	60.0	47	89.4	0.8	0.4	0.2	0.1	0.2	5.8
Decatur County	9 249	73.4	7	100.0	2	0.0	84	82.1	22	100.0	1.6	0.3	1.1	0.0	0.7	4.5
DeKalb County	14 869	72.5	31	29.0	12	75.0	41	63.4	123	87.0	0.8	0.2	0.2	0.2	0.4	4.7
Delaware County	43 104	63.9	3 005	58.6	121	76.9	220	45.9	383	65.5	1.5	0.3	0.6	0.3	0.3	6.3
Dubois County	14 416	73.2	5	100.0	5	0.0	4	50.0	268	64.6	2.1	0.2	0.1	1.8	1.6	7.2
Elkhart County	57 764	72.4	3 310	66.3	221	70.1	471	78.8	3 796	83.6	7.1	0.7	0.8	5.3	4.8	14.5
Fayette County	9 950	70.6	165	54.5	13	69.2	11	100.0	47	31.9	0.5	0.2	0.1	0.1	0.2	3.7
Floyd County	25 733	71.8	1 275	73.6	46	58.7	110	91.8	186	76.9	1.2	0.4	0.4	0.2	0.2	5.9
Fountain County	6 931	72.0	4	0.0	19	73.7	16	68.8	58	34.5	1.0	0.4	0.2	0.3	0.4	6.5
Franklin County	7 773	78.0	1	0.0	12	100.0	5	100.0	17	70.6	0.6	0.3	0.2	0.2	0.0	6.5
Fulton County	7 769	70.4	45	68.9	28	100.0	11	81.8	129	89.1	2.0	0.5	0.2	1.2	0.8	7.6
Gibson County	12 421	71.3	220	60.9	4	0.0	63	55.6	79	73.4	0.9	0.2	0.3	0.4	0.1	6.0
Grant County	25 495	69.4	1 847	69.1	127	73.2	150	60.7	452	70.8	1.2	0.4	0.4	0.2	0.5	6.9
Greene County	13 139	70.4	8	0.0	66	75.8	15	100.0	73	65.8	0.5	0.3	0.1	0.0	0.1	4.8
Hamilton County	62 344	77.3	852	76.8	175	73.1	1 339	86.4	816	82.2	4.0	1.1	1.8	0.6	0.7	9.0
Hancock County	20 452	78.3	5	100.0	54	88.9	80	70.0	86	79.1	0.9	0.5	0.2	0.1	0.1	6.3
Harrison County	12 680	76.5	90	65.6	50	100.0	27	51.9	70	82.1	0.5	0.2	0.2	0.3	0.2	5.1
Hendricks County	36 244	78.1	149	79.2	70	92.9	188	95.7	245	86.9	1.6	0.5	0.6	0.3	0.3	5.4
Henry County	19 175	72.0	151	53.6	23	91.3	25	72.0	95	76.8	0.5	0.3	0.1	0.1	0.2	4.1
Howard County	31 426	68.5	2 177	64.2	171	49.7	260	66.9	505	66.7	1.8	0.5	0.7	0.4	0.4	7.2
Huntington County	14 018	72.5	31	90.3	47	70.2	30	83.3	70	82.9	0.8	0.2	0.2	0.1	0.2	6.9
Jackson County	15 393	72.6	144	60.4	40	77.5	140	60.0	240	62.5	2.4	0.3	0.7	1.3	1.5	5.9
Jasper County	10 341	77.0	5	100.0	23	100.0	0	X	204	77.9	1.5	0.7	0.1	0.5	0.7	6.3
Jay County	8 221	71.3	19	63.2	8	0.0	24	75.0	83	96.4	1.5	0.3	0.3	0.9	1.1	7.7
Jefferson County	11 697	70.0	151	67.5	42	85.7	33	90.9	124	71.8	1.2	0.5	0.3	0.3	0.1	6.8
Jennings County	9 917	75.2	98	66.3	34	67.6	8	100.0	67	82.1	0.7	0.2	0.2	0.2	0.2	5.3
Johnson County	41 336	74.9	212	68.4	90	71.1	342	63.7	326	72.4	1.7	0.5	0.6	0.4	0.4	6.1
Knox County	15 080	65.5	127	52.0	55	70.9	104	34.6	86	77.9	1.1	0.3	0.5	0.3	0.5	6.2
Kosciusko County	25 782	73.4	131	74.0	94	69.1	108	76.9	965	84.5	2.9	0.3	0.4	2.0	2.2	10.5
LaGrange County	10 837	79.4	25	100.0	17	82.4	49	73.5	278	78.4	2.1	0.2	0.4	1.5	9.4	27.1
Lake County	116 196	69.4	45 242	68.2	396	71.5	1 318	84.4	16 915	81.7	5.3	1.9	0.8	2.5	2.1	17.9
LaPorte County	36 680	69.5	3 033	74.9	59	66.1	106	74.5	842	79.6	2.5	0.9	0.4	0.9	1.0	9.3
Lawrence County	18 057	70.6	83	65.1	40	35.0	46	89.1	104	64.4	0.9	0.3	0.3	0.2	0.1	4.6
Madison County	48 402	69.2	3 450	68.8	259	75.3	190	44.7	381	92.9	1.2	0.2	0.3	0.5	0.4	5.3
Marion County	255 496	59.3	78 891	65.0	1 060	63.1	4 375	65.8	9 151	70.5	4.6	0.8	1.2	2.1	2.0	9.5
Marshall County	15 639	73.7	21	85.7	33	100.0	36	72.2	669	80.7	4.4	0.6	0.3	3.2	2.7	11.5
Martin County	4 147	69.0	0	X	20	65.0	0	X	10	0.0	0.3	0.1	0.0	0.1	0.0	3.3
Miami County	12 900	71.9	261	64.0	150	74.0	27	100.0	183	73.2	1.0	0.5	0.2	0.3	0.2	7.0
Monroe County	42 472	54.5	1 304	43.3	130	88.5	1 631	33.4	757	40.2	5.4	1.4	3.0	0.5	1.3	9.8
Montgomery County	14 239	71.2	116	58.6	12	66.7	7	0.0	147	78.9	1.5	0.3	0.1	0.9	0.7	4.5
Morgan County	24 082	77.9	12	75.0	52	78.8	76	71.1	81	77.8	0.9	0.4	0.3	0.1	0.1	4.9
Newton County	5 182	75.3	10	40.0	47	74.5	20	75.0	91	85.7	2.3	0.5	0.3	1.4	0.7	9.1
Noble County	15 856	73.3	19	94.7	8	100.0	60	88.3	696	88.8	4.9	0.2	0.4	4.1	3.3	9.6
Ohio County	2 150	73.4	17	23.5	0	X	0	X	21	100.0	0.1	0.0	0.0	0.1	0.0	3.5
Orange County	7 513	71.2	19	26.3	32	59.4	7	100.0	41	48.8	0.8	0.3	0.0	0.4	0.2	6.3
Owen County	8 136	74.7	14	57.1	27	100.0	9	100.0	28	100.0	0.4	0.2	0.1	0.0	0.1	6.5
Parke County	6 364	72.7	5	80.0	22	90.9	0	X	7	71.4	0.5	0.3	0.1	0.0	0.7	5.2
Perry County	7 195	70.0	13	0.0	3	100.0	2	100.0	32	81.3	0.4	0.2	0.0	0.2	0.3	5.1
Pike County	5 016	72.2	2	100.0	5	20.0	9	77.8	33	90.9	0.6	0.2	0.1	0.1	0.1	4.4
Porter County	51 240	72.7	510	71.8	124	60.5	328	78.4	2 006	79.5	3.0	1.3	0.7	0.6	0.6	10.9
Posey County	10 013	75.2	79	75.9	13	100.0	3	100.0	45	82.2	0.5	0.2	0.1	0.1	0.1	5.4
Pulaski County	5 035	73.5	35	85.7	23	17.4	0	X	49	100.0	0.8	0.3	0.1	0.4	0.5	5.0

[1]Hispanic or Latino persons may be of any race.

STATE/ County code	MSA/PMSA/ NECMA code[1]	STATE County	Total population	Under 5 years	5 to 17 years	18 to 24 years	25 to 44 years	45 to 64 years	65 years and over	Median age	+/− U.S. percent under 18 years	+/− U.S. percent 65 years and over	Total population	Under 18 years	65 years and over
													Non-Hispanic White — Age (percent)		
			1	2	3	4	5	6	7	8	9	10	11	12	13
		INDIANA—Cont'd													
18 133	...	Putnam County	36 019	6.0	17.7	13.2	29.3	21.4	12.4	35.1	-2.0	0.0	33 821	23.9	13.0
18 135	...	Randolph County	27 401	6.7	18.6	7.9	27.4	23.6	15.8	38.2	-0.4	3.4	26 799	25.0	15.9
18 137	...	Ripley County	26 523	7.5	20.5	7.7	28.8	22.0	13.4	35.7	2.3	1.0	26 066	28.0	13.5
18 139	...	Rush County	18 261	6.9	19.8	7.5	28.9	22.1	14.8	36.9	1.0	2.4	17 651	26.3	14.9
18 141	7800	St. Joseph County	265 559	7.0	18.7	11.7	28.2	20.8	13.6	34.4	0.0	1.2	214 495	23.0	15.4
18 143	4520	Scott County	22 960	7.5	18.8	9.5	30.0	23.2	11.1	35.1	0.6	-1.3	22 434	25.8	11.1
18 145	3480	Shelby County	43 445	6.7	19.9	8.1	30.7	22.4	12.1	36.2	0.9	-0.3	42 046	26.3	12.4
18 147	...	Spencer County	20 391	6.2	20.3	7.3	29.1	24.1	12.9	37.3	0.8	0.5	19 890	26.4	13.1
18 149	...	Starke County	23 556	6.5	20.2	8.4	27.8	23.3	13.8	37.0	1.0	1.4	22 732	25.8	14.2
18 151	...	Steuben County	33 214	6.6	19.0	10.6	28.4	23.4	11.9	35.5	-0.1	-0.5	31 955	25.3	12.2
18 153	...	Sullivan County	21 751	5.7	16.9	9.4	30.7	23.2	14.1	37.3	-3.1	1.7	20 315	23.4	14.9
18 155	...	Switzerland County	9 065	6.2	20.0	8.8	27.7	24.6	12.7	36.8	0.5	0.3	8 932	26.0	12.8
18 157	3920	Tippecanoe County	148 955	5.9	14.9	25.5	27.4	17.2	9.0	27.2	-4.9	-3.4	128 788	20.4	10.2
18 159	3850	Tipton County	16 577	6.0	19.0	7.1	28.0	25.3	14.6	38.4	-0.7	2.2	16 202	25.0	14.6
18 161	...	Union County	7 349	6.8	20.4	7.7	28.4	23.8	12.9	36.5	1.5	0.5	7 239	26.9	12.9
18 163	2440	Vanderburgh County	171 922	6.2	16.9	11.6	28.0	22.0	15.3	36.9	-2.6	2.9	152 442	21.6	16.2
18 165	8320	Vermillion County	16 788	6.5	17.3	8.2	27.3	24.8	15.9	38.9	-1.9	3.5	16 366	23.3	16.3
18 167	8320	Vigo County	105 848	6.1	16.7	14.2	27.4	21.3	14.3	34.9	-2.9	1.9	95 153	22.2	15.1
18 169	...	Wabash County	34 960	5.8	18.7	10.4	26.2	23.2	15.6	37.5	-1.2	3.2	33 722	24.3	16.1
18 171	...	Warren County	8 419	6.0	20.3	6.7	27.7	25.5	14.0	38.2	0.6	1.6	8 302	26.3	14.2
18 173	2440	Warrick County	52 383	6.6	20.3	7.2	29.7	25.5	10.8	37.3	1.2	-1.6	51 157	26.6	10.9
18 175	...	Washington County	27 223	6.7	19.8	8.7	29.8	23.0	12.1	35.8	0.8	-0.3	26 792	26.3	12.2
18 177	...	Wayne County	71 097	6.1	18.0	9.3	27.5	23.3	15.9	37.7	-1.6	3.5	65 023	23.4	16.3
18 179	2760	Wells County	27 600	6.7	20.7	8.3	28.0	22.2	14.1	36.8	1.7	1.7	26 800	26.9	14.4
18 181	...	White County	25 267	6.3	19.4	7.7	27.9	23.8	14.9	37.6	0.0	2.5	23 470	24.9	15.8
18 183	2760	Whitley County	30 707	6.7	20.1	8.1	28.9	23.1	13.1	36.9	1.1	0.7	30 112	26.6	13.3
19 000	...	IOWA............................	2 926 324	6.4	18.6	10.2	27.7	22.2	14.9	36.6	-0.7	2.5	2 713 026	24.1	15.8
19 001	...	Adair County	8 243	5.5	18.5	7.0	24.2	22.8	22.1	41.8	-1.7	9.7	8 132	24.0	22.1
19 003	...	Adams County	4 482	5.8	18.0	6.4	24.1	24.5	21.3	41.9	-1.9	8.9	4 439	23.8	21.5
19 005	...	Allamakee County	14 675	5.9	19.6	6.7	25.7	23.6	18.4	39.7	-0.2	6.0	13 928	24.8	19.3
19 007	...	Appanoose County	13 721	5.6	18.2	7.7	25.1	23.5	20.0	40.6	-1.9	7.6	13 316	23.3	20.5
19 009	...	Audubon County	6 830	5.7	20.1	5.4	22.2	23.0	23.6	42.4	0.1	11.2	6 747	25.3	23.9
19 011	...	Benton County	25 308	6.5	20.9	7.2	28.9	21.1	15.4	37.2	1.7	3.0	24 991	27.0	15.6
19 013	8920	Black Hawk County	128 012	6.1	17.0	15.7	25.2	22.0	14.0	34.4	-2.6	1.6	112 282	20.9	15.1
19 015	...	Boone County	26 224	6.1	18.7	8.4	27.2	23.2	16.4	38.6	-0.9	4.0	25 696	24.4	16.7
19 017	...	Bremer County	23 325	5.6	18.5	12.3	23.6	24.0	15.9	38.1	-1.6	3.5	22 783	23.7	16.2
19 019	...	Buchanan County	21 093	6.8	21.7	8.0	26.5	22.5	14.5	36.4	2.8	2.1	20 576	28.1	14.8
19 021	...	Buena Vista County	20 411	5.8	19.5	12.3	25.6	19.9	16.8	36.4	-0.4	4.4	16 660	23.3	20.1
19 023	...	Butler County	15 305	5.6	18.9	6.4	24.8	24.1	20.2	41.3	-1.2	7.8	15 131	24.3	20.3
19 025	...	Calhoun County	11 115	5.0	17.9	6.2	25.3	23.5	22.1	42.4	-2.8	9.7	10 854	22.8	22.4
19 027	...	Carroll County	21 421	6.0	20.9	7.3	25.8	21.2	18.7	38.7	1.2	6.3	21 126	26.7	18.9
19 029	...	Cass County	14 684	5.4	18.3	6.2	25.5	23.8	20.8	41.6	-2.0	8.4	14 423	23.6	21.1
19 031	...	Cedar County	18 187	6.0	19.2	7.2	27.5	23.8	16.2	39.2	-0.5	3.8	17 829	25.0	16.5
19 033	...	Cerro Gordo County	46 447	6.1	17.9	8.8	26.3	23.1	17.7	39.3	-1.7	5.3	44 078	22.9	18.3
19 035	...	Cherokee County	13 035	5.3	19.1	7.1	23.7	24.4	20.3	41.7	-1.3	7.9	12 793	24.2	20.7
19 037	...	Chickasaw County	13 095	5.7	20.3	6.8	25.8	23.5	17.9	39.7	0.3	5.5	12 898	25.6	18.1
19 039	...	Clarke County	9 133	6.2	20.0	7.3	26.8	22.7	17.0	38.6	0.5	4.6	8 678	25.7	17.7
19 041	...	Clay County	17 372	6.2	18.4	8.0	26.9	22.4	18.0	39.4	-1.1	5.6	16 873	24.0	18.5
19 043	...	Clayton County	18 678	5.7	19.6	6.5	26.1	23.6	18.6	40.2	-0.4	6.2	18 349	25.0	18.8
19 045	...	Clinton County	50 149	6.4	19.2	8.3	27.0	23.3	15.8	38.2	-0.1	3.4	47 846	24.9	16.3
19 047	...	Crawford County	16 942	6.5	20.1	8.1	26.0	22.1	17.3	38.2	0.9	4.9	15 104	25.4	19.1
19 049	2120	Dallas County	40 750	8.1	20.1	6.8	32.1	21.7	11.1	35.1	2.5	-1.3	37 706	27.2	11.8
19 051	...	Davis County	8 541	7.1	20.1	7.5	25.1	22.8	17.4	38.5	1.5	5.0	8 397	27.0	17.3
19 053	...	Decatur County	8 689	5.5	17.6	16.1	21.8	21.4	17.6	36.4	-2.6	5.2	8 381	23.3	18.2
19 055	...	Delaware County	18 404	6.4	22.6	7.0	27.7	21.3	15.0	37.1	3.3	2.6	18 144	28.7	15.2
19 057	...	Des Moines County	42 351	6.1	18.2	8.6	25.8	24.6	16.7	38.9	-1.4	4.3	39 489	23.0	17.5
19 059	...	Dickinson County	16 424	5.3	16.6	6.7	23.8	27.0	20.6	43.3	-3.8	8.2	16 165	21.6	20.9
19 061	2200	Dubuque County	89 143	6.7	18.8	10.3	27.2	22.3	14.8	36.5	-0.2	2.4	86 204	25.1	15.2
19 063	...	Emmet County	11 027	5.3	18.5	10.3	23.9	22.7	19.2	39.6	-1.9	6.8	10 470	23.0	20.2
19 065	...	Fayette County	22 008	5.9	19.1	8.5	25.2	22.2	19.0	39.4	-0.7	6.6	21 327	24.7	19.4
19 067	...	Floyd County	16 900	6.1	19.1	7.1	24.4	24.3	19.1	40.3	-0.5	6.7	16 560	24.8	19.5
19 069	...	Franklin County	10 704	5.7	18.5	7.0	24.4	23.8	20.5	41.3	-1.5	8.1	9 966	23.2	21.9
19 071	...	Fremont County	8 010	5.4	19.5	5.7	24.9	24.8	19.8	41.2	-0.8	7.4	7 762	24.8	20.3
19 073	...	Greene County	10 366	5.9	19.7	6.4	24.0	22.3	21.7	41.0	-0.1	9.3	10 104	25.1	22.2
19 075	...	Grundy County	12 369	5.4	19.8	6.3	25.0	24.1	19.3	40.8	-0.5	6.9	12 192	24.8	19.5

[1]MSA = Metropolitan Statistical Area. PMSA = Primary MSA. NECMA = New England County Metropolitan Area. See the Appendix A for explanation of these concepts. See Appendix B for list of metropolitan areas identified by type, with component counties.

STATE County	Black or African American Total population	Age (percent) Under 18 years	65 years and over	American Indian and Alaska Native Total population	Age (percent) Under 18 years	65 years and over	Asian, Hawaiian, and Pacific Islander Total population	Age (percent) Under 18 years	65 years and over	Hispanic or Latino[1] Total population	Age (percent) Under 18 years	65 years and over	Two or more races Total population	Age (percent) Under 18 years	65 years and over
	14	15	16	17	18	19	20	21	22	23	24	25	26	27	28
INDIANA—Cont'd															
Putnam County	1 041	10.4	2.6	96	21.9	0.0	240	11.3	6.7	507	29.0	0.0	323	44.0	7.4
Randolph County	45	4.4	17.8	33	6.1	51.5	44	40.9	9.1	268	42.2	1.1	219	38.4	16.0
Ripley County	8	87.5	0.0	86	18.6	15.1	62	43.5	1.6	166	38.6	4.2	131	34.4	10.7
Rush County	174	44.8	13.8	70	41.4	0.0	23	17.4	0.0	126	28.6	10.3	217	42.4	14.7
St. Joseph County........	29 652	35.7	7.9	904	44.0	0.9	3 579	21.8	3.7	12 343	38.4	2.2	5 655	52.1	5.8
Scott County...............	64	42.2	10.9	110	39.1	0.0	24	54.2	0.0	183	52.5	8.7	162	50.0	11.1
Shelby County..............	273	28.2	8.8	89	39.3	0.0	191	30.9	0.0	464	37.9	0.0	516	41.1	6.0
Spencer County	94	25.5	3.2	85	30.6	24.7	33	27.3	0.0	228	30.3	2.6	64	42.2	10.9
Starke County	40	57.5	0.0	42	0.0	0.0	165	41.8	6.7	456	42.8	3.1	139	30.2	3.6
Steuben County	168	21.4	14.3	122	23.8	0.0	145	43.4	3.7	589	37.4	3.7	320	38.8	6.6
Sullivan County	921	0.4	0.9	89	18.0	6.7	22	54.5	0.0	205	33.7	7.3	247	28.7	4.0
Switzerland County	4	100.0	0.0	7	0.0	0.0	33	27.3	12.1	59	59.3	0.0	28	10.7	0.0
Tippecanoe County	3 362	27.4	2.6	637	33.1	2.0	6 818	12.7	1.2	7 752	29.5	0.7	2 352	35.6	5.4
Tipton County	1	100.0	0.0	29	13.8	44.8	104	31.7	5.8	134	38.1	3.0	112	14.3	31.3
Union County	26	46.2	34.6	12	0.0	0.0	27	59.3	0.0	6	100.0	0.0	29	37.9	17.2
Vanderburgh County	13 586	32.9	9.5	365	26.0	0.0	1 644	24.5	2.6	1 688	35.0	3.6	2 138	54.6	4.3
Vermillion County	46	76.1	0.0	53	39.6	0.0	30	13.3	0.0	154	39.0	0.0	169	43.8	0.0
Vigo County.................	6 464	24.4	8.4	297	24.6	7.1	1 106	18.4	7.5	1 258	28.5	5.9	1 699	46.4	4.5
Wabash County.............	96	36.5	0.0	307	28.3	6.5	251	19.9	1.6	305	31.1	1.3	310	36.8	3.2
Warren County	2	100.0	0.0	13	0.0	0.0	8	0.0	0.0	56	19.6	0.0	50	28.0	0.0
Warrick County	333	34.8	18.3	112	49.1	15.2	301	32.2	3.0	330	36.1	5.8	187	38.0	2.1
Washington County	66	43.9	0.0	13	0.0	0.0	42	23.8	0.0	165	43.0	1.2	169	43.2	13.6
Wayne County	3 261	25.8	15.9	239	39.7	0.0	505	27.5	7.7	919	30.8	4.5	1 201	53.5	4.6
Wells County	43	18.6	0.0	63	36.5	3.2	51	0.0	9.8	420	48.8	4.8	231	45.0	5.2
White County	13	23.1	0.0	89	22.5	14.6	104	11.5	15.4	1 345	39.5	0.7	327	33.6	2.1
Whitley County	84	44.0	0.0	66	30.3	13.6	151	37.1	0.0	196	37.2	0.5	108	21.3	0.0
IOWA.......................	59 758	34.7	6.3	9 263	35.0	3.2	35 978	27.4	3.2	81 501	38.9	2.8	33 624	51.8	3.8
Adair County	8	0.0	0.0	10	0.0	0.0	13	46.2	0.0	56	21.4	28.6	25	20.0	8.0
Adams County	13	0.0	0.0	13	84.6	0.0	11	0.0	0.0	7	0.0	0.0	6	0.0	33.3
Allamakee County	19	52.6	0.0	42	14.3	0.0	40	41.7	0.0	542	33.9	1.1	103	45.7	7.6
Appanoose County........	75	37.3	1.3	13	30.8	46.2	63	22.2	0.0	157	47.1	0.0	110	53.6	7.3
Audubon County	11	63.6	0.0	8	0.0	0.0	27	88.9	0.0	11	0.0	0.0	26	69.2	7.7
Benton County	39	10.3	0.0	13	69.2	0.0	46	60.9	0.0	100	72.0	0.0	133	48.9	9.8
Black Hawk County	9 871	37.2	7.8	276	26.4	4.7	1 372	22.7	1.2	2 396	42.7	4.2	2 037	54.4	3.1
Boone County	148	39.9	5.4	33	0.0	0.0	28	17.9	0.0	192	63.0	0.0	198	55.6	3.5
Bremer County	88	54.5	0.0	12	25.0	41.7	163	30.1	0.0	183	35.5	6.0	156	55.1	3.8
Buchanan County..........	66	39.4	0.0	42	42.9	0.0	95	42.1	11.6	205	45.9	1.0	123	49.6	1.6
Buena Vista County	97	44.3	0.0	47	74.5	0.0	887	32.1	2.9	2 555	40.7	2.0	323	35.6	4.3
Butler County	12	100.0	0.0	3	33.3	0.0	23	34.8	0.0	70	48.6	5.7	69	47.8	2.9
Calhoun County	83	9.6	0.0	12	33.3	0.0	16	87.5	0.0	102	26.5	10.8	49	24.5	28.6
Carroll County	28	67.9	0.0	26	50.0	0.0	68	36.8	0.0	124	40.3	4.8	65	63.1	9.2
Cass County.................	30	50.0	0.0	16	0.0	56.3	48	25.0	0.0	113	17.7	0.9	50	66.0	0.0
Cedar County	13	38.5	0.0	26	0.0	7.7	71	25.4	0.0	171	42.7	3.5	83	39.8	12.0
Cerro Gordo County......	408	45.8	3.4	77	18.2	0.0	327	36.4	0.0	1 187	43.1	10.3	457	59.3	10.9
Cherokee County	77	48.1	0.0	0	X	X	50	26.0	0.0	81	40.7	4.9	34	38.2	0.0
Chickasaw County	7	28.6	28.6	2	0.0	0.0	63	77.8	0.0	46	58.7	0.0	81	35.8	2.5
Clarke County	0	X	X	38	42.1	0.0	18	0.0	16.7	314	34.1	1.3	98	49.0	11.2
Clay County.................	34	50.0	0.0	1	0.0	0.0	169	60.4	3.6	204	24.0	2.5	70	52.9	7.1
Clayton County..............	78	46.2	0.0	23	34.8	0.0	35	37.1	0.0	109	32.1	6.4	82	53.7	11.0
Clinton County..............	797	34.6	5.8	127	26.8	21.3	316	38.9	0.6	868	46.0	3.0	309	51.8	5.5
Crawford County	143	25.9	0.0	237	60.8	0.0	17	35.3	29.4	1 524	35.0	1.8	116	63.8	0.0
Dallas County	400	31.8	9.5	50	32.0	2.0	169	27.8	0.0	2 176	40.4	0.2	333	56.8	3.9
Davis County	8	37.5	62.5	19	57.9	0.0	0	X	X	65	35.4	43.1	64	43.8	3.1
Decatur County	67	11.9	0.0	14	7.1	0.0	45	8.9	0.0	111	25.2	0.9	88	29.5	2.3
Delaware County	6	100.0	0.0	32	65.6	0.0	39	33.3	2.6	105	50.5	3.8	77	46.8	0.0
Des Moines County.......	1 378	39.0	7.3	112	20.5	7.1	236	44.9	7.2	722	42.5	5.0	466	49.6	4.1
Dickinson County	51	54.9	0.0	10	0.0	0.0	25	24.0	16.0	91	29.7	0.0	90	52.2	2.2
Dubuque County	717	35.3	2.9	139	36.7	0.0	367	24.0	6.3	1 066	34.4	0.0	774	52.7	5.7
Emmet County..............	27	22.2	14.8	16	81.3	0.0	11	63.6	0.0	480	38.3	0.8	44	59.1	0.0
Fayette County	102	4.9	0.0	25	40.0	0.0	118	23.7	5.1	325	37.5	11.1	131	42.7	1.5
Floyd County	20	0.0	0.0	16	68.8	12.5	48	41.7	0.0	183	42.1	0.0	73	50.7	2.7
Franklin County	3	100.0	0.0	18	0.0	33.3	39	48.7	0.0	651	37.0	1.1	39	61.5	5.1
Fremont County	2	0.0	0.0	11	0.0	0.0	46	28.3	4.3	141	29.1	2.8	50	36.0	8.0
Greene County..............	14	42.9	0.0	30	53.3	0.0	12	33.3	0.0	135	51.9	0.7	75	25.3	8.0
Grundy County	6	33.3	0.0	14	42.9	0.0	36	52.8	11.1	76	63.2	0.0	49	53.1	20.4

[1] Hispanic or Latino persons may be of any race.

STATE County	Total households	Family households (percent)						Nonfamily households (percent)						Percent of householders 65 years and over who live alone	Grandparents who are responsible for the care of their grandchildren
		Married-couple family households			Other family households			Two or more unrelated persons		Male living alone		Female living alone			
		Total	With children	Householder 65 years or over	Total	With children	Householder 65 years or over	Total	Householder 65 years or over	Total	Householder 65 years or over	Total	Householder 65 years or over		
	29	30	31	32	33	34	35	36	37	38	39	40	41	42	43
INDIANA—Cont'd															
Putnam County	12 451	63.8	28.0	11.1	10.5	6.7	1.1	3.4	0.1	9.1	2.8	13.1	7.4	45.3	120
Randolph County	10 919	59.4	24.9	12.1	12.0	7.2	2.0	3.6	0.3	10.5	2.7	14.5	9.0	45.0	166
Ripley County..............	9 814	61.1	28.9	10.4	13.0	7.9	2.0	3.0	0.3	9.7	2.3	13.1	7.9	44.4	207
Rush County................	6 960	60.4	27.9	11.0	13.0	8.1	2.0	3.3	0.2	9.4	2.9	13.8	8.5	46.2	90
St. Joseph County........	100 629	51.2	23.3	9.9	15.4	9.5	2.1	5.6	0.3	11.6	2.4	16.3	8.6	47.3	2 205
Scott County................	8 832	58.7	26.4	8.4	15.2	9.0	2.3	3.5	0.1	9.3	1.9	13.2	7.0	45.2	221
Shelby County	16 577	59.5	26.7	9.5	13.6	7.8	2.4	4.3	0.3	10.8	1.7	11.8	6.8	41.0	304
Spencer County	7 557	66.0	29.7	10.7	10.8	6.2	1.9	2.5	0.3	8.3	2.1	12.4	8.0	43.9	104
Starke County	8 729	61.0	26.0	11.0	13.1	7.9	2.3	3.5	0.3	9.6	2.6	12.8	8.5	44.9	222
Steuben County	12 721	56.8	25.1	9.7	13.2	8.2	1.6	5.7	0.3	11.5	2.2	12.8	6.6	43.0	141
Sullivan County	7 777	58.4	25.5	11.1	12.5	6.4	2.2	3.8	0.5	10.1	2.7	15.2	10.4	48.6	171
Switzerland County	3 470	60.2	25.0	10.2	13.8	8.0	2.4	4.4	0.4	11.9	2.8	9.6	6.3	41.2	100
Tippecanoe County	55 239	47.5	21.8	6.8	11.6	7.5	0.9	12.8	0.2	13.2	1.6	14.8	5.9	48.7	462
Tipton County	6 499	63.7	26.9	10.8	10.3	6.0	1.9	3.0	0.4	9.5	2.4	13.6	9.2	47.1	143
Union County	2 798	63.5	28.2	10.6	10.4	7.0	1.0	3.4	0.1	9.2	2.3	13.4	8.6	48.3	73
Vanderburgh County	70 549	48.7	20.2	9.9	14.5	8.9	1.9	5.7	0.3	12.2	2.4	18.8	9.6	49.8	1 185
Vermillion County	6 778	58.1	24.5	10.9	12.0	6.4	1.8	3.5	0.5	9.8	2.1	16.7	10.9	49.8	132
Vigo County.................	41 046	48.9	21.0	9.6	15.1	9.5	2.0	6.2	0.3	12.2	2.5	17.7	9.8	50.7	910
Wabash County............	13 260	59.2	24.9	12.3	12.7	7.6	1.9	3.5	0.4	9.3	2.1	15.3	9.2	43.7	213
Warren County.............	3 239	66.7	27.9	10.7	8.6	4.9	1.2	3.5	0.2	9.1	3.3	12.1	8.3	48.6	52
Warrick County............	19 466	67.5	31.6	8.5	10.9	6.2	1.5	3.0	0.3	7.3	1.7	11.4	6.0	42.9	509
Washington County.......	10 245	62.4	28.0	9.3	12.0	7.3	1.7	3.4	0.2	9.6	2.4	12.6	6.8	45.1	229
Wayne County.............	28 463	54.3	21.5	11.5	13.7	8.8	1.8	4.7	0.4	10.2	2.6	17.1	9.8	47.6	554
Wells County...............	10 432	61.6	28.4	11.1	12.1	7.4	1.6	3.1	0.4	9.4	2.0	13.8	7.9	43.3	108
White County	9 732	60.4	25.7	11.7	12.7	6.9	2.0	4.3	0.4	8.2	1.8	14.3	9.8	45.1	136
Whitley County	11 725	61.8	27.5	10.9	12.5	7.9	2.0	3.2	0.1	9.8	1.9	12.6	6.9	40.3	125
IOWA......................	1 150 197	55.9	24.6	11.1	11.4	7.2	1.5	5.5	0.3	11.1	2.4	16.0	9.0	47.1	13 073
Adair County	3 398	60.8	23.5	16.5	8.6	5.4	1.8	2.7	0.3	11.9	4.2	16.0	11.7	45.9	17
Adams County..............	1 863	60.7	21.9	16.6	6.5	5.0	0.8	2.6	0.4	10.3	2.4	19.9	14.8	49.2	26
Allamakee County	5 730	59.2	25.2	14.2	9.4	4.8	1.8	3.9	0.2	11.8	3.2	15.7	10.2	45.2	44
Appanoose County........	5 792	54.3	22.2	13.4	12.3	7.2	2.0	3.7	0.3	11.5	3.3	18.1	10.8	47.5	88
Audubon County	2 767	60.3	24.8	17.8	9.1	5.9	1.1	2.0	0.1	12.6	4.4	16.0	11.9	46.1	5
Benton County.............	9 782	63.3	28.5	13.0	10.3	6.4	1.4	3.1	0.1	10.1	2.4	13.2	9.4	44.7	67
Black Hawk County	49 736	51.6	21.5	10.4	13.2	8.3	1.4	8.2	0.4	10.6	2.3	16.5	8.6	47.3	679
Boone County	10 415	58.6	24.7	12.0	10.8	6.9	1.3	4.1	0.2	10.7	2.6	15.8	9.1	46.4	102
Bremer County	8 834	62.7	26.8	12.9	8.9	5.9	1.1	3.7	0.3	9.4	2.4	15.3	10.9	48.0	54
Buchanan County.........	7 923	62.8	28.5	11.7	9.5	6.1	1.3	3.0	0.2	9.2	2.4	15.5	10.2	48.9	94
Buena Vista County	7 514	58.6	25.2	14.5	10.0	6.5	1.5	4.6	0.1	10.8	1.8	16.1	10.1	42.5	54
Butler County	6 139	63.1	25.4	15.0	9.2	5.5	1.9	2.5	0.2	9.8	2.9	15.5	11.8	46.4	38
Calhoun County	4 496	58.8	22.2	15.9	9.1	6.0	1.0	2.2	0.0	10.2	3.5	19.7	14.6	51.7	35
Carroll County	8 480	58.3	26.7	13.8	8.8	6.1	1.4	3.3	0.2	11.7	2.7	17.9	12.4	49.7	52
Cass County................	6 115	56.8	23.2	13.2	10.7	7.0	1.2	3.1	0.3	11.9	3.6	17.5	12.4	52.1	53
Cedar County	7 159	62.5	27.5	12.9	9.6	5.8	1.4	4.3	0.1	10.2	2.9	13.4	9.3	46.1	70
Cerro Gordo County......	19 354	52.6	21.6	12.1	11.7	7.6	1.6	4.9	0.4	11.6	3.0	19.2	10.3	48.7	218
Cherokee County	5 377	58.4	23.5	15.6	8.8	6.0	1.3	3.4	0.0	12.7	3.3	16.7	11.7	46.9	57
Chickasaw County	5 188	62.0	26.4	15.0	8.4	5.5	1.2	3.5	0.3	12.1	2.9	14.0	9.6	43.2	49
Clarke County	3 588	58.9	23.9	11.9	11.7	8.2	2.3	3.6	0.4	11.2	3.7	14.6	9.2	47.0	33
Clay County.................	7 274	56.0	23.3	13.0	11.1	7.3	1.2	3.3	0.1	11.0	2.2	18.7	11.6	49.3	25
Clayton County............	7 381	59.7	24.3	14.1	10.6	6.7	2.0	3.3	0.2	12.1	3.1	14.3	10.1	44.8	66
Clinton County	20 156	56.0	23.9	11.9	12.4	7.4	1.5	4.3	0.6	11.3	2.4	16.0	9.7	46.5	234
Crawford County	6 458	60.5	26.1	14.6	10.1	5.9	1.9	3.3	0.3	11.3	2.3	14.8	10.1	42.6	83
Dallas County..............	15 592	61.3	30.0	8.6	10.8	7.5	1.0	4.5	0.4	9.8	2.1	13.7	6.2	45.4	178
Davis County...............	3 205	62.4	26.6	12.6	8.5	5.4	1.0	3.7	0.5	9.1	3.4	16.2	11.9	52.2	49
Decatur County	3 352	55.9	22.6	12.8	9.4	6.7	1.0	4.9	0.4	11.9	3.3	17.9	11.7	51.6	55
Delaware County..........	6 861	64.4	31.5	13.1	9.4	5.7	1.8	3.4	0.2	9.2	2.0	13.6	8.9	41.7	62
Des Moines County.......	17 293	54.0	21.4	11.7	13.3	8.7	1.7	4.2	0.3	11.2	2.4	17.2	10.2	48.0	150
Dickinson County	7 094	57.9	20.5	15.2	9.1	5.8	1.1	4.0	0.4	11.8	3.0	17.1	10.8	45.3	48
Dubuque County	33 703	57.7	26.5	10.9	11.1	6.6	1.7	4.5	0.2	11.6	2.5	15.1	8.3	45.5	208
Emmet County	4 446	55.7	21.7	14.4	10.1	6.3	1.7	3.8	0.1	13.4	2.4	17.0	11.8	46.7	56
Fayette County............	8 833	55.6	23.1	14.0	12.1	7.4	1.7	4.1	0.3	11.2	3.3	17.0	12.2	49.3	95
Floyd County...............	6 807	57.8	23.9	14.1	10.8	7.9	1.4	3.3	0.0	11.8	2.9	16.3	11.7	48.5	21
Franklin County	4 370	59.8	23.0	14.1	9.3	6.2	0.9	3.1	0.3	11.0	3.1	16.8	13.2	51.6	33
Fremont County	3 208	59.3	23.0	14.0	11.0	6.5	2.2	3.5	0.5	10.1	3.3	16.1	11.8	47.4	58
Greene County	4 202	56.1	21.9	15.2	12.6	8.2	2.2	2.2	0.3	10.8	3.3	18.3	13.3	48.5	52
Grundy County	4 964	65.0	25.4	15.3	7.4	4.8	1.1	2.1	0.0	9.9	2.8	15.7	11.7	47.0	44

Table A-3. States and Counties — Age, Ethnicity, and Household Structure

STATE County	Households with Non-Hispanic White householder — Number of households	Percent that are family households	Households with Black or African American householder — Number of households	Percent that are family households	Households with American Indian and Alaska Native householder — Number of households	Percent that are family households	Households with Asian, Hawaiian, and Pacific Islander householder — Number of households	Percent that are family households	Households with Hispanic or Latino[1] householder — Number of households	Percent that are family households	Foreign-born population — Percent of total population that is foreign-born	Place of birth (percent) — Europe	Asia	Latin America	Percent in non-English speaking households — Linguistically isolated	Not linguistically isolated
	44	45	46	47	48	49	50	51	52	53	54	55	56	57	58	59
INDIANA—Cont'd																
Putnam County	12 145	74.6	86	53.5	16	50.0	37	78.4	101	73.3	1.1	0.3	0.4	0.3	0.2	4.7
Randolph County	10 762	71.4	16	6.3	18	61.1	14	100.0	50	72.0	0.7	0.1	0.1	0.4	0.1	4.7
Ripley County	9 679	74.3	0	X	45	42.2	9	66.7	39	87.2	0.7	0.2	0.2	0.2	0.2	4.0
Rush County	6 777	73.3	60	76.7	20	100.0	13	30.8	40	92.5	0.3	0.1	0.1	0.0	0.1	3.9
St. Joseph County	84 462	66.1	10 411	68.5	302	73.2	1 254	62.7	3 188	76.2	4.6	1.2	1.1	1.7	1.6	11.4
Scott County	8 728	73.9	0	X	17	100.0	0	X	26	80.8	0.4	0.1	0.1	0.1	0.1	5.3
Shelby County	16 097	73.5	119	60.5	24	79.2	77	53.2	123	57.7	1.6	0.4	0.4	0.7	0.8	4.6
Spencer County	7 366	76.9	42	71.4	42	71.4	13	100.0	69	87.0	0.9	0.1	0.1	0.6	0.5	6.0
Starke County	8 493	74.2	9	100.0	38	50.0	37	83.8	87	89.7	2.6	1.5	0.3	0.7	1.0	8.3
Steuben County	12 336	70.2	61	49.2	50	48.0	36	72.2	167	73.7	1.4	0.4	0.3	0.5	0.5	7.6
Sullivan County	7 629	70.7	11	100.0	20	100.0	1	100.0	43	95.3	0.3	0.1	0.1	0.1	0.0	5.1
Switzerland County	3 427	74.0	0	X	7	100.0	12	100.0	6	100.0	0.5	0.1	0.2	0.1	0.0	5.1
Tippecanoe County	48 653	59.6	1 213	45.5	223	50.2	2 523	47.0	2 198	71.8	8.2	1.0	3.8	2.8	3.3	12.0
Tipton County	6 372	73.9	0	X	21	38.1	15	80.0	29	100.0	1.0	0.3	0.6	0.1	0.2	5.2
Union County	2 773	73.9	8	100.0	0	X	7	100.0	0	X	0.4	0.1	0.1	0.1	0.0	9.6
Vanderburgh County	63 543	63.3	5 254	63.8	158	62.0	513	71.7	540	54.4	1.6	0.4	0.8	0.3	0.6	7.0
Vermillion County	6 661	70.3	5	100.0	16	43.8	7	0.0	59	61.0	0.8	0.3	0.1	0.3	0.3	5.6
Vigo County	37 551	64.6	2 114	57.4	120	55.0	427	40.7	307	58.3	2.0	0.5	0.9	0.3	0.6	6.0
Wabash County	12 948	71.6	9	55.6	107	97.2	58	56.9	77	97.4	0.7	0.2	0.4	0.1	0.2	6.0
Warren County	3 214	75.3	0	X	0	X	0	X	10	100.0	0.3	0.0	0.1	0.2	0.2	4.1
Warrick County	19 109	78.3	114	69.3	30	100.0	67	89.6	80	81.3	1.3	0.3	0.4	0.3	0.2	6.2
Washington County	10 116	74.3	19	100.0	13	53.8	16	100.0	34	79.4	0.5	0.2	0.1	0.1	0.4	4.8
Wayne County	26 274	68.2	1 392	60.3	78	89.7	131	71.0	296	79.4	1.5	0.4	0.5	0.5	0.8	6.9
Wells County	10 186	73.6	13	100.0	30	100.0	8	100.0	143	76.9	0.8	0.4	0.2	0.2	0.3	7.1
White County	9 284	72.3	1	100.0	16	93.8	51	68.6	307	92.5	3.5	0.2	0.3	2.7	2.2	9.8
Whitley County	11 601	74.4	9	66.7	17	52.9	26	100.0	50	62.0	0.8	0.3	0.2	0.2	0.2	6.8
IOWA	1 088 899	67.2	20 969	65.0	2 792	71.0	10 693	68.5	20 905	76.3	3.1	0.7	1.0	1.1	1.4	8.2
Adair County	3 363	69.2	0	X	2	100.0	4	100.0	27	92.6	0.7	0.3	0.2	0.1	0.0	4.6
Adams County	1 863	67.3	0	X	0	X	0	X	0	X	0.2	0.0	0.2	0.0	0.2	3.4
Allamakee County	5 581	68.3	9	100.0	18	72.2	6	66.7	89	77.5	5.5	1.5	0.8	3.1	3.9	8.0
Appanoose County	5 680	66.7	36	30.6	8	0.0	14	57.1	37	83.8	1.0	0.3	0.4	0.1	0.3	4.2
Audubon County	2 752	69.4	4	100.0	2	100.0	1	0.0	6	100.0	0.7	0.2	0.4	0.1	0.2	4.1
Benton County	9 723	73.5	18	100.0	0	X	0	X	21	100.0	0.6	0.3	0.2	0.0	0.1	6.2
Black Hawk County	44 558	64.5	3 633	68.8	96	40.6	441	62.6	611	69.6	3.7	2.0	0.9	0.6	1.7	8.6
Boone County	10 270	69.6	34	38.2	32	34.4	14	35.7	20	100.0	0.8	0.5	0.1	0.1	0.4	4.9
Bremer County	8 750	71.6	12	83.3	4	100.0	22	50.0	26	92.3	1.2	0.5	0.5	0.2	0.4	7.1
Buchanan County	7 818	72.3	9	11.1	10	100.0	12	100.0	49	59.2	0.9	0.2	0.3	0.3	1.5	8.4
Buena Vista County	6 557	67.1	64	91.2	12	100.0	242	79.0	604	77.0	12.4	0.0	0.0	0.0	7.2	14.5
Butler County	6 091	72.3	0	X	0	X	2	100.0	19	57.9	0.9	0.5	0.1	0.2	0.5	6.9
Calhoun County	4 451	68.1	4	100.0	3	33.3	2	0.0	20	75.0	0.5	0.3	0.2	0.0	0.1	5.6
Carroll County	8 428	66.9	3	100.0	10	100.0	6	66.7	29	100.0	0.6	0.2	0.2	0.2	0.4	5.1
Cass County	6 063	67.7	15	26.7	2	0.0	15	53.3	20	45.0	0.8	0.2	0.2	0.2	0.3	6.5
Cedar County	7 069	72.3	1	100.0	5	100.0	7	57.1	61	59.0	0.7	0.2	0.3	0.1	0.3	7.0
Cerro Gordo County	18 633	64.0	106	75.5	42	76.2	98	84.7	378	61.9	1.4	0.5	0.5	0.2	0.5	5.9
Cherokee County	5 319	67.4	9	100.0	0	X	18	38.9	23	13.0	0.9	0.3	0.3	0.2	0.2	7.2
Chickasaw County	5 148	70.2	2	100.0	2	0.0	10	100.0	6	100.0	0.9	0.2	0.5	0.3	0.3	6.2
Clarke County	3 474	70.0	0	X	8	100.0	0	X	90	86.7	2.5	0.1	0.2	2.2	2.2	6.3
Clay County	7 176	66.8	7	100.0	1	0.0	31	87.1	44	90.9	1.8	0.3	0.7	0.8	1.0	5.5
Clayton County	7 304	70.3	22	68.2	6	66.7	7	100.0	22	63.6	1.2	0.4	0.3	0.3	0.8	5.1
Clinton County	19 503	68.2	301	68.8	29	93.1	43	83.7	208	75.0	1.4	0.4	0.4	0.4	0.5	6.5
Crawford County	5 993	70.1	28	100.0	56	100.0	2	100.0	396	75.5	6.1	0.4	0.1	5.6	4.1	11.0
Dallas County	14 820	71.7	129	71.3	13	84.6	64	73.4	520	86.3	4.0	0.4	0.3	3.0	1.8	8.6
Davis County	3 152	71.2	5	0.0	2	0.0	0	X	26	46.2	0.4	0.3	0.0	0.0	4.3	12.5
Decatur County	3 253	65.4	17	100.0	11	100.0	16	0.0	49	67.3	2.0	0.5	0.5	0.3	0.4	8.7
Delaware County	6 824	73.8	0	X	0	X	8	87.5	19	52.6	0.6	0.3	0.2	0.1	0.1	5.5
Des Moines County	16 420	67.2	525	70.1	27	25.9	45	77.8	169	75.7	1.6	0.6	0.5	0.3	0.6	5.3
Dickinson County	7 041	66.9	6	100.0	3	0.0	7	100.0	31	100.0	0.7	0.2	0.2	0.2	0.3	4.0
Dubuque County	32 902	68.8	256	68.8	40	80.0	74	78.4	261	68.6	1.9	0.7	0.3	0.5	0.7	6.6
Emmet County	4 328	65.7	14	50.0	0	X	4	0.0	90	81.1	2.3	0.2	0.1	1.9	0.9	6.7
Fayette County	8 670	67.8	7	42.9	13	23.1	27	66.7	103	71.8	1.1	0.2	0.5	0.1	0.3	6.3
Floyd County	6 741	68.8	11	27.3	4	50.0	10	100.0	31	51.6	1.1	0.2	0.3	0.5	0.8	6.7
Franklin County	4 203	68.9	0	X	5	100.0	10	100.0	142	69.7	4.4	0.2	0.3	3.8	2.2	9.9
Fremont County	3 142	70.3	2	0.0	5	20.0	17	70.6	31	77.4	1.7	0.2	0.2	1.0	0.4	7.4
Greene County	4 129	68.6	0	X	11	100.0	5	100.0	20	75.0	1.2	0.6	0.1	0.5	0.3	8.6
Grundy County	4 935	72.3	4	0.0	8	100.0	0	X	9	100.0	0.8	0.4	0.2	0.2	0.3	7.5

[1] Hispanic or Latino persons may be of any race.

STATE/ County code	MSA/PMSA/ NECMA code[1]	STATE County	Population by age (percent)										Non-Hispanic White		
														Age (percent)	
			Total population	Under 5 years	5 to 17 years	18 to 24 years	25 to 44 years	45 to 64 years	65 years and over	Median age	+/− U.S. percent under 18 years	+/− U.S. percent 65 years and over	Total population	Under 18 years	65 years and over
			1	2	3	4	5	6	7	8	9	10	11	12	13
		IOWA—Cont'd													
19 077	...	Guthrie County	11 353	5.4	18.1	6.2	24.8	24.9	20.6	41.9	-2.2	8.2	11 084	23.1	21.0
19 079	...	Hamilton County	16 438	6.4	19.0	7.1	27.2	22.3	18.0	39.1	-0.3	5.6	15 883	25.0	18.5
19 081	...	Hancock County	12 100	6.0	20.7	6.5	25.6	23.4	17.8	39.7	1.0	5.4	11 647	25.9	18.4
19 083	...	Hardin County	18 812	5.8	18.8	8.4	23.9	22.4	20.7	40.6	-1.1	8.3	18 158	23.8	21.4
19 085	...	Harrison County	15 666	6.0	20.2	6.9	27.0	22.3	17.7	38.9	0.5	5.3	15 420	25.9	17.9
19 087	...	Henry County	20 336	5.9	18.7	8.9	29.2	22.5	14.8	37.1	-1.1	2.4	19 005	24.0	15.5
19 089	...	Howard County	9 932	5.7	20.5	6.9	25.5	21.4	20.0	39.5	0.5	7.6	9 866	26.0	20.1
19 091	...	Humboldt County	10 381	5.4	19.5	7.0	24.5	22.7	21.0	41.3	-0.8	8.6	10 082	24.2	21.6
19 093	...	Ida County	7 837	5.6	19.9	6.3	24.2	22.4	21.6	41.5	-0.2	9.2	7 728	25.0	21.8
19 095	...	Iowa County	15 671	6.1	20.2	6.3	28.0	22.3	17.1	38.8	0.6	4.7	15 448	26.1	17.3
19 097	...	Jackson County	20 296	5.9	20.1	7.0	26.6	23.1	17.3	39.1	0.3	4.9	20 079	25.8	17.4
19 099	...	Jasper County	37 213	6.3	18.3	7.4	28.7	23.2	16.0	38.5	-1.1	3.6	36 036	24.3	16.4
19 101	...	Jefferson County	16 181	5.4	19.1	8.1	23.8	29.8	13.7	41.1	-1.2	1.3	15 446	24.3	14.3
19 103	3500	Johnson County	111 006	5.6	14.4	23.3	30.7	18.4	7.5	28.4	-5.7	-4.9	98 789	19.2	8.2
19 105	...	Jones County	20 221	5.6	18.5	7.7	29.0	23.3	15.8	38.5	-1.6	3.4	19 355	24.1	16.4
19 107	...	Keokuk County	11 400	5.9	19.9	7.0	25.4	21.6	20.2	40.0	0.1	7.8	11 235	25.5	20.5
19 109	...	Kossuth County	17 163	5.7	20.0	6.2	24.5	23.5	20.1	41.3	0.0	7.7	16 862	25.4	20.4
19 111	...	Lee County	38 052	6.0	18.4	7.8	26.8	24.6	16.5	39.5	-1.3	4.1	35 397	23.8	17.1
19 113	1360	Linn County	191 701	6.9	18.3	10.2	30.1	22.2	12.2	35.2	-0.5	-0.2	178 584	24.2	12.9
19 115	...	Louisa County	12 183	7.1	20.6	8.0	28.5	21.8	13.9	35.9	2.0	1.5	10 527	25.3	16.0
19 117	...	Lucas County	9 422	6.1	19.3	7.4	24.3	23.7	19.3	39.9	-0.3	6.9	9 255	24.8	19.4
19 119	...	Lyon County	11 763	6.7	21.3	7.9	24.7	20.7	18.7	38.1	2.3	6.3	11 667	28.1	18.8
19 121	...	Madison County	14 019	6.9	20.1	7.0	27.5	23.3	15.2	37.9	1.3	2.8	13 744	26.8	15.4
19 123	...	Mahaska County	22 335	6.7	19.0	9.4	26.9	21.7	16.3	37.2	0.0	3.9	21 502	25.1	16.9
19 125	...	Marion County	32 052	6.1	19.3	10.1	26.7	21.9	16.0	37.2	-0.3	3.6	31 134	25.0	16.3
19 127	...	Marshall County	39 311	6.4	18.9	8.1	26.6	23.4	16.6	38.6	-0.4	4.2	34 672	23.1	18.5
19 129	...	Mills County	14 547	6.4	20.3	6.9	28.5	25.4	12.6	38.1	1.0	0.2	14 137	26.4	12.9
19 131	...	Mitchell County	10 874	6.2	20.2	6.3	24.0	21.8	21.5	40.6	0.7	9.1	10 848	26.3	21.6
19 133	...	Monona County	10 020	5.3	17.9	6.1	23.3	23.3	23.9	43.0	-2.5	11.5	9 846	23.0	24.2
19 135	...	Monroe County	8 016	6.5	18.9	7.2	24.9	22.8	19.6	39.7	-0.3	7.2	7 856	24.6	20.0
19 137	...	Montgomery County	11 771	6.1	18.6	6.3	25.7	23.1	20.2	40.4	-1.0	7.8	11 506	24.5	20.6
19 139	...	Muscatine County	41 722	7.0	19.9	8.7	28.8	22.8	12.9	36.1	1.2	0.5	35 725	24.6	14.7
19 141	...	O'Brien County	15 102	5.9	18.9	7.8	24.2	22.0	21.2	40.7	-0.9	8.8	14 650	24.4	21.8
19 143	...	Osceola County	7 003	6.1	19.9	7.6	26.0	21.3	19.1	39.7	0.3	6.7	6 792	25.4	19.2
19 145	...	Page County	16 976	5.5	17.9	8.0	26.1	22.8	19.7	40.2	-2.3	7.3	16 285	22.9	20.4
19 147	...	Palo Alto County	10 147	5.8	18.4	9.8	22.3	22.2	21.4	40.7	-1.5	9.0	9 948	23.7	21.6
19 149	...	Plymouth County	24 849	6.6	21.6	7.4	26.5	22.0	15.9	37.8	2.5	3.5	24 342	27.8	16.2
19 151	...	Pocahontas County	8 662	4.9	20.6	5.2	23.5	24.1	21.7	42.5	-0.2	9.3	8 577	25.5	21.9
19 153	2120	Polk County	374 601	7.5	18.1	9.4	32.4	21.5	11.1	34.4	-0.1	-1.3	324 011	23.9	12.0
19 155	5920	Pottawattamie County	87 704	6.5	19.3	9.1	28.6	22.6	13.8	36.5	0.1	1.4	82 747	25.4	14.3
19 157	...	Poweshiek County	18 815	5.6	17.0	12.6	24.5	22.6	17.6	38.4	-3.1	5.2	18 136	22.7	18.1
19 159	...	Ringgold County	5 469	6.0	18.0	6.9	21.5	23.5	24.1	43.2	-1.7	11.7	5 393	23.8	24.2
19 161	...	Sac County	11 529	5.7	18.4	7.0	23.3	22.9	22.7	42.1	-1.6	10.3	11 229	23.2	23.2
19 163	1960	Scott County	158 668	7.0	19.4	9.3	29.5	23.1	11.9	35.4	0.7	-0.5	137 731	24.3	12.9
19 165	...	Shelby County	13 173	5.8	20.4	5.7	25.1	22.4	20.5	40.5	0.5	8.1	12 959	26.1	20.7
19 167	...	Sioux County	31 589	6.5	20.7	15.3	23.5	19.0	15.0	32.8	1.5	2.6	30 441	26.5	15.6
19 169	...	Story County	79 981	5.2	13.8	28.3	25.5	17.5	9.7	26.5	-6.7	-2.7	72 269	18.8	10.6
19 171	...	Tama County	18 103	6.9	19.7	7.1	25.2	22.4	18.7	39.1	0.9	6.3	16 266	24.5	20.5
19 173	...	Taylor County	6 958	5.5	18.5	7.5	23.6	22.8	22.1	41.6	-1.7	9.7	6 641	23.0	23.1
19 175	...	Union County	12 309	6.1	17.2	8.9	25.0	24.1	18.7	40.1	-2.4	6.3	12 017	23.2	19.1
19 177	...	Van Buren County	7 809	5.5	19.2	7.2	24.8	24.4	18.9	40.8	-1.0	6.5	7 729	24.5	19.0
19 179	...	Wapello County	36 051	5.8	17.4	9.9	25.9	23.2	17.8	39.2	-2.5	5.4	34 323	22.7	18.4
19 181	2120	Warren County	40 671	6.8	20.2	9.7	28.4	23.1	11.8	36.0	1.3	-0.6	39 538	26.6	12.1
19 183	...	Washington County	20 670	6.7	19.4	6.8	26.9	22.4	17.8	38.8	0.4	5.4	19 912	25.4	18.4
19 185	...	Wayne County	6 730	5.0	18.8	6.1	23.6	22.9	23.6	43.0	-1.9	11.2	6 603	23.7	23.9
19 187	...	Webster County	40 235	6.4	18.1	10.9	25.7	21.5	17.4	37.7	-1.2	5.0	37 230	23.7	18.5
19 189	...	Winnebago County	11 723	5.4	18.5	9.8	24.3	23.1	18.9	39.8	-1.8	6.5	11 334	23.7	19.6
19 191	...	Winneshiek County	21 310	5.0	17.8	16.9	24.2	20.4	15.8	35.7	-2.9	3.4	20 696	22.7	16.1
19 193	7720	Woodbury County	103 877	7.4	19.9	10.2	28.3	20.9	13.4	34.2	1.6	1.0	87 084	24.6	15.6
19 195	...	Worth County	7 909	5.6	18.5	6.6	26.1	23.7	19.4	40.7	-1.6	7.0	7 672	23.8	19.6
19 197	...	Wright County	14 334	5.6	18.9	6.5	24.5	23.4	21.1	41.4	-1.2	8.7	13 549	23.7	22.2
20 000	...	KANSAS	2 688 418	7.0	19.5	10.3	28.7	21.3	13.2	35.2	0.8	0.8	2 234 488	24.6	14.9
20 001	...	Allen County	14 385	6.2	19.1	10.0	23.9	22.7	18.0	38.8	-0.4	5.6	13 488	24.6	18.6
20 003	...	Anderson County	8 110	6.2	19.5	7.1	24.8	22.3	20.2	39.6	0.0	7.8	7 879	25.5	20.3
20 005	...	Atchison County	16 774	6.3	20.4	11.5	24.2	21.3	16.3	36.2	1.0	3.9	15 052	25.1	17.0

[1]MSA = Metropolitan Statistical Area. PMSA = Primary MSA. NECMA = New England County Metropolitan Area. See the Appendix A for explanation of these concepts. See Appendix B for list of metropolitan areas identified by type, with component counties.

STATE County	Black or African American			American Indian and Alaska Native			Asian, Hawaiian, and Pacific Islander			Hispanic or Latino[1]			Two or more races		
		Age (percent)			Age (percent)			Age (percent)			Age (percent)			Age (percent)	
	Total population	Under 18 years	65 years and over	Total population	Under 18 years	65 years and over	Total population	Under 18 years	65 years and over	Total population	Under 18 years	65 years and over	Total population	Under 18 years	65 years and over
	14	15	16	17	18	19	20	21	22	23	24	25	26	27	28
IOWA—Cont'd															
Guthrie County	23	78.3	0.0	8	0.0	0.0	4	50.0	0.0	179	34.6	3.9	64	50.0	3.1
Hamilton County	11	81.8	0.0	7	42.9	0.0	283	33.2	4.6	164	49.4	1.2	108	25.9	11.1
Hancock County	0	X	X	8	25.0	0.0	39	71.8	0.0	376	44.1	0.0	62	61.3	22.6
Hardin County	106	50.9	0.0	0	X	X	67	46.3	0.0	388	41.8	3.4	159	40.9	3.8
Harrison County	25	48.0	0.0	56	39.3	1.8	50	16.0	0.0	77	58.4	9.1	41	46.3	9.8
Henry County	305	14.4	5.2	51	27.5	3.9	389	35.7	3.9	329	29.2	3.6	256	50.4	0.4
Howard County	6	33.3	0.0	0	X	X	14	57.1	0.0	15	60.0	20.0	37	62.2	5.4
Humboldt County	35	0.0	0.0	5	0.0	0.0	46	65.2	4.3	141	7.1	3.5	119	84.0	0.0
Ida County	33	72.7	0.0	13	0.0	30.8	4	0.0	0.0	34	64.7	8.8	25	60.0	8.0
Iowa County	24	54.2	0.0	7	57.1	14.3	28	21.4	14.3	111	36.0	6.3	65	35.4	0.0
Jackson County	17	47.1	0.0	34	64.7	0.0	14	0.0	14.3	105	40.0	14.3	49	57.1	0.0
Jasper County	250	13.6	0.0	58	13.8	3.4	181	38.7	2.2	493	37.7	6.1	272	52.9	4.8
Jefferson County	219	33.8	0.0	47	4.3	0.0	127	13.4	0.0	183	19.1	4.4	170	56.5	0.0
Johnson County	3 120	30.5	2.4	251	28.3	0.0	4 488	20.1	1.8	2 925	30.6	1.8	1 720	37.0	2.2
Jones County	340	4.7	0.0	59	5.1	0.0	74	31.1	0.0	261	41.4	9.6	162	55.6	4.3
Keokuk County	29	89.7	0.0	8	62.5	0.0	24	0.0	20.8	66	37.9	0.0	45	55.6	0.0
Kossuth County	32	71.9	6.3	18	22.2	11.1	37	45.9	5.4	151	31.8	4.0	84	40.5	2.4
Lee County	872	20.8	14.0	129	38.8	0.0	311	37.0	6.1	783	29.2	9.8	613	48.6	6.4
Linn County	4 506	34.9	5.9	430	22.3	0.0	2 740	28.4	2.6	2 852	34.6	4.0	2 903	62.6	2.5
Louisa County	21	38.1	0.0	9	11.1	0.0	53	17.0	3.8	1 542	43.7	0.5	86	51.2	0.0
Lucas County	15	66.7	0.0	10	0.0	0.0	45	35.6	17.8	48	89.6	0.0	59	59.3	13.6
Lyon County	27	25.9	0.0	4	0.0	0.0	12	0.0	0.0	32	28.1	12.5	25	24.0	16.0
Madison County	12	16.7	16.7	11	45.5	0.0	52	28.8	3.8	83	34.9	15.7	126	37.3	11.1
Mahaska County	63	39.7	1.6	74	12.2	5.4	225	33.8	7.1	291	46.4	0.0	216	41.2	0.0
Marion County	208	38.5	1.9	44	22.7	0.0	320	35.0	9.7	227	51.1	0.0	130	36.9	7.7
Marshall County	316	28.2	10.8	91	36.3	0.0	349	40.4	2.6	3 481	42.8	1.7	642	51.2	0.5
Mills County	33	24.2	0.0	42	4.8	0.0	57	42.1	0.0	171	42.1	1.2	94	54.3	2.1
Mitchell County	8	75.0	25.0	9	0.0	0.0	0	X	X	7	71.4	0.0	7	71.4	0.0
Monona County	4	0.0	0.0	40	51.0	2.0	6	33.3	0.0	36	30.6	16.7	79	43.0	7.6
Monroe County	18	50.0	0.0	68	61.8	5.9	2	100.0	0.0	30	63.3	0.0	42	78.6	0.0
Montgomery County	3	100.0	0.0	0	X	X	35	37.1	0.0	157	30.6	1.3	51	29.4	9.8
Muscatine County	337	36.8	3.3	166	44.6	0.0	285	32.6	5.3	4 983	41.2	2.0	623	47.5	1.1
O'Brien County	45	40.0	0.0	23	43.5	0.0	52	25.0	13.5	253	35.2	0.0	82	69.5	3.7
Osceola County	28	60.7	3.6	9	0.0	44.4	7	0.0	100.0	136	39.0	12.5	47	91.5	0.0
Page County	228	26.8	0.9	76	13.2	0.0	103	55.3	7.8	232	36.2	8.2	83	42.2	4.8
Palo Alto County	0	X	X	14	28.6	0.0	5	60.0	0.0	128	53.1	5.5	56	32.1	25.0
Plymouth County	68	63.2	0.0	20	75.0	0.0	67	40.3	0.0	272	49.3	1.1	125	64.8	1.6
Pocahontas County	2	0.0	0.0	3	0.0	33.3	14	57.1	0.0	62	29.0	0.0	6	0.0	66.7
Polk County	17 472	34.5	8.5	1 311	34.1	3.4	9 395	27.3	4.9	16 354	37.9	2.1	7 092	53.2	3.5
Pottawattamie County	646	33.9	4.6	265	19.0	2.3	577	24.1	6.4	2 839	33.6	2.7	871	46.5	10.6
Poweshiek County	74	10.8	2.7	57	17.5	0.0	195	7.2	8.7	223	32.7	0.0	209	25.8	0.0
Ringgold County	5	100.0	0.0	20	20.0	0.0	16	18.8	37.5	18	61.1	11.1	17	47.1	23.5
Sac County	33	66.7	0.0	8	75.0	0.0	42	40.5	9.5	94	50.0	0.0	126	72.2	6.3
Scott County	9 565	37.8	4.9	691	32.1	6.7	2 284	29.1	4.3	6 282	39.9	6.4	3 066	61.0	2.8
Shelby County	17	0.0	0.0	5	0.0	0.0	44	31.8	15.9	92	48.9	3.3	64	43.8	0.0
Sioux County	97	24.7	0.0	47	53.2	0.0	203	38.4	0.0	664	42.5	0.3	202	60.4	2.0
Story County	1 505	24.3	1.1	209	20.6	0.0	3 658	15.8	1.2	1 321	21.7	3.4	1 079	35.3	3.6
Tama County	20	65.0	0.0	1 055	41.1	3.4	95	38.9	6.3	576	52.1	0.7	195	58.5	6.2
Taylor County	0	X	X	23	39.1	0.0	19	57.9	0.0	251	44.2	0.0	26	53.8	11.5
Union County	9	0.0	0.0	6	0.0	0.0	44	29.5	0.0	89	27.0	0.0	147	33.3	0.0
Van Buren County	11	100.0	0.0	11	45.5	18.2	14	64.3	0.0	19	15.8	10.5	28	17.9	14.3
Wapello County	348	31.6	6.0	29	58.6	0.0	220	23.6	0.9	876	37.2	6.1	366	29.8	12.0
Warren County	95	23.2	0.0	119	31.9	2.5	221	39.4	1.8	461	46.0	3.9	317	53.0	0.9
Washington County	74	28.4	0.0	29	48.3	0.0	11	27.3	0.0	551	46.6	3.4	182	42.9	0.0
Wayne County	24	54.2	0.0	7	0.0	0.0	25	32.0	20.0	43	34.9	18.6	34	50.0	0.0
Webster County	1 140	23.5	5.4	108	29.6	0.0	443	37.2	0.0	788	37.2	5.6	563	52.6	2.1
Winnebago County	16	0.0	0.0	24	0.0	0.0	34	11.8	0.0	267	29.6	0.7	58	65.5	0.0
Winneshiek County	145	20.7	0.0	8	25.0	0.0	192	14.1	1.6	170	35.3	0.6	129	38.0	14.0
Woodbury County	2 074	41.0	0.6	1 667	44.0	2.9	2 417	34.1	1.0	9 337	41.4	1.2	2 017	53.3	0.6
Worth County	22	9.1	54.5	23	34.8	0.0	25	20.0	0.0	84	33.3	11.9	88	52.3	11.4
Wright County	31	6.5	0.0	26	46.2	0.0	31	41.9	0.0	654	37.8	0.3	57	54.4	19.3
KANSAS	150 584	32.4	7.7	24 723	30.5	5.4	45 980	25.3	4.0	186 299	39.0	3.0	63 823	48.3	4.2
Allen County	332	33.4	11.1	124	22.6	6.5	9	0.0	22.2	262	32.1	9.2	200	53.0	4.0
Anderson County	22	18.2	0.0	28	21.4	0.0	11	0.0	0.0	103	24.3	20.4	80	55.0	20.0
Atchison County	1 011	37.4	12.0	201	53.7	8.0	33	18.2	0.0	386	37.8	10.4	216	60.6	0.0

[1] Hispanic or Latino persons may be of any race.

STATE County	Total households	Family households (percent)						Nonfamily households (percent)						Percent of householders 65 years and over who live alone	Grandparents who are responsible for the care of their grandchildren
		Married-couple family households			Other family households			Two or more unrelated persons		Male living alone		Female living alone			
		Total	With children	Householder 65 years or over	Total	With children	Householder 65 years or over	Total	Householder 65 years or over	Total	Householder 65 years or over	Total	Householder 65 years or over		
	29	30	31	32	33	34	35	36	37	38	39	40	41	42	43
IOWA—Cont'd															
Guthrie County	4 656	59.7	21.4	14.6	10.4	6.3	2.0	3.8	0.7	10.2	2.9	15.8	11.6	45.7	26
Hamilton County	6 689	59.6	24.3	14.2	9.7	5.8	1.5	3.2	0.1	11.1	2.9	16.4	10.3	45.6	89
Hancock County	4 792	61.9	26.4	13.5	9.1	6.2	1.2	2.8	0.2	10.7	3.4	15.5	11.0	49.1	59
Hardin County	7 636	57.7	23.5	14.7	9.2	6.3	1.2	3.7	0.3	11.8	3.0	17.6	12.1	48.5	137
Harrison County	6 104	60.4	25.8	13.0	10.1	5.7	1.5	3.5	0.2	10.1	3.3	15.9	11.3	49.7	129
Henry County	7 627	57.2	25.1	11.2	12.0	8.1	1.2	4.0	0.3	10.3	2.2	16.4	10.1	49.1	138
Howard County	3 982	57.8	26.6	14.5	9.0	5.2	1.8	3.7	0.2	12.3	3.4	17.2	11.7	47.7	11
Humboldt County	4 305	58.3	24.3	15.7	9.4	6.1	1.3	2.5	0.2	11.5	3.4	18.3	12.4	48.0	24
Ida County	3 197	59.5	24.4	16.4	8.6	5.2	2.0	2.6	0.0	12.0	3.2	17.3	12.7	46.4	33
Iowa County	6 186	61.8	28.2	13.2	8.3	5.2	1.3	4.1	0.0	10.8	2.5	15.1	9.9	46.0	61
Jackson County	8 096	58.5	25.5	12.6	10.8	6.8	1.1	3.7	0.5	10.9	2.7	16.2	11.6	50.3	77
Jasper County	14 694	59.2	24.8	12.8	10.8	7.2	1.6	3.9	0.1	10.3	2.3	15.8	9.4	44.6	170
Jefferson County	6 651	52.8	23.0	8.8	11.9	9.1	0.5	4.8	0.3	13.5	2.2	16.9	8.9	53.7	33
Johnson County	44 074	44.7	21.6	5.6	9.4	5.4	0.6	15.7	0.3	14.1	1.3	16.1	4.7	48.0	216
Jones County	7 577	59.6	23.8	13.0	10.6	6.5	1.4	4.6	0.2	10.5	2.5	14.8	10.1	46.3	92
Keokuk County	4 574	59.5	24.2	15.2	9.5	5.9	1.3	3.0	0.3	10.9	3.4	17.2	13.2	49.9	69
Kossuth County	6 959	61.1	26.0	15.3	7.8	4.8	1.3	2.6	0.2	11.8	4.0	16.8	12.1	48.8	18
Lee County	15 186	55.0	22.5	11.8	12.8	7.8	1.9	3.9	0.4	11.3	2.5	16.9	10.5	48.0	262
Linn County	76 806	54.3	25.0	9.0	11.8	7.5	1.4	6.6	0.2	11.8	2.2	15.7	7.2	47.0	765
Louisa County	4 526	62.9	29.6	11.8	11.2	7.4	1.1	3.7	0.1	10.3	2.8	12.0	8.0	45.4	112
Lucas County	3 776	57.5	22.0	14.9	10.2	6.9	1.1	3.6	0.3	12.2	2.4	16.6	10.8	44.9	31
Lyon County	4 395	67.6	31.2	16.4	6.5	3.9	1.5	1.8	0.0	9.6	2.5	14.5	10.5	42.2	30
Madison County	5 315	63.3	27.7	11.9	7.0	7.1	1.1	3.1	0.0	9.2	3.0	13.7	9.8	49.6	70
Mahaska County	8 881	58.3	25.3	12.5	11.1	7.6	1.5	4.1	0.2	11.9	2.9	14.6	9.1	45.8	83
Marion County	12 055	61.8	27.0	12.0	9.4	6.5	1.0	3.3	0.5	10.6	2.2	14.9	9.8	47.1	135
Marshall County	15 323	55.3	23.3	11.3	13.3	8.7	1.5	4.6	0.2	11.7	2.7	15.1	9.2	47.9	229
Mills County	5 336	63.5	27.3	10.7	11.3	7.0	1.6	3.3	0.3	8.6	2.2	13.3	8.1	45.1	105
Mitchell County	4 317	60.5	24.3	16.5	9.2	5.2	1.9	2.8	0.3	10.8	3.5	16.7	13.1	47.1	18
Monona County	4 206	54.5	21.4	16.1	11.2	5.9	3.0	3.5	0.2	12.1	3.9	18.7	14.1	48.2	51
Monroe County	3 222	58.0	23.9	15.2	10.7	7.0	1.5	3.7	0.4	11.2	3.8	16.3	11.1	46.6	78
Montgomery County	4 892	53.6	21.9	13.4	13.2	8.4	2.4	3.5	0.2	11.0	3.0	18.6	11.5	47.7	46
Muscatine County	15 883	58.6	27.5	10.3	12.9	8.3	1.4	4.5	0.2	10.4	2.2	13.6	7.6	44.9	205
O'Brien County	5 997	63.1	26.9	17.0	6.1	3.7	0.7	2.9	0.1	9.6	2.1	18.3	12.2	44.6	56
Osceola County	2 778	62.5	27.8	14.5	7.5	4.7	1.5	2.3	0.1	10.7	2.5	17.1	12.1	47.6	21
Page County	6 709	56.0	21.5	15.2	11.2	7.3	1.7	3.0	0.2	12.1	2.7	17.8	11.5	45.5	59
Palo Alto County	4 119	56.4	23.7	15.5	8.8	5.4	1.5	4.3	0.5	12.0	2.8	18.6	12.9	47.3	15
Plymouth County	9 385	64.2	30.6	14.0	8.9	5.7	1.3	3.0	0.2	9.5	2.5	14.4	9.1	42.7	85
Pocahontas County	3 623	59.5	24.6	14.9	8.1	5.4	1.0	2.1	0.1	12.3	4.2	17.9	13.8	53.1	8
Polk County	149 316	52.0	24.8	7.6	13.1	8.0	1.6	6.9	0.3	11.0	1.8	17.1	6.8	47.6	1 946
Pottawattamie County	33 896	54.1	23.1	10.1	15.9	9.6	2.1	5.1	0.2	10.2	2.5	14.6	8.3	46.4	715
Poweshiek County	7 421	55.7	22.9	13.4	10.4	6.9	1.3	4.7	0.3	12.8	2.9	16.5	10.5	47.2	25
Ringgold County	2 232	58.9	21.6	17.4	9.7	6.3	1.1	2.8	0.3	10.3	4.5	18.2	14.3	50.1	31
Sac County	4 748	58.2	22.9	16.2	9.5	5.8	1.9	2.8	0.3	12.0	3.5	17.5	13.0	47.3	19
Scott County	62 367	53.6	24.5	8.8	14.0	9.2	1.7	5.6	0.4	11.6	1.9	15.3	7.0	45.0	1 143
Shelby County	5 202	64.2	28.1	16.7	7.7	4.7	1.4	3.1	0.3	9.7	3.2	15.3	10.2	42.1	21
Sioux County	10 682	69.8	33.8	14.7	5.9	3.8	0.9	2.1	0.1	8.5	2.2	13.7	9.5	42.8	45
Story County	29 386	49.4	22.5	8.0	8.7	5.1	0.8	15.2	0.3	12.1	1.4	14.6	6.0	44.8	143
Tama County	7 020	60.5	25.7	14.6	10.7	6.4	1.4	3.5	0.0	10.7	3.5	14.7	10.6	46.7	151
Taylor County	2 817	60.1	22.9	15.9	8.0	5.5	1.2	4.2	0.5	11.2	4.0	16.4	12.4	48.2	33
Union County	5 278	54.9	21.4	12.1	9.5	7.4	0.7	4.3	0.6	12.7	3.2	18.5	12.1	53.4	37
Van Buren County	3 180	59.0	22.5	14.6	9.4	6.5	1.3	3.8	0.4	12.8	4.3	15.0	11.1	48.5	76
Wapello County	14 789	53.0	20.4	12.8	13.3	8.5	1.8	5.5	0.4	11.5	2.6	16.7	10.0	45.6	173
Warren County	14 709	64.9	30.3	9.8	11.7	8.0	1.1	3.6	0.2	7.4	2.0	12.4	6.9	44.5	157
Washington County	8 069	60.1	26.9	12.5	10.1	6.1	1.9	3.4	0.1	9.9	2.7	16.5	10.5	47.5	77
Wayne County	2 829	58.2	20.7	16.0	9.8	6.4	1.6	2.2	0.7	11.8	4.5	18.1	13.3	49.3	52
Webster County	15 862	52.5	22.3	11.9	12.4	8.5	1.5	4.7	0.5	12.6	3.2	17.8	10.5	49.4	235
Winnebago County	4 746	58.7	24.2	13.7	8.3	5.8	1.0	3.5	0.2	11.4	3.0	18.0	12.5	50.9	46
Winneshiek County	7 762	60.0	27.1	14.0	7.6	4.2	1.5	4.9	0.2	12.0	2.3	15.6	9.8	43.4	50
Woodbury County	39 256	53.5	25.3	9.9	14.7	9.4	1.8	5.3	0.2	10.3	2.4	16.2	9.1	49.1	635
Worth County	3 280	58.7	24.2	13.0	10.1	5.9	1.7	3.5	0.3	12.2	3.7	15.5	11.3	49.9	21
Wright County	5 972	58.5	23.5	14.5	8.2	5.8	1.4	3.3	0.4	11.5	3.5	18.6	13.1	50.5	44
KANSAS	1 038 940	55.7	25.9	10.0	12.4	7.9	1.4	5.0	0.2	11.5	2.3	15.4	8.0	47.0	17 873
Allen County	5 764	54.5	21.7	12.4	13.1	8.8	2.1	4.0	0.2	11.1	3.7	17.4	11.0	50.2	125
Anderson County	3 218	60.4	25.6	15.8	10.2	5.7	1.2	2.6	0.2	10.8	3.4	15.9	11.7	46.7	24
Atchison County	6 270	54.6	24.2	12.4	13.8	9.0	1.5	4.1	0.4	11.1	3.3	16.3	9.7	47.6	84

Table A-3. States and Counties — Age, Ethnicity, and Household Structure

STATE County	Households with Non-Hispanic White householder		Households with Black or African American householder		Households with American Indian and Alaska Native householder		Households with Asian, Hawaiian, and Pacific Islander householder		Households with Hispanic or Latino[1] householder		Foreign-born population	Place of birth (percent)			Percent in non-English speaking households	
	Number of households	Percent that are family households	Number of households	Percent that are family households	Number of households	Percent that are family households	Number of households	Percent that are family households	Number of households	Percent that are family households	Percent of total population that is foreign-born	Europe	Asia	Latin America	Linguistically isolated	Not linguistically isolated
	44	45	46	47	48	49	50	51	52	53	54	55	56	57	58	59
IOWA—Cont'd																
Guthrie County	4 579	69.9	3	100.0	5	60.0	2	100.0	59	83.1	1.2	0.4	0.1	0.7	0.5	5.2
Hamilton County	6 557	69.2	2	0.0	0	X	81	80.2	30	66.7	2.1	0.5	1.2	0.3	0.5	7.7
Hancock County	4 683	70.9	0	X	2	100.0	7	0.0	83	85.5	2.2	0.2	0.3	1.4	0.8	7.1
Hardin County	7 491	66.8	7	28.6	0	X	28	92.9	84	83.3	1.7	0.4	0.3	1.0	0.7	7.5
Harrison County	6 054	70.6	0	X	7	100.0	17	29.4	12	50.0	0.8	0.4	0.2	0.1	0.1	4.7
Henry County	7 357	69.6	25	92.0	8	100.0	120	58.3	61	63.9	1.8	0.2	1.3	0.2	0.4	7.2
Howard County	3 971	66.8	2	100.0	0	X	4	50.0	3	100.0	0.4	0.2	0.2	0.0	1.3	8.5
Humboldt County	4 231	67.4	8	100.0	0	X	11	81.8	56	92.9	1.4	0.2	0.3	0.8	0.8	5.7
Ida County	3 185	68.3	4	0.0	4	0.0	0	X	0	X	0.2	0.2	0.1	0.0	0.1	6.4
Iowa County	6 113	70.1	8	100.0	3	100.0	5	80.0	39	56.4	0.8	0.3	0.3	0.1	0.5	8.9
Jackson County	8 036	69.3	0	X	2	100.0	6	66.7	39	66.7	0.7	0.5	0.1	0.2	0.2	5.5
Jasper County	14 453	69.9	18	61.1	22	81.8	31	80.6	130	80.0	1.5	0.4	0.5	0.5	0.3	5.9
Jefferson County	6 492	65.0	83	44.6	0	X	20	45.0	28	92.9	4.0	1.5	1.1	0.3	0.0	7.6
Johnson County	39 503	54.0	1 256	49.8	138	47.8	1 790	55.8	888	67.3	6.4	1.0	3.7	0.9	2.3	12.6
Jones County	7 489	70.2	1	100.0	3	100.0	5	100.0	48	87.5	0.8	0.2	0.4	0.2	0.2	6.7
Keokuk County	4 534	68.9	3	100.0	3	100.0	6	100.0	26	69.2	0.4	0.1	0.1	0.2	0.0	4.1
Kossuth County	6 890	68.9	5	60.0	9	100.0	3	100.0	38	44.7	0.9	0.2	0.2	0.4	0.1	6.7
Lee County	14 334	67.7	338	59.2	25	92.0	122	72.1	268	80.2	1.1	0.2	0.6	0.2	0.4	5.8
Linn County	73 176	65.7	1 532	67.6	162	72.8	875	75.8	710	73.8	2.6	0.6	1.3	0.4	0.7	8.1
Louisa County	4 146	72.7	4	50.0	1	100.0	16	100.0	354	89.0	6.8	0.1	0.3	6.3	5.1	11.9
Lucas County	3 747	67.6	0	X	0	X	9	22.2	2	100.0	0.7	0.2	0.3	0.1	0.4	7.5
Lyon County	4 372	74.3	4	0.0	2	0.0	5	0.0	5	100.0	0.9	0.6	0.1	0.1	0.4	8.6
Madison County	5 249	74.2	2	0.0	0	X	10	70.0	14	57.1	0.6	0.1	0.2	0.0	0.2	4.6
Mahaska County	8 673	69.5	30	23.3	28	100.0	63	73.0	57	45.6	1.6	0.4	0.8	0.2	0.5	7.2
Marion County	11 797	71.1	73	60.3	22	90.9	90	78.9	38	84.7	1.7	0.7	0.6	0.2	0.8	6.8
Marshall County	14 180	68.0	116	49.1	18	61.1	95	74.7	805	81.6	6.6	0.5	0.6	5.3	3.7	11.4
Mills County	5 237	74.6	13	100.0	19	89.5	12	58.3	32	81.3	1.0	0.6	0.2	0.1	0.1	4.4
Mitchell County	4 317	69.8	0	X	0	X	0	X	0	X	0.5	0.3	0.0	0.0	1.2	5.4
Monona County	4 178	65.6	0	X	9	33.3	0	X	6	100.0	0.4	0.2	0.1	0.1	0.0	4.9
Monroe County	3 179	68.5	9	100.0	18	100.0	0	X	7	100.0	0.6	0.3	0.1	0.1	0.3	8.4
Montgomery County	4 791	66.9	0	X	0	X	14	85.7	42	90.5	1.2	0.0	0.3	0.9	0.8	4.2
Muscatine County	14 308	70.1	93	75.3	44	75.0	96	56.3	1 264	86.7	5.9	0.5	0.6	4.5	2.6	13.9
O'Brien County	5 875	69.3	9	44.4	2	0.0	19	78.9	78	62.8	2.0	0.5	0.2	1.0	1.0	7.0
Osceola County	2 740	69.9	4	0.0	2	0.0	0	X	28	82.1	1.2	0.3	0.1	0.8	0.8	4.7
Page County	6 582	67.4	3	100.0	6	100.0	42	31.0	49	49.0	1.0	0.3	0.2	0.4	0.4	4.9
Palo Alto County	4 079	65.0	0	X	0	X	0	X	22	63.6	0.9	0.6	0.0	0.0	0.4	6.0
Plymouth County	9 272	73.0	19	26.3	5	100.0	13	84.6	58	87.9	1.2	0.2	0.3	0.4	0.5	7.1
Pocahontas County	3 599	67.7	0	X	1	0.0	3	100.0	20	65.0	0.9	0.3	0.1	0.2	0.2	6.0
Polk County	134 008	64.4	6 664	62.8	404	67.8	2 584	79.7	4 370	79.8	5.9	1.5	2.0	1.0	2.0	10.4
Pottawattamie County	32 451	70.2	198	64.6	71	88.7	195	62.6	856	66.4	2.0	0.4	0.5	0.9	0.8	7.9
Poweshiek County	7 271	66.1	13	61.5	23	91.3	45	46.7	48	75.0	2.1	0.7	0.9	0.3	0.5	6.4
Ringgold County	2 219	68.7	0	X	4	100.0	4	50.0	3	33.3	0.5	0.2	0.3	0.0	2.0	7.9
Sac County	4 697	67.5	9	100.0	2	0.0	2	100.0	17	82.4	1.3	0.5	0.3	0.4	0.2	6.3
Scott County	56 041	67.1	3 312	73.0	262	73.3	659	70.3	1 702	69.7	3.1	0.8	1.2	0.8	1.3	8.1
Shelby County	5 141	71.9	5	100.0	2	100.0	20	65.0	21	66.7	0.6	0.2	0.3	0.1	0.2	7.4
Sioux County	10 407	75.6	13	84.6	14	100.0	57	75.4	164	78.7	2.9	0.8	0.6	1.0	1.1	8.3
Story County	26 777	58.5	526	48.5	67	50.7	1 353	50.6	395	61.3	6.9	1.1	4.2	0.8	2.4	11.0
Tama County	6 510	70.6	2	100.0	307	73.6	28	78.6	134	89.6	2.0	0.3	0.3	1.3	1.1	11.7
Taylor County	2 751	67.8	0	X	5	100.0	2	0.0	53	84.9	2.0	0.0	0.2	1.8	0.7	6.6
Union County	5 210	64.4	0	X	0	X	12	41.7	29	51.7	0.9	0.3	0.2	0.3	0.3	4.8
Van Buren County	3 166	68.5	0	X	4	50.0	0	X	2	100.0	0.6	0.3	0.2	0.1	0.7	6.7
Wapello County	14 228	66.2	138	61.6	2	100.0	73	68.5	268	69.8	1.9	0.3	0.4	1.0	0.6	6.0
Warren County	14 450	76.6	32	62.5	44	88.6	44	84.1	96	76.0	1.1	0.4	0.4	0.2	0.2	6.6
Washington County	7 859	70.1	24	20.8	12	100.0	1	100.0	136	80.1	1.5	0.5	0.1	0.9	1.2	9.8
Wayne County	2 783	67.9	11	100.0	7	0.0	6	66.7	17	82.4	0.6	0.1	0.3	0.1	0.3	3.9
Webster County	15 119	64.8	331	67.4	31	74.2	94	62.8	244	69.7	2.0	0.5	0.8	0.6	1.1	6.3
Winnebago County	4 647	67.4	12	41.7	10	100.0	0	X	69	42.0	1.8	0.8	0.3	0.7	1.3	5.9
Winneshiek County	7 644	67.6	10	100.0	4	50.0	25	36.0	39	48.7	2.1	0.5	0.9	0.4	0.3	8.1
Woodbury County	34 963	67.2	712	60.5	444	70.5	578	84.9	2 226	81.1	7.2	0.3	1.9	4.7	4.4	12.3
Worth County	3 213	69.0	8	0.0	4	50.0	7	100.0	22	54.5	1.1	0.4	0.4	0.2	0.7	5.0
Wright County	5 768	66.2	12	33.3	9	100.0	0	X	174	85.1	3.0	0.3	0.2	2.4	2.5	8.5
KANSAS	899 972	67.5	54 464	67.1	8 420	71.7	14 376	69.9	49 451	78.7	5.0	0.6	1.4	2.7	2.4	10.7
Allen County	5 528	67.4	82	68.3	38	81.6	0	X	70	72.9	0.9	0.4	0.1	0.3	0.3	8.2
Anderson County	3 153	70.6	12	16.7	4	100.0	0	X	30	70.0	0.6	0.3	0.2	0.1	0.4	7.9
Atchison County	5 749	68.0	368	67.4	19	100.0	8	100.0	129	82.2	0.7	0.1	0.2	0.2	0.2	4.7

[1]Hispanic or Latino persons may be of any race.

Table A-3. States and Counties — Age, Ethnicity, and Household Structure

STATE/ County code	MSA/PMSA/ NECMA code[1]	STATE County	Total population	Under 5 years	5 to 17 years	18 to 24 years	25 to 44 years	45 to 64 years	65 years and over	Median age	+/− U.S. percent under 18 years	+/− U.S. percent 65 years and over	Total population	Under 18 years	65 years and over
			1	2	3	4	5	6	7	8	9	10	11	12	13
		KANSAS—Cont'd													
20 007	...	Barber County	5 307	5.0	19.8	6.4	22.4	24.8	21.5	42.6	−0.9	9.1	5 127	24.0	21.9
20 009	...	Barton County	28 205	6.4	19.6	9.2	25.1	21.8	17.9	38.6	0.3	5.5	25 047	23.9	19.7
20 011	...	Bourbon County	15 379	5.9	19.8	9.4	24.3	22.2	18.2	38.0	0.0	5.8	14 428	25.3	18.8
20 013	...	Brown County	10 724	6.3	20.1	7.6	23.8	22.4	19.8	39.8	0.7	7.4	9 208	23.9	21.4
20 015	9040	Butler County	59 482	6.9	21.7	8.3	29.1	21.6	12.5	35.9	2.9	0.1	55 670	28.2	13.1
20 017	...	Chase County	3 030	5.8	18.3	7.3	26.0	24.0	18.7	40.3	−1.6	6.3	2 917	23.6	19.1
20 019	...	Chautauqua County	4 359	4.7	18.7	6.4	20.7	25.0	24.4	44.7	−2.3	12.0	4 050	22.3	25.4
20 021	...	Cherokee County	22 605	6.8	19.7	8.4	26.6	23.3	15.2	37.0	0.8	2.8	20 651	25.4	15.9
20 023	...	Cheyenne County	3 165	4.7	18.9	5.1	22.8	21.9	26.6	44.2	−2.1	14.2	3 064	23.2	27.4
20 025	...	Clark County	2 390	5.8	20.5	5.1	23.3	23.7	21.6	42.1	0.6	9.2	2 247	25.4	22.4
20 027	...	Clay County	8 822	5.5	19.5	6.7	23.8	23.8	20.8	41.3	−0.7	8.4	8 541	24.3	21.3
20 029	...	Cloud County	10 268	4.8	17.6	10.4	22.1	21.9	23.2	41.4	−3.3	10.8	10 013	22.1	23.7
20 031	...	Coffey County	8 865	5.8	21.0	6.3	26.6	24.0	16.3	39.2	1.1	3.9	8 467	25.4	16.9
20 033	...	Comanche County	1 967	5.5	16.8	4.5	20.9	26.6	25.7	46.9	−3.4	13.3	1 911	21.5	26.4
20 035	...	Cowley County	36 291	6.4	19.5	10.7	25.6	21.8	15.9	37.0	0.2	3.5	31 977	24.7	17.1
20 037	...	Crawford County	38 242	6.2	16.6	16.0	25.3	20.5	15.5	33.8	−2.9	3.1	35 265	22.3	16.5
20 039	...	Decatur County	3 472	4.7	18.9	5.0	22.1	23.0	26.3	44.3	−2.1	13.9	3 366	22.6	26.9
20 041	...	Dickinson County	19 344	5.7	20.1	6.2	26.2	23.2	18.6	40.0	0.1	6.2	18 331	25.1	19.1
20 043	...	Doniphan County	8 249	6.3	18.9	12.0	24.7	22.0	16.1	36.8	−0.5	3.7	7 826	24.6	16.5
20 045	4150	Douglas County	99 962	5.6	14.8	26.4	28.3	17.0	8.0	26.6	−5.3	−4.4	84 601	19.3	8.7
20 047	...	Edwards County	3 449	5.7	18.9	6.5	25.4	22.3	21.3	41.0	−1.1	8.9	3 027	22.3	23.3
20 049	...	Elk County	3 261	4.0	18.6	5.3	20.2	26.4	25.6	46.0	−3.1	13.2	3 085	22.0	26.3
20 051	...	Ellis County	27 507	5.7	16.5	18.6	25.2	19.7	14.3	32.7	−3.5	1.9	26 432	22.1	14.9
20 053	...	Ellsworth County	6 525	4.2	16.6	7.8	27.2	24.0	20.2	41.8	−4.9	7.8	5 926	21.5	21.9
20 055	...	Finney County	40 523	10.5	23.8	10.9	31.5	16.6	6.7	28.1	8.6	−5.7	20 935	27.0	11.5
20 057	...	Ford County	32 458	9.3	21.6	11.7	28.6	17.8	11.0	29.9	5.2	−1.4	18 558	24.1	17.7
20 059	...	Franklin County	24 784	6.8	20.7	9.0	28.5	21.2	13.9	36.0	1.8	1.5	23 300	27.0	14.5
20 061	...	Geary County	27 947	9.2	20.4	14.0	29.3	17.5	9.5	29.1	3.9	−2.9	17 226	24.8	12.7
20 063	...	Gove County	3 068	5.6	20.1	5.1	22.2	24.1	22.8	42.6	0.0	10.4	2 980	25.0	23.4
20 065	...	Graham County	2 946	4.3	18.1	5.5	23.3	25.4	23.5	44.4	−3.3	11.1	2 787	22.3	23.1
20 067	...	Grant County	7 909	8.4	24.3	7.7	29.0	21.2	9.4	31.4	7.0	−3.0	5 009	26.6	13.7
20 069	...	Gray County	5 904	8.0	23.6	8.5	26.9	20.6	12.4	33.0	5.9	0.0	5 249	29.8	13.9
20 071	...	Greeley County	1 534	6.4	22.4	7.2	25.9	20.1	18.1	38.6	3.1	5.7	1 348	26.6	20.1
20 073	...	Greenwood County	7 673	5.9	17.9	6.5	23.1	23.8	22.7	42.6	−1.9	10.3	7 324	23.3	23.4
20 075	...	Hamilton County	2 670	7.2	20.8	7.3	26.1	20.3	18.2	37.6	2.3	5.8	2 070	24.1	23.3
20 077	...	Harper County	6 536	5.6	19.0	7.1	21.6	23.5	23.1	42.9	−1.1	10.7	6 321	24.0	23.4
20 079	9040	Harvey County	32 869	6.6	19.4	9.3	26.4	21.3	17.0	37.6	0.3	4.6	28 983	24.5	18.1
20 081	...	Haskell County	4 307	8.9	24.0	8.9	28.0	19.5	10.6	30.8	7.2	−1.8	3 157	28.9	13.4
20 083	...	Hodgeman County	2 085	4.8	24.3	4.9	25.4	21.5	19.0	39.8	3.4	6.6	1 985	28.0	19.8
20 085	...	Jackson County	12 657	6.9	21.4	6.7	26.9	23.2	14.9	37.4	2.6	2.5	11 346	27.4	15.8
20 087	...	Jefferson County	18 426	6.4	20.9	6.9	28.2	24.8	12.8	38.0	1.6	0.4	17 764	27.4	13.0
20 089	...	Jewell County	3 791	4.5	17.3	4.4	21.4	26.4	26.0	46.2	−3.9	13.6	3 701	21.4	26.5
20 091	3760	Johnson County	451 086	7.5	19.5	7.5	33.0	22.6	10.0	35.2	1.3	−2.4	401 454	26.3	10.8
20 093	...	Kearny County	4 531	9.0	25.4	8.4	26.8	19.0	11.4	31.6	8.7	−1.0	3 231	29.3	14.4
20 095	...	Kingman County	8 673	5.9	21.5	5.6	24.8	22.6	19.6	40.2	1.7	7.2	8 386	26.5	20.2
20 097	...	Kiowa County	3 278	5.6	18.2	8.3	22.1	24.6	21.3	42.1	−1.9	8.9	3 157	23.2	21.9
20 099	...	Labette County	22 835	6.0	19.5	8.8	25.9	22.3	17.5	37.9	−0.2	5.1	20 023	24.5	18.6
20 101	...	Lane County	2 155	5.5	19.8	5.5	24.5	24.1	20.6	41.6	−0.4	8.2	2 069	24.5	21.3
20 103	3760	Leavenworth County	68 691	7.0	19.6	8.2	33.3	22.0	9.9	35.6	0.9	−2.5	56 272	26.1	11.0
20 105	...	Lincoln County	3 578	5.1	17.9	5.7	23.1	24.7	23.4	43.7	−2.7	11.0	3 496	22.9	23.7
20 107	...	Linn County	9 570	6.2	18.7	6.8	24.4	25.6	18.3	40.8	−0.8	5.9	9 238	23.9	18.7
20 109	...	Logan County	3 046	6.6	18.8	7.1	24.1	22.6	20.8	40.7	−0.3	8.4	2 955	25.1	20.8
20 111	...	Lyon County	35 935	6.9	18.9	17.0	27.0	18.7	11.5	30.9	0.1	−0.9	27 795	22.0	14.4
20 113	...	McPherson County	29 554	5.8	19.5	10.2	25.4	21.9	17.3	38.1	−0.4	4.9	28 284	24.9	17.9
20 115	...	Marion County	13 361	5.6	19.3	7.7	23.5	22.7	21.1	41.0	−0.8	8.7	12 888	24.5	21.7
20 117	...	Marshall County	10 965	4.9	20.1	6.9	23.3	22.6	22.1	41.7	−0.7	9.7	10 685	24.7	22.5
20 119	...	Meade County	4 631	8.0	21.7	6.7	26.8	19.0	17.8	36.1	4.0	5.4	3 997	27.1	20.2
20 121	3760	Miami County	28 351	6.7	21.2	7.0	30.0	23.1	11.9	36.7	2.2	−0.5	26 904	27.3	12.2
20 123	...	Mitchell County	6 932	5.1	19.5	8.4	22.4	23.3	21.3	41.1	−1.1	8.9	6 745	23.7	21.8
20 125	...	Montgomery County	36 252	6.1	18.9	8.5	24.8	23.4	18.3	39.2	−0.7	5.9	30 486	22.8	19.8
20 127	...	Morris County	6 104	5.6	19.5	5.7	23.9	24.4	21.0	42.0	−0.6	8.6	5 799	24.8	21.6
20 129	...	Morton County	3 496	8.0	21.5	8.5	26.7	21.5	13.8	36.2	3.8	1.4	2 866	27.1	16.3
20 131	...	Nemaha County	10 717	7.1	21.3	5.9	24.2	19.5	22.0	39.1	2.7	9.6	10 489	28.3	22.3
20 133	...	Neosho County	16 997	6.1	19.5	9.0	25.4	22.7	17.3	38.4	−0.1	4.9	15 844	24.7	18.1
20 135	...	Ness County	3 454	5.2	17.6	4.9	24.0	24.1	24.2	43.9	−2.9	11.8	3 363	22.2	24.9
20 137	...	Norton County	5 953	4.7	17.2	7.9	28.6	22.1	19.5	40.1	−3.8	7.1	5 476	22.8	21.0

[1]MSA = Metropolitan Statistical Area. PMSA = Primary MSA. NECMA = New England County Metropolitan Area. See the Appendix A for explanation of these concepts. See Appendix B for list of metropolitan areas identified by type, with component counties.

Table A-3. States and Counties — Age, Ethnicity, and Household Structure

STATE County	Black or African American			American Indian and Alaska Native			Asian, Hawaiian, and Pacific Islander			Hispanic or Latino[1]			Two or more races		
	Total population	Under 18 years	65 years and over	Total population	Under 18 years	65 years and over	Total population	Under 18 years	65 years and over	Total population	Under 18 years	65 years and over	Total population	Under 18 years	65 years and over
	14	15	16	17	18	19	20	21	22	23	24	25	26	27	28
KANSAS—Cont'd															
Barber County	20	45.0	15.0	32	56.3	0.0	2	0.0	0.0	83	53.0	7.2	43	41.9	20.9
Barton County	350	35.7	13.1	147	27.9	0.0	72	22.2	0.0	2 343	44.4	1.7	688	60.0	4.5
Bourbon County	406	12.3	19.7	42	19.0	40.5	11	18.2	0.0	146	43.2	0.0	362	54.4	0.0
Brown County	210	31.4	21.9	992	44.7	5.8	39	20.5	41.0	221	49.8	8.1	165	49.7	9.7
Butler County	806	18.2	2.9	709	27.2	5.5	212	26.9	3.8	1 140	44.9	1.8	1 031	45.1	5.6
Chase County	20	0.0	25.0	15	66.7	0.0	5	40.0	0.0	49	42.9	12.2	28	32.1	0.0
Chautauqua County	0	X	X	170	37.1	8.8	8	0.0	62.5	60	60.0	10.0	83	32.5	13.3
Cherokee County	172	45.9	11.0	698	39.7	4.7	71	43.7	0.0	233	42.1	8.2	837	35.8	9.4
Cheyenne County	0	X	X	9	0.0	22.2	5	20.0	0.0	78	42.3	0.0	13	46.2	15.4
Clark County	12	25.0	50.0	11	0.0	18.2	9	0.0	0.0	86	50.0	4.7	30	50.0	6.7
Clay County	20	35.0	20.0	16	25.0	0.0	12	0.0	0.0	92	47.8	2.2	163	54.6	4.9
Cloud County	23	17.4	0.0	23	26.1	0.0	27	0.0	3.7	78	24.4	17.9	109	49.5	1.8
Coffey County	22	72.7	0.0	80	50.0	0.0	70	57.1	5.7	122	54.9	0.0	113	54.9	3.5
Comanche County	0	X	X	0	X	X	10	50.0	0.0	25	48.0	8.0	21	52.4	0.0
Cowley County	847	22.7	7.8	793	37.3	5.7	552	30.4	6.7	1 216	39.9	3.9	1 061	40.3	9.9
Crawford County	693	31.0	5.5	353	22.9	0.0	402	8.0	1.5	977	33.5	2.3	725	37.4	5.1
Decatur County	13	76.9	0.0	26	42.3	0.0	20	40.0	30.0	34	41.2	0.0	20	100.0	0.0
Dickinson County	56	44.6	12.5	79	26.6	7.6	47	46.8	21.3	429	39.9	6.5	391	40.7	11.0
Doniphan County	138	32.6	7.2	82	15.9	20.7	20	20.0	15.0	58	29.3	3.4	127	58.3	3.1
Douglas County	4 184	26.4	5.9	2 305	24.1	2.2	3 335	11.7	1.8	3 146	28.3	3.3	3 038	46.6	4.6
Edwards County	10	20.0	0.0	17	47.1	0.0	15	26.7	0.0	348	39.9	7.2	39	48.7	20.5
Elk County	0	X	X	41	31.7	19.5	0	X	X	79	31.6	8.9	74	29.7	9.5
Ellis County	103	3.9	0.0	22	68.2	0.0	186	15.6	0.0	570	20.5	1.4	170	48.8	1.2
Ellsworth County	235	0.0	0.0	41	7.3	0.0	21	0.0	9.5	251	21.9	6.4	98	28.6	5.1
Finney County	450	39.8	2.0	384	31.3	0.0	1 027	26.8	2.0	17 553	43.2	1.5	1 284	50.4	2.8
Ford County	401	23.2	7.2	123	24.4	5.7	727	31.8	2.8	12 251	40.9	1.8	1 122	49.0	2.9
Franklin County	269	39.0	2.2	166	23.5	10.2	101	28.7	6.9	576	36.6	3.5	393	37.9	1.3
Geary County	5 990	36.2	5.5	271	31.7	0.0	890	17.1	11.9	2 400	38.6	1.1	1 601	53.8	1.2
Gove County	12	58.3	0.0	6	0.0	0.0	0	X	X	26	42.3	3.8	44	52.3	2.3
Graham County	82	20.7	45.1	9	0.0	33.3	15	20.0	13.3	24	33.3	0.0	33	39.4	21.2
Grant County	9	100.0	0.0	60	45.0	0.0	0	X	X	2 760	42.8	2.3	125	41.6	0.0
Gray County	6	33.3	0.0	20	10.0	0.0	4	100.0	0.0	688	42.0	0.7	70	47.1	1.4
Greeley County	0	100.0	0.0	4	0.0	0.0	0	X	X	174	43.1	3.4	24	50.0	0.0
Greenwood County	3	66.7	0.0	44	20.5	25.0	46	37.0	15.2	175	40.6	1.1	102	27.5	8.9
Hamilton County	4	0.0	0.0	18	55.6	0.0	1	0.0	0.0	563	43.3	0.5	48	29.2	2.1
Harper County	36	30.6	11.1	39	20.5	5.1	21	42.9	19.0	47	27.7	25.5	86	67.4	10.5
Harvey County	449	18.5	10.0	148	25.0	25.0	229	36.7	3.9	2 629	37.8	9.3	726	55.4	6.3
Haskell County	6	33.3	0.0	17	11.8	0.0	37	27.0	13.5	1 025	45.6	2.2	113	45.1	10.6
Hodgeman County	10	20.0	0.0	8	50.0	0.0	0	X	X	60	46.7	6.7	22	77.3	0.0
Jackson County	82	32.9	0.0	821	36.2	9.0	36	50.0	0.0	175	37.1	3.4	252	34.5	3.2
Jefferson County	55	16.4	30.9	197	26.4	4.1	28	3.6	0.0	163	33.1	4.3	259	26.3	8.9
Jewell County	2	0.0	0.0	22	45.5	0.0	12	0.0	0.0	33	51.5	0.0	25	52.0	16.0
Johnson County	11 038	30.5	3.9	1 679	24.7	3.8	12 721	25.0	3.7	17 873	32.9	2.7	7 859	46.6	4.2
Kearny County	31	67.7	0.0	31	41.9	0.0	10	80.0	0.0	1 204	46.1	3.9	101	54.5	7.9
Kingman County	43	76.7	0.0	23	13.0	30.4	16	12.5	0.0	144	63.9	0.0	71	35.2	1.4
Kiowa County	0	X	X	28	35.7	0.0	18	44.4	0.0	62	43.5	9.7	13	23.1	0.0
Labette County	1 067	28.2	8.2	527	28.8	9.3	139	35.3	7.2	574	36.9	10.5	662	45.3	10.9
Lane County	1	0.0	100.0	0	X	X	7	42.9	0.0	29	44.8	0.0	58	53.4	3.4
Leavenworth County	6 982	24.3	6.2	620	15.5	4.7	779	18.1	5.1	2 615	33.0	2.6	1 724	50.5	3.1
Lincoln County	8	75.0	0.0	9	0.0	22.2	3	0.0	66.7	30	43.3	13.3	30	20.0	6.7
Linn County	82	84.1	11.0	50	16.0	0.0	9	22.2	0.0	63	54.0	0.0	133	47.4	11.3
Logan County	8	25.0	50.0	4	0.0	0.0	4	0.0	0.0	41	29.3	34.1	34	44.1	5.9
Lyon County	692	29.0	3.5	284	25.4	0.0	425	30.4	5.9	6 068	40.2	1.8	911	50.3	0.4
McPherson County	293	21.8	4.4	45	8.9	0.0	15	6.7	0.0	473	37.0	1.5	558	40.1	4.7
Marion County	74	31.1	8.1	50	30.0	0.0	19	31.6	0.0	224	42.9	5.8	155	40.6	6.5
Marshall County	12	33.3	66.7	25	32.0	0.0	89	31.5	0.0	94	48.9	5.3	80	52.5	2.5
Meade County	13	15.4	0.0	30	13.3	10.0	11	18.2	27.3	492	48.0	1.4	115	60.0	3.5
Miami County	372	19.6	16.1	176	48.3	0.0	57	10.5	7.0	392	39.5	3.3	467	54.4	1.3
Mitchell County	54	40.7	0.0	18	77.8	0.0	13	0.0	0.0	54	83.3	0.0	79	67.1	5.1
Montgomery County	2 112	36.0	14.3	1 130	35.2	7.1	235	13.2	5.1	1 092	42.6	6.9	1 464	41.8	9.0
Morris County	29	37.9	17.2	34	11.8	5.9	15	13.3	40.0	175	37.7	3.4	54	25.9	16.7
Morton County	12	58.3	0.0	54	18.5	3.7	59	20.3	3.4	495	43.8	2.2	34	47.1	0.0
Nemaha County	56	23.2	10.7	16	18.8	0.0	8	0.0	37.5	44	25.0	0.0	104	47.1	9.6
Neosho County	133	28.6	9.8	146	44.5	6.8	50	18.0	0.0	440	34.5	7.3	417	48.2	4.1
Ness County	2	0.0	0.0	5	100.0	0.0	4	0.0	0.0	47	59.6	0.0	44	36.4	0.0
Norton County	226	0.0	0.0	31	0.0	0.0	23	0.0	0.0	154	12.3	4.5	56	64.3	12.5

[1] Hispanic or Latino persons may be of any race.

Items 14—28

STATE County	Total households	Family households (percent)						Nonfamily households (percent)						Percent of householders 65 years and over who live alone	Grandparents who are responsible for the care of their grandchildren
		Married-couple family households			Other family households			Two or more unrelated persons		Male living alone		Female living alone			
		Total	With children	Householder 65 years or over	Total	With children	Householder 65 years or over	Total	Householder 65 years or over	Total	Householder 65 years or over	Total	Householder 65 years or over		
	29	30	31	32	33	34	35	36	37	38	39	40	41	42	43
KANSAS—Cont'd															
Barber County	2 256	60.4	23.6	15.1	7.8	4.3	1.7	1.8	0.1	11.3	4.2	18.6	13.5	51.2	18
Barton County	11 391	55.2	24.4	12.8	11.3	7.7	1.1	3.3	0.2	12.1	2.7	18.0	12.2	51.5	131
Bourbon County	6 136	55.9	24.4	12.5	11.5	7.3	1.4	3.6	0.3	10.5	3.1	18.5	12.8	52.7	77
Brown County	4 306	55.6	22.6	15.0	13.2	9.4	1.0	2.4	0.5	10.1	2.7	18.6	12.3	47.6	50
Butler County	21 582	64.0	31.2	10.5	11.1	7.2	1.4	3.0	0.3	9.6	1.9	12.3	6.7	41.4	515
Chase County	1 255	56.3	23.8	14.2	10.2	6.4	1.5	3.3	0.2	15.0	4.0	15.3	9.7	46.4	26
Chautauqua County	1 793	59.3	20.5	18.7	9.9	5.0	2.2	1.2	0.0	11.2	4.5	18.3	12.0	44.2	35
Cherokee County	8 894	56.7	25.1	9.5	14.1	8.6	2.2	2.9	0.2	10.0	3.2	16.3	11.3	55.1	244
Cheyenne County	1 374	59.5	21.6	21.3	8.9	6.3	1.4	1.0	0.0	13.2	3.4	17.3	13.1	42.1	20
Clark County	980	61.6	25.7	16.4	8.2	4.9	0.9	1.0	0.2	10.6	3.3	18.6	12.2	46.9	15
Clay County	3 654	60.9	24.3	14.6	8.6	6.9	1.1	3.0	0.4	11.6	4.8	15.9	12.3	51.6	18
Cloud County	4 184	56.1	22.2	14.6	8.9	5.4	2.0	4.4	0.3	11.3	3.5	19.3	12.6	49.0	47
Coffey County	3 505	62.1	26.4	12.2	9.5	6.7	1.4	2.6	0.2	10.4	2.3	15.4	10.1	47.3	36
Comanche County	876	56.5	20.8	16.3	6.8	4.3	1.3	1.0	0.1	14.0	5.3	21.6	14.4	52.6	6
Cowley County	14 073	56.8	25.1	11.2	12.1	7.9	1.3	3.3	0.3	11.1	3.2	16.7	10.8	52.2	216
Crawford County	15 516	48.6	20.6	9.9	12.6	8.4	1.4	8.2	0.3	12.8	2.5	17.8	10.6	53.1	221
Decatur County	1 501	57.2	21.4	18.7	8.1	5.5	1.4	2.3	0.0	12.9	4.0	19.5	13.7	46.9	10
Dickinson County	7 916	59.3	24.6	13.0	9.3	6.3	1.0	3.4	0.5	10.7	3.3	17.3	11.7	50.9	118
Doniphan County	3 174	57.1	24.7	11.6	11.5	7.5	1.9	3.6	0.4	13.5	4.5	14.3	10.1	51.3	58
Douglas County	38 526	44.7	20.8	6.5	10.7	6.7	0.9	16.0	0.3	13.0	1.1	15.5	4.5	42.3	319
Edwards County	1 465	56.6	23.9	14.7	8.6	4.4	1.2	2.1	0.3	13.2	3.3	19.5	13.7	51.3	13
Elk County	1 418	57.3	19.0	18.5	8.5	5.0	1.7	1.2	0.1	15.2	4.9	17.8	12.3	45.9	31
Ellis County	11 204	49.7	22.8	10.2	11.4	7.1	1.6	8.9	0.1	13.4	2.4	16.6	7.9	46.3	90
Ellsworth County	2 495	58.0	22.4	14.5	8.3	5.3	1.5	2.2	0.0	13.0	4.2	18.4	13.4	52.4	6
Finney County	12 987	61.2	36.5	5.9	14.9	10.8	0.9	4.7	0.3	8.5	1.4	10.6	5.3	47.9	400
Ford County	10 861	58.1	31.8	8.8	14.9	9.0	1.5	4.2	0.0	10.3	2.4	12.5	7.3	48.2	211
Franklin County	9 457	58.6	26.4	10.4	13.6	9.2	1.6	3.2	0.2	10.2	2.5	14.4	8.5	47.6	178
Geary County	10 474	57.8	29.5	6.0	15.2	10.4	1.3	4.4	0.4	9.5	2.2	13.0	6.7	53.5	169
Gove County	1 254	62.8	25.4	17.0	6.8	4.1	1.2	1.1	0.3	11.2	3.4	18.0	13.1	47.2	9
Graham County	1 257	59.3	23.1	17.5	8.1	5.0	1.7	2.5	0.3	13.1	3.7	16.9	12.4	45.2	8
Grant County	2 748	67.6	35.4	8.2	9.9	7.8	0.5	1.5	0.0	9.2	1.9	11.7	6.4	48.7	77
Gray County	2 076	67.8	37.1	9.6	8.8	5.9	1.3	2.3	0.3	10.4	2.5	10.7	6.5	44.3	30
Greeley County	592	61.1	28.9	14.4	6.6	4.6	0.8	2.5	0.8	13.5	3.2	16.2	9.0	43.1	8
Greenwood County	3 234	58.5	20.9	16.8	8.3	6.0	1.1	3.0	0.3	11.8	3.6	18.3	12.7	47.2	56
Hamilton County	1 058	56.5	27.0	14.3	11.1	7.8	1.1	2.7	0.0	12.1	2.6	17.6	11.4	47.8	3
Harper County	2 765	56.1	21.8	16.4	9.4	5.0	1.6	2.4	0.4	12.9	3.2	19.3	12.9	46.7	62
Harvey County	12 607	60.6	26.7	13.7	10.6	6.5	1.5	3.2	0.2	10.1	2.3	15.5	9.4	43.3	203
Haskell County	1 477	70.5	39.1	9.3	7.9	5.6	1.1	1.6	0.1	9.3	2.0	10.6	7.8	48.2	22
Hodgeman County	787	63.4	28.3	15.8	9.1	5.8	1.8	2.2	0.3	11.1	4.3	14.2	9.9	44.4	9
Jackson County	4 734	62.5	29.2	11.6	12.3	7.4	2.0	2.5	0.3	9.6	3.8	13.1	7.9	45.6	79
Jefferson County	6 842	66.8	30.1	11.6	9.9	6.3	1.3	3.2	0.2	9.4	2.3	10.7	6.8	41.0	222
Jewell County	1 681	58.6	20.5	19.3	5.5	3.2	1.0	3.2	0.1	15.1	4.7	17.5	12.8	46.2	18
Johnson County	174 631	60.1	30.4	7.9	9.9	6.0	1.0	5.5	0.2	9.8	1.3	14.7	5.6	43.3	1 443
Kearny County	1 522	66.1	37.1	10.6	11.1	7.2	1.1	2.2	0.3	8.9	1.8	11.8	7.2	42.8	29
Kingman County	3 364	61.8	26.8	14.3	10.4	6.7	1.9	1.9	0.1	11.2	4.3	14.8	10.0	46.7	31
Kiowa County	1 363	60.5	22.5	16.8	7.1	5.4	0.4	1.8	0.0	11.7	3.6	18.9	11.9	47.4	22
Labette County	9 206	53.0	22.7	11.9	14.3	9.0	2.0	3.0	0.2	11.4	3.0	18.4	11.5	50.5	119
Lane County	915	61.6	24.9	15.4	6.8	5.0	1.0	2.1	0.7	12.8	4.5	16.7	11.7	48.7	14
Leavenworth County	23 087	62.0	31.1	8.4	13.0	8.5	1.5	3.4	0.2	9.5	2.0	12.2	6.3	44.9	571
Lincoln County	1 531	59.0	21.9	16.7	8.9	5.5	1.4	2.3	0.5	13.8	4.9	15.9	12.2	48.0	21
Linn County	3 814	63.9	25.2	15.8	9.3	5.3	1.2	2.8	0.4	10.4	3.6	13.6	9.4	43.0	93
Logan County	1 238	58.6	25.1	14.7	9.5	4.1	2.4	2.8	0.8	11.9	2.9	17.1	11.1	43.8	12
Lyon County	13 717	52.3	25.5	8.5	11.3	8.2	0.9	8.0	0.2	11.9	1.8	16.4	8.3	51.3	229
McPherson County	11 204	63.7	28.3	13.8	7.7	5.1	1.0	3.2	0.2	10.5	2.4	15.0	9.5	44.1	85
Marion County	5 082	64.0	25.8	16.7	8.2	5.1	1.7	2.8	0.7	10.2	2.8	14.9	10.2	40.6	45
Marshall County	4 465	60.0	26.7	16.0	7.7	4.0	1.3	2.9	0.1	10.9	3.6	18.5	14.2	50.5	68
Meade County	1 736	65.3	32.4	14.7	7.5	4.6	1.6	1.7	0.3	10.9	2.8	14.6	10.5	44.5	36
Miami County	10 397	64.7	30.3	9.6	10.7	7.1	1.1	3.7	0.3	9.0	2.2	11.9	7.5	46.8	167
Mitchell County	2 867	57.8	23.3	15.3	8.2	5.7	1.8	3.1	0.1	12.8	3.0	18.1	13.3	48.8	0
Montgomery County	14 902	54.2	22.0	12.6	13.3	8.6	1.8	2.8	0.0	11.7	3.1	18.0	11.5	50.5	296
Morris County	2 556	61.2	25.4	16.5	9.0	6.0	1.1	1.8	0.4	11.3	3.1	16.8	11.5	44.9	18
Morton County	1 282	63.7	29.6	12.7	10.1	6.8	1.0	2.0	0.3	11.3	1.6	12.9	8.0	40.4	13
Nemaha County	3 983	62.3	30.0	14.8	7.6	3.8	1.6	2.4	0.3	12.6	4.4	15.2	12.5	50.4	35
Neosho County	6 760	58.9	25.1	12.4	11.4	7.3	1.7	2.8	0.1	10.9	2.9	16.0	10.7	49.1	108
Ness County	1 515	57.2	21.7	15.4	7.1	4.7	1.6	1.9	0.3	16.0	6.1	17.8	13.5	53.1	18
Norton County	2 267	55.8	22.7	14.4	9.1	5.6	2.2	2.9	0.4	12.5	3.9	19.8	15.3	53.0	20

Table A-3. States and Counties — Age, Ethnicity, and Household Structure

STATE County	Households with Non-Hispanic White householder		Households with Black or African American householder		Households with American Indian and Alaska Native householder		Households with Asian, Hawaiian, and Pacific Islander householder		Households with Hispanic or Latino[1] householder		Foreign-born population	Place of birth (percent)			Percent in non-English speaking households	
	Number of households	Percent that are family households	Number of households	Percent that are family households	Number of households	Percent that are family households	Number of households	Percent that are family households	Number of households	Percent that are family households	Percent of total population that is foreign-born	Europe	Asia	Latin America	Linguistically isolated	Not linguistically isolated
	44	45	46	47	48	49	50	51	52	53	54	55	56	57	58	59
KANSAS—Cont'd																
Barber County	2 198	68.0	8	62.5	8	100.0	0	X	28	67.9	0.5	0.2	0.0	0.2	0.2	7.3
Barton County	10 568	65.6	121	43.0	56	85.7	26	100.0	554	87.0	4.4	0.3	0.2	3.8	3.5	8.3
Bourbon County	5 803	68.0	172	51.7	26	42.3	0	X	45	40.0	0.7	0.2	0.1	0.3	0.3	6.0
Brown County	3 759	68.6	109	67.0	345	72.8	19	68.4	46	87.0	1.3	0.4	0.4	0.4	0.6	6.3
Butler County	20 669	75.1	117	74.4	205	87.8	53	77.4	308	74.7	1.3	0.4	0.3	0.4	0.3	7.1
Chase County	1 217	66.3	8	75.0	5	100.0	0	X	17	47.1	1.1	0.1	0.0	0.6	0.0	5.0
Chautauqua County	1 698	69.1	0	X	40	75.0	6	50.0	16	56.3	0.8	0.3	0.1	0.3	0.3	5.7
Cherokee County	8 266	71.1	58	56.9	184	63.0	10	100.0	72	75.0	0.8	0.3	0.1	0.2	0.3	4.4
Cheyenne County	1 348	68.2	0	X	0	X	0	X	21	90.5	2.5	0.3	0.1	1.8	1.4	6.8
Clark County	947	69.7	3	100.0	7	28.6	0	X	16	87.5	2.8	0.1	0.3	2.4	1.4	6.3
Clay County	3 565	69.6	5	80.0	11	18.2	0	X	26	92.3	1.0	0.8	0.1	0.1	0.4	7.1
Cloud County	4 090	65.5	5	0.0	8	37.5	7	0.0	44	59.1	1.4	0.6	0.2	0.2	0.1	5.2
Coffey County	3 403	71.0	1	100.0	22	100.0	14	78.6	35	88.6	0.8	0.2	0.3	0.3	0.1	6.8
Comanche County	861	63.4	0	X	0	X	2	0.0	6	33.3	1.1	0.4	0.2	0.4	0.4	5.0
Cowley County	12 846	68.3	216	72.2	296	74.3	132	79.5	300	79.7	2.5	0.2	1.0	0.6	1.0	6.2
Crawford County	14 500	61.8	208	62.5	134	63.4	176	17.0	317	49.5	2.7	0.3	1.3	1.0	1.1	6.6
Decatur County	1 485	65.1	3	0.0	8	100.0	0	X	5	100.0	1.2	0.0	0.3	0.5	0.2	5.0
Dickinson County	7 598	68.6	25	52.0	39	79.5	16	0.0	143	74.1	1.7	0.9	0.2	0.4	0.5	7.5
Doniphan County	3 065	68.8	40	72.5	39	43.6	6	60.0	11	90.9	0.8	0.3	0.3	0.0	0.1	5.2
Douglas County	33 572	55.5	1 478	58.7	642	60.1	1 205	49.2	967	57.6	5.2	0.9	2.9	0.7	1.3	12.2
Edwards County	1 349	63.8	5	100.0	2	0.0	3	100.0	99	84.8	6.7	0.5	0.3	5.1	2.4	10.3
Elk County	1 361	65.2	0	X	7	100.0	0	X	29	75.9	0.7	0.3	0.1	0.4	0.1	5.1
Ellis County	10 837	61.3	57	0.0	0	X	71	83.1	185	62.7	2.3	0.1	0.7	1.2	1.0	10.9
Ellsworth County	2 397	66.4	0	X	3	100.0	4	100.0	69	60.9	1.3	0.6	0.2	0.5	0.5	8.7
Finney County	8 153	70.3	106	52.8	93	94.6	279	78.5	4 287	87.3	22.7	0.2	2.1	20.1	14.5	31.5
Ford County	7 532	67.3	153	62.7	54	98.1	191	85.9	2 847	87.6	22.5	0.1	1.8	20.6	13.0	28.2
Franklin County	9 014	71.9	89	78.7	67	70.1	16	100.0	168	69.0	1.3	0.2	0.4	0.6	0.6	6.2
Geary County	7 016	70.8	2 170	77.2	106	61.3	311	56.9	670	85.2	7.3	2.6	2.4	1.9	2.1	19.3
Gove County	1 227	69.4	3	100.0	2	0.0	0	X	12	91.7	0.5	0.3	0.1	0.0	0.5	6.8
Graham County	1 186	67.5	45	53.3	5	100.0	5	100.0	7	71.4	0.9	0.1	0.4	0.3	0.4	6.7
Grant County	1 988	74.1	0	X	14	57.1	0	X	728	87.6	12.3	0.1	0.0	12.0	5.9	30.0
Gray County	1 918	75.6	0	X	11	100.0	0	X	140	90.7	9.5	0.2	0.0	9.2	6.8	10.3
Greeley County	532	66.9	0	X	4	50.0	0	X	55	76.4	8.5	0.0	0.0	8.5	5.5	10.2
Greenwood County	3 132	67.1	0	X	22	36.4	8	100.0	38	68.4	1.0	0.2	0.4	0.4	0.1	5.3
Hamilton County	893	64.3	2	100.0	8	25.0	1	100.0	146	87.7	13.5	0.1	0.2	12.7	11.3	10.9
Harper County	2 691	66.2	10	100.0	21	28.6	8	0.0	18	33.3	0.4	0.2	0.2	0.0	0.4	5.3
Harvey County	11 493	70.8	138	43.5	70	91.4	41	95.1	796	78.9	3.7	0.5	0.6	2.2	1.7	10.1
Haskell County	1 203	74.5	2	0.0	11	100.0	11	100.0	229	96.5	13.4	0.0	0.9	12.4	5.8	22.3
Hodgeman County	764	72.0	4	100.0	0	X	0	X	15	100.0	1.0	0.0	0.0	1.0	0.7	6.4
Jackson County	4 329	74.2	27	77.8	280	81.8	8	100.0	30	96.7	0.5	0.0	0.2	0.2	0.1	5.7
Jefferson County	6 667	76.8	15	53.3	40	57.5	11	90.9	34	94.1	0.6	0.2	0.1	0.2	0.2	4.9
Jewell County	1 656	63.8	2	100.0	7	100.0	2	100.0	7	100.0	0.9	0.4	0.3	0.0	0.3	4.1
Johnson County	158 582	69.8	4 438	68.5	631	66.1	4 197	77.2	5 039	75.6	5.7	1.1	2.5	1.6	1.8	10.8
Kearny County	1 208	74.3	5	100.0	7	100.0	2	100.0	293	88.1	12.7	0.4	0.1	11.8	9.1	19.3
Kingman County	3 289	72.2	0	X	14	100.0	13	15.4	21	57.1	0.3	0.1	0.0	0.2	0.1	7.2
Kiowa County	1 329	67.9	0	X	1	100.0	4	100.0	25	44.0	1.0	0.4	0.3	0.8	0.4	6.5
Labette County	8 199	67.1	435	62.1	221	82.4	34	100.0	186	62.9	1.0	0.2	0.6	0.2	0.3	5.9
Lane County	892	68.0	0	X	0	X	0	X	10	80.0	0.5	0.1	0.2	0.0	0.3	3.9
Leavenworth County	20 010	75.3	1 890	70.6	145	77.2	167	68.3	593	70.3	2.7	1.0	0.9	0.6	0.7	10.4
Lincoln County	1 503	67.9	2	100.0	2	0.0	1	0.0	8	87.5	0.5	0.3	0.1	0.2	0.3	5.7
Linn County	3 755	73.2	3	66.7	26	100.0	2	100.0	14	42.9	0.3	0.1	0.1	0.0	0.0	4.5
Logan County	1 220	68.2	4	0.0	0	X	0	X	12	100.0	0.6	0.2	0.4	0.0	0.1	5.5
Lyon County	11 506	62.7	281	47.3	74	63.5	115	74.8	1 618	73.5	9.0	0.4	0.8	7.6	5.7	14.3
McPherson County	10 835	71.4	126	74.6	17	94.1	7	42.9	98	83.7	0.6	0.2	0.1	0.1	0.2	6.5
Marion County	4 936	72.2	17	52.9	14	50.0	9	44.4	71	80.3	1.1	0.5	0.2	0.2	0.7	9.9
Marshall County	4 376	68.0	8	0.0	13	53.8	18	55.6	31	54.8	1.1	0.2	0.5	0.1	0.7	4.8
Meade County	1 602	72.2	1	100.0	9	66.7	3	0.0	107	84.1	8.9	0.3	0.2	7.9	3.2	16.0
Miami County	10 001	76.0	132	59.1	58	74.1	21	57.1	77	41.6	0.6	0.2	0.1	0.2	0.2	5.6
Mitchell County	2 837	65.9	0	X	4	100.0	0	X	9	55.6	0.3	0.1	0.2	0.0	0.2	6.6
Montgomery County	12 877	67.5	831	59.8	422	82.9	52	59.6	287	76.0	1.3	0.3	0.5	0.4	0.3	7.0
Morris County	2 442	70.6	11	63.6	19	68.4	2	0.0	62	51.6	1.5	0.3	0.2	1.0	0.2	7.3
Morton County	1 109	72.8	4	100.0	22	59.1	21	81.0	122	83.6	9.5	0.1	1.1	7.5	3.7	15.8
Nemaha County	3 900	69.8	30	53.3	9	100.0	3	100.0	18	77.8	0.4	0.2	0.1	0.0	0.1	5.8
Neosho County	6 377	70.5	44	54.5	59	67.8	16	62.5	166	66.3	0.7	0.3	0.2	0.1	0.2	5.9
Ness County	1 488	63.7	2	100.0	0	X	0	X	15	100.0	0.9	0.2	0.1	0.5	0.1	7.0
Norton County	2 205	66.2	0	X	0	X	5	100.0	48	12.5	0.6	0.2	0.2	0.1	0.6	4.6

[1] Hispanic or Latino persons may be of any race.

STATE/ County code	MSA/PMSA/ NECMA code[1]	STATE County	Total population	Under 5 years	5 to 17 years	18 to 24 years	25 to 44 years	45 to 64 years	65 years and over	Median age	+/− U.S. percent under 18 years	+/− U.S. percent 65 years and over	Total population	Under 18 years	65 years and over
						Population by age (percent)							Non-Hispanic White — Age (percent)		
			1	2	3	4	5	6	7	8	9	10	11	12	13
		KANSAS—Cont'd													
20 139	...	Osage County	16 712	6.8	20.2	6.4	27.2	23.5	15.8	38.9	1.3	3.4	16 202	26.7	16.1
20 141	...	Osborne County	4 452	4.5	19.3	6.2	21.9	22.3	25.8	44.0	-1.9	13.4	4 347	23.5	26.2
20 143	...	Ottawa County	6 163	5.6	20.0	5.8	27.2	23.8	17.6	40.1	-0.1	5.2	6 016	25.4	17.8
20 145	...	Pawnee County	7 233	5.5	18.6	8.5	24.5	24.2	18.7	40.5	-1.6	6.3	6 455	23.4	19.9
20 147	...	Phillips County	6 001	5.6	19.1	5.6	23.1	24.7	21.9	42.5	-1.0	9.5	5 880	24.6	22.2
20 149	...	Pottawatomie County	18 209	7.3	21.9	8.0	27.6	21.8	13.4	35.9	3.5	1.0	17 353	28.7	13.8
20 151	...	Pratt County	9 647	6.3	18.5	9.2	23.5	23.2	19.3	40.2	-0.9	6.9	9 129	23.8	19.8
20 153	...	Rawlins County	2 966	4.3	19.6	3.6	21.8	24.7	26.0	45.4	-1.8	13.6	2 846	22.9	26.4
20 155	...	Reno County	64 790	6.4	18.0	9.1	27.3	23.0	16.3	38.2	-1.3	3.9	57 752	23.3	17.6
20 157	...	Republic County	5 835	4.5	17.8	4.8	22.1	24.6	26.2	45.7	-3.4	13.8	5 693	21.9	26.6
20 159	...	Rice County	10 761	6.0	18.6	13.2	22.4	21.7	18.1	37.6	-1.1	5.7	9 879	23.0	19.1
20 161	...	Riley County	62 843	5.6	13.2	34.5	25.7	13.5	7.5	23.9	-6.9	-4.9	52 156	17.0	8.7
20 163	...	Rooks County	5 685	5.6	19.6	6.1	25.6	21.5	21.5	40.5	-0.5	9.1	5 479	24.7	21.8
20 165	...	Rush County	3 551	4.8	17.3	5.5	22.9	23.9	25.5	44.6	-3.6	13.1	3 499	22.1	25.8
20 167	...	Russell County	7 370	4.9	17.2	5.7	23.2	24.8	24.3	44.1	-3.6	11.9	7 168	21.6	24.7
20 169	...	Saline County	53 597	6.8	19.4	9.1	28.9	22.0	13.8	36.1	0.5	1.4	46 660	24.3	15.3
20 171	...	Scott County	5 120	6.7	20.2	7.1	25.9	23.6	16.4	39.2	1.2	4.0	4 738	25.5	17.7
20 173	9040	Sedgwick County	452 869	7.8	20.3	9.5	30.5	20.5	11.4	33.6	2.4	-1.0	346 100	25.3	13.3
20 175	...	Seward County	22 510	9.5	22.5	11.6	31.2	16.8	8.4	29.0	6.3	-4.0	11 142	23.2	15.8
20 177	8440	Shawnee County	169 871	6.8	18.4	9.0	28.4	23.6	13.7	37.1	-0.5	1.3	135 843	22.7	15.5
20 179	...	Sheridan County	2 813	5.0	21.4	5.9	23.3	24.2	20.2	41.5	0.7	7.8	2 783	26.1	20.4
20 181	...	Sherman County	6 760	6.1	18.4	11.6	23.9	23.0	17.0	37.8	-1.2	4.6	6 084	22.7	18.6
20 183	...	Smith County	4 536	4.2	17.6	4.6	22.5	23.5	27.6	46.0	-3.9	15.2	4 435	21.2	28.1
20 185	...	Stafford County	4 789	5.6	20.9	5.6	24.6	22.4	21.0	41.0	0.8	8.6	4 429	25.4	22.5
20 187	...	Stanton County	2 406	7.9	22.9	8.2	28.6	19.1	13.3	33.8	5.1	0.9	1 793	27.3	16.1
20 189	...	Stevens County	5 463	8.7	22.4	8.7	28.6	18.2	13.4	33.6	5.4	1.0	4 092	27.4	16.8
20 191	...	Sumner County	25 946	6.7	21.8	7.3	26.0	22.7	15.4	37.6	2.8	3.0	24 000	27.8	16.1
20 193	...	Thomas County	8 180	6.8	19.3	13.1	24.6	21.6	14.7	35.3	0.4	2.3	7 917	25.5	15.0
20 195	...	Trego County	3 319	5.0	18.9	5.5	23.3	23.0	24.3	43.5	-1.8	11.9	3 293	23.8	24.3
20 197	...	Wabaunsee County	6 885	6.1	20.5	6.2	26.6	25.0	15.6	39.5	0.9	3.2	6 704	26.5	15.8
20 199	...	Wallace County	1 749	5.3	23.7	6.3	24.2	22.5	18.1	39.5	3.3	5.7	1 612	28.1	18.9
20 201	...	Washington County	6 483	5.7	18.0	5.8	22.5	23.0	25.0	43.6	-2.0	12.6	6 387	23.6	25.2
20 203	...	Wichita County	2 531	8.1	20.4	7.3	26.6	21.4	16.2	36.7	2.8	3.8	2 013	25.6	18.7
20 205	...	Wilson County	10 332	5.9	19.5	7.4	23.9	23.3	19.9	40.6	-0.3	7.5	9 954	25.2	20.4
20 207	...	Woodson County	3 788	5.1	16.7	7.8	21.7	23.9	24.8	44.1	-3.9	12.4	3 652	21.7	25.6
20 209	3760	Wyandotte County	157 882	8.0	20.4	10.4	29.8	19.7	11.7	32.5	2.7	-0.7	81 462	22.0	16.2
21 000	...	**KENTUCKY**	4 041 769	6.6	18.0	9.9	30.0	23.0	12.5	35.9	-1.1	0.1	3 610 112	23.8	13.1
21 001	...	Adair County	17 244	6.3	17.2	11.2	27.2	23.6	14.6	36.9	-2.2	2.2	16 506	23.6	14.6
21 003	...	Allen County	17 800	6.7	19.2	8.7	28.7	23.0	13.7	36.2	0.2	1.3	17 376	26.0	13.7
21 005	...	Anderson County	19 111	7.5	19.1	7.4	32.4	22.9	10.6	35.5	0.9	-1.8	18 334	26.6	10.9
21 007	...	Ballard County	8 286	6.2	16.8	7.4	27.9	25.6	16.1	39.6	-2.7	3.7	7 754	22.1	16.8
21 009	...	Barren County	38 033	6.3	17.8	8.2	29.1	23.7	14.9	38.0	-1.6	2.5	35 743	23.8	15.2
21 011	...	Bath County	11 085	6.6	17.8	8.4	28.9	23.8	14.5	37.4	-1.3	2.1	10 726	24.1	14.7
21 013	...	Bell County	30 060	6.0	18.4	9.0	29.1	24.2	13.4	37.0	-1.3	1.0	28 805	24.3	13.6
21 015	1640	Boone County	85 991	7.9	20.5	8.6	33.3	21.6	8.1	33.4	2.7	-4.3	80 814	28.2	8.4
21 017	4280	Bourbon County	19 360	6.5	18.5	7.8	29.1	24.8	13.4	37.6	-0.7	1.0	17 343	24.6	13.4
21 019	3400	Boyd County	49 752	5.5	16.4	8.4	28.5	25.7	15.6	39.7	-3.8	3.2	47 272	22.0	16.1
21 021	...	Boyle County	27 697	5.5	17.1	10.6	29.3	23.3	14.2	36.9	-3.1	1.8	24 093	22.0	15.0
21 023	...	Bracken County	8 279	6.5	19.0	8.6	29.4	23.1	13.5	36.8	-0.2	1.1	8 159	25.1	13.6
21 025	...	Breathitt County	16 100	5.7	19.7	10.0	28.8	24.1	11.6	35.9	-0.3	-0.8	15 801	25.3	11.7
21 027	...	Breckinridge County	18 648	6.1	18.8	8.1	26.8	26.0	14.2	38.5	-0.8	1.8	17 821	24.6	14.3
21 029	4520	Bullitt County	61 236	7.2	19.9	8.6	32.7	23.7	7.8	34.5	1.4	-4.6	59 782	26.9	7.8
21 031	...	Butler County	13 010	6.4	18.9	9.4	29.4	22.9	12.9	36.3	-0.4	0.5	12 656	25.0	13.1
21 033	...	Caldwell County	13 060	5.3	17.0	6.7	26.6	26.4	18.0	41.2	-3.4	5.6	12 215	21.8	18.4
21 035	...	Calloway County	34 177	4.9	13.9	19.7	24.7	21.9	14.9	34.5	-6.9	2.5	31 706	18.6	15.7
21 037	1640	Campbell County	88 616	6.9	18.7	9.9	30.5	21.5	12.6	35.2	-0.1	0.2	84 944	25.3	13.0
21 039	...	Carlisle County	5 351	6.0	17.4	7.7	26.0	24.6	18.3	39.5	-2.3	5.9	5 230	22.6	18.6
21 041	...	Carroll County	10 155	6.9	18.1	9.2	30.0	23.1	12.8	35.9	-0.7	0.4	9 464	25.0	12.9
21 043	3400	Carter County	26 889	6.5	18.1	10.7	28.5	23.7	12.5	35.8	-1.1	0.1	26 529	24.5	12.5
21 045	...	Casey County	15 447	6.1	18.3	8.2	27.5	24.7	15.2	37.8	-1.3	2.8	14 963	24.1	15.4
21 047	1660	Christian County	72 265	9.9	18.3	16.0	30.4	15.8	9.7	27.9	2.5	-2.7	49 440	24.9	11.8
21 049	4280	Clark County	33 144	6.6	18.1	8.4	30.1	24.4	12.4	36.8	-1.0	0.0	30 764	24.3	12.5
21 051	...	Clay County	24 556	5.6	19.8	9.1	32.5	22.6	10.3	34.6	-0.3	-2.1	22 791	26.2	10.7
21 053	...	Clinton County	9 634	6.3	16.5	8.7	27.6	25.8	15.0	39.0	-2.9	2.6	9 369	23.2	15.2
21 055	...	Crittenden County	9 384	5.3	17.9	8.0	26.2	26.4	16.3	40.1	-2.5	3.9	9 223	23.2	16.2

[1]MSA = Metropolitan Statistical Area. PMSA = Primary MSA. NECMA = New England County Metropolitan Area. See the Appendix A for explanation of these concepts. See Appendix B for list of metropolitan areas identified by type, with component counties.

STATE County	Black or African American Total population	Under 18 years	65 years and over	American Indian and Alaska Native Total population	Under 18 years	65 years and over	Asian, Hawaiian, and Pacific Islander Total population	Under 18 years	65 years and over	Hispanic or Latino[1] Total population	Under 18 years	65 years and over	Two or more races Total population	Under 18 years	65 years and over
	14	15	16	17	18	19	20	21	22	23	24	25	26	27	28
KANSAS—Cont'd															
Osage County	42	50.0	0.0	64	26.6	9.4	49	24.5	16.3	203	44.8	3.9	187	39.6	4.8
Osborne County	0	X	X	16	56.3	0.0	20	0.0	15.0	25	48.0	16.0	46	45.7	6.5
Ottawa County	20	0.0	0.0	20	50.0	10.0	11	27.3	0.0	44	25.0	27.3	56	51.8	0.0
Pawnee County	338	28.7	14.5	54	20.4	0.0	43	30.2	0.0	295	39.3	4.7	131	38.2	0.0
Phillips County	23	26.1	8.7	23	52.2	0.0	20	25.0	0.0	44	38.6	0.0	20	5.0	20.0
Pottawatomie County	123	59.3	0.0	123	31.7	7.3	31	22.6	6.5	332	44.6	4.5	308	39.3	7.5
Pratt County	73	38.4	0.0	3	0.0	0.0	9	66.7	0.0	361	46.3	12.5	85	31.8	3.5
Rawlins County	10	10.0	40.0	12	58.3	16.7	3	66.7	0.0	47	48.9	10.6	58	53.4	15.5
Reno County	1 840	28.4	4.2	438	38.6	3.4	401	19.0	3.5	3 556	37.2	6.0	1 135	44.5	7.3
Republic County	31	77.4	22.6	20	30.0	0.0	20	25.0	20.0	43	23.3	14.0	31	38.7	0.0
Rice County	75	26.7	22.7	59	49.2	0.0	50	8.0	10.0	617	46.2	6.5	155	56.1	0.0
Riley County	4 168	26.9	2.3	267	18.0	5.6	2 078	17.8	1.9	2 989	27.7	1.0	1 512	47.8	0.7
Rooks County	52	46.2	11.5	11	18.2	0.0	12	58.3	0.0	78	25.6	0.0	55	50.9	34.5
Rush County	0	X	X	9	0.0	33.3	4	0.0	0.0	30	30.0	13.3	19	36.8	0.0
Russell County	0	X	X	70	34.3	0.0	8	0.0	100.0	69	34.8	13.0	55	49.1	5.5
Saline County	1 587	31.3	10.6	253	23.7	5.5	877	27.5	1.7	3 197	39.4	1.9	1 200	59.3	2.3
Scott County	10	0.0	0.0	6	83.3	0.0	7	0.0	0.0	307	41.0	0.0	52	76.9	0.0
Sedgwick County	40 626	35.0	7.5	4 932	31.3	5.4	14 606	28.8	4.3	36 016	40.6	3.0	14 856	51.0	3.4
Seward County	847	33.9	0.8	160	51.9	0.0	447	30.2	5.8	9 518	41.0	0.9	751	45.7	1.3
Shawnee County	14 642	31.0	9.5	2 018	27.8	8.8	1 555	20.6	3.4	12 142	38.5	4.8	5 487	52.4	3.0
Sheridan County	0	X	X	2	0.0	0.0	15	53.3	0.0	10	40.0	0.0	3	100.0	0.0
Sherman County	25	0.0	0.0	37	40.5	5.4	0	X	X	604	40.0	2.3	61	65.6	0.0
Smith County	9	55.6	0.0	2	0.0	0.0	40	50.0	0.0	22	50.0	9.1	27	37.0	3.7
Stafford County	18	27.8	16.7	21	0.0	9.5	36	30.6	5.6	256	43.4	0.8	52	55.8	3.8
Stanton County	8	0.0	0.0	20	10.0	35.0	7	0.0	0.0	563	41.7	3.7	40	67.5	5.0
Stevens County	0	X	X	56	28.6	5.4	40	30.0	0.0	1 202	44.1	3.3	136	39.7	7.4
Sumner County	228	43.0	5.3	294	24.5	3.1	52	32.7	0.0	866	42.0	9.4	648	42.3	6.0
Thomas County	10	0.0	0.0	0	X	X	43	0.0	0.0	126	55.6	11.1	92	51.1	2.2
Trego County	4	100.0	0.0	2	0.0	0.0	5	60.0	0.0	11	0.0	45.5	4	100.0	0.0
Wabaunsee County	23	47.8	8.7	18	38.9	0.0	14	35.7	0.0	83	34.9	12.0	58	31.0	3.4
Wallace County	5	0.0	0.0	5	0.0	0.0	4	50.0	0.0	104	43.3	3.8	34	26.5	20.6
Washington County	8	50.0	0.0	19	36.8	0.0	0	X	X	46	37.0	17.4	32	37.5	18.8
Wichita County	0	X	X	19	36.8	21.1	1	0.0	0.0	470	38.1	6.2	76	56.6	0.0
Wilson County	38	42.1	7.9	86	27.9	0.0	23	21.7	0.0	82	43.9	0.0	142	29.6	19.0
Woodson County	19	0.0	0.0	37	32.4	5.4	20	0.0	0.0	43	48.8	7.0	40	47.5	5.0
Wyandotte County	44 768	33.8	9.0	1 116	31.8	6.9	2 319	36.5	5.5	25 182	36.7	3.1	4 702	45.7	4.5
KENTUCKY	293 915	30.0	8.7	9 080	22.5	5.6	30 149	23.9	3.5	56 414	31.6	3.5	47 341	43.8	5.9
Adair County	515	22.1	13.2	16	0.0	0.0	27	0.0	14.8	103	35.0	25.2	86	2.3	16.3
Allen County	145	24.1	16.6	10	0.0	0.0	26	0.0	0.0	119	12.6	12.6	145	39.3	10.3
Anderson County	446	21.5	4.0	11	0.0	54.5	118	35.6	5.9	96	19.8	6.3	121	47.1	0.0
Ballard County	261	34.9	6.1	3	0.0	0.0	37	40.5	0.0	44	36.4	4.5	189	37.6	7.9
Barren County	1 557	29.0	11.2	22	54.5	9.1	138	8.7	1.4	428	30.1	6.1	171	59.1	7.0
Bath County	191	22.0	14.7	6	0.0	0.0	15	0.0	0.0	118	56.8	0.0	67	43.3	6.0
Bell County	745	21.5	10.1	30	0.0	0.0	78	23.1	0.0	138	26.1	3.6	235	35.7	6.8
Boone County	1 420	27.2	2.8	242	28.1	9.9	1 049	29.3	2.2	1 512	26.7	2.6	1 025	45.1	3.9
Bourbon County	1 284	22.0	18.6	7	0.0	57.1	81	70.4	0.0	526	36.5	0.0	240	48.8	7.1
Boyd County	1 126	13.7	6.6	89	0.0	6.7	168	32.7	0.0	555	15.9	4.1	618	33.8	6.1
Boyle County	2 574	21.1	9.4	57	12.3	0.0	209	49.3	0.0	468	38.9	6.2	374	54.5	7.8
Bracken County	67	41.8	6.0	1	0.0	0.0	0	X	X	7	71.4	0.0	28	32.1	0.0
Breathitt County	33	93.9	0.0	27	70.4	0.0	43	37.2	0.0	72	37.5	2.8	135	15.6	8.1
Breckinridge County	484	28.3	12.4	27	22.2	48.1	22	13.6	18.2	139	33.8	8.6	166	33.7	17.5
Bullitt County	253	30.8	19.0	213	16.9	7.0	83	37.3	4.8	383	48.8	6.0	546	38.6	2.6
Butler County	57	61.4	28.1	0	X	X	88	48.9	8.0	176	25.0	3.4	41	46.3	0.0
Caldwell County	595	23.2	15.8	19	0.0	0.0	26	38.5	0.0	104	43.3	11.5	91	62.6	0.0
Calloway County	1 248	18.9	4.9	53	17.0	0.0	469	9.4	2.8	352	33.8	0.0	468	29.5	5.1
Campbell County	1 451	32.5	4.0	155	19.4	0.0	587	29.3	2.9	784	33.5	3.8	722	41.4	7.5
Carlisle County	54	59.3	11.1	6	0.0	0.0	0	X	X	26	84.6	0.0	35	31.4	0.0
Carroll County	206	28.6	29.1	69	0.0	0.0	45	0.0	0.0	138	12.3	0.0	239	37.2	9.2
Carter County	50	60.0	14.0	41	29.3	22.0	79	27.8	11.4	114	40.4	7.9	78	16.7	6.4
Casey County	63	31.7	11.1	40	0.0	0.0	10	0.0	0.0	320	41.6	1.9	69	21.7	47.8
Christian County	16 986	34.7	6.5	298	18.8	0.0	820	27.4	2.2	3 324	35.6	0.7	1 946	48.5	2.6
Clark County	1 695	28.0	14.9	44	34.1	0.0	189	23.3	0.0	203	30.0	2.5	248	42.3	2.8
Clay County	1 184	11.7	3.5	58	31.0	0.0	36	5.6	0.0	298	11.4	6.4	247	30.8	17.8
Clinton County	18	0.0	0.0	0	X	X	59	0.0	0.0	151	6.0	0.0	101	16.8	24.8
Crittenden County	64	21.9	29.7	14	0.0	0.0	20	0.0	0.0	37	21.6	32.4	32	50.0	12.5

[1] Hispanic or Latino persons may be of any race.

STATE County	Total households	Married-couple family households			Other family households			Two or more unrelated persons		Male living alone		Female living alone		Percent of householders 65 years and over who live alone	Grandparents who are responsible for the care of their grandchildren
		Total	With children	Householder 65 years or over	Total	With children	Householder 65 years or over	Total	Householder 65 years or over	Total	Householder 65 years or over	Total	Householder 65 years or over		
	29	30	31	32	33	34	35	36	37	38	39	40	41	42	43
KANSAS—Cont'd															
Osage County	6 471	61.9	25.9	12.9	11.3	8.3	1.1	3.1	0.3	9.9	2.4	13.7	8.6	43.5	143
Osborne County	1 951	55.5	21.6	18.1	7.3	4.2	1.3	2.4	0.3	15.4	3.6	19.4	14.6	48.0	22
Ottawa County	2 441	61.3	24.4	12.2	9.8	8.0	0.2	3.3	0.7	11.4	4.7	14.2	9.3	51.7	55
Pawnee County	2 751	57.3	25.0	13.7	9.4	6.9	1.2	1.5	0.5	15.0	2.9	16.8	9.7	44.9	22
Phillips County	2 495	62.7	23.4	17.1	6.7	3.9	1.6	2.3	0.0	12.5	2.7	15.8	11.8	43.5	11
Pottawatomie County	6 818	63.4	30.2	11.5	9.8	5.9	1.5	3.7	0.3	10.6	2.3	12.4	7.5	42.4	92
Pratt County	3 964	57.0	22.3	14.4	9.4	7.4	1.0	3.1	0.4	11.7	3.3	18.8	11.3	48.0	18
Rawlins County	1 298	57.4	22.5	17.1	9.3	4.5	2.9	1.9	0.7	13.3	4.7	18.1	13.5	46.8	8
Reno County	25 514	56.2	22.3	12.8	12.1	8.3	1.4	3.8	0.2	11.9	2.7	16.0	9.2	45.2	501
Republic County	2 549	60.5	20.6	18.5	5.3	4.0	0.5	2.4	0.3	12.1	3.9	19.7	14.9	49.4	7
Rice County	4 072	60.7	25.1	15.0	9.7	6.3	1.1	2.0	0.4	10.3	3.9	17.4	11.6	48.5	71
Riley County	22 120	46.6	22.4	6.3	9.5	5.9	0.7	16.5	0.1	12.6	1.8	14.8	5.5	50.7	201
Rooks County	2 365	55.4	22.3	15.1	10.4	5.8	1.7	2.4	0.0	12.9	4.1	18.8	13.9	51.8	18
Rush County	1 546	56.0	21.0	16.9	8.9	5.4	1.5	3.4	0.8	12.8	4.3	18.9	13.6	48.3	5
Russell County	3 225	53.8	17.6	18.0	9.9	6.8	1.8	3.7	0.2	12.8	3.8	19.8	13.0	45.7	41
Saline County	21 490	54.4	24.5	10.4	12.4	8.1	1.3	4.9	0.2	12.1	2.4	16.2	8.5	47.7	368
Scott County	2 047	59.6	25.5	10.8	11.1	7.7	1.0	2.2	0.0	12.6	4.2	14.5	10.7	55.8	0
Sedgwick County	176 600	52.7	25.8	8.4	14.5	9.2	1.7	4.7	0.2	13.3	2.1	14.8	6.6	45.9	4 066
Seward County	7 429	59.8	33.9	7.0	15.0	10.3	1.0	4.8	0.2	11.2	1.7	11.2	6.2	49.4	203
Shawnee County	69 007	51.1	22.2	9.5	14.3	9.0	1.8	4.9	0.3	12.1	2.5	17.5	8.2	48.1	1 351
Sheridan County	1 134	64.4	26.8	16.4	7.4	3.5	1.1	1.1	0.0	12.5	3.4	14.6	11.8	46.4	11
Sherman County	2 764	55.0	23.7	10.3	9.6	6.0	1.8	6.3	0.8	14.9	5.2	14.1	10.3	54.9	29
Smith County	1 953	60.5	22.6	19.2	7.9	4.7	1.4	1.5	0.1	13.6	6.1	16.5	12.7	47.7	7
Stafford County	1 999	56.1	24.1	13.8	8.7	6.7	1.2	2.4	0.1	11.9	4.0	21.1	15.4	56.2	13
Stanton County	852	64.0	34.4	13.4	11.4	7.4	1.6	2.7	0.6	12.8	2.1	9.2	5.5	32.8	13
Stevens County	1 984	63.5	31.3	10.6	10.8	6.0	2.0	1.3	0.1	8.5	1.2	16.0	9.2	45.1	36
Sumner County	9 920	61.0	28.3	12.3	10.8	6.8	1.5	2.6	0.2	10.7	2.1	14.8	9.8	45.9	222
Thomas County	3 217	58.7	29.2	12.0	8.6	4.9	0.6	4.1	0.4	13.8	1.7	14.8	7.8	42.3	3
Trego County	1 412	59.8	23.1	16.1	6.0	3.5	1.5	2.3	0.0	12.1	5.8	19.7	15.6	54.8	11
Wabaunsee County	2 640	64.5	27.3	12.8	9.6	5.3	1.4	2.9	0.0	11.6	4.1	11.5	8.3	46.7	63
Wallace County	684	64.9	29.1	15.9	6.3	4.5	0.6	2.0	0.9	11.7	1.6	15.1	11.4	42.8	10
Washington County	2 665	58.8	23.1	17.6	7.3	3.7	1.4	2.5	0.5	13.7	5.3	17.7	13.4	49.0	27
Wichita County	976	64.9	28.6	15.2	11.4	7.8	1.8	1.0	0.0	12.0	2.6	10.8	7.7	37.6	8
Wilson County	4 214	57.5	23.1	14.0	10.1	6.8	1.1	3.4	0.4	11.5	4.1	17.5	11.5	50.3	69
Woodson County	1 642	54.4	17.8	18.8	10.2	7.6	1.5	2.3	0.7	14.4	4.4	18.6	13.6	46.3	37
Wyandotte County	59 710	43.4	19.7	7.5	22.7	13.7	2.8	5.0	0.5	12.7	2.5	16.1	7.7	48.6	2 301
KENTUCKY	1 591 739	54.7	24.2	8.8	15.0	8.8	2.2	4.2	0.3	10.8	2.2	15.2	7.6	46.5	35 818
Adair County	6 733	58.3	24.3	9.9	12.7	7.2	2.8	2.6	0.7	9.8	2.8	16.6	9.7	48.4	180
Allen County	6 889	61.1	26.0	11.1	13.6	8.2	1.6	2.0	0.1	10.7	2.5	12.6	8.2	45.5	143
Anderson County	7 314	63.4	29.5	8.7	12.6	7.6	1.2	3.4	0.1	7.6	1.1	12.9	6.8	44.1	77
Ballard County	3 416	61.5	25.2	11.0	10.4	6.5	1.3	2.6	0.2	9.7	2.1	15.9	10.9	51.0	84
Barren County	15 355	59.2	24.9	10.3	12.8	7.5	2.1	2.5	0.2	9.9	2.0	15.6	9.5	47.7	211
Bath County	4 460	58.9	25.4	9.6	13.2	7.6	2.8	2.6	0.2	12.2	3.3	13.1	8.2	47.7	57
Bell County	12 031	52.0	22.0	8.4	19.4	10.4	3.3	1.8	0.3	10.4	2.2	16.4	8.5	47.0	277
Boone County	31 331	62.6	32.7	6.5	12.9	7.8	1.4	4.4	0.2	8.6	1.3	11.5	5.0	43.8	481
Bourbon County	7 705	54.7	23.1	10.0	16.8	10.3	2.3	3.9	0.6	9.1	1.7	15.6	8.4	44.0	175
Boyd County	20 077	57.1	21.1	11.4	14.0	8.2	2.1	2.6	0.3	9.5	2.5	16.8	9.8	47.0	416
Boyle County	10 589	54.7	23.0	10.6	14.8	8.4	2.1	3.5	0.3	9.2	2.3	17.9	9.9	48.4	274
Bracken County	3 223	58.8	25.9	9.3	13.9	7.9	2.8	3.4	0.2	11.2	3.4	12.7	8.9	50.0	136
Breathitt County	6 181	55.2	25.4	7.8	18.4	9.0	3.9	2.4	0.2	9.3	2.0	14.6	7.2	43.4	181
Breckinridge County	7 335	60.8	24.7	11.1	12.2	6.9	2.3	2.5	0.4	10.0	2.8	14.6	8.5	44.8	194
Bullitt County	22 248	66.0	30.7	6.9	14.3	8.7	1.6	3.4	0.3	7.4	1.3	8.9	4.0	37.7	575
Butler County	5 054	61.2	27.4	10.0	12.4	7.0	2.1	2.6	0.2	10.5	2.5	13.3	8.1	46.5	126
Caldwell County	5 419	59.6	22.0	13.5	11.2	6.8	2.2	1.6	0.0	11.1	2.8	16.5	10.6	45.9	168
Calloway County	13 822	52.6	20.8	11.5	10.0	5.6	1.5	7.8	0.1	11.8	1.9	17.8	9.1	45.4	165
Campbell County	34 831	51.4	24.1	8.4	15.5	8.8	2.4	4.6	0.1	11.6	2.4	16.9	7.7	48.1	639
Carlisle County	2 212	58.0	22.6	14.1	13.7	8.0	3.0	2.1	0.0	11.8	2.4	14.5	8.9	39.7	36
Carroll County	3 948	53.4	23.7	8.8	17.0	10.4	2.6	4.4	0.3	12.1	3.7	13.0	7.3	48.5	193
Carter County	10 356	61.7	26.8	9.6	13.4	7.1	2.6	2.7	0.2	8.9	2.8	13.4	8.1	46.8	163
Casey County	6 273	57.4	25.5	9.8	13.4	7.0	2.9	2.4	0.3	12.0	3.5	14.8	9.1	49.5	131
Christian County	24 887	57.8	31.0	7.7	16.3	10.8	1.7	3.5	0.2	9.7	2.0	12.6	6.8	47.7	485
Clark County	13 039	58.1	25.2	9.3	14.9	8.7	2.2	4.2	0.5	8.9	2.2	13.9	7.0	43.4	295
Clay County	8 573	58.6	29.5	8.3	16.6	8.1	4.0	2.4	0.1	8.9	2.0	13.6	6.3	40.0	338
Clinton County	4 075	56.9	22.5	11.2	11.7	7.6	1.1	3.0	0.6	11.8	2.8	16.6	9.9	49.7	91
Crittenden County	3 862	59.9	22.9	12.6	11.2	6.7	1.5	2.1	0.4	10.9	2.4	15.9	10.6	47.1	99

STATE County	Households with Non-Hispanic White householder		Households with Black or African American householder		Households with American Indian and Alaska Native householder		Households with Asian, Hawaiian, and Pacific Islander householder		Households with Hispanic or Latino[1] householder		Foreign-born population	Place of birth (percent)			Percent in non-English speaking households	
	Number of households	Percent that are family households	Number of households	Percent that are family households	Number of households	Percent that are family households	Number of households	Percent that are family households	Number of households	Percent that are family households	Percent of total population that is foreign-born	Europe	Asia	Latin America	Linguistically isolated	Not linguistically isolated
	44	45	46	47	48	49	50	51	52	53	54	55	56	57	58	59
KANSAS—Cont'd																
Osage County	6 319	73.2	7	71.4	19	78.9	22	100.0	61	59.0	0.6	0.2	0.1	0.1	0.1	5.7
Osborne County	1 920	63.3	0	X	5	60.0	12	8.3	6	0.0	0.7	0.1	0.4	0.2	0.2	4.9
Ottawa County	2 399	71.5	0	X	9	77.8	3	0.0	20	40.0	0.7	0.3	0.2	0.1	0.1	4.4
Pawnee County	2 549	66.2	74	37.8	17	100.0	13	100.0	98	91.8	1.4	0.2	0.6	0.2	0.7	4.4
Phillips County	2 460	69.8	8	25.0	9	44.4	7	42.9	7	42.9	0.4	0.2	0.2	0.0	0.0	5.4
Pottawatomie County	6 539	73.7	38	47.4	49	53.1	15	100.0	111	79.3	1.0	0.4	0.1	0.2	0.1	6.8
Pratt County	3 792	66.4	34	47.1	0	X	0	X	107	73.8	1.2	0.2	0.0	1.0	0.8	5.4
Rawlins County	1 259	66.8	6	100.0	2	100.0	1	100.0	12	58.3	0.4	0.1	0.1	0.1	0.1	7.7
Reno County	23 549	67.8	444	64.9	117	88.0	142	65.5	1 060	75.0	2.0	0.2	0.4	1.1	0.8	8.9
Republic County	2 500	65.9	3	100.0	11	100.0	10	60.0	20	70.0	0.8	0.2	0.3	0.2	0.5	5.9
Rice County	3 842	69.4	22	50.0	1	0.0	11	100.0	169	92.9	2.2	0.0	0.3	1.8	1.6	6.4
Riley County	19 038	54.5	1 265	71.1	75	68.0	653	63.6	764	63.5	6.1	1.7	2.8	1.2	1.6	13.7
Rooks County	2 325	65.7	10	20.0	2	100.0	2	100.0	13	100.0	0.2	0.1	0.1	0.1	0.1	6.2
Rush County	1 527	65.2	0	X	5	60.0	2	100.0	9	66.7	0.5	0.2	0.1	0.2	1.0	11.1
Russell County	3 146	63.5	0	X	34	100.0	8	100.0	14	100.0	0.7	0.2	0.0	0.4	1.4	4.4
Saline County	19 407	66.1	630	65.7	106	72.6	256	74.6	914	78.1	4.0	0.3	1.2	2.4	1.8	9.5
Scott County	1 948	70.5	10	100.0	1	0.0	7	100.0	81	69.1	2.6	0.0	0.0	2.5	1.6	6.9
Sedgwick County	143 153	66.1	14 923	68.4	1 866	71.7	4 529	71.4	9 485	79.8	6.6	0.5	2.6	3.1	3.1	12.3
Seward County	4 573	69.3	299	72.9	29	89.7	79	100.0	2 312	85.1	27.4	0.1	1.6	25.2	19.2	27.1
Shawnee County	57 351	65.4	5 733	64.6	694	69.2	559	67.6	3 816	68.9	2.7	0.3	0.7	1.5	1.1	9.1
Sheridan County	1 126	71.6	0	X	0	X	4	100.0	4	100.0	0.4	0.1	0.3	0.0	0.3	4.8
Sherman County	2 590	62.6	11	100.0	7	100.0	0	X	156	93.6	1.8	0.0	0.0	1.7	0.9	13.6
Smith County	1 930	68.8	2	0.0	0	X	3	100.0	9	0.0	0.6	0.4	0.2	0.0	0.5	4.0
Stafford County	1 895	64.3	8	100.0	12	41.7	8	75.0	69	81.2	3.6	0.3	0.4	2.7	2.1	6.2
Stanton County	697	74.0	0	X	11	54.5	4	50.0	140	85.7	12.7	0.0	0.1	12.4	7.0	17.2
Stevens County	1 622	71.6	0	X	25	64.0	9	100.0	292	86.6	12.0	0.2	0.4	10.7	6.6	16.6
Sumner County	9 320	71.7	78	73.1	128	75.8	8	25.0	220	70.0	0.8	0.2	0.1	0.4	0.4	6.8
Thomas County	3 122	67.9	10	0.0	0	X	0	X	42	38.1	0.4	0.0	0.2	0.2	0.4	7.3
Trego County	1 404	66.2	0	X	0	X	0	X	8	0.0	0.5	0.3	0.2	0.0	0.4	8.2
Wabaunsee County	2 596	74.3	5	60.0	2	100.0	2	0.0	22	63.6	0.7	0.2	0.1	0.4	0.1	5.9
Wallace County	638	70.7	3	100.0	5	60.0	0	X	30	93.3	2.2	0.2	0.2	1.8	1.8	7.7
Washington County	2 630	66.0	4	100.0	8	100.0	0	X	12	41.7	0.5	0.1	0.0	0.4	0.7	5.0
Wichita County	819	74.6	0	X	9	100.0	0	X	144	83.3	8.0	0.2	0.1	7.5	4.9	19.1
Wilson County	4 102	67.7	3	0.0	26	46.2	11	63.6	11	81.8	0.6	0.2	0.2	0.1	0.2	4.7
Woodson County	1 618	64.9	0	X	7	57.1	0	X	7	57.1	0.8	0.2	0.5	0.1	0.0	4.9
Wyandotte County	34 563	63.1	16 703	67.2	399	59.4	655	58.9	6 461	82.4	9.5	0.5	1.1	7.7	6.1	15.0
KENTUCKY	1 439 760	70.2	111 437	64.7	3 597	63.2	9 739	67.0	15 340	69.4	2.0	0.5	0.7	0.6	0.8	6.1
Adair County	6 498	71.1	145	67.6	7	100.0	5	100.0	24	58.3	0.6	0.1	0.1	0.0	1.2	5.8
Allen County	6 737	75.0	76	48.7	4	100.0	5	100.0	35	68.6	0.8	0.3	0.2	0.2	0.2	6.0
Anderson County	7 051	76.3	169	66.9	11	0.0	29	100.0	21	71.4	0.9	0.3	0.3	0.2	0.6	4.3
Ballard County	3 231	71.8	92	63.0	3	0.0	7	100.0	15	86.7	0.8	0.2	0.3	0.3	0.3	4.4
Barren County	14 482	72.5	662	64.8	3	33.3	51	56.9	111	72.1	1.2	0.1	0.4	0.4	0.5	5.4
Bath County	4 321	72.3	87	51.7	2	100.0	7	100.0	30	96.7	0.7	0.0	0.1	0.4	0.2	3.5
Bell County	11 553	71.7	296	60.5	13	38.5	18	100.0	59	78.0	0.7	0.1	0.3	0.2	0.3	4.6
Boone County	29 690	75.7	545	68.6	93	50.5	309	78.3	452	69.7	3.0	0.7	1.1	0.8	1.1	8.0
Bourbon County	6 945	71.8	591	64.6	5	100.0	10	100.0	123	82.9	2.0	0.2	0.1	1.6	1.0	7.4
Boyd County	19 515	71.4	215	64.2	34	55.9	39	74.4	56	60.7	1.1	0.2	0.2	0.6	0.2	4.8
Boyle County	9 506	69.8	815	69.6	25	100.0	42	83.3	151	58.3	1.8	0.4	0.6	0.8	0.8	4.1
Bracken County	3 186	72.6	23	82.6	0	X	0	X	2	0.0	0.3	0.2	0.0	0.0	0.2	2.8
Breathitt County	6 086	73.8	0	X	2	100.0	13	84.6	29	58.6	0.4	0.1	0.3	0.0	0.2	5.3
Breckinridge County	7 052	73.1	172	72.7	8	50.0	0	X	32	56.3	0.5	0.2	0.1	0.2	0.2	4.3
Bullitt County	21 843	80.5	81	69.1	74	73.0	13	53.8	83	83.1	0.6	0.3	0.1	0.2	0.1	4.5
Butler County	4 969	73.8	3	100.0	0	X	29	62.1	42	61.9	1.8	0.1	0.6	0.9	0.9	4.3
Caldwell County	5 103	70.9	255	68.6	0	X	5	100.0	38	52.6	0.5	0.3	0.2	0.0	0.1	5.2
Calloway County	13 005	63.7	469	43.5	25	24.0	163	33.7	65	73.8	2.7	0.6	1.3	0.5	0.9	7.1
Campbell County	33 596	67.2	466	65.9	70	65.7	181	75.1	300	46.0	1.4	0.4	0.6	0.3	0.5	6.1
Carlisle County	2 176	71.5	19	57.9	6	100.0	0	X	4	100.0	0.2	0.2	0.0	0.0	0.0	1.7
Carroll County	3 619	73.0	103	38.8	39	84.6	45	0.0	79	16.5	1.9	0.5	0.1	1.1	0.5	3.7
Carter County	10 253	75.1	0	X	9	100.0	23	73.9	29	75.9	0.4	0.1	0.2	0.0	0.1	4.7
Casey County	6 140	70.7	14	100.0	21	61.9	10	0.0	68	100.0	1.2	0.1	0.1	1.0	1.5	7.1
Christian County	17 742	73.7	5 806	73.7	108	71.3	169	86.4	749	82.9	2.5	0.6	0.6	1.0	1.1	10.2
Clark County	12 191	73.9	641	60.7	9	0.0	56	100.0	59	32.2	1.0	0.3	0.4	0.3	0.6	4.8
Clay County	8 388	75.1	95	66.3	5	0.0	4	100.0	45	93.3	0.7	0.1	0.1	0.4	0.1	2.5
Clinton County	3 978	68.6	9	100.0	0	X	7	0.0	37	48.6	0.8	0.0	0.0	0.7	1.4	5.4
Crittenden County	3 776	71.8	32	18.8	14	100.0	7	100.0	23	21.7	0.4	0.1	0.1	0.1	2.5	6.2

[1] Hispanic or Latino persons may be of any race.

Table A-3. States and Counties — Age, Ethnicity, and Household Structure

STATE/ County code	MSA/PMSA/ NECMA code[1]	STATE County	Total population	Under 5 years	5 to 17 years	18 to 24 years	25 to 44 years	45 to 64 years	65 years and over	Median age	+/− U.S. percent under 18 years	+/− U.S. percent 65 years and over	Non-Hispanic White Total population	Under 18 years	65 years and over
			1	2	3	4	5	6	7	8	9	10	11	12	13
		KENTUCKY—Cont'd													
21 057	...	Cumberland County	7 147	5.6	18.0	6.8	26.9	24.8	17.8	40.1	-2.1	5.4	6 797	23.2	17.7
21 059	5990	Daviess County	91 545	6.8	18.9	9.0	28.6	22.8	13.9	36.8	0.0	1.5	85 555	25.1	14.2
21 061	...	Edmonson County	11 644	5.9	17.6	9.0	27.8	25.3	14.4	38.0	-2.2	2.0	11 419	23.6	14.6
21 063	...	Elliott County	6 748	6.5	18.8	9.2	27.5	24.7	13.4	37.0	-0.4	1.0	6 708	25.2	13.4
21 065	...	Estill County	15 307	6.1	18.2	9.1	29.2	23.9	13.5	36.7	-1.4	1.1	15 161	24.1	13.6
21 067	4280	Fayette County	260 512	6.2	15.1	14.5	33.3	20.9	10.0	33.0	-4.4	-2.4	206 238	19.5	11.0
21 069	...	Fleming County	13 792	6.6	18.7	8.3	29.1	23.9	13.4	36.3	-0.4	1.0	13 383	25.0	13.5
21 071	...	Floyd County	42 441	6.1	17.6	9.5	30.3	24.4	12.2	36.7	-2.0	-0.2	41 211	23.5	12.3
21 073	...	Franklin County	47 687	6.1	16.7	9.3	30.8	24.9	12.3	37.0	-2.9	-0.1	41 740	22.1	13.3
21 075	...	Fulton County	7 752	6.1	18.8	9.2	25.6	22.9	17.4	38.5	-0.8	5.0	5 787	21.2	20.9
21 077	1640	Gallatin County	7 870	7.7	20.9	7.8	30.8	22.5	10.3	34.6	2.9	-2.1	7 671	28.5	10.2
21 079	...	Garrard County	14 792	6.0	18.4	8.3	30.6	23.5	13.1	37.1	-1.3	0.7	13 903	24.1	13.3
21 081	1640	Grant County	22 384	8.0	20.6	9.4	31.7	20.7	9.5	32.7	2.9	-2.9	21 946	28.5	9.6
21 083	...	Graves County	37 028	6.6	17.8	8.2	27.2	23.9	16.2	38.1	-1.3	3.8	34 085	23.6	16.8
21 085	...	Grayson County	24 053	6.4	18.3	9.1	27.7	24.6	14.0	37.5	-1.0	1.6	23 524	24.4	14.2
21 087	...	Green County	11 518	5.2	17.5	8.0	27.3	25.1	16.9	40.0	-3.0	4.5	11 138	22.4	17.0
21 089	3400	Greenup County	36 891	5.8	17.8	7.7	28.1	26.0	14.6	39.2	-2.1	2.2	35 872	23.3	14.8
21 091	...	Hancock County	8 392	7.1	19.7	8.6	29.1	24.7	10.9	35.9	1.1	-1.5	8 127	26.2	11.2
21 093	...	Hardin County	94 174	7.2	20.3	10.5	31.7	20.6	9.7	33.5	1.8	-2.7	76 097	25.8	11.0
21 095	...	Harlan County	33 202	6.1	18.9	8.6	27.3	25.1	13.9	37.8	-0.7	1.5	31 635	24.8	13.9
21 097	...	Harrison County	17 983	6.5	18.6	8.1	30.2	23.2	13.4	37.1	-0.6	1.0	17 089	24.8	13.7
21 099	...	Hart County	17 445	6.5	19.1	8.6	28.2	23.7	13.8	36.9	-0.1	1.4	16 129	25.5	14.0
21 101	2440	Henderson County	44 829	6.3	18.4	8.5	30.0	23.6	13.2	37.2	-1.0	0.8	40 499	23.7	13.6
21 103	...	Henry County	15 060	6.9	18.5	7.9	29.6	24.8	12.2	37.3	-0.3	-0.2	14 021	25.3	12.4
21 105	...	Hickman County	5 262	5.3	16.7	7.1	26.6	25.7	18.7	40.9	-3.7	6.3	4 631	20.5	19.8
21 107	...	Hopkins County	46 519	6.0	18.0	8.3	28.3	24.7	14.7	38.3	-1.7	2.3	42 523	23.0	15.2
21 109	...	Jackson County	13 495	6.5	19.5	10.2	29.0	22.9	11.9	34.9	0.3	-0.5	13 321	25.9	11.9
21 111	4520	Jefferson County	693 604	6.7	17.5	8.8	30.6	22.8	13.5	36.7	-1.5	1.1	530 648	21.8	15.2
21 113	4280	Jessamine County	39 041	7.4	18.9	11.8	31.1	21.4	9.5	32.9	0.6	-2.9	36 540	25.8	9.7
21 115	...	Johnson County	23 445	6.1	17.8	9.0	28.8	25.7	12.7	37.4	-1.8	0.3	23 095	23.9	12.7
21 117	1640	Kenton County	151 464	7.3	19.0	9.2	32.0	21.5	11.0	34.5	0.6	-1.4	141 427	25.6	11.5
21 119	...	Knott County	17 649	5.9	18.7	10.7	29.0	24.3	11.4	35.9	-1.1	-1.0	17 174	24.1	11.4
21 121	...	Knox County	31 795	7.0	19.1	9.7	28.1	23.4	12.7	35.3	0.4	0.3	31 011	26.3	12.7
21 123	...	Larue County	13 373	6.0	19.0	7.6	28.2	24.2	15.1	38.2	-0.7	2.7	12 514	24.6	15.4
21 125	...	Laurel County	52 715	7.1	18.3	9.3	30.4	23.5	11.4	35.5	-0.3	-1.0	51 259	25.3	11.5
21 127	...	Lawrence County	15 569	5.8	19.3	9.0	28.8	24.8	12.3	36.5	-0.6	-0.1	15 458	25.2	12.3
21 129	...	Lee County	7 916	5.1	17.5	9.5	30.2	23.4	14.4	37.4	-3.1	2.0	7 575	23.5	14.7
21 131	...	Leslie County	12 401	6.1	18.5	9.2	30.9	23.9	11.5	36.4	-1.1	-0.9	12 233	24.8	11.3
21 133	...	Letcher County	25 277	5.6	18.2	9.3	28.6	25.9	12.5	37.9	-1.9	0.1	24 853	23.7	12.5
21 135	...	Lewis County	14 092	6.2	19.0	9.1	29.5	23.6	12.5	35.9	-0.5	0.1	13 899	25.2	12.4
21 137	...	Lincoln County	23 361	6.9	18.9	8.2	29.7	23.3	13.1	36.0	0.1	0.7	22 379	25.6	12.9
21 139	...	Livingston County	9 804	5.3	17.2	7.6	28.1	26.8	15.0	39.8	-3.2	2.6	9 635	22.1	15.0
21 141	...	Logan County	26 573	6.9	18.8	8.6	28.3	23.6	13.9	37.0	0.0	1.5	23 879	25.0	14.2
21 143	...	Lyon County	8 080	3.8	11.9	7.8	32.8	26.9	16.9	41.5	-10.0	4.5	7 408	16.4	17.9
21 145	...	McCracken County	65 514	6.0	17.3	7.9	28.3	24.5	15.9	39.2	-2.4	3.5	56 577	21.5	17.1
21 147	...	McCreary County	17 080	6.6	20.9	10.1	28.0	24.0	10.5	34.2	1.8	-1.9	16 628	27.5	10.7
21 149	...	McLean County	9 938	6.6	17.6	7.9	28.0	25.3	14.4	38.1	-1.5	2.0	9 661	24.1	14.7
21 151	4280	Madison County	70 872	6.4	15.5	18.7	29.6	20.0	9.8	30.7	-3.8	-2.6	65 494	21.4	9.9
21 153	...	Magoffin County	13 332	7.1	19.7	10.2	30.5	22.1	10.5	34.3	1.1	-1.9	13 254	26.8	10.6
21 155	...	Marion County	18 212	6.6	18.6	10.2	30.5	21.2	12.9	35.4	-0.5	0.5	16 154	25.1	13.3
21 157	...	Marshall County	30 125	5.3	16.5	7.6	26.7	26.4	17.5	40.9	-3.9	5.1	29 416	21.6	17.7
21 159	...	Martin County	12 578	7.1	21.0	9.6	29.4	23.1	9.7	34.1	2.4	-2.7	12 443	28.1	9.8
21 161	...	Mason County	16 800	6.4	17.9	8.1	28.5	23.8	15.4	38.1	-1.4	3.0	15 133	23.3	15.8
21 163	...	Meade County	26 349	8.8	20.9	9.1	33.1	19.9	8.2	32.2	4.0	-4.2	24 138	28.8	8.6
21 165	...	Menifee County	6 556	5.9	19.1	10.8	27.3	25.3	11.7	36.3	-0.7	-0.7	6 381	25.0	11.6
21 167	...	Mercer County	20 817	6.5	17.9	7.6	28.6	24.8	14.6	38.2	-1.3	2.2	19 347	23.9	14.9
21 169	...	Metcalfe County	10 037	6.4	18.3	8.3	28.7	23.4	15.0	37.7	-1.0	2.6	9 673	24.5	15.1
21 171	...	Monroe County	11 756	6.2	17.8	8.8	27.7	24.2	15.2	38.2	-1.7	2.8	11 151	23.4	15.5
21 173	...	Montgomery County	22 554	6.8	18.0	8.6	30.4	23.5	12.8	36.0	-0.9	0.4	21 256	24.6	12.8
21 175	...	Morgan County	13 948	5.4	16.9	10.8	32.6	22.5	11.8	35.8	-3.4	-0.6	13 109	23.4	12.5
21 177	...	Muhlenberg County	31 839	5.9	16.8	9.3	28.0	24.7	15.3	38.7	-3.0	2.9	29 904	22.5	15.7
21 179	...	Nelson County	37 477	7.3	20.3	8.9	30.5	22.4	10.6	34.9	1.9	-1.8	34 701	27.3	10.8
21 181	...	Nicholas County	6 813	6.3	17.2	8.4	28.3	24.3	15.5	38.4	-2.2	3.1	6 641	23.3	15.3
21 183	...	Ohio County	22 916	6.2	18.7	8.7	27.2	24.9	14.4	37.5	-0.8	2.0	22 348	24.9	14.4
21 185	4520	Oldham County	46 178	6.6	20.8	6.9	33.1	25.7	7.0	36.7	1.7	-5.4	42 927	27.6	7.2
21 187	...	Owen County	10 547	6.0	19.4	8.2	28.4	24.0	14.0	37.5	-0.3	1.6	10 183	25.5	13.9

[1]MSA = Metropolitan Statistical Area. PMSA = Primary MSA. NECMA = New England County Metropolitan Area. See the Appendix A for explanation of these concepts. See Appendix B for list of metropolitan areas identified by type, with component counties.

STATE County	Black or African American Total population	Age (percent) Under 18 years	Age (percent) 65 years and over	American Indian and Alaska Native Total population	Age (percent) Under 18 years	Age (percent) 65 years and over	Asian, Hawaiian, and Pacific Islander Total population	Age (percent) Under 18 years	Age (percent) 65 years and over	Hispanic or Latino[1] Total population	Age (percent) Under 18 years	Age (percent) 65 years and over	Two or more races Total population	Age (percent) Under 18 years	Age (percent) 65 years and over
	14	15	16	17	18	19	20	21	22	23	24	25	26	27	28
KENTUCKY—Cont'd															
Cumberland County	260	21.5	21.9	2	0.0	100.0	8	37.5	25.0	16	37.5	0.0	71	67.6	15.5
Daviess County	3 656	29.8	10.8	126	10.3	4.8	323	22.9	7.7	862	32.3	8.8	1 056	58.2	4.1
Edmonson County	85	18.8	0.0	28	35.7	0.0	22	0.0	31.8	41	19.5	22.0	49	6.1	0.0
Elliott County	0	X	X	0	X	X	0	X	X	0	X	X	40	32.5	0.0
Estill County	5	0.0	100.0	13	0.0	0.0	18	22.2	0.0	55	38.2	0.0	60	63.3	3.3
Fayette County	34 928	28.2	8.4	828	21.0	2.4	5 947	19.1	2.1	8 677	26.2	2.5	4 647	40.8	2.4
Fleming County	249	33.3	10.4	9	33.3	0.0	0	X	X	107	50.5	6.5	62	27.4	3.2
Floyd County	549	16.2	7.7	15	0.0	0.0	74	18.9	0.0	350	28.6	8.0	230	42.6	8.7
Franklin County	4 484	23.9	5.5	106	28.3	0.0	239	31.8	7.1	533	34.3	3.4	604	48.2	3.6
Fulton County	1 830	34.5	7.8	0	X	X	0	X	X	35	77.1	0.0	116	47.4	0.0
Gallatin County	94	20.2	21.3	1	0.0	0.0	1	0.0	0.0	36	22.2	13.9	66	50.0	4.5
Garrard County	475	26.7	16.0	12	50.0	0.0	26	0.0	0.0	233	31.8	7.3	126	39.7	0.0
Grant County	39	2.6	0.0	36	13.9	11.1	179	36.3	0.0	147	54.4	12.2	50	28.0	0.0
Graves County	1 519	31.6	15.5	71	21.1	0.0	133	23.3	6.0	867	36.1	1.2	460	53.0	5.9
Grayson County	207	38.2	0.0	15	0.0	0.0	9	0.0	0.0	202	28.2	2.5	97	34.0	16.5
Green County	228	31.6	15.8	9	0.0	0.0	49	18.4	40.8	47	44.7	0.0	54	46.3	0.0
Greenup County	233	40.8	12.9	38	0.0	0.0	166	12.7	6.0	280	43.2	7.1	312	38.8	12.8
Hancock County	105	35.2	2.9	27	51.9	0.0	7	0.0	0.0	95	34.7	0.0	28	89.3	3.6
Hardin County	10 970	34.4	3.7	423	28.6	5.0	1 966	22.8	8.1	2 998	31.7	3.3	2 258	50.7	2.4
Harlan County	721	20.0	19.7	105	38.1	6.7	146	27.4	4.1	240	26.7	11.3	402	46.3	9.7
Harrison County	382	28.0	14.4	98	35.7	10.2	24	29.2	0.0	264	42.0	1.9	139	23.7	0.0
Hart County	1 002	24.5	13.6	87	46.0	0.0	6	0.0	0.0	157	37.6	4.5	62	38.7	11.3
Henderson County	3 197	31.0	10.9	38	0.0	18.4	259	30.9	13.1	409	39.1	3.9	381	50.7	6.3
Henry County	580	22.6	14.3	12	8.3	16.7	66	36.4	4.5	211	22.7	1.9	187	48.1	6.4
Hickman County	538	34.4	11.3	5	20.0	0.0	14	0.0	0.0	27	40.7	0.0	51	21.6	13.7
Hopkins County	2 932	32.1	10.0	47	31.9	4.3	197	40.6	0.0	376	35.1	2.7	481	55.5	9.1
Jackson County	0	X	X	50	40.0	0.0	13	0.0	100.0	55	20.0	7.3	58	44.8	19.0
Jefferson County	130 153	31.9	8.7	1 625	16.1	6.6	9 315	22.9	3.7	11 501	31.5	3.3	11 741	45.4	4.9
Jessamine County	1 286	27.2	12.1	68	20.6	0.0	407	42.0	2.7	322	19.6	1.6	407	52.8	0.0
Johnson County	70	35.7	0.0	11	0.0	100.0	47	0.0	0.0	85	8.2	0.0	118	28.0	17.8
Kenton County	5 805	34.9	4.1	293	25.3	3.8	913	30.0	1.9	1 534	39.4	4.8	1 575	44.3	5.2
Knott County	164	40.2	11.0	21	19.0	9.5	26	0.0	0.0	133	54.9	6.8	127	44.1	17.3
Knox County	311	18.6	9.3	56	21.4	10.7	38	52.6	0.0	113	18.6	16.8	273	19.0	11.0
Larue County	438	19.6	18.9	50	44.0	0.0	41	12.2	0.0	119	49.6	6.7	193	35.2	0.0
Laurel County	325	27.7	5.5	163	16.6	4.9	139	30.2	3.6	215	35.3	6.5	623	31.0	5.3
Lawrence County	8	0.0	100.0	18	44.4	0.0	0	X	X	18	0.0	0.0	67	7.5	11.9
Lee County	283	0.7	7.4	13	0.0	0.0	5	0.0	0.0	21	28.6	0.0	24	0.0	4.2
Leslie County	17	0.0	0.0	24	0.0	33.3	6	0.0	0.0	78	10.3	41.0	49	12.2	16.3
Letcher County	144	33.3	7.0	22	0.0	9.1	85	29.4	5.9	104	26.0	20.2	91	37.4	26.4
Lewis County	41	34.1	0.0	38	18.4	31.6	0	X	X	54	14.8	9.3	56	26.8	25.0
Lincoln County	533	26.5	25.1	22	50.0	0.0	37	35.1	0.0	259	33.2	4.6	159	39.0	29.6
Livingston County	2	0.0	100.0	65	55.4	13.8	5	0.0	0.0	20	35.0	0.0	74	44.6	10.8
Logan County	2 110	30.5	11.3	42	0.0	14.3	49	24.5	0.0	256	27.3	2.3	265	60.8	15.8
Lyon County	537	6.1	5.8	2	0.0	0.0	45	17.8	0.0	59	5.1	5.1	35	14.3	8.6
McCracken County	7 220	33.2	9.6	208	17.8	14.9	172	19.8	0.6	623	35.8	2.2	826	58.4	3.1
McCreary County	136	22.8	1.5	26	0.0	0.0	23	0.0	0.0	155	44.5	4.5	164	38.4	4.3
McLean County	42	7.1	14.3	9	44.4	0.0	7	0.0	0.0	153	38.6	2.6	66	30.3	12.1
Madison County	3 018	20.3	11.5	223	19.7	2.7	567	21.9	0.0	639	33.3	8.3	893	48.6	2.9
Magoffin County	7	0.0	0.0	7	0.0	0.0	18	16.7	0.0	36	16.7	0.0	23	30.4	0.0
Marion County	1 666	23.3	10.9	12	41.7	0.0	69	23.2	21.7	210	27.6	6.7	104	46.2	4.8
Marshall County	54	13.0	0.0	85	31.8	31.8	107	30.8	0.0	239	37.7	8.8	266	25.2	12.8
Martin County	11	45.5	0.0	27	14.8	0.0	0	X	X	34	0.0	11.8	63	47.6	9.5
Mason County	1 059	24.7	15.6	25	0.0	28.0	76	21.1	9.2	231	38.1	3.5	252	57.9	5.2
Meade County	1 049	39.2	4.4	157	22.9	5.7	180	34.4	6.1	545	43.9	0.0	349	45.3	5.2
Menifee County	98	31.6	8.2	3	0.0	0.0	0	X	X	55	23.6	0.0	49	10.2	28.6
Mercer County	797	26.6	14.6	32	0.0	0.0	115	22.6	0.0	307	42.7	0.7	258	42.2	10.1
Metcalfe County	112	26.8	19.6	54	13.0	0.0	0	X	X	57	33.3	15.8	141	31.9	10.6
Monroe County	333	26.7	18.3	8	0.0	0.0	30	60.0	0.0	206	45.6	0.0	47	57.4	0.0
Montgomery County	837	25.8	13.3	55	20.0	3.6	39	28.2	12.8	197	30.5	2.5	163	35.0	22.7
Morgan County	565	2.1	0.0	34	0.0	0.0	34	61.8	5.9	78	6.4	1.3	139	12.2	2.9
Muhlenberg County	1 563	20.7	7.5	11	0.0	0.0	20	50.0	15.0	186	38.2	12.4	178	45.5	15.7
Nelson County	2 013	32.8	7.6	78	10.3	7.7	191	23.6	0.5	284	36.6	12.7	250	40.8	5.2
Nicholas County	97	28.9	22.7	4	0.0	0.0	0	X	X	70	35.7	0.0	15	0.0	100.0
Ohio County	214	17.8	7.9	63	28.6	0.0	9	0.0	0.0	158	31.0	0.0	121	21.5	54.5
Oldham County	1 716	8.6	4.9	110	28.2	0.0	213	29.6	1.9	623	35.2	1.6	588	53.9	3.7
Owen County	97	3.1	37.1	63	36.5	0.0	16	12.5	0.0	85	15.3	15.3	91	40.7	8.8

[1] Hispanic or Latino persons may be of any race.

Table A-3. States and Counties — Age, Ethnicity, and Household Structure

STATE County	Total households	Family households (percent) Married-couple family households Total	With children	Householder 65 years or over	Other family households Total	With children	Householder 65 years or over	Nonfamily households (percent) Two or more unrelated persons Total	Householder 65 years or over	Male living alone Total	Householder 65 years or over	Female living alone Total	Householder 65 years or over	Percent of householders 65 years and over who live alone	Grandparents who are responsible for the care of their grandchildren
	29	30	31	32	33	34	35	36	37	38	39	40	41	42	43
KENTUCKY—Cont'd															
Cumberland County	2 958	54.6	21.2	11.6	14.6	7.6	2.6	1.6	0.1	11.7	3.9	17.5	11.7	52.3	81
Daviess County	36 076	55.2	24.9	9.9	14.1	8.5	1.9	3.6	0.3	10.7	2.1	16.4	8.5	46.5	633
Edmonson County........	4 671	63.6	25.6	11.5	11.4	6.4	1.4	2.7	0.2	8.3	2.7	14.1	8.8	46.7	87
Elliott County	2 629	59.5	24.2	9.6	13.5	7.0	3.2	2.1	0.2	11.5	3.2	13.4	8.1	46.6	82
Estill County	6 090	56.0	23.4	9.1	17.0	9.5	3.6	2.2	0.3	11.1	2.7	13.7	7.7	44.5	138
Fayette County	108 411	44.6	19.4	6.5	14.1	8.4	1.6	9.6	0.2	13.6	1.5	18.0	6.3	48.4	1 946
Fleming County	5 376	60.4	28.1	9.9	13.4	7.6	2.2	3.1	0.4	9.5	2.0	13.7	8.7	46.1	48
Floyd County	16 869	58.3	25.4	8.5	15.0	8.2	2.8	1.5	0.1	10.5	2.6	14.6	7.4	46.5	434
Franklin County	19 890	50.2	21.0	8.2	14.3	8.7	1.9	4.9	0.3	11.8	2.3	18.8	8.5	50.8	378
Fulton County	3 235	46.9	17.7	11.6	18.4	12.4	2.4	2.4	0.3	11.2	2.4	21.1	13.6	52.8	102
Gallatin County	2 906	59.2	30.2	6.1	14.9	8.1	2.2	4.1	0.5	9.6	2.5	12.2	5.8	48.8	48
Garrard County	5 770	63.4	26.7	11.0	12.4	7.9	1.6	3.1	0.2	8.6	2.6	12.5	6.7	42.3	100
Grant County	8 209	60.3	29.0	7.0	16.3	10.2	2.3	3.7	0.3	9.3	2.0	10.4	5.4	43.8	267
Graves County	14 859	57.5	23.6	11.6	13.9	8.3	2.0	2.5	0.2	10.3	2.9	15.9	9.7	47.8	297
Grayson County	9 617	60.4	24.7	11.3	12.2	7.9	1.3	3.1	0.0	10.3	3.1	13.9	8.1	46.9	261
Green County	4 748	60.8	24.0	12.9	11.9	5.8	2.3	2.3	0.2	9.6	3.4	15.4	9.5	45.7	129
Greenup County...........	14 554	64.1	26.4	11.6	12.5	6.2	2.6	1.7	0.2	8.4	2.3	13.4	8.2	41.9	303
Hancock County...........	3 215	63.8	29.0	7.5	11.5	7.9	1.2	3.3	0.8	10.4	3.0	11.0	5.7	48.0	75
Hardin County	34 490	59.7	29.0	8.2	14.5	9.8	1.4	3.2	0.2	10.6	1.7	12.0	5.4	42.1	823
Harlan County	13 281	54.7	23.9	8.4	16.2	7.9	3.4	2.0	0.1	10.4	2.8	16.6	10.1	51.9	401
Harrison County	7 006	59.2	27.0	9.4	13.0	7.8	1.8	3.6	0.4	9.5	2.5	14.7	9.3	50.5	149
Hart County	6 761	57.2	24.2	10.4	14.2	7.9	2.4	3.3	0.4	10.6	2.2	14.7	9.0	45.9	234
Henderson County	18 056	55.7	24.1	9.5	14.2	9.3	1.6	3.7	0.4	10.9	1.9	15.6	8.1	46.7	443
Henry County	5 826	59.0	24.6	9.7	15.3	9.2	2.5	3.8	0.3	9.5	2.1	12.3	6.7	41.4	157
Hickman County	2 187	55.3	18.5	12.8	15.7	10.3	2.5	1.5	0.1	12.6	3.3	14.9	8.2	42.9	41
Hopkins County............	18 844	56.6	24.3	10.0	14.8	8.0	2.7	2.9	0.2	9.6	1.9	16.1	9.3	46.4	368
Jackson County............	5 310	59.9	28.2	9.5	14.6	8.5	2.7	2.3	0.2	10.3	2.6	12.9	6.2	41.3	181
Jefferson County..........	287 133	45.6	19.5	8.5	18.4	10.6	2.7	5.6	0.4	12.7	2.3	17.8	7.9	47.1	6 371
Jessamine County........	13 862	62.6	30.1	7.9	14.8	8.9	1.6	4.2	0.1	7.3	1.2	11.2	4.9	38.6	265
Johnson County...........	9 089	62.0	26.5	9.5	13.6	7.9	2.5	2.0	0.3	8.4	2.0	14.0	6.5	40.9	270
Kenton County	59 453	50.6	24.8	7.2	15.8	8.9	2.2	5.8	0.3	12.4	2.0	15.5	7.1	48.3	1 182
Knott County	6 720	59.3	26.9	8.9	15.3	8.0	2.6	1.8	0.2	10.4	2.1	13.2	6.4	42.0	122
Knox County	12 390	55.2	25.8	8.3	16.5	9.0	2.8	2.7	0.6	10.0	2.0	15.6	8.3	47.0	435
Larue County...............	5 289	60.3	24.3	10.9	13.0	8.2	2.6	3.0	0.9	10.8	2.5	12.9	8.1	42.5	103
Laurel County..............	20 375	61.7	28.1	8.5	14.0	8.0	2.3	2.8	0.1	9.0	2.6	12.6	6.7	46.4	571
Lawrence County	5 950	62.5	28.7	9.0	13.0	6.1	3.1	2.2	0.3	10.6	2.8	11.8	6.3	42.2	172
Lee County..................	3 001	57.3	23.0	11.7	14.1	8.5	2.3	1.7	0.1	11.2	3.4	15.7	10.4	49.3	96
Leslie County	4 912	58.0	26.8	7.5	17.7	9.0	3.1	2.0	0.1	9.8	3.0	12.6	6.8	47.7	126
Letcher County............	10 054	58.7	25.5	8.1	15.6	7.5	3.5	1.7	0.2	9.5	2.3	14.5	7.7	45.9	239
Lewis County...............	5 419	61.0	27.5	10.2	13.9	8.0	2.3	2.7	0.3	8.8	2.5	13.6	7.2	43.0	126
Lincoln County	9 210	59.9	25.8	9.8	13.5	7.6	2.2	3.0	0.2	10.0	3.1	13.7	7.7	46.8	188
Livingston County........	3 973	60.8	24.4	10.9	11.4	5.5	2.7	3.1	0.5	12.0	3.9	12.6	7.2	43.9	54
Logan County...............	10 504	56.8	24.3	9.8	15.6	9.5	2.4	2.7	0.4	9.8	2.6	15.1	8.7	47.2	313
Lyon County.................	2 913	59.8	19.6	14.5	11.4	5.8	2.3	2.3	0.2	12.3	3.4	14.3	7.8	39.7	68
McCracken County.......	27 741	51.4	20.5	10.4	15.3	9.5	1.8	3.6	0.2	11.6	2.6	18.1	10.2	50.8	540
McCreary County	6 543	55.8	26.7	7.6	17.2	10.2	3.1	2.4	0.0	11.0	1.6	13.6	6.6	43.5	190
McLean County	3 978	59.4	25.2	10.0	13.8	8.1	2.2	2.3	0.4	10.8	3.5	13.8	7.4	46.4	124
Madison County	27 181	53.7	23.7	7.0	13.6	8.3	1.5	7.5	0.3	11.0	1.7	14.2	6.3	47.8	546
Magoffin County	5 030	60.0	29.7	6.8	17.2	8.8	2.9	1.6	0.3	9.8	1.9	11.4	5.9	43.9	135
Marion County	6 603	54.8	25.7	9.6	17.6	10.6	2.5	3.3	0.4	10.6	1.9	13.7	8.0	44.4	133
Marshall County	12 412	63.4	22.8	14.5	9.4	5.8	1.3	2.3	0.3	9.6	2.2	15.3	9.5	42.0	282
Martin County	4 769	59.7	29.6	7.1	16.6	10.4	3.4	2.0	0.0	10.4	2.7	11.3	6.1	45.3	122
Mason County	6 836	54.5	24.3	9.7	14.9	7.5	3.2	3.0	0.0	10.2	3.3	17.5	9.5	49.8	140
Meade County	9 497	65.1	33.9	6.3	13.6	9.2	1.5	3.3	0.3	9.1	1.8	8.9	5.2	46.2	316
Menifee County	2 523	63.0	24.6	9.2	11.8	7.6	0.8	3.1	0.2	9.3	2.9	12.9	5.8	46.0	74
Mercer County.............	8 441	59.2	24.5	9.4	13.2	7.3	3.0	2.6	0.3	8.8	2.5	16.2	9.6	48.6	163
Metcalfe County	4 009	59.6	25.0	10.2	13.1	7.6	2.9	2.0	0.1	10.7	3.1	14.6	8.8	47.6	96
Monroe County	4 725	55.7	23.9	10.7	16.2	7.9	3.5	1.8	0.1	10.4	2.5	15.9	9.4	45.6	160
Montgomery County......	8 878	57.7	25.0	9.5	14.6	8.8	1.5	3.6	0.3	9.6	2.4	14.4	8.5	49.2	254
Morgan County	4 783	63.0	29.1	8.9	11.6	6.9	2.0	2.5	0.3	8.0	3.0	14.4	8.2	50.1	132
Muhlenberg County.......	12 395	60.5	24.3	11.7	12.9	7.0	2.3	2.3	0.3	9.0	2.2	15.3	10.3	46.6	353
Nelson County..............	13 967	57.2	27.8	7.8	16.7	11.0	1.6	3.7	0.2	10.9	1.5	11.5	6.0	43.8	363
Nicholas County	2 721	56.6	24.1	9.4	15.6	7.1	2.9	3.3	0.8	8.9	3.7	15.5	8.2	47.5	85
Ohio County	8 894	61.2	26.5	10.9	13.2	7.3	2.1	2.4	0.2	9.8	2.7	13.4	8.1	45.0	213
Oldham County	14 846	72.0	37.6	6.7	10.6	6.7	1.0	2.4	0.2	7.0	0.8	8.0	3.6	35.6	234
Owen County	4 099	61.2	26.9	10.7	12.5	6.8	2.2	3.3	0.2	11.6	3.3	11.4	6.8	43.3	96

STATE County	Households with Non-Hispanic White householder		Households with Black or African American householder		Households with American Indian and Alaska Native householder		Households with Asian, Hawaiian, and Pacific Islander householder		Households with Hispanic or Latino[1] householder		Foreign-born population	Place of birth (percent)			Percent in non-English speaking households	
	Number of households	Percent that are family households	Number of households	Percent that are family households	Number of households	Percent that are family households	Number of households	Percent that are family households	Number of households	Percent that are family households	Percent of total population that is foreign-born	Europe	Asia	Latin America	Linguistically isolated	Not linguistically isolated
	44	45	46	47	48	49	50	51	52	53	54	55	56	57	58	59
KENTUCKY—Cont'd																
Cumberland County	2 822	69.9	117	58.1	2	0.0	2	100.0	5	40.0	0.3	0.0	0.0	0.1	0.0	4.5
Daviess County	34 010	69.6	1 438	65.0	64	51.6	97	88.7	230	65.7	1.0	0.3	0.4	0.3	0.4	6.7
Edmonson County	4 595	74.8	15	86.7	11	100.0	11	45.5	23	91.3	0.4	0.2	0.1	0.0	0.0	2.6
Elliott County	2 622	72.9	0	X	0	X	0	X	0	X	0.2	0.2	0.0	0.0	0.0	2.5
Estill County	6 025	73.0	0	X	2	100.0	14	35.7	32	71.9	0.3	0.0	0.2	0.1	0.1	4.1
Fayette County	88 723	58.0	14 028	61.5	342	51.2	2 147	60.2	2 123	68.0	5.9	1.0	2.2	2.2	2.3	9.3
Fleming County	5 259	73.7	75	66.7	2	100.0	0	X	24	100.0	0.2	0.1	0.0	0.1	0.0	4.4
Floyd County	16 641	73.4	62	48.4	5	0.0	·31	54.8	74	89.2	0.6	0.2	0.2	0.1	0.2	2.9
Franklin County	17 902	65.6	1 588	51.9	40	65.0	78	69.2	139	78.4	1.9	0.4	0.4	0.7	0.6	6.1
Fulton County	2 558	64.3	640	68.3	0	X	0	X	0	X	0.4	0.3	0.0	0.1	0.0	4.9
Gallatin County	2 836	74.3	29	65.5	0	X	1	0.0	11	18.2	0.4	0.1	0.0	0.3	0.0	5.7
Garrard County	5 450	76.0	175	62.9	6	100.0	19	100.0	59	84.7	1.6	0.3	0.2	1.0	0.7	5.0
Grant County	8 089	77.0	14	14.3	27	63.0	28	50.0	43	37.2	1.0	0.3	0.5	0.2	0.6	5.5
Graves County	13 829	71.9	637	56.4	29	79.3	48	75.0	216	87.0	2.1	0.2	0.4	1.3	1.2	6.2
Grayson County	9 447	72.6	48	83.3	12	83.3	0	X	81	70.4	0.6	0.3	0.1	0.2	0.0	5.2
Green County	4 614	72.8	93	74.2	0	X	9	100.0	12	100.0	0.7	0.1	0.3	0.3	0.0	4.7
Greenup County	14 313	76.6	52	59.6	20	30.0	49	91.8	49	83.7	0.6	0.1	0.4	0.0	0.0	4.3
Hancock County	3 157	75.5	31	71.0	0	X	2	0.0	24	70.8	0.8	0.2	0.1	0.5	0.0	3.8
Hardin County	28 771	74.2	3 807	75.5	146	52.7	541	74.3	898	71.0	4.5	1.9	1.6	0.8	0.7	12.2
Harlan County	12 642	71.7	358	68.0	41	68.3	56	50.0	59	83.1	0.6	0.2	0.3	0.1	0.2	3.3
Harrison County	6 688	72.1	150	68.0	32	56.3	5	100.0	63	90.5	1.2	0.3	0.1	0.6	0.0	5.6
Hart County	6 239	72.5	467	58.0	5	100.0	3	100.0	22	68.2	0.6	0.1	0.0	0.3	0.3	9.7
Henderson County	16 431	70.1	1 302	66.1	13	46.2	78	80.8	138	65.9	1.1	0.3	0.5	0.3	0.3	5.5
Henry County	5 477	74.8	229	70.3	4	0.0	17	76.5	69	60.9	1.4	0.1	0.3	0.9	0.6	4.5
Hickman County	1 946	71.4	210	65.2	2	100.0	10	100.0	10	60.0	0.6	0.1	0.2	0.2	0.1	3.6
Hopkins County	17 421	71.6	1 160	66.1	17	52.9	41	87.8	107	72.9	0.6	0.1	0.2	0.1	0.2	6.0
Jackson County	5 238	74.5	0	X	14	100.0	7	100.0	28	75.0	0.4	0.1	0.1	0.2	0.3	4.8
Jefferson County	225 257	63.8	51 249	64.4	705	67.7	3 258	65.5	3 624	64.7	3.4	1.0	1.3	0.9	1.3	7.5
Jessamine County	13 027	77.3	501	77.6	39	69.2	103	74.8	92	100.0	1.8	0.3	0.8	0.4	0.4	6.5
Johnson County	8 982	75.8	10	40.0	11	45.5	9	100.0	41	63.4	0.5	0.0	0.3	0.1	0.1	4.0
Kenton County	55 955	66.9	2 222	59.9	126	44.0	276	73.0	426	68.8	1.6	0.6	0.5	0.0	0.0	7.1
Knott County	6 588	74.6	37	100.0	11	100.0	9	0.0	32	78.1	0.4	0.1	0.2	0.1	0.0	4.3
Knox County	12 081	72.2	108	12.9	31	12.9	8	0.0	62	75.8	0.4	0.0	0.1	0.1	0.1	4.5
Larue County	4 998	73.5	183	64.5	16	100.0	5	100.0	33	69.7	0.4	0.1	0.2	0.2	0.2	4.3
Laurel County	19 928	75.9	90	61.1	60	83.3	39	79.5	55	49.1	0.8	0.2	0.2	0.1	0.3	4.0
Lawrence County	5 906	75.7	8	0.0	4	100.0	0	X	1	0.0	0.1	0.1	0.0	0.0	0.0	3.7
Lee County	2 966	71.3	21	71.4	13	100.0	0	X	0	X	0.2	0.1	0.0	0.1	0.0	1.8
Leslie County	4 830	75.7	6	100.0	18	100.0	3	100.0	34	82.4	0.2	0.0	0.0	0.0	0.0	2.4
Letcher County	9 911	74.4	49	73.5	2	0.0	21	81.0	45	68.9	0.4	0.1	0.2	0.1	0.1	4.3
Lewis County	5 341	75.3	18	38.9	18	88.9	0	X	22	40.9	0.1	0.1	0.0	0.1	0.0	3.8
Lincoln County	8 826	74.1	251	52.2	11	100.0	9	100.0	71	71.8	0.7	0.0	0.1	0.5	0.3	4.5
Livingston County	3 928	72.2	2	0.0	20	100.0	0	X	3	100.0	0.2	0.1	0.0	0.1	0.4	4.4
Logan County	9 527	72.9	835	66.8	12	50.0	12	100.0	64	60.9	0.8	0.2	0.2	0.4	0.3	5.9
Lyon County	2 804	71.5	52	82.7	2	100.0	13	76.9	23	30.4	0.8	0.2	0.5	0.2	0.1	4.8
McCracken County	24 264	67.1	2 962	62.3	103	32.0	81	69.1	155	92.3	0.9	0.2	0.2	0.4	0.3	4.6
McCreary County	6 428	73.1	0	X	17	47.1	23	47.8	37	56.8	0.5	0.2	0.1	0.3	0.2	4.8
McLean County	3 887	73.0	23	73.9	2	0.0	0	X	39	97.4	0.7	0.2	0.1	0.4	0.0	3.9
Madison County	25 346	67.7	1 168	60.1	84	72.6	153	83.7	204	60.8	1.5	0.3	0.7	0.3	0.5	5.0
Magoffin County	4 995	77.2	0	X	0	X	10	80.0	14	78.6	0.2	0.1	0.1	0.0	0.0	2.6
Marion County	6 014	73.1	482	62.2	0	X	34	55.9	57	96.5	1.2	0.2	0.5	0.5	0.8	3.9
Marshall County	12 176	72.9	7	100.0	41	34.1	24	54.2	51	74.5	0.8	0.1	0.3	0.3	0.3	3.6
Martin County	4 694	76.7	3	100.0	17	29.4	0	X	22	72.7	0.1	0.1	0.0	0.0	0.0	3.3
Mason County	6 196	70.3	504	54.2	0	X	25	100.0	53	81.1	1.4	0.4	0.6	0.4	0.5	5.1
Meade County	8 778	78.5	383	82.5	80	90.0	43	90.7	134	91.0	2.0	0.8	0.6	0.5	0.5	8.2
Menifee County	2 483	75.3	0	X	3	100.0	0	X	5	100.0	0.4	0.1	0.0	0.2	0.1	4.0
Mercer County	7 904	72.3	344	72.1	17	64.7	32	100.0	53	86.8	1.7	0.3	0.6	0.7	0.6	5.0
Metcalfe County	3 868	72.3	50	70.0	26	100.0	0	X	14	100.0	0.2	0.1	0.0	0.0	0.0	5.4
Monroe County	4 542	71.9	125	77.6	8	0.0	12	0.0	36	100.0	1.4	0.2	0.2	1.0	0.6	5.2
Montgomery County	8 280	73.6	411	52.8	32	75.0	12	33.3	74	56.8	0.5	0.1	0.1	0.2	0.3	4.3
Morgan County	4 721	75.1	15	100.0	7	0.0	9	77.8	12	100.0	0.7	0.2	0.1	0.2	0.2	4.1
Muhlenberg County	11 827	73.9	489	64.4	11	100.0	0	X	41	90.2	0.3	0.1	0.1	0.1	0.1	4.6
Nelson County	12 970	73.9	755	72.6	42	100.0	64	81.3	82	67.1	1.2	0.4	0.5	0.2	0.4	5.1
Nicholas County	2 655	72.6	41	31.7	0	X	0	X	34	58.8	0.5	0.3	0.0	0.0	0.0	3.8
Ohio County	8 705	74.2	100	73.0	14	100.0	4	100.0	35	91.4	0.7	0.3	0.0	0.3	0.3	3.7
Oldham County	14 208	82.8	323	75.2	37	81.1	38	97.4	139	84.9	1.6	0.5	0.4	0.5	0.3	7.4
Owen County	3 920	74.4	56	33.9	36	66.7	8	100.0	55	67.3	0.7	0.4	0.1	0.1	0.1	4.1

[1]Hispanic or Latino persons may be of any race.

STATE/ County code	MSA/PMSA/ NECMA code[1]	STATE County	Total population	Under 5 years	5 to 17 years	18 to 24 years	25 to 44 years	45 to 64 years	65 years and over	Median age	+/− U.S. percent under 18 years	+/− U.S. percent 65 years and over	Non-Hispanic White Total population	Non-Hispanic White Under 18 years	Non-Hispanic White 65 years and over
			1	2	3	4	5	6	7	8	9	10	11	12	13
		KENTUCKY—Cont'd													
21 189	...	Owsley County	4 858	5.8	18.4	9.0	27.0	24.4	15.3	38.2	−1.5	2.9	4 802	24.2	14.8
21 191	1640	Pendleton County	14 390	6.9	21.5	8.6	31.2	21.5	10.4	34.5	2.7	−2.0	14 152	28.3	10.5
21 193	...	Perry County	29 390	5.8	18.4	9.0	30.9	24.6	11.3	36.3	−1.5	−1.1	28 500	24.1	11.3
21 195	...	Pike County	68 736	6.1	17.6	9.1	30.0	24.8	12.4	37.1	−2.0	0.0	67 399	23.6	12.3
21 197	...	Powell County	13 237	6.9	19.7	9.3	30.1	23.5	10.6	34.8	0.9	−1.8	13 001	26.6	10.6
21 199	...	Pulaski County	56 217	5.9	17.6	8.1	28.6	24.7	15.0	38.5	−2.2	2.6	54 405	23.2	15.3
21 201	...	Robertson County	2 266	5.8	18.4	6.8	26.4	25.8	16.9	39.5	−1.5	4.5	2 226	24.0	16.8
21 203	...	Rockcastle County	16 582	6.0	18.3	8.7	30.1	23.6	13.3	36.3	−1.4	0.9	16 338	24.4	13.3
21 205	...	Rowan County	22 094	5.3	15.0	23.4	25.9	20.0	10.4	29.8	−5.4	−2.0	21 012	20.3	10.6
21 207	...	Russell County	16 315	5.5	16.9	7.5	27.6	26.0	16.5	39.9	−3.3	4.1	15 967	22.3	16.6
21 209	4280	Scott County	33 061	7.5	18.8	11.9	32.7	20.2	9.0	32.4	0.6	−3.4	30 223	25.9	9.0
21 211	...	Shelby County	33 337	7.2	18.2	8.4	31.4	24.2	10.6	35.9	−0.3	−1.8	28 343	24.3	11.7
21 213	...	Simpson County	16 405	7.3	18.9	8.7	29.2	22.7	13.3	35.9	0.5	0.9	14 392	25.9	13.5
21 215	...	Spencer County	11 766	7.3	19.8	7.7	33.3	22.9	9.1	35.1	1.4	−3.3	11 395	26.7	9.1
21 217	...	Taylor County	22 927	5.8	17.6	10.1	27.3	23.9	15.3	38.1	−2.3	2.9	21 262	23.0	15.6
21 219	...	Todd County	11 971	7.4	19.2	8.6	28.6	22.2	14.0	35.9	0.9	1.6	10 633	26.1	14.1
21 221	...	Trigg County	12 597	6.0	16.7	6.7	26.8	27.0	16.8	40.5	−3.0	4.4	11 042	21.7	17.2
21 223	...	Trimble County	8 125	6.7	19.8	7.8	30.7	23.6	11.4	35.7	0.8	−1.0	7 909	25.8	11.6
21 225	...	Union County	15 637	6.1	19.0	13.9	25.2	22.9	12.8	34.5	−0.6	0.4	13 178	24.3	14.0
21 227	...	Warren County	92 522	6.3	16.8	16.3	29.2	20.9	10.4	32.3	−2.6	−2.0	79 656	22.0	11.3
21 229	...	Washington County	10 916	6.0	19.5	9.1	27.7	23.0	14.8	37.1	−0.2	2.4	9 809	25.0	15.2
21 231	...	Wayne County	19 923	6.7	18.7	8.6	28.6	24.0	13.4	36.6	−0.3	1.0	19 049	25.0	13.8
21 233	...	Webster County	14 120	6.2	18.0	9.0	27.6	24.2	14.9	37.8	−1.5	2.5	12 972	23.8	15.3
21 235	...	Whitley County	35 865	6.4	19.3	11.0	27.4	23.1	12.9	35.4	0.0	0.5	35 002	25.5	13.0
21 237	...	Wolfe County	7 065	6.5	19.5	9.3	28.3	23.7	12.7	36.4	0.3	0.3	7 013	25.9	12.7
21 239	4280	Woodford County	23 208	6.0	19.2	7.7	31.4	25.2	10.4	37.1	−0.5	−2.0	21 093	25.1	10.5
22 000	...	LOUISIANA	4 468 976	7.1	20.2	10.6	29.0	21.5	11.6	34.0	1.6	−0.8	2 794 348	23.8	13.8
22 001	3880	Acadia Parish	58 861	7.8	22.0	9.7	27.3	20.8	12.3	33.7	4.1	−0.1	47 069	28.1	13.2
22 003	...	Allen Parish	25 440	6.5	18.1	9.3	33.6	20.8	11.7	34.8	−1.1	−0.7	17 311	26.4	13.9
22 005	0760	Ascension Parish	76 627	8.1	22.0	9.5	32.8	19.9	7.6	32.0	4.4	−4.8	58 460	28.4	8.0
22 007	...	Assumption Parish	23 388	7.0	21.4	10.0	28.8	21.9	11.0	34.2	2.7	−1.4	15 473	25.3	12.5
22 009	...	Avoyelles Parish	41 481	6.9	19.9	9.1	29.5	20.9	13.8	35.2	1.1	1.4	28 134	24.4	16.2
22 011	...	Beauregard Parish	32 986	6.8	20.5	8.9	28.7	23.2	11.8	35.5	1.6	−0.6	27 527	26.9	12.6
22 013	...	Bienville Parish	15 752	6.4	20.8	8.2	24.7	22.2	17.7	38.0	1.5	5.3	8 588	23.1	20.9
22 015	7680	Bossier Parish	98 310	7.4	20.5	9.7	30.8	21.0	10.5	33.8	2.2	−1.9	71 755	25.4	12.0
22 017	7680	Caddo Parish	252 161	6.9	19.9	10.2	27.5	21.9	13.7	35.1	1.1	1.3	131 547	20.9	18.0
22 019	3960	Calcasieu Parish	183 577	7.3	20.1	10.2	28.9	21.6	11.9	34.5	1.7	−0.5	133 607	25.2	13.3
22 021	...	Caldwell Parish	10 560	6.2	18.7	9.6	28.5	23.3	13.8	36.7	−0.8	1.4	8 399	24.8	14.2
22 023	...	Cameron Parish	9 991	6.4	21.9	9.1	30.0	22.1	10.5	35.0	2.6	−1.9	9 266	28.0	10.8
22 025	...	Catahoula Parish	10 920	6.4	19.4	10.9	26.6	22.4	14.2	36.7	0.1	1.8	7 798	23.7	16.0
22 027	...	Claiborne Parish	16 851	5.9	19.6	8.2	27.4	21.5	17.4	37.7	−0.2	5.0	8 686	21.0	21.6
22 029	...	Concordia Parish	20 247	7.3	20.5	9.0	25.4	23.1	14.8	36.9	2.1	2.4	12 136	24.2	16.8
22 031	...	De Soto Parish	25 494	7.0	21.3	8.4	26.4	22.3	14.5	36.3	2.6	2.1	14 053	24.3	15.9
22 033	0760	East Baton Rouge Parish	412 852	7.0	19.1	14.5	28.8	20.7	9.9	31.5	0.4	−2.5	227 677	20.8	12.9
22 035	...	East Carroll Parish	9 421	7.6	22.8	10.8	28.9	16.9	13.0	30.9	4.7	0.6	2 925	20.9	20.1
22 037	...	East Feliciana Parish	21 360	6.5	19.2	9.3	31.0	22.9	11.1	35.8	0.0	−1.3	10 973	23.0	12.8
22 039	...	Evangeline Parish	35 434	8.0	21.5	9.8	27.7	20.3	12.8	33.7	3.8	0.4	24 763	26.9	15.2
22 041	...	Franklin Parish	21 263	7.2	20.8	8.9	26.0	21.5	15.7	35.9	2.3	3.3	14 170	23.7	17.1
22 043	...	Grant Parish	18 698	7.5	20.7	8.0	27.8	23.2	12.8	35.5	2.5	0.4	15 934	27.3	12.9
22 045	...	Iberia Parish	73 266	7.9	22.0	10.0	28.2	20.4	11.4	33.3	4.2	−1.0	47 109	26.3	13.4
22 047	...	Iberville Parish	33 320	6.6	19.6	10.5	31.4	21.0	11.0	34.4	0.5	−1.4	16 244	22.4	14.6
22 049	...	Jackson Parish	15 397	6.3	19.0	9.3	25.5	23.4	16.4	37.6	−0.4	4.0	10 879	23.7	17.1
22 051	5560	Jefferson Parish	455 466	6.6	18.6	9.2	30.3	23.3	11.9	35.9	−0.5	−0.5	298 244	21.3	15.0
22 053	...	Jefferson Davis Parish	31 435	7.6	21.7	9.1	27.2	21.2	13.2	34.5	3.6	0.8	25 118	27.7	14.1
22 055	3880	Lafayette Parish	190 503	7.2	20.1	11.7	31.3	20.2	9.5	32.4	1.6	−2.9	137 867	24.8	10.9
22 057	3350	Lafourche Parish	89 974	6.9	20.4	10.6	29.7	21.2	11.2	34.1	1.6	−1.2	73 973	25.1	12.4
22 059	...	La Salle Parish	14 282	6.0	20.0	9.4	27.4	22.5	14.6	36.4	0.3	2.2	12 200	24.5	16.1
22 061	...	Lincoln Parish	42 509	6.0	16.2	25.9	23.1	17.4	11.4	26.5	−3.5	−1.0	24 216	20.1	13.4
22 063	0760	Livingston Parish	91 814	7.4	22.0	9.0	31.5	21.4	8.7	32.8	3.7	−3.7	85 780	29.2	8.5
22 065	...	Madison Parish	13 728	8.1	24.8	11.2	25.8	18.6	11.4	29.8	7.2	−1.0	5 030	23.5	15.4
22 067	...	Morehouse Parish	31 021	6.9	20.6	9.8	26.4	20.9	15.4	35.6	1.8	3.0	17 172	22.3	19.0
22 069	...	Natchitoches Parish	39 080	7.1	18.9	17.7	24.5	19.7	12.2	30.2	0.3	−0.2	22 370	21.3	14.1
22 071	5560	Orleans Parish	484 674	6.8	19.9	11.3	29.4	20.9	11.7	33.1	1.0	−0.7	129 215	13.4	19.6
22 073	5200	Ouachita Parish	147 250	7.2	20.6	12.1	27.8	20.4	11.8	32.3	2.1	−0.6	93 967	23.3	14.3
22 075	5560	Plaquemines Parish	26 757	7.2	22.1	9.2	30.4	21.1	9.9	33.7	3.6	−2.5	18 401	27.1	10.8

[1]MSA = Metropolitan Statistical Area. PMSA = Primary MSA. NECMA = New England County Metropolitan Area. See the Appendix A for explanation of these concepts. See Appendix B for list of metropolitan areas identified by type, with component counties.

STATE County	Black or African American			American Indian and Alaska Native			Asian, Hawaiian, and Pacific Islander			Hispanic or Latino[1]			Two or more races		
		Age (percent)			Age (percent)			Age (percent)			Age (percent)			Age (percent)	
	Total population	Under 18 years	65 years and over	Total population	Under 18 years	65 years and over	Total population	Under 18 years	65 years and over	Total population	Under 18 years	65 years and over	Total population	Under 18 years	65 years and over
	14	15	16	17	18	19	20	21	22	23	24	25	26	27	28
KENTUCKY—Cont'd															
Owsley County	0	X	X	15	0.0	100.0	0	X	X	18	0.0	72.2	23	78.3	21.7
Pendleton County	50	12.0	12.0	14	0.0	0.0	11	45.5	0.0	121	30.6	2.5	46	41.3	6.5
Perry County	391	27.9	2.0	22	27.3	0.0	166	30.7	0.0	111	37.8	27.0	191	33.0	35.6
Pike County	289	26.6	24.9	132	40.2	14.4	141	14.2	8.5	400	36.8	3.0	419	32.2	14.8
Powell County	64	26.6	9.4	38	21.1	5.3	0	X	X	53	9.4	9.4	88	39.8	14.8
Pulaski County	746	35.9	7.8	103	25.2	0.0	313	23.3	7.3	215	20.0	13.5	396	38.6	3.3
Robertson County	2	0.0	0.0	0	X	X	11	0.0	0.0	16	81.3	6.3	16	31.3	43.8
Rockcastle County	14	21.4	35.7	57	.15.8	0.0	0	X	X	84	15.5	22.6	89	21.3	12.4
Rowan County	349	14.3	0.0	73	24.7	8.2	128	12.5	0.0	260	10.4	9.6	283	32.2	16.3
Russell County	72	20.8	25.0	31	0.0	12.9	59	20.3	0.0	130	31.5	14.6	83	25.3	4.8
Scott County	1 648	27.9	12.6	23	0.0	0.0	188	31.4	0.0	477	31.4	1.5	535	38.3	6.4
Shelby County	2 914	28.3	7.6	56	14.3	0.0	86	17.4	0.0	1 524	31.8	0.0	502	51.0	1.8
Simpson County	1 752	28.8	11.7	19	0.0	36.8	86	20.9	10.5	41	78.0	0.0	135	31.9	8.9
Spencer County	92	16.3	21.7	19	52.6	0.0	1	0.0	0.0	94	52.1	3.2	170	47.6	1.8
Taylor County	1 252	24.2	15.0	15	0.0	0.0	29	0.0	0.0	285	44.2	2.5	100	67.0	7.0
Todd County	1 019	29.4	16.0	26	0.0	15.4	5	0.0	0.0	228	43.0	0.0	102	39.2	6.9
Trigg County	1 209	29.9	14.7	4	0.0	0.0	39	38.5	5.1	163	35.0	6.7	168	19.0	19.0
Trimble County	19	42.1	0.0	9	0.0	0.0	0	X	X	113	57.5	4.4	63	38.1	9.5
Union County	2 028	29.2	6.9	28	17.9	0.0	37	0.0	0.0	221	28.5	1.8	204	30.4	7.8
Warren County	7 854	27.0	6.4	527	43.5	3.6	1 136	26.8	2.3	2 155	30.8	1.5	1 172	45.8	4.4
Washington County	769	20.7	15.2	99	46.5	0.0	34	14.7	0.0	125	48.0	0.0	76	65.8	5.3
Wayne County	283	24.7	8.8	119	37.8	0.0	5	0.0	0.0	325	24.6	2.8	172	70.3	0.0
Webster County	727	23.9	14.7	0	X	X	23	21.7	0.0	295	29.5	0.0	129	58.9	5.4
Whitley County	183	24.6	7.1	51	23.5	0.0	105	39.0	6.7	275	36.7	8.7	341	47.2	12.3
Wolfe County	6	0.0	0.0	0	X	X	28	53.6	0.0	18	27.8	0.0	0	X	X
Woodford County	1 212	24.2	14.0	14	28.6	0.0	60	66.7	0.0	550	23.6	0.0	305	40.0	8.5
LOUISIANA	1 444 566	33.5	8.1	25 833	32.3	6.5	56 871	27.3	4.9	107 854	28.1	7.7	53 939	36.5	7.5
Acadia Parish	10 949	36.6	8.7	127	40.2	11.8	131	23.7	8.4	351	37.0	6.6	263	51.7	2.7
Allen Parish	6 046	21.4	7.7	474	24.9	11.0	145	3.4	6.2	1 230	14.7	0.0	358	47.5	13.1
Ascension Parish	15 179	35.6	6.7	333	46.4	5.3	220	22.8	1.3	1 040	26.2	3.7	672	36.0	7.6
Assumption Parish	7 365	34.5	7.7	78	43.6	0.0	117	39.3	5.1	288	22.9	12.2	138	50.0	15.9
Avoyelles Parish	12 261	31.5	8.6	297	33.7	2.4	167	40.1	15.0	328	36.6	9.8	308	33.8	12.7
Beauregard Parish	3 937	28.8	9.7	169	32.5	0.0	323	10.8	0.0	554	43.1	3.6	543	40.1	4.6
Bienville Parish	6 954	32.4	13.9	44	15.9	11.4	19	31.6	5.3	116	25.0	16.4	67	17.9	10.4
Bossier Parish	20 354	35.2	6.8	534	36.1	5.8	1 225	26.9	2.8	3 105	33.2	3.8	1 672	42.8	6.3
Caddo Parish	112 219	33.5	9.0	995	26.7	8.8	2 015	24.7	6.7	3 518	30.7	5.0	2 386	33.2	10.6
Calcasieu Parish	43 529	32.8	8.4	620	37.9	9.4	1 167	21.2	4.3	3 166	37.7	3.9	2 055	43.5	7.0
Caldwell Parish	1 901	25.3	11.8	11	0.0	0.0	34	20.6	41.2	159	28.3	6.9	61	9.8	21.3
Cameron Parish	354	29.1	10.7	51	39.2	0.0	34	23.5	0.0	207	36.7	0.0	79	29.1	12.7
Catahoula Parish	3 011	31.1	9.3	19	0.0	0.0	0	X	X	44	27.3	9.1	73	46.6	16.4
Claiborne Parish	7 979	30.4	13.0	15	20.0	0.0	24	29.2	16.7	143	35.7	6.3	68	13.2	17.6
Concordia Parish	7 696	34.1	12.1	73	19.2	15.1	59	23.7	0.0	283	14.1	0.0	93	11.8	25.8
De Soto Parish	10 535	33.2	13.2	158	11.4	8.2	44	27.3	13.6	492	34.6	7.7	262	39.3	16.8
East Baton Rouge Parish	163 787	33.5	6.4	1 102	20.6	3.9	8 883	24.6	2.5	7 704	25.4	5.5	4 477	35.8	7.0
East Carroll Parish	6 397	34.8	9.8	22	50.0	0.0	35	34.3	14.3	116	9.5	9.5	0	X	X
East Feliciana Parish	10 079	28.6	9.6	6	0.0	0.0	70	18.6	8.6	130	10.8	3.1	128	41.4	1.6
Evangeline Parish	10 056	35.8	7.0	68	30.9	16.2	136	33.1	5.9	298	24.5	10.1	218	50.5	11.5
Franklin Parish	6 670	36.6	12.6	111	38.7	0.0	90	38.9	13.3	87	46.0	0.0	162	24.7	29.6
Grant Parish	2 183	31.2	13.9	198	49.5	3.5	69	15.9	0.0	125	56.0	2.4	173	29.5	5.8
Iberia Parish	22 091	36.3	7.7	377	39.8	8.8	1 489	37.9	5.8	1 062	33.8	9.8	1 255	38.2	12.1
Iberville Parish	16 569	30.0	7.2	65	13.8	9.2	33	18.2	33.3	429	28.7	17.0	139	38.1	10.8
Jackson Parish	4 315	28.7	14.7	47	27.7	31.9	58	36.2	0.0	43	53.5	4.7	59	45.8	22.0
Jefferson Parish	104 025	35.5	5.0	1 865	30.6	9.1	13 951	26.3	5.3	32 227	25.8	9.4	8 170	33.8	6.5
Jefferson Davis Parish	5 418	34.4	10.7	147	52.4	2.7	130	18.5	4.6	402	55.2	1.7	247	47.0	3.6
Lafayette Parish	45 067	34.5	6.0	434	25.1	2.8	2 188	23.5	2.4	3 400	29.8	4.5	1 904	34.4	5.8
Lafourche Parish	11 272	37.2	6.3	1 829	41.0	5.4	568	27.8	2.3	1 464	36.9	6.1	1 061	44.4	1.8
La Salle Parish	1 757	34.0	6.1	79	46.8	5.1	35	14.3	0.0	115	42.6	4.3	84	34.5	14.3
Lincoln Parish	16 808	25.1	9.3	131	23.7	0.0	572	24.1	1.9	398	23.9	0.0	381	25.5	7.9
Livingston Parish	3 778	31.6	13.9	383	40.7	0.0	297	23.2	3.4	880	36.7	6.4	712	38.9	6.5
Madison Parish	8 389	39.2	9.2	22	18.2	0.0	28	0.0	28.6	288	24.0	1.7	99	0.0	0.0
Morehouse Parish	13 386	33.7	11.1	46	26.1	4.3	94	41.5	0.0	204	39.2	3.9	193	31.1	10.4
Natchitoches Parish	14 766	33.1	9.5	474	29.1	10.5	237	18.1	0.0	486	22.2	2.1	697	27.3	13.8
Orleans Parish	325 216	32.1	8.8	1 495	28.2	9.6	10 615	26.5	6.6	15 032	21.2	11.8	6 731	31.3	8.2
Ouachita Parish	49 693	36.7	7.5	204	7.4	16.7	830	11.8	5.4	1 548	26.8	9.5	1 261	30.5	11.2
Plaquemines Parish	6 115	33.5	7.4	543	33.3	11.2	637	31.1	6.4	483	31.3	16.8	588	48.5	5.3

[1] Hispanic or Latino persons may be of any race.

STATE County	Total households	Married-couple family households			Other family households			Two or more unrelated persons		Male living alone		Female living alone		Percent of householders 65 years and over who live alone	Grandparents who are responsible for the care of their grandchildren
		Total	With children	Householder 65 years or over	Total	With children	Householder 65 years or over	Total	Householder 65 years or over	Total	Householder 65 years or over	Total	Householder 65 years or over		
	29	30	31	32	33	34	35	36	37	38	39	40	41	42	43
KENTUCKY—Cont'd															
Owsley County	1 913	53.5	22.6	9.3	20.1	10.8	4.7	2.0	0.3	11.6	2.9	12.8	7.2	41.5	140
Pendleton County	5 171	64.3	31.2	8.9	12.6	7.9	1.6	3.0	0.0	9.7	1.9	10.3	5.9	42.5	193
Perry County	11 480	57.8	26.0	6.8	17.0	8.8	2.6	1.9	0.3	8.9	3.0	14.4	8.0	53.3	380
Pike County	27 660	58.7	26.5	8.1	15.2	8.1	2.6	2.0	0.2	9.9	2.6	14.2	7.6	48.3	831
Powell County	5 062	59.5	26.8	9.8	15.6	9.8	2.0	3.0	0.3	10.5	1.7	11.4	5.3	36.4	145
Pulaski County	22 664	58.6	23.8	11.7	13.6	8.2	1.9	2.8	0.3	10.1	2.6	14.9	8.0	43.3	372
Robertson County	856	57.6	22.8	11.8	13.7	7.9	2.8	3.4	0.6	11.0	2.3	14.4	8.3	41.2	38
Rockcastle County	6 546	58.1	24.3	9.2	14.9	8.7	2.5	2.5	0.2	11.4	3.0	13.2	7.5	46.9	172
Rowan County	7 935	53.4	24.4	8.1	13.2	7.0	2.0	6.5	0.1	11.9	2.7	15.0	7.3	49.3	115
Russell County	6 957	57.2	22.7	11.8	12.4	6.5	1.9	2.5	0.1	11.1	3.3	16.9	9.9	49.1	152
Scott County	12 081	60.4	30.0	6.9	14.5	8.8	1.7	4.2	0.1	8.9	1.3	12.1	5.4	43.6	222
Shelby County	12 118	61.1	27.0	8.4	14.4	8.4	2.1	4.3	0.3	8.5	2.0	11.7	6.0	42.8	229
Simpson County	6 432	58.1	25.3	9.8	14.2	8.1	2.2	3.6	0.5	9.9	2.7	14.3	8.6	47.5	166
Spencer County	4 258	69.8	33.0	7.8	10.2	5.7	1.6	2.9	0.2	8.0	1.2	9.0	4.7	38.3	96
Taylor County	9 220	55.9	22.0	10.0	15.1	8.6	2.7	2.9	0.4	10.0	3.4	16.1	10.5	51.5	112
Todd County	4 574	57.7	26.3	8.6	14.6	9.7	3.1	2.6	0.4	8.2	2.5	14.9	9.2	49.1	123
Trigg County	5 237	60.6	22.1	12.3	11.4	6.2	2.1	2.9	0.3	10.2	3.9	14.9	8.2	45.1	109
Trimble County	3 119	60.1	27.6	8.5	13.8	7.1	2.2	4.0	0.4	10.2	2.1	11.9	6.2	42.9	126
Union County	5 721	56.5	24.7	9.9	14.9	8.7	1.8	2.6	0.0	10.0	2.7	16.0	10.5	52.9	65
Warren County	35 402	53.0	23.9	7.5	14.0	8.7	1.4	7.0	0.2	11.0	1.8	15.0	6.9	48.9	878
Washington County	4 112	60.8	25.8	11.3	12.7	7.6	2.1	2.6	0.4	9.0	1.9	14.9	10.3	47.1	88
Wayne County	7 899	59.7	25.7	10.1	14.3	8.4	2.5	2.2	0.3	9.7	2.5	14.1	7.8	44.5	253
Webster County	5 568	60.1	25.1	11.5	13.3	7.0	2.1	2.4	0.1	9.8	2.6	14.4	9.4	46.6	181
Whitley County	13 788	56.4	25.0	9.2	16.1	9.4	2.9	2.4	0.4	10.3	2.5	14.8	7.9	45.3	390
Wolfe County	2 841	55.0	23.6	9.4	16.7	9.5	2.3	1.5	0.1	13.3	3.1	13.4	7.1	46.2	41
Woodford County	8 925	62.0	28.4	8.2	13.3	7.2	1.4	3.7	0.3	9.0	2.5	12.0	4.8	42.4	153
LOUISIANA	1 657 107	49.6	23.3	8.2	20.6	11.9	3.0	4.5	0.3	11.0	2.3	14.3	6.8	43.9	67 058
Acadia Parish	21 171	55.5	27.6	9.0	19.0	11.6	2.7	3.0	0.4	8.6	2.3	14.0	7.9	45.8	863
Allen Parish	8 127	55.0	26.8	9.7	19.2	10.5	3.9	1.9	0.3	8.8	2.8	15.2	8.7	45.3	415
Ascension Parish	26 773	60.2	31.9	5.9	18.2	10.8	2.2	3.3	0.1	8.7	1.2	9.6	4.3	40.1	1 032
Assumption Parish	8 217	56.5	26.9	8.5	19.9	12.0	3.3	3.2	0.3	9.6	2.0	10.8	7.2	43.1	468
Avoyelles Parish	14 749	52.5	24.6	9.7	19.5	11.7	2.5	3.0	0.5	9.9	2.6	15.0	9.7	49.2	510
Beauregard Parish	12 130	60.3	28.1	9.5	14.7	8.1	2.2	2.9	0.1	9.1	2.3	13.0	7.7	45.7	449
Bienville Parish	6 106	47.9	19.6	11.1	21.7	11.6	4.7	1.9	0.2	12.2	3.3	16.5	10.6	46.6	345
Bossier Parish	36 671	55.3	26.5	8.5	18.0	11.0	2.2	3.9	0.3	10.1	1.7	12.7	5.7	40.2	986
Caddo Parish	98 066	43.0	17.9	8.6	23.8	13.6	3.6	4.4	0.5	12.0	2.3	16.8	8.0	45.0	4 421
Calcasieu Parish	68 757	53.4	25.4	9.1	18.2	10.7	2.6	4.4	0.2	10.6	2.2	13.3	6.6	42.3	2 565
Caldwell Parish	3 925	55.0	24.3	9.8	16.6	8.6	3.4	3.1	0.6	10.1	2.9	15.3	8.7	45.6	167
Cameron Parish	3 592	61.4	32.6	8.3	13.8	7.3	2.8	3.7	0.3	9.7	2.4	11.3	5.5	40.9	85
Catahoula Parish	4 088	55.7	23.7	11.4	18.7	11.1	3.0	1.4	0.0	9.8	2.7	14.4	8.3	43.3	236
Claiborne Parish	6 288	46.7	18.3	11.4	23.1	12.0	4.7	2.0	0.3	11.3	3.7	17.0	10.9	47.0	385
Concordia Parish	7 538	49.2	19.7	11.4	23.4	13.3	4.5	2.2	0.4	11.1	2.1	14.2	7.8	37.7	585
De Soto Parish	9 680	50.3	21.5	9.7	21.7	12.9	4.1	2.8	0.2	10.5	4.1	14.7	8.3	47.0	575
East Baton Rouge Parish	156 521	45.5	21.5	7.0	20.5	12.0	2.5	7.1	0.2	11.8	1.8	15.1	5.6	43.2	5 006
East Carroll Parish	2 968	42.3	17.4	10.5	30.4	19.3	5.7	1.7	0.3	11.8	3.5	13.8	9.8	44.4	219
East Feliciana Parish	6 687	52.1	23.6	7.2	23.6	12.9	4.5	2.1	0.4	11.1	2.5	11.2	6.3	42.1	406
Evangeline Parish	12 769	52.7	26.2	9.0	19.8	12.5	2.6	1.7	0.2	11.9	3.6	13.9	8.7	51.1	466
Franklin Parish	7 789	52.7	23.5	10.8	21.4	10.9	4.0	2.1	0.1	8.9	2.6	14.9	9.3	43.7	349
Grant Parish	7 056	56.7	25.4	10.2	17.3	10.8	2.1	3.3	0.4	10.9	3.0	11.7	6.7	43.5	300
Iberia Parish	25 319	53.9	27.4	8.7	21.6	12.7	3.3	3.3	0.4	9.9	2.6	11.3	6.3	41.8	1 315
Iberville Parish	10 672	49.1	23.3	9.0	26.1	13.2	4.9	2.8	0.4	9.5	2.0	12.5	6.1	36.3	772
Jackson Parish	6 114	53.2	23.0	11.5	18.1	9.7	3.7	1.8	0.2	11.3	3.1	15.6	10.1	46.1	240
Jefferson Parish	176 424	49.0	22.0	8.5	19.5	10.5	2.9	4.9	0.3	11.6	2.0	15.0	6.4	41.9	5 922
Jefferson Davis Parish	11 519	57.3	28.7	10.1	17.4	10.1	3.1	2.7	0.1	9.6	3.1	12.8	7.8	44.9	447
Lafayette Parish	72 412	49.6	25.2	6.9	18.2	11.6	1.9	6.9	0.3	11.3	1.7	14.0	5.6	44.5	1 762
Lafourche Parish	32 093	55.0	28.7	8.8	16.5	9.8	2.6	4.4	0.6	8.2	2.1	11.3	6.4	41.7	871
La Salle Parish	5 288	58.9	27.2	10.3	12.7	6.5	2.8	2.7	0.2	9.3	3.3	16.4	10.3	50.6	257
Lincoln Parish	15 249	45.1	20.1	8.0	18.7	10.6	2.4	9.1	0.1	11.6	2.5	15.4	7.9	49.8	443
Livingston Parish	32 654	63.8	32.6	7.5	14.7	9.3	2.3	3.3	0.3	8.0	1.5	10.2	4.9	39.3	1 227
Madison Parish	4 459	42.2	18.0	9.0	28.5	17.4	3.3	2.8	0.9	12.2	1.9	14.4	6.5	39.2	257
Morehouse Parish	11 410	50.0	20.5	11.1	23.6	13.5	4.0	2.1	0.2	9.6	2.7	14.8	9.2	43.9	658
Natchitoches Parish	14 254	46.6	21.7	8.2	20.5	11.9	4.0	5.9	0.4	11.0	2.7	16.0	8.4	46.6	660
Orleans Parish	188 365	31.7	13.8	6.1	28.8	16.3	4.3	6.4	0.4	15.4	2.6	17.7	6.8	46.6	9 478
Ouachita Parish	55 276	48.6	22.1	8.2	21.1	12.6	2.7	4.5	0.3	9.9	2.0	15.9	7.7	46.5	2 662
Plaquemines Parish	9 001	60.3	30.2	8.6	17.3	9.7	2.3	3.9	0.2	8.5	2.3	10.0	6.4	44.1	436

Table A-3. States and Counties — Age, Ethnicity, and Household Structure

STATE County	Households with Non-Hispanic White householder — Number of households (44)	Percent that are family households (45)	Households with Black or African American householder — Number of households (46)	Percent that are family households (47)	Households with American Indian and Alaska Native householder — Number of households (48)	Percent that are family households (49)	Households with Asian, Hawaiian, and Pacific Islander householder — Number of households (50)	Percent that are family households (51)	Households with Hispanic or Latino[1] householder — Number of households (52)	Percent that are family households (53)	Foreign-born population — Percent of total population that is foreign-born (54)	Place of birth (percent) Europe (55)	Asia (56)	Latin America (57)	Percent in non-English speaking households — Linguistically isolated (58)	Not linguistically isolated (59)
KENTUCKY—Cont'd																
Owsley County	1 886	73.8	0	X	11	54.5	0	X	11	100.0	0.1	0.0	0.0	0.1	0.3	1.9
Pendleton County	5 105	77.2	18	50.0	12	100.0	2	100.0	30	43.3	0.5	0.0	0.0	0.5	0.2	4.0
Perry County	11 112	74.8	156	76.9	9	100.0	67	65.7	49	26.5	0.6	0.2	0.4	0.0	0.1	4.3
Pike County	27 194	74.0	88	70.5	26	80.8	56	51.8	139	79.9	0.4	0.1	0.2	0.1	0.1	2.9
Powell County	4 944	75.1	35	71.4	21	85.7	0	X	36	50.0	0.2	0.1	0.1	0.0	0.0	1.5
Pulaski County	22 068	72.4	257	66.9	45	55.6	110	60.9	88	59.1	0.8	0.2	0.5	0.1	0.3	3.8
Robertson County	847	71.2	0	X	0	X	2	100.0	1	100.0	0.5	0.0	0.4	0.1	0.0	3.8
Rockcastle County	6 432	73.4	5	100.0	15	0	0	X	38	65.8	0.0	0.0	0.0	0.0	0.0	3.8
Rowan County	7 757	66.5	44	52.3	33	63.6	21	100.0	44	84.1	1.4	0.4	0.5	0.3	0.4	3.9
Russell County	6 858	69.7	41	41.5	4	0.0	16	87.5	18	33.3	1.0	0.7	0.3	0.0	0.2	6.1
Scott County	11 061	75.3	670	68.1	23	100.0	56	78.6	115	56.5	1.9	0.3	0.6	0.8	0.8	5.7
Shelby County	10 814	75.7	871	76.7	20	35.0	14	100.0	288	66.3	3.9	0.4	0.1	3.2	2.2	6.5
Simpson County	5 722	72.9	627	70.3	12	0.0	47	38.3	0	X	1.2	0.3	0.6	0.0	0.4	5.8
Spencer County	4 152	80.4	35	51.4	5	100.0	1	0.0	25	80.0	1.2	0.2	0.3	0.6	0.8	4.7
Taylor County	8 569	71.6	546	61.0	15	100.0	11	0.0	63	74.6	1.3	0.3	0.0	0.9	0.8	3.7
Todd County	4 058	75.4	439	65.6	11	18.2	0	X	50	76.0	1.3	0.1	0.1	1.0	1.5	8.5
Trigg County	4 636	71.5	475	70.5	0	X	7	57.1	45	100.0	0.8	0.3	0.2	0.2	0.6	7.2
Trimble County	3 076	73.6	0	X	0	X	0	X	22	100.0	1.1	0.0	0.1	1.0	0.3	5.7
Union County	5 255	72.3	416	60.1	8	0.0	7	100.0	12	100.0	1.4	0.2	0.3	0.9	0.1	4.9
Warren County	31 083	67.1	2 873	64.4	121	70.2	392	62.2	619	74.2	4.3	1.6	1.1	1.4	2.2	8.1
Washington County	3 747	73.4	281	71.5	26	61.5	14	100.0	28	89.3	0.7	0.0	0.3	0.2	0.4	4.7
Wayne County	7 580	74.8	160	53.1	58	56.9	0	X	76	44.7	1.3	0.3	0.0	1.0	1.1	3.3
Webster County	5 180	74.1	291	66.7	0	X	7	71.4	68	50.0	1.9	0.2	0.2	1.5	1.5	6.8
Whitley County	13 551	72.6	39	59.0	11	100.0	25	36.0	58	89.7	0.7	0.2	0.2	0.2	0.4	3.9
Wolfe County	2 829	71.6	0	X	0	X	7	100.0	5	100.0	0.7	0.1	0.4	0.3	0.3	3.4
Woodford County	8 151	76.4	520	62.3	10	30.0	0	X	136	83.8	2.7	0.3	0.2	1.8	1.5	5.9
LOUISIANA	1 105 452	69.4	478 950	71.9	8 590	75.6	16 831	74.5	34 051	72.2	2.6	0.4	1.0	1.0	1.3	14.0
Acadia Parish	17 257	75.3	3 662	70.7	35	57.1	53	90.6	92	68.5	0.4	0.1	0.2	0.1	2.1	31.9
Allen Parish	6 284	75.4	1 415	70.2	228	67.1	22	45.5	95	84.2	0.6	0.1	0.2	0.2	1.0	16.6
Ascension Parish	20 963	78.5	4 884	77.4	80	90.0	104	83.7	598	83.8	1.8	0.2	0.4	1.1	0.8	10.6
Assumption Parish	5 773	75.5	2 281	78.3	20	50.0	21	100.0	116	83.6	0.8	0.2	0.3	0.3	3.4	28.7
Avoyelles Parish	11 019	71.0	3 362	75.8	97	60.8	51	100.0	113	85.0	0.5	0.2	0.2	0.1	2.7	29.2
Beauregard Parish	10 386	75.1	1 296	72.7	55	100.0	42	78.6	149	76.5	1.1	0.4	0.5	0.2	0.3	8.6
Bienville Parish	3 442	70.8	2 611	68.0	11	63.6	3	66.7	28	71.4	0.4	0.1	0.1	0.1	0.1	4.4
Bossier Parish	28 115	73.2	6 775	72.4	163	84.0	322	74.2	871	78.4	2.5	0.5	1.0	0.8	0.9	9.1
Caddo Parish	56 422	64.4	38 806	70.1	395	71.1	655	75.9	1 087	69.3	1.5	0.4	0.6	0.4	0.5	7.4
Calcasieu Parish	51 690	71.6	15 040	72.3	210	74.8	327	67.0	953	65.7	1.4	0.3	0.5	0.4	0.9	15.6
Caldwell Parish	3 269	71.9	569	69.1	6	83.3	12	100.0	58	67.2	0.6	0.1	0.3	0.2	0.2	6.6
Cameron Parish	3 339	76.1	153	55.6	12	100.0	12	100.0	52	90.4	1.6	0.2	0.3	1.1	1.3	23.1
Catahoula Parish	3 061	77.5	993	64.9	11	100.0	0	X	21	57.1	0.1	0.0	0.0	0.1	0.2	4.3
Claiborne Parish	3 556	70.9	2 661	68.0	12	100.0	0	X	47	85.1	0.4	0.0	0.1	0.3	0.1	5.0
Concordia Parish	4 765	75.2	2 661	67.5	34	73.5	18	66.7	51	60.8	1.3	0.1	0.2	0.8	0.2	6.4
De Soto Parish	5 596	74.3	3 834	67.8	51	86.3	8	100.0	129	85.3	1.0	0.2	0.1	0.7	0.2	7.4
East Baton Rouge Parish	94 755	62.7	54 833	71.9	402	72.6	2 823	66.0	2 476	67.2	3.7	0.6	1.8	0.9	1.3	10.9
East Carroll Parish	1 188	71.5	1 749	74.3	0	X	11	45.5	44	61.4	0.9	0.0	0.7	0.1	1.0	5.3
East Feliciana Parish	3 862	74.4	2 735	77.3	3	100.0	23	73.9	43	83.7	0.6	0.1	0.2	0.2	0.5	7.3
Evangeline Parish	9 489	71.8	3 096	75.4	33	57.6	33	66.7	99	68.7	0.6	0.2	0.4	0.0	5.2	38.2
Franklin Parish	5 478	74.2	2 184	73.9	32	81.3	18	100.0	17	76.5	0.6	0.1	0.3	0.1	0.1	4.5
Grant Parish	6 106	74.2	800	69.5	61	93.4	17	100.0	26	96.2	0.5	0.2	0.2	0.0	0.2	6.3
Iberia Parish	17 483	74.6	6 837	77.0	134	92.5	328	91.8	261	69.7	2.0	0.1	1.4	0.5	2.4	23.4
Iberville Parish	6 007	73.3	4 474	78.0	25	100.0	3	0.0	128	80.5	0.7	0.2	0.1	0.3	0.3	10.0
Jackson Parish	4 395	72.6	1 646	67.9	34	79.4	11	45.5	7	71.4	0.4	0.1	0.1	0.2	0.0	4.9
Jefferson Parish	124 657	65.7	33 875	75.6	710	71.4	4 455	80.5	10 951	75.1	7.5	0.7	2.4	4.1	2.4	16.2
Jefferson Davis Parish	9 412	74.2	1 866	76.6	42	78.6	39	100.0	87	87.4	0.6	0.2	0.3	0.1	2.2	27.3
Lafayette Parish	55 072	66.8	14 947	72.2	179	72.6	698	67.2	957	66.0	2.5	0.5	1.0	0.7	2.1	27.4
Lafourche Parish	27 247	75.9	3 536	75.8	496	85.1	180	81.7	383	77.8	1.5	0.2	0.5	0.7	2.7	31.7
La Salle Parish	4 783	72.2	418	66.0	24	83.3	10	10.0	34	58.8	0.6	0.1	0.2	0.3	0.1	5.5
Lincoln Parish	9 134	66.0	5 647	60.5	58	82.8	183	66.7	106	42.5	2.1	0.2	1.1	0.5	0.8	7.1
Livingston Parish	30 721	78.8	1 299	75.1	85	90.6	61	67.2	254	76.0	0.8	0.3	0.2	0.2	0.3	8.0
Madison Parish	1 958	72.0	2 443	69.7	7	100.0	14	0.0	49	81.6	0.5	0.1	0.1	0.3	0.0	4.3
Morehouse Parish	6 879	73.9	4 412	72.8	14	85.7	17	100.0	52	90.4	0.4	0.0	0.1	0.2	0.3	3.9
Natchitoches Parish	8 636	66.4	4 952	67.4	136	73.5	88	55.7	108	81.5	1.5	0.3	0.7	0.1	0.5	6.1
Orleans Parish	63 960	45.2	113 437	69.3	613	52.2	3 201	69.2	5 700	58.6	4.2	0.6	1.6	1.8	1.5	10.9
Ouachita Parish	37 573	69.6	16 379	70.2	86	47.7	331	62.8	515	68.2	1.0	0.2	0.5	0.2	0.5	6.0
Plaquemines Parish	6 579	76.7	1 769	81.9	163	67.5	178	65.2	159	76.7	2.8	0.6	1.8	0.3	1.7	13.4

[1]Hispanic or Latino persons may be of any race.

STATE/ County code	MSA/PMSA/ NECMA code[1]	STATE County	Total population	Under 5 years	5 to 17 years	18 to 24 years	25 to 44 years	45 to 64 years	65 years and over	Median age	+/− U.S. percent under 18 years	+/− U.S. percent 65 years and over	Non-Hispanic White Total population	Under 18 years	65 years and over
			1	2	3	4	5	6	7	8	9	10	11	12	13
		LOUISIANA—Cont'd													
22 077	...	Pointe Coupee Parish.....	22 763	6.8	20.3	8.8	27.0	23.3	13.7	36.7	1.4	1.3	13 749	23.9	15.6
22 079	0220	Rapides Parish..............	126 337	7.0	20.3	9.6	28.0	22.1	13.0	35.5	1.6	0.6	83 032	24.0	15.5
22 081	...	Red River Parish............	9 622	7.7	22.4	9.7	24.7	21.0	14.5	34.6	4.4	2.1	5 518	24.2	17.7
22 083	...	Richland Parish..............	20 981	7.6	19.6	10.6	26.6	20.5	15.2	35.8	1.5	2.8	12 685	23.5	18.1
22 085	...	Sabine Parish...............	23 459	6.6	19.6	8.2	24.7	24.4	16.5	38.2	0.5	4.1	16 683	22.6	19.4
22 087	5560	St. Bernard Parish	67 229	6.2	19.1	9.1	29.5	22.5	13.7	36.6	-0.4	1.3	56 900	24.0	14.7
22 089	5560	St. Charles Parish	48 072	7.3	23.0	8.2	31.6	20.8	9.1	34.2	4.6	-3.3	33 949	28.4	10.1
22 091	...	St. Helena Parish	10 525	7.2	21.7	9.4	25.9	23.3	12.5	35.0	3.2	0.1	4 862	23.6	15.1
22 093	5560	St. James Parish............	21 216	7.0	22.5	10.0	28.0	21.2	11.3	34.0	3.8	-1.1	10 539	25.3	14.3
22 095	5560	St. John the Baptist Parish...................	43 044	8.1	23.1	9.9	30.0	20.9	8.1	32.0	5.5	-4.3	21 908	26.5	10.5
22 097	3880	St. Landry Parish	87 700	7.8	21.7	9.4	26.4	21.2	13.5	34.6	3.8	1.1	49 095	25.3	16.2
22 099	3880	St. Martin Parish	48 583	7.5	21.9	9.6	29.8	21.0	10.1	33.4	3.7	-2.3	31 761	26.4	11.4
22 101	...	St. Mary Parish	53 500	7.4	22.2	8.4	29.6	21.4	11.1	34.3	3.9	-1.3	33 053	25.8	13.1
22 103	5560	St. Tammany Parish	191 268	7.0	21.4	7.3	30.0	24.3	10.0	36.3	2.7	-2.4	162 632	27.4	10.5
22 105	...	Tangipahoa Parish	100 588	7.2	20.5	12.7	27.7	21.3	10.6	32.3	2.0	-1.8	69 090	24.2	12.3
22 107	...	Tensas Parish	6 618	6.6	19.8	10.0	25.3	22.8	15.5	37.3	0.7	3.1	2 848	20.6	19.7
22 109	3350	Terrebonne Parish	104 503	7.4	21.7	10.3	29.9	21.0	9.6	33.0	3.4	-2.8	76 392	26.1	11.2
22 111	...	Union Parish	22 803	7.1	18.6	9.3	26.4	23.8	14.8	37.3	0.0	2.4	15 826	22.1	16.8
22 113	...	Vermilion Parish	53 807	7.2	21.0	9.3	28.5	20.4	13.6	35.1	2.5	1.2	44 038	25.9	14.9
22 115	...	Vernon Parish	52 531	9.5	19.6	15.1	31.2	16.7	8.0	28.3	3.4	-4.4	37 567	27.1	9.8
22 117	...	Washington Parish	43 926	7.0	19.8	9.6	26.8	22.0	14.8	36.1	1.1	2.4	29 357	24.0	16.6
22 119	7680	Webster Parish	41 831	6.2	19.5	8.1	26.4	23.5	16.3	38.1	0.0	3.9	27 253	22.2	18.3
22 121	0760	West Baton Rouge Parish...................	21 601	7.0	21.0	10.2	30.9	21.1	9.8	34.0	2.3	-2.6	13 414	26.2	10.1
22 123	...	West Carroll Parish........	12 314	6.0	19.6	9.5	27.1	22.4	15.5	37.2	-0.1	3.1	9 749	24.7	17.1
22 125	...	West Feliciana Parish	15 111	4.4	16.0	8.4	40.7	23.4	7.0	36.6	-5.3	-5.4	7 255	23.4	8.8
22 127	...	Winn Parish	16 894	6.3	18.6	9.5	29.3	21.9	14.4	36.2	-0.8	2.0	11 157	23.1	16.3
23 000	...	MAINE......................	1 274 923	5.6	18.1	8.2	29.0	24.8	14.4	38.6	-2.0	2.0	1 230 645	23.2	14.7
23 001	4243	Androscoggin County.....	103 793	5.9	17.9	9.1	29.7	22.9	14.4	37.2	-1.9	2.0	100 004	23.3	14.8
23 003	...	Aroostook County	73 938	5.1	17.5	7.8	26.4	26.2	17.0	40.7	-3.1	4.6	71 417	22.0	17.5
23 005	6403	Cumberland County	265 612	5.8	17.5	8.4	31.3	23.6	13.3	37.6	-2.4	0.9	253 041	22.7	13.8
23 007	...	Franklin County	29 467	5.1	18.6	11.0	26.4	24.8	14.2	38.2	-2.0	1.8	28 797	23.5	14.4
23 009	...	Hancock County	51 791	4.8	17.5	7.4	27.5	26.9	15.9	40.7	-3.4	3.5	50 295	21.9	16.3
23 011	...	Kennebec County	117 114	5.5	18.4	8.4	28.6	24.9	14.2	38.7	-1.8	1.8	113 636	23.6	14.5
23 013	...	Knox County	39 618	5.2	17.2	6.2	27.5	26.6	17.3	41.4	-3.3	4.9	38 818	22.2	17.5
23 015	...	Lincoln County	33 616	4.9	17.7	5.8	25.6	27.9	18.1	42.6	-3.1	5.7	32 989	22.2	18.4
23 017	...	Oxford County...............	54 755	5.2	18.9	6.6	27.7	25.5	16.1	40.2	-1.6	3.7	53 382	23.7	16.3
23 019	0733	Penobscot County...........	144 919	5.3	17.5	11.3	28.9	23.9	13.1	37.2	-2.9	0.7	139 562	22.5	13.4
23 021	...	Piscataquis County	17 235	4.8	18.5	5.7	26.3	27.4	17.3	42.1	-2.4	4.9	16 814	23.0	17.5
23 023	...	Sagadahoc County	35 214	6.3	19.5	6.5	30.7	24.8	12.3	38.0	0.1	-0.1	33 855	25.0	12.6
23 025	...	Somerset County	50 888	5.7	19.0	7.1	28.6	25.3	14.3	38.9	-1.0	1.9	49 826	24.4	14.5
23 027	...	Waldo County	36 280	5.6	18.6	7.4	28.0	26.9	13.5	39.3	-1.5	1.1	35 288	23.8	13.8
23 029	...	Washington County........	33 941	5.0	17.9	7.9	26.4	25.5	17.3	40.5	-2.8	4.9	31 592	21.9	18.2
23 031	...	York County	186 742	5.9	18.8	6.9	29.9	24.7	13.6	38.5	-1.0	1.2	181 329	24.5	13.9
24 000	...	MARYLAND	5 296 486	6.6	18.9	8.4	31.6	23.1	11.3	36.0	-0.2	-1.1	3 287 071	23.0	14.1
24 001	1900	Allegany County.............	74 930	5.0	15.5	11.2	26.7	23.7	17.9	39.1	-5.2	5.5	69 214	20.6	19.0
24 003	0720	Anne Arundel County......	489 656	6.7	18.5	8.1	32.9	24.0	10.0	36.0	-0.5	-2.4	390 556	23.9	10.9
24 005	0720	Baltimore County	754 292	5.9	17.7	8.6	29.9	23.3	14.6	37.7	-2.1	2.2	554 287	21.1	17.9
24 009	8840	Calvert County	74 563	6.7	22.9	6.4	31.9	23.3	8.9	35.9	3.9	-3.5	61 946	29.2	9.0
24 011	...	Caroline County	29 772	6.2	20.7	7.5	28.9	23.2	13.6	37.0	1.2	1.2	24 029	25.4	14.2
24 013	0720	Carroll County	150 897	6.4	21.0	6.9	30.8	23.8	10.8	36.9	2.0	-1.6	143 299	27.5	11.0
24 015	9160	Cecil County.................	85 951	6.9	20.8	7.4	31.2	23.3	10.4	35.5	2.0	-2.0	79 720	27.1	10.8
24 017	8840	Charles County	120 546	7.2	21.6	7.4	33.6	22.5	7.8	34.6	3.1	-4.6	81 072	26.1	9.0
24 019	...	Dorchester County	30 674	5.4	17.9	6.8	26.9	25.1	17.9	40.7	-2.4	5.5	21 101	20.2	20.2
24 021	8840	Frederick County	195 277	7.2	20.3	7.3	32.7	22.8	9.6	35.6	1.8	-2.8	172 105	26.6	10.3
24 023	...	Garrett County	29 846	6.1	19.0	7.9	27.7	24.4	14.9	38.3	-0.6	2.5	29 539	25.1	14.9
24 025	0720	Harford County	218 590	7.1	20.7	6.8	31.6	23.7	10.1	36.2	2.1	-2.3	187 590	26.6	10.9
24 027	0720	Howard County	247 842	7.3	20.7	6.1	34.7	23.9	7.3	35.5	2.3	-5.1	179 679	26.8	8.3
24 029	...	Kent County	19 197	4.6	16.3	10.9	23.9	25.1	19.2	41.3	-4.8	6.8	15 062	19.2	20.9
24 031	8840	Montgomery County.......	873 341	6.9	18.4	6.7	32.7	24.1	11.2	36.8	-0.4	-1.2	518 456	23.0	14.9
24 033	8840	Prince George's County..	801 515	7.2	19.6	10.4	33.1	22.0	7.7	33.3	1.1	-4.7	195 222	17.4	16.4
24 035	0720	Queen Anne's County.....	40 563	6.4	18.9	5.6	30.3	26.0	12.8	38.8	-0.4	0.4	35 823	25.1	12.6
24 037	...	St. Mary's County	86 211	7.2	20.7	8.8	33.0	21.2	9.0	34.2	2.2	-3.4	69 320	26.9	9.3
24 039	...	Somerset County	24 747	4.7	13.8	15.6	29.9	21.8	14.3	36.5	-7.2	1.9	13 775	18.6	19.2
24 041	...	Talbot County................	33 812	5.2	16.4	5.0	25.9	27.0	20.5	43.3	-4.1	8.1	27 475	20.6	22.1

[1]MSA = Metropolitan Statistical Area. PMSA = Primary MSA. NECMA = New England County Metropolitan Area. See the Appendix A for explanation of these concepts. See Appendix B for list of metropolitan areas identified by type, with component counties.

STATE County	Black or African American			American Indian and Alaska Native			Asian, Hawaiian, and Pacific Islander			Hispanic or Latino[1]			Two or more races		
		Age (percent)			Age (percent)			Age (percent)			Age (percent)			Age (percent)	
	Total population	Under 18 years	65 years and over	Total population	Under 18 years	65 years and over	Total population	Under 18 years	65 years and over	Total population	Under 18 years	65 years and over	Total population	Under 18 years	65 years and over
	14	15	16	17	18	19	20	21	22	23	24	25	26	27	28
LOUISIANA—Cont'd															
Pointe Coupee Parish...	8 631	32.8	11.2	37	0.0	0.0	36	8.3	5.6	234	24.8	0.4	126	25.4	0.0
Rapides Parish............	38 768	33.8	8.6	698	20.8	7.7	1 162	30.9	5.1	1 338	25.7	6.2	1 440	37.0	8.8
Red River Parish.........	3 969	38.2	9.6	12	16.7	0.0	9	22.2	22.2	71	26.8	19.7	64	39.1	28.1
Richland Parish...........	7 959	33.6	10.9	10	0.0	30.0	88	17.0	0.0	211	27.5	2.8	75	30.7	22.7
Sabine Parish..............	3 829	36.5	9.5	1 844	33.1	10.0	116	31.9	5.2	649	29.3	10.6	573	39.6	8.4
St. Bernard Parish........	4 615	37.2	6.0	378	22.5	3.4	1 079	37.6	7.0	3 506	25.0	12.6	1 158	33.4	4.6
St. Charles Parish........	11 985	34.6	6.6	93	16.1	4.3	386	48.2	6.5	1 364	33.1	5.3	507	39.4	10.8
St. Helena Parish........	5 536	33.6	10.3	22	54.5	0.0	8	62.5	0.0	138	30.4	16.7	39	59.0	10.3
St. James Parish..........	10 526	33.8	8.3	18	22.2	33.3	28	0.0	0.0	71	38.0	7.0	49	32.7	24.5
St. John the Baptist Parish..........................	19 182	36.0	5.7	126	37.3	4.0	315	41.0	3.8	1 264	29.8	4.6	394	40.1	2.0
St. Landry Parish	37 049	34.8	10.2	148	42.6	8.1	230	28.3	0.0	655	36.3	6.4	627	36.8	9.1
St. Martin Parish	15 686	34.9	8.1	159	37.1	0.0	373	38.6	7.5	346	32.9	0.0	321	51.1	4.4
St. Mary Parish	16 603	35.4	8.1	700	32.3	6.1	1 011	47.7	4.1	1 448	36.3	5.8	793	34.0	11.0
St. Tammany Parish	18 295	34.2	7.3	872	28.0	4.7	1 497	31.1	4.3	5 078	34.6	6.4	3 269	39.2	5.4
Tangipahoa Parish........	28 561	36.2	7.3	345	24.1	4.6	263	15.2	9.9	1 425	28.2	2.0	1 128	37.2	2.9
Tensas Parish	3 599	30.3	12.9	10	0.0	50.0	3	0.0	0.0	150	51.3	2.0	41	24.4	0.0
Terrebonne Parish........	18 446	37.5	5.8	5 269	38.0	4.1	926	32.0	4.2	1 674	33.8	4.5	1 895	38.7	5.6
Union Parish................	6 424	33.6	10.8	71	18.3	0.0	18	50.0	0.0	414	35.7	2.2	92	52.2	8.7
Vermilion Parish	7 602	38.1	9.0	179	39.1	2.2	1 045	41.0	2.2	687	41.8	6.1	384	40.4	8.6
Vernon Parish	8 568	33.6	2.8	756	29.2	4.1	1 240	25.8	6.3	3 002	35.3	2.9	2 031	47.2	4.8
Washington Parish........	13 874	32.5	11.1	85	22.4	12.9	20	30.0	0.0	283	24.7	11.7	327	31.8	14.7
Webster Parish............	13 719	32.4	12.8	150	20.0	10.0	83	19.3	0.0	289	25.3	11.8	420	43.6	12.1
West Baton Rouge Parish..........................	7 659	31.0	9.7	55	25.5	3.6	2	0.0	0.0	288	31.9	3.5	204	28.9	4.4
West Carroll Parish......	2 371	29.2	9.5	18	22.2	0.0	23	21.7	0.0	107	14.0	5.6	71	39.4	4.2
West Feliciana Parish ...	7 594	17.3	5.5	44	31.8	0.0	21	19.0	0.0	186	9.1	12.9	84	54.8	3.6
Winn Parish.................	5 410	27.7	11.0	98	31.6	13.3	20	15.0	10.0	131	48.9	0.8	90	43.3	6.7
MAINE	6 047	35.1	3.9	7 521	32.0	5.6	8 560	31.3	5.1	9 226	37.3	4.2	13 736	39.9	5.9
Androscoggin County....	601	39.3	1.8	422	32.7	8.1	552	27.0	4.3	851	34.9	5.6	1 454	44.4	5.0
Aroostook County.........	224	35.3	3.1	1 040	45.3	1.6	408	29.2	2.2	345	34.8	1.7	569	39.0	3.0
Cumberland County	2 470	35.3	4.2	1 036	24.1	4.0	3 366	33.2	4.4	2 447	36.7	3.8	3 463	40.1	5.1
Franklin County	60	58.3	3.3	114	31.6	6.1	116	11.2	11.2	133	31.6	5.3	268	35.8	7.8
Hancock County	179	43.0	1.1	180	24.4	4.0	201	31.3	4.0	326	40.5	2.5	639	42.3	6.7
Kennebec County.........	410	34.1	7.4	457	28.7	10.9	662	28.7	4.2	651	40.4	3.2	1 333	33.4	7.1
Knox County	71	33.8	14.1	152	25.0	2.0	125	20.0	16.0	208	15.9	5.3	257	40.1	3.9
Lincoln County	30	40.0	6.7	96	34.4	5.2	127	34.6	7.1	147	56.5	8.8	237	43.0	3.4
Oxford County	53	41.5	0.0	215	41.4	10.2	257	36.6	5.4	386	40.7	10.4	512	38.9	3.1
Penobscot County........	676	24.0	4.9	1 355	29.0	5.0	1 066	29.5	6.0	830	35.9	4.1	1 391	35.9	7.5
Piscataquis County	36	27.8	22.2	95	25.3	11.6	40	32.5	0.0	85	50.6	0.0	167	40.7	7.2
Sagadahoc County.......	229	45.0	0.0	99	31.3	0.0	216	45.8	5.6	513	44.8	2.1	463	44.7	5.8
Somerset County	70	30.0	2.9	185	22.7	4.9	150	33.3	11.3	227	53.3	7.9	435	40.0	11.5
Waldo County	66	57.6	7.6	194	27.8	4.1	76	25.0	18.4	184	42.4	2.2	470	40.4	2.6
Washington County.......	111	18.0	2.7	1 386	38.3	5.1	180	30.0	5.6	302	33.8	1.0	422	42.7	7.6
York County	752	36.0	1.9	495	20.2	12.5	1 018	31.0	4.6	1 591	34.3	4.5	1 656	41.9	7.2
MARYLAND	1 468 243	29.5	7.4	15 651	23.5	6.3	211 743	23.6	6.5	227 105	31.3	3.5	113 055	42.2	4.1
Allegany County...........	4 006	12.2	4.4	116	12.9	12.9	454	33.5	4.2	639	21.4	5.2	606	50.3	7.6
Anne Arundel County....	65 280	28.8	7.1	1 533	27.3	3.5	11 632	23.4	5.9	13 191	32.9	3.2	9 311	47.8	2.5
Baltimore County..........	149 943	30.8	5.6	1 912	21.5	6.2	23 922	24.9	4.6	13 578	29.5	5.7	12 687	43.3	4.0
Calvert County	9 672	29.8	9.3	235	21.3	0.0	672	21.9	5.7	1 033	36.1	4.6	1 064	47.6	4.1
Caroline County	4 442	30.3	13.4	95	22.1	7.4	137	31.4	10.9	816	40.2	1.1	372	54.0	4.0
Carroll County	3 541	26.8	11.4	271	29.9	3.3	1 329	30.5	4.2	1 300	35.6	4.9	1 200	45.2	3.5
Cecil County	3 152	28.6	8.8	231	37.7	7.4	570	30.2	7.0	1 302	44.0	2.5	1 112	48.5	1.8
Charles County	31 425	32.9	5.9	1 114	23.9	4.0	1 906	28.6	5.9	2 660	41.2	3.5	2 650	49.3	1.7
Dorchester County	8 632	29.1	13.8	51	37.3	0.0	259	20.1	5.8	409	42.5	10.3	321	49.5	4.7
Frederick County	12 191	31.5	6.1	466	17.8	3.2	3 372	28.3	6.4	4 598	36.4	1.7	3 092	52.3	2.9
Garrett County.............	79	29.1	15.2	27	11.1	25.9	33	51.5	0.0	104	38.5	15.4	74	12.2	14.9
Harford County	19 831	33.3	6.8	657	25.4	3.7	3 306	28.0	4.3	3 965	35.4	3.8	3 782	52.2	2.4
Howard County	35 412	29.5	5.6	403	32.3	3.7	18 837	27.9	4.6	7 824	31.6	3.3	6 196	49.7	2.3
Kent County	3 316	27.2	16.1	45	22.2	0.0	100	6.0	1.0	534	21.2	2.2	262	41.2	0.0
Montgomery County......	130 849	28.6	6.1	2 593	23.3	6.6	98 483	23.6	7.3	100 309	30.4	3.8	32 250	39.8	4.5
Prince George's County	501 431	30.0	5.1	2 643	21.0	8.9	30 770	20.3	7.3	56 813	31.7	2.2	22 187	38.3	3.6
Queen Anne's County...	3 541	23.8	16.4	99	18.2	18.2	181	40.3	3.9	505	38.8	3.6	416	34.9	9.1
St. Mary's County	11 676	29.4	9.7	344	24.1	5.8	1 744	28.2	4.0	1 706	39.5	1.3	1 695	51.9	3.5
Somerset County	10 138	17.4	8.1	73	0.0	9.6	220	25.9	7.7	274	32.5	8.0	299	33.8	9.7
Talbot County..............	5 122	23.8	15.8	36	0.0	16.7	329	34.0	0.0	717	32.2	1.4	217	43.3	4.1

[1] Hispanic or Latino persons may be of any race.

Table A-3. States and Counties — Age, Ethnicity, and Household Structure

STATE County	Total households	Family households (percent)						Nonfamily households (percent)						Percent of householders 65 years and over who live alone	Grandparents who are responsible for the care of their grandchildren
		Married-couple family households			Other family households			Two or more unrelated persons		Male living alone		Female living alone			
		Total	With children	Householder 65 years or over	Total	With children	Householder 65 years or over	Total	Householder 65 years or over	Total	Householder 65 years or over	Total	Householder 65 years or over		
	29	30	31	32	33	34	35	36	37	38	39	40	41	42	43
LOUISIANA—Cont'd															
Pointe Coupee Parish...	8 453	54.8	25.8	9.5	18.8	9.9	3.9	3.4	0.4	11.0	3.1	12.1	7.2	42.6	458
Rapides Parish............	47 161	50.2	23.4	9.1	20.5	11.9	2.9	3.4	0.4	10.0	2.5	15.9	7.8	45.4	1 969
Red River Parish.........	3 409	51.4	23.4	10.0	22.7	13.0	3.7	2.9	0.9	9.9	3.8	13.1	8.2	45.0	222
Richland Parish	7 501	53.1	23.8	10.7	20.7	11.8	4.2	2.5	0.3	8.5	3.1	15.3	10.1	46.4	379
Sabine Parish..............	9 237	56.7	22.6	12.5	15.2	8.6	2.6	2.1	0.1	12.2	4.1	13.8	8.3	44.9	332
St. Bernard Parish........	25 065	54.0	24.0	9.9	19.3	9.5	3.8	3.8	0.3	8.8	2.8	14.1	7.7	42.9	832
St. Charles Parish	16 393	60.9	32.2	8.2	19.5	11.6	2.5	2.9	0.3	8.1	1.6	8.6	3.8	32.9	546
St. Helena Parish	3 865	49.3	21.7	8.6	22.5	11.6	5.6	2.6	0.3	13.1	3.2	12.6	6.2	39.5	332
St. James Parish..........	6 999	56.5	26.8	10.7	23.0	11.9	3.9	2.1	0.1	8.7	2.1	9.6	5.6	34.3	323
St. John the Baptist Parish	14 250	56.4	29.6	6.5	23.2	14.0	3.0	2.8	0.1	8.1	1.6	9.5	4.7	39.8	794
St. Landry Parish	32 332	50.1	24.0	9.4	22.2	12.7	3.8	2.4	0.3	11.3	2.9	14.1	8.5	46.0	1 437
St. Martin Parish	17 121	55.0	26.8	8.0	20.8	13.6	2.4	3.4	0.4	9.8	2.3	11.0	6.4	44.7	678
St. Mary Parish	19 271	51.4	25.0	8.1	21.7	13.0	3.1	3.6	0.2	10.4	2.6	12.9	6.9	45.4	915
St. Tammany Parish	69 281	62.2	31.2	8.4	14.2	8.5	1.9	3.9	0.3	8.4	1.7	11.3	5.1	39.0	1 667
Tangipahoa Parish	36 516	51.5	24.7	7.5	19.4	11.4	2.9	5.1	0.2	10.8	2.3	13.2	6.4	45.0	1 733
Tensas Parish	2 435	44.9	18.9	9.3	23.2	12.9	5.7	2.6	0.2	11.6	3.7	17.7	12.0	50.9	163
Terrebonne Parish	36 017	58.1	28.6	8.4	18.2	10.7	2.2	4.5	0.3	8.7	1.9	10.6	5.5	40.7	1 799
Union Parish.................	8 864	56.3	23.6	10.7	16.2	8.6	2.5	2.5	0.2	11.5	3.1	13.5	8.2	45.9	311
Vermilion Parish............	19 836	56.0	27.6	9.7	17.1	10.1	2.6	3.9	0.6	9.4	2.5	13.6	8.7	46.4	560
Vernon Parish	18 276	62.2	33.3	7.1	13.8	9.3	1.5	2.4	0.2	10.4	1.7	11.2	5.8	45.9	564
Washington Parish	16 454	49.2	21.3	10.4	21.7	11.3	4.2	2.5	0.2	10.5	2.8	16.1	9.3	45.1	821
Webster Parish.............	16 506	51.4	19.8	11.3	19.1	10.4	3.6	2.4	0.4	11.0	2.7	16.0	9.7	44.9	803
West Baton Rouge Parish	7 672	52.4	24.8	8.0	22.7	13.1	3.5	3.4	0.5	8.9	1.2	12.5	5.6	36.2	367
West Carroll Parish	4 468	59.1	25.4	11.5	13.9	7.8	2.1	2.4	0.4	8.4	3.0	16.2	10.9	50.0	162
West Feliciana Parish ...	3 622	56.9	28.5	7.9	18.2	11.3	3.4	1.8	0.1	11.1	2.3	12.0	4.6	37.7	219
Winn Parish.................	5 926	53.2	24.3	10.3	19.0	9.4	3.4	1.7	0.1	12.2	4.3	14.0	9.1	49.3	432
MAINE	518 372	53.4	22.5	9.8	12.7	8.2	1.6	7.0	0.6	11.0	2.7	16.0	8.2	47.6	5 074
Androscoggin County....	42 095	50.6	21.3	8.8	14.7	9.8	1.8	6.5	0.5	11.4	2.6	16.8	8.8	50.7	391
Aroostook County.........	30 317	56.2	21.6	12.1	11.4	7.2	1.8	4.7	0.5	11.3	3.2	16.4	9.7	47.2	259
Cumberland County	108 037	51.0	23.1	8.6	12.1	7.4	1.5	8.5	0.5	11.0	2.6	17.4	7.9	49.9	884
Franklin County	11 772	52.9	20.9	10.0	13.4	8.5	2.2	8.0	0.8	10.2	2.6	15.5	8.0	44.9	175
Hancock County	21 859	54.1	21.0	11.2	11.7	7.8	1.6	6.8	0.5	11.3	2.8	16.6	8.9	46.9	279
Kennebec County..........	47 738	51.9	22.3	9.4	13.9	9.4	1.7	6.6	0.5	11.3	2.7	16.3	8.2	48.3	353
Knox County................	16 608	53.0	20.6	11.8	11.9	8.4	1.3	6.1	0.7	11.1	3.2	17.9	10.0	49.0	145
Lincoln County	14 170	56.3	21.1	12.6	11.4	7.2	1.9	5.7	0.6	11.2	3.4	15.4	9.0	45.0	191
Oxford County	22 321	55.5	22.2	11.6	12.7	8.3	1.8	6.3	0.6	10.9	3.1	14.5	8.1	44.5	194
Penobscot County........	58 135	52.7	22.0	9.0	13.0	8.5	1.6	7.7	0.6	10.8	2.4	15.8	7.7	47.4	632
Piscataquis County	7 272	53.6	20.4	11.2	13.1	8.7	1.8	5.6	0.9	11.8	3.4	15.9	10.2	49.3	50
Sagadahoc County	14 159	55.2	24.2	8.6	13.3	9.0	1.7	6.2	0.4	11.0	2.1	14.2	7.3	46.9	119
Somerset County	20 519	55.3	23.0	10.1	13.6	8.9	1.9	6.6	0.8	11.2	2.7	13.3	7.4	44.1	169
Waldo County	14 724	56.1	22.3	10.0	12.5	8.6	1.5	6.5	0.9	10.6	2.4	14.3	7.3	43.8	154
Washington County.......	14 119	52.8	20.1	11.5	13.1	8.2	2.1	5.7	0.5	12.1	3.3	16.3	10.1	48.7	312
York County	74 527	56.4	24.7	9.7	11.9	7.6	1.4	6.8	0.6	10.4	2.6	14.5	7.3	45.9	767
MARYLAND	1 981 795	51.2	24.1	8.0	17.8	10.0	2.3	6.0	0.4	10.1	2.0	14.9	6.2	43.3	50 974
Allegany County	29 350	51.9	20.0	11.9	12.9	6.9	2.6	5.3	0.5	11.0	3.7	19.0	12.0	51.2	569
Anne Arundel County....	178 754	57.8	27.4	8.0	14.9	8.1	2.2	6.0	0.3	9.4	1.6	11.9	4.8	37.6	4 077
Baltimore County..........	300 020	50.5	22.0	10.3	16.1	8.9	2.4	6.1	0.4	10.3	2.3	16.9	8.0	43.9	6 087
Calvert County	25 428	65.4	34.5	7.4	14.1	8.2	2.0	4.2	0.3	7.7	1.6	8.7	4.2	37.6	502
Caroline County	11 098	54.4	23.7	9.8	19.0	11.0	2.6	5.1	0.5	8.9	2.3	12.6	7.0	42.0	350
Carroll County	52 601	67.8	33.7	8.8	11.0	6.7	1.4	3.8	0.2	6.8	1.7	10.7	6.0	42.3	627
Cecil County	31 257	59.9	28.5	7.9	14.8	9.5	1.8	5.4	0.5	9.6	2.2	10.4	5.0	41.4	744
Charles County	41 675	59.2	30.2	6.3	18.8	11.6	1.7	4.9	0.3	7.9	1.3	9.2	3.8	38.1	1 245
Dorchester County	12 712	49.6	17.8	11.7	17.9	10.2	3.2	4.4	0.3	10.6	3.3	17.4	10.3	47.2	351
Frederick County...........	70 115	62.3	31.5	7.5	12.2	7.5	1.6	5.4	0.3	8.6	1.5	11.5	5.2	41.8	912
Garrett County.............	11 470	61.1	26.0	11.7	12.2	7.3	2.0	3.2	0.3	10.1	2.8	13.3	7.1	41.4	194
Harford County	79 748	62.7	31.4	8.4	13.5	7.8	1.9	4.1	0.2	8.1	1.4	11.7	5.4	39.1	1 411
Howard County	90 102	61.1	33.3	5.5	12.5	7.7	1.1	5.6	0.2	9.0	1.1	11.7	3.5	40.0	1 220
Kent County	7 674	52.6	17.5	14.5	14.6	9.2	2.3	5.1	0.4	10.9	2.9	16.7	10.3	43.5	191
Montgomery County......	324 940	56.1	28.4	8.4	13.4	7.2	1.5	6.1	0.4	8.9	1.7	15.5	6.0	43.0	4 100
Prince George's County	286 650	44.9	22.1	5.6	24.7	14.0	2.1	6.3	0.3	9.9	1.3	14.1	3.7	38.3	10 508
Queen Anne's County...	15 346	63.7	26.8	11.3	11.9	7.5	1.4	4.9	0.4	8.5	2.3	11.0	5.5	37.4	303
St. Mary's County	30 736	59.2	30.4	7.3	14.3	9.0	1.5	5.4	0.3	10.8	1.6	10.3	4.3	38.9	789
Somerset County	8 366	46.2	16.8	10.9	19.6	10.2	4.0	4.7	0.3	13.0	4.1	16.4	8.3	45.0	295
Talbot County..............	14 320	54.8	19.7	14.8	12.5	6.7	2.6	4.8	0.6	10.0	2.9	17.9	10.7	43.0	364

Table A-3. States and Counties — Age, Ethnicity, and Household Structure

STATE County	Households with Non-Hispanic White householder		Households with Black or African American householder		Households with American Indian and Alaska Native householder		Households with Asian, Hawaiian, and Pacific Islander householder		Households with Hispanic or Latino[1] householder		Foreign-born population	Place of birth (percent)			Percent in non-English speaking households	
	Number of households	Percent that are family households	Number of households	Percent that are family households	Number of households	Percent that are family households	Number of households	Percent that are family households	Number of households	Percent that are family households	Percent of total population that is foreign-born	Europe	Asia	Latin America	Linguistically isolated	Not linguistically isolated
	44	45	46	47	48	49	50	51	52	53	54	55	56	57	58	59
LOUISIANA—Cont'd																
Pointe Coupee Parish ...	5 479	74.3	2 841	72.6	23	69.6	29	13.8	55	50.9	0.9	0.1	0.2	0.5	0.8	10.5
Rapides Parish	33 111	69.7	12 728	73.7	256	68.0	297	81.8	362	65.7	1.6	0.3	0.7	0.4	0.7	8.7
Red River Parish	2 121	72.2	1 226	78.7	10	100.0	0	X	30	40.0	0.4	0.1	0.0	0.3	0.2	4.3
Richland Parish	4 909	74.3	2 506	72.6	3	0.0	9	100.0	59	86.4	0.5	0.0	0.3	0.2	0.0	5.1
Sabine Parish	6 916	71.7	1 304	73.1	635	72.9	29	86.2	235	70.6	1.0	0.1	0.3	0.5	0.5	5.3
St. Bernard Parish........	21 781	72.6	1 431	75.7	145	89.7	277	85.2	1 244	80.5	3.0	0.4	1.2	1.4	1.2	11.2
St. Charles Parish	11 893	81.6	3 952	76.1	33	51.5	78	100.0	364	90.4	2.5	0.4	0.6	1.1	0.9	12.1
St. Helena Parish	1 974	70.4	1 835	72.9	0	X	1	100.0	56	85.7	0.3	0.0	0.0	0.2	0.0	5.6
St. James Parish	3 783	77.8	3 170	81.6	12	100.0	7	71.4	24	58.3	0.2	0.1	0.1	0.0	0.9	11.5
St. John the Baptist Parish	8 136	76.5	5 646	83.2	35	100.0	72	83.3	312	91.0	2.3	0.2	0.6	1.5	0.9	10.3
St. Landry Parish	19 129	72.1	12 684	72.6	35	48.6	68	82.4	228	77.2	0.5	0.1	0.2	0.1	2.7	28.5
St. Martin Parish	11 822	75.6	4 975	77.0	61	78.7	85	82.4	100	49.0	0.9	0.2	0.5	0.2	4.3	42.3
St. Mary Parish	12 601	72.7	5 446	75.2	309	72.5	239	80.3	391	77.7	2.0	0.2	0.9	0.9	1.4	15.9
St. Tammany Parish	60 598	76.3	5 903	76.8	278	75.5	317	84.5	1 401	80.4	2.4	0.7	0.5	0.9	0.5	9.6
Tangipahoa Parish........	26 450	70.4	9 163	72.3	154	67.5	87	70.1	399	72.7	0.8	0.2	0.2	0.4	0.4	7.1
Tensas Parish	1 172	69.3	1 214	66.1	5	100.0	2	100.0	29	96.6	1.2	0.1	0.1	1.1	1.1	5.6
Terrebonne Parish	27 808	75.9	5 669	74.7	1 322	90.3	226	80.1	477	74.0	1.5	0.2	0.6	0.5	1.7	22.6
Union Parish................	6 479	73.5	2 244	68.8	33	69.7	2	100.0	102	98.0	1.2	0.1	0.0	1.0	0.8	4.1
Vermilion Parish	16 751	72.5	2 559	75.4	55	94.5	230	86.1	177	77.4	2.0	0.2	1.4	0.4	4.4	39.1
Vernon Parish	13 885	74.9	2 687	74.7	240	79.6	349	86.8	755	89.9	4.1	1.4	1.5	1.1	0.7	14.1
Washington Parish	11 556	71.8	4 615	69.1	48	47.9	14	50.0	109	71.6	0.4	0.1	0.1	0.2	0.2	5.1
Webster Parish	11 220	72.3	4 998	66.5	66	48.5	29	72.4	72	77.8	0.7	0.3	0.1	0.2	0.2	5.0
West Baton Rouge Parish	5 184	74.2	2 375	77.3	23	47.8	0	X	64	71.9	0.9	0.1	0.0	0.7	0.5	10.1
West Carroll Parish	3 791	73.3	632	70.3	6	100.0	0	X	27	88.9	0.3	0.1	0.1	0.1	0.0	5.6
West Feliciana Parish ...	2 332	76.6	1 221	74.0	20	60.0	12	33.3	39	76.9	0.5	0.2	0.1	0.1	0.1	10.8
Winn Parish..................	4 260	74.2	1 589	67.1	26	80.8	0	X	24	62.5	0.5	0.2	0.1	0.3	0.1	4.1
MAINE	505 297	66.1	1 886	63.3	2 727	64.1	2 168	70.9	2 308	69.3	2.9	0.9	0.5	0.2	1.0	11.8
Androscoggin County....	41 027	65.3	232	62.5	173	68.8	86	86.0	221	60.2	2.6	0.6	0.4	0.2	2.3	23.6
Aroostook County.........	29 657	67.7	37	43.2	292	64.7	107	78.5	69	82.6	5.8	0.4	0.4	0.1	3.5	28.5
Cumberland County	104 283	63.1	834	65.6	405	53.1	916	70.1	617	60.8	3.8	1.4	1.2	0.3	0.9	8.8
Franklin County	11 564	66.4	11	36.4	31	67.7	37	100.0	30	86.7	1.6	0.5	0.4	0.1	0.2	8.6
Hancock County............	21 465	65.4	52	50.0	57	59.6	62	48.4	73	72.6	2.3	1.0	0.3	0.2	0.2	6.9
Kennebec County..........	46 770	65.8	93	68.8	161	70.8	162	75.9	124	79.8	2.2	0.5	0.5	0.1	1.0	12.3
Knox County	16 388	64.8	16	25.0	40	80.0	43	65.1	61	75.4	2.1	1.1	0.2	0.1	0.2	6.4
Lincoln County	13 985	67.6	10	80.0	39	74.4	36	63.9	27	85.2	2.0	1.1	0.3	0.1	0.1	6.1
Oxford County	21 955	68.4	16	100.0	77	66.2	53	45.3	84	73.8	1.8	0.6	0.4	0.2	0.3	8.3
Penobscot County........	56 411	65.8	209	52.2	540	62.8	272	74.3	214	57.0	2.5	0.7	0.6	0.1	0.5	8.1
Piscataquis County	7 132	66.5	11	81.8	44	72.7	6	100.0	20	80.0	1.9	0.5	0.1	0.2	0.2	6.6
Sagadahoc County.......	13 786	68.8	65	61.5	42	42.9	57	47.4	122	54.9	2.4	1.2	0.5	0.2	0.6	7.8
Somerset County	20 202	68.7	25	76.0	84	67.9	23	100.0	46	80.4	1.7	0.6	0.1	0.1	0.3	8.2
Waldo County	14 400	68.9	15	53.3	77	64.9	9	55.6	63	57.1	1.7	0.8	0.2	0.1	0.1	7.0
Washington County	13 395	65.8	29	89.7	461	70.3	46	65.2	71	59.2	4.1	0.6	0.4	0.3	0.5	8.2
York County	72 877	68.3	231	66.2	204	61.3	253	71.1	466	82.8	2.8	1.0	0.4	0.2	1.1	14.7
MARYLAND	1 302 282	68.3	525 794	68.7	5 812	71.6	65 010	78.1	59 669	79.6	9.8	1.6	3.4	3.3	2.6	15.3
Allegany County...........	28 395	64.9	585	57.8	46	54.3	116	87.1	111	83.8	1.2	0.3	0.4	0.4	0.3	5.0
Anne Arundel County....	148 107	72.5	21 615	73.1	583	66.6	3 511	72.1	3 391	79.2	4.7	1.3	1.8	1.1	1.1	11.6
Baltimore County..........	228 409	65.7	55 951	68.8	780	68.5	7 659	78.5	4 350	66.6	7.1	2.2	2.8	1.3	1.9	12.9
Calvert County	21 425	79.3	3 168	80.5	84	84.5	179	92.7	227	87.2	2.2	0.7	0.6	0.6	0.3	9.1
Caroline County	9 161	74.2	1 682	68.8	31	29.0	23	73.9	153	79.7	2.5	0.5	0.4	1.4	1.3	6.9
Carroll County	50 533	78.7	1 110	78.2	63	95.2	294	86.7	314	90.1	2.0	0.9	0.7	0.2	0.3	8.6
Cecil County	29 205	74.9	1 211	66.9	77	61.0	162	94.4	337	86.1	1.8	0.8	0.5	0.3	0.3	8.3
Charles County	29 096	77.5	10 536	78.5	373	86.3	419	85.4	730	82.3	2.9	0.8	1.2	0.7	0.3	10.2
Dorchester County	9 092	67.8	3 382	65.3	11	63.6	78	100.0	103	86.4	2.0	0.6	0.7	0.5	0.6	6.3
Frederick County..........	62 874	74.6	4 182	73.2	214	47.2	846	80.3	1 400	73.5	4.0	1.3	1.5	0.9	0.7	9.0
Garrett County..............	11 393	73.4	7	0.0	7	0.0	10	90.0	34	70.6	0.8	0.5	0.1	0.1	0.3	6.4
Harford County	69 674	76.5	7 021	72.5	266	86.5	864	82.2	1 185	79.3	3.4	1.4	1.1	0.6	0.6	10.1
Howard County	67 748	73.1	13 011	71.8	145	82.1	5 642	84.2	2 229	74.8	11.3	1.8	6.2	2.1	2.5	17.2
Kent County	6 161	66.9	1 330	67.4	15	86.7	13	0.0	115	83.5	2.9	0.8	0.3	1.6	0.7	6.2
Montgomery County......	213 637	66.3	47 781	67.4	865	70.1	30 740	81.9	25 750	85.1	26.7	3.7	10.2	9.4	7.0	31.2
Prince George's County...	79 894	62.9	179 325	71.3	995	74.8	8 637	78.0	13 557	82.2	13.8	0.8	3.2	6.8	4.2	18.4
Queen Anne's County...	13 701	76.7	1 280	64.8	44	100.0	42	71.4	130	84.6	2.4	0.8	0.7	0.6	0.6	8.2
St. Mary's County.........	25 198	73.8	4 326	71.1	135	90.4	401	73.8	429	85.3	2.8	0.7	1.4	0.5	0.7	10.5
Somerset County	5 634	67.7	2 503	62.6	23	73.9	69	91.3	61	55.7	2.5	0.3	0.8	0.7	0.6	7.0
Talbot County...............	11 911	68.3	2 084	60.4	11	100.0	77	70.1	198	68.7	3.3	1.3	0.6	1.3	1.0	8.0

[1]Hispanic or Latino persons may be of any race.

STATE/ County code	MSA/PMSA/ NECMA code[1]	STATE County	Total population	Under 5 years	5 to 17 years	18 to 24 years	25 to 44 years	45 to 64 years	65 years and over	Median age	+/− U.S. percent under 18 years	+/− U.S. percent 65 years and over	Non-Hispanic White Total population	Under 18 years	65 years and over
			1	2	3	4	5	6	7	8	9	10	11	12	13
		MARYLAND—Cont'd													
24 043	3180	Washington County........	131 923	6.2	17.3	8.1	31.4	23.0	14.2	37.4	-2.2	1.8	117 803	23.2	15.4
24 045	...	Wicomico County	84 644	6.1	18.6	12.0	28.0	22.5	12.8	35.8	-1.0	0.4	60 650	21.6	14.3
24 047	...	Worcester County	46 543	4.9	15.6	6.2	26.3	26.8	20.2	43.0	-5.2	7.8	37 467	18.4	21.8
24 510	0720	Baltimore city	651 154	6.4	18.3	10.8	30.1	21.1	13.2	35.0	-1.0	0.8	201 881	15.8	19.1
25 000	...	MASSACHUSETTS	6 349 097	6.2	17.3	9.1	31.4	22.3	13.5	36.5	-2.2	1.1	5 197 124	21.7	15.4
25 001	0743	Barnstable County	222 230	4.8	15.7	5.3	25.0	26.1	23.1	44.6	-5.2	10.7	207 587	19.7	24.1
25 003	6323	Berkshire County	134 953	5.2	17.3	8.4	26.3	24.9	18.0	40.5	-3.2	5.6	127 054	21.6	18.7
25 005	1123	Bristol County	534 678	6.3	18.2	8.5	30.7	22.1	14.2	36.7	-1.2	1.8	478 074	23.4	15.1
25 007	...	Dukes County	14 987	5.6	17.1	5.9	29.0	28.1	14.2	40.7	-3.0	1.8	13 393	22.4	15.0
25 009	1123	Essex County	723 419	6.6	18.5	7.6	30.4	23.1	13.9	37.5	-0.6	1.5	601 218	22.7	15.9
25 011	...	Franklin County	71 535	5.1	18.3	7.9	28.4	25.9	14.3	39.5	-2.3	1.9	67 840	22.8	14.8
25 013	8003	Hampden County	456 228	6.5	19.5	9.2	28.6	21.8	14.5	36.4	0.3	2.1	339 244	21.4	17.9
25 015	8003	Hampshire County	152 251	4.4	15.1	19.3	27.0	22.2	12.0	34.4	-6.2	-0.4	136 253	19.0	13.0
25 017	1123	Middlesex County	1 465 396	6.3	16.1	8.9	33.6	22.3	12.8	36.4	-3.3	0.4	1 224 516	21.3	14.4
25 019	...	Nantucket County	9 520	5.7	13.7	7.4	39.8	23.1	10.4	36.7	-6.3	-2.0	8 188	20.0	11.6
25 021	1123	Norfolk County	650 308	6.4	17.0	7.0	31.7	23.5	14.4	38.1	-2.3	2.0	571 701	22.8	15.6
25 023	1123	Plymouth County	472 822	7.0	19.8	7.1	30.5	23.9	11.8	36.8	1.1	-0.6	414 611	25.5	12.7
25 025	1123	Suffolk County...............	689 807	5.5	14.6	15.2	35.5	18.1	11.1	31.7	-5.6	-1.3	358 445	11.6	15.5
25 027	1123	Worcester County...........	750 963	6.6	18.9	8.4	31.2	21.8	13.0	36.3	-0.2	0.6	649 000	23.9	14.6
26 000	...	MICHIGAN	9 938 444	6.7	19.3	9.4	29.9	22.4	12.3	35.5	0.3	-0.1	7 805 325	24.1	13.7
26 001	...	Alcona County	11 719	4.4	14.8	4.4	20.9	31.0	24.5	49.0	-6.5	12.1	11 365	18.5	25.0
26 003	...	Alger County	9 862	4.4	16.1	6.9	29.2	26.4	17.1	41.2	-5.2	4.7	8 607	20.4	19.3
26 005	3000	Allegan County..............	105 665	7.2	21.5	7.9	30.2	22.0	11.1	35.2	3.0	-1.3	95 730	27.6	11.8
26 007	...	Alpena County	31 314	5.5	18.2	8.0	26.3	24.9	17.1	40.4	-2.0	4.7	30 506	23.3	17.4
26 009	...	Antrim County	23 110	5.6	18.7	6.3	25.1	26.7	17.6	41.1	-1.4	5.2	22 298	23.8	18.0
26 011	...	Arenac County	17 269	5.3	17.9	8.1	26.6	25.6	16.5	40.1	-2.5	4.1	16 307	23.1	17.2
26 013	...	Baraga County	8 746	5.4	17.4	7.5	28.6	24.8	16.3	39.0	-2.9	3.9	6 846	21.4	19.4
26 015	...	Barry County	56 755	6.8	20.4	7.4	29.1	24.6	11.7	36.9	1.5	-0.7	54 829	26.7	12.0
26 017	6960	Bay County	110 157	6.1	18.3	8.3	28.2	24.4	14.7	38.4	-1.3	2.3	102 198	23.2	15.4
26 019	...	Benzie County	15 998	5.9	17.4	6.2	27.1	25.9	17.5	40.8	-2.4	5.1	15 219	22.7	18.0
26 021	0870	Berrien County	162 453	6.5	19.4	8.4	27.5	23.6	14.5	37.4	0.2	2.1	127 017	22.8	16.6
26 023	...	Branch County	45 787	6.3	19.3	8.3	30.1	23.1	13.0	36.7	-0.1	0.6	42 194	25.7	13.9
26 025	3720	Calhoun County	137 985	6.5	19.4	8.8	28.6	23.0	13.8	36.4	0.2	1.4	113 765	23.9	15.1
26 027	...	Cass County	51 104	6.1	19.5	7.3	27.5	26.0	13.6	38.5	-0.1	1.2	45 314	24.4	13.8
26 029	...	Charlevoix County	26 090	6.6	19.4	6.8	27.2	25.2	14.8	39.1	0.3	2.4	25 029	25.3	15.2
26 031	...	Cheboygan County	26 448	5.9	17.8	6.2	25.9	26.4	17.9	41.3	-2.0	5.5	24 937	22.7	18.6
26 033	...	Chippewa County...........	38 543	5.3	16.0	12.0	32.0	21.9	12.7	36.2	-4.4	0.3	28 924	18.7	15.4
26 035	...	Clare County	31 252	5.8	18.7	7.3	24.7	26.2	17.3	40.5	-1.2	4.9	30 205	24.1	17.6
26 037	4040	Clinton County	64 753	6.9	21.2	7.3	29.3	24.6	10.8	36.7	2.4	-1.6	61 241	27.3	11.2
26 039	...	Crawford County	14 273	5.6	18.8	6.4	26.6	26.0	16.6	40.6	-1.3	4.2	13 622	24.2	17.2
26 041	...	Delta County	38 520	5.3	18.5	7.8	26.1	25.2	17.1	40.4	-1.9	4.7	36 698	23.0	17.6
26 043	...	Dickinson County	27 472	5.6	19.5	6.3	27.0	23.4	18.1	40.0	-0.6	5.7	26 796	24.5	18.5
26 045	4040	Eaton County	103 655	6.3	19.8	9.2	28.7	24.7	11.3	36.4	0.4	-1.1	91 863	25.1	12.2
26 047	...	Emmet County	31 437	6.2	19.1	7.0	28.1	25.2	14.3	38.9	-0.4	1.9	29 617	24.9	14.7
26 049	2640	Genesee County	436 141	7.2	20.1	9.0	29.8	22.3	11.6	35.0	1.6	-0.8	323 422	24.4	13.1
26 051	...	Gladwin County	26 023	5.5	17.7	6.4	24.3	27.7	18.3	42.3	-2.5	5.9	25 276	23.1	18.6
26 053	...	Gogebic County	17 370	4.6	15.9	8.6	24.0	24.2	22.6	42.9	-5.2	10.2	16 335	20.0	23.7
26 055	...	Grand Traverse County ..	77 654	6.2	19.2	7.9	29.6	24.1	13.1	37.7	-0.3	0.7	74 187	24.9	13.5
26 057	...	Gratiot County	42 285	5.9	17.8	11.6	29.6	21.5	13.5	35.6	-2.0	1.1	38 045	24.0	14.7
26 059	...	Hillsdale County	46 527	6.5	19.8	10.1	26.9	23.5	13.3	36.5	0.6	0.9	45 046	25.9	13.6
26 061	...	Houghton County	36 016	5.4	16.5	19.1	22.5	21.0	15.5	34.0	-3.8	3.1	34 260	21.7	16.2
26 063	...	Huron County	36 079	5.5	18.8	6.5	25.0	24.7	19.5	41.2	-1.4	7.1	34 920	23.8	19.9
26 065	4040	Ingham County	279 320	6.3	17.1	18.3	29.0	19.9	9.4	30.4	-2.3	-3.0	214 792	20.3	11.0
26 067	...	Ionia County	61 518	6.8	20.1	11.6	31.1	20.4	10.0	32.9	1.2	-2.4	56 007	27.9	10.9
26 069	...	Iosco County	27 339	4.8	17.6	5.4	23.4	27.4	21.5	44.2	-3.3	9.1	26 315	21.9	22.1
26 071	...	Iron County	13 138	4.3	16.2	5.8	22.9	25.5	25.1	45.4	-5.2	12.7	12 610	20.3	25.9
26 073	...	Isabella County	63 351	5.3	15.1	29.6	23.6	17.4	9.0	25.1	-5.3	-3.4	57 335	19.4	9.6
26 075	3520	Jackson County...........	158 422	6.6	19.0	8.2	30.3	22.9	12.9	36.6	-0.1	0.5	138 631	24.7	13.8
26 077	3720	Kalamazoo County........	238 603	6.4	17.6	15.2	28.4	21.1	11.3	32.7	-1.7	-1.1	199 058	21.8	12.7
26 079	...	Kalkaska County	16 571	6.5	19.1	7.6	28.6	24.4	13.8	38.0	-0.1	1.4	16 075	25.3	14.1
26 081	3000	Kent County	574 335	7.7	20.6	10.5	31.2	19.7	10.4	32.5	2.6	-2.0	461 310	25.8	12.0
26 083	...	Keweenaw County	2 301	4.6	17.9	6.5	21.0	29.8	20.2	44.9	-3.2	7.8	2 186	20.4	21.2
26 085	...	Lake County	11 333	5.2	16.7	7.8	22.4	28.2	19.6	43.1	-3.8	7.2	9 525	20.4	20.5
26 087	2160	Lapeer County	87 904	6.7	21.5	7.6	30.9	23.8	9.5	35.9	2.5	-2.9	83 307	27.7	9.9

[1]MSA = Metropolitan Statistical Area. PMSA = Primary MSA. NECMA = New England County Metropolitan Area. See the Appendix A for explanation of these concepts. See Appendix B for list of metropolitan areas identified by type, with component counties.

Table A-3. States and Counties — Age, Ethnicity, and Household Structure

STATE County	Black or African American Total population	Under 18 years	65 years and over	American Indian and Alaska Native Total population	Under 18 years	65 years and over	Asian, Hawaiian, and Pacific Islander Total population	Under 18 years	65 years and over	Hispanic or Latino[1] Total population	Under 18 years	65 years and over	Two or more races Total population	Under 18 years	65 years and over
	14	15	16	17	18	19	20	21	22	23	24	25	26	27	28
MARYLAND—Cont'd															
Washington County......	10 112	19.4	2.9	220	20.9	2.7	1 024	23.3	7.7	1 497	42.7	3.4	1 445	53.7	5.0
Wicomico County	19 613	32.9	9.6	145	9.7	9.7	1 768	25.3	6.1	1 640	29.1	3.8	1 016	51.4	4.4
Worcester County	7 608	28.3	14.7	95	9.5	0.0	311	27.3	12.2	590	26.8	11.2	613	44.2	7.5
Baltimore city...............	417 231	29.1	10.9	2 247	26.0	8.0	10 384	15.1	6.4	11 101	26.7	5.2	10 188	32.4	7.1
MASSACHUSETTS ...	337 157	31.4	6.8	15 305	27.9	6.6	240 081	24.6	5.2	427 340	36.3	3.0	154 532	36.4	5.3
Barnstable County........	3 397	22.7	11.0	1 448	35.6	12.4	1 395	27.4	7.9	2 916	35.9	5.8	4 045	35.6	9.0
Berkshire County..........	2 704	34.5	6.4	153	22.2	21.6	1 293	26.8	1.9	2 223	35.4	4.4	1 764	47.7	8.3
Bristol County	10 814	37.4	5.4	1 191	20.7	5.4	7 436	31.5	6.6	18 998	40.9	2.8	13 243	34.9	8.0
Dukes County	315	13.3	19.4	217	30.0	11.5	108	46.3	0.0	201	46.3	4.0	481	23.9	4.4
Essex County	17 868	33.5	4.8	1 623	33.0	7.6	17 483	32.0	4.5	79 629	38.4	2.8	16 536	40.6	5.3
Franklin County	531	27.3	16.0	169	26.0	2.4	652	24.4	7.4	1 227	36.9	4.6	1 086	41.2	3.0
Hampden County	36 662	34.9	7.5	1 024	24.9	3.3	6 258	27.3	5.1	69 046	42.9	2.8	11 543	44.0	4.9
Hampshire County	3 000	21.8	2.3	341	33.4	6.5	4 909	14.0	2.9	5 123	27.8	3.0	3 189	33.8	3.3
Middlesex County.........	48 093	27.3	6.8	2 643	24.4	6.7	92 080	24.7	4.3	66 436	31.2	2.7	33 826	34.4	4.0
Nantucket County.........	731	6.3	1.6	0	X	X	129	20.9	4.7	206	18.9	0.0	128	14.8	7.8
Norfolk County	19 931	29.8	5.7	926	23.0	4.5	36 272	24.0	5.6	11 533	27.5	4.9	9 649	40.4	5.2
Plymouth County	21 586	36.0	4.6	956	24.6	5.6	4 581	33.3	5.4	11 519	38.0	3.2	12 039	38.9	5.8
Suffolk County	150 969	31.3	7.8	3 010	32.3	6.5	48 342	18.4	7.9	107 352	32.4	3.4	32 342	28.8	5.1
Worcester County	20 556	31.5	4.3	1 604	25.1	3.4	19 143	31.1	2.7	50 931	39.5	2.4	14 661	43.5	5.2
MICHIGAN	1 401 723	32.1	8.5	60 842	31.1	5.2	177 493	26.9	3.9	322 160	37.6	4.0	207 041	44.6	4.5
Alcona County	18	22.2	0.0	75	56.0	8.0	30	43.3	0.0	102	47.1	9.8	133	32.3	15.8
Alger County	571	0.0	0.0	402	42.8	2.7	38	28.9	0.0	74	31.1	2.7	204	36.8	6.9
Allegan County	1 441	36.1	10.3	537	27.9	7.8	595	43.5	5.2	6 325	41.9	2.0	1 438	44.4	7.3
Alpena County	119	38.7	0.0	207	31.9	9.7	120	26.7	0.0	122	43.4	6.6	263	54.8	3.8
Antrim County	48	37.5	8.3	240	35.0	3.8	61	57.4	8.2	219	39.7	5.5	259	39.4	9.7
Arenac County	317	1.3	0.0	146	18.5	11.0	74	43.2	4.1	216	39.8	6.1	241	36.1	9.1
Baraga County	387	1.3	0.5	1 059	37.8	5.0	27	3.7	0.0	84	13.1	4.8	404	28.5	9.7
Barry County	201	16.9	5.0	308	40.9	0.0	123	30.9	0.0	654	48.3	1.2	699	50.5	2.3
Bay County..................	1 374	33.8	8.2	583	25.9	2.4	623	34.3	3.4	4 186	38.1	4.6	1 787	53.6	3.8
Benzie County	28	57.1	0.0	296	27.4	10.5	25	16.0	8.0	270	44.1	5.9	189	37.6	4.2
Berrien County	25 946	37.3	8.0	786	28.8	5.9	1 732	28.1	3.1	4 569	35.0	4.6	2 725	46.7	7.0
Branch County	1 015	4.0	0.0	205	27.3	3.4	244	44.7	3.3	1 310	28.7	2.0	927	35.8	3.5
Calhoun County	14 784	32.7	9.7	1 019	32.1	4.4	1 481	26.4	2.5	4 367	41.6	4.0	3 152	47.7	5.6
Cass County	2 831	27.8	17.8	392	40.8	4.1	326	28.2	7.7	1 177	44.4	5.2	1 242	48.0	7.3
Charlevoix County........	47	29.8	0.0	389	34.4	5.4	80	46.3	2.5	273	46.9	8.4	275	54.5	3.3
Cheboygan County	42	50.0	14.3	766	35.6	5.6	86	37.2	15.1	210	41.0	6.2	425	42.4	5.2
Chippewa County.........	2 038	0.7	0.6	6 138	00.1	0.2	214	32.2	3.7	630	27.3	2.1	1 812	36.0	5.4
Clare County	91	16.5	18.7	190	24.2	5.3	104	33.7	13.5	340	41.8	6.2	410	43.2	3.2
Clinton County.............	260	31.5	6.2	373	35.9	1.6	375	39.2	0.5	1 823	40.2	4.7	840	50.8	1.8
Crawford County	229	6.1	0.0	93	28.0	16.1	107	50.5	1.9	165	56.4	0.6	97	33.0	11.3
Delta County	39	20.5	15.4	1 021	40.4	4.3	108	42.6	9.3	163	52.1	6.7	502	33.7	10.0
Dickinson County	59	25.4	0.0	112	37.5	4.5	179	40.8	0.0	143	53.1	0.0	184	63.6	6.0
Eaton County	5 149	30.8	4.3	424	31.8	3.8	1 240	25.4	3.7	3 163	38.0	2.5	2 288	49.5	2.0
Emmet County	123	26.0	4.1	1 058	32.8	9.5	79	21.5	0.0	253	34.0	4.7	374	35.3	1.1
Genesee County	87 757	34.8	8.0	2 708	30.2	3.8	3 293	24.5	3.0	10 140	40.8	4.5	10 466	47.4	4.0
Gladwin County	24	41.7	0.0	128	13.3	8.6	47	8.5	10.6	229	36.7	7.4	301	26.2	10.6
Gogebic County	311	7.1	0.0	330	39.4	4.5	42	50.0	21.4	132	40.9	4.5	256	33.6	13.3
Grand Traverse County .	362	40.1	0.0	908	35.5	6.8	301	34.2	2.7	924	34.2	1.6	1 021	39.3	2.5
Gratiot County	1 648	3.0	0.0	221	15.4	3.6	179	19.0	1.1	1 814	36.4	4.6	637	37.8	3.3
Hillsdale County	243	38.3	2.1	158	40.5	1.9	173	20.8	5.8	525	39.4	4.4	411	47.7	6.1
Houghton County	385	17.4	0.0	207	27.1	3.9	529	21.9	0.6	264	35.2	0.0	395	35.7	5.3
Huron County	58	44.8	3.4	131	34.4	1.5	99	31.3	9.1	520	37.9	7.7	377	44.8	6.4
Ingham County	29 909	32.7	5.2	1 666	25.4	3.1	10 173	23.2	2.8	16 004	36.3	3.6	8 863	51.8	2.3
Ionia County................	2 754	1.9	0.8	272	23.2	2.2	224	33.5	2.7	1 483	33.9	1.3	966	33.3	2.7
Iosco County	124	36.3	0.0	199	21.6	9.5	50	22.0	0.0	214	36.4	9.8	466	38.6	4.1
Iron County..................	114	2.6	0.0	142	41.5	0.0	21	0.0	42.9	101	32.7	5.9	156	34.0	12.8
Isabella County	1 277	17.8	2.3	1 750	36.9	3.6	837	18.5	1.3	1 498	34.8	4.5	997	42.3	1.9
Jackson County............	12 000	26.7	7.0	677	38.4	5.0	770	27.5	5.8	3 723	39.5	5.2	2 972	52.9	4.9
Kalamazoo County........	21 748	34.7	5.2	1 094	21.8	4.7	4 526	19.2	4.5	6 476	38.5	2.4	6 276	48.7	4.3
Kalkaska County	39	35.9	5.1	180	32.2	2.2	34	38.2	8.8	125	46.4	0.0	170	38.2	8.2
Kent County.................	51 480	36.9	5.6	3 209	29.5	4.4	10 822	32.1	3.2	40 018	38.7	2.0	12 884	50.8	2.7
Keweenaw County	60	61.7	0.0	9	100.0	0.0	1	0.0	0.0	27	74.1	7.4	25	48.0	0.0
Lake County	1 210	25.3	19.8	134	25.4	6.0	23	13.0	4.3	178	51.1	6.7	341	48.4	3.5
Lapeer County	654	8.4	0.6	444	34.9	2.3	182	22.0	6.6	2 538	41.7	3.0	1 064	46.3	4.2

[1]Hispanic or Latino persons may be of any race.

Table A-3. States and Counties — Age, Ethnicity, and Household Structure

STATE County	Total households	Family households (percent) — Married-couple family households			Family households (percent) — Other family households			Nonfamily households (percent) — Two or more unrelated persons		Nonfamily households (percent) — Male living alone		Nonfamily households (percent) — Female living alone		Percent of householders 65 years and over who live alone	Grandparents who are responsible for the care of their grandchildren
		Total	With children	Householder 65 years or over	Total	With children	Householder 65 years or over	Total	Householder 65 years or over	Total	Householder 65 years or over	Total	Householder 65 years or over		
	29	30	31	32	33	34	35	36	37	38	39	40	41	42	43
MARYLAND—Cont'd															
Washington County	49 708	55.5	23.5	10.4	13.4	8.3	1.7	5.2	0.4	10.5	2.9	15.5	8.5	47.8	979
Wicomico County	32 231	50.1	21.4	9.0	17.9	11.2	2.0	7.2	0.4	9.0	2.1	15.9	7.9	46.8	898
Worcester County	19 706	53.8	17.4	15.4	14.3	7.9	2.3	5.8	0.9	11.4	3.3	14.8	8.4	38.8	551
Baltimore city	257 788	28.0	10.7	6.1	29.5	15.4	4.5	7.6	0.7	14.6	3.3	20.3	8.4	50.7	13 707
MASSACHUSETTS	2 444 588	50.0	23.2	8.9	15.0	8.0	2.4	7.1	0.4	11.2	2.6	16.8	8.1	47.6	27 915
Barnstable County	94 845	52.7	18.6	16.9	11.9	6.4	2.1	5.9	0.8	10.6	3.5	18.9	11.2	42.7	814
Berkshire County	55 874	48.7	18.9	11.6	14.3	8.6	2.2	5.4	0.4	12.5	3.2	19.0	10.6	49.2	322
Bristol County	205 556	52.7	24.2	9.1	16.1	9.4	2.4	4.6	0.3	10.5	2.7	16.0	8.8	49.1	2 925
Dukes County	6 431	45.8	20.0	8.7	13.9	8.5	1.5	8.3	0.5	13.2	2.6	18.8	8.1	49.9	42
Essex County	275 410	51.9	24.6	9.1	15.6	8.7	2.4	5.4	0.3	10.2	2.5	16.8	8.5	48.0	3 009
Franklin County	29 492	48.7	20.8	9.5	14.1	9.0	2.0	8.2	0.5	11.8	2.3	17.2	8.4	47.1	247
Hampden County	175 475	46.6	20.7	9.2	19.8	12.0	2.6	5.2	0.4	11.2	3.2	17.1	9.1	50.2	2 839
Hampshire County	55 955	48.3	21.2	8.5	12.3	7.3	1.9	10.7	0.5	11.1	2.5	17.6	7.7	48.7	310
Middlesex County	561 506	52.3	25.0	8.7	12.5	5.8	2.4	8.1	0.3	10.7	2.2	16.4	7.3	45.3	4 513
Nantucket County	3 701	47.1	21.7	7.7	10.0	5.5	0.8	12.9	0.6	12.9	1.7	17.1	6.7	47.9	0
Norfolk County	248 901	55.2	26.9	10.0	11.8	5.0	2.7	6.2	0.3	9.6	2.4	17.2	7.0	45.8	1 924
Plymouth County	168 448	58.1	28.8	8.6	15.0	8.0	2.3	4.8	0.4	8.6	2.3	13.6	7.0	45.2	2 529
Suffolk County	278 776	30.2	13.3	5.2	20.3	10.8	2.8	13.2	0.3	16.2	2.8	20.1	6.9	53.8	4 809
Worcester County	284 218	53.2	25.6	8.7	14.9	8.8	2.1	5.7	0.3	11.0	2.6	15.2	8.0	48.8	3 632
MICHIGAN	3 788 780	52.3	23.8	9.0	16.1	9.4	2.2	5.4	0.4	11.4	2.3	14.8	7.1	44.8	70 044
Alcona County	5 114	60.4	14.6	20.4	9.3	5.1	1.9	3.5	0.4	12.5	4.7	14.3	9.8	39.1	70
Alger County	3 797	58.9	21.0	14.4	9.6	5.6	1.6	4.6	0.5	13.0	3.7	13.9	8.9	43.3	54
Allegan County	38 245	62.3	30.1	9.4	12.5	8.4	1.2	4.5	0.4	9.8	2.0	10.9	6.0	42.0	603
Alpena County	12 877	55.7	22.0	12.2	12.5	7.2	2.6	4.3	0.4	11.2	3.3	16.3	10.4	47.2	83
Antrim County	9 254	61.5	22.4	15.3	11.3	7.4	1.7	3.7	0.2	10.8	3.4	12.7	7.6	39.1	136
Arenac County	6 732	57.8	20.5	13.4	12.7	8.3	1.7	3.9	0.4	12.4	3.5	13.2	8.2	43.0	92
Baraga County	3 371	52.2	20.3	10.4	14.4	8.6	3.0	4.1	0.3	13.7	4.1	15.6	9.8	50.4	28
Barry County	21 096	65.8	28.7	10.8	10.6	7.3	1.0	4.2	0.4	8.8	2.2	10.6	6.1	40.5	372
Bay County	44 026	54.4	22.4	10.4	14.3	8.6	2.2	4.2	0.3	11.0	2.5	16.1	9.2	47.4	562
Benzie County	6 498	59.7	22.9	14.6	10.6	6.6	1.4	5.4	0.3	11.3	3.2	13.0	7.8	40.3	90
Berrien County	63 644	52.1	21.7	10.7	16.4	10.1	2.2	4.5	0.5	11.3	2.6	15.7	8.4	45.2	1 470
Branch County	16 440	57.0	24.8	10.7	14.1	9.0	1.8	4.9	0.6	10.1	2.3	13.9	8.2	44.5	249
Calhoun County	54 161	50.7	21.9	9.5	16.6	10.5	2.5	4.9	0.3	11.6	2.6	16.2	8.3	47.0	977
Cass County	19 620	58.9	22.7	11.2	14.1	8.6	2.0	4.3	0.4	10.5	2.6	12.2	7.1	41.4	440
Charlevoix County	10 373	57.9	23.8	12.1	12.5	8.4	1.6	4.5	0.3	11.2	2.8	13.9	7.7	42.7	127
Cheboygan County	10 841	58.0	21.0	14.7	12.5	8.3	1.8	4.0	0.3	11.8	3.6	13.8	7.8	40.3	189
Chippewa County	13 491	52.2	21.1	10.8	14.8	10.2	1.5	5.7	0.3	13.3	3.4	14.1	7.7	46.6	139
Clare County	12 739	55.6	19.1	14.2	13.7	8.9	1.7	4.7	0.7	11.3	3.4	14.7	8.6	41.9	211
Clinton County	23 707	65.3	31.3	9.6	10.9	7.0	1.2	4.0	0.4	8.9	1.5	10.8	5.3	38.2	218
Crawford County	5 628	58.3	20.5	13.9	14.0	9.8	1.8	3.7	0.6	10.8	3.5	13.1	7.4	40.1	49
Delta County	15 820	57.2	23.7	12.9	10.4	6.4	1.4	4.2	0.3	12.6	3.8	15.6	9.2	46.9	148
Dickinson County	11 407	56.1	24.3	12.0	10.8	7.6	1.5	3.8	0.6	11.7	3.4	17.6	11.9	51.9	82
Eaton County	40 251	57.5	26.1	8.8	13.3	8.5	1.2	4.8	0.1	9.7	1.6	14.7	6.9	45.6	645
Emmet County	12 542	56.4	24.8	10.0	11.3	7.2	1.6	5.3	0.3	11.6	2.5	15.3	7.9	46.6	115
Genesee County	170 030	48.2	21.3	8.4	20.6	12.9	2.2	4.7	0.4	11.4	2.0	15.1	6.9	44.7	4 749
Gladwin County	10 565	61.3	20.8	15.2	11.2	7.0	1.8	3.7	0.6	11.0	3.8	12.7	7.8	39.8	147
Gogebic County	7 401	49.9	17.8	14.1	12.1	7.2	2.0	3.7	0.5	15.8	5.8	18.4	13.3	53.5	68
Grand Traverse County	30 486	56.5	25.2	10.2	12.2	8.0	1.4	6.4	0.2	9.4	1.8	15.5	7.2	43.2	220
Gratiot County	14 492	58.4	25.3	11.2	13.4	8.7	1.5	4.5	0.4	9.7	2.1	14.0	8.3	44.2	221
Hillsdale County	17 287	60.9	26.1	11.3	11.7	7.1	1.5	4.4	0.3	10.5	2.3	12.4	7.3	42.2	346
Houghton County	13 793	48.1	20.4	10.4	11.7	7.0	2.1	7.9	0.6	15.4	4.0	16.9	10.0	51.9	73
Huron County	14 582	58.8	23.4	15.0	11.1	5.9	2.2	2.8	0.2	11.8	3.8	15.5	10.2	44.6	136
Ingham County	108 567	43.9	20.7	6.7	15.2	9.7	1.5	10.7	0.3	12.8	1.7	17.3	6.1	47.8	1 351
Ionia County	20 612	59.2	28.4	8.5	14.5	10.1	1.6	4.5	0.4	9.7	2.0	12.1	6.7	45.0	322
Iosco County	11 755	55.5	17.4	16.6	11.5	7.8	1.5	4.4	0.7	12.6	4.0	16.0	9.9	42.7	242
Iron County	5 734	50.8	16.6	16.0	12.3	7.3	2.5	3.1	0.5	14.6	5.2	19.2	13.8	50.0	55
Isabella County	22 409	45.8	20.5	7.8	12.5	8.0	1.1	18.0	0.4	10.1	1.5	13.6	5.6	43.4	216
Jackson County	58 318	55.1	23.8	9.9	15.5	10.1	2.0	4.8	0.5	10.6	2.5	14.0	7.8	45.6	1 198
Kalamazoo County	93 495	48.3	21.8	8.2	14.0	9.0	1.4	9.6	0.3	12.0	1.8	16.1	6.8	46.6	1 208
Kalkaska County	6 397	59.7	23.8	12.0	12.5	8.5	1.3	5.3	0.7	11.8	2.7	10.7	5.7	37.4	110
Kent County	213 124	53.0	26.9	7.8	15.2	9.6	1.6	6.3	0.3	10.9	1.7	14.6	6.4	45.6	3 169
Keweenaw County	1 012	52.6	15.5	13.6	8.8	5.4	1.8	3.4	0.0	17.0	7.1	18.3	12.2	55.6	6
Lake County	4 682	52.5	16.0	14.3	12.7	7.7	2.2	5.2	0.9	16.6	5.6	12.9	7.6	42.9	113
Lapeer County	30 779	66.4	32.4	8.7	11.9	6.8	1.5	3.3	0.2	8.4	1.4	10.0	5.4	39.4	571

Table A-3. States and Counties — Age, Ethnicity, and Household Structure

STATE County	Households with Non-Hispanic White householder — Number of households (44)	Percent that are family households (45)	Households with Black or African American householder — Number of households (46)	Percent that are family households (47)	Households with American Indian and Alaska Native householder — Number of households (48)	Percent that are family households (49)	Households with Asian, Hawaiian, and Pacific Islander householder — Number of households (50)	Percent that are family households (51)	Households with Hispanic or Latino[1] householder — Number of households (52)	Percent that are family households (53)	Foreign-born population — Percent of total population that is foreign-born (54)	Place of birth (percent) — Europe (55)	Asia (56)	Latin America (57)	Percent in non-English speaking households — Linguistically isolated (58)	Not linguistically isolated (59)
MARYLAND—Cont'd																
Washington County	46 870	69.0	1 715	64.2	95	81.1	314	80.6	400	70.3	1.9	0.6	0.7	0.4	0.5	6.0
Wicomico County	24 178	66.8	6 769	70.7	88	58.0	544	86.0	480	67.1	3.9	0.6	1.8	1.2	2.0	7.4
Worcester County	16 563	67.4	2 727	72.8	27	63.0	104	80.8	192	46.9	2.7	1.1	0.6	0.7	1.0	7.8
Baltimore city	93 423	47.6	152 493	64.0	834	65.2	4 266	42.0	3 793	55.4	4.6	1.1	1.2	1.6	1.6	10.3
MASSACHUSETTS	2 085 454	64.0	115 736	66.6	5 538	67.2	73 735	70.9	123 443	75.0	12.2	3.9	3.2	3.7	4.6	20.0
Barnstable County	90 080	64.5	1 190	62.5	486	73.5	431	71.7	780	62.7	4.9	2.3	0.6	1.3	1.1	10.5
Berkshire County	53 717	63.0	721	76.1	66	60.6	348	61.5	625	61.4	3.7	1.8	0.7	0.6	0.9	9.4
Bristol County	187 200	68.7	3 840	69.1	484	73.8	2 227	77.3	5 478	75.0	11.7	8.6	1.2	1.0	4.3	24.0
Dukes County	5 851	59.5	149	40.9	108	60.2	24	100.0	33	81.8	6.3	1.7	0.8	3.1	2.1	10.0
Essex County	239 980	66.3	6 379	65.6	614	72.5	4 839	80.7	22 153	79.9	11.3	3.1	2.1	5.2	4.9	20.4
Franklin County	28 314	63.1	154	68.8	89	46.1	191	48.2	371	65.0	3.6	1.7	0.9	0.5	1.0	9.5
Hampden County	138 575	64.9	12 954	66.3	421	69.6	1 794	74.9	20 391	76.3	7.2	3.8	1.5	1.3	5.8	22.9
Hampshire County	51 783	60.7	821	60.4	74	48.6	1 197	58.4	1 354	63.3	6.6	2.0	2.7	0.9	1.6	14.6
Middlesex County	487 298	63.9	16 890	63.8	913	66.6	27 895	74.6	18 867	73.3	15.2	4.5	5.2	4.0	4.6	21.7
Nantucket County	3 467	57.3	59	62.7	0	X	34	58.8	34	67.6	8.0	3.7	1.0	2.7	2.7	11.1
Norfolk County	225 135	66.4	6 417	73.4	308	67.9	11 034	75.7	3 260	67.5	11.8	4.1	4.7	1.7	2.8	16.9
Plymouth County	152 203	72.7	6 336	75.7	351	68.7	1 104	85.0	2 944	75.6	6.3	1.7	0.7	1.7	2.1	13.3
Suffolk County	168 317	40.4	53 022	65.9	1 035	61.4	17 048	55.1	32 147	72.5	25.5	4.6	5.8	12.4	11.4	29.5
Worcester County	253 534	67.4	6 804	66.0	589	66.6	5 569	79.9	15 006	77.7	7.9	2.4	2.1	1.9	3.5	16.8
MICHIGAN	3 088 895	68.4	491 963	67.1	20 422	70.1	56 378	72.8	84 443	75.2	5.3	1.6	2.1	0.9	1.7	11.3
Alcona County	5 017	69.8	5	60.0	18	77.8	2	100.0	26	73.1	1.5	0.5	0.2	0.2	0.2	4.7
Alger County	3 605	68.8	0	X	110	75.5	7	71.4	12	50.0	1.0	0.4	0.3	0.1	0.3	8.9
Allegan County	35 611	75.0	486	71.8	166	59.6	141	49.6	1 523	76.4	2.9	0.6	0.4	1.7	1.4	8.9
Alpena County	12 653	68.0	26	80.8	73	78.1	30	73.3	32	81.3	1.2	0.4	0.4	0.1	0.4	7.8
Antrim County	9 053	72.8	19	15.8	61	82.0	9	100.0	38	73.7	1.5	0.7	0.2	0.2	0.2	7.3
Arenac County	6 544	70.5	14	78.6	60	78.3	12	83.3	54	61.1	1.1	0.4	0.3	0.1	0.3	6.9
Baraga County	2 914	65.9	2	100.0	332	73.5	4	100.0	12	83.3	0.8	0.4	0.1	0.1	0.6	12.7
Barry County	20 577	76.5	76	77.6	89	71.9	44	40.9	136	63.2	0.8	0.5	0.1	0.1	0.1	4.8
Bay County	41 789	68.5	447	60.9	194	82.5	175	70.3	1 116	76.3	1.4	0.5	0.4	0.3	0.5	8.3
Benzie County	6 274	70.3	5	100.0	92	81.5	6	33.3	53	73.6	1.7	0.6	0.1	0.6	0.2	7.0
Berrien County	52 414	67.8	8 891	71.2	301	62.1	504	77.4	954	74.3	4.9	1.3	0.9	1.6	1.1	9.9
Branch County	15 786	70.7	23	78.3	59	67.8	68	86.8	253	83.4	2.6	0.3	0.9	1.2	1.3	8.3
Calhoun County	45 926	67.6	5 660	62.5	281	69.0	524	73.1	1 032	76.5	2.4	0.6	0.9	0.6	1.0	8.2
Cass County	17 738	73.3	1 164	59.9	142	87.3	74	91.9	215	93.0	1.9	0.7	0.6	0.5	0.3	7.5
Charlevoix County	10 117	70.5	27	40.7	131	58.8	10	70.0	36	69.4	1.4	0.6	0.2	0.2	0.5	6.5
Cheboygan County	10 381	70.3	12	100.0	281	73.7	25	80.0	44	70.5	1.2	0.6	0.2	0.1	0.5	6.5
Chippewa County	11 401	65.8	38	28.9	1 582	73.5	31	100.0	92	80.4	3.0	0.7	0.3	0.1	0.5	8.0
Clare County	12 443	69.4	17	29.4	75	69.3	19	78.9	87	72.4	1.1	0.5	0.2	0.0	0.6	6.2
Clinton County	22 734	76.2	89	88.8	107	86.9	107	55.1	486	81.5	1.2	0.5	0.4	0.2	0.3	8.3
Crawford County	5 516	72.0	5	100.0	40	87.5	20	90.0	25	100.0	1.3	0.4	0.4	0.1	0.3	6.3
Delta County	15 235	67.9	9	33.3	313	60.7	28	64.3	42	83.3	1.0	0.4	0.2	0.0	0.2	5.6
Dickinson County	11 221	66.6	16	100.0	51	88.2	60	78.3	21	100.0	1.1	0.5	0.4	0.0	0.3	6.5
Eaton County	36 317	71.2	1 977	65.8	185	50.3	347	73.8	879	71.6	2.2	0.5	1.1	0.3	0.5	8.3
Emmet County	12 022	67.5	10	10.0	340	79.4	28	82.1	56	55.4	1.7	1.0	0.2	0.1	0.2	7.7
Genesee County	131 185	68.4	31 577	69.8	917	72.7	1 153	72.8	2 715	76.9	2.1	0.8	0.7	0.2	0.4	8.2
Gladwin County	10 358	72.5	3	100.0	58	75.9	11	63.6	43	95.3	1.3	0.7	0.1	0.1	0.5	7.5
Gogebic County	7 180	61.5	2	100.0	102	81.4	13	23.1	14	78.6	1.3	0.9	0.2	0.1	0.3	9.6
Grand Traverse County	29 667	68.6	55	70.9	261	64.0	85	74.1	198	76.8	2.1	0.9	0.5	0.4	0.4	7.8
Gratiot County	13 818	71.8	33	72.7	54	61.1	35	74.3	492	73.8	1.2	0.3	0.4	0.3	0.3	7.1
Hillsdale County	16 926	72.8	41	46.3	23	91.3	40	50.0	127	76.4	1.1	0.4	0.3	0.1	0.3	6.8
Houghton County	13 309	60.3	120	39.2	70	52.9	143	58.7	46	13.0	2.7	0.8	1.3	0.1	0.9	11.5
Huron County	14 316	69.6	11	100.0	37	91.9	31	100.0	100	72.0	1.4	0.5	0.3	0.2	0.4	7.3
Ingham County	87 026	58.2	11 230	62.8	659	66.8	3 354	57.9	4 650	68.6	6.3	1.1	3.2	1.1	2.4	12.6
Ionia County	20 058	73.7	52	63.5	72	70.8	44	27.3	255	85.1	1.2	0.3	0.3	0.5	0.3	7.0
Iosco County	11 446	67.0	28	85.7	91	73.6	24	20.8	51	90.2	1.3	0.6	0.2	0.2	0.3	6.1
Iron County	5 635	63.1	4	100.0	25	68.0	7	0.0	17	64.7	1.1	0.6	0.2	0.1	0.3	8.3
Isabella County	20 631	58.5	306	39.9	564	70.2	316	46.8	398	58.5	2.3	0.4	1.2	0.2	0.5	8.8
Jackson County	53 300	70.8	2 985	65.3	188	67.6	230	56.5	912	78.2	1.7	0.6	0.4	0.4	0.5	7.0
Kalamazoo County	80 338	62.4	8 033	63.8	392	56.4	1 583	51.6	1 649	67.0	4.0	1.2	1.6	0.7	1.0	10.3
Kalkaska County	6 243	72.1	7	100.0	68	77.9	2	0.0	26	80.8	0.8	0.4	0.1	0.1	0.0	4.4
Kent County	179 849	67.4	17 857	68.8	1 160	61.1	2 776	82.3	9 663	79.8	6.6	1.5	1.6	3.0	3.2	11.6
Keweenaw County	1 006	61.1	0	X	0	X	0	X	2	100.0	1.0	0.6	0.0	0.0	0.2	7.2
Lake County	4 061	66.3	466	56.0	45	80.0	2	0.0	30	50.0	1.0	0.5	0.1	0.2	0.1	5.8
Lapeer County	29 828	78.0	43	58.1	124	96.8	56	58.9	540	89.1	2.2	0.8	0.2	0.7	0.8	7.7

[1]Hispanic or Latino persons may be of any race.

STATE/ County code	MSA/PMSA/ NECMA code[1]	STATE County	Population by age (percent)								+/− U.S. percent under 18 years	+/− U.S. percent 65 years and over	Non-Hispanic White	Age (percent)	
			Total population	Under 5 years	5 to 17 years	18 to 24 years	25 to 44 years	45 to 64 years	65 years and over	Median age			Total population	Under 18 years	65 years and over
			1	2	3	4	5	6	7	8	9	10	11	12	13
		MICHIGAN—Cont'd													
26 089	...	Leelanau County	21 119	5.1	19.3	5.6	24.3	28.4	17.4	42.6	-1.3	5.0	19 498	23.0	18.5
26 091	0440	Lenawee County	98 890	6.3	19.7	9.1	28.6	23.7	12.7	36.4	0.3	0.3	88 303	24.8	13.6
26 093	0440	Livingston County	156 951	7.2	21.5	6.7	31.6	24.8	8.2	36.2	3.0	-4.2	150 876	28.4	8.4
26 095	...	Luce County	7 024	5.1	16.3	8.4	30.3	24.5	15.4	38.6	-4.3	3.0	5 757	21.9	18.1
26 097	...	Mackinac County	11 943	4.7	17.6	5.8	25.4	28.2	18.3	42.8	-3.4	5.9	9 474	18.4	20.9
26 099	2160	Macomb County	788 149	6.5	17.6	8.0	31.5	22.8	13.6	36.9	-1.6	1.2	720 462	23.2	14.5
26 101	...	Manistee County	24 527	5.2	17.6	6.7	26.2	26.2	18.1	41.5	-2.9	5.7	22 737	21.9	19.3
26 103	...	Marquette County	64 634	5.0	16.4	13.8	26.9	24.5	13.5	37.5	-4.3	1.1	61 313	21.1	14.0
26 105	...	Mason County	28 274	5.5	18.7	7.0	26.5	25.5	16.9	40.4	-1.5	4.5	26 437	23.1	17.7
26 107	...	Mecosta County	40 553	5.9	16.6	20.0	23.0	21.4	13.1	31.9	-3.2	0.7	37 336	22.3	13.9
26 109	...	Menominee County	25 326	6.0	18.1	7.5	26.3	24.8	17.3	40.4	-1.6	4.9	24 297	23.1	17.9
26 111	6960	Midland County	82 874	6.4	20.4	8.6	29.1	23.4	12.0	36.3	1.1	-0.4	78 246	26.3	12.5
26 113	...	Missaukee County	14 478	6.4	20.7	7.5	27.0	23.5	14.9	37.7	1.4	2.5	14 111	26.8	15.1
26 115	2160	Monroe County	145 945	6.6	20.7	8.1	30.1	23.4	11.1	36.0	1.6	-1.3	137 493	26.7	11.4
26 117	...	Montcalm County	61 266	6.6	20.6	8.3	30.2	22.2	12.1	35.6	1.5	-0.3	57 207	27.0	12.8
26 119	...	Montmorency County	10 315	4.4	16.0	5.9	20.7	29.1	23.8	47.0	-5.3	11.4	10 075	20.2	24.2
26 121	3000	Muskegon County	170 200	6.8	20.7	8.7	29.2	21.8	12.9	35.5	1.8	0.5	135 477	25.1	14.4
26 123	...	Newaygo County	47 874	6.8	22.3	7.5	27.4	23.1	12.8	36.4	3.4	0.4	44 500	28.0	13.3
26 125	2160	Oakland County	1 194 156	6.7	18.4	7.2	32.5	23.9	11.3	36.7	-0.6	-1.1	972 063	23.9	12.6
26 127	...	Oceana County	26 873	6.4	21.8	8.1	26.3	23.6	13.9	36.9	2.5	1.5	23 020	25.7	15.8
26 129	...	Ogemaw County	21 645	5.2	18.4	6.3	24.2	27.2	18.7	42.3	-2.1	6.3	20 910	23.2	19.2
26 131	...	Ontonagon County	7 818	4.3	15.9	4.3	23.8	30.1	21.6	45.9	-5.5	9.2	7 547	19.6	22.1
26 133	...	Osceola County	23 197	6.2	20.9	8.0	26.5	24.1	14.1	37.6	1.4	1.7	22 426	26.6	14.4
26 135	...	Oscoda County	9 418	5.1	18.2	5.4	22.8	28.2	20.3	43.7	-2.4	7.9	9 161	22.9	20.7
26 137	...	Otsego County	23 301	6.3	20.4	6.9	28.7	23.9	13.8	37.7	1.0	1.4	22 567	26.1	14.0
26 139	3000	Ottawa County	238 314	7.5	21.1	11.8	29.6	19.9	10.1	32.3	2.9	-2.3	210 837	27.2	11.1
26 141	...	Presque Isle County	14 411	4.9	16.0	6.5	22.4	27.8	22.5	45.1	-4.8	10.1	14 130	20.5	22.6
26 143	...	Roscommon County	25 469	4.3	15.6	5.8	21.3	29.3	23.7	47.2	-5.8	11.3	24 783	19.3	24.2
26 145	6960	Saginaw County	210 039	6.8	19.8	9.0	27.7	23.2	13.4	36.3	0.9	1.0	151 946	22.6	15.8
26 147	2160	St. Clair County	164 235	6.8	19.9	7.9	30.0	23.2	12.3	36.4	1.0	-0.1	153 740	25.9	12.6
26 149	...	St. Joseph County	62 422	7.2	20.2	8.8	28.2	22.5	13.0	35.6	1.7	0.6	56 901	26.5	13.6
26 151	...	Sanilac County	44 547	6.5	20.4	7.6	27.2	22.9	15.4	37.8	1.2	3.0	42 610	26.4	15.8
26 153	...	Schoolcraft County	8 903	5.6	17.3	6.7	26.2	25.6	18.6	41.4	-2.8	6.2	7 878	21.5	20.3
26 155	...	Shiawassee County	71 687	6.7	20.1	8.2	29.3	23.7	12.0	36.4	1.1	-0.4	68 969	26.4	12.3
26 157	...	Tuscola County	58 266	6.2	20.7	8.1	28.1	24.2	12.8	37.0	1.2	0.4	55 150	26.2	13.2
26 159	3720	Van Buren County	76 263	6.8	21.2	7.8	28.2	23.7	12.3	36.6	2.3	-0.1	64 381	25.8	13.1
26 161	0440	Washtenaw County	322 895	6.2	15.7	16.9	32.5	20.6	8.0	31.3	-3.8	-4.4	245 326	20.6	9.4
26 163	2160	Wayne County	2 061 162	7.4	20.6	8.7	30.4	20.8	12.1	34.0	2.3	-0.3	1 028 164	23.1	15.4
26 165	...	Wexford County	30 484	6.4	20.4	7.7	27.9	23.6	14.0	37.3	1.1	1.6	29 448	26.5	14.2
27 000	...	**MINNESOTA**	4 919 479	6.7	19.5	9.5	30.5	21.7	12.1	35.4	0.5	-0.3	4 340 672	24.4	13.3
27 001	...	Aitkin County	15 301	4.5	16.3	5.5	21.4	29.2	23.0	46.5	-4.9	10.6	14 656	19.6	23.7
27 003	5120	Anoka County	298 084	7.5	21.4	8.3	34.1	21.7	7.0	33.7	3.2	-5.4	276 231	28.0	7.3
27 005	...	Becker County	30 000	6.3	20.4	7.2	25.0	24.7	16.3	39.4	1.0	3.9	26 737	25.0	17.6
27 007	...	Beltrami County	39 650	7.1	21.7	13.9	25.4	20.4	11.6	31.5	3.1	-0.8	30 237	23.4	14.1
27 009	6980	Benton County	34 226	7.2	19.8	12.2	31.4	18.2	11.1	31.9	1.3	-1.3	32 628	26.4	11.6
27 011	...	Big Stone County	5 820	4.6	20.3	5.5	21.7	23.7	24.2	43.6	-0.8	11.8	5 735	24.5	24.3
27 013	...	Blue Earth County	55 941	5.6	15.7	22.1	25.7	18.9	12.1	29.9	-4.4	-0.3	52 768	20.7	12.7
27 015	...	Brown County	26 911	5.3	20.0	9.7	25.6	21.9	17.5	38.4	-0.4	5.1	25 968	24.4	18.1
27 017	...	Carlton County	31 671	5.9	19.5	7.6	28.4	23.5	15.1	38.4	-0.3	2.7	28 913	24.6	16.1
27 019	5120	Carver County	70 205	8.8	22.8	6.9	34.6	19.6	7.3	33.9	5.9	-5.1	66 261	30.9	7.6
27 021	...	Cass County	27 150	5.1	20.0	6.0	23.1	27.8	18.0	42.2	-0.6	5.6	23 493	22.5	19.7
27 023	...	Chippewa County	13 088	5.3	19.5	7.3	24.2	23.1	20.0	40.5	-0.4	7.6	12 601	24.3	20.7
27 025	5120	Chisago County	41 101	7.6	22.4	7.0	32.2	20.9	9.8	34.3	4.3	-2.6	39 586	29.6	10.1
27 027	2520	Clay County	51 229	6.2	18.9	17.2	25.5	19.3	13.0	32.3	-0.6	0.6	47 288	23.7	13.7
27 029	...	Clearwater County	8 423	5.9	20.2	7.7	24.6	24.3	17.3	39.7	0.4	4.9	7 594	24.7	18.4
27 031	...	Cook County	5 168	4.5	15.7	5.1	26.5	30.9	17.3	44.0	-5.5	4.9	4 622	19.0	18.1
27 033	...	Cottonwood County	12 167	5.8	19.2	6.5	23.4	23.2	22.0	41.7	-0.7	9.6	11 556	23.5	23.0
27 035	...	Crow Wing County	55 099	6.0	18.8	7.9	25.9	24.3	17.1	39.4	-0.9	4.7	53 618	24.4	17.4
27 037	5120	Dakota County	355 904	7.7	21.4	7.8	34.4	21.2	7.4	33.7	3.4	-5.0	320 576	28.0	8.0
27 039	...	Dodge County	17 731	7.6	22.7	7.7	29.8	20.1	12.1	34.8	4.6	-0.3	16 966	29.6	12.5
27 041	...	Douglas County	32 821	5.6	18.4	9.1	25.1	23.8	17.9	39.7	-1.7	5.5	32 237	23.8	18.2
27 043	...	Faribault County	16 181	5.3	19.1	6.8	22.9	23.5	22.3	42.4	-1.3	9.9	15 370	23.3	23.3
27 045	...	Fillmore County	21 122	5.9	20.3	7.1	25.2	22.3	19.3	39.8	0.5	6.9	20 834	25.8	19.5
27 047	...	Freeborn County	32 584	5.5	18.4	7.5	25.7	24.0	18.9	40.4	-1.8	6.5	29 997	22.4	20.1
27 049	...	Goodhue County	44 127	6.0	20.5	7.5	27.7	23.3	15.0	38.1	0.8	2.6	42 334	25.7	15.5

[1]MSA = Metropolitan Statistical Area. PMSA = Primary MSA. NECMA = New England County Metropolitan Area. See the Appendix A for explanation of these concepts. See Appendix B for list of metropolitan areas identified by type, with component counties.

STATE County	Black or African American Total population	Under 18 years	65 years and over	American Indian and Alaska Native Total population	Under 18 years	65 years and over	Asian, Hawaiian, and Pacific Islander Total population	Under 18 years	65 years and over	Hispanic or Latino[1] Total population	Under 18 years	65 years and over	Two or more races Total population	Under 18 years	65 years and over
	14	15	16	17	18	19	20	21	22	23	24	25	26	27	28
MICHIGAN—Cont'd															
Leelanau County	21	57.1	0.0	799	38.2	6.1	85	50.6	0.0	570	47.5	1.1	222	36.0	4.5
Lenawee County	2 056	19.8	2.0	392	28.8	0.5	541	24.2	18.5	6 797	39.2	6.1	1 481	50.2	4.5
Livingston County	787	30.5	5.6	759	38.9	5.0	1 118	36.9	3.2	1 802	36.7	3.1	1 704	41.4	2.8
Luce County	563	1.4	0.4	400	38.0	6.8	8	50.0	0.0	89	16.9	2.2	232	31.0	3.4
Mackinac County	6	0.0	33.3	1 759	36.5	8.4	34	20.6	5.9	71	32.4	1.4	597	40.7	10.4
Macomb County	20 328	29.5	5.2	2 824	31.0	5.8	17 511	26.8	4.5	12 510	36.9	5.3	15 721	41.5	5.0
Manistee County	349	4.9	0.9	327	26.0	2.1	74	37.8	1.4	692	44.2	3.9	491	48.5	1.4
Marquette County	777	7.7	1.5	874	31.0	3.2	316	22.8	7.3	450	36.0	6.4	1 022	38.3	1.6
Mason County	241	24.5	1.7	240	31.7	4.6	55	14.5	5.5	865	47.5	3.5	557	45.2	8.3
Mecosta County	1 416	20.0	2.5	252	21.4	12.7	286	29.7	0.0	484	33.1	5.4	831	34.8	5.2
Menominee County	42	59.5	4.8	576	38.2	4.2	35	51.4	0.0	129	63.6	0.0	254	52.0	3.5
Midland County	907	27.1	3.4	436	38.1	3.0	1 175	29.2	3.8	1 207	41.1	5.5	968	47.6	4.9
Missaukee County	13	61.5	23.1	63	39.7	0.0	50	34.0	8.0	124	39.5	2.4	136	36.0	11.0
Monroe County	2 564	35.3	9.9	338	20.7	6.8	987	32.6	4.1	2 626	33.1	6.4	2 197	48.6	6.4
Montcalm County	1 288	4.6	1.7	391	29.2	3.8	184	31.0	1.1	1 299	41.3	2.7	1 119	45.2	3.6
Montmorency County	20	65.0	0.0	28	7.1	7.1	13	53.8	0.0	55	36.4	9.1	133	21.1	15.0
Muskegon County	24 037	34.6	8.2	1 248	18.6	3.1	792	33.5	6.4	5 775	41.6	3.9	3 743	51.9	3.3
Newaygo County	463	28.3	17.5	274	24.5	9.5	172	45.9	3.5	1 892	48.6	4.3	776	51.7	6.4
Oakland County	119 393	28.7	6.6	3 114	24.3	4.2	48 666	27.5	4.4	29 327	35.3	3.9	23 806	41.1	4.7
Oceana County	83	44.6	0.0	294	25.2	5.4	47	44.7	6.4	3 212	45.1	1.8	610	48.0	3.8
Ogemaw County	10	60.0	0.0	109	8.3	3.7	89	27.0	9.0	215	35.3	7.9	334	41.6	5.7
Ontonagon County	0	X	X	96	35.4	6.3	15	40.0	26.7	60	43.3	0.0	97	40.2	4.1
Osceola County	79	48.1	5.1	97	34.0	7.2	56	42.9	0.0	222	42.3	8.6	353	49.9	5.4
Oscoda County	7	0.0	0.0	45	37.8	4.4	19	68.4	0.0	94	37.2	10.6	113	31.0	8.8
Otsego County	31	12.9	0.0	179	39.7	2.2	141	31.2	11.3	158	54.4	0.0	250	48.0	8.8
Ottawa County	2 266	29.8	3.5	762	31.4	4.1	5 208	38.1	1.8	17 036	40.9	2.1	4 044	49.2	3.8
Presque Isle County	21	71.4	14.3	91	48.4	12.1	5	0.0	0.0	59	39.0	15.3	121	30.6	19.8
Roscommon County	52	46.2	0.0	132	37.1	9.1	110	40.9	8.2	232	41.4	5.2	169	42.0	11.8
Saginaw County	38 701	35.7	7.8	863	28.2	6.4	1 768	31.9	4.4	14 048	39.5	5.5	4 396	53.2	4.3
St. Clair County	3 665	32.5	10.6	886	31.2	0.2	467	27.4	3.4	3 643	39.1	6.9	2 205	49.0	5.0
St. Joseph County	1 560	32.9	14.6	247	23.9	20.6	307	22.8	14.0	2 316	36.2	0.9	1 230	47.9	4.9
Sanilac County	114	60.5	0.0	149	30.9	13.4	141	22.0	2.8	1 179	37.6	7.9	447	48.3	5.6
Schoolcraft County	137	4.4	0.0	555	40.2	3.4	23	52.2	0.0	75	36.0	0.0	215	36.3	16.7
Shiawassee County	149	26.8	11.4	334	27.2	2.7	142	41.5	3.5	1 261	39.9	3.6	986	46.1	5.8
Tuscola County	655	29.8	9.9	322	45.3	5.3	153	15.7	10.5	1 251	41.3	2.8	854	48.8	4.0
Van Buren County	4 089	33.1	17.4	580	31.0	5.2	232	57.3	0.0	5 762	45.6	1.8	1 903	43.5	7.0
Washtenaw County	38 831	27.3	5.4	1 227	21.1	3.6	20 125	18.1	2.5	8 950	23.0	1.9	9 276	41.6	2.2
Wayne County	866 622	32.4	9.6	8 231	27.5	6.7	35 768	27.9	4.1	77 501	35.9	5.5	53 171	41.9	5.1
Wexford County	57	54.4	5.3	103	38.0	5.5	178	37.1	2.8	321	35.8	7.8	337	33.8	7.7
MINNESOTA	167 857	37.7	3.2	54 568	37.1	4.2	140 969	37.6	3.4	141 786	38.7	1.9	88 777	51.1	2.9
Aitkin County	25	52.0	12.0	352	48.6	6.0	56	48.2	7.1	113	61.1	7.1	123	40.7	8.9
Anoka County	4 572	39.2	1.4	2 316	29.5	3.4	4 998	35.1	5.5	4 805	39.1	2.2	5 418	55.0	2.0
Becker County	77	66.2	0.0	2 232	38.8	6.5	161	60.2	1.2	160	43.8	2.5	648	38.7	8.2
Beltrami County	141	51.8	1.4	7 699	46.1	3.4	519	32.9	2.7	386	50.8	3.4	799	50.4	6.1
Benton County	198	16.2	0.0	145	29.0	0.0	480	36.0	2.1	332	44.3	3.6	475	58.5	0.4
Big Stone County	4	25.0	0.0	27	18.5	11.1	0	X	X	10	60.0	20.0	40	57.5	20.0
Blue Earth County	797	43.8	0.0	131	26.7	1.5	898	12.9	1.4	836	32.9	1.9	575	43.7	1.9
Brown County	74	24.3	0.0	114	32.5	1.8	75	54.7	0.0	587	52.5	0.9	154	54.5	5.8
Carlton County	267	0.0	0.0	1 571	33.0	4.8	121	30.6	2.5	315	36.8	8.3	507	53.5	6.1
Carver County	409	48.4	0.7	126	23.8	6.3	1 039	34.0	3.7	1 828	43.5	0.9	636	65.9	2.0
Cass County	33	51.5	0.0	2 999	41.6	6.4	81	21.0	16.0	227	51.1	2.6	398	45.2	9.8
Chippewa County	32	68.8	0.0	157	44.6	2.5	26	46.2	0.0	220	57.7	0.9	90	46.7	4.4
Chisago County	163	20.2	0.6	393	38.4	2.0	280	47.1	1.8	359	44.8	0.3	366	44.8	3.3
Clay County	260	26.2	0.0	661	38.3	2.1	415	18.3	6.3	1 853	46.3	3.7	955	52.4	3.9
Clearwater County	11	100.0	0.0	607	35.6	9.6	30	36.7	0.0	47	66.0	0.0	149	47.7	1.3
Cook County	5	0.0	0.0	363	28.1	9.1	15	20.0	0.0	28	35.7	10.7	128	37.5	18.8
Cottonwood County	18	44.4	0.0	11	45.5	0.0	189	43.9	0.0	299	63.9	1.3	150	53.3	3.3
Crow Wing County	71	47.9	21.1	425	32.5	9.6	223	35.9	5.8	365	43.6	6.8	418	41.1	5.3
Dakota County	8 091	39.0	2.7	1 525	40.9	1.4	9 282	30.5	3.2	10 192	39.9	2.3	7 268	56.0	1.6
Dodge County	28	39.3	7.1	22	22.7	9.1	70	67.1	0.0	550	44.5	2.5	129	52.7	3.1
Douglas County	98	55.1	2.0	67	3.0	10.4	89	32.6	12.4	156	38.5	1.3	181	31.5	3.9
Faribault County	38	63.2	0.0	106	56.6	0.0	44	36.4	4.5	596	48.0	3.4	133	51.1	8.3
Fillmore County	51	62.7	3.9	23	43.5	0.0	27	29.6	22.2	99	42.4	6.1	92	57.6	0.0
Freeborn County	122	62.3	0.0	33	45.5	18.2	122	20.5	23.8	2 162	40.5	4.9	284	41.5	9.2
Goodhue County	264	47.3	0.0	616	46.3	4.4	185	41.1	5.9	443	39.7	3.2	301	49.8	4.0

[1] Hispanic or Latino persons may be of any race.

Table A-3. States and Counties — Age, Ethnicity, and Household Structure

STATE County	Total households	Family households (percent)						Nonfamily households (percent)						Percent of householders 65 years and over who live alone	Grandparents who are responsible for the care of their grandchildren
		Married-couple family households			Other family households			Two or more unrelated persons		Male living alone		Female living alone			
		Total	With children	Householder 65 years or over	Total	With children	Householder 65 years or over	Total	Householder 65 years or over	Total	Householder 65 years or over	Total	Householder 65 years or over		
	29	30	31	32	33	34	35	36	37	38	39	40	41	42	43
MICHIGAN—Cont'd															
Leelanau County	8 458	64.2	24.3	16.3	9.7	5.9	1.5	3.8	0.5	10.3	2.6	12.0	6.7	33.6	68
Lenawee County	35 943	59.9	26.9	10.2	13.3	8.0	2.0	3.9	0.3	9.3	2.0	13.6	7.8	44.1	777
Livingston County	55 331	68.7	34.2	7.3	10.2	5.8	1.3	4.0	0.2	8.2	1.4	8.9	4.0	37.5	655
Luce County	2 486	59.8	22.1	13.8	11.1	8.0	1.3	2.9	0.1	11.3	2.6	14.8	9.1	43.4	23
Mackinac County	5 072	55.8	19.2	14.0	11.4	7.3	1.7	4.7	0.6	12.7	3.3	15.4	8.7	42.4	34
Macomb County	309 502	55.0	25.2	9.7	13.5	6.3	2.5	4.6	0.3	11.4	2.3	15.5	8.0	45.4	3 600
Manistee County	9 829	55.5	20.3	14.0	12.7	7.5	2.2	4.5	0.5	11.8	3.5	15.5	9.7	44.0	121
Marquette County	25 738	51.9	21.5	9.5	12.1	7.6	1.6	7.1	0.3	13.1	2.6	15.9	7.7	47.7	191
Mason County	11 436	56.8	21.5	13.0	13.0	9.0	1.4	4.1	0.5	11.4	3.0	14.8	8.9	44.2	205
Mecosta County	14 898	53.8	21.0	12.4	12.7	8.8	1.3	9.0	0.4	10.3	2.2	14.2	6.5	38.0	192
Menominee County	10 541	54.7	21.1	11.8	11.9	7.6	1.9	4.3	0.4	14.0	4.0	15.1	9.2	48.5	69
Midland County	31 778	61.2	28.5	9.9	10.5	7.0	1.2	4.9	0.5	9.2	1.7	14.2	6.9	42.5	281
Missaukee County	5 467	63.0	26.9	13.3	11.3	7.0	1.7	4.0	0.5	10.7	2.3	11.0	7.0	37.7	95
Monroe County	53 850	61.2	29.1	8.6	13.5	7.6	2.1	3.7	0.2	9.7	2.3	11.9	6.4	44.3	920
Montcalm County	22 083	60.1	26.9	11.2	13.7	9.2	1.5	4.3	0.3	9.6	2.3	12.3	7.0	41.8	328
Montmorency County	4 477	58.3	16.8	17.8	10.4	5.8	2.3	4.0	0.8	12.5	5.1	14.8	9.6	41.2	59
Muskegon County	63 491	52.3	23.6	9.8	18.1	11.6	2.4	4.5	0.4	10.4	2.3	14.7	7.9	44.8	1 469
Newaygo County	17 639	60.7	26.7	11.3	13.1	8.9	1.4	4.0	0.4	10.6	2.5	11.6	6.6	41.1	295
Oakland County	471 390	54.9	26.3	8.1	12.3	6.4	1.7	5.5	0.3	11.8	1.8	15.6	6.6	45.4	5 805
Oceana County	9 826	60.1	25.0	12.9	14.5	9.4	1.6	3.8	0.5	9.7	2.3	12.0	7.3	38.9	141
Ogemaw County	8 843	58.1	19.8	14.8	12.4	7.2	2.3	3.9	0.4	11.2	4.0	14.4	8.2	40.8	80
Ontonagon County	3 443	54.0	17.5	14.4	10.1	5.9	1.7	4.3	0.8	15.8	4.9	15.8	10.5	47.7	39
Osceola County	8 863	59.2	24.3	12.8	13.5	9.4	1.3	4.8	0.3	10.1	2.4	12.4	6.9	39.2	126
Oscoda County	3 934	60.1	18.9	16.9	10.0	7.2	1.2	4.0	1.0	12.4	4.2	13.6	8.3	39.6	54
Otsego County	8 993	61.5	27.1	11.5	11.4	6.5	1.6	4.5	0.4	10.8	2.8	11.9	7.0	42.0	74
Ottawa County	81 878	65.5	33.3	9.3	10.2	6.4	1.0	4.9	0.2	8.2	1.4	11.2	5.9	41.3	1 152
Presque Isle County	6 172	59.3	19.0	16.8	9.2	5.6	1.8	3.0	0.5	12.7	4.5	15.7	10.6	44.2	56
Roscommon County	11 264	57.5	14.8	19.4	10.3	6.3	1.9	4.1	0.6	12.8	4.2	15.3	9.3	38.1	133
Saginaw County	80 509	51.0	21.5	9.6	18.8	11.8	2.4	4.2	0.3	10.4	2.5	15.6	8.1	46.3	1 959
St. Clair County	62 188	58.6	27.0	9.3	13.8	8.3	1.8	4.3	0.3	10.3	2.4	13.0	7.5	46.6	1 004
St. Joseph County	23 410	56.3	24.1	10.4	15.0	10.2	1.6	5.0	0.3	9.9	2.2	13.8	7.8	44.9	448
Sanilac County	16 902	60.1	26.1	12.4	12.2	7.0	2.1	3.4	0.3	10.5	3.1	13.8	8.4	43.8	223
Schoolcraft County	3 616	57.5	20.8	13.4	12.1	7.5	2.4	3.3	0.5	11.9	4.2	15.2	9.8	46.3	30
Shiawassee County	26 906	59.8	26.6	9.8	14.4	9.2	1.9	4.1	0.2	9.5	2.1	12.2	6.9	43.0	340
Tuscola County	21 508	61.6	27.1	10.5	13.1	8.2	1.9	3.5	0.4	9.7	2.3	12.2	7.1	42.2	222
Van Buren County	28 038	57.5	26.6	9.8	15.2	9.4	2.1	4.8	0.4	10.4	2.2	12.2	6.8	42.5	707
Washtenaw County	125 465	47.2	22.5	5.9	11.9	7.1	1.3	11.4	0.3	13.7	1.4	15.7	4.4	43.8	1 453
Wayne County	768 626	41.7	19.5	7.7	25.3	13.9	3.9	4.7	0.4	12.5	2.7	15.8	7.3	45.4	24 767
Wexford County	11 793	56.7	23.8	11.3	14.1	9.5	1.5	4.9	0.3	10.5	2.4	13.8	7.5	42.8	179
MINNESOTA	1 896 209	54.6	26.0	9.1	12.0	7.6	1.3	6.6	0.3	11.7	2.2	15.1	7.2	46.8	17 682
Aitkin County	6 664	57.8	17.8	17.9	9.3	5.3	1.7	4.1	0.8	14.4	4.6	14.3	9.4	40.8	62
Anoka County	106 468	61.8	32.1	6.3	13.3	8.3	1.0	5.7	0.1	9.0	1.1	10.2	4.3	42.4	1 473
Becker County	11 842	58.0	24.3	12.7	11.4	7.7	1.4	3.8	0.5	12.3	3.6	14.5	9.5	47.1	171
Beltrami County	14 397	50.4	23.4	9.1	17.9	11.7	2.1	6.9	0.2	11.4	2.4	13.4	7.4	46.2	430
Benton County	13 067	53.3	27.2	8.0	11.6	7.5	1.2	9.2	0.2	12.0	1.8	13.9	6.9	48.2	47
Big Stone County	2 407	59.2	23.1	18.2	9.0	5.9	1.0	1.5	0.2	12.1	4.0	18.2	13.5	47.4	2
Blue Earth County	21 127	49.6	22.9	8.9	11.2	7.2	1.2	12.2	0.3	12.2	1.9	14.8	7.5	47.5	119
Brown County	10 552	58.3	25.6	13.1	9.7	5.9	1.4	3.1	0.1	12.1	3.2	16.9	11.4	50.0	48
Carlton County	12 017	57.6	25.1	11.8	12.0	7.6	1.8	4.2	0.3	11.4	2.8	14.8	9.4	46.8	189
Carver County	24 334	67.6	38.9	6.5	9.6	6.3	0.9	4.5	0.2	8.5	1.4	9.7	4.7	44.8	146
Cass County	10 864	58.9	20.3	14.8	12.0	7.7	1.6	4.0	0.7	12.4	4.4	12.7	7.9	41.9	222
Chippewa County	5 363	57.5	24.4	13.2	9.6	6.2	1.6	3.4	0.2	11.6	4.2	17.9	12.4	52.5	11
Chisago County	14 517	64.4	32.3	8.9	12.4	8.5	1.4	4.8	0.3	8.9	2.1	9.4	5.6	42.1	200
Clay County	18 657	54.6	26.0	10.2	12.1	8.2	1.1	7.2	0.4	10.7	2.4	15.4	8.0	47.3	189
Clearwater County	3 325	57.4	24.0	12.5	11.7	7.1	1.5	3.1	0.5	13.5	4.7	14.2	10.2	50.8	55
Cook County	2 370	51.4	18.1	12.6	9.4	6.7	1.4	6.2	0.2	16.5	2.4	16.5	7.7	41.8	17
Cottonwood County	4 922	60.1	23.0	17.4	9.2	5.5	1.1	2.1	0.2	9.0	2.3	19.6	12.1	43.5	25
Crow Wing County	22 294	57.7	22.8	14.1	11.1	7.8	1.0	5.0	0.3	11.4	3.0	14.9	8.8	43.1	228
Dakota County	131 352	60.4	32.8	6.4	11.7	7.8	0.9	6.3	0.3	9.5	1.2	12.1	4.3	42.5	1 029
Dodge County	6 420	65.0	33.2	10.3	10.8	7.9	0.8	4.0	0.3	8.3	2.5	11.9	8.2	48.4	44
Douglas County	13 241	59.4	24.3	14.2	8.9	5.7	1.0	5.1	0.1	11.4	2.9	15.2	9.4	44.4	61
Faribault County	6 670	59.0	23.4	16.4	8.3	5.2	1.2	3.1	0.3	12.1	3.8	17.4	13.4	48.9	65
Fillmore County	8 212	60.5	25.7	14.5	9.0	5.4	1.6	4.0	0.5	11.7	3.5	14.8	10.7	46.2	42
Freeborn County	13 379	56.5	22.0	13.9	11.1	7.4	1.3	4.2	0.3	12.0	3.4	16.2	10.9	48.0	108
Goodhue County	16 996	59.9	27.5	11.5	10.4	6.8	1.3	4.5	0.4	10.7	2.3	14.5	8.8	45.5	95

Table A-3. States and Counties — Age, Ethnicity, and Household Structure

STATE County	Households with Non-Hispanic White householder — Number of households (44)	Percent that are family households (45)	Households with Black or African American householder — Number of households (46)	Percent that are family households (47)	Households with American Indian and Alaska Native householder — Number of households (48)	Percent that are family households (49)	Households with Asian, Hawaiian, and Pacific Islander householder — Number of households (50)	Percent that are family households (51)	Households with Hispanic or Latino[1] householder — Number of households (52)	Percent that are family households (53)	Foreign-born population — Percent of total population that is foreign-born (54)	Place of birth (percent) Europe (55)	Asia (56)	Latin America (57)	Percent in non-English speaking households — Linguistically isolated (58)	Not linguistically isolated (59)
MICHIGAN—Cont'd																
Leelanau County	7 996	73.8	2	100.0	266	71.4	14	71.4	104	91.3	2.2	0.8	0.3	0.8	0.6	9.1
Lenawee County	33 265	72.8	305	73.8	150	76.7	166	68.7	1 870	79.8	1.6	0.5	0.5	0.4	0.8	9.4
Livingston County	53 875	78.9	106	71.7	239	86.2	264	75.4	470	79.4	3.0	1.2	0.6	0.3	0.3	7.5
Luce County	2 304	71.1	3	100.0	136	67.6	4	100.0	4	100.0	1.1	0.3	0.1	0.3	0.1	6.2
Mackinac County	4 240	67.0	2	0.0	601	67.6	7	71.4	22	68.2	1.2	0.4	0.1	0.2	0.2	7.0
Macomb County	288 406	68.3	7 566	62.5	1 017	72.6	5 267	79.2	3 414	74.5	8.8	4.3	3.1	0.4	2.5	15.1
Manistee County	9 492	68.0	19	84.2	88	70.5	12	100.0	138	67.4	1.3	0.6	0.2	0.2	0.2	6.9
Marquette County	24 974	64.0	77	68.8	274	61.7	93	58.1	75	58.7	1.4	0.6	0.4	0.1	0.4	7.7
Mason County	10 939	69.5	60	96.7	94	78.7	13	30.8	203	81.3	1.6	0.5	0.3	0.4	0.3	8.1
Mecosta County	13 889	67.5	453	45.3	115	62.6	92	35.9	129	63.6	1.9	0.5	0.8	0.2	0.8	8.2
Menominee County	10 259	66.9	2	0.0	187	62.0	6	66.7	30	53.3	0.9	0.6	0.1	0.1	0.3	6.6
Midland County	30 351	71.5	268	74.6	156	80.1	410	78.3	341	72.7	3.2	0.9	1.1	0.4	0.5	7.0
Missaukee County	5 370	74.3	2	100.0	18	66.7	9	77.8	22	81.8	1.0	0.4	0.2	0.2	0.2	5.7
Monroe County	51 537	74.8	863	71.5	93	67.7	230	79.1	700	75.9	1.9	0.6	0.6	0.4	0.6	7.6
Montcalm County	21 349	73.9	52	46.2	109	75.2	45	91.1	326	71.8	1.1	0.4	0.3	0.3	0.7	6.9
Montmorency County	4 402	68.9	0	X	12	33.3	2	100.0	14	35.7	1.3	0.6	0.1	0.1	0.3	5.3
Muskegon County	52 842	70.3	7 928	70.2	436	71.6	199	71.4	1 477	77.3	1.9	0.5	0.5	0.7	0.9	7.4
Newaygo County	16 818	73.8	153	53.6	91	76.9	41	48.8	379	87.1	1.8	0.4	0.3	1.0	0.9	7.3
Oakland County	392 610	66.9	46 545	64.7	1 203	68.3	16 328	79.2	8 550	71.5	10.0	3.0	4.9	0.7	2.4	15.2
Oceana County	8 995	73.7	6	100.0	105	74.3	6	50.0	623	90.4	4.4	0.4	0.1	3.7	2.3	13.6
Ogemaw County	8 618	70.4	2	100.0	63	84.1	30	53.3	51	72.5	1.3	0.5	0.3	0.0	0.2	5.3
Ontonagon County	3 375	64.0	0	X	32	71.9	3	0.0	7	100.0	1.4	1.0	0.2	0.0	0.6	10.8
Osceola County	8 663	72.8	13	92.3	33	66.7	6	66.7	54	68.5	1.2	0.5	0.2	0.2	0.5	7.0
Oscoda County	3 840	70.1	7	42.9	6	100.0	6	100.0	38	52.6	1.5	0.6	0.2	0.3	1.6	9.4
Otsego County	8 827	72.7	4	50.0	50	82.0	19	73.7	37	97.3	1.6	0.7	0.3	0.0	0.4	7.2
Ottawa County	75 066	75.1	650	64.3	265	70.2	1 235	82.3	4 076	86.9	4.9	1.0	1.6	1.9	1.7	11.9
Presque Isle County	6 086	68.8	1	0.0	24	62.5	0	X	16	62.5	1.2	0.6	0.1	0.0	0.4	8.6
Roscommon County	11 071	67.8	4	100.0	47	78.7	26	65.4	73	84.9	1.7	0.9	0.2	0.1	0.2	6.9
Saginaw County	61 489	69.0	13 380	70.9	338	83.1	548	67.3	4 093	76.6	2.0	0.5	0.8	0.5	0.7	10.3
St. Clair County	59 081	72.2	1 356	71.3	263	76.4	131	80.9	872	78.8	2.7	0.9	0.4	0.3	0.5	7.3
St. Joseph County	21 757	71.4	618	59.1	98	77.6	109	60.6	548	74.8	3.4	0.6	0.4	2.2	2.4	9.2
Sanilac County	16 361	72.1	10	100.0	43	81.4	37	81.1	354	73.2	1.6	0.6	0.3	0.1	0.6	7.6
Schoolcraft County	3 350	69.9	2	0.0	159	64.8	4	100.0	13	53.8	1.0	0.5	0.1	0.0	0.1	4.4
Shiawassee County	26 146	74.3	50	58.0	101	80.2	50	54.0	358	77.4	1.2	0.6	0.1	0.2	0.3	6.4
Tuscola County	20 745	74.7	110	68.2	82	68.3	51	88.2	319	70.2	1.1	0.4	0.3	0.1	0.4	7.4
Van Buren County	24 914	72.4	1 482	67.4	149	65.8	21	90.5	1 104	86.5	3.5	0.7	0.3	2.4	1.7	10.9
Washtenaw County	98 193	59.6	14 310	60.7	372	55.9	7 471	55.4	2 765	53.2	10.3	2.4	5.4	1.2	2.5	15.8
Wayne County	416 435	65.8	303 661	67.5	2 874	68.3	11 204	78.3	21 532	74.7	6.7	1.7	3.0	1.2	2.5	13.4
Wexford County	11 497	70.8	20	75.0	40	77.5	30	87.2	90	00.9	1.8	0.6	0.5	0.3	0.4	5.9
MINNESOTA	1 735 421	66.3	55 913	66.0	16 579	70.7	35 604	74.8	35 171	75.4	5.3	0.9	2.1	1.3	2.1	10.8
Aitkin County	6 491	66.7	5	0.0	114	86.8	2	100.0	18	77.8	0.9	0.3	0.2	0.1	0.3	6.7
Anoka County	101 106	74.8	1 339	79.4	658	82.1	1 109	83.7	1 158	81.8	3.6	1.0	1.3	0.7	1.2	8.8
Becker County	10 838	69.1	17	88.2	710	72.0	25	100.0	37	62.2	1.0	0.3	0.4	0.0	0.6	8.0
Beltrami County	11 889	66.3	30	80.0	2 125	79.3	119	61.3	71	95.8	1.8	0.4	0.9	0.1	0.5	10.9
Benton County	12 621	65.2	94	39.4	33	51.5	139	32.4	86	94.2	2.1	0.4	1.1	0.4	1.1	8.5
Big Stone County	2 385	68.5	0	X	9	55.6	0	X	4	0.0	0.8	0.4	0.1	0.1	1.4	7.4
Blue Earth County	20 247	60.9	230	57.0	33	72.7	273	52.0	259	69.1	2.9	0.4	1.5	0.5	0.7	8.0
Brown County	10 334	67.7	17	88.2	37	78.4	8	100.0	136	86.8	1.3	0.3	0.2	0.5	0.8	10.1
Carlton County	11 290	69.7	2	0.0	539	74.6	16	37.5	51	51.0	1.6	0.5	0.4	0.3	0.4	8.3
Carver County	23 457	77.0	109	71.6	37	81.1	259	88.4	385	84.9	3.4	0.5	1.1	1.2	1.2	10.1
Cass County	9 728	71.0	7	28.6	933	71.6	21	61.9	52	76.9	0.8	0.3	0.2	0.1	0.1	10.3
Chippewa County	5 249	67.0	3	100.0	36	77.8	2	100.0	49	83.7	1.4	0.4	0.2	0.7	0.4	6.0
Chisago County	14 237	76.8	34	91.2	43	60.5	39	84.6	59	67.8	1.2	0.3	0.5	0.1	0.2	7.1
Clay County	17 694	66.3	62	53.2	186	84.4	92	56.5	437	80.8	2.6	0.4	1.1	0.6	1.6	10.2
Clearwater County	3 083	68.3	0	X	188	80.3	5	100.0	8	100.0	0.9	0.3	0.3	0.1	0.2	6.6
Cook County	2 097	62.9	2	100.0	191	49.2	5	100.0	11	81.8	2.7	1.3	0.3	0.4	0.2	7.1
Cottonwood County	4 797	69.0	0	X	0	X	42	78.6	46	84.8	2.2	0.3	1.3	0.4	1.3	9.0
Crow Wing County	21 904	68.9	18	61.1	143	65.7	54	63.0	101	51.5	1.2	0.4	0.4	0.2	0.2	7.0
Dakota County	121 690	71.7	2 735	72.2	438	85.8	2 571	79.9	2 677	80.5	5.1	1.1	2.2	1.1	1.6	10.9
Dodge County	6 241	75.7	9	55.6	10	40.0	4	100.0	139	84.9	2.5	0.5	0.3	1.5	1.1	9.5
Douglas County	13 080	68.3	27	48.1	26	80.8	20	90.0	45	75.6	0.9	0.3	0.2	0.2	0.4	6.7
Faribault County	6 490	67.0	4	50.0	15	100.0	5	100.0	137	82.5	1.6	0.2	0.3	0.9	0.5	6.7
Fillmore County	8 149	69.5	10	100.0	3	33.3	5	0.0	25	72.0	0.8	0.3	0.1	0.1	1.6	8.7
Freeborn County	12 729	67.6	15	100.0	10	40.0	59	49.2	524	72.9	3.1	0.5	0.3	2.2	2.2	9.2
Goodhue County	16 550	70.3	62	90.3	183	53.6	44	61.4	110	69.1	1.2	0.4	0.4	0.3	0.4	6.6

[1]Hispanic or Latino persons may be of any race.

STATE/ County code	MSA/PMSA/ NECMA code[1]	STATE County	Population by age (percent)							Median age	+/− U.S. percent under 18 years	+/− U.S. percent 65 years and over	Non-Hispanic White		
			Total population	Under 5 years	5 to 17 years	18 to 24 years	25 to 44 years	45 to 64 years	65 years and over				Total population	Under 18 years	65 years and over
			1	2	3	4	5	6	7	8	9	10	11	12	13
		MINNESOTA—Cont'd													
27 051	...	Grant County.............	6 289	5.1	18.6	6.8	23.2	23.3	23.0	42.5	−2.0	10.6	6 196	23.5	23.3
27 053	5120	Hennepin County	1 116 200	6.5	17.5	9.7	33.9	21.5	10.9	34.9	−1.7	−1.5	882 300	20.4	13.1
27 055	3870	Houston County	19 718	5.8	21.3	6.6	27.0	23.2	16.0	38.8	1.4	3.6	19 348	26.8	16.3
27 057	...	Hubbard County	18 376	5.5	19.1	6.3	24.2	27.0	17.9	41.8	−1.1	5.5	17 699	24.0	18.4
27 059	5120	Isanti County	31 287	6.4	22.1	7.8	30.6	22.2	10.9	35.7	2.8	−1.5	30 377	28.2	11.1
27 061	...	Itasca County	43 992	5.3	19.1	7.7	24.6	26.6	16.8	41.1	−1.3	4.4	41 511	23.3	17.5
27 063	...	Jackson County	11 268	5.2	19.4	6.5	26.0	22.5	20.5	40.8	−1.1	8.1	10 885	24.0	21.0
27 065	...	Kanabec County	14 996	5.9	21.6	7.1	27.5	23.7	14.1	38.0	1.8	1.7	14 577	27.0	14.3
27 067	...	Kandiyohi County	41 203	6.3	20.4	9.3	26.7	22.5	15.0	36.9	1.0	2.6	37 303	24.4	16.4
27 069	...	Kittson County	5 285	6.1	19.0	5.7	23.5	24.2	21.6	42.4	−0.6	9.2	5 105	24.3	22.3
27 071	...	Koochiching County	14 355	5.2	18.7	6.4	25.9	25.8	17.9	41.5	−1.8	5.5	13 730	23.0	18.5
27 073	...	Lac qui Parle County	8 067	5.0	19.5	5.5	22.6	24.1	23.3	43.4	−1.2	10.9	7 965	24.2	23.5
27 075	...	Lake County	11 058	5.1	17.2	6.8	24.5	26.4	20.1	42.9	−3.4	7.7	10 784	21.9	20.4
27 077	...	Lake of the Woods County ..	4 522	4.3	20.2	5.7	25.3	27.2	17.3	41.6	−1.2	4.9	4 377	23.9	17.8
27 079	...	Le Sueur County	25 426	6.3	21.2	7.7	27.4	23.4	14.0	37.3	1.8	1.6	24 083	26.6	14.7
27 081	...	Lincoln County	6 429	5.6	18.1	6.1	23.4	22.5	24.3	43.0	−2.0	11.9	6 372	23.5	24.5
27 083	...	Lyon County	25 425	6.6	19.5	13.5	26.8	19.0	14.6	34.0	0.4	2.2	23 354	24.6	15.7
27 085	...	McLeod County	34 898	7.0	20.9	7.7	29.4	21.2	13.9	35.6	2.2	1.5	33 286	26.9	14.5
27 087	...	Mahnomen County	5 190	7.3	22.1	7.1	23.6	23.0	16.9	38.2	3.7	4.5	3 252	21.7	22.7
27 089	...	Marshall County	10 155	5.8	19.5	6.6	24.6	24.9	18.6	40.5	−0.4	6.2	9 708	24.3	19.2
27 091	...	Martin County	21 802	5.2	19.8	6.5	24.7	24.0	19.8	41.5	−0.7	7.4	21 150	24.2	20.3
27 093	...	Meeker County	22 644	6.4	20.7	7.4	26.5	22.8	16.3	38.3	1.4	3.9	22 021	26.9	16.7
27 095	...	Mille Lacs County	22 330	6.1	21.0	7.5	26.8	22.5	16.1	38.0	1.4	3.7	20 813	25.8	16.8
27 097	...	Morrison County	31 712	6.8	21.2	7.9	26.7	21.8	15.6	36.9	2.3	3.2	31 139	27.8	15.8
27 099	...	Mower County	38 603	6.2	18.8	8.3	25.7	21.5	19.5	38.9	−0.7	7.1	36 064	24.0	20.7
27 101	...	Murray County	9 165	5.4	19.5	6.6	23.1	24.6	21.3	42.4	−0.8	8.9	8 909	24.5	21.8
27 103	...	Nicollet County	29 771	5.9	18.8	16.5	26.7	21.2	10.9	32.6	−1.0	−1.5	28 424	24.4	11.4
27 105	...	Nobles County	20 832	6.8	19.8	7.9	27.0	21.2	17.3	37.5	0.9	4.9	17 319	24.0	20.6
27 107	...	Norman County	7 442	5.8	19.8	5.8	24.5	23.1	21.0	40.9	−0.1	8.6	6 995	24.2	22.2
27 109	6820	Olmsted County	124 277	7.1	19.9	8.4	32.3	21.5	10.8	35.0	1.3	−1.6	110 855	25.6	11.7
27 111	...	Otter Tail County	57 159	5.6	19.4	7.3	24.2	24.6	18.9	41.1	−0.7	6.5	55 183	24.3	19.5
27 113	...	Pennington County	13 584	6.2	18.1	10.6	26.7	22.6	15.9	37.9	−1.4	3.5	13 184	24.0	16.3
27 115	...	Pine County	26 530	5.3	20.1	7.8	27.9	23.8	15.1	38.4	−0.3	2.7	24 617	25.2	15.8
27 117	...	Pipestone County	9 895	5.9	19.8	6.9	24.6	21.5	21.4	40.2	0.0	9.0	9 533	25.2	21.9
27 119	2985	Polk County	31 369	6.1	19.8	9.7	24.9	22.2	17.3	38.2	0.2	4.9	29 000	24.4	18.5
27 121	....	Pope County	11 236	4.9	19.9	6.5	23.2	23.9	21.6	42.1	−0.9	9.2	11 116	24.6	21.8
27 123	5120	Ramsey County	511 035	6.9	18.7	11.2	31.0	20.6	11.7	33.7	−0.1	−0.7	385 176	20.0	14.4
27 125	...	Red Lake County	4 299	5.5	19.9	7.6	24.7	23.3	19.0	40.4	−0.3	6.6	4 147	25.3	18.7
27 127	...	Redwood County	16 815	6.2	20.3	6.5	25.0	22.7	19.3	39.5	0.8	6.9	15 917	25.3	20.2
27 129	...	Renville County	17 154	5.8	20.8	6.5	25.3	21.8	19.8	39.7	0.9	7.4	16 076	25.0	21.0
27 131	...	Rice County	56 665	6.1	19.1	15.8	27.4	20.3	11.3	32.9	−0.5	−1.1	51 247	24.4	12.4
27 133	...	Rock County	9 721	5.7	20.5	7.0	24.4	21.9	20.5	39.9	0.5	8.1	9 416	25.3	21.1
27 135	...	Roseau County	16 338	7.4	22.4	6.8	30.1	20.7	12.6	35.3	4.1	0.2	15 564	28.9	13.1
27 137	2240	St. Louis County	200 528	5.2	17.2	11.4	25.8	24.3	16.1	39.0	−3.3	3.7	189 227	21.4	16.8
27 139	5120	Scott County	89 498	9.1	22.1	6.7	37.4	18.6	6.1	32.7	5.5	−6.3	82 864	30.6	6.4
27 141	5120	Sherburne County	64 417	8.3	22.6	9.6	33.9	18.5	7.1	31.4	5.2	−5.3	61 973	30.6	7.3
27 143	...	Sibley County	15 356	7.0	20.6	7.5	27.4	21.0	16.5	37.3	1.9	4.1	14 354	26.2	17.6
27 145	6980	Stearns County	133 166	6.5	19.3	16.1	28.2	19.0	11.0	31.6	0.1	−1.4	127 239	25.4	11.4
27 147	...	Steele County	33 680	6.9	20.9	8.2	29.1	21.8	13.1	35.7	2.1	0.7	31 476	26.4	13.9
27 149	...	Stevens County	10 053	5.3	16.3	20.8	21.6	19.1	16.9	33.9	−4.1	4.5	9 621	21.7	17.5
27 151	...	Swift County	11 956	5.4	17.6	7.3	29.4	21.6	18.7	39.3	−2.7	6.3	10 824	24.2	20.5
27 153	...	Todd County	24 426	5.8	21.6	8.0	24.6	23.8	16.1	38.5	1.7	3.7	23 503	26.9	16.6
27 155	...	Traverse County	4 134	5.6	19.9	5.6	21.4	21.0	26.5	42.9	−0.2	14.1	3 960	24.7	27.4
27 157	...	Wabasha County	21 610	5.7	21.4	7.3	27.0	23.7	14.9	38.0	1.4	2.5	20 990	26.7	15.3
27 159	...	Wadena County	13 713	6.3	19.5	8.2	23.7	22.5	19.7	39.9	0.1	7.3	13 276	25.0	20.3
27 161	...	Waseca County	19 526	6.7	19.1	8.6	29.9	21.6	14.2	36.3	0.1	1.8	18 117	25.2	15.2
27 163	5120	Washington County	201 130	7.6	21.8	6.8	32.9	23.3	7.5	35.1	3.7	−4.9	186 010	28.5	7.9
27 165	...	Watonwan County	11 876	6.7	21.0	7.1	24.9	21.8	18.6	38.6	2.0	6.2	9 840	24.2	22.0
27 167	...	Wilkin County	7 138	6.4	21.5	6.7	27.7	21.6	16.1	38.1	2.2	3.7	6 919	27.2	16.5
27 169	...	Winona County	49 985	5.6	17.3	18.8	24.8	20.4	13.1	32.8	−2.8	0.7	47 550	22.3	13.7
27 171	5120	Wright County	89 986	8.3	22.8	7.4	32.8	19.8	8.8	33.1	5.4	−3.6	87 564	30.7	9.0
27 173	...	Yellow Medicine County .	11 080	5.7	20.1	7.4	24.3	22.0	20.4	40.4	0.1	8.0	10 482	24.8	21.2

[1]MSA = Metropolitan Statistical Area. PMSA = Primary MSA. NECMA = New England County Metropolitan Area. See the Appendix A for explanation of these concepts. See Appendix B for list of metropolitan areas identified by type, with component counties.

Table A-3. States and Counties — Age, Ethnicity, and Household Structure

	Black or African American			American Indian and Alaska Native			Asian, Hawaiian, and Pacific Islander			Hispanic or Latino[1]			Two or more races		
		Age (percent)			Age (percent)			Age (percent)			Age (percent)			Age (percent)	
STATE County	Total population	Under 18 years	65 years and over	Total population	Under 18 years	65 years and over	Total population	Under 18 years	65 years and over	Total population	Under 18 years	65 years and over	Total population	Under 18 years	65 years and over
	14	15	16	17	18	19	20	21	22	23	24	25	26	27	28
MINNESOTA—Cont'd															
Grant County	3	100.0	0.0	7	28.6	0.0	11	27.3	18.2	44	40.9	2.3	29	41.4	0.0
Hennepin County	98 138	37.6	3.1	10 659	33.6	3.8	53 719	34.3	3.4	45 424	33.4	1.5	30 731	49.0	2.6
Houston County	35	37.1	0.0	16	25.0	0.0	137	52.6	0.0	129	37.2	0.0	84	53.6	0.0
Hubbard County	28	67.9	0.0	303	39.3	3.0	68	33.8	2.9	100	44.0	4.0	186	44.1	8.6
Isanti County	124	44.4	1.6	163	42.3	0.0	106	47.2	1.9	285	39.3	4.6	269	39.4	4.8
Itasca County	116	41.4	3.4	1 450	40.2	5.9	96	44.8	9.4	330	47.6	3.6	545	40.7	6.6
Jackson County	14	57.1	0.0	15	0.0	0.0	185	44.9	4.3	153	44.4	6.5	11	63.6	0.0
Kanabec County	14	21.4	0.0	96	40.6	0.0	59	40.7	11.9	116	45.7	7.8	154	55.2	7.8
Kandiyohi County	285	53.0	0.0	63	31.7	15.9	118	33.1	1.7	3 240	46.9	1.3	503	55.7	0.6
Kittson County	22	50.0	0.0	33	42.4	0.0	16	56.3	6.3	68	50.0	0.0	45	37.8	4.4
Koochiching County	49	87.8	0.0	340	28.2	9.4	32	53.1	0.0	70	58.6	0.0	137	56.9	1.5
Lac qui Parle County	8	50.0	0.0	15	33.3	13.3	31	25.8	0.0	19	52.0	10.5	32	62.5	9.4
Lake County	2	0.0	0.0	137	40.1	1.5	11	9.1	0.0	38	15.8	36.8	86	48.8	2.3
Lake of the Woods County	11	45.5	0.0	64	59.4	0.0	11	9.1	18.2	18	44.4	0.0	41	31.7	4.9
Le Sueur County	60	43.3	0.0	86	24.4	4.7	87	32.2	5.7	946	43.2	2.0	190	47.4	2.6
Lincoln County	0	X	X	6	66.7	0.0	17	35.3	0.0	34	44.1	5.9	0	X	X
Lyon County	343	28.6	0.0	85	51.8	0.0	456	47.6	3.3	1 014	45.3	0.7	271	43.9	6.3
McLeod County	56	44.6	0.0	75	40.0	6.7	223	35.9	5.4	1 116	47.2	0.2	197	49.2	1.0
Mahnomen County	3	0.0	0.0	1 379	41.0	6.5	54	35.2	22.2	52	44.2	0.0	454	47.6	7.5
Marshall County	17	29.4	0.0	28	46.4	0.0	35	71.4	0.0	282	42.6	4.3	103	49.5	6.8
Martin County	32	46.9	0.0	75	53.3	6.7	156	50.6	0.0	310	46.8	1.3	107	73.8	9.3
Meeker County	61	14.8	8.2	108	32.4	1.9	63	60.3	0.0	377	34.2	1.3	108	20.4	1.9
Mille Lacs County	45	51.1	6.7	873	42.5	7.0	83	38.6	7.2	271	46.5	4.8	284	56.0	6.3
Morrison County	72	56.9	2.8	79	17.7	2.5	113	26.5	0.0	189	42.9	3.2	121	49.6	7.4
Mower County	220	39.5	0.9	100	22.0	9.0	475	32.6	1.7	1 568	37.1	1.7	259	64.9	5.0
Murray County	30	66.7	0.0	24	54.2	12.5	22	13.6	9.1	144	34.0	0.0	38	55.3	15.8
Nicollet County	301	21.3	1.7	10	20.0	0.0	428	22.9	0.0	511	35.2	0.0	124	57.3	1.6
Nobles County	284	45.4	0.7	130	46.2	0.0	782	38.0	3.1	2 234	37.8	0.3	338	55.0	3.3
Norman County	13	76.9	0.0	86	39.5	4.7	13	0.0	0.0	199	50.3	0.5	139	54.0	5.0
Olmsted County	3 100	39.9	3.4	400	12.3	3.0	5 354	35.1	3.5	2 545	34.4	2.1	2 119	53.9	2.8
Otter Tail County	209	70.3	1.0	284	34.2	6.7	171	35.1	4.1	974	41.0	2.6	422	52.1	2.4
Pennington County	36	52.8	0.0	129	20.2	0.0	97	32.0	0.0	99	34.3	0.0	56	33.9	1.8
Pine County	332	12.3	3.6	761	32.7	6.8	84	30.3	9.5	482	18.9	3.5	289	51.9	5.2
Pipestone County	13	30.8	0.0	109	39.4	7.3	92	8.7	19.6	48	31.3	4.2	89	73.0	2.2
Polk County	142	33.8	0.0	300	40.0	4.7	193	36.3	1.0	1 436	46.3	2.1	378	54.2	2.9
Pope County	17	64.7	0.0	9	44.4	0.0	26	34.6	0.0	34	32.4	5.9	40	45.0	15.0
Ramsey County	37 414	39.0	4.2	4 581	34.8	2.5	44 300	46.0	3.3	27 210	38.8	2.4	16 532	53.2	2.4
Red Lake County	0	X	X	103	23.3	39.8	11	63.6	0.0	20	40.0	0.0	24	50.0	0.0
Redwood County	8	75.0	0.0	596	41.9	2.9	72	55.6	0.0	134	59.0	3.0	126	57.9	8.7
Renville County	15	40.0	0.0	62	53.2	6.5	37	43.2	8.1	880	50.6	0.7	132	52.3	3.0
Rice County	711	17.0	0.3	320	20.3	0.9	925	23.2	1.7	3 055	38.8	0.5	805	46.8	2.7
Rock County	131	60.3	3.8	39	64.1	0.0	38	52.6	0.0	69	37.7	0.0	50	60.0	0.0
Roseau County	25	64.0	0.0	226	37.6	2.7	349	46.4	2.9	67	50.7	0.0	115	61.7	0.0
St. Louis County	1 769	35.3	9.2	3 750	39.0	3.8	1 590	29.7	4.3	1 655	47.1	4.4	2 648	47.8	4.3
Scott County	668	34.4	1.8	788	33.9	1.3	1 876	31.7	4.2	2 450	42.4	0.9	928	54.6	2.7
Sherburne County	454	13.0	0.0	249	31.7	0.0	379	37.7	3.2	883	46.5	1.0	549	53.0	1.5
Sibley County	26	42.3	0.0	58	43.1	0.0	40	45.0	0.0	810	47.3	0.6	114	46.5	1.8
Stearns County	900	25.3	2.2	400	29.5	4.5	1 807	23.1	3.9	1 633	40.0	1.0	1 294	49.8	1.6
Steele County	311	52.4	0.0	36	50.0	22.2	223	30.5	4.0	1 231	43.7	1.9	517	61.9	3.3
Stevens County	137	14.6	8.0	70	27.1	5.7	67	14.9	0.0	97	30.9	0.0	85	28.2	3.5
Swift County	229	2.6	0.0	29	3.4	3.4	275	5.5	0.7	349	22.1	6.0	380	13.2	0.8
Todd County	49	22.4	10.2	140	39.3	4.3	100	39.0	2.0	477	45.1	1.0	195	46.7	4.6
Traverse County	0	X	X	97	37.1	2.1	21	52.4	47.6	44	47.7	0.0	19	42.1	0.0
Wabasha County	39	46.2	0.0	73	46.6	2.7	99	32.3	5.1	355	42.5	0.6	78	48.7	9.0
Wadena County	52	36.5	0.0	95	42.1	0.0	81	45.7	0.0	147	57.1	4.8	66	48.5	9.1
Waseca County	464	20.7	0.0	179	14.0	1.1	92	47.8	0.0	577	43.7	3.1	145	53.8	0.0
Washington County	3 469	31.2	0.5	745	20.9	5.2	4 379	39.8	3.4	3 940	44.3	1.7	3 159	55.0	2.8
Watonwan County	104	64.4	0.0	32	53.1	0.0	96	40.6	5.2	1 785	43.7	2.0	76	43.4	3.9
Wilkin County	8	75.0	0.0	46	34.8	0.0	11	36.4	0.0	124	55.6	2.4	30	43.3	13.3
Winona County	393	43.8	0.0	150	24.0	4.7	810	25.8	1.1	687	38.4	0.6	571	41.9	9.8
Wright County	374	47.1	0.0	254	29.5	2.0	211	43.6	0.0	1 015	53.8	1.3	652	51.4	4.0
Yellow Medicine County	23	39.1	52.2	232	40.9	9.1	31	32.3	6.5	225	44.0	2.7	91	56.0	0.0

[1] Hispanic or Latino persons may be of any race.

Table A-3. States and Counties — Age, Ethnicity, and Household Structure

STATE County	Total households	Family households (percent)						Nonfamily households (percent)						Percent of householders 65 years and over who live alone	Grandparents who are responsible for the care of their grandchildren
		Married-couple family households			Other family households			Two or more unrelated persons		Male living alone		Female living alone			
		Total	With children	Householder 65 years or over	Total	With children	Householder 65 years or over	Total	Householder 65 years or over	Total	Householder 65 years or over	Total	Householder 65 years or over		
	29	30	31	32	33	34	35	36	37	38	39	40	41	42	43
MINNESOTA—Cont'd															
Grant County	2 542	59.8	24.1	15.9	9.4	5.7	1.6	3.1	0.5	11.3	4.3	16.4	12.4	48.0	10
Hennepin County	456 278	46.0	21.7	7.1	12.9	7.8	1.3	9.3	0.4	13.8	1.8	18.0	6.6	49.3	4 429
Houston County	7 594	59.3	27.0	12.3	11.5	7.4	1.5	3.7	0.2	11.5	3.1	14.1	9.3	47.1	18
Hubbard County	7 428	61.1	23.2	15.0	11.1	6.5	1.4	3.5	0.3	11.9	3.7	12.4	8.0	41.2	112
Isanti County	11 266	62.4	29.3	9.6	12.9	8.8	1.3	4.6	0.1	9.6	2.2	10.4	6.1	42.8	136
Itasca County	17 818	58.9	22.3	12.8	10.9	6.9	1.5	4.1	0.6	12.2	3.7	13.9	8.5	45.1	196
Jackson County	4 576	61.0	25.2	16.3	7.9	5.5	1.1	2.9	0.3	13.7	3.3	14.4	9.0	41.0	23
Kanabec County	5 754	59.4	24.9	12.4	12.9	9.1	1.2	4.0	0.5	12.0	3.2	11.7	7.0	41.8	69
Kandiyohi County	15 973	58.2	26.3	11.9	10.9	7.3	1.3	5.2	0.6	11.0	2.5	14.6	8.2	43.6	189
Kittson County	2 169	56.9	24.1	14.9	10.0	5.2	2.5	2.5	0.2	15.1	4.3	15.5	11.4	47.2	21
Koochiching County	6 057	54.3	21.1	11.5	11.7	8.3	1.3	3.9	0.4	13.2	3.8	16.9	11.0	52.9	48
Lac qui Parle County	3 315	60.1	24.2	16.4	6.9	4.1	1.5	2.8	0.5	13.0	4.8	17.1	12.8	48.9	27
Lake County	4 655	57.6	20.8	15.5	10.3	7.2	0.8	4.1	0.4	14.0	3.1	14.1	9.3	42.6	12
Lake of the Woods County	1 913	57.3	23.1	10.2	8.6	5.0	1.6	4.5	1.6	15.6	4.4	13.9	9.1	50.3	16
Le Sueur County	9 626	61.7	28.7	11.5	10.9	6.3	1.6	3.9	0.3	11.5	2.8	12.0	8.2	45.1	66
Lincoln County	2 648	60.4	23.9	17.4	7.0	3.4	2.0	2.4	0.1	12.6	4.2	17.6	12.8	46.5	19
Lyon County	9 678	55.7	26.6	10.5	9.8	6.7	0.8	6.6	0.4	10.8	2.6	17.1	10.7	53.2	32
McLeod County	13 478	59.9	28.4	10.6	10.3	6.7	1.0	4.9	0.1	10.3	2.1	14.7	9.5	49.5	81
Mahnomen County	1 964	50.7	21.4	11.9	18.4	10.9	2.7	3.5	0.6	12.7	4.5	14.6	11.0	50.5	84
Marshall County	4 111	61.5	25.9	14.8	8.1	5.0	1.4	1.9	0.1	14.2	3.9	14.4	10.6	47.0	33
Martin County	9 062	57.2	23.1	14.2	10.1	6.6	1.6	2.8	0.3	12.3	2.6	17.6	12.6	48.8	23
Meeker County	8 563	62.1	27.0	12.7	9.9	6.7	1.3	3.8	0.2	11.0	3.3	13.2	9.1	46.7	63
Mille Lacs County	8 648	56.5	23.6	12.6	13.1	9.1	1.4	4.6	0.4	11.5	3.3	14.2	9.1	46.2	79
Morrison County	11 836	60.9	27.5	13.1	11.4	7.6	1.5	2.8	0.2	11.3	3.1	13.6	8.9	45.0	124
Mower County	15 606	54.6	22.9	14.1	12.2	7.8	1.5	4.1	0.3	11.6	3.3	17.5	11.6	48.6	163
Murray County	3 716	63.5	24.5	16.8	6.3	3.9	1.4	3.0	0.5	12.0	3.5	15.2	11.7	44.8	17
Nicollet County	10 647	59.0	28.9	9.2	9.8	7.1	0.5	7.2	0.5	10.1	1.8	13.9	6.8	45.7	66
Nobles County	7 961	60.7	26.7	14.6	9.7	6.2	1.1	3.3	0.2	10.0	2.3	16.3	12.0	47.3	94
Norman County	3 011	58.6	26.0	14.8	8.3	4.7	1.3	2.0	0.3	13.9	4.9	17.2	12.8	51.8	26
Olmsted County	47 894	57.3	28.6	8.6	10.7	7.3	0.8	6.2	0.3	10.8	1.8	15.0	6.3	45.6	334
Otter Tail County	22 662	60.6	24.6	15.2	9.2	6.0	1.3	3.7	0.4	11.9	3.4	14.6	9.9	44.2	217
Pennington County	5 505	52.8	22.8	11.5	12.0	7.4	1.4	5.5	0.1	12.7	2.3	17.0	9.5	47.6	19
Pine County	9 908	57.0	23.5	12.0	12.8	8.2	1.7	5.0	0.4	12.8	3.4	12.4	7.2	42.6	150
Pipestone County	4 082	58.0	24.5	15.4	9.2	6.9	0.9	2.5	0.0	11.8	3.8	18.4	13.4	51.3	28
Polk County	12 053	55.8	25.7	11.9	11.5	7.4	1.5	3.8	0.3	12.5	3.9	16.3	10.4	51.2	69
Pope County	4 520	61.0	25.8	15.5	7.6	4.6	1.0	2.6	0.4	12.5	4.3	16.2	12.1	49.3	31
Ramsey County	201 379	45.2	21.7	7.5	14.9	9.0	1.8	8.0	0.4	13.2	2.1	18.7	7.3	49.5	2 183
Red Lake County	1 710	55.8	25.2	12.2	9.8	6.3	0.9	3.7	0.2	13.5	3.9	17.1	11.5	53.6	6
Redwood County	6 704	58.2	24.8	14.5	9.5	6.5	1.2	3.5	0.5	11.6	3.0	17.2	12.0	48.0	14
Renville County	6 759	60.0	26.6	14.4	8.2	4.9	1.7	3.3	0.4	13.1	3.8	15.5	11.2	47.7	63
Rice County	18 922	58.9	28.7	9.5	12.1	8.1	1.1	5.3	0.2	11.1	2.2	12.7	7.6	47.5	158
Rock County	3 848	64.5	26.9	16.6	6.7	4.5	0.5	1.9	0.0	10.1	3.5	16.9	12.3	48.1	24
Roseau County	6 204	60.8	30.6	9.8	11.2	7.7	1.1	3.4	0.3	12.8	2.6	11.8	7.4	46.9	35
St. Louis County	82 720	50.2	20.2	10.6	12.5	8.0	1.5	6.2	0.4	13.6	3.2	17.5	9.6	50.5	770
Scott County	30 714	68.0	38.2	5.6	10.6	7.3	0.9	5.3	0.2	7.6	1.0	8.4	3.6	41.1	235
Sherburne County	21 625	67.0	37.7	6.5	10.7	7.3	0.7	6.7	0.1	7.7	1.0	7.8	3.9	40.5	220
Sibley County	5 798	61.8	28.6	13.7	9.3	5.8	1.3	3.4	0.3	11.4	3.4	14.1	10.0	46.7	40
Stearns County	47 627	57.3	28.9	9.7	10.6	6.7	1.2	8.5	0.3	10.9	2.1	12.7	6.3	42.8	262
Steele County	12 818	59.5	28.1	10.6	11.2	7.8	1.2	4.7	0.4	10.3	2.3	14.3	7.8	45.5	84
Stevens County	3 767	56.7	24.4	14.0	6.7	4.0	0.6	7.6	0.3	11.1	2.8	17.9	12.3	50.3	13
Swift County	4 368	58.0	25.4	14.1	8.6	5.1	1.5	2.6	0.3	11.8	3.8	18.9	14.6	53.9	9
Todd County	9 363	60.8	26.4	13.7	9.5	5.6	1.2	3.5	0.4	11.7	3.0	14.5	9.7	45.4	70
Traverse County	1 720	56.7	21.8	19.8	8.7	5.7	2.0	2.1	0.2	14.8	4.9	17.6	12.6	44.3	6
Wabasha County	8 267	61.6	28.0	12.0	9.8	6.5	1.3	4.3	0.4	11.6	2.9	12.7	7.7	43.7	51
Wadena County	5 404	56.0	23.3	15.1	11.4	7.4	1.4	3.5	0.3	12.2	3.3	16.9	11.3	46.6	27
Waseca County	7 055	61.6	27.9	11.4	10.4	6.8	1.2	4.0	0.3	11.9	2.6	13.0	7.1	43.1	91
Washington County	71 496	66.4	34.9	7.0	10.6	7.1	0.8	4.3	0.1	7.8	1.2	10.8	4.2	40.2	620
Watonwan County	4 614	56.9	25.2	14.3	11.5	8.0	1.2	2.9	0.4	13.5	3.8	15.2	10.7	47.9	62
Wilkin County	2 744	60.0	29.6	12.8	10.4	6.0	1.9	3.6	0.1	10.1	2.6	15.8	10.4	46.5	11
Winona County	18 753	52.3	24.4	9.7	10.2	6.4	1.7	9.3	0.3	11.9	2.1	16.3	8.8	48.3	150
Wright County	31 415	65.0	35.0	8.2	11.2	7.5	0.9	4.9	0.3	9.1	1.4	9.7	4.8	40.1	259
Yellow Medicine County	4 441	58.5	25.4	14.3	8.9	5.5	1.8	3.6	0.3	11.9	2.9	17.1	12.7	48.6	17

Table A-3. States and Counties — Age, Ethnicity, and Household Structure

STATE County	Households with Non-Hispanic White householder		Households with Black or African American householder		Households with American Indian and Alaska Native householder		Households with Asian, Hawaiian, and Pacific Islander householder		Households with Hispanic or Latino[1] householder		Foreign-born population	Place of birth (percent)			Percent in non-English speaking households	
	Number of households	Percent that are family households	Number of households	Percent that are family households	Number of households	Percent that are family households	Number of households	Percent that are family households	Number of households	Percent that are family households	Percent of total population that is foreign-born	Europe	Asia	Latin America	Linguistically isolated	Not linguistically isolated
	44	45	46	47	48	49	50	51	52	53	54	55	56	57	58	59
MINNESOTA—Cont'd																
Grant County	2 519	69.3	0	X	2	100.0	6	0.0	11	90.9	0.7	0.3	0.1	0.1	0.3	8.1
Hennepin County	386 138	57.7	33 875	63.8	3 309	63.6	14 874	69.4	11 569	73.7	9.9	1.6	3.7	2.4	3.9	13.6
Houston County	7 515	71.0	13	23.1	5	20.0	18	94.4	30	53.3	1.1	0.4	0.4	0.1	0.4	7.0
Hubbard County	7 227	72.1	3	100.0	81	71.6	23	78.3	31	77.4	1.1	0.5	0.3	0.1	0.2	6.9
Isanti County	11 052	75.3	32	81.3	33	87.9	17	82.4	52	59.6	1.3	0.6	0.2	0.2	0.3	7.1
Itasca County	17 092	69.6	16	87.5	432	74.3	12	100.0	73	79.5	1.3	0.5	0.2	0.2	0.2	8.2
Jackson County	4 464	68.9	3	100.0	2	100.0	61	55.7	39	79.5	1.5	0.2	0.9	0.3	0.7	6.6
Kanabec County	5 639	72.4	6	100.0	25	92.0	10	40.0	32	71.9	0.9	0.4	0.3	0.1	0.4	6.1
Kandiyohi County	15 039	68.8	43	62.8	15	53.3	40	70.0	803	79.8	3.8	0.3	0.2	2.7	2.2	12.3
Kittson County	2 124	66.6	3	100.0	10	100.0	0	X	14	85.7	2.0	0.3	0.3	0.2	0.4	7.0
Koochiching County	5 898	65.7	0	X	119	69.7	3	100.0	15	100.0	5.9	0.9	0.2	0.2	0.3	7.0
Lac qui Parle County	3 294	66.9	2	100.0	5	60.0	6	66.7	1	100.0	1.0	0.4	0.3	0.1	0.3	6.9
Lake County	4 579	67.8	2	0.0	35	77.1	0	X	16	43.8	1.7	0.8	0.1	0.1	0.5	7.9
Lake of the Woods County	1 883	65.7	5	60.0	11	100.0	2	0.0	8	87.5	2.9	0.5	0.2	0.0	0.5	9.0
Le Sueur County	9 327	72.3	10	100.0	36	80.6	18	72.2	209	80.4	1.8	0.2	0.2	1.3	1.1	10.2
Lincoln County	2 634	67.3	0	X	0	X	3	100.0	11	81.8	0.7	0.2	0.2	0.1	0.5	7.8
Lyon County	9 186	65.4	110	88.2	18	100.0	91	48.4	234	73.1	4.5	0.4	1.4	2.0	2.5	9.8
McLeod County	13 074	69.8	20	30.0	20	60.0	74	75.7	272	91.9	2.2	0.2	0.4	1.4	1.6	8.5
Mahnomen County	1 376	67.4	1	100.0	430	75.1	19	84.2	7	28.6	1.3	0.3	0.7	0.2	0.7	9.0
Marshall County	4 037	69.4	2	0.0	0	X	0	X	55	78.2	1.9	0.3	0.4	0.8	1.3	9.0
Martin County	8 881	67.4	17	100.0	18	72.2	35	100.0	105	51.4	1.4	0.2	0.5	0.6	0.8	6.1
Meeker County	8 422	71.8	12	75.0	10	80.0	7	100.0	111	89.2	0.8	0.3	0.2	0.3	0.4	7.7
Mille Lacs County	8 261	69.4	10	70.0	262	76.0	21	100.0	53	73.6	1.1	0.3	0.3	0.2	0.4	10.1
Morrison County	11 695	72.2	11	100.0	15	66.7	46	67.4	36	94.4	1.0	0.4	0.3	0.1	0.3	7.6
Mower County	14 974	66.4	49	81.6	44	72.7	133	87.2	396	73.7	3.6	0.5	1.0	1.9	2.4	8.3
Murray County	3 658	69.8	6	100.0	3	100.0	3	0.0	34	79.4	1.4	0.2	0.2	0.8	0.8	7.4
Nicollet County	10 350	68.9	50	68.0	2	100.0	89	61.8	137	64.2	2.7	0.4	1.0	0.8	0.7	9.4
Nobles County	7 043	69.3	100	62.0	34	73.5	202	72.8	559	86.4	9.0	0.2	2.3	6.0	6.3	13.9
Norman County	2 910	66.2	0	X	23	87.0	6	33.3	42	95.2	1.9	0.3	0.2	0.9	1.1	9.5
Olmsted County	43 906	67.7	979	70.9	186	79.6	1 676	71.5	681	72.4	7.9	1.5	3.4	0.9	2.6	11.2
Otter Tail County	22 238	69.7	26	96.2	47	51.1	48	58.3	215	80.9	2.0	0.7	0.3	0.8	1.2	8.2
Pennington County	5 395	64.9	5	60.0	52	48.1	31	51.6	16	87.5	1.6	0.3	0.5	0.4	0.3	6.5
Pine County	9 549	69.9	26	69.2	202	76.2	18	50.0	60	60.0	1.1	0.4	0.2	0.2	0.2	7.8
Pipestone County	4 007	67.5	2	100.0	24	50.0	22	63.6	18	22.2	1.4	0.5	0.8	0.1	0.3	7.3
Polk County	11 452	66.5	14	92.9	72	87.5	65	61.5	379	86.8	2.2	0.4	0.4	0.6	0.8	11.7
Pope County	4 485	68.8	4	25.0	2	100.0	7	57.1	9	33.3	0.9	0.5	0.2	0.0	0.2	7.1
Ramsey County	166 983	57.7	12 979	67.3	1 496	65.6	9 733	82.5	7 217	69.6	10.6	1.2	5.9	2.1	4.8	16.1
Red Lake County	1 686	65.9	0	X	10	30.0	2	100.0	3	100.0	1.1	0.4	0.1	0.1	0.4	8.7
Redwood County	6 422	67.8	0	X	214	65.0	17	88.2	28	60.7	0.7	0.4	0.3	0.0	0.1	6.5
Renville County	6 525	67.6	2	0.0	17	64.7	1	0.0	185	89.7	2.1	0.2	0.2	1.6	1.5	10.9
Rice County	17 838	70.5	114	78.9	59	81.4	163	84.0	662	82.5	4.8	0.4	1.1	2.7	3.3	10.2
Rock County	3 778	70.8	23	100.0	10	40.0	4	100.0	27	100.0	1.1	0.4	0.3	0.3	0.1	6.0
Roseau County	6 010	71.9	3	100.0	81	63.0	80	90.0	16	81.3	2.8	0.3	1.2	0.1	1.2	7.8
St. Louis County	79 360	62.6	607	58.8	1 282	64.2	407	71.5	359	58.5	1.9	0.8	0.6	0.2	0.5	8.6
Scott County	29 090	78.4	179	88.8	266	70.7	541	87.2	511	87.1	4.0	0.6	1.6	1.4	1.6	10.3
Sherburne County	21 141	77.8	57	57.9	56	82.1	99	73.7	181	78.5	1.5	0.3	0.4	0.5	0.4	8.2
Sibley County	5 577	71.1	6	66.7	22	72.7	10	50.0	170	77.1	2.6	0.2	0.3	1.9	2.9	10.1
Stearns County	46 030	68.3	299	44.1	146	54.8	509	49.3	370	70.8	2.4	0.4	1.2	0.5	1.0	9.4
Steele County	12 259	70.0	101	94.1	6	100.0	52	80.8	304	79.6	3.5	0.6	0.6	1.1	1.3	8.8
Stevens County	3 641	68.3	53	37.7	30	66.7	6	100.0	25	80.0	1.7	0.6	0.5	0.3	0.4	8.3
Swift County	4 314	66.5	1	0.0	5	20.0	6	66.7	29	82.8	1.2	0.2	0.4	0.5	0.4	6.8
Todd County	9 138	70.1	23	52.2	51	78.4	8	100.0	87	88.5	1.8	0.4	0.3	1.0	0.9	8.2
Traverse County	1 673	65.5	0	X	28	85.7	2	0.0	10	70.0	0.7	0.4	0.1	0.1	0.3	5.2
Wabasha County	8 122	71.2	20	80.0	16	100.0	25	72.0	70	78.6	2.0	0.8	0.4	0.8	1.0	6.6
Wadena County	5 305	67.4	9	100.0	20	80.0	29	31.0	27	92.6	1.0	0.3	0.4	0.2	0.8	9.0
Waseca County	6 817	70.9	47	100.0	12	58.3	11	36.4	152	72.4	1.3	0.2	0.2	0.5	0.4	7.0
Washington County	68 005	76.6	845	86.0	223	74.9	1 054	95.4	899	83.5	3.4	0.8	1.6	0.4	0.7	9.5
Watonwan County	4 109	67.1	23	87.0	11	81.8	23	82.6	442	79.6	8.0	0.3	0.6	6.8	6.0	14.1
Wilkin County	2 684	70.7	2	0.0	9	77.8	1	100.0	38	63.2	0.7	0.3	0.2	0.2	0.9	7.2
Winona County	18 092	62.8	111	63.1	68	33.8	180	40.6	155	74.2	2.7	0.5	1.4	0.4	0.9	9.4
Wright County	30 872	76.3	112	68.8	66	74.2	23	52.2	183	84.2	1.1	0.3	0.2	0.3	0.4	7.1
Yellow Medicine County	4 251	67.0	9	77.8	91	71.4	14	85.7	63	74.6	1.2	0.2	0.3	0.6	0.6	6.6

[1] Hispanic or Latino persons may be of any race.

STATE/ County code	MSA/PMSA/ NECMA code[1]	STATE County	Population by age (percent)										Non-Hispanic White		
															Age (percent)
			Total population	Under 5 years	5 to 17 years	18 to 24 years	25 to 44 years	45 to 64 years	65 years and over	Median age	+/− U.S. percent under 18 years	+/− U.S. percent 65 years and over	Total population	Under 18 years	65 years and over
			1	2	3	4	5	6	7	8	9	10	11	12	13
28 000	...	MISSISSIPPI.............	2 844 658	7.1	20.1	11.0	28.5	21.2	12.1	33.8	1.5	−0.3	1 728 608	23.2	14.7
28 001	...	Adams County	34 340	6.4	20.3	8.6	25.6	23.5	15.6	38.1	1.0	3.2	15 673	20.6	20.1
28 003	...	Alcorn County	34 558	6.6	17.2	9.1	27.6	24.6	14.8	37.6	−1.9	2.4	30 020	22.7	15.7
28 005	...	Amite County	13 599	6.1	19.7	8.1	26.1	24.3	15.6	38.3	0.1	3.2	7 622	21.4	18.1
28 007	...	Attala County	19 661	6.4	19.6	9.5	25.5	21.6	17.3	37.3	0.3	4.9	11 396	21.7	21.3
28 009	...	Benton County	8 026	7.3	19.6	9.9	28.0	19.8	15.4	35.6	1.2	3.0	4 973	22.0	18.7
28 011	...	Bolivar County..............	40 633	7.4	22.0	14.0	25.9	19.7	11.0	29.8	3.7	−1.4	13 445	18.2	16.1
28 013	...	Calhoun County	15 069	6.3	19.0	8.2	27.4	22.5	16.6	37.4	−0.4	4.2	10 316	21.4	19.6
28 015	...	Carroll County	10 769	5.3	19.0	9.5	28.0	24.0	14.1	38.1	−1.4	1.7	6 643	21.2	14.8
28 017	...	Chickasaw County	19 440	7.5	21.1	8.9	28.8	20.6	13.1	34.4	2.9	0.7	10 868	23.4	17.1
28 019	...	Choctaw County	9 758	6.8	21.0	8.9	24.8	23.7	14.8	36.9	2.1	2.4	6 603	24.0	17.1
28 021	...	Claiborne County	11 831	6.6	19.7	23.3	21.9	17.9	10.5	25.6	0.6	−1.9	1 803	17.0	23.4
28 023	...	Clarke County	17 955	6.9	20.0	8.9	26.4	22.4	15.4	36.8	1.2	3.0	11 441	22.9	17.3
28 025	...	Clay County	21 979	7.2	21.6	10.0	27.5	20.3	13.4	33.9	3.1	1.0	9 338	21.5	18.1
28 027	...	Coahoma County	30 622	9.0	24.0	10.2	25.9	18.6	12.3	30.5	7.3	−0.1	8 948	21.6	19.5
28 029	...	Copiah County	28 757	6.5	20.4	12.6	26.7	20.7	13.2	34.0	1.2	0.8	13 623	21.1	17.8
28 031	...	Covington County	19 407	7.7	20.9	9.9	27.4	21.2	12.9	33.8	2.9	0.5	12 250	23.8	15.5
28 033	4920	DeSoto County..............	107 199	7.8	20.4	8.1	32.6	22.2	8.9	33.7	2.5	−3.5	90 925	27.1	9.3
28 035	3285	Forrest County	72 604	6.6	17.9	18.4	27.5	18.5	11.2	29.7	−1.2	−1.2	46 101	19.8	14.0
28 037	...	Franklin County	8 448	6.6	20.8	8.9	25.9	22.5	15.2	37.0	1.7	2.8	5 284	22.7	18.8
28 039	...	George County	19 144	7.3	21.6	9.3	28.8	21.8	11.2	33.3	3.2	−1.2	16 976	28.5	11.3
28 041	...	Greene County	13 299	7.0	17.0	13.2	32.1	20.5	10.3	32.4	−1.7	−2.1	9 626	25.5	11.8
28 043	...	Grenada County	23 263	6.9	20.3	9.8	27.0	21.6	14.5	35.7	1.5	2.1	13 434	23.3	17.1
28 045	0920	Hancock County............	42 967	6.4	18.8	7.7	27.4	25.7	14.0	38.5	−0.5	1.6	38 370	24.3	14.6
28 047	0920	Harrison County	189 601	7.2	18.7	11.2	30.7	21.0	11.1	33.9	0.2	−1.3	136 107	23.3	13.0
28 049	3560	Hinds County	250 800	7.3	20.5	12.2	29.1	19.9	11.0	31.9	2.1	−1.4	93 059	19.0	18.5
28 051	...	Holmes County	21 609	7.8	24.3	12.0	25.0	18.4	12.5	29.7	6.4	0.1	4 369	17.8	22.6
28 053	...	Humphreys County	11 206	7.5	25.3	10.3	25.9	18.9	12.2	30.5	7.1	−0.2	3 027	22.5	18.2
28 055	...	Issaquena County	2 274	5.9	21.7	11.7	31.0	19.0	10.7	33.1	1.9	−1.7	820	19.1	14.5
28 057	...	Itawamba County	22 770	6.1	18.2	10.5	27.8	23.2	14.1	36.2	−1.4	1.7	20 912	24.0	14.7
28 059	0920	Jackson County	131 420	7.0	20.6	9.4	29.9	22.8	10.3	34.7	1.9	−2.1	97 482	25.4	12.0
28 061	...	Jasper County	18 149	6.8	21.1	10.0	26.7	21.2	14.2	35.1	2.2	1.8	8 373	21.6	19.2
28 063	...	Jefferson County	9 740	7.3	21.3	12.1	29.6	18.6	11.1	32.4	2.9	−1.3	1 288	17.9	23.7
28 065	...	Jefferson Davis County...	13 962	7.1	21.2	10.1	26.1	21.8	13.8	35.0	2.6	1.4	5 746	19.8	20.6
28 067	...	Jones County	64 958	7.0	18.8	10.5	27.5	22.0	14.2	35.8	0.1	1.8	45 768	22.6	16.6
28 069	...	Kemper County	10 453	6.8	18.5	12.5	24.5	22.5	15.1	35.2	−0.4	2.7	4 123	17.2	20.5
28 071	...	Lafayette County	38 744	5.3	14.3	27.2	26.4	17.0	9.9	26.9	−6.1	−2.5	27 600	16.3	11.1
28 073	3285	Lamar County	39 070	7.3	20.8	10.9	30.6	20.7	9.8	32.6	2.4	−2.6	33 218	26.9	10.6
28 075	...	Lauderdale County	78 161	7.2	19.4	10.1	27.8	21.4	14.2	35.0	0.9	1.8	46 640	21.7	17.7
28 077	...	Lawrence County	13 258	6.8	20.7	9.2	27.6	22.6	13.1	35.8	1.8	0.7	8 793	24.4	15.2
28 079	...	Leake County	20 940	7.1	20.0	10.0	26.7	21.7	14.5	34.8	1.4	2.1	11 675	22.1	18.3
28 081	...	Lee County	75 755	7.5	20.2	8.5	30.8	21.6	11.5	34.6	2.0	−0.9	55 299	24.5	13.4
28 083	...	Leflore County	37 947	7.8	22.0	13.4	27.0	17.8	12.1	30.1	4.1	−0.3	11 237	19.2	21.6
28 085	...	Lincoln County	33 166	6.9	19.9	9.7	27.8	21.9	13.9	35.8	1.1	1.5	22 952	24.6	16.0
28 087	...	Lowndes County	61 586	7.7	20.8	10.6	29.4	20.3	11.3	32.7	2.8	−1.1	34 502	23.2	14.6
28 089	3560	Madison County	74 674	7.8	20.8	8.8	32.5	20.4	9.7	33.4	2.9	−2.7	44 497	25.1	11.4
28 091	...	Marion County	25 595	6.7	21.1	9.6	27.2	21.4	14.1	35.1	2.1	1.7	17 039	23.9	16.6
28 093	...	Marshall County	34 993	7.1	19.5	12.0	29.1	21.0	11.4	33.9	0.9	−1.0	16 773	21.8	14.3
28 095	...	Monroe County	38 014	6.6	20.6	8.9	27.4	22.7	13.8	35.7	1.5	1.4	25 701	23.9	16.4
28 097	...	Montgomery County........	12 189	6.2	20.7	8.9	25.6	21.9	16.7	37.3	1.2	4.3	6 575	21.0	20.8
28 099	...	Neshoba County	28 684	7.7	20.7	9.6	26.5	21.4	14.2	34.7	2.7	1.8	18 845	23.5	17.7
28 101	...	Newton County	21 838	7.0	19.2	11.2	26.3	21.5	14.8	35.1	0.5	2.4	14 224	22.4	17.9
28 103	...	Noxubee County	12 548	8.1	22.6	9.9	27.0	19.5	12.9	32.3	5.0	0.5	3 668	23.1	20.1
28 105	...	Oktibbeha County	42 902	5.9	15.1	29.4	24.9	15.9	8.8	24.8	−4.7	−3.6	25 120	15.2	10.0
28 107	...	Panola County	34 274	7.5	21.9	10.2	27.3	20.5	12.4	33.0	3.7	0.0	17 085	22.4	16.5
28 109	...	Pearl River County..........	48 621	7.0	20.0	9.4	27.0	24.1	12.5	35.9	1.3	0.1	41 098	25.8	13.3
28 111	...	Perry County	12 138	7.5	21.1	10.4	27.6	22.3	11.1	33.5	2.9	−1.3	9 219	25.8	11.7
28 113	...	Pike County	38 940	7.4	20.3	10.3	25.8	21.9	14.3	35.2	2.0	1.9	19 849	22.1	18.8
28 115	...	Pontotoc County	26 726	7.4	20.2	8.6	29.5	21.7	12.7	34.8	1.9	0.3	22 341	26.6	13.8
28 117	...	Prentiss County	25 556	6.8	18.3	11.9	26.8	22.6	13.6	35.0	−0.6	1.2	21 945	24.1	15.0
28 119	...	Quitman County	10 117	8.0	23.9	9.7	25.7	19.4	13.3	31.8	6.2	0.9	3 064	21.0	21.5
28 121	3560	Rankin County	115 327	7.0	18.8	9.3	32.9	23.0	9.1	34.6	0.1	−3.3	92 473	24.9	9.9
28 123	...	Scott County	28 423	7.5	21.0	9.9	28.1	21.1	12.3	33.8	2.8	−0.1	15 565	24.3	15.5
28 125	...	Sharkey County	6 580	8.3	24.7	10.7	25.2	20.0	11.1	30.8	7.3	−1.3	1 895	21.1	14.8
28 127	...	Simpson County	27 639	7.0	20.9	9.6	27.9	21.6	13.0	35.0	2.2	0.6	17 626	23.6	15.8
28 129	...	Smith County	16 182	6.9	20.6	9.0	27.4	21.9	14.2	35.6	1.8	1.8	12 267	24.6	15.7
28 131	...	Stone County	13 622	6.8	20.2	12.4	26.9	22.5	11.2	33.6	1.3	−1.2	10 765	25.9	12.3

[1]MSA = Metropolitan Statistical Area. PMSA = Primary MSA. NECMA = New England County Metropolitan Area. See the Appendix A for explanation of these concepts. See Appendix B for list of metropolitan areas identified by type, with component counties.

Table A-3. States and Counties — Age, Ethnicity, and Household Structure

STATE County	Black or African American Total population	Age (percent) Under 18 years	65 years and over	American Indian and Alaska Native Total population	Age (percent) Under 18 years	65 years and over	Asian, Hawaiian, and Pacific Islander Total population	Age (percent) Under 18 years	65 years and over	Hispanic or Latino[1] Total population	Age (percent) Under 18 years	65 years and over	Two or more races Total population	Age (percent) Under 18 years	65 years and over
	14	15	16	17	18	19	20	21	22	23	24	25	26	27	28
MISSISSIPPI	1 033 437	33.7	8.3	11 836	34.1	5.9	18 386	25.2	5.0	37 790	30.6	4.4	21 950	38.8	8.0
Adams County	17 935	31.8	11.9	42	0.0	14.3	300	43.0	13.7	232	25.4	14.7	214	37.4	0.0
Alcorn County	3 824	30.5	9.1	42	31.0	7.1	60	35.0	0.0	390	33.8	9.7	265	39.2	9.1
Amite County	5 860	31.8	12.2	3	0.0	0.0	19	26.3	0.0	67	11.9	3.0	63	11.1	28.6
Attala County	7 984	32.2	11.8	25	56.0	0.0	11	0.0	0.0	162	25.3	6.2	97	21.6	33.0
Benton County	2 962	35.1	10.2	20	60.0	0.0	1	100.0	0.0	92	43.5	2.2	29	6.9	10.3
Bolivar County	26 660	35.1	8.4	35	17.1	5.7	122	23.0	18.9	380	36.8	11.3	127	28.3	12.6
Calhoun County	4 327	32.9	10.9	15	66.7	0.0	10	20.0	20.0	368	32.6	1.4	107	72.0	9.3
Carroll County	3 898	29.7	13.1	2	100.0	0.0	80	43.8	0.0	109	18.3	16.5	64	12.5	9.4
Chickasaw County	8 160	35.2	8.4	2	0.0	0.0	19	0.0	0.0	390	37.9	1.5	39	5.1	25.6
Choctaw County	3 020	36.3	10.1	11	0.0	81.8	0	X	X	96	30.2	3.1	43	30.2	2.3
Claiborne County	9 973	28.1	8.2	7	0.0	0.0	12	0.0	0.0	51	31.4	0.0	13	30.8	30.8
Clarke County	6 225	32.9	12.7	40	65.0	0.0	37	43.2	0.0	184	37.5	6.5	74	64.9	0.0
Clay County	12 325	34.4	9.7	32	0.0	46.9	22	0.0	0.0	210	39.0	15.7	134	31.3	23.9
Coahoma County	21 269	37.8	9.3	13	61.5	0.0	147	30.6	21.8	226	28.8	12.4	65	26.2	13.8
Copiah County	14 745	32.0	8.9	47	57.4	0.0	32	21.9	21.9	167	32.3	15.6	168	45.2	11.9
Covington County	6 872	36.9	8.1	18	0.0	33.3	12	0.0	0.0	240	40.0	3.3	199	45.2	16.1
DeSoto County	12 156	34.0	8.3	192	20.8	12.0	763	31.5	1.3	2 480	34.0	1.5	795	38.9	2.6
Forrest County	24 359	33.5	6.4	136	34.6	4.4	633	14.7	2.7	880	28.1	4.1	549	12.8	12.4
Franklin County	3 017	35.2	9.4	45	15.6	0.0	6	0.0	0.0	93	45.2	0.0	26	53.8	19.2
George County	1 836	34.3	10.5	9	33.3	0.0	39	30.8	0.0	251	18.7	0.0	34	0.0	67.6
Greene County	3 485	20.4	5.9	30	20.0	6.7	16	37.5	18.8	103	7.8	9.7	57	35.1	14.0
Grenada County	9 452	32.4	11.3	64	54.7	0.0	118	31.4	0.0	70	25.7	8.6	134	37.3	8.2
Hancock County	2 973	33.7	9.0	437	18.8	5.5	222	38.7	2.7	571	29.2	13.5	457	31.9	12.0
Harrison County	39 679	33.0	6.8	948	16.9	7.9	5 143	28.7	4.7	4 820	32.8	3.4	3 989	43.0	4.0
Hinds County	152 941	33.2	6.6	569	35.0	2.3	1 343	19.1	2.3	1 869	27.9	8.0	1 694	38.3	8.2
Holmes County	17 018	35.7	9.9	17	17.6	0.0	19	5.3	36.8	162	41.4	12.3	146	55.5	13.7
Humphreys County	8 022	37.0	9.9	46	30.4	8.7	5	0.0	20.0	119	14.3	9.2	46	0.0	32.6
Issaquena County	1 444	32.3	8.7	0	X	X	0	X	X	3	66.7	0.0	9	55.6	0.0
Itawamba County	1 479	26.6	7.8	7	0.0	0.0	53	20.8	0.0	250	34.4	3.6	95	38.9	15.8
Jackson County	27 064	34.3	5.6	795	34.5	4.7	1 957	25.8	6.1	2 681	30.7	4.2	1 719	40.3	6.6
Jasper County	9 538	33.5	10.1	25	36.0	0.0	11	27.3	0.0	140	25.7	1.4	148	30.4	1.4
Jefferson County	8 389	30.1	9.3	4	50.0	0.0	3	0.0	66.7	43	14.0	2.3	20	85.0	0.0
Jefferson Davis County	7 962	33.7	9.0	37	43.2	0.0	35	31.4	0.0	120	54.2	3.3	102	60.8	20.6
Jones County	17 234	34.9	9.1	280	29.5	11.8	179	17.9	12.3	1 301	17.1	0.2	287	27.9	7.7
Kemper County	6 060	30.2	12.1	181	43.6	0.0	7	0.0	0.0	33	24.2	3.0	56	44.6	8.9
Lafayette County	9 731	29.0	7.2	128	13.3	6.3	466	6.0	0.0	501	30.9	5.4	396	33.3	9.8
Lamar County	5 004	34.9	5.5	42	52.4	0.0	313	30.0	0.0	292	32.2	0.7	202	40.6	9.4
Lauderdale County	30 296	34.1	8.9	137	0.0	13.1	237	23.2	8.0	516	23.6	9.9	393	33.1	7.1
Lawrence County	4 310	33.3	9.4	9	0.0	0.0	51	27.5	0.0	132	30.3	6.1	61	75.4	0.0
Leake County	7 929	32.6	10.2	703	44.5	6.7	65	23.1	27.7	393	24.4	0.0	278	41.0	13.7
Lee County	18 494	36.1	6.4	167	44.3	4.8	275	17.1	0.0	954	35.8	0.7	717	47.6	8.2
Leflore County	25 869	34.4	8.2	44	36.4	4.5	158	13.9	9.5	584	24.1	5.5	166	33.7	13.3
Lincoln County	9 608	31.3	9.2	103	24.3	5.8	86	33.7	4.7	333	48.9	0.0	162	30.2	22.2
Lowndes County	25 533	35.3	7.5	136	22.8	0.0	267	15.4	1.5	684	30.1	1.8	588	46.4	1.7
Madison County	28 426	33.7	7.3	211	42.7	6.2	604	12.7	12.7	453	39.1	1.1	612	51.5	3.1
Marion County	8 112	35.6	9.3	24	0.0	0.0	80	17.5	0.0	230	34.8	5.7	153	56.9	4.6
Marshall County	17 721	30.9	8.9	81	27.2	0.0	43	0.0	0.0	256	28.9	3.1	229	41.0	14.0
Monroe County	11 601	33.9	8.0	27	25.9	0.0	118	44.1	18.6	460	47.8	4.8	232	39.2	25.0
Montgomery County	5 503	33.6	12.1	9	0.0	0.0	9	0.0	0.0	117	29.9	21.4	43	83.7	16.3
Neshoba County	5 693	34.9	7.6	3 421	42.1	6.1	193	19.7	4.1	182	44.5	20.3	381	49.3	12.1
Newton County	6 751	32.4	9.9	570	44.7	0.0	98	15.3	0.0	165	30.3	3.0	75	40.0	2.7
Noxubee County	8 660	33.6	9.9	11	27.3	27.3	12	0.0	8.3	141	22.7	8.5	85	58.8	7.1
Oktibbeha County	15 993	30.6	7.6	70	20.0	0.0	1 096	17.7	1.1	354	17.8	3.1	286	24.1	0.0
Panola County	16 466	36.5	8.4	52	61.5	21.2	87	3.4	6.9	456	43.9	5.0	227	41.9	3.5
Pearl River County	6 022	32.8	8.0	219	38.8	7.8	75	25.3	0.0	712	41.9	12.8	565	33.8	5.5
Perry County	2 744	38.0	9.2	35	17.1	0.0	68	45.6	10.3	81	17.3	3.7	15	40.0	20.0
Pike County	18 475	33.4	9.8	52	11.5	11.5	274	42.3	1.5	326	31.9	6.4	77	36.4	5.2
Pontotoc County	3 780	32.1	7.9	65	21.5	6.2	90	51.1	0.0	341	28.4	1.2	149	32.2	3.4
Prentiss County	3 225	29.7	5.7	26	0.0	0.0	14	14.3	0.0	198	33.3	6.1	146	45.2	0.0
Quitman County	6 943	36.9	9.5	10	20.0	0.0	14	14.3	50.0	57	31.6	22.8	55	36.4	14.5
Rankin County	19 534	28.8	6.3	189	22.2	11.1	588	25.9	4.6	1 806	34.7	2.4	880	43.8	4.4
Scott County	10 975	35.0	9.4	199	41.2	4.5	61	18.0	0.0	1 631	26.0	3.1	394	26.1	3.0
Sharkey County	4 609	38.1	8.1	0	X	X	23	26.1	39.1	49	22.4	4.1	27	48.1	7.4
Simpson County	9 512	35.7	8.0	25	0.0	36.0	75	20.0	4.0	297	30.3	0.3	169	33.7	16.6
Smith County	3 642	37.1	9.7	14	0.0	0.0	59	44.1	0.0	157	18.5	8.9	120	36.7	0.8
Stone County	2 473	33.4	7.8	35	25.7	25.7	48	0.0	0.0	251	20.3	0.0	94	28.7	0.0

[1] Hispanic or Latino persons may be of any race.

Table A-3. States and Counties — Age, Ethnicity, and Household Structure

STATE County	Total households	Family households (percent)						Nonfamily households (percent)						Percent of householders 65 years and over who live alone	Grandparents who are responsible for the care of their grandchildren
		Married-couple family households			Other family households			Two or more unrelated persons		Male living alone		Female living alone			
		Total	With children	Householder 65 years or over	Total	With children	Householder 65 years or over	Total	Householder 65 years or over	Total	Householder 65 years or over	Total	Householder 65 years or over		
	29	30	31	32	33	34	35	36	37	38	39	40	41	42	43
MISSISSIPPI	1 047 555	50.6	23.1	8.6	21.2	12.2	3.2	3.6	0.2	10.4	2.3	14.1	7.4	44.6	48 061
Adams County	13 693	42.9	17.7	9.1	26.4	14.4	5.2	2.7	0.3	11.5	3.1	16.5	9.1	45.5	787
Alcorn County	14 178	54.7	22.5	9.7	15.2	7.7	2.7	2.4	0.1	10.5	2.3	17.3	9.8	49.2	434
Amite County	5 290	54.0	21.4	11.7	19.7	9.1	4.3	1.9	0.1	10.6	2.9	13.9	8.8	42.1	276
Attala County	7 565	50.6	22.2	10.8	21.0	11.0	3.8	2.0	0.4	10.5	3.3	15.9	11.4	49.6	304
Benton County	3 017	53.7	22.9	12.2	19.6	11.5	4.4	2.9	0.5	10.0	2.9	13.9	9.0	41.1	114
Bolivar County	13 788	38.1	17.3	6.6	32.9	18.5	5.5	3.7	0.2	11.6	2.5	13.6	6.6	42.5	1 114
Calhoun County	5 995	49.9	19.5	10.4	21.1	12.3	3.9	2.0	0.3	10.2	3.2	16.9	11.0	49.4	276
Carroll County	4 068	57.0	22.5	10.7	19.0	8.7	4.0	1.4	0.2	10.6	3.9	12.1	8.2	44.8	104
Chickasaw County	7 268	50.9	24.4	8.2	22.8	12.7	4.0	1.6	0.2	9.9	2.9	14.9	9.2	49.5	397
Choctaw County	3 682	54.3	22.7	10.8	17.7	10.4	3.1	3.0	0.6	8.8	2.0	16.2	9.8	44.9	162
Claiborne County	3 686	41.2	20.6	7.2	27.9	16.0	4.6	2.8	0.2	12.6	3.5	15.4	9.0	51.2	349
Clarke County	6 971	52.8	22.5	11.3	19.5	11.1	3.8	2.2	0.1	10.5	2.2	15.0	8.8	41.9	251
Clay County	8 167	46.0	19.7	8.3	26.7	15.7	3.4	1.8	0.1	10.2	2.6	15.2	8.8	48.9	565
Coahoma County	10 581	37.1	17.0	7.1	33.9	20.2	5.4	3.1	0.4	10.6	3.2	15.4	8.4	47.2	835
Copiah County	10 196	49.2	22.4	9.7	25.5	13.7	4.4	2.3	0.1	9.3	2.5	14.0	8.0	42.5	581
Covington County	7 134	52.7	23.7	8.9	21.9	12.1	3.9	1.9	0.5	9.3	2.2	14.1	8.6	44.8	327
DeSoto County	38 821	62.8	31.0	7.9	15.3	9.1	1.7	3.8	0.2	7.5	1.1	10.6	4.6	36.4	1 279
Forrest County	27 225	42.9	19.2	7.6	21.3	12.3	2.9	7.4	0.3	11.5	1.8	16.9	7.6	46.8	1 008
Franklin County	3 228	54.6	24.7	10.5	17.5	9.9	3.1	1.2	0.4	12.2	4.7	13.5	9.0	49.4	174
George County	6 753	66.0	31.0	9.8	12.9	7.3	2.7	2.1	0.1	8.4	2.4	10.6	6.9	42.6	198
Greene County	4 143	61.8	29.1	9.3	14.3	8.3	2.3	1.6	0.1	9.2	2.4	13.1	7.2	45.0	168
Grenada County	8 797	49.4	21.5	9.1	22.7	13.0	3.5	2.6	0.2	10.5	2.4	14.8	8.7	46.5	544
Hancock County	16 892	55.2	23.2	11.3	15.1	8.7	2.0	4.9	0.7	11.7	3.0	13.0	5.9	38.8	592
Harrison County	71 618	49.2	22.5	7.9	19.2	11.6	2.3	5.9	0.4	12.5	2.5	13.3	6.4	45.7	2 543
Hinds County	91 073	42.0	19.8	7.2	27.0	15.4	3.3	4.4	0.2	11.2	2.0	15.4	6.8	45.3	4 593
Holmes County	7 374	35.0	16.4	7.1	36.9	20.6	6.6	2.1	0.4	11.3	3.1	14.7	9.2	46.5	579
Humphreys County	3 789	36.5	16.4	7.0	36.7	20.7	6.5	1.9	0.2	10.3	2.3	14.6	8.6	44.1	321
Issaquena County	733	45.6	21.3	8.0	24.0	14.2	4.2	4.0	0.4	12.7	2.6	13.8	8.7	47.2	42
Itawamba County	8 799	61.3	26.6	11.5	13.2	7.4	2.0	2.2	0.1	9.3	2.6	14.0	8.3	44.6	217
Jackson County	47 753	57.3	26.6	8.6	18.0	10.8	2.6	4.0	0.4	9.6	1.8	11.2	5.6	38.9	2 210
Jasper County	6 710	50.7	23.1	10.4	24.2	13.3	4.7	0.9	0.2	10.8	2.7	13.4	8.5	42.3	448
Jefferson County	3 289	36.0	18.3	7.1	34.7	19.5	6.4	1.9	0.1	13.5	4.1	14.0	5.7	41.6	242
Jefferson Davis County	5 185	47.7	20.2	9.6	25.0	13.0	4.8	2.1	0.2	10.7	2.9	14.4	9.0	45.0	420
Jones County	24 263	53.6	22.8	10.9	19.2	10.6	3.8	2.8	0.2	9.4	2.0	15.0	8.6	41.4	1 084
Kemper County	3 907	48.2	18.5	11.1	23.8	12.9	4.7	1.8	0.2	11.7	2.5	14.6	10.0	43.9	256
Lafayette County	14 390	45.5	20.2	7.2	12.8	8.1	1.5	12.7	0.2	13.8	1.4	15.2	5.9	45.1	232
Lamar County	14 358	61.5	31.4	8.0	13.1	7.7	1.7	4.8	0.1	8.5	1.7	12.0	5.3	41.6	344
Lauderdale County	30 036	47.1	21.3	8.4	21.8	12.8	3.1	3.2	0.3	10.0	2.4	18.0	9.8	50.9	991
Lawrence County	5 071	57.4	26.6	10.3	17.2	10.2	2.1	1.5	0.2	10.5	2.3	13.3	8.8	47.1	290
Leake County	7 624	53.0	25.5	10.5	20.8	11.3	4.5	2.0	0.2	10.4	3.7	13.8	8.6	44.7	305
Lee County	29 216	53.6	25.5	7.9	17.8	11.1	1.9	3.6	0.2	10.3	1.8	14.7	6.8	46.5	798
Leflore County	12 983	35.4	15.8	6.9	33.6	20.4	4.9	2.9	0.1	11.6	3.1	16.5	9.3	51.2	874
Lincoln County	12 517	56.1	25.7	9.4	17.2	9.4	3.0	2.4	0.3	10.4	2.5	14.0	8.6	46.6	539
Lowndes County	22 851	50.7	23.9	7.9	21.5	13.6	2.1	3.3	0.2	10.7	1.8	13.9	6.9	46.2	786
Madison County	27 301	52.1	26.7	6.5	19.4	11.6	2.5	3.6	0.1	10.7	1.4	14.2	5.1	41.7	984
Marion County	9 371	54.9	25.5	9.8	19.7	11.3	3.4	1.5	0.2	9.6	2.4	14.3	9.2	46.2	561
Marshall County	12 139	49.2	20.9	8.5	25.9	13.4	4.7	2.8	0.3	10.9	2.5	11.2	5.6	37.5	668
Monroe County	14 601	52.7	24.0	8.9	20.6	11.3	3.3	2.0	0.2	9.0	2.3	15.7	9.8	49.4	603
Montgomery County	4 707	49.3	20.2	10.4	23.2	12.7	4.4	1.5	0.5	8.9	2.3	17.1	11.6	47.7	300
Neshoba County	10 690	53.2	23.5	11.1	20.1	12.2	3.3	2.1	0.3	10.2	2.5	14.3	8.5	42.8	649
Newton County	8 186	54.0	24.4	10.3	19.5	9.9	4.0	1.8	0.3	11.2	3.1	13.5	7.3	41.4	346
Noxubee County	4 472	43.2	19.5	8.8	28.9	15.9	5.3	1.8	0.0	11.6	3.2	14.5	8.5	45.3	325
Oktibbeha County	16 014	40.7	18.3	6.4	18.0	10.8	2.5	13.7	0.2	13.1	1.8	14.5	5.2	43.7	335
Panola County	12 249	49.3	22.8	8.7	24.9	14.5	4.3	2.6	0.3	10.5	2.8	12.7	7.9	44.5	605
Pearl River County	18 102	59.3	25.7	9.7	16.6	9.7	2.6	2.6	0.3	9.0	2.5	12.5	6.7	42.2	703
Perry County	4 428	60.7	30.6	8.1	15.4	6.9	3.3	2.3	0.3	9.4	2.4	12.2	6.5	43.1	308
Pike County	14 818	47.3	20.0	9.4	24.2	14.1	3.8	1.9	0.1	11.8	3.4	14.7	8.5	47.1	786
Pontotoc County	10 129	60.3	28.8	9.7	15.0	8.6	2.2	1.8	0.2	9.7	2.0	13.2	7.9	44.9	469
Prentiss County	9 825	55.7	25.1	9.8	16.9	8.3	3.2	2.6	0.2	8.8	2.6	16.1	8.9	46.6	265
Quitman County	3 581	38.1	16.9	7.4	32.1	17.1	6.4	2.9	0.2	11.5	3.7	15.4	8.8	47.3	269
Rankin County	42 155	58.8	28.2	7.5	15.5	9.1	2.0	3.9	0.2	9.0	1.3	12.8	5.1	40.2	1 190
Scott County	10 226	50.8	23.7	9.0	23.7	13.3	3.2	3.4	0.3	9.2	2.8	12.8	8.1	46.5	652
Sharkey County	2 178	41.1	19.7	6.0	32.9	16.8	7.3	2.7	0.4	11.1	3.1	12.2	7.7	44.2	281
Simpson County	10 103	55.6	25.7	8.8	18.5	9.9	3.3	2.0	0.2	10.2	2.8	13.8	8.2	47.0	530
Smith County	6 083	60.5	28.4	10.4	15.8	7.3	3.6	1.1	0.2	8.5	2.6	14.1	9.8	46.8	243
Stone County	4 747	61.3	28.6	10.3	15.7	9.8	1.4	2.5	0.0	8.8	1.9	11.7	6.9	42.5	215

Table A-3. States and Counties — Age, Ethnicity, and Household Structure

STATE County	Households with Non-Hispanic White householder		Households with Black or African American householder		Households with American Indian and Alaska Native householder		Households with Asian, Hawaiian, and Pacific Islander householder		Households with Hispanic or Latino[1] householder		Foreign-born population				Percent in non-English speaking households	
												Place of birth (percent)				
	Number of households	Percent that are family households	Number of households	Percent that are family households	Number of households	Percent that are family households	Number of households	Percent that are family households	Number of households	Percent that are family households	Percent of total population that is foreign-born	Europe	Asia	Latin America	Linguistically isolated	Not linguistically isolated
	44	45	46	47	48	49	50	51	52	53	54	55	56	57	58	59
MISSISSIPPI	685 549	71.4	339 157	72.6	3 660	73.5	5 165	72.7	9 781	70.8	1.4	0.3	0.5	0.5	0.6	6.4
Adams County	6 671	69.8	6 809	68.8	12	50.0	75	100.0	66	45.5	1.4	0.3	0.7	0.3	1.1	6.3
Alcorn County	12 531	70.3	1 452	65.8	16	62.5	16	62.5	94	67.0	1.0	0.2	0.2	0.5	0.4	4.9
Amite County	3 177	72.4	2 050	75.4	2	100.0	11	45.5	34	85.3	0.4	0.1	0.1	0.1	0.1	5.0
Attala County	4 715	70.0	2 755	74.6	0	X	4	100.0	62	80.6	0.8	0.1	0.2	0.5	0.2	5.9
Benton County	2 034	70.7	942	78.0	6	100.0	0	X	33	90.9	0.7	0.3	0.0	0.3	0.4	2.3
Bolivar County	5 349	66.1	8 261	74.2	16	68.8	57	66.7	124	73.4	0.5	0.1	0.1	0.2	0.3	7.1
Calhoun County	4 302	70.8	1 588	72.3	2	100.0	2	100.0	107	63.6	1.6	0.2	0.0	1.3	1.0	4.6
Carroll County	2 660	78.5	1 331	70.4	0	X	14	100.0	31	93.5	0.8	0.0	0.4	0.3	0.3	4.0
Chickasaw County	4 525	71.5	2 647	77.4	2	0.0	7	100.0	80	90.0	1.3	0.1	0.1	1.1	1.0	3.8
Choctaw County	2 630	73.8	1 026	67.8	4	50.0	0	X	19	68.4	0.3	0.1	0.0	0.2	0.3	4.3
Claiborne County	843	66.3	2 824	69.9	1	100.0	0	X	16	100.0	0.6	0.1	0.1	0.1	0.0	5.9
Clarke County	4 600	74.2	2 305	68.2	7	0.0	6	100.0	38	89.5	0.3	0.1	0.1	0.1	0.1	4.6
Clay County	3 896	69.7	4 129	76.3	32	37.5	0	X	93	57.0	0.5	0.1	0.1	0.2	0.4	4.8
Coahoma County	3 776	68.1	6 695	72.4	1	100.0	36	55.6	53	90.6	0.9	0.1	0.3	0.4	0.5	5.5
Copiah County	5 322	73.8	4 734	75.3	16	100.0	19	31.6	51	90.2	0.8	0.3	0.2	0.2	0.2	5.1
Covington County	4 908	73.3	2 161	78.1	6	0.0	0	X	39	76.9	0.6	0.3	0.1	0.2	0.1	4.5
DeSoto County	33 874	78.3	3 947	76.6	76	63.2	182	84.6	571	78.5	1.9	0.3	0.5	1.0	0.8	6.0
Forrest County	18 796	61.9	7 748	69.8	40	85.0	207	42.5	239	75.7	2.0	0.6	0.9	0.4	0.8	6.4
Franklin County	2 121	74.7	1 060	69.4	17	100.0	6	0.0	27	92.6	0.3	0.0	0.1	0.2	0.1	5.4
George County	6 100	79.6	579	70.6	6	100.0	11	100.0	28	75.0	1.3	0.0	0.2	1.0	0.6	3.7
Greene County	3 447	76.4	653	74.7	9	55.6	3	100.0	19	73.7	0.3	0.1	0.0	0.1	0.1	4.3
Grenada County	5 318	73.8	3 355	68.8	20	100.0	41	78.0	28	67.9	1.0	0.2	0.6	0.2	0.2	5.8
Hancock County	15 318	70.6	993	68.4	201	71.6	42	85.7	218	55.5	1.4	0.4	0.3	0.4	0.5	9.0
Harrison County	54 100	67.9	13 681	70.5	348	60.1	1 334	72.9	1 347	66.6	3.6	0.7	1.9	0.6	1.1	10.1
Hinds County	38 623	65.5	50 991	71.7	193	72.5	463	68.3	509	51.5	1.1	0.2	0.5	0.3	0.3	7.1
Holmes County	1 796	68.7	5 517	72.8	2	0.0	11	100.0	39	84.6	0.3	0.1	0.1	0.1	0.1	6.2
Humphreys County	1 228	67.8	2 515	75.3	21	100.0	2	100.0	27	100.0	0.8	0.1	0.1	0.6	0.1	6.6
Issaquena County	322	73.6	408	66.2	0	X	0	X	1	100.0	0.2	0.2	0.0	0.0	0.0	1.8
Itawamba County	8 247	74.7	438	71.5	5	100.0	15	46.7	74	87.8	0.6	0.1	0.2	0.3	0.2	5.1
Jackson County	36 997	75.5	8 998	74.5	185	79.5	497	79.9	773	65.3	2.7	0.7	1.1	0.8	0.9	8.1
Jasper County	3 475	73.3	3 195	76.4	0	X	2	100.0	29	89.7	0.3	0.0	0.1	0.2	0.2	6.1
Jefferson County	523	71.1	2 755	70.5	2	100.0	2	100.0	10	60.0	0.3	0.1	0.0	0.1	0.1	3.8
Jefferson Davis County	2 450	71.0	2 665	74.2	8	100.0	10	100.0	23	91.3	0.3	0.1	0.2	0.0	0.0	5.3
Jones County	18 221	72.7	5 628	73.7	92	52.2	45	33.3	235	68.9	2.0	0.3	0.2	1.5	1.5	5.2
Kemper County	1 729	68.2	2 099	74.3	52	100.0	0	X	8	62.5	0.4	0.1	0.1	0.1	1.5	2.9
Lafayette County	10 792	55.4	3 216	68.1	41	100.0	118	48.3	130	57.7	2.4	0.3	1.1	0.6	0.3	6.7
Lamar County	12 322	75.6	1 770	68.5	11	72.7	95	90.5	98	44.9	1.1	0.2	0.6	0.1	0.2	6.6
Lauderdale County	19 225	68.5	10 438	70.0	66	72.7	84	67.9	111	47.7	0.7	0.2	0.2	0.3	0.2	5.5
Lawrence County	3 456	76.2	1 561	71.9	7	0.0	14	100.0	48	66.7	0.6	0.2	0.2	0.1	0.1	4.7
Leake County	4 685	73.6	2 552	74.4	188	77.1	21	76.2	142	56.3	1.4	0.2	0.2	0.9	1.7	6.8
Lee County	22 289	71.2	6 414	72.5	64	68.8	62	62.9	246	64.6	1.1	0.3	0.3	0.5	0.4	6.1
Leflore County	4 764	66.4	7 999	71.1	23	56.5	72	62.5	93	57.0	1.1	0.3	0.3	0.4	0.3	6.0
Lincoln County	8 980	74.7	3 343	69.5	36	58.3	29	65.5	64	87.5	0.6	0.1	0.2	0.3	0.6	4.0
Lowndes County	13 690	71.4	8 742	73.0	65	49.2	63	79.4	189	79.9	1.3	0.4	0.4	0.4	0.3	6.6
Madison County	17 822	70.5	8 952	73.3	70	62.9	223	78.0	111	82.0	1.7	0.3	0.8	0.2	0.4	6.8
Marion County	6 676	74.3	2 598	75.1	3	0.0	31	100.0	55	74.5	0.8	0.2	0.3	0.2	0.3	4.6
Marshall County	6 560	73.7	5 448	76.7	26	100.0	19	36.8	84	69.0	1.0	0.3	0.1	0.4	0.1	5.4
Monroe County	10 344	73.5	4 059	72.5	7	57.1	25	100.0	97	93.8	0.6	0.2	0.2	0.1	0.1	4.7
Montgomery County	2 786	70.0	1 897	76.2	1	100.0	0	X	37	75.7	0.2	0.2	0.0	0.1	0.2	6.1
Neshoba County	7 578	71.7	1 959	75.7	846	81.8	97	91.8	70	54.3	0.8	0.1	0.5	0.2	3.2	12.0
Newton County	5 559	74.5	2 357	70.0	163	81.0	43	100.0	56	91.1	0.5	0.2	0.2	0.1	1.6	5.5
Noxubee County	1 505	68.1	2 921	74.0	4	100.0	2	0.0	30	83.3	1.0	0.1	0.1	0.6	0.3	5.5
Oktibbeha County	10 140	52.8	5 251	70.3	35	40.0	367	52.9	146	56.2	3.3	0.3	2.4	0.3	1.5	6.8
Panola County	6 992	72.9	5 065	75.8	7	100.0	19	100.0	126	87.3	0.6	0.1	0.3	0.2	0.2	6.2
Pearl River County	15 588	76.0	2 062	74.4	75	77.3	22	68.2	175	70.9	1.2	0.5	0.3	0.4	0.3	7.2
Perry County	3 488	77.5	881	71.6	16	81.3	11	100.0	45	48.9	0.5	0.2	0.2	0.1	0.1	4.5
Pike County	8 189	71.2	6 470	71.9	15	100.0	43	100.0	99	71.7	0.9	0.2	0.4	0.3	0.4	7.1
Pontotoc County	8 608	75.8	1 341	73.8	27	66.7	21	100.0	94	73.4	1.1	0.2	0.1	0.7	0.8	4.9
Prentiss County	8 609	72.7	1 104	72.4	20	65.0	5	100.0	83	66.3	0.4	0.1	0.1	0.1	0.1	4.9
Quitman County	1 336	65.7	2 198	73.1	4	50.0	8	62.5	15	66.7	0.2	0.0	0.1	0.1	0.4	2.9
Rankin County	35 563	73.9	5 800	75.5	68	76.5	159	90.6	433	80.6	1.6	0.2	0.5	0.6	0.5	6.3
Scott County	6 018	75.5	3 733	73.4	46	91.3	19	100.0	426	70.2	4.2	0.2	0.2	3.9	2.5	8.2
Sharkey County	795	72.6	1 353	74.5	0	X	7	100.0	17	82.4	0.4	0.0	0.2	0.2	0.2	4.8
Simpson County	6 931	72.9	3 025	76.8	23	30.4	22	86.4	94	86.2	0.9	0.1	0.2	0.6	0.6	3.6
Smith County	4 897	75.1	1 130	80.2	0	X	8	100.0	35	100.0	0.5	0.1	0.2	0.1	0.0	4.7
Stone County	3 965	76.3	712	77.9	9	100.0	8	100.0	25	100.0	1.0	0.2	0.2	0.5	0.0	6.3

[1] Hispanic or Latino persons may be of any race.

STATE/ County code	MSA/PMSA/ NECMA code[1]	STATE County	Total population	Under 5 years	5 to 17 years	18 to 24 years	25 to 44 years	45 to 64 years	65 years and over	Median age	+/− U.S. percent under 18 years	+/− U.S. percent 65 years and over	Total population	Under 18 years	65 years and over
						Population by age (percent)							Non-Hispanic White	Age (percent)	
			1	2	3	4	5	6	7	8	9	10	11	12	13
		MISSISSIPPI—Cont'd													
28 133	...	Sunflower County............	34 369	7.0	21.0	14.0	30.7	17.7	9.7	30.2	2.3	-2.7	9 748	18.3	17.5
28 135	...	Tallahatchie County........	14 903	6.8	23.3	9.7	26.3	20.7	13.3	33.3	4.4	0.9	5 862	21.3	19.3
28 137	...	Tate County.................	25 370	7.2	20.0	11.9	27.1	22.5	11.3	34.2	1.5	-1.1	17 126	24.8	12.7
28 139	...	Tippah County...............	20 826	6.4	18.6	9.9	27.9	22.7	14.5	35.9	-0.7	2.1	16 885	23.6	15.8
28 141	...	Tishomingo County........	19 163	5.8	17.1	7.8	27.3	25.0	17.0	39.1	-2.8	4.6	18 161	23.0	17.3
28 143	...	Tunica County...............	9 227	8.4	23.0	11.5	27.9	19.3	9.8	30.6	5.7	-2.6	2 478	16.3	14.1
28 145	...	Union County................	25 362	7.3	18.7	9.0	28.4	22.3	14.4	35.6	0.3	2.0	20 984	24.4	15.5
28 147	...	Walthall County.............	15 156	7.1	21.4	9.7	26.0	21.9	14.0	35.1	2.8	1.6	8 213	21.7	18.4
28 149	...	Warren County...............	49 644	7.5	21.0	9.1	28.8	21.7	11.8	34.8	2.8	-0.6	27 085	23.9	13.9
28 151	...	Washington County........	62 977	8.3	23.1	10.1	26.6	20.2	11.7	31.5	5.7	-0.7	21 224	21.5	17.7
28 153	...	Wayne County...............	21 216	7.6	21.6	9.9	27.4	21.6	11.9	33.8	3.5	-0.5	12 972	24.4	14.2
28 155	...	Webster County.............	10 294	6.5	19.5	8.8	27.3	21.4	16.6	37.3	0.3	4.2	7 925	23.5	18.2
28 157	...	Wilkinson County...........	10 312	5.7	20.2	10.9	29.0	20.4	13.9	35.0	0.2	1.5	3 209	19.0	19.0
28 159	...	Winston County.............	20 160	6.8	20.0	9.2	26.4	22.4	15.1	36.3	1.1	2.7	11 047	21.4	19.7
28 161	...	Yalobusha County..........	13 051	6.5	19.1	9.0	26.5	22.9	16.1	37.7	-0.1	3.7	7 844	20.4	19.8
28 163	...	Yazoo County................	28 149	7.5	20.9	10.1	29.2	19.7	12.6	33.7	2.7	0.2	11 543	21.9	17.8
29 000		**MISSOURI**	5 595 211	6.6	18.9	9.5	29.2	22.3	13.5	36.1	-0.2	1.1	4 687 837	24.0	14.7
29 001	...	Adair County.................	24 977	5.2	14.0	27.5	23.1	18.0	12.2	27.9	-6.5	-0.2	23 726	19.1	12.6
29 003	7000	Andrew County..............	16 492	6.2	20.0	8.1	27.6	23.8	14.4	37.8	0.5	2.0	16 057	25.9	14.5
29 005	...	Atchison County............	6 430	4.4	19.7	5.9	24.8	24.2	21.1	41.7	-1.6	8.7	6 204	22.8	21.8
29 007	...	Audrain County.............	25 853	6.4	18.1	7.8	28.2	22.2	17.2	38.0	-1.2	4.8	23 445	24.4	17.7
29 009	...	Barry County................	34 010	6.7	19.5	8.0	25.8	23.9	16.1	38.2	0.5	3.7	31 427	25.2	17.2
29 011	...	Barton County...............	12 541	7.7	19.7	8.2	26.4	21.4	16.5	37.3	1.7	4.1	12 071	27.2	16.8
29 013	...	Bates County................	16 653	6.1	20.4	7.5	26.1	22.4	17.4	38.4	0.8	5.0	16 149	26.3	17.7
29 015	...	Benton County..............	17 180	4.7	15.8	5.7	21.6	29.8	22.4	46.3	-5.2	10.0	16 688	20.3	22.5
29 017	...	Bollinger County............	12 029	6.1	20.1	7.7	26.8	24.6	14.7	37.9	0.5	2.3	11 696	25.9	14.9
29 019	1740	Boone County...............	135 454	6.1	16.6	19.7	30.2	18.7	8.6	29.5	-3.0	-3.8	114 740	21.1	9.5
29 021	7000	Buchanan County	85 998	6.2	18.0	11.1	28.2	21.4	15.0	36.1	-1.5	2.6	78 394	23.6	15.8
29 023	...	Butler County................	40 867	6.3	17.8	8.4	26.6	24.2	16.7	38.7	-1.6	4.3	37 509	23.0	17.3
29 025	...	Caldwell County............	8 969	6.4	20.7	7.2	25.1	23.6	16.9	38.8	1.4	4.5	8 774	26.5	17.2
29 027	...	Callaway County............	40 766	6.0	19.5	11.2	31.1	21.4	10.9	34.7	-0.2	-1.5	37 208	25.5	11.3
29 029	...	Camden County.............	37 051	4.7	15.5	6.1	23.4	31.3	18.9	45.2	-5.5	6.5	36 003	19.9	19.0
29 031	...	Cape Girardeau County..	68 693	5.8	17.5	13.4	27.9	21.6	13.7	35.2	-2.4	1.3	62 972	22.4	14.6
29 033	...	Carroll County	10 285	6.3	18.9	7.4	25.2	22.2	20.1	40.0	-0.5	7.7	9 888	24.7	20.5
29 035	...	Carter County...............	5 941	6.0	19.2	8.2	25.6	25.2	15.9	38.9	-0.5	3.5	5 626	24.5	16.3
29 037	3760	Cass County.................	82 092	7.4	20.9	7.4	30.1	22.4	11.7	35.8	2.6	-0.7	77 259	27.7	12.2
29 039	...	Cedar County...............	13 733	5.5	19.1	6.5	22.7	25.5	20.8	42.2	-1.1	8.4	13 239	24.2	21.0
29 041	...	Chariton County............	8 438	5.1	18.7	6.3	23.9	23.6	22.4	42.5	-1.9	10.0	8 129	23.8	22.1
29 043	7920	Christian County	54 285	7.6	20.2	8.1	31.7	21.9	10.6	34.5	2.1	-1.8	52 380	27.5	10.8
29 045	...	Clark County................	7 416	6.1	18.8	7.9	25.2	25.2	16.7	39.2	-0.8	4.3	7 297	24.8	16.9
29 047	3760	Clay County.................	184 006	7.2	18.7	8.7	32.5	22.2	10.8	35.0	0.2	-1.6	166 549	24.8	11.5
29 049	3760	Clinton County..............	18 979	6.5	20.2	7.4	28.1	23.7	14.1	37.7	1.0	1.7	18 182	26.5	14.3
29 051	...	Cole County.................	71 397	6.7	17.5	9.6	32.4	22.5	11.3	35.5	-1.5	-1.1	61 750	24.2	12.7
29 053	...	Cooper County..............	16 670	5.9	16.9	13.9	27.3	20.6	15.4	35.2	-2.9	3.0	14 715	23.3	16.5
29 055	...	Crawford County	22 804	6.5	19.6	7.9	27.2	23.1	15.8	37.9	0.4	3.4	22 179	26.0	16.0
29 057	...	Dade County................	7 923	5.8	18.6	6.9	24.1	24.4	20.3	41.7	-1.3	7.9	7 671	24.1	20.7
29 059	...	Dallas County...............	15 661	6.5	20.7	7.3	26.7	23.5	15.2	37.9	1.5	2.8	15 161	27.1	15.4
29 061	...	Daviess County............	8 016	7.0	20.0	7.9	23.7	23.8	17.6	38.9	1.3	5.2	7 922	26.8	17.7
29 063	...	DeKalb County.............	11 597	5.3	15.3	8.2	36.6	20.6	14.0	37.7	-5.1	1.6	10 262	22.6	15.4
29 065	...	Dent County.................	14 927	6.4	18.3	7.6	25.8	24.1	17.8	39.6	-1.0	5.4	14 471	24.3	18.1
29 067	...	Douglas County	13 084	5.9	19.9	7.2	24.4	25.6	17.0	40.1	0.1	4.6	12 608	25.9	17.3
29 069	...	Dunklin County..............	33 155	7.2	18.8	8.0	26.1	23.3	16.6	37.8	0.3	4.2	29 007	23.6	17.9
29 071	7040	Franklin County.............	93 807	6.9	20.5	8.1	30.0	22.4	12.1	35.8	1.7	-0.3	90 812	27.1	12.2
29 073	...	Gasconade County.........	15 342	5.9	18.8	6.7	26.0	23.7	18.9	40.3	-1.0	6.5	15 099	24.5	19.2
29 075	...	Gentry County...............	6 861	6.3	19.7	6.9	23.8	21.6	21.7	40.2	0.3	9.3	6 769	25.9	21.8
29 077	7920	Greene County..............	240 391	6.1	16.1	13.8	28.7	21.7	13.7	35.1	-3.5	1.3	222 352	21.5	14.3
29 079	...	Grundy County..............	10 432	6.3	17.0	8.2	23.8	24.2	20.5	41.3	-2.4	8.1	10 013	22.3	21.2
29 081	...	Harrison County	8 850	6.6	17.3	7.2	23.8	23.1	22.1	41.7	-1.8	9.7	8 670	23.4	22.4
29 083	...	Henry County...............	21 997	6.1	17.7	7.9	25.6	24.5	18.3	40.0	-1.9	5.9	21 161	23.3	18.7
29 085	...	Hickory County.............	8 940	4.4	15.5	5.1	19.7	29.4	26.0	49.7	-5.8	13.6	8 563	19.6	26.8
29 087	...	Holt County.................	5 351	4.8	18.9	6.5	24.5	23.8	21.5	41.8	-2.0	9.1	5 267	23.7	21.8
29 089	...	Howard County..............	10 212	5.6	18.3	13.2	25.5	21.1	16.2	36.7	-1.8	3.8	9 267	23.6	16.5
29 091	...	Howell County...............	37 238	6.8	19.1	8.0	26.0	23.2	16.8	38.2	0.2	4.4	35 592	25.3	17.2
29 093	...	Iron County	10 697	5.8	19.1	7.7	25.2	25.1	17.1	39.7	-0.8	4.7	10 283	24.9	17.6
29 095	3760	Jackson County.............	654 880	7.0	18.8	9.1	31.3	21.4	12.5	35.2	0.1	0.1	443 586	22.0	14.8

[1]MSA = Metropolitan Statistical Area. PMSA = Primary MSA. NECMA = New England County Metropolitan Area. See the Appendix A for explanation of these concepts. See Appendix B for list of metropolitan areas identified by type, with component counties.

STATE County	Black or African American Total population 14	Age (percent) Under 18 years 15	65 years and over 16	American Indian and Alaska Native Total population 17	Age (percent) Under 18 years 18	65 years and over 19	Asian, Hawaiian, and Pacific Islander Total population 20	Age (percent) Under 18 years 21	65 years and over 22	Hispanic or Latino[1] Total population 23	Age (percent) Under 18 years 24	65 years and over 25	Two or more races Total population 26	Age (percent) Under 18 years 27	65 years and over 28
MISSISSIPPI—Cont'd															
Sunflower County	24 084	31.7	6.7	85	35.3	10.6	61	3.3	9.8	383	40.2	1.8	176	31.8	7.4
Tallahatchie County	8 879	36.0	9.3	11	45.5	0.0	52	9.6	38.5	132	46.2	0.0	60	30.0	3.3
Tate County	7 975	31.8	8.5	18	11.1	0.0	57	0.0	17.5	96	52.1	1.0	123	39.8	11.4
Tippah County	3 263	30.6	9.8	71	28.2	9.9	29	24.1	0.0	516	32.8	1.4	114	21.9	13.2
Tishomingo County	601	21.8	17.3	48	8.3	0.0	33	0.0	0.0	283	23.3	1.1	46	19.6	6.5
Tunica County	6 522	37.1	8.4	14	0.0	0.0	25	0.0	32.0	223	30.5	3.6	58	62.1	0.0
Union County	3 624	31.4	10.3	18	0.0	0.0	153	58.2	0.0	508	39.4	0.0	215	45.1	6.0
Walthall County	6 744	36.8	8.5	12	41.7	0.0	49	28.6	4.1	111	24.3	0.0	54	9.3	55.6
Warren County	21 318	33.8	9.6	131	38.2	0.0	352	38.6	3.7	545	31.0	1.7	354	40.1	13.3
Washington County	40 639	36.6	8.5	86	17.4	19.8	270	31.1	14.1	513	36.5	8.4	350	18.0	18.0
Wayne County	8 075	36.7	7.9	16	0.0	0.0	44	11.4	38.6	35	14.3	40.0	88	22.7	19.3
Webster County	2 213	35.6	10.7	4	0.0	0.0	8	0.0	0.0	134	17.2	18.7	16	37.5	12.5
Wilkinson County	7 032	29.1	11.3	25	8.0	32.0	0	X	X	46	13.0	50.0	19	0.0	31.6
Winston County	8 521	33.0	9.8	178	41.6	1.1	35	62.9	0.0	381	36.5	7.3	105	40.0	15.2
Yalobusha County	5 070	33.8	10.5	30	0.0	0.0	8	25.0	0.0	70	27.1	2.9	67	28.4	11.9
Yazoo County	15 096	35.2	9.7	99	42.4	0.0	83	22.9	4.8	1 352	7.9	1.5	64	25.0	35.9
MISSOURI	622 087	32.5	8.6	26 200	26.6	6.7	63 500	23.2	4.7	116 373	36.2	4.0	90 948	41.9	5.8
Adair County	300	18.0	3.3	104	26.0	0.0	362	8.6	2.2	298	28.9	9.1	223	33.6	2.2
Andrew County	64	14.1	1.6	32	53.1	18.8	47	25.5	0.0	228	43.4	7.5	92	43.5	14.1
Atchison County	140	70.7	0.0	14	0.0	14.3	14	7.1	0.0	24	62.5	0.0	27	51.9	7.4
Audrain County	1 696	20.9	14.4	100	7.0	9.0	102	51.0	1.0	142	28.2	5.6	369	44.4	7.6
Barry County	63	14.3	6.3	260	26.2	1.9	86	16.3	10.5	1 730	42.7	0.8	572	42.8	5.9
Barton County	13	0.0	0.0	74	32.4	0.0	50	32.0	14.0	153	48.4	0.7	272	32.4	11.4
Bates County	60	16.7	25.0	61	27.9	0.0	74	18.9	16.2	174	54.6	1.1	135	24.4	17.0
Benton County	46	45.7	19.6	99	4.0	13.1	9	55.6	0.0	131	47.3	4.6	214	28.5	23.8
Bollinger County	2	0.0	100.0	97	29.9	6.2	12	8.3	0.0	67	58.2	7.5	156	36.5	10.9
Boone County	11 351	33.2	5.0	663	18.3	3.6	3 899	20.8	1.5	2 611	34.1	2.4	2 407	45.2	3.3
Buchanan County	3 620	24.4	7.3	429	27.3	11.9	359	19.2	5.8	2 152	37.0	6.2	1 288	48.4	4.3
Butler County	2 112	34.5	11.6	204	38.2	7.8	234	7.3	5.6	372	52.4	0.0	461	44.9	10.0
Caldwell County	10	30.0	0.0	18	38.9	0.0	12	0.0	0.0	60	60.5	0.0	110	59.0	4.2
Callaway County	2 210	20.9	7.9	220	30.9	15.9	212	8.0	9.9	392	31.1	4.3	527	37.0	4.2
Camden County	118	12.7	26.3	188	15.4	22.9	77	19.5	5.2	225	32.9	7.6	458	42.8	12.4
Cape Girardeau County	3 672	37.0	4.1	238	17.2	9.2	477	16.6	1.7	509	32.6	0.2	862	38.3	4.6
Carroll County	139	40.3	12.2	63	36.5	0.0	4	0.0	100.0	117	29.1	6.0	86	39.5	15.1
Carter County	7	0.0	0.0	94	48.9	3.2	12	0.0	66.7	58	46.6	0.0	150	31.3	13.3
Cass County	1 345	33.8	6.5	450	26.2	2.0	378	28.8	6.3	1 605	42.2	2.9	1 259	49.6	3.2
Cedar County	58	72.4	0.0	57	26.3	22.8	83	16.9	20.5	59	28.8	15.3	222	40.1	14.0
Chariton County	244	17.2	30.7	5	0.0	100.0	7	0.0	100.0	23	65.2	0.0	25	48.0	16.0
Christian County	130	40.0	0.0	415	29.6	6.3	180	20.0	4.4	639	39.7	2.0	596	45.5	1.7
Clark County	13	100.0	0.0	17	41.2	0.0	6	50.0	0.0	27	33.3	25.9	73	28.8	0.0
Clay County	4 524	31.4	2.7	979	23.7	8.5	2 337	27.8	2.7	6 364	38.5	4.6	4 168	46.2	3.5
Clinton County	237	26.2	6.8	95	21.1	17.9	37	0.0	24.3	244	49.6	2.5	241	45.2	7.9
Cole County	6 844	22.3	2.6	246	26.4	2.8	715	20.7	1.8	795	32.1	4.4	1 056	24.6	2.5
Cooper County	1 605	15.9	8.1	40	7.5	0.0	36	25.0	0.0	84	26.2	0.0	202	42.1	5.0
Crawford County	13	61.5	15.4	59	5.1	22.0	60	25.0	10.0	251	27.9	9.2	268	34.7	2.2
Dade County	8	0.0	0.0	50	28.0	8.0	10	0.0	20.0	53	52.8	13.2	133	29.3	5.3
Dallas County	16	0.0	0.0	115	14.8	30.4	27	48.1	0.0	148	35.1	10.1	180	40.0	0.0
Daviess County	4	0.0	0.0	10	60.0	0.0	20	65.0	0.0	35	45.7	5.7	27	44.4	7.4
DeKalb County	1 003	2.5	1.9	41	26.8	46.3	55	20.0	0.0	100	28.0	2.0	141	4.3	0.7
Dent County	57	21.1	12.3	140	36.4	7.9	29	48.3	0.0	139	48.2	2.9	127	40.9	7.1
Douglas County	0	X	X	111	22.5	4.5	16	0.0	0.0	111	27.9	24.3	235	20.4	6.4
Dunklin County	2 936	42.2	8.6	100	11.0	19.0	89	19.1	9.0	717	49.2	3.6	320	48.4	5.6
Franklin County	850	37.3	6.2	259	19.7	4.2	333	33.6	4.8	608	33.1	1.6	971	41.6	12.2
Gasconade County	16	37.5	0.0	16	50.0	0.0	22	36.4	0.0	63	27.0	0.0	128	35.2	7.8
Gentry County	7	42.9	0.0	30	26.7	20.0	7	14.3	28.6	15	53.3	0.0	33	36.4	18.2
Greene County	4 956	28.1	6.0	2 033	30.8	5.6	2 335	22.9	4.7	4 171	32.0	3.8	4 795	38.5	6.1
Grundy County	8	0.0	0.0	39	33.3	0.0	23	0.0	43.5	260	51.9	0.8	130	65.4	0.0
Harrison County	27	33.3	0.0	11	18.2	0.0	34	35.3	0.0	57	50.9	0.0	58	53.4	12.1
Henry County	219	37.4	2.7	114	36.8	13.2	62	29.0	0.0	219	36.1	7.8	226	31.4	13.3
Hickory County	1	0.0	0.0	77	2.6	3.9	14	50.0	35.7	71	28.2	12.7	217	32.3	8.3
Holt County	0	X	X	29	3.4	3.4	4	0.0	0.0	14	42.9	14.3	37	35.1	5.4
Howard County	643	24.1	16.3	42	33.3	4.8	31	9.7	6.5	115	24.3	10.4	115	49.6	7.0
Howell County	87	44.8	18.4	343	30.3	9.9	238	34.0	5.5	395	48.9	5.1	606	36.8	9.4
Iron County	162	44.4	1.9	58	13.8	5.2	12	16.7	0.0	53	45.3	17.0	141	11.3	3.5
Jackson County	150 202	33.2	8.7	3 334	22.9	6.6	9 572	24.0	5.0	34 925	35.0	4.7	16 530	44.1	5.0

[1] Hispanic or Latino persons may be of any race.

STATE County	Total households	Family households (percent)						Nonfamily households (percent)						Percent of householders 65 years and over who live alone	Grandparents who are responsible for the care of their grandchildren
		Married-couple family households			Other family households			Two or more unrelated persons		Male living alone		Female living alone			
		Total	With children	Householder 65 years or over	Total	With children	Householder 65 years or over	Total	Householder 65 years or over	Total	Householder 65 years or over	Total	Householder 65 years or over		
	29	30	31	32	33	34	35	36	37	38	39	40	41	42	43

MISSISSIPPI—Cont'd

STATE County	Total households	Total	With children	Householder 65 yrs or over	Total	With children	Householder 65 yrs or over	Total	Householder 65 yrs or over	Total	Householder 65 yrs or over	Total	Householder 65 yrs or over	Pct 65+ alone	Grandparents
Sunflower County	9 654	43.1	20.0	7.1	32.8	19.0	6.1	2.9	0.2	9.4	2.4	11.9	6.0	38.5	1 060
Tallahatchie County	5 251	44.3	17.7	9.7	28.5	15.8	6.1	2.6	0.4	11.7	2.5	13.0	7.5	38.2	463
Tate County	8 834	57.7	26.5	9.6	18.3	9.8	3.1	2.6	0.3	9.5	1.8	11.9	7.1	40.7	417
Tippah County	8 120	56.9	25.0	10.2	15.9	8.7	3.0	2.4	0.4	9.8	2.2	15.1	8.4	43.8	245
Tishomingo County	7 959	58.8	24.9	11.5	11.9	6.2	2.3	1.9	0.1	10.4	3.2	16.9	10.1	48.9	214
Tunica County	3 261	33.7	15.9	5.2	34.3	17.7	4.8	5.2	0.0	13.1	3.0	13.8	8.0	52.4	243
Union County	9 796	60.8	26.6	10.8	13.7	8.5	2.5	2.1	0.1	9.4	2.4	14.0	8.8	45.5	269
Walthall County	5 572	54.2	24.0	10.7	19.9	11.2	3.1	1.8	0.0	8.8	2.2	15.2	8.2	42.8	336
Warren County	18 783	47.1	22.2	7.6	23.8	14.1	3.1	3.3	0.4	11.2	2.5	14.5	7.1	46.2	698
Washington County	22 151	41.6	18.6	7.8	30.7	18.0	4.0	3.1	0.2	10.5	2.3	14.0	7.6	45.0	1 704
Wayne County	7 871	54.6	26.7	8.7	21.1	11.3	3.7	1.2	0.0	10.0	2.7	13.1	6.8	43.4	446
Webster County	3 917	58.3	26.1	11.0	15.4	8.4	3.4	2.0	0.3	9.4	3.5	14.8	10.0	48.0	170
Wilkinson County	3 584	41.7	17.6	8.6	29.0	15.3	6.8	2.0	0.1	12.1	3.3	15.2	9.0	44.2	300
Winston County	7 574	50.5	21.9	10.9	22.3	12.4	3.9	2.1	0.1	9.7	2.0	15.4	9.7	44.1	359
Yalobusha County	5 282	46.9	18.6	10.1	22.2	11.0	4.7	2.3	0.3	12.4	3.5	16.3	10.0	47.3	275
Yazoo County	9 164	42.6	18.4	8.5	30.4	19.4	4.8	2.6	0.2	9.7	3.1	14.7	8.6	46.6	622
MISSOURI	2 197 214	52.7	23.3	9.8	15.0	9.1	1.9	5.1	0.3	11.4	2.4	15.8	8.0	46.3	43 907
Adair County	9 645	46.4	20.2	8.6	9.6	6.1	0.9	12.5	0.3	13.0	1.7	18.5	8.8	52.1	100
Andrew County	6 249	62.6	27.4	12.0	11.5	7.6	1.6	3.6	0.4	10.1	1.8	12.3	8.1	41.1	76
Atchison County	2 736	55.1	20.3	14.4	10.3	6.3	2.1	3.3	0.4	12.1	2.9	19.2	13.6	49.4	36
Audrain County	9 872	56.2	23.1	12.6	13.1	8.9	1.4	3.0	0.3	9.7	3.0	18.0	11.0	49.4	111
Barry County	13 371	60.1	24.1	12.8	12.4	7.8	2.0	2.9	0.3	11.2	3.3	13.4	8.2	43.2	291
Barton County	4 908	58.1	26.5	11.9	12.5	7.5	2.3	3.0	0.3	10.1	3.6	16.3	10.2	48.8	96
Bates County	6 521	60.0	25.7	12.9	10.6	7.4	1.4	3.6	0.3	10.6	3.7	15.2	10.0	48.3	126
Benton County	7 444	60.2	17.7	18.3	9.8	6.3	1.5	3.8	0.5	12.0	4.6	14.2	9.1	40.2	161
Bollinger County	4 589	65.2	27.1	12.4	10.9	6.7	2.2	2.4	0.2	8.6	2.3	13.0	8.8	43.0	107
Boone County	53 106	46.4	22.3	6.3	13.2	8.7	1.0	11.7	0.2	13.1	1.4	15.6	4.8	45.5	584
Buchanan County	33 592	50.4	21.9	10.1	15.4	10.0	2.0	5.4	0.4	11.4	2.7	17.4	10.4	51.2	772
Butler County	16 737	53.5	21.9	11.4	14.6	8.9	2.2	4.0	0.4	10.6	3.3	17.3	9.8	48.3	368
Caldwell County	3 522	59.2	25.2	13.0	12.0	8.1	1.6	3.4	0.7	11.7	3.4	13.9	9.1	45.0	64
Callaway County	14 449	58.2	26.6	9.4	13.9	9.5	1.4	5.1	0.4	9.8	1.9	13.1	7.4	45.2	358
Camden County	15 740	62.1	17.8	16.6	9.7	6.1	1.1	4.8	0.7	10.8	3.4	12.5	7.1	36.4	219
Cape Girardeau County	27 031	54.7	23.8	10.1	12.2	7.8	1.4	5.9	0.3	10.5	1.8	16.7	8.2	46.1	392
Carroll County	4 169	60.3	25.4	14.9	8.8	5.1	1.6	3.0	0.1	10.9	2.9	17.1	12.7	48.6	46
Carter County	2 377	56.7	22.7	11.0	13.4	8.9	2.0	3.1	1.3	11.4	3.6	15.4	8.9	46.6	17
Cass County	30 236	64.4	30.5	9.8	12.0	8.1	1.2	3.7	0.2	8.6	2.1	11.4	6.2	42.5	564
Cedar County	5 664	59.9	22.5	15.3	9.0	5.7	1.6	3.1	0.4	11.3	4.9	16.8	11.5	48.7	86
Chariton County	3 462	59.1	24.2	14.8	9.0	4.9	2.4	2.3	0.5	11.7	4.5	17.9	13.1	49.8	64
Christian County	20 473	65.8	31.1	9.1	11.8	8.2	1.2	3.4	0.1	7.2	1.6	11.8	5.5	40.3	249
Clark County	2 967	60.9	24.2	12.2	9.8	6.2	1.6	3.4	0.4	10.5	2.7	15.4	10.8	48.6	64
Clay County	72 613	56.1	26.1	8.2	13.4	8.3	1.3	5.4	0.2	11.0	1.6	14.1	5.6	42.5	1 487
Clinton County	7 170	63.0	27.5	11.0	11.5	7.6	1.3	3.6	0.3	8.9	2.5	13.0	8.6	46.8	152
Cole County	27 064	53.7	26.3	8.7	12.8	8.3	1.3	4.8	0.1	11.8	2.1	16.9	7.0	47.3	330
Cooper County	5 943	58.2	24.7	12.4	11.8	7.3	1.4	3.8	0.1	10.2	3.0	15.9	10.2	48.6	126
Crawford County	8 870	61.1	25.7	13.0	11.0	7.6	1.0	3.6	0.5	10.7	3.4	13.6	7.9	43.7	261
Dade County	3 222	59.4	22.1	15.8	11.4	6.8	0.9	2.2	0.0	11.4	4.2	15.3	11.1	47.8	51
Dallas County	6 063	62.2	27.5	11.9	11.2	7.0	1.3	3.1	0.5	10.0	3.4	13.5	9.5	48.4	112
Daviess County	3 184	61.9	25.2	16.1	9.5	5.9	1.6	2.9	0.2	10.5	2.3	15.2	10.2	41.1	51
DeKalb County	3 553	60.4	27.3	12.7	9.5	6.4	1.2	3.3	0.3	10.3	3.1	16.4	12.1	51.8	48
Dent County	6 017	59.8	24.7	13.3	11.8	6.5	1.8	3.2	0.4	9.4	3.5	15.7	10.0	46.7	96
Douglas County	5 214	61.0	24.1	13.6	10.0	6.4	1.9	2.7	0.2	11.4	3.5	14.8	8.8	43.9	105
Dunklin County	13 414	52.6	21.5	11.0	16.2	10.0	2.1	3.2	0.3	9.8	3.0	18.2	10.8	50.7	401
Franklin County	35 081	61.2	28.7	10.2	12.7	8.0	1.6	4.1	0.2	9.9	1.9	12.0	6.9	42.2	733
Gasconade County	6 188	59.3	24.4	13.4	10.6	7.2	1.7	3.2	0.4	11.3	4.3	15.6	11.2	49.8	112
Gentry County	2 745	60.3	25.6	16.1	9.2	6.0	1.5	1.4	0.3	10.5	3.1	18.7	14.0	48.9	35
Greene County	98 003	50.1	20.7	9.7	13.3	8.0	1.6	7.5	0.3	12.0	2.0	17.1	7.8	45.8	1 211
Grundy County	4 395	55.1	20.1	14.1	11.1	7.4	1.4	3.1	0.3	11.5	3.6	19.2	11.4	48.6	90
Harrison County	3 683	58.5	21.0	15.8	10.9	6.5	2.0	1.7	0.1	10.9	3.8	17.9	12.6	47.8	61
Henry County	9 192	55.8	20.7	13.2	13.2	8.9	1.6	3.5	0.6	12.3	3.2	15.1	9.5	45.3	209
Hickory County	3 947	62.1	17.4	21.5	7.8	4.8	1.5	3.7	1.0	11.5	4.5	14.9	11.0	39.2	95
Holt County	2 236	56.6	21.4	15.6	11.3	7.2	1.9	2.5	0.2	12.8	3.4	16.9	13.1	48.2	22
Howard County	3 838	56.1	23.9	12.2	13.2	7.7	2.0	3.6	0.4	11.8	3.0	15.3	9.5	46.4	70
Howell County	14 805	60.2	25.2	13.2	12.2	7.6	1.6	2.7	0.6	9.7	2.5	15.3	9.8	44.6	306
Iron County	4 209	58.2	23.1	13.0	12.5	8.8	1.6	3.5	0.5	11.1	3.1	14.7	8.6	43.6	102
Jackson County	266 501	44.0	19.3	8.0	18.8	11.2	2.2	6.1	0.3	13.4	2.3	17.8	7.7	48.6	6 426

Table A-3. States and Counties — Age, Ethnicity, and Household Structure

STATE County	Households with Non-Hispanic White householder — Number of households	Percent that are family households	Households with Black or African American householder — Number of households	Percent that are family households	Households with American Indian and Alaska Native householder — Number of households	Percent that are family households	Households with Asian, Hawaiian, and Pacific Islander householder — Number of households	Percent that are family households	Households with Hispanic or Latino[1] householder — Number of households	Percent that are family households	Foreign-born population — Percent of total population that is foreign-born	Place of birth (percent) — Europe	Asia	Latin America	Percent in non-English speaking households — Linguistically isolated	Not linguistically isolated
	44	45	46	47	48	49	50	51	52	53	54	55	56	57	58	59
MISSISSIPPI—Cont'd																
Sunflower County	3 509	73.2	6 025	77.2	25	100.0	29	79.3	107	73.8	0.6	0.0	0.1	0.4	0.3	7.6
Tallahatchie County	2 392	74.7	2 797	71.5	0	X	21	76.2	34	52.9	0.5	0.2	0.2	0.1	0.0	6.2
Tate County	6 393	76.3	2 367	75.3	8	100.0	9	0.0	34	76.5	0.2	0.1	0.1	0.1	0.1	5.1
Tippah County	6 742	72.0	1 196	76.8	18	100.0	6	100.0	140	73.6	1.9	0.1	0.1	1.7	1.0	5.5
Tishomingo County	7 595	71.3	218	54.6	34	50.0	19	68.4	82	70.7	1.0	0.0	0.1	0.9	0.7	3.9
Tunica County	1 147	57.3	2 043	73.4	0	X	8	100.0	77	79.2	0.9	0.0	0.2	0.6	0.6	3.6
Union County	8 264	75.3	1 384	67.3	5	100.0	21	71.4	93	100.0	1.8	0.0	0.4	1.2	0.8	6.1
Walthall County	3 328	73.8	2 188	74.6	7	0.0	14	100.0	26	100.0	0.5	0.1	0.3	0.1	0.1	5.2
Warren County	10 777	72.6	7 631	68.6	37	67.6	77	71.4	152	84.9	1.2	0.4	0.5	0.2	0.1	6.7
Washington County	8 714	71.4	13 041	73.3	51	29.4	76	72.4	147	65.3	0.8	0.1	0.3	0.3	0.4	6.8
Wayne County	5 126	77.2	2 662	72.7	10	100.0	24	70.8	16	100.0	0.3	0.1	0.2	0.0	0.0	3.2
Webster County	3 161	73.9	713	73.5	0	X	1	0.0	39	69.2	0.5	0.3	0.1	0.1	0.2	4.7
Wilkinson County	1 207	68.3	2 340	72.1	17	100.0	0	X	27	59.3	0.1	0.0	0.0	0.1	0.1	3.8
Winston County	4 519	71.8	2 901	73.7	34	82.4	4	100.0	108	90.7	1.1	0.2	0.2	0.7	0.6	5.2
Yalobusha County	3 387	67.4	1 848	72.1	22	77.3	1	100.0	13	38.5	0.4	0.1	0.2	0.1	0.1	3.5
Yazoo County	4 512	73.2	4 518	72.4	26	100.0	18	66.7	67	92.5	3.9	0.3	0.2	3.4	0.5	5.7
MISSOURI	1 882 812	67.9	227 340	65.9	10 006	67.9	21 131	65.7	32 361	72.2	2.7	0.8	0.9	0.7	1.0	7.7
Adair County	9 161	57.3	128	32.8	34	85.3	165	10.3	102	44.1	2.0	0.5	1.0	0.3	0.6	8.3
Andrew County	6 143	73.7	12	83.3	2	100.0	5	100.0	53	88.7	0.6	0.2	0.2	0.1	0.1	4.7
Atchison County	2 717	65.4	6	50.0	2	0.0	5	100.0	4	100.0	0.3	0.0	0.2	0.1	0.1	3.8
Audrain County	9 172	69.8	497	62.4	33	42.4	21	95.2	48	91.7	0.7	0.3	0.2	0.1	1.1	7.7
Barry County	12 642	72.3	20	70.0	79	74.7	24	87.5	412	82.0	3.5	0.4	0.2	2.8	1.8	7.7
Barton County	4 741	70.7	0	X	23	69.6	16	75.0	26	84.6	0.7	0.2	0.2	0.3	0.8	3.5
Bates County	6 367	70.7	29	51.7	15	80.0	21	47.6	27	70.4	0.9	0.4	0.3	0.2	0.3	5.4
Benton County	7 253	70.2	7	42.9	49	65.3	4	0.0	31	77.4	0.7	0.4	0.0	0.2	0.4	5.1
Bollinger County	4 470	76.2	2	0.0	30	83.3	9	22.2	21	71.4	0.4	0.2	0.0	0.0	0.0	4.1
Boone County	45 873	59.5	4 266	62.3	302	63.6	1 383	54.0	642	62.5	4.5	0.7	2.5	0.7	1.3	10.3
Buchanan County	31 403	66.0	1 059	55.4	150	65.3	144	50.0	561	76.1	1.1	0.4	0.3	0.2	0.3	6.2
Butler County	15 529	67.9	832	70.1	72	61.1	68	85.3	57	87.7	1.4	0.3	0.6	0.4	0.4	5.7
Caldwell County	3 479	71.0	2	100.0	2	100.0	2	0.0	15	80.0	0.4	0.3	0.1	0.1	0.3	3.3
Callaway County	13 470	72.7	631	62.4	80	78.8	58	37.9	75	66.7	1.1	0.4	0.4	0.2	0.4	4.4
Camden County	15 417	71.9	53	64.2	71	64.8	16	100.0	73	67.1	1.4	0.8	0.3	0.2	0.3	5.8
Cape Girardeau County	25 144	66.9	1 225	70.0	74	62.2	142	43.0	138	57.2	1.3	0.5	0.6	0.2	0.3	5.7
Carroll County	4 042	69.1	51	70.6	26	76.9	4	0.0	27	74.1	0.4	0.4	0.0	0.1	0.6	5.2
Carter County	2 290	69.6	0	X	22	81.8	3	33.3	20	80.0	0.3	0.2	0.0	0.1	0.1	6.5
Cass County	28 781	76.2	440	73.0	191	71.7	71	81.7	475	85.5	1.6	0.5	0.4	0.6	0.4	6.5
Cedar County	5 526	68.9	8	100.0	18	61.1	24	37.5	18	61.1	1.3	0.3	0.6	0.1	0.4	6.0
Chariton County	3 316	68.9	128	48.4	3	0.0	0	X	4	100.0	0.6	0.5	0.1	0.0	0.1	5.5
Christian County	19 828	77.7	53	71.7	136	80.9	50	68.0	244	70.9	0.9	0.3	0.2	0.2	0.2	5.3
Clark County	2 949	70.6	0	X	10	100.0	0	X	5	40.0	0.2	0.1	0.0	0.1	0.6	7.5
Clay County	66 891	69.5	1 752	62.6	440	73.2	812	67.2	1 875	74.1	2.9	0.6	1.1	0.7	0.9	8.2
Clinton County	6 949	74.1	94	91.5	21	71.4	13	100.0	38	100.0	0.5	0.2	0.2	0.1	0.2	5.4
Cole County	24 406	67.5	1 831	53.1	84	91.7	291	66.3	236	69.9	2.2	0.4	0.8	0.6	0.8	6.5
Cooper County	5 534	71.3	337	50.7	3	0.0	11	45.5	27	70.4	0.6	0.4	0.1	0.1	0.1	5.4
Crawford County	8 646	72.0	5	60.0	28	50.0	24	70.8	78	96.2	1.2	0.4	0.3	0.4	0.4	4.8
Dade County	3 129	71.1	4	50.0	17	70.6	2	100.0	9	55.6	1.0	0.5	0.1	0.2	0.1	5.7
Dallas County	5 893	74.0	16	25.0	40	87.5	3	100.0	39	61.5	0.5	0.2	0.1	0.2	0.4	6.5
Daviess County	3 153	71.4	2	100.0	2	100.0	5	100.0	11	81.8	0.2	0.1	0.0	0.1	3.7	7.3
DeKalb County	3 475	70.1	22	36.4	24	50.0	17	100.0	8	75.0	1.0	0.4	0.4	0.0	0.0	4.9
Dent County	5 866	71.7	22	50.0	55	60.0	5	60.0	29	100.0	0.6	0.4	0.1	0.1	0.3	4.9
Douglas County	5 029	70.9	0	X	50	72.0	0	X	30	83.3	0.9	0.6	0.2	0.2	0.5	5.5
Dunklin County	12 040	68.7	1 034	70.2	69	65.2	32	93.8	164	79.3	1.5	0.1	0.2	1.1	0.9	5.8
Franklin County	34 179	74.1	322	60.9	127	65.4	46	91.3	203	74.4	0.8	0.4	0.3	0.1	0.2	5.5
Gasconade County	6 101	70.0	7	71.4	5	100.0	4	100.0	36	55.6	0.5	0.4	0.1	0.0	0.5	5.4
Gentry County	2 715	69.7	4	0.0	6	100.0	4	0.0	3	33.3	0.6	0.5	0.1	0.0	0.1	7.0
Greene County	92 104	63.4	1 680	64.1	779	55.3	742	61.1	1 177	70.6	1.9	0.5	0.7	0.4	0.5	6.8
Grundy County	4 275	66.0	8	75.0	8	0.0	12	100.0	68	83.8	1.4	0.1	0.2	0.8	0.6	7.4
Harrison County	3 625	69.1	7	100.0	7	42.9	11	100.0	18	100.0	1.0	0.2	0.3	0.3	0.7	2.5
Henry County	8 877	69.2	97	46.4	35	100.0	11	100.0	74	68.9	0.8	0.3	0.1	0.3	0.3	4.6
Hickory County	3 794	70.3	0	X	52	46.2	2	100.0	23	78.3	1.0	0.5	0.1	0.3	0.3	3.9
Holt County	2 206	67.9	0	X	15	86.7	2	0.0	4	50.0	0.4	0.2	0.1	0.0	0.0	5.7
Howard County	3 524	69.2	256	68.4	11	81.8	0	X	23	60.9	1.0	0.2	0.3	0.2	0.1	4.2
Howell County	14 323	72.2	10	20.0	126	84.9	70	85.7	88	94.3	1.3	0.7	0.4	0.2	0.6	4.7
Iron County	4 068	70.8	53	69.8	22	50.0	7	57.1	10	80.0	0.4	0.1	0.1	0.1	0.2	4.9
Jackson County	190 908	61.7	57 131	64.7	1 392	55.7	3 013	64.6	10 002	73.8	4.3	0.6	1.2	2.0	1.9	10.3

[1] Hispanic or Latino persons may be of any race.

STATE/ County code	MSA/PMSA/ NECMA code[1]	STATE County	Total population	Under 5 years	5 to 17 years	18 to 24 years	25 to 44 years	45 to 64 years	65 years and over	Median age	+/− U.S. percent under 18 years	+/− U.S. percent 65 years and over	Total population	Under 18 years	65 years and over
						Population by age (percent)							Non-Hispanic White Age (percent)		
			1	2	3	4	5	6	7	8	9	10	11	12	13
		MISSOURI—Cont'd													
29 097	3710	Jasper County	104 686	7.2	18.5	11.0	28.2	21.2	13.8	34.9	0.0	1.4	95 375	24.9	14.6
29 099	7040	Jefferson County	198 099	7.2	20.7	8.5	31.9	22.5	9.2	34.9	2.2	-3.2	191 889	27.7	9.2
29 101	...	Johnson County	48 258	6.9	18.3	19.8	28.1	17.5	9.4	28.5	-0.5	-3.0	42 779	24.4	10.2
29 103	...	Knox County	4 361	6.4	18.4	6.6	23.3	23.9	21.3	41.6	-0.9	8.9	4 289	24.5	21.4
29 105	...	Laclede County	32 513	6.9	19.8	8.4	28.0	22.8	14.2	36.6	1.0	1.8	31 291	26.4	14.5
29 107	3760	Lafayette County	32 960	6.1	20.0	7.6	27.4	23.6	15.4	37.9	0.4	3.0	31 270	25.5	15.8
29 109	...	Lawrence County	35 204	7.1	20.1	7.8	27.4	22.1	15.6	36.9	1.5	3.2	33 173	26.4	16.3
29 111	...	Lewis County	10 494	7.0	18.1	12.6	24.7	21.4	16.1	36.0	-0.6	3.7	10 031	24.8	16.1
29 113	7040	Lincoln County	38 944	7.3	22.7	8.1	30.3	20.8	10.8	34.5	4.3	-1.6	37 161	29.7	10.9
29 115	...	Linn County	13 754	6.0	19.3	7.3	24.1	22.9	20.5	40.3	-0.4	8.1	13 379	25.0	20.6
29 117	...	Livingston County	14 558	6.1	18.0	7.6	26.2	23.2	19.0	39.7	-1.6	6.6	13 993	24.2	19.6
29 119	...	McDonald County	21 681	7.7	21.1	9.3	28.2	22.5	11.2	34.3	3.1	-1.2	18 231	27.0	12.6
29 121	...	Macon County	15 762	6.3	17.9	7.9	25.0	23.9	19.1	40.1	-1.5	6.7	15 161	23.6	19.5
29 123	...	Madison County	11 800	6.0	18.5	8.0	26.4	23.0	18.0	39.1	-1.2	5.6	11 514	24.5	18.2
29 125	...	Maries County	8 903	6.5	19.5	7.0	26.6	24.6	15.9	38.5	0.3	3.5	8 619	25.8	16.1
29 127	...	Marion County	28 289	6.6	19.2	9.4	26.5	21.7	16.7	37.1	0.1	4.3	26 331	25.1	16.9
29 129	...	Mercer County	3 757	5.5	17.3	6.7	24.8	23.8	21.9	42.4	-2.9	9.5	3 730	22.8	21.9
29 131	...	Miller County	23 564	6.8	19.4	8.5	27.4	22.6	15.3	37.2	0.5	2.9	22 776	26.0	15.6
29 133	...	Mississippi County	13 427	7.2	19.2	8.8	25.3	23.6	15.9	37.3	0.7	3.5	10 381	22.4	17.7
29 135	...	Moniteau County	14 827	6.7	19.1	8.4	31.1	20.7	14.0	35.9	0.1	1.6	13 707	26.5	14.9
29 137	...	Monroe County	9 311	6.5	19.4	7.4	24.9	24.1	17.7	39.4	0.2	5.3	8 795	25.4	18.1
29 139	...	Montgomery County	12 136	5.8	19.5	7.3	26.1	23.9	17.4	39.4	-0.4	5.0	11 581	25.2	17.5
29 141	...	Morgan County	19 309	5.9	17.9	6.4	23.0	27.1	19.6	42.6	-1.9	7.2	18 633	23.6	20.0
29 143	...	New Madrid County	19 760	6.6	19.8	8.5	26.9	22.8	15.4	37.4	0.7	3.0	16 365	24.0	16.4
29 145	3710	Newton County	52 636	6.9	19.3	8.8	27.1	23.8	14.1	37.1	0.5	1.7	48 765	25.6	14.7
29 147	...	Nodaway County	21 912	4.7	14.6	25.2	23.0	18.7	13.8	30.2	-6.4	1.4	21 125	19.6	14.1
29 149	...	Oregon County	10 344	6.1	18.1	6.8	24.5	26.6	17.9	41.0	-1.5	5.5	9 692	23.8	18.6
29 151	...	Osage County	13 062	6.6	19.8	9.5	27.6	21.8	14.7	36.1	0.7	2.3	12 869	26.3	14.9
29 153	...	Ozark County	9 542	5.2	16.7	6.9	23.0	28.7	19.5	43.6	-3.8	7.1	9 212	21.8	19.8
29 155	...	Pemiscot County	20 047	8.2	21.7	9.1	25.2	20.7	15.1	34.4	4.2	2.7	14 154	24.3	17.1
29 157	...	Perry County	18 132	6.8	19.2	8.5	28.3	21.4	15.7	36.8	0.3	3.3	17 584	25.3	16.1
29 159	...	Pettis County	39 403	7.0	19.3	9.3	28.1	20.7	15.5	36.4	0.6	3.1	35 931	25.3	16.5
29 161	...	Phelps County	39 825	5.7	18.1	14.2	26.5	21.5	13.9	34.9	-1.9	1.5	36 821	23.5	14.7
29 163	...	Pike County	18 351	5.3	18.2	9.8	28.7	23.5	14.6	37.7	-2.2	2.2	16 109	24.7	15.5
29 165	3760	Platte County	73 781	6.9	18.8	8.3	32.6	24.6	8.8	35.9	0.0	-3.6	66 248	24.9	9.4
29 167	...	Polk County	26 992	6.7	19.0	12.7	25.6	20.8	15.3	35.0	0.0	2.9	26 092	25.5	15.5
29 169	...	Pulaski County	41 165	7.7	19.9	16.4	32.3	15.8	7.9	28.5	1.9	-4.5	31 174	25.9	9.7
29 171	...	Putnam County	5 223	6.5	17.5	6.2	24.2	25.0	20.6	41.9	-1.7	8.2	5 147	23.8	20.9
29 173	...	Ralls County	9 626	5.7	19.5	7.2	26.8	26.5	14.3	39.3	-0.5	1.9	9 408	25.1	14.3
29 175	...	Randolph County	24 663	6.5	17.3	9.5	29.4	22.4	14.9	37.2	-1.9	2.5	22 122	23.6	15.7
29 177	3760	Ray County	23 354	6.6	21.0	7.5	28.2	24.0	12.7	37.1	1.9	0.3	22 437	27.2	13.0
29 179	...	Reynolds County	6 689	5.7	18.2	6.7	25.2	27.9	16.3	40.7	-1.8	3.9	6 302	23.3	16.9
29 181	...	Ripley County	13 509	6.0	18.8	7.9	25.3	24.7	17.3	39.4	-0.9	4.9	13 081	24.8	17.5
29 183	7040	St. Charles County	283 883	7.6	21.3	8.2	32.6	21.6	8.7	34.3	3.2	-3.7	266 259	28.4	9.1
29 185	...	St. Clair County	9 652	5.3	17.7	5.7	23.1	26.9	21.2	43.9	-2.7	8.8	9 268	22.8	21.6
29 186	...	Ste. Genevieve County	17 842	6.0	20.5	7.7	28.2	23.0	14.6	37.7	0.8	2.2	17 417	26.4	14.9
29 187	...	St. Francois County	55 641	6.0	17.9	9.2	29.5	22.5	15.0	37.2	-1.8	2.6	53 218	24.1	15.4
29 189	7040	St. Louis County	1 016 315	6.3	18.9	8.2	29.1	23.4	14.1	37.5	-0.5	1.7	772 793	22.8	16.6
29 195	...	Saline County	23 756	6.3	18.1	11.7	25.7	22.0	16.2	37.2	-1.3	3.8	21 006	23.0	17.6
29 197	...	Schuyler County	4 170	5.7	18.9	6.6	25.1	24.0	19.8	40.8	-1.1	7.4	4 112	24.8	19.7
29 199	...	Scotland County	4 983	7.1	21.7	7.6	24.0	20.7	18.9	37.4	3.1	6.5	4 880	28.5	19.3
29 201	...	Scott County	40 422	7.1	20.3	8.9	27.3	22.6	13.8	36.0	1.7	1.4	35 339	25.4	14.7
29 203	...	Shannon County	8 324	6.0	20.2	7.1	26.4	25.3	14.9	38.8	0.5	2.5	7 984	26.1	14.8
29 205	...	Shelby County	6 799	5.7	19.6	7.2	24.4	23.2	19.9	40.4	-0.4	7.5	6 663	25.0	19.7
29 207	...	Stoddard County	29 705	5.6	18.2	8.5	26.3	24.2	17.2	39.1	-1.9	4.8	28 701	23.2	17.4
29 209	...	Stone County	28 658	5.5	15.9	6.0	24.1	29.5	18.9	44.1	-4.3	6.5	27 855	21.4	19.2
29 211	...	Sullivan County	7 219	7.1	18.1	7.4	26.3	22.8	18.3	38.9	-0.5	5.9	6 542	24.3	20.0
29 213	...	Taney County	39 703	6.0	16.4	10.0	26.6	24.9	16.1	38.8	-3.3	3.7	37 609	21.7	16.8
29 215	...	Texas County	23 003	5.8	19.2	7.1	24.9	25.2	17.9	40.4	-0.7	5.5	21 887	24.3	18.3
29 217	...	Vernon County	20 454	7.0	19.6	9.1	25.6	22.5	16.3	37.1	0.9	3.9	19 768	26.1	16.6
29 219	7040	Warren County	24 525	6.5	20.3	7.4	29.2	23.7	13.0	37.4	1.1	0.6	23 209	26.3	13.3
29 221	...	Washington County	23 344	6.7	19.9	10.0	29.2	22.6	11.7	35.2	0.9	-0.7	22 132	26.9	12.0
29 223	...	Wayne County	13 259	5.3	18.0	6.6	23.5	26.8	19.9	42.5	-2.4	7.5	12 918	23.3	20.0
29 225	7920	Webster County	31 045	7.5	21.4	8.2	29.7	21.7	11.5	34.6	3.2	-0.9	29 615	28.9	11.7
29 227	...	Worth County	2 382	5.4	18.8	6.8	23.4	23.1	22.5	41.9	-1.5	10.1	2 348	24.1	22.6
29 229	...	Wright County	17 955	6.9	20.1	8.2	25.3	23.0	16.5	37.7	1.3	4.1	17 302	26.8	16.8

[1]MSA = Metropolitan Statistical Area. PMSA = Primary MSA. NECMA = New England County Metropolitan Area. See the Appendix A for explanation of these concepts. See Appendix B for list of metropolitan areas identified by type, with component counties.

STATE County	Black or African American Total population (14)	Under 18 years (15)	65 years and over (16)	American Indian and Alaska Native Total population (17)	Under 18 years (18)	65 years and over (19)	Asian, Hawaiian, and Pacific Islander Total population (20)	Under 18 years (21)	65 years and over (22)	Hispanic or Latino[1] Total population (23)	Under 18 years (24)	65 years and over (25)	Two or more races Total population (26)	Under 18 years (27)	65 years and over (28)
MISSOURI—Cont'd															
Jasper County	1 391	26.9	9.4	1 420	29.6	5.8	641	16.7	7.0	3 891	40.1	1.4	2 493	42.0	7.0
Jefferson County	1 296	30.2	14.7	515	13.4	9.9	745	27.4	7.9	1 792	42.6	3.0	1 995	37.3	4.1
Johnson County	1 918	27.5	5.7	345	35.9	1.7	669	16.3	3.6	1 477	36.4	0.9	1 129	39.8	2.7
Knox County	13	100.0	0.0	2	0.0	100.0	12	41.7	0.0	16	37.5	18.8	33	36.4	30.3
Laclede County	97	32.0	3.1	144	31.3	0.0	90	3.3	10.0	459	41.4	3.9	454	36.1	10.8
Lafayette County	712	26.3	8.8	81	37.0	0.0	76	35.5	1.3	328	44.5	6.4	543	45.7	5.9
Lawrence County	44	6.8	0.0	251	32.7	4.4	52	42.3	0.0	1 238	45.9	2.6	505	33.3	9.9
Lewis County	252	26.2	25.4	17	0.0	0.0	27	0.0	0.0	35	17.1	14.3	127	58.3	6.3
Lincoln County	765	34.9	12.5	163	29.4	0.0	39	28.2	0.0	370	33.8	2.2	479	47.6	6.3
Linn County	119	37.8	21.0	55	27.3	9.1	30	23.3	10.0	98	33.7	11.2	90	37.8	24.4
Livingston County	338	6.8	3.8	51	31.4	0.0	28	46.4	0.0	68	27.9	10.3	144	26.4	1.4
McDonald County	22	40.9	4.5	581	40.3	8.4	82	36.6	0.0	2 047	38.8	1.1	851	37.8	6.8
Macon County	360	33.3	9.4	61	32.8	0.0	23	8.7	0.0	75	60.0	2.7	88	54.5	20.5
Madison County	16	0.0	0.0	21	0.0	9.5	62	9.7	25.8	42	31.0	0.0	154	34.4	9.7
Maries County	15	20.0	0.0	24	0.0	0.0	0	X	X	73	52.1	5.5	174	29.3	13.8
Marion County	1 190	31.8	15.8	41	31.7	14.6	47	40.4	0.0	268	35.1	3.0	396	44.9	14.1
Mercer County	0	X	X	2	0.0	0.0	5	0.0	0.0	7	28.6	28.6	13	38.5	23.1
Miller County	53	5.7	17.0	121	28.9	5.0	125	42.4	0.0	252	36.1	12.7	317	41.3	6.3
Mississippi County	2 833	40.3	9.5	49	38.8	16.3	51	11.8	0.0	41	58.5	17.1	73	27.4	9.6
Moniteau County	492	0.0	2.0	63	6.3	0.0	68	13.2	2.9	393	39.9	2.3	134	27.6	6.0
Monroe County	382	36.4	11.8	54	24.1	16.7	30	20.0	16.7	27	18.5	0.0	24	41.7	16.7
Montgomery County	196	19.4	29.1	21	0.0	0.0	96	0.0	10.4	134	50.7	10.4	159	59.7	3.1
Morgan County	96	20.8	18.8	103	34.0	8.7	30	6.7	13.3	181	30.9	7.2	306	30.1	8.8
New Madrid County	3 103	38.1	9.8	23	4.3	52.2	12	0.0	0.0	151	39.1	17.9	149	46.3	17.4
Newton County	282	34.8	8.2	1 155	33.5	6.8	340	30.6	0.6	996	40.5	3.0	1 206	33.0	11.1
Nodaway County	311	2.3	0.0	46	6.5	0.0	200	12.0	10.0	101	11.9	12.9	137	35.8	9.5
Oregon County	9	22.2	0.0	181	17.1	14.9	22	0.0	0.0	102	39.2	2.0	342	36.8	4.4
Osage County	10	40.0	0.0	58	22.4	0.0	18	22.2	0.0	35	34.3	5.7	80	47.5	2.5
Ozark County	5	0.0	0.0	50	18.0	14.0	19	21.1	0.0	110	39.1	7.3	165	23.0	9.1
Pemiscot County	5 468	43.4	10.5	25	0.0	0.0	40	17.5	15.0	307	50.2	0.0	128	54.7	17.2
Perry County	30	23.3	6.7	58	34.5	0.0	122	43.1	0.0	101	40.0	0.0	104	58.2	11.4
Pettis County	1 260	34.8	11.0	106	28.3	2.8	153	22.2	3.9	1 367	36.5	1.2	685	50.2	5.3
Phelps County	696	35.2	5.9	296	20.9	4.4	883	16.2	4.5	490	42.2	3.1	693	33.9	5.3
Pike County	1 532	12.3	8.1	35	17.1	31.4	119	6.7	11.8	300	11.0	4.7	261	39.1	4.6
Platte County	2 395	27.4	1.8	430	27.2	4.7	1 155	27.9	5.7	2 212	35.6	4.5	1 540	43.1	2.1
Polk County	92	30.4	14.1	122	10.7	18.9	112	3.6	0.0	376	41.5	2.7	231	44.2	20.3
Pulaski County	4 928	33.1	2.0	488	33.6	1.8	1 019	18.0	5.6	2 465	31.7	1.4	1 299	39.0	2.3
Putnam County	3	0.0	0.0	4	50.0	0.0	6	66.7	0.0	35	57.1	0.0	48	41.7	0.0
Ralls County	86	20.9	19.8	10	0.0	20.0	19	10.5	42.1	47	42.6	10.6	52	34.6	3.8
Randolph County	1 543	17.4	9.3	133	27.8	8.3	175	41.7	0.0	266	38.7	2.3	455	37.1	7.0
Ray County	290	25.2	6.2	74	16.2	0.0	28	25.0	3.6	289	50.2	1.7	242	45.5	9.1
Reynolds County	43	83.7	0.0	151	25.8	9.9	15	40.0	0.0	66	45.5	1.5	122	18.0	12.3
Ripley County	9	0.0	0.0	137	25.5	10.2	66	10.6	19.7	139	32.4	8.6	81	19.8	7.4
St. Charles County	6 674	34.4	4.0	911	28.5	2.7	2 528	27.2	3.2	4 519	38.6	2.9	3 592	48.4	4.5
St. Clair County	11	18.2	36.4	83	20.5	4.8	27	0.0	33.3	149	43.0	10.1	112	35.7	13.4
Ste. Genevieve County	149	0.7	2.7	47	74.5	0.0	7	0.0	0.0	140	42.9	0.0	126	38.1	0.0
St. Francois County	1 169	12.3	1.0	154	11.0	9.1	265	29.4	8.3	379	29.8	6.1	521	26.9	11.3
St. Louis County	192 348	32.7	6.7	1 983	28.6	6.8	21 971	24.2	5.0	14 517	33.7	5.0	14 180	45.3	4.9
Saline County	1 136	26.5	9.9	112	33.9	0.0	142	21.1	2.8	1 000	40.8	0.7	515	46.2	5.4
Schuyler County	0	X	X	19	31.6	5.3	2	0.0	0.0	10	10.0	40.0	23	8.7	34.8
Scotland County	0	X	X	3	0.0	0.0	11	54.5	0.0	74	39.2	2.7	15	46.7	0.0
Scott County	4 239	42.2	6.6	73	21.9	12.3	99	22.2	18.2	381	48.3	1.8	329	39.8	16.1
Shannon County	16	56.3	0.0	143	25.2	16.8	13	0.0	0.0	49	40.8	26.5	134	32.1	20.9
Shelby County	50	20.0	52.0	18	77.8	5.6	11	36.4	0.0	28	35.7	17.9	24	45.8	16.7
Stoddard County	304	39.8	19.7	67	25.4	0.0	119	44.5	0.0	164	43.3	3.7	359	40.1	14.2
Stone County	15	53.3	0.0	154	15.6	10.4	75	4.0	17.3	199	24.6	4.0	399	26.3	12.3
Sullivan County	13	46.2	0.0	23	0.0	13.0	11	0.0	81.8	631	34.1	0.8	36	47.2	0.0
Taney County	99	7.1	14.1	311	33.1	3.9	304	25.7	4.6	774	39.4	1.0	640	41.4	6.9
Texas County	98	43.9	0.0	235	35.3	11.9	50	48.0	0.0	242	42.1	3.7	519	31.8	14.3
Vernon County	73	42.5	0.0	129	15.5	7.0	94	24.5	11.7	171	48.5	3.5	211	45.5	9.0
Warren County	589	34.6	8.5	75	0.0	5.3	18	38.9	0.0	350	48.0	0.0	287	33.4	11.8
Washington County	552	1.4	4.5	132	31.1	5.3	108	39.8	0.0	189	38.1	2.6	231	38.5	11.7
Wayne County	10	0.0	50.0	97	25.8	7.2	15	13.3	33.3	38	26.3	13.2	188	20.7	17.0
Webster County	312	3.8	0.6	190	32.6	4.2	73	26.0	8.2	364	40.7	6.9	512	36.1	7.2
Worth County	2	100.0	0.0	11	0.0	18.2	0	X	X	4	0.0	100.0	17	58.8	0.0
Wright County	68	42.6	22.1	140	17.1	4.3	12	16.7	25.0	214	39.3	3.3	230	33.5	14.8

[1] Hispanic or Latino persons may be of any race.

Table A-3. States and Counties — Age, Ethnicity, and Household Structure

STATE County	Total households	Family households (percent)						Nonfamily households (percent)						Percent of householders 65 years and over who live alone	Grandparents who are responsible for the care of their grandchildren
		Married-couple family households			Other family households			Two or more unrelated persons		Male living alone		Female living alone			
		Total	With children	Householder 65 years or over	Total	With children	Householder 65 years or over	Total	Householder 65 years or over	Total	Householder 65 years or over	Total	Householder 65 years or over		
	29	30	31	32	33	34	35	36	37	38	39	40	41	42	43
MISSOURI—Cont'd															
Jasper County	41 471	53.0	23.2	10.2	14.7	9.6	1.8	5.1	0.3	10.9	2.2	16.2	8.7	47.0	883
Jefferson County	71 567	61.7	30.2	7.6	15.0	9.5	1.6	4.4	0.2	9.4	1.7	9.5	4.5	39.6	1 620
Johnson County	17 390	56.8	27.9	8.2	11.4	8.0	0.8	9.3	0.4	10.1	1.7	12.5	5.8	44.3	192
Knox County	1 794	58.3	22.8	16.1	9.8	5.2	2.0	2.6	0.6	10.5	3.5	18.8	11.4	44.4	8
Laclede County	12 809	60.5	26.5	11.4	11.9	7.8	1.9	3.6	0.2	9.6	2.6	14.3	8.2	44.4	349
Lafayette County	12 584	59.6	25.4	11.3	12.8	8.4	1.7	3.6	0.3	9.8	2.9	14.2	9.3	47.9	163
Lawrence County	13 612	60.2	26.6	12.5	12.7	7.5	1.8	2.7	0.1	10.5	2.9	13.9	8.6	44.4	400
Lewis County	3 965	56.7	23.0	12.2	12.0	8.7	1.1	4.2	0.5	10.3	2.7	16.8	11.2	50.3	68
Lincoln County	13 882	62.4	30.9	9.1	13.9	9.8	1.5	4.0	0.2	9.6	2.2	10.1	6.0	42.9	285
Linn County	5 741	53.9	22.0	12.9	12.8	7.6	2.4	3.3	0.8	11.0	3.6	19.1	13.6	51.8	128
Livingston County	5 796	55.4	22.9	12.9	11.4	7.4	1.4	3.1	0.3	10.9	2.2	19.3	12.7	50.3	163
McDonald County	8 133	56.8	25.8	8.8	15.7	10.8	1.6	4.4	0.2	11.8	2.8	11.3	6.0	45.3	187
Macon County	6 494	54.7	21.6	12.9	12.4	7.5	1.9	3.7	0.4	11.7	3.6	17.6	11.5	49.7	109
Madison County	4 711	57.8	23.6	12.8	12.3	7.9	2.0	3.9	0.8	9.4	3.5	16.6	11.4	48.9	106
Maries County	3 536	61.1	25.4	12.6	10.8	6.8	1.6	2.4	0.1	12.5	3.9	13.2	7.7	44.7	76
Marion County	11 064	55.8	24.5	11.3	12.7	8.3	1.9	3.5	0.2	10.2	3.1	17.9	11.2	51.5	186
Mercer County	1 601	58.8	22.1	14.3	9.6	6.7	0.9	2.5	0.7	10.7	3.4	18.4	14.0	52.3	15
Miller County	9 288	55.7	24.7	10.6	13.7	8.6	2.2	4.3	0.7	11.7	3.7	14.6	9.4	49.3	147
Mississippi County	5 379	47.9	18.2	8.6	21.2	13.6	3.5	2.4	0.2	10.6	3.7	17.9	12.1	56.2	321
Moniteau County	5 264	59.3	27.2	10.8	11.6	8.5	1.1	3.4	0.1	10.2	2.8	15.5	10.4	52.3	70
Monroe County	3 640	58.9	24.5	14.1	11.3	6.5	2.4	3.3	0.4	12.1	2.6	14.5	10.0	42.7	64
Montgomery County	4 782	56.5	23.7	12.4	13.7	7.7	2.4	3.6	0.4	11.0	3.6	15.1	10.6	48.4	122
Morgan County	7 847	61.5	20.9	16.3	9.5	5.9	1.5	3.9	0.4	11.1	3.7	14.0	8.2	39.5	134
New Madrid County	7 831	52.5	21.9	9.4	18.0	12.0	2.4	2.9	0.2	10.8	3.2	15.7	10.2	52.5	313
Newton County	20 163	62.0	26.7	11.9	11.3	7.0	1.3	4.1	0.4	9.5	2.1	13.2	7.4	41.1	517
Nodaway County	8 164	50.7	22.6	10.0	9.3	5.6	1.4	10.2	0.3	13.1	3.3	16.7	9.2	51.8	46
Oregon County	4 269	58.6	22.9	13.3	12.2	7.2	2.0	2.9	0.2	10.9	4.1	15.4	10.0	47.6	71
Osage County	4 956	62.7	29.7	11.7	10.1	5.2	2.0	3.5	0.3	11.2	2.6	12.3	8.0	43.2	104
Ozark County	3 987	62.8	21.7	16.2	10.5	5.5	2.1	2.9	0.5	11.0	4.5	12.8	8.0	40.1	53
Pemiscot County	7 906	44.9	18.6	9.1	23.0	15.5	2.3	3.6	0.2	11.2	3.7	17.3	11.0	56.0	329
Perry County	6 929	60.6	27.3	12.0	10.9	6.8	1.3	4.0	0.4	11.6	2.9	12.9	9.6	47.7	115
Pettis County	15 616	54.0	24.6	10.8	14.6	8.9	2.2	4.7	0.4	11.1	3.1	15.6	9.1	47.7	320
Phelps County	15 677	53.8	23.1	10.6	11.9	7.8	1.5	5.8	0.4	12.9	2.2	15.7	8.6	46.6	299
Pike County	6 417	55.8	22.8	12.3	13.4	8.6	1.4	3.8	0.9	12.4	3.2	14.6	9.7	47.1	135
Platte County	29 317	57.3	26.6	6.5	12.4	8.1	1.0	5.5	0.2	11.4	1.7	13.4	4.9	46.7	323
Polk County	9 899	61.8	25.9	13.9	10.8	6.8	1.5	4.2	0.4	8.7	2.2	14.5	8.1	39.4	128
Pulaski County	13 456	62.2	33.5	7.5	12.3	8.9	1.4	3.6	0.3	10.2	1.4	11.6	5.4	42.5	214
Putnam County	2 240	59.2	21.8	14.4	9.0	6.5	1.4	3.5	0.5	11.7	2.9	16.7	12.5	48.6	34
Ralls County	3 725	66.6	28.6	12.1	8.2	5.0	1.1	4.0	0.4	10.1	3.4	11.1	6.8	42.9	40
Randolph County	9 217	53.9	22.8	10.4	14.2	8.8	1.8	3.8	0.4	11.5	3.7	16.6	10.2	52.4	178
Ray County	8 725	63.9	27.9	11.7	10.9	7.3	1.5	3.0	0.4	9.8	2.0	12.4	7.1	40.8	215
Reynolds County	2 735	60.3	21.8	13.5	10.7	6.1	2.2	3.1	0.5	12.5	2.8	13.3	8.8	41.9	76
Ripley County	5 438	59.1	23.9	12.9	12.3	7.0	1.8	2.6	0.1	11.4	4.8	14.5	8.8	47.9	169
St. Charles County	101 826	64.2	33.5	7.7	11.9	7.8	1.1	4.6	0.3	8.4	1.2	10.9	4.8	40.0	1 510
St. Clair County	4 031	57.5	17.7	16.6	11.7	7.9	1.8	3.6	0.5	11.2	3.7	16.0	11.4	44.5	114
Ste. Genevieve County	6 602	63.5	28.1	12.1	11.5	7.9	1.5	3.3	0.6	9.8	2.7	11.9	8.3	43.5	113
St. Francois County	20 788	54.0	23.7	12.1	15.3	9.4	1.7	3.8	0.5	9.7	2.2	15.1	8.7	43.3	421
St. Louis County	404 607	51.7	23.3	10.1	15.7	8.8	2.2	4.7	0.3	10.8	2.1	17.1	8.1	44.8	7 030
Saline County	8 984	52.1	21.6	10.2	14.5	9.2	2.1	5.1	0.5	11.5	3.8	16.8	11.2	53.8	241
Schuyler County	1 725	59.7	23.9	14.4	9.5	6.0	1.9	2.4	0.3	11.5	3.2	16.9	12.3	48.6	20
Scotland County	1 895	60.1	26.6	13.7	9.4	6.0	0.8	2.4	0.0	9.4	4.4	18.4	11.9	52.9	30
Scott County	15 689	55.4	24.0	10.3	17.0	11.2	2.0	2.7	0.2	8.5	1.5	16.4	9.8	47.3	372
Shannon County	3 329	59.1	24.8	12.8	12.6	8.0	1.3	2.8	0.4	9.4	2.6	16.0	9.2	44.9	96
Shelby County	2 754	58.7	24.7	14.5	9.1	6.6	1.3	2.5	0.1	11.7	3.2	18.0	12.5	49.8	27
Stoddard County	12 047	58.1	22.6	12.2	12.3	7.8	1.8	2.9	0.5	10.3	2.8	16.4	10.7	48.3	348
Stone County	11 824	64.8	20.0	17.5	10.1	5.6	1.6	3.7	0.5	8.8	2.4	12.6	7.6	33.9	218
Sullivan County	2 921	53.6	22.1	12.3	13.8	7.5	2.2	3.1	0.3	12.4	4.1	14.7	11.7	51.6	43
Taney County	16 175	57.3	20.9	13.9	11.3	7.3	1.6	5.7	0.3	9.8	2.3	15.8	7.8	39.2	258
Texas County	9 379	58.7	22.5	14.0	12.7	8.4	1.7	2.6	0.3	10.1	3.3	15.9	10.1	45.7	187
Vernon County	8 018	55.5	24.3	11.0	13.0	8.6	2.0	3.6	0.3	11.8	3.4	16.2	8.9	48.1	108
Warren County	9 210	62.8	27.3	11.1	12.1	8.0	1.3	4.3	0.4	9.2	2.3	11.6	7.1	42.2	156
Washington County	8 376	59.4	27.2	10.3	15.2	9.8	1.7	3.4	0.4	10.1	2.6	11.9	6.0	40.8	328
Wayne County	5 540	56.4	18.7	14.7	13.0	7.6	2.2	3.3	0.6	11.3	5.0	11.9	9.9	46.0	166
Webster County	11 080	65.4	31.3	9.7	11.0	7.4	1.4	3.1	0.2	8.9	2.5	11.5	6.9	45.5	180
Worth County	1 007	57.5	22.9	17.2	9.8	6.3	1.3	2.6	0.5	13.2	3.0	16.9	11.7	43.7	11
Wright County	7 094	58.7	24.6	13.1	12.8	9.1	1.2	2.6	0.1	10.0	2.9	16.0	10.3	47.8	141

Table A-3. States and Counties — **Age, Ethnicity, and Household Structure**

STATE County	Households with Non-Hispanic White householder		Households with Black or African American householder		Households with American Indian and Alaska Native householder		Households with Asian, Hawaiian, and Pacific Islander householder		Households with Hispanic or Latino[1] householder		Foreign-born population				Percent in non-English speaking households	
												Place of birth (percent)				
	Number of households	Percent that are family households	Number of households	Percent that are family households	Number of households	Percent that are family households	Number of households	Percent that are family households	Number of households	Percent that are family households	Percent of total population that is foreign-born	Europe	Asia	Latin America	Linguistically isolated	Not linguistically isolated
	44	45	46	47	48	49	50	51	52	53	54	55	56	57	58	59
MISSOURI—Cont'd																
Jasper County	38 497	67.7	545	60.4	550	67.6	172	60.5	1 042	75.6	2.6	0.3	0.5	1.7	1.3	6.8
Jefferson County	69 603	76.9	485	66.8	251	67.3	176	79.0	456	68.0	1.0	0.5	0.3	0.1	0.3	6.1
Johnson County	15 699	68.3	681	58.6	105	75.2	224	60.7	407	75.9	3.0	0.4	1.3	1.1	1.3	7.4
Knox County	1 769	68.1	0	X	2	100.0	6	100.0	5	40.0	0.3	0.2	0.0	0.0	0.0	4.6
Laclede County	12 438	72.6	18	50.0	50	78.0	21	38.1	120	70.8	0.9	0.4	0.1	0.3	0.4	5.1
Lafayette County	11 994	72.5	305	69.8	23	69.6	15	100.0	72	73.6	0.7	0.2	0.1	0.3	0.3	4.9
Lawrence County	13 088	72.4	6	100.0	86	80.2	8	100.0	288	94.1	2.3	0.3	0.1	1.5	1.3	5.6
Lewis County	3 835	68.7	92	63.0	6	83.3	0	X	9	100.0	0.6	0.2	0.2	0.1	0.1	7.6
Lincoln County	13 341	76.4	244	68.4	77	77.9	10	40.0	107	81.3	0.6	0.1	0.2	0.2	0.1	4.5
Linn County	5 632	66.5	32	81.3	21	61.9	5	100.0	24	75.0	0.6	0.3	0.2	0.1	0.2	5.9
Livingston County	5 674	66.8	48	66.7	20	90.0	0	X	19	57.9	0.4	0.2	0.1	0.2	0.1	5.8
McDonald County	7 191	71.9	7	57.1	187	72.7	18	100.0	497	81.3	5.6	0.4	0.2	4.9	4.2	7.9
Macon County	6 243	67.4	180	52.8	19	84.2	5	100.0	18	77.8	0.3	0.1	0.1	0.1	0.5	6.0
Madison County	4 589	69.8	8	100.0	8	50.0	27	100.0	11	72.7	0.8	0.2	0.4	0.1	0.2	4.6
Maries County	3 422	72.5	12	0.0	11	81.8	0	X	21	81.0	0.8	0.4	0.0	0.2	0.0	4.0
Marion County	10 345	68.7	480	61.5	20	70.0	0	X	94	64.9	0.8	0.3	0.1	0.4	0.3	4.7
Mercer County	1 586	68.3	0	X	2	100.0	3	100.0	5	20.0	0.4	0.2	0.1	0.0	0.0	4.4
Miller County	9 038	69.4	7	71.4	53	58.5	25	84.0	80	70.0	0.7	0.3	0.2	0.1	0.3	5.0
Mississippi County	4 328	68.9	968	70.6	24	75.0	15	60.0	11	18.2	0.5	0.2	0.3	0.0	0.0	1.5
Moniteau County	5 098	70.8	19	21.1	31	100.0	2	50.0	82	92.7	1.6	0.1	0.3	1.2	2.4	7.2
Monroe County	3 456	70.2	148	68.2	11	100.0	7	100.0	12	58.3	0.5	0.2	0.3	0.0	1.3	4.9
Montgomery County	4 635	69.9	72	83.3	2	0.0	29	75.9	27	66.7	1.2	0.4	0.8	0.1	0.5	5.0
Morgan County	7 583	71.3	43	46.5	43	86.0	20	80.0	71	54.9	1.0	0.7	0.1	0.0	1.8	8.8
New Madrid County	6 605	71.0	1 129	69.3	19	36.8	8	100.0	36	61.1	0.3	0.1	0.1	0.1	0.0	3.5
Newton County	18 925	73.4	109	46.8	369	79.9	97	82.5	303	66.0	1.4	0.3	0.3	0.6	0.6	6.2
Nodaway County	7 979	60.5	42	16.7	20	35.0	53	49.1	13	53.8	1.4	0.3	0.8	0.1	0.5	6.2
Oregon County	4 030	70.8	0	X	78	74.4	6	100.0	22	36.4	0.7	0.3	0.3	0.0	0.4	4.2
Osage County	4 886	73.1	4	50.0	21	61.9	12	25.0	10	0.0	0.5	0.2	0.1	0.1	0.3	6.2
Ozark County	3 854	73.9	0	X	25	76.0	5	60.0	34	85.3	1.0	0.6	0.1	0.2	0.1	4.2
Pemiscot County	5 832	67.7	1 953	68.5	13	38.5	16	62.5	85	81.2	0.9	0.3	0.3	0.3	0.5	4.2
Perry County	6 806	71.4	7	57.1	14	64.3	37	83.0	61	74.2	1.1	0.4	0.4	0.0	1.1	8.0
Pettis County	14 524	68.5	491	58.7	39	84.6	42	78.6	375	77.3	2.9	0.7	0.3	1.7	1.6	7.6
Phelps County	14 601	66.6	255	51.8	124	54.8	361	44.0	126	73.0	4.0	0.8	2.4	0.3	0.9	7.7
Pike County	6 013	69.8	295	59.7	14	42.9	19	63.2	44	43.2	1.6	0.2	0.3	1.0	1.2	6.4
Platte County	26 792	69.7	929	65.3	159	64.8	397	78.3	581	69.2	3.7	1.0	1.3	0.8	1.3	7.5
Polk County	9 667	72.9	15	100.0	50	54.0	33	60.6	75	56.0	1.5	0.7	0.3	0.2	0.5	6.8
Pulaski County	10 944	74.8	1 443	70.8	133	91.7	229	71.2	484	78.7	4.8	1.9	1.9	0.8	0.6	14.7
Putnam County	2 214	67.8	0	X	2	100.0	2	0.0	8	100.0	0.5	0.1	0.1	0.2	0.0	6.4
Ralls County	3 629	74.8	49	61.2	10	80.0	10	100.0	15	86.7	0.3	0.1	0.2	0.1	0.3	2.5
Randolph County	8 636	68.5	357	59.9	36	66.7	35	94.3	57	66.7	1.3	0.3	0.6	0.3	0.5	6.5
Ray County	8 397	74.4	119	80.7	45	86.7	13	100.0	71	100.0	0.4	0.1	0.0	0.2	0.1	5.2
Reynolds County	2 595	71.4	0	X	62	54.8	2	100.0	14	78.6	0.4	0.1	0.1	0.1	0.3	3.9
Ripley County	5 271	71.4	6	100.0	67	82.1	28	67.9	29	37.9	1.1	0.4	0.3	0.2	0.1	6.6
St. Charles County	96 592	76.1	2 271	76.9	332	74.7	712	73.3	1 172	77.6	2.1	0.8	0.7	0.4	0.4	7.6
St. Clair County	3 902	69.4	9	55.6	37	67.6	14	100.0	30	63.3	0.7	0.2	0.2	0.1	0.0	4.2
Ste. Genevieve County	6 500	74.8	36	77.8	10	100.0	0	X	34	100.0	0.6	0.4	0.0	0.2	0.0	5.0
St. Francois County	20 358	71.3	65	52.3	25	72.0	74	71.6	89	69.7	0.9	0.3	0.4	0.1	0.2	5.2
St. Louis County	318 469	66.2	70 325	71.9	757	82.3	7 684	72.2	4 211	68.6	4.2	1.4	1.9	0.5	1.1	9.4
Saline County	8 204	66.8	366	62.3	33	72.7	24	37.5	251	86.5	3.5	0.2	0.4	2.7	2.8	6.3
Schuyler County	1 689	69.4	0	X	5	40.0	2	100.0	8	50.0	0.4	0.2	0.0	0.0	0.1	3.2
Scotland County	1 875	69.4	0	X	0	X	3	0.0	14	100.0	0.3	0.2	0.2	0.0	0.4	14.7
Scott County	14 013	71.9	1 424	75.4	33	100.0	31	83.9	90	88.9	0.6	0.2	0.2	0.1	0.2	4.5
Shannon County	3 201	71.9	3	100.0	60	65.0	0	X	11	72.7	0.5	0.3	0.0	0.1	0.1	4.0
Shelby County	2 707	67.8	22	68.2	3	66.7	3	100.0	12	58.3	0.8	0.4	0.2	0.1	0.2	4.8
Stoddard County	11 739	70.6	98	55.1	20	90.0	25	100.0	25	68.0	0.5	0.1	0.2	0.1	0.1	5.4
Stone County	11 543	75.0	3	33.3	57	80.7	21	57.1	64	79.7	1.1	0.5	0.3	0.2	0.4	4.1
Sullivan County	2 737	66.8	3	100.0	14	71.4	7	28.6	169	81.1	5.8	0.1	0.1	5.6	5.1	5.1
Taney County	15 624	68.9	30	40.0	77	81.8	38	100.0	218	45.0	2.0	0.6	0.6	0.6	0.5	5.9
Texas County	9 025	71.5	24	58.3	81	71.6	7	100.0	56	67.9	0.8	0.4	0.2	0.1	0.2	5.0
Vernon County	7 790	68.3	10	100.0	79	64.6	29	72.4	49	73.5	1.3	0.5	0.3	0.1	0.2	6.1
Warren County	8 761	75.3	207	66.2	18	66.7	11	0.0	105	79.0	1.5	0.5	0.1	0.6	0.4	7.1
Washington County	8 173	74.8	41	7.3	26	92.3	32	62.5	56	76.8	0.7	0.1	0.3	0.2	0.2	4.9
Wayne County	5 412	69.8	0	X	48	22.9	4	100.0	10	100.0	0.3	0.1	0.1	0.1	0.0	4.3
Webster County	10 738	76.3	6	100.0	53	69.8	16	87.5	95	73.7	0.8	0.4	0.2	0.2	1.0	8.7
Worth County	998	67.4	0	X	7	42.9	0	X	0	X	0.2	0.1	0.1	0.0	0.0	4.4
Wright County	6 885	71.6	16	75.0	61	57.4	3	0.0	52	78.8	0.9	0.3	0.1	0.4	0.5	5.4

[1] Hispanic or Latino persons may be of any race.

STATE/ County code	MSA/PMSA/ NECMA code[1]	STATE County	Population by age (percent)										Non-Hispanic White		
														Age (percent)	
			Total population	Under 5 years	5 to 17 years	18 to 24 years	25 to 44 years	45 to 64 years	65 years and over	Median age	+/− U.S. percent under 18 years	+/− U.S. percent 65 years and over	Total population	Under 18 years	65 years and over
			1	2	3	4	5	6	7	8	9	10	11	12	13
		MISSOURI—Cont'd													
29 510	7040	St. Louis city	348 189	6.7	19.0	10.6	31.2	18.8	13.7	33.7	0.0	1.3	149 553	16.6	17.3
30 000	...	MONTANA	902 195	6.1	19.4	9.5	27.3	24.4	13.4	37.5	−0.2	1.0	807 588	23.9	14.4
30 001	...	Beaverhead County	9 202	5.9	18.6	12.2	25.0	24.9	13.4	37.6	−1.2	1.0	8 656	23.6	14.0
30 003	...	Big Horn County	12 671	9.4	26.5	8.5	26.7	20.7	8.2	29.8	10.2	−4.2	4 472	23.2	15.6
30 005	...	Blaine County	7 009	8.3	24.3	8.3	24.5	21.8	12.9	34.4	6.9	0.5	3 694	24.5	18.7
30 007	...	Broadwater County	4 385	5.2	20.1	4.9	25.9	27.5	16.4	41.3	−0.4	4.0	4 204	25.0	17.1
30 009	...	Carbon County	9 552	5.1	18.9	5.8	25.7	27.5	16.9	41.9	−1.7	4.5	9 265	23.4	17.2
30 011	...	Carter County	1 360	4.0	22.4	4.0	25.5	26.3	17.8	41.8	0.7	5.4	1 341	26.6	17.7
30 013	3040	Cascade County	80 357	6.7	19.3	8.9	28.4	22.7	14.1	36.7	0.3	1.7	71 918	24.7	15.1
30 015	...	Chouteau County	5 970	6.5	22.3	6.9	24.5	22.4	17.4	39.3	3.1	5.0	5 031	24.9	20.3
30 017	...	Custer County	11 696	5.9	19.0	8.2	25.7	24.1	17.1	39.3	−0.8	4.7	11 158	24.1	17.6
30 019	...	Daniels County	2 017	4.6	17.6	5.0	19.8	29.3	23.6	47.0	−3.5	11.2	1 941	20.9	24.4
30 021	...	Dawson County	9 059	5.4	17.9	8.7	25.0	25.4	17.6	41.0	−2.4	5.2	8 810	23.5	18.0
30 023	...	Deer Lodge County	9 417	4.1	18.1	7.9	23.9	27.1	18.8	42.3	−3.5	6.4	8 888	21.8	19.5
30 025	...	Fallon County	2 837	4.8	20.9	6.1	25.4	24.9	17.9	41.1	0.0	5.5	2 794	25.5	18.0
30 027	...	Fergus County	11 893	5.2	19.3	5.8	23.7	26.1	19.9	42.4	−1.2	7.5	11 467	23.9	20.3
30 029	...	Flathead County	74 471	6.0	19.9	7.5	27.3	26.4	12.9	39.0	0.2	0.5	70 997	25.3	13.3
30 031	...	Gallatin County	67 831	5.8	16.1	18.5	30.4	20.7	8.5	30.7	−3.8	−3.9	64 406	21.4	8.9
30 033	...	Garfield County	1 279	6.6	18.3	7.0	22.8	26.0	19.3	41.6	−0.8	6.9	1 270	24.6	19.4
30 035	...	Glacier County	13 247	8.1	27.1	9.1	26.9	19.4	9.5	30.6	9.5	−2.9	4 753	27.0	16.5
30 037	...	Golden Valley County	1 042	4.9	22.9	4.6	24.2	27.0	16.4	41.5	2.1	4.0	1 028	27.5	16.6
30 039	...	Granite County	2 830	4.9	19.6	5.3	24.1	30.4	15.7	42.8	−1.2	3.3	2 657	23.0	16.6
30 041	...	Hill County	16 673	7.3	20.8	11.7	25.8	21.6	12.8	34.5	2.4	0.4	13 175	24.4	14.8
30 043	...	Jefferson County	10 049	5.3	22.5	5.3	26.9	29.7	10.2	40.2	2.1	−2.2	9 566	26.8	10.6
30 045	...	Judith Basin County	2 329	5.2	21.8	4.5	22.9	28.4	17.2	42.0	1.3	4.8	2 280	26.8	17.5
30 047	...	Lake County	26 507	6.6	21.4	7.9	24.9	24.6	14.5	38.2	2.3	2.1	18 809	23.8	18.3
30 049	...	Lewis and Clark County..	55 716	6.3	19.3	8.6	28.1	26.0	11.7	38.0	−0.1	−0.7	52 503	24.8	12.2
30 051	...	Liberty County	2 158	5.1	20.9	5.9	24.3	24.3	19.5	41.5	0.3	7.1	2 140	25.7	19.7
30 053	...	Lincoln County	18 837	5.0	20.2	5.7	24.1	29.8	15.1	42.1	−0.5	2.7	17 953	24.9	15.4
30 055	...	McCone County	1 977	5.7	19.0	5.8	24.2	26.4	18.9	42.4	−1.0	6.5	1 893	23.0	19.8
30 057	...	Madison County	6 851	4.8	18.2	4.9	25.0	30.0	17.2	43.4	−2.7	4.8	6 556	21.9	17.8
30 059	...	Meagher County	1 932	5.3	19.9	5.7	22.7	28.1	18.3	42.8	−0.5	5.9	1 878	24.8	18.8
30 061	...	Mineral County	3 884	4.9	19.2	6.6	25.8	29.4	14.1	41.1	−1.6	1.7	3 662	23.3	14.7
30 063	5140	Missoula County	95 802	5.6	17.3	15.3	29.2	22.5	10.1	33.2	−2.8	−2.3	88 969	22.0	10.6
30 065	...	Musselshell County	4 497	5.1	18.5	5.6	23.7	29.5	17.5	43.2	−2.1	5.1	4 308	22.9	17.7
30 067	...	Park County	15 694	5.8	17.6	6.5	28.5	26.9	14.8	40.6	−2.3	2.4	15 039	22.9	15.1
30 069	...	Petroleum County	493	6.9	18.9	6.7	23.5	27.6	16.4	41.1	0.1	4.0	483	25.5	16.8
30 071	...	Phillips County	4 601	5.0	22.2	5.5	24.6	25.4	17.4	40.8	1.5	5.0	4 067	25.9	18.0
30 073	...	Pondera County	6 424	6.5	23.1	6.5	25.4	22.4	16.1	38.6	3.9	3.7	5 352	27.2	18.1
30 075	...	Powder River County	1 858	6.0	20.8	4.7	23.2	27.0	18.3	42.1	1.1	5.9	1 794	26.0	19.0
30 077	...	Powell County	7 180	4.6	16.6	7.7	31.0	25.6	14.3	39.7	−4.5	1.9	6 578	21.2	15.2
30 079	...	Prairie County	1 199	4.3	14.9	4.7	19.6	32.4	24.2	48.9	−6.5	11.8	1 178	19.4	24.4
30 081	...	Ravalli County	36 070	5.7	20.0	6.1	24.9	27.8	15.4	41.1	0.0	3.0	34 548	25.4	15.8
30 083	...	Richland County	9 667	6.2	21.1	6.5	26.6	23.9	15.7	39.2	1.6	3.3	9 200	26.9	16.0
30 085	...	Roosevelt County	10 620	8.1	26.5	7.9	25.1	20.8	11.6	32.3	8.9	−0.8	4 407	22.1	21.5
30 087	...	Rosebud County	9 383	8.2	25.4	7.4	25.5	24.8	8.7	34.5	7.9	−3.7	5 966	26.3	11.6
30 089	...	Sanders County	10 227	4.7	19.0	5.5	22.0	32.0	16.9	44.2	−2.0	4.5	9 304	23.0	17.5
30 091	...	Sheridan County	4 105	5.3	17.1	6.2	21.4	26.5	23.5	45.1	−3.3	11.1	3 879	21.2	24.7
30 093	...	Silver Bow County	34 606	5.6	18.1	9.6	26.9	24.0	15.9	38.9	−2.0	3.5	32 404	22.9	16.8
30 095	...	Stillwater County	8 195	5.4	19.8	6.1	26.6	27.7	14.5	40.8	−0.5	2.1	7 817	24.0	15.0
30 097	...	Sweet Grass County	3 609	6.0	19.8	5.3	24.9	26.5	17.6	41.2	0.1	5.2	3 488	25.1	18.0
30 099	...	Teton County	6 445	6.0	21.3	6.1	24.8	24.9	16.9	40.0	1.6	4.5	6 156	26.9	17.3
30 101	...	Toole County	5 267	5.1	20.5	6.6	28.7	23.4	15.7	39.1	−0.1	3.3	4 921	25.4	16.5
30 103	...	Treasure County	861	5.6	21.8	5.6	23.1	27.2	16.7	41.8	1.7	4.3	819	25.8	17.2
30 105	...	Valley County	7 675	5.1	20.1	5.1	24.8	25.9	19.0	41.7	−0.5	6.6	6 764	23.5	20.2
30 107	...	Wheatland County	2 259	5.8	20.8	6.6	22.0	25.6	19.1	41.4	0.9	6.7	2 181	26.8	19.6
30 109	...	Wibaux County	1 068	5.3	20.6	5.0	24.4	23.3	21.3	42.3	0.2	8.9	1 039	25.8	21.8
30 111	0880	Yellowstone County	129 352	6.5	19.1	9.3	28.8	23.0	13.3	36.9	−0.1	0.9	117 762	24.1	14.2
31 000	...	NEBRASKA.................	1 711 263	6.8	19.5	10.2	28.5	21.4	13.6	35.3	0.6	1.2	1 495 553	24.7	14.9
31 001	...	Adams County	31 151	6.6	17.7	12.1	26.2	21.5	15.9	36.5	−1.4	3.5	28 707	23.3	17.0
31 003	...	Antelope County	7 452	6.0	21.5	6.2	23.4	23.0	19.9	40.6	1.8	7.5	7 355	27.2	20.1
31 005	...	Arthur County	444	3.4	20.9	6.8	27.5	24.1	17.3	40.3	−1.4	4.9	432	24.1	17.8
31 007	...	Banner County	819	4.5	23.4	4.8	23.1	27.7	16.5	39.9	2.2	4.1	790	27.0	16.8

[1] MSA = Metropolitan Statistical Area. PMSA = Primary MSA. NECMA = New England County Metropolitan Area. See the Appendix A for explanation of these concepts. See Appendix B for list of metropolitan areas identified by type, with component counties.

STATE County	Black or African American			American Indian and Alaska Native			Asian, Hawaiian, and Pacific Islander			Hispanic or Latino[1]			Two or more races		
	Total population	Age (percent) Under 18 years	65 years and over	Total population	Age (percent) Under 18 years	65 years and over	Total population	Age (percent) Under 18 years	65 years and over	Total population	Age (percent) Under 18 years	65 years and over	Total population	Age (percent) Under 18 years	65 years and over
	14	15	16	17	18	19	20	21	22	23	24	25	26	27	28
MISSOURI—Cont'd															
St. Louis city	177 627	32.9	11.8	1 050	26.2	4.4	7 178	19.3	4.5	6 745	29.7	4.7	7 210	41.0	4.0
MONTANA	2 359	32.6	4.7	55 218	39.1	4.6	4 810	28.1	7.0	18 490	41.6	4.2	17 106	44.0	5.0
Beaverhead County	18	50.0	0.0	153	45.8	0.0	0	X	X	213	36.2	2.3	128	32.0	9.4
Big Horn County	3	100.0	0.0	7 569	42.9	3.8	75	34.7	22.7	518	49.4	4.4	296	44.9	6.1
Blaine County	7	57.1	0.0	3 145	41.6	6.3	14	14.3	57.1	112	67.0	1.8	128	41.4	4.7
Broadwater County	8	62.5	0.0	43	20.9	7.0	5	0.0	0.0	58	41.4	0.0	80	33.8	0.0
Carbon County	7	57.1	0.0	65	35.4	6.2	33	57.6	18.2	117	59.8	0.0	87	32.2	14.9
Carter County	4	50.0	0.0	3	0.0	0.0	4	0.0	0.0	0	X	X	8	0.0	62.5
Cascade County	882	27.7	5.6	3 061	33.8	5.7	559	14.0	8.8	1 984	39.4	4.8	2 315	48.3	3.4
Chouteau County	3	0.0	0.0	841	50.1	1.4	19	52.6	0.0	38	34.2	0.0	58	48.3	8.6
Custer County	6	100.0	0.0	222	39.2	4.5	32	15.6	0.0	150	36.7	12.7	155	52.9	0.0
Daniels County	0	X	X	24	62.5	0.0	5	40.0	0.0	39	53.8	5.1	30	63.3	0.0
Dawson County	46	15.2	0.0	87	8.0	0.0	5	0.0	0.0	69	44.9	4.3	54	14.8	16.7
Deer Lodge County	13	0.0	0.0	140	15.0	3.6	43	30.2	7.0	177	40.1	9.6	192	31.3	9.9
Fallon County	9	55.6	0.0	12	16.7	33.3	4	0.0	0.0	17	41.2	0.0	7	28.6	28.6
Fergus County	48	83.3	0.0	134	26.9	14.9	10	0.0	0.0	107	29.9	10.3	115	52.2	1.7
Flathead County	70	64.3	0.0	1 026	30.3	3.4	293	31.4	3.1	1 114	37.9	3.1	1 115	43.7	5.7
Gallatin County	127	15.7	10.2	621	23.7	1.0	748	31.6	2.0	1 213	37.5	2.0	926	36.0	0.4
Garfield County	3	100.0	0.0	0	X	X	0	X	X	6	50.0	0.0	3	100.0	0.0
Glacier County	9	44.4	0.0	7 859	39.4	5.4	40	32.5	12.5	128	60.9	5.5	571	45.9	5.4
Golden Valley County	0	X	X	5	0.0	0.0	0	X	X	9	77.8	0.0	0	X	X
Granite County	0	X	X	64	34.4	3.1	9	0.0	11.1	32	43.8	0.0	60	65.0	3.3
Hill County	8	0.0	0.0	2 810	40.9	4.7	62	9.7	16.1	155	47.7	0.0	525	50.3	7.2
Jefferson County	20	90.0	0.0	132	31.8	6.1	43	60.5	0.0	148	45.9	0.0	154	61.7	3.9
Judith Basin County	2	100.0	0.0	10	80.0	0.0	2	0.0	0.0	23	26.1	0.0	16	18.8	0.0
Lake County	22	45.5	0.0	6 124	37.7	4.6	158	38.0	2.5	643	46.7	4.5	946	42.8	9.8
Lewis and Clark County	107	19.6	12.1	1 160	31.5	5.8	195	9.7	8.2	848	51.5	2.2	1 147	47.6	1.6
Liberty County	1	100.0	0.0	0	X	X	8	75.0	0.0	2	0.0	0.0	5	60.0	0.0
Lincoln County	9	22.2	0.0	290	32.4	8.3	53	47.2	1.9	215	37.2	10.2	359	31.5	9.5
McCone County	11	63.6	0.0	27	59.3	0.0	2	0.0	0.0	24	66.7	0.0	30	73.3	0.0
Madison County	7	100.0	0.0	28	14.3	7.1	23	60.9	8.7	104	38.5	5.8	144	55.6	3.5
Meagher County	0	X	X	12	8.3	0.0	2	0.0	0.0	31	58.1	0.0	11	27.3	0.0
Mineral County	2	100.0	0.0	64	43.8	0.0	24	58.3	16.7	69	44.9	0.0	76	21.1	9.2
Missoula County	169	23.1	0.0	2 235	37.0	4.4	966	24.8	3.6	1 728	36.3	5.0	1 823	38.3	3.1
Musselshell County	0	X	X	64	32.8	10.9	8	0.0	0.0	76	53.9	0.0	55	38.2	30.9
Park County	53	39.6	3.8	103	19.4	11.7	55	40.0	29.1	308	34.1	8.8	141	35.5	0.0
Petroleum County	0	X	X	0	X	X	0	X	X	7	57.1	0.0	0	X	X
Phillips County	4	0.0	0.0	379	36.1	11.1	34	8.8	52.9	24	45.8	12.5	96	46.9	4.2
Pondera County	16	43.8	0.0	884	41.5	5.7	19	0.0	0.0	40	50.0	20.0	126	50.8	6.3
Powder River County	2	0.0	0.0	42	42.9	0.0	5	40.0	0.0	15	73.3	0.0	0	X	X
Powell County	24	8.3	0.0	282	14.5	9.2	31	19.4	22.6	136	33.1	0.0	149	25.5	0.0
Prairie County	0	X	X	11	18.2	18.2	2	0.0	0.0	4	0.0	0.0	4	0.0	0.0
Ravalli County	8	0.0	0.0	375	24.5	10.1	78	28.2	5.1	642	40.5	0.0	472	37.9	8.3
Richland County	6	16.7	0.0	126	40.5	1.6	0	X	X	208	33.7	13.0	133	37.6	11.3
Roosevelt County	8	100.0	0.0	5 837	43.4	4.1	79	36.7	11.4	78	47.4	6.4	251	45.4	9.6
Rosebud County	0	X	X	2 948	46.3	4.1	82	68.3	0.0	196	37.2	4.1	246	48.0	2.0
Sanders County	24	41.7	0.0	444	25.9	12.6	52	38.5	17.3	164	37.8	6.7	292	37.3	7.9
Sheridan County	2	0.0	0.0	75	29.3	0.0	21	28.6	14.3	72	65.3	0.0	87	55.2	3.4
Silver Bow County	67	46.3	0.0	619	25.5	1.8	88	12.5	20.5	1 117	43.1	3.8	410	34.6	2.4
Stillwater County	9	55.6	0.0	66	30.3	7.6	21	66.7	0.0	165	42.4	3.6	145	60.7	0.0
Sweet Grass County	3	100.0	0.0	5	0.0	60.0	17	41.2	11.8	54	50.0	0.0	45	51.1	4.4
Teton County	7	100.0	0.0	90	37.8	7.8	10	20.0	0.0	78	47.4	3.8	87	24.1	5.7
Toole County	8	0.0	0.0	174	21.8	5.7	5	0.0	0.0	34	20.6	0.0	125	41.6	3.2
Treasure County	2	100.0	0.0	12	75.0	25.0	3	0.0	0.0	23	65.2	0.0	9	66.7	0.0
Valley County	7	28.6	71.4	634	35.3	7.7	11	9.1	18.2	118	61.0	0.0	168	45.8	21.4
Wheatland County	2	100.0	0.0	13	0.0	15.4	0	X	X	15	20.0	20.0	51	29.4	0.0
Wibaux County	0	X	X	10	40.0	0.0	2	0.0	0.0	13	38.5	15.4	6	0.0	0.0
Yellowstone County	486	32.7	5.8	4 059	40.3	1.1	751	32.9	8.8	4 812	41.7	4.5	2 444	50.2	5.6
NEBRASKA	67 435	34.9	6.4	15 421	38.4	4.7	21 799	26.3	3.8	93 872	39.2	2.9	25 032	51.1	3.4
Adams County	183	20.8	3.3	98	9.2	9.2	652	32.7	4.1	1 292	40.4	0.0	281	44.1	12.1
Antelope County	5	60.0	0.0	29	31.0	6.9	7	57.1	0.0	37	59.5	0.0	19	73.7	26.3
Arthur County	0	X	X	2	0.0	0.0	0	X	X	7	57.1	0.0	0	X	X
Banner County	2	0.0	100.0	5	100.0	0.0	0	X	X	16	56.3	0.0	8	50.0	0.0

[1] Hispanic or Latino persons may be of any race.

STATE County	Total households	Married-couple family households Total	With children	Householder 65 years or over	Other family households Total	With children	Householder 65 years or over	Two or more unrelated persons Total	Householder 65 years or over	Male living alone Total	Householder 65 years or over	Female living alone Total	Householder 65 years or over	Percent of householders 65 years and over who live alone	Grandparents who are responsible for the care of their grandchildren
	29	30	31	32	33	34	35	36	37	38	39	40	41	42	43
MISSOURI—Cont'd															
St. Louis city	147 286	26.3	11.4	5.3	26.5	14.8	4.3	7.0	0.5	18.1	3.4	22.1	9.8	56.6	4 671
MONTANA	359 070	54.1	23.4	10.1	12.4	8.1	1.5	6.1	0.4	12.5	2.8	14.9	7.6	46.3	6 053
Beaverhead County	3 679	55.6	25.1	11.5	8.4	5.2	0.4	6.4	0.6	14.4	3.1	15.2	8.1	47.3	13
Big Horn County	3 910	55.3	29.6	8.3	22.8	12.6	2.7	2.5	0.4	9.4	1.6	10.0	5.1	36.8	588
Blaine County	2 531	52.5	25.6	10.5	19.1	11.2	2.7	2.5	0.4	12.4	3.3	13.4	8.3	45.8	198
Broadwater County	1 747	62.8	24.6	13.1	10.6	5.6	2.1	2.6	0.3	13.9	4.2	10.2	6.5	40.8	22
Carbon County	4 067	57.3	22.2	12.8	9.5	6.1	1.7	4.4	0.2	14.2	4.5	14.7	8.2	46.2	32
Carter County	547	62.9	26.0	11.7	8.4	4.6	1.6	2.0	0.4	11.3	3.8	15.4	11.5	52.8	0
Cascade County	32 633	52.9	23.6	9.8	13.5	9.3	1.7	4.9	0.5	13.2	3.2	15.6	8.2	48.7	322
Chouteau County	2 240	60.3	27.1	14.2	12.3	7.9	1.9	2.6	0.4	13.2	3.6	11.6	6.8	38.7	42
Custer County	4 778	50.9	21.0	12.2	14.4	9.1	2.6	4.8	0.6	11.8	2.5	18.1	9.2	43.2	104
Daniels County	897	55.5	19.6	15.6	6.9	5.2	0.2	4.0	1.2	15.1	6.0	18.5	12.2	51.6	10
Dawson County	3 619	56.7	23.1	13.3	12.1	7.7	1.2	3.0	0.3	11.7	2.9	16.5	9.3	45.3	52
Deer Lodge County	4 018	51.4	20.2	10.8	11.5	6.1	3.0	3.6	0.1	14.7	5.1	18.9	12.5	55.9	46
Fallon County	1 126	61.0	27.5	13.4	9.7	5.3	1.9	2.4	0.4	11.7	4.1	15.2	10.2	47.8	7
Fergus County	4 860	56.0	23.1	13.1	10.0	5.8	1.8	3.8	0.5	12.4	2.7	17.9	11.4	47.9	78
Flathead County	29 694	57.1	24.4	10.3	12.3	8.6	1.3	5.6	0.2	11.7	2.6	13.3	6.5	43.4	297
Gallatin County	26 357	52.2	23.8	7.0	9.8	6.3	0.6	13.9	0.3	12.3	1.3	11.8	4.7	43.1	148
Garfield County	533	63.0	25.3	16.9	6.8	4.5	1.3	2.6	0.8	13.1	2.1	14.4	12.2	42.9	0
Glacier County	4 313	53.2	30.0	8.2	22.8	13.4	3.5	2.4	0.4	9.6	2.0	12.0	4.9	36.6	377
Golden Valley County	360	64.4	18.1	19.2	6.1	4.7	0.8	3.6	0.6	8.6	2.8	17.2	10.6	39.3	0
Granite County	1 201	55.0	20.9	11.2	11.4	7.1	1.5	4.3	0.3	16.7	4.7	12.5	6.7	46.8	21
Hill County	6 457	52.8	24.6	9.9	13.1	9.6	1.1	5.4	0.1	12.5	2.2	16.2	9.2	50.8	201
Jefferson County	3 741	67.8	30.5	8.7	8.5	5.3	1.1	3.6	0.4	10.3	2.6	9.9	4.8	41.7	48
Judith Basin County	951	63.0	26.3	13.7	6.5	3.5	0.9	2.9	0.5	14.6	4.6	12.9	8.3	46.1	3
Lake County	10 233	54.7	22.2	12.4	16.4	10.8	2.0	4.3	0.3	11.1	3.0	13.5	5.4	36.5	274
Lewis and Clark County	22 855	52.9	24.0	8.5	12.4	8.3	1.2	5.6	0.2	13.0	2.2	16.1	6.8	47.7	134
Liberty County	829	63.6	26.8	14.1	6.9	4.3	1.1	1.6	0.0	12.3	4.3	15.7	10.5	49.4	12
Lincoln County	7 788	58.2	21.5	12.2	11.2	7.9	1.5	4.1	0.6	14.1	3.5	12.4	6.9	42.2	210
McCone County	809	66.7	27.1	16.4	6.9	3.2	2.2	2.1	0.6	11.9	4.0	12.4	8.7	39.5	2
Madison County	2 958	58.2	21.4	13.1	6.8	4.1	1.3	5.8	0.8	15.7	4.0	13.5	6.8	41.5	22
Meagher County	807	57.0	23.0	13.6	8.9	7.2	1.0	3.3	0.5	13.3	3.7	17.5	10.9	49.2	6
Mineral County	1 592	58.2	20.4	12.2	9.9	7.3	0.4	5.8	0.5	15.6	3.3	10.5	5.2	39.2	20
Missoula County	38 493	48.0	21.4	7.3	12.5	7.9	1.2	11.6	0.4	13.5	1.9	14.5	5.6	45.8	423
Musselshell County	1 865	55.7	21.1	12.7	9.4	6.3	1.6	4.5	0.9	13.1	3.5	17.2	10.1	47.5	30
Park County	6 820	52.2	22.0	10.3	9.7	6.6	1.1	5.8	0.4	13.7	2.3	18.7	9.3	49.5	105
Petroleum County	209	56.5	25.8	14.4	9.6	8.1	0.0	3.8	0.0	20.1	5.7	10.0	8.1	49.2	3
Phillips County	1 844	56.5	24.9	11.8	10.9	7.1	1.6	3.2	0.3	13.9	4.6	15.5	10.6	52.7	29
Pondera County	2 414	61.2	27.8	15.4	10.9	7.5	1.7	2.1	0.2	10.1	2.4	15.6	8.9	39.5	81
Powder River County	739	64.4	27.1	15.8	8.0	4.9	1.6	3.4	0.3	11.5	2.3	12.7	7.6	35.8	10
Powell County	2 433	55.7	19.9	12.7	11.5	7.9	2.4	4.2	0.3	10.7	2.6	17.9	10.6	46.2	36
Prairie County	537	61.1	19.9	16.2	4.8	3.5	1.1	3.0	0.0	16.6	5.6	14.5	11.2	49.2	4
Ravalli County	14 259	61.3	23.7	13.4	10.1	6.7	1.1	4.5	0.5	10.9	3.0	13.2	7.5	41.2	221
Richland County	3 894	57.8	26.2	10.9	10.1	6.9	1.3	3.1	0.5	12.5	3.1	16.4	9.8	50.6	76
Roosevelt County	3 608	46.3	22.4	9.0	27.2	18.7	1.9	3.1	0.3	10.8	3.2	12.7	7.6	49.0	369
Rosebud County	3 282	55.2	26.5	6.8	17.9	11.7	2.0	2.3	0.2	12.8	3.5	11.4	5.6	50.4	216
Sanders County	4 276	58.3	19.1	12.9	10.3	7.2	1.4	3.9	0.6	14.1	4.3	13.4	7.1	43.2	55
Sheridan County	1 748	57.8	24.0	15.6	7.7	3.0	3.1	2.2	0.3	11.4	3.5	20.8	13.7	47.6	28
Silver Bow County	14 465	49.0	20.6	9.1	13.0	8.1	2.1	5.3	0.4	13.8	3.8	18.9	10.8	55.6	272
Stillwater County	3 209	64.9	27.7	13.1	7.9	5.4	0.7	3.1	0.2	13.1	3.3	11.0	6.6	41.4	44
Sweet Grass County	1 477	60.1	26.9	12.3	7.4	3.8	1.4	4.4	0.5	12.3	3.9	15.8	10.4	50.0	22
Teton County	2 518	60.5	25.7	14.1	8.7	5.6	1.2	3.3	0.3	12.8	4.0	14.6	10.4	48.0	8
Toole County	1 971	57.9	26.6	11.6	9.2	5.8	1.3	3.2	0.4	12.6	4.2	17.1	9.5	51.0	26
Treasure County	363	54.5	27.3	12.7	8.5	5.5	1.1	3.0	0.6	14.0	4.7	14.9	9.9	50.5	2
Valley County	3 143	57.8	23.6	13.6	10.3	5.9	2.8	2.5	0.5	13.1	2.9	16.3	10.4	44.0	63
Wheatland County	835	50.8	16.2	15.6	10.5	5.3	1.4	2.4	0.2	14.3	5.0	22.0	14.3	52.8	8
Wibaux County	425	59.1	24.5	14.6	9.6	5.2	2.6	2.4	0.5	15.5	7.1	13.4	9.9	49.0	4
Yellowstone County	52 113	52.5	22.8	9.5	13.7	9.1	1.5	5.9	0.4	11.6	2.6	16.4	8.3	48.7	629
NEBRASKA	666 995	54.9	25.5	10.2	12.1	7.7	1.4	5.6	0.3	11.8	2.4	15.7	8.3	47.3	8 454
Adams County	12 186	55.2	23.9	11.3	11.1	6.8	1.7	5.2	0.3	11.5	2.9	17.0	11.0	50.9	151
Antelope County	2 966	62.5	26.7	15.7	8.5	5.3	1.6	1.6	0.0	11.4	4.4	16.0	12.6	49.5	13
Arthur County	185	59.5	19.5	9.2	15.7	8.1	5.9	1.1	0.0	13.5	7.6	10.3	6.5	48.1	4
Banner County	315	72.7	27.3	18.1	4.8	2.5	1.0	2.9	1.3	8.9	1.6	10.8	9.2	34.7	1

STATE County	Households with Non-Hispanic White householder		Households with Black or African American householder		Households with American Indian and Alaska Native householder		Households with Asian, Hawaiian, and Pacific Islander householder		Households with Hispanic or Latino[1] householder		Foreign-born population	Place of birth (percent)			Percent in non-English speaking households	
	Number of households	Percent that are family households	Number of households	Percent that are family households	Number of households	Percent that are family households	Number of households	Percent that are family households	Number of households	Percent that are family households	Percent of total population that is foreign-born	Europe	Asia	Latin America	Linguistically isolated	Not linguistically isolated
	44	45	46	47	48	49	50	51	52	53	54	55	56	57	58	59
MISSOURI—Cont'd																
St. Louis city	73 161	45.1	66 635	61.2	426	52.3	2 824	54.0	2 298	56.0	5.6	2.5	1.8	0.8	3.1	10.0
MONTANA	331 568	65.9	858	52.9	15 834	78.9	1 425	58.5	5 177	70.9	1.8	0.7	0.4	0.2	0.6	9.2
Beaverhead County	3 518	63.6	0	X	42	78.6	0	X	61	83.6	1.6	0.3	0.1	0.8	0.4	7.5
Big Horn County	1 904	67.7	0	X	1 820	88.0	21	52.4	142	94.4	0.8	0.1	0.3	0.2	5.0	47.2
Blaine County	1 572	66.5	1	100.0	905	80.4	2	0.0	19	78.9	1.4	0.3	0.1	0.0	1.6	14.4
Broadwater County	1 699	72.8	3	0.0	13	100.0	0	X	6	100.0	1.4	0.5	0.0	0.1	0.1	6.9
Carbon County	3 981	66.8	3	100.0	12	66.7	9	22.2	21	90.5	1.6	0.8	0.1	0.1	0.5	6.1
Carter County	541	72.1	0	X	3	0.0	0	X	0	X	1.0	0.7	0.3	0.0	0.2	6.1
Cascade County	30 029	66.0	373	59.0	967	68.6	181	55.2	584	82.9	2.4	1.1	0.5	0.2	0.6	9.2
Chouteau County	2 014	70.8	0	X	200	91.0	4	100.0	10	100.0	1.9	0.3	0.2	0.2	0.4	10.1
Custer County	4 645	65.3	0	X	43	62.8	13	46.2	41	73.2	1.4	0.5	0.2	0.1	0.4	9.0
Daniels County	885	62.1	0	X	2	100.0	1	100.0	9	77.8	4.7	0.4	0.4	0.3	0.5	5.8
Dawson County	3 553	68.8	7	100.0	18	61.1	0	X	20	70.0	1.1	0.6	0.1	0.0	0.5	6.8
Deer Lodge County	3 873	63.2	0	X	49	49.0	3	0.0	34	85.3	1.4	1.1	0.2	0.0	0.0	9.7
Fallon County	1 113	71.2	2	100.0	4	0.0	0	X	2	100.0	1.0	0.6	0.0	0.1	0.2	6.9
Fergus County	4 747	65.9	6	100.0	54	51.9	4	0.0	28	78.6	1.0	0.7	0.1	0.1	0.1	5.7
Flathead County	28 675	69.0	19	31.6	323	82.4	101	84.2	285	76.8	2.1	0.9	0.4	0.2	0.4	7.3
Gallatin County	25 388	62.1	43	44.2	217	76.0	185	56.2	331	65.6	2.7	1.0	0.9	0.2	0.6	8.6
Garfield County	533	69.8	0	X	0	X	0	X	0	X	1.1	0.5	0.0	0.2	0.2	4.3
Glacier County	1 819	69.2	5	0.0	2 305	82.0	22	45.5	15	53.3	2.1	0.2	0.2	0.0	3.5	17.2
Golden Valley County	354	70.9	0	X	5	40.0	0	X	1	100.0	2.6	0.6	0.1	0.0	0.0	6.2
Granite County	1 167	66.4	0	X	19	68.4	1	0.0	5	100.0	1.0	0.3	0.2	0.4	0.2	7.1
Hill County	5 582	63.7	2	0.0	715	84.6	35	48.6	30	73.3	2.0	0.4	0.3	0.0	1.3	12.2
Jefferson County	3 629	76.1	0	X	40	57.5	2	100.0	39	94.9	1.0	0.4	0.2	0.0	0.3	7.7
Judith Basin County	947	69.4	0	X	0	X	0	X	2	100.0	1.4	0.0	0.1	0.1	1.7	9.5
Lake County	7 687	69.7	4	25.0	2 029	76.8	42	88.1	176	77.8	1.6	0.6	0.3	0.1	0.5	10.6
Lewis and Clark County	21 827	65.3	75	44.0	390	68.5	78	52.6	200	66.5	1.6	0.7	0.3	0.2	0.2	8.3
Liberty County	827	70.4	0	X	0	X	0	X	2	100.0	1.4	0.2	0.2	0.1	6.0	15.7
Lincoln County	7 498	69.4	7	71.4	79	77.2	10	70.0	65	70.8	1.4	0.8	0.1	0.1	0.4	7.1
McCone County	785	73.4	3	100.0	9	77.8	2	0.0	6	100.0	0.7	0.6	0.0	0.1	0.1	4.3
Madison County	2 883	64.8	0	X	10	80.0	4	100.0	27	74.1	1.4	0.6	0.1	0.5	0.3	6.9
Meagher County	786	66.3	0	X	9	44.4	2	0.0	9	77.8	1.8	0.7	0.1	0.1	0.0	10.9
Mineral County	1 525	68.8	0	X	28	50.0	2	100.0	21	76.2	1.5	0.4	0.5	0.2	0.6	6.2
Missoula County	36 370	60.8	51	29.4	611	73.0	336	53.3	493	44.4	2.3	1.1	0.6	0.1	0.6	8.1
Musselshell County	1 815	65.2	0	X	23	65.2	3	100.0	12	75.0	2.0	0.9	0.4	0.2	0.3	11.2
Park County	6 610	62.0	27	59.3	40	85.0	17	11.8	90	61.1	2.7	1.4	0.2	0.2	0.2	6.8
Petroleum County	208	65.9	0	X	0	X	0	X	0	X	0.6	0.6	0.0	0.0	0.0	11.8
Phillips County	1 689	67.1	4	100.0	111	68.5	9	100.0	5	40.0	1.0	0.1	0.1	0.0	0.0	7.4
Pondera County	2 136	70.6	5	100.0	216	89.8	5	60.0	16	50.0	1.6	0.5	0.2	0.0	1.6	13.3
Powder River County	721	72.8	0	X	16	62.5	0	X	2	0.0	0.6	0.2	0.3	0.1	0.1	2.5
Powell County	2 338	66.6	0	X	25	72.0	17	88.2	14	100.0	0.6	0.3	0.2	0.0	0.2	5.1
Prairie County	529	66.2	0	X	2	100.0	0	X	4	0.0	1.2	0.8	0.3	0.0	0.4	5.3
Ravalli County	13 861	71.4	1	0.0	142	57.0	13	38.5	126	81.0	1.7	0.8	0.2	0.2	0.2	6.8
Richland County	3 751	68.1	3	100.0	26	38.5	0	X	70	72.9	1.4	0.5	0.0	0.2	0.3	6.1
Roosevelt County	1 823	68.5	0	X	1 638	80.3	40	82.5	26	26.9	0.9	0.2	0.2	0.1	0.3	12.9
Rosebud County	2 439	70.2	0	X	738	81.2	10	100.0	50	74.0	1.1	0.4	0.4	0.3	1.5	24.2
Sanders County	3 942	69.0	4	100.0	200	62.0	11	54.5	49	63.3	2.0	0.7	0.3	0.3	0.4	7.7
Sheridan County	1 679	66.1	2	0.0	26	69.2	9	22.2	20	65.0	1.9	0.3	0.1	0.1	0.4	7.8
Silver Bow County	13 755	61.7	16	0.0	227	64.8	42	35.7	326	77.3	1.6	0.7	0.2	0.3	0.5	7.5
Stillwater County	3 117	72.6	4	50.0	27	81.5	0	X	40	82.5	1.5	0.5	0.2	0.1	0.2	6.8
Sweet Grass County	1 444	67.7	0	X	5	40.0	2	0.0	11	81.8	1.7	0.6	0.3	0.4	0.4	5.6
Teton County	2 437	69.2	0	X	26	69.2	4	100.0	20	85.0	1.5	0.4	0.1	0.0	2.8	8.7
Toole County	1 904	67.8	0	X	17	58.8	4	0.0	9	100.0	3.6	0.8	0.1	0.1	2.1	10.1
Treasure County	352	67.6	0	X	0	X	0	X	8	75.0	0.8	0.5	0.0	0.0	0.0	6.0
Valley County	2 862	67.4	3	100.0	197	73.6	2	100.0	36	94.4	1.1	0.4	0.1	0.0	0.1	7.5
Wheatland County	815	61.3	0	X	9	22.2	0	X	2	100.0	2.9	0.4	0.0	0.0	0.1	3.6
Wibaux County	417	68.6	0	X	2	100.0	0	X	2	0.0	1.4	0.7	0.2	0.0	0.3	7.0
Yellowstone County	48 568	65.9	185	51.9	1 200	83.3	181	62.4	1 555	68.0	1.4	0.5	0.4	0.2	0.4	9.4
NEBRASKA	603 693	66.6	24 346	65.0	4 189	75.2	6 506	67.7	23 919	78.4	4.4	0.6	1.1	2.3	2.2	10.0
Adams County	11 590	65.7	38	34.2	19	89.5	131	89.3	330	77.6	4.4	0.3	1.8	2.2	3.0	8.2
Antelope County	2 944	70.9	2	0.0	8	75.0	0	X	9	100.0	0.4	0.1	0.1	0.1	0.3	6.6
Arthur County	183	74.9	0	X	0	X	0	X	0	X	0.7	0.2	0.0	0.0	0.0	6.3
Banner County	305	77.4	0	X	0	X	0	X	6	66.7	0.9	0.2	0.0	0.2	0.0	7.9

[1] Hispanic or Latino persons may be of any race.

STATE/ County code	MSA/PMSA/ NECMA code[1]	STATE County	Total population	Under 5 years	5 to 17 years	18 to 24 years	25 to 44 years	45 to 64 years	65 years and over	Median age	+/− U.S. percent under 18 years	+/− U.S. percent 65 years and over	Total population	Under 18 years	65 years and over
						Population by age (percent)							Non-Hispanic White	Age (percent)	
			1	2	3	4	5	6	7	8	9	10	11	12	13
		NEBRASKA—Cont'd													
31 009	...	Blaine County	583	5.8	21.1	3.3	26.9	26.4	16.5	39.8	1.2	4.1	581	27.0	16.5
31 011	...	Boone County	6 259	5.9	23.2	4.9	24.0	21.5	20.6	39.9	3.4	8.2	6 162	28.7	20.7
31 013	...	Box Butte County	12 158	6.5	21.7	7.1	27.2	23.0	14.4	38.2	2.5	2.0	10 690	25.9	15.9
31 015	...	Boyd County	2 438	4.9	19.9	5.5	21.2	24.2	24.2	43.8	-0.9	11.8	2 414	24.6	24.2
31 017	...	Brown County	3 525	5.3	19.2	5.2	23.0	24.8	22.5	43.1	-1.2	10.1	3 472	24.2	22.7
31 019	...	Buffalo County	42 259	6.6	18.2	18.0	26.8	18.8	11.6	30.0	-0.9	-0.8	39 497	24.0	12.2
31 021	...	Burt County	7 791	5.7	20.0	5.2	23.4	23.9	21.7	42.2	0.0	9.3	7 555	25.1	22.2
31 023	...	Butler County	8 767	7.0	20.9	6.6	25.2	22.6	17.7	38.8	2.2	5.3	8 607	27.6	18.0
31 025	5920	Cass County	24 334	7.0	20.9	6.8	29.1	23.9	12.3	36.9	2.2	-0.1	23 521	27.3	12.6
31 027	...	Cedar County	9 615	6.2	23.3	5.9	24.1	20.4	20.0	38.8	3.8	7.6	9 498	29.1	20.3
31 029	...	Chase County	4 068	5.6	19.8	6.0	23.5	24.1	21.0	42.1	-0.3	8.6	3 923	24.5	21.6
31 031	...	Cherry County	6 148	6.1	20.6	6.3	26.0	23.8	17.2	39.4	1.0	4.8	5 767	25.7	17.9
31 033	...	Cheyenne County	9 830	6.5	19.9	7.0	26.4	22.9	17.2	38.7	0.7	4.8	9 263	25.5	17.9
31 035	...	Clay County	7 039	5.7	21.7	6.0	24.8	23.6	18.2	39.9	1.7	5.8	6 719	26.5	19.0
31 037	...	Colfax County	10 441	6.7	22.2	8.2	28.3	18.5	16.0	35.0	3.2	3.6	7 594	25.4	21.7
31 039	...	Cuming County	10 203	6.4	20.6	6.7	25.3	20.6	20.3	39.2	1.3	7.9	9 580	26.2	21.5
31 041	...	Custer County	11 793	5.6	20.7	5.7	23.6	23.4	21.0	41.3	0.6	8.6	11 520	25.8	21.4
31 043	7720	Dakota County	20 253	8.4	22.2	9.7	29.9	20.0	9.9	31.4	4.9	-2.5	14 505	25.9	13.3
31 045	...	Dawes County	9 060	5.0	16.2	23.4	20.7	19.8	14.9	30.6	-4.5	2.5	8 387	19.9	15.6
31 047	...	Dawson County	24 365	8.4	20.9	8.4	27.2	20.7	14.3	34.3	3.6	1.9	17 760	25.4	18.8
31 049	...	Deuel County	2 098	4.3	19.0	4.5	25.2	24.1	23.0	43.5	-2.4	10.6	2 017	22.7	23.4
31 051	...	Dixon County	6 339	6.1	21.3	7.1	25.0	22.1	18.2	38.7	1.7	5.8	5 898	26.4	19.4
31 053	...	Dodge County	36 160	6.4	18.3	9.5	26.4	21.8	17.6	37.9	-1.0	5.2	34 140	23.8	18.4
31 055	5920	Douglas County	463 585	7.3	19.2	10.3	31.3	21.0	11.0	33.6	0.8	-1.4	362 461	23.8	12.5
31 057	...	Dundy County	2 292	5.4	17.8	5.7	23.6	25.2	22.3	43.5	-2.5	9.9	2 202	23.5	22.8
31 059	...	Fillmore County	6 634	5.8	20.5	5.0	24.2	23.1	21.4	41.4	0.6	9.0	6 466	25.6	21.9
31 061	...	Franklin County	3 574	5.5	19.0	4.6	23.8	23.3	23.7	42.8	-1.2	11.3	3 528	24.4	24.0
31 063	...	Frontier County	3 099	5.5	20.5	11.4	22.9	23.1	16.6	38.5	0.3	4.2	3 017	26.0	16.9
31 065	...	Furnas County	5 324	5.8	18.4	5.1	23.0	23.9	23.8	43.5	-1.5	11.4	5 216	24.0	24.1
31 067	...	Gage County	22 993	5.9	18.3	7.6	26.4	22.7	19.1	39.9	-1.5	6.7	22 370	23.6	19.6
31 069	...	Garden County	2 292	3.6	18.2	4.7	22.6	26.8	24.1	45.6	-3.9	11.7	2 206	21.2	24.7
31 071	...	Garfield County	1 902	4.7	18.6	4.4	20.8	26.6	24.9	45.9	-2.4	12.5	1 873	22.8	25.3
31 073	...	Gosper County	2 143	5.0	18.6	5.6	24.2	25.9	20.7	43.4	-2.1	8.3	2 097	23.2	20.7
31 075	...	Grant County	747	5.2	24.0	4.8	24.1	28.0	13.9	39.9	3.5	1.5	733	28.8	14.2
31 077	...	Greeley County	2 714	5.7	21.3	6.3	21.3	22.1	23.4	41.7	1.3	11.0	2 685	26.8	23.6
31 079	...	Hall County	53 534	7.6	19.5	8.7	28.5	21.6	14.1	35.6	1.4	1.7	44 825	24.7	16.3
31 081	...	Hamilton County	9 403	6.7	22.2	5.9	26.6	23.3	15.3	38.1	3.2	2.9	9 294	28.7	15.3
31 083	...	Harlan County	3 786	5.1	19.2	5.0	21.5	26.5	22.7	44.5	-1.4	10.3	3 719	24.1	22.9
31 085	...	Hayes County	1 068	3.9	22.6	5.4	21.7	26.0	20.3	42.5	0.8	7.9	1 033	26.1	21.0
31 087	...	Hitchcock County	3 111	4.2	19.9	5.9	22.7	25.3	22.1	43.6	-1.6	9.7	2 994	23.1	22.9
31 089	...	Holt County	11 551	5.8	21.2	5.9	24.6	22.7	19.8	40.5	1.3	7.4	11 418	26.8	20.0
31 091	...	Hooker County	783	4.5	19.4	4.3	21.7	23.4	26.7	45.3	-1.8	14.3	761	23.7	26.7
31 093	...	Howard County	6 567	5.9	22.2	6.0	26.1	22.5	17.2	38.1	2.4	4.8	6 446	27.9	17.4
31 095	...	Jefferson County	8 333	5.1	18.2	6.1	23.6	24.2	22.7	42.9	-2.4	10.3	8 153	23.0	22.9
31 097	...	Johnson County	4 488	5.1	19.0	5.8	24.3	23.7	22.1	42.4	-1.6	9.7	4 125	22.5	23.7
31 099	...	Kearney County	6 882	6.2	20.5	6.5	27.4	22.7	16.6	38.7	1.0	4.2	6 605	26.2	17.2
31 101	...	Keith County	8 875	5.8	19.5	5.9	24.9	25.4	18.4	41.1	-0.4	6.0	8 332	24.3	19.3
31 103	...	Keya Paha County	983	6.0	18.0	6.7	22.9	25.8	20.5	41.9	-1.7	8.1	959	23.9	21.1
31 105	...	Kimball County	4 089	5.4	19.3	5.7	23.1	25.4	21.2	42.8	-1.0	8.8	3 844	24.0	21.9
31 107	...	Knox County	9 374	5.6	20.0	5.4	22.1	23.7	23.1	43.0	-0.1	10.7	8 581	23.7	24.8
31 109	4360	Lancaster County	250 291	6.6	16.9	15.5	30.3	20.3	10.4	32.0	-2.2	-2.0	222 097	22.1	11.3
31 111	...	Lincoln County	34 632	6.6	19.5	8.3	26.7	23.7	15.3	37.8	0.4	2.9	32 237	25.4	15.7
31 113	...	Logan County	774	5.2	22.5	4.7	24.2	26.0	17.6	41.8	2.0	5.2	734	25.5	18.5
31 115	...	Loup County	712	6.6	20.6	4.4	21.9	27.1	19.4	42.9	1.5	7.0	698	26.2	19.8
31 117	...	McPherson County	533	6.8	20.6	5.1	28.9	20.3	18.4	40.6	1.7	6.0	521	26.9	18.8
31 119	...	Madison County	35 226	6.9	19.9	11.5	27.3	19.9	14.4	35.0	1.1	2.0	31 190	24.8	16.1
31 121	...	Merrick County	8 204	6.3	21.3	6.2	25.0	23.8	17.4	39.2	1.9	5.0	8 004	27.3	17.9
31 123	...	Morrill County	5 440	6.1	21.2	7.0	24.4	24.5	16.8	39.5	1.6	4.4	4 778	24.5	18.3
31 125	...	Nance County	4 038	6.1	21.5	6.8	23.9	22.2	19.6	40.1	1.9	7.2	3 953	27.4	19.7
31 127	...	Nemaha County	7 576	4.6	18.5	12.2	23.7	22.7	18.4	39.4	-2.6	6.0	7 425	23.3	18.4
31 129	...	Nuckolls County	5 057	5.2	18.5	5.8	22.0	24.1	24.5	44.1	-2.0	12.1	4 984	23.5	24.8
31 131	...	Otoe County	15 396	6.5	19.8	6.4	26.1	22.9	18.4	39.5	0.6	6.0	14 753	25.5	19.0
31 133	...	Pawnee County	3 087	4.6	17.9	5.3	20.6	24.5	27.1	45.9	-3.2	14.7	3 060	25.8	27.1
31 135	...	Perkins County	3 200	5.4	21.1	6.0	23.6	24.4	19.4	40.7	0.8	7.0	3 104	25.8	20.0
31 137	...	Phelps County	9 747	6.3	20.1	6.3	25.8	23.4	18.2	39.4	0.7	5.8	9 350	25.5	18.6
31 139	...	Pierce County	7 857	6.1	23.0	7.1	26.0	20.8	17.1	37.9	3.4	4.7	7 671	28.6	17.3

[1]MSA = Metropolitan Statistical Area. PMSA = Primary MSA. NECMA = New England County Metropolitan Area. See the Appendix A for explanation of these concepts. See Appendix B for list of metropolitan areas identified by type, with component counties.

Table A-3. States and Counties — Age, Ethnicity, and Household Structure

STATE County	Black or African American Total population	Under 18 years	65 years and over	American Indian and Alaska Native Total population	Under 18 years	65 years and over	Asian, Hawaiian, and Pacific Islander Total population	Under 18 years	65 years and over	Hispanic or Latino[1] Total population	Under 18 years	65 years and over	Two or more races Total population	Under 18 years	65 years and over
	14	15	16	17	18	19	20	21	22	23	24	25	26	27	28
NEBRASKA—Cont'd															
Blaine County	0	X	X	0	X	X	0	X	X	0	X	X	2	0.0	0.0
Boone County	0	X	X	7	28.6	0.0	8	50.0	50.0	59	59.3	5.1	29	62.1	6.9
Box Butte County	49	4.1	8.2	270	40.0	5.6	60	41.7	3.3	950	46.2	3.3	230	63.5	3.5
Boyd County	0	X	X	0	X	X	6	0.0	66.7	0	X	X	18	55.6	11.1
Brown County	0	X	X	11	81.8	0.0	1	0.0	0.0	28	35.7	7.1	12	33.3	16.7
Buffalo County	206	29.1	3.4	125	31.2	5.6	184	9.8	0.0	1 950	39.9	3.7	483	52.4	4.3
Burt County	4	0.0	0.0	82	51.2	2.4	5	40.0	0.0	107	42.1	10.3	40	40.0	7.5
Butler County	4	50.0	0.0	14	35.7	0.0	20	65.0	0.0	96	41.7	2.1	48	58.3	0.0
Cass County	46	32.6	0.0	112	37.5	1.8	76	34.2	5.3	460	47.2	2.4	151	45.7	2.6
Cedar County	4	100.0	0.0	14	35.7	0.0	8	75.0	0.0	48	56.3	0.0	47	78.7	0.0
Chase County	9	100.0	0.0	1	0.0	0.0	2	0.0	0.0	118	48.3	1.7	16	37.5	50.0
Cherry County	9	100.0	0.0	200	41.0	3.5	25	12.0	60.0	22	59.1	9.1	133	48.1	1.5
Cheyenne County	0	X	X	65	23.1	1.5	26	7.7	0.0	450	46.2	6.9	102	58.8	2.0
Clay County	12	75.0	8.3	37	40.5	0.0	28	25.0	10.7	243	49.8	0.4	20	45.0	0.0
Colfax County	0	X	X	20	20.0	0.0	32	34.4	0.0	2 773	38.3	0.9	281	55.2	1.1
Cuming County	9	33.3	0.0	59	54.2	0.0	13	84.6	0.0	524	38.0	1.3	40	50.0	20.0
Custer County	2	0.0	0.0	50	16.0	8.0	6	66.7	0.0	174	53.4	0.0	46	47.8	13.0
Dakota County	94	30.9	0.0	427	43.1	4.4	510	30.2	5.7	4 573	43.8	0.6	522	49.8	0.0
Dawes County	90	18.9	0.0	129	31.8	4.7	26	26.9	38.5	306	41.8	3.9	157	54.8	7.6
Dawson County	95	16.8	6.3	182	36.8	3.3	125	13.6	20.0	6 114	41.1	1.7	335	37.9	3.0
Deuel County	2	100.0	0.0	4	0.0	0.0	13	15.4	0.0	56	48.2	14.3	12	50.0	16.7
Dixon County	0	X	X	74	43.2	6.8	13	38.5	23.1	360	38.1	2.2	64	59.4	1.6
Dodge County	260	60.4	1.2	170	27.1	2.9	108	13.0	6.5	1 392	37.2	1.7	254	60.6	7.1
Douglas County	52 214	35.4	7.4	3 265	31.5	5.8	8 066	22.8	2.7	30 990	37.1	2.6	8 913	52.6	2.7
Dundy County	0	X	X	2	0.0	0.0	27	33.3	0.0	46	0.0	6.5	19	21.1	31.6
Fillmore County	2	0.0	0.0	33	39.4	0.0	10	20.0	0.0	76	50.0	6.6	46	54.3	0.0
Franklin County	0	X	X	12	0.0	0.0	1	0.0	100.0	23	73.9	0.0	16	37.5	0.0
Frontier County	3	0.0	0.0	16	25.0	0.0	12	41.7	0.0	35	25.7	5.7	25	32.0	8.0
Furnas County	3	100.0	0.0	7	0.0	42.9	9	44.4	0.0	33	36.4	6.1	58	24.1	6.9
Gage County	164	56.1	0.0	122	28.7	9.8	53	7.5	0.0	176	48.3	1.1	153	61.4	4.6
Garden County	0	X	X	6	0.0	0.0	17	41.2	17.6	41	31.7	7.3	12	50.0	16.7
Garfield County	0	X	X	3	100.0	0.0	2	0.0	0.0	20	65.0	0.0	9	44.4	0.0
Gosper County	0	X	X	0	X	X	4	50.0	0.0	38	47.4	18.4	4	0.0	50.0
Grant County	0	X	X	3	0.0	0.0	0	X	X	11	63.6	0.0	0	X	X
Greeley County	8	25.0	0.0	0	X	X	3	100.0	0.0	16	37.5	0.0	2	0.0	0.0
Hall County	263	44.1	4.6	233	22.3	6.0	617	34.5	0.6	7 466	40.6	2.4	629	39.7	4.3
Hamilton County	19	89.5	0.0	0	X	X	1	100.0	0.0	66	45.5	13.6	32	56.3	6.3
Harlan County	23	13.0	17.4	8	0.0	0.0	2	100.0	0.0	21	33.3	9.5	14	85.7	0.0
Hayes County	0	X	X	0	X	X	0	X	X	29	44.8	0.0	6	0.0	0.0
Hitchcock County	3	66.7	0.0	13	69.2	0.0	4	0.0	0.0	83	53.0	0.0	19	15.8	15.8
Holt County	2	0.0	0.0	34	50.0	20.6	11	36.4	0.0	72	47.2	0.0	19	26.3	10.5
Hooker County	0	X	X	4	0.0	100.0	0	X	X	7	28.6	28.6	11	45.5	0.0
Howard County	9	66.7	0.0	29	51.7	10.3	11	0.0	27.3	67	35.8	13.4	16	37.5	0.0
Jefferson County	3	0.0	0.0	38	28.9	0.0	8	75.0	0.0	74	27.0	25.7	57	50.9	14.0
Johnson County	2	100.0	0.0	22	50.0	0.0	114	39.5	5.3	158	46.2	1.9	71	40.8	2.8
Kearney County	25	48.0	0.0	9	0.0	55.6	23	0.0	0.0	201	44.8	0.0	43	46.5	7.0
Keith County	0	X	X	67	52.2	0.0	45	15.6	11.1	388	47.4	3.1	103	16.5	12.6
Keya Paha County	0	X	X	0	X	X	0	X	X	24	29.2	0.0	5	40.0	0.0
Kimball County	4	0.0	0.0	50	48.0	8.0	15	0.0	0.0	131	33.6	10.7	71	38.0	11.3
Knox County	4	50.0	0.0	596	44.8	5.2	44	59.1	0.0	73	68.5	0.0	86	36.0	9.3
Lancaster County	7 005	32.4	3.4	1 913	34.4	3.8	6 934	28.4	3.2	8 532	34.7	4.1	4 732	49.9	2.0
Lincoln County	243	35.0	6.2	159	34.0	2.5	83	20.5	25.3	1 749	37.7	9.9	437	49.4	6.6
Logan County	0	X	X	19	78.9	0.0	0	X	X	13	53.8	0.0	8	62.5	0.0
Loup County	0	X	X	0	X	X	3	100.0	0.0	11	72.7	0.0	0	X	X
McPherson County	0	X	X	10	60.0	0.0	0	X	X	3	0.0	0.0	2	0.0	0.0
Madison County	295	45.4	0.0	265	41.5	1.5	213	23.9	3.8	3 027	41.9	1.2	375	53.6	6.1
Merrick County	7	0.0	0.0	6	0.0	0.0	28	60.7	0.0	158	36.7	0.0	27	59.3	0.0
Morrill County	9	55.6	0.0	31	48.4	9.7	7	28.6	28.6	576	46.0	5.2	107	65.4	2.8
Nance County	0	X	X	6	0.0	33.3	8	25.0	25.0	49	34.7	14.3	37	54.1	16.2
Nemaha County	20	0.0	65.0	15	26.7	0.0	48	0.0	29.2	36	16.7	0.0	30	16.7	0.0
Nuckolls County	3	0.0	0.0	3	0.0	0.0	9	0.0	0.0	30	50.0	0.0	18	44.4	0.0
Otoe County	38	55.3	10.5	93	47.3	0.0	49	30.6	12.2	332	42.2	7.8	106	33.0	0.0
Pawnee County	0	X	X	13	23.1	15.4	3	0.0	100.0	6	16.7	50.0	9	33.3	22.2
Perkins County	3	66.7	0.0	0	X	X	6	50.0	0.0	72	51.4	0.0	15	40.0	0.0
Phelps County	17	100.0	0.0	63	36.5	12.7	24	75.0	0.0	242	40.9	7.9	67	59.7	7.5
Pierce County	8	50.0	0.0	30	23.3	20.0	22	40.9	13.6	70	52.9	0.0	68	63.2	2.9

[1] Hispanic or Latino persons may be of any race.

STATE County	Total households	Family households (percent)						Nonfamily households (percent)						Percent of householders 65 years and over who live alone	Grandparents who are responsible for the care of their grandchildren
		Married-couple family households			Other family households			Two or more unrelated persons		Male living alone		Female living alone			
		Total	With children	Householder 65 years or over	Total	With children	Householder 65 years or over	Total	Householder 65 years or over	Total	Householder 65 years or over	Total	Householder 65 years or over		
	29	30	31	32	33	34	35	36	37	38	39	40	41	42	43
NEBRASKA—Cont'd															
Blaine County	242	65.3	28.5	12.4	5.4	1.2	1.7	3.3	0.8	11.2	2.9	14.9	11.6	49.3	0
Boone County	2 468	61.8	29.2	15.6	7.8	4.6	1.7	1.6	0.6	12.4	4.2	16.3	12.3	47.8	4
Box Butte County	4 778	57.8	27.4	10.5	11.9	9.3	0.9	2.9	0.6	13.1	2.8	14.3	8.7	48.7	66
Boyd County	1 019	60.2	25.1	17.8	5.4	4.4	0.5	2.3	0.2	14.2	4.4	18.0	14.3	50.4	7
Brown County	1 541	55.9	20.6	15.8	9.3	5.8	1.6	3.2	0.4	13.9	3.7	17.7	12.3	47.4	10
Buffalo County	15 955	53.4	26.1	8.9	11.1	7.4	0.7	9.4	0.2	10.4	2.2	15.6	7.8	50.4	63
Burt County	3 175	62.1	23.7	17.4	9.2	6.3	1.4	2.4	0.4	10.7	3.4	15.7	11.9	44.3	25
Butler County	3 430	61.5	28.4	15.0	7.7	4.1	1.5	2.6	0.3	13.2	3.6	15.0	11.3	46.9	32
Cass County	9 175	63.1	28.0	10.1	11.5	7.8	1.4	3.7	0.3	9.7	2.4	11.9	6.6	43.2	197
Cedar County	3 640	64.3	31.4	16.8	6.8	4.0	1.4	2.3	0.0	11.9	3.1	14.8	11.8	45.0	26
Chase County	1 663	62.6	25.7	16.3	7.6	5.2	1.1	2.7	0.2	11.7	4.0	15.5	10.8	45.6	11
Cherry County	2 518	57.6	23.9	12.4	10.8	7.5	1.4	2.7	0.3	13.3	3.6	15.6	10.1	49.3	39
Cheyenne County	4 076	54.9	24.7	12.5	11.1	7.2	0.9	3.9	0.0	12.8	3.3	17.3	10.7	51.1	35
Clay County	2 775	64.5	28.5	14.3	8.0	5.1	1.2	1.9	0.1	11.6	3.6	13.9	10.0	46.5	52
Colfax County	3 674	61.8	31.9	13.2	9.4	5.9	1.8	3.1	0.1	10.6	2.5	15.1	11.0	47.3	45
Cuming County	3 960	62.0	28.1	15.6	7.9	5.2	1.4	3.1	0.0	13.0	4.6	14.0	10.1	46.3	16
Custer County	4 846	61.9	25.3	16.7	7.5	4.8	1.0	1.9	0.2	11.4	3.4	17.3	12.1	46.4	112
Dakota County	7 083	55.7	29.4	7.7	16.8	11.6	1.8	4.6	0.3	10.5	2.4	12.4	6.7	48.2	102
Dawes County	3 520	51.9	20.5	11.8	8.1	5.2	1.2	9.1	0.7	11.5	2.2	19.3	10.4	47.8	36
Dawson County	8 821	59.7	28.4	12.2	11.3	7.4	1.1	4.1	0.2	10.6	2.6	14.4	9.7	47.6	156
Deuel County	916	56.7	20.4	17.4	9.4	6.1	1.9	2.6	0.3	15.8	4.6	15.5	10.5	43.5	2
Dixon County	2 414	61.7	27.2	15.2	9.5	5.8	1.5	2.9	0.2	11.1	2.8	14.7	10.9	44.8	26
Dodge County	14 425	55.9	23.6	12.8	11.8	7.7	1.6	4.7	0.5	11.1	2.8	16.5	10.3	46.7	146
Douglas County	182 553	48.1	23.3	7.4	15.5	9.3	1.9	6.7	0.3	12.9	1.8	16.8	6.9	47.8	2 866
Dundy County	950	62.8	23.8	16.8	3.9	2.6	0.6	2.2	0.3	14.2	3.5	16.8	12.3	47.0	2
Fillmore County	2 679	58.9	26.4	14.6	8.5	5.2	1.9	2.3	0.1	12.4	3.6	17.9	12.6	49.4	23
Franklin County	1 485	59.7	23.1	17.4	9.2	5.7	1.5	2.1	0.0	12.1	3.8	17.0	11.9	45.2	8
Frontier County	1 188	63.6	27.4	14.2	6.1	4.9	0.5	3.8	0.6	12.8	2.5	13.6	8.2	41.3	25
Furnas County	2 285	57.3	23.1	15.2	8.9	6.0	1.9	1.8	0.3	12.8	4.9	19.3	14.0	52.0	23
Gage County	9 322	57.6	24.0	14.2	9.2	6.4	0.8	4.0	0.1	10.6	2.6	18.7	12.4	49.7	78
Garden County	1 020	55.6	19.4	15.9	9.8	5.2	1.8	2.6	0.4	12.2	4.1	19.8	13.1	48.9	10
Garfield County	818	61.0	22.0	16.4	4.5	3.3	0.5	2.0	0.5	10.3	4.4	22.2	17.4	55.6	7
Gosper County	875	68.7	25.0	17.5	7.5	4.3	2.3	0.9	0.0	11.7	3.8	11.2	7.5	36.4	10
Grant County	298	69.1	29.9	17.4	8.4	6.0	0.0	0.7	0.0	13.1	2.7	8.7	4.0	27.8	4
Greeley County	1 071	58.1	25.2	16.1	10.0	5.2	3.9	1.1	0.2	14.8	6.8	16.0	12.1	48.4	9
Hall County	20 348	56.5	26.3	10.8	13.2	9.3	1.4	4.8	0.3	11.1	1.9	14.5	8.3	45.1	340
Hamilton County	3 509	68.1	30.8	13.9	9.2	6.8	1.3	2.0	0.2	8.7	2.2	12.0	7.7	39.1	60
Harlan County	1 582	60.2	22.1	19.1	5.4	3.7	0.9	3.3	0.3	16.0	4.8	15.1	10.2	42.4	28
Hayes County	436	67.0	28.2	18.6	5.5	0.0	0.9	0.9	0.0	12.2	3.2	14.4	12.2	44.1	4
Hitchcock County	1 292	60.3	22.1	15.9	10.6	6.0	1.5	2.4	0.3	10.4	3.6	16.3	12.1	46.9	10
Holt County	4 598	60.6	27.6	15.4	7.9	4.1	1.4	2.4	0.4	11.9	3.5	17.1	11.4	46.5	40
Hooker County	337	63.5	27.0	17.2	2.7	1.5	0.6	0.6	0.0	10.4	2.1	22.8	16.9	51.6	6
Howard County	2 569	62.8	28.2	14.3	8.6	6.0	1.1	2.7	0.1	10.5	3.4	15.3	11.6	49.2	25
Jefferson County	3 528	57.2	21.2	15.0	10.3	6.0	1.8	2.8	0.9	12.2	4.3	17.4	13.0	49.4	39
Johnson County	1 881	58.8	24.0	15.6	8.3	5.4	1.2	2.9	0.4	11.0	3.6	19.0	14.7	51.5	21
Kearney County	2 635	63.4	28.0	13.5	9.5	7.7	0.9	3.0	0.1	12.3	2.5	11.8	9.1	44.2	32
Keith County	3 699	58.4	23.4	13.9	9.8	6.8	0.8	3.7	0.7	13.3	4.5	14.8	8.9	46.5	44
Keya Paha County	413	64.4	21.8	17.7	7.0	4.1	1.5	1.9	0.5	12.8	4.8	13.8	10.4	43.8	3
Kimball County	1 723	56.6	22.3	15.7	9.2	4.6	1.9	4.0	1.0	14.0	3.5	16.1	12.0	45.4	22
Knox County	3 800	60.6	25.0	16.9	7.5	4.6	1.6	1.9	0.4	12.4	5.1	17.5	12.3	47.9	54
Lancaster County	99 254	49.7	23.3	7.8	12.1	7.5	1.2	9.2	0.2	12.8	1.7	16.2	6.5	46.8	946
Lincoln County	14 091	56.7	25.0	11.0	10.2	6.8	0.8	4.8	0.3	11.9	3.2	16.4	9.9	50.6	155
Logan County	315	64.1	24.8	14.0	9.2	5.7	1.6	1.9	0.3	12.1	3.5	12.7	11.1	47.9	11
Loup County	282	63.5	26.6	11.7	6.4	2.1	1.1	2.1	0.0	12.8	8.5	15.2	9.6	58.6	10
McPherson County	213	72.8	37.1	16.9	8.0	4.2	3.8	0.0	0.0	6.6	5.6	12.7	9.9	42.9	0
Madison County	13 422	55.7	26.0	10.6	11.2	7.8	0.9	5.4	0.3	10.5	2.4	17.2	10.1	51.7	164
Merrick County	3 198	61.5	27.1	13.4	10.8	7.1	1.5	2.6	0.2	11.2	3.8	13.9	9.6	46.9	47
Morrill County	2 149	61.0	27.9	13.7	9.1	5.6	1.3	3.4	0.1	12.6	3.2	14.1	9.6	45.8	37
Nance County	1 595	61.8	27.2	16.2	8.8	5.6	1.2	2.1	0.3	12.6	4.0	14.7	10.2	44.5	11
Nemaha County	3 038	56.2	24.5	12.8	9.1	5.7	1.3	4.3	0.4	12.4	3.6	18.0	13.5	54.0	8
Nuckolls County	2 221	59.3	22.4	18.4	5.6	3.6	1.0	2.7	0.2	12.8	4.6	19.6	14.1	48.9	22
Otoe County	6 062	61.0	26.9	13.2	9.0	6.2	1.2	3.7	0.4	10.2	3.2	16.2	11.0	49.1	73
Pawnee County	1 344	55.7	20.1	18.8	8.6	4.9	1.9	3.1	0.3	13.7	5.3	18.9	14.4	48.4	4
Perkins County	1 277	64.0	28.7	14.3	6.7	5.2	0.2	2.0	0.2	12.1	4.5	15.3	11.5	52.2	15
Phelps County	3 840	62.3	28.1	13.3	7.7	5.7	0.5	3.2	0.3	13.1	2.7	13.6	8.9	45.1	29
Pierce County	2 982	63.1	30.6	13.7	8.6	5.2	1.7	2.6	0.1	10.5	3.3	15.1	9.5	45.2	31

Table A-3. States and Counties — Age, Ethnicity, and Household Structure

STATE County	Households with Non-Hispanic White householder		Households with Black or African American householder		Households with American Indian and Alaska Native householder		Households with Asian, Hawaiian, and Pacific Islander householder		Households with Hispanic or Latino[1] householder		Foreign-born population	Place of birth (percent)			Percent in non-English speaking households	
	Number of households	Percent that are family households	Number of households	Percent that are family households	Number of households	Percent that are family households	Number of households	Percent that are family households	Number of households	Percent that are family households	Percent of total population that is foreign-born	Europe	Asia	Latin America	Linguistically isolated	Not linguistically isolated
	44	45	46	47	48	49	50	51	52	53	54	55	56	57	58	59
NEBRASKA—Cont'd																
Blaine County	242	70.7	0	X	0	X	0	X	0	X	0.3	0.3	0.0	0.0	0.0	12.4
Boone County	2 450	69.6	0	X	1	100.0	2	100.0	9	66.7	0.9	0.4	0.2	0.3	0.3	6.6
Box Butte County	4 393	68.5	34	55.9	96	78.1	10	100.0	211	88.2	3.1	0.4	0.3	2.3	1.4	10.1
Boyd County	1 013	65.5	0	X	0	X	2	0.0	0	X	0.4	0.2	0.2	0.0	0.8	5.8
Brown County	1 519	65.4	0	X	0	X	0	X	16	43.8	0.7	0.3	0.1	0.1	0.1	5.8
Buffalo County	15 180	64.7	45	44.4	40	80.0	75	33.3	552	68.5	2.6	0.3	0.5	1.7	1.0	8.9
Burt County	3 107	71.0	2	0.0	21	81.0	0	X	27	92.6	1.1	0.4	0.1	0.5	0.3	4.7
Butler County	3 395	69.1	0	X	0	X	2	100.0	24	91.7	0.9	0.2	0.1	0.5	0.4	11.9
Cass County	8 985	74.5	16	87.5	30	66.7	22	100.0	93	81.7	1.2	0.6	0.2	0.3	0.2	7.0
Cedar County	3 621	70.9	0	X	6	100.0	0	X	8	87.5	0.4	0.2	0.0	0.1	0.0	6.2
Chase County	1 630	69.8	0	X	1	100.0	0	X	31	90.3	1.4	0.2	0.0	0.9	0.3	4.9
Cherry County	2 390	68.6	0	X	68	73.5	12	50.0	2	0.0	0.7	0.1	0.2	0.0	0.4	5.7
Cheyenne County	3 907	65.9	0	X	34	82.4	15	60.0	121	69.4	0.9	0.3	0.2	0.4	0.2	7.2
Clay County	2 701	72.0	1	100.0	10	80.0	4	100.0	62	90.3	2.6	0.3	0.2	1.9	2.0	9.6
Colfax County	3 038	68.8	0	X	14	100.0	8	50.0	611	82.5	18.2	0.1	0.0	17.9	14.7	18.2
Cuming County	3 789	69.2	0	X	24	100.0	0	X	137	89.1	3.8	0.2	0.2	3.3	2.3	9.4
Custer County	4 778	69.4	0	X	26	65.4	0	X	29	93.1	0.4	0.1	0.0	0.2	0.3	5.9
Dakota County	5 732	68.9	39	79.5	94	97.9	125	76.0	1 046	91.0	15.6	0.5	2.3	12.8	10.4	19.3
Dawes County	3 389	59.5	4	100.0	37	86.5	15	33.3	32	50.0	2.2	0.2	0.1	1.2	0.2	8.3
Dawson County	7 272	68.7	22	27.3	57	89.5	32	53.1	1 387	84.1	15.9	0.3	0.4	15.1	10.0	18.2
Deuel County	889	66.4	0	X	2	100.0	4	50.0	15	73.3	0.9	0.1	0.4	0.2	0.2	5.7
Dixon County	2 325	71.1	0	X	9	100.0	3	100.0	78	73.1	3.4	0.4	0.1	2.9	2.2	9.0
Dodge County	13 914	67.1	43	93.0	57	78.9	25	92.0	364	81.3	2.8	0.2	0.2	2.2	1.9	7.8
Douglas County	150 128	62.8	19 325	64.9	887	68.2	2 774	60.6	7 854	76.7	5.9	0.8	1.5	3.1	2.7	11.2
Dundy County	923	67.3	0	X	2	100.0	7	71.4	10	20.0	1.9	0.3	1.4	0.3	1.0	3.4
Fillmore County	2 644	67.5	0	X	7	100.0	6	66.7	16	37.5	0.8	0.0	0.1	0.5	0.8	7.2
Franklin County	1 474	68.8	0	X	3	0.0	1	100.0	3	100.0	0.6	0.2	0.1	0.2	0.2	5.4
Frontier County	1 160	69.8	1	100.0	7	57.1	0	X	10	40.0	1.0	0.3	0.3	0.4	0.1	8.2
Furnas County	2 254	66.2	0	X	5	20.0	3	100.0	13	84.6	0.3	0.3	0.0	0.0	0.0	6.3
Gage County	9 187	66.7	26	100.0	36	66.7	39	59.0	21	100.0	0.7	0.3	0.2	0.1	0.2	7.0
Garden County	996	65.1	0	X	0	X	6	83.3	11	81.8	0.9	0.3	0.5	0.2	0.5	5.4
Garfield County	815	65.5	0	X	0	X	0	X	2	100.0	0.7	0.3	0.1	0.3	0.1	3.7
Gosper County	862	76.2	0	X	0	X	2	100.0	11	72.7	0.5	0.1	0.3	0.1	0.1	4.7
Grant County	298	77.5	0	X	0	X	0	X	0	X	1.1	0.7	0.0	0.0	0.0	2.5
Greeley County	1 064	67.9	2	100.0	0	X	0	X	3	100.0	0.7	0.1	0.0	0.2	0.4	5.0
Hall County	18 102	67.8	63	81.0	56	67.9	157	85.4	1 843	84.0	8.3	0.3	0.8	7.2	5.2	12.8
Hamilton County	3 492	77.4	2	100.0	0	X	0	X	9	22.2	0.4	0.2	0.0	0.1	0.0	6.6
Harlan County	1 564	65.5	11	100.0	3	0.0	0	X	4	75.0	0.3	0.1	0.1	0.0	0.1	4.0
Hayes County	430	72.6	0	X	0	X	0	X	4	100.0	2.0	0.0	0.0	2.0	1.0	9.5
Hitchcock County	1 268	70.8	0	X	3	100.0	0	X	16	87.5	1.2	0.5	0.1	0.5	0.3	5.9
Holt County	4 564	68.5	0	X	9	22.2	1	0.0	16	100.0	0.8	0.5	0.1	0.1	0.1	6.6
Hooker County	326	65.6	0	X	2	100.0	0	X	3	100.0	0.0	0.0	0.0	0.0	0.0	0.6
Howard County	2 533	71.3	0	X	7	100.0	4	100.0	21	81.0	0.8	0.2	0.1	0.4	0.5	5.9
Jefferson County	3 466	68.2	0	X	10	100.0	0	X	36	19.4	0.4	0.3	0.0	0.1	0.0	5.6
Johnson County	1 790	65.8	0	X	6	100.0	31	90.3	38	97.4	4.3	0.3	2.0	2.0	2.9	7.0
Kearney County	2 579	72.4	0	X	5	100.0	0	X	48	93.8	1.6	0.3	0.2	1.0	1.0	7.4
Keith County	3 525	67.8	0	X	22	72.7	21	76.2	99	86.9	1.7	0.4	0.3	0.8	1.2	7.5
Keya Paha County	410	71.2	0	X	0	X	0	X	3	100.0	2.2	0.1	0.0	1.7	2.2	5.5
Kimball County	1 649	65.7	0	X	15	100.0	9	0.0	38	84.2	0.7	0.1	0.6	0.0	0.1	6.0
Knox County	3 562	68.0	0	X	186	71.0	10	80.0	8	75.0	1.0	0.4	0.4	0.1	0.3	5.7
Lancaster County	90 976	61.6	2 336	59.5	507	63.7	2 005	74.1	2 437	66.2	5.4	1.2	2.7	1.2	2.6	10.3
Lincoln County	13 322	66.8	66	65.2	44	93.2	27	100.0	557	70.9	1.2	0.3	0.2	0.3	0.4	7.4
Logan County	308	72.7	0	X	0	X	0	X	4	100.0	0.3	0.3	0.0	0.0	0.3	11.2
Loup County	280	70.4	0	X	0	X	0	X	2	0.0	1.0	0.0	0.4	0.6	0.0	6.5
McPherson County	211	80.6	0	X	2	100.0	0	X	0	X	0.0	0.0	0.0	0.0	0.0	3.6
Madison County	12 423	65.5	80	57.5	80	63.8	48	87.5	723	88.0	5.5	0.2	0.5	4.7	3.5	10.5
Merrick County	3 144	72.3	6	33.3	0	X	5	100.0	40	80.0	1.0	0.1	0.0	0.8	0.8	6.1
Morrill County	1 989	68.8	2	100.0	6	100.0	0	X	148	85.8	3.8	0.3	0.2	3.1	1.2	14.1
Nance County	1 571	70.1	0	X	4	100.0	4	100.0	12	100.0	0.8	0.5	0.1	0.1	0.6	8.5
Nemaha County	2 988	65.3	7	100.0	4	100.0	24	62.5	11	36.4	0.8	0.1	0.5	0.1	0.4	5.2
Nuckolls County	2 196	65.0	3	0.0	3	0.0	3	100.0	10	70.0	0.6	0.0	0.3	0.1	0.1	4.3
Otoe County	5 884	70.0	13	69.2	26	76.9	11	54.5	94	68.1	1.4	0.2	0.2	0.8	0.5	6.9
Pawnee County	1 335	64.5	0	X	5	80.0	0	X	0	X	0.4	0.2	0.1	0.1	0.2	6.1
Perkins County	1 253	70.6	1	0.0	0	X	1	100.0	20	80.0	1.4	0.5	0.2	0.3	0.0	9.4
Phelps County	3 762	69.5	0	X	19	100.0	6	100.0	48	100.0	0.8	0.1	0.2	0.6	0.6	5.9
Pierce County	2 943	71.7	0	X	4	100.0	4	50.0	18	88.9	0.8	0.3	0.2	0.2	0.0	6.9

[1] Hispanic or Latino persons may be of any race.

Table A-3. States and Counties — Age, Ethnicity, and Household Structure

STATE/ County code	MSA/PMSA/ NECMA code[1]	STATE County	Population by age (percent)										Non-Hispanic White	Age (percent)	
			Total population	Under 5 years	5 to 17 years	18 to 24 years	25 to 44 years	45 to 64 years	65 years and over	Median age	+/− U.S. percent under 18 years	+/− U.S. percent 65 years and over	Total population	Under 18 years	65 years and over
			1	2	3	4	5	6	7	8	9	10	11	12	13
		NEBRASKA—Cont'd													
31 141	...	Platte County	31 662	7.1	21.9	7.9	27.5	21.8	13.8	35.8	3.3	1.4	29 211	28.0	14.9
31 143	...	Polk County	5 639	5.6	19.5	6.0	24.4	23.2	21.3	41.6	-0.6	8.9	5 572	25.0	21.5
31 145	...	Red Willow County	11 448	6.2	18.7	9.7	23.8	22.6	19.0	39.9	-0.8	6.6	11 061	24.3	19.5
31 147	...	Richardson County	9 531	5.0	20.4	5.9	23.6	23.6	21.5	41.4	-0.3	9.1	9 111	25.0	22.2
31 149	...	Rock County	1 756	5.8	16.9	6.6	24.3	24.4	22.1	43.5	-3.0	9.7	1 710	22.3	22.5
31 151	...	Saline County	13 843	5.7	19.0	12.5	25.4	20.1	17.2	36.4	-1.0	4.8	12 569	24.2	18.7
31 153	5920	Sarpy County	122 595	8.2	22.3	9.3	33.8	19.8	6.6	31.5	4.8	-5.8	107 006	29.4	7.1
31 155	...	Saunders County	19 830	6.3	21.6	6.3	27.6	23.0	15.2	38.0	2.2	2.8	19 359	27.5	15.5
31 157	...	Scotts Bluff County	36 951	6.7	19.3	8.3	25.6	22.9	17.4	38.4	0.3	5.0	29 484	22.6	20.1
31 159	...	Seward County	16 496	5.7	19.2	14.4	24.2	21.3	15.2	35.7	-0.8	2.8	16 079	24.5	15.5
31 161	...	Sheridan County	6 198	5.9	19.5	6.3	23.2	23.4	21.6	42.0	-0.3	9.2	5 457	23.0	23.7
31 163	...	Sherman County	3 318	5.2	19.3	4.6	23.8	24.3	22.9	43.3	-1.2	10.5	3 249	23.9	23.2
31 165	...	Sioux County	1 475	5.4	19.2	7.1	24.9	27.2	16.3	41.5	-1.1	3.9	1 425	24.3	16.1
31 167	...	Stanton County	6 455	7.5	22.3	7.3	27.4	22.1	13.5	35.9	4.1	1.1	6 239	29.1	13.9
31 169	...	Thayer County	6 055	5.4	18.5	5.0	22.1	24.3	24.6	44.1	-1.8	12.2	5 955	23.4	24.9
31 171	...	Thomas County	729	5.8	18.1	3.7	24.3	27.6	20.6	44.2	-1.8	8.2	708	24.3	21.2
31 173	...	Thurston County	7 171	9.7	27.3	7.9	23.9	18.0	13.2	29.8	11.3	0.8	3 281	24.7	23.1
31 175	...	Valley County	4 647	5.5	19.2	4.6	22.8	23.8	24.1	43.5	-1.0	11.7	4 551	23.8	24.6
31 177	5920	Washington County	18 780	6.4	20.8	9.2	26.6	23.9	13.1	37.1	1.5	0.7	18 266	26.9	13.3
31 179	...	Wayne County	9 851	5.3	16.4	26.4	20.2	18.1	13.6	27.9	-4.0	1.2	9 495	21.5	14.1
31 181	...	Webster County	4 061	5.1	18.5	4.8	23.0	24.4	24.3	44.2	-2.1	11.9	3 961	23.3	24.7
31 183	...	Wheeler County	886	6.7	22.2	6.0	22.5	25.7	16.9	40.4	3.2	4.5	870	28.3	17.0
31 185	...	York County	14 598	5.8	19.5	9.1	25.4	22.9	17.4	38.8	-0.4	5.0	14 078	24.9	17.9
32 000	...	NEVADA	1 998 257	7.2	18.3	8.9	31.7	22.9	10.9	35.0	-0.2	-1.5	1 301 738	21.2	14.3
32 001	...	Churchill County	23 982	7.4	21.5	7.8	28.7	22.7	11.8	34.7	3.2	-0.6	19 161	26.6	13.7
32 003	4120	Clark County	1 375 765	7.5	18.0	9.1	32.6	22.2	10.7	34.4	-0.2	-1.7	827 342	20.3	14.5
32 005	...	Douglas County	41 259	5.1	18.9	5.1	27.1	28.6	15.2	41.7	-1.7	2.8	36 327	22.3	16.4
32 007	...	Elko County	45 291	8.4	23.9	8.5	32.1	20.9	6.2	31.2	6.6	-6.2	32 873	29.7	6.9
32 009	...	Esmeralda County	971	3.2	17.0	6.6	21.9	34.1	17.2	45.1	-5.5	4.8	790	17.2	18.7
32 011	...	Eureka County	1 651	5.7	22.2	5.2	28.5	25.9	12.5	38.3	2.2	0.1	1 408	26.3	13.5
32 013	...	Humboldt County	16 106	8.1	23.4	7.5	31.6	22.2	7.4	33.4	5.8	-5.0	11 941	28.6	8.6
32 015	...	Lander County	5 794	7.4	24.6	6.1	29.6	25.3	6.9	34.1	6.3	-5.5	4 349	29.6	7.5
32 017	...	Lincoln County	4 165	6.4	23.7	6.1	22.8	25.1	15.9	38.8	4.4	3.5	3 753	29.0	17.3
32 019	...	Lyon County	34 501	6.4	20.5	6.7	27.3	25.3	13.8	38.2	1.2	1.4	28 760	24.6	15.6
32 021	...	Mineral County	5 071	5.2	19.0	6.3	23.3	25.8	20.4	42.9	-1.5	8.0	3 569	19.9	22.9
32 023	4120	Nye County	32 485	5.8	17.6	5.1	24.6	28.7	18.3	42.9	-2.3	5.9	27 662	21.7	20.2
32 027	...	Pershing County	6 693	6.4	19.0	7.4	37.5	22.0	7.8	34.4	-0.3	-4.6	4 664	23.0	10.0
32 029	...	Storey County	3 399	4.4	14.9	6.1	24.6	36.8	13.4	44.5	-6.4	1.0	3 054	18.8	13.9
32 031	6720	Washoe County	339 486	6.8	18.0	9.9	31.2	23.7	10.5	35.6	-0.9	-1.9	247 668	21.3	12.9
32 033	...	White Pine County	9 181	6.0	18.1	8.6	29.6	24.3	13.5	37.7	-1.6	1.1	7 293	24.1	15.2
32 510	...	Carson City	52 457	6.2	17.1	8.2	28.7	25.0	14.9	38.7	-2.4	2.5	41 124	20.8	18.0
33 000	...	NEW HAMPSHIRE	1 235 786	6.1	18.9	8.3	30.9	23.8	12.0	37.1	-0.7	-0.4	1 175 083	24.6	12.4
33 001	...	Belknap County	56 325	5.3	18.4	6.6	28.2	26.4	15.1	40.1	-2.0	2.7	54 445	23.4	15.4
33 003	...	Carroll County	43 666	4.8	17.8	5.2	26.6	27.7	17.8	42.5	-3.1	5.4	42 765	22.4	18.1
33 005	...	Cheshire County	73 825	5.2	18.0	11.8	26.9	24.5	13.7	37.6	-2.5	1.3	71 919	23.1	13.9
33 007	...	Coos County	33 111	5.1	17.8	6.2	26.9	25.6	18.5	41.5	-2.8	6.1	32 411	22.6	18.6
33 009	...	Grafton County	81 743	5.2	16.7	13.5	26.8	24.3	13.5	37.0	-3.8	1.1	77 611	21.6	13.9
33 011	1123	Hillsborough County	380 841	6.8	19.5	7.6	32.8	22.7	10.6	35.9	0.6	-1.8	351 507	25.5	11.2
33 013	...	Merrimack County	136 225	5.9	19.0	8.1	30.5	24.1	12.4	37.7	-0.8	0.0	131 395	24.7	12.7
33 015	1123	Rockingham County	277 359	6.5	19.8	6.2	32.9	24.5	10.1	37.2	0.6	-2.3	266 243	26.1	10.4
33 017	1123	Strafford County	112 233	5.9	17.7	13.8	30.5	20.9	11.2	34.4	-2.1	-1.2	107 253	23.2	11.6
33 019	...	Sullivan County	40 458	5.6	18.2	6.5	28.0	25.9	15.8	40.0	-1.9	3.4	39 554	23.8	16.0
34 000	...	NEW JERSEY	8 414 350	6.6	18.1	8.0	31.4	22.7	13.2	36.7	-1.0	0.8	5 554 478	22.3	16.7
34 001	0560	Atlantic County	252 552	6.4	18.9	7.9	30.9	22.4	13.5	37.0	-0.4	1.1	160 988	21.4	17.5
34 003	0875	Bergen County	884 118	6.2	16.7	6.6	30.9	24.4	15.2	39.1	-2.8	2.8	637 644	21.2	18.8
34 005	6160	Burlington County	423 394	6.3	18.8	7.4	31.6	23.2	12.6	37.1	-0.6	0.2	323 273	23.8	14.2
34 007	6160	Camden County	508 932	6.7	20.0	8.1	30.6	22.1	12.5	35.8	1.0	0.1	345 222	23.3	15.4
34 009	0560	Cape May County	102 326	5.1	17.2	6.5	25.3	25.7	20.3	42.3	-3.4	7.9	92 346	20.9	21.4
34 011	8760	Cumberland County	146 438	6.0	19.3	8.4	31.5	21.8	12.9	35.6	-0.4	0.5	85 635	21.0	18.1
34 013	5640	Essex County	793 633	7.2	18.8	9.3	31.3	21.5	11.9	34.7	0.3	-0.5	298 726	20.4	19.0
34 015	6160	Gloucester County	254 673	6.5	19.9	9.0	30.4	22.7	11.6	36.1	0.7	-0.8	218 249	25.3	12.2
34 017	3640	Hudson County	608 975	6.2	16.3	10.4	35.8	19.9	11.5	33.6	-3.2	-0.9	214 797	14.8	19.5
34 019	5015	Hunterdon County	121 989	6.7	19.0	5.8	31.5	27.0	10.0	38.8	0.0	-2.4	112 770	25.8	10.5

[1] MSA = Metropolitan Statistical Area. PMSA = Primary MSA. NECMA = New England County Metropolitan Area. See the Appendix A for explanation of these concepts. See Appendix B for list of metropolitan areas identified by type, with component counties.

Table A-3. States and Counties — Age, Ethnicity, and Household Structure

STATE County	Black or African American Total population (14)	Under 18 years (15)	65 years and over (16)	American Indian and Alaska Native Total population (17)	Under 18 years (18)	65 years and over (19)	Asian, Hawaiian, and Pacific Islander Total population (20)	Under 18 years (21)	65 years and over (22)	Hispanic or Latino[1] Total population (23)	Under 18 years (24)	65 years and over (25)	Two or more races Total population (26)	Under 18 years (27)	65 years and over (28)
NEBRASKA—Cont'd															
Platte County	105	48.6	0.0	60	28.3	0.0	136	49.3	6.6	2 010	40.6	0.1	356	40.4	5.3
Polk County	2	0.0	0.0	5	20.0	0.0	0	X	X	40	45.0	5.0	20	25.0	10.0
Red Willow County	24	45.8	0.0	13	0.0	0.0	2	0.0	0.0	259	41.3	5.0	91	53.8	3.3
Richardson County	17	52.9	17.6	135	16.3	11.9	85	35.3	0.0	42	40.5	2.4	150	50.7	4.7
Rock County	0	X	X	26	46.2	0.0	5	0.0	0.0	11	36.4	27.3	8	0.0	0.0
Saline County	49	12.2	0.0	120	33.3	0.0	158	33.5	1.3	879	28.2	3.3	89	33.7	3.4
Sarpy County	5 310	31.9	2.2	587	37.1	4.3	2 249	24.2	4.6	5 227	41.4	2.4	2 789	56.7	1.8
Saunders County	13	38.5	0.0	49	24.5	0.0	116	56.9	3.4	185	34.6	1.6	128	46.9	6.3
Scotts Bluff County	122	53.3	0.0	616	48.7	0.8	171	25.1	24.6	6 364	38.9	6.6	807	47.6	5.7
Seward County	54	22.2	0.0	38	28.9	21.1	83	25.3	0.0	182	53.3	0.0	84	48.8	8.3
Sheridan County	5	40.0	0.0	530	43.6	3.8	20	50.0	10.0	103	50.5	4.9	113	38.9	16.8
Sherman County	2	0.0	0.0	13	100.0	0.0	16	43.8	6.3	31	74.2	0.0	23	39.1	17.4
Sioux County	0	X	X	4	0.0	0.0	7	0.0	57.1	27	40.7	18.5	12	41.7	16.7
Stanton County	4	100.0	0.0	44	9.1	9.1	20	0.0	0.0	105	54.3	0.0	62	95.2	0.0
Thayer County	1	100.0	0.0	22	54.5	0.0	0	X	X	57	56.1	7.0	22	54.5	27.3
Thomas County	0	X	X	6	0.0	0.0	0	X	X	15	13.3	0.0	0	X	X
Thurston County	40	47.5	20.0	3 601	47.4	4.8	33	39.4	3.0	154	56.5	1.3	146	52.7	3.4
Valley County	0	X	X	15	73.3	0.0	5	60.0	0.0	52	61.5	0.0	24	83.3	0.0
Washington County	64	10.9	18.8	43	11.6	0.0	77	9.1	6.5	248	42.7	5.2	97	66.0	0.0
Wayne County	40	0.0	0.0	69	26.1	0.0	30	6.7	10.0	173	30.1	0.0	44	45.5	9.1
Webster County	2	0.0	0.0	5	0.0	100.0	34	20.6	11.8	20	35.0	0.0	39	56.4	0.0
Wheeler County	2	100.0	0.0	5	100.0	0.0	0	X	X	7	42.9	0.0	2	0.0	100.0
York County	93	20.4	0.0	30	46.7	0.0	62	41.9	0.0	258	43.8	4.7	99	34.3	0.0
NEVADA	132 490	30.8	6.9	26 485	29.6	6.2	96 927	21.2	7.9	393 539	37.0	3.0	81 171	42.2	4.4
Churchill County	241	19.9	4.6	1 154	33.4	6.3	861	29.4	2.8	2 053	40.5	3.5	766	58.7	4.7
Clark County	122 836	31.4	7.0	11 045	25.4	5.2	77 413	20.7	7.9	301 830	36.5	3.0	59 997	42.3	4.2
Douglas County	145	39.3	6.2	621	28.0	7.4	503	17.9	10.1	3 031	37.9	6.6	945	51.1	3.4
Elko County	294	46.9	4.8	2 397	32.2	7.5	358	30.7	12.0	8 917	42.1	2.4	1 279	39.7	5.8
Esmeralda County	0	X	X	41	22.0	9.8	1	0.0	0.0	87	41.4	2.3	58	31.0	22.4
Eureka County	4	0.0	100.0	21	14.3	19.0	27	25.9	0.0	130	43.8	3.1	55	30.9	9.1
Humboldt County	106	16.0	2.8	729	38.0	8.0	64	0.0	15.6	3 065	41.7	1.9	548	44.0	8.4
Lander County	0	X	X	281	35.2	6.8	17	0.0	0.0	1 086	42.9	3.8	173	37.6	13.9
Lincoln County	77	16.9	0.0	31	54.8	0.0	32	50.0	0.0	207	46.4	3.9	82	52.4	3.7
Lyon County	121	39.7	5.8	763	31.6	7.2	240	4.2	12.1	3 814	42.3	3.1	1 377	44.7	4.0
Mineral County	218	16.1	35.3	746	35.7	12.2	16	12.5	0.0	429	39.4	11.9	171	53.2	4.7
Nye County	309	21.7	6.8	732	28.3	12.4	314	21.7	11.8	2 686	37.5	5.4	1 042	30.8	7.4
Pershing County	333	3.0	0.0	220	29.5	14.1	47	0.0	0.0	1 296	39.3	1.1	198	38.4	6.6
Storey County	0	X	X	64	7.8	14.1	49	0.0	24.5	166	27.7	0.0	79	26.6	11.4
Washoe County	6 581	26.7	6.2	6 212	34.3	5.0	15 829	23.6	7.7	56 304	37.9	2.6	12 827	40.8	3.9
White Pine County	419	6.2	0.0	312	30.8	5.4	72	0.0	30.6	979	28.1	5.8	146	36.3	26.7
Carson City	806	5.3	0.0	1 116	26.0	5.8	1 084	26.3	8.6	7 459	36.7	2.5	1 428	45.9	4.4
NEW HAMPSHIRE	8 984	31.3	4.7	2 660	23.9	4.7	15 679	26.6	4.7	19 910	36.4	3.4	14 574	38.4	5.6
Belknap County	138	30.4	6.5	232	29.3	8.2	354	31.1	7.1	366	30.6	8.2	805	38.1	5.1
Carroll County	34	14.7	14.7	149	24.2	8.1	138	39.1	7.2	212	43.4	6.1	379	35.6	8.7
Cheshire County	190	11.6	1.1	135	25.2	11.1	486	25.3	1.9	464	25.9	6.9	597	28.0	13.1
Coos County	28	35.7	25.0	67	13.4	4.5	89	41.6	2.2	172	43.6	6.4	369	36.0	20.3
Grafton County	470	19.6	7.2	306	19.9	4.9	1 263	19.5	2.3	954	33.4	5.2	1 197	33.2	6.6
Hillsborough County	4 875	34.1	3.7	783	27.3	3.4	7 445	25.7	5.2	11 744	38.3	2.9	5 207	43.6	4.6
Merrimack County	904	36.6	2.9	228	23.7	0.0	1 164	24.8	5.0	1 077	28.5	3.3	1 597	34.8	3.9
Rockingham County	1 546	28.7	7.8	443	23.3	1.6	3 003	31.6	4.4	3 503	32.8	2.7	2 623	38.8	4.4
Strafford County	702	24.4	6.1	209	19.1	12.4	1 540	26.8	4.5	1 244	42.8	3.5	1 474	34.5	4.7
Sullivan County	97	30.9	0.0	108	14.8	1.9	197	16.2	8.6	174	27.6	10.9	326	31.3	7.1
NEW JERSEY	1 127 266	29.9	8.4	17 987	27.5	6.5	484 503	25.9	5.1	1 116 149	30.1	5.0	228 326	35.7	5.1
Atlantic County	43 895	32.0	9.6	655	24.1	4.3	13 046	27.1	3.8	30 610	34.5	3.1	7 417	40.5	5.2
Bergen County	46 028	24.9	10.1	1 168	27.6	7.1	94 292	27.0	4.8	91 466	27.5	5.2	21 661	34.3	5.4
Burlington County	62 935	28.0	8.4	1 070	25.9	5.0	11 283	24.7	8.7	17 511	30.1	3.8	9 959	44.7	4.0
Camden County	90 311	33.0	8.0	1 251	31.0	9.5	19 952	27.4	5.1	48 809	38.2	3.5	10 637	43.5	4.5
Cape May County	5 078	30.6	14.7	99	0.0	12.1	623	18.9	7.4	3 209	39.2	4.7	1 291	55.8	3.6
Cumberland County	29 591	29.2	6.3	1 345	21.3	12.1	1 193	25.5	10.9	27 712	34.5	3.9	4 412	42.0	4.3
Essex County	325 185	29.7	9.1	1 870	29.1	8.0	29 926	25.4	5.2	122 770	29.6	4.8	29 381	30.9	5.3
Gloucester County	22 356	30.8	10.3	633	25.6	6.8	4 214	28.3	5.5	6 234	33.6	3.7	3 914	47.6	4.9
Hudson County	81 072	29.4	7.1	1 911	26.0	6.3	57 619	21.2	5.7	242 234	27.0	7.5	35 662	29.4	6.4
Hunterdon County	2 431	11.4	3.5	260	15.4	1.5	2 614	29.6	1.8	3 234	27.3	2.4	1 207	31.7	7.7

[1] Hispanic or Latino persons may be of any race.

STATE County	Total households	Married-couple family households			Other family households			Two or more unrelated persons		Male living alone		Female living alone		Percent of householders 65 years and over who live alone	Grandparents who are responsible for the care of their grandchildren
		Total	With children	Householder 65 years or over	Total	With children	Householder 65 years or over	Total	Householder 65 years or over	Total	Householder 65 years or over	Total	Householder 65 years or over		
	29	30	31	32	33	34	35	36	37	38	39	40	41	42	43
NEBRASKA—Cont'd															
Platte County	12 135	60.5	30.7	11.6	9.7	6.0	1.1	3.9	0.2	11.2	2.7	14.6	8.7	47.0	46
Polk County	2 252	63.4	25.4	15.6	6.0	4.3	0.5	2.9	0.3	13.1	4.1	14.6	10.9	47.8	14
Red Willow County	4 731	57.7	24.6	14.5	9.7	6.8	1.5	3.9	0.2	11.7	2.8	17.0	10.4	44.8	69
Richardson County	3 997	52.7	22.2	12.7	11.5	7.4	1.8	3.5	0.8	11.9	3.8	20.4	14.8	55.0	38
Rock County	755	55.1	21.3	15.4	11.7	6.6	3.3	2.6	0.0	12.5	2.5	18.1	12.7	44.9	3
Saline County	5 192	55.6	25.1	11.3	11.7	8.0	1.6	5.2	0.3	12.2	3.9	15.4	11.4	53.6	49
Sarpy County	43 495	64.4	35.1	6.2	12.4	8.6	0.8	4.8	0.1	8.5	1.1	9.8	3.7	40.1	673
Saunders County	7 477	63.2	28.6	11.9	9.6	6.0	1.8	3.4	0.4	10.6	2.6	13.2	9.1	45.4	68
Scotts Bluff County	14 890	54.9	23.0	13.5	14.0	9.7	1.7	3.4	0.4	10.8	2.5	17.0	9.9	44.4	257
Seward County	6 005	63.5	28.4	12.6	6.9	4.6	0.8	4.6	0.2	11.0	2.8	14.0	10.4	49.5	54
Sheridan County	2 555	57.7	23.6	15.8	10.5	6.5	2.0	2.3	0.5	12.8	4.5	16.6	11.6	46.9	25
Sherman County	1 389	60.7	22.4	18.6	7.1	3.7	1.9	2.2	0.4	12.0	4.0	18.1	12.6	44.3	15
Sioux County	601	65.2	23.6	16.0	6.5	2.7	2.3	4.5	0.0	13.6	3.7	10.1	6.3	35.3	13
Stanton County	2 299	68.3	34.8	12.5	10.1	5.8	1.5	2.6	0.1	9.5	1.7	9.4	5.8	34.5	11
Thayer County	2 556	59.7	23.1	16.6	7.6	5.2	1.3	1.6	0.2	12.0	4.6	19.1	14.2	51.0	29
Thomas County	324	59.9	24.4	13.0	6.2	4.3	1.2	1.9	0.0	11.7	5.2	20.4	15.1	58.9	3
Thurston County	2 242	51.7	25.1	12.4	24.4	13.8	4.5	2.5	0.4	10.1	3.3	11.3	6.7	36.5	229
Valley County	1 961	57.7	22.4	16.5	8.9	5.9	1.6	2.5	0.4	12.6	4.2	18.3	13.5	48.9	2
Washington County	6 954	64.4	30.5	9.7	10.6	7.0	1.5	3.4	0.2	8.9	2.6	12.7	8.8	49.9	45
Wayne County	3 458	56.5	25.5	12.7	7.7	4.7	1.0	10.7	0.1	9.9	2.5	15.2	8.8	45.2	35
Webster County	1 708	58.6	22.2	16.5	6.4	4.2	1.1	2.2	0.1	12.3	4.7	20.5	14.2	51.7	2
Wheeler County	358	63.4	27.4	15.9	7.3	5.3	0.6	1.7	0.0	13.1	3.1	14.5	10.1	44.3	0
York County	5 718	61.1	24.5	14.1	8.2	5.7	0.8	3.0	0.1	11.4	2.7	16.3	11.1	48.0	41
NEVADA	751 977	50.6	23.0	8.5	16.2	9.6	1.7	8.4	0.8	13.0	2.6	11.9	4.7	39.9	18 685
Churchill County	8 934	60.9	29.3	9.8	12.5	8.7	2.1	4.2	0.5	11.0	2.8	11.3	6.4	42.7	243
Clark County	512 714	49.6	22.5	8.3	17.1	10.0	1.8	8.8	0.8	12.8	2.5	11.6	4.3	38.5	13 508
Douglas County	16 428	61.5	23.3	14.4	11.6	7.9	1.6	6.2	0.7	11.1	2.3	9.6	4.4	28.6	282
Elko County	15 689	60.5	34.5	5.0	13.3	9.0	0.9	5.4	0.3	12.2	2.0	8.6	3.0	45.0	395
Esmeralda County	453	47.5	15.7	12.4	8.4	4.9	2.0	7.3	0.2	24.9	8.4	11.9	4.6	47.2	11
Eureka County	663	57.9	30.2	10.1	8.3	4.8	1.2	5.1	0.9	17.2	4.2	11.5	6.3	46.4	5
Humboldt County	5 744	59.2	32.5	5.7	13.3	9.4	1.1	4.7	0.7	14.0	2.3	8.8	3.6	43.7	157
Lander County	2 116	61.8	30.7	5.6	12.3	8.8	0.9	4.0	0.0	14.1	2.1	7.7	2.9	43.4	79
Lincoln County	1 556	56.4	25.6	12.7	9.6	6.6	1.1	3.3	1.5	14.1	5.8	16.5	11.6	53.4	46
Lyon County	13 023	59.2	26.4	11.9	14.1	7.9	2.5	5.3	0.6	11.7	3.7	9.7	4.6	35.8	320
Mineral County	2 201	45.2	16.0	13.0	18.2	10.3	3.7	5.0	0.6	16.7	7.1	14.9	7.6	45.8	90
Nye County	13 312	57.3	20.2	14.5	10.9	6.7	1.4	6.1	1.9	14.5	5.0	11.1	6.0	38.0	309
Pershing County	1 962	56.4	28.5	6.6	14.9	11.2	1.0	4.7	0.8	13.9	3.5	10.1	4.8	49.7	65
Storey County	1 468	57.5	18.1	9.3	9.3	4.8	0.0	7.6	1.0	13.8	4.5	11.6	4.2	45.7	44
Washoe County	132 192	48.9	23.0	7.3	15.1	9.0	1.4	9.1	0.7	13.6	2.6	13.4	5.3	45.6	2 662
White Pine County	3 285	50.4	20.5	11.9	15.1	10.7	1.9	4.8	0.0	14.4	3.9	15.3	8.9	48.3	123
Carson City	20 237	50.1	20.2	11.4	16.2	10.4	1.4	5.9	0.8	12.8	3.2	14.9	7.6	44.2	346
NEW HAMPSHIRE	474 750	56.2	26.1	8.8	12.4	7.7	1.5	7.0	0.4	10.9	2.2	13.5	6.5	44.9	4 534
Belknap County	22 444	56.9	22.8	11.4	12.5	7.9	1.7	6.3	0.4	10.9	2.8	13.4	7.3	42.7	226
Carroll County	18 387	55.7	20.2	13.5	11.7	7.4	1.7	6.1	0.7	11.6	2.9	14.9	8.1	41.0	169
Cheshire County	28 321	54.2	23.0	10.1	12.4	7.5	1.9	7.7	0.5	10.8	2.8	14.8	7.3	44.8	231
Coos County	13 977	52.1	20.0	11.4	13.7	8.5	1.9	5.4	0.4	12.7	4.3	16.1	10.6	52.1	123
Grafton County	31 608	53.0	22.7	10.1	11.6	7.5	1.4	8.1	0.5	12.0	2.4	15.3	7.3	44.6	207
Hillsborough County	144 477	56.0	27.8	7.5	12.8	7.9	1.5	6.8	0.3	11.1	2.0	13.2	6.1	46.6	1 502
Merrimack County	51 892	55.8	25.9	8.8	13.2	8.5	1.6	6.5	0.5	9.9	2.1	14.6	7.0	45.5	518
Rockingham County	104 586	60.2	29.9	7.7	11.3	6.6	1.4	6.5	0.4	10.3	2.0	11.7	5.2	42.8	873
Strafford County	42 531	51.9	23.9	8.6	13.5	9.1	1.3	9.9	0.4	11.5	1.8	13.2	6.3	44.0	506
Sullivan County	16 527	55.6	21.8	11.6	12.3	7.6	1.4	6.4	0.5	11.5	3.2	14.2	7.6	44.5	179
NEW JERSEY	3 065 774	54.4	26.2	9.4	16.3	7.9	2.8	4.8	0.4	9.7	2.4	14.8	7.5	44.1	58 789
Atlantic County	95 025	47.8	21.9	9.0	19.0	10.1	2.6	6.2	0.6	10.9	2.7	16.1	8.2	47.1	2 681
Bergen County	330 891	58.7	27.8	11.2	12.7	4.7	3.1	4.0	0.5	9.3	2.4	15.4	7.8	40.9	3 269
Burlington County	154 571	58.9	27.9	10.1	13.8	7.1	2.3	4.5	0.4	9.3	1.9	13.6	6.4	39.6	3 176
Camden County	185 837	50.8	24.6	8.6	19.5	10.6	3.1	4.6	0.4	9.8	2.4	15.2	7.4	44.9	5 041
Cape May County	42 140	52.1	19.7	13.9	13.1	6.8	2.3	4.7	0.5	11.3	3.8	18.9	11.0	47.1	722
Cumberland County	49 096	49.2	21.9	9.3	22.9	13.1	3.6	4.4	0.5	9.3	2.7	14.3	7.9	44.0	1 658
Essex County	283 692	43.4	21.4	7.2	25.2	13.2	3.4	4.7	0.4	10.7	2.6	16.1	7.3	47.1	9 273
Gloucester County	90 755	59.5	29.8	8.7	14.9	7.8	2.5	4.4	0.2	8.7	2.1	12.5	6.6	42.9	1 773
Hudson County	230 698	40.4	19.3	6.2	22.4	11.0	3.2	7.7	0.4	13.4	2.5	16.1	7.1	49.6	5 599
Hunterdon County	43 730	67.0	33.6	8.1	8.4	4.2	1.6	4.7	0.3	8.2	1.8	11.7	5.0	40.3	289

STATE County	Households with Non-Hispanic White householder		Households with Black or African American householder		Households with American Indian and Alaska Native householder		Households with Asian, Hawaiian, and Pacific Islander householder		Households with Hispanic or Latino[1] householder		Foreign-born population	Place of birth (percent)			Percent in non-English speaking households	
	Number of households	Percent that are family households	Number of households	Percent that are family households	Number of households	Percent that are family households	Number of households	Percent that are family households	Number of households	Percent that are family households	Percent of total population that is foreign-born	Europe	Asia	Latin America	Linguistically isolated	Not linguistically isolated
	44	45	46	47	48	49	50	51	52	53	54	55	56	57	58	59
NEBRASKA—Cont'd																
Platte County	11 515	70.1	29	69.0	17	82.4	25	60.0	508	73.0	4.1	0.4	0.4	3.1	2.7	9.4
Polk County	2 228	69.3	0	X	2	100.0	0	X	15	66.7	0.8	0.2	0.0	0.5	0.2	6.1
Red Willow County	4 583	68.1	7	0.0	13	38.5	0	X	102	44.1	1.2	0.5	0.0	0.3	0.3	4.3
Richardson County	3 838	64.8	6	50.0	72	55.6	18	100.0	9	66.7	1.2	0.2	0.9	0.0	0.3	5.9
Rock County	742	67.4	0	X	7	42.9	3	33.3	3	0.0	0.3	0.0	0.3	0.0	0.2	6.2
Saline County	4 852	67.5	3	100.0	30	96.7	59	74.6	238	57.6	6.0	0.9	0.7	4.3	3.6	13.5
Sarpy County	39 079	77.2	1 983	72.4	174	76.4	577	66.0	1 371	86.1	3.7	1.1	1.5	0.9	1.1	10.7
Saunders County	7 377	72.8	0	X	10	100.0	7	71.4	48	68.8	1.2	0.3	0.4	0.4	0.4	8.4
Scotts Bluff County	12 620	66.9	36	36.1	174	82.8	65	64.6	1 900	81.7	4.1	0.3	0.3	3.2	3.0	16.7
Seward County	5 913	70.3	24	75.0	8	0.0	21	85.7	25	100.0	1.7	0.5	0.5	0.4	0.0	8.3
Sheridan County	2 340	67.8	3	100.0	159	76.7	1	100.0	23	87.0	0.7	0.3	0.2	0.2	0.2	8.8
Sherman County	1 372	67.5	0	X	0	X	0	X	7	100.0	0.4	0.2	0.2	0.0	0.3	6.8
Sioux County	584	72.8	0	X	2	0.0	2	100.0	11	36.4	1.3	0.5	0.0	0.7	0.5	4.4
Stanton County	2 264	78.1	0	X	12	100.0	0	X	23	100.0	1.2	0.3	0.1	0.7	0.2	10.1
Thayer County	2 535	67.2	0	X	4	75.0	0	X	15	73.3	0.8	0.4	0.0	0.4	0.5	7.4
Thomas County	317	65.9	0	X	0	X	0	X	7	71.4	1.6	0.7	0.0	1.0	0.0	3.5
Thurston County	1 354	70.2	6	100.0	835	85.6	8	100.0	16	50.0	1.6	0.3	0.6	0.5	0.7	14.1
Valley County	1 949	66.4	0	X	0	X	0	X	10	100.0	1.1	0.4	0.2	0.4	0.5	6.6
Washington County	6 845	74.8	28	92.9	25	48.0	10	100.0	44	95.5	1.6	0.8	0.4	0.2	0.0	7.8
Wayne County	3 360	64.1	18	100.0	14	21.4	5	0.0	42	81.0	1.7	0.2	0.3	1.0	1.1	5.8
Webster County	1 689	65.3	2	0.0	0	X	8	75.0	0	X	1.3	0.4	0.7	0.0	0.1	7.5
Wheeler County	354	70.3	0	X	0	X	0	X	2	100.0	0.0	0.0	0.0	0.0	0.5	5.3
York County	5 652	69.3	11	0.0	2	0.0	1	0.0	36	94.4	1.7	0.5	0.4	0.7	0.9	8.3
NEVADA	550 056	64.0	49 184	66.2	9 055	69.4	30 531	71.9	99 288	81.3	15.8	1.6	3.6	9.7	6.9	23.3
Churchill County	7 666	73.0	96	52.1	382	69.1	183	89.1	536	86.8	6.0	0.5	2.0	3.0	1.8	15.8
Clark County	351 972	63.5	45 802	66.8	3 588	69.4	24 858	72.0	76 310	80.7	18.0	1.8	4.3	11.0	8.0	25.5
Douglas County	15 092	72.9	42	76.2	270	62.2	135	75.6	765	79.0	5.7	1.8	0.7	2.4	2.3	13.2
Elko County	12 221	72.0	60	63.6	916	65.1	108	81.5	2 127	87.4	10.2	0.6	0.6	8.2	5.2	22.1
Esmeralda County	390	53.1	0	X	18	77.8	1	100.0	23	95.7	6.5	1.4	0.2	4.1	1.8	10.7
Eureka County	588	67.2	4	50.0	7	85.7	9	22.2	38	55.3	7.8	0.7	0.9	5.1	2.8	13.2
Humboldt County	4 574	70.0	21	57.1	238	70.6	6	100.0	832	87.4	10.4	1.0	0.2	8.8	4.7	21.1
Lander County	1 673	73.9	0	X	109	78.0	10	40.0	292	77.4	9.6	0.8	0.2	8.0	3.7	20.7
Lincoln County	1 491	65.7	6	100.0	5	100.0	2	100.0	37	70.3	3.5	0.6	0.4	2.1	0.0	9.5
Lyon County	11 342	72.7	41	68.3	269	74.0	61	45.9	1 037	82.6	6.0	0.9	0.4	4.3	2.7	14.1
Mineral County	1 655	64.6	119	43.7	289	63.7	9	33.3	104	69.2	2.4	0.7	0.4	1.2	0.8	10.1
Nye County	11 887	67.2	126	78.6	238	66.8	68	83.8	755	76.0	5.0	1.3	0.6	2.8	1.5	13.0
Pershing County	1 587	68.6	7	71.4	87	63.2	5	0.0	243	92.6	7.0	0.2	0.1	6.6	5.5	18.0
Storey County	1 333	68.4	0	X	45	55.6	25	28.0	51	74.5	2.2	1.1	0.6	0.6	0.2	15.6
Washoe County	106 441	61.1	2 739	58.0	2 042	70.7	4 744	70.9	14 111	83.7	14.1	1.4	3.4	8.4	5.8	20.5
White Pine County	2 778	65.3	28	75.0	120	61.7	13	0.0	271	72.7	2.9	1.1	0.6	1.0	1.4	14.2
Carson City	17 366	64.4	84	54.8	432	80.1	294	75.5	1 756	82.6	9.9	1.0	1.5	6.8	4.6	15.9
NEW HAMPSHIRE	456 148	68.5	3 151	65.2	947	69.4	4 669	75.1	5 772	71.0	4.4	1.5	1.1	0.6	1.2	12.4
Belknap County	21 860	69.2	37	78.4	90	91.1	84	76.2	102	69.6	2.5	1.2	0.5	0.2	0.7	10.0
Carroll County	18 100	67.4	12	33.3	50	70.0	28	82.1	48	77.1	2.4	1.4	0.3	0.2	0.3	7.9
Cheshire County	27 756	66.9	71	67.6	61	45.9	102	69.6	131	55.0	2.2	1.1	0.5	0.1	0.5	8.0
Coos County	13 768	65.7	9	100.0	32	56.3	12	83.3	40	85.0	4.0	0.7	0.3	0.1	2.3	23.8
Grafton County	30 462	65.1	132	37.1	87	41.4	306	58.5	259	56.4	3.9	1.6	1.1	0.4	0.5	8.2
Hillsborough County	135 437	68.6	1 696	69.3	258	80.2	2 435	73.3	3 385	72.4	6.8	1.9	1.7	1.4	2.4	16.6
Merrimack County	50 245	69.1	304	63.2	107	81.3	395	72.4	341	63.9	3.2	1.1	0.7	0.2	0.7	11.0
Rockingham County	101 238	71.5	610	62.0	151	58.9	813	88.6	1 061	74.7	3.7	1.4	1.0	0.5	0.6	11.0
Strafford County	41 040	65.4	249	60.6	91	60.4	414	72.7	346	68.2	3.4	1.3	1.1	0.2	0.8	10.8
Sullivan County	16 242	67.9	31	64.5	20	100.0	80	83.8	59	71.2	2.9	1.4	0.5	0.1	0.4	7.8
NEW JERSEY	2 182 369	68.8	382 711	68.9	5 674	74.4	145 230	83.0	315 560	80.3	17.5	4.2	4.9	7.5	6.3	25.6
Atlantic County	66 132	65.0	15 622	65.3	289	65.4	3 599	80.7	8 375	78.1	11.8	2.1	4.3	4.8	5.6	20.9
Bergen County	254 521	69.1	16 453	67.6	376	69.4	29 014	83.9	26 450	81.0	25.1	7.7	10.0	6.7	7.6	31.8
Burlington County	123 546	72.0	20 837	74.3	338	80.5	3 494	82.8	4 529	76.2	6.3	2.1	2.3	1.3	1.5	14.0
Camden County	134 470	68.6	30 736	71.2	358	83.0	5 633	86.9	13 440	80.3	6.9	1.6	3.0	1.8	1.3	17.7
Cape May County	38 883	65.0	1 846	65.0	46	30.4	206	82.5	963	69.4	3.2	1.7	0.6	0.6	3.4	17.7
Cumberland County	32 973	69.8	7 726	75.1	468	69.0	414	74.6	7 229	79.4	6.2	1.6	0.6	3.9	4.6	22.6
Essex County	119 076	67.0	113 530	65.9	554	76.0	8 932	82.4	36 287	78.4	21.2	4.5	3.0	12.1	7.5	28.9
Gloucester County	79 146	74.6	7 974	72.6	230	78.7	1 102	85.5	1 580	72.4	3.4	1.3	1.3	0.6	0.8	10.9
Hudson County	100 524	50.2	29 087	64.3	523	80.7	18 807	72.4	77 810	76.0	38.5	4.5	8.1	23.7	17.1	45.9
Hunterdon County	41 641	75.4	295	61.7	85	87.1	759	81.3	746	81.5	6.3	3.2	1.7	1.0	0.9	12.8

[1] Hispanic or Latino persons may be of any race.

STATE/ County code	MSA/PMSA/ NECMA code[1]	STATE County	Population by age (percent)										Non-Hispanic White Age (percent)		
			Total population	Under 5 years	5 to 17 years	18 to 24 years	25 to 44 years	45 to 64 years	65 years and over	Median age	+/− U.S. percent under 18 years	+/− U.S. percent 65 years and over	Total population	Under 18 years	65 years and over
			1	2	3	4	5	6	7	8	9	10	11	12	13
		NEW JERSEY— Cont'd													
34 021	8480	Mercer County	350 761	6.3	17.5	10.2	30.8	22.6	12.5	36.0	-1.9	0.1	225 079	20.5	15.9
34 023	5015	Middlesex County	750 162	6.5	17.1	9.6	32.9	21.6	12.3	35.7	-2.1	-0.1	463 779	20.4	17.1
34 025	5190	Monmouth County	615 301	6.8	19.2	6.8	30.6	24.0	12.6	37.7	0.3	0.2	495 716	24.8	13.8
34 027	5640	Morris County	470 212	6.9	17.8	6.4	32.1	25.2	11.6	37.8	-1.0	-0.8	385 451	24.1	13.0
34 029	5190	Ocean County	510 916	6.3	17.0	6.6	26.1	21.9	22.2	41.0	-2.4	9.8	459 135	22.1	23.9
34 031	0875	Passaic County	489 049	7.4	18.5	9.3	31.5	21.1	12.1	34.8	0.2	-0.3	251 713	20.9	18.6
34 033	6160	Salem County	64 285	6.0	19.6	7.9	27.9	24.3	14.4	38.0	-0.1	2.0	51 117	23.3	15.5
34 035	5015	Somerset County	297 490	7.4	18.1	5.8	34.0	23.5	11.2	37.2	-0.2	-1.2	220 274	23.9	13.6
34 037	5640	Sussex County	144 166	6.8	21.1	6.2	31.7	25.2	9.0	37.1	2.2	-3.4	134 707	27.4	9.4
34 039	5640	Union County	522 541	6.9	17.9	7.9	31.7	21.9	13.8	36.6	-0.9	1.4	283 293	21.4	19.7
34 041	5640	Warren County	102 437	6.9	19.1	6.2	31.4	23.6	12.9	37.6	0.3	0.5	94 564	25.4	13.5
35 000	...	**NEW MEXICO**	1 819 046	7.1	20.8	9.7	28.6	22.1	11.7	34.6	2.2	-0.7	813 380	20.3	16.8
35 001	0200	Bernalillo County	556 678	6.9	18.4	10.3	30.6	22.3	11.5	35.0	-0.4	-0.9	268 967	18.7	16.2
35 003	...	Catron County	3 543	4.2	16.7	4.1	20.0	36.2	18.8	47.8	-4.8	6.4	2 699	19.2	19.0
35 005	...	Chaves County	61 382	7.2	21.8	9.4	25.2	21.6	14.8	35.2	3.3	2.4	31 849	21.3	22.4
35 006	...	Cibola County	25 595	7.9	22.8	9.7	27.6	21.0	11.1	33.1	5.0	-1.3	6 318	20.1	17.6
35 007	...	Colfax County	14 189	5.4	19.7	7.8	24.0	25.7	17.4	40.8	-0.6	5.0	7 116	19.1	21.3
35 009	...	Curry County	45 044	8.2	21.8	11.3	29.1	18.1	11.4	30.8	4.3	-1.0	26 450	24.2	15.7
35 011	...	De Baca County	2 240	5.0	18.9	5.4	22.0	22.5	26.3	43.8	-1.8	13.9	1 445	21.5	27.5
35 013	4100	Dona Ana County	174 682	7.7	21.9	13.1	27.6	18.9	10.7	30.2	3.9	-1.7	56 757	18.2	18.1
35 015	...	Eddy County	51 658	7.2	21.5	8.2	26.6	21.8	14.7	36.4	3.0	2.3	29 656	23.2	19.4
35 017	...	Grant County	31 002	6.7	19.4	8.2	24.4	24.9	16.4	38.8	0.4	4.0	15 066	19.8	21.1
35 019	...	Guadalupe County	4 680	5.5	19.0	9.4	30.7	22.4	13.1	37.5	-1.2	0.7	765	15.8	12.5
35 021	...	Harding County	810	3.0	17.2	4.7	17.8	28.0	29.4	48.7	-5.5	17.0	412	18.9	26.0
35 023	...	Hidalgo County	5 932	7.7	24.0	7.6	25.1	21.9	13.5	34.8	6.0	1.1	2 531	25.2	18.4
35 025	...	Lea County	55 511	7.6	22.5	9.9	27.5	20.0	12.5	33.1	4.4	0.1	30 055	22.5	18.4
35 027	...	Lincoln County	19 411	5.0	17.7	6.0	23.3	30.1	18.0	43.8	-3.0	5.6	13 766	18.4	21.5
35 028	7490	Los Alamos County	18 343	5.8	20.1	4.2	27.5	30.0	12.4	40.8	0.2	0.0	15 073	24.4	13.0
35 029	...	Luna County	25 016	7.5	22.4	7.0	23.4	21.5	18.2	36.7	4.2	5.8	9 992	15.9	34.2
35 031	...	McKinley County	74 798	9.3	28.7	9.9	27.8	17.5	6.8	26.9	12.3	-5.6	9 005	20.4	12.6
35 033	...	Mora County	5 180	6.2	20.6	8.5	24.1	23.5	17.1	39.6	1.1	4.7	904	18.0	20.5
35 035	...	Otero County	62 298	7.1	22.3	9.4	28.5	21.1	11.5	33.8	3.7	-0.9	34 392	22.4	15.7
35 037	...	Quay County	10 155	5.5	19.4	6.5	22.5	26.8	19.4	41.5	-0.8	7.0	5 979	20.1	24.6
35 039	...	Rio Arriba County	41 190	6.7	21.8	8.5	29.0	23.2	10.8	34.5	2.8	-1.6	5 648	15.1	15.2
35 041	...	Roosevelt County	18 018	7.5	20.3	15.3	26.8	17.9	12.1	29.5	2.1	-0.3	11 315	22.8	16.3
35 043	0200	Sandoval County	89 908	7.3	22.3	7.6	30.3	22.0	10.5	35.1	3.9	-1.9	45 198	23.3	14.5
35 045	...	San Juan County	113 801	7.9	24.7	10.1	27.8	20.5	9.0	31.0	6.9	-3.4	52 587	25.7	12.6
35 047	...	San Miguel County	30 126	6.4	21.1	10.9	27.3	22.4	11.8	35.1	1.8	-0.6	5 725	16.8	16.4
35 049	7490	Santa Fe County	129 292	6.0	18.0	8.1	29.9	27.4	10.7	37.9	-1.7	-1.7	58 761	16.8	13.7
35 051	...	Sierra County	13 270	4.5	15.4	5.4	19.6	27.1	27.9	48.9	-5.8	15.5	9 366	14.2	33.6
35 053	...	Socorro County	18 078	6.8	21.4	12.9	26.2	21.6	11.1	32.4	2.5	-1.3	6 817	19.0	14.6
35 055	...	Taos County	29 979	5.4	19.1	7.0	27.4	28.9	12.2	39.5	-1.2	-0.2	10 248	16.2	12.2
35 057	...	Torrance County	16 911	7.0	23.3	7.3	29.4	22.9	10.1	34.8	4.6	-2.3	9 709	26.9	11.6
35 059	...	Union County	4 174	5.5	21.9	5.8	24.5	24.4	17.8	39.9	1.7	5.4	2 627	23.4	21.8
35 061	0200	Valencia County	66 152	7.6	22.4	8.2	30.4	21.2	10.3	33.8	4.3	-2.1	26 182	22.6	15.3
36 000	...	**NEW YORK**	18 976 457	6.5	18.2	9.3	30.9	22.3	12.9	35.9	-1.0	0.5	11 761 679	21.8	16.4
36 001	0160	Albany County	294 565	5.6	16.8	11.2	29.1	22.6	14.6	36.8	-3.3	2.2	240 921	20.2	16.5
36 003	...	Allegany County	49 927	5.6	18.7	15.6	23.9	22.2	14.0	35.0	-1.4	1.6	48 158	24.3	14.3
36 005	5600	Bronx County	1 332 650	8.1	21.6	10.7	30.7	18.8	10.1	31.2	4.0	-2.3	194 312	14.5	28.1
36 007	0960	Broome County	200 536	5.6	17.3	10.9	26.9	22.7	16.5	38.2	-2.8	4.1	181 437	22.1	17.7
36 009	...	Cattaraugus County	83 955	6.2	20.0	9.3	26.4	23.4	14.7	37.4	0.5	2.3	78 982	25.3	15.2
36 011	8160	Cayuga County	81 963	5.8	19.2	8.3	29.6	22.6	14.4	37.3	-0.7	2.0	75 600	25.0	15.4
36 013	3610	Chautauqua County	139 750	5.8	18.6	10.3	26.3	23.0	16.0	37.9	-1.3	3.6	128 574	23.4	17.0
36 015	2335	Chemung County	91 070	5.9	18.4	8.9	28.3	22.9	15.6	37.9	-1.4	3.2	81 877	23.8	16.7
36 017	...	Chenango County	51 401	6.0	20.2	7.0	27.6	24.3	14.9	38.4	0.5	2.5	49 779	26.0	15.1
36 019	...	Clinton County	79 894	5.1	17.8	12.5	30.6	22.1	11.9	35.7	-2.8	-0.5	73 737	23.5	12.7
36 021	...	Columbia County	63 094	5.3	18.5	6.4	27.0	26.3	16.5	40.5	-1.9	4.1	57 565	22.8	17.4
36 023	...	Cortland County	48 599	5.9	17.7	15.6	26.6	21.7	12.5	34.2	-2.1	0.1	46 787	23.4	12.8
36 025	...	Delaware County	48 055	5.1	18.0	8.1	24.1	26.1	18.6	41.4	-2.6	6.2	45 795	22.5	19.1
36 027	2281	Dutchess County	280 150	6.1	18.8	9.5	30.2	23.3	12.0	36.7	-0.8	-0.4	224 979	23.6	13.7
36 029	1280	Erie County	950 265	6.0	18.2	8.7	28.5	22.7	16.0	38.0	-1.5	3.6	768 476	22.0	17.8
36 031	...	Essex County	38 851	5.0	17.8	6.9	29.8	24.5	16.1	39.4	-2.9	3.7	36 275	23.4	17.0
36 033	...	Franklin County	51 134	4.9	17.7	9.9	32.9	21.7	12.8	36.3	-3.1	0.4	42 680	24.1	14.7
36 035	...	Fulton County	55 073	5.6	19.2	7.2	28.2	23.6	16.3	38.6	-0.9	3.9	52 392	24.2	16.9

[1]MSA = Metropolitan Statistical Area. PMSA = Primary MSA. NECMA = New England County Metropolitan Area. See the Appendix A for explanation of these concepts. See Appendix B for list of metropolitan areas identified by type, with component counties.

STATE County	Black or African American Total population	Age (percent) Under 18 years	65 years and over	American Indian and Alaska Native Total population	Age (percent) Under 18 years	65 years and over	Asian, Hawaiian, and Pacific Islander Total population	Age (percent) Under 18 years	65 years and over	Hispanic or Latino[1] Total population	Age (percent) Under 18 years	65 years and over	Two or more races Total population	Age (percent) Under 18 years	65 years and over
	14	15	16	17	18	19	20	21	22	23	24	25	26	27	28
NEW JERSEY—Cont'd															
Mercer County	68 582	30.5	8.4	786	27.4	7.0	17 698	25.4	5.0	34 140	30.1	3.3	7 990	38.1	4.6
Middlesex County	67 346	28.7	6.1	1 290	32.7	4.1	104 268	25.7	4.4	102 116	31.5	3.9	20 801	34.7	3.6
Monmouth County	48 883	30.7	10.4	769	26.0	3.3	24 234	27.1	5.7	38 076	31.7	4.6	11 264	42.8	4.7
Morris County	12 215	24.9	7.9	499	20.8	11.8	30 244	26.3	5.3	36 246	27.1	3.6	8 122	38.3	4.9
Ocean County	14 968	33.6	7.4	806	28.0	10.2	6 749	28.2	7.5	25 377	33.9	6.2	7 224	42.8	7.2
Passaic County	63 537	31.2	7.0	1 539	34.4	2.3	18 593	27.2	6.3	146 679	31.9	4.1	19 193	33.6	4.7
Salem County	9 471	32.8	12.0	265	39.2	12.8	386	23.6	6.5	2 358	39.1	4.4	1 031	48.3	5.2
Somerset County	22 143	29.2	5.6	429	15.2	6.1	25 156	28.9	4.3	25 868	30.1	3.2	5 761	41.2	4.6
Sussex County	1 324	30.4	5.4	191	26.2	1.6	1 668	34.1	3.8	5 030	34.0	2.7	1 631	41.6	4.0
Union County	107 984	29.8	8.7	973	30.3	1.7	19 524	24.8	5.7	102 851	28.0	5.2	18 513	31.8	4.9
Warren County	1 931	31.8	9.3	178	37.6	0.0	1 221	31.9	2.9	3 619	33.7	3.6	1 255	39.3	2.3
NEW MEXICO	33 513	30.4	8.9	172 276	37.3	5.8	19 534	24.2	6.7	765 610	33.8	7.9	70 080	42.3	6.7
Bernalillo County	15 303	29.8	7.1	22 964	30.1	4.3	10 396	23.5	7.5	233 527	31.8	7.3	25 946	41.5	5.6
Catron County	7	71.4	0.0	107	38.3	16.8	12	41.7	0.0	668	24.9	20.5	90	21.1	8.9
Chaves County	1 226	32.1	15.9	621	39.8	7.2	437	26.5	0.0	27 016	37.9	6.1	2 113	43.4	8.4
Cibola County	217	8.8	21.2	10 276	37.2	8.3	151	45.7	4.6	8 441	31.4	10.0	791	39.7	9.7
Colfax County	88	29.5	4.5	152	22.4	23.0	27	29.6	0.0	6 742	31.3	13.5	585	26.8	20.3
Curry County	2 825	36.6	7.6	501	28.3	6.4	1 078	26.3	1.3	13 683	39.7	5.1	1 686	57.9	3.0
De Baca County	0	X	X	36	41.7	11.1	4	0.0	0.0	775	28.9	23.6	46	43.5	21.7
Dona Ana County	2 444	27.9	10.2	2 523	30.4	5.4	1 494	24.8	6.0	110 807	35.8	7.2	6 359	38.7	6.8
Eddy County	959	35.7	12.4	396	23.5	8.8	244	20.1	0.0	20 130	37.0	8.0	1 404	44.9	7.4
Grant County	175	28.6	4.6	358	23.2	6.1	128	14.1	0.0	15 153	32.5	12.0	987	35.3	12.1
Guadalupe County	47	0.0	0.0	87	8.0	0.0	3	0.0	0.0	3 792	26.6	13.4	169	33.7	13.6
Harding County	0	X	X	8	25.0	25.0	0	X	X	370	21.6	33.5	36	13.9	38.9
Hidalgo County	14	21.4	0.0	36	22.2	13.9	5	40.0	60.0	3 337	36.6	9.6	223	40.4	13.5
Lea County	2 440	32.8	15.1	536	28.0	4.7	236	31.4	15.3	21 973	39.9	4.4	1 656	54.5	5.4
Lincoln County	65	23.1	16.9	311	31.5	5.8	66	16.7	10.6	4 978	33.5	9.3	522	42.0	7.7
Los Alamos County	43	0.0	48.8	95	25.3	9.5	798	34.2	0.0	2 158	33.7	12.5	316	44.3	5.7
Luna County	165	30.9	20.0	353	37.1	4.5	91	22.2	23.6	14 470	00.7	7.2	766	35.5	10.8
McKinley County	305	30.5	20.0	55 732	40.8	5.7	367	19.9	11.2	9 303	38.6	7.1	2 028	64.1	2.5
Mora County	8	0.0	0.0	48	39.6	16.7	0	X	X	4 236	28.5	16.5	207	46.9	6.3
Otero County	2 211	30.3	5.7	3 624	41.3	3.3	731	18.6	8.6	19 980	38.9	6.8	2 899	49.7	5.0
Quay County	65	27.7	30.8	73	23.3	2.7	122	23.0	23.8	3 861	32.1	11.2	362	42.5	14.4
Rio Arriba County	146	36.3	8.9	5 571	36.6	6.9	89	13.5	14.6	30 060	30.0	10.7	1 551	30.8	9.4
Roosevelt County	347	40.6	2.3	146	29.5	6.8	88	5.7	0.0	6 057	36.7	5.1	518	45.9	4.1
Sandoval County	1 366	27.2	15.6	14 821	38.1	5.7	796	26.0	6.9	26 426	35.4	6.4	3 058	46.8	4.8
San Juan County	504	30.2	6.4	42 051	38.5	6.0	297	39.7	4.4	16 984	38.4	5.3	3 252	52.6	4.5
San Miguel County	235	37.9	6.0	430	21.6	7.0	146	17.1	0.0	23 469	30.1	10.9	1 244	33.5	14.8
Santa Fe County	974	27.6	3.1	3 950	33.2	4.6	1 024	25.0	6.1	63 461	30.2	8.6	5 263	32.2	7.8
Sierra County	39	53.8	0.0	194	39.7	14.4	18	0.0	0.0	3 477	34.6	14.0	304	24.7	19.4
Socorro County	119	35.3	0.0	2 017	38.3	6.0	167	4.2	6.6	8 782	33.5	10.0	748	43.2	7.8
Taos County	101	2.0	2.0	1 892	29.1	12.9	85	2.4	1.2	17 388	29.0	12.3	1 191	35.2	10.8
Torrance County	276	25.4	1.4	290	36.6	5.9	86	44.2	5.8	6 282	35.4	8.5	745	41.6	7.2
Union County	0	X	X	23	30.4	0.0	8	0.0	0.0	1 453	33.7	11.8	112	52.7	4.5
Valencia County	769	20.5	10.1	2 054	30.4	6.9	350	23.1	16.6	36 363	35.6	6.8	2 883	41.5	8.4
NEW YORK	2 986 242	29.8	8.7	79 314	31.7	6.7	1 052 326	22.6	6.8	2 865 016	30.9	5.8	615 062	33.2	6.1
Albany County	31 611	33.1	6.9	891	28.6	6.5	7 918	22.5	4.4	9 271	35.2	3.9	5 587	43.1	5.1
Allegany County	329	12.2	5.8	120	18.3	9.2	437	20.8	4.3	393	28.0	4.8	515	32.6	7.6
Bronx County	473 407	31.1	8.4	10 429	41.0	4.9	40 175	24.8	6.3	645 222	34.2	6.0	78 528	32.1	6.4
Broome County	6 708	34.2	5.1	440	21.4	11.6	5 359	20.0	2.5	4 069	34.9	4.4	3 102	44.8	4.9
Cattaraugus County	865	37.1	7.4	2 033	35.6	8.5	456	30.5	4.2	771	43.1	3.2	882	56.1	6.7
Cayuga County	3 029	17.0	2.1	283	13.4	7.1	401	23.7	13.7	1 741	20.4	2.5	1 075	53.8	3.4
Chautauqua County	3 036	22.9	4.0	630	24.1	13.2	482	30.7	5.4	5 836	39.1	4.2	1 856	52.3	2.6
Chemung County	5 177	22.5	7.3	321	32.1	3.4	816	27.7	3.9	1 581	24.0	4.4	1 580	58.2	5.3
Chenango County	375	27.5	5.9	189	25.4	4.8	171	14.0	8.2	562	28.3	8.7	391	51.4	9.5
Clinton County	2 940	11.3	1.8	219	9.6	5.0	721	16.4	4.0	1 754	14.1	0.4	846	40.2	4.6
Columbia County	2 792	34.0	6.9	126	11.9	17.5	502	30.3	1.6	1 456	39.8	6.1	876	48.9	6.4
Cortland County	347	21.3	0.0	171	9.9	21.6	96	1.0	11.5	584	32.5	4.1	628	35.5	4.9
Delaware County	535	35.7	7.9	169	26.0	8.3	284	22.9	4.2	713	32.8	7.4	585	41.7	6.7
Dutchess County	25 687	29.0	5.9	512	11.1	9.0	7 145	25.6	4.1	17 617	30.9	3.5	6 039	44.2	5.0
Erie County	122 928	32.7	9.9	6 032	30.3	7.6	13 131	22.4	4.5	30 760	38.9	4.8	13 143	47.7	5.0
Essex County	1 144	6.5	0.2	136	26.5	9.6	208	15.9	6.3	856	9.8	2.0	388	39.2	5.2
Franklin County	3 111	1.2	1.0	3 207	34.0	7.7	67	6.0	1.5	2 054	5.5	0.1	229	36.2	6.6
Fulton County	999	35.5	5.4	182	20.9	6.6	244	31.1	3.7	896	37.7	3.3	455	44.8	6.8

[1] Hispanic or Latino persons may be of any race.

Table A-3. States and Counties — Age, Ethnicity, and Household Structure

STATE County	Total households	Family households (percent) Married-couple family households Total	With children	Householder 65 years or over	Other family households Total	With children	Householder 65 years or over	Nonfamily households (percent) Two or more unrelated persons Total	Householder 65 years or over	Male living alone Total	Householder 65 years or over	Female living alone Total	Householder 65 years or over	Percent of householders 65 years and over who live alone	Grandparents who are responsible for the care of their grandchildren
	29	30	31	32	33	34	35	36	37	38	39	40	41	42	43
NEW JERSEY— Cont'd															
Mercer County	125 787	52.0	25.0	8.6	17.0	8.7	2.7	5.4	0.5	9.8	2.5	15.8	7.8	46.8	2 506
Middlesex County	265 898	58.2	28.5	9.3	14.2	6.5	2.6	5.3	0.4	8.9	2.0	13.4	6.7	41.6	4 105
Monmouth County	224 447	58.9	30.0	9.0	12.9	6.0	2.4	4.4	0.4	9.4	2.3	14.4	7.3	44.8	3 170
Morris County	169 794	63.8	31.4	9.2	10.3	4.5	1.9	4.4	0.4	8.6	1.6	12.9	5.7	38.9	1 368
Ocean County	200 553	57.3	23.2	16.3	11.8	5.2	2.6	3.9	0.6	8.8	3.7	18.3	12.8	45.8	2 612
Passaic County	163 917	52.6	25.8	8.6	20.9	10.4	3.1	4.4	0.4	8.9	2.4	13.2	7.3	44.7	4 229
Salem County	24 316	54.8	23.4	10.1	17.1	9.5	2.8	3.8	0.5	9.3	2.5	15.0	8.3	44.7	672
Somerset County	109 070	61.4	31.7	8.2	11.0	5.2	2.1	4.9	0.3	8.8	1.6	13.9	5.5	40.2	1 292
Sussex County	50 789	65.5	34.4	6.7	11.1	5.7	1.7	4.5	0.4	8.7	1.7	10.2	4.9	43.2	416
Union County	186 093	53.6	26.1	9.6	18.5	8.3	3.5	4.4	0.4	9.0	2.6	14.5	8.0	43.9	4 576
Warren County	38 675	59.1	28.5	8.6	12.3	6.5	2.2	4.7	0.6	9.9	2.6	14.1	7.3	46.5	362
NEW MEXICO	678 032	51.1	24.1	9.3	18.1	11.2	2.3	5.5	0.4	11.7	2.4	13.7	6.0	41.4	24 041
Bernalillo County	220 939	46.5	21.4	8.1	17.8	10.7	2.1	7.3	0.4	13.0	2.1	15.4	6.0	43.4	5 761
Catron County	1 587	55.3	17.3	14.4	11.1	5.5	2.8	4.0	0.1	17.0	3.9	12.7	7.2	38.9	33
Chaves County	22 559	54.3	24.1	11.9	17.8	12.1	1.9	3.1	0.4	9.9	3.5	14.9	8.6	45.9	863
Cibola County	8 335	51.7	25.0	9.9	24.3	14.0	4.0	3.1	0.7	10.8	2.8	10.1	5.0	34.8	530
Colfax County	5 799	53.4	20.2	13.8	15.7	10.0	2.4	3.3	0.4	13.2	3.5	14.5	8.6	42.0	142
Curry County	16 813	54.1	26.7	8.8	17.1	11.8	1.5	3.3	0.4	12.6	2.5	12.9	6.9	46.7	538
De Baca County	924	55.4	20.0	18.1	11.5	5.2	3.8	1.9	0.5	14.3	5.8	16.9	12.9	45.5	26
Dona Ana County	59 479	53.2	26.7	10.2	19.1	12.4	1.9	6.4	0.4	10.1	2.1	11.3	4.9	35.8	2 455
Eddy County	19 410	57.0	25.5	12.0	15.7	10.5	2.1	3.1	0.2	11.0	2.8	13.2	7.7	42.4	782
Grant County	12 138	52.7	20.4	13.1	17.6	11.7	2.9	3.9	0.6	11.7	3.5	14.1	7.2	39.2	460
Guadalupe County	1 661	50.0	22.8	11.3	20.5	12.9	3.3	1.7	0.2	12.8	3.7	15.0	7.0	41.9	36
Harding County	366	47.5	17.2	17.8	13.7	5.7	6.8	2.5	0.5	21.9	10.9	14.5	10.7	46.2	3
Hidalgo County	2 152	53.6	25.7	10.0	18.2	12.0	1.8	2.7	0.6	13.3	5.0	12.2	6.9	49.1	60
Lea County	19 720	58.9	29.2	10.5	16.1	11.1	1.8	2.6	0.1	9.8	2.9	12.5	8.0	46.9	799
Lincoln County	8 206	55.7	18.3	15.7	13.2	8.3	1.8	4.4	0.5	11.4	2.9	15.4	7.2	36.1	147
Los Alamos County	7 495	64.1	28.4	11.1	7.9	5.7	1.1	3.1	0.1	13.5	1.9	11.3	4.4	34.2	41
Luna County	9 387	52.4	22.9	15.7	18.0	11.7	2.4	3.2	0.5	13.5	5.8	12.8	7.8	42.2	594
McKinley County	21 441	47.5	28.7	5.7	30.0	17.4	4.7	3.0	0.1	9.7	2.0	9.8	3.7	35.0	2 179
Mora County	2 015	48.3	17.6	14.8	21.2	13.9	2.0	3.5	1.2	14.9	4.4	12.1	5.4	35.2	60
Otero County	22 984	58.4	27.5	10.0	15.4	10.5	1.8	3.0	0.4	11.2	2.7	12.0	6.1	42.2	849
Quay County	4 208	53.2	20.5	14.6	14.8	8.2	3.1	3.1	0.7	10.9	3.3	18.0	10.9	43.6	93
Rio Arriba County	15 015	49.4	23.9	8.6	22.7	13.4	3.3	4.3	0.2	12.1	2.9	11.5	5.1	39.9	694
Roosevelt County	6 630	54.4	26.7	10.8	14.3	8.8	2.2	6.4	0.8	9.8	2.2	15.0	6.2	37.7	180
Sandoval County	31 412	58.8	29.0	9.1	16.7	9.9	2.4	4.6	0.4	8.7	1.9	11.2	5.1	36.8	1 264
San Juan County	37 740	57.2	30.5	8.3	20.2	12.6	2.2	3.5	0.3	9.3	1.7	9.9	4.8	37.3	1 877
San Miguel County	11 133	44.0	21.4	7.0	23.9	14.3	4.1	5.5	0.8	13.8	2.6	12.9	5.4	40.1	502
Santa Fe County	52 481	46.8	20.8	7.4	16.1	10.1	2.1	7.7	0.7	12.2	2.1	17.2	5.7	43.3	1 297
Sierra County	6 103	47.7	14.4	17.5	11.3	6.3	2.7	5.0	0.9	17.0	8.9	18.9	11.5	49.2	138
Socorro County	6 690	48.5	21.1	8.7	19.7	13.7	2.9	5.5	0.2	13.9	2.4	12.4	6.1	41.6	317
Taos County	12 701	42.9	19.8	7.4	18.7	11.5	2.5	6.5	0.7	13.7	2.9	18.3	7.2	49.0	318
Torrance County	6 067	56.1	27.9	9.5	16.9	10.0	2.3	4.0	0.2	11.6	2.7	11.3	5.1	39.6	183
Union County	1 728	55.4	22.7	14.3	12.6	8.4	2.1	2.0	0.5	14.5	4.2	15.6	9.8	45.4	29
Valencia County	22 714	57.9	28.6	9.5	18.5	11.6	2.1	4.8	0.4	9.3	1.8	9.5	4.7	34.9	791
NEW YORK	7 060 595	47.6	22.4	8.5	18.6	9.8	2.7	5.7	0.5	11.4	2.5	16.7	7.8	46.8	143 014
Albany County	120 645	43.7	19.4	8.5	15.3	9.1	2.3	7.9	0.4	13.9	2.9	19.1	8.6	50.4	1 292
Allegany County	18 056	55.1	23.9	11.3	12.5	7.8	1.7	6.2	0.6	11.3	3.1	14.8	8.5	46.1	266
Bronx County	463 242	32.2	16.8	5.0	36.3	22.1	3.7	4.2	0.4	11.0	2.4	16.4	7.2	51.5	18 970
Broome County	80 917	48.4	20.3	10.8	14.3	8.5	2.3	6.5	0.5	12.7	3.1	18.1	9.5	48.2	1 221
Cattaraugus County	32 055	53.4	23.6	10.4	14.6	9.3	2.0	5.2	0.7	12.0	3.0	14.9	8.9	47.8	576
Cayuga County	30 589	53.4	23.6	10.6	15.2	9.5	2.0	5.3	0.5	10.8	2.9	15.3	9.0	47.7	359
Chautauqua County	54 488	52.0	21.8	11.4	14.3	9.0	1.8	5.5	0.5	11.6	2.9	16.5	9.8	48.2	840
Chemung County	35 076	50.5	21.2	10.6	16.4	10.5	2.4	5.3	0.4	10.9	3.0	16.8	9.0	47.4	712
Chenango County	19 892	53.5	22.8	10.6	14.7	9.9	1.7	5.8	0.5	11.1	3.0	14.9	8.8	47.9	314
Clinton County	29 479	52.2	23.5	8.7	13.5	9.2	1.5	8.0	0.5	11.4	2.6	14.9	7.9	49.4	452
Columbia County	24 852	53.4	22.0	11.1	13.6	7.9	2.4	5.9	0.7	11.3	3.2	15.8	8.6	45.3	313
Cortland County	18 249	49.4	21.5	8.6	14.8	9.4	1.6	9.4	0.7	11.4	2.6	15.0	7.8	48.8	229
Delaware County	19 245	53.3	20.5	12.8	13.2	7.7	2.3	5.3	0.6	12.1	4.0	16.1	9.7	46.8	207
Dutchess County	99 719	56.6	27.8	9.1	13.4	7.5	2.0	5.5	0.5	10.6	2.3	14.0	7.0	44.5	1 505
Erie County	380 890	47.5	20.7	10.2	16.7	9.4	2.7	5.3	0.4	12.1	3.1	18.4	9.0	49.4	5 049
Essex County	15 015	52.8	21.7	11.6	13.2	7.8	2.7	5.9	0.6	12.0	3.2	16.2	9.1	45.4	201
Franklin County	17 985	50.0	22.7	8.9	16.2	9.9	2.5	5.7	0.4	12.0	3.1	16.0	9.2	50.9	206
Fulton County	21 879	51.6	20.7	12.0	15.4	10.0	1.5	5.4	0.3	10.7	2.6	16.8	10.6	49.0	308

Table A-3. States and Counties — Age, Ethnicity, and Household Structure

STATE County	Households with Non-Hispanic White householder — Number of households	Percent that are family households	Households with Black or African American householder — Number of households	Percent that are family households	Households with American Indian and Alaska Native householder — Number of households	Percent that are family households	Households with Asian, Hawaiian, and Pacific Islander householder — Number of households	Percent that are family households	Households with Hispanic or Latino[1] householder — Number of households	Percent that are family households	Foreign-born population — Percent of total population that is foreign-born	Place of birth (percent) Europe	Asia	Latin America	Percent in non-English speaking households — Linguistically isolated	Not linguistically isolated
	44	45	46	47	48	49	50	51	52	53	54	55	56	57	58	59
NEW JERSEY— Cont'd																
Mercer County............	87 600	67.2	22 538	68.3	242	81.4	5 082	82.3	8 936	81.0	13.9	3.8	3.8	5.1	5.1	21.9
Middlesex County.........	182 422	68.5	22 311	71.6	376	83.8	31 058	85.6	26 158	84.3	24.2	4.6	11.0	7.1	7.2	33.1
Monmouth County........	188 186	71.1	16 592	69.7	283	55.8	7 174	83.5	10 450	80.9	10.4	3.2	3.1	3.5	2.8	18.2
Morris County	145 389	73.0	4 350	65.2	144	84.7	8 996	86.9	9 483	81.0	15.4	4.7	5.2	4.7	4.0	22.0
Ocean County	185 891	68.3	4 806	77.3	307	71.3	1 859	82.0	6 738	81.5	6.5	3.2	1.2	1.7	2.2	14.9
Passaic County	98 727	68.3	20 218	72.1	388	85.8	5 011	85.8	37 323	86.5	26.6	5.3	4.5	16.4	12.3	36.4
Salem County	19 976	72.2	3 334	69.3	108	48.1	107	79.4	604	82.3	2.5	0.9	0.6	0.8	1.3	10.0
Somerset County	86 171	70.3	7 616	72.3	126	54.0	7 451	86.1	6 687	85.2	18.1	4.6	6.4	5.9	4.7	24.3
Sussex County	48 106	76.7	412	70.9	73	86.3	414	85.5	1 427	74.4	5.7	3.0	1.0	1.2	0.8	13.5
Union County	112 523	68.6	35 753	72.9	327	67.9	5 820	83.8	29 385	82.1	25.1	6.8	3.1	14.1	9.5	32.4
Warren County	30 400	71.1	675	66.8	33	54.5	298	93.0	960	76.5	5.8	2.7	1.1	1.7	1.3	12.0
NEW MEXICO..........	362 890	64.0	12 895	64.6	47 487	79.1	6 284	69.1	242 878	75.5	8.2	0.8	0.8	6.3	6.2	42.5
Bernalillo County	125 233	59.6	6 289	60.7	7 494	68.0	3 451	68.8	76 404	72.1	8.6	1.0	1.4	5.8	5.0	36.0
Catron County	1 250	65.7	0	X	29	75.9	0	X	278	68.7	1.6	0.4	0.0	1.0	2.5	22.5
Chaves County	13 829	66.9	499	62.9	187	75.4	130	76.2	7 811	81.5	11.2	0.6	0.6	9.9	7.2	36.2
Cibola County	2 715	69.8	89	56.2	2 689	81.7	38	81.6	2 719	75.8	2.3	0.3	0.2	1.5	5.2	58.6
Colfax County	3 318	67.3	10	30.0	63	44.4	14	14.3	2 361	72.5	2.2	0.7	0.4	1.1	2.8	35.3
Curry County	11 030	68.9	1 038	74.9	225	85.8	329	64.7	4 053	76.7	5.9	0.6	1.9	3.2	3.4	30.7
De Baca County	632	65.7	0	X	14	71.4	2	100.0	282	69.9	3.7	0.2	0.2	3.3	7.0	31.9
Dona Ana County.........	25 569	63.1	957	66.1	782	76.0	507	76.9	31 507	80.3	18.7	0.6	0.6	17.3	11.5	53.9
Eddy County	12 467	70.4	338	64.8	177	63.3	87	92.0	6 186	78.2	5.3	0.5	0.3	4.4	4.3	35.3
Grant County	6 671	66.7	73	64.4	106	89.6	62	32.3	5 148	75.9	3.3	0.4	0.1	2.6	4.3	44.6
Guadalupe County	279	69.2	0	X	15	100.0	3	100.0	1 366	70.4	4.0	0.2	0.1	3.5	8.0	76.0
Harding County	188	61.7	0	X	6	66.7	0	X	165	61.2	2.5	0.9	0.0	1.6	6.7	44.7
Hidalgo County	1 046	68.5	9	44.4	15	33.3	3	0.0	1 075	75.5	11.1	0.2	0.1	10.8	7.3	49.5
Lea County	12 547	71.9	881	68.0	194	49.0	83	68.7	5 957	83.8	11.3	0.2	0.3	10.7	6.8	33.6
Lincoln County	6 333	68.7	24	91.7	109	79.8	15	100.0	1 662	68.6	6.1	0.8	0.2	4.9	4.0	24.5
Los Alamos County.......	6 481	72.0	32	31.3	42	78.6	271	76.0	581	74.0	6.7	2.6	2.9	0.6	1.6	17.5
Luna County	4 844	63.0	60	80.0	152	50.7	28	21.4	4 287	80.3	19.5	0.4	0.3	18.6	12.6	45.8
McKinley County	4 154	61.8	122	62.3	14 157	82.7	141	68.8	2 759	76.0	1.8	0.1	0.3	1.3	10.1	69.3
Mora County	421	72.2	0	X	7	100.0	0	X	1 585	68.6	1.7	0.1	0.0	1.3	14.5	69.7
Otero County	14 733	71.1	792	79.8	1 027	80.1	159	50.9	5 857	79.5	11.1	3.3	0.8	6.8	6.4	34.9
Quay County	2 687	65.9	37	78.4	29	44.8	27	100.0	1 414	70.9	3.4	0.3	0.8	2.4	2.6	36.7
Rio Arriba County.........	2 735	59.5	47	89.4	1 711	76.2	32	93.8	10 520	74.8	3.7	0.2	0.0	3.4	9.7	71.4
Roosevelt County	4 666	65.9	122	72.1	51	58.8	13	100.0	1 758	76.9	6.2	0.3	0.4	5.5	5.2	30.8
Sandoval County	18 532	72.3	535	69.5	3 405	86.6	187	75.9	8 246	79.3	4.3	1.1	0.8	2.1	3.6	38.8
San Juan County	20 770	74.0	107	62.0	11 200	84.0	100	87.0	5 069	77.0	2.4	0.2	0.2	1.8	4.2	43.4
San Miguel County........	2 486	55.4	45	60.0	121	71.9	25	68.0	8 430	71.4	2.5	0.7	0.3	1.2	7.6	70.3
Santa Fe County	28 446	54.8	316	54.7	1 399	66.7	362	61.0	21 426	73.6	10.1	1.7	0.6	7.4	6.3	44.2
Sierra County	4 754	57.0	10	50.0	72	52.8	9	100.0	1 153	70.0	6.6	0.8	0.2	5.6	3.8	25.2
Socorro County	3 125	60.2	11	100.0	470	82.1	83	67.5	2 857	75.6	6.4	0.5	0.7	4.7	8.1	48.9
Taos County	5 288	51.4	43	39.5	725	67.6	36	8.3	6 492	70.2	4.1	0.8	0.3	2.7	7.3	58.9
Torrance County	3 978	69.3	22	100.0	54	81.5	0	X	1 916	79.6	4.2	0.4	0.3	3.4	2.3	36.5
Union County	1 145	66.2	0	X	13	30.8	4	0.0	648	71.9	2.2	0.0	0.1	2.0	5.2	28.0
Valencia County	10 530	73.0	307	59.3	687	72.6	83	75.9	11 006	80.7	6.4	0.3	0.3	5.7	5.2	43.0
NEW YORK..........	4 763 779	63.8	1 031 866	66.8	25 618	69.3	323 779	74.9	840 357	75.9	20.4	4.6	4.8	10.0	7.8	27.2
Albany County.............	101 741	58.9	12 016	59.4	309	49.2	2 556	64.9	2 766	58.8	6.5	2.3	2.3	1.2	1.6	13.3
Allegany County	17 614	68.1	60	35.0	53	50.9	102	63.7	83	56.6	1.8	0.6	0.8	0.2	0.4	6.6
Bronx County	86 457	54.5	169 483	66.5	3 033	76.5	12 063	79.7	201 106	75.8	29.0	3.0	2.2	21.7	15.8	46.1
Broome County	75 009	62.9	2 379	61.9	145	55.9	1 466	57.6	1 240	61.6	5.3	2.1	2.1	0.6	1.5	11.4
Cattaraugus County	30 545	67.9	261	64.8	739	72.0	139	78.4	175	67.4	1.4	0.6	0.4	0.1	1.0	8.2
Cayuga County	29 502	68.6	341	76.8	126	61.1	55	49.1	352	53.4	2.3	1.1	0.4	0.5	0.5	10.0
Chautauqua County	51 436	66.2	835	54.9	260	54.2	117	85.5	1 534	78.7	1.9	0.9	0.3	0.4	1.3	10.5
Chemung County	33 030	66.7	1 198	68.4	116	62.9	215	90.7	236	61.0	2.2	0.9	0.7	0.4	0.3	8.1
Chenango County	19 446	68.3	74	33.8	51	80.4	56	66.1	186	72.0	1.7	1.0	0.3	0.1	0.3	8.1
Clinton County	28 531	65.9	264	56.8	77	67.5	213	62.9	183	67.2	4.5	1.0	0.8	0.8	0.5	10.4
Columbia County..........	23 384	67.0	743	64.2	42	59.5	139	74.1	379	74.4	4.4	2.4	0.6	1.0	1.2	10.0
Cortland County	17 619	64.9	124	43.5	72	54.2	41	63.4	162	53.1	2.2	1.6	0.2	0.2	0.6	8.0
Delaware County	18 570	66.5	114	53.5	87	69.0	98	68.4	218	63.8	3.4	2.3	0.5	0.4	0.6	10.0
Dutchess County	84 778	69.6	7 343	69.5	133	71.4	2 233	76.0	4 226	76.4	8.4	3.1	2.0	2.8	1.7	17.1
Erie County	314 770	64.5	47 922	61.0	2 198	65.0	4 308	64.7	9 439	68.0	4.5	2.0	1.3	0.4	1.5	12.7
Essex County	14 697	66.3	46	73.9	59	44.1	32	56.3	69	43.5	3.4	1.3	0.4	0.9	0.5	6.7
Franklin County	16 635	65.6	80	66.3	1 066	74.4	15	53.3	115	80.0	3.7	0.6	0.1	1.4	0.4	9.7
Fulton County..............	21 339	67.0	192	67.2	70	82.9	88	56.8	114	77.2	1.9	1.2	0.4	0.1	0.4	8.7

[1] Hispanic or Latino persons may be of any race.

STATE/ County code	MSA/PMSA/ NECMA code[1]	STATE County	Population by age (percent)										Non-Hispanic White		
														Age (percent)	
			Total population	Under 5 years	5 to 17 years	18 to 24 years	25 to 44 years	45 to 64 years	65 years and over	Median age	+/− U.S. percent under 18 years	+/− U.S. percent 65 years and over	Total population	Under 18 years	65 years and over
			1	2	3	4	5	6	7	8	9	10	11	12	13
		NEW YORK—Cont'd													
36 037	6840	Genesee County	60 370	6.0	19.9	7.6	29.4	22.8	14.3	37.4	0.2	1.9	57 045	25.5	14.7
36 039	...	Greene County	48 195	5.2	17.6	9.6	27.1	24.9	15.6	39.1	-2.9	3.2	42 719	23.2	17.0
36 041	...	Hamilton County	5 379	4.3	15.6	5.4	23.9	30.8	20.1	45.4	-5.8	7.7	5 263	19.7	20.2
36 043	8680	Herkimer County	64 427	5.5	18.8	8.2	26.6	23.9	16.9	39.0	-1.4	4.5	62 787	24.1	17.2
36 045	...	Jefferson County	111 738	7.3	19.1	11.8	31.3	19.0	11.4	32.5	0.7	-1.0	97 489	25.8	12.8
36 047	5600	Kings County	2 465 326	7.3	19.4	10.3	30.9	20.6	11.5	33.1	1.0	-0.9	854 653	20.9	19.0
36 049	...	Lewis County	26 944	6.1	21.6	7.8	28.1	22.6	13.8	36.8	2.0	1.4	26 445	27.5	13.9
36 051	6840	Livingston County	64 328	5.5	17.8	14.4	28.7	22.2	11.4	35.3	-2.4	-1.0	59 828	23.6	12.0
36 053	8160	Madison County	69 441	5.9	19.1	11.9	27.6	23.0	12.5	36.1	-0.7	0.1	66 289	25.0	13.0
36 055	6840	Monroe County	735 343	6.3	19.2	9.5	29.4	22.6	13.0	36.1	-0.2	0.6	566 424	22.2	15.4
36 057	0160	Montgomery County	49 708	5.9	18.6	7.3	26.3	22.8	19.1	39.7	-1.2	6.7	45 127	22.9	20.6
36 059	5380	Nassau County	1 334 544	6.4	18.2	7.3	29.0	24.0	15.0	38.5	-1.1	2.6	986 378	22.8	18.2
36 061	5600	New York County	1 537 195	4.9	11.7	10.1	38.6	22.5	12.1	35.7	-9.1	-0.3	703 462	9.0	14.1
36 063	1280	Niagara County	219 846	6.0	18.7	8.4	28.5	23.0	15.5	38.2	-1.0	3.1	197 431	23.2	16.5
36 065	8680	Oneida County	235 469	5.7	18.2	8.6	28.2	22.7	16.5	38.2	-1.8	4.1	208 198	22.9	18.0
36 067	8160	Onondaga County	458 336	6.5	19.3	9.5	29.0	21.9	13.8	36.3	0.1	1.4	383 642	23.3	15.6
36 069	6840	Ontario County	100 224	6.1	19.3	8.2	28.5	24.7	13.2	37.9	-0.3	0.8	94 334	24.5	13.6
36 071	5660	Orange County	341 367	7.6	21.4	8.7	30.1	21.9	10.3	34.7	3.3	-2.1	265 003	27.3	12.0
36 073	6840	Orleans County	44 171	6.3	19.9	8.0	31.8	21.6	12.4	36.2	0.5	0.0	38 656	26.5	13.6
36 075	8160	Oswego County	122 377	6.2	20.6	11.0	28.9	22.0	11.3	35.0	1.1	-1.1	118 029	26.4	11.6
36 077	...	Otsego County	61 676	4.7	17.9	14.5	24.6	23.2	15.1	37.1	-3.1	2.7	58 587	22.2	15.8
36 079	5600	Putnam County	95 745	6.9	19.4	6.2	32.3	25.6	9.6	37.4	0.6	-2.8	85 774	25.9	10.2
36 081	5600	Queens County	2 229 379	6.3	16.5	9.5	33.3	21.7	12.7	35.4	-2.9	0.3	732 968	15.6	24.0
36 083	0160	Rensselaer County	152 538	6.1	18.1	10.1	29.2	23.0	13.6	36.7	-1.5	1.2	138 002	23.3	14.5
36 085	5600	Richmond County	443 728	6.6	18.8	8.4	31.0	23.6	11.6	35.9	-0.3	-0.8	316 600	22.5	14.1
36 087	5600	Rockland County	286 753	7.6	20.4	7.8	28.2	24.3	11.7	36.2	2.3	-0.7	205 288	26.8	14.1
36 089	...	St. Lawrence County	111 931	5.3	18.1	13.9	27.5	22.2	13.0	35.4	-2.3	0.6	104 910	23.9	13.6
36 091	0160	Saratoga County	200 635	6.5	18.5	7.7	31.7	24.2	11.4	36.9	-0.7	-1.0	190 358	24.6	11.8
36 093	0160	Schenectady County	146 555	6.1	18.2	7.8	28.5	22.9	16.6	38.6	-1.4	4.2	126 516	22.0	18.6
36 095	0160	Schoharie County	31 582	5.6	18.4	10.5	26.3	24.4	14.9	38.0	-1.7	2.5	30 077	23.9	15.2
36 097	...	Schuyler County	19 224	5.8	19.4	7.9	26.8	25.3	14.7	38.8	-0.5	2.3	18 403	24.9	15.1
36 099	...	Seneca County	33 342	5.5	19.4	7.4	28.8	23.8	15.1	38.2	-0.8	2.7	31 195	24.7	15.9
36 101	...	Steuben County	98 726	6.1	19.8	7.5	27.3	24.1	15.2	38.2	0.2	2.8	95 033	25.7	15.5
36 103	5380	Suffolk County	1 419 369	7.0	19.0	7.6	31.4	23.2	11.8	36.5	0.3	-0.6	1 117 720	24.4	13.6
36 105	...	Sullivan County	73 966	5.8	19.1	7.2	28.2	25.4	14.3	38.8	-0.8	1.9	59 092	23.6	16.4
36 107	0960	Tioga County	51 784	6.3	20.7	7.0	29.0	23.9	13.1	38.0	1.3	0.7	50 014	26.6	13.2
36 109	...	Tompkins County	96 501	4.4	14.7	25.9	26.3	19.1	9.6	28.6	-6.6	-2.8	81 031	18.8	10.9
36 111	...	Ulster County	177 749	5.4	18.0	8.7	30.0	24.6	13.3	38.2	-2.3	0.9	152 218	22.7	14.7
36 113	2975	Warren County	63 303	5.5	18.6	7.5	28.3	25.0	15.1	39.0	-1.6	2.7	61 343	23.7	15.3
36 115	2975	Washington County	61 042	5.6	19.0	8.3	29.4	23.7	14.0	37.5	-1.1	1.6	57 295	25.3	14.8
36 117	6840	Wayne County	93 765	6.4	20.9	6.8	30.2	23.6	12.1	36.9	1.6	-0.3	87 030	26.5	12.6
36 119	5600	Westchester County	923 459	6.9	18.0	7.0	30.7	23.4	14.0	37.6	-0.8	1.6	591 526	22.3	18.2
36 121	...	Wyoming County	43 424	5.3	18.8	8.0	32.9	23.0	12.1	36.7	-1.6	-0.3	39 343	25.8	13.2
36 123	...	Yates County	24 621	6.6	20.0	9.5	24.5	23.8	15.6	37.9	0.9	3.2	23 828	26.4	15.8
37 000		NORTH CAROLINA	8 049 313	6.7	17.7	10.0	31.2	22.4	12.0	35.3	-1.3	-0.4	5 648 953	21.8	14.1
37 001	3120	Alamance County	130 800	6.4	17.4	9.9	30.0	22.2	14.1	36.3	-1.9	1.7	94 679	21.3	16.5
37 003	3290	Alexander County	33 603	6.8	17.5	8.0	30.9	24.9	11.8	36.6	-1.4	-0.6	30 643	23.6	12.2
37 005	...	Alleghany County	10 677	5.2	14.1	7.4	26.3	27.7	19.3	43.0	-6.4	6.9	9 881	18.9	20.4
37 007	...	Anson County	25 275	6.3	18.9	8.2	29.6	22.5	14.4	36.6	-0.5	2.0	12 472	20.3	19.4
37 009	...	Ashe County	24 384	5.3	14.6	7.4	27.1	27.7	17.9	42.1	-5.8	5.5	23 474	19.5	18.3
37 011	...	Avery County	17 167	5.0	14.4	10.3	30.0	24.6	15.7	38.4	-6.3	3.3	15 884	19.8	16.8
37 013	...	Beaufort County	44 958	6.0	17.6	7.8	26.0	26.7	16.0	40.2	-2.1	3.6	30 145	20.3	17.8
37 015	...	Bertie County	19 773	6.1	20.0	7.5	26.8	23.6	16.0	38.6	0.4	3.6	7 116	19.0	20.7
37 017	...	Bladen County	32 278	6.9	17.8	9.0	27.0	24.7	14.6	37.9	-1.0	2.2	18 066	20.7	16.6
37 019	9200	Brunswick County	73 143	5.5	15.7	6.9	25.7	29.3	16.9	42.2	-4.5	4.5	59 277	18.9	18.7
37 021	0480	Buncombe County	206 330	5.6	16.3	8.5	29.5	24.7	15.4	38.9	-3.8	3.0	180 882	20.7	16.3
37 023	3290	Burke County	89 148	6.2	17.9	8.8	30.0	23.8	13.4	36.9	-1.6	1.0	75 794	22.1	14.7
37 025	1520	Cabarrus County	131 063	7.1	18.8	7.9	32.6	22.0	11.6	35.4	0.2	-0.8	106 182	24.2	12.8
37 027	3290	Caldwell County	77 415	6.3	17.0	7.5	30.7	25.1	13.4	37.5	-2.4	1.0	70 441	22.7	13.7
37 029	...	Camden County	6 885	5.5	19.2	6.0	31.5	24.4	13.4	39.1	-1.0	1.0	5 565	24.9	12.7
37 031	...	Carteret County	59 383	4.9	15.7	6.2	27.5	28.6	17.1	42.3	-5.1	4.7	52 927	19.6	18.2
37 033	...	Caswell County	23 501	5.8	17.5	7.7	30.1	25.8	13.1	38.2	-2.4	0.7	14 285	22.7	13.8
37 035	3290	Catawba County	141 685	6.6	17.7	8.8	31.0	23.6	12.2	36.1	-1.4	-0.2	116 583	22.3	13.8
37 037	6640	Chatham County	49 329	6.1	16.3	6.8	30.9	24.3	15.6	38.8	-3.3	3.2	35 337	20.3	17.9
37 039	...	Cherokee County	24 298	5.4	15.2	6.5	24.0	29.2	19.8	44.0	-5.1	7.4	22 808	20.2	20.3

[1]MSA = Metropolitan Statistical Area. PMSA = Primary MSA. NECMA = New England County Metropolitan Area. See the Appendix A for explanation of these concepts. See Appendix B for list of metropolitan areas identified by type, with component counties.

Table A-3. States and Counties — Age, Ethnicity, and Household Structure

STATE County	Black or African American	Age (percent)		American Indian and Alaska Native	Age (percent)		Asian, Hawaiian, and Pacific Islander	Age (percent)		Hispanic or Latino[1]	Age (percent)		Two or more races	Age (percent)	
	Total population	Under 18 years	65 years and over	Total population	Under 18 years	65 years and over	Total population	Under 18 years	65 years and over	Total population	Under 18 years	65 years and over	Total population	Under 18 years	65 years and over
	14	15	16	17	18	19	20	21	22	23	24	25	26	27	28
NEW YORK—Cont'd															
Genesee County	1 193	31.2	7.4	529	25.9	12.7	257	20.2	1.2	724	34.8	0.8	741	41.4	8.0
Greene County	2 659	10.9	4.9	117	5.1	12.0	233	21.9	9.4	2 070	24.3	2.8	582	50.5	5.2
Hamilton County	9	77.8	22.2	20	0.0	35.0	7	0.0	0.0	37	21.6	0.0	37	32.4	21.6
Herkimer County	320	41.6	10.9	72	34.7	4.2	265	15.8	3.0	502	32.3	5.0	593	39.1	9.6
Jefferson County	6 310	27.7	0.3	682	28.3	4.0	1 314	29.8	1.4	4 479	30.4	0.8	2 211	51.0	4.3
Kings County	893 000	30.1	8.4	8 533	33.5	6.9	187 363	24.7	7.0	488 163	31.5	6.0	108 854	29.6	7.1
Lewis County	102	49.0	4.9	93	17.2	1.1	58	41.4	8.6	133	43.6	6.0	121	49.6	3.3
Livingston County	1 783	3.5	6.7	154	38.3	4.5	685	20.3	1.9	1 389	22.6	2.7	681	44.5	2.9
Madison County	887	12.2	4.1	326	32.8	1.8	501	20.2	0.2	845	28.5	0.4	644	38.0	6.5
Monroe County	99 183	36.9	5.4	2 409	25.7	7.3	17 913	26.9	4.7	38 546	40.2	4.2	16 828	47.5	4.1
Montgomery County	528	27.1	8.5	73	5.5	5.5	356	40.2	1.1	3 438	40.3	3.8	504	49.8	8.1
Nassau County	133 525	30.0	7.9	1 841	32.0	8.1	62 946	28.5	5.8	133 041	29.7	4.2	30 087	31.9	5.7
New York County	265 682	23.9	13.0	6 904	28.5	7.2	144 980	13.1	10.4	418 005	26.6	9.1	63 335	24.0	8.3
Niagara County	13 434	35.5	7.6	2 053	37.1	4.7	1 237	24.6	6.5	2 879	37.8	7.1	3 353	54.0	3.0
Oneida County	13 398	27.5	6.3	495	15.4	7.5	2 795	30.5	4.9	7 414	32.0	3.1	4 173	45.1	3.4
Onondaga County	42 096	38.5	5.7	4 104	34.4	5.5	9 697	24.9	3.8	10 726	42.2	3.5	10 119	51.1	4.0
Ontario County	1 852	31.4	10.3	196	11.2	8.2	700	39.3	5.3	2 185	44.7	3.7	1 229	52.2	7.6
Orange County	26 621	32.6	6.5	1 187	32.4	1.6	5 558	26.3	4.5	39 840	36.3	3.3	8 531	48.6	2.8
Orleans County	3 140	16.3	5.4	195	22.6	6.7	107	39.3	2.8	1 747	25.9	2.3	521	57.6	4.8
Oswego County	630	22.4	4.9	441	35.1	3.9	556	21.9	3.6	1 401	37.3	1.9	1 476	48.2	1.9
Otsego County	1 090	28.4	2.6	95	15.8	1.1	312	20.5	7.7	1 106	31.4	2.0	634	37.5	2.2
Putnam County	1 219	21.4	7.5	262	30.2	2.3	1 225	24.5	2.3	5 973	28.9	4.6	1 467	44.9	3.8
Queens County	441 601	27.8	10.1	9 925	31.6	6.4	395 708	22.8	6.6	556 486	27.5	5.4	139 197	27.5	5.8
Rensselaer County	7 192	33.7	6.6	190	20.0	4.7	2 459	23.1	1.5	2 802	36.8	3.0	2 277	40.1	4.7
Richmond County	42 689	35.3	5.3	866	29.8	10.3	24 754	24.9	7.6	53 654	34.7	4.4	12 042	39.1	5.0
Rockland County	30 696	31.9	6.6	601	20.3	10.8	16 383	27.7	6.0	29 055	30.5	4.3	7 787	38.0	5.1
St. Lawrence County	2 628	5.9	1.4	1 037	32.2	5.5	674	21.5	2.1	1 923	15.5	2.0	965	26.9	11.5
Saratoga County	2 581	22.2	5.1	439	26.0	4.6	2 229	31.9	5.8	3 000	33.6	1.1	2 190	46.1	5.9
Schenectady County	9 538	38.8	5.3	407	36.6	5.2	2 912	25.3	2.4	4 620	45.0	2.5	3 265	47.7	4.5
Schoharie County	497	16.7	8.5	120	51.7	1.7	89	11.2	0.0	546	21.4	11.9	350	33.1	3.7
Schuyler County	252	22.2	2.8	65	26.2	13.8	38	10.5	23.7	193	37.8	2.1	297	43.8	4.4
Seneca County	792	15.5	2.7	138	53.6	7.2	345	26.7	0.0	640	25.8	0.8	326	45.1	11.3
Steuben County	1 083	20.9	12.9	302	17.2	4.3	838	31.1	5.7	628	38.2	5.1	922	41.1	6.3
Suffolk County	97 215	33.4	6.7	4 009	29.7	8.6	34 570	23.7	5.0	149 422	32.2	4.0	30 754	39.6	5.3
Sullivan County	6 155	25.5	8.1	200	23.5	5.0	911	25.8	4.9	7 041	33.4	4.5	1 531	47.0	4.6
Tioga County	311	25.1	23.2	115	23.5	1.7	376	23.1	17.0	482	43.6	3.9	549	46.6	2.4
Tompkins County	3 312	28.8	6.3	245	13.5	0.0	7 181	10.8	1.3	2 935	24.3	1.4	2 166	34.2	3.2
Ulster County	9 640	23.9	5.4	511	19.8	4.3	1 847	19.9	3.4	10 846	30.0	4.9	3 801	40.9	5.8
Warren County	320	33.4	10.0	79	2.5	6.3	548	33.0	11.3	509	41.3	5.1	592	38.7	8.1
Washington County	1 832	7.2	1.3	217	24.0	0.0	226	30.5	0.4	1 156	11.8	1.0	486	37.9	8.2
Wayne County	2 735	34.1	8.4	193	26.9	5.7	394	40.1	1.3	2 218	40.3	3.7	1 450	48.5	2.3
Westchester County	128 916	28.8	9.5	2 633	31.5	8.4	41 941	26.4	5.4	144 550	30.6	4.0	29 960	34.2	5.8
Wyoming County	2 475	1.1	1.3	94	9.6	2.1	139	28.1	1.4	1 268	11.0	0.8	277	35.7	7.2
Yates County	101	34.7	8.9	57	47.4	0.0	86	40.7	0.0	263	24.0	8.4	303	37.0	10.6
NORTH CAROLINA	1 734 154	29.8	8.9	100 956	30.1	6.4	114 991	27.0	3.7	372 964	31.4	1.5	111 909	42.7	3.6
Alamance County	24 493	28.5	10.3	715	29.2	9.2	1 211	29.6	2.4	8 759	33.6	0.6	1 608	41.9	4.5
Alexander County	1 587	24.3	11.8	56	32.1	0.0	345	55.4	0.0	715	31.0	2.5	317	46.1	6.3
Alleghany County	121	4.1	23.1	36	0.0	0.0	65	30.8	0.0	454	26.2	3.3	141	27.0	0.0
Anson County	12 413	29.8	9.8	149	20.8	0.7	32	40.6	6.3	134	29.9	2.2	97	67.0	2.1
Ashe County	235	25.1	20.0	64	23.4	0.0	56	28.6	12.5	484	24.8	1.2	121	68.6	2.5
Avery County	588	2.4	1.4	36	0.0	5.6	106	15.1	3.8	422	27.7	0.7	118	42.4	11.0
Beaufort County	13 217	29.5	13.7	94	27.7	11.7	116	23.3	1.7	1 223	35.7	0.0	271	46.1	2.6
Bertie County	12 364	30.0	13.4	66	40.9	0.0	39	15.4	0.0	156	25.6	17.9	86	55.8	12.8
Bladen County	12 274	29.5	13.1	604	32.8	8.4	22	45.5	0.0	1 178	33.9	1.8	274	31.4	6.6
Brunswick County	10 575	30.6	10.6	422	31.5	4.3	149	17.4	14.1	2 018	28.2	2.0	829	39.9	4.6
Buncombe County	15 063	29.6	12.1	833	27.1	4.9	1 907	23.6	4.2	5 469	31.5	2.5	2 454	37.9	6.0
Burke County	5 894	24.4	9.4	397	35.0	2.0	3 034	52.9	2.7	3 050	32.7	1.5	1 281	44.7	4.5
Cabarrus County	16 025	30.4	9.5	445	17.1	2.9	1 083	34.8	2.5	6 623	37.9	0.8	1 192	55.0	3.2
Caldwell County	4 466	30.1	13.5	173	18.5	1.2	250	26.8	8.0	1 731	28.4	3.5	562	47.5	7.5
Camden County	1 043	18.5	19.8	22	59.1	0.0	22	54.5	0.0	108	43.5	0.0	125	40.8	11.2
Carteret County	4 191	28.8	8.6	341	10.3	3.8	282	18.8	13.1	929	28.2	5.8	734	42.1	8.9
Caswell County	8 621	23.8	12.7	35	11.4	0.0	33	0.0	33.3	340	30.9	0.0	217	41.9	5.1
Catawba County	12 004	32.5	7.8	592	30.2	1.0	3 798	44.3	2.2	7 812	27.6	1.5	1 554	46.9	2.8
Chatham County	8 337	24.1	15.6	199	41.7	4.5	251	25.9	4.4	4 813	31.2	0.9	457	49.2	2.6
Cherokee County	415	31.1	10.8	362	13.8	18.5	88	34.1	25.0	199	12.1	0.0	449	37.9	10.0

[1] Hispanic or Latino persons may be of any race.

Table A-3. States and Counties — Age, Ethnicity, and Household Structure

STATE County	Total households	Family households (percent)						Nonfamily households (percent)						Percent of householders 65 years and over who live alone	Grandparents who are responsible for the care of their grandchildren
		Married-couple family households			Other family households			Two or more unrelated persons		Male living alone		Female living alone			
		Total	With children	Householder 65 years or over	Total	With children	Householder 65 years or over	Total	Householder 65 years or over	Total	Householder 65 years or over	Total	Householder 65 years or over		
	29	30	31	32	33	34	35	36	37	38	39	40	41	42	43

NEW YORK—Cont'd															
Genesee County	22 804	55.8	25.6	9.7	13.9	8.2	2.4	5.5	0.5	9.9	2.6	14.8	8.5	47.0	360
Greene County	18 276	51.8	20.9	10.5	14.4	8.6	2.1	5.8	0.9	12.2	4.0	15.8	8.2	47.7	235
Hamilton County	2 382	55.8	18.3	14.5	10.3	5.5	1.5	4.4	0.5	13.5	5.1	16.0	9.6	47.2	28
Herkimer County	25 740	51.4	21.2	11.0	15.4	9.7	2.2	5.6	0.6	10.9	3.9	16.6	10.7	51.4	381
Jefferson County	40 108	56.8	28.3	8.8	13.6	9.3	1.7	5.1	0.4	10.1	2.1	14.4	7.8	47.4	623
Kings County	881 006	39.7	20.0	6.7	27.1	14.0	3.6	5.4	0.5	10.9	2.5	16.9	7.4	47.9	29 285
Lewis County	10 058	60.1	27.8	10.6	12.6	7.8	2.3	4.7	0.3	9.9	3.0	12.7	8.1	45.8	126
Livingston County	22 149	55.3	25.3	9.3	14.4	9.4	1.8	7.2	0.5	10.1	2.3	13.0	7.2	44.8	245
Madison County	25 392	55.7	25.3	9.8	13.5	8.7	1.9	6.2	0.4	9.9	2.4	14.7	8.3	46.6	340
Monroe County	286 820	48.2	22.2	8.6	16.6	10.2	2.0	6.6	0.3	11.9	2.5	16.7	7.6	48.0	4 963
Montgomery County	20 028	49.4	20.4	12.3	16.1	9.3	2.9	5.1	0.4	11.4	3.3	18.0	12.0	49.6	265
Nassau County	447 803	64.2	30.8	12.9	13.9	5.1	3.5	3.1	0.5	6.5	2.1	12.3	7.4	36.0	6 776
New York County	739 167	25.8	10.2	4.4	15.6	7.5	2.4	10.7	0.6	20.6	3.2	27.3	8.0	60.2	12 451
Niagara County	87 877	51.2	22.1	10.8	15.8	9.2	2.5	4.5	0.3	12.0	2.9	16.6	9.3	47.5	1 216
Oneida County	90 507	50.0	21.7	11.0	15.6	9.3	2.5	4.9	0.4	12.0	3.3	17.5	10.2	49.3	1 251
Onondaga County	181 369	47.8	22.3	9.3	16.2	10.2	2.1	6.6	0.4	11.8	2.6	17.6	8.4	48.4	2 829
Ontario County	38 392	55.6	25.1	9.9	13.5	8.5	1.6	6.2	0.4	10.2	2.4	14.5	7.6	45.6	376
Orange County	114 809	58.9	31.3	8.1	15.2	8.9	2.0	4.5	0.3	9.2	2.0	12.2	6.2	44.0	1 904
Orleans County	15 350	54.2	24.8	9.7	16.7	11.0	1.8	5.5	0.4	10.3	2.5	13.4	8.1	47.0	260
Oswego County	45 525	53.8	25.3	8.5	14.9	10.3	1.6	7.0	0.4	11.0	2.5	13.2	7.3	48.5	736
Otsego County	23 279	51.8	21.3	11.3	13.3	8.5	2.1	7.9	0.7	10.7	3.2	16.2	8.5	45.2	257
Putnam County	32 742	66.4	34.7	8.2	11.3	5.1	2.0	4.3	0.3	7.9	1.5	10.1	4.4	35.6	334
Queens County	782 646	48.1	23.3	8.3	21.3	8.9	3.4	5.1	0.5	10.1	2.4	15.4	7.6	45.0	20 986
Rensselaer County	59 830	50.0	22.3	9.1	15.5	9.4	2.4	6.5	0.4	11.9	2.7	16.1	7.5	46.0	768
Richmond County	156 416	56.4	28.4	7.9	16.9	8.1	2.8	3.5	0.3	9.3	2.1	13.9	6.6	44.3	2 254
Rockland County	92 744	64.2	32.5	10.0	13.1	6.1	2.3	3.5	0.4	6.9	1.7	12.2	6.2	38.6	1 174
St. Lawrence County	40 527	52.4	22.5	10.0	14.5	9.9	1.5	6.6	0.6	10.8	2.7	15.6	8.3	47.6	720
Saratoga County	78 226	57.5	27.0	8.9	11.6	7.4	1.4	6.5	0.4	10.4	1.9	14.0	6.5	44.2	716
Schenectady County	59 732	48.5	20.9	10.6	15.7	9.4	2.4	5.4	0.3	11.9	2.9	18.6	9.7	48.8	726
Schoharie County	12 011	55.0	23.2	11.3	13.5	8.5	2.1	5.8	1.0	11.5	3.3	14.3	8.5	45.0	195
Schuyler County	7 375	55.7	23.2	11.0	14.8	9.8	1.9	5.7	0.4	9.9	2.8	13.8	8.1	44.9	211
Seneca County	12 619	53.9	22.7	10.8	14.5	9.3	2.1	6.3	0.8	9.9	2.9	15.3	9.1	46.9	128
Steuben County	39 093	52.5	22.5	10.4	14.9	9.9	1.9	5.4	0.4	11.4	3.2	15.8	8.9	48.5	563
Suffolk County	469 535	63.2	31.3	9.8	14.1	6.4	2.6	4.4	0.4	7.3	1.9	11.0	6.0	38.1	7 777
Sullivan County	27 681	51.0	21.8	10.9	15.6	10.0	2.1	5.4	0.6	12.6	3.6	15.3	8.2	46.5	482
Tioga County	19 779	59.2	26.9	10.8	13.4	8.9	1.4	4.9	0.4	9.8	2.5	12.6	7.2	43.5	394
Tompkins County	36 464	41.9	18.8	6.8	11.0	7.7	1.1	14.7	0.5	15.1	1.9	17.4	6.3	49.6	276
Ulster County	67 501	50.3	22.9	9.3	14.6	8.6	2.1	7.3	0.5	12.1	2.9	15.7	7.6	46.8	1 147
Warren County	25 729	52.5	22.9	10.5	14.2	8.8	1.8	6.1	0.5	11.7	2.8	15.5	8.1	46.0	209
Washington County	22 442	56.3	24.3	10.6	14.5	8.9	2.2	5.2	0.7	9.7	2.6	14.3	8.0	43.9	414
Wayne County	34 970	57.0	26.4	9.1	14.9	10.0	1.9	5.7	0.5	9.6	2.4	12.8	7.2	45.6	539
Westchester County	337 486	54.9	27.5	10.1	15.3	7.5	2.7	4.1	0.5	9.3	2.3	16.3	8.0	43.7	4 709
Wyoming County	14 877	58.9	26.1	9.7	13.4	8.1	2.5	4.6	0.3	10.8	2.7	12.3	7.2	44.3	212
Yates County	9 056	55.6	23.2	11.5	14.1	9.3	2.1	5.7	0.9	10.4	2.8	14.1	9.2	45.3	153
NORTH CAROLINA	3 133 282	53.4	23.3	8.7	16.0	9.1	2.2	5.3	0.3	10.6	2.0	14.8	6.8	43.9	79 810
Alamance County	51 722	52.6	22.6	9.8	16.6	9.3	2.7	5.0	0.3	10.4	2.0	15.4	7.8	43.2	1 220
Alexander County	13 177	61.6	26.0	9.3	13.2	7.6	1.6	3.4	0.2	10.0	1.9	11.8	6.0	41.6	355
Alleghany County	4 601	59.1	20.5	13.4	9.9	4.0	2.7	3.4	0.8	9.7	3.1	18.0	11.5	46.2	58
Anson County	9 213	47.9	18.0	9.3	25.0	13.1	5.4	2.2	0.2	10.3	3.2	14.6	8.9	44.9	450
Ashe County	10 394	60.0	21.0	13.2	11.5	5.3	3.1	2.7	0.4	10.8	2.9	15.0	8.9	41.2	105
Avery County	6 521	57.2	20.4	12.5	12.3	5.8	3.0	3.7	0.4	10.5	2.9	16.3	9.1	43.2	95
Beaufort County	18 295	54.4	20.0	11.3	16.6	9.2	3.2	3.1	0.3	10.6	2.4	15.3	9.0	43.6	537
Bertie County	7 734	47.1	19.3	10.8	23.6	11.5	4.4	2.3	0.3	11.1	3.7	15.9	10.5	47.8	388
Bladen County	12 873	48.0	19.3	8.8	21.2	11.6	4.0	3.1	0.3	11.1	3.3	16.7	9.1	48.8	598
Brunswick County	30 455	58.9	18.6	15.0	13.8	7.7	2.0	4.4	0.5	10.0	2.4	12.8	6.5	33.7	849
Buncombe County	85 743	51.3	20.3	10.5	13.9	7.8	2.3	5.9	0.3	11.1	2.2	17.8	8.4	44.8	1 665
Burke County	34 566	55.4	23.1	9.3	15.4	8.4	2.5	3.7	0.2	10.5	2.2	15.0	7.3	44.1	1 088
Cabarrus County	49 584	59.3	27.7	8.4	14.8	7.8	2.3	4.2	0.3	9.4	1.9	12.4	6.2	42.3	1 062
Caldwell County	30 822	57.6	22.3	9.9	15.7	8.9	2.3	3.7	0.2	10.1	1.8	12.9	7.0	41.6	978
Camden County	2 669	64.3	25.7	12.8	12.1	7.1	1.4	3.3	0.0	9.1	1.9	11.1	6.4	37.0	66
Carteret County	25 225	57.5	19.8	12.9	11.9	7.1	1.4	4.5	0.3	11.2	3.3	14.8	8.2	44.1	542
Caswell County	8 670	56.4	23.6	9.3	18.1	7.6	4.3	2.2	0.0	9.3	2.4	14.0	8.8	45.1	171
Catawba County	55 540	55.7	23.4	9.3	15.0	8.6	2.2	4.7	0.2	10.1	1.7	14.5	7.2	43.4	1 261
Chatham County	19 742	56.8	22.7	11.4	13.7	6.8	2.5	5.1	0.2	9.8	2.5	14.6	8.2	43.1	361
Cherokee County	10 301	60.1	20.1	14.4	11.6	5.7	2.9	2.5	0.5	10.4	3.1	15.4	8.9	40.2	222

STATE County	Households with Non-Hispanic White householder		Households with Black or African American householder		Households with American Indian and Alaska Native householder		Households with Asian, Hawaiian, and Pacific Islander householder		Households with Hispanic or Latino[1] householder		Foreign-born population				Percent in non-English speaking households	
											Percent of total population that is foreign-born	Place of birth (percent)				
	Number of households	Percent that are family households	Number of households	Percent that are family households	Number of households	Percent that are family households	Number of households	Percent that are family households	Number of households	Percent that are family households		Europe	Asia	Latin America	Linguistically isolated	Not linguistically isolated
	44	45	46	47	48	49	50	51	52	53	54	55	56	57	58	59
NEW YORK—Cont'd																
Genesee County	21 865	70.1	314	57.6	203	66.0	96	65.6	125	60.0	2.2	0.9	0.4	0.5	0.4	7.0
Greene County	17 280	66.1	365	63.6	53	86.8	54	100.0	389	74.6	6.4	4.3	0.5	1.2	1.2	13.1
Hamilton County	2 341	66.2	2	0.0	11	81.8	2	0.0	6	33.3	1.5	1.0	0.1	0.1	0.2	6.7
Herkimer County	25 264	66.8	87	70.1	12	100.0	107	57.0	133	79.7	2.0	1.4	0.4	0.0	0.7	9.0
Jefferson County	37 053	69.6	1 307	84.4	189	78.8	276	76.1	912	85.7	3.7	1.0	0.7	1.1	0.7	11.3
Kings County	352 542	59.4	312 261	68.7	2 641	71.5	52 552	81.6	149 247	75.8	37.8	9.7	7.5	19.5	15.1	39.5
Lewis County	9 926	72.7	20	70.0	31	83.9	18	88.9	23	73.9	1.1	0.4	0.2	0.1	0.2	6.3
Livingston County	21 476	69.8	224	52.7	30	76.7	150	73.3	163	81.6	2.6	0.8	0.8	0.7	0.4	8.7
Madison County	24 839	69.4	103	46.6	81	69.1	84	46.4	159	73.0	2.2	0.9	0.7	0.3	0.3	8.7
Monroe County	230 624	63.9	34 824	67.8	910	67.3	5 217	71.7	12 047	72.0	7.3	3.1	2.2	1.1	2.5	14.9
Montgomery County	18 612	64.9	209	62.7	40	70.0	98	86.7	1 071	73.3	3.2	1.6	0.5	0.9	2.3	14.0
Nassau County	357 560	76.2	37 442	81.5	595	77.1	16 625	91.8	30 954	87.7	17.9	4.7	4.4	8.3	4.2	27.0
New York County	419 015	30.6	113 651	49.8	2 485	56.1	59 862	48.9	140 680	66.4	29.4	5.4	8.0	14.2	13.0	35.1
Niagara County	80 330	67.1	5 141	64.0	627	69.9	325	71.1	866	71.9	3.9	1.7	0.5	0.3	0.8	9.8
Oneida County	83 462	65.6	3 689	63.3	173	65.3	748	74.7	1 585	71.5	5.2	3.2	1.1	0.7	2.5	11.8
Onondaga County	156 281	63.9	15 196	64.6	1 321	70.2	3 373	62.3	3 076	70.4	5.7	2.3	2.1	0.6	1.9	11.8
Ontario County	36 654	69.2	633	76.0	90	50.0	225	52.0	541	68.4	2.7	1.3	0.6	0.5	0.6	8.7
Orange County	93 556	73.7	8 137	68.9	387	71.6	1 575	83.3	10 223	81.3	8.4	2.9	1.4	3.8	4.4	21.3
Orleans County	14 486	70.6	444	65.5	75	82.7	31	100.0	232	85.8	2.7	0.6	0.2	1.5	0.4	8.2
Oswego County	44 322	68.9	260	49.2	108	77.8	143	45.5	336	67.6	1.6	0.7	0.3	0.3	0.3	8.5
Otsego County	22 584	65.5	175	45.1	47	53.2	83	44.6	270	54.8	2.3	1.2	0.4	0.4	0.4	9.0
Putnam County	30 187	77.6	362	67.7	58	69.0	353	81.3	1 432	82.8	8.8	5.0	1.0	2.4	2.2	19.6
Queens County	329 200	58.1	145 071	71.9	2 613	78.7	117 419	81.6	158 698	79.5	46.1	7.6	14.9	22.6	16.8	44.4
Rensselaer County	54 845	66.0	2 809	60.1	89	69.7	700	55.0	868	66.7	3.7	1.4	1.5	0.5	1.2	10.9
Richmond County	118 332	72.0	13 883	71.2	258	77.1	7 258	86.1	14 875	79.8	16.4	5.9	4.6	4.1	5.0	30.9
Rockland County	71 097	75.3	8 547	79.8	222	77.9	4 420	91.0	7 094	85.7	19.1	5.0	5.0	8.4	6.1	32.3
St. Lawrence County	39 244	67.1	178	55.1	390	57.7	205	66.8	223	61.9	3.4	0.9	0.5	0.6	0.7	8.4
Saratoga County	75 171	69.0	833	57.4	162	69.1	646	81.0	862	67.0	3.1	1.2	1.0	0.4	0.3	9.3
Schenectady County	53 274	63.7	3 337	66.9	177	57.1	904	75.2	1 305	68.0	5.3	2.5	1.5	0.9	1.6	13.9
Schoharie County	11 581	68.7	104	50.0	27	88.9	33	27.3	197	71.6	2.4	1.6	0.3	0.4	0.3	8.9
Schuyler County	7 210	70.6	32	68.8	20	80.0	15	80.0	27	44.4	1.2	0.8	0.1	0.1	0.4	7.1
Seneca County	12 227	68.4	108	71.3	50	76.0	105	68.6	57	61.4	2.4	0.8	0.5	0.3	0.9	9.2
Steuben County	37 800	67.7	431	62.4	112	42.9	280	70.4	170	54.7	1.9	0.9	0.6	0.2	0.4	7.5
Suffolk County	395 179	76.1	26 158	81.9	1 236	72.2	9 103	85.7	33 646	85.8	11.2	3.2	2.2	5.4	3.0	21.7
Sullivan County	23 575	66.3	1 689	63.6	88	59.1	272	75.4	1 828	70.2	7.9	3.7	1.0	3.0	3.2	17.9
Tioga County	19 259	72.9	117	41.9	49	61.2	90	76.7	147	68.7	1.7	0.8	0.5	0.2	0.5	7.5
Tompkins County	31 629	54.6	1 003	55.6	118	37.3	2 296	36.2	881	37.7	10.5	2.9	5.2	1.2	2.8	17.0
Ulster County	60 590	64.9	2 613	62.7	154	59.1	563	60.0	2 649	69.4	5.9	2.8	1.0	1.8	1.6	14.2
Warren County	25 165	66.6	99	78.8	25	48.0	171	78.9	113	56.6	2.4	1.2	0.6	0.2	0.6	8.0
Washington County	22 014	70.8	77	72.7	72	61.1	67	67.2	113	67.3	1.9	0.7	0.3	0.6	0.3	6.2
Wayne County	33 133	72.2	886	58.8	75	32.0	59	78.0	505	76.0	2.3	1.0	0.4	0.5	0.6	9.0
Westchester County	234 431	68.5	45 488	66.9	821	72.6	13 206	81.6	38 806	81.3	22.2	6.1	4.0	11.2	7.1	29.2
Wyoming County	14 659	72.3	37	75.7	34	50.0	25	80.0	69	58.0	2.3	0.5	0.3	1.2	0.2	6.1
Yates County	8 802	69.6	45	84.4	23	100.0	9	44.4	91	75.8	2.3	1.3	0.3	0.4	2.3	11.5
NORTH CAROLINA	2 321 636	68.9	627 854	69.1	34 775	75.1	33 599	75.7	93 499	80.3	5.3	0.7	1.2	3.0	2.5	9.4
Alamance County	39 362	68.3	9 473	68.6	268	78.7	313	90.4	2 008	85.8	6.3	0.6	0.8	4.8	4.2	8.5
Alexander County	12 213	75.0	623	64.7	10	100.0	65	90.8	204	80.9	2.4	0.2	0.6	1.4	1.1	5.8
Alleghany County	4 376	68.8	66	59.1	5	100.0	18	72.2	106	84.0	4.1	0.4	0.5	3.3	3.2	5.4
Anson County	5 105	71.2	4 036	74.8	41	80.5	9	100.0	25	96.0	0.7	0.2	0.1	0.4	0.3	5.9
Ashe County	10 164	71.3	83	80.7	15	46.7	12	100.0	108	66.7	1.9	0.3	0.1	1.4	0.9	5.1
Avery County	6 339	69.6	16	31.3	2	100.0	41	78.0	86	58.1	2.6	0.5	0.4	1.5	1.8	4.7
Beaufort County	12 939	70.8	4 910	70.9	27	85.2	21	100.0	352	77.8	2.6	0.3	0.3	2.0	1.5	6.3
Bertie County	3 174	68.2	4 473	72.4	11	100.0	14	64.3	47	89.4	0.7	0.1	0.1	0.4	0.1	5.8
Bladen County	7 684	70.0	4 643	67.5	193	66.8	10	100.0	284	73.9	2.3	0.4	0.1	1.8	1.3	7.7
Brunswick County	25 679	72.5	3 851	72.8	148	75.7	58	75.9	519	79.6	2.9	0.9	0.2	1.6	1.3	6.5
Buncombe County	76 983	65.3	5 786	61.6	267	69.3	539	75.7	1 431	76.5	3.9	1.3	0.7	1.6	1.7	7.5
Burke County	31 000	70.8	1 829	64.6	142	78.9	547	95.4	770	67.8	4.8	0.2	2.2	2.3	2.4	8.8
Cabarrus County	41 661	73.9	5 792	70.6	183	72.7	261	90.4	1 487	87.8	4.7	0.4	0.6	3.5	2.9	8.4
Caldwell County	28 267	73.6	1 819	69.4	102	70.6	63	100.0	468	73.9	1.9	0.3	0.2	1.5	0.9	5.3
Camden County	2 122	76.9	468	76.7	0	X	10	100.0	24	75.0	0.7	0.0	0.0	0.4	0.0	5.2
Carteret County	23 049	69.6	1 475	69.4	119	65.5	88	44.3	274	68.6	2.0	0.7	0.4	0.7	0.6	7.1
Caswell County	5 560	74.9	2 950	73.8	7	100.0	9	100.0	109	71.6	1.6	0.3	0.1	1.0	0.3	6.8
Catawba County	47 982	69.8	4 209	72.1	198	79.8	857	88.6	2 029	80.0	6.5	0.6	1.6	4.0	3.6	9.4
Chatham County	15 101	68.9	3 249	70.7	85	89.4	98	55.1	1 090	87.2	8.7	0.6	0.5	7.5	5.3	10.0
Cherokee County	9 678	71.8	167	82.6	210	71.0	32	21.9	71	95.8	1.2	0.4	0.3	0.3	0.4	6.5

[1] Hispanic or Latino persons may be of any race.

Table A-3. States and Counties — Age, Ethnicity, and Household Structure

STATE/ County code	MSA/PMSA/ NECMA code[1]	STATE County	Population by age (percent)								+/– U.S. percent under 18 years	+/– U.S. percent 65 years and over	Non-Hispanic White	Age (percent)	
			Total population	Under 5 years	5 to 17 years	18 to 24 years	25 to 44 years	45 to 64 years	65 years and over	Median age			Total population	Under 18 years	65 years and over
			1	2	3	4	5	6	7	8	9	10	11	12	13
		NORTH CAROLINA— Cont'd													
37 041	...	Chowan County	14 526	6.0	18.1	9.9	23.0	24.8	18.1	39.8	-1.6	5.7	8 746	19.7	21.6
37 043	...	Clay County	8 775	4.1	14.4	6.5	22.5	29.8	22.6	46.7	-7.2	10.2	8 586	18.4	22.7
37 045	...	Cleveland County	96 287	6.7	18.5	9.0	28.7	23.5	13.7	36.5	-0.5	1.3	73 509	22.9	15.1
37 047	...	Columbus County	54 749	6.6	19.2	8.6	27.6	24.1	13.9	36.9	0.1	1.5	34 405	21.8	15.7
37 049	...	Craven County	91 436	7.3	17.2	13.2	27.8	21.3	13.2	34.4	-1.2	0.8	62 624	21.8	15.7
37 051	2560	Cumberland County	302 963	8.1	19.8	13.8	32.8	17.8	7.7	29.6	2.2	-4.7	159 127	23.5	9.9
37 053	5720	Currituck County	18 190	6.0	19.2	6.8	30.1	25.9	11.9	38.3	-0.5	-0.5	16 290	24.9	12.0
37 055	...	Dare County...................	29 967	5.1	16.2	6.2	31.0	27.7	13.8	40.4	-4.4	1.4	28 019	20.8	14.4
37 057	3120	Davidson County............	147 246	6.5	17.6	7.8	31.2	24.1	12.7	37.1	-1.6	0.3	125 909	22.9	13.8
37 059	3120	Davie County	34 835	6.4	17.9	7.2	29.2	25.3	13.9	38.4	-1.4	1.5	30 886	23.7	14.6
37 061	...	Duplin County	49 063	6.9	19.3	9.2	29.9	22.1	12.6	34.9	0.5	0.2	27 122	22.2	16.1
37 063	6640	Durham County	223 314	6.9	15.9	12.8	35.1	19.6	9.6	32.2	-2.9	-2.8	107 572	17.6	13.8
37 065	6895	Edgecombe County	55 606	6.5	20.6	8.6	28.2	23.4	12.6	36.2	1.4	0.2	21 822	20.4	17.0
37 067	3120	Forsyth County	306 067	6.6	17.3	9.4	31.4	22.5	12.7	36.0	-1.8	0.3	202 388	20.7	15.6
37 069	6640	Franklin County	47 260	7.1	18.2	8.1	33.0	22.5	11.1	35.8	-0.4	-1.3	30 323	23.1	12.0
37 071	1520	Gaston County	190 365	6.7	17.9	8.3	30.9	23.5	12.7	36.2	-1.1	0.3	155 254	23.0	13.9
37 073	...	Gates County.................	10 516	5.7	20.9	6.0	29.5	23.7	14.3	38.1	0.9	1.9	6 167	25.2	15.3
37 075	...	Graham County..............	7 993	5.8	16.1	7.7	25.4	26.8	18.1	41.5	-3.8	5.7	7 259	20.6	19.3
37 077	...	Granville County	48 498	6.1	17.8	8.8	33.5	22.4	11.4	36.2	-1.8	-1.0	28 718	23.0	12.2
37 079	...	Greene County	18 974	6.7	18.4	9.7	31.1	22.3	11.9	35.5	-0.6	-0.5	9 525	20.8	15.8
37 081	3120	Guilford County..............	421 048	6.5	17.1	10.9	31.6	22.1	11.7	34.9	-2.1	-0.7	264 997	20.5	15.0
37 083	...	Halifax County................	57 370	6.2	20.0	8.1	27.7	23.1	14.9	37.2	0.5	2.5	24 247	20.4	20.1
37 085	...	Harnett County...............	91 025	7.5	19.3	10.4	32.8	19.6	10.4	32.5	1.1	-2.0	62 574	23.9	12.2
37 087	...	Haywood County.............	54 033	5.2	15.5	6.0	27.0	27.2	19.1	42.3	-5.0	6.7	51 830	20.2	19.4
37 089	...	Henderson County	89 173	5.5	15.3	6.2	26.1	25.1	21.7	42.7	-4.9	9.3	80 032	19.5	23.5
37 091	...	Hertford County..............	22 601	5.5	20.0	8.3	25.5	24.7	16.1	39.2	-0.2	3.7	8 371	18.7	19.9
37 093	...	Hoke County	33 646	8.9	20.9	10.9	34.4	17.1	7.6	30.0	4.1	-4.6	14 073	25.5	9.4
37 095	...	Hyde County	5 826	4.5	15.9	7.7	31.7	23.1	17.2	39.7	-5.3	4.8	3 614	19.3	18.3
37 097	...	Iredell County................	122 660	6.9	18.6	7.6	31.4	23.2	12.3	36.5	-0.2	-0.1	99 100	23.8	13.5
37 099	...	Jackson County..............	33 121	5.0	14.0	17.9	24.3	24.8	14.0	36.2	-6.7	1.6	28 233	17.2	15.0
37 101	6640	Johnston County	121 965	8.1	18.2	7.9	34.3	21.7	9.9	34.2	0.6	-2.5	91 855	24.0	11.0
37 103	...	Jones County	10 381	6.0	19.7	6.9	26.9	25.2	15.3	39.1	0.0	2.9	6 267	23.3	16.2
37 105	...	Lee County	49 040	6.9	18.7	9.1	30.3	22.0	13.0	35.9	-0.1	0.6	32 365	22.2	16.1
37 107	...	Lenoir County.................	59 648	6.4	18.9	7.9	27.8	24.3	14.7	38.1	-0.4	2.3	33 046	21.2	17.3
37 109	1520	Lincoln County................	63 780	6.4	18.4	7.4	32.0	24.2	11.6	36.4	-0.9	-0.8	55 384	23.6	12.4
37 111	...	McDowell County	42 151	6.1	16.8	7.9	29.9	25.0	14.2	38.0	-2.8	1.8	38 255	22.1	15.0
37 113	...	Macon County	29 811	5.0	15.3	6.2	23.4	27.7	22.4	45.2	-5.4	10.0	28 510	19.6	23.1
37 115	0480	Madison County	19 635	6.1	15.2	10.4	26.7	25.7	15.9	39.3	-4.4	3.5	18 929	21.1	16.2
37 117	...	Martin County.................	25 593	6.1	19.5	8.0	26.4	24.7	15.4	38.7	-0.1	3.0	13 215	20.6	18.1
37 119	1520	Mecklenburg County	695 454	7.2	17.7	9.6	36.5	20.4	8.5	33.1	-0.8	-3.9	425 279	21.8	11.0
37 121	...	Mitchell County	15 687	4.9	16.1	6.8	26.4	27.1	18.6	42.0	-4.7	6.2	15 220	20.8	19.0
37 123	...	Montgomery County........	26 822	6.8	18.1	9.1	28.3	23.7	14.0	36.7	-0.8	1.6	17 598	20.7	17.5
37 125	...	Moore County	74 769	5.6	16.5	6.5	25.9	23.4	22.0	41.8	-3.6	9.6	58 983	19.5	24.8
37 127	6895	Nash County...................	87 420	6.6	18.8	8.8	29.9	23.4	12.6	36.5	-0.3	0.2	53 244	21.8	15.2
37 129	9200	New Hanover County......	160 307	5.8	15.1	12.0	30.6	23.8	12.8	36.3	-4.8	0.4	126 487	18.5	13.8
37 131	...	Northampton County.......	22 086	5.7	18.8	6.8	26.6	24.6	17.6	40.0	-1.2	5.2	8 620	18.5	22.1
37 133	3605	Onslow County...............	150 355	8.8	17.4	23.7	29.4	14.3	6.4	25.0	0.5	-6.0	104 457	23.8	7.4
37 135	6640	Orange County...............	118 227	4.9	15.4	20.9	30.0	20.4	8.3	30.4	-5.4	-4.1	89 587	18.7	9.1
37 137	...	Pamlico County..............	12 934	5.2	15.9	6.8	26.1	27.4	18.7	42.9	-4.6	6.3	9 385	19.6	20.0
37 139	...	Pasquotank County........	34 897	6.1	18.7	11.5	28.4	21.2	14.1	35.9	-0.9	1.7	19 715	22.0	16.6
37 141	...	Pender County	41 082	5.7	17.5	7.2	29.9	25.6	14.0	38.8	-2.5	1.6	29 404	21.4	15.1
37 143	...	Perquimans County	11 368	5.0	17.9	7.0	24.4	25.9	19.8	42.2	-2.8	7.4	8 050	20.8	20.4
37 145	...	Person County	35 623	6.4	17.7	7.2	31.1	23.7	13.9	38.0	-1.6	1.5	24 270	21.6	15.1
37 147	3150	Pitt County	133 798	6.4	17.1	17.4	30.1	19.3	9.6	30.4	-2.2	-2.8	81 543	18.9	10.8
37 149	...	Polk County	18 324	5.4	14.6	5.4	24.7	26.1	23.7	44.9	-5.7	11.3	16 508	18.9	25.0
37 151	3120	Randolph County	130 454	6.8	18.3	7.9	31.6	23.3	12.1	36.2	-0.6	-0.3	112 337	23.7	13.2
37 153	...	Richmond County	46 564	6.8	18.9	10.1	27.9	22.6	13.6	35.5	0.0	1.2	29 610	21.9	16.5
37 155	...	Robeson County	123 339	7.8	21.1	10.7	29.5	20.9	9.9	32.0	3.2	-2.5	38 049	21.0	15.6
37 157	...	Rockingham County........	91 928	6.3	17.0	7.6	29.5	24.7	14.8	38.5	-2.4	2.4	69 972	21.7	16.3
37 159	1520	Rowan County	130 340	6.6	18.0	9.2	29.8	22.4	14.0	36.4	-1.1	1.6	101 814	22.7	15.8
37 161	...	Rutherford County..........	62 899	6.3	17.6	7.9	27.8	24.4	16.0	38.3	-1.8	3.6	54 132	22.5	17.0
37 163	...	Sampson County	60 161	7.4	18.4	9.7	29.9	21.8	12.8	35.0	0.1	0.4	34 247	22.3	15.2
37 165	...	Scotland County	35 998	7.3	20.9	9.2	28.6	23.0	11.0	34.6	2.5	-1.4	18 509	22.6	13.8
37 167	...	Stanly County	58 100	6.2	18.7	8.4	28.9	23.4	14.3	36.9	-0.8	1.9	48 547	23.2	15.6
37 169	3120	Stokes County................	44 711	6.4	18.0	7.1	31.7	25.0	11.7	37.2	-1.3	-0.7	41 376	24.1	11.9
37 171	...	Surry County	71 219	6.0	17.6	7.6	29.3	24.1	15.4	38.0	-2.1	3.0	62 896	22.0	16.6

[1]MSA = Metropolitan Statistical Area. PMSA = Primary MSA. NECMA = New England County Metropolitan Area. See the Appendix A for explanation of these concepts. See Appendix B for list of metropolitan areas identified by type, with component counties.

STATE County	Black or African American Total population 14	Under 18 years 15	65 years and over 16	American Indian and Alaska Native Total population 17	Under 18 years 18	65 years and over 19	Asian, Hawaiian, and Pacific Islander Total population 20	Under 18 years 21	65 years and over 22	Hispanic or Latino[1] Total population 23	Under 18 years 24	65 years and over 25	Two or more races Total population 26	Under 18 years 27	65 years and over 28
NORTH CAROLINA—Cont'd															
Chowan County	5 486	30.6	13.4	22	0.0	0.0	47	27.7	17.0	179	35.8	0.0	82	34.1	0.0
Clay County	11	18.2	0.0	53	28.3	18.9	14	0.0	0.0	54	11.1	24.1	43	48.8	7.0
Cleveland County	19 953	31.3	10.0	245	40.4	0.0	785	33.1	0.6	1 083	37.9	2.3	744	50.0	1.7
Columbus County	17 039	31.4	11.8	1 609	33.3	9.1	135	26.7	10.4	1 168	44.3	2.7	577	46.3	4.7
Craven County	22 698	29.8	9.2	358	25.4	6.7	1 186	18.5	7.3	3 761	31.9	1.7	1 372	49.6	2.8
Cumberland County	105 730	31.8	6.1	4 696	28.9	6.8	6 629	22.5	5.3	20 637	34.3	2.4	9 718	51.1	1.5
Currituck County	1 187	23.5	16.0	79	17.7	15.2	163	34.4	4.9	223	39.0	0.0	279	39.1	2.2
Dare County	831	26.0	7.8	105	33.3	0.0	101	13.9	2.0	551	26.9	5.3	351	39.6	5.1
Davidson County	13 495	29.4	8.9	503	19.9	4.4	1 290	31.5	1.1	4 935	35.2	1.8	1 388	44.1	2.8
Davie County	2 366	26.1	13.2	79	11.4	8.9	48	14.6	0.0	1 238	36.1	0.7	241	36.5	5.8
Duplin County	14 116	29.3	12.4	72	25.0	0.0	197	22.8	2.5	7 318	34.9	0.4	758	42.9	4.1
Durham County	87 424	28.8	7.2	778	22.5	4.0	7 119	16.8	3.4	16 994	24.7	0.7	4 554	34.8	2.5
Edgecombe County	32 138	31.1	10.3	51	15.7	19.6	169	44.4	0.0	1 483	35.8	2.4	173	54.3	3.5
Forsyth County	78 270	29.9	8.8	919	20.2	7.9	3 311	19.1	4.7	19 687	32.0	1.3	4 331	40.3	3.0
Franklin County	14 097	28.5	10.8	342	26.0	8.8	193	21.8	16.6	1 991	32.8	0.7	349	46.4	10.0
Gaston County	26 198	31.8	8.7	731	13.1	6.8	1 534	29.6	3.7	5 520	27.7	1.2	1 994	47.7	4.0
Gates County	4 024	27.2	13.6	86	48.8	0.0	120	43.3	0.0	21	23.8	0.0	103	51.5	5.8
Graham County	0	X	X	501	33.9	8.2	38	31.6	0.0	133	48.1	0.0	75	14.7	0.0
Granville County	16 710	24.0	12.0	234	18.8	5.6	254	33.9	2.8	2 102	29.4	0.7	528	39.4	0.0
Greene County	7 798	28.6	9.3	125	22.4	0.0	17	0.0	29.4	1 524	35.0	0.3	97	22.7	14.4
Guilford County	122 923	28.2	6.9	2 054	22.5	5.4	9 470	28.8	3.3	16 183	28.9	1.7	7 320	39.9	3.9
Halifax County	30 325	30.4	11.2	1 628	28.9	10.1	390	39.0	2.6	365	26.8	16.7	429	30.1	20.5
Harnett County	20 297	32.5	8.1	1 093	35.1	3.5	702	12.1	5.4	5 179	34.7	1.0	1 812	50.1	2.5
Haywood County	833	26.9	19.8	377	41.9	6.4	96	17.7	0.0	580	38.1	5.2	348	35.3	5.7
Henderson County	2 514	27.8	12.7	422	24.6	6.9	463	21.4	4.1	4 882	35.3	2.7	1 231	39.2	6.1
Hertford County	13 610	29.7	13.0	250	25.1	22.8	69	14.5	7.2	267	18.0	9.0	127	30.7	7.1
Hoke County	12 653	31.8	7.8	3 695	33.6	5.0	550	30.4	14.9	2 357	33.4	1.3	746	59.4	1.6
Hyde County	1 968	21.2	16.9	5	0.0	0.0	6	0.0	0.0	194	36.1	3.1	39	15.4	0.0
Iredell County	16 947	31.3	9.4	595	33.8	0.8	1 256	33.2	1.2	4 163	34.4	2.4	1 033	38.5	5.9
Jackson County	518	7.1	9.1	3 060	31.5	8.1	321	34.3	0.9	433	30.0	8.5	573	38.6	11.0
Johnston County	19 214	31.2	9.0	509	32.8	4.3	617	29.3	1.1	9 014	35.6	1.5	1 242	41.8	3.6
Jones County	3 741	28.5	14.5	9	0.0	77.8	65	18.5	20.0	285	43.5	2.8	30	20.0	0.0
Lee County	10 288	29.9	11.2	285	50.9	0.0	221	34.8	0.0	5 665	34.1	0.7	455	46.6	3.7
Lenoir County	24 188	29.9	12.3	110	19.1	2.7	392	35.5	3.6	1 852	36.1	1.5	322	50.9	4.3
Lincoln County	4 369	30.7	9.2	151	17.2	15.2	88	47.7	0.0	3 517	34.1	0.8	491	45.4	8.4
McDowell County	1 957	21.1	9.2	127	40.9	6.3	408	45.1	2.5	1 081	38.3	1.3	408	48.0	4.4
Macon County	300	37.7	12.0	41	7.3	17.1	263	33.8	0.0	435	35.9	6.2	277	30.7	6.5
Madison County	176	6.8	6.1	5	40.0	60.0	144	23.0	4.9	237	38.0	7.2	162	40.1	14.2
Martin County	11 762	30.4	13.1	42	35.7	0.0	57	21.1	0.0	475	38.1	3.2	123	53.7	0.0
Mecklenburg County	192 666	30.8	5.6	3 250	28.0	3.1	21 217	26.9	3.5	44 954	29.7	1.7	12 108	37.8	2.1
Mitchell County	54	42.6	11.1	31	0.0	16.1	30	0.0	0.0	273	31.5	0.0	106	33.8	11.8
Montgomery County	5 898	28.0	10.8	135	35.6	2.2	385	41.6	3.1	2 729	41.6	1.4	320	35.3	0.6
Moore County	11 596	30.5	14.5	524	30.7	2.9	264	17.8	3.0	2 896	37.6	1.7	704	46.9	4.4
Nash County	29 665	29.8	9.4	274	24.1	5.1	436	32.1	3.2	2 888	40.9	1.5	990	38.7	5.6
New Hanover County	26 655	30.1	10.5	832	18.0	2.4	1 491	20.8	5.0	3 425	27.6	2.4	1 780	44.3	2.9
Northampton County	13 113	28.2	14.6	53	24.5	22.6	32	6.3	0.0	128	32.0	28.1	167	34.1	6.0
Onslow County	27 426	30.7	5.4	1 157	27.1	2.3	2 966	20.4	6.7	10 766	29.6	1.1	5 283	50.5	0.9
Orange County	15 895	24.7	9.2	635	22.8	4.3	4 673	20.5	2.6	5 477	26.5	1.1	2 400	32.8	2.9
Pamlico County	3 145	24.9	16.3	45	20.0	11.1	41	36.6	17.1	203	25.1	0.5	135	23.0	11.1
Pasquotank County	13 947	27.6	11.2	153	12.4	12.4	376	19.7	12.0	420	40.5	4.3	369	63.7	4.1
Pender County	9 561	26.2	13.4	242	27.3	2.9	134	23.9	4.5	1 521	33.4	0.2	373	50.1	11.5
Perquimans County	3 144	27.4	18.9	72	36.1	19.4	0	X	X	67	29.9	0.0	70	52.9	0.0
Person County	10 126	28.7	11.4	163	3.7	34.4	104	0.0	11.5	603	40.8	5.6	386	47.2	5.4
Pitt County	45 095	30.8	8.6	550	26.0	1.1	1 377	20.4	3.2	4 088	31.7	2.0	1 502	36.8	3.9
Polk County	984	27.1	15.3	94	23.4	16.0	27	0.0	0.0	639	40.2	4.5	153	25.5	20.3
Randolph County	7 146	29.4	9.8	651	20.4	6.0	819	35.8	2.1	8 593	37.2	1.1	1 505	43.7	2.5
Richmond County	14 249	32.9	9.6	871	28.4	5.7	255	16.9	2.0	1 111	30.0	3.0	603	43.4	3.6
Robeson County	31 414	33.2	9.1	45 341	31.8	7.0	1 060	33.4	4.3	5 608	31.2	0.8	2 260	46.5	7.0
Rockingham County	17 735	27.1	12.3	369	20.6	4.9	297	29.6	1.0	2 991	33.7	1.6	781	40.1	1.2
Rowan County	20 876	30.2	9.2	667	34.0	3.3	868	33.8	8.6	4 892	32.5	1.6	1 583	43.0	4.0
Rutherford County	6 831	29.2	11.8	185	39.5	0.0	143	4.9	11.2	1 139	44.8	2.0	464	48.9	6.5
Sampson County	17 932	28.9	12.6	1 208	31.0	11.7	355	20.8	5.1	6 390	35.1	0.9	598	43.9	4.5
Scotland County	13 429	33.4	8.6	2 935	34.2	6.3	238	38.7	2.9	325	41.8	6.5	693	43.9	6.6
Stanly County	6 844	32.1	9.3	193	19.2	3.1	760	51.3	5.5	1 363	34.4	2.2	589	37.4	2.4
Stokes County	2 108	24.4	13.3	108	38.9	0.0	121	36.4	0.0	838	36.4	2.4	228	41.2	1.3
Surry County	2 753	28.3	15.3	352	39.5	6.3	478	61.7	1.7	4 378	38.0	1.0	709	26.2	6.9

[1] Hispanic or Latino persons may be of any race.

Table A-3. States and Counties — Age, Ethnicity, and Household Structure

STATE County	Total households	Married-couple family households Total	With children	Householder 65 years or over	Other family households Total	With children	Householder 65 years or over	Two or more unrelated persons Total	Householder 65 years or over	Male living alone Total	Householder 65 years or over	Female living alone Total	Householder 65 years or over	Percent of householders 65 years and over who live alone	Grandparents who are responsible for the care of their grandchildren
	29	30	31	32	33	34	35	36	37	38	39	40	41	42	43
NORTH CAROLINA—Cont'd															
Chowan County	5 554	52.9	20.3	14.8	19.0	11.0	3.3	2.7	0.8	10.6	2.0	14.8	9.8	38.4	197
Clay County	3 842	61.2	19.5	16.4	10.0	4.8	3.4	2.5	0.5	9.9	3.7	16.3	9.7	39.7	70
Cleveland County	37 047	55.9	22.8	10.0	17.5	10.0	2.6	3.1	0.2	9.5	1.9	14.0	7.9	43.4	1 241
Columbus County	21 305	51.6	21.7	9.2	19.5	10.8	3.3	2.5	0.2	10.6	2.7	15.7	9.2	48.3	1 055
Craven County	34 686	58.0	24.9	11.3	14.9	9.4	2.1	3.8	0.3	9.4	1.9	13.8	6.9	39.0	940
Cumberland County	107 391	54.0	28.1	5.7	18.9	12.1	2.0	4.8	0.3	10.3	1.5	12.1	4.6	43.3	3 433
Currituck County	6 896	62.0	25.1	9.9	13.8	9.0	2.3	4.7	0.6	9.6	2.2	9.9	5.6	37.7	271
Dare County	12 685	56.6	21.5	11.1	10.5	6.6	1.5	7.8	0.5	12.8	2.4	12.4	5.5	37.6	111
Davidson County	58 132	58.9	24.4	9.4	14.4	8.3	1.6	3.8	0.3	9.9	2.1	13.0	6.7	43.7	1 233
Davie County	13 724	61.9	25.5	11.2	13.0	7.8	1.9	2.8	0.1	9.4	2.6	12.8	7.0	42.2	304
Duplin County	18 283	53.6	24.7	8.9	18.7	9.3	2.8	3.3	0.2	9.8	2.3	14.7	8.7	48.1	479
Durham County	89 001	42.9	19.3	5.8	18.5	10.5	2.1	8.6	0.3	12.3	1.7	17.8	5.6	46.7	2 026
Edgecombe County	20 412	46.0	19.2	8.3	26.9	14.3	3.6	3.0	0.2	9.3	2.3	14.8	8.0	46.1	1 175
Forsyth County	124 023	49.8	21.4	8.6	16.6	9.7	2.2	4.7	0.3	11.3	2.0	17.6	7.6	46.4	2 725
Franklin County	17 843	56.4	25.4	7.7	16.4	8.7	2.5	3.7	0.3	10.4	2.2	13.1	6.4	45.3	615
Gaston County	73 836	56.1	23.4	8.9	16.6	9.0	2.7	4.0	0.1	9.5	2.0	13.9	7.0	43.6	2 464
Gates County	3 890	59.7	27.2	11.6	15.7	7.4	3.8	2.7	1.0	8.8	2.2	13.1	8.9	40.5	109
Graham County	3 375	60.0	21.4	13.5	12.0	5.8	3.3	2.0	0.2	8.8	1.8	17.2	11.7	44.3	113
Granville County	16 663	52.8	22.9	8.3	20.0	11.0	3.4	3.3	0.3	10.8	2.5	13.0	7.1	44.3	543
Greene County	6 681	52.7	24.0	7.7	22.5	11.9	4.8	2.3	0.0	8.0	1.7	14.5	8.1	43.9	275
Guilford County	168 710	48.8	21.4	8.1	16.7	9.6	2.0	6.6	0.2	11.4	1.9	16.5	6.5	44.6	3 271
Halifax County	22 134	44.9	18.0	9.4	24.5	13.2	4.2	2.9	0.5	11.5	2.9	16.2	9.5	46.8	1 032
Harnett County	33 837	53.6	25.3	7.1	18.0	11.1	2.2	5.1	0.3	10.4	1.7	12.9	6.7	46.7	1 148
Haywood County	23 113	57.4	20.0	13.5	12.5	6.3	3.0	3.4	0.3	9.8	2.7	16.9	9.3	41.7	435
Henderson County	37 467	59.4	20.1	17.2	11.5	6.2	1.9	3.4	0.5	9.0	2.4	16.7	10.0	38.8	469
Hertford County	8 945	46.3	17.0	10.2	23.6	13.2	4.3	3.1	0.2	10.6	2.9	16.4	8.6	43.8	494
Hoke County	11 374	54.1	27.9	5.1	23.6	13.0	3.3	3.3	0.2	8.5	1.0	10.5	3.9	36.1	649
Hyde County	2 179	47.8	18.1	8.1	18.2	7.1	7.5	3.3	0.3	14.9	5.4	15.9	9.7	48.6	81
Iredell County	47 375	59.0	26.1	9.2	14.5	8.3	2.1	3.9	0.2	9.8	2.0	12.8	6.4	42.2	1 220
Jackson County	13 168	52.0	18.7	10.5	13.6	7.3	2.3	7.6	0.3	10.8	2.2	16.1	8.0	43.6	292
Johnston County	46 700	58.4	27.8	6.8	14.3	8.4	1.8	4.2	0.1	9.0	1.7	14.1	7.1	50.5	1 076
Jones County	4 092	52.6	23.7	9.0	19.9	10.0	4.3	3.1	0.0	10.7	3.4	13.7	8.2	46.5	136
Lee County	18 504	54.9	24.2	10.2	17.6	10.2	2.9	4.1	0.4	9.9	1.8	13.5	6.8	39.0	700
Lenoir County	23 874	47.8	19.8	8.6	20.4	11.9	2.7	3.5	0.4	11.3	2.9	17.1	9.7	51.8	757
Lincoln County	24 060	62.9	28.0	8.7	13.1	7.1	1.9	3.8	0.1	8.9	2.1	11.2	6.3	43.9	604
McDowell County	16 586	58.5	23.6	10.6	13.9	7.6	1.9	3.3	0.3	10.1	2.4	14.2	8.2	45.4	516
Macon County	12 855	58.0	18.2	17.9	11.7	6.9	2.2	3.5	0.4	10.1	3.0	16.7	10.7	40.0	252
Madison County	7 996	56.5	21.4	10.4	13.5	7.2	2.6	3.8	0.3	11.9	3.4	14.3	9.0	48.2	120
Martin County	10 029	50.6	20.2	9.7	21.7	11.1	3.9	2.0	0.2	8.8	2.2	16.8	10.0	46.8	440
Mecklenburg County	273 561	48.7	23.5	5.9	15.8	9.0	1.6	7.9	0.2	12.1	1.3	15.5	4.6	43.7	5 985
Mitchell County	6 580	61.9	23.1	13.7	10.7	5.1	2.8	2.4	0.3	9.8	3.0	15.2	8.6	40.8	93
Montgomery County	9 855	56.5	22.2	10.3	17.0	8.9	3.4	2.5	0.2	10.5	2.9	13.6	8.4	44.8	337
Moore County	30 807	59.0	20.2	18.2	13.0	7.4	2.2	3.3	0.4	9.0	2.2	15.7	8.9	34.9	596
Nash County	33 629	54.0	24.1	8.6	17.4	9.1	2.5	3.6	0.2	9.9	2.3	15.2	7.9	47.4	941
New Hanover County	68 241	47.7	18.9	9.1	13.8	7.9	1.9	9.6	0.3	12.0	1.9	16.8	6.5	42.6	1 173
Northampton County	8 678	46.2	16.5	10.4	22.9	11.6	4.7	2.4	0.3	12.3	3.5	16.1	10.4	47.4	466
Onslow County	48 107	61.9	33.6	5.9	14.8	9.9	1.4	4.7	0.2	9.4	1.4	9.2	4.0	41.9	1 206
Orange County	45 916	45.2	21.6	5.8	12.3	7.3	1.3	14.5	0.3	11.7	1.5	16.4	5.3	47.8	358
Pamlico County	5 154	57.2	18.6	14.9	14.7	6.9	3.0	3.1	0.5	11.7	3.0	13.4	8.5	38.4	298
Pasquotank County	12 925	49.3	20.2	9.4	21.2	13.5	2.7	4.2	0.7	9.9	2.9	15.4	8.5	47.2	426
Pender County	16 057	59.4	22.5	11.5	13.9	7.2	2.4	3.8	0.2	10.4	2.4	12.5	6.4	38.5	614
Perquimans County	4 662	55.9	19.9	15.2	16.9	9.0	3.3	3.1	0.5	8.4	2.6	15.7	9.7	39.2	121
Person County	14 093	54.5	23.6	9.3	18.4	9.5	3.6	3.0	0.2	11.0	2.6	13.1	7.5	43.6	420
Pitt County	52 603	43.9	20.1	6.0	18.2	10.5	2.2	9.7	0.2	11.9	1.6	16.3	6.2	48.2	1 427
Polk County	7 887	57.8	19.1	17.1	9.5	4.9	2.5	3.7	0.4	10.0	2.8	19.1	11.4	41.7	220
Randolph County	50 637	59.4	25.8	9.0	14.6	8.4	2.1	3.5	0.3	9.6	1.9	12.8	6.6	42.5	1 141
Richmond County	17 913	48.2	20.0	9.3	22.5	12.7	3.3	3.1	0.2	11.0	2.9	15.2	8.2	46.6	872
Robeson County	43 628	48.0	22.8	6.7	25.9	15.2	3.3	3.4	0.3	9.2	2.1	13.5	6.9	46.5	1 962
Rockingham County	37 048	54.4	22.5	10.3	16.4	8.6	2.7	3.0	0.3	10.1	2.3	15.6	8.8	45.6	1 117
Rowan County	50 005	55.6	23.9	9.8	16.0	9.3	2.0	3.7	0.2	10.7	2.4	13.9	7.5	45.2	1 792
Rutherford County	25 174	56.7	22.7	11.3	15.1	7.9	2.6	2.8	0.2	9.4	2.1	16.0	9.4	45.1	840
Sampson County	22 226	54.5	24.0	8.9	18.6	9.8	3.6	3.2	0.3	9.6	2.2	14.1	8.3	44.9	650
Scotland County	13 407	49.5	21.5	7.3	23.5	14.0	3.4	2.6	0.3	9.7	2.1	14.7	6.4	43.9	540
Stanly County	22 203	59.1	25.1	10.5	13.9	7.7	2.4	2.8	0.3	9.4	2.3	14.8	9.0	46.2	524
Stokes County	17 577	62.2	27.6	8.6	12.7	7.3	2.0	2.3	0.1	9.4	1.6	13.4	7.3	45.5	355
Surry County	28 392	58.6	24.5	10.6	13.9	6.7	2.6	2.6	0.3	9.9	2.4	15.0	9.1	46.1	651

Table A-3. States and Counties — Age, Ethnicity, and Household Structure

	Households with Non-Hispanic White householder		Households with Black or African American householder		Households with American Indian and Alaska Native householder		Households with Asian, Hawaiian, and Pacific Islander householder		Households with Hispanic or Latino[1] householder		Foreign-born population	Place of birth (percent)			Percent in non-English speaking households	
STATE County	Number of households	Percent that are family households	Number of households	Percent that are family households	Number of households	Percent that are family households	Number of households	Percent that are family households	Number of households	Percent that are family households	Percent of total population that is foreign-born	Europe	Asia	Latin America	Linguistically isolated	Not linguistically isolated
	44	45	46	47	48	49	50	51	52	53	54	55	56	57	58	59
NORTH CAROLINA—Cont'd																
Chowan County	3 576	71.8	1 925	72.2	0	X	8	100.0	33	75.8	0.9	0.2	0.2	0.5	0.5	5.4
Clay County	3 785	71.0	9	100.0	8	100.0	0	X	14	92.9	1.2	0.8	0.2	0.1	0.2	4.8
Cleveland County	29 339	72.9	7 011	74.6	129	82.9	185	87.0	263	80.2	1.7	0.3	0.6	0.7	0.7	6.4
Columbus County	14 143	72.8	6 161	67.1	587	69.7	50	80.0	268	77.6	1.4	0.2	0.2	1.0	0.9	5.5
Craven County	24 717	73.6	8 485	69.9	126	79.4	277	70.4	885	85.4	3.4	0.6	1.1	1.4	1.0	9.3
Cumberland County	60 068	72.4	37 030	72.3	1 627	69.4	1 858	76.0	5 863	80.9	5.3	1.5	1.6	1.8	1.3	16.0
Currituck County	6 248	76.6	445	65.4	31	100.0	62	90.3	65	66.2	1.4	0.5	0.5	0.3	0.4	5.8
Dare County	11 991	66.9	323	65.9	27	92.6	45	73.3	177	75.7	2.5	1.1	0.3	1.0	0.8	6.1
Davidson County	50 876	73.3	5 158	70.7	187	77.5	324	76.9	1 289	83.9	3.6	0.4	0.6	2.4	1.9	7.0
Davie County	12 360	75.7	945	61.9	40	55.0	14	21.4	299	88.3	3.4	0.5	0.3	2.4	1.6	7.3
Duplin County	11 200	71.2	5 192	69.7	8	62.5	40	90.0	1 783	85.6	11.3	0.2	0.3	10.6	7.7	12.3
Durham County	47 646	58.3	33 092	64.5	304	53.9	2 604	57.9	4 257	76.3	10.9	1.0	2.6	5.9	4.9	13.5
Edgecombe County	9 095	70.2	10 986	74.8	14	14.3	29	100.0	321	79.4	2.1	0.2	0.2	1.6	0.9	7.7
Forsyth County	87 313	65.5	29 606	66.7	317	64.7	1 160	69.5	4 963	84.0	6.5	0.7	0.9	4.5	3.9	8.9
Franklin County	12 335	71.8	4 790	74.7	95	87.4	64	53.1	476	84.0	3.6	0.3	0.3	2.8	2.0	8.8
Gaston County	61 726	72.6	9 471	70.9	338	80.2	442	75.8	1 542	79.4	3.3	0.5	0.6	2.0	1.9	7.6
Gates County	2 435	75.8	1 386	74.0	23	100.0	23	91.3	3	0.0	1.1	0.2	0.6	0.2	0.5	4.8
Graham County	3 158	71.1	0	X	181	84.5	11	100.0	23	91.3	1.3	0.5	0.3	0.4	1.1	5.8
Granville County	10 963	71.5	5 189	74.2	65	80.0	42	100.0	356	88.2	4.0	0.2	0.4	3.2	2.5	6.1
Greene County	3 850	73.7	2 480	75.6	11	0.0	3	33.3	338	92.6	4.9	0.0	0.1	4.8	3.0	8.3
Guilford County	112 930	64.8	46 403	65.4	840	70.0	2 655	83.5	4 372	74.7	6.5	0.9	2.0	2.6	2.9	10.3
Halifax County	10 526	67.7	10 608	70.7	608	68.9	88	90.9	109	68.8	1.1	0.2	0.4	0.3	0.4	5.1
Harnett County	24 907	70.7	6 805	72.7	331	76.7	163	69.3	1 274	82.7	4.6	0.5	0.6	3.2	2.4	10.3
Haywood County	22 359	69.8	304	67.4	108	75.9	29	69.0	176	84.7	1.6	0.6	0.2	0.6	0.6	6.1
Henderson County	34 656	70.5	952	72.0	168	86.9	115	91.3	1 215	83.0	5.9	1.2	0.5	3.9	2.6	9.0
Hertford County	3 562	67.2	5 126	72.6	138	51.4	10	100.0	75	52.0	1.2	0.2	0.2	0.7	0.8	5.5
Hoke County	5 383	77.5	4 136	75.9	1 136	76.8	112	88.4	550	93.1	5.8	0.8	1.2	3.6	2.9	14.3
Hyde County	1 487	68.1	636	62.6	0	X	0	X	10	54.0	2.0	0.2	0.0	2.0	0.3	9.2
Iredell County	39 421	73.3	6 293	72.4	207	75.4	321	85.4	1 024	81.2	3.6	0.4	0.6	2.3	1.8	6.8
Jackson County	11 526	64.8	148	31.1	1 053	78.2	75	73.3	133	77.4	1.7	0.5	0.5	0.4	0.8	8.9
Johnston County	37 335	72.1	6 657	72.4	169	81.7	117	86.3	2 207	82.4	5.9	0.3	0.3	5.1	3.7	9.1
Jones County	2 475	75.0	1 520	68.0	4	100.0	23	100.0	62	74.2	2.1	0.2	0.7	1.2	1.0	7.5
Lee County	13 358	71.5	3 702	71.9	81	76.5	50	72.0	1 294	84.4	9.5	0.6	0.4	8.2	6.2	9.6
Lenoir County	13 937	69.8	9 258	65.6	51	39.2	94	89.4	503	69.0	2.7	0.4	0.5	1.8	1.2	8.4
Lincoln County	21 522	75.4	1 436	76.3	69	79.7	23	100.0	949	90.9	4.8	0.4	0.1	4.1	2.2	8.2
McDowell County	15 494	72.6	610	67.4	37	83.8	70	70.0	275	76.0	2.7	0.3	0.6	1.8	1.6	5.8
Macon County	12 533	69.5	42	61.9	23	69.6	47	93.6	132	77.3	2.6	0.9	0.7	0.8	1.0	4.4
Madison County	7 805	69.8	26	61.5	1	100.0	45	66.7	40	90.0	1.7	0.5	0.5	0.4	0.5	5.7
Martin County	5 548	72.2	4 327	71.9	18	55.6	15	100.0	126	92.9	1.5	0.1	0.2	1.1	0.4	5.4
Mecklenburg County	180 580	62.5	70 816	66.5	1 183	69.8	6 510	78.4	11 908	77.0	9.8	1.4	2.6	4.8	4.6	13.0
Mitchell County	6 445	72.9	24	100.0	13	46.2	0	X	65	73.8	1.5	0.2	0.1	0.9	0.5	6.6
Montgomery County	7 269	71.7	1 862	74.5	40	85.0	95	86.3	543	89.5	8.0	0.2	1.0	6.8	5.5	9.3
Moore County	25 334	72.6	4 400	67.1	187	75.9	77	46.8	671	87.5	4.2	1.0	0.3	2.5	1.7	7.6
Nash County	21 813	71.1	10 629	70.6	92	93.5	145	94.5	694	82.7	3.0	0.3	0.6	2.0	1.3	7.9
New Hanover County	55 689	60.8	10 279	65.6	310	46.5	486	61.9	1 065	67.6	3.2	1.1	0.7	1.1	1.0	8.3
Northampton County	3 589	71.6	4 989	67.0	17	100.0	11	100.0	39	76.9	0.7	0.2	0.2	0.3	0.4	4.5
Onslow County	35 310	76.9	8 667	75.6	350	79.4	676	60.1	2 391	82.5	4.1	0.7	1.4	1.8	0.9	13.5
Orange County	36 020	56.0	6 058	60.4	238	82.4	1 607	63.9	1 478	74.5	9.1	1.8	3.2	3.1	3.0	13.8
Pamlico County	4 018	72.0	1 023	71.9	18	50.0	13	100.0	41	61.0	1.8	0.6	0.1	0.9	0.5	8.4
Pasquotank County	7 851	70.3	4 706	71.0	66	84.8	111	71.2	113	69.9	2.3	0.5	1.0	0.6	0.8	7.0
Pender County	12 077	73.8	3 445	69.9	89	71.9	59	83.1	344	89.0	3.6	0.8	0.3	2.3	1.5	7.9
Perquimans County	3 385	73.9	1 218	69.7	28	100.0	0	X	26	34.6	0.7	0.6	0.0	0.1	0.1	5.2
Person County	10 019	72.8	3 703	72.4	80	83.8	38	76.3	161	86.3	1.3	0.1	0.4	0.6	0.5	6.9
Pitt County	34 140	59.2	16 401	67.9	232	59.1	522	63.6	980	66.2	3.6	0.6	0.8	1.8	1.6	7.8
Polk County	7 269	67.4	384	54.7	29	75.9	5	100.0	140	90.0	3.7	1.7	0.2	1.6	1.4	7.8
Randolph County	45 093	73.5	2 701	71.3	257	72.8	188	89.9	2 074	87.0	5.7	0.3	0.5	4.7	3.7	6.9
Richmond County	12 146	70.5	4 922	69.6	362	84.0	78	83.3	287	80.8	2.2	0.3	0.5	1.4	1.0	6.7
Robeson County	15 834	69.9	10 540	73.7	15 220	77.3	275	92.0	1 297	76.1	4.2	0.4	0.7	3.1	2.2	9.0
Rockingham County	29 197	70.8	6 716	73.2	135	70.4	90	100.0	723	81.2	2.7	0.3	0.3	2.1	1.6	6.3
Rowan County	40 031	71.6	7 203	69.2	173	74.6	200	86.0	1 143	88.3	3.7	0.4	0.5	2.7	2.3	6.8
Rutherford County	22 072	72.1	2 564	69.3	59	67.8	64	53.1	287	81.9	1.4	0.3	0.2	0.8	0.9	5.3
Sampson County	13 862	72.6	6 383	71.4	385	82.1	87	86.2	1 464	83.9	7.1	0.2	0.3	6.5	5.0	10.4
Scotland County	7 332	71.9	4 756	73.9	984	75.3	89	87.6	100	50.0	1.3	0.5	0.3	0.3	0.4	7.0
Stanly County	19 350	72.7	2 216	73.0	77	90.9	131	90.1	308	86.4	2.6	0.2	0.9	1.5	1.6	5.5
Stokes County	16 389	74.9	835	70.8	36	75.0	34	100.0	235	89.4	1.5	0.5	0.1	0.9	0.7	5.6
Surry County	25 830	72.0	1 104	68.8	155	70.3	58	96.6	1 147	86.8	5.3	0.4	0.4	4.4	3.3	7.8

[1] Hispanic or Latino persons may be of any race.

STATE/County code	MSA/PMSA/NECMA code[1]	STATE County	Population by age (percent)										Non-Hispanic White		
														Age (percent)	
			Total population	Under 5 years	5 to 17 years	18 to 24 years	25 to 44 years	45 to 64 years	65 years and over	Median age	+/− U.S. percent under 18 years	+/− U.S. percent 65 years and over	Total population	Under 18 years	65 years and over
			1	2	3	4	5	6	7	8	9	10	11	12	13
		NORTH CAROLINA—Cont'd													
37 173	...	Swain County	12 968	6.0	18.4	8.3	26.6	25.7	15.1	38.8	-1.3	2.7	8 704	19.5	19.4
37 175	...	Transylvania County	29 334	4.9	15.4	8.1	23.0	27.1	21.4	43.9	-5.4	9.0	27 173	19.2	22.6
37 177	...	Tyrrell County	4 149	4.6	17.9	9.3	29.5	21.9	16.8	38.7	-3.2	4.4	2 307	20.2	19.6
37 179	1520	Union County	123 677	8.0	19.9	8.2	33.1	21.6	9.1	34.0	2.2	-3.3	98 742	26.5	9.9
37 181	...	Vance County	42 954	7.2	19.9	9.2	28.6	22.3	12.8	35.0	1.4	0.4	19 930	20.8	17.2
37 183	6640	Wake County	627 846	7.1	17.9	10.7	36.6	20.3	7.3	32.9	-0.7	-5.1	438 938	23.3	8.5
37 185	...	Warren County	19 972	5.6	17.8	8.4	26.6	24.1	17.4	39.7	-2.3	5.0	7 715	17.7	22.8
37 187	...	Washington County	13 723	6.6	19.3	7.9	24.9	25.9	15.5	39.2	0.2	3.1	6 562	19.3	20.7
37 189	...	Watauga County	42 695	3.9	12.3	27.7	23.6	21.4	11.1	29.9	-9.5	-1.3	40 658	16.1	11.4
37 191	2980	Wayne County	113 329	6.8	19.4	9.5	30.8	22.0	11.5	34.8	0.5	-0.9	67 789	22.8	13.5
37 193	...	Wilkes County	65 632	6.3	16.3	8.1	29.6	25.6	14.2	38.5	-3.1	1.8	59 847	22.0	14.7
37 195	...	Wilson County	73 814	6.7	18.7	9.4	28.7	23.6	12.8	36.2	-0.3	0.4	39 485	20.3	16.6
37 197	3120	Yadkin County	36 348	6.6	17.3	7.6	30.3	24.0	14.2	37.6	-1.8	1.8	32 614	22.6	15.1
37 199	...	Yancey County	17 774	5.5	15.8	7.2	26.2	27.1	18.1	41.9	-4.4	5.7	17 061	20.9	18.6
38 000	...	NORTH DAKOTA	642 200	6.1	19.0	11.3	27.3	21.6	14.7	36.2	-0.6	2.3	589 853	23.7	15.7
38 001	...	Adams County	2 593	4.3	19.1	3.9	21.2	27.3	24.2	45.6	-2.3	11.8	2 526	23.5	24.5
38 003	...	Barnes County	11 775	5.3	16.9	11.6	23.0	23.5	19.7	40.6	-3.5	7.3	11 522	22.0	20.0
38 005	...	Benson County	6 964	9.1	27.2	7.7	23.4	18.8	13.8	31.4	10.6	1.4	3 558	23.4	24.3
38 007	...	Billings County	888	4.3	20.3	2.9	28.3	28.4	15.9	41.9	-1.1	3.5	885	24.6	15.9
38 009	...	Bottineau County	7 149	4.0	18.1	8.3	22.2	26.1	21.2	43.4	-3.6	8.8	6 944	21.3	21.6
38 011	...	Bowman County	3 242	4.6	19.4	5.4	24.3	24.5	21.9	43.0	-1.7	9.5	3 210	23.7	22.0
38 013	...	Burke County	2 242	3.6	17.3	3.9	21.8	28.7	24.8	47.5	-4.8	12.4	2 205	20.2	25.1
38 015	1010	Burleigh County	69 416	6.2	18.6	10.9	29.2	22.5	12.5	35.9	-0.9	0.1	65 850	23.9	13.0
38 017	2520	Cass County	123 138	6.6	16.9	15.9	31.4	19.6	9.6	31.3	-2.2	-2.8	116 106	22.6	10.1
38 019	...	Cavalier County	4 831	4.3	20.1	4.0	21.5	27.3	22.9	45.2	-1.3	10.5	4 772	23.9	23.2
38 021	...	Dickey County	5 757	5.6	18.1	10.0	22.6	22.4	21.3	40.7	-2.0	8.9	5 597	23.2	21.8
38 023	...	Divide County	2 283	3.0	17.1	3.6	20.1	26.7	29.4	49.0	-5.6	17.0	2 247	19.6	29.8
38 025	...	Dunn County	3 600	5.6	22.1	5.8	23.5	25.6	17.3	40.9	2.0	4.9	3 120	25.6	19.0
38 027	...	Eddy County	2 757	5.4	18.2	6.2	22.3	23.1	24.7	43.8	-2.1	12.3	2 684	23.0	25.3
38 029	...	Emmons County	4 331	5.5	19.4	3.0	23.0	23.6	25.6	44.5	-0.8	13.2	4 286	24.9	25.6
38 031	...	Foster County	3 759	5.3	20.8	5.5	26.4	20.7	21.3	40.5	0.4	8.9	3 706	25.9	21.5
38 033	...	Golden Valley County	1 924	5.5	23.0	5.0	22.3	23.1	21.0	41.2	2.8	8.6	1 881	27.6	21.4
38 035	2985	Grand Forks County	66 109	6.3	17.5	19.7	28.7	18.1	9.7	29.2	-1.9	-2.7	60 719	22.7	10.3
38 037	...	Grant County	2 841	4.5	19.1	4.5	20.7	26.8	24.5	46.5	-2.1	12.1	2 753	22.5	24.9
38 039	...	Griggs County	2 754	4.6	18.1	4.9	20.7	26.0	25.6	45.8	-3.0	13.2	2 738	22.8	25.7
38 041	...	Hettinger County	2 715	4.5	18.8	3.8	20.8	26.7	25.3	46.2	-2.4	12.9	2 684	23.4	25.5
38 043	...	Kidder County	2 753	4.6	18.6	4.7	22.5	25.4	24.1	44.5	-2.5	11.7	2 712	22.9	24.4
38 045	...	LaMoure County	4 701	4.4	19.8	5.6	22.9	23.9	23.3	43.3	-1.5	10.9	4 651	24.1	23.6
38 047	...	Logan County	2 308	5.6	17.3	3.8	21.5	24.7	27.1	46.4	-2.8	14.7	2 275	22.7	27.2
38 049	...	McHenry County	5 987	5.1	18.9	6.0	23.3	25.0	21.7	43.0	-1.7	9.3	5 903	23.8	21.9
38 051	...	McIntosh County	3 390	4.2	15.1	4.6	19.4	22.5	34.2	51.0	-6.4	21.8	3 345	19.2	34.6
38 053	...	McKenzie County	5 737	6.0	24.7	5.8	23.1	24.5	15.9	39.5	5.0	3.5	4 432	26.0	18.8
38 055	...	McLean County	9 311	4.8	18.8	5.3	22.7	28.0	20.3	44.1	-2.1	7.9	8 577	22.1	21.7
38 057	...	Mercer County	8 644	4.6	24.4	4.1	27.7	25.0	14.2	40.1	3.3	1.8	8 280	28.3	14.6
38 059	1010	Morton County	25 303	6.4	20.6	7.7	28.2	22.4	14.7	37.4	1.3	2.3	24 201	26.1	15.1
38 061	...	Mountrail County	6 631	6.5	21.6	6.9	23.3	24.1	17.6	39.6	2.4	5.2	4 343	21.9	23.9
38 063	...	Nelson County	3 715	3.9	18.4	3.6	20.4	26.2	27.5	47.2	-3.4	15.1	3 659	22.1	27.7
38 065	...	Oliver County	2 065	4.9	22.7	4.5	23.8	29.5	14.6	42.0	1.9	2.2	2 007	27.7	14.7
38 067	...	Pembina County	8 585	5.1	19.7	6.4	24.5	24.8	19.5	41.6	-0.9	7.1	8 101	24.2	20.4
38 069	...	Pierce County	4 675	5.6	18.2	5.6	24.6	22.1	24.0	42.9	-1.9	11.6	4 605	23.5	24.3
38 071	...	Ramsey County	12 066	5.5	19.5	7.7	26.3	22.1	18.9	39.5	-0.7	6.5	11 078	23.7	20.0
38 073	...	Ransom County	5 890	5.9	19.3	5.8	25.2	22.7	21.1	40.7	-0.5	8.7	5 742	24.5	21.5
38 075	...	Renville County	2 610	4.5	18.7	5.1	24.5	25.3	21.9	43.6	-2.5	9.5	2 526	23.1	22.3
38 077	...	Richland County	17 998	5.9	18.7	14.4	25.5	20.1	15.4	35.4	-1.1	3.0	17 316	24.1	15.7
38 079	...	Rolette County	13 674	8.5	28.0	9.3	25.8	18.6	9.8	28.9	10.8	-2.6	3 503	22.2	21.2
38 081	...	Sargent County	4 366	5.8	20.5	5.3	25.7	25.7	17.1	40.3	0.6	4.7	4 300	26.4	17.2
38 083	...	Sheridan County	1 710	3.2	18.0	3.9	19.8	28.2	26.8	48.1	-4.5	14.4	1 692	21.3	26.9
38 085	...	Sioux County	4 044	10.8	29.9	11.8	26.2	15.4	5.8	23.9	15.0	-6.6	670	22.2	16.6
38 087	...	Slope County	767	5.0	20.9	4.0	25.3	27.0	17.9	42.5	0.2	5.5	767	25.8	17.9
38 089	...	Stark County	22 636	5.7	19.7	11.6	26.4	21.1	15.5	36.9	-0.3	3.1	21 927	25.2	15.8
38 091	...	Steele County	2 258	5.8	21.9	4.7	23.3	24.8	19.6	41.4	2.0	7.2	2 226	27.6	19.8
38 093	...	Stutsman County	21 908	5.2	17.7	10.4	25.6	23.5	17.6	39.6	-2.8	5.2	21 404	22.7	18.0
38 095	...	Towner County	2 876	4.5	20.3	3.7	23.9	24.3	23.4	44.0	-0.9	11.0	2 792	24.7	23.6
38 097	...	Traill County	8 477	6.1	18.8	9.8	24.7	21.5	19.2	39.0	-0.8	6.8	8 213	24.4	19.7
38 099	...	Walsh County	12 389	5.7	19.1	6.4	25.1	24.2	19.5	40.9	-0.9	7.1	11 521	23.7	20.7

[1]MSA = Metropolitan Statistical Area. PMSA = Primary MSA. NECMA = New England County Metropolitan Area. See the Appendix A for explanation of these concepts. See Appendix B for list of metropolitan areas identified by type, with component counties.

Table A-3. States and Counties — Age, Ethnicity, and Household Structure

STATE County	Black or African American Total population	Under 18 years	65 years and over	American Indian and Alaska Native Total population	Under 18 years	65 years and over	Asian, Hawaiian, and Pacific Islander Total population	Under 18 years	65 years and over	Hispanic or Latino[1] Total population	Under 18 years	65 years and over	Two or more races Total population	Under 18 years	65 years and over
	14	15	16	17	18	19	20	21	22	23	24	25	26	27	28
NORTH CAROLINA—Cont'd															
Swain County	288	22.2	10.1	3 498	35.3	6.1	22	0.0	0.0	115	19.1	0.0	368	38.0	6.8
Transylvania County	1 404	34.7	6.1	97	17.5	6.2	114	7.0	9.6	214	41.1	8.4	341	40.2	4.4
Tyrrell County	1 593	25.2	15.1	7	28.6	0.0	21	0.0	0.0	195	24.1	1.5	33	63.6	0.0
Union County	15 381	33.7	7.9	508	34.3	0.0	603	34.2	1.7	7 726	32.0	1.6	1 173	44.7	5.8
Vance County	20 791	31.8	9.9	105	22.9	6.7	137	32.8	0.0	1 831	37.0	0.5	424	46.0	3.1
Wake County	123 058	29.0	6.2	2 271	23.9	3.0	21 039	25.0	3.0	34 135	28.0	1.3	11 066	41.3	2.4
Warren County	10 826	27.4	14.6	819	26.4	9.9	97	9.3	3.1	365	29.0	1.6	205	25.4	17.6
Washington County	6 856	31.5	11.2	0	X	X	80	22.5	0.0	159	28.9	0.0	105	62.9	0.0
Watauga County	679	16.6	11.5	174	6.3	0.0	199	17.1	0.0	591	15.4	2.5	444	28.8	5.2
Wayne County	37 586	30.0	9.9	330	24.2	3.6	1 145	25.2	2.5	5 300	37.0	0.9	1 505	48.3	2.1
Wilkes County	2 808	24.4	15.3	95	31.6	6.3	347	24.5	1.2	2 187	34.6	2.0	457	54.3	7.9
Wilson County	29 350	31.4	9.4	125	23.2	1.6	341	20.2	6.7	4 122	31.0	1.2	771	44.5	7.4
Yadkin County	1 081	25.1	15.1	67	37.3	13.4	50	14.0	18.0	2 432	39.6	2.1	259	45.2	9.3
Yancey County	86	24.4	17.4	74	56.8	0.0	32	25.0	0.0	504	33.5	1.2	57	14.0	38.6
NORTH DAKOTA.......	3 673	36.5	2.3	31 308	41.4	4.5	3 529	26.8	3.5	7 568	39.7	4.0	7 545	48.0	4.2
Adams County	22	0.0	18.2	31	19.4	9.7	0	X	X	5	0.0	0.0	9	77.8	0.0
Barnes County	21	28.6	0.0	98	42.9	0.0	18	0.0	0.0	41	7.3	0.0	75	36.0	13.3
Benson County	2	100.0	0.0	3 306	49.9	2.7	2	0.0	0.0	56	55.4	12.5	82	43.9	7.3
Billings County	0	X	X	0	X	X	0	X	X	0	X	X	3	0.0	0.0
Bottineau County	0	X	X	135	42.2	9.6	11	63.6	0.0	9	0.0	66.7	53	77.4	3.8
Bowman County	4	0.0	100.0	4	0.0	0.0	0	X	X	20	75.0	0.0	7	57.1	0.0
Burke County	2	0.0	100.0	13	46.2	0.0	3	0.0	0.0	4	100.0	0.0	19	84.2	0.0
Burleigh County............	204	21.1	15.2	2 079	45.0	0.6	279	27.6	5.7	516	36.4	9.3	545	42.0	5.7
Cass County..................	1 027	50.1	0.0	1 666	20.2	2.8	1 432	25.9	2.0	1 430	40.5	3.8	1 502	50.1	1.8
Cavalier County............	5	100.0	0.0	15	46.7	13.3	6	83.3	0.0	29	69.0	0.0	12	66.7	0.0
Dickey County............	7	71.4	0.0	44	47.7	4.5	20	60.0	10.0	68	32.4	2.9	24	41.7	0.0
Divide County	0	X	X	6	66.7	0.0	18	55.6	0.0	10	30.0	20.0	2	100.0	0.0
Dunn County	2	0.0	0.0	430	41.6	6.0	8	0.0	25.0	10	20.0	0.0	32	65.6	6.3
Eddy County	0	X	X	37	32.4	5.4	2	0.0	0.0	14	57.1	0.0	20	75.0	0.0
Emmons County	2	0.0	0.0	4	0.0	50.0	2	0.0	0.0	41	22.0	14.6	4	0.0	0.0
Foster County	6	100.0	0.0	0	X	X	10	30.0	0.0	15	0.0	13.3	18	83.3	0.0
Goldon Valley County ...	0	X	X	10	100.0	0.0	3	0.0	0.0	15	73.3	0.0	20	70.0	10.0
Grand Forks County......	867	29.2	1.4	1 612	38.8	1.7	662	15.3	0.9	1 408	36.0	3.9	1 023	51.2	2.5
Grant County	0	X	X	38	60.5	0.0	9	88.9	0.0	13	61.5	0.0	28	39.3	35.7
Griggs County	0	X	X	8	0.0	0.0	3	0.0	0.0	1	100.0	0.0	4	0.0	50.0
Hettinger County	0	X	X	12	25.0	16.7	2	0.0	0.0	11	18.2	18.2	8	12.5	0.0
Kidder County	2	100.0	0.0	4	0.0	0.0	0	X	X	28	50.0	7.1	10	00.0	0.0
LaMoure County............	0	X	X	10	10.0	0.0	0	X	X	24	41.7	0.0	16	50.0	0.0
Logan County	0	X	X	0	X	X	18	66.7	0.0	11	0.0	36.4	2	0.0	0.0
McHenry County	12	33.3	0.0	18	27.8	0.0	5	0.0	0.0	26	53.8	7.7	30	46.7	6.7
McIntosh County	0	X	X	5	20.0	0.0	8	37.5	0.0	20	20.0	5.0	15	46.7	13.3
McKenzie County	4	25.0	0.0	1 097	47.5	6.1	36	19.4	16.7	34	38.2	5.9	139	48.9	1.4
McLean County	3	100.0	0.0	589	39.7	4.6	7	28.6	0.0	62	53.2	0.0	118	48.3	4.2
Mercer County..............	2	100.0	0.0	139	49.6	8.6	39	66.7	0.0	67	47.8	0.0	146	41.1	5.5
Morton County..............	65	49.2	0.0	587	39.2	7.0	47	63.8	17.0	171	46.2	1.2	288	64.2	0.7
Mountrail County..........	3	0.0	0.0	1 986	41.6	4.6	41	22.0	7.3	77	71.4	6.5	236	30.1	11.9
Nelson County	2	0.0	0.0	24	20.8	25.0	13	30.8	0.0	2	100.0	0.0	15	73.3	0.0
Oliver County	0	X	X	28	10.7	14.3	4	100.0	0.0	12	66.7	0.0	14	0.0	14.3
Pembina County	4	0.0	0.0	119	25.2	3.4	18	44.4	0.0	242	42.1	2.5	143	37.8	4.9
Pierce County..............	12	41.7	0.0	32	40.6	0.0	5	0.0	0.0	3	100.0	0.0	12	25.0	0.0
Ramsey County..............	0	X	X	675	39.0	5.5	27	44.4	3.7	133	52.6	4.5	204	39.7	4.9
Ransom County	12	66.7	0.0	47	40.4	23.4	5	0.0	0.0	38	50.0	0.0	53	62.3	0.0
Renville County	11	45.5	0.0	24	8.3	25.0	11	36.4	18.2	17	52.9	0.0	18	11.1	0.0
Richland County	43	23.3	0.0	321	31.2	9.7	68	32.4	25.0	121	38.0	5.0	138	45.7	7.2
Rolette County	14	0.0	0.0	9 710	41.4	5.9	148	48.6	0.0	66	65.2	6.1	286	44.4	9.4
Sargent County	4	25.0	0.0	23	17.4	0.0	0	X	X	6	0.0	83.3	33	24.2	3.0
Sheridan County	0	X	X	5	0.0	0.0	0	X	X	8	0.0	50.0	5	40.0	0.0
Sioux County	2	100.0	0.0	3 240	44.1	3.7	31	41.9	0.0	86	58.1	5.8	86	59.3	0.0
Slope County................	0	X	X	0	X	X	0	X	X	0	X	X	0	X	X
Stark County	35	42.9	0.0	263	36.9	2.7	42	28.6	9.5	226	31.0	4.9	180	40.0	6.1
Steele County	1	0.0	0.0	21	33.3	9.5	0	X	X	3	0.0	0.0	8	25.0	0.0
Stutsman County	18	0.0	0.0	234	29.9	0.0	46	21.7	13.0	167	34.7	3.6	107	57.9	0.0
Towner County............	2	0.0	0.0	55	25.5	20.0	0	X	X	6	33.3	66.7	21	42.9	0.0
Traill County	14	28.6	0.0	76	46.1	5.3	16	37.5	12.5	139	31.7	0.0	26	57.7	0.0
Walsh County	4	50.0	0.0	134	36.6	0.0	7	0.0	0.0	646	39.8	2.8	130	52.3	6.9

[1] Hispanic or Latino persons may be of any race.

Table A-3. States and Counties — Age, Ethnicity, and Household Structure

STATE County	Total households	Family households (percent)						Nonfamily households (percent)						Percent of householders 65 years and over who live alone	Grandparents who are responsible for the care of their grandchildren
		Married-couple family households			Other family households			Two or more unrelated persons		Male living alone		Female living alone			
		Total	With children	Householder 65 years or over	Total	With children	Householder 65 years or over	Total	Householder 65 years or over	Total	Householder 65 years or over	Total	Householder 65 years or over		
	29	30	31	32	33	34	35	36	37	38	39	40	41	42	43
NORTH CAROLINA—Cont'd															
Swain County	5 131	54.0	19.7	11.2	17.8	10.0	4.0	2.4	0.0	10.3	2.6	15.4	6.9	38.3	228
Transylvania County	12 370	59.3	19.4	17.8	11.1	6.3	1.9	3.6	0.3	8.7	2.5	17.3	9.7	38.0	184
Tyrrell County	1 545	50.4	18.1	13.9	19.5	9.4	2.5	1.6	0.3	12.9	4.5	15.5	9.3	45.2	31
Union County	43 370	66.3	32.5	7.9	13.4	7.6	1.5	3.4	0.1	6.8	1.3	10.1	5.3	40.7	919
Vance County	16 173	47.3	20.3	8.0	24.8	13.9	3.8	3.7	0.4	9.2	2.5	15.0	7.8	45.7	628
Wake County	242 133	53.2	27.0	5.5	12.8	7.7	1.1	8.3	0.1	11.8	1.2	13.9	3.9	42.9	3 603
Warren County	7 715	50.2	19.2	12.5	21.1	10.4	4.1	2.5	0.4	12.0	2.8	14.2	8.7	40.3	306
Washington County	5 382	51.2	18.5	11.8	21.5	12.9	4.1	2.8	0.2	8.2	2.0	16.4	9.0	40.5	376
Watauga County	16 552	48.1	18.6	9.5	9.1	4.9	1.0	14.2	0.3	13.4	1.9	15.2	5.9	42.0	173
Wayne County	42 541	53.2	24.3	8.6	18.0	10.8	2.0	4.2	0.2	10.0	2.0	14.6	7.3	46.2	1 250
Wilkes County	26 667	60.6	24.2	10.7	12.4	6.0	2.7	2.5	0.3	10.1	2.3	14.5	7.9	42.8	451
Wilson County	28 660	47.9	20.6	7.7	21.6	11.8	2.7	4.1	0.2	10.6	2.6	15.8	8.5	51.2	1 026
Yadkin County	14 487	61.4	25.7	10.3	12.0	6.8	2.3	2.5	0.1	9.2	2.5	14.9	8.9	47.5	212
Yancey County	7 477	60.3	22.0	13.7	11.5	5.8	2.2	2.7	0.1	10.4	3.5	15.1	9.7	45.1	156
NORTH DAKOTA	257 234	54.1	24.7	10.8	10.8	6.9	1.3	5.8	0.2	13.1	2.8	16.2	8.7	48.3	2 547
Adams County	1 122	57.4	20.5	16.0	7.6	5.8	1.3	2.5	0.7	11.4	3.3	21.1	14.3	49.4	10
Barnes County	4 886	53.6	20.7	13.5	11.1	6.5	2.5	4.1	0.2	14.1	4.1	17.2	11.5	49.0	40
Benson County	2 338	49.3	21.4	12.1	24.5	16.1	3.2	2.1	0.3	12.6	4.1	11.6	7.7	43.4	159
Billings County	362	60.8	25.1	14.4	9.1	3.3	3.9	3.0	0.8	16.9	1.4	10.2	3.0	18.8	4
Bottineau County	2 967	58.5	23.7	15.0	7.4	4.3	1.6	2.7	0.3	13.2	4.1	18.1	12.2	49.2	11
Bowman County	1 372	60.2	26.7	13.8	6.6	4.4	1.4	2.1	0.4	14.7	5.5	16.4	12.1	53.1	6
Burke County	1 018	56.8	19.1	17.6	9.7	4.3	2.7	1.9	0.6	14.0	5.4	17.6	13.6	47.7	12
Burleigh County	27 737	55.2	26.1	9.5	10.8	6.6	1.0	6.0	0.2	10.7	1.7	17.3	7.6	46.5	152
Cass County	51 293	47.9	23.6	6.8	10.7	6.9	0.7	10.2	0.2	14.1	1.7	17.0	5.9	49.7	292
Cavalier County	2 007	60.8	24.1	16.5	6.7	3.7	1.4	1.1	0.4	14.1	3.9	17.3	13.2	48.2	3
Dickey County	2 290	57.7	24.5	14.1	8.5	4.8	1.6	2.1	0.1	13.3	4.6	18.4	13.5	53.5	7
Divide County	1 011	57.1	18.0	19.5	7.3	4.2	1.4	1.7	0.2	13.4	5.0	20.6	16.6	50.7	0
Dunn County	1 389	59.8	25.8	14.4	11.2	6.6	2.4	3.7	0.3	13.1	4.1	12.2	8.0	41.4	19
Eddy County	1 141	57.7	22.3	15.6	5.6	2.7	1.3	1.7	0.3	14.6	5.1	20.4	14.8	53.7	4
Emmons County	1 767	60.7	23.0	19.1	9.1	5.3	1.6	2.1	0.6	13.6	5.2	14.5	11.8	44.3	12
Foster County	1 551	58.5	26.6	17.5	9.2	6.0	1.1	2.5	0.1	12.7	2.6	17.2	11.6	43.2	0
Golden Valley County	759	60.7	23.3	17.1	6.5	4.7	1.4	1.3	0.0	11.5	2.0	20.0	12.5	43.8	9
Grand Forks County	25 451	50.2	25.2	6.9	11.7	7.6	1.2	9.8	0.2	14.0	2.0	14.3	6.4	50.6	157
Grant County	1 199	60.3	22.4	17.4	6.3	3.3	1.4	1.8	0.4	14.4	4.8	17.2	13.6	48.9	5
Griggs County	1 177	60.7	24.9	17.6	5.4	2.2	1.9	2.4	0.3	14.3	4.8	17.2	13.4	47.9	0
Hettinger County	1 161	62.5	23.4	19.0	5.1	2.8	1.3	1.0	0.3	13.8	4.7	17.6	13.4	46.9	12
Kidder County	1 164	60.7	23.5	18.6	7.6	4.1	2.4	2.0	0.3	12.9	4.4	16.8	12.9	44.8	8
LaMoure County	1 937	61.0	23.5	18.6	6.3	3.9	1.3	1.4	0.2	15.0	4.3	16.3	12.6	45.7	11
Logan County	959	63.2	23.3	21.6	4.8	1.3	1.0	2.7	0.5	12.7	2.5	16.6	13.6	41.0	0
McHenry County	2 524	58.0	24.2	16.0	9.5	4.6	2.1	2.9	0.8	14.5	5.2	15.1	10.5	45.2	29
McIntosh County	1 468	62.2	19.8	24.3	4.8	2.5	1.0	1.4	0.8	13.6	6.2	18.1	14.3	44.0	4
McKenzie County	2 161	58.3	25.5	12.6	13.1	8.5	2.5	2.3	0.2	12.8	4.2	13.4	9.5	47.2	86
McLean County	3 848	63.1	24.7	15.6	8.5	5.4	1.1	1.9	0.4	14.6	4.0	14.6	10.8	46.4	45
Mercer County	3 354	65.6	30.8	11.8	7.5	5.1	0.7	1.9	0.1	12.5	2.3	12.5	8.3	45.6	20
Morton County	9 883	59.0	27.3	12.2	11.4	7.9	0.8	3.8	0.3	11.9	2.1	13.9	8.4	44.2	128
Mountrail County	2 573	53.2	22.7	12.5	15.5	8.7	1.8	2.8	0.2	13.7	3.8	14.8	10.4	49.7	59
Nelson County	1 629	52.0	19.8	15.5	10.2	5.0	3.7	1.4	0.3	15.8	6.0	20.6	16.2	53.2	5
Oliver County	781	70.4	31.2	12.8	6.0	3.1	1.5	2.3	0.3	10.6	3.6	10.6	8.3	44.9	18
Pembina County	3 535	58.4	24.6	13.9	8.8	4.7	2.3	2.6	0.2	13.7	4.0	16.5	11.8	48.9	19
Pierce County	1 964	56.3	22.9	15.6	9.2	6.2	1.9	2.6	0.3	12.7	3.5	19.2	13.6	49.1	31
Ramsey County	4 950	51.8	22.0	12.4	12.6	8.5	1.6	4.3	0.3	12.4	3.2	18.9	11.0	49.9	53
Ransom County	2 343	60.0	26.8	14.6	6.8	4.6	1.3	2.8	0.3	12.2	2.4	18.2	13.3	49.3	4
Renville County	1 087	61.6	24.1	16.9	8.0	5.3	2.3	1.9	0.0	14.1	3.7	14.4	10.3	42.1	7
Richland County	6 848	54.5	26.7	10.5	9.7	5.7	1.7	6.3	0.3	13.8	2.8	15.7	9.2	49.0	57
Rolette County	4 557	45.6	24.3	6.8	28.3	19.7	2.9	3.6	0.1	10.8	3.9	11.8	6.7	51.7	339
Sargent County	1 783	62.2	27.3	13.5	7.6	3.9	1.0	2.7	0.1	14.4	3.3	13.1	10.4	48.3	6
Sheridan County	727	62.6	21.5	20.5	7.7	3.2	3.3	1.8	0.7	13.9	7.0	14.0	11.1	42.6	13
Sioux County	1 091	36.8	22.5	4.9	42.8	27.5	5.3	3.5	0.2	12.4	2.8	4.6	2.7	34.5	157
Slope County	312	64.1	27.9	18.6	6.7	4.8	1.3	1.3	0.6	18.6	3.2	9.3	6.7	32.6	2
Stark County	8 919	57.0	27.4	11.0	9.3	5.7	1.4	4.6	0.1	12.7	3.1	16.3	9.1	49.3	99
Steele County	925	64.0	25.9	17.4	5.1	3.5	1.2	2.5	0.0	16.8	5.5	11.7	8.0	42.1	2
Stutsman County	8 996	53.3	22.1	12.3	10.1	6.7	1.2	4.1	0.3	12.6	3.0	19.9	11.6	51.5	84
Towner County	1 204	56.6	21.4	15.7	7.8	5.0	1.4	2.0	0.0	16.5	4.8	17.0	13.7	52.0	10
Traill County	3 362	57.4	25.8	13.7	9.3	5.5	1.7	4.3	0.1	13.2	4.4	15.8	10.9	49.5	13
Walsh County	5 028	55.4	24.5	13.4	10.6	6.4	2.4	2.7	0.0	13.4	3.8	17.9	11.2	48.8	65

Table A-3. States and Counties — Age, Ethnicity, and Household Structure

STATE County	Households with Non-Hispanic White householder — Number of households	Percent that are family households	Households with Black or African American householder — Number of households	Percent that are family households	Households with American Indian and Alaska Native householder — Number of households	Percent that are family households	Households with Asian, Hawaiian, and Pacific Islander householder — Number of households	Percent that are family households	Households with Hispanic or Latino[1] householder — Number of households	Percent that are family households	Foreign-born population — Percent of total population that is foreign-born	Place of birth (percent) — Europe	Asia	Latin America	Percent in non-English speaking households — Linguistically isolated	Not linguistically isolated
	44	45	46	47	48	49	50	51	52	53	54	55	56	57	58	59
NORTH CAROLINA—Cont'd																
Swain County	3 578	70.4	76	38.2	1 278	77.1	17	100.0	7	57.1	1.0	0.3	0.2	0.5	0.6	9.6
Transylvania County	11 771	70.3	412	76.7	45	71.1	14	100.0	44	52.3	2.3	1.0	0.6	0.4	0.2	7.2
Tyrrell County	1 006	68.0	491	72.3	0	X	11	90.9	34	85.3	4.0	0.2	0.6	3.1	3.2	3.9
Union County	36 290	79.5	4 926	77.8	117	94.9	162	72.8	1 632	92.0	5.7	0.5	0.4	4.4	2.7	10.1
Vance County	8 254	71.2	7 381	72.4	41	48.8	32	93.8	411	87.3	3.4	0.1	0.3	3.0	1.8	7.9
Wake County	178 565	64.8	44 907	67.6	729	68.0	6 691	75.7	8 803	77.2	9.7	1.4	3.0	3.8	3.8	12.8
Warren County	3 291	73.9	3 902	70.0	320	68.8	20	80.0	106	76.4	2.3	0.4	0.3	1.3	0.5	7.6
Washington County	2 823	72.7	2 497	73.2	0	X	18	50.0	26	61.5	1.4	0.1	0.5	0.8	0.7	6.2
Watauga County	15 906	57.4	234	53.8	65	76.9	74	29.7	142	42.3	1.9	0.7	0.4	0.5	0.6	6.7
Wayne County	27 065	72.2	13 457	68.7	81	79.0	326	68.1	1 259	79.6	4.2	0.6	0.8	2.7	1.9	9.8
Wilkes County	24 720	73.3	1 215	63.5	23	100.0	103	70.9	490	84.9	3.0	0.2	0.4	2.2	1.9	6.3
Wilson County	16 685	70.0	10 745	67.8	36	61.1	111	89.2	929	82.1	4.9	0.1	0.6	4.1	3.1	9.0
Yadkin County	13 531	73.0	407	70.3	22	59.1	7	28.6	493	89.2	4.4	0.1	0.1	4.1	3.1	7.7
Yancey County	7 281	71.9	39	71.8	10	80.0	6	66.7	117	84.6	2.8	0.5	0.1	2.0	2.0	4.2
NORTH DAKOTA	242 300	64.4	1 153	66.3	8 925	76.7	1 111	73.0	2 137	68.7	1.9	0.6	0.4	0.2	0.9	10.0
Adams County	1 107	65.0	2	100.0	9	77.8	0	X	2	0.0	1.5	1.2	0.1	0.2	0.3	5.5
Barnes County	4 788	64.6	15	46.7	29	89.7	16	87.5	15	60.0	0.9	0.5	0.1	0.2	0.5	5.7
Benson County	1 517	66.6	0	X	797	87.3	2	100.0	7	71.4	0.5	0.2	0.0	0.0	0.5	17.7
Billings County	362	69.9	0	X	0	X	0	X	0	X	1.0	1.0	0.0	0.0	1.1	9.3
Bottineau County	2 927	65.9	0	X	32	68.8	2	100.0	3	100.0	2.1	0.8	0.2	0.1	0.3	7.8
Bowman County	1 364	66.9	4	0.0	2	100.0	0	X	2	100.0	0.4	0.2	0.0	0.2	0.3	1.7
Burke County	1 013	66.5	2	0.0	3	100.0	0	X	0	X	1.5	0.1	0.0	0.0	0.0	6.1
Burleigh County	26 838	65.9	57	64.9	508	79.7	119	78.2	105	39.0	1.5	0.6	0.4	0.3	1.1	11.0
Cass County	49 051	58.5	305	68.9	593	49.9	526	67.1	422	63.3	3.2	1.1	1.0	0.2	1.1	8.0
Cavalier County	1 993	67.4	0	X	6	50.0	0	X	4	100.0	2.5	0.5	0.1	0.2	0.3	4.3
Dickey County	2 256	65.8	2	100.0	15	86.7	3	100.0	13	84.6	1.6	0.8	0.3	0.2	1.2	11.6
Divide County	1 002	64.6	0	X	0	X	4	100.0	5	0.0	2.4	0.4	0.3	0.0	0.5	7.1
Dunn County	1 242	71.5	0	X	126	72.2	6	0.0	6	0.0	0.7	0.4	0.2	0.1	0.7	13.3
Eddy County	1 115	63.1	0	X	16	75.0	2	0.0	3	100.0	0.4	0.1	0.1	0.0	0.2	8.5
Emmons County	1 749	69.7	2	0.0	0	X	0	X	16	87.5	0.5	0.5	0.0	0.0	3.4	21.0
Foster County	1 546	67.5	0	X	0	X	3	100.0	2	100.0	1.5	0.5	0.2	0.3	0.8	6.3
Golden Valley County	750	67.2	0	X	0	X	3	0.0	2	100.0	0.6	0.2	0.2	0.0	0.2	6.0
Grand Forks County	23 869	61.6	313	60.1	449	63.7	188	86.7	474	65.8	3.2	0.9	0.8	0.3	0.8	9.9
Grant County	1 176	66.8	0	X	10	40.0	1	100.0	5	60.0	1.3	1.1	0.0	0.1	1.8	18.0
Griggs County	1 171	66.1	0	X	4	100.0	0	X	0	X	1.0	0.4	0.1	0.0	0.3	5.2
Hettinger County	1 150	68.0	0	X	7	42.9	0	X	4	0.0	0.1	0.1	0.1	0.0	0.6	9.2
Kidder County	1 158	68.4	0	X	0	X	0	X	6	66.7	0.9	0.9	0.0	0.0	1.6	11.4
LaMoure County	1 928	67.3	0	X	2	0.0	0	X	7	85.7	0.8	0.3	0.1	0.2	2.3	11.9
Logan County	952	68.0	0	X	0	X	5	60.0	2	100.0	0.6	0.3	0.3	0.0	5.8	28.8
McHenry County	2 500	67.7	4	50.0	4	100.0	3	0.0	6	0.0	1.0	0.4	0.0	0.0	0.4	9.2
McIntosh County	1 453	67.1	0	X	4	25.0	1	100.0	2	100.0	0.8	0.2	0.2	0.1	10.1	33.8
McKenzie County	1 832	68.4	3	33.3	283	89.0	11	54.5	7	100.0	1.4	0.2	0.5	0.0	0.4	13.6
McLean County	3 643	71.2	0	X	173	79.2	2	100.0	7	100.0	0.9	0.5	0.1	0.1	0.3	10.0
Mercer County	3 237	73.2	0	X	38	92.1	5	100.0	20	60.0	1.5	0.4	0.1	0.3	1.4	17.9
Morton County	9 651	70.3	12	58.3	154	74.7	0	X	42	81.0	0.9	0.4	0.1	0.1	0.7	11.9
Mountrail County	1 880	65.9	0	X	586	75.6	16	68.8	11	81.8	1.2	0.5	0.4	0.1	0.4	12.0
Nelson County	1 615	62.0	2	100.0	4	100.0	6	50.0	0	X	1.7	0.5	0.3	0.0	0.2	6.9
Oliver County	765	76.1	0	X	8	87.5	0	X	4	100.0	0.3	0.0	0.2	0.0	0.3	11.2
Pembina County	3 400	66.7	2	0.0	31	64.5	4	100.0	64	85.9	3.8	0.3	0.2	0.5	0.7	8.5
Pierce County	1 958	65.5	0	X	6	66.7	0	X	0	X	1.2	0.6	0.1	0.0	1.3	16.0
Ramsey County	4 692	63.6	0	X	185	82.7	10	0.0	6	100.0	1.5	0.3	0.2	0.4	0.1	7.5
Ransom County	2 319	66.5	3	100.0	6	100.0	2	100.0	6	100.0	0.9	0.3	0.2	0.2	0.9	8.2
Renville County	1 056	69.8	5	100.0	17	64.7	4	50.0	3	0.0	1.5	0.4	0.4	0.0	0.0	6.4
Richland County	6 665	63.9	0	X	127	77.2	0	X	30	93.3	1.1	0.6	0.2	0.1	0.2	7.9
Rolette County	1 470	65.3	5	100.0	2 947	78.3	37	83.8	13	30.8	1.3	0.2	0.7	0.0	0.2	12.4
Sargent County	1 756	70.2	3	0.0	6	100.0	0	X	6	16.7	0.5	0.3	0.0	0.0	0.0	6.6
Sheridan County	718	70.5	0	X	2	100.0	0	X	4	50.0	1.1	0.3	0.0	0.1	2.0	15.6
Sioux County	233	70.8	0	X	820	82.2	7	100.0	15	86.7	0.8	0.2	0.3	0.0	0.7	25.2
Slope County	312	70.8	0	X	0	X	0	X	0	X	0.3	0.3	0.0	0.0	0.0	7.1
Stark County	8 729	66.0	3	100.0	61	85.2	10	100.0	78	66.7	0.8	0.2	0.2	0.1	1.0	12.0
Steele County	916	69.1	0	X	5	40.0	0	X	0	X	0.3	0.1	0.0	0.1	0.2	7.1
Stutsman County	8 902	63.5	0	X	37	56.8	11	100.0	36	52.8	1.0	0.4	0.2	0.3	1.0	9.7
Towner County	1 186	64.7	2	0.0	12	58.3	0	X	2	100.0	0.8	0.2	0.0	0.1	0.1	5.3
Traill County	3 305	66.5	1	0.0	15	80.0	0	X	35	80.0	1.4	0.4	0.2	0.5	0.5	9.4
Walsh County	4 735	65.0	2	100.0	46	89.1	0	X	214	79.4	1.9	0.4	0.0	0.9	1.2	14.7

[1] Hispanic or Latino persons may be of any race.

STATE/ County code	MSA/PMSA/ NECMA code[1]	STATE County	Population by age (percent)										Non-Hispanic White		
														Age (percent)	
			Total population	Under 5 years	5 to 17 years	18 to 24 years	25 to 44 years	45 to 64 years	65 years and over	Median age	+/− U.S. percent under 18 years	+/− U.S. percent 65 years and over	Total population	Under 18 years	65 years and over
			1	2	3	4	5	6	7	8	9	10	11	12	13
		NORTH DAKOTA— Cont'd													
38 101	...	Ward County	58 795	7.2	19.0	12.7	29.4	19.3	12.5	32.4	0.5	0.1	53 765	25.2	13.4
38 103	...	Wells County	5 102	4.4	18.2	4.6	22.8	24.0	26.0	45.2	−3.1	13.6	5 026	22.2	26.2
38 105	...	Williams County	19 761	5.7	20.4	7.9	25.8	23.8	16.5	39.8	0.4	4.1	18 301	25.0	17.3
39 000	...	OHIO	11 353 140	6.6	18.8	9.3	29.4	22.6	13.3	36.2	−0.3	0.9	9 537 082	24.0	14.3
39 001	...	Adams County	27 330	6.3	20.0	8.7	28.5	23.2	13.4	36.3	0.6	1.0	26 674	26.0	13.6
39 003	4320	Allen County	108 473	6.6	19.2	9.9	27.7	22.3	14.1	36.3	0.1	1.7	91 193	24.2	15.5
39 005	...	Ashland County	52 523	6.7	19.2	10.7	26.4	23.1	14.0	36.3	0.2	1.6	51 105	25.5	14.1
39 007	1680	Ashtabula County	102 728	6.5	19.6	7.7	28.0	23.6	14.6	37.6	0.4	2.2	95 428	25.0	15.2
39 009	...	Athens County	62 223	4.8	13.5	31.0	23.4	18.0	9.3	25.7	−7.4	−3.1	57 696	18.1	9.7
39 011	4320	Auglaize County	46 611	6.7	20.9	7.9	28.1	22.1	14.4	36.5	1.9	2.0	45 493	27.4	14.7
39 013	9000	Belmont County	70 226	5.0	16.7	7.6	27.5	24.9	18.2	40.9	−4.0	5.8	66 320	21.7	18.7
39 015	1640	Brown County	42 285	7.0	20.5	8.1	30.3	22.4	11.6	35.4	1.8	−0.8	41 314	27.4	11.7
39 017	3200	Butler County	332 807	6.9	19.0	11.8	30.0	21.6	10.7	34.2	0.2	−1.7	300 629	25.1	11.2
39 019	1320	Carroll County	28 836	5.9	19.4	7.3	27.7	25.7	14.1	38.8	−0.4	1.7	28 299	25.0	14.3
39 021	...	Champaign County	38 890	6.6	19.6	7.9	28.8	24.5	12.6	37.0	0.5	0.2	37 217	25.8	12.7
39 023	2000	Clark County	144 742	6.7	18.5	9.0	26.9	24.2	14.7	37.6	−0.5	2.3	126 863	24.0	15.2
39 025	1640	Clermont County	177 977	7.6	20.2	8.4	31.7	22.6	9.4	34.8	2.1	−3.0	171 957	27.7	9.6
39 027	...	Clinton County	40 543	7.2	19.2	10.2	29.3	22.0	12.1	35.3	0.7	−0.3	38 636	25.7	12.3
39 029	9320	Columbiana County	112 075	5.9	18.5	7.8	28.6	24.3	15.0	38.5	−1.3	2.6	106 956	24.4	15.4
39 031	...	Coshocton County	36 655	6.4	19.8	7.9	27.3	23.9	14.7	37.8	0.5	2.3	35 539	25.9	14.8
39 033	4800	Crawford County	46 966	6.5	18.5	8.2	27.3	24.3	15.2	38.2	−0.7	2.8	45 607	24.6	15.4
39 035	1680	Cuyahoga County	1 393 978	6.5	18.4	7.9	29.5	22.1	15.6	37.3	−0.8	3.2	919 383	21.1	18.5
39 037	...	Darke County	53 309	6.7	19.5	7.8	27.5	23.3	15.2	37.4	0.5	2.8	52 086	25.9	15.4
39 039	...	Defiance County	39 500	6.9	19.6	9.2	27.4	24.2	12.8	36.5	0.8	0.4	35 489	25.2	13.9
39 041	1840	Delaware County	109 989	7.9	20.3	7.6	32.7	23.4	8.1	35.3	2.5	−4.3	102 991	27.7	8.4
39 043	...	Erie County	79 551	6.0	18.7	7.2	27.2	25.4	15.6	39.5	−1.0	3.2	69 596	23.0	16.5
39 045	1840	Fairfield County	122 759	7.0	19.8	8.1	30.1	23.8	11.2	36.2	1.1	−1.2	115 980	26.5	11.6
39 047	...	Fayette County	28 433	6.5	18.8	8.0	28.5	23.9	14.3	37.5	−0.4	1.9	27 064	25.1	14.6
39 049	1840	Franklin County	1 068 978	7.2	17.9	11.7	33.5	20.0	9.8	32.5	−0.6	−2.6	795 544	22.5	11.0
39 051	8400	Fulton County	42 084	7.2	21.0	7.9	28.4	22.7	12.8	36.1	2.5	0.4	39 009	27.4	13.3
39 053	...	Gallia County	31 069	6.3	18.7	10.0	27.5	24.1	13.4	37.4	−0.7	1.0	29 423	24.6	13.6
39 055	1680	Geauga County	90 895	6.7	21.6	6.6	26.5	26.7	11.9	38.7	2.6	−0.5	88 136	28.0	12.1
39 057	2000	Greene County	147 886	5.8	18.0	13.7	27.2	23.5	11.7	35.6	−1.9	−0.7	130 693	23.5	12.4
39 059	...	Guernsey County	40 792	6.8	19.4	8.0	27.4	23.9	14.4	37.7	0.5	2.0	39 022	25.6	14.7
39 061	1640	Hamilton County	845 303	6.7	19.1	9.6	29.7	21.4	13.5	35.5	0.1	1.1	612 104	23.1	15.3
39 063	...	Hancock County	71 295	6.9	18.8	10.0	28.6	22.5	13.2	36.0	0.0	0.8	66 870	25.2	13.8
39 065	...	Hardin County	31 945	6.5	17.8	15.5	26.0	21.2	13.0	33.3	−1.4	0.6	30 919	23.8	13.2
39 067	...	Harrison County	15 856	5.9	17.1	7.0	26.2	26.1	17.7	41.1	−2.7	5.3	15 296	22.5	18.0
39 069	...	Henry County	29 210	6.7	20.9	7.9	28.4	22.1	14.0	36.5	1.9	1.6	27 132	26.5	14.7
39 071	...	Highland County	40 875	7.2	19.8	8.5	27.8	23.0	13.7	36.1	1.3	1.3	39 488	26.8	13.9
39 073	...	Hocking County	28 241	6.7	18.8	8.3	28.2	25.1	13.1	37.7	−0.2	0.7	27 536	25.4	13.1
39 075	...	Holmes County	38 943	10.3	25.4	10.4	25.8	17.7	10.5	28.0	10.0	−1.9	38 287	35.6	10.4
39 077	...	Huron County	59 487	7.5	20.7	8.6	28.8	22.0	12.4	34.9	2.5	0.0	55 861	27.4	12.9
39 079	...	Jackson County	32 641	6.4	19.5	8.8	28.7	22.9	13.6	36.3	0.2	1.2	31 472	25.7	13.8
39 081	8080	Jefferson County	73 894	5.2	16.2	8.4	25.7	25.8	18.6	41.6	−4.3	6.2	68 041	20.7	19.1
39 083	...	Knox County	54 500	6.2	18.6	11.9	26.9	22.6	13.8	36.5	−0.9	1.4	52 956	24.5	14.0
39 085	1680	Lake County	227 511	6.1	18.1	7.2	29.9	24.6	14.1	38.6	−1.5	1.7	214 918	23.5	14.5
39 087	3400	Lawrence County	62 319	6.2	18.2	8.7	27.9	24.6	14.4	37.6	−1.3	2.0	59 726	24.0	14.6
39 089	1840	Licking County	145 491	6.8	19.2	8.7	29.5	23.9	11.9	36.6	0.3	−0.5	138 345	25.5	12.2
39 091	...	Logan County	46 005	6.9	19.8	8.2	28.0	23.2	13.9	36.9	1.0	1.5	43 845	26.0	14.3
39 093	1680	Lorain County	284 664	6.9	19.3	8.6	29.4	23.2	12.5	36.5	0.5	0.1	234 677	24.0	13.7
39 095	8400	Lucas County	455 054	6.8	19.4	9.8	29.3	21.5	13.1	35.0	0.5	0.7	343 116	23.0	14.9
39 097	1840	Madison County	40 213	6.3	18.4	9.1	32.7	22.6	10.9	35.8	−1.0	−1.5	36 706	25.3	11.5
39 099	9320	Mahoning County	257 555	5.9	17.7	8.5	26.5	23.6	17.8	39.7	−2.1	5.4	205 026	21.1	19.6
39 101	...	Marion County	66 217	5.9	18.5	8.4	30.4	23.4	13.4	37.2	−1.3	1.0	60 770	24.7	14.2
39 103	1680	Medina County	151 095	7.0	20.4	7.0	30.6	24.4	10.5	36.6	1.7	−1.9	145 469	27.0	10.7
39 105	...	Meigs County	23 072	5.6	18.3	8.5	27.8	25.1	14.8	38.6	−1.8	2.4	22 372	23.7	15.1
39 107	...	Mercer County	40 924	7.4	22.2	7.8	27.1	21.1	14.4	35.7	3.9	2.0	40 040	29.6	14.6
39 109	2000	Miami County	98 868	6.5	19.4	7.6	28.5	24.7	13.3	37.7	0.2	0.9	94 364	25.4	13.6
39 111	...	Monroe County	15 180	5.3	18.2	7.0	26.0	27.2	16.2	40.8	−2.2	3.8	14 926	23.4	16.5
39 113	2000	Montgomery County	559 062	6.6	18.0	9.7	29.2	22.8	13.7	36.4	−1.1	1.3	424 038	22.3	15.2
39 115	...	Morgan County	14 897	6.2	19.2	8.0	26.3	25.1	15.3	38.9	−0.3	2.9	13 976	24.9	16.1
39 117	...	Morrow County	31 628	6.6	20.7	7.6	29.5	24.1	11.4	36.5	1.6	−1.0	31 091	27.1	11.5
39 119	...	Muskingum County	84 585	6.6	19.3	9.5	27.7	22.5	14.3	36.5	0.2	1.9	79 045	25.1	14.4
39 121	...	Noble County	14 058	5.1	17.6	11.8	32.0	20.5	13.1	35.5	−3.0	0.7	12 951	24.3	14.0

[1]MSA = Metropolitan Statistical Area. PMSA = Primary MSA. NECMA = New England County Metropolitan Area. See the Appendix A for explanation of these concepts. See Appendix B for list of metropolitan areas identified by type, with component counties.

Table A-3. States and Counties — Age, Ethnicity, and Household Structure

STATE County	Black or African American			American Indian and Alaska Native			Asian, Hawaiian, and Pacific Islander			Hispanic or Latino[1]			Two or more races		
	Total population	Under 18 years	65 years and over	Total population	Under 18 years	65 years and over	Total population	Under 18 years	65 years and over	Total population	Under 18 years	65 years and over	Total population	Under 18 years	65 years and over
	14	15	16	17	18	19	20	21	22	23	24	25	26	27	28
NORTH DAKOTA— Cont'd															
Ward County	1 196	32.3	2.6	1 418	40.7	2.7	367	24.0	3.5	1 255	39.1	1.7	1 039	42.8	5.7
Wells County	22	77.3	0.0	35	22.9	28.6	3	100.0	0.0	10	40.0	0.0	6	33.3	0.0
Williams County	15	46.7	0.0	852	30.5	8.2	27	14.8	18.5	138	41.3	0.0	471	59.2	3.8
OHIO	1 288 359	31.9	9.5	26 999	25.3	4.8	134 772	23.5	5.0	213 889	36.6	4.5	173 338	46.2	5.0
Adams County	8	12.5	0.0	200	37.5	0.0	13	30.8	0.0	104	35.6	3.8	332	38.0	5.4
Allen County	13 145	32.5	8.0	225	28.0	4.4	543	26.3	1.8	1 538	32.8	4.9	2 071	55.0	2.8
Ashland County	467	44.5	6.9	96	26.0	11.5	246	22.4	12.2	314	42.0	4.5	287	30.3	9.4
Ashtabula County	3 104	35.9	10.5	228	26.3	7.9	310	20.3	16.5	2 545	42.9	1.8	1 303	54.0	4.5
Athens County	1 518	14.6	2.8	308	29.9	5.2	1 119	16.8	2.9	650	27.1	3.7	987	28.7	5.3
Auglaize County	78	34.6	7.7	66	17.0	17.0	106	23.1	6.0	204	00.0	2.5	514	45.9	0.0
Belmont County	2 430	14.8	9.1	259	47.9	10.4	203	20.2	11.8	351	27.4	17.7	618	37.2	9.7
Brown County	325	32.0	14.2	94	14.9	8.5	96	28.1	5.2	165	41.8	0.0	306	41.8	4.2
Butler County	17 924	32.1	8.1	838	29.7	1.9	5 139	29.1	4.0	4 312	30.7	2.7	4 096	47.4	2.6
Carroll County	145	37.9	15.9	56	10.7	0.0	34	35.3	11.8	139	38.1	5.0	173	38.2	5.8
Champaign County	755	25.4	16.3	136	17.6	0.7	58	13.8	12.1	262	39.3	4.2	491	49.9	3.5
Clark County	12 806	29.8	13.2	438	19.9	8.7	724	27.8	3.6	1 554	36.0	5.9	2 474	51.2	5.3
Clermont County	1 513	28.9	10.8	418	25.8	0.0	1 095	19.2	5.0	1 390	39.7	2.5	1 611	45.9	4.3
Clinton County	852	33.3	12.4	131	50.4	0.0	82	39.0	0.0	372	31.2	7.0	456	50.2	3.5
Columbiana County	2 349	15.9	8.3	240	32.9	6.3	331	21.1	0.0	1 283	21.1	2.5	1 104	42.0	7.5
Coshocton County	330	32.4	22.7	107	32.7	11.2	302	38.7	1.3	159	30.8	8.2	251	33.1	11.2
Crawford County	311	25.1	20.6	86	19.8	23.3	170	25.3	0.0	405	41.7	8.1	445	56.0	5.2
Cuyahoga County	380 189	31.9	11.0	2 429	26.9	5.2	26 137	21.8	6.4	46 484	37.4	4.4	24 380	43.5	6.3
Darke County	173	32.9	11.0	55	0.0	10.9	148	37.8	6.1	420	45.2	2.1	439	36.4	9.1
Defiance County	651	29.2	4.8	117	33.3	0.0	120	31.7	5.8	2 056	30.1	2.9	008	54.9	1.3
Delaware County	2 725	33.7	3.7	110	4.5	6.4	1 815	26.4	2.8	1 031	40.6	3.3	1 297	49.3	3.7
Erie County	6 863	34.2	10.4	163	30.1	3.7	338	31.4	5.0	1 453	32.7	6.4	1 319	50.4	4.9
Fairfield County	3 195	23.9	3.7	337	28.2	6.0	904	16.2	2.9	1 220	11.3	3.0	1 060	40.5	5.0
Fayette County	602	16.3	14.3	47	14.9	0.0	145	26.9	6.2	281	37.7	2.1	301	53.8	4.0
Franklin County	188 318	32.6	7.4	3 552	25.9	4.3	33 274	22.4	3.8	24 121	31.4	2.4	26 821	45.2	3.4
Fulton County	119	14.3	32.8	112	33.0	0.0	253	45.5	3.6	2 412	38.4	4.9	438	48.9	4.1
Gallia County	812	26.6	14.4	75	20.0	6.7	204	13.2	8.8	138	43.5	10.1	435	42.3	3.7
Geauga County	1 126	27.7	12.1	70	20.0	12.9	370	24.9	10.5	618	41.4	3.2	568	51.6	5.3
Greene County	9 174	22.1	7.5	412	28.9	1.5	2 945	17.7	4.8	1 889	35.5	4.9	3 020	44.4	5.9
Guernsey County	667	39.6	11.5	110	8.2	2.7	159	22.0	11.9	229	31.0	8.3	596	52.0	4.0
Hamilton County	197 718	33.0	9.3	1 710	25.8	5.4	12 897	21.6	5.4	9 143	31.7	4.1	11 687	43.0	5.6
Hancock County	713	30.3	4.5	215	23.7	2.3	780	22.2	0.3	2 180	36.9	6.7	750	51.6	4.1
Hardin County	229	28.8	10.9	102	20.6	0.0	126	18.3	22.2	378	46.0	1.6	269	46.0	0.0
Harrison County	316	22.8	12.3	15	0.0	0.0	0	X	X	38	55.3	0.0	189	56.6	8.5
Henry County	104	61.5	1.9	94	18.1	16.0	143	30.1	0.0	1 637	42.2	4.3	295	47.1	7.5
Highland County	605	23.5	9.8	188	26.1	8.5	175	45.1	5.1	157	49.0	8.3	312	44.6	5.4
Hocking County	298	10.4	21.1	55	23.6	0.0	63	44.4	0.0	80	27.5	15.0	221	47.5	1.8
Holmes County	80	50.0	8.8	53	37.7	0.0	75	44.0	9.3	283	30.4	21.2	197	38.1	7.6
Huron County	574	32.4	12.5	120	38.3	0.8	158	49.4	0.0	2 121	40.3	3.2	849	48.9	6.6
Jackson County	318	17.0	15.7	82	24.4	8.5	102	23.5	10.8	388	47.4	1.8	344	49.4	7.0
Jefferson County	4 190	28.7	13.7	122	16.4	4.9	124	20.2	15.3	582	36.8	15.8	877	46.0	4.8
Knox County	439	31.4	4.8	105	7.6	0.0	174	13.2	12.6	209	34.4	10.0	623	49.0	6.1
Lake County	3 914	27.0	10.1	178	28.1	13.5	2 251	25.7	8.9	3 999	38.2	2.3	2 428	50.7	6.1
Lawrence County	1 519	26.8	11.0	129	23.3	3.9	213	39.9	0.9	281	40.9	6.0	499	47.7	11.4
Licking County	3 179	30.5	6.7	345	24.3	5.8	705	14.9	7.0	940	46.3	2.8	1 923	46.9	4.7
Logan County	764	34.9	10.6	127	24.4	7.9	266	21.4	7.9	367	41.1	6.3	679	52.7	4.0
Lorain County	23 543	33.0	8.3	829	32.3	6.0	1 748	21.3	5.4	19 358	39.6	5.9	7 095	52.5	5.1
Lucas County	76 721	34.6	8.6	1 296	20.9	5.4	5 402	20.5	5.6	20 658	42.3	5.0	11 207	52.2	4.6
Madison County	2 412	11.7	5.2	94	5.3	5.3	215	27.0	4.7	294	33.0	0.0	620	41.5	4.0
Mahoning County	40 101	32.8	11.6	608	16.9	7.4	1 048	23.3	10.0	7 584	34.5	7.9	4 258	44.7	6.3
Marion County	3 563	15.9	4.0	108	4.6	7.4	381	29.7	3.1	830	24.6	3.9	704	45.5	5.1
Medina County	1 133	28.2	9.0	188	25.0	4.3	1 153	31.7	5.5	1 644	47.1	1.3	1 573	45.5	3.8
Meigs County	138	15.9	9.4	72	20.8	0.0	37	40.5	0.0	142	38.7	0.7	294	39.1	5.4
Mercer County	50	23.7	27.1	171	20.7	0.0	123	34.1	4.9	353	46.5	3.7	220	26.8	8.2
Miami County	1 818	31.6	10.0	135	13.3	0.0	856	23.2	6.0	640	36.4	1.3	1 097	56.4	4.5
Monroe County	16	56.3	0.0	40	32.5	0.0	20	0.0	0.0	69	55.1	0.0	118	16.9	5.1
Montgomery County	111 188	31.7	10.1	1 329	20.3	5.9	7 449	23.6	4.2	6 413	30.5	5.6	9 048	45.4	4.5
Morgan County	477	24.5	2.5	81	49.4	2.5	23	0.0	0.0	39	46.2	0.0	269	37.5	8.9
Morrow County	75	22.7	0.0	73	35.6	4.1	32	28.1	25.0	191	40.8	0.0	166	50.6	6.0
Muskingum County	3 386	33.4	10.8	106	25.5	0.0	312	35.6	1.3	416	41.6	2.9	1 176	48.2	8.3
Noble County	781	0.0	0.9	80	20.0	0.0	28	0.0	0.0	111	1.8	0.0	120	19.2	11.7

[1] Hispanic or Latino persons may be of any race.

STATE County	Total households	Family households (percent)						Nonfamily households (percent)						Percent of householders 65 years and over who live alone	Grandparents who are responsible for the care of their grandchildren
		Married-couple family households			Other family households			Two or more unrelated persons		Male living alone		Female living alone			
		Total	With children	Householder 65 years or over	Total	With children	Householder 65 years or over	Total	Householder 65 years or over	Total	Householder 65 years or over	Total	Householder 65 years or over		
	29	30	31	32	33	34	35	36	37	38	39	40	41	42	43

STATE County	29	30	31	32	33	34	35	36	37	38	39	40	41	42	43
NORTH DAKOTA—Cont'd															
Ward County	23 027	56.0	26.9	9.6	10.9	7.4	1.1	6.0	0.1	12.2	2.3	14.9	7.7	48.2	118
Wells County	2 216	59.1	22.1	17.1	6.4	3.9	1.7	1.9	0.1	13.9	4.7	18.8	15.7	52.1	22
Williams County	8 081	53.4	22.7	11.7	11.5	8.4	1.3	4.1	0.3	14.4	3.5	16.6	9.6	49.6	119
OHIO	4 446 621	52.2	23.1	9.4	15.5	9.1	2.2	5.1	0.3	11.4	2.4	15.9	7.8	46.1	86 009
Adams County	10 513	57.6	25.1	9.7	14.8	9.1	2.2	3.4	0.4	11.3	3.3	12.9	7.9	47.7	307
Allen County	40 625	53.7	22.7	10.7	16.4	10.7	1.9	3.6	0.3	10.4	2.4	15.9	8.8	46.5	822
Ashland County	19 489	60.9	25.6	11.7	11.4	7.3	1.3	3.6	0.3	9.2	2.1	14.8	8.6	44.6	365
Ashtabula County	39 437	55.6	24.0	10.6	15.2	9.1	2.4	4.3	0.4	10.6	2.8	14.2	8.1	44.9	913
Athens County	22 500	44.7	18.7	6.9	11.8	7.4	1.5	15.2	0.3	12.7	2.0	15.6	6.3	48.9	294
Auglaize County	17 441	62.1	28.7	11.3	11.5	7.2	1.9	3.0	0.3	9.8	2.3	13.5	8.6	44.8	233
Belmont County	28 363	54.2	21.5	11.7	14.2	7.8	2.8	3.0	0.3	10.1	3.2	18.6	11.9	50.3	474
Brown County	15 575	60.7	29.2	8.8	15.1	9.0	2.2	4.0	0.4	9.5	2.5	10.8	6.4	43.7	383
Butler County	123 125	58.1	27.9	8.5	13.9	8.5	1.8	5.5	0.2	9.9	1.8	12.7	5.8	42.0	2 746
Carroll County	11 161	62.3	25.9	11.4	11.2	6.5	1.6	3.6	0.3	10.8	2.4	12.1	7.6	42.7	227
Champaign County	15 010	60.7	26.7	9.6	12.3	7.7	1.7	3.6	0.2	9.2	2.0	14.2	7.9	46.3	263
Clark County	56 720	53.7	22.2	10.3	16.0	9.7	1.8	4.4	0.4	10.2	2.4	15.7	9.1	48.0	1 397
Clermont County	65 981	61.8	30.7	7.5	12.7	8.0	1.2	4.5	0.2	9.3	1.6	11.7	5.3	43.6	1 541
Clinton County	15 397	58.2	26.4	9.4	13.7	8.7	1.8	4.4	0.2	9.6	1.9	14.2	8.1	46.9	447
Columbiana County	42 968	58.4	24.3	11.7	13.7	7.7	2.0	3.3	0.3	10.1	2.7	14.8	8.9	45.6	770
Coshocton County	14 344	59.8	26.2	11.5	11.4	6.9	1.1	3.4	0.2	9.4	2.7	16.0	9.9	49.8	161
Crawford County	18 939	54.7	22.2	11.1	14.9	9.0	2.4	4.1	0.4	10.8	2.4	15.5	8.8	44.6	282
Cuyahoga County	571 606	43.1	18.5	9.3	19.3	10.5	3.2	4.9	0.4	13.4	3.0	19.4	9.2	48.5	12 256
Darke County	20 389	61.3	26.4	11.6	12.2	7.3	1.5	3.0	0.3	9.8	2.4	13.7	8.8	45.3	253
Defiance County	15 113	59.1	25.7	10.6	13.6	8.9	1.5	4.2	0.2	10.5	1.9	12.5	7.4	42.7	249
Delaware County	39 755	68.4	34.5	7.1	9.1	5.9	0.9	4.5	0.3	7.4	1.2	10.6	4.3	39.5	430
Erie County	31 756	54.9	22.4	10.4	14.2	8.8	2.2	3.9	0.4	11.7	2.9	15.3	8.2	46.2	844
Fairfield County	45 431	63.6	29.7	9.3	12.0	7.5	1.6	3.8	0.1	8.0	1.8	12.7	6.6	43.2	707
Fayette County	11 005	56.4	23.8	10.0	14.8	9.4	1.8	4.4	0.6	10.0	3.0	14.5	8.2	47.5	227
Franklin County	438 876	43.5	20.5	6.2	16.9	10.4	1.7	8.7	0.3	13.6	1.7	17.2	5.8	47.8	8 388
Fulton County	15 456	65.2	30.2	10.5	11.0	6.6	1.6	2.7	0.0	8.9	2.1	12.3	7.5	44.2	218
Gallia County	12 091	56.9	25.1	9.8	14.2	7.7	2.4	3.9	0.4	9.8	1.9	15.2	8.1	44.1	271
Geauga County	31 639	69.1	32.3	10.8	9.8	5.2	1.8	3.5	0.2	7.3	1.8	10.4	5.7	36.9	272
Greene County	55 298	58.3	25.7	9.7	12.7	7.9	1.4	5.9	0.2	10.2	1.9	12.8	5.8	40.5	940
Guernsey County	16 119	54.4	23.5	10.5	15.8	10.2	2.5	3.8	0.5	10.8	2.5	15.3	8.6	45.4	289
Hamilton County	346 831	44.1	20.1	8.2	17.4	10.6	2.4	5.5	0.3	13.8	2.4	19.1	8.3	49.5	6 733
Hancock County	27 906	57.0	25.4	10.4	12.1	7.6	1.2	4.8	0.2	11.4	1.8	14.7	8.0	45.5	374
Hardin County	11 995	55.3	24.1	10.3	13.3	7.9	1.6	4.8	0.2	11.2	2.8	15.4	8.7	48.8	275
Harrison County	6 404	60.2	23.6	12.2	10.4	5.7	2.1	3.6	0.3	10.3	3.5	15.5	10.2	48.4	151
Henry County	10 982	62.3	28.5	11.5	11.1	7.4	1.1	3.2	0.1	9.6	2.3	13.8	9.2	47.5	172
Highland County	15 607	59.8	26.6	10.5	13.8	8.6	2.1	3.2	0.2	9.5	3.0	13.7	8.1	46.5	368
Hocking County	10 816	60.2	25.7	10.7	12.2	7.9	1.2	3.9	0.3	10.2	2.4	13.5	6.7	42.8	197
Holmes County	11 354	71.8	39.6	11.1	9.4	4.9	2.2	2.7	0.3	7.1	1.4	8.8	5.2	32.7	133
Huron County	22 258	58.6	27.4	10.2	14.4	9.4	1.8	3.9	0.1	9.7	1.9	13.4	7.6	44.1	381
Jackson County	12 651	55.9	24.8	8.7	17.3	9.5	2.9	2.8	0.1	8.5	2.7	15.5	8.8	49.3	322
Jefferson County	30 373	54.2	19.6	12.8	15.0	7.5	2.7	3.3	0.4	10.8	3.2	17.6	10.5	46.4	597
Knox County	19 956	60.5	26.4	10.6	12.0	6.9	1.5	3.7	0.2	8.9	2.4	15.0	8.8	47.6	135
Lake County	89 729	58.4	24.6	10.5	13.2	6.8	2.2	4.4	0.5	10.3	2.2	15.3	7.5	42.5	1 035
Lawrence County	24 773	56.6	23.2	10.3	15.7	9.0	2.4	2.9	0.3	9.2	2.6	15.5	8.8	46.5	683
Licking County	55 588	59.0	26.6	9.1	13.4	8.2	1.7	4.4	0.3	9.9	2.3	13.3	6.9	45.3	1 017
Logan County	17 906	57.2	24.4	10.2	13.5	9.2	1.6	4.3	0.3	10.9	2.7	14.0	8.0	46.9	259
Lorain County	105 875	56.3	24.6	9.9	16.1	9.4	2.5	4.1	0.3	9.7	2.2	13.9	7.0	42.1	2 679
Lucas County	182 868	45.6	20.3	8.4	18.4	11.4	2.2	5.9	0.4	13.1	2.6	17.0	8.0	49.3	3 723
Madison County	13 690	60.3	27.6	8.9	13.3	8.5	2.1	4.1	0.4	9.2	2.2	13.1	7.4	46.0	205
Mahoning County	102 629	49.7	19.8	11.8	17.7	9.2	3.6	3.4	0.4	11.9	3.4	17.2	9.9	45.7	2 386
Marion County	24 626	55.8	23.8	10.7	15.0	9.2	1.7	4.1	0.4	9.3	1.6	15.8	8.9	45.0	561
Medina County	54 538	67.0	32.5	8.9	10.7	5.6	1.6	3.5	0.3	8.0	1.6	10.8	5.4	39.1	624
Meigs County	9 236	57.6	23.1	10.9	13.8	8.1	2.2	3.6	0.6	9.8	1.9	15.2	10.1	46.5	332
Mercer County	14 749	65.8	32.4	12.9	9.3	5.3	1.5	2.5	0.1	9.5	2.4	13.0	8.4	42.5	133
Miami County	38 525	59.8	25.4	10.2	13.3	8.6	1.7	3.9	0.3	9.6	2.0	13.5	7.9	44.8	729
Monroe County	6 030	62.3	23.7	14.1	11.0	5.3	2.0	2.7	0.1	10.8	2.5	13.1	8.7	40.9	92
Montgomery County	229 177	47.2	19.7	9.2	17.1	10.3	2.2	5.3	0.3	12.6	2.4	17.7	7.9	46.9	5 307
Morgan County	5 869	58.2	23.2	10.9	13.0	7.7	2.1	3.4	0.6	11.8	3.3	13.6	8.3	46.1	186
Morrow County	11 536	67.0	28.9	10.9	11.1	7.4	0.6	3.0	0.1	7.7	1.9	11.1	6.3	41.1	340
Muskingum County	32 447	55.4	24.4	10.3	14.8	9.4	2.0	4.8	0.4	9.6	2.5	15.4	9.2	47.9	484
Noble County	4 536	62.3	27.3	12.0	11.0	6.3	1.9	2.4	0.4	9.5	2.4	14.8	10.4	47.2	105

STATE County	Households with Non-Hispanic White householder		Households with Black or African American householder		Households with American Indian and Alaska Native householder		Households with Asian, Hawaiian, and Pacific Islander householder		Households with Hispanic or Latino[1] householder		Foreign-born population	Place of birth (percent)			Percent in non-English speaking households	
	Number of households	Percent that are family households	Number of households	Percent that are family households	Number of households	Percent that are family households	Number of households	Percent that are family households	Number of households	Percent that are family households	Percent of total population that is foreign-born	Europe	Asia	Latin America	Linguistically isolated	Not linguistically isolated
	44	45	46	47	48	49	50	51	52	53	54	55	56	57	58	59
NORTH DAKOTA—Cont'd																
Ward County	21 544	66.3	401	71.8	422	81.8	95	76.8	376	76.9	2.1	0.6	0.3	0.4	0.4	8.6
Wells County	2 198	65.5	3	0.0	8	100.0	0	X	3	0.0	0.8	0.4	0.1	0.0	1.0	10.1
Williams County	7 606	64.8	0	X	310	67.1	7	28.6	42	69.0	1.2	0.2	0.1	0.1	0.3	7.8
OHIO	3 797 198	68.1	489 208	64.0	10 348	65.1	46 043	69.1	62 102	70.9	3.0	1.2	1.1	0.4	1.1	9.0
Adams County	10 225	72.4	5	0.0	84	76.2	3	100.0	32	96.9	0.2	0.1	0.0	0.1	0.6	4.1
Allen County	35 264	70.1	4 469	68.3	61	72.1	184	83.7	376	73.7	1.0	0.3	0.4	0.2	0.2	6.3
Ashland County	19 179	72.3	45	42.2	28	100.0	81	71.6	77	74.0	1.1	0.4	0.5	0.1	0.5	7.3
Ashtabula County	37 295	71.1	1 075	63.0	86	59.3	103	59.2	627	76.6	1.6	0.7	0.2	0.5	1.0	8.1
Athens County	20 968	57.2	451	46.3	92	68.5	432	34.3	168	58.3	3.3	0.6	2.0	0.3	1.0	6.7
Auglaize County	17 109	73.6	22	68.2	20	80.0	61	82.0	73	82.2	1.1	0.4	0.4	0.1	0.3	5.4
Belmont County	27 387	68.4	560	64.5	50	70.0	65	89.2	119	68.1	1.0	0.5	0.3	0.1	0.2	7.5
Brown County	15 249	76.0	144	61.8	47	53.2	31	87.1	35	71.4	0.4	0.2	0.2	0.0	0.2	5.6
Butler County	112 367	72.3	6 774	66.7	354	57.3	1 474	82.1	1 156	65.7	2.7	0.6	1.2	0.6	0.7	8.2
Carroll County	10 967	73.6	48	56.3	31	64.5	3	100.0	43	72.1	0.6	0.2	0.1	0.1	0.2	5.5
Champaign County	14 431	73.4	337	59.3	43	74.4	22	95.5	59	72.9	0.7	0.3	0.1	0.2	0.1	4.6
Clark County	49 842	70.4	5 298	64.9	161	56.5	238	78.6	493	64.5	1.2	0.4	0.4	0.3	0.3	6.4
Clermont County	64 004	74.6	546	67.2	143	85.3	405	72.3	368	68.8	1.6	0.6	0.5	0.2	0.3	6.6
Clinton County	14 845	72.2	289	61.2	38	100.0	15	100.0	90	70.0	1.0	0.4	0.1	0.3	0.5	5.2
Columbiana County	41 982	71.9	532	70.3	71	60.6	67	79.1	138	83.3	1.4	0.4	0.3	0.6	0.2	6.1
Coshocton County	13 989	71.4	98	54.1	35	100.0	62	100.0	55	70.9	1.0	0.3	0.5	0.1	1.7	8.3
Crawford County	18 529	69.6	128	58.6	44	38.6	57	59.6	104	87.5	0.5	0.2	0.3	0.1	0.2	6.4
Cuyahoga County	395 316	61.0	146 078	64.4	963	70.8	9 241	70.4	14 142	72.7	6.4	3.4	1.9	0.6	2.4	13.5
Darke County	20 020	73.5	64	85.9	40	62.5	34	94.1	75	76.0	0.7	0.2	0.2	0.2	0.1	4.3
Defiance County	13 695	73.3	284	59.9	65	27.7	31	100.0	961	73.4	1.5	0.3	0.2	0.6	0.5	10.4
Delaware County	37 589	77.5	972	72.2	56	67.9	598	81.6	273	71.8	2.6	0.7	1.3	0.2	0.6	8.4
Erie County	28 370	69.3	2 546	67.9	51	72.5	113	64.6	435	62.5	1.5	0.8	0.4	0.2	0.6	7.2
Fairfield County	43 713	75.7	791	72.7	136	66.9	199	83.4	328	84.1	1.3	0.5	0.5	0.2	0.4	0.7
Fayette County	10 585	71.2	246	67.9	16	68.8	42	88.1	57	59.6	0.9	0.2	0.5	0.1	0.3	5.8
Franklin County	337 031	59.7	74 282	62.9	1 433	63.0	12 047	63.7	7 197	62.7	6.0	1.1	2.7	1.0	2.3	11.1
Fulton County	14 503	76.1	55	90.9	31	100.0	58	77.6	779	74.6	1.3	0.3	0.4	0.5	0.6	9.6
Gallia County	11 469	71.7	361	60.4	24	100.0	52	71.2	43	39.5	0.8	0.3	0.5	0.0	0.3	6.1
Geauga County	30 844	79.0	391	67.0	23	78.3	130	89.2	135	71.1	2.8	1.9	0.4	0.2	2.8	13.5
Greene County	49 950	71.8	2 942	61.6	159	45.3	1 043	67.1	504	67.9	3.4	0.9	1.9	0.3	0.9	8.4
Guernsey County	16 512	70.4	250	65.2	42	33.3	65	78.5	79	51.9	1.1	0.5	0.3	0.1	0.4	6.9
Hamilton County	255 634	62.0	79 241	60.6	747	59.4	4 856	59.7	2 831	60.0	3.4	1.1	1.3	0.5	1.0	8.5
Hancock County	26 496	69.5	273	44.7	103	75.7	287	62.0	619	65.4	2.0	0.4	1.0	0.3	0.8	7.0
Hardin County	11 668	68.9	85	69.4	55	45.5	49	24.5	73	61.6	1.0	0.4	0.4	0.1	1.0	5.0
Harrison County	6 191	70.3	150	88.0	15	13.3	0	X	2	100.0	0.5	0.3	0.1	0.0	0.2	4.5
Henry County	10 351	72.8	20	80.0	42	100.0	39	76.9	490	84.1	1.3	0.4	0.3	0.6	0.7	9.8
Highland County	15 111	73.7	227	65.2	90	56.7	45	86.7	39	84.6	0.6	0.2	0.3	0.0	0.1	5.0
Hocking County	10 646	72.2	55	89.1	39	76.9	15	100.0	25	100.0	0.6	0.3	0.2	0.1	0.3	5.2
Holmes County	11 180	81.7	15	100.0	11	100.0	9	100.0	101	61.4	0.7	0.3	0.1	0.2	16.0	35.6
Huron County	21 218	72.8	249	66.7	44	81.8	21	100.0	554	83.2	1.9	0.5	0.2	1.1	0.5	7.3
Jackson County	12 272	73.0	151	78.8	44	70.5	28	60.7	76	97.4	1.1	0.3	0.2	0.5	0.1	5.7
Jefferson County	27 989	68.8	1 824	61.8	55	38.2	27	81.5	203	65.5	1.3	0.9	0.2	0.1	0.4	7.4
Knox County	19 572	72.4	122	77.9	16	50.0	73	67.1	61	65.6	1.0	0.5	0.3	0.1	0.9	8.4
Lake County	86 018	69.9	1 582	65.5	53	69.8	679	79.1	819	77.8	4.3	2.3	0.8	0.9	1.4	9.7
Lawrence County	23 824	72.7	641	63.5	43	58.1	42	83.3	101	53.5	0.5	0.2	0.2	0.1	0.1	4.6
Licking County	53 332	72.4	1 137	69.7	140	63.6	235	73.2	254	80.7	1.1	0.5	0.4	0.2	0.2	6.0
Logan County	17 241	70.9	274	63.5	57	86.0	80	88.8	117	71.8	1.1	0.3	0.6	0.2	0.9	6.4
Lorain County	90 474	72.3	7 825	70.8	221	68.8	548	69.9	5 646	76.8	2.6	1.4	0.5	0.5	1.2	12.1
Lucas County	142 756	63.5	29 264	65.0	540	68.9	2 024	63.6	6 011	73.4	3.2	0.8	1.4	0.6	1.0	10.6
Madison County	13 117	73.8	297	55.2	29	93.1	61	100.0	57	70.2	1.1	0.6	0.3	0.1	0.7	7.6
Mahoning County	84 047	67.7	14 724	64.3	252	64.3	306	76.5	2 461	75.2	2.4	1.6	0.4	0.2	1.0	11.1
Marion County	23 472	71.1	660	62.4	29	0.0	122	75.4	234	69.2	1.1	0.3	0.4	0.3	0.5	4.9
Medina County	52 975	77.6	371	77.9	79	62.0	325	82.8	401	77.6	3.0	1.8	0.6	0.2	0.7	9.6
Meigs County	9 030	71.2	59	83.1	35	88.6	8	100.0	28	89.3	0.2	0.0	0.1	0.0	0.2	4.2
Mercer County	14 485	75.1	18	100.0	38	36.8	45	77.8	81	90.1	0.8	0.2	0.2	0.2	0.1	5.9
Miami County	37 010	73.4	748	63.2	87	100.0	311	62.4	146	65.8	1.5	0.5	0.7	0.2	0.3	5.5
Monroe County	5 959	73.2	3	100.0	11	63.6	6	100.0	14	71.4	0.3	0.2	0.1	0.0	1.0	5.3
Montgomery County	177 649	64.5	43 917	63.8	520	47.7	2 525	73.2	2 089	63.6	2.5	0.7	1.1	0.3	0.7	7.6
Morgan County	5 537	71.1	191	75.9	26	53.8	8	100.0	14	50.0	0.5	0.4	0.2	0.0	0.1	4.0
Morrow County	11 397	78.1	7	14.3	21	100.0	0	X	60	90.0	0.5	0.2	0.1	0.1	0.9	5.2
Muskingum County	30 681	70.1	1 224	73.4	40	82.5	75	85.3	126	73.0	0.7	0.4	0.3	0.1	0.4	5.1
Noble County	4 497	73.3	7	0.0	6	100.0	5	100.0	4	100.0	0.6	0.3	0.1	0.2	0.2	6.5

[1] Hispanic or Latino persons may be of any race.

STATE/ County code	MSA/PMSA/ NECMA code[1]	STATE County	Total population	Under 5 years	5 to 17 years	18 to 24 years	25 to 44 years	45 to 64 years	65 years and over	Median age	+/- U.S. percent under 18 years	+/- U.S. percent 65 years and over	Total population	Under 18 years	65 years and over
						Population by age (percent)							Non-Hispanic White Age (percent)		
			1	2	3	4	5	6	7	8	9	10	11	12	13
		OHIO—Cont'd													
39 123	...	Ottawa County	40 985	5.2	18.0	6.4	26.9	27.0	16.4	41.0	-2.5	4.0	38 740	22.5	16.8
39 125	...	Paulding County.............	20 293	6.6	20.1	8.8	28.2	23.9	12.5	36.5	1.0	0.1	19 289	26.4	12.7
39 127	...	Perry County.................	34 078	7.4	20.8	8.4	29.2	22.3	12.0	35.0	2.5	-0.4	33 463	27.9	12.1
39 129	1840	Pickaway County	52 727	5.9	18.1	9.1	32.7	23.3	10.8	36.0	-1.7	-1.6	48 333	25.4	11.5
39 131	...	Pike County..................	27 695	6.7	20.4	8.9	28.9	21.5	13.5	35.3	1.4	1.1	26 580	26.8	13.8
39 133	0080	Portage County.............	152 061	6.1	17.6	14.5	28.7	22.2	11.0	34.4	-2.0	-1.4	143 208	23.4	11.3
39 135	...	Preble County...............	42 337	6.4	19.6	7.7	28.7	24.4	13.1	37.5	0.3	0.7	41 566	26.0	13.2
39 137	...	Putnam County..............	34 726	7.3	22.4	8.4	28.1	20.6	13.3	35.0	4.0	0.9	32 931	28.9	13.8
39 139	4800	Richland County.............	128 852	6.4	18.4	8.3	28.6	24.2	14.1	37.7	-0.9	1.7	113 094	24.1	15.2
39 141	...	Ross County..................	73 345	6.2	17.8	8.6	31.6	23.7	12.1	36.9	-1.7	-0.3	67 094	24.3	12.6
39 143	...	Sandusky County............	61 792	6.6	19.5	8.3	28.0	23.1	14.5	37.3	0.4	2.1	55 050	24.5	15.5
39 145	...	Scioto County................	79 195	6.3	18.0	9.7	28.3	22.7	14.9	36.7	-1.4	2.5	74 800	24.2	15.4
39 147	...	Seneca County...............	58 683	6.2	19.8	10.5	27.2	22.2	14.1	36.3	0.3	1.7	54 914	25.1	14.6
39 149	...	Shelby County................	47 910	7.5	21.2	8.2	29.3	21.7	12.2	34.8	3.0	-0.2	45 675	27.9	12.6
39 151	1320	Stark County..................	378 098	6.4	18.4	8.3	27.8	23.9	15.1	38.2	-0.9	2.7	339 374	23.5	15.8
39 153	0080	Summit County................	542 899	6.6	18.4	8.2	29.7	22.9	14.1	37.2	-0.7	1.7	450 367	23.1	15.4
39 155	9320	Trumbull County..............	225 116	6.1	18.2	7.7	27.5	24.8	15.7	39.0	-1.4	3.3	201 798	23.2	16.5
39 157	...	Tuscarawas County	90 914	6.6	18.8	7.8	28.3	23.5	15.0	37.9	-0.3	2.6	88 474	25.1	15.1
39 159	...	Union County.................	40 909	7.5	20.0	7.6	33.9	21.2	9.7	34.5	1.8	-2.7	38 928	28.0	10.0
39 161	...	Van Wert County	29 659	6.4	19.7	8.4	27.2	22.9	15.4	37.6	0.4	3.0	28 582	25.5	16.0
39 163	...	Vinton County	12 806	7.3	19.8	8.7	28.8	23.2	12.2	35.5	1.4	-0.2	12 480	27.0	12.1
39 165	1640	Warren County	158 383	7.8	19.9	7.1	34.1	21.7	9.4	35.2	2.0	-3.0	148 528	27.8	9.9
39 167	6020	Washington County........	63 251	5.9	17.6	8.9	27.7	25.0	14.9	39.1	-2.2	2.5	61 223	23.3	15.2
39 169	...	Wayne County	111 564	7.0	20.4	9.8	27.9	22.6	12.2	35.4	1.7	-0.2	107 397	27.1	12.5
39 171	...	Williams County..............	39 188	6.3	19.8	8.3	28.8	22.9	13.9	36.9	0.4	1.5	37 324	25.8	14.4
39 173	8400	Wood County	121 065	5.8	17.8	17.3	27.0	21.2	10.9	32.6	-2.1	-1.5	112 901	23.0	11.4
39 175	...	Wyandot County	22 908	6.6	19.2	8.3	27.7	22.7	15.5	37.4	0.1	3.1	22 264	25.5	15.8
40 000	...	OKLAHOMA................	3 450 654	6.8	19.0	10.4	28.4	22.2	13.2	35.5	0.1	0.8	2 556 373	22.6	15.6
40 001	...	Adair County	21 038	7.6	22.9	8.9	27.3	21.3	12.1	33.2	4.8	-0.3	10 031	22.2	17.3
40 003	...	Alfalfa County	6 105	4.4	15.1	6.1	27.5	26.3	20.7	42.3	-6.2	8.3	5 438	20.2	22.6
40 005	...	Atoka County	13 879	5.8	17.9	8.7	28.3	24.3	14.9	38.3	-2.0	2.5	10 454	20.9	16.9
40 007	...	Beaver County	5 857	5.7	21.0	6.7	25.6	23.9	17.0	39.3	1.0	4.6	4 990	23.9	19.7
40 009	...	Beckham County.............	19 799	6.4	18.0	10.2	28.9	21.2	15.4	36.6	-1.3	3.0	16 839	23.8	17.4
40 011	...	Blaine County.................	11 976	5.9	18.1	8.2	29.8	21.4	16.6	37.6	-1.7	4.2	8 802	22.0	21.0
40 013	...	Bryan County.................	36 534	6.2	18.5	11.8	25.5	22.5	15.4	35.8	-1.0	3.0	28 849	22.1	17.4
40 015	...	Caddo County................	30 150	6.5	22.0	8.4	26.3	21.9	14.9	36.0	2.8	2.5	19 267	22.3	19.4
40 017	5880	Canadian County	87 697	6.8	21.1	8.0	31.2	23.5	9.5	35.4	2.2	-2.9	74 556	26.8	10.5
40 019	...	Carter County................	45 621	6.8	19.4	7.6	26.6	23.3	16.3	38.0	0.5	3.9	35 099	23.3	18.1
40 021	...	Cherokee County	42 521	6.8	19.4	14.5	26.3	21.0	12.1	32.3	0.5	-0.3	23 565	18.6	16.6
40 023	...	Choctaw County	15 342	6.4	19.5	7.5	25.3	23.8	17.4	38.7	0.2	5.0	10 383	21.3	19.9
40 025	...	Cimarron County.............	3 148	6.7	20.7	6.6	23.5	23.7	18.8	39.3	1.7	6.4	2 598	24.4	21.1
40 027	5880	Cleveland County...........	208 016	6.4	18.0	14.7	30.7	21.7	8.4	32.2	-1.3	-4.0	169 446	23.0	9.6
40 029	...	Coal County..................	6 031	6.5	20.1	7.7	25.6	22.4	17.8	38.1	0.9	5.4	4 494	22.8	20.0
40 031	4200	Comanche County	114 996	7.8	19.7	14.0	31.1	17.6	9.7	30.1	1.8	-2.7	71 214	23.2	12.9
40 033	...	Cotton County...............	6 614	6.6	18.9	7.5	26.3	22.8	18.0	38.6	-0.2	5.6	5 482	23.7	19.8
40 035	...	Craig County	14 950	5.8	18.2	7.8	28.1	23.7	16.5	39.3	-1.7	4.1	10 202	19.7	19.7
40 037	8560	Creek County	67 367	6.7	20.7	8.0	27.5	24.2	12.9	36.9	1.7	0.5	54 755	24.9	14.0
40 039	...	Custer County	26 142	5.9	18.3	17.8	24.4	19.9	13.7	32.7	-1.5	1.3	20 776	20.9	16.0
40 041	...	Delaware County	37 077	6.1	18.4	6.6	24.6	26.7	17.6	40.8	-1.2	5.2	25 727	19.0	21.8
40 043	...	Dewey County	4 743	5.0	18.2	7.1	23.1	25.4	21.3	43.0	-2.5	8.9	4 310	21.3	22.6
40 045	...	Ellis County	4 075	5.0	17.0	6.4	21.3	28.4	21.9	45.3	-3.7	9.5	3 867	21.0	22.7
40 047	2340	Garfield County	57 813	6.7	18.3	9.2	27.5	22.4	15.9	37.7	-0.7	3.5	50 219	23.0	17.6
40 049	...	Garvin County	27 210	6.3	18.4	8.1	26.0	23.3	17.8	39.0	-1.0	5.4	22 674	22.1	19.9
40 051	...	Grady County	45 516	6.7	19.9	9.3	28.0	23.1	13.0	36.5	0.9	0.6	39 201	24.7	14.1
40 053	...	Grant County.................	5 144	5.3	20.1	6.5	24.0	22.5	21.5	41.4	-0.3	9.1	4 899	24.7	22.3
40 055	...	Greer County	6 061	4.6	15.2	9.2	29.1	21.7	20.2	40.0	-5.9	7.8	4 781	19.1	24.3
40 057	...	Harmon County	3 283	5.1	20.6	7.6	25.9	20.5	20.4	39.9	0.0	8.0	2 162	18.4	28.4
40 059	...	Harper County	3 562	4.5	18.9	6.2	23.6	25.3	21.5	43.1	-2.3	9.1	3 314	22.0	23.0
40 061	...	Haskell County	11 792	6.7	19.3	8.1	24.8	24.0	17.0	38.6	0.3	4.6	9 192	22.5	19.7
40 063	...	Hughes County	14 154	5.8	17.1	8.1	27.4	23.2	18.5	39.3	-2.8	6.1	10 157	19.6	22.2
40 065	...	Jackson County	28 439	8.4	20.8	10.1	30.0	18.9	11.9	33.0	3.5	-0.5	20 405	25.7	14.8
40 067	...	Jefferson County.............	6 818	6.1	17.9	6.9	25.5	23.5	20.1	40.4	-1.7	7.7	5 703	22.0	22.3
40 069	...	Johnston County	10 513	6.3	19.3	10.1	24.4	24.4	15.5	38.0	-0.1	3.1	7 945	22.2	17.7
40 071	...	Kay County	48 080	7.0	19.3	8.9	24.9	22.9	16.9	38.1	0.6	4.5	39 758	24.0	19.1
40 073	...	Kingfisher County............	13 926	6.2	21.1	8.2	26.7	22.3	15.4	38.0	1.6	3.0	12 005	25.3	17.0

[1]MSA = Metropolitan Statistical Area. PMSA = Primary MSA. NECMA = New England County Metropolitan Area. See the Appendix A for explanation of these concepts. See Appendix B for list of metropolitan areas identified by type, with component counties.

Table A-3. States and Counties — Age, Ethnicity, and Household Structure

STATE County	Black or African American Total population	Age (percent) Under 18 years	65 years and over	American Indian and Alaska Native Total population	Age (percent) Under 18 years	65 years and over	Asian, Hawaiian, and Pacific Islander Total population	Age (percent) Under 18 years	65 years and over	Hispanic or Latino[1] Total population	Age (percent) Under 18 years	65 years and over	Two or more races Total population	Age (percent) Under 18 years	65 years and over
	14	15	16	17	18	19	20	21	22	23	24	25	26	27	28
OHIO—Cont'd															
Ottawa County	301	30.2	9.6	159	41.5	6.9	98	31.6	28.6	1 526	35.0	9.9	282	49.3	2.5
Paulding County	209	28.7	17.2	36	13.9	16.7	44	43.2	0.0	597	33.0	6.5	199	45.2	4.5
Perry County	90	32.2	6.7	20	0.0	0.0	84	22.6	20.2	183	43.2	0.0	241	52.7	2.9
Pickaway County	3 004	2.0	3.1	266	19.2	0.0	178	44.4	3.4	441	20.0	2.9	577	25.5	2.6
Pike County	222	35.6	18.5	285	18.2	5.6	111	20.7	0.0	146	58.9	2.7	351	42.5	6.3
Portage County	4 688	26.5	6.0	239	26.8	4.6	1 164	13.7	4.0	1 028	27.7	6.3	1 745	43.2	4.4
Preble County	80	26.3	5.0	191	16.8	10.5	159	42.1	1.3	173	28.9	5.8	166	24.1	22.9
Putnam County	29	31.0	0.0	56	25.0	0.0	80	40.0	16.3	1 494	42.2	4.8	268	53.4	2.6
Richland County	11 377	26.4	7.6	372	24.2	8.1	782	26.0	3.5	1 189	36.0	3.6	2 169	47.6	4.2
Ross County	4 166	14.4	8.7	267	25.8	0.0	245	38.8	13.5	588	32.3	0.0	1 058	35.3	5.5
Sandusky County	1 713	37.8	8.8	75	25.3	0.0	168	23.8	5.4	4 205	37.1	5.4	996	62.2	2.1
Scioto County	2 026	19.9	6.1	434	22.8	3.7	362	33.4	2.8	476	30.3	3.6	1 223	33.2	11.0
Seneca County	979	28.8	9.1	123	34.1	4.1	263	26.2	0.0	2 012	43.4	5.5	732	51.1	6.1
Shelby County	893	33.1	7.7	82	3.7	34.1	309	22.3	1.0	342	49.1	0.6	544	57.4	1.3
Stark County	27 099	34.8	9.8	777	26.6	2.7	1 880	19.7	6.3	3 418	36.0	8.3	5 668	47.8	6.1
Summit County	71 120	33.5	9.3	1 184	22.2	4.0	7 879	28.2	4.9	4 491	33.6	4.3	8 129	48.8	4.5
Trumbull County	17 198	32.4	10.2	484	29.5	4.1	1 072	21.0	3.3	1 762	34.1	4.0	2 910	46.7	4.7
Tuscarawas County	652	37.0	11.3	209	48.8	3.8	303	18.5	8.6	458	29.9	2.2	854	48.4	9.4
Union County	973	6.0	3.4	79	16.5	1.3	198	23.7	11.1	306	29.7	2.6	482	33.8	1.2
Van Wert County	233	43.8	2.6	38	0.0	0.0	58	10.3	3.4	554	38.8	2.0	225	50.7	0.0
Vinton County	19	31.6	0.0	50	18.0	0.0	0	X	X	77	7.8	33.8	184	40.8	13.6
Warren County	4 349	16.4	3.6	459	32.0	1.7	2 223	30.9	1.6	1 463	31.8	2.7	1 421	44.5	2.6
Washington County	481	23.9	12.5	159	13.8	0.0	269	17.1	6.7	263	27.0	2.3	805	39.6	8.1
Wayne County	1 367	32.0	7.2	156	18.6	9.6	796	29.9	6.4	671	38.7	5.5	1 232	49.3	4.0
Williams County	305	11.8	3.9	161	25.5	0.0	192	38.0	2.6	1 046	40.2	2.5	227	46.7	13.7
Wood County	1 733	24.9	1.4	241	28.2	11.6	1 187	29.1	2.9	4 047	37.1	3.1	1 404	38.7	2.6
Wyandot County	8	0.0	62.5	12	0.0	0.0	117	53.8	0.0	429	38.2	3.5	130	38.5	6.2
OKLAHOMA	258 532	32.4	7.3	266 801	35.7	6.9	47 386	23.1	4.5	177 768	39.0	2.8	168 426	39.7	7.4
Adair County	22	22.7	0.0	9 023	38.3	7.5	20	30.0	0.0	650	41.1	1.4	1 557	38.1	8.7
Alfalfa County	273	2.6	8.8	145	16.6	2.8	1	0.0	0.0	163	17.2	1.2	99	29.3	6.1
Atoka County	813	20.2	10.2	1 613	33.7	9.4	8	0.0	25.0	139	36.7	5.8	881	43.7	7.4
Beaver County	25	36.0	0.0	120	46.7	1.7	10	0.0	20.0	655	43.8	1.8	92	40.2	1.1
Beckham County	1 042	10.2	3.9	483	37.9	5.6	41	26.8	0.0	1 117	39.7	2.4	349	30.4	9.5
Blaine County	768	18.5	8.1	1 062	37.5	5.0	197	2.5	0.0	822	37.3	2.4	426	23.0	1.9
Bryan County	536	25.4	11.9	4 694	38.6	6.4	128	12.5	5.5	823	35.2	5.0	1 610	30.1	12.0
Caddo County	959	22.1	6.3	7 133	41.5	7.7	56	17.9	0.0	1 917	41.0	5.2	1 378	43.6	6.2
Canadian County	1 847	25.6	5.0	3 892	36.3	3.6	2 213	30.8	3.0	3 292	34.4	2.4	2 226	42.1	3.0
Carter County	3 514	31.9	14.1	3 706	36.4	7.7	198	29.3	14.1	1 188	38.7	7.7	2 087	42.3	9.7
Cherokee County	403	17.1	3.0	13 534	36.1	6.9	87	11.5	0.0	1 737	40.0	1.1	3 579	35.1	7.7
Choctaw County	1 591	30.7	16.1	2 349	37.2	9.6	34	20.6	5.9	240	42.1	9.6	883	42.7	11.6
Cimarron County	5	0.0	0.0	22	18.2	9.1	2	0.0	0.0	499	43.3	6.4	53	41.5	26.4
Cleveland County	7 181	25.5	1.6	8 667	30.5	3.9	5 979	20.6	3.0	8 332	35.2	2.9	9 770	38.3	3.9
Coal County	22	31.8	22.7	1 019	37.4	10.3	18	22.2	0.0	183	41.5	10.9	353	39.7	11.3
Comanche County	22 140	34.3	4.0	5 676	31.0	7.4	2 635	16.8	7.1	9 692	36.1	3.5	5 804	47.7	3.5
Cotton County	191	23.0	13.6	517	33.1	9.1	11	0.0	18.2	316	36.7	4.7	176	54.0	8.0
Craig County	478	18.2	8.4	2 484	36.4	7.9	24	0.0	0.0	128	47.7	0.0	1 679	32.8	12.7
Creek County	1 953	34.1	14.3	5 757	37.6	6.8	123	27.6	14.6	1 390	47.6	2.6	3 874	42.3	7.9
Custer County	780	34.2	6.3	1 495	36.2	4.5	236	10.2	0.0	2 289	41.0	4.7	973	45.6	2.4
Delaware County	65	80.0	0.0	7 878	36.2	8.2	89	43.8	0.0	867	44.4	1.4	2 649	38.0	9.6
Dewey County	7	57.1	28.6	221	38.9	9.0	3	33.3	0.0	124	44.4	6.5	102	50.0	6.9
Ellis County	0	X	X	39	33.3	0.0	0	X	X	97	34.0	11.3	75	50.7	5.3
Garfield County	1 824	34.9	6.2	1 345	36.6	4.6	747	25.6	9.1	2 260	40.2	2.4	1 691	45.8	4.9
Garvin County	662	32.8	8.3	2 032	39.5	6.5	82	22.0	6.1	869	42.1	1.5	999	39.1	12.8
Grady County	1 487	36.0	8.4	2 245	41.8	4.6	123	24.4	6.5	1 211	40.0	0.7	1 458	39.0	9.8
Grant County	2	0.0	0.0	106	44.3	5.7	11	18.2	0.0	56	37.5	3.6	70	42.9	8.6
Greer County	467	8.4	9.0	162	4.9	1.9	17	0.0	11.8	427	37.9	3.0	252	35.7	3.6
Harmon County	335	37.0	3.6	15	53.3	0.0	14	28.6	0.0	726	40.6	5.4	74	51.4	6.8
Harper County	0	X	X	33	24.2	0.0	3	33.3	0.0	195	49.2	1.0	25	4.0	8.0
Haskell County	92	35.9	15.2	1 615	37.0	5.8	29	20.7	34.5	239	59.0	5.0	681	38.2	11.3
Hughes County	645	11.3	6.7	2 230	32.5	10.3	16	37.5	12.5	310	41.0	5.8	851	39.8	7.8
Jackson County	2 184	33.6	7.1	378	31.7	6.9	363	28.9	8.5	4 426	40.9	3.1	1 065	46.1	3.2
Jefferson County	41	12.2	7.3	352	38.4	9.9	88	0.0	4.5	486	38.7	8.0	193	36.3	15.5
Johnston County	165	24.2	12.1	1 602	36.3	9.1	19	0.0	5.3	280	40.0	2.9	555	42.3	7.9
Kay County	821	28.4	8.9	3 520	38.7	6.0	282	20.2	1.4	2 008	44.0	2.1	2 043	40.7	8.5
Kingfisher County	216	30.1	15.7	299	43.8	2.0	3	0.0	0.0	973	41.6	1.8	489	39.9	9.4

[1] Hispanic or Latino persons may be of any race.

STATE County	Total households	Family households (percent)						Nonfamily households (percent)						Percent of householders 65 years and over who live alone	Grandparents who are responsible for the care of their grandchildren
		Married-couple family households			Other family households			Two or more unrelated persons		Male living alone		Female living alone			
		Total	With children	Householder 65 years or over	Total	With children	Householder 65 years or over	Total	Householder 65 years or over	Total	Householder 65 years or over	Total	Householder 65 years or over		
	29	30	31	32	33	34	35	36	37	38	39	40	41	42	43
OHIO—Cont'd															
Ottawa County	16 461	59.2	22.6	13.1	12.3	6.6	2.2	3.5	0.3	10.8	2.7	14.1	8.5	41.6	199
Paulding County	7 815	60.6	26.6	9.8	13.1	7.4	2.4	3.6	0.3	10.2	2.2	12.6	8.1	45.0	210
Perry County	12 519	62.0	28.8	9.7	13.2	8.6	1.6	3.5	0.4	8.3	2.3	13.1	8.3	47.5	353
Pickaway County	17 555	62.0	27.2	9.8	13.6	8.6	1.8	3.8	0.2	8.2	2.3	12.4	6.6	43.1	225
Pike County	10 436	56.5	25.5	10.1	16.6	10.8	2.5	4.0	0.2	9.3	1.9	13.6	8.2	44.1	289
Portage County	56 415	56.0	24.7	9.3	13.8	8.2	1.9	6.9	0.3	10.1	1.7	13.1	5.6	38.8	874
Preble County	15 946	63.8	27.8	10.9	12.2	7.1	1.8	3.3	0.3	9.4	2.3	11.3	7.1	41.9	232
Putnam County	12 191	65.8	33.5	12.0	10.6	6.1	1.8	2.3	0.1	9.4	2.1	11.9	8.1	42.3	125
Richland County	49 558	54.9	22.1	11.0	14.5	9.0	2.1	4.1	0.2	11.3	2.3	15.3	8.3	44.2	1 059
Ross County	27 148	56.1	24.7	8.6	14.7	8.5	2.2	4.4	0.4	10.0	2.6	14.8	8.2	49.2	635
Sandusky County	23 682	56.4	24.9	10.6	15.2	9.3	2.5	4.4	0.3	10.6	2.6	13.5	8.0	44.2	488
Scioto County	30 834	53.2	22.8	9.9	16.4	9.3	2.3	3.5	0.3	9.8	2.8	17.1	10.0	50.6	760
Seneca County	22 352	56.5	24.6	10.8	14.4	9.0	2.3	4.5	0.4	10.9	2.6	13.7	8.3	44.6	332
Shelby County	17 696	61.9	29.6	10.1	12.5	7.6	1.4	3.7	0.1	9.9	2.3	12.1	7.4	45.5	321
Stark County	148 323	54.7	23.1	10.9	14.8	8.3	2.4	4.4	0.3	10.3	2.5	15.8	8.5	44.7	2 771
Summit County	217 865	50.9	22.2	9.7	15.6	9.0	2.4	5.5	0.3	11.7	2.5	16.2	7.9	45.5	3 709
Trumbull County	88 981	53.7	21.7	11.0	15.9	8.8	2.7	3.5	0.5	11.1	2.9	15.8	8.8	45.1	1 712
Tuscarawas County	35 637	58.5	25.2	11.3	12.7	7.6	2.0	3.8	0.3	9.9	2.4	15.0	8.7	45.0	598
Union County	14 342	65.4	32.7	8.1	10.6	6.9	1.5	4.2	0.3	8.8	1.7	11.1	5.1	40.7	219
Van Wert County	11 569	60.7	26.5	12.0	12.2	7.1	1.7	2.6	0.2	9.9	2.4	14.6	8.7	44.2	102
Vinton County	4 906	57.3	23.8	9.6	15.6	10.2	1.3	3.3	0.2	9.9	2.7	13.9	6.9	46.3	181
Warren County	56 020	67.0	33.4	8.7	10.7	6.7	1.2	3.4	0.2	7.9	1.1	11.0	5.1	38.1	922
Washington County	25 162	57.8	23.2	10.9	12.8	7.7	2.1	4.0	0.3	10.7	2.8	14.7	8.3	45.5	452
Wayne County	40 486	62.0	28.6	10.4	11.5	6.7	1.6	3.8	0.2	9.6	1.8	13.2	7.0	41.9	571
Williams County	15 065	58.4	25.7	11.0	12.7	8.2	1.4	4.0	0.3	10.4	2.0	14.5	8.2	44.6	195
Wood County	45 192	54.3	25.1	8.3	11.8	7.4	1.1	8.1	0.3	11.2	1.9	14.5	7.4	48.9	639
Wyandot County	8 883	60.2	25.5	11.5	11.4	7.5	1.4	2.9	0.3	10.8	2.5	14.6	9.2	47.0	149
OKLAHOMA	1 343 506	54.3	24.0	9.9	14.7	8.9	1.9	4.3	0.3	11.3	2.4	15.3	7.8	45.7	39 279
Adair County	7 469	57.8	28.4	9.3	17.3	9.9	3.1	2.1	0.1	10.2	2.8	12.5	7.4	44.7	409
Alfalfa County	2 193	58.3	22.2	16.0	9.2	5.1	1.9	1.4	0.4	12.9	5.2	18.2	13.9	51.0	39
Atoka County	4 969	56.9	24.3	12.2	13.8	7.9	2.5	2.0	0.3	11.2	4.1	16.0	9.5	47.7	185
Beaver County	2 238	65.5	27.1	15.4	11.0	5.7	2.1	1.5	0.3	9.9	3.1	12.2	9.8	41.9	80
Beckham County	7 335	54.8	23.9	11.7	13.2	8.7	2.0	3.3	0.1	12.0	2.8	16.6	9.9	48.0	199
Blaine County	4 166	57.5	23.8	13.4	11.9	6.0	2.8	1.3	0.5	11.4	3.1	17.8	11.0	46.0	181
Bryan County	14 461	55.2	22.9	11.9	14.1	7.8	2.3	4.2	0.4	10.6	2.6	15.9	9.4	45.2	643
Caddo County	10 943	56.0	24.4	11.6	17.0	9.7	3.3	2.3	0.3	9.7	2.6	15.0	10.1	45.4	578
Canadian County	31 528	64.4	31.6	8.2	13.3	8.6	1.2	3.1	0.3	8.3	1.5	10.9	5.3	41.5	728
Carter County	17 981	56.2	24.2	12.3	14.6	8.4	2.3	2.6	0.2	9.4	2.2	17.2	9.3	43.7	660
Cherokee County	16 225	53.3	24.1	9.8	15.9	9.5	2.2	5.6	0.3	11.0	2.7	14.2	6.9	43.8	598
Choctaw County	6 236	52.2	20.8	11.5	17.3	10.3	3.4	2.5	0.4	11.0	3.7	17.1	10.4	48.1	248
Cimarron County	1 259	60.4	27.3	14.1	9.5	4.9	1.7	1.4	0.0	12.6	4.5	16.2	10.4	48.5	33
Cleveland County	79 210	55.1	26.3	6.7	13.3	7.7	1.4	7.2	0.2	11.4	1.5	13.0	4.6	42.5	1 514
Coal County	2 369	55.7	23.3	13.6	14.0	7.2	4.0	3.0	0.4	11.2	3.9	16.0	10.1	43.8	99
Comanche County	39 930	55.4	28.5	7.9	17.5	11.6	2.1	3.9	0.2	11.0	2.1	12.3	5.9	43.8	1 305
Cotton County	2 614	57.5	23.8	12.4	12.7	7.7	2.4	2.2	0.2	11.2	3.1	16.4	11.4	49.2	113
Craig County	5 606	57.8	24.4	11.9	12.7	7.8	2.3	2.5	0.3	10.0	2.9	16.9	10.6	48.3	219
Creek County	25 333	60.1	26.8	10.0	15.1	8.8	2.1	3.1	0.4	9.5	2.5	12.1	6.8	42.6	881
Custer County	10 157	50.9	22.4	9.0	14.3	8.0	1.9	7.1	0.1	11.8	2.7	15.9	8.5	50.5	250
Delaware County	14 876	60.7	21.9	14.3	12.1	7.9	1.4	3.3	0.5	10.3	3.8	13.6	8.0	42.1	565
Dewey County	1 969	61.9	24.1	15.0	6.9	3.3	1.8	1.7	0.1	10.9	3.6	18.6	12.5	48.8	42
Ellis County	1 774	60.3	19.4	15.5	8.9	5.9	1.4	1.9	0.6	11.8	4.0	17.1	12.1	47.8	20
Garfield County	23 220	55.8	24.2	11.2	12.6	8.2	1.7	4.0	0.2	10.9	2.8	16.7	9.0	47.5	519
Garvin County	10 903	57.0	23.2	13.5	13.2	7.4	2.1	2.9	0.5	9.3	2.8	17.6	11.6	47.1	279
Grady County	17 310	60.4	27.1	10.2	13.6	7.9	1.9	3.0	0.2	9.7	2.6	13.3	8.2	46.8	468
Grant County	2 087	60.2	25.4	15.9	9.8	6.3	1.4	1.4	0.2	11.5	3.6	17.1	13.2	48.9	32
Greer County	2 255	52.0	17.9	16.5	12.6	8.2	2.8	2.0	0.0	12.5	4.6	20.8	14.5	49.8	35
Harmon County	1 258	56.6	22.8	15.7	12.9	8.3	1.4	1.4	0.0	10.4	3.2	18.7	12.6	47.9	37
Harper County	1 529	59.3	23.5	15.6	9.4	5.6	1.4	2.7	0.1	12.2	5.2	16.4	11.6	49.4	34
Haskell County	4 627	60.9	25.7	11.8	13.2	6.7	2.3	1.2	0.4	9.7	3.7	15.0	9.5	47.7	192
Hughes County	5 345	55.0	22.7	12.9	14.4	7.3	2.8	2.1	0.5	10.8	4.1	17.7	12.5	50.7	170
Jackson County	10 622	58.9	29.1	9.3	13.8	9.6	1.7	3.2	0.2	11.3	2.0	12.7	8.3	47.8	367
Jefferson County	2 703	58.2	22.9	14.6	10.4	5.9	2.4	2.5	0.4	10.6	3.4	18.3	11.0	45.3	55
Johnston County	4 076	57.9	24.5	11.4	13.9	7.6	2.4	3.0	0.5	10.5	4.2	14.6	8.7	47.5	186
Kay County	19 138	55.1	23.9	12.5	13.6	8.0	2.1	3.5	0.2	10.9	2.7	17.0	10.6	47.4	592
Kingfisher County	5 244	62.6	29.7	12.4	11.7	6.9	1.7	2.2	0.2	9.1	2.1	14.3	10.1	46.1	104

Table A-3. States and Counties — **Age, Ethnicity, and Household Structure**

STATE County	Households with Non-Hispanic White householder		Households with Black or African American householder		Households with American Indian and Alaska Native householder		Households with Asian, Hawaiian, and Pacific Islander householder		Households with Hispanic or Latino[1] householder		Foreign-born population	Place of birth (percent)			Percent in non-English speaking households	
	Number of households	Percent that are family households	Number of households	Percent that are family households	Number of households	Percent that are family households	Number of households	Percent that are family households	Number of households	Percent that are family households	Percent of total population that is foreign-born	Europe	Asia	Latin America	Linguistically isolated	Not linguistically isolated
	44	45	46	47	48	49	50	51	52	53	54	55	56	57	58	59
OHIO—Cont'd																
Ottawa County	15 820	71.3	97	74.2	33	84.8	14	100.0	444	75.9	1.1	0.6	0.1	0.3	0.3	8.6
Paulding County	7 478	73.8	86	66.3	11	81.8	8	100.0	183	68.9	0.6	0.3	0.1	0.0	0.1	7.0
Perry County	12 375	75.1	28	50.0	9	100.0	39	79.5	19	100.0	0.6	0.2	0.2	0.1	0.1	5.3
Pickaway County	17 177	75.9	100	62.0	44	27.3	51	100.0	77	57.1	0.7	0.3	0.2	0.2	0.2	4.0
Pike County	10 114	73.3	67	47.8	99	63.6	36	86.1	32	90.6	0.6	0.2	0.3	0.1	0.2	5.6
Portage County	53 642	70.4	1 488	64.2	94	40.4	448	47.8	289	53.3	2.0	0.8	0.8	0.1	0.4	7.7
Preble County	15 632	76.1	42	45.2	93	91.4	42	64.3	62	72.6	0.6	0.2	0.4	0.0	0.2	4.8
Putnam County	11 707	76.6	11	100.0	32	46.9	26	88.5	399	70.7	0.7	0.1	0.2	0.3	0.6	7.9
Richland County	45 031	69.6	3 418	64.9	130	82.3	221	76.9	255	77.6	1.8	1.0	0.5	0.1	0.9	6.8
Ross County	25 636	70.9	925	70.7	109	60.6	64	81.3	168	89.3	0.7	0.2	0.3	0.2	0.2	5.3
Sandusky County	21 644	71.4	607	72.0	21	66.7	51	58.8	1 237	73.5	1.3	0.3	0.3	0.6	1.0	9.6
Scioto County	29 722	69.8	462	64.3	159	62.9	89	86.5	71	74.6	0.6	0.2	0.1	0.2	0.1	3.8
Seneca County	21 245	71.1	345	63.2	44	59.1	40	100.0	565	71.9	1.2	0.3	0.5	0.3	0.6	7.1
Shelby County	17 044	74.3	350	85.4	49	77.6	118	43.2	55	72.7	1.4	0.3	0.7	0.1	0.8	6.4
Stark County	134 933	69.8	10 043	66.7	317	55.5	606	78.1	996	63.6	1.8	1.0	0.5	0.2	0.5	7.5
Summit County	184 207	66.6	27 049	65.6	500	67.0	2 528	79.9	1 497	68.5	3.3	1.4	1.3	0.2	0.9	8.5
Trumbull County	81 048	69.6	6 224	69.0	217	85.3	325	75.4	535	74.0	1.8	1.1	0.5	0.1	0.8	8.9
Tuscarawas County	34 895	71.3	246	66.3	73	65.8	102	83.3	104	71.2	0.9	0.4	0.2	0.2	1.0	7.4
Union County	14 005	75.9	80	85.0	23	43.5	50	86.0	68	60.3	1.0	0.3	0.4	0.1	0.1	6.4
Van Wert County	11 260	72.7	62	66.1	20	100.0	16	56.3	147	81.6	0.7	0.3	0.2	0.2	0.2	6.1
Vinton County	4 785	73.1	7	0.0	14	100.0	0	X	39	56.4	0.3	0.2	0.0	0.1	0.1	4.6
Warren County	53 865	77.7	737	68.4	109	76.1	706	86.3	300	79.3	2.3	0.7	1.0	0.3	0.5	7.6
Washington County	24 551	70.5	231	72.3	53	62.3	48	83.3	63	52.4	0.6	0.2	0.3	0.0	0.1	5.3
Wayne County	39 226	73.6	520	63.8	55	80.0	196	81.6	183	84.2	1.7	0.6	0.6	0.3	2.2	11.5
Williams County	14 605	71.0	30	63.3	60	75.0	7	100.0	300	76.3	1.0	0.2	0.4	0.3	0.4	6.7
Wood County	42 781	66.2	506	50.8	58	75.9	379	78.1	1 161	68.0	2.4	0.8	0.9	0.4	0.4	9.2
Wyandot County	8 712	71.5	3	0.0	7	0.0	23	78.3	95	87.4	0.8	0.2	0.3	0.3	0.5	5.5
OKLAHOMA	1 056 941	68.5	92 704	66.8	85 177	74.4	14 862	67.2	47 397	78.1	3.8	0.5	1.2	1.9	1.8	9.8
Adair County	4 070	71.0	7	0.0	2 720	80.8	2	100.0	179	75.4	1.4	0.1	0.0	1.2	1.6	20.9
Alfalfa County	2 118	67.4	3	0.0	23	69.6	0	X	21	81.0	0.7	0.1	0.0	0.6	0.2	4.6
Atoka County	3 983	71.3	157	45.9	511	74.4	6	66.7	39	41.0	0.3	0.1	0.1	0.1	0.2	7.9
Beaver County	2 032	74.6	5	100.0	26	92.3	2	100.0	159	95.6	5.5	0.3	0.1	5.1	3.4	10.7
Beckham County	6 645	67.2	135	75.6	136	97.1	15	100.0	331	70.4	1.6	0.4	0.2	0.9	0.5	10.2
Blaine County	3 516	68.7	192	54.2	242	83.9	17	0.0	176	90.3	3.5	0.3	0.4	2.8	2.1	10.5
Bryan County	11 938	68.7	151	62.9	1 495	73.8	55	34.5	209	59.8	1.4	0.2	0.4	0.7	1.0	5.4
Caddo County	7 968	70.2	254	68.5	1 925	83.1	19	73.7	501	75.0	2.2	0.1	0.1	2.0	1.3	9.9
Canadian County	20 049	77.0	424	63.7	1 208	82.1	555	97.8	740	81.2	3.2	0.6	1.8	0.7	1.0	8.9
Carter County	14 558	71.2	1 321	63.8	1 164	73.3	51	88.2	317	80.8	1.3	0.3	0.3	0.6	0.6	7.4
Cherokee County	9 947	66.2	123	61.8	4 525	73.4	26	0.0	440	84.1	2.6	0.1	0.3	2.1	1.8	11.3
Choctaw County	4 481	69.0	643	67.8	787	76.0	11	36.4	49	71.4	0.5	0.1	0.1	0.3	0.4	7.0
Cimarron County	1 090	69.0	3	0.0	15	73.3	0	X	144	78.5	10.3	0.2	0.0	9.5	5.4	14.7
Cleveland County	66 905	68.7	2 374	61.0	2 830	72.5	2 090	61.8	2 434	73.4	4.4	0.7	2.4	0.9	1.5	10.5
Coal County	1 886	67.9	11	63.6	337	77.7	2	100.0	41	75.6	1.6	0.4	0.3	0.8	0.9	8.8
Comanche County	26 931	71.5	7 003	76.7	1 839	74.1	698	69.1	2 659	78.9	5.4	2.0	1.7	1.4	1.3	17.1
Cotton County	2 284	69.4	48	75.0	164	74.4	4	50.0	91	90.1	1.5	0.3	0.1	0.8	0.4	9.0
Craig County	3 987	69.4	129	66.7	840	77.0	14	57.1	36	88.9	0.5	0.2	0.2	0.1	0.3	5.0
Creek County	21 548	75.1	769	71.8	1 657	78.8	31	64.5	270	80.4	0.7	0.2	0.1	0.2	0.1	7.6
Custer County	8 592	63.6	248	62.5	363	79.6	83	50.6	676	81.2	3.4	0.2	0.5	2.4	1.9	11.4
Delaware County	11 214	72.0	6	100.0	2 627	75.9	19	89.5	133	85.0	1.3	0.3	0.1	0.9	0.9	11.2
Dewey County	1 838	68.4	1	0.0	63	63.5	2	0.0	33	93.9	1.3	0.2	0.0	1.1	0.9	4.9
Ellis County	1 707	68.9	0	X	14	85.7	0	X	31	61.3	0.8	0.2	0.0	0.5	0.7	6.1
Garfield County	20 937	68.0	609	65.4	433	73.0	219	71.7	675	83.6	2.7	0.4	0.7	1.3	1.1	8.9
Garvin County	9 472	69.6	258	74.4	651	74.7	14	100.0	229	83.8	1.6	0.1	0.1	1.3	0.7	5.7
Grady County	15 296	73.9	546	64.8	632	79.0	32	56.3	346	84.7	1.1	0.3	0.2	0.5	0.7	6.4
Grant County	2 021	69.5	2	100.0	30	80.0	3	100.0	19	78.9	0.9	0.4	0.3	0.3	0.5	5.5
Greer County	1 998	62.7	73	65.8	25	48.0	5	100.0	108	88.0	1.5	0.2	0.3	0.9	1.6	7.3
Harmon County	940	64.7	79	83.5	5	100.0	0	X	227	82.8	3.0	0.0	0.3	2.7	4.6	21.0
Harper County	1 462	68.3	0	X	17	52.9	0	X	48	81.3	3.5	0.3	0.2	3.0	1.9	5.2
Haskell County	3 786	73.3	42	71.4	510	81.4	10	80.0	63	88.7	0.8	0.3	0.0	0.3	0.3	5.1
Hughes County	4 185	68.1	118	45.8	707	77.7	5	20.0	82	75.6	1.1	0.1	0.0	0.8	0.5	10.3
Jackson County	8 139	71.7	838	67.5	121	75.2	66	80.3	1 286	82.7	4.7	0.8	0.9	2.8	2.0	17.7
Jefferson County	2 397	68.3	7	71.4	114	64.9	7	42.9	130	80.0	3.6	0.2	1.2	2.2	1.0	7.2
Johnston County	3 310	71.7	87	67.8	473	77.6	13	38.5	68	52.9	0.8	0.3	0.1	0.4	0.3	7.4
Kay County	16 526	67.9	361	59.6	1 093	75.2	81	75.3	499	80.8	2.3	0.3	0.5	1.5	1.3	7.1
Kingfisher County	4 752	73.8	75	57.3	66	86.4	2	100.0	213	92.5	4.1	0.1	0.0	3.9	2.7	8.1

[1] Hispanic or Latino persons may be of any race.

Table A-3. States and Counties — Age, Ethnicity, and Household Structure

STATE/ County code	MSA/PMSA/ NECMA code[1]	STATE County	Population by age (percent)								+/- U.S. percent under 18 years	+/- U.S. percent 65 years and over	Non-Hispanic White Age (percent)		
			Total population	Under 5 years	5 to 17 years	18 to 24 years	25 to 44 years	45 to 64 years	65 years and over	Median age			Total population	Under 18 years	65 years and over
			1	2	3	4	5	6	7	8	9	10	11	12	13
		OKLAHOMA—Cont'd													
40 075	...	Kiowa County............	10 227	5.8	18.2	7.9	24.2	23.5	20.3	40.9	-1.7	7.9	8 185	21.4	23.2
40 077	...	Latimer County............	10 692	6.7	18.9	11.6	24.3	22.5	16.0	36.8	-0.1	3.6	7 734	21.4	18.9
40 079	...	Le Flore County............	48 109	6.8	19.3	9.5	27.4	23.3	13.6	36.1	0.4	1.2	37 672	23.8	15.4
40 081	...	Lincoln County............	32 080	6.5	20.9	7.9	26.7	23.9	14.0	37.5	1.7	1.6	27 566	25.9	15.0
40 083	5880	Logan County............	33 924	6.0	19.4	12.1	26.7	23.8	12.0	36.1	-0.3	-0.4	27 208	24.8	13.6
40 085	...	Love County............	8 831	5.9	19.8	7.2	25.1	25.9	16.2	39.4	0.0	3.8	7 191	22.0	18.1
40 087	5880	McClain County............	27 740	6.5	20.2	8.2	29.5	23.7	11.9	36.9	1.0	-0.5	23 688	24.9	13.1
40 089	...	McCurtain County..........	34 402	7.5	20.4	8.5	26.2	23.4	13.9	36.0	2.2	1.5	23 902	23.6	16.2
40 091	...	McIntosh County............	19 456	5.3	17.3	6.5	23.1	26.2	21.6	44.1	-3.1	9.2	14 041	18.0	25.5
40 093	...	Major County............	7 545	5.7	18.9	6.6	24.6	24.9	19.3	41.6	-1.1	6.9	7 057	23.3	20.5
40 095	...	Marshall County............	13 184	6.4	17.1	7.6	23.5	26.0	19.4	41.3	-2.2	7.0	10 062	18.9	23.4
40 097	...	Mayes County............	38 369	6.8	19.8	8.6	25.9	24.1	14.7	37.2	0.9	2.3	27 434	22.0	17.9
40 099	...	Murray County............	12 623	6.3	17.4	8.4	25.3	24.2	18.4	39.8	-2.0	6.0	10 020	20.2	21.0
40 101	...	Muskogee County............	69 451	7.0	18.8	9.5	27.1	22.1	15.5	37.0	0.1	3.1	43 517	20.4	18.8
40 103	...	Noble County............	11 411	6.1	19.2	7.8	27.7	24.1	15.2	38.3	-0.4	2.8	9 798	23.5	16.4
40 105	...	Nowata County............	10 569	6.4	19.8	6.7	25.9	24.0	17.2	39.0	0.5	4.8	7 558	21.9	20.1
40 107	...	Okfuskee County............	11 814	6.2	18.5	8.4	26.8	23.8	16.3	38.6	-1.0	3.9	7 676	21.4	18.9
40 109	5880	Oklahoma County..........	660 448	7.2	18.3	10.8	30.3	21.2	12.2	34.2	-0.2	-0.2	442 945	21.1	15.6
40 111	...	Okmulgee County............	39 685	6.7	20.2	9.5	25.2	23.0	15.4	36.9	1.2	3.0	27 392	22.8	17.5
40 113	8560	Osage County............	44 437	6.0	20.3	7.5	27.9	25.2	13.1	38.1	0.6	0.7	29 305	22.5	15.8
40 115	...	Ottawa County............	33 194	6.7	19.0	9.5	24.9	23.1	16.8	37.3	0.0	4.4	24 266	22.1	19.7
40 117	...	Pawnee County............	16 612	6.2	20.4	7.2	26.3	25.2	14.7	38.5	0.9	2.3	13 584	23.8	16.2
40 119	...	Payne County............	68 190	5.2	14.2	25.9	26.1	17.7	10.8	27.6	-6.3	-1.6	56 750	18.6	12.2
40 121	...	Pittsburg County............	43 953	5.6	17.9	7.9	27.0	24.5	17.2	39.4	-2.2	4.8	33 529	20.4	19.5
40 123	...	Pontotoc County............	35 143	6.1	18.6	12.6	25.8	21.9	14.9	35.7	-1.0	2.5	26 326	20.5	17.7
40 125	5880	Pottawatomie County......	65 521	6.9	18.9	11.4	26.7	22.2	13.9	35.5	0.1	1.5	51 548	22.9	15.8
40 127	...	Pushmataha County	11 667	6.3	19.8	6.6	24.2	24.8	18.3	40.1	0.4	5.9	8 987	22.5	20.3
40 129	...	Roger Mills County	3 436	5.4	18.2	6.6	24.6	26.3	18.8	41.7	-2.1	6.4	3 089	21.5	20.7
40 131	8560	Rogers County............	70 641	7.0	21.7	7.4	28.5	24.1	11.3	36.2	3.0	-1.1	55 677	26.0	12.5
40 133	...	Seminole County............	24 894	6.5	19.8	9.4	24.1	23.3	16.8	38.1	0.6	4.4	17 398	21.6	19.7
40 135	2720	Sequoyah County	38 972	7.2	20.2	8.5	26.5	24.0	13.6	36.4	1.7	1.2	26 343	23.2	16.0
40 137	...	Stephens County............	43 182	6.5	18.0	8.1	24.9	24.1	18.4	40.1	-1.2	6.0	37 284	22.5	20.2
40 139	...	Texas County............	20 107	8.6	20.3	12.5	28.6	19.7	10.3	30.4	3.2	-2.1	13 403	24.3	14.2
40 141	...	Tillman County............	9 287	5.9	21.1	6.9	24.0	22.7	19.3	38.9	1.3	6.9	6 471	21.9	23.4
40 143	8560	Tulsa County............	563 299	7.3	18.9	10.0	30.6	21.5	11.8	34.4	0.5	-0.6	408 231	22.8	14.3
40 145	8560	Wagoner County............	57 491	7.1	21.0	7.7	28.6	25.5	10.1	36.2	2.4	-2.3	45 451	25.6	11.1
40 147	...	Washington County..........	48 996	5.9	19.2	7.8	25.0	24.5	17.7	40.1	-0.6	5.3	39 072	22.3	20.1
40 149	...	Washita County............	11 508	6.1	20.0	7.7	25.1	22.5	18.6	39.2	0.4	6.2	10 418	24.6	20.2
40 151	...	Woods County............	9 089	4.5	14.3	15.2	24.9	21.1	19.9	37.8	-6.9	7.5	8 307	18.4	21.3
40 153	...	Woodward County	18 486	6.6	19.3	9.2	27.8	22.8	14.2	37.4	0.2	1.8	16 729	24.8	15.3
41 000	...	OREGON	3 421 399	6.5	18.2	9.5	29.3	23.7	12.8	36.3	-1.0	0.4	2 857 100	22.6	14.5
41 001	...	Baker County	16 741	5.4	18.9	5.8	23.5	27.3	19.2	42.7	-1.4	6.8	15 929	23.7	19.6
41 003	1890	Benton County	78 153	5.0	16.4	20.1	26.7	21.7	10.2	31.1	-4.3	-2.2	67 739	20.5	11.3
41 005	6440	Clackamas County	338 391	6.5	19.6	8.0	28.8	26.1	11.1	37.5	0.4	-1.3	301 590	25.0	12.0
41 007	...	Clatsop County	35 630	5.6	17.9	8.9	25.5	26.6	15.5	40.0	-2.2	3.1	32 263	22.3	16.6
41 009	6440	Columbia County	43 560	6.5	20.8	6.8	28.2	26.0	11.7	37.7	1.6	-0.7	40 557	26.4	12.2
41 011	...	Coos County	62 779	4.9	16.9	7.1	24.2	27.9	19.1	43.1	-3.9	6.7	56 599	20.5	20.3
41 013	...	Crook County	19 182	6.4	20.1	7.3	25.8	25.8	14.5	38.6	0.8	2.1	17 454	25.1	15.8
41 015	...	Curry County	21 137	4.1	14.9	4.5	20.2	29.3	26.9	48.8	-6.7	14.5	19 239	17.6	28.3
41 017	...	Deschutes County............	115 367	6.1	18.5	7.8	28.6	25.9	13.0	38.3	-1.1	0.6	107 230	23.8	13.8
41 019	...	Douglas County	100 399	5.6	18.3	7.6	24.2	26.5	17.8	41.2	-1.8	5.4	92 395	22.9	18.7
41 021	...	Gilliam County	1 915	4.5	18.6	5.4	25.9	26.5	19.0	42.8	-2.6	6.6	1 846	22.8	19.7
41 023	...	Grant County................	7 935	5.7	20.2	5.7	23.8	27.9	16.7	41.7	0.2	4.3	7 511	25.2	17.3
41 025	...	Harney County	7 609	5.8	20.0	6.7	26.7	25.9	14.8	39.8	0.1	2.4	6 754	24.4	16.3
41 027	...	Hood River County	20 411	7.2	20.8	8.4	29.2	21.5	12.8	35.3	2.3	0.4	14 363	22.9	16.9
41 029	4890	Jackson County	181 269	6.0	18.3	8.8	25.4	25.4	16.0	39.2	-1.4	3.6	160 553	22.6	17.4
41 031	...	Jefferson County	19 009	7.4	22.3	7.4	27.1	23.5	12.4	34.8	4.0	0.0	12 286	23.0	17.5
41 033	...	Josephine County	75 726	5.3	17.7	6.4	23.4	27.0	20.1	43.1	-2.7	7.7	69 207	21.8	21.2
41 035	...	Klamath County	63 775	6.4	19.5	8.5	25.7	25.1	14.9	38.2	0.2	2.5	53 539	23.2	16.7
41 037	...	Lake County	7 422	5.1	19.5	5.3	24.2	28.2	17.7	42.7	-1.1	5.3	6 634	21.9	19.4
41 039	2400	Lane County................	322 959	5.7	17.1	12.0	27.6	24.4	13.3	36.6	-2.9	0.9	286 042	21.5	14.5
41 041	...	Lincoln County	44 479	4.8	16.6	6.7	23.3	29.2	19.4	44.1	-4.3	7.0	39 245	19.4	21.3
41 043	...	Linn County	103 069	6.8	19.1	8.5	27.0	24.1	14.4	37.4	0.2	2.0	93 984	24.9	15.4
41 045	...	Malheur County	31 615	7.4	20.1	10.6	27.2	21.2	13.6	34.0	1.8	1.2	21 710	22.5	17.1
41 047	7080	Marion County................	284 834	7.7	19.6	10.3	28.8	21.3	12.4	33.7	1.6	0.0	217 939	23.8	15.3

[1]MSA = Metropolitan Statistical Area. PMSA = Primary MSA. NECMA = New England County Metropolitan Area. See the Appendix A for explanation of these concepts. See Appendix B for list of metropolitan areas identified by type, with component counties.

STATE County	Black or African American Total population (14)	Age (percent) Under 18 years (15)	65 years and over (16)	American Indian and Alaska Native Total population (17)	Age (percent) Under 18 years (18)	65 years and over (19)	Asian, Hawaiian, and Pacific Islander Total population (20)	Age (percent) Under 18 years (21)	65 years and over (22)	Hispanic or Latino[1] Total population (23)	Age (percent) Under 18 years (24)	65 years and over (25)	Two or more races Total population (26)	Age (percent) Under 18 years (27)	65 years and over (28)
OKLAHOMA—Cont'd															
Kiowa County	497	31.8	12.1	609	29.4	12.2	2	100.0	0.0	721	37.4	4.6	362	50.0	6.4
Latimer County.............	107	32.7	12.1	2 004	37.0	7.5	39	51.3	20.5	201	33.8	10.4	662	37.5	8.0
Le Flore County	909	22.0	7.0	5 166	36.9	6.4	128	32.8	14.1	1 949	38.3	1.5	2 506	33.3	11.4
Lincoln County	636	25.6	15.7	2 086	39.2	6.2	103	21.4	18.4	334	37.4	6.3	1 448	38.2	6.2
Logan County...............	3 612	18.2	8.1	1 160	40.4	1.7	90	15.6	0.0	926	42.8	2.1	1 047	37.6	5.4
Love County	175	28.0	21.1	593	39.6	8.3	58	50.0	6.9	609	46.8	0.8	275	50.2	10.5
McClain County............	72	18.1	0.0	1 502	36.2	5.7	53	28.3	0.0	1 314	39.6	1.2	1 258	38.0	8.4
McCurtain County	3 045	33.9	12.9	4 527	36.7	7.6	49	38.8	4.1	1 146	41.0	4.6	1 954	47.8	6.3
McIntosh County	734	25.9	14.3	2 984	35.7	12.2	43	30.2	0.0	199	42.7	6.0	1 557	37.4	8.5
Major County	25	44.0	0.0	114	44.7	1.8	0	X	X	311	46.6	0.6	93	39.8	6.5
Marshall County	206	24.8	18.4	1 266	37.0	8.3	13	0.0	30.8	1 077	43.0	1.6	741	42.2	7.0
Mayes County	112	40.2	3.6	7 241	37.6	6.3	178	36.0	2.2	572	36.0	4.5	2 958	40.3	8.0
Murray County	197	16.2	16.2	1 232	39.6	8.2	22	0.0	0.0	497	36.6	1.4	678	40.0	11.2
Muskogee County	8 958	31.5	13.6	10 284	36.0	7.7	359	27.6	17.3	1 915	39.9	1.4	4 701	38.3	9.7
Noble County	181	22.7	16.0	913	35.7	8.8	85	32.9	3.5	139	48.9	7.9	335	45.1	2.4
Nowata County	292	35.3	16.1	1 783	39.1	8.5	0	X	X	118	36.4	1.7	861	33.2	12.1
Okfuskee County..........	1 194	18.2	19.2	2 160	36.2	7.6	15	33.3	33.3	215	36.3	3.3	602	35.4	12.0
Oklahoma County	98 107	33.8	6.9	21 088	31.5	4.9	18 454	22.2	5.0	56 990	39.3	2.5	29 920	42.1	6.4
Okmulgee County	4 044	30.2	16.4	4 757	36.1	8.2	85	24.7	9.4	761	52.2	3.7	2 907	42.8	8.4
Osage County	4 843	25.9	7.3	6 338	37.9	7.4	134	40.3	4.5	1 142	46.2	5.8	3 019	34.2	10.4
Ottawa County	193	7.3	0.0	5 298	36.5	8.6	92	17.4	6.5	1 109	46.2	1.9	2 342	33.6	12.1
Pawnee County	109	26.6	7.3	2 018	41.0	8.1	56	57.1	0.0	175	51.4	3.4	730	33.4	9.3
Payne County...............	2 550	21.6	2.5	3 000	26.4	4.4	1 906	8.9	1.0	1 640	31.5	1.1	2 580	30.5	6.1
Pittsburg County...........	1 671	22.1	8.4	5 250	35.0	9.6	242	23.1	6.2	1 138	39.0	6.6	2 279	37.7	12.4
Pontotoc County...........	835	30.7	4.4	5 469	39.3	5.9	122	9.0	15.6	637	36.6	3.3	1 949	38.6	9.5
Pottawatomie County	1 937	33.4	6.6	7 384	37.1	6.5	479	18.6	4.4	1 399	44.7	4.1	3 087	39.5	8.3
Pushmataha County......	132	25.8	37.9	1 743	39.4	9.8	33	42.4	0.0	214	45.8	1.9	642	36.8	13.4
Roger Mills County........	2	100.0	0.0	222	43.2	1.8	2	0.0	0.0	75	48.0	0.0	66	34.8	7.6
Rogers County	480	27.1	5.8	7 930	38.4	7.1	321	30.2	5.6	1 305	45.8	0.6	5 217	40.1	7.1
Seminole County	1 454	26.5	14.9	4 213	38.6	9.3	104	40.4	8.7	562	48.8	6.2	1 340	44.3	8.8
Sequoyah County..........	613	39.3	12.6	7 913	35.5	8.6	83	6.0	2.4	664	48.8	3.3	3 603	38.0	8.0
Stephens County...........	902	35.4	13.7	1 820	34.3	8.8	99	53.5	0.0	1 794	44.8	2.0	1 441	36.8	8.9
Texas County	162	31.5	3.7	266	31.2	0.0	167	25.1	12.6	5 971	39.5	1.9	438	33.1	6.6
Tillman County	651	30.9	20.3	244	34.4	11.5	146	46.6	1.4	1 610	40.1	6.2	327	49.2	9.8
Tulsa County	61 006	35.3	6.4	28 738	32.7	6.1	8 839	27.4	3.1	33 364	36.2	2.2	26 464	39.0	6.1
Wagoner County	2 400	33.5	7.8	5 054	37.3	4.5	493	43.8	2.6	1 164	44.3	3.6	3 104	37.6	8.7
Washington County.......	1 363	38.1	6.3	4 095	34.0	8.3	333	25.8	1.8	1 070	33.7	6.2	3 194	39.9	10.9
Washita County	68	29.4	16.2	292	41.1	0.7	11	9.1	0.0	518	45.9	2.1	233	39.1	3.0
Woods County..............	290	10.0	0.0	94	19.1	5.0	10	0.0	0.0	201	26.0	6.5	100	36.3	12.1
Woodward County.........	212	8.5	0.0	488	36.1	5.9	25	4.0	16.0	866	43.2	2.4	195	45.1	5.6
OREGON	53 032	31.0	6.6	43 434	30.3	4.8	106 719	24.9	6.5	273 938	39.0	2.0	113 867	42.9	4.6
Baker County	46	28.3	0.0	125	50.4	6.4	85	10.6	9.4	322	40.4	8.7	293	29.0	23.9
Benton County	761	21.6	0.0	538	30.7	1.9	3 404	18.0	4.0	3 622	32.2	2.2	2 494	34.5	3.6
Clackamas County	2 184	33.6	6.0	2 095	24.2	5.1	8 730	25.1	6.3	17 021	37.2	1.8	8 939	47.9	3.6
Clatsop County............	254	24.0	2.0	306	34.3	2.9	418	21.3	13.2	1 641	40.3	1.0	1 042	44.1	6.3
Columbia County	132	43.2	10.6	579	27.3	5.5	238	11.8	9.2	994	47.3	3.2	1 197	45.8	5.3
Coos County	131	25.2	22.1	1 604	33.3	5.5	411	23.1	7.1	1 989	39.3	6.2	2 422	37.2	9.3
Crook County	7	100.0	0.0	334	32.6	1.5	53	26.4	17.0	1 075	46.0	0.0	269	29.7	4.8
Curry County	25	0.0	48.0	509	30.8	9.8	173	47.4	3.5	707	37.2	9.6	553	32.2	19.0
Deschutes County........	266	34.2	0.0	998	30.9	6.2	702	22.8	8.7	4 366	38.8	2.5	2 306	45.5	2.3
Douglas County............	195	37.9	2.6	1 585	31.8	8.5	641	22.0	10.1	2 841	41.4	4.6	3 025	35.2	7.1
Gilliam County..............	2	0.0	0.0	19	47.4	0.0	6	33.3	0.0	26	30.8	0.0	16	18.8	0.0
Grant County	0	X	X	100	42.0	6.0	9	22.2	0.0	212	43.4	5.2	151	36.4	8.6
Harney County	7	0.0	0.0	275	34.9	4.7	78	19.2	10.3	341	46.9	0.0	301	45.2	0.7
Hood River County.......	51	33.3	0.0	179	40.2	16.2	307	10.7	28.3	5 128	41.7	1.2	520	48.1	5.0
Jackson County............	760	36.6	2.0	1 975	29.5	7.2	1 735	21.9	7.5	12 066	42.9	2.6	5 592	39.6	7.0
Jefferson County	12	0.0	0.0	2 913	41.9	4.5	121	8.3	17.4	3 351	44.6	1.3	645	43.6	2.8
Josephine County	119	30.3	5.0	1 007	20.1	8.7	428	25.2	12.1	3 210	42.2	6.8	2 244	39.3	7.9
Klamath County............	288	33.3	11.1	2 636	34.3	5.2	590	32.9	10.0	4 967	44.6	3.4	2 333	43.5	5.4
Lake County	2	100.0	0.0	238	38.2	2.1	59	45.8	10.2	360	45.8	2.5	200	45.5	5.0
Lane County	2 437	32.8	6.2	3 535	27.9	4.6	6 691	18.7	4.2	14 488	37.9	1.9	11 592	39.2	4.5
Lincoln County	98	29.6	0.0	1 213	29.1	7.2	414	33.1	9.9	2 099	37.1	1.9	1 737	42.8	5.1
Linn County	242	26.0	3.3	1 413	31.6	6.4	940	29.6	6.4	4 266	41.7	1.8	2 773	39.6	6.2
Malheur County............	427	10.5	2.6	286	14.0	5.2	557	8.4	49.0	8 110	42.4	2.8	897	45.9	7.7
Marion County..............	2 459	32.9	2.0	3 770	33.3	3.1	5 562	24.9	5.9	49 005	41.1	1.9	10 046	45.8	4.3

[1] Hispanic or Latino persons may be of any race.

STATE County	Family households (percent)						Nonfamily households (percent)						Percent of householders 65 years and over who live alone	Grandparents who are responsible for the care of their grandchildren
	Married-couple family households			Other family households			Two or more unrelated persons		Male living alone		Female living alone			
	Total households	Total	With children	Householder 65 years or over	Total	With children	Householder 65 years or over	Total	Householder 65 years or over	Total	Householder 65 years or over	Total	Householder 65 years or over		
	29	30	31	32	33	34	35	36	37	38	39	40	41	42	43
OKLAHOMA—Cont'd															
Kiowa County	4 214	52.0	19.6	11.9	14.9	7.7	4.3	2.5	0.3	11.9	4.2	18.7	12.8	50.9	174
Latimer County	3 974	55.8	21.4	11.7	17.0	11.4	2.5	2.4	0.2	10.8	4.3	14.0	8.6	47.4	230
Le Flore County	17 874	59.7	26.1	10.6	14.6	8.2	2.4	2.7	0.2	9.3	2.7	13.7	8.1	45.0	774
Lincoln County	12 196	62.4	26.8	11.8	12.9	7.4	2.1	2.4	0.3	9.6	2.4	12.7	7.7	41.5	409
Logan County	12 395	60.4	27.0	9.4	12.4	7.0	1.6	3.6	0.3	10.1	2.7	13.5	7.1	46.3	306
Love County	3 439	61.0	23.9	12.9	13.7	8.1	1.5	2.6	0.5	10.7	3.6	12.0	9.0	46.0	126
McClain County	10 334	66.1	29.0	10.5	12.2	7.7	1.3	2.4	0.2	8.7	2.3	10.6	6.5	42.4	270
McCurtain County	13 296	54.4	23.7	9.9	18.4	10.9	3.0	2.0	0.2	10.2	2.7	15.0	8.7	46.7	751
McIntosh County	8 095	58.0	18.4	16.4	12.6	7.1	2.5	2.7	0.6	11.8	5.0	14.8	10.1	43.5	342
Major County	3 056	65.4	26.7	15.6	7.4	5.9	0.5	2.3	0.1	9.4	2.6	15.4	11.6	46.6	57
Marshall County	5 374	57.3	20.4	14.9	13.5	7.4	2.2	2.7	0.6	10.4	3.7	16.1	10.9	45.2	248
Mayes County	14 809	60.9	25.6	11.5	12.2	7.2	1.6	2.9	0.2	10.3	3.3	13.7	8.6	47.1	481
Murray County	5 021	60.2	25.3	13.3	11.9	6.9	1.5	2.7	0.7	8.6	2.7	16.6	9.8	44.6	132
Muskogee County	26 453	53.9	22.8	11.4	16.1	9.4	2.9	3.4	0.2	10.3	2.6	16.3	9.6	45.4	1 087
Noble County	4 527	59.3	25.2	11.1	12.2	7.0	2.3	3.1	0.1	11.5	3.3	13.9	8.4	46.2	153
Nowata County	4 121	60.5	24.7	13.7	11.6	7.2	1.8	2.3	0.5	10.6	2.9	15.0	10.8	46.2	140
Okfuskee County	4 271	54.8	21.9	12.1	15.1	7.2	3.3	2.3	0.4	11.5	4.0	16.3	10.8	48.3	178
Oklahoma County	267 018	47.1	20.9	8.4	17.3	10.6	1.9	5.5	0.3	13.1	2.1	17.0	7.3	47.0	6 805
Okmulgee County	15 308	53.7	23.1	11.4	16.7	9.6	2.8	2.7	0.1	11.2	2.9	15.8	9.2	45.9	625
Osage County	16 656	60.3	25.4	11.0	13.7	8.3	1.9	2.8	0.3	10.9	2.7	12.3	7.0	42.5	680
Ottawa County	13 027	56.6	23.3	12.9	14.3	8.5	2.2	2.6	0.5	10.3	3.0	16.2	10.2	45.9	506
Pawnee County	6 372	62.8	26.0	12.6	12.0	7.0	1.8	2.6	0.2	9.7	2.4	12.9	8.5	42.6	204
Payne County	26 731	46.6	19.5	8.4	11.5	6.7	0.9	11.9	0.2	14.1	1.6	16.0	6.1	44.9	412
Pittsburg County	17 177	56.5	21.3	12.9	13.6	8.0	2.3	2.2	0.3	11.2	3.5	16.5	10.6	47.6	887
Pontotoc County	14 008	54.0	22.8	11.2	14.1	8.7	1.6	3.9	0.2	9.9	2.5	18.0	9.0	47.0	471
Pottawatomie County	24 575	57.2	23.9	10.8	15.4	8.9	2.7	3.4	0.4	9.5	2.7	14.6	8.3	44.3	1 010
Pushmataha County	4 712	56.6	22.4	12.5	13.1	8.1	2.3	2.5	0.5	12.0	4.4	15.8	10.4	49.2	174
Roger Mills County	1 430	60.9	25.1	14.2	8.5	4.9	1.5	1.7	0.1	11.6	4.3	17.3	12.9	52.1	39
Rogers County	25 747	66.8	31.3	10.0	12.0	7.5	1.3	2.3	0.2	8.0	1.5	10.9	6.0	39.8	774
Seminole County	9 580	55.4	21.9	12.5	16.1	9.3	3.0	2.8	0.4	9.9	3.5	15.8	9.8	45.5	411
Sequoyah County	14 765	60.7	26.3	10.9	14.1	8.4	1.8	2.8	0.4	9.0	2.8	13.4	7.5	44.2	591
Stephens County	17 486	60.5	23.5	14.2	12.2	7.2	2.0	1.9	0.4	9.4	3.1	16.0	10.2	44.4	493
Texas County	7 135	62.4	31.9	9.8	13.1	7.0	1.5	5.2	0.0	10.0	2.0	11.0	6.7	43.6	178
Tillman County	3 604	56.4	23.7	13.8	13.2	7.9	1.7	1.7	0.2	11.1	4.1	17.6	13.5	52.9	196
Tulsa County	226 988	50.0	23.1	8.2	15.3	9.6	1.7	5.1	0.3	12.8	1.9	16.8	7.1	47.2	4 742
Wagoner County	21 035	66.6	29.7	9.8	13.3	8.0	1.5	2.6	0.2	8.0	1.7	9.5	4.4	34.8	713
Washington County	20 207	57.6	23.1	13.7	12.6	7.8	1.7	2.3	0.3	10.0	2.9	17.4	10.1	45.4	446
Washita County	4 530	60.9	26.8	14.3	11.5	7.7	1.7	2.5	0.3	9.8	2.6	15.3	10.4	44.6	133
Woods County	3 703	50.6	19.0	13.9	11.6	6.5	1.7	5.0	0.3	13.3	2.6	20.1	10.9	45.9	53
Woodward County	7 105	59.8	25.7	11.5	11.6	7.6	1.1	3.1	0.1	9.8	2.4	15.7	8.4	45.8	219
OREGON	1 335 109	53.0	23.2	9.7	13.3	8.2	1.5	7.7	0.5	11.2	2.3	14.8	7.0	44.0	22 103
Baker County	6 893	56.7	21.0	14.6	11.2	7.4	1.9	4.2	0.7	11.9	3.7	16.0	9.2	42.9	77
Benton County	30 198	51.7	22.8	8.6	9.4	5.9	0.8	12.9	0.2	11.9	1.4	14.1	5.3	41.3	248
Clackamas County	128 360	59.8	27.4	8.9	12.2	7.3	1.4	6.0	0.4	8.8	1.7	13.2	6.3	42.6	2 207
Clatsop County	14 741	51.3	20.5	10.5	13.6	9.0	1.7	5.7	0.7	13.1	3.9	16.3	8.2	48.5	286
Columbia County	16 388	62.0	27.3	9.2	12.0	8.0	1.8	4.9	0.7	10.6	2.4	10.5	6.0	41.9	488
Coos County	26 181	54.0	18.8	14.1	12.8	8.1	1.8	5.9	1.1	11.9	4.1	15.3	8.3	42.2	477
Crook County	7 358	62.0	25.0	12.3	11.8	7.6	2.2	5.0	0.9	9.0	3.1	12.2	7.0	39.6	183
Curry County	9 554	55.9	15.9	19.5	9.3	5.8	1.7	5.2	1.4	13.2	5.7	16.5	10.7	42.0	128
Deschutes County	45 633	59.3	24.5	11.7	11.3	8.1	0.9	7.4	0.5	9.7	2.0	12.2	5.7	37.3	596
Douglas County	39 867	58.4	21.6	14.5	12.7	7.9	1.9	5.0	0.7	10.1	3.0	13.7	8.6	40.5	898
Gilliam County	830	57.2	23.1	13.5	9.4	5.4	1.7	4.0	0.5	12.9	2.2	16.5	10.7	45.1	26
Grant County	3 250	58.2	23.4	12.6	10.8	7.4	1.4	3.8	0.6	13.8	3.9	13.5	7.8	44.4	59
Harney County	3 043	58.0	22.2	11.5	11.1	7.0	1.3	4.9	0.4	13.6	2.7	12.3	7.2	43.0	34
Hood River County	7 260	59.5	29.2	11.1	12.9	8.1	1.9	5.0	0.4	9.8	2.0	12.8	7.3	40.9	97
Jackson County	71 575	54.3	22.0	12.4	13.8	9.1	1.7	6.8	0.7	9.6	2.5	15.4	8.5	42.5	1 060
Jefferson County	6 758	61.6	26.7	12.3	15.2	10.2	1.5	4.5	0.4	10.1	2.9	8.6	6.3	35.5	306
Josephine County	31 027	56.0	19.1	16.6	13.5	8.1	2.0	5.1	0.7	9.8	3.4	15.5	8.8	38.8	616
Klamath County	25 169	54.7	21.7	11.9	14.4	9.2	1.6	5.6	0.7	11.9	3.2	13.4	6.9	41.7	566
Lake County	3 098	58.0	21.3	13.9	11.4	7.5	0.9	4.2	0.5	13.1	4.5	13.3	6.6	42.1	53
Lane County	130 616	49.9	20.6	10.0	13.6	8.8	1.6	10.0	0.6	11.5	2.2	15.1	6.9	42.8	1 740
Lincoln County	19 352	50.2	16.1	13.8	14.1	9.4	1.8	6.5	1.1	12.1	3.6	17.1	9.1	43.1	413
Linn County	39 636	57.9	24.2	11.6	13.8	8.6	1.9	5.3	0.7	9.7	2.4	13.2	7.8	41.8	690
Malheur County	10 236	58.7	28.2	12.3	13.8	9.0	1.6	3.9	0.7	9.4	3.4	14.2	9.4	46.9	340
Marion County	101 791	54.2	25.0	9.8	15.6	9.9	1.6	6.3	0.6	9.2	2.1	14.8	7.5	44.3	2 212

Table A-3. States and Counties — Age, Ethnicity, and Household Structure

STATE County	Households with Non-Hispanic White householder		Households with Black or African American householder		Households with American Indian and Alaska Native householder		Households with Asian, Hawaiian, and Pacific Islander householder		Households with Hispanic or Latino[1] householder		Foreign-born population	Place of birth (percent)			Percent in non-English speaking households	
	Number of households	Percent that are family households	Number of households	Percent that are family households	Number of households	Percent that are family households	Number of households	Percent that are family households	Number of households	Percent that are family households	Percent of total population that is foreign-born	Europe	Asia	Latin America	Linguistically isolated	Not linguistically isolated
	44	45	46	47	48	49	50	51	52	53	54	55	56	57	58	59
OKLAHOMA—Cont'd																
Kiowa County	3 611	65.3	168	68.5	197	81.2	0	X	190	77.4	1.0	0.2	0.0	0.7	1.0	10.5
Latimer County	3 094	72.8	22	54.5	616	75.2	13	100.0	41	65.9	1.3	0.5	0.2	0.3	0.1	8.0
Le Flore County	14 691	73.4	230	79.1	1 592	80.8	36	61.1	498	89.8	2.5	0.2	0.2	2.1	1.7	7.2
Lincoln County	10 842	75.1	260	68.8	584	76.7	19	52.6	107	81.3	0.8	0.3	0.3	0.2	0.5	6.1
Logan County	10 660	73.9	1 022	59.0	341	78.6	16	100.0	171	75.4	1.5	0.2	0.2	0.6	0.6	7.3
Love County	2 974	74.5	79	57.0	178	78.7	4	100.0	137	92.7	3.2	0.1	0.3	2.9	1.1	9.3
McClain County	9 133	77.6	54	33.3	454	87.7	13	84.6	315	81.6	2.6	0.4	0.1	2.0	1.4	7.7
McCurtain County	9 828	72.1	1 175	66.7	1 508	78.6	11	72.7	299	83.3	1.8	0.2	0.1	1.3	0.9	10.1
McIntosh County	6 259	71.1	336	62.2	926	74.9	13	92.3	68	75.0	0.5	0.2	0.1	0.2	0.7	9.1
Major County	2 909	72.7	11	18.2	40	72.5	0	X	82	85.4	2.1	0.3	0.0	1.7	1.6	7.4
Marshall County	4 475	69.3	73	45.2	379	78.9	5	60.0	265	91.7	5.0	0.3	0.1	4.6	3.4	8.0
Mayes County	11 494	71.7	26	38.5	2 276	78.4	49	83.7	138	70.3	1.0	0.3	0.3	0.4	0.7	10.1
Murray County	4 143	72.4	71	43.7	456	67.1	2	100.0	123	82.1	2.8	0.3	0.1	2.0	1.4	7.2
Muskogee County	18 036	68.6	3 198	70.4	3 283	73.4	91	79.1	476	67.2	1.8	0.2	0.4	1.0	0.9	7.4
Noble County	4 035	71.2	82	56.1	283	77.7	25	100.0	38	44.7	1.1	0.2	0.6	0.2	0.5	5.8
Nowata County	3 111	71.1	120	51.7	576	77.6	0	X	47	51.1	0.2	0.1	0.0	0.0	0.5	5.0
Okfuskee County	2 991	70.9	355	57.2	689	74.0	3	0.0	26	76.9	1.7	0.4	0.1	1.0	1.4	11.2
Oklahoma County	193 635	62.8	36 805	66.8	7 062	67.4	6 173	65.7	15 509	78.3	7.2	0.5	2.5	3.8	3.6	12.6
Okmulgee County	11 147	70.8	1 604	63.7	1 602	70.4	23	91.3	139	79.1	0.7	0.2	0.1	0.3	0.5	6.9
Osage County	11 732	73.5	1 722	75.2	1 966	76.2	31	71.0	230	79.1	1.0	0.1	0.2	0.5	0.1	7.2
Ottawa County	10 131	69.2	18	77.8	1 660	77.7	26	100.0	273	89.7	1.7	0.2	0.1	1.1	0.9	6.9
Pawnee County	5 417	74.7	52	38.5	595	76.6	8	75.0	41	82.9	0.6	0.2	0.2	0.1	0.2	5.8
Payne County	22 985	58.8	825	54.1	1 058	56.8	700	37.7	443	56.9	4.6	0.4	2.9	0.7	1.5	7.7
Pittsburg County	13 936	70.3	439	66.3	1 737	70.0	59	83.1	262	82.8	1.1	0.2	0.4	0.3	0.4	6.0
Pontotoc County	11 202	67.7	293	69.6	1 714	71.4	47	55.3	172	82.6	1.2	0.1	0.3	0.5	0.6	6.9
Pottawatomie County	20 456	71.8	545	69.2	2 259	77.8	100	69.0	349	87.1	1.1	0.2	0.3	0.4	0.4	7.5
Pushmataha County	3 888	69.7	35	68.6	539	70.3	6	100.0	38	92.1	0.5	0.1	0.1	0.2	0.8	7.5
Roger Mills County	1 357	68.5	0	X	51	86.3	0	X	9	77.8	0.7	0.1	0.1	0.5	0.6	5.7
Rogers County	21 132	78.7	201	61.2	2 443	82.0	70	100.0	339	85.0	1.3	0.3	0.3	0.4	0.1	6.9
Seminole County	7 349	70.9	539	67.9	1 207	74.0	36	77.8	120	72.5	1.0	0.2	0.3	0.5	0.3	11.2
Sequoyah County	10 662	74.3	200	75.5	2 618	76.1	35	74.3	116	87.1	0.7	0.1	0.2	0.4	0.6	8.9
Stephens County	15 595	72.1	320	69.4	668	73.5	24	100.0	418	93.5	1.8	0.3	0.0	1.2	0.7	7.4
Texas County	5 472	72.4	27	96.3	99	98.0	35	77.1	1 418	78.3	16.9	0.4	0.6	15.8	9.6	22.2
Tillman County	2 715	68.3	261	57.5	61	78.7	26	61.5	505	80.6	4.3	0.3	0.5	2.8	1.5	18.5
Tulsa County	174 603	64.6	23 006	65.4	9 943	68.4	2 815	71.0	9 340	74.3	5.4	0.7	1.4	2.9	2.5	9.8
Wagoner County	17 428	80.0	886	71.6	1 471	84.2	110	100.0	287	78.4	1.8	0.4	0.6	0.6	0.7	6.9
Washington County	16 875	70.6	477	58.1	1 445	69.9	55	80.0	242	74.4	2.0	0.3	0.6	0.9	1.0	8.1
Washita County	4 252	72.1	15	66.7	82	72.0	2	0.0	120	84.2	1.6	0.2	0.1	1.2	1.1	7.1
Woods County	3 500	61.9	27	100.0	24	41.7	8	66.7	94	53.2	0.9	0.2	0.1	0.4	0.3	5.0
Woodward County	6 678	70.7	23	73.9	107	86.0	16	50.0	220	89.5	2.5	0.3	0.2	2.0	1.1	6.2
OREGON	1 177 750	65.5	18 618	63.4	14 746	68.6	33 763	69.8	64 749	79.7	8.5	1.6	2.3	3.8	3.7	13.4
Baker County	6 663	67.7	25	100.0	37	51.4	14	100.0	59	67.8	1.8	0.4	0.4	0.8	1.2	7.2
Benton County	26 755	61.7	334	45.2	177	69.5	1 262	51.0	1 042	65.5	7.6	2.0	3.2	1.7	2.9	12.0
Clackamas County	118 067	71.7	698	70.2	748	72.1	2 770	78.4	4 184	78.7	7.1	1.9	2.0	2.4	2.2	12.5
Clatsop County	13 828	64.2	59	47.5	97	90.7	134	72.4	375	83.2	4.2	0.7	0.7	2.2	2.1	8.9
Columbia County	15 490	73.7	43	100.0	243	80.7	86	54.7	271	86.3	1.8	0.7	0.4	0.3	0.4	8.3
Coos County	24 147	66.6	28	82.1	586	70.3	126	54.0	561	77.4	2.7	0.9	0.5	0.8	0.5	8.7
Crook County	6 916	73.3	0	X	88	73.9	23	60.9	261	90.8	3.3	0.4	0.1	2.7	1.6	9.8
Curry County	8 870	64.3	12	41.7	197	73.6	35	88.6	250	81.6	3.7	1.8	0.5	0.6	0.5	8.9
Deschutes County	43 348	70.9	77	26.0	375	70.9	194	39.7	1 100	69.2	2.8	0.8	0.5	1.0	0.7	9.1
Douglas County	37 365	71.0	71	80.3	590	72.5	155	58.7	791	75.2	2.1	0.6	0.4	0.5	0.3	8.0
Gilliam County	806	66.7	2	0.0	8	50.0	0	X	7	57.1	1.7	0.3	0.2	0.7	0.4	7.3
Grant County	3 151	68.9	0	X	24	79.2	0	X	30	70.0	1.4	0.3	0.1	0.7	0.4	5.0
Harney County	2 816	69.0	0	X	90	63.3	31	51.6	61	78.7	2.1	0.6	0.4	0.7	1.1	9.1
Hood River County	5 982	68.9	16	62.5	47	44.7	98	71.4	1 031	94.3	16.4	0.8	0.8	14.2	8.4	20.4
Jackson County	66 228	67.7	199	59.8	655	68.4	517	60.2	2 703	79.9	4.9	1.0	0.6	2.8	1.8	10.3
Jefferson County	5 071	74.4	10	50.0	744	81.5	29	82.8	820	85.7	9.9	0.4	0.6	8.6	5.9	20.1
Josephine County	29 156	69.1	26	57.7	356	71.1	143	67.1	791	81.5	3.1	1.2	0.4	0.8	0.7	8.0
Klamath County	22 194	68.8	107	60.7	905	69.9	167	62.9	1 152	84.9	4.8	0.9	0.6	2.9	2.1	10.5
Lake County	2 858	69.2	0	X	79	57.0	15	46.7	99	75.8	3.4	0.8	0.7	1.7	1.0	7.8
Lane County	119 340	63.8	846	60.3	1 176	63.5	2 373	43.1	3 883	70.3	4.9	1.1	1.6	1.6	1.5	11.7
Lincoln County	17 778	63.6	36	47.2	531	62.5	113	82.3	460	87.0	4.2	1.0	0.5	2.1	1.1	8.3
Linn County	37 145	71.4	90	36.7	509	71.5	283	78.8	918	89.8	3.5	0.9	0.6	1.6	1.5	9.1
Malheur County	7 818	70.0	37	56.8	61	78.7	243	67.9	1 923	84.6	8.2	0.4	0.4	7.1	6.1	24.4
Marion County	86 570	67.6	542	79.3	1 044	72.2	1 629	73.1	10 291	87.3	12.6	1.5	1.6	8.8	7.4	17.3

[1] Hispanic or Latino persons may be of any race.

STATE/ County code	MSA/PMSA/ NECMA code[1]	STATE County	Total population	Under 5 years	5 to 17 years	18 to 24 years	25 to 44 years	45 to 64 years	65 years and over	Median age	+/− U.S. percent under 18 years	+/− U.S. percent 65 years and over	Non-Hispanic White Total population	Age (percent) Under 18 years	Age (percent) 65 years and over
			1	2	3	4	5	6	7	8	9	10	11	12	13
		OREGON—Cont'd													
41 049	...	Morrow County	10 995	8.5	22.2	9.0	27.1	22.6	10.5	33.3	5.0	-1.9	7 817	25.0	14.0
41 051	6440	Multnomah County	660 486	6.3	15.9	10.2	34.0	22.4	11.2	34.9	-3.5	-1.2	505 016	19.2	13.0
41 053	7080	Polk County	62 380	6.6	18.8	11.5	25.0	23.3	14.7	36.5	-0.3	2.3	53 414	23.0	16.7
41 055	...	Sherman County	1 934	5.1	21.1	5.7	23.7	26.3	18.1	41.8	0.5	5.7	1 750	24.2	19.4
41 057	...	Tillamook County	24 262	5.1	17.1	7.1	23.0	28.1	19.6	43.5	-3.5	7.2	22 188	20.8	21.0
41 059	...	Umatilla County	70 548	7.4	20.3	9.1	28.6	22.3	12.2	34.6	2.0	-0.2	54 701	24.1	15.0
41 061	...	Union County	24 530	6.2	18.4	11.9	23.8	24.8	14.8	37.7	-1.1	2.4	22 945	24.2	15.4
41 063	...	Wallowa County	7 226	4.9	19.2	5.3	21.4	30.2	19.0	44.4	-1.6	6.6	7 035	23.7	19.3
41 065	...	Wasco County	23 791	6.4	18.8	7.5	25.0	25.6	16.7	39.9	-0.5	4.3	19 957	22.2	19.1
41 067	6440	Washington County	445 342	7.8	19.0	9.1	34.3	21.0	8.8	33.0	1.1	-3.6	346 419	24.7	10.5
41 069	...	Wheeler County	1 547	4.3	18.5	3.3	19.4	31.5	23.0	48.1	-2.9	10.6	1 461	22.4	24.4
41 071	6440	Yamhill County	84 992	6.8	19.8	11.4	28.8	21.4	11.7	34.1	0.9	-0.7	71 789	25.2	13.4
42 000	...	PENNSYLVANIA	12 281 054	5.9	17.9	8.9	28.6	23.0	15.6	38.0	-1.9	3.2	10 327 998	22.2	17.1
42 001	...	Adams County	91 292	5.9	18.9	9.3	28.9	23.1	13.9	37.0	-0.9	1.5	85 542	24.0	14.6
42 003	6280	Allegheny County	1 281 666	5.5	16.4	8.6	28.4	23.3	17.8	39.6	-3.8	5.4	1 074 037	20.1	19.4
42 005	...	Armstrong County	72 392	5.4	17.5	7.2	27.7	24.2	18.0	40.4	-2.8	5.6	70 899	22.7	18.2
42 007	6280	Beaver County	181 412	5.4	17.2	7.4	27.5	24.1	18.4	40.7	-3.1	6.0	167 086	21.5	19.1
42 009	...	Bedford County	49 984	6.1	17.5	7.2	28.1	24.6	16.4	39.5	-2.1	4.0	49 161	23.5	16.5
42 011	6680	Berks County	373 638	6.1	18.5	8.8	28.8	22.5	15.2	37.4	-1.1	2.8	317 659	22.1	17.0
42 013	0280	Blair County	129 144	5.6	17.0	8.9	27.1	24.0	17.3	39.5	-3.1	4.9	125 645	22.3	17.7
42 015	...	Bradford County	62 761	6.1	19.4	6.9	27.1	24.8	15.7	38.9	-0.2	3.3	61 394	25.2	15.9
42 017	6160	Bucks County	597 635	6.4	19.2	7.0	30.7	24.2	12.4	37.7	-0.1	0.0	545 162	25.0	13.1
42 019	6280	Butler County	174 083	6.4	18.3	8.7	29.4	23.0	14.3	37.6	-1.0	1.9	169 722	24.4	14.5
42 021	3680	Cambria County	152 598	5.1	15.9	9.1	26.1	24.2	19.7	41.2	-4.7	7.3	145 455	20.7	20.3
42 023	...	Cameron County	5 974	4.6	20.0	5.9	24.7	24.8	19.9	41.3	-1.1	7.5	5 913	24.4	20.1
42 025	0240	Carbon County	58 802	5.2	16.9	7.0	28.3	24.1	18.5	40.6	-3.6	6.1	57 048	21.6	18.8
42 027	8050	Centre County	135 758	4.6	13.3	27.0	26.5	18.3	10.3	28.7	-7.8	-2.1	123 267	18.3	11.2
42 029	6160	Chester County	433 501	6.7	19.5	7.9	30.4	23.8	11.8	36.9	0.5	-0.6	378 282	25.4	12.5
42 031	...	Clarion County	41 765	5.5	16.3	15.2	25.1	22.8	15.2	36.3	-3.9	2.8	40 906	21.5	15.4
42 033	...	Clearfield County	83 382	5.4	17.3	7.6	29.0	23.8	16.9	39.3	-3.0	4.5	80 913	22.9	17.3
42 035	...	Clinton County	37 914	5.4	16.0	13.4	25.8	22.6	16.7	37.8	-4.3	4.3	37 160	21.5	16.9
42 037	7560	Columbia County	64 151	4.9	15.9	14.3	26.0	23.0	15.9	37.5	-4.9	3.5	62 410	20.6	16.2
42 039	...	Crawford County	90 366	5.9	18.8	9.3	26.6	23.9	15.5	38.1	-1.0	3.1	87 190	23.4	15.8
42 041	3240	Cumberland County	213 674	5.5	16.5	10.6	28.6	24.0	14.9	38.1	-3.7	2.5	199 618	21.4	15.6
42 043	3240	Dauphin County	251 798	6.0	18.3	7.5	30.4	23.6	14.2	37.9	-1.4	1.8	190 620	20.9	16.5
42 045	6160	Delaware County	550 864	6.3	18.5	8.9	28.9	21.8	15.6	37.4	-0.9	3.2	438 290	22.9	17.6
42 047	...	Elk County	35 112	5.8	18.3	6.7	28.7	23.3	17.3	39.4	-1.6	4.9	34 617	23.9	17.5
42 049	2360	Erie County	280 843	6.1	18.9	10.8	27.6	22.2	14.3	36.2	-0.7	1.9	252 079	23.4	15.4
42 051	6280	Fayette County	148 644	5.6	17.1	7.9	27.1	24.1	18.2	40.2	-3.0	5.8	141 241	22.1	18.4
42 053	...	Forest County	4 946	3.7	19.1	5.6	23.1	28.9	19.5	44.2	-2.9	7.1	4 697	21.1	20.3
42 055	...	Franklin County	129 313	6.3	17.6	8.0	28.5	23.5	16.0	38.3	-1.8	3.6	122 106	23.2	16.6
42 057	...	Fulton County	14 261	6.2	18.2	7.6	28.5	24.9	14.5	38.2	-1.3	2.1	14 005	24.2	14.7
42 059	...	Greene County	40 672	5.2	16.9	9.7	29.2	23.8	15.2	38.2	-3.6	2.8	38 330	22.8	16.0
42 061	...	Huntingdon County	45 586	5.4	16.2	10.0	29.3	24.2	14.9	37.7	-4.1	2.5	42 362	22.4	15.8
42 063	...	Indiana County	89 605	4.9	16.1	16.5	24.9	22.7	14.9	36.2	-4.7	2.5	86 501	21.0	15.2
42 065	...	Jefferson County	45 932	5.5	18.0	7.7	27.3	23.6	17.9	39.8	-2.2	5.5	45 219	23.4	18.1
42 067	...	Juniata County	22 821	6.7	18.3	8.3	27.9	23.7	15.2	37.7	-0.7	2.8	22 233	24.5	15.5
42 069	7560	Lackawanna County	213 295	5.2	16.6	8.8	26.5	23.5	19.5	40.3	-3.9	7.1	205 041	21.1	20.0
42 071	4000	Lancaster County	470 658	6.9	19.7	9.1	28.4	21.8	14.0	36.1	0.9	1.6	420 994	25.1	15.2
42 073	...	Lawrence County	94 643	5.6	17.5	8.5	25.6	23.5	19.3	40.5	-2.6	6.9	89 391	22.3	19.9
42 075	3240	Lebanon County	120 327	6.1	17.6	8.2	28.1	23.7	16.4	38.7	-2.0	4.0	111 231	22.5	17.4
42 077	0240	Lehigh County	312 090	6.0	17.9	8.0	29.4	22.9	15.8	38.3	-1.8	3.4	259 812	21.0	18.3
42 079	7560	Luzerne County	319 250	5.0	16.0	8.1	27.2	24.0	19.6	40.8	-4.7	7.2	306 038	20.5	20.3
42 081	9140	Lycoming County	120 044	5.5	17.7	9.7	27.6	23.5	16.0	38.4	-2.5	3.6	112 316	22.3	16.8
42 083	...	McKean County	45 936	5.7	18.1	7.6	28.8	23.2	16.7	38.7	-1.9	4.3	43 854	23.8	17.2
42 085	7610	Mercer County	120 293	5.7	17.8	8.8	26.3	23.4	18.1	39.6	-2.2	5.7	111 455	22.4	18.8
42 087	...	Mifflin County	46 486	6.2	18.5	7.0	27.4	23.8	17.0	38.8	-1.0	4.6	45 716	24.4	17.2
42 089	...	Monroe County	138 687	6.0	20.7	8.6	29.0	23.6	12.2	37.2	1.0	-0.2	117 884	24.7	13.7
42 091	6160	Montgomery County	750 097	6.3	17.8	7.2	30.6	23.2	14.9	38.2	-1.6	2.5	640 575	23.2	16.3
42 093	...	Montour County	18 236	5.6	18.8	6.6	28.0	23.8	17.1	39.8	-1.3	4.7	17 615	23.8	17.6
42 095	0240	Northampton County	267 066	5.6	17.7	9.3	28.3	23.4	15.7	38.5	-2.4	3.3	235 408	21.6	17.2
42 097	...	Northumberland County	94 556	5.1	16.7	7.2	27.6	24.3	19.1	40.8	-3.9	6.7	91 203	21.5	19.6
42 099	3240	Perry County	43 602	6.1	19.4	7.4	29.7	25.1	12.2	37.5	-0.2	-0.2	42 805	25.2	12.4
42 101	6160	Philadelphia County	1 517 550	6.4	18.8	11.1	29.4	20.1	14.1	34.2	-0.5	1.7	645 973	17.3	20.1
42 103	5660	Pike County	46 302	5.8	20.8	5.4	27.9	25.2	15.1	39.6	0.9	2.7	41 607	25.6	16.2

[1]MSA = Metropolitan Statistical Area. PMSA = Primary MSA. NECMA = New England County Metropolitan Area. See the Appendix A for explanation of these concepts. See Appendix B for list of metropolitan areas identified by type, with component counties.

Table A-3. States and Counties — Age, Ethnicity, and Household Structure

STATE County	Black or African American			American Indian and Alaska Native			Asian, Hawaiian, and Pacific Islander			Hispanic or Latino[1]			Two or more races		
		Age (percent)			Age (percent)			Age (percent)			Age (percent)			Age (percent)	
	Total population	Under 18 years	65 years and over	Total population	Under 18 years	65 years and over	Total population	Under 18 years	65 years and over	Total population	Under 18 years	65 years and over	Total population	Under 18 years	65 years and over
	14	15	16	17	18	19	20	21	22	23	24	25	26	27	28
OREGON—Cont'd															
Morrow County	17	17.6	11.8	182	45.1	4.9	59	23.7	15.3	2 685	45.1	1.3	279	45.2	4.7
Multnomah County	35 854	31.7	8.0	6 674	24.7	3.8	39 791	25.5	7.5	49 474	35.0	2.2	29 812	42.9	3.7
Polk County	192	27.6	1.6	1 003	28.0	4.5	915	29.7	8.1	5 517	41.9	1.3	1 743	50.4	4.1
Sherman County	12	91.7	0.0	41	26.8	0.0	14	0.0	0.0	90	47.8	7.8	53	62.3	7.5
Tillamook County	47	31.9	17.0	121	19.8	1.7	149	19.5	10.7	1 229	44.7	0.4	633	30.8	9.8
Umatilla County	707	27.7	3.0	2 225	33.8	5.8	554	28.7	5.8	11 392	43.7	1.5	1 510	46.4	4.0
Union County	111	30.6	12.6	154	16.2	8.4	358	32.1	4.2	568	37.0	2.6	374	35.0	5.6
Wallowa County	0	X	X	26	26.9	0.0	6	0.0	0.0	54	57.4	0.0	110	40.9	10.0
Wasco County	105	58.1	2.9	843	41.8	5.8	234	21.4	5.6	2 214	42.5	2.3	635	41.9	7.9
Washington County	4 510	26.3	2.4	2 919	26.0	1.7	31 345	26.6	4.7	49 476	36.6	1.5	14 776	46.8	3.2
Wheeler County	2	0.0	0.0	8	25.0	0.0	0	X	X	52	36.5	0.0	37	29.7	0.0
Yamhill County	570	16.7	0.4	1 006	31.1	1.2	942	16.0	6.7	8 980	37.7	1.7	2 318	40.9	4.7
PENNSYLVANIA	1 211 669	30.8	10.2	19 511	27.3	7.2	220 352	25.3	4.7	392 121	37.6	3.8	155 159	44.1	5.4
Adams County	1 126	32.5	7.3	172	19.8	7.0	642	15.6	5.1	3 270	42.5	1.0	753	44.2	7.8
Allegheny County	158 002	32.0	11.3	1 644	24.1	9.8	21 501	20.2	3.1	11 617	29.0	7.1	15 301	44.6	6.0
Armstrong County	658	27.2	13.8	48	8.3	2.1	214	36.9	4.2	213	36.2	3.3	344	43.9	10.5
Beaver County	10 544	31.9	12.5	210	33.3	4.8	463	24.8	8.0	1 372	38.7	7.8	1 923	52.5	6.6
Bedford County	130	23.8	18.5	45	35.6	0.0	107	29.9	16.8	236	33.1	10.2	325	37.2	9.8
Berks County	13 057	33.1	9.9	852	32.3	5.0	3 863	29.6	6.0	36 096	42.4	2.9	6 284	50.3	3.7
Blair County	1 281	26.9	5.4	262	43.5	5.7	581	29.8	2.8	465	31.8	7.5	947	51.8	7.7
Bradford County	151	53.6	6.6	179	24.0	4.5	198	18.7	3.5	306	41.8	7.2	538	41.3	7.6
Bucks County	18 454	32.4	8.0	801	20.3	3.2	14 295	29.1	5.1	13 820	33.9	4.4	6 545	44.8	4.9
Butler County	1 125	34.8	6.9	147	17.0	0.0	971	16.3	8.0	1 208	45.6	2.6	1 095	47.2	4.7
Cambria County	4 407	23.8	7.8	120	10.8	3.3	606	21.0	4.0	1 151	17.2	8.4	962	55.4	3.0
Cameron County	16	37.5	0.0	0	X	X	3	0.0	0.0	20	20.0	20.0	26	76.9	0.0
Carbon County	354	42.1	15.0	65	35.4	0.0	157	19.7	0.6	884	41.5	6.0	339	41.3	12.4
Centre County	3 330	9.6	0.8	200	23.0	6.0	5 486	12.7	1.8	2 305	16.1	1.8	1 391	26.5	3.7
Chester County	26 421	28.5	11.0	814	38.5	4.1	8 863	28.7	4.0	16 016	34.4	2.7	5 032	45.6	5.0
Clarion County	236	14.0	0.8	41	26.8	9.8	160	19.4	2.5	124	32.3	0.8	300	47.3	5.3
Clearfield County	1 225	4.1	2.4	110	29.1	7.3	305	12.5	2.6	406	30.3	1.0	492	42.7	6.5
Clinton County	241	22.8	0.0	44	11.4	25.0	146	26.0	1.4	143	21.7	11.9	203	21.7	16.3
Columbia County	574	24.9	2.6	98	11.2	7.1	315	18.7	7.0	492	30.5	3.9	307	39.1	10.7
Crawford County	1 313	25.7	8.8	127	31.5	17.3	307	21.5	10.1	611	34.2	3.6	832	45.6	11.9
Cumberland County	5 111	22.1	5.2	260	26.9	6.9	3 492	28.1	6.2	2 986	31.8	4.2	2 346	48.6	5.2
Dauphin County	41 439	32.7	8.7	444	18.9	9.9	5 105	27.0	4.4	10 713	40.5	2.7	5 172	53.9	2.6
Delaware County	79 260	32.4	8.5	671	31.3	11.5	18 387	26.2	4.9	7 998	32.1	4.3	7 413	42.5	4.9
Elk County	33	45.5	0.0	39	25.6	2.6	204	28.9	0.0	101	40.6	5.9	125	50.4	5.6
Erie County	16 001	36.8	6.2	489	23.9	6.3	1 874	25.6	3.5	6 165	43.5	2.8	4 158	55.7	4.5
Fayette County	5 109	30.7	16.2	131	19.8	13.0	308	33.4	1.6	412	29.9	24.5	1 463	48.3	5.5
Forest County	108	79.6	0.0	32	0.0	6.3	12	16.7	16.7	42	50.0	11.9	38	34.2	10.5
Franklin County	3 087	32.7	8.2	161	17.4	0.0	981	36.1	3.6	2 251	36.8	2.7	1 025	52.8	6.6
Fulton County	86	33.7	10.5	19	5.3	10.5	24	58.3	0.0	28	21.4	7.1	102	51.0	8.8
Greene County	1 603	2.2	1.9	32	0.0	0.0	110	34.5	5.5	380	16.6	3.7	248	38.3	11.3
Huntingdon County	2 322	6.2	2.7	18	0.0	11.1	115	36.5	0.0	514	21.0	1.9	358	27.1	3.1
Indiana County	1 499	18.6	5.5	114	15.8	0.0	666	21.0	6.6	463	22.9	5.2	389	41.6	4.9
Jefferson County	46	54.3	8.7	61	32.8	4.9	177	37.3	1.1	149	15.4	22.1	287	39.7	8.4
Juniata County	51	72.5	0.0	34	29.4	0.0	118	44.1	2.5	347	40.6	1.4	133	39.1	4.5
Lackawanna County	2 432	37.0	6.1	182	22.0	2.2	1 818	29.2	8.5	2 695	37.1	3.2	1 487	48.9	4.8
Lancaster County	12 722	36.6	4.9	575	17.9	13.6	6 644	31.0	3.4	26 451	41.6	2.8	6 214	52.2	2.9
Lawrence County	3 568	41.3	11.0	129	25.6	0.0	306	28.1	2.0	496	41.9	5.4	760	44.1	10.4
Lebanon County	1 187	30.9	1.5	137	8.0	0.0	1 108	33.8	8.7	6 016	41.7	3.0	1 366	43.1	6.1
Lehigh County	10 449	38.4	3.2	721	35.8	4.9	6 971	27.2	2.8	31 811	40.5	2.9	6 009	46.0	4.8
Luzerne County	5 479	25.6	4.2	414	33.3	3.4	1 575	30.2	4.8	3 912	35.9	3.5	2 081	42.0	6.0
Lycoming County	4 988	33.8	3.1	298	14.1	1.3	520	31.2	3.8	915	39.7	2.6	998	51.1	4.8
McKean County	907	10.8	1.3	128	27.3	14.8	168	26.2	14.9	590	28.1	1.7	378	40.5	11.6
Mercer County	6 056	33.6	11.3	136	38.2	11.0	681	25.3	3.2	996	45.1	4.2	1 135	57.0	6.0
Mifflin County	221	46.6	7.2	31	3.2	0.0	87	37.9	8.0	248	41.9	3.2	180	42.2	11.1
Monroe County	8 291	34.6	4.3	249	33.7	2.8	1 417	32.7	3.1	9 183	39.3	2.9	2 892	50.4	3.6
Montgomery County	55 190	27.2	8.9	1 010	25.4	8.2	29 716	25.7	4.8	15 463	31.7	3.4	9 574	49.1	5.0
Montour County	135	68.1	0.0	19	0.0	0.0	228	28.5	6.6	205	40.0	0.0	115	44.3	0.0
Northampton County	7 258	33.8	5.7	328	28.7	1.8	3 811	29.5	3.1	17 708	38.1	4.3	3 931	37.7	5.0
Northumberland County	1 450	16.2	4.5	106	29.2	16.0	395	24.8	5.6	968	38.7	2.7	536	57.8	9.1
Perry County	126	51.6	6.3	57	40.4	5.3	130	38.5	3.8	269	42.4	2.2	220	38.6	1.8
Philadelphia County	653 364	30.7	11.2	4 413	31.1	10.5	65 961	23.8	5.5	128 300	37.6	4.4	37 219	35.3	6.1
Pike County	1 396	29.0	5.0	54	44.4	0.0	323	22.9	9.3	2 267	37.8	4.0	790	44.8	3.0

[1] Hispanic or Latino persons may be of any race.

STATE County	Total households	Family households (percent)						Nonfamily households (percent)						Percent of householders 65 years and over who live alone	Grandparents who are responsible for the care of their grandchildren
		Married-couple family households			Other family households			Two or more unrelated persons		Male living alone		Female living alone			
		Total	With children	Householder 65 years or over	Total	With children	Householder 65 years or over	Total	Householder 65 years or over	Total	Householder 65 years or over	Total	Householder 65 years or over		
	29	30	31	32	33	34	35	36	37	38	39	40	41	42	43
OREGON—Cont'd															
Morrow County	3 784	63.3	30.0	10.5	14.0	9.7	0.9	4.6	0.7	10.3	3.1	7.8	4.3	37.8	126
Multnomah County	272 356	42.0	18.9	6.5	14.5	8.3	1.7	11.1	0.5	14.6	2.2	17.8	6.8	50.6	3 843
Polk County	23 083	58.6	25.0	11.7	11.6	6.9	1.5	7.4	0.6	8.2	1.9	14.2	8.0	41.8	514
Sherman County	801	57.1	23.6	15.0	11.7	7.6	2.4	2.9	0.5	16.6	4.9	11.7	6.5	38.9	16
Tillamook County	10 214	55.5	18.5	14.6	11.2	6.6	2.1	5.5	1.1	11.7	3.9	16.1	9.5	43.0	272
Umatilla County	25 237	56.4	25.8	10.2	14.9	10.2	1.5	5.2	0.5	10.8	2.8	12.8	6.9	44.2	667
Union County	9 749	56.3	22.6	11.1	11.1	7.1	1.4	6.6	0.6	10.6	2.3	15.5	8.6	45.5	219
Wallowa County	3 045	59.0	22.0	14.9	10.1	7.0	1.0	3.9	1.2	14.2	4.2	12.6	8.4	42.3	31
Wasco County	9 390	55.1	21.5	12.2	14.6	9.3	2.1	4.2	0.5	10.7	3.3	15.4	8.7	44.8	190
Washington County	169 287	56.0	29.0	6.4	12.0	7.4	1.1	7.4	0.3	10.9	1.4	13.8	5.2	46.1	1 851
Wheeler County	649	59.9	17.4	19.6	7.9	4.9	1.2	5.1	1.5	11.6	3.1	15.6	7.7	32.6	8
Yamhill County	28 700	61.4	29.6	10.4	13.4	8.4	1.3	5.3	0.3	8.7	2.0	11.1	6.8	42.2	566
PENNSYLVANIA	4 779 186	52.4	22.5	10.7	15.1	8.0	2.8	4.9	0.4	11.1	2.8	16.5	8.9	46.0	80 423
Adams County	33 647	61.2	26.6	11.3	12.6	7.4	2.0	4.9	0.3	9.2	2.4	12.2	6.9	40.5	372
Allegheny County	537 405	46.6	19.0	10.9	15.5	7.8	3.3	5.2	0.3	12.7	3.2	20.0	10.2	47.9	6 900
Armstrong County	28 932	57.7	22.7	12.6	13.1	6.9	2.8	3.3	0.3	10.5	3.4	15.4	10.4	46.7	398
Beaver County	72 664	55.7	21.9	13.1	14.3	7.5	2.8	3.2	0.3	10.1	3.3	16.8	10.4	45.7	1 202
Bedford County	19 800	62.1	24.7	12.9	11.3	5.9	2.3	3.1	0.3	9.6	2.9	13.9	8.8	43.2	391
Berks County	141 609	56.2	24.2	11.2	13.6	7.8	2.1	5.6	0.5	10.3	2.9	14.3	8.0	44.1	2 378
Blair County	51 622	53.4	21.6	11.5	14.9	8.2	2.8	3.9	0.3	10.4	2.8	17.3	10.4	47.5	1 042
Bradford County	24 427	58.0	24.5	11.5	12.8	7.6	2.2	4.5	0.4	10.3	2.8	14.4	8.6	44.6	378
Bucks County	218 773	62.1	30.0	9.7	11.9	6.0	2.1	4.6	0.4	9.3	2.1	12.2	6.0	40.0	2 574
Butler County	65 929	60.5	27.4	10.4	10.8	5.9	1.8	4.5	0.2	9.9	2.4	14.3	8.2	46.2	773
Cambria County	60 568	53.1	20.4	13.2	14.4	6.8	3.7	2.8	0.4	10.7	3.4	19.0	12.4	47.8	1 028
Cameron County	2 468	52.9	20.2	15.2	12.9	7.0	2.9	3.9	0.2	13.7	2.6	16.6	10.9	42.3	37
Carbon County	23 729	55.4	22.1	12.2	13.9	7.2	3.1	4.7	0.4	11.2	3.7	14.8	10.2	46.9	484
Centre County	49 336	49.7	21.0	8.6	8.4	4.6	1.2	15.4	0.3	12.7	1.8	13.9	6.2	43.9	466
Chester County	158 025	61.6	30.2	9.4	10.6	5.6	1.7	5.2	0.3	8.9	1.8	13.7	6.1	40.8	1 807
Clarion County	16 011	55.4	22.5	12.0	11.9	6.5	1.9	6.5	0.3	11.6	3.2	14.5	8.3	44.7	122
Clearfield County	32 792	57.2	23.2	11.6	12.7	6.7	2.8	3.8	0.3	10.4	3.3	15.9	10.1	47.6	518
Clinton County	14 804	55.0	20.8	12.3	12.7	7.5	2.0	5.8	0.4	10.9	3.7	15.6	10.1	48.5	317
Columbia County	24 982	54.3	21.2	11.6	12.6	7.0	2.0	6.8	0.3	10.0	2.7	16.4	9.3	46.5	318
Crawford County	34 695	56.2	23.1	11.3	12.9	7.7	2.1	4.8	0.5	11.1	3.1	15.0	8.6	45.7	483
Cumberland County	83 047	56.7	23.6	10.7	11.0	6.5	1.6	5.5	0.4	10.6	2.2	16.1	8.3	45.0	821
Dauphin County	102 667	48.4	20.4	9.4	16.4	9.9	2.1	5.3	0.4	12.6	2.4	17.4	8.0	46.7	2 007
Delaware County	206 372	51.7	24.3	10.6	16.3	7.9	3.4	4.4	0.3	10.6	2.8	17.0	9.0	45.2	3 557
Elk County	14 105	56.4	24.8	11.9	12.6	6.3	2.4	3.7	0.2	11.5	3.8	15.8	10.3	49.2	147
Erie County	106 488	51.7	22.9	10.2	15.5	9.3	2.2	5.2	0.3	11.3	2.4	16.3	8.8	46.9	1 784
Fayette County	60 047	52.9	20.6	11.5	16.2	8.2	3.4	3.1	0.4	10.5	3.4	17.4	11.3	49.1	1 190
Forest County	1 996	55.7	18.3	13.6	10.5	5.1	1.5	4.6	1.1	14.1	6.0	15.2	10.0	49.7	32
Franklin County	50 574	61.1	24.8	12.6	11.1	6.5	1.5	4.1	0.4	9.4	2.5	14.4	8.4	43.0	810
Fulton County	5 659	59.6	23.8	11.6	12.8	7.7	1.7	3.4	0.4	10.8	2.4	13.4	8.0	43.3	93
Greene County	15 081	56.5	24.0	11.1	14.0	7.4	2.8	3.6	0.2	10.9	3.1	14.9	9.6	47.4	345
Huntingdon County	16 778	58.7	23.4	11.7	12.1	6.8	1.9	3.4	0.4	10.5	3.0	15.3	9.7	47.3	312
Indiana County	34 098	54.7	22.3	10.7	11.6	5.6	2.5	7.3	0.3	10.9	2.8	15.5	8.8	46.1	455
Jefferson County	18 396	57.5	23.7	12.2	12.9	7.1	2.5	3.0	0.2	11.2	3.6	15.4	10.0	47.6	262
Juniata County	8 580	65.4	27.4	12.5	10.2	5.7	1.6	3.4	0.1	8.5	2.2	12.5	8.8	43.7	137
Lackawanna County	86 204	50.3	20.9	11.3	14.7	6.6	3.6	3.7	0.3	11.7	3.8	19.6	12.3	51.3	891
Lancaster County	172 780	60.5	27.1	11.4	11.7	6.9	1.5	4.7	0.3	9.4	2.2	13.6	7.2	41.4	2 421
Lawrence County	37 136	55.5	22.1	13.4	14.6	7.2	3.4	2.9	0.2	9.8	3.5	17.2	11.4	46.7	593
Lebanon County	46 611	58.2	23.6	12.0	12.3	7.2	1.8	4.2	0.4	9.8	2.5	15.4	9.0	44.8	537
Lehigh County	121 947	56.3	23.0	10.9	13.9	7.9	2.1	5.4	0.5	11.1	2.6	16.0	9.0	46.2	1 829
Luzerne County	130 703	49.9	20.0	11.0	14.9	7.0	3.6	3.9	0.4	12.1	3.8	19.2	12.3	51.9	1 887
Lycoming County	47 040	54.0	21.8	12.0	13.9	8.4	1.9	5.3	0.4	11.0	2.7	15.8	9.1	45.2	618
McKean County	18 027	53.4	22.1	12.1	14.0	8.9	2.3	4.3	0.4	11.8	3.4	16.4	9.9	47.4	193
Mercer County	46 755	55.4	22.2	13.5	14.1	7.7	2.8	3.6	0.4	10.7	2.9	16.2	9.8	43.3	794
Mifflin County	18 446	58.1	24.5	11.8	12.5	6.3	2.3	3.5	0.3	9.4	2.9	16.5	10.3	47.8	334
Monroe County	49 508	61.3	28.9	10.6	12.6	7.4	1.7	5.9	0.6	9.4	2.3	10.8	5.6	38.3	1 019
Montgomery County	286 255	58.1	27.1	11.3	11.3	5.5	2.2	5.0	0.4	9.8	2.1	15.7	7.8	41.8	3 151
Montour County	7 107	57.4	24.4	10.9	10.4	6.1	1.7	4.2	0.5	10.4	2.9	17.6	7.8	44.9	99
Northampton County	101 631	57.1	24.7	11.3	13.2	7.0	2.5	4.9	0.4	9.9	2.7	14.8	8.5	44.3	1 374
Northumberland County	38 894	53.3	20.8	12.0	12.9	7.1	2.3	3.9	0.3	11.2	3.6	18.7	12.1	51.8	472
Perry County	16 742	62.0	26.5	9.4	12.3	7.0	1.8	4.1	0.5	9.5	2.4	12.1	7.1	44.6	271
Philadelphia County	590 283	32.7	14.0	7.1	27.5	14.3	4.7	6.0	0.6	13.9	3.2	19.9	8.9	49.4	21 123
Pike County	17 447	64.1	28.0	14.0	10.9	6.6	1.3	4.4	0.7	9.6	2.6	11.0	5.6	33.6	239

STATE County	Households with Non-Hispanic White householder		Households with Black or African American householder		Households with American Indian and Alaska Native householder		Households with Asian, Hawaiian, and Pacific Islander householder		Households with Hispanic or Latino[1] householder		Foreign-born population	Place of birth (percent)			Percent in non-English speaking households	
	Number of households	Percent that are family house-holds	Number of households	Percent that are family house-holds	Number of households	Percent that are family house-holds	Number of households	Percent that are family house-holds	Number of households	Percent that are family house-holds	Percent of total population that is foreign-born	Europe	Asia	Latin America	Linguis-tically isolated	Not linguis-tically isolated
	44	45	46	47	48	49	50	51	52	53	54	55	56	57	58	59
OREGON—Cont'd																
Morrow County	3 069	74.2	6	100.0	48	79.2	6	33.3	597	93.3	14.5	0.3	0.5	13.5	9.3	19.5
Multnomah County	224 803	54.5	13 256	63.2	2 463	56.6	12 287	70.4	12 773	69.4	12.7	3.1	4.4	3.9	5.9	15.9
Polk County	20 824	69.2	52	84.6	367	79.3	283	55.8	1 219	85.5	6.5	1.1	0.9	3.9	3.6	11.4
Sherman County	770	68.8	0	X	11	45.5	3	100.0	15	73.3	2.5	0.3	0.3	1.9	1.1	13.2
Tillamook County	9 596	66.2	12	100.0	53	86.8	41	58.5	320	73.1	4.2	0.7	0.5	2.3	1.9	8.0
Umatilla County	21 311	69.3	116	53.4	772	74.1	129	69.0	2 691	87.3	8.4	0.4	0.6	7.1	5.3	15.5
Union County	9 269	67.8	18	50.0	82	53.7	97	45.4	147	80.3	2.7	0.4	0.7	0.8	0.6	7.4
Wallowa County	2 999	69.5	0	X	7	0.0	0	X	9	100.0	0.8	0.3	0.1	0.2	0.1	5.1
Wasco County	8 366	68.7	33	69.7	233	78.5	61	75.4	540	83.1	6.2	0.6	0.6	4.4	3.3	11.1
Washington County	141 996	66.4	1 790	64.7	1 046	66.7	10 217	76.3	11 447	81.5	14.2	1.8	5.4	6.1	6.2	17.7
Wheeler County	617	67.9	2	100.0	3	100.0	0	X	14	64.3	2.1	1.0	0.0	1.0	1.0	5.6
Yamhill County	25 768	73.9	75	57.3	294	76.9	199	75.4	1 914	86.3	7.6	0.7	0.6	5.8	3.4	13.1
PENNSYLVANIA	4 129 114	67.5	434 217	64.9	7 184	66.7	68 958	72.0	109 484	75.1	4.1	1.5	1.5	0.8	1.7	11.0
Adams County	32 229	73.8	404	68.6	47	66.0	196	67.3	611	88.2	3.4	0.7	0.6	2.0	1.5	7.4
Allegheny County	458 900	62.2	61 689	62.4	599	67.9	8 219	58.4	3 868	58.3	3.8	1.7	1.4	0.3	1.0	9.8
Armstrong County	28 505	71.0	210	51.9	21	52.4	64	82.8	74	50.0	0.7	0.4	0.2	0.0	0.2	5.4
Beaver County	67 518	69.9	4 142	68.1	65	76.9	171	73.1	393	87.5	1.7	1.1	0.2	0.2	0.4	7.7
Bedford County	19 549	73.4	35	88.6	12	83.3	24	83.3	77	68.8	0.6	0.3	0.2	0.1	0.4	4.9
Berks County	125 465	69.3	4 467	67.3	327	69.7	1 092	79.1	9 624	77.6	4.3	1.2	0.8	2.0	2.9	15.3
Blair County	50 557	68.4	464	52.6	100	89.0	161	87.6	157	71.3	1.0	0.4	0.3	0.1	0.3	5.5
Bradford County	24 067	70.9	39	82.1	50	82.0	67	58.2	55	78.2	1.0	0.5	0.3	0.1	0.3	6.1
Bucks County	202 004	74.0	6 674	67.8	358	61.7	4 398	83.9	3 927	76.3	5.9	2.8	2.0	0.7	1.5	12.5
Butler County	64 624	71.4	369	57.5	79	69.6	323	79.6	272	72.4	1.4	0.6	0.5	0.2	0.2	6.0
Cambria County	58 760	67.7	1 180	62.7	42	47.6	191	77.0	251	51.8	1.3	0.5	0.4	0.3	0.4	6.4
Cameron County	2 450	65.0	5	100.0	0	X	3	100.0	8	100.0	0.6	0.5	0.1	0.0	0.0	5.3
Carbon County	23 223	69.1	117	69.2	33	63.6	24	75.0	230	80.0	1.8	1.2	0.3	0.3	0.7	9.3
Centre County	45 731	59.2	697	30.7	77	87.0	1 958	45.1	547	43.5	5.8	1.4	3.4	0.4	1.9	11.1
Chester County	141 711	72.3	8 973	67.6	181	56.4	2 658	79.7	3 665	78.0	5.5	1.8	1.6	1.6	1.8	11.6
Clarion County	15 785	67.6	72	45.8	18	88.9	54	33.3	23	87.0	1.0	0.4	0.5	0.0	0.1	4.5
Clearfield County	32 426	69.8	57	45.6	43	60.5	127	98.4	32	100.0	0.7	0.3	0.3	0.1	0.3	4.8
Clinton County	14 629	67.6	40	90.0	14	35.7	24	87.5	41	68.3	0.9	0.5	0.3	0.1	0.7	7.6
Columbia County	24 422	67.2	181	40.3	28	60.7	102	43.1	164	53.7	1.4	0.5	0.4	0.2	0.3	5.6
Crawford County	33 835	69.2	393	64.9	34	79.4	78	67.9	105	70.5	1.1	0.6	0.3	0.1	1.2	7.6
Cumberland County	79 439	67.8	1 248	62.3	117	46.2	1 004	77.9	774	60.3	3.2	1.2	1.5	0.3	1.2	7.7
Dauphin County	81 283	64.3	15 759	64.4	186	68.3	1 584	72.0	3 112	74.1	4.1	1.0	1.7	0.9	1.8	10.6
Delaware County	168 880	67.6	27 777	67.7	245	66.9	5 633	81.1	2 313	70.3	6.7	2.2	2.8	0.8	1.8	12.3
Elk County	13 951	68.8	0	X	21	61.9	44	96.4	44	72.7	1.1	0.4	0.5	0.1	0.3	7.3
Erie County	97 955	67.1	5 067	70.4	160	50.0	626	66.6	1 604	75.8	2.7	1.5	0.7	0.3	1.2	8.6
Fayette County	57 466	69.1	2 069	66.3	54	51.9	53	100.0	126	49.2	0.6	0.4	0.1	0.0	0.3	6.1
Forest County	1 961	66.1	0	X	17	82.4	2	0.0	12	58.3	0.6	0.2	0.0	0.2	0.2	6.1
Franklin County	48 335	72.5	1 169	60.5	74	62.2	229	67.7	688	72.1	2.0	0.6	0.6	0.7	1.0	6.9
Fulton County	5 570	72.3	37	75.7	12	75.0	4	75.0	11	100.0	0.7	0.4	0.1	0.1	0.2	3.9
Greene County	14 828	70.5	71	71.8	19	63.2	25	88.0	68	88.2	0.7	0.3	0.2	0.2	0.2	5.2
Huntingdon County	16 454	70.9	176	65.9	12	58.3	18	100.0	37	81.1	0.7	0.4	0.2	0.1	0.3	5.6
Indiana County	33 272	66.4	366	59.0	34	94.1	212	68.9	115	42.6	1.6	0.4	0.7	0.2	0.9	6.8
Jefferson County	18 193	70.6	15	20.0	24	54.2	41	68.3	57	49.1	0.6	0.3	0.3	0.0	0.4	5.8
Juniata County	8 438	75.5	4	50.0	5	100.0	29	86.2	94	85.1	1.0	0.3	0.3	0.4	1.1	8.7
Lackawanna County	83 936	64.9	739	63.7	84	45.2	481	79.0	671	76.8	2.3	1.0	0.7	0.3	0.8	8.8
Lancaster County	158 345	72.1	4 272	66.1	252	72.6	1 679	80.6	7 485	77.7	3.2	1.0	1.1	0.8	3.2	14.8
Lawrence County	35 591	70.0	1 097	72.5	57	100.0	102	69.6	149	75.2	1.3	0.8	0.4	0.1	0.7	8.0
Lebanon County	43 915	70.4	437	59.7	52	59.6	312	83.7	1 705	78.1	2.4	0.8	0.7	0.6	1.5	10.7
Lehigh County	106 199	66.5	3 445	70.5	245	57.1	2 256	74.6	9 004	77.7	6.2	1.6	2.4	1.8	3.2	17.4
Luzerne County	127 531	64.7	1 231	61.8	154	76.6	408	77.0	913	78.6	1.9	1.0	0.5	0.4	0.7	8.4
Lycoming County	44 964	67.8	1 367	70.2	125	68.8	152	47.4	174	64.4	1.2	0.5	0.3	0.1	0.4	6.0
McKean County	17 753	67.3	28	78.6	18	100.0	54	70.4	72	72.2	1.4	0.4	0.4	0.1	0.3	5.0
Mercer County	44 057	69.4	2 042	69.8	43	65.1	168	81.5	202	81.2	1.6	0.8	0.5	0.2	0.3	5.0
Mifflin County	18 277	70.6	55	70.9	8	12.5	18	38.9	60	86.7	0.8	0.5	0.1	0.1	1.9	9.4
Monroe County	43 605	72.8	2 530	82.0	126	71.4	346	87.6	2 402	85.3	5.8	2.8	0.7	1.8	1.1	14.9
Montgomery County	251 108	69.1	19 184	68.3	437	61.6	9 324	80.7	4 155	73.7	7.0	2.3	3.2	0.9	1.9	12.8
Montour County	6 942	68.0	24	0.0	17	88.2	90	61.1	54	70.4	2.2	0.6	1.1	0.3	1.3	6.9
Northampton County	92 394	69.8	2 373	70.7	112	77.7	964	83.3	5 126	79.3	4.6	1.7	1.4	1.2	2.0	13.9
Northumberland County	38 317	66.1	176	59.1	24	29.2	134	84.3	175	73.7	1.1	0.6	0.3	0.2	0.5	7.0
Perry County	16 565	74.3	17	88.2	6	66.7	21	81.0	54	79.6	0.9	0.3	0.3	0.2	0.3	6.8
Philadelphia County	282 063	54.5	240 006	64.3	1 630	62.5	20 886	66.2	38 509	74.6	9.0	2.7	3.5	2.1	4.8	18.7
Pike County	16 049	74.9	487	74.1	9	100.0	114	79.8	606	75.7	5.0	2.8	0.6	1.3	0.8	13.7

[1] Hispanic or Latino persons may be of any race.

STATE/ County code	MSA/PMSA/ NECMA code¹	STATE County	Total population	Under 5 years	5 to 17 years	18 to 24 years	25 to 44 years	45 to 64 years	65 years and over	Median age	+/− U.S. percent under 18 years	+/− U.S. percent 65 years and over	Non-Hispanic White Total population	Under 18 years	65 years and over
			1	2	3	4	5	6	7	8	9	10	11	12	13
		PENNSYLVANIA— Cont'd													
42 105	...	Potter County	18 080	6.1	19.8	6.9	26.2	24.4	16.6	39.1	0.2	4.2	17 628	25.4	16.7
42 107	...	Schuylkill County	150 336	4.9	16.0	7.3	28.3	23.7	19.9	40.9	−4.8	7.5	144 483	21.0	20.5
42 109	...	Snyder County	37 546	5.7	18.3	11.5	27.0	23.5	14.0	36.7	−1.7	1.6	36 647	23.8	14.2
42 111	3680	Somerset County	80 023	5.4	17.0	7.7	27.7	24.1	18.1	40.2	−3.3	5.7	77 575	22.5	18.5
42 113	...	Sullivan County	6 556	4.1	16.7	8.1	23.9	25.4	21.8	43.0	−4.9	9.4	6 232	19.5	22.7
42 115	...	Susquehanna County	42 238	5.7	19.8	6.8	27.0	25.1	15.6	39.5	−0.2	3.2	41 423	25.3	15.7
42 117	...	Tioga County	41 373	5.4	18.3	10.6	25.5	24.2	16.0	38.5	−2.0	3.6	40 439	23.4	16.3
42 119	...	Union County	41 624	4.8	15.3	13.8	31.1	21.6	13.4	35.8	−5.6	1.0	36 459	21.7	15.1
42 121	...	Venango County	57 565	5.7	18.6	7.4	26.5	25.1	16.8	40.2	−1.4	4.4	56 125	23.6	17.1
42 123	...	Warren County	43 863	5.6	18.6	6.3	27.1	25.9	16.6	40.5	−1.5	4.2	43 274	24.0	16.7
42 125	6280	Washington County	202 897	5.5	16.7	7.7	27.1	25.0	17.9	40.8	−3.5	5.5	192 657	21.7	18.2
42 127	...	Wayne County	47 722	5.6	18.4	6.1	26.8	25.5	17.5	40.8	−1.7	5.1	45 764	23.9	18.0
42 129	6280	Westmoreland County	369 993	5.2	16.8	6.8	27.5	25.4	18.3	41.3	−3.7	5.9	356 293	21.5	18.7
42 131	7560	Wyoming County	28 080	5.7	19.6	7.9	28.2	25.2	13.3	37.8	−0.4	0.9	27 531	25.1	13.5
42 133	9280	York County	381 751	6.1	18.6	7.5	30.4	24.0	13.5	37.8	−1.0	1.1	349 781	23.3	14.3
44 000	...	**RHODE ISLAND**	1 048 319	6.0	17.6	10.1	29.7	22.0	14.6	36.7	−2.1	2.2	858 665	21.0	16.7
44 001	6483	Bristol County	50 648	5.3	17.6	9.6	27.4	23.3	16.8	39.3	−2.8	4.4	48 668	22.5	17.2
44 003	6483	Kent County	167 090	5.9	17.2	7.1	30.5	24.1	15.2	38.9	−2.6	2.8	158 180	22.5	15.7
44 005	...	Newport County	85 433	5.9	16.6	8.3	30.0	24.8	14.4	38.6	−3.2	2.0	77 033	21.3	15.2
44 007	6483	Providence County	621 602	6.2	17.9	11.0	29.8	20.5	14.6	35.4	−1.6	2.2	458 796	19.8	18.1
44 009	6483	Washington County	123 546	5.8	17.4	11.3	28.3	24.5	12.7	37.4	−2.5	0.3	115 988	22.7	13.1
45 000	...	**SOUTH CAROLINA**	4 012 012	6.6	18.6	10.1	29.7	22.9	12.1	35.4	−0.5	−0.3	2 654 401	22.1	14.1
45 001	...	Abbeville County	26 167	6.7	18.5	9.5	26.7	23.6	14.9	36.9	−0.5	2.5	17 849	22.8	16.6
45 003	0600	Aiken County	142 552	6.6	19.5	8.7	29.2	23.1	12.9	36.4	0.4	0.5	100 438	23.6	14.8
45 005	...	Allendale County	11 211	6.6	19.7	10.3	28.1	22.3	12.8	35.1	0.8	0.4	3 011	15.6	20.6
45 007	3160	Anderson County	165 740	6.7	18.0	8.4	29.0	24.3	13.7	37.3	−1.0	1.3	134 107	23.0	14.8
45 009	...	Bamberg County	16 658	6.3	19.1	13.2	24.8	22.3	14.2	35.2	−0.3	1.8	6 083	21.1	19.7
45 011	...	Barnwell County	23 478	6.9	21.3	8.9	27.8	22.6	12.6	35.5	2.5	0.2	12 888	24.7	15.3
45 013	...	Beaufort County	120 937	6.7	16.4	11.9	27.4	21.8	15.6	35.8	−2.6	3.2	81 776	19.2	19.7
45 015	1440	Berkeley County	142 651	7.0	20.9	11.8	31.3	21.1	7.9	32.0	2.2	−4.5	95 324	25.5	8.4
45 017	...	Calhoun County	15 185	6.3	18.7	7.4	27.2	26.6	13.8	38.9	−0.7	1.4	7 505	19.4	16.6
45 019	1440	Charleston County	309 969	6.5	17.3	12.0	30.6	21.9	11.8	34.5	−1.9	−0.6	189 148	18.8	13.7
45 021	3160	Cherokee County	52 537	7.3	18.6	8.9	29.5	23.3	12.4	35.3	0.2	0.0	40 050	23.6	14.0
45 023	...	Chester County	34 068	6.6	20.2	8.4	28.5	23.5	12.7	36.0	1.1	0.3	20 298	22.3	15.7
45 025	...	Chesterfield County	42 768	6.8	19.9	8.4	29.2	23.5	12.2	35.7	1.0	−0.2	27 211	23.4	13.7
45 027	...	Clarendon County	32 502	6.1	19.8	10.5	25.2	24.3	14.2	37.0	0.2	1.8	14 443	20.3	17.6
45 029	...	Colleton County	38 264	6.9	20.5	8.1	27.1	24.5	13.0	36.5	1.7	0.6	20 993	22.9	14.7
45 031	...	Darlington County	67 394	6.6	19.4	9.2	28.1	24.3	12.1	36.0	0.5	−0.3	38 119	21.7	14.4
45 033	...	Dillon County	30 722	7.2	21.8	9.5	27.9	21.8	11.7	34.2	3.3	−0.7	15 311	22.7	15.0
45 035	1440	Dorchester County	96 413	6.7	22.1	7.6	31.6	22.9	9.1	34.7	3.1	−3.3	67 658	27.0	9.7
45 037	0600	Edgefield County	24 595	5.8	18.2	10.0	31.6	23.5	10.8	35.6	−1.7	−1.6	13 674	23.3	13.3
45 039	...	Fairfield County	23 454	6.6	19.6	8.8	27.6	24.2	13.2	36.9	0.5	0.8	9 177	19.0	18.2
45 041	2655	Florence County	125 761	6.5	19.5	9.8	29.0	23.5	11.8	35.5	0.3	−0.6	73 198	22.1	14.0
45 043	...	Georgetown County	55 797	6.2	19.0	7.9	26.2	25.5	15.2	39.1	−0.5	2.8	32 964	19.2	18.8
45 045	3160	Greenville County	379 616	6.7	17.9	9.5	31.4	22.7	11.8	35.5	−1.1	−0.6	287 093	22.6	13.4
45 047	...	Greenwood County	66 271	7.0	18.5	10.6	28.4	21.7	13.8	35.2	−0.2	1.4	42 506	22.0	16.9
45 049	...	Hampton County	21 386	6.7	21.0	8.4	29.8	22.1	12.0	34.8	2.0	−0.4	8 803	22.6	16.6
45 051	5330	Horry County	196 629	5.6	15.7	9.2	29.5	25.0	15.0	38.3	−4.4	2.6	157 151	18.8	17.1
45 053	...	Jasper County	20 678	7.3	19.5	9.8	31.5	21.0	10.9	33.8	1.1	−1.5	8 477	23.3	12.5
45 055	...	Kershaw County	52 647	6.4	19.7	7.7	28.9	24.5	12.8	37.4	0.4	0.4	37 253	24.2	13.7
45 057	...	Lancaster County	61 351	6.4	19.0	8.6	30.7	23.1	12.3	35.9	−0.3	−0.1	43 327	23.1	14.2
45 059	...	Laurens County	69 567	6.6	18.8	9.3	28.9	23.5	13.0	36.2	−0.3	0.6	49 404	23.0	14.7
45 061	...	Lee County	20 119	6.4	19.3	10.1	29.0	22.8	12.4	35.7	0.0	0.0	6 947	18.3	18.1
45 063	1760	Lexington County	216 014	6.8	19.3	8.2	31.7	23.8	10.2	35.7	0.4	−2.2	179 424	24.6	11.2
45 065	...	McCormick County	9 958	4.1	15.4	8.3	27.8	28.1	16.3	41.1	−6.2	3.9	4 448	12.2	24.8
45 067	...	Marion County	35 466	6.9	20.8	9.7	27.1	23.2	12.4	35.1	2.0	0.0	14 596	20.8	16.3
45 069	...	Marlboro County	28 818	6.8	19.4	9.6	29.2	22.6	12.3	35.4	0.5	−0.1	12 785	21.7	15.3
45 071	...	Newberry County	36 108	6.2	17.9	9.8	28.0	23.3	14.9	37.1	−1.6	2.5	22 327	19.7	18.8
45 073	...	Oconee County	66 215	6.1	16.7	7.8	27.6	26.2	15.5	39.5	−2.9	3.1	58 312	21.7	16.6
45 075	...	Orangeburg County	91 582	6.5	19.4	11.8	26.3	22.7	13.2	35.3	0.2	0.8	33 754	20.6	19.2
45 077	3160	Pickens County	110 757	6.1	16.1	17.4	27.7	21.3	11.3	32.7	−3.5	−1.1	99 059	22.0	11.9
45 079	1760	Richland County	320 677	6.3	18.0	13.8	31.6	20.7	9.7	32.6	−1.4	−2.7	157 862	18.9	13.4
45 081	...	Saluda County	19 181	6.5	18.5	9.1	27.8	23.5	14.6	37.0	−0.7	2.2	11 963	21.4	18.4
45 083	3160	Spartanburg County	253 791	6.7	18.1	9.1	30.2	23.4	12.5	36.1	−0.9	0.1	187 832	22.6	14.4

¹MSA = Metropolitan Statistical Area. PMSA = Primary MSA. NECMA = New England County Metropolitan Area. See the Appendix A for explanation of these concepts. See Appendix B for list of metropolitan areas identified by type, with component counties.

Table A-3. States and Counties — **Age, Ethnicity, and Household Structure**

STATE County	Black or African American Total population	Age (percent) Under 18 years	Age (percent) 65 years and over	American Indian and Alaska Native Total population	Age (percent) Under 18 years	Age (percent) 65 years and over	Asian, Hawaiian, and Pacific Islander Total population	Age (percent) Under 18 years	Age (percent) 65 years and over	Hispanic or Latino[1] Total population	Age (percent) Under 18 years	Age (percent) 65 years and over	Two or more races Total population	Age (percent) Under 18 years	Age (percent) 65 years and over
	14	15	16	17	18	19	20	21	22	23	24	25	26	27	28
PENNSYLVANIA— Cont'd															
Potter County	64	56.3	0.0	32	25.0	6.3	124	38.7	9.7	96	57.3	8.3	142	40.8	16.9
Schuylkill County	3 227	10.6	1.6	188	17.6	9.0	572	20.1	12.8	1 545	23.0	3.9	461	34.7	6.1
Snyder County	288	14.6	3.1	33	33.3	0.0	82	28.0	2.4	394	37.8	2.0	144	45.8	9.0
Somerset County	1 382	8.8	3.3	79	25.3	0.0	168	42.9	4.2	580	25.3	4.5	348	32.5	6.9
Sullivan County	137	58.4	3.6	46	45.7	0.0	4	50.0	0.0	56	33.9	1.8	94	41.5	10.6
Susquehanna County	125	35.2	10.4	41	26.8	0.0	114	31.6	3.5	260	36.5	8.1	301	36.2	8.6
Tioga County	253	31.6	0.0	75	24.0	9.3	109	26.6	8.3	204	48.0	5.4	318	43.4	2.5
Union County	2 826	4.1	0.1	87	6.9	0.0	414	12.3	4.1	1 721	11.8	1.5	578	15.1	4.8
Venango County	623	50.4	2.7	97	51.5	0.0	66	30.3	0.0	306	52.0	2.9	358	44.1	8.7
Warren County	51	39.2	0.0	58	3.4	8.6	114	31.6	0.0	147	17.0	18.4	232	38.4	10.8
Washington County	6 522	25.8	15.7	223	23.8	4.0	699	37.9	3.9	922	30.7	15.1	1 770	49.4	8.0
Wayne County	740	14.9	6.4	45	24.4	0.0	184	26.1	2.7	720	38.1	7.6	318	40.6	9.7
Westmoreland County	7 169	29.3	11.1	472	23.1	5.1	1 754	32.1	3.2	1 884	33.5	7.9	2 493	46.1	6.8
Wyoming County	138	55.1	0.0	35	17.1	5.7	88	39.8	0.0	178	38.8	5.1	140	33.6	1.4
York County	13 515	34.9	5.9	529	26.5	1.5	3 245	29.0	5.2	11 311	41.1	2.1	4 381	55.8	2.4
RHODE ISLAND	45 236	32.8	6.6	5 124	38.2	7.3	24 266	27.9	4.3	90 452	38.6	3.2	29 588	39.3	6.3
Bristol County	344	27.0	15.4	59	27.1	0.0	420	27.9	2.6	661	29.8	9.1	580	42.8	6.9
Kent County	1 406	23.5	3.4	343	36.4	3.2	2 203	26.4	6.1	2 746	34.0	3.5	2 405	42.8	8.2
Newport County	3 424	31.6	10.2	399	39.6	11.5	1 010	18.8	7.0	2 250	44.4	3.8	1 762	41.7	4.3
Providence County	38 908	33.6	6.4	3 245	41.4	6.3	18 694	28.9	3.7	83 004	38.8	3.2	23 113	38.0	6.4
Washington County	1 154	20.8	6.1	1 078	29.3	10.6	1 939	24.2	7.1	1 791	35.0	3.1	1 728	47.8	4.6
SOUTH CAROLINA	1 182 727	31.1	8.8	14 688	25.8	5.4	37 889	23.8	4.8	92 828	29.7	2.7	42 068	42.0	4.8
Abbeville County	7 925	30.2	11.1	24	0.0	0.0	50	0.0	20.0	215	47.0	0.0	136	39.7	22.1
Aiken County	36 158	31.8	8.7	465	28.0	9.5	953	24.1	11.0	3 087	34.0	3.1	1 829	46.3	4.6
Allendale County	7 920	30.2	10.2	9	0.0	0.0	22	45.5	0.0	204	35.3	5.4	53	45.3	3.8
Anderson County	27 792	31.1	9.5	277	23.5	9.7	868	34.9	4.0	1 599	30.1	6.0	1 253	41.8	5.1
Bamberg County	10 384	28.1	11.1	25	32.0	0.0	18	0.0	0.0	137	5.1	12.4	60	40.0	0.0
Barnwell County	10 148	32.3	9.5	119	16.8	8.4	86	46.5	0.0	142	44.4	4.9	97	24.7	0.0
Beaufort County	28 703	33.1	8.9	279	17.9	3.9	1 070	21.1	3.9	8 140	25.5	1.5	1 945	36.5	1.9
Berkeley County	37 403	33.3	7.6	1 031	25.5	4.4	3 054	18.0	7.6	3 834	33.5	2.1	2 758	50.8	2.5
Calhoun County	7 339	30.1	11.4	52	26.9	0.0	37	5.4	8.1	196	44.4	1.5	121	45.5	9.9
Charleston County	105 870	32.1	9.6	756	19.2	5.2	3 594	19.0	5.8	7 795	28.1	2.3	4 063	32.0	5.8
Cherokee County	11 054	31.3	7.7	138	34.1	0.0	59	28.8	16.9	790	44.4	1.8	508	51.4	10.4
Chester County	13 137	33.2	8.5	111	37.8	7.2	111	23.4	0.0	244	34.4	7.0	182	56.0	5.5
Chesterfield County	14 260	32.0	10.3	116	25.9	6.9	140	27.9	0.7	779	28.0	4.4	372	56.2	0.5
Clarendon County	17 318	30.1	11.6	125	34.4	8.8	130	25.2	6.5	475	41.5	0.1	157	54.1	8.3
Colleton County	16 301	33.4	10.9	222	11.3	15.3	83	10.8	0.0	451	17.7	12.2	270	34.8	24.1
Darlington County	27 902	31.8	9.4	186	39.8	5.9	299	39.5	3.3	672	36.3	3.0	382	53.1	10.2
Dillon County	13 911	35.0	8.9	706	36.3	3.8	77	39.0	0.0	505	35.8	1.2	249	41.4	8.0
Dorchester County	24 016	32.2	8.2	578	14.9	9.2	1 254	25.4	6.2	1 704	40.0	2.8	1 277	55.5	1.9
Edgefield County	10 189	25.2	8.0	120	3.3	2.5	131	28.2	6.1	407	21.9	2.9	165	26.7	3.0
Fairfield County	14 007	31.0	10.0	54	13.0	0.0	9	0.0	0.0	157	18.5	12.1	108	26.9	9.3
Florence County	49 405	30.9	9.0	248	22.2	16.5	1 026	26.0	5.6	1 157	38.5	4.9	1 045	48.0	4.7
Georgetown County	21 576	33.9	10.5	80	47.5	2.5	181	29.8	6.1	855	26.7	0.7	316	46.8	2.5
Greenville County	69 448	31.1	7.9	773	16.8	2.8	5 001	23.8	2.5	14 015	27.7	2.5	4 526	41.9	5.4
Greenwood County	20 933	31.4	9.1	173	35.8	0.0	525	32.0	1.1	1 859	31.7	3.4	666	36.9	7.1
Hampton County	12 013	31.7	9.1	38	0.0	0.0	43	7.0	0.0	468	15.0	0.4	108	45.4	7.4
Horry County	30 496	32.4	7.5	814	23.3	3.7	1 651	23.1	8.9	4 959	27.8	2.6	2 295	34.1	3.1
Jasper County	10 638	29.4	10.9	148	34.5	0.0	140	20.0	0.0	1 150	27.2	0.3	179	41.9	14.5
Kershaw County	13 859	29.9	11.4	183	25.1	0.0	219	24.7	2.3	852	43.3	2.1	328	31.4	10.1
Lancaster County	16 535	30.6	8.0	119	21.0	0.0	214	23.4	2.3	901	26.1	2.1	440	43.0	9.1
Laurens County	18 141	30.2	9.7	231	16.9	2.6	104	32.7	3.8	1 189	37.3	0.8	623	44.6	2.7
Lee County	12 586	29.6	9.6	11	45.5	0.0	15	0.0	100.0	607	27.0	2.5	92	37.0	15.2
Lexington County	27 145	33.9	6.0	861	27.6	2.0	2 117	27.3	6.1	4 848	32.3	3.1	1 972	39.4	2.7
McCormick County	5 394	25.0	9.6	8	100.0	0.0	5	0.0	0.0	93	37.6	0.0	50	44.0	4.0
Marion County	20 023	32.5	9.9	78	51.3	0.0	39	2.6	0.0	642	27.7	2.0	194	45.9	5.2
Marlboro County	14 643	29.9	10.3	957	28.9	7.4	151	17.9	0.0	152	25.7	9.9	197	43.1	8.6
Newberry County	11 930	31.3	9.5	129	29.5	0.0	45	15.6	0.0	1 613	30.3	2.4	377	41.1	0.5
Oconee County	5 432	30.9	9.7	162	17.9	8.0	272	17.3	9.2	1 478	33.6	1.9	827	44.4	5.3
Orangeburg County	55 950	28.8	9.8	409	28.9	12.5	265	25.7	1.5	661	40.1	8.9	783	41.8	10.7
Pickens County	7 503	25.5	9.0	165	15.2	3.6	1 332	13.3	0.8	1 914	26.0	1.1	977	36.0	4.3
Richland County	144 547	29.8	6.3	1 075	15.5	7.8	5 781	19.5	4.5	8 521	25.4	4.1	4 350	39.8	4.3
Saluda County	5 678	31.4	10.5	48	12.5	0.0	39	10.3	10.3	1 399	27.2	0.4	130	56.9	0.8
Spartanburg County	52 440	30.3	8.3	670	24.8	5.1	4 229	35.4	4.9	6 972	31.6	2.5	2 632	41.8	5.3

[1] Hispanic or Latino persons may be of any race.

STATE County	Total households	Married-couple family households			Other family households			Two or more unrelated persons		Male living alone		Female living alone		Percent of householders 65 years and over who live alone	Grandparents who are responsible for the care of their grandchildren
		Total	With children	Householder 65 years or over	Total	With children	Householder 65 years or over	Total	Householder 65 years or over	Total	Householder 65 years or over	Total	Householder 65 years or over		
	29	30	31	32	33	34	35	36	37	38	39	40	41	42	43
PENNSYLVANIA— Cont'd															
Potter County	6 988	59.8	24.7	12.8	12.0	7.1	2.1	3.6	0.5	10.6	2.9	14.0	8.9	43.4	118
Schuylkill County	60 500	52.4	20.4	12.3	14.1	6.7	3.3	3.6	0.4	11.6	3.9	18.3	12.5	50.6	856
Snyder County	13 643	62.6	26.4	12.3	10.6	5.9	1.5	4.5	0.3	8.2	2.1	14.1	8.3	42.4	159
Somerset County	31 193	59.3	23.9	12.8	11.7	5.8	2.8	2.9	0.3	10.1	3.3	16.1	10.6	46.5	408
Sullivan County	2 667	55.5	18.2	15.0	10.2	5.6	2.7	4.8	1.2	15.3	5.8	14.2	8.8	43.7	58
Susquehanna County	16 543	58.3	24.3	11.7	13.1	8.0	2.1	4.3	0.3	11.1	3.5	13.2	8.1	45.3	199
Tioga County	15 942	58.6	23.2	12.9	12.2	7.5	1.7	5.0	0.4	10.4	3.1	13.9	8.1	42.8	290
Union County	13 191	61.4	25.4	12.3	8.8	5.3	1.5	4.5	0.7	9.8	2.6	15.5	9.0	44.4	116
Venango County	22 788	55.7	22.0	11.5	14.5	8.9	2.5	3.6	0.4	10.2	3.2	16.0	9.8	47.5	263
Warren County	17 700	56.6	22.9	11.5	12.0	7.0	1.8	4.3	0.4	11.9	3.2	15.3	8.9	47.0	278
Washington County	81 129	56.4	22.5	12.1	13.0	6.0	3.2	3.6	0.4	10.0	3.0	17.0	10.4	45.9	1 110
Wayne County	18 300	57.6	23.2	13.4	13.2	7.0	2.4	4.0	0.5	10.6	3.3	14.6	8.9	42.9	255
Westmoreland County	149 870	57.8	22.9	13.0	12.3	5.9	2.9	3.1	0.3	10.2	3.1	16.7	10.2	45.1	1 994
Wyoming County	10 822	59.1	26.4	9.8	12.8	7.4	2.0	4.1	0.2	10.9	2.4	13.0	7.8	45.9	137
York County	148 288	58.7	25.1	10.2	12.7	7.6	1.8	5.3	0.4	10.3	2.1	13.0	7.1	42.7	2 397
RHODE ISLAND	408 412	49.1	21.8	9.4	16.1	9.3	2.4	6.2	0.4	11.5	2.8	17.0	8.9	49.1	5 060
Bristol County	19 051	58.6	26.1	12.3	12.0	6.0	2.4	4.4	0.6	8.3	2.3	16.7	9.1	42.7	222
Kent County	67 341	54.0	23.3	9.7	13.0	6.8	2.1	5.5	0.5	11.1	2.9	16.4	9.2	49.5	563
Newport County	35 212	50.6	21.7	9.2	13.0	7.3	2.6	6.6	0.4	12.5	2.7	17.4	8.6	48.2	370
Providence County	239 926	45.5	20.2	9.0	18.5	11.0	2.6	6.2	0.4	12.0	2.9	17.8	9.2	50.3	3 326
Washington County	46 882	55.9	25.6	9.6	12.5	7.1	1.4	7.5	0.4	10.3	2.3	13.7	7.0	44.9	579
SOUTH CAROLINA	1 534 334	52.0	22.6	8.8	18.3	10.3	2.7	4.7	0.3	10.6	2.1	14.4	6.7	42.9	51 755
Abbeville County	10 133	54.5	22.1	10.8	17.8	9.7	2.7	2.5	0.1	10.4	3.4	14.9	9.0	47.7	385
Aiken County	55 590	53.5	23.5	9.5	17.7	10.4	2.3	3.7	0.3	11.3	2.5	13.8	6.7	43.3	1 729
Allendale County	3 930	37.4	13.9	6.5	29.6	15.5	5.0	2.8	0.2	11.1	4.1	19.1	10.0	54.7	306
Anderson County	65 690	55.9	23.3	9.6	16.4	9.0	2.4	3.4	0.3	9.9	2.1	14.5	7.8	44.5	2 276
Bamberg County	6 104	43.2	17.6	8.8	26.8	13.5	5.5	2.3	0.4	12.8	3.3	15.0	9.1	45.8	331
Barnwell County	9 074	48.2	21.8	7.8	23.8	14.5	2.7	2.5	0.5	10.9	3.0	14.6	8.1	50.0	344
Beaufort County	45 518	59.5	22.7	15.2	13.9	8.6	1.6	5.1	0.4	8.7	2.3	12.8	6.4	33.5	1 160
Berkeley County	49 868	58.4	28.4	6.9	17.6	11.5	2.0	4.5	0.2	9.4	1.6	10.1	4.2	38.8	1 914
Calhoun County	5 946	52.4	21.6	8.9	20.0	9.5	4.0	3.1	0.6	11.4	2.8	13.0	7.0	42.0	300
Charleston County	123 260	44.2	18.8	7.9	18.9	10.3	2.8	8.6	0.3	11.9	2.1	16.4	6.2	43.0	3 544
Cherokee County	20 503	52.3	21.8	8.1	19.6	11.2	2.9	3.1	0.2	11.1	2.1	13.8	7.7	46.8	831
Chester County	12 878	49.5	20.7	8.4	23.4	13.2	3.4	2.9	0.4	10.7	2.3	13.4	7.2	43.9	553
Chesterfield County	16 598	50.3	23.6	7.7	20.9	11.2	3.4	2.9	0.2	12.0	2.7	13.8	7.3	46.8	564
Clarendon County	11 800	49.2	19.7	10.8	23.6	12.6	4.5	2.7	0.4	10.5	2.7	14.1	7.7	39.9	783
Colleton County	14 514	50.7	22.2	8.0	22.3	11.8	4.5	3.1	0.5	11.6	3.6	12.3	6.5	43.8	811
Darlington County	25 852	48.4	20.9	7.2	23.2	12.3	3.3	3.3	0.3	10.7	2.7	14.4	7.1	47.5	1 294
Dillon County	11 210	45.0	20.9	5.9	27.1	13.6	4.9	2.8	0.4	10.6	2.5	14.4	8.0	48.3	686
Dorchester County	34 688	58.8	29.8	7.0	17.6	10.8	2.0	3.5	0.2	8.9	1.4	11.3	5.3	42.3	1 145
Edgefield County	8 251	56.0	24.5	9.4	19.4	10.7	2.6	2.0	0.2	9.6	2.5	12.9	7.5	44.8	340
Fairfield County	8 757	48.8	19.3	9.6	24.0	13.3	4.3	2.8	0.1	11.8	2.5	12.7	7.0	40.3	408
Florence County	47 107	50.9	23.2	7.8	21.5	11.4	3.2	3.1	0.2	9.9	1.6	14.6	6.6	42.3	1 641
Georgetown County	21 720	54.9	20.6	12.8	18.2	10.0	3.4	3.6	0.4	9.9	2.3	13.4	6.7	35.3	868
Greenville County	149 681	53.1	23.7	8.3	15.5	8.7	2.0	4.7	0.3	11.2	1.9	15.6	6.9	45.3	4 070
Greenwood County	25 790	49.8	21.1	9.2	19.3	11.4	2.5	4.7	0.2	10.6	2.7	16.2	9.0	49.4	868
Hampton County	7 462	49.6	22.4	9.1	22.2	12.4	3.4	2.8	0.2	10.6	2.5	14.8	8.6	46.9	465
Horry County	81 785	52.1	18.6	12.1	14.9	8.3	2.2	7.3	0.6	11.2	2.3	14.5	6.4	36.9	1 930
Jasper County	7 025	50.7	24.2	8.3	22.1	11.5	4.1	3.8	0.3	11.2	3.3	12.2	6.2	42.7	335
Kershaw County	20 206	55.8	24.7	9.4	18.7	10.2	3.1	3.0	0.1	10.1	2.3	12.5	6.7	41.8	681
Lancaster County	23 227	54.3	22.8	8.9	19.2	11.3	3.4	3.5	0.2	10.3	2.2	13.4	7.5	43.6	845
Laurens County	26 279	51.8	21.7	8.4	20.2	11.1	3.2	3.4	0.3	10.6	2.5	14.0	7.6	45.7	1 028
Lee County	6 893	44.7	19.7	8.4	27.0	12.8	4.9	2.4	0.2	12.1	3.6	13.8	8.1	46.4	563
Lexington County	83 363	57.7	27.0	7.6	14.7	9.1	1.5	5.2	0.2	9.4	1.5	13.0	5.6	43.1	1 833
McCormick County	3 543	51.3	13.7	13.4	21.9	12.0	3.9	2.1	0.3	10.4	3.1	14.2	6.5	35.5	149
Marion County	13 277	44.8	17.9	7.8	27.1	14.9	4.6	2.7	0.2	9.2	2.0	16.2	7.7	43.6	798
Marlboro County	10 458	44.4	19.2	7.9	25.9	12.8	4.1	2.8	0.1	11.0	2.6	15.9	8.5	47.9	601
Newberry County	14 041	49.9	19.7	10.3	20.5	10.6	3.8	3.1	0.3	10.5	2.4	16.0	9.6	45.3	473
Oconee County	27 318	58.7	21.3	13.1	13.3	7.7	2.2	3.2	0.2	11.1	2.2	13.6	7.0	37.1	819
Orangeburg County	34 172	45.8	19.8	8.5	24.3	12.9	4.2	3.9	0.3	10.7	2.8	15.3	8.1	45.5	1 703
Pickens County	41 360	56.0	24.4	9.4	13.1	7.2	1.9	7.6	0.1	10.3	1.8	12.9	6.3	41.5	924
Richland County	120 034	44.7	20.8	6.6	19.3	11.4	2.5	6.9	0.3	12.2	1.7	16.9	5.6	43.5	3 533
Saluda County	7 141	55.4	22.5	11.0	19.2	9.3	3.7	3.0	0.1	8.8	2.7	13.6	8.2	42.4	303
Spartanburg County	97 658	53.9	23.4	8.7	17.5	9.5	2.5	3.7	0.3	10.2	2.0	14.7	7.3	44.6	2 893

Table A-3. States and Counties — Age, Ethnicity, and Household Structure

STATE County	Households with Non-Hispanic White householder — Number of households	Percent that are family households	Households with Black or African American householder — Number of households	Percent that are family households	Households with American Indian and Alaska Native householder — Number of households	Percent that are family households	Households with Asian, Hawaiian, and Pacific Islander householder — Number of households	Percent that are family households	Households with Hispanic or Latino[1] householder — Number of households	Percent that are family households	Foreign-born population — Percent of total population that is foreign-born	Place of birth (percent) Europe	Asia	Latin America	Percent in non-English speaking households — Linguistically isolated	Not linguistically isolated
	44	45	46	47	48	49	50	51	52	53	54	55	56	57	58	59
PENNSYLVANIA—Cont'd																
Potter County	6 869	71.8	23	78.3	10	80.0	33	93.9	19	31.6	1.1	0.5	0.4	0.1	0.4	7.0
Schuylkill County	59 718	66.6	195	57.9	61	54.1	127	66.9	281	57.3	1.0	0.6	0.3	0.1	0.4	7.2
Snyder County	13 478	73.4	31	25.8	2	100.0	2	100.0	89	56.2	0.9	0.4	0.2	0.2	1.7	11.0
Somerset County	30 971	71.0	47	48.9	27	88.9	34	94.1	66	74.2	0.7	0.3	0.2	0.2	0.8	5.8
Sullivan County	2 634	65.9	0	X	2	100.0	0	X	4	100.0	0.8	0.3	0.2	0.2	0.3	4.8
Susquehanna County	16 284	71.5	47	55.3	13	61.5	32	81.3	67	62.7	1.3	0.9	0.2	0.1	0.2	6.0
Tioga County	15 747	70.8	53	39.6	23	73.9	31	71.0	26	84.6	1.1	0.5	0.3	0.1	0.3	5.4
Union County	12 832	70.6	75	52.0	23	82.6	57	70.2	150	51.3	3.7	1.1	0.8	1.5	0.9	10.7
Venango County	22 481	70.2	116	62.9	30	86.7	9	88.9	50	70.0	0.6	0.4	0.1	0.1	0.3	5.0
Warren County	17 506	68.5	13	61.5	32	93.8	29	69.0	49	65.3	0.9	0.5	0.2	0.0	0.2	6.1
Washington County	77 494	69.8	2 609	61.0	98	70.4	214	81.3	328	61.9	1.2	0.7	0.3	0.1	0.3	7.0
Wayne County	17 884	70.7	102	81.4	10	80.0	47	61.7	173	84.4	3.0	2.1	0.3	0.4	1.0	8.6
Westmoreland County	145 461	70.1	2 619	61.7	170	81.8	491	91.0	485	74.0	1.4	0.8	0.4	0.1	0.4	6.9
Wyoming County	10 700	71.9	16	93.8	13	53.8	21	81.0	37	59.5	1.2	0.6	0.3	0.2	0.3	6.4
York County	139 029	71.1	4 495	70.3	160	80.0	873	80.8	2 965	82.0	2.2	0.7	0.6	0.6	1.0	7.7
RHODE ISLAND	351 002	64.0	15 828	66.2	1 607	64.5	7 056	69.9	24 939	82.3	11.4	3.7	1.9	4.2	5.1	21.4
Bristol County	18 473	70.9	92	79.3	17	100.0	124	83.1	202	47.0	10.0	8.2	0.7	0.6	2.7	18.0
Kent County	64 770	66.6	482	63.3	108	88.0	652	81.1	721	81.6	4.9	2.5	1.1	0.7	1.2	13.0
Newport County	32 486	63.3	1 317	62.8	104	60.6	286	65.4	581	83.6	4.9	2.6	0.9	0.7	1.2	13.4
Providence County	190 385	61.5	13 566	66.6	1 064	64.1	5 478	67.8	23 067	82.6	15.6	4.2	2.4	6.6	7.8	26.9
Washington County	44 888	68.3	371	63.3	314	57.0	516	77.3	368	84.0	4.2	1.9	1.4	0.4	0.8	12.2
SOUTH CAROLINA	1 076 317	69.7	408 372	71.7	5 374	71.5	11 850	72.1	24 259	74.3	2.9	0.7	0.7	1.2	1.2	7.9
Abbeville County	7 114	71.0	2 903	72.5	0	X	8	100.0	55	100.0	1.0	0.3	0.2	0.4	0.4	7.2
Aiken County	40 891	71.1	12 926	70.9	168	67.9	270	70.7	825	75.3	2.3	0.5	0.5	1.1	1.0	6.5
Allendale County	1 237	66.7	2 630	66.8	0	X	6	100.0	36	88.9	1.4	0.1	0.1	1.2	1.0	4.0
Anderson County	54 215	72.9	10 330	69.5	63	85.7	252	72.6	507	68.0	1.5	0.4	0.4	0.4	0.5	5.9
Bamberg County	2 591	68.4	3 425	71.1	7	100.0	5	100.0	77	66.2	0.9	0.5	0.1	0.4	0.1	5.4
Barnwell County	5 160	71.7	3 764	71.9	54	100.0	26	65.4	31	100.0	0.6	0.1	0.3	0.1	0.4	4.1
Beaufort County	33 556	72.6	9 494	73.8	67	77.6	301	78.7	1 900	85.1	6.3	1.3	0.7	3.8	3.1	11.5
Berkeley County	35 008	75.5	11 938	76.8	399	74.7	911	82.7	1 092	78.8	3.1	0.8	1.5	0.7	0.9	9.9
Calhoun County	3 288	71.1	2 582	73.7	13	100.0	12	33.3	49	89.8	1.0	0.2	0.2	0.6	0.5	4.3
Charleston County	81 094	60.0	37 373	69.9	343	44.3	1 335	58.2	2 230	67.8	3.6	1.1	0.9	1.2	1.4	9.5
Cherokee County	16 169	71.6	4 001	72.3	33	100.0	20	45.0	177	74.0	1.3	0.3	0.3	0.6	0.4	5.9
Chester County	8 263	71.3	4 431	75.8	28	46.4	55	85.5	70	88.6	0.8	0.2	0.3	0.2	0.2	5.9
Chesterfield County	11 205	70.8	5 048	72.0	43	90.7	42	76.2	195	73.8	1.6	0.2	0.3	1.1	0.8	5.7
Clarendon County	6 032	72.7	5 693	72.5	42	100.0	36	72.2	111	87.4	1.3	0.3	0.2	0.7	1.0	4.8
Colleton County	8 586	72.0	5 589	74.2	90	78.9	42	100.0	127	62.2	1.2	0.2	0.1	0.8	0.3	6.7
Darlington County	15 591	70.5	9 944	73.0	49	89.8	85	92.9	178	71.9	0.9	0.3	0.2	0.4	0.4	6.1
Dillon County	6 285	70.0	4 521	74.2	203	85.7	26	92.3	118	80.5	1.0	0.1	0.1	0.7	0.9	6.6
Dorchester County	25 380	76.3	8 021	75.9	274	70.1	361	82.5	448	81.7	2.8	1.0	0.9	0.5	0.4	10.2
Edgefield County	5 071	75.0	3 031	75.2	31	100.0	32	100.0	60	76.7	1.3	0.3	0.4	0.4	0.6	7.8
Fairfield County	3 919	71.4	4 739	74.3	12	41.7	9	0.0	41	70.0	0.5	0.1	0.0	0.3	0.4	5.6
Florence County	29 235	71.7	16 901	73.3	103	93.2	365	80.8	341	81.5	1.8	0.6	0.6	0.4	0.5	7.6
Georgetown County	14 269	72.6	7 113	74.2	29	75.9	50	64.0	194	76.3	2.2	0.6	0.2	1.0	0.6	6.0
Greenville County	116 627	68.7	26 019	67.6	417	53.5	1 610	71.9	4 101	72.9	4.9	1.0	1.1	2.4	2.1	8.6
Greenwood County	17 580	68.0	7 427	71.1	62	88.7	152	82.9	484	74.8	2.8	0.3	0.5	1.7	1.6	6.8
Hampton County	3 445	70.9	3 912	72.6	19	52.6	12	100.0	47	63.8	0.7	0.1	0.2	0.5	0.4	4.7
Horry County	68 793	66.1	10 340	73.2	374	66.6	474	77.0	1 248	66.9	4.0	1.0	0.9	1.7	1.6	8.8
Jasper County	3 182	70.8	3 513	73.6	43	100.0	31	100.0	223	78.5	5.4	0.1	0.4	4.7	3.1	9.5
Kershaw County	14 962	74.2	4 862	74.1	50	100.0	51	92.2	190	98.9	1.7	0.7	0.3	0.5	0.5	6.7
Lancaster County	17 420	73.1	5 470	71.8	27	37.0	70	60.0	180	71.7	1.3	0.2	0.2	0.9	0.5	6.5
Laurens County	19 371	71.3	6 381	73.9	68	79.4	29	100.0	242	80.6	1.6	0.3	0.2	1.1	1.2	5.6
Lee County	2 780	67.0	4 013	75.0	0	X	9	100.0	117	82.1	2.1	0.1	0.1	1.9	1.7	5.6
Lexington County	71 075	72.6	9 613	69.8	332	77.4	650	76.5	1 161	75.1	2.9	0.7	0.7	1.2	1.1	8.1
McCormick County	1 826	74.4	1 690	71.7	0	X	3	100.0	20	100.0	0.6	0.5	0.1	0.0	0.1	5.9
Marion County	6 138	71.7	6 959	72.4	4	0.0	10	100.0	129	58.1	1.4	0.1	0.2	1.2	0.9	7.1
Marlboro County	5 253	68.7	4 719	71.2	337	76.9	43	83.7	61	75.4	0.6	0.1	0.3	0.1	0.2	4.0
Newberry County	9 413	69.2	4 209	72.8	38	100.0	19	31.6	354	72.6	3.5	0.2	0.1	3.1	1.8	6.6
Oconee County	24 588	72.3	1 998	66.6	55	100.0	127	71.7	408	78.9	2.4	0.6	0.4	1.3	0.8	5.6
Orangeburg County	14 303	70.1	19 264	70.3	120	76.7	99	71.7	182	70.9	1.0	0.3	0.2	0.3	0.3	6.2
Pickens County	37 272	69.8	2 839	64.0	50	84.0	464	51.3	518	69.9	2.9	0.6	1.0	1.0	1.0	6.7
Richland County	66 149	59.5	48 485	70.0	449	69.3	1 945	60.8	2 346	69.7	3.9	1.0	1.5	1.1	1.2	10.8
Saluda County	4 853	73.9	1 937	76.1	19	52.6	24	66.7	299	76.9	5.9	0.1	0.2	5.7	4.8	5.8
Spartanburg County	75 281	71.1	18 817	71.4	237	66.2	1 074	84.5	1 811	75.9	3.7	0.8	1.1	1.6	1.7	8.3

[1] Hispanic or Latino persons may be of any race.

STATE/ County code	MSA/PMSA/ NECMA code[1]	STATE County	Total population	Under 5 years	5 to 17 years	18 to 24 years	25 to 44 years	45 to 64 years	65 years and over	Median age	+/− U.S. percent under 18 years	+/− U.S. percent 65 years and over	Total population	Under 18 years	65 years and over
			Population by age (percent)										Non-Hispanic White	Age (percent)	
			1	2	3	4	5	6	7	8	9	10	11	12	13
		SOUTH CAROLINA— Cont'd													
45 085	8140	Sumter County	104 646	7.4	20.7	10.6	29.3	20.7	11.3	33.4	2.4	-1.1	51 782	24.4	13.2
45 087	...	Union County	29 881	6.1	17.7	8.5	27.9	24.1	15.6	38.6	-1.9	3.2	20 172	21.0	18.4
45 089	...	Williamsburg County	37 217	6.8	21.9	9.0	25.7	23.4	13.1	35.5	3.0	0.7	12 110	21.1	17.2
45 091	1520	York County	164 614	6.7	19.6	9.5	31.2	22.8	10.3	34.9	0.6	-2.1	125 789	24.6	11.3
46 000	...	**SOUTH DAKOTA**	754 844	6.8	20.1	10.3	27.4	21.1	14.3	35.6	1.2	1.9	664 810	24.6	15.7
46 003	...	Aurora County	3 058	5.5	21.9	6.5	22.2	22.0	21.8	40.6	1.7	9.4	2 889	25.4	22.7
46 005	...	Beadle County	17 023	5.5	19.3	8.4	24.6	22.8	19.4	40.1	-0.9	7.0	16 435	24.3	19.9
46 007	...	Bennett County	3 574	8.8	27.5	8.6	25.7	18.6	11.0	29.2	10.6	-1.4	1 462	22.4	20.0
46 009	...	Bon Homme County	7 260	5.0	18.2	7.6	26.4	22.0	20.8	40.3	-2.5	8.4	6 895	22.4	21.8
46 011	...	Brookings County	28 220	5.7	15.0	26.7	24.0	17.5	11.0	26.6	-5.0	-1.4	27 129	20.3	11.2
46 013	...	Brown County	35 460	6.4	17.3	11.6	26.8	21.9	16.1	37.2	-2.0	3.7	33 812	22.9	16.8
46 015	...	Brule County	5 364	5.9	24.7	6.5	25.0	20.9	16.9	36.9	4.9	4.5	4 786	26.4	18.4
46 017	...	Buffalo County	2 032	10.3	31.4	11.6	25.6	14.8	6.3	23.4	16.0	-6.2	339	27.1	18.3
46 019	...	Butte County	9 094	6.1	22.1	7.3	26.2	23.2	15.0	38.0	2.5	2.6	8 570	27.3	15.7
46 021	...	Campbell County	1 782	5.3	20.9	3.6	24.7	23.5	21.9	41.9	0.5	9.5	1 766	26.1	21.8
46 023	...	Charles Mix County	9 350	8.6	23.6	7.1	23.3	20.1	17.3	35.7	6.5	4.9	6 428	25.7	23.2
46 025	...	Clark County	4 143	5.6	21.4	5.9	22.1	22.8	22.2	41.6	1.3	9.8	4 086	26.5	22.4
46 027	...	Clay County	13 537	5.4	13.5	31.4	23.4	16.1	10.2	24.9	-6.8	-2.2	12 530	17.9	10.7
46 029	...	Codington County	25 897	6.9	19.9	10.0	28.2	20.9	14.1	35.3	1.1	1.7	25 016	26.5	14.5
46 031	...	Corson County	4 181	9.2	27.5	9.8	24.2	18.7	10.7	28.3	11.0	-1.7	1 563	23.0	20.3
46 033	...	Custer County	7 275	4.7	19.3	5.9	23.0	30.8	16.4	43.2	-1.7	4.0	6 759	22.4	17.0
46 035	...	Davison County	18 741	6.5	18.9	12.1	25.7	20.6	16.3	36.0	-0.3	3.9	18 095	25.0	16.7
46 037	...	Day County	6 267	5.5	19.8	5.2	22.5	23.6	23.4	42.9	-0.4	11.0	5 665	23.2	25.5
46 039	...	Deuel County	4 498	5.8	19.7	5.8	25.6	22.6	20.6	40.8	-0.2	8.2	4 382	24.6	21.1
46 041	...	Dewey County	5 972	9.0	29.9	9.0	27.6	15.7	8.6	26.5	13.2	-3.8	1 445	23.0	18.5
46 043	...	Douglas County	3 458	5.9	21.7	4.9	22.4	22.3	22.8	41.8	1.9	10.4	3 395	27.0	23.2
46 045	...	Edmunds County	4 367	5.7	21.0	5.2	23.2	22.8	22.2	41.6	1.0	9.8	4 333	26.5	22.3
46 047	...	Fall River County	7 453	5.0	17.8	5.9	20.7	28.3	22.3	45.5	-2.9	9.4	6 649	20.8	23.6
46 049	...	Faulk County	2 640	5.2	21.4	5.2	23.5	22.0	22.8	41.5	0.9	10.4	2 604	26.3	23.0
46 051	...	Grant County	7 847	5.8	21.0	5.6	24.8	23.7	19.1	40.3	1.1	6.7	7 716	26.5	19.4
46 053	...	Gregory County	4 792	4.6	19.8	5.4	21.4	24.1	24.8	44.3	-1.3	12.4	4 436	23.3	25.7
46 055	...	Haakon County	2 196	5.5	19.8	7.5	24.6	24.8	17.9	41.3	-0.4	5.5	2 114	24.5	18.5
46 057	...	Hamlin County	5 540	6.5	23.2	7.0	23.7	20.4	19.2	38.0	4.0	6.8	5 414	29.4	19.4
46 059	...	Hand County	3 741	5.3	19.5	5.0	22.3	23.6	24.4	43.6	-0.9	12.0	3 702	24.7	24.5
46 061	...	Hanson County	3 139	7.6	22.1	7.8	25.8	21.7	15.0	36.0	4.0	2.6	3 118	29.5	15.0
46 063	...	Harding County	1 353	4.1	28.6	4.5	24.8	24.5	13.5	37.6	7.0	1.1	1 319	31.4	13.8
46 065	...	Hughes County	16 481	6.5	21.2	6.4	28.2	24.0	13.6	37.5	2.0	1.2	14 644	25.4	14.8
46 067	...	Hutchinson County	8 075	5.8	19.0	5.5	22.2	21.3	26.2	43.1	-0.9	13.8	7 950	24.2	26.7
46 069	...	Hyde County	1 671	8.5	17.3	5.6	23.4	22.9	22.3	42.2	0.1	9.9	1 567	25.0	23.2
46 071	...	Jackson County	2 930	8.8	27.4	7.1	24.4	20.3	12.0	30.6	10.5	-0.4	1 451	24.4	19.6
46 073	...	Jerauld County	2 295	3.6	17.8	6.3	20.1	26.8	25.5	46.3	-4.3	13.1	2 284	21.4	25.5
46 075	...	Jones County	1 193	4.8	21.0	6.3	26.0	24.4	17.6	41.1	0.1	5.2	1 141	25.3	18.4
46 077	...	Kingsbury County	5 815	5.3	19.4	5.8	22.7	22.0	24.3	42.7	-1.0	11.9	5 706	24.2	24.7
46 079	...	Lake County	11 276	5.4	18.3	14.9	23.7	21.3	16.3	36.5	-2.0	3.9	10 906	22.9	16.7
46 081	...	Lawrence County	21 802	4.8	18.4	13.8	25.5	23.0	14.5	37.2	-2.5	2.1	20 578	22.1	15.2
46 083	7760	Lincoln County	24 131	8.0	21.7	7.8	31.9	20.3	10.3	34.0	4.0	-2.1	23 495	29.2	10.5
46 085	...	Lyman County	3 895	8.5	23.7	7.5	25.6	21.0	13.6	34.5	6.5	1.2	2 551	24.1	18.8
46 087	...	McCook County	5 832	6.6	21.7	6.0	25.6	20.5	19.5	38.6	2.6	7.1	5 728	28.1	19.8
46 089	...	McPherson County	2 904	5.6	16.5	4.6	20.2	23.8	29.3	47.6	-3.6	16.9	2 887	21.9	29.4
46 091	...	Marshall County	4 576	5.9	21.3	4.9	23.4	23.5	21.1	41.6	1.5	8.7	4 207	25.6	22.6
46 093	...	Meade County	24 253	7.6	20.7	10.6	29.9	20.7	10.5	33.4	2.6	-1.9	22 262	27.6	11.0
46 095	...	Mellette County	2 083	9.1	26.2	7.2	23.5	21.1	12.9	32.1	9.6	0.5	929	21.9	18.9
46 097	...	Miner County	2 884	5.1	20.6	5.7	22.6	22.4	23.8	42.5	0.0	11.4	2 843	25.5	24.0
46 099	7760	Minnehaha County	148 281	7.3	18.8	10.9	32.1	19.9	11.0	33.5	0.4	-1.4	136 441	24.9	11.8
46 101	...	Moody County	6 595	6.4	22.8	7.3	26.5	21.9	15.2	37.0	3.5	2.8	5 567	26.9	16.9
46 103	6660	Pennington County	88 565	7.1	19.5	10.7	29.2	21.8	11.7	35.0	0.9	*-0.7	75 726	24.2	13.0
46 105	...	Perkins County	3 363	5.8	18.2	5.7	23.0	23.6	23.8	43.1	-1.7	11.4	3 236	23.1	24.4
46 107	...	Potter County	2 693	4.5	18.8	3.6	22.3	25.5	25.3	45.8	-2.4	12.9	2 662	23.0	25.5
46 109	...	Roberts County	10 016	6.8	23.2	7.1	24.3	21.7	16.9	37.1	4.3	4.5	6 851	23.1	22.7
46 111	...	Sanborn County	2 675	5.5	20.1	7.5	24.2	23.5	19.2	40.8	-0.1	6.8	2 584	24.5	19.4
46 113	...	Shannon County	12 466	11.1	33.9	10.7	26.0	13.6	4.7	20.6	19.3	-7.7	614	20.7	9.1
46 115	...	Spink County	7 454	6.1	19.8	6.7	26.1	22.4	19.0	39.9	0.2	6.6	7 236	25.5	19.5
46 117	...	Stanley County	2 772	5.5	21.6	7.1	28.1	26.7	11.0	37.6	1.4	-1.4	2 572	25.7	11.4
46 119	...	Sully County	1 556	5.3	19.7	6.1	26.0	24.9	17.5	40.0	-0.2	5.1	1 520	24.5	17.8
46 121	...	Todd County	9 050	12.4	31.6	10.0	25.6	14.3	6.2	21.7	18.3	-6.2	1 238	25.2	17.9

[1]MSA = Metropolitan Statistical Area. PMSA = Primary MSA. NECMA = New England County Metropolitan Area. See the Appendix A for explanation of these concepts. See Appendix B for list of metropolitan areas identified by type, with component counties.

Table A-3. States and Counties — Age, Ethnicity, and Household Structure

STATE County	Black or African American Total population	Under 18 years	65 years and over	American Indian and Alaska Native Total population	Under 18 years	65 years and over	Asian, Hawaiian, and Pacific Islander Total population	Under 18 years	65 years and over	Hispanic or Latino[1] Total population	Under 18 years	65 years and over	Two or more races Total population	Under 18 years	65 years and over
	14	15	16	17	18	19	20	21	22	23	24	25	26	27	28
SOUTH CAROLINA—Cont'd															
Sumter County	48 948	31.4	10.0	210	24.3	8.6	953	21.2	0.5	1 643	34.1	1.8	1 353	51.2	2.7
Union County	9 415	29.7	9.7	11	0.0	0.0	94	24.5	29.8	151	41.7	6.0	108	22.2	11.1
Williamsburg County	24 725	32.3	11.2	54	0.0	11.1	65	0.0	0.0	151	29.8	17.2	159	65.4	0.0
York County	31 587	31.1	7.7	1 640	40.9	3.7	1 329	26.0	2.5	3 045	30.1	2.3	1 356	48.1	5.6
SOUTH DAKOTA	4 518	34.8	3.2	61 724	44.6	4.2	4 972	30.2	4.0	10 386	41.4	3.9	10 711	51.1	4.4
Aurora County	27	100.0	0.0	62	90.3	3.2	6	0.0	0.0	51	21.6	3.9	25	48.0	24.0
Beadle County	64	9.4	0.0	201	47.8	2.5	61	14.8	9.8	101	36.6	18.8	178	55.6	0.0
Bennett County	19	31.6	36.8	1 852	46.4	3.7	0	X	X	114	52.6	18.4	216	44.0	8.3
Bon Homme County	66	56.1	0.0	230	29.6	0.9	3	100.0	0.0	41	39.0	12.2	34	73.5	0.0
Brookings County	80	45.0	0.0	250	31.2	3.6	443	22.8	9.0	179	43.6	1.1	189	48.7	0.0
Brown County	128	29.7	0.0	1 137	40.7	0.0	110	14.5	18.2	129	39.5	10.9	160	50.0	0.0
Brule County	0	X	X	487	66.7	4.5	13	7.7	0.0	35	62.9	11.4	64	70.3	0.0
Buffalo County	2	0.0	0.0	1 608	45.0	3.4	7	42.9	0.0	43	67.4	0.0	76	39.5	14.5
Butte County	2	100.0	0.0	86	36.0	5.8	48	45.8	0.0	309	43.0	4.5	127	59.8	1.6
Campbell County	0	X	X	2	0.0	0.0	4	100.0	0.0	0	X	X	10	20.0	60.0
Charles Mix County	9	44.4	0.0	2 681	46.4	4.7	11	36.4	0.0	184	52.2	4.3	123	54.5	0.8
Clark County	0	X	X	21	81.0	0.0	6	0.0	0.0	11	0.0	36.4	19	94.7	0.0
Clay County	103	35.0	0.0	456	35.5	7.2	208	5.8	3.8	111	10.8	0.0	186	54.3	0.0
Codington County	14	35.7	0.0	354	32.5	0.0	65	6.2	0.0	255	44.3	2.7	175	33.1	12.0
Corson County	3	0.0	0.0	2 510	44.7	5.1	6	0.0	0.0	75	52.0	0.0	82	65.9	2.4
Custer County	10	100.0	0.0	302	47.4	6.3	5	0.0	0.0	100	50.0	7.0	136	42.6	11.8
Davison County	132	33.3	18.2	332	32.2	0.0	27	0.0	0.0	112	40.2	7.1	69	53.6	0.0
Day County	0	X	X	474	42.4	4.0	22	27.3	9.1	11	63.6	18.2	97	58.8	2.1
Deuel County	5	80.0	0.0	16	18.8	12.5	3	33.3	0.0	43	48.8	0.0	44	70.5	4.5
Dewey County	16	68.8	0.0	4 297	44.0	5.4	30	10.0	26.7	56	64.3	0.0	174	48.9	4.0
Douglas County	0	X	X	51	66.7	0.0	0	X	X	18	50.0	0.0	5	0.0	0.0
Edmunds County	3	100.0	0.0	6	50.0	0.0	4	50.0	0.0	17	47.1	0.0	4	0.0	50.0
Fall River County	30	36.7	26.7	458	41.3	12.2	40	25.0	12.5	102	41.2	10.8	180	39.4	5.6
Faulk County	0	X	X	22	45.5	9.1	6	66.7	0.0	6	16.7	33.3	2	0.0	0.0
Grant County	0	X	X	72	44.4	0.0	10	50.0	0.0	34	50.0	0.0	24	66.7	0.0
Gregory County	7	42.9	0.0	262	36.3	13.0	9	22.2	0.0	42	54.8	9.5	47	40.4	21.3
Haakon County	0	X	X	57	52.6	0.0	14	42.9	0.0	3	0.0	0.0	8	25.0	0.0
Hamlin County	13	7.7	23.1	55	40.0	5.5	4	0.0	0.0	42	61.9	0.0	19	36.8	26.3
Hand County	2	0.0	100.0	7	0.0	0.0	7	0.0	28.6	12	58.3	0.0	11	45.5	0.0
Hanson County	2	100.0	0.0	0	X	X	5	0.0	40.0	5	20.0	0.0	9	100.0	0.0
Harding County	7	100.0	0.0	20	70.0	0.0	0	X	X	7	100.0	0.0	0	X	X
Hughes County	48	52.1	0.0	1 280	47.5	3.2	135	43.7	3.7	207	29.5	9.2	191	53.4	11.0
Hutchinson County	7	71.4	0.0	46	65.2	0.0	3	100.0	0.0	29	51.7	0.0	43	72.1	0.0
Hyde County	0	X	X	98	35.7	9.2	0	X	X	0	X	X	6	66.7	0.0
Jackson County	11	100.0	0.0	1 342	47.7	4.4	15	66.7	0.0	8	75.0	0.0	103	37.9	7.8
Jerauld County	0	X	X	5	20.0	0.0	0	X	X	7	0.0	28.6	1	100.0	0.0
Jones County	7	57.1	0.0	18	44.4	0.0	0	X	X	0	X	X	27	22.2	0.0
Kingsbury County	2	100.0	0.0	28	35.7	7.1	15	46.7	13.3	32	43.8	0.0	30	66.7	6.7
Lake County	23	73.9	0.0	88	44.3	0.0	53	17.0	9.4	140	61.4	0.0	77	37.7	10.4
Lawrence County	33	45.5	0.0	494	41.1	2.6	80	17.5	10.0	442	41.0	0.5	244	44.3	5.7
Lincoln County	114	32.5	0.0	105	52.4	0.0	113	44.2	0.0	157	55.4	0.0	191	51.8	6.3
Lyman County	2	0.0	0.0	1 249	47.7	3.4	8	0.0	37.5	1	0.0	0.0	85	55.3	3.5
McCook County	0	X	X	19	47.4	0.0	5	0.0	0.0	53	41.5	0.0	25	52.0	0.0
McPherson County	0	X	X	11	81.8	0.0	0	X	X	2	0.0	0.0	4	0.0	50.0
Marshall County	0	X	X	322	44.4	3.4	2	100.0	0.0	29	37.9	10.3	19	42.1	0.0
Meade County	331	25.4	0.9	549	47.7	4.9	178	28.1	11.8	435	29.2	0.0	573	40.3	7.9
Mellette County	0	X	X	1 078	44.9	8.6	3	0.0	0.0	41	75.6	0.0	52	65.4	0.0
Miner County	7	71.4	0.0	5	0.0	0.0	1	0.0	0.0	20	20.0	10.0	12	33.3	0.0
Minnehaha County	2 181	37.2	1.9	2 955	37.2	1.8	1 647	38.9	1.4	3 087	40.7	2.2	2 465	54.3	2.3
Moody County	19	31.6	31.6	764	40.4	4.8	67	34.3	0.0	56	67.9	10.7	156	48.7	10.3
Pennington County	677	28.8	5.3	6 748	40.9	4.3	954	25.7	3.1	2 335	42.8	4.6	2 707	54.0	2.9
Perkins County	3	0.0	66.7	70	52.9	2.9	13	30.8	0.0	3	0.0	100.0	34	32.4	17.6
Potter County	0	X	X	15	40.0	6.7	8	50.0	25.0	2	100.0	0.0	6	66.7	0.0
Roberts County	7	28.6	42.9	2 943	45.0	4.5	47	34.0	4.3	42	71.4	0.0	140	47.1	3.6
Sanborn County	3	100.0	0.0	23	60.9	8.7	14	28.6	14.3	41	51.2	17.1	10	100.0	0.0
Shannon County	15	46.7	0.0	11 678	46.4	4.5	48	47.9	0.0	171	26.9	5.8	56	62.5	0.0
Spink County	8	50.0	0.0	131	32.1	1.5	5	0.0	0.0	26	42.3	0.0	50	64.0	0.0
Stanley County	9	55.6	0.0	126	45.2	6.3	12	50.0	0.0	3	0.0	0.0	50	44.0	6.0
Sully County	2	100.0	0.0	9	44.4	0.0	4	100.0	0.0	3	0.0	0.0	18	77.8	11.1
Todd County	0	X	X	7 477	46.9	4.2	24	37.5	8.3	81	50.6	0.0	289	48.8	8.0

[1] Hispanic or Latino persons may be of any race.

STATE County	Total households	Family households (percent)								Nonfamily households (percent)						Percent of householders 65 years and over who live alone	Grandparents who are responsible for the care of their grandchildren
		Married-couple family households			Other family households			Two or more unrelated persons		Male living alone		Female living alone				
		Total	With children	Householder 65 years or over	Total	With children	Householder 65 years or over	Total	Householder 65 years or over	Total	Householder 65 years or over	Total	Householder 65 years or over		
	29	30	31	32	33	34	35	36	37	38	39	40	41	42	43
SOUTH CAROLINA—Cont'd															
Sumter County	37 719	51.3	24.4	7.8	22.4	12.7	3.4	3.1	0.2	10.0	2.2	13.3	6.9	44.4	1 600
Union County	12 081	49.3	18.7	10.3	21.3	11.2	3.5	2.3	0.3	11.6	2.2	15.5	9.0	44.5	448
Williamsburg County	13 736	48.4	21.9	9.0	25.0	13.3	4.6	1.8	0.1	9.4	2.1	15.5	8.3	43.3	786
York County	61 094	57.6	26.7	7.9	16.1	9.0	2.3	5.0	0.2	9.3	1.5	12.0	5.4	40.0	1 894
SOUTH DAKOTA	290 336	55.0	25.1	11.1	12.4	8.1	1.4	5.2	0.3	12.1	2.6	15.4	8.5	46.5	4 632
Aurora County	1 174	62.9	24.4	16.2	7.7	3.7	1.4	1.8	0.0	12.5	3.6	15.1	10.3	44.2	21
Beadle County	7 240	53.2	22.5	13.6	10.2	7.0	1.3	3.6	0.4	13.9	2.8	19.1	12.0	49.1	34
Bennett County	1 114	50.1	26.2	8.3	22.9	14.3	2.3	4.1	1.0	12.7	4.0	10.1	6.7	48.0	59
Bon Homme County	2 639	61.3	23.9	17.7	7.0	3.9	1.4	1.8	0.0	11.6	3.3	18.2	13.7	47.1	27
Brookings County	10 664	49.6	23.2	8.9	9.2	6.0	0.8	11.6	0.3	14.7	2.0	14.9	6.3	45.5	41
Brown County	14 695	53.2	23.2	10.6	11.0	7.3	1.3	5.2	0.3	13.3	3.0	17.3	9.2	50.1	166
Brule County	1 986	56.1	24.3	13.0	10.2	6.3	1.3	3.5	0.3	13.2	3.9	16.9	9.9	48.5	18
Buffalo County	520	39.6	22.1	7.5	40.8	27.9	2.5	2.5	0.0	9.8	2.3	7.3	3.3	35.8	70
Butte County	3 526	57.6	26.9	11.4	12.7	8.5	0.8	4.0	0.1	10.3	2.6	15.4	10.0	50.8	22
Campbell County	718	67.1	29.0	18.7	8.3	0.7	1.8	0.6	0.0	12.7	3.9	15.9	13.0	45.1	2
Charles Mix County	3 329	53.2	24.8	13.4	16.2	10.2	2.6	2.1	0.7	12.3	4.2	16.1	10.8	47.3	176
Clark County	1 590	62.3	26.4	18.3	7.3	4.0	2.1	1.9	0.3	13.0	3.9	15.5	12.0	43.5	4
Clay County	4 872	44.8	20.2	8.5	10.3	8.0	1.1	13.7	0.5	13.8	1.4	17.4	6.1	42.8	11
Codington County	10 360	55.5	26.4	10.4	11.4	6.3	1.2	5.3	0.3	11.2	2.3	16.6	9.6	50.1	74
Corson County	1 280	47.3	24.0	9.4	27.8	13.8	5.9	3.1	0.3	13.0	3.9	8.8	5.9	38.6	113
Custer County	2 975	62.3	22.4	14.4	7.7	6.2	0.6	4.4	0.6	11.5	3.5	14.1	7.7	41.9	44
Davison County	7 579	52.4	24.1	11.2	11.2	7.8	1.6	5.8	0.5	11.5	2.4	19.2	11.0	50.1	26
Day County	2 606	55.1	22.2	16.5	10.7	6.1	2.0	2.5	0.0	13.7	4.8	18.0	13.8	50.2	39
Deuel County	1 857	61.6	26.3	15.8	7.0	3.7	1.9	3.0	0.3	13.7	4.4	14.7	10.5	45.2	14
Dewey County	1 855	41.0	22.7	6.8	34.2	20.4	5.2	3.1	0.3	10.9	2.7	10.8	5.5	40.2	206
Douglas County	1 314	66.1	29.5	17.7	6.2	3.5	1.4	1.0	0.2	10.0	2.1	16.7	13.5	44.8	20
Edmunds County	1 659	65.5	27.8	17.3	6.8	3.5	1.4	1.9	0.2	11.5	3.8	14.3	11.4	44.4	14
Fall River County	3 109	52.7	16.4	15.1	10.7	7.1	1.7	3.7	0.6	16.9	4.6	16.0	9.4	44.4	60
Faulk County	1 017	63.7	25.5	20.8	6.0	3.3	0.4	1.6	0.2	13.2	3.8	15.5	11.6	41.9	15
Grant County	3 107	62.9	29.7	14.4	6.7	4.2	1.0	1.8	0.3	11.7	3.2	17.0	10.5	46.6	13
Gregory County	2 017	55.9	22.2	17.2	8.1	4.7	1.6	2.4	0.2	14.6	4.9	19.0	15.2	51.2	23
Haakon County	866	63.7	27.1	11.8	8.4	4.7	2.0	1.8	0.0	11.0	2.4	15.0	11.0	49.4	9
Hamlin County	2 032	64.3	29.5	14.4	7.0	4.8	0.7	1.9	0.4	11.7	3.5	15.1	10.8	48.0	18
Hand County	1 530	59.5	23.9	17.5	8.3	3.9	2.0	2.2	0.1	9.5	3.6	20.5	15.4	49.2	7
Hanson County	1 128	72.3	33.2	15.1	4.5	2.3	0.0	1.4	0.2	9.8	2.7	12.1	9.4	44.3	7
Harding County	522	60.3	30.1	9.2	5.9	3.8	1.9	2.1	0.6	16.3	4.2	15.3	12.1	58.2	4
Hughes County	6 522	56.5	26.1	10.1	7.4	4.7	1.3	3.7	0.2	12.5	1.6	17.1	8.6	46.9	41
Hutchinson County	3 197	61.9	25.6	18.6	7.2	3.5	2.2	1.5	0.1	11.2	3.7	18.2	14.7	46.9	15
Hyde County	680	58.1	23.8	16.8	7.2	6.3	0.9	2.4	0.0	11.3	4.3	18.7	12.9	49.4	5
Jackson County	944	49.0	25.3	9.2	22.1	14.7	4.7	3.0	0.4	13.5	4.2	12.4	8.1	46.2	62
Jerauld County	986	60.0	20.9	19.6	7.4	4.8	1.0	2.1	0.4	13.5	4.6	16.9	14.1	47.1	13
Jones County	502	51.4	22.3	12.4	12.4	8.8	1.2	2.4	0.4	19.9	6.0	13.9	9.8	53.0	1
Kingsbury County	2 405	59.8	23.0	17.8	7.7	5.0	1.7	1.4	0.2	14.3	5.3	16.8	12.9	48.1	29
Lake County	4 369	57.1	23.8	14.3	7.9	6.2	0.2	5.9	0.1	12.6	2.5	16.6	9.8	45.9	7
Lawrence County	8 871	51.7	20.9	10.6	11.3	7.5	1.3	7.5	0.5	12.4	3.0	17.1	9.0	49.0	102
Lincoln County	8 817	67.4	35.2	9.4	8.9	6.0	1.1	4.2	0.1	11.4	1.2	11.4	6.0	40.3	53
Lyman County	1 392	51.9	23.1	12.1	20.1	12.4	3.6	2.7	0.1	14.1	2.9	11.1	7.0	38.7	61
McCook County	2 200	62.5	29.1	15.0	8.0	4.7	0.9	2.5	0.1	12.1	4.6	14.8	10.9	49.2	9
McPherson County	1 239	63.4	21.5	23.9	4.5	1.6	0.9	1.5	0.4	11.3	4.0	19.3	14.9	42.9	0
Marshall County	1 833	56.6	24.3	16.0	11.3	6.3	2.1	1.9	0.0	15.0	4.4	15.2	11.3	46.5	28
Meade County	8 837	63.8	32.7	8.9	12.0	8.8	0.6	4.3	0.2	9.2	2.6	10.7	5.7	46.2	141
Mellette County	685	47.3	22.2	9.8	24.7	16.4	3.8	3.6	1.2	13.3	3.4	11.1	6.3	39.5	64
Miner County	1 220	58.0	23.9	18.8	7.7	4.0	2.5	2.4	0.0	16.5	5.0	15.4	10.7	42.6	11
Minnehaha County	58 019	52.7	25.8	8.4	12.6	8.4	1.0	7.0	0.2	11.6	1.6	16.1	7.0	47.1	602
Moody County	2 540	57.3	25.9	12.9	12.2	9.3	1.4	4.1	0.4	14.0	2.0	12.4	8.9	42.5	45
Pennington County	34 662	52.5	24.0	9.2	15.2	10.6	1.4	6.2	0.4	11.7	2.1	14.3	6.5	44.0	516
Perkins County	1 434	56.3	22.9	16.7	8.9	5.7	1.2	1.5	0.1	16.2	5.5	17.0	12.4	49.9	0
Potter County	1 130	58.6	22.5	17.2	8.2	4.3	1.9	1.4	0.0	13.2	4.6	18.6	13.5	48.7	2
Roberts County	3 684	53.0	23.3	13.0	18.3	11.6	2.6	2.0	0.4	12.4	2.8	14.3	9.9	44.2	126
Sanborn County	1 035	60.7	24.9	16.9	9.7	6.3	1.4	4.3	0.3	13.5	4.0	11.9	7.9	38.9	7
Shannon County	2 769	36.1	22.2	4.3	48.6	28.9	6.5	2.0	0.6	7.4	1.0	5.9	2.0	20.9	406
Spink County	2 847	58.7	24.8	15.8	9.1	5.8	1.1	3.0	0.3	11.8	4.3	17.5	12.4	49.2	28
Stanley County	1 124	57.3	24.8	8.7	13.0	9.0	2.1	4.8	1.1	12.4	2.5	12.5	5.9	41.2	23
Sully County	622	63.7	27.3	15.8	6.4	3.7	1.1	4.0	0.8	15.4	3.9	10.5	7.6	39.2	15
Todd County	2 474	32.3	18.6	5.6	45.5	30.1	5.3	3.4	0.0	11.5	2.6	7.4	3.6	36.4	462

Table A-3. States and Counties — Age, Ethnicity, and Household Structure

STATE County	Households with Non-Hispanic White householder		Households with Black or African American householder		Households with American Indian and Alaska Native householder		Households with Asian, Hawaiian, and Pacific Islander householder		Households with Hispanic or Latino[1] householder		Foreign-born population	Place of birth (percent)			Percent in non-English speaking households	
	Number of households	Percent that are family households	Number of households	Percent that are family households	Number of households	Percent that are family households	Number of households	Percent that are family households	Number of households	Percent that are family households	Percent of total population that is foreign-born	Europe	Asia	Latin America	Linguistically isolated	Not linguistically isolated
	44	45	46	47	48	49	50	51	52	53	54	55	56	57	58	59
SOUTH CAROLINA—Cont'd																
Sumter County	20 027	74.5	16 703	72.8	71	77.5	249	75.1	411	75.7	2.1	0.5	0.8	0.6	0.6	8.9
Union County	8 417	70.2	3 582	71.7	11	0.0	24	100.0	45	60.0	0.6	0.3	0.2	0.1	0.2	4.5
Williamsburg County	5 002	72.5	8 595	73.9	30	56.7	29	82.8	60	61.7	0.5	0.1	0.1	0.2	0.2	6.4
York County	48 501	73.9	10 638	73.4	510	68.8	395	84.1	760	74.2	2.4	0.6	0.6	1.0	0.9	7.7
SOUTH DAKOTA	267 618	66.6	1 349	68.3	15 422	78.8	1 288	61.7	2 658	74.7	1.8	0.6	0.5	0.3	1.2	10.5
Aurora County	1 158	70.6	0	X	4	50.0	0	X	12	83.3	1.5	0.2	0.2	1.1	1.2	6.4
Beadle County	7 069	63.6	41	70.7	39	69.2	21	28.6	27	77.8	1.2	0.4	0.4	0.0	1.7	6.8
Bennett County	629	63.1	6	100.0	418	85.2	0	X	16	100.0	0.4	0.1	0.0	0.2	0.8	25.9
Bon Homme County	2 603	68.5	7	71.4	16	62.5	0	X	9	77.8	0.7	0.3	0.2	0.1	1.6	9.3
Brookings County	10 328	59.1	29	24.1	94	62.8	135	52.6	32	50.0	2.3	0.4	1.5	0.2	0.8	8.1
Brown County	14 154	63.8	34	76.5	405	77.3	42	40.5	37	75.7	0.6	0.3	0.2	0.0	0.8	9.1
Brule County	1 876	66.4	0	X	99	68.7	5	100.0	0	X	0.4	0.2	0.2	0.0	2.0	11.3
Buffalo County	130	75.4	2	100.0	368	81.8	2	100.0	5	100.0	0.4	0.1	0.1	0.0	0.2	26.9
Butte County	3 392	70.5	0	X	20	80.0	9	100.0	94	58.5	1.2	0.1	0.5	0.4	0.1	7.0
Campbell County	712	71.5	0	X	0	X	0	X	0	X	0.4	0.0	0.2	0.0	0.4	12.4
Charles Mix County	2 597	66.4	2	0.0	683	79.4	0	X	41	85.4	0.8	0.2	0.0	0.4	2.7	15.6
Clark County	1 581	69.6	0	X	4	100.0	2	0.0	3	100.0	0.8	0.4	0.1	0.1	1.6	14.7
Clay County	4 549	55.4	22	100.0	164	51.2	82	43.9	41	53.7	2.6	0.5	1.3	0.5	0.7	7.1
Codington County	10 079	66.8	9	100.0	116	52.6	29	55.2	76	86.8	1.2	0.3	0.3	0.4	0.6	7.9
Corson County	667	69.3	0	X	590	83.4	4	0.0	20	50.0	0.3	0.1	0.1	0.0	1.2	32.3
Custer County	2 850	69.6	0	X	58	91.4	5	0.0	19	73.7	1.1	0.4	0.2	0.2	0.2	5.4
Davison County	7 417	63.8	37	78.4	93	47.3	10	0.0	22	54.5	1.0	0.3	0.1	0.4	0.6	5.7
Day County	2 446	65.0	0	X	129	80.6	5	100.0	2	0.0	0.9	0.3	0.3	0.0	0.6	7.5
Deuel County	1 832	68.5	1	100.0	9	77.8	0	X	8	75.0	0.7	0.2	0.1	0.4	0.8	7.9
Dewey County	585	68.7	5	0.0	1 220	78.1	13	100.0	14	100.0	0.6	0.0	0.4	0.1	0.8	33.6
Douglas County	1 300	72.3	0	X	10	70.0	0	X	7	100.0	0.4	0.2	0.0	0.0	3.4	7.8
Edmunds County	1 650	72.3	0	X	0	X	0	X	9	55.6	1.0	0.2	0.1	0.0	4.8	12.2
Fall River County	2 897	62.8	5	0.0	125	70.4	15	100.0	23	52.2	0.6	0.2	0.2	0.1	0.2	7.6
Faulk County	1 011	69.7	0	X	4	100.0	0	X	2	0.0	2.0	0.2	0.1	0.0	5.8	14.5
Grant County	3 093	69.4	0	X	5	100.0	0	X	9	100.0	1.1	0.6	0.1	0.0	0.0	6.4
Gregory County	1 903	63.9	0	X	90	65.6	1	100.0	8	100.0	0.7	0.4	0.2	0.0	0.1	4.6
Haakon County	838	71.5	0	X	17	88.2	5	100.0	3	100.0	1.0	0.4	0.4	0.0	0.6	5.0
Hamlin County	2 007	71.4	3	100.0	8	50.0	0	X	11	81.8	0.8	0.3	0.1	0.1	0.9	9.9
Hand County	1 524	67.9	0	X	2	0.0	0	X	0	X	1.0	0.6	0.2	0.0	2.5	5.9
Hanson County	1 123	77.1	0	X	0	X	3	0.0	2	0.0	0.5	0.1	0.1	0.1	4.9	10.9
Harding County	517	66.3	0	X	5	60.0	0	X	0	X	0.5	0.2	0.0	0.0	0.2	1.6
Hughes County	6 100	66.7	16	75.0	268	69.8	28	35.7	73	75.3	1.3	0.4	0.4	0.4	0.8	8.7
Hutchinson County	3 178	69.2	0	X	9	66.7	0	X	10	30.0	0.7	0.3	0.0	0.1	3.5	16.1
Hyde County	647	67.5	0	X	31	74.2	0	X	0	X	0.3	0.1	0.0	0.0	0.1	10.8
Jackson County	613	67.2	0	X	289	81.3	3	0.0	2	0.0	0.9	0.1	0.3	0.1	0.1	33.3
Jerauld County	982	67.5	0	X	2	0.0	0	X	2	100.0	0.3	0.2	0.0	0.0	0.2	11.0
Jones County	484	64.3	0	X	6	33.3	0	X	0	X	0.0	0.0	0.0	0.0	0.0	4.1
Kingsbury County	2 379	67.8	0	X	12	16.7	1	0.0	9	77.8	0.6	0.3	0.2	0.0	0.1	5.7
Lake County	4 259	64.6	0	X	33	93.9	14	35.7	41	73.2	0.9	0.1	0.4	0.3	0.9	7.9
Lawrence County	8 543	62.7	6	0.0	109	82.6	24	50.0	140	77.9	1.2	0.5	0.2	0.3	0.5	8.2
Lincoln County	8 711	76.2	22	100.0	13	100.0	24	62.5	31	93.5	1.1	0.5	0.3	0.1	0.5	5.8
Lyman County	1 057	70.7	2	0.0	312	78.2	3	66.7	1	100.0	0.6	0.2	0.3	0.0	0.2	13.4
McCook County	2 179	70.3	0	X	6	100.0	0	X	11	100.0	0.7	0.2	0.0	0.5	0.4	8.1
McPherson County	1 237	67.8	0	X	0	X	0	X	2	100.0	0.8	0.1	0.1	0.0	10.4	30.9
Marshall County	1 722	67.5	0	X	95	77.9	0	X	8	37.5	0.7	0.2	0.0	0.1	2.5	10.6
Meade County	8 356	74.9	96	90.6	156	85.9	14	100.0	102	96.1	1.4	0.5	0.5	0.3	0.2	8.4
Mellette County	405	67.4	0	X	263	81.0	3	0.0	9	66.7	0.4	0.2	0.1	0.1	1.1	27.4
Miner County	1 205	66.1	2	100.0	0	X	1	100.0	12	16.7	0.4	0.1	0.0	0.3	1.0	8.4
Minnehaha County	55 017	65.0	697	66.4	681	75.9	374	64.7	799	73.0	4.1	1.2	1.0	0.8	2.0	8.6
Moody County	2 195	69.9	6	100.0	265	62.6	15	66.7	7	100.0	1.4	0.3	0.7	0.3	1.2	10.4
Pennington County	31 055	67.2	240	61.7	1 957	76.2	246	67.5	662	77.0	2.1	0.8	0.7	0.3	0.7	8.7
Perkins County	1 403	65.3	2	0.0	20	70.0	3	100.0	0	X	1.3	0.4	0.3	0.1	0.5	4.5
Potter County	1 124	67.0	0	X	2	0.0	2	100.0	0	X	0.5	0.4	0.1	0.0	0.1	5.3
Roberts County	2 867	69.1	5	60.0	770	78.8	9	77.8	2	100.0	0.8	0.2	0.3	0.1	0.2	13.0
Sanborn County	1 027	70.3	0	X	3	100.0	2	100.0	3	33.3	0.6	0.1	0.3	0.0	2.2	7.8
Shannon County	266	57.1	0	X	2 451	87.7	17	100.0	31	67.7	0.6	0.4	0.1	0.1	1.6	59.7
Spink County	2 817	67.8	2	100.0	13	69.2	0	X	2	100.0	0.6	0.3	0.1	0.0	2.6	8.1
Stanley County	1 055	70.8	2	100.0	47	51.1	3	100.0	0	X	0.7	0.4	0.3	0.0	0.3	6.8
Sully County	618	70.2	0	X	1	100.0	0	X	3	33.3	0.8	0.5	0.3	0.0	0.8	6.5
Todd County	495	68.1	0	X	1 893	80.2	13	46.2	19	73.7	0.6	0.1	0.3	0.1	1.9	42.8

[1] Hispanic or Latino persons may be of any race.

STATE/ County code	MSA/PMSA/ NECMA code[1]	STATE County	Total population	Under 5 years	5 to 17 years	18 to 24 years	25 to 44 years	45 to 64 years	65 years and over	Median age	+/− U.S. percent under 18 years	+/− U.S. percent 65 years and over	Total population	Under 18 years	65 years and over
													Non-Hispanic White Age (percent)		
			1	2	3	4	5	6	7	8	9	10	11	12	13
		SOUTH DAKOTA— Cont'd													
46 123	...	Tripp County	6 430	6.2	21.7	6.5	24.1	21.9	19.6	39.5	2.2	7.2	5 637	25.0	21.6
46 125	...	Turner County	8 849	5.5	20.1	6.3	24.6	22.8	20.6	40.5	-0.1	8.2	8 749	25.4	20.7
46 127	...	Union County	12 584	6.8	20.2	7.4	28.6	23.5	13.5	36.9	1.3	1.1	12 009	26.2	14.1
46 129	...	Walworth County	5 974	6.0	18.3	7.3	22.3	24.1	21.9	42.8	-1.4	9.5	5 163	21.3	24.4
46 135	...	Yankton County	21 652	6.3	19.5	8.8	29.0	21.8	14.6	37.0	0.1	2.2	20 356	25.6	15.4
46 137	...	Ziebach County	2 519	10.8	29.7	10.9	24.3	16.7	7.6	23.8	14.8	-4.8	668	21.3	16.3
47 000	...	**TENNESSEE**	5 689 283	6.6	18.0	9.6	30.3	23.2	12.4	35.9	-1.1	0.0	4 508 623	22.7	13.7
47 001	3840	Anderson County	71 330	5.7	17.5	7.5	27.3	25.5	16.6	39.9	-2.5	4.2	66 165	22.5	17.2
47 003	...	Bedford County	37 586	7.3	18.4	9.9	29.3	22.5	12.7	34.9	0.0	0.3	31 105	24.8	13.9
47 005	...	Benton County	16 537	5.1	16.8	6.8	26.4	27.1	17.8	41.6	-3.8	5.4	15 814	21.5	18.0
47 007	...	Bledsoe County	12 367	5.8	17.3	8.5	31.2	25.6	11.6	37.4	-2.6	-0.8	11 687	23.1	11.8
47 009	3840	Blount County	105 823	5.8	17.0	8.3	29.5	25.3	14.1	38.4	-2.9	1.7	99 648	22.3	14.4
47 011	...	Bradley County	87 965	6.5	17.2	11.3	29.9	23.4	11.6	35.5	-2.0	-0.8	81 028	23.0	12.2
47 013	...	Campbell County	39 854	5.9	17.0	8.5	27.8	25.7	15.2	38.3	-2.8	2.8	38 725	22.9	15.2
47 015	...	Cannon County	12 826	6.9	18.7	8.3	28.8	23.7	13.6	36.8	-0.1	1.2	12 378	25.0	14.0
47 017	...	Carroll County	29 475	5.8	17.4	8.1	27.2	24.3	17.2	39.0	-2.5	4.8	25 799	22.4	18.0
47 019	3660	Carter County	56 742	5.5	15.8	9.1	29.1	25.4	15.0	38.5	-4.4	2.6	55 089	21.2	15.3
47 021	5360	Cheatham County	35 912	7.2	20.4	7.3	33.5	23.0	8.5	35.3	1.9	-3.9	34 454	27.6	8.6
47 023	3580	Chester County	15 540	6.7	17.7	14.3	25.7	21.9	13.8	34.1	-1.3	1.4	13 595	22.7	14.3
47 025	...	Claiborne County	29 862	5.6	18.0	8.8	28.7	25.5	13.5	37.4	-2.1	1.1	29 041	23.5	13.5
47 027	...	Clay County	7 976	5.0	16.2	8.2	27.3	27.4	15.8	39.9	-4.5	3.4	7 689	21.3	15.8
47 029	...	Cocke County	33 565	6.0	16.9	8.4	28.8	26.3	13.6	38.6	-2.8	1.2	32 001	22.3	13.8
47 031	...	Coffee County	48 014	6.7	18.2	8.3	28.6	23.6	14.7	37.5	-0.8	2.3	44 428	24.3	15.3
47 033	...	Crockett County	14 532	6.4	18.8	8.1	28.5	22.2	16.0	37.4	-0.5	3.6	11 536	23.3	17.6
47 035	...	Cumberland County	46 802	5.4	15.9	6.9	24.9	26.3	20.6	42.5	-4.4	8.2	45 605	21.0	20.8
47 037	5360	Davidson County	569 891	6.6	15.6	11.5	34.2	21.0	11.2	34.1	-3.5	-1.2	371 994	18.0	13.9
47 039	...	Decatur County	11 731	5.6	15.9	8.1	25.7	26.5	18.1	41.2	-4.2	5.7	10 910	21.1	18.5
47 041	...	DeKalb County	17 423	6.0	17.3	8.6	29.6	24.5	14.1	37.7	-2.4	1.7	16 323	23.0	14.6
47 043	5360	Dickson County	43 156	6.9	19.8	8.2	30.6	22.8	11.6	35.7	1.0	-0.8	40 202	26.2	12.0
47 045	...	Dyer County	37 279	6.6	19.1	9.0	28.5	23.4	13.4	36.5	0.0	1.0	31 723	24.3	14.3
47 047	4920	Fayette County	28 806	6.7	19.0	8.4	27.7	25.2	13.1	38.1	0.0	0.7	17 813	22.5	13.8
47 049	...	Fentress County	16 625	6.0	18.1	8.0	28.1	26.1	13.6	38.0	-1.6	1.2	16 439	23.9	13.7
47 051	...	Franklin County	39 270	6.0	17.0	10.9	26.5	24.4	15.3	38.1	-2.7	2.9	35 948	22.5	15.7
47 053	...	Gibson County	48 152	6.1	17.8	8.0	26.9	23.5	17.6	38.8	-1.8	5.2	37 755	22.0	19.5
47 055	...	Giles County	29 447	6.1	18.4	8.1	28.0	24.8	14.5	38.0	-1.2	2.1	25 412	24.0	14.8
47 057	...	Grainger County	20 659	6.1	16.8	8.3	30.4	25.8	12.6	37.7	-2.8	0.2	20 238	22.8	12.7
47 059	...	Greene County	62 909	5.9	16.4	8.1	28.5	26.2	14.8	38.9	-3.4	2.4	60 102	21.8	15.2
47 061	...	Grundy County	14 332	6.8	18.3	9.0	27.6	24.4	13.9	36.6	-0.6	1.5	14 070	25.1	14.0
47 063	...	Hamblen County	58 128	6.5	16.7	9.2	29.2	25.1	13.3	37.1	-2.5	0.9	51 611	22.6	14.3
47 065	1560	Hamilton County	307 896	5.9	17.2	9.5	29.3	24.2	13.8	37.4	-2.6	1.4	232 792	20.8	15.4
47 067	...	Hancock County	6 786	5.2	18.0	8.8	26.9	25.4	15.7	39.2	-2.5	3.3	6 573	23.0	15.8
47 069	...	Hardeman County	28 105	5.9	18.1	9.8	31.6	21.8	12.7	36.0	-1.7	0.3	15 937	20.6	16.3
47 071	...	Hardin County	25 578	5.9	17.3	7.8	26.7	26.2	16.1	39.8	-2.5	3.7	24 180	23.0	16.3
47 073	3660	Hawkins County	53 563	6.2	17.0	7.4	30.2	26.0	13.2	37.8	-2.5	0.8	51 898	23.0	13.3
47 075	...	Haywood County	19 797	7.1	19.9	10.2	27.5	21.4	13.8	35.3	1.3	1.4	9 077	22.0	17.8
47 077	...	Henderson County	25 522	6.5	17.9	8.5	28.9	24.0	14.2	37.3	-1.3	1.8	22 964	23.6	14.8
47 079	...	Henry County	31 115	5.4	16.8	7.7	25.8	26.2	18.1	40.9	-3.5	5.7	27 582	21.1	19.0
47 081	...	Hickman County	22 295	6.6	18.0	8.5	30.7	24.0	12.1	36.3	-1.1	-0.3	20 833	25.2	12.3
47 083	...	Houston County	8 088	6.6	17.7	7.2	26.1	25.7	16.7	39.5	-1.4	4.3	7 659	24.0	17.0
47 085	...	Humphreys County	17 929	5.8	17.9	7.8	27.7	26.0	14.8	39.0	-2.0	2.4	16 937	23.4	15.1
47 087	...	Jackson County	10 984	5.9	16.2	8.0	27.9	27.0	15.0	39.8	-3.6	2.6	10 630	22.1	15.4
47 089	...	Jefferson County	44 294	6.1	16.8	10.6	29.1	24.5	12.9	36.5	-2.8	0.5	42 087	22.7	13.0
47 091	...	Johnson County	17 499	4.9	14.7	7.4	30.8	27.1	15.0	40.0	-6.1	2.6	16 852	19.9	15.3
47 093	3840	Knox County	382 032	6.1	16.2	11.6	30.5	23.0	12.6	36.0	-3.4	0.2	333 879	21.1	13.4
47 095	...	Lake County	7 954	4.7	13.3	12.9	34.3	21.5	13.3	35.8	-7.7	0.9	5 261	19.2	16.5
47 097	...	Lauderdale County	27 101	6.8	18.1	10.5	31.2	21.5	11.9	34.9	-0.8	-0.5	17 169	22.4	14.0
47 099	...	Lawrence County	39 926	6.6	19.4	8.4	27.8	23.0	14.7	36.2	0.3	2.3	38 453	25.9	14.8
47 101	...	Lewis County	11 367	6.4	19.6	8.4	27.4	24.7	13.6	37.3	0.3	1.2	10 863	25.2	13.9
47 103	...	Lincoln County	31 340	6.0	17.8	8.1	27.4	25.2	15.5	38.9	-1.9	3.1	28 174	23.2	16.1
47 105	3840	Loudon County	39 086	5.8	16.0	6.8	27.5	27.9	16.0	41.0	-3.9	3.6	37 195	21.3	16.7
47 107	...	McMinn County	49 015	6.4	17.6	8.4	28.2	24.9	14.4	37.9	-1.7	2.0	45 121	23.2	14.9
47 109	...	McNairy County	24 653	6.2	17.5	8.2	26.7	25.7	15.8	39.1	-2.0	3.4	22 489	22.8	16.5
47 111	...	Macon County	20 386	7.2	18.9	8.5	29.6	23.1	12.7	35.5	0.4	0.3	19 724	26.0	13.0
47 113	3580	Madison County	91 837	6.9	18.9	11.0	29.1	21.7	12.3	34.7	0.1	-0.1	59 166	22.0	14.7
47 115	1560	Marion County	27 776	5.9	17.8	8.5	28.6	26.3	12.8	38.2	-2.0	0.4	26 195	23.5	12.8

[1]MSA = Metropolitan Statistical Area. PMSA = Primary MSA. NECMA = New England County Metropolitan Area. See the Appendix A for explanation of these concepts. See Appendix B for list of metropolitan areas identified by type, with component counties.

STATE County	Black or African American Total population	Under 18 years	65 years and over	American Indian and Alaska Native Total population	Under 18 years	65 years and over	Asian, Hawaiian, and Pacific Islander Total population	Under 18 years	65 years and over	Hispanic or Latino[1] Total population	Under 18 years	65 years and over	Two or more races Total population	Under 18 years	65 years and over
	14	15	16	17	18	19	20	21	22	23	24	25	26	27	28
SOUTH DAKOTA— Cont'd															
Tripp County	0	X	X	671	49.6	3.3	19	47.4	0.0	46	52.2	17.4	89	42.7	12.4
Turner County	5	60.0	0.0	32	50.0	6.3	8	62.5	0.0	15	46.7	13.3	43	46.5	7.0
Union County	32	15.6	12.5	104	57.7	1.0	216	31.9	0.9	168	37.5	0.6	56	85.7	7.1
Walworth County	0	X	X	691	45.6	2.6	14	28.6	0.0	56	12.5	35.7	71	45.1	14.1
Yankton County	228	14.0	1.3	381	32.3	1.3	75	18.7	0.0	384	26.8	2.3	257	34.2	7.8
Ziebach County	0	X	X	1 801	48.3	4.4	9	0.0	0.0	16	81.3	0.0	38	23.7	7.9
TENNESSEE	929 864	31.8	7.9	15 541	24.2	5.2	56 291	24.7	3.7	119 425	31.2	2.6	69 508	40.7	6.2
Anderson County	2 727	29.7	8.5	343	33.8	3.2	516	23.4	7.4	634	37.1	4.9	944	39.6	12.6
Bedford County	3 131	28.8	11.1	75	0.0	9.3	218	29.8	9.6	2 769	29.3	2.1	387	46.8	8.5
Benton County	404	41.6	9.7	55	18.2	7.3	53	22.6	28.3	82	17.1	19.5	137	20.4	21.2
Bledsoe County	436	13.5	7.1	8	0.0	37.5	9	0.0	22.2	116	36.2	6.9	127	38.6	8.7
Blount County	3 106	25.9	12.9	281	24.9	7.5	645	28.5	2.6	749	36.2	7.9	1 438	40.3	7.8
Bradley County	3 180	33.3	5.8	190	6.3	10.0	489	21.5	8.2	1 983	30.0	0.3	1 248	34.1	5.7
Campbell County	75	26.7	20.0	171	25.7	0.0	92	35.9	4.3	283	11.3	12.4	541	15.7	21.3
Cannon County	130	31.5	3.8	60	61.7	0.0	9	44.4	0.0	126	50.0	4.8	123	27.6	4.1
Carroll County	2 824	25.0	14.0	47	23.4	0.0	53	34.0	1.9	412	40.3	3.2	362	45.6	6.1
Carter County	474	13.9	9.5	69	14.5	14.5	114	16.7	0.0	480	31.9	2.7	508	33.5	4.1
Cheatham County	544	26.8	11.6	134	42.5	0.0	62	8.1	9.7	436	28.4	4.6	348	36.8	4.3
Chester County	1 635	34.1	11.7	5	100.0	0.0	17	58.8	0.0	54	38.9	0.0	265	49.1	1.9
Claiborne County	287	22.3	15.7	57	5.3	24.6	78	46.2	0.0	144	8.3	16.0	244	35.7	8.6
Clay County	149	24.8	19.5	20	0.0	50.0	33	0.0	12.1	46	43.5	4.3	68	32.4	2.9
Cocke County	749	27.5	13.4	116	30.2	11.2	68	8.8	0.0	261	43.3	3.8	442	50.0	6.1
Coffee County	1 620	31.5	8.3	169	24.9	8.3	436	23.2	3.9	1 036	21.9	3.9	439	48.1	7.7
Crockett County	2 094	29.7	13.1	29	27.6	0.0	22	9.1	9.1	776	36.9	1.7	105	71.4	7.6
Cumberland County	70	17.1	31.4	66	0.0	37.9	154	24.0	16.2	594	48.8	7.7	331	30.5	9.1
Davidson County	147 862	30.3	7.1	1 978	21.3	3.7	12 091	23.5	3.8	25 597	28.6	1.6	12 417	37.8	3.6
Decatur County	390	20.0	18.2	39	20.5	20.5	51	13.7	2.0	270	31.1	0.4	89	49.4	22.5
DeKalb County	323	20.1	10.5	21	14.3	0.0	90	57.8	0.0	501	24.0	3.0	163	40.5	7.4
Dickson County	1 952	31.1	7.3	136	22.8	6.6	62	32.3	0.0	363	38.0	3.0	487	43.9	5.1
Dyer County	4 704	34.7	7.7	49	44.9	14.3	112	20.5	3.6	418	27.0	8.6	288	36.1	17.7
Fayette County	10 467	30.6	12.4	54	9.3	5.6	74	40.5	4.1	186	36.0	0.0	218	43.6	3.2
Fentress County	23	8.7	0.0	11	100.0	0.0	1	0.0	100.0	118	56.8	0.0	36	22.2	25.0
Franklin County	2 042	26.8	12.1	101	21.8	0.0	164	20.7	4.3	502	29.3	6.2	592	41.0	8.3
Gibson County	9 435	31.0	11.4	38	7.9	0.0	138	18.8	0.0	511	29.7	0.6	358	35.5	8.7
Giles County	3 297	27.7	13.2	104	36.5	10.6	151	31.8	0.0	280	24.3	9.6	247	34.8	15.8
Grainger County	51	31.4	21.6	19	0.0	42.1	15	0.0	0.0	250	30.4	0.0	109	38.5	0.0
Greene County	1 352	26.9	12.6	104	19.2	4.8	230	27.0	7.4	740	40.5	0.0	547	54.3	4.9
Grundy County	9	0.0	44.4	32	25.0	6.3	5	20.0	0.0	138	32.6	2.9	79	22.8	10.1
Hamblen County	2 301	22.9	11.2	141	29.1	0.0	321	29.0	10.0	3 268	27.1	0.8	529	45.7	10.2
Hamilton County	61 850	31.0	9.7	944	21.6	3.8	3 918	24.2	4.1	5 329	27.2	4.8	3 531	35.2	9.3
Hancock County	33	48.5	12.1	4	50.0	0.0	26	30.8	0.0	30	0.0	33.3	101	23.8	7.9
Hardeman County	11 350	29.7	8.1	82	11.0	0.0	107	7.5	0.0	307	6.5	0.7	378	13.8	12.4
Hardin County	778	23.0	12.6	80	33.8	0.0	77	19.5	11.7	289	33.6	8.0	230	38.7	16.5
Hawkins County	853	26.4	10.2	99	21.2	13.1	171	42.1	0.0	355	33.5	3.4	231	40.3	12.1
Haywood County	10 130	31.4	10.8	47	40.4	31.9	23	0.0	0.0	475	30.1	1.7	72	18.1	15.3
Henderson County	2 071	28.8	8.4	59	25.4	15.3	23	0.0	0.0	195	35.4	10.3	231	50.6	15.2
Henry County	2 898	28.2	12.7	37	0.0	0.0	87	17.2	0.0	249	37.3	6.4	312	64.4	4.2
Hickman County	999	9.1	10.0	89	36.0	7.9	23	69.6	0.0	191	18.3	6.8	194	28.9	10.3
Houston County	194	26.8	13.4	20	0.0	45.0	36	33.3	5.6	86	29.1	4.7	88	36.4	12.5
Humphreys County	482	29.9	9.8	36	11.1	11.1	140	22.9	12.9	182	48.4	1.1	169	30.8	14.2
Jackson County	2	0.0	0.0	39	17.9	0.0	35	0.0	0.0	108	63.0	0.9	170	10.6	2.9
Jefferson County	1 088	23.5	14.7	122	8.2	5.7	84	13.1	8.3	687	32.2	4.1	292	41.8	7.2
Johnson County	323	0.0	4.0	61	24.6	4.9	31	0.0	45.2	145	35.2	5.5	91	37.4	12.1
Knox County	33 069	29.8	8.8	1 183	18.6	2.5	4 583	21.8	1.9	4 431	30.1	3.3	5 056	39.7	5.7
Lake County	2 546	15.2	7.1	28	0.0	0.0	0	X	X	61	44.3	0.0	68	25.0	10.3
Lauderdale County	9 464	29.2	8.5	61	13.1	0.0	108	24.1	0.0	238	31.1	8.0	175	32.0	11.4
Lawrence County	585	23.2	15.7	90	22.2	0.0	44	34.1	0.0	489	39.1	4.5	319	32.6	17.6
Lewis County	171	48.0	4.1	50	22.0	22.0	22	27.3	0.0	170	46.5	0.0	91	31.9	14.3
Lincoln County	2 294	28.0	11.2	97	30.9	34.0	94	30.9	0.0	371	30.2	3.8	288	32.6	11.8
Loudon County	423	32.2	5.9	95	14.7	1.1	82	26.8	0.0	847	41.1	0.0	441	22.9	6.3
McMinn County	2 278	31.1	13.5	137	13.9	2.2	205	33.7	0.0	823	40.8	4.0	579	39.0	2.8
McNairy County	1 431	31.2	8.2	118	70.3	0.0	81	30.9	11.1	267	35.6	5.2	304	28.6	10.2
Macon County	24	54.2	0.0	65	0.0	0.0	31	12.9	0.0	443	28.9	3.4	141	46.1	2.1
Madison County	29 671	32.4	8.5	224	40.2	0.0	576	39.4	5.0	1 502	28.6	2.4	832	46.0	9.4
Marion County	1 174	25.8	13.2	47	27.7	0.0	103	39.8	14.6	96	24.0	8.3	150	37.3	7.3

[1] Hispanic or Latino persons may be of any race.

STATE County	Total households	Married-couple family households			Other family households			Two or more unrelated persons		Male living alone		Female living alone		Percent of householders 65 years and over who live alone	Grandparents who are responsible for the care of their grandchildren
		Total	With children	Householder 65 years or over	Total	With children	Householder 65 years or over	Total	Householder 65 years or over	Total	Householder 65 years or over	Total	Householder 65 years or over		
	29	30	31	32	33	34	35	36	37	38	39	40	41	42	43
SOUTH DAKOTA— Cont'd															
Tripp County	2 528	57.6	25.6	15.0	10.0	6.1	1.4	2.8	0.1	12.1	3.8	17.4	11.9	48.8	55
Turner County	3 524	63.2	27.5	15.8	7.4	4.4	1.1	2.8	0.3	11.2	3.4	15.4	11.5	46.2	34
Union County	4 948	63.0	28.8	11.0	9.0	6.5	0.9	3.7	0.3	12.0	2.7	12.3	7.3	44.8	40
Walworth County	2 505	50.7	17.0	14.6	15.1	10.1	1.7	2.8	0.8	13.6	4.5	17.8	11.8	48.8	55
Yankton County	8 173	55.4	25.9	11.0	10.7	7.4	1.0	4.6	0.0	13.2	3.1	16.1	9.3	50.8	136
Ziebach County	739	45.3	23.7	9.9	34.6	23.8	3.9	2.4	0.3	11.2	1.8	6.4	2.6	23.5	81
TENNESSEE	2 234 229	53.5	23.1	8.8	16.3	9.2	2.4	4.5	0.3	10.8	2.0	15.0	7.1	44.4	61 252
Anderson County	29 773	54.3	21.8	11.1	14.8	8.5	2.0	3.3	0.3	10.5	2.9	17.2	9.8	48.6	652
Bedford County	13 933	58.5	25.1	10.0	16.1	9.4	2.2	4.0	0.2	8.6	1.9	12.8	8.1	44.7	457
Benton County	6 855	59.3	21.9	13.2	12.3	5.7	2.7	2.6	0.5	10.9	2.5	14.9	9.7	42.8	262
Bledsoe County	4 412	61.8	25.2	8.8	13.9	7.2	2.9	2.2	0.1	10.1	2.3	12.0	6.5	42.4	167
Blount County	42 834	59.4	24.3	10.5	12.8	6.6	2.3	3.6	0.3	9.6	2.1	14.6	7.4	42.1	1 104
Bradley County	34 255	58.4	24.9	9.0	13.9	7.6	2.1	4.3	0.2	10.0	1.9	13.4	6.4	42.3	952
Campbell County	16 119	56.5	22.6	10.4	15.5	7.0	3.4	2.7	0.1	10.2	2.5	15.1	9.0	45.2	381
Cannon County	4 996	60.2	27.1	10.4	13.6	7.0	3.1	2.0	0.3	10.4	2.8	13.7	7.6	42.9	116
Carroll County	11 812	56.4	21.9	11.9	14.9	8.1	2.2	3.0	0.2	9.5	3.0	16.3	10.2	48.0	320
Carter County	23 512	55.0	21.1	9.8	15.3	7.9	2.9	3.3	0.2	11.3	2.8	15.2	8.3	46.6	461
Cheatham County	12 869	65.5	31.4	7.2	13.9	8.1	1.9	3.6	0.4	8.1	1.2	8.8	4.1	35.6	389
Chester County	5 663	59.5	26.2	11.6	15.3	7.0	3.0	2.6	0.3	8.5	1.7	14.1	9.0	41.9	97
Claiborne County	11 774	59.3	25.2	9.5	14.7	7.3	3.3	2.7	0.2	10.6	2.9	12.7	7.3	44.0	315
Clay County	3 384	55.1	21.2	9.9	13.9	5.9	2.8	3.3	0.4	11.7	3.8	16.0	8.2	48.0	61
Cocke County	13 761	54.5	21.2	9.5	16.7	8.7	2.3	3.2	0.2	11.0	2.5	14.5	7.5	45.6	583
Coffee County	18 872	57.9	24.3	11.5	14.5	8.8	2.5	3.4	0.2	11.0	2.7	13.3	6.9	40.2	408
Crockett County	5 649	58.7	25.2	12.1	13.9	6.8	2.9	1.9	0.1	10.4	2.6	15.1	8.4	42.2	189
Cumberland County	19 510	62.1	19.8	18.5	12.5	6.9	2.2	2.9	0.5	9.1	2.7	13.4	8.1	33.7	461
Davidson County	237 432	40.9	17.3	6.6	17.7	10.1	2.2	8.0	0.4	14.0	1.8	19.3	6.6	47.9	5 550
Decatur County	4 938	57.5	20.9	12.4	12.6	7.1	2.3	2.2	0.2	11.1	2.4	16.6	11.1	47.5	165
DeKalb County	6 998	62.9	22.5	10.3	14.2	7.5	2.2	2.6	0.2	10.5	2.4	14.9	8.9	47.4	231
Dickson County	16 454	58.8	26.6	9.5	15.4	10.2	1.8	3.5	0.1	9.6	1.9	12.6	6.4	42.0	443
Dyer County	14 775	54.2	23.3	9.3	17.4	10.5	2.2	3.0	0.1	10.4	1.9	14.9	8.4	47.1	574
Fayette County	10 468	59.4	23.9	11.0	17.3	8.1	3.3	2.7	0.4	9.9	2.4	10.7	6.0	36.4	519
Fentress County	6 730	57.6	25.4	10.1	14.6	7.0	3.1	2.6	0.4	11.2	3.0	14.0	7.1	42.3	147
Franklin County	15 042	61.3	24.2	12.7	13.7	7.3	2.7	2.5	0.2	9.1	2.6	13.4	8.3	41.1	499
Gibson County	19 500	54.3	22.0	11.5	15.6	9.1	2.5	2.7	0.2	10.1	2.8	17.3	10.7	48.6	584
Giles County	11 697	56.1	24.5	9.7	15.1	7.5	3.4	3.0	0.3	11.2	2.7	14.6	8.1	44.9	200
Grainger County	8 298	62.9	26.0	8.5	12.1	6.3	2.8	2.7	0.3	10.5	2.9	11.9	6.7	45.4	285
Greene County	25 692	57.8	22.2	10.7	13.1	6.9	2.2	3.3	0.2	10.3	2.4	15.5	8.0	44.0	764
Grundy County	5 582	57.5	25.2	10.1	16.2	8.3	2.9	2.4	0.3	10.7	2.2	13.2	7.3	41.6	292
Hamblen County	23 245	56.6	22.8	9.1	14.8	8.1	2.2	3.9	0.2	10.0	2.1	14.7	7.5	45.3	689
Hamilton County	124 515	51.3	20.8	9.2	16.4	8.7	2.6	4.5	0.3	11.1	2.3	16.8	7.9	45.8	3 601
Hancock County	2 772	54.7	24.7	9.8	15.3	7.5	3.5	2.6	0.2	10.3	3.0	17.1	10.4	49.6	47
Hardeman County	9 384	49.9	21.1	10.1	22.1	11.5	3.5	2.6	0.3	10.9	3.3	14.4	8.9	46.7	583
Hardin County	10 445	58.2	23.1	11.0	13.2	7.0	3.0	3.1	0.1	10.6	3.0	14.9	8.8	45.4	221
Hawkins County	21 965	60.1	24.4	9.6	12.9	7.2	2.5	2.7	0.1	10.3	2.0	14.0	7.3	43.3	508
Haywood County	7 578	46.7	20.7	8.1	25.0	13.4	4.4	2.8	0.6	10.0	2.6	15.4	9.4	48.0	390
Henderson County	10 305	57.4	23.9	10.3	15.2	9.1	2.5	2.6	0.1	9.8	2.0	15.0	8.4	44.4	238
Henry County	13 078	56.0	21.3	12.2	13.5	6.6	2.4	3.6	0.6	11.3	3.1	15.6	9.9	46.2	369
Hickman County	8 087	61.2	27.6	9.7	13.0	6.9	2.2	3.2	0.6	10.4	2.1	12.3	8.1	44.7	69
Houston County	3 223	58.0	24.7	11.4	14.4	7.9	2.6	2.6	0.4	11.9	4.1	13.1	8.0	45.8	90
Humphreys County	7 231	59.1	22.8	11.1	12.9	7.9	1.9	3.0	0.4	10.7	2.3	14.2	8.8	45.3	147
Jackson County	4 472	55.6	22.1	10.1	15.2	6.9	3.4	3.8	0.8	12.8	2.7	12.6	7.2	40.8	78
Jefferson County	17 199	60.9	24.2	10.5	13.2	7.4	2.3	3.4	0.1	9.8	1.8	12.5	6.1	37.9	590
Johnson County	6 837	55.6	19.5	10.9	14.2	6.3	3.9	3.8	0.4	11.7	3.7	14.8	8.7	45.1	263
Knox County	157 758	50.4	21.3	8.3	13.6	7.5	2.2	6.5	0.3	12.4	1.9	17.2	7.2	45.4	2 654
Lake County	2 407	49.1	19.4	9.7	18.3	10.3	3.5	2.6	0.3	9.5	3.7	20.5	11.8	53.4	112
Lauderdale County	9 557	52.1	22.9	8.4	19.9	11.8	3.3	2.5	0.4	10.3	3.0	15.2	9.0	49.7	440
Lawrence County	15 537	60.3	26.3	10.9	13.6	7.7	2.0	2.4	0.4	9.0	2.5	14.7	9.4	47.6	474
Lewis County	4 380	58.0	25.6	9.4	14.8	7.7	2.6	3.5	0.5	10.2	3.2	13.5	7.6	46.2	107
Lincoln County	12 537	58.2	24.3	10.9	14.9	7.6	2.9	2.4	0.3	8.9	2.8	15.6	10.0	47.7	396
Loudon County	15 954	61.7	23.3	12.7	12.6	6.0	2.4	2.9	0.3	8.4	1.9	14.4	8.7	40.8	306
McMinn County	19 755	59.9	24.2	10.7	13.1	7.6	2.0	2.8	0.2	9.0	2.3	15.3	8.0	44.3	564
McNairy County	9 969	58.1	24.0	10.9	13.1	7.1	2.5	2.9	0.3	10.3	2.8	15.6	9.6	47.3	284
Macon County	7 942	59.9	27.6	8.3	13.5	7.3	2.8	2.8	0.4	9.5	2.5	14.3	8.6	49.2	132
Madison County	35 537	50.6	22.8	8.7	19.0	11.1	2.4	4.2	0.2	11.5	2.1	14.6	6.6	43.5	1 028
Marion County	11 034	59.1	23.4	9.7	15.1	8.1	2.1	2.3	0.1	9.1	2.2	14.4	8.2	46.4	419

Table A-3. States and Counties — Age, Ethnicity, and Household Structure

STATE County	Households with Non-Hispanic White householder		Households with Black or African American householder		Households with American Indian and Alaska Native householder		Households with Asian, Hawaiian, and Pacific Islander householder		Households with Hispanic or Latino[1] householder		Foreign-born population	Place of birth (percent)			Percent in non-English speaking households	
	Number of households	Percent that are family households	Number of households	Percent that are family households	Number of households	Percent that are family households	Number of households	Percent that are family households	Number of households	Percent that are family households	Percent of total population that is foreign-born	Europe	Asia	Latin America	Linguistically isolated	Not linguistically isolated
	44	45	46	47	48	49	50	51	52	53	54	55	56	57	58	59
SOUTH DAKOTA— Cont'd																
Tripp County	2 335	67.4	0	X	152	70.4	7	100.0	0	X	0.4	0.2	0.0	0.0	0.3	7.6
Turner County	3 507	70.7	0	X	6	66.7	2	100.0	3	0.0	0.5	0.2	0.1	0.0	0.2	6.8
Union County	4 810	71.7	16	62.5	16	93.8	69	82.6	35	88.6	2.4	0.4	1.4	0.6	0.5	6.8
Walworth County	2 261	64.7	0	X	199	80.4	10	0.0	24	58.3	0.7	0.3	0.2	0.0	0.8	12.9
Yankton County	7 918	66.1	32	81.3	100	53.0	8	100.0	63	76.2	1.5	0.4	0.5	0.4	0.9	8.0
Ziebach County	274	72.3	0	X	447	84.3	5	60.0	0	X	0.4	0.0	0.3	0.0	1.7	42.3
TENNESSEE	1 828 668	69.8	331 948	69.2	6 191	71.3	17 622	71.5	31 613	74.4	2.8	0.5	0.9	1.1	1.1	6.9
Anderson County	27 815	69.0	1 112	70.3	142	69.7	167	91.6	204	75.0	1.9	0.6	0.7	0.4	0.6	6.0
Bedford County	11 856	75.2	1 296	66.8	35	54.3	50	100.0	597	82.2	6.4	0.1	0.3	5.7	4.3	7.4
Benton County	6 592	71.4	131	71.8	24	100.0	15	100.0	37	86.5	0.7	0.3	0.1	0.3	0.0	5.1
Bledsoe County	4 311	75.9	45	62.2	2	100.0	4	100.0	28	82.1	0.4	0.1	0.0	0.2	0.4	4.8
Blount County	40 562	72.3	1 312	66.6	113	80.5	216	73.1	204	65.2	1.5	0.5	0.6	0.2	0.6	5.2
Bradley County	31 914	72.5	1 225	64.7	103	84.5	135	94.1	585	67.0	2.2	0.4	0.5	1.1	1.2	6.6
Campbell County	15 713	71.9	17	76.5	68	79.4	39	87.2	82	72.0	0.8	0.1	0.2	0.4	0.5	4.0
Cannon County	4 847	74.4	63	46.0	15	66.7	0	X	19	100.0	0.8	0.3	0.2	0.3	0.3	5.1
Carroll County	10 520	71.2	1 072	69.9	29	55.2	4	75.0	107	86.0	1.1	0.3	0.2	0.5	0.1	4.5
Carter County	22 915	70.4	166	71.7	37	16.2	30	100.0	179	74.9	0.8	0.3	0.2	0.3	0.4	5.2
Cheatham County	12 407	79.4	186	69.9	24	100.0	23	87.0	131	87.8	1.1	0.3	0.1	0.6	0.3	7.0
Chester County	5 082	75.0	505	73.9	0	X	0	X	8	100.0	0.5	0.1	0.1	0.1	0.1	5.4
Claiborne County	11 467	74.4	115	65.2	35	74.3	16	68.8	65	53.8	0.9	0.3	0.5	0.1	0.1	4.3
Clay County	3 271	68.9	56	53.6	16	87.5	15	100.0	18	88.9	1.1	0.3	0.4	0.4	0.5	2.8
Cocke County	13 229	71.3	290	64.5	34	55.9	35	60.0	43	76.7	0.8	0.2	0.2	0.3	0.2	5.8
Coffee County	17 683	72.4	634	66.4	73	83.6	100	70.0	300	79.7	2.3	0.3	0.6	1.3	0.9	6.1
Crockett County	4 659	73.4	800	65.9	15	0.0	7	28.6	146	90.4	3.9	0.2	0.1	3.6	2.8	5.9
Cumberland County	19 147	74.7	23	91.3	61	59.0	38	100.0	128	67.2	1.9	0.5	0.3	0.6	0.4	6.4
Davidson County	167 622	55.8	54 495	64.9	859	68.9	4 162	63.2	6 888	73.6	6.9	0.9	2.2	2.9	3.0	10.4
Decatur County	4 582	70.9	212	48.1	18	100.0	15	60.0	79	88.6	1.7	0.2	0.3	1.2	0.9	4.6
DeKalb County	6 674	72.2	147	64.6	2	100.0	12	75.0	103	66.0	2.7	0.2	0.6	1.9	0.9	4.2
Dickson County	15 458	74.2	686	73.2	76	64.5	25	68.0	106	91.5	0.7	0.3	0.2	0.2	0.3	5.5
Dyer County	12 595	72.1	1 090	67.0	10	50.0	64	100.0	122	70.7	1.3	0.1	0.3	0.7	0.8	6.1
Fayette County	6 965	76.2	3 373	77.4	20	90.0	14	85.7	52	92.3	0.7	0.2	0.2	0.2	0.1	4.3
Fentress County	6 674	72.0	0	X	0	X	1	100.0	33	100.0	0.4	0.2	0.0	0.1	0.2	2.6
Franklin County	13 886	75.8	810	68.3	35	71.4	41	53.7	124	60.5	1.4	0.3	0.5	0.5	0.5	5.1
Gibson County	15 724	70.0	3 446	69.5	25	60.0	35	94.3	175	82.9	0.8	0.1	0.2	0.4	0.4	4.2
Giles County	10 121	72.0	1 200	66.4	27	63.0	54	68.5	88	60.6	0.9	0.2	0.3	0.3	0.2	5.1
Grainger County	8 168	74.8	14	92.9	10	100.0	3	0.0	70	82.9	1.1	0.3	0.0	0.7	0.7	3.9
Greene County	24 796	71.0	510	66.9	45	46.7	68	66.2	145	74.5	1.3	0.4	0.3	0.5	0.6	5.5
Grundy County	5 514	73.6	0	X	6	100.0	4	100.0	32	100.0	0.7	0.2	0.1	0.4	0.2	3.6
Hamblen County	21 196	71.5	1 042	66.8	71	63.4	88	86.4	733	76.7	5.3	0.4	0.4	4.4	3.4	6.3
Hamilton County	97 207	67.9	23 290	67.0	394	73.9	1 258	66.8	1 540	66.8	3.0	0.7	1.1	0.9	0.9	7.7
Hancock County	2 684	69.6	9	77.8	2	100.0	6	100.0	15	86.7	0.3	0.1	0.2	0.0	0.0	4.2
Hardeman County	5 932	68.4	3 291	78.3	13	100.0	9	66.7	19	100.0	0.7	0.1	0.2	0.3	0.0	4.7
Hardin County	9 869	72.0	351	53.0	38	47.4	25	76.0	93	82.8	0.7	0.2	0.2	0.3	0.2	3.6
Hawkins County	21 398	72.8	322	74.5	35	100.0	50	100.0	95	90.5	0.7	0.2	0.2	0.2	0.1	4.0
Haywood County	3 665	72.4	3 738	71.2	22	36.4	12	0.0	130	73.1	1.7	0.1	0.1	1.4	0.7	5.8
Henderson County	9 298	72.5	855	75.8	30	33.3	9	100.0	61	73.8	0.7	0.3	0.1	0.3	0.1	3.8
Henry County	11 748	69.5	1 155	68.4	30	100.0	32	71.9	78	62.8	1.0	0.4	0.2	0.3	0.2	4.7
Hickman County	7 731	74.2	187	68.4	33	78.8	7	0.0	68	92.6	0.8	0.3	0.1	0.2	0.1	6.5
Houston County	3 074	72.7	67	65.7	7	100.0	11	100.0	37	64.9	1.6	0.4	0.3	0.6	0.9	4.8
Humphreys County	6 873	72.0	202	62.9	15	86.7	38	78.9	38	94.7	0.9	0.3	0.4	0.1	0.3	4.6
Jackson County	4 340	70.8	0	X	32	50.0	15	46.7	23	95.7	1.6	0.2	0.2	0.3	0.3	4.5
Jefferson County	16 513	74.5	407	66.8	37	100.0	27	29.6	151	74.8	1.5	0.2	0.2	0.9	0.8	4.0
Johnson County	6 727	69.9	8	100.0	15	20.0	11	100.0	56	66.1	0.6	0.1	0.2	0.2	0.2	4.7
Knox County	139 421	64.3	13 381	61.2	502	66.1	1 702	62.9	1 304	62.9	2.5	0.7	1.1	0.5	0.7	6.7
Lake County	1 930	66.7	442	70.6	3	100.0	0	X	16	75.0	0.5	0.2	0.0	0.3	0.4	7.0
Lauderdale County	6 626	72.0	2 800	71.8	12	41.7	35	100.0	60	85.0	0.7	0.1	0.4	0.2	0.4	4.6
Lawrence County	14 982	74.2	245	50.2	37	86.5	12	58.3	151	74.2	0.9	0.2	0.1	0.4	1.2	5.3
Lewis County	4 251	72.9	42	52.4	7	100.0	0	X	38	86.8	1.0	0.4	0.2	0.4	0.8	5.6
Lincoln County	11 294	74.4	954	61.2	25	76.0	27	100.0	104	73.1	0.9	0.2	0.2	0.3	0.4	6.0
Loudon County	15 388	74.5	169	56.8	29	55.2	30	23.3	162	98.1	1.8	0.4	0.2	1.1	0.9	4.1
McMinn County	18 369	73.6	873	58.2	85	90.6	61	72.1	188	87.8	1.3	0.1	0.3	0.7	0.5	5.4
McNairy County	9 183	71.5	573	67.7	4	100.0	19	73.7	102	67.6	0.9	0.3	0.2	0.5	0.4	4.6
Macon County	7 736	73.6	5	100.0	30	80.0	4	100.0	144	61.1	1.8	0.1	0.1	1.6	1.2	4.5
Madison County	23 804	70.1	10 925	68.2	90	81.1	141	90.8	392	69.6	2.3	0.4	0.6	1.0	0.9	6.0
Marion County	10 544	74.4	407	73.2	15	73.3	22	72.7	20	50.0	0.5	0.1	0.2	0.1	0.3	4.6

[1] Hispanic or Latino persons may be of any race.

STATE/ County code	MSA/PMSA/ NECMA code[1]	STATE County	Population by age (percent)										Non-Hispanic White		
															Age (percent)	
			Total population	Under 5 years	5 to 17 years	18 to 24 years	25 to 44 years	45 to 64 years	65 years and over	Median age	+/− U.S. percent under 18 years	+/− U.S. percent 65 years and over	Total population	Under 18 years	65 years and over
			1	2	3	4	5	6	7	8	9	10	11	12	13
		TENNESSEE—Cont'd													
47 117	...	Marshall County	26 767	6.5	19.0	8.6	30.1	23.2	12.5	36.3	-0.2	0.1	23 735	24.8	12.9
47 119	...	Maury County	69 498	7.0	19.3	8.6	30.2	23.0	12.0	36.3	0.6	-0.4	56 454	24.9	13.0
47 121	...	Meigs County	11 086	6.9	18.1	8.2	28.7	26.4	11.7	36.7	-0.7	-0.7	10 832	25.4	11.6
47 123	...	Monroe County	38 961	6.2	18.5	8.7	28.8	24.6	13.2	36.8	-1.0	0.8	36 690	24.2	13.5
47 125	1660	Montgomery County	134 768	8.3	20.0	12.4	34.5	17.0	7.7	30.0	2.6	-4.7	95 692	26.0	9.0
47 127	...	Moore County	5 740	5.3	18.0	8.1	27.0	26.6	15.1	39.7	-2.4	2.7	5 452	23.3	15.4
47 129	...	Morgan County	19 757	5.8	17.4	9.2	31.7	24.4	11.6	36.5	-2.5	-0.8	18 960	23.3	11.7
47 131	...	Obion County	32 450	6.3	17.1	8.4	27.6	25.3	15.2	38.7	-2.3	2.8	28 316	22.2	16.0
47 133	...	Overton County	20 118	6.1	17.0	8.5	27.5	25.9	15.0	38.8	-2.6	2.6	19 741	23.1	15.1
47 135	...	Perry County	7 631	6.1	18.3	7.4	25.4	26.5	16.3	39.8	-1.3	3.9	7 346	24.1	16.4
47 137	...	Pickett County	4 945	5.6	16.0	8.4	24.6	27.7	17.8	41.6	-4.1	5.4	4 876	21.4	17.9
47 139	...	Polk County	16 050	6.5	16.1	8.2	28.5	26.3	14.4	38.6	-3.1	2.0	15 706	22.8	14.4
47 141	...	Putnam County	62 315	6.1	16.2	14.6	28.1	22.0	13.2	34.4	-3.4	0.8	58 054	21.7	13.8
47 143	...	Rhea County	28 400	6.1	17.7	9.7	27.8	25.1	13.7	37.2	-1.9	1.3	26 940	23.0	14.1
47 145	...	Roane County	51 910	5.8	16.5	7.4	26.9	27.3	16.1	40.7	-3.4	3.7	49 278	21.9	16.3
47 147	5360	Robertson County	54 433	6.8	20.0	8.4	31.4	22.6	10.8	35.4	1.1	-1.6	47 580	26.2	11.1
47 149	5360	Rutherford County	182 023	7.5	18.9	13.2	33.5	19.3	7.5	31.2	0.7	-4.9	153 903	25.6	8.0
47 151	...	Scott County	21 127	6.9	19.1	10.2	28.8	23.6	11.4	34.7	0.3	-1.0	20 735	25.9	11.4
47 153	...	Sequatchie County	11 370	7.2	17.3	8.6	30.3	24.5	12.2	36.7	-1.2	-0.2	11 124	24.4	12.1
47 155	3840	Sevier County	71 170	5.9	17.1	8.4	29.8	26.2	12.6	38.1	-2.7	0.2	68 492	22.6	12.9
47 157	4920	Shelby County	897 472	7.6	20.6	9.6	31.3	21.0	10.0	32.9	2.5	-2.4	415 341	22.1	13.8
47 159	...	Smith County	17 712	6.6	18.9	7.9	30.2	23.0	13.4	36.8	-0.2	1.0	16 826	25.4	13.4
47 161	...	Stewart County	12 370	5.7	18.1	7.6	28.3	25.4	14.9	38.7	-1.9	2.5	11 783	23.6	15.1
47 163	3660	Sullivan County	153 048	5.5	16.2	7.2	28.6	26.4	15.9	40.1	-4.0	3.5	147 037	21.4	16.2
47 165	5360	Sumner County	130 449	6.6	19.6	8.1	30.7	24.3	10.6	36.1	0.5	-1.8	118 177	25.5	11.1
47 167	4920	Tipton County	51 271	7.0	22.2	8.6	30.6	21.7	9.9	34.4	3.5	-2.5	39 620	27.4	10.2
47 169	...	Trousdale County	7 259	6.3	17.7	9.1	28.3	24.1	14.4	38.1	-1.7	2.0	6 240	24.3	14.0
47 171	3660	Unicoi County	17 667	5.5	15.0	7.4	27.5	26.5	18.1	41.5	-5.2	5.7	17 100	19.8	18.6
47 173	3840	Union County	17 808	6.7	19.1	8.8	31.1	23.3	10.9	35.8	0.1	-1.5	17 520	25.9	11.0
47 175	...	Van Buren County	5 508	5.8	17.1	9.2	27.4	26.5	14.0	38.7	-2.8	1.6	5 433	23.2	14.0
47 177	...	Warren County	38 276	6.6	17.4	8.9	29.9	23.2	14.0	36.6	-1.7	1.6	34 685	23.8	14.8
47 179	3660	Washington County	107 198	6.0	15.3	10.7	30.2	23.9	13.9	37.1	-4.4	1.5	99 606	20.8	14.5
47 181	...	Wayne County	16 842	5.1	16.3	9.0	32.2	23.7	13.8	37.3	-4.3	1.4	15 394	22.6	14.5
47 183	...	Weakley County	34 895	5.8	15.8	15.6	26.3	22.3	14.2	34.8	-4.1	1.8	31 282	21.3	15.2
47 185	...	White County	23 102	6.0	17.6	8.0	27.8	25.4	15.3	38.8	-2.1	2.9	22 133	22.9	15.5
47 187	5360	Williamson County	126 638	7.3	22.2	6.0	31.9	24.8	7.7	36.2	3.8	-4.7	113 870	29.1	8.0
47 189	5360	Wilson County	88 809	6.8	19.5	7.7	31.9	24.6	9.7	36.3	0.6	-2.7	80 653	25.7	9.8
48 000	...	TEXAS	20 851 820	7.7	20.4	10.5	31.4	20.1	9.9	32.3	2.4	-2.5	10 927 538	22.9	13.8
48 001	...	Anderson County	55 109	5.7	15.0	9.5	37.7	20.7	11.5	35.8	-5.0	-0.9	34 832	21.3	15.1
48 003	...	Andrews County	13 004	7.1	24.3	8.5	28.1	19.9	12.1	34.1	5.7	-0.3	7 320	24.7	18.6
48 005	...	Angelina County	80 130	7.3	20.2	9.7	28.8	21.4	12.5	34.2	1.8	0.1	55 631	24.1	15.6
48 007	...	Aransas County	22 497	5.3	18.6	6.2	23.2	26.8	19.9	42.7	-1.8	7.5	16 483	19.2	24.5
48 009	9080	Archer County	8 854	6.3	21.8	7.2	27.4	23.3	14.0	38.1	2.4	1.6	8 285	27.3	14.7
48 011	...	Armstrong County	2 148	5.4	20.6	6.1	24.5	24.3	19.1	40.7	0.3	6.7	2 030	25.0	19.4
48 013	...	Atascosa County	38 628	8.2	23.5	9.4	27.3	20.6	11.0	32.3	6.0	-1.4	15 178	25.1	15.7
48 015	...	Austin County	23 590	6.5	20.5	8.2	26.5	23.5	14.8	37.6	1.3	2.4	16 947	23.3	18.0
48 017	...	Bailey County	6 594	8.0	22.3	9.7	23.4	21.9	14.8	34.9	4.6	2.4	3 241	20.1	24.7
48 019	...	Bandera County	17 645	5.4	19.2	5.7	25.7	27.8	16.1	41.3	-1.1	3.7	14 905	23.0	17.4
48 021	0640	Bastrop County	57 733	7.4	20.5	7.6	31.7	22.5	10.3	35.4	2.2	-2.1	37 796	24.5	12.2
48 023	...	Baylor County	4 093	5.4	17.5	5.3	22.2	24.7	24.9	44.8	-2.8	12.5	3 540	21.4	26.3
48 025	...	Bee County	32 359	5.9	17.4	13.2	35.7	17.5	10.4	31.8	-2.4	-2.0	11 299	19.0	16.0
48 027	3810	Bell County	237 974	8.9	20.0	13.4	32.0	17.0	8.7	29.2	3.2	-3.7	136 238	24.1	12.4
48 029	7240	Bexar County	1 392 931	7.8	20.5	10.7	30.8	19.8	10.4	32.1	2.6	-2.0	495 275	20.9	15.7
48 031	...	Blanco County	8 418	6.3	18.0	5.7	25.9	27.5	16.6	41.2	-1.4	4.2	6 910	22.3	18.9
48 033	...	Borden County	729	3.4	21.5	7.8	25.8	26.1	15.4	40.5	-0.8	3.0	581	21.3	18.2
48 035	...	Bosque County	17 204	5.7	18.6	6.4	23.8	24.7	20.7	41.7	-1.4	8.3	14 544	21.4	23.4
48 037	8360	Bowie County	89 306	6.5	18.4	9.3	29.6	22.2	14.0	36.3	-0.8	1.6	62 750	23.2	16.3
48 039	1145	Brazoria County	241 767	7.6	20.9	8.5	32.8	21.4	8.8	34.0	2.8	-3.6	157 936	25.7	11.2
48 041	1260	Brazos County	152 415	6.3	15.1	32.2	25.9	13.8	6.7	23.6	-4.3	-5.7	100 764	16.5	8.1
48 043	...	Brewster County	8 866	5.2	17.0	15.6	23.7	23.9	14.6	36.2	-3.5	2.2	4 763	16.3	18.2
48 045	...	Briscoe County	1 790	6.1	21.1	6.8	20.8	26.4	18.8	39.9	1.5	6.4	1 316	22.1	23.9
48 047	...	Brooks County	7 976	8.1	23.4	9.3	22.7	21.2	15.2	34.4	5.8	2.8	619	19.1	29.7
48 049	...	Brown County	37 674	6.2	19.6	10.5	24.7	22.7	16.3	37.2	0.1	3.9	29 792	22.6	19.2
48 051	...	Burleson County	16 470	7.0	19.8	7.7	26.3	23.3	15.9	37.9	1.1	3.5	11 351	22.6	18.5
48 053	...	Burnet County	34 147	6.6	18.0	6.8	26.3	24.6	17.7	40.2	-1.1	5.3	28 075	21.8	20.8

[1]MSA = Metropolitan Statistical Area. PMSA = Primary MSA. NECMA = New England County Metropolitan Area. See the Appendix A for explanation of these concepts. See Appendix B for list of metropolitan areas identified by type, with component counties.

STATE County	Black or African American Total population	Under 18 years	65 years and over	American Indian and Alaska Native Total population	Under 18 years	65 years and over	Asian, Hawaiian, and Pacific Islander Total population	Under 18 years	65 years and over	Hispanic or Latino[1] Total population	Under 18 years	65 years and over	Two or more races Total population	Under 18 years	65 years and over
	14	15	16	17	18	19	20	21	22	23	24	25	26	27	28
TENNESSEE—Cont'd															
Marshall County	2 122	30.0	11.2	16	0.0	0.0	18	33.3	0.0	663	35.9	1.5	220	41.4	5.9
Maury County	10 080	30.4	9.9	241	36.1	0.0	123	31.7	0.0	2 058	32.9	1.7	845	52.7	1.7
Meigs County	144	0.0	22.9	36	0.0	16.7	1	0.0	0.0	44	22.7	0.0	39	41.0	0.0
Monroe County	965	23.1	13.4	95	17.9	10.5	135	13.3	2.2	654	45.9	4.3	530	46.6	3.4
Montgomery County	25 365	32.9	5.7	628	26.0	4.5	2 723	18.9	4.4	7 125	35.8	1.8	4 298	55.5	0.5
Moore County	218	30.7	11.5	11	0.0	0.0	9	0.0	0.0	0	X	X	50	0.0	0.0
Morgan County	439	7.1	3.0	18	0.0	27.8	48	12.5	0.0	140	54.3	10.7	153	34.0	24.8
Obion County	3 132	29.6	11.4	28	0.0	0.0	77	22.1	0.0	571	29.2	2.1	291	55.3	10.0
Overton County	42	57.1	0.0	68	7.4	0.0	65	43.1	0.0	156	20.5	21.8	70	22.9	0.0
Perry County	115	23.5	27.0	30	20.0	0.0	0	X	X	77	49.4	0.0	63	31.7	12.7
Pickett County	15	93.3	0.0	16	0.0	25.0	0	X	X	26	34.6	0.0	12	0.0	25.0
Polk County	22	9.1	0.0	30	26.7	10.0	12	50.0	0.0	98	11.2	0.0	194	9.8	24.7
Putnam County	1 038	20.0	9.6	118	17.8	13.6	650	17.5	0.0	1 947	33.8	2.6	658	46.8	5.2
Rhea County	561	30.8	7.3	103	51.5	0.0	50	24.0	0.0	402	41.0	4.7	388	46.6	7.0
Roane County	1 336	24.3	11.0	220	45.5	8.6	244	19.3	15.6	350	30.0	18.3	498	44.4	6.2
Robertson County	4 674	30.4	12.6	125	34.4	0.0	182	29.7	0.0	1 474	27.6	0.9	509	50.7	5.3
Rutherford County	17 114	30.3	6.3	561	24.2	2.1	3 322	25.9	3.6	5 030	32.1	2.6	2 432	44.0	4.5
Scott County	4	0.0	0.0	101	29.7	3.0	34	0.0	5.9	76	50.0	3.9	184	25.5	18.5
Sequatchie County	14	0.0	42.9	0	X	X	73	20.5	0.0	40	20.0	37.5	127	46.5	13.4
Sevier County	520	35.4	9.0	314	20.4	4.5	418	33.5	1.9	706	29.7	6.1	802	34.0	7.2
Shelby County	434 127	33.7	7.1	1 722	21.9	7.4	15 418	26.1	3.7	22 322	30.3	1.7	10 684	43.7	5.6
Smith County	424	17.9	15.8	132	37.9	5.3	77	28.6	0.0	139	25.2	14.4	122	42.6	20.5
Stewart County	77	24.7	18.2	80	41.3	2.5	157	8.9	8.9	108	60.2	11.1	172	26.7	15.1
Sullivan County	2 940	29.1	9.9	409	33.7	6.8	610	26.9	5.2	1 065	33.8	6.1	1 054	32.3	11.9
Sumner County	7 636	33.7	7.8	452	38.5	6.2	922	19.4	4.2	2 227	33.9	2.8	1 179	41.2	5.3
Tipton County	10 263	34.9	9.7	201	29.9	0.0	198	36.4	0.0	546	42.7	5.1	517	41.8	4.4
Trousdale County	784	19.4	22.1	17	0.0	0.0	18	0.0	0.0	152	43.4	0.0	57	36.8	0.0
Unicoi County	0	X	X	24	37.5	0.0	27	59.3	0.0	417	43.9	4.3	101	40.6	0.0
Union County	7	0.0	28.6	22	0.0	0.0	20	60.0	0.0	63	0.0	4.8	172	29.1	5.8
Van Buren County	13	0.0	38.5	18	11.1	5.6	0	X	X	20	0.0	0.0	19	0.0	21.1
Warren County	1 190	20.5	13.1	105	20.0	3.8	184	37.5	4.3	1 848	27.2	2.4	393	36.4	13.0
Washington County	3 895	25.1	8.9	291	12.0	2.4	739	21.9	2.3	1 516	30.1	5.0	1 245	39.6	4.7
Wayne County	1 123	3.1	2.6	39	15.4	0.0	29	27.6	0.0	147	25.2	17.0	107	28.0	33.6
Weakley County	2 497	23.1	7.2	70	8.6	12.9	467	13.5	0.0	320	23.8	1.3	291	48.1	5.5
White County	410	31.7	11.7	73	9.6	17.8	121	38.0	0.0	210	58.6	5.7	176	52.3	11.9
Williamson County	6 843	30.0	8.7	260	20.0	0.0	1 534	32.0	3.1	3 124	38.0	1.2	1 103	40.9	3.4
Wilson County	5 691	28.9	9.9	231	40.3	0.0	303	28.1	6.9	1 075	36.7	3.3	1 003	46.7	5.0
TEXAS	2 305 554	31.0	7.4	113 755	28.6	5.3	568 392	25.3	4.5	6 670 122	35.7	5.1	530 162	39.9	4.9
Anderson County	12 997	17.1	7.1	175	18.9	9.1	433	29.1	7.4	6 614	22.6	1.3	419	53.0	8.1
Andrews County	330	30.3	6.4	60	10.0	0.0	54	35.2	25.9	5 216	41.3	3.3	371	57.7	2.7
Angelina County	11 851	31.4	8.8	277	18.4	11.6	548	33.6	5.8	11 282	38.8	1.9	1 245	50.3	5.5
Aransas County	266	30.1	10.9	141	29.1	14.2	667	35.8	5.5	4 593	37.3	7.2	499	33.3	4.4
Archer County	11	63.6	0.0	41	7.3	4.9	16	12.5	0.0	405	42.7	2.5	126	45.2	9.5
Armstrong County	7	100.0	0.0	13	69.2	15.4	0	X	X	84	48.8	7.1	36	47.2	22.2
Atascosa County	117	17.9	14.5	332	25.0	7.2	209	25.4	12.9	22 673	36.6	7.7	1 333	34.1	6.7
Austin County	2 501	30.7	13.0	34	70.6	0.0	30	16.7	0.0	3 788	40.1	2.5	416	41.1	5.8
Bailey County	74	36.5	8.1	60	21.7	0.0	0	X	X	3 147	40.3	5.1	167	43.7	12.0
Bandera County	50	58.0	22.0	118	16.9	11.0	54	29.6	0.0	2 374	34.6	8.5	259	34.4	13.1
Bastrop County	4 933	29.9	14.3	360	10.8	11.4	218	14.2	6.0	13 848	36.8	3.5	1 272	36.4	7.0
Baylor County	66	16.7	43.9	52	0.0	25.0	42	35.7	0.0	374	36.4	11.8	101	53.5	20.8
Bee County	3 251	5.1	2.3	96	24.0	3.1	140	22.9	22.1	17 459	29.3	8.2	471	46.5	3.0
Bell County	47 467	33.8	3.7	1 675	30.1	3.4	7 378	21.0	5.0	39 695	37.3	3.5	9 827	53.4	2.4
Bexar County	97 705	29.5	8.8	9 547	28.6	5.5	23 716	21.5	6.2	757 004	33.2	7.3	53 986	38.9	5.9
Blanco County	65	13.8	7.7	73	24.7	0.0	9	0.0	0.0	1 287	35.3	5.7	91	44.0	13.2
Borden County	5	100.0	0.0	3	0.0	0.0	9	0.0	0.0	133	39.8	4.5	15	20.0	6.7
Bosque County	279	29.7	23.7	142	31.7	1.4	19	26.3	57.9	2 121	44.1	3.9	259	40.2	4.6
Bowie County	20 811	30.5	9.7	450	25.6	2.4	471	24.4	10.0	3 810	18.7	2.6	1 302	40.1	3.8
Brazoria County	20 311	27.4	6.1	1 297	30.5	2.7	4 805	29.4	5.3	55 034	36.6	3.3	5 516	40.6	5.0
Brazos County	16 238	35.6	6.9	523	17.8	4.0	6 354	17.3	1.5	27 225	32.1	2.8	2 842	32.5	2.7
Brewster County	82	0.0	0.0	57	28.1	0.0	31	32.3	0.0	3 876	29.9	10.5	288	38.9	2.1
Briscoe County	52	30.8	15.4	0	X	X	0	X	X	407	42.8	2.2	33	54.5	6.1
Brooks County	16	0.0	50.0	55	0.0	0.0	0	X	X	7 338	32.7	14.0	123	36.6	20.3
Brown County	1 491	31.1	8.0	339	33.0	0.0	210	35.7	0.0	5 735	40.5	4.4	494	41.5	13.2
Burleson County	2 494	34.0	15.6	76	38.2	19.7	14	0.0	42.9	2 411	37.6	4.1	319	53.0	6.3
Burnet County	438	18.7	6.4	204	26.0	5.4	85	9.4	21.2	5 040	39.9	2.2	527	39.8	12.7

[1] Hispanic or Latino persons may be of any race.

Table A-3. States and Counties — Age, Ethnicity, and Household Structure

STATE County	Total households	Family households (percent)						Nonfamily households (percent)						Percent of householders 65 years and over who live alone	Grandparents who are responsible for the care of their grandchildren
		Married-couple family households			Other family households			Two or more unrelated persons		Male living alone		Female living alone			
		Total	With children	Householder 65 years or over	Total	With children	Householder 65 years or over	Total	Householder 65 years or over	Total	Householder 65 years or over	Total	Householder 65 years or over		
	29	30	31	32	33	34	35	36	37	38	39	40	41	42	43
TENNESSEE— Cont'd															
Marshall County	10 289	58.1	26.0	9.1	14.9	8.3	2.6	3.0	0.1	11.1	1.9	12.8	7.4	44.1	342
Maury County	26 511	56.7	25.9	8.6	17.1	9.8	2.3	3.1	0.2	9.5	2.2	13.6	6.9	45.2	774
Meigs County	4 304	63.9	27.4	10.2	12.2	6.9	1.3	3.1	0.4	8.9	1.3	11.8	6.4	39.3	124
Monroe County	15 324	59.8	24.5	10.8	13.6	7.8	2.5	3.2	0.2	10.6	2.0	12.8	6.8	39.7	511
Montgomery County	48 365	59.9	31.4	6.2	14.9	10.1	1.8	5.0	0.1	9.4	1.2	10.8	4.6	41.6	982
Moore County	2 200	64.0	24.6	10.6	13.0	6.5	2.9	1.7	0.0	9.8	4.0	11.5	8.3	47.6	67
Morgan County	7 026	60.7	26.6	9.5	14.6	7.4	3.0	2.6	0.3	9.4	2.6	12.6	6.2	40.7	250
Obion County	13 171	57.6	23.5	10.2	14.0	8.0	2.1	2.8	0.3	10.1	2.6	15.6	9.8	49.5	336
Overton County	8 112	58.5	23.7	10.2	14.8	6.4	3.6	2.7	0.3	9.5	2.5	14.5	8.8	44.3	192
Perry County	3 049	60.6	25.6	12.4	11.7	5.8	1.8	3.1	0.3	10.9	4.0	13.8	9.6	48.6	94
Pickett County	2 088	61.9	22.2	14.4	9.1	4.3	1.6	1.7	0.0	10.8	3.6	16.5	10.1	46.1	24
Polk County	6 458	62.0	24.9	10.2	12.3	4.7	4.7	2.5	0.6	10.1	2.3	13.1	6.7	36.8	194
Putnam County	24 874	53.3	22.8	9.8	12.9	7.3	1.7	6.8	0.2	11.0	2.1	15.9	8.2	46.7	467
Rhea County	11 179	58.5	22.8	9.8	14.2	8.7	2.0	3.4	0.6	9.7	2.1	14.2	7.6	43.9	280
Roane County	21 214	58.9	21.8	11.8	13.2	6.9	2.5	2.9	0.1	9.6	2.3	15.3	9.1	44.2	541
Robertson County	19 907	64.3	29.2	9.5	13.8	8.0	1.6	3.3	0.2	7.3	1.8	11.2	6.1	41.3	767
Rutherford County	66 464	57.2	29.2	6.0	14.6	8.9	1.4	7.4	0.2	9.9	1.0	10.8	4.0	39.7	1 846
Scott County	8 221	58.8	27.6	7.5	14.9	8.6	2.4	2.2	0.1	9.7	2.7	14.6	7.8	51.4	171
Sequatchie County	4 486	60.6	24.9	8.3	15.4	10.1	1.5	1.9	0.1	10.9	2.8	11.2	6.2	47.7	121
Sevier County	28 484	59.9	23.7	10.3	13.6	7.6	2.2	4.5	0.2	8.8	1.7	13.2	6.1	38.1	715
Shelby County	338 560	43.6	20.7	6.4	24.5	14.3	3.0	5.0	0.3	11.6	1.8	15.3	6.0	44.6	11 808
Smith County	6 878	62.1	28.0	10.3	12.2	6.7	2.1	2.3	0.0	9.7	2.0	13.7	8.3	45.4	170
Stewart County	4 955	64.5	25.8	12.6	10.6	6.5	1.4	1.9	0.3	10.7	3.0	12.4	7.5	42.6	141
Sullivan County	63 602	57.9	22.1	11.5	13.0	6.8	2.4	2.8	0.3	10.4	2.2	16.0	9.1	44.3	1 394
Sumner County	48 952	62.1	28.1	8.8	14.0	8.3	1.5	3.7	0.2	8.5	1.3	11.8	5.9	40.7	1 569
Tipton County	18 189	60.9	28.9	8.1	17.9	10.8	1.9	2.6	0.2	7.6	1.9	10.9	5.8	43.0	819
Trousdale County	2 787	58.0	24.6	8.6	15.0	7.6	2.5	4.2	0.1	10.0	3.8	12.8	7.2	49.6	104
Unicoi County	7 544	56.7	20.5	12.0	13.2	6.2	2.5	2.6	0.0	11.5	3.1	16.0	10.8	49.2	199
Union County	6 711	63.5	27.8	8.6	14.3	7.7	1.8	2.1	0.2	10.9	1.7	9.3	5.4	39.8	204
Van Buren County	2 176	58.4	21.5	9.4	15.9	9.1	2.9	3.7	0.2	9.7	3.1	12.2	6.5	43.5	132
Warren County	15 216	56.2	23.5	10.3	15.4	9.0	2.0	3.5	0.3	10.7	2.0	14.2	8.6	45.5	355
Washington County	44 211	53.8	21.2	9.4	13.1	7.3	2.2	5.4	0.2	11.2	2.1	16.5	8.0	46.1	923
Wayne County	5 909	59.0	23.4	11.5	13.8	7.3	3.1	2.8	0.3	9.8	2.4	14.5	8.9	43.1	186
Weakley County	13 635	54.8	22.0	10.7	13.0	7.8	1.6	5.4	0.2	11.9	2.3	14.9	8.2	45.5	359
White County	9 220	59.7	23.2	12.0	14.2	7.3	2.7	2.7	0.1	9.6	2.3	13.8	8.7	42.6	228
Williamson County	44 824	70.3	37.9	7.0	10.0	5.7	1.5	3.1	0.2	6.8	1.0	9.8	3.8	35.6	601
Wilson County	32 842	65.5	30.2	8.2	13.4	8.0	1.6	3.1	0.2	7.8	1.3	10.2	4.9	38.6	835
TEXAS	7 397 294	55.0	28.0	8.0	16.4	9.5	2.1	4.9	0.3	10.6	1.8	13.0	5.6	41.5	257 074
Anderson County	15 673	55.9	24.6	11.5	16.9	10.3	2.8	2.5	0.3	8.6	2.1	16.1	9.7	44.7	516
Andrews County	4 594	65.6	34.6	12.0	11.6	7.4	1.2	1.0	0.0	7.6	2.1	14.1	8.0	43.4	132
Angelina County	28 743	58.4	28.2	10.3	15.9	8.8	2.2	2.9	0.3	9.2	2.2	13.6	7.4	42.9	1 261
Aransas County	9 177	56.3	19.6	15.7	14.1	8.4	2.6	4.4	0.9	12.1	4.5	13.2	7.6	38.5	271
Archer County	3 350	66.7	31.0	12.9	9.2	5.9	1.1	2.4	0.2	9.5	2.9	12.3	8.2	43.7	104
Armstrong County	809	70.5	29.5	15.1	7.3	4.8	1.2	1.1	0.2	6.4	2.2	14.7	10.4	43.2	8
Atascosa County	12 828	61.6	32.6	9.8	16.9	9.3	2.5	2.6	0.4	8.7	2.5	10.3	6.2	40.5	754
Austin County	8 736	61.6	28.4	12.0	12.7	6.7	2.5	3.0	0.2	9.6	2.9	13.1	8.4	43.4	207
Bailey County	2 337	66.5	32.0	12.8	9.1	6.3	1.0	1.9	0.0	8.2	2.7	14.4	9.7	47.4	133
Bandera County	7 052	62.2	23.2	13.9	10.6	6.7	2.2	4.1	0.4	11.0	4.3	12.1	6.5	39.2	207
Bastrop County	20 067	59.8	27.9	8.7	14.1	8.3	1.8	4.7	0.4	10.2	2.4	11.2	5.5	42.0	722
Baylor County	1 789	55.6	20.0	16.6	10.2	5.8	2.1	0.7	0.3	13.0	4.0	20.5	15.1	50.1	50
Bee County	9 071	52.5	25.4	10.8	20.5	13.1	3.6	3.3	0.5	10.4	3.2	13.2	6.6	39.7	440
Bell County	85 382	57.8	30.2	7.0	15.1	10.6	1.3	4.9	0.2	10.8	1.5	11.5	5.0	43.0	2 401
Bexar County	489 252	56.1	26.1	8.1	19.5	11.1	2.8	5.0	0.4	10.5	1.9	13.4	5.5	39.9	18 066
Blanco County	3 312	61.7	24.1	14.0	10.7	6.7	1.4	3.6	0.5	11.1	2.6	12.9	7.2	38.0	70
Borden County	293	65.2	25.9	14.0	10.2	6.8	1.4	2.0	0.0	12.6	3.4	9.9	5.8	37.5	6
Bosque County	6 711	62.8	24.4	15.2	9.8	4.6	2.5	2.1	0.3	10.8	3.8	14.5	9.8	43.0	193
Bowie County	33 052	52.3	22.0	10.2	18.8	11.4	2.5	3.0	0.2	9.6	2.4	16.3	8.7	46.4	1 319
Brazoria County	82 020	63.1	32.7	7.8	14.4	8.9	1.8	3.5	0.2	8.8	1.7	10.3	4.8	39.9	2 887
Brazos County	55 188	43.0	21.8	5.5	12.7	7.0	1.2	18.8	0.1	12.4	0.9	13.1	4.1	42.7	1 278
Brewster County	3 674	48.1	20.4	10.3	13.0	7.2	1.9	6.2	0.5	14.5	2.9	18.1	8.6	47.5	96
Briscoe County	721	60.6	23.7	14.1	10.7	5.8	3.2	1.2	0.6	10.1	2.5	17.3	12.9	46.3	42
Brooks County	2 720	51.1	24.2	11.4	26.3	15.6	5.3	1.4	0.3	7.9	3.2	13.2	9.4	42.6	178
Brown County	14 344	56.1	23.4	12.3	14.1	9.0	1.9	3.4	0.5	10.4	2.7	15.9	10.2	46.6	443
Burleson County	6 362	58.3	23.6	12.5	14.1	8.1	2.4	2.7	0.9	9.9	2.9	14.9	9.6	44.1	254
Burnet County	13 150	62.2	23.5	16.4	11.4	7.0	1.4	4.0	0.6	8.8	2.0	13.6	8.6	36.6	243

Table A-3. States and Counties — Age, Ethnicity, and Household Structure

STATE County	Households with Non-Hispanic White householder — Number of households	Percent that are family households	Households with Black or African American householder — Number of households	Percent that are family households	Households with American Indian and Alaska Native householder — Number of households	Percent that are family households	Households with Asian, Hawaiian, and Pacific Islander householder — Number of households	Percent that are family households	Households with Hispanic or Latino[1] householder — Number of households	Percent that are family households	Foreign-born population — Percent of total population that is foreign-born	Place of birth (percent) — Europe	Asia	Latin America	Percent in non-English speaking households — Linguistically isolated	Not linguistically isolated
	44	45	46	47	48	49	50	51	52	53	54	55	56	57	58	59
TENNESSEE— Cont'd																
Marshall County	9 233	73.7	776	66.4	9	100.0	6	0.0	182	77.5	1.4	0.1	0.0	1.2	1.2	4.1
Maury County	21 885	74.3	3 832	69.7	89	95.5	52	71.2	527	81.2	2.1	0.3	0.2	1.5	1.0	6.1
Meigs County	4 181	76.8	76	52.6	17	82.4	1	100.0	21	14.3	0.6	0.4	0.0	0.2	0.1	6.5
Monroe County	14 612	73.6	371	65.5	27	70.4	48	35.4	134	88.8	1.2	0.2	0.3	0.6	0.4	4.7
Montgomery County......	35 913	75.0	9 029	74.3	250	66.4	503	65.2	1 962	79.7	4.4	1.5	1.5	1.1	0.8	14.5
Moore County	2 096	76.1	71	100.0	0	X	5	100.0	0	X	1.0	0.4	0.2	0.0	0.0	2.1
Morgan County	6 942	75.3	0	X	7	100.0	0	X	27	92.6	0.4	0.1	0.1	0.1	0.0	4.2
Obion County	11 610	72.4	1 268	65.5	24	29.2	21	100.0	172	57.6	1.3	0.1	0.1	1.1	0.8	4.8
Overton County	7 987	73.0	9	100.0	28	75.0	16	100.0	56	100.0	0.5	0.4	0.1	0.2	0.4	5.8
Perry County	2 942	72.5	54	51.9	14	28.6	0	X	20	100.0	0.5	0.1	0.0	0.2	0.0	5.9
Pickett County	2 065	70.9	1	100.0	4	100.0	0	X	10	100.0	0.3	0.3	0.0	0.0	0.3	3.5
Polk County	6 322	74.4	9	100.0	7	57.1	7	X	33	48.5	0.8	0.2	0.1	0.5	0.2	5.2
Putnam County	23 570	66.4	372	64.2	45	100.0	211	55.9	514	61.3	3.4	0.4	0.9	1.9	1.9	6.1
Rhea County	10 697	72.9	262	68.7	15	100.0	5	100.0	87	81.6	1.3	0.3	0.2	0.7	0.5	4.9
Roane County	20 229	72.4	598	62.5	71	84.5	73	68.5	112	67.9	1.2	0.5	0.3	0.2	0.2	3.9
Robertson County	17 728	78.9	1 703	71.2	35	85.7	37	100.0	303	75.9	2.5	0.3	0.2	1.9	1.8	6.1
Rutherford County	57 524	71.9	5 959	69.7	209	78.0	938	86.5	1 339	71.1	3.6	0.5	1.6	1.3	1.5	8.0
Scott County	8 059	73.8	0	X	43	44.2	6	100.0	26	88.5	0.4	0.1	0.3	0.1	0.0	3.9
Sequatchie County.......	4 426	76.1	0	X	0	X	18	100.0	14	28.6	1.2	0.1	0.8	0.2	0.2	4.1
Sevier County	27 668	73.8	141	56.7	124	48.4	116	89.7	202	64.4	1.6	0.5	0.4	0.5	0.6	4.9
Shelby County	174 142	65.1	150 421	71.1	781	64.9	4 965	76.3	5 715	75.3	3.8	0.5	1.5	1.5	1.6	9.0
Smith County...............	6 532	74.4	206	74.8	36	91.7	23	60.9	48	45.8	0.9	0.2	0.1	0.4	0.1	3.9
Stewart County	4 741	75.4	40	82.5	21	100.0	83	42.2	14	100.0	1.7	0.7	0.9	0.0	0.2	6.9
Sullivan County	61 465	71.0	1 134	58.8	122	85.2	172	79.1	293	76.1	1.3	0.5	0.4	0.2	0.3	4.4
Sumner County	45 194	76.0	2 588	78.5	132	69.7	302	69.2	516	84.3	2.4	0.5	0.6	0.9	0.8	6.5
Tipton County	14 461	79.0	3 431	78.3	61	82.0	46	69.6	109	71.6	0.8	0.3	0.1	0.3	0.1	5.2
Trousdale County	2 438	74.0	314	65.6	0	X	9	100.0	14	21.4	1.7	0.2	0.2	1.2	1.1	8.1
Unicoi County	7 368	69.9	0	X	8	100.0	6	100.0	136	70.6	1.4	0.3	0.1	1.1	0.5	4.0
Union County	6 584	78.3	0	X	18	88.9	3	33.3	34	47.1	0.3	0.1	0.1	0.0	0.1	3.4
Van Buren County........	2 146	74.3	0	X	13	46.2	0	X	6	100.0	0.2	0.2	0.0	0.0	0.0	2.6
Warren County	14 011	72.2	499	62.6	30	60.2	16	50.0	507	77.7	3.7	0.3	0.3	3.0	2.8	8.4
Washington County.......	41 556	66.9	1 513	61.4	134	71.6	183	83.1	465	78.1	1.9	0.4	0.6	0.6	0.5	5.3
Wayne County	5 736	73.2	37	51.4	23	60.9	7	100.0	56	58.9	0.4	0.0	0.1	0.2	0.1	3.6
Weakley County	12 346	68.8	924	61.0	47	83.0	164	53.0	107	40.2	2.0	0.2	1.3	0.3	0.9	4.5
White County...............	8 902	73.6	181	74.6	21	100.0	38	97.4	48	89.6	0.8	0.2	0.3	0.1	0.2	4.0
Williamson County	40 936	80.2	2 346	79.1	57	91.2	436	84.6	743	80.3	3.9	0.8	1.0	1.0	1.0	8.3
Wilson County	29 949	79.3	2 129	73.7	82	85.4	71	85.9	334	79.3	1.4	0.4	0.3	0.4	0.4	5.3
TEXAS....................	4 478 556	67.5	842 713	68.6	39 513	72.6	179 266	74.9	1 794 271	82.5	13.9	0.7	2.2	10.4	8.1	30.6
Anderson County	12 153	72.8	2 438	66.9	77	68.8	102	84.3	845	89.3	3.2	0.1	0.5	2.5	2.6	10.6
Andrews County	2 962	72.4	122	74.6	26	23.1	18	100.0	1 464	87.4	10.6	0.1	0.2	10.3	5.8	35.0
Angelina County	21 689	73.4	3 898	69.3	100	74.0	158	74.7	2 697	89.3	6.9	0.2	0.5	6.1	3.4	15.0
Aransas County	7 369	67.1	123	69.9	38	89.5	176	88.1	1 372	84.3	5.7	0.8	2.1	2.7	3.4	23.8
Archer County	3 189	75.8	2	100.0	14	85.7	6	66.7	110	81.8	2.3	0.2	0.2	1.7	1.5	6.6
Armstrong County	774	77.4	0	X	0	X	0	X	20	75.0	0.9	0.2	0.0	0.7	0.3	6.6
Atascosa County	6 091	74.0	50	36.0	135	81.5	53	94.3	6 429	82.7	5.1	0.2	0.3	4.5	7.8	53.7
Austin County	6 832	72.3	822	69.6	6	66.7	18	100.0	958	92.2	7.3	0.3	0.1	6.8	4.3	19.2
Bailey County	1 431	69.4	34	0.0	25	100.0	0	X	834	88.6	13.1	0.1	0.1	12.9	7.1	40.0
Bandera County	6 198	72.1	21	90.5	40	70.0	7	57.1	733	81.2	3.9	1.6	0.2	1.9	1.8	19.7
Bastrop County	14 867	72.0	1 663	65.4	114	92.1	58	87.9	3 105	86.7	8.1	0.6	0.4	6.9	4.5	25.2
Baylor County	1 580	65.8	40	15.0	32	81.3	9	100.0	120	86.7	2.0	0.4	0.2	0.7	1.0	14.1
Bee County	4 174	67.7	204	61.8	37	91.9	49	100.0	4 528	78.4	2.0	0.2	0.4	1.2	9.2	51.2
Bell County..................	53 180	71.2	17 048	73.0	570	75.6	2 053	73.0	11 451	80.1	7.3	1.7	2.1	3.2	2.4	24.8
Bexar County	211 245	65.2	36 385	68.0	3 339	71.5	8 009	66.7	227 172	77.6	10.9	0.8	1.4	8.4	7.0	49.7
Blanco County	2 866	71.2	24	91.7	29	82.8	9	11.1	346	81.8	5.0	0.4	0.1	4.5	3.3	20.7
Borden County	254	74.0	0	X	0	X	4	100.0	32	81.3	4.5	0.0	0.5	4.0	6.5	16.9
Bosque County............	5 960	71.7	109	68.8	50	82.0	0	X	548	84.9	4.4	0.4	0.1	3.8	2.2	14.2
Bowie County	24 626	72.0	7 331	66.6	175	63.4	114	77.2	510	87.5	1.5	0.2	0.3	0.8	0.6	7.0
Brazoria County	59 537	75.5	5 813	73.7	336	75.6	1 307	86.8	14 121	86.8	8.5	0.6	1.5	6.1	4.4	24.3
Brazos County	39 218	51.1	5 284	70.0	181	63.5	2 473	51.9	7 585	71.1	10.3	0.9	3.6	5.3	5.3	21.5
Brewster County..........	2 283	55.0	34	73.5	36	66.7	14	42.9	1 271	74.4	6.9	0.0	0.5	5.6	7.0	48.4
Briscoe County............	574	70.7	22	63.6	0	X	0	X	119	77.3	4.9	0.0	0.0	4.9	4.5	16.6
Brooks County	271	60.5	8	100.0	26	100.0	0	X	2 437	79.2	6.1	0.5	0.0	5.5	14.4	77.2
Brown County	12 040	69.9	537	57.2	121	54.5	62	69.4	1 536	82.2	3.1	0.2	0.3	2.4	2.0	15.4
Burleson County	4 717	71.4	874	67.8	34	58.8	9	66.7	682	87.2	3.0	0.3	0.1	2.6	2.8	19.4
Burnet County	11 612	72.6	97	73.2	84	81.0	27	100.0	1 241	85.3	5.4	0.4	0.3	4.4	3.1	16.0

[1]Hispanic or Latino persons may be of any race.

STATE/ County code	MSA/PMSA/ NECMA code[1]	STATE County	Population by age (percent)									Non-Hispanic White		
													Age (percent)	
			Total population	Under 5 years	5 to 17 years	18 to 24 years	25 to 44 years	45 to 64 years	65 years and over	Median age	+/− U.S. percent under 18 years	+/− U.S. percent 65 years and over	Total population	Under 18 years	65 years and over
			1	2	3	4	5	6	7	8	9	10	11	12	13
		TEXAS—Cont'd													
48 055	0640	Caldwell County	32 194	7.5	20.9	8.5	29.7	20.8	12.7	34.4	2.7	0.3	15 790	22.8	17.6
48 057	...	Calhoun County	20 647	7.6	21.0	8.4	27.5	22.2	13.4	35.3	2.9	1.0	10 797	22.4	19.0
48 059	...	Callahan County	12 905	5.4	20.7	6.8	24.9	25.0	17.2	39.8	0.4	4.8	11 857	25.0	18.0
48 061	1240	Cameron County	335 227	9.4	24.3	10.5	27.2	17.4	11.2	29.0	8.0	−1.2	48 551	16.9	32.4
48 063	...	Camp County	11 549	6.4	20.3	8.5	25.4	23.7	15.6	36.9	1.0	3.2	7 495	22.5	20.0
48 065	...	Carson County	6 516	5.8	22.1	6.1	26.5	24.2	15.4	38.9	2.2	3.0	5 877	26.6	16.5
48 067	...	Cass County	30 438	6.0	18.9	7.6	24.8	25.0	17.7	40.0	−0.8	5.3	23 545	22.5	18.7
48 069	...	Castro County	8 285	8.6	24.5	8.1	25.5	21.1	12.2	32.3	7.4	−0.2	3 626	23.6	21.4
48 071	3360	Chambers County	26 031	7.0	21.9	8.3	29.8	24.1	8.9	35.1	3.2	−3.5	20 298	27.4	9.6
48 073	...	Cherokee County	46 659	7.0	19.3	9.4	27.4	21.8	15.1	36.0	0.6	2.7	32 385	23.0	18.5
48 075	...	Childress County	7 688	4.9	17.3	10.5	31.2	21.0	15.0	36.6	−3.5	2.6	4 899	20.6	21.9
48 077	...	Clay County	11 006	5.9	19.0	6.6	26.7	25.9	16.0	40.2	−0.8	3.6	10 343	23.9	16.7
48 079	...	Cochran County	3 730	7.2	24.3	8.5	24.6	20.9	14.4	35.1	5.8	2.0	1 827	24.8	22.1
48 081	...	Coke County	3 864	4.0	20.3	7.9	20.3	23.6	23.9	43.3	−1.4	11.5	3 112	20.0	27.5
48 083	...	Coleman County	9 235	5.6	17.9	7.5	21.3	24.6	23.0	43.0	−2.2	10.6	7 622	21.0	26.3
48 085	1920	Collin County	491 675	8.6	20.1	7.2	38.4	20.6	5.2	32.9	3.0	−7.2	374 050	27.5	6.1
48 087	...	Collingsworth County	3 206	6.6	19.8	6.3	22.6	22.7	22.0	40.6	0.7	9.6	2 287	21.3	27.3
48 089	...	Colorado County	20 390	6.1	19.4	8.8	23.8	23.2	18.6	39.3	−0.2	6.2	13 152	21.3	23.6
48 091	7240	Comal County	78 021	6.2	19.4	7.0	27.6	25.0	14.7	39.0	−0.1	2.3	58 179	23.0	17.6
48 093	...	Comanche County	14 026	6.4	18.9	7.6	23.2	23.8	20.1	40.3	−0.4	7.7	10 788	21.0	25.2
48 095	...	Concho County	3 966	3.4	12.7	10.2	38.4	21.2	14.0	36.0	−9.6	1.6	2 247	16.1	20.9
48 097	...	Cooke County	36 363	7.0	20.5	8.9	26.1	22.7	14.8	36.7	1.8	2.4	30 798	25.1	17.0
48 099	3810	Coryell County	74 978	7.9	18.3	18.1	36.5	13.5	5.6	27.8	0.5	−6.8	45 283	24.0	8.3
48 101	...	Cottle County	1 904	5.0	19.2	5.3	21.3	23.6	25.6	43.9	−1.5	13.2	1 360	18.1	32.4
48 103	...	Crane County	3 996	6.8	24.8	8.5	26.2	22.9	10.8	34.2	5.9	−1.6	2 087	24.6	17.3
48 105	...	Crockett County	4 099	6.4	22.6	6.1	25.9	26.3	12.7	37.2	3.3	0.3	1 816	22.7	18.0
48 107	...	Crosby County	7 072	7.7	23.0	8.5	24.5	20.9	15.4	34.3	5.0	3.0	3 312	21.9	25.4
48 109	...	Culberson County	2 975	7.4	24.6	8.1	26.6	22.7	10.6	32.8	6.3	−1.8	746	19.0	18.4
48 111	...	Dallam County	6 222	8.6	23.4	8.5	27.9	21.2	10.4	31.4	6.3	−2.0	4 245	29.0	12.1
48 113	1920	Dallas County	2 218 899	8.1	19.7	10.6	34.8	18.8	8.0	31.1	2.1	−4.4	983 516	20.3	13.4
48 115	...	Dawson County	14 985	5.7	19.8	8.1	33.2	18.8	14.4	35.6	−0.2	2.0	6 375	19.6	24.6
48 117	...	Deaf Smith County........	18 561	8.7	24.7	9.8	26.1	18.9	11.8	30.6	7.7	−0.6	7 310	22.0	21.6
48 119	...	Delta County	5 327	5.2	20.2	6.6	26.8	23.2	17.9	38.8	−0.3	5.5	4 607	24.4	18.8
48 121	1920	Denton County	432 976	8.1	19.5	11.1	37.2	19.0	5.0	31.0	1.9	−7.4	328 989	26.2	5.9
48 123	...	DeWitt County	20 013	5.6	21.2	6.5	27.3	23.2	19.3	40.1	−1.9	6.9	12 146	20.3	24.2
48 125	...	Dickens County	2 762	4.6	13.8	11.4	30.3	21.1	18.8	39.2	−7.3	6.4	1 874	16.8	24.8
48 127	...	Dimmit County	10 248	8.1	24.9	8.6	26.3	19.1	12.9	31.6	7.3	0.5	1 318	21.4	23.0
48 129	...	Donley County	3 828	4.7	17.9	9.9	20.7	25.2	21.7	42.8	−3.1	9.3	3 387	21.1	23.9
48 131	...	Duval County	13 120	7.4	22.1	9.3	26.2	21.2	14.0	33.8	3.8	1.6	1 452	20.1	20.7
48 133	...	Eastland County	18 297	6.0	17.5	10.0	22.3	23.5	20.7	41.3	−2.2	8.3	15 724	22.0	23.3
48 135	5800	Ector County	121 123	7.9	22.5	10.4	28.0	20.5	10.7	32.0	4.7	−1.7	61 834	22.9	16.2
48 137	...	Edwards County	2 162	6.0	22.3	6.1	23.2	26.2	16.2	39.0	2.6	3.8	1 170	22.0	22.7
48 139	1920	Ellis County	111 360	7.6	22.3	9.3	30.0	21.3	9.2	33.2	4.4	−3.2	79 608	27.5	11.0
48 141	2320	El Paso County	679 622	8.6	23.3	10.5	29.5	18.4	9.8	30.0	6.2	−2.6	115 394	20.7	18.0
48 143	...	Erath County	33 001	6.4	18.2	16.7	25.9	19.4	13.4	31.4	−1.1	1.0	27 197	21.4	15.8
48 145	...	Falls County	18 576	5.8	21.8	7.7	26.9	21.0	16.8	36.5	1.9	4.4	10 352	21.2	22.3
48 147	...	Fannin County	31 242	5.9	17.4	9.1	28.5	23.1	16.0	38.0	−2.4	3.6	26 369	23.1	17.6
48 149	...	Fayette County	21 804	5.1	18.0	7.3	23.2	24.4	22.1	42.6	−2.6	9.7	17 395	20.5	25.1
48 151	...	Fisher County	4 344	5.7	18.3	6.1	23.1	23.9	22.9	42.9	−1.7	10.5	3 246	21.0	27.0
48 153	...	Floyd County	7 771	7.6	23.7	7.3	25.2	20.2	16.0	34.8	5.6	3.6	3 885	21.5	26.7
48 155	...	Foard County	1 622	5.8	20.2	5.2	23.3	22.3	23.2	41.7	0.3	10.8	1 294	23.3	26.7
48 157	3360	Fort Bend County	354 452	7.6	24.5	7.5	32.7	22.2	5.6	33.3	6.4	−6.8	163 771	28.9	7.7
48 159	...	Franklin County	9 458	5.9	18.6	7.6	24.3	25.2	18.3	40.3	−1.2	5.9	8 137	22.4	20.6
48 161	...	Freestone County	17 867	4.9	18.4	9.1	28.0	23.3	16.4	37.8	−2.4	4.0	12 827	22.3	18.1
48 163	...	Frio County	16 252	7.6	21.1	10.9	30.9	18.3	11.1	30.7	3.0	−1.3	3 386	18.4	19.7
48 165	...	Gaines County	14 467	8.1	26.6	9.9	27.0	18.2	10.2	29.7	9.0	−2.2	8 754	31.9	13.2
48 167	2920	Galveston County	250 158	6.9	19.7	8.8	30.4	23.2	11.0	35.9	0.9	−1.4	157 545	23.2	12.8
48 169	...	Garza County	4 872	6.6	21.4	7.7	29.4	20.8	14.1	35.1	2.3	1.7	2 724	22.5	21.6
48 171	...	Gillespie County	20 814	5.0	16.5	5.3	21.3	26.7	25.3	46.3	−4.2	12.9	17 199	18.4	29.7
48 173	...	Glasscock County	1 406	7.8	26.3	6.5	27.7	23.0	8.7	33.5	8.4	−3.7	964	30.4	11.7
48 175	...	Goliad County	6 928	6.2	19.8	7.5	24.0	24.8	17.6	40.2	0.3	5.2	4 116	21.2	20.5
48 177	...	Gonzales County	18 628	6.8	21.1	8.7	25.9	20.5	16.9	36.3	2.2	4.5	9 465	20.7	24.2
48 179	...	Gray County	22 744	5.8	18.0	8.4	27.6	22.0	18.2	38.9	−1.9	5.8	17 683	21.9	21.9
48 181	7640	Grayson County	110 595	6.5	18.7	9.4	27.6	22.8	15.1	37.2	−0.5	2.7	93 213	23.5	16.7
48 183	4420	Gregg County	111 379	6.9	19.8	10.4	28.1	21.3	13.5	35.0	1.0	1.1	76 866	23.2	16.1
48 185	...	Grimes County	23 552	5.9	18.8	7.0	30.9	23.6	13.8	38.1	−1.0	1.4	14 766	22.8	16.0

[1]MSA = Metropolitan Statistical Area. PMSA = Primary MSA. NECMA = New England County Metropolitan Area. See the Appendix A for explanation of these concepts. See Appendix B for list of metropolitan areas identified by type, with component counties.

Table A-3. States and Counties — Age, Ethnicity, and Household Structure

STATE County	Black or African American Total population	Under 18 years	65 years and over	American Indian and Alaska Native Total population	Under 18 years	65 years and over	Asian, Hawaiian, and Pacific Islander Total population	Under 18 years	65 years and over	Hispanic or Latino[1] Total population	Under 18 years	65 years and over	Two or more races Total population	Under 18 years	65 years and over
	14	15	16	17	18	19	20	21	22	23	24	25	26	27	28
TEXAS—Cont'd															
Caldwell County	2 658	24.9	11.1	164	28.0	11.6	183	31.7	17.5	13 072	35.1	7.4	890	47.1	2.5
Calhoun County	441	20.2	17.2	126	36.5	5.6	723	37.9	1.2	8 405	35.8	7.4	473	35.3	1.5
Callahan County	31	12.9	16.1	80	40.0	2.5	30	20.0	23.3	803	42.8	6.2	161	42.2	14.9
Cameron County	1 539	37.5	4.5	1 442	32.9	10.3	1 553	27.5	6.0	283 156	36.7	7.6	7 683	36.1	8.5
Camp County	2 189	28.0	13.7	63	60.3	0.0	97	45.4	0.0	1 669	41.2	0.0	149	43.0	1.3
Carson County	28	25.0	10.7	84	29.8	11.9	33	24.2	0.0	444	43.2	4.3	92	34.8	3.3
Cass County	5 804	30.8	16.0	97	49.5	7.2	118	55.9	5.1	494	46.2	0.2	471	41.0	10.0
Castro County	293	36.9	10.9	98	58.2	0.0	36	77.8	0.0	4 294	40.5	4.7	213	55.4	0.5
Chambers County	2 508	27.2	11.0	94	34.0	2.1	89	29.2	10.1	2 836	40.0	1.9	355	44.5	4.8
Cherokee County	7 689	29.9	11.6	126	10.3	22.2	88	18.2	0.0	6 183	39.3	1.9	462	36.1	9.3
Childress County	1 105	16.5	1.4	19	36.8	0.0	48	41.7	14.6	1 562	30.0	4.0	162	61.1	5.6
Clay County	51	62.7	0.0	112	34.8	3.6	6	0.0	0.0	338	47.9	3.6	189	24.9	11.6
Cochran County	159	28.3	15.7	40	20.0	10.0	0	X	X	1 680	39.2	6.4	93	35.5	7.5
Coke County	44	86.4	6.8	21	28.6	38.1	1	0.0	0.0	655	39.8	8.5	49	34.7	0.0
Coleman County	172	29.1	7.6	102	43.1	12.7	1	0.0	0.0	1 240	36.9	6.9	210	26.2	6.2
Collin County	22 811	30.9	2.7	2 521	21.6	2.9	33 854	28.4	3.0	50 262	33.9	1.6	11 117	46.2	3.0
Collingsworth County	150	29.3	19.3	48	31.3	16.7	20	45.0	10.0	660	39.8	6.5	64	48.4	6.3
Colorado County	3 128	29.4	16.4	54	33.3	11.1	39	0.0	0.0	4 029	37.1	3.9	254	28.7	6.7
Comal County	664	22.4	8.6	442	20.4	3.8	486	31.7	9.5	17 633	33.8	6.1	1 367	43.7	3.8
Comanche County	91	9.9	0.0	75	36.0	5.3	58	32.8	6.9	2 954	41.4	2.9	203	40.9	2.5
Concho County	37	10.8	0.0	17	17.6	5.9	16	0.0	0.0	1 652	16.4	5.1	63	27.0	3.2
Cooke County	1 093	39.2	6.2	386	35.8	1.6	99	14.1	0.0	3 570	41.8	1.5	616	47.4	5.7
Coryell County	15 942	25.6	1.2	604	40.2	0.5	1 813	24.3	5.1	9 391	31.3	1.3	3 183	55.7	1.8
Cottle County	181	43.6	12.2	0	X	X	0	X	X	360	38.9	6.4	18	50.0	16.7
Crane County	82	43.9	14.6	34	26.5	0.0	38	0.0	0.0	1 762	40.1	3.1	125	37.6	3.2
Crockett County	5	0.0	100.0	29	0.0	0.0	8	25.0	0.0	2 258	34.5	8.4	62	80.6	0.0
Crosby County	275	26.5	21.8	20	15.0	0.0	18	0.0	0.0	3 454	39.9	5.3	118	25.4	5.1
Culberson County	12	75.0	0.0	13	7.7	38.5	25	28.0	0.0	2 152	36.7	7.7	59	25.4	18.6
Dallam County	76	39.5	9.2	82	18.3	14.6	14	100.0	0.0	1 772	39.2	6.4	116	40.5	0.0
Dallas County	447 715	32.0	5.8	11 757	28.1	4.9	88 433	25.0	4.2	663 125	36.3	2.1	61 251	39.3	3.4
Dawson County	1 306	10.2	8.6	22	0.0	0.0	52	0.0	9.6	7 206	33.8	6.7	287	42.9	4.5
Deaf Smith County	386	37.6	19.9	101	12.9	17.8	128	18.0	11.7	10 711	41.3	4.8	386	41.2	2.8
Delta County	503	30.0	11.7	31	0.0	0.0	20	20.0	20.0	43	11.6	20.9	142	57.0	9.9
Denton County	25 126	30.9	2.5	2 825	22.1	5.1	17 312	26.4	2.8	52 365	34.5	1.6	10 082	41.6	2.3
DeWitt County	2 108	23.0	15.4	117	21.4	6.0	42	28.6	33.3	5 465	31.0	10.7	443	37.2	7.9
Dickens County	217	5.5	3.2	20	45.0	0.0	22	9.1	0.0	646	27.2	7.0	17	23.5	11.8
Dimmit County	130	37.7	7.7	00	24.2	0.0	30	0.0	0.0	8 743	34.9	11.5	226	38.1	12.8
Donley County	155	40.0	6.5	71	33.8	5.6	7	0.0	0.0	222	29.7	3.2	28	67.9	0.0
Duval County	51	0.0	0.0	36	19.4	13.9	8	0.0	0.0	11 566	30.7	13.2	462	35.9	14.9
Eastland County	255	3.9	4.7	106	25.5	0.0	12	0.0	0.0	1 967	36.1	4.7	364	35.2	5.2
Ector County	5 405	33.5	10.9	785	25.9	8.9	880	31.0	5.7	51 344	39.1	4.1	3 779	41.7	7.8
Edwards County	11	54.5	0.0	2	0.0	0.0	10	20.0	0.0	986	35.9	8.6	46	30.4	17.4
Ellis County	9 612	31.7	9.5	695	25.8	2.9	456	26.3	6.6	20 317	39.5	2.4	1 911	43.4	4.4
El Paso County	20 552	29.5	7.4	4 932	33.5	8.1	7 510	23.4	8.2	531 967	34.5	8.1	20 968	35.6	8.1
Erath County	221	21.3	1.8	223	21.1	9.0	267	33.3	0.7	4 943	42.2	1.6	517	37.7	3.9
Falls County	5 100	31.5	12.2	102	35.3	0.0	22	0.0	0.0	2 948	42.7	5.3	282	65.2	11.3
Fannin County	2 451	19.1	8.3	285	24.9	9.1	85	15.3	7.1	1 769	31.6	2.9	445	31.2	11.2
Fayette County	1 476	27.6	20.2	87	21.8	24.1	30	26.7	0.0	2 759	37.1	3.7	245	54.7	11.0
Fisher County	110	21.8	10.0	25	48.0	0.0	7	28.6	0.0	943	34.1	11.1	66	30.3	7.6
Floyd County	198	36.9	3.0	69	55.1	0.0	3	0.0	0.0	3 577	42.0	5.6	205	27.8	0.0
Foard County	40	25.0	17.5	4	0.0	0.0	5	40.0	0.0	263	39.2	6.8	28	39.3	21.4
Fort Bend County	70 812	34.2	3.4	1 328	41.9	4.6	38 963	30.4	4.7	74 786	36.8	3.8	9 078	41.8	3.8
Franklin County	380	25.0	11.1	73	37.0	2.7	8	0.0	0.0	830	44.0	1.4	61	39.3	0.0
Freestone County	3 301	21.7	16.4	53	22.6	15.1	36	25.0	0.0	1 507	32.1	2.6	209	54.1	4.3
Frio County	760	3.3	0.0	85	42.4	0.0	68	11.8	7.4	12 013	33.3	9.4	337	36.5	7.1
Gaines County	534	39.7	10.9	60	6.7	0.0	7	28.6	0.0	5 178	40.0	4.8	252	40.9	8.7
Galveston County	38 095	30.6	11.1	1 207	28.7	7.3	5 334	25.6	5.7	45 153	34.8	5.4	5 875	42.9	4.6
Garza County	302	47.7	11.3	0	X	X	0	X	X	1 810	32.4	3.4	109	62.4	7.3
Gillespie County	34	29.4	23.5	58	19.0	10.3	92	28.3	0.0	3 328	37.6	3.7	201	26.4	17.9
Glasscock County	1	0.0	0.0	4	0.0	0.0	0	X	X	420	41.7	2.4	29	69.0	0.0
Goliad County	336	32.4	16.4	11	9.1	0.0	4	50.0	0.0	2 404	33.7	13.2	233	50.2	10.3
Gonzales County	1 600	29.9	18.3	44	65.9	9.1	28	39.3	0.0	7 429	36.4	7.3	452	44.2	9.1
Gray County	1 300	14.9	6.2	158	21.5	17.7	90	7.8	0.0	2 953	37.4	3.0	769	40.2	8.7
Grayson County	6 550	32.0	8.9	1 446	27.4	7.7	694	28.0	6.8	7 071	38.3	2.8	2 345	35.5	7.3
Gregg County	22 518	32.3	9.9	497	28.2	8.5	693	30.2	2.5	9 873	40.1	2.2	1 673	42.0	6.8
Grimes County	4 689	25.9	13.4	70	5.7	24.3	107	16.8	6.5	3 827	30.8	5.3	369	37.9	7.3

[1]Hispanic or Latino persons may be of any race.

Items 14—28

Table A-3. States and Counties — Age, Ethnicity, and Household Structure

STATE County	Total households	Family households (percent)						Nonfamily households (percent)						Percent of householders 65 years and over who live alone	Grandparents who are responsible for the care of their grandchildren
		Married-couple family households			Other family households			Two or more unrelated persons		Male living alone		Female living alone			
		Total	With children	Householder 65 years or over	Total	With children	Householder 65 years or over	Total	Householder 65 years or over	Total	Householder 65 years or over	Total	Householder 65 years or over		
	29	30	31	32	33	34	35	36	37	38	39	40	41	42	43
TEXAS—Cont'd															
Caldwell County	10 777	57.3	27.5	10.4	17.6	9.9	2.4	3.7	0.3	9.9	2.3	11.4	6.8	41.0	452
Calhoun County	7 434	58.6	26.1	12.1	16.8	9.7	2.8	3.3	0.2	11.2	2.8	10.1	6.3	37.6	319
Callahan County	5 065	62.9	26.4	13.6	11.8	6.0	2.7	2.1	0.1	8.7	3.1	14.5	10.0	44.4	159
Cameron County	97 193	61.9	35.0	11.8	20.6	11.2	3.7	2.1	0.3	6.1	2.2	9.2	5.7	33.4	4 530
Camp County	4 354	57.8	22.1	13.0	16.1	8.8	2.2	1.8	0.0	10.5	3.4	13.8	8.5	43.7	221
Carson County	2 482	65.8	30.9	12.1	10.7	5.3	2.4	1.5	0.4	9.5	3.8	12.5	8.5	45.2	44
Cass County	12 186	56.1	22.0	12.2	15.2	8.5	2.9	2.4	0.1	9.9	3.2	16.4	10.9	48.3	491
Castro County	2 767	64.2	33.9	10.4	14.0	7.6	3.0	1.4	0.3	8.2	2.2	12.2	8.2	43.2	224
Chambers County	9 137	67.1	33.7	7.9	11.9	6.8	1.6	3.3	0.4	9.1	1.5	8.6	5.4	41.2	353
Cherokee County	16 658	57.1	25.1	11.4	16.5	9.0	2.9	2.3	0.5	8.7	2.9	15.3	9.9	46.6	522
Childress County	2 485	54.5	21.0	13.2	12.4	9.1	1.0	2.5	0.0	10.7	3.2	20.0	11.9	51.4	95
Clay County	4 336	64.7	25.8	13.3	9.6	5.3	2.6	2.5	0.3	8.7	2.9	14.5	8.7	41.8	130
Cochran County	1 315	63.7	30.5	15.0	14.1	7.7	2.7	1.4	0.0	8.9	2.3	12.0	8.4	37.6	110
Coke County	1 538	59.3	21.2	17.9	9.6	5.6	1.3	2.0	0.4	10.5	6.9	18.5	14.8	52.6	48
Coleman County	3 889	56.1	21.2	16.3	10.8	6.3	1.4	2.9	0.4	10.9	4.1	19.4	14.8	51.1	129
Collin County	182 245	63.2	35.1	4.2	9.9	6.3	0.6	4.9	0.1	10.4	0.7	11.6	2.5	38.5	2 658
Collingsworth County	1 291	58.9	23.4	15.7	12.0	6.9	2.8	1.1	0.4	9.5	2.4	18.5	15.6	48.8	48
Colorado County	7 624	57.9	25.1	14.0	12.7	6.0	2.9	3.0	0.4	12.1	4.6	14.2	10.2	46.2	291
Comal County	29 074	63.3	26.3	13.1	12.5	7.6	1.6	3.6	0.4	8.8	2.4	11.8	6.9	38.1	650
Comanche County	5 508	59.9	23.3	15.8	11.6	7.4	1.7	2.3	0.5	10.2	3.3	16.0	11.5	45.1	118
Concho County	1 053	59.7	23.2	14.7	12.1	6.1	2.6	1.1	0.0	10.4	2.2	16.6	12.4	45.8	33
Cooke County	13 649	61.0	26.6	12.2	12.5	7.3	1.9	3.2	0.4	9.4	2.4	13.9	8.8	43.5	410
Coryell County	19 955	64.7	37.3	6.6	14.8	11.0	1.0	3.5	0.2	7.6	1.0	9.4	4.2	40.1	454
Cottle County	820	54.8	21.3	15.6	12.9	7.7	2.9	0.7	0.2	10.2	4.6	21.3	17.3	53.9	36
Crane County	1 362	64.9	34.1	7.7	14.0	8.4	1.9	2.1	0.4	6.2	2.3	12.7	8.4	51.8	81
Crockett County	1 522	61.8	28.2	11.5	12.0	8.4	0.8	1.8	0.4	12.0	1.4	12.4	8.3	43.4	140
Crosby County	2 520	59.4	27.7	12.2	14.6	9.2	2.2	2.1	0.7	8.9	3.6	15.0	11.0	49.1	178
Culberson County	1 060	59.8	30.7	10.8	16.5	9.1	1.9	2.5	0.2	11.7	3.6	9.4	4.2	37.4	72
Dallam County	2 323	56.6	29.8	7.7	15.6	10.3	2.0	1.6	0.0	13.1	3.1	13.0	7.5	52.3	56
Dallas County	808 268	47.9	25.3	5.7	18.7	10.5	1.9	6.2	0.2	12.3	1.3	14.9	4.9	43.0	26 336
Dawson County	4 696	60.6	27.0	14.7	14.7	8.8	3.5	0.7	0.2	8.8	2.3	15.1	11.1	42.2	241
Deaf Smith County	6 155	60.6	30.2	10.9	18.2	11.0	2.4	1.4	0.1	7.3	1.2	12.5	8.2	41.1	389
Delta County	2 095	56.9	23.9	10.9	13.5	6.4	2.4	2.0	0.2	11.4	5.0	16.3	10.6	53.4	38
Denton County	159 062	58.9	32.3	4.0	11.6	7.4	0.7	7.3	0.1	10.5	0.7	11.6	2.5	39.7	3 001
DeWitt County	7 234	55.7	23.1	13.9	15.9	9.2	3.5	2.3	0.4	10.6	4.3	15.5	11.2	46.5	188
Dickens County	977	56.4	20.2	14.7	8.3	3.8	2.5	3.0	0.8	13.4	4.9	18.9	12.5	49.1	34
Dimmit County	3 298	58.1	31.1	10.6	22.1	11.7	6.5	1.8	0.5	8.3	3.8	9.7	6.1	36.0	207
Donley County	1 555	57.3	17.2	18.3	9.8	6.6	1.9	1.2	0.0	11.8	4.1	19.9	13.6	46.9	27
Duval County	4 351	54.9	26.9	11.7	20.1	9.9	4.8	2.2	0.3	11.5	3.1	11.4	7.9	39.7	346
Eastland County	7 324	56.8	20.9	15.3	12.2	6.9	2.4	2.4	0.5	10.6	3.6	17.9	12.8	47.3	208
Ector County	43 806	55.1	28.1	8.6	17.6	11.8	2.0	3.3	0.3	11.0	2.0	13.0	6.7	44.4	2 119
Edwards County	804	60.7	22.5	15.7	12.7	8.2	2.0	2.0	0.7	11.6	4.9	13.1	8.6	42.2	42
Ellis County	37 056	66.2	34.4	8.1	14.4	8.7	2.0	2.8	0.2	6.6	1.1	9.9	5.6	39.2	1 430
El Paso County	210 034	57.9	33.3	8.8	21.8	12.2	3.3	2.6	0.3	7.5	1.7	10.2	5.1	35.3	12 150
Erath County	12 567	54.9	26.0	10.1	10.1	6.0	1.1	7.3	0.4	11.6	2.0	16.1	8.5	47.3	279
Falls County	6 518	48.3	21.3	11.0	19.5	10.1	3.7	2.6	0.4	12.4	4.0	17.2	11.7	51.0	330
Fannin County	11 105	58.5	23.8	12.7	13.9	8.1	2.5	2.6	0.4	10.3	3.3	14.7	9.6	45.3	376
Fayette County	8 757	59.3	23.9	15.5	10.8	5.2	2.4	1.9	0.2	10.7	3.9	17.3	13.2	48.5	210
Fisher County	1 793	58.7	21.6	18.5	11.7	6.7	2.1	1.6	0.1	11.4	4.1	16.6	13.0	45.3	70
Floyd County	2 733	64.5	31.3	13.4	13.5	8.2	2.8	0.8	0.1	8.0	2.0	13.2	9.4	41.2	182
Foard County	669	56.1	22.9	16.1	10.6	6.0	2.2	2.1	0.9	9.7	3.4	21.5	16.6	51.0	12
Fort Bend County	111 164	69.2	41.5	4.9	15.2	9.2	1.1	2.2	0.1	6.1	0.9	7.3	2.4	34.4	3 800
Franklin County	3 739	63.4	24.0	14.8	9.8	6.3	1.5	2.2	0.3	9.8	3.0	14.8	10.6	45.1	102
Freestone County	6 588	57.4	23.0	12.6	13.8	7.7	3.0	2.4	0.3	10.8	3.9	15.6	10.0	46.8	238
Frio County	4 729	55.8	28.0	10.4	21.3	12.5	4.4	1.9	0.2	9.2	2.9	11.8	7.8	41.6	361
Gaines County	4 697	68.3	37.9	9.9	12.0	7.3	2.0	1.4	0.2	7.4	1.7	10.9	6.5	40.4	231
Galveston County	94 840	53.1	24.5	7.8	17.0	9.9	2.4	4.8	0.5	11.9	2.5	13.2	5.9	43.9	3 400
Garza County	1 686	59.4	29.3	11.7	15.4	7.1	1.6	2.3	1.1	8.6	2.6	14.4	9.7	46.0	82
Gillespie County	8 512	62.2	21.4	20.8	9.3	4.7	1.7	2.7	0.4	7.7	2.4	18.1	11.7	38.1	163
Glasscock County	473	69.3	36.4	9.7	4.2	3.4	0.2	2.7	0.0	14.2	2.1	9.5	4.7	40.5	6
Goliad County	2 638	63.0	26.2	14.9	11.3	6.3	2.5	2.5	0.9	10.4	4.2	12.8	9.0	41.8	57
Gonzales County	6 803	56.6	26.6	13.1	15.9	9.1	3.1	2.4	0.3	9.8	3.1	15.3	11.2	46.3	184
Gray County	8 789	59.2	23.4	13.9	10.3	6.6	1.3	1.9	0.2	10.7	3.9	17.9	11.9	50.4	350
Grayson County	42 834	56.2	24.2	11.0	14.5	8.7	2.4	3.9	0.3	10.4	2.6	15.0	8.9	45.5	1 378
Gregg County	42 647	53.1	23.7	9.7	16.9	10.0	2.5	3.8	0.3	10.1	2.4	16.0	8.6	46.8	1 566
Grimes County	7 714	55.8	27.0	9.1	17.1	9.4	3.0	3.3	0.1	11.1	3.5	12.7	8.1	48.6	254

STATE County	Households with Non-Hispanic White householder		Households with Black or African American householder		Households with American Indian and Alaska Native householder		Households with Asian, Hawaiian, and Pacific Islander householder		Households with Hispanic or Latino[1] householder		Foreign-born population				Percent in non-English speaking households	
												Place of birth (percent)				
	Number of households	Percent that are family households	Number of households	Percent that are family households	Number of households	Percent that are family households	Number of households	Percent that are family households	Number of households	Percent that are family households	Percent of total population that is foreign-born	Europe	Asia	Latin America	Linguistically isolated	Not linguistically isolated
	44	45	46	47	48	49	50	51	52	53	54	55	56	57	58	59
TEXAS—Cont'd																
Caldwell County	6 270	70.8	810	68.8	63	87.3	48	70.8	3 516	83.8	5.1	0.1	0.5	4.4	5.6	38.9
Calhoun County	4 519	71.9	224	53.6	48	68.8	205	85.4	2 409	83.8	8.5	0.1	2.5	5.9	4.4	39.1
Callahan County	4 785	74.6	5	60.0	24	79.2	2	100.0	219	76.3	1.4	0.1	0.2	1.1	0.9	9.2
Cameron County	21 943	69.0	432	81.7	466	82.4	498	65.1	73 958	86.8	25.6	0.3	0.4	24.7	17.5	69.5
Camp County	3 010	73.1	881	65.5	9	100.0	26	100.0	421	95.5	9.9	0.2	0.7	8.7	5.9	15.1
Carson County	2 315	76.0	7	100.0	34	64.7	8	100.0	104	85.6	2.7	0.3	0.2	2.2	1.4	9.4
Cass County	9 696	72.5	2 159	66.0	30	70.0	27	85.2	127	75.6	1.1	0.2	0.1	0.7	0.5	6.4
Castro County	1 584	69.9	79	84.8	26	100.0	0	X	1 092	89.4	12.1	0.2	0.0	11.9	8.2	45.4
Chambers County	7 393	77.9	940	78.3	26	69.2	17	58.8	727	93.7	5.1	0.1	0.3	4.6	2.6	16.0
Cherokee County	12 818	72.3	2 387	71.3	45	88.9	31	51.6	1 346	89.8	7.9	0.2	0.2	7.4	5.2	11.7
Childress County	2 018	62.3	113	78.8	4	100.0	14	50.0	326	90.5	4.7	0.3	0.4	4.1	4.5	18.8
Clay County	4 155	74.0	8	100.0	21	76.2	2	100.0	72	87.5	1.4	0.3	0.1	0.8	0.4	6.0
Cochran County	782	71.0	48	68.8	13	100.0	0	X	468	89.5	9.8	0.0	0.0	9.6	10.9	38.6
Coke County	1 344	68.4	3	100.0	10	50.0	0	X	173	73.4	2.8	0.3	0.0	2.4	2.2	15.3
Coleman County	3 381	64.8	55	76.4	22	68.2	0	X	392	79.6	3.4	0.2	0.0	2.8	1.4	15.1
Collin County	145 957	72.3	8 587	65.7	985	62.1	10 976	81.9	13 380	81.4	13.3	1.6	5.8	4.6	4.1	20.0
Collingsworth County	996	68.2	65	76.9	17	76.5	5	100.0	199	79.9	4.3	0.1	0.3	3.8	3.5	22.5
Colorado County	5 386	69.5	1 156	66.5	30	36.7	0	X	1 071	81.9	7.9	0.2	0.2	7.5	4.6	21.4
Comal County	23 554	74.5	263	77.9	157	62.4	151	73.5	4 807	83.6	4.8	0.9	0.4	3.2	3.2	25.1
Comanche County	4 630	69.0	11	100.0	27	96.3	9	100.0	797	84.6	7.1	0.3	0.3	6.5	4.7	19.9
Concho County	779	70.1	1	100.0	3	100.0	0	X	270	76.7	2.8	0.0	0.0	2.8	4.9	33.7
Cooke County	12 112	72.9	408	61.3	145	71.0	35	82.9	826	91.4	5.5	0.3	0.4	4.6	4.3	9.0
Coryell County	14 254	76.6	3 115	87.5	95	90.5	482	66.6	1 691	92.7	5.3	1.9	1.3	1.8	1.1	23.4
Cottle County	620	64.8	74	67.6	0	X	0	X	126	81.7	3.6	0.2	0.0	3.4	4.9	16.9
Crane County	834	73.6	22	45.5	9	100.0	24	100.0	471	89.2	14.4	0.0	1.0	13.1	7.7	42.3
Crockett County	760	75.0	5	0.0	14	50.0	6	0.0	744	73.5	10.5	0.2	0.0	10.4	9.9	49.1
Crosby County	1 481	67.5	108	55.6	6	50.0	4	100.0	929	86.9	3.9	0.1	0.1	3.6	6.2	47.0
Culberson County	357	65.3	1	100.0	12	50.0	10	60.0	668	82.8	15.6	0.2	0.6	14.7	12.8	67.9
Dallam County	1 001	70.0	10	00.0	10	77.0	0	X	500	77.1	7.0	0.0	0.0	7.0	1.7	01.0
Dallas County	437 571	59.2	165 616	68.3	3 877	70.5	28 956	74.1	163 542	83.4	20.9	0.8	3.4	15.6	12.2	26.4
Dawson County	2 647	68.5	172	63.4	16	100.0	21	76.2	1 833	86.5	4.2	0.1	0.3	3.7	8.0	42.9
Deaf Smith County	3 052	71.1	125	86.4	23	65.2	41	75.6	2 924	87.1	11.6	0.2	0.3	11.0	10.7	47.3
Delta County	1 866	70.7	177	66.1	8	100.0	0	X	21	100.0	0.5	0.0	0.3	0.2	0.0	4.9
Denton County	126 925	70.2	9 288	65.2	997	67.7	5 343	72.8	14 421	77.0	9.4	0.8	3.2	4.7	3.8	17.5
DeWitt County	4 972	70.0	591	60.2	30	53.3	4	0.0	1 591	81.2	2.6	0.3	0.0	2.2	4.3	28.6
Dickens County	818	62.3	17	52.9	6	100.0	7	57.1	131	80.2	2.0	0.0	0.1	1.9	1.8	22.1
Dimmit County	602	69.9	37	59.5	19	100.0	7	100.0	2 644	82.8	7.6	0.1	0.3	7.2	15.0	73.4
Donley County	1 451	66.4	33	72.7	14	57.1	0	X	53	86.8	1.6	0.1	0.3	1.3	0.3	7.4
Duval County	509	69.4	0	X	9	100.0	2	100.0	3 750	75.0	0.4	0.1	0.0	0.3	13.0	76.7
Eastland County	6 654	68.5	46	17.4	51	72.5	3	100.0	512	82.8	4.0	0.1	0.0	3.9	2.5	12.0
Ector County	26 197	67.1	2 079	65.7	271	79.7	237	80.2	14 652	83.3	10.6	0.1	0.6	9.8	6.7	37.5
Edwards County	506	71.5	1	100.0	2	100.0	3	100.0	293	76.1	10.8	0.6	0.1	10.0	9.7	46.0
Ellis County	28 686	79.7	2 986	75.7	236	72.0	84	86.9	4 835	89.4	7.1	0.4	0.3	6.2	3.9	18.7
El Paso County	50 772	68.4	7 254	71.4	1 594	78.9	2 521	66.2	147 951	84.3	27.4	0.9	0.9	25.5	16.1	66.8
Erath County	11 022	62.4	49	55.1	101	89.1	65	69.2	1 273	85.9	7.3	0.5	0.5	6.1	5.1	14.7
Falls County	4 186	66.2	1 577	66.7	27	88.9	0	X	717	79.6	4.6	0.1	0.0	4.4	5.2	12.1
Fannin County	10 045	72.4	495	69.7	98	73.5	33	75.8	321	81.9	3.1	0.4	0.2	2.5	1.4	7.4
Fayette County	7 290	69.8	647	59.5	46	47.8	7	42.9	746	85.1	5.6	0.4	0.2	4.9	5.3	23.1
Fisher County	1 409	68.8	55	60.0	9	100.0	2	100.0	311	78.8	2.3	0.0	0.1	2.1	4.6	20.4
Floyd County	1 639	73.5	67	76.1	23	65.2	3	100.0	986	86.1	5.9	0.2	0.0	5.8	7.9	39.3
Foard County	563	67.3	17	41.2	0	X	2	100.0	79	67.1	1.6	0.2	0.2	1.2	1.2	18.5
Fort Bend County	58 427	81.3	21 775	83.6	373	88.7	10 613	93.9	18 561	89.4	18.3	1.2	8.4	7.3	5.5	33.8
Franklin County	3 350	72.8	146	69.2	25	76.0	8	25.0	198	85.4	5.4	0.4	0.1	4.9	2.1	13.0
Freestone County	5 066	73.9	1 165	56.3	18	44.4	18	100.0	286	85.3	3.1	0.1	0.1	2.9	1.9	10.2
Frio County	1 419	66.2	9	0.0	33	60.6	17	29.4	3 278	82.4	5.8	0.0	0.1	5.6	13.8	65.3
Gaines County	3 101	77.3	153	88.9	19	100.0	2	100.0	1 421	85.9	18.9	0.0	0.0	17.9	11.5	44.7
Galveston County	64 546	68.7	14 192	69.4	519	71.9	1 735	72.0	13 017	78.3	8.3	0.8	1.8	5.3	4.0	20.0
Garza County	1 143	71.7	60	78.3	0	X	0	X	483	82.6	6.3	0.1	0.1	6.0	3.3	28.8
Gillespie County	7 543	70.2	24	29.2	31	64.5	25	76.0	821	84.9	7.0	1.0	0.2	5.7	5.3	28.7
Glasscock County	354	75.7	1	100.0	4	100.0	0	X	113	65.5	14.1	0.0	0.0	13.9	7.3	24.6
Goliad County	1 751	74.0	169	62.7	8	12.5	0	X	703	78.4	2.8	0.6	0.0	2.1	5.4	33.2
Gonzales County	4 007	70.7	638	56.1	6	33.3	6	100.0	2 117	80.8	11.0	0.2	0.1	10.5	8.3	34.8
Gray County	7 466	68.6	331	48.0	83	83.1	26	100.0	688	85.6	4.3	0.2	0.2	3.7	3.1	12.3
Grayson County	37 372	70.1	2 288	70.1	535	66.7	235	72.3	1 839	84.4	3.9	0.4	0.6	2.8	2.0	9.2
Gregg County	31 520	69.0	8 052	69.8	179	54.7	197	75.1	2 423	85.6	5.4	0.3	0.5	4.4	3.3	9.9
Grimes County	5 442	72.0	1 362	67.9	20	50.0	17	100.0	838	88.9	5.0	0.3	0.3	4.4	2.9	16.3

[1] Hispanic or Latino persons may be of any race.

STATE/ County code	MSA/PMSA/ NECMA code[1]	STATE County	Total population	Under 5 years	5 to 17 years	18 to 24 years	25 to 44 years	45 to 64 years	65 years and over	Median age	+/− U.S. percent under 18 years	+/− U.S. percent 65 years and over	Total population	Under 18 years	65 years and over
			1	2	3	4	5	6	7	8	9	10	11	12	13
		TEXAS—Cont'd													
48 187	7240	Guadalupe County	89 023	6.9	21.4	9.1	29.3	22.2	11.1	34.9	2.6	-1.3	52 918	23.5	14.7
48 189	...	Hale County	36 602	8.2	22.0	11.1	28.2	17.8	12.8	31.4	4.5	0.4	16 355	20.8	22.1
48 191	...	Hall County	3 782	7.3	19.9	6.0	23.1	22.8	21.0	40.2	1.5	8.6	2 407	18.7	29.5
48 193	...	Hamilton County	8 229	5.5	18.3	5.8	23.8	23.4	23.2	43.1	-1.9	10.8	7 541	22.5	25.2
48 195	...	Hansford County	5 369	6.7	22.4	7.2	26.0	22.4	15.3	36.5	3.4	2.9	3 571	22.9	21.3
48 197	...	Hardeman County	4 724	6.5	18.6	8.5	21.7	24.4	20.2	41.2	-0.6	7.8	3 664	21.2	23.7
48 199	0840	Hardin County	48 073	6.9	20.9	8.3	28.6	23.1	12.2	36.0	2.1	-0.2	42 714	26.6	12.8
48 201	3360	Harris County	3 400 578	8.2	20.7	10.3	33.7	19.7	7.4	31.2	3.2	-5.0	1 429 684	22.6	11.4
48 203	4420	Harrison County	62 110	6.5	20.3	10.1	27.0	22.9	13.1	36.1	1.1	0.7	42 994	24.7	13.9
48 205	...	Hartley County	5 537	5.9	14.8	4.6	36.4	26.5	11.8	39.6	-5.0	-0.6	4 284	22.9	14.8
48 207	...	Haskell County	6 093	4.8	18.8	5.6	22.3	23.0	25.5	43.9	-2.1	13.1	4 579	19.7	30.6
48 209	0640	Hays County	97 589	6.1	18.3	20.6	27.9	19.4	7.7	28.4	-1.3	-4.7	62 943	20.9	9.3
48 211	...	Hemphill County	3 351	5.8	21.8	7.0	25.5	25.0	14.9	38.6	1.9	2.5	2 752	24.1	16.8
48 213	1920	Henderson County	73 277	6.3	18.1	7.5	24.8	25.1	18.2	40.2	-1.3	5.8	62 135	22.3	20.2
48 215	4880	Hidalgo County	569 463	10.2	25.1	11.3	27.8	15.9	9.8	27.2	9.6	-2.6	59 009	15.3	37.4
48 217	...	Hill County	32 321	6.8	18.9	8.7	25.0	23.5	17.1	38.3	0.0	4.7	25 095	22.6	20.4
48 219	...	Hockley County	22 716	7.3	21.9	11.6	26.8	20.2	12.3	33.3	3.5	-0.1	13 141	22.8	17.6
48 221	2800	Hood County	41 100	5.8	18.0	6.6	25.1	26.8	17.8	41.5	-1.9	5.4	37 204	22.5	19.1
48 223	...	Hopkins County	31 960	6.4	19.8	8.1	27.5	23.1	15.1	36.9	0.5	2.7	25 976	24.1	17.1
48 225	...	Houston County	23 185	5.5	17.8	6.7	28.7	23.7	17.7	40.3	-2.4	5.3	14 777	20.3	22.6
48 227	...	Howard County	33 627	5.9	18.3	8.8	31.2	21.1	14.7	36.4	-1.5	2.3	19 188	21.6	20.7
48 229	...	Hudspeth County	3 344	8.6	25.5	8.7	26.9	20.3	10.0	30.2	8.4	-2.4	771	23.9	15.0
48 231	1920	Hunt County	76 596	6.6	19.9	10.2	28.0	22.7	12.7	35.5	0.8	0.3	61 167	24.5	14.3
48 233	...	Hutchinson County	23 857	6.9	20.6	8.5	25.7	22.9	15.4	37.5	1.8	3.0	19 115	24.5	18.2
48 235	...	Irion County	1 771	5.3	21.3	4.6	27.7	25.3	15.8	39.9	0.9	3.4	1 311	23.5	16.8
48 237	...	Jack County	8 763	5.7	17.8	10.0	30.0	21.5	15.1	37.0	-2.2	2.7	7 418	23.2	17.3
48 239	...	Jackson County	14 391	7.2	20.3	8.0	26.3	22.4	15.7	37.3	1.8	3.3	9 526	24.0	18.9
48 241	...	Jasper County	35 604	6.8	19.7	7.7	27.2	22.9	15.7	37.3	0.8	3.3	27 242	24.5	17.5
48 243	...	Jeff Davis County...........	2 207	3.8	20.8	4.8	24.6	29.7	16.4	42.5	-1.1	4.0	1 370	20.9	18.3
48 245	0840	Jefferson County	252 051	6.7	19.2	10.1	29.5	20.9	13.6	35.3	0.2	1.2	130 655	20.6	18.8
48 247	...	Jim Hogg County	5 281	8.0	23.6	7.7	26.4	20.1	14.1	33.9	5.9	1.7	472	26.5	23.1
48 249	...	Jim Wells County	39 326	8.1	23.3	8.8	26.6	20.9	12.3	32.8	5.7	-0.1	8 987	22.6	20.3
48 251	2800	Johnson County	126 811	7.3	21.4	8.7	30.6	21.9	10.1	34.3	3.0	-2.3	105 574	27.2	11.3
48 253	...	Jones County	20 785	5.0	17.5	11.3	32.0	20.4	13.9	36.0	-3.2	1.5	13 770	22.2	18.3
48 255	...	Karnes County	15 446	5.4	16.3	11.3	34.9	18.0	14.1	34.1	-4.0	1.7	6 283	18.5	23.3
48 257	1920	Kaufman County	71 313	7.2	21.8	8.1	29.5	22.7	10.7	34.9	3.3	-1.7	54 400	26.9	12.2
48 259	...	Kendall County	23 743	6.2	21.1	6.0	26.4	26.4	13.9	39.3	1.6	1.5	19 249	25.3	15.7
48 261	...	Kenedy County	414	8.7	21.5	6.8	29.2	22.2	11.6	34.2	4.5	-0.8	58	17.2	19.0
48 263	...	Kent County	859	3.1	17.3	4.7	22.9	26.7	25.3	47.1	-5.3	12.9	761	20.4	27.3
48 265	...	Kerr County	43 653	5.2	17.5	6.2	23.2	23.3	24.6	43.8	-3.0	12.2	33 904	18.9	29.5
48 267	...	Kimble County	4 468	6.2	17.8	5.7	22.5	26.7	21.2	43.1	-1.7	8.8	3 464	20.6	24.2
48 269	...	King County	356	7.0	26.4	2.5	30.3	23.0	10.7	37.0	7.7	-1.7	331	32.6	10.6
48 271	...	Kinney County	3 379	6.1	19.6	5.2	21.8	22.7	24.7	43.2	0.0	12.3	1 593	16.4	35.0
48 273	...	Kleberg County	31 549	7.6	19.7	16.0	28.1	17.7	10.9	29.2	1.6	-1.5	8 967	20.7	16.4
48 275	...	Knox County	4 253	6.3	21.5	5.9	22.4	21.4	22.5	40.5	2.1	10.1	2 809	21.1	29.1
48 277	...	Lamar County	48 499	7.0	19.1	8.7	26.5	22.9	15.8	36.9	0.4	3.4	39 191	24.3	17.3
48 279	...	Lamb County	14 709	7.6	22.0	7.8	24.7	20.6	17.2	36.2	3.9	4.8	7 490	21.5	26.4
48 281	...	Lampasas County	17 762	6.8	20.8	7.7	27.0	23.0	14.6	36.9	1.9	2.2	14 151	24.8	16.7
48 283	...	La Salle County	5 866	7.3	21.8	9.5	28.6	20.6	12.2	33.0	3.4	-0.2	1 074	17.0	21.5
48 285	...	Lavaca County	19 210	5.9	18.2	7.1	23.7	23.5	21.6	41.9	-1.6	9.2	15 507	21.8	24.4
48 287	...	Lee County.....................	15 657	7.0	21.7	8.6	27.1	21.2	14.3	35.6	3.0	1.9	10 727	24.1	17.7
48 289	...	Leon County	15 335	5.4	18.8	6.3	24.0	25.3	20.2	42.1	-1.5	7.8	12 447	22.4	21.3
48 291	3360	Liberty County	70 154	6.7	20.8	9.5	31.8	20.9	10.2	34.0	1.8	-2.2	52 397	26.8	11.6
48 293	...	Limestone County	22 051	6.4	18.8	8.7	26.8	22.9	16.4	37.4	-0.5	4.0	14 664	21.6	20.2
48 295	...	Lipscomb County	3 057	6.0	21.5	5.6	25.2	23.1	18.6	39.5	1.8	6.2	2 385	23.2	23.3
48 297	...	Live Oak County	12 309	4.8	17.5	9.4	26.8	25.0	16.4	39.2	-3.4	4.0	7 153	19.3	21.9
48 299	...	Llano County	17 044	3.6	12.3	4.5	18.7	30.4	30.6	53.0	-9.8	18.2	15 968	14.6	32.1
48 301	...	Loving County	67	0.0	20.9	3.0	20.9	40.3	14.9	45.8	-4.8	2.5	55	12.7	18.2
48 303	4600	Lubbock County	242 628	7.0	18.5	16.2	28.2	19.2	11.0	30.5	-0.2	-1.4	151 592	19.9	14.3
48 305	...	Lynn County	6 550	7.2	23.9	7.3	27.0	20.5	14.2	35.2	5.4	1.8	3 409	25.0	19.6
48 307	...	McCulloch County	8 205	6.4	20.1	5.9	24.0	23.7	20.0	40.4	0.8	7.6	5 833	22.9	23.5
48 309	8800	McLennan County...........	213 517	7.1	19.4	14.4	26.6	19.4	13.0	31.9	0.8	0.6	138 204	21.7	16.3
48 311	...	McMullen County	851	3.5	19.5	4.9	25.5	27.5	19.0	43.1	-2.7	6.6	547	19.4	23.2
48 313	...	Madison County	12 940	5.4	15.8	9.9	34.2	20.5	14.2	33.4	-4.5	1.8	7 726	20.5	19.5
48 315	...	Marion County	10 941	5.5	16.8	6.4	24.4	27.5	19.3	43.3	-3.4	6.9	7 854	20.0	20.0
48 317	...	Martin County.................	4 746	8.5	25.6	7.2	25.9	19.6	13.2	32.5	8.4	0.8	2 669	26.8	19.0

[1]MSA = Metropolitan Statistical Area. PMSA = Primary MSA. NECMA = New England County Metropolitan Area. See the Appendix A for explanation of these concepts. See Appendix B for list of metropolitan areas identified by type, with component counties.

Table A-3. States and Counties — Age, Ethnicity, and Household Structure

STATE County	Black or African American Total population	Under 18 years	65 years and over	American Indian and Alaska Native Total population	Under 18 years	65 years and over	Asian, Hawaiian, and Pacific Islander Total population	Under 18 years	65 years and over	Hispanic or Latino[1] Total population	Under 18 years	65 years and over	Two or more races Total population	Under 18 years	65 years and over
	14	15	16	17	18	19	20	21	22	23	24	25	26	27	28
TEXAS—Cont'd															
Guadalupe County	4 397	29.0	10.6	392	24.2	8.4	906	23.5	7.7	29 520	36.7	5.0	2 253	43.4	5.9
Hale County	2 072	28.5	9.3	233	30.5	11.2	329	37.7	7.0	17 565	39.2	4.5	753	35.7	6.0
Hall County	292	41.1	14.4	5	0.0	0.0	6	33.3	66.7	1 042	44.3	3.1	60	30.0	6.7
Hamilton County	0	X	X	18	27.8	0.0	3	100.0	0.0	617	40.5	1.0	67	28.4	7.5
Hansford County	0	X	X	74	40.5	0.0	8	100.0	0.0	1 709	41.8	2.9	125	45.6	10.4
Hardeman County	261	26.1	24.9	39	30.8	0.0	22	0.0	0.0	713	44.7	2.4	102	54.9	6.9
Hardin County	3 328	35.4	11.0	119	36.1	0.0	278	22.3	6.8	1 176	41.5	2.1	548	40.0	2.7
Harris County	627 111	31.4	6.9	14 670	29.8	3.9	173 491	24.5	5.3	1 120 625	36.0	2.9	102 669	37.1	3.2
Harrison County	14 892	29.2	13.5	144	25.7	7.6	201	18.4	10.0	3 354	45.0	1.4	870	34.1	10.0
Hartley County	438	0.9	0.7	21	0.0	0.0	18	0.0	0.0	763	17.7	2.0	110	47.3	0.0
Haskell County	194	21.6	18.0	23	8.7	47.8	9	22.2	0.0	1 256	37.5	8.4	110	46.4	5.5
Hayo County	3 580	24.0	2.6	500	26.0	3.0	916	23.5	0.7	28 738	32.0	5.2	2 500	30.3	6.2
Hemphill County	31	77.4	0.0	43	18.6	25.6	5	0.0	0.0	506	45.8	4.3	34	41.2	11.8
Henderson County	4 802	29.7	11.5	361	27.7	10.0	257	17.9	5.4	4 946	43.5	2.8	1 022	46.2	6.7
Hidalgo County	2 777	29.0	2.8	2 093	36.6	8.3	3 308	30.4	4.1	503 526	37.7	6.6	11 906	34.2	8.9
Hill County	2 419	35.4	7.3	160	27.5	5.0	66	0.0	9.1	4 343	39.0	4.2	537	38.7	6.3
Hockley County	773	33.6	11.9	212	42.5	0.9	64	42.2	9.4	8 453	38.4	4.3	473	29.2	8.5
Hood County	26	61.5	0.0	491	39.9	10.2	130	16.9	13.8	2 872	38.1	3.2	522	20.3	9.2
Hopkins County	2 415	29.2	13.3	283	31.4	2.8	117	43.6	0.0	2 960	40.9	1.4	498	36.9	6.4
Houston County	6 513	28.5	11.1	54	38.9	3.7	42	0.0	4.8	1 759	29.8	1.1	177	27.7	5.1
Howard County	1 370	30.6	11.6	135	14.1	12.6	140	16.4	6.4	12 630	27.7	5.9	715	34.3	7.1
Hudspeth County	15	20.0	0.0	54	27.8	5.6	5	0.0	60.0	2 523	37.7	8.4	64	29.7	20.3
Hunt County	7 126	32.1	9.2	607	27.0	6.1	557	24.6	1.8	6 271	37.8	2.6	1 442	43.6	11.0
Hutchinson County	524	33.8	12.6	304	31.6	5.6	49	22.4	12.2	3 451	43.1	1.5	626	35.9	8.9
Irion County	9	33.3	33.3	10	0.0	10.0	0	X	X	437	36.4	12.4	43	55.8	11.6
Jack County	535	11.2	0.7	35	62.9	0.0	45	35.6	17.8	694	34.1	3.0	69	24.6	10.1
Jackson County	1 094	27.8	15.1	28	28.6	0.0	35	25.7	0.0	3 608	36.2	7.7	533	55.9	5.3
Jasper County	6 351	32.1	11.4	79	10.1	5.1	149	31.5	6.0	1 409	37.1	3.5	453	40.0	11.3
Jeff Davis County	16	100.0	0.0	0	X	X	0	X	X	783	30.0	13.5	64	21.9	7.8
Jefferson County	84 970	31.1	9.3	996	11.0	10.0	7 159	34.2	4.0	26 664	32.6	5.0	3 707	37.8	7.5
Jim Hogg County	18	0.0	44.4	36	77.8	0.0	34	50.0	0.0	4 786	32.3	13.1	103	23.3	0.0
Jim Wells County	209	38.8	12.9	390	45.9	1.8	147	40.1	4.1	29 856	34.0	10.0	1 202	34.8	6.7
Johnson County	2 872	26.1	8.2	855	30.9	5.1	832	28.4	2.8	15 224	38.9	3.3	2 343	44.5	2.3
Jones County	2 354	11.4	4.8	75	40.0	14.7	39	0.0	7.7	4 385	28.7	5.2	368	47.0	5.2
Karnes County	1 723	6.3	2.2	182	6.6	0.0	16	0.0	0.0	7 369	28.3	9.1	359	22.3	6.7
Kaufman County	7 187	32.6	9.9	523	27.3	1.7	509	17.7	1.2	7 932	39.2	2.8	1 087	44.4	4.5
Kendall County	16	62.5	0.0	87	14.9	0.0	73	9.6	0.0	4 209	36.8	5.9	390	35.6	11.3
Kenedy County	2	0.0	0.0	0	X	X	0	X	X	356	32.3	10.4	5	80.0	0.0
Kent County	10	60.0	20.0	5	0.0	0.0	0	X	X	88	17.0	8.0	0	X	X
Kerr County	731	30.0	12.7	224	16.1	14.7	247	31.2	11.3	8 366	37.6	6.1	819	41.1	8.7
Kimble County	22	45.5	0.0	17	0.0	41.2	15	46.7	0.0	937	36.2	11.0	82	17.1	13.4
King County	0	X	X	0	X	X	0	X	X	22	50.0	0.0	6	0.0	50.0
Kinney County	39	12.8	15.4	13	0.0	0.0	17	17.6	0.0	1 693	34.7	15.6	141	36.2	10.6
Kleberg County	1 155	29.5	7.5	187	36.4	1.1	380	6.6	6.6	20 685	30.6	8.8	939	30.4	6.5
Knox County	304	42.8	13.5	36	38.9	0.0	18	0.0	33.3	1 086	41.3	8.7	82	37.8	17.1
Lamar County	6 257	32.1	11.1	530	33.4	5.7	164	16.5	1.8	1 715	38.6	3.4	770	40.4	11.9
Lamb County	713	27.2	18.4	113	20.4	1.8	27	11.1	11.1	6 430	39.5	6.4	227	49.3	5.3
Lampasas County	557	34.5	7.0	91	30.8	2.2	105	11.4	0.0	2 674	41.0	7.1	457	44.0	7.7
La Salle County	208	6.3	0.0	17	0.0	88.2	58	65.5	0.0	4 534	32.7	10.7	95	23.2	18.9
Lavaca County	1 321	32.3	15.1	50	16.0	12.0	13	0.0	0.0	2 192	36.4	6.3	299	29.1	16.4
Lee County	1 957	31.9	14.9	25	20.0	8.0	14	57.1	0.0	2 860	43.9	1.5	209	42.1	2.9
Leon County	1 537	25.5	25.2	30	20.0	0.0	17	17.6	17.6	1 206	41.9	1.3	158	31.6	18.4
Liberty County	8 884	24.5	9.6	341	15.8	3.2	241	10.4	7.1	7 661	36.0	1.2	1 102	42.4	10.1
Limestone County	4 242	30.4	12.5	63	55.6	3.2	89	16.9	0.0	2 862	36.2	3.3	277	35.4	8.7
Lipscomb County	10	20.0	30.0	45	37.8	4.4	5	X	X	587	43.6	1.7	76	47.4	0.0
Live Oak County	312	1.9	0.0	42	0.0	28.6	18	16.7	0.0	4 671	28.1	9.1	272	36.4	16.5
Llano County	22	0.0	0.0	25	0.0	0.0	23	21.7	30.4	876	41.0	4.8	150	15.3	24.0
Loving County	0	X	X	0	X	X	0	X	X	12	58.3	0.0	0	X	X
Lubbock County	18 779	33.3	7.8	1 405	29.1	4.1	3 043	20.0	4.4	66 568	36.2	4.7	4 800	40.0	5.4
Lynn County	203	39.9	10.3	46	54.3	0.0	13	53.8	0.0	2 903	37.3	7.9	158	60.8	8.9
McCulloch County	112	4.5	42.0	27	37.0	0.0	0	X	X	2 185	37.7	9.8	129	31.0	21.7
McLennan County	32 218	32.8	10.2	1 034	34.8	1.7	2 289	17.5	4.9	38 281	38.3	4.6	3 715	50.3	4.8
McMullen County	4	0.0	0.0	4	0.0	0.0	0	X	X	293	29.7	11.9	26	46.2	0.0
Madison County	3 094	18.1	9.0	15	26.7	0.0	41	29.3	0.0	2 044	27.1	2.3	110	48.2	7.3
Marion County	2 629	28.1	19.6	140	22.9	7.9	0	X	X	153	36.6	7.8	183	35.0	2.2
Martin County	80	37.5	15.0	22	31.8	0.0	13	15.4	7.7	1 969	43.6	5.6	77	44.2	0.0

[1] Hispanic or Latino persons may be of any race.

STATE County	Total households	Family households (percent)						Nonfamily households (percent)						Percent of householders 65 years and over who live alone	Grandparents who are responsible for the care of their grandchildren
		Married-couple family households			Other family households			Two or more unrelated persons		Male living alone		Female living alone			
		Total	With children	Householder 65 years or over	Total	With children	Householder 65 years or over	Total	Householder 65 years or over	Total	Householder 65 years or over	Total	Householder 65 years or over		
	29	30	31	32	33	34	35	36	37	38	39	40	41	42	43
TEXAS—Cont'd															
Guadalupe County	30 939	62.9	29.7	10.1	14.8	8.6	2.1	3.4	0.2	8.6	2.1	10.3	5.3	37.6	1 227
Hale County	11 950	61.5	31.7	11.4	15.5	9.4	2.2	2.0	0.2	8.1	2.5	12.9	7.6	42.1	565
Hall County	1 527	52.8	22.3	12.9	12.3	6.7	3.5	2.2	0.1	11.3	3.7	21.4	15.7	53.9	66
Hamilton County...........	3 368	60.0	22.4	16.3	9.9	5.8	1.9	1.7	0.2	10.5	4.3	17.9	13.1	48.5	73
Hansford County	2 023	66.0	31.3	12.6	8.2	5.2	1.3	1.9	0.4	9.8	2.9	14.1	9.9	47.3	68
Hardeman County	1 960	56.6	23.5	14.4	11.9	7.8	2.6	2.2	0.6	9.4	2.7	19.8	13.8	48.4	43
Hardin County	17 886	62.9	29.9	9.9	14.2	8.4	2.3	2.2	0.2	9.2	2.6	11.5	6.5	42.7	570
Harris County	1 206 423	51.6	28.2	5.5	18.1	10.3	1.9	5.3	0.3	12.0	1.3	13.0	4.0	41.3	39 104
Harrison County	23 141	57.2	25.2	9.6	16.7	9.0	2.9	2.6	0.3	10.0	2.9	13.6	8.1	46.1	783
Hartley County	1 590	70.5	31.1	11.6	5.3	3.3	0.6	2.5	0.5	7.5	1.6	14.2	11.3	50.2	24
Haskell County	2 571	60.1	22.7	18.7	9.5	6.0	1.9	1.4	0.1	9.7	3.4	19.3	13.7	45.2	86
Hays County	33 465	54.2	27.3	7.3	12.7	7.3	1.5	12.2	0.2	9.8	1.0	11.1	3.9	35.5	685
Hemphill County	1 275	65.3	27.8	11.8	8.8	5.3	1.6	1.6	0.4	9.6	2.0	14.6	9.8	46.2	35
Henderson County	28 830	59.5	21.9	15.3	13.6	7.6	2.3	3.2	0.4	9.9	3.0	13.8	8.4	38.8	1 261
Hidalgo County.............	156 708	66.0	39.6	11.7	19.0	10.6	3.1	2.0	0.3	5.1	1.7	7.9	4.7	29.5	8 736
Hill County	12 234	58.5	23.8	13.5	13.7	7.8	2.6	3.3	0.3	10.3	3.3	14.3	9.1	43.1	570
Hockley County	7 983	61.5	30.0	10.3	14.9	9.4	2.0	2.3	0.2	9.1	2.2	12.1	7.6	43.9	454
Hood County	16 135	65.1	23.6	16.8	10.1	5.7	2.1	3.3	0.5	9.2	2.6	12.4	7.2	33.6	627
Hopkins County	12 303	59.6	26.8	11.7	13.0	6.8	1.8	3.4	0.3	9.4	2.4	14.5	9.0	45.4	479
Houston County	8 268	53.1	19.8	14.1	16.9	8.3	4.0	2.3	0.2	10.6	3.7	17.1	11.2	44.9	341
Howard County	11 411	54.6	23.2	12.4	16.0	9.8	2.7	2.7	0.6	9.4	3.1	17.3	10.3	46.0	466
Hudspeth County	1 100	62.2	37.1	8.0	15.4	10.4	1.9	1.8	0.7	11.1	2.7	9.5	6.2	45.6	89
Hunt County	28 751	57.6	25.0	10.1	14.3	8.4	1.7	4.0	0.4	10.9	2.7	13.3	7.3	45.0	1 029
Hutchinson County........	9 282	61.9	28.3	12.5	12.0	6.7	1.8	2.2	0.1	9.4	3.4	14.4	9.0	46.2	317
Irion County	692	66.5	27.5	13.6	8.8	5.3	1.4	2.6	0.0	13.3	5.2	8.8	6.2	43.2	37
Jack County	3 040	62.0	26.4	13.4	11.7	6.9	2.0	1.8	0.0	10.3	3.8	14.2	9.1	45.6	93
Jackson County.............	5 340	60.4	28.6	11.4	13.8	7.9	2.7	1.7	0.4	10.3	3.4	13.8	9.2	46.3	239
Jasper County	13 443	59.5	25.5	12.7	14.8	8.3	2.4	2.5	0.5	9.5	3.0	13.7	8.4	43.3	560
Jeff Davis County........	895	60.8	24.2	13.6	9.5	4.7	2.2	2.9	0.0	14.9	3.5	12.0	6.7	39.1	39
Jefferson County	92 993	49.1	22.0	10.0	20.1	11.6	3.3	3.5	0.2	11.8	3.0	15.5	8.6	45.9	3 390
Jim Hogg County	1 816	58.5	32.9	10.8	17.5	9.1	4.7	0.8	0.0	11.1	4.4	12.1	9.4	47.0	103
Jim Wells County	12 971	60.6	30.0	11.4	17.8	9.7	3.5	1.9	0.2	9.6	3.1	10.1	6.1	37.8	687
Johnson County	43 626	66.5	33.3	9.2	12.9	7.9	1.6	3.3	0.3	7.4	1.7	9.9	5.4	39.1	1 579
Jones County	6 143	60.9	26.2	12.8	12.9	7.9	2.2	2.0	0.4	8.9	3.2	15.2	10.1	46.3	266
Karnes County	4 478	53.6	23.4	13.0	19.7	11.4	4.2	2.6	0.4	9.9	3.4	14.2	10.3	43.9	171
Kaufman County	24 363	64.5	32.2	9.3	14.7	8.5	2.3	2.9	0.3	7.6	1.6	10.3	5.6	37.6	1 163
Kendall County	8 622	67.6	30.8	12.9	9.7	6.1	1.1	3.6	0.1	7.9	1.6	11.3	6.7	37.0	135
Kenedy County.............	138	52.9	26.1	8.7	27.5	10.9	8.0	0.7	0.0	13.8	3.6	5.1	2.2	25.8	16
Kent County	351	62.7	22.5	17.9	8.3	4.6	3.1	1.1	0.0	14.0	3.4	14.0	8.0	35.1	4
Kerr County	17 765	57.2	18.9	19.6	12.0	7.0	1.8	3.2	0.7	9.2	3.8	18.3	12.4	42.2	636
Kimble County	1 879	58.8	21.3	16.0	11.3	7.4	1.5	1.6	0.5	10.7	4.0	17.5	12.0	46.9	65
King County	111	85.6	42.3	20.7	0.0	0.0	0.0	0.0	0.0	10.8	2.7	3.6	1.8	17.9	0
Kinney County	1 306	60.2	22.9	20.2	10.9	5.4	3.1	2.0	0.8	14.9	9.0	12.1	9.2	42.9	41
Kleberg County	10 918	52.3	25.2	9.0	19.4	10.7	2.6	6.0	0.3	10.0	1.5	12.2	6.3	39.4	470
Knox County................	1 671	57.9	23.6	15.9	11.4	7.4	2.3	1.3	0.1	10.6	4.2	18.9	12.9	48.4	81
Lamar County...............	19 048	54.7	22.9	10.7	16.6	10.2	2.4	2.6	0.3	9.9	2.9	16.2	9.7	48.4	755
Lamb County	5 361	59.4	27.7	14.0	15.2	8.6	3.0	1.8	0.3	8.8	2.7	14.8	10.2	42.7	248
Lampasas County	6 530	62.4	27.9	11.7	12.1	7.4	1.7	3.5	0.4	7.5	2.2	14.6	8.4	43.3	157
La Salle County	1 821	53.1	28.1	9.6	21.6	11.6	4.5	2.6	0.5	11.7	5.1	11.0	7.9	47.1	148
Lavaca County	7 660	58.1	23.7	15.2	12.3	6.5	2.8	1.9	0.4	10.4	3.8	17.3	12.6	47.0	205
Lee County..................	5 674	61.9	30.6	11.5	11.9	6.8	2.1	2.3	0.1	10.4	3.0	13.5	8.2	44.9	152
Leon County.................	6 212	62.5	23.1	17.4	11.2	6.3	2.3	1.9	0.4	10.0	3.1	14.4	9.9	39.4	268
Liberty County	23 238	61.1	30.0	8.5	16.1	9.2	2.6	2.5	0.1	9.0	2.5	11.3	6.7	45.2	1 043
Limestone County	7 908	54.5	22.5	11.8	16.6	9.9	2.2	3.0	0.7	10.3	3.5	15.5	10.3	48.4	271
Lipscomb County	1 209	62.3	28.9	12.7	7.0	4.2	1.4	2.2	0.2	9.8	3.3	18.7	13.7	54.4	36
Live Oak County	4 226	61.6	24.5	15.3	11.9	6.2	2.3	2.9	0.5	11.7	4.4	12.0	7.7	40.2	191
Llano County................	7 906	61.1	13.8	24.0	7.6	3.8	1.5	3.1	0.7	11.2	4.8	17.1	11.6	38.5	199
Loving County	30	56.7	23.3	10.0	0.0	0.0	0.0	0.0	0.0	20.0	0.0	23.3	10.0	50.0	0
Lubbock County	92 685	49.2	22.8	8.4	16.3	9.5	1.9	7.7	0.3	11.5	1.8	15.3	6.3	43.1	3 703
Lynn County	2 366	63.2	31.8	12.1	12.3	8.2	2.0	1.6	0.3	11.1	4.2	11.9	8.6	47.2	136
McCulloch County	3 288	57.8	24.7	15.2	11.5	7.0	1.3	2.8	0.6	10.6	3.7	17.3	12.3	48.2	90
McLennan County	78 926	51.1	23.8	9.6	16.2	9.5	2.3	6.7	0.4	10.7	2.0	15.3	7.9	44.5	2 730
McMullen County	358	60.3	22.3	14.2	8.4	4.2	1.4	0.6	0.6	19.3	8.4	11.5	8.1	50.4	2
Madison County	3 937	55.6	22.6	13.4	16.9	9.6	3.4	2.9	0.6	9.0	2.4	15.6	11.4	44.1	199
Marion County..............	4 605	51.8	16.2	14.0	16.4	8.8	3.6	3.0	0.7	14.0	4.9	14.8	9.0	43.1	208
Martin County...............	1 636	66.1	33.8	12.9	11.6	9.0	1.4	0.7	0.1	10.5	3.5	11.1	7.5	43.1	62

STATE County	Households with Non-Hispanic White householder		Households with Black or African American householder		Households with American Indian and Alaska Native householder		Households with Asian, Hawaiian, and Pacific Islander householder		Households with Hispanic or Latino[1] householder		Foreign-born population	Place of birth (percent)			Percent in non-English speaking households	
	Number of households	Percent that are family households	Number of households	Percent that are family households	Number of households	Percent that are family households	Number of households	Percent that are family households	Number of households	Percent that are family households	Percent of total population that is foreign-born	Europe	Asia	Latin America	Linguistically isolated	Not linguistically isolated
	44	45	46	47	48	49	50	51	52	53	54	55	56	57	58	59
TEXAS—Cont'd																
Guadalupe County	20 755	75.1	1 739	74.7	143	86.0	215	89.8	7 835	84.7	6.5	0.7	0.9	4.8	4.6	33.3
Hale County	6 538	70.8	576	68.2	105	74.3	89	89.9	4 676	87.0	8.2	0.1	0.5	7.5	8.5	41.0
Hall County	1 132	58.2	101	75.2	4	100.0	4	0.0	280	90.4	9.1	0.1	0.1	8.8	7.2	24.4
Hamilton County	3 217	69.7	0	X	4	100.0	0	X	132	72.0	3.7	0.5	0.0	3.1	2.2	11.0
Hansford County	1 537	69.1	0	X	13	100.0	0	X	457	92.3	15.6	0.1	0.5	15.0	9.0	25.5
Hardeman County	1 628	66.3	114	64.9	9	100.0	12	50.0	189	87.8	2.5	0.0	0.4	2.1	2.3	14.8
Hardin County	16 229	77.4	1 174	71.4	45	62.2	86	81.4	257	85.2	1.3	0.3	0.4	0.4	0.4	6.5
Harris County	609 381	63.6	229 194	67.8	4 858	75.1	55 719	76.8	293 972	82.8	22.2	1.1	4.3	15.9	11.4	31.7
Harrison County	16 704	76.0	5 428	65.8	52	90.4	36	94.4	750	82.9	3.3	0.3	0.3	2.6	1.4	8.7
Hartley County	1 481	75.6	6	100.0	0	X	0	X	98	75.5	2.6	0.2	0.1	2.1	2.0	6.3
Haskell County	2 070	67.7	92	55.4	11	100.0	2	100.0	393	81.9	3.6	0.3	0.1	3.2	3.1	21.1
Hays County	24 136	64.7	831	66.7	180	61.1	212	64.2	7 711	75.0	5.6	0.8	0.6	4.0	3.5	29.2
Hemphill County	1 123	72.5	3	0.0	18	61.1	0	X	125	92.0	6.5	0.3	0.0	6.2	3.0	16.2
Henderson County	25 351	72.4	1 776	69.7	135	88.9	86	77.9	1 217	90.7	3.8	0.2	0.2	3.2	1.7	9.6
Hidalgo County	27 565	70.8	553	68.7	710	82.1	1 099	73.9	126 900	88.3	29.5	0.2	0.4	28.7	20.0	69.9
Hill County	10 159	71.3	868	64.5	62	91.9	18	50.0	1 032	86.9	5.9	0.2	0.2	5.3	3.3	15.4
Hockley County	5 273	73.3	229	73.8	80	72.5	25	76.0	2 331	84.4	5.2	0.3	0.3	4.5	5.3	34.4
Hood County	15 059	75.3	7	0.0	92	90.2	47	74.5	725	73.4	3.3	0.4	0.2	2.5	1.4	9.4
Hopkins County	10 305	72.4	995	65.2	108	82.4	30	76.7	782	85.4	5.6	0.7	0.2	4.6	2.9	11.3
Houston County	5 974	71.6	1 937	64.5	24	33.3	22	77.3	269	77.7	3.0	0.2	0.3	2.4	1.4	7.6
Howard County	8 063	67.0	444	61.9	28	60.7	29	62.1	2 724	82.5	6.0	0.1	0.4	5.4	4.3	28.7
Hudspeth County	361	65.7	5	100.0	12	33.3	0	X	721	84.0	33.2	0.1	0.1	33.0	27.7	51.6
Hunt County	24 038	72.0	2 465	66.5	220	85.9	136	57.4	1 573	81.1	4.7	0.3	0.5	3.6	2.3	10.9
Hutchinson County	7 861	72.5	181	68.5	120	60.8	18	38.9	937	91.1	5.8	0.3	0.1	5.3	4.1	14.0
Irion County	554	74.5	6	50.0	3	0.0	0	X	125	82.4	3.5	0.2	0.0	3.3	3.5	28.3
Jack County	2 832	73.8	34	76.5	9	77.8	9	55.6	132	76.5	2.8	0.1	0.3	2.3	1.1	8.8
Jackson County	3 828	74.0	432	56.3	15	100.0	15	100.0	1 023	81.7	4.8	0.2	0.2	4.4	4.0	22.5
Jasper County	10 711	74.6	2 216	71.3	39	89.7	41	73.2	312	82.1	2.2	0.2	0.3	1.7	1.5	6.0
Jeff Davis County	607	68.0	0	X	0	X	0	X	265	77.7	10.9	0.9	0.1	8.9	9.0	33.8
Jefferson County	54 686	66.5	29 102	70.9	392	79.8	1 884	81.6	6 241	82.2	6.2	0.3	1.8	3.8	3.3	15.4
Jim Hogg County	167	72.5	13	0.0	8	100.0	13	100.0	1 636	77.0	5.1	0.0	0.1	4.9	13.1	81.2
Jim Wells County	3 691	71.9	55	74.5	103	98.1	45	77.8	9 115	81.1	3.6	0.1	0.3	3.1	12.0	64.6
Johnson County	38 091	79.1	810	72.1	308	65.9	189	92.6	3 824	84.8	5.2	0.3	0.4	4.1	2.5	14.7
Jones County	4 906	72.7	223	64.1	34	100.0	24	66.7	903	82.2	1.6	0.1	0.2	1.3	2.2	17.1
Karnes County	2 458	60.9	91	64.8	41	78.0	0	X	1 884	78.1	3.7	0.2	0.1	3.3	9.1	46.5
Kaufman County	19 648	78.8	2 353	75.6	167	68.9	147	87.1	1 860	90.2	5.7	0.3	0.6	4.7	3.2	12.5
Kendall County	7 292	75.8	6	100.0	43	72.1	35	51.4	1 207	87.2	5.6	1.0	0.3	4.0	2.6	22.6
Kenedy County	26	80.8	0	X	0	X	0	X	112	80.4	13.3	0.7	0.0	12.6	20.3	71.7
Kent County	312	70.2	4	50.0	3	100.0	0	X	65	90.0	1.7	0.2	0.0	1.5	1.4	12.8
Kerr County	15 001	68.0	281	56.9	87	74.7	26	100.0	2 292	78.9	6.6	0.7	0.4	5.1	3.6	20.8
Kimble County	1 589	67.8	5	100.0	13	76.9	4	100.0	261	84.7	5.5	0.4	0.1	4.8	4.0	20.9
King County	101	90.1	0	X	0	X	0	X	7	57.1	2.2	0.0	0.0	2.2	1.0	6.9
Kinney County	754	65.1	26	76.9	6	100.0	7	100.0	503	78.9	11.7	0.7	0.5	10.1	10.1	48.5
Kleberg County	3 924	67.3	322	63.4	65	76.9	79	39.2	6 468	75.5	6.5	0.3	1.2	4.8	8.7	61.1
Knox County	1 227	66.8	106	61.3	7	57.1	2	100.0	325	82.8	6.7	0.2	0.4	6.1	6.6	23.1
Lamar County	15 784	71.4	2 425	68.8	175	76.6	28	92.9	397	83.9	2.1	0.2	0.3	1.5	1.2	6.7
Lamb County	3 192	68.7	233	79.4	48	77.1	7	57.1	1 895	84.1	6.3	0.1	0.1	6.1	7.3	36.3
Lampasas County	5 483	73.6	201	73.1	17	82.4	28	67.9	750	82.9	6.0	2.2	0.4	3.1	3.2	22.5
La Salle County	404	58.4	0	X	8	100.0	7	71.4	1 407	79.5	4.0	0.3	0.6	3.0	20.5	63.6
Lavaca County	6 375	69.9	503	65.6	24	91.7	6	16.7	689	81.9	2.5	0.2	0.1	2.2	2.7	18.3
Lee County	4 291	72.4	706	69.0	16	75.0	2	100.0	638	89.2	6.1	0.3	0.0	5.7	4.1	22.2
Leon County	5 097	76.0	708	53.1	12	75.0	1	100.0	353	85.6	4.2	0.3	0.1	3.7	2.0	9.7
Liberty County	18 685	76.8	2 538	74.2	120	70.0	60	70.0	1 645	90.2	5.1	0.1	0.2	4.6	2.8	13.8
Limestone County	5 830	71.9	1 355	62.1	17	82.4	19	100.0	630	84.9	5.5	0.1	0.3	5.1	3.4	13.1
Lipscomb County	1 035	66.1	6	100.0	12	100.0	0	X	147	90.5	11.7	0.2	0.0	11.3	6.5	15.9
Live Oak County	2 945	70.6	11	63.6	24	45.8	1	100.0	1 216	81.3	2.3	0.2	0.0	1.9	3.4	37.8
Llano County	7 614	68.4	13	46.2	18	100.0	5	100.0	204	80.4	2.0	0.5	0.1	1.4	0.4	10.6
Loving County	29	55.2	0	X	0	X	0	X	1	100.0	0.0	0.0	0.0	0.0	17.9	25.4
Lubbock County	64 668	61.4	6 377	70.3	509	73.1	1 134	52.5	19 607	78.8	3.3	0.4	1.1	1.5	3.2	27.7
Lynn County	1 398	71.9	65	73.8	6	100.0	4	50.0	899	81.2	5.0	0.1	0.1	4.8	6.7	39.3
McCulloch County	2 481	68.1	72	38.9	10	100.0	0	X	691	75.7	3.2	0.0	0.0	3.2	3.1	25.1
McLennan County	55 495	65.2	11 734	66.3	355	83.4	778	50.1	10 199	80.6	6.1	0.4	0.7	4.9	4.0	17.5
McMullen County	247	66.0	2	100.0	0	X	0	X	109	74.3	4.2	0.2	0.0	4.0	5.5	36.2
Madison County	2 985	72.9	624	66.2	6	100.0	15	100.0	285	80.0	4.8	0.1	0.2	4.3	5.4	10.4
Marion County	3 433	68.8	1 016	63.8	57	70.2	0	X	42	85.7	0.9	0.3	0.0	0.6	0.5	5.9
Martin County	1 059	75.8	35	48.6	6	100.0	5	80.0	532	83.1	8.1	0.0	0.3	7.6	7.8	39.1

[1] Hispanic or Latino persons may be of any race.

STATE/ County code	MSA/PMSA/ NECMA code[1]	STATE County	Total population	Under 5 years	5 to 17 years	18 to 24 years	25 to 44 years	45 to 64 years	65 years and over	Median age	+/− U.S. percent under 18 years	+/− U.S. percent 65 years and over	Total population	Under 18 years	65 years and over
						Population by age (percent)							Non-Hispanic White Age (percent)		
			1	2	3	4	5	6	7	8	9	10	11	12	13
		TEXAS—Cont'd													
48 319	...	Mason County	3 738	5.1	17.4	5.3	19.8	29.0	23.5	46.7	-3.2	11.1	2 894	19.1	27.4
48 321	...	Matagorda County	37 957	7.0	22.8	8.2	28.0	21.0	12.9	34.8	4.1	0.5	19 932	23.5	17.0
48 323	...	Maverick County	47 297	10.0	27.0	9.1	26.9	17.4	9.6	27.8	11.3	-2.8	1 503	27.8	15.4
48 325	...	Medina County	39 304	6.9	22.1	8.4	29.6	20.8	12.3	34.4	3.3	-0.1	19 854	24.0	17.0
48 327	...	Menard County	2 360	4.6	19.7	5.3	22.2	26.0	22.1	44.1	-1.4	9.7	1 552	19.7	27.5
48 329	5800	Midland County	116 009	7.4	22.8	8.6	28.8	20.7	11.7	34.1	4.5	-0.7	71 856	25.1	15.5
48 331	...	Milam County	24 238	6.5	20.9	8.1	24.5	23.1	17.0	38.0	1.7	4.6	16 699	22.0	21.2
48 333	...	Mills County	5 151	5.5	20.1	4.8	21.0	25.6	23.0	44.4	-0.1	10.6	4 438	23.2	25.2
48 335	...	Mitchell County	9 698	4.7	15.5	11.4	31.7	22.3	14.4	38.6	-5.5	2.0	5 334	18.1	22.9
48 337	...	Montague County	19 117	5.9	18.1	6.9	24.3	24.9	19.8	41.3	-1.7	7.4	17 710	22.9	21.1
48 339	3360	Montgomery County	293 768	7.6	21.7	8.1	30.8	23.1	8.7	34.4	3.6	-3.7	238 587	27.7	9.8
48 341	...	Moore County	20 121	9.2	24.4	9.5	29.1	17.4	10.5	30.4	7.9	-1.9	10 045	24.3	18.5
48 343	...	Morris County	13 048	5.7	19.3	7.7	24.0	24.7	18.6	40.2	-0.7	6.2	9 182	21.5	20.6
48 345	...	Motley County	1 426	6.6	17.2	7.0	19.6	25.2	24.3	44.4	-1.9	11.9	1 170	21.0	26.9
48 347	...	Nacogdoches County	59 203	6.4	17.4	20.1	25.0	19.1	12.0	29.7	-1.9	-0.4	41 576	20.2	14.1
48 349	...	Navarro County	45 124	7.3	20.3	9.7	27.1	21.2	14.5	35.2	1.9	2.1	29 705	23.4	18.0
48 351	...	Newton County	15 072	6.5	19.7	9.2	26.2	24.3	14.1	36.9	0.5	1.7	11 187	24.4	15.4
48 353	...	Nolan County	15 802	6.2	20.8	8.4	26.0	21.8	16.8	37.4	1.3	4.4	10 515	22.5	21.0
48 355	1880	Nueces County	313 645	7.6	20.7	10.5	29.0	21.0	11.2	33.3	2.6	-1.2	118 136	21.2	16.2
48 357	...	Ochiltree County	9 006	8.2	22.5	8.9	28.2	20.7	11.5	33.7	5.0	-0.9	5 997	25.6	16.8
48 359	...	Oldham County	2 185	6.6	28.5	7.6	23.3	22.8	11.0	32.9	9.4	-1.4	1 823	31.7	12.9
48 361	0840	Orange County	84 966	6.7	20.5	8.9	28.2	23.0	12.6	36.1	1.5	0.2	72 921	25.8	13.4
48 363	...	Palo Pinto County	27 026	6.5	19.2	8.5	25.7	23.6	16.4	38.3	0.0	4.0	22 268	23.2	18.5
48 365	...	Panola County	22 756	5.6	19.8	9.3	25.0	24.2	16.1	38.8	-0.3	3.7	17 634	23.5	17.1
48 367	2800	Parker County	88 495	6.4	21.2	7.9	29.6	24.4	10.5	36.5	1.9	-1.9	79 044	27.0	11.4
48 369	...	Parmer County	10 016	7.9	25.1	8.4	26.5	19.4	12.7	32.1	7.3	0.3	4 855	24.9	21.7
48 371	...	Pecos County	16 809	6.3	21.2	13.7	27.2	19.9	11.6	31.2	1.8	-0.8	5 605	20.7	17.0
48 373	...	Polk County	41 133	5.5	17.2	8.1	26.5	24.7	18.0	39.3	-3.0	5.6	30 681	21.0	21.7
48 375	0320	Potter County	113 546	8.3	19.7	10.9	30.7	18.7	11.7	32.1	2.3	-0.7	65 492	21.4	17.0
48 377	...	Presidio County	7 304	7.7	25.2	8.2	25.2	19.5	14.2	32.8	7.2	1.8	1 041	19.4	19.1
48 379	...	Rains County	9 139	5.5	18.3	7.2	25.2	27.5	16.3	41.0	-1.9	3.9	8 219	22.7	17.0
48 381	0320	Randall County	104 312	6.9	19.0	11.2	28.7	22.3	11.9	34.9	0.2	-0.5	89 417	24.4	13.3
48 383	...	Reagan County	3 326	8.3	25.9	7.0	28.4	19.6	10.8	32.4	8.5	-1.6	1 531	26.0	17.6
48 385	...	Real County	3 047	4.6	19.1	5.8	21.4	28.7	20.5	44.6	-2.0	8.1	2 325	21.2	23.5
48 387	...	Red River County	14 314	5.7	18.2	7.6	25.2	23.7	19.5	40.4	-1.8	7.1	10 857	20.9	22.4
48 389	...	Reeves County	13 137	7.1	22.7	11.7	24.7	21.2	12.7	32.1	4.1	0.3	2 945	11.8	22.3
48 391	...	Refugio County	7 828	6.2	19.9	7.7	26.3	23.0	16.9	38.6	0.4	4.5	3 689	20.4	21.8
48 393	...	Roberts County	887	5.0	20.0	4.8	24.1	31.7	14.4	42.0	-0.7	2.0	864	24.1	14.6
48 395	...	Robertson County	16 000	7.2	21.1	7.9	24.1	23.0	16.7	37.6	2.6	4.3	9 608	22.4	20.7
48 397	1920	Rockwall County	43 080	7.3	22.8	7.0	31.0	23.5	8.4	35.3	4.4	-4.0	35 660	28.8	9.6
48 399	...	Runnels County	11 495	5.9	20.9	6.0	24.7	22.5	20.0	39.4	1.1	7.6	7 750	21.0	25.7
48 401	...	Rusk County	47 372	6.2	18.7	7.8	28.4	23.2	15.6	38.1	-0.8	3.2	33 701	22.4	18.0
48 403	...	Sabine County	10 469	5.2	15.8	5.6	20.9	27.6	24.9	47.0	-4.7	12.5	9 108	19.7	26.0
48 405	...	San Augustine County	8 946	5.7	18.0	6.8	23.2	25.1	21.3	42.1	-2.0	8.9	6 045	20.0	25.4
48 407	...	San Jacinto County	22 246	6.1	19.3	6.9	25.1	26.5	16.0	40.0	-0.3	3.6	17 986	23.1	17.4
48 409	1880	San Patricio County	67 138	7.9	23.0	10.1	28.2	20.3	10.4	32.0	5.2	-2.0	30 784	25.4	14.1
48 411	...	San Saba County	6 186	5.1	22.8	7.5	22.3	21.6	20.7	39.4	2.2	8.3	4 553	22.5	25.4
48 413	...	Schleicher County	2 935	6.3	21.4	7.1	24.0	24.9	16.2	38.8	2.0	3.8	1 584	19.5	23.7
48 415	...	Scurry County	16 361	6.3	18.8	10.0	27.6	22.0	15.3	37.0	-0.6	2.9	10 698	21.0	20.7
48 417	...	Shackelford County	3 302	5.1	21.9	5.7	24.9	24.3	18.0	40.1	1.3	5.6	3 003	25.6	19.4
48 419	...	Shelby County	25 224	6.7	19.8	9.0	26.0	21.9	16.5	36.9	0.8	4.1	17 549	23.0	20.0
48 421	...	Sherman County	3 186	7.0	24.0	7.2	26.3	21.8	13.6	34.4	5.3	1.2	2 256	27.0	17.8
48 423	8640	Smith County	174 706	7.1	19.5	9.8	27.6	22.0	14.0	35.5	0.9	1.6	118 784	22.7	17.3
48 425	...	Somervell County	6 809	6.5	21.7	7.6	26.9	24.1	13.2	36.8	2.5	0.8	5 806	26.4	15.2
48 427	...	Starr County	53 597	10.4	27.0	10.9	27.1	16.4	8.1	26.1	11.7	-4.3	847	20.1	17.4
48 429	...	Stephens County	9 674	5.4	18.9	8.7	26.6	22.8	17.6	38.9	-1.4	5.2	7 771	21.7	20.7
48 431	...	Sterling County	1 393	5.0	23.5	5.8	29.1	22.2	14.4	37.9	2.8	2.0	953	24.6	17.4
48 433	...	Stonewall County	1 693	4.8	17.5	6.1	23.0	24.6	24.0	43.7	-3.4	11.6	1 395	19.0	26.6
48 435	...	Sutton County	4 077	7.3	21.4	6.7	28.1	22.1	14.3	36.5	3.0	1.9	1 936	24.0	14.1
48 437	...	Swisher County	8 378	7.6	20.7	9.7	25.7	20.5	15.9	34.6	2.6	3.5	4 839	21.0	23.4
48 439	2800	Tarrant County	1 446 219	7.9	20.1	9.8	33.8	20.1	8.3	32.3	2.3	-4.1	895 446	23.9	11.0
48 441	0040	Taylor County	126 555	7.1	19.5	13.8	27.9	19.5	12.3	32.2	0.9	-0.1	92 004	22.6	15.3
48 443	...	Terrell County	1 081	5.3	21.3	5.4	23.8	26.2	18.1	42.0	0.9	5.7	512	22.1	19.5
48 445	...	Terry County	12 761	7.1	21.1	9.0	28.2	20.0	14.5	35.0	2.5	2.1	6 319	23.1	23.1
48 447	...	Throckmorton County	1 850	5.8	19.8	5.6	23.0	25.1	20.6	41.8	-0.1	8.2	1 684	24.4	22.4
48 449	...	Titus County	28 118	8.7	21.6	9.5	28.6	19.0	12.5	31.8	4.6	0.1	16 857	23.9	18.1

[1]MSA = Metropolitan Statistical Area. PMSA = Primary MSA. NECMA = New England County Metropolitan Area. See the Appendix A for explanation of these concepts. See Appendix B for list of metropolitan areas identified by type, with component counties.

STATE County	Black or African American Total population	Age (percent) Under 18 years	Age (percent) 65 years and over	American Indian and Alaska Native Total population	Age (percent) Under 18 years	Age (percent) 65 years and over	Asian, Hawaiian, and Pacific Islander Total population	Age (percent) Under 18 years	Age (percent) 65 years and over	Hispanic or Latino[1] Total population	Age (percent) Under 18 years	Age (percent) 65 years and over	Two or more races Total population	Age (percent) Under 18 years	Age (percent) 65 years and over
	14	15	16	17	18	19	20	21	22	23	24	25	26	27	28
TEXAS—Cont'd															
Mason County	8	0.0	50.0	49	0.0	14.3	0	X	X	793	36.1	8.8	25	20.0	0.0
Matagorda County	4 802	32.9	14.2	197	31.0	3.6	903	44.3	4.9	11 881	38.4	6.2	1 051	42.2	9.1
Maverick County	57	28.1	8.8	529	41.6	4.7	200	24.0	1.0	45 088	37.3	9.5	1 542	24.8	17.7
Medina County	785	7.6	2.8	255	33.7	6.7	90	7.8	0.0	17 880	35.5	7.7	1 333	45.6	5.3
Menard County	14	35.7	35.7	16	0.0	12.5	6	33.3	0.0	770	33.2	11.4	14	21.4	0.0
Midland County	8 204	33.6	10.7	757	34.6	6.5	1 076	31.4	5.3	33 557	39.8	4.3	2 417	50.0	5.6
Milam County	2 536	36.4	13.1	148	21.6	12.2	40	0.0	0.0	4 601	42.7	4.3	326	27.9	6.1
Mills County	41	65.9	0.0	5	0.0	0.0	4	100.0	0.0	643	40.7	9.8	55	23.6	7.3
Mitchell County	1 236	9.3	3.6	40	0.0	0.0	28	39.3	0.0	3 038	28.0	4.2	282	53.5	6.4
Montague County	71	35.2	0.0	70	17.1	14.3	34	5.9	0.0	1 050	46.7	2.3	280	25.7	8.2
Montgomery County	10 023	33.9	7.5	1 596	27.6	4.8	3 328	28.2	1.9	37 066	38.1	2.4	5 491	41.6	4.8
Moore County	114	45.6	0.0	147	46.9	4.1	217	30.4	0.0	9 536	43.3	2.1	472	45.8	6.1
Morris County	3 159	30.7	15.5	45	42.2	11.1	62	62.9	8.1	451	41.9	2.0	189	49.7	12.2
Motley County	46	28.3	28.3	12	50.0	0.0	0	X	X	193	40.4	8.8	16	0.0	12.5
Nacogdoches County	9 827	29.4	10.1	249	6.0	6.0	478	20.7	0.4	6 700	37.7	2.4	1 093	34.9	4.3
Navarro County	7 290	31.1	12.4	181	39.8	6.6	351	14.2	8.3	7 170	39.9	3.3	816	49.5	7.8
Newton County	3 131	31.4	12.3	61	18.0	4.9	67	62.7	4.5	559	27.9	0.0	96	54.2	7.3
Nolan County	614	36.3	11.9	52	30.8	11.5	72	0.0	8.3	4 409	36.1	7.5	269	46.1	11.5
Nueces County	13 239	31.9	10.5	1 911	31.2	4.0	3 602	22.7	7.1	174 743	32.9	8.0	9 972	38.4	7.2
Ochiltree County	0	X	X	73	16.4	0.0	45	48.9	0.0	2 854	41.1	1.0	216	41.2	4.2
Oldham County	37	73.0	0.0	25	12.0	0.0	0	X	X	280	50.0	2.1	23	91.3	0.0
Orange County	7 339	37.1	9.9	406	24.1	5.2	707	30.1	6.1	2 978	38.1	3.3	865	34.8	6.9
Palo Pinto County	571	29.1	16.3	139	18.0	9.4	181	15.5	8.3	3 574	41.1	3.8	466	36.9	12.4
Panola County	4 084	30.4	13.6	108	49.1	12.0	80	17.5	6.3	734	40.7	10.8	165	41.8	4.2
Parker County	1 573	13.9	0.9	544	20.0	7.2	242	20.2	7.0	6 163	38.5	2.8	1 405	40.0	4.1
Parmer County	118	26.3	7.6	74	29.7	14.9	22	0.0	22.7	4 991	41.5	4.1	184	39.1	2.2
Pecos County	719	2.5	3.9	36	27.8	0.0	63	44.4	0.0	10 268	32.6	9.5	487	41.9	9.7
Polk County	5 270	21.9	9.1	706	29.5	7.6	253	15.0	0.8	3 970	33.5	3.9	609	43.8	8.7
Potter County	10 739	29.7	7.8	934	28.3	8.4	3 030	29.2	4.1	32 001	40.0	3.4	3 145	49.4	3.7
Presidio County	12	0.0	0.0	20	55.0	0.0	26	3.8	15.4	6 191	35.4	13.3	55	23.6	32.7
Rains County	315	26.3	14.3	36	8.3	13.9	32	21.9	0.0	417	41.5	7.2	148	38.5	12.8
Randall County	1 430	37.5	1.0	623	21.3	12.5	1 152	19.0	8.4	10 719	37.8	2.2	1 912	43.8	7.8
Reagan County	96	44.8	6.3	19	0.0	42.1	18	61.1	0.0	1 652	41.1	4.8	55	50.9	0.0
Real County	3	0.0	0.0	23	21.7	0.0	6	66.7	0.0	659	32.8	9.9	55	29.1	23.6
Red River County	2 435	30.6	12.9	129	46.5	4.7	31	16.1	6.5	731	40.8	2.6	178	34.3	14.6
Reeves County	334	21.3	22.2	44	15.9	25.0	98	39.8	0.0	9 668	35.5	9.7	469	36.7	8.3
Refugio County	556	29.7	20.3	18	22.2	0.0	38	36.8	0.0	3 498	31.4	11.3	139	36.0	20.9
Roberts County	5	100.0	0.0	0	X	X	2	0.0	100.0	12	50.0	0.0	10	60.0	0.0
Robertson County	3 909	36.6	13.5	61	36.1	9.8	28	21.4	14.3	2 330	30.6	6.1	300	36.0	12.7
Rockwall County	1 369	36.2	3.9	122	17.2	4.1	726	30.0	7.0	4 795	38.1	1.2	572	42.1	7.2
Runnels County	133	23.3	5.3	69	14.5	24.6	13	0.0	0.0	3 380	39.4	8.6	296	38.9	12.8
Rusk County	9 175	27.2	13.3	174	32.2	1.7	130	25.4	3.8	3 934	39.9	1.4	476	42.9	5.0
Sabine County	1 080	30.9	18.4	29	37.9	34.5	12	0.0	0.0	168	33.9	3.0	88	26.1	23.9
San Augustine County	2 595	32.1	13.5	36	50.0	13.9	4	0.0	0.0	265	23.8	1.5	66	60.6	9.1
San Jacinto County	2 823	32.6	12.0	58	6.9	5.2	106	55.7	0.0	998	40.8	7.6	322	37.9	5.9
San Patricio County	1 932	33.4	4.7	466	21.5	6.9	477	22.4	3.6	33 167	36.1	7.4	1 770	44.4	8.7
San Saba County	139	57.6	0.0	54	27.8	13.0	30	50.0	0.0	1 340	41.3	8.2	55	40.0	20.0
Schleicher County	66	21.2	0.0	10	40.0	0.0	5	0.0	0.0	1 280	37.9	7.8	72	34.7	6.9
Scurry County	860	17.1	9.5	160	47.5	0.0	48	18.8	0.0	4 552	35.5	4.6	346	48.6	0.0
Shackelford County	10	60.0	0.0	13	15.4	15.4	6	0.0	0.0	272	43.0	4.0	11	45.5	0.0
Shelby County	4 968	32.6	12.6	63	25.4	7.9	103	17.5	0.0	2 391	39.2	0.8	568	42.8	2.3
Sherman County	14	42.9	0.0	11	63.6	0.0	16	62.5	0.0	891	40.9	3.4	26	38.5	7.7
Smith County	33 296	30.8	10.3	726	31.1	0.4	1 159	37.0	4.6	19 395	41.8	1.7	2 288	45.2	5.0
Somervell County	10	50.0	0.0	42	28.6	9.5	28	25.0	3.6	923	39.4	1.4	91	25.3	0.0
Starr County	43	0.0	20.9	144	22.9	13.2	146	28.8	0.0	52 581	37.7	8.0	621	31.2	6.1
Stephens County	320	16.6	15.6	24	0.0	0.0	91	28.6	0.0	1 371	41.1	1.2	185	37.3	13.0
Sterling County	0	X	X	4	50.0	0.0	0	X	X	436	36.7	8.0	27	66.7	0.0
Stonewall County	63	39.7	9.5	11	18.2	36.4	0	X	X	203	35.5	7.9	27	37.0	40.7
Sutton County	5	0.0	0.0	5	0.0	0.0	27	37.0	0.0	2 109	33.0	14.7	68	22.1	20.6
Swisher County	532	30.6	7.0	50	56.0	6.0	15	0.0	0.0	2 963	39.8	5.2	145	45.5	17.2
Tarrant County	182 365	32.7	5.9	8 809	26.8	4.0	52 848	27.0	3.9	285 338	37.1	2.4	38 464	44.1	3.0
Taylor County	8 284	32.7	7.0	818	30.1	2.9	1 752	26.2	3.7	22 200	38.9	3.7	3 462	51.5	2.6
Terrell County	0	X	X	2	0.0	0.0	2	100.0	0.0	555	31.0	16.6	25	32.0	24.0
Terry County	582	21.6	6.0	72	43.1	0.0	26	0.0	0.0	5 613	36.7	6.0	310	37.1	10.6
Throckmorton County	0	X	X	2	0.0	0.0	0	X	X	145	39.3	1.4	21	28.6	9.5
Titus County	2 947	30.1	13.2	191	32.5	0.0	79	30.4	3.8	7 986	43.7	0.9	537	52.9	2.6

[1] Hispanic or Latino persons may be of any race.

STATE County	Total households	Married-couple family households			Other family households			Two or more unrelated persons		Male living alone		Female living alone		Percent of householders 65 years and over who live alone	Grandparents who are responsible for the care of their grandchildren
		Total	With children	Householder 65 years or over	Total	With children	Householder 65 years or over	Total	Householder 65 years or over	Total	Householder 65 years or over	Total	Householder 65 years or over		
	29	30	31	32	33	34	35	36	37	38	39	40	41	42	43
TEXAS—Cont'd															
Mason County	1 592	61.6	18.7	18.5	7.9	4.0	2.8	1.6	0.3	8.6	3.1	20.4	15.1	45.8	27
Matagorda County	13 939	55.9	28.3	9.9	15.9	9.5	3.2	3.1	0.2	11.7	2.6	13.3	7.1	42.1	475
Maverick County	13 093	67.9	42.4	10.6	18.3	9.6	4.5	0.8	0.1	4.4	1.8	8.6	5.3	31.7	848
Medina County	12 898	66.2	31.8	11.7	13.5	7.8	2.2	2.2	0.5	8.5	3.0	9.6	5.7	37.7	525
Menard County	1 004	52.4	20.0	14.5	14.9	9.2	3.3	2.4	0.0	14.7	7.2	15.5	10.0	49.0	26
Midland County	42 751	58.5	30.3	9.6	14.3	9.3	1.7	2.9	0.2	10.0	1.8	14.2	6.5	42.2	1 451
Milam County	9 185	57.9	24.3	13.1	14.1	7.9	2.9	2.2	0.2	10.1	3.5	15.8	10.4	46.2	360
Mills County	2 000	60.8	22.9	17.5	9.7	6.4	1.9	2.1	0.2	13.3	5.7	14.2	11.2	46.2	37
Mitchell County	2 832	53.1	22.4	13.1	17.9	9.7	3.5	1.6	0.4	10.9	4.6	16.6	11.2	48.1	133
Montague County	7 759	59.6	22.8	14.3	11.1	6.4	1.9	2.0	0.4	10.2	3.9	17.1	11.6	48.5	196
Montgomery County	103 447	65.4	33.7	7.7	12.6	7.4	1.5	3.6	0.2	8.0	1.4	10.4	4.9	40.0	3 196
Moore County	6 810	65.2	35.1	10.1	14.1	9.3	1.7	2.6	0.1	9.0	1.4	9.2	5.7	37.4	272
Morris County	5 235	55.4	19.9	14.3	17.2	9.9	3.0	1.9	0.1	10.0	3.4	15.6	10.4	44.2	205
Motley County	593	61.2	21.9	18.0	10.1	4.4	3.4	2.7	1.3	9.3	2.7	16.7	13.3	41.3	26
Nacogdoches County	22 047	48.6	22.3	8.9	15.6	9.1	2.0	8.3	0.1	11.6	2.1	15.8	7.0	45.4	720
Navarro County	16 531	56.3	24.7	11.4	16.6	9.5	2.6	3.1	0.3	8.9	2.4	15.1	10.2	46.8	683
Newton County	5 598	58.2	24.8	11.9	15.6	7.7	2.6	2.0	0.2	12.0	3.9	12.1	7.1	42.7	274
Nolan County	6 169	52.6	21.9	10.3	17.4	10.9	3.1	3.0	0.4	9.6	3.1	17.4	12.2	52.5	229
Nueces County	110 316	52.4	25.4	9.0	20.2	11.4	2.8	4.8	0.3	10.3	1.9	12.3	5.9	39.1	6 031
Ochiltree County	3 275	67.2	34.1	9.9	9.4	6.4	1.0	2.5	0.2	8.9	1.9	12.1	7.5	45.9	115
Oldham County	741	70.6	31.8	11.7	7.7	4.0	1.6	1.6	0.0	7.7	1.9	12.4	6.3	38.1	29
Orange County	31 651	59.8	27.0	10.3	15.7	9.3	2.3	2.9	0.2	9.1	2.3	12.5	6.8	41.7	1 175
Palo Pinto County	10 618	55.6	22.0	12.2	15.0	8.6	2.8	3.3	0.5	10.8	3.6	15.4	9.6	45.9	543
Panola County	8 822	60.8	25.4	12.3	12.6	6.9	2.8	1.7	0.1	9.4	2.4	15.6	9.9	44.5	321
Parker County	31 151	66.1	30.8	9.9	12.4	7.6	1.7	3.2	0.3	8.0	1.5	10.2	5.4	36.8	1 139
Parmer County	3 307	70.1	37.4	12.3	8.8	6.1	0.9	1.9	0.3	6.5	1.0	12.7	9.0	42.5	135
Pecos County	5 156	63.8	30.9	13.6	14.1	8.8	2.9	2.6	0.3	8.7	2.1	10.9	5.6	31.6	254
Polk County	15 139	59.2	21.9	15.7	13.9	8.0	2.8	2.5	0.5	10.2	3.6	14.2	8.0	37.9	620
Potter County	40 756	48.9	23.4	8.4	19.2	11.8	2.4	4.3	0.3	11.7	2.4	15.8	7.7	47.7	1 395
Presidio County	2 508	58.1	30.2	12.4	16.0	9.7	3.9	2.0	0.6	12.5	5.4	11.4	7.1	42.4	181
Rains County	3 637	63.2	24.0	13.0	11.6	5.9	2.7	3.3	0.5	9.6	2.9	12.3	9.3	43.0	144
Randall County	41 242	58.5	27.3	10.0	11.2	7.2	1.2	4.9	0.4	10.7	1.9	14.7	6.8	42.8	1 023
Reagan County	1 115	69.4	41.7	10.1	10.4	6.4	2.1	0.6	0.4	10.8	3.2	8.8	3.3	34.3	44
Real County	1 231	60.2	20.1	16.2	9.8	6.0	2.1	1.5	0.2	12.8	4.3	15.6	10.2	44.0	50
Red River County	5 816	54.5	21.1	14.0	15.6	7.9	3.2	2.3	0.4	11.2	3.4	16.4	11.4	45.8	268
Reeves County	4 096	58.9	29.1	10.8	18.3	10.6	4.6	1.2	0.4	9.3	3.0	12.2	7.4	39.7	326
Refugio County	2 979	56.2	23.6	12.7	17.0	8.4	3.6	2.3	0.2	12.2	3.5	12.3	8.1	41.4	154
Roberts County	365	71.2	31.2	12.3	4.9	2.2	1.6	0.0	0.0	10.7	3.6	13.2	7.4	44.0	7
Robertson County	6 136	51.6	21.3	11.2	19.4	10.6	3.5	2.2	0.3	12.0	4.2	14.8	10.4	49.5	302
Rockwall County	14 581	72.8	38.8	8.0	10.2	6.9	1.0	2.8	0.2	6.3	0.4	8.0	3.3	28.8	342
Runnels County	4 442	60.0	24.0	15.2	12.1	6.8	1.9	1.4	0.2	8.2	3.3	18.3	13.8	49.6	153
Rusk County	17 336	58.9	24.9	11.7	14.7	7.8	3.3	2.2	0.4	9.1	2.7	15.1	10.2	45.6	771
Sabine County	4 494	60.6	19.3	20.1	10.0	5.2	2.8	2.6	0.5	12.2	5.4	14.6	9.7	39.1	217
San Augustine County	3 619	56.7	19.0	17.3	15.0	7.6	3.2	1.9	0.2	10.5	2.8	15.9	10.6	39.3	193
San Jacinto County	8 673	61.8	23.0	14.8	12.5	7.0	1.9	3.2	0.6	10.8	2.9	11.6	6.8	36.0	340
San Patricio County	22 037	61.1	31.6	9.6	17.2	9.9	3.0	2.9	0.2	8.9	2.3	9.9	5.5	37.7	1 034
San Saba County	2 290	60.0	23.4	16.6	11.1	6.2	2.4	1.4	0.2	11.3	3.5	16.2	11.3	43.5	79
Schleicher County	1 115	63.0	27.8	13.8	9.4	5.7	1.5	2.0	0.7	11.4	2.9	14.3	8.9	42.3	39
Scurry County	5 749	59.2	26.3	12.8	13.1	8.3	1.6	2.6	0.4	9.0	3.1	16.1	10.3	47.5	231
Shackelford County	1 292	61.5	27.8	13.6	11.3	5.6	1.9	1.1	0.2	9.1	1.5	17.0	12.6	47.4	32
Shelby County	9 644	55.4	24.3	11.7	16.9	8.5	3.5	2.4	0.5	10.0	3.2	15.2	10.0	45.6	376
Sherman County	1 129	67.1	34.3	12.9	9.8	7.1	1.5	1.3	0.0	11.0	2.5	10.7	6.3	37.8	41
Smith County	65 711	56.7	25.1	11.2	15.2	8.8	2.4	3.5	0.2	9.0	2.0	15.6	7.9	41.9	2 387
Somervell County	2 437	63.4	31.1	8.8	11.0	6.1	1.3	3.7	0.9	9.8	2.6	12.1	7.7	48.2	65
Starr County	14 378	67.2	43.2	9.3	21.0	11.5	4.2	0.6	0.3	4.1	1.5	7.1	4.6	30.4	945
Stephens County	3 668	57.0	24.0	14.2	13.7	9.0	2.0	3.0	0.1	9.4	2.9	16.8	9.9	43.7	100
Sterling County	515	67.0	32.2	12.0	9.7	6.0	1.0	0.8	0.4	10.7	2.5	11.8	9.3	46.9	18
Stonewall County	710	58.2	21.8	15.8	10.3	4.5	2.3	2.3	0.4	13.0	4.1	16.3	11.1	45.2	30
Sutton County	1 511	65.9	33.1	11.7	10.7	6.0	2.8	0.3	0.0	10.9	2.9	12.2	6.4	39.0	58
Swisher County	2 946	61.1	27.9	15.0	13.1	8.2	2.5	2.0	0.6	7.7	2.5	16.1	11.6	43.8	93
Tarrant County	534 019	53.6	28.1	6.2	16.0	9.6	1.7	5.5	0.2	11.8	1.3	13.1	4.6	41.9	15 697
Taylor County	47 269	54.8	25.8	9.6	14.4	9.4	1.6	5.2	0.3	10.6	2.1	15.0	7.9	46.8	1 649
Terrell County	441	54.6	22.7	11.8	12.7	7.3	2.0	0.7	0.0	13.2	5.2	18.8	13.2	57.0	12
Terry County	4 315	60.4	28.6	12.1	16.1	8.8	3.6	1.6	0.0	7.3	2.0	14.6	10.5	44.3	255
Throckmorton County	763	59.4	24.2	15.7	10.7	5.6	1.2	1.7	0.0	12.1	4.6	16.1	12.1	49.6	12
Titus County	9 565	59.9	30.9	10.6	16.0	9.0	2.1	2.0	0.3	8.1	2.6	14.0	8.2	45.4	360

Table A-3. States and Counties — Age, Ethnicity, and Household Structure

STATE County	Households with Non-Hispanic White householder		Households with Black or African American householder		Households with American Indian and Alaska Native householder		Households with Asian, Hawaiian, and Pacific Islander householder		Households with Hispanic or Latino[1] householder		Foreign-born population	Place of birth (percent)			Percent in non-English speaking households	
	Number of households	Percent that are family households	Number of households	Percent that are family households	Number of households	Percent that are family households	Number of households	Percent that are family households	Number of households	Percent that are family households	Percent of total population that is foreign-born	Europe	Asia	Latin America	Linguistically isolated	Not linguistically isolated
	44	45	46	47	48	49	50	51	52	53	54	55	56	57	58	59
TEXAS—Cont'd																
Mason County	1 345	67.5	4	100.0	22	100.0	0	X	221	78.7	4.7	0.3	0.0	4.4	3.2	23.1
Matagorda County	8 195	71.1	1 969	59.6	83	63.9	192	84.9	3 415	80.5	9.9	0.2	1.3	8.3	6.7	28.5
Maverick County	612	73.4	26	73.1	135	83.7	48	87.5	12 298	86.9	37.8	0.1	0.3	37.4	27.5	69.2
Medina County	7 636	76.7	84	64.3	69	69.6	11	100.0	4 966	84.9	4.1	0.4	0.2	3.4	5.1	44.5
Menard County	724	66.3	4	0.0	13	38.5	0	X	269	71.7	4.8	0.0	0.1	4.7	5.4	32.3
Midland County	29 435	70.2	3 129	63.6	291	74.6	290	83.4	9 433	83.8	7.6	0.3	0.8	6.2	4.6	29.0
Milam County	6 897	71.0	935	64.8	68	79.4	27	51.9	1 176	84.7	5.6	0.6	0.2	4.5	2.0	21.8
Mills County	1 785	69.0	0	X	5	100.0	0	X	192	84.4	4.4	0.0	0.0	4.3	3.3	13.8
Mitchell County	1 920	67.0	117	56.4	20	10.0	3	100.0	752	85.6	2.8	0.2	0.1	2.2	7.5	27.1
Montague County	7 396	70.2	19	100.0	31	67.7	15	53.3	232	87.9	2.4	0.2	0.1	2.0	1.0	9.2
Montgomery County	88 310	77.1	3 548	76.7	528	72.3	1 040	87.7	9 092	87.4	8.6	1.1	0.9	6.1	3.7	15.8
Moore County	4 153	73.8	25	100.0	42	95.2	71	84.5	2 498	88.4	20.9	0.1	0.7	20.0	14.0	32.6
Morris County	3 894	73.3	1 183	70.0	14	85.7	6	100.0	101	78.2	2.0	0.2	0.1	1.6	1.0	6.5
Motley County	517	71.4	22	54.5	2	0.0	0	X	45	82.2	3.3	0.1	0.0	2.9	3.6	11.1
Nacogdoches County	16 408	63.3	3 546	62.7	131	48.9	126	80.2	1 642	77.1	6.2	0.2	0.5	5.4	4.8	11.4
Navarro County	11 856	71.6	2 530	67.0	77	100.0	125	55.2	1 831	89.6	9.1	0.2	0.5	8.0	6.7	13.2
Newton County	4 444	74.1	1 048	72.1	30	60.0	11	100.0	52	98.1	0.9	0.1	0.2	0.5	0.5	6.3
Nolan County	4 477	66.9	227	66.5	27	100.0	13	100.0	1 406	79.4	4.2	0.2	0.4	3.6	4.4	28.7
Nueces County	50 626	65.7	4 777	68.6	599	76.3	1 109	77.9	52 585	79.6	6.5	0.5	0.9	4.8	6.2	50.7
Ochiltree County	2 522	71.5	0	X	25	40.0	12	100.0	706	95.5	16.1	0.2	0.3	15.6	9.8	23.7
Oldham County	666	76.9	4	100.0	8	100.0	0	X	64	89.1	5.4	0.2	0.0	4.2	2.4	16.2
Orange County	27 755	75.4	2 483	74.7	158	75.3	187	89.8	860	82.1	2.1	0.4	0.7	0.9	1.1	9.1
Palo Pinto County	9 220	69.4	266	62.4	79	51.9	44	75.0	871	88.2	4.4	0.3	0.5	3.6	3.9	11.9
Panola County	7 115	74.1	1 425	69.8	28	75.0	24	79.2	194	75.3	2.9	0.3	0.3	2.2	1.3	6.4
Parker County	28 924	78.5	209	67.0	228	76.8	68	82.4	1 398	80.8	2.6	0.5	0.2	1.7	1.2	10.7
Parmer County	1 946	73.0	45	62.2	27	77.8	13	7.7	1 289	89.1	20.1	0.2	0.2	19.7	9.8	43.4
Pecos County	2 061	70.8	42	38.1	17	100.0	20	100.0	2 992	82.8	13.5	0.3	0.2	12.8	12.2	55.5
Polk County	12 468	72.3	1 385	69.3	254	78.0	85	68.2	832	89.1	4.3	0.3	0.5	3.4	2.4	11.6
Potter County	27 616	63.1	3 087	68.2	320	71.9	847	90.1	8 553	82.5	9.4	0.3	2.1	7.0	5.7	26.8
Presidio County	517	55.9	7	28.6	3	100.0	13	69.2	1 954	79.1	35.8	0.4	0.3	35.1	33.6	56.2
Rains County	3 345	74.4	94	70.2	28	89.3	10	90.0	103	86.4	2.5	0.3	0.3	1.8	1.6	7.3
Randall County	36 412	69.5	478	67.4	313	59.4	455	57.6	3 147	76.8	2.6	0.7	0.9	0.9	1.3	12.1
Reagan County	607	76.3	19	84.2	17	23.5	3	100.0	470	85.3	16.4	0.0	0.2	16.2	10.0	43.5
Real County	972	70.0	3	100.0	6	66.7	0	X	226	75.2	4.0	0.2	0.1	3.5	3.3	23.2
Red River County	4 642	69.9	943	69.2	20	75.0	7	100.0	177	81.9	2.5	0.3	0.1	2.1	1.5	7.6
Reeves County	902	59.4	104	76.0	20	100.0	29	69.0	3 034	82.8	14.7	0.1	0.7	13.9	17.8	64.4
Refugio County	1 596	71.7	199	68.8	10	70.0	10	100.0	1 151	76.0	2.6	0.2	0.3	2.1	4.6	40.1
Roberts County	357	77.3	0	X	0	X	2	0.0	4	0.0	0.5	0.0	0.2	0.2	0.7	2.3
Robertson County	3 967	70.3	1 425	68.4	24	91.7	13	84.6	653	81.3	3.3	0.4	0.0	2.8	1.6	16.9
Rockwall County	12 722	82.1	436	81.0	67	65.7	185	91.9	1 095	92.5	7.8	0.9	1.4	5.0	3.1	15.1
Runnels County	3 309	69.3	40	75.0	33	63.6	7	100.0	1 015	80.1	4.5	0.1	0.0	4.3	5.9	26.4
Rusk County	13 207	73.6	3 140	70.4	60	53.3	34	50.0	776	89.0	4.4	0.2	0.2	3.9	3.1	8.8
Sabine County	3 964	71.5	440	61.8	8	100.0	0	X	51	78.4	1.1	0.4	0.2	0.4	0.7	4.9
San Augustine County	2 605	71.6	944	71.0	7	71.4	4	100.0	64	84.4	2.0	0.1	0.0	1.8	1.2	6.3
San Jacinto County	7 244	74.7	1 027	67.2	41	24.4	20	100.0	262	93.9	2.5	0.3	0.5	1.6	1.5	9.0
San Patricio County	11 776	74.2	598	82.1	165	87.3	69	63.8	9 335	83.4	3.3	0.2	0.4	2.5	5.9	46.3
San Saba County	1 898	70.2	2	100.0	19	100.0	7	100.0	344	75.9	5.5	0.1	0.3	5.1	4.5	21.5
Schleicher County	704	68.9	19	78.9	2	0.0	0	X	392	78.8	13.9	0.2	0.0	13.7	9.2	38.2
Scurry County	4 283	69.5	184	67.4	23	69.6	13	61.5	1 213	82.8	3.1	0.0	0.1	2.7	4.8	25.5
Shackelford County	1 211	72.1	1	100.0	6	83.3	4	0.0	69	91.3	2.9	0.2	0.3	2.5	2.1	12.3
Shelby County	7 172	71.5	1 781	70.1	7	28.6	30	100.0	608	88.0	6.6	0.2	0.3	6.0	3.8	10.0
Sherman County	894	72.8	4	100.0	2	0.0	4	100.0	223	93.3	12.4	0.0	0.3	12.1	7.0	24.0
Smith County	48 232	71.2	11 929	69.5	303	54.5	303	86.1	4 504	85.4	6.6	0.3	0.5	5.5	3.5	13.0
Somervell County	2 177	72.8	5	100.0	24	75.0	4	100.0	227	91.2	5.7	0.1	0.4	5.2	3.2	12.9
Starr County	299	85.6	19	100.0	45	66.7	65	58.5	14 000	88.4	36.9	0.0	0.2	36.6	28.1	68.5
Stephens County	3 182	68.4	63	54.0	17	100.0	38	100.0	334	90.4	6.6	0.1	0.7	5.6	2.9	15.6
Sterling County	366	75.1	0	X	2	0.0	0	X	147	81.6	9.2	0.5	0.0	8.7	10.5	21.4
Stonewall County	607	69.4	22	59.1	2	100.0	0	X	69	66.7	2.0	0.0	0.2	1.7	0.9	17.0
Sutton County	813	74.4	0	X	5	100.0	11	100.0	687	78.9	13.0	0.3	0.4	12.3	8.6	48.4
Swisher County	2 042	69.4	143	75.5	20	95.0	5	100.0	740	86.5	4.9	0.0	0.0	4.9	5.8	28.9
Tarrant County	367 809	67.1	67 402	68.1	3 195	69.3	15 578	75.9	73 682	82.2	12.7	0.8	3.0	8.1	6.8	21.3
Taylor County	36 776	67.6	3 005	68.5	284	79.2	544	60.5	6 313	79.8	4.0	0.6	1.1	2.0	1.8	20.4
Terrell County	247	60.3	0	X	2	100.0	0	X	182	76.9	9.9	0.4	0.2	9.3	9.7	58.8
Terry County	2 602	70.9	165	81.2	23	100.0	15	100.0	1 472	86.2	7.2	0.0	0.2	6.9	8.4	39.8
Throckmorton County	709	69.5	0	X	2	0.0	0	X	43	81.4	1.6	0.1	0.0	1.4	2.6	9.2
Titus County	6 755	72.5	1 007	69.5	52	100.0	17	100.0	1 706	92.6	17.4	0.1	0.3	16.9	12.2	19.3

[1] Hispanic or Latino persons may be of any race.

STATE/ County code	MSA/PMSA/ NECMA code[1]	STATE County	Total population	Under 5 years	5 to 17 years	18 to 24 years	25 to 44 years	45 to 64 years	65 years and over	Median age	+/− U.S. percent under 18 years	+/− U.S. percent 65 years and over	Non-Hispanic White Total population	Under 18 years	65 years and over
			1	2	3	4	5	6	7	8	9	10	11	12	13
		TEXAS—Cont'd													
48 451	7200	Tom Green County	104 010	6.7	19.3	13.0	27.4	20.1	13.5	33.8	0.3	1.1	65 541	21.1	17.6
48 453	0640	Travis County	812 280	7.2	16.5	14.6	36.9	18.2	6.7	30.4	-2.0	-5.7	457 910	18.5	9.0
48 455	...	Trinity County	13 779	5.9	17.0	7.3	22.7	25.1	22.0	43.3	-2.8	9.6	11 314	20.5	24.1
48 457	...	Tyler County	20 871	5.9	17.2	7.7	27.4	23.8	18.0	38.9	-2.6	5.6	17 373	23.1	19.6
48 459	4420	Upshur County	35 291	6.5	20.5	7.9	26.7	24.1	14.3	37.7	1.3	1.9	29 849	25.8	14.9
48 461	...	Upton County	3 404	5.6	23.5	7.3	25.4	24.6	13.7	38.1	3.4	1.3	1 852	23.9	17.8
48 463	...	Uvalde County	25 926	8.2	23.2	9.7	25.1	19.9	13.9	32.2	5.7	1.5	8 443	20.7	24.0
48 465	...	Val Verde County	44 856	8.6	23.4	9.4	28.2	19.6	10.8	30.8	6.3	-1.6	9 740	21.7	15.7
48 467	...	Van Zandt County	48 140	6.3	19.2	7.1	25.3	25.0	17.1	39.5	-0.2	4.7	42 556	24.3	18.4
48 469	8750	Victoria County	84 088	7.5	21.7	9.0	28.6	21.5	11.8	34.2	3.5	-0.6	44 487	23.6	16.0
48 471	...	Walker County	61 758	4.7	13.0	22.9	31.7	18.7	9.0	31.0	-8.0	-3.4	37 117	16.4	12.0
48 473	3360	Waller County	32 663	6.9	18.6	18.1	26.3	20.6	9.4	30.1	-0.2	-3.0	16 351	23.4	12.9
48 475	...	Ward County	10 909	6.4	24.1	7.5	25.9	22.1	14.0	36.0	4.8	1.6	5 650	24.9	19.6
48 477	...	Washington County	30 373	6.0	18.7	11.2	24.8	22.5	16.7	37.4	-1.0	4.3	21 480	21.0	20.6
48 479	4080	Webb County	193 117	10.5	25.7	11.4	29.4	15.3	7.7	26.5	10.5	-4.7	9 258	28.2	12.6
48 481	...	Wharton County	41 188	6.8	21.9	9.2	26.2	22.1	13.8	35.3	3.0	1.4	21 914	23.2	18.7
48 483	...	Wheeler County	5 284	5.5	19.4	6.9	22.1	25.1	20.9	42.5	-0.8	8.5	4 406	21.9	23.6
48 485	9080	Wichita County	131 664	6.9	18.1	13.7	29.1	19.5	12.7	33.2	-0.7	0.3	96 399	22.8	15.3
48 487	...	Wilbarger County	14 676	6.8	21.2	8.5	25.6	21.0	16.8	36.3	2.3	4.4	10 087	22.8	20.4
48 489	...	Willacy County	20 082	8.3	23.3	12.0	26.4	18.2	11.8	29.8	5.9	-0.6	2 256	17.1	27.7
48 491	0640	Williamson County	249 967	8.4	21.4	7.9	35.9	19.2	7.2	32.3	4.1	-5.2	183 705	27.5	8.8
48 493	7240	Wilson County	32 408	6.9	22.3	7.2	29.3	22.8	11.4	35.9	3.5	-1.0	19 701	26.0	13.7
48 495	...	Winkler County	7 173	7.0	22.9	9.0	25.7	21.0	14.4	35.2	4.2	2.0	3 815	23.7	19.8
48 497	...	Wise County	48 793	6.8	21.5	8.0	30.0	23.2	10.6	35.5	2.6	-1.8	42 109	26.7	11.7
48 499	...	Wood County	36 752	5.2	16.7	7.6	23.2	26.4	20.9	43.0	-3.8	8.5	31 874	20.6	22.6
48 501	...	Yoakum County	7 322	7.4	24.8	8.7	26.4	21.6	11.0	34.1	6.5	-1.4	3 872	24.7	18.0
48 503	...	Young County	17 943	5.9	19.0	6.7	25.3	23.4	19.7	40.7	-0.8	7.3	15 495	23.2	21.8
48 505	...	Zapata County	12 182	9.0	24.0	10.0	23.6	18.8	14.6	30.7	7.3	2.2	1 797	14.0	49.2
48 507	...	Zavala County	11 600	8.5	25.3	11.3	25.8	17.6	11.5	29.0	8.1	-0.9	862	16.7	26.2
49 000	...	**UTAH**	2 233 169	9.4	22.7	14.3	28.2	16.9	8.5	27.1	6.4	-3.9	1 905 227	31.1	9.4
49 001	...	Beaver County	6 005	9.5	23.9	9.3	24.2	19.2	13.9	30.8	7.7	1.5	5 440	32.8	15.1
49 003	...	Box Elder County	42 745	9.2	26.8	10.7	25.3	17.6	10.4	28.0	10.3	-2.0	38 885	35.2	10.9
49 005	...	Cache County	91 391	9.8	21.4	22.2	25.7	13.8	7.1	23.9	5.5	-5.3	82 184	30.5	7.8
49 007	...	Carbon County	20 422	7.3	21.0	12.5	24.8	21.3	13.2	33.6	2.6	0.8	17 613	27.7	13.7
49 009	...	Daggett County	921	6.7	16.4	8.3	30.3	24.4	13.9	39.2	-2.6	1.5	841	19.3	14.7
49 011	7160	Davis County	238 994	9.8	25.3	12.3	28.1	17.1	7.3	26.8	9.4	-5.1	214 408	34.6	7.8
49 013	...	Duchesne County	14 371	9.0	27.8	9.3	24.8	19.8	9.3	28.3	11.1	-3.1	12 861	35.8	10.0
49 015	...	Emery County	10 860	8.1	27.3	9.5	23.9	21.0	10.2	30.1	9.7	-2.2	10 065	34.5	10.7
49 017	...	Garfield County	4 735	8.6	23.7	7.9	23.2	22.5	14.1	33.8	6.6	1.7	4 514	32.5	14.3
49 019	...	Grand County	8 485	6.8	20.0	8.5	27.7	24.3	12.7	36.9	1.1	0.3	7 544	24.9	13.4
49 021	...	Iron County	33 779	9.4	21.8	20.5	23.7	16.1	8.5	24.2	5.5	-3.9	30 941	30.5	9.1
49 023	...	Juab County	8 238	10.9	27.6	9.4	25.2	17.0	9.8	26.5	12.8	-2.6	7 845	38.0	10.1
49 025	2620	Kane County	6 046	6.8	22.4	7.3	21.0	25.5	17.0	39.1	3.5	4.6	5 714	29.1	17.2
49 027	...	Millard County	12 405	8.1	29.2	8.2	22.9	19.2	12.5	29.9	11.6	0.1	11 224	36.7	13.6
49 029	...	Morgan County	7 129	8.1	28.8	9.7	24.5	20.1	8.8	28.5	11.2	-3.6	6 914	36.6	9.0
49 031	...	Piute County	1 435	8.3	22.8	6.7	19.4	25.9	17.0	38.9	5.4	4.6	1 369	30.2	17.1
49 033	...	Rich County	1 961	7.4	27.4	6.9	22.2	22.0	14.1	34.3	9.1	1.7	1 915	34.4	14.5
49 035	7160	Salt Lake County	898 387	8.9	21.4	13.0	30.7	17.9	8.1	28.9	4.6	-4.3	726 985	28.9	9.2
49 037	...	San Juan County	14 413	9.7	29.6	10.1	25.1	17.1	8.4	25.5	13.6	-4.0	5 689	32.7	11.8
49 039	...	Sanpete County	22 763	8.3	24.9	16.2	22.2	17.5	11.0	25.3	7.5	-1.4	20 611	32.4	11.9
49 041	...	Sevier County	18 842	8.8	25.7	9.9	23.1	19.5	13.0	30.3	8.8	0.6	17 861	33.9	13.5
49 043	...	Summit County	29 736	6.9	22.9	8.5	34.1	22.8	4.9	33.3	4.1	-7.5	26 614	29.6	5.3
49 045	...	Tooele County	40 735	11.0	24.1	11.5	29.8	16.2	7.5	27.1	9.4	-4.9	34 668	34.0	8.0
49 047	...	Uintah County	25 224	8.4	26.2	10.9	25.4	19.2	9.9	29.0	8.9	-2.5	21 557	33.4	10.8
49 049	6520	Utah County	368 536	10.9	23.0	20.9	26.0	12.7	6.4	23.3	8.2	-6.0	329 249	33.4	7.0
49 051	...	Wasatch County	15 215	9.1	25.1	10.3	28.9	18.3	8.4	29.5	8.5	-4.0	14 126	33.6	9.0
49 053	...	Washington County	90 354	9.1	21.9	11.6	22.6	17.8	17.0	31.0	5.3	4.6	82 550	30.2	18.3
49 055	...	Wayne County	2 509	8.4	23.9	8.1	22.7	22.5	14.3	34.1	6.6	1.9	2 428	31.7	14.7
49 057	7160	Weber County	196 533	8.8	22.1	12.5	28.2	18.0	10.4	29.3	5.2	-2.0	162 612	29.4	11.6
50 000	...	**VERMONT**	608 827	5.6	18.7	9.4	29.0	24.7	12.7	37.7	-1.4	0.3	585 217	23.8	13.0
50 001	...	Addison County	35 974	5.7	19.1	12.7	26.9	24.3	11.3	36.1	-0.9	-1.1	34 518	24.6	11.6
50 003	...	Bennington County	36 994	5.4	18.4	7.8	26.1	25.8	16.6	40.3	-1.9	4.2	35 906	23.5	16.9
50 005	...	Caledonia County	29 702	5.5	19.9	8.6	26.5	25.2	14.3	38.5	-0.3	1.9	28 771	24.8	14.7

[1]MSA = Metropolitan Statistical Area. PMSA = Primary MSA. NECMA = New England County Metropolitan Area. See the Appendix A for explanation of these concepts. See Appendix B for list of metropolitan areas identified by type, with component counties.

Table A-3. States and Counties — Age, Ethnicity, and Household Structure

STATE County	Black or African American			American Indian and Alaska Native			Asian, Hawaiian, and Pacific Islander			Hispanic or Latino[1]			Two or more races		
	\	Age (percent)			Age (percent)			Age (percent)			Age (percent)			Age (percent)	
	Total population	Under 18 years	65 years and over	Total population	Under 18 years	65 years and over	Total population	Under 18 years	65 years and over	Total population	Under 18 years	65 years and over	Total population	Under 18 years	65 years and over
	14	15	16	17	18	19	20	21	22	23	24	25	26	27	28
TEXAS—Cont'd															
Tom Green County	4 573	31.7	8.4	561	24.1	4.1	777	18.1	7.7	31 874	35.5	6.0	2 351	45.1	5.0
Travis County	73 809	29.7	6.8	4 490	26.7	2.9	36 795	19.1	2.1	229 106	32.4	3.0	24 404	38.0	2.3
Trinity County	1 693	32.5	15.4	49	18.4	8.2	30	40.0	16.7	561	36.5	1.8	161	40.4	19.9
Tyler County	2 475	24.9	8.3	99	8.1	59.6	12	0.0	0.0	761	20.8	4.3	238	33.2	21.4
Upshur County	3 529	31.4	14.6	150	18.0	6.7	104	23.1	0.0	1 336	40.5	2.5	394	30.2	5.1
Upton County	59	20.3	22.0	46	28.3	4.3	0	X	X	1 445	35.8	8.1	47	48.9	12.8
Uvalde County	83	41.0	0.0	191	37.7	5.2	150	30.7	0.0	17 142	36.6	9.1	619	36.5	13.6
Val Verde County	627	34.9	2.4	215	37.2	7.4	283	13.1	6.4	33 978	35.2	9.6	1 192	37.2	8.8
Van Zandt County	1 264	32.2	15.0	343	29.2	3.8	123	42.3	3.3	3 242	37.7	3.5	787	29.9	11.9
Victoria County	5 434	32.0	9.6	476	27.1	4.2	529	28.9	7.8	32 976	36.2	6.4	1 791	46.6	8.5
Walker County	14 792	18.3	6.1	318	19.5	1.3	417	20.6	3.4	8 660	21.0	2.1	745	37.7	2.4
Waller County	9 486	20.7	8.6	111	21.6	0.0	155	36.8	3.2	6 345	37.8	2.0	591	36.9	4.6
Ward County	507	47.9	11.8	80	22.5	0.0	3	0.0	0.0	4 626	35.8	7.7	325	35.7	0.6
Washington County	5 487	32.1	10.0	65	38.5	15.4	467	26.8	2.8	2 724	37.3	1.8	397	41.1	8.6
Webb County	738	47.6	3.4	841	30.3	8.7	816	30.8	6.0	182 296	36.7	7.5	4 688	33.3	9.0
Wharton County	6 094	31.7	13.5	136	48.5	0.0	175	17.7	5.7	12 861	37.2	5.6	597	37.9	7.9
Wheeler County	125	41.6	24.8	51	47.1	0.0	8	0.0	0.0	655	41.7	4.1	76	32.9	9.2
Wichita County	13 074	27.6	8.2	1 099	31.1	3.1	2 614	23.2	5.5	15 973	34.6	4.2	3 884	40.9	4.3
Wilbarger County	1 206	36.5	12.7	60	13.3	21.7	144	10.4	18.1	3 003	42.5	6.3	252	52.0	16.3
Willacy County	426	8.0	3.8	54	16.7	27.8	11	0.0	0.0	17 293	34.2	9.9	520	28.5	10.2
Williamson County	12 574	33.4	3.3	1 102	28.7	3.9	6 561	29.8	2.9	43 011	37.7	2.5	5 739	47.7	2.4
Wilson County	344	26.5	10.2	321	37.4	4.0	164	29.9	9.8	11 823	34.4	7.7	661	36.3	5.7
Winkler County	142	33.1	38.0	42	14.3	0.0	13	84.6	0.0	3 158	37.8	6.6	150	19.3	16.0
Wise County	409	14.2	2.0	375	22.4	7.2	125	18.4	2.4	5 250	40.8	2.5	844	46.7	6.0
Wood County	2 261	20.9	10.5	140	27.9	12.9	110	16.4	8.2	1 977	40.8	6.1	488	43.9	20.7
Yoakum County	55	0.0	0.0	50	20.0	24.0	3	0.0	0.0	3 362	41.3	2.9	121	38.0	9.9
Young County	209	17.7	19.6	131	29.8	0.0	29	0.0	20.7	1 884	37.8	4.1	294	42.2	11.6
Zapata County	0	X	X	6	100.0	0.0	15	0.0	0.0	10 347	36.9	8.5	273	25.3	9.5
Zavala County	99	61.6	16.2	58	11.8	1.7	17	0.0	41.2	10 001	35.1	10.2	175	30.0	17.1
UTAH	16 150	35.2	4.2	28 646	37.0	3.5	51 244	29.4	5.1	200 005	38.3	2.7	51 480	50.8	2.6
Beaver County	12	0.0	0.0	88	51.1	0.0	43	30.2	9.3	354	35.3	2.3	108	45.4	5.6
Box Elder County	84	85.7	0.0	329	29.5	14.9	373	24.9	18.5	2 721	44.3	2.6	721	68.1	2.2
Cache County	292	28.4	0.0	460	39.1	3.3	1 857	19.2	1.7	5 833	41.4	0.5	1 158	58.8	0.3
Carbon County	41	34.1	0.0	151	24.5	0.0	110	10.0	4.5	2 122	34.7	7.7	549	30.4	19.1
Daggett County	11	54.5	0.0	0	X	X	4	0.0	100.0	64	9.4	0.0	14	50.0	0.0
Davis County	2 555	33.5	2.2	1 279	32.4	2.7	4 425	24.7	6.0	12 780	41.0	3.4	5 226	59.7	1.6
Duchesne County	2	100.0	0.0	787	42.6	3.0	35	17.1	0.0	455	44.4	2.4	312	52.2	6.1
Emery County	12	91.7	0.0	58	44.8	5.2	47	40.0	4.0	503	47.9	2.0	213	50.2	3.3
Garfield County	15	0.0	0.0	60	30.0	5.0	6	0.0	100.0	88	33.0	8.0	73	28.8	12.3
Grand County	7	42.9	0.0	314	47.5	0.3	15	73.3	6.7	464	31.7	11.9	182	53.8	8.8
Iron County	72	48.6	0.0	627	42.4	2.6	383	13.8	0.8	1 365	42.1	1.7	654	46.0	4.1
Juab County	30	100.0	0.0	85	40.0	0.0	5	60.0	0.0	221	52.5	1.8	69	26.1	11.6
Kane County	10	0.0	60.0	56	32.1	23.2	7	0.0	100.0	182	37.4	8.8	103	38.8	1.9
Millard County	2	100.0	0.0	174	33.3	0.0	72	55.6	0.0	887	42.4	2.7	130	50.0	0.0
Morgan County	2	100.0	0.0	2	0.0	0.0	8	0.0	25.0	113	45.1	0.0	98	49.0	0.0
Piute County	2	100.0	0.0	7	71.4	28.6	7	28.6	71.4	50	50.0	6.0	5	60.0	0.0
Rich County	0	X	X	2	0.0	0.0	2	100.0	0.0	32	43.8	0.0	12	66.7	0.0
Salt Lake County	8 667	34.4	3.6	7 541	28.5	0.8	33 545	31.9	5.1	106 240	36.8	2.6	25 171	48.4	2.5
San Juan County	15	73.3	0.0	8 157	43.5	6.1	16	37.5	0.0	452	43.1	6.2	170	67.1	4.7
Sanpete County	81	8.6	0.0	123	36.6	0.0	202	42.1	0.0	1 534	42.3	2.1	391	47.6	3.6
Sevier County	61	42.6	0.0	321	48.0	5.3	39	23.1	0.0	476	47.7	2.9	146	65.1	6.8
Summit County	115	37.4	0.0	92	25.0	0.0	274	20.4	0.0	2 364	32.3	1.0	358	43.0	3.6
Tooele County	495	42.2	0.8	702	39.6	5.3	244	25.4	3.3	4 205	42.2	5.6	1 076	53.4	0.9
Uintah County	2	50.0	0.0	2 353	39.7	4.6	123	34.1	16.3	1 004	46.2	1.2	380	57.9	7.6
Utah County	1 054	51.8	0.4	2 286	40.0	1.6	5 764	25.3	3.4	25 134	38.2	1.5	7 384	50.6	1.9
Wasatch County	10	100.0	0.0	115	32.2	0.0	69	46.4	0.0	805	43.0	0.4	378	35.2	0.0
Washington County	105	21.9	0.0	894	39.0	1.6	921	36.6	5.9	4 550	37.7	3.5	1 913	54.5	3.5
Wayne County	8	75.0	0.0	18	33.3	0.0	2	0.0	0.0	37	56.8	0.0	12	58.3	0.0
Weber County	2 388	29.5	12.7	1 565	31.4	4.7	2 646	22.6	9.1	24 970	40.2	3.5	4 474	51.8	3.0
VERMONT	2 981	37.1	3.1	2 602	26.5	2.9	5 005	31.9	3.0	5 316	32.1	5.5	8 129	38.5	5.5
Addison County	217	19.4	0.0	62	9.7	4.8	254	37.0	7.5	381	30.4	3.7	573	37.0	5.1
Bennington County	107	17.8	6.5	89	25.8	7.9	146	23.3	1.4	363	31.4	7.2	404	40.3	7.2
Caledonia County	52	75.0	3.8	107	26.2	1.9	95	53.7	0.0	197	39.6	6.1	473	41.6	4.9

[1] Hispanic or Latino persons may be of any race.

STATE County	Total households	Family households (percent)						Nonfamily households (percent)						Percent of householders 65 years and over who live alone	Grandparents who are responsible for the care of their grandchildren
		Married-couple family households			Other family households			Two or more unrelated persons		Male living alone		Female living alone			
		Total	With children	Householder 65 years or over	Total	With children	Householder 65 years or over	Total	Householder 65 years or over	Total	Householder 65 years or over	Total	Householder 65 years or over		
	29	30	31	32	33	34	35	36	37	38	39	40	41	42	43
TEXAS—Cont'd															
Tom Green County	39 531	52.9	24.2	10.3	15.6	9.7	1.8	4.4	0.2	11.2	2.4	15.9	8.5	46.9	1 327
Travis County	320 883	43.5	21.9	4.7	14.4	8.0	1.2	12.0	0.2	15.2	1.0	14.9	3.5	42.9	6 230
Trinity County	5 730	55.6	17.9	17.0	15.0	8.9	2.6	2.7	0.5	10.4	3.8	16.4	10.8	42.1	238
Tyler County	7 770	61.8	23.5	16.3	11.4	5.5	2.1	2.4	0.4	10.2	3.6	14.1	8.8	39.7	380
Upshur County	13 296	61.2	26.9	11.8	14.0	7.3	2.3	3.0	0.3	9.1	2.2	12.7	8.4	42.5	513
Upton County	1 247	62.0	29.1	12.6	11.9	7.3	1.5	2.2	0.2	10.0	3.0	13.9	8.9	45.3	93
Uvalde County	8 546	62.2	31.5	12.4	16.1	9.7	3.2	1.8	0.4	8.9	3.2	11.0	6.8	38.6	416
Val Verde County	14 153	64.8	35.9	9.9	15.5	8.2	3.5	2.1	0.2	8.1	2.5	9.5	5.5	36.9	844
Van Zandt County	18 233	64.2	25.6	14.4	11.4	6.3	2.0	2.6	0.4	8.6	3.1	13.2	8.6	41.1	815
Victoria County	30 040	58.2	27.8	10.0	16.2	10.2	2.1	3.3	0.2	9.6	1.9	12.7	6.6	40.9	1 237
Walker County	18 331	48.6	20.9	8.6	14.3	7.9	1.9	10.2	0.7	11.8	2.0	15.1	6.3	42.7	492
Waller County	10 574	57.5	27.3	7.7	16.6	8.6	2.6	4.9	0.4	9.5	2.5	11.5	5.7	43.5	355
Ward County	3 982	60.6	28.1	11.3	14.1	8.6	2.6	1.7	0.4	10.3	4.9	13.3	7.7	46.7	162
Washington County	11 343	56.4	24.3	12.7	14.3	7.9	2.1	3.8	0.4	9.6	3.3	15.9	10.5	47.7	236
Webb County	50 647	65.0	42.0	7.8	21.3	11.4	4.0	1.4	0.2	5.5	1.2	6.8	3.6	28.8	3 404
Wharton County	14 807	56.6	26.6	10.9	16.2	9.3	2.6	2.8	0.3	10.0	2.7	14.3	8.9	45.8	720
Wheeler County	2 138	59.3	22.9	15.3	9.9	6.4	1.8	1.8	0.6	11.4	4.3	17.7	11.9	47.9	33
Wichita County	48 432	53.5	24.6	10.1	14.8	9.4	1.9	4.5	0.3	11.7	2.3	15.5	8.1	45.8	1 427
Wilbarger County	5 544	54.1	24.6	12.1	14.8	8.4	2.3	2.2	0.1	11.6	3.0	17.2	11.9	50.6	246
Willacy County	5 603	62.7	33.5	13.6	19.3	9.5	4.4	1.5	0.7	6.0	2.7	10.5	7.7	35.6	363
Williamson County	86 893	65.5	36.6	6.5	12.2	7.8	0.8	4.8	0.1	7.8	1.0	9.7	3.6	38.1	1 570
Wilson County	11 028	66.2	32.8	10.0	14.3	7.6	2.8	2.5	0.4	8.2	2.4	8.9	5.3	36.9	387
Winkler County	2 589	63.2	32.2	12.1	13.4	9.8	1.5	1.7	0.4	7.5	2.8	14.1	8.8	45.3	134
Wise County	17 180	67.5	32.2	9.8	10.9	6.5	1.4	3.2	0.2	8.6	1.6	9.8	5.8	39.4	568
Wood County	14 578	61.3	20.3	17.3	11.9	7.3	1.8	2.7	0.7	9.4	3.3	14.7	10.0	40.4	561
Yoakum County	2 473	69.4	35.9	12.3	12.5	7.6	0.6	1.0	0.0	5.3	1.3	11.7	6.5	37.7	142
Young County	7 161	60.0	24.3	14.3	11.5	6.5	2.4	2.2	0.3	9.3	2.7	17.0	11.0	44.6	223
Zapata County	3 927	64.3	34.4	15.0	17.0	8.8	3.6	1.2	0.6	8.4	4.3	9.0	7.1	37.0	274
Zavala County	3 399	56.5	32.5	11.8	24.8	13.0	5.2	1.9	0.6	6.2	2.3	10.6	7.8	36.5	220
UTAH	701 933	64.2	36.1	9.1	12.7	7.5	1.5	5.4	0.2	7.7	1.4	10.0	4.9	36.9	15 989
Beaver County	1 989	67.0	34.4	14.2	11.2	7.2	1.6	1.6	0.3	9.0	2.7	11.3	8.4	41.0	61
Box Elder County	13 211	72.1	41.1	12.2	10.6	6.5	1.9	1.6	0.0	6.6	2.1	9.1	5.8	36.0	330
Cache County	27 597	67.4	38.7	7.8	9.5	5.4	1.3	8.8	0.2	5.9	1.2	8.4	4.3	37.3	402
Carbon County	7 438	59.6	29.3	11.2	13.4	8.0	2.0	3.5	0.4	9.8	2.5	13.8	8.2	44.0	237
Daggett County	344	63.4	24.7	13.1	9.0	5.5	1.5	1.7	0.0	15.7	4.7	10.2	3.2	35.1	25
Davis County	71 115	71.5	42.6	8.7	12.2	7.6	1.4	2.9	0.2	6.0	1.0	7.4	3.6	31.1	1 660
Duchesne County	4 579	68.6	38.2	11.3	12.4	8.9	1.2	2.4	0.3	7.1	1.5	9.6	5.0	33.7	131
Emery County	3 471	71.5	38.4	10.9	9.0	6.3	1.1	1.5	0.1	7.6	1.9	10.4	6.9	42.4	99
Garfield County	1 588	67.3	31.7	16.4	9.1	5.9	1.3	3.3	0.1	9.2	2.1	11.0	7.7	35.7	45
Grand County	3 445	46.0	20.6	9.0	17.9	10.9	2.2	6.8	0.2	11.6	1.7	17.8	6.9	42.8	66
Iron County	10 676	66.6	35.5	9.9	10.2	6.0	1.3	7.4	0.1	7.1	1.4	8.7	5.0	36.1	164
Juab County	2 447	69.1	40.6	11.1	11.4	7.9	0.9	1.8	0.1	9.0	3.1	8.7	6.3	43.6	84
Kane County	2 236	65.1	29.2	16.8	8.1	5.1	1.8	3.3	0.5	10.4	2.5	13.2	6.8	32.9	47
Millard County	3 855	71.1	40.5	13.9	9.8	5.4	2.0	1.0	0.0	7.8	3.0	10.2	7.4	39.4	138
Morgan County	2 059	79.7	45.1	12.0	7.7	4.2	1.1	0.9	0.1	3.8	1.9	8.0	5.1	34.6	34
Piute County	503	67.4	27.8	18.7	9.3	4.6	2.8	0.8	0.0	8.5	2.0	13.9	11.1	37.9	28
Rich County	653	73.8	38.6	17.3	6.1	3.2	1.8	3.1	1.7	8.1	2.0	8.9	5.4	26.1	2
Salt Lake County	295 290	58.9	32.8	7.5	14.2	8.1	1.5	6.2	0.2	9.3	1.4	11.5	4.9	40.7	6 727
San Juan County	4 109	59.6	36.1	9.0	19.5	11.6	2.2	2.4	0.1	8.1	1.6	10.5	5.7	38.9	335
Sanpete County	6 549	68.3	37.6	13.6	9.5	6.2	1.3	4.2	0.1	6.4	2.2	11.5	8.3	41.1	165
Sevier County	6 104	71.0	37.5	14.4	10.2	6.7	1.6	1.3	0.1	7.8	2.5	9.6	6.8	36.9	178
Summit County	10 374	64.8	35.9	5.7	8.5	6.1	0.4	8.4	0.1	10.1	0.7	8.2	2.1	31.0	111
Tooele County	12 675	68.4	40.4	7.8	12.3	7.7	1.4	2.5	0.1	7.4	1.4	9.4	5.1	40.8	378
Uintah County	8 126	65.5	35.6	11.3	14.3	9.1	1.4	2.9	0.1	8.6	1.9	8.7	4.8	34.4	259
Utah County	100 164	71.1	43.6	8.3	10.4	5.7	1.1	7.5	0.2	4.1	0.8	6.9	3.7	31.7	1 960
Wasatch County	4 754	71.6	41.6	10.3	10.7	6.3	1.3	3.5	0.2	6.5	1.1	7.8	4.0	29.9	80
Washington County	29 970	68.6	31.4	20.4	10.3	6.5	1.4	3.6	0.3	6.7	2.2	10.8	7.1	29.4	556
Wayne County	904	68.3	30.8	16.2	6.9	5.5	0.7	3.2	0.0	11.2	2.9	10.5	6.4	35.6	19
Weber County	65 708	61.5	32.0	10.1	14.4	8.8	1.8	4.1	0.3	8.9	1.7	11.1	5.9	38.2	1 668
VERMONT	240 744	53.5	23.9	9.0	12.4	8.3	1.5	7.9	0.6	11.1	2.3	15.1	7.3	46.7	1 934
Addison County	13 077	58.0	26.7	9.2	12.0	7.8	1.7	6.6	0.3	10.0	2.3	13.3	6.8	45.2	96
Bennington County	14 822	54.2	22.4	11.4	13.0	8.8	1.6	6.1	0.7	10.1	2.1	16.6	8.9	44.5	150
Caledonia County	11 651	55.0	24.4	10.0	13.1	8.9	1.7	6.4	0.8	10.1	2.7	15.4	9.0	48.4	117

STATE County	Households with Non-Hispanic White householder		Households with Black or African American householder		Households with American Indian and Alaska Native householder		Households with Asian, Hawaiian, and Pacific Islander householder		Households with Hispanic or Latino[1] householder		Foreign-born population				Percent in non-English speaking households	
											Percent of total population that is foreign-born	Place of birth (percent)				
	Number of households	Percent that are family households	Number of households	Percent that are family households	Number of households	Percent that are family households	Number of households	Percent that are family households	Number of households	Percent that are family households		Europe	Asia	Latin America	Linguistically isolated	Not linguistically isolated
	44	45	46	47	48	49	50	51	52	53	54	55	56	57	58	59
TEXAS—Cont'd																
Tom Green County	27 519	65.8	1 546	67.6	223	70.0	257	59.9	9 753	77.2	5.9	0.5	0.6	4.7	4.0	32.1
Travis County	208 195	53.1	27 560	64.4	1 721	57.9	13 325	56.7	66 315	71.6	15.1	1.1	3.6	9.7	8.1	28.5
Trinity County	4 872	70.7	630	66.0	18	100.0	9	100.0	158	78.5	2.7	0.4	0.2	2.0	1.3	6.4
Tyler County	6 882	74.3	653	63.6	41	56.1	7	0.0	118	87.3	1.2	0.2	0.1	0.8	0.7	6.0
Upshur County	11 441	76.1	1 285	66.1	91	57.1	17	100.0	360	83.3	2.0	0.2	0.2	1.4	0.8	7.5
Upton County	785	68.7	29	48.3	10	80.0	0	X	423	85.8	11.2	0.0	0.0	11.2	8.4	38.2
Uvalde County	3 547	72.3	29	100.0	50	80.0	35	100.0	4 892	82.6	11.2	0.2	0.5	10.6	13.4	55.3
Val Verde County	4 155	71.1	226	81.9	46	84.8	85	58.8	9 622	84.6	23.4	0.3	0.4	22.5	14.2	63.8
Van Zandt County	16 591	75.4	481	68.2	117	76.1	28	92.9	781	83.6	3.6	0.3	0.2	3.0	2.2	9.3
Victoria County	17 994	71.4	2 027	66.7	167	86.2	137	86.1	9 623	81.5	4.3	0.3	0.6	3.0	4.0	34.5
Walker County	13 245	62.5	3 334	56.6	114	94.7	104	51.9	1 401	78.6	4.5	0.2	0.4	3.6	3.3	14.0
Waller County	6 313	74.9	2 611	63.8	42	71.4	43	93.0	1 524	88.1	9.4	0.3	0.2	8.7	5.0	21.2
Ward County	2 361	71.7	150	69.3	45	71.1	1	0.0	1 419	80.4	6.6	0.2	0.0	6.3	5.6	41.9
Washington County	8 634	70.9	1 918	64.8	19	68.4	105	90.5	628	78.7	5.4	0.5	1.2	3.3	2.3	16.4
Webb County	3 433	73.0	171	78.4	276	82.2	243	79.4	46 808	87.3	29.0	0.2	0.3	28.4	23.2	73.5
Wharton County	8 788	71.0	2 266	66.2	40	42.5	69	42.0	3 611	82.6	6.6	0.1	0.3	6.0	4.4	31.5
Wheeler County	1 866	68.2	44	68.2	17	100.0	0	X	190	74.7	5.4	0.1	0.2	4.9	2.5	12.9
Wichita County	38 047	67.3	4 144	67.2	324	67.9	741	75.4	4 395	78.5	5.1	1.0	1.5	2.5	2.4	15.9
Wilbarger County	4 139	67.5	372	67.2	38	31.6	56	64.3	900	79.1	4.2	0.1	0.8	3.0	3.0	20.1
Willacy County	916	71.0	21	100.0	35	65.7	0	X	4 629	84.4	13.3	0.1	0.0	13.0	17.0	72.1
Williamson County	68 351	76.6	4 236	76.0	381	71.7	1 916	82.5	11 154	84.3	7.4	0.8	2.2	3.9	3.0	22.0
Wilson County	7 205	80.2	122	81.1	100	60.0	45	80.0	3 523	82.4	3.3	0.2	0.3	2.6	4.9	36.7
Winkler County	1 625	71.1	65	76.9	16	100.0	0	X	872	88.0	14.3	0.0	0.3	13.9	10.3	34.7
Wise County	15 512	77.4	96	66.7	149	71.8	33	84.8	1 228	92.9	5.1	0.3	0.2	4.5	2.8	12.8
Wood County	13 154	73.0	673	75.5	46	93.5	29	100.0	553	75.8	3.8	0.5	0.1	2.7	1.7	6.8
Yoakum County	1 563	77.0	21	100.0	14	92.9	3	100.0	875	91.5	16.6	0.2	0.0	16.4	11.6	35.6
Young County	6 411	70.6	91	70.3	47	83.0	22	59.1	544	82.7	3.7	0.1	0.1	3.4	2.2	12.6
Zapata County	948	63.3	0	X	0	X	0	X	2 966	87.5	24.1	0.2	0.1	23.8	24.0	60.0
Zavala County	319	69.0	8	100.0	6	100.0	10	70.0	3 052	82.7	13.8	0.0	0.1	13.0	23.0	67.5
UTAH	620 009	76.6	5 112	69.5	7 729	78.0	13 951	76.6	48 190	82.7	7.1	1.1	1.3	3.9	2.9	17.4
Beaver County	1 870	77.5	0	X	12	100.0	17	64.7	78	88.5	4.4	0.3	0.8	3.1	3.6	8.5
Box Elder County	12 303	82.4	0	X	83	81.9	138	76.1	654	91.9	3.0	0.5	0.3	1.9	1.2	15.8
Cache County	25 367	77.0	115	41.7	137	70.8	615	62.4	1 227	87.0	6.7	0.6	1.7	3.5	3.0	14.8
Carbon County	6 510	73.1	4	100.0	35	77.1	40	67.5	684	72.7	2.0	0.5	0.3	0.9	0.9	12.0
Daggett County	339	72.9	0	X	0	X	0	X	5	40.0	2.7	1.1	0.4	1.2	1.2	5.1
Davis County	65 137	84.0	779	76.1	318	81.4	1 202	78.4	3 155	82.1	3.6	1.0	0.9	1.3	0.8	14.2
Duchesne County	4 200	81.5	0	X	219	77.2	7	85.7	97	74.2	1.3	0.2	0.1	0.7	0.3	8.1
Emery County	3 301	80.4	0	X	20	80.0	9	100.0	100	82.0	2.5	0.4	0.2	1.8	1.8	9.5
Garfield County	1 537	76.4	4	100.0	17	64.7	4	0.0	10	80.0	0.8	0.3	0.1	0.2	0.4	5.8
Grand County	3 194	63.5	0	X	91	83.5	1	100.0	130	56.2	3.0	1.3	0.1	1.3	1.0	12.5
Iron County	9 972	76.7	5	0.0	143	89.5	137	54.0	302	87.1	2.9	0.5	0.7	1.3	1.5	13.3
Juab County	2 382	80.5	0	X	24	83.3	0	X	18	55.6	1.4	0.5	0.0	0.5	0.2	9.4
Kane County	2 133	72.9	4	100.0	12	83.3	7	100.0	48	77.1	2.9	1.4	0.3	0.7	0.4	11.7
Millard County	3 561	80.8	0	X	60	88.3	13	100.0	215	80.9	5.1	0.5	0.3	4.1	3.1	12.7
Morgan County	2 009	87.0	0	X	2	100.0	0	X	22	100.0	2.7	1.0	0.3	1.0	0.7	14.0
Piute County	486	76.7	0	X	2	0.0	3	100.0	10	100.0	2.0	0.1	0.0	1.9	0.3	7.9
Rich County	644	79.8	0	X	0	X	0	X	7	85.7	1.9	0.4	0.1	0.8	0.4	8.3
Salt Lake County	251 627	72.2	2 845	68.6	2 199	71.4	9 087	79.6	25 934	81.5	10.4	1.8	2.0	5.5	4.2	19.9
San Juan County	2 002	74.7	2	100.0	1 974	83.6	3	33.3	116	89.7	0.9	0.0	0.1	0.6	7.3	52.2
Sanpete County	6 174	77.3	0	X	18	88.9	16	31.3	312	88.8	4.8	0.4	0.5	3.8	2.1	14.7
Sevier County	5 907	81.1	0	X	78	92.3	6	100.0	85	80.0	1.3	0.2	0.1	0.8	0.4	8.0
Summit County	9 565	72.8	60	63.3	41	75.6	62	50.0	548	85.2	7.7	1.3	0.4	5.2	4.2	11.6
Tooele County	11 158	81.2	72	79.2	177	79.1	60	48.3	1 131	78.9	3.7	0.6	0.3	2.5	2.4	12.2
Uintah County	7 150	79.8	0	X	640	79.5	49	81.6	214	89.7	1.4	0.3	0.2	0.7	0.5	13.3
Utah County	91 512	81.4	234	76.5	592	83.8	1 449	70.9	5 432	88.5	6.3	0.7	0.8	3.9	2.2	19.0
Wasatch County	4 519	81.8	0	X	29	100.0	18	77.8	150	96.0	4.2	0.5	0.2	3.2	2.7	10.5
Washington County	28 124	78.6	23	43.5	260	80.8	173	83.8	1 084	83.9	4.1	0.8	0.4	2.4	1.6	12.7
Wayne County	887	75.5	2	100.0	6	33.3	0	X	5	100.0	1.7	0.6	0.2	0.6	0.7	5.2
Weber County	56 439	75.6	963	68.3	540	66.1	835	67.8	6 417	82.1	6.4	0.7	0.9	4.6	3.0	16.9
VERMONT	233 583	66.0	878	55.5	1 038	63.8	1 270	70.5	1 567	61.3	3.8	1.5	0.7	0.2	0.7	9.6
Addison County	12 788	70.1	15	46.7	22	45.5	33	84.8	65	81.5	3.5	1.6	0.6	0.2	0.3	8.3
Bennington County	14 472	67.4	37	54.1	39	56.4	52	69.2	106	45.3	2.7	1.4	0.4	0.2	0.3	8.1
Caledonia County	11 379	67.9	5	100.0	50	70.0	25	72.0	49	67.3	2.5	1.1	0.3	0.0	0.5	7.9

[1] Hispanic or Latino persons may be of any race.

STATE/County code	MSA/PMSA/NECMA code[1]	STATE County	Total population	Under 5 years	5 to 17 years	18 to 24 years	25 to 44 years	45 to 64 years	65 years and over	Median age	+/− U.S. percent under 18 years	+/− U.S. percent 65 years and over	Non-Hispanic White Total population	Under 18 years	65 years and over
			1	2	3	4	5	6	7	8	9	10	11	12	13
		VERMONT—Cont'd													
50 007	1303	Chittenden County	146 571	5.8	17.7	13.3	32.0	21.8	9.4	34.2	-2.2	-3.0	138 418	22.9	9.8
50 009	...	Essex County	6 459	5.3	20.2	6.6	27.2	25.6	15.0	39.0	-0.2	2.6	6 220	25.5	15.3
50 011	1303	Franklin County	45 417	7.1	21.0	7.0	31.4	22.6	10.9	35.7	2.4	-1.5	43 498	27.8	11.2
50 013	1303	Grand Isle County	6 901	5.6	19.3	5.6	28.7	28.5	12.3	40.1	-0.8	-0.1	6 706	24.7	12.5
50 015	...	Lamoille County	23 233	5.6	18.7	9.9	29.9	24.6	11.3	36.5	-1.4	-1.1	22 380	24.1	11.4
50 017	...	Orange County	28 226	5.7	19.9	7.7	28.3	25.6	12.8	38.6	-0.1	0.4	27 506	25.3	13.0
50 019	...	Orleans County	26 277	5.6	19.5	7.1	26.9	25.9	15.1	39.3	-0.6	2.7	25 380	24.7	15.4
50 021	...	Rutland County	63 400	5.1	18.2	8.5	27.5	25.8	14.9	39.5	-2.4	2.5	61 859	23.0	15.2
50 023	...	Washington County........	58 039	5.4	18.1	9.0	28.7	26.0	12.8	38.5	-2.2	0.4	55 748	23.1	13.1
50 025	...	Windham County	44 216	5.3	18.4	7.3	27.9	27.2	14.0	40.5	-2.0	1.6	42 498	23.2	14.4
50 027	...	Windsor County	57 418	4.9	18.5	5.9	27.4	27.5	15.8	41.3	-2.3	3.4	55 809	22.9	16.2
51 000	...	VIRGINIA	7 078 515	6.5	18.0	9.6	31.8	23.0	11.2	35.7	-1.2	-1.2	4 963 910	22.4	12.9
51 001	...	Accomack County	38 305	6.0	18.3	8.1	26.4	24.4	16.9	39.4	-1.4	4.5	23 768	20.0	20.4
51 003	1540	Albemarle County	79 236	6.3	18.5	7.3	31.0	24.4	12.5	37.4	-0.9	0.1	66 270	23.9	13.4
51 005	...	Alleghany County	12 926	5.6	17.2	6.2	27.0	28.3	15.7	41.1	-2.9	3.3	12 458	22.6	15.5
51 007	...	Amelia County	11 400	6.2	19.2	6.3	29.7	25.4	13.2	38.5	-0.3	0.8	8 027	24.8	12.6
51 009	4640	Amherst County	31 894	5.6	17.9	9.8	27.8	25.2	13.7	38.0	-2.2	1.3	24 635	22.1	14.5
51 011	...	Appomattox County	13 705	6.1	18.6	6.6	28.2	25.5	15.0	39.1	-1.0	2.6	10 376	23.0	16.0
51 013	8840	Arlington County	189 453	5.5	10.8	10.4	42.8	21.4	9.1	34.0	-9.4	-3.3	114 696	12.4	12.0
51 015	...	Augusta County	65 615	5.6	18.1	6.8	29.7	27.0	12.8	39.0	-2.0	0.4	62 050	23.7	13.2
51 017	...	Bath County	5 048	4.5	16.2	5.9	28.1	28.2	17.1	41.8	-5.0	4.7	4 653	22.0	17.0
51 019	4640	Bedford County	60 371	5.8	18.3	5.7	29.9	27.5	12.9	39.7	-1.6	0.5	55 231	23.8	13.0
51 021	...	Bland County	6 871	4.5	14.8	8.2	29.1	28.8	14.8	40.3	-6.4	2.4	6 497	19.9	14.7
51 023	6800	Botetourt County	30 496	5.7	17.6	5.8	28.8	28.8	13.2	40.7	-2.4	0.8	28 864	23.3	13.1
51 025	...	Brunswick County	18 419	4.7	15.7	10.2	30.6	24.2	14.6	38.1	-5.3	2.2	7 653	17.1	19.1
51 027	...	Buchanan County	26 978	4.9	16.8	8.4	31.0	27.4	11.4	38.8	-4.0	-1.0	26 059	21.3	11.7
51 029	...	Buckingham County........	15 623	4.8	17.6	7.9	31.8	24.3	13.6	38.2	-3.3	1.2	9 220	21.8	15.4
51 031	4640	Campbell County	51 078	5.9	18.1	7.5	29.6	25.2	13.7	38.3	-1.7	1.3	42 337	23.0	14.0
51 033	...	Caroline County	22 121	6.1	18.6	7.1	30.3	24.8	13.1	37.7	-1.0	0.7	13 684	23.5	13.5
51 035	...	Carroll County	29 245	5.6	15.3	7.3	27.9	26.7	17.2	40.7	-4.8	4.8	28 326	20.4	17.2
51 036	6760	Charles City County........	6 926	5.5	16.4	8.1	29.1	27.5	13.3	39.9	-3.8	0.9	2 456	20.0	11.8
51 037	...	Charlotte County	12 472	5.3	19.1	6.9	27.1	23.8	17.8	40.0	-1.3	5.4	8 090	23.1	18.7
51 041	6760	Chesterfield County	259 903	6.6	21.6	7.5	31.3	24.9	8.1	35.7	2.5	-4.3	195 751	26.7	9.4
51 043	8840	Clarke County	12 652	5.1	18.2	5.4	29.4	27.2	14.7	40.6	-2.4	2.3	11 451	23.4	14.5
51 045	...	Craig County	5 091	5.2	18.5	6.4	29.8	26.4	13.7	39.6	-2.0	1.3	5 027	23.3	13.7
51 047	8840	Culpeper County	34 262	6.3	19.2	8.4	31.5	22.5	12.0	36.5	-0.2	-0.4	26 407	25.0	12.9
51 049	...	Cumberland County	9 017	6.1	18.6	6.7	29.2	24.4	15.0	38.4	-1.0	2.6	5 390	22.3	15.5
51 051	...	Dickenson County	16 395	5.4	16.6	9.0	27.6	26.9	14.5	39.7	-3.7	2.1	16 162	21.9	14.5
51 053	6760	Dinwiddie County	24 533	5.3	18.7	5.9	32.2	25.6	12.2	38.5	-1.7	-0.2	15 821	23.6	12.3
51 057	...	Essex County	9 989	4.7	18.3	6.4	27.7	25.5	17.3	40.3	-2.7	4.9	5 737	19.5	20.3
51 059	8840	Fairfax County	969 749	7.0	18.4	7.3	34.2	25.3	7.8	35.9	-0.3	-4.6	623 434	23.4	10.0
51 061	8840	Fauquier County	55 139	6.5	20.4	6.4	30.4	25.7	10.6	37.8	1.2	-1.8	48 028	26.7	10.3
51 063	...	Floyd County	13 874	5.7	16.6	6.8	27.5	27.6	15.8	40.5	-3.4	3.4	13 288	22.2	16.1
51 065	1540	Fluvanna County	20 047	6.2	17.5	5.8	31.6	25.0	13.9	38.3	-2.0	1.5	15 809	23.1	14.9
51 067	...	Franklin County	47 286	5.4	16.7	8.1	28.4	27.2	14.3	39.7	-3.6	1.9	41 725	21.4	14.8
51 069	...	Frederick County	59 209	6.5	19.9	7.3	31.6	24.1	10.7	36.7	0.7	-1.7	55 541	25.9	11.0
51 071	...	Giles County	16 657	5.6	16.3	6.9	28.3	26.2	16.6	40.2	-3.8	4.2	16 083	21.6	16.7
51 073	5720	Gloucester County	34 780	5.8	20.4	6.9	30.1	24.8	12.0	38.0	0.5	-0.4	29 704	25.6	11.6
51 075	6760	Goochland County	16 863	5.1	16.1	6.1	31.3	29.1	12.3	40.5	-4.5	-0.1	12 229	21.3	12.4
51 077	...	Grayson County	17 917	4.7	14.8	7.5	29.6	26.4	17.0	40.5	-6.2	4.6	16 199	19.9	18.3
51 079	1540	Greene County	15 244	7.3	19.8	6.5	33.9	22.8	9.8	35.5	1.4	-2.6	13 757	26.6	9.9
51 081	...	Greensville County..........	11 560	3.5	14.7	7.4	38.9	24.2	11.5	38.1	-7.5	-0.9	4 453	16.4	15.5
51 083	...	Halifax County	37 355	5.8	17.5	6.9	26.3	26.1	17.4	40.7	-2.4	5.0	22 391	21.1	19.2
51 085	6760	Hanover County	86 320	6.6	20.5	7.0	30.8	24.4	10.7	37.4	1.4	-1.7	75 685	26.7	10.6
51 087	6760	Henrico County	262 300	6.8	17.8	7.8	33.1	22.0	12.5	36.0	-1.1	0.1	177 643	22.1	15.6
51 089	...	Henry County	57 930	5.3	17.0	7.8	28.9	26.1	14.9	39.3	-3.4	2.5	42 110	20.4	17.0
51 091	...	Highland County	2 536	3.7	16.2	4.0	24.3	31.5	20.2	46.0	-5.8	7.8	2 519	19.8	20.2
51 093	5720	Isle of Wight County	29 728	6.0	19.4	6.9	29.9	25.8	12.0	38.9	-0.3	-0.4	21 038	24.6	11.9
51 095	5720	James City County	48 102	5.3	17.9	6.0	27.4	26.6	16.7	40.8	-2.5	4.3	38 911	21.7	18.6
51 097	...	King and Queen County .	6 630	5.4	17.4	6.9	26.9	26.5	16.9	40.9	-2.9	4.5	4 068	21.7	16.0
51 099	8840	King George County	16 803	7.1	20.6	8.0	31.6	23.0	9.6	35.1	2.0	-2.8	12 841	26.5	9.6
51 101	...	King William County	13 146	6.9	19.1	5.8	31.5	24.9	11.7	37.0	0.3	-0.7	9 636	25.7	10.6
51 103	...	Lancaster County	11 567	3.7	15.3	4.5	20.2	27.6	28.6	49.8	-6.7	16.2	8 038	14.9	33.9
51 105	...	Lee County	23 589	5.8	16.8	8.2	27.4	26.3	15.5	39.7	-3.1	3.1	23 060	22.5	15.6
51 107	8840	Loudoun County..............	169 599	9.6	20.1	5.7	39.0	20.1	5.5	33.6	4.0	-6.9	134 705	29.0	6.0

[1]MSA = Metropolitan Statistical Area. PMSA = Primary MSA. NECMA = New England County Metropolitan Area. See the Appendix A for explanation of these concepts. See Appendix B for list of metropolitan areas identified by type, with component counties.

	Black or African American			American Indian and Alaska Native			Asian, Hawaiian, and Pacific Islander			Hispanic or Latino[1]			Two or more races		
		Age (percent)			Age (percent)			Age (percent)			Age (percent)			Age (percent)	
STATE County	Total population	Under 18 years	65 years and over	Total population	Under 18 years	65 years and over	Total population	Under 18 years	65 years and over	Total population	Under 18 years	65 years and over	Total population	Under 18 years	65 years and over
	14	15	16	17	18	19	20	21	22	23	24	25	26	27	28
VERMONT—Cont'd															
Chittenden County	1 371	38.5	3.2	523	22.0	0.0	2 775	29.6	2.2	1 649	27.3	4.1	2 015	42.8	2.7
Essex County	8	37.5	0.0	48	18.8	8.3	16	18.8	12.5	20	40.0	0.0	145	24.8	8.3
Franklin County	159	53.5	0.0	656	26.4	2.9	129	43.4	0.0	224	40.6	4.9	789	35.1	7.2
Grand Isle County	4	0.0	0.0	38	42.1	0.0	18	33.3	5.6	19	36.8	5.3	119	31.1	6.7
Lamoille County	63	58.7	4.8	102	17.6	23.5	118	44.9	6.8	135	25.9	3.0	461	27.1	8.0
Orange County	65	40.0	4.6	86	24.4	2.3	76	35.5	3.9	173	42.2	6.9	283	36.4	4.6
Orleans County	71	70.4	8.5	179	17.9	3.9	145	33.8	11.0	140	42.1	1.4	395	38.2	6.1
Rutland County	213	29.6	4.7	228	36.8	0.0	221	30.8	8.6	454	36.8	4.2	466	36.9	7.7
Washington County	285	39.6	1.4	248	32.7	0.0	289	27.3	7.0	630	21.7	8.1	874	37.3	8.2
Windham County	208	21.6	5.3	112	29.5	1.8	277	26.7	4.0	536	44.0	7.3	626	38.7	3.5
Windsor County	158	35.4	1.3	124	40.3	4.0	446	40.6	0.9	395	33.7	8.6	506	45.5	5.9
VIRGINIA	1 384 008	29.2	8.9	22 394	22.7	5.8	259 972	23.3	5.3	327 273	31.0	2.6	156 831	42.0	3.5
Accomack County	11 998	31.0	12.8	41	24.4	4.9	118	24.6	2.5	2 072	31.4	1.6	515	45.6	9.1
Albemarle County	7 701	26.7	10.7	159	10.7	11.9	2 466	25.8	3.0	2 061	33.4	2.7	697	53.1	6.6
Alleghany County	328	26.5	22.6	0	X	X	73	35.6	16.4	17	0.0	0.0	50	44.0	16.0
Amelia County	3 242	26.7	14.8	32	34.4	0.0	28	75.0	0.0	5	0.0	0.0	66	9.1	24.2
Amherst County	6 204	27.5	11.6	230	24.3	10.4	94	17.0	5.3	446	31.2	5.6	320	35.0	10.0
Appomattox County	3 119	29.9	12.2	45	17.8	0.0	57	47.4	0.0	39	0.0	15.4	69	43.5	14.5
Arlington County	17 856	20.3	8.6	828	21.4	2.5	15 888	15.1	5.4	35 212	26.0	2.3	8 709	27.8	2.4
Augusta County	2 379	15.3	8.7	97	7.2	0.0	133	39.1	14.3	506	34.0	1.2	480	45.0	2.5
Bath County	290	2.4	12.8	0	X	X	16	0.0	0.0	79	11.4	35.4	18	22.2	33.3
Bedford County	3 586	21.8	14.7	137	18.2	8.8	590	24.9	4.1	240	22.1	3.3	565	50.8	2.3
Bland County	315	0.0	19.0	15	100.0	0.0	16	100.0	0.0	28	0.0	0.0	0	X	X
Botetourt County	1 118	20.1	17.7	46	30.4	0.0	120	31.7	14.2	120	24.2	8.3	206	33.5	6.3
Brunswick County	10 394	22.8	11.6	24	8.3	29.2	109	0.0	0.0	179	31.8	0.0	98	50.0	8.2
Buchanan County	630	33.5	0.0	0	X	X	63	17.5	14.3	170	31.2	8.8	79	45.6	0.0
Buckingham County	6 171	22.9	10.6	0	X	X	3	0.0	0.0	64	14.1	25.0	173	41.6	20.2
Campbell County	7 407	25.0	12.0	141	31.9	0.0	323	33.1	11.1	451	37.0	9.3	321	70.4	8.7
Caroline County	7 656	26.1	12.4	177	11.9	23.2	108	47.2	16.7	267	28.1	12.0	223	57.8	0.0
Carroll County	208	37.5	22.6	30	16.7	33.3	63	44.4	0.0	363	32.0	16.8	371	47.2	11.9
Charles City County	3 838	22.9	14.0	458	20.7	16.6	6	0.0	0.0	19	36.8	0.0	150	34.7	12.7
Charlotte County	4 223	27.0	16.4	0	X	X	4	25.0	0.0	127	22.8	0.8	37	37.8	16.2
Chesterfield County	46 134	32.4	4.0	832	19.8	2.2	6 460	30.1	5.8	7 063	32.0	2.6	4 464	44.1	3.4
Clarke County	854	19.3	20.8	40	15.0	10.0	57	10.5	5.3	197	32.0	11.2	59	50.8	0.0
Craig County	13	53.8	0.0	6	0.0	0.0	17	35.3	0.0	18	100.0	0.0	10	0.0	70.0
Culpeper County	5 880	24.3	11.3	144	30.6	13.2	366	25.4	0.0	1 042	31.4	1.8	583	51.5	0.9
Cumberland County	3 363	27.1	14.3	7	0.0	100.0	24	62.5	0.0	164	35.4	11.6	83	47.0	10.8
Dickenson County	50	24.0	14.0	14	0.0	14.3	26	50.0	0.0	64	14.1	4.7	84	36.9	29.8
Dinwiddie County	8 216	24.3	12.8	66	18.2	0.0	63	0.0	0.0	306	34.0	0.0	111	31.5	11.7
Essex County	3 951	27.0	14.3	8	0.0	0.0	86	26.7	1.2	20	0.0	0.0	170	45.9	0.0
Fairfax County	81 744	28.4	3.6	2 415	27.3	3.8	124 406	25.2	5.4	106 862	29.5	2.8	39 416	39.2	2.9
Fauquier County	4 646	24.3	17.1	163	16.0	8.6	484	27.3	2.5	1 131	32.6	1.6	899	42.4	5.3
Floyd County	185	27.6	20.5	0	X	X	21	0.0	0.0	193	27.5	5.7	183	25.7	4.9
Fluvanna County	3 747	24.2	10.6	25	0.0	0.0	78	32.1	3.8	196	27.6	8.2	201	55.7	4.0
Franklin County	4 516	25.7	12.0	53	0.0	1.9	91	0.0	9.9	488	34.4	0.0	473	34.0	4.0
Frederick County	1 600	29.6	8.5	82	18.3	13.4	521	32.8	3.1	1 006	38.8	2.4	524	40.1	3.4
Giles County	260	14.6	26.2	2	0.0	0.0	27	33.3	0.0	137	43.1	5.8	121	33.1	7.4
Gloucester County	3 339	23.2	20.4	155	18.7	3.9	323	18.0	5.6	644	43.0	4.3	645	58.8	2.0
Goochland County	4 356	21.2	12.1	43	72.1	0.0	99	6.1	0.0	80	0.0	20.0	61	19.7	0.0
Grayson County	1 234	5.7	5.7	16	50.0	0.0	31	41.9	0.0	319	41.4	1.6	226	50.0	1.8
Greene County	934	28.6	9.3	68	0.0	2.9	50	0.0	34.0	242	46.3	6.2	164	42.1	0.0
Greensville County	6 955	19.0	9.1	9	0.0	0.0	11	0.0	0.0	86	46.5	0.0	37	64.9	5.4
Halifax County	14 193	26.8	14.6	140	8.6	17.1	103	11.7	14.6	298	36.6	8.7	253	31.2	23.7
Hanover County	8 047	26.8	13.6	314	26.8	3.5	551	25.2	2.2	941	41.8	5.4	833	54.9	3.4
Henrico County	64 419	30.3	6.2	1 142	20.2	13.3	9 336	23.8	4.4	6 063	30.1	3.5	4 205	43.6	4.6
Henry County	13 256	26.3	10.6	213	47.9	3.8	156	32.1	3.8	1 901	28.1	1.3	400	49.3	7.0
Highland County	2	0.0	0.0	6	0.0	0.0	0	X	X	2	0.0	100.0	9	77.8	22.2
Isle of Wight County	8 050	26.9	12.8	46	17.4	0.0	87	27.6	12.6	271	24.0	0.0	274	49.6	3.6
James City County	6 832	27.0	10.1	241	49.8	4.6	832	28.0	9.1	875	44.9	4.3	570	40.9	2.5
King and Queen County	2 272	23.1	18.8	107	59.8	4.7	5	100.0	0.0	82	19.5	25.6	150	23.3	18.7
King George County	3 170	29.1	11.5	63	3.2	11.1	94	43.6	0.0	348	45.1	0.0	293	42.7	5.5
King William County	2 875	25.3	15.1	242	10.7	30.2	61	44.3	0.0	109	47.7	0.0	258	58.5	5.8
Lancaster County	3 348	27.6	17.1	9	0.0	0.0	49	8.2	14.3	93	75.3	6.5	30	36.7	16.7
Lee County	102	36.3	20.6	103	41.7	3.9	82	25.6	14.6	73	53.4	0.0	189	13.2	11.1
Loudoun County	11 541	29.2	5.5	441	21.3	6.6	9 052	28.4	3.7	10 117	33.4	2.2	4 485	46.9	2.4

[1] Hispanic or Latino persons may be of any race.

Table A-3. States and Counties — Age, Ethnicity, and Household Structure

	Total households	Family households (percent)						Nonfamily households (percent)						Percent of householders 65 years and over who live alone	Grandparents who are responsible for the care of their grandchildren
		Married-couple family households			Other family households			Two or more unrelated persons		Male living alone		Female living alone			
STATE County		Total	With children	Householder 65 years or over	Total	With children	Householder 65 years or over	Total	Householder 65 years or over	Total	Householder 65 years or over	Total	Householder 65 years or over		
	29	30	31	32	33	34	35	36	37	38	39	40	41	42	43
VERMONT—Cont'd															
Chittenden County	56 500	51.4	25.3	6.5	11.3	7.6	1.2	11.2	0.4	11.1	1.6	14.9	5.6	47.4	367
Essex County	2 597	55.3	23.3	10.2	14.6	9.0	2.1	6.3	1.0	12.4	3.9	11.4	7.2	45.5	42
Franklin County	16 767	59.4	28.6	8.0	13.6	9.1	1.6	6.3	0.5	9.2	2.4	11.6	6.4	46.6	177
Grand Isle County	2 776	59.9	24.7	10.5	10.7	6.8	1.6	7.4	0.3	10.7	2.0	11.2	6.1	39.3	39
Lamoille County	9 225	52.0	23.2	7.8	12.8	8.8	1.5	10.0	0.6	12.1	2.3	13.0	5.6	44.4	65
Orange County	10 979	57.3	25.0	10.1	12.9	8.4	1.7	6.5	0.8	10.1	2.2	13.3	7.2	42.7	56
Orleans County	10 475	55.0	23.3	10.7	13.9	9.5	1.8	5.9	0.4	10.5	2.1	14.7	8.6	45.5	142
Rutland County	25 686	51.7	21.9	9.9	13.8	8.4	2.2	6.6	0.6	12.0	2.9	15.8	8.1	46.4	186
Washington County	23 654	51.7	22.9	8.3	12.3	8.8	1.0	7.5	0.5	11.8	2.5	16.6	8.2	51.8	131
Windham County	18 369	50.2	21.3	9.2	12.5	8.9	1.2	7.6	0.7	12.7	2.5	17.0	7.9	48.3	185
Windsor County	24 166	53.8	21.8	11.5	11.5	7.4	1.5	6.5	0.6	11.5	2.8	16.7	8.5	45.2	181
VIRGINIA	2 700 335	53.7	24.6	8.2	15.2	8.6	2.1	6.1	0.3	10.5	1.9	14.5	6.2	43.3	59 464
Accomack County	15 270	50.6	19.1	12.4	17.3	10.0	3.1	4.3	0.5	11.5	3.9	16.2	8.7	43.9	629
Albemarle County	31 916	54.4	25.1	9.1	11.9	7.4	1.7	6.7	0.3	10.5	1.8	16.6	6.2	42.0	498
Alleghany County	5 145	65.6	25.1	11.9	10.2	6.0	2.4	2.0	0.3	8.7	3.2	13.5	8.8	45.2	169
Amelia County	4 240	58.6	25.3	10.4	16.4	8.0	3.2	4.2	0.5	9.3	1.6	11.5	5.6	33.6	104
Amherst County	11 928	57.3	23.0	10.6	15.8	8.9	2.7	2.9	0.4	10.2	2.5	13.8	7.5	42.2	324
Appomattox County	5 331	59.0	22.9	10.8	16.5	9.9	3.0	3.3	0.4	8.0	2.5	13.3	8.3	43.2	102
Arlington County	86 474	36.3	15.5	4.6	9.8	4.2	1.3	13.1	0.3	18.5	1.8	22.3	5.5	53.9	629
Augusta County	24 857	64.4	26.8	11.1	12.0	6.9	2.3	3.6	0.3	9.1	2.0	11.0	5.4	35.2	620
Bath County	2 053	60.8	21.2	12.7	10.2	4.2	2.7	2.6	0.3	13.9	3.1	12.5	6.8	38.5	75
Bedford County	23 798	66.7	27.1	11.1	9.5	5.5	1.7	3.5	0.5	9.5	2.0	10.8	6.3	38.8	460
Bland County	2 555	64.6	24.9	12.3	9.8	4.5	3.3	2.1	0.9	12.0	2.5	11.5	7.9	38.7	53
Botetourt County	11 662	69.3	28.1	12.4	9.3	4.5	1.6	2.2	0.3	8.7	1.9	10.4	5.6	34.2	194
Brunswick County	6 262	48.2	17.4	11.0	20.9	10.5	4.9	3.4	0.3	11.1	3.5	16.5	10.4	46.2	233
Buchanan County	10 496	62.3	24.8	8.0	13.5	6.1	2.5	1.8	0.1	8.7	2.6	13.6	7.5	48.8	313
Buckingham County	5 312	52.2	18.9	11.5	18.2	10.5	3.2	4.4	0.8	12.7	3.4	12.5	7.1	40.3	182
Campbell County	20 653	56.5	23.3	11.1	15.3	8.6	2.4	3.9	0.2	10.2	2.1	14.2	6.4	38.3	596
Caroline County	8 025	57.6	24.2	10.4	17.9	9.5	3.3	4.1	0.6	9.1	2.6	11.3	6.3	38.2	360
Carroll County	12 188	61.3	21.9	13.4	11.1	5.4	2.3	2.3	0.1	10.2	2.6	15.1	9.6	43.6	250
Charles City County	2 669	54.6	19.4	11.5	20.2	10.2	3.5	2.9	0.4	11.2	2.1	11.1	5.9	34.1	169
Charlotte County	4 954	54.2	21.6	13.7	15.4	7.1	3.6	3.4	0.6	10.1	2.2	17.0	10.7	41.8	255
Chesterfield County	93 807	63.4	32.5	7.2	13.9	8.5	1.3	4.3	0.2	7.8	0.9	10.7	3.9	35.6	1 672
Clarke County	4 950	57.3	22.8	11.0	13.9	7.6	2.9	4.8	0.2	11.0	2.4	13.1	7.8	41.8	54
Craig County	2 063	60.3	26.8	11.4	12.8	5.9	2.3	2.9	0.3	10.7	1.9	13.3	8.0	41.3	29
Culpeper County	12 151	58.3	26.3	10.2	16.0	8.8	2.5	5.1	0.3	9.2	2.1	11.4	5.8	38.0	369
Cumberland County	3 512	51.3	21.5	8.7	19.3	9.0	5.6	4.4	0.7	11.4	3.5	13.5	6.2	39.4	94
Dickenson County	6 742	57.6	24.0	10.2	15.2	7.4	3.4	1.9	0.1	10.4	2.3	14.8	9.1	45.3	194
Dinwiddie County	9 105	56.1	23.4	9.0	18.3	9.4	3.7	3.5	0.3	9.8	2.4	12.4	6.1	39.6	254
Essex County	3 981	53.2	21.6	12.6	16.4	7.9	2.6	4.6	0.4	11.2	3.8	14.6	8.7	44.3	124
Fairfax County	351 279	60.2	31.1	6.6	11.7	6.0	1.2	6.7	0.2	8.8	1.2	12.5	3.7	37.7	4 572
Fauquier County	19 889	64.7	30.5	8.8	11.7	5.8	2.3	4.9	0.4	8.2	1.6	10.4	4.3	34.0	451
Floyd County	5 803	61.6	23.8	13.4	10.9	5.7	1.8	2.7	0.1	11.6	1.8	13.1	7.8	38.5	86
Fluvanna County	7 369	63.1	24.5	13.9	14.4	8.3	2.4	3.7	0.4	7.2	2.1	11.5	4.7	29.0	105
Franklin County	18 954	60.6	22.9	11.7	13.1	7.0	2.0	3.7	0.3	11.2	2.4	11.4	6.9	40.0	201
Frederick County	22 124	63.4	29.5	9.4	12.4	7.5	1.5	5.0	0.3	8.6	1.7	10.6	5.3	38.4	553
Giles County	6 990	56.8	22.1	10.5	13.5	6.6	3.9	3.1	0.3	10.3	3.1	16.3	10.2	47.6	168
Gloucester County	13 133	62.4	28.2	9.9	13.0	7.3	2.1	4.3	0.1	9.0	2.1	11.3	6.0	40.1	222
Goochland County	6 178	65.2	25.7	11.3	11.7	4.9	3.5	3.5	0.0	10.0	1.8	9.7	4.8	30.9	141
Grayson County	7 261	59.2	21.0	12.6	11.0	5.3	2.6	2.9	0.2	11.1	2.9	15.8	10.6	46.8	99
Greene County	5 578	63.2	31.1	8.5	13.7	7.5	1.7	5.1	0.4	7.6	1.3	10.4	4.2	34.2	134
Greensville County	3 377	50.5	17.1	11.9	20.6	10.5	4.7	3.2	0.0	9.8	2.6	15.8	8.7	40.5	175
Halifax County	14 997	51.3	20.4	11.0	19.1	9.4	3.8	2.2	0.4	11.2	3.4	16.2	9.7	46.2	410
Hanover County	31 103	67.2	33.3	9.2	11.9	6.9	1.9	3.3	0.1	7.5	1.5	10.1	5.6	38.5	551
Henrico County	108 071	48.7	22.7	8.2	16.1	9.4	1.8	6.3	0.2	10.8	1.6	18.0	6.9	45.5	1 750
Henry County	23 946	55.5	21.0	10.7	15.6	8.0	2.9	3.1	0.3	10.8	2.7	15.0	8.3	44.1	630
Highland County	1 122	56.1	18.1	13.5	11.1	3.7	4.3	3.2	0.3	11.3	4.6	18.4	12.2	48.3	20
Isle of Wight County	11 307	61.6	26.6	9.5	15.7	8.8	2.6	2.7	0.1	9.5	1.9	10.5	6.3	40.3	388
James City County	19 049	61.8	23.5	14.9	11.6	7.0	1.3	5.1	0.3	8.1	1.9	13.3	7.4	35.9	284
King and Queen County	2 680	55.3	20.5	12.4	16.7	6.0	4.6	3.5	0.0	11.3	4.1	13.2	7.4	40.5	136
King George County	6 092	59.8	29.8	7.1	14.9	8.2	2.2	4.8	0.8	11.0	2.1	9.5	4.4	39.3	92
King William County	4 881	63.7	28.9	9.5	14.7	7.7	3.4	3.6	0.1	7.7	1.6	10.3	5.3	34.7	154
Lancaster County	5 012	57.2	15.2	20.7	12.1	6.7	2.6	2.2	0.3	10.2	3.4	18.2	13.1	41.1	107
Lee County	9 744	55.8	23.0	9.6	15.1	7.2	3.4	2.3	0.3	10.7	3.2	16.1	9.8	49.2	291
Loudoun County	59 921	65.3	36.9	4.5	10.3	6.1	0.8	6.0	0.3	8.3	0.8	10.2	2.8	39.8	891

Table A-3. States and Counties — Age, Ethnicity, and Household Structure

STATE County	Households with Non-Hispanic White householder		Households with Black or African American householder		Households with American Indian and Alaska Native householder		Households with Asian, Hawaiian, and Pacific Islander householder		Households with Hispanic or Latino[1] householder		Foreign-born population				Percent in non-English speaking households	
											Percent of total population that is foreign-born	Place of birth (percent)				
	Number of households	Percent that are family households	Number of households	Percent that are family households	Number of households	Percent that are family households	Number of households	Percent that are family households	Number of households	Percent that are family households		Europe	Asia	Latin America	Linguistically isolated	Not linguistically isolated
	44	45	46	47	48	49	50	51	52	53	54	55	56	57	58	59
VERMONT—Cont'd																
Chittenden County	53 947	62.8	494	54.5	218	56.9	770	70.4	527	54.8	5.9	2.3	1.7	0.3	1.4	11.3
Essex County	2 508	70.2	2	0.0	17	64.7	4	0.0	5	60.0	5.5	0.6	0.3	0.1	1.5	14.9
Franklin County	16 176	72.8	32	100.0	246	72.0	31	83.9	36	77.8	3.7	0.9	0.2	0.1	0.6	11.1
Grand Isle County	2 719	70.5	2	100.0	13	84.6	6	100.0	4	75.0	4.2	1.1	0.2	0.1	0.7	11.4
Lamoille County	8 965	65.0	11	45.5	60	71.7	21	66.7	31	58.1	3.8	1.6	0.4	0.1	0.4	8.7
Orange County	10 753	70.2	22	59.1	32	87.5	18	50.0	60	75.0	1.8	0.8	0.2	0.2	0.1	6.2
Orleans County	10 216	69.0	14	64.3	84	57.1	25	100.0	35	57.1	5.5	0.7	0.4	0.1	0.9	15.2
Rutland County	25 177	65.8	56	51.8	82	61.0	70	48.6	128	68.8	2.0	1.0	0.3	0.1	0.4	8.0
Washington County......	22 922	64.0	50	54.0	98	44.9	65	61.5	249	73.5	3.6	1.6	0.5	0.2	0.8	9.8
Windham County..........	17 846	62.8	82	54.9	31	71.0	70	80.0	150	48.0	3.1	1.4	0.6	0.4	0.5	7.7
Windsor County............	23 715	65.3	56	42.9	46	80.4	80	76.3	122	63.1	3.0	1.4	0.7	0.2	0.3	7.8
VIRGINIA................	2 004 156	68.0	493 797	69.4	8 274	70.5	78 401	76.7	83 553	79.6	8.1	1.2	3.3	2.7	2.5	13.4
Accomack County	10 513	66.0	4 230	71.6	20	60.0	27	85.2	397	76.6	4.2	0.3	0.3	3.5	2.5	6.7
Albemarle County	27 407	66.1	2 929	66.1	40	50.0	875	75.7	507	70.0	7.3	2.2	2.7	1.5	1.8	10.1
Alleghany County	4 987	76.2	105	54.3	0	X	24	100.0	8	100.0	0.9	0.3	0.5	0.0	0.1	4.3
Amelia County	3 049	76.3	1 131	71.4	13	100.0	0	X	5	100.0	0.7	0.3	0.2	0.1	0.0	7.3
Amherst County	9 327	72.6	2 296	74.5	85	71.8	17	64.7	102	75.5	1.2	0.4	0.2	0.6	0.4	4.8
Appomattox County	4 146	76.2	1 089	73.7	24	79.2	13	100.0	27	66.7	1.4	0.4	0.3	0.3	0.2	5.5
Arlington County	60 248	40.7	7 334	51.3	346	58.7	6 806	50.0	9 662	73.5	27.8	2.8	8.1	13.8	10.8	27.6
Augusta County............	23 821	76.7	646	62.7	67	91.0	25	60.0	187	79.7	1.4	0.7	0.2	0.4	0.3	5.1
Bath County	1 950	71.4	83	63.9	0	X	0	X	20	60.0	4.3	0.3	0.4	3.5	0.2	9.0
Bedford County	21 958	76.4	1 427	72.2	32	56.3	189	91.5	93	95.7	1.8	0.7	0.7	0.2	0.2	5.4
Bland County................	2 405	74.6	59	62.7	0	X	0	X	11	100.0	0.8	0.5	0.2	0.1	1.2	5.3
Botetourt County	11 153	78.8	351	72.4	18	61.1	20	100.0	34	55.9	0.9	0.4	0.3	0.2	0.1	4.7
Brunswick County	3 004	67.7	3 187	70.4	2	0.0	12	41.7	34	91.2	0.7	0.1	0.2	0.3	0.4	3.5
Buchanan County	10 397	75.9	5	60.0	0	X	33	57.6	42	83.3	0.3	0.1	0.1	0.0	0.0	3.3
Buckingham County	3 498	69.2	1 734	73.4	0	X	3	0.0	27	59.3	0.8	0.6	0.0	0.1	0.0	6.1
Campbell County...........	17 348	72.4	2 961	69.0	58	50.0	118	66.9	113	61.9	1.1	0.4	0.5	0.2	0.2	6.5
Caroline County	5 275	75.1	2 541	76.9	79	63.3	27	66.7	45	86.7	1.7	0.6	0.4	0.6	0.2	4.9
Carroll County	11 004	72.4	70	50.5	10	100.0	11	100.0	90	70.7	0.0	0.2	0.2	0.4	0.4	5.3
Charles City County	1 065	70.6	1 356	77.4	187	86.6	6	0.0	7	0.0	1.3	0.5	0.0	0.3	0.0	6.3
Charlotte County	3 409	69.7	1 521	70.0	0	X	1	0.0	5	100.0	0.8	0.2	0.1	0.3	0.4	7.0
Chesterfield County	73 507	77.2	15 257	76.0	363	78.0	1 770	84.0	1 940	83.0	5.2	1.1	2.0	1.5	1.6	10.5
Clarke County	4 515	71.6	335	62.4	23	34.8	20	100.0	48	100.0	2.5	1.0	0.5	0.7	0.4	6.9
Craig County	2 038	73.8	6	0.0	6	0.0	3	100.0	0	X	0.3	0.2	0.2	0.0	0.0	4.1
Culpeper County	9 768	74.7	1 866	72.7	48	83.3	89	67.4	251	76.1	3.5	0.7	0.8	1.9	1.0	9.1
Cumberland County	2 196	71.2	1 245	68.0	7	100.0	4	100.0	37	100.0	1.3	0.2	0.3	0.8	1.5	6.4
Dickenson County	6 659	72.9	23	47.8	8	75.0	6	100.0	16	81.3	0.2	0.0	0.2	0.0	0.2	3.5
Dinwiddie County	6 081	74.3	2 851	75.4	29	24.1	27	33.3	93	75.3	1.4	0.6	0.3	0.4	0.5	6.5
Essex County	2 447	71.6	1 447	65.4	0	X	23	91.3	12	75.0	1.4	0.4	0.7	0.1	0.4	5.9
Fairfax County	252 071	69.0	28 994	69.3	903	70.4	35 960	85.3	25 856	84.5	24.5	2.4	12.4	7.5	7.3	29.2
Fauquier County...........	17 628	77.3	1 663	68.8	45	100.0	112	83.0	324	66.7	3.6	1.4	0.9	0.9	0.9	9.2
Floyd County	5 558	73.0	104	41.3	0	X	9	100.0	51	74.5	1.5	0.3	0.1	0.9	0.7	4.7
Fluvanna County	6 184	77.4	1 064	80.1	11	0.0	16	56.3	60	71.7	2.3	1.3	0.4	0.4	0.2	6.8
Franklin County	16 874	74.3	1 756	69.2	47	34.0	35	42.9	147	83.7	1.4	0.6	0.3	0.4	0.2	5.9
Frederick County	21 007	75.6	526	79.8	27	40.7	140	82.9	252	89.7	2.4	0.5	0.8	0.9	0.5	8.0
Giles County................	6 804	70.7	130	50.8	2	100.0	0	X	23	82.6	0.8	0.3	0.3	0.1	0.0	5.1
Gloucester County	11 390	75.6	1 388	70.9	53	83.0	50	100.0	129	94.6	1.9	0.9	0.7	0.3	0.2	9.3
Goochland County	4 782	77.9	1 302	74.1	0	X	41	100.0	23	78.3	2.0	0.7	0.7	0.3	0.5	6.6
Grayson County	6 967	70.5	160	60.0	5	0.0	2	0.0	88	77.3	1.2	0.1	0.1	0.9	0.8	5.2
Greene County	5 064	76.4	343	81.9	47	78.7	16	100.0	81	82.7	1.6	0.7	0.4	0.4	0.2	5.5
Greensville County	1 510	70.1	1 834	72.0	2	0.0	11	100.0	15	60.0	0.3	0.1	0.1	0.2	0.1	3.7
Halifax County..............	9 303	70.6	5 403	70.5	58	74.1	47	44.7	89	56.2	1.0	0.2	0.2	0.5	0.4	5.5
Hanover County	27 872	78.8	2 570	79.8	114	78.1	157	94.3	263	94.3	1.8	0.6	0.5	0.4	0.3	8.0
Henrico County	76 832	62.7	24 667	70.3	500	64.4	3 139	70.3	1 828	71.0	6.7	1.4	3.1	1.5	2.2	10.8
Henry County	18 109	70.3	5 107	73.1	64	62.5	36	100.0	542	82.5	2.7	0.2	0.2	2.3	1.7	6.1
Highland County	1 116	66.9	0	X	4	100.0	0	X	2	100.0	0.4	0.4	0.0	0.0	0.0	5.0
Isle of Wight County......	8 082	78.0	2 998	73.9	25	72.0	31	83.9	85	100.0	1.1	0.4	0.3	0.2	0.2	7.3
James City County........	16 016	73.5	2 430	72.1	57	71.9	224	78.1	161	78.3	4.1	1.6	1.2	0.7	0.9	9.9
King and Queen County	1 656	72.2	901	68.9	43	74.4	0	X	34	100.0	0.9	0.6	0.0	0.2	0.0	3.5
King George County	4 706	74.1	1 134	76.4	24	66.7	22	22.7	93	87.1	1.3	0.5	0.4	0.3	0.1	8.0
King William County	3 553	80.0	1 056	71.6	148	81.1	29	72.4	31	100.0	1.2	0.4	0.4	0.3	0.5	7.3
Lancaster County	3 654	69.9	1 301	68.1	9	100.0	31	35.5	17	100.0	1.7	1.0	0.4	0.1	0.3	6.2
Lee County	9 545	70.8	45	55.6	38	73.7	18	100.0	17	100.0	0.5	0.2	0.2	0.1	0.0	5.2
Loudoun County............	49 970	74.6	4 154	73.2	139	71.9	2 469	87.0	2 321	87.9	11.3	2.0	4.7	3.5	2.8	18.4

[1] Hispanic or Latino persons may be of any race.

Table A-3. States and Counties — Age, Ethnicity, and Household Structure

STATE/ County code	MSA/PMSA/ NECMA code[1]	STATE County	Total population	Under 5 years	5 to 17 years	18 to 24 years	25 to 44 years	45 to 64 years	65 years and over	Median age	+/− U.S. percent under 18 years	+/− U.S. percent 65 years and over	Total population	Under 18 years	65 years and over
			1	2	3	4	5	6	7	8	9	10	11	12	13
		VIRGINIA—Cont'd													
51 109	...	Louisa County	25 627	6.0	18.4	6.6	29.8	26.3	12.9	38.8	−1.3	0.5	19 505	23.7	12.8
51 111	...	Lunenburg County	13 146	5.0	16.4	7.8	28.5	25.4	16.9	40.5	−4.3	4.5	7 666	20.4	18.8
51 113	...	Madison County	12 520	5.4	18.4	7.2	28.0	25.9	15.2	40.0	−1.9	2.8	10 829	23.6	15.2
51 115	5720	Mathews County	9 207	4.8	15.1	4.9	23.8	30.1	21.3	46.2	−5.8	8.9	7 941	19.0	21.8
51 117	...	Mecklenburg County	32 380	5.4	16.1	7.5	27.2	26.0	17.8	40.9	−4.2	5.4	18 993	18.8	20.7
51 119	...	Middlesex County	9 932	3.8	15.5	5.8	22.6	29.9	22.4	46.8	−6.4	10.0	7 729	18.0	23.1
51 121	...	Montgomery County	83 629	4.8	12.5	31.2	25.6	17.3	8.6	25.9	−8.4	−3.8	74 664	17.1	9.2
51 125	...	Nelson County	14 445	5.3	16.2	6.5	25.5	29.8	16.7	42.8	−4.2	4.3	11 776	20.8	16.9
51 127	6760	New Kent County	13 462	5.9	19.0	6.1	32.0	27.3	9.7	38.4	−0.8	−2.7	10 738	24.8	8.8
51 131	...	Northampton County	13 093	5.5	18.0	6.8	23.9	24.3	21.6	42.4	−2.2	9.2	6 867	18.4	24.5
51 133	...	Northumberland County ..	12 259	4.2	14.4	4.1	21.8	29.2	26.3	50.1	−7.1	13.9	8 834	14.9	29.6
51 135	...	Nottoway County	15 725	5.5	17.5	8.1	29.5	22.4	17.0	38.6	−2.7	4.6	8 918	22.0	19.0
51 137	...	Orange County	25 881	5.8	17.1	6.7	27.7	25.4	17.3	40.4	−2.8	4.9	21 588	21.9	18.3
51 139	...	Page County	23 177	5.8	17.4	7.7	28.3	25.3	15.8	39.0	−2.8	3.4	22 164	22.4	16.0
51 141	...	Patrick County	19 407	5.8	16.0	7.0	27.9	26.8	16.5	40.5	−3.9	4.1	17 621	21.1	17.1
51 143	1950	Pittsylvania County	61 745	5.7	17.3	7.1	29.2	26.4	14.3	39.6	−2.7	1.9	45 905	21.7	14.9
51 145	6760	Powhatan County............	22 377	5.8	18.1	7.2	34.7	25.8	8.4	36.8	−1.8	−4.0	18 169	25.3	8.3
51 147	...	Prince Edward County	19 720	4.6	15.6	23.5	22.3	19.8	14.1	31.5	−5.5	1.7	12 201	15.7	15.3
51 149	6760	Prince George County	33 047	6.0	19.2	13.5	33.5	20.7	7.2	32.1	−0.5	−5.2	19 464	24.2	9.4
51 153	8840	Prince William County.....	280 813	8.5	22.0	8.7	35.5	20.9	4.6	31.9	4.8	−7.8	181 477	27.5	5.8
51 155	...	Pulaski County	35 127	5.7	14.7	7.3	29.4	27.5	15.4	40.3	−5.3	3.0	32 415	20.2	15.6
51 157	...	Rappahannock County ...	6 983	5.1	14.9	5.0	27.2	31.5	13.8	42.6	−3.1	1.4	6 400	22.7	13.4
51 159	...	Richmond County	8 809	4.2	14.1	7.3	33.8	23.1	17.4	40.3	−7.4	5.0	5 572	18.2	21.1
51 161	6800	Roanoke County	85 778	5.3	17.5	6.4	27.8	27.3	15.8	40.9	−2.9	3.4	80 001	22.3	16.4
51 163	...	Rockbridge County	20 808	5.3	16.8	8.0	27.1	27.3	15.6	40.4	−3.6	3.2	19 767	21.7	15.8
51 165	...	Rockingham County........	67 725	6.3	18.4	8.7	29.0	23.8	13.9	37.5	−1.0	1.5	64 118	24.1	14.4
51 167	...	Russell County...............	30 308	5.2	16.0	8.3	30.8	26.3	13.3	38.7	−4.5	0.9	28 938	21.5	13.7
51 169	3660	Scott County..................	23 403	5.1	15.6	7.4	27.2	27.0	17.7	41.4	−5.0	5.3	22 927	20.4	18.0
51 171	...	Shenandoah County	35 075	5.7	16.6	6.6	27.7	26.2	17.2	40.9	−3.4	4.8	32 974	21.5	18.1
51 173	...	Smyth County	33 081	5.3	16.3	8.1	27.9	26.1	16.3	40.0	−4.1	3.9	31 887	21.4	16.5
51 175	...	Southampton County	17 482	5.2	17.6	8.1	30.5	24.2	14.4	38.6	−2.9	2.0	9 747	21.7	15.1
51 177	8840	Spotsylvania County	90 395	7.3	22.6	7.4	32.0	22.6	8.1	34.3	4.2	−4.3	73 437	28.7	8.9
51 179	8840	Stafford County	92 446	7.6	24.0	7.8	33.8	21.0	5.8	33.1	5.9	−6.6	74 042	30.0	6.5
51 181	...	Surry County	6 829	5.5	19.8	7.8	27.9	25.0	14.1	39.4	−0.4	1.7	3 170	22.4	16.3
51 183	...	Sussex County	12 504	4.6	15.0	9.1	34.5	23.3	13.4	37.6	−6.1	1.0	4 560	19.7	17.4
51 185	...	Tazewell County	44 598	5.4	16.1	8.4	27.2	27.6	15.4	40.7	−4.2	3.0	42 866	21.0	15.6
51 187	8840	Warren County	31 584	6.7	18.9	7.5	30.7	23.8	12.4	37.1	−0.1	0.0	28 837	24.8	12.7
51 191	3660	Washington County........	51 103	5.1	15.6	8.9	28.3	26.7	15.3	40.3	−5.0	2.9	49 585	20.4	15.5
51 193	...	Westmoreland County	16 718	5.2	17.9	6.3	24.6	26.8	19.2	42.8	−2.6	6.8	10 731	18.8	22.8
51 195	...	Wise County	40 123	5.7	17.3	10.4	27.8	24.8	14.0	37.8	−2.7	1.6	38 742	22.8	14.2
51 197	...	Wythe County	27 599	5.5	16.2	7.5	29.2	25.7	15.8	39.4	−4.0	3.4	26 287	21.4	16.1
51 199	5720	York County	56 297	6.6	22.5	6.6	30.9	24.2	9.2	36.5	3.4	−3.2	44 251	27.8	9.6
		Independent Cities													
51 510	8840	Alexandria city.................	128 283	6.2	10.5	8.6	44.1	21.6	8.9	34.4	−9.0	−3.5	68 937	10.6	12.2
51 515	4640	Bedford city....................	6 299	5.6	15.9	7.1	28.7	20.8	21.8	40.9	−4.2	9.4	4 706	18.9	26.0
51 520	3660	Bristol city......................	17 367	5.1	15.1	8.6	27.2	23.5	20.4	41.3	−5.5	8.0	15 974	19.5	21.5
51 530	...	Buena Vista city..............	6 349	5.8	16.5	10.7	26.1	24.6	16.2	37.9	−3.4	3.8	5 906	21.7	16.8
51 540	1540	Charlottesville city...........	45 049	4.4	10.7	34.1	25.7	15.1	10.0	25.6	−10.6	−2.4	30 900	11.0	11.8
51 550	5720	Chesapeake city	199 184	7.1	21.7	8.2	32.4	21.7	8.8	34.7	3.1	−3.6	131 138	26.9	9.7
51 560	...	Clifton Forge city	4 289	5.4	15.6	6.5	24.8	23.9	23.8	42.9	−4.7	11.4	3 529	19.8	24.9
51 570	6760	Colonial Heights city	16 897	4.9	17.7	8.4	26.6	23.8	18.7	39.9	−3.1	6.3	15 048	21.5	20.2
51 580	...	Covington city	6 303	6.4	14.9	7.6	27.2	23.5	20.5	40.5	−4.4	8.1	5 278	20.6	20.4
51 590	1950	Danville city....................	48 411	5.9	17.4	8.1	25.4	23.5	19.7	40.5	−2.4	7.3	25 795	15.7	28.1
51 595	...	Emporia city	5 665	5.6	19.7	8.0	25.3	21.4	20.0	38.8	−0.4	7.6	2 284	17.0	29.8
51 600	8840	Fairfax city.....................	21 498	5.9	14.2	9.1	34.1	24.1	12.6	37.0	−5.6	0.2	14 471	17.7	16.9
51 610	8840	Falls Church city	10 377	6.0	17.5	4.5	31.7	27.9	12.3	39.7	−2.2	−0.1	8 273	22.4	13.9
51 620	...	Franklin city....................	8 346	4.8	20.2	7.5	25.5	23.6	18.5	39.9	−0.7	6.1	3 816	18.6	24.5
51 630	8840	Fredericksburg city..........	19 279	5.7	12.0	24.2	26.8	18.3	13.1	30.3	−8.0	0.7	13 716	13.1	15.1
51 640	...	Galax city......................	6 837	5.5	17.7	6.9	27.2	24.1	18.6	39.8	−2.5	6.2	5 553	19.6	22.5
51 650	5720	Hampton city	146 437	6.2	17.9	12.7	32.7	20.1	10.4	34.0	−1.6	−2.0	70 792	20.0	13.3
51 660	...	Harrisonburg city............	40 468	4.8	10.3	41.7	20.9	13.0	9.3	22.6	−10.6	−3.1	32 542	12.8	11.0
51 670	6760	Hopewell city..................	22 354	7.6	19.2	9.1	29.0	20.6	14.5	35.0	1.1	2.1	13 689	21.1	19.5
51 678	...	Lexington city.................	6 867	3.1	7.4	41.6	14.2	17.3	16.4	23.3	−15.2	4.0	5 882	10.4	16.1
51 680	4640	Lynchburg city................	65 269	5.9	16.3	15.3	25.8	20.4	16.4	35.1	−3.5	4.0	43 065	17.9	20.1

[1]MSA = Metropolitan Statistical Area. PMSA = Primary MSA. NECMA = New England County Metropolitan Area. See the Appendix A for explanation of these concepts. See Appendix B for list of metropolitan areas identified by type, with component counties.

Table A-3. States and Counties — **Age, Ethnicity, and Household Structure**

STATE County	Black or African American			American Indian and Alaska Native			Asian, Hawaiian, and Pacific Islander			Hispanic or Latino[1]			Two or more races		
		Age (percent)			Age (percent)			Age (percent)			Age (percent)			Age (percent)	
	Total population	Under 18 years	65 years and over	Total population	Under 18 years	65 years and over	Total population	Under 18 years	65 years and over	Total population	Under 18 years	65 years and over	Total population	Under 18 years	65 years and over
	14	15	16	17	18	19	20	21	22	23	24	25	26	27	28
VIRGINIA—Cont'd															
Louisa County	5 582	25.2	14.2	111	66.7	1.8	142	31.7	2.8	135	37.8	0.7	231	42.9	5.6
Lunenburg County	5 068	22.9	14.6	47	53.2	8.5	11	36.4	36.4	178	12.9	11.8	200	26.0	8.0
Madison County	1 260	20.5	17.1	10	0.0	0.0	28	0.0	60.7	268	39.2	9.7	138	44.2	6.0
Mathews County	1 050	23.1	19.9	34	61.8	0.0	0	X	X	78	35.9	11.5	100	27.0	6.0
Mecklenburg County	12 599	24.6	14.1	26	42.3	0.0	159	17.6	5.7	451	38.1	3.1	214	50.9	10.7
Middlesex County	1 976	22.4	20.2	6	0.0	0.0	23	0.0	0.0	36	25.0	5.6	131	36.6	25.2
Montgomery County	3 252	24.8	6.1	159	11.9	17.0	3 154	10.5	1.0	1 225	20.6	4.0	1 238	21.5	1.3
Nelson County	2 249	23.4	18.1	0	X	X	22	0.0	22.7	306	34.6	1.6	142	36.6	3.5
New Kent County	2 258	25.3	14.0	215	16.3	13.5	29	13.8	20.7	89	30.3	4.5	163	46.0	3.7
Northampton County	5 581	28.0	20.1	19	15.8	10.5	24	41.7	0.0	528	34.7	3.4	171	31.6	12.3
Northumberland County	3 265	29.1	18.3	55	7.3	0.0	45	0.0	11.1	26	46.2	0.0	46	26.1	15.2
Nottoway County	6 421	23.8	15.2	45	15.6	0.0	69	33.3	5.8	235	29.8	0.0	62	56.5	0.0
Orange County	3 694	27.7	12.0	26	26.9	7.7	64	9.4	12.5	301	23.3	19.3	241	46.1	0.0
Page County	606	28.1	12.9	23	43.5	0.0	56	32.1	25.0	167	47.9	0.0	101	23.8	7.9
Patrick County	1 322	25.1	13.1	19	0.0	0.0	87	29.9	0.0	287	35.9	4.2	102	47.1	12.7
Pittsylvania County	14 609	26.0	13.0	104	0.0	0.0	94	20.2	5.5	726	35.7	5.5	441	51.2	3.6
Powhatan County	3 830	17.3	8.6	22	0.0	0.0	54	0.0	0.0	136	26.5	14.0	199	38.7	7.5
Prince Edward County	6 891	27.0	12.5	79	44.3	12.7	171	24.6	0.0	137	7.3	19.7	295	45.8	9.5
Prince George County	10 712	26.9	4.4	151	9.3	4.6	615	17.2	4.4	1 699	23.9	1.6	854	45.3	0.8
Prince William County	52 873	35.5	2.3	1 262	23.4	1.2	10 678	23.8	4.3	27 266	36.6	1.7	10 602	48.8	1.7
Pulaski County	1 984	21.8	15.2	103	4.9	0.0	23	0.0	39.1	195	10.8	2.6	417	40.3	4.3
Rappahannock County	348	22.4	28.2	31	0.0	0.0	26	42.3	0.0	144	32.6	7.6	66	3.0	0.0
Richmond County	2 877	17.1	12.1	9	22.2	77.8	35	20.0	11.4	304	28.3	0.0	61	24.6	0.0
Roanoke County	2 701	20.9	10.1	131	37.4	0.0	1 013	28.1	5.3	1 140	35.4	2.0	848	44.3	7.5
Rockbridge County	565	22.7	17.9	13	30.8	15.4	122	21.3	0.0	174	31.6	2.9	217	41.5	9.7
Rockingham County	854	24.0	12.1	126	27.0	3.2	223	35.9	2.7	2 101	40.3	0.7	525	33.9	4.6
Russell County	901	4.1	8.2	49	12.2	12.2	28	21.4	0.0	261	23.8	2.3	171	55.6	0.0
Scott County	204	22.1	8.8	63	54.0	0.0	17	0.0	0.0	70	47.1	14.3	124	38.7	8.1
Shenandoah County	487	26.1	9.4	40	10.0	0.0	161	34.2	0.0	1 204	30.7	0.2	310	45.5	1.6
Smyth County	663	21.9	9.5	81	17.3	0.0	38	15.8	47.4	204	27.9	15.7	196	44.9	12.2
Southampton County	7 522	23.9	13.5	48	25.0	0.0	7	0.0	0.0	75	57.3	6.7	140	41.4	21.4
Spotsylvania County	10 725	31.8	5.9	288	25.5	0.0	1 299	20.4	4.0	2 051	30.7	1.1	2 451	55.4	1.0
Stafford County	10 998	36.2	3.7	374	16.3	9.6	1 531	17.9	3.3	3 181	39.0	0.5	2 650	60.1	1.3
Surry County	3 515	27.7	12.5	9	11.1	0.0	9	0.0	0.0	67	32.8	10.4	84	36.9	2.4
Sussex County	7 788	19.6	11.3	6	0.0	0.0	29	6.9	0.0	96	30.2	0.0	60	23.3	6.7
Tazewell County	968	25.6	12.2	31	16.1	38.7	222	29.7	0.9	242	59.1	0.8	324	42.0	5.6
Warren County	1 835	32.6	11.3	62	17.7	0.0	215	29.3	3.3	366	28.7	5.5	333	45.9	7.8
Washington County	788	26.0	14.3	60	45.0	0.0	225	32.9	0.0	156	26.9	7.7	313	36.1	10.2
Westmoreland County	5 335	30.0	13.9	21	0.0	0.0	56	0.0	17.9	532	36.7	0.8	101	47.5	15.8
Wise County	631	24.9	10.0	70	15.7	14.3	108	25.0	0.0	220	31.4	7.7	334	31.1	9.9
Wythe County	728	27.9	11.4	32	0.0	0.0	118	16.9	5.1	158	35.4	12.7	353	39.4	5.9
York County	7 471	31.6	10.7	134	23.1	0.0	1 905	32.2	3.9	1 507	46.8	1.0	1 248	44.9	1.2
Independent Cities															
Alexandria city	28 444	23.6	6.6	384	16.1	4.4	7 114	15.3	7.6	18 747	26.8	2.0	5 962	29.1	3.0
Bedford city	1 439	26.8	9.5	8	0.0	0.0	32	37.5	0.0	19	0.0	52.6	95	73.7	7.4
Bristol city	903	26.1	9.2	23	0.0	0.0	72	0.0	0.0	173	42.2	11.6	207	39.6	0.0
Buena Vista city	392	35.2	9.9	7	0.0	0.0	13	0.0	0.0	9	0.0	0.0	22	0.0	0.0
Charlottesville city	9 882	28.3	7.7	36	13.9	22.2	2 187	8.5	0.8	1 229	24.2	1.0	919	22.7	3.7
Chesapeake city	56 448	31.5	8.0	1 177	25.3	2.0	3 583	23.0	3.7	3 893	37.8	3.7	3 780	53.6	4.4
Clifton Forge city	690	21.6	20.9	0	X	X	11	0.0	0.0	20	75.0	0.0	59	91.5	0.0
Colonial Heights city	1 019	34.2	4.5	72	40.3	9.7	368	21.7	8.4	293	24.6	6.8	107	45.8	15.9
Covington city	826	21.8	23.7	0	X	X	29	31.0	0.0	88	19.3	10.2	82	57.3	6.1
Danville city	21 391	31.8	10.1	143	25.2	16.8	248	13.7	8.5	566	35.3	10.8	375	49.6	6.4
Emporia city	3 138	31.5	14.3	0	X	X	14	0.0	0.0	223	29.6	0.0	47	48.9	0.0
Fairfax city	1 008	19.7	5.2	74	21.6	10.8	2 570	20.4	4.9	2 906	29.2	2.5	769	31.9	5.5
Falls Church city	256	16.8	8.2	25	0.0	0.0	674	17.8	7.0	892	29.8	6.4	264	59.1	5.3
Franklin city	4 411	30.6	13.2	18	0.0	61.1	18	61.1	0.0	43	0.0	16.3	46	23.9	19.6
Fredericksburg city	3 950	31.4	10.9	56	0.0	0.0	241	10.4	0.0	919	25.1	0.8	373	29.2	1.6
Galax city	499	39.3	4.4	8	0.0	0.0	16	0.0	0.0	759	38.5	0.0	40	62.5	0.0
Hampton city	65 665	27.7	8.1	731	37.3	5.1	2 708	19.3	5.6	3 871	30.2	3.4	3 568	39.1	3.4
Harrisonburg city	2 468	22.9	3.3	35	34.3	0.0	1 261	16.6	1.0	3 513	28.0	0.7	1 062	30.5	4.2
Hopewell city	7 365	36.2	6.9	51	15.7	0.0	158	15.8	13.9	644	37.3	2.0	571	45.7	5.4
Lexington city	705	12.3	22.4	13	0.0	100.0	75	0.0	0.0	133	11.3	6.0	82	29.3	0.0
Lynchburg city	19 274	30.5	9.7	192	10.4	19.3	1 001	15.1	5.3	981	29.7	4.5	1 040	51.5	5.6

[1] Hispanic or Latino persons may be of any race.

STATE County	Total households	Family households (percent) Married-couple family households Total	With children	Householder 65 years or over	Other family households Total	With children	Householder 65 years or over	Nonfamily households (percent) Two or more unrelated persons Total	Householder 65 years or over	Male living alone Total	Householder 65 years or over	Female living alone Total	Householder 65 years or over	Percent of householders 65 years and over who live alone	Grandparents who are responsible for the care of their grandchildren
	29	30	31	32	33	34	35	36	37	38	39	40	41	42	43
VIRGINIA—Cont'd															
Louisa County	9 975	57.5	22.9	9.6	15.9	8.8	2.4	4.5	0.4	10.7	3.0	11.4	6.4	43.0	326
Lunenburg County	4 996	50.5	18.0	12.1	18.0	9.6	3.5	2.8	1.0	11.8	3.3	17.0	11.2	46.8	180
Madison County	4 744	62.1	25.0	12.3	12.5	6.0	3.3	3.6	0.4	9.2	3.1	12.6	7.0	38.5	60
Mathews County	3 934	61.5	19.2	18.0	10.3	4.7	1.8	3.4	0.5	9.2	2.4	15.7	10.9	39.7	48
Mecklenburg County	12 901	51.5	18.2	11.9	17.5	8.2	3.9	3.7	0.6	10.1	2.9	17.3	11.0	45.9	363
Middlesex County	4 254	54.9	16.3	16.9	13.3	6.4	2.7	4.9	0.5	11.3	4.3	15.7	10.0	41.6	92
Montgomery County	31 054	45.9	19.9	6.6	10.2	5.8	1.4	18.4	0.2	12.0	1.7	13.6	5.3	46.1	406
Nelson County	5 887	55.3	21.0	12.2	15.4	7.5	3.6	4.3	0.5	12.0	3.2	12.9	6.5	37.4	207
New Kent County	4 913	65.9	28.2	9.0	13.0	7.0	2.9	4.4	0.2	8.4	1.6	8.2	4.3	32.9	171
Northampton County	5 319	46.7	16.4	14.6	20.2	9.6	4.6	3.6	0.6	10.8	5.1	18.6	10.6	44.3	219
Northumberland County	5 469	59.5	16.5	21.5	9.5	4.8	2.6	3.4	0.2	10.8	3.7	16.8	11.2	38.0	57
Nottoway County	5 670	50.9	20.1	11.4	18.8	10.1	5.0	2.9	0.1	8.6	3.0	18.8	11.1	46.1	364
Orange County	10 142	57.0	21.0	14.2	16.7	9.2	2.5	4.1	0.5	10.1	3.3	12.0	7.1	37.6	344
Page County	9 313	56.0	22.2	11.3	15.4	8.0	2.7	4.1	0.5	10.4	2.6	14.0	8.8	44.3	267
Patrick County	8 118	59.6	21.2	11.5	12.1	7.3	1.6	2.4	0.1	11.1	3.0	14.8	8.6	46.8	101
Pittsylvania County	24 666	59.1	23.7	10.7	15.1	7.2	3.0	2.5	0.2	10.4	2.4	12.9	7.6	42.0	858
Powhatan County	7 253	70.1	32.1	8.4	11.5	5.5	2.2	3.7	0.4	7.2	1.5	7.5	3.2	29.7	106
Prince Edward County	6 564	49.1	20.3	10.5	16.5	9.1	3.8	5.6	0.2	10.8	2.9	18.0	11.0	49.0	246
Prince George County	10 186	65.2	33.6	7.0	15.7	9.8	1.9	2.0	0.2	7.5	1.9	9.6	4.5	40.9	273
Prince William County	94 662	62.4	35.2	3.8	15.1	9.7	0.8	5.4	0.1	8.1	0.7	8.9	2.4	39.1	2 440
Pulaski County	14 626	55.4	19.6	10.0	13.9	7.5	2.4	3.7	0.1	10.7	2.4	16.2	9.6	48.8	259
Rappahannock County	2 796	60.7	24.1	10.7	11.7	5.4	2.6	4.4	0.0	12.7	3.9	10.4	4.1	37.7	25
Richmond County	2 922	52.6	19.0	13.6	16.3	8.7	2.7	2.9	0.2	11.4	3.0	16.7	11.4	46.6	83
Roanoke County	34 734	59.8	25.1	11.7	11.7	6.1	1.8	3.5	0.2	8.8	2.1	16.1	8.0	42.5	553
Rockbridge County	8 447	57.9	21.5	12.5	13.7	7.0	3.1	4.3	0.5	11.5	3.1	12.6	7.1	39.0	260
Rockingham County	25 352	62.6	27.1	11.5	12.3	6.4	2.6	4.0	0.4	8.6	2.0	12.5	7.0	38.2	588
Russell County	11 766	61.9	24.8	9.7	13.4	6.3	2.9	1.6	0.0	9.3	2.4	13.8	7.4	43.8	310
Scott County	9 851	60.4	22.7	11.7	11.9	5.4	3.1	1.7	0.1	9.5	3.3	16.5	10.4	47.9	201
Shenandoah County	14 284	57.5	21.3	12.8	13.1	7.5	1.9	4.2	0.3	10.6	2.6	14.5	8.6	42.9	274
Smyth County	13 497	56.7	22.5	11.0	14.4	7.6	2.5	2.8	0.2	10.3	2.8	15.8	9.9	48.2	340
Southampton County	6 299	53.2	21.8	11.2	19.3	10.3	3.6	2.7	0.6	11.4	2.6	13.4	8.7	42.4	194
Spotsylvania County	31 259	66.3	34.7	7.1	12.8	7.7	1.3	4.4	0.2	7.1	1.3	9.4	3.8	37.5	634
Stafford County	30 136	69.1	39.4	5.3	12.1	8.1	1.2	4.9	0.3	6.9	1.0	6.9	2.4	33.3	772
Surry County	2 603	55.7	22.3	11.2	17.4	8.2	3.0	3.2	0.6	10.6	3.5	13.0	6.1	39.1	213
Sussex County	4 124	46.7	17.6	10.7	22.0	11.7	4.6	3.2	0.6	11.7	2.6	16.3	10.0	44.0	133
Tazewell County	18 263	58.4	22.5	9.9	14.2	6.2	3.1	2.2	0.3	8.5	2.4	16.7	9.4	46.9	540
Warren County	12 125	55.3	24.2	8.2	15.2	9.4	2.3	5.5	0.6	10.9	2.4	13.1	6.7	44.9	393
Washington County	21 031	59.5	22.9	11.3	11.4	5.3	2.7	3.3	0.2	10.4	1.9	15.5	8.3	41.7	358
Westmoreland County	6 865	51.6	17.9	14.3	16.7	8.3	3.4	4.9	0.9	11.6	3.4	15.3	9.5	41.0	238
Wise County	16 047	57.7	23.5	9.8	14.7	8.0	3.0	2.1	0.1	10.4	2.6	15.1	8.2	45.7	459
Wythe County	11 517	56.8	21.5	11.1	14.2	7.3	2.3	2.9	0.3	9.9	1.9	16.2	8.8	43.8	340
York County	19 914	68.5	35.5	9.0	11.2	7.2	1.6	3.6	0.2	6.6	1.1	10.1	4.3	33.1	251
Independent Cities															
Alexandria city	61 968	33.3	13.3	4.0	12.2	6.2	1.2	11.2	0.3	18.6	1.5	24.8	5.1	54.5	622
Bedford city	2 520	43.1	14.6	12.3	20.2	13.9	1.7	3.5	0.3	12.2	2.5	20.9	12.2	50.6	47
Bristol city	7 714	48.0	17.5	11.0	14.9	8.3	3.4	3.0	0.3	9.3	3.1	24.7	15.1	55.2	140
Buena Vista city	2 542	53.9	20.9	9.2	14.8	9.0	2.4	3.8	0.2	7.0	3.1	20.5	12.2	56.2	84
Charlottesville city	16 861	30.9	12.1	6.3	15.3	9.8	1.8	18.9	0.4	14.9	2.0	20.0	6.2	49.1	216
Chesapeake city	69 835	60.3	30.8	7.3	17.4	10.6	1.8	4.3	0.2	7.1	1.2	10.9	4.6	38.2	2 184
Clifton Forge city	1 838	40.4	15.0	10.7	21.1	11.9	2.4	4.0	1.5	11.8	4.8	22.7	14.4	56.8	43
Colonial Heights city	7 037	51.5	20.4	14.1	16.3	8.9	1.7	4.8	0.3	8.5	1.4	18.9	10.3	42.1	109
Covington city	2 835	46.9	16.0	12.3	15.5	7.0	2.8	3.7	0.0	12.5	3.2	21.5	14.4	53.9	74
Danville city	20 608	38.7	13.7	10.5	24.2	13.3	4.1	3.2	0.4	12.5	3.1	21.3	12.7	51.3	670
Emporia city	2 222	40.3	18.8	8.3	22.5	12.8	3.2	5.0	1.1	8.8	3.2	23.3	15.0	59.2	138
Fairfax city	8 013	55.8	23.1	9.8	11.9	4.7	2.3	8.8	0.3	7.9	0.9	15.5	6.0	36.1	172
Falls Church city	4 472	46.0	23.1	5.6	12.6	7.4	2.3	7.4	0.5	14.5	2.6	19.5	8.2	56.2	5
Franklin city	3 395	43.3	17.2	9.8	24.7	14.1	4.6	3.3	0.6	8.2	2.1	20.5	9.8	44.2	111
Fredericksburg city	8 086	32.7	12.6	6.5	16.1	9.2	2.2	12.0	0.6	16.4	3.0	22.9	10.3	59.1	62
Galax city	2 938	47.8	19.8	9.9	15.1	8.4	2.0	3.0	0.2	12.2	3.7	21.9	10.8	54.3	75
Hampton city	53 954	47.2	20.8	7.7	20.0	12.4	2.4	6.3	0.3	12.2	1.9	14.3	5.9	42.8	1 613
Harrisonburg city	13 156	37.2	17.5	6.7	12.8	7.5	1.2	21.8	0.4	12.7	1.8	15.5	6.5	50.0	109
Hopewell city	9 053	42.3	16.5	9.3	24.3	15.6	2.8	5.8	0.4	10.3	2.1	17.3	9.2	47.2	220
Lexington city	2 223	39.4	14.2	10.2	9.8	4.3	3.3	10.1	0.9	14.5	4.3	26.3	12.4	53.5	20
Lynchburg city	25 465	41.1	16.4	10.1	21.0	12.6	3.2	5.3	0.4	12.4	2.4	20.2	9.8	47.2	660

Table A-3. States and Counties — **Age, Ethnicity, and Household Structure**

STATE County	Households with Non-Hispanic White householder — Number of households	Percent that are family households	Households with Black or African American householder — Number of households	Percent that are family households	Households with American Indian and Alaska Native householder — Number of households	Percent that are family households	Households with Asian, Hawaiian, and Pacific Islander householder — Number of households	Percent that are family households	Households with Hispanic or Latino[1] householder — Number of households	Percent that are family households	Foreign-born population — Percent of total population that is foreign-born	Place of birth (percent) — Europe	Asia	Latin America	Percent in non-English speaking households — Linguistically isolated	Not linguistically isolated
	44	45	46	47	48	49	50	51	52	53	54	55	56	57	58	59
VIRGINIA—Cont'd																
Louisa County	7 750	72.6	2 085	76.1	19	89.5	32	87.5	29	75.9	1.3	0.6	0.4	0.1	0.1	5.8
Lunenburg County........	3 228	66.9	1 647	70.9	16	68.8	1	100.0	39	74.4	1.2	0.4	0.1	0.7	0.7	7.7
Madison County	4 105	74.6	518	71.2	0	X	9	100.0	76	100.0	2.2	1.0	0.2	1.0	0.3	5.9
Mathews County	3 398	73.4	447	55.9	8	100.0	0	X	35	100.0	2.2	1.8	0.1	0.1	0.0	6.5
Mecklenburg County......	8 238	68.6	4 436	69.5	3	100.0	44	100.0	145	75.2	1.6	0.3	0.4	0.7	0.9	7.2
Middlesex County.........	3 389	68.5	806	66.5	0	X	0	X	14	100.0	2.1	1.3	0.4	0.3	0.2	8.4
Montgomery County......	28 161	56.6	1 191	57.0	47	83.0	978	45.2	381	54.1	5.8	1.1	3.3	0.6	1.2	9.6
Nelson County..............	4 894	72.0	900	64.4	0	X	10	100.0	25	72.0	1.9	1.0	0.0	0.7	0.4	5.7
New Kent County	4 035	78.6	742	80.3	68	92.6	17	64.7	17	76.5	0.9	0.5	0.1	0.2	0.0	5.3
Northampton County......	3 119	66.1	2 075	68.1	5	60.0	9	100.0	79	78.5	3.4	0.7	0.1	2.4	1.3	6.5
Northumberland County ..	4 154	69.8	1 244	67.4	7	100.0	39	12.8	0	X	1.6	0.8	0.3	0.0	0.6	4.6
Nottoway County...........	3 576	68.2	2 034	72.6	13	69.2	9	100.0	34	76.5	1.4	0.2	0.2	0.9	0.9	6.6
Orange County	8 758	74.2	1 265	71.8	8	62.5	5	60.0	89	60.7	1.9	0.9	0.3	0.5	0.3	6.3
Page County	8 965	71.5	215	68.4	11	100.0	6	100.0	59	67.8	1.5	0.5	0.2	0.5	0.4	6.0
Patrick County	7 429	72.5	531	67.0	17	52.9	36	44.4	94	63.8	1.5	0.3	0.3	0.8	1.2	5.9
Pittsylvania County.......	18 977	73.9	5 300	75.2	80	75.0	34	70.6	211	74.9	1.0	0.2	0.2	0.5	0.6	5.2
Powhatan County	6 333	81.8	815	81.8	11	0.0	0	X	34	100.0	1.5	0.4	0.2	0.4	0.2	5.9
Prince Edward County ..	3 987	62.3	2 413	70.1	26	96.2	43	86.0	33	84.8	1.4	0.4	0.5	0.2	0.6	7.9
Prince George County ..	6 924	80.3	2 805	81.7	23	34.8	66	90.9	294	85.0	4.5	1.3	1.4	1.7	0.7	13.1
Prince William County...	65 736	76.3	17 897	77.1	470	80.6	2 816	82.2	6 311	89.1	11.5	1.6	3.3	5.3	3.3	19.9
Pulaski County	13 632	69.8	705	55.7	53	67.9	0	X	87	88.5	0.6	0.2	0.1	0.2	0.7	4.4
Rappahannock County..	2 572	72.4	148	76.4	21	52.4	5	100.0	25	100.0	3.2	2.1	0.1	0.6	1.0	4.9
Richmond County.........	2 154	67.8	707	69.7	7	100.0	11	100.0	39	100.0	1.9	0.5	0.3	1.0	0.9	6.7
Roanoke County	32 674	71.8	1 132	61.0	38	52.6	331	85.5	313	85.3	3.1	0.9	1.1	0.6	0.7	8.0
Rockbridge County.......	8 103	72.0	209	58.9	7	71.4	33	100.0	68	80.7	2.0	0.8	0.7	0.4	0.3	5.8
Rockingham County......	24 361	74.7	294	66.7	53	84.9	58	75.9	472	86.2	3.3	0.9	0.4	1.8	1.7	7.0
Russell County	11 542	75.3	99	71.7	18	100.0	0	X	69	95.7	0.4	0.1	0.0	0.1	0.2	3.9
Scott County................	9 696	72.3	62	90.3	17	100.0	15	66.7	34	64.7	0.3	0.2	0.0	0.0	0.2	2.4
Shenandoah County	13 640	70.5	238	67.2	9	100.0	55	100.0	281	78.3	3.1	0.6	0.2	2.0	1.5	6.4
Smyth County...............	13 137	71.1	175	64.0	42	69.0	25	80.0	75	64.0	0.5	0.1	0.1	0.1	0.1	5.0
Southampton County	3 768	72.5	2 473	72.7	12	83.3	0	X	9	88.9	0.3	0.2	0.0	0.1	0.0	5.9
Spotsylvania County.....	25 924	78.8	3 765	78.3	83	100.0	343	88.0	673	80.0	3.2	0.0	1.2	0.8	0.6	10.0
Stafford County	24 861	81.6	3 559	80.1	143	71.3	464	64.2	699	92.6	4.0	1.1	1.5	1.1	0.6	13.6
Surry County	1 225	74.6	1 324	72.8	5	100.0	7	0.0	32	59.4	0.5	0.4	0.0	0.1	0.0	5.4
Sussex County	1 917	67.9	2 164	69.6	2	100.0	7	100.0	21	100.0	1.0	0.3	0.2	0.4	0.5	5.9
Tazewell County...........	17 594	72.9	437	67.5	22	18.2	64	84.4	70	77.1	1.0	0.3	0.5	0.1	0.3	5.0
Warren County	11 267	70.5	595	72.4	25	100.0	67	82.1	121	66.9	2.1	1.0	0.5	0.4	0.3	6.0
Washington County.......	20 494	71.1	285	57.5	20	100.0	67	82.1	70	80.0	0.9	0.4	0.4	0.1	0.1	4.7
Westmoreland County...	4 709	65.6	1 987	74.5	14	0.0	33	54.5	111	73.9	3.1	0.6	0.4	1.8	0.6	7.6
Wise County................	15 649	72.6	156	65.4	35	80.0	40	57.5	45	91.1	0.5	0.1	0.2	0.1	0.0	3.9
Wythe County..............	11 046	71.5	315	62.9	17	29.4	50	70.0	31	45.2	0.5	0.1	0.2	0.1	0.2	5.6
York County	16 289	79.1	2 607	81.8	46	87.0	439	82.7	326	89.3	5.2	1.7	2.5	0.7	0.8	12.8
Independent Cities																
Alexandria city.............	39 104	38.0	12 270	55.1	180	35.0	2 880	52.6	5 534	70.9	25.4	2.2	6.3	10.6	9.7	25.3
Bedford city	1 910	64.1	572	63.3	0	X	11	0.0	19	52.6	1.6	0.6	0.3	0.2	0.3	5.9
Bristol city	7 231	62.8	354	70.6	5	0.0	24	16.7	51	68.6	1.4	0.6	0.4	0.4	0.1	4.9
Buena Vista city	2 384	69.7	130	50.8	7	100.0	9	0.0	0	X	0.5	0.3	0.0	0.2	0.0	6.4
Charlottesville city	12 167	41.9	3 439	64.4	11	54.5	615	35.6	369	45.8	6.9	1.7	3.1	1.2	1.4	13.1
Chesapeake city...........	47 784	77.4	18 949	77.9	424	77.8	1 054	85.2	1 011	84.3	3.0	0.7	1.3	0.7	0.5	10.4
Clifton Forge city	1 514	60.6	314	64.6	0	X	5	100.0	5	100.0	0.3	0.0	0.3	0.0	0.5	4.0
Colonial Heights city	6 332	68.4	446	50.9	35	80.0	109	91.7	90	85.6	4.9	1.7	1.9	0.7	1.1	11.2
Covington city..............	2 409	62.1	356	62.6	0	X	16	25.0	27	66.7	2.3	0.1	0.4	1.6	0.4	5.4
Danville city	12 094	59.5	8 126	67.8	81	75.3	65	100.0	166	72.3	1.4	0.3	0.4	0.6	0.7	6.7
Emporia city	1 069	61.0	1 111	64.3	0	X	4	0.0	36	91.7	3.2	0.3	0.5	2.1	2.2	4.9
Fairfax city	6 089	64.1	365	59.2	26	84.6	764	82.9	637	87.0	25.4	2.7	12.0	9.6	7.7	29.3
Falls Church city	3 720	57.2	129	40.3	8	0.0	271	61.3	288	78.8	16.1	3.5	6.1	4.9	3.4	22.2
Franklin city	1 644	67.7	1 717	68.5	0	X	7	0.0	18	27.8	0.7	0.3	0.1	0.4	0.6	6.0
Fredericksburg city.......	6 155	43.9	1 457	63.5	44	59.1	34	58.8	274	82.1	5.2	1.1	0.6	3.0	2.5	10.6
Galax city	2 528	60.9	182	63.7	8	100.0	10	0.0	202	87.6	8.6	0.5	0.1	7.9	7.0	7.0
Hampton city	27 864	66.0	23 319	68.4	174	75.3	822	65.6	965	69.9	3.9	1.1	1.5	0.9	0.8	11.2
Harrisonburg city	11 041	47.4	773	49.3	5	100.0	314	59.6	846	79.6	9.2	1.2	2.5	4.8	6.7	13.2
Hopewell city	5 996	64.7	2 740	71.9	28	32.1	43	23.3	159	48.4	1.9	0.9	0.5	0.5	0.8	8.1
Lexington city	1 929	47.5	252	63.9	7	0.0	6	100.0	9	0.0	4.0	1.6	1.1	0.5	0.5	7.8
Lynchburg city	17 195	60.9	7 390	65.3	64	59.4	340	52.9	276	56.2	3.2	0.9	1.3	0.6	0.7	7.6

[1] Hispanic or Latino persons may be of any race.

STATE/ County code	MSA/PMSA/ NECMA code[1]	STATE County	Population by age (percent)										Non-Hispanic White		
														Age (percent)	
			Total population	Under 5 years	5 to 17 years	18 to 24 years	25 to 44 years	45 to 64 years	65 years and over	Median age	+/– U.S. percent under 18 years	+/– U.S. percent 65 years and over	Total population	Under 18 years	65 years and over
			1	2	3	4	5	6	7	8	9	10	11	12	13
		VIRGINIA—Cont'd													
51 683	8840	Manassas city	35 135	8.9	20.8	10.0	35.8	19.1	5.3	31.3	4.0	-7.1	23 292	27.3	6.9
51 685	8840	Manassas Park city	10 290	10.0	20.9	8.6	40.5	15.4	4.6	30.3	5.2	-7.8	6 891	28.7	5.6
51 690	...	Martinsville city	15 416	5.8	16.8	7.1	27.0	22.4	20.9	40.8	-3.1	8.5	8 320	16.9	28.2
51 700	5720	Newport News city	180 150	7.9	19.5	11.5	32.3	18.8	10.1	32.0	1.7	-2.3	93 842	22.0	13.4
51 710	5720	Norfolk city	234 403	7.1	16.9	18.3	29.9	16.9	10.9	29.6	-1.7	-1.5	109 980	17.7	14.1
51 720	...	Norton city	3 904	5.5	16.5	9.8	27.7	24.9	15.7	39.0	-3.7	3.3	3 520	19.9	16.5
51 730	6760	Petersburg city	33 740	6.6	18.3	9.1	27.7	22.7	15.6	36.9	-0.8	3.2	6 105	10.1	35.1
51 735	5720	Poquoson city	11 566	5.1	21.7	6.0	27.1	28.6	11.3	39.5	1.1	-1.1	10 995	26.6	11.5
51 740	5720	Portsmouth city	100 565	7.0	18.6	11.0	29.1	20.5	13.8	34.5	-0.1	1.4	45 574	20.1	16.9
51 750	...	Radford city	15 859	3.7	9.1	44.5	19.3	13.6	9.8	22.8	-12.9	-2.6	13 959	12.3	10.0
51 760	6760	Richmond city	197 790	6.3	15.6	13.1	31.8	19.8	13.4	33.9	-3.8	1.0	74 796	10.7	18.1
51 770	6800	Roanoke city	94 911	6.5	16.1	8.3	30.4	22.3	16.4	37.6	-3.1	4.0	65 104	18.6	19.6
51 775	6800	Salem city	24 747	4.9	15.9	11.9	26.6	23.7	16.9	39.2	-4.9	4.5	22 587	20.1	17.4
51 790	...	Staunton city	23 853	5.4	14.5	10.1	27.6	24.4	18.1	39.8	-5.8	5.7	19 868	18.7	19.6
51 800	5720	Suffolk city	63 677	7.2	20.5	6.8	31.5	22.3	11.6	36.0	2.0	-0.8	33 828	24.2	12.7
51 810	5720	Virginia Beach city	425 257	7.1	20.3	9.9	34.6	19.7	8.4	32.7	1.7	-4.0	295 080	24.6	10.3
51 820	...	Waynesboro city	19 520	6.3	17.5	8.0	27.1	23.5	17.5	38.9	-1.9	5.1	16 549	22.2	19.3
51 830	5720	Williamsburg city	11 998	2.7	7.2	45.4	17.7	15.1	11.9	22.6	-15.8	-0.5	9 360	7.0	12.6
51 840	...	Winchester city	23 585	6.1	15.7	13.3	29.3	21.3	14.3	35.2	-3.9	1.9	18 672	19.4	16.9
53 000	...	WASHINGTON	5 894 121	6.7	19.0	9.4	31.0	22.7	11.2	35.3	0.0	-1.2	4 649 156	23.2	13.0
53 001	...	Adams County	16 428	9.5	24.8	9.5	26.5	18.9	10.8	29.6	8.6	-1.6	8 294	26.2	17.4
53 003	...	Asotin County	20 551	6.8	18.6	8.3	26.2	23.9	16.2	38.8	-0.3	3.8	19 450	24.8	17.0
53 005	6740	Benton County	142 475	7.5	22.2	8.4	28.6	23.1	10.3	34.4	4.0	-2.1	116 379	27.0	11.9
53 007	...	Chelan County	66 616	7.1	20.8	8.4	27.0	22.7	14.0	36.3	2.2	1.6	51 545	23.6	17.5
53 009	...	Clallam County	64 525	5.1	16.7	7.3	22.8	26.7	21.3	43.8	-3.9	8.9	56 355	19.9	23.5
53 011	6440	Clark County	345 238	7.8	20.8	8.4	31.0	22.3	9.6	34.2	2.9	-2.8	298 602	27.2	10.5
53 013	...	Columbia County	4 064	5.6	18.4	6.5	23.1	27.7	18.8	42.4	-1.7	6.4	3 666	22.1	19.7
53 015	...	Cowlitz County	92 948	6.9	19.8	8.3	27.5	24.1	13.3	36.9	1.0	0.9	83 501	25.2	14.4
53 017	...	Douglas County	32 603	7.4	22.0	7.9	27.8	22.2	12.7	35.7	3.7	0.3	25 191	25.0	15.9
53 019	...	Ferry County	7 260	5.4	21.5	7.7	23.4	29.4	12.7	40.0	1.2	0.3	5 506	23.9	14.3
53 021	6740	Franklin County	49 347	9.8	24.7	11.2	28.0	17.9	8.4	28.0	8.8	-4.0	23 329	25.3	15.1
53 023	...	Garfield County	2 397	4.5	21.5	4.9	22.3	26.0	20.7	43.0	0.3	8.3	2 332	25.6	21.0
53 025	...	Grant County	74 698	8.7	23.4	9.9	27.3	19.0	11.6	31.1	6.4	-0.8	48 971	26.8	15.9
53 027	...	Grays Harbor County	67 194	6.3	19.4	7.9	25.9	25.1	15.4	38.8	0.0	3.0	58 231	23.5	16.9
53 029	7600	Island County	71 558	6.7	18.8	8.7	28.1	23.5	14.3	37.0	-0.2	1.9	60 936	23.6	16.1
53 031	...	Jefferson County	25 953	4.0	15.7	4.9	21.9	32.4	21.0	47.1	-6.0	8.6	23 667	18.4	22.3
53 033	7600	King County	1 737 034	6.0	16.4	9.2	35.0	23.0	10.5	35.7	-3.3	-1.9	1 273 696	20.0	12.1
53 035	1150	Kitsap County	231 969	6.6	20.1	9.2	29.9	23.7	10.5	35.8	1.0	-1.9	190 099	24.7	12.0
53 037	...	Kittitas County	33 362	5.1	15.5	21.6	24.8	21.4	11.6	31.4	-5.1	-0.8	29 875	19.8	12.8
53 039	...	Klickitat County	19 161	6.2	20.7	6.3	26.8	26.2	13.9	39.5	1.2	1.5	16 260	24.1	15.6
53 041	...	Lewis County	68 600	6.4	20.1	8.1	25.1	24.7	15.6	38.4	0.8	3.2	62 226	25.1	16.7
53 043	...	Lincoln County	10 184	5.7	19.5	4.9	23.7	27.2	18.9	42.8	-0.5	6.5	9 617	24.3	19.7
53 045	...	Mason County	49 405	5.4	18.1	7.9	26.6	25.7	16.4	40.3	-2.2	4.0	42 615	21.8	18.3
53 047	...	Okanogan County	39 564	6.4	21.3	7.1	25.9	25.3	14.1	38.2	2.0	1.7	28 267	22.7	18.1
53 049	...	Pacific County	20 984	4.4	17.0	5.7	21.4	29.1	22.4	45.8	-4.3	10.0	18 465	19.1	24.6
53 051	...	Pend Oreille County	11 732	5.4	20.8	5.6	23.8	29.3	15.1	41.9	0.5	2.7	10 755	25.1	15.8
53 053	8200	Pierce County	700 820	7.1	20.1	9.7	31.6	21.4	10.2	34.1	1.5	-2.2	532 530	24.3	11.9
53 055	...	San Juan County	14 077	3.8	15.6	4.6	21.4	35.4	19.1	47.4	-6.3	6.7	13 222	18.2	20.0
53 057	...	Skagit County	102 979	6.5	19.7	8.8	26.9	23.6	14.6	37.2	0.5	2.2	85 411	23.4	16.8
53 059	...	Skamania County	9 872	6.6	20.1	6.9	28.5	26.9	11.0	38.7	1.0	-1.4	9 044	25.4	11.7
53 061	7600	Snohomish County	606 024	7.1	20.2	8.5	33.1	22.0	9.1	34.7	1.6	-3.3	505 454	26.0	10.2
53 063	7840	Spokane County	417 939	6.6	19.0	10.6	29.1	22.3	12.5	35.4	-0.1	0.1	374 816	24.6	13.3
53 065	...	Stevens County	40 066	6.1	22.6	6.4	24.9	27.1	12.8	39.2	3.0	0.4	35 854	27.4	13.7
53 067	5910	Thurston County	207 355	6.1	19.1	9.3	29.4	24.8	11.3	36.5	-0.5	-1.1	172 797	23.3	12.8
53 069	...	Wahkiakum County	3 824	5.5	17.9	5.6	22.2	30.2	18.6	44.4	-2.3	6.2	3 567	22.5	19.5
53 071	...	Walla Walla County	55 180	6.2	18.1	13.4	26.8	20.8	14.7	34.9	-1.4	2.3	43 499	21.5	17.9
53 073	0860	Whatcom County	166 814	6.2	17.8	14.3	27.5	22.5	11.6	34.0	-1.7	-0.8	144 069	22.4	12.9
53 075	...	Whitman County	40 740	4.8	13.3	32.7	24.4	15.6	9.3	24.7	-7.6	-3.1	35 399	18.0	10.4
53 077	9260	Yakima County	222 581	8.6	23.1	9.6	28.1	19.4	11.2	31.2	6.0	-1.2	125 664	23.1	17.2
54 000	...	WEST VIRGINIA	1 808 344	5.6	16.6	9.6	27.7	25.2	15.3	38.9	-3.5	2.9	1 709 317	21.9	15.6
54 001	...	Barbour County	15 557	5.3	17.7	9.4	26.9	25.1	15.6	38.7	-2.7	3.2	15 156	23.1	15.8
54 003	8840	Berkeley County	75 905	6.5	19.2	8.3	31.3	23.6	11.1	35.8	0.0	-1.3	69 757	24.9	11.6
54 005	...	Boone County	25 535	6.4	16.9	9.1	28.0	26.1	13.6	38.8	-2.4	1.2	25 073	23.2	13.5

[1]MSA = Metropolitan Statistical Area. PMSA = Primary MSA. NECMA = New England County Metropolitan Area. See the Appendix A for explanation of these concepts. See Appendix B for list of metropolitan areas identified by type, with component counties.

Table A-3. States and Counties — Age, Ethnicity, and Household Structure

STATE County	Black or African American			American Indian and Alaska Native			Asian, Hawaiian, and Pacific Islander			Hispanic or Latino[1]			Two or more races		
		Age (percent)			Age (percent)			Age (percent)			Age (percent)			Age (percent)	
	Total population	Under 18 years	65 years and over	Total population	Under 18 years	65 years and over	Total population	Under 18 years	65 years and over	Total population	Under 18 years	65 years and over	Total population	Under 18 years	65 years and over
	14	15	16	17	18	19	20	21	22	23	24	25	26	27	28
VIRGINIA—Cont'd															
Manassas city	4 542	32.0	3.6	45	0.0	0.0	1 103	28.5	2.9	5 344	35.8	1.0	1 256	48.3	2.5
Manassas Park city	1 109	34.0	3.2	46	43.5	0.0	385	29.9	5.7	1 565	35.5	1.9	401	39.7	3.2
Martinsville city	6 450	28.2	13.1	10	0.0	0.0	69	18.8	0.0	458	43.4	1.5	145	33.8	9.7
Newport News city	70 149	33.2	7.1	803	27.3	5.2	4 405	22.1	5.3	7 441	34.9	2.7	5 263	47.9	2.1
Norfolk city	102 610	30.1	8.8	1 063	15.5	4.6	7 210	19.1	7.2	8 781	25.8	2.8	6 697	41.3	3.7
Norton city	233	36.5	9.9	6	0.0	0.0	42	28.6	14.3	13	38.5	15.4	90	58.9	0.0
Petersburg city	26 419	27.9	11.6	51	9.8	0.0	275	18.9	17.1	607	40.5	1.2	453	37.1	7.9
Poquoson city	55	27.3	29.1	34	11.8	23.5	185	23.8	9.2	137	50.4	3.6	143	42.0	0.0
Portsmouth city	50 742	30.3	11.9	495	19.6	4.0	992	20.8	1.6	1 745	25.4	3.6	1 445	44.1	2.9
Radford city	1 188	19.9	7.4	10	0.0	0.0	219	6.8	0.0	230	8.7	30.9	275	27.3	0.0
Richmond city	112 655	29.3	11.1	511	13.5	5.1	2 553	11.4	7.6	5 239	24.2	2.3	2 895	28.8	5.3
Roanoke city	25 387	30.5	10.2	263	17.9	1.9	1 063	29.4	6.4	1 198	33.2	3.5	1 886	41.7	6.5
Salem city	1 415	26.1	15.5	36	58.3	0.0	262	23.7	12.2	240	25.4	0.0	183	28.4	3.8
Staunton city	3 182	21.8	10.9	52	17.3	0.0	15	0.0	46.7	252	21.4	15.5	452	56.9	5.3
Suffolk city	27 612	31.3	10.7	171	13.5	2.9	553	16.6	9.4	853	38.9	1.1	717	46.6	10.6
Virginia Beach city	80 097	34.2	4.1	1 719	21.5	3.7	20 412	23.0	6.1	17 970	36.4	2.4	13 385	48.1	2.3
Waynesboro city	1 946	30.9	10.0	57	0.0	0.0	55	56.4	0.0	619	34.1	1.8	370	46.8	2.4
Williamsburg city	1 725	23.5	12.3	10	0.0	0.0	521	15.2	1.9	234	11.1	7.3	134	15.7	5.2
Winchester city	2 506	27.4	7.8	90	37.8	0.0	308	19.2	0.0	1 508	30.1	0.5	564	56.2	2.7
WASHINGTON	185 052	30.7	5.6	91 299	33.2	4.8	342 717	24.3	7.6	439 841	39.7	2.3	230 850	46.2	3.4
Adams County	51	37.3	15.7	61	34.4	3.3	131	19.1	15.3	7 754	43.1	3.8	472	41.3	6.1
Asotin County	21	23.8	28.6	184	20.1	0.0	110	22.7	5.5	374	44.7	2.4	478	50.4	4.0
Benton County	1 198	41.3	3.5	977	26.9	2.7	3 075	22.5	7.2	18 027	45.2	2.3	4 118	48.5	3.5
Chelan County	193	45.6	2.6	755	38.4	2.4	452	25.0	6.0	12 894	44.9	1.2	1 488	37.0	6.3
Clallam County	464	9.5	1.1	3 244	38.5	4.6	931	20.7	16.2	2 189	37.6	3.9	1 663	46.2	7.0
Clark County	5 199	34.6	3.7	3 148	34.5	4.0	11 951	27.9	6.4	16 091	41.2	2.0	11 841	49.6	2.6
Columbia County	3	0.0	0.0	38	26.3	39.5	41	48.8	0.0	269	46.8	6.3	69	23.2	13.0
Cowlitz County	418	44.3	1.0	1 511	31.0	6.1	1 404	34.4	6.0	4 213	45.3	1.3	2 518	46.7	4.1
Douglas County	175	36.6	1.7	325	33.5	1.8	274	44.5	12.8	6 490	45.7	0.9	737	44.8	2.8
Ferry County	35	60.0	0.0	1 289	34.9	8.8	19	31.6	0.0	126	33.3	11.1	309	44.3	4.2
Franklin County	1 080	26.8	14.3	306	28.4	0.3	962	30.8	4.7	23 154	44.5	1.8	2 171	43.4	2.0
Garfield County	0	X	X	6	0.0	50.0	7	42.9	0.0	22	31.8	0.0	34	58.8	14.7
Grant County	747	33.9	13.9	753	37.7	5.2	583	19.7	28.5	22 543	43.5	2.4	2 295	45.1	2.1
Grays Harbor County	172	42.4	2.3	3 325	38.9	4.6	762	28.2	12.3	3 244	47.4	1.4	2 078	43.9	8.1
Island County	1 743	35.4	0.8	632	24.2	5.5	3 108	26.6	5.3	2 961	37.8	3.1	2 614	52.1	3.8
Jefferson County	87	25.3	18.4	601	30.6	5.8	314	18.8	7.3	455	37.6	10.3	899	40.8	7.0
King County	91 538	29.2	6.9	15 728	25.9	4.8	196 058	23.4	7.9	95 250	31.9	2.5	76 641	43.0	3.2
Kitsap County	6 233	31.4	2.7	3 324	31.7	4.3	12 163	25.6	7.0	9 718	38.2	1.7	11 950	51.4	3.0
Kittitas County	247	29.6	0.0	256	18.4	4.7	735	14.0	1.1	1 668	35.0	1.4	676	27.7	2.2
Klickitat County	46	39.1	0.0	639	36.8	5.3	201	39.8	8.0	1 532	44.6	1.2	544	46.9	6.3
Lewis County	247	49.0	4.0	856	27.3	5.1	506	32.4	4.2	3 557	45.7	1.9	1 629	43.2	6.9
Lincoln County	30	40.0	40.0	153	30.7	3.9	31	29.0	0.0	168	55.4	0.0	199	40.2	8.0
Mason County	594	19.4	0.0	1 813	36.8	5.1	788	38.1	4.9	2 358	35.6	2.2	1 587	35.2	5.4
Okanogan County	133	48.1	0.0	4 524	38.1	6.0	256	30.5	2.3	5 754	44.1	1.3	998	43.2	6.9
Pacific County	32	68.8	0.0	441	30.4	12.5	501	35.7	2.6	1 102	45.1	4.2	606	39.8	8.7
Pend Oreille County	16	31.3	18.8	317	44.5	5.0	108	12.0	18.5	238	44.5	9.2	381	43.8	3.4
Pierce County	48 741	33.3	4.6	9 472	33.4	3.7	39 746	24.9	9.1	38 577	40.0	2.1	39 041	50.6	2.7
San Juan County	13	100.0	0.0	101	16.8	0.0	88	37.5	21.6	378	46.0	0.0	322	41.6	6.2
Skagit County	304	20.4	4.9	1 906	36.7	7.6	1 577	24.5	6.4	11 586	42.1	1.6	2 569	44.7	6.3
Skamania County	21	0.0	0.0	279	40.1	4.3	62	50.0	3.2	331	46.5	2.4	188	41.0	5.9
Snohomish County	9 587	28.5	2.4	8 127	32.9	4.0	36 784	26.9	5.2	27 340	36.1	1.8	22 118	49.4	2.6
Spokane County	6 325	30.3	6.8	5 740	30.7	4.8	8 139	21.4	9.6	11 465	37.3	3.2	13 004	46.5	4.1
Stevens County	79	40.5	8.9	2 331	38.9	5.8	188	27.7	6.4	661	47.4	2.6	1 069	46.8	6.3
Thurston County	4 783	30.8	1.6	3 144	34.2	3.3	10 629	27.8	6.1	9 067	36.3	2.5	8 121	49.1	3.0
Wahkiakum County	7	100.0	0.0	87	23.0	8.0	7	28.6	0.0	35	57.1	0.0	121	34.7	6.6
Walla Walla County	909	10.9	4.8	594	24.4	2.0	817	18.7	4.9	8 719	39.9	1.7	1 245	41.2	6.4
Whatcom County	1 014	23.6	1.9	4 699	36.4	5.8	4 535	21.1	4.7	8 316	38.6	2.0	5 054	42.6	2.6
Whitman County	624	22.1	1.0	217	26.3	6.5	2 343	13.7	1.7	1 263	20.9	2.5	1 118	26.2	1.1
Yakima County	1 943	36.5	9.6	9 396	39.1	4.8	2 331	25.2	8.5	79 952	44.4	2.7	7 885	45.0	5.5
WEST VIRGINIA	55 999	25.5	12.8	3 770	21.8	7.0	9 850	22.9	5.9	11 774	31.2	6.8	18 104	39.5	8.6
Barbour County	43	0.0	41.9	145	17.2	6.2	36	13.9	0.0	47	31.9	10.6	135	34.1	0.0
Berkeley County	3 519	31.7	5.1	250	39.2	2.8	293	5.8	13.3	1 043	32.8	4.2	1 036	49.7	5.8
Boone County	182	20.3	22.0	42	0.0	19.0	36	47.2	0.0	113	16.8	12.4	109	36.7	13.8

[1] Hispanic or Latino persons may be of any race.

Table A-3. States and Counties — Age, Ethnicity, and Household Structure

STATE County	Total households	Family households (percent)						Nonfamily households (percent)						Percent of householders 65 years and over who live alone	Grandparents who are responsible for the care of their grandchildren
		Married-couple family households			Other family households			Two or more unrelated persons		Male living alone		Female living alone			
		Total	With children	Householder 65 years or over	Total	With children	Householder 65 years or over	Total	Householder 65 years or over	Total	Householder 65 years or over	Total	Householder 65 years or over		
	29	30	31	32	33	34	35	36	37	38	39	40	41	42	43
VIRGINIA—Cont'd															
Manassas city	11 785	57.3	33.9	3.9	15.1	9.8	1.0	6.6	0.3	10.8	1.2	10.1	3.0	45.2	232
Manassas Park city	3 253	56.9	32.9	2.8	21.8	12.7	1.6	6.8	0.3	7.3	0.9	7.2	2.4	41.2	78
Martinsville city	6 506	40.0	14.3	10.8	22.4	12.1	5.4	3.5	0.2	12.0	3.1	22.0	12.7	49.0	213
Newport News city	69 750	45.6	22.4	6.6	21.4	13.8	2.2	6.0	0.3	12.0	1.7	15.0	6.2	46.5	1 754
Norfolk city	86 178	37.7	17.0	6.6	22.9	14.1	3.0	9.2	0.4	13.9	2.6	16.3	7.1	49.1	2 825
Norton city	1 730	42.4	12.8	5.8	19.4	13.2	2.1	2.9	0.6	11.8	2.7	23.5	12.5	64.1	60
Petersburg city	13 795	31.8	11.7	7.9	30.1	16.8	4.6	5.9	0.6	13.6	3.2	18.7	9.4	49.3	576
Poquoson city	4 166	70.3	31.8	10.0	10.9	6.8	1.7	3.0	0.1	6.7	1.4	9.1	5.8	37.9	32
Portsmouth city	38 137	41.5	17.0	8.4	25.7	14.2	4.4	5.3	0.6	11.9	2.9	15.7	7.8	44.3	1 858
Radford city	5 804	35.6	13.6	8.0	9.3	5.0	1.5	23.0	0.1	11.6	1.3	20.5	7.9	48.9	84
Richmond city	84 566	27.9	10.2	5.9	24.4	13.5	3.5	10.1	0.6	15.5	2.7	22.0	9.1	54.2	2 272
Roanoke city	42 026	37.7	14.2	8.7	20.4	11.5	2.9	5.9	0.5	14.5	2.6	21.5	10.1	51.6	983
Salem city	9 933	52.0	21.4	10.7	14.0	7.7	2.8	4.9	0.4	9.4	1.4	19.7	10.8	46.7	114
Staunton city	9 681	45.9	16.4	11.5	14.4	8.5	2.6	5.1	0.2	12.1	2.7	22.5	11.7	50.3	171
Suffolk city	23 290	55.2	25.6	8.4	21.0	12.1	3.2	3.6	0.3	9.3	2.3	10.9	5.5	39.3	605
Virginia Beach city	154 635	57.0	29.8	6.7	15.5	10.1	1.5	7.2	0.3	8.7	1.2	11.6	4.3	39.1	3 603
Waynesboro city	8 318	48.0	16.4	12.7	18.0	11.6	2.0	3.6	0.1	11.8	1.7	18.6	9.4	42.6	306
Williamsburg city	3 616	37.8	11.2	10.3	12.6	7.0	2.8	13.9	0.5	12.9	2.5	22.8	9.3	46.4	0
Winchester city	9 994	40.8	16.9	9.3	15.8	8.3	2.6	8.7	0.4	14.5	1.9	20.1	9.0	46.9	162
WASHINGTON	2 272 261	52.9	24.7	8.5	13.6	8.7	1.4	7.4	0.4	11.8	2.1	14.3	6.2	44.5	35 341
Adams County	5 217	64.1	35.2	11.8	15.5	9.8	1.7	2.0	0.3	8.4	1.5	10.0	5.6	33.9	147
Asotin County	8 352	51.1	19.8	11.4	16.8	12.2	1.5	5.0	0.7	11.1	2.4	16.0	8.4	44.4	203
Benton County	52 816	58.2	28.8	8.9	14.0	9.8	1.3	4.6	0.3	10.6	1.5	12.7	6.1	42.2	1 138
Chelan County	24 962	57.6	27.1	12.1	11.7	7.8	1.1	5.6	0.4	10.5	2.5	14.6	8.6	44.7	515
Clallam County	27 187	54.7	17.8	17.3	12.1	7.8	1.6	5.1	0.8	11.1	3.5	16.9	10.1	40.8	337
Clark County	127 290	57.2	28.4	7.7	14.7	9.5	1.3	6.3	0.4	10.0	1.8	11.8	5.1	42.3	1 856
Columbia County	1 688	56.8	20.1	14.4	11.1	7.5	1.3	3.1	1.0	12.4	3.6	16.5	9.7	44.3	49
Cowlitz County	35 883	55.6	23.4	10.5	14.8	10.3	1.2	5.4	0.5	10.9	2.4	13.4	7.6	45.1	707
Douglas County	11 724	62.6	29.3	12.5	13.4	9.4	1.3	4.2	0.5	8.6	1.8	11.3	5.6	34.0	193
Ferry County	2 814	55.1	19.8	11.7	14.9	10.7	1.6	5.0	0.3	13.2	2.7	11.8	6.0	39.0	54
Franklin County	14 870	60.5	33.1	8.9	18.1	11.6	1.6	3.7	0.2	7.8	2.1	9.8	5.0	39.6	340
Garfield County	999	57.2	21.6	16.1	11.3	7.9	1.4	3.3	0.5	12.4	4.1	15.8	9.9	43.8	24
Grant County	25 207	60.5	30.6	11.0	14.2	9.7	1.4	4.1	0.4	10.2	2.9	11.0	6.3	41.7	770
Grays Harbor County	26 807	50.9	20.3	11.3	16.4	10.8	1.8	6.1	0.6	12.1	3.6	14.6	8.2	46.2	579
Island County	27 756	63.2	27.1	13.5	9.6	6.3	0.7	5.7	0.7	9.0	1.8	12.4	6.4	35.4	289
Jefferson County	11 649	53.4	15.8	16.2	12.0	7.9	1.7	6.1	1.0	12.5	3.7	16.0	8.9	40.0	94
King County	711 235	47.2	22.1	6.8	12.3	7.0	1.4	9.9	0.4	14.1	1.9	16.4	5.7	46.8	7 903
Kitsap County	86 393	58.2	27.7	8.2	13.1	9.0	1.2	6.2	0.5	10.5	2.1	12.1	5.8	44.5	1 373
Kittitas County	13 405	48.2	20.6	8.6	10.2	6.5	1.1	13.1	0.4	13.1	3.0	15.3	6.4	48.2	93
Klickitat County	7 481	59.6	24.9	12.0	12.3	9.0	1.5	4.2	0.4	12.8	3.0	11.1	6.3	39.9	172
Lewis County	26 362	57.9	23.5	12.7	13.1	8.5	1.3	5.1	0.6	9.7	3.1	14.3	8.9	45.0	563
Lincoln County	4 180	61.9	23.4	15.4	8.6	6.3	0.9	3.8	0.5	11.5	3.7	14.2	9.0	43.0	65
Mason County	18 876	57.8	20.3	15.0	13.2	8.7	1.5	5.7	0.8	11.3	3.0	12.0	6.3	34.9	495
Okanogan County	15 018	54.3	22.9	11.8	16.4	10.9	1.8	4.8	0.7	12.2	3.0	12.3	6.4	39.7	338
Pacific County	9 089	54.7	16.9	17.0	10.3	6.0	2.2	5.6	1.1	12.9	4.9	16.6	9.9	42.1	252
Pend Oreille County	4 633	58.1	19.7	12.8	12.3	9.6	1.3	4.4	0.7	13.7	3.7	11.3	6.4	40.6	100
Pierce County	260 897	53.7	26.0	7.9	15.8	10.7	1.4	6.2	0.4	11.3	2.0	13.0	5.7	44.2	5 364
San Juan County	6 468	52.9	16.0	14.3	9.4	6.8	1.1	7.1	0.4	13.2	4.1	17.5	7.3	41.7	23
Skagit County	38 814	57.4	24.8	12.0	13.3	8.5	1.3	6.1	0.8	9.5	2.6	13.8	7.8	42.5	517
Skamania County	3 761	60.6	25.6	9.9	13.4	8.5	1.8	5.2	0.2	10.9	2.5	10.0	4.3	36.3	88
Snohomish County	224 966	56.8	29.0	7.1	13.8	8.8	1.2	6.8	0.3	10.4	1.5	12.1	5.2	43.6	3 270
Spokane County	163 826	51.1	23.4	9.0	14.4	9.7	1.3	6.4	0.3	12.0	2.3	16.0	7.7	48.6	2 072
Stevens County	15 048	60.9	26.2	10.7	12.6	8.6	1.6	4.5	0.7	10.2	2.9	11.7	6.4	41.5	406
Thurston County	81 666	53.7	24.4	8.8	13.9	9.1	1.3	7.3	0.4	10.4	1.9	14.6	6.1	43.4	1 242
Wahkiakum County	1 544	59.1	19.1	15.7	11.7	7.8	0.9	4.5	1.4	12.0	3.5	12.7	6.7	36.3	22
Walla Walla County	19 650	55.0	24.5	12.1	12.9	8.3	1.5	5.0	0.3	10.2	3.0	16.8	10.2	48.6	444
Whatcom County	64 464	52.1	23.0	9.5	12.0	7.6	1.1	10.3	0.5	11.9	2.0	13.7	6.5	43.3	769
Whitman County	15 247	45.3	20.0	8.1	7.8	5.1	0.8	17.6	0.2	13.7	2.0	15.6	5.0	43.8	95
Yakima County	74 017	57.1	29.5	9.7	17.1	11.8	1.8	4.3	0.4	8.7	2.2	12.8	7.5	45.2	2 380
WEST VIRGINIA	737 360	54.6	21.9	10.4	14.2	7.4	2.8	4.1	0.3	10.7	2.8	16.3	9.2	46.9	16 151
Barbour County	6 132	57.7	23.6	10.4	13.7	7.1	3.2	3.8	0.4	10.0	3.5	14.7	9.2	47.5	150
Berkeley County	29 616	55.1	24.4	8.5	15.3	9.6	1.9	5.4	0.4	11.2	1.9	13.0	6.1	42.6	717
Boone County	10 256	57.7	24.2	10.1	15.3	7.3	3.2	2.4	0.2	9.8	1.9	14.8	8.0	42.2	333

STATE County	Households with Non-Hispanic White householder — Number of households	Percent that are family households	Households with Black or African American householder — Number of households	Percent that are family households	Households with American Indian and Alaska Native householder — Number of households	Percent that are family households	Households with Asian, Hawaiian, and Pacific Islander householder — Number of households	Percent that are family households	Households with Hispanic or Latino[1] householder — Number of households	Percent that are family households	Foreign-born population — Percent of total population that is foreign-born	Place of birth (percent) Europe	Asia	Latin America	Percent in non-English speaking households — Linguistically isolated	Not linguistically isolated
	44	45	46	47	48	49	50	51	52	53	54	55	56	57	58	59
VIRGINIA—Cont'd																
Manassas city	8 670	69.7	1 466	74.7	16	100.0	326	92.6	1 121	86.7	14.2	1.3	2.2	10.2	5.8	19.4
Manassas Park city.......	2 440	76.6	305	83.0	17	29.4	103	75.7	338	92.9	15.0	0.6	4.3	9.9	7.5	18.2
Martinsville city	3 896	58.6	2 429	68.1	0	X	26	76.9	116	71.6	2.7	0.4	0.3	1.7	1.3	7.1
Newport News city	38 855	65.3	26 215	68.5	285	81.1	1 356	69.8	2 191	73.8	4.8	1.4	2.0	1.0	1.4	12.0
Norfolk city	45 015	56.3	35 068	65.7	381	63.3	2 244	69.8	2 203	62.5	5.0	0.9	2.5	1.2	1.2	12.6
Norton city	1 593	60.4	104	70.2	6	100.0	12	100.0	3	100.0	1.1	0.0	0.9	0.2	0.9	4.2
Petersburg city	3 131	52.8	10 222	64.4	40	37.5	91	57.1	197	80.7	2.3	1.0	0.6	0.6	0.9	8.9
Poquoson city..............	3 986	80.7	13	100.0	0	X	64	85.9	42	100.0	2.9	1.0	1.3	0.4	0.4	7.2
Portsmouth city	18 952	65.1	18 008	69.2	152	61.2	278	70.9	475	72.2	1.6	0.4	0.6	0.5	0.4	7.9
Radford city	5 159	44.3	391	52.7	0	X	89	39.3	72	41.7	2.5	0.7	0.8	0.5	0.7	7.9
Richmond city	38 284	40.4	42 440	63.3	228	41.7	1 020	36.6	1 656	66.5	3.9	0.7	1.0	1.8	1.8	9.0
Roanoke city	30 439	55.8	10 186	64.0	124	71.0	332	71.4	330	57.0	3.1	1.0	1.1	0.8	1.4	6.8
Salem city	9 234	66.0	522	63.4	7	100.0	69	87.0	47	78.7	2.1	0.8	0.9	0.4	0.3	6.3
Staunton city	8 359	60.6	1 123	56.6	9	100.0	0	X	72	79.2	2.0	0.9	0.2	0.7	0.3	6.1
Suffolk city	12 748	77.3	9 908	74.9	60	81.7	215	78.1	229	89.5	1.9	0.7	0.7	0.3	0.3	7.6
Virginia Beach city	114 901	70.9	26 779	75.6	458	79.5	5 532	85.5	4 822	80.1	6.6	1.5	3.6	1.1	1.1	16.2
Waynesboro city...........	7 323	65.5	717	63.2	9	100.0	16	100.0	167	88.6	2.4	0.6	0.2	1.6	1.7	6.5
Williamsburg city	2 785	47.9	652	56.7	0	X	83	74.7	81	45.7	5.2	1.8	2.0	0.4	1.6	11.7
Winchester city.............	8 379	55.5	932	61.3	24	100.0	130	42.3	395	80.5	6.8	0.7	1.1	4.7	4.0	9.3
WASHINGTON...........	1 907 298	65.5	68 959	64.8	29 399	71.1	106 931	72.1	110 036	78.5	10.4	2.1	4.1	2.9	3.8	15.8
Adams County..............	3 258	72.4	16	50.0	29	75.9	57	63.2	1 817	94.3	22.9	0.1	0.4	22.0	14.2	34.5
Asotin County...............	7 997	67.7	0	X	79	78.5	32	37.5	94	76.6	1.8	0.6	0.4	0.2	0.4	5.1
Benton County..............	45 736	71.0	378	69.0	311	81.7	1 096	74.3	4 382	85.3	8.5	1.5	1.5	4.9	3.6	16.5
Chelan County..............	21 459	67.3	27	100.0	228	53.1	152	52.0	2 761	88.1	12.9	0.7	0.4	11.1	7.2	17.1
Clallam County.............	24 956	66.2	60	73.3	1 112	75.4	199	70.4	475	71.4	4.5	1.5	0.9	1.0	0.9	9.5
Clark County................	114 173	71.4	1 905	66.7	997	78.8	3 592	79.3	4 153	75.4	8.5	3.4	2.6	1.0	3.6	13.4
Columbia County...........	1 557	67.4	0	X	17	76.5	12	100.0	74	77.0	3.2	0.2	0.6	2.0	0.9	9.4
Cowlitz County.............	33 508	69.9	141	71.6	514	74.3	355	86.8	899	76.9	3.7	0.7	1.0	1.4	1.6	8.2
Douglas County............	10 004	73.8	42	78.6	113	77.9	58	46.6	1 433	91.6	13.5	1.0	0.6	11.4	6.7	18.0
Ferry County................	2 197	70.7	6	50.0	488	69.1	0	X	30	46.7	2.5	0.6	0.2	0.4	0.2	6.9
Franklin County	8 856	72.8	361	67.6	91	83.5	310	81.0	5 079	90.0	25.2	0.9	1.6	22.4	15.6	36.4
Garfield County............	981	68.4	0	X	2	100.0	2	0.0	8	100.0	1.0	0.4	0.2	0.2	0.2	5.2
Grant County................	19 148	71.6	225	69.8	244	79.9	191	58.1	5 035	88.3	17.1	1.6	0.5	14.4	11.3	23.1
Grays Harbor County	24 325	66.7	59	30.5	1 015	74.3	259	68.0	651	81.0	4.2	0.9	0.7	2.0	1.9	8.9
Island County	24 918	72.8	566	77.7	233	75.1	745	71.7	779	79.1	6.4	1.6	3.1	0.6	1.0	13.5
Jefferson County	10 922	65.2	35	48.6	218	73.9	87	58.6	136	59.6	4.0	1.8	0.8	0.3	0.5	7.4
King County.................	559 007	58.1	36 047	59.3	5 654	57.0	64 684	70.2	27 778	66.4	15.4	3.0	7.9	2.4	5.3	19.0
Kitsap County..............	75 044	70.8	2 165	67.9	1 142	70.1	3 180	80.8	2 530	81.4	5.7	1.0	3.3	0.6	1.0	14.1
Kittitas County.............	12 365	58.6	76	36.8	93	73.1	206	36.9	474	66.2	5.3	1.0	1.4	2.3	2.4	8.6
Klickitat County............	6 721	71.0	19	78.9	175	85.1	32	100.0	383	78.3	6.0	0.6	0.3	4.5	3.1	12.0
Lewis County...............	24 678	70.7	67	61.2	335	69.3	97	82.5	803	77.3	4.1	0.9	0.3	2.4	1.8	9.5
Lincoln County	4 029	70.7	8	87.5	47	55.3	6	100.0	31	80.6	1.2	0.6	0.1	0.1	0.2	5.9
Mason County..............	17 114	70.3	76	92.1	557	82.8	174	78.7	555	76.9	4.4	1.1	0.7	1.9	1.2	8.4
Okanogan County	11 884	68.5	39	100.0	1 465	76.5	41	51.2	1 251	90.6	10.2	0.6	0.5	8.0	4.7	14.8
Pacific County..............	8 355	64.0	5	100.0	177	66.7	137	88.3	230	86.1	6.0	1.3	1.7	2.0	2.6	9.4
Pend Oreille County......	4 386	70.5	3	100.0	98	69.4	25	96.0	50	70.0	2.0	0.8	0.4	0.2	0.2	7.8
Pierce County...............	210 920	68.6	17 713	72.9	2 954	70.9	12 010	73.3	9 882	78.6	8.1	2.1	3.7	1.5	2.6	15.8
San Juan County	6 200	62.0	0	X	41	80.5	36	100.0	91	78.0	5.9	2.8	0.7	0.9	0.5	8.4
Skagit County	34 514	69.4	117	44.4	551	77.3	420	65.7	2 613	88.5	8.8	1.4	1.1	5.2	4.2	12.5
Skamania County..........	3 544	73.2	13	61.5	83	84.3	18	100.0	57	93.0	3.5	1.2	0.4	1.4	0.5	8.9
Snohomish County.........	197 050	69.8	3 293	72.4	2 473	74.0	10 376	81.4	7 214	76.3	9.7	2.4	4.5	1.6	3.0	14.6
Spokane County............	151 244	65.6	2 051	66.7	1 961	67.5	2 378	65.2	3 032	66.2	4.5	1.9	1.5	0.4	1.6	9.7
Stevens County............	13 790	73.4	18	88.9	746	75.9	38	63.2	171	66.7	2.4	1.2	0.3	0.2	0.4	5.7
Thurston County...........	71 322	66.6	1 907	73.4	1 086	75.6	2 942	81.6	2 621	72.9	6.1	1.3	3.2	0.9	1.6	13.2
Wahkiakum County	1 482	69.9	0	X	19	100.0	3	0.0	7	71.4	1.3	0.7	0.0	0.3	0.4	7.5
Walla Walla County.......	17 127	66.7	126	65.9	210	54.8	144	57.6	1 852	84.3	9.4	0.9	0.8	7.0	4.8	15.8
Whatcom County..........	57 940	63.8	477	54.7	1 325	79.7	1 293	63.1	2 338	69.2	9.8	2.6	2.2	1.5	2.2	12.0
Whitman County...........	13 382	55.4	233	36.5	82	76.8	793	36.8	411	39.9	7.7	1.1	4.7	0.8	2.2	12.1
Yakima County.............	51 205	69.0	685	61.0	2 434	81.0	751	72.7	17 856	89.4	16.9	0.4	0.6	15.4	9.9	29.5
WEST VIRGINIA	701 781	69.1	21 811	60.1	1 595	68.0	3 224	64.9	3 686	65.5	1.1	0.4	0.5	0.1	0.2	5.1
Barbour County............	5 964	71.9	24	12.5	62	54.8	10	50.0	24	58.3	0.5	0.2	0.2	0.0	0.2	3.2
Berkeley County...........	27 489	70.9	1 387	59.6	69	100.0	97	81.4	317	72.6	1.7	0.5	0.4	0.6	0.4	7.0
Boone County	10 062	73.0	83	73.5	23	78.3	6	100.0	48	77.1	0.4	0.1	0.1	0.1	0.1	2.8

[1] Hispanic or Latino persons may be of any race.

Table A-3. States and Counties — Age, Ethnicity, and Household Structure

STATE/County code	MSA/PMSA/NECMA code[1]	STATE County	Total population	Under 5 years	5 to 17 years	18 to 24 years	25 to 44 years	45 to 64 years	65 years and over	Median age	+/- U.S. percent under 18 years	+/- U.S. percent 65 years and over	Non-Hispanic White Total population	Under 18 years	65 years and over
			1	2	3	4	5	6	7	8	9	10	11	12	13
		WEST VIRGINIA— Cont'd													
54 007	...	Braxton County	14 702	5.0	17.6	7.5	28.2	25.8	15.9	39.6	-3.1	3.5	14 464	22.5	16.0
54 009	8080	Brooke County	25 447	4.9	15.5	9.4	25.8	26.0	18.3	41.2	-5.3	5.9	24 863	20.1	18.5
54 011	3400	Cabell County	96 784	5.5	14.4	13.5	26.9	23.7	16.1	37.5	-5.8	3.7	89 983	19.4	16.5
54 013	...	Calhoun County	7 582	5.1	17.2	8.1	25.9	27.1	16.7	41.3	-3.4	4.3	7 390	22.4	17.0
54 015	...	Clay County	10 330	6.1	19.4	9.0	27.5	24.2	13.7	36.8	-0.2	1.3	10 102	25.4	13.8
54 017	...	Doddridge County	7 403	6.0	19.4	8.5	26.3	25.0	14.9	38.7	-0.3	2.5	7 186	25.1	14.9
54 019	...	Fayette County	47 579	5.7	16.0	9.5	27.0	25.6	16.2	39.6	-4.0	3.8	43 767	21.5	16.4
54 021	...	Gilmer County	7 160	5.1	15.2	16.7	24.7	23.0	15.4	36.8	-5.4	3.0	6 951	20.4	15.7
54 023	...	Grant County	11 299	6.4	16.3	7.8	27.4	26.9	15.3	39.3	-3.0	2.9	11 173	22.7	15.2
54 025	...	Greenbrier County	34 453	5.4	16.1	7.7	26.3	26.8	17.6	41.6	-4.2	5.2	32 522	21.3	17.9
54 027	...	Hampshire County	20 203	6.3	18.7	7.3	27.6	25.6	14.5	38.5	-0.7	2.1	19 729	24.7	14.6
54 029	8080	Hancock County	32 667	5.3	15.7	7.1	27.1	26.4	18.4	41.7	-4.7	6.0	31 246	20.4	18.7
54 031	...	Hardy County	12 669	5.9	17.4	7.5	28.9	25.4	14.8	38.9	-2.4	2.4	12 171	23.2	15.0
54 033	...	Harrison County	68 652	5.6	17.5	8.7	27.3	24.4	16.5	39.2	-2.6	4.1	65 680	22.9	16.8
54 035	...	Jackson County	28 000	6.0	18.0	7.9	27.8	25.0	15.3	38.8	-1.7	2.9	27 662	23.8	15.5
54 037	8840	Jefferson County	42 190	6.3	17.3	10.2	30.1	24.9	11.2	36.8	-2.1	-1.2	38 007	23.3	11.5
54 039	1480	Kanawha County	200 073	5.7	15.6	8.5	28.1	25.7	16.5	40.2	-4.4	4.1	180 022	20.2	17.3
54 041	...	Lewis County	16 919	5.3	16.9	7.7	27.9	25.8	16.4	40.1	-3.5	4.0	16 713	22.2	16.5
54 043	...	Lincoln County	22 108	6.0	17.4	9.4	29.2	24.9	13.1	37.4	-2.3	0.7	21 862	23.1	13.1
54 045	...	Logan County	37 710	5.7	16.4	9.5	28.0	26.1	14.4	39.3	-3.6	2.0	36 042	21.8	14.3
54 047	...	McDowell County	27 329	5.2	18.1	7.9	26.7	26.0	16.1	40.5	-2.4	3.7	23 846	23.0	15.1
54 049	...	Marion County	56 598	5.0	15.5	10.6	26.2	24.8	17.8	39.9	-5.2	5.4	53 384	20.0	18.2
54 051	9000	Marshall County	35 519	5.4	17.5	7.6	26.8	26.5	16.3	40.4	-2.8	3.9	34 665	22.5	16.5
54 053	...	Mason County	25 957	5.7	16.9	8.2	27.8	26.1	15.3	39.7	-3.1	2.9	25 428	22.6	15.2
54 055	...	Mercer County	62 980	5.8	15.3	9.6	26.5	25.4	17.5	40.2	-4.6	5.1	57 862	20.3	17.7
54 057	1900	Mineral County	27 078	5.5	17.9	8.5	27.1	25.9	15.1	39.1	-2.3	2.7	25 894	23.0	15.2
54 059	...	Mingo County	28 253	5.8	18.5	9.2	29.3	24.7	12.5	37.2	-1.4	0.1	27 164	24.1	12.4
54 061	...	Monongalia County	81 866	5.0	13.2	23.3	27.7	20.2	10.7	30.4	-7.5	-1.7	75 076	17.9	11.3
54 063	...	Monroe County	14 583	5.0	15.1	8.0	30.9	25.6	15.3	39.7	-5.6	2.9	13 487	21.2	16.2
54 065	...	Morgan County	14 943	5.9	16.5	6.7	27.5	26.9	16.5	40.7	-3.3	4.1	14 550	22.4	16.6
54 067	...	Nicholas County	26 562	5.4	17.9	8.4	27.3	26.0	15.0	39.4	-2.4	2.6	26 191	23.3	14.9
54 069	9000	Ohio County	47 427	5.1	16.2	10.7	25.0	24.4	18.7	40.6	-4.4	6.3	44 522	20.4	19.4
54 071	...	Pendleton County	8 196	5.1	16.7	7.3	26.9	26.2	17.9	41.1	-3.9	5.5	7 890	21.8	18.2
54 073	...	Pleasants County	7 514	5.9	18.0	7.9	28.4	24.8	14.9	38.9	-1.8	2.5	7 339	24.0	15.1
54 075	...	Pocahontas County	9 131	4.9	16.1	7.2	27.1	27.4	17.2	41.9	-4.7	4.8	8 934	20.9	17.2
54 077	...	Preston County	29 334	5.5	18.2	8.0	28.0	25.5	14.9	39.1	-2.0	2.5	28 768	23.4	15.0
54 079	1480	Putnam County	51 589	6.5	18.4	7.5	30.5	25.5	11.6	37.7	-0.8	-0.8	50 254	24.6	11.8
54 081	...	Raleigh County	79 220	5.5	16.1	8.8	28.8	25.4	15.5	39.5	-4.1	3.1	70 511	21.2	15.9
54 083	...	Randolph County	28 262	5.2	17.1	8.7	28.4	25.5	15.1	38.8	-3.4	2.7	27 580	22.4	15.3
54 085	...	Ritchie County	10 343	5.5	17.4	7.7	28.0	26.1	15.2	39.9	-2.8	2.8	10 135	22.9	15.4
54 087	...	Roane County	15 446	5.8	17.5	9.1	26.6	26.3	14.8	39.5	-2.4	2.4	15 083	23.1	14.8
54 089	...	Summers County	12 999	4.6	15.8	8.0	24.3	27.4	19.9	43.4	-5.3	7.5	12 546	20.1	20.1
54 091	...	Taylor County	16 089	5.3	17.7	7.8	28.5	25.1	15.7	39.1	-2.7	3.3	15 542	22.6	15.9
54 093	...	Tucker County	7 321	4.6	16.6	6.4	27.0	27.3	18.1	42.0	-4.5	5.7	7 196	21.0	18.4
54 095	...	Tyler County	9 592	5.2	18.0	6.5	26.9	26.9	16.6	40.8	-2.5	4.2	9 463	23.1	16.8
54 097	...	Upshur County	23 404	5.4	17.2	12.4	25.7	24.6	14.8	37.4	-3.1	2.4	22 827	22.5	15.0
54 099	3400	Wayne County	42 903	5.8	17.5	8.6	27.9	25.3	14.9	38.4	-2.4	2.5	42 322	23.2	14.9
54 101	...	Webster County	9 719	5.3	17.7	8.0	26.7	27.1	15.2	40.4	-2.7	2.8	9 653	22.9	16.3
54 103	...	Wetzel County	17 693	5.5	18.2	6.8	26.5	26.8	16.2	40.4	-2.0	3.8	17 464	23.7	16.3
54 105	...	Wirt County	5 873	5.5	19.8	7.6	29.4	24.8	12.9	37.9	-0.4	0.5	5 802	25.4	12.5
54 107	6020	Wood County	87 986	5.8	17.2	8.0	27.8	25.7	15.5	39.3	-2.7	3.1	85 073	22.6	15.7
54 109	...	Wyoming County	25 708	5.7	16.7	8.7	27.6	27.4	14.0	40.1	-3.3	1.6	25 345	22.3	13.9
55 000	...	WISCONSIN	5 363 675	6.4	19.1	9.7	29.6	22.2	13.1	36.0	-0.2	0.7	4 687 649	23.5	14.4
55 001	...	Adams County	18 643	4.8	15.9	5.6	24.3	28.4	21.0	44.5	-5.0	8.6	18 005	20.0	21.5
55 003	...	Ashland County	16 866	6.3	19.2	11.3	25.7	21.6	16.0	36.9	-0.2	3.6	14 674	23.5	17.4
55 005	...	Barron County	44 963	5.6	19.7	8.1	27.0	23.2	16.4	38.8	-0.4	4.0	43 689	24.7	16.8
55 007	...	Bayfield County	15 013	5.4	19.3	5.2	25.4	28.3	16.4	42.1	-1.0	4.0	13 297	22.5	17.9
55 009	3080	Brown County	226 778	6.9	19.1	10.4	32.0	20.9	10.6	34.2	0.3	-1.8	203 437	24.3	11.6
55 011	...	Buffalo County	13 804	5.9	19.3	6.9	27.8	23.5	16.7	39.2	-0.5	4.3	13 589	24.8	16.9
55 013	...	Burnett County	15 674	5.0	17.1	6.0	23.1	28.5	20.3	44.1	-3.6	7.9	14 596	20.9	21.4
55 015	0460	Calumet County	40 631	7.0	21.6	7.2	32.0	21.3	10.8	35.2	2.9	-1.6	39 100	27.9	11.1
55 017	2290	Chippewa County	55 195	6.1	20.3	7.7	28.3	23.0	14.6	37.6	0.7	2.2	53 876	26.0	14.8
55 019	...	Clark County	33 557	7.6	22.3	7.5	26.3	20.2	16.1	35.9	4.2	3.7	32 712	29.5	16.3
55 021	...	Columbia County	52 468	6.2	19.0	7.1	29.9	23.4	14.4	38.0	-0.5	2.0	50 384	24.7	14.9
55 023	...	Crawford County	17 243	5.9	20.3	8.2	24.9	24.8	15.9	38.9	0.5	3.5	16 699	26.0	16.2

[1]MSA = Metropolitan Statistical Area. PMSA = Primary MSA. NECMA = New England County Metropolitan Area. See the Appendix A for explanation of these concepts. See Appendix B for list of metropolitan areas identified by type, with component counties.

STATE County	Black or African American			American Indian and Alaska Native			Asian, Hawaiian, and Pacific Islander			Hispanic or Latino[1]			Two or more races		
		Age (percent)			Age (percent)			Age (percent)			Age (percent)			Age (percent)	
	Total population	Under 18 years	65 years and over	Total population	Under 18 years	65 years and over	Total population	Under 18 years	65 years and over	Total population	Under 18 years	65 years and over	Total population	Under 18 years	65 years and over
	14	15	16	17	18	19	20	21	22	23	24	25	26	27	28
WEST VIRGINIA—Cont'd															
Braxton County	60	38.3	5.0	26	30.8	0.0	5	0.0	60.0	32	12.5	0.0	115	35.7	10.4
Brooke County	230	23.5	10.0	4	0.0	0.0	67	43.3	0.0	72	52.8	6.9	221	32.6	13.6
Cabell County	3 876	22.7	12.5	212	19.8	3.8	843	15.9	7.4	591	32.1	3.9	1 233	43.6	9.1
Calhoun County	4	100.0	0.0	62	12.9	0.0	21	38.1	0.0	82	17.1	7.3	68	13.2	5.9
Clay County	7	0.0	0.0	94	42.6	11.7	7	0.0	100.0	14	50.0	0.0	113	17.7	10.6
Doddridge County	20	100.0	0.0	31	0.0	16.1	23	0.0	65.2	42	47.6	0.0	101	32.7	10.9
Fayette County	2 451	20.5	19.6	194	32.5	1.0	203	22.2	2.0	332	36.4	2.1	638	29.6	5.0
Gilmer County	70	2.9	0.0	10	0.0	0.0	47	0.0	0.0	30	56.7	0.0	71	36.6	16.9
Grant County	72	15.3	31.9	9	22.2	0.0	0	X	X	26	34.6	23.1	19	0.0	21.1
Greenbrier County	1 057	20.2	16.7	110	20.9	6.4	59	18.6	0.0	258	30.2	10.1	446	37.4	8.5
Hampshire County	151	37.7	0.0	20	40.0	0.0	46	13.0	19.6	93	48.4	0.0	175	29.1	20.6
Hancock County	707	27.0	10.8	09	0.0	23.6	82	40.2	11.0	305	50.8	4.6	280	45.7	13.9
Hardy County	335	29.6	9.0	11	36.4	0.0	0	X	X	84	10.7	10.7	71	26.8	16.9
Harrison County	1 068	23.5	9.6	63	0.0	7.9	406	17.7	4.4	746	28.8	11.4	690	38.3	9.1
Jackson County	37	45.9	0.0	63	42.9	0.0	60	26.7	0.0	62	45.2	0.0	111	54.1	14.4
Jefferson County	2 364	22.3	13.4	170	19.4	2.4	354	22.0	4.8	671	33.8	0.9	760	39.3	0.4
Kanawha County	13 377	27.8	10.8	462	25.8	1.5	1 706	27.7	6.1	1 188	32.3	5.2	3 273	43.4	7.8
Lewis County	6	0.0	0.0	13	0.0	0.0	58	46.6	20.7	39	0.0	28.2	84	13.1	2.4
Lincoln County	8	100.0	0.0	13	30.8	0.0	15	6.7	0.0	130	60.8	0.0	105	34.3	31.4
Logan County	933	21.8	25.0	74	8.1	9.5	102	26.5	7.8	230	32.2	8.3	354	47.2	7.3
McDowell County	3 156	25.6	23.0	8	0.0	37.5	25	0.0	0.0	120	30.0	18.3	180	20.6	31.7
Marion County	2 055	30.5	12.8	115	26.1	0.9	194	16.5	5.7	451	25.5	15.1	488	36.3	11.1
Marshall County	111	33.3	0.0	61	0.0	0.0	76	18.4	9.2	218	34.9	18.3	411	50.1	3.2
Mason County	176	25.0	36.9	31	32.3	3.2	115	32.2	0.0	91	15.4	24.2	114	19.3	11.4
Mercer County	3 725	29.3	16.9	89	19.1	33.7	380	18.9	8.4	225	20.0	10.7	732	42.9	7.5
Mineral County	805	30.9	10.2	1	0.0	0.0	87	23.0	6.9	118	27.1	21.2	145	31.7	22.8
Mingo County	672	26.6	22.0	47	59.6	10.6	60	25.0	0.0	98	26.5	6.1	231	34.6	6.1
Monongalia County	2 512	17.4	5.3	295	12.5	7.8	1 948	18.3	2.5	941	15.3	1.8	1 128	35.0	4.2
Monroe County	912	3.8	0.4	10	0.0	0.0	33	45.7	0.0	28	0.0	42.3	104	19.2	2.9
Morgan County	94	12.8	24.5	43	11.6	0.0	5	40.0	0.0	160	25.6	6.3	87	40.2	0.0
Nicholas County	5	100.0	0.0	39	0.0	17.9	106	28.3	29.2	106	29.2	8.5	123	18.7	24.4
Ohio County	1 655	29.5	10.8	58	10.3	0.0	317	23.0	5.7	345	33.9	6.4	547	58.3	3.1
Pendleton County	190	15.8	8.9	5	0.0	0.0	26	7.7	0.0	42	26.2	0.0	52	40.4	19.2
Pleasants County	31	6.5	0.0	41	17.1	14.6	24	29.2	8.3	18	16.7	0.0	61	31.1	14.8
Pocahontas County	90	13.3	25.6	40	45.0	15.0	8	0.0	0.0	25	20.0	24.0	40	37.5	17.5
Preston County	120	13.3	21.7	0	X	X	50	62.0	0.0	183	45.9	3.8	233	43.8	14.2
Putnam County	332	32.8	2.4	70	47.1	10.0	306	38.6	1.6	351	47.0	1.1	330	37.9	7.0
Raleigh County	6 758	23.5	13.7	72	18.1	4.2	729	27.3	6.6	671	24.4	5.4	480	35.4	11.9
Randolph County	309	19.1	6.8	52	0.0	15.4	87	28.7	0.0	91	17.6	11.0	151	20.5	16.6
Ritchie County	18	11.1	0.0	27	7.4	0.0	21	57.1	4.8	38	28.9	0.0	104	27.9	12.5
Roane County	11	0.0	54.5	78	19.2	23.1	54	51.9	0.0	85	38.8	4.7	142	34.5	11.3
Summers County	294	26.5	17.7	5	0.0	0.0	11	0.0	0.0	46	34.8	15.2	60	46.7	0.0
Taylor County	210	15.2	23.8	31	0.0	6.5	21	23.8	0.0	107	42.1	1.9	187	60.4	0.0
Tucker County	0	X	X	16	0.0	0.0	20	70.0	0.0	11	72.7	0.0	76	27.6	2.6
Tyler County	5	0.0	0.0	2	0.0	100.0	10	30.0	0.0	36	44.4	0.0	78	17.9	6.4
Upshur County	106	17.9	6.6	23	0.0	0.0	75	8.0	0.0	186	36.0	13.4	184	34.2	6.0
Wayne County	57	43.9	14.0	99	34.3	9.1	92	0.0	35.9	120	34.2	17.5	218	41.3	6.4
Webster County	2	100.0	0.0	6	0.0	0.0	23	82.6	0.0	3	100.0	0.0	32	18.8	12.5
Wetzel County	7	0.0	0.0	44	40.9	0.0	6	66.7	0.0	40	0.0	65.0	137	27.7	0.0
Wirt County	0	X	X	21	0.0	57.1	12	0.0	83.3	15	46.7	0.0	23	0.0	43.5
Wood County	839	36.8	12.2	155	24.5	7.7	451	26.4	4.2	505	38.2	5.7	932	36.3	13.3
Wyoming County	165	26.1	20.6	19	0.0	42.1	7	0.0	100.0	72	31.9	0.0	86	52.3	27.9
WISCONSIN	300 355	37.8	5.2	49 661	36.3	4.7	84 654	38.7	3.7	191 049	38.7	2.8	71 171	50.9	3.7
Adams County	52	36.5	1.9	84	32.1	2.4	92	40.2	13.0	262	46.2	5.7	181	42.0	5.0
Ashland County	43	69.8	0.0	1 722	38.1	6.9	78	37.2	11.5	179	38.0	4.5	269	40.1	1.5
Barron County	69	20.3	5.8	342	36.3	2.3	140	52.1	0.7	441	47.6	5.0	292	46.9	8.6
Bayfield County	7	42.9	0.0	1 329	39.4	4.4	53	56.6	5.7	128	60.2	0.0	241	46.1	4.6
Brown County	2 619	31.3	0.3	5 193	35.0	4.9	4 609	47.9	2.4	8 798	38.9	1.0	3 054	56.6	2.1
Buffalo County	34	70.6	0.0	35	37.1	0.0	27	40.7	7.4	87	51.7	2.3	44	40.9	9.1
Burnett County	22	54.5	0.0	685	33.3	6.1	62	33.9	0.0	82	57.3	2.4	238	44.5	6.3
Calumet County	55	14.5	0.0	134	36.6	11.9	685	51.8	3.9	421	45.4	0.5	261	50.6	1.9
Chippewa County	64	62.5	0.0	178	31.5	11.2	469	50.1	3.6	306	42.8	5.2	307	37.8	10.1
Clark County	92	56.5	2.2	154	50.6	6.5	86	45.3	22.1	301	41.9	1.3	226	54.4	5.8
Columbia County	517	8.5	2.7	172	26.7	2.9	195	34.9	4.6	866	37.8	0.7	476	61.3	4.4
Crawford County	267	21.7	0.7	61	18.0	11.5	49	28.6	4.1	70	58.6	4.3	101	49.5	10.9

[1] Hispanic or Latino persons may be of any race.

Table A-3. States and Counties — Age, Ethnicity, and Household Structure

STATE County	Total households	Family households (percent) Married-couple family households Total	With children	Householder 65 years or over	Other family households Total	With children	Householder 65 years or over	Nonfamily households (percent) Two or more unrelated persons Total	Householder 65 years or over	Male living alone Total	Householder 65 years or over	Female living alone Total	Householder 65 years or over	Percent of householders 65 years and over who live alone	Grandparents who are responsible for the care of their grandchildren
	29	30	31	32	33	34	35	36	37	38	39	40	41	42	43
WEST VIRGINIA—Cont'd															
Braxton County	5 792	58.9	23.3	12.3	12.5	7.3	2.4	3.4	0.4	9.8	2.9	15.4	9.6	45.2	149
Brooke County	10 410	55.4	21.2	11.7	13.6	6.2	3.3	3.1	0.8	11.1	3.7	16.7	10.1	46.6	226
Cabell County	41 262	48.1	18.2	10.2	14.4	7.7	2.7	6.4	0.3	12.0	2.7	19.2	10.3	49.7	630
Calhoun County	3 084	58.9	23.7	12.0	13.8	5.7	4.1	2.5	0.7	11.2	2.7	13.6	8.3	39.5	112
Clay County	4 048	59.1	24.9	10.6	15.4	9.3	3.8	1.3	0.0	11.6	3.0	12.6	8.2	43.6	67
Doddridge County	2 852	58.7	26.3	12.1	14.7	7.0	4.5	3.9	0.1	9.6	2.8	13.1	8.0	39.4	91
Fayette County	19 006	52.3	20.8	10.1	17.4	8.9	4.3	3.5	0.3	10.4	3.2	16.4	10.5	48.2	698
Gilmer County	2 780	53.8	20.1	11.5	13.9	8.1	3.0	7.1	0.4	10.6	3.5	14.5	9.2	46.0	61
Grant County	4 608	60.1	23.7	11.0	11.6	6.9	1.7	4.0	0.4	10.9	3.0	13.5	8.8	47.4	76
Greenbrier County	14 616	54.5	20.5	11.4	14.2	7.5	2.9	2.9	0.3	10.8	3.2	17.7	10.3	47.9	282
Hampshire County	7 985	57.4	23.1	11.7	14.1	8.4	2.0	4.0	1.0	10.7	2.8	13.9	7.4	40.7	123
Hancock County	13 690	55.1	20.4	12.3	14.9	6.1	3.9	3.4	0.2	10.8	3.2	15.8	9.4	43.5	226
Hardy County	5 208	56.4	22.5	10.2	12.1	6.9	2.2	4.4	0.5	12.5	3.3	14.6	8.9	48.8	132
Harrison County	27 897	54.2	22.6	10.8	14.7	7.6	3.3	3.4	0.4	10.5	3.1	17.1	10.1	47.6	552
Jackson County	11 028	61.8	24.8	12.3	12.8	6.8	2.1	2.7	0.4	8.6	2.6	14.2	7.7	41.2	280
Jefferson County	16 179	56.3	24.0	8.3	14.1	8.0	2.1	6.5	0.6	11.0	2.3	12.2	6.0	42.9	400
Kanawha County	86 175	49.2	19.0	10.1	15.8	7.9	3.2	4.2	0.3	11.9	2.9	18.9	10.0	48.6	1 797
Lewis County	6 943	56.3	21.2	12.1	13.2	7.7	2.5	3.6	0.5	9.7	2.8	17.1	10.2	46.3	181
Lincoln County	8 688	60.7	25.4	10.4	15.1	8.4	2.6	2.0	0.1	9.3	2.2	13.0	7.8	43.2	310
Logan County	14 892	57.5	23.2	10.1	16.6	7.6	4.0	1.9	0.1	9.1	2.5	14.9	9.2	44.9	727
McDowell County	11 196	52.2	20.4	9.4	18.9	9.8	4.7	1.8	0.5	10.6	3.0	16.5	9.3	45.8	532
Marion County	23 649	52.3	19.8	11.0	13.7	6.6	3.3	5.1	0.2	10.1	3.2	18.7	11.2	49.9	324
Marshall County	14 208	56.6	22.4	10.4	14.6	7.4	3.5	3.2	0.2	9.8	3.7	15.8	9.4	48.1	229
Mason County	10 620	59.1	23.8	11.2	13.4	7.6	1.8	2.0	0.3	10.8	2.9	14.7	8.5	45.9	207
Mercer County	26 555	52.8	19.9	11.2	15.1	7.3	3.6	3.5	0.2	10.2	3.2	18.4	10.6	47.8	662
Mineral County	10 822	58.5	24.2	10.4	13.1	7.1	2.2	3.5	0.7	9.8	3.2	15.1	8.4	46.7	202
Mingo County	11 331	57.4	26.4	8.3	15.7	7.7	3.3	1.8	0.0	10.5	3.0	14.6	8.3	49.2	410
Monongalia County	33 477	44.6	19.3	7.2	11.2	5.6	2.0	13.0	0.3	13.2	1.9	18.1	6.5	47.0	468
Monroe County	5 465	59.2	23.9	12.6	12.2	5.4	3.1	3.0	0.0	10.3	2.9	15.4	9.9	44.9	77
Morgan County	6 144	59.7	22.3	13.0	11.0	6.1	2.3	4.8	0.4	11.1	2.5	13.3	7.0	37.8	115
Nicholas County	10 717	59.8	23.9	10.9	12.8	6.6	2.6	2.5	0.4	9.3	3.2	15.6	8.9	46.5	229
Ohio County	19 776	48.0	19.2	11.2	14.0	7.6	2.7	4.4	0.3	12.2	3.8	21.3	12.1	52.9	348
Pendleton County	3 364	56.6	22.9	13.7	13.9	4.8	2.9	3.9	0.0	11.1	3.4	14.4	8.5	41.7	43
Pleasants County	2 893	61.4	25.5	10.6	12.8	7.9	2.2	3.0	0.4	8.6	3.2	14.1	10.5	50.9	43
Pocahontas County	3 840	55.8	20.3	10.8	10.0	4.7	2.3	4.5	1.2	13.1	5.0	16.6	10.0	51.4	78
Preston County	11 551	60.3	25.2	10.6	12.4	6.4	2.6	3.6	0.3	10.4	2.9	13.4	8.5	45.6	182
Putnam County	20 043	65.0	28.7	9.6	11.5	6.5	1.7	2.9	0.4	8.8	1.8	11.9	5.8	39.2	298
Raleigh County	31 892	55.6	21.5	9.9	14.2	7.7	3.1	3.2	0.3	10.2	3.0	16.8	10.5	50.5	759
Randolph County	11 068	55.9	22.6	10.7	13.4	7.5	2.0	4.4	0.5	10.4	2.8	15.9	9.6	48.4	261
Ritchie County	4 181	59.1	23.3	10.1	12.3	5.7	2.9	3.3	0.5	10.3	3.2	15.0	9.7	48.6	129
Roane County	6 147	59.7	24.4	9.9	13.0	6.9	2.0	3.8	1.0	9.2	3.3	14.3	9.4	49.3	92
Summers County	5 541	54.7	19.3	13.7	14.1	7.0	2.6	2.1	0.4	12.1	3.3	17.0	11.3	46.7	190
Taylor County	6 316	56.9	23.5	10.9	14.0	6.3	4.1	3.8	0.1	10.4	2.6	15.0	9.7	44.8	57
Tucker County	3 068	57.0	22.6	11.2	13.1	5.9	4.5	3.1	1.2	11.0	2.8	15.9	10.0	43.0	85
Tyler County	3 842	61.9	23.1	13.1	11.9	6.5	2.5	3.0	0.4	9.4	3.3	13.7	8.5	42.3	94
Upshur County	9 021	58.3	23.7	11.5	13.4	8.0	2.6	3.1	0.2	10.4	3.1	14.7	9.3	46.4	80
Wayne County	17 244	60.4	25.2	11.0	13.3	6.6	2.7	2.1	0.2	9.8	2.7	14.3	7.9	43.1	472
Webster County	4 027	58.3	23.1	9.5	12.9	8.4	1.7	3.1	0.9	11.6	3.8	14.9	8.4	50.0	79
Wetzel County	7 170	58.2	23.8	11.7	12.7	6.5	2.4	3.5	0.7	8.5	2.2	17.0	10.8	46.9	126
Wirt County	2 304	62.2	28.3	8.8	12.2	6.4	3.2	3.3	0.0	10.5	4.7	11.6	8.5	52.4	95
Wood County	36 262	54.8	21.5	10.6	14.1	8.0	2.2	3.9	0.3	10.4	2.5	16.7	9.3	47.6	619
Wyoming County	10 479	61.5	24.9	9.6	12.9	7.1	2.4	1.3	0.2	9.4	2.5	14.9	8.7	47.8	246
WISCONSIN	2 086 304	54.0	24.4	9.7	12.8	7.9	1.5	6.4	0.3	11.5	2.4	15.2	7.7	46.4	23 687
Adams County	7 924	58.5	17.0	18.0	11.0	6.3	1.8	5.0	0.9	13.2	4.1	12.3	7.7	36.3	126
Ashland County	6 697	49.4	21.5	10.0	14.3	8.7	1.8	5.3	0.2	13.0	3.7	18.0	10.6	54.4	109
Barron County	17 816	58.1	24.6	12.6	11.6	7.4	1.3	4.9	0.5	10.4	2.8	15.0	9.3	45.9	175
Bayfield County	6 208	56.0	20.8	12.4	12.8	8.5	1.7	4.7	0.5	13.5	3.8	13.0	7.4	43.5	100
Brown County	87 356	54.0	26.3	8.1	12.3	8.2	1.0	7.2	0.2	11.4	1.7	15.1	7.0	48.5	578
Buffalo County	5 521	59.2	25.7	13.1	9.5	5.5	1.7	4.2	0.4	14.1	3.2	12.9	9.0	44.5	23
Burnett County	6 599	57.0	18.3	16.6	10.9	6.6	1.3	5.2	0.6	14.1	3.9	12.8	8.1	39.6	99
Calumet County	14 952	65.8	32.6	9.4	9.6	6.1	1.3	4.3	0.1	9.7	1.7	10.7	5.5	39.8	99
Chippewa County	21 408	58.0	26.1	11.6	12.3	7.7	1.5	5.0	0.4	11.0	2.3	13.7	8.2	43.5	270
Clark County	12 109	62.5	29.7	13.8	10.3	6.0	1.5	3.7	0.2	9.7	2.9	13.9	10.0	45.2	85
Columbia County	20 414	59.2	26.1	10.9	10.3	6.0	1.7	5.0	0.2	11.2	2.6	14.2	8.5	46.1	117
Crawford County	6 657	57.7	24.3	12.0	11.9	7.2	1.7	3.7	0.3	11.5	3.3	15.2	9.2	47.1	33

Table A-3. States and Counties — Age, Ethnicity, and Household Structure

STATE County	Households with Non-Hispanic White householder		Households with Black or African American householder		Households with American Indian and Alaska Native householder		Households with Asian, Hawaiian, and Pacific Islander householder		Households with Hispanic or Latino[1] householder		Foreign-born population	Place of birth (percent)			Percent in non-English speaking households	
	Number of households	Percent that are family households	Number of households	Percent that are family households	Number of households	Percent that are family households	Number of households	Percent that are family households	Number of households	Percent that are family households	Percent of total population that is foreign-born	Europe	Asia	Latin America	Linguistically isolated	Not linguistically isolated
	44	45	46	47	48	49	50	51	52	53	54	55	56	57	58	59
WEST VIRGINIA— Cont'd																
Braxton County	5 706	71.3	22	90.9	8	75.0	3	100.0	22	40.9	0.2	0.1	0.0	0.0	0.0	3.6
Brooke County	10 230	69.2	77	66.2	0	X	8	0.0	20	0.0	1.1	0.8	0.1	0.0	0.2	6.8
Cabell County	38 610	63.2	1 678	49.9	114	30.7	293	57.0	199	59.8	1.3	0.3	0.7	0.1	0.2	4.7
Calhoun County	3 007	73.6	0	X	13	0.0	7	100.0	27	40.7	0.6	0.1	0.3	0.1	0.0	4.3
Clay County	3 969	74.6	0	X	33	63.6	7	100.0	0	X	0.1	0.0	0.1	0.0	0.3	4.8
Doddridge County	2 798	72.9	0	X	13	100.0	5	100.0	5	100.0	0.6	0.3	0.3	0.0	0.1	7.2
Fayette County	17 638	69.7	932	66.7	86	91.9	70	67.1	113	72.6	0.8	0.2	0.3	0.1	0.2	4.4
Gilmer County	2 732	68.1	6	0.0	4	50.0	20	40.0	4	50.0	1.0	0.2	0.6	0.0	0.1	4.0
Grant County	4 555	71.8	35	54.3	2	0.0	0	X	7	57.1	0.5	0.3	0.0	0.1	0.0	5.0
Greenbrier County	13 803	69.4	526	53.8	44	52.3	25	40.0	97	71.1	0.6	0.3	0.1	0.1	0.0	4.9
Hampshire County	7 832	71.7	32	100.0	12	100.0	18	22.2	25	76.0	0.6	0.3	0.2	0.1	0.0	4.7
Hancock County	13 162	70.2	310	69.4	35	62.9	32	28.1	84	61.9	1.8	1.4	0.2	0.1	0.7	9.8
Hardy County	5 015	68.4	132	69.7	4	50.0	0	X	31	87.1	0.5	0.2	0.1	0.2	0.0	3.5
Harrison County	26 872	69.3	403	66.7	34	64.7	110	30.9	243	65.0	1.4	0.5	0.6	0.2	0.3	5.5
Jackson County	10 932	74.7	0	X	26	46.2	21	23.8	13	100.0	0.5	0.2	0.3	0.0	0.1	3.7
Jefferson County	14 688	71.3	986	62.0	79	43.0	92	80.4	175	60.6	2.1	0.7	0.7	0.5	0.7	7.1
Kanawha County	78 472	65.2	5 580	59.6	187	84.0	565	81.8	379	61.7	1.4	0.3	0.8	0.1	0.2	5.7
Lewis County	6 872	69.3	6	100.0	13	76.9	6	100.0	23	91.3	0.5	0.2	0.2	0.1	0.0	3.3
Lincoln County	8 628	75.8	0	X	7	0.0	6	100.0	22	100.0	0.0	0.0	0.0	0.0	0.1	3.5
Logan County	14 265	74.3	373	65.1	40	50.0	42	52.4	74	90.5	0.5	0.1	0.3	0.0	0.1	3.3
McDowell County	9 696	72.2	1 354	62.9	8	0.0	17	100.0	40	97.5	0.5	0.3	0.1	0.0	0.2	3.4
Marion County	22 417	65.8	773	69.0	50	68.0	52	71.2	195	72.8	1.0	0.4	0.3	0.2	0.2	5.4
Marshall County	13 986	71.2	29	86.2	25	100.0	29	44.8	67	70.1	0.7	0.4	0.1	0.1	0.1	5.1
Mason County	10 448	72.6	39	28.2	7	85.7	38	92.1	41	58.5	0.5	0.1	0.3	0.0	0.1	3.3
Mercer County	24 553	68.3	1 574	60.7	48	64.6	105	74.3	73	46.6	0.8	0.3	0.4	0.1	0.2	4.5
Mineral County	10 434	71.9	280	65.7	0	X	23	78.3	13	46.2	0.6	0.2	0.3	0.1	0.2	3.8
Mingo County	10 861	73.8	316	55.7	11	45.5	9	33.3	32	62.5	0.3	0.0	0.2	0.1	0.1	3.6
Monongalia County	31 076	56.1	811	48.1	158	63.3	813	53.4	361	49.2	3.8	1.0	2.1	0.3	1.1	9.2
Monroe County	5 350	71.3	49	73.5	10	100.0	1	100.0	20	100.0	0.5	0.3	0.1	0.1	0.1	4.7
Morgan County	6 027	70.5	27	81.5	11	18.2	0	X	55	87.3	1.4	0.8	0.0	0.2	0.3	5.9
Nicholas County	10 569	72.8	0	X	32	81.3	28	71.4	45	37.8	0.6	0.2	0.3	0.1	0.1	4.3
Ohio County	18 736	62.4	740	51.9	29	86.2	87	62.1	78	48.7	1.3	0.6	0.5	0.1	0.4	6.0
Pendleton County	3 271	70.7	77	64.9	5	60.0	4	100.0	2	0.0	0.7	0.4	0.1	0.1	0.1	7.1
Pleasants County	2 852	74.2	2	100.0	8	75.0	6	100.0	8	100.0	0.5	0.1	0.3	0.0	0.1	3.3
Pocahontas County	3 786	66.0	20	55.0	7	28.6	3	0.0	8	100.0	0.6	0.4	0.1	0.0	0.1	4.3
Preston County	11 353	72.7	56	76.8	0	X	8	100.0	56	73.2	0.6	0.3	0.1	0.0	0.2	3.8
Putnam County	19 687	76.4	126	71.4	27	66.7	51	90.2	70	91.4	1.0	0.3	0.5	0.1	0.1	4.9
Raleigh County	29 121	70.2	2 263	63.1	8	50.0	204	80.9	126	77.8	1.2	0.3	0.6	0.0	0.3	5.4
Randolph County	10 884	69.7	39	35.9	29	93.1	13	100.0	39	20.5	0.7	0.4	0.2	0.1	0.2	4.2
Ritchie County	4 108	71.6	9	77.8	8	87.5	7	85.7	16	56.3	0.3	0.1	0.1	0.1	0.0	2.7
Roane County	6 043	72.7	5	0.0	25	100.0	6	100.0	24	58.3	0.6	0.2	0.3	0.2	0.1	3.7
Summers County	5 350	69.3	146	46.6	0	X	0	X	19	63.2	0.4	0.2	0.1	0.0	0.0	3.8
Taylor County	6 160	71.0	77	64.9	13	46.2	5	0.0	34	67.6	0.6	0.2	0.2	0.1	0.1	5.3
Tucker County	3 007	70.4	0	X	11	27.3	3	100.0	2	100.0	0.2	0.2	0.0	0.0	0.1	6.1
Tyler County	3 815	73.7	0	X	2	100.0	3	100.0	9	77.8	0.3	0.1	0.1	0.0	0.0	2.9
Upshur County	8 849	71.8	27	59.3	10	100.0	19	0.0	71	84.5	0.4	0.2	0.2	0.0	0.0	4.9
Wayne County	17 034	73.9	19	52.6	38	76.3	38	36.8	52	61.5	0.6	0.3	0.2	0.1	0.1	3.4
Webster County	4 009	70.6	0	X	6	0.0	4	0.0	0	X	0.4	0.2	0.2	0.0	0.0	3.3
Wetzel County	7 073	70.8	7	0.0	21	57.1	2	100.0	23	100.0	0.4	0.1	0.2	0.0	0.1	4.2
Wirt County	2 267	74.3	0	X	12	100.0	10	100.0	8	100.0	0.3	0.1	0.2	0.0	0.0	2.1
Wood County	35 319	69.0	283	64.3	64	93.8	186	69.9	127	59.8	1.1	0.4	0.4	0.2	0.1	4.1
Wyoming County	10 339	74.6	71	74.6	4	100.0	7	0.0	27	37.0	0.2	0.1	0.0	0.0	0.0	3.9
WISCONSIN	1 888 577	66.4	98 260	68.7	16 033	71.8	21 877	71.3	49 345	77.5	3.6	1.0	1.2	1.2	1.5	10.3
Adams County	7 758	69.4	17	58.8	30	70.0	16	68.8	65	70.8	2.3	1.6	0.3	0.2	0.6	7.9
Ashland County	6 030	63.9	18	61.1	533	64.2	12	75.0	41	65.9	1.0	0.4	0.2	0.1	0.2	6.7
Barron County	17 519	69.6	18	77.8	93	87.1	24	70.8	111	84.7	1.2	0.4	0.2	0.4	0.5	7.2
Bayfield County	5 675	68.7	0	X	437	71.6	6	66.7	19	84.2	1.2	0.7	0.3	0.0	0.2	7.2
Brown County	81 315	65.6	484	64.9	1 792	68.1	1 014	85.7	2 254	79.9	3.9	0.4	1.4	2.1	2.1	9.0
Buffalo County	5 466	68.7	3	100.0	8	50.0	9	55.6	19	63.2	0.6	0.3	0.1	0.2	0.5	6.4
Burnett County	6 294	67.7	7	28.6	232	71.1	8	100.0	16	100.0	1.2	0.6	0.2	0.2	0.4	5.7
Calumet County	14 573	75.2	15	93.3	36	91.7	142	81.0	105	74.3	2.1	0.4	1.2	0.3	1.0	7.9
Chippewa County	21 064	70.5	14	42.9	55	63.6	89	88.8	93	46.2	0.9	0.3	0.3	0.1	0.4	5.7
Clark County	11 933	72.8	19	78.9	29	65.5	16	56.3	63	76.2	1.2	0.4	0.2	0.4	2.3	11.5
Columbia County	20 001	69.4	46	32.6	69	81.2	55	100.0	173	80.3	1.3	0.6	0.3	0.3	0.5	8.3
Crawford County	6 585	69.4	9	100.0	32	87.5	8	75.0	10	100.0	0.7	0.4	0.2	0.0	0.2	6.4

[1] Hispanic or Latino persons may be of any race.

Table A-3. States and Counties — Age, Ethnicity, and Household Structure

STATE/ County code	MSA/PMSA/ NECMA code[1]	STATE County	Population by age (percent)										Non-Hispanic White		
															Age (percent)
			Total population	Under 5 years	5 to 17 years	18 to 24 years	25 to 44 years	45 to 64 years	65 years and over	Median age	+/− U.S. percent under 18 years	+/− U.S. percent 65 years and over	Total population	Under 18 years	65 years and over
			1	2	3	4	5	6	7	8	9	10	11	12	13
		WISCONSIN—Cont'd													
55 025	4720	Dane County	426 526	6.0	16.5	14.3	32.6	21.3	9.3	33.2	−3.2	−3.1	373 075	20.9	10.3
55 027	...	Dodge County	85 897	5.9	18.8	8.3	31.1	21.8	14.0	37.0	−1.0	1.6	80 674	25.0	14.8
55 029	...	Door County	27 961	4.7	17.3	6.3	25.5	27.6	18.7	42.9	−3.7	6.3	27 202	21.6	19.1
55 031	2240	Douglas County	43 287	5.9	17.6	10.3	27.9	23.8	14.5	37.7	−2.2	2.1	41 145	22.9	15.1
55 033	...	Dunn County	39 858	5.8	17.6	19.9	25.7	19.9	11.2	30.6	−2.3	−1.2	38 135	22.5	11.7
55 035	2290	Eau Claire County	93 142	5.9	17.6	17.2	26.6	20.5	12.2	32.4	−2.2	−0.2	88 023	22.2	12.8
55 037	...	Florence County	5 088	4.6	18.4	5.4	26.9	27.1	17.6	41.9	−2.7	5.2	5 045	23.1	17.5
55 039	...	Fond du Lac County	97 296	5.9	19.3	9.5	28.7	22.3	14.3	36.9	−0.5	1.9	92 527	24.5	14.9
55 041	...	Forest County	10 024	5.7	19.8	7.8	23.7	23.8	19.3	39.9	−0.2	6.9	8 567	22.1	21.8
55 043	...	Grant County	49 597	5.2	18.4	14.6	24.8	21.6	15.3	35.9	−2.1	2.9	48 461	23.6	15.6
55 045	...	Green County	33 647	6.4	20.1	6.6	29.3	23.0	14.7	37.9	0.8	2.3	32 904	26.0	14.9
55 047	...	Green Lake County	19 105	5.7	18.3	6.7	26.2	24.2	18.8	40.9	−1.7	6.4	18 519	23.6	19.3
55 049	...	Iowa County	22 780	6.4	20.7	6.7	30.5	22.4	13.4	37.1	1.4	1.0	22 442	26.7	13.5
55 051	...	Iron County	6 861	3.8	15.6	5.9	24.8	26.7	23.2	45.0	−6.3	10.8	6 744	19.1	23.5
55 053	...	Jackson County	19 100	5.6	18.5	9.0	29.2	22.7	15.0	37.6	−1.6	2.6	16 980	23.7	16.2
55 055	...	Jefferson County	74 021	6.3	18.9	8.5	30.4	23.2	12.6	36.6	−0.5	0.2	69 849	24.5	13.3
55 057	...	Juneau County	24 316	5.9	19.6	6.8	26.5	24.3	16.8	39.4	−0.2	4.4	23 344	24.8	17.3
55 059	3800	Kenosha County	149 577	6.8	20.1	9.5	31.3	20.7	11.5	34.8	1.2	−0.9	127 676	24.8	12.9
55 061	...	Kewaunee County	20 187	5.9	19.8	8.2	28.1	22.7	15.3	37.5	0.0	2.9	19 797	25.5	15.5
55 063	3870	La Crosse County	107 120	6.0	17.6	15.5	27.6	20.7	12.6	33.5	−2.1	0.2	100 547	22.1	13.2
55 065	...	Lafayette County	16 137	5.9	21.3	7.5	27.2	22.3	15.8	38.1	1.5	3.4	15 978	27.1	15.9
55 067	...	Langlade County	20 740	5.6	18.7	6.4	26.2	24.2	19.0	40.5	−1.4	6.6	20 160	23.7	19.4
55 069	...	Lincoln County	29 641	5.6	19.9	6.6	28.3	23.3	16.3	38.9	−0.2	3.9	28 766	24.7	16.7
55 071	...	Manitowoc County	82 887	5.7	19.7	7.7	28.3	23.0	15.6	38.3	−0.3	3.2	78 824	24.4	16.3
55 073	8940	Marathon County	125 834	6.5	20.3	8.2	29.5	22.6	13.0	36.3	1.1	0.6	118 052	24.9	13.7
55 075	...	Marinette County	43 384	5.1	18.4	8.3	25.6	24.9	17.6	40.5	−2.2	5.2	42 499	23.3	17.8
55 077	...	Marquette County	15 832	4.7	16.4	6.7	28.9	25.2	18.1	40.9	−4.6	5.7	14 631	21.8	19.4
55 078	...	Menominee County	4 562	9.9	29.1	8.4	24.8	18.6	9.2	27.7	13.3	−3.2	554	11.0	38.4
55 079	5080	Milwaukee County	940 164	7.1	19.2	10.4	30.4	19.9	12.9	33.7	0.6	0.5	585 075	18.6	17.8
55 081	...	Monroe County	40 899	6.8	21.2	7.6	27.7	22.8	13.9	36.8	2.3	1.5	39 103	27.6	14.4
55 083	...	Oconto County	35 634	5.8	20.0	6.3	28.7	24.1	15.1	38.8	0.1	2.7	34 735	25.4	15.3
55 085	...	Oneida County	36 776	4.6	17.8	5.7	26.2	27.0	18.7	42.4	−3.3	6.3	35 825	22.1	18.9
55 087	0460	Outagamie County	160 971	6.9	20.6	8.9	32.0	20.6	10.9	34.4	1.8	−1.5	149 627	26.4	11.5
55 089	5080	Ozaukee County	82 317	6.2	20.4	6.7	28.3	25.8	12.6	38.9	0.9	0.2	79 082	26.2	12.9
55 091	...	Pepin County	7 213	5.9	20.5	8.0	26.0	22.8	16.9	38.7	0.7	4.5	7 112	26.2	17.1
55 093	5120	Pierce County	36 804	5.7	18.7	17.1	28.1	20.8	9.6	32.1	−1.3	−2.8	35 851	24.0	9.8
55 095	...	Polk County	41 319	5.9	20.3	6.7	27.7	24.2	15.2	38.7	0.5	2.8	40 108	25.6	15.6
55 097	...	Portage County	67 182	5.9	18.1	16.3	27.7	21.1	10.9	33.0	−1.7	−1.5	63 824	22.9	11.4
55 099	...	Price County	15 822	4.7	19.2	5.8	25.7	25.6	19.0	41.7	−1.8	6.6	15 551	23.6	19.2
55 101	6600	Racine County	188 831	7.0	20.1	8.2	30.0	22.4	12.4	36.1	1.4	0.0	150 968	24.3	14.2
55 103	...	Richland County	17 924	5.7	19.4	8.6	25.6	23.6	17.2	39.2	−0.6	4.8	17 485	24.6	17.5
55 105	3620	Rock County	152 307	6.8	19.7	8.7	29.8	22.2	12.8	35.9	0.8	0.4	135 964	24.9	13.8
55 107	...	Rusk County	15 347	5.5	19.3	8.2	24.7	23.9	18.5	40.0	−0.9	6.1	15 059	24.6	18.7
55 109	5120	St. Croix County	63 155	7.0	20.9	8.2	32.0	22.0	9.8	35.0	2.2	−2.6	61 422	27.4	10.0
55 111	...	Sauk County	55 225	6.5	19.6	7.4	29.2	22.7	14.5	37.3	0.4	2.1	53 323	25.5	15.0
55 113	...	Sawyer County	16 196	5.3	18.7	5.9	24.8	27.2	18.0	42.1	−1.7	5.6	13 191	20.8	20.4
55 115	...	Shawano County	40 664	6.2	19.5	6.7	27.8	23.1	16.8	38.5	0.0	4.4	37 055	24.3	17.8
55 117	7620	Sheboygan County	112 646	6.4	19.0	8.3	30.0	22.2	14.0	36.8	−0.3	1.6	102 643	23.8	15.1
55 119	...	Taylor County	19 680	5.7	21.4	7.5	28.4	21.8	15.2	37.4	1.4	2.8	19 292	26.9	15.4
55 121	...	Trempealeau County	27 010	6.0	19.3	6.9	28.2	23.2	16.4	38.3	−0.4	4.0	26 538	25.1	16.7
55 123	...	Vernon County	28 056	6.6	20.9	6.7	25.4	23.4	17.1	39.1	1.8	4.7	27 682	27.3	17.2
55 125	...	Vilas County	21 033	4.2	16.5	4.8	23.1	28.4	23.0	45.8	−5.0	10.6	18 802	18.1	25.1
55 127	...	Walworth County	93 759	5.8	18.3	13.9	27.4	21.8	12.8	35.1	−1.6	0.4	85 775	22.9	13.7
55 129	...	Washburn County	16 036	5.1	18.7	6.1	24.5	27.0	18.6	42.1	−1.9	6.2	15 488	23.2	19.0
55 131	5080	Washington County	117 493	6.8	19.8	7.3	31.5	23.4	11.2	36.6	0.9	−1.2	113 723	26.1	11.5
55 133	5080	Waukesha County	360 767	6.4	19.9	6.8	29.8	25.1	12.0	38.1	0.6	−0.4	340 155	25.5	12.5
55 135	...	Waupaca County	51 731	6.0	19.7	7.2	27.8	22.7	16.6	38.5	0.0	4.2	50 375	25.1	17.0
55 137	...	Waushara County	23 154	5.1	18.5	6.0	24.9	26.4	19.1	42.1	−2.1	6.7	22 042	22.8	19.8
55 139	0460	Winnebago County	156 763	6.0	17.9	11.7	30.6	21.3	12.5	35.4	−1.8	0.1	147 251	22.9	13.2
55 141	...	Wood County	75 555	6.2	19.5	7.8	28.2	22.9	15.4	38.0	0.0	3.0	72 345	24.7	15.9
56 000	...	WYOMING	493 782	6.3	19.7	10.1	28.2	24.1	11.6	36.2	0.3	−0.8	438 538	24.9	12.4
56 001	...	Albany County	32 014	5.1	13.2	28.5	26.1	18.8	8.2	26.7	−7.4	−4.2	28 075	17.2	8.7
56 003	...	Big Horn County	11 461	7.1	21.6	7.2	22.7	24.6	16.8	38.7	3.0	4.4	10 486	27.6	17.8
56 005	...	Campbell County	33 698	7.4	23.6	9.3	32.4	22.2	5.0	32.2	5.3	−7.4	31 524	30.6	5.3
56 007	...	Carbon County	15 639	5.8	18.2	8.8	28.5	26.7	12.0	38.9	−1.7	−0.4	12 823	22.8	12.7

[1]MSA = Metropolitan Statistical Area. PMSA = Primary MSA. NECMA = New England County Metropolitan Area. See the Appendix A for explanation of these concepts. See Appendix B for list of metropolitan areas identified by type, with component counties.

STATE County	Black or African American			American Indian and Alaska Native			Asian, Hawaiian, and Pacific Islander			Hispanic or Latino[1]			Two or more races		
	Total population	Age (percent) Under 18 years	65 years and over	Total population	Age (percent) Under 18 years	65 years and over	Total population	Age (percent) Under 18 years	65 years and over	Total population	Age (percent) Under 18 years	65 years and over	Total population	Age (percent) Under 18 years	65 years and over
	14	15	16	17	18	19	20	21	22	23	24	25	26	27	28
WISCONSIN—Cont'd															
Dane County	16 449	36.2	3.0	1 518	28.0	1.0	14 550	25.8	3.0	14 602	30.5	1.5	7 702	45.5	2.1
Dodge County	2 162	3.2	1.0	430	39.8	0.9	301	26.6	10.0	1 976	34.0	1.5	580	41.6	4.0
Door County	36	52.8	0.0	207	17.9	4.8	104	65.4	1.9	235	31.1	7.7	236	37.3	3.8
Douglas County	198	36.4	0.0	771	24.5	4.8	299	39.8	0.7	274	47.4	0.7	639	46.3	3.8
Dunn County	73	17.8	0.0	144	22.9	1.4	704	55.1	0.0	413	40.0	3.6	406	31.3	4.7
Eau Claire County	455	31.6	0.0	601	36.1	1.7	2 327	49.8	2.8	792	34.5	0.8	992	50.4	5.8
Florence County	14	14.3	42.9	11	0.0	0.0	4	0.0	50.0	6	33.3	0.0	8	0.0	25.0
Fond du Lac County	958	29.6	0.4	539	32.8	2.8	615	50.2	8.5	2 003	39.6	4.4	751	42.9	5.1
Forest County	86	36.0	0.0	1 088	45.4	4.7	40	40.0	5.0	162	53.7	2.5	133	48.9	1.5
Grant County	270	21.9	0.7	160	36.9	0.0	187	13.4	5.3	318	29.9	0.6	237	35.4	3.4
Green County	78	48.7	0.0	127	40.9	8.7	56	50.0	7.1	281	41.6	7.1	232	62.9	2.6
Green Lake County	53	52.8	3.8	23	8.7	0.0	22	63.6	0.0	398	34.4	5.5	93	39.8	5.4
Iowa County	13	69.2	0.0	82	50.0	2.4	55	76.4	0.0	70	47.1	7.1	134	42.5	0.7
Iron County	4	50.0	0.0	22	13.6	27.3	24	41.7	0.0	16	37.5	18.8	61	41.0	3.3
Jackson County	440	4.1	0.0	1 095	37.6	6.9	95	32.6	2.1	341	19.4	2.6	204	34.3	8.3
Jefferson County	244	35.2	2.5	223	26.0	6.3	220	36.8	4.5	2 991	37.0	1.0	873	42.7	2.7
Juneau County	75	49.3	5.3	306	37.3	6.2	97	47.4	6.2	321	44.5	3.1	213	42.3	4.7
Kenosha County	7 170	37.9	4.7	615	31.4	5.4	1 424	24.9	6.5	10 427	39.5	3.1	3 013	53.8	1.3
Kewaunee County	4	100.0	0.0	37	24.3	10.8	48	18.8	0.0	189	38.6	0.0	112	49.1	2.7
La Crosse County	934	28.2	1.4	652	35.0	5.4	2 882	53.1	2.1	850	36.1	4.5	1 323	55.6	2.0
Lafayette County	3	33.3	0.0	15	20.0	0.0	30	40.0	6.7	78	44.9	6.4	54	53.7	0.0
Langlade County	21	38.1	0.0	196	35.7	2.0	95	51.6	0.0	120	46.7	2.5	178	50.6	9.0
Lincoln County	128	64.1	0.0	164	47.6	0.6	137	32.8	1.5	293	59.0	5.5	211	53.1	5.2
Manitowoc County	124	19.4	0.0	450	26.4	1.3	1 494	49.7	2.3	1 470	45.6	1.3	645	52.1	4.7
Marathon County	260	50.8	0.0	549	38.6	3.1	5 174	58.7	2.2	932	39.9	3.0	982	55.7	2.9
Marinette County	39	59.0	0.0	282	37.2	3.5	116	37.1	16.4	234	29.1	7.3	224	41.5	9.8
Marquette County	482	0.8	0.0	156	7.7	4.5	30	30.0	0.0	404	21.5	3.7	207	24.2	3.4
Menominee County	18	44.4	33.3	3 701	42.9	5.0	144	42.4	3.5	100	53.0	0.0	103	55.3	5.8
Milwaukee County	229 203	39.1	5.0	8 245	30.4	4.3	22 070	04.2	4.0	00 000	00.0	0.0	00 070	51.1	1.1
Monroe County	209	41.6	1.0	336	37.5	10.1	231	28.1	2.2	770	36.6	1.2	302	48.0	0.0
Oconto County	50	54.0	8.0	292	33.9	5.5	106	51.9	4.7	175	39.4	6.3	299	46.8	7.4
Oneida County	73	6.8	2.7	300	29.0	13.0	83	39.8	14.5	232	58.6	0.0	347	45.2	13.5
Outagamie County	949	27.5	0.0	2 360	35.7	5.7	3 706	49.6	4.0	3 255	40.0	1.6	1 541	55.6	6.0
Ozaukee County	729	28.9	7.0	267	38.2	1.9	670	32.1	4.3	1 055	35.6	11.8	655	55.9	4.1
Pepin County	7	71.4	0.0	17	58.8	0.0	20	65.0	0.0	23	0.0	0.0	34	35.3	5.9
Pierce County	108	6.5	0.0	161	51.6	1.9	219	23.3	0.0	227	58.1	2.6	243	41.6	0.8
Polk County	79	55.7	2.5	429	38.9	2.3	105	46.7	0.0	303	45.5	6.6	328	52.4	3.4
Portage County	231	46.8	0.0	231	20.8	0.9	1 337	51.7	1.3	978	42.3	3.2	670	41.8	3.6
Price County	36	38.9	0.0	71	40.8	1.4	18	38.9	0.0	05	55.0	0.0	02	46.3	13.4
Racine County	19 155	35.1	6.3	749	39.5	2.3	1 366	29.2	3.6	14 706	39.7	3.7	3 630	59.3	2.4
Richland County	24	66.7	4.2	52	23.1	9.6	22	9.1	0.0	210	53.3	3.8	151	44.4	6.0
Rock County	6 704	37.4	7.2	513	28.3	1.9	1 380	27.8	7.5	5 982	39.1	1.8	2 023	58.8	2.5
Rusk County	30	26.7	0.0	37	21.6	5.4	43	9.3	25.6	116	49.1	4.3	84	33.3	10.7
St. Croix County	333	30.3	6.6	190	46.3	0.0	267	29.6	0.0	493	49.3	3.9	491	60.7	1.8
Sauk County	155	25.2	0.0	361	35.2	0.0	217	44.7	1.4	871	44.4	2.2	402	48.3	3.5
Sawyer County	55	3.6	0.0	2 489	39.4	7.1	86	40.7	24.4	133	50.4	0.8	253	37.5	9.9
Shawano County	88	86.4	4.5	2 442	36.4	6.3	186	29.6	6.5	350	47.1	2.0	628	47.3	6.2
Sheboygan County	1 364	20.4	0.2	326	36.2	0.0	3 596	52.7	3.1	3 680	39.1	4.0	1 510	53.5	2.2
Taylor County	38	63.2	0.0	67	19.4	0.0	26	15.4	15.4	141	38.3	9.2	112	44.6	5.4
Trempealeau County	24	16.7	0.0	71	36.6	11.3	27	37.0	0.0	258	40.3	0.0	114	43.0	4.4
Vernon County	25	36.0	0.0	80	33.8	1.3	36	33.3	8.3	136	44.9	11.8	106	45.3	7.5
Vilas County	19	26.3	0.0	1 638	42.1	6.2	172	34.9	2.3	268	46.3	5.2	208	51.9	1.9
Walworth County	672	28.4	7.9	474	37.6	0.4	584	23.1	4.6	5 991	38.6	2.7	796	50.6	2.5
Washburn County	11	27.3	27.3	163	23.9	18.4	43	48.8	0.0	160	41.9	2.5	177	59.9	5.1
Washington County	625	35.8	2.6	450	39.3	2.0	520	30.4	1.5	1 472	42.4	0.7	837	49.9	7.5
Waukesha County	2 555	40.3	2.4	1 036	30.6	6.0	5 076	31.5	3.3	8 962	39.5	2.9	3 869	55.0	4.4
Waupaca County	118	65.3	0.0	196	43.4	2.0	118	44.9	6.8	591	49.9	3.7	336	45.8	8.6
Waushara County	25	76.0	16.0	84	25.0	6.0	44	29.5	13.6	783	40.7	3.3	229	38.9	7.0
Winnebago County	1 729	20.0	1.0	781	31.1	2.2	2 480	45.0	2.4	3 169	38.8	2.5	1 681	51.1	4.3
Wood County	300	47.3	7.0	500	41.6	1.2	1 175	51.5	2.0	849	46.1	7.4	524	50.8	4.4
WYOMING	3 126	25.5	3.7	11 363	36.7	4.8	3 204	23.2	8.0	31 384	35.1	5.6	9 399	42.2	5.1
Albany County	284	24.3	0.0	291	16.2	3.8	554	17.0	5.2	2 356	28.0	5.5	656	35.7	4.1
Big Horn County	28	53.6	0.0	178	34.8	0.0	26	26.9	0.0	674	43.9	4.0	184	40.2	16.3
Campbell County	24	0.0	0.0	322	36.0	2.2	257	32.7	2.7	1 088	39.4	0.9	639	42.4	0.0
Carbon County	130	4.6	22.3	217	33.6	2.8	60	36.7	18.3	2 175	30.5	7.6	399	36.8	11.5

[1] Hispanic or Latino persons may be of any race.

Table A-3. States and Counties — Age, Ethnicity, and Household Structure

STATE County	Total households	Family households (percent)						Nonfamily households (percent)						Percent of householders 65 years and over who live alone	Grandparents who are responsible for the care of their grandchildren
		Married-couple family households			Other family households			Two or more unrelated persons		Male living alone		Female living alone			
		Total	With children	Householder 65 years or over	Total	With children	Householder 65 years or over	Total	Householder 65 years or over	Total	Householder 65 years or over	Total	Householder 65 years or over		
	29	30	31	32	33	34	35	36	37	38	39	40	41	42	43
WISCONSIN—Cont'd															
Dane County	173 710	48.1	22.9	6.7	10.4	6.6	0.9	12.1	0.2	12.7	1.5	16.7	5.5	47.4	957
Dodge County	31 513	60.2	27.7	11.5	11.2	6.7	1.6	4.4	0.2	10.9	2.7	13.3	8.2	45.1	245
Door County	11 811	58.3	21.9	14.0	9.4	5.5	1.1	4.2	0.3	10.9	3.0	17.2	10.7	47.0	109
Douglas County	17 787	50.5	20.4	9.9	13.1	8.6	1.4	6.6	0.4	13.3	2.7	16.5	9.0	49.9	262
Dunn County	14 404	54.7	25.5	10.0	10.7	6.8	1.1	10.4	0.4	11.9	2.3	12.4	6.2	42.6	165
Eau Claire County	35 872	51.9	23.8	9.2	10.5	6.7	1.2	10.5	0.3	11.4	2.1	15.7	8.0	48.7	312
Florence County	2 121	59.0	23.1	13.0	8.3	5.1	1.6	4.4	0.0	14.9	4.9	13.3	7.8	46.5	25
Fond du Lac County	36 894	58.8	26.7	10.7	10.7	6.5	1.4	5.0	0.3	10.9	2.4	14.5	8.4	46.5	302
Forest County	4 028	54.8	20.0	15.9	14.2	9.8	1.8	2.8	0.6	13.6	3.6	14.6	9.1	41.1	73
Grant County	18 515	56.9	24.6	12.0	10.9	6.4	1.4	6.3	0.3	10.6	2.6	15.3	9.6	47.1	141
Green County	13 231	58.1	26.4	10.6	12.0	7.9	1.5	5.0	0.6	10.1	2.1	14.8	9.3	47.4	131
Green Lake County	7 652	59.9	23.8	14.2	9.6	5.3	1.5	3.4	0.3	11.4	3.2	15.8	10.9	46.9	42
Iowa County	8 777	59.2	27.8	10.2	11.8	6.6	1.8	4.7	0.4	11.1	2.7	13.1	7.5	45.1	62
Iron County	3 094	53.5	17.0	15.3	9.7	4.9	2.2	4.7	0.4	15.0	4.4	17.2	12.2	48.0	36
Jackson County	7 103	57.2	23.9	12.4	11.7	7.2	1.6	5.1	0.3	12.0	3.3	14.0	9.1	46.3	79
Jefferson County	28 188	58.7	26.3	10.0	12.0	7.0	1.5	5.6	0.4	10.3	2.0	13.4	7.6	44.6	191
Juneau County	9 693	55.9	22.8	12.5	13.4	8.3	2.1	4.6	0.7	11.8	3.6	14.3	8.1	43.5	108
Kenosha County	56 093	53.9	26.1	8.4	15.1	9.3	1.9	5.6	0.4	11.2	2.3	14.2	6.9	46.3	944
Kewaunee County	7 643	62.3	27.3	11.9	10.8	6.2	1.7	3.5	0.3	10.0	2.5	13.4	9.2	45.5	57
La Crosse County	41 644	50.7	23.3	8.9	11.4	7.3	1.3	9.6	0.3	11.3	2.2	17.0	7.9	49.2	293
Lafayette County	6 214	59.4	27.0	12.3	11.2	6.5	1.9	3.9	0.3	11.2	3.8	14.3	9.9	48.4	60
Langlade County	8 494	57.7	22.5	14.2	11.1	6.8	1.7	4.5	0.7	11.0	3.3	15.8	10.5	45.4	185
Lincoln County	11 744	59.6	24.8	11.7	11.0	7.2	1.3	4.0	0.5	11.2	3.2	14.3	10.0	49.6	132
Manitowoc County	32 731	58.0	25.3	11.9	10.6	6.5	1.5	4.5	0.3	11.1	2.4	15.7	9.5	46.6	328
Marathon County	47 737	60.6	27.8	10.4	10.8	6.7	1.5	5.0	0.3	10.4	2.2	13.3	7.7	45.1	317
Marinette County	17 590	57.1	22.4	11.9	10.5	6.4	1.8	4.0	0.4	13.1	4.2	15.3	10.3	50.7	117
Marquette County	5 949	58.6	20.9	15.7	11.1	6.4	2.2	4.9	0.6	12.9	4.3	12.6	8.1	40.1	71
Menominee County	1 350	42.1	19.2	9.3	36.4	23.0	5.1	5.1	0.2	10.1	1.9	10.1	5.2	32.5	106
Milwaukee County	377 983	39.9	17.8	7.7	20.1	12.2	2.4	7.1	0.4	14.1	2.7	18.8	8.0	50.5	7 976
Monroe County	15 452	58.0	26.6	9.9	12.3	8.1	1.7	4.7	0.4	11.5	3.2	13.5	8.2	48.6	231
Oconto County	13 988	61.6	25.5	13.0	10.7	6.6	1.5	4.3	0.3	10.9	2.9	12.4	8.2	42.9	167
Oneida County	15 332	58.0	21.4	14.2	10.5	6.4	1.8	5.1	0.6	12.1	3.5	14.2	7.9	40.5	116
Outagamie County	60 578	60.1	29.9	8.9	10.0	6.6	1.1	5.8	0.2	10.5	1.6	13.6	6.8	45.1	476
Ozaukee County	30 887	66.5	31.5	11.4	8.5	5.2	1.0	3.7	0.2	8.5	1.9	12.8	6.3	39.5	156
Pepin County	2 778	60.7	27.1	13.3	9.3	5.2	1.3	3.9	0.2	10.7	3.0	15.4	10.3	47.3	24
Pierce County	13 041	59.3	28.6	8.5	10.3	6.5	1.3	9.0	0.3	10.3	2.0	11.1	5.1	41.7	115
Polk County	16 305	58.7	24.9	12.1	11.4	7.3	1.3	4.8	0.4	11.8	2.8	13.3	8.2	44.2	173
Portage County	25 112	56.2	26.2	8.5	10.0	6.0	1.2	9.2	0.3	11.2	2.3	13.3	6.8	47.4	111
Price County	6 558	55.9	22.4	12.8	11.1	6.7	2.0	4.5	0.4	13.5	4.5	15.0	10.2	49.3	68
Racine County	70 796	55.8	25.2	9.7	14.9	9.4	1.8	4.8	0.3	10.1	2.1	14.3	7.3	44.0	1 306
Richland County	7 118	56.0	23.6	12.7	12.2	8.0	1.7	4.5	0.6	11.8	2.5	15.5	10.6	46.7	44
Rock County	58 674	55.1	24.6	10.0	14.2	9.3	1.3	5.6	0.3	10.3	2.1	14.8	7.4	45.1	961
Rusk County	6 119	57.0	23.0	13.3	11.5	5.9	2.0	4.6	0.4	12.2	3.1	14.7	10.1	45.7	93
St. Croix County	23 428	63.4	31.5	7.8	9.6	6.5	0.9	5.9	0.2	9.2	1.7	11.9	6.1	46.9	127
Sauk County	21 647	57.3	25.4	11.2	11.4	7.5	1.2	6.0	0.5	10.5	2.3	14.8	8.6	45.9	260
Sawyer County	6 602	54.7	18.4	13.8	14.2	9.1	2.2	4.9	0.8	13.0	4.2	13.2	7.2	40.5	89
Shawano County	15 820	59.0	24.7	13.3	11.7	7.3	1.7	4.5	0.5	10.3	3.1	14.5	9.1	44.0	185
Sheboygan County	43 595	58.8	26.2	10.9	10.2	6.5	1.1	4.9	0.2	11.4	2.4	14.6	8.0	46.0	409
Taylor County	7 520	60.2	27.3	12.4	11.1	6.7	1.8	4.1	0.3	12.4	3.0	12.2	8.1	43.6	73
Trempealeau County	10 777	55.8	24.7	10.9	11.7	7.0	1.8	4.8	0.3	12.5	3.8	15.3	9.8	51.2	46
Vernon County	10 820	59.0	25.7	12.2	10.4	5.9	2.0	3.9	0.5	11.9	3.7	14.8	9.9	48.2	125
Vilas County	9 084	58.3	17.0	17.6	11.0	6.1	1.9	4.4	0.7	12.7	3.8	13.5	8.9	38.7	78
Walworth County	34 515	55.9	25.1	10.3	11.8	6.9	1.6	7.5	0.2	11.0	2.0	13.8	7.4	43.5	373
Washburn County	6 640	59.3	21.4	14.8	9.9	6.0	1.6	4.3	0.6	12.4	3.7	14.1	9.2	43.2	67
Washington County	43 910	64.8	30.6	9.4	10.3	6.1	1.3	4.7	0.3	8.9	1.5	11.3	6.1	40.8	240
Waukesha County	135 450	65.5	30.9	10.0	9.1	5.2	1.2	4.6	0.3	8.2	1.8	12.6	6.6	42.1	842
Waupaca County	19 909	59.2	26.2	11.3	11.0	6.7	1.6	4.6	0.4	10.7	2.6	14.4	9.6	47.8	205
Waushara County	9 312	60.2	21.3	15.3	10.3	6.3	1.9	4.4	0.8	11.8	3.4	13.3	8.1	39.0	107
Winnebago County	61 180	53.8	24.3	9.3	11.3	7.2	1.2	7.5	0.3	11.7	2.2	15.8	7.8	48.2	442
Wood County	30 131	58.3	26.1	11.3	10.2	6.5	1.3	4.3	0.5	10.9	2.4	16.2	9.2	47.1	338
WYOMING	193 959	55.7	25.1	9.1	12.1	8.1	1.1	5.9	0.3	12.6	2.3	13.7	6.6	45.6	3 582
Albany County	13 289	42.7	18.2	6.4	10.6	6.1	0.8	15.3	0.3	16.2	1.4	15.2	4.0	42.0	133
Big Horn County	4 315	60.5	25.3	13.8	11.1	7.0	1.7	3.4	0.5	11.6	3.3	13.4	8.7	42.9	91
Campbell County	12 242	62.1	34.5	4.0	12.4	9.3	0.3	5.4	0.2	10.7	1.0	9.4	3.2	48.1	236
Carbon County	6 159	56.6	24.2	9.5	11.3	7.9	1.1	4.9	0.6	13.9	2.7	13.3	6.7	45.5	98

Table A-3. States and Counties — Age, Ethnicity, and Household Structure

STATE County	Households with Non-Hispanic White householder		Households with Black or African American householder		Households with American Indian and Alaska Native householder		Households with Asian, Hawaiian, and Pacific Islander householder		Households with Hispanic or Latino[1] householder		Foreign-born population	Place of birth (percent)			Percent in non-English speaking households	
	Number of households	Percent that are family households	Number of households	Percent that are family households	Number of households	Percent that are family households	Number of households	Percent that are family households	Number of households	Percent that are family households	Percent of total population that is foreign-born	Europe	Asia	Latin America	Linguistically isolated	Not linguistically isolated
	44	45	46	47	48	49	50	51	52	53	54	55	56	57	58	59
WISCONSIN—Cont'd																
Dane County	156 539	58.3	5 500	62.5	568	59.9	5 144	55.7	4 266	67.3	6.3	1.1	2.7	1.8	2.2	11.9
Dodge County	30 770	71.3	88	78.4	58	96.6	98	87.8	409	74.1	1.6	0.6	0.3	0.7	0.8	8.1
Door County	11 606	67.6	9	77.8	67	76.1	20	55.0	52	88.5	1.5	0.8	0.2	0.3	0.3	7.9
Douglas County	17 143	63.7	51	96.1	320	66.9	67	67.2	51	33.3	1.6	0.6	0.6	0.1	0.5	6.6
Dunn County	13 969	64.9	14	21.4	59	84.7	126	72.2	93	83.9	2.1	0.4	1.1	0.2	0.8	8.1
Eau Claire County	34 835	62.1	123	64.2	149	51.7	412	79.1	186	63.4	2.2	0.4	1.5	0.2	1.0	9.3
Florence County	2 102	67.5	6	100.0	5	60.0	2	0.0	2	0.0	0.6	0.3	0.1	0.0	0.6	7.7
Fond du Lac County	35 793	69.6	122	68.9	183	59.0	140	57.9	461	77.9	2.0	0.6	0.5	0.7	0.5	8.0
Forest County	3 609	68.6	4	100.0	345	69.6	10	100.0	23	95.7	1.1	0.6	0.3	0.1	0.6	8.9
Grant County	18 284	67.9	37	32.4	50	88.0	35	45.7	65	63.1	1.0	0.3	0.4	0.2	0.4	7.7
Green County	13 030	70.1	21	14.3	47	74.5	11	63.6	92	84.8	1.3	0.7	0.2	0.2	0.3	7.6
Green Lake County	7 485	69.2	10	50.0	15	80.0	4	100.0	112	86.6	1.8	0.6	0.1	1.1	1.6	9.1
Iowa County	8 699	71.1	2	100.0	22	100.0	4	100.0	13	53.8	0.6	0.3	0.1	0.1	0.2	6.7
Iron County	3 057	63.1	0	X	8	100.0	3	100.0	3	100.0	1.8	1.3	0.2	0.0	0.4	6.7
Jackson County	6 646	68.8	5	100.0	325	68.9	19	100.0	54	66.7	1.9	0.4	0.5	1.0	0.9	9.7
Jefferson County	27 144	70.3	74	90.5	73	61.6	58	86.2	723	78.1	2.8	0.8	0.3	1.5	1.2	9.0
Juneau County	9 420	69.3	27	55.6	102	71.6	23	73.9	81	70.4	1.5	0.8	0.2	0.3	0.7	7.3
Kenosha County	50 214	68.1	2 183	72.3	278	68.7	418	68.2	2 590	83.2	4.8	1.8	0.8	1.9	1.7	13.7
Kewaunee County	7 554	73.1	0	X	13	30.8	15	86.7	43	83.7	0.9	0.4	0.1	0.4	0.4	7.7
La Crosse County	40 244	61.9	232	66.4	213	70.4	513	76.4	195	53.8	2.5	0.5	1.7	0.1	0.6	8.7
Lafayette County	6 167	70.7	2	100.0	8	50.0	8	75.0	23	47.8	0.8	0.4	0.2	0.1	0.2	6.0
Langlade County	8 322	68.8	7	100.0	62	67.7	19	100.0	35	100.0	1.0	0.6	0.2	0.1	0.4	5.9
Lincoln County	11 551	70.6	5	60.0	45	75.6	23	69.6	83	62.7	1.6	0.8	0.4	0.3	0.7	6.4
Manitowoc County	31 754	68.3	27	70.4	200	68.5	282	92.6	345	83.2	2.3	0.5	1.1	0.6	1.0	7.8
Marathon County	46 300	71.0	45	93.3	110	74.5	841	92.3	223	76.2	3.5	0.5	2.6	0.2	1.8	9.4
Marinette County	17 348	67.8	4	50.0	95	60.0	33	60.6	53	62.3	1.2	0.8	0.2	0.1	0.4	7.4
Marquette County	5 844	69.7	6	66.7	16	56.3	2	100.0	51	88.2	1.5	0.9	0.2	0.3	0.5	7.4
Menominee County	242	60.3	0	X	1 024	81.5	36	88.9	14	100.0	2.7	0.3	2.0	0.1	1.6	20.0
Milwaukee County	265 474	55.7	78 041	68.9	2 818	70.8	6 513	68.8	21 917	77.2	6.8	1.7	1.9	2.8	3.4	15.2
Monroe County	15 013	70.0	53	88.7	112	90.2	40	95.0	158	84.8	1.8	0.5	0.3	0.8	2.2	10.3
Oconto County	13 763	72.4	12	83.3	108	63.9	20	100.0	33	63.6	0.7	0.4	0.2	0.1	0.3	6.7
Oneida County	15 055	68.6	2	0.0	103	65.0	24	66.7	52	44.2	1.0	0.6	0.1	0.0	0.3	6.6
Outagamie County	57 782	69.9	252	77.8	765	80.3	737	79.5	758	71.8	3.1	0.6	1.5	0.7	1.3	9.0
Ozaukee County	30 002	74.8	240	80.4	106	80.2	175	90.9	290	73.4	3.3	1.8	0.8	0.3	0.5	10.0
Pepin County	2 748	69.9	0	X	2	100.0	4	100.0	11	81.8	0.6	0.1	0.2	0.1	1.5	8.1
Pierce County	12 793	69.8	32	50.0	50	58.0	51	49.0	46	78.3	1.0	0.3	0.5	0.1	0.2	6.7
Polk County	16 028	70.1	10	80.0	105	81.9	25	56.0	70	67.1	1.0	0.4	0.2	0.2	0.3	6.6
Portage County	24 349	66.3	42	54.8	95	49.5	199	69.8	254	67.7	2.2	0.5	1.2	0.4	1.1	9.9
Price County	6 480	66.9	9	33.3	27	77.8	4	100.0	12	50.0	0.6	0.4	0.1	0.1	0.3	6.3
Racine County	59 840	70.0	6 214	69.6	229	80.8	436	72.5	3 799	82.9	4.1	1.3	0.6	2.0	1.9	11.9
Richland County	7 014	68.3	5	40.0	29	34.5	6	100.0	43	81.4	1.0	0.4	0.2	0.4	0.4	5.9
Rock County	54 102	69.0	2 255	69.7	146	58.2	377	69.0	1 468	80.7	3.3	0.5	0.7	2.0	1.7	8.8
Rusk County	6 060	68.6	7	71.4	9	22.2	2	100.0	19	84.2	1.7	1.0	0.3	0.1	0.4	7.3
St. Croix County	23 051	72.8	86	81.4	53	88.7	78	89.7	92	69.6	1.1	0.4	0.3	0.2	0.2	7.2
Sauk County	21 123	68.9	70	30.0	121	52.1	44	90.9	233	70.0	1.9	1.0	0.2	0.6	0.9	8.0
Sawyer County	5 651	67.6	3	0.0	790	76.8	31	87.1	31	100.0	1.6	0.9	0.3	0.1	0.5	8.8
Shawano County	14 796	70.4	6	66.7	745	76.1	35	100.0	86	80.2	1.0	0.3	0.2	0.3	0.4	6.6
Sheboygan County	41 415	68.6	210	76.7	61	85.2	670	88.8	985	69.8	4.3	0.9	2.1	1.1	2.2	10.5
Taylor County	7 432	71.3	5	100.0	18	27.8	8	100.0	31	71.0	0.9	0.2	0.2	0.3	0.8	7.1
Trempealeau County	10 643	67.4	7	42.9	19	78.9	0	X	74	78.4	0.8	0.3	0.1	0.3	0.8	8.8
Vernon County	10 732	69.5	2	100.0	21	66.7	5	80.0	34	61.8	0.8	0.4	0.1	0.2	2.4	10.9
Vilas County	8 404	68.6	4	100.0	525	79.4	40	87.5	54	66.7	2.4	1.3	0.6	0.2	0.5	8.2
Walworth County	32 665	67.1	193	50.8	137	90.5	191	57.6	1 294	88.0	5.4	1.4	0.6	3.2	2.1	11.9
Washburn County	6 513	69.3	8	0.0	33	75.8	10	80.0	41	63.4	1.0	0.5	0.2	0.1	0.2	6.2
Washington County	42 989	74.7	145	94.5	116	100.0	116	98.3	366	86.9	1.9	0.9	0.5	0.4	0.6	9.1
Waukesha County	129 855	74.4	731	73.1	343	64.7	1 496	81.6	2 393	84.3	3.6	1.5	1.1	0.7	0.8	9.8
Waupaca County	19 594	70.2	13	61.5	67	74.6	17	52.9	143	79.7	1.0	0.4	0.2	0.2	0.3	7.1
Waushara County	9 045	70.3	4	0.0	18	72.2	14	85.7	184	78.8	2.0	0.8	0.2	0.9	1.2	9.0
Winnebago County	58 957	64.7	245	54.3	305	70.2	548	77.7	830	78.6	2.8	0.7	1.2	0.7	1.0	8.5
Wood County	29 325	68.2	100	78.0	151	63.6	196	92.9	234	82.5	2.1	0.3	1.0	0.2	0.6	7.6
WYOMING	176 982	67.7	1 154	64.1	3 353	74.5	845	64.5	9 570	69.0	2.3	0.6	0.4	0.9	0.8	10.4
Albany County	11 918	52.5	110	36.4	106	72.6	183	51.4	798	64.8	3.8	1.0	1.2	0.7	1.4	10.1
Big Horn County	4 047	71.0	8	100.0	43	81.4	3	100.0	185	78.9	2.2	0.4	0.2	1.3	1.0	9.6
Campbell County	11 682	74.7	0	X	98	83.7	69	91.3	255	60.0	1.7	0.2	0.5	0.6	1.0	8.5
Carbon County	5 246	67.9	24	50.0	52	75.0	15	100.0	741	68.4	2.9	0.6	0.2	1.8	1.0	13.0

[1]Hispanic or Latino persons may be of any race.

STATE/ County code	MSA/PMSA/ NECMA code[1]	STATE County	Total population	Under 5 years	5 to 17 years	18 to 24 years	25 to 44 years	45 to 64 years	65 years and over	Median age	+/− U.S. percent under 18 years	+/− U.S. percent 65 years and over	Total population	Under 18 years	65 years and over
						Population by age (percent)							Non-Hispanic White	Age (percent)	
			1	2	3	4	5	6	7	8	9	10	11	12	13
		WYOMING—Cont'd													
56 009	...	Converse County	12 052	6.5	21.7	6.8	28.3	25.3	11.3	37.5	2.5	-1.1	11 104	27.7	11.4
56 011	...	Crook County	5 887	5.0	22.0	7.0	24.5	26.8	14.7	40.2	1.3	2.3	5 780	26.6	14.8
56 013	...	Fremont County	35 804	6.7	20.7	8.2	26.1	25.2	13.1	37.7	1.7	0.7	26 695	23.1	15.8
56 015	...	Goshen County	12 538	5.9	18.0	9.1	24.8	25.0	17.3	40.0	-1.8	4.9	11 235	22.7	18.4
56 017	...	Hot Springs County	4 882	4.5	17.6	5.9	23.9	28.1	20.0	44.2	-3.6	7.6	4 602	21.5	20.8
56 019	...	Johnson County	7 075	4.9	19.4	5.3	23.7	28.6	18.1	43.0	-1.4	5.7	6 810	23.5	18.5
56 021	1580	Laramie County	81 607	6.5	18.9	9.7	30.6	23.0	11.4	35.3	-0.3	-1.0	67 807	23.9	12.5
56 023	...	Lincoln County	14 573	6.7	24.2	7.0	25.6	24.1	12.3	36.8	5.2	-0.1	13 962	30.7	12.6
56 025	1350	Natrona County	66 533	6.4	19.5	10.0	28.0	23.6	12.6	36.4	0.2	0.2	61 005	25.1	13.3
56 027	...	Niobrara County	2 407	4.7	17.7	5.7	26.3	26.8	18.9	42.8	-3.3	6.5	2 345	21.9	19.2
56 029	...	Park County	25 786	5.6	18.8	9.1	25.3	26.7	14.5	39.8	-1.3	2.1	24 368	23.8	15.0
56 031	...	Platte County	8 807	5.2	20.0	6.3	24.8	27.2	16.6	41.2	-0.5	4.2	8 175	24.3	17.2
56 033	...	Sheridan County	26 560	5.4	18.8	8.1	25.1	27.1	15.5	40.6	-1.5	3.1	25 139	23.4	15.9
56 035	...	Sublette County	5 920	6.0	19.9	5.8	27.5	28.9	12.0	39.8	0.2	-0.4	5 691	25.2	12.3
56 037	...	Sweetwater County	37 613	7.1	21.5	10.1	29.6	23.7	8.0	34.2	2.9	-4.4	32 586	27.7	8.5
56 039	...	Teton County	18 251	5.1	14.2	10.3	38.0	25.5	6.9	35.0	-6.4	-5.5	16 675	19.3	7.4
56 041	...	Uinta County	19 742	8.3	24.9	8.8	29.6	21.3	7.0	31.4	7.5	-5.4	18 129	32.6	7.3
56 043	...	Washakie County	8 289	5.6	21.5	7.0	25.6	24.5	15.7	39.4	1.4	3.3	7 224	25.4	17.2
56 045	...	Weston County	6 644	5.1	18.9	7.5	26.2	26.7	15.6	40.7	-1.7	3.2	6 298	23.9	16.1

[1]MSA = Metropolitan Statistical Area. PMSA = Primary MSA. NECMA = New England County Metropolitan Area. See the Appendix A for explanation of these concepts. See Appendix B for list of metropolitan areas identified by type, with component counties.

STATE County	Black or African American			American Indian and Alaska Native			Asian, Hawaiian, and Pacific Islander			Hispanic or Latino[1]			Two or more races		
		Age (percent)			Age (percent)			Age (percent)			Age (percent)			Age (percent)	
	Total population	Under 18 years	65 years and over	Total population	Under 18 years	65 years and over	Total population	Under 18 years	65 years and over	Total population	Under 18 years	65 years and over	Total population	Under 18 years	65 years and over
	14	15	16	17	18	19	20	21	22	23	24	25	26	27	28
WYOMING—Cont'd															
Converse County	21	47.6	14.3	143	38.5	1.4	20	35.0	30.0	658	33.9	10.9	132	52.3	4.5
Crook County	2	100.0	0.0	35	37.1	14.3	3	0.0	0.0	52	61.5	5.8	14	50.0	0.0
Fremont County	24	0.0	0.0	6 897	40.9	5.2	138	26.1	5.8	1 486	40.3	4.5	919	43.5	4.5
Goshen County	32	12.5	34.4	123	44.7	0.0	14	57.1	0.0	1 083	32.7	8.4	157	28.7	2.5
Hot Springs County	7	0.0	0.0	57	33.3	8.8	31	32.3	0.0	120	48.3	5.8	69	11.6	11.6
Johnson County	18	61.1	0.0	13	53.8	0.0	1	100.0	0.0	153	54.9	0.0	97	36.1	23.7
Laramie County	1 773	22.0	3.1	868	30.2	7.9	858	23.3	8.7	8 920	33.0	7.0	2 462	50.5	2.8
Lincoln County	4	50.0	0.0	95	30.5	2.1	55	14.5	18.2	325	37.8	5.2	169	45.0	5.3
Natrona County	346	30.6	2.6	852	29.8	5.4	432	31.3	4.4	3 201	37.9	5.1	1 039	41.0	5.0
Niobrara County	0	X	X	9	0.0	22.2	4	50.0	50.0	35	54.3	5.7	21	28.6	0.0
Park County	31	93.5	0.0	109	26.6	7.3	229	24.5	9.2	882	38.3	5.9	199	30.2	8.0
Platte County................	0	X	X	28	10.7	0.0	9	0.0	0.0	480	39.0	8.3	113	41.6	11.5
Sheridan County	30	43.3	6.7	350	38.3	2.6	93	8.6	41.9	673	41.9	5.6	330	40.6	6.7
Sublette County............	11	54.5	0.0	34	23.5	5.9	17	35.3	0.0	141	51.1	5.7	52	61.5	3.8
Sweetwater County	316	39.2	2.5	276	24.6	2.2	228	7.9	7.5	3 606	36.7	4.9	959	40.1	6.3
Teton County................	6	0.0	0.0	89	4.5	0.0	96	6.3	0.0	1 192	22.0	0.6	244	24.2	2.5
Uinta County	24	16.7	0.0	140	25.7	8.6	46	65.2	0.0	1 095	44.7	1.4	344	34.3	9.6
Washakie County	7	100.0	0.0	115	34.8	0.0	10	0.0	50.0	892	39.0	4.3	106	50.9	14.2
Weston County..............	8	0.0	0.0	122	28.7	0.0	23	17.4	30.4	97	21.6	14.4	95	34.7	0.0

[1] Hispanic or Latino persons may be of any race.

STATE County	Total households	Family households (percent)							Nonfamily households (percent)							Percent of householders 65 years and over who live alone	Grandparents who are responsible for the care of their grandchildren
		Married-couple family households			Other family households			Two or more unrelated persons		Male living alone		Female living alone				
		Total	With children	Householder 65 years or over	Total	With children	Householder 65 years or over	Total	Householder 65 years or over	Total	Householder 65 years or over	Total	Householder 65 years or over		
	29	30	31	32	33	34	35	36	37	38	39	40	41	42	43

WYOMING—Cont'd

STATE County	Total households	Total	With children	Householder 65 years or over	Total	With children	Householder 65 years or over	Total	Householder 65 years or over	Total	Householder 65 years or over	Total	Householder 65 years or over	65 yrs alone pct	Grandparents
Converse County	4 709	61.2	28.8	9.6	12.1	9.4	1.1	3.7	0.5	10.7	1.9	12.3	6.1	41.6	54
Crook County	2 306	61.4	25.5	13.8	10.1	7.2	1.2	3.5	0.1	14.4	2.6	10.6	7.0	38.8	35
Fremont County	13 553	54.0	22.7	10.6	16.0	9.9	1.9	4.4	0.5	11.0	2.8	14.5	7.0	43.0	588
Goshen County	5 067	57.1	23.5	14.1	11.2	6.0	1.7	4.2	0.1	10.3	2.4	17.1	10.2	44.3	69
Hot Springs County	2 117	57.2	22.1	12.8	7.7	3.9	1.3	3.5	0.2	13.3	4.2	18.4	10.4	50.3	30
Johnson County	2 972	57.4	21.6	13.5	10.9	7.1	2.1	3.2	0.6	10.6	3.5	17.8	11.1	47.4	39
Laramie County.............	32 032	54.5	24.7	8.5	13.7	9.3	1.3	4.8	0.3	12.5	2.3	14.6	6.8	47.4	546
Lincoln County	5 295	67.2	31.9	11.9	7.9	5.8	0.9	4.0	0.6	11.0	2.3	9.9	5.7	37.4	93
Natrona County	26 801	52.8	23.2	9.3	13.5	9.3	1.1	6.1	0.3	13.3	2.7	14.2	7.2	48.0	428
Niobrara County	1 023	57.6	21.9	15.7	9.9	6.2	1.6	2.9	0.6	11.7	3.3	17.9	11.2	44.9	11
Park County	10 321	59.6	24.1	11.6	9.2	6.6	0.9	5.0	0.2	11.4	2.7	14.7	6.9	43.1	159
Platte County................	3 635	61.4	24.3	13.6	8.5	5.3	1.8	2.7	0.2	13.6	3.6	13.8	7.5	41.6	53
Sheridan County	11 169	53.1	21.5	10.1	10.6	7.0	1.5	5.3	0.5	13.7	3.4	17.3	9.9	52.4	177
Sublette County	2 372	63.4	26.2	10.8	8.1	6.4	0.6	4.8	0.3	14.4	3.0	9.3	3.8	36.5	36
Sweetwater County	14 105	59.3	29.1	6.4	12.9	9.3	0.9	4.2	0.2	13.1	1.6	10.4	5.3	48.1	425
Teton County................	7 698	46.0	20.8	5.9	9.3	5.6	0.6	17.5	0.4	14.6	0.5	12.6	3.2	35.1	13
Uinta County	6 844	62.1	35.3	7.0	13.8	10.1	0.9	3.3	0.1	10.1	1.5	10.7	3.7	39.2	133
Washakie County	3 294	57.6	24.5	11.7	12.6	7.5	0.9	3.1	0.1	11.0	4.4	15.7	9.6	52.5	76
Weston County..............	2 641	62.5	25.9	12.1	9.5	5.9	0.8	3.1	0.5	11.1	2.5	13.9	9.9	48.2	59

STATE County	Households with Non-Hispanic White householder		Households with Black or African American householder		Households with American Indian and Alaska Native householder		Households with Asian, Hawaiian, and Pacific Islander householder		Households with Hispanic or Latino[1] householder		Foreign-born population	Place of birth (percent)			Percent in non-English speaking households	
	Number of households	Percent that are family house-holds	Number of households	Percent that are family house-holds	Number of households	Percent that are family house-holds	Number of households	Percent that are family house-holds	Number of households	Percent that are family house-holds	Percent of total population that is foreign-born	Europe	Asia	Latin America	Linguis-tically isolated	Not linguis-tically isolated
	44	45	46	47	48	49	50	51	52	53	54	55	56	57	58	59
WYOMING—Cont'd																
Converse County	4 360	73.3	8	100.0	42	66.7	9	33.3	249	70.3	1.9	0.1	0.2	1.2	0.9	8.9
Crook County	2 279	71.3	0	X	10	90.0	0	X	10	90.0	0.9	0.6	0.1	0.0	0.1	8.7
Fremont County	11 020	68.6	15	40.0	1 834	80.4	34	79.4	455	60.2	0.8	0.2	0.2	0.3	0.7	15.1
Goshen County	4 644	67.5	17	100.0	42	73.8	0	X	338	79.3	1.9	0.3	0.1	1.3	1.1	11.1
Hot Springs County	2 020	65.1	7	0.0	26	73.1	5	100.0	33	48.5	1.3	0.3	0.6	0.0	0.3	6.7
Johnson County	2 877	68.5	7	0.0	6	0.0	0	X	47	70.2	0.8	0.3	0.0	0.4	0.6	6.2
Laramie County............	27 534	68.3	640	66.3	313	70.0	204	50.0	2 967	68.0	2.9	0.9	0.7	1.0	0.8	13.2
Lincoln County	5 104	75.3	0	X	32	56.3	19	73.7	97	75.3	1.4	0.5	0.1	0.5	0.5	8.4
Natrona County	25 027	66.7	162	68.5	323	56.0	118	72.9	934	60.1	1.8	0.6	0.3	0.6	0.4	9.4
Niobrara County	1 003	67.5	0	X	5	60.0	0	X	5	100.0	0.7	0.5	0.2	0.0	0.2	7.8
Park County	9 904	68.5	2	100.0	37	100.0	39	100.0	273	74.0	1.8	0.4	0.7	0.2	0.7	6.9
Platte County................	3 443	69.5	0	X	14	85.7	4	50.0	147	74.1	1.5	0.2	0.2	1.2	0.7	7.3
Sheridan County	10 771	63.4	0	X	106	90.6	28	53.6	167	83.2	1.6	0.7	0.1	0.2	0.3	9.5
Sublette County............	2 296	71.5	5	100.0	21	42.9	4	100.0	35	94.3	1.6	0.7	0.3	0.3	0.4	6.9
Sweetwater County	12 610	72.4	135	74.8	82	34.1	54	81.5	1 026	70.7	2.7	0.8	0.5	1.2	0.8	12.2
Teton County	7 227	54.2	6	100.0	57	71.9	44	52.3	277	78.7	5.9	1.1	0.3	4.1	2.2	11.4
Uinta County	6 427	75.7	8	0.0	41	24.4	7	0.0	264	85.6	2.5	0.4	0.2	1.8	0.9	8.8
Washakie County	3 005	70.0	0	X	30	70.0	3	100.0	243	72.8	2.4	0.5	0.1	1.7	1.3	10.3
Weston County..............	2 538	71.7	0	X	33	87.9	3	100.0	24	75.0	0.8	0.2	0.3	0.2	0.2	3.2

[1] Hispanic or Latino persons may be of any race.

Table A-4. Metropolitan Areas — Age, Ethnicity, and Household Structure

CMSA/MSA/PMSA/NECMA code[1]	Area name	Population by age (percent)							Median age	+/- U.S. percent under 18 years	+/- U.S. percent 65 years and over	Non-Hispanic White	Age (percent)	
		Total population	Under 5 years	5 to 17 years	18 to 24 years	25 to 44 years	45 to 64 years	65 years and over				Total population	Under 18 years	65 years and over
		1	2	3	4	5	6	7	8	9	10	11	12	13
0040	Abilene, TX..................	126 555	7.1	19.5	13.8	27.9	19.5	12.3	32.2	0.9	-0.1	92 004	22.6	15.3
0120	Albany, GA...............	120 822	7.6	20.6	11.3	29.1	20.7	10.6	32.3	2.5	-1.8	55 934	22.9	14.7
0160	Albany-Schenectady-Troy, NY.............	875 583	6.0	17.8	9.4	29.3	23.2	14.3	37.3	-1.9	1.9	771 001	22.5	15.5
0200	Albuquerque, NM..........	712 738	7.0	19.2	9.8	30.5	22.2	11.3	34.9	0.5	-1.1	340 347	19.6	15.9
0220	Alexandria, LA.................	126 337	7.0	20.3	9.6	28.0	22.1	13.0	35.5	1.6	0.6	83 032	24.0	15.5
0240	Allentown-Bethlehem-Easton, PA.................	637 958	5.8	17.7	8.5	28.9	23.2	16.0	38.6	-2.2	3.6	552 268	21.3	17.9
0280	Altoona, PA................	129 144	5.6	17.0	8.9	27.1	24.0	17.3	39.5	-3.1	4.9	125 645	22.3	17.7
0320	Amarillo, TX.................	217 858	7.6	19.4	11.0	29.8	20.4	11.8	33.4	1.3	-0.6	154 909	23.1	14.8
0380	Anchorage, AK.............	260 283	7.6	21.5	9.5	34.2	21.9	5.3	32.4	3.4	-7.1	181 919	25.4	6.0
0450	Anniston, AL.................	112 249	6.2	17.4	10.5	27.7	24.1	14.1	37.2	-2.1	1.7	87 679	21.8	15.5
0460	Appleton-Oshkosh-Neenah, WI............	358 365	6.5	19.5	9.9	31.4	21.0	11.6	35.0	0.3	-0.8	335 978	25.1	12.2
0480	Asheville, NC.................	225 965	5.6	16.2	8.7	29.3	24.8	15.4	38.9	-3.9	3.0	199 811	20.7	16.3
0500	Athens, GA..................	153 444	5.9	15.5	23.1	28.8	18.2	8.6	28.1	-4.3	-3.8	108 572	17.9	9.9
0520	Atlanta, GA.................	4 112 198	7.5	19.1	9.4	35.7	20.7	7.6	32.9	0.9	-4.8	2 461 950	23.8	9.9
0580	Auburn-Opalika, AL......	115 092	6.2	17.1	22.7	28.1	17.8	8.1	27.5	-2.4	-4.3	84 196	20.6	8.6
0600	Augusta-Aiken, GA-SC .	477 441	6.9	20.1	9.8	30.1	22.0	11.0	34.6	1.3	-1.4	288 114	23.7	13.5
0640	Austin-San Marcos, TX .	1 249 763	7.4	17.9	13.2	35.5	18.7	7.2	30.9	-0.4	-5.2	758 144	21.3	9.3
0680	Bakersfield, CA	661 645	8.3	23.5	10.2	30.0	18.6	9.4	30.6	6.1	-3.0	326 523	25.0	14.4
0733	Bangor, ME..................	144 919	5.3	17.5	11.3	28.9	23.9	13.1	37.2	-2.9	0.7	139 562	22.5	13.4
0743	Barnstable-Yarmouth, MA..........................	222 230	4.8	15.7	5.3	25.0	26.1	23.1	44.6	-5.2	10.7	207 587	19.7	24.1
0760	Baton Rouge, LA...........	602 894	7.2	20.0	12.8	29.8	20.8	9.4	31.9	1.5	-3.0	385 331	24.0	11.1
0840	Beaumont-Port Arthur, TX..........................	385 090	6.7	19.7	9.7	29.1	21.6	13.2	35.6	0.7	0.8	246 290	23.2	16.2
0860	Bellingham, WA............	166 814	6.2	17.8	14.3	27.5	22.5	11.6	34.0	-1.7	-0.8	144 069	22.4	12.9
0870	Benton Harbor, MI........	162 453	6.5	19.4	8.4	27.5	23.6	14.5	37.4	0.2	2.1	127 017	22.8	16.6
0880	Billings, MT.................	129 352	6.5	19.1	9.3	28.8	23.0	13.3	36.9	-0.1	0.9	117 762	24.1	14.2
0920	Biloxi-Gulfport-Pascagoula, MS........	363 988	7.1	19.4	10.1	30.0	22.2	11.2	34.7	0.8	-1.2	271 959	24.2	12.9
0960	Binghamton, NY............	252 320	5.8	18.0	10.1	27.3	23.0	15.8	38.1	-1.9	3.4	231 451	23.1	16.8
1000	Birmingham, AL............	921 106	6.7	18.4	9.2	30.5	22.6	12.7	35.9	-0.6	0.3	612 165	22.6	14.4
1010	Bismarck, ND...............	94 719	6.3	19.1	10.0	29.0	22.5	13.1	36.3	-0.3	0.7	90 051	24.5	13.6
1020	Bloomington, IN............	120 563	5.0	12.9	27.8	27.2	17.9	9.1	27.6	-7.8	-3.3	108 470	17.6	9.9
1040	Bloomington-Normal, IL	150 433	6.4	17.0	18.6	29.2	19.0	9.8	30.5	-2.3	-2.6	132 511	22.2	10.7
1080	Boise City, ID	432 345	8.1	20.2	10.3	31.4	20.3	9.7	32.1	2.6	-2.7	374 503	26.8	10.7
1123	Boston-Worcester-Lawrence-Lowell-Brockton, MA-NH	6 057 826	6.4	17.6	8.9	32.3	22.2	12.7	36.2	-1.7	0.3	5 022 568	22.4	14.2
1240	Brownsville-Harlingen-San Benito, TX...........	335 227	9.4	24.3	10.5	27.2	17.4	11.2	29.0	8.0	-1.2	48 551	16.9	32.4
1260	Bryan-College Station, TX..........................	152 415	6.3	15.1	32.2	25.9	13.8	6.7	23.6	-4.3	-5.7	100 764	16.5	8.1
1280	Buffalo-Niagara Falls, NY..........................	1 170 111	6.0	18.3	8.6	28.5	22.7	15.9	38.0	-1.4	3.5	965 907	22.2	17.5
1303	Burlington, VT..............	198 889	6.1	18.5	11.6	31.8	22.2	9.8	34.8	-1.1	-2.6	188 622	24.1	10.2
1320	Canton-Massillon, OH ...	406 934	6.3	18.5	8.2	27.8	24.1	15.1	38.3	-0.9	2.7	367 673	23.6	15.7
1350	Casper, WY..................	66 533	6.4	19.5	10.0	28.0	23.6	12.6	36.4	0.2	0.2	61 005	25.1	13.3
1360	Cedar Rapids, IA..........	191 701	6.9	18.3	10.2	30.1	22.2	12.2	35.2	-0.5	-0.2	178 584	24.2	12.9
1400	Champaign-Urbana, IL..	179 669	5.8	15.3	23.0	28.3	17.8	9.8	28.6	-4.6	-2.6	139 527	19.6	11.5
1480	Charleston, WV............	251 662	5.9	16.2	8.3	28.6	25.7	15.5	39.6	-3.6	3.1	230 276	21.2	16.1
1440	Charleston-North Charleston, SC...........	549 033	6.7	19.0	11.1	31.0	21.9	10.3	33.9	0.0	-2.1	352 130	22.2	11.5
1520	Charlotte-Gastonia-Rock Hill, NC-SC	1 499 293	7.1	18.3	9.0	33.8	21.6	10.2	34.3	-0.3	-2.2	1 068 444	23.1	12.1
1540	Charlottesville, VA.........	159 576	5.8	16.3	14.6	29.9	21.7	11.7	34.3	-3.6	-0.7	126 736	20.9	12.8
1560	Chattanooga, TN-GA ...	465 161	6.1	17.6	9.3	29.3	24.2	13.5	37.2	-2.0	1.1	381 830	22.2	14.4
1580	Cheyenne, WY..............	81 607	6.5	18.9	9.7	30.6	23.0	11.4	35.3	-0.3	-1.0	67 807	23.9	12.5
14	Chicago-Gary-Kenosha, IL-IN-WI	9 157 540	7.4	19.5	9.4	31.8	21.1	10.9	33.9	1.2	-1.5	5 433 528	22.6	14.1
1600	Chicago, IL	8 272 768	7.4	19.4	9.4	32.1	20.9	10.7	33.7	1.1	-1.7	4 796 451	22.5	14.1
2960	Gary, IN......................	631 362	7.0	19.5	9.4	28.5	23.1	12.5	36.0	0.8	0.1	428 566	23.4	14.2
3740	Kankakee, IL	103 833	6.9	20.1	9.5	28.6	21.7	13.1	35.2	1.3	0.7	80 835	24.0	15.0
3800	Kenosha, WI................	149 577	6.8	20.1	9.5	31.3	20.7	11.5	34.8	1.2	-0.9	127 676	24.8	12.9
1620	Chico-Paradise, CA......	203 171	5.7	18.2	13.7	25.0	21.6	15.7	35.8	-1.8	3.3	162 142	20.6	18.4
21	Cincinnati-Hamilton, OH-KY-IN	1 979 202	7.0	19.4	9.5	30.7	21.7	11.7	35.0	0.7	-0.7	1 676 081	25.3	12.4
1640	Cincinnati, OH-KY-IN .	1 646 395	7.1	19.5	9.0	30.9	21.7	11.9	35.1	0.9	-0.5	1 375 452	25.3	12.7
3200	Hamilton-Middletown, OH........................	332 807	6.9	19.0	11.8	30.0	21.6	10.7	34.2	0.2	-1.7	300 629	25.1	11.2
1660	Clarksville-Hopkinsville, TN-KY....................	207 033	8.9	19.4	13.7	33.1	16.6	8.4	29.3	2.6	-4.0	145 132	25.6	10.0
28	Cleveland-Akron, OH ...	2 945 831	6.6	18.7	8.2	29.4	22.9	14.3	37.2	-0.4	1.9	2 291 580	23.0	15.7
0080	Akron, OH	694 960	6.5	18.3	9.5	29.5	22.8	13.4	36.6	-0.9	1.0	593 575	23.2	14.4
1680	Cleveland-Lorain-Elyria, OH..................	2 250 871	6.6	18.8	7.8	29.4	22.9	14.5	37.3	-0.3	2.1	1 698 011	22.9	16.2
1720	Colorado Springs, CO...	516 929	7.5	19.9	10.5	32.6	20.7	8.6	33.0	1.7	-3.8	393 713	25.2	10.0
1740	Columbia, MO	135 454	6.1	16.6	19.7	30.2	18.7	8.6	29.5	-3.0	-3.8	114 740	21.1	9.5

[1]MSA = Metropolitan Statistical Area. CMSA = Consolidated Metropolitan Area. PMSA = Primary MSA. NECMA = New England County Metropolitan Area. See the Appendix A for explanation of these concepts. See Appendix B for list of metropolitan areas identified by type, with component counties.

Table A-4. Metropolitan Areas — **Age, Ethnicity, and Household Structure**

Area name	Black or African American Total population	Under 18 years	65 years and over	American Indian and Alaska Native Total population	Under 18 years	65 years and over	Asian, Hawaiian, and Pacific Islander Total population	Under 18 years	65 years and over	Hispanic or Latino[1] Total population	Under 18 years	65 years and over	Two or more races Total population	Under 18 years	65 years and over
	Age (percent)			Age (percent)			Age (percent)			Age (percent)			Age (percent)		
	14	15	16	17	18	19	20	21	22	23	24	25	26	27	28
Abilene, TX..................	8 284	32.7	7.0	818	30.1	2.9	1 752	26.2	3.7	22 200	38.9	3.7	3 462	51.5	2.6
Albany, GA..................	61 663	32.8	7.3	220	28.6	0.0	842	22.1	3.6	1 597	32.5	3.8	890	48.2	5.1
Albany-Schenectady-Troy, NY	51 947	33.5	6.5	2 120	29.3	5.4	15 963	24.7	3.7	23 677	37.5	3.3	14 173	44.1	5.1
Albuquerque, NM	17 438	29.2	7.9	39 839	33.1	5.0	11 542	23.6	7.7	296 316	32.6	7.2	31 887	42.0	5.8
Alexandria, LA..............	38 768	33.8	8.6	698	20.8	7.7	1 162	30.9	5.1	1 338	25.7	6.2	1 440	37.0	8.8
Allentown-Bethlehem-Easton, PA	18 061	36.6	4.4	1 114	33.7	3.7	10 939	27.9	2.9	50 403	39.7	3.5	10 279	42.7	5.1
Altoona, PA..................	1 281	26.9	5.4	262	43.5	5.7	581	29.8	2.8	465	31.8	7.5	947	51.8	7.7
Amarillo, TX..................	12 169	30.6	7.0	1 557	25.5	10.0	4 182	26.4	5.3	42 720	39.4	3.1	5 057	47.3	5.2
Anchorage, AK	15 201	34.8	3.3	18 800	34.1	4.5	16 293	30.4	6.0	14 738	39.7	2.2	16 465	53.1	1.7
Anniston, AL	20 458	30.1	9.8	437	16.9	1.1	692	21.8	8.5	1 912	33.1	4.3	1 138	30.5	9.7
Appleton-Oshkosh-Neenah, WI	2 733	22.5	0.6	3 275	34.6	5.1	6 871	48.1	3.4	6 845	39.8	2.0	3 483	53.1	4.9
Asheville, NC	15 239	29.4	12.0	838	27.2	5.3	2 051	23.6	4.2	5 706	31.8	2.7	2 616	38.1	6.5
Athens, GA..................	31 700	30.3	7.0	413	27.4	6.1	3 919	22.1	1.1	7 619	31.4	1.8	1 732	36.5	1.0
Atlanta, GA..................	1 184 059	31.4	4.8	11 804	24.1	3.6	134 849	25.2	3.6	266 050	28.9	1.9	75 585	36.6	3.2
Auburn-Opalika, AL.......	25 753	30.7	7.7	305	37.7	0.0	1 875	19.4	4.3	1 944	28.9	3.3	1 265	44.5	1.5
Augusta-Aiken, GA-SC .	163 184	31.8	7.8	1 711	26.1	6.0	7 297	23.9	5.5	11 536	33.0	3.8	7 534	47.8	3.4
Austin-San Marcos, TX .	97 563	29.9	6.7	6 715	26.1	3.7	44 673	20.8	2.3	327 775	33.3	3.3	34 805	39.9	2.8
Bakersfield, CA	38 804	33.5	5.9	9 014	31.7	6.0	22 340	28.7	9.1	254 059	40.5	3.7	29 500	44.7	4.9
Bangor, ME..................	676	24.0	4.9	1 355	29.0	5.0	1 066	29.5	6.0	830	35.9	4.1	1 391	35.9	7.5
Barnstable-Yarmouth, MA..................	3 397	22.7	11.0	1 448	35.6	12.4	1 395	27.4	7.9	2 916	35.9	5.8	4 045	35.6	9.0
Baton Rouge, LA..........	190 403	33.5	6.7	1 863	29.4	3.3	9 502	24.9	2.5	10 812	28.3	5.0	5 965	35.9	6.9
Beaumont-Port Arthur, TX..................	95 637	31.7	9.4	1 521	16.5	8.0	8 144	33.5	4.3	30 818	33.5	4.7	5 120	37.6	6.9
Bellingham, WA............	1 014	23.6	1.9	4 699	36.4	5.8	4 535	21.1	4.7	8 316	38.6	2.0	5 054	42.6	2.6
Benton Harbor, MI........	25 946	37.3	8.0	786	28.8	5.9	1 732	28.1	3.1	4 569	35.0	4.6	2 725	46.7	7.0
Billings, MT..................	486	32.7	5.8	4 059	40.3	1.1	751	32.9	8.8	4 812	41.7	4.5	2 444	50.2	5.6
Biloxi-Gulfport-Pascagoula, MS	69 716	33.5	6.4	2 180	23.7	6.2	7 322	28.2	5.0	8 072	31.9	4.4	6 165	41.5	5.3
Binghamton, NY	7 019	33.8	5.9	555	21.8	9.5	5 735	20.2	3.4	4 551	35.8	4.3	3 651	45.1	4.5
Birmingham, AL	275 939	29.9	9.9	2 551	23.8	5.6	7 190	23.4	4.1	16 421	32.7	2.6	8 263	34.4	5.0
Bismarck, ND	269	27.9	11.5	2 666	43.7	2.0	326	32.8	7.4	687	38.9	7.3	833	49.7	4.0
Bloomington, IN............	3 611	23.0	2.2	274	17.5	5.5	3 954	9.6	1.2	2 034	15.4	1.2	2 220	38.9	2.9
Bloomington-Normal, IL	9 055	31.9	2.9	291	12.0	2.4	3 261	18.2	4.4	3 597	34.7	2.1	2 316	57.3	1.5
Boise City, ID	2 172	35.1	5.1	3 199	28.9	4.1	6 393	23.4	5.2	38 001	40.8	1.9	10 815	44.9	3.9
Boston-Worcester-Lawrence-Brockton, MA-NH	296 940	31.2	6.7	13 388	20.9	5.0	207 025	24.9	5.2	362 880	35.2	3.0	141 600	36.0	5.2
Brownsville-Harlingen-San Benito, TX	1 539	37.5	4.5	1 442	32.9	10.3	1 553	27.5	6.0	283 156	36.7	7.6	7 683	36.1	8.5
Bryan-College Station, TX..................	16 238	35.6	6.9	523	17.8	4.0	6 354	17.3	1.5	27 225	32.1	2.8	2 842	32.5	2.7
Buffalo-Niagara Falls, NY..................	136 362	32.9	9.7	8 085	32.0	6.9	14 368	22.6	4.7	33 639	38.8	5.0	16 496	49.0	4.6
Burlington, VT	1 534	40.0	2.9	1 217	25.0	1.6	2 922	30.2	2.1	1 892	29.0	4.2	2 923	40.2	4.1
Canton-Massillon, OH ...	27 244	34.8	9.8	833	25.6	2.5	1 914	20.0	6.4	3 557	36.1	8.1	5 841	47.5	6.1
Casper, WY	346	30.6	2.6	852	29.8	5.4	432	31.3	4.4	3 201	37.9	5.1	1 039	41.0	5.0
Cedar Rapids, IA..........	4 506	34.9	5.9	430	22.3	0.0	2 740	28.4	2.6	2 852	34.6	4.0	2 903	62.6	2.5
Champaign-Urbana, IL..	20 064	32.9	6.3	390	31.8	7.4	11 631	12.5	1.8	4 933	19.3	2.0	3 470	39.9	1.5
Charleston, WV	13 709	28.0	10.6	532	28.6	2.6	2 012	29.3	5.4	1 539	35.7	4.3	3 603	42.9	7.7
Charleston-North Charleston, SC	167 289	32.4	9.0	2 365	20.9	5.8	7 902	19.6	6.6	13 333	31.2	2.3	8 098	42.1	4.1
Charlotte-Gastonia-Rock Hill, NC-SC	307 102	31.0	6.7	7 392	29.5	3.6	26 722	27.8	3.6	76 277	28.6	1.6	19 897	41.5	3.1
Charlottesville, VA........	22 264	27.1	9.3	288	7.6	10.1	4 781	17.7	2.3	3 728	30.9	2.6	1 981	38.4	4.4
Chattanooga, TN-GA	66 172	30.9	9.7	1 415	24.3	3.9	4 787	24.3	4.7	6 750	28.9	5.0	4 881	34.7	12.0
Cheyenne, WY	1 773	22.0	3.1	868	30.2	7.9	858	23.3	8.7	8 920	33.0	7.0	2 462	50.5	2.8
Chicago-Gary-Kenosha, IL-IN-WI	1 698 040	32.2	8.8	23 075	30.1	4.0	392 394	23.6	6.3	1 497 832	36.0	3.2	213 220	39.8	4.9
Chicago, IL	1 551 203	32.2	8.7	20 621	30.5	3.8	384 955	23.5	6.3	1 416 605	35.9	3.1	196 636	39.3	4.9
Gary, IN..................	123 876	31.7	10.4	1 528	25.7	6.0	5 266	26.2	4.5	65 851	35.9	6.4	12 200	43.3	6.3
Kankakee, IL	15 792	36.8	7.8	311	23.2	6.1	749	32.0	7.7	4 949	39.9	1.8	1 551	53.8	2.9
Kenosha, WI..............	7 170	37.9	4.7	615	31.4	5.4	1 424	24.9	6.5	10 427	39.5	3.1	3 013	53.8	1.3
Chico-Paradise, CA	2 535	32.5	8.2	3 803	33.9	5.6	6 823	39.6	4.9	21 377	37.4	4.3	8 587	42.0	5.5
Cincinnati-Hamilton, OH-KY-IN	231 027	32.6	8.9	4 302	26.8	3.8	24 300	24.9	4.5	20 819	32.7	3.6	22 982	44.0	4.8
Cincinnati, OH-KY-IN .	213 103	32.6	8.9	3 464	26.0	4.3	19 161	23.7	4.7	16 507	33.2	3.8	18 886	43.3	5.2
Hamilton-Middletown, OH..................	17 924	32.1	8.1	838	29.7	1.9	5 139	29.1	4.0	4 312	30.7	2.7	4 096	47.4	2.6
Clarksville-Hopkinsville, TN-KY..................	42 351	33.6	6.0	926	23.7	3.0	3 543	20.9	3.9	10 449	35.7	1.5	6 244	53.3	1.1
Cleveland-Akron, OH	488 817	32.1	10.6	5 345	26.5	5.5	41 012	23.3	6.3	80 167	38.0	4.5	47 221	46.6	5.6
Akron, OH	75 808	33.1	9.1	1 423	23.0	4.1	9 043	26.3	4.8	5 519	32.5	4.7	9 874	47.8	4.5
Cleveland-Lorain-Elyria, OH..............	413 009	31.9	10.8	3 922	27.8	6.0	31 969	22.4	6.7	74 648	38.5	4.5	37 347	46.3	5.9
Colorado Springs, CO ...	31 940	31.9	4.3	4 812	31.6	3.6	14 445	22.4	6.9	58 419	36.4	3.8	21 841	50.0	2.7
Columbia, MO	11 351	33.2	5.0	663	18.3	3.6	3 899	20.8	1.5	2 511	34.1	2.4	2 487	45.2	3.3

[1] Hispanic or Latino persons may be of any race.

Table A-4. Metropolitan Areas — Age, Ethnicity, and Household Structure

Area name	Total households	Married-couple family households			Other family households			Two or more unrelated persons		Male living alone		Female living alone		Percent of householders 65 years and over who live alone	Grandparents who are responsible for the care of their grandchildren
		Total	With children	Householder 65 years or over	Total	With children	Householder 65 years or over	Total	Householder 65 years or over	Total	Householder 65 years or over	Total	Householder 65 years or over		
	29	30	31	32	33	34	35	36	37	38	39	40	41	42	43
Abilene, TX...............	47 269	54.8	25.8	9.6	14.4	9.4	1.6	5.2	0.3	10.6	2.1	15.0	7.9	46.8	1 649
Albany, GA.................	43 827	46.4	21.3	7.5	25.0	14.7	3.1	4.2	0.3	9.9	1.8	14.5	6.5	43.1	2 005
Albany-Schenectady-Troy, NY..................	350 472	49.4	22.0	9.4	14.6	8.8	2.2	6.7	0.4	12.2	2.7	17.1	8.3	48.0	3 962
Albuquerque, NM.........	275 065	48.8	22.9	8.3	17.7	10.7	2.2	6.7	0.4	12.2	2.1	14.5	5.8	42.0	7 816
Alexandria, LA............	47 161	50.2	23.4	9.1	20.5	11.9	2.9	3.4	0.4	10.0	2.5	15.9	7.8	45.4	1 969
Allentown-Bethlehem-Easton, PA..............	247 307	55.2	23.6	11.2	13.6	7.4	2.4	5.2	0.4	10.6	2.7	15.4	8.9	45.5	3 687
Altoona, PA..................	51 622	53.4	21.6	11.5	14.9	8.2	2.8	3.9	0.3	10.4	2.8	17.3	10.4	47.5	1 042
Amarillo, TX.................	81 998	53.7	25.4	9.2	15.2	9.5	1.8	4.6	0.3	11.2	2.1	15.3	7.3	45.3	2 418
Anchorage, AK.............	95 080	52.2	28.6	4.0	16.0	11.2	0.9	8.5	0.4	12.3	1.1	11.0	2.6	41.5	1 719
Anniston, AL................	45 380	52.9	21.3	9.8	16.4	8.8	2.9	3.9	0.3	10.5	2.0	16.4	8.6	44.9	1 723
Appleton-Oshkosh-Neenah, WI..............	136 710	57.9	27.7	9.1	10.5	6.8	1.2	6.4	0.2	10.9	1.9	14.3	7.1	46.1	1 017
Asheville, NC..............	93 739	51.8	20.4	10.5	13.9	7.8	2.3	5.7	0.3	11.2	2.3	17.5	8.5	45.2	1 785
Athens, GA.................	58 541	43.4	19.9	6.1	15.5	8.7	1.6	14.9	0.2	11.5	1.6	14.6	5.0	45.3	1 418
Atlanta, GA.................	1 505 564	52.4	26.7	5.6	17.3	9.7	1.7	7.0	0.2	10.1	1.1	13.2	4.0	40.6	36 993
Auburn-Opalika, AL......	45 751	45.1	21.9	5.8	15.3	8.7	1.9	12.0	0.2	13.7	1.2	14.0	4.5	41.9	1 088
Augusta-Aiken, GA-SC.	176 872	51.6	24.3	8.0	20.2	11.9	2.5	3.9	0.4	10.2	2.0	14.0	6.2	43.1	6 494
Austin-San Marcos, TX.	472 085	49.3	25.4	5.5	14.0	8.0	1.2	10.2	0.2	13.1	1.1	13.4	3.7	41.2	9 659
Bakersfield, CA............	208 786	56.1	30.4	8.4	19.4	12.6	2.2	4.2	0.5	8.9	2.1	11.3	5.6	41.1	8 273
Bangor, ME.................	58 135	52.7	22.0	9.0	13.0	8.5	1.6	7.7	0.6	10.8	2.4	15.8	7.7	47.4	632
Barnstable-Yarmouth, MA.........	94 845	52.7	18.6	16.9	11.9	6.4	2.1	5.9	0.8	10.6	3.5	18.9	11.2	42.7	814
Baton Rouge, LA.........	223 620	50.2	24.5	7.0	19.5	11.5	2.5	6.0	0.2	10.8	1.7	13.6	5.3	42.1	7 632
Beaumont-Port Arthur, TX..........	142 530	53.2	24.1	10.0	18.4	10.7	3.0	3.2	0.2	10.8	2.8	14.3	7.9	44.7	5 135
Bellingham, WA............	64 464	52.1	23.0	9.5	12.0	7.6	1.1	10.3	0.5	11.9	2.0	13.7	6.5	43.3	769
Benton Harbor, MI........	63 644	52.1	21.7	10.7	16.4	10.1	2.2	4.5	0.5	11.3	2.6	15.7	8.4	45.2	1 470
Billings, MT.................	52 113	52.5	22.8	9.5	13.7	9.1	1.5	5.9	0.4	11.6	2.6	16.4	8.3	48.7	629
Biloxi-Gulfport-Pascagoula, MS.......	136 263	52.8	24.0	8.6	18.2	11.0	2.4	5.1	0.4	11.4	2.3	12.5	6.1	42.4	5 345
Binghamton, NY...........	100 696	50.5	21.6	10.8	14.1	8.5	2.1	6.2	0.5	12.2	3.0	17.1	9.1	47.4	1 615
Birmingham, AL............	361 107	51.6	23.3	8.7	18.0	9.4	3.1	3.7	0.3	10.7	2.0	16.0	7.2	43.2	11 062
Bismarck, ND..............	37 620	56.2	26.4	10.2	11.0	6.9	1.0	5.4	0.3	11.0	1.8	16.4	7.8	45.8	280
Bloomington, IN............	46 939	42.4	17.8	6.6	10.7	6.9	1.0	14.6	0.3	14.3	1.8	18.0	5.8	49.1	544
Bloomington-Normal, IL	56 792	51.3	24.5	7.4	11.5	7.4	1.0	9.6	0.2	11.7	1.6	15.9	6.5	48.6	606
Boise City, ID..............	158 642	57.8	29.3	7.9	13.1	8.7	1.1	6.6	0.3	9.8	1.5	12.7	5.9	44.3	2 359
Boston-Worcester-Lawrence-Lowell-Brockton, MA-NH.......	2 314 409	51.1	24.4	8.4	14.5	7.7	2.3	7.2	0.3	11.1	2.4	16.1	7.5	47.4	26 222
Brownsville-Harlingen-San Benito, TX...........	97 193	61.9	35.0	11.8	20.6	11.2	3.7	2.1	0.3	6.1	2.2	9.2	5.7	33.4	4 530
Bryan-College Station, TX..........	55 188	43.0	21.8	5.5	12.7	7.0	1.2	18.8	0.1	12.4	0.9	13.1	4.1	42.7	1 278
Buffalo-Niagara Falls, NY.............	468 767	48.2	21.0	10.3	16.5	9.4	2.6	5.2	0.4	12.1	3.1	18.1	9.7	49.0	6 265
Burlington, VT..............	76 043	53.5	26.0	7.0	11.8	7.9	1.3	10.0	0.4	10.7	1.8	14.1	5.8	46.9	583
Canton-Massillon, OH...	159 484	55.3	23.3	10.9	14.5	8.2	2.3	4.4	0.3	10.4	2.5	15.5	8.4	44.6	2 998
Casper, WY.................	26 801	52.8	23.2	9.3	13.5	9.3	1.1	6.1	0.3	13.3	2.7	14.2	7.2	48.0	428
Cedar Rapids, IA..........	76 806	54.3	25.0	9.0	11.6	7.5	1.4	6.6	0.2	11.8	2.2	15.7	7.2	47.0	765
Champaign-Urbana, IL..	70 619	44.6	20.2	7.5	11.7	7.6	1.1	12.3	0.2	14.3	1.6	17.1	6.3	47.4	951
Charleston, WV............	106 218	52.2	20.8	10.0	14.9	7.6	2.9	4.0	0.3	11.3	2.7	17.6	9.2	47.2	2 095
Charleston-North Charleston, SC..........	207 816	50.0	23.0	7.5	18.4	10.7	2.5	6.8	0.2	10.8	1.9	14.1	5.6	42.1	6 603
Charlotte-Gastonia-Rock Hill, NC-SC.......	575 510	54.0	25.1	7.3	15.6	8.8	1.9	5.9	0.2	10.6	1.6	13.9	5.5	43.1	14 720
Charlottesville, VA........	61 724	49.8	22.0	8.8	13.3	8.1	1.8	9.5	0.4	11.0	1.9	16.3	5.8	41.2	953
Chattanooga, TN-GA....	185 305	54.2	22.4	9.5	15.8	8.5	2.5	3.9	0.2	10.2	2.2	15.8	7.9	45.2	5 395
Cheyenne, WY.............	32 032	54.5	24.7	8.5	13.7	9.3	1.3	4.8	0.3	12.5	2.3	14.6	6.8	47.4	546
Chicago-Gary-Kenosha, IL-IN-WI	3 302 985	51.4	25.9	7.7	17.1	8.7	2.6	5.3	0.3	11.2	2.1	15.0	6.5	44.8	81 927
Chicago, IL..................	2 972 373	51.2	26.1	7.5	17.1	8.6	2.6	5.4	0.3	11.3	2.1	15.1	6.4	44.9	73 245
Gary, IN.....................	236 310	52.4	23.7	9.2	18.6	10.1	3.0	4.2	0.4	10.9	2.4	14.0	7.0	42.9	6 712
Kankakee, IL	38 209	54.3	25.0	9.9	16.4	9.9	2.3	4.5	0.4	10.1	2.1	14.8	8.2	45.0	1 026
Kenosha, WI...............	56 093	53.9	26.1	8.4	15.1	9.3	1.9	5.6	0.4	11.2	2.3	14.2	6.9	46.3	944
Chico-Paradise, CA......	79 674	47.8	19.7	11.9	14.7	9.4	1.9	10.4	0.8	10.8	2.6	16.4	8.6	43.5	1 329
Cincinnati-Hamilton, OH-KY-IN	768 454	52.3	24.9	8.1	15.3	9.3	2.0	5.1	0.3	11.6	2.1	15.6	7.0	46.5	15 473
Cincinnati, OH-KY-IN.	645 329	51.2	24.4	8.1	15.6	9.5	2.1	5.0	0.3	12.0	2.1	16.2	7.2	47.3	12 727
Hamilton-Middletown, OH	123 125	58.1	27.9	8.5	13.9	8.5	1.8	5.5	0.2	9.9	1.8	12.7	5.8	42.0	2 746
Clarksville-Hopkinsville, TN-KY..............	73 252	59.2	31.2	6.7	15.4	10.3	1.7	4.5	0.2	9.5	1.5	11.4	5.3	44.0	1 467
Cleveland-Akron, OH....	1 167 104	49.7	21.7	9.6	16.8	9.3	2.7	4.9	0.4	11.8	2.6	16.9	8.1	45.9	22 362
Akron, OH..................	274 280	52.0	22.7	9.6	15.3	8.8	2.3	5.8	0.3	11.4	2.3	15.6	7.4	44.3	4 583
Cleveland-Lorain-Elyria, OH..............	892 824	48.9	21.4	9.6	17.2	9.5	2.8	4.6	0.4	12.0	2.7	17.2	8.3	46.3	17 779
Colorado Springs, CO...	192 599	56.6	28.5	7.0	13.5	8.9	1.3	6.1	0.3	11.1	1.5	12.7	4.8	42.6	3 489
Columbia, MO...............	53 106	46.4	22.3	6.3	13.2	8.7	1.0	11.7	0.2	13.1	1.4	15.6	4.8	45.5	584

Table A-4. Metropolitan Areas — Age, Ethnicity, and Household Structure

Area name	Households with Non-Hispanic White householder		Households with Black or African American householder		Households with American Indian and Alaska Native householder		Households with Asian, Hawaiian, and Pacific Islander householder		Households with Hispanic or Latino[1] householder		Foreign-born population				Percent in non-English speaking households	
												Place of birth (percent)				
	Number of households	Percent that are family households	Number of households	Percent that are family households	Number of households	Percent that are family households	Number of households	Percent that are family households	Number of households	Percent that are family households	Percent of total population that is foreign-born	Europe	Asia	Latin America	Linguistically isolated	Not linguistically isolated
	44	45	46	47	48	49	50	51	52	53	54	55	56	57	58	59
Abilene, TX..................	36 776	67.6	3 005	68.5	284	79.2	544	60.5	6 313	79.8	4.0	0.6	1.1	2.0	1.8	20.4
Albany, GA.................	22 783	71.7	20 120	71.1	79	54.4	232	69.8	479	73.5	1.7	0.2	0.7	0.6	0.3	8.4
Albany-Schenectady-Troy, NY	315 224	64.1	19 308	60.7	804	59.6	4 937	67.7	7 059	65.0	4.7	1.9	1.5	0.8	1.2	12.0
Albuquerque, NM	154 295	62.0	7 131	61.3	11 586	73.8	3 721	69.3	95 656	73.7	7.9	1.0	1.2	5.3	4.8	37.0
Alexandria, LA	33 111	69.7	12 728	73.7	256	68.0	297	81.8	362	65.7	1.6	0.3	0.7	0.4	0.7	8.7
Allentown-Bethlehem-Easton, PA	221 816	68.1	5 935	70.5	390	63.6	3 244	77.2	14 360	78.3	5.1	1.6	1.8	1.4	2.5	15.2
Altoona, PA	50 557	68.4	464	52.6	100	89.0	161	87.6	157	71.3	1.0	0.4	0.3	0.1	0.3	5.5
Amarillo, TX.................	64 028	66.7	3 565	68.1	633	65.7	1 302	78.7	11 700	81.0	6.2	0.5	1.5	4.0	3.5	19.5
Anchorage, AK	72 584	67.6	5 388	70.7	5 602	65.3	4 647	76.0	3 889	74.9	8.2	1.6	4.0	1.7	2.7	18.0
Anniston, AL	36 218	70.0	7 731	66.6	213	56.8	228	52.2	597	68.5	1.7	0.4	0.5	0.7	0.5	5.9
Appleton-Oshkosh-Neenah, WI	131 312	68.2	512	67.0	1 106	77.8	1 427	79.0	1 693	75.3	2.9	0.6	1.3	0.7	1.1	8.7
Asheville, NC..............	84 788	65.7	5 812	61.6	268	69.4	584	75.0	1 479	77.1	3.7	1.2	0.7	1.5	1.6	7.4
Athens, GA.................	43 583	56.0	11 375	67.9	157	74.5	1 279	61.3	1 844	76.2	6.6	0.7	1.9	3.3	3.2	10.7
Atlanta, GA.................	967 972	69.1	413 736	68.7	3 976	72.8	39 808	78.9	63 694	80.2	10.3	1.3	2.8	5.0	4.4	14.0
Auburn-Opalika, AL	34 307	58.6	9 690	67.3	88	42.0	683	63.5	718	54.6	2.7	0.6	1.3	0.5	0.7	8.1
Augusta-Aiken, GA-SC .	114 207	70.7	55 526	73.7	635	68.7	2 051	81.4	3 114	78.1	3.1	0.9	1.1	0.9	0.8	9.6
Austin-San Marcos, TX.	321 819	60.2	35 100	66.0	2 459	62.6	15 559	60.1	91 801	74.4	12.2	1.0	2.9	7.8	6.5	27.3
Bakersfield, CA	126 726	70.0	10 874	72.4	2 895	78.0	6 121	81.9	58 597	87.9	16.9	0.6	2.4	13.6	9.9	31.7
Bangor, ME	56 411	65.8	209	52.2	540	62.8	272	74.3	214	57.0	2.5	0.7	0.6	0.1	0.5	8.1
Barnstable-Yarmouth, MA	90 080	64.5	1 190	62.5	486	73.5	431	71.7	780	62.7	4.9	2.3	0.6	1.3	1.1	10.5
Baton Rouge, LA..........	151 623	68.5	63 391	72.6	590	76.6	2 988	66.7	3 392	70.8	2.9	0.5	1.3	0.8	1.0	10.4
Beaumont-Port Arthur, TX	98 670	70.8	32 759	71.2	595	77.3	2 157	82.3	7 358	82.3	4.7	0.4	1.4	2.8	2.5	12.8
Bellingham, WA............	57 940	63.8	477	54.7	1 325	79.7	1 293	63.1	2 338	69.2	9.8	2.6	2.2	1.5	2.2	12.0
Benton Harbor, MI........	52 414	67.8	8 891	71.2	301	62.1	504	77.4	954	74.3	4.9	1.3	0.9	1.6	1.1	9.9
Billings, MT.................	48 568	65.9	185	51.9	1 200	83.3	181	62.4	1 555	68.0	1.4	0.5	0.4	0.2	0.4	9.4
Biloxi-Gulfport-Pascagoula, MS	106 415	71.0	23 672	72.0	734	68.1	1 873	75.0	2 338	65.1	3.0	0.7	1.4	0.6	1.0	9.2
Binghamton, NY...........	94 200	64.0	2 406	61.0	194	57.2	1 556	58.7	1 387	62.4	4.5	1.8	1.8	0.5	1.3	10.5
Birmingham, AL...........	249 580	69.6	101 536	69.3	1 017	75.5	2 472	67.3	4 425	78.0	2.3	0.4	0.7	1.0	0.9	6.9
Bismarck, ND..............	36 489	67.0	69	63.8	662	78.5	119	78.2	147	51.0	1.3	0.5	0.3	0.2	1.0	11.3
Bloomington, IN............	42 472	54.5	1 304	43.3	130	88.5	1 631	33.4	757	40.2	5.4	1.4	3.0	0.5	1.3	9.8
Bloomington-Normal, IL	51 105	62.6	3 279	65.0	108	40.7	1 029	60.4	1 020	70.7	3.3	0.6	1.7	0.7	1.1	8.2
Boise City, ID	140 200	70.3	683	63.4	1 007	74.3	2 126	67.0	9 328	82.3	5.6	1.3	1.0	2.9	2.5	13.5
Boston-Worcester-Lawrence-Lowell-Brockton, MA-NH	1 991 382	64.8	102 243	66.8	4 794	67.6	73 378	71.4	104 647	75.0	12.4	3.8	3.3	3.7	4.5	10.8
Brownsville-Harlingen-San Benito, TX..........	21 943	69.0	432	81.7	466	82.4	498	65.1	73 958	86.8	25.6	0.3	0.4	24.7	17.5	69.5
Bryan-College Station, TX	39 218	51.1	5 284	70.0	181	63.5	2 473	51.9	7 585	71.1	10.3	0.9	3.6	5.3	5.3	21.5
Buffalo-Niagara Falls, NY	305 100	65.1	53 063	61.3	2 825	66.1	4 633	65.2	10 305	68.3	4.4	2.0	1.1	0.4	1.4	12.1
Burlington, VT..............	72 842	65.3	528	57.4	477	65.4	807	71.1	567	56.4	5.4	1.9	1.3	0.2	1.2	11.3
Canton-Massillon, OH ..	145 900	70.1	10 091	66.6	348	56.3	609	78.2	1 039	63.9	1.7	0.9	0.4	0.2	0.4	7.4
Casper, WY	25 027	66.7	162	68.5	323	56.0	118	72.9	934	60.1	1.8	0.6	0.3	0.6	0.4	9.4
Cedar Rapids, IA..........	73 176	65.7	1 532	67.6	162	72.8	875	75.8	710	73.8	2.6	0.6	1.3	0.4	0.7	8.1
Champaign-Urbana, IL..	56 681	56.9	7 141	60.7	159	52.2	4 092	47.2	1 476	47.3	8.0	1.5	4.7	1.1	2.5	13.0
Charleston, WV	98 159	67.5	5 706	59.9	214	81.8	616	82.5	449	66.4	1.3	0.3	0.8	0.1	0.2	5.5
Charleston-North Charleston, SC...........	141 482	66.8	57 332	72.2	1 016	63.2	2 607	70.1	3 770	72.6	3.3	1.0	1.0	0.9	1.1	9.7
Charlotte-Gastonia-Rock Hill, NC-SC	431 211	69.3	110 312	68.5	2 573	72.9	7 993	79.1	19 421	80.5	6.7	0.9	1.5	3.6	3.3	10.3
Charlottesville, VA.......	50 822	62.7	7 775	67.9	109	57.8	1 522	59.5	1 017	62.3	6.0	1.8	2.3	1.2	1.4	10.0
Chattanooga, TN-GA	155 347	70.6	24 764	67.4	548	75.4	1 529	67.7	1 906	68.0	2.4	0.5	0.9	0.8	0.7	7.1
Cheyenne, WY	27 534	68.3	640	66.3	313	70.0	204	50.0	2 967	68.0	2.9	0.9	0.7	1.0	0.8	13.2
Chicago-Gary-Kenosha, IL-IN-WI....................	2 191 527	65.4	577 604	68.7	7 521	72.9	124 872	76.0	367 005	84.7	16.0	4.1	3.6	7.8	7.0	24.1
Chicago, IL..................	1 942 661	64.8	524 476	68.7	6 609	73.8	122 584	75.9	344 308	84.8	17.2	4.4	3.9	8.4	7.6	25.0
Gary, IN.....................	167 436	70.4	45 752	68.2	520	68.8	1 646	83.2	18 921	81.4	4.8	1.7	0.8	2.0	1.7	16.3
Kankakee, IL..............	31 216	69.8	5 193	71.1	114	48.2	224	82.1	1 186	88.7	3.5	0.6	0.7	2.0	1.5	9.2
Kenosha, WI...............	50 214	68.1	2 183	72.3	278	68.7	418	68.2	2 590	83.2	4.8	1.8	0.8	1.9	1.7	13.7
Chico-Paradise, CA......	68 052	61.6	1 020	52.9	1 362	64.8	1 693	68.3	5 627	73.1	7.7	1.0	2.4	3.7	3.3	14.9
Cincinnati-Hamilton, OH-KY-IN..................	655 008	68.7	90 921	61.2	1 744	60.9	8 303	68.0	6 019	62.7	2.6	0.8	1.0	0.4	0.7	7.8
Cincinnati, OH-KY-IN .	542 641	67.9	84 147	60.7	1 390	61.8	6 829	65.0	4 863	61.9	2.6	0.8	1.0	0.4	0.7	7.7
Hamilton-Middletown, OH	112 367	72.3	6 774	66.7	354	57.3	1 474	82.1	1 156	65.7	2.7	0.6	1.2	0.6	0.7	8.2
Clarksville-Hopkinsville, TN-KY.......................	53 655	74.6	14 835	74.0	358	67.9	672	70.5	2 711	80.6	3.7	1.2	1.2	1.1	0.9	13.1
Cleveland-Akron, OH	930 771	66.5	185 859	64.9	2 019	67.5	14 000	72.2	23 556	73.5	4.6	2.4	1.3	0.5	1.7	11.5
Akron, OH	237 849	67.4	28 537	65.5	594	62.8	2 976	75.1	1 786	66.1	3.0	1.3	1.2	0.2	0.8	8.4
Cleveland-Lorain-Elyria, OH...............	692 922	66.2	157 322	64.8	1 425	69.4	11 026	71.4	21 770	74.1	5.1	2.8	1.4	0.6	2.0	12.5
Colorado Springs, CO ...	154 839	69.1	11 586	75.6	1 669	70.2	4 369	72.6	16 964	75.3	6.4	2.1	2.0	1.8	1.7	16.8
Columbia, MO..............	45 873	59.5	4 266	62.3	302	63.6	1 383	54.0	642	62.5	4.5	0.7	2.5	0.7	1.3	10.3

[1] Hispanic or Latino persons may be of any race.

Table A-4. Metropolitan Areas — Age, Ethnicity, and Household Structure

CMSA/MSA/PMSA/NECMA code[1]	Area name	Total population	Under 5 years	5 to 17 years	18 to 24 years	25 to 44 years	45 to 64 years	65 years and over	Median age	+/− U.S. percent under 18 years	+/− U.S. percent 65 years and over	Non-Hispanic White Total population	Under 18 years	65 years and over
		1	2	3	4	5	6	7	8	9	10	11	12	13
1760	Columbia, SC	536 691	6.5	18.5	11.6	31.7	21.9	9.9	33.9	-0.7	-2.5	337 286	21.9	12.2
1800	Columbus, GA-AL	274 624	7.2	19.5	11.8	29.9	20.1	11.4	32.7	1.0	-1.0	144 792	22.0	14.8
1840	Columbus, OH..............	1 540 157	7.1	18.3	10.7	32.7	21.1	10.0	33.6	-0.3	-2.4	1 237 899	23.9	11.0
1880	Corpus Christi, TX........	380 783	7.7	21.1	10.4	28.8	20.9	11.0	33.0	3.1	-1.4	148 920	22.1	15.7
1890	Corvallis, OR	78 153	5.0	16.4	20.1	26.7	21.7	10.2	31.1	-4.3	-2.2	67 739	20.5	11.3
1900	Cumberland, MD-WV	102 008	5.1	16.2	10.5	26.8	24.3	17.2	39.1	-4.4	4.8	95 108	21.3	18.0
31	Dallas-Fort Worth, TX ...	5 221 801	8.0	20.0	9.8	34.4	19.8	8.0	32.1	2.3	-4.4	3 096 793	23.8	11.0
1920	Dallas, TX..................	3 519 176	8.1	19.9	10.0	34.9	19.5	7.7	31.8	2.3	-4.7	1 979 525	23.4	10.8
2800	Fort Worth-Arlington, TX..............	1 702 625	7.7	20.2	9.5	33.1	20.6	8.8	32.8	2.2	-3.6	1 117 268	24.4	11.4
1950	Danville, VA..............	110 156	5.8	17.4	7.6	27.6	25.1	16.6	40.0	-2.5	4.2	71 700	19.6	19.7
1960	Davenport-Moline-Rock Island, IA-IL	359 062	6.6	18.5	9.4	28.2	23.5	13.8	36.9	-0.6	1.4	307 806	22.9	15.3
2000	Dayton-Springfield, OH .	950 558	6.5	18.2	10.0	28.4	23.3	13.5	36.6	-1.0	1.1	775 958	23.1	14.5
2020	Daytona Beach, FL	493 175	4.8	15.1	7.9	24.8	24.6	22.8	43.1	-5.8	10.4	404 923	17.9	25.4
2030	Decatur, AL	145 867	6.5	18.9	8.6	30.0	23.7	12.2	36.4	-0.3	-0.2	119 237	23.7	13.5
2040	Decatur, IL..............	114 706	6.4	18.2	9.9	26.4	23.8	15.3	38.0	-1.1	2.9	95 202	21.8	17.0
34	Denver-Boulder-Greeley, CO	2 581 506	7.1	18.5	9.7	34.0	21.8	8.9	33.8	-0.1	-3.5	1 853 158	22.4	10.6
1125	Boulder-Longmont, CO......................	291 288	6.0	16.8	13.3	34.0	22.1	7.8	33.4	-2.9	-4.6	243 414	21.0	8.8
2080	Denver, CO	2 109 282	7.1	18.6	8.9	34.4	21.9	9.0	34.1	0.0	-3.4	1 483 260	22.5	10.9
3060	Greeley, CO	180 936	7.7	20.5	13.1	29.7	20.0	9.0	30.9	2.5	-3.4	126 484	24.1	11.2
2120	Des Moines, IA.............	456 022	7.5	18.4	9.2	32.0	21.7	11.2	34.6	0.2	-1.2	401 255	24.4	12.0
35	Detroit-Ann Arbor-Flint, MI	5 456 428	6.9	19.4	8.7	31.1	22.2	11.7	35.3	0.6	-0.7	3 903 156	23.9	13.3
0440	Ann Arbor, MI	578 736	6.5	18.0	12.8	31.6	22.2	8.9	33.5	-1.2	-3.5	484 505	23.8	9.8
2160	Detroit, MI	4 441 551	7.0	19.5	8.1	31.1	22.2	12.1	35.5	0.8	-0.3	3 095 229	23.8	13.8
2640	Flint, MI	436 141	7.2	20.1	9.0	29.8	22.3	11.6	35.0	1.6	-0.8	323 422	24.4	13.1
2180	Dothan, AL	137 916	7.1	19.1	8.6	29.7	22.7	13.0	35.9	0.5	0.6	100 427	23.3	14.8
2190	Dover, DE	126 697	7.2	20.0	10.2	29.7	21.3	11.6	34.4	1.5	-0.8	91 515	25.2	13.4
2200	Dubuque, IA	89 143	6.7	18.8	10.3	27.2	22.3	14.8	36.5	-0.2	2.4	86 204	25.1	15.2
2240	Duluth-Superior, MN-WI	243 815	5.3	17.3	11.2	26.2	24.2	15.8	38.8	-3.1	3.4	230 372	21.6	16.5
2290	Eau Claire, WI	148 337	6.0	18.6	13.7	27.2	21.4	13.1	34.7	-1.1	0.7	141 899	23.6	13.5
2320	El Paso, TX	679 622	8.6	23.3	10.5	29.5	18.4	9.8	30.0	6.2	-2.6	115 394	20.7	18.0
2330	Elkhart-Goshen, IN........	182 791	8.1	20.8	9.4	29.9	21.0	10.9	33.0	3.2	-1.5	152 389	26.9	12.5
2335	Elmira, NY	91 070	5.9	18.4	8.9	28.3	22.9	15.6	37.9	-1.4	3.2	81 877	23.8	16.7
2340	Enid, OK..................	57 813	6.7	18.3	9.2	27.5	22.4	15.9	37.7	-0.7	3.5	50 219	23.0	17.6
2360	Erie, PA	280 843	6.1	18.9	10.8	27.6	22.2	14.3	36.2	-0.7	1.9	252 079	23.4	15.4
2400	Eugene-Springfield, OR	322 959	5.7	17.1	12.0	27.6	24.4	13.3	36.6	-2.9	0.9	286 042	21.5	14.5
2440	Evansville-Henderson, IN-KY	296 195	6.3	18.1	10.0	28.7	23.0	13.9	37.1	-1.3	1.5	270 509	23.4	14.5
2520	Fargo-Moorhead, ND-MN	174 367	6.4	17.5	16.3	29.6	19.5	10.6	31.5	-1.8	-1.8	163 394	22.9	11.1
2560	Fayetteville, NC............	302 963	8.1	19.8	13.8	32.8	17.8	7.7	29.6	2.2	-4.7	159 127	23.5	9.9
2580	Fayetteville-Springdale-Rogers, AR	311 121	7.5	18.3	12.0	30.0	20.1	12.1	33.0	0.1	-0.3	266 307	24.1	13.8
2620	Flagstaff, AZ-UT............	122 366	7.3	21.4	14.3	28.9	20.8	7.4	29.9	3.0	-5.0	72 802	21.6	8.7
2650	Florence, AL	142 950	6.0	17.4	9.3	28.0	24.2	15.2	38.0	-2.3	2.8	121 677	22.2	16.0
2655	Florence, SC	125 761	6.5	19.5	9.8	29.0	23.5	11.8	35.5	0.3	-0.6	73 198	22.1	14.0
2670	Fort Collins-Loveland, CO	251 494	6.0	17.6	14.2	30.9	21.8	9.6	33.2	-2.1	-2.8	220 432	22.4	10.4
2700	Fort Myers-Cape Coral, FL	440 888	5.2	14.3	6.1	24.2	24.7	25.4	45.2	-6.2	13.0	361 259	16.2	29.6
2710	Fort Pierce-Port St. Lucie, FL	319 426	5.0	15.9	6.2	24.3	23.7	24.9	44.0	-4.8	12.5	251 548	17.4	29.4
2720	Fort Smith, AR-OK........	207 290	7.4	19.4	8.9	28.9	22.8	12.6	35.6	1.1	0.2	166 845	24.6	14.3
2750	Fort Walton Beach, FL..	170 498	6.3	18.2	9.5	31.4	22.4	12.1	36.1	-1.2	-0.3	138 101	23.1	14.0
2760	Fort Wayne, IN............	502 141	7.5	20.3	9.2	29.5	21.5	12.0	34.6	2.1	-0.4	435 558	26.3	13.1
2840	Fresno, CA	922 516	8.3	23.4	10.9	28.9	18.6	10.0	30.2	6.0	-2.4	374 129	21.8	17.2
2880	Gadsden, AL	103 459	6.5	17.4	8.6	27.4	24.1	16.0	38.3	-1.8	3.6	85 000	21.9	17.4
2900	Gainesville, FL	217 955	5.1	15.0	23.2	27.8	19.4	9.5	29.0	-5.6	-2.9	151 933	16.9	11.1
2975	Glens Falls, NY	124 345	5.5	18.8	7.9	28.9	24.4	14.6	38.3	-1.4	2.2	118 638	24.5	15.1
2980	Goldsboro, NC............	113 329	6.8	19.4	9.5	30.8	22.0	11.5	34.8	0.5	-0.9	67 789	22.8	13.5
2985	Grand Forks, ND-MN	97 478	6.3	18.2	16.5	27.5	19.4	12.1	31.9	-1.2	-0.3	89 719	23.3	13.0
2995	Grand Junction, CO	116 255	6.1	18.8	9.4	26.8	23.8	15.1	38.1	-0.8	2.7	101 015	23.2	16.5
3000	Grand Rapids-Muskegon-Holland, MI	1 088 514	7.5	20.8	10.2	30.4	20.3	10.8	33.2	2.6	-1.6	903 354	26.2	12.1
3040	Great Falls, MT	80 357	6.7	19.3	8.9	28.4	22.7	14.1	36.7	0.3	1.7	71 918	24.7	15.1
3080	Green Bay, WI	226 778	6.9	19.1	10.4	32.0	20.9	10.6	34.2	0.3	-1.8	203 437	24.3	11.6
3120	Greensboro—Winston-Salem—High Point, NC	1 251 509	6.6	17.4	9.4	31.2	22.8	12.5	36.0	-1.7	0.1	905 186	21.7	14.8
3150	Greenville, NC.............	133 798	6.4	17.1	17.4	30.1	19.3	9.6	30.4	-2.2	-2.8	81 543	18.9	10.8
3160	Greenville-Spartanburg-Anderson, SC	962 441	6.7	17.8	10.1	30.1	23.0	12.3	35.7	-1.2	-0.1	748 141	22.6	13.7
3240	Harrisburg-Lebanon-Carlisle, PA	629 401	5.8	17.6	8.7	29.3	23.9	14.7	38.1	-2.3	2.3	544 274	21.7	16.0

[1]MSA = Metropolitan Statistical Area. CMSA = Consolidated Metropolitan Area. PMSA = Primary MSA. NECMA = New England County Metropolitan Area. See the Appendix A for explanation of these concepts. See Appendix B for list of metropolitan areas identified by type, with component counties.

Table A-4. Metropolitan Areas — Age, Ethnicity, and Household Structure

	Black or African American			American Indian and Alaska Native			Asian, Hawaiian, and Pacific Islander			Hispanic or Latino[1]			Two or more races		
	Age (percent)			Age (percent)			Age (percent)			Age (percent)			Age (percent)		
Area name	Total population	Under 18 years	65 years and over	Total population	Under 18 years	65 years and over	Total population	Under 18 years	65 years and over	Total population	Under 18 years	65 years and over	Total population	Under 18 years	65 years and over
	14	15	16	17	18	19	20	21	22	23	24	25	26	27	28
Columbia, SC	171 692	30.4	6.2	1 936	20.9	5.2	7 898	21.6	4.9	13 369	27.9	3.7	6 322	39.7	3.8
Columbus, GA-AL	109 724	32.0	8.3	1 548	23.8	4.5	4 105	24.6	4.9	10 919	31.4	3.7	5 222	43.7	4.1
Columbus, OH	202 833	31.7	7.2	4 704	24.7	4.3	37 091	23.0	3.7	28 047	32.5	2.5	32 506	44.9	3.5
Corpus Christi, TX	15 171	32.1	9.7	2 377	29.3	4.6	4 079	22.6	6.7	207 910	33.4	7.9	11 742	39.3	7.5
Corvallis, OR	761	21.6	0.0	538	30.7	1.9	3 404	18.0	4.0	3 622	32.2	2.2	2 494	34.5	3.6
Cumberland, MD-WV	4 811	15.4	5.4	117	12.8	12.8	541	31.8	4.6	757	22.3	7.7	751	46.7	10.5
Dallas-Fort Worth, TX	712 584	32.0	5.8	30 110	26.6	4.6	196 156	26.3	3.8	1 119 610	36.5	2.2	131 218	41.7	3.3
Dallas, TX	525 748	31.9	5.8	19 411	26.2	4.6	142 104	26.0	3.8	810 013	36.2	2.1	88 484	40.7	3.4
Fort Worth-Arlington, TX	186 836	32.4	5.9	10 699	27.4	4.5	54 052	27.0	3.9	309 597	37.2	2.4	42 734	43.7	3.1
Danville, VA	36 000	29.4	11.3	247	14.6	9.7	342	15.5	6.1	1 292	35.5	7.8	816	50.5	4.9
Davenport-Moline-Rock Island, IA-IL	20 603	34.8	6.1	1 390	35.1	5.0	3 887	28.6	3.8	20 712	39.4	4.6	6 893	56.6	3.5
Dayton-Springfield, OH	134 986	30.8	10.2	2 314	21.3	5.3	11 974	22.3	4.5	10 496	32.6	5.2	15 639	46.9	4.9
Daytona Beach, FL	44 208	29.5	11.5	1 497	12.3	8.7	5 586	21.0	9.7	31 825	30.4	10.3	7 811	35.9	9.5
Decatur, AL	16 950	32.0	8.3	2 621	32.2	2.3	642	40.2	1.4	3 851	35.7	1.9	2 969	36.2	6.2
Decatur, IL	15 941	36.0	7.7	133	24.1	0.0	790	25.7	2.7	1 083	35.1	4.9	1 746	60.0	3.4
Denver-Boulder-Greeley, CO	116 450	30.8	6.9	22 291	27.6	3.2	74 341	25.0	6.5	476 585	35.3	3.8	80 894	42.9	3.1
Boulder-Longmont, CO	2 321	20.1	3.7	1 935	33.9	4.0	9 375	24.1	3.0	30 368	35.1	2.7	6 206	35.1	3.3
Denver, CO	113 160	31.0	7.0	18 706	26.4	3.1	63 307	25.3	7.0	397 319	34.9	3.9	69 475	43.7	3.1
Greeley, CO	969	32.8	1.8	1 650	34.4	3.6	1 659	22.2	7.5	48 898	38.7	3.9	5 213	42.2	3.1
Des Moines, IA	17 967	34.3	8.5	1 480	33.9	3.3	9 785	27.6	4.8	18 991	38.3	1.9	7 742	53.3	3.4
Detroit-Ann Arbor-Flint, MI	1 142 657	31.9	8.9	20 923	28.1	5.1	128 658	26.0	4.0	155 834	35.7	4.9	121 091	42.5	4.6
Ann Arbor, MI	41 674	27.0	5.2	2 378	28.0	3.5	21 784	19.3	3.0	17 549	30.7	3.6	12 461	42.6	2.6
Detroit, MI	1 013 226	31.9	9.2	15 837	27.8	5.6	103 581	27.5	4.3	128 145	36.0	5.1	98 164	42.0	5.0
Flint, MI	87 757	34.8	8.0	2 708	30.2	3.8	3 293	24.5	3.0	10 140	40.8	4.5	10 466	47.4	4.0
Dothan, AL	31 717	33.9	8.4	646	19.5	3.1	1 068	20.4	8.4	2 576	38.5	3.6	1 903	43.7	5.9
Dover, DE	25 626	31.0	7.6	1 079	26.0	9.0	2 110	20.4	6.6	4 278	38.7	3.8	2 950	51.0	2.8
Dubuque, IA	717	35.3	2.9	139	36.7	0.0	367	24.0	6.3	1 066	34.4	0.0	774	52.7	5.7
Duluth-Superior, MN-WI	1 967	35.4	8.3	4 521	36.5	3.9	1 889	31.3	3.8	1 929	47.1	3.8	3 287	47.5	4.2
Eau Claire, WI	519	35.5	0.0	779	35.0	3.9	2 796	49.8	2.9	1 098	36.8	2.0	1 299	47.4	6.9
El Paso, TX	20 552	29.5	7.4	4 932	33.5	8.1	7 510	23.4	8.2	531 967	34.5	8.1	20 968	35.6	8.1
Elkhart-Goshen, IN	9 354	36.5	5.2	692	34.0	5.9	1 624	29.3	3.0	16 195	37.1	1.3	3 659	53.8	2.4
Elmira, NY	5 177	22.5	7.3	321	32.1	3.4	816	27.7	3.9	1 581	24.0	4.4	1 580	58.2	5.3
Enid, OK	1 824	34.9	6.2	1 345	36.6	4.6	747	25.6	9.1	2 260	42.0	2.4	1 691	45.8	4.9
Erie, PA	16 991	36.8	6.2	489	23.9	6.3	1 874	25.6	3.5	6 165	43.5	2.8	4 158	55.7	4.5
Eugene-Springfield, OR	2 437	32.8	6.2	3 535	27.9	4.6	6 691	18.7	4.2	14 488	37.9	1.9	11 592	39.2	4.5
Evansville-Henderson, IN-KY	17 382	32.6	9.8	561	27.6	4.5	2 235	26.9	3.8	2 573	35.6	4.0	2 889	52.0	4.9
Fargo-Moorhead, ND-MN	1 287	45.3	0.0	2 316	31.8	2.6	1 847	24.2	3.0	3 291	43.8	3.7	2 517	50.9	2.5
Fayetteville, NC	105 730	31.8	6.1	4 696	28.9	6.8	6 629	22.5	5.3	20 637	34.3	2.4	9 718	51.1	1.5
Fayetteville-Springdale-Rogers, AR	4 142	31.1	2.3	4 954	33.3	5.3	5 051	25.8	1.6	26 323	39.2	1.2	5 947	42.1	3.8
Flagstaff, AZ-UT	1 378	32.4	7.8	32 882	40.9	5.7	1 095	22.4	1.6	12 874	36.1	4.8	2 794	51.1	2.1
Florence, AL	18 029	29.7	11.2	358	27.7	1.1	503	23.9	6.6	1 358	28.9	8.2	1 176	36.0	9.4
Florence, SC	49 405	30.9	9.0	248	22.2	16.5	1 026	26.0	5.6	1 157	38.5	4.9	1 045	48.0	4.7
Fort Collins-Loveland, CO	1 736	29.7	0.6	1 875	28.9	3.4	3 752	24.6	5.0	20 631	33.5	3.2	5 918	41.2	5.2
Fort Myers-Cape Coral, FL	28 570	37.3	7.5	1 340	27.8	9.9	3 397	21.0	10.1	41 993	34.0	5.1	7 590	38.4	7.4
Fort Pierce-Port St. Lucie, FL	35 638	34.0	9.4	988	32.2	7.3	2 778	26.1	8.0	25 494	33.7	6.1	5 222	38.5	8.0
Fort Smith, AR-OK	8 112	33.7	7.3	10 865	35.2	7.4	4 395	29.3	5.4	9 769	39.8	2.1	8 320	41.1	6.0
Fort Walton Beach, FL	15 116	29.9	3.8	854	20.5	5.7	4 622	19.3	5.8	6 901	31.2	4.3	5 843	46.0	3.0
Fort Wayne, IN	37 427	36.4	5.8	1 598	27.2	3.8	5 189	28.3	3.8	16 454	37.5	2.6	7 194	51.1	3.7
Fresno, CA	45 923	33.7	7.2	15 754	35.2	4.8	66 387	39.3	7.7	406 688	38.9	4.2	46 875	43.0	5.4
Gadsden, AL	14 672	31.4	11.1	375	39.7	3.5	430	22.1	4.4	1 651	31.1	4.2	1 462	54.4	5.1
Gainesville, FL	40 994	32.0	7.3	420	12.9	2.1	7 908	12.9	2.6	12 333	19.2	3.8	5 262	33.7	3.8
Glens Falls, NY	2 152	11.1	2.6	296	18.2	1.7	774	32.3	8.1	1 665	20.8	2.2	1 078	38.3	8.2
Goldsboro, NC	37 586	30.0	9.9	330	24.2	3.6	1 145	25.2	2.5	5 300	37.0	0.9	1 505	48.3	2.1
Grand Forks, ND-MN	1 009	29.8	1.2	1 912	39.0	2.2	855	20.0	0.9	2 844	41.2	3.0	1 401	52.0	2.6
Grand Junction, CO	516	29.5	1.2	1 154	33.7	7.3	511	22.7	10.4	11 629	36.8	5.3	2 478	43.4	5.6
Grand Rapids-Muskegon-Holland, MI	79 224	36.0	6.4	5 756	27.3	4.4	17 417	34.4	3.0	69 154	39.8	2.2	22 109	50.3	3.3
Great Falls, MT	882	27.7	5.6	3 061	33.8	5.7	559	14.0	8.8	1 984	39.4	4.8	2 315	48.3	3.4
Green Bay, WI	2 619	31.3	0.3	5 193	35.0	4.9	4 609	47.9	2.4	8 798	38.9	1.0	3 054	56.6	2.1
Greensboro—Winston-Salem—High Point, NC	251 882	28.8	8.2	5 096	22.9	6.4	16 320	27.4	3.3	62 665	32.8	1.4	16 880	40.9	3.6
Greenville, NC	45 095	30.8	8.6	550	26.0	1.1	1 377	20.4	3.2	4 088	31.7	2.0	1 502	36.8	3.9
Greenville-Spartanburg-Anderson, SC	168 237	30.6	8.3	2 023	21.4	4.4	11 489	27.7	3.4	25 290	29.3	2.6	9 896	41.8	5.5
Harrisburg-Lebanon-Carlisle, PA	47 863	31.6	8.2	898	20.9	7.2	9 835	28.3	5.5	19 984	39.6	3.0	9 104	50.5	3.8

[1] Hispanic or Latino persons may be of any race.

Table A-4. Metropolitan Areas — Age, Ethnicity, and Household Structure

Area name	Total households	Family households (percent)						Nonfamily households (percent)						Percent of householders 65 years and over who live alone	Grandparents who are responsible for the care of their grandchildren
		Married-couple family households			Other family households			Two or more unrelated persons		Male living alone		Female living alone			
		Total	With children	Householder 65 years or over	Total	With children	Householder 65 years or over	Total	Householder 65 years or over	Total	Householder 65 years or over	Total	Householder 65 years or over		
	29	30	31	32	33	34	35	36	37	38	39	40	41	42	43
Columbia, SC	203 397	50.0	23.3	7.0	17.4	10.4	2.1	6.2	0.2	11.1	1.6	15.3	5.6	43.3	5 366
Columbus, GA-AL	101 317	48.1	22.6	7.7	21.9	12.7	3.1	4.2	0.3	10.3	2.0	15.4	7.4	45.9	3 482
Columbus, OH	610 895	48.9	23.0	6.9	15.6	9.6	1.6	7.4	0.3	12.2	1.8	15.9	5.9	46.5	10 972
Corpus Christi, TX	132 353	53.8	26.4	9.1	19.7	11.2	2.9	4.5	0.3	10.0	2.0	11.9	5.8	38.8	7 065
Corvallis, OR	30 198	51.7	22.8	8.6	9.4	5.9	0.8	12.9	0.2	11.9	1.4	14.1	5.3	41.3	248
Cumberland, MD-WV	40 172	53.7	21.1	11.5	12.9	7.0	2.5	4.8	0.6	10.6	3.6	18.0	11.1	50.2	771
Dallas-Fort Worth, TX	1 908 087	53.8	28.2	6.1	15.9	9.3	1.6	5.6	0.2	11.4	1.3	13.3	4.4	41.5	56 262
Dallas, TX	1 283 156	53.0	28.0	5.8	16.1	9.3	1.6	5.8	0.2	11.4	1.2	13.6	4.2	41.8	37 220
Fort Worth-Arlington, TX	624 931	55.4	28.5	6.9	15.4	9.3	1.7	5.2	0.2	11.2	1.4	12.7	4.8	41.0	19 042
Danville, VA	45 274	49.8	19.2	10.6	19.2	10.0	3.5	2.8	0.3	11.4	2.7	16.7	9.9	46.8	1 528
Davenport-Moline-Rock Island, IA-IL	143 110	52.9	22.6	9.9	14.0	8.8	1.8	5.0	0.4	11.7	2.4	16.4	8.7	48.0	2 670
Dayton-Springfield, OH	379 720	51.1	21.5	9.5	15.9	9.7	2.0	5.1	0.3	11.6	2.3	16.3	7.8	46.1	8 373
Daytona Beach, FL	206 005	52.5	16.7	17.4	13.7	7.5	2.4	6.5	0.9	10.9	3.6	16.4	10.1	39.9	4 376
Decatur, AL	57 070	59.5	26.4	9.4	13.9	7.9	2.0	2.3	0.2	10.3	2.0	14.0	7.1	44.1	1 626
Decatur, IL	46 518	50.9	19.9	10.8	16.0	10.4	2.1	4.3	0.4	12.3	2.4	16.6	9.3	46.7	906
Denver-Boulder-Greeley, CO	1 003 941	51.0	25.2	6.5	13.4	8.1	1.2	8.3	0.3	12.6	1.6	14.7	5.1	45.8	16 844
Boulder-Longmont, CO	114 793	49.8	24.7	5.9	10.8	7.0	0.8	13.2	0.2	12.3	1.2	13.9	4.6	45.7	1 031
Denver, CO	825 951	50.5	24.9	6.4	13.8	8.3	1.3	7.7	0.3	12.9	1.6	15.1	5.2	46.0	14 097
Greeley, CO	63 197	59.4	30.2	8.0	12.7	7.7	1.1	7.0	0.2	9.4	1.7	11.6	5.4	43.6	1 716
Des Moines, IA	179 617	53.9	25.7	7.9	12.8	8.0	1.5	6.4	0.3	10.6	1.8	16.4	6.8	47.1	2 281
Detroit-Ann Arbor-Flint, MI	2 083 104	49.9	23.4	8.1	18.0	9.8	2.7	5.2	0.3	11.8	2.2	15.1	6.9	45.0	44 301
Ann Arbor, MI	216 739	54.8	26.2	7.0	11.7	6.9	1.4	8.3	0.2	11.6	1.5	13.6	4.9	42.4	2 885
Detroit, MI	1 696 335	49.5	23.2	8.3	18.5	9.9	2.9	4.8	0.4	11.9	2.3	15.3	7.2	45.3	36 667
Flint, MI	170 030	48.2	21.3	8.4	20.6	12.9	2.2	4.7	0.4	11.4	2.0	15.1	6.9	44.7	4 749
Dothan, AL	54 751	54.3	23.9	9.5	16.9	10.6	2.1	3.1	0.3	10.8	2.3	14.9	7.5	45.2	1 514
Dover, DE	47 199	53.5	24.5	9.0	17.9	11.5	2.1	5.6	0.5	10.1	2.3	12.9	6.3	42.8	1 397
Dubuque, IA	33 703	57.7	26.5	10.9	11.1	6.6	1.7	4.5	0.2	11.6	2.5	15.1	8.3	45.5	208
Duluth-Superior, MN-WI	100 507	50.2	20.2	10.5	12.6	8.2	1.5	6.3	0.4	13.6	3.1	17.3	9.5	50.4	1 032
Eau Claire, WI	57 280	54.2	24.6	10.1	11.2	7.1	1.3	8.4	0.3	11.2	2.2	15.0	8.0	46.6	582
El Paso, TX	210 034	57.9	33.3	8.8	21.8	12.2	3.3	2.6	0.3	7.5	1.7	10.2	5.1	35.3	12 150
Elkhart-Goshen, IN	66 124	58.4	27.7	9.2	14.3	9.5	1.2	4.8	0.4	9.4	1.7	13.2	6.8	44.5	1 524
Elmira, NY	35 076	50.5	21.2	10.6	16.4	10.5	2.4	5.3	0.4	10.9	3.0	16.8	9.0	47.4	712
Enid, OK	23 220	55.8	24.2	11.2	12.6	8.2	1.7	4.0	0.2	10.9	2.8	16.7	9.0	47.5	519
Erie, PA	106 488	51.7	22.9	10.2	15.5	9.3	2.2	5.2	0.3	11.3	2.4	16.3	8.8	46.9	1 784
Eugene-Springfield, OR	130 616	49.9	20.6	10.0	13.6	8.8	1.6	10.0	0.6	11.5	2.2	15.1	6.9	42.8	1 740
Evansville-Henderson, IN-KY	118 294	54.2	23.5	9.6	13.5	8.3	1.7	4.7	0.3	10.9	2.2	16.5	8.6	48.3	2 360
Fargo-Moorhead, ND-MN	69 950	49.7	24.3	7.7	11.1	7.3	0.8	9.4	0.3	13.2	1.9	16.6	6.5	48.9	481
Fayetteville, NC	107 391	54.0	28.1	5.7	18.9	12.1	2.0	4.8	0.3	10.3	1.5	12.1	4.6	43.3	3 433
Fayetteville-Springdale-Rogers, AR	118 425	58.3	26.4	10.7	12.1	7.5	1.3	6.1	0.3	10.1	1.8	13.3	6.3	39.7	2 384
Flagstaff, AZ-UT	42 622	51.4	25.0	6.9	16.2	10.3	1.7	10.3	0.3	11.1	1.6	10.9	3.3	35.6	1 717
Florence, AL	58 616	56.6	23.5	11.3	14.0	7.6	2.3	3.1	0.2	10.8	2.4	15.5	8.5	44.1	1 284
Florence, SC	47 107	50.9	23.2	7.8	21.5	11.4	3.2	3.1	0.2	9.9	1.6	14.6	6.6	42.3	1 641
Fort Collins-Loveland, CO	97 128	55.0	25.5	7.8	10.6	6.6	0.8	11.1	0.2	10.3	1.4	13.0	5.3	43.0	978
Fort Myers-Cape Coral, FL	188 755	55.9	15.9	20.9	12.2	6.9	2.0	6.2	0.9	10.5	3.8	15.3	9.3	35.4	3 232
Fort Pierce-Port St. Lucie, FL	132 282	56.1	17.6	20.6	12.5	7.1	2.0	5.5	1.0	10.1	3.8	15.7	10.0	36.9	2 477
Fort Smith, AR-OK	79 818	56.8	25.6	9.4	14.8	9.1	2.0	3.8	0.3	10.3	2.3	14.3	7.5	45.7	2 483
Fort Walton Beach, FL	66 373	57.1	25.0	10.3	13.5	8.7	1.5	5.9	0.3	11.2	2.1	12.3	5.7	39.1	1 479
Fort Wayne, IN	192 274	55.1	26.2	9.0	14.1	9.0	1.5	4.7	0.3	11.4	2.0	14.7	7.2	46.1	3 210
Fresno, CA	289 591	55.0	29.5	9.0	20.1	12.4	2.3	4.9	0.4	8.3	2.0	11.8	6.1	40.8	10 530
Gadsden, AL	41 634	54.3	21.9	11.0	16.8	8.5	3.4	2.6	0.3	9.9	3.0	16.4	9.8	46.7	1 079
Gainesville, FL	87 536	39.7	17.1	6.4	15.2	8.7	1.7	16.0	0.4	13.2	1.5	15.9	4.9	43.0	1 654
Glens Falls, NY	48 171	54.2	23.6	10.6	14.4	8.9	2.0	5.7	0.6	10.8	2.7	14.9	8.1	45.0	623
Goldsboro, NC	42 541	53.2	24.3	8.6	18.0	10.8	2.0	4.2	0.2	10.0	2.0	14.6	7.3	46.2	1 250
Grand Forks, ND-MN	37 504	52.0	25.4	8.5	11.7	7.6	1.3	7.9	0.2	13.5	2.6	15.0	7.7	50.8	226
Grand Junction, CO	45 840	56.2	23.5	11.8	13.1	8.5	1.6	5.7	0.4	10.2	2.5	14.8	8.1	43.6	863
Grand Rapids-Muskegon-Holland, MI	396 738	56.4	28.0	8.6	14.3	9.2	1.6	5.6	0.3	10.2	1.8	13.6	6.5	44.2	6 393
Great Falls, MT	32 633	52.9	23.6	9.8	13.5	9.3	1.7	4.9	0.5	13.2	3.2	15.6	8.2	48.7	322
Green Bay, WI	87 356	54.0	26.3	8.1	12.3	8.2	1.0	7.2	0.2	11.4	1.7	15.1	7.0	48.5	578
Greensboro—Winston-Salem—High Point, NC	499 012	52.9	22.8	8.8	15.8	9.1	2.1	5.0	0.3	10.7	2.0	15.6	7.0	44.6	10 461
Greenville, NC	52 603	43.9	20.1	6.0	18.2	10.5	2.2	9.7	0.2	11.9	1.6	16.3	6.2	48.2	1 427
Greenville-Spartanburg-Anderson, SC	374 892	54.1	23.5	8.8	16.1	8.9	2.2	4.4	0.3	10.6	2.0	14.8	7.1	44.6	10 994
Harrisburg-Lebanon-Carlisle, PA	249 067	53.9	22.5	10.3	13.6	8.1	1.9	5.1	0.4	11.2	2.4	16.2	8.2	45.6	3 636

Area name	Households with Non-Hispanic White householder		Households with Black or African American householder		Households with American Indian and Alaska Native householder		Households with Asian, Hawaiian, and Pacific Islander householder		Households with Hispanic or Latino[1] householder		Foreign-born population				Percent in non-English speaking households	
											Percent of total population that is foreign-born	Place of birth (percent)				
	Number of households	Percent that are family households	Number of households	Percent that are family households	Number of households	Percent that are family households	Number of households	Percent that are family households	Number of households	Percent that are family households		Europe	Asia	Latin America	Linguistically isolated	Not linguistically isolated
	44	45	46	47	48	49	50	51	52	53	54	55	56	57	58	59
Columbia, SC	137 224	66.3	58 098	70.0	781	72.7	2 595	64.7	3 507	71.5	3.5	0.9	1.2	1.1	1.2	9.7
Columbus, GA-AL	57 249	68.8	38 710	71.5	543	70.9	1 097	85.6	2 902	73.5	4.0	1.2	1.0	1.5	1.1	10.6
Columbus, OH..............	501 959	64.7	77 579	63.2	1 838	63.1	13 191	65.3	8 186	64.4	4.6	0.9	2.1	0.7	1.7	9.7
Corpus Christi, TX.......	62 402	67.3	5 375	70.1	764	78.7	1 178	77.1	61 920	80.2	6.0	0.4	0.8	4.4	6.2	49.9
Corvallis, OR	26 755	61.7	334	45.2	177	69.5	1 262	51.0	1 042	65.5	7.6	2.0	3.2	1.7	2.9	12.0
Cumberland, MD-WV	38 829	66.7	865	60.3	46	54.3	139	85.6	124	79.8	1.1	0.3	0.4	0.3	0.2	4.7
Dallas-Fort Worth, TX ...	1 270 781	66.8	261 935	68.2	10 507	69.8	61 795	75.9	281 552	82.9	15.0	0.9	3.2	10.2	8.1	22.0
Dallas, TX....................	820 898	65.6	193 507	68.3	6 684	69.7	45 913	75.9	201 923	83.1	16.8	0.9	3.4	11.6	9.1	23.0
Fort Worth-Arlington, TX	449 883	69.1	68 428	68.2	3 823	70.0	15 882	76.1	79 629	82.2	11.4	0.8	2.6	7.3	6.0	19.9
Danville, VA.................	31 071	68.3	13 426	70.7	161	75.2	99	89.9	377	73.7	1.2	0.3	0.3	0.5	0.6	5.9
Davenport-Moline-Rock Island, IA-IL	127 592	66.6	7 294	67.9	460	74.8	1 116	74.1	5 621	75.5	3.5	0.8	0.9	1.6	1.5	8.9
Dayton-Springfield, OH.	314 451	67.6	52 905	63.8	927	53.7	4 117	71.2	3 232	64.5	2.3	0.7	1.1	0.3	0.6	7.3
Daytona Beach, FL	177 322	65.4	15 456	67.4	547	68.7	1 784	68.6	9 157	80.8	6.8	2.4	1.0	2.4	2.0	13.7
Decatur, AL	48 032	73.5	6 157	70.1	798	82.6	168	79.2	1 082	82.8	2.2	0.3	0.3	1.5	1.5	5.6
Decatur, IL	39 853	67.1	5 887	64.7	53	41.5	254	78.3	264	72.0	1.4	0.4	0.5	0.3	0.3	6.2
Denver-Boulder-Greeley, CO	783 960	62.1	45 677	62.8	7 671	69.7	23 847	70.2	131 288	77.5	10.7	1.7	2.2	6.1	5.2	18.3
Boulder-Longmont, CO...........................	101 048	59.3	825	61.3	522	77.0	3 134	65.0	7 979	76.3	9.4	2.1	2.5	4.0	3.5	15.8
Denver, CO	633 980	62.0	44 618	62.9	6 685	68.4	20 179	71.0	110 709	76.9	11.1	1.7	2.3	6.2	5.4	18.3
Greeley, CO	48 932	69.3	234	56.4	464	80.4	534	70.4	12 600	83.4	9.3	0.5	0.4	8.2	5.9	22.1
Des Moines, IA	163 278	66.1	6 825	63.0	461	70.3	2 692	79.6	4 986	80.4	5.3	1.3	1.7	1.8	2.5	9.9
Detroit-Ann Arbor-Flint, MI	1 554 415	67.8	406 332	67.1	7 252	70.4	42 270	74.5	43 428	73.4	7.0	2.2	3.1	0.8	2.1	13.1
Ann Arbor, MI..............	185 333	67.6	14 721	61.0	761	69.5	7 901	56.3	5 105	65.4	6.8	1.8	3.2	0.8	1.6	12.4
Detroit, MI...................	1 237 897	67.7	360 034	67.1	5 574	70.1	33 216	78.9	35 608	74.2	7.5	2.4	3.3	0.9	2.3	13.7
Flint, MI	131 185	68.4	31 577	69.8	917	72.7	1 153	72.8	2 715	76.9	2.1	0.8	0.7	0.2	0.4	8.2
Dothan, AL..................	41 257	71.4	11 751	69.9	304	57.6	282	72.3	671	83.2	2.1	0.7	0.6	0.6	0.5	6.7
Dover, DE....................	35 686	70.8	8 892	72.4	380	68.7	582	78.0	1 157	76.1	4.0	1.1	1.3	1.1	1.5	11.5
Dubuque, IA	32 902	68.8	256	68.8	40	80.0	74	78.4	261	68.6	1.9	0.7	0.3	0.5	0.7	6.6
Duluth-Superior, MN-WI	96 503	62.8	658	61.7	1 602	64.7	474	70.9	410	55.4	1.9	0.7	0.6	0.2	0.5	8.3
Eau Claire, WI.............	55 899	65.3	137	62.0	204	54.9	501	80.8	279	57.7	1.8	0.4	1.0	0.2	0.8	7.9
El Paso, TX	50 772	68.4	7 254	71.4	1 594	78.9	2 521	66.2	147 951	84.3	27.4	0.9	0.9	25.5	16.1	66.8
Elkhart-Goshen, IN.......	57 764	72.4	3 310	66.3	221	70.1	471	78.8	3 796	83.6	7.1	0.7	0.8	5.3	4.8	14.5
Elmira, NY...................	33 030	66.7	1 198	68.4	116	62.9	215	90.7	236	61.0	2.2	0.9	0.7	0.4	0.3	8.1
Enid, OK	20 937	68.0	609	65.4	433	73.0	219	71.7	675	83.6	2.7	0.4	0.7	1.3	1.1	8.9
Erie, PA......................	97 955	67.1	5 367	70.4	163	58.9	626	66.6	1 604	75.8	2.7	1.5	0.7	0.3	1.2	8.5
Eugene-Springfield, OR	119 340	63.8	846	60.3	1 176	63.5	2 373	43.1	3 883	70.3	4.9	1.1	1.6	1.6	1.5	11.7
Evansville-Henderson, IN-KY	109 096	68.0	6 749	64.5	214	68.7	661	74.7	803	60.6	1.4	0.4	0.6	0.3	0.4	6.5
Fargo-Moorhead, ND-MN	66 745	60.6	367	66.2	779	58.2	618	65.5	859	72.2	3.0	0.9	1.0	0.3	1.3	8.6
Fayetteville, NC............	60 068	72.4	37 030	72.3	1 627	69.4	1 858	76.0	5 863	80.9	5.3	1.5	1.6	1.8	1.3	16.0
Fayetteville-Springdale-Rogers, AR.................	106 204	69.9	1 296	54.9	1 552	70.7	1 480	68.4	6 483	85.1	6.9	0.5	1.0	5.0	4.0	10.3
Flagstaff, AZ-UT...........	29 489	62.7	505	66.9	8 250	83.9	371	56.3	3 665	74.1	4.3	0.7	0.7	2.4	4.5	34.1
Florence, AL	50 555	70.7	6 898	70.0	162	61.1	144	88.2	450	69.8	1.0	0.2	0.3	0.4	0.4	4.6
Florence, SC	29 235	71.7	16 901	73.3	103	93.2	365	80.8	341	81.5	1.8	0.6	0.6	0.4	0.5	7.6
Fort Collins-Loveland, CO.............................	87 874	65.3	542	65.3	671	66.5	1 281	62.9	5 839	72.6	4.3	1.0	1.2	1.5	1.5	12.8
Fort Myers-Cape Coral, FL..............................	165 098	66.8	9 245	74.0	471	69.0	1 077	66.9	11 458	80.2	9.2	2.4	0.7	5.0	3.6	14.7
Fort Pierce-Port St. Lucie, FL....................	112 735	67.3	11 321	73.6	221	67.4	804	80.1	6 339	83.0	9.5	2.3	0.7	5.8	3.3	14.4
Fort Smith, AR-OK	67 364	71.0	2 913	67.2	3 628	76.2	1 299	82.8	2 287	81.2	4.6	0.3	1.6	2.6	2.1	9.3
Fort Walton Beach, FL..	56 289	70.6	5 395	69.4	359	75.5	1 132	72.1	1 926	76.2	5.3	1.8	2.1	1.1	0.8	13.2
Fort Wayne, IN.............	170 785	69.1	13 373	68.1	629	65.3	1 659	74.6	4 335	78.0	3.0	0.7	0.8	1.1	1.4	9.5
Fresno, CA..................	152 311	68.2	14 326	72.0	4 363	78.2	15 522	82.4	98 649	85.4	21.0	0.7	4.6	15.2	11.8	38.7
Gadsden, AL	35 147	71.6	5 569	65.8	145	86.9	145	77.9	343	87.8	1.6	0.2	0.4	0.9	0.6	5.2
Gainesville, FL.............	64 129	53.9	14 220	64.6	191	56.5	3 069	48.3	4 310	46.1	7.3	1.4	2.9	2.2	1.6	15.2
Glens Falls, NY	47 179	68.5	176	76.1	97	57.7	238	75.6	226	61.9	2.2	1.0	0.4	0.4	0.4	7.1
Goldsboro, NC	27 065	72.2	13 457	68.7	81	79.0	326	68.1	1 259	79.6	4.2	0.6	0.8	2.7	1.9	9.8
Grand Forks, ND-MN ...	35 321	63.2	327	61.5	521	67.0	253	80.2	853	75.1	2.9	0.8	0.7	0.4	0.8	10.5
Grand Junction, CO......	41 295	68.6	166	59.6	366	69.7	108	80.6	3 455	77.7	3.0	0.6	0.3	1.7	1.2	12.1
Grand Rapids-Muskegon-Holland, MI...............................	343 368	70.3	26 921	69.2	2 027	64.4	4 351	80.7	16 739	81.0	5.2	1.1	1.3	2.3	2.3	10.7
Great Falls, MT	30 029	66.0	373	59.0	967	68.6	181	55.2	584	82.9	2.4	1.1	0.5	0.2	0.6	9.2
Green Bay, WI	81 315	65.6	484	64.9	1 792	68.1	1 014	85.7	2 254	79.9	3.9	0.4	1.4	2.1	2.1	9.0
Greensboro—Winston-Salem—High Point, NC	377 854	68.6	95 528	66.6	1 967	71.1	4 695	80.2	15 733	82.4	5.7	0.7	1.1	3.5	3.2	8.7
Greenville, NC	34 140	59.2	16 401	67.9	232	59.1	522	63.6	980	66.2	3.6	0.6	0.8	1.8	1.6	7.8
Greenville-Spartanburg-Anderson, SC.............	299 564	70.4	62 006	69.2	800	63.6	3 420	72.9	7 114	73.1	3.6	0.8	0.9	1.6	1.5	7.7
Harrisburg-Lebanon-Carlisle, PA	221 202	67.5	17 461	64.2	361	59.8	2 921	75.4	5 645	73.5	3.2	1.0	1.3	0.6	1.5	9.4

[1]Hispanic or Latino persons may be of any race.

CMSA/MSA/ PMSA/NECMA code[1]	Area name	Total population	Under 5 years	5 to 17 years	18 to 24 years	25 to 44 years	45 to 64 years	65 years and over	Median age	+/− U.S. percent under 18 years	+/− U.S. percent 65 years and over	Non-Hispanic White Total population	Age (percent) Under 18 years	65 years and over
		1	2	3	4	5	6	7	8	9	10	11	12	13
3283	Hartford, CT	1 148 618	6.3	17.9	8.3	30.2	23.3	13.9	37.6	−1.5	1.5	888 658	21.5	16.5
3285	Hattiesburg, MS	111 674	6.8	18.9	15.8	28.6	19.2	10.7	30.8	0.0	−1.7	79 319	22.8	12.6
3290	Hickory-Morganton-Lenoir, NC	341 851	6.5	17.6	8.4	30.7	24.1	12.8	36.7	−1.6	0.4	293 461	22.5	13.9
3320	Honolulu, HI	876 156	6.4	17.3	10.1	30.7	22.0	13.5	35.7	−2.0	1.1	175 331	16.1	12.6
3350	Houma, LA	194 477	7.2	21.1	10.4	29.8	21.1	10.4	33.5	2.6	−2.0	150 365	25.6	11.8
42	Houston-Galveston-Brazoria, TX	4 669 571	8.0	21.0	9.8	33.1	20.4	7.6	31.9	3.3	−4.8	2 236 569	24.0	11.0
1145	Brazoria, TX	241 767	7.6	20.9	8.5	32.8	21.4	8.8	34.0	2.8	−3.6	157 936	25.7	11.2
2920	Galveston-Texas City, TX ...	250 158	6.9	19.7	8.8	30.4	23.2	11.0	35.9	0.9	−1.4	157 545	23.2	12.8
3360	Houston, TX	4 177 646	8.1	21.1	10.0	33.3	20.2	7.4	31.6	3.5	−5.0	1 921 088	23.9	10.9
3400	Huntington-Ashland, WV-KY-OH	315 538	5.8	16.6	10.2	27.7	24.7	15.0	38.1	−3.3	2.6	301 704	22.2	15.3
3440	Huntsville, AL	342 376	6.8	18.6	9.2	31.8	22.7	10.9	35.7	−0.3	−1.5	250 552	23.7	12.8
3480	Indianapolis, IN	1 607 486	7.4	19.1	8.7	32.3	21.4	10.9	34.6	0.8	−1.5	1 299 515	25.1	11.9
3500	Iowa City, IA	111 006	5.6	14.4	23.3	30.7	18.4	7.5	28.4	−5.7	−4.9	98 789	19.2	8.2
3520	Jackson, MI	158 422	6.6	19.0	8.2	30.3	22.9	12.9	36.6	−0.1	0.5	138 631	24.7	13.8
3560	Jackson, MS	440 801	7.3	20.1	10.8	30.7	20.8	10.3	33.0	1.7	−2.1	230 029	22.5	13.6
3580	Jackson, TN	107 377	6.8	18.7	11.5	28.6	21.7	12.6	34.6	−0.2	0.2	72 761	22.2	14.6
3600	Jacksonville, FL............	1 100 491	6.8	19.3	9.0	31.5	22.4	11.1	35.3	0.4	−1.3	775 129	23.1	12.9
3605	Jacksonville, NC...........	150 355	8.8	17.4	23.7	29.4	14.3	6.4	25.0	0.5	−6.0	104 457	23.8	7.4
3610	Jamestown, NY	139 750	5.8	18.6	10.3	26.3	23.0	16.0	37.9	−1.3	3.6	128 574	23.4	17.0
3620	Janesville-Beloit, WI	152 307	6.8	19.7	8.7	29.8	22.2	12.8	35.9	0.8	0.4	135 964	24.9	13.8
3660	Johnson City-Kingsport-Bristol, TN-VA	480 091	5.6	15.9	8.5	29.0	25.7	15.3	39.2	−4.2	2.9	459 216	21.2	15.7
3680	Johnstown, PA	232 621	5.2	16.3	8.6	26.6	24.2	19.1	40.9	−4.2	6.7	223 030	21.3	19.7
3700	Jonesboro, AR	82 148	6.8	17.4	14.0	28.7	21.3	11.7	33.0	−1.5	−0.7	72 604	22.8	12.7
3710	Joplin, MO	157 322	7.1	18.8	10.3	27.9	22.1	13.9	35.6	0.2	1.5	144 140	25.1	14.6
3720	Kalamazoo-Battle Creek, MI	452 851	6.5	18.8	12.0	28.4	22.1	12.2	34.7	−0.4	−0.2	377 204	23.1	13.5
3760	Kansas City, MO-KS	1 776 062	7.2	19.3	8.5	31.6	22.0	11.4	35.2	0.8	−1.0	1 391 623	24.5	12.7
3810	Killeen-Temple, TX.......	312 952	8.7	19.6	14.5	33.1	16.2	8.0	28.8	2.6	−4.4	181 521	24.0	11.4
3840	Knoxville, TN	687 249	6.0	16.6	10.0	29.8	24.2	13.4	37.3	−3.1	1.0	622 899	21.8	14.1
3850	Kokomo, IN	101 541	6.9	18.6	8.0	28.3	24.6	13.6	37.3	−0.2	1.2	91 767	24.3	14.3
3870	La Crosse, WI-MN	126 838	6.0	18.2	14.1	27.5	21.1	13.1	34.4	−1.5	0.7	119 895	22.9	13.7
3920	Lafayette, IN	182 821	6.2	15.9	22.3	27.6	17.9	10.1	28.5	−3.6	−2.3	159 929	21.6	11.2
3880	Lafayette, LA	385 647	7.5	21.0	10.6	29.4	20.6	10.9	33.2	2.8	−1.5	265 792	25.7	12.4
3960	Lake Charles, LA	183 577	7.3	20.1	10.2	28.9	21.6	11.9	34.5	1.7	−0.5	133 607	25.2	13.3
3980	Lakeland-Winter Haven, FL	483 924	6.4	17.9	8.3	26.5	22.6	18.3	38.6	−1.4	5.9	361 079	20.7	22.3
4000	Lancaster, PA	470 658	6.9	19.7	9.1	28.4	21.8	14.0	36.1	0.9	1.6	420 994	25.1	15.2
4040	Lansing-East Lansing, MI	447 728	6.4	18.3	14.6	28.9	21.7	10.1	32.7	−1.0	−2.3	367 896	22.7	11.4
4080	Laredo, TX	193 117	10.5	25.7	11.4	29.4	15.3	7.7	26.5	10.5	−4.7	9 258	28.2	12.6
4100	Las Cruces, NM	174 682	7.7	21.9	13.1	27.6	18.9	10.7	30.2	3.9	−1.7	56 757	18.2	18.1
4120	Las Vegas, NV-AZ	1 563 282	7.3	17.9	8.7	31.5	22.8	11.8	35.2	−0.5	−0.6	985 291	20.4	15.8
4150	Lawrence, KS	99 962	5.6	14.8	26.4	28.3	17.0	8.0	26.6	−5.3	−4.4	84 601	19.3	8.7
4200	Lawton, OK	114 996	7.8	19.7	14.0	31.1	17.6	9.7	30.1	1.8	−2.7	71 214	23.2	12.9
4243	Lewiston-Auburn, ME....	103 793	5.9	17.9	9.1	29.7	22.9	14.4	37.2	−1.9	2.0	100 004	23.3	14.8
4280	Lexington, KY	479 198	6.4	16.3	13.7	32.0	21.4	10.2	33.3	−3.0	−2.2	407 695	21.7	10.7
4320	Lima, OH	155 084	6.7	19.7	9.3	27.8	22.3	14.2	36.4	0.7	1.8	136 686	25.3	15.2
4360	Lincoln, NE	250 291	6.6	16.9	15.5	30.3	20.3	10.4	32.0	−2.2	−2.0	222 097	22.1	11.3
4400	Little Rock-North Little Rock, AR	583 845	7.0	18.6	10.0	30.8	22.3	11.2	34.7	−0.1	−1.2	428 975	22.9	13.2
4420	Longview-Marshall, TX..	208 780	6.7	20.1	9.9	27.6	22.2	13.5	35.8	1.1	1.1	149 709	24.2	15.2
49	Los Angeles-Riverside-Orange County, CA....	16 373 645	7.7	20.8	9.9	32.3	19.4	9.9	32.3	2.8	−2.5	6 364 336	20.3	16.5
4480	Los Angeles-Long Beach, CA	9 519 338	7.7	20.3	10.3	32.8	19.2	9.7	32.0	2.3	−2.7	2 946 145	17.8	17.5
5945	Orange County, CA....	2 846 289	7.5	19.4	9.3	33.4	20.5	9.8	33.3	1.2	−2.6	1 455 470	21.0	14.9
6780	Riverside-San Bernardino, CA..........	3 254 821	8.0	23.3	9.7	29.9	18.6	10.5	31.6	5.6	−1.9	1 536 542	23.4	17.1
8735	Ventura, CA................	753 197	7.4	20.9	9.0	30.9	21.7	10.0	34.2	2.6	−2.4	426 179	23.5	13.9
4520	Louisville, KY-IN...........	1 025 598	6.7	18.0	8.7	30.8	23.2	12.5	36.5	−1.0	0.1	841 244	23.1	13.6
4600	Lubbock, TX	242 628	7.0	18.5	16.2	28.2	19.2	11.0	30.5	−0.2	−1.4	151 592	19.9	14.3
4640	Lynchburg, VA..............	214 911	5.8	17.5	9.7	28.2	24.3	14.5	38.0	−2.4	2.1	169 974	21.7	15.6
4680	Macon, GA	322 549	7.1	20.0	10.1	30.1	21.6	11.2	34.4	1.4	−1.2	187 501	23.3	14.0
4720	Madison, WI	426 526	6.0	16.5	14.3	32.6	21.3	9.3	33.2	−3.2	−3.1	373 075	20.9	10.3
4800	Mansfield, OH	175 818	6.4	18.5	8.2	28.2	24.2	14.4	37.8	−0.8	2.0	158 701	24.3	15.2
4880	McAllen-Edinburg-Mission, TX	569 463	10.2	25.1	11.3	27.8	15.9	9.8	27.2	9.6	−2.6	59 009	15.3	37.4
4890	Medford-Ashland, OR ...	181 269	6.0	18.3	8.8	25.4	25.4	16.0	39.2	−1.4	3.6	160 553	22.6	17.4
4900	Melbourne-Titusville-Palm Bay,FL............	476 230	5.2	16.7	6.8	27.2	24.3	19.9	41.4	−3.8	7.5	398 332	20.1	21.9
4920	Memphis, TN-AR-MS	1 135 614	7.6	20.7	9.4	31.2	21.2	9.9	33.2	2.6	−2.5	589 338	23.3	12.8

[1]MSA = Metropolitan Statistical Area. CMSA = Consolidated Metropolitan Area. PMSA = Primary MSA. NECMA = New England County Metropolitan Area. See the Appendix A for explanation of these concepts. See Appendix B for list of metropolitan areas identified by type, with component counties.

Area name	Black or African American			American Indian and Alaska Native			Asian, Hawaiian, and Pacific Islander			Hispanic or Latino[1]			Two or more races		
		Age (percent)			Age (percent)			Age (percent)			Age (percent)			Age (percent)	
	Total population	Under 18 years	65 years and over	Total population	Under 18 years	65 years and over	Total population	Under 18 years	65 years and over	Total population	Under 18 years	65 years and over	Total population	Under 18 years	65 years and over
	14	15	16	17	18	19	20	21	22	23	24	25	26	27	28
Hartford, CT	108 280	31.1	6.6	2 311	21.7	9.7	26 968	26.1	4.3	107 143	37.8	3.4	26 298	39.2	5.5
Hattiesburg, MS	29 363	33.8	6.2	178	38.8	3.4	946	19.8	1.8	1 172	29.1	3.2	751	20.2	11.6
Hickory-Morganton-Lenoir, NC	23 951	29.5	9.5	1 218	30.2	1.3	7 427	47.7	2.5	13 308	29.1	1.8	3 714	46.1	4.4
Honolulu, HI	19 688	24.9	2.2	1 881	16.4	4.5	481 668	19.9	17.7	58 731	38.2	4.2	176 540	41.2	5.2
Houma, LA	29 718	37.4	6.0	7 098	38.8	4.4	1 494	30.4	3.5	3 138	35.2	5.3	2 956	40.8	4.3
Houston-Galveston-Brazoria, TX	787 230	31.3	6.9	20 644	30.1	4.1	226 406	25.7	5.2	1 349 506	36.1	3.0	130 677	38.1	3.6
Brazoria, TX	20 311	27.4	6.1	1 297	30.5	2.7	4 805	29.4	5.3	55 034	36.6	3.3	5 516	40.6	5.6
Galveston-Texas City, TX..	38 095	30.6	11.1	1 207	28.7	7.3	5 334	25.6	5.7	45 153	34.8	5.4	5 875	42.9	4.6
Houston, TX	728 824	31.5	6.7	18 140	30.2	4.0	216 267	25.6	5.2	1 249 319	36.1	2.9	119 286	37.8	3.4
Huntington Ashland, WV-KY-OH	6 861	23.2	11.2	608	19.4	6.1	1 561	20.3	7.4	1 941	31.0	5.8	2 958	40.9	9.0
Huntsville, AL	71 081	28.9	6.3	2 734	31.5	1.6	5 118	24.7	4.3	6 938	36.3	3.0	6 630	38.5	4.8
Indianapolis, IN	222 703	32.2	8.3	4 456	24.5	7.9	19 101	24.4	4.6	41 056	32.1	1.9	23 324	47.0	3.4
Iowa City, IA	3 120	30.5	2.4	251	28.3	0.0	4 488	20.1	1.8	2 925	30.6	1.8	1 720	37.0	2.2
Jackson, MI	12 009	26.7	7.0	677	38.4	5.0	770	27.5	5.8	3 723	39.5	5.2	2 972	52.9	4.9
Jackson, MS................	200 901	32.9	6.7	969	34.2	4.9	2 535	19.2	5.3	4 128	32.1	4.8	3 186	42.3	6.2
Jackson, TN	31 306	32.5	8.7	229	41.5	0.0	593	40.0	4.9	1 556	29.0	2.3	1 097	46.8	7.6
Jacksonville, FL...........	237 336	33.7	7.5	3 828	23.9	4.1	25 736	23.7	5.2	42 633	31.7	4.8	21 403	42.6	3.6
Jacksonville, NC..........	27 426	30.7	5.4	1 157	27.1	2.3	2 966	20.4	6.7	10 766	29.6	1.1	5 283	50.5	0.9
Jamestown, NY.........	3 036	22.9	4.0	630	24.1	13.2	482	30.7	5.4	5 836	39.1	4.2	1 856	52.3	2.6
Janesville-Beloit, WI......	6 704	37.4	7.2	513	28.3	1.9	1 380	27.8	7.5	5 982	39.1	1.8	2 023	58.8	2.5
Johnson City-Kingsport-Bristol, TN-VA	10 057	25.9	9.8	1 038	26.4	5.6	1 975	25.7	2.5	4 232	33.6	5.3	3 783	36.5	7.2
Johnstown, PA	5 789	20.2	6.7	199	16.0	2.0	774	25.7	4.0	1 731	19.9	7.1	1 310	49.3	4.0
Jonesboro, AR	6 403	34.8	3.8	311	26.4	4.8	517	36.6	0.8	1 520	35.9	6.1	920	35.0	8.0
Joplin, MO	1 673	28.2	9.2	2 575	31.4	6.2	981	21.5	4.8	4 887	40.2	1.7	3 699	39.0	8.3
Kalamazoo-Battle Creek, MI..................	40 621	33.8	8.1	2 693	27.7	4.7	6 239	22.4	3.8	16 605	41.8	2.6	11 331	47.5	5.1
Kansas City, MO-KS	222 865	32.7	8.3	9 034	24.8	5.7	29 459	25.7	4.4	92 029	35.5	3.8	39 275	45.6	4.4
Killeen-Temple, TX.......	63 409	31.7	3.0	2 279	32.8	2.6	9 191	21.6	5.0	49 086	36.1	3.1	13 010	53.9	2.2
Knoxville, TN	39 852	29.6	9.1	2 238	21.6	3.4	6 264	23.6	2.4	7 430	32.2	3.8	8 853	38.2	7.0
Kokomo, IN	5 475	32.7	9.3	351	27.6	5.4	818	26.4	5.4	1 895	42.8	3.9	1 394	53.1	6.0
La Crosse, WI-MN	969	28.5	1.3	668	34.7	5.2	3 019	53.0	2.0	979	36.3	3.9	1 407	55.5	1.9
Lafayette, IN	3 414	27.2	2.5	658	33.1	2.0	6 857	12.8	1.2	10 200	31.4	1.2	2 566	35.7	5.4
Lafayette, LA..............	108 751	34.8	8.0	868	32.5	4.5	2 922	25.8	3.1	4 752	31.4	4.6	3 115	38.1	6.0
Lake Charles, LA	43 529	32.8	8.4	620	37.9	9.4	1 167	21.2	4.3	3 166	37.7	3.9	2 055	43.5	7.0
Lakeland-Winter Haven, FL..	63 709	34.6	8.4	2 172	30.2	7.3	5 964	29.3	7.1	45 650	35.9	4.0	8 820	38.5	6.3
Lancaster, PA.............	12 722	36.6	4.9	575	17.9	13.6	6 644	31.0	3.4	26 451	41.6	2.8	6 214	52.2	2.9
Lansing-East Lansing, MI	35 318	32.4	5.1	2 463	28.1	3.0	11 788	23.9	2.9	20 990	36.9	3.5	11 991	51.3	2.2
Laredo, TX.................	738	47.6	3.4	841	30.3	8.7	816	30.8	6.0	182 396	36.7	7.5	4 688	33.3	9.0
Las Cruces, NM	2 444	27.9	10.2	2 523	30.4	5.4	1 494	24.8	6.0	110 807	35.8	7.2	6 359	38.7	6.8
Las Vegas, NV-AZ	123 915	31.4	7.0	15 496	27.7	6.2	78 741	20.7	7.9	321 515	36.6	3.2	65 150	42.0	4.5
Lawrence, KS	4 184	26.4	5.9	2 305	24.1	2.2	3 335	11.7	1.8	3 146	28.3	3.3	3 038	46.6	4.6
Lawton, OK	22 140	34.3	4.0	5 676	31.0	7.4	2 635	16.8	7.1	9 692	36.1	3.5	5 804	47.7	3.5
Lewiston-Auburn, ME....	601	39.3	1.8	422	32.7	8.1	552	27.0	4.3	851	34.9	5.6	1 454	44.4	5.0
Lexington, KY	45 071	27.4	9.5	1 207	20.8	2.5	7 439	21.9	1.8	11 394	27.1	2.5	7 275	42.5	3.0
Lima, OH	13 223	32.5	8.0	281	26.0	7.1	738	25.5	3.0	1 822	33.6	4.5	2 585	53.2	2.4
Lincoln, NE...............	7 005	32.4	3.4	1 913	34.4	3.8	6 934	28.4	3.2	8 532	34.7	4.1	4 732	49.9	2.0
Little Rock-North Little Rock, AR..	127 681	33.6	6.2	2 539	28.2	3.5	5 730	21.6	3.7	12 263	33.6	2.0	8 117	38.1	6.2
Longview-Marshall, TX..	40 939	31.1	11.6	791	25.8	8.0	998	27.1	3.7	14 563	41.3	2.1	2 937	38.1	7.5
Los Angeles-Riverside-Orange County, CA....	1 222 728	30.8	8.5	129 749	31.3	5.4	1 739 698	22.8	9.4	6 601 133	37.0	4.1	804 620	38.9	5.1
Los Angeles-Long Beach, CA..	916 907	29.5	9.6	68 471	31.3	5.3	1 161 484	22.0	10.4	4 243 487	36.1	4.3	486 792	35.7	5.7
Orange County, CA....	44 256	29.6	4.0	17 664	29.0	5.1	394 874	24.1	7.5	876 451	37.2	3.1	121 239	40.1	4.1
Riverside-San Bernardino, CA..........	247 517	36.0	5.5	37 331	32.7	5.7	142 489	26.3	6.9	1 229 230	40.2	3.9	166 179	46.4	4.1
Ventura, CA	14 048	27.8	5.3	6 283	31.0	6.1	40 851	23.2	9.2	251 965	36.5	4.2	30 410	44.0	3.6
Louisville, KY-IN..........	141 623	31.6	8.8	2 633	17.8	5.2	10 530	22.8	3.9	15 542	33.5	3.1	15 694	46.2	4.8
Lubbock, TX	18 779	33.3	7.8	1 405	29.1	4.1	3 043	20.0	4.4	66 568	36.2	4.7	4 800	40.0	5.4
Lynchburg, VA............	37 990	28.1	11.1	708	20.6	10.3	2 040	21.2	5.8	2 137	30.4	6.0	2 341	52.6	5.9
Macon, GA	120 715	32.0	7.7	872	24.0	4.8	3 889	27.9	3.8	6 485	33.8	3.5	4 086	46.1	3.2
Madison, WI	16 449	36.2	3.0	1 518	28.0	1.0	14 550	25.8	3.0	14 602	30.5	1.5	7 702	45.5	2.1
Mansfield, OH	11 688	26.3	8.0	450	23.4	10.9	952	25.8	2.8	1 594	37.5	4.8	2 614	49.0	4.4
McAllen-Edinburg-Mission, TX	2 777	29.0	2.8	2 093	36.6	8.3	3 308	30.4	4.1	503 526	37.7	6.6	11 906	34.2	8.9
Medford-Ashland, OR ...	760	36.6	2.0	1 975	29.5	7.2	1 735	21.9	7.5	12 066	42.9	2.6	5 592	39.6	7.0
Melbourne-Titusville-Palm Bay, FL.............	38 680	32.9	10.4	2 070	18.7	9.4	7 400	20.0	8.4	21 902	30.0	8.4	10 093	40.2	7.5
Memphis, TN-AR-MS....	490 705	33.9	7.3	2 408	23.5	7.1	16 686	26.5	3.6	26 359	31.1	1.8	12 568	43.2	5.5

[1] Hispanic or Latino persons may be of any race.

Table A-4. Metropolitan Areas — Age, Ethnicity, and Household Structure

Area name	Total households	Married-couple family households — Total	With children	Householder 65 years or over	Other family households — Total	With children	Householder 65 years or over	Two or more unrelated persons — Total	Householder 65 years or over	Male living alone — Total	Householder 65 years or over	Female living alone — Total	Householder 65 years or over	Percent of householders 65 years and over who live alone	Grandparents who are responsible for the care of their grandchildren
	29	30	31	32	33	34	35	36	37	38	39	40	41	42	43
Hartford, CT	445 916	51.3	22.9	9.5	15.5	8.9	2.2	5.8	0.4	11.0	2.5	16.3	7.9	46.1	6 498
Hattiesburg, MS	41 583	49.3	23.4	7.7	18.5	10.7	2.5	6.5	0.2	10.5	1.8	15.2	6.8	45.2	1 352
Hickory-Morganton-Lenoir, NC	134 105	56.6	23.3	9.4	15.1	8.5	2.2	4.1	0.2	10.2	1.9	14.0	7.1	43.0	3 682
Honolulu, HI	286 731	55.4	25.3	11.2	16.9	7.0	4.1	6.2	0.5	10.6	2.2	11.0	4.9	30.8	10 302
Houma, LA	68 110	58.8	28.7	8.6	17.4	10.3	2.4	4.5	0.4	8.5	2.0	10.9	6.0	41.2	2 670
Houston-Galveston-Brazoria, TX	1 640 843	54.6	29.5	5.9	17.2	9.9	1.8	4.8	0.3	11.1	1.4	12.3	4.1	41.1	54 138
Brazoria, TX	82 020	63.1	32.7	7.8	14.4	8.9	1.8	3.5	0.2	8.8	1.7	10.3	4.8	39.9	2 887
Galveston-Texas City, TX...........................	94 840	53.1	24.5	7.8	17.0	9.9	2.4	4.8	0.5	11.9	2.5	13.2	5.9	43.9	3 400
Houston, TX	1 463 983	54.2	29.7	5.7	17.4	10.0	1.8	4.9	0.2	11.2	1.3	12.3	4.0	40.9	47 851
Huntington-Ashland, WV-KY-OH	128 266	55.7	22.2	10.6	14.1	7.6	2.5	3.7	0.3	10.1	2.6	16.3	9.2	46.7	2 667
Huntsville, AL	134 753	55.3	25.0	8.6	14.7	8.7	1.9	3.6	0.1	12.0	1.7	14.5	5.9	41.8	3 480
Indianapolis, IN	630 031	51.5	24.3	7.6	15.7	9.7	1.8	5.7	0.3	11.5	1.9	15.5	6.5	46.6	13 520
Iowa City, IA	44 074	44.7	21.6	5.6	9.4	5.4	0.6	15.7	0.3	14.1	1.3	16.1	4.7	48.0	216
Jackson, MI.................	58 318	55.1	23.8	9.9	15.5	10.1	2.0	4.8	0.5	10.6	2.5	14.0	7.8	45.6	1 198
Jackson, MS................	160 529	48.1	23.2	7.1	22.7	13.1	2.8	4.2	0.2	10.5	1.7	14.5	6.1	43.6	6 767
Jackson, TN	41 200	51.8	23.3	9.1	18.5	10.5	2.5	4.0	0.2	11.1	2.1	14.6	6.9	43.2	1 125
Jacksonville, FL............	425 809	51.5	23.6	8.0	17.5	10.5	2.0	6.3	0.4	10.9	1.9	13.9	6.0	43.2	12 342
Jacksonville, NC...........	48 107	61.9	33.6	5.9	14.8	9.9	1.4	4.7	0.2	9.4	1.4	9.2	4.0	41.9	1 206
Jamestown, NY	54 488	52.0	21.8	11.4	14.3	9.0	1.8	5.5	0.5	11.6	2.9	16.5	9.8	48.2	840
Janesville-Beloit, WI	58 674	55.1	24.6	10.0	14.2	9.3	1.3	5.6	0.3	10.3	2.1	14.8	7.4	45.1	961
Johnson City-Kingsport-Bristol, TN-VA	199 430	56.7	21.9	10.6	13.1	6.9	2.5	3.4	0.2	10.6	2.3	16.1	8.8	45.5	4 184
Johnstown, PA	91 761	55.2	21.6	13.1	13.5	6.4	3.4	2.8	0.4	10.5	3.3	18.0	11.8	47.4	1 436
Jonesboro, AR	32 301	53.5	24.3	8.0	15.5	8.6	1.7	5.8	0.3	10.3	1.7	14.9	7.2	47.1	852
Joplin, MO	61 634	55.9	24.3	10.8	13.6	8.8	1.7	4.7	0.3	10.5	2.2	15.2	8.3	45.0	1 400
Kalamazoo-Battle Creek, MI	175 694	50.5	22.6	8.8	15.0	9.5	1.8	7.4	0.4	11.6	2.1	15.5	7.3	46.1	2 892
Kansas City, MO-KS	694 971	52.4	24.5	8.2	15.2	9.3	1.7	5.4	0.3	11.5	2.0	15.6	6.7	46.2	13 812
Killeen-Temple, TX........	105 337	59.1	31.5	7.0	15.1	10.7	1.2	4.6	0.2	10.2	1.4	11.1	4.9	42.6	2 855
Knoxville, TN	281 514	54.1	22.3	9.4	13.6	7.4	2.2	5.2	0.3	11.2	2.0	16.0	7.4	44.2	5 635
Kokomo, IN	41 345	55.0	22.7	9.7	14.0	8.6	1.8	3.7	0.2	11.4	2.2	16.0	8.4	47.5	920
La Crosse, WI-MN	49 238	52.0	23.9	9.4	11.4	7.3	1.3	8.7	0.2	11.3	2.4	16.6	8.1	48.8	311
Lafayette, IN................	67 789	49.5	22.8	7.5	12.1	7.7	1.0	11.3	0.2	12.8	1.9	14.4	6.3	48.8	712
Lafayette, LA................	143 036	51.2	25.5	7.9	19.5	12.1	2.5	4.9	0.3	10.7	2.1	13.7	6.7	45.2	4 740
Lake Charles, LA	68 757	53.4	25.4	9.1	18.2	10.7	2.6	4.4	0.2	10.6	2.2	13.3	6.6	42.3	2 565
Lakeland-Winter Haven, FL	187 162	55.3	20.3	15.3	15.7	9.0	2.4	4.9	0.7	9.9	3.0	14.2	8.4	38.2	6 077
Lancaster, PA...............	172 780	60.5	27.1	11.4	11.7	6.9	1.5	4.7	0.3	9.4	2.2	13.6	7.2	41.4	2 421
Lansing-East Lansing, MI	172 525	50.0	23.4	7.6	14.2	9.1	1.4	8.4	0.3	11.5	1.7	15.8	6.2	45.9	2 214
Laredo, TX	50 647	65.0	42.0	7.8	21.3	11.4	4.0	1.4	0.2	5.5	1.2	6.8	3.6	28.8	3 404
Las Cruces, NM	59 479	53.2	26.7	10.2	19.1	12.4	1.9	6.4	0.4	10.1	2.1	11.3	4.9	35.8	2 455
Las Vegas, NV-AZ	588 822	50.5	21.9	9.4	16.6	9.7	1.8	8.4	0.9	12.7	2.7	11.7	4.7	38.0	15 628
Lawrence, KS................	38 526	44.7	20.8	6.5	10.7	6.7	0.9	16.0	0.3	13.0	1.1	15.5	4.5	42.3	319
Lawton, OK	39 930	55.4	28.5	7.9	17.5	11.6	2.1	3.9	0.2	11.0	2.1	12.3	5.9	43.8	1 305
Lewiston-Auburn, ME....	42 095	50.6	21.3	8.8	14.7	9.8	1.8	6.5	0.5	11.4	2.6	16.8	8.8	50.7	391
Lexington, KY...............	191 204	50.4	22.4	7.1	14.2	8.5	1.6	7.7	0.2	11.8	1.6	15.9	6.2	46.4	3 602
Lima, OH	58 066	56.2	24.5	10.9	14.9	9.7	1.9	3.4	0.3	10.2	2.4	15.2	8.7	46.0	1 055
Lincoln, NE..................	99 254	49.7	23.3	7.8	12.1	7.5	1.2	9.2	0.2	12.8	1.7	16.2	6.5	46.8	946
Little Rock-North Little Rock, AR	230 955	52.4	23.3	8.2	16.3	10.0	1.8	4.7	0.2	11.3	1.7	15.2	6.4	44.2	6 533
Longview-Marshall, TX..	79 084	55.6	24.7	10.0	16.3	9.3	2.6	3.3	0.3	9.9	2.5	14.8	8.4	45.8	2 862
Los Angeles-Riverside-Orange County, CA....	5 351 556	52.2	28.4	7.8	18.7	10.3	2.3	6.4	0.6	10.1	2.0	12.6	5.4	41.0	149 557
Los Angeles-Long Beach, CA	3 136 279	48.5	26.8	7.1	20.2	10.8	2.5	6.7	0.5	11.3	2.0	13.3	5.2	41.6	88 511
Orange County, CA....	936 154	57.0	30.0	8.1	15.0	7.8	1.9	7.0	0.5	8.8	1.6	12.3	5.5	40.7	18 792
Riverside-San Bernardino, CA...........	1 035 620	57.2	30.9	9.4	18.4	11.3	2.1	5.0	0.6	8.4	2.2	11.1	5.8	39.7	36 600
Ventura, CA...............	243 503	60.2	31.8	8.7	15.5	8.6	2.0	5.5	0.5	7.9	1.8	11.0	5.6	39.9	5 654
Louisville, KY-IN...........	412 289	49.9	21.9	8.3	17.2	10.1	2.4	5.1	0.3	11.6	2.2	16.2	7.4	46.4	8 900
Lubbock, TX	92 685	49.2	22.8	8.4	16.3	9.5	1.9	7.7	0.3	11.5	1.8	15.3	6.3	43.1	3 703
Lynchburg, VA..............	84 364	54.4	22.0	10.8	15.6	9.1	2.5	4.1	0.4	10.7	2.2	15.2	7.7	42.4	2 087
Macon, GA	121 456	49.7	22.5	8.3	21.2	12.8	2.5	4.1	0.3	10.4	1.7	14.6	6.7	43.2	4 415
Madison, WI	173 710	48.1	22.9	6.7	10.4	6.6	0.9	12.1	0.2	12.7	1.5	16.7	5.5	47.4	957
Mansfield, OH	68 497	54.8	22.1	11.0	14.6	9.0	2.2	4.1	0.3	11.1	2.4	15.3	8.4	44.3	1 341
McAllen-Edinburg-Mission, TX	156 708	66.0	39.6	11.7	19.0	10.6	3.1	2.0	0.3	5.1	1.7	7.9	4.7	29.5	8 736
Medford-Ashland, OR ...	71 575	54.3	22.0	12.4	13.8	9.1	1.7	6.8	0.7	9.6	2.5	15.4	8.5	42.5	1 060
Melbourne-Titusville-Palm Bay,FL.............	198 371	53.7	19.2	15.5	13.6	7.8	2.3	5.9	0.7	11.7	3.3	15.1	8.5	38.9	4 283
Memphis, TN-AR-MS	424 498	46.6	22.1	6.7	23.2	13.6	2.8	4.7	0.3	11.0	1.7	14.4	5.8	43.5	15 388

Area name	Households with Non-Hispanic White householder		Households with Black or African American householder		Households with American Indian and Alaska Native householder		Households with Asian, Hawaiian, and Pacific Islander householder		Households with Hispanic or Latino[1] householder		Foreign-born population				Percent in non-English speaking households	
												Place of birth (percent)				
	Number of households	Percent that are family households	Number of households	Percent that are family households	Number of households	Percent that are family households	Number of households	Percent that are family households	Number of households	Percent that are family households	Percent of total population that is foreign-born	Europe	Asia	Latin America	Linguistically isolated	Not linguistically isolated
	44	45	46	47	48	49	50	51	52	53	54	55	56	57	58	59
Hartford, CT	362 318	65.9	37 933	67.5	877	53.2	8 246	73.7	31 552	77.1	10.3	4.3	1.9	3.0	4.2	20.5
Hattiesburg, MS	31 118	67.3	9 518	69.6	51	82.4	302	57.6	337	66.8	1.7	0.5	0.8	0.3	0.6	6.5
Hickory-Morganton-Lenoir, NC	119 462	71.5	8 480	69.3	452	77.9	1 532	91.6	3 471	76.5	4.6	0.4	1.3	2.7	2.4	7.9
Honolulu, HI	75 887	63.8	6 887	73.9	620	75.6	156 354	75.4	14 303	75.8	19.2	0.8	16.4	0.5	6.4	36.8
Houma, LA	55 055	75.9	9 205	75.1	1 818	88.9	406	80.8	860	75.7	1.5	0.2	0.6	0.6	2.2	26.8
Houston-Galveston-Brazoria, TX	912 592	67.6	280 611	69.4	6 802	75.3	70 534	79.6	352 659	83.3	19.2	1.0	4.0	13.3	9.5	29.4
Brazoria, TX	59 537	75.5	5 813	73.7	336	75.6	1 307	86.8	14 121	86.8	8.5	0.6	1.5	6.1	4.4	24.3
Galveston-Texas City, TX.....................	64 546	68.7	14 192	69.4	519	71.9	1 735	72.0	13 017	78.3	8.3	0.8	1.8	5.3	4.0	20.0
Houston, TX	788 509	67.0	260 606	69.3	5 947	75.6	67 492	79.7	325 521	83.4	20.5	1.1	4.3	14.2	10.1	30.3
Huntington-Ashland, WV-KY-OH	123 549	70.3	2 605	54.7	258	47.7	484	63.4	486	62.1	0.9	0.2	0.4	0.2	0.1	4.5
Huntsville, AL	102 939	70.2	25 540	68.5	898	71.9	1 533	78.0	1 963	75.8	3.5	0.8	1.3	1.0	0.9	7.9
Indianapolis, IN	521 242	67.5	83 697	65.3	1 800	68.7	6 743	70.2	11 295	72.4	3.4	0.7	1.0	1.3	1.3	8.0
Iowa City, IA	39 503	54.0	1 256	49.8	138	47.8	1 790	55.8	888	67.3	6.4	1.0	3.7	0.9	2.3	12.6
Jackson, MI	53 300	70.8	2 985	65.3	188	67.6	230	56.5	912	78.2	1.7	0.6	0.4	0.4	0.5	7.0
Jackson, MS................	92 008	69.7	65 743	72.3	331	71.3	845	75.0	1 053	66.7	1.3	0.2	0.5	0.3	0.4	6.8
Jackson, TN	28 886	71.0	11 430	68.5	90	81.1	141	90.8	400	70.3	2.0	0.4	0.5	0.9	0.8	5.9
Jacksonville, FL.............	314 611	68.3	84 523	70.3	1 417	71.3	7 622	76.9	13 315	75.2	5.4	1.5	2.0	1.4	1.4	12.4
Jacksonville, NC............	35 310	76.9	8 667	75.6	350	79.4	676	60.1	2 391	82.5	4.1	0.7	1.4	1.8	0.9	13.5
Jamestown, NY	51 436	66.2	835	54.9	260	54.2	117	85.5	1 534	78.7	1.9	0.9	0.3	0.4	1.3	10.5
Janesville-Beloit, WI........	54 102	69.0	2 255	69.7	146	58.2	377	69.0	1 468	80.7	3.3	0.5	0.7	2.0	1.7	8.8
Johnson City-Kingsport-Bristol, TN-VA	192 123	70.0	3 836	63.2	378	75.7	547	81.0	1 323	76.7	1.2	0.4	0.3	0.3	0.3	4.6
Johnstown, PA	89 731	68.8	1 227	62.2	69	63.8	225	79.6	317	56.5	1.1	0.4	0.3	0.3	0.5	6.2
Jonesboro, AR	29 138	69.3	2 304	64.8	93	69.9	89	76.4	403	81.9	2.0	0.2	0.6	1.0	1.0	5.4
Joplin, MO	57 422	69.6	654	58.1	919	72.6	269	68.4	1 345	73.5	2.2	0.3	0.5	1.3	1.1	6.6
Kalamazoo-Battle Creek, MI................	151 178	65.6	15 175	63.7	822	62.4	2 128	57.3	3 785	75.3	3.4	0.9	1.1	1.0	1.1	9.7
Kansas City, MO-KS.......	563 868	67.4	83 933	65.6	3 504	63.2	9 374	71.0	25 284	76.4	4.5	0.7	1.4	2.0	1.9	10.1
Killeen-Temple, TX........	67 434	72.3	20 163	75.2	665	77.7	2 535	71.8	13 142	81.7	6.8	1.7	1.9	2.9	2.1	24.5
Knoxville, TN	257 438	68.0	16 115	62.2	928	66.2	2 234	66.8	2 110	66.9	2.1	0.6	0.8	0.5	0.6	6.0
Kokomo, IN	37 798	69.4	2 177	64.2	192	48.4	275	67.6	534	68.5	1.6	0.5	0.6	0.3	0.4	6.9
La Crosse, WI-MN	47 759	63.3	245	64.1	218	69.3	531	77.0	225	53.8	2.3	0.4	1.5	0.1	0.6	8.4
Lafayette, IN	60 490	62.0	1 247	44.3	234	52.1	2 545	47.4	2 779	73.9	7.5	0.9	3.1	3.1	3.1	11.6
Lafayette, LA	103 280	70.2	36 268	72.8	310	69.4	904	71.1	1 377	66.8	1.5	0.3	0.7	0.4	2.5	30.3
Lake Charles, LA	51 690	71.6	15 040	72.3	210	74.8	327	67.0	953	65.7	1.4	0.3	0.5	0.4	0.9	15.6
Lakeland-Winter Haven, FL........................	150 206	70.0	21 043	72.2	771	63.4	1 651	78.4	11 850	81.2	6.0	0.0	0.0	4.6	3.2	10.0
Lancaster, PA...............	158 345	72.1	4 272	66.1	252	72.6	1 679	80.6	7 485	77.7	3.2	1.0	1.1	0.8	3.2	14.8
Lansing-East Lansing, MI........................	146 077	64.2	13 296	63.4	951	65.8	3 808	59.2	6 015	70.0	4.6	0.9	2.3	0.8	1.6	10.9
Laredo, TX..................	3 433	73.0	171	78.4	276	82.2	243	79.4	46 800	87.3	29.0	0.2	0.3	28.4	23.2	73.5
Las Cruces, NM	25 569	63.1	957	66.1	782	76.0	507	76.9	31 507	80.3	18.7	0.6	0.6	17.3	11.5	53.9
Las Vegas, NV-AZ	419 291	64.3	46 204	66.8	5 055	70.2	25 267	72.0	81 849	80.8	16.5	1.7	3.8	10.1	7.2	24.1
Lawrence, KS..............	33 572	55.5	1 478	58.7	642	60.1	1 205	49.2	967	57.6	5.2	0.9	2.9	0.7	1.3	12.2
Lawton, OK	26 931	71.5	7 003	76.7	1 839	74.1	698	69.1	2 659	78.9	5.4	2.0	1.7	1.4	1.3	17.1
Lewiston-Auburn, ME......	41 027	65.3	232	62.5	173	68.8	86	86.0	221	69.2	2.6	0.6	0.4	0.2	2.3	22.6
Lexington, KY	165 444	64.8	18 119	62.2	512	57.4	2 525	63.6	2 852	68.7	4.0	0.7	1.4	1.5	1.6	7.6
Lima, OH	52 373	71.2	4 491	68.3	81	74.1	245	83.3	449	75.1	1.1	0.3	0.4	0.2	0.2	6.0
Lincoln, NE.................	90 976	61.6	2 336	59.5	507	63.7	2 005	74.1	2 437	66.2	5.4	1.2	2.7	1.2	2.6	10.3
Little Rock-North Little Rock, AR	176 780	68.6	45 627	68.7	990	69.8	1 768	69.2	3 657	74.0	2.4	0.5	0.9	0.8	0.9	7.7
Longview-Marshall, TX...	59 665	72.3	14 765	68.0	322	61.2	250	79.6	3 533	84.8	4.2	0.3	0.4	3.4	2.3	9.1
Los Angeles-Riverside-Orange County, CA	2 704 618	62.3	443 407	66.0	38 022	75.1	531 699	77.4	1 532 475	85.9	30.9	1.9	9.0	19.2	14.0	41.3
Los Angeles-Long Beach, CA	1 325 885	56.4	345 153	63.2	20 264	73.8	368 564	75.0	1 012 555	85.0	36.2	2.0	10.7	22.5	16.7	45.7
Orange County, CA......	603 927	65.4	15 740	69.6	5 002	74.7	111 836	83.0	182 929	87.5	29.9	2.0	10.9	15.8	13.0	36.0
Riverside-San Bernardino, CA..........	607 294	69.4	77 670	77.1	10 844	77.7	39 796	82.2	282 466	87.9	18.8	1.2	3.1	13.7	8.2	34.8
Ventura, CA.............	167 512	71.5	4 844	73.4	1 912	75.0	11 503	83.0	54 525	88.0	20.7	1.8	4.1	14.0	7.9	34.1
Louisville, KY-IN...........	343 589	67.5	55 285	64.9	1 101	68.2	3 626	65.6	4 667	67.7	2.7	0.8	1.0	0.7	1.0	6.9
Lubbock, TX................	64 668	61.4	6 377	70.3	509	73.1	1 134	52.5	19 607	78.8	3.3	0.4	1.1	1.5	3.2	27.7
Lynchburg, VA..............	67 738	70.6	14 646	68.1	239	61.1	675	65.6	603	66.5	2.0	0.6	0.8	0.4	0.4	6.2
Macon, GA	75 013	71.0	42 573	70.5	365	75.3	1 096	73.7	1 811	75.7	2.4	0.4	0.9	0.9	0.8	8.0
Madison, WI	156 539	58.3	5 500	62.5	568	59.9	5 144	55.7	4 266	67.3	6.3	1.1	2.7	1.8	2.2	11.9
Mansfield, OH	63 560	69.6	3 546	64.7	174	71.3	278	73.4	359	80.5	1.4	0.8	0.4	0.1	0.7	6.7
McAllen-Edinburg-Mission, TX	27 565	70.8	553	68.7	710	82.1	1 099	73.9	126 900	88.3	29.5	0.2	0.4	28.7	20.0	69.9
Medford-Ashland, OR ...	66 228	67.7	199	59.8	655	68.4	517	60.2	2 703	79.9	4.9	1.0	0.6	2.8	1.8	10.3
Melbourne-Titusville-Palm Bay,FL.............	172 246	66.7	13 792	70.6	903	66.7	2 257	69.0	6 810	75.3	6.5	2.1	1.4	2.2	1.2	12.7
Memphis, TN-AR-MS	239 823	68.4	168 795	71.6	1 048	67.7	5 256	76.8	6 661	75.6	3.3	0.5	1.2	1.3	1.4	8.3

[1]Hispanic or Latino persons may be of any race.

CMSA/MSA/PMSA/NECMA code[1]	Area name	Population by age (percent)								+/− U.S. percent under 18 years	+/− U.S. percent 65 years and over	Non-Hispanic White Age (percent)		
		Total population	Under 5 years	5 to 17 years	18 to 24 years	25 to 44 years	45 to 64 years	65 years and over	Median age			Total population	Under 18 years	65 years and over
		1	2	3	4	5	6	7	8	9	10	11	12	13
4940	Merced, CA	210 554	8.7	25.7	10.2	28.4	17.7	9.4	29.0	8.7	−3.0	84 807	24.7	16.3
56	Miami-Fort Lauderdale, FL	3 876 380	6.4	17.8	8.2	31.5	21.6	14.5	36.5	−1.5	2.1	1 406 586	20.5	21.4
2680	Fort Lauderdale, FL	1 623 018	6.3	17.2	7.1	31.8	21.6	16.0	37.8	−2.2	3.6	940 692	18.2	23.4
5000	Miami, FL	2 253 362	6.4	18.3	9.1	31.2	21.6	13.3	35.6	−1.0	0.9	465 894	25.2	17.5
63	Milwaukee-Racine, WI	1 689 572	6.9	19.6	9.0	30.2	21.8	12.5	35.5	0.8	0.1	1 269 003	22.3	15.1
5080	Milwaukee-Waukesha, WI	1 500 741	6.9	19.5	9.1	30.2	21.7	12.6	35.4	0.7	0.2	1 118 035	22.0	15.2
6600	Racine, WI	188 831	7.0	20.1	8.2	30.0	22.4	12.4	36.1	1.4	0.0	150 968	24.3	14.2
5120	Minneapolis-St. Paul, MN-WI	2 968 806	7.1	19.6	9.2	33.3	21.2	9.6	34.2	1.0	−2.8	2 516 191	24.4	10.8
5140	Missoula, MT	95 802	5.6	17.3	15.3	29.2	22.5	10.1	33.2	−2.8	−2.3	88 969	22.0	10.6
5160	Mobile, AL	540 258	7.0	19.7	9.2	28.6	22.6	12.9	35.7	1.0	0.5	370 794	23.6	14.8
5170	Modesto, CA	446 997	7.9	23.2	9.8	29.3	19.5	10.4	31.7	5.4	−2.0	254 650	24.8	14.8
5200	Monroe, LA	147 250	7.2	20.6	12.1	27.8	20.4	11.8	32.3	2.1	−0.6	93 967	23.3	14.3
5240	Montgomery, AL	333 055	6.8	19.3	10.2	30.8	21.5	11.4	34.2	0.4	−1.0	193 171	22.8	14.3
5280	Muncie, IN	118 769	5.9	16.2	16.9	25.7	21.8	13.5	33.8	−3.6	1.1	107 158	21.0	14.0
5330	Myrtle Beach, SC	196 629	5.6	15.7	9.2	29.5	25.0	15.0	38.3	−4.4	2.6	157 151	18.8	17.1
5345	Naples, FL	251 377	5.3	14.5	6.4	24.9	24.5	24.4	44.1	−5.9	12.0	185 063	15.2	31.6
5360	Nashville, TN	1 231 311	6.9	17.9	10.2	33.0	21.9	10.0	34.5	−0.9	−2.4	960 833	23.2	11.1
5523	New London-Norwich, CT	259 088	6.2	18.1	8.5	31.3	22.8	13.0	37.0	−1.4	0.6	219 195	22.7	14.5
5560	New Orleans, LA	1 337 726	6.8	19.9	9.7	29.9	22.3	11.4	34.8	1.0	−1.0	731 788	22.2	14.3
70	New York-Northern New Jersey-Long Island, NY-NJ-CT-PA	21 199 865	6.7	17.9	8.6	31.7	22.3	12.7	35.9	−1.1	0.3	11 949 107	21.3	17.1
0875	Bergen-Passaic, NJ	1 373 167	6.6	17.4	7.6	31.1	23.2	14.1	37.6	−1.7	1.7	889 357	21.1	18.7
2281	Dutchess County, NY	280 150	6.1	18.8	9.5	30.2	23.3	12.0	36.7	−0.8	−0.4	224 979	23.6	13.7
3640	Jersey City, NJ	608 975	6.2	16.3	10.4	35.8	19.9	11.5	33.6	−3.2	−0.9	214 797	14.8	19.5
5015	Middlesex-Somerset-Hunterdon, NJ	1 169 641	6.7	17.6	8.2	33.0	22.7	11.8	36.4	−1.4	−0.6	796 823	22.1	15.2
5190	Monmouth-Ocean, NJ	1 126 217	6.6	18.2	6.7	28.5	23.0	16.9	39.1	−0.9	4.5	954 851	23.5	18.7
5380	Nassau-Suffolk, NY	2 753 913	6.7	18.6	7.5	30.2	23.6	13.4	37.5	−0.4	1.0	2 104 098	23.7	15.7
5483	New Haven-Bridgeport-Stamford-Danbury-Waterbury, CT	1 706 575	6.8	18.2	7.7	30.6	22.8	13.8	37.1	−0.7	1.4	1 260 879	22.3	16.8
5600	New York, NY	9 314 235	6.7	17.6	9.6	32.6	21.5	11.9	34.6	−1.4	−0.5	3 684 583	18.0	18.5
5640	Newark, NJ	2 032 989	7.0	18.5	7.9	31.6	22.8	12.2	36.3	−0.2	−0.2	1 196 741	23.0	15.7
5660	Newburgh, NY-PA	387 669	7.4	21.3	8.3	29.8	22.3	10.9	35.3	3.0	−1.5	306 610	27.0	12.6
8480	Trenton, NJ	350 761	6.3	17.5	10.2	30.8	22.6	12.5	36.0	−1.9	0.1	225 079	20.5	15.9
5720	Norfolk-Virginia Beach-Newport News, VA-NC	1 569 541	6.9	19.4	11.1	31.9	20.4	10.3	33.6	0.6	−2.1	958 724	23.2	12.1
5790	Ocala, FL	258 916	5.1	16.3	6.4	23.9	23.8	24.5	43.8	−4.3	12.1	208 175	18.7	27.8
5800	Odessa-Midland, TX	237 132	7.7	22.6	9.5	28.4	20.6	11.2	33.0	4.6	−1.2	133 690	24.1	15.8
5880	Oklahoma City, OK	1 083 346	6.9	18.6	11.3	30.1	21.7	11.4	34.1	−0.2	−1.0	789 391	22.4	13.7
5920	Omaha, NE-IA	716 998	7.3	19.8	9.8	31.2	21.2	10.6	33.7	1.4	−1.8	594 001	25.3	11.8
5960	Orlando, FL	1 644 561	6.5	18.2	9.4	32.2	21.3	12.4	35.3	−1.0	0.0	1 071 277	21.1	15.6
5990	Owensboro, KY	91 545	6.8	18.9	9.0	28.6	22.8	13.9	36.8	0.0	1.5	85 555	25.1	14.2
6015	Panama City, FL	148 217	6.1	18.0	8.6	30.3	23.7	13.3	37.4	−1.6	0.9	122 663	22.3	14.6
6020	Parkersburg-Marietta, WV-OH	151 237	5.8	17.4	8.4	27.8	25.4	15.3	39.2	−2.5	2.9	146 296	22.9	15.5
6080	Pensacola, FL	412 153	6.2	18.2	10.7	29.8	22.5	12.6	35.9	−1.3	0.2	313 364	22.0	14.2
6120	Peoria-Pekin, IL	347 387	6.6	18.4	9.4	28.0	23.2	14.5	37.0	−0.7	2.1	303 068	23.1	15.8
77	Philadelphia-Wilmington-Atlantic City, PA-NJ-DE-MD	6 188 463	6.4	18.9	8.8	30.2	22.2	13.5	36.4	−0.4	1.1	4 358 653	22.7	15.7
0560	Atlantic-Cape May, NJ	354 878	6.0	18.5	7.5	29.3	23.3	15.5	38.4	−1.2	3.1	253 334	21.2	18.9
6160	Philadelphia, PA-NJ	5 100 931	6.4	18.9	8.8	30.1	22.2	13.6	36.4	−0.4	1.2	3 586 143	22.8	15.7
8760	Vineland-Millville-Bridgeton, NJ	146 438	6.0	19.3	8.4	31.5	21.8	12.9	35.6	−0.4	0.5	85 635	21.0	18.1
9160	Wilmington-Newark, DE-MD	586 216	6.6	18.6	9.8	31.6	21.9	11.4	35.1	−0.5	−1.0	433 541	23.0	13.4
6200	Phoenix-Mesa, AZ	3 251 876	7.7	19.0	10.1	31.4	19.8	11.9	33.2	1.0	−0.5	2 139 085	21.5	16.3
6240	Pine Bluff, AR	84 278	6.9	19.2	10.9	28.1	22.1	12.8	35.1	0.4	0.4	40 415	20.0	17.1
6280	Pittsburgh, PA	2 358 695	5.5	16.7	8.1	28.1	23.9	17.7	40.0	−3.5	5.3	2 101 036	21.1	18.7
6323	Pittsfield, MA	134 953	5.2	17.3	8.4	26.3	24.9	18.0	40.5	−3.2	5.6	127 054	21.6	18.7
6340	Pocatello, ID	75 565	8.1	19.9	14.7	27.2	19.8	10.3	29.8	2.3	−2.1	67 720	27.0	10.7
6403	Portland, ME	265 612	5.8	17.5	8.4	31.3	23.6	13.3	37.6	−2.4	0.9	253 041	22.7	13.8
79	Portland-Salem, OR-WA	2 265 223	7.1	18.6	9.4	31.6	22.6	10.7	34.7	0.0	−1.7	1 835 326	23.5	12.3
6440	Portland-Vancouver, OR-WA	1 918 009	7.0	18.4	9.2	32.3	22.7	10.4	34.8	−0.3	−2.0	1 563 973	23.5	11.8
7080	Salem, OR	347 214	7.5	19.5	10.5	28.1	21.6	12.8	34.2	1.3	0.4	271 353	23.6	15.6
6483	Providence-Warwick-Pawtucket, RI	962 886	6.0	17.7	10.3	29.6	21.8	14.6	36.6	−2.0	2.2	781 632	21.0	16.8
6520	Provo-Orem, UT	368 536	10.9	23.0	20.9	26.0	12.7	6.4	23.3	8.2	−6.0	329 249	33.4	7.0
6560	Pueblo, CO	141 472	6.6	19.0	9.3	27.6	22.2	15.3	36.7	−0.1	2.9	81 404	20.9	19.3
6580	Punta Gorda, FL	141 627	3.5	12.2	4.5	18.9	26.2	34.7	54.3	−10.0	22.3	128 021	14.5	36.5
6640	Raleigh-Durham-Chapel Hill, NC	1 187 941	6.9	17.3	11.6	35.1	20.6	8.6	33.0	−1.5	−3.8	793 612	22.0	10.1
6660	Rapid City, SD	88 565	7.1	19.5	10.7	29.2	21.8	11.7	35.0	0.9	−0.7	75 726	24.2	13.0

[1]MSA = Metropolitan Statistical Area. CMSA = Consolidated Metropolitan Area. PMSA = Primary MSA. NECMA = New England County Metropolitan Area. See the Appendix A for explanation of these concepts. See Appendix B for list of metropolitan areas identified by type, with component counties.

Area name	Black or African American Total population	Under 18 years	65 years and over	American Indian and Alaska Native Total population	Under 18 years	65 years and over	Asian, Hawaiian, and Pacific Islander Total population	Under 18 years	65 years and over	Hispanic or Latino[1] Total population	Under 18 years	65 years and over	Two or more races Total population	Under 18 years	65 years and over
	14	15	16	17	18	19	20	21	22	23	24	25	26	27	28
Merced, CA	7 838	35.0	9.7	2 207	29.2	1.7	14 858	45.2	5.9	95 610	41.4	3.9	12 982	43.2	6.1
Miami-Fort Lauderdale, FL	782 082	33.6	6.5	8 803	27.3	6.5	68 447	22.6	5.9	1 563 204	22.5	13.0	150 349	28.2	7.4
Fort Lauderdale, FL	329 749	34.2	5.4	3 962	28.6	5.5	37 150	24.3	4.9	271 523	27.4	6.7	58 884	31.5	5.8
Miami, FL	452 333	33.1	7.2	4 841	26.3	7.3	31 297	20.7	7.0	1 291 681	21.4	14.3	91 465	26.1	8.4
Milwaukee-Racine, WI	252 267	38.8	5.6	10 747	36.2	4.1	30 508	33.4	4.5	108 583	39.2	3.1	31 264	52.6	4.0
Milwaukee-Waukesha, WI	233 112	39.1	5.6	9 998	36.0	4.3	29 142	33.6	4.5	93 877	39.1	3.0	27 634	51.7	4.2
Racine, WI	19 155	35.1	6.3	749	39.5	2.3	1 366	29.2	3.6	14 706	39.7	3.7	3 630	59.3	2.4
Minneapolis-St. Paul, MN-WI	154 317	37.8	3.2	22 150	33.8	3.1	121 055	38.5	3.4	99 111	37.2	1.9	67 242	51.8	2.4
Missoula, MT	169	23.1	0.0	2 235	37.0	4.4	966	24.8	3.6	1 728	36.3	5.0	1 823	38.3	3.1
Mobile, AL	147 895	33.9	9.3	3 488	27.8	4.6	5 960	28.4	3.4	6 755	30.2	5.4	6 514	36.2	8.2
Modesto, CA	10 550	36.2	5.6	5 224	28.3	6.8	20 196	34.6	6.7	141 926	41.1	3.8	26 758	41.8	5.3
Monroe, LA	49 693	36.7	7.5	204	7.4	16.7	830	11.8	5.4	1 548	26.8	9.5	1 261	30.5	11.2
Montgomery, AL	129 865	30.7	7.7	1 190	27.1	2.8	2 387	18.0	4.9	3 616	27.4	3.2	3 412	37.3	5.7
Muncie, IN	7 761	31.5	10.3	259	24.7	5.8	766	17.5	1.7	1 546	40.0	5.4	1 461	43.5	7.7
Myrtle Beach, SC	30 496	32.4	7.5	814	23.3	3.7	1 651	23.1	8.9	4 959	27.8	2.6	2 295	34.1	3.1
Naples, FL	11 673	35.3	6.1	1 067	26.1	5.5	1 397	22.0	6.3	49 252	31.7	3.7	6 131	35.7	4.5
Nashville, TN	192 316	30.3	7.4	3 877	26.0	3.2	18 478	24.6	3.7	39 326	30.4	1.9	19 478	39.9	4.0
New London-Norwich, CT	13 269	28.3	6.0	2 293	33.8	6.7	5 077	29.7	4.1	13 531	36.2	2.4	7 901	42.5	5.2
New Orleans, LA	499 959	33.2	7.7	5 390	29.1	8.2	28 508	27.6	5.8	59 025	25.7	9.8	20 866	34.5	6.8
New York-Northern New Jersey-Long Island, NY-NJ-CT-PA	3 606 421	29.6	8.8	64 633	31.7	6.4	1 446 684	23.6	6.3	3 851 852	30.4	5.6	750 011	31.9	6.0
Bergen-Passaic, NJ	109 565	28.5	8.3	2 707	31.4	4.4	112 885	27.0	5.0	238 145	30.2	4.5	40 854	34.0	5.1
Dutchess County, NY	25 687	29.0	5.9	512	11.1	9.0	7 145	25.6	4.1	17 617	30.9	3.5	6 039	44.2	5.0
Jersey City, NJ	81 072	29.4	7.1	1 911	26.0	6.3	57 619	21.2	5.7	242 234	27.0	7.5	35 662	29.4	6.4
Middlesex-Somerset-Hunterdon, NJ	91 920	28.4	5.9	1 979	26.6	4.2	132 038	26.4	4.3	131 218	31.1	3.7	27 769	35.9	4.0
Monmouth-Ocean, NJ	63 851	31.4	9.7	1 575	27.0	6.8	30 983	27.4	6.1	63 453	32.6	5.2	18 488	42.8	5.7
Nassau-Suffolk, NY	230 740	31.5	7.4	5 850	30.4	8.4	97 516	26.8	5.5	282 463	31.0	4.1	60 841	35.8	5.5
New Haven-Bridgeport-Stamford-Danbury-Waterbury, CT	180 369	32.7	7.3	4 006	28.3	6.4	48 540	25.3	3.9	186 932	34.5	3.5	41 738	38.0	5.3
New York, NY	2 277 210	29.2	9.2	40 153	33.7	6.5	852 529	22.0	7.3	2 341 108	30.4	6.2	441 310	29.4	6.5
Newark, NJ	448 639	29.6	8.9	3 711	28.6	6.1	82 583	25.9	5.3	270 516	28.8	4.7	58 902	32.7	5.0
Newburgh, NY-PA	28 017	32.4	6.5	1 241	33.0	1.5	5 881	26.1	4.7	42 107	36.4	3.3	9 321	48.2	2.8
Trenton, NJ	68 582	30.5	8.4	786	27.4	7.0	17 698	25.4	5.0	34 140	30.1	3.3	7 990	38.1	4.6
Norfolk-Virginia Beach-Newport News, VA-NC	483 032	31.0	8.3	6 892	24.2	4.0	43 879	22.3	5.8	48 523	33.9	2.8	38 248	46.1	3.0
Ocala, FL	29 401	33.3	12.1	1 314	26.5	6.5	2 273	27.9	9.8	15 535	31.9	9.8	3 680	35.9	10.4
Odessa-Midland, TX	13 609	33.6	10.8	1 542	30.2	7.7	1 956	31.2	5.5	84 901	39.3	4.2	6 196	44.9	7.0
Oklahoma City, OK	112 756	32.6	6.5	43 693	33.0	4.8	27 268	22.4	4.4	72 253	38.7	2.5	47 308	40.9	5.9
Omaha, NE-IA	58 280	35.0	6.9	4 272	31.5	5.2	11 045	23.2	3.3	39 704	37.5	2.6	12 821	53.1	3.0
Orlando, FL	225 415	33.7	7.1	5 599	22.4	4.7	43 610	23.6	5.2	271 425	30.9	6.2	52 824	35.4	4.6
Owensboro, KY	3 656	29.8	10.8	126	10.3	4.8	323	22.9	7.7	862	32.3	8.8	1 056	58.2	4.1
Panama City, FL	15 944	32.9	7.6	1 130	22.2	4.8	2 494	21.8	3.7	3 534	30.2	6.9	2 946	44.8	5.9
Parkersburg-Marietta, WV-OH	1 320	32.1	12.3	314	19.1	3.8	720	22.9	5.1	768	34.4	4.6	1 737	37.8	10.9
Pensacola, FL	67 468	33.1	8.7	3 528	24.8	5.3	8 519	22.5	6.2	10 637	27.5	6.3	9 758	40.1	4.0
Peoria-Pekin, IL	30 411	38.4	5.7	642	22.9	5.5	3 899	21.9	5.5	5 345	37.1	4.1	4 545	52.8	6.1
Philadelphia-Wilmington-Atlantic City, PA-NJ-DE-MD	1 199 256	30.7	10.0	14 231	28.4	8.4	201 890	25.6	5.3	345 649	36.0	3.8	114 710	41.8	5.0
Atlantic-Cape May, NJ	48 973	31.9	10.1	754	21.0	5.3	13 669	26.7	4.0	33 819	35.0	3.3	8 708	42.7	5.0
Philadelphia, PA-NJ	1 017 762	30.7	10.3	10 928	29.7	8.5	173 057	25.6	5.4	256 509	36.2	4.0	91 324	41.2	5.3
Vineland-Millville-Bridgeton, NJ	29 591	29.2	6.3	1 345	21.3	12.1	1 193	25.5	10.9	27 712	34.5	3.9	4 412	42.0	4.3
Wilmington-Newark, DE-MD	102 930	30.6	7.1	1 204	29.6	4.5	13 971	23.4	4.5	27 609	36.6	2.5	10 266	45.8	3.0
Phoenix-Mesa, AZ	116 473	31.4	6.1	68 438	35.8	3.4	71 339	24.1	5.7	817 115	38.6	3.0	100 710	46.2	3.8
Pine Bluff, AR	41 667	31.6	9.1	259	23.9	18.1	443	27.1	5.6	878	36.6	6.4	737	38.0	3.4
Pittsburgh, PA	188 471	31.7	11.6	2 827	24.0	7.8	25 696	21.6	3.4	17 415	31.5	7.7	24 045	46.1	6.2
Pittsfield, MA	2 704	34.5	6.4	153	22.2	21.6	1 293	26.8	1.9	2 223	35.4	4.4	1 764	47.7	8.3
Pocatello, ID	424	19.6	16.3	2 284	35.6	6.6	936	19.0	9.3	3 560	42.4	3.5	1 342	54.8	3.4
Portland, ME	2 470	35.3	4.2	1 036	24.1	4.0	3 366	33.2	4.4	2 447	36.7	3.8	3 463	40.1	5.1
Portland-Salem, OR-WA	51 100	31.5	6.6	21 194	28.4	3.6	99 474	26.0	6.3	196 558	38.0	1.8	80 672	45.7	3.5
Portland-Vancouver, OR-WA	48 449	31.4	6.8	16 421	27.2	3.6	92 997	26.0	6.3	142 036	36.8	1.8	68 883	45.5	3.4
Salem, OR	2 651	32.5	2.0	4 773	32.2	3.4	6 477	25.6	6.2	54 522	41.2	1.8	11 789	46.5	4.2
Providence-Warwick-Pawtucket, RI	41 812	32.9	6.3	4 725	38.1	7.0	23 256	28.3	4.2	88 202	38.5	3.2	27 826	39.1	6.4
Provo-Orem, UT	1 054	51.8	0.4	2 286	40.0	1.6	5 764	25.3	3.4	25 134	38.2	1.5	7 384	50.6	1.9
Pueblo, CO	2 430	20.6	10.7	2 176	26.6	6.3	875	20.8	11.9	53 804	32.7	9.8	5 461	43.1	7.6
Punta Gorda, FL	6 384	27.3	19.5	405	8.9	19.5	889	17.5	20.0	4 585	27.9	11.8	1 804	32.1	21.6
Raleigh-Durham-Chapel Hill, NC	268 025	28.6	7.4	4 734	25.4	4.0	33 892	22.7	3.1	72 424	28.4	1.1	20 068	39.1	2.7
Rapid City, SD	677	28.8	5.3	6 748	40.9	4.3	954	25.7	3.1	2 335	42.8	4.6	2 707	54.0	2.9

[1] Hispanic or Latino persons may be of any race.

| Area name | Total households | Married-couple family households | | | Other family households | | | Two or more unrelated persons | | Male living alone | | Female living alone | | Percent of householders 65 years and over who live alone | Grandparents who are responsible for the care of their grandchildren |
| | | Total | With children | Householder 65 years or over | Total | With children | Householder 65 years or over | Total | Householder 65 years or over | Total | Householder 65 years or over | Total | Householder 65 years or over | | |
	29	30	31	32	33	34	35	36	37	38	39	40	41	42	43
Merced, CA	63 933	58.7	33.9	9.1	19.7	12.4	2.2	3.9	0.4	7.4	2.0	10.3	5.4	38.5	2 218
Miami-Fort Lauderdale, FL	1 432 165	47.8	22.2	9.7	19.7	10.3	2.7	6.4	0.8	11.3	2.7	14.9	7.8	44.5	39 998
Fort Lauderdale, FL	654 787	46.8	20.7	10.4	16.4	9.2	2.0	7.2	0.8	12.3	3.1	17.3	9.6	49.1	12 996
Miami, FL	777 378	48.7	23.4	9.1	22.4	11.2	3.3	5.6	0.8	10.5	2.4	12.8	6.3	39.9	27 002
Milwaukee-Racine, WI	659 026	49.8	22.8	8.7	16.1	9.8	1.9	6.0	0.4	11.9	2.3	16.3	7.4	47.1	10 520
Milwaukee-Waukesha, WI	588 230	49.0	22.5	8.6	16.2	9.8	1.9	6.1	0.4	12.1	2.3	16.5	7.5	47.4	9 214
Racine, WI	70 796	55.8	25.2	9.7	14.9	9.4	1.8	4.8	0.3	10.1	2.1	14.3	7.3	44.0	1 306
Minneapolis-St. Paul, MN-WI	1 137 313	53.2	26.7	7.0	12.7	7.9	1.2	7.5	0.3	11.6	1.7	15.0	5.9	46.8	11 172
Missoula, MT	38 493	48.0	21.4	7.3	12.5	7.9	1.2	11.6	0.4	13.5	1.9	14.5	5.6	45.8	423
Mobile, AL	205 611	53.1	23.6	9.8	18.8	10.7	3.0	3.7	0.3	10.3	2.3	14.0	6.9	41.4	7 822
Modesto, CA	145 253	57.2	30.8	9.0	18.7	11.1	2.3	4.7	0.4	7.8	1.9	11.6	6.1	40.6	4 894
Monroe, LA	55 276	48.6	22.1	8.2	21.1	12.6	2.7	4.5	0.3	9.9	2.0	15.9	7.7	46.5	2 662
Montgomery, AL	124 695	50.2	22.9	8.1	19.6	11.5	2.7	3.7	0.2	10.5	1.9	16.0	7.1	45.0	3 834
Muncie, IN	47 131	50.3	20.0	9.5	13.3	8.6	1.6	8.4	0.4	11.4	2.4	16.7	8.2	48.0	855
Myrtle Beach, SC	81 785	52.1	18.6	12.1	14.9	8.3	2.2	7.3	0.6	11.2	2.3	14.5	6.4	36.9	1 930
Naples, FL	103 126	58.5	16.7	22.3	11.1	6.4	1.5	5.9	1.0	9.5	3.4	14.9	8.6	32.7	1 346
Nashville, TN	479 744	52.0	24.0	7.1	15.5	9.0	1.9	6.2	0.3	11.2	1.5	15.0	5.7	43.8	12 000
New London-Norwich, CT	99 864	53.0	23.8	9.2	14.8	9.0	2.2	5.9	0.3	11.8	2.5	14.5	7.2	45.2	1 274
New Orleans, LA	505 778	45.5	21.1	7.6	22.3	12.5	3.3	5.1	0.3	12.1	2.2	15.0	6.3	43.0	19 998
New York-Northern New Jersey-Long Island, NY-NJ-CT-PA	7 738 759	49.5	24.0	8.5	18.6	9.1	2.9	5.3	0.5	10.6	2.4	16.0	7.4	45.4	161 649
Bergen-Passaic, NJ	494 808	56.7	27.2	10.3	15.4	6.6	3.1	4.1	0.5	9.1	2.4	14.7	7.6	42.0	7 498
Dutchess County, NY	99 719	56.6	27.8	9.1	13.4	7.5	2.0	5.5	0.5	10.6	2.3	14.0	7.0	44.5	1 505
Jersey City, NJ	230 698	40.4	19.3	6.2	22.4	11.0	3.2	7.7	0.4	13.4	2.5	16.1	7.1	49.6	5 599
Middlesex-Somerset-Hunterdon, NJ	418 698	59.9	29.9	8.9	12.7	5.9	2.4	5.1	0.3	8.8	1.9	13.4	6.2	41.1	5 686
Monmouth-Ocean, NJ	425 000	58.1	26.8	12.4	12.4	5.6	2.5	4.2	0.5	9.1	2.9	16.2	9.9	45.4	5 782
Nassau-Suffolk, NY	917 338	63.6	31.1	11.3	14.0	5.8	3.0	3.8	0.5	6.9	2.0	11.6	6.7	37.0	14 553
New Haven-Bridgeport-Stamford-Danbury-Waterbury, CT	643 712	53.0	25.1	9.5	15.6	8.3	2.5	5.3	0.4	10.3	2.6	15.8	7.8	45.3	9 858
New York, NY	3 485 449	40.8	19.8	6.8	22.5	11.4	3.1	6.0	0.5	12.4	2.5	18.3	7.5	49.0	90 163
Newark, NJ	729 043	53.1	26.2	8.3	18.4	9.1	2.9	4.5	0.4	9.6	2.3	14.4	6.9	44.2	15 995
Newburgh, NY-PA	132 256	59.6	30.8	8.9	14.6	8.6	1.9	4.5	0.4	9.2	2.1	12.1	6.1	42.3	2 143
Trenton, NJ	125 787	52.0	25.0	8.6	17.0	8.7	2.7	5.4	0.5	9.8	2.5	15.8	7.8	46.8	2 506
Norfolk-Virginia Beach-Newport News, VA-NC	577 794	52.0	24.9	7.7	18.4	11.4	2.2	6.3	0.3	10.2	1.8	13.1	5.7	42.1	15 938
Ocala, FL	106 707	56.2	17.4	20.3	14.0	7.7	2.5	4.8	1.0	9.5	4.0	15.5	9.5	36.2	2 511
Odessa-Midland, TX	86 557	56.8	29.2	9.1	16.0	10.6	1.8	3.1	0.3	10.5	1.9	13.6	6.6	43.3	3 570
Oklahoma City, OK	425 060	51.3	23.3	8.3	15.8	9.6	1.8	5.4	0.3	12.0	2.0	15.4	6.7	45.6	10 633
Omaha, NE-IA	276 073	52.3	25.5	7.7	14.8	9.1	1.7	6.0	0.2	11.7	1.8	15.2	6.6	46.7	4 496
Orlando, FL	625 346	52.1	23.1	9.8	16.4	9.5	1.9	8.0	0.5	10.4	1.9	13.1	5.8	38.8	16 200
Owensboro, KY	36 076	55.2	24.9	9.9	14.1	8.5	1.9	3.6	0.4	10.7	2.1	16.4	8.5	46.5	633
Panama City, FL	59 594	53.2	21.7	10.2	15.0	9.1	2.0	5.8	0.5	11.7	2.4	14.3	6.4	41.0	1 532
Parkersburg-Marietta, WV-OH	61 424	56.1	22.2	10.7	13.6	7.9	2.1	4.0	0.3	10.5	2.6	15.9	8.9	46.8	1 071
Pensacola, FL	154 851	52.3	21.9	10.2	17.5	10.5	2.4	5.5	0.4	10.8	2.1	13.9	6.5	39.9	3 876
Peoria-Pekin, IL	135 940	54.9	23.1	10.9	13.6	8.6	1.7	4.5	0.4	11.0	2.3	16.0	8.5	45.5	2 520
Philadelphia-Wilmington-Atlantic City, PA-NJ-DE-MD	2 321 679	49.9	23.2	9.1	18.0	9.4	3.0	5.2	0.4	10.8	2.5	16.0	7.7	44.7	52 977
Atlantic-Cape May, NJ	137 165	49.1	21.2	10.5	17.2	9.1	2.5	5.8	0.6	11.0	3.1	17.0	9.1	47.1	3 403
Philadelphia, PA-NJ	1 915 187	49.7	23.2	9.1	18.1	9.3	3.2	5.1	0.4	10.9	2.5	16.2	7.7	44.7	42 874
Vineland-Millville-Bridgeton, NJ	49 096	49.2	21.9	9.3	22.9	13.1	3.6	4.4	0.5	9.3	2.7	14.3	7.9	44.0	1 658
Wilmington-Newark, DE-MD	220 231	52.1	24.3	8.3	16.7	9.5	2.1	6.4	0.4	10.3	2.0	14.6	6.3	43.5	5 042
Phoenix-Mesa, AZ	1 194 461	53.0	24.3	10.2	15.2	9.1	1.5	7.5	0.5	10.8	2.0	13.5	6.1	39.8	28 153
Pine Bluff, AR	30 555	48.9	20.7	8.7	21.9	13.0	3.4	3.1	0.2	11.3	2.6	14.8	8.9	48.3	1 528
Pittsburgh, PA	967 044	51.2	20.8	11.5	14.4	7.2	3.1	4.4	0.3	11.6	3.1	18.4	10.1	47.1	13 169
Pittsfield, MA	55 874	48.7	18.9	11.6	14.3	8.6	2.2	5.4	0.4	12.5	3.2	19.0	10.6	49.2	322
Pocatello, ID	27 214	57.9	28.4	9.2	13.1	8.3	1.5	6.2	0.3	10.4	1.6	12.3	5.8	40.4	421
Portland, ME	108 037	51.0	23.1	8.6	12.1	7.4	1.5	8.5	0.4	11.0	2.6	17.4	7.9	49.9	884
Portland-Salem, OR-WA	867 255	52.5	24.9	7.7	13.7	8.3	1.5	7.9	0.4	11.3	1.9	14.6	6.3	45.8	13 537
Portland-Vancouver, OR-WA	742 381	52.0	24.9	7.3	13.5	8.1	1.4	8.2	0.4	11.7	1.8	14.6	6.0	46.2	10 811
Salem, OR	124 874	55.0	25.0	10.2	14.9	9.3	1.6	6.5	0.6	9.0	2.0	14.7	7.6	43.8	2 726
Providence-Warwick-Pawtucket, RI	373 200	49.0	21.8	9.4	16.4	9.5	2.4	6.1	0.4	11.4	2.8	17.0	8.9	49.2	4 690
Provo-Orem, UT	100 164	71.1	43.6	8.3	10.4	5.7	1.1	7.5	0.2	4.1	0.8	6.9	3.7	31.7	1 960
Pueblo, CO	54 618	51.0	21.6	11.5	17.9	10.6	2.7	4.6	0.5	11.0	3.0	15.5	8.6	44.2	1 980
Punta Gorda, FL	63 918	59.7	12.9	28.0	9.4	4.9	2.0	4.9	1.1	9.3	5.0	16.7	11.9	35.2	838
Raleigh-Durham-Chapel Hill, NC	461 335	51.2	24.8	6.0	14.2	8.3	1.5	8.3	0.2	11.4	1.4	14.9	5.0	45.3	8 039
Rapid City, SD	34 662	52.5	24.0	9.2	15.2	10.6	1.4	6.2	0.4	11.7	2.1	14.3	6.5	44.0	516

Table A-4. Metropolitan Areas — Age, Ethnicity, and Household Structure

Area name	Households with Non-Hispanic White householder		Households with Black or African American householder		Households with American Indian and Alaska Native householder		Households with Asian, Hawaiian, and Pacific Islander householder		Households with Hispanic or Latino[1] householder		Foreign-born population	Place of birth (percent)			Percent in non-English speaking households	
	Number of households	Percent that are family households	Number of households	Percent that are family households	Number of households	Percent that are family households	Number of households	Percent that are family households	Number of households	Percent that are family households	Percent of total population that is foreign-born	Europe	Asia	Latin America	Linguistically isolated	Not linguistically isolated
	44	45	46	47	48	49	50	51	52	53	54	55	56	57	58	59
Merced, CA	33 190	72.0	2 837	72.3	719	73.7	2 999	88.4	22 548	88.1	24.8	2.1	4.5	17.9	13.0	42.0
Miami-Fort Lauderdale, FL	626 033	56.2	241 518	75.3	3 085	68.5	22 643	74.7	524 207	77.1	40.2	2.6	1.5	35.0	15.0	43.0
Fort Lauderdale, FL	437 887	56.6	103 464	76.4	1 409	68.3	11 904	76.2	86 780	78.0	25.3	3.6	1.9	18.1	6.6	29.2
Miami, FL	188 146	55.0	138 054	74.4	1 676	68.7	10 739	73.2	437 427	76.9	50.9	2.0	1.3	47.2	21.0	53.1
Milwaukee-Racine, WI	528 160	64.5	85 371	69.1	3 612	72.1	8 736	72.0	28 765	78.6	5.3	1.6	1.4	2.0	2.3	13.0
Milwaukee-Waukesha, WI	468 320	63.8	79 157	69.0	3 383	71.5	8 300	72.0	24 966	78.0	5.4	1.6	1.5	2.0	2.4	13.1
Racine, WI	59 840	70.0	6 214	69.6	229	80.8	436	72.5	3 799	82.9	4.1	1.3	0.6	2.0	1.9	11.9
Minneapolis-St. Paul, MN-WI	1 009 615	65.4	52 414	66.0	6 728	68.6	30 448	76.4	25 029	74.5	7.1	1.1	3.0	1.6	2.7	12.1
Missoula, MT	36 370	60.8	51	29.4	611	73.0	336	53.3	493	44.4	2.3	1.1	0.6	0.1	0.6	8.1
Mobile, AL	147 827	71.5	51 231	73.0	1 330	78.7	1 613	72.3	1 914	70.5	2.2	0.6	0.9	0.5	0.6	7.6
Modesto, CA	97 654	71.2	3 550	71.4	1 673	77.9	5 088	86.3	32 967	88.3	18.3	1.6	3.8	12.0	8.5	32.3
Monroe, LA	37 573	69.6	16 379	70.2	86	47.7	331	62.8	515	68.2	1.0	0.2	0.5	0.2	0.5	6.0
Montgomery, AL	77 559	70.1	44 168	69.2	374	66.8	704	66.2	1 056	73.4	1.7	0.5	0.6	0.4	0.4	6.5
Muncie, IN	43 104	63.9	3 005	58.6	121	76.9	220	45.9	383	65.5	1.5	0.3	0.6	0.3	0.3	6.3
Myrtle Beach, SC	68 793	66.1	10 340	73.2	374	66.6	474	77.0	1 248	66.9	4.0	1.0	0.9	1.7	1.6	8.8
Naples, FL	86 494	67.0	3 134	78.4	321	81.3	415	65.3	11 838	86.1	18.3	3.1	0.5	13.6	8.4	21.3
Nashville, TN	386 738	67.5	70 092	66.8	1 474	72.7	5 993	69.3	10 360	75.6	4.7	0.7	1.5	1.9	1.9	8.5
New London-Norwich, CT	88 013	67.4	4 416	69.1	790	71.1	1 575	69.5	3 659	78.8	5.4	2.0	1.4	1.3	1.7	13.6
New Orleans, LA	301 387	65.3	169 183	71.9	1 989	67.4	8 585	76.5	20 155	71.7	4.8	0.6	1.6	2.3	1.6	12.6
New York-Northern New Jersey-Long Island, NY-NJ-CT-PA	4 813 584	65.1	1 245 539	67.7	19 797	71.9	443 372	77.8	1 124 034	77.5	24.4	5.5	5.9	12.0	9.2	31.6
Bergen-Passaic, NJ	353 248	68.9	36 671	70.1	764	77.7	34 025	84.2	63 773	84.2	25.7	6.8	8.0	10.1	9.3	33.4
Dutchess County, NY	84 778	69.6	7 343	69.5	133	71.4	2 233	76.0	4 226	76.4	8.4	3.1	2.0	2.8	1.7	17.1
Jersey City, NJ	100 524	50.2	29 087	64.3	523	80.7	18 807	72.4	77 810	76.0	38.5	4.5	8.1	23.7	17.1	45.9
Middlesex-Somerset-Hunterdon, NJ	310 234	69.9	30 222	71.6	587	77.9	39 268	85.6	33 591	84.4	20.8	4.4	8.9	6.2	5.9	28.8
Monmouth-Ocean, NJ	374 077	69.7	21 398	71.4	590	63.9	9 033	83.2	17 188	81.1	8.6	3.2	2.3	2.7	2.5	16.7
Nassau-Suffolk, NY	752 709	70.2	63 690	81.7	1 831	73.8	25 728	89.7	64 600	86.7	14.4	3.9	3.3	6.8	3.6	24.3
New Haven-Bridgeport-Stamford-Danbury-Waterbury, CT	503 261	67.4	62 316	68.8	1 355	65.2	15 637	72.6	52 875	79.3	13.1	4.7	2.4	5.2	5.1	22.4
New York, NY	1 641 261	54.8	808 746	66.2	12 131	71.4	267 133	74.5	712 028	75.3	33.7	6.8	7.9	17.6	13.6	39.0
Newark, NJ	461 560	70.6	154 720	67.5	1 131	74.8	24 460	84.6	77 542	80.0	19.0	4.9	3.3	9.6	6.4	26.3
Newburgh, NY-PA	109 605	73.8	8 624	69.2	396	72.2	1 689	83.1	10 829	81.0	8.0	2.9	1.3	3.5	3.9	20.4
Trenton, NJ	87 600	67.2	22 538	68.3	242	81.4	5 082	82.3	8 936	81.0	13.9	3.8	3.8	5.1	5.1	21.9
Norfolk-Virginia Beach-Newport News, VA-NC	374 313	69.8	169 226	70.8	2 154	75.3	12 454	78.9	12 820	75.7	4.5	1.1	2.1	0.9	0.9	12.2
Ocala, FL	90 048	69.3	9 815	72.4	419	76.1	699	86.7	4 990	80.9	5.2	1.3	0.7	2.5	1.7	11.5
Odessa-Midland, TX	55 632	68.8	5 208	64.4	562	77.0	527	82.0	24 085	83.5	9.1	0.2	0.7	8.1	5.6	33.4
Oklahoma City, OK	328 838	66.6	41 224	66.2	14 154	72.3	8 947	66.9	19 518	78.0	5.7	0.5	2.2	2.6	2.6	11.3
Omaha, NE-IA	237 488	67.0	21 550	65.6	1 187	70.2	3 578	61.9	10 218	77.2	4.8	0.8	1.3	2.3	2.0	10.5
Orlando, FL	444 032	65.6	73 452	72.5	2 071	72.8	13 681	77.4	83 299	79.3	12.0	1.6	2.1	7.3	4.8	23.5
Owensboro, KY	34 010	69.6	1 438	65.0	64	51.6	97	88.7	230	65.7	1.0	0.3	0.4	0.3	0.4	6.7
Panama City, FL	51 055	68.3	5 600	67.9	400	76.3	659	69.5	1 164	65.1	3.6	1.3	1.3	0.6	0.7	9.9
Parkersburg-Marietta, WV-OH	59 870	69.7	514	67.9	117	79.5	234	72.6	190	57.4	0.9	0.3	0.3	0.1	0.1	4.6
Pensacola, FL	123 317	69.4	23 021	71.0	1 199	65.1	2 235	77.0	2 811	73.6	3.5	0.9	1.5	0.8	0.7	9.8
Peoria-Pekin, IL	122 161	68.3	9 931	68.9	211	59.2	1 362	74.7	1 348	82.8	2.2	0.5	1.0	0.5	0.6	7.6
Philadelphia-Wilmington-Atlantic City, PA-NJ-DE-MD	1 710 193	67.5	427 201	66.6	5 174	66.2	62 214	76.6	96 628	76.5	7.0	2.2	2.7	1.6	2.8	14.9
Atlantic-Cape May, NJ	105 015	65.0	17 468	65.3	335	60.6	3 805	80.8	9 338	77.2	9.3	2.0	3.3	3.6	4.3	17.5
Philadelphia, PA-NJ	1 402 904	67.6	365 495	66.3	3 885	66.3	53 235	76.1	72 722	75.8	7.0	2.3	2.7	1.4	2.8	14.8
Vineland-Millville-Bridgeton, NJ	32 973	69.8	7 726	75.1	468	69.0	414	74.6	7 229	79.4	6.2	1.6	0.6	3.9	4.6	22.6
Wilmington-Newark, DE-MD	169 301	68.2	36 512	68.4	486	66.5	4 760	78.8	7 339	79.0	5.9	1.4	2.0	2.0	2.0	12.7
Phoenix-Mesa, AZ	900 204	65.0	41 720	65.1	18 950	75.8	22 996	72.1	198 831	82.4	14.1	1.5	1.8	9.9	7.1	24.6
Pine Bluff, AR	16 225	70.9	13 670	70.5	107	79.4	120	92.5	262	78.6	1.1	0.1	0.5	0.3	0.4	7.1
Pittsburgh, PA	871 463	65.9	73 497	62.7	1 065	70.2	9 471	61.8	5 472	62.5	2.6	1.3	0.9	0.2	0.7	8.4
Pittsfield, MA	53 717	63.0	721	76.1	66	60.6	348	61.5	625	61.4	3.7	1.8	0.7	0.6	0.9	9.4
Pocatello, ID	24 792	71.0	194	55.2	693	78.8	282	57.1	999	79.1	2.2	0.5	0.8	0.6	0.7	11.1
Portland, ME	104 283	63.1	834	65.6	405	53.1	916	70.1	617	60.8	3.8	1.4	1.2	0.3	0.9	8.8
Portland-Salem, OR-WA	747 691	65.0	18 361	64.6	7 202	67.8	31 063	74.1	46 252	79.0	11.0	2.3	3.3	4.4	5.0	15.2
Portland-Vancouver, OR-WA	640 297	64.6	17 767	64.1	5 791	66.3	29 151	74.4	34 742	76.3	10.8	2.5	3.6	3.8	4.7	15.0
Salem, OR	107 394	67.9	594	79.8	1 411	74.1	1 912	70.6	11 510	87.1	11.5	1.5	1.5	7.9	6.7	16.2
Providence-Warwick-Pawtucket, RI	318 516	64.0	14 511	66.5	1 503	64.7	6 770	70.1	24 358	82.3	11.9	3.8	2.0	4.5	5.5	22.1
Provo-Orem, UT	91 512	81.4	234	76.5	592	83.8	1 449	70.9	5 432	88.5	6.3	0.7	0.8	3.9	2.2	19.0
Pueblo, CO	34 513	65.9	920	62.1	865	69.5	286	68.2	17 884	75.0	3.0	0.5	0.4	1.9	2.3	23.4
Punta Gorda, FL	59 265	68.9	2 101	72.8	231	62.8	259	64.9	1 465	76.7	8.0	2.9	0.7	2.9	1.2	11.5
Raleigh-Durham-Chapel Hill, NC	327 002	64.2	98 753	66.9	1 620	71.2	11 181	69.7	18 311	78.1	9.2	1.2	2.5	4.4	3.9	12.4
Rapid City, SD	31 055	67.2	240	61.7	1 957	76.2	246	67.5	662	77.0	2.1	0.8	0.7	0.3	0.7	8.7

[1] Hispanic or Latino persons may be of any race.

Table A-4. Metropolitan Areas — Age, Ethnicity, and Household Structure

CMSA/MSA/ PMSA/NECMA code[1]	Area name	Total population	Under 5 years	5 to 17 years	18 to 24 years	25 to 44 years	45 to 64 years	65 years and over	Median age	+/- U.S. percent under 18 years	+/- U.S. percent 65 years and over	Non-Hispanic White Total population	Under 18 years	65 years and over
		1	2	3	4	5	6	7	8	9	10	11	12	13
6680	Reading, PA..............	373 638	6.1	18.5	8.8	28.8	22.5	15.2	37.4	-1.1	2.8	317 659	22.1	17.0
6690	Redding, CA..............	163 256	5.9	20.2	8.2	25.2	25.3	15.2	38.9	0.4	2.8	141 087	24.1	16.5
6720	Reno, NV...................	339 486	6.8	18.0	9.9	31.2	23.7	10.5	35.6	-0.9	-1.9	247 668	21.3	12.9
6740	Richland-Kennewick-Pasco, WA	191 822	8.1	22.9	9.1	28.4	21.7	9.8	32.7	5.3	-2.6	139 708	26.7	12.4
6760	Richmond-Petersburg, VA.	996 512	6.5	18.7	8.9	31.7	22.9	11.3	35.8	-0.5	-1.1	637 594	22.8	13.1
6800	Roanoke, VA...............	235 932	5.8	16.8	7.7	28.9	25.1	15.8	39.4	-3.1	3.4	196 556	21.0	17.1
6820	Rochester, MN............	124 277	7.1	19.9	8.4	32.3	21.5	10.8	35.0	1.3	-1.6	110 855	25.6	11.7
6840	Rochester, NY.............	1 098 201	6.2	19.4	9.2	29.4	22.8	12.9	36.3	-0.1	0.5	903 317	23.3	14.6
6880	Rockford, IL...............	371 236	7.0	20.0	8.1	29.7	22.7	12.6	35.9	1.3	0.2	303 368	24.3	14.5
6895	Rocky Mount, NC.........	143 026	6.6	19.5	8.7	29.2	23.4	12.6	36.4	0.4	0.2	75 066	21.4	15.7
82	Sacramento-Yolo, CA..	1 796 857	6.8	20.1	9.6	30.5	21.6	11.3	34.6	1.2	-1.1	1 143 214	22.7	14.2
6920	Sacramento, CA........	1 628 197	6.9	20.3	8.7	30.7	21.8	11.5	35.1	1.5	-0.9	1 045 663	22.9	14.4
9270	Yolo, CA	168 660	6.4	18.7	18.3	28.6	18.8	9.2	29.5	-0.6	-3.2	97 551	21.1	12.8
6960	Saginaw-Bay City-Midland, MI..	403 070	6.5	19.5	8.8	28.1	23.6	13.5	36.9	0.3	1.1	332 390	23.7	14.9
7120	Salinas, CA................	401 762	7.7	20.7	10.9	31.7	19.0	10.0	31.7	2.7	-2.4	161 630	18.8	17.7
7160	Salt Lake City-Ogden, UT...................	1 333 914	9.1	22.2	12.8	29.9	17.8	8.3	28.6	5.6	-4.1	1 104 005	30.1	9.3
7200	San Angelo, TX..........	104 010	6.7	19.3	13.0	27.4	20.1	13.5	33.8	0.3	1.1	65 541	21.1	17.6
7240	San Antonio, TX..........	1 592 383	7.7	20.6	10.3	30.6	20.2	10.6	32.7	2.6	-1.8	626 073	21.5	15.7
7320	San Diego, CA	2 813 833	7.0	18.6	11.4	32.3	19.6	11.1	33.2	-0.1	-1.3	1 544 484	19.3	15.8
84	San Francisco-Oakland-San Jose, CA....	7 039 362	6.4	17.2	8.8	34.0	22.5	11.1	35.6	-2.1	-1.3	3 550 121	18.5	14.9
5775	Oakland, CA............	2 392 557	6.8	18.5	8.7	32.9	22.5	10.6	35.3	-0.4	-1.8	1 137 080	19.9	14.6
7360	San Francisco, CA	1 731 183	5.1	13.5	8.0	36.6	23.6	13.2	37.3	-7.1	0.8	884 436	14.2	15.9
7400	San Jose, CA	1 682 585	7.0	17.7	9.2	35.8	20.9	9.5	34.0	-1.0	-2.9	741 000	19.1	14.0
7485	Santa Cruz-Watsonville, CA..........	255 602	6.0	17.6	11.8	31.1	23.5	9.9	35.0	-2.1	-2.5	167 347	18.7	12.9
7500	Santa Rosa, CA	458 614	5.9	18.4	8.9	29.4	24.9	12.5	37.5	-1.4	0.1	340 842	20.9	15.5
8720	Vallejo-Fairfield-Napa, CA...................	518 821	6.9	20.4	9.0	30.8	22.1	10.9	34.9	1.6	-1.5	279 416	22.1	15.2
7460	San Luis Obispo-Atascadero-Paso Robles, CA	246 681	4.9	16.6	14.0	26.9	23.1	14.5	37.3	-4.2	2.1	187 597	19.2	17.5
7480	Santa Barbara-Santa Maria-Lompoc, CA	399 347	6.4	18.4	13.5	29.1	20.1	12.7	33.4	-0.9	0.3	226 841	18.0	18.4
7490	Santa Fe, NM.............	147 635	6.0	18.2	7.6	29.6	27.7	10.9	38.3	-1.5	-1.5	73 834	18.3	13.5
7510	Sarasota-Bradenton, FL	589 959	4.7	13.5	5.6	23.2	24.5	28.5	47.3	-7.5	16.1	504 604	15.5	32.2
7520	Savannah, GA...............	293 000	6.8	19.3	10.6	30.0	21.4	11.9	34.2	0.4	-0.5	176 320	22.2	13.8
7560	Scranton—Wilkes-Barre—Hazleton, PA..	624 776	5.1	16.4	8.9	26.9	23.8	18.9	40.2	-4.2	6.5	601 020	21.0	19.5
91	Seattle-Tacoma-Bremerton, WA..........	3 554 760	6.5	18.2	9.2	33.2	22.6	10.3	35.3	-1.0	-2.1	2 735 512	22.5	11.9
1150	Bremerton, WA...........	231 969	6.6	20.1	9.2	29.9	23.7	10.5	35.8	1.0	-1.9	190 099	24.7	12.0
5910	Olympia, WA	207 355	6.1	19.1	9.3	29.4	24.8	11.3	36.5	-0.5	-1.1	172 797	23.3	12.8
7600	Seattle-Bellevue-Everett, WA...............	2 414 616	6.3	17.4	9.0	34.3	22.7	10.2	35.5	-2.0	-2.2	1 840 086	21.7	11.7
8200	Tacoma, WA...............	700 820	7.1	20.1	9.7	31.6	21.4	10.2	34.1	1.5	-2.2	532 530	24.3	11.9
7610	Sharon, PA.................	120 293	5.7	17.8	8.8	26.3	23.4	18.1	39.6	-2.2	5.7	111 455	22.4	18.8
7620	Sheboygan, WI...........	112 646	6.4	19.0	8.3	30.0	22.2	14.0	36.8	-0.3	1.6	102 643	23.8	15.1
7640	Sherman-Denison, TX...	110 595	6.5	18.7	9.4	27.6	22.8	15.1	37.2	-0.5	2.7	93 213	23.5	16.7
7680	Shreveport-Bossier City, LA...................	392 302	7.0	20.0	9.8	28.2	21.9	13.2	35.1	1.3	0.8	230 555	22.5	16.2
7720	Sioux City, IA-NE	124 130	7.6	20.3	10.1	28.5	20.7	12.8	33.7	2.2	0.4	101 589	24.8	15.2
7760	Sioux Falls, SD	172 412	7.4	19.2	10.4	32.1	20.0	10.9	33.6	0.9	-1.5	159 936	25.5	11.6
7800	South Bend, IN............	265 559	7.0	18.7	11.7	28.2	20.8	13.6	34.4	0.0	1.2	214 495	23.0	15.4
7840	Spokane, WA..............	417 939	6.6	19.0	10.6	29.1	22.3	12.5	35.4	-0.1	0.1	374 816	24.6	13.3
7880	Springfield, IL.............	201 437	6.3	18.7	8.0	29.7	23.6	13.6	37.4	-0.7	1.2	176 694	23.3	14.6
8003	Springfield, MA............	608 479	6.0	18.4	11.7	28.2	21.9	13.9	35.9	-1.3	1.5	475 497	20.8	16.5
7920	Springfield, MO	325 721	6.5	17.3	12.3	29.3	21.7	12.9	34.9	-1.9	0.5	304 347	23.2	13.5
6980	St. Cloud, MN..............	167 392	6.6	19.4	15.3	28.8	18.9	11.0	31.6	0.3	-1.4	159 867	25.6	11.4
7000	St. Joseph, MO	102 490	6.2	18.4	10.6	28.1	21.8	14.9	36.4	-1.1	2.5	94 451	24.0	15.6
7040	St. Louis, MO-IL	2 603 607	6.7	19.6	8.7	30.1	22.1	12.9	36.0	0.6	0.5	2 015 553	24.2	14.3
8050	State College, PA.........	135 758	4.6	13.3	27.0	26.5	18.3	10.3	28.7	-7.8	-2.1	123 267	18.3	11.2
8080	Steubenville-Weirton, OH-WV	132 008	5.2	16.0	8.3	26.1	26.0	18.5	41.5	-4.5	6.1	124 150	20.5	18.9
8120	Stockton-Lodi, CA........	563 598	7.8	23.1	9.9	29.2	19.5	10.6	31.9	5.2	-1.8	265 960	23.6	15.6
8140	Sumter, SC..................	104 646	7.4	20.7	10.6	29.3	20.7	11.3	33.4	2.4	-1.1	51 782	24.4	13.2
8160	Syracuse, NY	732 117	6.3	19.5	9.8	28.9	22.1	13.4	36.1	0.1	1.0	643 560	24.3	14.6
8240	Tallahassee, FL............	284 539	5.9	16.2	19.4	29.0	20.6	8.9	30.3	-3.6	-3.5	169 796	18.9	10.9
8280	Tampa-St. Petersburg-Clearwater, FL............	2 395 997	5.7	16.1	7.5	28.5	23.0	19.2	40.0	-3.9	6.8	1 821 488	18.7	22.8
8320	Terre Haute, IN	149 192	6.2	17.3	12.5	27.5	21.9	14.6	35.8	-2.2	2.2	137 533	23.1	15.2
8360	Texarkana, TX-Texarkana, AR	129 749	6.8	18.5	9.5	29.2	22.2	13.8	35.8	-0.4	1.4	92 424	23.4	15.8
8400	Toledo, OH	618 203	6.6	19.2	11.2	28.8	21.5	12.7	34.7	0.1	0.3	495 026	23.3	14.0
8440	Topeka, KS	169 871	6.8	18.4	9.0	28.4	23.6	13.7	37.1	-0.5	1.3	135 843	22.7	15.5

[1]MSA = Metropolitan Statistical Area. CMSA = Consolidated Metropolitan Area. PMSA = Primary MSA. NECMA = New England County Metropolitan Area. See the Appendix A for explanation of these concepts. See Appendix B for list of metropolitan areas identified by type, with component counties.

Table A-4. Metropolitan Areas — **Age, Ethnicity, and Household Structure**

Area name	Black or African American			American Indian and Alaska Native			Asian, Hawaiian, and Pacific Islander			Hispanic or Latino[1]			Two or more races		
		Age (percent)			Age (percent)			Age (percent)			Age (percent)			Age (percent)	
	Total population	Under 18 years	65 years and over	Total population	Under 18 years	65 years and over	Total population	Under 18 years	65 years and over	Total population	Under 18 years	65 years and over	Total population	Under 18 years	65 years and over
	14	15	16	17	18	19	20	21	22	23	24	25	26	27	28
Reading, PA..................	13 057	33.1	9.9	852	32.3	5.0	3 863	29.6	6.0	36 096	42.4	2.9	6 284	50.3	3.7
Redding, CA.................	655	24.0	12.8	3 897	37.1	4.8	3 354	36.0	7.8	8 827	40.8	5.0	6 874	45.6	6.3
Reno, NV....................	6 581	26.7	6.2	6 212	34.3	5.0	15 829	23.6	7.7	56 304	37.9	2.6	12 827	40.8	3.9
Richland-Kennewick-Pasco, WA..................	2 278	34.4	8.6	1 283	27.3	2.1	4 037	24.5	6.6	41 181	44.9	2.0	6 289	46.7	3.0
Richmond-Petersburg, VA..........................	299 268	29.4	8.8	3 928	19.8	8.3	20 567	23.7	5.5	23 179	29.7	2.9	15 066	41.2	4.4
Roanoke, VA................	30 621	29.1	10.7	476	27.5	1.1	2 458	28.4	7.0	2 698	33.1	2.8	3 123	41.1	6.6
Rochester, MN.............	3 100	39.9	3.4	400	12.3	3.0	5 354	35.1	3.5	2 545	34.4	2.1	2 119	53.9	2.8
Rochester, NY..............	109 886	35.6	5.6	3 676	25.4	7.9	20 056	27.4	4.5	46 809	39.3	4.0	21 450	47.7	4.3
Rockford, IL................	29 860	37.0	5.7	1 191	29.6	2.7	4 894	30.8	4.0	27 447	40.6	2.6	7 510	51.9	4.1
Rocky Mount, NC........	61 803	30.5	9.8	325	22.8	7.4	605	35.5	2.3	4 371	39.2	1.8	1 163	41.0	5.2
Sacramento-Yolo, CA..	125 719	34.1	6.5	18 306	28.8	5.6	168 522	28.5	8.8	277 574	37.1	4.7	99 586	44.6	4.2
Sacramento, CA........	122 457	34.3	6.4	16 592	29.0	5.6	152 015	29.7	9.4	233 827	37.3	4.8	90 080	45.3	4.3
Yolo, CA.................	3 262	25.4	7.6	1 714	27.5	5.5	16 507	16.8	3.5	43 747	36.1	4.5	9 506	38.1	3.4
Saginaw-Bay City-Midland, MI................	40 982	35.4	7.7	1 882	29.8	4.4	3 566	31.4	4.0	19 441	39.3	5.3	7 151	52.5	4.3
Salinas, CA.................	14 998	22.1	7.4	3 928	26.4	4.7	26 044	23.2	14.1	188 388	37.6	3.2	19 298	40.1	4.7
Salt Lake City-Ogden, UT.............................	13 610	33.4	4.9	10 385	29.4	1.6	40 616	30.5	5.5	143 990	37.8	2.8	34 871	50.5	2.4
San Angelo, TX..........	4 573	31.7	8.4	561	24.1	4.1	777	18.1	7.7	31 874	35.5	6.0	2 351	45.1	5.0
San Antonio, TX.........	103 110	29.5	8.8	10 702	20.4	5.5	25 272	21.8	6.3	815 980	33.3	7.2	58 267	39.1	5.9
San Diego, CA............	158 371	30.6	5.5	23 513	28.8	5.8	262 135	23.5	8.5	750 991	36.5	4.4	139 772	43.7	4.1
San Francisco-Oakland-San Jose, CA.............	503 464	27.5	9.3	45 059	26.3	5.5	1 332 091	22.7	9.6	1 384 506	33.2	4.7	367 574	40.0	4.7
Oakland, CA.............	299 886	28.9	9.4	14 596	27.2	5.2	409 584	24.1	8.7	441 946	34.4	4.5	139 405	42.1	4.2
San Francisco, CA	90 623	21.9	13.2	7 073	18.0	6.7	405 534	19.2	13.3	291 398	27.9	6.4	82 395	33.7	6.2
San Jose, CA...........	45 076	24.9	5.1	11 233	28.4	5.0	435 994	24.3	7.2	404 012	33.7	4.5	83 765	40.1	4.8
Santa Cruz-Watsonville, CA..........	2 751	27.0	3.8	2 679	24.7	5.9	8 812	16.1	10.5	68 572	35.9	3.2	10 467	33.9	4.2
Santa Rosa, CA	6 486	29.2	4.7	5 163	30.4	4.4	14 820	24.5	7.6	79 624	36.1	2.9	19 236	42.4	4.3
Vallejo-Fairfield-Napa, CA..................	58 642	31.1	6.4	4 315	27.4	7.5	57 347	25.5	9.4	98 954	37.2	3.7	32 306	47.7	3.7
San Luis Obispo-Atascadero-Paso Robles, CA.................	4 556	12.0	3.1	1 982	19.1	6.8	7 015	16.3	9.3	40 114	32.9	3.8	9 304	37.9	6.3
Santa Barbara-Santa Maria-Lompoc, CA	9 057	23.8	6.8	4 318	32.4	5.8	16 535	18.9	9.7	136 737	36.2	4.2	17 745	39.5	4.8
Santa Fe, NM.............	1 017	26.5	5.0	4 045	33.0	4.7	1 822	29.0	3.4	65 619	30.3	8.7	5 579	32.9	7.7
Sarasota-Bradenton, FL	35 257	34.8	8.5	1 553	24.5	6.7	5 011	20.0	8.6	38 874	33.5	5.2	7 221	42.0	7.0
Savannah, GA............	102 280	32.4	9.2	746	19.7	13.8	4 835	23.4	7.9	5 841	30.6	3.8	3 700	44.2	7.2
Scranton—Wilkes-Barre—Hazleton, PA..	8 623	29.2	4.5	729	26.7	3.7	3 796	29.0	6.7	7 277	36.1	3.4	4 015	44.1	5.8
Seattle-Tacoma-Bremerton, WA..........	162 625	30.6	5.6	40 427	30.2	4.2	298 488	24.3	7.6	182 913	34.9	2.3	160 485	46.8	3.0
Bremerton, WA..........	6 233	31.4	2.7	3 324	31.7	4.3	12 163	25.6	7.0	9 718	38.2	1.7	11 950	51.4	3.0
Olympia, WA.............	4 783	30.8	1.6	3 144	34.2	3.3	10 629	27.8	6.1	9 067	36.3	2.5	8 121	49.1	3.0
Seattle-Bellevue-Everett, WA..............	102 868	29.3	6.4	24 487	28.2	4.5	235 950	24.0	7.5	125 551	32.9	2.4	101 373	44.6	3.1
Tacoma, WA	48 741	33.3	4.6	9 472	33.4	3.7	39 746	24.9	9.1	38 577	40.0	2.1	39 041	50.6	2.7
Sharon, PA................	6 056	33.6	11.3	136	38.2	11.0	681	25.3	3.2	996	45.1	4.2	1 135	57.0	6.0
Sheboygan, WI...........	1 364	20.4	0.2	326	36.2	0.0	3 596	52.7	3.1	3 680	39.1	4.0	1 510	53.5	2.2
Sherman-Denison, TX...	6 550	32.0	8.9	1 446	27.4	7.7	694	28.0	6.8	7 071	38.3	2.8	2 345	35.5	7.3
Shreveport-Bossier City, LA...................	146 292	33.6	9.0	1 679	29.1	8.0	3 323	25.4	5.1	6 912	31.6	4.7	4 478	37.7	9.1
Sioux City, IA-NE	2 168	40.6	6.1	2 094	43.8	3.2	2 927	33.4	1.8	13 910	42.2	1.0	2 539	52.6	0.5
Sioux Falls, SD	2 295	36.9	1.8	3 060	37.7	1.8	1 760	39.3	1.3	3 244	41.4	2.1	2 656	54.1	2.6
South Bend, IN............	29 652	35.7	7.9	904	44.0	0.9	3 579	21.8	3.7	12 343	38.4	2.2	5 655	52.1	5.8
Spokane, WA..............	6 325	30.3	6.8	5 740	30.7	4.8	8 139	21.4	9.6	11 465	37.3	3.2	13 004	46.5	4.1
Springfield, IL.............	17 860	37.4	7.1	417	30.5	2.4	2 021	25.1	6.6	1 726	33.3	6.2	2 845	48.9	7.6
Springfield, MA...........	39 662	33.9	7.1	1 365	27.0	4.1	11 167	21.5	4.1	74 169	41.8	2.8	14 732	41.8	4.5
Springfield, MO	5 398	27.0	5.5	2 638	30.7	5.6	2 588	22.8	4.8	5 174	33.6	3.8	5 903	39.0	5.8
St. Cloud, MN.............	1 098	23.7	1.8	545	29.4	3.3	2 287	25.8	3.5	1 965	40.8	1.5	1 769	52.1	1.3
St. Joseph, MO...........	3 684	24.3	7.2	461	29.1	12.4	406	20.0	5.2	2 380	37.6	6.3	1 380	48.1	4.9
St. Louis, MO-IL..........	473 691	33.3	8.9	6 697	26.4	5.2	36 818	23.5	4.8	39 525	35.0	4.5	36 131	44.2	5.2
State College, PA........	3 330	9.6	0.8	200	23.0	6.0	5 486	12.7	1.8	2 305	16.1	1.8	1 391	26.5	3.7
Steubenville-Weirton, OH-WV	5 127	28.3	13.5	215	9.3	12.6	273	31.9	10.3	959	42.4	11.6	1 378	40.3	8.1
Stockton-Lodi, CA	36 829	35.0	6.9	5 679	27.9	5.0	66 850	36.0	9.0	172 027	38.7	4.6	34 867	45.1	4.5
Sumter, SC.................	48 948	31.4	10.0	210	24.3	8.6	953	21.2	0.5	1 643	34.1	1.8	1 353	51.2	2.7
Syracuse, NY	46 642	36.4	5.4	5 154	33.2	5.2	11 155	24.5	4.0	14 713	38.4	3.0	13 314	50.4	3.8
Tallahassee, FL...........	95 216	27.4	6.6	700	23.0	3.6	5 059	18.8	3.1	10 993	22.9	2.6	3 974	32.9	3.6
Tampa-St. Petersburg-Clearwater, FL............	242 307	34.1	7.4	8 496	22.0	5.2	45 486	24.5	6.0	248 037	30.2	8.9	51 129	36.9	6.6
Terre Haute, IN............	6 601	25.0	8.6	441	28.1	4.8	1 210	20.4	6.9	1 551	30.2	4.9	2 010	46.1	3.9
Texarkana, TX-Texarkana, AR	29 892	31.4	9.7	633	23.2	4.9	648	24.1	9.3	4 421	19.3	4.4	2 036	41.5	6.4
Toledo, OH.................	78 573	34.4	8.5	1 649	22.8	5.9	6 842	22.9	5.1	27 117	41.2	4.7	13 049	50.6	4.4
Topeka, KS	14 642	31.0	9.5	2 018	27.8	8.8	1 555	20.6	3.4	12 142	38.5	4.8	5 487	52.4	3.0

[1] Hispanic or Latino persons may be of any race.

Area name	Total households	Family households (percent)						Nonfamily households (percent)						Percent of householders 65 years and over who live alone	Grandparents who are responsible for the care of their grandchildren
		Married-couple family households			Other family households			Two or more unrelated persons		Male living alone		Female living alone			
		Total	With children	House-holder 65 years or over	Total	With children	House-holder 65 years or over	Total	House-holder 65 years or over	Total	House-holder 65 years or over	Total	House-holder 65 years or over		
	29	30	31	32	33	34	35	36	37	38	39	40	41	42	43
Reading, PA	141 609	56.2	24.2	11.2	13.6	7.8	2.1	5.6	0.5	10.3	2.9	14.3	8.0	44.1	2 378
Redding, CA	63 497	53.6	21.7	11.8	15.9	10.4	2.1	5.9	0.7	10.6	2.9	14.0	7.1	40.6	1 418
Reno, NV	132 192	48.9	23.0	7.3	15.1	9.0	1.4	9.1	0.7	13.6	2.6	13.4	5.3	45.6	2 662
Richland-Kennewick-Pasco, WA	67 686	58.7	29.7	8.9	14.9	10.2	1.4	4.4	0.3	10.0	1.7	12.1	5.9	41.7	1 478
Richmond-Petersburg, VA	387 736	50.0	23.2	7.7	17.6	10.1	2.3	6.0	0.3	10.7	1.8	15.7	6.5	44.6	8 264
Roanoke, VA	98 355	50.7	20.4	10.4	15.4	8.4	2.3	4.5	0.4	11.3	2.2	18.1	8.9	46.0	1 844
Rochester, MN	47 894	57.3	28.6	8.6	10.7	7.3	0.8	6.2	0.3	10.8	1.8	15.0	6.3	45.6	334
Rochester, NY	420 485	50.6	23.2	8.9	15.9	9.9	2.0	6.4	0.4	11.3	2.5	15.8	7.6	47.3	6 743
Rockford, IL	141 826	55.6	25.3	9.5	14.6	9.3	1.5	4.8	0.4	11.1	2.3	14.0	7.2	45.3	3 096
Rocky Mount, NC	54 041	50.9	22.2	8.5	21.0	11.1	2.9	3.4	0.2	9.6	2.3	15.1	8.0	46.9	2 116
Sacramento-Yolo, CA	665 722	50.5	24.5	8.7	16.9	10.3	1.9	7.5	0.5	10.7	2.0	14.3	5.9	41.8	14 588
Sacramento, CA	606 364	50.8	24.4	8.9	17.1	10.4	1.9	7.0	0.5	10.7	2.0	14.4	5.9	41.5	13 301
Yolo, CA	59 358	48.4	25.6	6.9	15.1	9.0	1.9	13.2	0.4	10.1	2.1	13.2	5.6	45.5	1 287
Saginaw-Bay City-Midland, MI	156 313	54.0	23.2	9.9	15.8	9.9	2.1	4.4	0.3	10.3	2.3	15.5	8.2	46.0	2 802
Salinas, CA	121 199	56.8	30.6	9.3	16.3	9.3	2.2	5.8	0.7	8.3	2.0	12.9	6.3	40.2	3 327
Salt Lake City-Ogden, UT	432 113	61.4	34.3	8.1	13.9	8.1	1.5	5.3	0.2	8.7	1.4	10.7	4.8	38.8	10 055
San Angelo, TX	39 531	52.9	24.2	10.3	15.6	9.7	1.8	4.4	0.2	11.2	2.4	15.9	8.5	46.9	1 327
San Antonio, TX	560 293	53.2	26.4	8.5	18.7	10.7	2.7	4.8	0.3	10.2	2.0	13.1	5.6	39.5	20 330
San Diego, CA	995 492	51.3	25.5	8.8	15.9	9.2	2.0	8.6	0.6	10.9	2.1	13.2	5.8	41.1	21 244
San Francisco-Oakland-San Jose, CA	2 559 268	50.3	24.6	7.8	14.8	7.5	2.2	9.1	0.6	11.4	2.0	14.4	5.9	43.0	50 754
Oakland, CA	868 209	51.0	25.7	7.4	16.5	8.6	2.3	7.8	0.5	10.5	2.0	14.2	5.8	43.2	19 013
San Francisco, CA	684 805	43.1	19.0	8.1	12.6	5.4	2.3	12.2	0.8	14.7	2.6	17.5	6.8	45.6	11 057
San Jose, CA	566 485	56.1	28.7	7.5	14.4	6.9	2.0	8.1	0.5	10.3	1.5	11.1	4.5	37.6	11 912
Santa Cruz-Watsonville, CA	91 244	48.3	23.7	7.3	15.1	9.0	1.9	11.5	0.6	11.0	1.8	14.1	6.1	44.8	1 463
Santa Rosa, CA	172 690	51.4	24.1	9.1	14.4	8.5	1.8	8.5	0.7	10.0	2.4	15.7	7.7	46.6	2 451
Vallejo-Fairfield-Napa, CA	175 835	56.5	28.4	8.6	16.9	9.9	2.1	5.5	0.4	8.6	1.9	12.5	6.0	41.2	4 858
San Luis Obispo-Atascadero-Paso Robles, CA	92 732	51.1	21.5	11.7	12.4	7.3	1.7	10.5	0.8	10.8	2.6	15.1	8.1	42.9	1 502
Santa Barbara-Santa Maria-Lompoc, CA	136 769	52.3	25.8	10.4	13.7	7.5	2.2	9.7	0.9	9.8	2.5	14.4	7.2	41.8	2 693
Santa Fe, NM	59 976	49.0	21.7	7.9	15.1	9.6	2.0	7.2	0.6	12.3	2.1	16.5	5.5	42.1	1 338
Sarasota-Bradenton, FL	262 622	53.3	14.5	21.3	11.2	6.1	1.9	6.0	1.1	10.4	4.0	19.2	12.4	40.4	3 756
Savannah, GA	111 080	49.9	22.3	8.7	19.3	11.1	2.9	5.7	0.3	10.5	2.0	14.7	6.9	42.9	3 908
Scranton—Wilkes-Barre—Hazleton, PA	252 711	50.9	20.7	11.1	14.5	6.9	3.4	4.1	0.3	11.7	3.7	18.8	11.8	51.0	3 233
Seattle-Tacoma-Bremerton, WA	1 392 913	51.4	24.5	7.4	13.3	8.2	1.3	8.3	0.4	12.5	1.9	14.6	5.7	45.2	19 441
Bremerton, WA	86 393	58.2	27.7	8.2	13.1	9.0	1.2	6.2	0.5	10.5	2.1	12.1	5.8	44.5	1 373
Olympia, WA	81 666	53.7	24.4	8.8	13.9	9.1	1.3	7.3	0.4	10.4	1.9	14.6	6.1	43.4	1 242
Seattle-Bellevue-Everett, WA	963 957	49.9	24.5	7.1	12.6	7.4	1.3	9.1	0.4	13.1	1.8	15.3	5.6	45.7	11 462
Tacoma, WA	260 897	53.7	26.0	7.9	15.8	10.7	1.4	6.2	0.4	11.3	2.0	13.0	5.7	44.2	5 364
Sharon, PA	46 755	55.4	22.2	13.5	14.1	7.7	2.8	3.6	0.4	10.7	2.9	16.2	9.8	43.3	794
Sheboygan, WI	43 595	58.8	26.2	10.9	10.2	6.5	1.1	4.9	0.2	11.4	2.4	14.6	8.0	46.0	409
Sherman-Denison, TX	42 834	56.2	24.2	11.0	14.5	8.7	2.4	3.9	0.3	10.4	2.6	15.0	8.9	45.5	1 378
Shreveport-Bossier City, LA	151 243	46.9	20.2	8.9	21.9	12.6	3.2	4.1	0.4	11.4	2.2	15.7	7.6	44.0	6 210
Sioux City, IA-NE	46 339	53.8	25.9	9.6	15.0	9.7	1.8	5.2	0.2	10.3	2.4	15.6	8.8	49.0	737
Sioux Falls, SD	66 836	54.6	27.0	8.5	12.1	8.1	1.0	6.6	0.2	11.2	1.5	15.5	6.9	46.2	655
South Bend, IN	100 629	51.2	23.3	9.9	15.4	9.5	2.1	5.6	0.3	11.6	2.4	16.3	8.6	47.3	2 205
Spokane, WA	163 826	51.1	23.4	9.0	14.4	9.7	1.3	6.4	0.3	12.0	2.3	16.0	7.7	48.6	2 072
Springfield, IL	83 656	49.2	22.0	8.8	14.9	9.5	1.7	5.4	0.4	12.3	2.4	18.2	8.5	49.9	1 204
Springfield, MA	231 430	47.0	20.8	9.0	18.0	10.8	2.4	6.6	0.4	11.2	3.0	17.2	8.8	49.9	3 149
Springfield, MO	129 556	53.9	23.2	9.6	12.9	8.0	1.5	6.5	0.2	11.0	2.0	15.8	7.3	45.0	1 640
St. Cloud, MN	60 694	56.4	28.5	9.3	10.8	6.9	1.2	8.7	0.2	11.1	2.0	13.0	6.4	43.9	309
St. Joseph, MO	39 841	52.3	22.7	10.4	14.8	9.6	1.9	5.1	0.4	11.2	2.6	16.6	10.0	49.7	848
St. Louis, MO-IL	1 013 341	50.8	23.6	8.9	17.0	9.9	2.4	4.9	0.3	11.5	2.3	15.9	7.7	46.3	21 229
State College, PA	49 336	49.7	21.0	8.6	8.4	4.6	1.2	15.4	0.3	12.7	1.8	13.9	6.2	43.9	466
Steubenville-Weirton, OH-WV	54 473	54.1	20.1	12.5	14.7	6.9	3.1	3.3	0.4	10.9	3.3	17.0	10.2	45.7	1 049
Stockton-Lodi, CA	181 612	55.6	29.7	8.6	19.0	11.6	2.2	4.8	0.5	8.5	2.1	12.2	6.5	43.2	6 666
Sumter, SC	37 719	51.3	24.4	7.8	22.4	12.7	3.4	3.1	0.2	10.0	2.2	13.3	6.9	44.4	1 600
Syracuse, NY	282 875	50.1	23.2	9.3	15.6	10.0	2.0	6.5	0.4	11.4	2.6	16.4	8.3	48.2	4 264
Tallahassee, FL	112 533	41.3	18.8	6.0	17.7	10.2	1.9	12.2	0.3	13.0	1.6	15.9	4.7	43.3	2 795
Tampa-St. Petersburg-Clearwater, FL	1 009 792	48.8	18.1	13.4	14.7	8.3	2.1	6.8	0.7	12.0	3.3	17.7	9.7	44.4	19 071
Terre Haute, IN	58 022	52.0	22.4	10.0	14.3	8.6	1.9	5.3	0.4	11.3	2.4	17.1	10.0	50.0	1 348
Texarkana, TX-Texarkana, AR	48 743	52.2	22.2	9.9	19.0	11.5	2.5	3.1	0.2	9.8	2.4	16.0	8.7	46.7	1 982
Toledo, OH	243 516	48.5	21.8	8.5	16.7	10.3	1.9	6.1	0.3	12.5	2.4	16.2	7.9	48.9	4 580
Topeka, KS	69 007	51.1	22.2	9.5	14.3	9.0	1.8	4.9	0.3	12.1	2.5	17.5	8.2	48.1	1 351

Table A-4. Metropolitan Areas — **Age, Ethnicity, and Household Structure**

Area name	Households with Non-Hispanic White householder		Households with Black or African American householder		Households with American Indian and Alaska Native householder		Households with Asian, Hawaiian, and Pacific Islander householder		Households with Hispanic or Latino[1] householder		Foreign-born population	Place of birth (percent)			Percent in non-English speaking households	
	Number of households	Percent that are family households	Number of households	Percent that are family households	Number of households	Percent that are family households	Number of households	Percent that are family households	Number of households	Percent that are family households	Percent of total population that is foreign-born	Europe	Asia	Latin America	Linguistically isolated	Not linguistically isolated
	44	45	46	47	48	49	50	51	52	53	54	55	56	57	58	59
Reading, PA	125 465	69.3	4 467	67.3	327	69.7	1 092	79.1	9 624	77.6	4.3	1.2	0.8	2.0	2.9	15.3
Redding, CA	57 117	69.0	259	64.9	1 244	76.9	801	82.4	2 381	73.7	4.0	0.8	1.5	1.1	1.2	10.1
Reno, NV	106 441	61.1	2 739	58.0	2 042	70.7	4 744	70.9	14 111	83.7	14.1	1.4	3.4	8.4	5.8	20.5
Richland-Kennewick-Pasco, WA	54 592	71.3	739	68.3	402	82.1	1 406	75.7	9 461	87.8	12.8	1.3	1.5	9.4	6.6	21.5
Richmond-Petersburg, VA	261 174	67.1	108 213	68.7	1 626	66.5	6 486	69.3	6 601	75.1	4.5	1.0	1.7	1.3	1.5	9.7
Roanoke, VA	83 500	66.2	12 191	63.9	187	67.4	752	79.8	724	70.6	2.7	0.8	1.0	0.6	0.9	6.9
Rochester, MN	43 906	67.7	979	70.9	186	79.6	1 676	71.5	681	72.4	7.9	1.5	3.4	0.9	2.6	11.2
Rochester, NY	358 238	66.2	37 325	67.6	1 383	65.1	5 778	71.0	13 613	72.3	5.7	2.4	1.7	1.0	1.9	12.8
Rockford, IL	121 580	69.3	10 354	71.1	428	78.7	1 490	75.5	7 016	83.0	6.0	1.4	1.1	3.4	2.6	12.3
Rocky Mount, NC	30 908	70.8	21 615	72.7	106	83.0	174	95.4	1 015	81.7	2.6	0.2	0.5	1.8	1.1	7.8
Sacramento-Yolo, CA	472 472	65.0	44 165	69.0	6 155	68.1	49 534	73.6	75 825	77.2	14.5	2.7	5.9	4.8	6.1	22.8
Sacramento, CA	432 964	65.4	43 047	69.2	5 623	68.1	44 539	76.5	64 371	76.7	13.9	2.7	5.9	4.2	5.8	21.9
Yolo, CA	39 508	60.9	1 118	61.0	532	68.4	4 995	48.3	11 454	80.2	20.3	2.8	6.0	10.3	9.2	31.5
Saginaw-Bay City-Midland, MI	133 629	69.4	14 095	70.6	688	82.3	1 133	71.8	5 550	76.3	2.1	0.6	0.7	0.4	0.6	9.1
Salinas, CA	68 367	63.8	4 002	69.7	1 154	77.2	8 211	75.0	37 387	90.3	29.0	1.9	3.9	22.6	15.4	41.5
Salt Lake City-Ogden, UT	373 203	74.8	4 587	69.8	3 057	71.5	11 124	78.6	35 506	81.7	8.6	1.5	1.7	4.6	3.4	18.5
San Angelo, TX	27 519	65.8	1 546	67.6	223	70.0	257	59.9	9 753	77.2	5.9	0.5	0.6	4.7	4.0	32.1
San Antonio, TX	262 759	67.2	38 509	68.4	3 739	71.4	8 420	67.5	243 337	78.1	10.2	0.8	1.3	7.8	6.6	47.3
San Diego, CA	657 282	61.9	54 826	68.4	7 522	69.8	74 052	77.4	182 122	82.2	21.5	2.0	7.0	11.4	8.1	34.0
San Francisco-Oakland-San Jose, CA	1 559 348	59.2	185 848	64.0	14 405	66.6	404 419	76.7	330 948	80.2	27.0	3.1	13.6	9.0	9.7	34.9
Oakland, CA	490 498	62.6	113 126	64.4	4 986	67.2	125 223	77.8	109 343	80.7	24.0	2.3	12.1	8.2	8.6	32.1
San Francisco, CA	427 710	48.1	34 787	55.2	2 560	45.8	128 620	71.2	75 179	73.2	32.0	4.5	16.6	9.3	11.2	37.6
San Jose, CA	315 370	63.4	16 087	67.1	3 094	75.6	127 964	80.5	91 466	82.7	34.1	3.4	19.5	9.8	12.2	42.5
Santa Cruz-Watsonville, CA	70 128	59.8	907	61.1	829	69.5	2 812	62.6	14 517	83.8	18.2	2.5	2.0	13.0	7.9	27.6
Santa Rosa, CA	143 605	63.5	2 038	67.6	1 559	75.5	4 337	75.6	17 272	83.7	14.3	2.3	2.4	8.8	5.4	21.3
Vallejo-Fairfield-Napa, CA	112 037	68.9	18 903	75.2	1 377	70.7	15 463	86.1	23 171	85.6	17.2	1.7	7.0	7.8	5.4	29.2
San Luis Obispo-Atascadero-Paso Robles, CA	77 781	62.6	767	50.3	831	59.2	2 190	56.8	9 479	76.2	8.9	1.5	1.7	5.0	3.3	18.1
Santa Barbara-Santa Maria-Lompoc, CA	93 985	60.5	3 101	65.6	1 350	77.7	5 154	64.9	31 405	84.1	21.2	2.6	2.8	15.0	9.9	31.8
Santa Fe, NM	34 927	58.0	348	52.6	1 441	67.0	633	67.5	22 007	73.6	9.7	1.8	0.9	6.5	5.7	40.8
Sarasota-Bradenton, FL	237 335	63.4	11 680	72.5	689	69.4	1 478	78.7	10 125	78.2	8.9	3.3	0.8	3.6	2.0	12.8
Savannah, GA	71 911	68.3	34 790	70.8	308	74.0	1 548	68.9	1 682	69.6	3.5	0.8	1.3	1.0	1.2	9.2
Scranton—Wilkes-Barre—Hazleton, PA	246 589	65.3	2 167	60.9	279	64.5	1 012	74.6	1 785	75.2	2.0	0.9	0.5	0.3	0.7	8.2
Seattle-Tacoma-Bremerton, WA	1 138 261	63.7	61 691	64.8	13 542	66.0	93 937	72.5	50 804	71.4	11.7	2.5	5.9	1.8	3.8	16.9
Bremerton, WA	75 044	70.8	2 165	67.9	1 142	70.1	3 180	80.8	2 530	81.4	5.7	1.0	3.3	0.6	1.0	14.1
Olympia, WA	71 322	66.6	1 907	73.4	1 086	75.6	2 942	81.6	2 621	72.9	6.1	1.3	3.2	0.9	1.6	13.2
Seattle-Bellevue-Everett, WA	780 975	61.5	39 906	60.7	8 360	62.5	75 805	71.7	35 771	68.6	13.7	2.8	6.9	2.1	4.6	17.7
Tacoma, WA	210 920	68.6	17 713	72.9	2 954	70.9	12 010	73.3	9 882	78.6	8.1	2.1	3.7	1.5	2.6	15.8
Sharon, PA	44 057	69.4	2 042	69.8	43	65.1	168	81.5	202	81.2	1.6	0.8	0.5	0.2	0.9	7.0
Sheboygan, WI	41 415	68.6	210	76.7	61	85.2	670	88.8	985	69.8	4.3	0.9	2.1	1.1	2.2	10.5
Sherman-Denison, TX	37 372	70.1	2 288	70.1	535	66.7	235	72.3	1 839	84.4	3.9	0.4	0.6	2.8	2.0	9.2
Shreveport-Bossier City, LA	95 757	67.9	50 579	70.1	624	72.1	1 006	75.2	2 030	73.5	1.7	0.4	0.7	0.5	0.5	7.6
Sioux City, IA-NE	40 695	67.4	751	61.5	538	75.3	703	83.4	3 272	84.3	8.6	0.3	1.9	6.0	5.4	13.5
Sioux Falls, SD	63 728	66.6	719	67.5	694	76.4	398	64.6	830	73.7	3.7	1.1	0.9	0.7	1.8	8.2
South Bend, IN	84 462	66.1	10 411	68.5	302	73.2	1 254	62.7	3 188	76.2	4.6	1.2	1.1	1.7	1.6	11.4
Spokane, WA	151 244	65.6	2 051	66.7	1 961	67.5	2 378	65.2	3 032	66.2	4.5	1.9	1.5	0.4	1.6	9.7
Springfield, IL	75 088	64.2	6 386	64.9	182	39.0	683	61.3	601	70.7	1.8	0.5	0.8	0.2	0.3	6.5
Springfield, MA	190 358	63.8	13 775	65.9	495	66.5	2 991	68.3	21 745	75.5	7.1	3.3	1.8	1.2	4.8	20.9
Springfield, MO	122 670	66.9	1 739	64.5	968	59.7	808	62.0	1 516	70.8	1.6	0.4	0.6	0.3	0.5	6.7
St. Cloud, MN	58 651	67.7	393	43.0	179	54.2	648	45.7	456	75.2	2.3	0.4	1.2	0.5	1.0	9.2
St. Joseph, MO	37 546	67.3	1 071	55.7	152	65.8	149	51.7	614	77.2	1.0	0.4	0.2	0.2	0.2	5.9
St. Louis, MO-IL	805 799	67.8	172 243	67.8	2 591	72.0	12 521	68.3	11 529	69.8	3.1	1.1	1.2	0.5	1.0	8.3
State College, PA	45 731	59.2	697	30.7	77	87.0	1 958	45.1	547	43.5	5.8	1.4	3.4	0.4	1.9	11.1
Steubenville-Weirton, OH-WV	51 381	69.3	2 211	63.0	90	47.8	67	46.3	307	60.3	1.4	1.0	0.2	0.1	0.5	7.9
Stockton-Lodi, CA	104 627	69.3	11 715	75.5	1 841	74.3	17 477	82.6	41 376	84.2	19.5	1.1	7.2	10.6	10.1	32.7
Sumter, SC	20 027	74.5	16 703	72.8	71	77.5	249	75.1	411	75.7	2.1	0.5	0.8	0.6	0.6	8.9
Syracuse, NY	254 944	65.8	15 900	64.5	1 636	69.9	3 655	61.1	3 923	68.7	4.3	1.8	1.5	0.5	1.3	10.7
Tallahassee, FL	71 649	58.1	34 412	60.9	232	59.5	1 855	64.0	3 393	56.6	4.6	0.9	1.4	1.8	1.2	10.8
Tampa-St. Petersburg-Clearwater, FL	818 466	61.8	85 174	68.3	3 324	62.8	13 818	75.9	78 984	73.9	9.8	2.6	1.7	4.4	3.4	17.4
Terre Haute, IN	54 198	66.9	2 155	57.1	179	56.4	448	42.0	423	61.2	1.6	0.4	0.7	0.4	0.4	5.7
Texarkana, TX-Texarkana, AR	36 431	71.8	10 598	68.3	280	65.4	194	63.9	744	83.2	1.4	0.2	0.3	0.7	0.6	6.6
Toledo, OH	200 040	65.0	29 825	64.8	629	71.1	2 461	66.2	7 951	72.7	2.9	0.8	1.2	0.6	0.8	10.3
Topeka, KS	57 351	65.4	5 733	64.6	694	69.2	559	67.6	3 816	68.9	2.7	0.3	0.7	1.5	1.1	9.1

[1] Hispanic or Latino persons may be of any race.

CMSA/MSA/ PMSA/NECMA code[1]	Area name	Total population	Population by age (percent)							Median age	+/- U.S. percent under 18 years	+/- U.S. percent 65 years and over	Non-Hispanic White		
			Under 5 years	5 to 17 years	18 to 24 years	25 to 44 years	45 to 64 years	65 years and over				Total population	Age (percent)	
													Under 18 years	65 years and over
		1	2	3	4	5	6	7	8	9	10	11	12	13
8520	Tucson, AZ..................	843 746	6.5	18.0	10.7	28.8	21.8	14.2	35.7	-1.2	1.8	517 982	18.3	19.4
8560	Tulsa, OK	803 235	7.1	19.5	9.3	29.8	22.4	11.8	35.1	0.9	-0.6	593 419	23.5	13.9
8600	Tuscaloosa, AL	164 875	6.3	17.1	16.5	28.1	20.8	11.2	31.9	-2.3	-1.2	111 273	20.4	12.8
8640	Tyler, TX.....................	174 706	7.1	19.5	9.8	27.6	22.0	14.0	35.5	0.9	1.6	118 784	22.7	17.3
8680	Utica-Rome, NY	299 896	5.7	18.3	8.5	27.9	23.0	16.6	38.4	-1.7	4.2	270 985	23.2	17.8
8750	Victoria, TX..................	84 088	7.5	21.7	9.0	28.6	21.5	11.8	34.2	3.5	-0.6	44 487	23.6	16.0
8780	Visalia-Tulare-Porterville, CA	368 021	8.9	24.9	10.6	27.8	18.1	9.7	29.2	8.1	-2.7	153 340	23.9	16.9
8800	Waco, TX	213 517	7.1	19.4	14.4	26.6	19.4	13.0	31.9	0.8	0.6	138 204	21.7	16.3
97	Washington-Baltimore, DC-MD-VA-WV	7 608 070	6.8	18.4	8.6	33.1	23.0	10.1	35.4	-0.5	-2.3	4 571 035	22.8	12.3
0720	Baltimore, MD	2 552 994	6.5	18.8	8.5	31.2	23.0	12.0	36.3	-0.4	-0.4	1 693 115	22.9	14.0
3180	Hagerstown, MD	131 923	6.2	17.3	8.1	31.4	23.0	14.2	37.4	-2.2	1.8	117 803	23.2	15.4
8840	Washington, DC-MD-VA-WV	4 923 153	6.9	18.3	8.6	34.1	23.0	9.0	34.9	-0.5	-3.4	2 760 117	22.6	11.1
8920	Waterloo-Cedar Falls, IA	128 012	6.1	17.0	15.7	25.2	22.0	14.0	34.4	-2.6	1.6	112 282	20.9	15.1
8940	Wausau, WI.................	125 834	6.5	20.3	8.2	29.5	22.6	13.0	36.3	1.1	0.6	118 052	24.9	13.7
8960	West Palm Beach-Boca Raton, FL	1 131 184	5.5	15.7	6.5	27.1	22.0	23.2	41.8	-4.5	10.8	798 753	16.7	30.2
9000	Wheeling, WV-OH........	153 172	5.1	16.7	8.5	26.6	25.1	17.9	40.7	-3.9	5.5	145 507	21.5	18.4
9080	Wichita Falls, TX..........	140 518	6.8	18.3	13.3	29.0	19.7	12.8	33.6	-0.6	0.4	104 684	23.1	15.2
9040	Wichita, KS..................	545 220	7.6	20.4	9.4	30.1	20.7	11.8	34.1	2.3	-0.6	430 753	25.6	13.6
9140	Williamsport, PA	120 044	5.5	17.7	9.7	27.6	23.5	16.0	38.4	-2.5	3.6	112 316	22.3	16.8
9200	Wilmington, NC	233 450	5.7	15.3	10.4	29.0	25.6	14.1	38.0	-4.7	1.7	185 764	18.6	15.4
9260	Yakima, WA	222 581	8.6	23.1	9.6	28.1	19.4	11.2	31.2	6.0	-1.2	125 664	23.1	17.2
9280	York, PA......................	381 751	6.1	18.6	7.5	30.4	24.0	13.5	37.8	-1.0	1.1	349 781	23.3	14.3
9320	Youngstown-Warren, OH	594 746	6.0	18.0	8.1	27.3	24.2	16.5	39.2	-1.7	4.1	513 780	22.6	17.5
9340	Yuba City, CA	139 149	7.5	22.2	9.7	28.5	20.8	11.3	32.9	4.0	-1.1	86 580	24.7	15.3
9360	Yuma, AZ	160 026	7.8	21.0	10.2	25.5	18.9	16.6	33.9	3.1	4.2	71 130	15.8	31.0

[1]MSA = Metropolitan Statistical Area. CMSA = Consolidated Metropolitan Area. PMSA = Primary MSA. NECMA = New England County Metropolitan Area. See the Appendix A for explanation of these concepts. See Appendix B for list of metropolitan areas identified by type, with component counties.

Table A-4. Metropolitan Areas — Age, Ethnicity, and Household Structure

Area name	Black or African American Total population	Under 18 years	65 years and over	American Indian and Alaska Native Total population	Under 18 years	65 years and over	Asian, Hawaiian, and Pacific Islander Total population	Under 18 years	65 years and over	Hispanic or Latino[1] Total population	Under 18 years	65 years and over	Two or more races Total population	Under 18 years	65 years and over
	14	15	16	17	18	19	20	21	22	23	24	25	26	27	28
Tucson, AZ	24 460	28.6	7.9	27 440	34.2	4.9	17 991	21.2	5.7	247 861	36.0	5.9	29 339	43.5	4.7
Tulsa, OK	70 682	34.5	6.7	53 817	35.1	6.3	9 910	28.5	3.3	38 365	37.5	2.3	41 678	39.0	6.9
Tuscaloosa, AL	47 935	29.6	8.3	648	21.1	5.2	1 561	15.8	3.8	2 062	36.2	3.2	1 602	36.5	6.1
Tyler, TX	33 296	30.8	10.3	726	31.1	0.4	1 159	37.0	4.6	19 395	41.8	1.7	2 288	45.2	5.0
Utica-Rome, NY	13 718	27.8	6.4	567	17.8	7.1	3 060	29.2	4.8	7 916	32.1	3.2	4 766	44.4	4.2
Victoria, TX	5 434	32.0	9.6	476	27.1	4.2	529	28.9	7.8	32 976	36.2	6.4	1 791	46.6	8.5
Visalia-Tulare-Porterville, CA	6 196	40.2	7.3	4 702	35.0	7.6	12 616	36.0	9.7	186 913	41.6	3.9	17 034	42.8	6.1
Waco, TX	32 218	32.8	10.2	1 034	34.8	1.7	2 289	17.5	4.9	38 281	38.3	4.6	3 715	50.3	4.8
Washington-Baltimore, DC-MD-VA-WV	1 980 986	28.8	8.1	23 529	23.6	. 5.7	397 857	23.1	5.9	483 549	30.2	3.0	202 430	39.9	3.7
Baltimore, MD	694 779	29.5	9.0	7 122	25.4	5.8	69 591	24.3	5.1	51 464	30.8	4.4	43 780	43.4	4.1
Hagerstown, MD	10 112	19.4	2.9	220	20.9	2.7	1 024	23.3	7.7	1 497	42.7	3.4	1 445	53.7	5.0
Washington, DC-MD-VA-WV	1 276 095	28.5	7.7	16 187	22.8	5.7	327 242	22.9	6.1	430 588	30.1	2.9	157 205	38.8	3.6
Waterloo-Cedar Falls, IA	9 871	37.2	7.8	276	26.4	4.7	1 372	22.7	1.2	2 396	42.7	4.2	2 037	54.4	3.1
Wausau, WI	260	50.8	0.0	549	38.6	3.1	5 174	58.7	2.2	932	39.9	3.0	982	55.7	2.9
West Palm Beach-Boca Raton, FL	156 496	35.6	5.9	2 706	30.7	4.7	17 318	23.6	5.9	140 568	29.0	6.8	27 518	32.0	6.2
Wheeling, WV-OH	4 196	21.1	9.5	378	34.4	7.1	596	21.5	8.2	914	31.6	13.6	1 576	47.9	5.7
Wichita Falls, TX	13 085	27.6	8.1	1 140	30.3	3.2	2 630	23.1	5.4	16 378	34.8	4.2	4 010	41.0	4.5
Wichita, KS	41 881	34.5	7.4	5 789	30.7	5.9	15 047	28.9	4.3	39 785	40.5	3.4	16 613	50.8	3.6
Williamsport, PA	4 988	33.8	3.1	298	14.1	1.3	520	31.2	3.8	915	39.7	2.6	998	51.1	4.8
Wilmington, NC	37 230	30.2	10.5	1 254	22.6	3.0	1 640	20.5	5.9	5 443	27.8	2.2	2 609	42.9	3.4
Yakima, WA	1 943	36.5	9.6	9 396	39.1	4.8	2 331	25.2	8.5	79 952	44.4	2.7	7 885	45.0	5.5
York, PA	13 515	34.9	5.9	529	26.5	1.5	3 245	29.0	5.2	11 311	41.1	2.1	4 381	55.8	2.4
Youngstown-Warren, OH	59 648	32.0	11.0	1 332	24.4	6.0	2 451	22.0	5.7	10 629	32.8	6.6	8 272	45.0	5.9
Yuba City, CA	3 631	32.6	7.2	2 768	29.6	5.8	13 712	36.0	6.9	27 872	40.2	2.8	7 512	43.8	4.6
Yuma, AZ	3 505	29.7	4.3	2 683	30.2	10.3	1 508	22.1	12.5	80 828	40.3	4.7	4 730	49.1	6.4

[1] Hispanic or Latino persons may be of any race.

Table A-4. Metropolitan Areas — Age, Ethnicity, and Household Structure

Area name	Total households	Family households (percent)						Nonfamily households (percent)						Percent of householders 65 years and over who live alone	Grandparents who are responsible for the care of their grandchildren
		Married-couple family households			Other family households			Two or more unrelated persons		Male living alone		Female living alone			
		Total	With children	Householder 65 years or over	Total	With children	Householder 65 years or over	Total	Householder 65 years or over	Total	Householder 65 years or over	Total	Householder 65 years or over		
	29	30	31	32	33	34	35	36	37	38	39	40	41	42	43
Tucson, AZ	332 497	48.7	20.8	10.9	15.6	9.2	1.9	7.3	0.6	12.7	2.6	15.8	7.1	41.8	8 471
Tulsa, OK	315 759	53.8	24.6	8.7	14.8	9.2	1.7	4.5	0.3	11.7	2.0	15.2	6.8	45.1	7 790
Tuscaloosa, AL	64 517	47.9	21.0	7.7	17.3	9.8	2.4	6.4	0.2	12.3	1.8	16.0	6.8	45.5	1 929
Tyler, TX	65 711	56.7	25.1	11.2	15.2	8.8	2.4	3.5	0.2	9.0	2.0	15.6	7.9	41.9	2 387
Utica-Rome, NY	116 247	50.3	21.6	11.0	15.6	9.4	2.4	5.1	0.4	11.8	3.4	17.3	10.3	49.8	1 632
Victoria, TX	30 040	58.2	27.8	10.0	16.2	10.2	2.1	3.3	0.2	9.6	1.9	12.7	6.6	40.9	1 237
Visalia-Tulare-Porterville, CA	110 356	59.2	32.8	9.2	20.3	12.9	2.5	3.5	0.4	6.7	2.0	10.3	5.8	38.9	4 078
Waco, TX	78 926	51.1	23.8	9.6	16.2	9.5	2.3	6.7	0.4	10.7	2.0	15.3	7.9	44.5	2 730
Washington-Baltimore, DC-MD-VA-WV	2 873 775	50.1	24.2	6.9	16.9	9.2	2.1	6.7	0.4	11.0	1.8	15.3	5.5	43.8	67 446
Baltimore, MD	974 359	49.0	22.5	8.1	18.6	10.1	2.7	6.1	0.4	10.8	2.2	15.6	6.7	44.3	27 432
Hagerstown, MD	49 708	55.5	23.5	10.4	13.4	8.3	1.7	5.2	0.4	10.5	2.9	15.5	8.5	47.8	979
Washington, DC-MD-VA-WV	1 849 708	50.5	25.1	6.2	16.1	8.8	1.9	7.1	0.4	11.2	1.6	15.2	4.8	43.3	39 035
Waterloo-Cedar Falls, IA	49 736	51.6	21.5	10.4	13.2	8.3	1.4	8.2	0.4	10.6	2.3	16.5	8.6	47.3	679
Wausau, WI	47 737	60.6	27.8	10.4	10.8	6.7	1.5	5.0	0.3	10.4	2.2	13.3	7.7	45.1	317
West Palm Beach-Boca Raton, FL	474 295	51.4	18.4	17.5	13.1	7.2	1.8	6.3	1.0	11.1	3.6	18.0	11.1	42.0	7 761
Wheeling, WV-OH	62 347	52.8	21.0	11.3	14.3	7.6	2.9	3.5	0.3	10.7	3.5	18.8	11.4	50.7	1 051
Wichita Falls, TX	51 782	54.4	25.0	10.2	14.4	9.2	1.9	4.4	0.3	11.6	2.4	15.3	8.1	45.7	1 531
Wichita, KS	210 789	54.3	26.4	9.0	13.9	8.9	1.6	4.4	0.2	12.7	2.1	14.6	6.8	45.2	4 784
Williamsport, PA	47 040	54.0	21.8	12.0	13.9	8.4	1.9	5.3	0.4	11.0	2.7	15.8	9.1	45.2	618
Wilmington, NC	98 696	51.2	18.8	10.9	13.8	7.8	1.9	8.0	0.4	11.4	2.0	15.5	6.5	39.3	2 022
Yakima, WA	74 017	57.1	29.5	9.7	17.1	11.8	1.8	4.3	0.4	8.7	2.2	12.8	7.5	45.2	2 380
York, PA	148 288	58.7	25.1	10.2	12.7	7.6	1.8	5.3	0.4	10.3	2.1	13.0	7.1	42.7	2 397
Youngstown-Warren, OH	234 578	52.8	21.3	11.5	16.3	8.8	3.0	3.4	0.4	11.3	3.1	16.2	9.3	45.5	4 868
Yuba City, CA	47 650	56.5	28.4	9.6	17.4	10.6	2.1	4.8	0.5	9.6	2.2	11.8	5.9	40.0	1 476
Yuma, AZ	53 904	63.6	28.0	17.9	14.3	9.1	1.9	3.8	1.0	8.0	3.4	10.4	6.2	31.5	1 916

Table A-4. Metropolitan Areas — **Age, Ethnicity, and Household Structure**

Area name	Households with Non-Hispanic White householder — Number of households	Percent that are family households	Households with Black or African American householder — Number of households	Percent that are family households	Households with American Indian and Alaska Native householder — Number of households	Percent that are family households	Households with Asian, Hawaiian, and Pacific Islander householder — Number of households	Percent that are family households	Households with Hispanic or Latino[1] householder — Number of households	Percent that are family households	Foreign-born population — Percent of total population that is foreign-born	Place of birth (percent) Europe	Asia	Latin America	Percent in non-English speaking households — Linguistically isolated	Not linguistically isolated
	44	45	46	47	48	49	50	51	52	53	54	55	56	57	58	59
Tucson, AZ	234 832	60.2	9 148	61.1	7 968	75.4	6 250	60.7	71 125	78.1	11.9	1.5	1.7	8.0	5.2	31.0
Tulsa, OK	246 443	68.2	26 584	66.4	17 480	73.5	3 057	72.6	10 466	75.0	4.1	0.6	1.1	2.2	1.8	9.0
Tuscaloosa, AL	45 342	64.7	17 445	67.1	220	63.6	531	57.1	538	69.0	2.1	0.6	0.8	0.6	0.7	7.2
Tyler, TX	48 232	71.2	11 929	69.5	303	54.5	303	86.1	4 504	85.4	6.6	0.3	0.5	5.5	3.5	13.0
Utica-Rome, NY	108 726	65.8	3 776	63.4	185	67.6	855	72.5	1 718	72.2	4.5	2.8	0.9	0.5	2.1	11.2
Victoria, TX	17 994	71.4	2 027	66.7	167	86.2	137	86.1	9 623	81.5	4.3	0.3	0.6	3.0	4.0	34.5
Visalia-Tulare-Porterville, CA	59 303	72.6	1 725	80.2	1 452	77.7	3 038	83.4	43 171	89.0	22.6	0.9	2.3	19.1	13.2	40.6
Waco, TX	55 495	65.2	11 734	66.3	355	83.4	778	50.1	10 199	80.6	6.1	0.4	0.7	4.9	4.0	17.5
Washington-Baltimore, DC-MD-VA-WV	1 844 182	65.9	727 992	66.1	8 792	68.8	123 650	76.3	126 948	78.4	12.9	1.9	4.7	4.7	3.8	18.3
Baltimore, MD	671 595	67.8	252 481	66.6	2 715	70.7	22 278	72.2	15 392	69.4	5.7	1.5	2.2	1.3	1.5	11.9
Hagerstown, MD	46 870	69.0	1 715	64.2	95	81.1	314	80.6	400	70.3	1.9	0.6	0.7	0.4	0.5	6.0
Washington, DC-MD-VA-WV	1 125 717	64.7	473 796	65.9	5 982	67.7	101 058	77.2	111 156	79.6	16.9	2.1	6.1	6.5	5.1	21.9
Waterloo-Cedar Falls, IA	44 558	64.5	3 633	68.8	96	40.6	441	62.6	611	69.6	3.7	2.0	0.9	0.6	1.7	8.6
Wausau, WI	46 300	71.0	45	93.3	110	74.5	841	92.3	223	76.2	3.5	0.5	2.6	0.2	1.8	9.4
West Palm Beach-Boca Raton, FL	373 870	61.2	47 553	76.3	767	64.8	5 681	75.9	41 303	79.3	17.4	3.5	1.5	11.2	6.0	21.4
Wheeling, WV-OH	60 109	67.2	1 329	57.9	104	81.7	181	69.1	264	62.9	1.0	0.5	0.3	0.1	0.2	6.5
Wichita Falls, TX	41 236	67.9	4 146	67.2	338	68.6	747	75.4	4 505	78.6	4.9	0.9	1.4	2.4	2.3	15.2
Wichita, KS	175 315	67.5	15 178	68.3	2 141	73.8	4 623	71.7	10 589	79.5	5.9	0.5	2.2	2.7	2.7	11.6
Williamsport, PA	44 964	67.8	1 367	70.2	125	68.8	152	47.4	174	64.4	1.2	0.5	0.3	0.1	0.4	6.0
Wilmington, NC	81 368	64.5	14 130	67.6	458	55.9	544	63.4	1 584	71.5	3.1	1.0	0.5	1.3	1.1	7.7
Yakima, WA	51 205	69.0	685	61.0	2 434	81.0	751	72.7	17 856	89.4	16.9	0.4	0.6	15.4	9.9	29.5
York, PA	139 029	71.1	4 495	70.3	160	80.0	873	80.8	2 965	82.0	2.2	0.7	0.6	0.6	1.0	7.7
Youngstown-Warren, OH	207 077	69.3	21 480	65.8	540	72.2	698	76.2	3 134	76.4	2.0	1.2	0.4	0.3	0.8	9.3
Yuba City, CA	34 441	70.5	1 253	72.2	965	77.3	3 034	87.2	6 679	85.1	16.6	1.1	6.3	8.9	8.3	24.9
Yuma, AZ	31 660	71.2	998	67.8	019	70.9	473	74.0	19 807	89.9	21.0	0.5	0.6	20.0	10.0	40.4

[1] Hispanic or Latino persons may be of any race.

STATE Place code	City	Total population	Population by age (percent)						Median age	+/− U.S. percent under 18 years	+/− U.S. percent 65 years and over	Non-Hispanic White		
			Under 5 years	5 to 17 years	18 to 24 years	25 to 44 years	45 to 64 years	65 years and over				Total population	Age (percent) Under 18 years	65 years and over
		1	2	3	4	5	6	7	8	9	10	11	12	13
00 00000	UNITED STATES....	281 421 906	6.8	18.9	9.6	30.4	21.9	12.4	35.3	0.0	0.0	194 514 140	22.6	15.0
01 00000	ALABAMA	4 447 100	6.6	18.6	9.8	29.1	22.8	13.0	35.8	-0.5	0.6	3 127 039	22.8	14.8
01 03076	Auburn city	42 896	4.0	11.6	44.6	21.3	11.8	6.6	22.6	-10.1	-5.8	32 915	12.6	6.9
01 05980	Bessemer city	29 949	8.3	19.0	9.7	26.4	20.0	16.7	35.9	1.6	4.3	8 595	15.2	28.8
01 07000	Birmingham city	243 072	6.8	18.3	11.2	30.0	20.1	13.6	34.3	-0.6	1.2	57 447	10.7	23.7
01 20104	Decatur city	53 953	6.6	18.7	9.0	29.4	23.4	12.9	36.3	-0.4	0.5	39 338	21.8	15.9
01 21184	Dothan city	57 652	6.8	18.3	8.3	28.5	23.4	14.6	37.2	-0.6	2.2	38 587	21.2	17.8
01 26896	Florence city	36 430	5.7	16.2	13.8	26.2	20.7	17.4	36.9	-3.8	5.0	28 266	19.4	19.9
01 28696	Gadsden city	38 836	6.7	16.3	9.4	25.5	21.8	20.3	39.0	-2.7	7.9	24 028	16.9	26.6
01 35800	Homewood city	24 878	5.7	14.7	18.0	33.7	17.2	10.7	30.5	-5.3	-1.7	19 391	18.8	12.5
01 35896	Hoover city	62 480	6.7	17.8	8.1	33.0	23.8	10.6	36.2	-1.2	-1.8	53 441	23.7	12.0
01 37000	Huntsville city	157 899	6.1	17.0	10.6	29.6	23.5	13.3	36.7	-2.6	0.9	100 033	19.4	17.7
01 45784	Madison city	29 089	7.8	21.6	6.8	36.2	22.2	5.4	34.5	3.7	-7.0	22 755	28.2	6.1
01 50000	Mobile city	198 887	7.3	19.2	10.8	28.1	20.8	13.8	34.3	0.8	1.4	99 182	19.5	18.5
01 51000	Montgomery city	201 609	7.0	18.8	11.4	30.5	20.4	11.9	32.9	0.1	-0.5	95 132	20.0	17.1
01 59472	Phenix City city	28 338	7.0	19.6	9.3	29.1	21.1	13.8	35.1	0.9	1.4	14 778	21.2	18.3
01 62496	Prichard city	28 903	8.1	23.3	11.9	24.4	20.9	11.4	31.8	5.7	-1.0	4 205	19.0	20.7
01 77256	Tuscaloosa city	78 265	5.4	14.7	24.3	25.7	18.2	11.7	28.4	-5.6	-0.7	41 924	13.2	15.4
02 00000	ALASKA	626 932	7.5	22.9	9.1	32.7	22.3	5.6	32.4	4.7	-6.8	423 660	26.5	6.1
02 03000	Anchorage municipality .	260 283	7.6	21.5	9.5	34.2	21.9	5.3	32.4	3.4	-7.1	181 919	25.4	6.0
02 24230	Fairbanks city	30 259	9.4	19.7	14.7	33.2	16.2	6.8	27.6	3.4	-5.6	19 636	25.2	8.0
02 36400	Juneau city and borough	30 711	6.5	21.0	7.6	33.2	25.4	6.2	35.3	1.8	-6.2	22 501	24.0	6.4
04 00000	ARIZONA	5 130 632	7.4	19.2	10.0	29.7	20.8	13.0	34.2	0.9	0.6	3 272 065	20.7	17.7
04 02830	Apache Junction city	31 281	6.9	13.5	7.1	23.8	23.2	25.5	44.1	-5.3	13.1	27 449	17.7	28.4
04 04720	Avondale city	35 802	9.4	24.7	9.4	33.1	18.0	5.4	29.0	8.4	-7.0	15 814	27.4	6.7
04 08220	Bullhead City city	33 852	6.3	16.0	7.4	25.0	26.1	19.2	41.8	-3.4	6.8	25 448	17.6	23.8
04 10530	Casa Grande city	25 321	9.0	22.8	9.0	27.9	18.2	13.2	32.3	6.1	0.8	12 657	22.2	20.4
04 12000	Chandler city	176 338	9.0	20.8	8.6	38.1	17.8	5.7	31.2	4.1	-6.7	120 929	26.2	7.0
04 23620	Flagstaff city	53 137	6.8	17.4	21.7	30.7	18.2	5.2	26.8	-1.5	-7.2	37 126	19.8	5.5
04 27400	Gilbert town	109 936	10.5	23.6	7.2	38.2	16.9	3.5	30.1	8.4	-8.9	87 237	32.8	3.9
04 27820	Glendale city	218 596	8.4	21.5	10.6	32.1	19.9	7.4	30.8	4.2	-5.0	141 000	25.4	9.6
04 39370	Lake Havasu City city ...	41 859	4.5	14.8	5.8	21.9	27.4	25.6	47.5	-6.4	13.2	37 305	17.3	27.6
04 46000	Mesa city	397 215	8.1	19.2	11.0	30.1	18.4	13.3	32.0	1.6	0.9	290 091	23.8	17.1
04 51600	Oro Valley town............	29 662	4.6	16.5	4.1	24.3	27.9	22.6	45.3	-4.6	10.2	26 059	19.7	24.8
04 54050	Peoria city	108 462	7.5	20.8	6.6	30.6	19.8	14.7	35.6	2.6	2.3	84 717	25.3	17.6
04 55000	Phoenix city	1 320 994	8.6	20.3	10.9	33.4	18.7	8.1	30.7	3.2	-4.3	737 369	21.8	11.9
04 57380	Prescott city	34 411	3.5	12.7	10.8	19.0	26.9	27.1	47.8	-9.5	14.7	30 429	14.7	29.3
04 65000	Scottsdale city	202 744	5.0	14.2	6.5	30.7	26.8	16.8	41.0	-6.5	4.4	178 332	17.8	18.4
04 66820	Sierra Vista city	37 287	7.3	18.1	13.3	29.0	20.2	12.0	32.0	-0.3	-0.4	24 395	21.2	15.9
04 71510	Surprise city	30 886	7.2	12.6	7.0	22.7	25.3	25.2	46.1	-5.9	12.8	22 227	12.9	33.0
04 73000	Tempe city	158 426	5.5	14.1	21.5	33.3	18.4	7.2	28.8	-6.1	-5.2	110 433	16.1	9.0
04 77000	Tucson city	486 591	7.1	17.3	13.7	31.0	19.0	12.0	32.1	-1.3	-0.4	263 269	16.9	16.8
04 85540	Yuma city	77 545	8.6	20.8	12.3	26.6	17.8	13.7	31.2	3.7	1.3	37 231	19.2	23.4
05 00000	ARKANSAS.............	2 673 400	6.8	18.7	9.8	28.1	22.6	14.0	36.0	-0.2	1.6	2 100 065	23.1	15.7
05 15190	Conway city	43 199	6.7	16.6	22.2	29.6	16.1	8.8	27.3	-2.4	-3.6	35 802	21.7	10.1
05 23290	Fayetteville city	57 783	6.8	13.0	25.7	30.1	15.6	8.9	26.9	-5.9	-3.5	48 756	18.4	10.3
05 24550	Fort Smith city	80 414	7.7	17.7	9.9	29.5	21.6	13.7	35.3	-0.3	1.3	59 581	21.9	17.0
05 33400	Hot Springs city	35 613	5.9	14.5	8.1	25.2	22.9	23.4	42.4	-5.3	11.0	27 318	16.5	27.3
05 34760	Jacksonville city	29 787	9.0	19.3	13.2	32.6	18.8	7.1	29.5	2.6	-5.3	20 087	24.1	9.5
05 35710	Jonesboro city	55 617	6.6	16.5	16.7	28.4	20.3	11.7	31.8	-2.6	-0.7	46 989	20.8	13.2
05 41000	Little Rock city	183 558	7.1	17.6	9.9	31.7	21.9	11.8	34.5	-1.0	-0.6	99 160	18.1	16.9
05 50450	North Little Rock city	60 432	7.1	18.4	8.9	28.5	22.1	14.8	36.5	-0.2	2.4	37 169	18.4	20.2
05 55310	Pine Bluff city	54 618	7.5	19.9	12.2	27.3	19.7	13.5	33.1	1.7	1.1	17 309	16.4	24.0
05 60410	Rogers city	38 761	8.8	20.6	8.8	32.3	17.7	11.8	32.3	3.7	-0.6	29 980	26.4	14.8
05 66080	Springdale city	46 060	9.4	19.8	10.8	31.7	18.2	10.1	31.0	3.5	-2.3	33 925	25.3	13.2
05 68810	Texarkana city	26 881	7.7	18.2	10.2	28.3	21.9	13.7	34.8	0.2	1.3	17 546	21.1	16.4
05 74540	West Memphis city	27 752	8.7	23.2	9.4	27.9	20.3	10.5	31.3	6.2	-1.9	11 454	20.7	15.3
06 00000	CALIFORNIA.............	33 871 648	7.2	20.0	9.9	31.9	20.4	10.6	33.3	1.5	-1.8	15 771 163	20.4	16.0
06 00562	Alameda city...............	72 259	5.6	15.6	6.9	33.8	24.9	13.1	38.3	-4.5	0.7	37 862	15.3	17.3
06 00884	Alhambra city	85 961	6.0	16.4	9.5	34.6	20.3	13.2	35.0	-3.3	0.8	11 879	10.3	35.3
06 02000	Anaheim city................	327 357	9.2	21.0	10.4	33.7	17.7	8.0	30.3	4.5	-4.4	116 951	20.0	16.2
06 02252	Antioch city	90 814	8.5	24.0	8.0	32.7	19.6	7.3	32.3	6.8	-5.1	50 673	27.6	9.8
06 02364	Apple Valley town	54 175	6.9	24.8	7.6	25.4	21.4	13.8	35.4	6.0	1.4	36 442	27.1	17.1
06 02462	Arcadia city.................	52 951	4.4	18.8	7.3	27.8	26.1	15.7	40.5	-2.5	3.3	21 365	15.9	28.6
06 03064	Atascadero city.............	26 431	5.0	20.9	8.1	29.3	25.2	11.4	38.2	0.2	-1.0	21 860	25.1	12.8

Table A-5. Cities — Age, Ethnicity, and Household Structure

City	Black or African American			American Indian and Alaska Native			Asian, Hawaiian, and Pacific Islander			Hispanic or Latino[1]			Two or more races		
		Age (percent)			Age (percent)			Age (percent)			Age (percent)			Age (percent)	
	Total population	Under 18 years	65 years and over	Total population	Under 18 years	65 years and over	Total population	Under 18 years	65 years and over	Total population	Under 18 years	65 years and over	Total population	Under 18 years	65 years and over
	14	15	16	17	18	19	20	21	22	23	24	25	26	27	28
UNITED STATES....	34 361 740	31.3	8.2	2 447 989	33.3	5.6	10 550 602	24.2	7.6	35 238 481	34.8	4.8	7 270 926	40.7	5.0
ALABAMA	1 153 044	31.0	9.5	22 897	28.2	4.4	31 095	23.8	4.4	72 627	33.4	3.3	49 238	36.9	6.4
Auburn city	7 186	27.5	6.4	207	39.6	0.0	1 364	16.1	3.7	807	15.2	4.5	507	37.9	3.7
Bessemer city	20 882	31.9	12.0	85	31.8	0.0	67	17.9	0.0	186	35.5	5.4	203	44.3	4.9
Birmingham city	178 244	29.6	10.7	476	16.2	5.9	1 806	17.6	4.4	3 694	26.5	4.6	1 971	37.4	4.4
Decatur city	10 357	34.7	5.9	462	26.2	7.6	364	32.7	1.6	2 840	34.5	0.9	761	35.3	6.7
Dothan city	17 305	33.3	8.6	282	21.6	0.7	460	29.1	7.2	618	38.8	6.8	514	28.6	4.7
Florence city	7 018	30.8	9.6	116	28.4	0.0	242	21.9	0.0	455	24.8	4.6	397	42.6	6.3
Gadsden city	12 687	31.8	10.8	116	45.7	0.0	188	18.6	3.2	964	29.5	4.4	950	55.2	6.6
Homewood city	3 867	25.6	4.7	78	25.6	16.7	612	14.1	4.2	729	37.3	2.5	267	33.3	1.9
Hoover city	3 933	27.4	1.3	166	25.9	0.0	1 784	28.5	3.7	2 476	25.3	2.1	757	51.1	1.6
Huntsville city	47 052	29.0	0.0	1 269	30.6	2.1	3 003	20.3	4.5	3 330	31.2	4.4	3 528	36.4	4.8
Madison city	3 830	32.3	3.4	218	39.0	0.0	1 041	26.9	3.7	666	46.2	0.0	594	39.6	2.2
Mobile city	91 741	34.1	9.3	729	27.8	7.8	2 955	22.1	4.2	2 717	25.5	6.9	2 318	35.5	7.8
Montgomery city	100 094	31.3	7.5	491	26.3	4.5	1 852	15.0	5.7	2 384	25.3	2.1	2 097	38.6	5.7
Phenix City city	12 692	32.5	9.5	142	25.4	0.0	128	9.4	8.6	394	35.8	2.8	235	44.7	4.7
Prichard city	24 088	33.7	9.9	106	41.5	0.0	48	29.2	0.0	154	33.1	0.0	324	26.2	11.1
Tuscaloosa city	33 391	28.4	7.6	224	17.9	10.7	996	10.8	5.2	1 055	32.3	2.5	819	34.2	7.1
ALASKA	21 968	35.1	3.2	97 012	38.4	5.9	28 618	28.1	5.5	25 765	39.5	2.1	35 240	52.3	2.3
Anchorage municipality .	15 201	34.8	3.3	18 800	34.1	4.5	16 293	30.4	6.0	14 738	39.7	2.2	16 465	53.1	1.7
Fairbanks city	3 279	35.3	3.5	2 932	33.8	7.0	1 109	23.2	7.8	1 838	39.8	2.4	1 919	54.4	2.1
Juneau city and borough	235	21.3	16.2	3 558	33.7	5.8	1 560	33.1	7.1	972	40.8	1.2	2 099	50.3	4.0
ARIZONA	154 010	30.7	8.3	253 542	38.8	5.6	97 389	23.3	5.9	1 295 317	38.0	4.2	156 497	45.7	4.4
Apache Junction city	158	31.0	6.3	245	29.8	11.0	218	20.2	0.0	2 674	40.1	3.4	908	50.1	4.2
Avondale city	1 760	30.0	0.0	403	42.7	0.7	843	35.3	1.3	16 529	39.7	4.7	1 719	52.8	3.3
Bullhead City city	252	32.1	8.3	388	22.2	18.3	284	15.8	10.2	6 818	39.2	4.0	1 059	34.5	7.1
Casa Grande city	1 006	44.2	11.9	1 019	36.9	4.7	304	57.2	3.9	10 094	41.0	5.4	1 013	50.9	10.6
Chandler city	6 195	29.9	4.9	1 977	32.1	4.3	7 694	26.9	3.4	36 925	39.7	2.5	5 862	55.2	2.5
Flagstaff city	1 047	33.9	8.5	4 936	36.5	2.1	765	17.9	0.9	8 572	34.9	5.2	1 477	42.6	2.0
Gilbert town	2 350	33.1	2.2	932	42.2	0.0	4 025	32.6	3.2	13 310	40.5	2.2	3 554	55.0	1.1
Glendale city	10 358	34.5	4.2	2 570	36.5	1.6	6 032	24.5	5.8	54 324	39.9	3.0	8 321	47.4	3.8
Lake Havasu City city ...	115	21.7	23.5	378	38.1	10.6	264	13.6	5.3	3 424	38.1	7.2	816	46.6	11.0
Mesa city	9 607	32.7	3.9	6 220	34.7	1.2	6 669	20.7	5.8	78 589	38.2	2.4	12 450	47.2	3.2
Oro Valley town	408	20.8	2.0	157	29.3	10.8	518	23.6	6.8	2 184	34.5	7.8	399	33.6	7.0
Peoria city	3 017	36.6	5.1	692	29.9	4.9	1 969	32.1	4.1	16 816	39.9	3.7	2 499	53.9	4.8
Phoenix city	65 312	32.1	6.6	26 127	32.9	2.5	27 358	24.6	7.0	450 423	39.4	2.4	44 594	45.9	3.3
Prescott city	160	38.8	6.3	352	22.2	11.6	391	12.8	6.9	2 664	28.7	11.6	598	32.1	4.0
Scottsdale city	2 269	23.0	7.3	1 218	26.7	8.9	4 404	19.3	6.4	13 773	31.4	4.9	3 682	38.5	5.1
Sierra Vista city	4 051	30.1	1.9	276	19.9	12.0	1 508	15.1	11.8	5 722	35.8	4.2	1 871	54.2	4.8
Surprise city	874	35.2	9.4	91	18.7	7.7	266	21.4	9.8	7 189	38.4	4.1	463	41.3	9.7
Tempe city.................	5 659	25.9	4.2	3 315	28.0	1.1	8 243	16.5	3.1	28 302	30.7	3.2	5 403	33.4	2.1
Tucson city	20 620	28.8	7.7	10 983	27.9	4.2	12 375	18.9	5.6	174 354	35.0	6.2	19 688	42.6	5.1
Yuma city	2 512	33.4	4.5	1 231	30.7	12.2	1 159	23.2	11.6	35 088	40.4	4.3	2 755	50.3	5.0
ARKANSAS...............	417 881	33.6	8.9	18 492	30.6	5.8	20 615	25.1	4.5	85 576	36.8	2.5	38 082	38.1	7.9
Conway city	5 217	32.3	2.4	171	17.0	0.0	442	13.8	0.0	1 067	31.6	1.4	573	36.1	7.7
Fayetteville city	2 795	24.3	2.7	566	26.5	0.0	1 769	17.9	0.7	2 838	30.8	1.1	1 176	42.2	2.3
Fort Smith city	6 899	33.0	6.4	1 659	34.5	4.0	3 363	29.2	5.4	6 877	37.9	1.4	2 506	46.8	3.2
Hot Springs city	6 028	32.5	11.8	275	16.7	1.8	196	27.6	3.1	1 230	38.8	7.1	723	40.4	13.1
Jacksonville city	7 176	37.8	1.5	160	38.1	0.0	454	14.1	3.7	1 219	34.9	0.7	893	44.2	8.0
Jonesboro city	6 265	34.9	3.7	221	13.6	5.9	455	35.2	0.9	1 172	35.4	4.9	588	38.4	6.5
Little Rock city	74 195	32.8	6.2	751	32.6	2.7	2 899	21.2	3.5	4 908	31.1	1.9	2 297	39.9	2.2
North Little Rock city	20 422	38.2	6.3	236	28.0	0.0	368	15.2	18.2	1 420	34.4	2.3	921	28.9	11.4
Pine Bluff city	36 128	32.5	8.6	90	17.8	12.2	304	27.0	8.2	434	32.5	10.8	447	42.1	3.4
Rogers city	338	36.1	0.0	628	37.7	2.1	296	25.0	4.7	7 329	40.3	1.5	654	49.5	2.1
Springdale city	435	63.0	0.0	537	22.2	12.7	1 433	35.9	0.1	9 089	40.2	0.9	1 117	44.1	5.5
Texarkana city	7 974	35.5	8.3	99	12.1	15.2	153	23.5	0.0	523	22.8	17.2	609	44.7	11.0
West Memphis city.......	15 706	39.8	7.2	83	60.2	10.8	165	20.0	11.5	267	40.1	4.1	132	46.2	8.3
CALIFORNIA............	2 219 190	30.2	8.2	312 215	30.7	5.7	3 796 833	23.9	9.3	10 969 132	36.8	4.2	1 694 607	40.5	4.9
Alameda city	4 194	29.6	5.9	464	20.7	4.5	19 494	23.8	10.7	6 577	27.5	6.8	4 588	45.1	4.9
Alhambra city	1 307	24.5	5.4	396	14.4	6.6	40 747	19.3	10.9	30 546	30.6	8.1	3 623	37.3	7.5
Anaheim city...............	8 054	31.8	3.7	2 594	32.6	3.4	40 684	24.7	7.2	153 319	39.2	2.4	16 389	38.9	3.7
Antioch city	8 652	38.6	2.5	746	22.0	4.8	7 082	29.6	7.0	20 024	40.0	3.5	6 772	51.0	3.2
Apple Valley town	4 184	39.9	7.8	408	15.4	10.5	1 305	23.4	10.4	10 083	43.7	5.9	2 742	48.8	8.6
Arcadia city................	467	29.8	7.7	156	27.6	5.8	24 068	27.7	7.1	5 240	28.3	6.1	1 960	37.0	6.3
Atascadero city............	569	8.6	2.6	163	3.1	0.0	357	24.4	3.9	2 783	35.4	4.1	903	41.4	9.3

[1] Hispanic or Latino persons may be of any race.

City	Total households	Family households (percent)						Nonfamily households (percent)						Percent of householders 65 years and over who live alone	Grandparents who are responsible for the care of their grandchildren
		Married-couple family households			Other family households			Two or more unrelated persons		Male living alone		Female living alone			
		Total	With children	House-holder 65 years or over	Total	With children	House-holder 65 years or over	Total	House-holder 65 years or over	Total	House-holder 65 years or over	Total	House-holder 65 years or over		
	29	30	31	32	33	34	35	36	37	38	39	40	41	42	43
UNITED STATES....	105 539 122	52.5	24.3	9.2	15.9	9.1	2.2	5.8	0.4	11.0	2.3	14.8	7.1	44.2	2 426 730
ALABAMA	1 737 385	53.0	23.2	9.3	17.4	9.6	2.8	3.5	0.3	10.8	2.2	15.3	7.6	44.4	56 369
Auburn city	18 398	28.9	14.3	4.4	10.9	5.4	1.2	23.6	0.0	19.7	1.2	16.9	3.5	45.1	105
Bessemer city	11 750	34.4	14.0	8.1	33.9	17.4	7.5	2.1	0.2	11.6	3.8	17.9	9.9	46.3	813
Birmingham city...........	98 748	31.7	13.3	6.9	28.8	15.1	5.2	5.2	0.4	14.7	2.4	19.7	7.8	45.0	4 764
Decatur city	21 812	51.7	22.3	8.6	16.7	10.2	2.4	2.9	0.2	11.8	1.9	17.0	7.9	46.8	443
Dothan city	23 746	49.6	20.6	9.3	18.5	11.3	2.6	3.4	0.3	11.4	2.6	17.1	8.4	47.2	644
Florence city	15 795	44.1	16.6	11.1	16.8	9.9	2.4	5.3	0.1	13.6	2.3	20.2	10.4	48.3	283
Gadsden city	16 403	40.2	14.5	11.2	22.4	11.5	4.3	3.3	0.5	11.8	3.9	22.3	13.7	52.6	557
Homewood city	10 609	42.3	20.1	6.6	13.8	7.3	1.6	8.5	0.3	13.6	1.4	21.8	7.8	51.8	75
Hoover city	25 070	61.4	29.6	8.5	8.5	4.4	1.0	4.1	0.1	10.2	1.0	15.7	5.6	41.0	105
Huntsville city	66 709	46.3	18.2	9.7	16.5	9.9	1.9	4.7	0.2	14.3	1.9	18.1	7.0	43.1	1 524
Madison city	11 134	60.5	34.0	3.3	11.9	8.2	0.5	3.7	0.1	12.0	1.0	11.9	2.7	48.8	160
Mobile city	78 548	42.0	18.3	8.4	23.0	13.2	3.7	4.8	0.4	12.4	2.6	17.8	8.2	46.2	2 825
Montgomery city	78 436	43.3	19.4	7.4	22.0	13.1	2.8	4.5	0.3	11.6	2.0	18.5	7.7	47.9	2 325
Phenix City city	11 525	40.9	19.0	7.4	24.9	14.4	4.0	3.5	0.4	13.2	2.9	17.4	7.8	47.6	276
Prichard city	9 896	35.5	14.9	6.9	39.5	22.5	6.5	2.3	0.4	10.3	2.9	12.4	7.1	42.0	1 033
Tuscaloosa city	31 602	36.5	14.2	7.3	18.3	10.2	2.5	10.0	0.2	15.7	1.8	19.6	7.8	49.0	945
ALASKA	221 804	53.3	29.3	4.5	15.9	11.2	1.3	7.3	0.3	13.4	1.4	10.0	2.6	39.4	5 419
Anchorage municipality .	95 080	52.2	28.6	4.0	16.0	11.2	0.9	8.5	0.4	12.3	1.1	11.0	2.6	41.5	1 719
Fairbanks city	11 132	49.6	27.8	4.3	15.7	11.8	1.6	7.4	0.4	14.7	1.8	12.7	3.7	46.4	177
Juneau city and borough	11 534	52.6	26.3	4.7	14.6	10.3	1.3	8.4	0.2	11.2	1.2	13.2	3.0	40.8	174
ARIZONA	1 901 625	52.9	23.5	11.2	15.3	9.2	1.7	7.0	0.6	11.1	2.4	13.7	6.3	39.3	52 210
Apache Junction city	13 559	52.8	15.6	19.7	13.2	7.4	2.4	7.0	1.9	12.5	4.4	14.5	8.4	34.8	228
Avondale city	10 654	63.5	36.3	4.8	18.9	11.6	1.7	4.7	0.3	6.6	0.9	6.3	2.3	32.3	616
Bullhead City city	13 902	49.6	15.6	14.5	17.0	10.2	2.7	8.3	1.8	12.3	3.7	12.8	6.7	35.4	445
Casa Grande city	8 834	53.7	24.6	12.5	19.7	13.8	1.7	4.6	1.1	8.5	1.8	13.5	7.5	37.7	317
Chandler city	62 289	58.7	32.2	4.7	14.5	9.4	0.9	7.5	0.3	8.9	1.1	10.4	2.6	38.6	1 164
Flagstaff city	19 355	45.4	22.6	4.2	15.8	10.9	0.9	15.5	0.2	12.1	1.1	11.2	3.0	43.1	427
Gilbert town	35 512	70.2	43.2	3.7	11.9	7.6	0.5	5.1	0.1	6.2	0.4	6.5	1.4	29.4	434
Glendale city	75 697	54.4	29.0	5.6	17.9	11.3	1.4	6.4	0.3	10.0	1.3	11.3	4.5	44.4	2 340
Lake Havasu City city ...	17 837	60.3	15.9	22.8	11.1	6.6	1.6	5.9	0.9	9.0	3.2	13.6	9.5	33.4	286
Mesa city	146 700	54.2	25.2	11.2	14.4	8.8	1.2	7.2	0.5	10.2	2.0	13.9	7.2	41.5	2 875
Oro Valley town...........	12 307	70.3	24.5	22.1	5.6	2.9	0.8	4.4	0.8	7.7	2.6	12.0	6.3	27.4	92
Peoria city	39 286	62.4	30.0	12.4	12.4	8.1	1.0	4.7	0.4	6.9	2.3	13.5	8.1	42.8	826
Phoenix city................	466 114	48.2	25.4	6.1	18.4	11.1	1.7	8.1	0.4	12.3	1.7	13.1	4.6	43.5	13 262
Prescott city	15 405	48.6	12.0	19.0	11.0	6.7	1.9	8.1	0.7	12.8	4.6	19.5	11.6	42.8	220
Scottsdale city	90 602	50.1	17.7	12.0	10.4	5.7	1.5	8.8	0.6	11.8	2.3	18.9	7.7	41.2	739
Sierra Vista city	14 083	56.2	24.9	10.5	14.2	10.2	1.3	4.5	0.3	11.8	2.0	13.2	5.2	37.5	313
Surprise city	12 474	70.5	17.3	27.1	7.9	4.3	0.7	3.9	0.7	6.5	3.0	11.1	6.1	24.2	273
Tempe city	63 486	39.6	17.5	5.3	13.8	7.5	1.0	18.0	0.2	15.1	1.0	13.4	3.6	42.0	873
Tucson city	192 884	40.8	19.0	7.8	18.1	10.8	2.1	8.8	0.5	14.7	2.5	17.5	7.1	48.1	4 995
Yuma city	26 740	57.6	28.0	11.7	16.2	10.8	2.0	4.5	0.9	8.9	3.2	12.8	7.6	42.4	660
ARKANSAS...............	1 042 807	55.1	23.4	10.6	15.5	9.1	2.2	3.9	0.3	10.6	2.4	14.9	8.1	44.3	33 618
Conway city................	16 072	49.8	24.7	6.3	14.6	9.5	0.9	9.7	0.3	10.5	1.2	15.3	6.2	49.7	179
Fayetteville city............	23 691	39.2	17.4	5.8	12.3	7.6	0.8	14.6	0.2	16.7	1.2	17.2	4.6	45.9	249
Fort Smith city	32 445	47.9	21.3	8.3	16.4	10.3	2.2	5.3	0.2	13.0	2.4	17.5	8.9	51.1	760
Hot Springs city	16 048	40.5	13.7	11.9	16.2	8.8	3.2	4.9	0.7	13.7	4.1	24.6	14.7	54.4	475
Jacksonville city	10 910	55.5	28.2	6.1	18.8	13.1	1.3	3.7	0.1	10.0	0.8	11.9	5.4	45.7	308
Jonesboro city	22 244	48.8	22.2	7.5	16.4	9.0	1.6	7.4	0.3	11.1	1.6	16.4	7.3	48.7	448
Little Rock city............	77 521	42.1	18.0	7.2	18.7	11.5	2.0	5.6	0.2	13.9	1.8	19.7	6.9	48.2	2 271
North Little Rock city.....	25 561	43.1	16.6	9.4	20.3	12.6	2.6	4.6	0.2	12.1	2.3	19.8	9.7	49.4	853
Pine Bluff city	19 768	40.2	16.7	7.7	27.0	16.6	3.8	3.7	0.2	12.0	2.7	17.2	10.3	52.3	993
Rogers city	14 061	58.4	31.9	9.8	15.0	9.0	1.3	4.5	0.2	8.4	1.5	13.8	7.2	43.5	416
Springdale city	16 287	59.2	30.7	8.4	14.6	9.0	1.6	4.1	0.3	8.8	1.5	13.2	7.4	46.3	399
Texarkana city.............	10 540	46.9	19.2	8.3	21.5	13.2	2.5	3.6	0.4	11.1	2.4	16.9	9.3	51.0	379
West Memphis city.......	10 015	41.7	18.4	6.9	29.9	18.5	3.6	3.7	0.5	10.1	1.4	14.7	6.9	43.2	455
CALIFORNIA.............	11 512 020	52.1	26.9	8.3	17.3	9.6	2.2	7.1	0.6	10.4	2.1	13.1	5.8	41.5	294 969
Alameda city...............	30 259	43.9	20.8	6.9	15.3	7.4	2.0	8.6	0.7	13.8	2.5	18.4	6.8	48.9	360
Alhambra city	29 126	50.0	24.9	8.5	21.6	9.1	2.9	5.8	0.3	9.2	2.0	13.4	5.9	40.2	660
Anaheim city...............	96 902	57.9	33.9	6.6	18.8	10.4	2.1	5.6	0.4	7.7	1.3	10.0	4.6	39.5	2 548
Antioch city................	29 351	61.5	35.7	6.1	17.9	11.8	1.5	4.8	0.4	6.1	1.2	9.7	4.2	40.5	925
Apple Valley town	18 592	59.3	27.6	13.6	18.4	12.3	2.3	4.3	0.8	6.6	2.5	11.4	6.4	34.4	745
Arcadia city.................	19 073	58.1	28.9	11.1	16.2	7.3	2.4	3.6	0.5	7.6	2.2	14.6	7.6	41.0	393
Atascadero city............	9 498	55.4	26.7	8.6	16.5	11.6	1.2	6.3	0.7	10.6	3.0	11.2	6.4	47.4	213

City	Households with Non-Hispanic White householder		Households with Black or African American householder		Households with American Indian and Alaska Native householder		Households with Asian, Hawaiian, and Pacific Islander householder		Households with Hispanic or Latino¹ householder		Foreign-born population	Place of birth (percent)			Percent in non-English speaking households	
	Number of households	Percent that are family households	Number of households	Percent that are family households	Number of households	Percent that are family households	Number of households	Percent that are family households	Number of households	Percent that are family households	Percent of total population that is foreign-born	Europe	Asia	Latin America	Linguistically isolated	Not linguistically isolated
	44	45	46	47	48	49	50	51	52	53	54	55	56	57	58	59
UNITED STATES....	78 983 497	66.8	12 023 966	68.3	770 334	73.2	3 229 278	75.2	9 272 610	80.7	11.1	1.7	2.9	5.7	4.7	18.9
ALABAMA	1 273 242	70.5	413 673	69.8	8 368	73.6	9 558	70.0	19 798	76.0	2.0	0.4	0.6	0.8	0.7	6.4
Auburn city	14 268	37.1	3 004	50.4	71	28.2	560	58.6	376	36.4	4.9	0.9	2.7	0.7	1.4	10.9
Bessemer city	4 084	58.1	7 545	73.5	29	79.3	22	100.0	56	87.5	0.9	0.1	0.2	0.4	0.3	3.7
Birmingham city..............	29 250	44.4	67 008	67.5	203	57.6	653	55.0	1 163	69.6	2.1	0.3	0.6	1.0	1.2	6.9
Decatur city	16 699	67.3	3 828	69.7	187	72.2	115	71.3	805	83.4	4.5	0.4	0.6	3.4	3.3	5.9
Dothan city	16 544	68.2	6 576	68.0	158	50.0	126	78.6	162	69.8	2.0	0.6	0.7	0.6	0.4	5.2
Florence city	12 658	59.8	2 708	66.1	70	47.1	69	91.3	178	57.3	1.6	0.2	0.6	0.7	0.6	5.6
Gadsden city	11 119	60.6	4 807	65.0	40	82.5	55	80.0	186	88.2	2.6	0.2	0.5	1.7	1.1	6.3
Homewood city..............	8 313	56.1	1 751	54.1	18	100.0	252	50.0	205	78.0	6.4	0.9	2.6	1.5	2.2	11.3
Hoover city	21 943	70.2	1 728	57.9	68	75.0	564	85.5	623	81.1	6.4	0.8	2.5	2.7	2.1	9.7
Huntsville city	45 733	61.7	17 349	64.7	481	70.7	1 004	73.7	1 064	73.1	4.9	1.3	1.7	1.3	1.2	8.7
Madison city	8 817	72.6	1 515	73.0	78	74.4	315	77.1	189	65.6	5.6	1.0	3.3	0.4	0.7	11.9
Mobile city	43 298	60.5	32 642	71.0	310	66.1	899	61.7	893	58.8	2.9	0.6	1.4	0.6	0.9	8.3
Montgomery city...........	40 892	63.1	35 514	67.7	231	60.2	596	69.3	693	67.2	2.1	0.6	0.8	0.4	0.5	7.2
Phenix City city	6 484	63.8	4 780	69.2	59	28.8	31	51.6	120	59.2	1.7	0.4	0.4	0.7	0.6	6.0
Prichard city	1 502	73.8	8 197	75.0	31	100.0	8	100.0	41	65.9	0.7	0.1	0.1	0.4	0.1	7.4
Tuscaloosa city	18 480	48.4	12 099	64.8	91	64.8	364	45.6	301	58.5	2.5	0.6	1.2	0.7	0.9	8.0
ALASKA	166 838	68.3	7 508	71.4	26 616	72.3	7 206	77.6	6 407	75.5	5.9	1.2	3.0	1.1	2.3	19.3
Anchorage municipality .	72 584	67.6	5 388	70.7	5 602	65.3	4 647	76.0	3 889	74.9	8.2	1.6	4.0	1.7	2.7	18.0
Fairbanks city	7 873	64.2	1 096	78.8	945	60.6	320	67.2	524	70.2	5.1	1.1	2.4	0.8	1.6	16.7
Juneau city and borough	9 186	66.6	116	69.0	1 129	63.9	402	81.1	275	78.9	5.7	0.9	3.1	0.8	1.1	15.6
ARIZONA	1 397 040	64.7	55 071	64.7	67 858	78.7	31 575	69.5	331 850	81.7	12.8	1.4	1.5	9.1	6.7	27.2
Apache Junction city	12 390	65.0	84	56.0	100	92.0	83	65.1	768	81.5	4.6	0.6	0.5	2.3	2.0	11.2
Avondale city................	5 743	77.8	637	87.3	89	92.1	202	76.2	3 907	88.5	17.1	1.0	1.7	14.0	8.1	42.4
Bullhead City city	11 471	63.6	87	65.5	137	72.3	113	49.6	1 908	85.6	10.3	0.8	0.7	8.2	4.5	20.4
Casa Grande city	5 455	69.3	329	71.4	296	82.8	63	77.8	2 032	81.2	8.5	0.1	0.8	7.4	4.0	35.1
Chandler city	47 233	70.6	2 367	70.6	607	81.5	2 426	80.3	9 092	84.2	12.9	1.2	3.4	7.5	5.4	24.3
Flagstaff city	14 645	57.6	367	70.3	1 356	81.2	269	48.3	2 503	73.7	6.1	0.9	1.2	3.3	2.6	23.9
Gilbert town..................	29 536	81.6	845	74.4	251	70.5	1 139	91.2	3 367	85.1	6.6	1.2	2.7	2.1	1.5	18.9
Glendale city	54 264	70.0	3 720	72.0	747	75.6	1 932	77.8	13 785	81.9	12.7	1.5	2.3	8.2	6.0	25.1
Lake Havasu City city ...	16 533	71.4	61	65.6	115	82.0	08	77.9	942	80.1	5.6	1.7	0.5	2.4	1.5	11.4
Mesa city	117 837	66.5	3 548	63.1	1 875	70.5	2 116	78.0	19 650	82.0	11.2	1.1	1.3	7.9	5.6	20.9
Oro Valley town............	11 175	75.3	140	77.1	87	50.6	176	76.7	617	87.6	6.2	2.2	1.2	1.4	0.5	15.8
Peoria city	33 063	72.9	972	79.3	220	89.5	494	82.2	4 283	87.4	6.2	1.5	1.4	2.7	1.5	20.2
Phoenix city	314 493	61.1	23 365	62.8	7 784	71.0	8 796	71.5	107 197	83.2	19.5	1.6	1.7	15.5	11.2	28.7
Prescott city	14 147	59.0	16	62.5	138	54.3	130	63.1	851	70.4	5.6	2.1	1.0	2.0	1.5	10.8
Scottsdale city.............	82 676	59.9	1 029	59.3	439	68.3	1 623	65.5	3 868	69.8	9.5	2.9	2.0	2.8	2.2	14.4
Sierra Vista city	10 104	69.1	1 503	72.8	137	62.8	368	63.0	1 716	79.1	9.1	2.7	3.0	2.8	1.9	26.5
Surprise city	10 435	76.8	304	77.6	25	80.0	44	68.2	1 593	89.1	11.2	2.2	0.8	7.0	5.4	21.4
Tempe city	48 004	50.7	2 373	52.3	1 006	69.2	3 144	55.5	8 067	67.8	12.9	1.5	4.4	6.1	5.5	23.4
Tucson city	123 797	51.9	7 767	60.5	3 504	70.6	4 472	55.1	51 234	76.1	14.3	1.4	2.0	10.3	6.9	34.5
Yuma city	16 007	67.8	813	64.9	431	59.2	381	69.6	8 977	86.8	18.1	0.6	1.0	15.7	8.6	40.0
ARKANSAS.................	852 927	70.6	145 438	69.5	6 468	70.8	6 010	72.1	21 674	80.6	2.8	0.4	0.6	1.6	1.4	6.9
Conway city	13 657	64.5	1 773	63.2	82	79.3	120	67.5	304	62.2	2.6	0.4	0.6	1.2	1.3	7.6
Fayetteville city............	20 703	51.5	954	48.6	221	55.7	619	50.2	826	64.2	6.4	0.8	2.4	2.7	2.8	10.9
Fort Smith city	26 042	62.3	2 521	65.7	582	72.2	1 032	83.4	1 659	80.0	9.2	0.3	3.2	5.4	4.4	12.1
Hot Springs city	13 025	55.2	2 243	65.5	133	34.6	62	30.6	377	64.5	3.7	1.6	0.5	1.3	2.1	7.0
Jacksonville city	7 882	72.8	2 375	81.3	51	74.5	82	62.2	289	74.4	3.5	0.8	1.2	1.2	1.0	11.1
Jonesboro city	19 319	65.2	2 257	64.8	84	66.7	79	73.4	320	79.7	2.6	0.2	0.8	1.2	1.3	6.0
Little Rock city..............	46 866	56.8	27 142	67.2	331	60.4	1 081	63.5	1 562	70.7	3.8	0.7	1.4	1.3	1.5	8.5
North Little Rock city.....	17 313	61.0	7 327	68.3	69	71.0	115	56.5	424	82.8	2.2	0.3	0.6	1.1	1.3	7.9
Pine Bluff city	7 384	61.5	11 996	70.5	46	67.4	84	90.5	148	73.6	1.1	0.1	0.5	0.3	0.4	6.5
Rogers city	11 873	70.9	113	84.1	185	76.8	94	78.7	1 719	89.6	13.0	0.3	0.6	12.0	9.5	14.7
Springdale city.............	13 361	70.7	64	100.0	205	59.5	323	89.5	2 120	92.2	15.7	0.4	1.1	12.9	9.4	15.7
Texarkana city	7 267	66.9	2 791	73.2	54	50.0	67	53.7	203	73.4	1.6	0.1	0.5	0.7	0.6	6.5
West Memphis city........	4 871	68.2	4 962	75.0	33	72.7	35	100.0	76	69.7	1.0	0.1	0.6	0.3	0.9	5.9
CALIFORNIA...............	6 673 836	62.7	788 392	66.3	96 479	72.7	1 136 310	77.2	2 574 994	84.7	26.2	2.1	8.6	14.5	11.3	36.6
Alameda city	19 130	51.9	1 758	58.9	191	62.8	6 089	80.1	2 139	60.2	26.1	2.9	18.6	2.9	8.7	34.6
Alhambra city	5 874	51.3	432	63.2	181	65.2	12 988	77.6	9 335	76.8	50.8	1.0	37.4	12.0	26.7	54.4
Anaheim city	47 801	67.3	3 064	63.1	749	74.5	11 677	83.7	31 883	89.7	37.9	1.5	10.0	25.4	18.9	43.6
Antioch city..................	18 669	76.6	2 724	80.3	299	71.6	1 903	86.2	5 047	87.4	13.2	1.1	4.7	6.8	5.1	25.4
Apple Valley town	13 731	76.2	1 301	78.6	196	77.6	400	79.8	2 491	86.5	7.6	1.3	1.8	3.8	2.3	19.7
Arcadia city	9 623	63.9	163	65.0	45	100.0	7 197	87.6	1 558	78.8	43.6	2.2	36.3	3.8	17.2	44.3
Atascadero city............	8 260	71.6	67	37.3	78	73.1	124	69.4	729	81.1	4.4	1.0	0.9	1.8	1.3	12.6

¹Hispanic or Latino persons may be of any race.

Table A-5. Cities — Age, Ethnicity, and Household Structure

STATE Place code	City	Total population	Under 5 years	5 to 17 years	18 to 24 years	25 to 44 years	45 to 64 years	65 years and over	Median age	+/− U.S. percent under 18 years	+/− U.S. percent 65 years and over	Non-Hispanic White Total population	Under 18 years	65 years and over
		1	2	3	4	5	6	7	8	9	10	11	12	13
	CALIFORNIA—Cont'd													
06 03386	Azusa city	44 371	9.2	21.7	15.6	31.6	14.9	7.0	27.1	5.2	−5.4	10 459	15.9	13.3
06 03526	Bakersfield city	247 385	8.6	24.0	10.0	30.1	18.6	8.8	30.1	6.9	−3.6	125 829	25.7	12.9
06 03666	Baldwin Park city	75 753	9.7	25.3	11.6	30.7	16.6	6.1	26.9	9.3	−6.3	5 583	17.2	22.2
06 04870	Bell city	36 667	10.5	24.5	13.0	32.6	14.2	5.1	25.9	9.3	−7.3	2 146	21.4	23.3
06 04982	Bellflower city	72 829	9.2	22.5	10.2	31.9	17.9	8.2	29.7	6.0	−4.2	22 464	20.8	18.2
06 04996	Bell Gardens city	44 054	11.4	28.0	13.1	30.9	12.6	4.0	23.8	13.7	−8.4	2 050	16.6	27.2
06 05108	Belmont city	25 138	5.8	13.3	6.1	36.3	24.5	13.9	38.8	−6.6	1.5	17 793	17.9	16.0
06 05290	Benicia city	26 967	5.0	22.3	6.2	28.2	29.0	9.3	38.9	1.6	−3.1	20 016	24.9	10.4
06 06000	Berkeley city	102 743	3.8	10.2	21.6	31.9	22.2	10.3	32.5	−11.7	−2.1	56 670	11.8	10.7
06 06308	Beverly Hills city	33 829	3.4	16.3	6.1	29.5	26.9	17.7	41.3	−6.0	5.3	27 678	19.4	19.6
06 08100	Brea city	35 122	5.8	19.4	9.0	30.4	24.4	11.0	36.4	−0.5	−1.4	23 320	22.3	14.1
06 08786	Buena Park city	78 358	7.9	21.4	9.4	33.2	19.0	9.1	32.0	3.6	−3.3	30 230	22.8	15.2
06 08954	Burbank city	100 316	5.4	16.7	7.5	36.0	21.4	12.9	36.4	−3.6	0.5	58 936	17.8	17.4
06 09066	Burlingame city	27 975	5.1	13.8	5.7	37.6	22.6	15.3	38.4	−6.8	2.9	19 904	17.3	18.6
06 09710	Calexico city	27 042	7.7	27.2	9.8	26.8	17.5	11.0	29.2	9.2	−1.4	501	37.9	12.0
06 10046	Camarillo city	57 122	6.8	18.3	6.7	28.1	23.1	17.0	38.9	−0.6	4.6	41 099	21.8	21.3
06 10345	Campbell city	38 187	5.9	15.5	7.4	40.0	21.2	10.1	35.2	−4.3	−2.3	25 257	18.1	12.1
06 11194	Carlsbad city	77 998	6.4	17.0	6.5	31.3	24.7	14.1	38.9	−2.3	1.7	62 532	21.4	16.1
06 11530	Carson city	89 549	6.8	21.4	10.1	28.6	22.6	10.5	33.7	2.5	−1.9	10 723	11.8	24.6
06 12048	Cathedral City city	42 919	8.7	22.5	9.0	30.4	17.2	12.3	32.0	5.5	−0.1	18 182	20.1	23.7
06 12524	Ceres city	34 534	9.2	25.4	10.0	30.2	16.9	8.3	29.4	8.9	−4.1	17 198	27.8	12.1
06 12552	Cerritos city	51 507	4.6	19.8	8.9	25.9	31.3	9.5	39.3	−1.3	−2.9	10 786	13.1	15.8
06 13014	Chico city	59 444	6.0	14.6	27.1	27.0	15.2	10.1	25.9	−5.1	−2.3	45 996	17.6	12.2
06 13210	Chino city	67 600	7.0	21.4	12.4	34.0	19.4	5.8	30.9	2.7	−6.6	25 191	23.1	8.9
06 13214	Chino Hills city	66 716	8.4	24.4	7.1	36.3	19.8	3.9	32.3	7.1	−8.5	29 190	30.6	3.7
06 13392	Chula Vista city	173 860	7.7	21.2	9.3	31.8	18.8	11.2	33.0	3.2	−1.2	54 707	18.7	20.1
06 13588	Citrus Heights city	85 230	6.7	18.5	10.2	30.5	21.2	12.9	34.9	−0.5	0.5	67 907	23.1	14.8
06 13756	Claremont city	33 978	3.7	16.5	18.5	22.7	23.7	15.0	35.8	−5.5	2.6	21 831	16.2	19.3
06 14218	Clovis city	68 197	7.3	23.2	9.1	30.7	20.1	9.5	32.8	4.8	−2.9	46 032	26.9	11.8
06 14890	Colton city	48 011	9.7	24.9	11.8	31.9	14.8	6.9	26.8	8.9	−5.5	9 864	22.1	12.1
06 15044	Compton city	93 226	10.3	28.1	11.6	28.8	14.1	7.2	25.0	12.7	−5.2	747	15.9	14.5
06 16000	Concord city	121 710	7.0	18.2	9.0	33.1	21.9	10.8	35.1	−0.5	−1.6	73 588	21.1	14.6
06 16350	Corona city	124 935	9.6	23.8	8.6	35.5	16.7	5.8	29.9	7.7	−6.6	58 841	28.3	8.0
06 16532	Costa Mesa city	108 785	7.0	16.1	11.1	39.0	18.3	8.5	32.0	−2.6	−3.9	61 445	16.6	12.8
06 16742	Covina city	47 144	7.6	20.4	9.6	31.4	20.3	10.6	33.5	2.3	−1.8	19 775	20.2	18.1
06 17568	Culver City city	38 816	5.1	15.6	6.4	33.9	25.2	13.9	39.1	−5.0	1.5	18 759	15.6	19.0
06 17610	Cupertino city	50 657	6.2	20.7	5.0	33.7	23.6	10.8	38.0	1.2	−1.6	24 350	20.6	17.0
06 17750	Cypress city	46 534	5.8	21.3	8.1	30.5	23.8	10.5	36.7	1.4	−1.9	26 563	23.8	13.1
06 17918	Daly City city	103 549	6.0	16.3	10.4	32.8	22.4	12.1	35.4	−3.4	−0.3	18 271	11.8	26.1
06 17946	Dana Point city	34 851	5.4	14.9	7.3	32.0	27.7	12.7	39.8	−5.4	0.3	27 258	17.5	14.9
06 17988	Danville town	42 127	6.8	21.7	3.9	27.7	29.5	10.3	39.9	2.8	−2.1	35 041	27.4	11.3
06 18100	Davis city	60 341	4.6	14.1	31.0	27.5	16.4	6.5	25.2	−7.0	−5.9	39 540	18.9	8.7
06 18394	Delano city	38 981	9.2	23.3	11.7	33.9	14.2	7.8	27.9	6.8	−4.6	3 840	12.0	20.9
06 19192	Diamond Bar city	56 349	5.6	21.1	8.8	30.2	27.1	7.3	36.5	1.0	−5.1	17 499	21.2	10.9
06 19766	Downey city	107 323	8.0	21.2	9.5	31.8	18.3	11.2	31.6	3.5	−1.2	30 668	17.7	26.4
06 20018	Dublin city	30 036	5.9	14.8	9.4	43.6	21.3	5.0	34.3	−5.0	−7.4	18 577	21.4	6.2
06 20956	East Palo Alto city	29 450	9.6	25.6	13.3	32.2	14.6	4.7	25.8	9.5	−7.7	1 776	11.3	4.9
06 21712	El Cajon city	94 819	8.0	19.8	11.2	31.5	18.2	11.3	31.9	2.1	−1.1	60 678	22.1	15.1
06 21782	El Centro city	37 801	8.4	25.1	9.4	29.7	17.8	9.6	30.0	7.8	−2.8	6 943	19.2	19.3
06 22230	El Monte city	116 249	9.6	24.3	12.4	32.0	15.1	6.6	27.1	8.2	−5.8	8 501	15.8	24.1
06 22678	Encinitas city	58 195	6.1	16.9	7.1	34.0	25.8	10.2	37.9	−2.7	−2.2	46 041	21.0	11.5
06 22804	Escondido city	133 528	8.8	21.0	10.6	31.3	17.1	11.3	31.2	4.1	−1.1	69 396	21.7	18.3
06 23042	Eureka city	25 929	5.8	16.4	12.1	28.3	23.4	14.0	36.6	−3.5	1.6	20 599	18.9	16.1
06 23182	Fairfield city	96 168	8.1	21.4	11.7	30.9	18.7	9.2	31.1	3.8	−3.2	47 072	23.9	12.8
06 24638	Folsom city	51 912	6.7	17.6	6.3	39.6	21.5	8.3	35.9	−1.4	−4.1	38 454	25.0	10.2
06 24680	Fontana city	128 174	10.0	28.0	10.0	32.9	14.5	4.6	26.2	12.3	−7.8	30 279	27.4	9.6
06 25338	Foster City city	28 803	5.7	15.3	5.2	36.5	27.1	10.1	38.1	−4.7	−2.3	16 023	19.0	12.5
06 25380	Fountain Valley city	54 995	6.1	17.4	8.3	30.1	26.6	11.6	38.1	−2.2	−0.8	32 071	20.6	13.8
06 26000	Fremont city	203 413	7.4	18.4	7.3	37.3	21.3	8.4	34.5	0.1	−4.0	84 047	21.4	12.1
06 27000	Fresno city	427 224	9.0	23.8	11.8	29.2	17.1	9.1	28.5	7.1	−3.3	158 199	20.8	16.6
06 28000	Fullerton city	126 246	7.2	18.0	11.4	32.4	19.8	11.2	32.9	−0.5	−1.2	61 197	17.8	18.3
06 28168	Gardena city	57 818	7.6	17.8	8.5	33.2	20.3	12.6	34.4	−0.3	0.2	7 184	13.3	24.7
06 29000	Garden Grove city	165 710	7.9	20.6	9.1	34.0	19.0	9.5	32.3	2.8	−2.9	54 321	20.5	17.8
06 29504	Gilroy city	41 587	9.2	23.4	9.4	33.3	17.9	6.8	29.9	6.9	−5.6	15 738	25.9	10.2
06 30000	Glendale city	195 047	5.7	16.6	8.5	32.7	22.6	13.9	37.5	−3.4	1.5	105 444	19.2	19.2
06 30014	Glendora city	49 719	6.2	21.0	7.9	28.6	23.7	12.6	36.9	1.5	0.2	33 380	24.3	15.5
06 31960	Hanford city	41 729	8.3	23.0	9.7	30.5	18.2	10.4	30.9	5.6	−2.0	20 511	23.8	15.4
06 32548	Hawthorne city	83 963	9.8	21.6	11.0	35.4	16.1	6.1	28.7	5.7	−6.3	10 940	17.5	20.5
06 33000	Hayward city	139 895	7.8	18.9	10.5	33.7	18.9	10.1	31.9	1.0	−2.3	40 624	14.7	21.4
06 33182	Hemet city	58 770	6.5	15.8	6.9	21.3	16.3	33.2	44.6	−3.4	20.8	41 233	15.1	43.9
06 33434	Hesperia city	62 578	7.9	24.6	9.1	28.3	19.3	10.8	32.0	6.8	−1.6	38 971	28.0	13.7

Table A-5. Cities — Age, Ethnicity, and Household Structure

City	Black or African American — Total population (14)	Under 18 years (15)	65 years and over (16)	American Indian and Alaska Native — Total population (17)	Under 18 years (18)	65 years and over (19)	Asian, Hawaiian, and Pacific Islander — Total population (20)	Under 18 years (21)	65 years and over (22)	Hispanic or Latino[1] — Total population (23)	Under 18 years (24)	65 years and over (25)	Two or more races — Total population (26)	Under 18 years (27)	65 years and over (28)
CALIFORNIA—Cont'd															
Azusa city	1 603	33.3	3.4	555	31.2	5.2	2 520	22.0	9.8	28 702	37.4	4.5	2 652	36.7	5.4
Bakersfield city	22 186	39.7	7.3	3 205	32.2	5.4	10 967	29.7	7.0	79 914	41.1	3.2	12 353	46.0	3.6
Baldwin Park city	1 174	33.1	7.8	1 073	33.8	0.0	9 154	25.4	9.9	59 654	38.2	3.9	3 424	37.4	4.4
Bell city	422	11.1	6.6	330	37.3	1.5	465	12.7	31.2	33 273	36.4	3.6	1 710	32.9	6.0
Bellflower city	9 103	37.5	2.5	700	46.7	4.0	7 441	24.6	7.0	31 202	38.9	3.2	4 107	41.8	3.9
Bell Gardens city	376	39.6	18.9	649	36.7	1.4	281	36.7	2.8	41 290	40.7	2.7	1 672	35.0	6.3
Belmont city	417	10.8	5.5	15	0.0	0.0	3 984	17.7	10.6	2 012	23.5	8.2	1 164	41.8	4.6
Benicia city	1 181	24.1	14.1	67	25.4	0.0	1 991	23.5	7.7	2 467	39.0	3.3	1 751	52.0	2.4
Berkeley city	13 885	21.6	19.9	447	19.9	1.1	16 821	7.0	7.5	10 031	21.8	3.0	5 906	25.6	3.2
Beverly Hills city	461	17.1	8.5	110	10.9	7.3	2 621	23.1	6.4	1 613	13.6	11.5	1 486	27.4	13.8
Brea city	517	20.5	0.0	134	29.9	3.7	3 176	27.3	4.8	7 129	32.9	5.0	1 582	36.4	3.4
Buena Park city	2 411	33.0	2.1	543	33.1	5.5	17 188	25.4	6.6	26 081	37.9	4.7	4 635	44.1	4.7
Burbank city	1 801	21.3	2.2	439	12.5	2.3	9 378	22.9	7.2	24 882	31.0	6.3	7 070	34.2	6.1
Burlingame city	205	14.6	12.7	13	0.0	30.8	3 810	18.8	7.7	2 988	23.4	6.7	1 313	35.8	4.9
Calexico city	77	36.4	7.8	217	35.5	11.1	468	28.8	7.3	25 847	35.1	11.0	975	33.6	14.1
Camarillo city	959	30.3	5.0	256	32.8	0.0	4 104	25.6	8.7	9 122	35.4	5.3	2 081	48.4	4.4
Campbell city	857	30.3	4.1	258	26.4	3.1	5 777	19.5	8.3	4 883	32.3	4.6	1 951	46.8	4.0
Carlsbad city	913	36.4	4.7	378	23.5	10.3	3 221	20.5	7.1	9 103	32.7	5.0	2 523	42.9	6.0
Carson city	22 458	27.9	9.0	353	26.1	4.2	22 085	25.1	12.2	31 256	35.6	5.6	5 315	38.1	7.3
Cathedral City city	949	29.0	9.2	314	42.4	6.1	1 380	25.1	10.1	21 537	39.9	3.3	1 812	51.3	3.0
Ceres city	926	38.7	6.0	399	33.6	6.0	1 821	35.9	7.1	13 061	43.3	3.5	1 875	42.1	6.5
Cerritos city	3 332	26.7	7.6	150	26.0	21.3	30 231	26.5	7.9	5 344	26.0	8.4	2 235	44.3	6.0
Chico city	880	27.6	1.5	844	23.9	3.3	2 378	29.5	1.8	7 237	31.8	3.2	2 880	38.4	3.4
Chino city	4 981	15.4	2.3	500	36.2	1.8	3 491	25.2	6.7	32 641	34.2	3.9	3 266	43.8	5.2
Chino Hills city	3 825	33.1	1.4	598	33.4	10.0	14 418	29.4	6.3	17 106	38.1	2.6	3 522	52.2	3.0
Chula Vista city	7 858	31.6	4.9	1 272	33.4	5.1	19 603	24.8	10.1	86 500	34.9	6.7	10 659	45.6	5.7
Citrus Heights city	2 640	34.7	5.7	922	28.2	8.1	2 558	17.0	11.0	8 427	37.1	4.8	4 258	42.9	2.6
Claremont city	1 629	23.7	10.4	67	34.3	0.0	4 010	22.8	6.3	5 323	32.0	7.0	1 518	28.0	6.4
Clovis city	1 155	33.4	4.1	1 195	27.4	3.8	4 475	37.7	5.4	13 948	38.0	4.9	3 225	45.5	2.6
Colton city	5 555	37.7	1.5	444	33.8	5.2	2 595	25.6	7.4	29 116	38.8	6.2	2 407	48.8	8.6
Compton city	37 045	32.1	13.8	744	42.1	4.7	1 448	45.0	8.8	53 302	43.2	2.3	2 955	37.0	4.9
Concord city	3 751	31.9	4.1	742	29.2	6.3	11 585	22.7	8.7	26 713	33.8	3.5	8 166	42.8	4.8
Corona city	8 165	36.2	3.3	1 152	28.0	2.6	9 649	30.1	6.3	44 645	39.9	3.4	6 597	48.3	2.6
Costa Mesa city	1 354	23.3	3.5	685	27.7	1.6	8 530	17.0	6.7	34 587	35.5	1.8	4 369	30.5	5.1
Covina city	2 290	34.8	1.8	390	27.9	9.2	4 602	24.4	11.1	18 711	36.2	4.3	2 413	32.1	5.1
Culver City city	4 189	17.4	9.5	196	23.0	6.1	4 813	16.0	13.9	9 227	30.2	7.3	2 392	42.3	5.0
Cupertino city	301	18.9	3.3	203	31.0	6.4	22 795	31.9	5.0	1 863	30.0	7.2	1 442	47.1	4.4
Cypress city	1 338	28.0	2.2	189	19.6	10.6	9 593	27.2	8.7	7 421	35.9	5.8	2 423	46.0	4.0
Daly City city	4 649	21.0	11.8	351	23.9	8.3	53 155	22.6	9.5	23 139	28.4	7.6	6 819	34.2	7.7
Dana Point city	171	10.5	0.0	175	26.3	6.9	1 047	20.2	13.0	5 396	32.6	2.6	1 028	29.3	9.6
Danville town	432	29.6	8.3	64	29.7	15.6	3 623	31.2	5.1	2 070	35.2	6.3	1 249	49.0	2.6
Davis city	1 477	21.8	1.2	304	20.1	2.0	10 364	9.2	2.1	5 813	26.9	3.1	3 434	35.0	1.0
Delano city	1 901	6.4	3.8	352	36.1	9.1	6 067	30.8	12.4	26 749	37.6	4.9	1 861	46.2	7.3
Diamond Bar city	2 630	27.0	5.3	90	8.9	0.0	23 906	28.3	5.6	10 501	30.1	5.8	2 655	44.9	5.8
Downey city	3 881	34.7	4.0	855	34.6	4.6	8 053	23.0	7.4	62 049	35.2	4.7	5 590	37.0	5.5
Dublin city	3 005	5.9	1.8	281	21.4	3.9	3 014	20.9	5.0	4 134	22.1	2.8	1 328	43.8	0.5
East Palo Alto city	6 893	28.5	13.6	130	23.1	4.6	2 774	36.7	4.3	17 301	40.3	1.3	1 488	40.3	1.5
El Cajon city	4 778	38.0	2.1	924	27.6	6.0	2 925	22.4	9.4	21 273	39.5	4.1	7 148	47.1	4.0
El Centro city	1 082	22.9	19.1	450	25.1	12.9	1 180	24.8	5.8	28 218	37.7	7.0	1 203	45.1	3.7
El Monte city	836	43.2	5.0	1 070	34.0	4.8	21 689	24.6	10.0	84 231	38.2	4.0	4 817	37.4	4.6
Encinitas city	398	34.4	0.0	224	17.4	5.8	1 775	15.5	8.2	8 608	31.9	5.1	1 690	39.8	2.5
Escondido city	2 694	28.4	4.1	1 466	36.2	4.0	5 950	24.8	7.5	51 661	40.3	3.1	7 373	46.4	4.0
Eureka city	306	45.8	5.2	1 086	20.4	8.6	788	37.1	3.7	1 867	33.7	4.4	1 677	42.3	6.9
Fairfield city	13 939	34.2	5.5	880	30.6	6.3	11 633	25.3	9.1	17 813	38.2	4.0	7 687	50.7	3.3
Folsom city	3 091	4.4	0.9	272	21.7	9.9	3 650	24.7	3.3	4 885	24.4	2.3	1 998	48.8	5.2
Fontana city	14 673	39.4	4.1	1 524	42.3	5.2	6 502	32.1	5.2	73 681	42.4	2.5	7 525	48.7	2.9
Foster City city	570	24.2	6.8	22	0.0	0.0	9 566	21.6	7.6	1 510	23.4	9.1	1 332	40.6	2.8
Fountain Valley city	522	29.5	1.5	241	24.1	14.1	14 548	24.3	9.5	6 026	31.6	6.7	2 155	41.2	5.4
Fremont city	5 780	27.1	3.5	1 084	30.0	5.4	75 423	26.2	6.1	27 453	31.7	5.8	13 067	43.5	4.6
Fresno city	34 794	37.5	7.3	6 305	38.3	5.0	48 768	42.2	5.5	170 330	39.8	3.8	24 254	45.7	4.2
Fullerton city	2 429	28.5	4.3	956	27.4	5.8	20 575	24.5	6.9	38 260	36.4	3.3	5 219	38.9	3.5
Gardena city	14 477	29.4	7.0	451	48.8	1.8	15 797	14.1	22.0	18 407	34.7	4.5	3 086	44.4	7.0
Garden Grove city	1 536	32.2	3.5	1 139	28.3	5.9	52 295	25.7	8.1	53 841	38.9	2.6	6 563	42.0	6.1
Gilroy city	752	34.0	0.0	431	29.2	7.7	1 923	26.6	11.0	22 497	37.6	4.1	2 631	47.2	3.1
Glendale city	2 430	20.8	6.7	668	30.7	3.7	32 124	22.9	7.6	38 186	29.3	6.9	19 540	26.3	9.5
Glendora city	692	30.5	5.9	379	25.9	6.3	3 310	24.1	9.3	11 017	36.4	5.7	2 188	44.4	3.9
Hanford city	1 976	34.8	7.7	362	31.5	8.6	1 384	27.1	13.2	16 329	40.2	4.6	2 722	45.4	4.4
Hawthorne city	27 539	33.4	3.5	466	38.0	3.4	6 494	22.6	8.5	37 148	35.5	3.4	4 303	36.6	2.8
Hayward city	15 161	30.8	3.8	1 054	26.4	4.9	28 463	24.9	8.0	47 973	35.2	4.8	11 281	40.3	4.4
Hemet city	1 512	37.5	9.4	762	26.1	14.6	826	30.6	9.9	13 489	41.2	6.8	2 162	42.7	8.7
Hesperia city	2 505	41.3	7.6	571	33.3	12.3	883	26.5	12.6	18 474	41.4	4.9	3 197	43.4	6.0

[1] Hispanic or Latino persons may be of any race.

Table A-5. Cities — Age, Ethnicity, and Household Structure

| | | Family households (percent) | | | | | | Nonfamily households (percent) | | | | | | | |
| | | Married-couple family households | | | Other family households | | | Two or more unrelated persons | | Male living alone | | Female living alone | | | |
City	Total households	Total	With children	House-holder 65 years or over	Total	With children	House-holder 65 years or over	Total	House-holder 65 years or over	Total	House-holder 65 years or over	Total	House-holder 65 years or over	Percent of householders 65 years and over who live alone	Grandparents who are responsible for the care of their grandchildren
	29	30	31	32	33	34	35	36	37	38	39	40	41	42	43
CALIFORNIA—Cont'd															
Azusa city	12 389	50.5	31.5	5.6	24.9	13.8	3.3	6.1	0.4	7.0	1.6	11.4	4.8	40.4	495
Bakersfield city	83 601	53.9	30.1	6.9	20.0	13.2	1.7	4.6	0.4	8.7	1.6	12.7	5.6	44.1	2 684
Baldwin Park city	16 953	62.7	42.6	5.7	26.4	14.0	2.8	2.8	0.4	3.3	1.0	4.8	3.1	31.9	927
Bell city	8 932	58.1	42.8	3.6	28.7	17.1	2.0	2.4	0.4	5.2	1.9	5.6	3.0	44.5	348
Bellflower city	23 394	49.5	29.2	5.8	24.3	15.0	2.2	5.3	0.6	9.5	2.0	11.4	5.2	45.6	720
Bell Gardens city	9 470	61.2	47.9	3.1	29.7	20.0	1.4	2.5	0.3	3.6	1.2	3.0	1.6	37.0	538
Belmont city	10 401	55.0	22.3	10.6	8.6	4.1	1.1	9.4	0.6	10.9	1.6	16.1	6.8	40.5	29
Benicia city	10 350	54.7	27.5	7.6	15.7	10.1	1.8	6.4	0.4	9.8	1.2	13.4	4.6	37.4	141
Berkeley city	45 007	29.5	12.7	5.0	12.7	5.8	2.4	19.7	0.8	17.7	2.3	20.4	6.2	50.7	361
Beverly Hills city	15 038	45.6	19.7	12.5	10.0	5.0	1.8	6.4	1.1	13.2	2.7	24.8	9.1	43.4	113
Brea city	12 994	57.3	27.5	8.4	13.8	7.1	2.2	5.7	0.3	9.1	1.5	14.0	6.6	42.5	264
Buena Park city	23 454	57.9	31.4	7.7	22.0	11.4	3.8	5.2	0.3	6.4	1.0	8.5	4.1	29.9	839
Burbank city	41 656	44.2	21.4	7.2	14.8	7.7	2.1	7.6	0.6	15.0	2.6	18.5	7.3	49.9	472
Burlingame city	12 503	44.8	19.4	9.8	10.3	4.1	1.6	9.1	0.4	14.9	2.2	20.9	7.7	45.7	49
Calexico city	6 828	62.4	41.5	11.5	26.0	13.1	5.9	1.6	0.7	3.5	2.0	6.5	4.6	26.9	306
Camarillo city	21 434	61.4	27.8	13.2	10.0	5.8	1.5	4.5	0.8	8.6	3.0	15.5	10.1	45.9	383
Campbell city	15 973	43.4	20.4	5.8	14.3	7.6	1.4	12.1	0.7	14.8	1.2	15.4	5.9	47.3	136
Carlsbad city	31 410	54.0	24.2	10.7	13.0	6.7	1.6	8.3	0.7	10.1	2.2	14.5	6.1	38.8	337
Carson city	24 618	59.7	30.4	9.5	22.7	9.3	4.2	3.6	0.6	5.4	1.6	8.7	4.5	30.1	1 716
Cathedral City city	14 104	52.5	30.6	10.0	16.7	10.3	1.7	8.0	1.5	9.7	3.5	13.0	7.0	44.1	296
Ceres city	10 421	61.5	36.2	8.2	19.8	12.6	2.2	4.5	0.4	6.3	1.3	7.9	4.6	35.1	505
Cerritos city	15 383	74.0	36.9	9.5	14.7	4.9	1.8	2.5	0.3	3.4	0.8	5.5	2.2	20.4	512
Chico city	23 424	35.8	18.0	6.0	13.9	9.9	1.0	20.9	0.4	12.2	1.5	17.2	6.2	50.9	123
Chino city	17 408	64.0	37.3	5.4	18.0	10.0	1.7	3.8	0.2	5.6	1.2	8.6	5.1	46.1	762
Chino Hills city	19 988	73.7	47.3	3.0	11.5	6.7	0.6	4.1	0.1	5.3	0.4	5.5	1.4	32.4	388
Chula Vista city	57 626	56.5	30.5	9.4	19.8	11.0	2.6	4.5	0.5	8.3	2.1	10.9	5.8	38.4	1 885
Citrus Heights city	33 457	47.7	22.4	8.7	17.4	9.9	1.7	8.3	0.6	10.9	2.1	15.7	7.7	46.9	710
Claremont city	11 344	55.5	24.2	12.4	13.9	6.8	2.2	5.5	0.8	9.6	2.8	15.4	8.6	42.5	177
Clovis city	24 154	55.2	30.4	7.1	18.0	11.4	1.8	4.8	0.4	8.2	1.4	13.9	6.7	46.5	531
Colton city	14 741	50.7	31.3	5.3	25.3	16.2	2.6	4.7	0.2	9.3	1.0	10.0	3.3	34.9	608
Compton city	22 272	49.0	32.1	7.2	34.8	18.9	5.7	3.0	0.4	5.7	1.9	7.5	3.9	30.0	1 929
Concord city	44 111	52.5	26.8	7.8	16.9	8.9	2.2	7.4	0.5	9.5	1.9	13.7	5.5	41.1	848
Corona city	37 917	65.1	41.2	4.9	15.9	9.8	1.3	4.7	0.2	6.7	0.7	7.7	3.0	36.5	1 209
Costa Mesa city	39 207	43.7	22.2	5.7	15.2	7.7	1.8	13.0	0.7	13.7	1.7	14.4	4.8	44.0	414
Covina city	15 953	50.4	26.5	7.7	24.1	13.7	2.3	5.0	0.5	8.1	2.1	12.3	5.3	41.2	419
Culver City city	16 636	41.8	19.0	8.3	15.5	7.7	2.1	8.3	0.6	12.8	2.3	21.7	7.0	45.9	298
Cupertino city	18 206	64.7	37.6	7.7	10.3	4.6	2.1	5.7	0.4	9.2	1.8	10.2	5.3	40.9	182
Cypress city	15 695	61.5	31.1	9.3	17.7	8.8	1.9	3.6	0.5	6.6	1.4	10.7	5.3	36.4	408
Daly City city	30 794	55.1	27.3	9.3	19.7	7.5	3.1	6.8	0.5	8.1	1.9	10.3	4.5	33.3	1 167
Dana Point city	14 449	52.1	20.3	10.3	12.1	6.9	1.4	9.4	0.8	11.8	1.5	14.5	5.3	35.2	161
Danville town	15 014	71.5	36.9	8.8	8.8	4.9	1.2	4.0	0.6	5.1	1.4	10.6	4.6	36.2	74
Davis city	22 959	38.8	20.8	4.5	10.7	6.3	0.6	25.5	0.4	10.5	1.1	14.6	4.5	50.6	114
Delano city	8 485	62.7	42.2	8.2	24.3	15.5	3.1	2.7	1.0	4.3	1.4	6.1	3.6	29.0	591
Diamond Bar city	17 733	68.3	37.3	6.2	15.7	6.8	1.4	3.1	0.2	5.2	0.8	7.6	2.3	28.4	492
Downey city	34 014	54.2	29.7	9.0	22.6	12.3	2.7	4.2	0.4	7.6	1.9	11.4	6.5	40.9	1 130
Dublin city	9 332	56.6	28.2	4.2	13.7	7.7	1.6	8.6	0.3	9.1	0.8	12.0	1.7	29.5	146
East Palo Alto city	6 953	48.7	33.3	4.3	27.4	14.9	3.3	5.5	0.4	8.5	1.4	9.9	3.1	35.6	493
El Cajon city	34 370	46.6	23.9	7.3	21.5	13.8	1.6	7.7	0.5	10.7	2.2	13.4	6.3	47.3	710
El Centro city	11 449	54.7	33.3	7.8	23.8	14.8	3.1	2.6	0.4	8.9	2.4	10.1	5.1	39.7	539
El Monte city	27 094	57.1	38.1	5.3	28.6	15.3	3.1	3.7	0.4	4.5	1.3	6.1	3.2	34.0	1 508
Encinitas city	22 970	50.9	24.8	6.8	11.5	6.3	1.4	11.9	0.4	11.4	1.5	14.3	5.3	44.4	226
Escondido city	43 870	54.7	29.2	8.9	17.0	10.6	1.5	5.9	0.5	8.6	2.4	13.8	8.0	48.6	1 075
Eureka city	10 834	35.9	13.4	7.8	18.4	12.1	1.8	10.5	0.6	14.8	3.6	20.5	8.9	54.9	188
Fairfield city	30 959	59.6	32.1	8.0	18.5	11.3	2.1	4.8	0.4	7.2	1.5	9.9	4.1	34.5	1 003
Folsom city	17 220	62.6	33.1	7.4	10.2	6.9	0.8	5.4	0.3	9.4	1.3	12.4	5.6	44.7	163
Fontana city	33 942	65.1	45.2	4.2	20.8	13.7	1.5	3.5	0.4	5.0	1.0	5.6	2.3	35.4	1 625
Foster City city	11 611	59.3	26.5	7.9	9.1	4.5	1.0	8.1	0.6	9.6	0.9	14.0	3.2	30.3	69
Fountain Valley city	18 139	64.5	29.7	10.2	14.4	5.3	2.5	5.1	0.6	7.3	1.9	8.8	3.9	30.2	489
Fremont city	68 302	63.7	34.6	6.6	13.4	6.1	1.7	6.4	0.2	8.0	1.0	8.4	3.1	32.3	1 605
Fresno city	139 969	47.8	26.9	6.9	22.9	14.7	2.1	6.2	0.4	9.7	2.0	13.5	6.2	46.5	4 672
Fullerton city	43 678	52.9	26.1	9.4	15.5	7.8	1.8	8.2	0.4	10.9	2.0	12.5	5.0	37.8	831
Gardena city	20 404	46.6	23.0	8.3	22.9	11.4	3.3	5.0	0.4	11.7	2.6	13.7	6.0	42.0	619
Garden Grove city	45 945	61.0	34.7	8.5	19.4	8.8	2.8	4.5	0.5	6.2	1.3	8.9	4.7	34.0	1 558
Gilroy city	11 933	60.7	36.2	5.5	21.2	12.9	2.0	3.8	0.4	5.6	1.7	8.7	4.4	43.2	382
Glendale city	71 872	53.1	26.8	9.2	16.3	6.5	2.6	5.0	0.6	10.3	2.0	15.3	6.9	41.9	809
Glendora city	16 940	60.6	29.9	9.8	16.0	8.5	2.3	4.1	0.5	7.2	1.8	12.0	6.4	39.5	376
Hanford city	13 989	55.5	29.3	8.4	19.4	13.2	1.9	4.8	0.6	7.7	2.1	12.7	6.8	45.0	471
Hawthorne city	28 510	40.2	25.8	3.7	29.3	18.9	1.9	5.9	0.4	11.8	1.3	12.8	3.0	42.2	750
Hayward city	44 809	51.2	27.6	7.3	20.7	10.4	2.4	7.2	0.6	9.5	2.2	11.3	5.4	42.7	1 368
Hemet city	25 325	46.2	14.4	21.5	14.5	8.8	2.5	4.8	1.5	11.0	5.4	23.5	17.5	47.3	478
Hesperia city	19 978	59.7	30.9	9.7	20.1	12.7	3.1	3.8	0.5	7.5	2.0	9.0	5.1	35.0	819

City	Households with Non-Hispanic White householder		Households with Black or African American householder		Households with American Indian and Alaska Native householder		Households with Asian, Hawaiian, and Pacific Islander householder		Households with Hispanic or Latino[1] householder		Foreign-born population				Percent in non-English speaking households	
											Percent of total population that is foreign-born	Place of birth (percent)				
	Number of households	Percent that are family households	Number of households	Percent that are family households	Number of households	Percent that are family households	Number of households	Percent that are family households	Number of households	Percent that are family households		Europe	Asia	Latin America	Linguistically isolated	Not linguistically isolated
	44	45	46	47	48	49	50	51	52	53	54	55	56	57	58	59
CALIFORNIA—Cont'd																
Azusa city	4 083	55.9	634	63.9	177	67.8	722	75.8	6 621	89.1	34.0	0.6	5.1	27.8	16.8	53.3
Bakersfield city	49 673	69.2	7 630	71.3	1 118	77.7	3 232	80.2	20 522	85.5	13.6	0.6	3.0	9.4	6.8	29.0
Baldwin Park city	2 078	67.3	356	80.3	213	100.0	2 311	88.4	12 197	93.2	45.7	0.2	8.7	36.6	19.7	69.7
Bell city	887	55.4	38	78.9	85	78.8	126	77.0	7 749	91.2	53.3	0.4	1.8	51.0	31.5	62.7
Bellflower city	9 815	61.5	3 223	71.9	148	71.6	2 029	84.2	7 604	88.0	28.4	1.2	7.6	18.3	12.8	42.8
Bell Gardens city	730	54.7	57	100.0	170	81.2	78	66.7	8 566	94.3	50.4	0.3	0.4	49.7	28.3	66.7
Belmont city	7 809	62.4	177	55.4	15	100.0	1 515	66.5	643	73.4	22.6	5.5	11.6	3.3	4.0	30.4
Benicia city	8 250	68.9	530	63.8	31	25.8	572	85.5	628	89.5	9.4	1.9	4.5	2.2	2.0	20.1
Berkeley city	27 159	42.8	5 873	51.1	140	26.4	7 005	29.9	3 032	51.5	20.4	4.7	9.7	4.2	4.3	31.7
Beverly Hills city	12 883	53.7	241	50.2	44	79.5	896	79.7	514	55.3	38.2	8.4	24.2	3.4	7.3	46.1
Brea city	9 642	67.9	200	84.5	34	82.4	1 026	81.0	1 843	82.0	17.2	2.2	7.1	7.0	4.0	28.5
Buena Park city	11 418	73.5	902	76.6	182	75.3	4 651	87.3	5 711	86.9	33.0	1.6	16.5	13.8	13.2	46.0
Burbank city	28 272	63.5	627	40.7	102	74.7	3 137	69.5	7 394	75.2	31.1	3.0	15.1	11.7	10.3	39.3
Burlingame city	9 475	52.8	87	43.7	13	69.2	1 534	60.3	1 068	65.7	24.6	5.1	11.8	5.6	5.8	30.6
Calexico city	157	79.0	13	46.2	63	79.4	118	96.6	6 472	88.7	51.2	0.0	1.2	49.9	28.4	69.4
Camarillo city	17 176	68.5	340	77.4	59	100.0	1 134	83.8	2 264	83.1	13.3	2.7	4.7	5.0	3.5	24.3
Campbell city	11 728	54.2	376	53.5	82	61.0	1 975	71.3	1 459	64.4	21.7	4.3	11.4	4.8	6.8	28.2
Carlsbad city	26 956	65.8	283	72.8	142	50.7	1 123	72.7	2 321	79.7	12.7	3.2	3.3	4.8	3.8	20.3
Carson city	4 690	61.5	7 086	82.4	111	87.4	5 380	90.0	6 812	90.9	32.9	0.5	16.2	15.4	8.8	54.1
Cathedral City city	8 316	56.1	367	65.4	77	96.1	332	85.5	4 875	89.9	29.5	1.5	2.7	24.4	13.5	42.2
Ceres city	6 387	75.4	322	68.3	125	88.0	394	96.7	2 925	92.7	19.0	0.8	4.2	13.6	7.6	35.7
Cerritos city	4 308	79.5	1 088	85.6	51	74.5	8 239	94.3	1 331	87.4	45.5	1.1	39.6	3.6	12.6	57.7
Chico city	19 176	48.6	395	47.3	298	59.7	770	52.3	2 173	59.5	9.0	1.0	3.2	4.2	4.0	16.2
Chino city	8 511	77.5	874	78.3	101	92.1	919	85.5	6 795	88.3	20.4	1.7	3.4	14.7	8.4	45.7
Chino Hills city	10 165	81.1	1 307	86.1	144	94.4	3 988	89.2	3 993	90.2	22.7	1.2	14.3	6.4	6.0	42.5
Chula Vista city	24 522	67.8	2 902	72.6	392	72.7	5 707	82.7	23 122	84.4	28.7	1.1	7.6	19.7	8.3	55.7
Citrus Heights city	27 930	64.5	1 014	72.0	277	65.7	839	67.2	2 545	68.0	9.2	3.9	2.4	2.2	2.8	15.7
Claremont city	8 137	65.1	534	78.7	20	100.0	966	84.4	1 412	80.9	15.8	2.8	7.7	3.8	5.3	29.7
Clovis city	17 856	71.0	378	67.2	419	71.8	1 165	85.5	3 959	80.4	8.0	1.0	3.8	2.8	3.2	21.8
Colton city	4 222	61.1	2 142	70.5	101	86.0	774	80.2	7 303	86.2	24.0	0.6	4.0	18.6	11.7	50.1
Compton city	219	63.0	11 928	75.0	177	74.6	300	94.7	9 632	95.1	31.4	0.0	0.3	30.7	18.7	42.1
Concord city	30 974	65.8	1 424	64.8	242	63.2	3 767	76.2	6 336	81.6	23.4	2.3	8.0	11.9	8.7	28.3
Corona city	21 087	75.8	2 587	81.7	384	88.0	2 609	89.4	10 579	89.6	21.4	1.1	5.3	13.8	8.7	37.5
Costa Mesa city	27 358	52.6	524	58.8	149	69.1	3 076	64.2	7 223	83.0	29.2	2.1	6.2	19.3	13.1	32.0
Covina city	8 186	68.3	825	69.8	118	73.7	1 346	83.4	5 084	83.9	20.0	1.2	7.4	10.5	5.7	42.2
Culver City city	9 533	53.5	2 200	44.2	70	51.4	1 759	69.5	2 659	71.7	26.6	3.3	8.5	12.4	8.5	35.2
Cupertino city	10 246	66.8	133	72.2	55	80.0	6 921	87.5	520	71.2	42.8	5.7	34.0	1.4	12.1	45.0
Cypress city	10 039	75.4	464	83.0	66	89.4	2 834	89.6	1 934	83.3	21.3	2.1	14.4	3.5	5.6	34.2
Daly City city	8 628	55.6	1 874	65.7	129	73.6	13 385	85.1	5 900	83.1	52.4	2.1	36.3	12.9	13.1	65.6
Dana Point city	12 323	63.0	77	48.1	59	28.8	386	66.6	1 329	78.5	15.7	3.9	2.3	7.9	5.0	18.2
Danville town	13 050	79.5	152	90.1	12	100.0	1 059	86.3	555	82.9	11.0	3.7	5.2	0.9	1.1	18.6
Davis city	16 359	52.0	488	56.1	102	55.9	3 375	35.7	1 796	54.0	17.2	2.7	9.7	2.7	3.1	30.9
Delano city	1 011	64.9	165	60.0	107	88.8	1 404	90.9	6 766	90.5	38.2	0.2	11.3	26.6	26.1	63.0
Diamond Bar city	6 833	76.2	927	81.3	36	66.7	6 872	92.1	2 693	83.5	38.3	1.4	30.5	4.8	12.7	52.0
Downey city	13 480	65.3	1 450	68.2	312	73.7	2 401	88.7	15 886	85.4	35.3	1.7	5.8	26.6	11.8	57.4
Dublin city	7 048	68.4	225	54.7	85	91.8	873	86.1	849	71.5	13.6	2.1	7.3	2.4	3.2	24.5
East Palo Alto city	895	33.3	2 310	70.4	30	66.7	577	79.5	2 956	92.6	43.8	0.3	1.3	36.6	19.0	53.2
El Cajon city	24 679	63.9	1 693	70.7	435	67.6	874	72.4	5 564	84.2	17.5	1.8	6.2	8.9	6.8	27.7
El Centro city	3 216	64.3	443	71.3	158	80.4	388	67.8	7 244	85.7	34.4	0.3	2.2	31.7	18.2	61.1
El Monte city	3 523	59.0	189	77.2	252	84.9	5 351	88.9	17 746	90.3	51.3	0.3	14.5	36.3	32.3	56.9
Encinitas city	19 858	60.6	143	79.7	86	38.4	690	67.2	1 895	79.8	13.9	2.8	2.3	7.7	4.1	23.2
Escondido city	29 166	65.3	1 053	64.5	409	70.4	1 653	78.9	11 115	88.3	25.5	1.5	3.4	19.9	13.0	32.6
Eureka city	9 234	52.1	111	73.9	391	59.6	209	73.7	579	65.8	5.5	1.1	1.9	2.1	3.2	11.0
Fairfield city	17 531	75.8	4 645	78.8	268	68.7	3 258	81.5	4 323	85.2	16.3	1.6	7.3	6.6	4.7	31.0
Folsom city	14 242	71.5	312	60.9	114	67.5	1 284	84.9	911	79.5	8.8	1.4	5.2	1.4	1.3	17.5
Fontana city	10 743	77.0	4 525	84.1	428	80.8	1 594	92.7	16 307	92.0	26.9	0.5	3.3	22.5	12.3	49.6
Foster City city	7 071	64.6	237	62.4	22	81.8	3 446	76.1	545	76.9	35.2	6.2	24.1	2.3	7.5	40.2
Fountain Valley city	12 074	73.9	207	52.2	77	94.8	3 931	90.9	1 474	88.8	27.6	2.7	19.7	3.8	9.8	33.3
Fremont city	33 365	70.9	2 131	69.5	367	75.2	22 921	85.6	6 987	81.1	37.1	2.7	28.9	4.3	10.8	45.4
Fresno city	68 292	61.7	11 911	72.0	1 971	73.2	10 880	82.3	44 360	81.7	20.3	0.7	7.7	11.4	11.2	38.7
Fullerton city	26 389	61.6	950	66.7	234	71.4	6 360	78.0	8 817	82.6	28.9	1.8	12.2	13.9	12.6	36.8
Gardena city	3 542	52.1	5 362	71.1	105	50.5	6 376	68.8	4 565	83.7	32.8	0.7	14.6	16.5	16.7	40.2
Garden Grove city	20 850	69.3	543	69.4	331	88.2	12 733	90.0	10 727	90.7	43.1	1.2	24.7	16.5	23.8	43.3
Gilroy city	6 082	75.3	248	91.9	103	77.7	567	81.8	4 864	89.9	24.1	1.1	2.5	20.1	14.2	41.2
Glendale city	42 832	65.0	996	58.5	198	65.7	10 704	77.7	11 824	73.9	54.4	3.7	39.1	10.6	20.2	52.7
Glendora city	12 626	74.2	234	72.6	133	100.0	956	87.1	2 760	83.2	14.1	1.6	6.5	5.2	3.2	29.5
Hanford city	8 369	70.4	686	74.6	161	71.4	428	73.4	4 069	83.4	13.6	0.9	2.3	10.2	6.0	32.9
Hawthorne city	5 068	58.4	11 019	60.7	159	84.9	2 020	74.5	9 791	85.0	33.3	0.6	5.4	25.4	15.6	41.6
Hayward city	18 049	59.3	5 559	71.3	341	66.3	8 155	81.1	10 947	85.7	34.8	1.7	13.8	16.2	13.5	46.2
Hemet city	20 253	57.1	585	64.8	266	70.7	238	72.7	3 655	79.5	11.5	1.7	1.1	7.5	5.3	21.3
Hesperia city	13 841	77.2	745	82.3	204	60.8	224	68.3	4 527	90.1	9.8	0.7	1.0	7.5	3.6	26.4

[1] Hispanic or Latino persons may be of any race.

Table A-5. Cities — Age, Ethnicity, and Household Structure

STATE Place code	City	Total population	Population by age (percent)						Median age	+/- U.S. percent under 18 years	+/- U.S. percent 65 years and over	Non-Hispanic White	Age (percent)	
			Under 5 years	5 to 17 years	18 to 24 years	25 to 44 years	45 to 64 years	65 years and over				Total population	Under 18 years	65 years and over
		1	2	3	4	5	6	7	8	9	10	11	12	13
	CALIFORNIA—Cont'd													
06 33588	Highland city	44 629	8.8	26.9	9.1	29.8	18.7	6.7	29.3	10.0	-5.7	18 719	27.6	10.5
06 34120	Hollister city	34 614	9.7	25.0	9.5	34.3	15.3	6.1	29.0	9.0	-6.3	13 233	30.5	8.1
06 36000	Huntington Beach city	189 940	6.1	16.2	8.2	35.1	23.9	10.4	36.0	-3.4	-2.0	136 299	19.6	12.1
06 36056	Huntington Park city	61 370	10.4	25.2	13.2	32.4	13.5	5.2	25.6	9.9	-7.2	1 848	20.6	23.9
06 36294	Imperial Beach city	26 980	8.2	21.1	13.9	32.6	16.3	7.8	28.6	3.6	-4.6	11 698	20.3	11.3
06 36448	Indio city	49 159	10.2	25.2	11.1	30.2	14.5	8.8	27.3	9.7	-3.6	9 487	17.2	28.1
06 36546	Inglewood city	112 482	9.0	23.3	10.3	32.3	18.1	7.0	29.6	6.6	-5.4	4 448	10.6	31.5
06 36770	Irvine city	143 034	5.6	17.8	14.4	32.4	22.6	7.2	33.1	-2.3	-5.2	81 030	22.4	9.5
06 39220	Laguna Hills city	31 277	6.0	20.1	6.7	28.8	25.8	12.6	37.7	0.4	0.2	21 766	24.0	16.1
06 39248	Laguna Niguel city	61 963	7.4	19.2	5.8	33.0	25.7	8.9	37.5	0.9	-3.5	47 846	25.6	10.2
06 39290	La Habra city	59 191	8.0	21.2	9.8	31.9	18.1	11.0	31.5	3.5	-1.4	24 471	19.8	20.0
06 39486	Lake Elsinore city	29 290	9.6	26.6	9.0	31.9	15.7	7.2	28.7	10.5	-5.2	14 866	29.9	9.8
06 39496	Lake Forest city	58 806	6.9	20.0	8.4	33.1	23.0	8.5	35.1	1.2	-3.9	39 158	24.4	10.6
06 39892	Lakewood city	79 412	7.0	20.4	8.2	31.2	21.6	11.6	35.3	1.7	-0.8	41 498	21.6	17.1
06 40004	La Mesa city	54 751	5.6	14.1	10.1	32.6	20.4	17.1	37.3	-6.0	4.7	40 130	16.4	21.0
06 40032	La Mirada city	46 782	5.8	20.3	10.8	28.3	21.2	13.5	35.4	0.4	1.1	21 944	19.9	20.9
06 40130	Lancaster city	118 783	8.0	24.3	9.3	31.8	17.7	8.8	31.1	6.6	-3.6	62 101	26.3	13.0
06 40340	La Puente city	41 009	9.0	24.7	11.6	31.6	15.4	7.7	27.7	8.0	-4.7	2 754	18.2	24.8
06 40830	La Verne city	31 845	5.6	20.3	10.0	27.5	24.1	12.6	37.7	0.2	0.2	20 443	23.3	15.9
06 40886	Lawndale city	31 729	9.1	22.7	10.4	36.4	16.4	5.0	29.3	6.1	-7.4	7 007	19.8	12.6
06 41992	Livermore city	73 436	7.6	20.6	7.2	35.1	22.1	7.4	35.0	2.5	-5.0	54 652	26.0	8.4
06 42202	Lodi city	57 037	7.8	20.5	10.3	27.8	19.4	14.3	34.1	2.6	1.9	35 668	22.6	19.9
06 42524	Lompoc city	41 078	7.6	22.2	9.4	32.9	18.3	9.5	32.2	4.1	-2.9	19 863	22.5	15.3
06 43000	Long Beach city	461 381	8.2	20.8	10.8	33.3	17.8	9.0	30.8	3.3	-3.4	153 009	14.4	18.6
06 43280	Los Altos city	27 585	5.7	18.0	3.4	24.1	29.1	19.7	44.2	-2.0	7.3	21 536	21.5	22.6
06 44000	Los Angeles city	3 694 834	7.6	18.9	11.0	34.3	18.5	9.7	31.6	0.8	-2.7	1 093 447	15.2	17.6
06 44028	Los Banos city	25 878	9.5	25.4	8.3	31.4	15.9	9.5	29.7	9.2	-2.9	10 361	26.0	16.5
06 44112	Los Gatos town	28 683	5.4	15.7	4.2	31.5	27.8	15.3	41.2	-4.6	2.9	23 639	19.7	16.6
06 44574	Lynwood city	69 899	10.6	27.4	13.3	31.4	13.2	4.1	24.4	12.3	-8.3	1 996	16.0	27.6
06 45022	Madera city	43 370	10.8	24.6	12.2	31.4	15.4	8.2	26.2	9.7	-4.2	10 847	20.7	20.0
06 45400	Manhattan Beach city	34 039	6.5	15.7	4.2	38.0	25.4	10.2	37.7	-3.5	-2.2	29 100	21.5	11.1
06 45484	Manteca city	49 201	7.4	23.9	8.7	31.0	20.1	8.9	32.5	5.6	-3.5	31 577	27.3	11.6
06 45778	Marina city	25 052	5.4	16.1	13.4	39.6	18.3	7.3	32.3	-4.2	-5.1	9 399	16.4	11.3
06 46114	Martinez city	36 167	5.7	17.0	7.6	33.1	26.4	10.2	38.6	-3.0	-2.2	27 326	20.9	11.3
06 46492	Maywood city	28 083	11.4	25.8	13.8	31.5	13.2	4.3	24.9	11.5	-8.1	778	23.5	26.6
06 46870	Menlo Park city	30 786	6.3	15.2	5.5	35.3	21.5	16.1	37.4	-4.2	3.7	20 417	17.6	20.3
06 46898	Merced city	63 991	8.9	25.6	11.7	27.1	17.5	9.2	27.8	8.8	-3.2	23 875	22.4	16.5
06 47766	Milpitas city	62 714	7.2	17.4	9.9	37.8	20.7	7.1	33.4	-1.1	-5.3	14 929	19.0	8.7
06 48256	Mission Viejo city	92 780	6.8	20.3	6.6	30.9	24.6	10.8	37.5	1.4	-1.6	70 570	25.5	12.5
06 48354	Modesto city	189 460	7.4	22.5	9.6	29.0	20.5	11.0	32.7	4.2	-1.4	112 069	23.7	15.5
06 48648	Monrovia city	36 817	7.8	19.6	8.4	33.4	20.1	10.7	33.7	1.7	-1.7	17 017	20.5	15.3
06 48788	Montclair city	33 119	8.6	24.3	10.5	30.9	17.1	8.6	29.0	7.2	-3.8	7 914	19.2	21.3
06 48816	Montebello city	61 960	8.2	20.5	10.2	30.2	18.4	12.5	31.4	3.0	0.1	6 757	16.2	29.4
06 48872	Monterey city	29 773	5.0	11.5	13.6	34.1	20.6	15.2	36.1	-9.2	2.8	22 147	14.6	17.2
06 48914	Monterey Park city	59 933	5.4	15.6	8.5	30.2	22.2	18.1	38.4	-4.7	5.7	4 462	9.2	40.5
06 49138	Moorpark city	31 274	7.9	26.0	8.7	32.7	20.2	4.5	31.5	8.2	-7.9	19 513	32.6	5.1
06 49270	Moreno Valley city	142 584	8.7	28.1	10.6	29.7	17.9	5.0	27.1	11.1	-7.4	46 128	28.8	8.3
06 49278	Morgan Hill city	33 635	8.4	22.3	7.8	32.2	22.1	7.1	34.0	5.0	-5.3	20 720	26.8	8.7
06 49670	Mountain View city	70 467	6.0	11.7	8.0	44.4	19.6	10.3	34.6	-8.0	-2.1	38 679	14.3	13.4
06 50076	Murrieta city	44 350	7.5	26.1	6.3	31.2	17.7	11.3	34.4	7.9	-1.1	31 591	31.1	13.6
06 50258	Napa city	72 781	6.8	19.1	8.2	30.2	22.0	13.7	36.1	0.2	1.3	49 448	20.8	18.6
06 50398	National City city	54 405	7.9	22.3	14.1	28.4	16.2	11.2	28.7	4.5	-1.2	7 736	12.6	25.4
06 50916	Newark city	42 471	6.9	20.4	10.1	34.0	20.7	8.0	33.1	1.6	-4.4	16 763	22.1	10.0
06 51182	Newport Beach city	70 022	4.2	11.7	5.9	33.5	27.3	17.4	41.6	-9.8	5.0	61 946	15.5	18.9
06 52526	Norwalk city	103 223	8.6	23.5	10.6	30.9	17.4	9.1	29.7	6.4	-3.3	19 579	19.2	22.2
06 52582	Novato city	47 795	5.9	17.5	6.3	30.4	27.1	12.8	39.6	-2.3	0.4	36 489	21.3	14.9
06 53000	Oakland city	399 477	7.0	17.9	9.7	34.2	20.8	10.5	33.3	-0.8	-1.9	93 613	11.2	15.2
06 53070	Oakley city	25 465	8.1	25.9	7.8	34.3	18.1	5.8	31.5	8.3	-6.6	16 440	30.2	5.8
06 53322	Oceanside city	160 905	7.6	19.8	10.0	31.8	17.2	13.6	33.3	1.7	1.2	85 914	19.7	21.4
06 53896	Ontario city	157 339	9.6	24.6	11.3	32.6	16.1	5.7	27.6	8.5	-6.7	41 607	23.0	12.7
06 53980	Orange city	128 438	7.4	19.2	9.5	34.1	20.3	9.6	33.2	0.9	-2.8	69 940	21.0	13.9
06 54652	Oxnard city	170 595	8.9	22.8	11.9	31.3	17.4	7.8	28.9	6.0	-4.6	34 853	17.1	18.5
06 54806	Pacifica city	38 413	5.1	18.1	8.0	32.5	26.3	10.0	37.6	-2.5	-2.4	23 484	19.9	11.5
06 55156	Palmdale city	116 573	9.2	28.5	8.3	31.6	16.7	5.8	28.2	12.0	-6.6	47 512	30.9	8.7
06 55184	Palm Desert city	41 284	4.4	12.3	6.2	23.4	26.0	27.6	48.0	-9.0	15.2	31 953	12.7	34.0
06 55254	Palm Springs city	42 848	4.8	12.3	6.4	23.6	26.5	26.4	46.9	-8.6	14.0	28 714	9.4	35.8
06 55282	Palo Alto city	58 783	5.0	16.0	4.8	32.2	26.3	15.6	40.2	-4.7	3.2	42 673	18.8	18.1
06 55520	Paradise town	26 451	4.5	16.3	6.0	21.8	24.8	26.6	46.6	-4.9	14.2	24 148	19.6	28.3
06 55618	Paramount city	55 319	10.9	26.0	12.2	31.7	14.0	5.1	25.6	11.2	-7.3	4 938	16.2	23.9
06 56000	Pasadena city	133 871	6.9	16.0	9.2	35.4	20.5	12.0	34.5	-2.8	-0.4	51 998	13.9	19.1
06 56700	Perris city	36 203	10.8	28.7	9.8	31.5	13.1	6.1	25.4	13.8	-6.3	7 832	26.4	13.9

City	Black or African American Total population	Under 18 years	65 years and over	American Indian and Alaska Native Total population	Under 18 years	65 years and over	Asian, Hawaiian, and Pacific Islander Total population	Under 18 years	65 years and over	Hispanic or Latino[1] Total population	Under 18 years	65 years and over	Two or more races Total population	Under 18 years	65 years and over
		Age (percent)			Age (percent)			Age (percent)			Age (percent)			Age (percent)	
	14	15	16	17	18	19	20	21	22	23	24	25	26	27	28
CALIFORNIA—Cont'd															
Highland city	5 142	43.6	3.5	477	36.3	1.9	2 939	29.1	5.9	16 410	43.3	4.0	2 164	47.5	3.0
Hollister city	508	36.6	0.0	493	46.0	6.9	821	26.4	7.9	18 992	37.7	5.0	1 999	46.1	2.1
Huntington Beach city	1 262	22.6	4.8	979	15.9	3.3	17 995	21.7	9.1	28 012	33.2	4.4	8 120	36.7	4.5
Huntington Park city	501	27.9	3.6	656	33.2	3.2	525	26.5	9.1	58 387	36.4	4.5	2 566	30.7	5.4
Imperial Beach city	1 376	33.4	2.6	311	26.0	3.5	1 927	21.5	10.5	10 732	38.9	4.2	1 881	46.8	6.4
Indio city	1 329	30.6	11.4	612	22.2	10.1	809	21.9	14.0	37 043	40.7	3.7	2 282	48.4	1.2
Inglewood city	52 803	27.9	9.0	789	36.4	9.8	1 268	24.5	7.9	51 751	39.0	2.6	4 681	35.2	6.3
Irvine city	1 958	22.8	3.5	322	28.9	9.9	42 715	22.2	4.1	10 415	27.2	3.7	7 765	38.0	3.9
Laguna Hills city	309	20.1	4.2	65	21.5	0.0	3 293	21.9	5.3	5 034	34.2	3.3	1 047	50.6	7.3
Laguna Niguel city	769	25.7	3.6	180	15.0	0.0	4 714	22.5	6.0	6 552	33.5	3.3	2 449	42.0	3.9
La Habra city	979	33.4	2.2	434	37.8	3.7	3 542	22.8	8.2	29 126	37.4	4.2	2 610	47.6	4.4
Lake Elsinore city	1 861	38.9	8.4	536	51.3	1.3	416	27.4	3.6	11 213	43.9	3.8	1 525	55.4	4.1
Lake Forest city	1 051	40.1	3.8	237	28.7	7.2	5 614	21.9	6.8	10 973	34.5	2.9	2 951	44.3	4.1
Lakewood city	5 628	34.9	2.7	477	35.2	2.1	11 194	27.0	6.6	18 172	36.2	5.2	4 544	45.2	5.4
La Mesa city	2 641	27.1	8.0	278	19.1	2.5	2 515	16.7	8.1	7 354	31.6	5.1	2 693	41.0	5.9
La Mirada city	824	35.3	5.8	371	29.4	5.1	7 046	23.6	9.6	15 675	34.6	6.0	2 236	38.0	4.8
Lancaster city	18 846	39.1	4.3	1 356	22.3	8.7	4 826	22.9	8.0	28 846	41.7	3.5	6 402	50.1	2.9
La Puente city	830	35.2	4.1	477	39.2	3.1	3 054	22.6	12.8	33 915	36.2	5.8	2 117	38.5	6.2
La Verne city	928	27.2	5.4	89	50.6	9.0	2 410	21.5	5.4	7 230	32.2	7.0	1 242	43.6	6.7
Lawndale city	3 746	37.2	0.4	233	24.9	2.6	3 391	24.5	6.0	16 628	37.1	2.7	1 901	37.5	3.6
Livermore city	1 256	35.7	5.9	411	31.6	1.0	4 399	23.0	8.5	10 560	36.5	2.9	3 485	49.8	2.1
Lodi city	591	44.5	6.9	405	25.7	3.7	3 141	30.5	13.3	15 436	40.0	3.0	3 046	44.0	4.1
Lompoc city	2 797	24.3	7.6	728	29.8	4.0	1 728	25.4	7.2	15 102	39.9	3.2	2 479	52.0	3.2
Long Beach city	68 594	35.3	4.5	3 749	28.6	2.9	60 185	30.0	8.6	164 927	39.4	2.5	25 334	39.3	4.5
Los Altos city	80	25.0	0.0	103	29.1	0.0	4 239	26.6	10.0	949	30.0	9.0	762	64.4	5.5
Los Angeles city	411 089	27.0	11.5	26 696	30.9	5.4	375 089	18.1	12.1	1 719 916	35.4	3.7	191 299	31.6	5.8
Los Banos city	1 086	37.5	8.8	235	34.9	3.8	737	26.3	11.9	12 904	41.8	3.8	1 983	51.1	4.4
Los Gatos town	101	12.9	3.0	119	33.6	25.2	2 375	25.9	5.9	1 552	27.8	11.3	1 021	38.4	10.0
Lynwood city	9 497	30.3	7.7	515	41.0	7.6	1 053	26.0	8.5	57 320	40.2	2.6	2 602	36.9	2.6
Madera city	1 377	29.3	12.8	1 177	30.0	1.4	973	32.5	7.9	29 443	41.0	3.7	2 487	52.3	4.1
Manhattan Beach city	165	24.8	3.6	89	20.2	2.2	2 122	19.2	5.7	1 751	22.7	6.2	937	46.0	3.4
Manteca city	1 327	37.2	4.2	671	26.7	3.0	1 907	29.5	6.3	12 209	40.7	4.2	3 432	46.4	1.8
Marina city	3 636	15.7	2.4	110	11.8	9.1	4 727	23.6	10.9	5 836	28.6	1.2	1 776	44.0	4.2
Martinez city	1 200	22.7	5.3	304	32.6	2.0	2 357	20.2	11.7	3 828	30.6	5.8	1 812	43.1	1.7
Maywood city	33	18.2	51.5	324	38.6	0.0	102	43.1	19.6	27 083	37.7	3.6	1 099	36.0	4.1
Menlo Park city	2 094	27.0	17.4	97	23.7	0.0	2 491	19.9	8.4	4 955	34.5	4.0	1 000	30.3	5.8
Merced city	4 146	37.0	7.6	799	28.5	0.5	7 266	52.4	4.3	26 529	40.0	4.6	3 600	43.8	5.8
Milpitas city	1 889	22.4	7.9	332	8.1	4.2	33 397	25.1	7.3	10 370	28.4	4.1	2 794	42.7	2.2
Mission Viejo city	971	25.3	5.5	325	31.4	3.4	7 498	26.1	7.8	11 118	34.6	4.2	3 458	44.7	2.5
Modesto city	6 762	30.9	5.0	2 194	30.8	4.7	12 436	35.7	5.6	49 115	40.8	3.9	12 141	42.9	4.0
Monrovia city	3 083	31.3	12.1	435	27.1	10.1	2 516	18.7	10.3	12 977	36.8	4.5	2 103	40.0	7.0
Montclair city	2 187	32.6	7.7	251	41.4	4.4	2 747	25.7	6.7	19 912	39.6	3.9	1 403	35.0	6.0
Montebello city	396	39.4	9.3	664	31.9	13.7	7 146	15.4	18.0	46 257	32.7	9.0	3 416	30.4	10.7
Monterey city	748	20.5	11.5	167	0.0	0.0	2 392	15.1	13.1	3 285	24.7	8.1	1 210	33.2	5.1
Monterey Park city	111	7.2	0.0	377	35.5	13.0	36 863	18.5	17.9	17 269	28.9	12.9	2 346	29.8	8.9
Moorpark city	670	32.2	0.9	99	19.2	20.2	1 404	23.6	2.8	8 651	38.1	3.6	1 312	45.7	2.6
Moreno Valley city	28 298	41.0	4.0	1 314	38.7	8.3	8 294	27.1	5.6	54 713	42.3	2.8	8 875	48.0	1.7
Morgan Hill city	451	24.8	0.0	163	25.2	0.0	2 140	25.1	10.3	9 237	39.3	3.5	1 926	49.2	5.0
Mountain View city	1 813	15.8	4.5	283	11.0	0.0	14 795	15.1	8.1	12 767	28.6	5.0	2 886	34.1	6.9
Murrieta city	1 505	33.8	4.3	450	42.0	3.6	1 598	25.0	8.8	7 961	41.3	5.5	2 383	53.8	2.8
Napa city	349	48.4	2.6	641	27.9	7.3	1 495	21.5	8.6	19 651	38.0	2.5	2 593	39.9	5.6
National City city	3 042	25.4	5.1	603	41.3	6.0	10 312	21.6	17.2	32 253	37.1	6.6	3 069	41.7	6.1
Newark city	1 591	27.7	5.9	490	39.4	2.9	9 323	24.3	9.7	12 070	34.8	4.9	3 797	41.9	3.4
Newport Beach city	329	25.2	4.9	328	13.7	10.7	2 896	14.7	5.7	3 262	17.4	7.1	1 632	26.4	6.0
Norwalk city	4 684	35.0	3.6	1 065	26.7	12.7	12 353	23.9	10.1	64 808	37.2	5.3	5 267	39.0	5.3
Novato city	1 014	25.6	7.7	175	13.7	2.3	2 644	24.3	10.3	6 174	31.3	4.2	1 803	47.4	4.8
Oakland city	141 294	27.8	11.1	2 482	24.5	6.4	62 691	23.4	13.2	87 443	34.5	3.1	20 817	35.3	4.6
Oakley city	754	39.0	7.7	166	27.1	0.0	770	26.8	7.4	6 259	42.1	5.3	1 671	48.5	4.8
Oceanside city	10 225	33.5	3.0	1 252	30.7	7.1	11 265	25.0	10.7	48 684	38.8	3.4	8 162	47.0	3.4
Ontario city	11 205	34.5	4.1	1 322	35.1	3.0	6 674	26.4	6.7	94 100	39.8	2.8	8 260	43.0	2.6
Orange city	2 008	33.3	4.6	796	23.7	3.1	11 978	22.6	9.0	41 380	36.1	2.9	5 024	39.3	5.2
Oxnard city	6 014	28.4	7.3	1 614	32.5	7.7	13 510	23.4	12.6	113 182	37.1	4.1	8 213	40.4	3.9
Pacifica city	1 351	25.7	10.3	116	2.6	5.2	6 068	22.0	7.8	5 643	32.5	7.9	2 750	45.0	3.8
Palmdale city	16 685	43.1	5.0	896	31.6	3.8	4 707	26.9	8.2	43 725	43.8	2.8	7 072	51.6	2.4
Palm Desert city	493	17.6	17.0	130	7.7	20.0	1 061	16.4	7.4	7 081	33.7	4.6	1 246	34.8	3.2
Palm Springs city	1 714	27.5	16.2	322	29.2	6.8	1 849	22.5	12.2	9 869	36.5	4.8	1 186	27.2	10.4
Palo Alto city	1 220	23.7	12.7	210	21.4	15.7	10 372	24.0	9.8	2 738	23.9	7.0	1 824	50.7	5.6
Paradise town	38	0.0	0.0	237	41.4	11.8	263	11.4	18.6	1 179	39.8	4.1	628	31.8	13.1
Paramount city	6 725	36.2	3.3	371	27.2	4.6	2 386	31.8	5.6	40 312	39.9	3.1	2 931	41.9	4.3
Pasadena city	19 258	27.7	11.7	931	32.7	6.0	13 488	14.0	10.7	44 804	33.3	4.6	7 495	32.4	6.3
Perris city	5 810	40.8	6.0	439	44.0	1.1	1 068	34.6	8.5	20 759	43.9	3.1	2 223	47.5	2.2

[1] Hispanic or Latino persons may be of any race.

City	Total households	Family households (percent)							Nonfamily households (percent)							Percent of householders 65 years and over who live alone	Grandparents who are responsible for the care of their grandchildren
		Married-couple family households				Other family households			Two or more unrelated persons		Male living alone		Female living alone				
		Total	With children	House-holder 65 years or over	Total	With children	House-holder 65 years or over	Total	House-holder 65 years or over	Total	House-holder 65 years or over	Total	House-holder 65 years or over			
	29	30	31	32	33	34	35	36	37	38	39	40	41	42	43

City															
CALIFORNIA—Cont'd															
Highland city	13 414	55.7	34.0	6.0	25.3	16.1	2.6	3.9	0.4	7.1	1.4	8.0	3.2	33.7	594
Hollister city	9 791	65.1	41.1	6.1	18.2	12.9	2.0	3.9	0.3	5.5	0.8	7.4	4.0	36.5	280
Huntington Beach city	73 874	51.3	22.5	7.9	14.0	7.0	1.7	10.3	0.5	11.3	1.6	13.2	5.1	39.7	1 107
Huntington Park city	14 893	58.1	42.7	3.8	27.4	16.7	2.0	3.5	0.5	5.5	1.6	5.6	3.2	43.2	649
Imperial Beach city	9 274	45.8	24.3	6.8	25.2	16.4	2.1	7.7	0.1	11.3	1.6	10.0	3.3	35.3	243
Indio city	13 977	57.5	34.8	8.3	23.3	14.4	2.3	3.2	0.5	6.3	1.8	9.8	5.8	40.8	890
Inglewood city	36 834	39.6	24.9	4.0	30.8	18.7	2.5	4.2	0.4	10.8	1.9	14.6	4.5	48.0	1 457
Irvine city	51 144	54.6	29.4	6.0	13.0	7.0	0.7	9.6	0.3	9.7	1.0	13.1	4.0	41.1	485
Laguna Hills city	11 028	62.2	32.1	9.3	11.1	4.9	1.1	4.6	0.5	6.1	1.2	16.1	8.7	47.6	214
Laguna Niguel city	23 230	62.1	32.3	7.2	10.5	6.4	0.8	6.9	0.5	8.3	1.3	12.3	3.9	38.0	75
La Habra city	19 013	55.2	29.0	8.9	19.2	10.2	2.3	4.9	0.5	9.0	2.0	11.8	6.7	42.8	400
Lake Elsinore city	8 872	59.0	36.4	6.4	20.1	12.4	2.1	5.2	0.6	7.6	1.4	8.1	3.7	35.7	313
Lake Forest city	20 042	59.7	31.4	6.3	14.3	7.7	1.2	6.4	0.5	7.7	1.0	11.8	4.2	39.4	452
Lakewood city	26 790	57.9	30.6	9.0	19.3	8.6	4.0	4.4	0.4	7.5	1.8	10.8	6.2	37.3	942
La Mesa city	24 126	40.0	17.5	8.4	16.1	8.6	2.8	9.9	0.6	13.7	3.2	20.3	9.6	52.0	199
La Mirada city	14 567	65.0	32.4	12.7	14.6	5.3	3.1	3.2	0.7	5.2	1.9	12.0	8.5	38.4	427
Lancaster city	38 157	50.1	28.1	6.9	23.2	16.0	1.8	4.9	0.4	10.2	2.1	11.7	5.6	45.9	1 325
La Puente city	9 444	60.4	38.5	8.7	27.1	12.9	4.4	3.4	0.4	4.3	1.0	4.8	3.1	23.2	598
La Verne city	11 070	61.7	29.8	11.1	14.6	7.4	2.2	4.7	0.6	6.4	1.8	12.6	7.6	40.2	165
Lawndale city	9 567	45.8	30.4	3.8	28.8	15.3	2.2	6.7	0.7	10.0	1.3	8.7	2.7	37.4	441
Livermore city	26 149	61.4	33.0	6.1	13.9	7.8	1.2	6.0	0.3	9.0	1.2	9.7	4.0	41.0	493
Lodi city	20 567	51.7	25.9	10.1	17.8	10.8	2.4	5.3	0.4	9.4	2.2	15.8	9.2	47.2	378
Lompoc city	13 062	52.1	29.2	8.2	19.2	12.5	2.3	5.2	0.8	10.1	2.4	13.4	5.5	41.1	429
Long Beach city	163 279	39.7	22.0	5.1	22.1	13.7	2.1	8.7	0.5	14.4	2.2	15.1	5.1	48.8	4 099
Los Altos city	10 455	70.0	31.0	17.0	6.8	3.1	2.5	4.4	1.0	6.9	2.6	11.8	7.3	32.4	58
Los Angeles city	1 276 609	42.9	23.5	6.4	20.3	10.9	2.4	8.3	0.6	13.7	2.2	14.8	5.3	44.3	30 511
Los Banos city	7 758	64.4	38.6	9.0	17.5	12.1	2.1	2.6	0.2	5.8	1.5	9.7	4.9	35.8	255
Los Gatos town	12 007	51.2	22.3	9.6	10.1	5.1	1.5	8.8	0.6	12.5	2.5	17.3	7.8	46.9	12
Lynwood city	14 432	62.0	46.5	2.9	28.3	17.6	2.4	2.1	0.3	3.2	0.4	4.4	2.2	31.9	938
Madera city	11 971	55.3	33.3	8.2	23.9	15.0	2.2	3.8	0.4	6.1	1.5	11.0	5.7	40.2	511
Manhattan Beach city	14 491	50.9	25.3	7.6	7.7	3.9	1.2	12.2	0.6	15.0	1.9	14.2	4.6	40.9	41
Manteca city	16 360	58.9	32.6	7.4	17.8	10.7	1.4	4.7	0.4	7.5	1.5	11.1	5.5	43.1	559
Marina city	6 730	52.0	25.3	8.1	20.4	12.2	2.2	6.5	0.2	8.8	1.2	12.3	5.2	37.8	145
Martinez city	14 323	50.9	23.6	6.7	13.9	7.5	1.9	7.9	0.5	11.7	1.6	15.6	5.3	43.3	274
Maywood city	6 482	63.0	48.3	3.9	26.5	16.7	1.8	3.1	0.1	4.1	0.8	3.2	2.1	33.1	299
Menlo Park city	12 481	47.8	22.3	9.1	10.9	5.6	2.4	9.2	1.1	12.7	2.9	19.5	8.5	47.7	222
Merced city	20 465	47.3	27.7	6.6	24.7	16.4	2.8	5.4	0.5	9.6	2.2	12.9	6.1	45.4	634
Milpitas city	17 158	67.8	37.2	6.1	15.0	7.1	1.7	5.8	0.0	5.4	0.6	6.0	2.3	26.3	594
Mission Viejo city	32 379	67.0	34.3	9.8	11.3	6.0	1.1	4.7	0.3	6.4	0.9	10.6	5.1	34.8	406
Modesto city	65 192	52.5	27.5	8.2	19.8	11.9	2.1	5.2	0.4	8.6	2.0	13.8	6.8	44.9	1 824
Monrovia city	13 451	47.0	24.4	6.8	20.9	11.9	2.9	6.1	0.4	11.0	2.5	15.0	5.8	44.9	276
Montclair city	8 831	59.1	36.4	7.5	22.0	12.0	3.0	3.6	0.5	6.1	1.1	9.3	4.6	34.0	491
Montebello city	18 851	51.9	26.8	10.5	27.0	13.7	4.3	4.1	0.6	7.1	2.1	10.0	6.1	34.8	718
Monterey city	12 656	41.0	16.0	9.1	11.9	6.6	2.4	10.2	1.1	16.3	2.6	20.6	8.2	45.8	37
Monterey Park city	19 563	56.9	23.7	16.3	21.7	8.5	3.9	4.2	0.6	6.6	2.2	10.5	6.8	30.1	363
Moorpark city	8 981	73.9	48.7	4.5	12.0	7.4	1.2	4.1	0.1	4.1	0.7	5.9	1.9	31.3	208
Moreno Valley city	39 341	63.1	40.3	5.1	22.6	14.7	1.8	3.2	0.3	5.1	0.8	6.0	2.2	29.6	2 410
Morgan Hill city	10 813	65.2	35.7	6.5	14.5	8.9	1.2	4.8	0.2	6.7	1.0	8.8	4.4	40.4	218
Mountain View city	31 229	41.4	18.8	5.7	10.1	4.5	1.3	12.9	0.5	19.0	1.6	16.7	5.4	48.3	214
Murrieta city	14 325	71.7	41.0	12.4	10.8	6.8	1.2	3.2	0.4	5.9	1.8	8.4	4.4	30.4	330
Napa city	27 032	52.5	25.8	9.7	14.2	8.1	1.7	6.5	0.6	9.2	2.6	17.6	9.3	49.9	505
National City city	15 144	51.1	29.5	8.6	27.1	15.5	4.2	4.4	0.9	7.7	2.8	9.7	5.8	38.6	801
Newark city	13 024	63.0	32.7	7.2	17.2	7.7	1.9	5.6	0.3	6.3	0.9	7.9	3.1	29.9	421
Newport Beach city	33 148	43.1	14.7	11.3	8.7	3.5	1.7	12.8	0.9	16.3	2.7	19.0	7.7	42.8	127
Norwalk city	26 930	61.8	36.6	8.8	22.1	10.7	3.4	3.1	0.3	5.2	1.3	7.7	4.3	31.0	1 667
Novato city	18 554	53.6	25.1	8.3	14.2	8.8	1.8	6.9	0.7	9.3	2.0	15.9	6.7	44.6	69
Oakland city	150 971	35.0	17.3	5.6	22.9	12.1	3.4	9.7	0.6	14.1	2.6	18.4	6.3	48.2	4 079
Oakley city	7 833	71.5	45.2	6.1	11.3	7.3	0.8	4.4	0.4	5.8	1.0	7.0	3.1	36.0	235
Oceanside city	56 547	55.3	27.1	11.5	14.8	9.2	1.8	7.2	0.8	9.4	2.5	13.2	7.8	42.1	1 438
Ontario city	43 367	57.9	37.0	5.0	22.6	13.3	2.0	4.4	0.3	6.7	1.3	8.3	3.3	39.1	1 864
Orange city	41 030	58.5	29.6	8.3	16.1	8.5	2.0	6.0	0.3	7.1	1.4	12.3	5.2	38.4	728
Oxnard city	43 577	59.9	36.0	7.4	21.0	11.0	3.1	4.8	0.4	6.6	1.7	7.7	4.1	33.9	1 743
Pacifica city	13 975	55.1	25.7	7.5	14.0	6.5	2.1	9.5	0.4	9.4	1.7	12.0	4.9	39.9	294
Palmdale city	34 387	59.9	39.5	5.2	22.2	15.6	1.8	4.1	0.2	6.7	1.1	7.1	2.9	36.2	1 522
Palm Desert city	19 370	48.5	13.5	20.1	10.6	6.0	0.9	7.9	1.5	11.5	3.7	21.5	11.7	40.7	247
Palm Springs city	20 476	35.3	11.1	12.7	11.4	5.6	2.2	11.8	2.8	19.9	6.4	21.6	12.1	51.3	245
Palo Alto city	25 308	50.0	22.9	10.0	8.7	4.5	1.9	9.0	1.0	14.0	2.7	18.4	8.2	45.7	156
Paradise town	11 567	49.5	16.6	16.9	13.3	8.1	2.8	5.3	1.4	10.5	4.6	21.5	14.6	47.6	88
Paramount city	13 963	52.2	39.9	3.4	29.2	18.1	2.4	4.0	0.3	6.3	1.3	8.3	3.6	44.0	464
Pasadena city	51 809	41.5	19.5	6.9	16.0	7.8	2.3	8.7	0.6	14.7	2.2	19.1	6.8	48.2	904
Perris city	9 665	59.9	41.9	5.4	24.7	16.6	1.9	3.3	0.3	5.8	1.8	6.3	2.5	36.5	533

City	Households with Non-Hispanic White householder		Households with Black or African American householder		Households with American Indian and Alaska Native householder		Households with Asian, Hawaiian, and Pacific Islander householder		Households with Hispanic or Latino[1] householder		Foreign-born population	Place of birth (percent)			Percent in non-English speaking households	
	Number of households	Percent that are family households	Number of households	Percent that are family households	Number of households	Percent that are family households	Number of households	Percent that are family households	Number of households	Percent that are family households	Percent of total population that is foreign-born	Europe	Asia	Latin America	Linguistically isolated	Not linguistically isolated
	44	45	46	47	48	49	50	51	52	53	54	55	56	57	58	59
CALIFORNIA—Cont'd																
Highland city	6 869	76.4	1 636	80.2	146	89.0	724	91.4	3 745	88.8	19.1	0.8	4.3	13.4	9.3	33.3
Hollister city	4 698	78.8	181	83.4	125	75.2	285	89.8	4 327	87.6	20.8	0.6	1.4	18.5	8.6	45.0
Huntington Beach city ...	58 502	63.1	518	57.7	421	54.6	5 927	76.7	6 835	77.2	16.9	2.6	7.0	6.0	5.8	23.0
Huntington Park city	935	49.8	150	51.3	170	78.8	122	94.3	13 644	88.5	55.9	0.2	0.6	55.1	34.8	61.3
Imperial Beach city	5 146	62.3	487	64.7	106	100.0	592	83.4	2 722	84.3	20.4	0.8	5.3	13.9	6.5	44.1
Indio city	4 193	66.3	379	78.6	153	81.7	284	73.9	8 967	87.8	33.2	0.5	0.9	31.0	19.7	54.5
Inglewood city	2 220	46.2	21 959	62.9	229	65.9	374	74.3	11 471	90.2	29.5	0.4	0.8	27.2	16.0	36.2
Irvine city	33 143	64.2	772	73.4	81	70.4	12 589	75.9	2 852	69.9	32.1	3.1	24.3	2.4	8.4	39.0
Laguna Hills city	8 521	70.4	133	54.9	29	65.5	920	85.5	1 262	86.8	22.3	3.4	9.2	8.1	6.5	29.6
Laguna Niguel city	18 940	71.1	307	75.2	54	66.7	1 650	80.2	1 759	80.0	17.5	3.5	8.6	4.1	3.4	25.0
La Habra city	10 341	64.8	336	69.3	95	90.5	1 155	83.5	6 858	87.3	27.0	1.5	4.3	20.3	12.6	41.2
Lake Elsinore city	5 419	73.8	580	75.3	117	100.0	108	100.0	2 498	89.3	17.2	1.4	0.9	14.5	8.8	32.4
Lake Forest city	15 117	70.7	285	82.5	88	64.0	1 728	81.3	2 370	89.7	21.1	2.1	8.7	9.1	7.1	28.8
Lakewood city	16 536	72.7	1 976	75.1	136	94.1	3 072	85.0	4 543	88.8	19.0	1.4	9.8	6.7	5.7	32.7
La Mesa city	19 180	54.1	1 063	58.2	128	96.9	917	58.6	2 299	67.7	11.6	2.9	4.2	3.7	3.3	21.6
La Mirada city	8 173	72.1	244	81.1	109	97.2	2 086	88.0	3 804	90.2	22.7	1.6	10.7	9.3	5.3	43.6
Lancaster city	23 825	67.7	5 220	81.2	436	77.8	1 444	82.5	6 496	85.8	13.0	1.1	2.9	8.3	4.6	25.1
La Puente city	1 087	66.8	260	78.8	97	100.0	876	87.1	7 087	91.0	43.5	0.2	5.6	37.5	17.7	68.3
La Verne city	7 779	73.7	322	73.3	30	66.7	747	81.5	2 012	84.8	14.5	1.8	6.7	4.8	2.5	30.2
Lawndale city	2 954	59.7	1 321	70.3	78	80.8	990	78.8	3 934	87.8	38.7	0.9	7.7	28.8	16.6	49.8
Livermore city	21 145	73.8	422	75.4	179	86.6	1 424	76.3	2 425	86.4	12.2	2.2	4.0	5.4	3.4	19.3
Lodi city	14 972	64.5	113	93.8	171	57.9	999	81.8	3 730	86.0	18.8	1.4	3.9	12.7	10.2	26.8
Lompoc city	7 839	65.0	868	68.5	220	85.5	413	72.4	3 523	86.0	17.9	1.5	2.6	13.2	9.6	28.9
Long Beach city	75 409	48.1	25 129	64.7	1 318	61.8	16 512	75.2	41 017	80.9	28.6	1.2	8.6	17.9	14.7	37.2
Los Altos city	8 594	75.7	32	75.0	6	100.0	1 429	82.9	255	86.3	17.6	5.1	9.9	1.0	2.2	25.9
Los Angeles city	522 105	49.7	164 955	57.2	7 872	71.6	132 667	64.5	420 825	82.8	40.9	2.7	10.2	27.0	20.3	45.0
Los Banos city	3 876	76.0	376	82.4	50	72.9	206	92.7	3 071	89.1	18.9	1.7	1.7	15.2	9.4	42.9
Los Gatos town	10 370	59.4	41	65.9	30	73.3	780	81.0	514	62.5	14.9	5.3	7.0	1.2	2.2	21.0
Lynwood city	687	57.8	2 663	80.4	142	100.0	197	94.9	10 820	95.0	43.6	0.1	0.7	42.6	23.8	61.9
Madera city	4 583	64.2	521	74.3	209	95.2	218	86.7	6 495	89.7	31.7	0.5	1.3	29.7	20.7	45.2
Manhattan Beach city ...	12 972	58.7	53	67.9	58	25.9	787	65.9	507	44.8	9.1	2.7	3.7	1.4	0.9	18.9
Manteca city	11 708	73.8	433	78.8	249	74.3	562	85.6	3 049	87.5	10.7	1.5	2.5	6.0	4.2	23.5
Marina city	3 471	67.0	649	65.5	18	61.1	1 433	80.0	915	82.5	22.8	2.5	11.5	7.5	11.2	35.6
Martinez city	11 750	64.1	295	58.0	99	61.6	753	80.5	1 125	66.8	9.5	2.5	4.4	2.0	2.0	18.3
Maywood city	311	42.1	5	0.0	93	87.1	24	58.3	6 107	92.1	55.2	0.1	0.2	54.8	35.2	61.5
Menlo Park city	9 657	54.4	679	75.7	68	85.3	867	65.2	986	86.1	22.8	4.6	5.7	10.2	4.7	29.1
Merced city	10 206	63.7	1 431	72.7	276	64.5	1 297	89.4	6 853	83.0	22.1	0.9	7.4	13.6	12.5	39.1
Milpitas city	5 622	71.9	524	77.3	99	100.0	8 682	88.2	1 895	89.6	47.3	1.2	39.9	5.5	15.0	57.0
Mission Viejo city	26 394	76.6	317	79.8	91	72.5	2 243	87.7	2 807	87.1	16.5	3.0	7.8	4.4	3.0	26.0
Modesto city	45 155	67.6	2 414	72.2	711	73.1	3 053	88.0	11 900	85.5	15.8	1.6	5.1	7.7	6.6	29.6
Monrovia city	7 557	60.4	1 126	67.7	116	70.7	890	78.2	3 465	81.0	21.5	1.8	5.7	13.5	8.6	34.6
Montclair city	3 071	69.1	753	69.7	52	100.0	730	90.1	4 170	90.6	34.1	0.5	6.9	26.0	18.2	48.3
Montebello city	2 793	64.2	144	80.6	204	64.2	2 550	76.8	12 901	82.7	38.0	1.5	9.1	26.9	17.4	66.6
Monterey city	10 076	50.7	286	48.3	65	76.9	946	52.6	966	75.2	17.8	5.8	6.4	4.4	5.6	27.2
Monterey Park city	2 334	58.6	48	33.3	113	80.5	11 756	81.0	5 018	83.4	53.6	0.8	43.8	8.7	28.7	56.1
Moorpark city	6 372	84.7	240	82.1	72	47.2	444	88.5	1 677	91.5	19.2	2.2	3.8	11.9	4.8	33.2
Moreno Valley city	15 665	80.3	8 232	84.2	375	87.7	2 173	88.5	11 962	94.1	20.0	1.0	4.3	14.2	7.5	39.0
Morgan Hill city	7 692	77.4	183	74.9	29	89.7	688	84.0	2 027	87.7	15.2	2.3	3.7	7.8	5.0	29.9
Mountain View city	20 067	45.8	881	46.1	122	52.5	6 038	59.6	3 422	72.5	35.0	6.8	16.1	10.4	12.9	33.6
Murrieta city	11 142	81.5	510	85.3	121	86.8	486	80.2	1 850	87.0	8.6	1.4	2.7	3.9	2.4	22.8
Napa city	21 442	62.6	33	54.5	206	85.0	496	70.2	4 435	86.0	19.3	2.0	1.5	15.3	8.6	23.9
National City city	2 913	60.0	999	63.1	151	63.6	3 072	78.5	7 898	87.1	41.3	0.3	14.5	26.2	18.3	64.8
Newark city	6 514	74.7	535	78.7	94	94.7	2 681	84.7	2 606	88.7	31.6	2.6	16.4	11.4	10.2	43.9
Newport Beach city	30 194	52.0	137	54.0	127	50.4	1 084	58.2	1 183	40.0	10.7	3.2	4.3	1.4	1.8	16.9
Norwalk city	7 433	70.9	1 554	74.6	321	88.8	3 341	87.2	14 029	91.7	36.4	0.6	8.8	26.3	14.6	57.9
Novato city	15 467	65.9	330	83.0	65	38.5	827	79.4	1 534	78.9	17.2	4.0	4.4	7.5	5.9	22.3
Oakland city	49 550	41.6	55 745	60.6	832	56.3	19 981	70.4	20 907	78.6	26.6	1.4	11.0	12.7	14.2	29.5
Oakley city	5 575	80.7	212	84.0	74	79.7	219	79.0	1 518	88.9	9.6	1.0	1.9	6.4	2.5	25.3
Oceanside city	37 759	64.9	3 626	73.8	370	70.8	2 995	77.9	10 810	86.1	20.5	2.0	4.1	13.4	7.9	33.9
Ontario city	16 210	69.3	3 683	76.5	344	90.1	1 860	84.5	20 552	89.8	31.0	0.8	3.1	26.5	15.5	47.6
Orange city	27 556	69.1	574	85.4	209	75.5	3 520	81.5	8 602	88.5	25.1	1.4	7.5	15.4	11.1	33.4
Oxnard city	14 886	66.9	2 081	73.6	448	79.7	3 531	85.9	22 273	90.6	36.9	0.5	5.4	30.6	17.7	55.8
Pacifica city	9 853	66.5	497	63.8	54	38.9	1 704	78.1	1 486	82.6	18.7	3.2	9.9	4.4	2.6	33.1
Palmdale city	16 823	77.8	5 236	77.3	294	73.5	1 276	85.3	9 869	91.5	19.8	1.0	3.2	14.8	7.3	37.3
Palm Desert city	16 511	56.8	210	75.7	56	89.3	368	69.0	2 031	74.6	16.0	3.6	2.3	7.8	5.3	20.1
Palm Springs city	16 206	41.0	674	55.9	139	66.9	541	73.0	2 734	72.5	21.4	4.1	3.4	11.9	8.2	25.6
Palo Alto city	19 757	55.7	509	55.6	60	78.3	3 740	75.2	851	62.4	26.5	9.1	12.8	2.3	5.2	30.8
Paradise town	10 788	62.4	16	0.0	87	66.7	116	73.3	336	74.1	3.7	1.7	0.8	0.6	0.9	9.9
Paramount city	2 274	53.8	2 404	72.2	76	61.8	650	76.6	8 416	92.1	40.6	0.2	2.6	37.3	21.6	57.0
Pasadena city	25 274	49.3	7 604	59.9	325	76.6	5 675	55.1	11 578	75.3	32.3	2.6	10.2	18.1	13.1	40.2
Perris city	2 771	74.6	1 797	77.0	107	86.9	243	88.5	4 657	93.4	27.0	0.2	1.7	24.9	14.4	44.9

[1] Hispanic or Latino persons may be of any race.

STATE Place code	City	Population by age (percent)								+/− U.S. percent under 18 years	+/− U.S. percent 65 years and over	Non-Hispanic White		
													Age (percent)	
		Total population	Under 5 years	5 to 17 years	18 to 24 years	25 to 44 years	45 to 64 years	65 years and over	Median age			Total population	Under 18 years	65 years and over
		1	2	3	4	5	6	7	8	9	10	11	12	13
	CALIFORNIA—Cont'd													
06 56784	Petaluma city	54 538	6.6	19.5	7.3	31.7	24.1	10.9	37.1	0.4	-1.5	41 717	23.9	13.0
06 56924	Pico Rivera city	63 151	8.0	23.0	10.3	30.0	17.3	11.3	30.6	5.3	-1.1	4 754	15.7	32.7
06 57456	Pittsburg city	56 820	8.0	22.7	10.6	30.7	19.8	8.2	30.9	5.0	-4.2	17 763	20.4	12.3
06 57526	Placentia city	47 099	7.2	19.9	9.2	32.2	22.2	9.1	33.3	1.4	-3.3	25 482	21.7	12.4
06 57764	Pleasant Hill city	32 847	6.1	15.1	7.0	33.0	25.6	13.1	39.0	-4.5	0.7	25 118	19.8	15.3
06 57792	Pleasanton city	63 569	6.8	21.1	5.4	33.9	25.3	7.4	36.9	2.2	-5.0	48 010	26.3	8.6
06 58072	Pomona city	149 644	9.4	25.1	12.9	31.0	15.0	6.6	26.5	8.8	-5.8	25 189	17.4	18.2
06 58240	Porterville city	40 025	9.6	25.1	10.8	28.1	17.0	9.4	28.6	9.0	-3.0	16 548	24.0	17.2
06 58520	Poway city	48 295	6.0	24.5	7.8	27.5	25.6	8.5	36.9	4.8	-3.9	37 230	29.4	9.8
06 59451	Rancho Cucamonga city	128 161	6.8	23.0	9.9	33.5	20.7	6.1	32.2	4.1	-6.3	69 400	26.3	7.7
06 59514	Rancho Palos Verdes city	41 301	4.4	18.5	4.5	23.4	30.6	18.7	44.7	-2.8	6.3	25 926	19.4	25.3
06 59587	Rancho Santa Margarita city	47 718	10.3	23.4	5.6	41.7	15.6	3.4	31.9	8.0	-9.0	35 124	33.0	3.6
06 59920	Redding city	81 198	6.6	19.6	9.7	26.4	22.3	15.5	36.7	0.5	3.1	69 457	23.9	17.0
06 59962	Redlands city	63 672	6.2	19.7	10.8	28.3	22.5	12.5	35.1	0.2	0.1	40 414	20.8	16.2
06 60018	Redondo Beach city	63 261	5.8	12.8	5.7	43.8	23.6	8.2	36.7	-7.1	-4.2	44 557	16.2	9.8
06 60102	Redwood City city	75 447	7.4	15.7	8.4	37.5	21.0	10.0	34.8	-2.6	-2.4	40 658	17.7	15.0
06 60466	Rialto city	91 711	9.4	28.2	10.4	29.8	15.9	6.4	26.4	11.9	-6.0	19 503	23.2	15.8
06 60620	Richmond city	99 716	7.7	19.9	9.6	32.0	21.2	9.6	32.8	1.9	-2.8	21 228	12.9	17.2
06 62000	Riverside city	255 093	7.7	22.3	12.7	30.4	18.1	8.8	29.8	4.3	-3.6	116 149	22.8	14.5
06 62364	Rocklin city	36 563	7.8	22.3	7.0	33.4	21.2	8.3	34.5	4.4	-4.1	30 545	28.7	9.2
06 62546	Rohnert Park city	42 388	6.5	18.6	14.7	32.1	20.1	8.0	31.5	-0.6	-4.4	31 147	22.5	9.4
06 62896	Rosemead city	53 280	7.3	20.1	10.9	31.2	19.9	10.5	32.3	1.7	-1.9	4 272	12.3	33.6
06 62938	Roseville city	80 092	7.2	19.7	6.9	31.0	20.9	14.3	36.4	1.2	1.9	63 740	24.8	16.3
06 64000	Sacramento city	407 075	7.0	20.2	10.2	31.2	20.0	11.4	32.8	1.5	-1.0	165 297	16.4	16.9
06 64224	Salinas city	150 724	9.2	22.9	11.9	33.8	15.1	7.1	28.5	6.4	-5.3	36 183	19.2	17.4
06 65000	San Bernardino city	185 388	9.8	25.5	11.2	29.8	15.8	8.0	27.6	9.6	-4.4	53 900	21.7	16.0
06 65028	San Bruno city	40 164	5.9	16.9	8.3	34.7	22.8	11.4	36.3	-2.9	-1.0	19 081	17.6	16.9
06 65042	San Buenaventura (Ventura) city	101 155	6.7	18.3	8.0	31.8	22.6	12.5	36.8	-0.7	0.1	68 700	20.5	16.3
06 65070	San Carlos city	27 697	7.0	15.4	4.0	33.6	26.0	14.0	39.9	-3.3	1.6	22 132	21.4	16.1
06 65084	San Clemente city	49 861	6.3	17.7	6.6	32.2	24.0	13.2	38.0	-1.7	0.8	38 976	21.2	15.6
06 66000	San Diego city	1 223 341	6.7	17.2	12.4	34.4	18.9	10.4	32.5	-1.8	-2.0	602 799	15.7	15.1
06 66070	San Dimas city	35 064	5.8	19.9	8.5	28.2	25.6	12.0	37.3	0.0	-0.4	21 306	21.3	15.2
06 67000	San Francisco city	776 733	4.0	10.4	8.9	41.0	22.0	13.8	36.5	-11.3	1.4	338 886	7.6	13.9
06 67042	San Gabriel city	39 306	6.3	16.9	8.2	34.3	20.9	13.4	35.6	-2.5	1.0	6 838	14.4	30.2
06 68000	San Jose city	893 889	7.6	18.8	9.8	35.9	19.8	8.1	32.6	0.7	-4.3	320 070	19.5	12.5
06 68028	San Juan Capistrano city	33 945	6.9	21.3	7.7	27.5	23.4	13.2	36.4	2.5	0.8	21 211	23.0	18.3
06 68084	San Leandro city	79 286	6.1	16.0	7.4	32.4	22.1	15.9	37.7	-3.6	3.5	33 501	14.3	26.9
06 68154	San Luis Obispo city	44 148	3.6	10.5	33.3	23.8	16.5	12.3	26.2	-11.6	-0.1	34 641	13.0	14.4
06 68196	San Marcos city	55 160	8.5	20.3	9.5	32.3	17.3	12.1	32.1	3.1	-0.3	29 619	21.7	19.4
06 68252	San Mateo city	92 372	6.0	14.3	7.0	35.8	21.8	15.1	37.5	-5.4	2.7	52 027	16.2	20.6
06 68294	San Pablo city	30 121	8.5	23.4	10.5	31.9	16.8	8.9	29.5	6.2	-3.5	4 856	15.0	25.8
06 68364	San Rafael city	56 132	5.9	13.4	8.2	33.1	25.3	14.1	38.5	-6.4	1.7	36 800	15.0	19.7
06 68378	San Ramon city	44 477	7.2	18.9	5.7	35.9	26.0	6.2	36.5	0.4	-6.2	31 941	24.6	6.8
06 69000	Santa Ana city	337 512	10.2	23.9	12.9	34.0	13.5	5.4	26.5	8.4	-7.0	41 798	15.3	19.4
06 69070	Santa Barbara city	92 196	5.5	14.2	14.0	32.0	20.5	13.7	34.6	-6.0	1.3	53 849	12.3	19.2
06 69084	Santa Clara city	102 104	6.4	13.3	11.6	39.2	18.8	10.6	33.4	-6.0	-1.8	49 136	15.8	15.5
06 69088	Santa Clarita city	151 381	7.9	22.3	7.9	34.3	20.7	6.9	33.4	4.5	-5.5	104 729	28.1	8.3
06 69112	Santa Cruz city	54 364	4.9	12.4	20.3	32.8	21.1	8.4	31.7	-8.4	-4.0	39 132	14.5	10.7
06 69196	Santa Maria city	77 113	8.8	22.5	11.9	29.8	15.8	11.2	29.2	5.6	-1.2	24 636	17.6	25.6
06 70000	Santa Monica city	84 084	4.0	10.3	5.8	40.9	24.6	14.3	39.3	-11.4	1.9	59 975	12.2	16.4
06 70042	Santa Paula city	28 631	8.9	22.4	10.9	29.4	17.8	10.6	29.6	5.6	-1.8	7 382	18.4	24.9
06 70098	Santa Rosa city	147 532	6.2	18.1	9.6	30.3	21.9	13.8	36.2	-1.4	1.4	104 450	19.7	18.1
06 70224	Santee city	53 090	6.6	21.7	8.4	32.6	21.8	8.9	34.8	2.6	-3.5	42 781	26.8	10.0
06 70280	Saratoga city	29 855	5.3	20.7	3.8	23.9	29.7	16.6	43.2	0.3	4.2	19 436	21.6	21.7
06 70742	Seaside city	31 786	9.4	20.6	10.7	35.3	15.3	8.6	29.5	4.3	-3.8	11 412	23.8	10.6
06 72016	Simi Valley city	111 547	7.3	21.0	7.9	33.0	23.1	7.6	34.7	2.6	-4.8	81 032	26.5	8.7
06 73080	South Gate city	96 418	10.0	25.6	12.5	32.0	14.4	5.4	26.0	9.9	-7.0	5 663	14.5	31.7
06 73262	South San Francisco city	60 727	6.6	17.5	9.4	31.9	21.7	12.9	35.7	-1.6	0.5	18 565	15.1	24.4
06 73962	Stanton city	36 934	9.2	21.3	10.0	33.8	16.2	9.6	30.0	4.8	-2.8	10 908	18.5	22.5
06 75000	Stockton city	242 714	8.3	23.9	10.8	27.8	18.8	10.4	29.8	6.5	-2.0	78 575	20.6	17.8
06 75630	Suisun City city	26 050	7.7	25.1	9.0	32.4	20.4	5.6	31.7	7.1	-6.8	9 808	26.3	5.9
06 77000	Sunnyvale city	131 905	7.0	13.3	7.5	41.9	19.7	10.7	34.3	-5.4	-1.7	61 535	16.1	16.0
06 78120	Temecula city	57 425	9.1	25.3	8.4	32.7	17.6	7.0	31.3	8.7	-5.4	39 622	32.4	8.4
06 78148	Temple City city	33 296	5.9	18.2	8.9	28.0	25.2	13.8	38.6	-1.6	1.4	12 694	17.4	23.3
06 78582	Thousand Oaks city	116 725	6.5	19.2	7.0	30.2	26.0	10.9	37.7	0.0	-1.5	90 658	24.2	12.9
06 80000	Torrance city	137 933	5.5	17.3	6.8	32.5	23.7	14.1	38.7	-2.9	1.7	71 813	18.9	19.5
06 80238	Tracy city	56 839	9.0	25.3	7.5	35.3	16.6	6.3	30.9	8.6	-6.1	30 909	30.8	7.8
06 80644	Tulare city	43 915	9.3	25.2	9.6	29.8	16.7	9.4	28.5	8.8	-3.0	19 455	25.8	15.1
06 80812	Turlock city	55 488	7.9	21.7	11.6	28.6	18.2	12.0	30.9	3.9	-0.4	33 224	23.6	16.9
06 80854	Tustin city	67 551	8.0	18.7	9.7	38.1	18.5	7.0	31.8	1.0	-5.4	30 668	19.3	11.8
06 81204	Union City city	66 861	7.5	20.4	9.3	33.5	21.0	8.3	32.8	2.2	-4.1	13 611	19.2	13.5

Table A-5. Cities — Age, Ethnicity, and Household Structure

City	Black or African American — Total population	Under 18 years	65 years and over	American Indian and Alaska Native — Total population	Under 18 years	65 years and over	Asian, Hawaiian, and Pacific Islander — Total population	Under 18 years	65 years and over	Hispanic or Latino[1] — Total population	Under 18 years	65 years and over	Two or more races — Total population	Under 18 years	65 years and over
	14	15	16	17	18	19	20	21	22	23	24	25	26	27	28
CALIFORNIA—Cont'd															
Petaluma city	534	17.2	6.9	407	25.6	6.6	2 292	26.9	8.5	8 305	35.2	3.2	2 362	42.0	2.4
Pico Rivera city	411	19.7	16.8	497	27.4	8.7	1 640	28.4	9.1	55 499	32.6	9.4	4 704	32.2	8.2
Pittsburg city	10 338	35.3	8.8	308	28.9	4.9	7 802	26.6	7.6	18 171	37.8	4.8	4 220	48.9	4.2
Placentia city	589	24.6	6.5	433	29.1	6.0	5 307	24.2	7.8	14 547	37.2	4.5	1 699	38.3	2.9
Pleasant Hill city	377	16.2	16.7	173	15.6	15.0	3 390	23.6	5.9	2 690	27.7	5.6	1 426	34.9	1.8
Pleasanton city	736	24.0	3.8	225	37.8	3.1	7 445	29.9	3.9	5 164	33.0	5.0	2 673	50.5	1.6
Pomona city	13 962	30.1	9.0	1 376	33.9	3.2	10 998	25.3	5.9	96 517	40.6	3.4	8 149	42.6	4.4
Porterville city	529	32.7	14.9	403	25.3	6.9	2 160	33.8	7.6	19 859	44.0	3.2	1 784	39.5	5.1
Poway city	834	35.0	5.0	206	24.8	3.4	3 604	26.4	4.8	5 028	37.6	3.4	1 902	43.6	3.4
Rancho Cucamonga city	9 867	29.6	4.0	1 142	23.2	4.6	7 502	24.4	5.3	35 558	36.0	3.9	8 514	48.2	3.5
Rancho Palos Verdes city	878	21.9	8.5	66	36.4	0.0	10 410	26.8	7.9	2 314	26.3	9.2	1 819	45.3	3.9
Rancho Santa Margarita city	936	35.0	0.9	157	14.6	0.0	3 879	26.5	4.0	6 280	36.9	2.1	1 954	55.6	1.7
Redding city	449	18.5	14.7	1 514	42.5	4.4	2 767	37.9	7.6	4 429	40.8	6.0	3 415	48.0	4.5
Redlands city	2 851	37.0	4.7	566	36.0	6.5	3 362	21.0	5.5	15 054	36.6	7.0	3 148	47.3	2.8
Redondo Beach city	1 496	24.2	2.5	266	23.3	2.3	6 189	16.9	3.8	8 495	26.3	5.9	3 158	38.2	3.3
Redwood City city	1 824	16.8	5.7	406	26.8	3.4	7 498	19.8	6.9	23 439	32.5	3.1	3 557	39.7	3.2
Rialto city	20 918	40.2	4.4	775	26.5	5.5	2 280	31.4	8.1	46 865	42.8	3.3	5 199	46.2	5.0
Richmond city	35 700	30.4	10.6	674	35.5	6.8	12 489	24.1	8.7	26 773	36.1	3.5	5 357	40.1	4.2
Riverside city	18 222	33.1	6.1	2 692	31.1	2.6	15 246	19.3	5.4	97 539	39.3	3.4	13 963	43.8	4.9
Rocklin city	490	28.8	3.7	248	26.6	0.0	1 370	26.4	5.8	2 905	38.2	3.5	1 395	48.7	3.8
Rohnert Park city	838	20.2	4.8	412	25.0	0.0	2 567	25.1	5.0	5 707	34.5	3.9	2 433	44.5	4.0
Rosemead city	469	41.2	7.2	256	43.8	2.7	26 002	24.6	10.0	21 846	33.3	7.0	1 699	37.1	4.4
Roseville city	968	32.6	8.3	426	40.1	9.9	3 480	28.1	5.6	9 341	36.6	7.2	2 883	45.3	4.7
Sacramento city	62 468	34.9	7.9	4 940	26.7	6.1	71 092	31.9	11.1	87 968	36.6	5.3	27 185	41.9	4.7
Salinas city	4 781	19.5	2.1	1 986	33.2	2.8	9 638	26.6	13.5	97 030	38.1	2.9	7 580	40.9	3.7
San Bernardino city	29 541	39.3	6.1	2 485	33.4	3.4	8 249	30.1	5.9	87 654	42.4	4.3	11 273	47.7	3.1
San Bruno city	683	22.1	10.0	199	14.6	7.5	6 510	22.1	7.0	9 648	30.9	5.8	3 143	39.1	5.0
San Buenaventura (Ventura) city	1 362	23.5	7.1	942	27.4	6.1	3 308	20.0	8.1	24 586	36.8	4.1	4 491	43.3	3.6
San Carlos city	354	14.7	1.7	5	0.0	0.0	2 010	19.9	6.8	2 172	28.0	7.3	1 384	39.7	2.7
San Clemente city	419	26.7	1.7	398	24.6	2.5	1 293	23.8	5.0	7 885	36.7	4.0	1 348	37.9	7.6
San Diego city	94 539	30.4	7.0	7 573	23.8	5.7	172 542	23.8	7.9	310 533	35.8	4.5	60 952	42.0	3.7
San Dimas city	992	28.5	14.6	177	19.8	6.2	3 188	22.4	6.2	8 235	35.1	7.4	2 342	49.9	3.4
San Francisco city	59 060	21.7	15.0	3 524	14.6	6.8	243 519	17.4	16.2	109 565	22.4	8.8	35 015	27.1	7.7
San Gabriel city	413	31.4	2.9	224	9.8	5.8	19 304	22.0	10.2	11 940	29.5	9.6	1 503	38.7	4.6
San Jose city	30 107	26.4	5.2	7 340	30.7	4.4	242 699	25.4	7.5	269 908	34.5	4.2	48 474	38.8	4.6
San Juan Capistrano city	321	41.7	5.6	306	16.7	18.3	679	17.5	12.4	11 196	37.7	3.8	1 008	48.6	2.8
San Leandro city	7 526	26.5	3.8	717	24.3	7.1	18 925	24.3	9.6	15 933	32.5	7.5	4 722	40.5	7.7
San Luis Obispo city	549	17.3	3.3	225	12.9	8.9	2 339	5.6	5.2	5 061	23.4	4.2	2 032	24.0	5.5
San Marcos city	1 419	29.3	4.3	418	23.4	9.8	2 593	21.1	8.8	20 251	39.7	2.7	2 325	40.3	4.7
San Mateo city	2 304	23.3	10.6	488	31.1	4.9	15 590	17.5	12.1	18 970	30.3	4.6	4 491	37.8	6.9
San Pablo city	5 499	32.9	6.3	323	21.7	6.2	4 974	28.7	10.8	13 413	38.2	3.1	2 117	41.4	6.1
San Rafael city	1 301	29.0	4.0	223	16.1	4.5	3 207	21.4	5.6	13 113	28.6	2.4	2 811	30.3	2.8
San Ramon city	950	24.4	5.2	203	34.0	1.5	6 909	27.8	5.5	3 212	29.4	4.5	1 686	50.0	2.6
Santa Ana city	5 466	32.1	7.6	3 010	39.3	4.1	31 078	24.1	9.5	256 708	38.5	2.5	15 417	37.0	3.5
Santa Barbara city	1 690	17.6	10.1	819	21.7	10.1	2 502	13.9	9.3	32 290	32.2	5.4	3 277	31.0	6.3
Santa Clara city	2 462	20.9	4.2	541	24.8	5.9	29 577	19.7	6.0	16 634	28.5	6.4	5 324	31.6	5.6
Santa Clarita city	3 128	31.1	3.2	606	25.4	6.1	7 889	26.3	5.9	31 243	36.6	3.1	5 963	46.0	3.8
Santa Cruz city	918	17.0	5.6	759	27.5	1.1	2 850	11.6	5.1	9 402	28.6	1.5	2 259	28.2	1.8
Santa Maria city	1 291	22.9	7.6	1 077	39.6	4.3	3 739	25.2	14.1	45 805	39.4	3.4	4 127	43.2	3.9
Santa Monica city	3 117	18.4	10.6	348	22.1	10.1	6 033	10.1	9.4	11 351	24.0	9.3	4 264	27.7	7.3
Santa Paula city	111	47.7	0.0	324	41.0	6.8	298	29.5	5.7	20 452	35.9	5.6	1 263	40.8	2.2
Santa Rosa city	3 421	32.9	4.3	1 970	33.1	4.2	5 786	25.6	6.4	27 991	37.3	2.1	6 623	43.5	5.4
Santee city	725	30.2	0.0	437	13.5	12.4	1 303	15.6	8.0	6 001	36.1	4.2	2 541	50.3	2.2
Saratoga city	158	20.3	12.7	10	0.0	0.0	8 616	33.0	6.6	852	23.9	14.6	867	57.7	4.5
Seaside city	4 037	27.6	16.3	272	13.2	13.6	3 592	23.3	16.7	10 959	38.1	1.7	2 406	45.5	2.2
Simi Valley city	1 205	28.3	4.6	1 042	32.1	6.2	6 890	23.3	7.4	18 843	35.2	3.8	4 257	46.5	3.5
South Gate city	966	31.6	10.2	664	33.3	4.2	895	26.0	4.8	88 844	37.2	3.7	4 742	32.6	5.2
South San Francisco city	1 723	22.6	8.5	467	20.8	13.9	18 492	23.6	8.9	19 245	31.3	6.9	4 572	39.7	5.5
Stanton city	752	30.2	0.0	393	45.3	1.8	5 982	24.5	7.4	18 062	39.1	3.5	1 950	40.5	2.3
Stockton city	26 584	37.3	7.9	2 476	25.7	5.3	49 717	36.8	8.7	78 232	38.5	5.3	16 534	46.4	4.6
Suisun City city	5 196	35.6	5.4	219	33.8	0.0	4 946	29.7	7.9	4 653	42.7	4.0	2 003	52.4	1.8
Sunnyvale city	2 849	20.8	5.3	563	23.4	7.6	43 140	19.6	6.1	20 101	30.1	6.5	5 699	41.1	4.1
Temecula city	1 866	31.2	2.3	454	32.4	4.2	2 784	27.5	6.3	10 903	40.8	3.6	2 792	55.2	1.5
Temple City city	291	38.5	11.3	91	8.8	20.9	12 957	24.9	9.1	6 749	33.7	5.3	1 063	37.4	8.5
Thousand Oaks city	1 291	27.7	5.3	591	30.6	2.7	6 492	22.0	5.8	15 124	32.3	3.5	3 572	46.4	3.5
Torrance city	2 710	25.5	3.1	504	27.6	4.2	39 714	24.1	8.8	17 761	30.3	8.2	7 463	41.8	5.3
Tracy city	3 127	36.2	1.7	506	33.4	9.3	5 051	34.8	7.2	15 731	40.3	3.9	3 610	46.2	2.0
Tulare city	2 588	43.0	5.1	388	34.3	4.6	824	42.5	8.9	19 834	42.1	4.2	2 679	47.7	5.5
Turlock city	777	25.0	3.9	267	20.2	8.6	2 600	30.0	8.9	16 481	41.2	3.4	3 299	36.8	7.3
Tustin city	1 909	25.6	1.8	577	26.9	3.3	9 639	23.0	5.8	23 340	37.5	1.7	2 835	40.0	1.7
Union City city	4 516	32.1	6.0	203	38.4	2.0	30 076	26.9	7.5	15 843	34.4	6.7	4 545	42.2	3.2

[1] Hispanic or Latino persons may be of any race.

City	Total households	Family households (percent)						Nonfamily households (percent)						Percent of householders 65 years and over who live alone	Grandparents who are responsible for the care of their grandchildren
		Married-couple family households			Other family households			Two or more unrelated persons		Male living alone		Female living alone			
		Total	With children	House-holder 65 years or over	Total	With children	House-holder 65 years or over	Total	House-holder 65 years or over	Total	House-holder 65 years or over	Total	House-holder 65 years or over		
	29	30	31	32	33	34	35	36	37	38	39	40	41	42	43
CALIFORNIA—Cont'd															
Petaluma city	19 958	56.3	28.4	7.5	13.8	7.6	1.7	7.1	0.7	7.7	2.3	15.1	7.6	50.1	225
Pico Rivera city	16 490	59.9	33.2	11.6	25.3	11.1	5.1	2.0	0.4	6.0	2.8	6.8	5.0	31.2	695
Pittsburg city	17 821	55.3	30.7	6.6	20.5	11.1	2.3	6.0	0.7	8.4	1.4	9.9	4.1	36.2	743
Placentia city	15 136	62.8	31.6	8.8	15.5	6.7	2.6	5.7	0.5	5.8	1.0	10.2	4.3	30.7	443
Pleasant Hill city	13 663	49.7	22.6	8.3	12.0	6.4	1.8	9.3	0.6	11.0	2.0	17.9	7.5	46.9	84
Pleasanton city	23 280	64.8	35.2	6.1	10.2	5.9	0.7	5.8	0.4	8.3	1.0	10.9	4.3	42.5	211
Pomona city	37 997	55.8	37.0	5.5	23.3	14.0	2.2	5.6	0.6	6.7	1.7	8.5	4.3	42.0	1 956
Porterville city	11 963	53.8	31.7	8.0	24.0	17.7	2.6	3.6	0.6	6.4	1.5	12.2	5.8	39.6	378
Poway city	15 588	69.1	39.0	7.9	14.3	8.8	1.6	3.9	0.3	5.6	0.7	7.1	3.9	32.0	407
Rancho Cucamonga city	41 067	60.3	34.7	4.7	18.3	11.0	1.5	4.6	0.3	7.5	0.9	9.3	3.4	40.0	870
Rancho Palos Verdes city	15 353	70.7	28.7	19.1	9.0	3.8	2.0	3.2	1.2	6.7	1.8	10.3	5.4	24.5	95
Rancho Santa Margarita city	16 440	65.0	44.4	2.3	11.9	8.2	0.2	5.3	0.2	7.7	0.5	10.0	2.1	48.7	149
Redding city	32 191	48.5	20.8	10.8	17.3	11.9	2.2	6.7	0.8	11.3	2.6	16.2	8.4	44.3	609
Redlands city	23 590	51.0	23.6	8.9	17.3	10.5	2.0	5.7	0.3	10.0	2.2	16.0	7.6	46.7	468
Redondo Beach city	28 594	40.9	17.5	4.5	12.7	5.8	1.8	13.4	0.5	16.8	1.6	16.3	4.2	46.1	262
Redwood City city	28 153	50.2	24.5	6.9	14.2	7.8	1.4	8.5	0.5	12.1	1.6	14.9	6.5	47.9	362
Rialto city	24 534	58.2	37.4	5.6	26.0	16.7	2.3	3.0	0.4	5.0	0.9	7.8	4.2	38.4	1 583
Richmond city	34 752	42.7	21.6	6.2	24.7	12.7	3.8	6.8	0.5	10.7	1.9	15.2	5.2	40.4	1 350
Riverside city	82 128	50.7	28.8	6.6	20.7	12.3	2.5	7.2	0.4	9.0	1.6	12.3	5.8	43.5	2 478
Rocklin city	13 293	62.8	33.7	7.5	13.1	8.4	1.0	5.6	0.2	8.1	1.2	10.4	5.1	42.1	363
Rohnert Park city	15 615	47.6	26.1	4.9	15.9	9.5	1.6	12.0	0.5	9.8	1.5	14.6	6.7	54.0	192
Rosemead city	13 930	59.0	34.5	8.2	25.1	10.2	3.8	3.2	0.5	5.2	1.4	7.5	4.5	31.9	555
Roseville city	30 790	58.6	28.1	12.1	13.2	8.3	1.5	5.2	0.5	8.8	1.8	14.3	7.1	38.6	360
Sacramento city	154 893	39.6	19.1	7.3	19.9	11.9	2.4	8.3	0.5	13.9	2.6	18.2	6.7	47.9	4 103
Salinas city	38 151	58.6	37.6	6.6	19.8	12.0	2.2	4.4	0.5	6.8	1.7	10.4	5.1	42.4	1 393
San Bernardino city	56 391	46.4	27.5	6.3	27.1	17.8	2.8	5.5	0.3	9.4	2.0	11.7	5.6	44.5	2 419
San Bruno city	14 558	53.8	25.9	8.3	14.9	6.4	3.0	6.2	0.3	11.0	2.1	14.0	5.3	39.1	328
San Buenaventura (Ventura) city	38 675	49.5	23.2	9.0	16.5	9.5	2.1	7.6	0.6	11.1	2.4	15.3	7.4	45.8	810
San Carlos city	11 376	57.7	26.4	10.3	9.7	4.6	1.6	7.3	1.1	8.3	1.6	16.9	8.4	43.5	56
San Clemente city	19 457	56.6	25.1	11.1	11.2	6.2	1.3	8.9	0.6	11.0	2.1	12.3	6.5	39.9	249
San Diego city	451 126	45.4	22.4	7.4	15.4	8.6	1.9	11.3	0.6	13.3	2.1	14.6	5.4	42.9	8 840
San Dimas city	12 206	58.9	28.2	8.5	15.1	7.7	2.3	4.8	0.2	6.6	1.2	14.6	7.6	44.7	395
San Francisco city	329 850	32.7	13.0	6.8	12.0	4.2	2.6	16.8	0.9	19.1	3.1	19.5	7.0	49.3	5 474
San Gabriel city	12 554	54.9	27.2	8.5	21.9	9.6	2.7	5.0	0.6	7.6	1.9	10.6	5.3	37.8	335
San Jose city	276 408	57.4	30.9	6.6	17.1	8.3	2.1	7.3	0.4	8.8	1.2	9.5	3.7	34.9	8 080
San Juan Capistrano city	10 982	62.5	31.1	11.8	13.1	7.7	2.5	4.6	0.3	6.4	2.1	13.4	7.6	39.7	321
San Leandro city	30 596	47.9	21.4	10.1	17.1	8.1	2.8	6.5	1.0	11.6	2.8	16.9	8.2	44.0	764
San Luis Obispo city	18 656	32.2	13.8	7.4	9.8	4.9	1.1	25.3	0.6	14.6	2.2	18.2	7.8	52.3	72
San Marcos city	18 228	60.5	32.5	10.5	13.6	7.9	2.0	5.8	0.6	6.6	2.1	13.5	8.3	44.2	460
San Mateo city	37 362	47.7	21.5	9.5	12.5	5.6	2.2	8.3	0.7	12.8	2.7	18.7	9.5	49.7	580
San Pablo city	9 089	46.3	29.0	4.5	27.1	15.9	2.1	4.2	0.3	10.1	2.6	12.3	6.7	57.5	420
San Rafael city	22 378	44.9	20.0	8.7	12.5	6.8	1.4	10.4	0.5	12.3	2.3	19.9	8.7	51.0	153
San Ramon city	16 855	61.7	32.2	5.0	9.9	6.0	0.6	7.3	0.4	9.3	0.8	11.8	3.0	38.9	81
Santa Ana city	72 993	62.3	44.0	5.3	20.6	11.2	2.1	4.8	0.4	5.2	1.3	7.2	3.1	35.8	3 204
Santa Barbara city	35 720	41.2	18.7	8.3	12.8	6.7	1.8	13.0	0.9	13.2	3.0	19.8	9.2	52.6	440
Santa Clara city	38 564	49.7	22.6	7.2	13.7	5.6	2.2	10.7	0.4	12.7	1.8	13.3	5.5	42.6	589
Santa Clarita city	50 697	61.7	37.0	5.1	13.8	8.3	1.1	5.5	0.3	7.7	1.1	11.3	5.0	48.1	914
Santa Cruz city	20 368	38.0	17.8	6.0	14.4	8.9	1.6	18.4	0.6	14.0	1.7	15.3	5.6	47.1	144
Santa Maria city	22 111	57.6	32.0	10.1	18.1	10.6	2.5	4.4	0.6	7.9	2.1	12.0	7.2	41.5	648
Santa Monica city	44 503	28.3	11.6	5.3	9.7	4.9	1.1	10.8	0.8	23.7	3.2	27.5	7.4	59.5	257
Santa Paula city	8 231	61.0	34.5	10.2	18.2	11.0	2.4	3.6	0.5	5.2	2.5	12.0	7.6	43.6	318
Santa Rosa city	56 066	47.8	22.3	9.5	15.3	9.3	1.5	9.0	0.7	9.9	2.5	17.9	9.2	50.0	723
Santee city	18 487	58.7	30.2	7.1	18.1	11.3	2.3	5.1	0.3	7.0	1.3	11.1	5.1	39.8	454
Saratoga city	10 484	75.8	36.7	15.8	6.3	2.5	1.9	3.2	0.6	5.8	2.3	8.9	5.2	29.2	89
Seaside city	9 872	55.6	32.9	6.0	20.2	10.1	3.3	6.2	0.8	7.8	1.9	10.2	4.9	40.0	334
Simi Valley city	36 543	64.1	33.7	6.5	15.7	8.8	1.3	5.6	0.6	6.4	1.0	8.2	3.7	35.9	679
South Gate city	23 165	62.6	44.9	4.4	24.9	14.5	2.3	2.4	0.3	4.2	1.1	5.9	3.7	40.7	1 126
South San Francisco city	19 749	57.4	29.0	10.4	17.9	7.7	2.7	4.9	0.3	8.3	2.8	11.4	6.7	41.6	688
Stanton city	10 769	52.3	31.6	6.7	20.0	10.4	2.7	5.9	0.4	7.8	1.7	14.0	7.4	48.3	215
Stockton city	78 594	49.7	27.4	7.5	22.5	14.2	2.4	5.0	0.6	9.3	2.3	13.6	6.6	45.9	3 310
Suisun City city	7 941	64.2	38.0	4.6	17.9	10.6	2.2	3.8	0.3	6.5	0.7	7.6	2.1	28.3	450
Sunnyvale city	52 610	51.2	23.0	7.4	11.4	5.1	1.8	10.3	0.6	14.2	1.5	12.8	5.1	40.3	642
Temecula city	18 249	69.5	43.4	7.7	13.7	9.3	1.2	4.1	0.5	5.7	0.8	7.1	2.4	25.5	410
Temple City city	11 393	57.6	28.7	9.8	18.5	8.7	2.3	3.8	0.2	8.2	1.7	11.9	5.6	37.2	173
Thousand Oaks city	41 792	63.6	32.0	9.4	11.6	6.2	1.5	5.3	0.4	8.0	1.5	11.5	5.5	38.3	600
Torrance city	54 540	52.7	24.9	9.5	13.9	6.5	2.7	5.9	0.5	12.0	2.3	15.5	7.1	42.5	803
Tracy city	17 529	66.5	42.8	4.8	14.7	9.2	1.4	4.5	0.1	6.3	1.2	8.1	4.4	46.9	553
Tulare city	13 514	57.4	32.0	8.8	22.2	14.7	2.0	3.6	0.4	6.2	1.8	10.4	6.4	42.3	432
Turlock city	18 385	55.9	30.4	9.6	17.4	10.6	2.0	5.4	0.3	8.5	2.2	12.8	6.7	42.8	510
Tustin city	23 853	51.3	28.3	4.7	16.3	9.3	1.6	8.4	0.3	10.4	1.2	13.6	4.2	44.8	361
Union City city	18 633	67.2	37.5	6.4	17.4	7.9	2.2	4.1	0.1	5.2	1.1	6.1	3.4	34.1	808

City	Households with Non-Hispanic White householder		Households with Black or African American householder		Households with American Indian and Alaska Native householder		Households with Asian, Hawaiian, and Pacific Islander householder		Households with Hispanic or Latino[1] householder		Foreign-born population	Place of birth (percent)			Percent in non-English speaking households	
	Number of households	Percent that are family households	Number of households	Percent that are family households	Number of households	Percent that are family households	Number of households	Percent that are family households	Number of households	Percent that are family households	Percent of total population that is foreign-born	Europe	Asia	Latin America	Linguistically isolated	Not linguistically isolated
	44	45	46	47	48	49	50	51	52	53	54	55	56	57	58	59
CALIFORNIA—Cont'd																
Petaluma city	16 812	68.2	178	75.3	108	85.2	660	82.0	1 775	85.2	14.4	3.0	3.0	7.5	4.8	20.3
Pico Rivera city	2 105	61.6	117	81.2	175	90.9	446	83.2	13 506	89.0	33.9	0.3	1.8	31.4	12.2	72.8
Pittsburg city	7 405	67.2	3 478	74.5	113	59.3	2 043	89.5	4 228	85.6	24.8	0.9	8.9	13.8	9.4	39.6
Placentia city	9 970	73.8	186	76.9	90	92.2	1 605	87.2	3 131	87.7	24.5	1.9	8.3	13.4	9.7	35.4
Pleasant Hill city	10 973	60.4	181	43.1	91	49.5	1 153	70.3	927	68.5	14.0	3.2	7.3	2.5	3.9	19.9
Pleasanton city	18 571	73.7	270	80.7	46	34.8	2 385	85.9	1 537	73.2	14.2	3.3	7.8	2.1	3.1	21.6
Pomona city	10 066	59.9	4 568	69.4	337	77.2	2 671	78.8	19 800	91.6	36.7	0.5	5.0	30.7	18.6	54.5
Porterville city	6 333	72.0	128	91.4	157	75.2	492	89.8	4 660	84.5	22.6	0.4	4.1	17.9	14.4	39.5
Poway city	12 962	82.6	251	84.5	48	89.6	910	89.7	1 026	92.0	10.6	1.7	4.9	3.3	2.4	21.3
Rancho Cucamonga city	25 268	75.6	3 409	73.8	271	82.3	2 288	88.9	8 787	86.0	13.8	1.1	5.1	6.6	3.4	32.1
Rancho Palos Verdes city	10 786	76.1	282	83.3	14	57.1	3 271	92.1	665	74.6	26.8	5.0	18.9	1.5	6.4	34.2
Rancho Santa Margarita city	12 854	75.3	338	80.5	49	100.0	1 206	88.1	1 638	83.0	13.2	1.7	5.8	4.8	2.6	23.8
Redding city	28 787	65.2	206	65.0	444	79.5	691	82.8	1 274	67.4	5.1	0.8	2.5	1.0	1.5	10.6
Redlands city	16 864	65.1	1 004	68.9	178	78.7	1 083	71.3	4 115	80.5	12.8	1.9	4.3	5.6	4.1	27.1
Redondo Beach city	21 992	51.6	593	52.3	111	64.9	2 446	59.7	2 786	66.8	17.0	3.5	6.9	4.8	3.7	25.9
Redwood City city	18 461	58.4	716	58.7	121	74.4	2 801	66.9	5 645	83.3	30.0	3.9	6.7	18.1	11.6	35.0
Rialto city	7 322	73.5	6 140	83.0	225	68.0	512	94.7	10 014	92.8	22.3	0.5	1.4	19.6	9.9	43.0
Richmond city	10 520	52.2	12 954	69.4	204	84.3	3 849	75.4	6 255	83.5	25.8	1.1	8.7	15.3	11.5	31.9
Riverside city	45 854	66.1	6 356	69.7	752	74.2	4 713	66.4	22 812	84.2	19.9	1.1	3.9	14.2	8.5	36.5
Rocklin city	11 499	75.2	170	80.6	65	73.8	472	76.7	804	79.5	5.2	1.4	1.9	1.2	0.7	14.2
Rohnert Park city	12 564	62.3	290	67.6	144	65.3	772	72.7	1 397	77.9	12.3	1.7	4.8	4.9	2.9	21.7
Rosemead city	1 972	56.5	126	90.5	70	94.3	6 236	90.7	5 371	86.9	56.4	0.5	37.1	18.2	31.0	57.8
Roseville city	25 954	70.7	377	62.6	132	84.1	1 015	82.1	2 700	77.7	9.0	2.3	2.9	3.0	2.5	17.1
Sacramento city	80 528	49.2	22 407	66.3	1 767	58.9	20 254	73.5	25 433	74.1	20.3	2.0	9.9	6.9	9.8	30.0
Salinas city	14 569	63.5	1 034	67.9	461	79.2	2 867	79.9	18 807	91.1	35.2	0.6	3.3	30.9	21.0	50.3
San Bernardino city	21 935	61.5	9 672	74.1	658	72.9	2 194	80.0	20 758	85.5	20.6	0.8	3.4	16.0	11.4	40.1
San Bruno city	8 464	62.0	286	50.4	77	36.4	3 616	70.5	2 508	81.7	32.4	4.5	12.4	11.6	8.8	42.9
San Buenaventura (Ventura) city	29 721	63.2	551	61.5	339	62.5	1 060	70.3	6 352	81.0	13.0	1.7	2.6	7.9	4.8	23.8
San Carlos city	9 490	67.1	155	58.1	5	100.0	696	70.1	747	70.4	15.6	5.2	5.6	2.9	2.8	23.8
San Clemente city	16 424	67.3	188	38.8	130	65.4	461	72.2	1 889	77.1	13.5	2.2	2.2	7.7	5.0	19.3
San Diego city	277 282	52.7	34 138	65.5	2 559	65.1	48 364	76.6	79 175	77.8	25.7	2.4	10.5	11.3	9.8	36.8
San Dimas city	8 208	70.4	413	64.4	84	56.0	1 033	85.6	2 194	81.0	15.4	1.4	7.2	5.7	3.1	33.9
San Francisco city	184 523	31.6	24 273	50.3	1 321	33.8	79 765	67.3	31 874	61.0	36.8	5.1	22.6	7.8	15.0	39.0
San Gabriel city	3 059	63.8	130	82.3	102	97.1	5 537	80.6	3 578	81.8	52.6	1.1	39.3	11.8	27.8	51.1
San Jose city	132 609	66.3	10 513	70.0	1 908	77.7	65 569	83.9	59 174	84.2	36.9	2.5	20.4	12.8	14.8	46.2
San Juan Capistrano city	8 588	71.5	39	82.1	71	83.1	159	84.3	2 066	91.3	23.7	2.3	1.8	18.9	9.7	29.9
San Leandro city	16 109	56.2	3 291	60.3	303	73.9	5 268	82.4	4 669	77.7	27.4	3.3	16.4	6.6	10.7	36.8
San Luis Obispo city	15 252	42.7	220	35.0	141	36.9	880	35.5	1 689	43.8	9.5	2.0	3.5	3.3	2.0	19.8
San Marcos city	12 499	67.9	512	77.0	111	65.8	726	83.1	4 091	91.4	25.6	2.1	3.5	19.2	12.4	31.4
San Mateo city	25 037	54.6	933	61.3	153	41.8	5 588	68.3	4 723	79.5	30.2	4.6	11.2	11.8	9.7	35.5
San Pablo city	2 358	50.1	2 102	69.4	63	76.2	1 318	84.7	2 779	89.3	40.9	0.5	12.6	26.8	22.0	44.2
San Rafael city	17 310	52.4	457	62.4	80	56.3	1 123	67.8	2 949	81.6	28.1	4.3	5.3	17.3	13.7	26.0
San Ramon city	13 050	69.4	368	70.4	77	75.3	2 143	86.3	898	71.6	16.4	2.9	10.3	1.6	1.8	27.2
Santa Ana city	17 558	55.4	1 552	72.1	643	87.4	7 689	83.9	45 309	93.9	53.3	0.4	7.0	45.5	30.0	56.6
Santa Barbara city	25 171	47.4	710	49.6	318	67.0	867	46.9	8 154	77.3	25.3	4.0	2.3	17.9	11.0	33.8
Santa Clara city	22 031	56.0	920	65.3	167	68.9	9 757	73.4	4 474	78.2	35.0	4.6	23.0	5.5	10.5	40.4
Santa Clarita city	38 628	73.1	1 103	82.2	180	66.7	2 256	82.0	7 511	85.7	16.3	2.0	4.2	9.0	5.7	26.3
Santa Cruz city	16 278	50.3	348	55.5	225	73.8	842	47.1	2 133	74.0	15.1	3.2	3.3	7.8	6.0	25.5
Santa Maria city	10 631	62.4	451	64.1	332	87.3	1 052	85.9	9 509	89.7	32.0	0.9	3.2	27.5	19.8	41.8
Santa Monica city	34 771	35.5	1 443	39.8	119	46.2	2 793	43.5	3 978	56.3	24.8	8.4	7.9	6.2	6.2	29.7
Santa Paula city	3 268	64.0	35	57.1	104	91.3	75	90.7	4 748	90.1	29.5	0.4	0.5	28.4	19.3	48.2
Santa Rosa city	45 643	60.2	1 059	68.6	575	72.7	1 679	71.4	5 917	82.3	16.3	2.0	3.1	9.9	6.3	22.4
Santee city	16 079	76.1	171	77.8	150	84.0	332	86.4	1 317	81.9	6.6	1.6	2.0	2.5	1.3	17.8
Saratoga city	7 638	78.9	36	86.1	10	0.0	2 456	93.4	218	69.3	25.6	5.1	18.6	0.5	5.3	35.3
Seaside city	4 623	69.0	1 494	72.2	101	82.2	1 048	81.6	2 230	89.2	31.2	2.2	6.9	20.9	16.6	37.0
Simi Valley city	29 078	78.1	402	80.8	349	83.1	1 890	86.3	4 326	88.3	15.1	2.3	5.1	6.6	3.2	26.7
South Gate city	2 778	55.4	336	63.1	203	76.8	261	69.7	19 733	92.9	49.3	0.4	0.6	40.1	23.9	68.2
South San Francisco city	8 436	63.7	639	75.0	182	49.5	5 247	84.9	4 719	86.7	39.1	2.4	19.7	15.2	10.9	56.2
Stanton city	4 885	56.8	268	57.8	68	79.4	1 680	85.7	3 681	86.6	41.3	1.3	12.8	26.5	21.0	46.4
Stockton city	33 522	62.2	9 380	73.3	789	75.2	12 790	82.5	20 199	81.3	24.5	0.6	12.6	10.7	13.5	38.5
Suisun City city	3 741	77.0	1 642	80.9	34	76.5	1 162	90.8	1 067	89.8	19.8	1.0	13.0	5.1	4.4	36.8
Sunnyvale city	29 287	55.0	1 189	59.5	236	66.1	15 607	72.1	5 226	76.6	39.4	4.6	26.6	6.9	11.8	41.4
Temecula city	13 598	81.1	679	97.2	133	90.2	794	85.5	2 738	88.6	12.0	1.8	3.5	5.9	3.6	24.5
Temple City city	5 435	67.0	99	72.7	48	58.3	3 734	86.7	1 915	81.1	38.6	1.9	30.0	5.8	17.0	43.2
Thousand Oaks city	34 862	73.9	473	74.0	210	77.6	2 043	80.8	3 656	86.5	15.6	3.2	4.6	6.4	4.0	22.8
Torrance city	32 457	61.8	1 223	59.0	163	74.2	13 792	75.8	5 416	73.8	27.6	2.7	18.9	4.6	9.5	34.4
Tracy city	10 957	78.4	979	87.7	185	84.3	1 229	81.9	3 748	87.3	16.8	1.7	5.3	9.0	6.4	29.8
Tulare city	7 198	74.2	780	81.7	142	81.7	137	86.1	4 931	87.9	17.6	3.0	1.5	13.0	8.4	41.2
Turlock city	12 646	69.5	218	50.9	100	75.0	726	72.5	3 870	86.5	21.5	2.7	6.9	11.0	8.3	37.6
Tustin city	14 089	58.6	798	64.4	192	56.8	2 932	80.2	5 313	86.0	33.3	1.9	11.9	18.5	13.4	40.8
Union City city	5 363	73.8	1 486	83.4	65	81.5	7 420	92.1	3 669	87.4	44.0	1.2	32.7	8.6	12.3	59.1

[1] Hispanic or Latino persons may be of any race.

STATE Place code	City	Total population	Under 5 years	5 to 17 years	18 to 24 years	25 to 44 years	45 to 64 years	65 years and over	Median age	+/− U.S. percent under 18 years	+/− U.S. percent 65 years and over	Non-Hispanic White Total population	Age (percent) Under 18 years	65 years and over
		1	2	3	4	5	6	7	8	9	10	11	12	13
	CALIFORNIA—Cont'd													
06 81344	Upland city	68 427	6.9	20.4	9.4	29.5	23.0	10.8	34.5	1.6	−1.6	37 435	21.8	15.7
06 81554	Vacaville city	88 644	6.9	20.0	8.7	36.4	19.8	8.2	33.9	1.2	−4.2	55 827	25.1	10.6
06 81666	Vallejo city	116 351	6.9	20.5	8.9	29.9	22.6	11.2	34.9	1.7	−1.2	35 533	16.7	19.6
06 82590	Victorville city	64 516	8.7	25.7	8.6	28.8	16.8	11.4	30.7	8.7	−1.0	30 213	27.6	16.1
06 82954	Visalia city	91 513	8.2	23.1	9.7	28.6	19.4	10.9	31.7	5.6	−1.5	49 979	23.9	16.1
06 82996	Vista city	90 131	8.6	21.1	11.5	32.9	16.0	9.9	30.3	4.0	−2.5	45 016	21.7	16.8
06 83332	Walnut city	30 004	4.7	22.9	10.1	27.3	27.8	7.2	37.2	1.9	−5.2	5 547	22.9	11.4
06 83346	Walnut Creek city	64 583	4.6	13.0	4.9	27.8	24.6	25.0	45.1	−8.1	12.6	52 199	16.2	28.8
06 83668	Watsonville city	44 475	9.1	24.7	12.1	30.5	14.8	8.8	27.4	8.1	−3.6	8 450	16.0	26.4
06 84200	West Covina city	104 893	7.5	20.7	9.8	30.8	20.5	10.7	32.7	2.5	−1.7	24 510	16.7	25.0
06 84410	West Hollywood city	35 716	1.6	3.9	5.7	49.3	22.6	16.9	39.4	−20.2	4.5	28 995	4.6	19.3
06 84550	Westminster city	87 884	7.2	18.9	8.8	32.4	21.8	11.0	34.1	0.4	−1.4	31 707	19.4	18.2
06 84816	West Sacramento city	31 604	7.7	22.3	9.3	27.6	20.5	12.7	34.0	4.3	0.3	17 274	23.0	17.5
06 85292	Whittier city	83 838	7.8	20.6	10.1	30.9	18.2	12.5	32.8	2.7	0.1	31 144	17.8	24.5
06 86328	Woodland city	49 132	8.0	21.7	9.4	30.3	20.2	10.4	32.4	4.0	−2.0	25 802	23.1	15.6
06 86832	Yorba Linda city	58 595	5.8	23.3	7.0	29.2	27.1	7.6	37.4	3.4	−4.8	43 393	27.9	8.6
06 86972	Yuba City city	36 586	7.7	21.2	10.5	29.7	18.6	12.3	31.8	3.2	−0.1	21 379	23.3	17.8
06 87042	Yucaipa city	41 299	6.5	22.3	7.6	27.5	20.8	15.2	36.8	3.1	2.8	31 519	25.5	18.3
08 00000	COLORADO	4 301 261	6.9	18.6	9.9	32.8	22.1	9.7	34.3	−0.2	−2.7	3 201 519	22.7	11.3
08 03455	Arvada city	102 505	6.4	19.8	8.0	30.4	24.8	10.6	37.2	0.5	−1.8	87 440	24.4	11.8
08 04000	Aurora city	275 936	8.0	19.6	10.0	34.9	20.2	7.4	31.7	1.9	−5.0	163 406	22.4	10.3
08 07850	Boulder city	94 510	3.9	10.7	25.9	33.1	18.4	8.0	29.0	−11.1	−4.4	79 713	13.2	9.0
08 09280	Broomfield city	38 297	7.7	21.6	7.2	36.1	20.7	6.7	33.2	3.6	−5.7	31 980	27.7	7.4
08 16000	Colorado Springs city	360 798	7.5	19.0	10.2	32.9	20.9	9.6	33.6	0.8	−2.8	271 968	24.0	11.3
08 20000	Denver city	554 636	6.7	15.1	10.7	36.5	19.8	11.2	33.1	−3.9	−1.2	287 857	12.4	16.1
08 24785	Englewood city	31 589	5.4	14.3	9.9	36.1	19.7	14.6	36.2	−6.0	2.2	25 673	17.8	16.9
08 27425	Fort Collins city	118 440	6.0	15.3	22.0	31.8	17.0	7.8	28.2	−4.4	−4.6	101 184	20.2	8.6
08 31660	Grand Junction city	42 225	5.8	15.5	12.0	26.2	22.5	18.0	38.8	−4.4	5.6	35 984	19.2	19.9
08 32155	Greeley city	76 818	7.5	18.2	19.2	26.8	18.1	10.2	28.5	0.0	−2.2	51 480	20.2	13.6
08 43000	Lakewood city	144 089	6.0	16.1	9.8	32.1	23.9	12.1	36.5	−3.6	−0.3	113 810	19.4	14.1
08 45255	Littleton city	40 416	5.5	17.6	8.5	29.9	24.6	14.0	38.6	−2.6	1.6	35 098	21.7	15.4
08 45970	Longmont city	71 303	7.8	20.1	8.7	33.3	21.0	9.1	34.0	2.2	−3.3	54 756	25.1	11.0
08 46465	Loveland city	50 680	7.0	19.8	7.6	31.1	21.7	12.7	36.0	1.1	0.3	44 939	25.5	13.7
08 54330	Northglenn city	31 635	7.4	19.1	9.8	33.6	19.6	10.4	33.2	0.8	−2.0	22 986	23.4	12.2
08 62000	Pueblo city	102 235	6.6	18.5	10.2	27.0	21.1	16.7	36.5	−0.6	4.3	52 188	18.6	22.9
08 77290	Thornton city	82 433	8.5	21.3	9.8	35.9	18.8	5.7	30.8	4.1	−6.7	59 627	27.1	6.7
08 83835	Westminster city	101 197	7.1	19.8	9.3	36.7	20.8	6.4	32.6	1.2	−6.0	76 681	24.7	7.5
08 84440	Wheat Ridge city	33 015	6.3	14.9	7.3	29.3	23.0	19.2	40.0	−4.5	6.8	27 096	18.4	22.2
09 00000	CONNECTICUT	3 405 565	6.5	18.2	7.9	30.5	23.1	13.8	37.4	−1.0	1.4	2 637 525	22.2	16.3
09 08000	Bridgeport city	139 529	8.0	20.2	11.2	31.0	18.1	11.4	31.4	2.5	−1.0	43 174	14.2	25.3
09 08420	Bristol city	60 062	6.3	16.9	7.2	32.8	22.1	14.8	37.6	−2.5	2.4	53 512	21.4	16.2
09 18430	Danbury city	74 848	6.6	15.0	10.0	35.8	21.5	11.1	35.2	−4.1	−1.3	50 732	18.9	14.5
09 37000	Hartford city	121 578	8.4	21.6	12.5	30.0	17.7	9.7	29.7	4.3	−2.7	21 513	9.6	25.6
09 46450	Meriden city	58 244	6.8	18.8	8.3	29.7	22.4	14.0	36.2	−0.1	1.6	40 761	20.2	18.4
09 47290	Middletown city	43 167	6.5	15.3	7.6	35.5	21.6	13.4	36.3	−3.9	1.0	33 317	18.2	15.9
09 47500	Milford city	52 305	5.8	16.5	6.0	31.5	25.3	14.9	39.4	−3.4	2.5	47 515	21.3	15.8
09 49880	Naugatuck borough	30 989	6.9	20.0	7.1	33.6	20.8	11.6	35.5	1.2	−0.8	27 404	25.6	12.8
09 50370	New Britain city	71 538	6.2	17.9	13.0	28.8	18.4	15.7	33.9	−1.6	3.3	42 418	14.9	24.0
09 52000	New Haven city	123 626	6.9	18.4	16.3	31.4	16.7	10.3	29.3	−0.4	−2.1	44 074	11.3	19.0
09 52280	New London city	25 671	6.6	16.1	17.5	30.2	17.4	12.1	31.2	−3.0	−0.3	14 300	12.6	17.3
09 55990	Norwalk city	82 951	6.6	15.3	7.1	35.7	22.4	12.8	36.6	−3.8	0.4	53 283	18.2	16.6
09 56200	Norwich city	36 117	5.9	18.3	9.0	29.7	21.9	15.1	36.9	−1.5	2.7	29 048	20.7	18.0
09 68100	Shelton city	38 101	6.2	17.2	5.7	30.3	25.9	14.7	39.8	−2.3	2.3	35 041	22.8	15.5
09 73000	Stamford city	117 083	6.7	15.3	7.2	35.4	21.5	13.9	36.4	−3.7	1.5	71 474	18.4	18.7
09 76500	Torrington city	35 202	5.9	17.1	6.2	31.2	22.1	17.5	39.1	−2.7	5.1	32 275	21.9	18.7
09 80000	Waterbury city	107 271	7.7	18.8	8.5	30.4	19.7	15.0	34.9	0.8	2.6	62 485	18.2	21.9
09 82800	West Haven city	52 360	6.1	16.9	9.5	31.8	21.3	14.4	36.4	−2.7	2.0	36 466	19.1	18.7
10 00000	DELAWARE	783 600	6.5	18.2	9.6	30.3	22.4	13.0	36.0	−1.0	0.6	568 356	22.0	15.5
10 21200	Dover city	32 470	6.8	16.7	15.4	28.2	19.5	13.4	32.9	−2.2	1.0	17 510	18.9	18.5
10 50670	Newark city	28 570	3.1	8.9	43.9	19.8	15.3	9.0	22.6	−13.7	−3.4	24 649	11.5	9.5
10 77580	Wilmington city	72 664	6.7	18.9	9.8	32.1	19.8	12.6	33.7	−0.1	0.2	23 304	12.4	21.7
11 00000	DISTRICT OF COLUMBIA	572 059	5.7	14.3	12.8	33.2	21.8	12.3	34.6	−5.7	−0.1	158 617	8.5	11.4
11 50000	Washington city	572 059	5.7	14.3	12.8	33.2	21.8	12.3	34.6	−5.7	−0.1	158 617	8.5	11.4

City	Black or African American			American Indian and Alaska Native			Asian, Hawaiian, and Pacific Islander			Hispanic or Latino[1]			Two or more races		
		Age (percent)			Age (percent)			Age (percent)			Age (percent)			Age (percent)	
	Total population	Under 18 years	65 years and over	Total population	Under 18 years	65 years and over	Total population	Under 18 years	65 years and over	Total population	Under 18 years	65 years and over	Total population	Under 18 years	65 years and over
	14	15	16	17	18	19	20	21	22	23	24	25	26	27	28
CALIFORNIA—Cont'd															
Upland city	4 924	34.7	3.9	653	28.5	4.4	5 068	24.7	5.9	18 781	36.5	4.5	3 189	39.9	5.6
Vacaville city	8 270	18.8	3.2	908	24.8	6.9	4 101	21.6	8.4	15 901	34.9	4.0	5 655	50.1	2.3
Vallejo city	26 976	32.3	7.8	865	27.4	8.1	29 028	26.0	9.6	18 292	37.7	4.1	8 409	45.7	5.1
Victorville city	7 112	38.5	9.4	884	32.1	9.7	2 460	28.7	9.5	22 023	42.5	6.2	4 359	54.1	5.2
Visalia city	1 629	41.7	7.9	1 060	25.7	11.2	5 123	40.8	5.8	32 448	40.7	4.2	3 958	43.5	4.9
Vista city	3 516	35.4	2.9	630	27.5	5.9	3 742	20.4	6.5	35 119	40.0	2.4	4 970	40.7	4.1
Walnut city	1 144	20.7	2.1	56	50.0	8.9	16 908	28.6	7.0	5 729	31.0	4.8	848	28.9	7.0
Walnut Creek city	613	9.8	6.5	187	15.0	13.4	6 255	19.0	10.9	3 752	26.3	6.4	2 077	42.0	5.5
Watsonville city	404	33.4	8.4	713	31.0	8.7	1 379	14.2	29.4	33 530	39.2	3.5	2 100	37.5	5.6
West Covina city	6 664	29.7	7.1	790	28.4	10.0	24 198	24.7	8.9	47 748	36.1	4.7	5 574	40.5	5.1
West Hollywood city	1 022	6.8	8.3	178	20.2	3.9	1 429	4.2	3.6	3 203	10.8	4.7	1 272	13.1	11.2
Westminster city	664	31.3	2.0	706	38.2	4.5	33 786	25.7	8.7	18 833	35.9	3.9	3 959	38.4	4.0
West Sacramento city	835	32.6	12.7	570	28.8	5.3	2 327	41.8	8.2	9 404	38.7	5.6	2 039	44.1	8.9
Whittier city	919	35.7	2.4	1 114	30.1	0.7	3 374	21.6	12.3	46 791	35.7	4.9	4 364	39.4	4.8
Woodland city	512	37.5	10.0	617	29.3	6.0	1 992	32.1	6.0	19 180	37.9	4.3	2 460	42.4	3.0
Yorba Linda city	657	32.6	2.9	332	20.8	10.5	6 444	29.0	5.3	6 096	33.7	3.9	2 356	45.5	3.2
Yuba City city	1 077	26.6	8.4	687	33.3	6.7	3 171	27.6	8.4	9 072	40.7	1.9	2 171	43.9	6.0
Yucaipa city	343	42.6	0.0	434	27.6	6.9	502	22.1	11.8	7 830	41.0	4.2	1 648	50.5	5.2
COLORADO	159 279	30.1	6.1	43 101	28.7	3.9	97 604	24.5	6.6	735 099	34.9	4.0	132 146	43.6	3.7
Arvada city	542	33.8	2.0	658	27.7	1.1	2 406	30.0	4.3	9 995	38.1	3.7	2 651	48.5	2.1
Aurora city	36 419	34.0	3.8	2 196	25.7	2.0	11 722	23.3	8.9	54 783	36.6	1.9	13 287	49.9	2.1
Boulder city	1 012	18.1	5.1	455	24.0	6.6	3 731	16.4	2.4	7 694	26.4	1.7	2 464	20.0	2.6
Broomfield city	397	30.5	1.3	148	15.5	5.4	1 648	34.6	4.9	3 587	38.7	2.3	869	44.0	1.6
Colorado Springs city	22 860	31.4	4.6	3 343	30.8	3.9	11 093	23.6	6.4	42 848	35.3	4.0	14 713	49.3	2.5
Denver city	60 599	29.5	9.8	7 330	28.4	3.4	15 619	19.8	8.5	176 063	33.9	4.6	21 346	36.2	4.8
Englewood city	408	24.0	0.7	360	25.3	4.7	464	9.3	3.4	4 188	31.2	5.5	1 002	34.1	3.3
Fort Collins city	1 355	26.4	0.4	932	20.6	2.8	2 676	20.7	5.0	10 307	28.7	3.2	3 209	36.7	4.2
Grand Junction city	323	28.5	1.9	393	29.3	3.1	232	23.3	12.5	4 835	35.1	6.7	968	42.1	5.4
Greeley city	681	28.9	2.5	704	35.2	0.0	1 039	20.8	3.7	22 535	38.7	3.4	2 154	37.3	3.1
Lakewood city	1 846	26.3	2.0	1 595	24.1	4.5	3 931	26.6	7.1	20 714	32.8	4.6	4 541	43.1	3.5
Littleton city	443	35.2	1.1	189	6.3	0.0	726	31.5	6.5	3 347	31.1	4.9	904	37.1	3.3
Longmont city	407	34.2	2.7	601	42.9	2.0	1 571	28.7	3.7	13 697	38.6	2.6	1 304	36.5	5.4
Loveland city	143	39.2	0.0	373	35.4	3.5	382	39.0	4.7	4 430	37.0	4.7	1 054	46.4	7.9
Northglenn city	462	37.9	11.9	266	32.3	2.3	920	29.1	8.0	6 352	34.9	5.0	1 015	38.9	5.0
Pueblo city	2 317	20.5	11.1	1 707	25.6	6.2	637	20.3	11.9	45 137	32.7	10.2	4 122	43.4	7.2
Thornton city	1 398	34.5	2.0	787	29.9	3.4	1 927	31.0	3.9	17 420	37.3	3.0	2 904	46.7	0.4
Westminster city	923	23.6	2.6	792	22.7	4.3	5 570	31.0	4.8	15 536	34.3	2.7	3 225	46.9	1.8
Wheat Ridge city	281	28.1	13.5	332	28.3	4.6	389	19.5	23.7	4 477	35.1	3.5	823	43.9	3.4
CONNECTICUT	305 902	31.9	7.0	9 419	27.2	7.3	83 634	26.0	4.0	318 947	35.8	3.4	80 007	39.1	5.3
Bridgeport city	42 478	34.2	6.8	486	32.1	3.3	4 551	26.1	2.7	44 568	36.3	4.0	8 477	36.3	4.2
Bristol city	1 486	27.6	5.0	119	4.2	19.3	882	31.2	2.8	3 325	41.7	2.4	1 016	49.0	3.6
Danbury city	5 361	25.3	7.6	192	18.8	7.8	3 677	27.1	3.1	11 903	27.6	3.2	3 037	35.6	2.3
Hartford city	46 144	32.4	8.0	466	14.8	8.6	2 004	18.8	6.6	49 323	38.2	4.3	7 305	32.2	7.7
Meriden city	4 065	39.0	4.9	313	41.2	0.0	556	18.3	4.1	12 279	39.2	3.0	1 670	42.2	5.1
Middletown city	5 117	34.7	5.7	128	12.5	25.0	1 209	23.7	4.9	2 264	39.4	2.8	1 298	42.1	3.5
Milford city	1 040	27.8	9.5	57	0.0	0.0	1 415	25.1	5.6	1 795	40.9	3.2	579	37.5	8.3
Naugatuck borough	831	31.5	3.0	45	75.6	0.0	782	24.9	0.0	1 323	40.1	4.0	560	52.1	1.1
New Britain city	7 191	32.4	5.3	187	15.5	18.2	1 835	21.8	3.7	19 109	41.2	2.6	2 614	43.4	4.3
New Haven city	45 561	34.2	7.4	753	25.4	8.4	4 636	11.9	2.0	26 498	36.6	2.5	5 057	31.3	4.8
New London city	4 745	33.0	8.2	123	22.8	14.6	568	22.0	1.9	5 079	38.5	3.0	1 715	42.4	6.1
Norwalk city	12 651	29.4	8.7	149	8.7	18.1	2 621	23.5	5.3	12 918	28.1	3.3	2 473	37.1	6.7
Norwich city	2 320	35.9	4.2	394	34.3	3.0	672	33.8	4.9	2 312	41.3	0.5	1 774	45.5	3.6
Shelton city	390	35.4	4.4	16	0.0	0.0	865	28.3	4.2	1 256	32.4	2.7	592	29.2	18.6
Stamford city	17 918	30.3	9.5	232	23.3	14.7	5 885	20.1	4.3	19 569	26.8	3.7	3 822	30.5	5.9
Torrington city	787	32.0	5.8	28	32.1	32.1	705	31.9	1.7	1 176	41.0	4.4	305	37.4	7.2
Waterbury city	17 177	35.7	7.9	490	20.8	6.7	1 774	26.4	3.7	23 430	41.3	3.2	3 887	42.1	7.0
West Haven city	8 195	32.8	4.8	131	31.3	6.1	1 525	18.6	2.2	4 764	33.8	3.8	1 683	38.7	4.4
DELAWARE	148 823	30.9	7.6	3 111	26.3	9.1	16 388	22.6	4.6	37 321	36.1	2.8	14 353	47.5	3.0
Dover city	11 639	27.4	8.1	347	21.3	2.3	912	25.0	8.3	1 432	33.5	5.7	1 071	52.3	1.9
Newark city	1 517	21.7	9.4	48	0.0	0.0	1 285	10.9	1.2	602	6.5	6.0	466	20.0	5.4
Wilmington city	40 819	31.0	9.2	198	24.7	4.5	616	18.8	8.6	7 151	36.8	3.8	1 691	49.7	4.9
DISTRICT OF COLUMBIA	343 213	25.1	14.1	2 006	22.1	9.3	15 145	11.5	6.0	45 015	24.8	4.0	14 661	22.3	7.1
Washington city	343 213	25.1	14.1	2 006	22.1	9.3	15 145	11.5	6.0	45 015	24.8	4.0	14 661	22.3	7.1

[1] Hispanic or Latino persons may be of any race.

Table A-5. Cities — Age, Ethnicity, and Household Structure

City	Total households	Married-couple family households Total	With children	Householder 65 years or over	Other family households Total	With children	Householder 65 years or over	Two or more unrelated persons Total	Householder 65 years or over	Male living alone Total	Householder 65 years or over	Female living alone Total	Householder 65 years or over	Percent of householders 65 years and over who live alone	Grandparents who are responsible for the care of their grandchildren
	29	30	31	32	33	34	35	36	37	38	39	40	41	42	43
CALIFORNIA—Cont'd															
Upland city	24 609	55.4	27.2	8.7	17.6	10.4	1.8	6.0	0.5	8.2	1.5	12.8	5.9	40.5	517
Vacaville city	28 088	58.6	31.1	7.3	16.5	10.9	1.7	5.7	0.4	8.4	1.2	10.9	5.4	41.1	614
Vallejo city	39 592	50.7	25.5	7.7	21.2	11.5	2.8	5.3	0.3	9.7	2.2	13.2	6.2	43.7	1 501
Victorville city	21 041	53.4	29.4	9.9	23.0	15.1	2.8	4.3	0.5	7.9	2.2	11.4	6.7	40.4	910
Visalia city	30 848	56.4	29.6	8.5	18.3	12.4	1.9	4.5	0.3	7.6	1.9	13.3	6.5	43.9	771
Vista city	28 900	54.1	29.9	8.8	18.6	11.9	2.2	7.0	0.4	8.8	1.6	11.5	5.0	36.4	625
Walnut city	8 256	77.9	46.1	7.0	14.7	5.5	1.0	1.9	0.2	2.7	0.4	2.8	0.6	11.4	312
Walnut Creek city	30 515	46.6	17.4	13.8	8.2	4.1	1.4	7.1	0.9	12.0	3.7	26.1	16.1	55.1	128
Watsonville city	11 478	55.8	36.6	8.1	22.2	13.1	2.6	4.1	0.5	6.5	1.6	11.4	7.0	43.5	489
West Covina city	31 409	60.5	32.7	8.5	20.1	9.3	3.1	4.8	0.7	5.8	1.6	8.9	4.6	33.4	1 612
West Hollywood city	23 110	16.9	4.2	5.2	5.8	2.2	1.0	16.8	1.1	32.8	3.5	27.7	8.3	62.0	8
Westminster city	26 358	59.8	30.7	9.8	17.8	7.9	2.7	5.5	0.7	7.2	1.7	9.8	5.9	36.7	920
West Sacramento city	11 429	46.4	23.7	8.3	20.9	12.2	3.2	5.6	0.6	13.2	4.0	13.9	7.1	47.6	461
Whittier city	28 273	53.1	27.3	9.8	19.9	10.9	2.9	4.6	0.2	9.2	2.6	13.2	7.4	43.5	589
Woodland city	16 726	56.7	31.0	7.7	16.9	10.1	2.4	5.2	0.3	8.3	2.0	12.8	6.9	45.8	476
Yorba Linda city	19 184	74.1	39.9	7.5	10.1	5.4	1.2	3.5	0.2	4.7	0.8	7.6	3.5	32.8	321
Yuba City city	13 352	49.1	24.9	8.5	18.8	12.1	2.0	5.1	0.3	10.8	1.9	16.1	7.2	45.7	361
Yucaipa city	15 156	55.4	27.6	11.3	15.2	8.9	2.0	4.3	0.6	9.6	3.0	15.5	10.1	48.5	320
COLORADO	1 659 308	52.8	25.4	7.3	13.1	8.1	1.3	7.9	0.3	12.1	1.8	14.1	5.4	44.7	28 524
Arvada city	38 981	58.8	27.1	8.8	12.9	8.0	1.2	5.5	0.3	9.3	1.6	13.5	5.9	42.0	597
Aurora city	105 526	48.0	24.9	5.0	17.6	11.1	1.2	7.0	0.3	12.1	1.3	15.2	4.7	47.8	2 278
Boulder city	39 610	33.7	15.3	5.1	9.2	5.5	0.8	23.4	0.3	16.4	1.3	17.3	5.0	50.6	147
Broomfield city	13 833	63.3	34.5	6.0	11.5	7.9	1.1	6.3	0.2	8.8	0.7	10.1	4.1	39.2	170
Colorado Springs city	141 757	52.5	25.7	6.9	13.7	9.0	1.3	6.8	0.3	12.4	1.7	14.6	5.5	45.6	2 164
Denver city	239 415	35.3	15.6	6.0	15.0	8.3	1.8	10.5	0.4	18.4	2.4	20.9	7.1	53.7	4 710
Englewood city	14 328	36.9	15.4	7.5	14.7	8.0	2.0	10.2	0.2	19.1	2.8	19.1	7.3	51.0	180
Fort Collins city	45 769	46.0	23.0	5.7	10.7	6.4	0.7	17.2	0.2	11.6	1.1	14.5	5.3	49.6	279
Grand Junction city	17 948	46.9	18.0	11.6	12.6	8.1	1.6	7.2	0.5	12.7	2.9	20.6	11.3	51.0	185
Greeley city	27 685	51.0	25.7	8.1	13.6	8.6	1.0	9.7	0.2	10.3	1.7	15.5	7.0	48.4	702
Lakewood city	60 653	46.6	19.7	8.7	14.0	8.7	1.3	8.7	0.3	13.9	1.9	16.7	5.8	42.8	793
Littleton city	17 396	48.3	20.9	8.7	11.6	7.5	0.8	6.5	0.5	13.6	2.1	19.9	8.6	51.9	111
Longmont city	26 771	55.6	29.0	6.3	14.3	9.7	0.9	6.4	0.3	10.0	1.6	13.7	6.3	51.3	467
Loveland city	19 855	59.8	27.9	10.1	11.8	7.7	1.2	4.9	0.3	8.9	1.9	14.7	7.5	44.9	286
Northglenn city	11 688	55.2	25.1	9.4	16.2	9.5	1.7	5.5	0.6	11.2	1.4	11.9	4.4	32.9	262
Pueblo city	40 365	45.2	18.9	11.0	20.1	11.9	3.1	4.8	0.5	12.2	3.4	17.8	10.1	48.2	1 531
Thornton city	29 018	59.2	32.3	4.3	15.9	10.2	0.6	6.3	0.2	9.3	1.1	9.3	3.7	48.6	766
Westminster city	38 493	54.3	28.5	4.9	13.7	8.2	0.9	8.0	0.2	10.9	0.8	13.0	3.8	43.4	621
Wheat Ridge city	14 653	43.0	16.8	10.1	15.0	9.0	2.5	6.4	0.3	13.9	3.4	21.5	11.7	53.9	170
CONNECTICUT	1 302 227	52.7	24.3	9.5	15.3	8.5	2.3	5.6	0.4	10.6	2.5	15.8	7.8	45.6	18 898
Bridgeport city	50 305	36.1	17.9	6.4	29.6	17.5	3.2	5.4	0.3	12.2	3.1	16.7	8.2	53.5	1 757
Bristol city	24 887	49.4	20.7	9.2	15.8	9.3	2.0	6.0	0.4	11.5	2.8	17.3	8.9	50.1	315
Danbury city	27 198	52.4	25.4	7.2	14.3	6.3	2.3	7.1	0.3	11.8	2.3	14.4	6.1	46.4	325
Hartford city	45 036	25.0	11.2	4.5	36.0	24.1	2.9	5.9	0.5	16.3	3.3	16.9	6.6	55.9	2 157
Meriden city	22 958	47.4	20.4	9.1	18.3	11.4	2.0	5.4	0.2	12.5	2.4	16.3	8.1	48.0	364
Middletown city	18 542	42.3	18.3	6.8	14.1	7.8	2.2	8.7	0.4	14.0	2.2	21.0	7.9	52.2	267
Milford city	20 909	55.0	23.9	10.3	12.4	5.7	2.5	6.0	0.4	10.0	2.1	16.6	8.3	44.0	297
Naugatuck borough	11 821	53.7	27.3	7.4	16.4	9.5	1.9	5.0	0.4	10.4	2.5	14.5	7.2	50.1	178
New Britain city	28 596	37.2	15.4	9.2	22.6	13.6	2.6	7.1	0.4	14.6	3.3	18.4	9.4	51.0	645
New Haven city	47 193	29.2	13.5	4.8	26.5	16.9	2.5	8.3	0.4	15.7	3.0	20.4	7.6	57.9	1 641
New London city	10 193	29.3	12.3	6.1	23.9	16.2	2.9	9.2	0.4	18.9	3.9	18.7	7.1	53.7	220
Norwalk city	32 703	48.4	22.5	8.2	16.2	7.6	2.7	7.3	0.7	11.4	2.5	16.7	6.4	43.5	578
Norwich city	15 086	40.5	17.3	7.7	20.3	13.3	2.3	7.2	0.4	14.0	3.2	18.0	9.9	55.9	218
Shelton city	14 180	63.0	27.3	10.4	11.4	4.6	2.7	3.7	0.3	7.8	2.2	14.0	7.1	41.2	111
Stamford city	45 454	48.3	21.9	8.9	16.0	7.4	2.7	7.0	0.3	11.4	2.7	17.2	7.5	46.1	724
Torrington city	14 730	48.4	20.8	9.5	13.6	7.8	2.6	5.9	0.6	13.4	3.6	18.7	11.0	53.7	91
Waterbury city	42 655	39.9	17.2	7.9	23.4	14.4	3.0	5.3	0.5	13.6	3.6	17.8	9.0	52.6	941
West Haven city	21 105	43.1	18.3	8.1	19.3	10.5	3.0	6.6	0.4	13.4	2.9	17.6	7.9	48.5	414
DELAWARE	298 755	52.3	22.8	9.9	16.5	9.6	2.1	6.2	0.5	10.2	2.3	14.7	6.9	42.4	7 204
Dover city	12 460	39.9	17.6	8.3	20.1	13.0	1.9	7.9	0.7	13.4	2.4	18.7	8.2	49.1	332
Newark city	8 959	43.6	17.8	8.2	8.4	3.7	1.2	21.0	0.3	10.5	1.2	16.6	6.8	45.5	7
Wilmington city	28 661	27.7	11.4	5.2	28.0	16.0	3.4	7.4	0.5	14.8	3.5	22.2	10.0	59.6	1 118
DISTRICT OF COLUMBIA	248 590	23.4	8.7	4.7	23.3	11.8	4.0	9.7	0.7	19.2	3.0	24.5	7.3	52.2	8 183
Washington city	248 590	23.4	8.7	4.7	23.3	11.8	4.0	9.7	0.7	19.2	3.0	24.5	7.3	52.2	8 183

City	Households with Non-Hispanic White householder		Households with Black or African American householder		Households with American Indian and Alaska Native householder		Households with Asian, Hawaiian, and Pacific Islander householder		Households with Hispanic or Latino[1] householder		Foreign-born population	Place of birth (percent)			Percent in non-English speaking households	
	Number of households	Percent that are family households	Number of households	Percent that are family households	Number of households	Percent that are family households	Number of households	Percent that are family households	Number of households	Percent that are family households	Percent of total population that is foreign-born	Europe	Asia	Latin America	Linguistically isolated	Not linguistically isolated
	44	45	46	47	48	49	50	51	52	53	54	55	56	57	58	59
CALIFORNIA—Cont'd																
Upland city	15 302	70.8	1 872	68.1	172	56.4	1 600	81.4	5 035	81.3	16.2	1.1	6.5	7.8	6.2	29.0
Vacaville city	20 123	73.5	1 803	70.1	290	69.3	1 181	78.4	3 677	83.8	9.0	1.4	2.6	4.6	3.4	21.0
Vallejo city	16 153	59.9	9 495	74.1	359	66.9	7 683	89.8	4 615	81.5	24.7	1.2	16.3	6.5	5.8	39.3
Victorville city	11 658	70.6	2 446	79.7	288	66.3	625	82.9	5 495	86.5	12.3	1.1	2.5	8.1	4.8	30.5
Visalia city	19 969	69.7	484	72.9	364	64.3	1 146	84.3	8 477	85.5	12.8	0.7	3.8	7.9	6.9	31.6
Vista city	18 337	66.3	1 302	75.0	225	77.3	1 320	66.2	7 182	89.7	24.4	1.6	3.0	19.1	12.3	33.8
Walnut city	1 919	87.8	328	98.2	23	100.0	4 458	93.7	1 326	94.2	46.2	0.9	39.6	4.9	14.2	61.2
Walnut Creek city	26 005	53.3	296	43.9	97	40.2	2 394	68.1	1 197	65.7	18.2	5.5	8.2	2.7	3.6	21.5
Watsonville city	3 927	59.8	115	46.1	172	68.0	500	79.2	6 684	90.3	44.2	1.6	1.7	40.7	25.2	53.8
West Covina city	10 479	69.5	2 240	77.0	217	92.2	6 481	85.8	11 527	88.2	32.5	0.9	16.8	13.8	9.5	56.1
West Hollywood city	19 443	22.1	581	15.8	94	26.6	792	28.8	1 679	27.0	35.9	22.8	6.4	4.5	15.2	26.0
Westminster city	13 055	66.6	240	71.7	185	93.0	8 340	89.0	3 949	89.2	42.6	1.4	30.0	10.6	22.4	41.0
West Sacramento city	7 479	62.3	333	64.9	146	82.2	582	78.7	2 400	79.5	25.1	7.2	6.4	10.3	16.0	30.2
Whittier city	13 467	64.9	196	77.6	383	68.4	1 048	78.3	12 960	81.4	18.3	1.2	2.5	14.1	6.9	44.7
Woodland city	10 324	67.1	158	67.1	189	64.6	629	78.1	5 092	86.8	19.4	0.6	2.5	15.7	10.8	33.4
Yorba Linda city	15 125	82.6	210	75.2	105	82.9	1 899	94.0	1 502	86.2	13.9	2.2	7.8	2.5	2.3	24.6
Yuba City city	9 253	63.5	422	56.4	239	74.9	934	79.3	2 185	83.8	19.5	0.9	6.3	12.0	10.8	24.3
Yucaipa city	12 602	68.5	118	55.9	188	68.1	174	95.4	1 847	84.7	8.2	1.5	0.8	5.3	3.1	18.3
COLORADO	1 327 444	64.1	59 518	65.2	14 528	70.0	31 027	69.8	208 192	76.7	8.6	1.5	1.7	4.8	4.1	17.5
Arvada city	34 868	70.9	206	61.2	261	70.9	653	80.6	2 704	80.5	4.8	2.1	1.6	0.7	1.9	12.7
Aurora city	71 325	61.8	14 144	67.2	748	70.7	3 709	74.7	13 770	80.4	16.2	2.0	3.4	9.8	8.1	21.0
Boulder city	34 875	41.7	361	42.7	159	68.6	1 343	51.8	2 091	61.2	11.5	2.8	3.2	4.2	4.1	16.4
Broomfield city	12 085	74.1	149	71.1	40	85.0	437	88.3	962	80.1	6.6	1.2	3.2	1.7	2.6	13.2
Colorado Springs city	112 804	65.1	8 869	71.7	1 265	65.5	3 495	70.1	13 274	71.8	7.0	2.1	2.2	2.1	2.1	16.5
Denver city	153 669	41.0	24 362	59.4	2 502	63.2	6 049	55.8	49 870	73.9	17.4	1.8	2.3	12.3	9.8	24.1
Englewood city	12 267	50.1	174	51.7	129	78.3	210	53.8	1 404	65.2	7.0	1.1	1.5	3.6	3.8	13.0
Fort Collins city	40 317	55.9	424	62.3	300	68.7	1 005	59.5	3 178	64.7	5.3	1.4	1.9	1.4	1.6	14.0
Grand Junction city	15 911	58.0	109	56.0	176	50.5	59	88.1	1 544	74.2	4.1	0.9	0.4	2.5	1.6	13.3
Greeley city	20 672	60.1	166	49.4	228	77.6	338	63.9	6 084	80.9	9.7	0.4	0.6	8.3	7.1	22.9
Lakewood city	50 858	59.0	738	51.5	633	70.5	1 215	66.6	6 505	73.1	7.1	1.8	2.0	2.8	2.7	15.7
Littleton city	15 662	59.8	171	49.7	98	44.9	209	67.9	1 056	66.7	5.7	1.3	1.4	2.3	2.1	11.9
Longmont city	22 475	67.4	116	72.4	170	77.1	463	68.7	3 408	84.4	10.6	1.2	1.6	7.4	5.5	17.8
Loveland city	18 249	71.0	49	100.0	186	52.7	75	100.0	1 173	81.5	3.4	0.7	0.5	1.9	1.7	11.3
Northglenn city	9 227	68.8	157	71.3	74	59.5	264	85.6	1 796	82.9	8.3	1.6	2.4	3.9	3.8	18.9
Pueblo city	23 290	59.7	871	60.5	685	65.5	240	72.1	15 257	73.9	3.3	0.5	0.4	2.2	2.8	25.8
Thornton city	22 738	72.6	443	81.9	284	75.4	546	82.8	4 729	85.6	6.8	1.2	1.4	3.8	3.2	17.4
Westminster city	31 075	66.8	399	63.7	367	68.9	1 499	80.4	4 718	73.2	9.0	1.5	3.8	3.2	4.2	16.1
Wheat Ridge city	12 679	55.5	96	51.0	134	62.7	141	80.1	1 450	70.3	6.0	1.9	0.9	2.9	2.9	12.8
CONNECTICUT	1 059 715	67.1	105 870	68.3	3 278	63.0	26 265	72.9	91 298	78.4	10.9	4.1	2.1	3.8	4.2	20.3
Bridgeport city	20 141	52.1	14 364	71.0	91	65.9	1 187	77.0	13 013	79.6	20.5	4.7	2.9	11.9	12.9	39.6
Bristol city	22 745	64.2	579	69.8	48	58.3	306	73.9	1 009	82.1	7.8	3.3	1.1	1.2	2.6	19.9
Danbury city	20 635	63.7	1 562	71.3	54	70.4	1 132	79.8	2 981	80.2	27.0	5.3	4.1	16.9	13.4	28.0
Hartford city	10 336	38.5	17 150	63.0	195	43.1	642	46.7	15 296	76.2	18.6	4.5	1.4	12.2	13.9	39.3
Meriden city	17 440	62.6	1 314	71.8	124	79.0	236	41.1	3 743	80.5	6.5	2.1	0.9	2.5	5.3	26.2
Middletown city	15 132	54.3	1 907	65.9	39	20.5	423	63.6	653	73.5	9.6	4.4	2.3	2.1	3.3	17.7
Milford city	19 413	67.0	373	72.9	28	10.7	515	73.8	489	74.0	8.1	3.5	2.6	1.2	1.4	15.2
Naugatuck borough	10 679	69.2	331	80.4	4	100.0	268	89.9	371	76.3	11.3	6.1	2.3	2.2	3.1	20.9
New Britain city	19 010	53.5	2 676	67.7	76	61.8	723	62.8	5 790	76.8	18.0	12.1	2.3	2.6	13.4	38.5
New Haven city	20 281	41.9	16 418	64.5	294	54.1	1 689	44.6	5 939	77.2	11.6	2.6	2.7	5.5	7.7	28.1
New London city	6 236	45.1	1 856	64.9	62	51.6	224	31.3	1 562	75.7	9.7	2.6	1.6	4.9	6.3	23.7
Norwalk city	23 568	60.9	4 482	70.1	91	45.1	825	71.4	3 419	81.3	20.3	5.0	2.7	11.8	7.2	25.7
Norwich city	12 774	59.2	859	67.8	115	76.5	221	66.5	715	82.1	6.6	1.7	1.6	1.9	3.0	17.3
Shelton city	13 172	74.0	117	83.8	5	100.0	252	78.2	429	86.0	9.5	5.5	2.0	1.5	2.3	20.3
Stamford city	30 724	61.3	6 368	67.4	63	90.5	2 292	63.0	5 169	80.2	29.6	8.1	4.2	16.4	9.8	31.7
Torrington city	13 767	61.4	304	71.4	19	52.6	182	88.5	369	65.0	5.9	2.8	1.6	1.1	2.7	14.4
Waterbury city	27 872	58.6	6 120	68.7	182	77.5	605	66.9	7 132	76.1	12.1	5.2	1.6	4.5	8.5	29.1
West Haven city	15 587	59.1	2 935	70.9	79	78.5	606	63.9	1 498	75.1	11.4	3.2	3.1	3.9	5.0	19.1
DELAWARE	227 711	68.0	52 362	69.9	1 175	64.3	5 434	78.4	9 662	79.8	5.7	1.3	1.7	2.2	2.1	12.3
Dover city	7 495	56.4	3 995	64.0	102	69.6	289	70.9	438	70.3	6.1	1.3	2.2	1.4	1.9	14.7
Newark city	7 611	52.9	614	45.6	27	0.0	380	53.4	164	57.9	7.4	2.1	3.6	1.0	1.7	13.9
Wilmington city	12 060	40.1	14 180	65.9	73	89.0	235	60.0	1 952	78.3	5.0	1.1	0.6	3.2	3.6	14.3
DISTRICT OF COLUMBIA	83 742	30.8	139 143	55.5	763	43.6	6 502	40.7	14 449	59.6	12.9	2.3	2.2	6.5	4.7	17.7
Washington city	83 742	30.8	139 143	55.5	763	43.6	6 502	40.7	14 449	59.6	12.9	2.3	2.2	6.5	4.7	17.7

[1]Hispanic or Latino persons may be of any race.

STATE Place code	City	Total population	Under 5 years	5 to 17 years	18 to 24 years	25 to 44 years	45 to 64 years	65 years and over	Median age	+/− U.S. percent under 18 years	+/− U.S. percent 65 years and over	Non-Hispanic White Total population	Under 18 years	65 years and over
		1	2	3	4	5	6	7	8	9	10	11	12	13
12 00000	FLORIDA..................	15 982 378	5.9	16.9	8.3	28.8	22.6	17.6	38.7	-2.9	5.2	10 456 458	19.3	22.3
12 00950	Altamonte Springs city ..	41 402	6.0	14.5	10.1	38.4	20.3	10.7	33.8	-5.2	-1.7	28 551	17.5	12.7
12 01700	Apopka city..............	26 082	8.8	19.3	8.4	33.7	20.3	9.6	33.3	2.4	-2.8	16 217	23.8	12.8
12 02681	Aventura city.............	25 267	3.5	6.5	4.1	27.0	23.6	35.3	52.8	-15.7	22.9	18 915	8.2	42.6
12 07300	Boca Raton city..........	75 594	4.5	14.2	8.3	26.5	26.6	19.9	42.9	-7.0	7.5	63 677	18.0	22.3
12 07525	Bonita Springs city	32 914	4.1	9.9	5.5	20.7	28.4	31.5	54.1	-11.7	19.1	26 677	9.7	38.2
12 07875	Boynton Beach city	59 951	5.8	13.6	6.2	29.2	19.9	25.2	41.8	-6.3	12.8	39 023	12.2	36.5
12 07950	Bradenton city	49 908	6.1	15.4	7.5	26.0	19.8	25.1	41.5	-4.2	12.7	35 632	15.8	32.9
12 10275	Cape Coral city	102 206	5.6	16.9	5.7	27.0	25.3	19.6	41.6	-3.2	7.2	89 564	21.1	21.0
12 12875	Clearwater city	107 925	5.1	14.0	7.7	28.1	23.7	21.4	41.8	-6.6	9.0	84 283	15.4	25.8
12 13275	Coconut Creek city.......	43 327	6.3	11.8	5.3	32.3	18.3	26.1	41.3	-7.6	13.7	33 755	15.2	32.2
12 14125	Cooper City city..........	27 685	5.6	25.8	6.3	30.0	25.7	6.5	36.7	5.7	-5.9	20 960	31.6	6.5
12 14250	Coral Gables city.........	42 202	4.9	12.6	14.4	28.9	23.4	15.7	38.1	-8.2	3.3	20 176	19.1	16.6
12 14400	Coral Springs city........	117 482	6.9	23.7	7.8	32.5	23.1	5.9	33.8	4.9	-6.5	81 841	29.1	7.0
12 16475	Davie town	75 685	6.8	19.3	8.1	33.5	23.0	9.3	35.5	0.4	-3.1	54 563	24.5	11.0
12 16525	Daytona Beach city	64 070	4.9	12.4	17.1	25.3	20.4	19.9	37.2	-8.4	7.5	38 839	10.3	26.8
12 16725	Deerfield Beach city	64 716	4.8	10.8	6.3	29.2	19.8	29.1	44.6	-10.1	16.7	46 393	10.4	38.2
12 17100	Delray Beach city	59 941	4.7	12.9	6.5	27.5	22.5	25.9	43.8	-8.1	13.5	37 141	9.6	37.8
12 17200	Deltona city	69 818	6.3	20.8	7.4	29.3	21.0	15.3	37.1	1.4	2.9	50 937	25.5	16.8
12 18575	Dunedin city	35 926	3.8	11.7	5.0	24.2	25.1	30.1	48.2	-10.2	17.7	32 984	14.3	31.8
12 24000	Fort Lauderdale city	152 125	5.1	14.1	7.6	33.0	24.8	15.4	39.3	-6.5	3.0	88 225	11.5	21.8
12 24125	Fort Myers city	48 046	7.8	18.2	11.8	30.4	17.6	14.1	32.4	0.3	1.7	23 453	14.5	23.3
12 24300	Fort Pierce city	37 489	7.5	19.0	10.4	25.7	19.5	17.8	35.4	0.8	5.4	15 566	14.2	32.5
12 25175	Gainesville city	95 605	4.6	13.2	29.4	27.0	16.1	9.8	26.4	-7.9	-2.6	61 108	12.8	11.9
12 27322	Greenacres city	27 269	5.9	14.5	7.8	28.1	18.8	24.9	39.6	-5.3	12.5	18 785	14.6	33.2
12 28450	Hallandale city	34 551	3.8	9.5	4.8	24.1	22.1	35.7	52.7	-12.4	23.3	21 761	6.6	49.4
12 30000	Hialeah city	226 411	5.8	17.2	8.2	29.3	22.9	16.5	37.7	-2.7	4.1	18 448	49.0	13.3
12 32000	Hollywood city	139 261	5.8	15.4	7.0	31.6	22.9	17.3	39.2	-4.5	4.9	85 619	16.9	23.5
12 32275	Homestead city	32 046	10.5	22.6	12.1	32.8	14.4	7.6	27.2	7.4	-4.8	7 340	18.1	17.8
12 35000	Jacksonville city	735 503	7.3	19.4	9.7	32.4	21.0	10.3	33.8	1.0	-2.1	457 686	22.7	12.5
12 35875	Jupiter city	39 314	5.3	15.3	5.1	29.0	26.5	18.8	42.4	-5.1	6.4	35 302	20.2	20.1
12 36550	Key West city	25 480	4.5	11.4	8.1	37.3	27.2	11.6	38.9	-9.8	-0.8	18 145	13.4	11.7
12 36950	Kissimmee city	47 558	7.3	19.1	12.7	35.2	18.5	7.2	30.6	0.7	-5.2	21 144	20.4	10.7
12 38250	Lakeland city	78 162	6.1	15.1	10.3	24.8	20.8	22.9	39.7	-4.5	10.5	54 440	15.8	29.3
12 39075	Lake Worth city	35 237	6.8	16.2	10.6	32.8	19.2	14.4	35.2	-2.7	2.0	17 035	13.8	25.6
12 39425	Largo city...............	69 470	4.3	11.2	5.9	25.5	22.9	30.2	47.5	-10.2	17.8	62 669	14.1	32.8
12 39525	Lauderdale Lakes city ...	31 517	7.5	19.9	9.2	27.0	18.5	17.8	35.7	1.7	5.4	6 665	3.4	58.5
12 39550	Lauderhill city	57 254	7.6	18.9	8.5	30.3	18.5	16.2	34.9	0.8	3.8	16 968	11.0	42.5
12 43125	Margate city.............	53 852	5.6	14.9	6.2	29.7	21.4	22.2	40.4	-5.2	9.8	36 708	16.4	29.3
12 43975	Melbourne city...........	71 371	5.3	15.4	9.4	28.6	22.0	19.4	39.8	-5.0	7.0	57 518	18.8	22.1
12 45000	Miami city	362 563	5.9	15.8	8.6	30.8	21.8	17.0	37.7	-4.0	4.6	43 195	25.5	15.2
12 45025	Miami Beach city..........	88 061	3.6	9.8	7.9	37.9	21.3	19.4	39.0	-12.3	7.0	36 009	13.5	21.3
12 45975	Miramar city	72 674	8.8	22.1	8.4	35.5	18.6	6.5	31.8	5.2	-5.9	15 297	25.4	13.1
12 49425	North Lauderdale city	32 323	8.2	22.0	10.9	35.5	16.3	7.1	30.5	4.5	-5.3	11 525	22.3	14.4
12 49450	North Miami city	60 036	8.1	20.4	11.0	32.1	19.5	9.0	31.8	2.8	-3.4	10 770	15.0	25.5
12 49475	North Miami Beach city .	40 673	6.7	20.1	9.6	31.1	20.6	11.9	34.5	1.1	-0.5	10 180	18.2	26.2
12 50575	Oakland Park city	31 205	6.4	14.4	9.3	38.9	21.3	9.7	35.8	-4.9	-2.7	16 745	13.6	15.2
12 50750	Ocala city	45 622	6.0	16.8	10.1	25.6	21.0	20.6	39.0	-2.9	8.2	31 709	18.2	25.0
12 53000	Orlando city	185 984	6.5	15.5	10.5	37.7	18.4	11.4	32.9	-3.7	-1.0	94 328	14.4	15.0
12 53150	Ormond Beach city	36 348	4.1	14.8	4.7	22.4	26.7	27.2	47.5	-6.8	14.8	33 590	18.2	28.3
12 53575	Oviedo city	27 023	8.2	23.9	7.4	36.6	18.6	5.4	32.8	6.4	-7.0	20 112	31.4	5.4
12 54000	Palm Bay city	79 455	6.2	20.2	7.8	29.7	21.3	14.9	37.2	0.7	2.5	60 412	24.8	15.5
12 54075	Palm Beach Gardens city	34 472	4.3	14.6	5.6	26.1	28.7	20.8	45.0	-6.8	8.4	30 678	17.8	22.8
12 54200	Palm Coast city	33 504	4.6	14.0	4.5	20.2	26.8	29.8	51.2	-7.1	17.4	26 794	17.5	30.6
12 54700	Panama City city	36 371	5.7	17.1	9.4	29.9	21.8	16.1	37.2	-2.9	3.7	26 513	20.0	18.3
12 55775	Pembroke Pines city	137 112	7.0	18.5	6.2	34.0	19.1	15.1	36.5	-0.2	2.7	72 364	22.2	22.9
12 55925	Pensacola city	56 288	5.9	17.0	9.1	26.8	24.0	17.2	39.4	-2.8	4.8	35 689	17.6	19.7
12 56975	Pinellas Park city..........	45 414	6.0	15.4	6.4	29.8	22.1	20.4	40.2	-4.3	8.0	38 843	19.5	23.2
12 57425	Plantation city	83 274	5.9	17.1	6.7	32.7	24.7	12.9	37.9	-2.7	0.5	56 439	20.5	16.1
12 57550	Plant City city	30 106	8.3	21.2	8.8	29.1	20.8	11.9	33.3	3.8	-0.5	19 596	24.8	15.1
12 58050	Pompano Beach city	78 301	5.1	12.6	7.3	29.4	22.0	23.5	42.2	-8.0	11.1	47 386	9.4	34.6
12 58575	Port Orange city	45 370	4.5	15.4	5.7	25.4	25.3	23.7	44.6	-5.8	11.3	42 382	19.1	24.9
12 58715	Port St. Lucie city.........	88 796	5.9	18.2	6.1	28.1	23.0	18.8	39.9	-1.6	6.4	73 332	22.4	20.4
12 60975	Riviera Beach city	30 414	7.4	22.2	8.0	25.9	20.9	15.7	35.6	3.9	3.3	7 672	9.4	36.8
12 63000	St. Petersburg city........	247 793	5.6	15.9	7.8	30.1	23.1	17.5	39.3	-4.2	5.1	170 652	16.8	21.7
12 63650	Sanford city	37 597	7.7	19.0	10.4	33.3	19.2	10.5	32.5	1.0	-1.9	20 726	19.7	14.0
12 64175	Sarasota city	52 537	5.0	13.2	8.8	28.3	22.4	22.3	41.1	-7.5	9.9	36 548	12.1	28.7
12 69700	Sunrise city..............	85 636	6.4	18.5	7.2	31.8	18.7	17.5	36.6	-0.8	5.1	48 622	20.0	26.9
12 70600	Tallahassee city	150 581	5.1	12.3	29.6	27.7	17.2	8.2	26.3	-8.3	-4.2	86 941	14.1	10.6
12 70675	Tamarac city	56 081	4.4	9.2	5.1	24.4	19.9	36.9	52.9	-12.1	24.5	39 725	9.1	48.9
12 71000	Tampa city..............	303 512	6.7	17.9	9.9	32.4	20.5	12.5	34.7	-1.1	0.1	154 748	18.4	14.9
12 71900	Titusville city.............	40 662	5.8	17.2	7.2	25.6	23.5	20.7	41.0	-2.7	8.3	32 882	20.3	23.6

City	Black or African American Total population	Under 18 years	65 years and over	American Indian and Alaska Native Total population	Under 18 years	65 years and over	Asian, Hawaiian, and Pacific Islander Total population	Under 18 years	65 years and over	Hispanic or Latino[1] Total population	Under 18 years	65 years and over	Two or more races Total population	Under 18 years	65 years and over
	14	15	16	17	18	19	20	21	22	23	24	25	26	27	28
FLORIDA..................	2 312 105	33.1	7.4	54 428	24.0	6.2	271 189	22.9	6.0	2 680 314	25.9	10.4	409 021	33.7	6.5
Altamonte Springs city ..	4 335	29.7	4.2	96	0.0	6.3	1 232	18.2	7.2	6 665	27.2	7.0	1 257	33.9	3.7
Apopka city..................	4 083	35.7	5.2	61	14.8	0.0	495	37.6	0.0	4 809	33.3	4.8	1 013	36.5	1.8
Aventura city...............	458	12.2	17.0	38	21.1	26.3	392	15.6	21.7	5 212	15.8	12.7	446	12.3	9.4
Boca Raton city............	2 977	26.2	5.1	147	19.0	9.5	1 216	15.1	3.2	6 368	22.2	8.4	1 525	25.4	4.6
Bonita Springs city	106	41.5	14.2	54	0.0	18.5	146	8.9	18.5	5 649	32.7	1.3	631	41.8	8.1
Boynton Beach city	14 470	35.9	3.8	134	30.6	0.0	951	20.8	6.1	5 000	28.3	3.7	1 039	27.0	7.8
Bradenton city	7 632	37.1	7.5	104	18.3	11.5	381	14.7	8.7	5 618	36.5	3.1	851	33.5	4.5
Cape Coral city	1 884	32.9	9.4	231	26.0	19.0	1 153	26.4	13.3	8 355	32.3	9.2	1 494	33.9	8.0
Clearwater city	10 178	36.3	7.5	535	17.2	3.7	1 605	23.6	4.2	9 615	29.0	5.1	2 609	36.4	3.6
Coconut Creek city.......	2 516	28.1	2.6	45	0.0	8.9	1 047	20.9	3.8	5 111	27.9	6.2	1 093	41.6	5.9
Cooper City city...........	1 033	29.8	6.5	24	29.2	0.0	1 257	31.3	5.4	4 122	30.6	6.6	337	30.0	8.6
Coral Gables city	1 531	15.2	2.2	58	12.1	13.8	633	11.7	4.6	19 623	16.3	16.4	500	13.4	9.2
Coral Springs city.........	11 147	36.8	3.3	327	00.0	0.0	3 999	26.6	4.7	18 279	33.0	3.4	3 149	38.0	3.5
Davie town	3 198	33.9	4.8	271	32.5	13.7	2 082	24.0	0.9	14 384	29.4	5.6	2 214	37.6	2.8
Daytona Beach city.......	20 689	29.8	9.6	207	9.7	16.4	1 140	14.5	4.5	2 275	25.1	8.1	1 208	20.9	5.8
Deerfield Beach city	10 283	33.6	6.2	128	11.7	3.1	691	16.8	3.9	5 517	20.3	7.0	1 971	31.3	3.3
Delray Beach city.........	16 050	33.1	7.4	123	13.8	7.3	601	13.1	3.5	4 165	25.2	5.1	2 196	27.0	3.6
Deltona city	4 166	34.0	10.4	228	16.7	9.6	964	28.0	2.7	12 855	29.7	12.5	2 003	41.7	7.6
Dunedin city	712	22.6	15.6	95	12.6	0.0	442	33.5	6.1	1 321	32.1	11.1	569	30.1	16.7
Fort Lauderdale city	42 466	34.1	6.1	291	21.0	0.0	1 805	19.0	6.6	13 894	19.7	8.9	6 265	28.3	3.9
Fort Myers city	16 130	38.5	6.7	413	40.7	2.4	606	24.3	1.7	6 836	34.0	3.2	1 476	37.1	2.2
Fort Pierce city	15 154	35.4	9.6	96	42.7	6.3	376	21.3	4.8	5 817	35.3	2.0	973	39.1	4.7
Gainesville city	22 049	31.9	7.3	242	12.0	3.7	4 447	10.8	3.0	5 962	15.7	4.4	2 354	28.2	6.0
Greenacres city	1 487	36.5	5.5	166	37.3	0.0	474	28.9	8.9	6 064	32.5	6.6	901	39.2	5.4
Hallandale city	5 577	34.3	9.0	40	50.0	0.0	358	10.3	12.8	6 469	18.4	14.5	698	20.3	11.7
Hialeah city	5 088	28.4	11.6	423	20.1	13.5	592	10.8	18.4	204 808	20.5	17.0	8 630	23.2	10.9
Hollywood city	16 546	32.6	6.1	182	40.7	3.3	3 000	23.2	6.0	31 380	25.9	7.9	5 117	27.5	8.4
Homestead city	6 984	42.2	4.6	158	37.3	5.7	216	22.7	3.2	17 137	35.4	4.8	1 531	41.1	1.9
Jacksonville city	213 258	33.9	7.2	2 892	26.5	3.6	20 335	23.9	5.0	30 414	30.7	4.6	15 165	42.9	3.4
Jupiter town	301	20.5	11.3	29	0.0	0.0	497	23.1	4.2	2 755	22.4	6.4	537	36.9	4.1
Key West city	2 335	21.6	12.3	131	14.5	0.0	199	20.6	0.0	4 314	21.4	13.0	702	32.2	3.1
Kissimmee city	4 895	30.8	6.6	182	23.1	6.0	1 406	24.3	0.0	19 652	32.0	4.3	2 330	33.6	4.5
Lakeland city	16 343	35.2	8.2	362	38.7	1.9	1 082	20.9	9.2	5 050	29.3	8.9	1 341	42.5	8.1
Lake Worth city	6 626	37.2	3.9	379	43.3	0.0	378	25.7	10.1	10 408	29.7	3.5	1 722	27.1	6.0
Largo city	1 468	32.0	3.0	257	12.8	4.7	1 353	20.0	3.5	2 849	26.6	9.7	1 224	40.8	8.8
Lauderdale Lakes city ..	21 256	36.0	6.0	6	0.0	0.0	359	28.7	7.0	1 827	21.4	11.8	1 549	21.4	13.0
Lauderhill city	33 387	34.4	4.5	26	0.0	0.0	883	24.7	7.6	3 015	25.9	7.9	2 530	27.0	7.4
Margate city	6 055	35.0	5.2	82	17.1	17.1	1 703	24.9	3.3	8 222	26.0	8.0	2 109	31.8	8.5
Melbourne city.............	6 337	29.3	11.0	338	16.6	5.6	1 580	15.6	4.2	3 807	27.7	6.8	2 182	40.3	4.9
Miami city	79 351	30.7	10.0	818	29.0	4.9	2 290	14.5	8.5	238 461	17.7	20.1	18 391	22.3	10.0
Miami Beach city..........	3 612	16.1	8.8	326	8.9	8.3	977	8.1	5.8	46 980	13.1	19.4	3 045	15.5	15.2
Miramar city	31 379	35.1	4.0	177	11.9	11.9	2 145	27.6	5.3	21 536	28.7	6.0	3 946	32.1	4.8
North Lauderdale city....	11 212	38.6	2.5	27	29.6	0.0	996	22.4	2.5	7 024	30.2	4.8	1 768	33.1	1.1
North Miami city	32 573	34.9	3.9	88	19.3	11.4	1 370	26.3	5.0	14 311	24.1	8.5	2 807	28.6	4.8
North Miami Beach city .	15 561	34.5	5.4	159	15.1	7.5	1 710	25.4	5.0	12 312	24.4	9.9	2 211	24.6	9.1
Oakland Park city	7 027	35.3	2.2	37	0.0	0.0	605	18.2	6.8	5 622	22.7	4.3	1 551	28.6	5.3
Ocala city	10 126	33.4	11.8	266	15.8	12.8	505	27.7	5.9	2 515	33.2	7.2	662	38.2	5.1
Orlando city	49 471	33.3	8.6	493	19.9	6.3	5 010	17.3	6.0	32 897	27.7	7.0	7 043	28.0	4.9
Ormond Beach city	970	28.5	16.5	76	0.0	0.0	599	27.5	9.7	805	25.6	14.0	272	41.5	16.9
Oviedo city	2 218	32.8	7.8	109	45.9	0.0	613	25.4	1.5	3 402	35.2	4.9	699	35.9	2.1
Palm Bay city	8 692	32.5	15.6	446	24.4	4.3	1 313	14.8	14.6	6 968	31.8	10.4	2 571	44.4	7.2
Palm Beach Gardens city	706	34.3	1.0	47	27.7	0.0	911	22.8	2.7	1 926	26.1	4.8	197	39.1	9.6
Palm Coast city	3 146	17.7	34.8	88	20.5	0.0	562	31.1	11.4	2 284	26.1	20.0	783	36.4	26.8
Panama City city..........	7 735	31.0	11.2	248	5.6	18.1	505	21.0	6.9	908	26.1	3.7	742	35.8	5.1
Pembroke Pines city	17 737	30.5	5.2	146	15.8	4.8	5 004	24.2	4.9	38 348	28.8	7.2	5 452	33.7	6.5
Pensacola city	17 198	32.4	13.1	247	11.3	12.6	1 090	28.8	10.7	1 198	25.0	15.3	1 013	45.0	7.6
Pinellas Park city.........	1 123	37.3	1.9	139	5.8	4.3	1 822	26.3	5.9	2 720	32.5	2.9	1 154	40.5	3.5
Plantation city.............	11 453	31.6	5.6	188	27.1	0.0	2 227	20.0	5.9	10 999	25.8	6.6	2 693	33.5	5.3
Plant City city	4 904	36.2	10.1	59	18.6	30.5	295	25.1	5.8	5 187	40.9	1.6	472	39.2	2.3
Pompano Beach city	19 896	32.1	7.0	101	5.0	9.4	536	27.2	1.5	7 710	25.5	6.6	3 260	34.4	3.7
Port Orange city	852	41.1	0.0	84	13.1	20.2	529	24.4	13.4	1 156	32.8	6.9	348	31.0	8.6
Port St. Lucie city........	6 214	33.8	13.1	273	12.5	6.6	1 101	27.0	7.8	6 822	30.8	11.1	1 723	36.6	9.7
Riviera Beach city	20 612	37.0	8.5	21	0.0	0.0	352	27.6	11.4	1 494	31.5	9.8	643	33.9	5.8
St. Petersburg city........	55 260	33.2	8.9	835	16.5	2.0	6 820	24.1	4.7	9 878	26.3	9.9	5 398	41.1	4.9
Sanford city	11 959	35.9	7.2	189	27.5	2.1	487	18.5	5.3	3 711	33.0	4.7	1 035	39.4	0.4
Sarasota city	8 492	33.7	10.0	131	25.2	4.6	601	19.1	0.0	6 390	30.3	5.1	1 068	42.6	4.9
Sunrise city	17 494	34.9	3.9	201	35.3	0.0	2 943	25.9	3.8	14 542	27.7	6.7	2 556	35.0	8.6
Tallahassee city	51 732	23.0	5.5	315	19.0	4.1	3 498	13.6	2.3	6 077	13.5	2.2	2 585	29.4	8.6
Tamarac city...............	5 954	28.2	4.9	103	24.3	25.2	975	24.5	6.9	7 969	23.6	7.7	1 989	19.0	13.6
Tampa city..................	78 497	34.6	8.3	1 333	27.4	4.3	6 669	18.2	5.7	58 571	27.2	13.3	9 766	35.8	6.4
Titusville city	4 816	36.7	8.5	203	14.3	10.3	489	15.5	9.8	1 579	30.1	7.9	858	38.6	10.0

[1]Hispanic or Latino persons may be of any race.

Table A-5. Cities — Age, Ethnicity, and Household Structure

City	Total households	Family households (percent)						Nonfamily households (percent)						Percent of householders 65 years and over who live alone	Grandparents who are responsible for the care of their grandchildren
		Married-couple family households			Other family households			Two or more unrelated persons		Male living alone		Female living alone			
		Total	With children	House-holder 65 years or over	Total	With children	House-holder 65 years or over	Total	House-holder 65 years or over	Total	House-holder 65 years or over	Total	House-holder 65 years or over		
	29	30	31	32	33	34	35	36	37	38	39	40	41	42	43
FLORIDA	6 341 121	51.1	19.9	13.4	15.7	8.8	2.2	6.6	0.7	11.1	3.0	15.5	8.4	41.1	147 893
Altamonte Springs city	18 939	37.6	17.2	5.9	15.6	9.1	1.7	10.1	0.5	16.5	1.3	20.2	5.8	46.5	317
Apopka city	9 549	55.5	29.2	7.4	19.1	10.5	1.3	6.6	0.3	7.5	1.9	11.3	4.5	41.5	225
Aventura city	14 006	40.1	9.0	17.2	7.7	3.3	1.5	6.9	1.5	15.1	4.8	30.1	18.5	53.5	26
Boca Raton city	32 086	53.7	20.2	15.1	10.2	4.9	1.6	7.3	1.0	12.4	2.7	16.4	8.4	38.6	333
Bonita Springs city	14 821	61.5	11.1	28.3	8.1	3.5	1.4	6.5	1.0	10.3	4.1	13.5	7.9	28.2	230
Boynton Beach city	26 055	46.5	15.7	16.1	13.9	7.1	2.1	6.6	0.9	11.5	4.3	21.4	13.9	48.8	315
Bradenton city	21 526	44.4	14.4	16.0	15.8	9.2	2.3	6.3	0.7	11.1	3.8	22.4	14.6	49.2	400
Cape Coral city	40 848	61.3	22.5	17.1	13.2	7.3	2.3	5.7	0.8	8.4	2.7	11.4	6.5	31.3	756
Clearwater city	48 159	42.0	13.6	13.0	15.0	8.7	1.9	7.6	0.7	14.7	3.8	20.7	11.5	49.4	829
Coconut Creek city	20 075	50.9	18.3	17.0	9.7	4.6	1.3	6.8	0.8	10.5	3.8	22.2	14.3	48.6	176
Cooper City city	9 059	72.9	44.4	6.5	13.5	8.3	1.6	2.9	0.1	4.3	0.6	6.4	2.6	28.0	150
Coral Gables city	16 729	48.8	19.5	11.1	12.1	4.9	3.0	7.2	0.7	12.8	2.7	19.1	7.6	41.0	59
Coral Springs city	39 549	61.2	36.9	4.5	18.3	12.0	1.2	5.1	0.2	6.9	1.0	8.5	2.9	40.2	579
Davie town	28 618	51.2	27.0	6.2	17.9	10.3	2.0	8.7	0.6	11.0	2.1	11.2	4.6	43.3	517
Daytona Beach city	28 561	31.1	8.5	10.7	18.1	10.3	2.5	11.5	1.0	18.2	4.4	21.1	10.5	51.2	835
Deerfield Beach city	31 394	39.4	11.0	14.8	12.2	5.9	2.0	8.1	1.0	14.2	5.9	26.1	17.7	57.0	403
Delray Beach city	26 854	42.9	12.5	16.3	13.4	6.9	2.1	8.2	1.5	13.2	4.9	22.3	14.0	48.6	521
Deltona city	24 906	62.4	28.0	15.1	16.2	9.4	2.6	4.9	0.7	7.1	1.9	9.4	5.4	28.3	708
Dunedin city	17 377	44.2	12.4	16.7	11.4	6.1	2.1	6.7	0.6	12.4	4.1	25.3	16.2	51.2	106
Fort Lauderdale city	68 510	33.2	11.8	8.6	15.3	8.4	1.9	11.0	1.3	21.3	3.5	19.2	8.0	49.7	1 564
Fort Myers city	19 139	32.8	13.9	7.3	23.9	15.1	2.2	9.4	0.7	15.8	3.6	18.1	8.8	54.9	553
Fort Pierce city	14 379	38.4	14.7	11.8	23.4	13.7	3.3	7.1	1.0	13.0	4.1	18.2	10.0	46.6	669
Gainesville city	37 361	33.3	13.9	6.3	16.3	9.1	1.9	17.7	0.3	14.6	1.8	18.1	5.8	47.1	769
Greenacres city	12 000	46.5	15.4	17.7	16.5	9.3	2.0	7.5	1.0	10.3	4.0	19.2	11.9	43.4	112
Hallandale city	18 178	36.5	7.5	17.8	11.8	5.6	2.5	6.5	1.4	16.4	6.6	28.7	19.3	54.4	153
Hialeah city	70 664	58.1	26.7	13.5	23.5	10.2	4.5	3.7	0.9	5.6	1.9	9.1	5.5	28.4	2 637
Hollywood city	59 645	42.2	16.4	9.7	15.8	8.5	2.0	7.4	1.0	15.5	3.6	19.1	10.3	52.4	1 136
Homestead city	10 077	40.1	23.3	4.6	30.9	20.1	2.1	8.1	0.5	10.4	2.5	10.6	4.7	49.7	392
Jacksonville city	284 661	47.7	22.5	6.9	19.8	11.9	2.2	6.4	0.4	11.6	1.9	14.6	6.1	45.3	8 695
Jupiter town	16 938	56.7	20.8	15.6	10.6	6.0	0.9	6.7	1.0	10.9	2.6	15.0	7.5	36.4	115
Key West city	11 019	37.4	15.1	5.8	13.1	5.9	2.3	18.1	1.0	18.5	3.1	12.9	5.0	47.3	109
Kissimmee city	17 209	46.6	23.4	5.6	23.2	14.3	1.6	9.6	0.4	9.3	1.1	11.2	3.6	38.3	427
Lakeland city	33 480	43.7	14.2	14.7	17.0	10.1	2.6	6.2	0.7	13.5	3.7	19.6	11.4	45.5	915
Lake Worth city	13 906	37.7	17.3	7.7	18.9	10.3	2.2	9.6	1.2	17.1	3.7	16.6	8.1	51.5	181
Largo city	34 095	42.3	11.2	16.9	11.5	5.8	2.1	7.4	1.2	13.8	4.5	25.0	15.4	49.6	362
Lauderdale Lakes city	12 024	36.9	16.6	9.9	27.3	16.9	2.2	5.6	1.3	10.1	3.7	20.1	14.1	57.0	431
Lauderhill city	22 636	38.2	17.4	9.4	24.7	15.7	2.3	6.4	1.3	11.6	3.1	19.2	10.3	50.9	645
Margate city	22 737	49.0	19.3	13.5	14.2	7.3	2.2	6.1	0.8	10.6	4.2	20.2	13.9	52.3	269
Melbourne city	30 698	45.4	16.6	12.4	14.7	7.8	2.7	7.1	0.5	13.7	3.3	19.2	9.8	45.8	636
Miami city	134 344	37.8	15.3	9.7	24.9	11.6	4.7	6.9	1.0	14.9	4.0	15.5	8.8	45.3	4 810
Miami Beach city	46 242	28.0	9.6	7.4	12.3	5.4	1.8	11.1	1.0	25.5	4.3	23.1	11.2	60.1	464
Miramar city	23 007	58.0	35.2	5.0	23.9	13.6	2.3	4.1	0.3	6.2	1.0	7.8	2.5	31.7	528
North Lauderdale city	10 731	46.7	25.5	4.9	26.7	18.5	1.6	7.4	0.4	7.7	0.8	11.4	5.0	45.4	362
North Miami city	20 427	39.7	22.5	4.7	27.0	15.7	2.4	6.4	0.5	13.4	2.0	13.6	4.5	46.1	716
North Miami Beach city	14 019	44.9	24.7	6.8	25.8	13.1	2.4	5.9	0.7	9.8	3.0	13.7	6.5	48.8	461
Oakland Park city	13 507	33.2	15.2	5.1	19.5	10.6	1.5	13.2	0.7	18.4	2.2	15.7	5.7	52.1	243
Ocala city	18 704	40.6	14.8	11.0	19.5	12.1	2.9	6.2	0.9	11.7	3.6	22.0	12.6	52.2	408
Orlando city	80 996	33.3	13.7	5.5	19.7	11.8	2.1	12.0	0.5	15.7	1.9	19.3	6.7	51.4	2 126
Ormond Beach city	15 776	55.9	17.9	19.6	11.5	5.9	2.7	5.1	1.0	9.0	3.1	18.5	12.2	39.5	89
Oviedo city	8 667	72.0	44.5	4.8	13.0	7.6	1.7	5.5	0.4	4.4	0.5	5.1	1.3	20.5	156
Palm Bay city	30 397	56.0	24.8	12.9	16.3	10.1	1.7	5.9	0.5	8.8	2.2	12.9	6.9	37.7	878
Palm Beach Gardens city	15 216	55.3	18.6	16.3	11.1	6.5	1.8	6.2	0.8	9.6	2.3	17.8	7.6	34.5	63
Palm Coast city	13 943	68.0	18.4	27.5	8.9	5.0	1.6	3.9	1.2	6.3	3.2	12.9	10.0	30.3	262
Panama City city	14 831	43.8	16.9	9.2	17.6	10.6	2.2	6.5	0.8	12.5	2.8	19.6	10.0	51.0	344
Pembroke Pines city	51 964	57.0	29.1	10.8	13.9	7.7	1.6	5.1	0.6	7.7	2.3	16.4	10.2	49.0	656
Pensacola city	24 467	39.9	14.5	11.2	20.3	10.6	4.3	7.0	0.6	13.6	2.6	19.2	8.4	40.5	548
Pinellas Park city	19 424	47.1	17.9	13.0	15.5	8.6	2.1	6.9	0.9	11.7	3.2	18.7	11.0	46.9	361
Plantation city	33 379	52.5	22.8	9.4	14.7	8.2	1.5	7.3	0.4	9.9	1.9	15.6	6.8	43.7	511
Plant City city	10 924	53.0	25.5	9.0	19.9	12.8	2.6	4.3	0.2	9.2	1.6	13.6	7.0	41.9	370
Pompano Beach city	35 217	38.3	10.4	14.6	14.3	7.1	2.4	8.7	1.1	16.1	3.9	22.6	12.8	48.1	1 054
Port Orange city	19 433	54.7	17.8	17.5	13.0	7.6	1.7	6.5	0.8	10.0	3.9	15.8	9.7	40.4	447
Port St. Lucie city	33 917	62.5	24.0	17.7	13.5	7.8	1.8	5.8	0.9	7.2	2.3	11.0	6.3	29.7	618
Riviera Beach city	11 515	38.0	13.4	11.8	29.2	17.6	3.9	5.8	0.8	13.2	4.1	13.9	7.4	41.0	729
St. Petersburg city	109 608	39.1	14.5	9.4	17.4	9.8	2.6	7.9	0.7	15.5	3.5	20.2	9.9	51.4	2 358
Sanford city	13 974	41.8	18.4	7.3	22.5	13.8	2.0	8.3	0.4	12.0	2.1	15.4	7.4	49.7	455
Sarasota city	23 534	35.7	10.9	11.9	16.1	8.6	2.3	9.6	0.9	15.5	4.7	23.1	12.6	53.5	472
Sunrise city	33 289	49.4	23.6	11.0	17.4	10.2	1.8	5.8	0.4	9.3	3.1	18.0	11.9	53.2	494
Tallahassee city	63 165	31.0	13.4	4.8	16.1	9.2	1.5	18.3	0.3	15.5	1.4	19.1	4.5	47.0	971
Tamarac city	27 736	45.2	10.4	21.8	12.5	5.8	2.3	6.3	1.0	10.2	5.1	25.8	17.9	47.8	218
Tampa city	124 594	37.2	16.8	6.9	20.3	11.6	2.9	8.8	0.7	15.0	2.6	18.7	8.0	50.1	3 524
Titusville city	17 183	48.2	16.7	14.1	16.7	10.4	2.5	5.3	0.6	12.4	3.7	17.5	10.7	45.6	427

City	Households with Non-Hispanic White householder		Households with Black or African American householder		Households with American Indian and Alaska Native householder		Households with Asian, Hawaiian, and Pacific Islander householder		Households with Hispanic or Latino[1] householder		Foreign-born population	Place of birth (percent)			Percent in non-English speaking households	
	Number of households	Percent that are family households	Number of households	Percent that are family households	Number of households	Percent that are family households	Number of households	Percent that are family households	Number of households	Percent that are family households	Percent of total population that is foreign-born	Europe	Asia	Latin America	Linguistically isolated	Not linguistically isolated
	44	45	46	47	48	49	50	51	52	53	54	55	56	57	58	59
FLORIDA	4 566 541	64.0	752 783	71.9	19 623	67.7	85 036	74.4	851 742	77.2	16.7	2.2	1.5	12.2	6.1	22.6
Altamonte Springs city	14 034	49.2	1 774	58.2	36	33.3	498	64.1	2 299	72.6	12.7	2.3	2.5	6.8	4.0	21.3
Apopka city	6 475	72.5	1 378	74.7	34	100.0	170	81.8	1 419	83.1	11.8	1.4	1.6	8.2	5.0	22.4
Aventura city	11 274	45.5	200	50.0	10	0.0	135	71.9	2 241	60.5	36.8	10.2	4.1	19.7	7.8	38.7
Boca Raton city	28 171	63.2	791	82.3	46	45.7	478	66.1	2 207	68.2	18.0	5.1	2.4	8.5	4.5	22.4
Bonita Springs city	13 270	68.8	36	44.4	15	66.7	71	67.6	1 344	78.4	16.0	2.6	0.5	11.0	7.5	15.0
Boynton Beach city	19 909	54.2	4 119	83.1	47	59.6	287	75.6	1 542	76.9	17.4	3.4	1.1	11.6	5.4	21.4
Bradenton city	17 352	56.9	2 481	76.0	49	75.5	129	62.0	1 336	76.9	8.5	1.5	0.8	5.4	3.2	16.3
Cape Coral city	36 839	74.0	679	80.1	74	71.6	318	80.5	2 584	79.1	8.7	3.3	0.9	3.6	2.6	17.1
Clearwater city	40 509	54.7	3 657	67.0	211	61.6	524	70.0	2 697	77.9	13.2	4.8	1.6	5.1	4.5	17.2
Coconut Creek city	16 874	57.7	929	66.4	20	100.0	344	73.8	1 619	80.7	18.3	5.2	2.1	9.5	4.0	24.5
Cooper City city	7 083	84.5	352	91.8	0	X	355	100.0	1 171	93.0	16.9	2.9	4.1	8.8	2.9	30.1
Coral Gables city	8 160	55.3	329	58.4	34	26.5	137	55.5	7 984	67.1	37.9	4.4	1.2	31.5	9.1	57.8
Coral Springs city	29 267	77.5	3 308	85.1	63	100.0	1 204	85.9	5 150	85.4	21.3	2.9	2.8	14.3	5.3	29.4
Davie town	21 839	66.7	1 195	68.7	122	92.6	670	74.2	4 509	80.5	17.5	2.4	2.0	11.6	4.4	28.2
Daytona Beach city	19 438	43.9	7 266	63.6	75	46.7	481	46.6	879	53.4	7.7	2.6	1.9	2.0	1.8	13.7
Deerfield Beach city	25 569	47.0	3 074	74.2	47	34.0	284	54.9	1 823	69.8	22.7	5.1	1.1	13.9	7.0	23.0
Delray Beach city	20 290	49.5	4 552	80.0	51	37.3	195	65.1	1 272	75.0	21.5	3.5	0.9	15.7	7.8	22.8
Deltona city	19 204	76.1	1 329	88.4	56	100.0	236	74.6	3 931	88.2	7.1	1.8	1.0	3.8	3.0	23.9
Dunedin city	16 442	55.5	243	70.4	22	0.0	101	60.4	447	59.5	9.7	4.6	1.4	1.6	1.8	12.5
Fort Lauderdale city	47 793	41.2	12 893	69.9	151	11.3	664	50.9	5 188	57.0	21.7	3.8	1.3	15.0	7.1	23.4
Fort Myers city	11 595	45.9	5 187	72.3	95	57.9	207	56.0	1 838	77.5	13.4	1.4	0.9	10.5	7.6	18.5
Fort Pierce city	7 634	55.4	5 245	66.8	29	48.3	102	69.6	1 240	77.1	18.4	1.1	0.8	16.2	8.9	20.1
Gainesville city	25 798	45.6	7 116	67.0	137	64.2	1 795	44.6	1 866	45.4	8.7	1.7	3.8	2.3	2.2	16.4
Greenacres city	9 492	58.3	512	83.2	75	100.0	147	75.5	1 677	81.8	19.3	3.6	1.2	13.9	8.0	25.3
Hallandale city	13 186	42.3	1 902	68.1	6	0.0	174	50.6	2 707	64.6	36.1	12.9	1.7	16.0	13.7	32.0
Hialeah city	3 535	63.1	1 483	75.9	91	81.3	212	73.6	66 225	82.7	72.1	0.5	0.3	71.2	38.4	57.9
Hollywood city	41 348	52.5	5 846	68.6	139	88.5	985	72.2	10 512	72.7	26.3	4.8	1.9	17.2	7.8	33.2
Homestead city	3 245	57.4	2 159	71.0	52	84.6	63	55.6	4 509	80.8	36.0	0.8	0.7	34.4	26.9	36.9
Jacksonville city	188 746	65.8	76 041	70.0	956	73.3	6 154	76.9	9 847	73.7	5.9	1.5	2.4	1.0	1.8	13.1
Jupiter town	15 726	66.5	106	75.5	6	100.0	107	79.0	849	77.5	10.5	3.3	1.2	4.9	3.5	15.4
Key West city	9 527	48.2	734	58.9	26	23.1	60	55.0	1 488	72.4	15.8	4.9	1.4	8.8	5.8	27.1
Kissimmee city	8 713	62.5	1 511	76.4	51	90.2	449	70.6	6 360	79.9	19.5	2.1	2.9	13.2	11.7	41.4
Lakeland city	25 163	58.8	5 848	66.4	109	79.8	378	72.0	1 728	66.0	5.7	1.2	1.1	2.7	2.4	12.5
Lake Worth city	8 574	44.8	1 948	72.0	64	100.0	70	65.7	2 969	78.3	35.6	4.2	1.2	28.7	20.8	28.9
Largo city	31 649	53.1	569	55.2	127	70.1	406	91.4	1 045	58.5	9.4	3.6	1.7	2.0	2.2	13.1
Lauderdale Lakes city	4 068	39.2	6 674	78.3	6	100.0	132	65.9	656	66.2	40.5	2.3	0.8	35.1	9.6	26.2
Lauderhill city	8 869	50.3	11 202	72.0	26	100.0	287	79.4	1 407	67.2	33.8	2.3	1.4	28.4	6.1	22.5
Margate city	17 460	57.4	1 816	86.0	33	75.8	556	85.1	2 456	82.5	22.0	3.3	2.3	15.0	7.0	24.4
Melbourne city	25 894	59.2	2 400	64.6	147	61.2	545	61.1	1 245	67.5	7.8	2.5	2.3	2.1	1.7	13.8
Miami city	17 987	41.5	26 748	64.1	239	55.6	922	56.5	89 431	66.5	59.5	1.2	0.6	57.4	33.1	47.1
Miami Beach city	20 401	32.4	1 773	39.1	194	34.5	495	22.4	23 285	47.6	55.5	7.6	1.6	45.1	25.7	47.8
Miramar city	5 830	70.8	9 499	84.3	53	84.9	552	88.8	6 487	87.3	40.7	1.5	1.7	36.4	6.4	43.5
North Lauderdale city	4 789	62.5	3 244	83.7	11	0.0	317	71.3	1 931	82.8	34.9	1.8	2.1	30.4	9.8	32.1
North Miami city	5 388	41.3	9 404	79.5	28	0.0	404	66.3	4 981	69.9	48.5	1.8	1.8	44.4	17.2	55.6
North Miami Beach city	4 691	55.0	4 417	78.5	88	60.2	535	82.1	3 975	79.8	49.7	3.3	4.0	41.3	14.6	55.6
Oakland Park city	8 650	43.6	2 261	69.9	19	0.0	252	56.3	1 917	69.2	29.6	2.8	2.2	23.4	13.3	27.9
Ocala city	13 949	57.5	3 495	66.9	67	46.3	154	87.0	899	73.7	4.6	0.9	1.1	2.0	2.4	9.2
Orlando city	47 988	44.7	17 535	65.8	173	46.8	1 825	64.2	11 975	65.8	14.4	1.3	2.4	9.6	6.6	24.5
Ormond Beach city	14 865	67.1	365	62.2	18	33.3	231	85.7	226	82.7	7.0	3.0	1.3	1.1	1.1	11.7
Oviedo city	6 662	83.5	660	81.1	19	100.0	184	93.5	999	95.8	9.2	2.0	1.7	4.4	1.5	23.6
Palm Bay city	23 807	71.9	3 268	71.6	162	67.3	461	70.5	2 153	82.6	9.5	1.7	1.6	5.4	2.1	16.7
Palm Beach Gardens city	13 966	65.5	263	70.7	0	X	379	72.6	554	81.6	10.8	3.4	2.0	3.8	1.4	16.6
Palm Coast city	11 392	77.2	1 425	65.6	55	74.5	155	97.4	747	88.9	12.5	5.2	1.5	5.0	2.1	18.4
Panama City city	11 343	60.8	2 780	63.2	81	61.7	183	58.5	227	68.3	3.2	1.1	1.3	0.4	0.6	9.0
Pembroke Pines city	31 084	63.7	5 873	77.1	53	100.0	1 694	82.2	12 266	84.3	29.0	2.9	2.9	22.0	5.1	41.1
Pensacola city	16 791	56.9	6 513	67.7	98	42.9	311	74.6	497	70.6	3.6	1.0	1.5	0.7	1.2	9.5
Pinellas Park city	17 312	61.1	347	70.9	68	70.6	536	83.0	947	76.0	9.5	3.1	3.4	2.0	3.3	14.5
Plantation city	24 393	64.2	3 826	76.8	81	77.8	787	64.5	3 595	74.8	22.4	2.9	2.4	15.5	4.3	25.8
Plant City city	7 807	70.7	1 644	72.3	14	21.4	80	77.5	1 302	88.5	9.8	0.6	0.7	8.1	6.7	15.5
Pompano Beach city	25 830	46.6	5 722	73.0	60	38.3	176	73.3	2 519	65.0	20.3	4.5	0.9	12.9	7.1	22.6
Port Orange city	18 445	67.3	265	75.5	17	64.7	140	71.4	398	76.9	5.7	2.8	1.2	0.7	1.1	11.5
Port St. Lucie city	29 463	74.8	1 894	85.3	74	60.8	312	92.3	1 874	85.8	9.6	2.6	1.1	5.4	1.8	16.9
Riviera Beach city	4 113	54.5	6 707	74.5	21	0.0	108	86.1	456	73.0	10.1	1.5	1.3	6.7	3.3	11.4
St. Petersburg city	81 865	53.4	20 274	66.7	324	50.3	2 171	72.9	3 612	59.1	9.1	3.3	2.3	2.5	3.0	13.7
Sanford city	8 725	60.6	3 843	69.8	56	82.1	157	80.3	1 099	73.9	5.9	0.8	1.0	3.6	3.6	15.5
Sarasota city	18 383	46.8	3 032	67.4	70	55.7	163	70.6	1 796	75.7	13.9	3.1	1.0	8.9	7.7	15.3
Sunrise city	21 442	59.8	5 467	79.7	74	78.4	845	83.7	4 860	79.9	28.1	3.7	2.7	20.8	5.8	30.4
Tallahassee city	38 918	45.7	19 956	49.5	117	41.0	1 375	57.3	2 023	40.7	5.5	1.1	1.9	1.8	1.3	12.4
Tamarac city	21 714	53.8	2 211	71.1	31	58.1	304	70.7	2 801	75.9	21.3	4.3	1.4	14.5	5.2	22.6
Tampa city	72 255	51.8	27 433	66.2	553	56.2	2 155	65.9	20 940	65.6	12.2	1.3	1.9	8.4	6.3	23.4
Titusville city	14 366	64.5	1 854	65.3	107	74.8	144	67.4	498	72.7	4.8	1.5	0.9	1.8	0.7	10.8

[1]Hispanic or Latino persons may be of any race.

STATE Place code	City	Total population	Under 5 years	5 to 17 years	18 to 24 years	25 to 44 years	45 to 64 years	65 years and over	Median age	+/- U.S. percent under 18 years	+/- U.S. percent 65 years and over	Non-Hispanic White Total population	Under 18 years	65 years and over
		1	2	3	4	5	6	7	8	9	10	11	12	13
	FLORIDA—Cont'd													
12 75812	Wellington village	38 036	6.6	24.2	6.2	29.5	24.6	8.9	36.9	5.1	-3.5	30 394	30.1	9.4
12 76582	Weston city..................	49 133	8.8	23.7	4.8	36.4	19.4	6.9	34.1	6.8	-5.5	30 018	32.2	8.4
12 76600	West Palm Beach city...	81 539	5.6	15.3	9.7	31.7	21.4	16.3	36.7	-4.8	3.9	37 646	10.8	24.4
12 78275	Winter Haven city.........	25 944	5.5	14.2	7.5	22.0	22.3	28.4	44.0	-6.0	16.0	18 114	14.1	36.2
12 78325	Winter Springs city........	31 424	6.4	21.0	6.9	29.9	24.7	11.0	37.4	1.7	-1.4	25 660	26.2	11.9
13 00000	GEORGIA..................	8 186 453	7.2	19.2	10.2	32.6	21.1	9.6	33.4	0.7	-2.8	5 129 727	23.5	12.0
13 01052	Albany city....................	77 053	7.8	20.0	12.8	28.1	19.3	12.0	31.1	2.1	-0.4	25 080	17.6	21.1
13 01696	Alpharetta city	34 611	8.8	18.7	7.2	40.3	19.4	5.6	33.3	1.8	-6.8	27 827	26.8	6.6
13 03436	Athens-Clarke County ...	101 489	5.4	12.5	31.0	28.0	15.1	8.0	25.4	-7.8	-4.4	62 893	10.9	9.6
13 04000	Atlanta city....................	416 629	6.4	15.9	13.3	35.4	19.1	9.9	31.9	-3.4	-2.5	130 417	11.1	11.2
13 04200	Augusta-Richmond County	199 775	7.2	19.7	11.8	30.4	20.0	10.9	32.3	1.2	-1.5	88 675	19.8	15.9
13 19000	Columbus city	186 291	7.3	19.5	12.0	29.8	19.7	11.7	32.6	1.1	-0.7	90 547	21.1	16.4
13 21380	Dalton city	28 233	8.6	18.3	12.3	29.9	19.1	11.8	31.1	1.2	-0.6	14 092	19.1	20.7
13 25720	East Point city	39 429	8.9	20.6	11.6	31.4	19.4	8.1	30.0	3.8	-4.3	5 097	9.6	33.8
13 31908	Gainesville city	25 454	8.5	16.4	15.7	29.8	17.0	12.6	29.9	-0.8	0.2	12 312	16.1	21.8
13 38964	Hinesville city	30 534	10.4	23.5	14.0	36.3	12.7	3.1	25.9	8.2	-9.3	12 120	27.8	5.2
13 44340	LaGrange city	26 393	7.8	20.8	11.8	26.7	19.0	13.9	32.8	2.9	1.5	12 442	21.1	20.4
13 49000	Macon city	97 719	7.9	19.1	11.5	27.6	20.0	14.0	33.6	1.3	1.6	34 073	15.2	24.3
13 49756	Marietta city	58 374	7.5	14.5	14.6	39.3	16.0	8.1	30.0	-3.7	-4.3	28 229	16.1	14.1
13 59724	Peachtree City city	31 896	6.2	25.1	5.3	29.1	26.5	7.8	37.5	5.6	-4.6	27 391	30.8	8.4
13 66668	Rome city	35 055	6.3	17.4	12.4	28.0	19.9	15.9	34.6	-2.0	3.5	20 982	17.8	21.8
13 67284	Roswell city	79 844	6.7	17.8	8.2	35.3	24.6	7.3	35.2	-1.2	-5.1	60 381	23.3	8.9
13 69000	Savannah city	131 603	7.0	18.6	13.4	28.2	19.4	13.4	32.3	-0.1	1.0	49 983	15.3	19.0
13 71492	Smyrna city	40 780	6.2	13.1	10.4	44.0	17.7	8.7	32.0	-6.4	-3.7	22 062	12.5	14.1
13 78800	Valdosta city.................	43 823	7.7	18.5	18.5	27.0	17.8	10.6	28.2	0.5	-1.8	20 521	17.4	14.3
13 80508	Warner Robins city........	48 885	7.3	20.0	9.4	32.8	19.5	10.9	33.3	1.6	-1.5	29 340	21.5	15.7
15 00000	HAWAII.....................	1 211 537	6.4	17.9	9.5	30.1	22.9	13.3	36.2	-1.4	0.9	276 191	16.0	12.9
15 14650	Hilo CDP	40 798	5.6	19.1	10.2	24.5	24.0	16.6	38.6	-1.0	4.2	6 315	12.3	21.1
15 17000	Honolulu CDP	371 619	5.0	14.1	8.9	29.9	24.1	18.0	39.7	-6.6	5.6	69 202	11.8	18.0
15 23150	Kailua CDP	36 585	5.5	18.6	7.2	28.6	26.3	13.6	39.1	-1.6	1.2	15 436	17.5	15.8
15 28250	Kaneohe CDP	34 976	5.2	19.3	7.8	29.1	23.3	15.2	38.0	-1.2	2.8	6 729	14.5	17.7
15 51050	Mililani Town CDP........	28 565	6.3	20.9	8.9	28.7	28.7	6.5	36.2	1.5	-5.9	5 440	20.0	6.3
15 62600	Pearl City CDP	30 818	4.9	13.3	14.4	26.6	23.1	17.8	37.0	-7.5	5.4	4 890	12.1	11.0
15 77750	Waimalu CDP	29 504	5.6	15.9	9.8	31.5	27.3	9.9	37.8	-4.2	-2.5	4 788	10.5	9.3
15 79700	Waipahu CDP	33 109	6.7	19.8	9.8	27.3	20.6	15.8	35.5	0.8	3.4	1 406	12.4	18.8
16 00000	IDAHO.......................	1 293 953	7.5	20.9	10.7	28.2	21.4	11.3	33.2	2.7	-1.1	1 138 460	27.0	12.3
16 08830	Boise City city	185 937	7.0	18.2	11.5	32.7	20.5	10.0	32.8	-0.5	-2.4	167 306	24.4	10.8
16 12250	Caldwell city	25 720	9.4	21.6	13.0	27.1	17.9	11.0	28.8	5.3	-1.4	17 270	25.3	15.4
16 16750	Coeur d'Alene city........	34 785	7.0	18.2	11.5	28.3	20.4	14.6	34.8	-0.5	2.2	32 658	24.6	15.2
16 39700	Idaho Falls city	50 484	8.0	21.9	9.7	28.2	20.9	11.3	32.3	4.2	-1.1	45 167	28.9	12.2
16 46540	Lewiston city.................	31 047	5.8	17.6	10.7	26.5	22.1	17.3	37.9	-2.3	4.9	29 325	22.9	17.9
16 52120	Meridian city	34 858	11.5	22.5	7.0	37.1	15.6	6.3	30.1	8.3	-6.1	32 227	33.3	6.7
16 56260	Nampa city	52 416	10.5	20.7	12.3	30.6	14.7	11.1	28.5	5.5	-1.3	40 761	28.5	13.5
16 64090	Pocatello city	51 565	8.4	18.1	16.8	27.4	18.7	10.6	28.8	0.8	-1.8	46 620	25.5	11.0
16 82810	Twin Falls city	34 164	8.0	18.1	12.2	25.9	20.6	15.2	33.8	0.4	2.8	29 987	24.3	16.7
17 00000	ILLINOIS....................	12 419 293	7.0	19.1	9.7	30.7	21.4	12.1	34.7	0.4	-0.3	8 423 408	22.8	14.9
17 00243	Addison village	35 709	7.7	18.9	10.8	32.4	21.9	8.3	32.2	0.9	-4.1	21 094	20.4	12.6
17 01114	Alton city	30 425	6.9	18.9	8.7	29.9	19.6	16.1	35.4	0.1	3.7	21 847	21.1	18.9
17 02154	Arlington Heights village	76 098	6.2	17.0	5.9	30.2	25.0	15.8	39.7	-2.5	3.4	66 666	22.6	17.6
17 03012	Aurora city	143 609	10.5	21.2	10.0	36.4	15.9	5.9	29.3	6.0	-6.5	74 593	26.1	9.5
17 04013	Bartlett village	36 840	10.9	21.3	5.1	38.5	18.6	5.6	33.5	6.5	-6.8	30 930	31.1	6.3
17 04845	Belleville city................	42 165	6.1	17.4	8.7	31.0	19.8	17.0	37.2	-2.2	4.6	33 899	20.9	20.0
17 05573	Berwyn city	54 016	7.9	18.1	9.8	32.3	18.4	13.5	33.8	0.3	1.1	30 493	18.5	21.3
17 06613	Bloomington city	65 046	7.3	17.4	12.3	33.5	19.3	10.1	32.4	-1.0	-2.3	54 347	22.6	11.4
17 07133	Bolingbrook village	56 454	9.6	22.6	8.1	35.5	19.8	4.3	31.0	6.5	-8.1	32 452	28.3	5.1
17 09447	Buffalo Grove village.....	42 591	6.5	22.1	5.6	32.3	24.4	9.1	37.4	2.9	-3.3	36 616	27.7	9.9
17 09642	Burbank city	27 825	5.8	19.0	10.0	28.0	23.1	14.1	36.9	-0.9	1.7	23 447	23.3	15.9
17 10487	Calumet City city	38 992	8.0	20.9	8.2	31.3	18.7	12.8	33.7	3.2	0.4	13 523	16.0	27.2
17 11332	Carol Stream village	39 790	7.5	22.7	8.9	37.8	17.7	5.5	31.3	4.5	-6.9	29 168	29.4	6.5
17 11358	Carpentersville village ...	30 287	10.4	22.6	10.9	35.2	15.5	5.4	28.1	7.3	-7.0	15 475	25.7	9.0
17 12385	Champaign city	67 873	4.8	13.1	31.5	26.8	15.1	8.8	25.3	-7.8	-3.6	48 497	14.7	10.4
17 14000	Chicago city..................	2 895 964	7.5	18.6	11.2	33.6	18.8	10.3	31.5	0.4	-2.1	907 734	13.5	16.4
17 14026	Chicago Heights city	33 045	9.0	22.8	9.4	28.6	18.4	11.8	30.6	6.1	-0.6	12 164	19.7	22.1
17 14351	Cicero town	85 616	10.8	23.8	13.0	31.8	13.6	7.0	26.4	8.9	-5.4	16 859	15.5	27.3
17 17887	Crystal Lake city...........	37 836	8.3	23.7	6.5	33.4	19.3	8.8	34.1	6.3	-3.6	33 919	31.2	9.6

Table A-5. Cities — Age, Ethnicity, and Household Structure

City	Black or African American Total population	Under 18 years	65 years and over	American Indian and Alaska Native Total population	Under 18 years	65 years and over	Asian, Hawaiian, and Pacific Islander Total population	Under 18 years	65 years and over	Hispanic or Latino[1] Total population	Under 18 years	65 years and over	Two or more races Total population	Under 18 years	65 years and over
	14	15	16	17	18	19	20	21	22	23	24	25	26	27	28
FLORIDA—Cont'd															
Wellington village	2 057	39.5	4.9	28	21.4	0.0	766	23.8	11.2	4 314	31.8	7.1	678	43.5	7.2
Weston city	2 046	34.4	4.6	73	19.2	0.0	1 562	33.9	4.5	15 060	32.7	4.7	1 380	42.8	2.7
West Palm Beach city	25 996	33.3	8.8	223	39.0	12.6	1 317	22.5	3.8	15 007	23.9	10.9	3 101	29.4	8.8
Winter Haven city	5 855	32.7	10.7	32	100.0	0.0	403	29.5	10.2	1 182	32.0	10.9	573	34.0	8.7
Winter Springs city	1 597	38.4	5.9	71	7.0	0.0	495	27.7	3.2	3 251	32.4	8.7	649	37.0	4.9
GEORGIA	2 342 110	31.7	6.6	23 688	24.5	4.8	175 329	25.2	3.8	429 976	31.0	2.0	124 217	39.4	4.1
Albany city	50 315	32.7	7.6	115	19.1	0.0	510	25.1	2.7	720	21.5	5.3	435	57.7	10.3
Alpharetta city	2 405	30.8	1.1	119	26.1	0.0	1 709	28.6	3.0	1 820	30.4	1.1	626	34.8	1.8
Athens-Clarke County	27 978	30.3	6.7	240	29.2	6.7	3 298	19.5	1.1	6 170	29.6	1.7	1 321	30.4	1.3
Atlanta city	254 914	28.4	10.0	854	23.4	6.4	8 360	12.9	3.3	18 582	21.7	2.8	5 005	21.8	7.0
Augusta-Richmond County	98 824	32.2	7.4	606	24.7	7.2	3 235	20.4	3.8	5 637	32.2	3.4	3 912	49.4	3.4
Columbus city	80 509	32.4	7.7	1 048	24.2	6.1	3 368	26.1	5.2	8 459	30.5	4.4	3 650	43.3	4.7
Dalton city	2 149	26.9	9.5	145	40.0	0.0	461	21.9	2.4	11 344	37.0	1.2	797	40.4	5.0
East Point city	30 758	32.2	4.5	115	43.5	14.8	162	21.0	0.0	2 942	33.9	2.1	734	41.8	4.1
Gainesville city	3 760	29.4	10.1	34	0.0	20.6	755	30.2	3.4	8 423	34.7	1.3	576	49.5	6.1
Hinesville city	13 697	37.5	1.7	161	21.1	0.0	745	13.6	2.6	2 815	39.0	1.6	1 390	60.7	0.6
LaGrange city	12 618	35.3	8.8	67	28.4	0.0	216	10.6	0.0	784	26.8	1.8	419	60.9	5.5
Macon city	61 080	33.1	8.7	151	44.4	11.9	795	28.9	0.8	866	39.1	2.7	960	46.3	6.7
Marietta city	17 316	29.2	3.3	197	21.3	0.0	1 382	13.0	5.9	9 929	25.2	1.0	2 013	32.9	2.7
Peachtree City city	1 835	39.2	3.3	63	22.2	0.0	1 263	29.8	1.6	1 133	26.7	7.4	362	40.3	5.8
Rome city	9 642	31.3	9.2	169	23.7	3.6	547	29.4	4.4	3 509	34.6	1.3	660	47.3	6.8
Roswell city	6 328	28.7	3.4	271	38.0	11.1	2 994	23.9	3.7	8 449	25.9	1.2	1 763	43.1	0.9
Savannah city	75 172	32.4	10.2	288	11.1	23.3	2 284	21.3	7.7	2 779	26.3	3.4	1 460	34.5	9.5
Smyrna city	10 945	28.0	2.3	145	26.9	0.0	1 619	16.0	3.5	5 386	27.7	1.7	990	35.4	3.9
Valdosta city	21 573	34.4	7.3	163	51.5	0.0	258	7.0	8.1	813	22.5	7.4	681	40.7	4.6
Warner Robins city	15 311	36.5	3.8	245	9.8	4.9	1 199	25.9	5.0	2 208	32.8	2.5	932	54.1	1.8
HAWAII	20 945	25.0	2.4	3 216	20.8	4.3	616 511	20.4	17.8	87 582	39.3	4.4	263 587	41.9	5.0
Hilo CDP	312	36.2	2.2	154	17.5	0.0	20 318	18.4	22.7	3 624	43.6	4.4	12 824	40.9	5.7
Honolulu CDP	5 566	22.8	3.8	676	16.6	8.1	233 884	17.1	21.2	16 360	32.2	6.2	55 647	35.9	7.6
Kailua CDP	272	22.1	3.3	150	21.3	4.7	10 615	18.7	18.9	2 175	39.1	4.4	9 205	41.0	6.1
Kaneohe CDP	340	19.1	4.1	0	0.0	0.0	17 847	19.6	19.4	2 564	38.5	4.4	9 494	41.3	6.5
Mililani Town CDP	928	33.8	2.4	19	0.0	0.0	14 368	19.9	9.2	2 235	45.8	0.9	7 143	46.8	2.3
Pearl City CDP	878	18.9	0.0	56	10.7	0.0	18 673	14.1	24.4	2 342	32.6	5.0	5 616	37.7	5.8
Waimalu CDP	402	10.2	3.0	122	12.3	0.0	17 413	18.8	12.9	1 859	33.9	3.6	6 289	30.9	3.0
Waipahu CDP	252	30.2	5.6	16	0.0	0.0	25 683	23.7	17.7	2 036	38.8	6.9	5 386	43.9	6.6
IDAHO	5 244	35.8	4.4	17 528	34.5	5.0	12 553	23.3	7.7	101 594	41.8	2.2	26 990	44.7	5.0
Boise City city	1 417	32.5	6.4	1 523	30.9	5.1	3 721	22.4	3.4	8 405	34.7	2.5	4 613	41.9	3.1
Caldwell city	74	54.1	0.0	255	36.9	6.7	249	17.3	6.4	7 400	43.4	1.4	751	52.6	5.6
Coeur d'Alene city	79	26.6	0.0	303	27.4	5.9	255	29.0	14.9	755	36.2	3.6	799	42.6	2.8
Idaho Falls city	406	46.8	0.0	450	34.9	3.1	359	21.7	6.7	3 473	37.8	3.0	788	42.8	5.2
Lewiston city	115	35.7	13.0	374	37.2	1.3	291	16.8	5.5	546	37.2	9.2	455	34.3	12.3
Meridian city	43	9.3	11.6	117	17.1	6.8	582	23.7	2.6	1 128	46.2	0.0	861	54.9	2.7
Nampa city	181	31.5	7.7	363	35.8	2.8	655	27.6	4.0	9 529	42.0	2.4	1 542	44.7	4.5
Pocatello city	407	19.4	17.0	753	31.9	8.1	700	18.4	5.9	2 656	41.6	4.2	966	50.1	3.6
Twin Falls city	30	0.0	0.0	190	32.1	4.2	325	26.5	5.5	3 185	41.2	3.0	826	42.5	6.9
ILLINOIS	1 864 619	32.3	8.3	30 407	29.2	4.1	427 251	23.3	6.1	1 529 141	36.0	3.1	249 431	41.2	5.0
Addison village	966	47.2	1.7	27	0.0	0.0	2 954	24.0	4.5	10 353	37.9	1.3	900	38.4	3.6
Alton city	7 163	36.4	9.7	123	21.1	4.1	62	21.0	0.0	539	40.8	4.1	751	50.9	4.5
Arlington Heights village	793	37.2	0.5	93	59.1	0.0	4 682	22.2	4.0	3 287	26.8	1.7	994	41.6	4.3
Aurora city	15 589	37.0	3.0	493	28.4	1.4	4 465	29.3	1.6	47 192	38.4	1.7	4 215	51.0	2.2
Bartlett village	595	36.6	0.0	0	X	X	2 934	32.7	4.3	2 002	41.3	0.9	493	57.2	0.0
Belleville city	6 421	33.8	4.9	96	29.2	17.7	289	13.1	1.4	959	41.9	2.2	662	44.3	7.1
Berwyn city	745	37.0	2.6	199	31.7	9.0	1 292	14.9	7.6	20 543	37.5	2.8	1 953	38.7	3.7
Bloomington city	5 480	35.5	4.0	128	7.8	3.9	1 915	22.1	3.9	2 135	35.6	1.7	1 423	60.0	2.1
Bolingbrook village	11 334	38.1	2.0	134	37.3	0.0	3 858	28.7	7.2	7 338	38.3	3.2	1 810	53.6	2.9
Buffalo Grove village	277	36.5	6.5	55	32.7	0.0	3 687	31.7	3.7	1 524	34.8	6.1	595	57.5	3.9
Burbank city	45	20.0	13.3	77	40.3	0.0	535	32.5	6.9	3 131	32.5	3.9	751	39.5	3.9
Calumet City city	20 507	35.4	5.2	30	33.3	0.0	278	36.0	9.4	4 243	36.5	4.3	706	47.2	7.5
Carol Stream village	1 652	33.1	1.5	108	32.4	0.0	4 071	28.1	3.6	4 033	33.6	2.4	1 024	42.6	2.5
Carpentersville village	1 153	45.9	1.2	109	17.4	0.0	640	38.1	4.1	12 510	40.4	1.2	1 328	41.8	3.6
Champaign city	10 531	33.5	6.9	182	23.1	5.5	4 625	12.0	1.8	2 899	16.3	1.9	1 315	34.8	1.9
Chicago city	1 059 594	31.6	10.1	9 498	29.5	5.0	128 117	18.4	9.2	753 835	35.2	3.6	87 381	33.1	6.2
Chicago Heights city	12 397	39.6	6.9	69	42.0	11.6	223	27.8	6.3	7 784	38.2	3.7	1 092	40.3	7.4
Cicero town	1 002	29.3	3.2	633	48.2	0.0	854	28.6	2.6	66 188	39.7	1.8	3 175	38.2	3.7
Crystal Lake city	313	54.3	0.0	48	27.1	0.0	554	31.2	3.1	2 584	36.0	1.1	435	60.7	1.4

[1] Hispanic or Latino persons may be of any race.

Table A-5. Cities — Age, Ethnicity, and Household Structure

City	Total households	Family households (percent)						Nonfamily households (percent)						Percent of householders 65 years and over who live alone	Grandparents who are responsible for the care of their grandchildren
		Married-couple family households			Other family households			Two or more unrelated persons		Male living alone		Female living alone			
		Total	With children	House-holder 65 years or over	Total	With children	House-holder 65 years or over	Total	House-holder 65 years or over	Total	House-holder 65 years or over	Total	House-holder 65 years or over		
	29	30	31	32	33	34	35	36	37	38	39	40	41	42	43
FLORIDA—Cont'd															
Wellington village	12 877	70.8	39.2	9.4	11.9	8.0	1.0	4.1	0.3	5.3	1.0	7.9	2.7	26.1	178
Weston city	16 525	71.9	44.6	6.9	10.6	6.8	0.9	3.6	0.3	6.2	0.9	7.7	2.9	31.8	196
West Palm Beach city	34 679	35.1	13.3	8.4	18.1	9.6	2.2	9.4	0.5	17.3	3.7	20.1	8.6	52.7	839
Winter Haven city	11 847	42.4	12.3	16.2	16.0	8.3	2.5	5.4	1.1	13.1	4.8	23.1	14.4	49.2	320
Winter Springs city	11 740	63.2	31.1	9.5	13.8	8.5	1.4	4.7	0.6	6.1	1.9	12.2	4.8	37.2	192
GEORGIA	3 007 678	52.5	25.2	7.1	18.2	10.4	2.2	5.7	0.3	9.9	1.6	13.7	5.6	42.7	92 265
Albany city	28 747	37.0	15.5	7.2	28.9	16.8	3.7	5.1	0.4	11.4	2.0	17.6	7.9	46.9	1 391
Alpharetta city	13 705	55.4	31.9	3.8	9.3	5.1	0.6	7.8	0.1	11.0	0.8	16.6	3.6	49.2	110
Athens-Clarke County	39 678	33.3	14.2	5.3	16.7	9.3	1.8	20.2	0.2	13.1	1.5	16.6	4.8	46.7	925
Atlanta city	168 341	25.1	9.9	4.4	25.1	13.5	3.7	11.4	0.5	17.8	2.2	20.6	6.4	50.4	5 947
Augusta-Richmond County	73 939	42.7	19.9	7.1	24.9	14.8	2.9	4.8	0.5	11.1	2.0	16.5	6.6	44.8	3 312
Columbus city	69 787	45.5	21.4	7.7	23.1	13.6	3.1	4.7	0.3	10.3	1.9	16.4	7.7	46.2	2 571
Dalton city	9 850	54.3	27.9	7.5	15.4	7.7	1.8	3.8	0.4	9.5	2.0	17.0	8.1	51.2	369
East Point city	14 484	30.9	13.7	5.9	33.9	21.1	2.3	7.6	0.4	13.0	1.1	14.6	4.4	39.4	648
Gainesville city	8 430	46.0	22.0	9.0	18.0	9.4	2.4	6.0	0.3	11.3	2.1	18.7	9.4	49.7	241
Hinesville city	10 611	56.3	35.2	2.3	21.0	16.0	0.9	5.7	0.0	9.2	0.4	7.7	1.4	36.7	386
LaGrange city	10 069	37.6	17.3	7.9	28.0	15.9	4.3	4.5	0.3	11.0	1.9	18.8	9.2	47.0	446
Macon city	38 594	34.4	13.8	8.0	29.1	17.4	3.9	5.0	0.5	11.9	2.5	19.7	9.6	49.5	1 766
Marietta city	23 945	36.3	16.9	4.2	18.6	11.0	1.3	11.7	0.3	14.0	1.3	19.4	5.4	54.0	363
Peachtree City city	10 974	72.9	41.5	7.3	8.7	6.1	0.7	2.3	0.0	5.9	0.6	10.2	5.0	41.5	107
Rome city	13 159	43.3	18.5	9.4	21.7	11.6	3.1	5.0	0.5	10.4	2.5	19.6	11.5	51.8	449
Roswell city	30 326	59.1	29.3	5.6	10.7	5.8	0.7	7.3	0.1	9.4	0.8	13.4	3.8	41.8	200
Savannah city	51 378	36.6	15.0	7.7	24.9	14.1	4.3	7.2	0.4	12.4	2.5	19.0	9.2	48.6	2 318
Smyrna city	18 551	36.0	15.2	5.2	15.3	8.2	0.9	10.0	0.2	15.2	1.1	23.4	4.4	46.7	193
Valdosta city	16 695	37.5	17.5	6.0	23.9	14.1	3.0	9.8	0.5	11.2	2.0	17.6	7.0	48.7	590
Warner Robins city	19 655	47.2	21.0	8.3	20.7	14.3	1.8	4.2	0.2	13.2	1.9	14.7	6.2	44.1	522
HAWAII	403 572	54.5	24.8	11.1	17.1	7.8	3.8	6.6	0.5	10.7	2.3	11.1	4.9	31.8	14 029
Hilo CDP	14 593	49.6	19.6	13.4	20.4	11.1	3.1	6.0	0.7	10.7	3.5	13.4	7.5	38.9	523
Honolulu CDP	140 401	46.2	18.2	12.3	16.3	5.9	4.6	7.7	0.7	13.9	3.0	15.8	7.2	36.9	3 260
Kailua CDP	12 238	60.5	25.7	12.7	16.1	7.3	3.8	6.9	0.9	7.3	1.6	9.2	4.1	24.9	451
Kaneohe CDP	10 984	62.1	26.6	15.6	18.2	7.5	5.7	4.3	0.4	6.8	1.6	8.6	4.3	21.4	549
Mililani Town CDP	9 049	71.8	36.5	7.3	13.8	6.7	1.4	3.6	0.1	5.1	0.4	5.7	1.2	15.4	210
Pearl City CDP	8 872	63.5	20.1	20.2	19.3	4.4	7.1	2.3	0.3	6.8	2.4	8.2	4.9	20.8	330
Waimalu CDP	10 599	57.5	23.9	8.6	14.6	6.2	1.8	6.9	0.1	13.8	1.4	7.3	1.9	24.2	369
Waipahu CDP	7 582	61.9	26.4	17.2	23.9	10.0	5.9	3.5	0.7	5.0	2.1	5.7	3.6	19.3	740
IDAHO	470 133	59.6	28.9	10.0	12.3	8.0	1.2	5.8	0.3	10.0	2.1	12.3	6.3	42.0	8 110
Boise City city	74 609	49.8	24.3	7.0	13.2	8.6	1.0	9.0	0.3	12.4	1.6	15.6	6.5	49.4	717
Caldwell city	8 931	52.8	27.3	8.4	18.3	12.0	1.3	5.3	0.3	9.1	2.1	14.4	8.8	52.0	346
Coeur d'Alene city	14 001	47.9	21.6	10.2	16.1	10.7	1.5	8.0	0.3	10.1	1.7	17.8	9.3	47.8	239
Idaho Falls city	18 805	56.5	28.6	9.1	13.7	9.2	1.4	4.6	0.2	11.1	2.4	14.2	7.0	47.0	206
Lewiston city	12 820	51.6	20.7	12.4	13.5	8.3	1.7	7.1	0.6	11.8	2.9	16.0	8.5	43.8	163
Meridian city	11 753	67.3	40.5	5.6	13.7	9.7	0.7	4.5	0.3	6.1	0.6	8.4	4.3	42.6	125
Nampa city	18 270	56.7	30.9	8.5	15.5	10.7	1.5	5.3	0.3	7.9	1.9	14.6	7.9	48.6	359
Pocatello city	19 423	53.7	25.6	8.9	13.7	8.7	1.4	7.6	0.3	11.5	1.7	13.5	6.1	42.3	233
Twin Falls city	13 273	51.4	22.9	10.8	15.7	10.1	1.2	6.0	0.4	10.7	2.2	16.3	8.9	47.1	254
ILLINOIS	4 592 740	52.2	25.1	8.6	15.9	8.5	2.3	5.2	0.3	11.3	2.3	15.5	7.4	46.2	103 717
Addison village	11 623	63.7	31.8	8.7	14.8	7.4	1.7	5.0	0.3	7.6	1.4	8.9	3.8	32.5	186
Alton city	12 520	39.8	17.4	8.5	21.2	13.2	3.1	5.4	0.3	14.0	3.4	19.5	11.4	55.5	334
Arlington Heights village	30 844	58.8	26.6	11.4	7.9	3.0	1.8	3.9	0.3	10.5	2.0	18.8	9.3	45.6	160
Aurora city	46 649	57.8	34.9	4.4	16.2	10.1	1.1	5.4	0.3	9.7	1.3	10.8	3.9	47.4	1 225
Bartlett village	12 157	73.3	45.5	5.2	8.9	5.5	0.5	4.1	0.1	5.7	0.7	8.0	3.0	39.4	116
Belleville city	17 895	43.3	18.9	9.3	17.2	10.3	2.7	4.7	0.3	13.6	2.6	21.3	11.9	54.1	261
Berwyn city	19 707	48.3	26.1	7.6	17.4	7.1	4.0	4.9	0.5	12.6	3.6	16.8	8.8	50.6	586
Bloomington city	26 734	47.2	22.9	6.3	12.4	8.1	1.1	8.0	0.3	13.6	1.8	18.9	6.8	52.6	278
Bolingbrook village	17 401	67.1	39.2	3.3	15.8	9.6	0.8	3.0	0.0	7.2	0.4	7.0	2.5	41.7	541
Buffalo Grove village	15 565	67.2	38.3	7.5	7.6	4.2	0.7	3.6	0.2	8.0	1.5	13.6	4.9	43.5	146
Burbank city	9 273	59.0	28.3	11.4	19.3	6.9	5.1	2.5	0.5	7.8	2.8	11.4	7.4	37.4	226
Calumet City city	15 141	40.2	19.8	8.2	27.0	16.1	3.6	2.9	0.2	12.1	2.9	17.8	8.3	48.4	517
Carol Stream village	13 800	60.9	39.3	2.7	12.6	7.2	0.7	5.3	0.3	9.2	1.0	12.0	4.9	61.6	126
Carpentersville village	8 681	63.7	38.3	5.0	19.2	11.0	2.2	3.6	0.1	6.5	1.0	7.1	2.7	33.9	300
Champaign city	27 187	35.8	16.3	6.1	10.7	6.4	1.2	16.9	0.2	17.8	1.5	18.8	5.7	48.5	313
Chicago city	1 061 964	36.3	17.8	5.7	23.8	11.8	3.7	7.4	0.5	14.5	2.5	18.0	6.4	47.3	41 328
Chicago Heights city	10 736	46.9	23.0	10.5	27.5	15.3	3.9	3.5	0.2	9.9	2.8	12.3	6.4	38.7	501
Cicero town	23 124	57.5	40.4	5.2	21.3	11.4	2.4	3.6	0.2	8.5	2.7	9.0	6.1	53.0	966
Crystal Lake city	12 900	66.0	39.3	6.9	10.0	6.0	1.1	3.8	0.5	6.8	1.6	13.4	7.2	50.9	131

Table A-5. Cities — Age, Ethnicity, and Household Structure

City	Households with Non-Hispanic White householder		Households with Black or African American householder		Households with American Indian and Alaska Native householder		Households with Asian, Hawaiian, and Pacific Islander householder		Households with Hispanic or Latino[1] householder		Foreign-born population				Percent in non-English speaking households	
												Place of birth (percent)				
	Number of households	Percent that are family households	Number of households	Percent that are family households	Number of households	Percent that are family households	Number of households	Percent that are family households	Number of households	Percent that are family households	Percent of total population that is foreign-born	Europe	Asia	Latin America	Linguistically isolated	Not linguistically isolated
	44	45	46	47	48	49	50	51	52	53	54	55	56	57	58	59
FLORIDA—Cont'd																
Wellington village	10 738	82.6	569	81.0	8	0.0	232	79.7	1 226	85.2	13.4	2.7	1.8	7.9	2.0	25.7
Weston city	10 804	79.6	686	88.9	51	62.7	413	96.6	4 446	88.6	28.0	2.5	2.8	21.2	5.7	40.6
West Palm Beach city	19 696	41.9	9 021	67.8	67	50.7	515	55.7	4 857	71.5	24.7	2.7	1.6	19.4	10.8	23.6
Winter Haven city	8 995	55.6	2 153	66.5	0	X	82	65.9	452	70.8	5.9	1.0	1.1	3.3	2.4	13.4
Winter Springs city	9 824	75.8	516	72.9	59	62.7	187	82.4	1 019	88.6	8.1	1.9	1.5	3.8	2.2	19.0
GEORGIA	2 017 242	70.2	803 387	70.2	8 251	74.5	51 421	78.3	102 650	80.5	7.1	0.9	1.8	3.7	3.1	11.3
Albany city	11 628	61.5	16 582	69.2	56	35.7	149	65.8	301	58.5	1.5	0.2	0.6	0.4	0.4	9.0
Alpharetta city	11 363	63.4	985	61.4	56	85.7	577	70.4	523	80.1	11.7	2.2	3.9	4.0	2.8	15.9
Athens-Clarke County	26 589	42.3	10 077	66.5	89	62.9	1 143	57.3	1 541	72.6	8.4	0.8	2.4	4.2	4.3	12.6
Atlanta city	66 985	34.8	91 921	61.1	298	58.7	2 557	48.8	4 962	60.3	6.6	0.9	1.4	3.3	3.3	12.6
Augusta-Richmond County	37 278	61.7	33 470	73.8	265	56.6	944	72.5	1 514	75.4	3.4	1.0	1.2	0.9	0.7	11.2
Columbus city	36 848	66.1	28 604	71.2	359	75.5	936	87.0	2 457	71.9	4.7	1.4	1.2	1.8	1.3	11.7
Dalton city	6 184	60.3	805	65.2	40	100.0	135	100.0	2 621	91.8	30.5	0.4	1.6	28.2	21.5	21.5
East Point city	2 537	47.6	11 106	67.6	43	79.1	54	53.7	635	84.6	7.9	0.4	0.4	6.4	4.4	12.4
Gainesville city	5 286	55.8	1 400	66.4	6	100.0	129	93.0	1 542	88.5	29.3	0.7	2.8	25.0	20.8	19.0
Hinesville city	4 700	75.0	4 633	79.2	78	85.9	232	78.4	818	80.8	6.7	1.7	1.9	2.7	1.7	22.2
LaGrange city	5 312	62.0	4 377	69.8	40	100.0	51	37.3	217	63.6	2.9	0.4	0.7	1.7	1.3	7.0
Macon city	15 808	55.5	22 032	69.3	46	87.0	262	65.3	271	66.4	1.3	0.2	0.6	0.3	0.6	6.3
Marietta city	13 527	50.6	7 057	56.3	75	84.0	507	63.9	2 320	72.6	19.7	1.3	2.5	14.0	12.0	18.2
Peachtree City city	9 694	81.1	575	85.0	13	100.0	329	84.2	299	86.0	7.8	2.3	2.9	1.4	1.7	13.5
Rome city	8 573	61.6	3 520	68.0	59	100.0	147	78.9	830	87.8	8.9	0.4	1.3	7.0	6.2	10.7
Roswell city	24 380	68.9	2 469	64.4	86	54.7	935	79.9	2 077	82.5	15.7	2.4	3.7	8.7	7.9	16.8
Savannah city	22 819	53.3	26 405	68.4	101	81.2	765	60.8	886	64.6	3.8	0.8	1.3	1.3	1.3	9.8
Smyrna city	11 306	47.0	4 801	54.6	65	41.5	690	57.2	1 453	72.3	17.6	1.7	3.7	10.6	6.8	19.1
Valdosta city	9 060	53.8	7 229	70.5	42	92.9	63	63.5	210	80.0	2.3	0.6	0.5	1.2	0.9	6.3
Warner Robins city	12 740	66.0	5 600	69.9	138	69.6	329	81.5	640	83.6	4.2	0.6	1.9	1.6	1.3	10.9
HAWAII	122 694	62.7	7 327	73.5	1 109	69.8	201 643	75.6	21 490	76.0	17.5	0.9	14.6	0.6	5.8	34.5
Hilo CDP	3 106	56.4	100	70.0	83	62.7	7 807	72.5	896	76.6	7.2	0.5	5.0	0.3	3.3	25.1
Honolulu CDP	35 398	51.2	2 257	63.9	273	74.7	84 459	67.6	5 068	61.7	25.3	1.1	21.7	0.5	10.5	37.7
Kailua CDP	6 202	71.0	107	44.9	47	74.5	3 628	82.5	484	76.4	7.2	1.4	4.1	0.5	1.6	22.0
Kaneohe CDP	2 978	71.1	134	67.2	4	0.0	5 648	84.2	506	86.4	6.3	0.7	4.7	0.3	0.8	28.6
Mililani Town CDP	2 377	78.9	311	82.3	4	100.0	4 654	87.8	546	91.8	10.9	0.7	9.0	0.5	1.6	28.7
Pearl City CDP	1 373	74.9	197	68.0	16	43.8	6 023	85.1	454	89.6	13.4	0.5	12.2	0.2	2.9	36.9
Waimalu CDP	2 611	61.9	302	48.3	55	72.7	5 907	77.9	551	67.5	14.6	0.3	13.0	0.4	3.0	34.7
Waipahu CDP	505	71.9	80	68.8	7	0.0	5 851	88.5	437	88.8	37.7	0.2	34.4	0.3	9.8	62.3
IDAHO	428 555	71.3	1 402	62.5	5 462	76.2	3 911	65.5	25 016	83.1	5.0	0.9	0.6	3.0	2.2	12.3
Boise City city	68 646	63.0	466	47.6	499	70.5	1 389	63.6	2 533	66.7	4.8	2.0	1.4	1.0	1.7	11.7
Caldwell city	6 927	67.2	22	100.0	76	48.7	114	64.9	1 688	87.5	11.5	0.3	0.6	10.3	6.3	28.3
Coeur d'Alene city	13 273	63.4	37	62.2	122	73.8	84	50.0	241	82.2	2.4	0.8	0.5	0.3	0.4	6.7
Idaho Falls city	17 289	69.8	95	85.3	102	81.4	152	50.0	981	75.1	4.4	0.5	0.4	3.1	2.3	10.5
Lewiston city	12 231	65.8	29	20.7	151	35.1	83	31.3	182	55.5	2.1	0.6	0.8	0.3	0.5	6.4
Meridian city	11 031	81.2	27	81.5	30	83.3	184	85.3	293	66.2	3.2	1.1	1.1	0.6	1.0	9.8
Nampa city	15 453	69.9	61	67.2	93	75.3	156	78.8	2 246	89.2	8.3	0.6	0.8	6.6	4.8	19.1
Pocatello city	17 723	67.6	194	55.2	312	69.2	219	59.4	771	75.6	2.6	0.6	0.9	0.7	0.7	10.5
Twin Falls city	12 100	66.7	13	23.1	68	54.4	72	88.9	844	77.4	6.3	2.4	0.8	2.8	2.7	14.2
ILLINOIS	3 405 787	66.0	624 639	68.5	10 180	71.1	136 187	74.5	373 499	84.2	12.3	3.1	2.9	5.9	5.4	19.2
Addison village	8 142	73.3	291	86.3	15	100.0	857	91.8	2 279	90.7	34.3	9.4	6.7	17.8	17.2	36.7
Alton city	9 396	58.5	2 712	69.8	70	50.0	25	40.0	132	82.6	0.9	0.3	0.2	0.3	0.2	7.1
Arlington Heights village	27 728	66.3	307	43.3	17	100.0	1 780	71.1	816	79.7	13.9	6.0	5.1	2.2	4.4	19.2
Aurora city	28 939	68.8	5 253	72.6	148	70.3	1 333	85.7	10 698	87.5	21.5	1.2	2.4	17.4	12.4	28.2
Bartlett village	10 631	80.6	200	91.5	0	X	773	93.3	497	93.8	10.9	3.2	5.7	1.7	2.1	22.2
Belleville city	14 984	59.9	2 351	63.5	39	82.1	85	83.5	264	61.0	1.9	0.8	0.6	0.3	0.4	7.8
Berwyn city	13 570	57.4	199	71.4	59	91.5	393	83.2	5 138	87.0	25.1	5.7	2.5	16.6	9.2	42.4
Bloomington city	23 053	58.2	2 229	65.2	37	51.4	673	67.3	619	82.2	4.5	0.6	2.4	1.3	1.9	8.9
Bolingbrook village	11 018	80.2	3 561	84.1	52	100.0	979	94.7	1 542	91.8	14.4	1.5	5.5	6.2	3.8	24.0
Buffalo Grove village	13 759	73.7	127	41.7	32	100.0	1 142	90.5	419	69.5	20.4	10.5	7.4	1.9	5.4	25.1
Burbank city	8 110	76.8	4	100.0	10	100.0	136	93.4	870	86.9	21.8	14.1	4.0	3.5	8.6	29.8
Calumet City city	6 173	61.6	7 606	69.4	12	0.0	100	69.0	1 097	83.0	7.3	1.3	0.9	4.6	3.3	17.7
Carol Stream village	10 738	69.2	653	75.2	30	70.0	1 136	94.2	1 113	92.1	16.8	3.6	8.0	4.6	6.3	22.9
Carpentersville village	5 660	76.9	340	94.4	32	84.4	142	84.5	2 435	95.4	26.4	1.4	1.2	23.7	20.6	28.0
Champaign city	20 233	44.9	3 802	58.7	89	46.1	1 703	41.0	933	47.8	9.4	1.7	5.1	1.8	3.4	13.9
Chicago city	444 580	45.3	361 626	66.5	3 189	69.0	46 000	61.9	191 357	82.4	21.7	5.0	3.9	12.2	11.2	30.7
Chicago Heights city	4 898	69.4	3 857	74.7	21	61.9	67	86.6	1 803	88.4	11.2	1.3	0.4	9.5	6.3	25.4
Cicero town	7 890	54.9	348	62.9	142	93.0	276	92.0	14 293	92.4	43.6	1.6	1.0	41.0	24.7	56.3
Crystal Lake city	12 078	75.2	59	81.4	23	30.4	149	77.9	510	93.3	7.4	1.7	1.3	3.8	2.7	11.4

[1] Hispanic or Latino persons may be of any race.

STATE Place code	City	Total population	Under 5 years	5 to 17 years	18 to 24 years	25 to 44 years	45 to 64 years	65 years and over	Median age	+/− U.S. percent under 18 years	+/− U.S. percent 65 years and over	Non-Hispanic White Total population	Under 18 years	65 years and over
		1	2	3	4	5	6	7	8	9	10	11	12	13
	ILLINOIS—Cont'd													
17 18563	Danville city	33 865	7.2	17.5	10.2	27.2	21.3	16.6	36.6	-1.0	4.2	23 107	20.5	21.4
17 18823	Decatur city	82 113	6.7	17.3	11.4	25.9	22.2	16.5	37.2	-1.7	4.1	63 436	20.0	19.4
17 19161	DeKalb city	38 840	5.4	11.9	38.7	24.0	11.9	8.1	23.1	-8.4	-4.3	29 479	15.9	10.2
17 19642	Des Plaines city	58 695	5.6	16.3	7.3	29.7	23.6	17.5	39.7	-3.8	5.1	44 539	19.0	21.7
17 20292	Dolton village	25 740	7.1	24.6	8.8	29.4	20.7	9.3	33.3	6.0	-3.1	3 354	6.9	40.7
17 20591	Downers Grove village ..	48 638	6.2	18.2	6.8	29.1	25.3	14.3	39.1	-1.3	1.9	42 464	24.0	15.7
17 22255	East St. Louis city	31 530	8.8	24.3	9.6	24.5	20.3	12.6	31.2	7.4	0.2	421	13.8	37.3
17 23074	Elgin city	93 895	9.1	19.7	10.1	33.7	18.6	8.8	30.9	3.1	-3.6	50 982	21.9	14.3
17 23256	Elk Grove Village village	34 758	6.3	18.5	7.0	31.8	24.6	11.9	37.7	-0.9	-0.5	28 510	24.0	13.5
17 23620	Elmhurst city	42 959	7.1	18.8	6.8	28.3	22.8	16.2	38.7	0.2	3.8	38 971	25.2	17.4
17 23724	Elmwood Park village	25 405	5.6	16.4	8.5	30.4	22.5	16.6	38.6	-3.7	4.2	21 381	20.4	18.6
17 24582	Evanston city	74 239	5.7	14.5	16.1	32.4	20.4	10.9	32.5	-5.5	-1.5	46 456	15.8	13.1
17 27884	Freeport city	26 440	6.6	17.8	8.7	28.1	20.7	18.1	37.9	-1.3	5.7	21 310	20.6	21.1
17 28326	Galesburg city	33 827	5.9	15.2	12.0	27.4	21.6	17.9	38.1	-4.6	5.5	27 803	19.8	20.5
17 29730	Glendale Heights village	31 676	8.0	18.9	11.6	37.1	19.7	4.8	30.5	1.2	-7.6	17 589	22.7	6.5
17 29756	Glen Ellyn village	27 040	8.3	19.9	6.3	30.4	23.8	11.2	37.0	2.5	-1.2	23 558	28.1	12.2
17 29938	Glenview village	41 679	6.7	18.9	5.1	25.6	27.7	15.9	41.3	-0.1	3.5	34 212	24.1	18.4
17 30926	Granite City city	31 632	6.0	18.9	8.5	29.0	21.5	16.1	37.6	-0.8	3.7	29 527	23.7	16.8
17 32018	Gurnee village	28 615	9.5	21.2	5.2	37.5	19.7	7.0	34.2	5.0	-5.4	22 549	28.9	7.7
17 32746	Hanover Park village	38 366	9.0	22.2	10.7	35.0	19.1	4.0	29.7	5.5	-8.4	21 075	27.4	5.0
17 33383	Harvey city	30 106	9.6	25.7	10.8	26.8	18.2	8.9	27.9	9.6	-3.5	1 738	9.8	39.4
17 34722	Highland Park city	31 379	7.4	19.8	4.3	25.9	27.7	15.0	40.6	1.5	2.6	27 161	26.5	16.8
17 35411	Hoffman Estates village	50 352	7.2	21.2	8.9	34.2	21.9	6.6	33.6	2.7	-5.8	34 486	26.8	8.2
17 38570	Joliet city	106 157	9.2	20.1	9.9	33.6	16.2	11.0	31.0	3.6	-1.4	64 680	24.6	15.5
17 38934	Kankakee city	27 561	8.2	21.5	9.8	29.5	17.6	13.3	32.3	4.0	0.9	13 210	20.3	22.2
17 42028	Lansing village	28 161	6.5	17.8	8.2	28.5	23.6	15.5	38.4	-1.4	3.1	23 022	22.3	18.4
17 44407	Lombard village	41 859	6.0	16.4	7.9	33.4	21.3	14.9	36.7	-3.3	2.5	35 206	21.8	16.6
17 47774	Maywood village	26 987	7.9	23.8	10.8	27.4	20.4	9.7	30.7	6.0	-2.7	1 476	16.6	27.8
17 49867	Moline city	43 717	6.5	17.4	9.3	27.8	23.6	15.3	37.9	-1.8	2.9	36 061	21.1	17.8
17 51089	Mount Prospect village ..	56 706	6.4	16.3	8.1	31.3	23.0	14.8	37.2	-3.0	2.4	41 384	20.5	18.9
17 51349	Mundelein village	30 588	9.2	21.8	8.2	36.2	18.1	6.5	31.7	5.3	-5.9	20 463	29.0	8.5
17 51622	Naperville city	128 300	8.3	23.7	6.6	33.4	21.8	6.2	34.2	6.3	-6.2	106 772	31.5	6.7
17 53000	Niles village	30 144	3.9	13.0	7.5	23.6	25.0	27.0	46.8	-8.8	14.6	24 423	14.9	31.8
17 53234	Normal town	45 337	4.9	12.4	38.3	22.8	13.8	7.7	23.0	-8.4	-4.7	39 101	16.1	8.7
17 53481	Northbrook village	33 425	5.7	19.4	4.4	22.0	29.4	19.1	44.1	-0.6	6.7	29 332	24.8	21.0
17 53559	North Chicago city	36 001	7.8	16.3	34.4	27.6	9.7	4.2	22.0	-1.6	-8.2	14 178	15.3	3.8
17 54638	Oak Forest city	27 955	6.5	19.8	8.9	31.3	24.7	8.9	35.6	0.6	-3.5	24 524	26.3	9.4
17 54820	Oak Lawn village	55 391	5.3	16.6	7.4	26.1	22.9	21.7	41.5	-3.8	9.3	49 764	20.8	23.3
17 54885	Oak Park village	52 524	6.9	17.2	6.5	35.8	24.0	9.6	36.0	-1.6	-2.8	34 793	22.1	11.6
17 56640	Orland Park village	51 103	5.2	19.3	7.3	24.5	27.0	16.7	41.4	-1.2	4.3	46 280	23.7	17.9
17 57225	Palatine village	65 156	7.3	17.2	8.7	35.6	22.4	8.8	34.3	-1.2	-3.6	48 311	21.9	11.0
17 57875	Park Ridge city	37 735	5.8	18.3	5.7	25.1	25.7	19.5	42.5	-1.6	7.1	35 106	23.6	20.5
17 58447	Pekin city	33 840	6.6	16.7	9.2	30.4	21.5	15.6	37.1	-2.4	3.2	32 006	23.7	16.3
17 59000	Peoria city	112 892	7.4	18.3	12.0	27.6	20.5	14.1	33.8	0.0	1.7	77 099	19.2	18.1
17 62367	Quincy city	40 277	6.1	17.5	10.2	26.0	20.6	19.7	38.4	-2.1	7.3	37 219	22.3	20.8
17 65000	Rockford city	149 704	7.6	18.9	9.2	29.8	20.2	14.2	34.4	0.8	1.8	102 753	20.8	18.7
17 65078	Rock Island city	39 723	6.4	16.7	13.6	25.2	21.9	16.2	36.4	-2.6	3.8	29 610	18.3	19.6
17 66040	Round Lake Beach village	25 659	11.2	23.9	9.5	36.2	14.6	4.6	28.5	9.4	-7.8	15 991	31.3	6.4
17 66703	St. Charles city	27 955	6.1	21.7	7.3	29.7	25.2	10.0	36.6	2.1	-2.4	25 264	26.8	10.8
17 68003	Schaumburg village	74 511	5.8	15.9	8.3	36.3	24.3	9.4	35.3	-4.0	-3.0	56 308	19.5	11.4
17 70122	Skokie village	63 320	5.1	17.7	7.2	25.3	25.1	19.6	41.9	-2.9	7.2	41 456	19.7	26.3
17 72000	Springfield city	112 201	6.4	17.6	8.9	30.0	22.6	14.5	36.9	-1.7	2.1	90 418	20.9	16.3
17 73157	Streamwood village	36 732	8.2	19.7	8.0	37.1	20.9	6.0	32.5	2.2	-6.4	24 966	24.5	7.4
17 75484	Tinley Park village	48 327	6.4	19.9	8.0	31.1	23.6	11.0	36.5	0.6	-1.4	43 863	25.8	11.7
17 77005	Urbana city	36 196	4.4	10.3	36.2	26.5	13.1	9.4	24.6	-11.0	-3.0	23 575	12.1	12.9
17 79293	Waukegan city	87 969	9.6	20.9	12.0	33.4	16.4	7.8	29.0	4.8	-4.6	27 183	18.3	17.6
17 81048	Wheaton city	55 439	6.4	19.8	10.1	29.2	23.3	11.2	35.8	0.5	-1.2	48 635	25.6	12.3
17 81087	Wheeling village	34 411	6.9	16.6	9.9	35.1	20.9	10.6	34.5	-2.2	-1.8	22 769	18.8	14.2
17 82075	Wilmette village	27 684	7.1	23.0	3.4	21.9	28.0	16.5	42.2	4.4	4.1	24 334	29.7	18.0
17 83245	Woodridge village	31 075	7.2	19.5	9.2	35.8	22.4	5.8	32.8	1.0	-6.6	21 837	25.6	6.8
18 00000	**INDIANA**	6 080 485	7.0	18.9	10.1	29.5	22.1	12.4	35.2	0.2	0.0	5 220 722	24.6	13.3
18 01468	Anderson city	59 636	6.8	16.5	11.4	27.9	21.1	16.4	36.1	-2.4	4.0	48 372	20.8	18.5
18 05860	Bloomington city	69 229	3.9	8.5	42.4	24.4	12.9	8.0	23.3	-13.3	-4.4	59 608	11.8	9.0
18 10342	Carmel city	37 802	7.9	22.4	4.7	30.3	25.0	9.8	37.2	4.6	-2.6	34 630	29.9	10.5
18 14734	Columbus city	39 137	7.7	18.0	8.2	29.7	22.8	13.7	36.4	0.0	1.3	35 261	25.0	14.7
18 19486	East Chicago city	32 414	9.0	21.6	11.5	26.4	17.8	13.8	30.8	4.9	1.4	3 946	12.2	38.2
18 20728	Elkhart city	51 701	9.7	18.8	10.4	31.9	17.7	11.5	30.8	2.8	-0.9	34 226	23.6	15.7
18 22000	Evansville city	121 877	6.4	16.4	11.5	28.5	20.9	16.3	36.5	-2.9	3.9	104 262	20.6	17.7
18 23278	Fishers town	38 937	11.9	20.2	5.2	45.0	14.3	3.3	30.7	6.4	-9.1	35 332	31.7	3.5

Table A-5. Cities — Age, Ethnicity, and Household Structure

City	Black or African American			American Indian and Alaska Native			Asian, Hawaiian, and Pacific Islander			Hispanic or Latino[1]			Two or more races		
		Age (percent)			Age (percent)			Age (percent)			Age (percent)			Age (percent)	
	Total population	Under 18 years	65 years and over	Total population	Under 18 years	65 years and over	Total population	Under 18 years	65 years and over	Total population	Under 18 years	65 years and over	Total population	Under 18 years	65 years and over
	14	15	16	17	18	19	20	21	22	23	24	25	26	27	28
ILLINOIS—Cont'd															
Danville city	8 136	31.5	8.0	44	11.4	0.0	433	38.1	1.6	1 589	36.9	1.3	713	53.4	1.0
Decatur city	15 777	36.0	7.7	66	15.2	0.0	634	24.8	0.9	875	32.1	4.5	1 485	61.5	3.3
DeKalb city	3 388	16.5	1.9	39	12.8	10.3	1 911	12.0	0.4	3 420	29.1	1.3	1 175	41.9	2.5
Des Plaines city	455	16.7	7.3	154	37.7	11.0	4 382	26.1	6.6	8 427	33.9	2.4	1 414	37.3	4.7
Dolton village	21 144	35.4	4.6	34	0.0	0.0	235	20.4	11.1	674	39.0	4.0	344	46.5	2.0
Downers Grove village ..	807	22.6	5.1	93	46.2	0.0	2 984	24.1	5.7	1 821	30.1	2.5	582	46.6	7.6
East St. Louis city	30 802	33.4	12.2	15	0.0	60.0	33	24.2	0.0	114	4.4	27.2	171	31.6	17.5
Elgin city	6 415	34.3	3.7	435	31.3	0.0	3 295	28.3	2.2	31 926	38.0	1.8	3 493	45.1	3.1
Elk Grove Village village	368	23.4	0.0	22	63.6	0.0	3 334	25.4	4.4	2 027	28.1	6.7	499	43.5	0.0
Elmhurst city	391	18.2	3.6	64	23.4	0.0	1 412	31.0	3.8	1 673	37.2	5.6	581	43.2	5.0
Elmwood Park village....	121	23.1	38.0	234	44.9	5.6	462	20.3	9.3	2 752	31.3	4.4	676	35.1	3.0
Evanston city	16 412	29.6	10.4	114	23.7	0.0	4 510	9.5	3.4	4 633	32.1	2.2	2 443	38.1	4.5
Freeport city	3 648	36.2	6.9	132	25.0	0.0	139	34.5	0.0	545	46.6	2.8	668	62.0	0.9
Galesburg city	3 433	22.9	6.8	95	28.4	0.0	366	19.4	1.6	1 667	29.6	6.6	618	56.8	0.0
Glendale Heights village	1 448	33.4	0.0	104	3.8	0.0	6 357	28.6	4.2	5 686	35.1	1.3	990	38.3	2.7
Glen Ellyn village	510	19.4	4.9	36	0.0	0.0	1 325	28.8	3.7	1 208	30.3	1.4	525	41.9	9.3
Glenview village	816	41.8	4.0	25	44.0	0.0	4 254	27.2	5.0	1 923	36.8	3.4	568	45.1	6.2
Granite City city	675	50.2	0.0	94	24.5	10.6	105	25.7	20.0	923	42.0	5.0	368	39.7	16.0
Gurnee village	1 220	29.2	4.4	26	0.0	0.0	2 461	33.4	4.1	1 788	43.7	5.5	618	51.1	1.6
Hanover Park village.....	2 420	43.0	1.7	30	63.3	0.0	4 249	29.0	5.3	10 075	36.4	1.8	1 121	46.8	2.1
Harvey city	23 835	36.1	7.9	73	35.6	0.0	134	26.9	0.0	4 096	40.7	2.4	667	46.0	5.8
Highland Park city	383	30.5	10.7	55	5.5	0.0	804	22.9	5.8	2 940	33.2	1.3	383	43.3	3.7
Hoffman Estates village	2 091	35.4	2.2	140	29.3	0.0	7 485	27.8	3.8	5 238	34.3	2.8	1 356	47.0	2.4
Joliet city	19 403	35.8	5.2	447	44.3	4.0	1 464	30.3	5.1	19 328	37.3	2.5	2 205	47.5	4.0
Kankakee city	11 131	38.3	6.3	81	29.6	0.0	156	57.7	0.0	2 511	36.0	1.1	563	51.2	0.0
Lansing village	3 074	33.3	1.9	46	28.3	0.0	223	33.6	1.3	1 587	34.7	3.5	346	30.9	6.9
Lombard village	1 075	25.5	4.7	78	0.0	9.0	2 920	21.2	5.0	1 965	31.6	4.9	758	36.3	12.5
Maywood village	22 352	31.9	9.2	19	47.4	31.6	58	27.6	8.6	2 930	28.1	5.0	381	26.5	9.7
Moline city	1 218	32.8	4.8	131	40.0	12.2	534	26.8	0.0	5 271	38.0	4.0	871	51.1	3.7
Mount Prospect village..	1 207	26.8	1.7	105	18.1	11.4	6 507	22.9	6.2	6 633	33.3	2.3	1 506	37.5	3.5
Mundelein village	227	25.1	3.5	165	41.8	0.0	2 054	30.7	0.3	7 396	36.2	1.3	760	47.0	0.8
Naperville city	3 578	31.0	3.3	196	43.9	0.0	11 747	32.6	4.7	4 493	37.7	2.0	1 842	45.3	4.0
Niles village	287	23.0	15.7	94	55.3	0.0	3 381	21.8	6.2	1 403	29.8	5.4	589	32.6	8.1
Normal town	3 427	25.8	1.0	95	8.4	0.0	1 232	11.1	5.4	1 040	29.4	1.9	641	54.9	0.0
Northbrook village	235	28.9	8.9	24	75.0	0.0	2 920	24.2	4.8	538	29.2	6.9	462	46.8	9.5
North Chicago city.........	13 032	30.2	6.9	254	14.6	2.8	1 185	16.9	0.5	6 545	31.1	1.0	1 325	31.8	0.4
Oak Forest city.............	959	13.7	9.5	0	X	X	745	22.3	3.0	1 437	31.3	4.2	419	38.7	0.0
Oak Lawn village...........	676	16.7	9.2	82	15.9	0.0	1 015	33.9	7.4	2 981	33.0	7.9	942	40.6	5.4
Oak Park village	11 799	27.3	6.2	40	20.0	0.0	2 282	19.8	3.5	2 087	28.9	4.3	1 576	46.1	4.6
Orland Park village	293	32.1	6.5	63	9.5	0.0	2 132	28.1	5.3	1 908	35.7	4.5	491	46.4	4.3
Palatine village	1 371	28.6	1.9	142	25.4	0.0	5 225	25.5	3.6	9 479	34.6	2.3	1 162	42.5	3.3
Park Ridge city	151	41.7	5.3	55	60.0	0.0	987	17.5	7.1	1 157	34.1	5.9	428	55.8	2.3
Pekin city	945	3.6	1.5	119	18.5	0.0	79	16.5	0.0	457	36.3	2.4	263	34.2	13.7
Peoria city	27 601	40.3	5.8	232	33.2	5.6	2 776	20.7	5.5	2 792	36.8	2.4	2 640	55.5	5.0
Quincy city	1 865	36.2	8.2	97	33.0	9.3	185	23.8	3.2	377	44.6	0.0	515	50.3	4.9
Rockford city	25 870	38.1	5.5	478	28.2	2.7	3 039	30.8	3.5	15 301	41.1	2.9	4 031	51.1	3.7
Rock Island city	6 429	35.0	7.4	222	43.2	0.5	248	9.3	16.5	2 468	36.9	3.4	965	59.5	3.6
Round Lake Beach village	708	51.7	0.0	72	29.2	0.0	563	30.6	7.8	8 045	40.4	1.4	913	61.0	1.5
St. Charles city.............	502	59.4	0.0	92	7.6	5.4	408	16.9	4.2	1 528	36.4	3.5	247	41.3	2.4
Schaumburg village.......	2 515	32.2	1.1	100	9.0	0.0	10 293	24.0	3.7	4 008	30.4	4.0	1 704	49.4	1.4
Skokie village	2 955	33.2	5.3	150	44.0	4.7	13 395	25.7	6.8	3 554	29.3	8.8	2 121	42.1	5.2
Springfield city	16 905	36.8	7.2	205	24.4	0.0	1 579	24.8	7.0	1 095	26.1	7.8	2 057	49.3	8.8
Streamwood village.......	1 710	40.1	1.3	131	28.2	0.0	3 314	24.2	5.9	6 031	38.3	2.3	786	52.9	2.3
Tinley Park village.........	908	27.6	1.4	21	66.7	0.0	1 254	25.8	5.7	1 889	34.7	3.7	452	39.8	3.5
Urbana city	5 315	30.2	5.4	46	8.7	13.0	5 283	8.6	1.2	1 126	14.3	0.6	887	28.5	1.8
Waukegan city..............	16 487	33.3	5.8	273	23.1	4.0	3 090	25.3	8.5	39 706	37.7	1.8	3 002	41.9	3.7
Wheaton city	1 401	31.5	3.7	78	21.8	0.0	2 711	26.8	4.2	2 163	31.0	3.5	639	48.2	3.1
Wheeling village	872	35.1	3.8	106	23.6	0.0	2 968	24.2	7.0	7 199	35.1	2.2	951	43.5	1.1
Wilmette village	104	40.4	11.5	26	23.1	0.0	2 218	31.3	4.8	738	34.4	8.8	315	57.5	2.5
Woodridge village.........	2 549	32.6	2.4	110	20.9	5.5	3 503	26.1	5.0	2 780	30.4	2.4	532	36.8	3.4
INDIANA....................	504 449	32.2	8.6	17 168	26.7	5.7	58 955	22.7	3.9	210 538	35.3	3.5	84 487	46.5	4.8
Anderson city	8 846	32.2	8.0	229	9.6	19.2	345	46.4	1.7	1 157	34.1	1.8	699	46.5	11.7
Bloomington city	2 874	19.7	2.0	219	15.1	6.8	3 477	7.5	0.9	1 555	10.8	0.8	1 473	31.8	2.4
Carmel city	439	33.7	0.0	101	20.8	0.0	1 636	32.0	3.1	560	39.1	0.0	403	45.7	4.5
Columbus city	1 045	20.3	7.0	74	25.7	0.0	1 106	22.5	4.1	1 142	33.1	3.6	443	48.3	1.4
East Chicago city	11 655	33.7	11.2	156	28.8	3.2	61	45.9	4.9	16 720	33.2	9.6	866	35.1	12.4
Elkhart city	7 747	37.8	5.5	343	32.4	12.0	534	29.2	0.9	8 126	36.6	1.3	1 465	51.1	3.4
Evansville city..............	12 812	33.6	9.8	291	22.3	0.0	1 072	24.1	2.5	1 429	34.5	3.1	1 914	57.1	3.9
Fishers town................	1 060	32.1	1.4	60	0.0	0.0	1 153	29.1	2.3	822	42.6	0.0	585	59.7	0.0

[1] Hispanic or Latino persons may be of any race.

City	Total households	Family households (percent)						Nonfamily households (percent)						Percent of householders 65 years and over who live alone	Grandparents who are responsible for the care of their grandchildren
		Married-couple family households			Other family households			Two or more unrelated persons		Male living alone		Female living alone			
		Total	With children	House-holder 65 years or over	Total	With children	House-holder 65 years or over	Total	House-holder 65 years or over	Total	House-holder 65 years or over	Total	House-holder 65 years or over		
	29	30	31	32	33	34	35	36	37	38	39	40	41	42	43
ILLINOIS—Cont'd															
Danville city	13 252	43.7	16.4	10.9	18.5	12.1	2.2	4.0	0.3	13.1	3.3	20.6	11.8	52.8	322
Decatur city	34 084	44.1	16.6	10.6	18.1	11.8	2.3	5.1	0.6	13.6	2.7	19.0	10.5	49.7	716
DeKalb city	12 980	39.0	18.7	5.8	12.5	8.1	1.5	19.3	0.3	14.4	2.0	14.8	5.6	49.9	90
Des Plaines city	22 369	55.8	25.0	11.3	12.3	4.6	2.6	3.8	0.5	11.1	3.6	17.0	10.1	48.7	236
Dolton village	8 516	45.6	23.9	6.2	31.8	18.1	2.9	2.1	0.2	6.1	1.5	14.4	6.4	45.8	399
Downers Grove village..	18 968	59.3	28.4	9.4	9.3	4.3	1.6	4.0	0.4	9.9	2.1	17.6	10.1	51.6	125
East St. Louis city	11 144	22.6	7.8	6.1	46.9	25.0	8.4	2.8	1.0	11.9	3.5	15.9	7.3	41.0	750
Elgin city	31 563	55.6	31.5	6.5	15.8	9.1	1.2	5.2	0.4	9.8	1.8	13.6	6.0	48.8	617
Elk Grove Village village	13 271	60.4	29.7	9.4	9.9	4.4	1.6	4.2	0.1	9.0	1.7	16.6	7.5	45.5	119
Elmhurst city	15 714	63.0	31.3	11.2	8.9	3.7	2.4	3.1	0.3	9.9	2.6	15.1	9.2	46.0	88
Elmwood Park village....	9 852	49.1	22.9	8.6	16.6	7.2	3.9	5.1	0.9	12.1	3.6	17.0	10.1	50.6	173
Evanston city	29 675	41.3	18.7	5.9	12.9	7.1	1.8	9.7	0.3	14.1	2.3	22.1	7.4	54.8	502
Freeport city	11 231	45.9	17.9	11.3	15.4	10.4	2.1	5.0	0.3	12.4	2.7	21.3	11.3	50.4	199
Galesburg city	13 201	45.1	17.5	11.2	15.0	9.8	2.3	5.7	0.3	12.3	3.8	21.9	13.4	55.4	204
Glendale Heights village	10 866	57.0	32.4	3.2	13.8	6.6	1.4	6.5	0.1	12.9	0.9	9.8	2.3	41.2	255
Glen Ellyn village	10 212	63.0	34.1	9.0	8.4	4.0	0.8	3.6	0.3	8.8	1.9	16.1	8.0	49.3	58
Glenview village	15 407	68.3	32.0	14.0	8.8	4.3	1.5	2.1	0.3	6.5	2.0	14.3	7.6	37.9	61
Granite City city	12 862	47.1	19.8	10.5	18.8	10.7	2.4	4.4	0.4	11.4	2.7	18.3	11.2	51.2	257
Gurnee village	10 536	63.0	39.1	5.0	8.8	5.5	0.5	4.7	0.2	9.8	1.5	13.7	4.7	52.5	55
Hanover Park village.....	11 271	64.6	40.3	3.6	17.5	9.2	0.6	3.7	0.1	7.6	0.7	6.6	1.3	32.1	304
Harvey city	9 018	40.2	20.7	6.6	35.7	19.8	4.2	3.0	0.4	9.3	3.0	11.8	5.7	43.5	952
Highland Park city	11 500	71.2	33.8	15.0	6.7	4.0	1.1	2.4	0.7	6.5	2.0	13.2	7.6	36.6	34
Hoffman Estates village	17 096	61.6	35.5	4.7	13.3	7.4	1.0	5.5	0.3	10.1	0.9	9.5	3.0	39.4	305
Joliet city	36 332	53.6	30.5	7.0	17.0	9.6	2.0	5.0	0.4	9.6	2.3	14.8	8.3	52.9	988
Kankakee city	9 995	37.5	18.5	7.0	25.8	17.0	2.9	5.3	0.3	12.4	3.2	19.0	11.3	58.8	401
Lansing village	11 333	53.8	22.8	11.6	14.4	7.6	2.1	4.1	0.3	10.7	2.8	17.0	9.6	46.9	172
Lombard village	16 391	54.1	25.3	8.7	10.6	4.4	2.0	5.8	0.2	12.5	2.0	17.1	8.4	48.6	203
Maywood village	7 934	41.2	19.4	7.2	36.8	17.5	5.7	3.0	0.8	8.1	2.4	11.0	5.4	36.3	675
Moline city	18 468	49.0	20.2	10.7	14.2	8.8	1.6	4.8	0.4	13.2	2.5	18.8	9.9	49.3	331
Mount Prospect village..	21 648	60.2	26.3	13.2	10.6	3.5	1.9	4.4	0.2	11.0	2.3	13.9	7.5	39.0	328
Mundelein village	9 784	67.3	41.4	5.3	11.5	6.2	0.9	4.4	0.2	7.6	1.0	9.2	4.0	43.8	113
Naperville city	43 667	70.0	43.7	4.8	7.4	4.5	0.6	3.9	0.1	7.5	0.8	11.2	3.8	45.6	402
Niles village	12 012	54.1	20.4	16.6	12.2	3.6	3.5	3.0	0.6	10.0	4.1	20.7	14.5	47.4	85
Normal town	15 207	42.9	20.3	6.9	11.5	7.7	0.8	19.0	0.0	10.8	1.1	15.8	6.4	49.2	185
Northbrook village	12 336	72.7	32.0	18.6	6.9	3.2	1.8	1.5	0.3	5.2	2.1	13.8	8.9	34.8	88
North Chicago city	7 723	50.3	32.4	3.0	22.9	15.0	2.7	4.7	0.2	11.7	2.2	10.4	3.9	50.4	300
Oak Forest city	9 722	62.8	32.4	7.6	12.4	5.0	2.2	3.9	0.3	10.1	1.6	10.7	5.0	39.3	165
Oak Lawn village..........	22 293	53.0	22.5	14.3	13.1	3.9	4.6	3.1	0.6	9.9	3.4	21.0	13.1	45.8	273
Oak Park village	23 107	42.5	22.5	4.4	13.9	7.7	1.6	6.6	0.3	14.2	2.1	22.8	6.8	58.7	235
Orland Park village........	18 657	67.3	29.4	15.1	10.4	4.0	2.0	2.2	0.1	6.2	2.1	13.8	7.3	35.4	174
Palatine village	25 385	55.1	27.3	6.3	10.3	4.8	1.1	7.0	0.3	12.4	1.5	15.3	5.3	47.0	282
Park Ridge city	14 287	63.6	28.9	15.7	9.9	3.8	3.2	2.1	0.2	7.8	2.5	16.6	10.0	39.4	54
Pekin city	13 378	52.4	22.7	11.4	13.5	8.9	1.6	4.8	0.4	10.7	2.5	18.6	10.2	48.7	217
Peoria city	45 094	42.0	17.4	8.8	18.6	12.7	2.0	6.4	0.5	13.0	2.5	20.0	9.0	50.2	1 044
Quincy city	16 469	48.1	21.1	10.8	13.5	8.7	1.7	4.8	0.5	12.6	3.3	21.1	12.8	55.3	263
Rockford city	59 114	44.8	20.0	9.0	18.9	12.4	1.8	5.7	0.4	12.7	2.5	17.9	8.9	50.4	1 576
Rock Island city	16 122	42.6	16.5	10.0	16.5	9.8	2.3	5.9	0.4	14.5	3.8	20.4	10.6	53.3	400
Round Lake Beach village	7 349	67.3	45.2	2.9	15.1	10.5	0.8	3.9	0.2	6.4	1.6	7.3	2.9	53.5	327
St. Charles city	10 337	60.9	30.5	7.7	10.7	5.0	1.5	4.7	0.1	9.4	1.3	14.3	6.6	45.8	85
Schaumburg village.......	31 585	50.1	23.4	5.3	11.2	5.4	0.8	6.5	0.2	13.7	1.3	18.5	6.4	55.2	328
Skokie village	23 208	60.5	27.6	15.4	13.2	4.7	2.6	2.8	0.3	7.2	3.0	16.3	11.1	43.5	188
Springfield city	48 753	41.7	18.2	7.8	16.3	10.1	1.9	6.0	0.4	14.4	2.7	21.6	9.6	54.9	735
Streamwood village.......	12 146	63.6	32.9	5.0	14.1	7.6	1.0	4.0	0.2	9.4	0.9	8.9	1.6	28.7	226
Tinley Park village	17 496	62.0	31.7	8.3	11.1	4.9	2.0	3.7	0.1	8.1	1.5	15.0	7.5	46.3	142
Urbana city	14 247	32.4	13.4	5.9	11.6	7.3	0.9	19.0	0.3	16.5	2.0	20.4	6.3	54.0	229
Waukegan city	27 676	50.5	29.8	5.9	20.6	12.1	1.9	5.1	0.4	11.0	1.8	12.8	5.4	46.5	981
Wheaton city	19 427	62.8	32.8	8.7	8.7	4.3	1.0	3.9	0.1	9.2	1.1	15.5	6.7	44.3	100
Wheeling village	13 237	52.4	26.9	6.1	11.5	5.4	1.1	5.6	0.5	11.9	1.2	18.6	7.4	52.9	44
Wilmette village	9 994	69.0	37.9	15.3	8.0	3.9	1.9	1.9	0.5	6.8	2.6	14.3	9.0	39.5	49
Woodridge village........	11 474	56.6	30.5	3.9	15.2	8.9	0.9	4.9	0.0	11.4	0.7	12.0	3.1	44.1	128
INDIANA	2 337 229	54.5	24.6	9.1	14.5	8.8	1.8	5.2	0.3	11.0	2.2	14.9	7.5	46.2	48 181
Anderson city	25 193	42.9	15.9	9.7	18.9	11.7	2.4	5.1	0.5	12.9	3.2	20.3	11.7	54.1	631
Bloomington city...........	26 403	30.3	11.7	5.5	9.6	6.1	0.9	21.2	0.3	17.6	1.5	21.4	5.9	52.7	116
Carmel city	13 682	69.6	38.8	7.4	8.4	5.2	0.8	3.1	0.5	8.0	1.8	10.9	5.2	44.4	54
Columbus city	15 986	52.2	23.7	8.3	14.0	9.0	1.8	5.0	0.2	12.2	2.6	16.6	8.9	52.6	277
East Chicago city	11 689	36.8	18.2	9.5	31.4	18.3	5.3	3.1	0.5	12.9	3.7	15.8	7.6	42.7	579
Elkhart city	20 107	42.2	21.0	6.8	19.9	13.9	1.4	6.7	0.6	13.0	2.7	18.1	9.0	56.8	559
Evansville city..............	52 373	42.2	16.8	9.2	16.6	10.4	2.1	6.1	0.3	13.8	2.5	21.3	10.8	53.5	984
Fishers town................	14 387	66.0	41.5	2.5	8.2	5.6	0.1	5.5	0.0	7.9	0.3	12.5	2.3	49.9	116

Table A-5. Cities — Age, Ethnicity, and Household Structure

City	Households with Non-Hispanic White householder — Number of households	Percent that are family households	Households with Black or African American householder — Number of households	Percent that are family households	Households with American Indian and Alaska Native householder — Number of households	Percent that are family households	Households with Asian, Hawaiian, and Pacific Islander householder — Number of households	Percent that are family households	Households with Hispanic or Latino[1] householder — Number of households	Percent that are family households	Foreign-born population — Percent of total population that is foreign-born	Place of birth (percent) Europe	Asia	Latin America	Percent in non-English speaking households — Linguistically isolated	Not linguistically isolated
	44	45	46	47	48	49	50	51	52	53	54	55	56	57	58	59
ILLINOIS—Cont'd																
Danville city	10 102	61.5	2 543	60.5	39	69.2	138	67.4	313	88.2	2.9	0.3	0.7	1.7	1.0	9.5
Decatur city	27 614	61.6	5 818	64.7	27	37.0	217	77.4	235	69.4	1.6	0.5	0.6	0.3	0.4	6.4
DeKalb city	10 452	51.6	1 148	47.6	3	100.0	436	44.7	761	64.0	9.1	1.4	3.0	3.7	3.1	18.2
Des Plaines city	18 867	65.1	189	45.0	47	89.4	1 118	88.5	1 989	88.4	23.9	9.5	6.0	8.2	8.0	30.5
Dolton village	1 701	58.3	6 527	82.1	16	62.5	57	91.2	158	89.2	3.7	0.3	0.7	1.9	0.7	14.0
Downers Grove village..	17 036	67.3	365	51.0	30	60.0	881	88.2	526	79.8	9.8	3.1	4.4	1.7	1.6	16.5
East St. Louis city	146	58.9	10 894	69.7	6	0.0	7	100.0	50	56.0	0.3	0.0	0.1	0.1	0.1	6.6
Elgin city	21 035	64.1	2 228	73.5	142	95.1	837	83.9	7 088	91.0	23.7	1.3	3.0	19.1	14.2	28.1
Elk Grove Village village	11 334	68.2	172	48.8	8	0.0	1 096	84.6	559	88.4	14.3	4.1	7.6	2.2	4.0	23.4
Elmhurst city	14 666	71.1	111	75.7	17	100.0	406	89.7	382	77.2	8.0	3.8	2.6	1.3	2.0	16.8
Elmwood Park village....	8 681	64.0	44	38.6	42	76.2	140	66.4	774	81.9	24.3	18.9	1.9	3.2	10.5	30.7
Evanston city	20 625	49.7	5 709	70.0	50	86.0	1 509	41.9	1 227	69.9	15.4	3.7	4.4	6.3	3.2	21.5
Freeport city	9 556	59.9	1 200	69.0	67	58.2	38	86.8	137	77.4	2.7	1.0	0.5	1.2	1.2	7.9
Galesburg city	11 762	59.7	790	62.2	40	32.5	55	63.6	451	74.3	2.2	0.5	0.5	1.0	0.6	8.4
Glendale Heights village	7 081	62.8	577	64.1	30	100.0	1 768	86.8	1 281	93.4	30.3	4.3	15.7	9.9	11.9	35.8
Glen Ellyn village	9 202	70.6	225	54.2	24	70.8	353	91.5	300	84.0	10.7	3.2	4.1	2.7	2.8	16.1
Glenview village	13 333	74.9	244	91.4	0	X	1 261	94.2	459	85.0	19.5	9.1	7.7	2.1	4.8	28.5
Granite City city	12 214	65.2	171	81.9	58	100.0	45	28.9	258	97.7	1.1	0.3	0.2	0.5	0.4	6.3
Gurnee village	8 812	69.1	486	76.3	26	53.8	667	92.1	430	88.1	11.7	3.1	6.0	1.9	1.7	22.0
Hanover Park village.....	7 178	76.5	702	84.5	11	100.0	1 159	91.7	2 116	94.6	28.4	3.3	8.6	16.0	11.7	33.3
Harvey city	798	54.1	7 211	76.5	6	100.0	19	100.0	912	91.6	8.2	0.2	0.3	7.8	5.3	16.6
Highland Park city	10 551	76.8	141	100.0	7	100.0	217	97.7	574	89.2	15.3	5.7	2.5	6.3	5.5	18.8
Hoffman Estates village	12 607	72.7	814	64.9	35	100.0	2 174	89.0	1 269	83.8	23.1	4.0	12.6	6.0	8.2	28.5
Joliet city	24 896	67.0	6 023	71.7	124	78.2	426	78.4	4 630	89.0	10.9	1.1	1.0	8.7	6.2	18.5
Kankakee city	5 564	54.6	3 695	71.2	29	48.3	38	100.0	566	94.5	6.7	0.4	0.8	5.4	3.0	14.0
Lansing village	9 605	68.1	1 167	63.3	13	61.5	59	76.3	404	77.0	5.6	2.7	1.0	1.3	1.3	14.2
Lombard village	14 221	63.2	449	60.8	33	100.0	970	79.0	539	78.1	11.6	3.5	5.6	1.8	1.8	18.1
Maywood village	527	54.1	6 750	78.6	0	X	12	100.0	576	95.8	7.2	0.3	0.2	6.7	2.7	16.4
Moline city	15 971	62.0	601	59.6	54	74.1	168	89.3	1 538	75.9	7.1	0.9	1.0	4.9	3.2	11.9
Mount Prospect village..	17 246	67.9	535	49.0	33	45.5	2 111	85.3	1 485	88.4	26.7	9.2	9.4	7.5	11.4	29.3
Mundelein village	7 408	75.4	82	91.5	36	72.2	565	89.4	1 616	91.5	23.8	3.5	4.8	15.2	12.9	24.8
Naperville city	37 116	70.0	1 303	73.2	66	80.3	3 345	90.7	1 163	78.8	11.7	2.6	6.9	1.2	2.3	18.6
Niles village	10 375	63.4	72	72.2	11	100.0	1 017	86.9	338	88.2	33.7	20.0	11.0	2.3	12.1	39.8
Normal town	13 407	54.4	1 011	63.9	57	29.8	337	46.6	315	45.1	3.6	0.8	1.9	0.4	0.7	9.7
Northbrook village	11 255	78.1	21	100.0	0	X	876	97.4	113	83.2	15.2	7.1	7.0	0.6	0.3	23.2
North Chicago city	2 792	64.0	3 515	74.9	24	70.8	185	85.5	1 130	91.2	12.9	0.4	2.3	9.7	6.8	24.1
Oak Forest city	8 605	75.4	307	54.4	0	X	221	90.0	444	79.3	5.8	1.6	2.6	1.6	1.5	13.3
Oak Lawn village	20 587	65.6	324	39.2	36	100.0	285	69.1	856	80.0	11.5	6.2	3.5	1.6	3.9	19.2
Oak Park village	15 968	56.2	5 097	66.0	27	18.5	924	61.6	741	54.7	9.8	3.0	3.8	1.9	1.3	17.0
Orland Park village	17 467	77.2	91	74.7	22	100.0	554	93.3	413	78.7	9.4	4.7	3.5	1.1	2.3	19.1
Palatine village	20 810	62.1	490	71.0	32	100.0	1 821	74.4	2 075	89.5	21.9	5.2	6.6	9.4	9.2	24.4
Park Ridge city	13 606	73.0	21	100.0	7	100.0	322	85.4	258	77.1	12.7	8.5	2.6	1.3	3.0	22.3
Pekin city	13 116	65.8	0	X	39	71.8	14	100.0	114	73.7	0.8	0.4	0.2	0.2	0.3	4.6
Peoria city	33 230	57.6	9 493	68.9	81	51.9	1 069	71.7	709	78.6	4.4	0.8	2.3	0.9	1.4	11.1
Quincy city	15 461	61.6	722	62.5	32	81.3	58	39.7	82	73.2	1.0	0.3	0.3	0.2	0.2	5.2
Rockford city	44 622	60.5	8 854	71.2	169	76.3	924	77.8	3 988	81.3	8.7	1.9	1.6	4.9	4.1	15.2
Rock Island city	12 816	57.7	2 371	65.2	39	64.1	76	65.8	678	69.0	3.2	0.9	0.4	1.6	1.0	8.9
Round Lake Beach village	5 366	77.7	195	89.7	8	87.5	151	92.7	1 572	96.0	21.5	1.9	1.8	17.7	10.9	28.1
St. Charles city	9 726	71.0	65	73.8	32	53.1	128	95.3	346	78.3	6.6	2.4	1.1	2.7	2.5	11.9
Schaumburg village	25 328	58.3	1 021	67.7	31	100.0	3 636	76.2	1 218	72.7	19.1	4.5	11.5	2.4	5.1	25.8
Skokie village	17 040	68.7	853	81.6	44	84.1	3 836	90.1	1 019	86.8	37.0	12.7	19.7	3.9	9.4	43.1
Springfield city	41 031	57.0	6 141	64.7	110	41.8	547	55.6	383	69.5	2.3	0.6	1.1	0.3	0.4	7.2
Streamwood village	9 262	74.1	566	74.6	50	86.0	942	89.9	1 243	95.5	19.9	4.6	7.2	7.7	5.9	30.9
Tinley Park village	16 288	72.9	290	49.7	7	0.0	334	94.9	492	81.7	5.8	2.1	2.3	1.2	1.6	12.8
Urbana city	9 862	42.2	1 883	58.6	18	33.3	1 839	41.7	294	31.3	15.8	2.9	10.2	1.5	5.1	22.2
Waukegan city	11 852	60.1	5 656	68.4	96	56.3	965	73.0	8 691	88.3	30.2	1.1	2.9	25.9	17.7	35.9
Wheaton city	17 546	70.9	453	58.9	21	61.9	795	84.2	503	79.7	9.5	2.9	4.1	1.7	2.7	14.3
Wheeling village	10 259	58.6	315	75.2	51	86.3	946	77.4	1 545	89.9	31.4	9.9	7.6	13.5	15.5	29.7
Wilmette village	9 144	75.5	19	73.7	5	100.0	644	92.5	150	96.7	13.2	5.2	6.2	1.3	2.5	18.8
Woodridge village	8 505	70.0	1 033	65.6	28	78.6	1 066	85.4	735	83.5	17.3	3.0	8.9	4.7	4.0	23.7
INDIANA	2 050 401	69.0	184 808	66.1	6 546	69.0	20 022	64.8	56 960	77.1	3.1	0.7	0.8	1.3	1.3	9.0
Anderson city	21 257	60.2	3 295	68.9	157	80.3	63	100.0	293	90.8	1.8	0.3	0.3	1.0	0.7	6.1
Bloomington city	22 778	40.7	995	39.1	105	85.7	1 488	29.2	590	33.2	8.1	2.0	4.7	0.7	2.3	13.6
Carmel city	12 618	77.7	198	61.1	54	85.2	534	87.1	151	82.1	7.3	2.4	3.6	0.8	1.1	12.3
Columbus city	14 720	66.0	387	62.5	28	100.0	448	74.1	295	64.4	5.5	1.1	2.2	1.9	1.6	9.2
East Chicago city	2 072	51.8	4 427	64.7	48	85.4	12	100.0	5 112	78.3	14.7	1.2	0.1	13.3	8.6	45.8
Elkhart city	14 815	59.2	2 856	65.4	100	80.0	166	81.3	1 984	80.0	11.4	0.7	1.1	9.2	7.3	14.4
Evansville city	45 910	58.4	5 003	63.8	158	62.0	346	60.7	452	49.8	1.6	0.4	0.7	0.3	0.7	6.9
Fishers town	13 264	73.4	389	75.1	33	100.0	390	88.7	218	81.2	4.0	0.9	2.0	0.6	1.0	10.1

[1]Hispanic or Latino persons may be of any race.

STATE Place code	City	Population by age (percent) Total population	Under 5 years	5 to 17 years	18 to 24 years	25 to 44 years	45 to 64 years	65 years and over	Median age	+/− U.S. percent under 18 years	+/− U.S. percent 65 years and over	Non-Hispanic White Total population	Age (percent) Under 18 years	65 years and over
		1	2	3	4	5	6	7	8	9	10	11	12	13
	INDIANA—Cont'd													
18 25000	Fort Wayne city	205 941	7.9	19.2	10.8	30.2	19.5	12.4	32.8	1.4	0.0	150 843	23.5	15.1
18 27000	Gary city	102 746	8.3	21.6	9.9	25.4	22.0	12.7	33.6	4.2	0.3	10 219	19.2	19.4
18 28386	Goshen city	29 288	7.5	18.1	12.9	29.7	18.2	13.6	31.5	−0.1	1.2	22 317	22.5	17.4
18 29898	Greenwood city	35 767	7.8	17.3	9.7	31.9	21.2	12.1	34.1	−0.6	−0.3	34 193	24.9	12.4
18 31000	Hammond city	83 048	8.0	19.3	9.8	30.1	20.0	12.8	33.9	1.6	0.4	51 877	21.1	17.7
18 34114	Hobart city	25 400	5.7	17.9	9.0	29.5	22.7	15.3	37.7	−2.1	2.9	22 493	22.0	16.1
18 36000	Indianapolis city	792 217	7.4	18.3	10.1	33.0	20.3	11.1	33.6	0.0	−1.3	536 890	22.2	12.8
18 38358	Jeffersonville city	27 463	6.5	17.2	8.7	31.2	23.6	12.7	36.7	−2.0	0.3	22 363	21.2	13.8
18 40392	Kokomo city	45 967	8.0	16.9	9.3	29.4	22.0	14.3	35.7	−0.8	1.9	38 678	22.5	15.6
18 40788	Lafayette city	56 244	7.1	16.0	14.1	32.0	18.7	12.1	31.7	−2.6	−0.3	47 770	21.5	13.9
18 42426	Lawrence city	39 237	8.7	20.8	8.2	36.1	18.2	8.0	32.4	3.8	−4.4	29 604	27.4	9.9
18 46908	Marion city	31 125	6.7	16.4	13.0	25.4	21.8	16.6	36.3	−2.6	4.2	24 126	19.7	19.3
18 48528	Merrillville town	30 712	6.2	18.3	8.6	30.3	22.0	14.8	37.0	−1.2	2.4	20 095	20.1	20.3
18 48798	Michigan City city	32 822	7.2	17.6	9.3	31.3	20.1	14.4	35.2	−0.9	2.0	22 239	20.5	18.2
18 49932	Mishawaka city	46 796	7.2	16.7	11.8	31.1	19.0	14.1	33.5	−1.8	1.7	42 162	22.9	15.2
18 51876	Muncie city	67 468	5.9	14.0	24.4	24.2	18.1	13.4	28.9	−5.8	1.0	57 515	17.9	14.2
18 52326	New Albany city	37 366	6.5	17.3	9.6	29.5	21.8	15.3	36.6	−1.9	2.9	33 524	22.4	16.4
18 54180	Noblesville city	28 953	9.3	19.9	7.2	34.3	20.6	8.6	33.0	3.5	−3.8	27 882	29.1	8.7
18 61092	Portage city	33 548	7.3	18.6	10.0	29.6	22.7	11.7	35.4	0.2	−0.7	28 990	24.7	12.7
18 64260	Richmond city	39 138	6.9	16.5	11.1	27.9	21.2	16.5	36.3	−2.3	4.1	33 678	22.0	17.3
18 71000	South Bend city	107 045	8.4	18.9	10.4	29.3	18.2	14.8	32.7	1.6	2.4	67 933	20.9	19.7
18 75428	Terre Haute city	59 563	6.0	15.4	18.4	26.7	18.5	14.9	32.1	−4.3	2.5	50 811	20.3	16.3
18 78326	Valparaiso city	27 498	5.8	15.5	17.4	27.9	20.2	13.2	32.7	−4.4	0.8	25 376	20.7	14.0
18 82862	West Lafayette city	28 949	2.5	7.8	54.6	17.0	10.2	7.8	22.3	−15.4	−4.6	23 773	10.2	9.3
19 00000	**IOWA**	2 926 324	6.4	18.6	10.2	27.7	22.2	14.9	36.6	−0.7	2.5	2 713 026	24.1	15.8
19 01855	Ames city	50 656	4.5	10.1	40.1	23.5	14.3	7.4	23.6	−11.1	−5.0	43 711	13.7	8.4
19 02305	Ankeny city	26 923	8.2	19.0	11.6	33.6	19.8	7.9	31.9	1.5	−4.5	25 998	26.9	8.0
19 06355	Bettendorf city	31 321	6.2	20.2	6.7	28.3	26.5	12.2	38.7	0.7	−0.2	29 315	25.8	12.6
19 09550	Burlington city	26 817	6.3	17.8	8.7	26.2	23.6	17.3	37.9	−1.6	4.9	24 433	22.5	18.3
19 11755	Cedar Falls city	36 257	4.1	13.5	30.6	20.5	19.4	11.8	26.0	−8.1	−0.6	34 384	16.9	12.3
19 12000	Cedar Rapids city	120 563	6.9	17.5	10.8	30.5	21.2	13.1	34.7	−1.3	0.7	109 795	23.0	14.0
19 14430	Clinton city	27 806	6.5	18.2	9.2	26.6	22.6	16.9	38.3	−1.0	4.5	25 885	23.5	17.9
19 16860	Council Bluffs city	58 249	7.0	18.9	10.4	29.7	20.7	13.4	34.6	0.2	1.0	54 030	25.3	14.1
19 19000	Davenport city	98 357	7.5	18.5	10.7	30.0	21.0	12.3	33.6	0.3	−0.1	80 386	22.6	14.0
19 21000	Des Moines city	198 688	7.6	17.0	10.6	32.1	20.3	12.4	33.8	−1.1	0.0	158 585	21.6	14.0
19 22395	Dubuque city	57 468	6.2	17.3	11.7	26.5	21.5	16.7	36.9	−2.2	4.3	54 994	22.9	17.4
19 28515	Fort Dodge city	25 125	6.9	17.5	10.8	24.9	21.3	18.6	38.0	−1.3	6.2	23 028	23.1	19.9
19 38595	Iowa City city	62 381	4.4	11.8	32.6	28.1	15.9	7.2	25.4	−9.5	−5.2	53 547	14.8	8.1
19 49485	Marion city	26 477	7.3	19.1	8.4	31.9	22.2	11.2	35.1	0.7	−1.2	25 439	25.8	11.6
19 49755	Marshalltown city	26 032	6.5	18.0	9.0	26.3	22.1	18.0	38.4	−1.2	5.6	21 814	21.4	21.1
19 50160	Mason City city	29 179	6.6	17.2	10.0	26.5	21.8	17.9	38.2	−1.9	5.5	27 203	22.4	18.6
19 73335	Sioux City city	85 040	7.6	19.4	10.8	28.4	20.4	13.3	33.4	1.3	0.9	68 814	23.7	16.0
19 79950	Urbandale city	29 066	6.4	19.9	7.1	31.0	25.0	10.5	37.0	0.6	−1.9	27 295	25.7	11.1
19 82425	Waterloo city	68 636	7.1	17.7	10.4	27.6	21.9	15.4	35.9	−0.9	3.0	55 315	21.1	17.5
19 83910	West Des Moines city ...	46 300	7.7	17.2	9.4	35.8	20.3	9.6	33.0	−0.8	−2.8	42 083	23.9	10.3
20 00000	**KANSAS**	2 688 418	7.0	19.5	10.3	28.7	21.3	13.2	35.2	0.8	0.8	2 234 488	24.6	14.9
20 18250	Dodge City city	25 065	9.7	21.6	12.5	29.3	16.9	9.9	28.9	5.6	−2.5	13 060	23.9	16.9
20 21275	Emporia city	26 702	7.3	18.1	20.4	26.7	16.4	11.0	28.4	−0.3	−1.4	19 018	20.1	14.7
20 25325	Garden City city	28 060	10.0	22.9	11.4	31.4	16.8	7.5	28.6	7.2	−4.9	13 708	24.2	13.5
20 33625	Hutchinson city	40 737	6.6	16.8	10.5	28.4	21.1	16.7	37.1	−2.3	4.3	34 748	21.7	18.6
20 36000	Kansas City city	146 867	8.0	20.5	10.5	29.9	19.6	11.5	32.3	2.8	−0.9	71 729	21.4	16.5
20 38900	Lawrence city	80 083	5.4	13.2	30.5	28.5	15.2	7.2	25.3	−7.1	−5.2	65 701	17.1	8.0
20 39000	Leavenworth city	35 304	8.3	18.9	8.9	35.1	18.8	10.0	34.1	1.5	−2.4	26 120	25.8	11.6
20 39075	Leawood city	27 870	6.5	23.9	4.1	23.7	29.6	12.2	41.3	4.7	−0.2	26 200	30.1	12.6
20 39350	Lenexa city	40 097	7.0	19.0	9.1	32.9	23.3	8.8	35.1	0.3	−3.6	35 485	25.3	9.5
20 44250	Manhattan city	44 823	4.2	11.4	39.2	24.0	13.4	7.9	23.5	−10.1	−4.5	38 426	14.3	8.8
20 52575	Olathe city	93 013	9.2	21.7	9.1	36.7	18.1	5.2	30.8	5.2	−7.2	79 964	30.2	5.7
20 53775	Overland Park city	148 848	7.1	18.5	6.8	32.9	23.1	11.5	36.3	−0.1	−0.9	131 458	25.1	12.5
20 62700	Salina city	45 634	7.0	18.8	9.8	29.0	21.2	14.1	35.3	0.1	1.7	39 033	23.7	15.8
20 64500	Shawnee city	48 152	7.7	18.9	7.8	34.1	23.0	8.5	34.8	0.9	−3.9	42 329	25.8	9.1
20 71000	Topeka city	122 045	7.1	17.1	10.1	28.7	21.9	15.0	36.3	−1.5	2.6	91 795	20.5	17.6
20 79000	Wichita city	343 997	7.9	19.1	10.1	31.0	20.0	11.9	33.4	1.3	−0.5	246 553	23.2	14.5
21 00000	**KENTUCKY**	4 041 769	6.6	18.0	9.9	30.0	23.0	12.5	35.9	−1.1	0.1	3 610 112	23.8	13.1
21 08902	Bowling Green city	49 125	6.0	14.2	23.7	26.7	17.3	12.1	28.6	−5.5	−0.3	39 224	18.1	13.8
21 17848	Covington city	43 348	7.6	18.4	9.8	33.0	19.4	11.7	33.1	0.3	−0.7	37 286	24.0	12.9
21 28900	Frankfort city	27 509	6.3	15.3	11.2	30.7	22.4	14.0	35.9	−4.1	1.6	22 221	20.3	16.1
21 35866	Henderson city	27 385	6.7	16.9	9.2	29.9	22.1	15.3	37.0	−2.1	2.9	23 535	21.8	16.1

Table A-5. Cities — Age, Ethnicity, and Household Structure

City	Black or African American Total population	Under 18 years	65 years and over	American Indian and Alaska Native Total population	Under 18 years	65 years and over	Asian, Hawaiian, and Pacific Islander Total population	Under 18 years	65 years and over	Hispanic or Latino[1] Total population	Under 18 years	65 years and over	Two or more races Total population	Under 18 years	65 years and over
	14	15	16	17	18	19	20	21	22	23	24	25	26	27	28
INDIANA—Cont'd															
Fort Wayne city	35 534	36.5	6.0	886	23.6	4.2	3 161	25.9	3.2	11 752	36.1	1.9	4 799	54.0	3.2
Gary city	86 337	30.9	12.0	261	47.5	6.5	241	39.0	5.4	4 806	32.7	12.4	1 604	40.0	9.3
Goshen city	354	23.2	0.0	50	8.0	0.0	373	21.2	2.1	5 846	36.9	1.1	675	48.7	1.9
Greenwood city	199	19.6	0.0	34	20.6	0.0	359	23.4	8.6	641	30.1	2.3	366	43.4	9.3
Hammond city	11 729	36.1	5.4	313	28.1	3.8	491	9.6	10.4	17 459	39.0	3.7	2 622	50.0	4.2
Hobart city	393	29.3	8.9	79	45.6	0.0	135	21.5	11.9	2 058	37.0	8.8	415	44.6	7.2
Indianapolis city	199 569	32.4	8.7	2 713	28.1	5.2	10 837	20.8	5.3	29 732	30.9	1.7	14 238	48.7	2.8
Jeffersonville city	3 720	31.4	9.5	90	0.0	0.0	143	19.6	7.0	487	39.4	3.1	609	59.8	1.8
Kokomo city	4 691	32.5	9.7	202	30.7	3.0	354	31.9	9.0	1 215	42.7	1.4	866	56.7	3.9
Lafayette city	1 406	29.1	4.3	308	34.7	4.2	832	15.4	0.0	5 309	33.3	0.8	1 150	43.7	4.8
Lawrence city	6 102	37.0	2.1	132	29.5	4.5	602	23.9	7.3	1 889	30.1	0.9	1 138	50.2	0.6
Marion city	4 800	32.2	8.4	186	19.4	3.2	230	8.7	7.0	1 066	41.1	5.4	853	60.4	6.0
Merrillville town	6 990	32.3	3.8	112	0.0	0.0	422	32.0	5.9	2 890	37.2	5.2	581	30.6	4.6
Michigan City city	8 616	32.9	7.3	128	27.3	0.0	69	43.5	0.0	939	41.3	2.3	1 067	40.8	2.3
Mishawaka city	1 608	30.0	2.5	218	42.2	0.0	707	21.9	3.4	1 269	36.1	2.9	1 042	48.1	8.3
Muncie city	7 095	31.2	10.9	161	22.4	3.7	611	11.3	0.8	1 162	35.9	4.0	1 021	41.7	5.5
New Albany city	2 624	34.9	6.9	84	0.0	0.0	256	12.9	5.9	286	48.6	0.0	668	57.5	6.4
Noblesville city	311	23.8	8.7	21	0.0	28.6	130	35.4	0.0	485	37.9	3.1	216	49.5	3.2
Portage city	569	30.2	2.6	45	0.0	22.2	108	16.7	7.4	3 492	33.2	5.8	827	45.5	4.2
Richmond city	3 114	25.6	15.6	194	45.4	0.0	477	26.4	7.8	726	25.8	5.6	968	53.8	3.8
South Bend city	25 989	36.8	8.2	415	39.3	1.7	1 241	13.0	3.2	9 117	41.0	1.9	3 067	57.5	4.4
Terre Haute city	5 902	23.7	8.4	226	28.8	9.3	568	10.6	0.5	891	29.4	3.9	1 314	50.2	2.7
Valparaiso city	425	22.8	5.6	46	26.1	0.0	452	26.5	2.0	872	29.8	0.7	431	40.6	1.9
West Lafayette city	750	15.2	1.6	46	19.6	0.0	3 177	7.7	1.1	778	9.0	0.0	470	23.0	2.6
IOWA	59 758	34.7	6.3	9 263	35.0	3.2	35 978	27.4	3.2	81 501	38.9	2.8	33 624	51.8	3.8
Ames city	1 370	23.4	0.3	147	18.4	0.0	3 509	14.6	1.2	1 116	18.8	4.0	837	33.5	2.0
Ankeny city	121	47.1	0.0	11	45.5	0.0	201	10.4	4.0	330	47.6	0.0	296	36.8	10.1
Bettendorf city	467	30.4	12.4	50	20.0	0.0	430	27.0	2.6	811	30.2	8.3	314	66.2	0.0
Burlington city	1 255	39.2	8.0	92	25.0	8.7	194	44.8	8.8	513	44.2	7.0	332	46.7	3.9
Cedar Falls city	400	25.8	5.0	166	25.9	4.2	591	20.8	0.7	336	39.3	3.0	405	45.9	3.7
Cedar Rapids city	4 126	34.7	6.3	307	24.1	0.0	2 219	28.0	2.3	2 160	33.8	4.7	2 170	64.6	2.1
Clinton city	776	35.1	5.9	91	33.0	0.0	220	47.7	0.0	725	44.1	3.3	205	53.7	2.0
Council Bluffs city	585	34.5	4.6	218	17.9	2.8	403	21.8	6.7	2 632	33.6	2.1	584	44.3	12.0
Davenport city	8 957	38.3	4.5	549	33.9	8.4	1 736	30.7	4.6	5 075	40.8	5.8	2 511	60.5	3.0
Des Moines city	15 459	35.0	9.3	937	37.4	3.2	6 551	28.2	6.5	12 820	37.9	1.8	5 069	51.8	3.7
Dubuque city	705	35.3	3.0	116	39.7	0.0	269	30.9	7.4	951	34.6	0.0	568	52.3	6.5
Fort Dodge city	796	28.6	7.7	32	56.3	0.0	305	33.4	0.0	647	38.5	5.6	328	62.2	1.2
Iowa City city	2 283	31.1	2.5	124	7.3	0.0	3 547	19.5	1.8	1 790	25.4	1.6	1 259	34.2	1.7
Marion city	171	52.6	0.0	75	13.3	0.0	219	21.5	6.0	283	36.4	0.0	304	49.3	3.3
Marshalltown city	300	27.0	11.0	65	30.8	0.0	275	38.5	2.5	3 254	42.3	1.8	557	49.2	0.0
Mason City city	387	47.3	3.6	53	17.0	0.0	248	31.9	0.0	971	41.4	11.6	364	58.2	11.5
Sioux City city	2 020	40.5	6.5	1 575	45.0	2.7	2 268	33.8	1.0	9 202	41.2	1.2	1 870	52.6	0.7
Urbandale city	541	28.7	2.6	94	31.9	0.0	376	31.9	0.0	498	35.1	2.4	300	57.3	0.0
Waterloo city	9 375	37.6	8.0	77	28.6	5.2	692	24.7	1.9	1 874	44.1	3.3	1 469	56.8	2.3
West Des Moines city	836	28.1	2.3	125	6.4	6.4	1 236	24.4	0.0	1 522	37.1	5.7	572	59.4	4.0
KANSAS	150 584	32.4	7.7	24 723	30.5	5.4	45 980	25.3	4.0	186 299	39.0	3.0	63 823	48.3	4.2
Dodge City city	390	22.8	7.4	86	12.8	7.0	655	31.1	3.1	10 614	40.3	2.1	882	50.8	3.4
Emporia city	676	29.0	3.6	207	20.8	0.0	410	31.0	6.1	5 770	39.9	1.9	840	50.2	0.0
Garden City city	343	30.6	2.6	304	36.5	0.0	916	25.8	2.3	12 653	42.7	1.7	871	49.0	3.3
Hutchinson city	1 728	28.6	4.3	303	37.6	1.0	340	19.4	0.0	3 098	36.9	6.4	791	45.3	5.3
Kansas City city	44 364	34.0	8.8	1 040	29.7	7.4	2 259	35.8	5.7	24 597	36.7	3.1	4 504	45.5	4.4
Lawrence city	4 011	26.2	6.2	2 213	23.9	2.3	3 296	11.4	1.9	2 811	26.6	3.1	2 635	46.9	3.9
Leavenworth city	5 762	26.8	6.6	321	19.0	3.1	458	20.3	6.6	1 740	34.4	3.0	1 122	54.8	2.8
Leawood city	422	26.3	1.9	50	14.0	0.0	698	31.5	6.2	299	36.5	8.4	167	53.3	12.0
Lenexa city	1 268	30.8	3.7	178	17.4	7.3	1 206	21.9	3.6	1 584	32.8	0.6	488	51.0	3.9
Manhattan city	2 006	24.1	4.6	176	10.8	8.5	1 765	17.7	2.0	1 654	21.9	1.5	880	38.1	0.0
Olathe city	3 396	33.3	3.9	506	31.6	1.0	2 502	26.7	2.5	5 060	34.3	0.9	1 966	52.3	3.1
Overland Park city	3 531	29.0	4.2	460	28.0	4.1	5 738	23.9	4.1	5 559	30.2	2.8	2 586	41.9	5.0
Salina city	1 576	30.9	10.7	219	17.8	6.4	852	27.8	1.8	3 022	39.3	1.9	1 098	59.2	2.6
Shawnee city	1 300	28.8	1.9	105	23.8	11.4	1 460	27.1	4.0	2 092	30.5	5.7	966	47.7	2.4
Topeka city	13 740	31.1	9.9	1 462	28.9	9.6	1 237	21.6	3.0	10 674	38.2	4.7	4 755	54.0	2.7
Wichita city	38 796	35.1	7.7	4 076	31.4	5.3	13 041	28.5	4.3	33 002	40.1	3.1	12 377	49.0	3.3
KENTUCKY	293 915	30.0	8.7	9 080	22.5	5.6	30 149	23.9	3.5	56 414	31.6	3.5	47 341	43.8	5.9
Bowling Green city	6 038	26.5	7.2	350	41.1	5.4	942	27.3	1.7	1 764	29.5	0.6	816	40.0	3.7
Covington city	4 183	35.6	4.9	141	27.7	7.8	221	31.2	4.5	763	41.3	3.4	824	52.3	1.3
Frankfort city	4 174	23.4	5.9	77	10.4	0.0	201	28.9	8.5	442	36.7	0.0	433	55.2	5.1
Henderson city	2 926	31.1	10.6	32	0.0	21.9	248	30.6	13.7	332	46.1	3.0	271	51.7	7.4

[1] Hispanic or Latino persons may be of any race.

Table A-5. Cities — Age, Ethnicity, and Household Structure

City	Total households	Family households (percent)						Nonfamily households (percent)						Percent of householders 65 years and over who live alone	Grandparents who are responsible for the care of their grandchildren
		Married-couple family households			Other family households			Two or more unrelated persons		Male living alone		Female living alone			
		Total	With children	Householder 65 years or over	Total	With children	Householder 65 years or over	Total	Householder 65 years or over	Total	Householder 65 years or over	Total	Householder 65 years or over		
	29	30	31	32	33	34	35	36	37	38	39	40	41	42	43
INDIANA—Cont'd															
Fort Wayne city	83 416	42.5	20.4	7.6	18.4	11.7	1.7	6.4	0.3	14.2	2.4	18.4	8.3	52.5	1 832
Gary city	38 281	31.3	12.1	7.8	36.2	19.9	6.0	3.6	0.5	12.8	2.9	16.0	6.5	39.5	2 408
Goshen city	10 642	54.2	24.2	10.1	13.2	8.0	1.2	5.1	0.3	10.4	1.8	17.1	10.0	50.4	201
Greenwood city	14 876	51.9	23.9	7.1	12.8	8.3	1.0	5.3	0.5	11.5	1.4	18.5	8.6	54.0	161
Hammond city	31 968	44.4	20.5	8.5	21.1	11.9	3.3	4.7	0.4	13.9	2.9	15.8	8.1	47.4	849
Hobart city	9 866	56.0	24.6	11.3	14.7	7.6	2.7	4.8	0.3	9.3	2.5	15.1	8.4	43.5	179
Indianapolis city	324 583	41.5	18.9	6.7	19.1	11.7	2.2	7.4	0.3	13.8	2.1	18.1	6.7	49.0	8 141
Jeffersonville city	11 704	45.2	19.0	6.6	17.6	11.0	1.9	5.1	0.3	13.8	2.8	18.3	7.5	53.9	262
Kokomo city	20 239	42.3	17.3	7.7	17.6	10.6	2.2	4.4	0.2	14.4	2.7	21.3	10.4	56.4	442
Lafayette city	24 055	43.6	19.6	7.3	13.8	9.0	1.4	9.5	0.2	15.2	2.1	17.9	7.7	52.4	243
Lawrence city	14 932	52.2	27.5	5.7	17.0	11.9	1.1	6.1	0.3	11.5	1.6	13.2	4.6	46.7	348
Marion city	12 378	43.1	16.1	8.7	18.0	10.8	2.2	4.9	0.4	11.4	2.9	22.7	14.0	60.0	444
Merrillville town	11 780	54.1	25.0	10.1	15.1	7.0	2.1	4.6	0.4	9.6	2.4	16.6	9.6	48.8	361
Michigan City city	12 610	40.8	17.2	9.1	22.7	14.5	2.8	5.4	0.5	13.3	2.1	17.7	9.2	47.6	387
Mishawaka city	20 299	40.8	18.4	7.9	16.8	11.0	2.1	6.7	0.2	14.9	2.4	20.8	9.8	54.2	382
Muncie city	27 322	38.1	14.3	7.8	15.9	10.0	2.1	12.0	0.6	13.3	2.7	20.8	9.7	54.0	478
New Albany city	15 862	44.3	18.1	9.0	19.1	11.9	2.2	5.6	0.3	12.1	2.2	18.9	9.2	49.6	251
Noblesville city	10 780	63.5	34.8	5.9	11.2	7.7	0.6	3.7	0.2	8.5	1.8	13.2	6.2	54.1	109
Portage city	12 756	54.2	25.6	7.1	16.8	10.2	2.4	5.3	0.5	11.5	3.0	12.2	7.5	51.2	375
Richmond city	16 329	45.4	17.9	10.1	15.4	10.3	1.9	5.7	0.4	12.4	3.0	21.1	11.6	54.2	337
South Bend city	42 627	40.4	18.5	9.0	20.2	12.7	2.6	6.6	0.4	13.0	2.8	19.7	10.3	52.3	1 189
Terre Haute city	22 849	38.8	16.6	8.1	18.4	11.7	2.5	8.0	0.4	13.2	2.9	21.6	11.9	57.2	498
Valparaiso city	10 919	46.9	21.6	7.6	11.8	7.8	1.5	7.9	0.2	14.5	2.4	19.0	9.3	55.3	31
West Lafayette city	10 522	28.9	12.8	5.8	6.2	2.2	0.3	32.5	0.3	15.3	1.0	17.2	6.4	53.8	7
IOWA	1 150 197	55.9	24.6	11.1	11.4	7.2	1.5	5.5	0.3	11.1	2.4	16.0	9.0	47.1	13 073
Ames city	18 066	41.5	18.3	6.2	8.2	4.4	0.5	21.7	0.4	13.2	1.1	15.5	4.9	46.0	43
Ankeny city	10 250	59.9	31.6	6.1	10.9	7.8	0.7	7.4	0.1	8.8	0.4	13.0	5.1	44.2	54
Bettendorf city	12 459	61.0	29.4	9.4	9.1	6.2	0.8	3.8	0.2	11.1	1.9	15.0	7.6	47.6	165
Burlington city	11 167	49.9	19.8	11.0	14.5	9.4	1.8	4.6	0.4	11.7	2.8	19.3	11.4	51.9	107
Cedar Falls city	12 896	50.1	21.2	10.1	9.2	5.8	0.6	15.1	0.3	9.8	1.5	15.8	7.1	44.0	97
Cedar Rapids city	49 879	49.8	22.6	8.9	12.6	8.1	1.6	7.4	0.2	13.0	2.5	17.2	7.9	49.1	509
Clinton city	11 439	50.3	20.8	11.4	14.6	9.1	1.8	5.0	0.6	12.8	2.9	17.3	10.7	49.6	170
Council Bluffs city	22 913	47.3	20.6	8.9	18.7	11.8	2.2	6.0	0.2	11.4	2.6	16.5	8.8	50.3	444
Davenport city	39 238	47.4	21.0	8.4	16.4	10.7	2.0	6.7	0.5	12.2	1.8	17.3	7.6	46.4	805
Des Moines city	80 621	45.0	20.6	7.6	15.8	9.5	2.1	7.3	0.4	12.8	2.3	19.1	8.0	50.7	1 484
Dubuque city	22 612	51.0	22.4	10.8	12.4	7.4	1.9	5.4	0.3	13.3	2.8	17.9	9.4	48.5	123
Fort Dodge city	10 454	46.9	19.8	10.5	14.1	9.8	1.7	5.1	0.4	13.5	3.6	20.4	11.5	54.6	164
Iowa City city	25 187	36.4	17.6	4.7	8.9	4.6	0.5	21.0	0.3	15.4	1.4	18.3	5.2	54.6	103
Marion city	10 448	57.1	27.8	8.6	11.4	7.1	1.0	5.6	0.2	9.6	1.5	16.2	6.7	45.6	101
Marshalltown city	10 187	50.8	21.5	10.5	14.7	9.7	1.8	5.0	0.1	12.1	3.0	17.5	10.5	51.9	182
Mason City city	12 373	47.9	20.0	10.9	12.6	8.4	1.7	5.9	0.5	11.9	3.2	21.8	11.4	52.5	168
Sioux City city	32 158	50.9	24.1	9.5	15.5	10.1	1.9	6.0	0.2	10.5	2.3	17.1	9.3	50.2	532
Urbandale city	11 503	62.1	30.4	8.3	8.7	4.9	0.9	5.4	0.0	7.2	1.1	16.7	6.6	45.6	3
Waterloo city	28 192	48.0	19.5	9.9	15.6	9.9	1.8	6.5	0.5	11.4	2.6	18.5	9.7	50.4	457
West Des Moines city	19 811	50.8	24.6	6.7	9.6	6.3	0.6	9.2	0.2	10.8	1.1	19.7	5.9	48.3	57
KANSAS	1 038 940	55.7	25.9	10.0	12.4	7.9	1.4	5.0	0.2	11.5	2.3	15.4	8.0	47.0	17 873
Dodge City city	8 376	55.1	31.0	7.6	16.6	10.2	1.6	4.9	0.1	10.4	2.5	12.9	7.3	51.4	171
Emporia city	10 266	47.3	24.0	7.5	12.1	8.8	0.7	9.6	0.2	12.6	1.5	18.4	8.8	55.0	161
Garden City city	9 248	56.9	33.2	5.5	15.4	10.8	1.2	5.3	0.4	9.4	1.4	13.0	6.6	52.9	317
Hutchinson city	16 310	49.1	19.7	12.1	14.2	9.9	1.6	4.6	0.2	13.2	2.8	18.8	10.5	49.1	290
Kansas City city	55 533	42.6	19.3	7.4	23.3	14.0	2.8	5.0	0.4	12.9	2.5	16.2	7.6	48.6	2 210
Lawrence city	31 435	39.5	18.5	5.5	11.2	7.0	0.8	18.7	0.3	14.1	1.0	16.5	4.4	44.6	226
Leavenworth city	12 076	53.1	29.2	6.7	15.1	10.0	1.8	4.3	0.3	11.7	2.4	15.8	8.0	54.0	280
Leawood city	9 841	76.8	37.9	14.0	6.3	3.1	1.2	1.7	0.0	5.4	0.9	9.8	5.8	30.7	44
Lenexa city	15 572	59.5	30.0	5.9	9.1	5.7	0.5	7.0	0.1	10.4	1.0	14.0	4.9	48.4	86
Manhattan city	16 981	39.8	17.2	5.8	9.8	5.7	0.8	20.1	0.1	13.5	1.7	16.8	6.1	53.9	169
Olathe city	32 271	64.9	38.0	4.1	12.2	8.4	0.5	4.8	0.1	7.8	1.1	10.3	3.1	46.8	340
Overland Park city	59 895	57.4	28.7	8.5	9.0	5.1	1.1	6.1	0.2	10.4	1.4	17.1	6.7	45.6	369
Salina city	18 537	51.3	23.4	9.8	13.3	8.6	1.4	5.3	0.2	12.6	2.5	17.4	8.7	50.0	347
Shawnee city	18 623	61.5	30.3	7.3	10.3	5.8	1.1	5.5	0.1	10.2	1.0	12.5	4.2	37.6	225
Topeka city	52 143	43.3	18.2	8.9	16.1	10.1	2.0	5.7	0.3	14.2	2.9	20.7	9.7	52.8	931
Wichita city	139 127	48.3	23.1	8.2	15.3	9.6	1.7	5.3	0.2	14.7	2.2	16.4	7.1	48.1	3 303
KENTUCKY	1 591 739	54.7	24.2	8.8	15.0	8.8	2.2	4.2	0.3	10.8	2.2	15.2	7.6	46.5	35 818
Bowling Green city	19 241	39.6	17.3	7.1	16.7	10.5	1.4	10.3	0.3	13.5	2.1	20.0	8.9	55.6	373
Covington city	18 211	34.6	16.3	4.9	21.3	12.8	2.8	7.8	0.4	17.3	2.9	19.1	9.1	59.6	560
Frankfort city	12 250	39.8	16.3	7.4	16.1	10.1	2.1	5.8	0.3	14.3	2.7	24.0	10.9	57.9	148
Henderson city	11 682	45.5	19.4	9.0	17.3	11.6	1.8	4.7	0.3	13.1	2.4	19.4	10.2	53.0	263

Table A-5. Cities — Age, Ethnicity, and Household Structure

City	Households with Non-Hispanic White householder		Households with Black or African American householder		Households with American Indian and Alaska Native householder		Households with Asian, Hawaiian, and Pacific Islander householder		Households with Hispanic or Latino[1] householder		Foreign-born population	Place of birth (percent)			Percent in non-English speaking households	
	Number of households	Percent that are family households	Number of households	Percent that are family households	Number of households	Percent that are family households	Number of households	Percent that are family households	Number of households	Percent that are family households	Percent of total population that is foreign-born	Europe	Asia	Latin America	Linguistically isolated	Not linguistically isolated
	44	45	46	47	48	49	50	51	52	53	54	55	56	57	58	59
INDIANA—Cont'd																
Fort Wayne city	65 075	58.9	12 794	67.5	391	64.7	1 078	66.4	3 152	77.7	4.9	1.0	1.4	2.2	2.5	10.5
Gary city	4 382	54.9	31 880	68.8	72	76.4	101	83.2	1 511	79.0	1.6	0.4	0.2	0.8	1.1	10.3
Goshen city	9 135	64.9	53	24.5	17	58.8	121	71.1	1 244	89.2	15.8	0.6	1.2	13.6	9.1	16.8
Greenwood city	14 292	64.9	87	49.4	18	100.0	180	43.9	190	69.5	2.4	0.6	0.9	0.7	0.8	5.8
Hammond city	22 191	60.6	4 326	68.4	101	79.2	196	82.7	4 793	84.6	7.3	1.3	0.7	5.1	3.4	23.1
Hobart city	8 995	70.3	145	62.8	21	71.4	34	82.4	602	81.2	2.9	1.9	0.6	0.3	1.0	11.9
Indianapolis city	232 057	58.9	75 981	65.1	992	61.3	4 060	64.8	8 472	70.3	4.6	0.8	1.2	2.1	2.0	9.5
Jeffersonville city	9 807	62.2	1 447	68.1	77	48.1	87	52.9	143	84.6	1.7	0.6	0.3	0.3	0.4	5.5
Kokomo city	17 500	59.5	1 932	62.4	117	46.2	119	71.4	350	63.4	2.0	0.6	0.6	0.5	0.5	7.4
Lafayette city	21 279	56.5	612	48.2	150	41.3	368	46.2	1 480	80.5	7.9	0.8	1.2	5.7	4.2	11.2
Lawrence city	11 852	68.5	2 161	67.8	48	85.4	171	93.0	503	79.7	5.5	0.7	1.6	2.7	2.8	10.5
Marion city	9 981	59.3	1 756	68.3	65	49.2	98	62.2	315	65.4	1.8	0.5	0.6	0.4	0.8	8.3
Merrillville town	8 121	65.0	2 507	74.1	32	31.3	115	91.3	893	90.7	7.0	3.8	1.3	1.3	2.6	21.4
Michigan City city	9 463	59.7	2 686	74.3	31	77.4	16	100.0	238	78.2	2.1	0.6	0.6	0.7	1.3	8.6
Mishawaka city	18 530	57.6	715	49.0	105	80.0	278	65.8	392	63.0	4.4	1.2	1.6	0.9	1.5	8.9
Muncie city	23 786	53.5	2 762	57.7	73	61.6	182	39.0	292	61.3	1.9	0.3	0.8	0.5	0.5	6.8
New Albany city	14 439	62.4	1 042	74.3	42	54.8	78	88.5	110	60.9	1.3	0.4	0.5	0.3	0.3	5.5
Noblesville city	10 466	74.6	100	87.0	6	100.0	61	67.2	115	70.4	2.0	0.5	0.7	0.5	0.7	6.8
Portage city	11 339	70.3	214	64.5	31	25.8	14	100.0	1 040	80.0	3.0	1.1	0.6	1.2	0.7	13.5
Richmond city	14 282	60.4	1 364	59.9	55	85.5	129	70.5	251	78.9	2.4	0.5	0.9	0.8	1.2	7.5
South Bend city	30 158	56.7	9 041	69.7	157	62.4	468	47.4	2 342	78.9	6.4	1.2	1.1	3.4	2.8	14.4
Terre Haute city	20 159	57.4	1 832	57.8	78	37.2	238	27.3	168	61.9	2.1	0.5	0.9	0.4	0.7	6.3
Valparaiso city	10 213	58.6	133	55.6	10	100.0	148	64.2	304	64.8	4.1	1.1	1.6	1.0	1.0	10.1
West Lafayette city	8 633	36.2	320	23.8	9	100.0	1 172	29.1	276	30.4	13.3	2.0	9.1	1.3	4.0	17.9
IOWA	1 088 899	67.2	20 969	65.0	2 792	71.0	10 693	68.5	20 905	76.3	3.1	0.7	1.0	1.1	1.4	8.2
Ames city	15 643	49.1	474	51.1	53	47.2	1 307	50.7	351	59.0	10.3	1.6	6.4	1.1	3.8	14.3
Ankeny city	9 989	71.0	32	100.0	5	0.0	48	54.2	81	55.6	3.0	1.8	0.8	0.3	1.5	8.6
Bettendorf city	11 802	69.5	181	79.0	23	78.3	117	96.6	282	73.0	2.9	0.8	1.2	0.4	0.5	8.4
Burlington city	10 411	64.0	480	60.0	19	36.8	36	91.7	127	78.7	1.6	0.5	0.7	0.2	0.6	5.9
Cedar Falls city	12 338	59.8	116	58.6	72	23.6	180	46.7	72	40.3	2.7	0.8	1.4	0.3	0.6	8.8
Cedar Rapids city	46 794	62.0	1 423	67.1	131	69.5	701	74.8	559	71.7	3.3	0.7	1.7	0.6	0.9	8.8
Clinton city	10 863	64.4	292	69.2	27	100.0	31	87.1	181	77.3	1.5	0.3	0.6	0.6	0.7	7.6
Council Bluffs city	21 642	66.1	183	66.1	58	89.7	162	58.6	786	66.7	2.6	0.5	0.5	1.4	1.2	8.7
Davenport city	33 798	62.8	3 086	72.7	221	73.3	511	63.4	1 335	69.4	3.7	1.0	1.4	1.1	1.9	8.5
Des Moines city	68 435	59.1	5 870	62.1	268	68.3	1 669	77.7	3 403	81.9	7.9	1.6	2.6	3.1	4.1	11.9
Dubuque city	21 909	63.2	253	68.4	30	73.3	67	80.6	223	73.5	2.5	1.1	0.3	0.8	1.1	6.6
Fort Dodge city	9 783	60.7	331	67.4	14	57.1	80	56.3	211	70.1	2.3	0.6	0.8	0.8	1.5	6.6
Iowa City city	21 839	44.1	914	51.0	86	37.2	1 403	55.6	581	60.6	8.2	1.3	4.0	1.0	3.0	14.0
Marion city	10 199	68.3	44	65.9	16	75.0	93	88.2	49	83.7	1.6	0.3	0.9	0.2	0.4	6.6
Marshalltown city	9 132	64.4	108	45.4	16	56.3	82	73.2	752	81.4	9.2	0.5	0.7	7.6	5.2	13.6
Mason City city	11 741	60.1	106	75.5	23	56.5	82	81.7	351	64.7	1.5	0.5	0.6	0.3	0.7	6.1
Sioux City city	27 990	64.9	703	60.2	416	69.2	556	84.7	2 196	81.1	8.6	0.3	2.1	5.7	5.4	13.6
Urbandale city	10 923	70.0	219	81.7	27	66.7	120	81.7	158	87.3	4.1	2.2	1.0	0.5	1.6	8.4
Waterloo city	23 747	62.6	3 484	68.9	8	100.0	240	71.3	485	71.5	5.2	3.2	0.8	1.0	2.7	9.5
West Des Moines city	18 360	59.9	406	56.7	72	56.9	449	80.8	469	60.8	5.4	1.4	2.3	1.0	1.6	10.7
KANSAS	899 972	67.5	54 464	67.1	8 420	71.7	14 376	69.9	49 451	78.7	5.0	0.6	1.4	2.7	2.4	10.7
Dodge City city	5 449	64.4	148	61.5	50	100.0	175	84.6	2 486	87.6	25.3	0.1	2.2	23.0	13.7	31.4
Emporia city	8 148	57.5	276	46.4	56	53.6	115	74.8	1 553	72.5	11.6	0.5	1.1	9.9	7.5	17.2
Garden City city	5 661	65.2	97	48.5	62	91.9	242	83.5	3 131	84.8	22.8	0.2	2.8	19.7	13.7	33.4
Hutchinson city	14 630	62.4	406	61.6	68	100.0	133	63.9	942	75.2	2.4	0.2	0.5	1.6	0.9	8.1
Kansas City city	30 761	62.2	16 526	67.4	388	58.2	643	58.2	6 330	82.1	10.0	0.5	1.2	8.1	6.5	15.5
Lawrence city	26 719	50.3	1 445	58.5	609	58.0	1 199	49.1	919	55.4	6.2	1.1	3.6	0.9	1.7	14.0
Leavenworth city	9 656	68.1	1 690	69.6	81	67.9	90	50.0	399	61.4	3.2	1.2	1.1	0.7	0.9	11.3
Leawood city	9 342	83.1	173	73.4	11	100.0	194	87.6	74	94.6	3.6	1.3	1.6	0.2	0.9	9.4
Lenexa city	13 895	69.0	517	64.6	74	75.7	431	72.4	536	62.1	6.1	1.0	2.8	1.6	1.6	11.9
Manhattan city	14 698	48.3	831	59.3	52	65.4	587	59.8	542	53.5	6.5	1.4	3.4	1.0	1.8	13.2
Olathe city	28 610	76.7	1 217	76.7	154	81.2	717	93.0	1 260	81.7	5.9	0.6	2.3	2.5	2.5	10.6
Overland Park city	53 935	65.9	1 545	63.4	165	68.5	2 025	76.8	1 615	73.7	7.4	1.5	3.6	1.8	2.2	12.3
Salina city	16 520	63.6	628	65.9	99	70.7	253	74.3	878	77.2	4.5	0.3	1.4	2.7	2.1	10.1
Shawnee city	16 749	71.3	518	71.6	43	62.8	457	77.0	599	84.6	5.2	0.8	2.5	1.4	1.4	10.3
Topeka city	41 606	58.3	5 440	63.7	519	65.7	446	62.8	3 421	66.9	3.3	0.3	0.7	1.9	1.5	9.8
Wichita city	108 054	61.4	14 340	67.7	1 569	71.3	4 066	70.4	8 787	79.7	8.1	0.6	3.1	3.9	3.9	13.9
KENTUCKY	1 439 760	70.2	111 437	64.7	3 597	63.2	9 739	67.0	15 340	69.4	2.0	0.5	0.7	0.6	0.8	6.1
Bowling Green city	15 870	54.6	2 201	61.4	92	66.3	314	63.1	507	74.6	7.0	2.8	1.6	2.3	4.2	10.1
Covington city	16 049	55.3	1 667	60.5	72	43.1	47	78.7	202	58.9	1.5	0.4	0.4	0.6	0.7	7.4
Frankfort city	10 458	56.3	1 483	50.3	33	78.8	68	64.7	115	77.4	2.4	0.5	0.5	0.9	0.9	6.8
Henderson city	10 224	62.5	1 199	65.0	7	0.0	76	80.3	111	58.6	1.3	0.2	0.7	0.3	0.5	6.0

[1]Hispanic or Latino persons may be of any race.

Table A-5. Cities — Age, Ethnicity, and Household Structure

STATE Place code	City	Total population	Population by age (percent)						Median age	+/− U.S. percent under 18 years	+/− U.S. percent 65 years and over	Non-Hispanic White		
			Under 5 years	5 to 17 years	18 to 24 years	25 to 44 years	45 to 64 years	65 years and over				Total population	Under 18 years	65 years and over
		1	2	3	4	5	6	7	8	9	10	11	12	13
	KENTUCKY—Cont'd													
21 37918	Hopkinsville city............	30 222	7.5	18.9	9.8	28.5	20.2	15.1	35.1	0.7	2.7	19 769	21.9	18.5
21 40222	Jeffersontown city	26 610	7.8	17.8	7.3	33.4	22.8	10.9	35.7	-0.1	-1.5	22 825	23.9	12.0
21 46027	Lexington-Fayette..........	260 512	6.2	15.1	14.5	33.3	20.9	10.0	33.0	-4.4	-2.4	206 238	19.5	11.0
21 48000	Louisville city...............	256 420	6.6	17.1	10.2	30.7	20.8	14.6	35.8	-2.0	2.2	158 784	18.5	17.7
21 58620	Owensboro city.............	54 138	6.6	17.1	9.7	27.6	22.4	16.5	37.4	-2.0	4.1	48 917	22.7	17.2
21 58836	Paducah city.................	26 275	6.6	16.1	8.5	26.8	22.2	19.9	39.9	-3.0	7.5	19 037	18.1	23.8
21 65226	Richmond city...............	27 091	6.1	11.3	32.0	27.7	13.8	9.2	25.3	-8.3	-3.2	23 708	16.0	9.4
22 00000	**LOUISIANA**	4 468 976	7.1	20.2	10.6	29.0	21.5	11.6	34.0	1.6	-0.8	2 794 348	23.8	13.8
22 00975	Alexandria city..............	46 738	7.5	20.6	9.7	26.4	21.2	14.8	35.6	2.4	2.4	19 421	19.4	22.9
22 05000	Baton Rouge city...........	227 920	6.8	17.6	17.4	27.4	19.3	11.5	30.4	-1.3	-0.9	101 886	16.0	16.8
22 08920	Bossier City city	56 349	7.9	20.2	11.1	30.7	19.3	10.9	32.1	2.4	-1.5	39 120	24.4	14.0
22 36255	Houma city	32 124	7.5	20.3	10.2	29.3	20.9	11.9	34.3	2.1	-0.5	21 112	23.0	15.0
22 39475	Kenner city...................	70 517	6.9	20.4	9.4	30.8	23.8	8.8	34.5	1.6	-3.6	41 943	23.6	10.8
22 40735	Lafayette city................	110 261	6.4	18.8	13.1	29.7	20.8	11.2	33.1	-0.5	-1.2	74 337	21.9	13.6
22 41155	Lake Charles city	71 519	6.9	18.6	11.8	26.7	21.0	14.9	35.3	-0.2	2.5	35 612	18.9	21.0
22 51410	Monroe city..................	53 091	7.7	21.8	15.0	25.3	17.3	12.8	29.1	3.8	0.4	19 283	17.3	21.2
22 54035	New Iberia city..............	32 606	8.1	21.6	9.7	27.5	19.4	13.7	33.6	4.0	1.3	18 473	23.4	18.2
22 55000	New Orleans city...........	484 674	6.8	19.9	11.3	29.4	20.9	11.7	33.1	1.0	-0.7	129 215	13.4	19.6
22 70000	Shreveport city.............	200 549	7.1	19.9	10.7	27.4	21.1	13.9	34.3	1.3	1.5	92 103	19.3	19.9
22 70805	Slidell city....................	25 588	6.4	20.0	7.6	28.2	23.8	14.0	37.0	0.7	1.6	20 959	24.3	15.1
23 00000	**MAINE**	1 274 923	5.6	18.1	8.2	29.0	24.8	14.4	38.6	-2.0	2.0	1 230 645	23.2	14.7
23 02795	Bangor city...................	31 473	5.6	15.5	12.7	29.8	22.3	14.1	36.1	-4.6	1.7	29 877	20.7	14.6
23 38740	Lewiston city................	35 690	5.4	15.1	12.7	26.7	22.2	17.8	37.6	-5.2	5.4	33 871	19.8	18.4
23 60545	Portland city	64 257	5.0	13.9	10.6	36.1	20.6	13.8	35.7	-6.8	1.4	58 237	17.1	14.9
24 00000	**MARYLAND**	5 296 486	6.6	18.9	8.4	31.6	23.1	11.3	36.0	-0.2	-1.1	3 287 071	23.0	14.1
24 01600	Annapolis city	35 806	6.5	15.4	9.4	33.0	23.3	12.5	35.7	-3.8	0.1	21 183	14.8	14.7
24 04000	Baltimore city...............	651 154	6.4	18.3	10.8	30.1	21.1	13.2	35.0	-1.0	0.8	201 881	15.8	19.1
24 08775	Bowie city....................	49 866	7.4	19.0	5.9	35.1	23.3	9.2	36.3	0.7	-3.2	30 788	23.8	12.1
24 30325	Frederick city................	52 693	7.6	17.6	9.0	35.6	19.0	11.3	33.8	-0.5	-1.1	39 411	22.3	13.5
24 31175	Gaithersburg city	52 780	8.5	16.6	8.7	38.3	19.8	8.2	33.6	-0.6	-4.2	25 501	20.5	13.3
24 36075	Hagerstown city............	36 739	8.0	17.4	9.2	30.9	20.2	14.3	34.8	-0.3	1.9	31 264	22.6	15.9
24 67675	Rockville city................	47 257	6.2	17.1	6.4	33.0	24.5	12.8	37.8	-2.4	0.4	29 448	20.4	16.9
25 00000	**MASSACHUSETTS** ...	6 349 097	6.2	17.3	9.1	31.4	22.3	13.5	36.5	-2.2	1.1	5 197 124	21.7	15.4
25 00765	Agawam city.................	28 144	5.5	16.4	6.5	29.9	25.2	16.6	40.3	-3.8	4.2	26 862	21.5	17.1
25 02690	Attleboro city................	42 068	6.9	18.3	6.8	34.6	20.8	12.6	36.1	-0.5	0.2	37 505	24.2	13.9
25 03600	Barnstable Town city.....	47 821	5.2	16.7	5.5	27.4	25.1	20.0	42.3	-3.8	7.6	43 429	21.0	21.3
25 05595	Beverly city..................	39 862	6.2	15.7	8.9	31.0	22.8	15.6	38.3	-3.8	3.2	37 720	21.1	16.3
25 07000	Boston city...................	589 141	5.4	14.3	16.2	35.9	17.7	10.5	31.1	-6.0	-1.9	290 972	10.2	14.3
25 09000	Brockton city................	94 304	7.0	20.9	9.1	30.3	20.9	11.7	34.0	2.2	-0.7	55 164	20.8	16.9
25 11000	Cambridge city	101 355	4.1	9.1	21.3	38.7	17.5	9.2	30.4	-12.5	-3.2	65 439	9.6	11.4
25 13205	Chelsea city..................	35 080	7.9	19.4	11.2	34.2	16.0	11.4	31.3	1.6	-1.0	13 206	16.5	24.4
25 13660	Chicopee city................	54 653	5.2	17.3	8.5	28.7	22.7	17.6	38.7	-3.2	5.2	47 335	19.6	19.8
25 21990	Everett city...................	38 037	5.9	15.6	9.1	35.0	19.7	14.8	35.6	-4.2	2.4	28 547	18.9	18.6
25 23000	Fall River city...............	91 938	6.3	17.9	9.3	29.8	19.8	16.9	35.7	-1.5	4.5	82 335	21.9	18.4
25 23875	Fitchburg city................	39 102	6.1	19.5	10.8	29.5	19.5	14.6	34.1	-0.1	2.2	29 222	19.9	18.6
25 25100	Franklin city..................	29 560	9.6	20.8	6.2	35.2	19.8	8.4	34.8	4.7	-4.0	28 079	30.1	8.6
25 26150	Gloucester city.............	30 273	5.7	16.2	6.7	29.7	26.1	15.6	40.2	-3.8	3.2	29 061	21.5	15.9
25 29405	Haverhill city................	58 969	7.2	18.3	7.8	33.6	20.3	12.8	35.5	-0.2	0.4	51 007	23.7	14.3
25 30840	Holyoke city.................	39 838	7.8	21.7	9.0	26.9	19.2	15.4	34.0	3.8	3.0	21 632	17.4	25.7
25 34550	Lawrence city...............	72 043	8.8	23.1	11.3	30.6	16.7	9.6	29.5	6.2	-2.8	24 520	19.6	22.0
25 35075	Leominster city.............	41 303	7.2	18.3	7.2	32.8	21.0	13.5	36.3	-0.2	1.1	33 604	22.7	16.1
25 37000	Lowell city...................	105 167	7.3	19.6	11.8	33.2	17.4	10.6	31.4	1.2	-1.8	65 523	20.2	15.5
25 37490	Lynn city......................	89 122	7.4	19.4	9.1	31.3	20.0	12.8	34.2	1.1	0.4	55 423	19.8	18.3
25 37875	Malden city...................	56 340	5.8	14.1	8.0	37.0	21.1	13.9	35.7	-5.8	1.5	39 206	16.9	17.8
25 38715	Marlborough city............	36 255	6.5	16.6	6.5	37.2	21.5	11.6	36.1	-2.6	-0.8	30 882	21.9	13.1
25 39835	Medford city.................	55 765	4.9	13.3	10.6	32.7	21.2	17.3	37.5	-7.5	4.9	47 400	16.6	19.2
25 40115	Melrose city.................	27 134	6.7	15.3	5.4	32.5	23.5	16.5	39.4	-3.7	4.1	25 599	21.6	16.9
25 40710	Methuen city.................	43 789	6.2	18.4	7.0	31.2	21.9	15.3	37.5	-1.1	2.9	37 532	22.5	17.4
25 45000	New Bedford city..........	93 768	6.6	18.1	9.5	29.5	19.5	16.8	35.9	-1.0	4.4	70 614	21.3	19.6
25 45560	Newton city..................	83 829	5.5	15.7	10.0	28.6	25.1	15.1	38.7	-4.5	2.7	72 546	20.6	16.4
25 46330	Northampton city...........	28 978	3.8	13.0	15.1	30.4	23.8	13.7	37.3	-8.9	1.3	25 397	15.6	15.2
25 52490	Peabody city.................	48 129	5.8	16.5	6.5	29.3	24.4	17.5	40.3	-3.4	5.1	44 581	21.6	18.3
25 53960	Pittsfield city................	45 793	6.0	17.2	6.8	28.2	23.2	18.7	39.6	-2.5	6.3	41 923	21.8	19.9
25 55745	Quincy city...................	88 025	5.0	12.5	8.1	36.0	22.2	16.3	37.6	-8.2	3.9	69 098	15.6	18.9
25 56585	Revere city	47 283	5.6	15.1	7.9	32.8	21.9	16.6	37.6	-5.0	4.2	37 236	17.9	20.3
25 59105	Salem city....................	40 407	5.5	14.5	10.3	34.0	21.7	14.0	36.4	-5.7	1.6	33 283	16.7	16.4

Table A-5. Cities — Age, Ethnicity, and Household Structure

City	Black or African American Total population	Age (percent) Under 18 years	65 years and over	American Indian and Alaska Native Total population	Age (percent) Under 18 years	65 years and over	Asian, Hawaiian, and Pacific Islander Total population	Age (percent) Under 18 years	65 years and over	Hispanic or Latino[1] Total population	Age (percent) Under 18 years	65 years and over	Two or more races Total population	Age (percent) Under 18 years	65 years and over
	14	15	16	17	18	19	20	21	22	23	24	25	26	27	28
KENTUCKY—Cont'd															
Hopkinsville city	9 278	34.4	9.5	90	18.9	0.0	294	42.2	2.0	472	40.5	4.2	432	42.4	4.6
Jeffersontown city	2 287	29.5	6.5	37	13.5	24.3	359	21.7	1.7	620	47.1	0.0	550	57.5	1.8
Lexington-Fayette	34 928	28.2	8.4	828	21.0	2.4	5 947	19.1	2.1	8 677	26.2	2.5	4 647	40.8	2.4
Louisville city	84 298	32.2	10.5	876	14.0	7.3	3 309	24.7	2.1	4 618	27.5	4.8	5 078	41.2	4.8
Owensboro city	3 461	29.6	11.0	113	5.3	5.3	280	18.2	8.9	577	31.9	9.7	761	63.7	4.1
Paducah city	6 499	33.9	9.9	74	21.6	29.7	72	34.7	0.0	297	30.6	4.7	346	62.7	4.6
Richmond city	2 091	22.1	11.0	101	18.8	5.9	327	19.3	0.0	361	35.7	5.3	482	47.9	2.3
LOUISIANA	1 444 566	33.5	8.1	25 833	32.3	6.5	56 871	27.3	4.9	107 854	28.1	7.7	53 939	36.5	7.5
Alexandria city	26 053	34.4	9.1	104	11.5	13.5	464	25.0	3.7	306	14.1	8.2	435	44.8	6.2
Baton Rouge city	113 225	32.0	7.4	516	11.8	5.0	5 842	22.3	2.6	4 239	22.4	7.0	2 671	36.2	7.9
Bossier City city	12 906	38.2	3.7	343	36.7	5.8	991	24.6	3.1	2 077	32.2	3.6	1 000	42.0	7.2
Houma city	8 682	37.4	6.2	918	39.2	4.7	670	33.5	5.9	538	28.8	7.1	572	28.5	4.7
Kenner city	16 140	36.5	4.2	160	46.3	3.1	1 886	27.9	6.1	9 732	27.5	8.7	1 518	34.1	5.7
Lafayette city	31 139	32.8	6.7	193	14.5	0.0	1 703	22.0	0.8	2 007	28.3	5.6	1 067	27.7	6.8
Lake Charles city	33 077	32.3	8.9	149	16.8	21.5	720	21.4	4.3	1 272	33.1	6.9	888	41.4	8.7
Monroe city	32 728	37.3	8.2	68	5.9	20.6	480	5.6	1.9	364	20.1	14.0	354	30.8	11.0
New Iberia city	12 421	37.7	7.5	105	46.7	4.8	740	37.4	10.1	461	40.8	8.9	451	41.9	11.8
New Orleans city	325 216	32.1	8.8	1 495	28.2	9.6	10 615	26.5	6.6	15 032	21.2	11.8	6 731	31.3	8.2
Shreveport city	101 838	33.8	8.8	682	23.2	9.4	1 811	26.1	5.4	2 704	27.6	5.3	1 818	34.7	9.4
Slidell city	3 305	35.7	8.6	99	23.2	9.1	206	32.5	3.4	678	39.5	9.0	425	39.1	8.9
MAINE	6 047	35.1	3.9	7 521	32.0	5.6	8 560	31.3	5.1	9 226	37.3	4.2	13 736	39.9	5.9
Bangor city	280	25.4	10.7	244	30.3	0.0	461	35.1	5.0	264	34.8	0.0	351	28.8	13.4
Lewiston city	320	36.9	1.3	162	33.3	0.0	321	19.0	7.2	365	33.7	5.8	699	40.3	9.0
Portland city	1 451	36.0	4.0	425	22.4	2.4	1 930	37.9	2.2	858	35.0	4.3	1 343	38.9	2.8
MARYLAND	1 468 243	29.5	7.4	15 651	23.5	6.3	211 743	23.6	6.5	227 105	31.3	3.5	113 055	42.2	4.1
Annapolis city	11 026	32.8	10.9	71	15.5	0.0	580	15.0	11.6	2 286	24.7	2.4	754	47.6	4.6
Baltimore city	417 231	29.1	10.9	2 247	26.0	8.0	10 384	15.1	6.4	11 101	26.7	5.2	10 188	32.4	7.1
Bowie city	15 202	30.3	4.3	116	22.4	3.4	1 587	27.0	7.3	1 355	29.9	4.5	982	40.3	1.9
Frederick city	7 765	31.5	6.2	174	8.0	0.0	1 617	27.1	5.6	2 520	34.3	1.2	1 538	57.7	1.6
Gaithersburg city	7 646	30.0	3.2	140	39.3	6.4	6 970	23.2	5.1	10 698	31.0	2.3	2 930	37.1	4.3
Hagerstown city	3 716	40.0	5.8	103	30.1	0.0	333	15.3	6.6	771	50.1	2.2	644	61.0	4.2
Rockville city	4 260	30.2	8.5	296	17.2	3.0	6 687	25.1	6.9	5 415	28.5	3.2	1 639	36.2	4.8
MASSACHUSETTS	337 157	31.4	6.8	15 305	27.9	6.6	240 081	24.6	5.2	427 340	30.3	3.0	154 532	36.4	5.3
Agawam city	304	34.5	7.2	70	35.7	18.6	362	24.3	0.0	392	28.8	3.3	202	23.8	7.9
Attleboro city	801	34.1	3.9	57	10.5	0.0	1 222	36.6	1.4	1 723	32.8	0.6	963	33.6	4.6
Barnstable Town city	1 058	20.5	11.6	297	30.0	10.4	376	38.3	0.0	885	29.4	8.7	1 286	34.1	5.9
Beverly city	434	33.4	0.0	37	16.2	0.0	506	24.7	0.0	764	35.9	3.9	405	50.4	4.2
Boston city	146 958	31.3	8.0	2 581	30.2	7.0	44 563	17.3	8.3	85 199	32.1	3.5	27 631	27.8	5.2
Brockton city	16 430	38.1	4.2	278	32.7	5.0	2 505	35.7	4.0	7 512	40.4	2.8	7 227	40.2	4.7
Cambridge city	12 040	26.8	9.1	427	17.1	8.4	12 159	10.5	2.6	7 440	22.6	3.1	4 661	24.9	4.0
Chelsea city	2 552	31.3	4.1	128	50.8	0.0	1 464	32.2	2.2	16 964	34.3	3.3	2 576	38.0	3.8
Chicopee city	1 148	33.7	3.9	53	20.8	0.0	626	23.0	11.2	4 830	46.5	2.2	1 123	44.1	2.5
Everett city	2 329	27.4	3.7	68	45.6	0.0	1 242	33.1	4.3	3 668	28.8	1.8	2 275	31.1	4.0
Fall River city	2 526	50.2	0.8	186	29.6	0.0	1 957	41.7	3.2	2 995	51.7	2.1	2 298	33.8	10.4
Fitchburg city	1 207	33.3	2.0	85	24.7	0.0	1 802	46.4	2.4	5 796	41.8	2.7	1 630	50.8	3.2
Franklin city	357	41.5	0.0	28	0.0	0.0	600	26.8	6.8	271	32.5	14.4	293	64.8	3.4
Gloucester city	217	28.1	6.5	12	100.0	0.0	180	11.1	22.8	563	41.0	2.5	263	28.5	10.3
Haverhill city	1 231	37.1	5.2	209	28.7	6.2	712	23.0	3.8	5 150	40.1	2.2	1 457	40.2	5.5
Holyoke city	1 672	37.1	6.4	56	3.6	0.0	441	39.7	10.2	16 349	45.1	2.4	939	43.0	5.5
Lawrence city	3 030	32.1	5.8	445	48.3	0.9	2 047	32.0	5.7	43 098	38.4	2.9	5 082	42.2	3.7
Leominster city	1 695	37.4	2.4	20	70.0	0.0	1 094	32.4	3.2	4 558	40.5	2.0	733	40.2	4.1
Lowell city	4 390	30.9	2.1	376	39.1	1.6	17 184	36.9	3.6	14 530	40.6	1.7	4 488	45.3	1.2
Lynn city	9 362	35.6	3.8	397	32.7	17.1	6 049	39.4	3.1	16 393	39.1	3.0	4 360	40.5	5.5
Malden city	4 493	29.6	6.7	197	27.9	11.2	7 879	24.0	5.5	2 677	31.2	2.5	1 861	28.9	3.8
Marlborough city	682	23.6	6.2	62	19.4	12.9	1 605	25.2	1.7	2 136	34.8	2.9	1 001	30.3	4.6
Medford city	3 308	30.0	9.6	87	10.3	9.2	2 338	20.8	3.5	1 394	23.1	4.7	1 192	34.1	8.2
Melrose city	227	38.3	18.9	26	0.0	30.8	570	28.2	15.3	245	19.6	4.9	502	33.9	2.8
Methuen city	528	26.1	3.8	173	38.2	14.5	1 206	27.4	4.1	4 177	39.6	1.5	819	43.8	5.3
New Bedford city	4 175	35.2	7.4	447	20.8	8.3	768	22.9	10.7	9 454	41.2	3.4	5 703	34.7	8.7
Newton city	1 564	19.4	7.0	103	22.3	12.6	6 323	24.9	7.1	2 123	21.6	6.1	1 184	39.7	6.2
Northampton city	542	22.0	2.6	76	31.6	7.9	951	15.8	3.3	1 483	33.2	3.6	653	27.4	5.1
Peabody city	372	35.2	10.5	51	0.0	0.0	625	24.3	5.6	1 699	37.9	5.3	812	28.0	14.4
Pittsfield city	1 651	34.9	7.6	52	44.2	9.6	514	20.8	1.4	924	41.0	2.4	825	56.6	5.9
Quincy city	1 595	25.6	3.4	180	28.0	2.6	14 007	24.2	6.7	1 545	17.5	8.6	1 675	27.9	5.6
Revere city	1 258	25.5	0.8	244	45.1	2.9	2 161	32.3	3.7	4 572	32.5	1.8	1 901	31.7	5.2
Salem city	1 170	27.4	4.6	67	25.4	0.0	990	22.0	3.6	4 461	39.5	2.1	951	41.0	4.6

[1] Hispanic or Latino persons may be of any race.

City	Total households	Family households (percent)						Nonfamily households (percent)						Percent of householders 65 years and over who live alone	Grandparents who are responsible for the care of their grandchildren
		Married-couple family households			Other family households			Two or more unrelated persons		Male living alone		Female living alone			
		Total	With children	Householder 65 years or over	Total	With children	Householder 65 years or over	Total	Householder 65 years or over	Total	Householder 65 years or over	Total	Householder 65 years or over		
	29	30	31	32	33	34	35	36	37	38	39	40	41	42	43
KENTUCKY—Cont'd															
Hopkinsville city	12 197	45.6	19.2	8.8	21.5	13.6	2.6	3.2	0.3	11.3	2.7	18.4	10.1	52.4	279
Jeffersontown city	10 563	55.1	25.6	7.4	14.3	8.1	1.3	5.0	0.4	9.9	1.0	15.6	5.7	42.3	173
Lexington-Fayette	108 411	44.6	19.4	6.5	14.1	8.4	1.6	9.6	0.2	13.6	1.5	18.0	6.3	48.4	1 946
Louisville city	111 384	32.1	12.8	7.0	23.2	13.6	3.5	6.8	0.5	16.4	3.0	21.5	9.4	53.0	3 061
Owensboro city	22 778	46.7	19.3	10.0	15.9	9.3	2.2	4.3	0.3	12.5	2.5	20.7	10.5	50.8	393
Paducah city	11 771	36.9	14.4	9.2	19.9	12.1	2.4	4.6	0.3	13.8	3.5	24.7	14.8	60.6	250
Richmond city	10 801	35.6	15.7	4.9	15.8	9.6	1.5	13.9	0.4	15.6	2.1	19.1	7.0	57.3	85
LOUISIANA	1 657 107	49.6	23.3	8.2	20.6	11.9	3.0	4.5	0.3	11.0	2.3	14.3	6.8	43.9	67 058
Alexandria city	17 822	39.2	16.7	8.6	26.9	15.7	3.8	3.6	0.6	11.0	2.9	19.3	9.2	48.1	900
Baton Rouge city	88 913	37.0	16.0	7.4	22.8	12.9	3.2	8.7	0.4	14.2	2.3	17.4	6.6	45.0	2 979
Bossier City city	21 167	51.0	24.7	8.3	19.5	12.7	2.0	4.6	0.2	10.7	1.7	14.2	6.5	43.6	470
Houma city	11 587	49.8	23.0	9.3	21.2	11.9	2.8	4.8	0.4	9.4	2.4	14.7	8.3	46.1	539
Kenner city	25 638	51.6	25.8	6.0	20.7	11.0	2.4	4.6	0.1	10.1	1.3	13.1	5.0	42.7	1 134
Lafayette city	43 306	44.9	20.9	7.6	17.8	10.9	2.1	8.1	0.4	12.7	1.8	16.5	6.8	46.1	967
Lake Charles city	27 965	42.6	18.3	9.9	22.2	12.7	3.3	5.4	0.4	12.7	2.3	17.1	8.2	43.6	1 149
Monroe city	19 447	34.1	15.7	6.4	28.7	17.1	3.9	5.7	0.4	12.2	2.7	19.3	9.6	53.4	1 098
New Iberia city	11 720	45.9	22.7	8.1	24.8	14.4	3.9	3.8	0.6	11.2	3.2	14.3	8.5	48.0	643
New Orleans city	188 365	31.7	13.8	6.1	28.8	16.3	4.3	6.4	0.4	15.4	2.6	17.7	6.8	46.6	9 478
Shreveport city	78 735	39.0	16.2	8.1	25.7	14.6	3.8	4.7	0.5	12.5	2.3	18.1	8.4	46.4	3 633
Slidell city	9 504	57.4	25.8	10.7	17.2	10.5	2.5	3.9	0.2	8.3	2.1	13.2	7.0	40.3	339
MAINE	518 372	53.4	22.5	9.8	12.7	8.2	1.6	7.0	0.6	11.0	2.7	16.0	8.2	47.6	5 074
Bangor city	13 738	38.6	17.6	6.1	14.7	9.7	1.6	9.4	0.5	14.6	2.5	22.7	10.1	60.7	89
Lewiston city	15 291	41.5	15.3	9.6	15.4	10.2	2.2	7.1	0.5	13.9	3.3	22.0	11.3	54.4	115
Portland city	29 722	33.3	14.3	6.0	12.7	7.9	1.5	13.9	0.5	16.7	3.0	23.3	8.7	59.4	257
MARYLAND	1 981 795	51.2	24.1	8.0	17.8	10.0	2.3	6.0	0.4	10.1	2.0	14.9	6.2	43.3	50 974
Annapolis city	15 231	37.4	13.9	7.0	20.3	11.6	3.0	10.0	0.5	12.7	1.6	19.5	7.1	45.4	367
Baltimore city	257 788	28.0	10.7	6.1	29.5	15.4	4.5	7.6	0.7	14.6	3.3	20.3	8.4	50.7	13 707
Bowie city	18 155	61.4	30.5	7.8	13.1	7.2	1.3	5.8	0.3	6.5	0.9	13.3	3.8	33.3	301
Frederick city	20 886	46.0	23.0	6.0	15.5	10.2	1.7	8.6	0.4	12.6	1.8	17.4	6.7	51.3	288
Gaithersburg city	19 686	49.6	26.9	4.1	15.6	9.6	0.7	7.3	0.2	10.4	1.4	17.1	5.6	58.6	271
Hagerstown city	15 802	39.8	17.2	7.2	18.7	12.9	1.6	6.7	0.3	13.5	3.2	21.3	10.1	59.3	304
Rockville city	17 222	56.8	27.0	8.9	13.0	6.6	2.1	6.3	0.5	8.7	1.9	15.1	7.2	44.3	197
MASSACHUSETTS	2 444 588	50.0	23.2	8.9	15.0	8.0	2.4	7.1	0.4	11.2	2.6	16.8	8.1	47.6	27 915
Agawam city	11 271	53.7	23.0	10.3	12.3	6.4	2.2	5.9	0.3	10.2	2.4	17.8	9.1	47.1	77
Attleboro city	16 021	54.7	25.6	8.4	14.2	7.9	2.0	5.4	0.3	11.0	1.8	14.7	7.0	45.0	184
Barnstable Town city	19 647	52.7	20.7	15.6	14.0	7.4	2.1	5.7	0.6	9.9	3.1	17.7	10.2	42.0	195
Beverly city	15 736	51.7	23.3	9.1	11.4	5.9	2.2	7.0	0.5	11.2	2.2	18.7	8.1	46.6	79
Boston city	239 603	28.3	12.4	4.6	20.4	10.9	2.6	14.2	0.3	16.7	2.7	20.4	6.6	54.9	4 142
Brockton city	33 672	44.1	21.1	7.5	23.4	14.5	2.7	5.9	0.4	11.6	2.6	15.0	6.9	47.4	781
Cambridge city	42 635	30.5	12.6	4.5	11.6	6.3	1.5	16.6	0.5	18.3	2.3	23.0	6.6	58.0	286
Chelsea city	11 908	38.7	21.1	5.6	25.9	15.3	3.0	6.7	0.3	13.1	3.4	15.6	7.8	55.7	411
Chicopee city	23 115	43.9	17.3	10.0	17.8	10.3	3.2	5.7	0.6	13.3	3.9	19.4	10.3	50.9	285
Everett city	15 433	43.3	18.5	9.3	18.9	9.9	2.5	6.5	0.3	12.0	2.8	19.2	9.3	49.7	164
Fall River city	38 775	40.5	17.5	8.2	20.7	13.0	2.6	4.6	0.3	13.5	3.4	20.6	11.6	57.5	525
Fitchburg city	14 982	43.8	19.4	9.0	19.4	12.4	2.2	6.6	0.2	13.4	3.1	16.9	9.6	52.6	163
Franklin city	10 153	67.6	40.5	6.7	10.1	5.1	1.9	4.0	0.5	7.5	1.9	10.8	5.1	43.6	47
Gloucester city	12 588	48.5	20.4	9.6	14.4	7.7	2.6	6.5	0.3	12.0	2.6	18.7	8.8	47.7	92
Haverhill city	22 999	48.4	23.3	7.6	16.6	10.6	1.5	6.4	0.1	11.3	2.1	17.3	8.7	54.3	271
Holyoke city	15 000	37.2	16.3	7.8	26.3	17.5	2.8	5.5	0.4	11.9	3.6	19.1	10.3	55.8	316
Lawrence city	24 477	37.3	20.1	5.5	32.1	22.1	2.4	5.3	0.1	10.8	2.6	14.6	7.7	56.2	824
Leominster city	16 496	50.2	23.7	8.7	16.4	10.5	1.7	5.5	0.2	11.3	2.4	16.5	8.2	49.5	279
Lowell city	37 992	41.1	21.3	5.8	22.7	13.9	2.6	7.3	0.3	13.7	2.3	15.1	6.7	51.2	577
Lynn city	33 649	40.4	19.7	7.3	22.5	13.4	2.7	5.7	0.4	12.9	2.9	18.5	8.7	52.7	733
Malden city	23 028	43.9	19.1	7.3	15.5	6.3	2.9	8.5	0.2	13.5	3.5	18.6	8.1	52.6	123
Marlborough city	14 516	53.8	25.5	7.5	10.8	5.6	1.6	7.0	0.2	13.0	1.9	15.4	6.5	47.6	178
Medford city	22 081	46.0	18.6	10.6	15.4	4.8	4.4	10.0	0.4	10.1	2.9	18.6	9.5	44.5	203
Melrose city	10 971	54.8	25.0	10.7	9.9	3.9	2.5	5.6	0.3	9.8	2.6	19.9	11.1	50.3	88
Methuen city	16 527	54.9	25.4	9.9	15.4	7.6	2.9	4.4	0.3	8.8	2.2	16.4	9.7	47.6	142
New Bedford city	38 240	40.8	17.5	9.3	22.7	14.8	2.9	5.0	0.2	12.4	3.6	19.1	11.1	54.3	780
Newton city	31 221	56.9	27.6	11.5	9.2	3.7	2.6	8.5	0.7	7.2	2.2	18.3	9.4	43.7	82
Northampton city	11 863	37.4	16.2	6.3	12.3	7.2	2.2	12.8	0.3	14.3	2.7	23.1	8.3	55.5	51
Peabody city	18 578	56.6	24.2	12.4	13.3	5.5	3.2	4.6	0.6	9.9	2.9	15.5	9.0	42.5	104
Pittsfield city	19 653	42.9	16.1	11.3	17.2	11.0	2.4	5.9	0.3	13.6	3.0	20.5	11.2	50.6	98
Quincy city	38 893	39.5	16.1	8.0	13.7	5.3	2.8	9.3	0.3	14.8	3.5	22.8	10.6	56.0	334
Revere city	19 422	42.2	17.4	9.8	18.9	8.4	4.0	6.3	0.4	14.0	3.4	18.7	9.1	46.7	229
Salem city	17 477	40.3	16.2	8.3	15.5	8.2	2.1	9.2	0.7	12.7	2.4	22.2	9.1	50.9	141

City	Households with Non-Hispanic White householder		Households with Black or African American householder		Households with American Indian and Alaska Native householder		Households with Asian, Hawaiian, and Pacific Islander householder		Households with Hispanic or Latino[1] householder		Foreign-born population	Place of birth (percent)			Percent in non-English speaking households	
	Number of households	Percent that are family households	Number of households	Percent that are family households	Number of households	Percent that are family households	Number of households	Percent that are family households	Number of households	Percent that are family households	Percent of total population that is foreign-born	Europe	Asia	Latin America	Linguistically isolated	Not linguistically isolated
	44	45	46	47	48	49	50	51	52	53	54	55	56	57	58	59
KENTUCKY—Cont'd																
Hopkinsville city	8 327	66.5	3 537	68.1	40	77.5	65	75.4	136	57.4	1.6	0.6	0.5	0.2	0.4	7.0
Jeffersontown city	9 257	68.3	852	75.6	29	100.0	137	55.5	189	85.2	5.3	1.8	1.6	1.2	1.9	8.0
Lexington-Fayette	88 723	58.0	14 028	61.5	342	51.2	2 147	60.2	2 123	68.0	5.9	1.0	2.2	2.2	2.3	9.3
Louisville city	73 510	52.1	33 374	61.8	386	67.4	1 082	61.6	1 571	59.9	3.8	1.0	1.3	1.1	2.0	7.5
Owensboro city	20 911	62.3	1 374	65.2	58	46.6	97	88.7	165	64.2	1.2	0.3	0.5	0.3	0.5	6.4
Paducah city	8 916	54.5	2 633	63.8	51	45.1	31	100.0	76	93.4	1.1	0.2	0.3	0.6	0.5	5.8
Richmond city	9 619	50.2	827	60.0	37	62.2	93	73.1	89	58.4	2.1	0.2	1.1	0.5	0.6	6.0
LOUISIANA	1 105 452	69.4	478 950	71.9	8 590	75.6	16 831	74.5	34 051	72.2	2.6	0.4	1.0	1.0	1.3	14.0
Alexandria city	8 633	58.7	8 772	73.7	62	66.1	138	88.4	97	41.2	1.7	0.3	1.0	0.3	0.6	8.1
Baton Rouge city	45 779	51.9	38 871	69.1	246	67.5	1 900	60.9	1 409	61.7	4.4	0.7	2.2	1.0	1.6	11.3
Bossier City city	15 834	69.6	4 141	72.9	100	80.0	277	70.4	544	74.6	3.2	0.5	1.4	1.1	1.2	10.8
Houma city	8 366	70.2	2 650	72.6	202	91.1	66	100.0	151	59.6	2.3	0.3	1.0	0.9	1.6	18.4
Kenner city	16 378	69.3	5 191	77.0	42	69.0	603	87.7	3 149	79.7	11.3	0.7	2.3	8.2	3.2	21.0
Lafayette city	31 291	60.5	10 392	70.0	101	68.3	564	63.5	586	62.5	3.2	0.6	1.5	0.7	2.0	23.6
Lake Charles city	15 285	60.6	11 689	71.0	61	60.7	219	54.8	451	56.3	2.1	0.4	0.9	0.7	1.5	15.3
Monroe city	8 545	53.8	10 464	70.8	38	10.5	199	55.3	134	48.5	1.3	0.2	0.8	0.2	0.6	5.8
New Iberia city	7 398	67.4	3 916	76.1	40	100.0	151	82.1	135	65.2	2.3	0.1	1.6	0.6	2.8	20.6
New Orleans city	63 960	45.2	113 437	69.3	613	52.2	3 201	69.2	5 700	58.6	4.2	0.6	1.6	1.8	1.5	10.9
Shreveport city	41 172	60.5	35 318	69.7	297	62.6	581	75.2	876	66.1	1.6	0.4	0.7	0.4	0.5	7.5
Slidell city	7 976	74.3	1 184	76.1	37	81.1	35	80.0	197	84.8	2.2	0.7	0.3	0.8	0.6	9.5
MAINE	505 297	66.1	1 886	63.3	2 727	64.1	2 168	70.9	2 308	69.3	2.9	0.9	0.5	0.2	1.0	11.8
Bangor city	13 240	53.3	86	52.3	91	41.8	107	84.1	63	63.5	3.4	0.8	1.1	0.2	0.5	8.5
Lewiston city	14 738	56.9	127	42.5	80	66.3	30	100.0	106	68.9	3.7	0.6	0.6	0.1	4.5	35.7
Portland city	27 679	45.2	515	62.9	224	31.3	558	68.5	234	43.2	7.6	2.5	2.9	0.5	2.8	10.5
MARYLAND	1 302 282	68.3	525 794	68.7	5 812	71.6	65 010	78.1	59 669	79.6	9.8	1.6	3.4	3.3	2.6	15.3
Annapolis city	10 092	52.4	4 276	67.5	23	100.0	208	59.6	628	77.7	9.7	2.3	1.6	5.1	4.0	13.4
Baltimore city	93 423	47.6	152 493	64.0	604	65.2	4 266	42.0	3 793	55.4	4.6	1.1	1.2	1.6	1.6	10.3
Bowie city	11 615	76.0	5 420	71.2	70	87.1	453	83.7	410	68.0	7.4	1.5	2.8	2.1	0.8	14.7
Frederick city	16 351	59.3	2 844	71.4	95	42.1	441	68.3	873	65.9	7.3	1.7	2.8	2.1	1.7	12.8
Gaithersburg city	11 389	57.1	2 818	67.0	48	58.3	2 376	77.5	2 562	86.9	34.3	2.7	12.7	15.4	12.1	35.6
Hagerstown city	13 934	58.2	1 353	61.1	35	100.0	149	70.5	224	64.7	2.7	0.7	0.8	0.8	1.1	6.4
Rockville city	11 958	66.2	1 273	71.2	64	85.9	2 186	80.4	1 440	82.2	31.0	4.9	14.9	9.3	10.6	32.6
MASSACHUSETTS	2 085 454	64.0	115 736	66.6	5 538	67.2	73 735	70.9	123 443	75.0	12.2	3.9	3.2	3.7	4.6	20.0
Agawam city	10 840	66.4	108	60.2	29	17.2	119	56.3	110	61.8	5.3	3.1	1.1	0.3	1.0	13.5
Attleboro city	14 589	68.3	294	75.9	35	100.0	369	83.7	477	70.0	8.9	3.3	2.4	2.0	2.3	18.4
Barnstable Town city	18 240	66.6	366	55.7	124	75.8	98	54.1	261	67.0	6.9	2.3	0.8	2.9	2.3	12.1
Beverly city	15 000	63.4	182	78.6	0	X	185	62.2	260	45.0	5.3	2.7	0.9	1.0	1.2	12.4
Boston city	138 545	36.9	51 485	66.0	929	62.4	16 071	53.4	26 294	70.5	25.8	4.5	6.2	12.3	11.4	29.1
Brockton city	22 283	62.4	5 139	76.3	117	45.3	627	88.8	2 173	74.4	18.4	2.2	1.8	6.8	8.4	27.5
Cambridge city	30 503	37.8	4 417	58.0	149	55.7	3 929	47.3	2 258	55.9	25.9	6.5	9.1	7.3	7.3	30.6
Chelsea city	5 877	47.8	921	68.4	33	100.0	352	92.9	4 495	82.5	36.1	3.8	3.7	26.2	20.3	45.4
Chicopee city	20 866	60.5	426	55.4	17	100.0	205	67.8	1 383	79.6	8.2	5.3	1.0	0.5	5.7	21.7
Everett city	12 485	59.6	828	71.0	27	77.8	327	81.7	988	79.9	21.9	4.3	2.9	12.7	10.2	26.9
Fall River city	35 768	60.3	804	76.7	82	61.0	491	73.7	820	74.9	19.8	16.2	1.8	1.3	8.4	33.9
Fitchburg city	12 230	60.4	321	67.3	34	73.5	365	73.7	1 818	77.4	8.3	1.6	2.6	1.8	5.4	25.4
Franklin city	9 840	77.4	99	89.9	10	100.0	121	90.1	57	82.5	5.3	2.3	1.7	0.4	1.4	11.6
Gloucester city	12 215	62.8	99	56.6	0	X	80	60.0	131	69.5	5.3	3.2	0.7	0.7	1.4	15.1
Haverhill city	20 602	64.0	416	65.9	96	78.1	243	61.3	1 418	77.0	6.9	1.9	1.3	3.0	3.0	16.4
Holyoke city	9 454	55.1	515	77.9	30	46.7	177	72.3	4 873	79.3	5.4	2.4	0.8	1.6	12.1	39.1
Lawrence city	10 827	54.6	1 049	67.8	133	77.4	599	84.6	12 313	81.5	30.6	1.3	2.7	25.7	19.4	52.4
Leominster city	14 016	65.3	650	65.5	0	X	337	79.5	1 415	77.0	10.4	1.6	2.1	4.2	5.8	20.0
Lowell city	26 998	57.5	1 417	68.7	89	58.4	4 240	86.4	4 398	77.3	22.1	3.5	11.9	4.9	11.1	36.8
Lynn city	23 876	58.7	3 370	65.5	119	73.1	1 430	85.0	4 431	79.2	22.8	5.1	5.2	10.6	11.8	27.8
Malden city	17 340	55.8	1 739	60.5	55	74.5	2 386	79.3	898	70.9	25.7	4.3	11.9	7.1	10.5	27.9
Marlborough city	12 737	63.6	274	60.9	28	100.0	608	75.8	539	71.2	16.2	2.8	4.0	8.0	6.2	18.5
Medford city	19 474	60.3	1 110	72.7	27	29.6	719	70.1	383	60.3	16.2	6.6	3.4	5.2	5.1	22.5
Melrose city	10 374	64.8	78	62.8	19	42.1	161	90.7	111	40.5	6.1	2.8	1.7	0.6	1.8	11.2
Methuen city	14 854	68.6	139	95.7	60	80.0	308	90.9	1 144	85.0	11.2	2.4	3.5	4.3	3.7	23.7
New Bedford city	29 899	61.7	1 521	67.9	204	76.5	236	63.6	2 907	76.2	19.6	14.6	0.8	2.1	10.0	36.1
Newton city	28 365	64.2	344	84.6	32	40.6	1 824	85.4	461	83.9	18.0	8.3	6.3	1.9	3.7	23.8
Northampton city	10 729	49.7	149	49.0	21	0.0	311	57.2	436	58.0	6.5	2.2	2.5	0.9	1.6	14.6
Peabody city	17 444	69.9	157	85.4	22	100.0	164	68.9	465	80.0	11.2	6.7	1.2	2.7	3.8	18.6
Pittsfield city	18 484	59.8	496	73.8	23	21.7	195	60.0	271	56.8	3.9	1.9	0.9	0.4	1.3	10.4
Quincy city	32 837	50.1	617	48.3	62	56.5	4 096	79.9	632	49.5	20.0	4.6	12.6	1.5	7.6	21.0
Revere city	16 485	59.4	506	56.1	59	39.0	568	80.5	1 198	78.5	21.0	6.6	4.7	7.8	8.8	28.2
Salem city	15 257	53.7	439	53.3	13	69.2	322	74.5	1 313	77.8	11.9	3.2	2.1	5.9	4.6	21.9

[1] Hispanic or Latino persons may be of any race.

STATE Place code	City	Total population	Under 5 years	5 to 17 years	18 to 24 years	25 to 44 years	45 to 64 years	65 years and over	Median age	+/− U.S. percent under 18 years	+/− U.S. percent 65 years and over	Total population	Under 18 years	65 years and over
						Population by age (percent)						Non-Hispanic White	Age (percent)	
		1	2	3	4	5	6	7	8	9	10	11	12	13
	MASSACHUSETTS—Cont'd													
25 62535	Somerville city	77 478	4.4	10.0	16.2	43.1	15.9	10.4	31.1	-11.3	-2.0	56 222	11.5	13.1
25 67000	Springfield city	152 082	7.6	21.2	11.5	28.7	18.6	12.4	31.9	3.1	0.0	73 933	18.2	20.0
25 69170	Taunton city	55 976	6.9	17.7	7.8	33.3	21.3	13.0	35.7	-1.1	0.6	50 072	23.4	13.8
25 72600	Waltham city	59 226	4.6	10.8	17.1	34.2	20.0	13.2	34.2	-10.3	0.8	46 139	13.4	15.6
25 73440	Watertown city	32 986	4.4	9.8	9.1	40.2	19.8	16.6	36.7	-11.5	4.2	29 592	13.4	18.2
25 76030	Westfield city	40 072	6.4	17.4	12.8	28.5	21.5	13.6	35.8	-1.9	1.2	36 925	22.5	14.4
25 81035	Woburn city	37 258	5.4	15.5	7.0	34.6	22.2	15.3	37.7	-4.8	2.9	33 136	20.2	16.8
25 82000	Worcester city	172 648	6.4	17.1	13.5	30.2	18.6	14.2	33.4	-2.2	1.8	122 112	18.3	18.5
26 00000	**MICHIGAN**	9 938 444	6.7	19.3	9.4	29.9	22.4	12.3	35.5	0.3	-0.1	7 805 325	24.1	13.7
26 01380	Allen Park city	29 376	5.6	16.5	6.4	28.4	22.0	21.1	41.0	-3.6	8.7	27 033	21.3	21.9
26 03000	Ann Arbor city	114 110	5.1	11.5	26.7	31.6	17.2	7.9	28.1	-9.1	-4.5	83 491	15.3	9.3
26 05920	Battle Creek city	53 251	7.3	19.8	8.5	30.0	20.6	13.7	34.7	1.4	1.3	38 448	23.3	16.2
26 06020	Bay City city	36 817	6.9	18.5	9.4	30.5	20.5	14.2	35.2	-0.3	1.8	32 223	23.0	15.6
26 12060	Burton city	30 308	7.3	20.2	8.5	31.7	21.2	11.2	34.6	1.8	-1.2	27 586	26.5	11.7
26 21000	Dearborn city	97 775	8.2	19.5	8.1	29.3	19.2	15.6	34.5	2.0	3.2	82 649	26.1	17.5
26 21020	Dearborn Heights city ...	58 264	6.4	16.1	7.5	29.6	21.7	18.7	38.9	-3.2	6.3	51 857	21.5	20.2
26 22000	Detroit city	951 270	8.0	23.1	9.6	29.6	19.2	10.5	30.9	5.4	-1.9	100 371	16.2	20.5
26 24120	East Lansing city	46 704	2.5	6.7	58.1	16.4	10.2	6.1	21.7	-16.5	-6.3	36 840	7.8	7.5
26 24290	Eastpointe city	34 077	6.3	18.0	7.3	32.4	19.4	16.6	36.6	-1.4	4.2	31 022	23.3	17.7
26 27440	Farmington Hills city	82 111	5.8	17.3	6.8	31.0	24.7	14.4	38.6	-2.6	2.0	67 304	22.1	16.6
26 29000	Flint city	124 939	8.9	21.7	10.4	29.4	19.1	10.5	30.8	4.9	-1.9	50 384	22.2	14.1
26 31420	Garden City city	30 047	6.1	19.0	7.4	33.1	21.0	13.5	36.5	-0.6	1.1	28 515	24.7	13.9
26 34000	Grand Rapids city	197 846	8.1	19.8	13.1	31.7	16.6	11.6	30.4	1.3	-0.8	123 474	20.4	16.0
26 38640	Holland city	35 211	7.8	18.4	16.7	28.1	15.5	13.5	29.2	0.5	1.1	24 495	20.3	18.1
26 40680	Inkster city	30 115	8.0	21.9	9.1	30.6	19.7	10.6	31.8	4.2	-1.8	7 405	20.0	15.9
26 41420	Jackson city	36 316	9.1	20.6	9.9	30.5	17.9	12.0	31.3	4.0	-0.4	26 255	25.1	13.7
26 42160	Kalamazoo city	77 092	6.1	14.2	27.9	26.5	15.2	10.0	26.1	-5.4	-2.4	53 502	14.0	12.5
26 42820	Kentwood city	45 239	7.5	19.1	10.3	33.2	19.8	10.1	32.4	0.9	-2.3	35 762	24.1	11.7
26 46000	Lansing city	118 920	8.0	18.8	11.2	33.2	19.0	9.8	31.4	1.1	-2.6	73 234	19.6	12.8
26 47800	Lincoln Park city	40 008	6.9	17.3	8.4	32.9	20.4	14.2	35.5	-1.5	1.8	35 714	23.1	15.0
26 49000	Livonia city	100 545	5.6	18.3	6.2	28.9	24.2	16.9	40.2	-1.8	4.5	94 662	23.5	17.5
26 50560	Madison Heights city	31 101	6.3	15.6	8.0	35.8	20.2	14.1	36.1	-3.8	1.7	27 816	22.3	15.1
26 53780	Midland city	41 663	6.3	19.3	10.2	28.0	22.3	13.9	36.2	-0.1	1.5	38 368	24.8	14.7
26 56020	Mount Pleasant city	26 101	3.8	7.8	54.4	16.4	10.4	7.3	21.8	-14.1	-5.1	22 956	10.3	7.9
26 56320	Muskegon city	40 136	7.4	18.3	11.7	32.4	17.8	12.4	32.3	0.0	0.0	23 294	19.7	17.0
26 59440	Novi city	47 459	7.3	20.1	6.8	35.7	21.8	8.2	35.2	1.7	-4.2	40 785	26.5	9.0
26 59920	Oak Park city	29 793	6.6	21.6	8.3	29.9	21.6	12.1	34.6	2.5	-0.3	13 981	24.6	19.6
26 65440	Pontiac city	66 337	8.8	21.6	10.3	32.7	18.3	8.3	30.0	4.7	-4.1	22 922	19.7	12.3
26 65560	Portage city	44 926	6.9	19.6	8.1	30.2	23.5	11.8	35.8	0.8	-0.6	40 408	25.4	12.6
26 65820	Port Huron city	32 363	8.0	18.8	9.9	29.6	19.5	14.1	34.0	1.1	1.7	27 314	24.5	15.4
26 69035	Rochester Hills city	68 840	6.4	19.5	6.7	30.4	26.5	10.4	38.1	0.2	-2.0	59 984	24.8	11.8
26 69800	Roseville city	48 129	6.4	16.8	8.1	33.2	20.1	15.4	36.2	-2.5	3.0	44 432	22.3	16.2
26 70040	Royal Oak city	60 062	5.2	12.6	7.3	38.6	21.3	15.0	36.9	-7.9	2.6	56 094	17.3	15.6
26 70520	Saginaw city	61 842	8.6	23.0	9.8	28.9	18.4	11.3	30.7	5.9	-1.1	26 304	20.7	16.9
26 70760	St. Clair Shores city	63 124	5.1	15.0	6.2	29.0	22.9	21.8	42.0	-5.6	9.4	60 433	19.6	22.5
26 74900	Southfield city	78 296	5.5	16.0	7.7	31.1	24.5	15.1	38.3	-4.2	2.7	30 115	14.9	27.6
26 74960	Southgate city	30 136	5.4	16.0	8.4	30.6	23.2	16.3	38.5	-4.3	3.9	27 171	20.6	17.4
26 76460	Sterling Heights city	124 471	6.3	17.8	8.6	30.4	25.2	11.7	37.0	-1.6	-0.7	111 257	23.3	12.6
26 79000	Taylor city	65 868	7.4	19.8	9.2	31.1	21.4	11.0	33.9	1.5	-1.4	55 254	24.5	12.4
26 80700	Troy city	80 959	6.1	20.0	6.9	29.7	27.2	10.2	38.1	0.4	-2.2	65 928	25.2	11.5
26 84000	Warren city	138 276	6.2	16.7	7.7	30.5	21.6	17.2	37.9	-2.8	4.8	124 623	21.9	18.6
26 86000	Westland city	86 660	7.0	16.2	9.1	33.9	20.6	13.2	35.2	-2.5	0.8	74 159	22.6	14.3
26 88900	Wyandotte city	28 006	5.6	17.0	8.6	31.5	21.6	15.8	38.0	-3.1	3.4	26 415	22.0	16.5
26 88940	Wyoming city	69 366	7.9	20.2	10.7	33.7	18.2	9.3	31.2	2.4	-3.1	55 816	25.7	10.9
27 00000	**MINNESOTA**	4 919 479	6.7	19.5	9.5	30.5	21.7	12.1	35.4	0.5	-0.3	4 340 672	24.4	13.3
27 01486	Andover city	26 588	8.9	26.6	6.3	36.6	18.9	2.7	31.9	9.8	-9.7	25 451	35.4	2.8
27 01900	Apple Valley city...........	45 527	7.2	22.6	7.3	32.9	24.5	5.5	34.5	4.1	-6.9	41 324	28.6	5.9
27 06382	Blaine city	44 934	7.6	21.6	8.6	34.7	22.4	5.1	32.7	3.5	-7.3	41 627	28.2	5.3
27 06616	Bloomington city	85 202	5.3	15.2	7.9	29.7	26.2	15.8	40.1	-5.2	3.4	73 990	18.4	17.6
27 07948	Brooklyn Center city	29 061	6.6	18.3	9.5	30.7	19.4	15.5	35.3	-0.8	3.1	20 536	17.7	21.0
27 07966	Brooklyn Park city	67 388	8.1	20.8	9.9	34.7	21.2	5.4	31.9	3.2	-7.0	47 546	24.8	7.0
27 08794	Burnsville city	60 148	7.0	19.3	10.3	33.5	22.5	7.3	33.0	0.6	-5.1	52 130	24.6	8.1
27 13114	Coon Rapids city...........	61 627	7.5	21.1	9.4	32.9	21.9	7.1	33.3	2.9	-5.3	56 952	27.1	7.5
27 13456	Cottage Grove city	30 557	8.7	24.0	7.1	34.9	20.6	4.8	31.9	7.0	-7.6	28 304	31.5	5.0
27 17000	Duluth city	86 810	5.4	15.8	16.2	26.0	21.4	15.2	35.4	-4.5	2.8	79 908	19.7	16.1
27 17288	Eagan city	63 629	8.1	21.6	7.1	38.6	20.5	4.1	32.8	4.0	-8.3	55 123	28.5	4.4
27 18116	Eden Prairie city	54 901	7.9	22.5	6.1	35.6	23.1	4.7	34.2	4.7	-7.7	49 191	29.4	5.1
27 18188	Edina city	47 509	5.4	17.6	4.6	23.6	26.1	22.7	44.5	-2.7	10.3	44 341	21.8	23.9
27 22814	Fridley city	27 449	6.4	16.1	9.7	31.4	24.6	11.8	36.3	-3.2	-0.6	23 857	19.9	13.2

Table A-5. Cities — Age, Ethnicity, and Household Structure

City	Black or African American Total population	Age (percent) Under 18 years	65 years and over	American Indian and Alaska Native Total population	Age (percent) Under 18 years	65 years and over	Asian, Hawaiian, and Pacific Islander Total population	Age (percent) Under 18 years	65 years and over	Hispanic or Latino[1] Total population	Age (percent) Under 18 years	65 years and over	Two or more races Total population	Age (percent) Under 18 years	65 years and over
	14	15	16	17	18	19	20	21	22	23	24	25	26	27	28
MASSACHUSETTS— Cont'd															
Somerville city	4 938	28.7	4.9	294	23.1	8.8	5 107	14.4	3.4	6 689	23.8	0.6	3 691	21.1	4.5
Springfield city	31 472	35.2	7.9	590	33.9	2.9	2 951	25.3	4.3	41 359	42.8	3.1	6 924	45.2	4.5
Taunton city	1 188	32.2	5.5	115	29.6	2.6	467	24.0	11.3	2 308	37.6	3.0	1 205	35.2	9.2
Waltham city	2 450	25.3	4.7	153	20.9	3.3	4 647	16.2	5.4	5 046	28.5	3.5	1 300	23.2	7.6
Watertown city	573	12.0	1.6	16	37.5	0.0	1 183	18.9	4.6	961	28.6	0.0	793	20.2	3.8
Westfield city	339	49.9	0.0	60	0.0	0.0	244	34.4	0.0	2 126	41.4	4.6	565	35.4	4.6
Woburn city	577	32.4	6.9	117	30.8	6.0	1 852	19.9	4.2	1 258	30.8	0.0	398	35.9	1.3
Worcester city	12 285	33.1	5.2	391	26.9	3.8	7 940	29.2	3.0	26 456	39.8	2.5	6 180	39.9	6.6
MICHIGAN	1 401 723	32.1	8.5	60 842	31.1	5.2	177 493	26.9	3.9	322 160	37.6	4.0	207 041	44.6	4.5
Allen Park city	245	11.0	15.5	155	31.0	7.1	302	25.8	7.9	1 345	33.8	12.7	325	40.6	6.2
Ann Arbor city	9 835	23.4	7.1	460	14.1	5.4	13 416	15.8	2.3	3 708	15.5	1.1	3 471	32.4	2.9
Battle Creek city	9 599	34.8	8.8	478	25.9	5.6	978	29.8	3.6	2 404	43.0	3.7	1 699	53.0	5.7
Bay City city	977	31.3	8.1	340	26.2	3.5	240	36.7	0.0	2 455	42.4	3.5	970	65.8	0.3
Burton city	960	29.8	4.1	250	39.2	6.4	266	38.7	3.8	820	42.4	9.9	577	48.9	5.9
Dearborn city	1 178	23.1	8.8	423	25.1	10.9	1 497	24.0	4.8	2 936	34.7	9.8	9 115	41.8	3.2
Dearborn Heights city ...	1 243	24.6	6.9	369	30.4	3.5	1 175	22.4	5.4	2 265	32.5	9.4	1 563	42.9	3.1
Detroit city	774 175	32.5	9.7	3 273	25.1	9.1	9 739	30.8	5.0	47 257	35.9	4.4	21 814	41.6	6.5
East Lansing city	3 353	13.6	1.0	265	14.0	0.0	3 931	13.3	0.5	1 393	11.1	1.2	1 016	25.6	2.3
Eastpointe city	1 578	31.0	3.9	173	23.7	5.8	185	9.2	5.4	385	33.5	7.8	778	49.7	7.3
Farmington Hills city......	5 743	27.9	4.3	93	10.8	0.0	5 767	22.4	4.5	1 245	32.3	4.1	2 004	41.3	5.4
Flint city	65 430	35.6	8.5	1 134	34.5	3.4	457	24.7	7.2	3 735	40.4	3.8	4 541	47.0	4.7
Garden City city	323	34.1	5.6	86	23.3	0.0	238	13.0	4.6	581	36.5	5.7	364	35.7	10.2
Grand Rapids city	40 330	37.7	6.2	1 623	30.0	4.1	3 500	29.2	3.1	25 814	37.7	1.7	6 747	50.9	2.5
Holland city	866	42.5	0.6	159	45.3	4.4	1 271	32.1	2.2	7 880	40.2	2.9	1 102	46.9	4.3
Inkster city	19 973	33.0	9.8	145	29.0	13.1	1 148	16.8	1.0	544	38.4	0.9	926	53.6	2.9
Jackson city	6 898	39.6	9.1	237	39.2	3.4	156	34.6	3.8	1 624	42.2	3.6	1 363	59.0	4.4
Kalamazoo city	15 213	35.9	5.6	470	14.0	5.3	1 828	6.6	1.9	3 362	39.3	1.2	3 170	46.7	3.4
Kentwood city	4 111	34.5	4.8	270	30.7	9.6	2 504	29.0	4.4	1 723	40.2	1.7	1 013	57.1	3.6
Lansing city	25 674	36.2	5.9	931	26.1	4.1	3 237	33.3	4.0	11 739	38.9	4.1	5 913	58.2	2.3
Lincoln Park city	794	22.0	12.1	185	17.3	6.5	169	33.7	0.0	2 531	34.8	6.4	824	37.5	4.4
Livonia city	847	19.8	13.8	234	29.5	3.0	2 122	26.2	5.6	1 767	36.1	7.2	1 113	42.1	6.1
Madison Heights city	552	7.8	7.8	111	19.8	0.0	1 609	16.7	7.8	443	28.2	0.0	446	28.9	5.4
Midland city	828	25.6	3.1	79	16.5	6.3	1 084	30.1	3.7	773	40.6	7.9	517	45.5	5.8
Mount Pleasant city.......	970	14.8	2.6	494	38.1	1.8	684	15.2	1.6	690	21.9	6.1	434	24.7	0.0
Muskegon city	12 439	32.5	6.9	443	11.5	1.4	257	22.2	9.3	2 427	37.4	3.4	1 679	51.5	3.3
Novi city.....................	959	25.5	2.2	38	0.0	0.0	3 993	32.1	4.2	1 012	37.1	0.7	754	45.8	0.9
Oak Park city	13 432	30.4	5.4	50	22.0	28.0	786	30.0	6.5	367	49.3	3.5	1 166	36.3	5.7
Pontiac city.................	31 655	34.3	6.8	369	43.4	1.4	1 563	47.7	3.6	8 401	36.6	4.4	2 607	52.7	5.2
Portage city.................	1 401	30.4	4.4	183	26.8	5.5	1 164	28.6	5.2	963	41.2	3.1	792	54.7	1.5
Port Huron city	2 555	37.3	7.5	259	27.0	0.0	129	20.9	1.6	1 339	39.0	9.9	957	53.1	4.1
Rochester Hills city	1 437	27.0	0.0	113	20.4	6.2	4 631	30.3	1.6	1 569	36.6	0.8	1 217	49.8	2.5
Roseville city	1 217	30.5	6.8	126	35.7	7.1	883	28.8	5.5	710	32.8	9.3	828	48.2	1.3
Royal Oak city	1 105	24.0	11.9	141	17.0	0.0	949	17.8	9.2	838	32.3	3.1	892	29.6	2.0
Saginaw city	26 691	38.3	7.8	337	42.1	7.1	188	33.5	2.7	7 364	42.0	5.1	1 797	58.9	4.1
St. Clair Shores city	419	24.8	7.9	225	33.3	9.8	516	23.4	2.7	775	30.8	5.8	818	37.0	8.7
Southfield city	41 743	25.6	7.2	242	30.6	7.9	2 419	13.8	5.1	1 010	26.0	6.2	2 865	34.6	8.0
Southgate city	591	20.3	2.9	233	18.9	8.6	489	19.4	2.0	1 165	33.3	10.9	640	43.8	4.7
Sterling Heights city	1 387	22.6	3.5	458	34.5	4.8	6 514	26.0	4.1	1 581	39.3	7.0	3 309	40.1	4.8
Taylor city...................	5 864	44.5	2.0	401	38.7	5.5	926	23.2	7.8	2 197	39.1	7.6	1 570	46.7	2.2
Troy city.....................	1 831	27.4	5.6	143	11.2	7.7	10 400	29.7	3.6	1 158	32.6	5.6	1 580	37.5	5.9
Warren city	3 437	30.5	2.0	382	30.6	9.9	4 358	28.0	4.4	1 954	37.2	7.9	3 685	37.3	5.0
Westland city................	5 524	23.2	10.2	476	35.1	4.6	2 386	19.7	2.5	2 198	28.3	6.1	2 174	38.9	4.2
Wyandotte city	210	24.3	1.9	119	12.6	0.0	146	36.3	3.4	631	36.9	6.3	587	34.2	2.6
Wyoming city...............	3 259	33.3	2.6	347	22.2	1.4	2 032	33.1	3.1	6 722	39.5	2.5	2 079	48.3	3.2
MINNESOTA	167 857	37.7	3.2	54 568	37.1	4.2	140 969	37.6	3.4	141 786	38.7	1.9	88 777	51.1	2.9
Andover city	76	50.0	0.0	177	27.1	0.0	239	23.0	10.5	279	51.6	0.0	406	46.6	0.0
Apple Valley city...........	874	46.0	2.2	114	26.3	0.0	1 505	34.8	3.1	877	40.7	1.6	980	50.1	0.0
Blaine city	419	43.0	0.0	416	34.6	5.0	959	28.8	4.7	876	47.7	1.0	818	62.3	0.0
Bloomington city	3 048	33.6	3.5	461	29.7	0.0	4 259	27.0	5.7	2 200	36.2	2.4	1 601	55.1	3.5
Brooklyn Center city......	4 012	39.7	1.9	119	24.4	15.1	2 611	43.1	2.5	984	38.7	2.0	925	54.2	1.8
Brooklyn Park city	9 025	39.0	1.2	448	44.2	0.0	6 216	34.7	2.5	1 946	28.7	2.1	2 425	51.7	2.1
Burnsville city	2 142	35.3	5.4	442	45.5	0.0	2 075	28.7	1.3	1 802	32.7	1.6	1 579	55.1	0.0
Coon Rapids city	1 151	46.7	1.0	424	31.1	5.7	944	42.3	3.8	945	38.3	1.6	1 242	57.2	3.5
Cottage Grove city	751	48.2	0.0	135	25.2	5.2	375	35.7	1.3	616	48.2	2.3	483	60.9	1.2
Duluth city...................	1 450	33.7	9.4	1 901	38.4	3.2	1 248	26.9	5.2	928	48.4	5.5	1 475	50.3	3.1
Eagan city...................	2 495	38.2	1.1	273	36.6	2.2	3 116	30.5	3.7	1 324	37.0	1.1	1 381	54.9	2.8
Eden Prairie city...........	1 140	45.2	0.0	153	26.8	7.8	2 793	33.6	3.2	867	40.6	0.0	786	49.0	0.0
Edina city....................	503	31.0	7.6	169	32.0	11.2	1 260	30.2	6.6	552	41.3	7.4	661	54.8	6.7
Fridley city..................	998	35.6	1.3	180	31.7	0.0	825	39.4	2.8	616	41.1	2.4	915	47.9	3.1

[1] Hispanic or Latino persons may be of any race.

Table A-5. Cities — Age, Ethnicity, and Household Structure

City	Total households	Married-couple family households			Other family households			Two or more unrelated persons		Male living alone		Female living alone		Percent of householders 65 years and over who live alone	Grandparents who are responsible for the care of their grandchildren
		Total	With children	Householder 65 years or over	Total	With children	Householder 65 years or over	Total	Householder 65 years or over	Total	Householder 65 years or over	Total	Householder 65 years or over		
	29	30	31	32	33	34	35	36	37	38	39	40	41	42	43
MASSACHUSETTS—Cont'd															
Somerville city	31 535	33.3	14.0	5.5	14.1	5.3	3.0	21.6	0.3	13.4	2.2	17.6	6.3	49.1	289
Springfield city	57 178	36.0	16.1	7.4	28.3	18.3	2.8	5.6	0.3	12.1	3.2	18.0	8.8	53.4	1 470
Taunton city	22 071	48.9	22.8	8.5	17.0	9.9	2.6	5.9	0.2	12.3	2.5	15.8	7.7	47.3	328
Waltham city	23 157	42.1	17.0	7.9	12.1	3.5	3.4	11.5	0.5	14.7	2.4	19.6	7.6	46.0	216
Watertown city	14 645	38.4	14.1	7.7	12.2	4.0	3.7	15.1	0.4	12.6	3.4	21.6	9.4	52.1	143
Westfield city	14 798	53.3	24.8	8.9	14.5	7.4	2.6	6.3	0.5	10.9	3.0	15.0	8.1	48.2	163
Woburn city	15 029	51.4	22.1	10.9	13.1	5.6	3.0	6.8	0.2	12.6	2.3	16.0	7.8	42.0	142
Worcester city	67 083	38.9	18.2	7.8	20.3	12.1	2.6	7.8	0.3	14.5	3.1	18.5	8.8	52.8	1 120
MICHIGAN	3 788 780	52.3	23.8	9.0	16.1	9.4	2.2	5.4	0.4	11.4	2.3	14.8	7.1	44.8	70 044
Allen Park city	11 984	55.9	24.6	14.1	12.9	4.6	4.1	3.1	0.4	10.4	3.2	17.8	12.3	45.4	131
Ann Arbor city	45 744	38.5	17.9	5.5	9.3	5.3	1.1	16.8	0.3	16.0	1.2	19.3	5.0	47.3	339
Battle Creek city	21 372	42.7	19.3	8.1	20.1	13.5	2.6	5.6	0.3	12.2	2.9	19.5	9.7	53.2	388
Bay City city	15 252	43.5	19.3	8.6	18.3	11.6	2.6	5.3	0.4	13.5	2.6	19.5	10.9	53.6	158
Burton city	11 701	52.8	24.0	8.0	17.7	11.2	2.1	4.3	0.2	10.7	2.6	14.5	7.2	48.8	270
Dearborn city	36 713	51.4	26.1	10.7	13.8	5.7	3.3	3.9	0.4	13.2	3.6	17.7	11.2	50.8	386
Dearborn Heights city	23 270	53.4	22.8	13.6	14.7	5.3	4.3	3.9	0.3	11.9	3.1	16.0	9.4	40.9	305
Detroit city	336 482	27.8	13.1	5.3	37.7	21.5	5.4	4.8	0.6	13.6	3.0	16.0	6.2	44.9	17 086
East Lansing city	14 401	27.8	12.6	5.2	8.3	4.1	0.8	28.0	0.3	15.2	1.3	20.8	6.0	54.1	54
Eastpointe city	13 609	50.3	24.3	10.1	16.2	6.6	4.2	4.7	0.4	12.0	3.7	16.7	10.9	49.7	277
Farmington Hills city	33 538	56.2	25.7	9.9	8.9	4.6	1.3	5.3	0.3	12.1	2.2	17.5	8.3	47.7	233
Flint city	48 818	30.4	13.8	5.9	32.4	20.8	3.2	5.4	0.5	14.3	2.5	17.5	7.4	50.9	2 033
Garden City city	11 493	56.1	25.2	10.9	15.9	8.1	2.8	4.0	0.2	10.5	2.4	13.5	7.6	41.8	149
Grand Rapids city	73 336	41.4	20.4	7.0	19.8	12.3	2.3	7.9	0.3	12.9	2.0	17.9	7.8	50.5	1 542
Holland city	12 044	52.2	26.4	10.5	14.3	8.9	1.5	6.9	0.2	10.3	1.7	16.3	9.2	47.3	345
Inkster city	11 166	35.9	15.3	6.6	31.7	18.8	4.2	4.5	0.4	12.7	2.9	15.2	6.4	45.7	714
Jackson city	14 215	37.1	17.5	6.1	24.0	16.5	2.2	6.9	0.5	13.1	3.3	18.9	8.7	57.6	298
Kalamazoo city	29 415	30.7	13.2	5.4	18.4	12.1	1.5	16.2	0.4	15.2	2.3	19.6	7.5	57.2	463
Kentwood city	18 448	49.2	25.3	6.6	13.4	8.4	1.1	6.5	0.2	12.6	1.7	18.4	7.2	52.8	201
Lansing city	49 458	36.6	17.0	5.8	21.1	13.7	1.9	9.1	0.4	14.3	1.9	18.8	6.3	50.5	897
Lincoln Park city	16 201	47.1	21.5	9.4	18.7	9.4	3.4	5.0	0.3	13.4	2.3	15.8	8.1	44.4	361
Livonia city	38 129	62.9	28.2	13.1	11.0	4.5	3.0	3.3	0.3	9.1	2.7	13.8	8.4	40.4	473
Madison Heights city	13 307	46.7	20.6	8.2	13.5	6.4	2.4	6.1	0.2	15.3	2.4	18.4	9.5	52.6	189
Midland city	16 787	55.2	26.2	10.4	10.6	7.2	1.1	5.6	0.4	9.8	1.6	18.8	9.3	47.8	86
Mount Pleasant city	8 475	26.6	11.9	4.7	11.2	7.1	0.8	33.6	0.2	9.4	1.2	19.2	7.1	59.3	54
Muskegon city	14 567	34.8	16.4	6.8	24.7	16.0	3.2	6.3	0.6	13.9	2.9	20.3	9.5	53.9	514
Novi city	18 710	58.0	31.5	5.4	7.9	4.0	0.8	6.0	0.2	13.0	1.3	15.1	4.7	48.2	218
Oak Park city	11 091	45.5	22.8	9.3	23.3	11.6	3.4	4.6	0.1	8.6	2.1	18.1	8.1	44.4	387
Pontiac city	24 274	32.7	16.2	4.3	30.7	18.8	3.4	7.2	0.3	13.2	1.7	16.2	6.0	49.2	1 023
Portage city	18 094	55.6	26.7	9.2	12.2	7.8	1.3	5.4	0.3	10.9	1.5	16.0	6.9	43.7	156
Port Huron city	12 938	41.1	18.9	7.6	21.3	14.4	2.0	5.9	0.6	12.9	3.3	18.9	10.3	57.3	173
Rochester Hills city	26 363	63.7	31.1	7.8	8.8	4.4	1.4	3.6	0.3	9.5	1.3	14.4	7.1	46.8	185
Roseville city	19 999	45.9	20.9	9.5	18.1	8.2	3.9	5.4	0.3	13.1	2.7	17.5	9.4	47.0	223
Royal Oak city	28 850	40.3	16.5	7.8	9.9	3.7	2.1	8.8	0.2	17.4	2.9	23.5	8.7	53.3	94
Saginaw city	23 196	33.6	15.6	6.3	32.1	21.3	3.5	4.8	0.3	12.9	2.8	16.6	7.7	51.0	960
St. Clair Shores city	27 495	50.6	19.9	13.6	12.8	4.9	3.8	3.9	0.4	12.6	3.6	20.1	12.3	47.1	240
Southfield city	33 971	40.3	16.6	8.3	18.0	9.0	2.3	5.4	0.4	13.5	2.4	22.8	9.3	51.5	699
Southgate city	12 822	49.7	21.3	10.4	13.0	5.8	3.2	5.0	0.5	13.1	2.8	19.2	10.9	49.3	239
Sterling Heights city	46 381	61.0	28.5	8.7	11.3	4.7	1.8	3.7	0.2	9.9	1.8	14.1	6.8	44.4	641
Taylor city	24 766	49.9	22.3	8.1	22.1	13.9	2.3	5.0	0.3	10.7	2.3	12.3	5.6	42.3	652
Troy city	30 043	64.7	34.0	7.8	8.5	3.5	1.4	4.1	0.3	10.0	1.8	12.9	6.1	45.4	207
Warren city	55 619	49.6	20.7	12.2	16.7	7.2	3.5	5.1	0.5	12.8	2.9	15.9	8.9	42.1	944
Westland city	36 699	46.1	21.0	7.6	15.0	8.0	2.0	6.3	0.4	13.3	2.3	19.3	9.3	53.8	618
Wyandotte city	11 818	46.2	20.5	9.7	17.1	8.2	3.2	4.9	0.2	13.5	3.5	18.3	10.7	51.9	141
Wyoming city	26 549	49.8	26.3	7.0	16.6	10.3	1.6	7.1	0.3	12.5	1.6	13.9	5.9	46.0	463
MINNESOTA	1 896 209	54.6	26.0	9.1	12.0	7.6	1.3	6.6	0.3	11.7	2.2	15.1	7.2	46.8	17 682
Andover city	8 124	82.0	51.9	2.8	6.6	4.3	0.2	3.5	0.1	4.9	0.8	3.0	1.6	43.5	85
Apple Valley city	16 348	65.0	35.5	4.9	11.2	7.0	0.4	4.6	0.2	7.2	0.6	12.1	3.5	42.8	112
Blaine city	15 821	62.1	32.4	5.3	14.6	9.1	0.6	6.2	0.1	7.9	0.6	9.1	2.7	35.5	232
Bloomington city	36 459	52.1	19.4	11.6	10.9	6.1	1.5	7.4	0.5	11.2	2.1	18.4	7.9	42.6	348
Brooklyn Center city	11 422	48.2	20.0	11.5	17.0	10.8	2.0	6.7	0.3	10.9	2.8	17.3	8.6	45.3	170
Brooklyn Park city	24 440	55.8	29.6	4.8	15.7	10.7	0.7	6.4	0.1	10.0	0.8	12.0	3.0	40.3	364
Burnsville city	23 617	53.6	26.6	6.4	12.6	8.4	0.6	8.9	0.2	11.1	1.0	13.7	4.0	40.7	207
Coon Rapids city	22 625	58.8	29.7	6.3	15.2	9.9	1.1	6.0	0.1	8.2	0.8	11.9	4.5	41.8	425
Cottage Grove city	9 902	75.5	42.3	6.1	11.0	7.4	0.7	2.7	0.1	4.9	0.5	5.8	2.0	26.6	91
Duluth city	35 547	42.6	18.2	8.9	14.0	9.2	1.5	9.0	0.5	14.0	2.7	20.3	9.9	53.4	226
Eagan city	23 922	59.0	35.1	3.7	10.3	6.9	0.5	7.8	0.1	11.2	0.8	11.6	1.9	38.2	181
Eden Prairie city	20 473	63.2	37.0	4.3	9.2	6.2	0.2	6.4	0.2	9.1	0.5	13.0	2.8	41.5	85
Edina city	21 038	54.8	23.2	15.3	6.8	3.4	1.4	4.4	0.5	9.3	3.0	24.7	14.8	50.8	82
Fridley city	11 331	49.4	19.0	10.4	15.3	9.0	1.4	8.4	0.2	12.4	1.3	14.5	4.8	33.8	142

City	Households with Non-Hispanic White householder		Households with Black or African American householder		Households with American Indian and Alaska Native householder		Households with Asian, Hawaiian, and Pacific Islander householder		Households with Hispanic or Latino[1] householder		Foreign-born population	Place of birth (percent)			Percent in non-English speaking households	
	Number of households	Percent that are family households	Number of households	Percent that are family households	Number of households	Percent that are family households	Number of households	Percent that are family households	Number of households	Percent that are family households	Percent of total population that is foreign-born	Europe	Asia	Latin America	Linguistically isolated	Not linguistically isolated
	44	45	46	47	48	49	50	51	52	53	54	55	56	57	58	59
MASSACHUSETTS— Cont'd																
Somerville city	24 563	42.8	1 721	65.6	118	94.9	1 649	51.7	2 078	66.9	29.3	8.8	5.4	13.3	9.7	33.7
Springfield city	31 879	58.2	11 272	66.8	207	89.4	723	83.4	12 561	76.0	8.0	2.6	1.9	2.7	8.4	31.0
Taunton city	19 906	66.2	498	52.2	16	100.0	189	72.5	795	68.8	10.1	7.6	0.7	1.0	3.8	21.9
Waltham city	19 086	51.1	790	55.1	70	68.6	1 503	69.0	1 415	80.7	20.2	4.0	7.3	5.3	5.4	27.5
Watertown city	13 524	49.3	210	61.9	10	100.0	400	58.0	280	65.0	20.3	7.9	8.5	2.3	5.7	26.5
Westfield city	13 892	67.7	82	67.1	31	16.1	71	47.9	623	74.0	7.1	5.4	1.0	0.2	4.4	12.1
Woburn city	13 617	64.1	191	57.6	45	80.0	693	65.5	370	76.5	9.6	2.7	4.5	1.7	2.3	17.7
Worcester city	50 875	55.1	4 509	63.2	157	67.5	2 377	76.0	8 154	77.7	14.5	4.1	4.2	4.0	8.5	26.4
MICHIGAN	3 088 895	68.4	491 963	67.1	20 422	70.1	56 378	72.8	84 443	75.2	5.3	1.6	2.1	0.9	1.7	11.3
Allen Park city	11 247	68.4	95	50.5	42	45.2	93	93.5	434	78.1	4.7	2.0	1.1	0.6	1.0	9.8
Ann Arbor city	34 237	47.2	3 970	54.2	147	56.5	5 089	40.0	1 304	42.6	16.6	3.7	9.6	1.5	4.6	22.1
Battle Creek city	16 467	61.9	3 570	62.2	118	57.6	343	84.8	538	79.0	3.4	0.5	1.4	1.2	1.7	9.4
Bay City city	14 018	61.1	329	62.3	140	77.1	72	45.8	617	75.9	1.4	0.4	0.6	0.3	0.4	10.3
Burton city	10 885	70.8	364	58.2	89	95.5	69	66.7	165	70.3	2.2	0.9	0.8	0.2	0.8	8.0
Dearborn city	32 187	64.3	435	32.0	156	67.9	510	70.8	920	67.6	25.4	3.2	19.7	0.7	8.5	35.9
Dearborn Heights city	21 201	67.7	486	49.4	150	79.3	341	84.8	639	78.1	12.4	5.1	5.2	0.6	3.7	21.6
Detroit city	44 789	48.5	270 292	67.8	1 125	71.2	2 839	71.6	12 446	75.9	4.8	0.6	1.6	2.1	2.6	12.0
East Lansing city	11 248	34.4	1 061	39.7	91	62.6	1 384	43.7	391	33.8	11.7	1.6	7.5	1.0	4.6	17.0
Eastpointe city	12 708	65.5	526	82.3	60	50.0	55	80.0	111	85.6	4.9	2.9	0.9	0.3	1.1	10.2
Farmington Hills city	28 114	64.0	2 299	62.7	30	53.3	2 146	81.0	403	67.5	15.7	4.3	9.1	0.7	2.8	20.7
Flint city	22 650	55.4	23 539	69.6	365	82.2	155	60.6	1 017	76.0	1.5	0.5	0.3	0.3	0.4	8.0
Garden City city	10 957	72.9	104	60.6	37	75.7	83	47.0	190	60.0	3.3	1.3	1.0	0.2	0.8	10.4
Grand Rapids city	51 636	56.3	13 503	70.8	605	56.0	927	76.9	5 868	81.3	10.5	1.7	1.6	6.5	6.0	15.1
Holland city	9 163	62.6	271	81.9	53	45.3	332	69.6	2 089	81.8	10.7	1.0	3.0	6.5	6.0	23.6
Inkster city	3 173	57.6	7 087	72.4	54	66.7	480	66.7	158	79.7	5.4	0.6	3.4	0.7	1.8	10.2
Jackson city	10 994	59.5	2 450	65.3	71	57.7	17	0.0	436	75.9	1.8	0.5	0.3	0.8	0.8	8.3
Kalamazoo city	21 623	45.7	5 378	63.6	205	54.1	695	26.5	768	60.4	5.2	1.1	2.2	1.4	1.9	12.2
Kentwood city	15 211	61.8	1 755	61.4	101	65.3	666	87.1	554	69.7	9.3	2.5	4.9	1.0	4.0	12.6
Lansing city	33 928	53.7	9 746	66.7	339	66.9	951	67.9	3 458	70.7	5.9	0.9	2.3	1.9	3.1	14.6
Lincoln Park city	14 067	66.4	412	32.3	61	47.5	80	65.0	803	72.2	4.0	1.9	0.5	1.0	1.5	10.1
Livonia city	36 335	73.7	295	55.3	125	78.4	689	85.3	451	79.2	6.7	3.0	2.3	0.2	1.4	12.4
Madison Heights city	11 766	61.9	401	19.5	58	12.1	693	55.8	169	79.3	14.4	4.4	8.4	0.3	6.4	14.3
Midland city	15 691	65.4	248	74.6	57	68.4	384	78.6	248	65.3	5.0	1.1	2.0	0.6	0.8	8.7
Mount Pleasant city	7 565	37.2	202	38.1	132	57.6	277	40.8	215	47.0	4.0	0.6	2.6	0.2	1.1	11.8
Muskegon city	9 720	54.5	3 782	69.3	140	77.9	74	56.8	581	73.1	2.0	0.4	0.6	1.9	2.4	8.1
Novi city	16 519	65.3	353	60.1	23	26.1	1 003	79.0	280	61.4	12.7	3.2	6.8	1.1	3.2	16.0
Oak Park city	5 498	64.6	4 904	72.6	25	48.0	176	96.6	74	100.0	14.9	3.7	0.4	0.5	6.4	16.4
Pontiac city	9 811	53.2	11 492	67.8	128	85.2	343	79.0	2 281	79.1	6.2	0.4	2.1	3.2	4.6	14.8
Portage city	16 531	67.5	652	60.4	54	66.7	411	82.0	238	71.4	4.8	1.3	1.9	0.7	0.5	10.6
Port Huron city	11 413	60.7	912	71.2	83	83.1	34	85.3	343	80.8	3.2	0.9	0.6	0.3	1.1	5.7
Rochester Hills city	23 612	71.5	542	74.7	28	100.0	1 488	87.2	464	67.9	12.2	3.7	5.6	0.9	1.8	18.6
Roseville city	18 736	63.7	476	58.4	61	67.2	282	80.9	242	66.5	5.4	2.7	1.6	0.3	1.9	11.0
Royal Oak city	27 415	50.2	391	39.9	52	67.3	399	54.9	313	51.8	6.3	2.8	1.7	0.3	1.4	10.1
Saginaw city	11 472	59.6	9 175	71.0	97	73.2	54	57.4	2 184	75.8	1.6	0.4	0.2	0.9	1.0	12.5
St. Clair Shores city	26 620	63.1	157	70.7	82	80.5	140	75.7	274	81.0	5.7	2.9	1.1	0.3	1.2	10.9
Southfield city	13 964	52.4	17 663	62.5	103	59.2	985	62.2	321	72.9	14.0	3.4	7.9	0.7	4.3	17.7
Southgate city	11 849	62.6	263	41.8	63	38.1	140	67.9	370	75.9	5.7	2.9	1.4	0.6	1.2	14.4
Sterling Heights city	42 395	72.1	594	55.4	150	54.0	1 978	80.4	419	77.1	17.0	7.0	8.7	0.3	5.0	24.2
Taylor city	21 248	72.0	2 115	73.4	106	85.8	264	83.7	696	64.8	4.0	1.5	1.4	0.4	0.8	8.4
Troy city	25 148	71.1	680	69.4	57	87.7	3 376	88.3	336	72.6	19.6	4.6	12.3	0.7	3.2	26.5
Warren city	51 199	66.5	1 520	49.0	169	74.0	1 236	75.6	496	69.2	10.3	4.3	4.6	0.3	3.0	16.6
Westland city	31 831	61.0	2 390	53.9	173	73.4	966	73.1	758	63.1	6.8	2.0	3.2	0.6	2.0	11.1
Wyandotte city	11 358	63.0	62	80.6	47	66.0	40	85.0	154	75.3	3.6	1.9	0.5	0.3	1.4	10.8
Wyoming city	22 491	65.2	1 324	62.3	133	74.4	526	89.9	1 821	79.1	7.9	1.3	2.5	3.7	4.0	13.6
MINNESOTA	1 735 421	66.3	55 913	66.0	16 579	70.7	35 604	74.8	35 171	75.4	5.3	0.9	2.1	1.3	2.1	10.8
Andover city	7 822	88.9	23	65.2	70	100.0	42	100.0	72	77.8	2.5	0.9	0.9	0.3	0.4	10.3
Apple Valley city	15 238	75.8	290	73.8	14	100.0	400	87.0	238	76.5	5.4	1.0	2.7	0.9	1.5	10.2
Blaine city	15 038	76.1	123	93.5	112	88.4	257	82.5	182	92.3	3.4	1.0	1.6	0.5	1.0	8.6
Bloomington city	33 148	62.1	1 126	63.8	133	73.7	1 217	80.8	562	73.0	7.7	1.1	4.2	1.3	2.9	11.0
Brooklyn Center city	9 063	62.4	1 425	70.4	41	82.9	462	91.6	281	79.4	11.3	1.4	4.4	1.3	3.3	18.4
Brooklyn Park city	18 640	69.6	3 234	75.4	123	78.9	1 430	84.3	573	82.9	13.3	1.0	6.2	1.6	3.7	16.6
Burnsville city	21 403	65.0	814	76.2	143	83.2	559	82.8	434	81.3	7.4	1.4	2.9	2.0	2.4	12.3
Coon Rapids city	21 474	73.4	385	83.9	121	62.8	192	78.6	242	94.6	3.7	1.3	1.2	0.7	1.2	7.9
Cottage Grove city	9 316	86.2	225	92.0	58	100.0	79	100.0	155	89.0	2.8	0.5	1.2	0.3	0.3	9.6
Duluth city	33 460	56.4	494	58.9	647	59.5	353	73.4	208	55.8	2.8	1.0	1.1	0.2	0.6	8.7
Eagan city	21 383	68.7	812	72.2	107	71.0	938	74.0	372	79.0	7.7	1.6	4.0	1.0	1.8	13.2
Eden Prairie city	18 760	70.5	392	75.3	34	17.6	883	86.7	216	81.5	8.9	2.0	4.4	0.8	2.8	12.9
Edina city	19 972	61.6	170	55.3	83	54.2	425	64.7	220	64.1	6.0	1.9	2.8	0.5	0.8	12.4
Fridley city	10 260	63.9	401	71.8	73	45.2	180	88.3	154	83.1	7.2	1.6	2.6	1.3	3.1	10.8

[1] Hispanic or Latino persons may be of any race.

Table A-5. Cities — Age, Ethnicity, and Household Structure

STATE Place code	City	Total population	Under 5 years	5 to 17 years	18 to 24 years	25 to 44 years	45 to 64 years	65 years and over	Median age	+/− U.S. percent under 18 years	+/− U.S. percent 65 years and over	Non-Hispanic White Total population	Under 18 years	65 years and over
		1	2	3	4	5	6	7	8	9	10	11	12	13
	MINNESOTA—Cont'd													
27 31076	Inver Grove Heights city	29 724	7.1	20.2	9.3	33.9	21.5	7.9	33.8	1.6	−4.5	26 741	25.6	8.5
27 35180	Lakeville city	43 128	10.3	25.8	5.5	38.1	17.4	3.0	31.5	10.4	−9.4	40 464	35.5	3.0
27 39878	Mankato city	32 357	4.9	11.9	32.4	24.1	15.6	11.2	25.3	−8.9	−1.2	29 722	15.9	12.1
27 40166	Maple Grove city	50 343	7.5	23.1	6.4	35.1	23.8	4.0	34.4	4.9	−8.4	47 235	30.0	4.1
27 40382	Maplewood city	34 942	6.5	18.3	7.4	30.0	22.6	15.1	37.8	−0.9	2.7	30 530	22.3	16.6
27 43000	Minneapolis city	382 452	6.4	15.5	14.4	36.9	17.7	9.1	31.2	−3.8	−3.3	239 771	12.8	12.7
27 43252	Minnetonka city	51 299	5.3	17.8	6.0	28.7	28.3	13.9	40.8	−2.6	1.5	48 199	22.3	14.7
27 43864	Moorhead city	32 161	5.7	16.9	23.4	24.0	17.2	12.8	28.7	−3.1	0.4	29 033	20.9	13.8
27 47680	Oakdale city	26 669	7.8	21.2	7.5	34.1	21.1	8.4	34.3	3.3	−4.0	24 179	27.4	9.0
27 51730	Plymouth city	65 903	6.9	20.1	7.1	33.6	24.8	7.6	36.1	1.3	−4.8	59 521	26.0	8.1
27 54214	Richfield city	34 441	6.3	14.0	9.1	33.7	20.6	16.3	37.1	−5.4	3.9	27 078	17.3	19.9
27 54880	Rochester city	85 392	7.5	18.4	9.1	33.5	20.1	11.4	34.3	0.2	−1.0	73 631	24.0	12.8
27 55852	Roseville city	33 757	4.8	13.5	11.4	26.3	23.8	20.2	41.0	−7.4	7.8	30 057	16.7	22.1
27 56896	St. Cloud city	58 978	5.6	15.1	24.1	27.8	17.3	10.2	28.2	−5.0	−2.2	53 958	20.0	11.0
27 57220	St. Louis Park city	44 120	5.6	13.2	8.4	38.2	19.8	14.7	35.7	−6.9	2.3	38 773	16.9	16.1
27 58000	St. Paul city	287 151	7.5	19.5	12.3	32.5	17.8	10.4	31.0	1.3	−2.0	184 191	17.7	14.3
27 59998	Shoreview city	25 924	5.6	20.5	7.1	28.6	28.4	9.7	39.2	0.4	−2.7	23 961	25.1	10.3
27 71032	Winona city	26 989	4.3	13.5	27.9	21.9	18.0	14.5	28.8	−7.9	2.1	25 290	17.0	15.2
27 71428	Woodbury city	46 464	9.6	21.2	5.8	36.8	20.6	6.0	33.4	5.1	−6.4	41 163	29.2	6.4
28 00000	**MISSISSIPPI**	2 844 658	7.1	20.1	11.0	28.5	21.2	12.1	33.8	1.5	−0.3	1 728 608	23.2	14.7
28 06220	Biloxi city	50 713	7.4	17.0	14.4	30.3	18.9	12.0	32.5	−1.3	−0.4	35 420	21.3	15.0
28 15380	Columbus city	26 032	7.2	18.7	12.4	26.4	20.1	15.2	33.8	0.2	2.8	11 341	16.2	23.9
28 29180	Greenville city	41 623	8.5	22.6	10.4	26.5	20.1	11.8	31.5	5.4	−0.6	11 910	18.8	20.1
28 29700	Gulfport city	70 986	7.2	18.6	11.1	30.6	20.7	11.8	33.6	0.1	−0.6	43 271	21.2	14.8
28 31020	Hattiesburg city	44 697	6.3	15.2	24.7	26.2	15.8	11.8	27.1	−4.2	−0.6	22 019	11.1	17.4
28 36000	Jackson city	184 032	7.8	20.7	12.5	29.3	18.9	10.9	31.0	2.8	−1.5	50 522	15.9	22.9
28 46640	Meridian city	40 035	7.4	19.7	9.8	26.6	19.5	17.0	34.6	1.4	4.6	17 426	16.8	26.3
28 55360	Pascagoula city	26 222	7.9	18.9	11.9	29.6	19.9	11.8	32.6	1.1	−0.6	17 119	22.1	16.0
28 69280	Southaven city	29 086	7.7	19.4	9.2	32.3	23.1	8.4	33.1	1.4	−4.0	26 176	26.3	9.0
28 74840	Tupelo city	34 418	7.6	20.0	8.0	31.3	20.5	12.7	34.9	1.9	0.3	23 772	23.4	15.7
28 76720	Vicksburg city	26 170	8.0	20.1	9.4	28.6	18.7	15.3	34.3	2.4	2.9	10 052	20.4	22.4
29 00000	**MISSOURI**	5 595 211	6.6	18.9	9.5	29.2	22.3	13.5	36.1	−0.2	1.1	4 687 837	24.0	14.7
29 03160	Ballwin city	31 223	7.0	20.0	6.5	30.2	24.4	12.0	37.6	1.3	−0.4	28 980	26.4	12.7
29 06652	Blue Springs city	47 990	7.6	21.6	9.1	31.8	22.5	7.4	33.1	3.5	−5.0	43 907	28.5	7.7
29 11242	Cape Girardeau city	35 319	5.4	15.2	18.4	25.8	19.9	15.4	33.6	−5.1	3.0	30 626	18.4	17.3
29 13600	Chesterfield city	46 973	5.6	19.1	5.7	25.2	29.8	14.6	41.8	−1.0	2.2	42 115	24.1	15.7
29 15670	Columbia city	84 780	5.8	13.7	26.7	28.9	16.2	8.7	26.8	−6.2	−3.7	68 474	17.1	9.9
29 24778	Florissant city	50 229	6.4	18.6	8.0	30.6	19.5	17.0	37.1	−0.7	4.6	42 844	23.0	19.3
29 27190	Gladstone city	26 339	5.7	15.4	8.6	28.3	26.1	15.9	40.0	−4.6	3.5	23 973	19.8	16.9
29 31276	Hazelwood city	26 174	6.1	18.3	9.9	31.5	23.1	11.1	35.6	−1.3	−1.3	20 689	22.6	13.1
29 35000	Independence city	113 207	6.6	17.2	8.5	29.3	22.9	15.5	37.8	−1.9	3.1	101 865	22.2	16.7
29 37000	Jefferson City city..........	39 521	6.1	14.1	11.0	32.7	21.9	14.1	36.5	−5.5	1.7	32 058	19.8	16.8
29 37592	Joplin city	45 566	7.0	16.2	13.4	27.6	20.3	15.6	34.7	−2.5	3.2	41 147	22.3	16.5
29 38000	Kansas City city	441 269	7.1	18.2	9.6	32.8	20.6	11.7	34.0	−0.4	−0.7	255 383	19.9	14.4
29 39044	Kirkwood city	27 270	6.0	16.9	6.1	27.6	25.0	18.4	41.1	−2.8	6.0	24 454	21.5	18.9
29 41348	Lee's Summit city..........	71 074	8.1	21.2	6.4	32.8	21.4	10.1	35.1	3.6	−2.3	65 451	28.6	10.7
29 42032	Liberty city	26 034	6.4	21.1	10.1	30.5	21.2	10.7	34.0	1.8	−1.7	24 009	26.7	11.1
29 46586	Maryland Heights city....	25 937	5.7	16.0	9.5	37.5	21.8	9.5	34.2	−4.0	−2.9	21 651	20.7	10.7
29 54074	O'Fallon city	45 888	10.4	23.0	6.5	38.4	15.1	6.5	31.1	7.7	−5.9	43 420	33.2	6.7
29 60788	Raytown city	30 401	5.8	16.0	7.8	28.1	22.4	19.1	39.8	−3.1	6.7	25 101	19.7	22.1
29 64082	St. Charles city	59 997	6.3	16.9	12.2	30.3	22.0	12.3	35.4	−2.5	−0.1	54 977	22.4	13.1
29 64550	St. Joseph city	73 829	6.4	17.7	11.8	28.2	20.6	15.4	35.6	−1.6	3.0	66 592	23.3	16.4
29 65000	St. Louis city	348 189	6.7	19.0	10.6	31.2	18.8	13.7	33.7	0.0	1.3	149 553	16.6	17.3
29 65126	St. Peters city	51 332	7.4	22.8	7.4	33.7	21.2	7.6	34.2	4.5	−4.8	48 239	29.8	7.9
29 70000	Springfield city	151 823	5.9	14.0	17.4	28.2	19.5	15.0	33.5	−5.8	2.6	137 202	18.8	16.0
29 75220	University City city.........	37 462	5.9	16.1	10.8	31.3	22.6	13.3	35.4	−3.7	0.9	18 313	17.4	14.2
29 79820	Wildwood city	33 445	8.5	25.0	4.6	32.1	24.5	5.4	36.1	7.8	−7.0	31 500	33.2	5.6
30 00000	**MONTANA**	902 195	6.1	19.4	9.5	27.3	24.4	13.4	37.5	−0.2	1.0	807 588	23.9	14.4
30 06550	Billings city	89 362	6.4	17.6	10.2	28.9	22.1	14.8	36.8	−1.7	2.4	80 580	22.4	16.0
30 08950	Bozeman city	28 003	5.0	11.4	32.5	28.9	14.5	7.7	25.4	−9.3	−4.7	26 081	15.6	8.2
30 11390	Butte-Silver Bow	34 606	5.6	18.1	9.6	26.9	24.0	15.9	38.9	−2.0	3.5	32 404	22.9	16.8
30 32800	Great Falls city	56 644	6.4	18.7	8.6	28.1	22.4	15.7	37.8	−0.6	3.3	50 421	23.8	17.0
30 35600	Helena city	25 563	5.8	16.3	11.4	26.4	26.1	14.0	38.8	−3.6	1.6	24 010	21.3	14.6
30 50200	Missoula city	56 968	5.3	14.5	20.6	29.5	19.6	10.6	30.3	−5.9	−1.8	52 553	18.9	11.2

City	Black or African American			American Indian and Alaska Native			Asian, Hawaiian, and Pacific Islander			Hispanic or Latino[1]			Two or more races		
		Age (percent)			Age (percent)			Age (percent)			Age (percent)			Age (percent)	
	Total population	Under 18 years	65 years and over	Total population	Under 18 years	65 years and over	Total population	Under 18 years	65 years and over	Total population	Under 18 years	65 years and over	Total population	Under 18 years	65 years and over
	14	15	16	17	18	19	20	21	22	23	24	25	26	27	28
MINNESOTA—Cont'd															
Inver Grove Heights city	631	44.5	1.0	173	39.9	3.5	477	23.3	1.7	1 209	44.5	2.9	682	62.0	0.0
Lakeville city	448	31.3	0.9	183	51.9	0.0	765	33.1	5.9	560	46.8	0.0	704	68.9	1.1
Mankato city	721	41.3	0.0	96	14.6	0.0	823	9.2	0.7	612	28.8	0.8	422	39.6	1.4
Maple Grove city	738	37.4	4.1	109	35.8	0.0	1 165	35.8	1.5	612	45.6	0.0	589	53.8	1.0
Maplewood city	992	36.0	7.6	217	21.2	5.5	1 358	37.3	3.4	1 003	47.2	3.6	1 091	56.4	3.5
Minneapolis city	67 262	37.8	3.5	7 576	34.7	3.4	24 276	38.1	3.0	29 085	31.8	1.2	17 771	46.1	2.6
Minnetonka city	831	37.5	1.3	99	35.4	0.0	1 035	29.5	4.1	739	35.7	1.1	496	52.4	0.0
Moorhead city	229	19.7	0.0	473	34.9	0.0	383	16.2	6.8	1 415	43.5	4.6	758	50.3	3.7
Oakdale city	602	43.0	0.0	90	11.1	21.1	581	41.8	3.8	713	41.4	1.5	606	54.6	1.3
Plymouth city	1 725	28.4	3.9	271	22.1	0.0	2 467	32.5	2.5	1 096	40.8	1.9	884	56.0	0.0
Richfield city	2 461	29.9	1.7	212	28.8	2.8	1 760	24.1	5.0	2 119	33.4	0.6	1 010	50.2	5.5
Rochester city	2 763	39.6	2.2	369	10.8	3.3	4 814	35.1	3.3	2 192	33.2	2.3	1 690	53.8	2.0
Roseville city	816	26.0	5.0	152	3.9	3.3	1 635	29.5	5.0	603	27.5	3.3	512	56.1	1.4
St. Cloud city	1 139	20.1	1.1	467	25.1	0.6	1 654	23.6	2.5	771	28.1	1.7	1 066	48.6	0.7
St. Louis Park city	2 046	36.2	1.7	186	26.9	5.9	1 292	20.0	8.9	1 229	35.6	2.7	679	50.4	5.0
St. Paul city	32 394	38.9	4.4	3 413	37.1	2.6	35 479	49.9	3.2	22 696	38.4	2.4	12 426	53.3	2.5
Shoreview city	307	39.1	5.9	55	16.4	0.0	768	28.5	2.2	500	44.4	3.6	404	52.0	2.5
Winona city	299	39.1	0.0	92	9.8	7.6	598	21.2	0.0	431	39.2	0.0	443	41.5	10.4
Woodbury city	968	30.5	1.7	80	10.0	0.0	2 382	37.8	3.5	1 076	47.6	0.0	883	67.5	3.3
MISSISSIPPI	1 033 437	33.7	8.3	11 836	34.1	5.9	18 386	25.2	5.0	37 790	30.6	4.4	21 950	38.8	8.0
Biloxi city	9 543	30.7	5.5	366	10.9	2.2	2 467	30.8	5.5	1 807	31.5	3.2	1 556	46.7	4.4
Columbus city	14 118	33.6	8.8	18	0.0	0.0	138	8.0	2.9	240	28.8	0.0	246	38.2	2.0
Greenville city	29 034	36.2	8.4	66	22.7	25.8	223	31.8	12.6	302	34.8	14.2	178	11.2	19.7
Gulfport city	24 049	33.6	7.3	360	15.3	8.9	751	21.3	4.4	1 645	26.7	4.7	1 330	41.4	3.6
Hattiesburg city	21 258	32.8	6.6	67	19.4	0.0	495	9.7	0.0	459	18.3	3.3	423	12.3	9.9
Jackson city	129 862	33.3	6.3	473	37.8	2.7	1 008	19.0	3.1	1 290	24.2	8.8	1 283	38.3	6.9
Meridian city	22 060	35.4	9.6	56	0.0	0.0	168	29.2	11.3	156	25.0	23.7	193	20.7	14.5
Pascagoula city	7 476	36.9	3.8	152	33.2	4.6	260	00.4	0.0	1 009	26.5	3.1	315	37.8	7.0
Southaven city	1 670	00.0	4.4	90	24.4	0.0	329	35.6	3.0	684	33.3	2.2	202	25.7	0.0
Tupelo city	9 529	36.3	6.4	127	48.0	0.0	141	17.0	0.0	522	38.5	0.8	445	57.1	1.1
Vicksburg city	15 535	32.9	10.9	71	35.2	0.0	211	43.1	6.2	239	25.5	3.8	125	20.0	24.0
MISSOURI	622 087	32.5	8.6	26 200	26.6	6.7	63 500	23.2	4.7	116 373	36.2	4.0	90 948	41.9	5.8
Ballwin city	329	41.0	0.0	49	26.5	10.2	900	27.9	2.6	493	28.4	7.3	552	52.7	0.0
Blue Springs city	1 393	35.7	4.0	316	25.6	8.5	510	26.5	8.2	1 170	40.8	2.5	827	49.5	0.8
Cape Girardeau city	3 337	37.8	4.0	186	16.7	4.8	330	12.7	0.0	328	29.0	0.0	563	36.8	4.3
Chesterfield city	1 084	30.3	7.6	61	42.6	6.6	2 509	27.8	5.2	678	32.0	2.4	468	44.3	5.9
Columbia city	9 102	31.8	5.4	422	10.0	5.0	3 588	19.7	1.1	1 802	29.5	2.1	1 557	44.3	3.7
Florissant city	5 675	35.9	3.3	129	5.4	11.6	261	49.0	5.4	608	35.0	9.7	777	44.8	4.0
Gladstone city	426	28.4	0.0	235	20.4	16.6	238	32.8	2.9	941	33.9	7.7	611	39.6	6.2
Hazelwood city	4 095	30.1	2.7	4	0.0	0.0	570	27.4	9.3	424	32.5	1.2	392	48.0	6.4
Independence city	2 596	36.3	3.1	612	26.1	5.7	1 427	30.3	6.3	4 010	38.0	3.9	2 927	50.5	6.3
Jefferson City city	5 522	21.8	2.7	154	18.8	3.2	574	20.9	1.0	487	25.3	3.3	734	20.4	2.6
Joplin city	1 044	24.2	11.2	762	27.0	7.9	358	15.6	4.2	1 222	43.5	2.4	1 189	39.8	7.3
Kansas City city	135 671	32.8	9.1	2 308	20.1	7.5	8 803	23.5	3.9	30 374	34.0	5.1	11 870	41.6	4.5
Kirkwood city	2 004	31.9	17.7	41	0.0	0.0	156	23.7	4.5	314	51.0	0.0	324	47.2	11.1
Lee's Summit city	2 453	34.6	2.6	331	33.8	5.7	512	28.1	4.1	1 434	40.9	0.6	1 019	46.3	5.4
Liberty city	612	30.6	9.8	117	27.4	0.0	153	45.1	3.3	788	43.9	5.6	474	42.8	3.0
Maryland Heights city	1 418	33.9	4.3	42	0.0	14.3	1 846	19.6	3.0	629	27.8	1.4	372	45.2	3.5
O'Fallon city	949	41.3	1.3	39	0.0	0.0	558	26.0	2.9	590	36.9	3.9	403	41.2	3.2
Raytown city	3 599	32.7	5.1	86	16.3	7.0	319	22.9	1.9	727	50.1	1.7	768	58.6	6.4
St. Charles city	2 040	30.9	4.3	492	28.9	3.7	528	28.2	3.4	1 427	34.3	1.5	764	37.8	3.3
St. Joseph city	3 620	24.4	7.3	416	27.2	11.1	282	14.9	5.0	1 938	36.4	6.2	1 216	48.9	4.4
St. Louis city	177 627	32.9	11.8	1 050	26.2	4.4	7 178	19.3	4.5	6 745	29.7	4.7	7 210	41.0	4.0
St. Peters city	1 005	26.2	3.8	91	15.4	0.0	663	30.8	2.6	668	40.6	0.6	731	53.1	3.7
Springfield city	4 674	27.2	6.3	1 423	27.1	5.6	1 996	22.0	5.0	3 266	30.7	3.1	3 531	38.7	7.1
University City city	16 572	26.4	13.4	75	33.3	0.0	1 164	18.1	6.2	624	27.7	5.0	850	37.2	5.5
Wildwood city	373	28.7	0.0	39	41.0	0.0	667	28.6	3.3	417	38.8	1.9	457	59.3	0.0
MONTANA	2 059	32.6	4.7	55 218	39.1	4.6	4 810	28.1	7.0	18 490	41.6	4.2	17 106	44.0	5.0
Billings city	416	29.6	6.7	3 045	38.5	0.7	560	28.2	9.5	3 692	39.0	3.9	1 847	50.4	4.8
Bozeman city	48	0.0	27.1	401	24.4	0.0	531	23.5	0.8	575	37.0	1.2	484	35.7	0.0
Butte-Silver Bow	67	46.3	0.0	619	25.5	1.8	88	12.5	20.5	1 117	43.1	3.8	410	34.6	2.4
Great Falls city	563	24.7	8.7	2 579	34.3	5.5	359	11.4	8.9	1 303	39.1	5.8	1 630	47.8	3.8
Helena city	60	0.0	10.0	451	26.6	9.8	141	8.5	11.3	534	58.4	0.6	542	41.3	0.0
Missoula city	127	18.9	0.0	1 489	36.3	2.7	667	22.0	4.0	1 110	30.1	6.6	1 064	35.3	1.4

[1] Hispanic or Latino persons may be of any race.

City	Total households	Married-couple family households			Other family households			Two or more unrelated persons		Male living alone		Female living alone		Percent of householders 65 years and over who live alone	Grandparents who are responsible for the care of their grandchildren
		Total	With children	House-holder 65 years or over	Total	With children	House-holder 65 years or over	Total	House-holder 65 years or over	Total	House-holder 65 years or over	Total	House-holder 65 years or over		
	29	30	31	32	33	34	35	36	37	38	39	40	41	42	43
MINNESOTA—Cont'd															
Inver Grove Heights city	11 227	57.1	28.3	6.7	13.4	9.5	0.9	7.9	0.6	10.5	0.9	11.0	2.6	30.1	48
Lakeville city	13 633	75.1	48.8	3.6	10.2	7.8	0.2	4.1	0.0	6.1	0.7	4.5	1.4	34.5	87
Mankato city	12 362	37.7	16.5	7.3	12.4	8.0	1.0	17.7	0.4	14.4	1.8	17.7	7.9	52.6	65
Maple Grove city	17 527	70.5	41.0	4.1	9.7	6.0	0.4	4.3	0.1	6.5	0.7	8.9	2.3	38.7	128
Maplewood city	13 794	54.2	25.1	10.9	12.7	6.9	1.7	6.1	0.3	10.3	1.6	16.7	8.6	44.2	164
Minneapolis city	162 382	29.9	13.6	4.0	16.0	9.8	1.5	13.7	0.3	19.7	2.1	20.7	6.0	57.8	2 250
Minnetonka city	21 426	57.2	25.0	10.1	9.1	5.2	1.2	6.5	0.5	10.4	2.1	16.9	8.0	46.1	134
Moorhead city	11 679	47.9	22.7	9.5	13.1	9.0	0.9	9.7	0.5	10.6	2.0	18.6	8.8	49.6	150
Oakdale city	10 229	57.1	30.1	6.7	13.0	9.1	0.7	4.8	0.0	9.9	1.5	15.3	5.8	49.8	141
Plymouth city	24 869	60.9	32.0	7.1	10.2	6.2	0.7	7.3	0.2	8.7	0.8	13.0	4.0	37.8	93
Richfield city	15 077	44.5	17.7	10.1	14.2	7.8	2.2	7.8	0.4	13.9	2.8	19.6	9.3	48.8	126
Rochester city	34 009	52.4	26.0	8.3	11.1	7.5	0.9	6.8	0.3	11.8	1.8	17.9	7.2	48.9	212
Roseville city	14 630	49.8	18.2	13.9	9.5	4.9	1.3	7.1	0.5	12.5	2.9	21.0	10.8	46.3	91
St. Cloud city	22 580	42.4	20.1	7.2	12.0	8.1	1.2	15.5	0.3	13.8	1.6	16.4	6.2	47.1	112
St. Louis Park city	20 777	39.8	16.1	8.0	11.4	6.3	1.4	11.1	0.7	14.7	1.8	23.0	8.2	49.9	93
St. Paul city	112 128	37.4	19.2	5.5	17.5	10.8	2.1	9.2	0.4	15.5	2.3	20.4	7.2	54.3	1 514
Shoreview city	10 116	60.3	29.5	8.6	10.7	6.6	1.1	4.9	0.2	8.0	1.3	16.1	5.9	42.3	49
Winona city	10 337	41.6	18.4	8.6	10.1	6.1	2.0	12.9	0.3	13.8	2.4	21.5	11.2	55.5	92
Woodbury city	16 675	67.6	38.2	5.4	8.5	5.5	0.4	5.1	0.2	7.3	0.8	11.5	2.6	36.0	100
MISSISSIPPI	1 047 555	50.6	23.1	8.6	21.2	12.2	3.2	3.6	0.2	10.4	2.3	14.1	7.4	44.6	48 061
Biloxi city	19 606	45.4	20.6	7.5	18.3	11.7	2.4	6.1	0.4	14.3	3.3	15.8	8.1	52.5	561
Columbus city	10 011	39.4	17.1	8.2	24.7	14.8	3.2	4.7	0.1	12.0	2.4	19.1	10.1	51.9	408
Greenville city	14 746	39.3	17.3	7.2	31.4	18.7	3.8	3.5	0.2	10.8	2.4	15.0	7.7	47.3	1 081
Gulfport city	27 054	43.5	19.3	7.5	22.3	13.3	2.8	6.2	0.4	13.2	2.8	14.7	7.1	47.9	1 159
Hattiesburg city	17 199	32.6	12.4	6.6	23.0	13.3	3.0	10.6	0.4	14.4	1.9	19.4	7.8	49.4	674
Jackson city	67 782	36.2	17.0	6.5	29.9	17.5	3.5	5.1	0.3	12.1	2.1	16.7	7.0	47.1	3 700
Meridian city	16 062	36.2	14.8	9.2	26.7	16.4	3.9	3.8	0.3	11.6	2.7	21.7	11.9	52.3	623
Pascagoula city	9 802	46.5	20.8	8.8	22.2	14.0	2.8	4.8	0.6	11.6	2.3	14.9	7.8	45.1	377
Southaven city	11 037	58.7	28.0	6.5	16.1	9.9	1.7	4.2	0.0	8.5	0.9	12.5	4.9	40.8	401
Tupelo city	13 495	49.2	22.9	8.1	19.2	12.5	1.8	3.9	0.1	10.8	1.6	16.9	7.0	46.2	356
Vicksburg city	10 316	36.0	16.2	8.2	28.7	17.1	4.2	3.1	0.3	13.7	3.4	18.4	9.7	50.9	408
MISSOURI	2 197 214	52.7	23.3	9.8	15.0	9.1	1.9	5.1	0.3	11.4	2.4	15.8	8.0	46.3	43 907
Ballwin city	11 834	66.4	32.1	11.7	9.0	5.4	1.0	3.1	0.1	8.2	1.5	13.2	6.6	38.9	83
Blue Springs city	17 384	62.9	33.4	5.7	14.6	9.6	0.6	4.5	0.4	7.2	0.8	10.8	4.5	44.3	420
Cape Girardeau city	14 409	45.2	18.0	9.8	13.2	8.0	1.7	8.3	0.4	12.6	2.0	20.8	9.5	49.1	220
Chesterfield city	18 108	66.5	29.8	11.5	6.9	3.6	0.9	3.5	0.2	8.6	2.1	14.6	7.0	42.1	146
Columbia city	33 819	38.9	18.4	5.8	13.0	8.1	1.1	15.0	0.2	15.2	1.5	17.8	5.2	48.6	295
Florissant city	20 232	49.9	21.6	12.5	16.9	9.3	2.6	4.1	0.2	10.6	2.6	18.5	10.3	45.5	255
Gladstone city	11 512	51.9	19.3	11.6	12.6	7.0	1.8	5.7	0.2	12.6	1.9	17.1	7.5	41.0	238
Hazelwood city	10 935	44.8	20.2	7.2	17.3	9.9	1.7	6.0	0.4	14.7	1.9	17.2	7.2	49.3	188
Independence city	47 415	49.0	19.2	10.9	15.8	9.3	2.0	5.2	0.3	11.6	2.2	18.4	9.2	46.5	1 236
Jefferson City city	15 870	44.8	19.9	9.4	13.3	8.7	1.5	5.8	0.2	14.3	2.2	21.8	9.0	50.3	149
Joplin city	19 196	45.6	18.6	10.5	15.0	9.7	1.7	6.9	0.2	13.1	2.1	19.5	9.6	48.5	367
Kansas City city	184 028	38.8	16.7	6.9	20.1	12.1	2.4	7.1	0.3	15.2	2.5	18.8	7.0	50.0	4 411
Kirkwood city	11 844	49.9	21.9	11.3	11.6	5.7	2.5	5.0	0.5	10.1	2.5	23.5	12.0	50.4	61
Lee's Summit city	26 546	62.4	33.3	7.5	11.4	7.9	0.7	3.9	0.1	8.4	1.4	13.8	7.4	51.5	250
Liberty city	9 464	57.5	29.0	7.7	15.3	10.3	1.4	4.5	0.1	9.4	1.9	13.3	6.7	48.3	143
Maryland Heights city	11 410	44.5	18.8	6.6	12.8	7.5	1.3	8.1	0.0	17.7	1.4	16.8	4.8	44.0	192
O'Fallon city	15 369	70.0	43.9	6.4	11.8	8.0	0.9	3.6	0.1	7.6	0.9	7.1	2.5	31.7	301
Raytown city	12 871	49.1	19.2	13.2	15.9	8.1	2.9	4.6	0.4	11.1	2.0	19.3	10.3	42.8	327
St. Charles city	24 068	51.7	23.0	8.6	12.3	7.8	1.3	6.8	0.5	12.3	1.7	16.9	8.2	48.9	165
St. Joseph city	29 022	47.8	20.6	9.9	16.3	10.6	2.1	5.5	0.4	11.8	2.8	18.6	11.0	52.6	668
St. Louis city	147 286	26.3	11.4	5.3	26.5	14.8	4.3	7.0	0.5	18.1	3.4	22.1	9.8	56.6	4 671
St. Peters city	18 482	63.6	34.9	6.2	11.6	7.4	1.0	4.4	0.3	8.0	0.9	12.5	5.4	45.7	366
Springfield city	64 779	40.4	15.5	9.0	15.1	8.9	1.9	9.5	0.3	14.6	2.3	20.5	9.3	50.8	740
University City city	16 448	36.7	15.1	6.9	19.0	9.2	3.2	10.1	0.2	13.5	2.4	20.6	8.1	50.2	442
Wildwood city	11 003	80.7	48.4	6.0	6.1	4.0	0.3	1.3	0.1	4.3	0.4	7.6	3.8	39.6	70
MONTANA	359 070	54.1	23.4	10.1	12.4	8.1	1.5	6.1	0.4	12.5	2.8	14.9	7.6	46.3	6 053
Billings city	37 470	47.9	20.3	9.6	14.2	9.5	1.6	6.5	0.4	12.3	2.6	19.2	9.5	51.0	419
Bozeman city	11 001	36.4	17.5	4.6	10.8	6.5	0.5	22.9	0.4	15.0	1.2	14.8	5.8	56.0	22
Butte-Silver Bow	14 465	49.0	20.6	9.1	13.0	8.1	2.1	5.3	0.4	13.8	3.8	18.9	10.8	55.6	272
Great Falls city	23 811	48.0	20.8	9.7	14.8	10.3	1.8	5.5	0.5	13.5	3.4	18.2	9.6	52.0	209
Helena city	11 476	42.6	18.2	7.7	12.8	8.5	1.3	6.6	0.2	15.5	2.6	22.5	9.0	55.5	48
Missoula city	24 014	38.2	16.4	6.7	13.3	8.4	1.2	15.3	0.4	15.2	1.9	18.0	7.0	51.9	176

Table A-5. Cities — **Age, Ethnicity, and Household Structure**

City	Households with Non-Hispanic White householder		Households with Black or African American householder		Households with American Indian and Alaska Native householder		Households with Asian, Hawaiian, and Pacific Islander householder		Households with Hispanic or Latino[1] householder		Foreign-born population	Place of birth (percent)			Percent in non-English speaking households	
	Number of households	Percent that are family households	Number of households	Percent that are family households	Number of households	Percent that are family households	Number of households	Percent that are family households	Number of households	Percent that are family households	Percent of total population that is foreign-born	Europe	Asia	Latin America	Linguistically isolated	Not linguistically isolated
	44	45	46	47	48	49	50	51	52	53	54	55	56	57	58	59
MINNESOTA—Cont'd																
Inver Grove Heights city	10 394	70.2	201	62.2	56	100.0	146	76.7	323	74.9	4.4	1.1	1.5	1.0	0.8	12.5
Lakeville city	12 980	85.5	168	77.4	27	100.0	189	89.4	134	80.6	3.0	0.8	1.5	0.5	1.0	8.8
Mankato city	11 581	49.7	215	54.4	25	80.0	260	52.3	212	69.8	4.3	0.5	2.4	0.7	1.0	9.5
Maple Grove city	16 706	79.9	238	78.2	33	100.0	291	96.6	154	83.1	4.3	1.3	1.8	0.3	1.0	9.3
Maplewood city	12 653	65.3	352	79.0	66	78.8	322	94.1	191	88.5	4.6	0.9	2.8	0.5	1.3	11.7
Minneapolis city	119 132	40.3	23 046	61.3	2 302	61.9	6 696	58.3	7 168	70.7	14.5	1.4	4.5	4.8	7.3	17.1
Minnetonka city	20 556	66.2	272	71.7	23	69.6	285	65.6	233	71.2	5.7	2.5	1.9	0.6	1.1	10.8
Moorhead city	10 876	60.2	56	51.8	140	89.3	85	52.9	352	80.4	3.4	0.5	1.7	0.7	2.0	11.2
Oakdale city	9 671	69.6	164	76.2	32	40.6	122	100.0	161	71.4	3.0	0.5	1.7	0.3	0.7	9.6
Plymouth city	23 100	71.0	473	65.8	52	80.8	782	82.1	307	68.7	7.4	2.5	3.0	0.8	1.8	12.2
Richfield city	12 726	57.3	965	53.5	81	51.9	552	72.8	540	86.9	11.4	1.4	4.1	4.0	5.3	12.5
Rochester city	30 436	62.6	891	70.3	178	79.8	1 560	70.3	573	70.2	10.1	1.0	4.0	1.2	3.6	12.3
Roseville city	13 410	59.1	331	63.1	61	57.1	491	70.9	188	51.1	6.5	1.0	3.9	1.0	1.1	12.6
St. Cloud city	21 149	55.0	323	37.5	143	53.1	531	37.7	210	66.2	3.8	0.5	2.5	0.5	1.4	9.2
St. Louis Park city	18 895	49.9	799	62.3	68	57.4	470	60.6	332	78.0	8.7	2.8	2.7	1.6	3.1	11.0
St. Paul city	84 406	49.7	11 284	65.9	1 036	65.7	7 102	83.5	6 122	69.6	14.3	1.1	8.1	3.2	7.6	19.9
Shoreview city	9 565	70.8	82	81.7	32	78.1	285	72.6	85	78.8	5.5	1.3	2.8	0.7	0.8	9.9
Winona city	9 845	52.0	95	56.8	58	22.4	141	29.1	97	61.9	3.5	0.5	2.1	0.4	1.0	10.0
Woodbury city	15 235	74.8	375	86.1	41	80.5	646	93.8	247	89.1	6.6	1.2	3.7	0.6	1.4	12.2
MISSISSIPPI	685 549	71.4	339 157	72.6	3 660	73.5	5 165	72.7	9 781	70.8	1.4	0.3	0.5	0.5	0.6	6.4
Biloxi city	14 637	62.6	3 428	67.7	152	57.2	596	76.5	481	63.2	5.4	1.0	3.3	0.7	2.0	14.4
Columbus city	4 937	57.4	4 896	70.5	18	0.0	46	84.8	69	63.8	1.4	0.4	0.4	0.4	0.5	6.0
Greenville city	5 131	67.9	9 389	72.5	34	17.6	56	75.0	88	56.8	0.7	0.1	0.3	0.2	0.3	7.2
Gulfport city	17 785	63.8	8 138	70.7	148	50.0	214	50.9	515	65.4	2.6	0.7	1.0	0.6	0.8	8.5
Hattiesburg city	9 793	47.1	6 891	67.5	22	100.0	190	37.4	145	62.8	2.6	0.7	1.2	0.5	1.0	6.7
Jackson city	22 992	56.8	43 674	71.1	135	77.0	339	67.6	418	49.8	1.1	0.2	0.5	0.3	0.4	7.3
Meridian city	8 039	57.6	7 819	68.7	20	100.0	53	49.1	56	57.1	0.7	0.2	0.3	0.2	0.2	6.0
Pascagoula city	6 916	68.9	2 499	67.2	26	100.0	66	72.7	259	69.9	3.4	0.5	0.7	2.1	1.9	8.3
Southaven city	10 093	74.7	556	77.5	31	67.7	99	71.7	181	80.1	2.2	0.3	0.7	1.2	0.9	6.8
Tupelo city	9 912	67.0	3 287	72.3	45	60.0	39	64.1	131	65.6	1.6	0.5	0.4	0.6	0.6	7.3
Vicksburg city	4 371	61.0	5 749	67.1	27	55.6	53	58.5	72	68.1	1.6	0.6	0.7	0.2	0.3	6.8
MISSOURI	1 882 812	67.9	227 340	65.9	10 006	67.9	21 131	65.7	32 361	72.2	2.7	0.8	0.9	0.7	1.0	7.7
Ballwin city	11 236	75.0	108	89.8	15	100.0	259	87.6	125	55.2	5.1	2.3	2.1	0.5	0.6	10.8
Blue Springs city	16 191	77.0	450	79.1	111	79.3	149	75.2	301	90.7	1.7	0.4	0.7	0.3	0.3	7.4
Cape Girardeau city	12 830	57.4	1 104	71.0	50	48.0	123	39.8	102	54.9	2.0	0.8	0.8	0.3	0.4	6.5
Chesterfield city	16 597	72.6	421	74.1	21	100.0	750	87.2	212	71.2	8.0	1.0	4.0	0.7	1.7	12.7
Columbia city	27 885	50.8	3 489	59.8	230	61.7	1 303	52.2	495	56.2	6.4	1.0	3.6	1.0	2.0	12.1
Florissant city	17 558	66.8	2 176	65.4	69	79.7	65	52.3	232	78.0	1.3	0.4	0.5	0.4	0.4	6.9
Gladstone city	10 752	64.8	191	38.7	116	73.3	64	78.1	283	59.4	2.0	0.5	0.7	0.4	0.9	6.8
Hazelwood city	8 806	62.2	1 726	60.7	0	X	132	81.8	167	61.1	3.1	0.7	1.6	0.3	0.8	8.5
Independence city	43 824	64.5	1 031	62.0	278	51.8	439	81.8	1 166	76.2	2.6	0.5	0.8	0.9	0.7	8.2
Jefferson City city	13 745	58.7	1 512	51.1	67	92.5	236	67.8	164	58.5	2.9	0.5	1.2	0.6	1.0	7.8
Joplin city	17 590	60.4	434	56.0	285	66.7	142	59.9	387	67.4	1.9	0.4	0.7	0.7	0.7	7.6
Kansas City city	115 894	55.8	52 282	63.6	1 003	52.3	2 951	62.3	8 942	71.9	5.8	0.7	1.7	2.8	2.7	11.8
Kirkwood city	10 821	60.4	783	72.0	0	X	58	70.7	74	100.0	1.6	0.6	0.5	0.4	0.3	7.4
Lee's Summit city	24 688	73.6	894	76.5	104	66.3	153	76.5	434	86.2	2.0	0.7	0.6	0.4	0.2	8.1
Liberty city	8 911	72.5	221	68.3	46	87.0	36	100.0	185	82.7	1.4	0.3	0.6	0.4	0.6	8.3
Maryland Heights city	9 792	56.4	592	60.0	30	73.3	752	62.6	178	70.2	10.2	1.5	6.8	1.3	3.7	12.6
O'Fallon city	14 620	81.6	319	85.0	19	100.0	144	100.0	148	79.7	2.1	0.9	0.8	0.2	0.2	6.9
Raytown city	11 182	63.7	1 317	73.7	48	81.3	59	91.5	162	64.8	2.0	0.7	0.8	0.3	0.9	7.5
St. Charles city	22 521	63.9	640	70.0	169	69.8	171	43.3	378	78.6	2.6	0.9	0.6	0.8	1.0	7.2
St. Joseph city	26 924	64.3	1 059	55.4	148	64.9	125	45.6	509	74.3	1.0	0.4	0.3	0.2	0.3	6.3
St. Louis city	73 161	45.1	66 635	61.2	426	52.3	2 824	54.0	2 298	56.0	5.6	2.5	1.8	0.8	3.1	10.0
St. Peters city	17 505	75.0	398	80.2	51	74.5	185	71.4	214	85.0	1.8	0.5	1.0	0.2	0.3	8.1
Springfield city	59 860	55.1	1 595	62.8	588	52.0	637	57.8	954	66.4	2.4	0.6	0.9	0.5	0.8	7.4
University City city	8 820	46.0	6 599	70.7	30	0.0	511	45.8	260	45.8	7.1	2.4	2.8	0.7	2.3	11.8
Wildwood city	10 526	86.5	131	95.4	9	100.0	218	91.3	46	100.0	3.6	0.8	1.7	0.6	0.3	8.7
MONTANA	331 568	65.9	858	52.9	15 834	78.9	1 425	58.5	5 177	70.9	1.8	0.7	0.4	0.2	0.6	9.2
Billings city	34 662	61.5	163	58.3	926	81.4	127	58.3	1 311	65.1	1.5	0.5	0.4	0.3	0.4	9.7
Bozeman city	10 439	47.3	14	0.0	132	72.0	133	47.4	161	38.5	3.7	1.3	1.6	0.2	1.3	9.3
Butte-Silver Bow	13 755	61.7	16	0.0	227	64.8	42	35.7	326	77.3	1.6	0.7	0.2	0.3	0.5	7.5
Great Falls city	21 749	62.4	276	54.0	832	65.6	141	48.2	450	78.7	2.5	1.3	0.5	0.2	0.5	9.0
Helena city	10 899	55.4	60	43.3	184	50.5	64	53.1	115	61.7	1.7	0.8	0.5	0.2	0.4	8.0
Missoula city	22 523	51.8	39	15.4	417	67.4	268	50.4	377	37.9	2.5	1.2	0.7	0.2	0.7	8.5

[1] Hispanic or Latino persons may be of any race.

Table A-5. Cities — Age, Ethnicity, and Household Structure

STATE Place code	City	Total population	Under 5 years	5 to 17 years	18 to 24 years	25 to 44 years	45 to 64 years	65 years and over	Median age	+/- U.S. percent under 18 years	+/- U.S. percent 65 years and over	Non-Hispanic White Total population	Non-Hispanic White Under 18 years	Non-Hispanic White 65 years and over
		1	2	3	4	5	6	7	8	9	10	11	12	13
31 00000	NEBRASKA..............	1 711 263	6.8	19.5	10.2	28.5	21.4	13.6	35.3	0.6	1.2	1 495 553	24.7	14.9
31 03950	Bellevue city	44 320	7.0	20.2	10.2	31.1	22.2	9.3	33.5	1.5	-3.1	36 712	25.5	10.4
31 17670	Fremont city	25 157	6.6	17.7	10.7	26.9	20.7	17.4	37.0	-1.4	5.0	23 579	23.3	18.4
31 19595	Grand Island city	42 819	7.8	19.2	9.2	28.8	20.9	14.1	34.8	1.3	1.7	34 840	24.1	16.8
31 25055	Kearney city	27 035	6.5	15.0	24.4	26.7	16.7	10.7	27.3	-4.2	-1.7	25 299	21.0	11.2
31 28000	Lincoln city	225 442	6.7	16.3	16.5	30.5	19.5	10.4	31.3	-2.7	-2.0	197 951	21.4	11.4
31 37000	Omaha city	390 112	7.2	18.4	11.1	31.0	20.6	11.8	33.5	-0.1	-0.6	293 812	22.3	13.9
32 00000	NEVADA..................	1 998 257	7.2	18.3	8.9	31.7	22.9	10.9	35.0	-0.2	-1.5	1 301 738	21.2	14.3
32 09700	Carson City	52 457	6.2	17.1	8.2	28.7	25.0	14.9	38.7	-2.4	2.5	41 124	20.8	18.0
32 31900	Henderson city	176 048	6.8	18.2	7.6	33.0	24.4	10.0	35.9	-0.7	-2.4	137 401	22.9	11.1
32 40000	Las Vegas city..............	478 868	7.6	18.1	8.8	32.4	21.6	11.5	34.5	0.0	-0.9	277 357	20.2	16.0
32 51800	North Las Vegas city.....	115 489	10.3	23.5	9.5	35.1	15.9	5.8	28.8	8.1	-6.6	42 758	25.5	9.3
32 60600	Reno city	180 658	6.7	16.5	11.8	31.6	22.1	11.3	34.5	-2.5	-1.1	124 799	18.9	14.6
32 68400	Sparks city	66 532	7.2	19.4	9.7	31.6	21.8	10.3	34.5	0.9	-2.1	45 875	22.5	12.8
33 00000	NEW HAMPSHIRE.....	1 235 786	6.1	18.9	8.3	30.9	23.8	12.0	37.1	-0.7	-0.4	1 175 083	24.6	12.4
33 14200	Concord city	40 687	5.7	17.3	8.3	32.9	22.1	13.7	37.0	-2.7	1.3	38 613	22.7	14.2
33 18820	Dover city	26 884	5.7	15.0	11.3	34.0	20.2	13.8	35.5	-5.0	1.4	25 106	20.1	14.5
33 45140	Manchester city	107 006	6.8	17.0	9.4	33.4	20.5	13.0	34.9	-1.9	0.6	95 663	22.4	14.1
33 50260	Nashua city	86 605	6.4	18.3	8.0	33.3	22.4	11.6	35.8	-1.0	-0.8	74 976	23.2	13.0
33 65140	Rochester city	28 461	6.7	18.7	7.5	31.6	22.2	13.4	36.7	-0.3	1.0	27 562	25.0	13.6
34 00000	NEW JERSEY............	8 414 350	6.6	18.1	8.0	31.4	22.7	13.2	36.7	-1.0	0.8	5 554 478	22.3	16.7
34 02080	Atlantic City city	40 517	7.3	18.4	8.8	31.3	20.0	14.1	34.7	0.0	1.7	7 609	7.6	34.8
34 03580	Bayonne city	61 842	5.9	16.1	7.9	31.3	22.0	16.8	38.1	-3.7	4.4	43 303	18.2	21.4
34 05170	Bergenfield borough......	26 247	6.9	17.8	7.3	31.5	22.6	13.8	37.6	-1.0	1.4	14 194	19.5	20.6
34 10000	Camden city	79 904	9.1	25.5	12.0	29.7	16.2	7.5	27.2	8.9	-4.9	5 985	12.3	21.1
34 13690	Clifton city	78 672	5.9	15.6	7.7	30.6	22.7	17.6	38.8	-4.2	5.2	53 346	17.2	23.7
34 19390	East Orange city	69 904	8.1	20.1	9.6	30.3	20.6	11.3	33.0	2.5	-1.1	2 103	9.2	37.9
34 21000	Elizabeth city	120 568	7.5	18.8	10.8	34.1	18.9	10.0	32.6	0.6	-2.4	32 351	20.0	20.6
34 21480	Englewood city	26 203	7.2	16.7	7.4	30.7	24.5	13.6	37.4	-1.8	1.2	8 306	19.5	21.9
34 22470	Fair Lawn borough	31 637	5.4	17.4	6.3	26.9	25.4	18.7	41.8	-2.9	6.3	27 735	21.7	20.6
34 24420	Fort Lee borough	35 461	5.2	12.4	4.9	33.5	24.0	20.0	41.6	-8.1	7.6	20 404	11.7	30.8
34 25770	Garfield city	29 786	5.8	16.6	9.5	32.8	21.5	13.7	35.6	-3.3	1.3	21 464	18.1	18.0
34 28680	Hackensack city	42 677	5.9	12.1	8.1	39.3	22.4	12.1	36.2	-7.7	-0.3	17 042	9.9	21.3
34 32250	Hoboken city	38 669	3.2	7.0	15.7	51.5	13.0	9.6	30.4	-15.5	-2.8	27 116	5.8	9.3
34 36000	Jersey City city	240 055	6.7	17.9	10.6	35.0	20.0	9.7	32.4	-1.1	-2.7	56 644	11.5	22.0
34 36510	Kearny town	40 513	5.7	15.5	10.5	36.0	21.2	11.1	34.7	-4.5	-1.3	24 447	20.1	15.3
34 40350	Linden city	39 394	6.1	16.2	8.6	30.4	22.2	16.6	38.0	-3.4	4.2	22 886	17.6	22.6
34 41310	Long Branch city	31 340	6.4	17.3	10.0	33.5	19.8	13.0	34.7	-2.0	0.6	17 981	17.4	18.1
34 46680	Millville city	26 847	6.9	21.1	8.7	29.1	21.3	12.9	35.0	2.3	0.5	19 258	22.5	16.8
34 51000	Newark city	273 546	7.6	20.2	12.1	32.1	18.6	9.3	30.8	2.1	-3.1	39 131	17.0	17.6
34 51210	New Brunswick city	48 573	6.8	13.3	34.4	28.3	11.1	6.1	23.6	-5.6	-6.3	15 906	5.2	10.7
34 55950	Paramus borough..........	25 737	5.2	18.1	5.7	24.4	24.9	21.7	42.9	-2.4	9.3	19 451	20.6	26.0
34 56550	Passaic city	67 861	10.0	20.9	12.5	32.7	15.8	8.2	28.6	5.2	-4.2	12 430	24.4	23.7
34 57000	Paterson city	149 222	8.4	21.3	11.3	32.1	18.6	8.4	30.5	4.0	-4.0	19 678	17.5	27.4
34 58200	Perth Amboy city	47 303	7.9	20.8	11.5	31.5	18.2	10.1	31.2	3.0	-2.3	9 020	12.7	30.8
34 59190	Plainfield city	47 829	7.6	19.9	10.2	32.8	20.3	9.3	32.8	1.8	-3.1	5 700	13.4	25.7
34 61530	Rahway city	26 500	6.2	17.7	7.7	32.2	21.5	14.7	37.1	-1.8	2.3	13 985	18.0	21.0
34 65790	Sayreville borough	40 377	6.7	16.8	7.5	34.0	22.4	12.6	36.5	-2.2	0.2	29 017	20.7	16.0
34 74000	Trenton city	85 258	7.7	19.8	10.3	31.8	19.0	11.3	32.2	1.8	-1.1	21 053	13.7	24.1
34 74630	Union City city	67 088	7.2	18.1	11.1	34.6	19.0	9.9	32.5	-0.4	-2.5	8 962	22.4	22.6
34 76070	Vineland city	56 271	5.9	19.7	8.1	29.6	22.9	13.9	36.5	-0.1	1.5	30 911	19.5	20.9
34 79040	Westfield town..............	29 644	8.1	20.4	3.9	30.3	23.8	13.5	38.6	2.8	1.1	26 242	28.2	14.0
34 79610	West New York town	45 768	6.6	15.5	10.9	34.9	19.1	13.1	34.0	-3.6	0.7	6 817	18.9	23.4
35 00000	NEW MEXICO...........	1 819 046	7.1	20.8	9.7	28.6	22.1	11.7	34.6	2.2	-0.7	813 380	20.3	16.8
35 01780	Alamogordo city	35 392	7.3	21.4	9.3	29.9	19.7	12.5	33.5	3.0	0.1	20 414	22.7	16.5
35 02000	Albuquerque city	448 627	6.9	17.5	10.6	31.2	21.9	11.9	34.9	-1.3	-0.5	223 882	18.1	17.0
35 12150	Carlsbad city	25 947	7.3	20.1	8.1	26.5	21.2	16.8	37.7	1.7	4.4	15 238	21.7	22.2
35 16420	Clovis city	32 540	7.8	22.1	9.2	28.7	19.1	13.0	33.1	4.2	0.6	18 160	23.0	18.7
35 25800	Farmington city.............	37 612	7.3	22.0	9.8	28.4	21.7	10.7	33.6	3.6	-1.7	23 436	24.5	14.5
35 32520	Hobbs city	28 475	8.1	22.9	10.1	27.4	18.6	12.9	32.1	5.3	0.5	14 203	22.4	19.7
35 39380	Las Cruces city	74 483	7.1	18.0	15.9	27.4	18.5	13.1	31.2	-0.6	0.7	30 957	16.3	20.2
35 63460	Rio Rancho city	51 722	7.4	21.9	7.1	32.1	19.9	11.7	35.1	3.6	-0.7	33 315	24.9	15.4
35 64930	Roswell city	45 451	7.4	21.1	9.8	24.6	20.8	16.3	35.2	2.8	3.9	22 680	20.1	25.9
35 70500	Santa Fe city	61 805	5.4	14.7	8.7	29.1	27.9	14.1	39.8	-5.6	1.7	29 491	13.2	17.3

City	Black or African American — Total population	Under 18 years	65 years and over	American Indian and Alaska Native — Total population	Under 18 years	65 years and over	Asian, Hawaiian, and Pacific Islander — Total population	Under 18 years	65 years and over	Hispanic or Latino[1] — Total population	Under 18 years	65 years and over	Two or more races — Total population	Under 18 years	65 years and over
	14	15	16	17	18	19	20	21	22	23	24	25	26	27	28
NEBRASKA.............	67 435	34.9	6.4	15 421	38.4	4.7	21 799	26.3	3.8	93 872	39.2	2.9	25 032	51.1	3.4
Bellevue city	2 813	29.6	2.9	274	41.2	2.2	890	14.4	8.8	2 604	39.6	3.1	1 248	50.3	3.4
Fremont city	253	62.1	0.0	151	26.5	0.0	80	0.0	0.0	1 039	35.9	1.7	198	58.6	9.1
Grand Island city	242	43.8	5.0	216	24.1	6.5	586	36.2	0.7	6 809	40.4	2.2	574	38.7	4.7
Kearney city	143	10.5	4.9	73	5.5	8.2	160	8.1	0.0	1 119	33.8	5.2	352	54.3	4.8
Lincoln city	6 876	32.5	3.4	1 824	34.4	3.8	6 866	28.4	3.2	8 299	34.8	4.2	4 529	49.7	1.9
Omaha city	51 173	35.4	7.5	3 065	31.8	6.0	7 303	20.9	3.0	29 006	36.7	2.5	7 900	51.2	3.0
NEVADA.....	132 490	30.8	6.9	26 485	29.6	6.2	96 927	21.2	7.9	393 539	37.0	3.0	81 171	42.2	4.4
Carson City	806	5.3	0.0	1 116	26.0	5.8	1 084	26.3	8.6	7 459	36.7	2.5	1 428	45.9	4.4
Henderson city	6 889	27.3	11.3	1 271	21.9	7.9	7 441	20.2	6.7	18 614	35.3	4.5	6 035	50.4	2.9
Las Vegas city	49 071	31.6	8.0	3 548	24.6	5.1	23 307	19.7	10.0	113 237	36.6	3.0	20 852	40.9	4.4
North Las Vegas city.....	21 791	35.8	6.4	950	45.6	1.6	4 592	23.7	7.8	43 503	40.8	1.7	5 351	48.9	5.2
Reno city	4 183	25.6	6.2	2 306	31.4	3.8	10 390	21.9	7.6	34 762	37.1	2.4	7 544	38.9	4.5
Sparks city	1 681	28.1	5.1	1 030	36.9	6.8	3 491	27.3	8.7	13 056	38.3	3.3	2 821	43.6	4.0
NEW HAMPSHIRE.....	8 984	31.3	4.7	2 660	23.9	4.7	15 679	26.6	4.7	19 910	36.4	3.4	14 574	38.4	5.6
Concord city	487	41.9	0.0	43	16.3	0.0	564	20.7	7.8	353	24.4	5.4	658	35.1	2.9
Dover city	292	32.5	6.8	82	6.1	0.0	712	26.1	5.9	273	39.9	0.0	466	32.4	0.0
Manchester city	2 498	38.8	3.7	316	29.4	3.2	2 275	22.2	6.5	4 840	38.5	3.4	1 978	42.0	3.9
Nashua city	1 528	29.9	3.9	183	30.6	0.0	3 387	23.9	3.6	5 153	39.2	2.3	1 508	46.0	3.6
Rochester city	110	42.7	5.5	5	0.0	0.0	202	22.3	5.4	332	55.1	0.9	315	26.7	11.4
NEW JERSEY...........	1 127 266	29.9	8.4	17 987	27.5	6.5	484 503	25.9	5.1	1 116 149	30.1	5.0	228 326	35.7	5.1
Atlantic City city............	18 134	32.3	12.7	98	5.1	14.3	4 186	21.5	4.3	10 105	31.7	3.2	1 998	25.7	12.1
Bayonne city................	3 119	27.3	9.7	137	39.4	0.0	2 613	29.3	6.8	11 002	31.4	4.7	2 374	40.5	6.6
Bergenfield borough......	1 752	30.7	7.9	43	69.8	0.0	5 347	30.8	5.5	4 422	30.6	5.5	841	39.1	3.9
Camden city	41 795	35.4	8.3	449	25.2	12.7	2 337	24.2	6.1	30 869	30.5	3.4	3 116	42.8	4.7
Clifton city	2 168	29.8	3.9	138	23.9	3.6	5 433	27.9	7.0	15 608	31.6	3.8	3 355	31.1	5.2
East Orange city	61 828	28.8	10.9	289	39.1	11.4	282	11.7	16.0	3 295	32.6	4.7	2 875	26.4	6.2
Elizabeth city	23 744	30.0	7.2	444	38.5	2.5	2 699	19.6	6.7	59 746	28.1	5.7	7 675	30.4	4.8
Englewood city	10 064	26.3	12.9	53	24.5	0.0	1 388	19.2	6.4	5 670	25.2	5.3	1 274	35.6	3.9
Fair Lawn borough	181	16.6	2.2	32	15.6	15.6	1 829	31.8	6.9	1 724	29.5	2.8	170	33.5	8.8
Fort Lee borough	685	22.0	6.7	45	0.0	0.0	11 032	26.3	4.7	2 740	22.7	7.7	846	24.5	4.6
Garfield city	885	32.0	4.9	23	0.0	30.4	683	32.5	3.8	6 023	34.1	1.9	1 244	35.5	3.5
Hackensack city	10 376	23.6	8.2	142	19.0	0.0	3 217	16.2	4.2	11 133	24.6	4.5	2 188	33.1	5.1
Hoboken city	1 665	22.3	8.3	74	0.0	23.0	1 717	6.1	2.4	7 920	22.4	12.3	1 026	29.5	13.4
Jersey City city	67 225	31.0	7.1	608	28.9	5.9	39 228	21.5	5.9	68 032	31.4	4.6	14 772	30.7	5.8
Kearny town	1 528	4.5	0.9	142	30.3	4.9	2 300	17.9	5.7	11 065	25.7	4.9	1 805	25.7	5.8
Linden city	8 855	29.1	10.0	54	35.2	0.0	841	26.9	6.1	5 556	28.4	7.2	1 414	28.9	7.6
Long Branch city	5 575	34.1	8.9	129	43.4	0.0	553	20.1	8.9	6 490	33.3	3.1	1 399	34.6	5.4
Millville city	4 186	41.9	2.5	162	11.7	11.1	150	30.7	0.0	2 973	43.2	3.5	483	65.8	3.1
Newark city	145 953	30.3	9.8	820	21.0	7.0	3 189	20.3	4.2	80 451	29.6	5.0	13 592	29.1	4.4
New Brunswick city	10 908	28.0	7.5	137	41.6	2.9	2 758	4.4	2.9	18 971	30.5	1.9	1 966	34.9	0.6
Paramus borough.........	267	21.0	33.3	13	0.0	0.0	4 413	31.9	7.0	1 200	29.3	10.7	439	35.3	1.4
Passaic city	9 180	30.9	8.2	335	40.3	1.5	3 854	22.1	7.2	42 410	33.5	3.6	3 278	33.3	6.1
Paterson city	48 557	31.6	6.8	560	43.0	2.1	2 816	32.6	6.8	74 869	31.4	4.5	8 982	31.7	4.9
Perth Amboy city..........	4 767	31.8	7.7	446	39.0	2.5	596	21.5	5.4	33 042	33.2	4.6	2 648	34.0	7.1
Plainfield city	29 644	30.4	8.9	163	25.2	0.0	261	21.8	8.4	12 073	27.5	2.0	2 337	25.5	4.5
Rahway city	7 073	30.2	9.5	17	0.0	0.0	1 149	25.8	5.3	3 777	31.0	4.7	896	33.5	4.2
Sayreville borough	3 377	32.9	2.5	56	42.9	0.0	4 184	27.3	2.8	2 898	31.5	6.3	1 193	37.6	4.0
Trenton city	43 868	32.4	8.6	284	25.7	10.6	751	25.3	3.2	18 502	31.7	3.3	2 823	35.9	5.6
Union City city	2 273	26.0	7.4	358	34.6	6.7	1 758	22.5	6.5	55 241	25.6	8.1	4 677	27.9	6.3
Vineland city	7 340	30.0	6.0	341	23.8	5.9	603	32.3	6.0	16 867	34.4	5.0	2 030	40.4	3.9
Westfield town	1 112	23.7	20.9	26	26.9	23.1	1 109	25.8	4.3	783	34.0	5.9	382	59.9	0.0
West New York town	1 818	24.1	8.0	177	12.4	8.5	1 304	13.9	3.1	36 042	23.1	11.8	3 870	23.9	7.0
NEW MEXICO...........	33 513	30.4	8.9	172 276	37.3	5.8	19 534	24.2	6.7	765 610	33.8	7.9	70 080	42.3	6.7
Alamogordo city	1 808	32.2	6.5	407	33.2	8.6	516	19.4	6.4	11 124	37.3	7.7	2 027	53.6	3.3
Albuquerque city	13 797	28.7	7.2	17 519	29.6	3.6	9 700	23.1	7.7	178 904	31.2	7.1	21 274	41.5	5.5
Carlsbad city	671	33.2	17.0	167	29.9	7.8	157	15.9	0.0	9 425	36.2	8.3	688	42.3	13.1
Clovis city	2 182	37.9	9.7	364	23.4	8.0	804	25.9	1.7	10 849	40.3	5.1	1 156	57.9	4.3
Farmington city............	295	28.8	3.7	6 289	36.5	3.6	173	46.2	7.5	6 654	36.3	5.3	1 149	48.3	4.9
Hobbs city	1 900	34.8	17.1	217	6.5	7.4	138	16.7	24.6	11 915	41.0	4.2	969	52.5	6.4
Las Cruces city	1 512	26.2	12.5	1 437	26.5	6.8	988	21.7	5.7	38 890	32.4	8.0	3 210	37.7	8.9
Rio Rancho city	1 154	27.6	18.5	1 330	38.6	2.0	707	26.9	7.8	14 285	38.3	4.2	2 202	51.1	3.9
Roswell city	1 159	32.8	16.8	547	41.9	7.1	390	23.8	0.0	20 499	37.5	6.2	1 762	43.2	7.6
Santa Fe city...............	385	14.3	6.2	1 393	29.6	4.2	565	20.5	5.7	29 367	26.8	11.7	2 974	27.9	9.8

[1] Hispanic or Latino persons may be of any race.

Table A-5. Cities — Age, Ethnicity, and Household Structure

City	Total households	Family households (percent)						Nonfamily households (percent)						Percent of householders 65 years and over who live alone	Grandparents who are responsible for the care of their grandchildren
		Married-couple family households			Other family households			Two or more unrelated persons		Male living alone		Female living alone			
		Total	With children	House-holder 65 years or over	Total	With children	House-holder 65 years or over	Total	House-holder 65 years or over	Total	House-holder 65 years or over	Total	House-holder 65 years or over		
	29	30	31	32	33	34	35	36	37	38	39	40	41	42	43
NEBRASKA	666 995	54.9	25.5	10.2	12.1	7.7	1.4	5.6	0.3	11.8	2.4	15.7	8.3	47.3	8 454
Bellevue city	17 007	56.6	26.5	8.7	14.5	9.8	1.3	5.7	0.2	10.9	1.4	12.4	5.0	38.5	252
Fremont city	10 162	52.7	22.3	12.2	12.9	8.6	1.7	5.1	0.5	11.0	2.7	18.2	11.0	48.7	91
Grand Island city	16 382	53.6	25.1	10.3	14.1	10.1	1.5	5.1	0.3	11.7	2.0	15.5	8.9	47.5	302
Kearney city	10 461	46.1	22.3	7.4	12.9	8.6	0.7	12.4	0.1	11.0	2.2	17.7	7.8	55.0	36
Lincoln city	90 560	47.2	22.2	7.5	12.6	7.8	1.3	9.8	0.3	13.3	1.6	17.1	6.8	48.2	873
Omaha city	157 034	44.3	20.7	7.5	16.7	10.0	2.1	7.2	0.3	13.8	1.9	18.1	7.6	48.9	2 592
NEVADA	751 977	50.6	23.0	8.5	16.2	9.6	1.7	8.4	0.8	13.0	2.6	11.9	4.7	39.9	18 685
Carson City	20 237	50.1	20.2	11.4	16.2	10.4	1.4	5.9	0.8	12.8	3.2	14.9	7.6	44.2	346
Henderson city	66 555	56.8	24.9	8.8	14.4	8.8	1.3	8.6	0.6	10.1	1.6	10.1	3.6	32.5	1 365
Las Vegas city	177 223	49.1	22.2	9.1	17.8	10.3	1.9	8.1	0.8	12.5	2.7	12.5	4.9	39.1	4 812
North Las Vegas city	34 093	57.8	34.7	5.0	22.1	13.5	1.9	6.5	0.3	7.2	1.6	6.5	1.8	31.9	1 810
Reno city	73 859	41.5	19.2	6.7	15.4	9.3	1.4	10.6	0.8	16.3	3.1	16.1	6.3	51.7	1 292
Sparks city	24 698	51.4	26.7	7.1	17.2	10.1	1.6	7.3	0.6	11.9	2.4	12.2	5.5	45.7	550
NEW HAMPSHIRE	474 750	56.2	26.1	8.8	12.4	7.7	1.5	7.0	0.4	10.9	2.2	13.5	6.5	44.9	4 534
Concord city	16 325	44.9	21.3	7.5	14.8	10.1	2.0	7.8	0.5	12.7	2.2	19.9	9.0	52.8	143
Dover city	11 542	43.0	18.8	7.9	13.5	8.3	1.2	12.4	0.2	15.1	2.0	16.0	6.8	48.5	82
Manchester city	44 254	43.6	20.2	7.3	15.8	9.8	1.9	8.9	0.4	14.2	2.5	17.5	8.2	52.6	436
Nashua city	34 630	50.6	23.8	7.8	13.5	8.0	1.4	7.6	0.4	13.3	2.0	15.1	6.8	47.9	418
Rochester city	11 397	52.5	23.1	9.6	14.8	9.9	1.4	7.1	0.7	11.0	2.1	14.6	8.1	46.6	214
NEW JERSEY	3 065 774	54.4	26.2	9.4	16.3	7.9	2.8	4.8	0.4	9.7	2.4	14.8	7.5	44.1	58 789
Atlantic City city	15 886	25.8	11.2	5.4	29.7	16.8	3.7	7.3	0.7	16.3	5.0	20.8	11.2	62.3	616
Bayonne city	25 581	44.2	20.4	9.2	19.3	8.7	4.7	3.7	0.5	13.1	3.8	19.7	11.0	50.7	368
Bergenfield borough	8 977	59.8	31.5	10.6	15.4	5.0	4.0	4.0	0.6	7.4	2.2	13.4	7.7	39.4	116
Camden city	24 233	26.1	13.6	4.2	46.7	30.1	4.7	4.7	0.6	9.1	2.5	13.3	5.4	45.2	1 769
Clifton city	30 242	51.9	23.1	11.2	15.6	6.0	4.0	4.5	0.5	10.7	3.4	17.3	10.8	47.5	304
East Orange city	26 076	26.9	12.4	5.0	35.1	19.6	4.3	5.0	0.5	12.4	2.9	20.6	8.4	53.7	1 511
Elizabeth city	40 489	42.5	23.2	5.7	27.6	14.4	3.3	5.3	0.4	11.7	2.6	12.9	6.2	48.5	1 445
Englewood city	9 291	49.3	24.2	9.0	20.7	7.9	4.8	5.3	0.9	8.1	2.9	16.6	7.0	40.0	299
Fair Lawn borough	11 824	64.1	29.0	15.2	11.2	4.1	3.0	3.4	0.6	7.1	3.0	14.2	9.4	39.7	13
Fort Lee borough	16 533	48.0	19.5	12.7	9.2	3.6	1.9	3.8	0.7	15.2	3.0	23.8	10.6	47.1	187
Garfield city	11 218	48.7	23.3	8.0	17.5	7.0	4.0	6.3	0.3	11.2	3.1	16.2	9.0	49.7	139
Hackensack city	18 114	35.0	15.0	5.8	18.1	8.0	2.5	7.1	0.6	17.2	2.3	22.5	6.8	50.7	262
Hoboken city	19 462	24.7	7.1	3.6	11.2	5.0	1.8	22.4	0.2	20.0	2.0	21.7	6.3	59.8	185
Jersey City city	88 617	37.2	18.1	4.7	26.1	13.7	3.4	7.5	0.3	13.9	2.2	15.3	5.8	49.0	2 996
Kearny town	13 561	54.1	27.2	7.2	19.5	8.3	3.4	4.6	0.4	9.4	2.4	12.4	6.7	45.3	219
Linden city	15 029	49.2	22.0	10.6	18.1	7.4	3.9	4.7	0.3	10.3	3.2	17.7	10.6	48.0	510
Long Branch city	12 594	37.9	17.1	7.9	20.5	11.2	2.7	7.5	0.6	16.0	2.6	18.1	7.4	47.3	248
Millville city	10 072	48.5	22.0	8.2	21.5	14.2	2.6	4.9	0.5	9.6	3.0	15.5	8.3	50.0	249
Newark city	91 366	32.4	16.1	4.6	36.0	19.9	3.8	4.9	0.4	11.7	2.8	14.9	6.4	51.0	4 832
New Brunswick city	13 053	30.1	16.2	4.3	26.2	15.4	2.7	19.3	0.5	11.9	1.6	12.4	5.4	48.0	520
Paramus borough	8 076	75.1	35.7	19.0	9.2	2.9	3.3	1.3	0.4	3.9	2.0	10.5	7.7	30.0	62
Passaic city	19 499	44.2	26.5	5.0	30.5	16.2	2.6	5.0	0.5	7.4	2.3	12.8	6.8	53.0	767
Paterson city	44 760	41.1	22.5	5.6	34.4	19.5	3.3	4.1	0.4	8.9	2.3	11.5	5.7	46.2	2 537
Perth Amboy city	14 563	47.9	26.0	6.5	27.2	15.3	3.1	4.3	0.6	8.2	2.4	12.3	6.5	46.5	549
Plainfield city	15 149	39.6	19.3	5.7	33.0	16.9	4.3	6.4	0.4	8.6	2.3	12.4	6.0	44.3	798
Rahway city	10 028	48.4	21.6	9.8	18.8	8.4	3.5	4.8	0.1	10.7	2.8	17.3	9.1	46.9	311
Sayreville borough	14 964	59.8	28.7	9.1	13.6	5.8	2.9	4.4	0.3	8.7	2.1	13.6	6.5	41.0	168
Trenton city	29 370	30.9	15.2	5.2	33.5	18.7	4.2	5.8	0.6	12.4	3.3	17.4	8.9	55.1	1 439
Union City city	22 913	42.4	22.2	6.2	28.5	15.4	2.7	6.2	0.5	11.9	2.5	11.1	5.8	47.2	750
Vineland city	19 876	48.8	22.6	8.9	22.6	12.1	3.5	4.8	0.7	9.3	2.5	14.5	7.8	44.0	485
Westfield town	10 639	68.1	36.3	11.3	9.1	4.1	2.8	3.5	0.3	6.3	1.7	13.1	7.7	39.3	60
West New York town	16 768	40.3	19.0	8.1	25.9	12.2	3.3	6.3	0.4	11.6	2.7	15.9	9.2	50.2	486
NEW MEXICO	678 032	51.1	24.1	9.3	18.1	11.2	2.3	5.5	0.4	11.7	2.4	13.7	6.0	41.4	24 041
Alamogordo city	13 632	56.6	26.6	9.4	15.3	10.4	2.3	2.8	0.2	12.4	2.8	12.9	7.3	45.8	389
Albuquerque city	183 625	44.1	20.2	8.0	17.6	10.7	2.0	7.8	0.4	13.7	2.2	16.8	6.4	45.5	4 272
Carlsbad city	10 080	51.9	21.5	12.6	17.7	12.1	2.3	3.5	0.2	11.8	2.6	15.1	8.7	42.8	413
Clovis city	12 468	49.8	23.4	9.3	19.5	13.7	1.7	3.7	0.4	12.1	2.9	14.9	8.1	49.2	421
Farmington city	13 983	56.5	27.1	9.5	17.1	11.9	1.2	4.0	0.2	9.4	1.5	12.9	6.2	41.1	395
Hobbs city	10 092	55.3	28.1	9.6	17.9	12.8	1.9	2.8	0.0	10.0	3.1	14.1	8.8	50.8	364
Las Cruces city	29 101	43.1	18.7	10.2	19.6	12.6	1.8	9.6	0.5	12.1	2.4	15.6	6.5	41.6	730
Rio Rancho city	18 971	60.7	31.8	9.5	14.0	9.0	1.7	4.5	0.4	8.4	2.0	12.4	5.6	39.5	302
Roswell city	17 089	50.7	22.1	11.9	18.7	12.8	2.0	3.3	0.6	10.3	4.1	17.0	10.1	49.5	603
Santa Fe city	27 493	38.5	15.3	7.8	16.1	9.3	2.9	8.6	0.7	14.4	2.6	22.4	7.7	47.3	504

City	Households with Non-Hispanic White householder		Households with Black or African American householder		Households with American Indian and Alaska Native householder		Households with Asian, Hawaiian, and Pacific Islander householder		Households with Hispanic or Latino[1] householder		Foreign-born population				Percent in non-English speaking households	
											Percent of total population that is foreign-born	Place of birth (percent)				
	Number of households	Percent that are family households	Number of households	Percent that are family households	Number of households	Percent that are family households	Number of households	Percent that are family households	Number of households	Percent that are family households		Europe	Asia	Latin America	Linguistically isolated	Not linguistically isolated
	44	45	46	47	48	49	50	51	52	53	54	55	56	57	58	59
NEBRASKA.............	603 693	66.6	24 346	65.0	4 189	75.2	6 506	67.7	23 919	78.4	4.4	0.6	1.1	2.3	2.2	10.0
Bellevue city	14 433	71.7	1 143	65.3	122	66.4	309	57.3	786	83.2	5.7	1.7	2.0	1.6	1.5	13.2
Fremont city	9 755	65.1	37	100.0	52	76.9	16	87.5	279	75.6	3.0	0.2	0.3	2.4	2.0	7.9
Grand Island city	14 310	65.3	62	80.6	51	70.6	145	84.1	1 685	83.7	9.6	0.3	1.0	8.3	6.0	13.8
Kearney city	9 889	59.2	41	43.9	33	75.8	75	33.3	373	62.5	2.6	0.3	0.7	1.4	1.0	7.8
Lincoln city	82 430	59.4	2 303	60.0	496	63.5	1 987	74.0	2 395	65.8	5.9	1.2	3.0	1.3	2.8	10.4
Omaha city	125 872	59.7	18 971	64.8	812	65.3	2 609	58.7	7 349	76.1	6.6	0.9	1.6	3.6	3.1	11.6
NEVADA...................	550 056	64.0	49 184	66.2	9 055	69.4	30 531	71.9	99 288	81.3	15.8	1.6	3.6	9.7	6.9	23.3
Carson City	17 366	64.4	84	54.8	432	80.1	294	75.5	1 756	82.6	9.9	1.0	1.5	6.8	4.6	15.9
Henderson city	55 172	70.3	2 707	71.9	430	78.4	2 227	75.7	5 135	78.1	8.3	1.7	3.1	2.6	1.8	18.6
Las Vegas city.............	118 601	63.6	18 520	65.6	1 098	67.8	7 845	71.7	27 460	81.4	18.9	1.9	3.6	12.6	8.6	25.6
North Las Vegas city.....	15 844	74.5	7 012	77.7	213	76.5	1 167	87.1	9 456	89.8	25.1	0.8	2.6	21.3	14.1	31.1
Reno city	57 785	52.7	1 771	50.9	795	62.0	3 262	66.5	8 828	80.7	17.3	1.6	4.2	10.4	7.7	22.2
Sparks city	10 025	64.9	686	67.5	322	77.6	997	77.8	3 292	87.6	15.6	1.3	3.7	9.6	6.5	23.1
NEW HAMPSHIRE.....	456 148	68.5	3 151	65.2	947	69.4	4 669	75.1	5 772	71.0	4.4	1.5	1.1	0.6	1.2	12.4
Concord city	15 638	59.5	145	60.7	18	33.3	221	71.0	113	66.4	4.3	1.4	1.3	0.3	0.9	10.5
Dover city	10 991	56.5	98	45.9	33	21.2	193	66.3	103	59.2	5.0	1.6	2.2	0.2	1.5	11.6
Manchester city	40 782	58.6	726	64.9	128	71.1	774	68.9	1 392	69.1	9.4	2.9	2.2	1.9	4.5	22.1
Nashua city	30 804	63.0	634	71.6	63	81.0	1 229	76.3	1 526	73.7	10.1	1.9	3.5	3.0	3.9	19.8
Rochester city	11 115	67.1	42	50.0	5	100.0	53	58.5	70	100.0	2.5	0.9	0.6	0.1	0.6	10.3
NEW JERSEY..........	2 182 369	68.8	382 711	68.9	5 674	74.4	145 230	83.0	315 560	80.3	17.5	4.2	4.9	7.5	6.3	25.6
Atlantic City city............	4 238	38.0	7 164	56.4	55	34.5	1 283	73.0	2 906	74.0	24.7	1.6	9.9	12.2	14.1	29.8
Bayonne city	19 575	60.0	1 367	60.4	70	90.0	780	80.8	3 321	80.3	20.2	6.5	3.7	7.0	7.6	31.9
Bergenfield borough.......	5 738	67.7	578	77.2	7	100.0	1 281	91.9	1 225	90.5	32.1	4.4	16.4	10.4	6.5	40.6
Camden city	2 315	49.0	13 102	72.1	106	77.4	590	86.1	8 810	81.0	8.9	0.2	2.3	6.1	11.3	34.9
Clifton city	23 009	62.5	821	77.3	67	83.6	1 400	88.4	4 201	86.7	29.2	10.7	7.4	10.3	10.9	39.3
East Orange city	909	36.5	23 230	62.3	89	59.6	129	51.9	964	69.2	18.3	0.5	0.5	15.1	2.7	18.6
Elizabeth city	12 990	59.6	8 200	63.1	121	86.8	885	77.3	17 867	80.3	43.9	7.9	2.1	33.0	23.5	50.6
Englewood city	3 586	60.9	3 601	71.4	0	X	437	84.9	1 488	83.1	30.8	3.0	4.9	22.0	8.7	31.3
Fair Lawn borough........	10 815	74.0	65	47.7	16	68.8	429	92.3	476	92.4	26.8	15.4	8.3	2.5	5.2	33.4
Fort Lee borough	10 896	50.3	340	38.2	30	66.7	4 042	74.1	981	67.5	44.7	10.5	28.6	4.4	18.3	41.6
Garfield city	8 863	61.6	286	83.2	23	30.4	191	97.0	1 000	83.7	39.1	24.9	3.3	10.3	16.9	45.3
Hackensack city	9 103	41.1	4 095	58.7	31	74.2	1 300	68.3	3 196	75.0	33.8	4.0	7.5	20.8	12.4	34.1
Hoboken city	14 992	29.8	585	55.9	27	74.1	702	29.1	3 049	65.4	14.5	5.6	3.3	4.7	6.3	28.3
Jersey City city............	27 656	47.2	24 029	65.8	170	80.0	12 516	74.4	21 100	74.6	34.0	2.7	13.8	13.8	12.2	45.4
Kearny town	9 248	69.0	158	61.4	31	77.4	759	70.8	3 044	88.6	38.2	13.4	5.0	18.7	13.6	47.7
Linden city	9 717	62.0	2 916	72.7	27	63.0	280	73.2	1 679	85.6	20.3	12.9	2.0	10.8	8.9	35.4
Long Branch city	8 245	52.4	2 027	63.8	49	69.4	196	54.6	1 955	79.1	19.7	4.7	1.8	12.7	10.0	29.7
Millville city	7 693	68.0	1 385	75.8	71	62.0	54	83.3	897	78.8	2.2	1.2	0.3	0.6	2.3	15.8
Newark city	14 494	64.2	49 825	65.1	242	78.1	1 073	64.3	23 954	78.2	24.1	6.1	0.9	15.4	13.9	35.2
New Brunswick city	5 089	30.6	3 403	68.2	20	35.0	657	43.4	3 788	84.5	33.4	2.0	4.0	25.7	20.4	36.6
Paramus borough..........	6 584	81.9	45	82.2	13	100.0	1 088	95.2	279	93.2	25.1	6.1	16.2	2.2	6.5	33.6
Passaic city	4 861	56.3	3 359	62.8	50	90.0	1 001	85.3	10 265	86.9	45.8	4.0	5.0	36.4	29.3	47.9
Paterson city	8 655	55.0	15 024	73.6	122	75.4	663	85.8	19 410	86.0	32.8	2.0	3.1	27.3	17.6	44.7
Perth Amboy city..........	4 131	55.2	1 587	67.1	149	83.9	181	72.4	8 552	87.2	35.7	3.5	1.1	30.7	24.4	55.9
Plainfield city	2 477	54.5	9 634	74.7	60	48.3	77	68.8	2 869	83.9	23.7	1.0	0.4	21.5	11.5	22.4
Rahway city	5 992	62.7	2 507	73.6	9	0.0	357	72.8	971	78.3	17.2	3.8	3.4	8.8	5.9	26.0
Sayreville borough	11 158	72.3	1 247	64.6	25	100.0	1 374	82.3	871	85.9	20.1	5.1	9.2	3.2	4.6	29.7
Trenton city	9 581	50.6	14 351	67.6	75	78.7	207	80.2	4 782	82.2	14.1	2.1	0.6	9.8	9.4	26.1
Union City city	3 851	48.0	864	65.0	109	64.2	581	69.4	18 098	76.0	58.7	1.7	2.1	54.5	36.3	54.9
Vineland city	12 119	67.7	2 331	74.6	111	67.6	179	78.8	5 068	78.9	8.1	2.7	0.9	4.4	7.5	33.4
Westfield town..............	9 646	76.4	372	80.1	13	100.0	347	89.3	218	80.3	9.1	4.3	3.0	1.3	1.9	15.6
West New York town	3 423	39.0	763	53.5	17	100.0	535	67.1	12 122	75.1	65.2	2.0	3.3	59.2	36.5	52.4
NEW MEXICO...........	362 890	64.0	12 895	64.6	47 487	79.1	6 284	69.1	242 878	75.5	8.2	0.8	0.8	6.3	6.2	42.5
Alamogordo city	8 966	69.5	702	79.9	155	67.1	111	52.3	3 394	77.1	12.1	5.0	1.0	5.9	6.3	33.6
Albuquerque city	106 831	57.2	5 811	59.7	5 751	66.6	3 259	68.1	59 979	69.6	8.9	1.1	1.6	5.7	4.8	33.8
Carlsbad city	6 585	67.2	257	65.8	84	53.6	62	88.7	2 966	75.5	4.0	0.6	0.4	2.6	3.9	32.8
Clovis city	7 982	66.6	832	74.4	182	86.8	263	58.9	3 170	75.5	5.5	0.6	1.8	3.0	3.5	31.7
Farmington city.............	9 746	71.8	149	57.0	1 760	82.3	42	83.3	2 115	75.3	3.3	0.3	0.3	2.4	1.8	28.0
Hobbs city	5 972	68.7	752	66.9	79	38.0	58	55.2	3 227	83.7	10.9	0.3	0.3	10.2	5.7	36.4
Las Cruces city	15 025	56.4	659	64.3	485	67.4	357	74.2	12 389	70.8	10.5	0.9	0.9	8.4	6.3	46.2
Rio Rancho city	13 356	72.2	472	66.9	380	82.6	146	80.8	4 297	82.3	4.8	1.4	1.3	1.7	1.0	26.4
Roswell city	10 302	62.8	471	63.9	151	75.5	122	74.6	5 964	81.0	10.8	0.6	0.7	9.2	7.0	36.7
Santa Fe city................	15 577	45.2	166	42.2	485	54.2	238	66.4	10 736	68.3	11.6	2.1	0.9	8.1	6.6	42.5

[1] Hispanic or Latino persons may be of any race.

STATE Place code	City	Total population	Under 5 years	5 to 17 years	18 to 24 years	25 to 44 years	45 to 64 years	65 years and over	Median age	+/− U.S. percent under 18 years	+/− U.S. percent 65 years and over	Non-Hispanic White Total population	Under 18 years	65 years and over
		1	2	3	4	5	6	7	8	9	10	11	12	13
36 00000	NEW YORK..............	18 976 457	6.5	18.2	9.3	30.9	22.3	12.9	35.9	-1.0	0.5	11 761 679	21.8	16.4
36 01000	Albany city.................	95 658	5.7	14.0	19.3	29.8	17.6	13.6	31.4	-6.0	1.2	58 555	11.5	18.6
36 03078	Auburn city	28 574	6.2	16.4	9.6	30.2	19.7	18.0	36.9	-3.1	5.6	24 840	21.9	20.1
36 06607	Binghamton city.............	47 380	6.1	15.4	13.4	26.5	20.7	17.8	36.7	-4.2	5.4	38 802	18.3	20.6
36 11000	Buffalo city.................	292 648	7.1	19.2	11.2	29.5	19.5	13.5	33.6	0.6	1.1	152 109	18.5	17.8
36 24229	Elmira city..................	30 940	6.9	18.2	13.1	30.0	18.1	13.8	33.4	-0.6	1.4	25 071	23.6	15.5
36 27485	Freeport village	43 783	7.0	19.4	9.3	32.3	21.7	10.4	34.6	0.7	-2.0	13 922	16.9	21.0
36 29113	Glen Cove city..............	26 622	5.6	15.6	8.3	30.9	22.0	17.7	38.6	-4.5	5.3	17 945	17.9	22.7
36 33139	Hempstead village........	56 544	8.1	18.4	16.3	31.9	16.9	8.4	29.4	0.8	-4.0	7 354	7.6	24.4
36 38077	Ithaca city..................	29 006	2.4	6.4	54.2	20.8	10.0	6.3	22.0	-16.9	-6.1	20 818	7.8	7.8
36 38264	Jamestown city..............	31 730	7.4	18.0	9.0	28.7	20.9	15.9	36.2	-0.3	3.5	28 349	23.7	17.3
36 42554	Lindenhurst village	27 933	6.9	19.8	7.4	33.8	20.9	11.3	35.8	1.0	-1.1	25 073	26.2	11.6
36 43335	Long Beach city	35 462	4.5	13.8	6.0	34.9	24.1	16.7	39.6	-7.4	4.3	27 260	15.8	19.6
36 47042	Middletown city.............	25 329	7.8	20.1	9.7	31.0	19.3	12.1	33.4	2.2	-0.3	14 566	20.0	18.4
36 49121	Mount Vernon city........	68 381	7.0	18.3	7.9	31.6	22.4	12.9	35.8	-0.4	0.5	16 505	13.9	26.3
36 50034	Newburgh city...............	28 233	9.6	23.6	12.7	28.3	17.0	8.9	27.8	7.5	-3.5	7 936	19.0	21.1
36 50617	New Rochelle city	72 182	6.6	17.2	8.5	29.8	22.3	15.6	37.0	-1.9	3.2	40 447	20.6	21.0
36 51000	New York city..............	8 008 278	6.7	17.5	10.0	33.0	21.2	11.7	34.2	-1.5	-0.7	2 801 995	16.2	19.2
36 51055	Niagara Falls city	55 677	6.5	18.3	8.4	28.0	20.2	18.5	38.0	-0.9	6.1	42 014	20.5	22.1
36 53682	North Tonawanda city ...	33 262	5.7	17.9	8.6	28.9	23.3	15.6	38.4	-2.1	3.2	32 164	23.3	16.0
36 59223	Port Chester village.......	27 867	7.2	15.4	10.2	36.1	18.1	13.1	34.0	-3.1	0.7	11 721	15.7	23.8
36 59641	Poughkeepsie city..........	29 871	7.3	18.4	12.7	28.5	19.3	13.7	32.7	0.0	1.3	14 863	15.6	21.6
36 63000	Rochester city..............	219 766	7.8	20.3	11.5	32.3	18.2	9.9	30.8	2.4	-2.5	96 915	14.9	16.1
36 63418	Rome city...................	34 922	6.0	16.0	8.4	30.4	22.1	17.1	38.2	-3.7	4.7	29 765	21.9	19.2
36 65255	Saratoga Springs city	26 187	5.4	13.9	15.2	27.9	23.3	14.2	36.3	-6.4	1.8	24 308	18.7	14.7
36 65508	Schenectady city	61 908	6.9	17.4	11.5	30.4	18.8	15.0	34.8	-1.4	2.6	46 195	19.0	18.9
36 70420	Spring Valley village......	25 374	9.4	22.7	11.1	31.5	18.6	6.7	29.4	6.4	-5.7	7 616	33.7	11.8
36 73000	Syracuse city...............	147 326	6.9	18.0	16.6	28.3	17.2	12.9	30.5	-0.8	0.5	91 879	16.9	17.7
36 75484	Troy city....................	49 170	6.3	15.8	17.5	28.7	18.0	13.8	31.7	-3.6	1.4	38 966	19.3	16.1
36 76540	Utica city...................	60 679	6.7	17.5	9.7	27.1	19.9	19.0	37.0	-1.5	6.6	46 406	19.2	23.1
36 76705	Valley Stream village	36 394	5.7	18.1	7.9	28.9	23.1	16.3	39.0	-1.9	3.9	26 035	19.9	21.0
36 78608	Watertown city..............	26 705	7.6	18.3	10.4	29.3	18.8	15.7	34.0	0.2	3.3	23 544	23.9	17.4
36 81677	White Plains city..........	53 077	6.0	15.2	7.2	33.5	23.1	14.9	38.1	-4.5	2.5	28 875	17.5	22.0
36 84000	Yonkers city.................	196 086	6.9	17.3	8.6	30.9	21.3	15.1	35.8	-1.5	2.7	99 414	15.5	24.6
37 00000	NORTH CAROLINA ...	8 049 313	6.7	17.7	10.0	31.2	22.4	12.0	35.3	-1.3	-0.4	5 648 953	21.8	14.1
37 02140	Asheville city	68 952	5.2	14.2	10.5	28.9	22.7	18.5	39.2	-6.3	6.1	52 331	16.2	21.0
37 09060	Burlington city..............	45 363	6.6	17.4	8.9	29.5	21.0	16.7	36.9	-1.7	4.3	28 229	19.6	22.8
37 10740	Cary town..................	94 530	8.1	21.0	6.3	39.1	20.2	5.3	33.7	3.4	-7.1	74 981	28.7	6.0
37 11800	Chapel Hill town	48 796	3.2	11.6	36.7	25.0	15.5	8.0	24.0	-10.9	-4.4	36 934	12.3	9.2
37 12000	Charlotte city..............	542 131	7.1	17.6	10.3	36.4	20.0	8.7	32.7	-1.0	-3.7	298 501	20.5	11.9
37 14100	Concord city................	55 941	7.8	18.5	8.4	34.0	19.9	11.4	33.6	0.6	-1.0	42 119	24.3	13.1
37 19000	Durham city................	187 183	7.1	15.8	14.0	35.9	17.9	9.3	31.0	-2.8	-3.1	79 346	16.5	14.1
37 22920	Fayetteville city............	120 843	7.5	17.9	12.7	31.0	19.9	11.0	31.9	-0.3	-1.4	55 959	19.5	15.0
37 25580	Gastonia city	66 298	6.8	18.2	8.7	30.7	21.7	13.8	35.6	-0.7	1.4	44 747	21.5	17.1
37 26880	Goldsboro city..............	38 731	7.0	17.9	11.5	29.7	20.2	13.7	34.3	-0.8	1.3	16 454	19.4	19.0
37 28000	Greensboro city	223 299	6.2	16.1	14.0	31.8	20.1	11.9	33.0	-3.4	-0.5	119 660	17.8	17.0
37 28080	Greenville city..............	60 385	5.4	13.0	28.7	28.4	15.3	9.1	26.0	-7.3	-3.3	36 467	12.3	10.3
37 31060	Hickory city.................	37 511	7.0	16.7	11.3	30.4	21.1	13.4	34.6	-2.0	1.0	27 012	19.7	16.9
37 31400	High Point city.............	85 949	7.3	18.4	9.5	32.0	21.0	11.8	34.4	0.0	-0.6	50 173	20.9	16.2
37 34200	Jacksonville city	66 751	9.6	14.9	36.2	25.7	8.8	4.8	22.4	-1.2	-7.6	40 478	20.9	5.7
37 35200	Kannapolis city	36 699	6.9	17.3	9.3	30.2	20.6	15.6	36.0	-1.5	3.2	27 645	20.9	18.3
37 43920	Monroe city.................	25 953	8.4	17.6	12.2	31.5	19.2	11.1	30.9	0.3	-1.3	12 731	18.7	18.0
37 55000	Raleigh city.................	276 579	6.3	14.5	16.1	36.6	18.2	8.3	30.9	-4.9	-4.1	166 680	16.8	10.7
37 57500	Rocky Mount city..........	56 244	7.1	20.6	9.4	28.2	21.6	13.1	35.2	2.0	0.7	22 566	19.7	19.7
37 58860	Salisbury city	26 676	6.2	15.6	12.2	26.0	19.9	20.2	37.1	-3.9	7.8	14 881	15.1	29.1
37 74440	Wilmington city	75 542	5.3	12.8	17.2	28.6	20.5	15.5	34.1	-7.6	3.1	52 227	13.2	17.9
37 74540	Wilson city.................	44 308	7.3	18.8	10.3	28.5	21.8	13.3	35.1	0.4	0.9	19 252	18.9	19.7
37 75000	Winston-Salem city	185 480	6.6	16.6	11.6	30.6	20.6	14.0	34.6	-2.5	1.6	97 426	17.2	19.9
38 00000	NORTH DAKOTA.......	642 200	6.1	19.0	11.3	27.3	21.6	14.7	36.2	-0.6	2.3	589 853	23.7	15.7
38 07200	Bismarck city...............	55 284	5.8	17.7	11.2	28.7	22.9	13.8	36.5	-2.2	1.4	52 318	22.5	14.4
38 25700	Fargo city	90 787	6.4	14.8	19.0	31.2	18.6	10.1	30.1	-4.5	-2.3	84 738	20.1	10.6
38 32060	Grand Forks city...........	49 282	5.7	15.6	23.0	27.5	18.3	9.8	28.3	-4.4	-2.6	45 475	20.2	10.4
38 53380	Minot city	36 580	6.5	16.6	12.9	28.0	20.6	15.4	35.0	-2.6	3.0	33 828	22.0	16.3
39 00000	OHIO	11 353 140	6.6	18.8	9.3	29.4	22.6	13.3	36.2	-0.3	0.9	9 537 082	24.0	14.3
39 01000	Akron city...................	217 088	7.1	18.2	10.4	30.5	20.2	13.6	34.2	-0.4	1.2	144 939	21.0	16.1
39 03828	Barberton city	27 995	7.7	17.2	8.5	28.3	21.2	17.0	37.2	-0.8	4.6	25 078	23.0	18.0
39 04720	Beavercreek city...........	38 183	5.2	20.0	6.2	26.9	29.5	12.1	40.5	-0.5	-0.3	35 371	24.8	12.8
39 07972	Bowling Green city	29 562	3.5	9.6	47.0	19.5	12.9	7.5	22.4	-12.6	-4.9	26 735	12.4	8.1

City	Black or African American			American Indian and Alaska Native			Asian, Hawaiian, and Pacific Islander			Hispanic or Latino[1]			Two or more races		
		Age (percent)			Age (percent)			Age (percent)			Age (percent)			Age (percent)	
	Total population	Under 18 years	65 years and over	Total population	Under 18 years	65 years and over	Total population	Under 18 years	65 years and over	Total population	Under 18 years	65 years and over	Total population	Under 18 years	65 years and over
	14	15	16	17	18	19	20	21	22	23	24	25	26	27	28
NEW YORK	2 986 242	29.8	8.7	79 314	31.7	6.7	1 052 326	22.6	6.8	2 865 016	30.9	5.8	615 062	33.2	6.1
Albany city	26 221	34.1	6.6	510	39.4	6.5	2 915	13.3	3.4	5 387	34.1	2.6	3 485	43.0	3.5
Auburn city	1 919	21.6	2.9	136	8.1	13.2	237	8.0	21.1	951	19.7	2.5	505	62.0	0.0
Binghamton city	4 002	37.3	6.3	184	26.1	9.2	1 511	28.9	2.6	1 860	37.2	4.0	1 312	43.8	5.0
Buffalo city	108 933	33.8	10.0	2 288	28.8	6.3	3 938	18.0	4.5	21 699	41.2	4.9	7 112	48.6	4.8
Elmira city	3 961	24.7	8.2	218	44.0	0.0	184	14.1	8.7	801	24.0	3.6	871	68.2	3.9
Freeport village	13 927	29.9	8.0	75	24.0	14.7	542	14.8	10.0	14 707	31.6	3.0	2 639	37.7	2.3
Glen Cove city	1 904	28.8	12.1	168	50.6	3.0	1 053	26.4	9.0	5 409	28.7	4.3	989	24.8	8.4
Hempstead village	29 759	30.0	8.0	183	33.9	5.5	603	13.3	12.9	18 081	29.2	2.5	2 544	29.6	4.1
Ithaca city	1 783	21.4	9.8	115	7.8	0.0	4 067	3.2	0.3	1 546	14.7	2.3	971	21.0	1.0
Jamestown city	1 098	30.3	5.7	249	27.3	9.6	60	25.0	8.3	1 473	40.0	3.1	878	59.6	0.7
Lindenhurst village	201	31.3	24.4	59	18.6	55.9	265	25.3	4.9	1 926	30.4	6.8	461	36.9	5.4
Long Beach city	2 261	28.5	10.3	39	15.4	0.0	806	17.7	6.0	4 448	26.3	5.5	1 034	36.4	8.8
Middletown city	3 660	35.6	4.8	193	48.2	0.0	424	35.8	1.9	6 346	40.0	0.7	1 309	51.0	0.5
Mount Vernon city	40 401	29.1	9.6	294	32.7	12.6	1 680	25.7	5.5	7 030	30.3	4.5	3 401	27.4	4.8
Newburgh city	9 061	39.0	6.1	364	36.0	3.8	292	19.2	3.8	10 208	38.2	2.2	1 711	50.9	3.5
New Rochelle city	13 676	25.6	14.0	169	12.4	3.0	2 704	23.6	5.8	14 378	30.7	3.6	2 273	30.3	11.1
New York city	2 116 379	29.2	9.3	36 657	34.1	6.3	792 980	21.6	7.4	2 161 530	30.4	6.4	401 956	28.8	6.6
Niagara Falls city	10 453	36.8	8.4	791	36.2	2.4	315	39.0	4.1	1 050	36.4	9.0	1 271	56.3	2.4
North Tonawanda city	68	39.7	13.2	95	22.1	7.4	176	0.0	6.8	425	39.8	5.2	358	47.2	4.7
Port Chester village	1 751	25.8	14.3	125	35.2	0.0	707	24.2	4.8	12 953	27.7	4.0	2 124	26.6	6.1
Poughkeepsie city	10 692	37.3	6.0	77	10.4	9.1	388	13.9	16.0	3 136	31.6	2.9	1 275	44.0	6.9
Rochester city	82 980	38.4	5.3	1 269	29.7	9.1	4 790	21.5	4.6	27 869	41.7	3.8	10 681	47.0	4.5
Rome city	2 714	20.1	4.6	67	13.4	11.9	295	19.7	6.1	1 550	20.5	4.6	826	36.3	3.3
Saratoga Springs city	685	22.9	12.4	71	19.7	0.0	270	22.2	8.9	568	33.6	1.1	390	51.8	7.2
Schenectady city	8 832	39.8	4.6	311	35.7	2.6	1 359	23.2	1.9	3 544	44.2	2.0	2 247	49.8	2.6
Spring Valley village	11 065	34.1	5.0	78	21.8	0.0	1 507	27.3	6.6	3 854	25.1	1.5	1 714	30.4	6.4
Syracuse city	36 945	39.2	5.7	1 790	31.6	5.7	4 937	18.0	3.8	7 648	40.5	2.0	5 817	50.6	3.2
Troy city	5 489	34.6	6.6	117	32.5	0.0	1 704	17.4	2.1	1 957	37.2	1.7	1 178	40.4	4.8
Utica city	7 542	37.7	8.3	147	23.1	5.4	1 349	29.5	5.6	3 457	46.4	2.7	2 062	50.1	1.8
Valley Stream village	2 643	36.5	3.0	45	15.6	11.1	2 575	32.0	6.3	4 450	33.0	4.4	810	34.6	3.0
Watertown city	1 122	39.1	1.1	183	20.2	1.1	438	28.5	2.5	853	44.2	2.9	713	57.4	4.6
White Plains city	8 176	24.3	12.5	221	33.9	7.7	2 199	17.0	2.0	12 620	27.6	3.5	2 149	31.5	5.7
Yonkers city	32 122	34.2	6.0	785	33.1	8.9	9 644	25.0	7.3	50 954	34.5	4.2	8 854	34.2	5.6
NORTH CAROLINA	1 734 154	29.8	8.9	100 956	30.1	6.4	114 991	27.0	3.7	372 964	31.4	1.5	111 909	42.7	3.6
Asheville city	11 882	29.9	13.0	333	24.9	7.8	798	22.3	3.8	2 713	28.3	3.2	1 137	38.2	8.0
Burlington city	11 401	30.3	9.5	289	27.3	4.8	829	28.1	1.4	4 287	32.3	0.1	691	39.7	3.9
Cary town	5 783	30.6	2.8	431	25.5	0.7	7 570	29.0	3.0	4 029	29.4	1.1	2 110	43.0	1.2
Chapel Hill town	5 538	22.0	6.1	311	25.1	3.9	3 357	18.3	2.6	1 660	24.5	2.5	1 170	31.5	1.5
Charlotte city	170 047	31.0	5.6	2 340	23.9	3.6	17 903	26.4	3.4	40 008	25.1	1.7	10 259	36.7	2.1
Concord city	8 323	29.8	9.1	334	21.3	0.0	665	35.6	2.9	4 346	35.8	0.6	490	56.7	7.8
Durham city	81 586	28.9	7.2	574	17.8	5.4	6 579	16.2	3.1	15 922	23.9	0.6	4 226	34.9	2.2
Fayetteville city	51 211	29.6	8.4	1 211	28.3	7.8	3 080	22.2	5.5	6 843	32.8	4.7	3 371	46.5	2.6
Gastonia city	17 249	33.7	8.0	230	10.0	10.4	502	22.1	4.4	3 560	25.3	1.5	748	46.3	4.0
Goldsboro city	20 150	28.3	10.7	163	20.2	4.3	572	28.1	0.0	846	36.5	0.7	731	44.9	1.6
Greensboro city	83 500	26.8	6.8	1 197	25.6	3.7	5 644	29.2	3.2	10 143	27.2	1.5	4 513	36.9	4.0
Greenville city	20 639	28.6	8.1	279	25.8	2.2	999	17.2	1.1	1 214	19.9	3.6	855	30.9	4.7
Hickory city	5 354	33.1	6.8	94	17.0	6.4	1 622	45.5	1.0	2 974	27.9	2.3	612	42.3	4.4
High Point city	27 244	32.9	6.5	437	16.7	14.0	2 839	28.1	3.6	4 302	31.0	2.0	1 418	41.8	3.5
Jacksonville city	16 018	31.0	4.8	505	17.0	1.6	1 609	21.3	3.2	6 720	25.4	0.5	2 491	47.0	0.0
Kannapolis city	6 201	32.5	10.1	63	31.7	20.6	187	32.1	0.0	2 381	38.6	0.9	319	51.7	0.9
Monroe city	7 275	36.6	7.0	218	27.5	0.0	100	8.0	0.0	5 692	29.7	1.1	274	28.5	5.5
Raleigh city	76 069	27.5	5.9	1 065	19.1	0.9	9 237	20.6	2.6	19 522	25.4	1.2	5 467	35.6	3.0
Rocky Mount city	31 634	32.7	9.0	101	15.8	14.9	396	33.6	3.5	1 057	38.5	3.5	637	41.0	6.1
Salisbury city	10 081	29.5	10.2	108	17.6	0.0	397	34.3	1.8	1 001	28.3	1.7	352	44.9	1.4
Wilmington city	19 487	30.4	11.7	499	24.4	4.0	673	13.4	1.2	1 945	23.2	1.1	893	30.7	3.1
Wilson city	21 278	31.7	9.5	72	19.4	0.0	264	25.0	8.0	3 175	28.9	0.6	598	45.5	4.0
Winston-Salem city	69 169	29.8	9.1	622	15.6	6.3	2 190	15.3	3.6	15 839	31.3	1.1	2 991	39.8	2.6
NORTH DAKOTA	3 673	36.5	2.3	31 308	41.4	4.5	3 529	26.8	3.5	7 568	39.7	4.0	7 545	48.0	4.2
Bismarck city	172	22.1	18.0	1 717	44.0	0.6	259	26.6	6.2	431	39.0	11.1	427	39.6	5.6
Fargo city	973	49.0	0.0	1 387	25.4	3.1	1 339	25.3	1.3	1 085	36.9	2.9	1 319	49.1	1.1
Grand Forks city	397	25.7	2.0	1 416	39.3	1.7	472	14.2	0.0	995	34.7	5.5	654	47.2	2.9
Minot city	449	25.8	6.2	1 085	42.6	3.1	172	17.4	4.7	642	42.1	1.7	518	38.0	6.9
OHIO	1 288 359	31.9	9.5	26 999	25.3	4.8	134 772	23.5	5.0	213 889	36.6	4.5	173 338	46.2	5.0
Akron city	61 287	33.5	9.5	563	16.9	3.6	3 254	24.5	4.8	2 367	34.5	3.0	4 944	48.0	4.3
Barberton city	1 667	44.6	7.1	43	44.2	11.6	69	13.0	4.3	159	28.3	15.1	304	59.9	0.7
Beavercreek city	560	33.4	2.7	111	27.9	0.0	1 231	21.6	4.4	397	43.8	4.8	532	35.9	4.5
Bowling Green city	947	11.5	0.0	34	14.7	0.0	524	24.4	1.3	965	24.6	3.3	429	26.1	1.6

[1] Hispanic or Latino persons may be of any race.

City	Total households	Family households (percent)						Nonfamily households (percent)						Percent of householders 65 years and over who live alone	Grandparents who are responsible for the care of their grandchildren
		Married-couple family households			Other family households			Two or more unrelated persons		Male living alone		Female living alone			
		Total	With children	House-holder 65 years or over	Total	With children	House-holder 65 years or over	Total	House-holder 65 years or over	Total	House-holder 65 years or over	Total	House-holder 65 years or over		
	29	30	31	32	33	34	35	36	37	38	39	40	41	42	43
NEW YORK...............	7 060 595	47.6	22.4	8.5	18.6	9.8	2.7	5.7	0.5	11.4	2.5	16.7	7.8	46.8	143 014
Albany city....................	40 772	25.6	10.3	5.9	19.9	12.6	2.3	12.6	0.4	19.4	3.2	22.5	8.6	57.8	625
Auburn city..................	11 437	39.2	17.2	8.6	18.7	11.8	2.7	6.0	0.7	14.1	3.8	22.0	12.8	57.9	114
Binghamton city............	21 113	33.1	13.6	8.2	16.7	10.2	2.9	10.0	0.7	16.7	3.6	23.6	11.9	56.9	304
Buffalo city..................	122 672	28.5	12.5	6.0	26.4	16.7	3.3	7.4	0.5	16.9	3.5	20.7	8.9	56.0	2 987
Elmira city..................	11 486	36.4	16.2	7.4	22.5	15.9	2.4	6.7	0.6	13.2	3.1	21.2	10.3	56.2	250
Freeport village	13 547	50.4	26.2	7.3	24.0	11.7	3.0	4.6	0.6	8.3	2.1	12.7	6.3	43.1	506
Glen Cove city..............	9 456	54.3	23.3	11.7	16.5	7.0	4.2	5.0	0.8	8.5	2.6	15.7	9.9	43.0	230
Hempstead village.........	15 204	40.9	22.3	4.7	34.1	16.6	4.0	4.3	0.5	7.1	1.8	13.7	5.2	43.3	718
Ithaca city...................	10 236	18.6	7.5	3.8	9.9	7.0	0.8	28.3	0.6	22.3	1.6	21.0	5.6	58.0	33
Jamestown city.............	13 532	40.0	17.2	9.2	18.2	12.7	1.8	6.7	0.5	14.7	3.0	20.4	10.9	55.0	225
Lindenhurst village	9 060	63.8	34.7	9.0	14.9	5.9	3.0	4.4	0.6	7.7	2.4	9.2	5.0	37.1	110
Long Beach city	14 938	40.9	15.6	8.0	14.2	6.3	2.0	8.3	0.4	17.0	2.5	19.7	9.0	52.6	134
Middletown city.............	9 440	41.1	19.8	7.2	22.5	13.9	2.5	6.0	0.4	12.1	2.8	18.3	8.7	53.2	235
Mount Vernon city	25 722	38.3	18.1	6.6	27.1	14.0	3.6	4.6	0.5	11.5	2.3	18.5	7.8	48.5	987
Newburgh city..............	9 139	36.3	20.6	5.2	30.5	21.1	2.4	6.2	0.1	12.1	3.1	14.9	6.8	56.4	313
New Rochelle city	26 235	50.8	26.3	10.3	16.6	7.4	2.9	4.7	0.5	9.9	2.5	18.0	9.5	46.8	449
New York city	3 022 477	38.2	18.4	6.3	23.7	12.0	3.2	6.3	0.5	13.0	2.6	18.8	7.5	50.2	83 946
Niagara Falls city	24 071	37.4	15.3	10.6	22.3	13.8	3.5	4.4	0.3	14.9	3.8	20.9	11.8	52.1	446
North Tonawanda city ...	13 681	53.6	22.6	11.2	12.7	7.2	2.7	4.2	0.2	11.6	2.9	17.9	10.0	47.7	92
Port Chester village......	9 553	49.6	25.3	8.3	18.7	7.3	3.8	5.1	0.3	10.4	3.1	16.2	9.0	49.3	205
Poughkeepsie city	12 024	30.3	13.0	6.2	25.2	16.4	2.6	9.2	0.4	15.3	3.6	20.0	10.2	60.0	404
Rochester city	89 093	25.7	12.3	3.7	27.8	18.6	2.5	9.5	0.4	17.7	2.7	19.2	6.8	58.8	2 924
Rome city	13 653	43.6	16.2	10.5	17.4	11.4	2.7	5.6	0.2	13.5	3.3	19.9	11.6	52.8	147
Saratoga Springs city....	10 777	44.8	18.7	7.6	11.1	7.2	1.4	9.1	0.4	14.9	2.3	20.0	9.7	55.8	58
Schenectady city...........	26 297	32.6	14.2	7.1	21.3	13.7	2.9	7.5	0.2	16.4	3.3	22.1	10.4	57.3	376
Spring Valley village......	7 549	46.2	28.9	4.2	28.9	15.2	2.2	4.6	0.0	8.6	1.5	11.7	4.7	49.1	167
Syracuse city...............	59 568	28.7	12.9	6.2	22.9	15.4	2.3	10.3	0.4	17.0	3.2	21.2	9.0	57.8	1 352
Troy city.....................	19 963	33.1	13.9	7.0	21.3	14.1	2.9	9.0	0.5	16.5	3.1	20.1	9.0	53.5	256
Utica city....................	25 093	36.6	15.6	9.7	20.7	12.7	3.2	5.4	0.5	15.7	4.1	21.5	11.7	54.2	424
Valley Stream village ...	12 508	62.3	28.9	13.1	15.3	5.3	4.5	2.2	0.1	6.6	2.5	13.6	9.2	39.7	195
Watertown city..............	11 039	42.5	20.4	8.3	16.9	12.2	1.9	6.1	0.3	13.2	2.0	21.3	10.7	54.9	135
White Plains city...........	20 951	47.5	21.8	9.1	13.6	6.1	2.3	5.6	0.5	11.7	2.1	21.6	9.1	48.5	287
Yonkers city..................	74 358	44.9	20.2	9.7	21.7	11.7	3.4	4.2	0.4	10.9	2.8	18.3	9.2	47.2	1 442
NORTH CAROLINA ...	3 133 282	53.4	23.3	8.7	16.0	9.1	2.2	5.3	0.3	10.6	2.0	14.8	6.8	43.9	79 810
Asheville city	30 688	39.2	14.4	10.6	15.4	8.6	2.5	8.4	0.3	13.6	3.0	23.3	11.1	51.2	535
Burlington city..............	18 397	45.9	19.6	10.5	19.1	10.7	2.9	5.0	0.2	10.9	2.2	19.2	9.7	46.8	448
Cary town	34 867	64.0	37.1	4.6	8.3	5.4	0.3	6.6	0.0	9.8	0.6	11.3	2.3	36.3	206
Chapel Hill town	17 982	37.1	16.9	5.5	9.1	5.5	0.6	22.7	0.3	11.9	1.6	19.2	6.5	55.8	102
Charlotte city...............	215 803	44.7	21.4	5.7	17.4	9.8	1.7	8.5	0.2	12.8	1.4	16.6	4.9	45.0	5 175
Concord city	20 917	56.1	26.8	7.5	16.3	9.4	2.5	4.4	0.2	10.0	1.5	13.2	6.1	42.8	412
Durham city.................	74 993	39.4	18.2	5.3	19.6	11.2	2.1	9.2	0.3	13.1	1.6	18.8	5.7	48.7	1 661
Fayetteville city.............	48 399	45.7	20.5	6.8	20.1	12.0	2.6	6.0	0.5	12.4	1.8	15.8	6.1	44.6	1 507
Gastonia city................	25 891	49.6	20.8	8.8	19.9	10.7	3.1	4.3	0.1	10.1	2.1	16.1	7.9	45.6	1 027
Goldsboro city..............	14 566	43.1	18.7	8.8	21.7	13.8	2.0	4.4	0.4	11.0	2.2	19.8	10.4	53.0	620
Greensboro city............	92 084	40.6	17.5	7.3	18.1	10.5	2.0	8.6	0.3	13.2	1.9	19.5	7.0	48.0	1 817
Greenville city..............	25 187	31.6	13.6	5.0	16.8	9.8	1.8	16.3	0.2	15.2	1.5	20.2	5.6	50.3	473
Hickory city..................	15 500	44.6	19.5	7.9	16.1	9.2	2.7	6.8	0.2	13.0	1.9	19.5	8.9	49.8	239
High Point city	33 626	47.3	21.9	7.3	19.9	11.4	2.4	5.6	0.3	10.6	2.3	16.6	7.5	49.6	687
Jacksonville city	17 127	63.8	39.1	4.8	15.4	11.4	1.2	4.2	0.1	7.3	1.0	9.3	4.4	47.2	440
Kannapolis city	14 753	50.0	21.0	9.7	19.6	9.6	3.6	4.6	0.4	9.7	2.8	16.1	9.3	46.9	382
Monroe city	8 960	49.7	21.8	7.8	21.9	12.9	2.4	5.0	0.1	8.9	2.1	14.5	7.6	48.5	227
Raleigh city..................	112 727	40.2	18.5	5.4	14.9	9.0	1.2	11.8	0.2	14.8	1.4	18.2	4.8	47.8	1 654
Rocky Mount city..........	21 610	44.7	20.2	8.5	24.4	13.9	2.8	3.7	0.2	9.7	2.4	17.5	8.5	48.6	785
Salisbury city...............	10 376	40.3	15.6	10.2	20.8	12.4	2.4	4.7	0.3	13.3	2.9	20.8	10.1	50.4	324
Wilmington city.............	34 268	34.6	11.6	8.7	16.9	9.6	2.6	12.0	0.3	14.5	2.2	22.0	8.9	49.1	671
Wilson city	17 340	41.4	18.6	7.1	24.7	13.7	3.0	4.6	0.1	11.3	2.8	18.0	9.0	53.6	583
Winston-Salem city	76 340	41.0	16.8	8.6	20.1	11.8	2.6	5.4	0.4	12.5	2.2	21.0	8.9	49.0	1 788
NORTH DAKOTA.......	257 234	54.1	24.7	10.8	10.8	6.9	1.3	5.8	0.2	13.1	2.8	16.2	8.7	48.3	2 547
Bismarck city................	23 163	51.2	22.9	9.8	11.2	6.9	1.0	6.7	0.3	11.3	1.8	19.5	8.6	48.5	75
Fargo city....................	39 354	42.4	20.2	6.5	10.9	6.9	0.6	12.0	0.3	15.4	1.7	19.2	6.3	51.9	223
Grand Forks city...........	19 658	44.2	20.9	6.3	12.7	8.2	1.3	11.8	0.1	15.0	1.8	16.3	7.0	53.5	105
Minot city....................	15 495	47.9	20.2	10.2	12.0	8.0	1.2	7.6	0.2	13.5	2.5	18.9	10.0	51.8	33
OHIO	4 446 621	52.2	23.1	9.4	15.5	9.1	2.2	5.1	0.3	11.4	2.4	15.9	7.8	46.1	86 009
Akron city....................	90 143	38.3	16.0	7.8	21.7	13.1	3.1	7.0	0.5	14.3	3.0	18.6	8.3	49.7	2 101
Barberton city...............	11 561	45.8	18.8	10.4	19.0	11.5	2.9	5.2	0.5	11.6	2.8	18.3	10.9	49.7	277
Beavercreek city...........	14 143	71.1	31.7	10.8	8.3	4.2	1.3	3.2	0.1	9.0	1.6	8.4	4.0	31.5	177
Bowling Green city........	10 199	33.5	14.5	5.7	10.0	6.8	0.4	22.6	0.3	15.3	1.0	18.6	5.3	49.7	100

Table A-5. Cities — Age, Ethnicity, and Household Structure

City	Households with Non-Hispanic White householder		Households with Black or African American householder		Households with American Indian and Alaska Native householder		Households with Asian, Hawaiian, and Pacific Islander householder		Households with Hispanic or Latino[1] householder		Foreign-born population	Place of birth (percent)			Percent in non-English speaking households	
	Number of households	Percent that are family households	Number of households	Percent that are family households	Number of households	Percent that are family households	Number of households	Percent that are family households	Number of households	Percent that are family households	Percent of total population that is foreign-born	Europe	Asia	Latin America	Linguistically isolated	Not linguistically isolated
	44	45	46	47	48	49	50	51	52	53	54	55	56	57	58	59
NEW YORK............	4 763 779	63.8	1 031 866	66.8	25 618	69.3	323 779	74.9	840 357	75.9	20.4	4.6	4.8	10.0	7.8	27.2
Albany city..............	27 211	39.9	10 208	58.1	151	52.3	901	49.6	1 646	53.3	8.6	2.7	2.5	2.3	2.8	15.7
Auburn city..............	10 721	57.3	292	80.1	67	53.7	29	55.2	241	50.2	3.3	1.5	0.8	0.7	0.7	12.5
Binghamton city............	18 087	48.9	1 513	61.2	63	55.6	520	46.2	659	55.5	8.5	3.6	2.9	1.2	3.4	16.0
Buffalo city..............	68 646	50.1	43 499	60.5	896	59.8	1 355	54.5	7 197	67.0	4.4	1.6	1.3	0.7	2.8	15.0
Elmira city..............	10 166	57.9	987	68.0	61	70.5	40	100.0	100	52.0	2.2	0.8	0.6	0.6	0.3	8.7
Freeport village	5 748	62.1	4 247	77.1	39	87.2	103	95.1	3 278	91.8	29.9	1.6	1.3	26.6	12.7	32.0
Glen Cove city............	7 143	66.4	557	77.9	29	100.0	294	88.4	1 366	87.3	27.9	9.3	4.3	14.0	10.8	37.4
Hempstead village........	1 951	54.1	9 072	75.0	69	24.6	216	65.7	3 656	88.7	33.2	1.4	0.7	30.5	13.4	33.3
Ithaca city..............	7 764	28.8	567	46.7	63	0.0	1 087	18.5	524	25.8	16.0	4.1	8.1	2.3	4.7	28.1
Jamestown city............	12 380	57.7	474	51.9	134	56.0	17	100.0	428	75.7	2.2	1.6	0.1	0.2	1.9	11.1
Lindenhurst village........	8 401	78.4	31	100.0	31	77.4	62	91.9	428	81.8	10.8	6.1	1.2	3.4	3.2	20.1
Long Beach city............	12 467	51.6	677	75.5	25	20.0	251	64.9	1 351	72.5	15.3	5.4	2.5	7.1	4.6	24.0
Middletown city............	6 340	50.0	1 255	63.1	38	100.0	113	69.9	1 629	81.6	13.5	2.9	1.4	9.1	7.9	27.5
Mount Vernon city........	7 732	54.3	14 264	69.1	108	75.0	547	74.4	2 122	75.4	29.1	4.4	1.8	21.7	5.0	25.7
Newburgh city	3 333	57.2	2 965	66.8	142	51.4	44	84.1	2 529	80.9	20.3	1.0	0.4	18.3	12.8	31.4
New Rochelle city........	16 290	64.8	5 038	64.5	78	93.6	852	70.2	3 735	81.5	27.3	5.6	3.2	17.1	10.1	30.8
New York city............	1 305 546	50.6	754 349	66.0	11 030	71.2	249 154	73.8	664 696	74.8	35.9	7.0	8.6	18.9	14.7	40.6
Niagara Falls city	18 988	58.6	4 128	64.8	258	60.1	78	52.6	358	58.9	5.0	2.2	0.5	0.4	1.2	10.7
North Tonawanda city ...	13 363	66.3	19	47.4	28	100.0	49	55.1	137	85.4	3.6	2.0	0.6	0.1	1.0	10.0
Port Chester village.......	5 087	59.0	763	63.7	38	100.0	199	78.4	3 226	85.8	41.4	5.2	1.9	34.0	22.3	40.0
Poughkeepsie city........	7 082	46.8	3 567	70.0	14	100.0	178	36.0	919	70.3	13.9	2.4	1.4	9.6	4.2	17.7
Rochester city............	47 011	41.9	29 447	66.6	488	61.9	1 437	64.0	8 729	71.2	7.3	2.1	2.1	2.2	4.5	19.2
Rome city	12 584	60.3	527	72.1	46	87.0	88	70.5	273	78.4	3.8	1.5	0.7	1.1	1.0	11.0
Saratoga Springs city....	10 129	55.7	287	54.7	45	71.1	78	67.9	168	60.7	3.2	1.3	0.9	0.5	0.5	10.5
Schenectady city..........	21 062	51.3	3 105	66.9	143	53.8	420	55.0	1 060	64.2	6.5	2.6	1.5	1.6	2.6	16.7
Spring Valley village......	2 612	59.2	3 187	80.7	24	100.0	470	90.0	808	93.6	43.0	5.1	6.3	31.0	19.7	46.4
Syracuse city............	40 185	46.0	13 410	63.4	652	63.0	1 905	47.2	2 224	66.0	7.6	2.5	3.3	1.2	3.9	14.1
Troy city..................	16 351	53.5	2 159	58.6	64	60.9	497	50.7	656	67.7	5.8	1.7	2.9	0.9	3.1	13.8
Utica city..................	20 195	55.8	2 864	60.5	58	51.7	405	73.1	1 097	69.9	11.9	8.8	2.2	0.7	8.1	18.1
Valley Stream village	9 912	73.4	694	93.5	27	100.0	604	100.0	1 135	90.8	19.6	4.8	5.5	8.6	3.1	33.2
Watertown city............	10 019	58.2	409	75.3	75	62.7	134	68.7	266	77.8	4.0	1.2	1.0	0.8	0.9	14.2
White Plains city........	13 126	56.5	3 323	56.6	56	46.4	929	63.0	3 140	84.0	29.3	5.6	4.1	18.8	10.8	32.6
Yonkers city..................	43 428	61.1	11 869	67.9	287	69.7	2 798	83.6	14 712	79.3	26.4	7.4	4.7	13.3	9.7	37.6
NORTH CAROLINA ...	2 321 636	68.9	627 854	69.1	34 775	75.1	33 599	75.7	93 499	80.3	5.3	0.7	1.2	3.0	2.5	9.4
Asheville city	24 531	52.6	4 764	61.0	95	80.0	227	80.6	736	66.3	5.2	1.7	0.9	2.3	2.8	9.4
Burlington city..............	12 556	61.9	4 421	67.5	120	75.8	227	90.3	943	84.3	9.6	0.6	1.5	7.1	5.7	10.5
Cary town	28 475	71.5	2 249	68.3	145	71.0	2 450	83.6	1 075	80.9	14.0	2.8	6.5	2.7	3.0	18.4
Chapel Hill town	14 145	43.7	2 028	45.2	82	78.0	1 071	66.9	477	63.7	11.2	2.7	5.2	2.1	3.4	17.1
Charlotte city	131 536	58.3	65 071	65.9	913	66.6	5 499	78.1	10 612	76.4	11.0	1.4	2.9	5.6	5.4	13.6
Concord city	16 629	71.8	2 931	68.3	144	86.1	160	94.4	998	87.9	7.1	0.5	0.8	5.6	4.5	9.4
Durham city	36 270	53.2	31 072	63.8	261	49.0	2 407	57.8	3 990	75.9	12.0	1.0	2.9	6.7	5.5	14.3
Fayetteville city............	24 496	64.1	19 480	66.5	521	61.6	953	70.9	2 396	75.1	5.6	1.7	2.0	1.6	1.3	16.0
Gastonia city	18 410	67.8	6 095	72.6	126	76.2	190	74.7	1 024	76.5	5.6	0.7	0.7	3.9	3.5	9.4
Goldsboro city	8 572	65.4	7 416	64.2	25	36.0	166	62.7	213	69.5	2.4	0.5	1.1	0.5	0.6	10.3
Greensboro city............	54 341	55.6	31 997	61.9	473	65.1	1 631	79.3	2 747	70.8	8.1	1.1	2.2	3.2	3.6	11.8
Greenville city..............	16 174	42.0	7 837	61.3	159	43.4	381	63.3	378	44.7	3.9	0.9	1.3	1.0	1.2	8.7
Hickory city	12 195	57.0	1 915	72.1	33	87.9	390	85.4	784	80.0	9.9	1.1	2.8	5.6	5.4	12.8
High Point city	21 395	64.0	9 879	71.2	183	73.2	748	87.7	1 130	79.9	7.5	0.8	2.8	3.5	4.4	10.2
Jacksonville city............	10 715	79.4	4 499	76.4	111	85.6	345	69.6	1 234	89.1	5.0	0.5	1.8	2.4	0.8	16.6
Kannapolis city	11 761	68.3	2 348	71.5	8	0.0	76	78.9	499	91.6	5.5	0.2	0.4	4.7	4.3	8.5
Monroe city	5 409	66.5	2 342	75.0	30	100.0	44	0.0	1 100	92.5	17.6	0.3	0.3	16.9	10.7	15.2
Raleigh city..................	74 863	50.7	28 245	62.8	351	56.4	3 000	65.5	4 965	75.1	11.7	1.4	3.2	5.3	5.7	13.6
Rocky Mount city..........	9 644	66.9	11 367	70.4	44	72.7	133	96.2	287	70.7	2.2	0.4	0.7	1.0	1.0	8.1
Salisbury city	6 376	58.6	3 587	64.2	37	70.3	111	82.9	240	74.6	4.9	0.5	1.0	2.9	3.6	7.9
Wilmington city	25 141	47.9	7 813	62.2	177	45.8	228	46.1	671	60.8	3.7	1.0	0.7	1.6	1.3	8.3
Wilson city	8 351	65.7	8 060	65.2	12	58.3	80	87.5	715	80.7	6.6	0.2	0.8	5.4	4.3	10.2
Winston-Salem city	44 709	56.8	26 379	65.5	238	63.4	847	64.8	3 922	83.5	8.3	0.8	0.9	6.1	5.4	9.8
NORTH DAKOTA.......	242 300	64.4	1 153	66.3	8 925	76.7	1 111	73.0	2 137	68.7	1.9	0.6	0.4	0.2	0.0	10.0
Bismarck city	22 378	62.2	43	53.5	436	77.1	115	77.4	99	39.4	1.6	0.6	0.4	0.3	1.3	11.0
Fargo city	37 340	53.0	298	68.1	526	47.7	509	66.6	339	61.7	4.0	1.4	1.3	0.2	1.4	8.4
Grand Forks city...........	18 446	56.6	176	38.6	392	63.8	147	89.8	380	60.8	3.3	0.9	0.9	0.3	0.8	9.5
Minot city	14 633	59.4	170	48.8	306	79.1	66	66.7	197	72.1	2.1	0.6	0.2	0.3	0.5	7.9
OHIO	3 797 198	68.1	489 208	64.0	10 348	65.1	46 043	69.1	62 102	70.9	3.0	1.2	1.1	0.4	1.1	9.0
Akron city	63 076	58.1	23 575	64.6	283	62.9	1 069	68.6	807	67.0	3.2	1.2	1.4	0.3	1.1	8.3
Barberton city	10 801	64.6	594	71.5	9	0.0	40	57.5	33	57.6	1.9	1.6	0.2	0.1	0.8	7.4
Beavercreek city............	13 294	79.2	192	77.6	39	46.2	401	80.5	87	89.7	4.7	1.1	3.1	0.3	1.1	9.2
Bowling Green city........	9 340	43.2	255	38.0	5	100.0	174	68.4	306	41.2	3.6	0.8	1.8	0.5	0.6	10.8

[1] Hispanic or Latino persons may be of any race.

Table A-5. Cities — **Age, Ethnicity, and Household Structure**

STATE Place code	City	Total population	Population by age (percent) Under 5 years	5 to 17 years	18 to 24 years	25 to 44 years	45 to 64 years	65 years and over	Median age	+/− U.S. percent under 18 years	+/− U.S. percent 65 years and over	Non-Hispanic White Total population	Age (percent) Under 18 years	65 years and over
		1	2	3	4	5	6	7	8	9	10	11	12	13
	OHIO—Cont'd													
39 09680	Brunswick city	33 391	7.2	20.6	8.2	32.3	23.5	8.2	34.6	2.1	-4.2	32 097	27.0	8.4
39 12000	Canton city	81 118	7.8	18.6	9.9	29.0	20.2	14.4	34.4	0.7	2.0	59 714	22.2	16.4
39 15000	Cincinnati city	330 662	7.2	17.3	12.8	31.8	18.6	12.3	32.1	-1.2	-0.1	173 427	17.0	15.2
39 16000	Cleveland city	478 393	8.1	20.4	9.5	30.7	18.8	12.6	33.0	2.8	0.2	186 368	20.2	15.7
39 16014	Cleveland Heights city ..	49 984	6.2	17.7	9.0	32.0	23.4	11.7	35.2	-1.8	-0.7	26 012	18.1	14.5
39 18000	Columbus city	711 644	7.4	16.7	13.9	35.4	17.8	8.8	30.6	-1.6	-3.6	476 117	20.2	10.0
39 19778	Cuyahoga Falls city.......	49 358	6.6	15.8	8.1	32.0	21.2	16.3	37.2	-3.3	3.9	46 989	21.9	16.8
39 21000	Dayton city	166 193	7.0	18.0	14.4	29.0	19.6	12.0	32.4	-0.7	-0.4	87 558	18.8	13.2
39 21434	Delaware city................	25 216	8.3	16.5	14.4	31.1	18.9	10.7	31.6	-0.9	-1.7	23 225	24.1	11.2
39 22694	Dublin city....................	31 478	8.7	24.0	4.7	32.9	24.1	5.7	35.4	7.0	-6.7	27 855	32.2	6.0
39 23380	East Cleveland city	27 217	7.4	22.2	9.0	26.7	21.4	13.3	33.9	3.9	0.9	1 235	6.0	48.7
39 25256	Elyria city....................	55 882	8.0	18.4	9.0	30.4	21.1	13.1	34.8	0.7	0.7	44 755	23.5	14.4
39 25704	Euclid city....................	52 717	6.3	16.0	6.8	30.8	20.9	19.2	38.9	-3.4	6.8	34 848	18.4	24.7
39 25914	Fairborn city	31 991	5.6	15.3	18.4	29.5	20.0	11.3	31.3	-4.8	-1.1	27 615	20.2	12.4
39 25970	Fairfield city.................	41 972	6.0	18.2	9.2	32.7	23.3	10.7	35.2	-1.5	-1.7	37 420	23.5	11.6
39 27048	Findlay city	39 241	7.3	16.6	12.0	28.8	21.2	14.0	35.1	-1.8	1.6	36 155	23.2	14.9
39 29106	Gahanna city................	32 523	7.3	21.6	6.8	31.8	24.1	8.5	36.5	3.2	-3.9	27 851	28.3	9.0
39 29428	Garfield Heights city......	30 621	6.1	18.0	7.5	28.7	21.0	18.6	38.3	-1.6	6.2	24 531	22.2	21.4
39 32592	Grove City city..............	27 020	7.7	21.1	7.5	31.7	21.3	10.7	35.0	3.1	-1.7	25 944	28.4	10.9
39 33012	Hamilton city................	60 662	7.4	18.4	9.9	29.7	20.2	14.4	34.9	0.1	2.0	53 404	24.6	15.3
39 36610	Huber Heights city........	38 272	7.3	20.0	8.3	31.4	23.7	9.3	34.4	1.6	-3.1	31 997	25.9	10.2
39 39872	Kent city......................	27 994	5.0	11.2	39.9	23.4	13.1	7.4	22.9	-9.5	-5.0	23 831	14.5	8.4
39 40040	Kettering city................	57 531	5.8	16.8	7.6	29.7	22.1	18.1	38.9	-3.1	5.7	54 485	22.1	18.8
39 41664	Lakewood city	56 646	6.0	15.1	9.2	37.6	19.9	12.2	34.2	-4.6	-0.2	51 730	20.0	12.9
39 41720	Lancaster city	35 266	7.7	16.7	9.4	29.4	20.7	16.2	35.9	-1.3	3.8	34 051	23.7	16.5
39 43554	Lima city......................	40 263	8.3	19.0	11.7	28.6	19.2	13.3	32.9	1.6	0.9	27 338	22.6	16.0
39 44856	Lorain city....................	68 655	7.8	20.6	8.9	28.2	20.5	13.9	34.4	2.7	1.5	42 109	21.5	18.2
39 47138	Mansfield city...............	49 402	7.3	16.6	8.8	30.4	21.3	15.6	36.4	-1.8	3.2	37 693	21.4	18.2
39 47306	Maple Heights city........	26 156	6.1	19.7	6.5	30.8	20.5	16.3	37.4	0.1	3.9	13 388	16.1	27.4
39 47754	Marion city...................	35 299	7.0	18.0	9.7	30.6	21.5	13.2	35.2	-0.7	0.8	31 509	24.9	14.2
39 48244	Massillon city................	31 384	6.9	18.5	7.6	28.4	22.3	16.3	37.6	-0.3	3.9	27 495	23.7	17.2
39 48790	Medina city	25 070	9.4	21.0	7.2	34.4	17.9	10.1	33.2	4.7	-2.3	23 362	29.8	10.6
39 49056	Mentor city...................	50 278	6.0	19.9	6.4	29.1	26.3	12.3	38.9	0.2	-0.1	48 725	25.7	12.4
39 49840	Middletown city.............	51 795	7.3	17.6	9.3	29.3	21.3	15.2	36.2	-0.8	2.8	44 866	23.3	16.0
39 54040	Newark city...................	46 115	7.3	17.8	9.4	29.2	21.5	14.8	35.9	-0.6	2.4	43 394	24.6	15.3
39 56882	North Olmsted city........	34 113	5.6	18.1	7.3	27.7	26.5	14.8	39.9	-2.0	2.4	31 514	22.9	15.8
39 57008	North Royalton city.......	28 648	5.2	19.0	7.8	30.4	25.6	12.0	38.6	-1.5	-0.4	27 279	23.9	12.3
39 61000	Parma city....................	85 655	5.8	16.4	7.0	29.6	21.6	19.6	39.4	-3.5	7.2	81 380	21.9	20.3
39 66390	Reynoldsburg city.........	32 225	7.4	19.2	7.9	32.2	22.9	10.4	35.4	0.9	-2.0	27 053	24.4	11.6
39 70380	Sandusky city	28 000	6.9	18.8	9.3	29.1	21.0	14.9	36.2	0.0	2.5	20 425	21.7	17.4
39 71682	Shaker Heights city	29 415	6.1	20.0	4.7	27.8	25.5	15.8	39.6	0.4	3.4	17 678	25.1	16.5
39 74118	Springfield city.............	65 322	7.7	17.9	11.6	27.0	20.3	15.4	34.5	-0.1	3.0	50 625	23.4	16.5
39 74944	Stow city......................	32 139	6.6	19.5	7.2	31.5	23.4	11.8	36.9	0.4	-0.6	30 456	25.7	12.3
39 75098	Strongsville city............	43 861	6.2	19.9	6.1	28.7	27.7	11.4	39.1	0.4	-1.0	40 918	25.8	11.9
39 77000	Toledo city....................	313 587	7.2	18.9	11.0	30.1	19.6	13.2	33.2	0.4	0.8	212 710	21.4	15.8
39 77554	Trotwood city................	27 545	6.4	19.9	7.2	27.1	23.2	16.2	38.4	0.6	3.8	10 559	16.7	30.1
39 79002	Upper Arlington city.......	33 605	5.6	19.1	4.4	25.2	27.1	18.6	42.6	-1.0	6.2	31 403	24.1	19.4
39 80892	Warren city	46 886	7.8	18.5	8.4	27.7	20.6	17.0	36.3	0.6	4.6	33 596	21.6	19.8
39 83342	Westerville city	35 408	6.1	21.0	9.1	27.4	25.9	10.6	37.8	1.4	-1.8	32 849	26.3	11.0
39 83622	Westlake city................	31 856	5.2	17.5	5.3	27.0	26.9	18.0	42.0	-3.0	5.6	29 165	22.0	19.4
39 88000	Youngstown city	82 026	7.1	18.6	10.1	26.6	20.2	17.4	36.4	0.0	5.0	40 217	17.3	24.0
39 88084	Zanesville city..............	25 690	8.0	19.0	9.1	28.5	20.0	15.3	34.8	1.3	2.9	21 694	24.7	16.4
40 00000	OKLAHOMA	3 450 654	6.8	19.0	10.4	28.4	22.2	13.2	35.5	0.1	0.8	2 556 373	22.6	15.6
40 04450	Bartlesville city	34 733	6.2	18.8	8.1	24.7	23.8	18.5	40.0	-0.7	6.1	27 870	22.0	21.1
40 09050	Broken Arrow city.........	74 956	8.0	22.9	7.9	32.4	21.3	7.5	33.3	5.2	-4.9	62 596	29.3	8.3
40 23200	Edmond city..................	68 514	7.1	20.3	11.2	30.3	22.3	8.8	33.6	1.7	-3.6	58 201	26.9	9.8
40 23950	Enid city.......................	47 094	7.0	17.8	9.6	27.8	21.5	16.3	37.2	-0.9	3.9	40 113	22.5	18.3
40 41850	Lawton city...................	93 030	8.1	19.4	15.5	31.8	15.9	9.3	28.9	1.8	-3.1	53 727	22.5	12.9
40 48350	Midwest City city	54 202	7.2	19.4	10.5	29.5	20.3	13.1	34.2	0.9	0.7	36 723	21.8	17.2
40 49200	Moore city....................	40 879	7.8	21.6	9.4	32.5	21.7	7.0	32.0	3.7	-5.4	33 636	27.4	7.9
40 50050	Muskogee city	38 317	7.3	18.4	9.5	26.2	20.8	17.9	36.9	0.0	5.5	22 935	19.2	22.5
40 52500	Norman city	95 693	5.9	15.2	21.3	29.2	19.4	9.0	29.3	-4.6	-3.4	76 913	19.9	10.4
40 55000	Oklahoma City city	505 963	7.3	18.2	10.6	30.9	21.4	11.5	34.0	-0.2	-0.9	326 949	20.6	14.9
40 59850	Ponca City city.............	25 960	7.6	18.6	8.7	25.2	22.3	17.7	38.2	0.5	5.3	21 473	24.0	20.0
40 66800	Shawnee city................	28 687	7.3	16.9	15.5	24.8	19.5	16.1	33.3	-1.5	3.7	21 727	20.5	18.9
40 70300	Stillwater city	38 968	4.3	10.6	38.0	24.7	13.7	8.7	23.9	-10.8	-3.7	31 667	14.1	10.1
40 75000	Tulsa city.....................	393 051	7.2	17.4	11.0	30.3	21.3	12.8	34.5	-1.1	0.4	263 992	20.1	16.4

Table A-5. Cities — Age, Ethnicity, and Household Structure

City	Black or African American Total population	Under 18 years	65 years and over	American Indian and Alaska Native Total population	Under 18 years	65 years and over	Asian, Hawaiian, and Pacific Islander Total population	Under 18 years	65 years and over	Hispanic or Latino[1] Total population	Under 18 years	65 years and over	Two or more races Total population	Under 18 years	65 years and over
	14	15	16	17	18	19	20	21	22	23	24	25	26	27	28
OHIO—Cont'd															
Brunswick city	262	42.0	3.8	35	34.3	8.6	347	37.2	2.0	306	48.4	0.0	369	58.8	5.7
Canton city	17 206	36.9	9.2	282	28.7	0.0	336	11.6	14.3	1 058	37.1	9.5	2 610	50.6	4.9
Cincinnati city	141 616	33.2	9.7	788	20.1	3.6	5 084	14.0	3.9	4 089	27.5	3.5	5 648	38.4	6.0
Cleveland city	242 481	33.3	11.7	1 406	32.6	3.1	7 074	18.3	7.6	34 554	38.5	4.0	10 604	44.6	6.2
Cleveland Heights city ..	20 717	30.4	9.2	90	34.4	17.8	1 358	11.8	6.5	672	31.3	3.0	1 100	43.2	4.3
Columbus city	171 493	32.5	7.4	2 666	27.2	4.1	24 998	20.2	3.4	17 368	30.1	2.8	21 068	44.3	3.1
Cuyahoga Falls city	1 033	39.7	4.8	133	22.6	4.5	461	28.0	2.4	354	26.8	7.3	398	32.2	8.0
Dayton city	71 860	32.0	11.2	529	15.9	5.3	1 064	12.7	6.2	2 079	28.1	2.9	3 221	42.0	4.7
Delaware city	944	28.8	6.0	41	0.0	17.1	301	25.6	3.0	192	22.4	7.3	479	42.6	2.5
Dublin city	453	34.4	0.9	22	54.5	0.0	2 497	33.1	3.3	275	45.8	3.3	438	55.9	3.0
East Cleveland city	25 291	30.9	11.5	21	0.0	28.6	141	5.7	7.8	150	14.7	34.0	422	32.5	11.4
Elyria city	8 300	34.2	9.5	211	48.3	0.0	183	7.1	16.4	1 396	48.3	1.5	1 277	62.6	3.1
Euclid city	16 114	28.5	8.8	17	0.0	0.0	304	20.1	7.6	716	44.3	2.5	829	44.4	6.4
Fairborn city	1 945	22.7	2.9	145	22.1	0.0	899	11.1	2.9	577	30.0	5.2	906	39.4	8.6
Fairfield city	2 580	27.2	3.7	116	12.1	0.0	966	22.2	3.3	516	40.1	2.5	394	54.8	6.1
Findlay city	462	21.9	3.7	111	22.5	0.0	617	21.1	0.0	1 525	37.9	6.5	536	51.9	4.3
Gahanna city	2 772	29.7	7.2	71	0.0	11.3	1 000	29.0	3.0	374	47.1	0.0	463	47.7	3.9
Garfield Heights city	5 039	31.8	7.7	80	18.8	10.0	383	20.9	7.6	348	36.8	2.9	269	40.5	3.7
Grove City city	385	42.1	4.2	95	16.8	0.0	89	9.0	15.7	302	40.4	3.0	266	49.6	7.1
Hamilton city	4 470	33.2	10.6	266	29.7	1.5	345	34.2	6.1	1 403	33.9	2.6	901	46.9	3.0
Huber Heights city	3 656	29.7	6.3	121	9.9	3.3	928	29.5	2.7	699	42.1	2.0	914	57.5	2.7
Kent city	2 618	25.6	2.4	81	19.8	0.0	625	12.3	0.0	343	22.7	1.5	464	41.4	0.0
Kettering city	939	34.0	3.1	130	26.2	16.2	783	16.3	4.9	519	29.3	9.6	722	45.6	3.9
Lakewood city	943	20.7	6.3	80	22.5	6.3	804	22.9	5.2	1 248	33.7	6.0	1 922	40.9	3.5
Lancaster city	220	32.7	15.0	186	30.6	3.8	227	57.7	0.0	284	35.9	8.1	383	53.0	5.2
Lima city	10 771	35.2	8.3	84	4.8	3.6	205	28.8	0.0	701	35.1	5.4	1 181	61.8	1.5
Lorain city	10 505	39.4	7.4	215	45.6	5.6	350	10.4	0.4	14 189	39.2	6.9	3 404	55.0	4.4
Mansfield city	9 183	29.2	8.2	210	40.0	1.9	371	22.1	6.7	570	32.6	6.7	1 465	49.3	4.2
Maple Heights city	11 624	35.7	4.8	66	42.4	0.0	478	26.2	2.1	372	50.5	4.8	326	43.6	10.1
Marion city	2 304	21.0	4.9	103	4.9	7.8	280	29.3	2.5	621	27.5	5.2	491	45.6	5.9
Massillon city	2 932	32.7	10.8	53	7.5	15.1	111	4.5	12.6	342	54.4	4.7	462	61.5	5.2
Medina city	581	27.5	11.0	31	0.0	0.0	327	35.5	2.8	383	49.1	0.0	342	47.4	0.0
Mentor city	300	28.3	11.7	12	50.0	0.0	572	27.3	10.8	429	28.7	0.7	198	48.5	5.1
Middletown city	5 591	33.1	12.3	86	37.2	0.0	137	22.6	3.6	362	37.0	8.8	757	50.3	0.8
Newark city	1 274	27.2	10.0	94	42.6	5.3	304	16.1	6.6	313	34.5	8.3	676	50.3	2.8
North Olmsted city	314	18.8	4.8	73	15.1	5.5	946	31.7	3.7	549	32.2	0.7	685	43.6	3.2
North Royalton city	264	35.6	0.0	22	59.1	0.0	549	20.9	7.5	246	21.1	0.0	267	47.9	10.1
Parma city	690	31.6	1.4	68	2.9	10.3	1 424	17.6	5.5	1 268	28.9	6.0	950	43.2	7.7
Reynoldsburg city	3 427	36.2	4.1	82	30.5	0.0	416	20.0	2.4	593	43.5	3.5	735	61.6	2.7
Sandusky city	5 924	34.9	9.6	71	29.6	8.5	80	24.7	5.0	600	33.4	3.3	795	55.5	3.4
Shaker Heights city	9 882	27.0	16.3	28	46.4	0.0	819	26.3	4.4	276	29.3	8.3	706	41.4	6.4
Springfield city	11 706	30.5	13.3	284	20.1	7.0	370	28.6	2.2	838	34.7	7.4	1 560	57.9	4.9
Stow city	475	36.2	3.2	119	20.2	0.0	569	23.9	0.0	265	29.4	7.5	303	58.7	5.9
Strongsville city	662	30.7	3.9	4	0.0	0.0	1 494	26.6	6.1	464	40.5	2.2	390	39.2	3.6
Toledo city	73 421	34.8	8.6	1 139	22.0	5.2	3 059	15.4	4.3	17 241	42.6	4.8	9 219	52.6	4.9
Trotwood city	16 206	31.9	7.3	53	0.0	9.4	21	0.0	33.3	120	14.2	5.0	586	41.8	11.1
Upper Arlington city	201	30.3	5.5	64	7.8	21.9	1 020	25.8	8.7	376	42.3	0.0	556	45.0	3.6
Warren city	11 607	36.9	10.5	62	0.0	6.5	224	28.1	3.6	390	33.1	4.4	1 081	53.5	4.0
Westerville city	1 090	32.8	6.1	40	27.5	0.0	444	14.4	9.5	389	49.1	4.9	591	55.2	6.3
Westlake city	363	32.2	0.0	36	16.7	0.0	1 359	23.0	5.2	392	37.2	2.6	592	50.2	2.5
Youngstown city	35 194	33.0	11.6	256	19.1	4.3	330	29.7	6.1	4 088	35.7	9.1	2 630	46.9	6.9
Zanesville city	2 774	35.0	10.6	70	25.7	0.0	119	45.4	0.0	203	43.8	2.5	732	46.4	7.2
OKLAHOMA	258 532	32.4	7.3	266 801	35.7	6.9	47 386	23.1	4.5	177 768	39.0	2.8	168 426	39.7	7.4
Bartlesville city	1 293	38.3	6.1	2 358	33.5	8.3	256	22.3	2.3	849	33.0	4.8	2 180	43.3	9.8
Broken Arrow city	2 792	35.7	1.4	3 018	37.7	4.4	1 418	33.5	2.3	2 770	44.9	2.2	2 644	43.1	4.6
Edmond city	2 884	33.8	1.9	1 248	29.9	5.6	2 126	12.6	2.6	2 052	38.1	2.6	2 267	37.6	5.9
Enid city	1 796	34.7	6.1	1 081	35.0	5.4	725	25.7	9.0	2 126	41.8	2.4	1 502	46.7	4.7
Lawton city	21 790	34.3	4.0	3 323	29.9	6.4	2 463	16.6	7.0	8 768	35.4	3.6	4 823	47.5	3.3
Midwest City city	10 394	38.7	3.2	1 904	34.0	5.9	1 080	17.8	7.0	2 123	32.3	5.3	2 435	46.6	6.9
Moore city	1 004	37.1	2.4	1 518	34.1	3.9	585	26.2	5.8	2 133	42.3	2.7	2 523	45.9	1.9
Muskogee city	6 844	34.3	13.8	4 688	35.4	9.0	252	30.2	21.4	1 263	34.9	1.1	2 450	39.2	10.4
Norman city	3 881	25.1	1.1	3 908	25.1	4.5	3 481	14.1	1.7	3 629	30.5	2.8	4 399	34.6	5.2
Oklahoma City city	76 478	32.9	7.6	16 945	31.7	4.3	17 476	25.3	4.6	50 849	39.5	2.3	22 988	41.8	5.9
Ponca City city	743	29.5	8.2	1 505	36.3	6.2	183	21.9	1.1	1 138	44.0	2.2	1 116	43.4	9.3
Shawnee city	1 217	35.7	7.1	3 710	38.2	6.6	346	19.4	1.4	520	35.2	7.5	1 302	38.6	8.9
Stillwater city	1 763	22.0	1.9	1 497	20.0	3.9	1 869	8.3	1.0	1 097	25.3	1.3	1 241	22.8	5.8
Tulsa city	60 286	34.7	6.7	17 642	29.9	6.3	6 954	25.4	2.8	28 097	34.9	2.2	18 856	38.1	6.5

[1] Hispanic or Latino persons may be of any race.

Table A-5. Cities — **Age, Ethnicity, and Household Structure**

City	Total households	Family households (percent)						Nonfamily households (percent)						Percent of householders 65 years and over who live alone	Grandparents who are responsible for the care of their grandchildren
		Married-couple family households			Other family households			Two or more unrelated persons		Male living alone		Female living alone			
		Total	With children	Householder 65 years or over	Total	With children	Householder 65 years or over	Total	Householder 65 years or over	Total	Householder 65 years or over	Total	Householder 65 years or over		
	29	30	31	32	33	34	35	36	37	38	39	40	41	42	43
OHIO—Cont'd															
Brunswick city	11 885	64.8	31.9	6.9	12.9	7.0	1.7	4.3	0.2	8.2	1.2	9.7	4.1	37.6	104
Canton city	32 564	38.5	16.5	7.4	22.6	13.8	3.3	5.9	0.3	13.1	2.9	20.0	9.7	53.3	789
Cincinnati city	147 979	27.1	11.4	4.9	22.1	14.4	2.6	8.0	0.4	19.0	2.8	23.8	8.5	59.3	3 202
Cleveland city	190 725	29.3	12.9	5.9	29.9	17.7	4.3	5.7	0.6	16.2	3.3	19.0	7.8	50.9	7 039
Cleveland Heights city	20 932	41.8	18.5	7.2	17.0	9.2	2.6	8.6	0.5	13.3	1.9	19.3	6.6	45.1	530
Columbus city	301 800	36.4	17.0	4.8	18.6	11.6	1.7	10.7	0.3	15.6	1.6	18.6	5.5	51.1	6 263
Cuyahoga Falls city	21 706	49.3	20.5	10.4	12.4	7.1	2.3	5.7	0.2	12.2	2.7	20.4	9.9	49.4	244
Dayton city	67 476	31.5	13.0	6.0	24.6	14.7	3.0	7.0	0.4	16.2	3.1	20.7	8.8	55.9	2 402
Delaware city	9 552	51.8	24.5	7.4	14.5	10.4	1.1	6.8	0.6	10.3	1.7	16.6	7.0	49.1	139
Dublin city	11 232	71.3	43.3	5.4	6.6	4.0	0.4	3.4	0.2	9.0	0.6	9.8	3.3	38.8	24
East Cleveland city	11 222	22.5	8.0	6.0	34.9	21.1	4.4	4.6	0.7	15.7	3.2	22.3	8.4	51.0	390
Elyria city	22 462	47.4	20.1	9.0	18.8	11.5	2.4	5.2	0.4	12.0	2.6	16.5	7.9	47.0	714
Euclid city	24 312	36.3	15.5	9.3	19.2	10.3	3.2	4.7	0.5	15.5	4.0	24.3	11.9	55.2	286
Fairborn city	13 575	42.5	17.1	8.2	16.0	9.9	1.3	10.6	0.2	14.3	2.1	16.6	6.8	47.9	245
Fairfield city	16 959	55.2	24.9	8.2	11.9	8.0	0.8	6.1	0.1	11.9	1.0	14.9	4.9	39.4	223
Findlay city	15 998	50.5	21.7	10.1	13.0	8.5	1.0	6.3	0.2	13.1	1.6	17.1	8.4	46.8	145
Gahanna city	11 971	62.9	34.1	6.5	11.7	7.0	1.1	4.5	0.1	7.5	1.2	13.4	5.5	46.5	143
Garfield Heights city	12 333	48.3	20.6	11.1	18.0	8.1	4.1	3.7	0.3	10.7	3.3	19.3	11.7	49.2	354
Grove City city	10 223	59.4	29.9	7.4	13.7	8.8	1.6	3.9	0.3	9.3	1.8	13.7	6.7	47.9	151
Hamilton city	24 246	46.7	20.5	9.3	19.0	11.9	2.8	4.7	0.4	12.5	2.9	17.1	8.8	48.4	749
Huber Heights city	14 415	59.6	27.8	7.5	15.4	9.1	1.7	4.6	0.1	8.3	1.8	12.1	5.0	42.4	350
Kent city	9 784	34.4	15.0	5.7	16.6	12.2	0.9	17.1	0.1	11.1	1.3	20.7	6.4	53.4	66
Kettering city	25 651	49.2	20.1	12.5	12.3	7.1	1.8	5.2	0.3	13.1	2.7	20.2	10.1	46.8	302
Lakewood city	26 721	34.0	15.8	4.9	12.9	7.3	1.7	9.5	0.3	18.9	2.9	24.7	9.0	63.2	125
Lancaster city	14 791	48.5	21.0	9.7	16.2	10.4	2.2	5.1	0.2	11.1	2.8	19.2	11.1	53.4	161
Lima city	15 446	37.1	15.0	8.3	25.6	17.6	2.4	5.0	0.3	12.7	2.8	19.6	10.0	53.6	439
Lorain city	26 422	44.5	18.8	9.5	24.0	15.3	3.7	4.3	0.4	11.0	2.3	16.3	8.2	43.6	776
Mansfield city	20 182	41.8	16.4	9.3	18.2	12.0	2.5	5.5	0.3	13.6	3.1	20.8	11.2	54.1	540
Maple Heights city	10 493	46.0	20.6	10.3	20.9	11.1	3.6	3.2	0.2	12.3	3.4	17.6	9.4	47.7	380
Marion city	13 570	47.0	20.7	9.0	18.3	11.5	1.8	5.1	0.4	10.6	1.8	19.1	10.1	51.4	385
Massillon city	12 720	50.2	20.2	11.0	16.3	10.0	2.2	4.2	0.3	10.7	2.6	18.6	10.2	48.8	307
Medina city	9 377	60.1	34.6	6.3	11.4	7.8	0.7	3.3	0.0	9.2	2.0	16.1	8.2	58.8	73
Mentor city	18 758	64.3	30.1	10.3	11.6	5.7	1.7	3.6	0.4	8.3	1.9	12.3	6.5	40.2	205
Middletown city	21 538	46.1	19.2	9.7	19.1	11.8	3.0	5.1	0.4	12.1	2.4	17.5	9.1	46.6	597
Newark city	19 280	46.0	20.4	8.6	17.5	10.7	2.3	5.3	0.2	12.4	3.0	18.8	9.7	53.1	295
North Olmsted city	13 574	58.2	24.4	11.6	11.5	5.6	2.0	3.9	0.4	10.3	2.0	16.2	8.3	42.3	273
North Royalton city	11 266	58.8	27.4	8.7	9.9	4.0	2.2	4.7	0.2	11.0	2.1	15.6	5.8	41.5	37
Parma city	35 178	53.6	22.2	13.3	13.1	5.8	2.9	4.2	0.3	11.3	3.1	17.8	11.0	46.0	377
Reynoldsburg city	12 788	53.8	25.2	8.2	15.6	10.6	1.7	5.6	0.2	9.8	1.5	15.2	5.5	40.8	165
Sandusky city	11 884	41.0	17.3	7.6	19.8	13.2	2.6	5.3	0.5	15.0	3.5	18.9	9.4	54.7	371
Shaker Heights city	12 266	49.8	24.2	10.3	15.7	9.0	2.2	4.1	0.4	9.8	2.7	20.6	10.6	50.9	156
Springfield city	26 229	41.4	17.8	8.5	20.8	13.0	2.2	5.7	0.4	12.8	2.9	19.3	11.2	55.8	617
Stow city	12 288	61.8	30.5	8.7	9.5	5.5	1.5	4.9	0.2	10.2	1.8	13.6	6.5	44.5	108
Strongsville city	16 207	67.9	31.7	9.8	8.7	4.2	1.1	3.5	0.2	8.2	1.8	11.7	5.8	40.5	187
Toledo city	128 842	39.2	17.1	7.8	21.2	13.4	2.4	6.9	0.4	14.5	2.8	18.2	8.4	51.3	2 893
Trotwood city	11 146	42.4	16.2	9.2	24.0	15.3	3.4	3.8	0.5	11.4	2.6	18.5	8.8	46.4	495
Upper Arlington city	14 002	59.2	27.0	14.2	9.0	4.4	1.8	3.7	0.4	8.7	2.6	19.4	10.2	43.8	126
Warren city	19 292	39.3	16.1	9.5	23.6	15.0	3.7	4.1	0.3	13.7	3.5	19.3	10.7	51.1	503
Westerville city	12 678	65.7	33.2	8.0	10.4	6.6	0.9	3.0	0.2	7.0	1.2	14.0	6.8	47.1	106
Westlake city	12 845	57.8	25.3	10.5	6.7	3.1	1.2	3.9	0.5	10.9	2.8	20.6	10.4	52.0	63
Youngstown city	32 207	34.0	12.5	9.9	27.9	15.5	5.1	4.2	0.5	14.8	4.2	19.1	10.5	48.8	1 339
Zanesville city	10 593	40.1	18.2	8.0	20.6	14.0	2.4	6.0	0.4	11.4	2.4	21.8	12.4	57.8	217
OKLAHOMA	1 343 506	54.3	24.0	9.9	14.7	8.9	1.9	4.3	0.3	11.3	2.4	15.3	7.8	45.7	39 279
Bartlesville city	14 584	55.4	22.6	13.9	12.6	8.0	1.5	2.4	0.3	10.7	3.0	18.8	10.7	46.6	215
Broken Arrow city	26 125	69.8	38.3	6.8	11.8	8.2	0.8	2.8	0.2	5.8	1.0	9.7	4.0	39.0	554
Edmond city	25 353	62.7	32.4	7.6	12.2	7.6	0.9	4.6	0.0	8.0	1.1	12.5	5.0	41.9	429
Enid city	18 987	53.3	23.1	10.9	13.1	8.5	1.6	4.6	0.2	11.2	2.7	17.9	9.4	48.9	421
Lawton city	31 869	52.4	28.1	7.1	18.8	12.7	2.2	4.4	0.2	11.6	2.0	12.8	5.9	45.2	1 033
Midwest City city	22 259	46.8	19.6	9.2	20.4	12.9	2.3	4.4	0.2	12.9	2.4	15.5	7.6	46.1	642
Moore city	14 841	60.5	31.2	5.9	17.5	10.9	1.7	3.4	0.3	8.2	1.3	10.5	3.8	39.5	403
Muskogee city	15 531	46.1	18.8	10.9	18.5	10.6	3.6	4.2	0.2	11.3	2.6	19.9	11.9	49.8	442
Norman city	38 864	46.1	21.3	6.0	12.4	7.1	1.2	11.2	0.1	14.4	1.7	15.9	5.4	49.1	465
Oklahoma City city	204 493	46.4	20.8	7.8	17.1	10.5	1.8	5.7	0.3	13.7	2.0	17.0	6.9	47.5	5 218
Ponca City city	10 667	51.6	22.8	11.9	14.7	8.6	2.3	3.9	0.1	11.0	3.0	18.9	11.5	50.3	309
Shawnee city	11 369	47.0	19.0	10.5	18.1	10.4	2.8	4.6	0.6	11.0	3.1	19.2	10.9	50.2	453
Stillwater city	15 601	36.7	15.4	5.6	10.5	6.2	0.5	18.1	0.3	16.9	1.1	17.8	5.4	50.4	143
Tulsa city	165 881	43.9	19.0	8.3	16.3	10.1	1.8	6.0	0.3	14.9	2.2	19.0	7.6	48.9	3 482

Table A-5. Cities — Age, Ethnicity, and Household Structure

City	Households with Non-Hispanic White householder — Number of households	Percent that are family households	Households with Black or African American householder — Number of households	Percent that are family households	Households with American Indian and Alaska Native householder — Number of households	Percent that are family households	Households with Asian, Hawaiian, and Pacific Islander householder — Number of households	Percent that are family households	Households with Hispanic or Latino[1] householder — Number of households	Percent that are family households	Foreign-born population — Percent of total population that is foreign-born	Place of birth (percent) Europe	Asia	Latin America	Percent in non-English speaking households — Linguistically isolated	Not linguistically isolated
	44	45	46	47	48	49	50	51	52	53	54	55	56	57	58	59
OHIO—Cont'd																
Brunswick city	11 582	77.7	54	92.6	15	60.0	90	76.7	69	76.8	4.3	2.6	0.9	0.3	1.3	10.6
Canton city	24 969	60.1	6 374	65.4	130	34.6	90	78.9	309	62.5	1.7	0.7	0.4	0.4	0.6	7.8
Cincinnati city	83 124	44.6	58 579	56.2	377	40.3	2 331	41.5	1 479	44.4	3.8	1.2	1.3	0.6	1.5	9.1
Cleveland city	83 827	51.8	91 266	64.3	495	65.5	2 529	61.5	10 485	74.4	4.5	1.8	1.3	1.0	3.0	13.8
Cleveland Heights city ..	12 309	50.9	7 411	73.7	52	71.2	615	31.4	232	66.8	8.3	3.9	2.7	0.8	2.8	13.9
Columbus city	212 423	52.2	67 738	62.8	1 065	60.5	9 501	58.4	5 359	60.7	6.7	1.0	3.1	1.0	2.6	11.7
Cuyahoga Falls city	20 829	61.8	424	56.6	62	62.9	151	88.1	124	47.6	3.1	1.6	1.1	0.2	0.9	7.1
Dayton city	36 975	52.4	28 361	61.3	198	40.4	387	45.7	630	57.3	2.0	0.5	0.5	0.5	0.7	7.2
Delaware city	8 847	66.6	375	53.3	21	100.0	99	67.7	76	42.1	1.6	0.5	0.6	0.2	0.8	5.2
Dublin city	10 089	77.6	199	58.8	10	100.0	804	85.3	65	56.9	9.1	1.5	6.6	0.1	2.9	13.4
East Cleveland city	654	39.9	10 280	58.8	14	0.0	67	43.3	63	58.7	2.9	1.7	0.6	0.4	1.9	7.0
Elyria city	18 631	65.5	3 062	73.2	66	60.6	84	46.4	386	53.6	1.5	0.7	0.3	0.3	0.5	7.1
Euclid city	16 405	56.3	7 373	53.7	17	100.0	112	57.1	157	65.0	5.3	3.8	0.6	0.4	2.2	12.3
Fairborn city	12 043	59.5	671	51.4	64	29.7	368	44.0	184	53.8	4.6	0.9	2.9	0.4	1.9	8.5
Fairfield city	15 173	67.5	1 083	62.0	50	48.0	354	74.6	177	54.8	3.6	0.7	2.1	0.5	0.7	8.3
Findlay city	14 956	64.0	202	32.2	72	68.1	242	63.6	445	58.9	2.7	0.4	1.5	0.4	1.2	7.8
Gahanna city	10 485	73.6	929	79.5	51	84.3	318	86.5	91	84.6	4.9	1.5	2.3	0.6	1.2	9.6
Garfield Heights city	10 100	65.1	1 891	72.0	17	52.9	123	77.2	110	72.7	4.4	2.7	1.1	0.3	1.1	11.9
Grove City city	9 879	73.3	131	68.7	25	100.0	40	77.5	104	63.5	1.2	0.4	0.3	0.3	0.2	7.3
Hamilton city	21 698	65.9	1 753	62.9	131	48.1	109	78.9	337	73.9	2.2	0.3	0.4	1.4	1.2	7.2
Huber Heights city	12 342	74.1	1 381	81.0	35	74.3	308	83.8	193	81.3	3.2	1.0	1.7	0.3	0.7	9.6
Kent city	8 575	49.9	749	65.6	39	15.4	222	46.4	82	46.3	4.4	1.2	2.5	0.3	1.0	10.0
Kettering city	24 552	61.6	373	53.9	61	73.8	263	73.0	178	52.2	2.7	1.2	1.2	0.2	0.8	7.8
Lakewood city	24 854	46.8	501	32.7	48	50.0	346	47.1	393	52.4	8.7	4.9	2.7	0.5	2.7	14.5
Lancaster city	14 420	64.8	71	60.6	94	66.0	45	40.0	95	75.8	0.9	0.5	0.3	0.1	0.3	6.2
Lima city	11 236	60.6	3 775	67.2	37	54.1	54	88.9	209	71.8	1.1	0.3	0.4	0.2	0.3	6.2
Lorain city	17 760	65.9	3 705	69.0	61	88.5	119	79.0	4 332	78.5	3.6	1.6	0.5	1.4	3.6	22.7
Mansfield city	16 392	59.0	3 132	63.0	53	84.9	121	90.1	149	73.2	2.2	1.3	0.6	0.1	0.6	7.3
Maple Heights city	6 093	62.2	4 102	73.3	31	100.0	134	82.1	106	78.3	2.9	1.2	1.4	0.3	1.6	9.6
Marion city	12 629	65.4	562	62.1	27	0.0	86	81.4	199	67.3	1.5	0.5	0.5	0.5	0.7	5.1
Massillon city	11 480	66.5	1 025	68.4	24	0.0	46	76.1	69	60.9	1.3	0.9	0.4	0.1	0.5	7.2
Medina city	8 854	71.4	225	68.0	23	43.5	77	100.0	107	73.8	2.7	1.3	0.9	0.2	0.3	8.2
Mentor city	18 348	75.5	99	91.9	6	100.0	153	92.8	98	93.9	3.8	2.1	0.9	0.2	0.7	9.8
Middletown city	18 914	65.2	2 227	65.5	43	83.7	61	52.5	116	70.7	1.0	0.4	0.5	0.3	0.2	6.2
Newark city	18 314	63.5	555	58.4	18	44.4	113	58.4	106	60.4	1.1	0.4	0.5	0.1	0.3	6.0
North Olmsted city	12 726	69.8	178	47.8	18	100.0	303	83.8	193	60.1	7.8	3.8	3.2	0.5	1.8	13.8
North Royalton city	10 909	68.5	59	49.2	9	100.0	137	94.2	70	71.4	6.8	4.9	1.7	0.1	2.0	15.0
Parma city	33 637	66.7	289	43.3	21	100.0	547	69.8	436	75.0	9.1	6.7	1.7	0.3	3.4	15.2
Reynoldsburg city	11 060	68.5	1 224	76.6	32	71.9	138	75.4	178	70.2	3.6	1.2	1.2	0.4	0.5	10.1
Sandusky city	9 173	68.6	2 246	66.9	26	76.9	42	38.1	257	68.1	1.7	1.0	0.3	0.3	0.7	7.3
Shaker Heights city	7 502	63.4	4 100	68.3	8	100.0	308	74.4	108	56.5	7.2	2.6	2.7	0.6	1.3	11.8
Springfield city	20 496	61.9	4 837	64.2	91	46.2	135	68.1	239	60.3	1.2	0.4	0.4	0.2	0.2	7.4
Stow city	11 700	71.0	187	62.6	68	83.8	228	90.8	84	67.9	3.7	1.2	1.9	0.3	0.7	8.3
Strongsville city	15 318	76.2	251	82.1	4	100.0	412	87.4	123	91.9	6.5	3.1	2.6	0.3	0.8	14.2
Toledo city	92 309	58.6	27 992	64.6	501	69.9	1 223	55.5	4 997	72.3	3.0	0.6	1.2	0.7	1.1	11.3
Trotwood city	4 735	58.7	6 119	72.9	39	28.2	17	58.8	78	44.9	1.2	0.5	0.1	0.2	0.4	7.9
Upper Arlington city	13 327	67.6	69	73.9	26	73.1	341	85.3	111	82.9	6.3	2.0	3.1	0.5	1.0	12.3
Warren city	14 636	60.4	4 206	71.2	46	50.0	59	62.7	128	71.9	1.9	1.4	0.3	0.1	0.8	8.5
Westerville city	11 979	75.9	334	78.4	0	X	140	77.1	111	68.5	3.2	1.1	1.4	0.3	0.6	8.4
Westlake city	12 011	63.2	136	86.8	12	100.0	451	90.7	115	65.2	8.4	3.6	4.0	0.4	1.4	16.9
Youngstown city	17 539	59.1	12 667	64.5	96	67.7	77	76.6	1 302	71.1	2.0	1.1	0.4	0.4	1.5	12.7
Zanesville city	9 203	59.1	1 027	72.2	33	78.8	46	84.8	79	75.9	0.9	0.3	0.4	0.1	0.3	5.0
OKLAHOMA	1 056 941	68.5	92 704	66.8	85 177	74.4	14 862	67.2	47 397	78.1	3.8	0.5	1.2	1.9	1.8	9.8
Bartlesville city	12 262	68.2	444	58.6	879	68.1	51	78.4	201	77.1	2.2	0.4	0.7	1.0	1.2	8.3
Broken Arrow city	22 592	81.4	932	79.7	952	85.9	351	92.3	695	83.5	4.1	1.0	1.4	1.1	0.8	10.6
Edmond city	22 135	76.1	869	78.4	453	72.8	758	44.1	442	79.2	5.2	0.7	3.1	0.8	1.7	10.3
Enid city	16 878	65.7	601	65.2	362	74.3	215	71.2	638	82.9	3.1	0.5	0.8	1.5	1.4	9.7
Lawton city	20 151	69.0	6 888	76.6	1 110	66.8	673	70.0	2 452	78.7	6.2	2.2	1.9	1.7	1.5	18.9
Midwest City city	16 029	66.7	3 832	71.4	646	73.4	362	58.8	780	59.0	3.3	0.8	1.6	0.7	0.8	10.1
Moore city	12 721	77.3	329	83.0	488	77.7	218	94.5	609	83.7	2.9	0.5	1.3	0.9	0.8	9.0
Muskogee city	10 200	61.8	2 563	68.6	1 617	69.1	64	84.4	353	64.0	2.4	0.3	0.6	1.4	1.1	7.7
Norman city	32 279	59.0	1 414	53.2	1 358	64.3	1 329	46.2	1 141	59.5	6.0	0.9	3.2	1.1	2.2	12.0
Oklahoma City city	144 390	61.4	29 134	65.1	5 713	66.7	5 625	72.5	13 753	80.0	8.5	0.9	2.9	4.6	4.3	13.7
Ponca City city	9 150	65.3	342	59.9	503	74.2	60	73.3	305	78.7	2.4	0.3	0.6	1.4	1.6	6.4
Shawnee city	9 128	64.2	413	64.4	1 190	70.3	79	73.4	163	72.4	1.6	0.2	0.6	0.5	0.8	8.1
Stillwater city	12 995	47.9	675	51.4	589	43.5	693	37.1	311	47.9	7.3	0.6	4.9	0.9	2.6	10.3
Tulsa city	120 707	58.2	23 022	65.2	6 495	61.8	2 376	67.3	8 011	73.0	6.5	0.7	1.7	3.8	3.3	10.4

[1] Hispanic or Latino persons may be of any race.

Table A-5. Cities — Age, Ethnicity, and Household Structure

STATE Place code	City	Population by age (percent) Total population	Under 5 years	5 to 17 years	18 to 24 years	25 to 44 years	45 to 64 years	65 years and over	Median age	+/- U.S. percent under 18 years	+/- U.S. percent 65 years and over	Non-Hispanic White Total population	Under 18 years	65 years and over
		1	2	3	4	5	6	7	8	9	10	11	12	13
41 00000	OREGON	3 421 399	6.5	18.2	9.5	29.3	23.7	12.8	36.3	-1.0	0.4	2 857 100	22.6	14.5
41 01000	Albany city..................	40 848	7.9	18.3	9.4	29.5	22.1	12.7	34.6	0.5	0.3	36 387	25.1	13.9
41 05350	Beaverton city	75 918	7.1	18.0	10.5	34.9	20.8	8.7	32.6	-0.6	-3.7	56 248	23.0	10.7
41 05800	Bend city	51 808	6.8	17.6	10.1	31.0	22.3	12.2	34.8	-1.3	-0.2	47 321	23.1	13.1
41 15800	Corvallis city	49 184	4.5	13.3	28.2	26.9	17.3	9.8	27.0	-7.9	-2.6	41 013	16.7	11.2
41 23850	Eugene city.................	137 799	5.3	15.3	17.0	28.6	21.7	12.1	33.0	-5.1	-0.3	118 429	19.0	13.5
41 31250	Gresham city	90 158	8.0	19.4	11.0	30.4	21.3	9.9	32.5	1.7	-2.5	70 554	24.4	11.8
41 34100	Hillsboro city................	69 883	9.2	19.0	10.9	37.7	17.0	6.2	29.7	2.5	-6.2	49 244	25.4	8.2
41 38500	Keizer city...................	32 494	8.1	20.4	7.7	30.6	21.4	11.8	34.4	2.8	-0.6	26 661	25.5	13.9
41 40550	Lake Oswego city..........	35 222	4.9	19.8	5.4	26.8	31.6	11.5	41.2	-1.0	-0.9	31 946	23.8	12.3
41 45000	McMinnville city	26 552	7.3	18.8	14.5	27.1	17.9	14.4	31.5	0.4	2.0	21 306	23.3	17.2
41 47000	Medford city.................	63 436	7.1	18.2	8.7	27.2	22.1	16.6	37.0	-0.4	4.2	54 199	22.8	18.8
41 55200	Oregon City city	25 533	8.1	18.2	10.6	32.0	21.1	9.8	32.7	0.6	-2.6	23 019	25.2	10.5
41 59000	Portland city	529 025	6.0	15.0	10.2	34.9	22.3	11.6	35.2	-4.7	-0.8	399 054	17.7	13.5
41 64900	Salem city...................	136 694	7.5	17.9	11.5	30.0	20.5	12.5	33.6	-0.3	0.1	105 790	21.9	15.4
41 69600	Springfield city..............	52 729	8.2	18.6	11.8	30.8	20.2	10.4	32.1	1.1	-2.0	45 574	25.2	11.5
41 73650	Tigard city....................	41 261	7.8	17.6	8.8	34.3	21.2	10.4	34.5	-0.3	-2.0	33 096	23.7	12.0
42 00000	PENNSYLVANIA.......	12 281 054	5.9	17.9	8.9	28.6	23.0	15.6	38.0	-1.9	3.2	10 327 998	22.2	17.1
42 02000	Allentown city	106 632	6.9	17.7	10.9	30.0	19.3	15.1	34.5	-1.1	2.7	68 673	16.8	21.8
42 02184	Altoona city.................	49 525	6.3	16.6	10.9	27.5	21.9	16.7	37.4	-2.8	4.3	47 387	22.4	17.3
42 06064	Bethel Park borough	33 556	5.3	18.1	5.1	27.0	26.3	18.2	42.1	-2.3	5.8	32 426	23.1	18.5
42 06088	Bethlehem city..............	71 329	5.3	15.4	14.6	26.9	20.0	17.8	36.2	-5.0	5.4	53 211	15.7	22.4
42 13208	Chester city	36 854	8.2	21.3	13.0	27.5	18.0	12.0	30.6	3.8	-0.4	6 554	11.1	23.7
42 21648	Easton city..................	26 263	6.5	16.7	16.6	29.9	18.5	11.8	32.0	-2.5	-0.6	19 184	18.8	14.4
42 24000	Erie city	103 725	7.0	18.4	11.7	28.5	19.1	15.4	34.1	-0.3	3.0	81 699	20.8	18.0
42 32800	Harrisburg city	49 100	7.9	20.1	9.4	31.5	20.2	10.9	33.0	2.3	-1.5	14 331	10.6	18.6
42 41216	Lancaster city	56 347	7.7	19.9	13.5	31.1	17.6	10.2	30.4	1.9	-2.2	29 428	16.3	16.6
42 52330	Municipality of Monroeville borough...	29 349	4.7	15.4	6.3	27.8	25.7	20.1	42.6	-5.6	7.7	24 919	18.7	22.4
42 53368	New Castle city	26 311	6.7	17.1	8.1	25.7	21.3	21.1	39.4	-1.9	8.7	22 618	20.7	23.0
42 54656	Norristown borough.......	31 284	6.5	18.1	11.1	32.7	19.5	12.1	33.7	-1.1	-0.3	15 427	17.1	17.6
42 60000	Philadelphia city	1 517 550	6.4	18.8	11.1	29.4	20.1	14.1	34.2	-0.5	1.7	645 973	17.3	20.1
42 61000	Pittsburgh city..............	334 563	5.3	14.5	14.7	28.6	20.4	16.4	35.5	-5.9	4.0	224 341	15.2	19.1
42 61536	Plum borough...............	26 940	6.4	18.6	6.1	30.9	24.8	13.2	38.4	-0.7	0.8	25 417	24.1	13.7
42 63624	Reading city.................	81 201	8.4	21.6	11.5	29.2	16.8	12.6	30.6	4.3	0.2	39 320	18.2	22.1
42 69000	Scranton city................	76 415	5.0	15.7	12.2	25.7	21.3	20.1	38.8	-5.0	7.7	70 803	19.5	21.4
42 73808	State College borough ..	38 420	2.0	3.5	66.1	16.4	6.3	5.8	21.8	-20.2	-6.6	31 885	5.1	6.8
42 85152	Wilkes-Barre city	43 123	4.8	15.1	12.6	26.1	20.8	20.6	38.8	-5.8	8.2	39 360	18.4	22.1
42 85312	Williamsport city	30 706	6.1	16.2	17.8	27.3	19.3	13.3	32.4	-3.4	0.9	25 741	19.1	15.4
42 87048	York city	40 889	7.8	20.6	11.4	30.4	18.9	10.9	31.3	2.7	-1.5	22 299	17.5	16.5
44 00000	RHODE ISLAND	1 048 319	6.0	17.6	10.1	29.7	22.0	14.6	36.7	-2.1	2.2	858 665	21.0	16.7
44 19180	Cranston city	79 269	5.3	16.5	7.7	31.0	22.0	17.4	39.0	-3.9	5.0	68 980	20.2	19.3
44 22960	East Providence city	48 688	5.3	16.3	7.6	29.3	22.7	18.8	39.6	-4.1	6.4	41 636	20.2	20.0
44 49960	Newport city	26 475	6.0	13.8	14.4	31.7	21.2	12.9	34.9	-5.9	0.5	21 707	16.4	14.3
44 54640	Pawtucket city..............	72 958	6.7	18.2	9.2	30.9	20.3	14.8	35.4	-0.8	2.4	50 484	20.0	19.4
44 59000	Providence city	173 618	6.9	19.1	18.6	29.0	15.8	10.6	28.1	0.3	-1.8	80 082	13.9	17.4
44 74300	Warwick city	85 808	5.5	16.3	6.8	30.1	24.3	17.0	40.0	-3.9	4.6	80 889	21.2	17.8
44 80780	Woonsocket city	43 224	7.6	18.3	9.1	30.5	19.4	15.1	34.8	0.2	2.7	34 489	21.3	18.5
45 00000	SOUTH CAROLINA ...	4 012 012	6.6	18.6	10.1	29.7	22.9	12.1	35.4	-0.5	-0.3	2 654 401	22.1	14.1
45 00550	Aiken city....................	25 340	6.4	16.4	9.5	26.0	24.1	17.6	39.5	-2.9	5.2	16 638	19.5	21.3
45 01360	Anderson city	25 236	6.5	15.3	10.3	26.0	20.3	21.7	38.0	-3.9	9.3	15 778	16.7	27.8
45 13330	Charleston city	96 086	5.6	14.4	17.2	28.8	20.4	13.7	33.2	-5.7	1.3	60 048	15.1	14.2
45 16000	Columbia city................	115 994	5.4	14.7	23.1	29.8	16.8	10.2	28.6	-5.6	-2.2	55 651	13.4	12.8
45 25810	Florence city................	30 306	6.3	18.8	8.6	27.9	23.3	15.1	36.8	-0.6	2.7	16 185	21.1	18.5
45 29815	Goose Creek city	29 162	8.9	20.5	18.2	33.1	14.9	4.3	26.3	3.7	-8.1	22 206	27.8	4.9
45 30850	Greenville city...............	56 334	5.6	14.4	14.0	31.1	20.6	14.2	34.6	-5.7	1.8	34 007	15.1	17.4
45 34045	Hilton Head Island town .	33 775	4.6	12.5	7.0	25.0	26.9	24.0	46.0	-8.6	11.6	26 678	14.5	29.0
45 48535	Mount Pleasant town	47 386	7.7	17.3	6.5	35.0	23.3	10.1	35.9	-0.7	-2.3	42 553	24.9	10.1
45 50875	North Charleston city	79 442	8.2	19.6	13.2	32.9	17.2	9.0	29.9	2.1	-3.4	34 584	18.5	14.3
45 61405	Rock Hill city	50 209	6.8	18.4	14.6	30.6	18.3	11.3	31.0	-0.5	-1.1	28 923	20.5	14.5
45 68290	Spartanburg city	39 407	6.5	18.0	12.1	26.9	20.7	15.8	34.7	-1.2	3.4	18 378	15.6	24.0
45 70270	Summerville town.........	28 269	7.0	21.6	8.1	31.4	21.9	9.9	34.4	2.9	-2.5	21 690	26.9	10.8
45 70405	Sumter city..................	40 213	8.1	19.9	12.3	27.9	18.0	13.9	31.9	2.3	1.5	19 744	24.1	17.7
46 00000	SOUTH DAKOTA.......	754 844	6.8	20.1	10.3	27.4	21.1	14.3	35.6	1.2	1.9	664 810	24.6	15.7
46 52980	Rapid City city	59 507	6.9	18.1	12.0	28.8	20.9	13.3	34.8	-0.7	0.9	49 595	22.0	15.0
46 59020	Sioux Falls city	124 096	7.3	17.9	11.8	32.4	19.6	11.0	33.0	-0.5	-1.4	112 798	23.8	11.9

Table A-5. Cities — Age, Ethnicity, and Household Structure

City	Black or African American			American Indian and Alaska Native			Asian, Hawaiian, and Pacific Islander			Hispanic or Latino[1]			Two or more races		
	Total population	Age (percent) Under 18 years	65 years and over	Total population	Age (percent) Under 18 years	65 years and over	Total population	Age (percent) Under 18 years	65 years and over	Total population	Age (percent) Under 18 years	65 years and over	Total population	Age (percent) Under 18 years	65 years and over
	14	15	16	17	18	19	20	21	22	23	24	25	26	27	28
OREGON	53 032	31.0	6.6	43 434	30.3	4.8	106 719	24.9	6.5	273 938	39.0	2.0	113 867	42.9	4.6
Albany city....................	172	27.9	4.7	445	24.9	7.9	614	32.9	5.7	2 402	39.9	1.9	1 070	41.0	5.2
Beaverton city	952	17.0	2.0	489	30.3	0.0	7 645	25.5	5.1	8 335	32.6	1.3	3 023	50.2	3.7
Bend city......................	190	31.6	0.0	554	35.9	6.0	453	26.7	3.8	2 449	39.2	2.4	1 091	49.1	0.0
Corvallis city.................	655	18.3	0.0	226	24.8	3.1	3 076	16.2	3.6	2 738	28.1	1.9	1 851	31.1	2.7
Eugene city..................	1 622	28.5	5.1	1 096	25.1	2.3	4 713	17.2	2.7	6 851	36.2	2.6	5 977	37.1	3.6
Gresham city................	1 621	37.8	2.8	829	17.2	5.2	2 887	28.5	7.1	11 084	38.6	2.2	4 523	47.2	3.4
Hillsboro city................	753	29.6	3.1	422	19.4	0.0	4 723	23.7	2.6	13 230	37.6	1.2	2 482	46.8	0.0
Keizer city....................	289	45.0	8.3	393	40.2	3.8	491	18.9	6.3	3 848	43.9	0.4	1 390	51.5	4.7
Lake Oswego city..........	229	27.5	4.8	85	8.2	0.0	1 556	28.7	5.7	900	36.0	2.0	607	51.6	2.8
McMinnville city	113	46.9	0.0	243	34.6	0.0	416	16.1	8.4	3 929	39.0	1.8	870	45.5	5.6
Medford city.................	293	49.5	2.7	734	29.2	11.0	799	26.8	4.0	5 975	43.0	2.0	2 413	44.1	4.8
Oregon City city	111	41.4	6.3	230	24.3	0.0	292	29.5	12.3	1 365	36.0	2.7	718	46.4	2.6
Portland city.................	33 725	31.4	8.3	5 418	24.9	3.8	35 693	25.1	7.6	35 791	33.7	2.1	23 911	41.9	3.7
Salem city....................	1 559	26.6	1.0	1 963	28.3	2.7	3 692	24.5	7.9	20 078	40.7	1.5	5 227	46.2	2.7
Springfield city..............	277	36.1	3.6	747	32.5	3.5	870	26.6	5.9	3 475	39.5	1.0	2 177	44.0	4.4
Tigard city....................	530	23.0	2.1	290	36.6	0.0	2 700	29.4	6.1	3 661	32.6	1.6	1 258	43.4	5.4
PENNSYLVANIA	1 211 669	30.8	10.2	19 511	27.3	7.2	220 352	25.3	4.7	392 121	37.6	3.8	155 159	44.1	5.4
Allentown city...............	7 790	37.8	3.1	460	39.1	4.6	2 753	22.5	4.0	25 970	41.0	2.6	3 995	47.3	4.6
Altoona city..................	1 035	25.7	3.7	165	49.1	3.0	167	13.2	2.4	295	34.9	5.1	494	55.9	3.4
Bethel Park borough	358	33.2	14.5	59	5.1	0.0	366	26.0	7.1	145	41.4	0.0	226	42.0	2.7
Bethlehem city..............	2 573	30.5	4.0	116	32.8	0.0	1 583	22.9	2.5	13 028	38.8	4.1	1 926	35.5	5.5
Chester city..................	27 795	33.6	9.9	50	44.0	14.0	342	19.3	2.0	2 003	36.4	4.1	488	38.3	1.2
Easton city...................	3 325	35.1	5.6	29	44.8	0.0	363	21.8	1.9	2 512	34.7	2.5	1 003	36.2	6.8
Erie city.......................	14 520	40.1	6.6	293	22.2	6.8	570	23.5	3.9	4 708	47.7	2.1	2 754	59.0	4.1
Harrisburg city..............	26 167	34.2	8.8	120	6.7	20.0	1 432	22.7	7.3	5 780	40.1	3.2	2 272	50.0	2.8
Lancaster city...............	8 037	38.6	4.3	142	26.1	2.8	1 233	27.4	3.7	17 224	41.6	2.8	2 354	48.0	1.6
Municipality of Monroeville borough...	2 494	28.0	7.8	41	36.6	0.0	1 188	23.1	0.9	228	21.1	9.6	459	41.2	18.1
New Castle city.............	2 875	42.2	10.7	28	17.9	0.0	129	28.7	0.0	225	33.8	3.6	415	52.3	9.4
Norristown borough.......	10 763	33.3	8.1	77	33.8	6.5	949	15.3	3.8	3 419	30.1	2.3	1 112	47.3	6.3
Philadelphia city...........	653 364	30.7	11.2	4 413	31.1	10.5	65 961	23.8	5.5	128 300	37.6	4.4	37 219	35.3	6.1
Pittsburgh city..............	89 517	31.2	12.4	672	21.1	12.8	9 249	12.0	2.1	4 522	20.8	6.0	6 239	37.6	5.6
Plum borough................	869	41.2	6.2	0	X	X	226	23.0	5.8	211	46.0	0.0	198	46.5	8.6
Reading city..................	9 262	35.2	6.7	542	35.1	6.5	1 483	30.5	3.2	30 181	43.1	2.6	3 966	53.9	2.0
Scranton city................	2 087	36.0	4.3	112	10.1	0.0	770	20.0	10.0	1 937	37.6	1.4	943	44.4	3.1
State College borough ..	1 303	3.8	0.0	37	0.0	32.4	3 516	7.7	1.2	1 204	7.1	0.6	615	12.0	0.0
Wilkes-Barre city	2 494	34.3	5.5	26	65.4	0.0	217	18.4	5.1	508	35.0	4.5	511	43.8	7.4
Williamsport city...........	3 853	39.8	2.9	183	7.7	0.0	184	27.7	0.0	280	45.4	0.0	493	46.9	1.8
York city......................	9 846	38.3	6.1	139	40.3	0.0	694	30.7	2.7	7 034	43.6	1.7	1 659	60.9	1.8
RHODE ISLAND	45 236	32.8	6.6	5 124	38.2	7.3	24 266	27.9	4.3	90 452	38.6	3.2	29 588	39.3	6.3
Cranston city	2 525	24.7	5.9	223	43.0	5.4	2 507	25.0	4.8	3 627	40.0	2.6	1 812	42.9	6.9
East Providence city	2 364	27.4	11.5	204	10.7	17.3	560	22.9	0.9	889	35.4	10.1	2 342	30.6	12.4
Newport city.................	2 000	30.0	11.4	231	50.6	4.3	321	7.5	7.8	1 433	48.3	2.6	1 070	42.6	3.9
Pawtucket city..............	5 209	37.4	4.5	162	34.0	3.7	666	27.3	3.0	10 166	37.4	2.0	4 000	34.7	7.1
Providence city.............	24 124	34.6	6.9	2 020	44.7	5.7	10 985	29.2	3.6	52 047	39.2	3.4	10 057	38.3	5.3
Warwick city.................	924	21.1	2.2	225	31.6	1.3	1 296	25.2	5.1	1 367	32.1	3.3	1 285	45.4	4.8
Woonsocket city............	1 685	34.8	3.0	194	52.1	0.0	1 658	35.2	2.5	4 032	49.0	1.1	1 609	51.8	2.2
SOUTH CAROLINA ...	1 182 727	31.1	8.8	14 688	25.8	5.4	37 889	23.8	4.8	92 828	29.7	2.7	42 068	42.0	4.8
Aiken city.....................	7 606	28.8	11.2	88	0.0	10.2	322	24.5	4.7	401	33.4	6.0	345	49.9	2.0
Anderson city	8 649	29.9	11.9	21	19.0	42.9	221	54.3	3.6	423	24.6	5.0	153	52.3	11.8
Charleston city..............	32 106	28.8	13.7	162	22.8	9.9	1 405	21.0	4.3	1 462	21.9	3.6	1 104	21.5	8.9
Columbia city................	53 303	27.2	8.6	407	10.6	4.4	2 145	13.0	1.8	3 371	18.7	2.6	1 655	35.7	2.2
Florence city.................	13 446	29.8	11.3	42	21.4	42.9	214	15.4	3.3	261	34.1	13.4	269	39.8	8.2
Goose Creek city	3 993	37.0	2.6	258	22.9	0.0	829	23.0	2.2	1 216	29.5	2.0	942	51.2	2.2
Greenville city...............	19 335	28.7	10.4	139	12.2	2.9	653	15.8	1.7	1 840	20.2	4.0	658	26.7	2.0
Hilton Head Island town .	2 600	32.1	9.7	103	19.4	10.7	290	10.0	5.5	3 904	23.5	1.8	427	29.5	3.0
Mount Pleasant town	3 149	27.0	13.7	76	0.0	0.0	538	21.4	5.0	766	16.1	0.8	455	45.1	2.9
North Charleston city	38 954	36.4	5.2	236	10.2	6.4	1 342	17.7	5.2	3 329	27.6	1.1	1 590	36.9	2.4
Rock Hill city	18 770	31.3	7.5	352	50.6	0.0	669	21.8	1.8	1 108	30.4	1.9	436	46.1	7.1
Spartanburg city............	19 464	32.7	8.7	91	29.7	18.7	505	22.2	3.2	762	26.0	6.6	344	27.3	11.6
Summerville town..........	5 397	32.8	7.8	88	0.0	33.0	318	34.9	0.0	343	31.5	6.1	434	59.7	0.0
Sumter city	18 604	31.2	11.0	74	20.3	13.5	476	22.7	0.0	757	32.5	1.3	710	50.0	2.3
SOUTH DAKOTA.......	4 518	34.8	3.2	61 724	44.6	4.2	4 972	30.2	4.0	10 386	41.4	3.9	10 711	51.1	4.4
Rapid City city	469	26.2	5.5	5 519	40.5	4.7	786	25.3	2.4	1 596	41.4	5.8	1 939	54.5	2.3
Sioux Falls city	2 201	37.2	1.9	2 817	35.7	1.8	1 530	36.9	1.4	2 898	40.2	2.2	2 289	52.9	2.1

[1] Hispanic or Latino persons may be of any race.

City	Total households	Family households (percent) Married-couple family households Total	With children	House-holder 65 years or over	Other family households Total	With children	House-holder 65 years or over	Nonfamily households (percent) Two or more unrelated persons Total	House-holder 65 years or over	Male living alone Total	House-holder 65 years or over	Female living alone Total	House-holder 65 years or over	Percent of householders 65 years and over who live alone	Grandparents who are responsible for the care of their grandchildren
	29	30	31	32	33	34	35	36	37	38	39	40	41	42	43
OREGON	1 335 109	53.0	23.2	9.7	13.3	8.2	1.5	7.7	0.5	11.2	2.3	14.8	7.0	44.0	22 103
Albany city..................	16 189	52.4	23.9	8.8	15.5	10.3	1.5	6.4	0.5	10.7	2.2	15.0	8.5	49.7	243
Beaverton city	30 833	47.7	25.0	5.0	13.4	8.7	1.0	8.9	0.2	13.4	1.2	16.7	5.4	51.9	143
Bend city	21 050	51.9	23.6	9.1	12.5	9.4	0.6	9.4	0.3	10.1	1.9	16.1	7.5	48.2	106
Corvallis city	19 555	41.7	18.4	6.9	9.6	6.0	0.7	17.1	0.2	14.5	1.6	17.1	6.0	49.3	119
Eugene city	57 996	41.5	18.0	7.8	13.0	8.7	1.2	14.0	0.5	13.3	1.8	18.2	7.7	50.0	424
Gresham city	33 407	52.5	26.1	6.4	16.1	10.4	1.2	7.0	0.6	9.9	1.3	14.5	6.5	48.5	408
Hillsboro city	25 028	56.4	30.8	4.4	12.1	7.9	0.8	7.9	0.2	11.0	1.0	12.6	4.4	50.0	360
Keizer city...................	12 110	56.6	26.0	9.6	16.0	10.2	1.3	5.9	0.8	7.1	1.5	14.5	7.1	42.5	247
Lake Oswego city..........	14 824	57.2	27.1	8.5	8.7	5.4	0.8	6.4	0.4	9.2	1.3	18.5	7.5	47.3	49
McMinnville city	9 356	53.9	25.8	11.8	16.0	9.9	1.3	6.5	0.5	8.7	2.1	14.9	9.5	46.1	157
Medford city	25 250	51.5	21.9	11.6	14.8	10.3	1.3	6.1	0.6	10.2	2.6	17.4	10.7	49.7	293
Oregon City city	9 493	53.2	24.8	6.6	17.8	11.6	2.0	6.6	0.6	9.2	1.0	13.2	5.8	42.2	141
Portland city	223 987	39.1	17.2	6.5	14.4	8.0	1.8	12.0	0.4	15.7	2.4	18.8	7.0	51.9	3 112
Salem city...................	50 585	48.7	22.4	8.6	15.6	10.4	1.3	7.3	0.6	10.7	2.1	17.7	8.5	50.2	900
Springfield city..............	20 423	46.0	22.3	6.8	20.0	13.5	1.7	8.7	0.7	11.1	1.9	14.3	5.8	45.4	276
Tigard city...................	16 499	53.8	26.3	7.4	12.2	8.2	0.7	6.9	0.3	10.6	1.8	16.4	6.0	48.3	202
PENNSYLVANIA........	4 779 186	52.4	22.5	10.7	15.1	8.0	2.8	4.9	0.4	11.1	2.8	16.5	8.9	46.0	80 423
Allentown city...............	42 051	40.2	16.8	9.0	20.1	12.6	2.5	6.6	0.4	13.8	2.9	19.3	10.3	52.8	1 022
Altoona city..................	20 091	45.2	18.8	10.2	18.1	10.1	3.5	5.2	0.4	11.2	2.8	20.3	11.9	51.2	589
Bethel Park borough	13 421	62.0	26.7	13.7	9.7	3.9	2.6	2.4	0.3	8.8	2.9	17.1	9.9	43.6	49
Bethlehem city..............	28 106	45.0	17.3	11.4	16.3	9.5	2.5	6.4	0.4	11.6	3.3	20.7	12.1	51.9	482
Chester city	12 797	26.7	11.8	4.8	37.0	22.0	5.2	5.0	0.7	13.4	3.7	17.9	8.2	52.7	723
Easton city	9 545	37.9	18.0	6.2	22.3	12.5	3.5	8.1	0.3	15.6	2.7	16.1	7.4	50.1	225
Erie city	40 908	39.6	17.1	8.9	20.9	12.9	3.0	6.1	0.4	13.3	2.8	20.1	10.3	51.6	845
Harrisburg city..............	20 613	23.6	10.0	4.3	30.1	19.5	2.7	7.2	0.5	18.2	3.2	20.9	7.7	59.4	882
Lancaster city...............	20 928	33.9	16.3	5.7	24.2	15.9	2.2	8.5	0.2	14.8	2.4	18.5	7.5	55.2	792
Municipality of Monroeville borough...	12 398	52.3	20.2	12.6	13.4	6.7	3.0	3.7	0.1	12.2	2.4	18.4	9.7	43.5	109
New Castle city	10 760	42.3	16.1	11.5	20.9	11.3	4.3	3.6	0.2	11.7	4.2	21.6	13.3	52.2	179
Norristown borough.......	12 036	32.6	14.3	5.9	27.6	14.3	4.5	7.1	0.7	15.6	2.8	17.1	7.0	46.9	430
Philadelphia city	590 283	32.7	14.0	7.1	27.5	14.3	4.7	6.0	0.6	13.9	3.2	19.9	8.9	49.4	21 123
Pittsburgh city..............	143 752	32.1	11.9	8.0	19.9	10.4	3.8	8.7	0.5	16.4	3.6	22.9	10.4	53.4	2 699
Plum borough...............	10 242	63.1	29.2	11.1	11.7	5.7	2.2	3.6	0.1	9.7	2.1	11.9	6.6	39.0	138
Reading city	30 104	35.4	17.1	6.9	26.4	17.2	3.0	6.5	0.6	13.9	3.7	17.8	8.8	54.4	1 079
Scranton city	31 307	41.3	17.1	9.8	17.0	8.1	3.8	4.9	0.4	13.8	4.7	22.9	13.9	57.1	381
State College borough ..	12 059	22.6	8.0	5.1	4.9	2.5	0.4	38.9	0.2	18.4	1.2	15.3	4.8	51.3	17
Wilkes-Barre city	17 919	37.7	14.6	9.1	17.4	8.5	4.4	5.8	0.6	15.1	4.9	24.0	13.9	57.3	340
Williamsport city	12 213	36.3	15.7	7.6	19.5	12.4	1.7	9.1	0.5	15.3	2.7	19.8	10.2	56.9	147
York city	16 098	31.2	13.8	5.2	26.9	17.4	3.2	8.8	0.4	15.7	2.7	17.4	7.7	54.0	692
RHODE ISLAND	408 412	49.1	21.8	9.4	16.1	9.3	2.4	6.2	0.4	11.5	2.8	17.0	8.9	49.1	5 060
Cranston city	30 971	50.1	21.5	11.8	15.7	7.3	3.4	4.9	0.3	9.8	2.3	19.5	10.6	45.4	386
East Providence city	20 547	46.0	19.0	9.8	16.6	8.4	3.6	4.9	0.3	12.2	3.7	20.2	12.2	53.5	189
Newport city	11 562	33.1	13.3	6.3	16.7	10.5	2.5	10.8	0.5	17.8	3.4	21.6	8.4	55.7	137
Pawtucket city	30 042	41.6	18.2	8.5	20.1	12.9	1.8	6.0	0.4	13.4	3.2	18.9	10.0	55.0	317
Providence city.............	62 327	32.6	16.6	5.9	25.4	16.6	2.7	9.7	0.5	14.3	2.9	17.9	7.4	53.2	1 219
Warwick city	35 543	51.8	21.6	10.5	13.1	6.2	2.4	5.4	0.6	11.0	3.1	18.8	10.8	50.8	376
Woonsocket city	17 771	41.1	17.4	7.9	19.8	14.2	1.9	6.4	0.2	14.4	3.4	18.2	9.9	57.3	265
SOUTH CAROLINA ...	1 534 334	52.0	22.6	8.8	18.3	10.3	2.7	4.7	0.3	10.6	2.1	14.4	6.7	42.9	51 755
Aiken city....................	10 284	49.6	18.8	11.5	16.2	8.9	2.5	4.6	0.4	11.3	3.1	18.5	8.9	45.5	229
Anderson city	10 578	38.4	13.1	10.7	20.6	11.1	3.2	4.4	0.4	13.1	3.5	23.4	13.9	54.8	287
Charleston city	40 550	36.6	14.6	7.7	18.0	9.0	3.4	11.5	0.3	13.3	2.5	20.6	7.7	47.2	944
Columbia city...............	41 960	32.6	14.1	6.0	20.3	11.8	3.1	10.1	0.4	14.6	1.9	22.4	7.8	50.4	931
Florence city................	12 031	42.6	18.0	8.4	24.0	12.4	3.9	3.8	0.2	10.7	1.8	18.9	8.6	45.1	426
Goose Creek city	8 921	68.7	40.5	3.9	13.9	9.9	1.2	4.1	0.0	5.7	0.9	7.6	2.7	41.8	162
Greenville city..............	24 330	33.9	13.0	7.1	18.8	10.1	2.5	6.7	0.4	15.9	2.5	24.7	10.2	56.1	762
Hilton Head Island town	14 409	61.3	17.3	22.1	9.0	5.0	1.0	6.1	0.3	8.8	3.1	14.7	9.0	34.2	70
Mount Pleasant town	18 911	57.8	28.6	7.1	10.4	6.1	1.3	8.2	0.2	8.1	1.3	15.5	5.3	43.5	149
North Charleston city	29 811	36.8	17.4	5.8	27.5	17.5	2.5	6.9	0.2	14.1	1.8	14.7	4.8	43.6	1 073
Rock Hill city	18 953	44.1	20.5	6.7	20.9	12.5	2.3	7.7	0.1	11.0	1.7	16.2	6.8	48.3	715
Spartanburg city	15 935	34.8	12.9	7.7	26.6	15.9	3.4	4.8	0.4	11.7	3.0	22.1	10.7	54.2	524
Summerville town..........	10 476	57.3	29.3	6.7	15.8	10.9	1.3	3.9	0.0	8.2	1.0	14.8	7.6	51.5	234
Sumter city	14 781	46.6	23.5	8.0	22.8	13.0	3.4	3.0	0.1	10.5	2.9	17.1	9.9	52.6	597
SOUTH DAKOTA.......	290 336	55.0	25.1	11.1	12.4	8.1	1.4	5.2	0.3	12.1	2.6	15.4	8.5	46.5	4 632
Rapid City city	24 054	47.9	20.9	9.3	16.0	10.9	1.5	6.5	0.4	12.6	2.4	17.0	8.0	48.0	385
Sioux Falls city	49 740	49.6	24.0	8.0	12.8	8.5	1.0	7.7	0.3	12.3	1.6	17.5	7.3	48.9	537

Table A-5. Cities — Age, Ethnicity, and Household Structure

City	Households with Non-Hispanic White householder		Households with Black or African American householder		Households with American Indian and Alaska Native householder		Households with Asian, Hawaiian, and Pacific Islander householder		Households with Hispanic or Latino[1] householder		Foreign-born population	Place of birth (percent)			Percent in non-English speaking households	
	Number of households	Percent that are family households	Number of households	Percent that are family households	Number of households	Percent that are family households	Number of households	Percent that are family households	Number of households	Percent that are family households	Percent of total population that is foreign-born	Europe	Asia	Latin America	Linguistically isolated	Not linguistically isolated
	44	45	46	47	48	49	50	51	52	53	54	55	56	57	58	59
OREGON	1 177 750	65.5	18 618	63.4	14 746	68.6	33 763	69.8	64 749	79.7	8.5	1.6	2.3	3.8	3.7	13.4
Albany city	14 953	67.0	67	41.8	146	73.3	180	82.8	525	93.3	4.4	0.7	1.0	2.3	2.4	9.0
Beaverton city	24 826	58.5	492	47.4	169	66.9	2 622	75.9	2 171	74.0	18.4	2.2	9.0	6.2	7.4	21.6
Bend city	19 858	64.2	43	46.5	185	63.2	116	57.8	636	68.2	3.7	0.8	0.5	1.6	1.0	9.1
Corvallis city	16 747	51.3	296	46.3	70	44.3	1 154	47.6	830	61.8	9.7	2.0	4.7	2.2	4.2	13.4
Eugene city	51 673	54.9	582	56.4	383	51.7	1 864	35.9	1 931	63.2	6.6	1.3	2.7	1.6	2.1	13.5
Gresham city	28 474	67.6	501	70.7	331	56.2	840	72.4	2 437	78.9	13.1	2.3	2.5	7.4	6.8	16.5
Hillsboro city	19 828	66.5	263	72.2	160	81.9	1 723	61.5	2 717	86.9	18.0	1.2	4.9	11.1	9.8	19.2
Keizer city	10 629	70.9	68	100.0	116	78.4	183	79.8	862	91.4	8.2	1.4	1.3	4.9	4.3	14.7
Lake Oswego city	13 696	65.2	93	68.8	39	100.0	544	85.7	312	65.4	9.5	2.5	4.3	1.0	1.1	14.4
McMinnville city	8 113	67.9	36	58.3	52	82.7	108	75.9	887	85.1	10.3	0.6	1.0	8.4	6.2	14.8
Medford city	23 029	65.1	73	89.0	227	77.1	235	63.8	1 291	84.2	6.3	0.8	0.8	4.1	2.8	10.7
Oregon City city	8 755	70.1	30	50.0	74	64.9	92	68.5	399	90.7	5.3	1.9	1.1	2.0	2.7	12.0
Portland city	182 890	51.1	12 619	62.8	1 995	53.8	11 044	69.7	9 851	66.1	13.0	3.3	5.0	3.3	6.1	15.9
Salem city	43 384	62.1	345	80.9	563	68.6	1 030	70.1	4 391	82.5	11.7	1.4	2.0	7.5	6.6	16.0
Springfield city	18 393	65.4	103	77.7	291	73.2	213	75.1	959	73.2	4.9	0.5	0.8	2.7	2.0	11.1
Tigard city	14 143	64.7	197	76.1	131	45.0	775	79.1	955	78.2	12.7	2.2	4.4	5.2	5.2	16.7
PENNSYLVANIA	4 129 114	67.5	434 217	64.9	7 184	66.7	68 958	72.0	109 484	75.1	4.1	1.5	1.5	0.8	1.7	11.0
Allentown city	30 609	55.0	2 605	70.0	167	67.1	845	62.7	7 489	78.2	9.6	1.4	3.5	4.4	7.5	26.8
Altoona city	19 416	63.5	394	48.2	67	91.0	54	77.8	75	88.0	1.1	0.5	0.3	0.2	0.3	5.8
Bethel Park borough	13 128	71.4	114	72.8	18	72.2	101	100.0	23	100.0	2.9	1.7	0.8	0.2	0.3	9.0
Bethlehem city	22 562	58.1	892	68.8	54	53.7	452	65.3	3 952	78.6	6.1	1.9	2.0	1.6	4.9	22.6
Chester city	2 428	50.7	9 631	66.6	14	50.0	94	64.9	615	75.4	2.5	0.4	0.7	0.8	2.1	10.7
Easton city	7 504	58.4	1 060	64.5	3	100.0	90	75.6	639	74.2	8.6	2.0	1.4	4.7	4.5	16.9
Erie city	33 972	58.6	4 947	70.6	110	66.4	222	44.6	1 240	76.7	4.2	2.4	0.8	0.6	2.6	11.1
Harrisburg city	7 780	34.7	10 164	63.4	67	77.6	400	68.1	1 794	75.7	5.8	0.4	2.5	2.0	4.6	16.4
Lancaster city	12 938	49.4	2 675	66.5	77	57.1	325	78.5	4 941	76.4	6.6	1.0	1.9	3.3	9.5	28.6
Municipality of Monroeville borough	10 752	64.3	986	75.1	11	100.0	452	79.9	59	83.1	6.4	1.9	3.6	0.5	1.3	13.1
New Castle city	9 618	62.6	919	70.0	7	100.0	62	67.7	100	65.0	1.8	1.1	0.5	0.1	0.6	10.3
Norristown borough	6 538	54.5	3 983	65.6	31	100.0	318	69.8	944	72.8	10.2	1.3	2.6	5.8	6.6	15.0
Philadelphia city	282 063	54.5	240 006	64.3	1 630	62.5	20 886	66.2	38 509	74.6	9.0	2.7	3.5	2.1	4.8	18.7
Pittsburgh city	101 229	49.7	34 943	60.2	193	57.5	3 056	38.8	1 586	44.6	5.6	2.2	2.4	0.6	1.8	12.2
Plum borough	9 759	75.1	298	74.2	0	X	83	63.9	56	64.3	2.3	1.3	0.6	0.2	0.5	5.8
Reading city	17 791	53.2	3 389	65.7	183	70.5	392	78.8	8 301	77.5	10.5	1.4	1.2	7.4	10.2	34.5
Scranton city	29 754	57.9	636	65.3	48	43.8	207	74.9	444	76.8	3.1	1.3	1.0	0.7	1.4	9.9
State College borough	9 987	27.3	363	14.3	22	54.5	1 259	34.8	297	24.6	11.1	2.4	6.9	0.8	3.9	18.7
Wilkes-Barre city	16 804	54.8	830	61.4	5	100.0	63	33.3	111	66.7	2.3	1.0	0.6	0.5	1.1	9.5
Williamsport city	10 618	53.9	1 268	69.6	85	68.2	61	70.5	52	51.9	1.4	0.5	0.5	0.2	0.7	6.0
York city	10 458	48.9	3 422	70.5	43	100.0	201	74.1	1 853	83.2	4.9	0.7	1.1	2.9	5.5	19.0
RHODE ISLAND	351 002	64.0	15 828	66.2	1 607	64.5	7 056	69.9	24 939	82.3	11.4	3.7	1.9	4.2	5.1	21.4
Cranston city	28 540	64.9	535	72.9	65	35.4	691	79.6	773	79.8	9.0	3.8	2.7	2.0	2.5	20.4
East Providence city	17 735	62.4	1 058	65.8	164	62.2	229	69.4	217	64.1	16.0	12.0	1.2	1.0	5.0	27.0
Newport city	9 986	47.4	788	60.2	58	62.1	99	49.5	368	89.1	5.6	2.5	1.0	1.1	2.4	11.7
Pawtucket city	22 838	56.8	1 925	70.5	64	65.6	219	67.1	3 075	81.7	23.4	6.9	1.0	7.3	11.4	31.1
Providence city	34 027	45.6	8 329	65.3	558	64.3	3 204	61.0	14 430	83.6	25.3	3.0	4.5	15.6	14.9	37.5
Warwick city	34 152	64.5	316	58.9	64	79.7	400	77.0	351	76.9	4.8	2.3	1.3	0.6	0.8	13.1
Woonsocket city	15 024	57.8	734	68.3	63	55.6	492	81.7	1 158	86.1	7.5	1.5	3.0	1.2	5.8	27.8
SOUTH CAROLINA	1 076 317	69.7	408 372	71.7	5 374	71.5	11 850	72.1	24 259	74.3	2.9	0.7	0.7	1.2	1.2	7.9
Aiken city	7 146	65.1	2 750	66.8	58	41.4	97	66.0	139	70.5	2.6	0.7	0.9	0.7	0.7	8.1
Anderson city	6 927	58.4	3 401	60.5	0	X	51	74.5	151	68.2	2.3	0.5	0.4	1.0	0.7	7.6
Charleston city	26 723	49.5	12 358	65.4	69	59.4	572	54.2	536	63.1	3.5	1.4	1.1	0.6	1.3	9.9
Columbia city	23 372	45.0	16 735	63.8	166	54.2	771	45.1	643	61.7	4.1	0.9	1.5	1.3	1.5	10.7
Florence city	6 946	63.4	4 815	70.7	16	100.0	107	71.0	106	74.5	2.0	0.5	0.6	0.4	0.9	8.0
Goose Creek city	7 068	81.9	1 164	85.0	71	84.5	197	84.3	297	91.6	4.0	1.1	1.6	0.8	0.9	11.9
Greenville city	15 791	49.5	7 548	59.5	83	61.4	259	38.6	515	56.5	4.3	0.9	0.9	1.9	2.0	8.8
Hilton Head Island town	12 312	68.5	899	81.3	34	67.6	125	88.8	988	83.3	12.7	2.1	0.9	8.8	7.9	11.8
Mount Pleasant town	17 264	68.0	1 084	71.1	37	0.0	183	69.4	292	71.2	4.3	2.0	0.9	0.8	0.3	10.2
North Charleston city	14 512	60.2	13 514	69.2	134	59.0	501	57.7	808	65.3	4.5	0.7	1.3	2.2	2.4	10.1
Rock Hill city	11 781	62.0	6 500	69.6	78	51.3	179	92.7	307	74.3	3.2	0.4	1.0	1.3	1.8	8.0
Spartanburg city	8 084	54.9	7 341	68.4	30	56.7	142	81.7	237	55.3	3.3	0.7	1.1	1.1	1.1	7.8
Summerville town	8 282	73.5	1 882	70.5	57	59.6	85	70.6	105	85.7	3.2	1.3	0.8	0.5	0.9	9.0
Sumter city	7 882	69.3	6 443	68.9	24	79.2	134	87.3	189	75.7	2.4	0.6	0.9	0.7	0.6	11.1
SOUTH DAKOTA	267 618	66.6	1 349	68.3	15 422	78.8	1 288	61.7	2 658	74.7	1.8	0.6	0.5	0.3	1.2	10.5
Rapid City city	21 149	63.0	171	55.6	1 634	74.1	223	66.8	491	71.7	2.4	1.0	0.9	0.3	0.9	8.8
Sioux Falls city	46 853	62.0	688	67.4	647	76.0	358	63.1	766	71.8	4.6	1.4	1.1	0.9	2.4	8.9

[1] Hispanic or Latino persons may be of any race.

STATE Place code	City	Total population	Under 5 years	5 to 17 years	18 to 24 years	25 to 44 years	45 to 64 years	65 years and over	Median age	+/− U.S. percent under 18 years	+/− U.S. percent 65 years and over	Total population	Under 18 years	65 years and over
		1	2	3	4	5	6	7	8	9	10	11	12	13
47 00000	TENNESSEE............	5 689 283	6.6	18.0	9.6	30.3	23.2	12.4	35.9	−1.1	0.0	4 508 623	22.7	13.7
47 03440	Bartlett city	40 309	6.8	22.1	6.8	29.6	26.0	8.7	36.6	3.2	−3.7	36 983	28.5	9.1
47 14000	Chattanooga city	155 509	5.9	16.4	10.7	29.0	22.7	15.3	36.8	−3.4	2.9	91 685	16.8	19.2
47 15160	Clarksville city	103 766	8.8	20.0	13.8	35.0	15.3	7.1	28.8	3.1	−5.3	67 792	25.8	8.8
47 15400	Cleveland city	37 136	6.6	15.5	15.2	27.9	21.1	13.7	34.0	−3.6	1.3	32 505	20.9	15.1
47 16420	Collierville town	31 877	7.7	25.7	5.4	33.3	21.9	6.0	35.2	7.7	−6.4	28 257	33.3	5.9
47 16540	Columbia city	33 058	7.5	18.3	9.5	28.8	21.1	14.8	35.7	0.1	2.4	24 130	23.4	17.4
47 27740	Franklin city	41 756	8.6	19.6	7.1	38.3	19.0	7.5	33.0	2.5	−4.9	34 094	27.2	7.9
47 28960	Germantown city	37 281	5.5	22.5	5.6	24.0	33.4	9.1	41.3	2.3	−3.3	34 356	27.8	9.5
47 33280	Hendersonville city	40 537	6.5	19.2	7.9	31.3	24.9	10.1	36.2	0.0	−2.3	37 223	25.1	10.7
47 37640	Jackson city	59 673	7.2	18.7	12.6	28.9	19.3	13.3	32.8	0.2	0.9	32 250	19.8	18.2
47 38320	Johnson City city	55 323	5.5	14.3	13.7	28.6	22.1	15.8	36.9	−5.9	3.4	49 252	18.9	16.8
47 39560	Kingsport city	44 560	5.6	16.3	6.4	26.7	25.0	20.0	41.9	−3.8	7.6	41 324	21.0	20.8
47 40000	Knoxville city	173 680	5.8	13.8	16.8	29.6	19.5	14.4	33.4	−6.1	2.0	137 162	16.9	16.1
47 48000	Memphis city	649 845	7.7	20.1	10.8	30.8	19.6	10.9	31.9	2.1	−1.5	216 447	16.7	18.8
47 51560	Murfreesboro city	68 957	6.5	16.0	20.6	30.7	17.2	9.1	28.7	−3.2	−3.3	54 134	20.9	10.1
47 52004	Nashville-Davidson.......	569 891	6.6	15.6	11.5	34.2	21.0	11.2	34.1	−3.5	−1.2	371 994	18.0	13.9
47 55120	Oak Ridge city	27 413	5.1	17.3	6.5	23.8	26.1	21.1	43.4	−3.3	8.7	23 691	21.0	22.9
47 69420	Smyrna town	25 383	8.5	18.7	11.0	35.4	19.8	6.6	31.7	1.5	−5.8	21 473	26.4	7.1
48 00000	TEXAS............	20 851 820	7.7	20.4	10.5	31.4	20.1	9.9	32.3	2.4	−2.5	10 927 538	22.9	13.8
48 01000	Abilene city	115 794	7.0	18.5	15.2	28.9	18.5	11.9	31.1	−0.2	−0.5	79 594	21.5	15.4
48 01924	Allen city	43 457	10.6	24.1	5.0	41.5	15.9	2.9	31.4	9.0	−9.5	36 338	34.4	3.1
48 03000	Amarillo city	173 526	8.0	19.8	10.0	29.3	20.2	12.7	33.5	2.1	0.3	118 794	22.8	16.3
48 04000	Arlington city	332 695	8.2	20.0	10.7	36.1	19.0	6.1	30.7	2.5	−6.3	198 950	23.9	8.9
48 05000	Austin city	656 302	7.1	15.4	16.4	37.5	17.0	6.7	29.6	−3.2	−5.7	347 533	16.1	9.2
48 06128	Baytown city	66 944	8.7	21.2	11.4	29.9	19.1	9.7	30.6	4.2	−2.7	33 634	21.9	15.9
48 07000	Beaumont city	113 888	7.1	20.0	10.4	28.1	21.0	13.4	34.5	1.4	1.0	48 690	18.7	20.2
48 07132	Bedford city	47 072	5.9	16.2	9.7	33.2	26.4	8.6	36.2	−3.6	−3.8	39 404	20.9	9.8
48 08236	Big Spring city	25 346	6.1	17.6	9.7	33.0	19.3	14.2	35.1	−2.0	1.8	12 346	20.5	22.0
48 10768	Brownsville city	140 075	10.0	24.7	11.0	28.0	16.7	9.6	27.7	9.0	−2.8	10 859	21.2	25.8
48 10912	Bryan city	66 069	8.2	18.8	18.5	29.8	15.5	9.2	27.6	1.3	−3.2	34 291	19.2	13.5
48 13024	Carrollton city	109 215	7.8	20.1	7.9	37.2	21.7	5.2	33.0	2.2	−7.2	67 013	24.4	6.8
48 13492	Cedar Hill city	32 147	8.2	24.1	7.5	36.7	19.3	4.2	31.5	6.6	−8.2	16 396	26.4	6.8
48 13552	Cedar Park city	25 776	10.7	22.4	6.1	40.7	15.9	4.2	31.1	7.4	−8.2	20 159	31.7	4.8
48 15364	Cleburne city	26 204	7.8	20.0	9.8	29.1	19.7	13.5	33.2	2.1	1.1	19 379	24.0	16.8
48 15976	College Station city	67 900	4.6	9.9	51.2	21.1	9.4	3.8	21.9	−11.2	−8.6	51 283	12.3	4.3
48 16432	Conroe city	36 660	8.6	18.9	14.4	31.0	17.0	10.0	29.4	1.8	−2.4	19 822	21.2	15.3
48 16612	Coppell city	35 955	9.8	24.8	4.3	39.3	18.9	2.9	33.5	8.9	−9.5	28 346	34.1	2.9
48 16624	Copperas Cove city.......	29 998	10.8	21.6	14.5	33.7	14.6	4.9	26.9	6.7	−7.5	18 377	28.6	6.1
48 17000	Corpus Christi city........	277 569	7.6	20.4	10.6	29.2	21.0	11.1	33.2	2.3	−1.3	106 891	21.1	16.1
48 19000	Dallas city	1 188 204	8.3	18.2	11.8	35.6	17.6	8.6	30.5	0.8	−3.8	411 172	14.6	16.4
48 19624	Deer Park city	28 392	6.1	22.9	9.6	30.1	24.3	7.0	34.7	3.3	−5.4	23 015	27.8	7.9
48 19792	Del Rio city	34 082	8.3	23.5	8.6	27.5	20.6	11.5	31.7	6.1	−0.9	5 668	22.7	16.0
48 19972	Denton city	80 578	6.0	14.7	24.8	31.2	15.3	8.0	26.8	−5.0	−4.4	55 741	17.8	10.4
48 20092	DeSoto city	37 623	6.8	21.0	7.5	30.8	24.4	9.5	36.1	2.1	−2.9	16 655	20.9	17.2
48 21628	Duncanville city	35 989	6.5	21.7	8.3	28.7	25.1	9.8	35.8	2.5	−2.6	20 053	20.9	15.3
48 22660	Edinburg city	48 863	9.9	23.4	12.7	30.0	15.7	8.3	27.2	7.6	−4.1	4 865	21.1	17.8
48 24000	El Paso city	564 280	8.3	22.6	9.8	29.3	19.2	10.7	31.1	5.2	−1.7	103 458	20.4	18.9
48 24768	Euless city	46 088	7.6	17.5	9.3	40.4	19.3	5.9	32.2	−0.6	−6.5	31 302	21.5	7.2
48 25452	Farmers Branch city	28 325	7.6	18.8	9.6	31.2	21.3	11.5	34.7	0.7	−0.9	15 605	19.4	18.7
48 26232	Flower Mound town	51 203	10.4	24.1	4.3	39.4	19.2	2.6	33.3	8.8	−9.8	44 478	34.3	2.7
48 27000	Fort Worth city	535 420	8.4	19.7	11.2	33.1	18.0	9.5	30.9	2.4	−2.9	245 492	20.2	14.9
48 27648	Friendswood city	28 734	6.5	23.0	6.4	29.2	26.3	8.6	37.2	3.8	−3.8	24 168	29.0	9.3
48 27684	Frisco city	33 501	12.9	17.9	4.6	46.6	14.7	3.3	30.9	5.1	−9.1	27 237	29.7	3.8
48 28068	Galveston city	57 186	6.4	16.9	11.3	30.7	21.3	13.4	35.5	−2.4	1.0	25 350	15.2	17.8
48 29000	Garland city	215 991	8.2	21.6	9.4	33.5	20.2	7.2	31.7	4.1	−5.2	114 875	23.7	11.1
48 29336	Georgetown city	28 230	6.0	16.8	11.8	26.1	21.5	17.8	36.9	−2.9	5.4	21 868	19.6	21.5
48 30464	Grand Prairie city	127 049	8.7	21.8	10.1	34.5	18.6	6.4	30.5	4.8	−6.0	59 869	23.0	10.5
48 30644	Grapevine city	42 131	7.3	21.9	7.2	36.8	22.0	4.8	34.3	3.5	−7.6	34 536	28.4	5.4
48 31928	Haltom City city	39 229	8.2	18.6	10.0	33.3	19.7	10.3	32.3	1.1	−2.1	26 502	22.6	13.9
48 32372	Harlingen city	57 624	9.1	21.5	9.8	26.9	17.4	15.3	31.8	4.9	2.9	14 163	16.3	35.6
48 35000	Houston city	1 954 848	8.2	19.2	11.2	34.1	19.0	8.4	30.9	1.7	−4.0	601 105	16.9	15.4
48 35528	Huntsville city	34 985	4.6	10.4	28.9	31.9	15.6	8.6	28.3	−10.7	−3.8	19 409	12.7	11.7
48 35576	Hurst city	36 303	7.1	18.3	8.7	29.9	23.5	12.5	36.6	−0.3	0.1	29 332	22.7	14.8
48 37000	Irving city	191 611	8.0	17.1	11.7	39.9	17.3	5.9	30.3	−0.6	−6.5	92 483	18.1	10.6
48 38632	Keller city	27 310	8.4	25.8	4.3	35.1	22.3	4.0	35.0	8.5	−8.4	24 568	33.4	4.2
48 39148	Killeen city	86 822	10.2	19.6	16.1	35.6	13.7	4.8	26.7	4.1	−7.6	34 398	22.9	7.8
48 39352	Kingsville city	25 541	8.0	18.6	17.8	27.7	17.0	10.9	28.4	0.9	−1.5	6 610	19.8	16.6
48 40588	Lake Jackson city	26 515	7.4	23.2	8.2	29.7	21.3	10.2	34.5	4.9	−2.2	20 691	28.7	11.9
48 41212	Lancaster city	25 893	7.7	22.7	8.9	32.0	20.0	8.8	32.3	4.7	−3.6	8 665	18.6	21.0

City	Black or African American			American Indian and Alaska Native			Asian, Hawaiian, and Pacific Islander			Hispanic or Latino[1]			Two or more races		
		Age (percent)			Age (percent)			Age (percent)			Age (percent)			Age (percent)	
	Total population	Under 18 years	65 years and over	Total population	Under 18 years	65 years and over	Total population	Under 18 years	65 years and over	Total population	Under 18 years	65 years and over	Total population	Under 18 years	65 years and over
	14	15	16	17	18	19	20	21	22	23	24	25	26	27	28
TENNESSEE............	929 864	31.8	7.9	15 541	24.2	5.2	56 291	24.7	3.7	119 425	31.2	2.6	69 508	40.7	6.2
Bartlett city..............	1 783	29.3	5.7	128	21.1	0.0	487	36.1	4.1	496	35.1	0.0	483	49.1	6.0
Chattanooga city..........	56 331	30.7	10.4	471	15.1	2.3	2 654	22.0	3.7	2 703	24.3	2.8	2 039	35.1	9.0
Clarksville city............	23 694	33.7	4.8	467	25.5	0.0	2 494	19.4	4.8	6 471	35.4	1.7	3 828	55.5	0.5
Cleveland city.............	2 528	32.7	5.7	35	17.1	0.0	396	18.4	10.1	1 219	27.9	0.0	563	31.3	4.3
Collierville town...........	2 466	31.8	8.4	33	0.0	27.3	435	30.3	4.4	361	41.3	2.2	381	53.0	0.0
Columbia city.............	7 116	31.4	9.5	66	24.2	0.0	57	26.3	0.0	1 384	31.3	1.7	511	48.7	0.0
Franklin city...............	4 322	29.2	8.6	89	41.6	0.0	670	28.4	5.4	2 041	34.3	1.0	624	45.2	4.8
Germantown city..........	733	23.5	1.4	66	39.4	0.0	1 387	28.9	3.7	363	26.2	9.6	385	46.0	4.4
Hendersonville city.......	1 581	35.1	2.3	96	6.3	16.7	459	22.4	4.1	780	35.9	4.4	427	42.4	6.6
Jackson city..............	25 220	33.1	7.6	150	30.7	0.0	363	37.7	8.0	1 175	27.7	2.7	631	50.1	9.5
Johnson City city.........	3 406	24.5	8.8	114	6.1	14.9	707	22.8	2.4	1 151	29.2	5.2	732	48.9	5.9
Kingsport city.............	1 932	32.7	11.0	277	31.0	11.9	281	31.0	4.3	373	34.0	1.9	402	41.3	10.9
Knoxville city.............	20 322	30.2	9.7	563	12.8	2.7	2 295	17.5	1.6	2 591	28.9	2.1	2 888	38.4	4.8
Memphis city.............	397 702	33.8	7.3	1 216	21.2	7.0	10 246	24.4	3.4	18 751	28.9	1.5	7 379	41.3	6.5
Murfreesboro city	9 547	27.9	6.3	167	4.8	1.8	1 765	24.4	3.7	2 385	28.6	2.9	1 053	42.8	3.1
Nashville-Davidson........	147 862	30.3	7.1	1 978	21.3	3.7	12 091	23.5	3.8	25 597	28.6	1.6	12 417	37.8	3.6
Oak Ridge city............	2 136	31.7	9.0	137	17.5	2.2	486	23.7	11.1	463	33.3	6.5	501	44.7	16.0
Smyrna town..............	1 909	32.5	5.6	112	19.6	0.0	398	26.9	1.5	1 123	23.1	1.4	576	46.4	3.0
TEXAS....................	2 385 554	31.0	7.4	113 755	28.6	5.3	568 392	25.3	4.5	6 670 122	35.7	5.1	530 162	39.9	4.9
Abilene city................	9 960	27.7	6.2	686	29.2	3.5	1 678	26.5	3.8	22 575	37.0	3.4	3 199	52.8	2.2
Allen city..................	1 819	33.4	1.6	158	25.9	0.0	1 643	32.0	0.9	2 945	37.5	2.4	708	58.5	1.7
Amarillo city..............	9 789	37.4	8.6	1 266	23.2	11.2	3 696	27.5	5.8	38 058	40.8	3.2	4 247	49.0	5.4
Arlington city.............	44 621	35.0	1.6	1 731	23.2	2.1	19 642	26.6	3.3	60 977	36.4	1.4	10 713	45.0	2.9
Austin city................	64 822	29.2	7.2	3 466	27.2	2.9	31 311	17.6	1.9	201 040	31.8	3.0	19 675	35.5	2.3
Baytown city..............	8 994	35.0	4.8	310	21.0	8.7	667	36.4	1.0	22 792	39.4	2.9	1 854	46.2	3.1
Beaumont city............	52 239	33.4	8.9	322	7.8	19.3	2 723	30.0	3.6	9 126	35.5	5.3	1 486	37.9	7.7
Bedford city..............	1 742	28.2	1.4	268	22.4	5.6	1 795	30.9	3.2	3 093	24.8	3.1	915	33.4	1.4
Big Spring city............	1 357	30.9	10.8	123	13.0	13.8	117	19.7	0.0	11 298	26.8	6.1	573	31.1	7.2
Brownsville city...........	517	33.1	8.7	458	32.1	7.9	579	24.0	7.1	128 127	35.9	8.2	3 477	36.3	7.7
Bryan city................	11 630	36.5	6.5	228	19.7	6.6	1 071	11.2	0.9	19 397	36.5	3.4	1 260	40.2	4.0
Carrollton city.............	6 916	32.5	1.5	673	24.7	4.5	11 468	30.1	4.2	21 158	35.6	1.9	3 231	40.2	3.8
Cedar Hill city............	10 877	38.1	1.4	221	59.7	0.0	466	30.9	10.3	3 676	37.1	1.3	786	53.6	0.0
Cedar Park city	1 024	41.4	0.0	117	32.5	10.3	669	29.4	3.3	3 678	39.7	2.0	412	40.0	4.9
Cleburne city	1 105	35.4	10.4	120	23.3	0.0	132	30.3	0.0	5 167	39.9	3.0	579	55.3	1.4
College Station city	3 513	33.4	6.7	246	11.8	2.4	5 255	18.6	1.6	6 812	17.8	1.1	1 365	22.3	0.7
Conroe city...............	4 031	33.7	9.8	153	14.4	2.6	370	23.5	3.8	12 035	35.8	1.5	1 216	40.2	3.8
Coppell city...............	906	34.3	1.1	124	19.4	0.0	3 469	35.4	3.9	2 487	36.9	2.3	739	49.7	4.7
Copperas Cove city.......	5 920	37.4	2.4	185	43.2	0.0	1 085	23.6	7.6	3 264	39.5	2.0	1 656	52.7	3.4
Corpus Christi city........	12 901	31.8	10.3	1 735	31.6	4.1	3 492	22.2	7.2	150 620	32.7	7.8	8 761	38.6	7.2
Dallas city................	306 122	30.4	7.5	5 832	26.1	4.4	32 806	21.0	4.6	423 178	35.5	2.3	32 040	36.0	3.4
Deer Park city............	296	24.7	0.0	127	28.3	0.0	304	19.7	3.6	4 389	36.2	3.4	640	39.4	3.4
Del Rio city...............	355	26.8	3.4	168	36.9	9.5	173	13.9	10.4	27 728	33.9	10.7	882	36.2	11.3
Denton city	7 275	25.6	4.6	420	18.6	5.7	2 724	13.4	0.7	13 198	31.4	1.2	1 866	29.2	3.3
DeSoto city...............	16 986	33.2	3.3	107	15.0	0.0	742	27.9	7.3	2 861	34.5	4.0	493	41.8	0.0
Duncanville city...........	9 003	37.6	2.7	169	14.2	7.7	789	22.8	8.0	5 249	37.9	2.5	1 014	47.8	2.0
Edinburg city..............	186	27.4	9.1	142	30.3	21.1	355	30.7	2.3	43 258	34.8	7.3	884	33.4	5.8
El Paso city...............	17 322	30.5	8.4	4 232	33.0	8.6	7 101	23.6	8.3	432 544	33.6	8.9	18 530	35.9	8.6
Euless city................	3 026	28.8	3.1	454	23.6	0.0	3 461	29.3	4.5	6 353	35.2	1.9	1 966	43.6	5.4
Farmers Branch city.......	709	28.3	0.8	82	0.0	0.0	1 066	22.4	3.3	10 640	37.3	2.8	588	34.9	5.4
Flower Mound town.......	1 506	34.4	2.1	193	22.3	4.7	1 372	26.9	1.2	2 844	39.2	2.5	1 076	52.9	0.4
Fort Worth city............	107 549	32.0	8.4	3 517	27.4	4.3	14 393	25.3	4.4	159 212	37.6	2.9	14 102	41.5	3.5
Friendswood city	705	33.2	0.0	109	17.4	4.6	662	33.2	11.9	2 554	33.0	3.8	580	32.9	9.1
Frisco city................	1 226	33.6	0.0	98	13.3	0.0	732	19.1	2.7	3 697	38.5	1.2	631	42.6	1.1
Galveston city............	14 456	29.2	13.2	276	33.3	2.9	1 846	20.2	4.3	14 730	31.7	7.4	1 473	37.2	6.6
Garland city..............	25 124	37.3	2.5	1 380	27.3	8.1	15 699	29.6	4.7	55 547	38.3	1.9	6 384	42.5	3.9
Georgetown city...........	777	27.7	9.0	26	26.9	0.0	179	2.8	17.9	5 039	35.4	4.6	721	45.4	2.6
Grand Prairie city.........	17 063	33.9	3.0	719	23.8	4.3	5 339	28.0	3.7	42 050	39.5	2.2	4 620	45.2	3.7
Grapevine city............	1 041	32.9	3.6	215	50.2	0.0	875	24.3	4.9	4 810	31.6	1.5	673	45.3	0.0
Haltom City city..........	972	32.6	0.8	515	27.4	3.1	3 145	30.2	4.8	7 596	37.9	2.1	985	43.7	2.4
Harlingen city.............	571	35.9	1.6	385	29.9	8.8	543	30.6	5.7	42 176	35.3	8.7	1 342	37.6	14.8
Houston city..............	493 149	30.3	8.1	8 266	31.9	3.9	103 360	22.0	5.9	731 680	34.8	3.2	61 206	33.5	3.6
Huntsville city............	9 325	17.5	6.1	190	24.7	0.0	317	16.1	3.5	5 565	17.5	2.7	410	33.9	2.4
Hurst city.................	1 503	37.5	2.0	257	23.0	14.8	605	32.1	5.1	3 992	35.5	2.1	750	52.9	2.9
Irving city.................	19 277	30.0	1.0	1 344	27.5	3.5	15 722	21.2	2.6	59 932	34.8	1.3	5 864	43.0	2.6
Keller city.................	351	37.9	2.3	100	41.0	0.0	541	28.1	2.2	1 358	46.7	2.1	547	53.6	4.4
Killeen city...............	28 426	33.1	2.4	649	27.0	1.7	4 851	21.7	5.3	15 450	35.9	2.9	5 226	55.3	1.2
Kingsville city.............	1 117	30.3	7.8	138	37.0	0.0	337	2.7	6.8	17 222	29.8	9.1	803	30.8	3.6
Lake Jackson city.........	924	34.0	0.9	76	38.2	14.5	665	28.7	4.4	3 857	40.0	3.6	579	45.6	8.5
Lancaster city............	13 722	35.2	2.6	90	27.8	0.0	98	22.4	0.0	3 156	41.6	2.2	462	39.8	5.0

[1]Hispanic or Latino persons may be of any race.

City	Total households	Family households (percent)						Nonfamily households (percent)						Percent of householders 65 years and over who live alone	Grandparents who are responsible for the care of their grandchildren
		Married-couple family households			Other family households			Two or more unrelated persons		Male living alone		Female living alone			
		Total	With children	House-holder 65 years or over	Total	With children	House-holder 65 years or over	Total	House-holder 65 years or over	Total	House-holder 65 years or over	Total	House-holder 65 years or over		
	29	30	31	32	33	34	35	36	37	38	39	40	41	42	43
TENNESSEE............	2 234 229	53.5	23.1	8.8	16.3	9.2	2.4	4.5	0.3	10.8	2.0	15.0	7.1	44.4	61 252
Bartlett city	13 724	75.3	38.0	8.4	10.9	6.2	1.4	1.8	0.1	4.3	1.1	7.7	3.6	32.1	362
Chattanooga city	65 513	40.1	14.5	8.5	20.9	11.1	3.2	5.5	0.4	13.5	2.8	20.1	9.2	49.9	1 956
Clarksville city	36 987	57.5	31.2	5.5	15.8	11.2	1.5	5.5	0.1	9.9	1.0	11.2	4.3	43.3	795
Cleveland city	15 114	48.0	20.5	8.6	16.1	9.0	2.7	5.3	0.3	11.8	2.2	18.8	8.9	49.0	341
Collierville town	10 324	76.3	46.5	6.3	10.0	6.9	0.7	1.9	0.1	5.0	0.5	6.9	2.8	31.7	173
Columbia city	13 124	46.9	20.6	8.9	21.0	12.2	2.5	4.1	0.3	10.0	2.6	18.1	9.2	50.1	257
Franklin city	16 092	56.7	32.1	4.7	13.1	7.5	1.4	4.8	0.2	10.1	1.0	15.3	5.3	50.3	180
Germantown city	13 231	76.3	38.0	10.0	7.6	4.4	1.0	1.4	0.2	4.7	0.5	10.1	4.0	28.5	108
Hendersonville city	15 798	60.3	27.9	8.5	13.2	8.3	1.0	4.0	0.2	8.8	1.1	13.7	5.9	41.9	256
Jackson city.................	23 523	42.0	18.5	7.9	22.5	13.8	2.6	5.0	0.2	12.7	2.4	17.8	7.6	48.1	696
Johnson City city..........	23 677	44.5	17.5	9.1	14.5	8.1	2.3	7.1	0.2	13.4	2.3	20.5	9.7	50.6	377
Kingsport city	19 530	47.6	18.2	11.2	16.4	9.4	2.7	3.3	0.5	11.2	2.4	21.5	11.8	49.6	423
Knoxville city	76 550	35.7	13.7	7.1	17.0	9.5	2.9	8.9	0.4	16.1	2.4	22.3	9.1	52.5	1 289
Memphis city	250 907	34.7	15.4	6.1	29.1	16.9	3.6	5.7	0.4	13.4	2.1	17.1	6.8	47.0	9 660
Murfreesboro city	26 724	45.7	22.1	6.1	14.3	8.8	1.3	11.8	0.3	12.3	1.1	16.0	6.2	48.8	419
Nashville-Davidson.......	237 432	40.9	17.3	6.6	17.7	10.1	2.2	8.0	0.4	14.0	1.8	19.3	6.6	47.9	5 550
Oak Ridge city	12 056	49.9	19.3	13.6	14.4	8.8	1.7	3.2	0.3	12.7	3.8	19.9	12.1	50.3	196
Smyrna town	9 579	55.2	28.2	4.8	17.5	11.2	1.6	5.5	0.3	10.6	0.6	11.2	3.1	35.3	294
TEXAS....................	7 397 294	55.0	28.0	8.0	16.4	9.5	2.1	4.9	0.3	10.6	1.8	13.0	5.6	41.5	257 074
Abilene city..................	41 535	53.4	25.3	9.5	14.6	9.6	1.6	5.5	0.2	10.9	2.0	15.6	8.1	47.2	1 406
Allen city.....................	14 219	75.6	49.3	3.2	9.9	7.0	0.5	2.8	0.0	6.3	0.3	5.4	1.1	26.5	187
Amarillo city.................	67 559	52.0	24.7	9.3	16.0	10.0	1.9	4.4	0.3	11.6	2.2	16.0	7.8	46.6	2 015
Arlington city................	124 852	53.2	28.9	4.8	15.4	9.9	1.0	6.6	0.2	12.5	0.7	12.3	3.1	38.4	2 758
Austin city...................	265 594	39.0	19.3	4.2	14.9	8.2	1.2	13.3	0.2	16.5	1.1	16.2	3.7	46.2	5 105
Baytown city	23 608	54.2	27.8	7.3	19.3	11.6	2.1	4.0	0.2	9.9	1.3	12.6	6.2	43.9	789
Beaumont city	44 333	44.2	19.8	8.7	21.9	12.9	3.4	4.4	0.3	12.6	2.7	16.9	8.5	47.6	1 696
Bedford city	20 317	50.3	22.8	5.4	12.0	7.1	1.2	6.1	0.0	14.2	1.1	17.4	4.8	47.4	218
Big Spring city..............	8 179	48.8	21.1	11.1	18.7	11.7	3.4	3.5	0.7	9.7	3.3	19.3	11.5	49.3	338
Brownsville city............	38 286	60.8	37.5	9.2	24.0	12.8	4.5	1.9	0.3	4.8	1.7	8.5	5.1	32.9	2 087
Bryan city....................	23 855	46.3	23.5	7.0	16.8	10.4	1.9	10.7	0.1	10.9	1.3	15.2	6.3	45.7	777
Carrollton city	39 166	60.8	32.8	3.8	13.6	8.4	0.8	5.6	0.2	9.4	0.7	10.6	2.3	38.6	812
Cedar Hill city	10 741	62.6	37.5	2.9	19.5	12.6	1.2	3.2	0.1	5.8	0.6	8.9	2.4	42.4	313
Cedar Park city	8 655	70.6	44.4	3.5	12.2	8.8	0.3	4.2	0.0	6.7	0.9	6.3	1.7	40.4	134
Cleburne city	9 350	58.0	28.4	9.8	15.3	9.1	2.5	3.2	0.4	8.5	2.0	15.1	8.8	46.1	375
College Station city	24 599	33.2	17.5	3.5	9.3	4.2	0.4	30.5	0.1	14.7	0.3	12.3	2.3	39.8	294
Conroe city..................	13 218	47.9	24.8	6.9	19.3	11.2	1.9	5.8	0.3	10.6	1.6	16.4	8.3	52.0	476
Coppell city..................	12 227	71.2	48.0	2.3	9.7	7.0	0.2	3.3	0.1	7.3	0.6	8.5	1.1	39.8	100
Copperas Cove city.......	10 355	61.8	35.8	4.5	16.6	12.9	0.7	5.1	0.1	8.6	0.5	7.9	2.2	34.0	182
Corpus Christi city........	98 779	51.4	25.1	8.6	20.3	11.5	2.8	5.1	0.4	10.4	1.9	12.8	6.0	40.1	5 170
Dallas city...................	452 009	39.8	20.4	5.4	19.9	10.6	2.3	7.5	0.3	15.5	1.6	17.4	5.0	45.0	15 019
Deer Park city	9 579	68.6	35.5	7.2	14.0	8.2	1.4	3.4	0.0	6.4	0.9	7.6	2.9	30.6	346
Del Rio city	10 769	62.5	34.2	9.5	17.7	9.1	4.3	1.7	0.2	7.9	2.6	10.2	5.8	37.8	631
Denton city	30 932	41.0	19.5	5.8	13.0	7.6	1.2	14.7	0.3	14.1	0.8	17.3	4.8	43.3	673
DeSoto city..................	13 749	61.1	29.3	7.8	16.1	10.6	1.2	2.0	0.1	7.0	1.4	13.8	5.0	41.5	520
Duncanville city............	12 884	60.7	27.9	8.4	19.1	11.3	2.1	2.8	0.2	5.0	1.1	12.4	5.3	37.8	580
Edinburg city	14 251	54.3	34.3	7.7	23.3	12.6	3.3	4.1	0.5	6.4	1.4	8.6	4.3	33.4	855
El Paso city	182 237	55.8	30.8	9.1	22.2	12.3	3.5	2.9	0.3	8.0	1.8	11.1	5.6	36.2	10 055
Euless city	19 234	46.6	23.2	4.1	14.2	9.4	0.8	7.9	0.1	16.8	0.9	14.5	2.5	40.3	309
Farmers Branch city......	9 885	58.0	28.1	11.2	13.7	7.5	1.7	5.4	0.3	9.9	1.9	13.0	5.0	34.1	378
Flower Mound town.......	16 396	81.0	52.0	2.1	7.8	5.2	0.3	2.0	0.0	4.7	0.4	4.4	0.7	31.1	248
Fort Worth city.............	195 309	46.6	24.5	6.4	19.1	11.0	2.4	5.7	0.3	13.0	1.8	15.5	6.0	46.0	7 574
Friendswood city	10 030	68.3	37.3	7.0	11.7	7.4	1.4	2.9	0.3	6.1	1.0	11.0	5.2	41.6	147
Frisco city....................	11 994	71.8	42.7	3.3	8.3	5.5	0.5	4.0	0.1	6.7	0.2	9.3	1.6	32.0	120
Galveston city	23 791	37.6	14.9	7.5	20.5	12.2	3.2	6.3	0.5	15.7	3.3	19.9	8.1	50.3	890
Garland city.................	73 279	58.0	31.8	6.0	18.2	10.8	1.4	4.1	0.1	8.0	0.9	11.7	4.0	39.6	2 324
Georgetown city	10 397	62.4	24.5	17.0	12.4	7.1	1.4	3.6	0.1	6.4	1.6	15.2	8.0	34.1	155
Grand Prairie city	43 566	58.8	31.0	5.2	18.3	11.6	1.6	5.4	0.2	9.6	0.8	10.8	4.0	40.8	1 631
Grapevine city..............	15 746	61.0	34.9	3.4	11.4	7.7	0.5	5.7	0.0	10.6	0.7	11.2	3.2	49.6	120
Haltom City city	15 014	48.8	24.9	7.0	18.4	9.9	2.3	6.1	0.3	13.1	1.7	13.7	6.0	44.7	580
Harlingen city	18 997	57.3	29.5	13.5	18.9	10.3	3.4	2.8	0.4	8.2	2.8	12.7	8.2	38.9	661
Houston city................	718 897	44.2	23.1	5.7	20.1	10.8	2.3	6.2	0.3	14.3	1.7	15.3	4.7	43.3	25 347
Huntsville city	10 239	39.1	17.2	7.3	15.0	8.5	1.4	15.0	0.8	13.3	2.1	17.5	6.3	46.9	197
Hurst city....................	14 088	58.0	25.2	10.6	15.6	9.5	1.8	4.4	0.2	8.5	1.1	13.4	6.1	36.4	371
Irving city....................	76 373	45.2	22.7	4.4	15.9	9.6	1.0	7.7	0.1	15.4	0.8	15.8	2.9	40.2	1 796
Keller city	8 811	83.3	49.8	4.9	5.8	3.4	0.4	1.7	0.2	4.6	0.3	4.7	1.6	25.6	170
Killeen city	32 514	54.4	29.7	3.5	16.9	12.6	0.8	6.3	0.1	12.8	0.9	9.5	2.8	46.5	904
Kingsville city	8 954	49.2	23.9	8.5	20.5	11.4	2.7	6.6	0.3	10.4	1.3	13.3	6.6	40.4	349
Lake Jackson city.........	9 610	64.7	35.3	9.1	12.5	8.4	1.3	2.9	0.1	8.9	1.9	11.0	6.0	43.0	190
Lancaster city	9 167	50.1	25.3	6.1	25.6	15.8	2.2	3.1	0.1	7.6	1.1	13.5	4.6	40.2	514

Table A-5. Cities — Age, Ethnicity, and Household Structure

City	Households with Non-Hispanic White householder		Households with Black or African American householder		Households with American Indian and Alaska Native householder		Households with Asian, Hawaiian, and Pacific Islander householder		Households with Hispanic or Latino[1] householder		Foreign-born population	Place of birth (percent)			Percent in non-English speaking households	
	Number of households	Percent that are family households	Number of households	Percent that are family households	Number of households	Percent that are family households	Number of households	Percent that are family households	Number of households	Percent that are family households	Percent of total population that is foreign-born	Europe	Asia	Latin America	Linguistically isolated	Not linguistically isolated
	44	45	46	47	48	49	50	51	52	53	54	55	56	57	58	59
TENNESSEE............	1 828 668	69.8	331 948	69.2	6 191	71.3	17 622	71.5	31 613	74.4	2.8	0.5	0.9	1.1	1.1	6.9
Bartlett city	12 795	85.8	515	93.0	57	68.4	111	89.2	147	89.1	1.7	0.4	0.8	0.3	0.4	6.9
Chattanooga city	41 821	58.0	21 335	66.8	217	61.8	919	61.2	780	62.9	3.4	0.6	1.5	1.1	1.1	8.1
Clarksville city	25 522	72.7	8 343	74.4	184	65.8	454	67.4	1 823	80.1	5.0	1.6	1.8	1.4	0.9	16.2
Cleveland city	13 466	63.5	983	62.8	21	57.1	124	93.5	383	72.1	3.7	0.6	1.0	1.8	2.0	7.4
Collierville town	9 339	87.2	723	78.1	16	31.3	115	90.4	94	69.1	2.8	0.5	1.1	0.5	0.5	7.0
Columbia city	9 906	67.1	2 733	69.2	34	100.0	25	40.0	351	79.2	3.4	0.4	0.2	2.6	1.8	7.3
Franklin city	13 696	68.5	1 566	74.8	25	80.0	203	75.4	456	86.8	5.9	0.8	1.6	3.0	2.0	9.3
Germantown city	12 334	84.0	262	76.7	21	33.3	389	90.0	120	81.7	5.3	1.6	2.8	0.3	0.8	10.7
Hendersonville city	14 772	73.0	532	86.5	57	49.1	166	74.1	141	85.8	2.9	0.9	1.0	0.8	0.8	7.3
Jackson city.................	13 576	62.7	9 325	66.6	69	100.0	95	91.6	324	67.3	2.8	0.3	0.6	1.5	1.3	6.2
Johnson City city	21 501	58.8	1 380	58.3	79	48.1	179	86.0	354	72.3	3.0	0.6	0.9	1.0	0.7	6.3
Kingsport city	18 318	64.1	790	57.7	91	86.8	74	83.8	95	66.3	2.1	0.7	0.5	0.4	0.6	4.0
Knoxville city	62 183	51.6	11 524	59.1	238	61.8	958	41.4	758	52.9	3.0	0.9	1.2	0.7	1.0	6.9
Memphis city	101 854	54.3	138 455	70.3	538	67.1	3 453	71.9	4 782	74.2	4.0	0.4	1.4	1.8	1.9	9.2
Murfreesboro city	21 887	59.4	3 326	60.7	69	88.4	538	79.9	682	58.9	4.9	0.5	2.2	1.8	2.3	9.2
Nashville-Davidson........	167 622	55.8	54 495	64.9	859	68.9	4 162	63.2	6 888	73.6	6.9	0.9	2.2	2.9	3.0	10.4
Oak Ridge city..............	10 555	64.0	898	67.3	82	52.4	182	84.1	166	76.5	4.5	1.6	1.5	0.9	1.2	8.7
Smyrna town	8 314	72.1	722	76.3	66	75.8	112	94.6	286	75.2	4.7	0.4	1.4	2.7	2.3	8.3
TEXAS....................	4 478 556	67.5	842 713	68.6	39 513	72.6	179 266	74.9	1 794 271	82.5	13.9	0.7	2.2	10.4	8.1	30.6
Abilene city..................	31 519	65.8	2 967	68.3	255	76.9	533	59.7	6 000	79.8	4.1	0.5	1.1	2.1	2.0	21.8
Allen city......................	12 193	84.9	561	88.9	49	71.4	477	93.1	799	90.2	7.3	1.3	2.6	1.9	1.0	18.3
Amarillo city.................	51 055	65.0	3 472	68.2	543	65.6	1 157	82.5	10 732	81.8	7.3	0.5	1.7	4.9	4.0	21.5
Arlington city................	82 665	66.6	17 078	64.7	763	70.1	5 730	75.9	16 567	80.5	15.3	0.8	5.3	8.0	8.0	22.4
Austin city....................	165 648	47.4	24 452	62.8	1 403	52.6	11 880	52.9	58 848	70.1	16.6	1.1	3.8	11.0	9.3	29.7
Baytown city................	14 384	67.7	3 045	74.0	119	68.1	188	93.1	5 686	87.5	16.0	0.3	0.9	14.6	7.8	30.6
Beaumont city	21 877	60.0	18 702	70.9	179	77.7	761	78.2	2 465	79.9	5.7	0.5	1.6	3.3	2.3	14.1
Bedford city	17 626	61.8	782	63.7	117	55.6	526	73.4	1 003	69.6	7.0	1.5	2.6	1.9	1.6	15.1
Big Spring city	5 298	61.6	438	61.4	19	42.1	19	63.2	2 315	82.5	7.1	0.1	0.4	6.5	5.5	32.9
Brownsville city	4 500	69.4	140	95.7	114	79.8	185	60.5	33 378	87.1	31.5	0.2	0.4	30.7	20.2	73.6
Bryan city	14 730	55.9	3 687	71.7	81	61.7	478	45.8	4 701	82.0	11.1	0.6	1.7	8.5	6.7	25.2
Carrollton city	27 225	70.4	2 623	69.2	206	84.0	3 005	91.9	5 478	85.8	20.0	0.9	8.5	9.9	8.9	26.0
Cedar Hill city	6 036	79.5	3 544	84.0	26	100.0	114	89.5	876	92.9	4.3	0.3	1.2	2.3	0.9	18.8
Cedar Park city	7 086	81.8	335	85.4	43	69.8	175	93.1	944	91.0	6.1	1.0	2.3	2.4	1.2	19.3
Cleburne city	7 410	70.8	383	68.7	61	100.0	33	100.0	1 380	86.2	8.3	0.1	0.2	7.7	5.2	18.4
College Station city	18 725	39.8	1 214	64.6	83	57.8	1 978	53.5	2 368	44.0	11.1	1.2	6.4	2.8	4.9	20.0
Conroe city	8 724	60.5	1 504	72.4	48	70.8	121	88.4	2 752	85.5	22.3	0.5	0.8	20.6	13.9	24.1
Coppell city	10 030	80.0	342	78.1	32	65.6	952	92.6	692	78.2	11.9	1.7	7.0	2.3	3.9	19.5
Copperas Cove city......	6 850	76.4	1 982	83.9	52	100.0	396	59.3	867	89.9	7.5	3.3	2.1	1.8	1.1	26.6
Corpus Christi city........	46 002	65.0	4 651	68.8	553	75.0	1 070	78.7	45 898	78.8	6.7	0.5	1.0	4.8	5.9	49.4
Dallas city....................	211 215	46.0	116 711	65.1	1 983	59.4	12 509	61.7	105 354	81.4	24.4	0.9	2.6	19.8	15.3	27.6
Deer Park city	8 233	82.0	70	100.0	37	83.8	93	94.6	1 065	87.3	4.9	0.3	1.0	3.5	1.9	18.8
Del Rio city	2 451	70.3	154	73.4	37	81.1	54	51.9	8 063	83.5	24.1	0.3	0.3	23.4	15.4	67.4
Denton city	23 196	52.7	2 394	52.6	156	43.6	1 170	34.0	3 473	72.2	11.2	0.6	2.8	7.4	6.7	17.8
DeSoto city	6 756	73.8	5 889	80.7	50	100.0	241	80.5	757	77.8	4.8	0.6	1.4	2.3	1.2	15.0
Duncanville city	8 031	77.0	3 083	81.2	58	75.9	209	88.5	1 358	91.2	8.0	0.6	2.2	4.7	3.5	19.4
Edinburg city	2 096	67.7	68	38.2	53	71.7	139	74.8	11 839	83.5	21.5	0.2	0.6	20.6	15.3	75.7
El Paso city	46 934	67.8	6 732	69.3	1 395	77.7	2 422	65.4	124 705	82.8	26.1	1.0	1.0	24.0	14.7	66.6
Euless city	14 359	58.4	1 255	57.6	214	60.7	1 065	77.1	1 936	72.0	14.1	1.5	6.0	4.7	5.3	21.5
Farmers Branch city......	6 789	65.6	323	72.8	67	38.8	390	57.9	2 238	93.1	25.2	0.5	3.6	20.6	13.2	31.2
Flower Mound town.......	14 472	88.8	528	87.1	80	100.0	379	91.6	770	85.2	5.4	1.2	2.3	1.2	0.8	14.1
Fort Worth city..............	108 765	58.3	39 542	68.1	1 196	69.1	4 463	70.6	39 630	83.2	16.3	0.8	2.2	12.9	10.0	25.7
Friendswood city	8 785	79.1	246	74.8	39	69.2	173	88.4	660	92.4	5.7	1.3	1.7	2.1	1.0	16.1
Frisco city	10 188	79.7	408	78.7	39	38.5	266	87.6	954	88.1	7.8	1.2	1.8	3.9	2.1	17.0
Galveston city..............	12 234	51.0	5 660	62.5	117	69.2	811	54.7	4 747	73.2	12.8	0.8	2.8	8.6	6.8	27.3
Garland city	46 167	70.8	8 694	79.4	427	79.6	4 241	86.8	12 723	89.1	20.2	0.7	5.7	13.0	10.8	27.5
Georgetown city............	8 699	73.9	242	72.7	13	100.0	72	23.6	1 273	84.2	6.7	1.0	0.4	4.9	4.4	18.1
Grand Prairie city	24 116	68.9	6 285	70.5	302	55.6	1 509	85.6	10 776	86.3	16.4	0.7	3.2	11.7	8.2	32.2
Grapevine city	13 388	72.6	401	73.6	51	33.3	320	69.7	1 368	74.0	9.4	0.9	1.8	5.8	4.1	15.4
Haltom City city	11 254	63.6	432	63.4	168	83.9	898	74.3	2 101	82.1	14.1	0.5	6.1	6.9	8.6	21.1
Harlingen city	6 373	65.5	202	75.2	172	84.3	193	68.4	12 117	82.1	17.3	0.4	0.7	15.8	11.7	64.8
Houston city.................	292 549	52.1	184 163	65.5	2 598	73.3	36 320	70.2	195 594	80.6	26.4	1.2	4.7	19.4	14.5	33.3
Huntsville city	6 857	51.8	2 218	51.1	66	95.5	81	42.0	960	75.2	5.6	0.3	0.6	4.5	4.4	16.6
Hurst city	12 109	72.1	516	78.1	74	87.8	177	85.9	1 067	84.9	8.0	1.1	1.3	4.5	3.2	14.5
Irving city	44 204	54.6	8 629	53.9	473	70.8	6 019	68.7	16 052	79.8	26.5	1.0	7.2	16.8	14.8	29.3
Keller city.....................	8 065	89.2	128	83.6	30	100.0	162	94.4	300	86.0	5.2	1.9	1.8	0.8	0.8	12.0
Killeen city...................	14 731	68.2	10 858	72.5	246	77.2	1 378	70.8	4 803	76.9	10.3	2.8	3.6	3.4	2.6	31.3
Kingsville city...............	3 006	64.2	314	63.7	53	71.7	75	36.0	5 469	73.9	6.7	0.4	1.5	4.8	7.9	63.6
Lake Jackson city..........	7 844	75.3	305	87.5	15	60.0	186	93.5	1 127	85.1	5.1	0.9	1.7	2.0	1.4	20.1
Lancaster city	3 633	70.2	4 690	78.7	30	100.0	28	60.7	736	87.5	5.2	0.3	0.5	4.3	2.7	15.8

[1] Hispanic or Latino persons may be of any race.

Table A-5. Cities — Age, Ethnicity, and Household Structure

STATE Place code	City	Population by age (percent)								+/− U.S. percent under 18 years	+/− U.S. percent 65 years and over	Non-Hispanic White		
		Total population	Under 5 years	5 to 17 years	18 to 24 years	25 to 44 years	45 to 64 years	65 years and over	Median age			Total population	Under 18 years	65 years and over
		1	2	3	4	5	6	7	8	9	10	11	12	13
	TEXAS—Cont'd													
48 41440	La Porte city	31 899	7.3	22.1	9.4	32.6	22.2	6.3	32.6	3.7	-6.1	22 433	26.9	8.0
48 41464	Laredo city	176 807	10.4	25.1	11.4	29.6	15.5	7.9	26.9	9.8	-4.5	8 737	27.7	12.5
48 41980	League City city	45 282	8.1	21.1	6.5	36.0	22.3	6.0	34.4	3.5	-6.4	34 788	27.9	6.5
48 42508	Lewisville city	77 514	9.1	17.2	11.8	41.4	16.1	4.3	29.8	0.6	-8.1	53 620	23.5	5.6
48 43888	Longview city	73 158	7.4	19.4	11.0	28.4	20.2	13.6	34.0	1.1	1.2	48 038	22.5	17.2
48 45000	Lubbock city	199 556	7.0	17.7	17.8	28.0	18.5	11.1	29.7	-1.0	-1.3	122 193	18.5	14.7
48 45072	Lufkin city	32 623	7.5	19.3	10.5	27.9	19.8	15.0	34.0	1.1	2.6	17 500	19.7	22.0
48 45384	McAllen city	106 211	8.6	22.0	10.3	30.0	18.5	10.6	30.5	4.9	-1.8	18 154	21.0	23.0
48 45744	McKinney city	54 384	10.1	20.8	9.3	36.4	16.6	6.9	30.6	5.2	-5.5	38 933	29.3	8.5
48 46452	Mansfield city	28 988	8.6	23.3	7.6	35.0	19.9	5.5	32.3	6.2	-6.9	23 371	31.0	6.3
48 47892	Mesquite city	124 578	7.5	22.8	9.1	34.6	19.1	6.9	31.9	4.6	-5.5	81 617	26.6	9.3
48 48072	Midland city	95 155	7.4	22.5	8.7	28.7	20.4	12.4	34.1	4.2	0.0	57 816	24.7	16.6
48 48768	Mission city	45 920	9.2	22.8	9.9	26.8	16.7	14.5	30.5	6.3	2.1	8 057	13.2	44.2
48 48804	Missouri City city	52 477	7.3	23.4	6.5	31.7	25.8	5.3	35.5	5.0	-7.1	20 449	26.5	8.7
48 50256	Nacogdoches city	30 314	5.6	15.0	30.7	22.8	15.5	10.3	24.4	-5.1	-2.1	18 967	14.8	12.7
48 50820	New Braunfels city	36 884	7.2	18.9	8.2	29.0	20.2	16.5	36.2	0.4	4.1	23 058	21.5	22.3
48 52356	North Richland Hills city	55 490	6.9	20.3	9.0	33.0	22.2	8.6	34.7	1.5	-3.8	46 206	25.9	10.0
48 53388	Odessa city	91 053	8.1	21.7	10.6	27.8	20.2	11.6	32.3	4.1	-0.8	46 122	22.3	17.6
48 55080	Paris city	25 885	7.5	18.0	9.9	25.8	20.6	18.3	36.5	-0.2	5.9	18 508	22.3	21.8
48 56000	Pasadena city	141 731	9.1	22.4	11.6	31.1	17.8	7.9	29.2	5.8	-4.5	66 869	23.2	14.2
48 56348	Pearland city	37 596	7.7	20.7	6.8	35.1	21.4	8.3	34.3	2.7	-4.1	27 910	26.3	10.1
48 57200	Pharr city	46 616	10.5	24.2	11.4	25.9	15.9	12.1	27.4	9.0	-0.3	4 183	17.6	58.9
48 58016	Plano city	222 301	8.2	20.3	6.7	37.4	22.6	4.8	34.1	2.8	-7.6	161 462	27.0	5.7
48 58820	Port Arthur city	57 756	7.7	21.0	9.7	26.5	19.3	15.8	34.6	3.0	3.4	18 410	16.1	28.9
48 61796	Richardson city	91 635	6.7	18.1	8.7	32.9	23.8	9.7	35.8	-0.9	-2.7	63 769	22.4	12.6
48 63500	Round Rock city	60 407	9.8	22.1	8.1	38.5	17.0	4.5	30.1	6.2	-7.9	39 279	28.7	5.9
48 63572	Rowlett city	44 326	8.7	24.7	5.3	37.5	18.5	5.3	32.8	7.7	-7.1	34 102	31.8	6.3
48 64472	San Angelo city	88 609	6.8	18.9	13.9	27.4	19.0	14.0	32.8	0.0	1.6	53 065	19.8	19.0
48 65000	San Antonio city	1 144 554	8.0	20.4	10.7	31.2	19.2	10.4	31.7	2.7	-2.0	363 870	20.3	16.1
48 65516	San Juan city	26 107	11.1	26.5	11.8	27.6	15.0	8.1	25.5	11.9	-4.3	1 236	16.0	36.3
48 65600	San Marcos city	34 005	4.9	9.8	42.0	24.5	11.3	7.6	23.3	-11.0	-4.8	18 886	8.2	8.4
48 67496	Sherman city	34 957	7.1	17.1	13.4	27.3	19.8	15.3	34.0	-1.5	2.9	25 550	20.9	18.8
48 68636	Socorro city	27 840	9.4	26.9	11.6	28.0	17.6	6.3	26.6	10.6	-6.1	759	29.8	18.4
48 70808	Sugar Land city	63 507	6.1	25.1	6.2	29.1	26.8	6.7	37.4	5.5	-5.7	38 590	30.6	7.9
48 72176	Temple city	54 437	7.6	18.6	9.2	28.8	20.1	15.7	35.2	0.5	3.3	34 157	20.7	20.7
48 72368	Texarkana city	34 898	7.3	19.0	9.8	28.0	20.1	15.9	35.7	0.6	3.5	20 399	20.1	21.5
48 72392	Texas City city	41 391	6.6	20.2	9.4	27.9	22.7	13.2	35.5	1.1	0.8	20 340	20.8	17.6
48 72530	The Colony city	26 661	8.2	25.3	7.1	38.3	18.3	2.8	30.8	7.8	-9.6	20 688	32.3	2.8
48 74144	Tyler city	83 861	7.4	18.5	11.9	27.0	20.1	15.1	34.1	0.2	2.7	47 010	19.3	21.4
48 75428	Victoria city	60 463	7.6	21.1	9.5	28.6	20.8	12.3	33.9	3.0	-0.1	28 863	22.1	18.2
48 76000	Waco city	114 032	7.5	18.0	19.9	25.4	15.6	13.7	27.9	-0.2	1.3	58 289	16.1	19.8
48 77272	Weslaco city	26 802	9.2	22.1	9.8	26.2	16.6	16.1	30.8	5.6	3.7	4 026	11.6	45.9
48 79000	Wichita Falls city	103 921	7.1	17.3	15.3	29.5	18.5	12.3	31.9	-1.3	-0.1	71 492	21.7	15.3
49 00000	UTAH	2 233 169	9.4	22.7	14.3	28.2	16.9	8.5	27.1	6.4	-3.9	1 905 227	31.1	9.4
49 07690	Bountiful city	41 392	8.4	21.3	12.1	23.8	20.1	14.3	32.5	4.0	1.9	38 998	28.9	15.0
49 13850	Clearfield city	25 918	12.4	24.2	15.2	30.4	12.0	5.8	24.0	10.9	-6.6	20 405	35.6	6.8
49 20120	Draper city	25 436	10.2	21.2	11.5	38.4	15.3	3.4	28.6	5.7	-9.0	22 630	32.7	3.7
49 43660	Layton city	58 678	10.2	24.9	12.0	31.0	16.3	5.6	26.8	9.4	-6.8	51 008	34.5	5.7
49 45860	Logan city	42 725	9.4	13.7	34.4	25.4	10.2	6.9	23.5	-2.6	-5.5	36 630	21.6	7.9
49 49710	Midvale city	27 039	9.7	15.6	16.9	31.6	17.0	9.2	28.1	-0.4	-3.2	19 821	22.6	11.3
49 53230	Murray city	33 911	7.6	19.1	13.5	29.3	19.3	11.3	31.0	1.0	-1.1	29 862	25.9	12.3
49 55980	Ogden city	77 240	9.4	19.3	14.5	29.3	16.0	11.5	28.6	3.0	-0.9	54 125	24.7	14.4
49 57300	Orem city	84 333	10.6	24.5	17.4	25.7	14.7	7.0	23.9	9.4	-5.4	72 940	34.4	7.7
49 62470	Provo city	105 258	8.6	13.5	40.0	23.6	8.5	5.7	22.9	-3.6	-6.7	88 800	20.4	6.5
49 64340	Riverton city	25 140	12.2	30.3	8.5	32.3	12.9	3.8	23.7	16.8	-8.6	23 800	42.0	3.9
49 65110	Roy city	32 744	9.7	23.6	11.1	31.0	16.3	8.3	28.0	7.6	-4.1	28 713	32.5	9.0
49 65330	St. George city	49 621	8.6	19.5	13.8	21.9	16.9	19.3	31.4	2.4	6.9	44 195	26.8	21.3
49 67000	Salt Lake City city	181 456	7.8	15.6	15.5	33.8	16.3	11.1	30.0	-2.3	-1.3	127 780	19.1	14.0
49 67440	Sandy city	88 259	7.8	26.8	11.2	27.3	21.6	5.4	29.1	8.9	-7.0	80 444	34.1	5.6
49 70850	South Jordan city	29 461	8.8	30.5	10.8	26.9	18.5	4.5	25.3	13.6	-7.9	27 517	38.9	4.7
49 75360	Taylorsville city	57 878	8.5	22.3	14.7	28.9	19.6	6.0	27.8	5.1	-6.4	45 872	29.2	7.0
49 82950	West Jordan city	68 216	11.2	26.5	12.3	31.9	14.8	3.3	25.0	12.0	-9.1	57 931	37.2	3.5
49 83470	West Valley City city	108 823	10.8	22.8	13.0	30.6	17.5	5.3	26.8	7.9	-7.1	76 502	31.0	6.5
50 00000	VERMONT	608 827	5.6	18.7	9.4	29.0	24.7	12.7	37.7	-1.4	0.3	585 217	23.8	13.0
50 10675	Burlington city	38 889	4.3	12.0	25.5	31.1	16.6	10.5	29.2	-9.4	-1.9	35 659	15.1	11.2

Table A-5. Cities — Age, Ethnicity, and Household Structure

City	Black or African American			American Indian and Alaska Native			Asian, Hawaiian, and Pacific Islander			Hispanic or Latino[1]			Two or more races		
		Age (percent)			Age (percent)			Age (percent)			Age (percent)			Age (percent)	
	Total population	Under 18 years	65 years and over	Total population	Under 18 years	65 years and over	Total population	Under 18 years	65 years and over	Total population	Under 18 years	65 years and over	Total population	Under 18 years	65 years and over
	14	15	16	17	18	19	20	21	22	23	24	25	26	27	28
TEXAS—Cont'd															
La Porte city	2 181	33.0	3.4	179	11.7	5.0	231	29.0	6.1	6 507	37.1	1.9	846	32.6	2.6
Laredo city	704	47.6	3.6	756	29.1	9.4	810	30.5	6.0	166 544	36.0	7.7	4 197	32.4	9.5
League City city	2 280	34.1	4.4	235	26.4	7.7	1 422	27.6	6.0	6 096	35.2	3.7	904	40.9	0.7
Lewisville city	5 768	33.0	1.4	586	29.0	4.8	3 055	26.8	2.4	13 699	33.7	1.1	2 091	42.6	2.2
Longview city	16 523	33.4	8.6	292	25.7	4.5	532	35.7	1.1	7 297	39.1	2.2	1 048	41.8	7.6
Lubbock city	17 397	34.0	7.6	1 139	29.0	4.8	2 900	20.1	4.2	54 946	35.9	4.6	3 922	37.9	5.9
Lufkin city	8 716	32.1	10.2	80	0.0	0.0	478	34.5	4.6	5 757	39.6	1.8	350	41.1	7.4
McAllen city	711	37.7	2.0	484	35.5	5.8	2 007	29.8	2.6	85 064	32.8	8.2	2 583	31.4	11.1
McKinney city	3 770	34.6	5.8	287	34.8	1.7	829	30.5	2.1	9 951	34.5	2.0	1 180	50.3	2.1
Mansfield city	1 214	31.6	4.9	144	31.9	7.6	399	27.6	1.8	3 608	37.6	1.3	493	39.6	2.2
Mesquite city	16 438	38.3	1.3	619	33.9	1.1	4 594	32.5	3.0	19 128	37.7	2.5	3 530	43.6	3.5
Midland city	7 883	32.6	11.1	547	33.5	9.0	1 025	31.6	5.6	27 441	39.5	4.5	2 006	49.5	5.5
Mission city	207	27.5	4.8	137	21.2	17.5	160	20.6	5.0	37 333	36.2	8.1	1 148	37.0	14.9
Missouri City city	20 141	34.6	2.1	98	14.3	6.1	5 746	28.7	6.2	5 358	33.7	4.1	1 256	38.5	1.3
Nacogdoches city	7 444	29.6	8.7	125	8.8	8.0	356	15.7	0.0	3 083	33.0	1.1	710	32.7	2.0
New Braunfels city	378	21.7	10.8	104	29.8	6.7	279	29.0	10.4	12 746	33.7	6.7	779	42.9	4.4
North Richland Hills city	1 427	32.3	2.8	189	32.8	1.6	1 286	28.1	1.3	5 457	33.5	1.3	1 376	40.9	0.7
Odessa city	5 152	33.4	11.1	588	24.1	7.7	741	28.3	6.7	37 754	38.4	4.4	2 967	42.0	6.8
Paris city	5 549	33.1	10.4	243	28.8	9.1	111	18.9	0.0	1 035	35.9	3.7	474	39.7	10.5
Pasadena city	2 036	38.3	4.8	818	27.8	3.1	2 746	29.4	2.9	68 439	39.5	2.1	4 720	42.7	2.8
Pearland city	2 236	35.1	2.4	222	42.3	0.0	1 109	24.9	3.8	5 812	36.7	2.9	762	44.9	7.3
Pharr city	164	73.8	0.0	226	21.7	6.2	144	38.2	13.9	42 195	37.3	7.5	912	29.3	8.2
Plano city	11 066	32.2	2.7	886	21.8	5.6	22 618	30.7	3.1	22 359	32.7	1.3	5 249	45.4	3.7
Port Arthur city	25 005	32.1	11.7	294	12.2	9.2	3 433	38.3	5.2	10 121	39.6	6.3	1 334	39.4	6.3
Richardson city	5 710	34.0	1.9	485	22.5	15.1	10 261	23.5	4.8	9 336	33.7	1.7	2 994	43.7	2.0
Round Rock city	4 687	37.3	1.6	334	36.8	3.9	1 756	29.7	2.2	13 536	37.9	2.2	1 697	50.1	1.5
Rowlett city	4 007	37.9	1.5	220	48.2	0.0	1 689	32.1	3.1	3 879	41.9	1.6	871	54.4	3.4
San Angelo city	4 433	32.4	8.1	456	24.8	2.9	701	17.8	7.4	29 410	35.4	6.1	2 067	44.3	4.0
San Antonio city	75 804	29.1	10.2	7 848	29.4	6.2	18 792	21.1	6.5	671 200	32.9	7.0	44 210	37.0	6.1
San Juan city	99	40.4	25.3	23	30.4	34.8	0	X	X	24 871	38.6	6.7	648	43.2	10.0
San Marcos city	1 794	18.3	3.4	248	20.6	4.8	411	12.9	0.0	12 379	24.1	7.2	902	28.4	6.8
Sherman city	3 996	32.6	7.0	371	31.3	8.6	372	27.4	10.8	4 151	36.6	3.0	863	32.4	10.2
Socorro city	137	44.5	4.4	294	37.8	5.1	62	12.9	27.4	26 887	36.6	5.9	823	31.5	4.3
Sugar Land city	3 139	33.9	5.4	236	47.9	5.5	14 468	30.4	4.8	5 250	33.7	4.8	2 049	40.3	6.0
Temple city	8 796	35.0	9.4	364	36.0	3.8	865	19.0	5.9	9 733	37.5	5.2	1 327	43.6	5.6
Texarkana city	13 009	34.4	8.5	91	24.2	0.0	303	29.7	6.3	775	34.2	4.3	492	57.3	1.2
Texas City city	11 235	28.8	11.6	211	29.9	9.0	540	29.4	5.6	8 565	36.2	6.0	1 139	46.1	6.4
The Colony city	1 331	35.4	1.7	162	25.3	0.0	569	27.4	2.8	3 393	38.9	3.7	651	54.4	2.5
Tyler city	22 021	30.1	10.2	325	18.8	0.0	723	37.1	2.6	13 193	41.1	2.2	1 236	46.3	4.4
Victoria city	4 690	32.3	9.4	358	29.9	4.2	495	29.9	8.3	25 920	35.4	6.4	1 291	45.8	8.4
Waco city	25 758	33.7	10.0	582	36.8	1.9	1 581	11.7	5.7	26 876	37.9	4.8	2 423	49.2	5.1
Weslaco city	43	79.1	0.0	141	30.5	9.2	251	15.1	3.6	22 385	35.1	10.9	497	31.2	15.7
Wichita Falls city	12 558	27.2	8.1	806	30.4	2.5	2 450	24.1	4.5	14 460	33.5	4.3	3 429	39.8	4.2
UTAH	16 150	35.2	4.2	28 646	37.0	3.5	51 244	29.4	5.1	200 005	38.3	2.7	51 480	50.8	2.6
Bountiful city	78	75.6	0.0	70	62.9	0.0	583	29.3	2.4	1 199	39.3	4.6	597	56.3	2.0
Clearfield city	943	39.1	1.2	438	33.1	0.0	902	25.8	5.9	2 810	42.3	2.1	964	61.6	2.3
Draper city	388	13.9	0.0	227	12.3	0.0	379	21.1	7.1	1 466	18.9	0.0	553	36.3	0.0
Layton city	903	25.2	5.1	337	29.1	7.1	1 442	25.9	6.3	4 140	42.2	5.2	1 466	59.1	0.3
Logan city	221	20.8	0.0	359	40.1	3.6	1 557	17.1	1.2	3 607	37.5	0.8	574	50.9	0.0
Midvale city	206	19.9	4.4	237	31.6	0.0	774	26.2	5.7	5 615	33.3	3.2	834	49.8	2.6
Murray city	253	23.7	3.2	389	29.8	0.0	473	15.0	12.5	2 406	31.8	3.2	666	53.3	0.8
Ogden city	1 688	28.6	14.1	940	35.9	4.8	1 190	22.1	10.7	18 369	40.3	3.5	2 373	45.3	3.4
Orem city	312	63.5	0.0	508	42.3	1.8	1 933	27.9	5.2	7 080	39.5	1.6	2 256	52.3	2.7
Provo city	366	29.5	1.1	790	26.8	2.2	2 640	14.8	3.0	10 937	34.0	1.4	2 488	43.4	0.8
Riverton city	153	71.2	0.0	45	55.6	0.0	266	32.7	4.9	776	51.2	0.6	247	68.0	4.0
Roy city	225	31.1	2.7	268	23.1	3.4	542	27.9	6.3	2 467	38.9	2.6	672	51.3	1.0
St. George city	73	17.0	0.0	586	38.7	0.0	806	36.1	6.0	3 220	36.1	2.9	1 252	54.6	2.7
Salt Lake City city	3 510	34.6	5.9	2 423	23.9	0.2	9 799	28.6	8.0	34 102	35.5	2.9	6 753	41.9	4.1
Sandy city	312	42.9	1.3	189	22.8	3.7	1 927	33.2	3.3	4 016	37.1	3.9	1 727	52.2	2.5
South Jordan city	124	51.6	0.0	115	46.1	0.0	422	42.7	4.7	959	46.0	1.4	411	43.6	0.0
Taylorsville city	595	32.8	0.0	596	41.6	0.0	2 449	33.5	3.8	7 366	37.6	2.2	1 764	43.0	1.4
West Jordan city	254	52.8	2.0	214	22.4	3.7	1 897	35.1	2.0	6 750	40.3	1.7	1 857	55.0	3.3
West Valley City city	1 167	42.6	4.9	1 242	34.6	0.4	7 890	35.9	2.5	19 860	39.9	2.5	4 195	54.8	0.6
VERMONT	2 981	37.1	3.1	2 602	26.5	2.9	5 005	31.9	3.0	5 316	32.1	5.5	8 129	38.5	5.5
Burlington city	753	42.6	3.5	171	14.6	0.0	1 014	26.8	1.2	647	20.6	4.2	726	32.1	4.0

[1] Hispanic or Latino persons may be of any race.

City	Total households	Family households (percent)						Nonfamily households (percent)						Percent of householders 65 years and over who live alone	Grandparents who are responsible for the care of their grandchildren
		Married-couple family households			Other family households			Two or more unrelated persons		Male living alone		Female living alone			
		Total	With children	House-holder 65 years or over	Total	With children	House-holder 65 years or over	Total	House-holder 65 years or over	Total	House-holder 65 years or over	Total	House-holder 65 years or over		
	29	30	31	32	33	34	35	36	37	38	39	40	41	42	43
TEXAS—Cont'd															
La Porte city	10 918	65.6	35.4	5.4	14.1	8.4	1.0	3.5	0.3	8.8	0.7	8.1	2.6	33.1	469
Laredo city	46 908	64.5	41.2	7.7	21.6	11.3	4.1	1.3	0.2	5.5	1.2	7.0	3.8	29.1	3 092
League City city	16 129	66.7	35.9	4.7	10.7	7.3	0.6	4.2	0.2	10.9	1.0	7.4	2.6	39.3	320
Lewisville city	30 119	53.4	28.8	3.1	12.9	8.1	0.9	8.3	0.1	11.6	0.5	13.8	2.3	41.1	521
Longview city	28 362	49.3	22.2	9.3	18.4	11.1	2.6	4.0	0.2	11.2	2.3	17.1	8.8	47.8	1 014
Lubbock city	77 648	46.8	21.3	8.1	16.4	9.5	2.0	8.6	0.3	12.0	1.7	16.3	6.3	43.8	2 855
Lufkin city	12 262	49.8	23.8	9.8	18.5	10.5	2.1	3.9	0.2	9.6	2.3	18.2	10.0	50.6	616
McAllen city	33 038	59.6	33.5	9.7	19.0	10.1	3.0	3.3	0.4	7.3	1.6	10.7	5.3	34.7	1 510
McKinney city	18 277	65.4	37.9	5.2	12.5	7.9	1.1	3.2	0.3	8.0	1.2	10.8	4.0	44.1	422
Mansfield city	9 173	75.5	44.3	5.5	10.9	6.6	1.0	2.7	0.2	5.1	0.7	5.8	2.3	31.2	366
Mesquite city	43 993	57.4	32.4	5.2	17.5	10.7	1.4	4.5	0.2	8.3	0.9	12.2	3.9	41.7	1 213
Midland city	35 717	56.3	29.3	9.7	14.9	9.5	1.8	3.0	0.2	10.3	1.9	15.4	7.1	43.3	1 154
Mission city	13 947	64.5	34.2	15.8	18.3	10.4	3.1	1.7	0.6	5.5	2.6	10.0	6.3	31.2	540
Missouri City city	17 003	70.9	40.1	4.8	15.0	8.5	0.9	2.0	0.2	4.4	0.6	7.6	1.7	27.8	548
Nacogdoches city	11 312	36.4	16.1	6.9	17.8	11.3	1.7	13.0	0.1	13.4	1.8	19.4	6.9	49.8	367
New Braunfels city	13 641	56.2	25.6	12.1	15.5	9.2	1.9	3.6	0.2	9.2	2.7	15.5	9.7	46.7	376
North Richland Hills city	20 757	59.9	30.0	6.7	14.3	8.6	1.4	5.3	0.1	9.8	1.5	10.7	4.5	42.4	401
Odessa city	33 644	52.9	26.8	8.9	18.0	12.0	2.2	3.4	0.3	11.3	1.9	14.4	7.2	44.7	1 489
Paris city	10 577	43.5	17.5	9.5	20.9	13.2	2.7	3.3	0.3	11.5	3.5	20.8	12.1	55.4	435
Pasadena city	47 164	56.8	32.6	6.2	18.6	11.1	1.9	4.3	0.4	9.8	1.6	10.7	4.8	43.1	1 509
Pearland city	13 290	69.1	37.5	7.3	12.5	7.2	2.3	2.9	0.3	5.9	1.0	9.6	3.0	28.6	215
Pharr city	12 812	67.1	37.7	16.3	18.8	9.4	3.0	1.1	0.1	4.5	2.2	8.5	5.6	28.5	718
Plano city	81 179	65.6	36.7	3.8	9.7	6.2	0.4	4.6	0.1	9.1	0.5	11.1	2.5	41.4	971
Port Arthur city	21 869	43.3	19.6	10.0	24.6	14.0	4.8	2.8	0.3	13.0	4.3	16.3	9.9	48.6	1 054
Richardson city	35 109	59.7	28.2	8.4	11.1	6.4	1.0	6.4	0.1	10.1	1.1	12.7	4.6	37.2	573
Round Rock city	20 926	62.0	38.4	3.3	13.7	9.6	0.5	5.7	0.1	9.3	0.3	9.2	2.5	41.9	427
Rowlett city	14 286	76.9	46.4	5.5	10.6	7.6	0.5	2.0	0.1	4.3	0.5	6.2	2.2	30.4	310
San Angelo city	34 100	50.6	23.2	10.3	16.2	10.1	1.7	4.6	0.2	11.5	2.4	17.1	9.2	48.5	1 071
San Antonio city	405 887	49.1	25.0	7.7	20.5	11.6	3.0	5.4	0.4	10.9	2.0	14.1	5.7	40.8	15 075
San Juan city	6 618	70.1	45.3	10.8	19.6	11.8	2.9	1.5	0.4	3.6	1.8	5.2	3.3	26.3	377
San Marcos city	12 666	29.5	12.9	5.3	14.1	6.6	1.8	25.2	0.1	15.2	1.2	16.0	4.4	43.8	199
Sherman city	13 804	48.4	21.6	9.8	15.8	9.7	2.4	5.1	0.2	12.5	2.5	18.2	10.3	50.6	469
Socorro city	6 923	71.7	46.4	8.0	20.9	11.4	3.1	1.2	0.2	2.5	0.6	3.8	1.6	16.3	501
Sugar Land city	20 560	74.1	44.8	6.0	11.5	7.3	0.9	2.1	0.1	5.2	0.8	7.2	2.5	32.0	400
Temple city	21 508	49.6	22.9	10.2	16.1	10.5	1.9	4.5	0.3	11.8	2.2	17.9	9.1	47.6	568
Texarkana city	13 593	42.1	16.7	9.5	24.0	15.3	2.4	4.1	0.1	11.2	2.6	18.5	9.6	50.3	662
Texas City city	15 482	50.2	21.9	9.6	20.9	11.1	3.0	4.0	0.8	10.9	2.8	14.0	7.1	42.7	832
The Colony city	8 532	71.4	45.1	2.6	12.5	8.3	0.3	4.6	0.2	5.4	0.5	6.0	1.4	38.0	212
Tyler city	32 643	47.6	21.1	10.0	17.4	10.1	2.7	4.7	0.2	10.2	2.1	20.1	9.7	48.0	986
Victoria city	22 045	53.9	25.3	9.6	18.1	11.8	2.3	3.6	0.1	10.1	1.8	14.3	7.4	43.2	986
Waco city	42 279	39.8	18.4	8.4	19.2	11.4	2.7	10.0	0.5	12.7	2.1	18.4	8.8	48.3	1 446
Weslaco city	8 213	58.0	30.1	15.0	21.5	11.0	5.5	1.7	0.3	7.1	3.6	11.7	7.8	35.3	315
Wichita Falls city	37 908	51.0	24.2	9.4	15.2	9.6	1.9	5.1	0.2	12.4	2.3	16.2	8.2	47.9	1 036
UTAH	701 933	64.2	36.1	9.1	12.7	7.5	1.5	5.4	0.2	7.7	1.4	10.0	4.9	36.9	15 989
Bountiful city	13 319	71.2	33.4	16.4	10.3	5.5	2.0	2.2	0.4	5.4	1.2	10.9	6.6	29.3	248
Clearfield city	7 838	61.2	40.0	5.5	19.1	13.7	1.6	4.0	0.2	7.9	0.9	7.9	3.4	36.9	233
Draper city	6 413	78.4	48.9	4.7	8.4	5.3	0.2	2.3	0.1	5.7	0.9	5.2	0.7	24.0	73
Layton city	18 364	67.1	41.4	5.9	13.6	8.5	1.2	4.3	0.3	8.8	1.1	6.2	2.2	30.8	469
Logan city	13 910	56.3	27.8	6.0	10.3	5.5	1.4	15.7	0.2	8.1	1.2	9.6	4.3	42.2	133
Midvale city	10 205	46.9	21.9	7.6	19.4	10.8	2.6	8.6	0.4	11.2	1.5	14.0	5.2	38.7	196
Murray city	12 700	54.8	26.9	10.0	14.0	7.8	1.6	6.5	0.3	10.1	1.9	14.6	6.2	40.3	232
Ogden city	27 379	50.2	25.1	9.0	17.6	10.9	1.9	6.1	0.4	12.0	2.5	14.1	7.3	46.6	801
Orem city	23 479	69.5	43.1	8.4	12.9	7.2	1.7	5.2	0.1	4.6	0.8	7.8	3.7	30.3	476
Provo city	29 266	58.6	30.2	6.8	10.5	4.4	0.7	19.3	0.4	4.5	0.7	7.1	3.8	36.4	453
Riverton city	6 416	84.0	60.3	5.8	8.9	7.2	0.5	1.1	0.4	2.6	0.5	3.3	1.5	23.6	100
Roy city	10 608	67.0	38.5	8.5	13.8	8.3	1.7	3.5	0.2	7.0	1.4	8.7	3.8	33.3	245
St. George city	17 359	64.7	27.8	21.2	11.0	7.2	1.3	4.8	0.4	7.0	2.2	12.4	8.7	32.4	346
Salt Lake City city	71 492	42.1	20.3	7.1	14.4	7.5	1.9	10.3	0.3	15.3	2.2	17.9	7.6	51.6	1 300
Sandy city	25 678	74.0	45.1	5.7	11.3	7.1	0.8	3.6	0.2	4.5	0.6	6.7	2.9	34.3	631
South Jordan city	7 473	84.5	55.8	6.5	7.1	4.0	1.2	1.2	0.0	2.7	0.9	4.4	2.6	31.3	173
Taylorsville city	18 513	61.2	33.7	6.4	16.5	9.8	1.1	5.5	0.1	7.5	0.9	9.4	3.4	35.9	478
West Jordan city	18 920	72.6	49.4	4.0	13.1	8.3	0.9	3.6	0.2	5.7	0.4	5.0	1.7	29.5	543
West Valley City city	32 233	62.1	36.5	5.3	18.6	11.1	1.5	4.6	0.2	6.8	1.0	7.9	3.0	36.4	1 278
VERMONT	240 744	53.5	23.9	9.0	12.4	8.3	1.5	7.9	0.6	11.1	2.3	15.1	7.3	46.7	1 934
Burlington city	15 869	32.3	13.9	5.7	12.6	8.1	1.4	19.6	0.2	15.0	1.6	20.6	6.6	52.6	74

Table A-5. Cities — Age, Ethnicity, and Household Structure

City	Households with Non-Hispanic White householder: Number of households	Percent that are family households	Households with Black or African American householder: Number of households	Percent that are family households	Households with American Indian and Alaska Native householder: Number of households	Percent that are family households	Households with Asian, Hawaiian, and Pacific Islander householder: Number of households	Percent that are family households	Households with Hispanic or Latino[1] householder: Number of households	Percent that are family households	Foreign-born population: Percent of total population that is foreign-born	Place of birth (percent): Europe	Asia	Latin America	Percent in non-English speaking households: Linguistically isolated	Not linguistically isolated
	44	45	46	47	48	49	50	51	52	53	54	55	56	57	58	59
TEXAS—Cont'd																
La Porte city	8 242	77.4	707	80.2	71	66.2	43	93.0	1 667	90.1	5.7	0.5	0.6	4.4	2.6	22.7
Laredo city	3 262	73.0	158	76.6	256	82.8	241	79.3	43 247	87.2	28.4	0.2	0.3	27.8	22.6	74.1
League City city	13 034	76.2	797	83.7	107	57.0	375	85.6	1 658	83.4	8.9	1.3	2.6	4.3	3.0	20.4
Lewisville city	22 727	63.3	2 269	68.8	188	63.3	920	82.8	3 684	78.6	12.7	0.7	3.0	8.1	7.0	18.7
Longview city	20 319	65.5	5 851	70.9	89	41.6	164	73.8	1 808	85.1	5.8	0.4	0.5	4.7	3.8	10.9
Lubbock city	53 475	58.4	6 006	70.6	437	69.3	1 102	51.5	16 332	77.5	3.5	0.5	1.2	1.5	3.1	27.9
Lufkin city	7 618	64.9	3 093	67.9	20	55.0	138	78.3	1 361	88.7	10.0	0.3	1.0	8.5	5.5	17.8
McAllen city	8 062	68.4	263	60.5	210	80.5	682	68.5	23 880	82.7	27.7	0.3	1.4	25.5	14.3	70.4
McKinney city	14 451	77.3	1 019	70.6	64	53.1	202	100.0	2 353	85.9	12.6	1.1	1.4	9.1	7.1	18.1
Mansfield city	7 807	85.9	349	87.4	41	78.0	89	100.0	797	93.6	8.2	0.9	0.9	5.8	3.7	15.8
Mesquite city	31 260	73.2	5 609	74.0	224	83.9	1 206	89.5	5 074	84.4	9.2	0.4	3.0	5.1	3.4	19.7
Midland city	24 170	68.5	3 083	63.1	211	69.6	283	83.0	7 828	82.5	7.5	0.4	0.9	6.1	4.4	28.8
Mission city	3 937	69.2	75	76.0	67	100.0	33	100.0	9 816	88.3	25.1	0.2	0.3	24.4	16.7	66.1
Missouri City city	7 432	84.6	6 317	85.0	55	100.0	1 565	90.7	1 430	91.8	17.6	1.3	8.7	5.1	3.3	28.1
Nacogdoches city	7 571	50.0	2 653	61.6	81	37.0	99	74.7	783	65.6	6.0	0.3	0.8	4.8	5.2	10.6
New Braunfels city	9 731	67.3	159	81.8	35	71.4	60	91.7	3 571	83.3	6.6	1.0	0.6	4.9	5.8	33.2
North Richland Hills city	17 990	73.9	435	75.4	91	69.2	397	85.1	1 596	75.4	6.2	0.6	1.8	2.9	2.2	15.4
Odessa city	19 843	65.4	2 007	65.3	228	75.9	225	79.1	11 067	81.6	9.8	0.2	0.7	8.9	6.4	37.1
Paris city	7 898	62.6	2 145	69.2	114	72.8	23	100.0	229	76.0	2.2	0.3	0.3	1.5	1.4	6.4
Pasadena city	27 127	68.2	693	63.8	304	74.7	816	84.7	17 932	86.5	21.7	0.3	1.6	19.6	13.5	38.0
Pearland city	10 520	80.9	687	82.5	65	100.0	281	89.7	1 631	82.7	6.7	1.1	2.0	3.2	2.5	20.7
Pharr city	2 145	70.3	6	100.0	65	73.8	42	100.0	10 596	89.0	33.2	0.2	0.3	32.5	23.7	67.6
Plano city	62 932	73.4	4 180	68.7	346	69.1	6 789	90.1	5 872	82.7	17.1	2.1	8.4	5.2	4.8	22.9
Port Arthur city	8 636	58.7	9 487	70.3	110	88.2	863	82.6	2 573	84.6	12.4	0.2	3.6	8.5	8.2	20.9
Richardson city	26 679	68.8	2 027	73.3	214	76.6	3 374	76.1	2 252	83.6	18.9	1.8	10.2	5.5	6.9	22.8
Round Rock city	14 827	73.6	1 645	80.7	119	71.4	518	78.0	3 633	81.6	9.2	0.8	2.3	5.4	4.3	25.5
Rowlett city	11 524	86.3	1 208	88.8	67	88.1	435	97.7	927	94.1	6.4	0.7	2.8	2.1	1.6	17.1
San Angelo city	22 899	63.1	1 509	66.9	198	66.2	233	60.5	9 078	76.9	6.3	0.5	0.6	5.0	4.3	33.8
San Antonio city	160 321	62.1	29 700	64.4	2 821	71.4	6 745	65.4	203 889	76.8	11.7	0.7	1.4	9.3	7.8	52.6
San Juan city	619	63.8	17	100.0	16	50.0	0	X	3 633	92.4	34.4	0.1	0.0	34.2	22.5	73.4
San Marcos city	7 838	33.2	535	61.1	100	45.0	130	52.3	3 920	62.1	4.9	0.6	0.8	3.3	4.3	36.3
Sherman city	10 837	61.4	1 335	70.6	157	61.8	109	72.5	1 142	82.3	8.0	0.5	1.0	6.3	4.1	13.1
Socorro city	303	77.9	44	100.0	98	80.8	27	100.0	6 530	93.5	36.9	0.1	0.2	36.7	24.8	72.6
Sugar Land city	13 533	82.7	1 016	85.1	80	83.8	3 945	95.4	1 436	84.0	23.5	1.9	17.6	2.2	5.1	34.3
Temple city	14 513	63.4	3 371	66.4	156	51.9	316	75.9	2 949	75.6	5.8	0.8	1.1	3.6	3.0	20.5
Texarkana city	8 433	65.0	4 830	67.4	40	22.5	68	76.5	196	88.8	1.9	0.3	0.5	0.9	0.8	6.8
Texas City city	8 522	66.9	4 125	73.3	108	75.0	130	96.2	2 503	80.1	6.0	0.4	0.9	4.5	3.2	19.3
The Colony city	7 057	82.7	435	85.5	44	100.0	156	94.9	744	90.2	6.5	1.0	1.7	3.2	1.1	19.8
Tyler city	20 886	60.9	8 101	67.4	160	45.6	205	83.4	3 145	84.3	9.6	0.3	0.7	8.2	5.2	15.6
Victoria city	12 212	67.9	1 770	64.6	115	80.0	137	86.1	7 750	79.8	4.9	0.3	0.7	3.4	4.4	37.0
Waco city	24 888	50.7	9 116	65.9	172	74.4	571	41.9	7 261	78.9	8.4	0.4	0.9	6.9	5.8	20.8
Weslaco city	1 943	64.7	9	100.0	66	81.8	93	88.2	6 100	84.0	20.5	0.2	0.8	19.2	15.6	69.1
Wichita Falls city	28 321	64.4	3 985	67.4	265	68.7	680	74.4	3 959	78.3	6.0	1.1	1.8	3.0	2.9	17.6
UTAH	620 009	76.6	5 112	69.5	7 729	78.0	13 951	76.6	48 190	82.7	7.1	1.1	1.3	3.9	2.9	17.4
Bountiful city	12 851	81.4	12	58.3	7	100.0	141	95.0	203	73.4	3.3	1.4	0.6	0.9	0.5	14.7
Clearfield city	6 524	80.4	241	72.2	114	92.1	236	79.2	680	78.8	5.1	0.6	2.0	2.2	1.5	16.7
Draper city	6 081	86.7	38	100.0	16	100.0	90	93.3	137	83.9	3.7	1.2	0.9	0.9	1.1	13.7
Layton city	16 145	81.1	418	74.6	130	69.2	425	76.5	1 125	82.1	4.4	1.2	1.4	1.2	0.9	16.1
Logan city	12 278	66.2	99	37.4	125	71.2	534	56.7	784	83.9	9.8	0.6	3.2	5.0	4.9	17.1
Midvale city	8 383	64.6	95	48.4	99	78.8	261	73.6	1 299	73.1	15.2	1.3	1.6	11.5	10.4	18.3
Murray city	11 353	68.6	113	77.0	133	51.9	158	74.1	838	72.4	4.5	1.1	0.8	2.3	2.2	16.3
Ogden city	21 173	65.6	657	70.0	276	58.0	393	53.9	4 555	81.1	12.2	0.6	1.1	10.1	6.9	21.6
Orem city	21 002	82.1	54	85.2	125	91.2	518	74.5	1 551	88.3	8.2	0.7	1.2	5.3	2.9	21.0
Provo city	25 286	67.8	109	56.9	237	79.7	731	61.6	2 510	86.7	9.6	0.9	1.5	6.1	3.9	25.6
Riverton city	6 182	92.8	25	100.0	17	100.0	67	100.0	117	91.5	2.0	0.3	0.7	0.5	0.3	13.4
Roy city	9 416	80.5	118	66.9	104	100.0	133	76.7	726	83.6	3.2	0.7	1.0	1.1	1.0	13.4
St. George city	16 039	75.3	18	38.9	163	75.5	151	82.8	815	82.1	5.5	0.9	0.7	3.3	2.3	14.2
Salt Lake City city	56 710	53.2	1 181	62.5	749	67.6	3 040	66.4	8 561	75.6	18.3	3.1	3.0	10.2	8.9	24.0
Sandy city	23 774	85.1	80	80.0	74	82.4	447	93.7	1 023	85.7	5.2	1.6	1.3	1.5	1.2	15.8
South Jordan city	7 074	91.5	23	100.0	10	100.0	126	93.7	187	100.0	3.1	1.0	0.8	0.6	0.6	13.6
Taylorsville city	15 434	77.0	253	48.2	190	68.4	599	93.0	1 831	84.5	9.8	1.0	2.2	5.7	3.7	21.1
West Jordan city	16 403	85.6	76	100.0	75	38.7	469	93.4	1 683	87.5	5.5	0.7	1.2	2.9	1.3	18.7
West Valley City city	24 762	78.7	396	72.0	358	87.2	1 730	89.2	4 621	89.4	14.4	1.1	3.4	8.3	5.4	25.1
VERMONT	233 583	66.0	878	55.5	1 038	63.8	1 270	70.5	1 567	61.3	3.8	1.5	0.7	0.2	0.7	9.6
Burlington city	14 770	44.6	303	51.5	70	27.1	283	72.1	193	35.8	8.1	4.0	2.5	0.3	2.6	12.4

[1]Hispanic or Latino persons may be of any race.

Table A-5. Cities — Age, Ethnicity, and Household Structure

STATE Place code	City	Population by age (percent)							Median age	+/- U.S. percent under 18 years	+/- U.S. percent 65 years and over	Non-Hispanic White		
													Age (percent)	
		Total population	Under 5 years	5 to 17 years	18 to 24 years	25 to 44 years	45 to 64 years	65 years and over	Median age	+/- U.S. percent under 18 years	+/- U.S. percent 65 years and over	Total population	Under 18 years	65 years and over
		1	2	3	4	5	6	7	8	9	10	11	12	13
51 00000	VIRGINIA..................	7 078 515	6.5	18.0	9.6	31.8	23.0	11.2	35.7	-1.2	-1.2	4 963 910	22.4	12.9
51 01000	Alexandria city............	128 283	6.2	10.5	8.6	44.1	21.6	8.9	34.4	-9.0	-3.5	68 937	10.6	12.2
51 07784	Blacksburg town.........	39 393	3.1	6.6	57.6	18.8	8.7	5.1	21.9	-16.0	-7.3	32 714	8.8	5.8
51 14968	Charlottesville city.........	45 049	4.4	10.7	34.1	25.7	15.1	10.0	25.6	-10.6	-2.4	30 900	11.0	11.8
51 16000	Chesapeake city..........	199 184	7.1	21.7	8.2	32.4	21.7	8.8	34.7	3.1	-3.6	131 138	26.9	9.7
51 21344	Danville city..............	48 411	5.9	17.4	8.1	25.4	23.5	19.7	40.5	-2.4	7.3	25 795	15.7	28.1
51 35000	Hampton city.............	146 437	6.2	17.9	12.7	32.7	20.1	10.4	34.0	-1.6	-2.0	70 792	20.0	13.3
51 35624	Harrisonburg city.........	40 468	4.8	10.3	41.7	20.9	13.0	9.3	22.6	-10.6	-3.1	32 542	12.8	11.0
51 44984	Leesburg town............	28 237	9.6	19.6	6.1	39.4	19.4	5.9	33.1	3.5	-6.5	22 654	28.4	6.4
51 47672	Lynchburg city............	65 269	5.9	16.3	15.3	25.8	20.4	16.4	35.1	-3.5	4.0	43 065	17.9	20.1
51 48952	Manassas city	35 135	8.9	20.8	10.0	35.8	19.1	5.3	31.3	4.0	-7.1	23 292	27.3	6.9
51 56000	Newport News city	180 150	7.9	19.5	11.5	32.3	18.8	10.1	32.0	1.7	-2.3	93 842	22.0	13.4
51 57000	Norfolk city..............	234 403	7.1	16.9	18.3	29.9	16.9	10.9	29.6	-1.7	-1.5	109 980	17.7	14.1
51 61832	Petersburg city...........	33 740	6.6	18.3	9.1	27.7	22.7	15.6	36.9	-0.8	3.2	6 105	10.1	35.1
51 64000	Portsmouth city...........	100 565	7.0	18.6	11.0	29.1	20.5	13.8	34.5	-0.1	1.4	45 574	20.1	16.9
51 67000	Richmond city.............	197 790	6.3	15.6	13.1	31.8	19.8	13.4	33.9	-3.8	1.0	74 796	10.7	18.1
51 68000	Roanoke city	94 911	6.5	16.1	8.3	30.4	22.3	16.4	37.6	-3.1	4.0	65 104	18.6	19.6
51 76432	Suffolk city...............	63 677	7.2	20.5	6.8	31.5	22.3	11.6	36.0	2.0	-0.8	33 828	24.2	12.7
51 82000	Virginia Beach city	425 257	7.1	20.3	9.9	34.6	19.7	8.4	32.7	1.7	-4.0	295 080	24.6	10.3
53 00000	WASHINGTON..........	5 894 121	6.7	19.0	9.4	31.0	22.7	11.2	35.3	0.0	-1.2	4 649 156	23.2	13.0
53 03180	Auburn city...............	40 279	7.9	18.7	9.9	31.5	20.3	11.7	34.1	0.9	-0.7	32 030	24.1	13.7
53 05210	Bellevue city..............	109 189	5.6	15.5	7.5	33.0	25.0	13.4	38.2	-4.6	1.0	78 419	18.8	16.6
53 05280	Bellingham city...........	66 815	5.1	11.9	24.3	26.5	19.4	12.8	30.4	-8.7	0.4	57 346	15.7	14.2
53 07380	Bothell city...............	29 869	6.5	18.5	8.5	32.6	24.2	9.6	36.0	-0.7	-2.8	24 939	23.1	10.8
53 07695	Bremerton city............	37 054	8.2	16.3	16.0	30.7	16.3	12.6	30.9	-1.2	0.2	26 517	20.2	16.1
53 08850	Burien city................	31 744	5.6	16.5	7.4	31.2	25.2	14.0	38.4	-3.6	1.6	22 691	18.0	18.2
53 17635	Des Moines city..........	29 409	6.5	17.5	8.0	31.7	21.4	14.9	37.0	-1.7	2.5	21 262	19.1	18.7
53 20750	Edmonds city.............	39 610	5.1	15.6	7.3	27.9	27.6	16.6	42.0	-5.0	4.2	34 299	19.6	18.4
53 22640	Everett city................	91 290	7.9	17.0	12.6	33.1	19.2	10.3	32.2	-0.8	-2.1	71 179	22.7	12.3
53 23515	Federal Way city	83 233	7.8	20.1	9.8	33.3	21.2	7.7	32.5	2.2	-4.7	54 726	24.5	9.8
53 35275	Kennewick city	55 090	8.2	21.6	10.3	28.9	21.1	9.8	32.3	4.1	-2.6	42 985	26.1	11.8
53 35415	Kent city	79 325	8.3	19.2	10.3	35.1	19.7	7.3	31.8	1.8	-5.1	53 933	23.6	9.3
53 35940	Kirkland city..............	44 986	5.5	12.6	9.0	38.8	24.0	10.1	36.1	-7.6	-2.3	37 452	16.8	11.4
53 36745	Lacey city	31 107	8.0	17.6	9.6	30.9	19.8	14.0	34.2	-0.1	1.6	23 642	23.0	17.4
53 38038	Lakewood city	58 317	7.3	17.1	11.1	30.1	20.9	13.4	35.0	-1.3	1.0	35 545	18.8	17.6
53 40245	Longview city.............	34 804	7.3	18.5	9.0	27.1	22.5	15.6	36.6	0.1	3.2	30 274	23.5	17.4
53 40840	Lynnwood city............	33 730	6.8	17.4	10.2	32.4	21.3	11.9	34.9	-1.5	-0.5	24 012	21.7	14.8
53 43955	Marysville city............	25 221	8.3	21.9	7.7	33.4	17.0	11.8	33.0	4.5	-0.6	21 753	28.7	13.1
53 47560	Mount Vernon city	26 297	8.2	20.5	12.0	29.0	17.8	12.5	31.1	3.0	0.1	17 982	23.2	17.4
53 51300	Olympia city..............	42 345	5.6	16.1	11.7	30.8	22.8	13.1	36.0	-4.0	0.7	35 012	19.2	15.0
53 53545	Pasco city................	31 976	10.9	24.6	12.4	28.4	15.4	8.3	26.6	9.8	-4.1	11 754	22.6	18.3
53 56695	Puyallup city..............	32 682	7.3	20.2	10.1	31.5	20.3	10.7	34.1	1.8	-1.7	27 768	25.5	12.1
53 57535	Redmond city.............	45 389	6.1	15.3	9.5	37.9	21.9	9.3	34.0	-4.3	-3.1	34 751	19.9	11.2
53 57745	Renton city...............	49 894	6.8	15.0	10.0	37.0	21.0	10.1	34.0	-3.9	-2.3	32 755	17.8	12.7
53 58235	Richland city..............	38 653	6.5	20.8	7.2	27.4	25.0	13.1	37.7	1.6	0.7	33 565	25.8	14.2
53 61115	Sammamish city..........	34 119	7.8	25.3	4.4	33.9	24.9	3.6	35.3	7.4	-8.8	29 297	32.5	3.9
53 62288	SeaTac city	25 523	6.1	18.0	11.0	33.6	21.6	9.7	33.9	-1.6	-2.7	14 410	18.7	14.7
53 63000	Seattle city...............	563 375	4.6	10.9	11.8	38.9	21.7	12.1	35.4	-10.2	-0.3	382 170	11.7	13.7
53 63960	Shoreline city............	52 954	5.2	17.2	7.7	30.6	24.9	14.3	39.3	-3.3	1.9	39 941	20.0	17.4
53 67000	Spokane city.............	196 143	7.0	17.6	11.2	30.0	20.3	14.0	34.7	-1.1	1.6	171 537	23.1	15.1
53 70000	Tacoma city..............	193 177	7.0	18.8	10.0	32.3	20.1	11.8	33.9	0.1	-0.6	128 518	20.7	15.1
53 73465	University Place city......	30 120	6.2	19.8	9.4	28.2	25.5	10.9	36.5	0.3	-1.5	22 404	22.6	13.5
53 74060	Vancouver city............	143 226	8.2	18.6	9.6	32.6	20.1	10.8	33.1	1.1	-1.6	117 042	24.4	12.4
53 75775	Walla Walla city..........	29 792	5.9	16.9	15.1	27.6	19.4	15.1	33.8	-2.9	2.7	22 642	20.3	19.1
53 77105	Wenatchee city...........	28 098	8.0	20.0	9.8	28.4	19.2	14.7	34.0	2.3	2.3	21 156	23.6	19.0
53 80010	Yakima city...............	72 294	8.7	20.7	10.0	29.1	17.5	14.1	31.4	3.7	1.7	43 325	20.4	21.6
54 00000	WEST VIRGINIA........	1 808 344	5.6	16.6	9.6	27.7	25.2	15.3	38.9	-3.5	2.9	1 709 317	21.9	15.6
54 14600	Charleston city	53 196	5.4	14.8	8.6	27.8	25.4	17.9	40.8	-5.5	5.5	42 576	17.3	19.9
54 39460	Huntington city...........	51 529	5.0	12.7	17.5	24.9	21.9	18.0	36.7	-8.0	5.6	46 117	16.9	18.8
54 55756	Morgantown city..........	27 161	2.9	7.9	45.0	20.3	13.5	10.5	23.1	-14.9	-1.9	24 099	10.2	11.1
54 62140	Parkersburg city..........	33 158	5.7	15.7	9.0	27.0	23.7	18.9	39.9	-4.3	6.5	31 567	20.7	19.3
54 86452	Wheeling city.............	31 301	4.8	15.8	9.2	24.2	24.7	21.3	42.4	-5.1	8.9	28 852	19.4	22.4
55 00000	WISCONSIN.............	5 363 675	6.4	19.1	9.7	29.6	22.2	13.1	36.0	-0.2	0.7	4 687 649	23.5	14.4
55 02375	Appleton city..............	70 124	6.9	20.5	9.6	31.9	19.9	11.3	33.8	1.7	-1.1	63 419	25.3	12.2
55 06500	Beloit city.................	35 653	7.6	20.1	11.1	29.0	19.0	13.3	32.7	2.0	0.9	25 664	23.2	16.6
55 10025	Brookfield city............	38 807	5.6	21.0	4.7	22.9	28.0	17.8	42.5	0.9	5.4	36 507	25.9	18.6
55 22300	Eau Claire city............	61 516	5.5	16.1	22.4	26.0	18.2	11.9	29.4	-4.1	-0.5	57 197	19.8	12.6
55 26275	Fond du Lac city	42 296	6.1	18.0	11.0	29.2	20.4	15.4	35.7	-1.6	3.0	38 972	23.0	16.3

Table A-5. Cities — Age, Ethnicity, and Household Structure

City	Black or African American Total population	Under 18 years	65 years and over	American Indian and Alaska Native Total population	Under 18 years	65 years and over	Asian, Hawaiian, and Pacific Islander Total population	Under 18 years	65 years and over	Hispanic or Latino[1] Total population	Under 18 years	65 years and over	Two or more races Total population	Under 18 years	65 years and over
	14	15	16	17	18	19	20	21	22	23	24	25	26	27	28
VIRGINIA	1 384 008	29.2	8.9	22 394	22.7	5.8	259 972	23.3	5.3	327 273	31.0	2.6	156 831	42.0	3.5
Alexandria city	28 444	23.6	6.6	384	16.1	4.4	7 114	15.3	7.6	18 747	26.8	2.0	5 962	29.1	3.0
Blacksburg town	1 871	20.4	3.1	82	0.0	29.3	2 895	9.7	0.6	891	11.1	2.8	959	17.0	0.4
Charlottesville city	9 882	28.3	7.7	36	13.9	22.2	2 187	8.5	0.8	1 229	24.2	1.0	919	22.7	3.7
Chesapeake city	56 448	31.5	8.0	1 177	25.3	2.0	3 583	23.0	3.7	3 893	37.8	3.7	3 780	53.6	4.4
Danville city	21 391	31.8	10.1	143	25.2	16.8	248	13.7	8.5	566	35.3	10.8	375	49.6	6.4
Hampton city	65 665	27.7	8.1	731	37.3	5.1	2 708	19.3	5.6	3 871	30.2	3.4	3 568	39.1	3.4
Harrisonburg city	2 468	22.9	3.3	35	34.3	0.0	1 261	16.6	1.0	3 513	28.0	0.7	1 062	30.5	4.2
Leesburg town	2 532	30.2	5.8	133	31.6	0.0	815	25.2	4.3	1 696	31.2	2.0	640	46.7	3.9
Lynchburg city	19 274	30.5	9.7	192	10.4	19.3	1 001	15.1	5.3	981	29.7	4.5	1 040	51.5	5.6
Manassas city	4 542	32.0	3.6	45	0.0	0.0	1 103	28.5	2.9	5 344	35.8	1.0	1 256	48.3	2.5
Newport News city	70 149	33.2	7.1	803	27.3	5.2	4 405	22.1	5.3	7 441	34.9	2.7	5 263	47.9	2.1
Norfolk city	102 610	30.1	8.8	1 063	15.5	4.6	7 210	19.1	7.2	8 781	25.8	2.8	6 697	41.3	3.7
Petersburg city	26 419	27.9	11.6	51	9.8	0.0	275	18.9	17.1	607	40.5	1.2	453	37.1	7.9
Portsmouth city	50 742	30.3	11.9	495	19.6	4.0	992	20.8	1.6	1 745	25.4	3.6	1 445	44.1	2.9
Richmond city	112 655	29.3	11.1	511	13.5	5.1	2 553	11.4	7.6	5 239	24.2	2.3	2 895	28.8	5.3
Roanoke city	25 387	30.5	10.2	263	17.9	1.9	1 063	29.4	6.4	1 198	33.2	3.5	1 886	41.7	6.5
Suffolk city	27 612	31.3	10.7	171	13.5	2.9	553	16.6	9.4	853	38.9	1.1	717	46.6	10.6
Virginia Beach city	80 097	34.2	4.1	1 719	21.5	3.7	20 412	23.0	6.1	17 970	36.4	2.4	13 385	48.1	2.3
WASHINGTON	185 052	30.7	5.6	91 299	33.2	4.8	342 717	24.3	7.6	439 841	39.7	2.3	230 850	46.2	3.4
Auburn city	1 064	38.6	1.1	887	33.5	5.1	1 606	27.3	5.5	2 971	39.5	2.7	2 008	40.5	3.9
Bellevue city	1 936	25.6	7.6	639	34.0	3.6	19 086	23.3	6.5	5 717	27.3	2.8	3 670	45.4	1.8
Bellingham city	532	8.1	0.0	1 006	27.8	8.7	2 760	14.7	5.5	3 186	30.4	2.6	2 299	34.6	1.8
Bothell city	249	20.1	6.8	223	12.1	13.9	2 361	31.8	2.5	1 340	38.7	3.5	867	50.5	1.0
Bremerton city	2 614	29.3	3.0	759	28.6	2.1	2 320	24.4	8.1	2 396	36.7	0.6	3 008	54.8	2.1
Burien city	1 610	37.8	3.0	395	31.6	6.6	2 493	22.3	3.6	3 418	34.8	2.5	1 537	41.6	3.6
Des Moines city	2 164	41.5	3.0	217	24.0	9.2	2 855	31.1	6.3	1 950	37.3	4.4	1 294	46.4	3.8
Edmonds city	900	0.0	0.6	020	0.0	0.7	2 040	22.0	7.0	1 240	20.1	1.4	1 150	40.7	3.9
Everett city	2 867	27.8	3.3	1 691	34.1	1.7	6 300	27.4	5.2	6 273	33.1	0.5	3 689	44.4	3.9
Federal Way city	6 240	35.3	2.0	714	29.7	1.5	11 057	28.5	5.9	6 360	36.9	2.2	5 204	47.9	3.2
Kennewick city	668	39.2	2.2	550	28.5	0.0	1 038	20.8	7.2	8 726	46.8	2.0	1 806	49.3	2.4
Kent city	6 386	36.4	2.4	783	26.4	2.6	7 978	27.8	6.0	6 456	37.8	1.0	4 473	49.5	2.2
Kirkland city	558	19.9	3.0	248	22.2	0.0	3 552	17.5	4.8	1 928	29.0	2.0	1 486	42.6	2.4
Lacey city	1 297	31.8	2.5	510	39.0	2.0	2 866	26.9	4.7	1 753	29.3	3.5	1 332	52.9	2.4
Lakewood city	7 433	33.8	4.6	848	31.7	2.0	5 927	20.5	14.7	5 010	36.7	3.2	4 493	48.1	3.7
Longview city	228	53.9	0.0	647	30.4	3.1	896	35.0	6.0	2 129	44.8	1.9	873	46.6	7.3
Lynnwood city	1 194	29.3	4.5	322	35.7	6.8	4 878	26.3	6.5	2 257	33.8	2.2	1 427	44.5	1.5
Marysville city	264	31.8	2.3	825	25.1	11.1	970	20.5	4.5	1 170	37.4	2.7	938	58.8	1.7
Mount Vernon city	97	35.1	7.2	391	46.5	5.4	687	22.0	3.2	6 606	41.6	0.8	718	50.1	7.1
Olympia city	811	21.9	1.2	569	33.0	2.3	2 423	29.2	8.2	1 958	37.8	1.7	1 905	46.7	2.6
Pasco city	887	29.2	14.3	222	29.7	0.0	732	34.3	4.1	18 035	44.5	1.9	1 366	46.7	1.0
Puyallup city	427	36.1	1.2	234	44.0	0.0	1 243	21.6	8.8	1 663	46.1	0.6	1 560	48.8	0.3
Redmond city	555	33.5	3.4	204	19.6	0.0	6 129	22.2	3.0	2 597	28.4	2.2	1 571	40.2	2.5
Renton city	4 018	28.0	6.3	266	24.4	2.6	6 827	23.8	6.8	3 745	35.5	1.4	2 646	42.7	4.1
Richland city	430	41.2	6.3	179	29.6	0.0	1 591	22.6	8.7	1 850	45.5	4.9	1 217	51.8	4.8
Sammamish city	194	43.8	0.0	145	27.6	0.0	2 588	28.6	1.9	894	41.3	1.3	1 127	57.0	2.7
SeaTac city	2 388	32.7	2.1	336	28.0	6.5	3 559	27.0	5.5	3 425	31.9	1.0	1 627	40.4	3.0
Seattle city	46 716	25.7	10.0	5 645	18.1	6.5	76 363	18.9	11.4	29 655	24.9	3.6	27 137	33.5	4.1
Shoreline city	1 444	29.6	0.3	552	40.0	2.7	6 816	23.5	6.5	1 974	29.9	2.1	2 520	48.4	3.5
Spokane city	3 877	32.4	8.0	3 495	29.7	4.9	4 801	23.6	12.3	5 766	38.3	2.7	7 635	45.3	4.4
Tacoma city	21 667	32.3	6.8	3 739	35.7	4.1	15 683	27.1	8.2	13 232	41.1	1.8	13 105	51.6	2.3
University Place city	2 597	34.4	4.7	241	32.8	6.6	2 481	27.4	3.7	1 126	43.8	1.5	1 568	49.8	0.6
Vancouver city	3 272	35.0	4.7	1 502	31.8	6.8	7 098	27.5	6.2	9 013	40.3	2.4	6 279	51.2	2.2
Walla Walla city	694	1.0	2.4	354	24.0	3.4	479	19.2	4.2	5 219	37.4	1.7	777	37.7	6.0
Wenatchee city	137	36.5	3.6	328	31.4	0.0	284	25.0	1.4	5 854	43.3	1.1	822	39.8	3.2
Yakima city	1 287	37.9	10.2	1 360	28.9	7.6	861	27.4	4.8	24 418	45.1	1.9	2 880	44.2	4.4
WEST VIRGINIA	55 999	25.5	12.8	3 770	21.8	7.0	9 850	22.9	5.9	11 774	31.2	6.8	18 104	39.5	8.6
Charleston city	7 735	30.6	10.7	184	20.1	2.7	1 055	29.5	6.9	374	20.6	7.5	1 265	47.0	8.6
Huntington city	3 408	21.1	13.8	151	19.2	5.3	514	10.7	6.0	385	23.6	2.6	909	45.9	8.5
Morgantown city	1 086	19.4	10.2	137	5.1	12.4	939	8.5	1.1	503	14.7	1.6	385	24.9	2.9
Parkersburg city	537	30.0	13.8	23	0.0	0.0	163	30.1	0.0	321	41.7	3.7	502	36.7	15.3
Wheeling city	1 564	29.5	10.5	54	11.1	0.0	265	24.9	5.3	250	34.4	4.8	323	63.8	3.1
WISCONSIN	300 355	37.8	5.2	49 661	36.3	4.7	84 654	38.7	3.7	191 049	38.7	2.8	71 171	50.9	3.7
Appleton city	678	32.9	0.0	479	41.8	3.5	3 236	53.4	3.2	1 738	37.1	1.8	756	53.7	4.1
Beloit city	5 345	38.4	7.0	169	26.6	0.0	560	29.8	7.9	3 220	38.1	0.6	880	56.5	2.8
Brookfield city	266	33.8	9.8	109	24.8	8.3	1 312	37.0	2.9	303	36.0	5.9	313	59.1	8.3
Eau Claire city	369	28.7	0.0	472	38.3	1.3	2 218	50.8	2.4	548	29.4	0.0	760	48.4	7.0
Fond du Lac city	868	28.0	0.5	291	35.1	3.1	405	47.4	6.4	1 370	37.6	5.0	441	45.6	5.7

[1] Hispanic or Latino persons may be of any race.

Table A-5. Cities — Age, Ethnicity, and Household Structure

City	Total households	Family households (percent)						Nonfamily households (percent)						Percent of householders 65 years and over who live alone	Grandparents who are responsible for the care of their grandchildren
		Married-couple family households			Other family households			Two or more unrelated persons		Male living alone		Female living alone			
		Total	With children	Householder 65 years or over	Total	With children	Householder 65 years or over	Total	Householder 65 years or over	Total	Householder 65 years or over	Total	Householder 65 years or over		
	29	30	31	32	33	34	35	36	37	38	39	40	41	42	43
VIRGINIA	2 700 335	53.7	24.6	8.2	15.2	8.6	2.1	6.1	0.3	10.5	1.9	14.5	6.2	43.3	59 464
Alexandria city	61 968	33.3	13.3	4.0	12.2	6.2	1.2	11.2	0.3	18.6	1.5	24.8	5.1	54.5	622
Blacksburg town	13 174	28.7	12.1	4.6	7.3	4.1	0.6	36.9	0.2	13.9	0.8	13.1	2.8	39.1	13
Charlottesville city	16 861	30.9	12.1	6.3	15.3	9.8	1.8	18.9	0.4	14.9	2.0	20.0	6.2	49.1	216
Chesapeake city	69 835	60.3	30.8	7.3	17.4	10.6	1.8	4.3	0.2	7.1	1.2	10.9	4.6	38.2	2 184
Danville city	20 608	38.7	13.7	10.5	24.2	13.3	4.1	3.2	0.4	12.5	3.1	21.3	12.7	51.3	670
Hampton city	53 954	47.2	20.8	7.7	20.0	12.4	2.4	6.3	0.3	12.2	1.9	14.3	5.9	42.8	1 613
Harrisonburg city	13 156	37.2	17.5	6.7	12.8	7.5	1.2	21.8	0.4	12.7	1.8	15.5	6.5	50.0	109
Leesburg town	10 339	57.7	33.9	3.2	12.7	7.5	0.7	6.5	0.2	10.1	0.9	13.0	3.9	53.6	220
Lynchburg city	25 465	41.1	16.4	10.1	21.0	12.6	3.2	5.3	0.4	12.4	2.4	20.2	9.8	47.2	660
Manassas city	11 785	57.3	33.9	3.9	15.1	9.8	1.0	6.6	0.3	10.8	1.2	10.1	3.0	45.2	232
Newport News city	69 750	45.6	22.4	6.6	21.4	13.8	2.2	6.0	0.3	12.0	1.7	15.0	6.2	46.5	1 754
Norfolk city	86 178	37.7	17.0	6.6	22.9	14.1	3.0	9.2	0.4	13.9	2.6	16.3	7.1	49.1	2 825
Petersburg city	13 795	31.8	11.7	7.9	30.1	16.8	4.6	5.9	0.6	13.6	3.2	18.7	9.4	49.3	576
Portsmouth city	38 137	41.5	17.0	8.4	25.7	14.2	4.4	5.3	0.6	11.9	2.9	15.7	7.8	44.3	1 858
Richmond city	84 566	27.9	10.2	5.9	24.4	13.5	3.5	10.1	0.6	15.5	2.7	22.0	9.1	54.2	2 272
Roanoke city	42 026	37.7	14.2	8.7	20.4	11.5	2.9	5.9	0.5	14.5	2.6	21.5	10.1	51.6	983
Suffolk city	23 290	55.2	25.6	8.4	21.0	12.1	3.2	3.6	0.3	9.3	2.3	10.9	5.5	39.3	605
Virginia Beach city	154 635	57.0	29.8	6.7	15.5	10.1	1.5	7.2	0.3	8.7	1.2	11.6	4.3	39.1	3 603
WASHINGTON	2 272 261	52.9	24.7	8.5	13.6	8.7	1.4	7.4	0.4	11.8	2.1	14.3	6.2	44.5	35 341
Auburn city	16 091	44.3	20.7	7.5	18.2	12.8	1.3	8.4	0.5	13.5	2.0	15.5	6.7	48.5	254
Bellevue city	45 787	53.8	23.6	10.3	9.8	4.6	1.5	7.8	0.5	12.3	1.4	16.3	6.5	39.1	334
Bellingham city	28 012	38.0	15.6	8.2	11.9	7.1	1.2	16.7	0.5	14.6	2.1	18.8	8.0	50.4	160
Bothell city	11 868	53.6	27.7	6.2	12.8	6.6	1.7	7.8	0.3	9.8	1.3	15.9	5.1	43.8	102
Bremerton city	15 025	38.4	18.8	6.4	17.7	12.7	1.2	8.1	0.7	17.3	3.2	18.5	8.9	59.3	172
Burien city	13 356	44.7	18.5	8.1	15.9	8.7	1.9	7.0	0.6	14.0	3.6	18.3	7.4	50.9	168
Des Moines city	11 324	47.6	20.7	8.5	16.9	10.6	2.1	7.6	0.2	13.8	1.4	14.1	4.9	37.1	215
Edmonds city	16 925	52.5	20.4	12.4	12.2	6.3	2.0	6.4	0.7	9.4	1.7	19.5	8.7	41.0	209
Everett city	36 255	43.3	21.2	6.4	17.2	11.2	1.2	8.2	0.3	15.4	2.0	15.9	6.5	51.8	519
Federal Way city	31 473	50.7	26.6	5.8	17.2	11.8	1.0	7.5	0.2	11.6	1.5	12.9	4.2	44.7	440
Kennewick city	20 765	52.2	26.5	7.7	16.4	12.0	1.3	5.9	0.2	11.2	1.8	14.3	6.8	48.3	465
Kent city	31 053	45.8	24.3	4.6	17.2	11.7	1.0	8.6	0.3	14.3	1.6	14.1	4.5	50.9	486
Kirkland city	20 631	41.7	17.0	5.8	11.3	6.7	1.0	11.1	0.2	15.5	1.3	20.3	4.9	46.6	138
Lacey city	12 351	50.2	24.2	9.7	15.3	10.3	0.9	5.6	0.3	10.6	2.5	18.2	8.7	50.9	175
Lakewood city	23 902	45.2	18.3	9.6	18.4	13.0	1.6	6.8	0.7	14.1	2.2	15.5	6.9	43.4	465
Longview city	14 090	48.2	19.8	10.5	16.8	12.0	1.0	5.4	0.4	11.6	2.3	18.1	10.5	51.6	243
Lynnwood city	13 298	47.7	24.2	6.9	14.9	9.0	1.9	8.1	0.5	12.3	2.1	16.9	7.5	50.7	136
Marysville city	9 348	56.2	31.7	8.3	14.7	9.4	1.4	5.5	0.3	9.6	1.9	14.0	8.6	51.1	176
Mount Vernon city	9 253	52.5	27.0	9.1	14.6	9.6	0.6	6.7	0.4	9.8	2.4	16.4	9.7	54.9	94
Olympia city	18 673	40.2	19.2	7.1	13.3	8.8	1.4	10.7	0.4	14.4	2.0	21.4	8.8	54.8	121
Pasco city	9 625	53.0	30.4	7.3	22.7	14.7	2.0	4.0	0.3	8.3	2.5	11.9	5.8	46.3	280
Puyallup city	12 749	50.7	27.0	6.8	14.9	10.5	0.9	7.3	0.0	11.6	2.1	15.5	7.0	53.9	134
Redmond city	19 182	49.3	22.9	4.7	10.5	5.9	0.7	10.0	0.6	14.9	1.2	15.2	4.6	49.6	68
Renton city	21 618	42.2	18.6	5.5	14.1	8.6	1.0	9.4	0.4	16.2	1.6	18.1	6.4	53.9	350
Richland city	15 464	56.5	25.9	10.8	12.0	8.2	1.3	4.1	0.3	12.1	1.3	15.3	7.6	41.5	166
Sammamish city	11 172	79.9	48.6	4.1	7.3	4.8	0.5	3.5	0.1	5.0	0.4	4.3	1.5	28.3	71
SeaTac city	9 783	44.1	21.4	6.7	17.9	11.2	1.4	7.9	0.5	16.5	2.1	13.6	4.9	45.1	103
Seattle city	258 635	33.7	13.4	6.0	11.0	5.4	1.7	14.6	0.5	18.9	2.5	21.8	7.0	53.8	2 180
Shoreline city	20 746	52.1	23.7	9.4	13.7	7.1	1.8	7.7	0.3	10.5	1.8	16.0	7.9	45.5	274
Spokane city	81 762	42.7	19.3	8.3	16.0	10.7	1.5	7.5	0.4	13.9	2.7	19.8	9.5	54.7	948
Tacoma city	76 127	43.1	20.0	7.0	17.9	11.6	1.7	7.3	0.4	14.6	2.7	17.1	7.5	53.0	1 856
University Place city	12 203	52.0	23.9	8.4	15.8	11.9	1.0	6.5	0.3	11.1	1.8	14.6	5.0	41.2	107
Vancouver city	56 605	48.0	23.1	7.4	16.7	10.9	1.3	7.7	0.3	12.2	2.0	15.4	6.5	48.5	746
Walla Walla city	10 629	47.5	21.3	11.2	14.4	9.9	1.3	6.1	0.3	11.9	3.8	20.1	12.4	55.8	207
Wenatchee city	10 744	50.5	24.8	11.4	13.5	9.0	1.2	6.2	0.2	11.2	2.1	18.6	11.0	50.6	214
Yakima city	26 706	45.9	22.8	9.2	18.5	13.4	2.0	5.6	0.4	11.3	2.7	18.8	11.3	54.9	598
WEST VIRGINIA	737 360	54.6	21.9	10.4	14.2	7.4	2.8	4.1	0.3	10.7	2.8	16.3	9.2	46.9	16 151
Charleston city	24 522	38.6	14.8	9.0	17.0	9.2	3.1	5.3	0.2	15.0	3.2	24.1	11.6	54.4	417
Huntington city	23 067	37.5	13.0	9.3	16.3	8.1	3.2	8.3	0.3	13.8	3.0	24.0	12.9	55.5	431
Morgantown city	11 065	29.4	12.0	6.5	9.3	3.9	2.3	23.3	0.3	16.4	2.0	21.6	7.1	50.0	73
Parkersburg city	14 479	42.7	14.8	10.5	18.1	10.1	2.9	5.2	0.3	12.0	3.1	22.0	12.4	52.8	283
Wheeling city	13 713	42.0	16.4	10.8	15.2	8.0	3.0	4.7	0.3	13.1	4.2	25.1	14.7	57.3	227
WISCONSIN	2 086 304	54.0	24.4	9.7	12.8	7.9	1.5	6.4	0.3	11.5	2.4	15.2	7.7	46.4	23 687
Appleton city	26 899	55.1	27.9	8.4	11.1	7.5	1.0	6.0	0.1	11.4	1.7	16.4	7.3	48.6	242
Beloit city	13 424	47.1	20.8	9.7	19.7	13.4	1.5	5.3	0.3	10.8	2.4	17.2	8.7	49.0	398
Brookfield city	13 985	73.7	33.0	16.9	7.3	3.5	1.3	2.2	0.4	5.6	1.8	11.3	6.6	31.1	73
Eau Claire city	23 997	45.3	20.9	8.3	11.5	7.5	1.2	13.2	0.2	11.9	1.9	18.0	8.5	51.7	208
Fond du Lac city	16 676	50.0	22.4	9.7	12.8	8.7	0.9	6.4	0.3	12.7	2.5	18.1	9.8	52.7	92

Table A-5. Cities — **Age, Ethnicity, and Household Structure**

City	Households with Non-Hispanic White householder		Households with Black or African American householder		Households with American Indian and Alaska Native householder		Households with Asian, Hawaiian, and Pacific Islander householder		Households with Hispanic or Latino[1] householder		Foreign-born population	Place of birth (percent)			Percent in non-English speaking households	
	Number of households	Percent that are family households	Number of households	Percent that are family households	Number of households	Percent that are family households	Number of households	Percent that are family households	Number of households	Percent that are family households	Percent of total population that is foreign-born	Europe	Asia	Latin America	Linguistically isolated	Not linguistically isolated
	44	45	46	47	48	49	50	51	52	53	54	55	56	57	58	59
VIRGINIA..............	2 004 156	68.0	493 797	69.4	8 274	70.5	78 401	76.7	83 553	79.6	8.1	1.2	3.3	2.7	2.5	13.4
Alexandria city............	39 104	38.0	12 270	55.1	180	35.0	2 880	52.6	5 534	70.9	25.4	2.2	6.3	10.6	9.7	25.3
Blacksburg town.........	11 117	35.0	653	44.6	22	63.6	879	42.0	262	43.5	10.8	2.1	6.4	1.2	2.6	17.3
Charlottesville city........	12 167	41.9	3 439	64.4	11	54.5	615	35.6	369	45.8	6.9	1.7	3.1	1.2	1.4	13.1
Chesapeake city..........	47 784	77.4	18 949	77.9	424	77.8	1 054	85.2	1 011	84.3	3.0	0.7	1.3	0.7	0.5	10.4
Danville city..............	12 094	59.5	8 126	67.8	81	75.3	65	100.0	166	72.3	1.4	0.3	0.4	0.6	0.7	6.7
Hampton city..............	27 864	66.0	23 319	68.4	174	75.3	822	65.6	965	69.9	3.9	1.1	1.5	0.9	0.8	11.2
Harrisonburg city..........	11 041	47.4	773	49.3	5	100.0	314	59.6	846	79.6	9.2	1.2	2.5	4.8	6.7	13.2
Leesburg town............	8 736	70.0	906	73.5	12	100.0	252	60.3	321	79.4	8.6	2.1	2.5	3.2	3.0	13.6
Lynchburg city............	17 195	60.9	7 390	65.3	64	59.4	340	52.9	276	56.2	3.2	0.9	1.3	0.6	0.7	7.6
Manassas city............	8 670	69.7	1 466	74.7	16	100.0	326	92.6	1 121	86.7	14.2	1.3	2.2	10.2	5.8	19.4
Newport News city.......	38 855	65.3	26 215	68.5	285	81.1	1 356	69.8	2 191	73.8	4.8	1.4	2.0	1.0	1.4	12.0
Norfolk city...............	45 015	56.3	35 068	65.7	381	63.3	2 244	69.8	2 203	62.5	5.0	0.9	2.5	1.2	1.2	12.6
Petersburg city............	3 131	52.8	10 222	64.4	40	37.5	91	57.1	197	80.7	2.0	1.0	0.0	0.0	0.0	0.0
Portsmouth city	18 952	65.1	18 008	69.2	152	61.2	278	70.9	475	72.2	1.6	0.4	0.6	0.5	0.4	7.9
Richmond city.............	38 284	40.4	42 440	63.3	228	41.7	1 020	36.6	1 656	66.5	3.9	0.7	1.0	1.8	1.8	9.0
Roanoke city	30 439	55.8	10 186	64.0	124	71.0	332	71.4	330	57.0	3.1	1.0	1.1	0.8	1.4	6.8
Suffolk city...............	12 748	77.3	9 908	74.9	60	81.7	215	78.1	229	89.5	1.9	0.7	0.7	0.3	0.3	7.6
Virginia Beach city	114 901	70.9	26 779	75.6	458	79.5	5 532	85.5	4 822	80.1	6.6	1.5	3.6	1.1	1.1	16.2
WASHINGTON..........	1 907 298	65.5	68 959	64.8	29 399	71.1	106 931	72.1	110 036	78.5	10.4	2.1	4.1	2.9	3.8	15.8
Auburn city...............	13 718	60.9	316	80.1	322	61.5	497	75.9	794	75.8	11.2	3.2	3.6	2.9	5.7	12.1
Bellevue city..............	35 441	61.4	760	60.3	150	71.3	6 950	71.8	1 655	80.3	24.5	5.3	13.6	3.1	7.7	25.0
Bellingham city...........	25 039	49.9	261	36.4	313	53.4	851	51.8	1 029	52.9	9.1	2.3	3.2	1.5	2.4	12.3
Bothell city...............	10 408	65.7	120	62.5	103	69.9	716	76.5	342	71.6	11.2	2.7	5.0	2.0	2.2	16.0
Bremerton city............	11 990	53.7	896	61.7	260	72.3	734	74.5	558	74.7	7.2	0.7	4.6	0.9	2.3	15.5
Burien city................	10 569	57.5	601	64.9	166	67.5	778	82.5	905	77.9	15.2	2.9	5.5	5.2	5.5	20.2
Des Moines city...........	8 756	63.3	823	68.0	92	60.9	842	71.1	557	74.0	12.3	1.2	0.2	3.0	3.0	19.9
Edmonds city..............	15 149	64.1	176	65.9	96	65.6	861	71.2	351	76.9	11.0	3.4	4.3	1.4	3.0	13.7
Everett city................	30 477	50.9	904	64.5	400	61.0	1 046	77.0	1 700	60.0	10.1	0.0	6.0	0.0	0.0	16.7
Federal Way city..........	22 347	66.3	2 413	62.7	215	72.6	3 445	81.0	1 797	69.1	17.5	3.8	9.3	2.9	8.0	19.3
Kennewick city............	17 590	66.5	201	79.6	169	88.8	397	75.1	2 047	84.5	9.6	1.5	1.3	6.2	4.9	17.4
Kent city..................	23 335	60.2	2 539	67.8	337	65.6	2 358	73.8	1 614	80.4	16.9	4.0	7.3	3.8	7.7	19.9
Kirkland city..............	17 950	52.4	284	36.3	78	48.7	1 339	63.6	575	62.8	14.4	3.5	6.7	1.8	3.1	17.1
Lacey city.................	10 115	62.7	546	77.3	150	77.3	753	83.3	545	75.0	9.4	1.6	5.9	1.4	2.7	17.0
Lakewood city	16 054	61.7	3 033	69.7	353	60.9	2 008	64.4	1 511	76.3	12.7	2.7	6.6	2.6	5.1	22.8
Longview city..............	12 862	63.8	63	58.7	239	73.2	224	93.3	504	78.6	5.5	0.9	1.7	2.3	2.6	9.4
Lynnwood city.............	10 372	58.6	490	81.4	113	77.0	1 303	82.9	678	73.2	21.4	4.9	11.6	3.1	8.2	21.4
Marysville city............	8 436	69.7	103	100.0	56	57.1	318	81.1	264	83.0	7.4	1.5	2.6	2.0	2.1	12.3
Mount Vernon city	7 386	62.9	56	42.9	76	60.5	174	56.3	1 458	91.4	19.5	2.2	2.0	14.2	11.9	19.5
Olympia city...............	16 164	51.9	371	56.3	215	74.9	836	75.7	588	57.3	6.6	1.1	3.9	0.8	1.9	12.8
Pasco city................	4 832	65.6	311	66.2	79	84.8	237	77.2	4 050	89.2	30.5	1.1	1.9	27.2	20.2	41.7
Puyallup city..............	11 400	65.0	165	50.3	73	65.8	373	74.5	414	75.4	4.8	1.4	2.2	0.9	0.8	12.1
Redmond city.............	15 519	58.1	240	47.5	99	53.5	2 277	68.0	684	76.0	20.6	4.3	10.9	3.2	5.6	22.4
Renton city	15 631	53.1	1 823	53.9	104	39.4	2 332	72.6	997	74.7	19.2	3.9	9.2	3.9	8.6	20.1
Richland city..............	13 787	68.9	163	57.1	51	80.4	561	74.9	569	67.5	7.2	2.7	2.9	1.0	1.3	15.1
Sammamish city..........	9 818	87.4	77	63.6	33	100.0	798	86.0	254	76.8	9.9	1.9	5.3	0.4	0.7	16.4
SeaTac city	6 568	57.9	914	59.6	66	65.2	961	74.7	862	80.9	22.6	2.4	8.4	7.4	10.3	26.2
Seattle city...............	193 456	41.4	18 526	53.9	2 226	40.2	26 765	59.9	10 094	49.5	16.9	2.7	9.4	2.2	5.9	20.2
Shoreline city.............	16 903	63.5	590	70.2	153	67.3	1 970	79.9	557	74.0	16.9	3.0	10.1	1.3	5.4	20.4
Spokane city..............	74 048	58.6	1 397	61.9	1 236	63.6	1 404	65.5	1 703	59.6	5.7	2.7	1.8	0.4	2.4	10.1
Tacoma city...............	55 566	57.4	8 275	68.4	1 195	67.4	4 959	74.5	3 684	74.9	11.9	3.0	5.7	2.4	4.9	18.8
University Place city......	9 632	66.7	998	71.7	94	61.7	770	73.4	328	69.2	10.0	2.4	5.9	0.9	3.1	15.0
Vancouver city............	48 816	63.5	1 281	62.3	512	70.1	2 338	76.9	2 333	73.0	12.2	5.0	3.7	2.5	6.0	15.2
Walla Walla city..........	9 026	59.5	68	52.9	149	51.7	79	58.2	1 159	82.7	9.3	0.7	0.7	7.4	5.3	17.4
Wenatchee city...........	9 159	61.3	24	100.0	107	41.1	93	53.8	1 198	86.6	13.4	0.7	0.6	11.6	7.3	18.6
Yakima city...............	19 497	58.1	491	63.1	410	72.7	285	63.9	5 602	86.6	17.4	0.6	0.8	15.6	10.7	26.7
WEST VIRGINIA	701 781	69.1	21 811	60.1	1 595	68.0	3 224	64.9	3 686	65.5	1.1	0.4	0.5	0.1	0.2	5.1
Charleston city............	20 345	54.6	3 225	56.5	108	87.0	337	87.2	128	61.7	3.2	0.6	2.0	0.3	0.4	8.3
Huntington city	20 852	54.3	1 541	48.7	84	31.0	188	48.4	144	57.6	1.5	0.3	0.8	0.1	0.4	5.2
Morgantown city	9 843	38.2	412	47.8	80	50.0	434	41.0	196	38.8	5.9	1.5	3.0	0.7	2.2	11.6
Parkersburg city..........	13 979	60.9	197	56.3	17	76.5	56	44.6	64	71.9	0.9	0.3	0.3	0.2	0.1	4.7
Wheeling city..............	12 801	57.3	690	51.0	29	86.2	78	61.5	50	56.0	1.7	0.7	0.7	0.1	0.5	6.1
WISCONSIN.............	1 888 577	66.4	98 260	68.7	16 033	71.8	21 877	71.3	49 345	77.5	3.6	1.0	1.2	1.2	1.5	10.3
Appleton city..............	25 429	65.3	166	95.8	141	91.5	583	85.2	388	70.1	5.1	0.7	3.0	0.8	2.3	10.6
Beloit city.................	10 559	64.5	1 847	70.5	53	66.0	143	72.7	679	89.7	7.2	0.6	1.0	5.4	4.3	11.7
Brookfield city.............	13 350	80.6	89	93.3	31	54.8	359	87.7	73	91.8	6.3	3.1	2.4	0.4	1.2	12.4
Eau Claire city............	23 156	56.3	101	66.3	101	45.5	391	77.7	125	52.8	2.7	0.4	1.9	0.2	1.2	9.7
Fond du Lac city	15 914	62.4	104	73.1	107	51.4	102	62.7	327	79.5	3.3	0.7	0.9	1.4	1.0	8.9

[1]Hispanic or Latino persons may be of any race.

STATE Place code	City	Population by age (percent)										Non-Hispanic White		
										+/− U.S. percent under 18 years	+/− U.S. percent 65 years and over		Age (percent)	
		Total population	Under 5 years	5 to 17 years	18 to 24 years	25 to 44 years	45 to 64 years	65 years and over	Median age			Total population	Under 18 years	65 years and over
		1	2	3	4	5	6	7	8	9	10	11	12	13
	WISCONSIN—Cont'd													
55 27300	Franklin city	29 556	5.9	17.5	8.2	32.8	25.7	9.9	37.9	-2.3	-2.5	26 452	23.6	10.8
55 31000	Green Bay city	102 368	7.2	18.2	11.6	32.0	19.3	11.7	33.2	-0.3	-0.7	85 585	22.2	13.6
55 31175	Greenfield city	35 478	4.8	14.2	8.1	28.5	24.3	20.2	41.7	-6.7	7.8	32 591	17.7	21.8
55 37825	Janesville city	59 366	7.1	18.9	8.4	30.8	21.9	12.9	35.3	0.3	0.5	55 749	25.0	13.5
55 39225	Kenosha city	90 668	7.5	19.7	10.2	31.7	18.8	12.2	33.6	1.5	-0.2	72 380	23.8	14.3
55 40775	La Crosse city	51 638	4.9	14.0	24.1	25.0	16.9	15.0	30.1	-6.8	2.6	47 228	16.6	16.1
55 48000	Madison city	207 525	5.1	12.4	21.4	32.4	19.4	9.3	30.6	-8.2	-3.1	170 522	14.7	10.7
55 48500	Manitowoc city	33 996	6.0	18.3	8.2	27.9	21.1	18.4	38.6	-1.4	6.0	31 221	22.4	19.9
55 51000	Menomonee Falls village	32 646	6.7	18.1	5.2	30.7	23.6	15.7	39.2	-0.9	3.3	31 254	24.1	16.1
55 53000	Milwaukee city	596 956	7.9	20.8	12.1	30.4	18.0	10.9	30.6	3.0	-1.5	273 056	15.6	18.0
55 56375	New Berlin city	38 362	5.9	19.1	6.4	29.0	27.0	12.5	39.8	-0.7	0.1	36 408	24.2	13.0
55 58800	Oak Creek city	28 456	6.7	17.8	9.3	35.7	21.4	9.0	34.5	-1.2	-3.4	25 486	23.6	9.5
55 60500	Oshkosh city	62 943	5.6	15.1	18.2	30.3	17.9	13.0	32.4	-5.0	0.6	57 685	19.3	14.0
55 66000	Racine city	81 827	8.1	20.9	9.9	29.7	18.8	12.6	33.1	3.3	0.2	52 139	23.0	16.8
55 72975	Sheboygan city	50 801	7.0	18.7	8.8	30.6	19.2	15.8	35.4	0.0	3.4	43 173	21.9	18.0
55 78650	Superior city	27 382	6.1	16.6	12.8	27.8	21.7	15.0	35.9	-3.0	2.6	25 780	21.9	15.7
55 84250	Waukesha city	64 372	7.3	16.8	11.0	33.7	20.4	10.8	33.4	-1.6	-1.6	56 077	22.5	12.1
55 84475	Wausau city	38 404	6.3	18.7	9.5	27.3	20.9	17.3	36.5	-0.7	4.9	32 945	19.8	19.8
55 84675	Wauwatosa city	47 271	6.4	16.9	5.6	31.0	21.8	18.3	39.1	-2.4	5.9	43 860	22.2	19.3
55 85300	West Allis city	61 295	5.8	15.6	8.4	32.3	20.7	17.3	37.8	-4.3	4.9	56 339	20.0	18.5
55 85350	West Bend city	28 133	7.5	18.6	8.8	30.8	19.7	14.6	35.3	0.4	2.2	26 982	25.3	15.1
56 00000	WYOMING	493 782	6.3	19.7	10.1	28.2	24.1	11.6	36.2	0.3	-0.8	438 538	24.9	12.4
56 13150	Casper city	49 855	6.4	19.3	10.3	27.7	22.6	13.6	36.1	0.0	1.2	45 565	24.9	14.4
56 13900	Cheyenne city	52 763	6.1	18.2	9.0	29.7	23.2	13.8	36.6	-1.4	1.4	42 877	22.7	15.3
56 45050	Laramie city	27 213	5.3	11.9	32.0	25.9	16.9	8.0	25.3	-8.5	-4.4	23 828	16.3	8.3

Table A-5. Cities — Age, Ethnicity, and Household Structure

City	Black or African American Total population	Age (percent) Under 18 years	Age (percent) 65 years and over	American Indian and Alaska Native Total population	Age (percent) Under 18 years	Age (percent) 65 years and over	Asian, Hawaiian, and Pacific Islander Total population	Age (percent) Under 18 years	Age (percent) 65 years and over	Hispanic or Latino[1] Total population	Age (percent) Under 18 years	Age (percent) 65 years and over	Two or more races Total population	Age (percent) Under 18 years	Age (percent) 65 years and over
	14	15	16	17	18	19	20	21	22	23	24	25	26	27	28
WISCONSIN—Cont'd															
Franklin city	1 479	6.2	1.1	118	17.8	6.8	685	30.2	2.8	686	44.8	3.2	222	49.1	0.0
Green Bay city	1 313	46.2	0.0	3 274	34.7	3.9	3 480	51.1	2.7	7 440	37.9	0.7	2 121	57.3	2.0
Greenfield city	411	49.4	0.0	196	27.0	0.0	753	23.1	2.4	1 335	35.0	4.3	459	48.6	1.1
Janesville city	700	41.3	3.3	214	29.0	0.0	489	24.1	5.5	1 623	40.5	4.1	650	60.9	1.2
Kenosha city	6 713	39.9	4.7	391	28.4	7.7	884	25.3	8.0	8 734	39.4	3.3	2 159	56.5	1.1
La Crosse city	814	26.9	1.6	474	36.9	5.9	1 970	51.6	2.2	401	19.7	8.5	776	61.9	2.3
Madison city	11 553	35.9	3.1	835	27.8	0.0	11 817	23.3	3.0	8 638	26.8	1.7	4 974	42.0	1.4
Manitowoc city	98	20.4	0.0	278	27.0	2.2	1 160	51.9	2.2	946	43.1	1.0	354	46.0	4.2
Menomonee Falls village	557	44.2	2.3	46	47.8	0.0	205	29.3	0.0	337	41.2	4.7	347	53.0	17.0
Milwaukee city	220 770	39.6	5.6	6 388	38.6	3.6	16 482	37.6	4.8	71 032	39.1	2.7	17 452	50.9	4.2
New Berlin city	102	22.1	0.0	106	42.1	3.8	933	32.6	4.8	426	40.3	4.2	326	49.1	2.2
Oak Creek city	670	31.6	1.5	136	16.2	24.3	629	32.9	5.2	1 211	34.8	5.2	361	38.2	0.0
Oshkosh city	1 281	6.6	1.3	327	29.1	2.4	1 653	51.1	2.3	1 364	39.2	2.6	774	52.7	1.9
Racine city	16 365	37.3	6.4	395	48.6	2.0	547	32.7	1.6	11 385	40.8	4.0	2 371	60.2	2.2
Sheboygan city	539	41.7	0.0	225	36.9	0.0	3 310	54.7	3.4	2 818	38.0	4.2	1 147	52.6	1.1
Superior city	144	35.4	0.0	577	23.4	5.7	256	42.2	0.0	191	42.9	0.0	467	47.5	4.3
Waukesha city	720	31.3	0.3	252	15.1	3.2	1 228	25.2	0.0	5 385	36.4	2.7	1 186	49.0	1.9
Wausau city	159	52.2	0.0	325	44.0	0.0	4 181	59.2	2.0	395	43.3	3.3	442	57.7	3.2
Wauwatosa city	1 097	37.7	4.7	234	45.7	0.0	850	22.6	11.5	844	34.8	2.6	582	58.4	4.3
West Allis city	766	43.5	1.2	380	27.4	3.7	1 035	25.1	4.6	2 058	39.1	3.3	1 012	51.8	2.3
West Bend city	129	45.0	12.4	140	37.9	0.0	220	30.9	2.7	480	38.3	1.7	229	74.2	3.9
WYOMING	3 126	25.5	3.7	11 363	36.7	4.8	3 204	23.2	8.0	31 384	35.1	5.6	9 399	42.2	5.1
Casper city	282	29.1	3.2	592	27.2	4.6	385	33.2	4.2	2 645	37.5	5.1	623	43.2	4.8
Cheyenne city	1 262	24.0	3.4	530	27.0	0.2	514	26.1	13.6	6 809	31.3	8.2	1 611	51.4	3.3
Laramie city	271	20.7	0.0	204	16.2	5.4	534	16.5	5.4	2 022	25.5	6.2	478	31.4	4.2

[1] Hispanic or Latino persons may be of any race.

City		Family households (percent)						Nonfamily households (percent)							
		Married-couple family households			Other family households			Two or more unrelated persons		Male living alone		Female living alone			
	Total households	Total	With children	House- holder 65 years or over	Total	With children	House- holder 65 years or over	Total	House- holder 65 years or over	Total	House- holder 65 years or over	Total	House- holder 65 years or over	Percent of householders 65 years and over who live alone	Grandparents who are responsible for the care of their grandchildren
	29	30	31	32	33	34	35	36	37	38	39	40	41	42	43
WISCONSIN—Cont'd															
Franklin city	10 637	63.3	29.5	8.8	9.7	4.4	1.8	4.3	0.4	9.7	1.3	13.0	5.0	36.6	25
Green Bay city	41 656	44.7	21.1	7.5	15.0	10.3	1.0	8.6	0.3	14.0	1.9	17.8	8.3	53.7	401
Greenfield city	15 702	47.5	17.5	11.4	11.0	5.2	2.2	6.8	0.5	12.0	2.8	22.7	11.5	50.4	122
Janesville city	24 009	51.8	23.0	9.8	14.2	9.7	0.9	6.6	0.2	10.9	1.8	16.5	7.3	45.5	256
Kenosha city	34 503	48.1	23.7	7.9	17.8	11.2	2.2	5.8	0.4	11.9	2.5	16.4	7.8	49.3	614
La Crosse city	21 043	37.5	15.6	8.7	11.7	7.1	1.2	13.7	0.2	13.7	2.7	23.4	11.4	57.9	133
Madison city	89 267	37.6	16.4	5.8	10.3	6.0	1.0	16.7	0.3	15.5	1.4	19.9	5.6	49.7	487
Manitowoc city	14 165	50.4	21.5	12.1	12.2	7.8	1.8	5.0	0.4	11.6	2.5	20.8	12.2	50.8	114
Menomonee Falls village	12 874	63.7	28.8	12.3	8.9	4.5	1.9	3.6	0.3	8.2	2.6	15.4	9.4	45.2	28
Milwaukee city	232 312	33.2	15.2	6.1	25.5	16.1	2.6	7.9	0.4	15.2	2.6	18.3	6.9	51.0	7 052
New Berlin city	14 499	68.2	30.6	11.6	7.6	3.7	1.6	5.1	0.3	7.4	1.3	11.7	5.2	32.9	109
Oak Creek city	11 277	58.0	30.2	6.6	9.0	4.9	1.0	7.8	0.2	11.5	2.1	13.7	4.6	46.0	60
Oshkosh city	24 019	45.5	20.4	8.6	11.7	7.6	1.2	10.5	0.3	12.9	2.5	19.4	9.5	54.4	96
Racine city	31 358	44.2	20.0	9.0	20.9	13.8	2.3	5.5	0.4	12.0	2.5	17.3	8.2	48.0	925
Sheboygan city	20 799	49.2	22.2	10.0	12.8	8.5	1.3	5.7	0.1	13.9	3.0	18.4	9.7	52.6	244
Superior city	11 606	42.5	17.5	8.6	15.4	10.5	1.5	7.9	0.4	14.1	2.8	20.1	10.6	56.2	144
Waukesha city	25 624	51.5	25.4	7.0	11.9	7.4	0.9	7.5	0.3	11.8	1.8	17.3	7.5	53.0	251
Wausau city	15 743	47.6	20.2	10.4	12.2	7.5	1.8	6.5	0.3	12.8	2.9	20.9	11.9	54.1	153
Wauwatosa city	20 430	50.7	23.5	10.5	9.8	4.9	1.7	5.6	0.3	10.6	3.0	23.3	12.7	55.5	117
West Allis city	27 640	42.2	17.4	9.2	14.0	8.3	2.1	6.7	0.4	15.8	3.1	21.4	10.9	54.1	154
West Bend city	11 366	55.1	25.7	10.3	11.6	8.0	1.2	6.1	0.3	9.8	1.8	17.4	10.2	50.3	47
WYOMING	193 959	55.7	25.1	9.1	12.1	8.1	1.1	5.9	0.3	12.6	2.3	13.7	6.6	45.6	3 582
Casper city	20 436	50.8	22.3	9.4	14.0	9.6	1.1	6.0	0.2	13.3	2.8	15.9	8.1	50.2	267
Cheyenne city	22 346	49.7	21.8	8.7	13.9	9.5	1.4	5.1	0.4	13.9	2.6	17.5	8.2	50.7	340
Laramie city	11 364	39.4	17.1	6.0	10.7	6.2	0.7	17.0	0.3	16.6	1.3	16.3	4.0	43.1	61

City	Households with Non-Hispanic White householder		Households with Black or African American householder		Households with American Indian and Alaska Native householder		Households with Asian, Hawaiian, and Pacific Islander householder		Households with Hispanic or Latino[1] householder		Foreign-born population	Place of birth (percent)			Percent in non-English speaking households	
	Number of households	Percent that are family house-holds	Number of households	Percent that are family house-holds	Number of households	Percent that are family house-holds	Number of households	Percent that are family house-holds	Number of households	Percent that are family house-holds	Percent of total population that is foreign-born	Europe	Asia	Latin America	Linguis-tically isolated	Not linguis-tically isolated
	44	45	46	47	48	49	50	51	52	53	54	55	56	57	58	59
WISCONSIN—Cont'd																
Franklin city	10 086	72.9	73	47.9	50	60.0	171	95.3	218	73.4	4.3	1.9	1.9	0.3	1.3	14.1
Green Bay city	37 233	57.7	380	60.8	1 160	66.9	678	91.2	1 885	80.6	6.8	0.4	2.2	4.1	3.9	12.1
Greenfield city	14 853	58.1	138	70.3	75	54.7	211	82.0	377	64.2	5.8	2.8	1.8	0.8	1.4	12.2
Janesville city	22 916	66.2	220	55.0	59	62.7	183	58.5	521	69.1	2.4	0.5	0.7	1.1	1.1	7.9
Kenosha city................	29 475	64.3	2 066	73.4	212	68.4	292	64.0	2 201	82.0	5.9	1.9	0.9	3.0	2.4	15.8
La Crosse city	20 068	48.6	202	61.4	158	66.5	376	68.1	114	30.7	3.3	0.5	2.4	0.1	1.0	9.8
Madison city	76 631	46.4	4 013	60.9	311	44.4	4 417	52.8	2 700	63.0	9.1	1.4	4.7	2.1	3.2	14.7
Manitowoc city............	13 465	61.5	21	61.9	142	69.7	221	96.4	229	80.3	4.0	0.7	2.2	1.0	1.8	10.0
Menomonee Falls village	12 457	72.7	154	81.8	11	100.0	69	55.1	118	83.1	2.9	1.8	0.6	0.2	0.6	8.4
Milwaukee city.............	129 043	49.5	75 603	69.0	2 204	71.5	4 374	67.7	18 689	77.9	7.7	1.3	2.0	4.1	4.6	17.0
New Berlin city	13 046	75.8	00	48.0	37	51.4	268	85.4	91	80.2	4.4	2.0	1.8	0.3	0.9	9.5
Oak Creek city	10 319	66.8	206	54.9	48	87.5	208	63.0	400	83.3	4.4	0.9	2.1	0.8	0.8	12.8
Oshkosh city................	22 933	56.8	137	35.8	121	70.2	352	75.6	366	70.2	3.4	0.8	1.9	0.6	1.8	8.9
Racine city..................	22 401	61.8	5 551	69.5	141	72.3	152	53.3	2 983	82.6	5.7	1.2	0.6	3.8	3.6	14.8
Sheboygan city............	18 903	60.6	184	77.7	49	89.8	613	90.4	843	66.2	7.7	1.3	4.3	2.0	4.2	13.6
Superior city	11 112	57.7	40	100.0	249	64.3	59	66.1	36	27.8	2.0	0.7	0.8	0.2	0.6	6.2
Waukesha city..............	23 129	61.9	214	66.8	135	65.2	456	71.1	1 546	85.1	5.4	0.8	1.6	2.6	2.0	12.5
Wausau city..................	14 733	58.1	30	100.0	69	66.7	694	91.6	99	76.8	8.4	0.7	7.1	0.4	4.4	12.2
Wauwatosa city	19 459	60.4	299	63.5	48	64.6	354	47.7	217	86.2	3.8	1.7	1.2	0.4	0.8	10.4
West Allis city..............	26 171	55.3	226	62.4	109	78.9	347	66.6	598	78.6	3.6	1.6	1.4	0.5	1.0	10.5
West Bend city	11 063	66.2	29	100.0	45	100.0	49	100.0	154	78.6	1.4	0.8	0.2	0.3	0.6	9.6
WYOMING	176 982	67.7	1 154	64.1	3 353	74.5	845	64.5	9 570	69.0	2.3	0.6	0.4	0.9	0.8	10.4
Casper city	18 971	65.3	144	68.1	223	52.5	104	69.2	847	58.0	2.0	0.7	0.4	0.7	0.4	9.7
Cheyenne city	10 767	60.5	532	65.4	221	63.3	124	39.5	2 458	65.0	3.3	1.1	0.8	1.0	1.0	14.1
Laramie city.................	10 127	49.1	110	36.4	80	63.8	183	51.4	737	63.0	4.0	1.0	1.4	0.8	1.7	10.2

[1]Hispanic or Latino persons may be of any race.

Education, Labor Force, and Income

(For explanation of symbols, see page xi.)

Population With Bachelor's Degree or Higher
2000

Percent Population with
Bachelor's Degree or Higher

Less than 10.0%

10.0% to 14.9%

15.0% to 24.3%

24.4% or more

(U.S. = 24.4%)

Note: Includes persons 25 years and over.

Population With High School Diploma or Less
2000

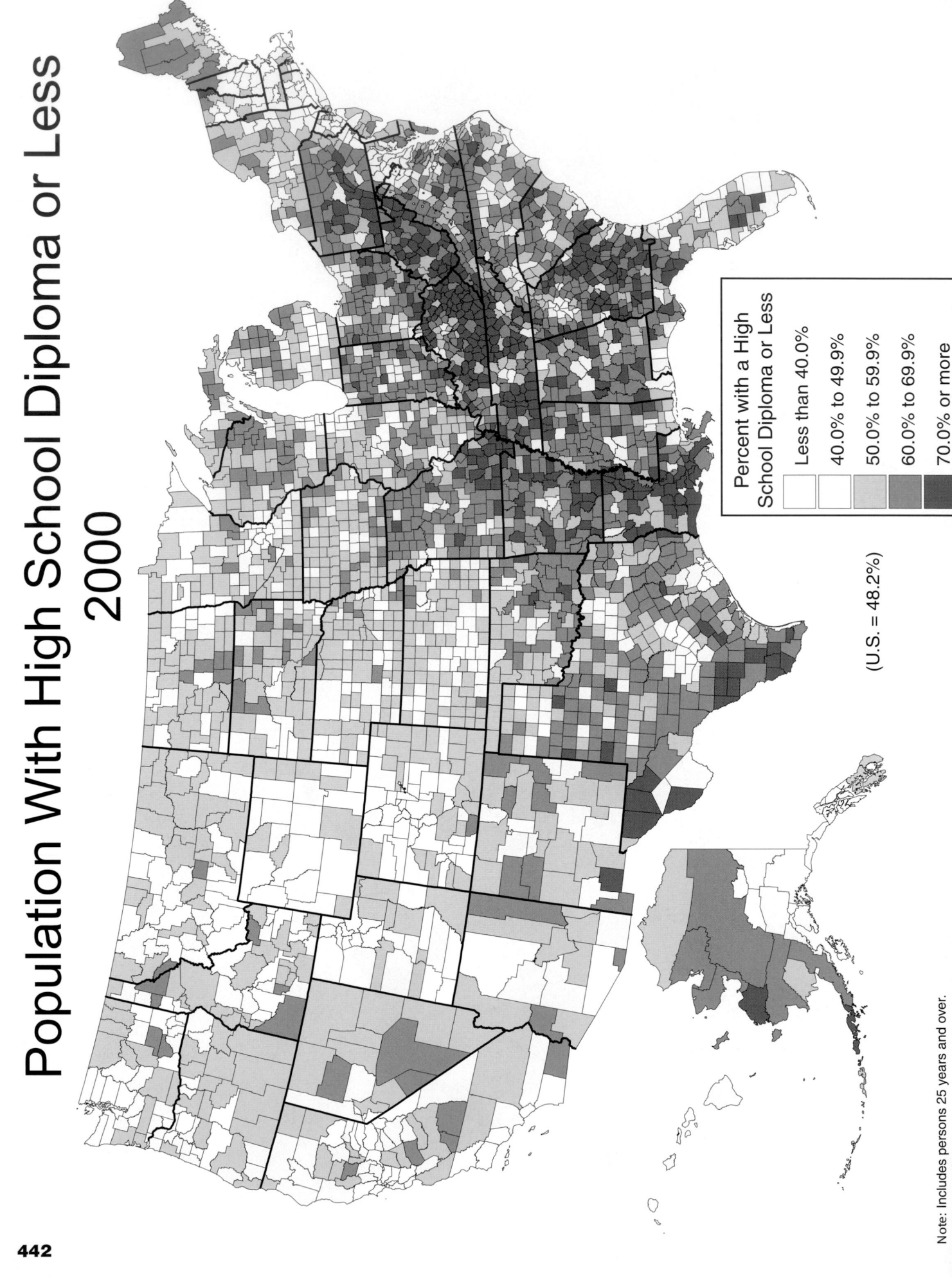

Percent with a High School Diploma or Less

- Less than 40.0%
- 40.0% to 49.9%
- 50.0% to 59.9%
- 60.0% to 69.9%
- 70.0% or more

(U.S. = 48.2%)

Note: Includes persons 25 years and over.

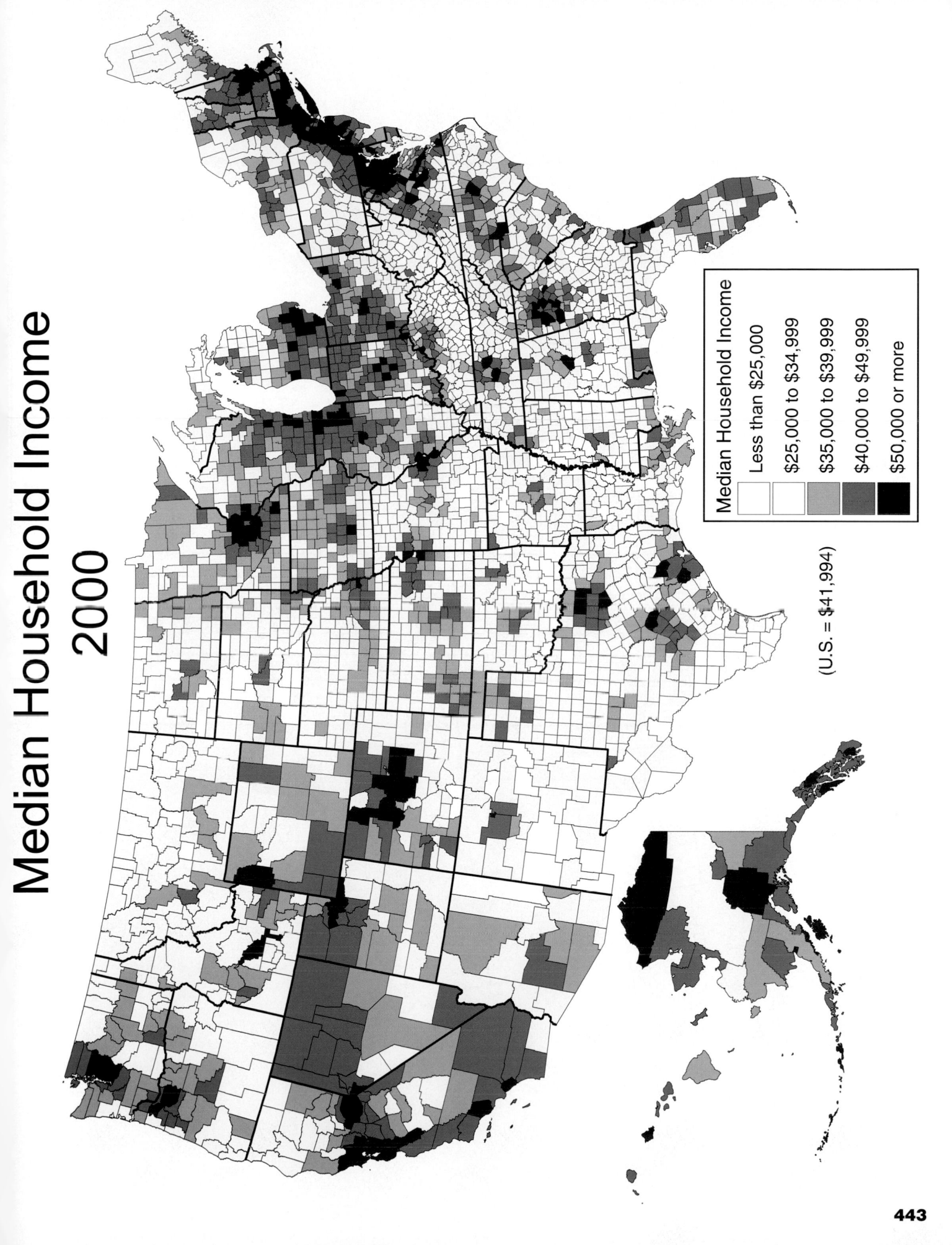

Median Household Income 2000

Median Household Income

- Less than $25,000
- $25,000 to $34,999
- $35,000 to $39,999
- $40,000 to $49,999
- $50,000 or more

(U.S. = $41,994)

443

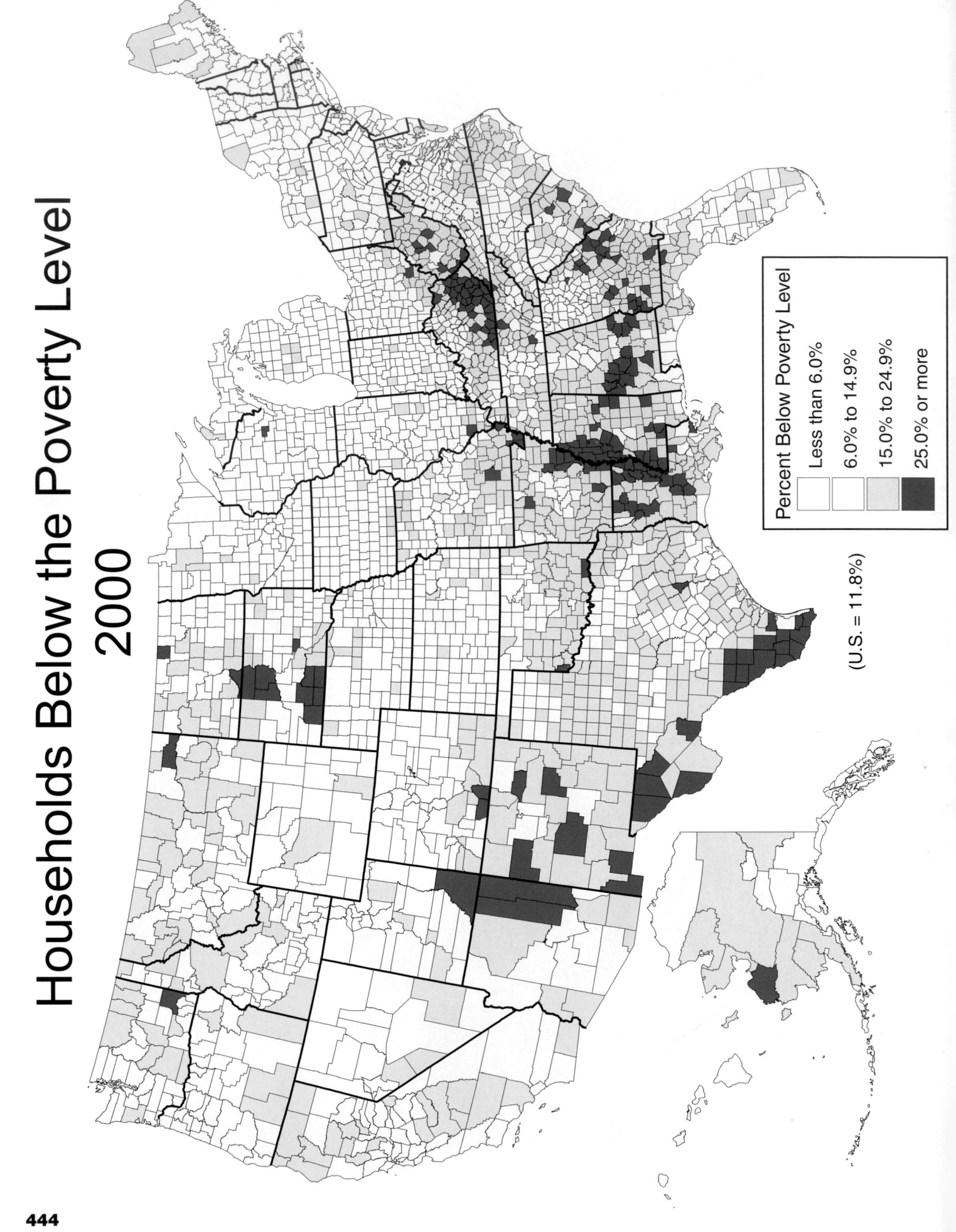

Households Below the Poverty Level
2000

Percent Below Poverty Level

Less than 6.0%

6.0% to 14.9%

15.0% to 24.9%

25.0% or more

(U.S. = 11.8%)

Full-Time Workers
2000

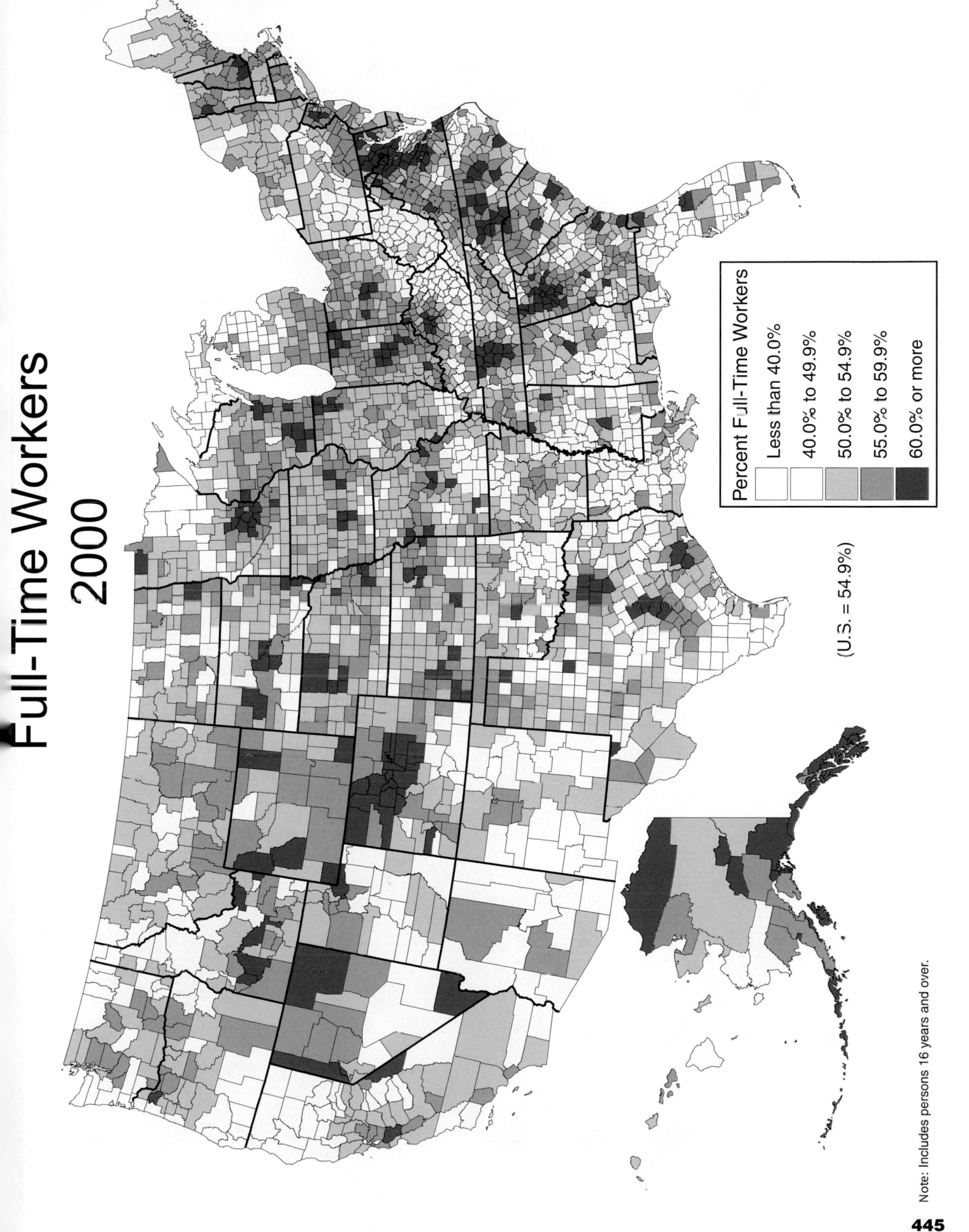

Percent Full-Time Workers

Less than 40.0%
40.0% to 49.9%
50.0% to 54.9%
55.0% to 59.9%
60.0% or more

(U.S. = 54.9%)

Note: Includes persons 16 years and over.

445

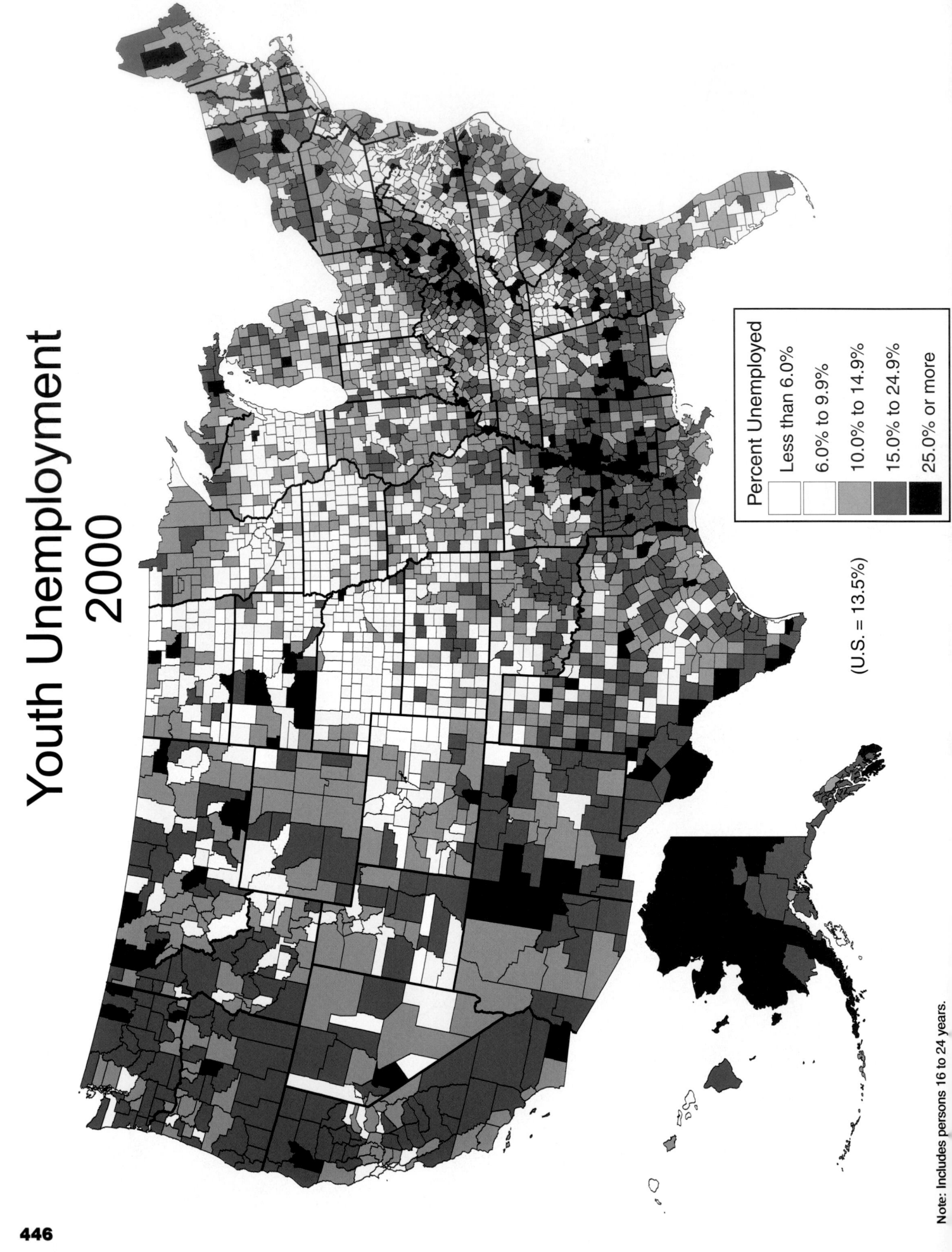

Youth Unemployment 2000

Percent Unemployed

Less than 6.0%

6.0% to 9.9%

10.0% to 14.9%

15.0% to 24.9%

25.0% or more

(U.S. = 13.5%)

Note: Includes persons 16 to 24 years.

446

Children With No "Stay-At-Home" Parent
2000

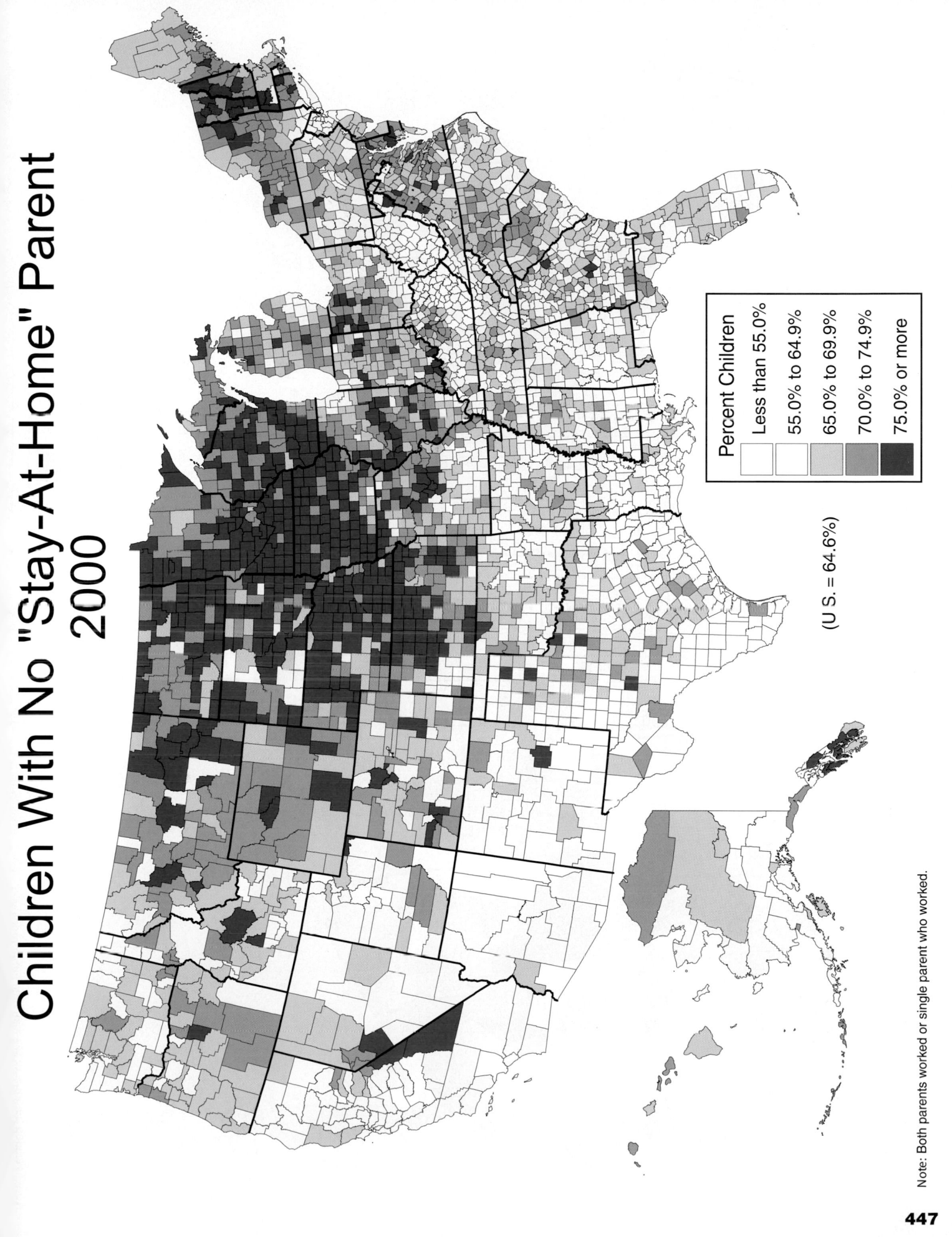

Percent Children

- Less than 55.0%
- 55.0% to 64.9%
- 65.0% to 69.9%
- 70.0% to 74.9%
- 75.0% or more

(U.S. = 64.6%)

Note: Both parents worked or single parent who worked.

447

Children in "Traditional" Families
2000

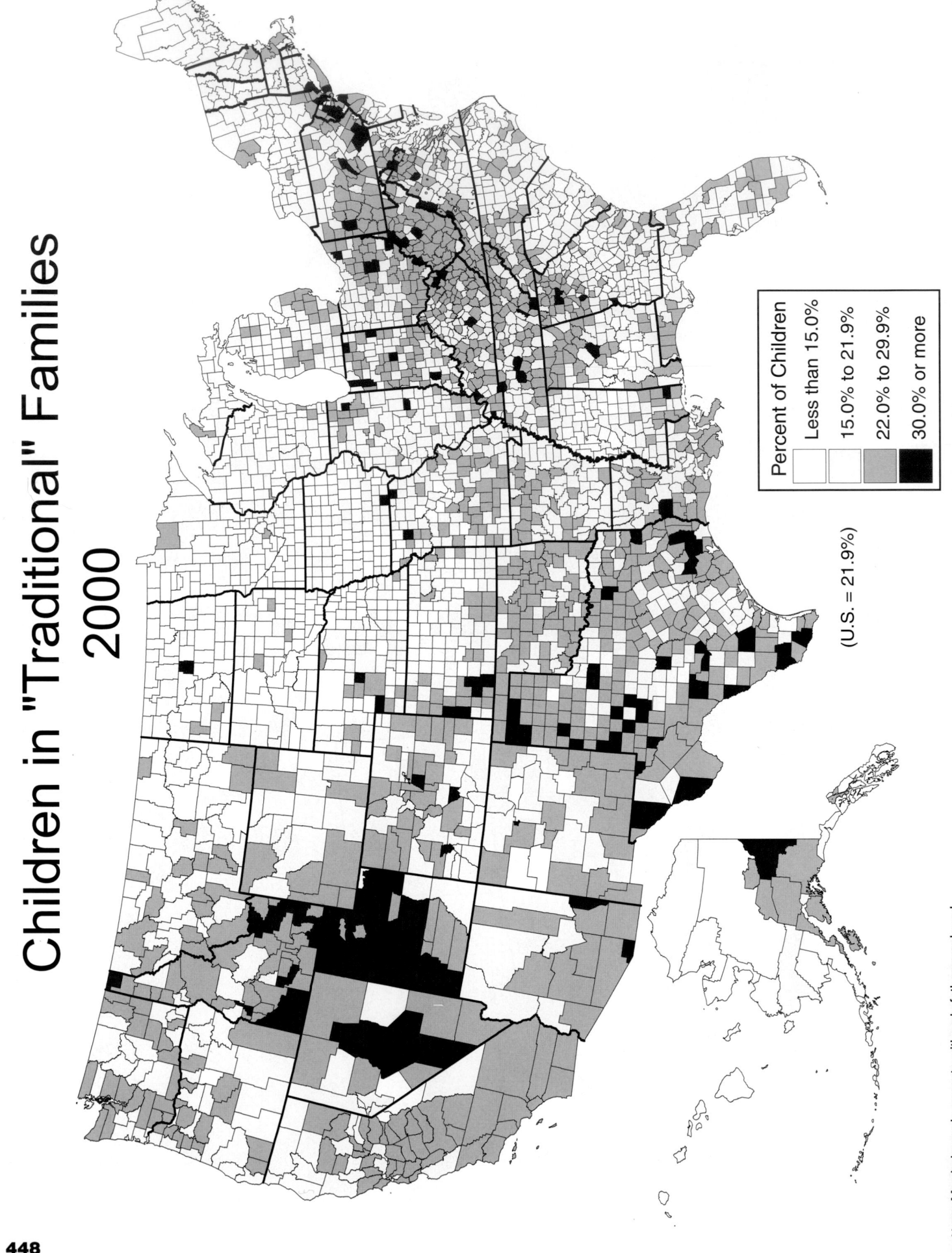

Percent of Children
- Less than 15.0%
- 15.0% to 21.9%
- 22.0% to 29.9%
- 30.0% or more

(U.S. = 21.9%)

Note: Married couple parents with only father employed.

Education, Labor Force, and Income

Americans' employment and income potential are closely related to their educational attainment. According to Census 2000, Americans seem to have reached a plateau in that both younger and older working age adults have pretty much the same education credentials. However, pronounced geographic differences continue to influence the location of economic activities. Whether workers or employers, decisions about moving to or from states where the work force has relatively low educational attainment tend to be made in a low-wage context. In contrast, workers or employers make decisions about moving to or from states where the work force has relatively high educational attainment in a context of relatively high incomes.

Education Milestones

Census 2000 paints a generally positive picture of the population's educational base and its economic potential. Perhaps the most dramatic change is the "aging out" of the working ages by Americans who grew up before a high school diploma was considered an essential credential. In 2000, less than half as many Americans in the prime working ages, 25 to 64, lacked a high school diploma as Americans aged 65 and over. (See Table B-1.1.)

This shift has significant implications for social policies that have been based on the income needs of people who exhausted their health in physically demanding

Table B-1.1. Educational Attainment by Age, United States, 2000

(Number, percent.)

Age	Total	Less than high school	High school graduate	Some college/associate degree	Bachelor's degree or higher
Total Population 18 Years and Over	209 279 149	20.3	28.6	28.8	22.3
18 to 24 years	27 067 510	25.3	28.6	38.4	7.8
25 years and over	182 211 639	19.6	28.6	27.4	24.4
25 to 44 years	85 482 828	15.5	27.2	30.6	26.7
45 to 64 years	61 749 839	16.8	28.7	28.1	26.4
65 years and over	34 978 972	34.5	32.0	18.1	15.4
Male Population 18 Years and Over	100 909 272	21.1	28.0	27.6	23.4
18 to 24 years	13 831 586	28.6	30.2	34.9	6.4
25 years and over	87 077 686	19.9	27.6	26.4	26.1
25 to 44 years	42 700 352	17.3	28.5	28.5	25.8
45 to 64 years	29 994 964	17.1	26.4	27.3	29.3
65 years and over	14 382 370	33.6	27.5	18.4	20.5
Female Population 18 Years and Over	108 369 877	19.6	29.2	29.9	21.2
18 to 24 years	13 235 924	21.8	26.9	42.0	9.3
25 years and over	95 133 953	19.3	29.6	28.2	22.8
25 years to 44 years	42 782 476	13.7	26.0	32.7	27.5
45 to 64 years	31 754 875	16.6	30.8	28.9	23.7
65 years and over	20 596 602	35.1	35.1	18.0	11.8
In Central City of a Metropolitan Area					
Total population 18 years and over	63 997 079	23.0	24.9	28.7	23.4
Male	30 511 507	23.4	24.4	27.6	24.6
Female	33 485 572	22.6	25.5	29.6	22.3
In a Metropolitan Area, Not in Central City					
Total population 18 years and over	103 835 067	17.3	28.3	29.6	24.9
Male	50 127 233	18.0	27.2	28.4	26.4
Female	53 707 834	16.7	29.3	30.7	23.4
Not in a Metropolitan Area					
Total population 18 years and over	41 447 003	23.8	35.2	27.1	14.0
Male	20 270 532	25.2	35.2	25.5	14.1
Female	21 176 471	22.4	35.1	28.6	13.9

Source: Census 2000 Summary File 3—United States, U.S. Census Bureau, 2002. Table PCT25.

occupations, but lacked the basic education needed for service jobs in demand, such as sales clerks or cashiers. Research has found that people who take early retirement have tended to have these characteristics. Now, a larger share of the work force has some capacity to shift occupations, at whatever rung of the ladder, at the same time as a declining share of jobs are physically demanding.

The data also suggest that young Americans, young men especially, are taking several years to complete their basic education. In 2000, a quarter of adults aged 18 to 25 still lacked a high school diploma, compared with 15 percent of adults aged 25 to 44. Research indicates that many of these young adults are "stopping out," not dropping out, but policymakers need to make sure that the way is clear for them to acquire a diploma or its equivalent, once they perceive its advantages.

In general, today's working age Americans, whether in the early or the later stages of work life, have similar educational levels, with more than a quarter of people aged 25 to 64 having a bachelor's degree or higher. The major difference between generations is that more men than women have higher education credentials among those aged 45 to 64, while the reverse is true among those aged 25 to 44.

Labor force quality is primarily measured by educational attainment, so it is somewhat surprising to still find large variations from state to state in this key characteristic. (See Table B-1.2.) Southern states have typically lagged in basic education; one reason is because so much of their economy was agricultural until recent decades. Many of these states have closed the gap with the rest of the country, but other, poorer states have not.

Geographic differences are even more pronounced among the college-educated population. (See Table B-1.3.) In part, this is because higher educated people tend to cluster where there are good jobs to be had, while people with less education have relatively less to gain from moving. And in part it reflects the quality of a state's higher education, since students are likely to attend college in a different state if they deem it a superior option. Thus a state like Massachusetts, where higher education is an important product, has a particularly large college-educated population among people aged 25 and older, as students often remain in the state where they go to college.

Over the last several decades, policymakers have paid particular attention to closing educational gaps between the nation's racial and ethnic populations. To a large extent, these gaps have narrowed, especially for African Americans. (See Table B-1.4.) In 2000, 85 percent of all non-Hispanic whites aged 25 and over had a high school diploma, compared with 72 percent of African-Americans, and 71 percent of American Indians and Alaska Natives. Among younger people, however, the gaps have almost disappeared.

Immigration has complicated progress toward equalizing educational attainment among the nation's racial and ethnic groups, as new immigrants tend to have either very low or very high educational attainment. As a result, in 2000 only 52 percent of the nation's Hispanic population had a high school diploma, compared with 80 percent for Asian-Americans. Native Hawaiian and other Pacific Islanders are just behind—78 percent were high school graduates in 2000.

Table B-1.2.
High school graduation is more common in some states than in others.
Population with a High School Diploma or Higher, Selected States, 2000

(Percentage of graduates among population 25 years and over.)

State	Low proportion	State	High proportion
Mississippi	72.9	Alaska	88.3
Kentucky	74.1	Minnesota	87.9
Louisiana	74.8	Wyoming	87.9
West Virginia	75.2	Utah	87.7
Alabama	75.3	Montana	87.2
Arkansas	75.3	Washington	87.1

Source: Census 2000 Summary File 3—United States, U.S. Census Bureau, 2002. Table P37.

Table B-1.3.
The location of college-educated people varies widely.
Population with a Bachelor's Degree or Higher, Selected States, 2000

(Percentage of graduates among population 25 years and over.)

State	Low proportion	State	High proportion
West Virginia	14.8	Massachusetts	33.2
Arkansas	16.7	Colorado	32.7
Mississippi	16.9	Connecticut	31.4
Kentucky	17.1	Maryland	31.4
Nevada	18.2	New Jersey	29.8

Source: Census 2000 Summary File 3—United States, U.S. Census Bureau, 2002. Table P37.

Table B-1.4. Educational Attainment by Race and Hispanic Origin, United States, 2000

(Number, percent.)

Age, race and Hispanic origin	Total	Less than high school	High school graduate	Some college/associate degree	Bachelor's degree or higher
Total Population 25 Years and Over					
One race only					
White	143 085 659	16.4	29.5	28.0	26.1
Black or African American	19 858 095	27.7	29.8	28.2	14.3
American Indian and Alaska Native	1 350 998	29.1	29.2	30.2	11.5
Asian	6 640 671	19.6	15.8	20.5	44.1
Native Hawaiian and Other Pacific					
Islander	206 675	21.7	33.7	30.8	13.8
Some other race	7 611 121	53.2	21.8	17.8	7.3
Two or more races	3 458 420	26.7	25.2	28.5	19.6
Hispanic or Latino[1]	18 270 377	47.6	22.1	19.9	10.4
White alone, not Hispanic or Latino	133 786 263	14.5	30.0	28.5	27.0
Male Population 25 Years and Over					
One race only					
White	68 622 786	16.6	28.1	27.2	28.2
Black or African American	8 980 716	29.1	31.4	26.5	13.1
American Indian and Alaska Native	655 259	30.0	30.2	28.5	11.4
Asian	3 099 433	16.6	14.4	20.8	48.2
Native Hawaiian and Other Pacific					
Islander	103 072	21.9	32.7	30.9	14.5
Some other race	3 921 838	54.7	21.7	16.7	6.9
Two or more races	1 694 582	27.1	25.1	27.3	20.6
Hispanic or Latino[1]	9 186 431	49.2	21.8	18.8	10.2
White alone, not Hispanic or Latino	64 027 316	14.6	28.5	27.6	29.3
Female Population 25 Years and Over					
One race only					
White	74 462 873	16.3	30.8	28.8	24.1
Black or African American	10 877 379	26.6	28.4	29.7	15.2
American Indian and Alaska Native	695 739	28.3	28.3	31.8	11.6
Asian	3 541 238	22.2	17.1	20.3	40.4
Native Hawaiian and Other Pacific					
Islander	103 603	21.6	34.6	30.8	13.1
Some other race	3 689 283	51.6	21.8	18.9	7.7
Two or more races	1 763 838	26.3	25.2	29.7	18.7
Hispanic or Latino[1]	9 083 946	46.0	22.4	20.9	10.7
White alone, not Hispanic or Latino	69 758 947	14.5	31.4	29.3	24.8

Source: Census 2000 Summary File 3—United States, U.S. Census Bureau, 2002. Table P148A-I.
[1]Hispanic or Latino persons may be of any race.

Again, higher education varies even more. Only 10 percent of Hispanics have a bachelor's degree or higher, compared with 44 percent of Asian-Americans. In comparison, 27 percent of non-Hispanic whites have at least one degree, almost twice the 14 percent share of African Americans and 12 percent of American Indians and Alaska Natives.

The uneven location of the nation's racial and ethnic groups contributes to variation in statewide educational levels. For instance, California has an above-average rate of high school completion among non-Hispanic whites, as well as among blacks. But large numbers of Mexican immigrants swell the state's population of high school dropouts, putting the state well below the national average for high school completion.

These differences are less stark for younger adults, who have benefited from initiatives designed to equalize their educational preparation. However, many young people are not following the standard path of high school completion, and are at risk of stagnating in low-wage jobs when they enter the labor force. Looking just at the population aged 16 to 19—key transition years—Census 2000 found that nearly 10 percent of Americans this age both lacked a diploma and were not enrolled in school. (See Table B-1.5.) (About half were working, and about half were unemployed or not in the labor force.)

Only 4 percent of Asian youth, and 7 percent of non-Hispanic white youth are neither high school graduates or enrolled in school, compared with 21 percent of Hispanic youth. Fully 12 percent of African-American youth and 16 percent of American Indian youth are in this uncertain state. To some extent, the uneven location of these population groups is reflected in state portraits of this key age group. (See Table B-1.6.)

Policymakers should note that three of the eight in 10 Americans ages 16 to 19 enrolled in school are combining

Table B-1.5. School Enrollment and Labor Force Status for the Population 16 to 19 Years, United States, 2000

(Number, percent.)

Enrollment and employment status	Total population 16 to 19 years	White alone	Black or African American alone	American Indian and Alaska Native alone	Asian alone	Native Hawaiian and Other Pacific Islander alone	Some other race	Two or more races	Hispanic or Latino[1]	White alone, not Hispanic or Latino
Total population 16 to 19 years	15 930 458	11 134 041	2 284 042	178 590	590 880	29 478	1 189 313	524 114	2 518 961	10 026 825
PERCENT										
In Armed Forces	0.6	0.6	0.8	0.6	0.5	0.9	0.7	0.8	0.6	0.6
Civilian	99.4	99.4	99.2	99.4	99.5	99.1	99.3	99.2	99.4	99.4
Enrolled in school	79.7	81.2	77.4	72.1	90.7	75.0	66.1	78.0	68.1	82.5
Employed	29.8	33.7	19.8	18.6	24.1	19.6	18.9	26.9	19.9	35.1
Unemployed	6.4	5.9	9.2	6.7	5.9	10.0	6.2	7.0	6.0	5.9
Not in labor force	43.5	41.7	48.4	46.8	60.7	45.5	41.0	44.1	42.2	41.5
Not enrolled in school	19.7	18.1	21.7	27.3	8.9	24.1	33.3	21.2	31.3	16.8
High school graduate	9.9	10.0	10.0	11.2	4.9	13.1	10.4	10.2	10.3	9.9
Employed	6.4	7.0	4.8	5.8	2.7	7.6	6.2	6.4	6.1	7.1
Unemployed	1.2	1.1	2.0	2.1	0.5	1.9	1.2	1.4	1.2	1.1
Not in labor force	2.2	1.9	3.3	3.3	1.6	3.7	3.0	2.5	3.0	1.8
Not high school graduate	9.8	8.2	11.7	16.1	4.0	11.0	22.9	11.0	21.0	6.9
Employed	4.3	4.0	2.9	5.4	1.6	4.7	11.0	4.8	9.9	3.4
Unemployed	1.6	1.3	2.6	3.0	0.5	1.7	2.8	1.9	2.6	1.2
Not in labor force	3.9	2.9	6.1	7.7	1.9	4.6	9.1	4.4	8.5	2.4

Source: Census 2000 Summary File 3—United States, U.S. Census Bureau, 2002. Tables P38 and P149A-I.
[1]Hispanic or Latino persons may be of any race.

Table B-1.6.
Youth who are neither in school nor high school graduates are at economic risk.
Population 16 to 19 Years Who Are Not Enrolled in School and Not High School Graduates, Selected States, 2000

(Percentage of population 16 to 19 years.)

State	High proportion	State	Low proportion
Nevada	16.0	North Dakota	4.8
Arizona	14.8	Hawaii	5.8
Georgia	13.5	Iowa	5.8
North Carolina	12.5	Minnesota	5.9
Texas	12.5	Vermont	5.9

Source: Census 2000 Summary File 3—United States, U.S. Census Bureau, 2002. Table P38.

Table B-1.7.
Adult education is a way for Americans to increase their human capital.
Population 25 Years and Over Enrolled in School, United States, 2000

(Percentage of population 25 years and over.)

State	Low adult enrollment	State	High adult enrollment
West Virginia	3.2	California	7.3
Arkansas	3.5	New Mexico	6.7
Mississippi	3.7	Arizona	6.2
South Dakota	3.7	Utah	6.2
Tennessee	3.7		

Source: Census 2000 Summary File 3—United States, U.S. Census Bureau, 2002. Tables PCT 23 and PCT 24.

school with work. Asians are least likely to combine work with schooling; non-Hispanic whites are most likely to work while attending school. Across all groups, unemployment rates are high for young students, but in the spring of 2000 at least, they were very low for those who weren't continuing their schooling, whether they were high school graduates or not.

Combining work and education is increasingly important for older people. In 2000, one in 20 Americans aged 25 and older was enrolled in school, mostly in college or graduate school. (See Table B-1.7 and Table B-1.8.) With so many jobs requiring specific educational skills,

working Americans are looking for ways to prepare themselves for new careers or to keep current with their existing jobs. Adult education is also a way for young adults who stopped out of school to re-enter and gain credentials for better jobs. Thus, the lengthening life span, combined with rapid economic evolution, is making life-long education an important focus for policymakers.

Working Americans

Census 2000 took place toward the end of a long period of economic prosperity, so it depicts a full-employment America. The census questions about work

Table B-1.8. Enrollment in School, College, or Graduate School by Age, United States, 2000

(Number, percent.)

Enrollment status	Total population 15 years and over	15 to 17 years	Population 18 years and over		
			18 years and over	18 to 24 years	25 years and over
Total Population 15 Years and Over	221 148 671	11 869 522	209 279 149	27 067 510	182 211 639
Percent enrolled in school	14.8	94.9	10.2	44.7	5.1
Percent enrolled in college or graduate school ..	7.9	0.6	8.3	34.0	4.5
Male Population 15 Years and Over	107 027 405	6 118 133	100 909 272	13 831 586	87 077 686
Percent enrolled in school	14.8	94.4	10.0	42.3	4.8
Percent enrolled in college or graduate school ..	7.4	0.5	7.8	30.7	4.2
Female Population 15 Years and Over	114 121 266	5 751 389	108 369 877	13 235 924	95 133 953
Percent enrolled in school	14.8	95.3	10.5	47.2	5.4
Percent enrolled in college or graduate school ..	8.4	0.7	8.8	37.5	4.8

Source: Census 2000 Summary File 3—United States, U.S. Census Bureau, 2002. Tables PCT23 and PCT24.

and employment focused on the previous full year—1999. Fully 55 percent of the total population aged 16 and over worked full-time in 1999, over 40 percent full-time and all year. Nearly 15 percent worked part-time, two-thirds for part of the year and one-third all year. (See Table B-1.10.)

Since jobs were relatively plentiful in 1999, state and local differences in the size of the employed population in large part reflect divergent age structures. (See Table B-1.11.) States like Florida and Pennsylvania, with large numbers of older, mostly retired people, had a smaller share of their population employed. Similarly, states with relatively young populations, like Colorado and Nevada, had a large share of their population employed. Thus, age differences that reflect previous trends in migration, whether in or out, resonate throughout state and local economies.

Nationally, two-thirds of men aged 16 and older worked full-time in 1999, as did 45 percent of women aged

Table B-1.9. School Enrollment, United States, 2000

(Number.)

Characteristic	Total enrolled in school	Nursery School/ Pre-school	Kindergarten	Grades 1–8	Grades 9–12	College or Graduate School
Total Population 3 Years and Over	76 632 927	4 957 582	4 157 491	33 653 641	16 380 951	17 483 262
Public	64 083 103	2 666 606	3 536 045	29 989 966	14 848 628	13 041 858
Private	12 549 824	2 290 976	621 446	3 663 675	1 532 323	4 441 404
Male Population 3 Years and Over	38 321 493	2 560 768	2 146 927	17 298 311	8 395 859	7 919 628
Public	32 172 925	1 390 894	1 832 507	15 450 855	7 610 678	5 887 991
Private	6 148 568	1 169 874	314 420	1 847 456	785 181	2 031 637
Female Population 3 Years and Over	38 311 434	2 396 814	2 010 564	16 355 330	7 985 092	9 563 634
Public	31 910 178	1 275 712	1 703 538	14 539 111	7 237 950	7 153 867
Private	6 401 256	1 121 102	307 026	1 816 219	747 142	2 409 767
Race and Hispanic Origin						
One race only	53 140 018	3 454 118	2 791 195	23 113 764	11 278 192	12 502 749
White	11 399 015	787 932	641 575	5 210 408	2 534 919	2 224 181
Black or African American	813 485	49 282	45 968	393 045	186 290	138 900
American Indian and Alaska Native	3 277 991	162 879	140 100	1 102 964	619 459	1 252 589
Asian	127 293	5 725	6 842	54 709	30 095	29 922
Native Hawaiian and Other Pacific Islander	5 113 338	279 039	346 578	2 505 364	1 180 691	801 666
Some other race	2 761 787	218 607	185 233	1 273 387	551 305	533 255
Two or more races	11 395 650	617 730	776 894	5 564 414	2 567 913	1 868 699
Hispanic or Latino[1]	47 911 074	3 142 406	2 438 997	20 592 972	10 132 266	11 604 433

Source: Census 2000 Summary File 3—United States, U.S. Census Bureau, 2002. Tables P36 and P147A-I.
[1]Hispanic or Latino persons may be of any race.

Table B-1.10. Work Experience in 1999 by Sex, Race, and Hispanic Origin, United States, 2000

(Number, percent.)

Race, Hispanic origin, and sex	Total population 16 years and over	Worked in 1999 (percent)				Did not work in 1999 (percent)
		Worked full-time		Worked part-time		
		Total	Full-year	Total	Full-year	
Total Population 16 Years and Over	217 168 077	54.9	40.5	14.6	5.5	30.5
Male	104 982 282	65.7	50.0	10.7	3.7	23.6
Female	112 185 795	44.8	31.6	18.3	7.2	36.9
White Alone	167 359 106	54.9	41.8	15.1	5.9	30.0
Male	81 072 654	66.8	52.5	10.7	3.9	22.5
Female	86 286 452	43.8	31.8	19.2	7.9	37.1
Black or African American Alone	24 744 502	53.4	36.3	12.6	4.0	33.9
Male	11 399 924	56.6	39.0	10.7	3.3	32.7
Female	13 344 578	50.7	34.0	14.3	4.7	35.0
American Indian and Alaska Native Alone	1 725 321	54.2	33.6	13.3	4.0	32.5
Male	846 909	61.7	38.8	10.3	3.0	28.0
Female	878 412	46.9	28.6	16.2	5.0	36.9
Asian Alone	8 020 330	55.9	38.9	13.9	4.6	30.3
Male	3 793 543	65.9	47.1	11.7	3.8	22.3
Female	4 226 787	46.9	31.5	15.8	5.2	37.3
Native Hawaiian and Other Pacific Islander Alone	272 266	55.9	38.3	14.1	4.6	29.9
Male	136 941	63.6	44.2	11.9	3.9	24.5
Female	135 325	48.2	32.4	16.4	5.4	35.4
Some Other Race	10 472 197	58.0	34.4	11.8	3.7	30.2
Male	5 470 803	70.2	42.8	8.8	2.8	21.0
Female	5 001 394	44.7	25.3	15.1	4.7	40.2
Two or More Races	4 574 355	54.3	36.2	15.9	5.2	29.7
Male	2 261 508	63.9	43.6	12.6	3.9	23.5
Female	2 312 847	45.0	28.9	19.1	6.3	35.9
Hispanic or Latino[1]	24 169 746	56.6	34.8	12.1	3.9	31.3
Male	12 383 364	68.6	43.1	9.2	2.9	22.2
Female	11 786 382	43.9	26.1	15.2	4.9	40.9
White Alone, Not Hispanic or Latino	155 509 898	54.9	42.3	15.3	6.1	29.8
Male	75 086 359	66.7	53.1	10.9	3.9	22.4
Female	80 423 539	43.8	32.1	19.5	8.1	36.7

Source: Census 2000 Summary File 3—United States, U.S. Census Bureau, 2002. Tables P47 and PCT71A-I.
[1]Hispanic or Latino persons may be of any race.

16 and older. Women were twice as likely as men to work part-time year-round. Non-Hispanic white women were most likely to work part-time, and black women were most likely to work full-time—fully half of black women worked full-time in 1999. Meanwhile, a relatively low share of black men were employed in 1999—indeed, women's and men's employment experience in 1999 was very similar for blacks, in contrast to the other racial and ethnic groups.

Another way to look at employment is via labor force participation rates, that is, the proportion of the population that is in the labor force, whether in the military, employed in a civilian job, or unemployed. (See Table B-1.12.) For two reasons, Census 2000 reported very high labor force participation rates. First, women's participation rates have continued to increase, reaching 57.5 percent in 2000. Second, thanks to the Baby Boom, a relatively high proportion of the population was working age in 2000.

Table B-1.11.
The share of the population working full-time differs geographically.

Population 16 Years and Over Who Worked Full-Time, Selected States, 2000

(Percentage of population 16 years and over.)

State	Below average population working full-time	State	Above average population working full-time
West Virginia	46.8	Alaska	63.2
Louisiana	51.2	Colorado	60.7
Florida	51.5	Nevada	59.9
Pennsylvania	51.9	Maryland	59.6
New Mexico	52.2	Virginia	59.6

Source: Census 2000 Summary File 3—United States, U.S. Census Bureau, 2002. Table P47.

Table B-1.12. Employment Status by Age, Sex, Race and Hispanic Origin, United States, 2000

(Number, percent.)

Age, sex, race, and Hispanic origin	Total population	In labor force						Not in labor force
		Total in civilian and military labor force	Labor force participation rate	In armed forces	Civilian			
					Employed	Unemployed	Percent unemployed	
Total Population 16 years and over	217 168 077	138 820 935	63.9	1 152 137	129 721 512	7 947 286	5.8	78 347 142
Male	104 982 282	74 273 203	70.7	987 898	69 091 443	4 193 862	5.7	30 709 079
Female	112 185 795	64 547 732	57.5	164 239	60 630 069	3 753 424	5.8	47 638 063
Metropolitan Status								
Population 16 years and over in Central Cities of Metropolitan Areas	66 199 592	41 776 980	63.1	446 849	38 221 336	3 108 795	7.5	24 422 602
Male	31 638 331	21 991 104	69.5	377 162	20 000 988	1 612 954	7.5	9 647 227
Female	34 561 261	19 785 876	57.2	69 687	18 220 348	1 495 841	7.6	14 775 375
Population 16 years and over in Metropolitan Areas, not in Central City	107 833 265	71 108 636	65.9	533 089	67 305 478	3 270 069	4.6	36 724 632
Male	52 196 573	38 282 152	73.3	460 274	36 090 881	1 730 997	4.6	13 914 421
Female	55 636 692	32 826 484	59.0	72 815	31 214 597	1 539 072	4.7	22 810 211
Population 16 years and over not in Metropolitan Areas	43 135 220	25 935 312	60.1	172 202	24 194 698	1 568 412	6.1	17 199 908
Male	21 147 378	13 999 947	66.2	150 462	12 999 574	849 911	6.1	7 147 431
Female	21 987 842	11 935 365	54.3	21 740	11 195 124	718 501	6.0	10 052 477
Age								
Total 16 to 24 years	34 956 438	22 281 754	63.7	450 248	18 889 736	2 941 770	13.5	12 674 684
Male	17 904 596	11 678 835	65.2	376 422	9 728 834	1 573 579	13.9	6 225 761
Female	17 051 842	10 602 919	62.2	73 826	9 160 902	1 368 191	13.0	6 448 923
Total 25 to 44 years	85 482 828	68 097 242	79.7	642 550	64 278 465	3 176 227	4.7	17 385 586
Male	42 700 352	36 692 381	85.9	559 768	34 507 096	1 625 517	4.5	6 007 971
Female	42 782 476	31 404 861	73.4	82 782	29 771 369	1 550 710	5.0	11 377 615
Total 45 to 64 years	61 749 839	43 803 194	70.9	59 339	42 184 413	1 559 442	3.6	17 946 645
Male	29 994 964	23 257 053	77.5	51 708	22 334 387	870 958	3.8	6 737 911
Female	31 754 875	20 546 141	64.7	7 631	19 850 026	688 484	3.4	11 208 734
Total 65 years and over	34 978 972	4 638 745	13.3	0	4 368 898	269 847	5.8	30 340 227
Male	14 382 370	2 644 934	18.4	0	2 521 126	123 808	4.7	11 737 436
Female	20 596 602	1 993 811	9.7	0	1 847 772	146 039	7.3	18 602 791
Race and Hispanic Origin								
White alone	167 359 106	108 079 326	64.6	811 022	102 324 962	4 943 342	4.6	59 279 780
Male	81 072 654	58 495 465	72.2	714 774	55 099 441	2 681 250	4.6	22 577 189
Female	86 286 452	49 583 861	57.5	96 248	47 225 521	2 262 092	4.6	36 702 591
Black or African American alone	24 744 502	14 905 895	60.2	205 683	13 001 795	1 698 417	11.6	9 838 607
Male	11 399 924	6 947 332	60.9	158 558	5 953 284	835 490	12.3	4 452 592
Female	13 344 578	7 958 563	59.6	47 125	7 048 511	862 927	10.9	5 386 015
American Indian and Alaska Native alone	1 725 321	1 054 768	61.1	10 901	914 484	129 383	12.4	670 553
Male	846 909	555 757	65.6	8 926	475 372	71 459	13.1	291 152
Female	878 412	499 011	56.8	1 975	439 112	57 924	11.7	379 401
Asian Alone	8 020 330	5 077 701	63.3	32 305	4 786 782	258 614	5.1	2 042 630
Male	3 793 543	2 693 069	71.0	27 787	2 532 334	132 948	5.0	1 100 474
Female	4 226 787	2 384 722	56.4	4 608	2 254 448	125 666	5.3	1 842 065
Native Hawaiian and Other Pacific Islander alone	272 266	180 331	66.2	4 065	157 119	19 147	10.9	91 935
Male	136 941	97 907	71.5	3 461	84 262	10 184	10.8	39 034
Female	135 325	82 424	60.9	604	72 857	8 963	11.0	52 901
Some other race	10 472 197	6 589 301	62.9	54 644	5 886 427	648 230	9.9	3 882 896
Male	5 470 803	3 895 708	71.2	46 884	3 516 412	332 412	8.6	1 575 095
Female	5 001 394	2 693 593	53.9	7 760	2 370 015	315 818	11.8	2 307 801
Two or more races	4 574 355	2 933 523	64.1	33 427	2 649 943	250 153	8.6	1 640 832
Male	2 261 508	1 587 965	70.2	27 508	1 430 338	130 119	8.3	673 543
Female	2 312 847	1 345 558	58.2	5 919	1 219 605	120 034	9.0	967 289
Hispanic or Latino[1]	24 169 746	14 835 741	61.4	116 024	13 347 876	1 371 841	9.3	9 334 005
Male	12 383 364	8 589 271	69.4	99 010	7 782 049	708 212	8.3	3 794 093
Female	11 786 382	6 246 470	53.0	17 014	5 565 827	663 629	10.7	5 539 912
White Alone, not Hispanic or Latino	155 509 898	100 942 871	64.9	764 881	95 834 018	4 343 972	4.3	54 567 027
Male	75 086 359	54 409 342	72.5	675 097	51 366 266	2 367 979	4.4	20 677 017
Female	80 423 539	46 533 529	57.9	89 784	44 467 752	1 975 993	4.3	33 890 010

Source: Census 2000 Summary File 3—United States, U.S. Census Bureau, 2002. Tables P43, PCT35 and P150A-I.
[1]Hispanic or Latino persons may be of any race.

Overall, 63.9 percent of Americans aged 16 and older were in the labor force in 2000. Men aged 25 to 44 had the highest participation rates (86 percent), followed by men aged 45 to 64 (78 percent). In perhaps a harbinger of the future, nearly 20 percent of men aged 65 and older were in the labor force, as were nearly 10 percent of women in this age group.

Nationally, Census 2000 found 5.8 percent of the population unemployed in 1999—a rate so low that many economists feared a return of inflationary pressures. In that context, high rates of unemployment for young adults aged 16 to 24 suggest how much more complex the school-to-work transition has become. Fully 14 percent of young men, and 13 percent of young women were unemployed, compared with less than 5 percent of people in the prime working ages of 25 to 64. Unemployment rates for people aged 65 and older were slightly higher, especially for women. With Americans' increasing need to support themselves over longer lives, this development also bears watching.

Not surprisingly, states with high unemployment rates for adults had particularly high youth unemployment rates. So did states with large youth populations. Conversely, young people found employment relatively easily in states that have been losing population, since young adults are those that tend to leave. (See Table B-1.13.)

Unemployment also varies by racial and ethnic group, largely because of differences in educational investment, and also because the nation's minority populations are relatively younger than the non-Hispanic majority. In 1999, fewer than 5 percent of non-Hispanic whites aged 16 and older were unemployed. Black and American Indian men

Table B-1.13.
It takes time for young people to become established in the work force.
Unemployment Rates for Population 16 to 24 Years, Selected States, 2000

(Percentage of population 16 to 24 years.)

State	High youth unemployment	State	Low youth unemployment
Mississippi	18.8	Nebraska	8.3
Alaska	18.6	Minnesota	8.5
West Virginia	18.3	Iowa	9.4
Louisiana	17.5	North Dakota	9.5
New York	17.4	Wisconsin	9.5

Source: Census 2000 Summary File 3—United States, U.S. Census Bureau, 2002. Table PCT35.

Table B-1.14. Employment Status of Parents by Age of Child, Race, and Hispanic Origin, United States, 2000

(Number, percent.)

Employment status	Total children	White alone	Black or African American alone	American Indian or Alaska Native alone	Asian alone	Native Hawaiian or Other Pacific Islander alone	Some other race alone	Two or more races	Hispanic or Latino[1]	White alone, not Hispanic or Latino
Total Own Children Under 18 Years in Families and Subfamilies	67 882 626	47 467 606	9 464 953	724 603	2 334 006	107 630	5 025 140	2 758 688	11 223 036	42 383 794
Living with two parents	71.8	78.9	38.8	57.2	85.9	68.6	67.1	64.1	67.8	80.0
Both parents in labor force	43.2	48.6	25.4	31.0	46.5	38.2	29.8	36.1	30.8	50.6
Father only in labor force	21.9	24.7	7.3	16.0	26.4	19.1	23.0	20.3	23.0	24.8
Mother only in labor force	3.0	2.7	3.3	4.5	4.8	5.3	4.4	3.3	4.3	2.5
Neither parent in labor force	3.7	2.9	2.8	5.7	8.2	5.9	9.9	4.5	9.7	2.1
Living with one parent	28.2	21.1	61.2	42.8	14.1	31.4	32.9	35.9	32.2	20.0
Living with father	6.1	5.5	7.8	10.7	3.9	8.2	8.4	7.6	8.0	5.2
Father in labor force	5.0	4.7	5.8	8.0	3.0	6.3	6.4	6.2	6.1	4.6
Living with mother	22.0	15.6	53.4	32.1	10.3	23.2	24.5	28.3	24.2	14.8
Mother in labor force	16.3	12.2	37.9	21.6	7.0	15.8	15.4	21.2	15.7	12.0
Total Own Children Under 6 Years in Families and Subfamilies	21 833 613	14 967 661	2 975 987	223 035	760 575	34 059	1 790 405	1 081 891	4 042 687	13 146 910
Living with two parents	72.2	80.4	36.1	53.6	87.0	66.6	65.7	62.7	66.9	81.9
Both parents in labor force	38.5	43.5	23.0	26.3	41.8	31.4	26.1	32.3	27.1	45.6
Father only in labor force	27.5	31.6	8.2	18.4	33.7	24.2	26.3	23.5	26.6	32.1
Mother only in labor force	2.5	2.2	2.5	3.6	3.9	4.8	3.6	2.7	3.5	2.0
Neither parent in labor force	3.8	3.1	2.4	5.3	7.6	6.3	9.7	4.2	9.7	2.1
Living with one parent	27.8	19.6	63.9	46.4	13.0	33.4	34.3	37.3	33.1	18.1
Living with father	6.7	5.6	9.0	12.6	3.9	10.1	10.6	8.4	9.8	5.2
Father in labor force	5.4	4.8	6.5	9.3	3.0	7.6	8.0	6.8	7.4	4.5
Living with mother	21.1	13.9	54.9	33.8	9.1	23.3	23.8	28.9	23.3	13.0
Mother in labor force	14.7	10.1	37.8	21.1	6.1	14.9	14.0	21.0	14.2	9.7
Total Own Children 6 to 17 Years in Families and Subfamilies	46 049 013	32 499 945	6 488 966	501 568	1 573 431	73 571	3 234 735	1 676 797	7 180 349	29 236 884
Living with two parents	71.7	78.2	40.0	58.7	85.4	69.5	67.8	65.1	68.3	79.1
Both parents in labor force	45.5	51.0	26.4	33.1	48.9	41.4	31.8	38.5	32.9	52.9
Father only in labor force	19.3	21.5	6.9	15.0	22.9	16.8	21.1	18.1	21.0	21.5
Mother only in labor force	3.3	2.9	3.7	4.9	5.2	5.5	4.9	3.7	4.7	2.7
Neither parent in labor force	3.6	2.8	3.0	5.9	8.4	5.8	10.0	4.7	9.7	2.0
Living with one parent	28.3	21.8	60.0	41.3	14.6	30.5	32.2	34.9	31.7	20.9
Living with father	5.8	5.4	7.3	9.9	3.8	7.3	7.2	7.0	7.0	5.3
Father in labor force	4.9	4.7	5.4	7.4	3.0	5.7	5.5	5.8	5.3	4.7
Living with mother	22.5	16.4	52.7	31.4	10.8	23.2	25.0	27.9	24.7	15.6
Mother in labor force	17.1	13.2	38.0	21.8	7.4	16.2	16.2	21.2	16.6	12.9

Source: Census 2000 Summary File 3—United States, U.S. Census Bureau, 2002. Tables P46 and PCT70A-I.
[1]Hispanic or Latino persons may be of any race.

Table B-1.15.
Children's "work-family" situation varies across the country.
Family Structure and Employment Status of Parents, Selected States, 2000

(Percentage of children.)

State	Traditional families	State	Both parents working	State	Single parent who works
Utah	32.9	North Dakota	60.2	Mississippi	27.7
Idaho	26.9	Iowa	59.1	Louisiana	26.7
Texas	25.2	South Dakota	57.8	South Carolina	25.8
West Virginia	25.1	Minnesota	57.3	Delaware	25.1
Arizona	24.8	Nebraska	56.7	Florida	24.8
New Jersey	24.6				

Source: Census 2000 Summary File 3—United States, U.S. Census Bureau, 2002. Table P46.

had the highest unemployment rates—over 12 percent—followed closely by American Indian, black, and Hispanic women. Asian-American men and women had unemployment rates almost as low as non-Hispanic whites did. Again, the clustering of minority populations in particular locations tends to be reflected in place-based differences in unemployment.

Work and family. At the end of the twentieth century, issues of blending work and family were a prime concern for many Americans, especially those in the first half of work life, ages 25 to 44. On the one hand, research has shown that even with more mothers in the work force, Americans are spending more time with each of their children than they did at the beginning of the century. Working mothers are spending a few minutes more per week with each child,

and fathers and stay-at-home mothers are spending quite a bit more time.[1] With smaller families, there are simply fewer children to share parents' attention; also, housework demands far less time than it used to. On the other hand, parents' expectations for their children's development have grown, so working parents in particular tell pollsters that they are too short of time with their children.

Census 2000 found that over 40 percent of American children under age 18 lived with two parents who were both in the labor force. (See Table B-1.14.) This is twice the share of children living in the traditional configuration of a working father and a stay-at-home mother. About the same proportion of children lived with a single, working parent as lived in a traditional family. Across all children,

Table B-1.16. Employment Status of Mothers by Age of Children, United States, 2000

(Number, percent.)

Employment status	All women 16 years and over	With children under 18 years				Women with no children under 18 years
		Total women with children under 18 years	Women with children under 6 years only	Women with children under 6 and 6 to 17 years	Women with children 6 to 17 years only	
All Women	112 185 795	34 926 892	8 445 132	7 144 068	19 337 692	77 258 903
In labor force	64 547 732	24 150 847	5 362 352	4 289 258	14 499 237	40 396 885
Employed or in armed forces	60 794 308	22 844 047	4 973 569	3 995 025	13 875 453	37 950 261
Unemployed	3 753 424	1 306 800	388 783	294 233	623 784	2 446 624
Not in labor force	47 638 063	10 776 045	3 082 780	2 854 810	4 838 455	36 862 018
All Women	100.0	100.0	100.0	100.0	100.0	100.0
In labor force	57.5	69.1	63.5	60.0	75.0	52.3
Employed or in armed forces	54.2	65.4	58.9	55.9	71.8	49.1
Unemployed	3.3	3.7	4.6	4.1	3.2	3.2
Not in labor force	42.5	30.9	36.5	40.0	25.0	47.7

Source: Census 2000 Summary File 3—United States, U.S. Census Bureau, 2002. Table P45.

[1]Bianchi, Suzanne M. "Maternal Employment and Time with Children: Dramatic Change or Surprising Continuity." *Demography* 37 (November 2000): 401-414.

Table B-1.17. Employment Status by Family Type, United States, 2000

(Number, percent.)

Employment status	Number	Percent
TOTAL FAMILIES	72 261 780	100.0
MARRIED-COUPLE FAMILIES	55 458 451	100.0
Husband in Labor Force	41 686 722	75.2
Husband employed or in armed forces	40 619 663	73.2
Wife in labor force	28 442 464	51.3
Wife employed or in armed forces	27 626 749	49.8
Wife unemployed	815 715	1.5
Wife not in labor force	12 177 199	22.0
Husband unemployed	1 067 059	1.9
Wife in labor force	709 398	1.3
Wife employed or in armed forces	626 227	1.1
Wife unemployed	83 171	0.1
Wife not in labor force	357 661	0.6
Husband Not in Labor Force	13 771 729	24.8
Wife in labor force	3 742 571	6.7
Wife employed or in armed forces	3 556 221	6.4
Wife unemployed	186 350	0.3
Wife not in labor force	10 029 158	18.1
OTHER FAMILIES	16 803 329	100.0
Male Householder, No Wife	4 302 568	25.6
In labor force	3 249 123	19.3
Employed or in armed forces	3 072 462	18.3
Unemployed	176 661	1.1
Not in labor force	1 053 445	6.3
Female Householder, No Husband	12 500 761	74.4
In labor force	8 288 381	49.3
Employed or in armed forces	7 680 727	45.7
Unemployed	607 654	3.6
Not in labor force	4 212 380	25.1

Source: Census 2000 Summary File 3—United States, U.S. Census Bureau, 2002. Table P44.

almost 60 percent of children under age 6 lacked a full-time stay-at-home parent, as did more than two-thirds of all children aged 6 to 17.

Over half of all non-Hispanic white children live with two parents who are both working, as do almost as many Asian-American children. Asian-American children are most likely to live in traditional families—over 25 percent

Table B-1.18.
Some states have relatively large numbers of self-employed people.
Self-Employed Persons, United States, 2000

(Percentage of employed civilians 16 years and over.)

State	Percent
Montana	16.7
South Dakota	14.7
Vermont	14.1
North Dakota	13.9
Idaho	13.2

Source: Census 2000 Summary File 3—United States, U.S. Census Bureau, 2002. Table P51.

do, followed closely by non-Hispanic white and Hispanic children. The same two-to-one ratio holds for American Indian and Alaska Native children too, only at lower levels due to their relatively higher levels of single parenting. In contrast, only 7 percent of black children are in a traditional family, and a quarter in two-working-parent families. Fully three out of five black children live with just one parent, most with a single working parent.

With or without children in the home, both partners are in the labor force in more than half of married-couple families, compared with 22 percent in the traditional configuration. (See Table B-1.17.) And more than two-thirds of "other" families are working families. (The bulk of the remainder consists of older, retired people.)

Occupations and Industry. Three out of four Americans work for employers in the private sector, and another 10 percent are self-employed. In a distinct change from earlier times—and a direct reflection of Americans' upgraded education credentials—fully one in three Americans work in management, professional, and related occupations. (See Table B-1.20.) More than four in 10 work in sales, service, and office occupations.

Table B-1.19.
Newer industries tend to offer higher paid jobs, raising state income levels.
Selected Industries, Selected States, 2000

(Percentage of labor force.)

State	Professional, scientific, and management	State	Information	State	Finance, insurance, and real estate
Maryland	12.4	Colorado	4.9	Delaware	11.6
Colorado	11.7	New Jersey	4.4	Connecticut	9.8
California	11.6	New York	4.1	New Jersey	8.9
Massachusetts	11.6	Maryland	4.0	New York	8.8
Virginia	11.6	California	3.9	Massachusetts	8.2

Source: Census 2000 Summary File 3—United States, U.S. Census Bureau, 2002.

Table B-1.20. Class of Worker, Occupation, and Industry, by Sex, United States, 2000

(Number, percent.)

Class of worker, occupation, and industry	Total		Male		Female	
	Number	Percent	Number	Percent	Number	Percent
Total Employed Civilian Population 16 Years and Over ...	129 721 512	100.0	69 091 443	100.0	60 630 069	100.0
Percent who worked at home	...	3.3	...	...	...	...
Class of Worker						
Private	97 704 854	75.3	52 103 337	25.4	45 601 517	75.2
Government	18 923 353	14.6	8 376 235	12.1	10 547 118	17.4
Self-employed	12 693 268	9.8	84 281 132	12.2	4 265 136	7.1
Unpaid family workers	400 037	0.3	183 739	0.3	216 298	0.4
Occupation						
Management, professional, and related occupations	43 646 731	33.6	21 708 758	31.4	21 937 973	36.2
Service occupations	19 276 947	14.9	8 346 408	12.1	10 930 539	18.0
Sales and office occupations	34 621 390	26.7	12 341 968	17.9	22 279 422	36.7
Farming, fishing, and forestry occupations	951 810	0.7	750 915	1.1	200 895	0.3
Construction, extraction, and maintenance occupations	12 256 138	9.4	11 802 699	17.1	453 439	0.7
Production, transportation, and material moving occupations	18 968 496	14.6	14 140 695	20.5	4 827 801	8.0
Industry						
Agriculture, forestry, fishing and hunting, and mining	2 426 053	1.9	1 986 285	2.9	439 768	0.7
Construction	8 801 507	6.8	7 919 645	11.5	881 862	1.5
Manufacturing	18 286 005	14.1	12 534 909	18.1	5 751 096	9.5
Wholesale trade	4 666 757	3.6	3 260 178	4.7	1 406 579	2.3
Retail trade	15 221 716	11.7	7 678 162	11.1	7 543 554	12.4
Transportation and warehousing, and utilities	6 740 102	5.2	5 025 989	7.3	1 714 113	2.8
Information	3 996 564	3.1	2 161 769	3.1	1 834 795	3.0
Finance, insurance, real estate, and rental and leasing	8 934 972	6.9	3 785 972	5.5	5 149 000	8.5
Professional, scientific, management, administrative, and waste management services	12 061 865	9.3	6 697 970	9.7	5 363 895	8.8
Educational, health and social services	25 843 029	19.9	6 539 753	9.5	19 303 276	31.8
Arts, entertainment, recreation, accommodation, and food services	10 210 295	7.9	4 929 179	7.1	5 281 116	8.7
Other services	6 320 632	4.9	3 174 397	4.6	3 146 235	5.2
Public administration	6 212 015	4.8	3 397 235	4.9	2 814 780	4.6

Source: Census 2000 Summary File 3—United States, U.S. Census Bureau, 2002. Tables P30, P49, P50, P51.
. . . = Not available.

In another sign of the times, the largest single industry is education, health, and social services. Nearly a third of working women are in this industry, compared with less than 10 percent of working men. Less than 10 percent of working women are in manufacturing; while the proportion of men working in manufacturing is down to less than 20 percent.

The rise of white collar and service jobs has combined with the rapid spread of computing and communications technology to allow more people to work at home. This development is also related to the large numbers of people who are self-employed. Census 2000 found that 3.3 percent of the population primarily worked at home. States with large proportions of self-employed people also had relatively large proportions of people who worked primarily at home. (See Table B-1.18.)

For a variety of reasons, different industries thrive in different parts of the country, and to the extent that they offer attractive jobs at attractive pay, they can be a magnet

for qualified people. In general, occupations with the highest pay are management, professional, and related occupations. So it is no surprise that states with relatively high incomes have a high proportion of their residents working in these occupations. Similarly, states with relatively low incomes have a low proportion of residents in these occupations.

Newer industries, especially those that rely on new technology, tend to pay their employees relatively well. Consequently, states and communities compete to attract employers in professional, scientific, and management-related industries; the information industry; and finance, insurance, and real estate. (See Table B-1.19.)

Incomes and Income Sources

Census 2000 found that American households had a record-high median income of $41,994 in 1999. (See Table B-1.21.) Family households reported a median of $50,046,

Table B-1.21. Median Incomes in 1999, United States

(Dollars.)

Characteristic	Income
Median household income	41 994
Metropolitan Status	
In central city of a metropolitan area	36 964
In a metropolitan area, not in central city	50 147
Not in a metropolitan area	33 687
Age	
Householder under 25 years	22 679
Householder 25 to 34 years	41 414
Householder 35 to 44 years	50 654
Householder 45 to 54 years	56 300
Householder 55 to 64 years	47 447
Householder 65 to 74 years	31 368
Householder 75 years and over	22 259
Family	
Median family income	50 046
Families with own children under 18 years	48 196
Married couple family	59 461
Female family householder	20 284
Male family householder	29 907
Families with no own children under 18 years	51 425
Married couple family	55 644
Female family householder	35 230
Male family householder	42 078
Nonfamily	
Median nonfamily household income	25 705
Householder living alone	
Male	27 022
15 to 64 years	29 970
65 years and over	18 574
Female	19 473
15 to 64 years	25 929
65 years and over	14 653
Householder not living alone	
Male householder	48 023
15 to 64 years	48 749
65 years and over	37 755
Female householder	44 460
15 to 64 years	45 359
65 years and over	35 808
Median income of persons 15 years and older	
Male	27 932
Full-year full-time	38 349
Female	16 327
Full-year full-time	28 135

Source: Census 2000 Summary File 3—United States, U.S. Census Bureau, 2002. Tables P53, P56, PCT39, PCT40, PCT42, and PCT45.

while non-family households reported a median of $25,705. This two-to-one ratio is a direct reflection of two important demographic trends discussed earlier: the majority of married couples below retirement age contain two earners, and the great majority of non-family households consist of just one person.

Median household income peaked at $56,300 for householders in the 45-to-55 age group, but was almost as high—$50,654—for the 35-to-44 age group. These decades are the prime earning ages, as early retirement holds down incomes for people over age 55, while many people under age 35 are still finding their feet in the economy.

Men's and women's incomes differed appreciably; on average, men's median income exceeded women's by over $10,000, whether they worked full- or part-time. These differences are not as great among single-person households, presumably because single people with low incomes are likely to share living costs and space with others. Among people aged 15 to 64 and living alone, men earned $29,970, while women earned $25,929. Men and women sharing households with other people had median incomes nearly as high as family households did.

State-by-state differences in average income are of great import, as they determine the resources the state has for increasing its economic potential. (See Table B-1.22 and Table B-1.23.) In particular, states invest in the human capital of their population via their educational systems. Employers that are willing to pay qualified people good salaries are likely to shun states with low educational attainment, while employers looking for cheap labor are likely to seek out such states. These employers tend to move away—often to other countries—when they find a source of even cheaper labor.

Americans tend to be touchy about reporting their income on the census, and it is the question they most often leave blank. Still, the census long form goes to so many households—roughly one in six—that the data are reliable even for a sub-set of the population, like the one in eight households that reported earning more than $100,000 in 1999. (See Table B-1.24.) People who are in late middle age, between 45 and 65, were most likely to be in this group, as they tend to have climbed the career ladders they have chosen. Nearly 20 percent of households in this age group had incomes over $100,000 in 1999.

Table B-1.22.
Household income makes some states rich, and others relatively poor.

Median Household Income in 1999, Selected States

(Dollars.)

State	High median income	State	Low median income
New Jersey	55 146	West Virginia	29 696
Connecticut	53 935	Mississippi	31 330
Maryland	52 868	Arkansas	32 182
Alaska	51 571	Louisiana	32 566
Massachusetts	50 502	Montana	33 024

Source: Census 2000 Summary File 3—United States, U.S. Census Bureau, 2002. Table P53.

Table B-1.23. High and Low Income Housholders by Age of Householder and Family Type, United States 2000

(Number, percent.)

Household type	Total Households	Householder under 25 years	Householder 25 to 44 years	Householder 45 to 64 years	Householder 65 years and over
NUMBER					
Total Households	105 539 122	5 435 076	42 414 484	35 414 109	22 275 453
Households with Income Over $100,000	12 972 539	88 139	4 926 460	6 487 075	1 470 865
Households with Income Below the Poverty Level	12 404 237	1 809 800	4 862 716	3 196 135	2 535 586
Family households	6 620 945	809 929	3 632 256	1 528 712	650 048
Married-couple family households	2 719 059	185 036	1 339 338	798 293	396 392
Other family households	3 901 886	624 893	2 292 918	730 419	253 656
Male householder, no wife present	585 970	97 640	312 713	135 273	40 344
Female householder, no husband present	3 315 916	527 253	1 980 205	595 146	213 312
Nonfamily households	5 783 292	999 871	1 230 460	1 667 423	1 885 538
Male householder	2 280 334	472 590	721 291	703 040	383 413
Female householder	3 502 958	527 281	509 169	964 383	1 502 125
PERCENT					
Total Households	100.0	100.0	100.0	100.0	100.0
Households with Income Over $100,000	12.3	1.6	11.6	18.3	6.6
Households with Income Below the Poverty Level	11.8	33.3	11.5	9.0	11.4
Family households	6.3	14.9	8.6	4.3	2.9
Married-couple family households	2.6	3.4	3.2	2.3	1.8
Other family households	3.7	11.5	5.4	2.1	1.1
Male householder, no wife present	0.6	1.8	0.7	0.4	0.2
Female householder, no husband present	3.1	9.7	4.7	1.7	1.0
Nonfamily households	5.5	18.4	2.9	4.7	8.5
Male householder	2.2	8.7	1.7	2.0	1.7
Female householder	3.3	9.7	1.2	2.7	6.7

Source: Census 2000 Summary File 3 United States, U.S. Census Bureau, 2002. Table P55 and P92.

Income differences persist across the nation's racial and ethnic groups. Still, each group has thousands of households with incomes of $100,000 or higher. (See Table B-1.25.) Over 10 million white non-Hispanic households surpassed this income level in 1999, according to Census 2000, as did nearly 700,000 African Americans, over 600,000 Asians, and nearly as many Hispanics. Over 40,000 American Indian households reported this level of income.

However, minority households are still far more likely to be in poverty than to have high incomes. For example, 44,000 American Indian married couples had income below the poverty level in 1999, as did nearly 80,000 "other families" in this population. Among African Americans and Hispanics, almost three times as many families reported poverty level incomes as reported $100,000+ incomes. Asian American and non-Hispanic white families reported just the opposite.

Poverty tends to be concentrated in specific household and family types. In particular, households headed by women without a husband present are far more likely to have incomes below the poverty line than married couple families are. This holds true across the country. With less earning ability, women who are not in a married couple have generally low incomes, and having children to care for too increases their challenge. Single mothers, generally aged between 25 and 44, account for the largest single group of poor families.

Table B-1.24.

Where the well-off are, and aren't.

Households With Income Exceeding $100,000, Selected States, 2000

(Percent.)

State	Percent	State	Percent
New Jersey	21.3	West Virginia	5.0
Connecticut	20.2	Montana	5.6
Maryland	18.1	North Dakota	5.7
Massachusetts	17.7	South Dakota	5.9
California	17.3	Arkansas	6.0
		Mississippi	6.0

Source: Census 2000 Summary File 3—United States, U.S. Census Bureau, 2002. Table P55.

Table B-1.25. High and Low Income Families by Race, Hispanic Origin, and Family Type, United States, 2000

(Number, percent.)

Household type	Total families	White alone	Black or African American alone	American Indian and Alaska Native alone	Asian alone	Native Hawaiian and Other Pacific Islander alone	Some other race	Two or more races	Hispanic or Latino[1]	White alone, not Hispanic or Latino
NUMBER										
Total Families	72 261 780	56 470 094	8 209 432	563 651	2 350 399	79 254	3 206 531	1 382 419	7 483 038	52 769 534
Total Families with Over $100,000	11 032 447	9 570 800	580 016	34 444	543 169	8 899	157 722	137 397	503 653	9 259 371
Families With Income Below Poverty	6 620 945	3 548 532	1 777 105	122 927	226 915	11 584	706 479	227 403	1 495 297	2 889 096
Married-couple family	2 719 059	1 763 072	321 952	43 963	151 560	5 424	336 294	96 794	738 200	1 412 212
With related children under 18 years	1 767 368	1 042 811	211 419	33 254	105 866	4 564	295 836	73 618	624 197	758 291
Under 5 years only	329 946	205 185	31 724	5 174	20 389	771	52 741	13 962	113 689	151 689
Under 5 years and 5 to 17 years	618 283	345 986	69 542	12 534	28 922	1 954	130 945	28 400	270 715	225 048
5 to 17 years only	819 139	491 640	110 153	15 546	56 555	1 839	112 150	31 256	239 793	381 554
No related children under 18 years	951 691	720 261	110 533	10 709	45 694	860	40 458	23 176	114 003	653 921
Other family	3 901 886	1 785 460	1 455 153	78 964	75 355	6 160	370 185	130 609	757 097	1 476 884
Male householder, no wife	585 970	310 676	140 595	14 965	18 853	1 395	74 859	24 627	150 303	248 935
With related children under 18 years	448 039	239 093	106 211	12 219	9 974	1 172	61 161	18 209	120 887	190 556
Under 5 years only	113 215	61 802	25 026	2 819	1 886	364	16 454	4 864	32 173	49 257
Under 5 years and 5 to 17 years	99 326	46 199	23 400	3 182	1 862	319	19 813	4 551	38 628	30 932
5 to 17 years only	235 498	131 092	57 785	6 218	6 226	489	24 894	8 794	50 086	110 367
No related children under 18 years	137 931	71 583	34 384	2 746	8 879	223	13 698	6 418	29 416	58 379
Female householder, no husband	3 315 916	1 474 784	1 314 558	63 999	56 502	4 765	295 326	105 982	606 794	1 227 949
With related children under 18 years	2 940 459	1 292 158	1 176 153	57 053	42 952	4 381	272 388	95 374	550 489	1 073 236
Under 5 years only	589 201	290 847	214 612	10 344	6 178	796	46 545	19 879	94 098	253 560
Under 5 years and 5 to 17 years	812 292	302 035	359 360	18 248	8 785	1 396	94 977	27 491	183 192	233 003
5 to 17 years only	1 538 966	699 276	602 181	28 461	27 989	2 189	130 866	48 004	273 199	586 673
No related children under 18 years	375 457	182 626	138 405	6 946	13 550	384	22 938	10 608	56 305	154 713
PERCENT										
Total Families	100.0	100.0	100.0	100.0	100.0	100.0	100.0	100.0	100.0	100.0
Total Families with Over $100,000	15.3	16.9	7.1	6.1	23.1	11.2	4.9	9.9	6.7	17.5
Families with Income Below Poverty	9.2	6.3	21.6	21.8	9.7	14.6	22.0	16.4	20.0	5.5
Married-couple family	3.8	3.1	3.9	7.8	6.4	6.8	10.5	7.0	9.9	2.7
With related children under 18 years	2.4	1.8	2.6	5.9	4.5	5.8	9.2	5.3	8.3	1.4
Under 5 years only	0.5	0.4	0.4	0.9	0.9	1.0	1.6	1.0	1.5	0.3
Under 5 years and 5 to 17 years	0.9	0.6	0.8	2.2	1.2	2.5	4.1	2.1	3.6	0.4
5 to 17 years only	1.1	0.9	1.3	2.8	2.4	2.3	3.5	2.3	3.2	0.7
No related children under 18 years	1.3	1.3	1.3	1.9	1.9	1.1	1.3	1.7	1.5	1.2
Other family	5.4	3.2	17.7	14.0	3.2	7.8	11.5	9.4	10.1	2.8
Male householder, no wife	0.8	0.6	1.7	2.7	0.8	1.8	2.3	1.8	2.0	0.5
With related children under 18 years	0.6	0.4	1.3	2.2	0.4	1.5	1.9	1.3	1.6	0.4
Under 5 years only	0.2	0.1	0.3	0.5	0.1	0.5	0.5	0.4	0.4	0.1
Under 5 years and 5 to 17 years	0.1	0.1	0.3	0.6	0.1	0.4	0.6	0.3	0.5	0.1
5 to 17 years only	0.3	0.2	0.7	1.1	0.3	0.6	0.8	0.6	0.7	0.2
No related children under 18 years	0.2	0.1	0.4	0.5	0.4	0.3	0.4	0.5	0.4	0.1
Female householder, no husband	4.6	2.6	16.0	11.4	2.4	6.0	9.2	7.7	8.1	2.3
With related children under 18 years	4.1	2.3	14.3	10.1	1.8	5.5	8.5	6.9	7.4	2.0
Under 5 years only	0.8	0.5	2.6	1.8	0.3	1.0	1.5	1.4	1.3	0.5
Under 5 years and 5 to 17 years	1.1	0.5	4.4	3.2	0.4	1.8	3.0	2.0	2.4	0.4
5 to 17 years only	2.1	1.2	7.3	5.0	1.2	2.8	4.1	3.5	3.7	1.1
No related children under 18 years	0.5	0.3	1.7	1.2	0.6	0.5	0.7	0.8	0.8	0.3

Source: Census 2000 Summary File 3—United States, U.S. Census Bureau, 2002. Tables P76, P90, P154A-I, and P160A-I.
[1] Hispanic or Latino persons may be of any race.

Women over age 65 are the other large demographic group in poverty; whether widowed or divorced, today's typical older woman tends to have fewer resources to fall back on than tomorrow's will have, since this is the last generation of women to have spent relatively little time working for pay. Among householders aged 65 and older, one in five women who are not living in a family live in poverty, as do one in eight women that age who are heading a family household. These households are especially numerous in Mississippi, Louisiana, Alabama, and other poor states in the Southeast.

Income sources. The vast majority of American households—four in five households in 1999—get income through work. But other sources of income are important for many households. Over a third reported getting income from interest, dividends, or rental, and over a quarter reported getting Social Security. (See Table B-1.26.)

In general, states have roughly similar profiles of residents' income sources. But states like Alaska, Colorado, and Utah that tend to have young populations have relatively more households with earnings. And states that have relatively old populations have higher proportions of households with income from Social Security or pensions. West Virginia, for example, has the lowest proportion of households with earnings, and the highest proportion of households with Social Security or other retirement income. Differences like these help determine the policies states and communities use to raise revenue from their residents effectively.

Veteran and Disability Status. People's ability to work can be compromised by physical disabilities. And, until the advent of the All-Volunteer Force in 1973, men could be called away from work to defend the country. In both cases, the public offers some compensation in the form of income, such as disability payments or veterans' benefits.

The bulk of the nation's surviving veterans earned that status in wars conducted in decades past, so veterans as a whole have been aging. Nationally, nearly 13 percent of the population ages 18 years and older reported in 2000 that they were veterans. However, less than 10 percent of people ages 18 to 64 are veterans, compared with nearly 28 percent of people ages 65 and older. (See Table B-1.27.) As a result, veterans make up a larger than average share of the population in states where the population is disproportionately older.

For instance, veterans make up a relatively small share of the population in very youthful states like Utah. They

also make up a relatively small proportion of the population in states like New York and California that are traditionally immigrant-receiving states. (Immigrants tend to arrive here past military age.) In contrast, they make up a large share of the population in states that attract migrants from other states, including retirees. Over 35 percent of Nevada's population ages 65 and older are veterans.

The same pattern applies to the population with disabilities, with relatively older states having a larger share of their population ages 5 and older reporting disabilities. Nationally, nearly 20 percent of the population this age reported one or more disabilities. (See Table B-1.28.) However, less than 15 percent of the population ages 5 and older had disabilities in very youthful states like Utah and Alaska, compared with nearly 25 percent in states where people are both relatively older, relatively less well-educated, and relatively poor: West Virginia, Kentucky, Arkansas, Mississippi, and Alabama.

Table B-1.26. Households by Sources of Income in 1999, United States

(Number, percent.)

Income source	Number	Percent
Total Households	105 539 122	100.0
With earnings	84 962 743	80.5
With wage and salary income	82 024 820	77.7
With self-employment income	12 556 526	11.9
With interest, dividends, or net rental income	37 860 638	35.9
With social security	27 084 417	25.7
With supplemental security	4 615 885	4.4
With public assistance	3 629 732	3.4
With retirement income	17 659 058	16.7
With other type of income	13 888 738	13.2

Source: Census 2000 Summary File 3—United States, U.S. Census Bureau, 2002. Tables P58, P59, P60, P61, P62, P63, P64, P65, and P66.

Table B-1.27. Veteran Status, United States, 2000

(Number, percent.)

Veteran status	Total	Male	Female
Total Population 18 Years and Over	209 279 149	100 909 272	108 369 877
NUMBER			
18 to 64 Years	174 300 177	86 526 902	87 773 275
In Armed Forces	1 148 797	985 393	163 404
Civilian	173 151 380	85 541 509	87 609 871
Veteran	16 740 194	15 494 594	1 245 600
Nonveteran	156 411 186	70 046 915	86 364 271
65 Years and Over	34 978 972	14 382 370	20 596 602
In Armed Forces	0	0	0
Civilian	34 978 972	14 382 370	20 596 602
Veteran	9 663 509	9 315 855	347 654
Nonveteran	25 315 463	5 066 515	20 248 948
PERCENT			
18 to 64 Years	174 300 177	86 526 902	87 773 275
In Armed Forces	0.7	1.1	0.2
Civilian	99.3	98.9	99.8
Veteran	9.6	17.9	1.4
Nonveteran	89.7	81.0	98.4
65 Years and Over	34 978 972	14 382 370	20 596 602
In Armed Forces	0.0	0.0	0.0
Civilian	100.0	100.0	100.0
Veteran	27.6	64.8	1.7
Nonveteran	72.4	35.2	98.3

Source: Census 2000 Summary File 3—United States, U.S. Census Bureau, 2002. Table P39.

Table B-1.28. Disability Status, United States, 2000

(Number, percent.)

Disability status	Total	Male	Female
Total population 5 years and over	257 167 527	124 636 825	132 530 702
Percent with a disability	19.3	19.6	19.1
5 to 15 years	45 133 667	23 125 324	22 008 343
Percent with a disability	5.8	7.2	4.3
With one type of disability	4.6	5.8	3.3
Sensory disability	0.5	0.5	0.5
Physical disability	0.4	0.4	0.4
Mental disability	3.6	4.7	2.3
Self-care disability	0.2	0.2	0.2
With two or more types of disability	1.2	1.4	1.0
Includes self-care disability	0.8	0.9	0.6
Does not include self-care disability	0.4	0.5	0.3
No disability	94.2	92.8	95.7
16 to 20 years	19 555 690	9 904 704	9 650 986
Percent with a disability	13.3	14.5	12.0
With one type of disability	8.8	9.5	8.0
Sensory disability	0.6	0.7	0.6
Physical disability	0.5	0.4	0.6
Mental disability	2.1	2.7	1.6
Self-care disability	0.0	0.1	0.0
Go-outside-home disability	1.7	1.7	1.8
Employment disability	3.7	4.0	3.4
With two or more types of disability	4.5	5.0	4.0
Includes self-care disability	0.7	0.8	0.6
Does not include self-care disability	3.8	4.2	3.4
Go-outside home and employment only	2.1	2.3	2.0
Other combination	1.7	1.9	1.5
No disability	86.7	85.5	88.0
21 to 64 years	159 131 544	77 665 879	81 465 665
Percent with a disability	19.2	20.2	18.2
With one type of disability	10.2	10.8	9.6
Sensory disability	1.1	1.3	0.8
Physical disability	2.1	2.0	2.2
Mental disability	0.8	0.8	0.7
Self-care disability	0.0	0.0	0.0
Go-outside-home disability	0.8	0.6	1.1
Employment disability	5.4	6.1	4.7
With two or more types of disability	9.0	9.4	8.6
Includes self-care disability	1.8	1.7	1.9
Does not include self-care disability	7.2	7.7	6.7
Go-outside home and employment only	2.8	3.2	2.5
Other combination	4.3	4.5	4.2
No disability	80.8	79.8	81.8
65 years and over	33 346 626	13 940 918	19 405 708
Percent with a disability	41.9	40.4	43.0
With one type of disability	20.1	21.3	19.3
Sensory disability	4.0	5.5	2.9
Physical disability	9.7	9.6	9.9
Mental disability	1.1	1.2	1.0
Self-care disability	0.2	0.1	0.2
Go-outside-home disability	5.1	4.9	5.3
With two or more types of disability	21.8	19.1	23.7
Includes self-care disability	9.4	7.4	10.9
Does not include self-care disability	12.4	11.8	12.9
No disability	58.1	59.6	57.0

Source: Census 2000 Summary File 3—United States, U.S. Census Bureau, 2002. Table PCT26.

Table B-2. States — **Education, Labor Force, and Income**

FIPS CODE	STATE	Total population 25 years and over	Percent with a high school diploma or less	Percent with a high school diploma or more (25 years and over)								
				Total	+/− U.S.	Male	Female	Non-Hispanic White	Black or African American	American Indian and Alaska Native	Asian, Hawaiian, and Pacific Islander	Hispanic or Latino[1]
		1	2	3	4	5	6	7	8	9	10	11
00	UNITED STATES....	182 211 639	48.2	80.4	0.0	80.1	80.7	85.5	72.3	70.9	80.4	52.4
01	ALABAMA	2 887 400	55.1	75.3	-5.1	75.1	75.4	78.1	66.9	72.4	80.7	56.9
02	ALASKA	379 556	39.5	88.3	7.9	88.3	88.4	92.7	88.7	71.8	73.2	78.3
04	ARIZONA	3 256 184	43.3	81.0	0.6	80.4	81.5	89.4	81.7	61.9	83.4	52.5
05	ARKANSAS..............	1 731 200	58.8	75.3	-5.1	74.9	75.7	77.8	65.8	72.5	72.7	41.2
06	CALIFORNIA..............	21 298 900	43.3	76.8	-3.6	76.8	76.8	89.8	80.5	67.5	80.4	46.7
08	COLORADO..............	2 776 632	36.3	86.9	6.5	86.5	87.4	92.2	84.4	76.2	81.9	58.1
09	CONNECTICUT	2 295 617	44.5	84.0	3.6	83.9	84.1	87.3	73.9	67.8	84.9	58.5
10	DELAWARE	514 658	48.8	82.6	2.2	81.7	83.4	85.5	74.2	65.2	87.6	57.1
11	DISTRICT OF COLUMBIA.............	384 535	42.8	77.8	-2.6	77.9	77.7	97.5	70.4	71.8	82.0	47.8
12	FLORIDA................	11 024 645	48.9	79.9	-0.5	79.4	80.3	85.6	67.0	73.5	80.5	63.3
13	GEORGIA................	5 185 905	50.1	78.6	1.8	78.1	79.0	82.7	72.5	73.9	79.4	48.5
15	HAWAII................	802 477	43.9	84.6	4.2	85.6	83.6	93.2	92.9	91.0	80.1	81.5
16	IDAHO................	787 505	43.8	84.7	4.3	84.3	85.1	87.4	82.5	75.6	81.9	44.4
17	ILLINOIS................	7 973 671	46.3	81.4	1.0	81.1	81.8	87.0	73.0	69.5	86.8	48.5
18	INDIANA................	3 893 278	55.1	82.1	1.7	82.1	82.2	83.5	74.9	73.3	86.0	57.9
19	IOWA................	1 895 856	50.0	86.1	5.7	85.4	86.8	87.1	77.3	76.9	74.4	52.3
20	KANSAS................	1 701 207	43.8	86.0	5.6	85.5	86.5	88.6	79.7	81.3	75.2	51.7
21	KENTUCKY.............	2 646 397	59.4	74.1	-6.3	73.1	75.0	74.3	73.2	72.5	85.9	59.1
22	LOUISIANA.............	2 775 468	57.6	74.8	-5.6	73.7	75.8	80.1	63.1	60.5	67.7	69.0
23	MAINE................	869 893	50.8	85.4	5.0	84.4	86.3	85.5	84.7	76.0	74.8	79.2
24	MARYLAND.............	3 495 595	42.9	83.8	3.4	83.5	84.1	86.8	78.9	75.5	85.5	61.9
25	MASSACHUSETTS ...	4 273 275	42.5	84.8	4.4	84.6	84.9	87.4	76.3	72.5	76.2	57.3
26	MICHIGAN	6 415 941	47.9	83.4	3.0	82.9	83.8	85.6	74.1	76.4	85.5	62.3
27	MINNESOTA	3 164 345	40.9	87.9	7.5	87.4	88.4	89.5	79.0	74.5	71.2	58.1
28	MISSISSIPPI	1 757 517	56.5	72.9	-7.5	71.0	73.7	79.0	60.4	64.0	72.8	59.1
29	MISSOURI.............	3 634 906	51.4	81.3	0.9	81.4	81.2	82.5	73.9	74.3	82.3	65.7
30	MONTANA................	580 021	44.1	87.2	6.8	86.6	87.6	87.9	91.2	75.5	84.8	78.0
31	NEBRASKA..............	1 087 241	44.7	86.6	6.2	85.8	87.3	88.8	78.6	75.9	77.2	46.6
32	NEVADA................	1 310 176	48.7	80.7	0.3	80.7	80.6	87.6	78.9	75.2	81.9	47.3
33	NEW HAMPSHIRE.....	823 987	42.7	87.4	7.0	86.6	88.2	87.7	84.4	76.5	84.9	73.6
34	NEW JERSEY..........	5 657 799	47.3	82.1	1.7	82.3	81.9	86.5	74.5	70.4	88.4	59.5
35	NEW MEXICO...........	1 134 801	47.7	78.9	-1.5	78.5	79.1	90.6	79.4	67.1	82.8	64.4
36	NEW YORK..............	12 542 536	48.7	79.1	-1.3	78.9	79.2	86.0	70.6	66.4	73.3	55.0
37	NORTH CAROLINA ...	5 282 994	50.3	78.1	-2.3	77.0	79.1	81.7	70.7	62.7	79.4	44.5
38	NORTH DAKOTA.......	408 585	44.0	83.9	3.5	83.0	84.7	84.3	92.6	74.8	84.1	73.0
39	OHIO	7 411 740	53.1	83.0	2.6	83.0	83.0	84.3	73.9	73.2	86.4	67.1
40	OKLAHOMA.............	2 203 173	50.9	80.6	0.2	80.6	80.6	82.6	78.5	76.5	77.1	50.9
41	OREGON	2 250 990	41.1	85.1	4.7	84.4	85.9	87.8	79.8	77.5	79.6	48.8
42	PENNSYLVANIA.......	8 266 284	56.2	81.9	1.5	82.0	81.8	83.6	71.8	73.2	78.4	56.9
44	RHODE ISLAND	694 573	49.8	78.0	-2.4	78.1	77.8	80.8	71.0	68.3	69.0	50.4
45	SOUTH CAROLINA ...	2 596 010	53.6	76.3	-4.1	75.7	76.9	81.1	64.9	64.2	79.3	56.4
46	SOUTH DAKOTA.......	474 359	48.3	84.6	4.2	83.4	85.7	85.7	84.1	70.9	72.5	64.9
47	TENNESSEE.............	3 744 928	55.7	75.9	-4.5	75.5	76.3	77.1	70.8	74.9	81.8	55.4
48	TEXAS................	12 790 893	49.2	75.7	-4.7	75.5	75.8	87.2	75.8	71.5	80.6	49.3
49	UTAH................	1 197 892	36.9	87.7	7.3	87.3	88.1	91.0	83.2	68.7	79.2	56.5
50	VERMONT	404 223	45.9	86.4	6.0	85.0	87.7	86.6	84.2	76.9	79.1	85.6
51	VIRGINIA................	4 666 574	44.5	81.5	1.1	80.8	82.1	84.6	71.6	78.5	84.2	62.9
53	WASHINGTON...........	3 827 507	37.8	87.1	6.7	86.9	87.3	90.0	84.0	77.4	80.7	53.0
54	WEST VIRGINIA	1 233 581	64.2	75.2	-5.2	74.6	75.8	75.1	76.6	73.5	90.2	74.2
55	WISCONSIN.............	3 475 878	49.5	85.1	4.7	84.5	85.6	86.9	68.5	77.3	73.3	54.6
56	WYOMING	315 663	43.1	87.9	7.5	87.2	88.5	89.3	86.7	77.2	81.7	66.3

[1] Hispanic or Latino persons may be of any race.

STATE	Percent with a high school diploma by age				Percent with bachelor's degree or more (25 years and over)								
	18 to 24 years	25 to 44 years	45 to 64 years	65 years and over	Total	+/− U.S.	Male	Female	Non-Hispanic White	Black or African American	American Indian and Alaska Native	Asian, Hawaiian, and Pacific Islander	Hispanic or Latino[1]
	12	13	14	15	16	17	18	19	20	21	22	23	24
UNITED STATES....	74.7	84.5	83.2	65.5	24.4	0.0	26.1	22.8	27.0	14.3	11.5	43.1	10.4
ALABAMA	72.2	82.3	78.2	54.6	19.0	-5.4	20.3	17.9	21.2	11.5	13.0	47.2	14.6
ALASKA	76.9	90.9	89.9	67.4	24.7	0.3	24.1	25.4	29.5	14.9	6.0	20.4	15.3
ARIZONA	69.2	80.9	84.7	75.1	23.5	-0.9	25.7	21.5	28.1	18.6	7.3	43.2	8.1
ARKANSAS	75.4	82.8	78.6	55.0	16.7	-7.7	17.5	15.9	17.9	10.2	12.1	31.5	7.1
CALIFORNIA	70.7	76.6	80.5	70.1	26.6	2.2	28.6	24.7	33.8	17.2	11.4	40.9	7.7
COLORADO	75.1	88.2	90.1	75.4	32.7	8.3	34.5	30.9	37.0	20.5	14.1	41.9	10.4
CONNECTICUT	78.2	89.2	86.7	67.8	31.4	7.0	33.5	29.5	34.2	13.7	15.7	57.2	11.3
DELAWARE	77.6	87.5	85.0	67.1	25.0	0.6	26.8	23.5	26.9	14.4	13.2	61.0	13.5
DISTRICT OF COLUMBIA	79.4	82.8	79.0	62.2	39.1	14.7	41.7	36.8	80.6	17.5	28.1	58.1	24.8
FLORIDA	71.7	83.5	82.0	71.2	22.3	-2.1	24.7	20.2	24.7	12.4	14.9	40.3	17.5
GEORGIA	70.0	83.9	79.9	57.5	24.3	-0.1	25.7	23.0	27.7	15.5	18.1	43.8	13.6
HAWAII	85.8	91.6	87.0	64.6	26.2	1.8	26.9	25.5	37.3	21.0	21.5	24.5	13.3
IDAHO	77.3	86.9	88.3	72.5	21.7	-2.7	24.0	19.4	22.6	22.4	9.5	36.8	6.6
ILLINOIS	76.0	85.6	84.3	65.7	26.1	1.7	27.8	24.5	28.8	14.7	13.3	57.4	9.1
INDIANA	76.5	87.3	84.6	65.5	19.4	-5.0	20.9	18.1	19.9	12.1	10.3	57.0	11.3
IOWA	81.4	91.5	89.8	70.6	21.2	-3.2	22.1	20.4	21.3	14.7	9.9	42.4	11.0
KANSAS	78.3	89.0	89.6	73.7	25.8	1.4	27.3	24.4	27.2	14.9	14.9	40.0	9.7
KENTUCKY	74.9	83.1	75.2	50.4	17.1	-7.3	18.0	16.4	17.4	10.7	13.9	52.0	13.0
LOUISIANA	72.3	80.5	77.5	55.7	18.7	-5.7	19.4	18.2	21.7	10.9	9.2	35.2	19.5
MAINE	78.9	91.6	87.4	69.2	22.9	-1.5	23.3	22.5	22.9	22.5	12.1	31.7	21.6
MARYLAND	79.6	88.8	85.9	65.7	31.4	7.0	33.5	29.6	34.9	20.3	21.2	54.7	21.4
MASSACHUSETTS	82.2	89.9	86.2	70.3	33.2	8.8	35.2	31.4	34.6	19.7	19.2	49.6	14.1
MICHIGAN	76.5	88.6	86.6	64.9	21.8	-2.6	23.4	20.2	22.7	12.8	10.3	60.5	12.9
MINNESOTA	79.3	92.9	91.8	68.6	27.4	3.0	28.7	26.2	28.0	18.7	8.8	36.1	14.0
MISSISSIPPI	71.3	80.2	74.0	53.5	16.9	-7.5	17.3	16.6	20.1	10.1	9.1	35.2	12.1
MISSOURI	76.5	87.4	84.7	62.7	21.6	-2.8	23.0	20.3	22.3	13.2	12.9	50.1	16.1
MONTANA	78.6	91.5	90.5	72.1	24.4	0.0	25.4	23.4	25.2	33.2	10.5	38.9	15.4
NEBRASKA	80.0	90.5	90.7	71.9	23.7	-0.7	24.7	22.9	24.6	14.1	8.8	41.6	8.5
NEVADA	66.7	80.1	84.8	73.6	18.2	-6.2	19.6	16.7	20.7	12.0	8.6	27.1	6.4
NEW HAMPSHIRE	77.8	91.9	89.2	72.2	28.7	4.3	30.6	26.8	28.5	27.8	17.0	54.2	22.7
NEW JERSEY	76.3	87.7	84.3	64.9	29.8	5.4	32.4	27.4	32.3	16.2	16.4	61.9	12.5
NEW MEXICO	70.5	81.9	82.4	64.8	23.5	-0.9	24.7	22.3	34.3	18.8	7.7	43.0	10.8
NEW YORK	76.1	84.1	80.6	64.3	27.4	3.0	28.8	26.1	31.8	15.8	14.4	41.2	11.5
NORTH CAROLINA	74.2	84.3	80.1	58.4	22.5	-1.9	23.2	21.8	25.2	13.1	10.4	43.0	10.5
NORTH DAKOTA	84.4	94.1	88.7	57.8	22.0	-2.4	22.1	21.9	22.4	20.5	9.7	47.4	16.3
OHIO	76.8	88.9	85.2	66.1	21.1	-3.3	23.0	19.4	21.8	11.9	12.4	58.0	15.2
OKLAHOMA	74.8	85.3	84.2	64.5	20.3	-4.1	21.8	18.9	21.7	13.7	13.2	36.7	9.6
OREGON	74.2	86.1	89.6	74.7	25.1	0.7	26.8	23.5	26.0	17.8	12.2	37.2	9.6
PENNSYLVANIA	79.8	89.2	85.5	63.2	22.4	-2.0	24.3	20.6	23.2	12.0	13.2	48.8	12.0
RHODE ISLAND	81.3	85.2	81.8	57.3	25.6	1.2	27.8	23.7	27.3	16.7	14.1	35.9	8.6
SOUTH CAROLINA	74.3	83.1	77.4	57.7	20.4	-4.0	21.6	19.4	24.3	9.9	11.2	39.8	14.1
SOUTH DAKOTA	78.2	91.0	88.9	65.8	21.5	-2.9	22.3	20.8	22.3	19.3	8.5	39.2	11.7
TENNESSEE	75.1	83.5	78.0	53.4	19.6	-4.8	20.9	18.3	20.5	12.9	14.0	46.7	14.1
TEXAS	68.6	78.2	78.5	61.7	23.2	-1.2	25.1	21.5	30.0	15.3	15.7	47.2	8.9
UTAH	80.3	88.3	90.8	79.6	26.1	1.7	30.0	22.3	27.7	19.8	9.1	31.1	9.8
VERMONT	83.0	92.0	88.6	69.5	29.4	5.0	29.3	29.5	29.4	34.8	18.1	46.1	36.8
VIRGINIA	79.4	87.2	82.6	62.7	29.5	5.1	31.5	27.6	32.4	15.1	19.6	48.5	20.7
WASHINGTON	75.3	88.5	90.3	76.7	27.7	3.3	29.7	25.8	28.9	19.4	12.4	35.5	11.1
WEST VIRGINIA	78.2	83.9	78.0	54.8	14.8	-9.6	15.8	14.0	14.6	11.5	12.8	62.1	19.7
WISCONSIN	78.9	90.2	89.2	66.7	22.4	-2.0	23.2	21.7	23.1	10.5	10.4	42.5	11.4
WYOMING	79.0	91.2	90.5	74.4	21.9	-2.5	23.0	20.8	23.0	18.6	8.1	34.3	7.8

[1] Hispanic or Latino persons may be of any race.

STATE	18 to 24 years			25 to 44 years			45 to 64 years			65 years and over		
	Total	Male	Female	Total	Male	Female	Total	Male	Female	Total	Male	Female
	25	26	27	28	29	30	31	32	33	34	35	36
UNITED STATES....	7.8	6.4	9.3	26.7	25.8	27.5	26.4	29.3	23.7	15.4	20.5	11.8
ALABAMA	5.9	4.6	7.1	21.3	20.1	22.5	20.1	22.5	17.9	12.0	16.1	9.3
ALASKA	4.0	2.8	5.4	22.2	20.2	24.4	30.2	30.7	29.6	17.3	19.3	15.5
ARIZONA	5.7	4.4	7.1	23.4	22.9	23.8	26.5	30.2	23.1	19.1	25.1	14.4
ARKANSAS.............	4.8	3.8	5.7	18.2	16.7	19.7	18.2	20.0	16.6	11.0	14.6	8.5
CALIFORNIA	6.7	5.5	8.1	26.7	26.2	27.2	30.1	33.7	26.7	19.8	26.4	15.0
COLORADO..............	8.9	7.0	11.1	34.1	33.0	35.3	35.6	39.2	32.1	21.1	28.2	16.0
CONNECTICUT	11.2	9.5	13.0	34.9	33.5	36.2	34.5	37.9	31.3	18.6	24.7	14.4
DELAWARE	8.1	6.7	9.5	27.7	26.7	28.7	25.9	28.6	23.4	17.4	23.5	12.9
DISTRICT OF COLUMBIA............	19.4	15.8	22.4	44.7	45.2	44.3	38.7	41.2	36.6	24.4	30.5	20.6
FLORIDA..................	6.4	5.2	7.7	23.5	22.7	24.3	24.5	28.1	21.2	17.6	23.6	13.0
GEORGIA.................	7.2	5.5	9.0	26.9	25.7	28.2	24.9	28.0	21.9	14.1	19.2	10.8
HAWAII....................	5.9	4.3	7.9	27.3	25.5	29.1	30.6	32.1	29.1	16.1	20.5	12.6
IDAHO	3.7	2.7	4.8	22.0	22.1	21.9	25.0	29.0	21.0	14.4	18.6	11.1
ILLINOIS..................	10.0	8.3	11.8	30.1	29.4	30.9	27.3	30.1	24.8	13.4	17.9	10.5
INDIANA..................	6.7	5.7	7.8	22.1	21.7	22.6	20.5	22.7	18.5	11.0	14.6	8.5
IOWA.......................	7.9	6.6	9.4	25.0	23.5	26.4	23.1	24.9	21.3	11.5	13.9	9.9
KANSAS...................	7.6	6.6	8.6	28.9	27.6	30.3	28.3	31.2	25.5	14.9	18.9	12.2
KENTUCKY..............	5.8	4.7	7.0	19.4	18.4	20.3	18.0	19.7	16.4	10.2	12.9	8.4
LOUISIANA	5.5	4.2	6.8	19.8	18.3	21.2	20.5	22.3	18.9	12.8	16.2	10.5
MAINE	6.5	5.0	8.1	23.5	21.2	25.7	26.4	27.7	25.1	15.6	19.3	13.0
MARYLAND	10.6	8.5	12.7	33.8	32.5	35.0	33.8	37.3	30.6	20.0	27.5	14.9
MASSACHUSETTS ...	14.9	13.0	16.8	38.8	37.5	40.0	34.8	37.5	32.2	17.7	24.1	13.5
MICHIGAN	7.1	5.9	8.2	24.2	23.9	24.6	23.5	25.9	21.1	12.6	16.5	9.9
MINNESOTA	9.5	7.7	11.4	31.7	30.5	32.9	28.7	30.9	26.6	14.2	18.4	11.3
MISSISSIPPI............	5.0	3.9	6.1	17.8	16.1	19.5	18.6	19.9	17.4	11.8	15.1	9.6
MISSOURI................	7.8	6.3	9.3	25.0	23.9	26.0	23.1	25.6	20.7	11.8	15.7	9.1
MONTANA	6.5	5.2	7.9	25.5	23.9	27.0	28.1	30.4	25.8	15.3	18.5	12.8
NEBRASKA..............	7.9	6.4	9.5	27.6	25.8	29.4	26.2	28.5	24.0	11.7	14.3	10.0
NEVADA...................	4.0	3.1	5.0	17.6	16.8	18.4	20.7	23.7	17.8	14.4	19.5	10.0
NEW HAMPSHIRE.....	8.6	6.9	10.4	30.1	29.4	30.8	31.5	34.5	28.5	19.4	25.4	15.0
NEW JERSEY...........	11.8	10.1	13.6	34.1	33.4	34.8	32.1	36.1	28.4	15.7	22.3	11.2
NEW MEXICO...........	4.0	3.1	5.0	21.2	20.3	22.1	28.8	31.1	26.7	18.7	23.3	15.2
NEW YORK................	11.8	9.7	13.8	31.0	29.9	32.1	28.7	30.9	20.0	10.4	21.3	10.1
NORTH CAROLINA ...	7.9	6.0	9.8	25.4	23.7	27.1	22.6	24.4	20.9	14.7	19.2	11.7
NORTH DAKOTA.......	6.7	5.7	8.0	26.4	23.7	29.3	24.7	26.3	23.1	9.8	11.2	8.8
OHIO	7.4	6.2	8.6	24.2	23.9	24.4	22.1	24.8	19.7	12.5	16.7	9.6
OKLAHOMA	5.5	4.7	6.5	21.3	20.1	22.5	22.7	25.6	20.0	13.9	18.5	10.7
OREGON	6.9	5.6	8.3	25.8	25.0	26.5	28.4	31.1	25.8	17.3	22.2	13.7
PENNSYLVANIA.......	9.5	7.9	11.1	26.7	25.9	27.5	24.0	26.8	21.4	11.9	16.3	9.0
RHODE ISLAND	9.5	8.4	10.6	28.5	27.7	29.3	29.5	32.9	26.4	13.7	18.6	10.5
SOUTH CAROLINA ...	6.9	5.4	8.5	21.8	20.3	23.3	21.2	23.8	18.9	15.5	20.5	12.1
SOUTH DAKOTA.......	6.8	5.7	8.0	24.8	22.7	26.9	24.2	26.7	21.7	11.2	13.4	9.7
TENNESSEE.............	6.6	5.2	8.0	22.1	21.0	23.1	20.4	23.0	18.0	11.8	15.9	9.0
TEXAS.....................	5.9	4.8	7.1	24.0	23.5	24.6	25.7	29.3	22.2	15.7	21.4	11.8
UTAH.......................	4.8	2.8	6.7	25.8	27.6	24.0	30.1	35.6	24.7	19.2	26.8	13.3
VERMONT	9.3	7.7	11.1	29.9	27.1	32.7	33.6	34.1	33.2	20.1	24.2	17.2
VIRGINIA..................	10.1	8.3	12.1	32.1	30.9	33.3	31.4	35.3	27.7	18.0	24.5	13.6
WASHINGTON..........	7.0	5.5	8.5	28.5	27.8	29.1	30.8	34.1	27.6	19.5	25.6	15.0
WEST VIRGINIA	5.6	4.5	6.7	16.6	16.2	17.0	16.4	17.6	15.1	9.1	11.1	7.7
WISCONSIN.............	7.4	6.1	8.8	25.4	23.8	27.1	24.2	26.1	22.3	12.7	15.6	10.7
WYOMING	5.3	4.1	6.7	21.6	20.5	22.8	25.5	27.8	23.1	15.2	18.5	12.6

Table B-2. States — Education, Labor Force, and Income

STATE	Total population 3 years and over — Number enrolled	Percent enrolled in public schools	Enrolled in nursery school — Number enrolled	Percent enrolled in public schools	Enrolled in kindergarten through 12th grade (percent, except where noted) — Number enrolled	Enrolled in public schools	Non-Hispanic White enrolled in public schools	Black or African American enrolled in public schools	American Indian and Alaska Native enrolled in public schools	Asian, Hawaiian, and Pacific Islander enrolled in public schools	Hispanic or Latino[1] enrolled in public schools
	37	38	39	40	41	42	43	44	45	46	47
UNITED STATES....	76 632 927	83.6	4 957 582	53.8	54 192 083	89.3	86.8	93.7	94.4	89.1	93.9
ALABAMA	1 155 504	86.1	74 879	51.9	837 350	89.4	85.9	95.9	92.3	87.1	91.5
ALASKA	185 760	89.9	10 804	60.1	142 653	93.2	91.2	95.0	97.8	95.4	94.2
ARIZONA	1 401 840	89.4	81 923	59.0	988 818	93.6	91.6	95.5	95.6	91.1	96.1
ARKANSAS	675 109	89.3	43 353	62.5	503 693	92.6	90.8	97.9	94.2	88.3	96.4
CALIFORNIA..............	10 129 990	85.9	547 066	53.5	7 026 326	90.5	85.5	91.2	94.6	88.9	95.0
COLORADO...............	1 166 004	86.1	79 064	55.2	804 108	91.2	89.7	94.1	93.8	91.7	94.8
CONNECTICUT	910 869	80.3	66 689	48.5	639 968	89.5	87.9	92.8	89.6	90.5	94.9
DELAWARE	209 979	78.2	14 792	47.8	143 780	82.7	77.3	94.0	92.5	79.1	91.6
DISTRICT OF COLUMBIA.............	157 475	67.3	9 409	68.1	88 568	84.9	38.3	90.5	92.3	80.1	90.3
FLORIDA....................	3 933 279	82.8	271 313	46.5	2 775 141	88.5	84.8	95.5	90.8	86.3	90.9
GEORGIA..................	2 211 688	85.6	176 842	59.1	1 598 291	91.3	87.6	96.4	93.4	92.5	95.2
HAWAII.....................	320 842	79.5	17 909	42.0	223 185	84.5	75.4	94.0	91.3	86.0	89.7
IDAHO......................	368 579	87.8	20 764	52.9	270 423	93.0	92.4	97.2	93.9	90.8	96.8
ILLINOIS....................	3 450 604	80.8	253 102	59.1	2 387 464	86.9	84.6	91.6	87.9	87.9	90.3
INDIANA	1 603 554	83.4	108 711	50.9	1 142 156	88.7	88.1	92.7	89.8	84.3	90.5
IOWA........................	792 057	84.6	52 114	62.0	552 637	90.3	89.8	95.9	94.5	94.4	95.0
KANSAS....................	756 960	86.5	51 305	58.0	529 202	89.6	88.6	95.3	93.5	94.1	92.2
KENTUCKY................	1 007 452	85.3	62 338	63.0	738 747	89.8	87.3	96.7	89.3	84.2	91.4
LOUISIANA	1 271 299	81.1	89 597	58.0	923 702	83.1	75.0	94.1	90.6	78.6	81.4
MAINE......................	321 041	85.7	17 558	53.8	236 267	92.2	92.3	93.9	95.9	89.3	90.9
MARYLAND	1 475 484	79.6	96 052	45.6	1 024 955	85.1	81.1	91.0	88.0	87.8	88.6
MASSACHUSETTS ...	1 726 111	74.0	122 930	46.5	1 129 778	88.4	87.3	89.8	91.0	90.4	94.0
MICHIGAN	2 780 378	86.2	173 083	64.2	1 971 459	89.4	88.3	93.2	92.4	87.9	92.1
MINNESOTA..............	1 362 507	84.2	90 516	61.8	975 733	89.6	88.7	94.8	95.0	94.7	92.9
MISSISSIPPI	789 903	87.2	54 058	64.0	582 848	89.5	82.6	97.5	62.2	82.8	91.2
MISSOURI.................	1 479 573	81.5	102 502	56.2	1 057 556	86.8	85.4	93.7	89.8	86.4	87.8
MONTANA.................	241 754	89.8	13 694	59.4	176 805	92.7	92.5	95.3	95.3	88.7	92.0
NEBRASKA................	480 705	82.8	30 386	55.7	338 004	86.5	85.3	94.7	95.9	89.2	92.8
NEVADA...................	492 885	90.9	27 345	55.5	366 909	94.7	93.2	96.8	95.2	94.4	97.2
NEW HAMPSHIRE.....	332 888	79.4	20 868	38.9	237 188	89.1	88.9	89.1	91.3	88.2	94.1
NEW JERSEY............	2 217 832	78.2	181 423	42.2	1 566 107	86.3	85.0	88.6	92.9	85.8	89.1
NEW MEXICO............	533 786	89.2	28 597	65.7	384 924	91.7	87.4	92.6	93.6	89.6	94.2
NEW YORK................	5 217 030	76.4	331 376	50.4	3 584 279	85.9	82.9	89.3	91.6	89.2	90.1
NORTH CAROLINA ...	2 043 225	86.2	135 315	51.7	1 445 635	92.0	89.1	97.3	95.7	93.3	95.9
NORTH DAKOTA.......	179 667	91.1	8 725	70.5	123 939	93.3	92.9	94.4	97.6	90.4	92.7
OHIO	3 014 460	82.1	204 086	56.7	2 157 981	86.6	85.5	92.6	90.5	85.4	87.4
OKLAHOMA	930 865	89.4	60 100	69.1	667 503	93.4	92.1	95.9	97.2	89.5	96.3
OREGON	876 492	86.0	50 273	47.3	621 408	90.6	89.6	93.5	95.2	90.2	95.8
PENNSYLVANIA........	3 135 934	76.5	203 934	45.7	2 228 837	84.6	83.3	90.0	88.0	84.7	90.2
RHODE ISLAND	290 605	75.6	16 207	47.0	190 389	87.1	85.2	90.4	91.5	93.1	94.2
SOUTH CAROLINA ...	1 053 152	85.9	68 727	56.4	767 586	90.4	85.7	97.2	94.3	88.6	92.6
SOUTH DAKOTA.......	208 229	88.6	12 693	62.0	152 642	92.6	92.2	94.0	95.3	89.9	93.6
TENNESSEE..............	1 415 105	85.1	90 016	56.4	1 037 539	90.1	88.0	96.7	90.9	86.7	92.1
TEXAS......................	5 948 260	88.6	390 094	57.0	4 355 276	93.1	89.6	95.8	94.8	91.9	96.1
UTAH.......................	741 524	87.1	46 057	52.1	508 724	95.7	95.6	94.6	97.7	94.9	96.3
VERMONT	164 156	81.9	9 520	55.9	114 318	91.6	91.7	85.9	93.2	92.0	88.2
VIRGINIA..................	1 868 101	83.8	125 701	43.1	1 291 600	90.4	88.1	95.8	91.6	90.6	93.2
WASHINGTON...........	1 584 701	86.3	98 839	48.4	1 127 448	91.1	90.0	94.2	95.3	92.8	96.3
WEST VIRGINIA	418 553	91.0	22 008	67.1	304 216	94.7	94.6	97.0	96.3	87.3	92.0
WISCONSIN..............	1 463 038	82.7	85 045	55.6	1 049 456	85.8	84.7	90.7	90.7	93.4	89.1
WYOMING	136 139	92.9	7 880	64.6	98 562	95.6	95.7	93.8	96.0	96.4	95.2

[1] Hispanic or Latino persons may be of any race.

STATE	Enrolled in college or graduate school (percent, except where noted)							Adult school enrollment					
								18 to 24 years			25 years and over		
	Number enrolled	Enrolled in public schools	Non-Hispanic White enrolled in public schools	Black or African American enrolled in public schools	American Indian and Alaska Native enrolled in public schools	Asian, Hawaiian, and Pacific Islander enrolled in public schools	Hispanic or Latino[1] enrolled in public schools	Total population	Percent enrolled in all school levels	Percent enrolled in college or graduate school	Total population	Percent enrolled in all school levels	Percent enrolled in college or graduate school
	48	49	50	51	52	53	54	55	56	57	58	59	60
UNITED STATES....	17 483 262	74.6	74.1	75.8	81.9	71.2	78.6	27 067 510	44.7	34.0	182 211 639	5.1	4.5
ALABAMA	243 275	85.3	87.1	81.4	87.7	90.1	78.1	437 088	43.3	33.3	2 887 400	3.8	3.3
ALASKA	32 303	85.3	85.8	83.2	90.2	75.1	78.1	56 869	31.7	19.2	379 556	6.0	5.6
ARIZONA	331 099	84.5	84.0	83.1	86.3	84.1	86.6	511 747	39.7	29.2	3 256 184	6.2	5.5
ARKANSAS.............	128 063	85.2	84.4	89.6	83.1	82.4	85.4	262 142	38.7	28.6	1 731 200	3.5	3.0
CALIFORNIA	2 556 598	80.3	78.4	79.7	83.2	78.6	85.7	3 351 285	46.1	35.4	21 298 900	7.3	6.4
COLORADO..............	282 832	80.2	80.2	77.5	82.8	77.8	82.5	427 839	40.8	31.1	2 776 632	5.8	5.4
CONNECTICUT	204 212	61.8	61.6	69.2	74.1	47.7	64.7	270 374	49.6	38.3	2 295 617	5.0	4.4
DELAWARE	51 407	74.4	73.2	79.5	63.1	76.2	72.0	74 980	46.8	37.8	514 658	5.0	4.5
DISTRICT OF COLUMBIA	59 498	41.0	35.6	49.8	55.8	28.6	40.4	73 192	54.0	46.1	384 535	7.7	6.7
FLORIDA..................	886 825	76.2	76.8	77.2	76.6	74.8	74.0	1 323 161	43.7	31.7	11 024 645	4.9	4.2
GEORGIA.................	436 555	75.2	77.0	72.5	74.7	60.7	70.5	834 714	38.6	27.9	5 185 965	4.5	3.9
HAWAII....................	79 748	74.0	68.8	63.3	69.1	76.6	75.2	114 735	40.2	32.5	802 477	6.0	5.2
IDAHO.....................	77 392	79.2	78.6	88.2	87.8	83.6	84.3	138 317	41.1	30.7	787 505	4.8	4.4
ILLINOIS..................	810 038	69.4	69.6	73.8	68.4	59.6	69.4	1 206 393	44.6	34.8	7 973 671	5.4	4.8
INDIANA..................	352 687	76.4	76.3	77.9	76.1	80.7	72.9	614 401	44.5	34.3	3 893 278	4.1	3.6
IOWA......................	187 306	74.0	73.8	72.4	80.4	78.1	73.8	298 134	51.1	40.1	1 895 856	3.9	3.6
KANSAS..................	176 453	85.3	85.3	83.2	76.1	89.7	84.4	275 991	47.6	36.5	1 701 207	4.8	4.4
KENTUCKY..............	206 367	81.2	81.0	83.6	68.7	82.4	78.7	401 531	39.4	29.5	2 646 397	3.8	3.3
LOUISIANA	258 000	81.7	82.3	82.1	80.3	75.9	71.4	475 055	43.2	32.3	2 775 468	4.4	3.7
MAINE.....................	67 216	71.0	71.3	71.4	81.9	49.7	70.0	104 052	46.1	33.0	869 893	4.2	3.7
MARYLAND	354 477	72.9	72.0	76.0	67.7	69.4	70.2	447 472	45.8	36.3	3 495 595	6.0	5.4
MASSACHUSETTS ...	473 403	46.7	47.7	54.3	44.4	31.5	49.2	579 855	54.3	44.1	4 273 275	5.7	5.0
MICHIGAN	635 836	82.5	83.3	78.6	85.0	82.6	79.7	929 908	47.9	36.7	6 415 941	5.1	4.6
MINNESOTA............	296 258	72.9	72.6	73.2	83.9	76.4	72.3	468 595	48.6	36.1	3 164 345	4.4	4.0
MISSISSIPPI............	152 997	86.7	85.5	89.1	84.5	87.3	76.3	312 737	42.3	31.3	1 757 517	3.7	3.1
MISSOURI................	319 515	71.8	71.8	75.9	72.5	63.8	66.8	534 203	43.6	32.9	3 634 906	4.4	3.9
MONTANA................	51 255	88.0	88.1	77.1	88.0	84.3	85.0	85 630	45.9	33.8	586 621	4.1	3.8
NEBRASKA..............	112 315	79.0	70.0	76.0	77.7	66.7	77.5	174 407	49.6	38.5	1 087 241	4.6	4.1
NEVADA..................	98 631	86.5	87.2	83.4	85.7	83.8	86.6	178 350	31.9	22.3	1 310 176	5.1	4.5
NEW HAMPSHIRE	74 832	60.2	61.8	44.9	50.9	33.9	44.0	102 898	51.2	38.6	823 987	4.6	4.3
NEW JERSEY...........	470 302	65.4	65.1	69.6	63.6	61.1	64.9	675 077	46.9	35.1	5 657 799	4.8	4.1
NEW MEXICO...........	120 265	86.8	85.8	87.6	88.0	86.1	87.9	176 677	41.8	29.1	1 134 801	6.7	6.0
NEW YORK...............	1 301 375	57.0	54.5	63.3	62.7	53.1	63.2	1 759 730	50.0	39.5	12 542 536	5.5	4.8
NORTH CAROLINA ...	462 275	78.5	78.3	79.8	84.6	74.9	74.6	805 002	39.7	30.9	5 282 994	4.6	4.0
NORTH DAKOTA.......	47 003	89.2	89.2	92.5	89.8	90.4	83.3	72 716	55.1	44.1	408 585	4.0	3.7
OHIO......................	652 393	75.1	74.7	78.6	73.3	73.3	75.0	1 056 259	45.2	34.2	7 411 740	4.4	3.9
OKLAHOMA.............	203 262	82.3	82.5	81.8	88.4	76.1	76.6	357 217	43.5	31.8	2 203 173	4.5	4.0
OREGON	204 811	81.7	81.0	84.1	86.7	81.4	85.0	326 131	40.8	30.8	2 250 998	5.0	4.6
PENNSYLVANIA........	703 163	59.7	60.1	65.2	58.5	46.0	55.3	1 095 782	49.8	39.0	8 266 284	3.8	3.3
RHODE ISLAND	84 009	55.0	56.2	53.4	59.6	34.3	58.4	106 237	56.1	47.7	694 573	5.5	4.8
SOUTH CAROLINA ...	216 839	79.4	79.0	80.1	83.9	86.2	75.2	406 909	40.9	31.0	2 596 010	4.1	3.5
SOUTH DAKOTA.......	42 894	82.0	82.2	56.0	88.1	79.2	66.3	77 759	47.0	34.6	474 359	3.7	3.4
TENNESSEE.............	287 550	75.9	75.7	79.3	78.2	66.5	64.9	547 119	39.8	30.0	3 744 928	3.7	3.3
TEXAS....................	1 202 890	82.6	81.6	82.6	80.4	81.0	85.4	2 186 997	40.5	28.8	12 790 893	5.2	4.4
UTAH......................	186 743	72.3	72.0	79.4	80.1	76.4	72.6	318 446	45.5	36.6	1 197 892	6.2	5.8
VERMONT................	40 318	60.4	61.5	36.6	45.1	46.6	53.5	57 025	52.6	43.1	404 223	4.2	3.9
VIRGINIA.................	450 800	76.3	77.3	75.7	69.7	73.7	70.4	676 117	43.1	34.0	4 666 574	5.2	4.7
WASHINGTON..........	358 414	81.7	81.4	85.3	84.1	80.2	84.9	556 834	42.5	30.9	3 827 507	5.2	4.8
WEST VIRGINIA	92 329	84.6	85.0	86.1	81.7	74.3	68.6	172 988	42.9	33.2	1 233 581	3.2	2.8
WISCONSIN.............	328 537	79.7	80.1	73.8	81.7	79.6	76.9	520 411	47.8	36.5	3 475 878	4.4	4.0
WYOMING	29 697	91.2	91.4	93.9	90.0	90.7	87.5	50 022	43.3	31.6	315 663	4.7	4.4

[1] Hispanic or Latino persons may be of any race.

	Total Population			Non-Hispanic White		Black or African American		American Indian and Alaska Native		Asian, Hawaiian, and Pacific Islander		Hispanic or Latino[1]	
STATE	Number	Percent not enrolled in school/ not high school graduate	Percent not enrolled in school/not high school graduate/not employed	Number	Percent not enrolled in school/ not high school graduate	Number	Percent not enrolled in school/ not high school graduate	Number	Percent not enrolled in school/ not high school graduate	Number	Percent not enrolled in school/ not high school graduate	Number	Percent not enrolled in school/ not high school graduate
	61	62	63	64	65	66	67	68	69	70	71	72	73
UNITED STATES....	15 930 458	9.8	5.5	10 026 825	6.9	2 284 042	11.7	178 590	16.1	620 358	4.3	2 518 961	21.0
ALABAMA	255 315	12.0	7.1	159 996	10.7	83 305	13.0	1 909	15.1	1 782	7.5	5 615	37.0
ALASKA	38 321	8.7	5.2	23 526	6.2	1 521	7.1	7 149	15.2	1 932	11.1	1 819	13.2
ARIZONA	288 587	14.8	8.4	152 353	8.3	10 057	12.6	19 923	18.0	5 916	4.2	96 190	25.5
ARKANSAS.............	156 258	9.5	5.4	111 565	7.5	32 797	10.9	1 344	15.3	1 476	9.7	6 929	34.8
CALIFORNIA	1 925 479	10.1	5.8	710 670	4.6	132 880	8.4	20 532	14.6	222 906	3.5	781 832	17.7
COLORADO............	243 396	12.1	5.9	165 437	7.4	9 829	11.5	3 300	18.4	5 838	5.9	54 546	27.7
CONNECTICUT	169 277	7.4	4.4	118 197	4.4	20 141	10.7	588	13.8	4 582	2.5	22 512	21.2
DELAWARE	44 154	10.3	5.6	29 568	8.0	10 032	12.4	209	12.9	702	2.8	2 762	30.6
DISTRICT OF COLUMBIA.........	32 400	10.1	6.7	9 040	0.7	18 896	11.8	103	10.7	1 005	6.0	2 861	30.5
FLORIDA.................	794 066	11.9	6.3	438 427	9.6	164 835	11.8	3 442	19.8	15 591	6.1	158 321	18.7
GEORGIA...............	471 799	13.5	7.3	261 261	10.5	158 733	12.8	1 414	15.7	10 874	6.4	33 720	44.3
HAWAII..................	64 343	5.8	3.6	9 784	5.2	1 076	0.0	252	4.0	30 361	5.7	6 764	7.0
IDAHO...................	87 734	8.2	4.0	75 397	6.2	356	5.9	1 314	16.9	856	4.2	8 610	25.6
ILLINOIS.................	704 632	9.9	5.7	433 951	5.7	122 493	13.5	2 118	15.1	24 098	2.6	112 827	23.9
INDIANA.................	360 606	9.8	5.1	300 131	8.8	34 852	12.7	927	18.9	4 009	3.0	15 826	24.6
IOWA....................	178 931	5.8	2.8	163 010	4.9	4 281	8.4	689	20.8	2 645	4.7	6 096	27.2
KANSAS.................	166 014	8.0	4.0	132 669	6.0	10 594	9.3	1 842	16.3	3 140	7.4	14 374	25.3
KENTUCKY.............	228 979	11.5	7.1	199 776	10.8	20 171	14.4	617	20.1	1 472	2.3	4 249	31.2
LOUISIANA.............	289 111	11.7	8.0	162 111	9.7	111 033	14.7	2 121	16.8	3 853	4.6	7 189	14.3
MAINE..................	69 770	6.2	3.4	66 161	5.9	567	15.0	562	11.7	757	10.6	811	10.5
MARYLAND.............	277 834	8.4	4.8	156 476	6.5	87 836	10.2	1 023	14.6	11 373	3.3	15 272	20.9
MASSACHUSETTS ...	330 827	6.6	3.7	248 110	4.9	22 226	8.0	1 036	18.1	16 380	4.5	32 802	18.9
MICHIGAN..............	566 976	8.7	4.9	429 730	7.2	86 092	12.0	4 290	13.9	10 706	4.2	24 550	23.5
MINNESOTA............	293 223	5.9	2.8	250 095	4.5	11 372	12.0	4 095	18.0	11 521	7.3	10 530	25.8
MISSISSIPPI............	184 029	12.2	7.8	96 161	11.0	81 464	13.0	892	12.1	1 116	11.0	3 263	31.3
MISSOURI..............	323 992	10.2	5.6	261 693	9.4	41 712	12.2	1 773	16.7	4 016	3.6	8 752	23.6
MONTANA..............	55 369	7.9	4.4	47 519	6.6	191	14.7	4 556	19.5	249	0.0	1 692	13.8
NEBRASKA.............	107 180	7.0	3.4	91 068	4.8	4 780	11.6	1 159	21.7	1 483	8.0	7 356	28.7
NEVADA................	98 513	16.0	8.3	55 666	10.2	7 475	14.6	1 680	19.2	4 956	8.8	25 533	30.3
NEW HAMPSHIRE.....	67 668	7.3	3.1	63 342	6.9	702	10.0	244	18.9	802	7.2	1 435	17.9
NEW JERSEY..........	408 187	7.2	4.3	236 590	3.5	68 051	11.1	1 095	14.8	23 513	2.0	72 587	17.5
NEW MEXICO...........	113 028	12.1	7.5	39 981	7.1	2 298	8.1	13 288	14.1	1 025	2.0	55 409	15.8
NEW YORK.............	1 017 375	8.7	5.6	564 489	5.3	187 816	11.3	5 042	16.0	58 178	4.7	189 545	18.0
NORTH CAROLINA ...	428 384	12.5	6.4	270 116	9.4	110 644	11.5	6 767	19.2	7 383	8.4	28 975	46.8
NORTH DAKOTA......	43 073	4.8	2.6	38 712	3.8	308	7.8	2 614	18.3	258	4.7	691	10.7
OHIO....................	639 825	8.3	4.6	521 870	7.2	81 905	13.3	1 865	14.3	6 895	4.3	16 425	18.8
OKLAHOMA.............	213 273	9.9	5.6	143 743	8.0	19 397	9.8	20 995	12.3	3 279	4.0	14 863	26.7
OREGON...............	191 546	10.4	5.4	151 837	8.1	3 347	10.4	3 423	16.2	6 505	6.5	19 687	29.2
PENNSYLVANIA.......	672 849	7.1	4.0	540 145	5.9	76 508	11.0	1 345	13.0	15 867	4.6	30 153	20.6
RHODE ISLAND	61 409	8.2	4.6	45 578	5.8	3 924	9.5	485	28.9	2 490	6.5	7 190	21.7
SOUTH CAROLINA ...	235 984	11.1	6.4	137 886	9.1	84 867	12.5	841	18.4	2 549	4.6	7 790	34.1
SOUTH DAKOTA......	49 305	7.9	4.7	41 883	5.8	458	12.7	5 222	23.8	224	5.8	853	15.7
TENNESSEE............	312 760	9.8	5.2	231 632	8.1	63 387	11.8	1 080	23.5	3 492	6.6	9 230	40.5
TEXAS..................	1 289 185	12.5	7.1	577 408	6.5	160 212	10.5	7 473	15.7	33 207	3.9	499 514	20.7
UTAH...................	173 747	8.7	3.9	147 140	6.5	1 290	12.4	2 643	18.1	4 165	6.8	15 852	28.6
VERMONT	36 432	5.9	2.5	34 228	5.7	360	7.5	204	13.2	446	4.9	627	8.5
VIRGINIA................	382 918	7.7	4.0	246 722	6.0	89 421	9.7	1 395	13.0	14 603	3.2	22 402	21.8
WASHINGTON..........	335 082	8.7	4.6	245 871	6.9	11 835	9.4	6 685	15.5	21 914	4.1	33 510	23.5
WEST VIRGINIA	99 445	9.0	6.4	92 636	8.9	3 636	9.6	328	14.9	580	3.3	859	16.8
WISCONSIN............	319 738	6.4	3.4	267 583	4.5	21 833	14.3	3 797	13.8	7 135	7.9	15 347	24.8
WYOMING	32 130	7.5	3.8	27 885	6.5	246	11.0	900	16.7	253	12.3	2 414	14.1

[1]Hispanic or Latino persons may be of any race.

	Work status in 1999 by sex, race, and Hispanic origin										
	Total population 16 years and over						Male population 16 years and over					
		Worked full-time (percent)		Worked part-time (percent)				Worked full-time (percent)		Worked part-time (percent)		
STATE	Number	Total	Full-year	Total	Full-year	Did not work in 1999 (percent)	Number	Total	Full-year	Total	Full-year	Did not work in 1999 (percent)
	74	75	76	77	78	79	80	81	82	83	84	85
UNITED STATES....	217 168 077	54.9	40.5	14.6	5.5	30.5	104 982 282	65.7	50.0	10.7	3.7	23.6
ALABAMA	3 450 542	52.9	39.6	12.1	4.4	35.1	1 634 366	63.4	49.9	9.0	3.1	27.5
ALASKA	458 054	63.2	38.1	15.7	4.7	21.1	237 360	72.9	43.9	11.0	3.0	16.2
ARIZONA	3 907 229	53.4	38.4	13.4	4.7	33.2	1 929 472	63.4	47.1	10.3	3.5	26.2
ARKANSAS	2 072 068	53.5	38.8	12.4	4.6	34.2	994 985	63.1	47.8	9.3	3.3	27.6
CALIFORNIA	25 596 144	53.5	36.5	14.6	5.2	31.9	12 597 735	64.6	45.1	11.2	3.8	24.2
COLORADO	3 325 197	60.7	44.9	16.1	5.8	23.2	1 663 537	71.9	54.6	11.3	3.8	16.8
CONNECTICUT	2 652 316	55.4	43.4	16.2	6.7	28.4	1 262 269	67.3	54.0	10.9	3.9	21.8
DELAWARE	610 289	57.3	43.9	14.6	5.7	28.1	291 135	67.1	52.9	10.7	3.9	22.2
DISTRICT OF COLUMBIA	469 041	55.8	38.5	13.1	3.7	31.1	216 954	61.2	42.9	11.3	3.3	27.5
FLORIDA	12 744 825	51.5	38.2	12.5	4.7	36.0	6 129 759	60.3	46.3	10.1	3.7	29.6
GEORGIA	6 250 687	59.0	44.3	12.5	4.4	28.5	3 032 442	68.9	54.0	9.3	3.2	21.8
HAWAII	950 055	53.4	39.6	15.2	6.0	31.4	473 542	61.2	46.1	12.4	5.1	26.4
IDAHO	969 872	55.2	38.0	17.9	6.3	26.8	481 578	68.5	48.3	12.0	3.9	19.5
ILLINOIS	9 530 946	56.0	41.6	15.2	5.9	28.9	4 595 958	67.1	51.1	10.9	3.8	22.0
INDIANA	4 683 717	57.0	43.4	15.8	6.0	27.2	2 264 556	68.6	54.1	11.2	3.8	20.3
IOWA	2 281 274	56.1	43.3	18.2	7.6	25.7	1 104 397	67.1	52.9	13.3	5.0	19.5
KANSAS	2 059 160	57.5	43.9	16.2	6.3	26.2	1 004 208	68.7	54.5	11.9	4.4	19.4
KENTUCKY	3 161 542	52.4	38.7	13.6	5.1	34.0	1 523 013	62.5	48.1	10.3	3.6	27.3
LOUISIANA	3 394 546	51.2	36.4	13.0	4.7	35.8	1 611 901	61.2	45.0	9.7	3.4	29.1
MAINE	1 010 318	53.7	40.6	17.4	7.1	28.9	484 628	65.5	50.4	11.7	4.1	22.8
MARYLAND	4 085 942	59.6	46.5	13.8	5.4	26.6	1 935 130	68.8	55.3	10.2	3.7	21.0
MASSACHUSETTS ...	5 010 241	54.4	42.3	17.4	7.3	28.1	2 370 006	66.7	53.2	11.5	4.1	21.8
MICHIGAN	7 630 645	53.9	40.1	16.5	6.2	29.6	3 687 508	65.7	50.5	11.1	3.7	23.2
MINNESOTA	3 781 756	57.9	44.7	19.2	8.2	22.9	1 850 659	69.4	54.6	13.2	4.9	17.3
MISSISSIPPI	2 158 941	52.4	36.9	11.9	4.0	35.7	1 020 250	61.3	46.1	9.4	3.1	29.3
MISSOURI	4 331 369	55.7	42.1	15.0	5.7	29.3	2 071 280	65.4	51.3	11.6	4.0	23.0
MONTANA	701 168	53.1	36.4	18.6	7.0	28.2	346 102	64.6	45.0	12.9	4.5	22.5
NEBRASKA	1 315 715	58.2	45.2	17.7	7.5	24.0	640 600	69.7	55.8	12.5	4.8	17.9
NEVADA	1 538 516	59.9	42.4	12.0	4.3	28.1	780 044	68.9	49.7	9.2	3.2	21.9
NEW HAMPSHIRE	960 498	58.6	46.5	17.7	7.1	23.7	467 062	70.9	58.0	11.6	4.1	17.5
NEW JERSEY	6 546 155	55.7	42.4	13.7	5.5	30.5	3 120 943	67.5	53.0	9.6	3.5	22.9
NEW MEXICO	1 369 176	52.2	36.4	14.7	5.2	33.0	663 095	62.4	45.1	11.2	3.8	26.3
NEW YORK	14 805 912	51.7	38.2	14.1	5.5	34.2	6 995 476	62.4	47.1	10.5	3.8	27.2
NORTH CAROLINA ...	6 290 618	58.1	43.8	13.0	4.6	28.9	3 039 013	68.0	53.6	9.8	3.3	22.2
NORTH DAKOTA	502 306	55.7	40.4	18.7	8.0	25.5	248 683	67.8	49.6	12.8	4.8	19.4
OHIO	8 788 494	54.5	42.0	15.9	6.5	29.6	4 196 673	66.1	52.4	11.1	4.0	22.8
OKLAHOMA	2 666 724	54.2	39.6	13.8	5.0	32.0	1 292 958	64.4	49.2	10.6	3.8	25.0
OREGON	2 673 782	53.7	37.3	17.2	6.2	29.1	1 311 960	65.6	46.7	12.0	3.9	22.4
PENNSYLVANIA	9 693 040	51.9	40.0	15.2	6.2	32.9	4 598 907	63.9	50.4	10.6	3.8	25.4
RHODE ISLAND	827 797	52.6	40.0	17.4	7.4	30.0	389 042	64.2	50.2	12.3	4.7	23.6
SOUTH CAROLINA ...	3 114 016	55.8	41.7	12.8	4.6	31.5	1 487 654	65.1	51.0	9.3	3.3	25.2
SOUTH DAKOTA	577 129	57.0	42.8	17.4	7.3	25.5	283 240	66.8	51.7	12.9	5.0	20.3
TENNESSEE	4 445 909	55.9	41.8	13.0	4.7	31.1	2 130 176	66.0	51.6	10.1	3.5	23.9
TEXAS	15 617 373	57.3	41.0	12.5	4.3	30.3	7 656 473	68.0	50.4	9.7	3.3	22.3
UTAH	1 600 279	54.5	39.3	20.9	7.3	24.5	793 083	68.3	51.4	14.7	5.1	17.1
VERMONT	479 140	56.8	42.7	18.8	7.3	24.4	231 856	68.4	52.6	12.8	4.4	18.8
VIRGINIA	5 529 980	59.6	45.6	13.6	4.9	26.8	2 675 692	70.1	55.6	9.8	3.3	20.1
WASHINGTON	4 553 591	55.5	39.4	16.5	6.0	27.9	2 243 278	67.4	49.3	11.3	3.7	21.3
WEST VIRGINIA	1 455 101	46.8	33.2	12.3	4.5	40.9	697 967	57.7	42.0	8.9	2.9	33.4
WISCONSIN	4 157 030	57.1	43.8	18.1	8.0	24.8	2 030 019	68.4	53.6	12.3	4.7	19.3
WYOMING	381 912	58.0	40.6	16.9	5.9	25.1	190 649	70.7	51.1	11.0	3.6	18.4

	Work status in 1999 by sex, race, and Hispanic origin											
	Female population 16 years and over						Non-Hispanic White population 16 years and over					
STATE		Worked full-time (percent)		Worked part-time (percent)		Did not work in 1999 (percent)		Worked full-time (percent)		Worked part-time (percent)		Did not work in 1999 (percent)
	Number	Total	Full-year	Total	Full-year		Number	Total	Full-year	Total	Full-year	
	86	87	88	89	90	91	92	93	94	95	96	97
UNITED STATES....	112 185 795	44.8	31.6	18.3	7.2	36.9	155 509 898	54.9	42.3	15.3	6.1	29.8
ALABAMA	1 816 176	43.3	30.4	14.8	5.5	41.8	2 496 136	54.1	42.0	12.1	4.6	33.8
ALASKA	220 694	52.8	31.9	20.7	6.4	26.5	324 720	65.6	41.9	15.2	4.8	19.2
ARIZONA	1 977 757	43.7	29.9	16.4	5.9	40.0	2 668 560	52.5	40.0	14.3	5.3	33.3
ARKANSAS	1 077 083	44.6	30.5	15.2	5.7	40.2	1 670 414	53.8	40.2	12.5	4.8	33.7
CALIFORNIA	12 998 409	42.7	28.1	17.9	6.5	39.5	12 916 610	52.7	39.5	15.9	6.1	31.4
COLORADO	1 661 660	49.5	35.2	20.8	7.9	29.6	2 556 644	60.8	46.3	16.8	6.3	22.4
CONNECTICUT	1 390 047	44.7	33.7	21.0	9.3	34.3	2 113 840	55.3	44.4	16.4	7.1	28.3
DELAWARE	319 154	48.3	35.7	18.3	7.4	33.4	456 820	56.5	44.5	15.1	6.1	28.5
DISTRICT OF COLUMBIA	252 087	51.1	34.8	14.7	4.1	34.2	146 266	67.3	49.2	15.4	3.8	17.4
FLORIDA	6 615 066	43.4	30.8	14.7	5.6	42.0	8 658 205	49.5	38.4	12.8	5.0	37.7
GEORGIA	3 218 245	49.8	35.1	15.5	5.6	34.7	4 055 860	59.1	46.7	12.9	4.8	28.0
HAWAII	476 513	45.7	33.2	18.0	6.8	36.3	236 305	57.3	43.2	16.2	6.3	26.5
IDAHO	488 294	42.2	27.8	23.8	8.6	34.0	868 708	54.6	38.5	18.3	6.6	27.0
ILLINOIS	4 934 988	45.6	32.7	19.1	7.8	35.3	6 723 212	56.1	43.8	16.2	6.7	27.7
INDIANA	2 419 161	46.1	33.3	20.2	8.1	33.7	4 082 797	57.1	44.2	16.0	6.3	26.9
IOWA	1 176 877	45.8	34.3	22.7	10.0	31.6	2 140 492	56.0	43.8	18.2	7.7	25.7
KANSAS	1 054 952	46.9	33.8	20.3	8.2	32.8	1 752 105	57.3	44.7	16.5	6.6	26.2
KENTUCKY	1 638 529	43.0	30.0	16.8	6.5	40.3	2 851 060	52.2	39.0	13.6	5.1	34.2
LOUISIANA	1 782 645	42.2	28.6	15.9	5.8	41.9	2 209 083	53.3	39.7	13.0	5.0	33.7
MAINE	525 690	42.9	31.6	22.7	9.9	34.4	980 004	53.8	40.8	17.4	7.1	28.9
MARYLAND	2 150 812	51.3	38.6	17.1	7.0	31.6	2 611 274	58.5	47.4	14.7	6.1	26.9
MASSACHUSETTS	2 640 235	43.4	32.5	22.7	10.2	33.8	4 189 315	54.6	43.3	17.8	7.8	27.6
MICHIGAN	3 943 137	42.8	30.5	21.5	8.6	35.7	6 141 644	54.1	41.6	17.1	6.7	28.8
MINNESOTA	1 931 097	46.8	35.2	24.9	11.4	28.2	3 410 493	57.8	45.5	19.5	8.5	22.7
MISSISSIPPI	1 135 691	44.3	29.3	14.2	4.9	41.5	1 374 323	54.5	40.8	12.0	4.4	33.5
MISSOURI	2 260 089	46.7	33.7	18.2	7.3	35.0	3 692 302	55.7	43.0	15.2	6.0	29.0
MONTANA	355 066	42.0	28.1	24.2	9.4	33.8	639 293	53.3	37.2	18.8	7.2	27.9
NEBRASKA	675 106	47.3	35.2	22.6	10.0	30.1	1 172 720	58.0	46.0	18.0	7.8	23.9
NEVADA	758 472	50.7	34.9	14.9	5.4	34.4	1 055 018	58.4	43.7	12.9	4.9	28.7
NEW HAMPSHIRE	493 436	46.9	35.7	23.5	10.0	29.6	917 783	58.5	46.7	17.7	7.2	23.7
NEW JERSEY	3 425 212	45.0	32.6	17.5	7.4	37.5	4 444 303	54.4	43.0	14.8	6.3	30.7
NEW MEXICO	706 081	42.6	28.2	18.0	6.4	39.4	668 674	52.4	39.1	15.7	5.8	31.9
NEW YORK	7 810 436	42.1	30.1	17.4	7.1	40.5	9 481 062	52.2	40.3	15.3	6.3	32.5
NORTH CAROLINA	3 251 605	48.9	34.7	16.0	5.8	35.1	4 549 492	58.1	45.4	13.5	5.0	28.4
NORTH DAKOTA	253 623	43.9	31.4	24.6	11.2	31.5	468 956	55.8	40.9	19.0	8.3	25.3
OHIO	4 591 821	43.9	32.5	20.3	8.7	35.8	7 512 545	54.8	42.9	16.1	6.7	29.1
OKLAHOMA	1 373 766	44.5	30.5	16.8	6.1	38.7	2 051 302	53.9	40.5	13.7	5.2	32.3
OREGON	1 361 822	42.2	28.2	22.2	8.5	35.6	2 288 321	52.8	37.6	17.5	6.5	29.7
PENNSYLVANIA	5 094 133	40.9	30.6	19.4	8.4	39.6	8 305 457	52.1	41.0	15.5	6.5	32.4
RHODE ISLAND	438 755	42.3	31.0	22.0	9.9	35.7	698 518	52.5	41.0	17.9	7.9	29.6
SOUTH CAROLINA	1 626 362	47.2	33.2	15.6	5.8	37.1	2 132 183	56.8	44.2	13.1	4.9	30.1
SOUTH DAKOTA	293 889	47.6	34.2	21.8	9.6	30.5	522 083	57.6	44.3	17.9	7.7	24.6
TENNESSEE	2 315 733	46.7	32.7	15.7	5.8	37.6	3 602 136	55.8	42.6	13.1	4.8	31.1
TEXAS	7 960 900	47.0	31.9	15.1	5.3	37.9	8 714 168	58.0	44.6	13.1	4.8	28.9
UTAH	807 196	41.0	27.4	27.1	9.5	31.9	1 384 274	53.8	39.6	21.8	7.7	24.4
VERMONT	247 284	45.9	33.3	24.5	10.1	29.6	462 639	56.9	42.9	18.7	7.4	24.4
VIRGINIA	2 854 288	49.8	36.2	17.2	6.4	33.1	3 973 735	59.4	46.9	13.8	5.1	26.9
WASHINGTON	2 310 313	44.0	29.8	21.6	8.2	34.4	3 694 690	54.8	40.2	16.9	6.3	28.3
WEST VIRGINIA	757 134	36.7	25.1	15.5	6.0	47.9	1 381 211	46.9	33.4	12.2	4.5	40.9
WISCONSIN	2 127 011	46.3	34.6	23.7	11.2	30.0	3 718 446	57.2	44.9	18.4	8.4	24.4
WYOMING	191 263	45.5	30.2	22.8	8.1	31.7	343 697	58.1	41.1	17.0	6.0	24.9

STATE	Black or African American population 16 years and over						American Indian and Alaska Native population 16 years and over					
		Worked full-time (percent)		Worked part-time (percent)		Did not work in 1999 (percent)		Worked full-time (percent)		Worked part-time (percent)		Did not work in 1999 (percent)
	Number	Total	Full-year	Total	Full-year		Number	Total	Full-year	Total	Full-year	
	98	99	100	101	102	103	104	105	106	107	108	109
UNITED STATES....	24 744 502	53.4	36.3	12.6	4.0	33.9	1 725 321	54.2	33.6	13.3	4.0	32.5
ALABAMA	835 045	48.5	32.8	11.9	3.8	39.5	17 359	54.3	37.7	13.9	5.2	31.8
ALASKA	15 094	69.8	47.3	13.3	3.4	16.9	63 934	50.0	20.1	19.2	4.3	30.8
ARIZONA	111 529	58.3	40.5	12.5	4.1	29.2	165 587	49.3	26.8	8.5	2.2	42.2
ARKANSAS	294 095	49.6	31.3	12.2	3.6	38.2	13 568	57.1	38.0	12.4	2.9	30.5
CALIFORNIA	1 617 340	51.6	34.3	12.9	4.1	35.5	226 434	53.1	32.3	14.5	4.6	32.3
COLORADO	116 301	63.6	44.6	13.4	4.3	23.0	32 235	60.5	39.4	16.5	5.6	23.0
CONNECTICUT	218 396	55.1	39.4	16.0	5.9	28.9	7 119	53.3	38.8	15.5	4.3	31.2
DELAWARE	107 765	59.4	41.7	13.4	4.7	27.1	2 390	57.3	43.2	14.1	3.8	28.6
DISTRICT OF COLUMBIA............	265 830	48.1	32.8	11.6	3.5	40.3	1 608	59.8	39.4	14.4	5.0	25.9
FLORIDA.................	1 629 041	54.3	37.0	12.1	3.8	33.6	43 123	57.8	38.8	11.8	3.5	30.4
GEORGIA................	1 677 435	57.7	39.4	12.2	3.8	30.1	18 557	60.7	41.2	12.3	3.6	27.0
HAWAII..................	16 038	71.8	54.4	12.6	5.5	15.6	2 673	55.6	41.8	18.0	5.3	26.4
IDAHO...................	3 520	65.1	40.9	15.8	3.2	19.1	12 164	58.6	33.1	14.4	3.5	27.0
ILLINOIS.................	1 324 414	50.1	32.9	13.5	4.0	36.4	22 600	59.0	37.9	14.4	4.8	26.6
INDIANA..................	359 134	54.6	37.0	14.2	4.1	31.2	12 977	59.2	39.5	13.4	4.1	27.4
IOWA.....................	40 970	52.5	33.0	17.9	5.5	29.6	6 359	53.0	30.3	18.6	4.5	28.4
KANSAS..................	106 705	56.9	38.4	13.9	4.3	29.2	18 005	60.4	40.4	15.0	4.3	24.7
KENTUCKY	215 138	53.1	35.9	14.0	4.5	32.9	7 308	52.3	34.5	13.1	4.4	34.6
LOUISIANA	1 016 357	46.5	29.5	12.7	3.8	40.8	18 501	51.9	32.1	13.3	4.1	34.8
MAINE	4 127	55.2	38.3	20.1	6.5	24.7	5 396	51.2	34.1	17.2	4.9	31.6
MARYLAND	1 080 251	61.4	45.2	11.6	3.9	26.9	12 513	64.5	47.3	11.6	4.0	23.9
MASSACHUSETTS ...	242 121	54.3	38.7	15.3	5.2	30.5	11 520	48.8	33.9	16.5	6.2	34.7
MICHIGAN	995 314	51.1	32.8	13.2	3.8	35.7	44 005	56.5	37.1	16.5	5.2	27.0
MINNESOTA	110 193	58.6	37.1	16.1	4.4	25.3	36 590	55.4	34.1	15.6	5.1	29.1
MISSISSIPPI	725 315	48.1	29.8	11.8	3.4	40.0	8 232	55.0	36.7	8.8	2.8	36.2
MISSOURI...............	440 785	54.1	36.0	13.5	4.1	32.4	20 064	57.8	38.4	14.4	3.9	27.8
MONTANA...............	1 657	58.1	34.6	22.3	5.7	19.6	36 092	51.5	25.7	13.2	3.5	35.3
NEBRASKA..............	48 291	50.0	30.2	15.5	4.9	28.5	10 140	54.2	32.8	15.7	4.2	30.1
NEVADA.................	95 442	61.7	40.3	10.5	2.8	27.8	19 551	62.0	40.2	10.7	3.2	27.3
NEW HAMPSHIRE.....	6 421	61.3	44.3	16.8	5.3	21.9	2 125	58.1	37.9	17.7	5.9	24.2
NEW JERSEY...........	825 798	55.3	39.5	11.9	4.1	32.8	13 569	56.0	36.6	12.3	4.5	31.7
NEW MEXICO...........	24 364	55.4	38.2	14.4	4.8	30.2	115 003	48.9	28.0	10.5	2.9	40.6
NEW YORK..............	2 190 706	49.7	34.5	11.8	4.2	38.5	56 635	50.1	33.0	13.3	4.6	36.6
NORTH CAROLINA ...	1 269 882	56.2	39.0	12.3	3.8	31.5	74 108	58.1	38.3	9.8	3.0	32.1
NORTH DAKOTA.......	2 439	64.2	40.9	19.3	8.0	16.5	19 719	54.5	30.8	11.2	2.7	34.4
OHIO.....................	918 715	51.9	35.5	14.0	4.5	34.1	21 046	52.2	36.4	15.7	5.7	32.1
OKLAHOMA	184 077	53.1	34.6	14.4	4.5	32.4	182 254	55.0	36.7	13.7	4.4	31.4
OREGON	38 410	55.2	34.0	16.0	4.4	28.9	32 025	57.3	34.5	16.6	5.6	26.1
PENNSYLVANIA........	876 277	49.4	33.4	13.0	4.2	37.5	14 770	52.2	34.9	13.8	4.5	34.0
RHODE ISLAND	31 895	51.4	33.8	16.6	6.2	32.0	3 442	47.3	34.7	14.8	4.0	38.0
SOUTH CAROLINA ...	855 740	52.6	35.8	12.0	3.9	35.3	11 308	59.0	42.5	10.0	3.7	31.1
SOUTH DAKOTA.......	3 186	59.7	33.4	16.7	4.6	23.6	37 023	47.5	24.6	11.5	2.9	41.0
TENNESSEE............	664 914	55.7	38.1	12.6	3.9	31.7	12 369	60.1	42.2	13.6	4.9	26.2
TEXAS...................	1 725 126	56.6	38.1	11.8	3.8	31.6	85 039	58.9	39.4	13.0	4.1	28.1
UTAH....................	11 058	61.2	40.8	15.7	4.3	23.1	19 242	52.3	28.5	16.0	4.6	31.7
VERMONT	1 994	57.3	34.4	19.7	3.9	23.1	2 028	56.9	41.6	15.7	4.7	27.4
VIRGINIA.................	1 023 750	58.5	41.4	13.2	4.3	28.3	17 950	64.5	45.8	13.4	4.7	22.1
WASHINGTON..........	134 174	60.3	40.8	14.5	4.5	25.3	64 543	53.9	33.3	14.8	4.4	31.3
WEST VIRGINIA	43 292	42.3	28.6	13.4	4.1	44.3	3 110	41.4	26.9	12.8	4.9	45.9
WISCONSIN............	198 169	52.7	32.8	15.0	4.4	32.2	33 758	59.7	38.5	15.9	5.0	24.3
WYOMING	2 472	60.8	39.2	17.9	4.9	21.3	7 651	51.5	28.2	15.2	3.9	33.4

Table B-2. States — Education, Labor Force, and Income

	Work status in 1999 by sex, race, and Hispanic origin											
	Asian, Hawaiian, and Pacific Islander population 16 years and over						Hispanic or Latino[1] population 16 years and over					
		Worked full-time (percent)		Worked part-time (percent)				Worked full-time (percent)		Worked part-time (percent)		
STATE	Number	Total	Full-year	Total	Full-year	Did not work in 1999 (percent)	Number	Total	Full-year	Total	Full-year	Did not work in 1999 (percent)
	110	111	112	113	114	115	116	117	118	119	120	121
UNITED STATES....	8 292 596	55.9	38.9	13.9	4.6	30.2	24 169 746	56.6	34.8	12.1	3.9	31.3
ALABAMA	24 521	52.8	37.6	15.7	5.4	31.5	50 834	60.6	39.4	10.5	3.4	28.8
ALASKA	21 587	60.3	32.0	15.0	4.9	24.7	16 600	64.7	37.5	15.9	3.9	19.4
ARIZONA	77 304	56.6	39.4	14.9	5.0	28.5	848 427	56.3	35.3	11.5	3.5	32.2
ARKANSAS.............	16 088	59.2	38.2	12.6	4.2	28.2	57 303	62.2	37.6	9.0	3.0	28.8
CALIFORNIA.............	2 998 070	53.7	36.9	13.6	4.5	32.7	7 304 131	55.4	31.4	12.8	4.0	31.8
COLORADO................	76 499	60.1	42.5	14.4	5.0	25.5	504 271	59.8	38.6	13.1	4.2	27.1
CONNECTICUT	64 152	60.9	44.6	13.9	4.3	25.2	215 260	55.5	37.4	14.5	5.0	30.0
DELAWARE	12 976	60.8	44.2	14.1	5.0	25.1	25 058	61.2	41.6	11.6	3.7	27.1
DISTRICT OF COLUMBIA	13 561	58.1	35.3	17.2	4.7	24.7	34 935	64.5	39.1	13.5	4.2	22.0
FLORIDA..................	216 928	57.8	41.3	14.2	5.0	28.0	2 062 177	56.5	38.0	11.0	3.9	32.4
GEORGIA..................	136 352	60.2	41.5	13.5	4.1	26.3	309 943	65.5	39.9	8.0	2.5	26.5
HAWAII....................	506 514	51.2	38.0	13.9	5.7	34.9	56 434	53.4	37.3	18.0	6.1	28.6
IDAHO.....................	10 035	54.5	36.3	19.3	5.2	26.2	63 534	62.5	32.7	13.4	3.4	24.1
ILLINOIS..................	338 808	59.7	41.8	14.1	4.4	26.2	1 030 821	61.5	38.1	10.7	3.5	27.9
INDIANA...................	46 958	54.8	37.1	18.2	4.7	27.0	143 240	61.7	38.6	13.0	4.0	25.3
IOWA.......................	27 365	54.8	38.5	22.0	7.2	23.2	52 336	63.7	38.1	12.6	4.2	23.7
KANSAS...................	35 784	57.3	40.0	16.1	5.5	26.6	120 530	61.8	40.1	13.0	4.1	25.2
KENTUCKY..............	23 588	57.0	39.7	15.4	5.8	27.6	40 290	60.4	37.3	11.3	3.3	28.3
LOUISIANA	43 232	50.6	34.3	15.7	5.5	33.8	80 880	53.6	35.5	13.6	4.5	32.8
MAINE	6 227	52.4	36.8	19.0	5.8	28.6	6 181	55.9	35.4	18.7	7.1	25.4
MARYLAND..............	167 318	60.6	44.5	13.9	4.9	25.5	162 674	64.0	42.5	13.8	4.6	22.2
MASSACHUSETTS ...	187 271	55.7	39.3	15.3	4.7	29.0	287 055	51.9	34.0	15.2	5.1	32.9
MICHIGAN	134 749	57.6	39.3	15.5	4.5	27.0	212 851	59.5	36.6	14.4	4.4	26.1
MINNESOTA	93 813	55.5	38.5	17.4	5.5	27.0	91 695	63.0	37.8	14.5	4.6	22.4
MISSISSIPPI	14 246	55.8	36.7	14.9	4.9	29.3	27 518	56.3	35.6	10.6	3.1	33.1
MISSOURI................	50 527	56.5	40.0	16.6	5.3	26.9	78 362	61.5	40.1	13.2	3.8	25.4
MONTANA	3 582	47.4	28.5	25.4	8.8	27.2	11 666	52.3	33.1	21.3	6.9	26.4
NEBRASKA..............	16 795	56.6	40.4	19.3	6.7	24.1	60 607	63.7	40.2	12.2	3.8	24.2
NEVADA..................	78 938	63.9	43.4	10.6	3.4	25.5	260 014	64.1	37.7	9.2	2.7	26.7
NEW HAMPSHIRE.....	11 937	59.9	44.3	15.6	4.8	24.4	13 237	62.5	43.7	14.9	3.6	22.6
NEW JERSEY...........	371 457	62.6	46.1	10.9	3.8	26.5	814 474	60.0	39.7	10.9	3.7	29.2
NEW MEXICO...........	15 311	54.3	39.7	17.1	6.2	28.6	535 176	52.6	34.5	14.2	4.8	33.1
NEW YORK...............	841 102	54.9	36.9	12.1	3.8	33.0	2 070 755	49.9	32.6	11.7	4.2	38.4
NORTH CAROLINA ...	87 231	61.6	42.7	13.2	4.6	25.1	266 410	66.5	40.8	8.2	2.4	25.3
NORTH DAKOTA......	2 723	49.5	30.9	29.1	12.0	21.4	4 836	61.2	39.1	19.1	5.6	19.7
OHIO......................	106 352	56.6	40.8	16.4	5.7	27.0	143 507	57.7	38.6	15.3	5.1	27.0
OKLAHOMA	37 930	51.6	36.9	17.1	4.9	31.3	115 504	60.4	38.1	12.2	3.6	27.4
OREGON..................	83 068	57.1	38.5	15.9	4.5	27.0	176 163	62.6	34.5	13.8	4.2	23.6
PENNSYLVANIA	171 280	54.4	36.7	15.2	4.2	30.5	259 321	52.0	33.2	12.9	4.0	35.1
RHODE ISLAND	18 374	51.8	34.0	17.2	4.6	31.0	58 954	53.4	33.0	12.8	4.0	33.8
SOUTH CAROLINA ...	29 981	57.0	40.3	15.2	5.2	27.8	67 919	62.2	39.8	10.3	3.1	27.5
SOUTH DAKOTA.......	3 598	61.6	39.4	16.2	4.3	22.2	6 522	63.9	38.4	15.9	5.3	20.2
TENNESSEE.............	43 963	58.5	40.5	14.2	3.7	27.4	85 779	65.4	40.0	9.8	3.0	24.8
TEXAS....................	441 245	59.0	41.6	13.2	4.3	27.8	4 530 356	55.9	35.0	11.5	3.6	32.7
UTAH......................	38 021	55.7	39.0	17.7	5.0	26.6	130 696	62.3	37.8	13.7	4.5	24.0
VERMONT	3 577	53.1	35.1	22.4	5.1	24.4	3 869	55.2	32.7	23.8	7.0	21.0
VIRGINIA..................	206 469	61.9	44.3	13.5	4.4	24.6	235 965	66.2	43.5	12.3	4.0	21.5
WASHINGTON..........	269 323	56.4	37.4	15.2	4.9	28.5	280 614	63.1	32.6	13.2	3.8	23.8
WEST VIRGINIA	7 837	47.7	31.6	19.4	5.3	32.9	8 491	48.9	34.3	15.4	3.8	35.8
WISCONSIN..............	55 452	53.5	35.1	19.9	5.7	26.6	124 166	61.5	37.0	13.8	4.3	24.7
WYOMING	2 577	53.1	34.3	17.5	5.8	29.4	21 405	59.9	37.8	15.5	4.5	24.6

[1] Hispanic or Latino persons may be of any race.

Table B-2. States — **Education, Labor Force, and Income**

STATE	Employment status by sex and age, 2000										
	Total population 16 years and over			Male population 16 years and over			Female population 16 years and over			Total population 16 to 24 years		
	Number	Labor force participation rate	Unemployment rate	Number	Labor force participation rate	Unemployment rate	Number	Labor force participation rate	Unemployment rate	Number	Labor force participation rate	Unemployment rate
	122	123	124	125	126	127	128	129	130	131	132	133
UNITED STATES....	217 168 077	63.9	5.8	104 982 282	70.7	5.7	112 185 795	57.5	5.8	34 956 438	63.7	13.5
ALABAMA	3 450 542	59.7	6.2	1 634 366	67.4	5.5	1 816 176	52.8	7.0	563 142	59.3	15.4
ALASKA	458 054	71.3	9.0	237 360	76.3	10.5	220 694	65.9	7.3	78 498	63.6	18.6
ARIZONA	3 907 229	61.1	5.6	1 929 472	68.0	5.6	1 977 757	54.3	5.6	651 045	64.0	11.9
ARKANSAS	2 072 068	60.6	6.1	994 985	67.3	5.8	1 077 083	54.4	6.4	340 868	63.2	15.7
CALIFORNIA	25 596 144	62.4	7.0	12 597 735	69.6	6.8	12 998 409	55.5	7.3	4 297 244	58.8	14.4
COLORADO	3 325 197	70.1	4.3	1 663 537	76.6	4.3	1 661 660	63.7	4.3	548 565	68.7	10.7
CONNECTICUT	2 652 316	66.6	5.3	1 262 269	73.3	5.5	1 390 047	60.4	5.0	356 699	66.0	15.7
DELAWARE	610 289	65.7	5.2	291 135	71.8	5.3	319 154	60.2	5.0	95 631	66.1	14.0
DISTRICT OF COLUMBIA	469 041	63.6	10.8	216 954	67.5	10.6	252 087	60.2	11.0	84 506	61.7	27.3
FLORIDA	12 744 825	58.6	5.6	6 129 759	64.9	5.2	6 615 066	52.8	5.9	1 720 180	63.7	13.3
GEORGIA	6 250 687	66.1	5.5	3 032 442	73.1	5.0	3 218 245	60.4	6.1	1 064 722	64.0	14.2
HAWAII	950 055	64.5	6.3	473 542	69.9	6.8	476 513	59.1	5.6	147 578	62.2	14.6
IDAHO	969 872	66.1	5.8	481 578	73.2	6.0	488 294	59.1	5.5	182 367	67.0	11.9
ILLINOIS	9 530 946	65.4	6.0	4 595 958	72.2	6.2	4 934 988	59.0	5.8	1 557 275	65.5	13.7
INDIANA	4 683 717	66.6	4.9	2 264 556	73.7	4.9	2 419 161	60.0	4.9	790 439	68.3	12.0
IOWA	2 281 274	68.2	4.2	1 104 397	74.2	4.5	1 176 877	62.7	3.8	385 418	72.9	9.4
KANSAS	2 059 160	67.5	4.2	1 004 208	74.4	4.3	1 054 952	60.9	4.2	357 953	69.2	10.6
KENTUCKY	3 161 542	60.9	5.7	1 523 013	68.0	5.7	1 638 529	54.4	5.8	515 145	64.5	13.9
LOUISIANA	3 394 546	59.4	7.3	1 611 901	66.2	7.0	1 782 645	53.2	7.6	619 078	56.8	17.5
MAINE	1 010 318	65.3	4.8	484 628	71.2	5.0	525 690	59.8	4.5	140 425	66.4	11.6
MARYLAND	4 085 942	67.8	4.7	1 935 130	73.3	4.6	2 150 812	62.8	4.8	590 347	64.7	12.7
MASSACHUSETTS ...	5 010 241	66.2	4.6	2 370 006	72.6	4.7	2 640 235	60.4	4.4	736 966	65.5	11.1
MICHIGAN	7 630 645	64.6	5.8	3 687 508	71.1	6.1	3 943 137	58.5	5.5	1 214 704	67.8	12.4
MINNESOTA	3 781 756	71.2	4.1	1 850 659	76.5	4.6	1 931 097	66.0	3.4	617 411	73.3	8.5
MISSISSIPPI	2 158 941	59.4	7.4	1 023 250	66.0	6.6	1 135 691	53.5	8.0	401 424	57.6	18.8
MISSOURI	4 331 369	65.2	5.3	2 071 280	71.6	5.2	2 260 089	59.2	5.4	696 463	68.7	12.9
MONTANA	701 168	65.4	6.3	346 102	71.0	7.2	355 066	59.9	5.3	114 547	65.7	14.5
NEBRASKA	1 315 715	69.7	3.5	640 000	76.0	3.5	675 106	63.0	3.6	228 474	72.1	8.3
NEVADA	1 538 516	65.2	6.2	780 044	71.0	6.2	758 472	59.2	6.3	228 340	65.3	12.4
NEW HAMPSHIRE	960 498	70.5	3.8	467 062	76.9	3.9	493 436	64.4	3.6	136 511	70.3	11.4
NEW JERSEY	6 546 155	64.2	5.8	3 120 943	71.6	5.7	3 425 212	57.5	5.9	888 356	61.1	13.7
NEW MEXICO	1 369 176	61.0	7.3	663 095	67.6	7.4	706 081	54.7	7.2	234 375	60.2	16.1
NEW YORK	14 805 912	61.1	7.1	6 995 476	67.8	7.1	7 810 436	55.1	7.0	2 263 376	56.8	17.4
NORTH CAROLINA ...	6 290 618	65.7	5.3	3 039 013	72.7	4.9	3 251 605	59.0	5.8	1 007 624	67.0	13.7
NORTH DAKOTA	502 306	67.5	4.6	248 683	72.7	5.5	253 623	62.4	3.5	93 721	69.5	9.5
OHIO	8 788 494	64.8	5.0	4 196 673	71.7	5.1	4 591 821	58.5	4.8	1 376 754	67.6	11.7
OKLAHOMA	2 666 724	62.1	5.3	1 292 958	69.6	5.2	1 373 766	55.1	5.5	463 551	64.1	12.5
OREGON	2 673 782	65.2	6.5	1 311 900	72.0	6.7	1 361 822	58.6	6.1	422 784	65.8	13.3
PENNSYLVANIA	9 693 040	61.9	5.7	4 598 907	69.2	5.7	5 094 133	55.3	5.6	1 426 756	62.9	14.0
RHODE ISLAND	827 797	64.6	5.6	389 042	71.2	5.7	438 755	58.7	5.6	133 224	66.5	12.4
SOUTH CAROLINA ...	3 114 016	63.4	5.9	1 487 654	69.8	5.3	1 626 362	57.5	6.4	518 006	64.1	14.7
SOUTH DAKOTA	577 129	68.4	4.4	283 240	73.3	4.7	293 889	63.7	4.1	102 770	70.4	10.4
TENNESSEE	4 445 909	63.5	5.5	2 130 176	71.1	5.1	2 315 733	56.5	5.9	700 981	65.3	13.1
TEXAS	15 617 373	63.6	6.1	7 656 473	71.4	5.7	7 960 900	56.2	6.5	2 826 480	60.6	14.4
UTAH	1 600 279	69.0	5.0	793 083	77.2	4.8	807 196	61.0	5.2	402 387	71.5	9.6
VERMONT	479 140	69.3	4.2	231 856	74.6	4.4	247 284	64.3	4.0	74 917	65.8	11.3
VIRGINIA	5 529 980	66.8	4.2	2 675 692	73.4	4.1	2 854 288	60.6	4.4	863 406	64.7	12.1
WASHINGTON	4 553 591	66.5	6.2	2 243 278	73.3	6.4	2 310 313	59.9	6.1	726 084	66.4	13.7
WEST VIRGINIA	1 455 101	54.5	7.3	697 967	61.9	8.0	757 134	47.6	6.6	221 520	57.0	18.3
WISCONSIN	4 157 030	69.1	4.7	2 030 019	74.3	5.1	2 127 011	64.1	4.2	681 152	72.8	9.5
WYOMING	381 912	67.5	5.3	190 649	73.7	5.6	191 263	61.3	4.9	66 249	66.6	12.9

Table B-2. States — **Education, Labor Force, and Income**

STATE	Employment status by sex and age, 2000								
	Total population 25 to 44 years			Total population 45 to 64 years			Total population 65 years and over		
	Number	Labor force participation rate	Unemployment rate	Number	Labor force participation rate	Unemployment rate	Number	Labor force participation rate	Unemployment rate
	134	135	136	137	138	139	140	141	142
UNITED STATES....	85 482 828	79.7	4.7	61 749 839	70.9	3.6	34 978 972	13.3	5.8
ALABAMA	1 294 710	77.5	5.0	1 012 662	64.7	3.5	580 028	11.8	5.3
ALASKA	204 903	81.7	8.1	139 560	74.5	6.4	35 093	15.4	8.5
ARIZONA	1 523 018	77.2	4.6	1 065 559	67.3	3.6	667 607	11.5	6.9
ARKANSAS..............	752 410	79.1	4.7	604 061	66.1	3.2	374 729	12.4	4.4
CALIFORNIA............	10 811 836	75.3	6.0	6 900 270	69.9	4.8	3 586 794	13.6	7.8
COLORADO.............	1 409 857	82.9	3.2	950 993	75.9	2.7	415 782	15.5	5.7
CONNECTICUT	1 038 361	82.7	4.0	787 969	76.7	3.3	469 287	14.3	4.0
DELAWARE	237 498	83.0	3.9	175 490	72.4	3.0	101 670	13.5	4.2
DISTRICT OF COLUMBIA............	189 647	78.7	8.0	124 800	69.1	6.3	70 088	15.1	6.8
FLORIDA.................	4 601 680	78.7	4.4	3 616 828	66.8	3.7	2 806 137	12.0	6.5
GEORGIA................	2 668 138	79.7	4.2	1 729 921	69.9	2.9	787 906	14.3	7.3
HAWAII..................	364 429	81.0	5.7	276 907	73.3	3.9	161 141	14.3	5.1
IDAHO...................	364 414	81.6	4.5	277 146	73.4	3.9	145 945	12.4	6.3
ILLINOIS.................	3 815 155	80.1	5.1	2 659 587	73.1	3.7	1 498 929	13.9	4.5
INDIANA.................	1 796 028	82.9	3.9	1 344 365	73.4	2.7	752 885	13.9	3.4
IOWA.....................	809 243	86.7	3.4	650 236	78.2	2.4	436 377	15.0	3.5
KANSAS..................	771 963	83.4	3.4	573 563	77.0	2.2	355 681	15.9	2.7
KENTUCKY..............	1 213 784	78.0	4.7	928 945	63.3	3.2	503 668	11.9	3.1
LOUISIANA.............	1 297 462	75.8	5.8	959 909	64.3	4.2	518 097	12.1	5.2
MAINE	370 360	84.2	3.8	315 891	73.0	3.1	183 642	12.9	6.4
MARYLAND..............	1 674 507	82.5	3.8	1 223 084	75.1	2.8	598 004	14.6	5.4
MASSACHUSETTS ...	1 996 306	82.1	3.6	1 417 368	76.0	3.2	859 601	13.8	3.3
MICHIGAN	2 968 963	81.1	4.9	2 227 746	69.8	3.6	1 219 232	11.4	7.1
MINNESOTA	1 502 342	87.1	3.2	1 068 588	79.1	2.8	593 415	14.4	5.2
MISSISSIPPI	810 365	76.7	5.9	602 864	64.3	3.5	344 288	12.2	4.4
MISSOURI................	1 632 448	82.4	4.2	1 246 420	71.7	3.0	756 038	13.8	4.8
MONTANA...............	245 973	84.0	5.2	219 717	72.3	4.0	120 931	14.6	5.9
NEBRASKA..............	487 862	86.0	2.8	367 020	79.4	1.9	232 359	18.0	3.8
NEVADA..................	634 425	78.7	5.3	457 254	70.3	4.7	218 497	15.4	7.0
NEW HAMPSHIRE.....	381 572	86.0	2.5	294 376	78.4	2.3	148 039	15.1	5.5
NEW JERSEY..........	2 638 465	79.4	4.9	1 906 299	74.0	4.0	1 113 035	14.1	6.1
NEW MEXICO...........	520 069	76.6	6.3	402 242	66.6	4.4	212 490	12.6	5.9
NEW YORK..............	5 856 084	77.0	5.9	4 235 755	69.3	4.6	2 450 697	12.8	6.3
NORTH CAROLINA	2 510 345	81.7	4.0	1 802 827	70.2	2.9	969 822	14.4	8.3
NORTH DAKOTA......	175 257	87.4	3.7	138 731	77.2	3.1	94 597	14.3	4.3
OHIO	3 335 997	82.1	4.1	2 567 648	71.5	3.0	1 508 095	12.6	3.7
OKLAHOMA	980 231	78.5	4.4	767 242	68.7	3.0	455 700	13.6	3.8
OREGON	1 000 959	81.9	5.7	812 152	73.1	4.3	437 887	11.5	7.6
PENNSYLVANIA........	3 515 992	81.2	4.5	2 830 035	71.5	3.5	1 920 257	11.7	7.2
RHODE ISLAND	310 942	81.9	4.7	230 912	74.4	3.7	152 719	12.5	4.8
SOUTH CAROLINA ...	1 191 564	80.1	4.5	918 601	67.8	3.3	485 845	13.5	7.3
SOUTH DAKOTA.......	206 623	86.5	3.4	159 620	78.0	2.5	108 116	18.0	3.2
TENNESSEE..............	1 724 588	79.9	4.4	1 317 501	67.8	3.2	702 839	13.2	5.6
TEXAS....................	6 537 409	76.6	4.7	4 186 017	69.6	3.7	2 067 467	14.5	4.7
UTAH......................	628 873	80.5	3.6	378 488	75.0	2.8	190 531	13.8	3.3
VERMONT	176 278	86.3	3.1	150 650	78.2	2.6	77 295	16.4	4.9
VIRGINIA.................	2 249 249	81.9	3.2	1 626 758	72.6	2.3	790 567	14.2	5.1
WASHINGTON..........	1 828 473	81.5	5.2	1 336 872	73.2	4.0	662 162	11.7	9.5
WEST VIRGINIA	501 526	74.5	6.2	455 229	59.0	4.0	276 826	8.7	3.8
WISCONSIN..............	1 585 067	85.8	3.9	1 188 143	77.4	3.0	702 668	13.8	7.3
WYOMING	139 178	83.7	4.1	119 018	74.2	3.3	57 467	15.3	3.2

Table B-2. States — Education, Labor Force, and Income

STATE	Children under 18 years in families				Children under 6 years in families				Children 6 to 7 years in families			
	Number	Percent living with two parents, both in the labor force	Percent living with two parents, father only in the labor force	Percent living with one parent, who is in the labor force	Number	Percent living with two parents, both in the labor force	Percent living with two parents, father only in the labor force	Percent living with one parent, who is in the labor force	Number	Percent living with two parents, both in the labor force	Percent living with two parents, father only in the labor force	Percent living with one parent, who is in the labor force
	143	144	145	146	147	148	149	150	151	152	153	154
UNITED STATES....	67 882 626	43.2	21.9	21.4	21 833 613	38.5	27.5	20.1	46 049 013	45.5	19.3	22.0
ALABAMA	1 049 873	40.4	21.4	22.9	336 150	36.1	26.5	22.3	713 723	42.4	18.9	23.2
ALASKA	180 009	45.4	21.4	20.7	54 369	38.8	27.8	20.9	125 640	48.3	18.6	20.6
ARIZONA	1 270 112	37.6	24.8	22.1	429 041	32.6	30.2	20.8	841 071	40.1	22.0	22.8
ARKANSAS	633 653	43.1	20.2	22.3	206 090	38.1	25.5	22.0	427 563	45.6	17.6	22.4
CALIFORNIA	8 565 858	37.1	24.3	20.1	2 782 416	33.5	29.0	18.3	5 783 442	38.8	22.0	20.9
COLORADO	1 043 072	47.2	22.9	19.6	339 553	41.4	29.9	17.5	703 519	50.1	19.5	20.6
CONNECTICUT	802 658	48.0	21.2	20.7	258 382	43.1	27.9	18.8	544 276	50.3	18.0	21.6
DELAWARE	181 743	45.8	18.5	25.1	57 950	41.2	24.0	24.0	123 793	48.0	16.0	25.5
DISTRICT OF COLUMBIA	99 374	23.1	9.1	41.0	34 987	23.5	11.0	38.7	64 387	22.8	8.0	42.3
FLORIDA	3 383 513	40.4	20.0	24.8	1 069 643	36.9	25.1	23.4	2 313 870	42.0	17.7	25.5
GEORGIA	2 015 574	41.2	21.3	24.1	668 530	36.8	27.2	22.4	1 347 044	43.4	10.0	25.0
HAWAII	271 881	46.8	17.5	21.3	86 956	40.9	23.6	20.8	184 925	49.5	14.6	21.5
IDAHO	352 685	48.7	26.9	16.7	112 639	42.0	34.4	15.7	240 046	51.8	23.4	17.2
ILLINOIS	3 046 677	44.1	22.1	20.8	996 903	38.7	28.0	19.7	2 049 774	46.8	19.2	21.3
INDIANA	1 493 290	47.6	21.7	21.3	486 912	41.1	27.2	21.6	1 006 378	50.8	19.0	21.1
IOWA	703 382	59.1	15.3	17.9	219 439	53.7	19.6	17.7	483 943	61.5	13.3	17.9
KANSAS	680 064	51.6	20.8	18.9	217 901	45.2	27.5	17.5	462 163	54.6	17.7	19.6
KENTUCKY	939 639	43.1	21.8	19.7	305 950	39.2	26.9	19.4	633 689	45.0	19.4	19.9
LOUISIANA	1 126 561	36.3	19.8	26.7	353 949	32.5	23.2	26.6	772 612	38.1	18.2	26.8
MAINE	287 045	51.4	18.0	20.3	82 970	46.0	24.2	19.5	204 075	53.7	15.4	20.7
MARYLAND	1 267 484	46.3	18.7	24.2	402 876	42.6	24.2	22.0	864 608	48.0	16.2	25.2
MASSACHUSETTS	1 434 842	48.2	20.1	19.1	461 589	44.6	26.9	16.2	973 253	49.9	16.9	20.4
MICHIGAN	2 456 837	44.2	21.9	22.8	775 738	38.6	27.8	22.3	1 681 099	46.8	19.2	23.1
MINNESOTA	1 239 179	57.3	16.9	17.7	384 991	52.2	22.6	16.6	854 188	59.6	14.4	18.2
MISSISSIPPI	711 441	37.3	17.2	27.7	226 744	33.5	20.6	28.2	484 697	39.1	15.0	27.5
MISSOURI	1 350 334	47.2	19.4	22.5	426 489	42.6	24.7	21.7	923 845	49.3	17.0	22.9
MONTANA	218 232	51.2	18.9	20.4	63 486	45.2	25.0	19.7	154 746	53.6	16.4	20.7
NEBRASKA	430 210	56.7	16.7	18.3	135 904	52.0	21.3	17.8	294 000	58.6	14.6	19.6
NEVADA	475 371	39.6	21.8	23.9	164 695	34.7	27.0	22.6	310 676	42.2	19.1	24.5
NEW HAMPSHIRE	297 516	53.7	20.7	18.4	88 817	48.1	28.1	15.8	208 699	56.0	17.6	19.5
NEW JERSEY	1 981 051	44.4	24.6	18.6	647 086	39.7	31.4	16.3	1 333 965	46.7	21.3	19.8
NEW MEXICO	475 039	36.6	21.7	24.4	147 072	31.1	26.1	24.3	327 967	39.1	19.7	24.4
NEW YORK	4 383 249	38.9	22.1	21.7	1 405 240	34.7	28.1	19.7	2 978 009	40.9	19.3	22.7
NORTH CAROLINA	1 837 327	44.2	20.5	23.1	613 366	39.3	26.5	21.9	1 223 961	46.6	17.5	23.8
NORTH DAKOTA	155 201	60.2	14.0	17.0	46 413	54.9	18.6	17.7	108 788	62.4	13.3	16.6
OHIO	2 744 090	45.8	21.2	22.3	869 999	40.3	26.4	21.8	1 874 091	48.3	18.7	22.6
OKLAHOMA	832 936	42.9	23.1	21.9	267 950	37.3	29.1	21.0	564 986	45.6	20.2	22.3
OREGON	796 563	45.7	23.8	20.7	254 587	39.5	30.1	19.4	541 976	48.6	20.8	21.3
PENNSYLVANIA	2 774 571	45.4	22.7	20.7	845 915	40.2	28.2	19.9	1 928 656	47.7	20.3	21.1
RHODE ISLAND	237 201	46.6	17.0	21.0	74 194	41.6	22.4	20.1	163 007	48.9	14.5	21.4
SOUTH CAROLINA	937 333	41.4	18.6	25.8	297 176	37.8	23.3	24.8	640 157	43.1	16.5	26.3
SOUTH DAKOTA	191 501	57.8	13.4	19.5	58 823	52.5	17.4	20.5	132 678	60.2	11.7	19.0
TENNESSEE	1 308 500	42.6	21.4	22.9	425 940	38.1	26.8	21.9	882 659	44.8	18.9	23.4
TEXAS	5 503 509	39.0	25.2	20.6	1 827 869	34.1	30.6	19.2	3 675 640	41.4	22.5	21.3
UTAH	689 581	46.5	32.9	13.2	241 072	40.6	39.6	11.8	448 509	49.7	29.3	14.0
VERMONT	141 993	55.5	16.1	19.9	40 561	50.5	22.3	17.6	101 432	57.4	13.6	20.8
VIRGINIA	1 639 504	46.4	21.4	21.5	531 130	42.4	27.1	19.8	1 108 374	48.3	18.7	22.3
WASHINGTON	1 433 592	45.0	24.2	20.1	454 165	39.1	31.4	18.5	979 427	47.8	20.9	20.9
WEST VIRGINIA	380 926	39.5	25.1	18.6	118 161	35.8	30.0	18.4	262 765	41.2	22.8	18.7
WISCONSIN	1 308 767	55.0	16.5	19.4	399 076	49.6	21.9	18.8	909 691	57.4	14.2	19.7
WYOMING	121 984	51.3	21.3	20.1	35 759	43.5	28.4	20.3	86 225	54.5	18.4	20.0

STATE	Total families	Total married-couple families	Employment status of family householders — Percent of married-couple families with both in the labor force	Employment status of family householders — +/− U.S. percent of couples with both employed	Total other families	Percent of other family householders in labor force	Women 16 years and over by presence of children and employment status — Total women 16 years and over	Women 16 years and over by presence of children and employment status — Percent with children under 18 years	Women 16 years and over by presence of children and employment status — Percent with children under 18 years and in the labor force
	155	156	157	158	159	160	161	162	163
UNITED STATES....	72 261 780	55 458 451	51.3	0.0	16 803 329	68.7	112 185 795	31.1	21.5
ALABAMA	1 223 185	921 298	48.1	-3.4	301 887	61.7	1 816 176	31.5	21.3
ALASKA	153 611	118 332	57.0	5.0	35 279	75.6	220 694	38.5	27.4
ARIZONA	1 296 593	1 005 901	44.8	-6.3	290 692	71.3	1 977 757	30.8	19.8
ARKANSAS.............	736 063	574 619	48.8	-2.4	161 444	66.2	1 077 083	31.0	21.8
CALIFORNIA............	7 985 489	5 995 225	47.2	-4.5	1 990 264	68.3	12 998 409	32.5	20.3
COLORADO.............	1 092 352	875 669	56.9	5.8	216 683	76.5	1 661 660	32.5	23.0
CONNECTICUT	885 747	686 713	55.6	4.6	199 034	70.1	1 390 047	30.5	22.2
DELAWARE	205 775	156 351	54.2	3.2	49 424	71.6	319 154	29.8	22.3
DISTRICT OF COLUMBIA	115 963	58 050	51.1	-0.6	57 913	59.2	252 087	21.2	14.4
FLORIDA.................	4 238 409	3 242 027	44.2	-7.0	996 382	68.8	6 615 066	27.1	18.8
GEORGIA................	2 126 360	1 579 407	53.6	2.3	546 953	68.9	3 218 245	33.3	23.1
HAWAII..................	289 012	220 144	51.7	0.2	68 868	63.5	476 513	29.4	21.3
IDAHO...................	337 884	280 206	52.9	1.6	57 678	77.4	488 294	34.4	24.0
ILLINOIS.................	3 125 318	2 396 891	53.0	1.8	728 427	68.8	4 934 988	31.4	21.8
INDIANA.................	1 611 045	1 272 826	54.7	3.6	338 219	73.3	2 419 161	31.4	22.9
IOWA.....................	774 246	643 097	59.9	9.1	131 149	75.6	1 176 877	30.0	24.2
KANSAS.................	706 786	578 340	57.3	6.3	128 446	76.3	1 054 952	32.2	24.0
KENTUCKY.............	1 110 426	870 930	48.4	-2.9	239 496	63.0	1 638 529	31.5	21.4
LOUISIANA	1 163 191	822 374	47.1	-4.3	340 817	63.3	1 782 645	32.8	22.1
MAINE	342 431	276 856	55.3	4.2	65 575	71.5	525 690	28.7	21.9
MARYLAND	1 368 647	1 015 033	57.5	6.5	353 614	72.2	2 150 812	31.5	23.5
MASSACHUSETTS ...	1 587 537	1 221 127	55.9	4.9	366 410	66.2	2 640 235	28.7	20.6
MICHIGAN	2 591 312	1 980 112	51.2	0.1	611 200	69.9	3 943 137	31.3	22.3
MINNESOTA	1 262 953	1 035 612	61.8	11.0	227 341	77.8	1 931 097	31.8	25.2
MISSISSIPPI	752 234	529 852	49.2	-2.5	222 382	61.8	1 135 691	33.0	22.9
MISSOURI................	1 486 546	1 157 550	53.7	2.7	328 996	71.3	2 260 089	30.8	22.7
MONTANA	238 733	194 207	54.2	3.1	44 526	75.2	355 066	30.4	23.1
NEBRASKA..............	446 551	365 981	61.3	10.5	80 570	76.8	675 106	31.7	25.0
NEVADA.................	502 508	380 469	48.6	-3.1	122 039	74.9	758 472	31.1	21.1
NEW HAMPSHIRE.....	325 581	266 624	60.1	9.3	58 957	76.0	493 436	31.2	23.7
NEW JERSEY..........	2 167 577	1 668 616	51.7	0.3	498 961	66.5	3 425 212	30.7	20.7
NEW MEXICO...........	468 899	346 478	45.8	-5.8	122 421	67.2	706 081	33.0	21.6
NEW YORK..............	4 673 485	3 359 150	48.6	-2.8	1 314 335	62.6	7 810 436	29.3	19.2
NORTH CAROLINA ...	2 173 346	1 672 543	53.4	2.2	500 803	69.0	3 251 605	30.9	22.1
NORTH DAKOTA......	166 963	139 203	59.5	8.8	27 760	75.8	253 623	30.6	24.9
OHIO	3 007 207	2 319 012	52.8	1.8	688 195	69.4	4 591 821	30.6	22.1
OKLAHOMA	927 703	729 743	49.5	-1.7	197 960	70.2	1 373 766	31.5	21.7
OREGON	884 875	707 602	51.4	-0.1	177 273	74.7	1 361 822	29.7	21.0
PENNSYLVANIA........	3 225 707	2 504 664	50.8	-0.3	721 043	65.4	5 094 133	28.1	19.9
RHODE ISLAND	266 655	200 729	54.7	3.3	65 926	64.2	438 755	28.5	20.6
SOUTH CAROLINA ...	1 078 736	797 922	51.4	0.1	280 814	66.0	1 626 362	31.0	22.2
SOUTH DAKOTA.......	195 455	159 559	61.5	10.7	35 896	76.0	293 889	31.4	25.7
TENNESSEE.............	1 557 620	1 194 205	51.0	-0.4	363 415	66.4	2 315 733	30.9	21.5
TEXAS...................	5 283 474	4 068 697	49.0	-2.5	1 214 777	69.9	7 960 900	35.2	22.6
UTAH.....................	539 728	450 765	53.4	2.2	88 963	75.7	807 196	38.0	24.7
VERMONT	158 684	128 731	61.1	10.2	29 953	73.8	247 284	29.7	23.4
VIRGINIA.................	1 859 983	1 449 217	55.3	4.3	410 766	70.7	2 854 288	31.3	22.6
WASHINGTON..........	1 509 395	1 201 324	52.2	0.6	308 071	75.4	2 310 313	31.6	22.0
WEST VIRGINIA	507 255	402 781	40.7	-10.5	104 474	57.4	757 134	28.0	17.7
WISCONSIN.............	1 395 037	1 127 613	59.5	8.6	267 424	74.6	2 127 011	30.6	24.1
WYOMING	131 508	108 074	56.1	4.8	23 434	78.9	191 263	32.1	23.9

Table B-2. States — Education, Labor Force, and Income

STATE	Total employed civilian population 16 years and over	Class of worker for employed civilians 16 years and over					
		Percent private wage and salary workers	Percent government workers	Percent self-employed workers, including incorporated business owners	Percent unpaid family workers	Percent who worked at home	+/− U.S. percent worked at home
	164	165	166	167	168	169	170
UNITED STATES....	129 721 512	75.3	14.6	9.8	0.3	3.3	0.0
ALABAMA	1 920 189	75.0	15.5	9.2	0.3	2.1	-1.2
ALASKA	281 532	62.4	26.8	10.6	0.3	4.1	0.8
ARIZONA	2 233 004	74.6	15.2	9.9	0.3	3.7	0.4
ARKANSAS..............	1 173 399	73.6	14.9	11.1	0.4	2.6	-0.7
CALIFORNIA............	14 718 928	73.7	14.7	11.2	0.4	3.8	0.5
COLORADO.............	2 205 194	73.7	13.9	12.0	0.3	4.9	1.6
CONNECTICUT	1 664 440	76.7	13.3	9.8	0.2	3.1	-0.2
DELAWARE	376 811	77.7	13.8	8.3	0.2	3.0	-0.3
DISTRICT OF COLUMBIA.............	263 108	66.7	25.9	7.3	0.1	3.8	0.5
FLORIDA.................	6 995 047	74.8	13.7	11.1	0.3	3.0	-0.3
GEORGIA...............	3 839 756	75.3	14.9	9.5	0.3	2.8	-0.5
HAWAII..................	537 909	67.8	21.0	10.8	0.4	3.6	0.3
IDAHO...................	599 453	70.0	16.4	13.2	0.5	4.7	1.4
ILLINOIS.................	5 833 185	78.6	12.7	8.4	0.3	3.1	-0.2
INDIANA.................	2 965 174	80.6	10.9	8.2	0.3	2.9	-0.4
IOWA....................	1 489 816	74.8	13.6	11.1	0.4	4.7	1.4
KANSAS.................	1 316 283	73.3	15.5	10.8	0.4	4.0	0.7
KENTUCKY.............	1 798 264	75.5	14.4	9.6	0.4	2.7	-0.6
LOUISIANA.............	1 851 777	72.8	17.4	9.4	0.3	2.1	-1.2
MAINE	624 011	72.8	14.5	12.4	0.3	4.4	1.1
MARYLAND.............	2 608 457	68.9	22.3	8.5	0.2	3.3	0.0
MASSACHUSETTS ...	3 161 087	77.3	13.5	9.0	0.2	3.1	-0.2
MICHIGAN	4 637 461	79.9	11.4	8.4	0.3	2.8	-0.5
MINNESOTA............	2 580 046	77.1	12.4	10.2	0.3	4.6	1.3
MISSISSIPPI...........	1 173 314	72.7	17.6	9.3	0.4	1.9	-1.4
MISSOURI..............	2 657 924	77.2	12.8	9.7	0.4	3.5	0.2
MONTANA	425 977	64.3	18.3	16.7	0.7	6.4	3.1
NEBRASKA.............	877 237	73.7	13.7	12.1	0.5	4.6	1.3
NEVADA.................	933 280	79.6	12.5	7.7	0.3	2.6	-0.7
NEW HAMPSHIRE.....	650 871	76.5	12.8	10.5	0.2	4.0	0.7
NEW JERSEY..........	3 950 029	77.1	13.9	8.8	0.2	2.7	-0.6
NEW MEXICO...........	763 116	65.1	22.7	11.8	0.4	4.2	0.9
NEW YORK.............	8 382 988	73.4	17.0	9.4	0.2	3.0	-0.3
NORTH CAROLINA ...	3 824 741	75.6	14.5	9.6	0.3	2.7	-0.6
NORTH DAKOTA......	316 632	69.1	16.5	13.9	0.6	6.0	2.7
OHIO....................	5 402 175	79.5	12.2	8.0	0.3	2.8	-0.5
OKLAHOMA	1 545 296	71.3	16.8	11.4	0.5	3.1	-0.2
OREGON................	1 627 769	72.5	14.4	12.7	0.4	5.0	1.7
PENNSYLVANIA.......	5 653 500	80.0	11.3	8.4	0.3	3.0	-0.3
RHODE ISLAND	500 731	77.3	13.8	8.7	0.2	2.2	-1.1
SOUTH CAROLINA ...	1 824 700	75.0	15.9	8.8	0.3	2.1	-1.2
SOUTH DAKOTA.......	374 373	69.2	15.3	14.7	0.8	6.5	3.2
TENNESSEE............	2 651 638	76.2	13.9	9.6	0.3	2.6	-0.7
TEXAS..................	9 234 372	75.3	14.6	9.8	0.3	2.8	-0.5
UTAH....................	1 044 362	74.3	15.7	9.7	0.3	4.2	0.9
VERMONT	317 134	71.5	14.2	14.1	0.3	5.7	2.4
VIRGINIA................	3 412 647	71.6	19.6	8.6	0.2	3.2	-0.1
WASHINGTON..........	2 793 722	72.8	16.5	10.4	0.3	4.3	1.0
WEST VIRGINIA.......	732 673	73.5	17.9	8.2	0.4	2.4	-0.9
WISCONSIN.............	2 734 925	78.2	12.5	9.0	0.3	3.9	0.6
WYOMING	241 055	66.1	20.4	13.0	0.5	4.3	1.0

Items 164—170

STATE	Employed civilian population 16 years and over	Percent management, professional, and related occupations	Percent service occupations	Percent sales and office occupations	Percent farming, fishing, and forestry occupations	Percent construction, extraction, and maintenance occupations	Percent production, transportation, and material moving occupations
	171	172	173	174	175	176	177
UNITED STATES....	129 721 512	33.6	14.9	26.7	0.7	9.4	14.6
ALABAMA	1 920 189	29.5	13.5	25.9	0.8	11.3	19.0
ALASKA	281 532	34.4	15.6	26.1	1.5	11.6	10.8
ARIZONA	2 233 004	32.7	16.2	28.5	0.6	11.0	10.9
ARKANSAS...............	1 173 399	27.7	14.1	25.1	1.5	10.6	21.0
CALIFORNIA..............	14 718 928	36.0	14.8	26.8	1.3	8.4	12.7
COLORADO...............	2 205 194	37.4	13.9	27.2	0.6	10.5	10.5
CONNECTICUT	1 664 440	39.1	14.3	26.5	0.2	8.0	12.0
DELAWARE	376 811	35.3	14.6	27.6	0.5	9.5	12.5
DISTRICT OF COLUMBIA.............	263 108	51.1	16.1	22.8	0.1	4.8	5.2
FLORIDA....................	6 995 047	31.5	16.9	29.5	0.9	10.3	10.8
GEORGIA..................	3 839 756	32.7	13.4	26.8	0.6	10.8	15.7
HAWAII.....................	537 909	32.2	20.9	28.1	1.3	8.6	8.9
IDAHO......................	599 453	31.4	15.6	25.3	2.7	10.8	14.2
ILLINOIS...................	5 833 185	34.2	13.9	27.6	0.3	8.2	15.7
INDIANA...................	2 965 174	28.7	14.2	25.3	0.4	10.0	21.4
IOWA.......................	1 489 816	31.3	14.8	25.9	1.1	8.9	18.1
KANSAS...................	1 316 283	33.9	14.4	25.8	1.0	9.9	15.0
KENTUCKY...............	1 798 264	28.7	14.3	25.4	0.9	11.0	19.7
LOUISIANA	1 851 777	29.9	16.7	26.8	0.8	11.7	14.1
MAINE	624 011	31.5	15.3	25.9	1.7	10.3	15.3
MARYLAND...............	2 608 457	41.3	13.9	26.4	0.3	8.6	9.5
MASSACHUSETTS ...	3 161 087	41.1	14.1	25.9	0.2	7.5	11.3
MICHIGAN	4 637 461	31.5	14.8	25.6	0.5	9.2	18.5
MINNESOTA.............	2 580 046	35.8	13.7	26.5	0.7	8.4	14.9
MISSISSIPPI.............	1 173 314	27.4	14.9	24.9	1.2	11.2	20.4
MISSOURI................	2 657 924	31.5	15.0	26.9	0.6	9.8	16.3
MONTANA	425 977	33.1	17.2	25.5	2.2	10.7	11.2
NEBRASKA..............	877 237	33.0	14.6	26.4	1.6	9.3	15.1
NEVADA..................	933 280	25.7	24.6	27.6	0.3	11.4	10.4
NEW HAMPSHIRE.....	650 871	35.8	13.0	26.6	0.4	9.4	14.8
NEW JERSEY...........	3 950 029	38.0	13.6	28.5	0.2	7.8	12.0
NEW MEXICO...........	763 116	34.0	17.0	25.9	1.0	11.4	10.7
NEW YORK...............	8 382 988	36.7	16.6	27.1	0.3	7.6	11.7
NORTH CAROLINA ...	3 824 741	31.2	13.5	24.8	0.8	11.0	18.7
NORTH DAKOTA......	316 632	33.3	16.7	26.1	1.7	9.8	12.4
OHIO........................	5 402 175	31.0	14.6	26.4	0.3	8.7	19.0
OKLAHOMA..............	1 545 296	30.3	15.5	26.6	0.9	11.3	15.4
OREGON	1 627 769	33.1	15.3	26.1	1.7	9.1	14.7
PENNSYLVANIA........	5 653 500	32.6	14.8	27.0	0.5	8.9	16.3
RHODE ISLAND	500 731	33.9	15.7	27.1	0.3	7.7	15.2
SOUTH CAROLINA ...	1 824 700	29.1	14.7	25.2	0.6	11.5	19.0
SOUTH DAKOTA.......	374 373	32.6	15.6	26.5	1.9	9.1	14.2
TENNESSEE.............	2 651 638	29.5	13.7	26.1	0.6	10.3	19.9
TEXAS......................	9 234 372	33.3	14.6	27.2	0.7	10.9	13.2
UTAH.......................	1 044 362	32.5	14.0	28.9	0.5	10.6	13.5
VERMONT	317 134	36.3	14.6	24.5	1.3	9.3	14.0
VIRGINIA..................	3 412 647	38.2	13.7	25.5	0.5	9.6	12.5
WASHINGTON..........	2 793 722	35.6	14.9	25.9	1.6	9.4	12.7
WEST VIRGINIA	732 673	27.9	16.6	26.1	0.7	12.3	16.4
WISCONSIN..............	2 734 925	31.3	14.0	25.2	0.9	8.7	19.8
WYOMING	241 055	30.0	16.7	24.2	1.5	14.8	12.8

STATE	Number of employed civilian population 16 years and over	Industry for employed population 16 years and over (percent, except where noted)												
		Agriculture, forestry, fishing and hunting, mining	Construc-tion	Manufac-turing	Whole-sale trade	Retail trade	Transpor-tation and ware-housing, and utilities	Information	Finance, insurance, real estate, rental and leasing	Professional, scientific, management, adminis-trative, and waste management services	Educational, health, and social services	Arts, enter-tainment, recreation, accom-modation, and food services	Other services (except public adminis-tration)	Public adminis-tration
	178	179	180	181	182	183	184	185	186	187	188	189	190	191
UNITED STATES....	129 721 512	1.9	6.8	14.1	3.6	11.7	5.2	3.1	6.9	9.3	19.9	7.9	4.9	4.8
ALABAMA	1 920 189	1.9	7.6	18.4	3.6	12.2	5.3	2.2	5.8	7.1	19.3	6.4	5.1	5.2
ALASKA	281 532	4.9	7.3	3.3	2.6	11.6	8.9	2.7	4.6	7.6	21.7	8.6	5.6	10.7
ARIZONA	2 233 004	1.5	8.7	10.2	3.3	12.3	5.0	2.8	7.9	10.3	18.0	10.1	4.6	5.4
ARKANSAS	1 173 399	3.7	7.0	19.4	3.3	13.0	5.9	2.2	4.8	5.4	19.6	6.3	5.0	4.3
CALIFORNIA............	14 718 928	1.9	6.2	13.1	4.1	11.2	4.7	3.9	6.9	11.6	18.5	8.2	5.2	4.5
COLORADO..............	2 205 194	2.0	9.1	9.1	3.5	11.8	4.9	4.9	7.7	11.7	17.0	9.0	4.8	4.6
CONNECTICUT	1 664 440	0.4	6.0	14.8	3.2	11.2	3.9	3.3	9.8	10.1	22.0	6.7	4.5	4.0
DELAWARE	376 811	1.1	7.4	13.2	2.8	11.6	4.8	1.9	11.6	9.3	19.4	7.7	4.2	5.2
DISTRICT OF COLUMBIA............	263 108	0.1	3.9	1.5	0.9	6.0	3.6	6.4	7.4	18.8	18.0	9.1	9.3	15.0
FLORIDA.................	6 995 047	1.3	8.0	7.3	4.0	13.5	5.3	3.1	8.1	10.6	18.1	10.5	5.1	5.2
GEORGIA.................	3 839 756	1.4	7.9	14.8	3.9	12.0	6.0	3.5	6.5	9.4	17.6	7.1	4.7	5.0
HAWAII....................	537 909	2.3	6.0	3.5	3.2	12.2	6.2	2.5	7.0	9.5	19.0	16.0	4.4	8.1
IDAHO......................	599 453	5.8	8.1	13.1	3.6	12.6	4.7	2.3	5.1	8.0	19.2	8.0	4.5	5.1
ILLINOIS..................	5 833 185	1.1	5.7	16.0	3.8	11.0	6.0	3.0	7.9	10.1	19.4	7.2	4.7	4.0
INDIANA..................	2 965 174	1.4	6.6	22.9	3.4	11.8	5.2	2.1	5.7	6.3	19.3	7.3	4.7	3.3
IOWA.......................	1 489 816	4.4	6.2	17.0	3.6	12.0	4.9	2.8	6.7	6.1	21.8	6.6	4.4	3.4
KANSAS...................	1 316 283	3.8	6.5	15.0	3.3	11.5	5.2	3.3	6.1	7.2	21.9	7.0	4.6	4.4
KENTUCKY..............	1 798 264	3.3	7.2	17.6	3.4	12.1	6.0	2.2	5.4	6.2	20.3	7.2	4.7	4.3
LOUISIANA..............	1 851 777	4.2	7.9	10.1	3.5	11.9	5.3	2.0	5.7	7.6	21.7	9.1	5.2	5.8
MAINE.....................	624 011	2.6	6.9	14.2	3.4	13.5	4.3	2.5	6.2	6.9	23.2	7.1	4.7	4.5
MARYLAND	2 608 457	0.6	6.9	7.3	2.8	10.5	4.9	4.0	7.1	12.4	20.6	6.8	5.6	10.5
MASSACHUSETTS ...	3 161 087	0.4	5.5	12.8	3.3	11.2	4.2	3.7	8.2	11.6	23.7	6.8	4.4	4.3
MICHIGAN	4 637 461	1.1	6.0	22.5	3.3	11.9	4.1	2.1	5.3	8.0	19.9	7.6	4.6	3.6
MINNESOTA.............	2 580 046	2.6	5.9	16.3	3.6	11.9	5.1	2.5	7.2	8.8	20.9	7.2	4.6	3.4
MISSISSIPPI.............	1 173 314	3.4	7.6	18.3	3.4	11.8	5.4	1.8	4.8	5.2	20.1	8.3	4.8	5.1
MISSOURI................	2 657 924	2.2	6.9	14.8	3.7	11.9	5.7	3.0	6.7	7.5	20.4	7.8	5.0	4.6
MONTANA................	425 977	7.9	7.4	6.0	3.0	12.8	5.4	2.2	5.5	6.5	21.7	10.4	5.3	5.9
NEBRASKA..............	877 237	5.6	6.5	12.2	3.6	12.1	6.1	2.5	7.7	7.3	20.7	7.3	4.6	3.9
NEVADA..................	933 200	1.0	9.2	4.8	2.7	11.3	5.2	2.2	6.5	8.8	12.9	26.3	3.9	4.5
NEW HAMPSHIRE.....	650 871	0.9	6.8	18.1	3.6	13.7	4.1	2.7	6.3	8.8	20.0	6.9	4.3	3.8
NEW JERSEY...........	3 950 029	0.3	5.6	12.0	4.4	11.3	5.9	4.4	8.9	11.5	19.8	6.9	4.4	4.5
NEW MEXICO...........	763 116	4.0	7.9	6.5	2.7	12.2	4.7	2.4	5.5	9.4	21.7	9.8	5.1	8.0
NEW YORK...............	8 382 988	0.6	5.2	10.0	3.4	10.5	5.5	4.1	8.8	10.1	24.3	7.3	5.1	5.2
NORTH CAROLINA ...	3 824 741	1.6	8.2	19.7	3.4	11.5	4.6	2.3	6.0	7.7	19.2	6.9	4.6	4.1
NORTH DAKOTA......	316 632	8.2	6.2	7.1	3.7	12.7	5.7	2.3	5.9	6.0	24.2	8.2	4.0	4.8
OHIO	5 402 175	1.1	6.0	20.0	3.6	11.9	4.9	2.4	6.3	8.0	19.7	7.5	4.5	4.1
OKLAHOMA..............	1 545 296	4.1	6.9	12.5	3.4	12.0	5.6	2.7	6.0	7.3	20.5	7.5	5.6	5.9
OREGON	1 627 769	3.2	6.9	14.4	4.1	12.5	4.7	2.4	6.1	8.9	19.3	8.2	4.9	4.4
PENNSYLVANIA........	5 653 500	1.3	6.0	16.0	3.6	12.1	5.4	2.6	6.6	8.5	21.9	7.0	4.8	4.2
RHODE ISLAND	500 731	0.5	5.4	16.4	3.4	12.1	3.9	2.3	6.9	8.3	23.0	8.6	4.7	4.5
SOUTH CAROLINA ...	1 824 700	1.1	8.3	19.4	3.3	11.9	5.0	2.1	5.6	6.9	18.6	8.3	4.7	4.7
SOUTH DAKOTA.......	374 373	8.1	6.3	11.1	3.3	12.0	4.7	2.1	7.4	5.0	22.0	8.3	5.1	4.8
TENNESSEE.............	2 651 638	1.4	7.3	18.9	3.8	11.8	6.3	2.4	5.8	7.4	18.6	7.5	4.8	4.0
TEXAS.....................	9 234 372	2.7	8.1	11.8	3.9	12.0	5.8	3.1	6.8	9.5	19.3	7.3	5.2	4.5
UTAH.......................	1 044 362	1.9	8.2	12.1	3.5	12.8	4.9	3.3	6.8	9.4	19.2	8.0	4.4	5.5
VERMONT	317 134	3.0	6.7	15.1	3.1	12.0	3.7	2.7	4.7	7.1	24.1	8.6	4.7	4.6
VIRGINIA.................	3 412 647	1.3	7.3	11.3	2.7	11.4	4.6	3.8	6.6	11.6	18.3	7.2	5.4	8.3
WASHINGTON..........	2 793 722	2.5	7.0	12.5	4.1	12.1	5.4	3.4	6.1	9.8	19.4	7.9	4.8	5.0
WEST VIRGINIA........	732 673	4.1	7.0	11.9	2.8	13.1	6.0	2.2	4.6	6.7	23.0	8.0	5.0	5.8
WISCONSIN.............	2 734 925	2.8	5.9	22.2	3.2	11.6	4.5	2.2	6.1	6.6	20.0	7.3	4.1	3.5
WYOMING	241 055	10.7	8.7	4.9	2.3	11.8	6.6	2.2	4.7	5.9	21.5	9.6	4.9	6.3

| STATE | Percent of the population 5 years and over with a disability | Veteran status | | | Median household income | +/− U.S. median income |
| | | Total population 18 years and over | Veterans 18 years and over (percent) | Veterans 18 to 64 years (percent) | Veterans 65 years and over (percent) | | |
	192	193	194	195	196	197	198
UNITED STATES....	19.3	209 279 149	12.6	9.6	27.6	41 994	0
ALABAMA	23.2	3 324 488	13.5	10.6	26.9	34 135	-7 859
ALASKA	14.9	436 425	16.4	14.9	33.8	51 571	9 577
ARIZONA	19.3	3 767 931	14.9	11.1	32.9	40 558	-1 436
ARKANSAS..............	23.6	1 993 342	14.1	11.0	27.5	32 182	-9 812
CALIFORNIA............	19.2	24 650 185	10.4	7.7	26.5	47 493	5 499
COLORADO..............	16.3	3 204 471	13.9	11.3	31.5	47 203	5 209
CONNECTICUT	17.5	2 565 991	12.1	8.5	28.1	53 935	11 941
DELAWARE	18.4	589 638	14.3	11.1	29.4	47 381	5 387
DISTRICT OF COLUMBIA............	21.9	457 727	9.7	6.8	25.9	40 127	-1 867
FLORIDA..................	22.2	12 347 806	15.2	11.0	29.4	38 819	-3 175
GEORGIA.................	19.7	6 020 679	12.8	10.7	26.4	42 433	439
HAWAII....................	18.4	917 212	13.1	10.6	25.3	49 820	7 826
IDAHO	17.1	925 822	14.8	11.7	31.2	37 572	-4 422
ILLINOIS...................	17.6	9 180 064	10.9	8.0	26.1	46 590	4 596
INDIANA..................	19.0	4 507 679	13.1	10.2	27.4	41 567	-427
IOWA......................	16.6	2 193 990	13.3	10.0	26.5	39 469	-2 525
KANSAS..................	17.6	1 977 198	13.5	10.4	27.8	40 624	-1 370
KENTUCKY..............	23.7	3 047 928	12.5	9.8	26.2	33 672	-8 322
LOUISIANA..............	21.8	3 250 523	12.1	9.4	26.4	32 566	-9 428
MAINE	20.0	973 945	15.9	12.5	30.2	37 240	-4 754
MARYLAND..............	17.6	3 943 067	13.3	10.6	28.5	52 868	10 874
MASSACHUSETTS ...	18.5	4 853 130	11.5	7.9	28.1	50 502	8 508
MICHIGAN	18.7	7 345 849	12.4	9.5	27.3	44 667	2 673
MINNESOTA.............	15.0	3 632 940	12.8	9.8	28.4	47 111	5 117
MISSISSIPPI............	23.6	2 070 254	12.0	9.3	25.7	31 330	-10 664
MISSOURI................	19.0	4 169 109	14.2	11.0	28.8	37 934	-4 060
MONTANA................	17.5	672 251	16.1	12.9	31.1	33 024	-8 970
NEBRASKA..............	16.0	1 261 648	13.7	10.6	27.6	39 250	-2 744
NEVADA..................	20.6	1 488 526	16.0	12.7	35.4	44 581	2 587
NEW HAMPSHIRE.....	16.9	926 885	15.0	11.8	32.0	49 467	7 473
NEW JERSEY...........	18.0	6 332 876	10.6	7.2	26.6	55 146	13 152
NEW MEXICO...........	20.4	1 311 478	14.5	11.4	30.8	34 133	-7 861
NEW YORK...............	20.6	14 302 266	9.5	6.6	23.6	43 393	1 399
NORTH CAROLINA ...	21.1	6 087 996	13.0	10.4	26.8	39 184	-2 810
NORTH DAKOTA......	16.7	481 301	12.7	10.2	23.2	34 604	-7 390
OHIO......................	18.3	8 467 999	13.5	10.4	28.1	40 956	-1 038
OKLAHOMA.............	21.6	2 560 390	14.7	11.6	28.8	33 400	-8 594
OREGON	18.8	2 577 129	15.1	11.8	31.1	40 916	-1 078
PENNSYLVANIA.......	18.6	9 362 066	13.7	9.9	28.4	40 106	-1 888
RHODE ISLAND	20.2	800 810	12.8	9.2	28.1	42 090	96
SOUTH CAROLINA ...	22.2	3 002 919	14.0	11.4	27.6	37 082	-4 912
SOUTH DAKOTA......	16.7	552 118	14.4	11.2	27.4	35 282	-6 712
TENNESSEE............	22.0	4 292 047	13.1	10.5	26.0	36 360	-5 634
TEXAS....................	19.2	14 977 890	11.7	9.2	27.5	39 927	-2 067
UTAH......................	14.9	1 516 338	10.6	7.6	31.6	45 726	3 732
VERMONT	17.1	461 248	13.6	10.6	28.8	40 856	-1 138
VIRGINIA.................	18.1	5 342 691	14.7	12.3	28.7	46 677	4 683
WASHINGTON..........	18.2	4 384 341	15.3	12.5	30.8	45 776	3 782
WEST VIRGINIA.......	24.4	1 406 569	14.3	11.1	27.7	29 696	-12 298
WISCONSIN.............	16.0	3 996 289	12.9	9.8	27.1	43 791	1 797
WYOMING	17.1	365 685	15.8	12.9	31.3	37 892	-4 102

STATE	Median household income by age of householder							Median family income by family type						
	Under 25 years	25 to 34 years	35 to 44 years	45 to 54 years	55 to 64 years	65 to 74 years	75 years and over	All families	Married-couple families with children	Married-couple families without children	Male family householder with children	Male family householder without children	Female family householder with children	Female family householder without children
	199	200	201	202	203	204	205	206	207	208	209	210	211	212
UNITED STATES...	22 679	41 414	50 654	56 300	47 447	31 368	22 259	50 046	59 461	55 644	29 907	42 078	20 284	35 230
ALABAMA	16 907	34 473	42 035	46 705	37 934	25 676	17 729	41 657	51 129	47 996	26 284	33 994	15 403	25 967
ALASKA	27 595	44 378	55 401	66 008	59 296	40 906	32 033	59 036	65 353	71 155	35 386	49 878	25 203	42 827
ARIZONA	23 844	40 042	48 518	52 470	45 607	33 437	25 841	46 723	53 815	52 798	28 171	39 193	21 517	34 309
ARKANSAS	19 447	33 094	39 149	42 699	35 699	25 757	17 903	38 663	46 222	42 561	23 707	32 124	15 497	26 252
CALIFORNIA	24 742	44 424	54 365	61 312	55 742	37 000	27 081	53 025	60 318	64 760	31 161	.45 136	22 200	39 657
COLORADO	26 037	45 635	55 597	60 649	52 249	34 493	24 707	55 883	63 532	61 702	33 223	45 387	24 551	39 580
CONNECTICUT	26 572	51 273	64 150	72 370	63 667	38 282	24 415	65 521	78 589	71 466	36 199	55 102	24 626	45 554
DELAWARE	26 309	46 460	55 974	62 308	51 965	35 091	24 584	55 257	67 131	60 342	31 963	48 407	23 690	41 625
DISTRICT OF COLUMBIA	20 422	39 709	44 617	52 837	48 077	32 356	28 172	46 283	73 909	78 366	27 385	41 231	19 656	38 501
FLORIDA	22 861	39 021	46 291	50 347	42 971	32 398	25 085	45 625	55 511	50 262	27 357	38 315	20 553	33 301
GEORGIA	23 271	42 097	50 720	55 327	46 056	29 366	19 760	49 280	59 178	57 175	29 371	40 130	20 011	31 563
HAWAII	22 126	41 042	52 083	62 029	62 216	46 980	35 958	56 961	61 332	66 228	30 830	51 979	21 954	47 606
IDAHO	22 064	36 307	45 313	50 176	42 835	29 591	21 084	43 490	49 381	46 538	27 714	36 902	18 494	31 191
ILLINOIS	24 427	46 057	55 877	62 053	52 275	33 419	23 363	55 545	65 628	61 212	32 231	47 067	22 200	39 194
INDIANA	23 468	41 914	50 792	56 875	46 554	29 284	20 774	50 261	59 025	53 726	30 623	43 813	20 793	35 128
IOWA	23 184	40 787	48 204	53 264	44 241	29 804	21 230	48 005	55 946	49 513	28 788	40 069	20 453	34 854
KANSAS	21 621	40 023	49 354	55 671	46 946	31 565	22 189	49 624	56 918	52 644	29 587	40 906	21 194	35 115
KENTUCKY	20 232	35 294	41 932	45 977	35 120	24 531	17 780	40 939	49 851	45 006	24 350	33 525	15 713	28 252
LOUISIANA	16 905	33 155	40 067	44 805	35 724	24 566	17 681	39 774	51 507	47 326	25 613	31 994	14 101	24 707
MAINE	22 809	37 939	45 462	49 684	39 541	26 046	18 956	45 179	53 839	47 446	27 407	37 603	17 632	32 135
MARYLAND	27 015	48 851	61 027	68 364	60 585	38 607	27 246	61 876	74 531	70 277	36 405	51 467	27 166	43 651
MASSACHUSETTS...	27 364	51 855	61 304	67 287	56 699	33 589	21 522	61 664	74 589	66 847	34 532	53 703	22 138	44 195
MICHIGAN	24 436	44 420	53 725	61 791	50 228	31 574	22 114	53 457	65 021	58 476	32 208	46 717	21 208	37 894
MINNESOTA	26 585	47 442	56 902	62 245	52 450	33 041	21 165	56 874	66 428	58 488	32 454	48 788	24 335	41 709
MISSISSIPPI	18 156	31 765	37 619	41 582	34 225	24 061	15 994	37 406	47 589	45 239	23 153	31 492	14 655	23 262
MISSOURI	21 403	37 851	46 463	51 486	42 480	28 999	20 643	46 044	55 854	49 764	28 804	39 531	19 014	30 031
MONTANA	17 446	31 708	39 007	43 373	37 311	27 865	20 312	40 487	46 202	43 814	25 095	35 456	16 203	28 207
NEBRASKA	22 771	39 271	47 436	53 195	44 595	30 765	21 400	48 032	55 343	50 228	27 526	39 612	20 480	35 991
NEVADA	20 705	40 005	50 470	54 774	40 542	34 001	20 142	50 040	57 707	56 707	32 114	45 444	21 110	40 000
NEW HAMPSHIRE ...	27 718	49 047	59 054	62 125	51 647	32 944	22 065	57 575	67 028	60 232	35 036	48 590	24 774	41 278
NEW JERSEY	30 108	53 612	65 149	73 188	63 775	38 155	24 700	65 370	77 760	72 214	35 172	52 473	25 473	45 938
NEW MEXICO	18 048	31 671	38 988	44 981	38 777	28 433	22 431	39 425	46 011	47 504	23 054	31 882	16 453	27 582
NEW YORK	21 730	42 868	51 082	57 309	50 737	32 349	21 617	51 691	63 281	60 836	30 373	45 425	18 992	38 000
NORTH CAROLINA..	23 201	39 763	46 595	51 070	42 250	28 521	19 307	46 335	55 255	52 165	27 115	36 471	19 250	30 396
NORTH DAKOTA	19 571	35 478	43 637	47 782	38 454	27 450	19 580	43 654	51 447	44 701	26 194	34 139	16 538	29 852
OHIO	21 948	40 964	50 282	56 136	46 223	29 792	21 551	50 037	60 491	54 039	30 270	42 694	19 627	35 137
OKLAHOMA	18 650	32 592	40 682	45 650	37 304	26 962	19 627	40 709	47 652	45 647	24 745	32 731	16 657	28 069
OREGON	22 636	40 325	48 538	53 916	46 535	31 518	23 783	48 680	56 294	53 241	29 546	40 692	19 921	34 741
PENNSYLVANIA	20 947	41 057	49 814	56 076	44 876	28 639	20 359	49 184	60 167	51 981	29 595	42 756	19 585	35 363
RHODE ISLAND	20 885	41 660	51 916	59 448	50 132	30 557	19 034	52 781	63 706	58 894	29 776	46 878	17 252	40 405
SOUTH CAROLINA	22 072	37 242	43 569	48 128	40 275	28 293	19 525	44 227	53 649	51 237	27 291	35 462	17 982	28 562
SOUTH DAKOTA	20 685	36 782	43 344	46 760	39 876	28 845	19 106	43 237	50 872	44 956	24 255	36 130	17 977	31 008
TENNESSEE	21 146	36 431	43 627	48 742	39 587	26 939	18 598	43 517	52 047	48 599	26 932	35 759	17 912	30 510
TEXAS	21 570	37 732	47 418	52 926	44 905	30 296	21 734	45 861	52 372	54 374	27 667	36 962	19 769	31 095
UTAH	27 873	41 958	54 126	63 095	54 256	37 159	25 572	51 022	56 556	52 993	32 364	44 597	22 090	38 290
VERMONT	23 835	39 701	47 624	52 738	45 594	29 877	20 985	48 625	56 642	51 646	28 817	40 694	19 973	34 796
VIRGINIA	25 023	44 534	53 670	61 601	52 121	34 346	24 419	54 169	63 157	61 405	31 274	43 182	21 602	35 587
WASHINGTON	24 481	43 570	53 202	59 445	51 896	34 849	25 659	53 760	61 575	59 933	32 356	44 745	21 832	37 835
WEST VIRGINIA	14 442	29 818	36 662	41 677	32 199	23 768	18 336	36 484	42 228	40 273	21 310	29 342	12 861	25 913
WISCONSIN	25 157	44 296	52 953	58 888	49 274	31 328	21 046	52 911	61 834	55 394	31 599	45 387	22 057	37 357
WYOMING	19 300	35 643	46 165	51 731	42 253	29 686	21 286	45 685	51 815	49 324	29 194	40 924	17 122	29 954

STATE	Median nonfamily household income by household type							Median income for population 15 years and over with income				
	All nonfamily households	Male householder not living alone	Male householder living alone	Male householder living alone, 65 years or over	Female householder not living alone	Female householder living alone	Female householder living alone, 65 years or over	Males 15 years and over	Males 15 years and over who worked full-year, full-time	Females 15 years and over	Females 15 years and over who worked full-year, full-time	Per capita income
	213	214	215	216	217	218	219	220	221	222	223	224
UNITED STATES....	25 705	48 023	27 022	18 574	44 460	19 473	14 653	27 932	38 349	16 327	28 135	21 587
ALABAMA	17 866	32 655	21 156	14 121	29 799	14 039	11 544	25 327	33 992	13 513	23 585	18 189
ALASKA	33 796	54 580	31 284	22 075	51 390	26 476	18 916	30 493	43 856	18 107	32 624	22 660
ARIZONA	26 828	46 087	26 146	20 110	43 627	21 145	16 801	26 669	36 110	16 393	27 570	20 275
ARKANSAS................	17 999	33 626	20 067	13 895	30 892	14 130	11 678	22 478	30 623	13 091	21 837	16 904
CALIFORNIA	32 024	58 271	31 944	21 613	52 915	23 887	16 853	28 120	41 526	17 216	32 432	22 711
COLORADO..............	30 728	52 387	30 604	20 937	48 756	23 365	16 398	30 594	40 105	18 512	30 268	24 049
CONNECTICUT	30 873	62 545	32 209	20 525	59 442	22 760	16 085	35 845	47 156	20 692	34 929	28 766
DELAWARE	29 891	53 911	32 203	21 738	49 804	21 715	15 639	30 819	40 442	18 921	30 394	23 305
DISTRICT OF COLUMBIA	34 130	67 243	31 779	18 335	57 539	29 691	17 464	26 884	41 567	21 994	37 236	28 659
FLORIDA...................	24 799	44 418	25 430	20 156	41 595	19 217	15 857	26 112	33 980	16 035	26 236	21 557
GEORGIA..................	26 509	48 709	27 521	15 439	44 357	19 891	12 579	27 727	36 710	16 853	27 336	21 154
HAWAII	30 272	54 636	29 391	22 044	49 396	22 115	17 037	27 453	36 808	19 225	29 831	21 525
IDAHO	21 861	37 935	23 262	17 526	35 164	16 557	13 981	25 248	34 323	12 713	23 991	17 841
ILLINOIS...................	28 368	53 833	30 855	20 200	49 062	21 719	16 135	30 868	41 870	17 568	30 081	23 104
INDIANA....................	23 689	43 004	26 727	18 333	39 957	18 123	14 630	29 092	38 138	15 874	26 046	20 397
IOWA.......................	22 454	41 519	24 623	18 759	35 871	17 833	15 101	26 557	34 320	15 571	24 987	19 674
KANSAS...................	23 002	40 144	25 231	18 651	34 693	18 746	15 592	27 509	36 188	15 881	25 978	20 506
KENTUCKY...............	18 972	38 008	21 150	14 247	35 320	14 628	12 239	24 047	33 836	13 387	24 194	18 093
LOUISIANA	18 393	35 386	20 761	13 397	29 934	13 812	11 417	24 765	35 108	12 446	22 778	16 912
MAINE	21 715	41 571	22 155	16 336	41 127	15 977	12 874	25 538	34 180	14 636	25 151	19 533
MARYLAND	32 654	58 498	33 152	22 157	55 629	25 975	17 170	33 323	42 857	21 748	33 301	25 614
MASSACHUSETTS ...	29 774	61 945	30 106	17 974	58 940	20 908	14 328	32 406	45 130	19 173	33 281	25 952
MICHIGAN	26 194	47 805	29 592	19 926	42 185	19 646	15 248	30 963	42 962	16 300	29 256	22 168
MINNESOTA.............	27 913	52 523	29 056	18 969	48 472	20 972	15 267	30 949	40 408	18 107	29 670	23 198
MISSISSIPPI.............	16 616	31 524	19 224	12 003	28 750	12 542	10 633	22 366	31 246	12 415	22 109	15 853
MISSOURI................	22 293	41 537	24 238	17 139	36 924	17 732	14 300	26 263	35 604	15 486	25 552	19 936
MONTANA................	19 484	33 113	20 540	17 718	29 828	15 495	14 260	22 831	31 591	12 493	21 679	17 151
NEBRASKA..............	22 985	41 383	24 561	17 968	36 344	18 470	15 461	26 271	33 399	15 484	24 635	19 613
NEVADA..................	30 088	51 235	28 006	20 158	47 612	21 575	15 813	28 706	36 812	18 832	28 019	21 989
NEW HAMPSHIRE.....	28 945	54 653	29 969	18 632	49 496	20 238	15 308	31 781	40 819	18 032	28 669	23 844
NEW JERSEY...........	31 298	63 091	34 652	20 632	59 702	23 041	16 132	35 416	48 027	20 232	34 636	27 006
NEW MEXICO...........	21 791	36 804	21 626	16 995	37 644	17 464	14 102	22 914	32 232	13 617	24 532	17 261
NEW YORK	27 073	54 073	28 603	19 020	51 165	20 445	14 395	28 967	41 188	17 296	31 800	23 389
NORTH CAROLINA ...	23 240	43 127	25 137	15 176	40 393	17 723	12 351	26 173	33 398	16 321	25 631	20 307
NORTH DAKOTA.......	20 296	34 503	21 990	17 281	29 220	15 744	13 975	24 072	31 410	13 324	21 552	17 769
OHIO	24 005	44 886	26 819	19 219	40 289	18 516	14 728	29 091	38 977	15 886	27 152	21 003
OKLAHOMA..............	19 331	32 561	20 933	15 605	30 581	15 844	13 662	23 889	31 973	13 582	23 450	17 646
OREGON	25 761	43 796	25 830	19 184	40 467	19 945	15 937	27 467	37 680	15 817	27 915	20 940
PENNSYLVANIA........	22 205	45 419	25 549	17 814	40 875	16 919	13 777	27 706	38 176	15 092	27 365	20 880
RHODE ISLAND	23 561	48 414	25 857	16 448	44 577	17 306	13 122	28 090	39 202	15 984	28 472	21 688
SOUTH CAROLINA ...	21 508	40 018	23 595	15 338	37 014	16 178	12 148	25 824	33 279	15 194	24 187	18 795
SOUTH DAKOTA.......	20 672	37 629	21 900	15 729	33 237	16 223	13 835	23 712	30 723	14 179	22 172	17 562
TENNESSEE.............	21 032	38 776	22 775	14 749	36 717	16 154	12 022	25 396	33 643	14 839	24 832	19 393
TEXAS.....................	25 623	44 309	26 937	16 855	39 728	19 991	13 683	26 023	35 893	15 515	26 827	19 617
UTAH.......................	26 405	44 538	27 342	20 116	37 117	19 949	15 907	27 445	38 046	13 485	25 579	18 185
VERMONT	24 557	44 600	24 146	17 779	40 686	18 399	14 664	26 142	34 148	16 074	26 223	20 625
VIRGINIA..................	29 642	52 094	30 562	20 158	48 366	22 484	15 667	30 286	39 613	17 882	29 164	23 975
WASHINGTON...........	29 394	51 988	30 215	21 808	46 986	22 005	16 882	31 346	41 774	17 336	30 787	22 973
WEST VIRGINIA	16 007	28 622	17 894	15 893	27 037	13 486	12 688	21 787	32 044	11 805	21 767	16 477
WISCONSIN..............	25 837	48 283	27 530	18 841	42 189	19 388	15 088	29 723	38 180	16 635	26 644	21 271
WYOMING	21 689	38 585	23 455	17 585	35 939	16 279	14 184	26 794	35 831	12 834	22 397	19 134

STATE	Total households	Percent with earnings	Percent with wage or salary income	Percent with self-employment income	Percent with interest, dividends, or net rental income	Percent with Social Security income	Percent with Supplemental Security income	Percent with public assistance	Percent with retirement income	Percent with other types of income
	225	226	227	228	229	230	231	232	233	234
UNITED STATES....	105 539 122	80.5	77.7	11.9	35.9	25.7	4.4	3.4	16.7	13.2
ALABAMA	1 737 385	77.0	74.4	9.8	27.1	28.0	6.0	2.2	17.9	14.0
ALASKA	221 804	89.5	86.1	17.9	72.4	13.7	3.1	8.7	14.7	22.3
ARIZONA	1 901 625	78.7	75.9	10.9	34.6	27.1	3.6	2.9	18.5	12.7
ARKANSAS	1 042 807	76.8	73.4	12.2	28.3	30.4	5.8	2.9	16.3	14.1
CALIFORNIA...........	11 512 020	82.5	78.7	14.4	35.0	22.3	5.3	4.9	15.4	13.2
COLORADO.............	1 659 308	85.8	82.5	15.5	40.6	19.9	3.0	2.5	14.6	11.9
CONNECTICUT	1 302 227	81.2	78.6	11.6	44.4	27.0	3.3	3.7	17.6	11.6
DELAWARE............	298 755	81.3	79.4	9.5	39.0	26.9	3.5	2.7	21.0	13.4
DISTRICT OF COLUMBIA.............	248 590	78.6	76.3	9.5	31.4	19.5	4.6	5.5	17.9	10.6
FLORIDA................	6 341 121	74.7	72.0	10.3	35.3	32.7	4.2	2.8	19.9	13.3
GEORGIA................	3 007 678	83.8	81.3	10.9	28.8	21.9	4.5	2.9	14.4	12.4
HAWAII..................	403 572	82.9	79.5	14.8	45.5	27.8	3.6	7.2	21.2	13.7
IDAHO...................	470 133	82.2	78.4	17.6	36.4	25.2	3.5	3.4	15.6	16.3
ILLINOIS................	4 592 740	81.7	79.6	10.6	39.7	24.7	3.9	3.3	15.4	11.6
INDIANA................	2 337 229	81.8	79.7	11.0	35.6	26.0	3.5	2.6	17.0	12.7
IOWA....................	1 150 197	80.4	77.3	16.3	43.5	28.6	3.2	2.9	14.6	14.3
KANSAS.................	1 038 940	81.8	78.6	15.0	39.1	26.2	3.1	2.4	14.8	13.0
KENTUCKY.............	1 591 739	76.5	73.6	11.9	29.0	28.5	7.2	3.8	17.5	14.4
LOUISIANA	1 657 107	78.1	75.4	9.8	25.9	25.2	6.1	3.3	14.8	13.5
MAINE	518 372	78.5	74.7	15.8	37.8	28.9	4.6	4.8	17.4	15.0
MARYLAND	1 981 795	83.8	81.7	11.1	39.2	22.5	3.4	2.4	18.7	12.2
MASSACHUSETTS ...	2 444 588	80.1	77.7	11.7	42.1	26.2	4.9	2.9	16.5	12.9
MICHIGAN..............	3 788 780	80.2	78.1	10.1	38.0	26.2	4.2	3.6	19.2	13.9
MINNESOTA............	1 896 209	83.4	80.8	14.8	44.0	23.9	2.9	3.4	13.7	13.0
MISSISSIPPI............	1 047 555	77.2	74.5	10.1	22.6	27.9	7.6	3.5	15.6	14.4
MISSOURI..............	2 197 214	79.5	76.7	12.4	36.2	27.6	4.1	3.4	17.0	13.1
MONTANA	359 070	79.6	74.6	19.8	40.0	27.7	3.6	3.3	16.3	15.4
NEBRASKA	666 995	82.5	79.0	16.9	41.6	26.4	3.0	2.8	12.8	13.4
NEVADA.................	751 977	83.5	81.5	9.5	29.0	23.0	0.0	2.0	17.4	10.1
NEW HAMPSHIRE.....	474 750	83.8	80.8	14.1	41.9	24.7	3.0	3.0	16.4	12.5
NEW JERSEY...........	3 065 774	81.4	79.4	9.7	42.4	26.9	3.5	2.8	17.1	12.1
NEW MEXICO...........	678 032	79.5	75.8	13.5	30.2	25.5	4.9	4.7	17.4	13.7
NEW YORK..............	7 060 595	78.1	75.6	10.4	36.5	26.0	5.5	4.9	16.9	12.2
NORTH CAROLINA ...	3 133 282	81.5	78.8	11.2	30.5	25.3	4.2	2.8	16.4	12.6
NORTH DAKOTA......	257 234	80.7	76.2	20.0	42.4	27.5	3.0	2.9	10.8	15.4
OHIO....................	4 446 621	79.6	77.4	10.2	36.6	26.4	4.2	3.2	18.9	13.3
OKLAHOMA.............	1 343 506	78.6	75.1	13.5	30.5	27.2	4.5	5.1	16.4	13.4
OREGON	1 335 109	80.2	76.5	15.5	39.6	25.8	3.5	3.6	17.2	15.6
PENNSYLVANIA.......	4 779 186	76.7	74.3	9.9	40.4	30.4	4.3	3.1	19.7	13.3
RHODE ISLAND	408 412	77.4	75.2	9.9	37.0	27.9	5.2	4.6	17.4	14.5
SOUTH CAROLINA ...	1 534 334	79.9	77.5	9.9	27.2	26.5	4.7	2.5	17.9	13.2
SOUTH DAKOTA......	290 336	81.4	76.8	20.4	41.0	28.0	3.4	3.0	12.7	14.7
TENNESSEE............	2 234 229	79.7	76.6	12.2	29.4	26.5	5.2	3.5	16.2	13.1
TEXAS...................	7 397 294	83.9	80.6	12.5	29.2	21.6	3.9	3.2	13.2	12.5
UTAH....................	701 933	86.1	84.0	15.0	37.5	20.6	2.8	3.1	15.7	13.9
VERMONT	240 744	82.2	78.1	18.6	45.0	26.5	4.1	4.8	15.5	14.5
VIRGINIA................	2 700 335	83.4	81.2	11.0	38.2	23.4	3.5	2.5	18.8	12.9
WASHINGTON.........	2 272 261	81.9	79.0	13.1	40.0	22.9	3.7	3.8	17.1	15.4
WEST VIRGINIA.......	737 360	70.6	68.2	8.7	28.7	33.9	6.9	4.0	22.0	15.6
WISCONSIN............	2 086 304	81.8	79.6	12.0	47.2	26.4	3.4	1.7	15.7	14.9
WYOMING	193 959	82.5	78.8	16.7	38.2	24.5	2.8	2.6	14.6	14.7

STATE	Percent of all households with income over $100,000	+/− U.S. for income >$100,000	Households with income over $100,000 by age of householder (percent)				
			Householder under 25 years	Householder 25 to 44 years	Householder 45 to 64 years	Householder 65 to 74 years	Householder 75 years or over
	235	236	237	238	239	240	241
UNITED STATES....	12.3	0.0	7.5	11.6	18.3	7.9	5.1
ALABAMA	7.6	-4.7	2.2	6.4	12.1	5.6	3.8
ALASKA	16.1	3.8	16.7	12.3	24.6	11.5	9.3
ARIZONA	10.8	-1.5	6.6	10.2	16.3	7.7	5.4
ARKANSAS	6.0	-6.3	2.7	5.1	9.4	4.4	3.4
CALIFORNIA............	17.3	5.0	15.1	16.6	24.1	12.0	8.0
COLORADO..............	14.2	1.9	12.7	13.5	20.9	8.3	5.3
CONNECTICUT	20.2	7.9	15.0	19.7	29.2	12.4	6.7
DELAWARE	14.0	1.7	11.6	13.1	21.3	8.0	5.8
DISTRICT OF COLUMBIA	16.4	4.1	9.2	15.0	23.6	14.1	10.7
FLORIDA..................	10.4	-1.9	6.3	9.7	15.3	8.2	6.2
GEORGIA.................	12.3	0.0	8.4	11.6	18.3	7.3	4.7
HAWAII....................	16.6	4.3	10.2	11.7	24.1	17.1	12.0
IDAHO.....................	7.3	-5.0	3.4	6.2	11.7	5.1	3.7
ILLINOIS..................	14.4	2.1	10.2	14.2	21.2	8.5	5.1
INDIANA	9.2	-3.1	4.9	8.1	15.0	5.3	3.2
IOWA	7.3	-5.0	4.1	6.6	11.8	4.8	3.1
KANSAS..................	9.3	-3.0	4.4	8.3	15.0	6.4	4.1
KENTUCKY..............	7.2	-5.1	3.0	6.5	10.9	4.7	3.4
LOUISIANA	7.4	-4.9	2.2	6.3	11.7	5.5	3.8
MAINE	7.1	-5.2	3.1	6.3	10.8	4.6	3.5
MARYLAND	18.1	5.8	11.4	16.2	26.5	12.1	7.6
MASSACHUSETTS ...	17.7	5.4	17.2	18.4	25.3	9.8	5.1
MICHIGAN	12.7	0.4	7.3	11.5	20.1	6.9	4.2
MINNESOTA............	12.6	0.3	10.7	12.5	19.4	6.5	3.6
MISSISSIPPI............	6.0	-6.3	2.4	4.9	9.3	4.9	3.4
MISSOURI...............	8.8	-3.5	4.3	7.9	13.8	5.5	4.0
MONTANA...............	5.6	-6.7	1.4	4.5	8.8	4.2	2.8
NEBRASKA..............	8.1	-4.2	4.0	7.3	13.3	5.5	3.5
NEVADA..................	11.3	-1.0	19.3	10.2	16.2	7.5	5.7
NEW HAMPSHIRE.....	13.8	1.5	8.1	13.5	19.5	7.4	4.9
NEW JERSEY...........	21.3	9.0	25.7	21.5	30.2	12.3	6.3
NEW MEXICO...........	7.6	-4.7	2.6	5.8	12.0	6.4	4.7
NEW YORK...............	15.3	3.0	11.9	15.0	21.3	10.4	6.0
NORTH CAROLINA ...	9.4	-2.9	5.9	8.6	14.3	6.3	4.4
NORTH DAKOTA.......	5.7	-6.6	2.5	5.0	9.3	4.1	2.9
OHIO	9.8	-2.5	3.8	8.8	15.6	5.9	3.8
OKLAHOMA	6.6	-5.7	2.5	5.5	10.7	5.1	3.9
OREGON	10.0	-2.3	5.3	9.1	15.3	6.5	4.5
PENNSYLVANIA........	10.3	-2.0	4.6	9.9	16.0	5.8	3.6
RHODE ISLAND	11.5	-0.8	5.2	10.3	18.5	7.8	4.1
SOUTH CAROLINA ...	8.1	-4.2	3.7	6.7	12.5	6.1	4.3
SOUTH DAKOTA.......	5.9	-6.4	3.0	5.3	9.6	4.5	2.9
TENNESSEE.............	8.3	-4.0	4.1	7.2	12.9	5.8	4.1
TEXAS.....................	11.5	-0.8	5.5	10.6	17.6	7.7	5.3
UTAH......................	11.2	-1.1	11.8	9.2	19.4	8.4	4.5
VERMONT	8.7	-3.6	5.5	6.8	13.6	7.0	3.8
VIRGINIA.................	15.1	2.8	10.1	13.3	22.7	10.1	6.7
WASHINGTON..........	12.6	0.3	9.9	11.7	18.8	7.6	5.3
WEST VIRGINIA	5.0	-7.3	1.8	4.2	7.7	3.8	2.9
WISCONSIN.............	9.4	-2.9	5.9	8.4	15.3	5.8	3.5
WYOMING	6.7	-5.6	1.5	5.1	10.9	4.6	3.7

STATE	Percent of all households with income below poverty	Married-couple family households	Male householder family households	Female householder family households	Male householder nonfamily households	Female householder nonfamily households	Householder under 25 years	Householder 25 to 44 years	Householder 45 to 54 years	Householder 65 years and over
	242	243	244	245	246	247	248	249	250	251
UNITED STATES....	11.8	4.9	13.6	26.5	15.1	19.3	33.3	11.5	9.0	11.4
ALABAMA	16.7	6.2	17.6	35.6	22.7	29.5	41.6	15.1	13.1	18.3
ALASKA	8.3	3.4	13.0	20.0	12.0	12.0	19.4	8.7	6.4	7.0
ARIZONA	11.8	6.2	15.7	25.8	14.7	16.8	30.8	12.4	9.2	9.1
ARKANSAS..............	15.8	6.8	18.4	34.7	20.7	28.0	35.3	15.1	12.4	16.5
CALIFORNIA..............	11.8	6.8	15.0	25.0	13.5	15.6	33.6	13.1	9.1	8.5
COLORADO..............	8.8	3.4	9.6	20.6	12.0	15.4	28.2	7.8	6.3	8.8
CONNECTICUT	8.0	2.3	9.0	19.6	11.0	14.3	29.0	7.8	5.9	8.3
DELAWARE	8.8	2.9	9.4	20.4	11.0	16.0	27.9	8.0	6.5	9.5
DISTRICT OF COLUMBIA............	17.1	5.7	17.0	30.0	16.2	18.5	40.3	15.7	13.6	17.9
FLORIDA...................	11.7	4.9	13.8	25.3	14.9	19.0	33.3	11.9	9.8	10.4
GEORGIA...................	12.6	4.6	13.7	28.5	15.9	22.1	32.9	11.0	9.7	15.9
HAWAII......................	10.5	4.2	13.4	20.6	15.6	19.6	33.6	11.5	8.4	8.2
IDAHO	11.2	5.3	12.8	27.7	16.1	20.9	32.1	10.9	8.1	9.6
ILLINOIS...................	10.1	3.8	12.1	24.1	13.2	16.6	32.2	9.8	7.6	9.8
INDIANA....................	9.5	3.1	11.0	23.4	13.5	17.4	31.2	8.8	6.7	9.0
IOWA........................	9.3	3.2	11.2	23.4	14.6	17.3	31.1	8.5	6.4	8.8
KANSAS...................	10.1	3.7	12.0	23.5	15.3	18.8	32.3	9.0	7.0	9.3
KENTUCKY...............	16.2	8.0	18.8	33.1	21.1	27.1	35.6	15.2	13.8	16.6
LOUISIANA	19.1	7.2	20.3	40.6	22.8	30.6	44.1	18.3	15.4	19.4
MAINE......................	11.5	3.9	13.5	28.1	15.8	21.1	31.7	11.1	9.2	12.0
MARYLAND	8.3	2.6	9.0	18.4	11.7	14.5	28.3	7.7	6.1	9.7
MASSACHUSETTS ...	9.8	2.9	9.2	22.1	13.4	17.2	33.2	9.2	7.3	10.6
MICHIGAN	10.1	3.2	11.5	24.0	13.7	17.8	31.6	10.0	7.6	9.4
MINNESOTA..............	7.9	2.6	9.1	19.3	11.8	15.1	26.1	6.7	5.4	9.3
MISSISSIPPI.............	19.7	7.3	21.5	40.2	24.9	32.9	40.3	18.5	16.2	22.0
MISSOURI................	11.8	4.4	14.5	26.1	16.1	20.4	32.7	11.3	8.8	11.7
MONTANA................	14.1	6.4	17.1	33.2	19.6	22.7	40.4	14.8	10.9	10.6
NEBRASKA...............	9.7	3.6	11.5	24.0	13.7	17.5	28.3	9.1	6.5	9.5
NEVADA...................	9.4	4.3	11.6	20.5	11.6	15.2	24.1	9.9	7.3	8.2
NEW HAMPSHIRE.....	6.9	2.0	7.6	17.6	9.6	15.1	25.9	6.0	4.9	8.6
NEW JERSEY...........	8.3	3.0	9.9	19.4	10.9	14.9	26.4	8.4	6.3	9.1
NEW MEXICO............	16.8	8.7	22.9	34.1	19.9	23.5	40.3	17.5	13.1	14.7
NEW YORK................	13.9	5.9	14.0	29.2	16.5	20.4	38.5	14.6	11.1	13.0
NORTH CAROLINA ...	12.4	4.5	13.6	27.4	16.2	22.8	30.9	10.6	9.4	15.5
NORTH DAKOTA.......	12.5	4.7	16.0	30.6	17.3	23.2	35.7	10.4	8.8	13.0
OHIO........................	10.7	3.4	12.1	26.3	14.3	18.6	34.2	10.4	8.0	9.6
OKLAHOMA..............	14.6	6.5	18.5	32.0	20.1	24.2	36.7	14.5	11.1	13.3
OREGON	10.8	4.4	12.8	25.9	15.4	17.4	32.8	11.2	8.0	8.2
PENNSYLVANIA........	11.0	3.8	11.9	24.9	15.1	19.7	37.9	10.7	8.6	10.4
RHODE ISLAND........	12.4	3.5	11.9	29.1	16.1	21.1	41.9	12.1	8.2	12.6
SOUTH CAROLINA ...	14.1	5.0	14.4	30.6	18.1	25.3	33.2	12.7	11.5	16.2
SOUTH DAKOTA.......	12.5	5.3	19.7	30.4	16.6	21.4	33.0	11.1	9.4	12.6
TENNESSEE.............	14.0	5.5	15.2	29.5	18.7	25.2	33.7	12.6	10.9	16.2
TEXAS.....................	14.0	7.7	16.3	29.5	16.0	21.7	33.8	13.2	10.6	14.8
UTAH.......................	8.9	4.1	10.6	22.1	14.6	18.8	24.6	8.7	5.7	6.9
VERMONT	9.7	3.0	11.5	24.1	13.9	18.5	33.6	9.0	7.2	9.9
VIRGINIA..................	9.6	3.3	10.4	23.0	13.0	17.4	29.8	8.4	7.2	11.4
WASHINGTON..........	9.8	4.0	11.9	24.1	13.2	16.2	30.5	9.7	7.4	8.2
WEST VIRGINIA	18.0	9.1	23.8	35.5	25.3	28.3	48.8	19.5	15.1	13.8
WISCONSIN..............	8.4	2.6	9.8	21.7	12.0	15.7	30.2	7.5	5.7	8.2
WYOMING	11.2	4.4	11.3	30.9	14.6	21.5	34.1	10.6	8.0	10.1

STATE	Total families	Total families with income below poverty as a percent of all families in group					
		Total families	Non-Hispanic White	Black or African American	American Indian and Alaska Native	Asian, Hawaiian, and Pacific Islander	Hispanic or Latino[1]
	252	253	254	255	256	257	258
UNITED STATES....	72 261 780	9.2	5.5	21.6	21.8	9.8	20.0
ALABAMA	1 223 185	12.5	7.4	28.1	17.8	11.4	21.3
ALASKA	153 611	6.7	4.3	7.7	17.9	11.2	10.3
ARIZONA	1 296 593	9.9	4.8	15.6	33.3	8.9	21.6
ARKANSAS..............	736 063	12.0	8.6	29.9	16.3	11.4	24.4
CALIFORNIA	7 985 489	10.6	5.0	18.7	18.6	9.8	19.5
COLORADO..............	1 092 352	6.2	3.8	13.0	14.9	8.6	16.2
CONNECTICUT	885 747	5.6	2.7	16.5	12.1	5.8	23.0
DELAWARE	205 775	6.5	3.6	15.4	10.7	7.3	20.5
DISTRICT OF COLUMBIA............	115 963	16.7	1.9	21.7	22.2	19.0	17.0
FLORIDA..................	4 238 409	9.0	5.2	22.3	15.0	9.8	14.6
GEORGIA..................	2 126 360	9.9	5.3	20.4	12.6	8.4	17.2
HAWAII....................	289 012	7.6	5.1	5.6	12.7	7.2	16.8
IDAHO	337 884	8.3	7.2	10.3	21.3	7.6	21.3
ILLINOIS...................	3 125 318	7.8	4.1	22.3	14.6	7.0	14.3
INDIANA..................	1 611 045	6.7	5.2	20.2	13.3	10.0	15.0
IOWA	774 246	6.0	5.3	26.8	22.1	10.2	17.1
KANSAS..................	706 786	6.7	5.1	19.1	12.1	10.8	16.9
KENTUCKY..............	1 110 426	12.7	11.7	24.7	25.2	10.2	18.9
LOUISIANA..............	1 163 191	15.8	7.9	33.2	18.8	16.8	15.2
MAINE	342 431	7.8	7.5	22.6	26.0	15.1	15.8
MARYLAND	1 368 647	6.1	3.3	12.2	9.4	6.5	9.6
MASSACHUSETTS ...	1 587 537	6.7	4.1	18.3	18.9	12.4	28.5
MICHIGAN	2 591 312	7.4	4.8	21.1	13.3	7.6	15.7
MINNESOTA............	1 262 953	5.1	3.6	23.5	24.9	14.9	17.5
MISSISSIPPI............	752 234	16.0	7.9	31.6	29.5	15.1	22.3
MISSOURI................	1 486 546	8.6	6.7	22.0	16.3	10.4	17.3
MONTANA................	238 733	10.5	8.8	19.4	34.1	17.0	21.3
NEBRASKA..............	446 551	6.7	5.3	22.8	29.3	10.0	17.8
NEVADA..................	502 508	7.5	4.7	17.9	15.1	6.3	15.0
NEW HAMPSHIRE.....	325 581	4.3	4.0	14.2	5.5	9.2	13.9
NEW JERSEY...........	2 167 577	6.3	3.0	15.7	13.1	5.6	15.6
NEW MEXICO...........	468 899	14.5	6.8	17.8	33.2	9.0	20.7
NEW YORK...............	4 673 485	11.5	5.7	22.3	23.8	14.8	26.0
NORTH CAROLINA ...	2 173 346	9.0	5.3	19.9	18.1	8.2	21.1
NORTH DAKOTA.......	166 963	8.3	6.9	15.3	35.5	10.6	19.3
OHIO	3 007 207	7.8	5.7	23.1	18.9	9.1	17.4
OKLAHOMA	927 703	11.2	8.5	25.6	19.1	12.2	23.8
OREGON	884 875	7.9	6.5	20.0	17.7	8.6	21.3
PENNSYLVANIA........	3 225 707	7.8	5.5	22.8	19.9	12.5	29.3
RHODE ISLAND	266 655	8.9	5.1	27.2	33.2	16.7	35.3
SOUTH CAROLINA ...	1 078 736	10.7	5.5	23.5	14.9	9.2	20.3
SOUTH DAKOTA.......	195 455	9.3	6.6	15.5	44.5	10.4	21.1
TENNESSEE............	1 557 620	10.3	7.9	22.6	14.6	9.8	18.3
TEXAS....................	5 283 474	12.0	5.2	20.4	17.0	9.5	22.8
UTAH.......................	539 728	6.5	5.1	15.5	30.0	10.4	16.6
VERMONT	158 684	6.3	6.1	17.2	23.4	9.9	9.6
VIRGINIA.................	1 859 983	7.0	4.4	16.4	9.3	7.5	10.0
WASHINGTON...........	1 509 395	7.3	5.5	14.9	18.9	10.8	21.9
WEST VIRGINIA	507 255	13.9	13.4	28.1	20.1	11.5	17.9
WISCONSIN.............	1 395 037	5.6	3.7	28.4	19.8	15.7	18.6
WYOMING	131 508	8.0	7.0	13.5	31.8	8.8	16.3

[1]Hispanic or Latino persons may be of any race.

Table B-3. States and Counties — Education, Labor Force, and Income

STATE/ County code	MSA/PMSA/ NECMA code[1]	STATE County	High school graduates			College graduates		College graduates (percent)				
			Total population 25 years and over	Percent with a high school diploma or less	Percent with a high school diploma or more	Percent with a bachelor's degree or more	+/− U.S. percent with bachelor's degree or more	Non-Hispanic White	Black or African American	American Indian and Alaska Native	Asian, Hawaiian, and Pacific Islander	Hispanic or Latino[2]
			1	2	3	4	5	6	7	8	9	10
00 000	...	UNITED STATES....	182 211 639	48.2	80.4	24.4	0.0	27.0	14.3	11.5	43.1	10.4
01 000	...	ALABAMA	2 887 400	55.1	75.3	19.0	-5.4	21.2	11.5	13.0	47.2	14.6
01 001	5240	Autauga County	27 589	55.1	78.7	18.0	-6.4	20.0	7.6	12.3	16.7	15.1
01 003	5160	Baldwin County	96 010	47.6	82.0	23.1	-1.3	24.8	7.5	14.2	29.2	17.9
01 005	...	Barbour County	18 896	67.8	64.7	10.9	-13.5	16.5	3.8	0.0	0.0	9.7
01 007	...	Bibb County..................	13 540	72.5	63.2	7.1	-17.3	8.5	1.2	11.5	0.0	16.2
01 009	1000	Blount County...............	33 702	65.6	70.4	9.6	-14.8	9.8	2.5	2.6	62.7	4.4
01 011	...	Bullock County	7 570	74.8	60.5	7.7	-16.7	15.8	4.4	0.0	0.0	8.3
01 013	...	Butler County	13 767	66.7	67.8	10.4	-14.0	13.3	4.8	0.0	91.3	0.0
01 015	0450	Calhoun County	74 015	58.3	73.9	15.2	-9.2	16.4	8.9	13.2	31.7	9.5
01 017	...	Chambers County	24 497	67.9	64.2	9.5	-14.9	12.2	4.3	0.0	40.0	15.9
01 019	...	Cherokee County	16 825	71.3	63.5	9.7	-14.7	9.8	7.2	14.0	46.9	5.0
01 021	...	Chilton County	25 902	69.6	66.2	9.9	-14.5	10.6	5.4	0.0	17.2	4.3
01 023	...	Choctaw County............	10 569	69.8	65.0	9.6	-14.8	13.1	4.4	0.0	40.0	13.4
01 025	...	Clarke County	17 702	66.8	70.8	12.1	-12.3	16.4	5.2	22.2	34.5	0.0
01 027	...	Clay County..................	9 767	71.8	66.0	7.8	-16.6	8.8	2.7	0.0	0.0	0.7
01 029	...	Cleburne County	9 533	72.9	62.9	9.2	-15.2	9.5	4.2	6.7	X	13.3
01 031	...	Coffee County	28 885	53.1	73.2	19.3	-5.1	21.5	8.5	13.8	21.7	26.5
01 033	2650	Colbert County	37 384	60.6	73.3	14.1	-10.3	15.2	7.6	8.4	37.0	16.5
01 035	...	Conecuh County	9 230	70.4	67.7	9.2	-15.2	10.4	7.6	0.0	0.0	15.0
01 037	...	Coosa County	8 255	72.6	65.7	8.0	-16.4	10.4	3.1	0.0	X	0.0
01 039	...	Covington County..........	25 705	64.5	68.4	12.2	-12.2	12.9	5.8	8.6	20.8	14.4
01 041	...	Crenshaw County	9 268	68.9	60.1	11.2	-13.2	13.0	5.4	40.0	X	3.8
01 043	...	Cullman County	51 787	61.6	70.4	11.9	-12.5	12.1	8.6	4.3	16.2	4.2
01 045	2180	Dale County	31 390	51.4	77.8	14.0	-10.4	15.1	7.9	12.1	18.8	15.8
01 047	...	Dallas County	28 742	63.2	70.3	13.9	-10.5	20.4	9.0	7.9	40.7	14.9
01 049	...	DeKalb County	42 740	70.2	63.8	8.3	-16.1	8.4	2.5	11.3	27.1	1.9
01 051	5240	Elmore County	43 177	56.2	77.6	16.6	-7.8	18.9	6.5	12.6	34.2	12.7
01 053	...	Escambia County	25 510	66.2	68.5	10.6	-13.8	12.7	6.1	2.6	8.1	9.8
01 055	2880	Etowah County..............	69 829	58.2	74.1	13.4	-11.0	14.3	7.4	8.0	33.8	7.8
01 057	...	Fayette County..............	12 579	68.9	66.1	9.2	-15.2	9.2	8.7	0.0	46.9	0.0
01 059	...	Franklin County	20 860	68.4	62.1	9.7	-14.7	9.9	9.3	24.7	0.0	6.2
01 061	...	Geneva County	17 588	66.4	65.6	8.7	-15.7	9.4	1.4	9.0	76.7	1.4
01 063	...	Greene County	6 204	70.1	64.8	10.5	-13.9	15.8	8.6	X	100.0	30.0
01 065	...	Hale County	10 591	70.7	65.2	8.1	-16.3	11.1	5.2	47.4	100.0	9.2
01 067	...	Henry County	10 967	62.4	66.7	14.1	-10.3	17.6	5.8	66.7	X	3.8
01 069	2180	Houston County	58 671	53.8	76.5	18.4	6.0	21.1	0.0	9.0	34.8	13.1
01 071	...	Jackson County............	36 435	67.8	67.0	10.4	-14.0	10.7	5.2	9.7	19.0	5.7
01 073	1000	Jefferson County	434 158	47.0	80.9	24.6	0.2	30.0	14.3	23.0	63.9	18.8
01 075	...	Lamar County	10 758	72.5	65.1	7.8	-16.6	8.1	5.3	0.0	31.8	7.1
01 077	2650	Lauderdale County	58 894	57.8	76.4	18.5	-5.9	19.3	9.5	17.3	50.8	16.0
01 079	2030	Lawrence County	22 894	73.8	65.6	7.5	-16.9	7.4	5.2	10.4	30.2	18.2
01 081	0580	Lee County	82 170	45.3	81.4	27.9	3.5	31.9	12.2	25.9	64.7	23.8
01 083	3440	Limestone County	43 456	58.0	74.5	16.9	-7.5	18.2	8.8	14.7	41.0	3.3
01 085	...	Lowndes County	8 183	69.1	64.3	11.0	-13.4	21.4	6.1	0.0	X	20.0
01 087	...	Macon County	13 955	55.0	70.0	18.8	-5.6	15.2	18.7	10.7	90.1	4.0
01 089	3440	Madison County	180 389	36.5	85.4	34.3	9.9	36.8	23.9	21.4	52.9	26.5
01 091	...	Marengo County	14 326	65.4	71.9	12.1	-12.3	18.4	4.9	0.0	0.0	17.2
01 093	...	Marion County	21 611	69.7	63.2	8.0	-16.4	8.2	3.5	0.0	0.0	6.4
01 095	...	Marshall County	54 961	61.1	69.4	13.9	-10.5	14.4	5.4	12.2	32.8	2.9
01 097	5160	Mobile County	250 122	55.2	76.7	18.6	-5.8	21.9	10.7	33.9	33.9	21.5
01 099	...	Monroe County	15 378	66.5	67.9	11.8	-12.6	15.6	5.0	11.1	25.0	11.6
01 101	5240	Montgomery County......	141 342	44.1	80.3	28.5	4.1	36.5	18.2	11.3	32.7	25.2
01 103	2030	Morgan County	73 331	54.0	76.3	18.4	-6.0	19.6	7.4	23.7	54.3	10.9
01 105	...	Perry County	6 978	68.0	62.4	10.0	-14.4	16.4	6.4	0.0	0.0	3.4
01 107	...	Pickens County	13 536	68.1	69.7	9.8	-14.6	12.3	5.7	0.0	35.3	0.0
01 109	...	Pike County	17 703	60.9	69.1	18.4	-6.0	24.7	6.6	8.3	35.0	4.6
01 111	...	Randolph County	14 762	70.1	61.9	10.0	-14.4	10.8	6.2	0.0	48.1	6.7
01 113	1800	Russell County	32 107	66.5	66.5	9.7	-14.7	11.1	6.4	22.8	36.5	11.2
01 115	1000	St. Clair County	43 101	63.3	71.3	11.1	-13.3	11.5	6.0	6.1	34.9	12.9
01 117	1000	Shelby County	94 185	36.2	86.8	36.8	12.4	37.8	24.9	19.7	72.3	22.0
01 119	...	Sumter County	8 731	66.4	64.8	12.4	-12.0	27.4	6.1	0.0	0.0	12.8
01 121	...	Talladega County	53 060	64.8	69.7	11.2	-13.2	13.0	6.4	21.8	34.1	12.9
01 123	...	Tallapoosa County	28 373	62.9	70.1	14.1	-10.3	16.4	6.3	16.7	38.6	34.3
01 125	8600	Tuscaloosa County	99 039	49.6	78.8	24.0	-0.4	27.9	12.1	15.7	65.6	22.7
01 127	...	Walker County..............	47 919	67.5	67.2	9.1	-15.3	9.0	8.4	7.8	37.3	5.0

[1]MSA = Metropolitan Statistical Area. PMSA = Primary MSA. NECMA = New England County Metropolitan Area. See the Appendix A for explanation of these concepts. See Appendix B for list of metropolitan areas identified by type, with component counties.
[2]Hispanic or Latino persons may be of any race.

STATE County	School enrollment			Population 16 to 19 years				Employment status, 2000			Work status in 1999 of the population 16 years and over (percent)		
											Worked in 1999		
	Grades kindergarten through 12	College or graduate school	Percent private	Number	Percent in armed forces	Percent high school graduates	Percent not enrolled, not grads, not in armed forces, not employed	Total population 16 years and over	Percent in labor force	Unemployment rate	Full-time	Part-time	Did not work in 1999
	11	12	13	14	15	16	17	18	19	20	21	22	23
UNITED STATES....	54 192 083	17 483 262	14.3	15 930 458	0.6	10.5	5.5	217 168 077	63.9	5.7	54.9	14.6	30.5
ALABAMA	837 350	243 275	11.5	255 315	0.2	9.6	7.1	3 450 542	59.7	6.2	52.9	12.1	35.1
Autauga County	9 502	1 695	13.7	2 390	0.0	13.5	7.1	32 490	65.1	4.8	58.5	11.8	29.7
Baldwin County	25 805	4 708	12.5	7 374	0.0	10.2	6.1	110 255	59.8	4.3	53.1	12.5	34.5
Barbour County	5 760	743	9.9	1 664	0.0	10.7	11.4	22 546	48.0	5.7	46.3	8.7	44.9
Bibb County.................	4 142	500	10.6	1 144	0.0	15.1	8.0	16 111	52.9	6.2	48.6	10.5	40.9
Blount County	9 431	1 600	5.6	2 764	0.2	10.6	9.2	39 450	60.6	4.8	54.0	10.9	35.0
Bullock County	2 414	282	14.4	654	0.0	8.4	12.5	9 069	41.6	8.5	41.9	7.1	51.0
Butler County	4 552	673	14.5	1 406	0.0	6.0	9.5	16 480	54.5	10.6	45.7	10.5	43.7
Calhoun County	19 267	7 129	7.7	6 252	0.2	8.9	7.2	88 878	57.8	6.6	51.2	12.2	36.6
Chambers County	6 548	1 122	12.7	2 082	0.0	11.8	7.1	28 703	58.6	6.5	51.9	10.1	38.0
Cherokee County	3 836	571	4.7	1 136	0.0	12.5	10.7	19 300	55.0	3.9	51.6	8.8	39.7
Chilton County	7 509	935	6.6	2 150	0.0	16.6	7.3	30 545	59.7	4.3	54.2	10.3	35.4
Choctaw County...........	3 156	424	20.8	951	0.0	6.8	6.6	12 369	48.7	8.7	44.3	8.8	46.9
Clarke County	5 962	559	12.3	1 624	0.0	10.8	8.9	20 937	54.3	8.9	48.2	9.5	42.3
Clay County.................	2 567	357	7.5	655	0.5	9.9	4.9	11 243	55.9	5.5	50.3	8.2	41.5
Cleburne County	2 432	501	6.1	768	0.0	9.0	8.6	11 135	58.7	5.3	52.2	10.6	37.2
Coffee County	8 284	1 991	5.5	2 525	0.2	11.7	8.8	34 099	59.6	5.3	53.3	11.0	35.7
Colbert County	9 836	1 904	6.5	2 876	0.0	9.8	6.2	43 398	56.2	5.2	49.0	12.2	38.8
Conecuh County	2 810	385	11.4	751	0.0	8.0	8.3	10 877	49.6	9.8	44.3	9.1	46.7
Coosa County	2 300	247	8.9	668	0.0	15.7	6.3	9 609	54.3	7.1	54.8	8.3	37.0
Covington County..........	6 710	1 166	2.7	1 972	0.7	11.8	8.5	29 740	55.9	7.6	49.3	10.9	39.8
Crenshaw County	2 599	425	9.2	728	0.0	6.3	6.5	10 717	54.1	5.3	48.7	9.3	42.0
Cullman County	13 754	3 327	6.0	4 283	0.0	11.9	7.9	60 901	60.2	4.1	53.6	11.3	35.0
Dale County	9 468	2 353	6.8	2 775	6.0	16.6	5.7	37 429	62.3	6.7	54.4	11.8	33.7
Dallas County	10 258	1 870	14.2	3 125	0.0	6.6	10.1	34 701	50.0	11.1	43.2	9.4	47.4
DeKalb County	11 435	1 696	4.3	3 343	0.0	10.7	9.1	50 247	61.5	5.1	55.0	10.7	34.3
Elmore County	12 967	2 245	11.7	3 608	0.2	13.1	8.4	50 934	59.0	4.9	55.6	10.4	34.0
Escambia County	6 955	1 296	7.2	2 147	0.0	12.0	12.2	30 201	52.0	7.0	47.0	10.0	43.0
Etowah County	17 868	4 130	8.9	5 786	0.0	10.1	10.5	81 735	56.6	6.0	49.4	11.8	38.8
Fayette County.............	3 301	663	3.1	992	0.0	7.0	11.8	14 603	54.9	7.7	50.4	9.4	40.2
Franklin County	5 687	945	4.3	1 675	0.0	13.6	7.9	24 493	56.6	5.6	51.9	10.3	37.8
Geneva County	4 715	625	4.5	1 295	0.5	7.3	6.2	20 345	58.0	7.9	51.2	9.1	39.7
Greene County	2 181	225	8.4	694	0.0	9.1	16.9	7 464	47.9	13.1	42.9	9.2	47.9
Hale County	3 799	467	8.3	1 193	0.0	11.1	9.5	12 747	49.8	8.0	44.8	10.1	45.1
Henry County	3 026	488	6.7	893	0.0	8.4	8.0	12 880	56.5	6.3	51.1	9.6	39.3
Houston County	17 275	3 113	13.3	4 832	0.0	8.9	5.5	68 505	62.4	5.2	55.8	11.5	32.6
Jackson County.............	9 368	1 435	3.9	2 794	0.0	14.2	6.4	42 472	62.0	5.1	55.9	10.8	33.3
Jefferson County	124 485	38 365	13.1	36 688	0.0	10.2	6.4	516 341	61.5	6.3	53.9	12.3	33.8
Lamar County	2 890	443	3.1	917	0.0	13.8	6.3	12 622	55.9	7.1	50.8	10.1	39.1
Lauderdale County........	15 145	5 618	8.5	4 930	0.0	7.1	5.7	70 064	58.9	5.6	49.6	14.6	35.8
Lawrence County	6 667	997	7.0	1 982	0.0	11.5	10.6	26 933	58.6	6.2	53.0	10.0	37.1
Lee County	19 485	24 433	7.1	10 016	0.0	5.0	2.9	91 203	62.0	5.7	53.8	20.1	26.1
Limestone County	12 113	2 898	7.8	3 229	0.3	12.0	7.9	51 118	60.8	4.3	54.5	10.9	34.7
Lowndes County	3 192	348	11.8	905	0.1	11.0	11.3	9 902	51.1	11.9	45.6	9.6	44.8
Macon County	4 702	3 440	35.6	2 192	0.5	5.7	5.1	18 695	49.7	12.3	42.9	14.8	42.3
Madison County	51 678	21 212	13.8	15 636	1.3	8.5	5.7	213 615	67.6	5.7	58.8	13.8	27.4
Marengo County	4 999	707	9.4	1 322	0.1	10.5	7.7	16 849	52.4	8.7	45.8	10.4	43.8
Marion County	5 123	932	5.6	1 508	0.0	10.4	7.4	24 951	56.1	8.1	50.9	9.8	39.2
Marshall County	14 556	2 441	4.0	4 270	0.1	7.8	9.3	64 209	60.6	5.7	53.3	11.0	35.7
Mobile County	82 148	20 709	19.2	23 622	0.1	9.1	7.2	301 859	59.4	7.6	51.7	12.7	35.6
Monroe County.............	5 059	768	12.2	1 505	0.0	8.8	10.6	18 216	55.0	8.4	49.6	8.8	41.6
Montgomery County......	43 518	16 879	18.3	12 924	0.2	8.7	8.3	171 966	61.3	6.5	55.7	12.9	31.4
Morgan County.............	20 603	3 925	7.4	5 898	0.2	10.0	8.4	86 074	62.2	5.4	55.5	11.7	32.8
Perry County	2 585	551	12.1	852	0.0	10.8	9.6	8 764	46.6	14.7	40.5	10.2	49.2
Pickens County	4 382	641	9.3	1 254	0.0	7.4	7.1	15 911	52.4	8.2	47.0	9.4	43.6
Pike County	5 330	3 315	11.8	2 161	0.0	5.5	6.2	23 243	60.6	9.2	48.6	16.0	35.4
Randolph County	4 290	745	6.7	1 188	0.0	8.7	8.4	17 282	55.8	5.3	49.8	10.0	40.1
Russell County	9 866	1 766	7.4	2 663	0.6	9.4	6.8	37 952	57.1	6.2	52.9	9.0	38.1
St. Clair County	12 249	1 905	10.0	3 147	0.0	10.8	7.3	50 004	59.0	4.2	55.4	10.4	34.2
Shelby County..............	26 646	7 321	16.2	7 202	0.0	7.7	4.0	109 617	70.3	3.0	61.7	13.1	25.2
Sumter County	3 291	1 075	11.1	949	0.0	6.1	6.7	10 977	47.6	11.4	42.1	12.1	45.8
Talladega County	15 320	2 625	8.5	4 591	0.2	12.5	7.6	62 620	55.2	7.7	49.2	10.4	40.4
Tallapoosa County	7 677	1 221	4.3	2 056	0.0	10.9	7.3	32 480	56.7	6.0	53.1	8.8	38.0
Tuscaloosa County	28 564	21 141	9.2	12 685	0.0	7.2	4.4	130 752	60.7	6.2	51.6	16.5	31.9
Walker County..............	12 057	2 581	7.9	3 756	0.0	9.6	7.9	56 066	53.3	6.4	47.3	10.3	42.4

STATE County	Total (24)	Men (25)	Women (26)	Non-Hispanic White (27)	Black or African American (28)	American Indian and Alaska Native (29)	Asian, Hawaiian, and Pacific Islander (30)	Hispanic or Latino[1] (31)	Number (32)	Both in labor force (33)	Father only in labor force (34)	With one parent who is in labor force (percent) (35)	+/- U.S. percent of children with no stay-at-home parent (percent) (36)	+/- U.S. percent two-income couples (37)	Private (38)	Government (39)	Self-employed (40)	Unpaid family worker (41)
UNITED STATES....	40.5	50.0	31.6	42.3	36.3	33.6	38.9	34.8	67 882 626	43.2	21.9	21.4	0.0	0.0	75.3	14.6	9.8	0.3
ALABAMA	39.6	49.9	30.4	42.0	32.8	37.7	37.6	39.4	1 049 873	40.4	21.4	22.9	-1.3	-3.4	75.0	15.5	9.2	0.3
Autauga County	46.7	58.5	35.9	49.2	35.4	46.9	47.1	46.8	11 903	46.3	22.3	18.4	0.1	-0.9	72.8	18.6	8.3	0.3
Baldwin County	40.6	51.2	30.7	40.8	37.2	45.1	31.7	45.6	32 894	47.3	23.8	18.1	0.8	-5.2	72.9	13.8	13.0	0.3
Barbour County	32.4	36.7	27.7	38.9	24.6	11.7	45.0	28.9	6 806	36.5	14.6	24.7	-3.4	-2.1	74.4	14.4	10.8	0.5
Bibb County................	34.4	42.1	26.2	38.2	19.4	75.0	100.0	46.2	4 881	41.3	26.7	18.3	-5.0	-7.9	77.7	13.9	8.1	0.3
Blount County.............	40.9	52.7	29.4	41.7	31.3	37.6	28.4	27.3	12 446	46.7	25.7	13.7	-4.2	-3.5	76.0	13.2	10.3	0.5
Bullock County	29.2	31.9	26.2	36.3	24.9	9.6	0.0	62.8	2 664	21.8	8.6	33.0	-9.8	-15.6	70.9	21.3	7.5	0.2
Butler County	33.4	42.8	25.6	39.4	24.2	40.0	26.9	17.9	5 337	37.4	13.4	32.5	5.3	-8.9	75.3	14.8	9.4	0.6
Calhoun County	38.3	49.4	28.3	39.1	33.8	28.4	31.3	45.9	24 403	38.2	22.3	23.2	-3.2	-8.0	73.4	18.0	8.3	0.4
Chambers County	39.9	47.8	33.1	42.7	35.3	38.8	0.0	44.8	8 223	41.1	12.0	30.5	7.0	-0.1	81.7	10.9	7.4	0.1
Cherokee County	37.2	47.5	27.6	37.4	34.8	13.1	18.8	49.3	4 982	47.3	20.7	13.5	-3.8	-7.7	74.8	13.2	11.3	0.8
Chilton County	40.6	53.3	28.7	42.0	31.0	45.6	26.2	31.7	9 475	43.1	28.5	16.1	-5.4	-6.1	76.9	11.9	10.9	0.3
Choctaw County	28.7	38.3	20.6	32.4	23.3	57.1	20.0	38.4	3 688	29.9	23.9	23.9	-10.8	-16.6	75.6	12.9	11.1	0.5
Clarke County	35.7	48.7	24.5	42.0	26.6	0.0	30.9	27.4	7 348	38.4	19.5	21.1	-5.1	-7.0	78.8	13.6	7.4	0.1
Clay County................	38.2	50.3	27.1	39.2	32.5	29.2	0.0	31.7	3 170	45.8	16.7	22.3	3.5	-6.5	76.3	13.8	9.1	0.8
Cleburne County	40.0	52.3	28.0	40.0	35.7	24.4	X	58.8	3 248	44.9	28.8	14.3	-5.4	-8.1	75.1	14.2	10.5	0.2
Coffee County	40.9	52.6	30.2	43.2	31.5	28.1	43.5	35.7	10 038	40.8	23.0	22.0	-1.8	-4.4	70.2	19.2	10.4	0.2
Colbert County	36.2	47.7	25.9	37.2	30.9	25.6	44.5	42.2	12 329	41.5	25.0	18.6	4.5	8.6	74.6	15.8	9.2	0.4
Conecuh County	32.4	41.6	24.6	36.1	26.5	57.1	33.3	56.9	3 393	33.4	13.6	24.5	-6.7	-13.6	75.0	14.0	10.8	0.2
Coosa County	39.3	47.1	31.5	42.3	33.3	55.0	X	44.4	2 620	37.3	19.9	26.2	-1.1	-8.8	80.5	12.5	7.0	0.0
Covington County	35.5	45.2	27.0	35.9	33.6	41.7	18.5	18.7	8 351	43.5	19.9	21.6	0.5	-7.1	72.6	14.2	12.7	0.5
Crenshaw County	36.0	46.8	27.0	39.1	26.6	40.0	X	28.1	3 073	42.4	16.1	22.9	0.7	-7.8	72.2	15.4	12.1	0.3
Cullman County............	40.4	52.3	29.1	40.5	35.3	35.5	28.9	39.4	17 729	47.1	25.9	15.7	-1.8	-4.8	75.7	11.5	12.3	0.5
Dale County	41.4	54.2	29.3	43.0	36.2	28.9	37.7	38.3	12 393	37.7	25.5	22.0	-4.9	-6.7	70.2	20.5	9.0	0.3
Dallas County	30.9	39.0	24.5	41.0	24.1	41.3	68.6	15.5	11 742	26.8	12.1	29.0	-9.0	-0.0	74.7	16.7	8.4	0.2
DeKalb County	41.3	52.6	31.1	41.1	40.4	38.9	30.8	46.4	14 884	46.7	24.7	16.0	-1.9	-2.8	77.7	10.2	11.6	0.6
Elmore County	43.2	50.8	35.5	47.6	27.5	23.0	58.4	29.7	16 140	48.8	21.6	19.2	3.4	2.8	71.1	19.4	9.3	0.2
Escambia County	33.1	38.7	27.3	35.9	26.1	36.4	35.2	41.0	8 501	40.8	17.8	24.9	1.1	-5.9	74.7	15.8	9.1	0.4
Etowah County	35.7	46.6	26.2	36.7	30.5	31.6	42.9	24.9	22 854	37.9	23.7	22.2	-4.5	-8.0	77.6	12.7	9.4	0.3
Fayette County	35.5	49.4	22.9	36.3	32.0	0.0	0.0	19.5	4 203	46.6	26.4	13.5	-4.5	-8.2	76.9	13.0	10.0	0.2
Franklin County	37.7	48.5	27.7	37.7	30.4	27.1	56.0	43.1	7 077	42.7	22.4	18.4	-3.5	-5.2	77.6	12.2	9.9	0.4
Geneva County	39.1	48.9	30.3	40.6	28.1	17.2	36.7	52.8	5 779	47.0	19.2	19.0	1.4	-4.0	74.1	14.0	11.4	0.5
Greene County	28.2	33.4	24.1	43.9	23.9	X	100.0	28.2	2 531	25.0	10.5	32.8	-6.8	-8.0	69.5	22.6	7.6	0.3
Hale County	31.2	39.9	23.7	39.4	24.7	52.6	100.0	14.3	4 629	32.7	17.4	23.0	-8.9	-7.0	74.7	16.7	8.2	0.3
Henry County	38.4	47.3	30.4	39.7	35.7	20.0	X	34.1	3 597	41.7	19.1	21.5	-1.4	-5.6	73.3	16.6	9.9	0.3
Houston County	43.7	55.0	33.9	46.2	35.9	51.9	45.6	32.1	21 695	41.7	19.3	24.0	1.1	1.0	77.4	12.4	9.9	0.3
Jackson County...........	40.3	51.1	30.3	40.8	36.1	35.3	47.8	38.0	12 090	47.0	20.0	21.4	4.4	2.1	76.3	14.2	9.2	0.4
Jefferson County	41.1	50.0	33.6	44.5	35.8	45.1	39.3	37.6	152 343	38.1	19.3	26.9	0.4	-0.9	77.6	14.4	7.8	0.3
Lamar County	35.9	46.3	26.4	36.5	32.9	18.5	44.8	21.6	3 505	46.3	20.9	17.7	-0.6	-7.9	77.8	11.8	10.1	0.3
Lauderdale County	36.7	48.7	25.9	37.3	31.2	35.2	26.3	37.6	19 498	40.5	27.3	19.3	-4.8	-7.9	74.2	16.0	9.6	0.3
Lawrence County	38.6	50.7	27.4	39.0	35.9	39.9	37.7	41.9	8 484	47.6	22.2	17.7	0.7	-5.3	78.6	11.1	9.8	0.5
Lee County	37.2	45.4	29.4	37.8	35.3	33.2	30.4	39.2	25 210	44.5	21.3	23.9	3.8	5.0	69.8	20.6	8.9	0.7
Limestone County	40.6	50.7	30.3	42.3	31.6	31.7	40.3	41.8	15 622	44.6	24.5	19.1	-0.9	-0.3	75.8	15.4	8.5	0.3
Lowndes County	31.1	37.9	25.5	42.9	26.3	0.0	X	31.6	3 665	25.4	7.2	34.0	-5.2	-8.4	70.4	19.7	9.5	0.3
Macon County	27.7	31.3	24.8	40.7	25.4	17.9	25.4	13.3	5 306	23.2	7.6	43.6	2.2	-5.7	64.5	28.1	7.3	0.1
Madison County	45.6	56.6	35.5	47.4	40.5	44.2	38.9	45.3	67 467	46.2	22.3	21.9	3.5	2.0	72.2	19.3	8.3	0.2
Marengo County	33.3	44.1	24.4	43.6	22.8	70.4	0.0	29.0	5 851	33.2	18.1	23.3	-8.1	-9.8	78.7	14.0	7.0	0.2
Marion County	36.1	46.7	26.1	36.6	29.1	29.2	34.6	28.8	6 613	46.4	19.2	18.9	0.7	-7.9	77.6	10.5	11.6	0.3
Marshall County	41.1	54.0	29.2	40.8	45.2	36.2	51.6	46.3	19 073	44.9	25.6	17.6	-2.1	-5.1	74.4	12.7	12.4	0.5
Mobile County	38.1	48.4	29.2	41.5	31.7	29.3	32.4	35.4	101 714	34.7	21.2	26.6	-3.3	-6.1	76.8	14.2	8.8	0.2
Monroe County	36.7	48.3	26.5	40.5	30.8	30.9	25.0	78.9	6 389	37.9	19.6	25.6	-1.1	-8.7	76.3	13.9	9.2	0.6
Montgomery County	42.9	51.3	35.5	48.5	36.4	40.0	49.5	53.5	53 512	36.2	15.5	29.5	1.1	1.9	67.0	24.2	8.5	0.3
Morgan County	42.0	54.4	30.4	42.9	37.2	43.6	39.6	33.8	26 946	43.2	26.8	19.0	-2.4	-3.6	77.6	12.5	9.7	0.2
Perry County	26.8	33.0	21.9	34.8	22.7	0.0	0.0	20.8	3 135	24.1	11.4	27.2	-13.3	-11.0	75.7	16.7	7.2	0.4
Pickens County	34.2	46.0	24.4	40.6	24.7	36.1	4.5	49.2	5 211	35.8	15.9	24.3	-4.5	-6.3	71.7	16.4	11.7	0.3
Pike County	35.4	46.8	25.7	40.8	26.4	39.6	14.9	25.8	6 586	37.5	17.4	24.8	-2.3	-3.6	68.7	20.9	10.1	0.2
Randolph County	36.2	45.7	27.7	38.0	29.3	0.0	3.7	35.3	5 199	39.5	22.6	23.2	-1.9	-6.7	75.6	12.1	11.7	0.6
Russell County	38.9	48.3	30.9	41.6	34.6	43.2	46.9	39.2	12 099	35.1	16.6	26.6	-2.9	-2.8	77.9	15.2	6.6	0.4
St. Clair County	42.2	52.4	32.0	43.5	28.1	39.2	36.9	35.1	15 565	42.9	27.1	17.0	-4.7	-4.9	77.4	11.0	11.1	0.5
Shelby County.............	50.2	64.8	36.6	50.5	45.2	51.2	60.9	50.5	36 303	48.4	32.9	12.1	-4.1	4.6	78.5	11.0	10.4	0.2
Sumter County	26.2	33.9	20.3	38.5	21.0	77.8	55.6	11.2	3 803	21.7	10.0	31.6	-11.3	-11.3	72.8	19.8	7.2	0.2
Talladega County	36.9	46.3	28.2	40.0	30.5	36.3	28.8	15.0	18 187	40.9	18.5	22.9	-0.8	-5.5	75.4	16.9	7.4	0.2
Tallapoosa County	40.0	48.0	33.0	42.2	32.8	56.1	38.8	46.0	9 320	40.3	16.7	24.4	0.1	-3.5	77.1	12.9	9.7	0.3
Tuscaloosa County	37.5	47.1	28.8	39.6	33.0	44.3	22.5	29.3	36 506	38.7	20.1	26.4	0.5	-2.1	72.3	20.0	7.3	0.4
Walker County..............	34.8	46.9	23.8	35.2	28.1	38.2	56.1	43.4	15 466	36.7	28.0	19.0	-8.9	-12.8	77.7	13.3	8.5	0.4

[1]Hispanic or Latino persons may be of any race.

STATE County	Percent who worked at home	Percent of the population 5 years and over with a disability	Veterans as a percent of the population 18 years and over	Occupation for employed population 16 years and over (percent)						Industry for employed population 16 years and over (percent)					
				Management, professional, and related occupations	Service occupa-tions	Sales and office occupa-tions	Farming, fishing, and forestry occupa-tions	Con-struction, extraction, and main-tenance occupa-tions	Production, transporta-tion and material moving occupa-tions	Agricul-ture, forestry, fishing, and mining	Construc-tion and manufac-turing	Whole-sale and retail trade	Trans-porta-tion and ware-housing, and utilities	Service industries	Public adminis-tration
	42	43	44	45	46	47	48	49	50	51	52	53	54	55	56
UNITED STATES....	3.3	19.3	12.6	33.6	14.9	26.7	0.7	9.4	14.6	1.9	20.9	15.3	5.2	51.9	4.8
ALABAMA	2.1	23.2	13.5	29.5	13.5	25.9	0.8	11.3	19.0	1.9	26.0	15.8	5.3	45.8	5.2
Autauga County	1.9	21.6	16.8	27.1	14.1	28.7	0.8	11.3	18.0	2.3	24.0	17.1	4.8	41.4	10.4
Baldwin County	3.5	22.1	17.7	29.5	14.5	27.5	1.0	13.8	13.7	1.9	23.3	18.0	5.2	47.5	4.2
Barbour County	2.1	27.2	12.8	23.3	13.5	22.0	1.2	10.9	29.1	4.2	38.0	13.6	6.3	33.1	4.8
Bibb County.................	1.5	25.7	10.3	22.1	11.9	21.3	2.5	15.8	26.4	5.6	32.8	14.2	7.6	36.0	3.7
Blount County	2.5	24.9	12.3	23.6	11.8	23.6	1.0	18.1	21.8	3.1	31.6	16.7	7.2	37.8	3.5
Bullock County	3.1	29.5	11.9	18.0	18.8	17.1	4.7	10.4	31.0	10.5	28.8	10.5	7.1	33.7	9.3
Butler County	3.0	29.3	13.4	20.9	14.4	24.7	2.2	11.9	25.9	5.2	30.1	18.5	4.7	35.3	6.2
Calhoun County	1.7	24.8	16.3	25.5	14.6	25.0	0.5	11.2	23.2	0.9	28.3	16.4	4.7	41.6	8.0
Chambers County	1.2	27.4	13.5	19.6	12.2	23.6	0.6	12.3	31.7	1.5	44.0	12.5	3.7	35.0	3.2
Cherokee County	2.3	26.0	12.9	19.0	9.9	21.3	2.2	14.8	32.8	3.6	44.1	14.5	5.5	29.0	3.3
Chilton County	2.3	24.5	12.5	22.0	12.4	25.6	1.4	18.7	20.0	3.4	30.0	16.7	7.2	39.4	3.4
Choctaw County	2.4	29.2	10.3	21.9	12.9	20.4	2.4	16.6	25.9	6.7	37.6	11.6	5.1	35.6	3.5
Clarke County	1.3	25.3	11.2	23.9	12.9	21.9	2.3	13.7	25.3	4.6	37.5	13.8	6.3	34.5	3.2
Clay County	1.9	25.2	12.9	19.4	10.9	20.8	2.2	11.5	35.1	4.1	42.7	12.3	5.4	30.5	4.9
Cleburne County	1.2	24.3	11.3	21.3	10.6	21.0	1.6	16.6	28.8	4.3	41.5	13.9	4.5	31.6	4.1
Coffee County	1.9	23.6	18.0	29.9	13.3	23.9	1.4	11.9	19.5	3.6	23.3	15.7	7.7	42.7	7.0
Colbert County	1.1	26.1	13.5	24.0	13.7	24.7	0.5	13.7	23.3	1.8	30.4	16.5	7.1	40.7	3.5
Conecuh County	3.3	28.5	13.6	19.4	11.8	25.6	1.4	13.8	28.1	5.7	34.1	16.2	9.3	29.9	4.9
Coosa County	1.4	32.2	13.3	16.3	14.6	19.8	0.7	14.3	34.3	2.9	44.8	12.8	5.3	29.8	4.3
Covington County.........	2.9	28.0	14.5	26.3	13.5	23.0	1.7	13.7	21.8	4.9	28.0	15.4	8.4	38.9	4.4
Crenshaw County	3.1	28.5	12.1	22.4	14.2	21.7	3.9	13.4	24.3	9.1	24.9	17.7	6.4	36.0	6.0
Cullman County...........	3.4	22.9	13.4	24.5	10.7	23.8	1.9	13.8	25.2	4.4	31.4	18.6	5.7	36.8	3.1
Dale County	1.9	24.2	20.1	24.0	18.1	24.6	0.6	14.8	17.9	1.5	21.2	16.1	10.3	43.4	7.5
Dallas County	1.2	28.1	11.2	24.6	15.9	23.9	0.9	10.8	23.9	2.1	30.5	14.2	4.8	42.3	6.2
DeKalb County	2.9	25.5	11.0	19.7	10.7	18.6	1.6	12.2	37.3	3.8	46.6	11.7	4.9	30.3	2.7
Elmore County	2.2	21.2	16.1	29.1	12.5	27.7	0.7	13.4	16.6	1.4	24.4	15.8	5.2	43.6	9.6
Escambia County	1.1	26.9	13.1	22.6	13.9	24.3	1.9	12.0	25.4	5.0	29.7	15.6	6.0	37.9	5.8
Etowah County	1.9	25.6	14.1	25.3	13.7	25.0	0.7	12.2	23.2	1.1	28.8	16.9	5.1	43.6	4.5
Fayette County.............	1.3	24.6	11.9	20.7	11.4	20.8	2.5	14.2	30.4	6.1	37.1	14.6	5.9	32.4	4.0
Franklin County	2.5	26.4	10.0	20.0	11.3	18.7	1.7	13.5	34.8	4.3	41.7	14.8	5.6	31.0	2.7
Geneva County	3.2	28.2	14.3	22.2	14.5	23.2	2.9	14.4	22.8	6.3	27.3	17.5	9.0	35.5	4.3
Greene County	3.4	30.0	9.7	20.8	20.6	21.5	1.9	9.5	25.7	6.5	24.7	12.9	6.0	43.0	6.8
Hale County	2.6	29.7	9.4	19.6	15.4	22.1	2.3	13.2	27.4	4.8	33.8	15.6	5.2	36.4	4.2
Henry County	2.6	29.3	15.0	24.9	11.1	24.7	2.1	14.0	23.2	4.5	31.6	16.1	7.1	36.6	4.1
Houston County	1.5	21.9	14.5	29.5	14.7	27.4	0.6	10.9	17.0	1.4	21.3	19.1	8.4	45.8	4.0
Jackson County............	1.7	23.7	12.0	21.7	11.5	20.7	1.1	13.1	31.9	2.6	42.9	12.6	6.5	32.3	3.2
Jefferson County	1.9	22.4	12.7	34.0	13.7	30.7	0.1	8.8	12.7	0.6	16.2	16.5	5.5	56.9	4.2
Lamar County	1.1	27.7	12.7	19.8	10.8	21.1	3.2	10.8	34.3	4.4	40.2	12.6	6.4	33.1	3.3
Lauderdale County........	2.1	22.8	12.8	26.2	14.0	26.6	0.7	11.1	21.5	1.3	29.1	17.9	6.3	41.7	3.7
Lawrence County	1.9	26.2	9.1	18.1	14.6	20.5	0.8	16.5	29.6	2.5	43.0	14.3	4.4	33.0	2.8
Lee County	1.8	17.7	11.0	33.9	15.2	25.8	0.6	9.2	15.4	1.1	21.7	14.7	3.3	55.2	4.1
Limestone County	2.0	22.7	13.3	27.0	12.4	22.2	0.9	13.6	24.0	1.7	35.9	15.6	4.2	37.8	4.8
Lowndes County	2.2	31.8	8.9	23.4	12.7	19.2	2.9	14.9	26.9	5.6	31.8	14.0	5.0	35.4	8.2
Macon County	2.0	29.6	11.6	29.6	22.9	22.9	0.6	8.6	15.3	2.4	17.6	10.6	3.7	58.8	7.0
Madison County	2.3	17.8	16.0	43.3	12.4	23.8	0.2	7.5	12.8	0.5	24.5	13.1	3.1	49.2	9.7
Marengo County...........	1.4	28.5	11.1	23.0	13.3	22.0	2.5	11.4	27.8	4.7	34.3	14.3	6.0	37.1	3.7
Marion County	1.8	25.9	11.8	19.9	12.0	21.0	1.3	13.6	32.1	3.3	41.6	14.0	6.6	31.4	3.0
Marshall County	2.7	22.5	13.4	25.1	11.6	24.4	1.0	12.7	25.1	2.4	35.9	17.3	4.2	35.8	4.4
Mobile County	1.8	23.8	13.6	29.0	15.2	26.9	0.6	12.1	16.2	1.1	22.6	17.2	5.5	49.7	4.0
Monroe County	2.1	22.4	11.6	21.5	12.6	22.0	1.8	11.9	30.2	4.1	37.2	16.2	7.0	31.9	3.7
Montgomery County......	1.7	21.8	14.4	36.6	15.7	29.0	0.2	6.9	11.6	0.7	13.4	15.0	4.1	55.0	11.9
Morgan County.............	1.9	21.8	13.4	27.1	12.6	23.6	0.6	11.7	24.4	1.5	36.1	14.7	4.5	39.3	3.9
Perry County	1.6	28.1	10.0	23.3	15.3	16.2	2.6	9.1	33.4	4.8	34.5	10.9	4.4	41.0	4.4
Pickens County	2.0	27.8	12.1	22.9	12.5	23.2	2.9	12.3	26.1	6.0	33.3	14.5	5.9	36.5	3.8
Pike County	2.0	24.3	11.1	24.8	18.0	26.4	1.6	11.0	18.3	3.5	22.7	17.4	5.9	43.5	7.0
Randolph County	2.1	25.3	12.3	20.2	12.5	19.0	1.6	14.5	32.3	4.1	44.6	12.2	3.7	32.2	3.2
Russell County	1.0	26.3	14.6	22.6	14.5	26.3	0.8	13.3	22.5	1.4	30.6	13.6	4.4	44.6	5.4
St. Clair County	2.2	21.9	14.0	25.0	11.3	27.7	0.7	16.0	19.3	1.6	29.3	17.4	5.9	42.1	3.7
Shelby County..............	3.2	15.2	12.1	42.9	9.5	28.8	0.3	9.7	8.9	1.0	18.8	16.6	5.0	55.7	3.0
Sumter County	1.7	26.2	8.0	22.5	17.4	24.8	2.3	7.9	25.2	5.0	26.5	15.5	5.8	42.4	4.8
Talladega County	1.2	27.7	13.4	24.3	12.5	23.1	0.5	14.0	25.6	2.5	33.4	14.8	4.8	38.9	5.6
Tallapoosa County	1.9	28.7	13.7	23.7	12.8	24.9	0.7	12.9	25.0	1.7	40.0	13.3	4.1	36.4	4.4
Tuscaloosa County	2.0	20.9	12.1	32.0	14.1	27.1	0.4	9.7	16.7	2.1	21.5	16.7	3.5	52.7	3.6
Walker County..............	1.4	29.4	13.6	22.4	13.7	24.3	1.1	16.8	21.7	5.8	22.6	18.2	8.9	40.6	3.9

STATE County	Median household income	Median family income: All families	Median family income: Families with children: Married-couple	Median family income: Families with children: Male householder	Median family income: Families with children: Female householder	Median nonfamily household income	Median income for full-year, full-time workers: Men	Median income for full-year, full-time workers: Women	Per capita income	Households by source of income (percent): With earnings	Households by source of income (percent): With interest, dividend, or rental income	Households by source of income (percent): With Social Security income	Households by source of income (percent): With public assistance income	Households by source of income (percent): With retirement income	Households with income over $100,000 (percent)	+/– U.S. percent for income over $100,000	Households with income below poverty (percent)	Families with children with income below poverty (percent)
	57	58	59	60	61	62	63	64	65	66	67	68	69	70	71	72	73	74
UNITED STATES	41 994	50 046	59 461	29 907	20 284	25 705	38 349	28 135	21 587	80.5	35.9	25.7	3.4	16.7	12.3	0.0	11.8	13.6
ALABAMA	34 135	41 657	51 129	26 284	15 403	17 866	33 992	23 585	18 189	77.0	27.1	28.0	2.2	17.9	7.6	-4.7	16.7	18.2
Autauga County	42 013	48 458	55 462	31 063	18 951	19 117	36 575	23 682	18 518	83.3	28.9	24.9	2.1	19.7	7.6	-4.7	11.5	10.8
Baldwin County	40 250	47 028	54 446	29 868	18 404	21 811	35 889	24 423	20 826	76.2	35.7	31.3	1.4	22.3	9.5	-2.8	10.3	11.5
Barbour County	25 101	31 877	42 625	18 309	11 847	11 403	29 363	20 270	13 316	68.9	18.7	31.3	2.9	15.8	5.0	-7.3	26.8	32.0
Bibb County	31 420	37 230	42 515	26 964	11 947	14 266	30 982	21 571	14 105	75.0	18.7	29.9	3.0	18.9	3.5	-8.8	19.4	24.4
Blount County	35 241	41 573	46 723	24 875	18 456	13 750	32 006	23 496	16 325	78.4	25.7	29.4	1.7	16.9	5.0	-7.3	13.6	12.1
Bullock County	20 605	23 990	38 977	22 450	11 555	11 263	23 908	20 308	10 163	68.6	12.7	29.4	3.2	17.1	2.6	-9.7	33.6	41.2
Butler County	24 791	30 915	41 572	25 781	14 040	12 500	29 845	19 737	15 715	71.3	19.7	33.4	3.2	17.9	4.8	-7.5	24.7	26.6
Calhoun County	31 768	39 908	45 553	24 425	13 440	16 629	31 839	21 641	17 367	74.8	26.2	29.6	2.3	22.9	5.9	-6.4	16.9	19.5
Chambers County	29 667	36 598	47 472	28 517	14 762	14 730	29 455	21 481	15 147	73.4	19.8	33.1	2.7	13.8	3.3	0.0	18.7	10.0
Cherokee County	30 874	36 920	41 431	24 760	14 286	14 892	30 488	21 340	15 543	71.3	25.0	35.6	2.3	18.4	3.6	-8.7	16.4	18.1
Chilton County	32 588	39 505	45 472	34 219	14 932	15 386	31 408	21 662	15 303	76.5	23.9	31.1	2.4	16.5	4.0	-8.3	16.4	16.2
Choctaw County	24 749	31 870	42 133	13 500	11 747	12 688	34 884	19 302	14 635	69.0	19.4	33.4	2.3	17.3	4.9	-7.4	24.9	29.7
Clarke County	27 388	34 546	45 506	29 844	13 992	12 657	35 544	19 710	14 581	71.7	20.9	29.3	4.3	13.5	5.0	-7.3	22.5	24.0
Clay County	27 885	34 033	40 712	19 550	15 000	14 315	26 578	19 175	13 785	71.2	20.4	33.2	2.7	19.5	2.0	-10.3	18.9	18.7
Cleburne County	30 820	35 579	40 117	18 500	15 093	14 048	30 235	19 689	14 762	76.4	21.1	29.6	2.0	17.1	3.5	-8.8	16.4	15.4
Coffee County	33 664	39 664	46 160	22 120	14 060	17 996	32 758	21 232	18 321	77.5	28.0	29.8	2.6	21.7	6.6	-5.7	14.5	18.7
Colbert County	31 954	39 294	47 099	28 565	14 269	16 477	33 439	20 630	17 533	72.7	30.3	32.3	1.8	22.0	5.8	-6.5	15.4	16.4
Conecuh County	22 111	31 424	41 250	25 625	10 612	10 669	29 535	19 734	12 964	65.2	15.2	34.3	4.2	16.6	3.6	-8.7	28.7	29.5
Coosa County	29 873	36 082	45 136	26 125	15 102	14 608	26 079	18 881	14 875	75.8	21.6	32.2	2.4	18.8	3.5	-8.8	16.6	16.6
Covington County	26 336	33 201	41 615	21 179	12 946	12 831	28 491	20 563	15 365	70.4	24.0	35.9	2.4	16.4	4.3	-8.0	19.6	20.5
Crenshaw County	26 054	31 724	42 010	21 964	13 534	12 649	28 248	18 460	14 565	70.5	19.5	34.4	3.3	15.6	3.7	-8.6	23.4	25.1
Cullman County	32 256	39 341	42 974	27 348	18 718	15 251	30 864	21 083	16 922	77.0	25.3	30.2	1.5	16.5	5.5	-6.8	14.5	12.6
Dale County	31 998	37 806	44 240	21 757	12 468	17 574	31 165	20 644	16 010	77.5	23.7	25.4	2.6	22.1	3.9	-8.4	16.1	17.6
Dallas County	23 370	29 906	47 263	23 086	9 279	11 948	32 563	19 347	13 638	65.4	17.4	30.4	5.2	17.1	4.2	8.1	31.0	38.3
DeKalb County	30 137	35 801	40 517	25 000	15 744	14 073	29 527	19 654	15 818	76.4	22.3	29.4	2.0	14.4	4.3	-8.0	17.0	15.6
Elmore County	41 243	47 155	53 575	30 357	19 567	20 436	34 427	25 259	17 650	82.0	28.4	25.9	1.3	20.5	8.2	-4.1	10.7	11.2
Escambia County	28 319	36 086	44 159	26 607	12 235	13 393	31 371	18 900	14 396	71.8	21.4	32.9	2.9	17.0	4.8	-7.5	19.9	21.3
Etowah County	31 170	38 697	46 806	23 750	14 608	15 628	32 255	21 834	16 783	72.0	25.3	34.1	2.3	21.2	5.6	-6.7	16.2	18.9
Fayette County	28 539	35 291	40 997	26 190	12 446	11 877	29 685	21 193	14 439	69.9	24.8	34.0	2.2	18.2	2.7	-9.6	19.1	17.8
Franklin County	27 177	34 274	39 148	22 813	13 384	11 654	28 793	19 439	14 814	71.5	22.7	33.2	2.3	15.8	3.9	-8.4	21.1	22.0
Geneva County	26 448	32 563	40 814	20 673	11 830	12 483	27 065	19 992	14 620	72.2	21.0	33.3	2.1	18.1	0.6	0.7	20.4	20.7
Greene County	19 819	24 604	40 855	16 944	12 658	10 322	26 706	19 386	13 686	68.0	13.3	32.0	3.2	15.8	3.3	-9.0	34.6	39.9
Hale County	25 807	31 875	45 153	17 750	11 453	9 886	29 160	19 830	12 661	69.2	17.6	30.2	3.3	17.1	3.3	-9.0	28.3	29.2
Henry County	30 353	36 555	47 917	23 750	14 028	11 451	30 438	21 170	15 681	70.3	26.0	35.7	2.1	17.0	4.8	-7.5	20.0	22.8
Houston County	34 401	42 407	52 003	27 371	14 441	17 893	33 764	22 018	18 759	77.3	28.3	27.6	1.9	15.5	8.0	-4.3	15.8	18.2
Jackson County	32 020	38 082	43 348	27 929	16 190	14 982	30 383	21 430	16 000	77.6	23.6	29.4	1.7	15.9	4.6	-7.7	15.5	13.9
Jefferson County	36 868	45 951	59 872	28 951	18 468	22 033	36 760	27 311	20 892	78.0	28.8	28.3	2.2	16.9	10.1	-2.2	14.7	17.0
Lamar County	28 059	33 050	41 139	28 125	14 271	12 826	31 138	19 668	14 435	71.5	24.3	34.8	2.2	17.4	2.7	-9.6	18.3	18.3
Lauderdale County	33 354	41 438	47 541	21 633	15 411	16 474	35 189	21 382	18 626	74.8	31.9	30.5	1.9	21.5	7.1	-5.2	15.5	16.0
Lawrence County	31 549	38 565	46 346	28 426	16 397	14 167	32 181	21 067	16 515	75.3	20.5	27.9	2.3	16.7	5.8	-6.5	17.6	15.2
Lee County	30 952	46 781	56 256	27 936	16 280	12 643	35 137	24 217	17 158	84.5	26.9	17.9	1.5	13.0	7.2	-5.1	25.2	14.1
Limestone County	37 405	45 146	54 224	28 359	16 420	18 224	36 825	24 370	17 782	79.7	29.1	25.7	3.0	18.4	8.0	-4.3	13.2	14.2
Lowndes County	23 050	28 035	43 303	28 750	10 616	9 300	29 422	20 571	12 457	70.2	15.9	29.6	3.5	15.5	4.2	-8.1	33.2	37.1
Macon County	21 180	28 511	43 429	19 688	13 355	12 096	27 029	22 549	13 714	69.1	14.3	27.6	3.3	20.2	3.9	-8.4	32.0	38.1
Madison County	44 704	54 360	64 231	27 061	19 458	26 187	42 139	27 406	23 091	83.6	38.5	21.1	2.0	19.7	13.3	1.0	10.8	12.2
Marengo County	27 025	35 475	44 838	22 500	10 567	11 675	36 603	20 112	15 308	68.9	19.3	31.9	2.6	16.8	5.9	-6.4	26.7	29.9
Marion County	27 475	34 359	38 903	23 750	14 244	12 473	27 829	19 707	15 321	71.1	22.9	33.2	2.6	18.2	4.0	-8.3	17.7	16.8
Marshall County	32 167	38 788	43 656	23 107	12 411	16 047	31 141	21 327	17 089	76.1	27.1	29.5	2.5	19.6	6.4	-5.9	16.4	16.8
Mobile County	33 710	40 378	50 565	25 800	12 796	18 926	33 925	22 517	17 178	77.6	24.8	27.3	2.6	17.2	6.7	-5.6	18.3	22.8
Monroe County	29 093	34 569	45 217	21 417	11 161	13 531	31 800	19 350	14 862	72.0	19.1	30.0	2.5	16.6	4.4	-7.9	22.9	24.9
Montgomery County	35 962	44 669	56 444	25 885	16 761	23 052	33 377	25 847	19 358	79.9	30.2	25.6	2.4	18.9	9.7	-2.6	15.7	20.1
Morgan County	37 803	45 827	52 645	32 813	16 185	19 622	36 588	22 437	19 223	80.2	30.6	25.9	1.6	17.6	8.6	-3.7	13.1	14.3
Perry County	20 200	26 150	39 139	15 455	11 009	10 845	27 011	17 250	10 948	63.8	15.8	30.8	3.6	16.4	3.1	-9.2	33.4	43.4
Pickens County	26 254	32 938	45 784	25 966	12 234	11 937	29 593	21 216	13 746	68.3	21.8	33.7	3.3	16.8	3.7	-8.6	24.5	29.7
Pike County	25 551	34 132	42 515	23 542	10 461	13 425	27 574	19 354	14 904	74.6	19.3	28.2	3.2	13.9	4.7	-7.6	24.8	25.7
Randolph County	28 675	34 684	42 258	23 750	16 156	12 379	27 565	20 820	14 147	73.5	22.6	31.4	2.4	19.1	3.5	-8.8	17.8	19.5
Russell County	27 492	34 004	43 790	26 161	13 682	14 991	29 638	21 370	14 015	73.4	16.2	29.7	3.6	16.5	2.5	-9.8	20.7	22.9
St. Clair County	37 285	43 152	48 443	29 567	19 838	20 130	35 221	25 380	17 060	70.2	25.8	27.2	2.0	18.3	7.1	-5.2	12.8	12.8
Shelby County	55 440	64 105	71 756	39 444	25 579	32 733	47 282	31 928	27 176	87.2	39.8	18.3	1.0	13.7	19.4	7.1	6.8	6.3
Sumter County	18 911	23 176	41 538	17 639	10 453	9 799	28 895	18 500	11 491	66.1	14.8	27.0	5.2	15.3	2.2	-10.1	38.2	42.5
Talladega County	31 628	38 004	44 729	28 140	13 194	13 885	30 929	21 416	15 704	73.0	21.6	30.8	2.4	19.7	5.2	-7.1	18.5	19.7
Tallapoosa County	30 745	38 148	46 751	25 433	12 278	14 733	29 715	20 621	16 909	72.4	24.4	34.0	2.1	20.8	6.2	-6.1	17.1	20.4
Tuscaloosa County	34 436	45 485	56 523	30 210	17 226	16 729	35 973	25 219	18 998	79.3	28.4	24.2	1.6	17.6	7.8	-4.5	18.8	16.2
Walker County	29 076	35 221	41 919	24 024	12 797	13 590	31 948	20 610	15 546	71.1	20.2	32.3	2.0	21.1	4.7	-7.6	18.1	18.5

STATE/ County code	MSA/PMSA/ NECMA code[1]	STATE County	High school graduates			College graduates		College graduates (percent)				
			Total population 25 years and over	Percent with a high school diploma or less	Percent with a high school diploma or more	Percent with a bachelor's degree or more	+/− U.S. percent with bachelor's degree or more	Non-Hispanic White	Black or African American	American Indian and Alaska Native	Asian, Hawaiian, and Pacific Islander	Hispanic or Latino[2]
			1	2	3	4	5	6	7	8	9	10
		ALABAMA—Cont'd										
01 129	...	Washington County......	11 240	71.3	72.3	8.6	-15.8	9.8	6.6	4.5	0.0	0.0
01 131	...	Wilcox County	7 979	70.7	59.5	10.1	-14.3	18.0	6.1	0.0	0.0	0.0
01 133	...	Winston County............	17 078	71.7	62.6	8.3	-16.1	7.9	0.0	34.7	82.6	13.3
02 000	...	ALASKA	379 556	39.5	88.3	24.7	0.3	29.5	14.9	6.0	20.4	15.3
02 013	...	Aleutians East Borough	2 007	74.2	74.7	4.9	-19.5	17.5	0.0	1.4	1.3	0.0
02 016	...	Aleutians West Census Area...............	4 251	55.9	78.5	11.0	-13.4	22.9	0.8	3.2	3.4	6.8
02 020	0380	Anchorage Municipality .	159 931	33.9	90.3	28.9	4.5	33.0	15.5	10.6	23.1	16.3
02 050	...	Bethel Census Area......	8 026	67.6	71.0	13.1	-11.3	46.5	7.4	4.5	24.7	30.9
02 060	...	Bristol Bay Borough	782	45.1	88.9	21.1	-3.3	28.9	0.0	8.9	22.2	40.0
02 068	...	Denali Borough	1 316	38.7	91.7	22.7	-1.7	24.2	11.8	6.7	23.5	23.5
02 070	...	Dillingham Census Area	2 655	57.3	76.6	16.4	-8.0	39.6	33.3	4.6	45.0	20.4
02 090	...	Fairbanks North Star Borough................	47 974	33.7	91.8	27.0	2.6	30.0	12.5	9.8	24.6	15.5
02 100	...	Haines Borough	1 660	42.2	88.9	23.8	-0.6	26.3	0.0	8.5	20.0	31.3
02 110	...	Juneau City and Borough..................	19 899	28.8	93.2	36.0	11.6	41.5	23.0	7.9	32.1	19.9
02 122	...	Kenai Peninsula Borough..................	31 388	43.3	88.5	20.3	-4.1	22.1	5.4	3.4	20.5	14.1
02 130	...	Ketchikan Gateway Borough..................	8 999	40.1	89.6	20.2	-4.2	22.9	0.0	4.3	23.5	28.1
02 150	...	Kodiak Island Borough..	8 187	45.9	85.4	18.7	-5.7	24.7	16.2	5.4	9.8	10.6
02 164	...	Lake and Peninsula Borough..................	981	67.1	72.2	12.4	-12.0	40.2	X	2.0	0.0	0.0
02 170	...	Matanuska-Susitna Borough..................	35 721	43.2	88.1	18.3	-6.1	19.3	19.8	5.9	17.4	9.0
02 180	...	Nome Census Area......	4 916	63.3	74.8	14.7	-9.7	42.4	25.0	3.3	24.5	6.5
02 185	...	North Slope Borough	3 883	57.6	77.4	17.0	-7.4	48.0	39.5	3.3	24.7	13.8
02 188	...	Northwest Arctic Borough..................	3 498	68.4	72.0	12.7	-11.7	44.8	0.0	3.3	39.5	34.8
02 201	...	Prince of Wales-Outer Ketchikan Cens	3 797	57.0	84.1	14.2	-10.2	19.7	33.3	5.1	12.5	7.7
02 220	...	Sitka City and Borough .	5 608	34.7	90.6	29.5	5.1	36.6	45.2	8.2	20.4	14.7
02 232	...	Skagway-Hoonah-Angoon Census Area.	2 273	46.1	84.4	21.6	-2.8	27.4	0.0	6.7	15.4	44.7
02 240	...	Southeast Fairbanks Census Area	3 693	48.3	86.8	18.2	-6.2	20.6	11.9	4.4	0.0	20.6
02 261	...	Valdez-Cordova Census Area	6 441	41.4	88.5	21.2	-3.2	23.8	20.8	5.7	24.2	17.4
02 270	...	Wade Hampton Census Area.................	3 082	74.9	66.3	9.1	-15.3	68.1	42.9	2.8	55.6	16.7
02 280	...	Wrangell-Petersburg Census Area	4 359	50.6	85.8	16.3	-8.1	19.2	X	2.0	16.5	13.2
02 282	...	Yakutat City and Borough..................	522	49.0	84.3	17.6	-6.8	20.4	100.0	10.9	20.0	0.0
02 290	...	Yukon-Koyukuk Census Area.................	3 707	65.0	74.3	14.2	-10.2	35.0	0.0	4.3	33.3	24.2
04 000	...	ARIZONA	3 256 184	43.3	81.0	23.5	-0.9	28.1	18.6	7.3	43.2	8.1
04 001	...	Apache County.............	36 217	61.2	63.6	11.3	-13.1	25.4	8.3	6.7	51.1	7.9
04 003	...	Cochise County............	75 774	45.2	79.5	18.8	-5.6	23.7	18.9	6.9	18.1	5.8
04 005	2620	Coconino County..........	65 976	37.9	83.8	29.9	5.5	40.2	21.8	7.8	45.3	15.3
04 007	...	Gila County	35 150	50.5	78.2	13.9	-10.5	16.6	9.3	1.9	41.6	6.3
04 009	...	Graham County............	19 302	54.5	75.6	11.8	-12.6	17.6	4.0	2.5	27.5	2.2
04 011	...	Greenlee County	5 207	52.6	82.5	12.2	-12.2	16.0	6.9	0.0	0.0	7.3
04 012	...	La Paz County	14 389	64.6	69.3	8.7	-15.7	9.8	16.9	6.5	16.9	3.8
04 013	6200	Maricopa County	1 934 957	40.6	82.5	25.9	1.5	30.2	19.9	11.2	45.7	8.1
04 015	4120	Mohave County	109 347	57.4	77.5	9.9	-14.5	10.3	6.2	6.0	22.8	6.0
04 017	...	Navajo County	54 215	56.6	71.2	12.3	-12.1	19.9	6.4	4.2	25.9	4.8
04 019	8520	Pima County.................	546 200	39.9	83.4	26.7	2.3	32.5	16.8	9.4	42.2	10.9
04 021	6200	Pinal County	119 102	57.7	72.7	11.9	-12.5	15.6	7.4	2.0	22.6	3.9
04 023	...	Santa Cruz County.......	22 445	62.2	60.7	15.2	-9.2	37.5	11.2	6.3	16.5	7.9
04 025	...	Yavapai County	120 223	43.5	84.7	21.1	-3.3	22.3	39.5	9.7	42.4	7.7
04 027	9360	Yuma County	97 680	59.9	65.8	11.8	-12.6	16.6	12.6	6.2	23.4	4.7
05 000	...	ARKANSAS............	1 731 200	58.8	75.3	16.7	-7.7	17.9	10.2	12.1	31.5	7.1
05 001	...	Arkansas County...........	13 888	67.4	72.4	12.2	-12.2	14.0	4.8	0.0	31.1	0.0
05 003	...	Ashley County	15 722	70.7	72.5	10.1	-14.3	11.8	4.6	12.3	44.4	3.2
05 005	...	Baxter County	28 861	60.0	77.5	12.8	-11.6	12.8	0.0	13.1	18.8	5.4
05 007	2580	Benton County	99 436	52.4	80.4	20.3	-4.1	21.3	27.2	11.7	35.9	6.2
05 009	...	Boone County	23 070	58.2	76.8	12.7	-11.7	12.7	0.0	5.9	30.0	16.2
05 011	...	Bradley County	8 368	70.2	66.6	11.9	-12.5	14.9	6.0	X	0.0	5.1
05 013	...	Calhoun County	3 906	74.8	68.7	7.3	-17.1	8.4	3.1	0.0	0.0	7.1
05 015	...	Carroll County..............	17 207	62.3	71.8	13.8	-10.6	14.5	0.0	17.8	18.2	4.8
05 017	...	Chicot County..............	9 062	71.0	64.2	11.7	-12.7	15.9	7.2	0.0	27.5	7.5
05 019	...	Clark County	13 735	57.1	75.3	19.8	-4.6	23.1	8.7	35.6	56.8	7.3
05 021	...	Clay County	12 175	77.2	60.6	7.4	-17.0	7.3	0.0	3.8	100.0	0.0
05 023	...	Cleburne County	17 299	61.6	74.8	13.9	-10.5	14.0	20.0	14.3	55.6	4.7
05 025	...	Cleveland County	5 659	70.3	73.1	10.0	-14.4	11.1	2.7	0.0	10.0	0.0
05 027	...	Columbia County..........	16 039	61.7	74.1	16.8	-7.6	22.0	6.5	4.2	33.3	7.2

[1]MSA = Metropolitan Statistical Area. PMSA = Primary MSA. NECMA = New England County Metropolitan Area. See the Appendix A for explanation of these concepts. See Appendix B for list of metropolitan areas identified by type, with component counties.
[2]Hispanic or Latino persons may be of any race.

Table B-3. States and Counties — Education, Labor Force, and Income

STATE County	School enrollment			Population 16 to 19 years				Employment status, 2000			Work status in 1999 of the population 16 years and over (percent)		
											Worked in 1999		
	Grades kindergarten through 12	College or graduate school	Percent private	Number	Percent in armed forces	Percent high school graduates	Percent not enrolled, not grads, not in armed forces, not employed	Total population 16 years and over	Percent in labor force	Unemploy- ment rate	Full-time	Part-time	Did not work in 1999
	11	12	13	14	15	16	17	18	19	20	21	22	23

STATE County	11	12	13	14	15	16	17	18	19	20	21	22	23
ALABAMA—Cont'd													
Washington County......	3 845	441	4.3	1 212	0.0	17.2	6.3	13 497	54.5	7.7	48.6	10.0	41.4
Wilcox County	3 095	328	10.8	941	0.0	5.4	13.9	9 668	42.0	15.2	36.2	8.5	55.3
Winston County............	4 311	709	3.9	1 145	0.0	11.7	7.7	19 544	58.2	6.2	53.3	9.5	37.2
ALASKA................	142 653	32 303	8.3	38 321	2.3	15.1	5.2	458 054	71.3	8.6	63.2	15.7	21.1
Aleutians East Borough	342	28	1.4	116	0.0	24.1	3.4	2 337	79.3	41.4	67.2	14.7	18.1
Aleutians West Census Area...............	698	161	11.8	156	0.0	13.5	1.3	4 637	81.7	12.5	73.3	12.6	14.1
Anchorage Municipality .	55 296	15 169	10.2	15 210	3.1	16.6	4.7	192 782	74.4	6.4	66.0	14.7	19.3
Bethel Census Area......	4 814	375	2.8	1 175	0.0	14.6	8.6	10 269	62.8	14.5	47.6	25.5	26.9
Bristol Bay Borough	306	54	4.7	75	0.0	18.7	9.3	908	71.5	10.5	76.4	10.6	13.0
Denali Borough	344	88	6.7	104	6.7	18.3	5.8	1 505	70.8	10.3	71.0	11.8	17.3
Dillingham Census Area	1 434	176	2.4	310	0.0	16.1	8.7	3 216	62.4	11.5	57.2	18.7	24.1
Fairbanks North Star Borough....................	18 063	6 952	8.6	5 230	5.6	16.1	4.7	60 618	74.2	7.9	65.4	15.6	18.9
Haines Borough	486	60	16.8	125	0.0	10.4	4.0	1 864	61.6	13.7	55.5	18.3	26.2
Juneau City and Borough....................	6 210	1 890	6.9	1 692	0.4	13.2	1.2	23 342	75.5	5.3	67.2	15.2	17.6
Kenai Peninsula Borough....................	11 739	1 623	7.9	3 224	0.9	12.4	2.8	36 781	62.8	11.4	56.0	17.2	26.8
Ketchikan Gateway Borough....................	3 051	456	8.5	866	2.5	14.3	7.0	10 567	73.5	7.5	66.8	14.9	18.3
Kodiak Island Borough..	3 150	543	10.7	727	2.1	19.5	2.2	9 794	74.1	4.6	67.7	15.7	16.6
Lake and Peninsula Borough....................	555	39	7.1	149	0.0	16.1	8.1	1 224	55.4	14.3	57.2	19.9	23.0
Matanuska-Susitna Borough....................	14 884	2 100	7.0	3 925	0.2	11.4	5.0	42 705	66.1	10.2	58.6	14.9	26.4
Nome Census Area.......	2 659	278	1.5	644	0.0	13.0	14.8	6 176	60.6	16.2	50.9	19.6	29.5
North Slope Borough	2 148	250	2.1	556	0.0	17.6	7.2	4 875	72.2	14.9	69.0	9.1	21.9
Northwest Arctic Borough....................	2 202	121	1.3	539	0.0	16.0	20.4	4 535	63.4	15.5	59.0	12.6	28.4
Prince of Wales-Outer Ketchikan Cens	1 473	109	3.8	361	0.0	11.1	4.2	4 477	68.7	15.0	62.0	17.3	20.8
Sitka City and Borough .	1 864	575	11.5	501	5.8	19.8	3.0	6 700	73.6	7.4	62.6	18.6	18.8
Skagway-Hoonah- Angoon Census Area.	732	104	10.6	188	0.0	10.6	8.5	2 624	66.8	15.6	61.1	17.0	22.0
Southeast Fairbanks Census Area	1 574	286	14.2	405	2.0	16.5	6.4	4 385	57.8	16.4	53.1	14.8	32.1
Valdez-Cordova Census Area	2 337	416	6.8	611	0.8	12.9	5.9	7 567	66.6	9.4	63.0	15.6	21.4
Wade Hampton Census Area........................	2 583	119	0.7	573	0.0	12.7	10.8	4 094	58.6	23.9	42.0	27.1	30.8
Wrangell-Petersburg Census Area	1 542	140	4.8	345	0.0	13.0	3.5	4 928	69.1	11.0	62.6	17.0	20.5
Yakutat City and Borough....................	173	27	0.0	46	0.0	13.0	6.5	613	77.8	7.8	72.1	18.1	9.8
Yukon-Koyukuk Census Area........................	1 994	164	2.9	468	0.0	9.8	10.0	4 531	62.8	19.9	50.0	22.1	27.9
ARIZONA..................	988 818	331 099	8.7	288 587	0.6	11.1	8.4	3 907 229	61.1	5.6	53.4	13.4	33.2
Apache County.............	21 435	3 235	4.2	5 232	0.0	9.7	11.9	45 710	46.1	21.8	44.1	9.2	46.7
Cochise County............	23 733	7 459	7.5	7 562	10.4	19.8	6.1	90 424	56.4	6.0	47.7	13.9	38.3
Coconino County..........	25 217	14 842	5.5	8 192	0.0	7.9	6.6	86 977	68.6	6.9	56.5	19.2	24.3
Gila County	10 261	1 886	6.4	2 558	0.0	10.4	9.6	39 890	50.1	9.7	41.9	12.6	45.4
Graham County............	7 879	2 540	5.5	2 653	0.0	10.8	7.9	24 541	49.3	11.6	45.5	14.0	40.6
Greenlee County..........	2 070	222	3.6	538	0.0	10.0	2.2	6 159	60.0	6.3	53.1	11.5	35.5
La Paz County	3 303	437	4.6	923	0.0	10.9	8.2	16 134	44.3	8.0	40.2	9.0	50.8
Maricopa County	584 324	197 913	9.7	168 713	0.2	11.3	8.4	2 327 675	64.6	4.7	56.9	13.0	30.1
Mohave County	25 729	5 259	6.3	7 038	0.0	13.9	11.8	123 257	52.8	7.0	45.7	11.7	42.6
Navajo County.............	26 882	3 956	4.5	7 191	0.0	10.3	10.5	66 857	50.5	12.3	47.0	10.8	42.1
Pima County................	153 693	69 727	8.9	49 172	0.7	10.0	6.8	658 638	60.3	5.3	51.0	15.9	33.1
Pinal County................	33 416	6 840	6.4	9 460	0.0	10.9	14.5	139 536	47.9	8.1	45.0	10.2	44.7
Santa Cruz County.......	10 092	1 314	3.8	2 215	0.0	8.2	8.4	26 674	52.4	7.7	47.5	11.8	40.7
Yavapai County	26 770	8 408	11.8	7 946	0.1	10.5	6.0	136 294	52.7	5.0	42.9	15.4	41.7
Yuma County	34 014	7 061	3.7	9 194	3.3	11.4	9.6	118 463	50.3	11.4	47.3	10.5	42.3
ARKANSAS...............	503 693	128 063	8.9	156 258	0.2	13.2	5.4	2 072 068	60.6	6.1	53.5	12.4	34.2
Arkansas County..........	3 938	743	7.4	1 142	0.0	11.6	6.5	16 236	61.1	6.2	54.7	11.4	33.9
Ashley County	5 065	671	3.9	1 373	0.0	9.7	4.4	18 483	56.0	6.9	50.6	10.2	39.2
Baxter County	5 533	911	3.5	1 655	0.0	22.9	2.8	31 998	49.2	4.0	41.1	11.4	47.6
Benton County.............	29 280	5 637	11.3	8 071	0.0	13.8	4.4	116 881	63.8	3.3	56.7	12.3	31.0
Boone County..............	6 016	988	7.5	1 867	0.0	15.3	4.2	26 819	59.6	5.0	51.7	12.3	36.0
Bradley County............	2 383	345	3.0	679	1.2	23.3	3.5	10 039	51.9	10.8	45.4	10.8	43.8
Calhoun County	1 159	115	4.3	273	0.0	13.9	0.0	4 479	55.5	5.3	50.8	8.7	40.5
Carroll County	4 297	398	7.9	1 457	0.0	21.4	6.2	19 991	62.1	5.5	53.1	13.2	33.7
Chicot County..............	2 961	348	9.4	916	0.0	12.1	6.6	10 781	51.1	10.2	45.3	10.6	44.1
Clark County	3 821	3 738	21.0	2 054	0.0	5.9	1.3	18 964	59.3	4.7	48.5	18.8	32.7
Clay County.................	2 960	402	2.5	777	0.0	18.5	1.3	13 980	57.0	5.6	52.0	9.7	38.3
Cleburne County..........	3 905	538	6.3	1 131	0.0	14.1	4.7	19 560	52.5	4.9	47.2	10.7	42.2
Cleveland County	1 697	253	3.1	453	0.0	19.9	3.5	6 553	59.0	5.5	53.8	9.3	36.9
Columbia County..........	4 889	2 082	3.5	1 800	0.0	7.9	5.2	20 006	57.3	7.6	47.8	12.7	39.5

Table B-3. States and Counties — Education, Labor Force, and Income

STATE County	Full-year full-time employed (percent)								Children under 18 years in families						Total employed by class of worker (percent)			
										With two parents (percent)		With one parent who is in labor force (percent)	+/− U.S. percent of children with no stay-at-home parent (percent)	+/− U.S. percent two-income couples				
	Total	Men	Women	Non-Hispanic White	Black or African American	American Indian and Alaska Native	Asian, Hawaiian, and Pacific Islander	Hispanic or Latino[1]	Number	Both in labor force	Father only in labor force				Private	Government	Self-employed	Unpaid family worker
	24	25	26	27	28	29	30	31	32	33	34	35	36	37	38	39	40	41
ALABAMA—Cont'd																		
Washington County	33.9	45.8	23.0	36.7	27.4	28.5	41.2	23.2	4 906	38.8	29.1	17.2	-8.6	-12.4	74.8	16.3	8.5	0.5
Wilcox County	25.0	33.0	18.4	36.7	19.7	22.7	80.0	15.8	3 610	24.9	10.5	25.7	-14.0	-15.1	69.2	19.9	10.4	0.5
Winston County	37.7	48.3	27.6	37.5	35.9	31.9	41.3	55.4	5 655	44.6	20.2	20.4	0.4	-5.7	74.5	11.6	13.4	0.4
ALASKA	38.1	43.9	31.9	41.9	47.3	20.1	32.0	37.5	180 009	45.4	21.4	20.7	1.5	5.0	62.4	26.8	10.6	0.3
Aleutians East Borough	18.3	18.0	18.8	28.7	50.0	17.5	11.3	12.3	414	28.0	8.5	27.3	-9.3	-4.1	70.4	20.7	8.7	0.2
Aleutians West Census Area	32.5	31.2	35.2	44.9	1.6	28.1	23.4	25.8	889	58.4	16.1	15.5	9.3	20.3	79.2	17.8	2.8	0.2
Anchorage Municipality	44.6	51.9	37.1	47.5	46.0	29.0	33.5	39.6	71 592	46.4	21.2	21.1	2.9	9.3	67.9	22.0	9.9	0.2
Bethel Census Area	19.9	22.2	17.3	43.8	47.9	14.0	34.0	51.9	5 858	43.4	15.7	19.8	-1.4	-2.1	42.6	53.0	4.2	0.2
Bristol Bay Borough	40.0	44.6	34.0	49.6	100.0	22.4	77.8	50.0	389	59.1	19.0	13.6	8.1	8.2	55.8	37.0	7.2	0.0
Denali Borough	38.3	49.0	22.5	39.5	77.3	21.2	27.5	35.0	444	40.5	26.1	24.1	0.0	-5.4	54.2	32.7	12.8	0.2
Dillingham Census Area	23.1	23.6	22.7	42.3	66.7	14.4	50.0	37.9	1 758	45.6	10.5	18.7	-0.3	-1.8	43.6	47.5	8.2	0.8
Fairbanks North Star Borough	42.1	50.8	32.5	43.4	53.4	23.7	33.2	44.0	23 861	48.1	24.7	18.3	1.8	7.5	60.3	30.7	8.7	0.3
Haines Borough	25.3	30.9	19.6	26.7	40.0	13.7	53.8	8.7	585	40.9	25.3	16.6	-7.1	-10.0	52.6	23.5	21.9	2.0
Juneau City and Borough	45.0	50.3	39.8	46.5	44.8	35.8	44.1	42.3	7 951	53.4	16.3	22.8	11.6	13.8	49.2	39.8	10.7	0.3
Kenai Peninsula Borough	27.4	31.4	23.1	28.5	28.6	16.4	27.3	24.8	14 192	40.9	27.9	18.3	-5.4	-8.2	64.3	19.5	15.5	0.6
Ketchikan Gateway Borough	39.8	47.1	32.4	42.1	72.5	25.7	36.9	51.2	3 771	55.1	14.9	21.8	12.3	11.3	61.5	26.9	11.3	0.3
Kodiak Island Borough	36.5	43.2	28.7	45.1	59.2	18.9	25.7	25.9	4 301	46.2	22.2	20.2	1.8	7.6	64.0	23.6	12.3	0.1
Lake and Peninsula Borough	16.3	15.9	16.9	38.5	X	8.6	20.0	0.0	638	33.7	8.6	21.9	-9.0	-12.7	26.7	65.4	7.6	0.3
Matanuska-Susitna Borough	32.8	37.8	27.2	33.8	33.7	18.8	21.4	32.1	18 261	42.9	27.0	18.4	-3.3	-1.7	65.2	20.8	13.5	0.5
Nome Census Area	24.0	26.4	21.1	50.0	70.8	14.3	42.4	42.6	3 097	34.7	9.3	28.9	-1.0	-5.2	46.2	48.9	4.5	0.5
North Slope Borough	32.6	35.0	29.7	52.2	84.8	22.9	55.3	42.2	2 552	40.8	17.2	29.4	5.6	5.1	35.8	61.5	2.5	0.2
Northwest Arctic Borough	23.2	23.0	23.6	40.8	15.0	19.0	40.9	35.1	2 637	35.5	10.9	27.9	-1.2	-3.9	54.9	41.0	4.0	0.1
Prince of Wales-Outer Ketchikan Cens	24.5	27.0	21.2	27.8	46.2	19.5	15.8	29.8	1 744	47.6	18.3	19.7	2.7	-2.0	53.6	32.7	13.5	0.3
Sitka City and Borough	36.3	40.9	31.4	37.8	67.7	28.9	33.2	29.1	2 243	55.7	10.0	25.5	16.6	14.4	56.3	27.4	16.0	0.4
Skagway-Hoonah-Angoon Census Area	21.0	22.7	19.0	26.8	40.0	10.3	23.1	16.7	864	44.7	20.6	19.7	-0.2	-4.0	54.3	29.2	16.2	0.3
Southeast Fairbanks Census Area	26.3	32.1	20.2	28.1	70.9	12.8	15.6	25.3	1 858	29.8	33.7	14.5	-20.3	-15.8	47.8	39.6	12.3	0.3
Valdez-Cordova Census Area	30.5	34.9	25.3	32.9	45.8	18.5	19.7	33.0	2 909	39.8	28.4	18.6	-6.2	-5.0	58.3	27.0	14.2	0.4
Wade Hampton Census Area	9.6	11.3	7.7	29.5	28.6	7.7	66.7	14.3	3 017	38.9	11.2	24.7	-1.0	-13.1	39.9	57.7	2.2	0.1
Wrangell-Petersburg Census Area	28.6	31.3	25.6	31.1	X	18.2	20.0	30.6	1 908	57.2	11.8	21.1	13.7	3.6	47.1	29.9	22.8	0.2
Yakutat City and Borough	28.2	27.4	29.6	35.1	100.0	18.0	28.6	0.0	200	40.5	16.0	31.5	7.4	8.9	63.6	23.2	13.2	0.0
Yukon-Koyukuk Census Area	18.8	19.5	17.9	30.9	40.0	13.3	23.5	14.6	2 076	35.0	12.3	32.7	3.1	-5.8	37.1	55.8	6.4	0.7
ARIZONA	38.4	47.1	29.9	40.0	40.5	26.8	39.4	35.3	1 270 112	37.6	24.8	22.1	-4.9	-6.3	74.6	15.2	9.9	0.3
Apache County	22.1	25.4	19.0	32.0	14.9	19.2	34.7	23.2	24 535	27.5	18.3	20.9	-16.2	-19.6	47.3	45.0	7.4	0.2
Cochise County	33.5	42.1	24.8	34.6	48.1	25.2	32.6	28.9	28 568	37.0	24.8	23.1	-4.5	-10.1	60.1	28.2	11.3	0.4
Coconino County	36.5	44.1	29.1	40.3	40.0	25.5	46.9	38.1	30 714	42.0	17.2	22.4	-0.2	3.6	61.3	28.0	10.3	0.3
Gila County	28.8	36.2	21.8	29.4	13.1	16.9	34.9	34.4	11 763	37.7	20.5	22.9	-4.0	-16.5	62.1	23.3	14.1	0.5
Graham County	27.2	34.5	19.1	28.5	25.4	19.6	22.6	27.7	9 377	33.3	26.8	23.6	-7.7	-12.8	61.7	28.4	9.6	0.3
Greenlee County	37.7	51.2	23.4	40.2	44.1	38.0	27.3	33.6	2 583	36.4	35.6	18.1	-10.1	-10.6	78.8	14.8	5.9	0.5
La Paz County	27.1	32.3	21.6	23.0	43.4	35.7	39.0	37.7	3 771	37.1	19.8	29.8	2.3	-21.3	58.9	29.3	11.7	0.2
Maricopa County	42.2	51.6	33.0	43.8	42.6	39.0	41.9	37.1	771 629	38.5	25.9	21.4	-4.7	-3.1	78.3	12.1	9.4	0.2
Mohave County	31.9	37.6	26.3	31.3	29.1	33.0	37.7	37.2	32 849	38.4	21.7	25.5	-0.7	-15.0	76.2	13.1	10.3	0.4
Navajo County	26.9	33.4	20.6	32.5	23.5	19.9	37.9	33.3	31 230	30.2	23.3	22.3	-12.1	-14.6	58.8	30.4	10.3	0.5
Pima County	36.3	45.2	28.1	36.9	36.5	30.1	32.3	35.8	194 133	37.8	22.5	24.1	-2.7	-6.2	71.0	18.7	10.0	0.3
Pinal County	30.0	34.1	25.3	30.9	21.2	23.6	34.1	30.1	40 874	33.2	22.0	26.1	-5.3	-16.5	70.0	20.5	8.9	0.5
Santa Cruz County	29.4	41.6	18.9	35.1	10.0	42.9	29.0	27.7	12 176	26.0	32.2	18.6	-20.0	-19.0	63.5	19.5	16.2	0.8
Yavapai County	30.6	38.9	22.9	29.8	18.5	34.9	26.8	38.7	32 800	40.4	26.7	21.4	-2.8	-15.1	67.7	14.2	17.7	0.4
Yuma County	28.1	36.0	20.2	28.6	36.3	27.1	38.2	26.9	43 110	34.3	27.1	19.2	-11.1	-19.5	68.1	22.4	8.9	0.6
ARKANSAS	38.8	47.8	30.5	40.2	31.3	38.0	38.2	37.6	633 653	43.1	20.2	22.3	0.8	-2.4	73.6	14.9	11.1	0.4
Arkansas County	40.6	51.4	31.4	42.7	32.5	41.4	62.2	58.5	4 696	36.7	21.8	27.4	-0.5	-1.6	68.5	16.8	14.3	0.4
Ashley County	35.3	48.2	23.5	38.7	26.2	3.6	36.9	35.2	5 911	39.1	24.6	20.3	-5.2	-9.5	77.0	12.7	10.0	0.3
Baxter County	30.8	36.1	26.2	30.7	47.1	41.3	25.9	44.3	6 853	48.9	20.0	17.6	1.9	-14.5	73.3	11.7	14.4	0.6
Benton County	43.5	53.2	34.3	43.3	70.0	45.2	50.1	42.7	38 911	47.3	25.2	17.1	-0.2	-1.2	80.7	8.2	10.8	0.3
Boone County	37.7	46.5	29.7	37.8	50.0	35.7	22.5	38.8	7 691	50.5	18.9	16.5	2.4	-2.7	72.8	12.0	14.6	0.6
Bradley County	28.6	34.5	22.9	32.6	21.6	X	66.7	20.3	2 683	36.1	20.3	25.4	-3.1	-10.7	69.2	17.0	13.2	0.6
Calhoun County	37.0	48.7	26.4	39.0	30.8	0.0	100.0	35.7	1 340	50.1	19.8	19.3	4.8	-2.7	69.9	19.2	9.7	1.2
Carroll County	37.8	45.9	30.0	37.0	27.3	59.9	45.5	43.2	5 692	42.7	18.2	24.4	2.5	-5.5	71.4	9.8	18.0	0.8
Chicot County	28.3	33.0	23.9	35.8	21.5	20.0	40.5	24.1	3 297	30.2	12.9	31.4	-3.0	-8.0	64.1	20.3	15.2	0.4
Clark County	32.4	40.4	25.1	32.7	31.2	14.4	21.4	43.5	4 811	50.2	14.1	23.9	9.5	1.6	72.0	18.0	9.7	0.3
Clay County	36.0	43.7	29.0	36.1	100.0	23.6	47.4	32.2	3 858	55.3	16.4	17.2	7.9	-3.9	74.5	12.5	12.8	0.3
Cleburne County	32.9	42.5	24.0	33.1	29.4	16.9	35.1	24.2	4 837	46.3	26.3	15.9	-2.4	-13.0	69.6	14.3	15.8	0.3
Cleveland County	39.2	49.7	29.4	41.2	25.1	20.0	16.3	53.8	2 065	47.6	21.5	16.7	-0.3	-4.2	68.9	18.7	11.8	0.6
Columbia County	33.6	43.4	25.1	37.7	26.6	17.7	32.5	21.9	5 770	39.4	16.8	25.3	0.1	-3.6	73.4	16.9	9.3	0.4

[1] Hispanic or Latino persons may be of any race.

Table B-3. States and Counties — Education, Labor Force, and Income

STATE County	Percent who worked at home	Percent of the population 5 years and over with a disability	Veterans as a percent of the population 18 years and over	Occupation for employed population 16 years and over (percent)						Industry for employed population 16 years and over (percent)					
				Management, professional, and related occupations	Service occupations	Sales and office occupations	Farming, fishing, and forestry occupations	Construction, extraction, and maintenance occupations	Production, transportation and material moving occupations	Agriculture, forestry, fishing, and mining	Construction and manufacturing	Wholesale and retail trade	Transportation and warehousing, and utilities	Service industries	Public administration
	42	43	44	45	46	47	48	49	50	51	52	53	54	55	56
ALABAMA—Cont'd															
Washington County	1.9	22.9	10.5	19.6	12.5	18.3	3.5	17.4	28.7	7.4	39.2	13.2	7.0	28.8	4.4
Wilcox County	1.7	29.9	8.2	20.6	15.9	21.8	4.8	11.0	26.0	7.6	27.8	17.3	7.4	35.6	4.3
Winston County	3.0	24.7	11.8	19.6	10.2	21.6	1.6	13.7	33.2	4.2	41.1	14.8	7.9	29.3	2.7
ALASKA	4.1	14.9	16.4	34.4	15.6	26.1	1.5	11.6	10.8	4.9	10.6	14.2	8.9	50.8	10.7
Aleutians East Borough	0.8	14.1	9.3	16.4	12.1	12.0	11.1	6.4	42.1	9.6	47.6	6.4	8.7	21.1	6.5
Aleutians West Census Area	1.2	17.3	11.1	19.1	11.5	17.9	11.3	10.1	30.2	13.5	37.4	10.1	8.5	21.8	8.7
Anchorage Municipality	3.7	14.9	16.7	36.8	15.1	28.5	0.3	9.7	9.6	3.1	8.4	15.7	9.4	53.8	9.7
Bethel Census Area	2.9	18.0	11.9	37.9	19.0	23.0	0.8	8.9	10.5	0.9	4.4	10.1	11.9	56.4	16.3
Bristol Bay Borough	4.6	25.6	18.6	34.1	17.0	24.6	0.7	15.1	8.4	0.9	12.9	8.1	17.4	46.0	14.8
Denali Borough	9.2	12.0	18.8	30.2	17.5	17.5	0.7	20.8	13.3	15.0	9.9	8.6	11.3	47.3	8.0
Dillingham Census Area	3.7	20.3	10.1	38.8	16.4	21.8	3.8	10.5	8.8	3.9	6.1	10.6	9.9	55.8	13.7
Fairbanks North Star Borough	3.8	13.0	18.1	35.8	15.3	25.4	0.3	13.5	9.6	2.6	10.8	14.5	8.7	53.5	9.8
Haines Borough	11.6	14.8	19.2	31.9	13.1	26.2	2.9	16.1	9.8	5.7	16.0	12.5	7.2	51.2	7.4
Juneau City and Borough	4.3	13.7	12.4	42.3	13.4	26.8	1.8	8.6	7.0	5.2	7.5	11.3	6.5	47.0	22.6
Kenai Peninsula Borough	5.5	16.0	17.1	27.4	17.0	23.3	2.4	16.7	13.2	10.6	14.5	14.5	6.5	46.5	7.5
Ketchikan Gateway Borough	4.3	16.0	16.9	28.5	17.0	27.6	2.3	11.1	13.6	4.7	13.9	13.1	10.9	46.4	11.1
Kodiak Island Borough	2.7	12.3	14.6	23.3	14.0	24.5	7.0	8.6	22.6	9.8	22.2	12.7	7.1	37.3	11.0
Lake and Peninsula Borough	9.1	19.0	12.7	35.5	19.1	17.7	1.4	13.4	12.9	1.4	6.0	6.2	10.2	51.6	24.6
Matanuska-Susitna Borough	6.3	16.5	19.2	30.1	16.2	25.3	0.9	17.6	9.9	5.7	13.8	15.3	8.2	49.2	7.9
Nome Census Area	3.2	17.4	13.5	36.6	21.1	23.9	0.5	7.9	9.9	1.5	3.9	9.7	10.3	58.1	16.4
North Slope Borough	2.3	12.2	9.6	34.1	18.0	22.1	0.2	15.2	10.4	2.1	8.3	6.6	9.4	50.4	23.1
Northwest Arctic Borough	4.5	12.6	13.3	33.9	19.0	19.8	0.1	15.3	11.9	14.3	4.7	7.1	11.1	50.5	12.4
Prince of Wales-Outer Ketchikan Cens	3.9	14.2	15.4	24.8	13.8	21.8	11.5	12.0	16.1	19.4	15.3	13.5	6.5	37.2	8.1
Sitka City and Borough	4.1	14.9	14.4	33.8	17.8	22.1	6.3	9.6	10.4	9.4	10.2	12.2	5.6	56.8	5.9
Skagway-Hoonah-Angoon Census Area	4.8	13.6	14.4	25.9	15.0	22.0	8.9	15.8	12.4	14.5	14.1	9.4	14.1	40.0	7.9
Southeast Fairbanks Census Area	3.3	13.2	19.6	32.6	17.4	22.9	1.4	13.9	11.7	4.7	9.1	10.5	10.1	48.0	17.6
Valdez-Cordova Census Area	5.6	12.6	17.5	30.0	15.3	23.1	3.3	14.5	13.8	6.7	12.8	12.8	14.1	44.3	9.3
Wade Hampton Census Area	3.0	18.6	8.4	36.6	22.2	24.1	0.3	9.0	7.8	1.2	4.7	14.5	8.5	53.4	17.7
Wrangell-Petersburg Census Area	4.6	15.0	16.5	27.2	16.8	21.7	11.0	10.5	12.9	17.9	15.0	10.0	7.2	40.3	9.5
Yakutat City and Borough	5.5	9.7	16.2	26.6	12.5	15.2	23.4	9.8	12.5	30.9	13.0	4.8	14.5	30.0	6.8
Yukon-Koyukuk Census Area	4.4	14.0	14.3	36.1	20.5	19.9	1.3	10.4	11.9	3.0	7.1	7.5	10.3	52.9	19.2
ARIZONA	3.7	19.3	14.9	32.7	16.2	28.5	0.6	11.0	10.9	1.5	18.9	15.6	5.0	53.7	5.4
Apache County	3.4	24.4	10.4	33.2	17.9	21.7	0.7	16.3	10.2	3.1	13.5	9.1	7.2	54.5	12.6
Cochise County	3.9	22.1	21.9	30.2	21.3	27.1	1.3	10.7	9.4	3.3	11.3	16.1	4.9	50.0	14.3
Coconino County	3.8	16.3	11.7	34.8	19.1	25.7	0.5	10.0	10.0	1.7	12.9	14.8	5.4	58.4	6.8
Gila County	4.2	24.9	19.6	24.3	22.8	24.8	0.8	16.4	10.9	7.6	15.3	13.6	4.5	49.4	9.6
Graham County	3.6	18.6	13.5	25.9	20.8	23.5	1.9	16.4	11.5	13.4	11.8	14.4	3.1	46.2	11.1
Greenlee County	2.7	21.0	16.4	23.0	11.6	15.8	1.2	30.0	18.4	48.1	11.1	6.5	3.2	26.0	5.1
La Paz County	3.8	29.1	23.1	23.8	23.4	23.8	5.3	11.1	12.6	8.8	10.7	13.9	4.9	49.1	12.6
Maricopa County	3.7	18.0	13.7	33.9	14.6	29.7	0.4	10.5	11.0	0.6	20.2	15.9	5.1	53.7	4.4
Mohave County	2.8	26.1	21.4	20.4	25.2	27.9	0.4	13.2	12.8	1.0	16.7	15.9	5.7	56.1	4.5
Navajo County	3.5	22.4	12.5	27.2	17.8	24.1	1.3	16.0	13.7	3.7	16.6	14.7	7.0	48.8	9.2
Pima County	3.6	20.1	16.0	35.0	17.6	27.1	0.2	10.7	9.4	0.9	17.5	14.4	4.5	56.9	5.8
Pinal County	3.3	22.9	17.8	22.1	21.9	24.4	2.7	14.2	14.7	6.3	21.6	13.3	4.0	44.8	10.0
Santa Cruz County	4.0	18.3	8.3	25.1	16.4	32.6	1.3	9.8	14.8	2.8	15.1	26.3	6.3	41.3	8.2
Yavapai County	5.9	21.9	20.4	28.3	19.2	26.9	0.8	13.2	11.6	3.2	18.7	16.1	4.1	53.5	4.6
Yuma County	1.9	20.8	16.0	26.7	17.7	26.4	6.3	10.7	12.2	8.8	12.5	18.4	5.0	44.5	10.7
ARKANSAS	2.6	23.6	14.1	27.7	14.1	25.1	1.5	10.6	21.0	3.7	26.4	16.3	5.9	43.4	4.3
Arkansas County	2.9	26.4	11.6	26.2	11.9	24.5	4.8	10.0	22.5	11.6	27.3	15.1	4.5	35.3	6.2
Ashley County	1.7	24.0	12.2	21.6	13.2	20.5	3.4	14.6	26.9	7.4	37.6	13.8	5.4	32.7	3.1
Baxter County	2.7	26.0	20.8	24.2	16.6	26.3	0.7	11.8	20.5	1.5	28.6	15.8	3.4	47.9	2.8
Benton County	3.3	19.8	15.5	29.7	12.3	27.0	1.2	9.8	20.2	3.2	27.1	25.1	5.4	36.8	2.3
Boone County	4.0	24.8	15.3	24.4	13.2	29.1	1.0	10.8	21.5	3.1	24.8	19.1	9.1	41.4	2.5
Bradley County	2.5	27.6	12.5	25.6	15.2	20.2	7.5	8.7	22.7	10.7	25.9	14.9	4.1	40.0	4.4
Calhoun County	1.0	26.9	13.9	20.3	13.1	19.2	3.4	14.8	29.3	8.2	36.1	11.6	8.4	29.4	6.3
Carroll County	7.2	22.1	14.9	25.8	16.9	20.7	2.4	10.1	24.1	6.6	32.4	15.5	4.0	38.9	2.7
Chicot County	2.1	32.4	10.6	30.4	16.4	23.0	4.7	7.2	18.3	12.5	18.3	14.7	5.3	43.7	5.4
Clark County	2.2	23.0	11.0	29.4	13.3	24.8	2.9	8.7	20.8	4.5	25.4	14.0	3.8	49.5	2.8
Clay County	2.6	27.8	13.9	20.7	11.9	20.1	3.3	9.6	34.3	8.3	37.5	13.0	6.2	32.2	2.7
Cleburne County	3.1	24.6	19.9	25.5	12.0	23.1	1.2	15.0	23.2	3.2	32.3	16.7	6.4	37.1	4.4
Cleveland County	3.2	22.2	13.4	24.5	11.6	22.0	4.3	12.3	25.2	9.4	32.5	11.9	7.7	33.2	5.3
Columbia County	1.6	23.4	11.3	26.3	15.2	22.1	1.7	10.9	23.7	5.3	29.9	15.3	4.2	42.1	3.3

STATE County	Median house-hold income	Median family income All families	Families with children Married-couple	Families with children Male house-holder	Families with children Female house-holder	Median nonfamily house-hold income	Median income for full-year, full-time workers Men	Median income for full-year, full-time workers Women	Per capita income	With earnings	With interest, dividend, or rental income	With Social Security income	With public assis-tance income	With retire-ment income	House-holds with income over $100,000 (percent)	+/– U.S. percent for income over $100,000	House-holds with income below poverty (percent)	Families with children with income below poverty (percent)
	57	58	59	60	61	62	63	64	65	66	67	68	69	70	71	72	73	74
ALABAMA—Cont'd																		
Washington County	30 815	37 881	44 394	25 469	12 034	11 839	35 987	19 402	14 081	73.9	19.5	30.4	2.8	17.5	2.8	-9.5	19.9	19.3
Wilcox County	16 646	22 200	38 750	4 732	6 949	8 600	26 466	18 225	10 903	58.2	16.7	34.1	6.8	14.4	3.1	-9.2	40.5	45.3
Winston County	28 435	32 628	37 165	24 313	14 478	12 036	26 610	18 478	15 738	73.5	19.7	29.9	2.3	14.9	4.5	-7.8	19.2	17.9
ALASKA	51 571	59 036	65 353	35 386	25 203	33 796	43 856	32 624	22 660	89.5	72.4	13.7	8.7	14.7	16.1	3.8	8.3	9.3
Aleutians East Borough	47 875	50 625	65 208	75 518	25 000	32 109	23 438	25 625	18 421	92.7	75.4	9.0	7.8	4.0	15.8	3.5	9.5	7.1
Aleutians West Census Area	61 406	72 500	76 972	63 125	30 625	50 208	41 667	31 314	24 037	94.5	78.7	5.2	4.9	8.6	21.0	8.7	4.8	4.5
Anchorage Municipality	55 546	63 682	69 621	38 140	26 325	37 503	43 971	33 606	25 287	90.8	69.6	12.4	7.0	14.4	18.8	6.5	6.4	7.4
Bethel Census Area	35 701	36 250	44 139	24 821	24 265	26 250	38 700	37 218	12 603	90.1	83.2	13.8	26.1	12.3	9.7	-2.6	19.8	21.1
Bristol Bay Borough	52 167	59 868	67 750	43 125	12 188	36 912	47 321	36 172	22 210	95.7	88.0	12.2	4.9	10.6	9.6	-2.7	7.7	10.3
Denali Borough	53 654	70 000	75 121	68 750	24 375	35 833	56 042	31 458	26 251	93.3	83.1	7.4	4.2	11.0	14.6	2.3	7.1	7.2
Dillingham Census Area	43 079	45 391	54 107	21 250	20 000	30 069	48 661	37 458	16 021	90.7	84.2	13.8	18.5	8.4	13.3	1.0	19.2	23.0
Fairbanks North Star Borough	49 076	56 478	59 275	39 841	22 989	32 004	39 496	30 618	21 553	91.2	68.3	11.5	7.1	14.9	14.1	1.8	7.9	7.6
Haines Borough	40 772	50 580	55 357	22 500	20 625	26 250	44 853	31 406	22 090	84.4	78.5	20.8	7.3	16.9	9.5	-2.8	9.2	11.9
Juneau City and Borough	62 034	70 284	77 664	38 750	29 634	37 363	50 000	35 533	26 719	89.9	78.1	13.1	5.7	17.0	19.7	7.4	5.1	5.5
Kenai Peninsula Borough	46 397	54 106	63 081	36 389	21 662	27 500	46 731	30 057	20 949	85.4	73.4	18.3	10.2	15.5	12.9	0.6	9.5	10.8
Ketchikan Gateway Borough	51 344	59 583	67 944	36 250	23 788	35 211	46 863	33 125	23 994	88.5	71.4	16.8	8.1	15.8	14.1	1.8	5.9	6.1
Kodiak Island Borough	54 636	58 834	60 179	47 794	23 398	32 381	38 364	32 780	22 195	92.0	79.7	11.5	7.7	13.0	19.4	7.1	5.6	5.8
Lake and Peninsula Borough	36 442	42 313	54 583	21 042	26 250	16 563	38 977	32 266	15 361	87.7	92.3	14.5	20.8	8.2	10.1	-2.2	20.1	18.8
Matanuska-Susitna Borough	51 221	56 939	64 241	37 212	24 275	29 483	48 077	30 861	21 105	86.4	69.4	15.7	8.9	16.5	13.8	1.5	9.7	11.3
Nome Census Area	41 250	44 189	58 611	21 250	24 375	26 667	45 719	35 544	15 476	86.3	86.7	17.8	20.6	13.8	11.8	-0.5	16.7	17.9
North Slope Borough	63 173	63 810	84 680	36 250	37 589	45 750	50 673	46 250	20 540	92.7	86.4	11.9	8.6	11.1	22.6	10.3	9.9	10.4
Northwest Arctic Borough	45 976	45 230	60 750	30 833	22 400	30 139	41 471	36 755	15 286	90.4	87.3	17.8	17.5	13.4	12.4	0.1	15.9	17.7
Prince of Wales-Outer Ketchikan Cens	40 636	46 944	57 135	30 417	16 328	25 833	41 875	26 106	18 395	89.1	78.2	16.5	12.5	9.0	6.8	-5.5	12.4	12.8
Sitka City and Borough	51 901	62 361	73 542	33 906	26 116	28 317	42 642	32 804	23 622	90.2	67.6	15.5	8.4	18.9	14.8	2.5	8.0	6.0
Skagway-Hoonah-Angoon Census Area	40 879	47 946	56 406	29 167	18 500	30 262	45 000	30 469	19 974	86.0	74.2	17.7	7.9	13.3	9.0	-3.3	12.6	14.1
Southeast Fairbanks Census Area	38 776	48 208	50 054	27 344	23 125	20 583	40 833	31 652	16 679	81.3	84.8	16.5	14.8	18.3	9.0	-3.3	15.1	15.8
Valdez-Cordova Census Area	48 734	60 497	65 303	30 156	28 500	29 450	49 125	31 754	23 046	89.1	77.2	13.7	8.3	13.0	16.3	4.0	10.1	9.2
Wade Hampton Census Area	30 184	29 867	38 796	15 833	19 740	20 972	29 531	25 500	8 717	89.2	95.8	16.8	36.9	11.5	3.4	-8.9	25.8	26.7
Wrangell-Petersburg Census Area	46 434	54 046	61 838	32 500	25 278	28 077	46 111	30 313	23 494	85.0	73.6	19.3	8.1	14.3	13.6	1.3	8.6	8.2
Yakutat City and Borough	46 786	51 875	66 000	27 083	21 875	31 875	45 114	27 917	22 579	97.4	76.7	11.7	10.9	8.6	6.4	-5.9	13.9	17.3
Yukon-Koyukuk Census Area	28 666	33 832	48 542	13 542	23 894	15 397	41 047	29 837	13 720	82.9	91.9	17.8	18.7	14.0	5.5	-6.8	23.3	22.7
ARIZONA	40 558	46 723	53 815	28 171	21 517	26 828	36 110	27 570	20 275	78.7	34.6	27.1	2.9	18.5	10.8	-1.5	11.8	15.2
Apache County	23 344	26 315	34 943	11 927	13 836	10 465	30 529	22 768	8 986	70.2	11.4	22.1	13.4	12.3	3.0	-9.3	36.7	37.8
Cochise County	32 105	38 005	43 203	25 812	15 677	20 100	32 113	23 337	15 988	73.7	31.0	31.9	4.1	26.5	5.4	-6.9	15.7	21.6
Coconino County	38 256	45 873	53 461	26 068	17 299	25 388	33 652	25 767	17 139	86.8	30.4	17.2	3.8	12.6	8.5	-3.8	16.1	18.8
Gila County	30 917	36 593	42 629	25 203	15 887	17 377	33 350	23 466	16 315	65.8	32.0	40.7	4.7	28.4	5.3	-7.0	14.8	22.0
Graham County	29 668	34 417	43 066	19 563	13 352	13 877	31 106	21 332	12 139	74.0	25.3	31.7	6.9	18.6	3.3	-9.0	19.9	24.9
Greenlee County	39 384	43 523	48 938	34 286	16 458	23 144	39 845	24 519	15 814	79.2	21.0	22.8	3.9	18.8	2.9	-9.4	10.9	9.5
La Paz County	25 839	29 141	38 425	21 563	17 821	16 644	27 536	21 566	14 916	58.7	26.2	45.6	3.1	28.1	3.6	-8.7	17.5	22.6
Maricopa County	45 358	51 827	59 779	30 703	24 873	30 457	37 833	29 813	22 251	81.7	35.3	24.3	2.2	16.3	13.3	1.0	9.7	12.3
Mohave County	31 521	36 311	44 249	25 685	17 326	19 453	29 584	21 315	16 788	67.9	30.9	41.2	3.6	26.3	4.7	-7.6	12.3	16.5
Navajo County	28 569	32 409	39 473	18 575	14 335	14 785	31 170	22 222	11 609	74.0	20.0	25.8	9.3	17.0	4.3	-8.0	25.9	30.6
Pima County	36 758	44 446	50 767	26 241	18 917	23 936	33 839	25 789	19 785	77.7	37.8	28.0	3.1	19.7	9.0	-3.3	13.3	16.4
Pinal County	35 856	39 548	45 584	24 086	17 473	21 853	32 069	24 893	16 025	70.8	30.7	36.9	4.1	25.2	6.3	-6.0	14.0	21.0
Santa Cruz County	29 710	32 057	33 793	23 618	15 863	16 353	29 225	21 513	13 278	80.7	21.3	25.1	4.6	12.8	7.1	-5.2	22.9	26.0
Yavapai County	34 901	40 910	45 247	18 096	21 199	21 736	31 666	23 092	19 727	67.8	41.1	40.1	2.1	27.3	7.4	-4.9	11.0	14.5
Yuma County	32 182	34 659	36 340	23 426	16 228	21 736	29 143	23 379	14 802	70.3	31.0	35.8	3.5	25.1	6.0	-6.3	15.8	24.4
ARKANSAS	32 182	38 663	46 222	23 707	15 497	17 999	30 623	21 837	16 904	76.8	28.3	30.4	2.9	16.3	6.0	-6.3	15.8	18.1
Arkansas County	30 316	36 472	42 431	26 339	16 840	16 817	29 749	21 805	16 401	77.6	25.0	31.9	3.5	11.7	4.6	-7.7	17.4	20.1
Ashley County	31 758	37 370	44 244	26 818	10 380	14 262	35 436	20 181	15 702	75.1	20.9	32.3	3.9	14.9	4.7	-7.6	17.7	22.0
Baxter County	29 106	34 578	42 377	20 234	16 099	16 469	27 072	19 381	16 859	61.5	40.4	47.0	2.3	29.5	4.1	-8.2	12.0	13.4
Benton County	40 281	45 235	50 273	25 015	20 025	23 694	31 140	23 429	19 377	79.2	35.7	29.7	2.0	17.3	8.9	-3.4	9.3	11.2
Boone County	29 988	34 974	40 160	27 500	15 574	14 659	27 963	19 889	16 175	73.6	33.4	36.5	3.0	17.3	4.5	-7.8	15.9	15.8
Bradley County	24 821	30 753	40 083	28 571	11 607	12 274	28 762	19 239	13 895	67.7	23.4	35.3	3.3	19.4	5.6	-6.7	25.7	29.3
Calhoun County	28 438	34 647	41 193	32 917	14 306	14 561	31 044	17 997	15 555	70.4	18.7	36.5	2.1	17.2	4.8	-7.5	17.8	17.8
Carroll County	27 924	33 218	36 289	17 639	16 064	16 287	22 393	18 634	16 003	76.1	35.2	34.1	2.5	14.2	5.8	-6.5	15.6	18.3
Chicot County	22 024	27 960	39 776	23 214	13 056	11 633	26 854	17 867	12 825	69.8	17.3	36.3	5.3	13.6	3.9	-8.4	27.5	33.6
Clark County	28 845	37 092	46 120	22 333	13 873	13 307	29 709	20 654	14 533	74.2	27.4	31.3	2.5	16.9	3.9	-8.4	21.2	19.0
Clay County	25 345	32 558	37 516	20 234	12 156	12 328	25 323	17 740	14 512	67.9	26.0	38.7	2.9	15.5	2.9	-9.4	20.2	18.8
Cleburne County	31 531	37 273	43 552	22 102	14 205	15 166	29 472	20 510	17 250	67.8	34.7	40.9	2.0	22.3	4.9	-7.4	14.1	14.9
Cleveland County	32 405	38 164	44 343	35 147	14 375	12 786	31 669	21 982	15 362	75.0	24.2	33.9	2.1	14.6	3.9	-8.4	15.5	16.6
Columbia County	27 640	36 271	47 669	25 446	14 464	14 123	31 877	20 854	15 322	70.8	26.0	33.5	2.4	15.4	5.2	-7.1	21.1	22.9

Table B-3. States and Counties — Education, Labor Force, and Income

			High school graduates			College graduates		College graduates (percent)				
STATE/ County code	MSA/PMSA/ NECMA code[1]	STATE County	Total population 25 years and over	Percent with a high school diploma or less	Percent with a high school diploma or more	Percent with a bachelor's degree or more	+/− U.S. percent with bachelor's degree or more	Non-Hispanic White	Black or African American	American Indian and Alaska Native	Asian, Hawaiian, and Pacific Islander	Hispanic or Latino[2]
			1	2	3	4	5	6	7	8	9	10
		ARKANSAS—Cont'd										
05 029	...	Conway County............	13 480	68.2	73.2	11.5	-12.9	12.3	7.5	23.8	19.4	4.6
05 031	3700	Craighead County	50 725	55.5	77.3	20.9	-3.5	21.5	14.4	8.6	22.0	11.6
05 033	2720	Crawford County	33 765	64.5	71.5	9.7	-14.7	9.9	8.7	4.6	7.0	9.4
05 035	4920	Crittenden County	30 251	64.0	69.2	12.8	-11.6	18.0	5.4	11.3	15.4	0.0
05 037	...	Cross County	12 412	69.8	68.3	9.9	-14.5	10.8	6.4	14.5	22.2	0.0
05 039	...	Dallas County	5 989	74.3	66.8	9.6	-14.8	14.8	1.6	0.0	X	0.0
05 041	...	Desha County	9 574	71.0	65.0	11.1	-13.3	14.1	6.9	0.0	45.9	0.0
05 043	...	Drew County	11 553	61.3	73.1	17.3	-7.1	20.6	8.2	0.0	13.0	9.1
05 045	4400	Faulkner County............	50 849	47.9	83.3	25.2	0.8	26.2	14.9	18.3	41.1	15.4
05 047	...	Franklin County	11 654	64.3	71.1	11.0	-13.4	11.2	0.0	13.8	9.1	0.0
05 049	...	Fulton County	8 243	66.9	72.2	10.5	-13.9	10.5	X	5.0	27.8	6.1
05 051	...	Garland County	62 094	54.5	70.0	10.0	0.4	10.0	0.2	18.3	34.0	11.6
05 053	...	Grant County	10 824	65.1	77.2	11.0	-13.4	11.0	14.7	23.6	16.1	0.0
05 055	...	Greene County	24 510	68.5	72.1	10.9	-13.5	11.1	0.0	10.1	0.0	0.0
05 057	...	Hempstead County	14 869	69.2	69.2	11.0	-13.4	13.2	7.2	0.0	41.7	2.0
05 059	...	Hot Spring County........	20 260	66.4	73.3	11.2	-13.2	11.7	7.2	15.4	22.0	4.1
05 061	...	Howard County	9 271	67.1	70.7	11.6	-12.8	13.1	6.8	6.3	5.7	8.2
05 063	...	Independence County ...	22 705	64.2	75.5	13.7	-10.7	13.8	11.1	23.8	11.4	3.1
05 065	...	Izard County	9 524	63.2	73.3	11.7	-12.7	11.8	0.0	7.5	62.5	30.4
05 067	...	Jackson County	12 204	72.3	66.0	10.3	-14.1	10.8	6.4	4.9	47.8	5.3
05 069	6240	Jefferson County	53 132	60.0	74.8	15.7	-8.7	15.6	15.7	8.6	49.5	5.2
05 071	...	Johnson County	14 901	69.0	67.6	13.1	-11.3	13.5	10.0	7.6	0.0	8.3
05 073	...	Lafayette County	5 692	70.7	65.3	9.5	-14.9	13.0	2.9	0.0	6.7	0.0
05 075	...	Lawrence County	11 824	73.5	63.3	8.5	-15.9	8.6	0.0	2.4	11.5	0.0
05 077	...	Lee County	7 924	73.4	56.2	7.3	-17.1	8.1	6.8	23.2	0.0	0.0
05 079	...	Lincoln County	9 533	72.8	65.0	7.6	-16.8	9.5	4.0	0.0	0.0	1.5
05 081	...	Little River County........	9 009	64.7	73.4	9.9	-14.5	11.7	3.4	8.4	0.0	5.0
05 083	...	Logan County	15 004	68.6	69.8	9.4	-15.0	9.1	4.0	24.5	68.9	12.3
05 085	4400	Lonoke County.............	33 160	58.0	77.6	11.6	0.8	16.2	6.5	3.3	7.7	17.7
05 087	...	Madison County	9 327	71.0	67.8	10.1	-14.3	10.3	0.0	9.4	7.1	2.6
05 089	...	Marion County	11 593	62.3	76.0	10.4	-14.0	10.3	X	10.9	6.8	8.2
05 091	8360	Miller County	25 790	61.5	74.3	12.5	-11.9	14.2	6.0	0.0	50.4	9.6
05 093	...	Mississippi County	31 612	67.4	64.7	11.3	-13.1	13.5	5.5	1.8	44.8	7.0
05 095	...	Monroe County	6 602	74.4	63.8	8.4	-16.0	9.6	6.1	0.0	0.0	2.2
05 097	...	Montgomery County......	6 464	69.4	69.8	8.8	-15.6	8.8	X	27.0	0.0	3.1
05 099	...	Nevada County	6 575	70.2	69.1	10.7	-13.7	13.3	5.1	0.0	X	1.2
05 101	...	Newton County	5 814	67.6	70.2	11.8	-12.6	11.7	0.0	32.7	X	6.9
05 103	...	Ouachita County	18 975	61.4	73.5	12.7	-11.7	15.6	7.2	23.4	41.5	12.0
05 105	...	Perry County	6 850	67.6	73.8	11.1	-13.3	10.7	11.3	4.4	62.5	4.8
05 107	...	Phillips County	15 420	64.3	62.2	12.4	-12.0	16.6	8.0	0.0	40.5	5.1
05 109	...	Pike County................	7 653	70.3	68.8	10.1	-14.3	10.1	6.5	20.7	15.4	7.6
05 111	...	Poinsett County	16 674	77.5	62.0	6.3	-18.1	6.7	2.2	0.0	0.0	0.0
05 113	...	Polk County	13 505	63.6	72.6	10.9	-13.5	11.2	0.0	0.0	24.0	6.3
05 115	...	Pope County	34 297	56.1	77.4	19.0	-5.4	19.3	14.8	14.1	12.4	12.8
05 117	...	Prairie County	6 550	70.6	68.2	9.0	-15.4	9.7	3.6	0.0	0.0	3.8
05 119	4400	Pulaski County	235 921	42.7	84.4	28.1	3.7	32.9	15.5	21.3	47.1	16.2
05 121	...	Randolph County	12 207	69.1	69.2	10.6	-13.8	10.6	0.0	0.0	0.0	12.0
05 123	...	St. Francis County	18 173	67.6	65.1	9.6	-14.8	13.0	6.4	16.7	22.0	0.3
05 125	4400	Saline County..............	55 796	55.4	82.3	16.4	-8.0	16.4	11.9	13.9	24.0	9.6
05 127	...	Scott County	7 141	71.8	65.4	8.4	-16.0	8.6	X	0.0	28.6	0.0
05 129	...	Searcy County.............	5 792	72.6	68.0	8.4	-16.0	8.4	0.0	8.8	11.1	20.8
05 131	2720	Sebastian County.........	74 601	54.6	76.6	16.6	-7.8	18.3	7.9	15.3	7.0	4.6
05 133	...	Sevier County	9 828	69.2	64.6	9.2	-15.2	10.9	4.8	2.8	0.0	1.8
05 135	...	Sharp County	12 294	65.4	72.9	10.3	-14.1	10.4	0.0	9.8	7.7	12.2
05 137	...	Stone County	8 119	70.4	68.0	9.8	-14.6	9.9	0.0	0.0	100.0	0.0
05 139	...	Union County	29 986	61.0	74.5	14.9	-9.5	18.5	5.7	2.2	43.7	8.6
05 141	...	Van Buren County........	11 602	65.2	71.6	11.5	-12.9	11.5	38.5	23.2	0.0	12.1
05 143	2580	Washington County.......	94 019	51.0	79.5	24.5	0.1	25.3	25.0	13.0	50.6	6.1
05 145	...	White County	42 366	62.8	72.9	15.5	-8.9	15.8	12.6	2.1	14.4	11.3
05 147	...	Woodruff County	5 716	76.1	60.6	8.0	-16.4	8.7	6.4	0.0	0.0	9.7
05 149	...	Yell County.................	13 659	71.6	64.1	10.9	-13.5	12.1	2.7	11.5	1.0	1.2
06 000	...	CALIFORNIA............	21 298 900	43.3	76.8	26.6	2.2	33.8	17.2	11.4	40.9	7.7
06 001	5775	Alameda County...........	953 716	36.7	82.4	34.9	10.5	42.7	18.8	16.7	45.3	12.7
06 003	...	Alpine County..............	797	37.6	88.3	28.2	3.8	34.1	X	3.0	0.0	8.7
06 005	...	Amador County............	25 549	46.3	84.0	16.6	-7.8	18.0	0.5	14.4	32.9	7.8

[1]MSA = Metropolitan Statistical Area. PMSA = Primary MSA. NECMA = New England County Metropolitan Area. See the Appendix A for explanation of these concepts. See Appendix B for list of metropolitan areas identified by type, with component counties.
[2]Hispanic or Latino persons may be of any race.

STATE County	School enrollment			Population 16 to 19 years				Employment status, 2000			Work status in 1999 of the population 16 years and over (percent)		
											Worked in 1999		
	Grades kindergarten through 12	College or graduate school	Percent private	Number	Percent in armed forces	Percent high school graduates	Percent not enrolled, not grads, not in armed forces, not employed	Total population 16 years and over	Percent in labor force	Unemployment rate	Full-time	Part-time	Did not work in 1999
	11	12	13	14	15	16	17	18	19	20	21	22	23
ARKANSAS—Cont'd													
Conway County	3 877	712	7.2	1 158	0.0	14.6	5.4	15 797	58.0	6.5	51.7	11.9	36.4
Craighead County	14 353	6 945	5.6	5 400	0.0	14.2	2.0	64 417	66.0	5.7	55.9	15.6	28.6
Crawford County	10 961	1 655	4.9	3 033	0.0	12.2	4.0	39 946	62.0	6.1	54.3	12.3	33.4
Crittenden County	11 592	1 928	6.0	3 230	0.0	9.2	7.5	36 786	60.1	6.9	54.8	11.2	34.0
Cross County	4 316	645	3.0	1 232	0.0	13.3	6.7	14 763	58.9	7.6	53.5	9.1	37.4
Dallas County	2 015	212	1.6	602	0.0	11.3	11.8	7 117	54.4	7.4	49.5	8.1	42.4
Desha County	3 406	457	2.8	963	0.1	9.9	4.0	11 473	52.3	8.8	48.9	9.2	41.9
Drew County	3 633	1 484	1.8	1 343	0.0	10.3	3.9	14 510	60.7	8.9	52.2	14.8	33.0
Faulkner County	16 292	9 182	13.1	6 320	0.2	9.6	1.2	66 339	68.8	6.7	57.9	16.3	25.8
Franklin County	3 379	466	4.0	1 195	0.0	16.5	6.1	13 888	58.3	5.9	49.9	11.0	39.0
Fulton County	2 031	276	4.8	552	0.0	10.5	3.8	9 321	52.3	5.9	45.0	12.0	43.0
Garland County	14 253	2 731	7.5	4 158	0.0	15.6	6.3	71 338	54.1	5.1	46.7	12.9	40.4
Grant County	3 194	539	3.8	885	0.0	16.9	2.0	12 683	62.3	4.2	56.4	11.1	32.4
Greene County	6 798	1 233	7.7	2 054	0.0	15.9	6.4	29 044	62.0	5.6	54.6	11.6	33.8
Hempstead County	4 618	932	4.4	1 363	0.0	13.4	10.4	17 899	61.5	6.5	53.0	11.2	35.8
Hot Spring County	5 578	1 005	4.5	1 662	0.0	16.3	5.1	23 624	60.1	4.9	52.4	11.7	35.9
Howard County	2 847	328	5.1	855	0.0	11.6	9.6	10 922	61.2	4.9	54.6	11.0	34.5
Independence County	6 268	1 382	10.6	2 132	0.7	15.1	3.0	26 922	60.8	5.9	54.6	11.6	33.8
Izard County	2 093	457	6.6	610	0.0	15.1	5.9	10 810	47.4	4.1	44.5	10.2	45.3
Jackson County	3 200	545	3.1	1 108	0.2	7.3	15.2	14 856	50.2	6.9	47.8	9.7	42.5
Jefferson County	16 558	4 998	5.1	5 609	0.0	12.9	6.0	64 892	56.0	8.3	51.6	11.1	37.3
Johnson County	4 256	841	4.2	1 393	0.4	12.3	8.0	17 833	58.7	7.8	51.3	11.1	37.6
Lafayette County	1 706	218	2.5	513	0.0	9.4	4.5	6 709	51.3	7.9	45.4	10.5	44.1
Lawrence County	3 181	809	11.2	1 107	0.0	13.2	4.2	14 048	54.7	5.6	49.6	12.6	37.7
Lee County	2 646	361	11.0	818	0.0	10.9	9.5	9 741	42.6	13.2	42.6	7.6	49.8
Lincoln County	2 397	307	5.3	804	0.0	18.0	6.6	11 676	42.7	7.0	53.1	7.9	39.0
Little River County	2 481	385	5.5	695	0.0	19.9	3.3	10 568	60.0	6.5	53.0	11.0	36.0
Logan County	4 293	508	5.8	1 234	0.1	17.8	5.2	17 404	56.0	5.3	50.5	10.1	39.5
Lonoke County	11 362	1 678	3.9	3 102	0.7	15.0	5.6	39 473	66.9	3.8	59.5	11.5	29.0
Madison County	2 875	182	3.6	813	0.0	15.0	4.4	10 905	61.2	2.7	52.3	13.1	34.5
Marion County	2 770	400	7.4	774	0.0	11.1	1.7	13 035	49.7	5.1	45.0	10.8	44.2
Miller County	7 692	1 392	8.0	2 225	0.0	14.7	8.6	30 854	58.7	6.8	50.5	12.1	37.4
Mississippi County	11 331	1 655	6.0	3 268	0.0	14.4	10.4	38 274	58.6	8.8	52.9	10.1	37.0
Monroe County	2 218	208	11.1	566	0.0	14.1	4.9	7 705	52.0	5.3	48.1	9.9	42.0
Montgomery County	1 589	185	5.2	459	0.0	10.5	6.8	7 315	54.8	6.3	47.3	11.2	41.5
Nevada County	1 927	366	1.7	480	0.0	12.3	2.1	7 700	59.4	6.3	49.7	11.2	39.1
Newton County	1 656	156	5.3	500	0.0	14.6	4.4	6 770	54.3	4.5	45.7	12.2	42.1
Ouachita County	5 915	965	5.4	1 647	0.0	11.8	6.1	22 199	56.0	8.5	49.8	9.2	41.0
Perry County	1 958	257	6.9	579	0.0	15.4	8.8	7 954	58.6	4.7	52.6	10.2	37.2
Phillips County	6 506	923	9.4	1 854	0.2	8.0	7.2	18 966	53.1	11.3	46.5	10.0	43.5
Pike County	2 111	357	4.9	609	0.0	8.5	3.0	8 860	58.0	4.3	49.4	11.2	39.4
Poinsett County	4 997	678	3.0	1 520	0.0	12.4	8.8	19 765	57.7	6.2	51.4	10.1	38.5
Polk County	3 852	711	6.4	1 142	0.4	14.1	4.0	15 734	56.6	5.8	49.1	10.4	40.5
Pope County	10 420	3 951	4.6	3 688	0.1	10.9	5.4	42 190	62.1	5.8	52.5	14.8	32.7
Prairie County	1 761	167	4.9	490	0.0	12.9	3.9	7 551	56.5	4.5	52.1	11.0	36.9
Pulaski County	66 912	20 254	17.9	19 002	1.3	13.3	5.9	280 470	66.5	5.2	59.1	13.4	27.6
Randolph County	3 368	571	5.0	1 000	0.0	19.5	9.6	14 239	57.0	6.4	51.3	10.2	38.6
St. Francis County	6 323	1 147	5.2	1 853	0.0	12.3	6.4	22 104	50.7	11.8	46.7	10.2	43.1
Saline County	15 742	3 030	8.2	4 127	0.0	14.4	4.6	64 643	64.6	3.9	58.8	11.6	29.6
Scott County	2 123	177	3.1	604	0.0	15.2	6.5	8 399	58.1	3.9	52.6	10.6	36.8
Searcy County	1 471	208	3.2	473	0.0	17.3	3.2	6 647	49.3	4.7	43.5	11.4	45.1
Sebastian County	21 543	4 352	9.2	6 418	0.3	12.8	6.6	88 555	63.2	4.7	56.1	12.0	31.9
Sevier County	3 254	479	2.7	968	0.0	14.7	6.1	11 833	60.2	4.7	53.4	12.0	34.7
Sharp County	2 774	391	6.8	870	0.0	16.7	9.3	13 850	46.4	6.4	40.9	10.4	48.7
Stone County	1 962	263	5.8	587	0.0	25.6	4.1	9 209	49.7	4.3	44.8	11.6	43.6
Union County	9 106	1 427	7.4	2 802	0.0	14.2	7.1	35 344	56.8	6.9	50.3	10.5	39.3
Van Buren County	2 688	363	5.1	730	0.0	20.1	5.3	13 107	49.7	6.7	41.8	12.1	46.1
Washington County	27 413	16 443	6.5	10 993	0.0	11.7	4.5	122 584	68.3	7.9	58.1	16.1	25.8
White County	12 232	5 349	24.0	4 613	0.0	10.0	5.4	52 588	62.7	11.3	53.7	14.3	32.1
Woodruff County	1 674	229	3.0	498	0.0	8.6	11.8	6 754	55.9	8.0	50.7	9.3	40.0
Yell County	4 062	439	4.2	1 328	0.0	16.9	6.8	16 396	58.8	5.2	53.3	10.4	36.4
CALIFORNIA	7 026 326	2 556 598	12.2	1 925 479	0.8	9.9	5.8	25 596 144	62.4	6.9	53.5	14.6	31.9
Alameda County	264 846	126 921	14.7	71 920	0.1	8.7	5.1	1 124 967	65.3	5.5	56.4	14.7	25.3
Alpine County	208	67	9.5	86	0.0	34.9	7.0	984	69.4	8.1	55.7	19.0	25.3
Amador County	6 659	1 063	10.4	2 350	0.0	10.5	8.1	29 086	48.9	4.4	47.3	15.4	37.3

Table B-3. States and Counties — Education, Labor Force, and Income

STATE County	Full-year full-time employed (percent)								Children under 18 years in families					+/− U.S. percent two-income couples	Total employed by class of worker (percent)			
	Total	Men	Women	Non-Hispanic White	Black or African American	American Indian and Alaska Native	Asian, Hawaiian, and Pacific Islander	Hispanic or Latino[1]	Number	With two parents (percent) Both in labor force	Father only in labor force	With one parent who is in labor force (percent)	+/− U.S. percent of children with no stay-at-home parent (percent)		Private	Government	Self-employed	Unpaid family worker
	24	25	26	27	28	29	30	31	32	33	34	35	36	37	38	39	40	41
ARKANSAS—Cont'd																		
Conway County	35.8	45.3	27.1	37.7	25.6	18.5	37.5	32.7	4 844	42.6	15.8	22.3	0.3	−7.9	71.5	15.6	12.2	0.7
Craighead County	40.8	51.6	31.1	42.0	32.3	33.3	27.6	22.6	18 911	46.4	21.3	21.0	2.8	2.6	74.5	14.0	11.2	0.2
Crawford County	40.8	50.7	31.4	41.1	32.2	30.4	24.9	44.5	14 310	44.8	20.5	18.2	−1.6	−3.2	77.0	11.5	10.9	0.5
Crittenden County	39.7	48.2	32.5	46.5	30.9	54.6	40.2	39.0	14 270	31.7	15.0	30.9	−2.0	−1.5	78.2	14.1	7.5	0.2
Cross County	37.8	46.8	29.7	41.2	26.1	20.3	27.7	36.5	4 994	38.3	19.0	24.6	−1.7	−3.7	70.8	16.2	13.0	0.0
Dallas County	33.9	41.4	27.0	36.0	31.3	0.0	X	22.6	1 974	42.1	16.1	26.6	4.1	−3.4	70.4	16.7	12.5	0.4
Desha County	31.8	39.9	25.1	37.5	24.3	56.8	42.6	36.4	3 997	27.9	17.1	27.3	−9.4	−5.4	66.9	19.3	13.4	0.4
Drew County	36.0	43.3	29.1	38.2	29.8	47.6	39.1	38.8	4 465	40.0	20.0	23.8	−0.8	−3.7	68.8	19.7	11.4	0.2
Faulkner County	42.1	52.9	32.2	42.6	39.1	53.8	19.5	42.8	20 950	49.7	21.2	20.2	5.3	6.7	73.1	17.2	9.3	0.4
Franklin County	36.8	44.8	29.0	37.4	0.0	47.8	27.2	39.4	4 318	51.5	21.1	17.1	4.3	−4.3	72.5	16.0	11.3	0.2
Fulton County	32.5	39.1	26.2	32.6	X	21.4	33.3	20.0	2 502	50.7	18.0	17.0	3.1	−10.4	67.7	15.2	16.5	0.6
Garland County	34.0	42.1	26.8	34.3	32.5	33.1	23.8	32.2	17 597	41.8	19.6	25.0	2.2	−10.5	73.3	12.1	13.9	0.6
Grant County	43.3	54.4	32.7	43.3	49.7	19.8	53.1	41.5	4 066	56.0	22.7	12.9	4.3	−1.9	74.1	15.4	10.4	0.1
Greene County	39.8	50.4	30.1	40.1	5.3	30.2	29.4	36.3	8 755	51.6	20.8	16.8	3.8	0.1	77.3	11.6	10.8	0.4
Hempstead County	40.4	51.1	30.8	41.3	37.3	61.5	33.3	44.3	5 833	40.2	19.9	24.7	0.3	−0.5	75.0	14.0	10.6	0.3
Hot Spring County	39.3	48.9	30.1	40.1	32.1	52.3	24.5	46.4	7 012	49.4	17.5	20.3	5.1	−2.8	73.9	16.0	9.9	0.2
Howard County	41.2	51.9	31.4	42.1	36.2	31.3	57.1	47.8	3 546	45.9	21.2	22.8	4.1	0.2	72.9	11.7	15.2	0.3
Independence County	39.3	46.4	32.6	39.5	35.2	18.9	43.2	44.2	7 961	49.6	20.4	16.6	1.6	−1.6	76.8	12.5	10.1	0.6
Izard County	30.5	36.7	24.2	31.3	0.0	41.1	16.7	21.1	2 611	46.3	22.3	16.5	−1.8	−12.8	66.1	17.9	15.6	0.4
Jackson County	32.2	39.6	25.9	34.4	22.2	21.1	78.3	31.4	3 813	41.6	17.5	23.7	0.7	−9.0	71.7	16.6	11.6	0.1
Jefferson County	34.8	41.0	29.0	40.8	28.0	33.5	45.5	31.4	20 023	36.0	14.1	28.1	−0.5	−2.6	69.6	21.6	8.3	0.5
Johnson County	36.4	45.1	28.1	36.4	34.2	25.5	7.7	39.2	5 403	44.7	22.5	17.6	−0.3	−6.4	76.5	10.6	12.4	0.6
Lafayette County	32.0	42.1	23.2	35.2	26.2	14.3	20.0	45.9	1 914	34.5	16.0	29.6	−0.5	−11.2	68.2	17.4	13.8	0.5
Lawrence County	33.4	42.6	25.1	33.5	27.3	23.1	36.6	34.5	4 009	39.8	27.7	18.3	−6.5	−9.7	70.2	13.6	15.6	0.6
Lee County	22.4	23.5	21.1	31.9	15.5	51.8	100.0	5.5	2 786	21.7	19.8	35.9	−7.0	−8.8	64.0	20.9	14.3	0.8
Lincoln County	27.1	26.8	27.5	34.0	13.2	27.6	0.0	28.0	2 890	44.6	18.2	21.5	1.5	−5.7	68.2	21.1	10.2	0.5
Little River County	38.4	50.0	27.8	40.3	32.9	26.6	50.0	44.8	3 230	41.6	22.4	23.3	0.3	−5.3	74.4	15.0	9.8	0.8
Logan County	37.3	45.5	29.3	37.4	24.1	44.2	36.0	45.5	5 470	47.0	19.5	17.6	0.0	−3.9	69.3	15.5	15.0	0.2
Lonoke County	47.0	59.0	35.9	48.1	36.8	41.1	30.8	41.2	14 354	52.5	21.7	17.0	4.9	5.8	71.7	17.5	10.6	0.2
Madison County	38.5	48.0	29.1	38.6	20.0	26.0	35.5	47.2	3 630	47.0	25.0	14.7	−2.9	−1.5	66.6	13.1	19.5	0.8
Marion County	31.9	38.3	25.7	31.8	X	20.3	6.6	53.3	3 313	45.8	22.0	15.3	−3.5	−14.8	74.7	11.6	13.3	0.5
Miller County	37.2	47.5	27.9	40.0	27.6	49.0	51.8	30.8	9 852	35.6	21.1	28.1	−0.9	−4.0	74.9	15.1	9.5	0.4
Mississippi County	36.7	47.0	27.6	39.9	28.2	38.5	68.5	39.4	13 783	32.7	20.0	28.6	−3.3	−3.8	76.5	14.2	8.8	0.4
Monroe County	32.3	40.5	25.3	38.5	21.4	100.0	0.0	27.1	2 608	28.9	20.9	25.1	−10.6	−6.9	66.6	17.0	15.4	1.1
Montgomery County	33.5	41.6	25.9	33.5	X	30.8	54.5	37.7	2 078	49.4	23.8	16.3	1.1	−9.1	66.0	14.7	18.0	1.3
Nevada County	35.0	43.6	27.1	36.3	32.2	50.0	X	25.0	2 272	40.4	19.1	26.3	2.1	2.0	70.2	18.4	11.1	0.3
Newton County	31.2	39.7	22.5	31.2	68.8	42.9	0.0	30.2	2 031	45.2	22.6	14.2	−5.2	−11.5	64.2	16.6	17.9	1.3
Ouachita County	36.6	45.4	29.1	40.6	29.7	42.1	17.7	42.7	6 907	41.3	15.0	25.7	2.4	−5.1	73.8	16.9	8.9	0.3
Perry County	39.0	48.8	29.5	39.1	31.6	40.3	33.3	51.8	2 393	47.9	22.1	14.2	−2.5	−5.6	71.0	16.1	12.5	0.4
Phillips County	31.2	38.6	25.4	37.8	25.4	0.0	38.5	40.8	7 586	25.9	11.0	39.0	0.3	−7.0	68.5	20.3	10.8	0.4
Pike County	35.9	47.5	25.0	35.9	34.6	46.2	11.5	42.9	2 693	48.2	24.1	17.2	0.8	−4.5	70.2	14.3	15.2	0.3
Poinsett County	37.6	48.4	27.7	38.5	26.8	35.1	50.0	33.5	6 119	43.4	18.7	22.0	0.8	−5.2	75.5	11.7	12.7	0.1
Polk County	34.5	43.5	26.1	34.9	23.1	14.6	24.0	42.3	4 799	45.1	28.4	14.5	−5.0	−6.8	66.9	14.2	17.9	1.0
Pope County	37.9	49.2	27.3	38.1	39.0	30.1	30.5	33.5	13 159	48.1	21.8	17.4	0.9	−2.8	73.5	15.1	10.9	0.5
Prairie County	36.9	48.4	26.2	38.1	28.1	50.0	14.3	41.4	2 111	35.9	27.6	20.4	−8.3	−7.1	65.7	17.5	16.3	0.5
Pulaski County	44.5	53.4	36.7	47.4	38.5	38.5	38.8	30.5	84 023	38.4	18.0	28.5	2.3	2.6	71.5	19.5	8.8	0.2
Randolph County	36.9	45.5	29.0	37.4	6.0	27.4	100.0	45.2	4 227	48.9	17.6	20.2	4.5	−6.6	71.7	13.7	13.8	0.8
St. Francis County	30.3	33.7	26.8	38.2	25.2	33.3	32.1	6.2	7 487	30.5	15.4	33.3	−0.8	−5.2	69.4	19.3	10.9	0.4
Saline County	47.2	56.1	38.5	47.4	30.8	54.2	52.5	52.2	20 149	53.8	20.0	17.6	6.8	2.9	74.6	15.4	9.8	0.2
Scott County	36.5	45.5	27.6	37.3	50.0	35.9	27.9	27.0	2 748	51.7	20.3	15.4	2.5	−3.1	69.6	12.9	16.2	1.3
Searcy County	28.4	34.8	22.2	28.1	0.0	30.8	40.9	50.0	1 808	40.9	28.2	15.5	−8.2	−12.6	58.8	17.7	22.6	0.9
Sebastian County	41.6	52.3	31.8	42.3	36.7	41.9	45.6	36.4	28 207	43.9	20.6	21.4	0.7	0.2	80.9	9.7	9.1	0.4
Sevier County	36.4	47.9	25.2	37.0	33.7	23.1	33.3	35.8	4 088	38.6	20.2	22.7	−3.3	−5.5	73.5	13.0	12.9	0.6
Sharp County	29.2	37.3	21.8	29.2	10.0	33.7	71.4	31.1	3 499	40.7	23.1	18.8	−5.1	−16.3	68.4	13.2	17.9	0.5
Stone County	30.5	38.4	22.8	30.7	33.3	20.0	100.0	27.9	2 466	47.7	27.1	10.9	−6.0	−12.8	61.8	14.9	22.6	0.8
Union County	36.2	46.5	27.3	39.6	28.6	27.2	16.3	29.6	10 902	40.2	18.1	25.1	0.7	−4.1	76.3	13.8	9.5	0.4
Van Buren County	29.0	37.3	21.2	29.0	0.0	31.1	11.5	27.5	3 236	43.0	23.1	21.0	−0.6	−17.1	68.4	13.9	17.5	0.3
Washington County	41.0	50.1	31.9	41.5	34.3	43.1	35.4	38.3	37 564	46.0	23.4	18.5	−0.1	2.9	75.0	14.2	10.5	0.3
White County	36.8	46.3	28.0	37.1	34.8	25.9	25.7	34.1	15 545	45.5	25.3	17.7	−1.4	−3.7	75.0	12.7	11.9	0.4
Woodruff County	33.4	41.1	26.6	36.4	26.2	0.0	50.0	18.9	2 061	36.4	13.4	28.3	0.1	−4.7	72.3	16.7	10.6	0.4
Yell County	37.7	47.0	28.8	37.2	37.8	13.9	27.5	43.3	5 092	45.8	18.5	21.7	2.9	−2.3	74.1	12.5	12.9	0.6
CALIFORNIA	36.5	45.1	28.1	39.5	34.3	32.3	36.9	31.4	8 565 858	37.1	24.3	20.1	−7.4	−4.5	73.7	14.7	11.2	0.4
Alameda County	40.1	48.3	32.4	43.7	35.4	39.4	39.4	35.5	330 922	39.6	22.0	21.1	−3.9	0.9	75.7	15.0	9.1	0.3
Alpine County	36.3	43.6	27.8	39.6	X	21.3	100.0	39.5	229	38.0	12.2	32.8	6.2	−4.0	64.2	28.7	6.8	0.3
Amador County	32.2	37.3	25.7	31.8	36.7	31.7	30.8	33.8	6 589	46.3	22.7	22.4	4.1	−8.5	61.7	20.8	17.4	0.1

[1]Hispanic or Latino persons may be of any race.

Table B-3. States and Counties — Education, Labor Force, and Income

				Occupation for employed population 16 years and over (percent)						Industry for employed population 16 years and over (percent)					
STATE County	Percent who worked at home	Percent of the population 5 years and over with a disability	Veterans as a percent of the population 18 years and over	Management, professional, and related occupations	Service occupations	Sales and office occupations	Farming, fishing, and forestry occupations	Construction, extraction, and maintenance occupations	Production, transportation and material moving occupations	Agriculture, forestry, fishing, and mining	Construction and manufacturing	Wholesale and retail trade	Transportation and warehousing, and utilities	Service industries	Public administration
	42	43	44	45	46	47	48	49	50	51	52	53	54	55	56
ARKANSAS—Cont'd															
Conway County	3.4	26.4	14.0	23.9	15.0	23.8	1.9	12.4	23.1	5.4	28.7	14.2	6.5	42.1	3.0
Craighead County	2.6	22.7	12.1	28.5	14.4	26.0	1.0	9.8	20.5	2.6	24.7	17.7	4.7	47.3	3.0
Crawford County	2.0	24.6	15.1	21.3	14.8	24.8	1.2	11.4	26.5	2.8	33.2	16.1	5.8	38.8	3.3
Crittenden County	1.1	23.4	11.3	25.3	14.8	27.2	1.7	11.4	19.6	3.1	21.2	17.3	9.3	44.9	4.1
Cross County	2.0	27.2	10.2	26.2	13.6	22.6	3.1	9.9	24.8	8.7	27.5	17.1	5.9	36.1	4.7
Dallas County	1.4	28.8	11.8	21.2	10.8	20.7	6.9	9.1	31.3	10.2	38.7	11.1	3.9	32.4	3.7
Desha County	2.6	28.7	11.1	24.6	17.3	20.2	5.2	9.1	23.6	12.1	25.6	12.4	6.7	35.4	7.9
Drew County	1.6	22.3	12.5	26.8	12.8	24.9	3.2	10.4	21.9	6.6	29.1	15.7	4.2	38.4	5.9
Faulkner County	2.8	19.6	12.5	31.3	13.9	26.7	0.4	11.0	16.7	1.1	24.6	15.2	4.8	50.2	4.2
Franklin County	2.4	26.0	14.9	25.5	12.1	21.0	2.3	12.0	27.2	7.3	30.1	13.0	9.8	35.1	4.8
Fulton County	4.4	26.7	17.0	24.6	14.8	21.6	2.2	11.9	25.0	5.4	26.6	16.6	7.6	40.2	3.6
Garland County	2.7	25.1	17.5	27.7	19.3	24.9	0.8	12.4	14.8	1.9	22.1	16.8	4.2	52.1	2.9
Grant County	1.2	23.3	13.9	21.9	10.8	25.9	1.5	15.5	24.4	3.6	35.6	15.7	6.4	33.2	5.6
Greene County	2.3	26.2	13.3	22.4	11.7	23.1	1.2	10.3	31.3	3.1	38.5	15.8	4.4	35.8	2.4
Hempstead County	2.9	23.8	11.8	23.0	12.9	18.6	2.6	9.2	33.6	6.7	39.4	11.6	4.4	34.2	3.7
Hot Spring County	2.1	24.7	15.6	23.1	15.9	22.4	1.6	14.1	23.0	3.5	30.6	15.6	5.5	40.7	4.1
Howard County	2.7	23.2	12.0	22.5	12.9	16.5	3.5	11.8	32.9	10.0	42.2	11.0	3.4	29.5	3.9
Independence County	2.7	23.4	14.4	24.5	13.2	21.5	1.1	10.6	29.2	3.8	33.8	12.9	7.6	38.4	3.6
Izard County	4.2	26.5	17.5	26.9	15.8	19.7	1.8	14.5	21.4	7.0	28.1	12.5	4.7	41.5	6.3
Jackson County	1.6	29.3	10.9	24.8	16.3	24.6	3.3	9.3	21.7	8.2	23.7	17.9	5.9	37.9	6.4
Jefferson County	1.8	25.0	14.0	27.2	15.6	25.3	0.7	9.3	21.8	1.7	26.3	15.0	6.1	41.9	8.9
Johnson County	3.1	27.3	13.3	21.0	14.9	20.5	2.2	10.9	30.5	5.9	36.5	14.5	5.7	35.1	2.3
Lafayette County	4.1	29.5	13.2	21.3	14.3	20.4	3.2	12.4	28.4	9.9	33.0	12.4	6.0	33.9	4.9
Lawrence County	2.9	30.5	13.0	21.8	13.4	21.8	3.2	11.2	28.8	7.9	29.0	15.9	9.2	35.2	2.8
Lee County	1.7	30.4	9.9	23.8	21.7	21.1	4.0	7.1	22.3	10.7	22.2	12.8	6.9	39.4	8.0
Lincoln County	1.3	27.6	12.4	24.4	15.7	19.1	3.8	13.5	23.4	8.8	29.6	11.7	5.9	34.3	9.7
Little River County	1.4	24.4	13.5	20.8	13.2	23.1	3.1	13.4	26.4	5.5	34.3	12.6	6.7	34.8	6.1
Logan County	3.9	26.7	15.2	22.9	13.5	19.6	1.6	14.1	28.3	7.9	37.5	11.9	5.2	33.3	4.2
Lonoke County	2.0	22.7	15.5	28.3	12.2	28.2	1.6	11.7	17.9	4.2	21.6	18.5	8.1	41.2	6.5
Madison County	8.0	23.2	12.6	25.0	13.4	18.3	3.3	13.3	26.7	10.4	35.4	14.1	6.4	30.9	2.8
Marion County	3.7	26.6	21.0	21.1	14.2	22.0	1.1	11.7	29.9	3.5	36.8	13.6	5.7	37.0	3.4
Miller County	1.3	23.7	13.7	26.4	16.1	24.9	1.0	12.0	19.6	2.1	24.2	18.2	6.5	43.0	5.9
Mississippi County	1.0	26.4	12.2	21.1	13.7	21.6	3.0	10.1	30.5	5.7	39.2	12.6	4.4	34.3	3.8
Monroe County	2.8	28.1	12.1	22.4	17.1	20.8	6.3	8.1	25.2	10.8	22.9	17.5	5.6	37.4	5.8
Montgomery County	4.4	26.9	17.1	23.3	16.1	19.4	5.0	14.5	21.7	11.5	26.9	14.2	5.5	37.9	4.0
Nevada County	1.7	29.7	12.7	21.9	14.0	20.6	3.4	12.4	27.6	7.6	32.9	13.7	5.2	34.6	6.1
Newton County	5.2	27.0	13.5	23.1	14.1	20.7	3.8	11.8	26.5	8.7	30.3	15.1	7.0	36.1	2.8
Ouachita County	1.8	27.0	14.3	24.3	14.1	23.6	1.8	9.5	26.7	2.6	36.1	14.8	5.2	37.5	3.8
Perry County	3.4	27.9	16.2	22.0	16.7	23.1	1.6	17.4	19.2	5.8	30.7	14.7	4.2	38.0	6.5
Phillips County	1.3	28.4	10.1	26.9	20.1	24.6	3.1	8.9	16.5	7.8	18.2	15.2	5.1	48.5	5.2
Pike County	3.6	24.7	13.3	21.4	13.1	20.8	5.3	12.3	27.1	10.8	30.3	13.8	7.4	33.4	4.3
Poinsett County	1.8	30.5	12.2	18.7	12.9	21.5	3.0	12.5	31.4	7.6	35.0	15.9	7.1	31.0	3.5
Polk County	3.7	26.0	17.4	25.3	12.0	22.6	3.8	12.0	24.2	10.3	29.2	13.4	7.6	36.1	3.5
Pope County	2.2	22.6	14.3	27.7	15.2	23.8	1.0	10.1	22.2	3.0	26.5	16.6	9.6	41.1	3.3
Prairie County	3.3	29.4	14.1	26.0	13.2	21.3	5.5	8.1	25.9	15.0	24.4	15.3	7.2	31.3	6.7
Pulaski County	2.2	21.1	14.8	36.4	13.8	29.8	0.2	8.3	11.5	0.5	14.1	15.8	6.1	56.6	6.9
Randolph County	3.5	26.4	14.8	24.7	11.2	19.9	1.7	10.6	31.9	5.1	36.7	13.3	7.4	35.1	2.4
St. Francis County	1.8	26.6	11.5	23.8	14.8	25.4	2.0	10.6	23.5	4.9	25.9	18.5	6.7	37.8	6.2
Saline County	2.3	22.1	15.8	27.8	13.2	30.1	0.4	13.6	15.0	0.9	21.3	19.0	6.7	47.0	5.2
Scott County	6.0	25.8	14.8	25.0	11.4	14.2	6.4	10.9	32.1	12.6	39.4	10.1	5.4	29.6	2.9
Searcy County	4.2	28.7	15.5	22.4	14.0	20.7	3.6	14.7	24.6	8.5	31.9	14.6	5.3	36.0	3.7
Sebastian County	2.1	22.4	14.2	27.5	13.3	24.2	0.5	8.7	25.8	1.4	31.6	15.4	5.2	43.6	2.8
Sevier County	2.8	24.2	12.5	20.9	13.8	18.2	4.9	11.2	31.0	10.8	36.1	12.4	5.6	32.4	2.8
Sharp County	4.2	30.2	18.8	25.2	13.2	22.5	2.5	13.8	22.7	5.2	27.8	15.7	8.2	39.9	3.2
Stone County	6.4	29.2	16.5	24.3	15.4	20.7	2.7	14.8	22.1	7.0	31.9	16.3	3.9	37.1	3.7
Union County	1.6	25.2	12.7	25.6	13.4	23.8	1.4	11.3	24.5	4.5	32.2	14.0	4.6	41.3	3.4
Van Buren County	3.4	28.6	19.4	22.7	18.1	21.2	1.7	14.3	21.9	5.0	27.6	14.9	8.7	40.0	3.9
Washington County	3.5	18.1	12.1	31.8	14.3	26.4	0.9	9.5	17.0	2.3	24.5	17.0	5.7	48.2	2.3
White County	2.8	21.5	13.5	24.6	13.8	24.9	1.2	12.5	22.9	2.3	27.9	17.1	7.7	41.6	3.3
Woodruff County	1.7	28.6	11.3	22.1	14.7	21.5	7.9	8.2	25.6	15.2	23.5	18.4	6.8	30.4	5.7
Yell County	2.8	26.6	12.5	22.1	15.5	18.7	4.3	10.1	29.3	7.9	38.9	14.1	5.3	30.7	3.2
CALIFORNIA	3.8	19.2	10.4	36.0	14.8	26.8	1.3	8.4	12.7	1.9	19.3	15.2	4.7	54.3	4.5
Alameda County	3.5	18.7	9.2	42.3	11.9	26.3	0.2	7.5	11.8	0.3	19.8	14.9	5.8	55.5	3.7
Alpine County	4.6	15.9	13.9	26.6	26.8	24.8	2.9	9.9	9.1	3.7	12.6	8.6	4.0	57.8	13.4
Amador County	5.3	22.6	19.2	30.0	22.3	23.9	1.5	11.2	11.1	3.9	15.6	14.3	4.3	51.7	10.2

STATE County	Median house-hold income	Median family income — All families	Families with children — Married-couple	Families with children — Male house-holder	Families with children — Female house-holder	Median nonfamily house-hold income	Median income for full-year, full-time workers — Men	Median income for full-year, full-time workers — Women	Per capita income	With earnings	With interest, dividend, or rental income	With Social Security income	With public assis-tance income	With retire-ment income	House-holds with income over $100,000 (percent)	+/- U.S. percent for income over $100,000 (percent)	House-holds with income below poverty (percent)	Families with children with income below poverty (percent)
	57	58	59	60	61	62	63	64	65	66	67	68	69	70	71	72	73	74
ARKANSAS—Cont'd																		
Conway County	31 209	38 179	46 126	21 250	16 652	15 140	29 529	20 753	16 056	74.6	26.8	35.3	3.7	19.0	5.0	-7.3	15.6	19.3
Craighead County	32 425	40 688	47 290	26 495	13 902	17 774	31 134	21 716	17 091	81.7	27.2	25.3	2.8	13.3	6.2	-6.1	16.0	16.9
Crawford County	32 871	36 741	42 517	26 806	15 807	16 776	30 325	20 915	15 015	78.9	25.7	29.5	3.7	14.3	4.4	-7.9	14.1	15.8
Crittenden County	30 109	34 982	46 946	25 298	14 087	18 893	32 173	22 362	14 424	80.3	17.8	24.2	4.4	12.6	5.1	-7.2	23.1	29.0
Cross County	29 362	34 044	41 250	20 379	13 386	17 096	28 376	20 599	15 726	76.2	21.6	30.0	4.0	15.3	4.8	-7.5	19.0	23.9
Dallas County	26 608	32 630	39 259	21 625	15 221	12 101	28 929	18 553	14 610	71.4	20.2	34.4	3.4	14.0	3.6	-8.7	19.5	19.6
Desha County	24 121	30 028	40 743	17 143	10 777	11 934	30 220	19 425	13 446	71.7	16.0	29.9	5.6	10.6	4.4	-7.9	28.1	33.8
Drew County	28 627	37 317	47 308	30 804	13 319	14 492	31 589	20 934	16 264	77.1	23.1	25.8	3.1	13.5	5.7	-6.6	19.4	18.9
Faulkner County	38 204	45 946	53 649	29 770	19 000	20 081	33 044	25 079	17 988	83.9	28.2	21.7	2.0	12.8	7.7	-4.6	13.3	11.4
Franklin County	30 848	36 189	44 117	19 773	18 750	13 789	28 846	19 688	14 616	71.2	29.0	34.7	2.9	17.7	3.6	-8.7	16.0	13.6
Fulton County	25 529	29 952	36 169	23 750	16 094	14 301	24 478	19 517	15 712	66.7	30.3	43.0	5.1	22.8	3.3	-9.0	16.9	19.6
Garland County	31 724	38 079	43 880	21 849	14 343	19 000	29 070	21 290	19 031	69.0	35.0	36.0	2.7	23.8	6.1	-6.2	14.0	19.6
Grant County	37 182	42 901	46 476	22 083	19 000	17 827	32 680	22 895	17 547	79.7	25.5	30.5	2.1	17.4	5.4	-6.9	11.0	9.5
Greene County	30 828	37 316	43 017	20 323	16 514	15 202	28 158	20 755	16 403	76.1	26.2	31.5	2.5	17.9	3.9	-8.4	14.7	14.5
Hempstead County	28 622	34 082	41 814	17 174	13 888	14 148	26 431	18 203	14 103	75.4	20.4	30.0	4.3	13.4	3.6	-8.7	19.6	24.1
Hot Spring County	31 543	37 077	42 086	30 368	14 504	15 110	29 424	20 121	15 216	74.6	27.3	33.5	2.0	20.4	2.9	-9.4	15.1	16.4
Howard County	28 699	34 510	43 482	21 406	17 134	15 162	29 667	18 093	15 586	77.1	23.7	32.0	2.2	13.7	5.1	-7.2	16.0	17.5
Independence County	31 920	38 444	43 325	22 273	12 391	15 805	28 209	20 466	16 163	75.7	29.5	33.3	2.8	16.0	4.1	-8.2	14.3	14.3
Izard County	25 670	32 313	34 665	18 571	14 194	13 140	23 424	19 238	14 397	63.6	31.3	43.6	2.7	22.2	2.8	-9.5	18.7	20.7
Jackson County	25 081	32 661	38 865	23 864	14 792	12 841	27 446	18 860	14 564	72.1	21.4	37.5	3.8	14.9	4.7	-7.6	18.2	19.2
Jefferson County	31 327	38 252	49 758	25 068	15 787	17 113	32 824	22 711	15 417	76.8	24.1	30.3	3.9	15.5	5.6	-6.7	19.5	24.1
Johnson County	27 910	33 630	38 944	20 208	14 483	14 776	26 441	20 241	15 097	71.6	28.0	36.2	2.2	16.7	3.6	-8.7	16.9	16.9
Lafayette County	24 831	30 720	41 949	23 000	13 839	12 074	27 055	17 397	14 128	69.1	23.2	38.1	4.4	16.0	3.6	-8.7	23.2	29.5
Lawrence County	27 139	32 163	38 776	21 838	15 116	13 590	27 020	19 471	13 785	72.8	24.7	36.4	3.6	16.6	2.9	-9.4	19.2	20.1
Lee County	20 510	25 846	36 354	25 208	12 776	10 281	29 000	19 834	10 983	66.1	14.4	37.5	5.7	13.3	3.1	-9.2	30.7	34.3
Lincoln County	29 607	35 408	42 750	31 442	12 328	15 136	30 041	20 433	12 479	74.4	20.1	33.6	3.7	14.7	3.7	-8.6	19.1	24.3
Little River County	29 417	36 207	46 121	25 096	14 398	14 679	33 452	19 086	15 899	75.6	22.3	30.0	3.2	15.8	5.2	-7.1	17.3	17.3
Logan County	28 344	33 732	38 818	20 250	15 396	13 268	25 336	19 492	14 527	71.3	26.4	36.6	3.0	17.3	3.6	-8.7	16.9	16.1
Lonoke County	40 314	46 173	52 205	21 008	18 427	19 004	34 400	24 125	17 007	86.0	26.6	23.8	1.7	16.1	6.1	-5.9	11.4	11.9
Madison County	27 895	32 910	36 652	18 750	15 298	12 715	25 572	19 386	14 736	77.2	29.2	32.3	2.9	13.8	3.5	-8.8	19.6	21.1
Marion County	26 737	32 181	36 982	28 750	12 284	14 237	23 987	18 163	14 588	65.3	31.1	42.8	2.5	24.7	3.0	-9.3	16.0	20.6
Miller County	30 951	36 665	47 117	24 596	12 559	17 552	34 334	21 832	16 444	75.9	25.0	29.4	3.0	16.1	5.5	-6.8	18.0	22.8
Mississippi County	27 479	32 648	44 184	25 734	12 539	14 089	30 539	20 414	13 978	75.1	19.7	30.0	4.8	13.9	4.4	-7.9	22.5	26.7
Monroe County	22 632	28 915	36 250	26 607	12 108	11 237	25 685	17 650	13 096	69.0	18.2	36.7	4.8	13.6	3.1	-9.2	27.9	32.1
Montgomery County	28 421	32 769	39 611	21 250	14 028	14 865	26 752	19 099	14 668	70.5	29.3	39.9	2.9	19.0	3.6	-8.7	17.0	18.7
Nevada County	26 962	33 095	41 797	23 750	11 085	11 588	28 607	18 559	14 184	70.8	20.7	35.7	3.0	15.2	3.4	-8.9	23.7	25.1
Newton County	24 756	30 134	33 101	21 154	10 598	11 984	22 910	18 534	13 788	70.1	27.8	37.2	3.8	18.7	3.0	-9.3	21.5	22.6
Ouachita County	29 341	35 736	46 155	23 994	13 553	15 498	31 668	19 608	15 118	70.8	25.5	37.8	2.9	19.0	3.9	-8.4	19.4	23.2
Perry County	31 083	37 170	42 397	17 917	16 875	15 583	28 721	22 070	16 216	73.8	21.4	36.5	2.7	17.9	5.2	-7.1	14.8	14.1
Phillips County	22 231	26 570	41 736	20 000	11 206	12 036	25 547	18 112	12 288	70.6	15.8	32.0	5.9	13.3	3.9	-8.4	30.7	40.8
Pike County	27 695	32 882	37 234	19 615	11 728	12 086	28 718	17 941	15 385	71.5	24.9	34.7	1.6	16.4	3.8	-8.5	18.0	18.3
Poinsett County	26 558	32 257	40 395	21 643	12 483	12 674	27 194	20 063	13 087	74.0	18.2	32.7	4.3	14.9	2.8	-9.5	22.1	24.1
Polk County	25 180	31 379	37 421	18 309	16 000	13 722	24 078	18 322	14 063	70.5	26.2	37.4	2.5	17.4	3.4	-8.9	17.9	19.5
Pope County	32 069	39 055	45 258	29 085	13 530	17 885	30 794	19 862	15 918	78.5	29.7	29.0	2.5	15.2	5.6	-6.7	15.5	16.9
Prairie County	29 990	36 131	40 895	22 500	14 489	14 915	29 750	19 477	15 907	75.2	25.1	35.1	2.5	14.7	4.1	-8.2	17.1	17.3
Pulaski County	38 120	46 523	56 753	26 842	18 601	24 976	35 073	26 650	21 466	82.9	31.6	23.1	2.6	15.5	10.0	-2.3	12.4	16.3
Randolph County	27 583	33 535	38 408	20 926	13 021	12 750	25 856	19 037	14 502	71.0	30.0	36.7	3.5	16.9	3.2	-9.1	17.2	18.8
St. Francis County	26 146	30 324	40 940	20 221	10 941	12 355	28 866	21 120	12 483	73.7	16.7	29.9	6.7	11.9	4.0	-8.3	26.8	32.9
Saline County	42 569	48 717	53 272	31 175	20 160	23 254	32 911	24 124	19 214	81.3	32.1	28.0	1.6	20.4	6.8	-5.5	7.4	7.8
Scott County	26 412	30 311	34 771	12 321	13 606	15 110	24 296	17 481	13 609	75.1	22.6	35.3	3.4	16.1	2.6	-9.7	17.8	20.1
Searcy County	21 397	27 580	33 200	18 333	11 375	10 113	22 255	17 044	12 536	66.1	22.1	41.1	2.9	16.6	1.7	-10.6	25.3	26.4
Sebastian County	33 889	41 303	48 530	21 641	16 408	20 506	30 878	22 097	18 424	74.8	30.8	27.9	2.9	15.3	7.2	-5.1	13.3	16.5
Sevier County	30 144	34 560	36 687	20 804	17 125	14 583	26 541	18 261	14 122	78.5	24.9	31.1	3.4	15.6	3.8	-8.5	18.0	21.5
Sharp County	25 152	29 691	34 409	16 250	13 370	14 046	24 629	17 294	14 143	62.3	29.7	47.6	3.4	24.9	3.7	-8.6	17.5	20.8
Stone County	22 209	28 009	30 732	30 804	12 188	11 777	21 500	15 669	14 134	68.0	27.0	40.2	3.0	21.5	4.0	-8.3	18.3	22.1
Union County	29 809	36 805	49 746	24 651	12 824	15 391	32 737	20 263	16 063	73.9	26.2	32.9	2.6	15.8	5.4	-6.9	18.5	21.4
Van Buren County	27 004	32 284	37 121	21 823	17 344	15 641	27 158	19 785	16 603	64.9	31.0	44.5	2.7	23.2	4.7	-7.6	15.6	18.8
Washington County	34 691	42 795	48 871	23 137	18 538	20 624	30 428	22 161	17 347	84.1	30.9	22.1	1.9	12.1	6.7	-5.6	14.8	14.2
White County	32 203	38 782	43 222	25 604	15 429	15 896	30 564	20 902	15 890	77.1	28.2	30.8	2.7	15.3	5.0	-7.3	14.6	15.1
Woodruff County	22 099	27 824	34 327	21 250	12 147	11 833	25 037	18 292	13 269	68.8	18.1	36.1	4.9	11.3	2.5	-9.8	27.0	30.9
Yell County	28 916	33 409	42 083	26 406	16 734	14 045	24 421	19 022	15 383	74.7	25.0	35.3	3.0	10.1	3.9	-0.4	15.7	16.2
CALIFORNIA	47 493	53 025	60 318	31 161	22 200	32 024	41 526	32 432	22 711	82.5	35.0	22.3	4.9	15.4	17.3	5.0	11.8	15.3
Alameda County	55 946	65 857	78 889	40 725	28 167	36 795	49 391	37 872	26 680	84.3	40.0	19.5	4.2	14.9	22.2	9.9	9.8	10.9
Alpine County	41 875	50 250	58 750	14 375	14 375	29 688	39 464	26 136	24 431	85.8	29.7	21.7	5.3	18.5	9.8	-2.5	15.4	21.5
Amador County	42 280	51 226	62 138	35 833	22 529	24 474	40 665	30 596	22 412	72.1	43.6	37.7	2.3	29.9	10.7	-1.6	8.7	12.0

STATE/ County code	MSA/PMSA/ NECMA code[1]	STATE County	High school graduates			College graduates		College graduates (percent)				
			Total population 25 years and over	Percent with a high school diploma or less	Percent with a high school diploma or more	Percent with a bachelor's degree or more	+/- U.S. percent with bachelor's degree or more	Non-Hispanic White	Black or African American	American Indian and Alaska Native	Asian, Hawaiian, and Pacific Islander	Hispanic or Latino[2]
			1	2	3	4	5	6	7	8	9	10
		CALIFORNIA—Cont'd										
06 007	1620	Butte County	126 736	42.1	82.3	21.8	-2.6	23.2	14.6	10.5	25.6	11.7
06 009	...	Calaveras County..........	29 201	42.9	85.7	17.1	-7.3	17.9	25.2	7.4	54.7	5.5
06 011	...	Colusa County.............	10 912	60.1	64.0	10.6	-13.8	16.5	0.0	6.0	10.0	2.3
06 013	5775	Contra Costa County	625 641	32.9	86.9	35.0	10.6	40.1	18.3	17.7	48.0	12.5
06 015	...	Del Norte County.........	18 459	55.8	71.6	11.0	-13.4	13.2	1.3	6.0	12.5	4.2
06 017	6920	El Dorado County.........	105 034	33.1	89.1	26.5	2.1	27.6	50.6	11.9	35.5	10.7
06 019	2840	Fresno County.............	455 540	53.6	67.5	17.5	-6.9	26.2	11.8	7.5	24.5	5.6
06 021	...	Glenn County..............	16 099	58.3	68.5	10.7	-13.7	12.8	11.0	6.7	9.6	2.8
06 023	...	Humboldt County.........	81 501	40.8	84.9	23.0	-1.4	24.2	11.4	12.4	28.9	15.4
06 025	...	Imperial County	83 632	62.9	59.0	10.3	-14.1	19.7	4.5	5.4	30.7	6.4
06 027	...	Inyo County	12 566	49.0	82.3	17.1	-7.3	20.0	0.0	4.1	20.9	3.0
06 029	0680	Kern County................	383 667	56.9	68.5	13.5	-10.9	18.6	7.4	6.9	28.0	3.7
06 031	...	Kings County...............	77 095	60.1	68.8	10.4	-14.0	16.7	3.3	4.0	21.1	3.3
06 033	...	Lake County................	40 717	52.5	77.3	12.1	-12.3	12.9	5.8	1.8	31.2	5.0
06 035	...	Lassen County	22 963	51.2	79.6	10.7	-13.7	13.9	0.3	3.0	13.3	2.2
06 037	4480	Los Angeles County......	5 882 948	48.9	69.9	24.9	0.5	37.7	17.8	11.6	42.4	6.8
06 039	2840	Madera County............	74 830	59.9	65.4	12.0	-12.4	17.2	7.2	9.3	27.6	3.7
06 041	7360	Marin County...............	183 694	21.2	91.2	51.3	26.9	56.0	16.8	26.2	54.7	18.1
06 043	...	Mariposa County	12 196	41.2	85.1	20.2	-4.2	20.8	51.6	7.8	25.4	19.6
06 045	...	Mendocino County	56 886	45.2	80.8	20.2	-4.2	22.6	14.7	4.9	35.5	7.1
06 047	4940	Merced County.............	116 725	60.1	63.8	11.0	-13.4	16.6	11.1	7.4	13.2	3.5
06 049	...	Modoc County	6 464	52.3	77.1	12.4	-12.0	13.4	0.0	0.0	7.1	11.4
06 051	...	Mono County	8 674	32.7	87.9	28.9	4.5	32.8	58.3	12.2	46.8	4.9
06 053	7120	Monterey County	244 128	50.1	68.4	22.5	-1.9	36.4	11.3	8.7	26.5	4.6
06 055	8720	Napa County...............	83 938	40.1	80.4	26.4	2.0	30.5	11.3	12.1	40.0	7.4
06 057	...	Nevada County	65 148	33.5	90.3	26.1	1.7	26.8	37.2	14.1	23.8	15.0
06 059	5945	Orange County.............	1 813 456	38.0	79.5	30.8	6.4	37.6	27.6	13.3	40.9	8.5
06 061	6920	Placer County..............	165 894	30.8	90.5	30.3	5.9	31.1	39.4	20.3	45.4	15.7
06 063	...	Plumas County.............	14 786	39.7	88.0	17.5	-6.9	18.2	5.2	2.2	32.3	3.9
06 065	6780	Riverside County	936 024	49.7	75.0	16.6	-7.8	20.7	15.1	9.5	36.7	5.8
06 067	6920	Sacramento County	772 488	39.6	83.3	24.8	0.4	28.2	15.4	13.6	29.7	12.0
06 069	...	San Benito County	31 401	48.3	74.9	17.1	-7.3	25.5	16.3	15.5	27.3	5.6
06 071	6780	San Bernardino County .	983 273	50.8	74.2	15.9	-8.5	19.2	14.8	9.0	42.0	6.4
06 073	7320	San Diego County	1 773 327	37.3	82.6	29.5	5.1	36.1	16.3	13.8	36.0	10.7
06 075	7360	San Francisco County...	595 805	32.7	81.2	45.0	20.6	63.2	18.1	28.0	31.6	20.3
06 077	8120	San Joaquin County......	333 572	54.0	71.2	14.5	-9.9	18.2	9.7	6.4	20.7	5.3
06 079	7460	San Luis Obispo County	159 196	36.2	85.6	26.7	2.3	29.8	7.6	11.6	34.1	8.9
06 081	7360	San Mateo County........	490 285	32.2	85.3	39.0	14.6	45.2	20.0	20.4	48.3	12.3
06 083	7480	Santa Barbara County ..	246 729	39.8	79.2	29.4	5.0	38.9	16.9	12.3	37.1	7.0
06 085	7400	Santa Clara County.......	1 113 058	32.5	83.4	40.5	16.1	47.1	29.7	16.3	50.9	11.0
06 087	7485	Santa Cruz County........	164 999	33.3	83.2	34.2	9.8	41.0	22.7	18.1	40.7	9.3
06 089	6690	Shasta County.............	107 272	44.4	83.3	16.6	-7.8	17.2	12.7	5.4	17.3	10.8
06 091	...	Sierra County	2 540	43.5	85.2	17.2	-7.2	18.0	X	8.3	100.0	5.9
06 093	...	Siskiyou County	30 682	44.4	83.8	17.7	-6.7	19.2	5.0	7.2	10.5	6.7
06 095	8720	Solano County..............	246 488	40.7	83.8	21.4	-3.0	23.9	14.7	8.2	31.1	9.8
06 097	7500	Sonoma County	306 564	35.5	84.9	28.5	4.1	31.7	21.6	10.6	35.3	9.6
06 099	5170	Stanislaus County	264 578	55.7	70.4	14.1	-10.3	17.2	14.7	7.4	21.0	5.1
06 101	9340	Sutter County	49 071	50.6	73.0	15.3	-9.1	17.3	12.6	11.3	19.2	5.3
06 103	...	Tehama County............	36 261	55.1	75.7	11.3	-13.1	12.5	10.0	6.9	38.5	2.4
06 105	...	Trinity County	9 433	48.6	81.0	15.5	-8.9	16.6	0.0	1.4	6.8	5.5
06 107	8780	Tulare County..............	204 888	61.3	61.7	11.5	-12.9	17.5	6.7	4.6	18.4	3.6
06 109	...	Tuolumne County..........	38 977	45.4	84.3	16.1	-8.3	17.4	2.5	5.3	46.5	4.8
06 111	8735	Ventura County............	471 756	39.6	80.1	26.9	2.5	33.3	27.1	15.1	46.3	7.6
06 113	9270	Yolo County................	95 423	40.0	79.8	34.1	9.7	40.7	22.3	14.2	55.3	9.6
06 115	9340	Yuba County	35 218	55.4	71.8	10.3	-14.1	11.6	14.6	4.5	10.2	3.7
08 000	...	COLORADO..............	2 776 632	36.3	86.9	32.7	8.3	37.0	20.5	14.1	41.9	10.4
08 001	2080	Adams County..............	223 094	51.9	78.8	17.4	-7.0	20.8	16.9	6.2	24.0	6.8
08 003	...	Alamosa County............	8 567	44.5	82.6	27.0	2.6	33.8	42.6	13.8	40.5	16.4
08 005	2080	Arapahoe County	316 560	29.9	90.7	37.0	12.6	40.7	24.5	19.5	40.1	15.2
08 007	...	Archuleta County	6 821	39.5	87.3	29.0	4.6	32.2	0.0	14.1	33.3	9.7
08 009	...	Baca County................	3 152	55.8	78.5	14.0	-10.4	14.6	X	13.2	71.4	3.4
08 011	...	Bent County................	4 037	57.9	77.2	11.5	-12.9	15.8	2.5	0.0	21.9	1.3
08 013	1125	Boulder County	186 126	22.3	92.8	52.4	28.0	55.2	45.0	31.2	64.9	18.2
08 015	...	Chaffee County	11 837	41.4	88.5	24.3	-0.1	26.4	0.0	8.4	40.0	7.3
08 017	...	Cheyenne County	1 431	50.7	84.1	14.2	-10.2	14.6	X	0.0	X	8.3

[1]MSA = Metropolitan Statistical Area. PMSA = Primary MSA. NECMA = New England County Metropolitan Area. See the Appendix A for explanation of these concepts. See Appendix B for list of metropolitan areas identified by type, with component counties.
[2]Hispanic or Latino persons may be of any race.

Table B-3. States and Counties — Education, Labor Force, and Income

STATE County	School enrollment			Population 16 to 19 years				Employment status, 2000			Work status in 1999 of the population 16 years and over (percent)		
											Worked in 1999		
	Grades kindergarten through 12	College or graduate school	Percent private	Number	Percent in armed forces	Percent high school graduates	Percent not enrolled, not grads, not in armed forces, not employed	Total population 16 years and over	Percent in labor force	Unemployment rate	Full-time	Part-time	Did not work in 1999
	11	12	13	14	15	16	17	18	19	20	21	22	23
CALIFORNIA—Cont'd													
Butte County	38 232	25 780	5.7	13 482	0.1	8.2	2.7	160 320	56.8	9.3	42.7	20.0	37.3
Calaveras County.........	7 597	1 426	6.1	2 061	0.0	12.8	5.1	32 543	54.0	7.7	43.2	17.2	39.6
Colusa County............	4 635	722	4.8	1 480	0.0	8.6	11.8	13 632	59.5	10.7	52.8	14.2	33.1
Contra Costa County	189 347	61 975	13.5	48 997	0.0	9.1	3.9	724 451	65.5	4.8	55.6	15.2	29.2
Del Norte County	5 685	1 127	11.6	1 693	0.0	13.2	7.2	21 624	46.6	10.6	42.2	13.0	44.8
El Dorado County..........	32 460	9 288	8.1	8 592	0.0	11.7	2.2	120 392	64.9	5.4	53.2	17.1	29.7
Fresno County.............	197 351	54 663	5.9	54 287	0.0	9.1	6.9	571 317	59.9	11.8	50.4	15.0	34.6
Glenn County	6 253	1 058	3.8	1 596	0.0	10.8	4.2	19 300	60.0	9.1	49.8	15.0	35.2
Humboldt County	22 774	13 891	5.5	7 987	0.3	11.8	4.0	100 662	60.4	8.6	45.4	21.0	33.7
Imperial County	36 443	8 705	4.4	9 576	0.2	9.1	6.7	102 881	49.4	12.6	49.1	11.9	39.0
Inyo County	3 460	546	5.9	934	0.0	14.6	2.9	14 156	60.1	5.9	46.5	17.4	36.1
Kern County	161 296	34 561	6.9	42 920	0.5	11.6	7.2	473 552	56.5	11.8	51.1	12.6	36.4
Kings County	29 332	6 475	9.0	7 867	4.1	14.5	8.6	95 979	51.1	12.7	56.3	13.6	30.1
Lake County	11 232	2 295	5.7	2 895	0.0	11.8	7.1	45 977	50.2	10.9	40.1	14.8	45.1
Lassen County	6 518	2 013	7.1	1 735	0.0	16.4	4.8	27 365	41.1	9.4	48.5	12.7	38.8
Los Angeles County......	2 041 738	730 314	14.2	539 900	0.1	8.0	7.1	7 122 525	60.5	8.2	52.4	13.6	33.9
Madera County	28 604	5 995	6.6	8 045	0.0	11.1	9.1	90 917	53.5	13.2	47.5	13.4	39.1
Marin County...............	37 704	14 513	21.3	9 466	0.1	8.2	3.6	202 668	65.7	3.0	53.7	18.2	28.1
Mariposa County	3 096	819	10.2	863	0.0	18.4	4.1	13 798	57.7	14.1	46.4	16.3	37.3
Mendocino County	17 157	4 500	6.5	5 310	0.3	14.3	6.8	67 115	62.1	7.2	48.1	19.1	32.8
Merced County	55 741	11 077	5.8	14 424	0.0	10.2	7.2	145 720	59.5	13.1	51.0	13.8	35.2
Modoc County	2 005	192	2.4	517	0.0	14.5	3.9	7 325	56.4	11.9	47.8	13.6	38.5
Mono County...............	2 210	601	9.6	680	5.3	30.6	4.3	10 281	75.6	5.7	62.9	18.3	18.8
Monterey County..........	86 811	24 295	9.5	25 375	3.6	11.9	7.6	299 991	61.6	8.5	54.5	14.3	31.1
Napa County	23 590	7 765	16.1	6 854	0.0	9.5	3.5	97 675	62.7	4.3	51.5	16.4	32.1
Nevada County	17 457	4 524	6.9	4 998	0.0	8.2	4.1	73 812	59.2	4.7	46.4	19.0	34.6
Orange County............	569 481	230 740	12.1	151 675	0.1	8.0	4.9	2 153 952	65.5	5.0	56.5	14.7	28.8
Placer County	50 421	14 728	9.8	13 370	0.0	10.0	2.7	190 295	65.1	4.0	54.0	16.5	29.6
Plumas County	3 071	922	5.0	1 109	0.0	11.0	1.5	10 708	50.1	9.5	44.8	17.0	38.3
Riverside County	356 146	88 703	9.3	93 272	0.1	12.4	6.0	1 124 807	58.2	7.5	49.6	13.5	36.9
Sacramento County	253 944	93 272	10.5	67 282	0.4	11.8	5.6	921 897	63.7	6.6	53.9	14.7	31.4
San Benito County	12 580	2 570	8.8	2 807	0.0	14.9	4.5	37 663	67.3	6.6	59.8	13.8	26.4
San Bernardino County.	420 751	108 262	9.6	109 876	1.8	12.9	6.7	1 214 368	60.6	8.1	51.8	13.8	34.4
San Diego County.........	539 834	242 117	11.3	158 984	5.9	14.7	4.6	2 165 034	65.0	5.6	54.6	15.4	30.0
San Francisco County...	88 461	85 159	24.9	26 234	0.2	8.5	4.2	676 376	66.3	4.6	57.5	14.2	28.3
San Joaquin County......	133 856	33 087	11.1	37 229	0.0	10.7	7.0	408 554	59.8	10.3	51.3	13.7	35.0
San Luis Obispo County	42 791	31 338	7.2	18 175	0.1	8.8	2.3	200 572	58.3	5.9	47.2	19.6	33.2
San Mateo County	121 187	51 250	19.9	32 251	0.0	7.4	4.4	562 287	66.5	3.3	58.5	14.2	27.3
Santa Barbara County ..	74 970	46 317	11.8	26 449	0.3	7.3	4.2	310 929	63.1	6.6	49.1	19.1	31.8
Santa Clara County.......	305 563	141 601	17.2	85 189	0.0	7.9	4.5	1 308 666	67.2	3.9	60.0	13.2	26.7
Santa Cruz County.......	46 143	27 005	11.1	15 913	0.0	8.1	4.6	201 874	68.2	6.1	53.6	20.8	25.5
Shasta County	33 592	8 952	10.4	9 897	0.0	10.3	4.1	125 913	57.3	8.7	44.4	16.7	38.9
Sierra County	699	124	1.8	206	0.0	19.9	0.0	2 843	58.8	9.4	46.0	19.3	34.7
Siskiyou County	8 563	2 109	5.8	2 597	0.0	9.5	3.6	35 200	54.3	9.6	42.3	16.7	41.0
Solano County.............	85 648	24 612	11.2	22 795	1.8	12.8	4.2	294 773	64.5	5.9	56.0	14.4	29.6
Sonoma County............	86 107	32 351	11.0	25 183	0.5	11.3	4.5	359 736	66.8	4.3	53.3	18.5	28.2
Stanislaus County	106 277	24 120	7.8	28 694	0.0	12.5	6.4	322 469	61.2	11.6	51.3	14.6	34.1
Sutter County	17 600	4 072	6.5	4 725	0.0	11.7	5.8	58 728	60.4	11.6	53.0	13.2	33.8
Tehama County............	12 146	2 501	4.7	3 288	0.0	12.3	3.2	42 573	54.7	9.7	45.2	14.7	40.0
Trinity County	2 548	441	5.3	628	0.0	10.4	2.5	10 449	50.4	13.9	40.6	15.5	43.9
Tulare County..............	94 339	17 959	5.6	25 935	0.0	10.0	7.5	257 320	59.8	12.7	50.7	13.3	36.0
Tuolumne County..........	9 741	2 825	9.5	2 911	0.0	10.3	4.6	44 782	49.4	7.7	44.6	17.2	38.1
Ventura County	162 520	48 445	11.7	43 659	0.8	9.5	4.6	562 080	66.2	5.1	56.3	14.9	28.7
Yolo County	32 000	30 104	6.1	14 269	0.0	6.5	3.0	130 589	63.3	7.1	50.5	22.2	27.3
Yuba County	14 106	3 732	5.9	3 927	3.6	13.0	6.7	43 708	57.6	10.3	49.4	12.7	37.9
COLORADO............	804 108	282 832	11.7	243 396	0.9	12.4	5.9	3 325 197	70.1	4.3	60.7	16.1	23.2
Adams County.............	73 319	15 697	9.3	20 522	0.1	15.5	9.7	270 484	70.6	4.6	63.9	13.3	22.8
Alamosa County...........	3 079	1 945	7.0	1 396	0.0	10.7	6.9	11 324	66.3	8.8	53.5	19.5	27.0
Arapahoe County	97 404	27 529	12.8	26 415	0.3	12.8	4.3	372 885	73.3	3.2	64.7	14.7	20.6
Archuleta County..........	1 975	141	9.8	543	0.0	11.0	5.5	7 736	63.2	4.9	54.2	19.0	26.8
Baca County................	909	112	4.8	277	0.0	7.6	1.4	3 595	57.6	2.4	46.9	16.2	36.9
Bent County................	1 197	232	5.8	306	0.0	11.4	5.9	4 739	48.6	5.3	48.1	11.8	40.1
Boulder County............	48 758	35 657	10.9	18 302	0.0	8.2	3.1	231 690	73.4	4.4	59.2	21.2	19.6
Chaffee County	2 620	507	13.4	798	0.0	14.3	4.8	13 484	53.0	4.7	50.8	15.7	33.5
Cheyenne County	508	51	3.4	155	0.0	3.9	6.5	1 680	63.5	1.1	55.4	15.2	29.4

STATE County	Full-year full-time employed (percent)								Children under 18 years in families						Total employed by class of worker (percent)			
										With two parents (percent)		With one parent who is in labor force (percent)	+/- U.S. percent of children with no stay-at-home parent (percent)	+/- U.S. percent two-income couples				Unpaid family worker
	Total	Men	Women	Non-Hispanic White	Black or African American	American Indian and Alaska Native	Asian, Hawaiian, and Pacific Islander	Hispanic or Latino[1]	Number	Both in labor force	Father only in labor force				Private	Government	Self-employed	
	24	25	26	27	28	29	30	31	32	33	34	35	36	37	38	39	40	41
CALIFORNIA—Cont'd																		
Butte County	27.5	34.3	21.1	28.2	27.1	28.6	19.4	23.6	45 378	39.3	19.7	21.6	-3.7	-8.4	66.9	19.2	13.3	0.6
Calaveras County	29.3	36.5	22.3	29.5	51.0	24.3	39.7	23.5	8 360	43.8	22.2	20.1	-0.7	-12.3	60.2	20.3	19.0	0.5
Colusa County	26.3	32.6	19.7	34.0	3.1	28.1	10.1	17.6	5 355	44.0	18.5	15.3	-5.3	-9.4	66.5	17.9	14.1	1.5
Contra Costa County	41.4	51.8	31.8	43.0	39.2	41.4	41.2	36.5	237 116	42.3	25.9	18.8	-3.5	-0.1	74.6	13.9	11.2	0.3
Del Norte County	27.0	30.5	22.4	29.2	17.7	27.7	26.2	21.0	6 329	34.0	17.2	25.8	-4.8	-10.6	52.2	35.1	12.2	0.5
El Dorado County	38.9	48.4	29.7	38.8	47.5	36.2	43.1	38.7	38 631	47.2	25.7	17.8	0.4	-1.6	65.7	19.1	14.7	0.5
Fresno County	30.2	37.3	23.3	36.6	26.0	26.4	22.4	25.1	237 551	33.7	22.3	21.0	-9.9	-7.8	70.0	19.7	9.8	0.5
Glenn County	31.1	40.4	21.9	33.5	36.5	37.0	17.8	26.3	7 635	40.1	24.1	20.6	-3.9	-5.8	65.6	18.2	15.3	0.9
Humboldt County	28.9	34.8	23.2	29.4	21.3	26.1	26.3	28.2	27 144	38.0	18.3	25.9	-0.7	-4.6	61.2	23.1	15.0	0.6
Imperial County	27.0	34.3	18.8	33.2	32.8	29.3	41.3	23.6	41 594	32.3	24.6	20.7	-11.6	-14.6	62.7	27.7	9.2	0.4
Inyo County	34.3	43.7	25.6	33.4	30.0	31.9	62.2	38.5	4 202	50.4	16.1	24.8	10.6	-1.2	57.3	30.8	11.4	0.4
Kern County	30.8	39.3	21.8	35.5	27.5	28.7	29.4	23.9	195 676	35.5	23.6	21.2	-7.9	-9.6	69.0	20.6	9.9	0.5
Kings County	29.3	34.1	22.3	37.2	23.6	26.8	28.4	21.9	34 805	37.6	26.0	19.8	-7.2	-7.1	63.8	26.6	9.0	0.6
Lake County	25.9	31.2	21.0	25.8	19.0	24.4	27.1	32.1	12 814	31.4	19.0	27.7	-5.5	-16.5	63.0	21.1	15.2	0.6
Lassen County	27.5	28.6	25.5	30.1	15.8	23.3	29.2	25.4	6 995	44.3	22.3	18.7	-1.6	-5.7	44.4	42.6	12.3	0.6
Los Angeles County	34.1	34.0	26.7	38.4	32.1	31.4	34.7	30.7	2 448 852	31.9	23.5	20.8	-11.9	-8.1	75.2	12.6	11.8	0.4
Madera County	26.7	36.6	18.2	31.8	16.1	18.3	26.4	21.2	33 347	35.9	25.6	20.1	-8.6	-12.6	69.5	17.8	12.2	0.5
Marin County	39.2	47.9	30.8	40.2	28.4	41.7	41.2	32.8	48 015	44.9	27.2	18.1	-1.6	1.5	66.3	10.5	22.8	0.4
Mariposa County	29.3	36.6	21.6	29.3	22.5	24.4	39.4	34.3	3 611	37.8	26.1	22.8	-4.0	-11.7	58.4	25.1	16.0	0.5
Mendocino County	30.9	38.5	23.5	31.0	17.8	27.4	33.5	31.9	19 889	42.6	16.3	24.7	2.7	-4.0	63.8	18.0	17.6	0.5
Merced County	29.6	38.8	20.6	35.0	27.0	33.4	21.1	24.8	67 821	35.3	24.7	19.2	-10.1	-10.3	73.1	16.8	9.6	0.6
Modoc County	29.9	34.9	25.1	31.3	16.2	12.7	20.0	22.5	2 191	47.6	18.8	18.0	1.0	-8.0	46.9	33.4	18.5	1.2
Mono County	40.3	45.3	33.9	40.9	0.0	40.7	61.4	36.1	2 767	53.6	11.7	22.2	11.2	8.9	65.2	19.3	14.6	0.9
Monterey County	30.7	36.9	24.1	37.7	31.8	27.8	33.2	22.3	103 507	40.6	21.7	18.3	-5.7	-5.3	71.6	16.3	11.8	0.4
Napa County	35.9	43.9	28.1	37.0	29.5	40.4	37.8	32.1	28 218	44.6	23.8	17.9	-2.1	-1.8	71.3	13.9	14.2	0.6
Nevada County	32.4	40.5	24.8	32.4	42.9	33.5	31.2	34.5	19 930	47.1	21.1	21.3	3.8	-5.7	64.5	14.6	20.5	0.4
Orange County	40.9	51.5	30.7	44.0	46.7	36.3	37.9	36.0	714 668	39.4	28.1	16.9	-8.3	-2.1	77.0	11.1	11.6	0.4
Placer County	40.9	51.6	30.9	41.1	46.8	41.9	39.3	39.6	62 987	46.5	27.6	17.8	-0.3	-1.2	69.5	17.0	13.1	0.4
Plumas County	28.8	36.4	21.2	29.2	3.2	25.7	28.7	20.7	4 483	43.9	26.1	19.0	-1.7	-11.2	59.4	24.2	15.0	1.4
Riverside County	33.5	42.8	24.6	34.8	34.6	30.1	33.7	31.0	433 985	37.0	26.2	19.7	-7.9	-8.7	73.3	15.5	10.9	0.4
Sacramento County	38.8	45.7	32.4	41.3	35.6	35.8	33.7	35.0	313 381	36.8	21.0	23.8	-4.0	-1.4	68.1	23.0	8.7	0.2
San Benito County	39.8	51.2	28.6	44.0	38.5	38.9	39.5	34.5	16 036	42.9	25.0	17.5	-4.2	-0.1	74.2	15.2	10.1	0.5
San Bernardino County	35.8	45.9	26.0	37.7	35.8	32.1	36.5	33.2	509 823	34.5	24.9	21.1	-9.0	-6.1	72.6	17.9	9.1	0.4
San Diego County	39.2	49.1	29.3	41.7	41.4	36.1	36.9	33.5	676 014	38.3	25.7	20.8	-5.5	-2.8	72.3	16.0	11.4	0.3
San Francisco County	39.1	44.6	33.5	45.8	27.2	34.7	34.4	33.1	101 572	42.0	18.6	19.3	-3.3	-0.9	76.8	11.7	11.2	0.2
San Joaquin County	33.2	41.4	25.3	37.7	30.1	29.5	27.2	27.9	161 571	35.6	23.6	20.4	-8.6	-6.7	75.4	15.8	8.4	0.3
San Luis Obispo County	31.7	39.7	23.3	32.0	25.3	35.1	28.3	32.0	50 070	44.7	25.0	19.9	0.0	-4.1	63.2	20.6	15.7	0.5
San Mateo County	43.0	52.0	34.6	44.1	40.2	36.4	44.9	38.6	151 222	46.3	23.4	16.6	-1.7	2.1	77.2	11.2	11.3	0.3
Santa Barbara County	33.5	42.2	25.0	34.2	36.6	30.1	31.6	32.5	91 811	43.1	24.1	18.2	-3.3	-3.5	69.8	16.3	13.6	0.3
Santa Clara County	43.8	54.0	33.5	46.1	47.2	36.9	44.6	37.8	387 650	42.6	26.4	17.2	-4.8	0.4	82.1	9.2	8.4	0.3
Santa Cruz County	35.4	44.8	26.2	38.0	36.6	30.2	32.0	28.0	56 258	42.2	23.1	21.7	-0.7	1.7	69.8	15.4	14.4	0.4
Shasta County	30.4	38.3	23.1	30.8	32.3	26.4	24.1	27.9	39 363	38.7	21.2	22.4	-3.5	-9.3	68.5	18.4	12.6	0.5
Sierra County	28.8	39.0	19.1	28.9	X	28.6	100.0	24.2	788	49.0	19.2	21.3	5.7	-4.0	57.2	32.1	10.4	0.4
Siskiyou County	26.5	33.0	20.4	27.4	21.4	19.2	16.7	22.9	10 036	40.9	20.6	21.2	-2.5	-10.8	57.0	23.6	18.5	1.0
Solano County	40.5	48.0	32.9	42.4	39.4	34.2	40.1	35.2	104 010	42.9	21.8	21.9	0.2	1.8	71.8	20.4	7.6	0.2
Sonoma County	38.8	48.6	29.6	39.0	35.8	40.3	41.6	37.1	104 433	46.0	23.1	20.2	1.6	2.2	71.4	13.6	14.5	0.4
Stanislaus County	32.9	43.0	23.4	35.8	31.8	36.2	29.8	26.5	128 843	38.8	23.8	18.8	-7.0	-7.5	74.5	14.7	10.4	0.5
Sutter County	32.7	41.7	24.2	36.5	37.5	31.3	27.0	24.3	21 413	42.0	23.1	18.9	-3.7	-7.8	69.5	18.2	11.8	0.6
Tehama County	29.7	37.9	21.9	30.9	36.5	19.0	21.3	26.0	14 113	36.7	23.1	21.9	-6.0	-12.1	68.5	16.9	13.7	0.9
Trinity County	24.1	28.4	19.7	23.8	11.9	11.4	34.2	44.2	2 707	37.2	19.3	22.2	-5.2	-17.2	48.2	33.3	17.9	0.6
Tulare County	28.9	36.9	21.1	34.3	22.0	23.4	23.5	23.7	114 629	36.2	22.2	21.1	-7.3	-9.3	70.5	18.4	10.6	0.5
Tuolumne County	29.1	36.6	20.8	28.2	40.3	34.1	39.9	34.0	10 484	38.9	24.8	22.6	-3.1	-14.0	60.7	21.6	17.3	0.4
Ventura County	40.3	50.6	30.1	42.9	44.9	37.6	43.1	34.0	200 721	42.0	26.7	17.5	-5.1	-0.4	73.0	14.4	12.2	0.4
Yolo County	32.9	40.9	25.5	36.9	24.5	33.6	19.8	30.1	40 010	42.7	22.3	20.1	-1.8	0.9	61.2	29.7	8.7	0.3
Yuba County	31.9	41.2	22.6	33.8	37.4	27.0	23.0	26.6	17 304	35.2	23.6	19.5	-9.9	-10.5	68.3	19.0	11.7	0.9
COLORADO	44.9	54.6	35.2	46.3	44.6	39.4	42.5	38.6	1 043 072	47.2	22.9	19.6	2.2	5.8	73.7	13.9	12.0	0.3
Adams County	48.1	57.3	38.8	51.3	42.1	48.7	48.1	40.6	97 046	43.6	20.1	22.4	1.4	5.2	81.4	11.0	7.4	0.3
Alamosa County	35.4	44.4	26.9	36.3	55.2	29.9	34.2	33.2	3 961	45.6	19.1	24.4	5.4	3.6	64.6	22.1	12.8	0.5
Arapahoe County	50.2	59.9	41.1	51.4	52.4	46.3	44.3	43.5	124 803	48.6	22.7	20.1	4.1	8.8	77.7	11.1	10.9	0.3
Archuleta County	32.6	40.2	24.8	32.0	0.0	37.2	100.0	34.1	2 385	50.4	20.8	20.6	6.4	-3.0	54.5	17.3	27.5	0.7
Baca County	32.5	42.8	22.6	32.4	X	37.5	22.2	33.2	1 077	55.3	19.8	16.1	6.8	-1.5	48.0	21.0	29.5	1.4
Bent County	31.2	34.7	26.8	34.6	9.3	40.3	28.8	27.5	1 333	51.3	15.7	20.4	7.1	-2.6	52.0	28.9	17.9	1.2
Boulder County	43.1	53.4	32.7	43.9	43.0	31.3	41.9	38.3	63 936	48.5	26.2	18.1	2.0	7.5	72.0	15.0	12.8	0.3
Chaffee County	31.8	38.4	24.1	31.9	27.0	25.0	34.0	27.9	3 090	45.9	23.2	21.0	2.3	-6.1	56.4	20.1	22.6	1.0
Cheyenne County	42.1	57.6	26.9	43.3	X	50.0	0.0	25.7	625	60.2	22.4	9.6	5.2	7.1	53.3	20.2	24.7	1.8

[1]Hispanic or Latino persons may be of any race.

Table B-3. States and Counties — Education, Labor Force, and Income

STATE County	Percent who worked at home	Percent of the population 5 years and over with a disability	Veterans as a percent of the population 18 years and over	Occupation for employed population 16 years and over (percent)						Industry for employed population 16 years and over (percent)					
				Management, professional, and related occupations	Service occupations	Sales and office occupations	Farming, fishing, and forestry occupations	Construction, extraction, and maintenance occupations	Production, transportation and material moving occupations	Agriculture, forestry, fishing, and mining	Construction and manufacturing	Wholesale and retail trade	Transportation and warehousing, and utilities	Service industries	Public administration
	42	43	44	45	46	47	48	49	50	51	52	53	54	55	56
CALIFORNIA—Cont'd															
Butte County	4.3	21.5	14.9	31.7	18.7	26.7	2.0	9.3	11.6	3.7	13.7	16.0	4.1	57.9	4.6
Calaveras County..........	7.0	21.3	21.0	31.1	18.2	23.9	0.7	14.5	11.5	2.7	18.3	15.4	7.1	49.0	7.5
Colusa County	3.6	19.7	12.0	22.9	18.0	20.7	14.8	9.6	14.0	26.0	12.1	13.5	5.4	37.4	5.5
Contra Costa County	4.3	16.8	11.6	41.0	13.4	28.0	0.2	8.9	8.5	0.5	16.1	15.3	5.4	58.5	4.2
Del Norte County.........	3.6	25.0	16.6	24.3	31.5	21.7	4.3	8.8	9.4	6.2	9.8	12.8	2.9	48.3	20.0
El Dorado County.........	5.8	17.4	15.9	37.3	19.1	25.1	0.6	10.4	7.6	1.8	16.5	13.5	4.0	56.4	7.9
Fresno County..............	3.1	21.3	10.2	29.5	16.2	26.0	6.6	8.5	13.3	8.4	14.0	16.2	4.5	50.1	6.8
Glenn County	6.2	18.4	12.7	24.4	17.6	21.9	12.1	8.4	15.6	20.9	14.6	13.3	6.6	38.6	6.1
Humboldt County	5.6	21.2	14.4	31.5	19.6	24.9	2.6	8.8	12.6	4.9	14.5	15.6	3.8	55.4	5.7
Imperial County	3.0	20.4	8.8	24.7	19.7	25.6	9.3	9.0	11.7	11.7	10.1	17.7	6.4	43.1	11.0
Inyo County	3.8	19.1	17.2	27.6	23.3	24.9	1.5	12.0	10.8	3.7	11.9	14.4	7.0	52.9	10.1
Kern County.................	2.7	22.5	12.1	27.0	17.6	24.1	6.7	11.0	13.5	12.3	12.9	15.5	5.3	45.8	8.2
Kings County	2.6	19.7	12.6	25.9	19.7	22.8	9.4	8.5	13.7	14.5	13.1	13.5	4.0	41.0	13.2
Lake County	7.3	29.8	20.1	27.2	21.6	23.6	2.5	13.8	11.3	4.6	14.1	14.1	5.1	55.9	6.3
Lassen County	5.0	19.8	16.5	30.0	28.1	20.7	2.3	10.0	9.0	6.8	9.1	12.3	3.2	41.8	26.9
Los Angeles County......	3.5	20.4	7.4	34.3	14.7	27.6	0.2	7.8	15.5	0.3	20.0	15.2	5.0	56.4	3.2
Madera County.............	4.2	22.6	11.8	24.7	16.8	23.5	9.7	10.2	15.2	14.0	16.7	14.2	5.0	44.4	5.7
Marin County...............	8.8	15.4	11.4	52.5	12.0	24.7	0.3	6.0	4.5	0.5	10.8	13.7	2.7	69.0	3.2
Mariposa County	5.4	21.9	20.6	28.7	21.8	25.1	0.4	12.0	12.0	2.7	15.0	10.0	5.4	58.8	8.2
Mendocino County	6.9	22.9	15.0	29.6	19.5	23.0	4.0	10.9	12.9	7.1	17.9	14.8	3.6	51.0	5.6
Merced County	3.2	20.9	11.1	25.6	15.8	22.0	8.7	10.5	17.4	12.5	19.7	15.2	4.8	43.6	4.2
Modoc County	8.1	27.7	17.7	29.9	21.1	22.5	7.3	8.5	10.7	18.2	10.6	13.0	5.8	42.3	10.1
Mono County	7.5	13.8	11.9	35.4	23.0	21.7	0.3	13.0	6.7	2.8	14.2	11.2	2.3	63.9	5.7
Monterey County	3.6	19.8	11.0	29.2	16.8	23.2	11.2	8.5	11.1	12.4	12.0	17.2	3.3	49.7	5.5
Napa County	5.1	19.0	13.8	34.6	18.0	23.6	3.0	9.3	11.4	4.5	21.8	13.9	3.2	52.3	4.3
Nevada County	7.6	18.5	18.1	34.3	16.4	26.8	0.7	12.3	9.5	2.0	20.7	15.1	3.7	53.9	4.6
Orange County..............	3.7	16.6	9.3	38.1	13.2	28.7	0.3	7.3	12.5	0.4	23.1	16.3	3.6	53.7	2.9
Placer County..............	5.9	16.4	15.9	39.7	13.2	28.0	0.5	9.9	8.7	0.9	19.1	15.8	4.6	52.1	7.4
Plumas County	5.5	21.8	19.3	30.0	19.7	22.7	2.0	12.2	13.5	6.0	18.5	13.5	5.7	50.0	6.4
Riverside County..........	3.9	20.0	13.4	27.8	17.5	27.1	1.6	11.8	14.3	2.2	21.3	16.2	5.3	50.2	4.8
Sacramento County	3.4	20.0	13.6	36.3	14.5	29.9	0.4	8.7	10.2	0.7	14.0	14.9	4.6	53.4	12.3
San Benito County	3.0	17.1	10.3	30.2	14.7	25.1	4.7	12.0	13.3	6.4	23.2	18.3	4.5	41.9	5.7
San Bernardino County.	3.1	19.8	12.1	28.1	15.8	27.3	0.5	11.3	17.0	0.9	20.2	16.9	7.1	49.4	5.6
San Diego County	4.4	17.9	14.0	37.7	16.1	27.2	0.5	8.7	9.9	0.7	17.6	14.5	3.8	57.9	5.4
San Francisco County...	4.6	20.3	7.0	48.3	14.3	25.6	0.1	4.2	7.5	0.2	10.1	12.8	4.5	69.1	3.3
San Joaquin County......	2.9	21.4	11.4	27.1	14.6	27.1	4.1	10.2	16.8	5.4	19.6	16.6	6.2	46.8	5.3
San Luis Obispo County	5.6	17.6	14.4	34.3	18.8	25.3	2.1	9.8	9.8	3.8	15.0	14.8	4.5	55.7	6.2
San Mateo County	3.6	16.4	9.2	42.7	13.5	27.3	0.3	7.5	8.6	0.4	16.5	15.3	6.8	57.7	3.2
Santa Barbara County ..	4.6	17.7	12.0	35.4	17.1	25.3	4.9	7.7	9.6	6.7	15.6	14.5	2.9	56.0	4.2
Santa Clara County.......	3.1	16.4	8.4	48.5	10.5	22.7	0.4	6.6	11.2	0.5	32.5	12.9	2.8	48.8	2.5
Santa Cruz County........	5.3	15.9	9.8	40.3	14.8	23.4	3.7	8.9	8.9	4.4	20.3	14.8	2.8	54.3	3.4
Shasta County..............	4.1	22.8	17.0	30.4	19.6	27.0	0.9	9.8	12.3	2.5	13.8	17.2	5.7	55.1	5.8
Sierra County	4.3	21.6	19.4	34.7	20.8	17.3	1.2	13.9	12.1	4.0	22.3	6.5	4.5	53.5	9.2
Siskiyou County	8.4	22.0	18.2	30.8	19.5	24.3	4.6	9.1	11.7	10.1	11.9	14.9	5.7	50.4	6.9
Solano County..............	3.1	19.1	16.1	30.9	16.4	28.0	0.6	11.0	13.0	1.1	18.0	15.2	7.1	50.9	7.7
Sonoma County	5.4	17.7	12.7	35.0	15.1	26.6	1.6	10.2	11.4	2.6	21.1	15.0	4.1	53.3	3.9
Stanislaus County	3.2	21.5	10.6	26.5	15.4	25.6	3.6	11.4	17.5	5.6	22.6	16.7	5.3	46.0	3.9
Sutter County	3.0	20.4	14.5	28.5	14.8	24.5	5.8	11.0	15.5	9.4	18.3	16.4	5.1	44.9	5.9
Tehama County.............	6.0	23.1	17.7	25.3	18.8	22.7	4.3	9.3	19.7	7.7	18.3	18.0	5.1	46.6	4.3
Trinity County	8.4	24.0	20.5	28.3	21.4	22.8	2.8	10.8	13.9	7.8	14.4	13.7	4.5	51.1	8.6
Tulare County...............	3.5	21.1	9.6	25.3	16.2	22.7	13.2	8.4	14.2	15.2	14.7	16.8	4.2	43.3	5.7
Tuolumne County	5.7	21.8	19.1	29.7	21.4	24.7	0.9	12.1	11.3	3.1	15.6	15.3	4.9	53.5	7.5
Ventura County	4.2	17.7	11.8	36.5	13.4	27.3	3.1	8.2	11.5	4.1	20.1	15.0	3.3	52.0	5.4
Yolo County.................	3.8	16.7	9.1	41.4	14.2	23.8	2.6	7.1	10.9	3.9	11.3	14.3	4.5	58.4	7.7
Yuba County	4.1	26.1	16.0	23.0	18.6	24.7	4.6	12.5	16.6	6.7	18.4	16.6	6.1	47.0	5.2
COLORADO..............	4.9	16.3	13.9	37.4	13.9	27.2	0.6	10.5	10.5	2.0	18.2	15.2	4.9	55.1	4.6
Adams County..............	3.1	18.6	13.2	26.7	13.0	29.2	0.3	14.3	16.5	0.9	23.3	17.9	8.1	46.1	3.7
Alamosa County	4.5	17.9	11.8	34.6	14.5	28.1	3.8	10.5	8.5	6.5	10.6	15.7	3.6	57.5	6.1
Arapahoe County	4.6	14.8	14.2	39.6	11.7	31.3	0.1	8.7	8.6	0.7	13.8	16.4	5.6	59.3	4.1
Archuleta County..........	8.4	20.9	16.3	26.6	17.2	27.6	0.7	19.0	8.8	3.4	20.9	14.9	3.9	52.3	4.6
Baca County................	10.2	21.6	13.5	39.1	15.1	17.0	7.0	11.0	10.9	27.5	9.6	10.6	6.9	41.0	4.4
Bent County	6.2	25.1	17.7	33.5	16.9	24.0	10.1	7.6	8.0	23.1	8.6	14.8	3.8	41.5	8.2
Boulder County............	6.4	11.8	10.0	50.2	12.1	23.7	0.2	6.3	7.6	0.7	20.0	13.8	2.7	59.6	3.2
Chaffee County	8.3	18.5	17.1	30.1	21.6	24.6	0.8	14.0	8.9	3.2	16.3	14.4	4.3	51.6	10.2
Cheyenne County	12.4	16.1	12.0	35.3	16.7	17.8	4.6	15.1	10.4	28.3	11.4	10.8	5.7	38.6	5.2

STATE County	Median house-hold income	All families	Married-couple	Male house-holder	Female house-holder	Median nonfamily house-hold income	Men	Women	Per capita income	With earnings	With interest, dividend, or rental income	With Social Security income	With public assis-tance income	With retire-ment income	House-holds with income over $100,000 (percent)	+/– U.S. percent for income over $100,000	House-holds with income below poverty (percent)	Families with children with income below poverty (percent)
	57	58	59	60	61	62	63	64	65	66	67	68	69	70	71	72	73	74
CALIFORNIA—Cont'd																		
Butte County	31 924	41 010	49 906	24 981	16 684	19 339	35 675	26 211	17 517	72.5	33.8	31.3	6.5	20.8	6.7	-5.6	17.6	19.8
Calaveras County	41 022	47 379	57 793	21 917	16 678	22 801	45 069	29 404	21 420	71.0	41.3	36.7	3.7	28.7	10.1	-2.2	11.3	13.2
Colusa County	35 062	40 138	41 480	29 091	16 080	20 057	33 544	22 106	14 730	79.2	28.7	28.5	4.6	16.0	6.3	-6.0	14.8	18.1
Contra Costa County	63 675	73 039	84 397	42 619	31 659	40 722	55 364	40 144	30 615	83.6	44.5	22.6	2.8	17.8	26.7	14.4	6.6	7.9
Del Norte County	29 642	36 056	48 361	28 854	12 500	16 473	40 324	23 519	14 573	71.7	28.5	32.7	8.9	17.4	5.8	-6.5	18.2	24.0
El Dorado County	51 484	60 250	70 845	37 813	26 690	29 945	48 767	32 212	25 560	80.7	41.3	25.9	2.8	21.2	17.2	4.9	7.0	7.1
Fresno County	34 725	38 455	43 478	22 425	16 316	22 277	34 763	27 296	15 495	80.6	26.8	23.6	8.5	14.2	8.6	-3.7	18.2	24.8
Glenn County	32 107	37 023	39 222	21 205	16 855	16 756	30 989	22 347	14 069	76.9	28.9	28.8	6.8	16.3	4.8	-7.5	15.4	19.4
Humboldt County	31 226	39 370	46 161	23 111	14 186	19 111	33 572	25 027	17 203	76.8	36.6	26.3	6.1	17.0	5.8	-6.5	18.7	20.8
Imperial County	31 870	35 226	40 666	21 782	15 057	16 549	34 237	24 586	13 239	79.3	19.3	28.9	10.3	13.6	7.2	-5.1	20.1	24.6
Inyo County	35 006	44 970	55 147	22 981	18 384	19 010	38 998	26 483	19 639	71.7	34.7	33.7	3.8	22.7	8.4	-3.9	12.5	14.4
Kern County	35 446	39 403	45 817	23 835	14 858	21 286	39 696	26 599	15 760	78.9	25.0	24.8	7.5	15.9	8.3	-4.0	17.7	22.9
Kings County	35 749	38 111	42 118	25 038	15 552	22 441	32 587	25 615	15 848	83.5	24.6	22.0	7.6	15.3	7.5	-4.8	15.8	22.2
Lake County	29 627	35 818	47 470	25 582	17 159	17 208	36 906	25 681	16 825	64.6	28.6	40.3	8.3	24.8	5.5	-6.8	15.8	21.6
Lassen County	36 310	43 398	51 788	26 136	16 944	19 938	38 767	27 179	14 749	76.6	30.1	27.5	6.5	19.9	6.6	-5.7	13.6	15.5
Los Angeles County	42 189	46 452	51 165	27 278	20 044	30 917	37 089	31 583	20 683	83.3	29.7	19.7	6.4	12.1	15.1	2.8	15.1	19.9
Madera County	36 286	39 226	42 350	24 852	17 001	19 227	34 757	25 276	14 682	78.5	24.9	29.0	8.0	17.5	8.2	-4.1	16.5	23.1
Marin County	71 306	88 934	108 095	51 449	36 740	48 823	65 481	47 440	44 962	83.1	56.6	23.5	1.4	16.1	35.1	22.8	5.5	6.1
Mariposa County	34 626	42 655	47 212	23 750	17 375	20 815	31 698	26 439	18 190	69.3	35.5	37.5	5.0	24.3	7.1	-5.2	12.1	16.4
Mendocino County	35 996	42 168	48 943	22 181	17 590	22 327	35 029	25 326	19 443	77.1	36.7	28.7	5.9	18.2	8.5	-3.8	13.7	17.6
Merced County	35 532	38 009	42 519	23 691	15 129	21 465	32 540	24 994	14 257	81.2	24.7	24.0	9.1	16.4	6.9	-5.4	17.8	22.8
Modoc County	27 522	35 978	42 386	22 321	14 554	15 795	31 975	23 980	17 285	70.0	28.8	33.6	8.0	20.7	5.1	-7.2	18.1	25.7
Mono County	44 992	50 487	48 182	21 964	17 283	33 820	33 289	26 998	23 422	88.2	37.0	16.0	2.5	13.5	11.6	-0.7	8.9	10.9
Monterey County	48 305	51 169	52 342	30 832	23 662	33 014	40 169	30 775	20 165	83.7	36.3	24.6	4.0	17.7	15.2	2.9	10.3	14.0
Napa County	51 738	61 410	67 833	39 410	28 476	32 361	44 290	32 969	26 395	78.7	44.5	28.7	2.5	22.9	18.6	6.3	6.9	8.8
Nevada County	45 864	52 697	64 586	30 154	24 348	27 299	41 919	28 786	24 007	73.4	45.0	32.9	2.5	25.7	13.5	1.2	7.9	8.7
Orange County	58 820	64 611	69 855	37 506	31 285	40 152	46 263	35 268	25 826	86.3	39.5	20.2	2.7	14.1	23.5	11.2	7.7	10.1
Placer County	57 535	65 858	79 989	40 921	28 724	32 766	51 348	35 136	27 963	81.0	44.7	26.0	2.4	20.4	20.5	8.2	5.8	6.0
Plumas County	36 351	46 119	51 551	35 313	17 371	18 387	40 119	27 031	19 391	71.6	36.2	33.3	4.1	22.5	7.4	-4.9	13.3	15.9
Riverside County	42 887	48 409	55 526	28 983	20 319	25 209	40 039	29 182	18 689	77.9	30.0	28.9	4.3	18.4	12.2	-0.1	12.0	15.1
Sacramento County	43 816	50 717	59 686	31 793	23 259	30 739	40 514	32 251	21 142	81.5	33.1	22.4	6.6	18.4	12.3	0.0	11.5	15.4
San Benito County	57 469	60 665	66 206	39 643	28 594	32 479	45 475	30 426	20 932	87.4	31.6	20.7	4.0	14.6	19.8	7.5	7.7	8.6
San Bernardino County	42 066	46 574	53 319	29 304	19 611	25 144	37 902	28 903	16 856	82.4	24.8	22.1	6.5	15.9	11.0	-1.3	13.5	16.8
San Diego County	47 067	53 438	60 332	31 338	23 092	32 044	38 160	31 095	22 926	82.6	37.5	22.5	3.6	17.7	15.7	3.4	10.3	13.3
San Francisco County	55 221	63 545	72 158	34 770	27 433	46 457	48 203	40 938	34 556	81.3	46.3	21.0	3.9	13.0	24.7	12.4	10.2	11.8
San Joaquin County	41 282	46 919	54 871	29 061	18 286	23 873	40 324	28 677	17 365	79.9	28.1	24.6	7.2	17.1	10.6	-1.7	14.5	19.0
San Luis Obispo County	42 428	52 447	60 919	33 832	23 185	25 261	41 857	28 975	21 864	76.9	43.2	29.2	2.3	20.3	12.0	-0.3	11.8	9.9
San Mateo County	70 819	80 737	91 921	48 090	38 791	46 093	52 353	41 215	36 045	84.7	50.1	23.4	1.6	16.4	32.3	20.0	4.9	4.9
Santa Barbara County	46 677	54 042	57 996	31 643	22 160	30 309	39 862	30 611	23 059	80.5	42.4	26.8	3.1	18.1	16.0	3.7	11.6	13.0
Santa Clara County	74 335	81 717	93 371	47 972	35 375	51 732	58 224	41 379	32 795	87.7	45.9	18.2	2.7	13.6	34.6	22.3	6.1	6.8
Santa Cruz County	53 998	61 941	70 496	41 033	28 545	35 297	48 103	35 404	26 396	84.9	43.4	21.3	2.7	14.4	21.9	9.6	9.5	9.8
Shasta County	34 335	40 491	49 712	26 058	16 353	19 535	36 925	25 704	17 738	73.0	31.6	32.1	6.9	21.4	7.2	-5.1	13.9	18.1
Sierra County	35 827	42 756	45 529	39 500	15 250	22 697	37 100	30 000	18 815	74.9	34.1	32.1	3.6	21.8	6.1	-6.2	13.7	17.5
Siskiyou County	29 530	36 890	42 179	17 282	14 197	16 647	33 954	24 003	17 570	68.3	35.9	36.6	5.4	22.9	5.7	-6.6	16.9	23.8
Solano County	54 099	60 597	69 001	35 685	27 002	32 926	43 425	32 693	21 731	84.5	32.2	20.9	3.9	21.2	16.5	4.2	7.4	8.5
Sonoma County	53 076	61 921	70 829	41 567	29 530	33 047	44 038	33 500	25 724	81.2	44.1	25.5	2.3	18.1	18.1	5.8	7.0	6.9
Stanislaus County	40 101	44 703	51 669	28 810	17 068	26 262	37 795	27 315	16 913	80.6	27.7	25.1	6.3	16.3	9.1	-3.2	13.6	17.3
Sutter County	38 375	44 330	48 921	27 188	17 625	22 071	36 956	26 400	17 428	80.7	29.2	26.6	5.1	19.6	9.1	-3.2	13.3	17.9
Tehama County	31 206	37 277	43 093	20 036	17 125	17 347	31 774	24 012	15 793	71.0	30.2	35.6	6.6	22.4	5.1	-7.2	15.3	20.5
Trinity County	27 711	34 343	37 344	16 964	12 418	15 952	32 447	24 848	16 868	67.4	35.3	35.4	5.0	25.1	5.5	-6.8	17.8	26.1
Tulare County	33 983	36 297	38 960	22 143	15 092	20 526	31 524	25 445	14 006	80.6	23.6	25.3	8.6	14.6	7.6	-4.7	19.0	26.6
Tuolumne County	38 725	44 327	52 493	27 045	17 074	23 727	36 160	27 006	21 015	69.5	40.3	38.5	4.3	29.1	8.6	-3.7	10.5	15.3
Ventura County	59 666	65 285	71 930	40 902	29 864	36 651	46 937	33 737	24 600	85.2	40.2	23.2	2.9	17.5	22.8	10.5	7.2	9.1
Yolo County	40 769	51 623	59 134	29 643	24 134	22 194	40 079	31 228	19 365	83.7	38.1	19.8	4.4	14.9	13.0	0.7	16.8	13.3
Yuba County	30 460	34 103	39 165	26 250	13 742	18 258	28 699	22 113	14 124	76.7	23.3	25.9	9.5	16.9	4.6	-7.7	18.7	23.1
COLORADO	47 203	55 883	63 532	33 223	24 551	30 728	40 105	30 268	24 049	85.8	40.6	19.9	2.5	14.6	14.2	1.9	8.8	9.2
Adams County	47 323	52 517	58 391	35 705	25 910	31 597	37 089	28 855	19 944	88.1	30.4	18.6	2.2	13.6	10.0	-2.3	7.7	9.2
Alamosa County	29 447	38 389	40 471	15 667	12 566	16 214	29 462	23 659	15 037	80.3	28.8	21.1	6.2	11.0	6.5	-5.8	20.6	23.5
Arapahoe County	53 570	63 875	72 444	38 757	30 651	35 116	42 944	32 335	28 147	88.7	42.4	17.0	1.7	13.9	17.9	5.6	5.6	6.2
Archuleta County	37 901	43 259	49 896	20 046	17 188	21 563	30 631	21 996	21 683	82.8	38.0	24.4	3.7	19.1	8.3	-4.0	12.6	14.9
Baca County	28 099	34 018	35 550	38 125	16 000	14 159	25 106	19 313	15 068	72.9	34.4	38.0	5.6	11.6	2.8	-9.5	18.2	20.1
Bent County	28 125	34 096	39 583	22 500	13 000	16 154	24 592	24 942	13 567	76.5	30.1	33.5	5.2	18.5	3.8	-8.5	18.1	24.5
Boulder County	55 861	70 572	81 942	39 750	29 066	35 276	50 054	33 541	28 976	88.3	51.4	15.0	1.6	12.6	21.7	9.4	9.2	6.5
Chaffee County	34 368	42 043	45 515	24 125	15 078	20 261	31 665	23 325	19 430	73.5	43.4	34.5	3.6	23.2	7.1	-5.2	12.0	14.7
Cheyenne County	37 054	44 394	49 028	40 000	15 938	19 583	34 330	19 844	17 850	79.2	39.0	31.5	3.0	11.2	7.1	-5.2	12.0	11.8

Table B-3. States and Counties — Education, Labor Force, and Income

STATE/ County code	MSA/PMSA/ NECMA code[1]	STATE County	High school graduates			College graduates		College graduates (percent)				
			Total population 25 years and over	Percent with a high school diploma or less	Percent with a high school diploma or more	Percent with a bachelor's degree or more	+/- U.S. percent with bachelor's degree or more	Non-Hispanic White	Black or African American	American Indian and Alaska Native	Asian, Hawaiian, and Pacific Islander	Hispanic or Latino[2]
			1	2	3	4	5	6	7	8	9	10
		COLORADO—Cont'd										
08 019	...	Clear Creek County	6 702	28.1	93.4	38.8	14.4	39.7	0.0	20.4	32.6	14.5
08 021	...	Conejos County............	4 979	61.8	72.1	14.4	-10.0	22.5	0.0	1.0	33.3	9.1
08 023	...	Costilla County	2 506	59.2	68.2	12.8	-11.6	23.0	0.0	16.7	16.3	7.3
08 025	...	Crowley County............	3 897	57.0	77.5	11.9	-12.5	16.7	0.0	1.1	9.1	1.6
08 027	...	Custer County	2 548	37.8	90.3	26.7	2.3	27.4	0.0	0.0	X	22.6
08 029	...	Delta County	19 330	53.9	80.1	17.6	-6.8	19.0	0.0	15.4	23.6	3.9
08 031	2080	Denver County	374 478	41.1	78.9	34.5	10.1	47.8	17.8	13.7	40.3	7.8
08 033	...	Dolores County	1 323	57.2	76.0	13.5	-10.9	13.8	X	0.0	57.1	15.0
08 035	2080	Douglas County............	112 436	16.2	97.0	51.9	27.5	52.4	57.0	36.9	59.0	37.6
08 037	...	Eagle County...............	27 178	29.9	86.6	42.6	18.2	51.0	14.3	23.5	47.8	6.7
08 039	...	Elbert County	12 814	34.9	92.5	26.6	2.2	26.7	25.9	31.3	66.7	17.4
08 041	1720	El Paso County	320 420	31.6	91.3	31.8	7.4	34.9	19.0	13.3	33.7	14.1
08 043	...	Fremont County	00 214	50.2	00.5	13.5	-10.9	15.9	0.2	4.9	6.1	3.8
08 045	...	Garfield County	27 884	41.5	85.4	23.8	-0.6	26.2	0.0	9.5	34.3	6.5
08 047	...	Gilpin County	3 501	31.5	94.1	31.2	6.8	31.9	65.5	0.0	36.7	3.6
08 049	...	Grand County	8 571	31.7	92.3	34.5	10.1	35.1	0.0	9.8	72.7	17.6
08 051	...	Gunnison County	8 504	23.7	94.1	43.6	19.2	45.0	23.7	31.4	7.7	20.1
08 053	...	Hinsdale County	593	27.7	93.1	34.9	10.5	35.5	X	0.0	100.0	0.0
08 055	...	Huerfano County	5 647	54.5	77.8	16.1	-8.3	21.4	3.4	4.6	48.5	5.7
08 057	...	Jackson County	1 098	49.8	86.2	19.9	-4.5	20.2	0.0	0.0	100.0	13.2
08 059	2080	Jefferson County	351 579	30.8	91.8	36.5	12.1	38.2	33.2	21.3	47.8	17.5
08 061	...	Kiowa County	1 085	49.2	86.3	16.1	-8.3	16.1	0.0	0.0	X	26.7
08 063	...	Kit Carson County	5 254	54.6	77.0	15.4	-9.0	16.9	12.1	0.0	0.0	4.8
08 065	...	Lake County	4 710	47.8	79.5	19.5	-4.9	26.8	X	0.0	77.8	2.2
08 067	...	La Plata County	27 973	31.7	91.4	36.4	12.0	39.7	21.1	14.3	32.4	14.3
08 069	2670	Larimer County	156 426	29.0	92.3	39.5	15.1	40.8	39.4	16.9	61.9	17.4
08 071	...	Las Animas County.......	10 279	50.0	70.9	10.2	-8.2	21.2	0.0	4.1	33.3	7.9
08 073	...	Lincoln County	4 214	53.2	81.8	13.2	-11.2	14.5	10.3	13.9	0.0	4.1
08 075	...	Logan County	13 074	49.7	82.3	14.6	-9.8	15.8	20.3	0.0	5.9	2.6
08 077	2006	Mesa County...............	76 259	45.0	86.0	20.0	-2.4	20.2	10.0	4.7	24.3	5.5
08 079	...	Mineral County	631	36.8	91.6	31.2	6.8	31.7	X	0.0	X	0.0
08 081	...	Moffat County	8 404	53.8	79.6	12.5	-11.9	13.1	48.0	12.2	33.3	3.1
08 083	...	Montezuma County	15 512	51.9	81.1	21.0	-3.4	23.7	0.0	5.4	12.5	8.4
08 085	...	Montrose County	22 089	52.7	80.7	18.7	-5.7	20.2	8.5	21.0	13.4	6.1
08 087	...	Morgan County	16 661	59.6	71.4	13.5	-10.9	16.8	21.1	12.1	18.8	2.4
08 089	...	Otero County...............	13 172	55.0	75.7	15.4	-9.0	20.7	68.8	0.8	41.2	4.3
08 091	...	Ouray County	2 741	28.2	93.4	36.8	12.4	37.6	0.0	10.0	0.0	19.7
08 093	...	Park County	10 371	33.4	93.3	30.3	5.9	30.6	34.5	27.3	51.9	18.9
08 095	...	Phillips County	2 999	50.6	81.6	19.9	-4.5	21.3	0.0	50.0	25.0	5.7
08 097	...	Pitkin County	11 322	14.6	96.3	57.1	32.7	60.1	82.7	23.5	38.3	13.9
08 099	...	Prowers County	8 545	56.9	72.0	11.9	-12.5	14.4	100.0	3.6	23.5	4.7
08 101	6560	Pueblo County	92 080	49.7	81.3	18.3	-6.1	22.8	15.7	11.0	42.1	9.5
08 103	...	Rio Blanco County	3 857	43.6	88.4	19.5	-4.9	19.8	X	15.8	66.7	9.0
08 105	...	Rio Grande County	7 959	51.9	78.1	18.8	-5.6	26.6	X	4.5	16.7	5.4
08 107	...	Routt County	13 267	22.4	95.3	42.5	18.1	43.3	77.8	22.0	14.7	23.2
08 109	...	Saguache County	3 760	54.8	70.0	19.6	-4.8	29.2	0.0	8.7	50.0	4.5
08 111	...	San Juan County	428	22.4	92.1	43.7	19.3	45.8	X	0.0	50.0	20.0
08 113	...	San Miguel County........	4 762	21.4	93.6	48.5	24.1	50.6	20.0	15.4	49.0	11.3
08 115	...	Sedgwick County	1 938	56.2	79.3	13.4	-11.0	14.8	0.0	0.0	0.0	2.4
08 117	...	Summit County.............	15 795	24.4	93.3	48.3	23.9	51.7	21.7	26.1	42.4	14.8
08 119	...	Teller County	14 240	29.5	94.0	31.7	7.3	32.3	31.4	9.5	31.0	15.8
08 121	...	Washington County.......	3 314	51.9	81.7	14.3	-10.1	14.3	0.0	27.8	75.0	7.6
08 123	3060	Weld County	106 245	47.2	79.6	21.6	-2.8	25.7	23.4	13.0	48.4	6.5
08 125	...	Yuma County	6 340	54.3	79.5	15.5	-8.9	16.5	100.0	25.0	X	4.1
09 000	...	CONNECTICUT	2 295 617	44.5	84.0	31.4	7.0	34.2	13.7	15.7	57.2	11.3
09 001	5483	Fairfield County	596 371	39.2	84.4	39.9	15.5	45.8	13.9	23.3	59.2	11.7
09 003	3283	Hartford County	579 839	46.3	82.4	29.6	5.2	33.2	13.3	15.3	50.7	10.0
09 005	...	Litchfield County...........	127 305	45.5	85.9	27.5	3.1	27.5	20.4	15.0	42.4	24.1
09 007	3283	Middlesex County	108 106	39.8	88.7	33.8	9.4	34.4	18.5	22.8	53.0	29.7
09 009	5480	New Haven County	551 042	47.8	83.0	27.6	3.2	29.9	13.6	14.9	65.7	10.0
09 011	5523	New London County	173 910	46.0	86.0	26.2	1.8	27.5	12.5	10.9	42.8	11.9
09 013	3283	Tolland County	87 202	39.8	89.2	32.8	8.4	32.5	20.9	18.9	70.9	21.6
09 015	...	Windham County...........	71 242	56.1	79.6	19.0	-5.4	19.5	9.8	10.7	35.5	10.3

[1]MSA = Metropolitan Statistical Area. PMSA = Primary MSA. NECMA = New England County Metropolitan Area. See the Appendix A for explanation of these concepts. See Appendix B for list of metropolitan areas identified by type, with component counties.
[2]Hispanic or Latino persons may be of any race.

Table B-3. States and Counties — Education, Labor Force, and Income

STATE County	School enrollment			Population 16 to 19 years				Employment status, 2000			Work status in 1999 of the population 16 years and over (percent)		
											Worked in 1999		
	Grades kindergarten through 12	College or graduate school	Percent private	Number	Percent in armed forces	Percent high school graduates	Percent not enrolled, not grads, not in armed forces, not employed	Total population 16 years and over	Percent in labor force	Unemploy-ment rate	Full-time	Part-time	Did not work in 1999
	11	12	13	14	15	16	17	18	19	20	21	22	23
COLORADO—Cont'd													
Clear Creek County	1 570	300	11.1	447	0.0	9.8	3.8	7 472	77.3	2.0	66.6	16.8	16.5
Conejos County	2 119	320	1.7	619	0.0	9.2	4.7	6 035	55.1	6.0	48.0	14.2	37.8
Costilla County	733	100	6.4	245	0.8	19.2	9.8	2 873	45.7	13.2	36.8	13.4	49.9
Crowley County	930	370	9.7	231	0.0	12.1	5.6	4 602	31.9	5.7	45.7	12.5	41.8
Custer County	579	63	13.1	127	0.0	5.5	6.3	2 801	56.3	3.7	46.8	17.4	35.8
Delta County	5 042	538	10.9	1 402	0.0	13.0	5.5	22 032	54.9	5.6	46.7	15.6	37.8
Denver County	83 908	38 309	18.3	26 299	0.0	13.3	12.6	445 977	67.7	5.7	60.7	13.4	25.9
Dolores County	312	33	6.4	88	0.0	12.5	1.1	1 501	58.0	6.1	48.8	15.8	35.4
Douglas County	37 565	8 719	13.8	7 620	0.0	7.7	2.0	125 260	79.0	1.7	68.2	15.8	16.0
Eagle County	6 782	1 625	10.6	1 872	0.0	9.4	13.5	32 878	80.9	3.3	73.6	13.1	13.4
Elbert County	4 876	655	10.7	1 308	0.0	7.0	4.4	14 653	75.5	2.4	64.3	17.2	18.5
El Paso County	103 247	33 737	14.2	30 763	6.7	18.6	5.0	389 986	71.9	4.3	62.4	15.4	22.2
Fremont County	7 865	1 820	11.2	2 245	0.0	9.4	6.4	37 959	45.1	4.1	53.5	11.4	35.1
Garfield County	8 442	1 676	8.0	2 408	0.3	14.4	6.3	33 162	71.1	2.7	61.6	15.5	22.9
Gilpin County	732	210	13.5	186	0.0	9.7	0.0	3 873	81.3	2.1	68.7	17.1	14.2
Grand County	2 038	301	7.6	627	0.0	20.1	1.0	10 076	77.1	3.2	67.4	16.9	15.7
Gunnison County	1 918	2 556	6.4	1 116	0.0	7.9	0.4	11 770	73.4	5.3	59.6	25.8	14.6
Hinsdale County	111	16	21.3	30	0.0	6.7	0.0	651	70.5	2.2	57.5	19.5	23.0
Huerfano County	1 349	255	16.4	348	0.0	11.8	4.9	6 450	48.8	8.6	44.8	14.1	41.1
Jackson County	303	26	6.4	99	0.0	11.1	3.0	1 242	66.7	4.3	61.4	16.7	22.0
Jefferson County	100 325	31 045	13.5	28 334	0.0	10.9	3.6	409 449	73.4	3.2	62.8	16.4	20.9
Kiowa County	341	49	1.3	119	0.0	7.6	0.0	1 280	60.6	3.0	52.3	17.1	30.6
Kit Carson County	1 743	204	4.9	464	0.0	8.0	3.0	6 143	61.0	2.2	51.9	19.6	28.5
Lake County	1 521	403	3.3	468	0.0	12.4	9.0	5 927	72.7	6.0	64.1	13.9	22.0
La Plata County	7 778	4 732	7.9	3 309	0.0	9.9	3.3	35 325	69.0	5.7	57.1	20.8	22.1
Larimer County	44 334	31 384	8.2	17 029	0.1	9.2	2.9	198 990	71.9	4.2	57.8	21.8	20.5
Las Animas County	2 816	885	8.9	875	0.0	9.6	8.6	11 995	54.7	5.7	45.3	15.4	39.3
Lincoln County	1 323	166	11.6	367	0.0	7.1	4.9	4 835	52.4	2.3	55.3	13.3	31.4
Logan County	4 078	1 291	7.7	1 477	0.0	11.8	3.0	16 084	60.7	3.8	54.4	18.6	27.1
Mesa County	21 719	5 836	8.8	7 200	0.0	13.8	6.9	90 939	64.2	5.7	51.4	18.1	30.5
Mineral County	138	25	3.7	31	0.0	0.0	0.0	687	62.3	2.8	50.8	23.9	25.3
Moffat County	2 835	496	6.0	830	0.0	15.4	12.7	9 925	69.3	5.5	60.8	15.1	24.1
Montezuma County	4 789	723	4.9	1 337	0.0	14.7	5.9	18 049	63.3	6.9	54.1	15.8	30.2
Montrose County	6 780	498	7.1	1 904	0.0	15.1	8.2	25 532	62.6	5.0	51.5	16.0	32.5
Morgan County	5 760	796	4.7	1 682	0.0	10.0	8.4	19 905	62.4	4.2	55.9	13.9	30.3
Otero County	4 069	963	4.9	1 281	0.0	11.5	5.3	15 598	58.4	8.3	50.3	14.3	35.4
Ouray County	664	56	4.9	161	0.0	1.2	0.0	2 993	63.0	3.6	52.8	19.5	27.7
Park County	2 589	432	12.1	710	0.0	10.4	1.3	11 570	70.3	2.9	61.8	14.6	23.5
Phillips County	905	116	4.0	240	0.0	10.4	0.0	3 418	59.7	2.8	53.1	16.8	30.1
Pitkin County	1 922	659	14.7	516	0.0	8.5	3.1	12 705	79.9	3.2	68.2	16.6	15.1
Prowers County	3 164	599	2.1	997	0.7	8.0	8.5	10 663	65.4	3.9	56.1	15.7	28.3
Pueblo County	27 023	8 081	6.7	8 387	0.0	9.9	8.6	109 584	58.3	6.3	49.1	15.3	35.6
Rio Blanco County	1 269	385	2.7	531	0.0	10.5	5.3	4 651	67.6	5.9	57.6	16.4	26.0
Rio Grande County	2 585	500	5.4	687	0.0	10.8	6.3	9 321	61.5	6.1	52.6	16.4	31.1
Routt County	3 316	1 014	9.6	979	0.0	14.6	1.3	15 781	80.4	3.1	69.1	19.0	11.9
Saguache County	1 277	166	7.1	392	0.0	9.9	8.9	4 455	59.8	6.1	52.1	16.4	31.4
San Juan County	88	14	6.9	31	0.0	0.0	0.0	473	69.6	3.0	59.0	28.3	12.7
San Miguel County	873	182	15.7	263	0.0	16.3	4.2	5 567	83.8	2.6	71.3	17.9	10.8
Sedgwick County	488	69	3.6	133	0.0	14.3	0.0	2 201	60.9	1.4	51.2	16.3	32.6
Summit County	2 878	1 056	9.9	912	0.0	32.9	3.0	19 840	86.1	2.8	76.4	13.6	10.1
Teller County	4 209	635	9.7	1 130	0.0	14.1	4.9	15 884	72.4	4.0	64.1	15.6	20.2
Washington County	1 034	116	3.3	312	0.0	5.8	1.3	3 819	62.8	1.6	52.7	16.3	31.0
Weld County	37 126	15 531	6.9	12 913	0.0	9.0	6.2	135 308	68.6	5.4	59.0	17.5	23.6
Yuma County	2 159	225	4.9	601	0.0	7.8	1.8	7 431	66.2	2.4	54.6	16.8	28.6
CONNECTICUT	639 968	204 212	17.2	169 277	0.6	8.9	4.4	2 652 316	66.6	5.2	55.4	16.2	28.4
Fairfield County	167 739	44 981	20.5	39 493	0.0	7.5	3.6	678 639	66.0	4.8	56.2	14.9	28.9
Hartford County	162 211	48 436	13.1	42 608	0.1	8.6	5.5	668 892	65.5	6.2	54.6	15.6	29.7
Litchfield County	34 508	7 392	13.5	8 090	0.0	12.1	2.4	142 506	69.8	3.8	56.8	17.5	25.7
Middlesex County	26 978	9 945	20.6	7 196	0.0	6.9	3.1	122 797	70.3	4.8	58.0	17.1	25.0
New Haven County	154 863	55 307	21.6	42 794	0.1	8.7	5.4	643 641	65.5	5.9	54.3	16.3	29.4
New London County	48 220	14 440	15.1	13 209	6.6	17.1	3.4	202 798	67.8	3.9	56.4	17.0	26.6
Tolland County	24 004	16 790	7.0	9 564	0.1	4.4	1.6	108 302	69.8	3.7	56.2	21.2	22.6
Windham County	21 445	6 921	10.0	6 323	0.3	8.7	4.6	84 741	69.2	5.8	55.2	18.1	26.7

Table B-3. States and Counties — Education, Labor Force, and Income

STATE County	Full-year full-time employed (percent)								Children under 18 years in families					+/− U.S. percent two-income couples	Total employed by class of worker (percent)			
										With two parents (percent)		With one parent who is in labor force (percent)	+/− U.S. percent of children with no stay-at-home parent (percent)					
	Total	Men	Women	Non-Hispanic White	Black or African American	American Indian and Alaska Native	Asian, Hawaiian, and Pacific Islander	Hispanic or Latino[1]	Number	Both in labor force	Father only in labor force				Private	Government	Self-employed	Unpaid family worker
	24	25	26	27	28	29	30	31	32	33	34	35	36	37	38	39	40	41
COLORADO—Cont'd																		
Clear Creek County	49.2	58.1	39.4	49.2	42.9	47.6	30.4	50.8	2 042	49.2	22.1	18.9	3.5	12.3	65.7	16.3	17.9	0.1
Conejos County............	31.6	39.7	23.6	37.3	0.0	15.8	25.0	28.2	2 581	40.1	21.9	20.9	-3.6	-7.7	57.7	23.3	17.9	1.1
Costilla County	21.1	29.7	12.9	24.6	0.0	4.2	12.5	19.9	836	30.7	19.1	17.6	-16.3	-18.5	54.6	28.8	15.6	1.0
Crowley County	23.3	23.4	23.2	27.5	4.2	18.4	3.0	19.8	992	40.2	24.6	16.5	-7.9	-6.8	52.9	28.0	18.3	0.8
Custer County	29.9	36.3	23.3	30.7	100.0	23.9	X	2.8	730	37.0	35.1	11.0	-16.6	-7.6	51.3	16.0	31.1	1.6
Delta County	31.4	40.7	22.3	31.3	49.6	43.4	32.2	29.7	6 352	43.5	28.3	17.4	-3.7	-9.3	62.0	15.6	21.4	0.9
Denver County	42.8	49.5	36.1	47.1	38.5	35.2	37.4	36.1	110 483	32.7	19.3	26.7	-5.2	-0.4	76.8	13.4	9.5	0.2
Dolores County	29.4	38.5	19.6	30.6	X	18.0	0.0	17.5	379	46.4	18.5	27.7	9.5	-9.6	58.1	20.8	20.5	0.6
Douglas County............	56.4	72.0	41.1	56.4	63.0	50.0	53.3	57.5	54 346	56.0	31.7	9.1	0.5	14.7	76.6	10.2	12.9	0.3
Eagle County	48.8	56.5	39.1	51.2	65.3	59.2	43.8	40.0	8 936	53.3	23.6	15.1	3.8	15.2	74.6	8.4	16.7	0.4
Elbert County	50.9	63.0	38.9	51.0	63.0	44.4	40.5	52.4	5 781	54.2	28.5	11.3	0.9	11.6	65.1	14.0	19.7	1.2
El Paso County	47.3	59.4	35.3	47.6	50.9	44.9	42.4	44.9	136 188	47.0	25.5	19.5	1.9	5.8	74.6	14.5	10.6	0.3
Fremont County	37.4	44.3	27.5	36.6	47.9	36.0	27.8	37.1	8 911	50.4	19.9	20.1	5.9	-5.6	60.9	25.1	13.7	0.3
Garfield County	42.3	52.5	31.7	43.9	9.1	40.1	36.6	34.4	11 395	48.9	23.3	18.1	2.4	7.2	69.6	12.6	17.7	0.2
Gilpin County	51.5	58.5	43.4	50.8	69.1	50.0	46.7	73.3	968	65.7	12.7	19.1	20.2	24.4	69.0	14.2	16.4	0.4
Grand County	46.4	54.9	36.6	47.1	0.0	42.0	39.6	33.4	2 497	60.2	17.8	15.4	11.0	12.8	66.6	13.4	19.3	0.7
Gunnison County	33.7	39.3	26.8	34.2	27.9	36.3	12.2	22.7	2 448	59.7	18.6	13.7	8.8	11.3	61.7	17.5	20.0	0.8
Hinsdale County	37.5	42.2	32.3	37.3	X	50.0	0.0	71.4	156	58.3	17.9	23.7	17.4	-0.3	46.5	14.0	36.7	2.7
Huerfano County	27.3	28.9	25.4	27.4	8.9	43.7	24.2	28.5	1 524	41.1	19.6	23.1	-0.4	-9.7	57.1	21.4	19.6	1.9
Jackson County	41.1	53.2	28.5	41.0	0.0	41.7	100.0	36.0	390	50.8	22.8	13.3	-0.5	2.9	48.2	21.2	29.1	1.5
Jefferson County	49.6	60.3	39.2	50.0	51.0	44.6	45.5	47.0	128 014	52.0	23.2	18.4	5.8	9.6	74.5	13.7	11.6	0.2
Kiowa County	38.0	53.0	23.5	37.8	0.0	33.3	X	57.1	393	47.3	29.5	19.1	1.8	-1.5	48.6	28.0	22.2	1.2
Kit Carson County	37.7	45.8	28.5	40.5	15.0	6.5	0.0	24.2	2 100	52.5	25.0	11.9	-0.2	6.5	57.3	20.9	20.5	1.2
Lake County	41.2	47.3	34.0	42.6	X	44.0	28.1	38.9	1 980	46.5	21.3	21.4	3.3	4.7	74.3	13.7	11.8	0.2
La Plata County	36.7	43.5	29.7	37.6	21.2	28.0	24.1	36.0	9 556	50.1	21.3	20.4	5.9	6.5	63.7	18.0	17.9	0.4
Larimer County	41.8	53.1	30.7	42.2	40.3	41.7	32.6	39.4	57 552	52.2	25.1	16.1	3.7	7.8	70.7	16.1	12.7	0.4
Las Animas County	30.2	38.6	22.5	31.6	70.6	15.1	4.4	28.9	3 497	43.0	19.0	20.8	-0.2	-7.4	59.6	23.2	16.4	0.8
Lincoln County	36.8	38.9	34.1	39.9	8.7	36.2	25.8	28.3	1 414	56.5	14.9	20.0	11.9	9.4	49.1	28.8	20.0	2.1
Logan County	37.7	47.8	26.3	37.4	19.4	80.0	81.3	40.7	4 861	54.6	17.7	14.5	4.5	6.4	64.5	18.2	16.4	0.9
Mesa County	30.7	43.5	20.4	30.0	37.0	40.0	35.5	35.0	27 002	40.1	21.1	21.0	5.0	0.1	71.0	14.0	13.4	0.9
Mineral County	30.6	39.3	22.0	31.3	X	50.0	X	0.0	156	51.3	26.3	6.4	-6.9	-6.0	52.4	23.3	23.6	0.7
Moffat County	44.2	56.1	31.6	45.7	0.0	43.9	100.0	31.5	3 566	48.3	24.7	20.1	3.8	5.1	70.6	17.6	11.6	0.2
Montezuma County	33.5	40.9	26.6	33.6	0.0	33.6	41.7	32.3	6 248	45.1	18.8	24.2	4.7	-1.3	62.0	21.3	16.3	0.4
Montrose County	37.1	47.6	27.1	37.5	25.6	32.8	42.5	32.9	8 475	53.3	22.9	15.4	4.1	-1.5	66.0	13.5	19.8	0.7
Morgan County............	41.5	54.6	28.5	42.5	36.4	11.9	15.9	39.2	7 660	43.7	23.7	18.2	-2.7	-0.8	68.8	14.8	15.9	0.5
Otero County	35.2	44.3	26.7	38.2	29.2	26.5	40.3	29.6	5 099	43.2	16.7	23.2	1.8	-2.6	60.6	23.7	15.2	0.4
Ouray County	34.2	44.4	23.8	33.9	100.0	25.0	50.0	27.6	836	45.8	32.9	11.6	-7.2	-4.3	55.8	13.1	30.6	0.5
Park County	46.1	57.3	34.1	46.5	40.8	47.7	34.2	44.1	3 272	49.8	28.6	14.9	0.1	5.2	65.8	14.3	19.6	0.3
Phillips County	37.9	50.3	26.5	38.5	57.1	56.5	0.0	32.0	1 156	52.8	21.9	14.6	2.8	-0.2	55.4	15.7	27.1	1.8
Pitkin County	42.5	50.5	33.3	42.4	21.4	0.0	51.9	42.1	2 358	53.6	22.3	15.9	4.9	8.8	66.5	9.1	24.1	0.2
Prowers County	38.3	48.9	27.8	40.1	28.9	29.2	25.6	34.4	4 100	45.5	26.5	14.7	-4.4	0.9	69.1	15.8	14.8	0.4
Pueblo County	35.6	42.0	29.5	37.0	29.3	37.3	36.2	33.3	33 775	41.8	15.0	26.8	4.0	-4.8	72.3	18.3	8.9	0.5
Rio Blanco County	40.2	50.3	30.0	40.8	X	37.3	26.7	32.4	1 495	52.8	22.9	19.7	7.9	4.6	57.5	25.9	15.9	0.7
Rio Grande County	34.7	44.6	25.2	39.5	X	14.7	49.2	28.1	3 310	48.5	15.8	18.7	2.6	1.3	58.3	21.0	19.3	1.4
Routt County	47.6	55.7	37.9	48.0	45.5	53.2	66.3	33.9	4 308	56.0	21.4	16.9	8.3	14.2	67.1	11.7	20.7	0.5
Saguache County	29.8	38.9	20.6	28.6	0.0	25.4	33.3	31.2	1 557	40.7	24.6	19.1	-4.8	-6.0	58.6	17.2	23.0	1.2
San Juan County	31.1	33.7	27.9	33.1	X	0.0	0.0	16.0	95	26.3	16.8	50.5	12.2	4.3	44.2	25.1	30.1	0.6
San Miguel County	42.7	47.8	36.2	43.6	70.0	50.0	41.1	30.4	1 107	48.8	18.6	26.6	10.8	17.2	65.6	11.9	21.8	0.7
Sedgwick County	38.3	49.5	27.3	39.1	20.0	75.0	5.9	32.1	589	63.5	17.0	11.2	10.1	2.9	58.4	16.4	23.6	1.6
Summit County.............	51.2	56.1	44.0	51.9	37.7	62.7	57.5	42.3	3 745	59.5	19.9	15.5	10.4	20.8	77.3	8.2	14.3	0.2
Teller County	47.1	57.2	37.0	47.1	67.4	39.7	54.3	55.1	5 125	51.6	24.6	15.9	2.9	8.5	69.4	15.2	15.0	0.5
Washington County.......	41.2	54.7	27.9	41.5	100.0	18.2	40.0	33.1	1 277	58.0	20.4	13.3	6.7	2.6	48.7	18.3	31.9	1.1
Weld County	41.9	52.7	31.3	43.9	40.5	40.0	29.8	36.3	48 270	49.7	21.3	16.9	2.0	5.7	72.4	15.2	12.0	0.4
Yuma County	40.8	54.3	28.0	40.5	0.0	100.0	0.0	43.7	2 653	57.9	22.3	12.5	5.8	9.3	59.7	13.1	25.7	1.5
CONNECTICUT	43.4	54.0	33.7	44.4	39.4	38.8	44.6	37.4	802 658	48.0	21.2	20.7	4.1	4.6	76.7	13.3	9.8	0.2
Fairfield County	43.6	55.7	32.7	44.2	41.5	42.0	47.4	40.0	216 341	43.6	30.2	16.7	-4.3	0.5	77.3	9.7	12.7	0.2
Hartford County	42.9	52.3	34.5	44.4	40.0	29.6	45.7	34.0	200 430	47.1	16.8	24.2	6.7	4.8	77.6	14.2	8.0	0.2
Litchfield County..........	45.5	58.3	33.6	45.4	48.5	43.7	45.2	52.2	43 030	57.4	21.8	14.8	7.6	8.3	74.1	12.2	13.3	0.4
Middlesex County	46.4	57.3	36.3	46.9	40.7	28.2	38.0	48.0	34 391	57.6	18.4	17.8	10.8	10.3	75.7	14.2	9.9	0.2
New Haven County	42.1	51.8	33.4	43.3	37.4	42.0	41.9	36.5	191 339	46.8	17.7	23.3	5.5	4.6	77.3	14.0	8.5	0.2
New London County	44.4	55.9	33.3	45.1	37.8	39.3	49.4	41.0	60 353	51.7	18.6	21.9	9.0	6.1	76.1	15.2	8.5	0.2
Tolland County.............	44.0	54.1	33.9	45.4	22.6	44.0	31.2	27.0	30 766	58.4	19.6	15.3	9.1	11.7	71.0	19.5	9.2	0.2
Windham County..........	43.7	53.6	34.5	44.5	31.7	43.6	30.2	37.2	26 008	51.5	16.2	24.0	10.9	7.9	74.8	17.1	7.9	0.2

[1] Hispanic or Latino persons may be of any race.

Table B-3. States and Counties — Education, Labor Force, and Income

				Occupation for employed population 16 years and over (percent)						Industry for employed population 16 years and over (percent)					
STATE County	Percent who worked at home	Percent of the population 5 years and over with a disability	Veterans as a percent of the population 18 years and over	Management, professional, and related occupations	Service occupa-tions	Sales and office occupa-tions	Farming, fishing, and forestry occupa-tions	Con-struction, extraction, and main-tenance occupa-tions	Production, transporta-tion and material moving occupa-tions	Agricul-ture, forestry, fishing, and mining	Construc-tion and manufac-turing	Whole-sale and retail trade	Transporta-tion and ware-housing, and utilities	Service industries	Public adminis-tration
	42	43	44	45	46	47	48	49	50	51	52	53	54	55	56
COLORADO—Cont'd															
Clear Creek County	7.6	15.6	15.1	39.6	16.4	22.6	0.6	12.3	8.5	3.2	16.1	12.9	5.3	55.5	6.9
Conejos County.............	6.9	22.8	13.1	27.5	14.5	22.2	5.3	14.9	15.7	14.6	14.6	14.5	6.9	44.7	4.7
Costilla County	4.6	30.5	14.4	23.1	19.3	22.1	6.1	15.9	13.5	10.6	16.5	9.8	6.8	45.2	11.1
Crowley County.............	6.1	26.3	16.9	31.0	17.0	19.1	5.5	14.2	13.3	15.8	16.1	12.1	6.6	35.7	13.6
Custer County	10.8	18.9	21.8	32.3	15.9	22.9	1.9	17.3	9.7	10.3	20.9	13.1	5.1	42.1	8.5
Delta County	9.5	21.5	18.1	28.0	17.3	21.8	2.9	15.6	14.4	13.4	18.3	16.6	4.0	43.7	4.0
Denver County...............	3.7	20.7	11.2	37.9	15.2	26.3	0.2	10.0	10.4	0.6	15.1	13.3	4.8	61.7	4.6
Dolores County	6.8	22.1	15.0	27.8	13.9	23.5	1.8	22.9	10.1	12.3	20.3	16.7	4.3	40.6	5.7
Douglas County..............	7.9	8.3	12.2	51.8	8.1	29.7	0.1	5.5	4.7	1.0	14.2	15.9	4.1	61.0	3.8
Eagle County.................	5.1	10.4	7.5	33.3	20.9	22.9	0.6	15.0	7.3	1.2	20.4	12.3	3.4	59.5	3.3
Elbert County.................	6.8	11.8	16.2	36.2	11.2	26.7	1.8	13.8	10.3	6.6	21.1	16.9	5.3	44.9	5.2
El Paso County	4.0	15.7	20.0	37.2	14.5	27.7	0.1	9.8	10.7	0.5	19.2	15.0	3.9	56.5	4.9
Fremont County	5.3	22.0	21.3	28.1	22.5	22.5	0.5	14.2	12.3	3.3	18.5	13.7	4.4	44.6	15.6
Garfield County	5.2	14.3	12.7	26.9	15.8	26.8	0.9	20.5	9.1	2.4	23.5	16.9	5.5	47.7	4.0
Gilpin County.................	5.2	11.8	16.5	35.0	19.0	22.7	0.2	14.9	8.2	1.1	18.9	10.4	3.7	60.5	5.5
Grand County.................	7.7	13.1	13.8	30.0	17.7	24.0	2.7	16.5	9.1	6.8	17.4	13.2	4.3	54.1	4.2
Gunnison County	6.7	9.8	10.0	32.6	21.1	24.6	1.4	14.9	5.4	3.7	16.0	15.3	3.1	58.5	3.4
Hinsdale County............	18.5	10.9	12.3	31.2	11.1	27.6	1.8	21.2	7.1	3.6	21.2	16.7	3.8	50.3	4.5
Huerfano County............	8.5	22.6	18.9	32.2	17.5	21.2	2.3	16.3	10.5	7.0	17.2	12.5	5.3	49.5	8.5
Jackson County..............	19.6	13.9	16.5	33.7	8.4	23.0	12.2	12.7	10.0	30.5	13.7	12.1	4.8	32.8	6.1
Jefferson County............	5.1	14.1	13.9	41.3	11.5	28.8	0.1	9.6	8.7	0.9	17.8	15.6	4.9	55.2	5.5
Kiowa County	9.2	21.3	13.2	35.7	15.8	17.7	10.9	10.1	9.8	33.2	8.8	11.6	6.2	34.0	6.2
Kit Carson County........	8.1	18.3	13.9	33.7	15.4	24.4	7.4	8.7	10.3	18.9	8.2	14.8	6.5	44.0	7.5
Lake County	3.3	16.6	12.3	23.7	23.4	19.4	0.0	24.5	9.0	2.3	23.6	13.0	2.9	53.9	4.3
La Plata County	8.4	13.4	12.6	36.0	17.3	26.3	0.8	11.9	7.7	4.5	14.1	14.3	5.0	57.7	4.4
Larimer County..............	5.1	13.3	12.1	39.6	13.9	24.8	0.5	9.6	11.5	1.5	23.8	15.4	3.4	52.5	3.4
Las Animas County.......	5.1	25.9	16.0	30.8	21.6	20.4	1.6	14.6	11.1	6.9	16.5	13.0	6.4	51.4	5.7
Lincoln County	10.1	19.1	15.9	32.2	24.0	20.5	3.3	10.1	10.0	14.3	10.4	11.9	6.9	41.8	14.6
Logan County................	5.6	19.3	13.5	28.4	19.7	23.5	2.9	11.0	14.5	10.3	14.4	13.8	6.1	48.0	7.4
Mesa County	5.3	21.1	17.1	29.3	17.2	27.9	0.9	11.8	12.9	3.0	17.6	17.2	5.5	52.2	4.4
Mineral County	8.0	16.9	17.3	27.9	20.7	23.6	1.0	19.5	7.5	3.4	18.3	17.8	4.3	49.8	6.5
Moffat County	3.4	17.2	16.0	20.9	17.3	22.2	1.9	23.3	14.4	16.2	15.0	15.4	10.3	37.8	5.3
Montezuma County........	4.7	19.1	16.1	32.1	16.1	24.6	1.1	15.3	10.8	5.4	18.7	16.6	5.4	48.6	5.3
Montrose County............	7.2	19.9	16.1	25.9	17.9	24.2	1.8	16.9	13.4	6.0	23.4	16.1	5.1	44.8	4.6
Morgan County..............	3.8	17.3	11.9	24.4	15.0	20.9	4.0	13.8	21.9	10.6	26.3	13.8	5.5	38.5	5.3
Otero County	4.8	24.8	15.7	32.1	17.8	24.6	3.1	10.1	12.4	7.8	15.1	15.3	6.5	46.7	8.6
Ouray County	13.8	13.0	16.2	37.2	15.6	22.0	1.7	16.7	6.9	6.2	24.2	10.8	2.1	52.4	4.2
Park County	8.1	14.1	19.2	33.2	13.2	26.4	0.6	16.7	9.9	3.3	23.5	15.3	4.6	48.8	4.5
Phillips County	10.7	17.1	12.7	35.3	13.8	21.5	10.8	10.9	7.7	26.4	8.1	12.0	8.5	39.6	5.5
Pitkin County	10.2	14.4	9.0	42.1	19.0	23.7	1.6	9.6	4.1	3.1	10.8	12.0	3.1	67.9	3.1
Prowers County	3.5	20.3	10.2	26.3	15.9	22.8	6.8	11.7	16.5	14.0	18.8	16.7	6.7	38.9	4.9
Pueblo County..............	3.3	23.5	16.7	28.2	18.2	28.2	0.4	11.7	13.3	1.4	17.5	16.1	5.3	52.9	6.8
Rio Blanco County	4.6	14.3	15.3	29.8	17.2	21.3	3.1	18.6	10.1	22.7	9.7	12.4	5.8	40.9	8.6
Rio Grande County	8.0	20.8	15.3	30.2	14.7	24.8	6.0	11.8	12.4	11.0	12.1	20.4	5.2	45.9	5.3
Routt County	6.0	9.7	10.2	34.5	16.6	24.3	1.2	15.8	7.6	5.9	18.1	12.9	5.0	54.3	3.8
Saguache County.........	9.4	21.1	13.0	27.9	13.4	21.0	14.3	11.7	11.7	22.0	13.0	17.1	4.3	38.9	4.7
San Juan County	12.7	12.0	19.6	37.6	12.2	18.8	0.0	21.3	10.0	3.1	23.2	9.1	3.4	53.3	7.8
San Miguel County........	8.3	8.0	8.8	35.8	19.6	23.2	0.5	14.4	6.5	2.5	18.9	11.9	4.0	58.4	4.2
Sedgwick County	10.4	20.4	16.2	31.7	15.1	22.0	8.0	10.1	13.1	23.9	11.8	16.9	6.7	36.0	4.6
Summit County.............	5.9	10.6	8.7	30.8	20.2	27.3	2.2	12.8	6.8	2.8	15.8	13.3	3.2	61.2	3.8
Teller County	5.8	15.4	19.8	36.6	14.0	25.4	0.2	14.8	9.0	2.6	20.5	13.3	5.0	54.2	4.4
Washington County........	15.4	18.7	15.5	37.9	11.3	20.2	5.3	11.1	14.3	25.4	14.0	12.4	8.5	34.7	5.0
Weld County.................	4.2	17.9	11.7	29.5	14.6	25.2	2.0	12.8	15.9	5.1	24.5	15.5	4.9	46.0	4.0
Yuma County	11.2	18.5	12.6	34.0	13.4	22.2	8.7	11.2	10.6	29.1	11.1	12.9	5.6	38.1	3.4
CONNECTICUT	3.1	17.5	12.1	39.1	14.3	26.5	0.2	8.0	12.0	0.4	20.8	14.4	3.9	56.5	4.0
Fairfield County	4.5	16.4	10.3	43.7	12.7	26.7	0.1	7.6	9.3	0.2	19.7	14.3	3.2	60.0	2.6
Hartford County.............	2.4	18.5	11.9	38.8	13.9	27.7	0.2	6.9	12.5	0.3	19.4	14.0	4.1	57.2	4.9
Litchfield County............	3.9	16.3	13.9	35.8	14.4	24.3	0.3	10.7	14.5	0.9	27.1	14.5	3.3	50.5	3.9
Middlesex County..........	3.3	15.3	13.6	42.1	13.0	25.2	0.2	8.6	11.0	0.5	22.3	14.0	4.4	54.3	4.5
New Haven County........	2.5	18.7	11.9	37.0	14.5	26.7	0.1	8.1	13.6	0.3	21.4	14.8	4.2	55.2	4.1
New London County	2.6	17.9	16.3	35.6	19.9	24.4	0.4	8.9	10.8	0.8	20.5	13.8	4.7	54.5	5.6
Tolland County	2.8	13.7	12.3	41.3	13.2	25.9	0.3	8.7	10.6	0.9	19.5	14.5	3.8	56.8	4.6
Windham County...........	2.6	19.3	14.1	28.8	17.2	24.7	0.9	9.9	18.5	1.8	24.6	15.4	4.0	49.7	4.4

STATE County	Median house-hold income (57)	Median family income — All families (58)	Married-couple (59)	Male house-holder (60)	Female house-holder (61)	Median nonfamily house-hold income (62)	Men (63)	Women (64)	Per capita income (65)	With earnings (66)	With interest, dividend, or rental income (67)	With Social Security income (68)	With public assis-tance income (69)	With retire-ment income (70)	House-holds with income over $100,000 (percent) (71)	+/- U.S. percent for income over $100,000 (72)	House-holds with income below poverty (percent) (73)	Families with children with income below poverty (percent) (74)
COLORADO—Cont'd																		
Clear Creek County	50 997	61 400	67 841	36 094	27 115	32 318	43 145	31 292	28 160	90.0	44.2	15.0	1.1	10.8	17.7	5.4	6.2	5.8
Conejos County	24 744	29 066	33 963	20 764	12 356	10 833	27 375	20 684	12 050	72.1	19.6	33.1	12.7	14.8	3.7	-8.6	25.0	26.7
Costilla County	19 531	25 509	31 823	15 962	10 268	9 797	23 563	16 121	10 748	63.2	19.1	39.6	16.0	17.9	1.9	-10.4	29.7	29.1
Crowley County	26 803	32 162	36 375	17 222	12 981	13 500	21 174	22 457	12 836	74.4	26.6	34.9	10.0	14.2	3.1	-9.2	18.5	22.2
Custer County	34 731	41 198	40 500	24 750	16 250	17 727	34 330	21 281	19 817	74.8	40.6	33.7	3.8	21.7	8.1	-4.2	14.5	15.9
Delta County	32 785	37 748	46 262	27 870	18 159	17 417	32 799	20 944	17 152	72.1	39.1	37.6	4.0	23.2	5.0	-7.3	11.5	13.5
Denver County	39 500	48 195	53 613	31 064	21 171	31 233	35 316	31 432	24 101	82.9	35.2	21.0	3.4	12.9	11.5	-0.8	12.1	16.6
Dolores County	32 196	38 000	40 956	21 875	19 688	13 875	31 681	21 250	17 106	75.0	34.5	34.2	6.4	15.6	3.8	-8.5	15.7	9.0
Douglas County............	82 929	88 482	92 429	52 098	40 964	52 679	61 943	40 275	34 848	94.7	51.8	9.2	0.5	9.6	36.7	24.4	2.2	1.9
Eagle County	62 682	68 226	71 685	36 941	34 250	51 075	38 994	30 940	32 011	95.1	43.0	8.0	1.3	5.1	23.7	11.4	5.6	5.5
Elbert County	62 480	66 740	70 769	39 028	30 313	33 177	47 254	31 129	24 960	92.6	40.5	15.8	0.9	13.9	21.0	8.7	3.8	3.7
El Paso County	46 844	53 995	59 931	32 062	22 592	28 712	37 776	26 898	22 005	86.9	40.3	19.1	2.6	19.0	12.2	-0.1	7.9	8.6
Fremont County	34 150	42 303	48 542	18 750	10 778	18 541	34 770	24 002	17 420	70.1	38.0	34.0	3.0	22.3	4.4	-7.9	12.0	14.7
Garfield County	47 016	53 840	56 140	34 926	26 351	30 431	38 770	28 131	21 341	86.8	37.1	18.7	1.8	11.0	10.8	-1.5	6.7	7.5
Gilpin County	51 942	61 859	65 625	51 000	26 964	33 807	40 104	31 359	26 148	91.1	42.4	14.7	0.9	9.6	12.5	0.2	4.1	1.0
Grand County	47 759	55 217	54 425	32 188	17 750	34 561	36 370	27 717	25 198	89.8	45.7	14.8	1.2	12.3	12.5	0.2	7.2	8.2
Gunnison County	36 916	51 950	52 388	30 694	25 750	25 297	31 911	25 753	21 407	90.3	43.4	14.2	2.2	10.3	8.9	-3.4	14.8	8.7
Hinsdale County	37 279	42 159	45 625	28 333	32 500	23 500	28 125	27 692	22 360	85.2	55.7	23.8	1.7	13.7	10.1	-2.2	9.0	0.0
Huerfano County	25 775	32 664	34 698	23 750	17 188	14 583	24 928	22 021	15 242	68.8	29.5	34.9	8.6	21.1	4.3	-8.0	18.8	23.6
Jackson County............	31 821	37 361	38 889	24 583	12 292	21 648	27 639	19 135	17 826	84.0	40.6	27.4	3.4	12.1	4.5	-7.8	12.1	15.9
Jefferson County	57 339	67 310	75 931	39 382	30 123	36 420	46 617	33 890	28 066	87.6	46.8	18.4	1.4	14.9	19.1	6.8	4.9	5.1
Kiowa County	30 494	35 536	37 143	25 000	23 125	17 813	28 194	19 135	16 382	79.1	39.8	31.8	3.8	13.9	7.2	-5.1	13.1	11.3
Kit Carson County	33 152	41 867	45 588	28 654	12 500	18 500	30 099	20 799	16 964	80.9	38.8	30.3	3.8	10.6	6.1	-6.2	12.0	14.7
Lake County	37 691	41 652	44 028	30 250	20 444	27 500	32 134	25 902	18 524	87.7	17.4	17.4	3.1	15.4	6.7	-5.6	11.3	12.4
La Plata County	40 159	50 446	55 712	33 125	22 966	23 048	34 467	26 220	21 534	85.7	41.0	19.7	2.0	12.8	10.9	-1.4	12.4	9.1
Larimer County	48 655	58 866	66 937	35 453	25 385	28 303	41 792	28 958	23 689	86.8	47.8	19.1	1.8	13.8	13.9	1.6	9.1	6.1
Las Animas County	28 273	34 072	40 927	18 068	16 250	14 105	28 265	21 029	16 029	70.2	27.0	35.2	7.0	19.9	4.4	-7.9	19.3	20.4
Lincoln County	31 914	39 738	46 382	35 000	25 250	19 583	27 402	24 191	15 510	79.5	35.7	29.9	3.2	13.1	5.8	-6.5	11.4	11.5
Logan County	32 724	42 241	46 532	30 284	14 476	17 793	28 926	21 779	16 721	78.2	39.9	31.9	2.6	13.8	5.2	-7.1	13.1	13.5
Mesa County	35 884	43 009	51 210	27 134	18 513	20 697	34 001	23 531	19 716	79.0	37.0	30.0	3.0	17.0	7.1	-5.2	10.2	11.0
Mineral County	34 844	40 833	47 500	11 250	9 750	24 821	29 375	20 536	24 475	84.3	45.9	27.8	2.6	18.9	5.2	-7.1	10.2	12.6
Moffat County	41 528	45 511	52 732	37 083	19 939	25 779	40 123	22 457	18 540	85.5	29.6	20.6	2.4	12.3	2.8	-9.5	8.7	9.1
Montezuma County	32 083	38 071	43 910	29 722	13 662	20 116	31 653	21 833	17 003	80.5	31.0	28.3	4.8	15.3	5.8	-6.5	15.7	20.0
Montrose County	35 234	40 849	45 636	22 219	16 788	20 646	30 880	21 915	17 158	77.3	36.9	31.1	3.6	18.3	5.2	-7.1	11.8	13.4
Morgan County	34 568	39 102	42 688	26 319	20 903	10 597	28 008	22 342	15 492	81.6	33.6	26.5	4.3	11.9	5.1	-7.2	11.5	11.9
Otero County	29 738	35 906	41 686	18 651	15 100	16 443	29 012	21 734	15 113	75.1	32.1	33.2	6.1	16.8	4.5	-7.8	17.4	22.4
Ouray County	42 019	49 776	49 615	31 250	19 375	25 143	35 841	27 407	24 335	82.7	46.7	22.3	1.8	17.6	12.1	-0.2	7.8	9.5
Park County	51 899	57 025	63 528	40 156	29 750	33 454	43 674	28 560	25 019	86.0	43.2	17.4	2.0	17.1	12.7	0.4	5.6	4.6
Phillips County	32 177	38 144	41 098	25 000	14 779	18 000	30 818	19 386	16 394	76.5	44.0	33.8	3.6	11.8	5.3	-7.0	11.1	12.4
Pitkin County	59 375	75 048	79 117	46 563	37 069	42 134	41 471	35 349	40 811	93.2	48.7	10.4	1.0	5.0	23.1	10.8	5.2	4.2
Prowers County............	29 935	34 202	33 635	20 441	14 138	17 002	26 043	21 304	14 150	82.2	28.4	26.4	5.7	9.7	4.0	-8.3	17.8	22.0
Pueblo County..............	32 775	40 130	48 940	26 533	17 193	19 254	32 344	23 823	17 163	74.0	31.9	31.9	4.9	22.5	5.8	-6.5	14.5	17.5
Rio Blanco County	37 711	44 425	54 100	25 625	16 442	22 163	39 828	20 332	17 344	84.9	36.3	23.5	1.6	14.5	4.2	-8.1	8.8	10.2
Rio Grande County	31 836	36 809	42 450	27 500	12 813	17 239	30 697	23 736	15 650	78.7	32.9	28.6	7.3	14.4	4.7	-7.6	14.5	16.6
Routt County	53 612	61 927	73 383	35 167	26 250	38 000	39 553	27 429	28 792	93.7	47.1	11.7	2.0	8.6	15.9	3.6	5.6	4.3
Saguache County	25 495	29 405	31 308	16 875	16 591	16 756	25 870	19 583	13 121	80.7	28.6	25.1	7.4	10.9	3.2	-9.1	21.8	26.2
San Juan County	30 764	40 000	55 625	28 750	11 875	16 750	31 324	25 313	17 584	88.8	42.0	19.3	1.5	13.4	4.5	-7.8	20.1	24.3
San Miguel County	48 514	60 417	63 750	42 750	24 147	36 793	37 019	30 916	35 329	94.4	41.5	7.4	2.2	6.1	17.8	5.5	9.7	9.2
Sedgwick County	28 278	33 953	34 792	14 250	15 208	17 051	26 454	17 788	16 125	76.7	39.0	39.0	3.4	17.1	4.4	-8.3	10.2	14.7
Summit County	56 587	66 914	72 174	36 250	30 635	42 696	35 420	27 961	28 676	95.8	37.1	7.7	0.9	7.6	19.9	7.6	6.3	4.6
Teller County	50 165	57 071	60 836	41 875	33 182	31 118	40 222	28 117	23 412	88.4	42.8	17.9	1.9	16.7	12.9	0.6	5.4	4.7
Washington County.......	32 431	37 287	40 543	25 625	21 250	21 141	27 926	22 058	17 788	79.7	45.5	32.6	2.9	14.1	6.1	-6.2	9.9	13.5
Weld County	42 321	49 569	54 465	27 656	19 943	23 967	35 886	26 415	18 957	85.9	36.5	21.2	2.9	12.6	9.5	-2.8	11.7	11.9
Yuma County	33 169	39 814	44 861	35 625	19 643	18 484	28 310	20 146	16 005	80.4	45.4	30.2	2.9	10.7	4.7	-7.6	13.1	12.7
CONNECTICUT	53 935	65 521	78 589	36 199	24 626	30 873	47 156	34 929	28 766	81.2	44.4	27.0	3.7	17.6	20.2	7.9	8.0	8.6
Fairfield County	65 249	77 690	97 749	37 389	27 851	36 385	55 047	38 621	38 350	83.4	48.1	25.9	2.7	15.9	31.0	18.7	6.9	7.2
Hartford County	50 756	62 144	76 695	35 524	23 123	30 274	45 670	34 530	26 047	79.4	43.2	27.7	4.6	19.3	17.1	4.8	9.1	10.9
Litchfield County..........	56 273	66 445	74 596	37 160	28 434	29 823	46 829	33 442	28 408	82.5	48.7	27.6	2.2	17.8	18.7	6.4	5.0	3.7
Middlesex County	59 175	71 319	82 316	40 787	28 164	35 037	50 096	35 544	28 251	83.4	49.4	26.0	2.1	17.5	20.6	8.3	4.8	3.6
New Haven County	48 834	60 540	72 766	35 669	22 090	27 043	45 291	32 956	24 439	79.4	40.4	28.2	4.7	17.1	15.8	3.5	9.7	11.0
New London County	50 646	59 857	68 559	35 537	25 120	30 486	42 286	31 339	24 678	81.6	44.0	26.5	3.1	20.1	14.5	2.2	6.7	7.3
Tolland County	59 044	70 856	78 679	39 643	30 375	32 930	48 295	35 262	25 474	85.4	48.2	22.3	1.7	17.2	19.4	7.1	5.7	3.9
Windham County..........	45 115	52 490	61 922	31 722	21 927	24 506	39 490	27 452	20 443	81.6	37.3	26.4	4.1	17.0	9.5	-2.8	8.6	9.1

Table B-3. States and Counties — Education, Labor Force, and Income

STATE/ County code	MSA/PMSA/ NECMA code[1]	STATE County	High school graduates			College graduates		College graduates (percent)				
			Total population 25 years and over	Percent with a high school diploma or less	Percent with a high school diploma or more	Percent with a bachelor's degree or more	+/− U.S. percent with bachelor's degree or more	Non-Hispanic White	Black or African American	American Indian and Alaska Native	Asian, Hawaiian, and Pacific Islander	Hispanic or Latino[2]
			1	2	3	4	5	6	7	8	9	10
10 000	...	DELAWARE	514 658	48.8	82.6	25.0	0.6	26.9	14.4	13.2	61.0	13.5
10 001	2190	Kent County	79 249	53.5	79.4	18.6	-5.8	19.4	15.6	9.4	33.9	11.8
10 003	9160	New Castle County	324 810	44.2	85.5	29.5	5.1	32.1	16.0	26.3	67.3	14.3
10 005	...	Sussex County	110 599	59.1	76.5	16.6	-7.8	18.3	6.5	5.5	35.6	11.2
11 000	...	DISTRICT OF COLUMBIA...............	384 535	42.8	77.8	39.1	14.7	80.6	17.5	28.1	58.1	24.8
11 001	8840	District of Columbia.......	384 535	42.8	77.8	39.1	14.7	80.6	17.5	28.1	58.1	24.8
12 000	...	FLORIDA....................	11 024 645	48.9	79.9	22.3	-2.1	24.7	12.4	14.9	40.3	17.5
12 001	2900	Alachua County............	123 524	32.2	88.1	38.7	14.3	42.2	14.3	35.3	78.6	47.0
12 003	...	Baker County	13 953	69.5	71.9	8.2	-16.2	8.9	5.6	0.0	0.0	5.1
12 005	6015	Bay County	99 771	49.6	81.0	17.7	-6.7	18.5	9.5	9.8	22.5	19.0
12 007	...	Bradford County	17 883	66.0	74.2	8.4	-16.0	10.2	2.2	0.0	30.4	5.4
12 009	4900	Brevard County	339 738	42.5	86.3	23.6	-0.8	24.3	12.1	10.3	37.0	22.9
12 011	2680	Broward County	1 126 502	46.4	82.0	24.5	0.1	27.2	14.7	15.2	38.4	23.0
12 013	...	Calhoun County	8 884	69.4	69.1	7.7	-16.7	8.6	3.3	15.8	31.7	0.0
12 015	6580	Charlotte County	113 071	53.5	82.1	17.6	-6.8	17.6	14.0	8.8	42.7	17.3
12 017	...	Citrus County	92 594	59.7	78.3	13.2	-11.2	13.1	9.1	15.0	42.1	11.0
12 019	3600	Clay County.................	90 382	45.3	86.4	20.1	-4.3	20.2	17.6	11.4	31.0	17.9
12 021	5345	Collier County	185 357	44.5	81.8	27.9	3.5	32.4	8.9	8.5	43.8	7.1
12 023	...	Columbia County	36 880	60.2	74.7	10.9	-13.5	11.2	6.0	33.6	50.8	16.1
12 027	...	DeSoto County	21 222	71.8	63.5	8.4	-16.0	10.7	2.8	0.0	33.6	2.3
12 029	...	Dixie County................	9 643	73.5	65.9	6.8	-17.6	7.1	1.9	0.0	20.0	4.8
12 031	3600	Duval County	499 602	46.3	82.7	21.9	-2.5	24.6	13.1	17.9	34.0	21.8
12 033	6080	Escambia County	189 710	46.3	82.1	21.0	-3.4	23.9	9.8	9.3	23.2	22.8
12 035	2020	Flagler County	38 616	46.1	85.9	21.2	-3.2	21.4	18.9	26.3	37.2	17.1
12 037	...	Franklin County	8 202	68.1	68.3	12.4	-12.0	14.0	3.7	18.5	63.2	7.2
12 039	8240	Gadsden County	28 932	65.2	70.7	12.9	-11.5	20.8	6.8	18.8	43.5	4.3
12 041	...	Gilchrist County	8 866	63.7	72.4	9.4	-15.0	9.6	4.3	0.0	0.0	7.1
12 043	...	Glades County	7 403	67.0	69.8	9.8	-14.6	11.2	3.2	14.3	48.6	3.1
12 045	...	Gulf County	9 527	64.6	72.6	10.1	-14.3	11.1	6.6	8.2	23.5	6.4
12 047	...	Hamilton County...........	8 758	72.2	62.9	7.3	-17.1	9.3	3.9	0.0	16.0	3.0
12 049	...	Hardee County	16 509	73.5	58.0	8.4	-16.0	11.3	6.2	8.7	43.3	1.4
12 051	...	Hendry County	20 551	74.9	54.2	8.2	-16.2	12.4	3.8	9.4	36.5	2.7
12 053	8280	Hernando County	99 082	59.3	78.5	12.7	-11.7	12.9	10.0	2.9	28.2	8.9
12 055	...	Highlands County..........	65 087	60.1	74.5	13.6	-10.8	14.2	5.1	22.9	48.5	9.2
12 057	8280	Hillsborough County......	653 841	45.9	80.8	25.1	0.7	28.5	14.6	21.1	42.7	15.7
12 059	...	Holmes County.............	12 659	72.6	65.2	8.8	-15.6	9.1	2.2	12.0	21.6	3.3
12 061	...	Indian River County	84 531	47.5	81.6	23.1	-1.3	24.8	7.6	19.2	44.9	9.1
12 063	...	Jackson County	31 771	63.5	69.1	12.8	-11.6	14.9	7.1	6.7	44.7	11.6
12 065	...	Jefferson County	8 911	59.1	73.2	16.9	-7.5	23.3	6.7	0.0	30.8	6.9
12 067	...	Lafayette County	4 745	71.9	68.2	7.2	-17.2	9.2	0.4	0.0	0.0	1.4
12 069	5960	Lake County	155 572	54.5	79.8	16.6	-7.8	17.3	7.3	1.7	33.5	14.5
12 071	2700	Lee County..................	327 672	50.2	82.3	21.1	-3.3	22.6	8.9	11.4	40.7	8.9
12 073	8240	Leon County	137 537	29.8	89.1	41.7	17.3	46.2	27.3	28.0	65.5	38.2
12 075	...	Levy County	24 030	64.3	73.9	10.6	-13.8	10.6	8.0	12.8	57.1	14.0
12 077	...	Liberty County..............	4 828	74.9	65.6	7.4	-17.0	8.9	1.8	0.0	17.6	0.0
12 079	...	Madison County	12 254	66.7	67.5	10.2	-14.2	13.5	4.7	0.0	0.0	6.9
12 081	7510	Manatee County...........	192 789	50.4	81.4	20.8	-3.6	22.3	10.9	10.9	32.6	8.3
12 083	5790	Marion County	187 187	57.7	78.2	13.7	-10.7	14.0	10.5	16.5	34.9	9.5
12 085	2710	Martin County...............	96 467	43.0	85.3	26.3	1.9	27.7	7.4	4.3	42.9	14.1
12 086	5000	Miami-Dade County	1 491 789	54.5	67.9	21.7	-2.7	38.0	11.5	15.8	44.7	18.1
12 087	...	Monroe County	61 161	44.0	84.9	25.5	1.1	28.2	8.8	13.0	47.3	13.9
12 089	3600	Nassau County.............	38 972	53.4	81.0	18.9	-5.5	19.8	8.4	12.7	26.1	10.8
12 091	2750	Okaloosa County..........	112 429	39.1	88.0	24.2	-0.2	26.1	11.9	15.4	14.8	19.6
12 093	...	Okeechobee County	23 388	68.8	65.1	8.9	-15.5	9.1	6.4	21.1	51.3	5.0
12 095	5960	Orange County	574 101	44.0	81.8	26.1	1.7	30.7	14.7	14.5	40.6	17.0
12 097	5960	Osceola County	110 607	54.8	79.1	15.7	-8.7	16.3	11.6	6.3	40.0	12.5
12 099	8960	Palm Beach County	817 899	43.3	83.6	27.7	3.3	31.3	11.4	16.5	47.3	15.3
12 101	8280	Pasco County...............	255 472	59.2	77.6	13.1	-11.3	12.7	13.0	5.9	45.2	14.2
12 103	8280	Pinellas County	686 094	45.6	84.0	22.9	-1.5	23.8	10.5	18.1	33.6	20.0
12 105	3980	Polk County.................	326 208	58.9	74.8	14.9	-9.5	16.0	8.9	13.0	40.0	8.6
12 107	...	Putnam County	47 761	67.0	70.4	9.4	-15.0	10.1	6.6	9.2	24.3	2.1
12 109	3600	St. Johns County..........	86 199	37.3	87.2	33.1	8.7	34.2	12.6	50.0	58.7	25.9
12 111	2710	St. Lucie County...........	136 448	55.0	77.7	15.1	-9.3	16.2	8.9	7.9	30.2	11.5
12 113	6080	Santa Rosa County.......	78 166	43.8	85.4	22.9	-1.5	23.7	6.2	11.3	28.8	23.9

[1]MSA = Metropolitan Statistical Area. PMSA = Primary MSA. NECMA = New England County Metropolitan Area. See the Appendix A for explanation of these concepts. See Appendix B for list of metropolitan areas identified by type, with component counties.
[2]Hispanic or Latino persons may be of any race.

Table B-3. States and Counties — **Education, Labor Force, and Income**

STATE County	School enrollment			Population 16 to 19 years				Employment status, 2000			Work status in 1999 of the population 16 years and over (percent)		
											Worked in 1999		
	Grades kindergarten through 12	College or graduate school	Percent private	Number	Percent in armed forces	Percent high school graduates	Percent not enrolled, not grads, not in armed forces, not employed	Total population 16 years and over	Percent in labor force	Unemployment rate	Full-time	Part-time	Did not work in 1999
	11	12	13	14	15	16	17	18	19	20	21	22	23
DELAWARE	143 780	51 407	19.5	44 154	0.3	11.5	5.6	610 289	65.7	5.1	57.3	14.6	28.1
Kent County	25 303	8 588	11.5	7 812	1.3	11.1	5.1	95 895	67.1	5.3	58.3	14.2	27.6
New Castle County	92 041	37 364	24.1	29 102	0.1	11.4	5.4	389 036	67.7	5.2	59.1	15.0	25.8
Sussex County	26 436	5 455	9.4	7 240	0.1	12.2	7.2	125 358	58.5	4.9	50.8	13.8	35.4
DISTRICT OF COLUMBIA..............	88 568	59 498	32.7	32 400	1.0	8.2	6.7	469 041	63.6	10.7	55.8	13.1	31.1
District of Columbia.......	88 568	59 498	32.7	32 400	1.0	8.2	6.7	469 041	63.6	10.7	55.8	13.1	31.1
FLORIDA..................	2 775 141	886 825	14.5	794 066	0.7	10.2	6.3	12 744 825	58.6	5.5	51.5	12.5	36.0
Alachua County...........	32 792	53 371	6.4	19 335	0.0	5.6	1.9	179 084	63.3	7.0	49.1	23.2	27.7
Baker County	4 509	723	6.8	1 315	0.0	11.6	14.1	16 835	58.3	4.5	53.3	9.7	37.0
Bay County.................	27 420	6 965	7.8	7 949	2.3	13.4	5.2	116 666	61.8	4.7	53.8	12.8	33.4
Bradford County	4 735	795	8.8	1 382	0.4	12.9	7.7	21 092	47.8	4.8	46.0	10.5	43.5
Brevard County	80 722	23 877	15.6	22 865	0.2	9.1	6.1	384 076	57.4	4.9	48.7	13.2	38.1
Broward County	290 350	88 536	17.2	73 499	0.0	9.3	5.4	1 281 478	62.7	5.3	55.2	11.8	32.9
Calhoun County	2 364	397	2.0	663	0.0	16.6	5.3	10 394	47.5	6.5	45.4	9.1	45.4
Charlotte County	17 899	3 279	9.5	4 880	0.0	13.7	4.9	122 061	43.0	3.5	35.8	12.4	51.8
Citrus County	16 026	2 722	8.5	4 639	0.0	12.1	7.1	100 484	41.4	6.7	35.1	11.2	53.7
Clay County................	30 688	6 892	9.8	8 239	0.3	9.8	4.8	106 017	67.9	4.5	59.6	12.6	27.8
Collier County	36 873	6 692	11.3	10 207	0.1	11.1	8.9	206 955	52.9	3.7	46.5	12.3	41.1
Columbia County..........	11 213	1 874	8.2	3 592	0.1	12.0	10.2	44 067	55.6	6.0	49.1	10.9	40.0
DeSoto County	5 087	556	5.8	2 042	0.0	9.2	14.7	25 862	52.1	5.3	46.1	9.0	44.9
Dixie County	2 350	358	6.7	736	0.0	20.5	7.7	11 165	44.6	7.4	39.8	10.2	50.0
Duval County	151 264	43 351	15.8	42 483	2.0	12.2	6.5	595 693	67.4	4.8	61.0	12.0	27.0
Escambia County	53 184	20 805	17.5	19 846	15.0	23.7	4.4	232 862	59.9	6.1	52.5	14.0	33.5
Flagler County	6 882	1 784	9.7	1 749	0.0	13.0	4.5	41 870	47.0	4.3	39.9	12.5	47.6
Franklin County	1 583	246	4.9	517	0.0	19.3	4.6	9 290	44.0	3.6	41.4	10.2	48.3
Gadsden County	9 547	1 599	10.3	2 664	0.1	8.5	8.9	34 547	56.6	7.6	52.2	9.5	38.2
Gilchrist County...........	2 968	431	5.4	917	0.0	14.6	11.0	11 370	53.0	4.4	45.8	10.8	43.4
Glades County	1 757	285	6.7	491	0.0	19.1	5.3	8 483	47.6	8.8	44.6	8.2	47.2
Gulf County	2 321	592	3.8	559	0.0	13.4	4.5	10 770	46.2	6.0	43.2	9.1	47.6
Hamilton County...........	2 466	232	7.4	797	0.0	13.3	13.8	10 658	41.8	7.1	38.2	7.9	53.9
Hardee County	5 483	627	4.8	1 801	0.0	12.8	11.0	20 364	54.1	9.7	48.9	9.3	41.8
Hendry County	8 191	873	5.1	2 700	0.0	8.8	11.8	26 600	59.8	7.8	57.3	9.2	33.6
Hernando County	18 867	3 490	12.3	5 403	0.0	14.0	6.2	109 225	42.6	5.2	35.9	11.3	52.8
Highlands County.........	12 420	2 080	8.2	3 531	0.0	13.2	7.4	72 351	43.5	4.4	36.5	10.8	52.6
Hillsborough County......	187 070	60 920	15.1	52 941	0.2	10.7	7.5	773 033	65.9	5.6	58.6	12.8	28.7
Holmes County............	3 444	524	7.0	1 011	0.0	10.2	6.8	14 835	49.9	6.2	45.4	9.5	45.1
Indian River County	17 024	3 733	15.0	4 932	0.6	11.2	6.8	93 974	50.8	4.5	42.0	13.1	44.9
Jackson County	8 562	2 115	9.3	2 608	0.0	10.8	6.2	37 680	48.8	5.7	45.4	9.7	44.8
Jefferson County	2 422	392	20.1	691	0.0	8.1	8.4	10 283	56.2	4.8	51.7	10.1	38.2
Lafayette County	1 052	226	4.9	375	0.0	6.7	15.5	5 707	46.6	4.5	46.6	7.0	46.4
Lake County	32 307	5 504	11.5	8 260	0.0	11.0	6.6	172 274	50.1	3.9	44.0	11.5	44.5
Lee County	62 918	12 539	12.7	17 053	0.4	14.5	7.2	363 694	53.3	3.7	46.5	11.9	41.6
Leon County	38 023	50 886	7.8	21 304	0.1	5.4	1.9	194 247	69.1	8.3	55.4	20.3	24.4
Levy County	6 303	930	5.4	1 968	0.5	10.2	9.8	27 396	50.4	6.1	44.8	10.6	44.6
Liberty County	1 217	218	6.5	372	0.0	2.7	8.6	5 699	43.8	5.0	49.9	8.3	41.8
Madison County	3 840	597	10.4	1 005	0.0	6.6	10.6	14 536	50.5	5.4	44.4	9.8	45.7
Manatee County..........	40 225	8 183	11.5	10 524	0.6	11.6	6.8	215 081	54.4	3.5	47.9	11.6	40.5
Marion County	42 621	8 078	12.3	11 281	0.1	10.9	7.5	209 732	49.8	5.8	43.0	11.5	45.5
Martin County..............	18 261	4 372	14.0	4 579	0.0	6.1	9.2	105 653	50.5	4.2	42.9	12.3	44.7
Miami-Dade County	443 852	160 435	17.2	123 037	0.1	7.7	6.8	1 758 374	57.5	8.7	53.0	11.4	35.6
Monroe County............	10 266	3 028	11.0	2 776	1.7	17.0	4.3	67 582	64.9	3.1	57.9	11.7	30.4
Nassau County............	10 897	2 188	8.3	2 900	0.0	11.2	5.5	44 957	63.9	4.7	55.1	13.3	31.6
Okaloosa County..........	31 577	9 816	7.8	9 554	5.7	17.8	3.0	133 583	65.1	4.1	56.3	13.9	29.8
Okeechobee County	6 898	1 136	4.7	2 304	0.0	7.6	12.8	28 097	52.9	4.7	47.2	10.5	42.3
Orange County............	167 077	64 155	14.6	49 260	0.1	10.1	6.2	693 426	68.1	5.0	60.7	13.4	25.9
Osceola County	35 247	7 092	11.2	9 337	0.0	10.1	6.2	131 277	64.1	5.0	58.3	12.1	29.6
Palm Beach County	183 941	50 064	17.0	49 015	0.0	8.5	6.9	917 453	55.6	5.0	48.1	12.5	39.4
Pasco County	51 677	11 290	10.8	14 076	0.1	11.7	5.8	282 735	49.8	4.6	42.9	11.4	45.8
Pinellas County	133 945	41 446	17.5	36 204	0.2	11.2	5.9	763 594	58.3	4.3	50.3	12.5	37.2
Polk County................	88 103	18 134	13.2	25 278	0.0	9.9	8.1	379 236	57.8	5.7	51.1	11.4	37.5
Putnam County	13 307	1 984	6.9	3 725	0.0	10.2	9.1	55 103	50.7	5.7	44.6	10.2	45.2
St. Johns County..........	22 042	6 425	19.5	5 896	0.0	10.4	2.0	98 092	63.1	3.3	53.4	14.8	31.7
St. Lucie County...........	33 356	7 060	11.1	8 988	0.0	9.7	9.3	154 078	53.4	5.1	45.4	12.2	42.4
Santa Rosa County.......	23 695	5 600	8.9	6 309	0.2	9.1	3.6	90 261	61.5	5.0	53.0	13.3	33.8

Table B-3. States and Counties — **Education, Labor Force, and Income**

STATE County	Full-year full-time employed (percent)								Children under 18 years in families					Total employed by class of worker (percent)				
										With two parents (percent)								
	Total	Men	Women	Non-Hispanic White	Black or African American	American Indian and Alaska Native	Asian, Hawaiian, and Pacific Islander	Hispanic or Latino[1]	Number	Both in labor force	Father only in labor force	With one parent who is in labor force (percent)	+/− U.S. percent of children with no stay-at-home parent (percent)	+/− U.S. percent two-income couples	Private	Government	Self-employed	Unpaid family worker
	24	25	26	27	28	29	30	31	32	33	34	35	36	37	38	39	40	41
DELAWARE	43.9	52.9	35.7	44.5	41.7	43.2	44.2	41.6	181 743	45.8	18.5	25.1	6.3	3.2	77.7	13.8	8.3	0.2
Kent County	44.8	54.9	35.8	46.4	39.8	42.7	39.9	44.6	32 338	44.0	19.1	26.2	5.6	3.7	68.3	22.4	9.0	0.3
New Castle County	45.6	54.5	37.4	46.5	43.2	51.5	45.1	41.1	116 775	46.9	18.2	24.6	6.9	6.3	81.5	11.6	6.7	0.1
Sussex County	37.9	46.3	30.2	37.8	37.5	36.7	40.3	41.7	32 630	44.0	19.3	25.4	4.8	−5.5	72.3	14.4	13.1	0.2
DISTRICT OF COLUMBIA	38.5	42.9	34.8	49.2	32.8	39.4	35.3	39.1	99 374	23.1	9.1	41.0	−0.5	−0.6	66.7	25.9	7.3	0.1
District of Columbia	38.5	42.9	34.8	49.2	32.8	39.4	35.3	39.1	99 374	23.1	9.1	41.0	−0.5	−0.6	66.7	25.9	7.3	0.1
FLORIDA	38.2	46.3	30.8	38.4	37.0	38.8	41.3	38.0	3 383 513	40.4	20.0	24.8	0.6	−7.0	74.8	13.7	11.1	0.3
Alachua County	34.0	40.3	28.1	36.0	30.9	44.8	25.8	24.2	40 825	39.8	19.7	26.8	2.0	3.3	59.6	31.6	8.5	0.3
Baker County	41.3	47.9	34.1	44.6	26.1	44.1	14.3	24.2	5 558	46.1	19.6	19.0	0.5	0.9	66.4	26.9	6.2	0.5
Bay County	40.1	49.3	31.3	40.8	36.0	36.3	32.6	38.1	33 366	41.5	22.7	22.9	−0.2	−4.6	71.7	17.7	10.4	0.2
Bradford County	33.1	34.4	31.3	37.3	19.2	25.0	10.1	13.5	5 198	43.2	12.1	27.2	5.8	−4.0	57.2	32.8	9.6	0.4
Brevard County	37.4	46.3	28.9	37.5	35.3	41.1	35.8	39.4	97 602	42.2	23.2	24.0	1.6	−9.0	74.0	15.4	10.3	0.3
Broward County	42.0	51.0	33.9	41.2	43.1	42.8	44.1	43.7	357 728	41.5	19.8	25.2	2.1	−2.1	76.7	11.7	11.3	0.2
Calhoun County	28.7	32.9	23.7	33.0	15.2	18.2	18.3	9.5	2 760	39.3	27.1	20.8	−4.5	−10.8	67.2	23.7	8.4	0.7
Charlotte County	26.5	31.3	22.2	26.0	28.5	32.5	41.5	35.6	20 879	46.1	19.1	23.2	4.7	−21.3	72.9	12.6	14.1	0.4
Citrus County	25.1	30.5	20.3	24.9	32.6	34.5	39.3	23.5	18 888	38.9	22.1	24.8	−0.9	−24.4	72.1	13.4	14.0	0.4
Clay County	47.5	59.6	36.1	47.6	48.7	44.7	45.3	45.3	37 306	48.5	23.9	19.6	3.5	1.4	73.4	17.8	8.4	0.4
Collier County	32.4	39.7	25.1	31.2	35.2	32.8	56.8	35.7	45 804	39.7	22.6	23.2	−1.7	−15.8	74.6	9.2	15.9	0.3
Columbia County	36.7	42.5	30.7	38.0	30.4	46.1	29.5	30.3	13 148	42.4	19.1	21.6	−0.6	−5.5	64.8	25.0	10.0	0.2
DeSoto County	28.8	33.1	22.9	29.4	26.5	30.7	59.5	27.2	6 140	33.6	25.7	23.7	−7.3	−17.8	72.7	17.5	9.7	0.1
Dixie County	28.6	34.6	21.7	29.8	16.0	0.0	38.0	20.2	2 803	34.8	23.2	23.0	−6.8	−17.9	65.5	20.4	13.7	0.3
Duval County	46.7	55.8	38.4	48.8	41.5	44.3	47.8	45.4	191 011	39.1	18.7	27.8	2.3	2.5	78.7	12.9	8.2	0.2
Escambia County	38.0	46.3	30.0	39.4	33.6	33.9	37.8	34.7	64 217	36.0	19.1	30.4	1.8	−6.0	71.8	18.4	9.6	0.2
Flagler County	28.9	35.1	23.3	29.5	22.9	49.6	29.9	28.8	8 426	48.1	18.0	21.7	5.2	−19.6	70.8	14.9	14.0	0.3
Franklin County	27.8	29.1	26.0	31.2	12.5	11.1	22.7	21.6	1 889	38.4	20.8	28.3	2.1	−12.0	58.1	18.5	22.9	0.5
Gadsden County	37.6	42.4	33.4	43.9	32.1	29.4	59.2	46.1	10 795	32.6	12.0	33.6	1.6	−1.7	60.0	32.5	7.1	0.3
Gilchrist County	34.5	40.9	27.1	36.7	15.1	64.0	100.0	22.2	3 259	49.6	18.5	20.0	5.0	−4.9	60.3	25.5	13.5	0.7
Glades County	30.6	32.9	27.9	31.1	24.5	31.9	18.9	33.6	2 065	35.2	25.1	26.1	−3.3	−15.6	66.6	23.4	9.5	0.5
Gulf County	31.1	34.0	27.7	32.9	23.1	32.1	39.1	20.8	2 605	41.6	16.4	26.0	3.0	−9.6	59.4	25.7	14.4	0.5
Hamilton County	27.8	27.4	28.2	34.7	19.9	4.9	48.0	12.9	2 746	30.2	17.5	26.0	−8.4	−11.3	65.3	24.5	9.4	0.8
Hardee County	30.2	36.3	22.9	32.6	25.9	19.1	26.5	26.9	6 627	33.2	27.7	20.2	−11.2	−11.7	72.9	16.7	9.8	0.6
Hendry County	36.8	43.0	28.7	42.1	31.6	40.3	22.5	31.8	9 629	35.7	19.3	24.4	−4.5	−7.8	73.8	17.8	7.8	0.6
Hernando County	26.1	32.4	20.6	25.6	28.1	36.0	27.5	32.0	23 079	39.7	24.6	21.5	−3.4	−23.2	73.3	14.3	12.0	0.4
Highlands County	25.9	31.2	20.9	24.1	31.7	34.7	40.3	33.2	15 404	38.3	20.2	25.8	−0.5	−22.6	71.3	15.7	12.5	0.6
Hillsborough County	43.6	52.4	35.4	45.8	39.6	48.3	40.1	40.2	234 187	39.9	19.6	25.7	1.0	0.4	78.0	12.8	9.0	0.2
Holmes County	31.0	34.6	26.9	33.5	5.4	23.4	26.6	17.6	4 053	39.0	28.6	20.5	−5.1	−12.5	62.8	24.2	12.5	0.4
Indian River County	31.3	38.0	25.1	30.6	37.0	46.2	31.8	30.9	19 811	44.5	19.4	25.0	4.9	−15.2	73.2	12.7	13.7	0.4
Jackson County	32.6	35.2	29.8	35.5	26.7	12.8	40.9	19.5	9 574	38.2	16.3	28.5	2.1	−4.5	54.4	35.9	9.4	0.4
Jefferson County	37.3	41.0	33.4	43.3	29.2	0.0	15.4	24.9	2 661	44.2	12.7	28.6	8.2	2.3	54.2	34.1	11.3	0.4
Lafayette County	32.3	35.9	26.8	35.2	13.8	25.9	50.0	41.1	1 353	42.5	20.3	23.1	1.0	−4.8	57.6	27.5	14.0	0.9
Lake County	33.0	41.3	25.4	32.2	31.6	43.3	42.3	45.3	40 147	43.4	21.6	22.6	1.4	−13.7	75.1	12.3	12.2	0.4
Lee County	34.9	41.9	28.4	34.1	38.3	38.9	45.7	40.3	80 672	44.2	18.8	26.0	5.6	−12.9	75.5	11.5	12.7	0.3
Leon County	40.2	46.8	34.5	43.9	33.1	50.8	39.3	28.3	47 879	45.1	16.7	27.2	7.7	10.2	54.9	36.7	8.2	0.3
Levy County	32.6	39.4	26.4	33.5	28.6	31.5	34.4	25.1	7 412	34.1	22.5	26.4	−4.1	−14.6	65.7	20.4	13.3	0.6
Liberty County	37.0	39.3	33.3	41.2	21.3	17.2	58.8	47.3	1 391	39.9	18.1	22.5	−2.2	1.2	52.9	34.9	11.4	0.8
Madison County	32.8	37.2	28.2	37.6	26.8	56.5	0.0	18.7	4 139	36.3	11.3	30.1	1.8	−3.6	66.7	21.7	11.3	0.3
Manatee County	36.2	44.2	28.9	35.2	40.8	35.6	40.8	42.1	49 963	43.4	19.5	25.4	4.2	−10.8	76.0	12.4	11.4	0.3
Marion County	31.1	38.2	24.7	31.1	30.7	33.2	34.2	33.1	50 719	40.0	20.8	24.9	0.3	−15.6	73.9	13.4	12.4	0.4
Martin County	32.2	40.2	24.6	31.5	33.4	30.8	36.6	40.0	22 162	42.4	25.4	20.2	−2.0	−15.3	72.8	10.9	16.0	0.3
Miami-Dade County	36.8	44.6	29.9	39.3	34.2	29.4	39.6	36.6	513 035	35.0	17.3	25.0	−4.6	−8.1	75.2	12.7	11.7	0.3
Monroe County	43.2	48.9	36.7	43.3	45.4	39.3	39.3	46.6	12 776	48.3	18.7	20.3	4.0	−2.3	66.5	15.8	17.2	0.5
Nassau County	43.1	55.0	31.8	44.4	31.2	29.5	26.6	27.1	13 329	44.8	25.5	19.7	−0.1	−1.8	73.3	15.6	11.0	0.1
Okaloosa County	43.8	55.3	32.0	44.0	44.9	49.4	39.3	41.9	39 540	43.8	26.4	20.3	−0.5	−2.4	69.7	20.0	10.2	0.2
Okeechobee County	31.5	36.8	25.3	33.3	22.0	11.8	46.9	28.0	7 853	39.6	26.1	19.4	−5.6	−11.4	70.7	16.7	11.9	0.7
Orange County	45.1	53.7	36.9	47.7	40.9	38.9	42.2	40.9	210 165	39.4	19.8	26.3	1.1	2.0	80.8	10.6	8.4	0.2
Osceola County	43.4	51.4	35.9	45.5	41.0	33.0	39.2	39.2	43 189	40.7	19.0	24.4	0.5	−1.5	82.0	9.9	7.9	0.2
Palm Beach County	36.4	45.4	28.2	35.1	39.7	38.8	44.4	39.8	224 561	41.0	22.1	23.3	−0.3	−11.1	73.9	11.8	14.0	0.3
Pasco County	32.6	40.2	25.8	32.1	31.8	43.1	39.9	38.8	65 210	43.1	20.9	22.4	0.9	−14.4	75.9	12.6	11.2	0.3
Pinellas County	38.7	46.5	31.9	38.6	38.1	47.3	44.6	39.8	166 547	42.6	18.4	27.4	5.4	−5.6	77.0	10.8	11.9	0.3
Polk County	38.1	45.8	30.8	38.2	36.2	34.0	41.5	38.5	107 722	40.9	19.7	24.7	1.0	−7.7	77.9	13.0	8.9	0.3
Putnam County	31.8	39.8	24.2	32.8	26.2	20.7	37.5	31.3	15 798	36.4	19.6	24.8	−3.4	−13.7	70.0	19.4	10.2	0.3
St. Johns County	40.9	52.1	30.7	41.5	33.0	51.3	46.4	35.9	27 064	46.0	25.1	19.8	1.2	−3.8	73.9	12.5	13.2	0.4
St. Lucie County	33.9	41.0	27.4	34.2	29.7	44.7	42.5	37.4	39 702	40.4	17.7	25.3	1.1	−12.1	75.7	13.4	10.6	0.3
Santa Rosa County	39.8	50.2	29.6	40.3	30.4	44.0	34.7	34.2	29 502	43.5	27.1	18.1	−3.0	−5.6	70.8	17.0	11.9	0.3

[1] Hispanic or Latino persons may be of any race.

Table B-3. States and Counties — Education, Labor Force, and Income

				Occupation for employed population 16 years and over (percent)						Industry for employed population 16 years and over (percent)					
STATE County	Percent who worked at home	Percent of the population 5 years and over with a disability	Veterans as a percent of the population 18 years and over	Management, professional, and related occupations	Service occupations	Sales and office occupations	Farming, fishing, and forestry occupations	Construction, extraction, and maintenance occupations	Production, transportation and material moving occupations	Agriculture, forestry, fishing, and mining	Construction and manufacturing	Wholesale and retail trade	Transportation and warehousing, and utilities	Service industries	Public administration
	42	43	44	45	46	47	48	49	50	51	52	53	54	55	56
DELAWARE	3.0	18.4	14.3	35.3	14.6	27.6	0.5	9.5	12.5	1.1	20.6	14.3	4.8	54.0	5.2
Kent County	3.1	19.2	18.0	28.5	17.0	26.9	0.7	11.6	15.3	1.6	20.9	15.5	5.3	45.7	10.8
New Castle County	2.6	16.9	12.5	39.1	13.4	28.4	0.3	8.1	10.7	0.5	19.2	13.0	4.8	58.6	3.9
Sussex County	4.1	22.4	17.1	27.2	16.7	25.3	1.3	12.8	16.6	2.7	25.1	18.0	4.2	44.7	5.2
DISTRICT OF COLUMBIA................	3.8	21.9	9.7	51.1	16.1	22.8	0.1	4.8	5.2	0.1	5.5	6.9	3.6	69.0	15.0
District of Columbia.......	3.8	21.9	9.7	51.1	16.1	22.8	0.1	4.8	5.2	0.1	5.5	6.9	3.6	69.0	15.0
FLORIDA..................	3.0	22.2	15.2	31.5	16.9	29.5	0.9	10.3	10.8	1.3	15.3	17.5	5.3	55.4	5.2
Alachua County............	3.2	16.1	11.2	44.0	16.2	26.3	0.6	6.2	6.7	1.1	9.1	12.7	2.8	68.8	5.5
Baker County	2.0	21.6	15.0	23.6	19.6	24.3	1.4	14.4	16.6	2.7	19.9	14.1	8.5	43.9	11.0
Bay County	2.3	22.0	20.1	28.5	19.7	28.1	0.6	12.3	10.8	0.9	15.6	16.8	4.7	54.2	7.7
Bradford County	2.9	25.6	17.3	23.1	23.4	23.7	1.3	13.8	14.8	3.5	16.2	11.6	8.1	43.7	16.9
Brevard County	2.7	21.9	21.3	34.9	16.5	26.9	0.3	10.5	10.8	0.5	21.5	15.9	4.1	50.8	7.3
Broward County	2.9	20.6	11.5	33.3	16.3	31.0	0.2	9.8	9.3	0.3	14.1	18.6	5.7	56.8	4.5
Calhoun County	2.1	26.0	14.2	24.9	21.8	21.0	4.0	15.1	13.2	6.7	17.4	15.7	7.1	40.8	12.4
Charlotte County	3.2	24.9	22.8	27.2	20.9	29.6	0.5	12.6	9.3	0.7	14.5	19.9	3.8	56.3	4.9
Citrus County	3.1	28.3	24.3	25.8	20.6	26.6	1.2	13.7	12.2	1.5	16.9	17.4	6.9	51.9	5.4
Clay County.................	2.3	18.8	21.9	31.2	14.0	30.4	0.3	12.8	11.4	0.9	16.2	17.8	7.4	49.8	7.9
Collier County	4.7	20.8	17.6	28.4	19.9	27.9	2.8	12.9	8.1	3.5	16.6	17.6	3.4	55.5	3.3
Columbia County..........	2.3	26.8	19.1	23.1	20.8	26.6	1.1	14.5	13.9	2.7	17.0	17.1	7.4	44.6	11.2
DeSoto County	2.7	23.6	15.0	18.5	18.7	16.8	24.9	11.1	10.0	29.4	10.2	12.1	3.5	38.6	6.3
Dixie County	5.2	33.5	20.0	18.0	21.4	23.7	6.3	13.5	17.2	8.9	21.2	18.3	4.3	37.6	9.8
Duval County	2.0	21.3	17.3	31.7	14.1	32.2	0.3	9.6	12.1	0.4	14.3	16.3	7.8	56.4	4.9
Escambia County	2.4	22.5	21.1	30.0	17.9	28.4	0.5	11.5	11.7	0.8	15.2	17.0	5.4	54.3	7.4
Flagler County	3.4	22.0	22.6	29.3	19.1	28.7	0.3	11.6	11.0	1.3	19.9	18.5	4.3	51.3	4.7
Franklin County	2.8	25.8	18.8	21.2	21.0	23.2	9.7	13.0	11.9	9.2	16.9	20.3	2.0	41.0	10.6
Gadsden County	1.0	25.0	12.4	20.0	21.0	25.1	3.1	11.2	13.0	4.4	14.1	13.5	3.8	48.7	15.4
Gilchrist County	4.4	25.1	15.5	24.3	17.2	25.1	3.5	14.9	15.1	7.7	19.0	14.5	5.3	42.4	11.1
Glades County	2.9	27.6	17.4	23.3	17.6	22.9	6.5	15.1	14.6	12.5	15.4	12.0	6.6	42.5	10.9
Gulf County	3.8	26.6	17.6	23.7	22.1	22.9	1.6	16.0	13.7	2.8	18.7	12.6	5.6	46.8	13.5
Hamilton County...........	1.7	27.3	12.6	20.7	22.8	21.8	5.3	13.5	15.9	10.6	18.7	12.8	5.7	39.9	12.3
Hardee County	2.7	24.2	11.7	20.7	15.8	18.6	19.1	12.3	13.5	26.0	13.2	14.5	3.9	37.4	5.0
Hendry County	1.9	22.7	9.6	18.7	15.0	19.3	18.2	14.1	14.7	25.0	18.0	13.2	4.4	33.4	8.3
Hernando County	2.9	27.2	23.1	25.3	18.8	28.6	0.6	13.6	13.1	1.8	16.9	18.9	6.2	50.9	5.3
Highlands County.........	2.6	27.9	21.3	24.6	19.4	26.3	8.1	10.1	11.6	10.3	11.8	18.3	3.6	49.5	6.6
Hillsborough County......	2.9	21.5	14.3	33.8	14.0	31.7	0.7	8.7	11.0	1.1	14.0	18.5	5.3	57.1	4.0
Holmes County............	4.8	27.8	16.7	19.1	19.4	22.1	2.2	16.0	21.2	4.5	26.1	14.7	5.3	37.9	11.3
Indian River County	3.8	23.0	20.5	20.0	21.0	27.2	2.0	11.8	9.4	3.2	15.1	18.5	3.3	55.4	4.5
Jackson County	3.2	28.3	15.4	28.6	24.0	23.5	1.3	10.3	12.3	3.3	14.2	14.4	5.0	47.6	15.5
Jefferson County	2.3	24.4	15.5	29.0	18.1	27.6	3.6	12.5	9.2	6.1	12.5	12.1	4.0	47.0	18.3
Lafayette County	2.7	21.6	14.1	23.7	22.4	18.4	10.3	9.1	16.2	16.4	13.7	15.5	4.4	33.0	16.9
Lake County.................	3.2	25.2	21.2	28.6	18.4	27.1	1.9	12.4	11.7	2.8	16.7	17.6	4.9	52.9	5.2
Lee County..................	3.5	22.0	19.2	28.1	18.5	29.7	0.8	13.5	9.3	1.1	17.1	19.1	4.0	54.4	4.1
Leon County................	2.5	14.0	10.9	45.3	14.2	28.7	0.1	6.0	5.7	0.4	7.3	13.1	2.4	57.0	19.7
Levy County	4.0	28.0	19.3	23.9	19.1	25.3	3.2	14.9	13.6	6.2	17.3	15.9	6.0	48.0	6.6
Liberty County	2.0	28.4	13.2	22.1	17.7	22.6	3.2	19.2	15.2	5.1	26.1	10.7	5.6	31.7	20.8
Madison County	2.9	29.0	14.3	23.5	20.2	19.4	2.9	10.9	23.1	6.2	27.9	14.2	3.3	39.4	9.0
Manatee County...........	3.4	23.3	18.6	29.1	16.9	28.2	1.4	11.2	13.2	1.6	21.0	17.9	3.8	51.1	4.6
Marion County..............	3.1	25.9	21.3	26.4	17.5	28.2	1.3	12.1	14.5	3.5	19.6	18.9	4.9	48.5	4.7
Martin County	4.9	21.2	19.9	32.8	18.6	27.3	1.3	11.2	8.7	2.1	17.1	16.3	5.3	54.9	4.4
Miami-Dade County	2.7	22.8	5.4	30.2	16.9	31.0	0.6	9.5	11.9	0.7	13.9	18.3	7.5	55.4	4.1
Monroe County............	5.0	23.7	19.0	27.3	23.4	25.3	3.2	12.2	8.6	3.5	11.3	15.1	5.9	56.3	7.9
Nassau County............	3.4	19.6	18.6	27.2	14.6	26.9	0.6	14.1	16.5	1.4	23.4	15.4	7.8	46.1	6.0
Okaloosa County..........	2.1	20.1	25.0	32.0	19.0	26.9	0.5	12.3	9.2	0.7	13.8	15.6	4.0	55.0	10.9
Okeechobee County	2.3	27.4	15.8	21.5	17.5	21.7	12.2	14.5	12.6	17.5	14.3	14.8	5.1	40.9	7.4
Orange County............	2.5	20.2	12.7	32.4	17.9	29.7	0.4	8.9	10.6	0.5	13.9	16.0	5.5	60.7	3.4
Osceola County	1.9	22.0	13.6	23.0	23.8	29.0	0.3	12.0	11.8	0.6	14.2	16.5	5.9	59.7	3.1
Palm Beach County	4.1	21.2	15.1	34.4	17.7	29.0	0.8	9.7	8.4	1.1	14.6	16.8	4.5	58.5	4.4
Pasco County	2.9	27.2	20.2	27.4	17.3	30.2	0.8	12.5	11.8	1.1	16.1	19.7	4.9	53.9	4.3
Pinellas County	3.5	23.9	17.8	34.2	15.5	31.0	0.2	8.1	11.0	0.2	16.2	17.6	4.1	58.0	4.0
Polk County.................	2.1	24.6	17.0	26.2	16.7	27.1	2.0	11.8	16.1	3.4	17.7	19.8	6.1	48.3	4.8
Putnam County	2.0	30.3	19.0	22.2	17.5	24.9	3.3	13.9	18.2	4.9	23.2	15.8	5.9	42.5	7.7
St. Johns County..........	3.7	18.7	17.9	37.0	16.2	29.1	0.5	8.9	8.4	0.8	15.4	17.8	5.4	56.1	4.6
St. Lucie County...........	2.5	25.0	18.1	25.3	17.8	28.8	2.6	13.6	12.0	2.8	17.2	20.2	5.0	49.2	5.6
Santa Rosa County.......	3.0	21.2	20.9	32.5	14.8	27.1	0.4	13.5	11.7	1.3	18.2	16.7	6.0	51.1	6.8

Table B-3. States and Counties — **Education, Labor Force, and Income**

STATE County	Median household income	Median family income: All families	Median family income: Families with children: Married-couple	Median family income: Families with children: Male householder	Median family income: Families with children: Female householder	Median nonfamily household income	Median income for full-year, full-time workers: Men	Median income for full-year, full-time workers: Women	Per capita income	Households by source of income (percent): With earnings	Households by source of income (percent): With interest, dividend, or rental income	Households by source of income (percent): With Social Security income	Households by source of income (percent): With public assistance income	Households by source of income (percent): With retirement income	Households with income over $100,000 (percent)	+/– U.S. percent for income over $100,000	Households with income below poverty (percent)	Families with children with income below poverty (percent)
	57	58	59	60	61	62	63	64	65	66	67	68	69	70	71	72	73	74
DELAWARE	47 381	55 257	67 131	31 963	23 690	29 891	40 442	30 394	23 305	81.3	39.0	26.9	2.7	21.0	14.0	1.7	8.8	9.9
Kent County	40 950	46 504	53 856	30 731	20 443	24 698	35 197	25 429	18 662	82.1	33.0	25.7	3.3	21.9	8.1	-4.2	10.2	12.3
New Castle County	52 419	62 144	75 691	35 057	26 402	32 824	44 501	32 473	25 413	83.5	40.8	24.2	2.4	18.9	17.4	5.1	8.0	8.4
Sussex County	39 208	45 203	52 919	27 936	19 916	22 640	31 988	24 797	20 328	73.8	38.1	36.0	3.2	26.8	8.4	-3.9	10.1	12.5
DISTRICT OF COLUMBIA	40 127	46 283	73 909	27 385	19 656	34 130	41 567	37 236	28 659	78.6	31.4	19.5	5.5	17.9	16.4	4.1	17.1	24.5
District of Columbia	40 127	46 283	73 909	27 385	19 656	34 130	41 567	37 236	28 659	78.6	31.4	19.5	5.5	17.9	16.4	4.1	17.1	24.5
FLORIDA	38 819	45 625	55 511	27 357	20 553	24 799	33 980	26 236	21 557	74.7	35.3	32.7	2.8	19.9	10.4	-1.9	11.7	14.2
Alachua County	31 426	46 587	57 211	25 935	17 758	18 982	33 661	26 885	18 465	83.4	34.2	19.0	2.7	13.4	8.7	-3.6	23.2	16.9
Baker County	40 035	43 503	49 954	22 315	15 306	19 031	30 844	21 900	15 164	81.6	21.7	23.9	3.5	17.1	5.3	-7.0	13.9	16.2
Bay County	36 092	42 729	50 302	24 033	16 621	21 747	31 571	22 541	18 700	77.6	34.8	28.0	3.2	22.7	6.6	-5.7	12.7	15.9
Bradford County	33 140	39 123	48 929	25 850	15 903	18 041	30 397	21 385	14 226	75.1	23.7	30.4	3.5	22.4	3.6	-8.7	15.2	14.7
Brevard County	40 099	47 571	57 702	30 930	20 145	24 911	38 090	25 551	21 484	72.3	40.7	35.8	2.3	27.2	9.3	-3.0	9.1	11.2
Broward County	41 691	50 531	63 460	30 181	24 093	27 417	37 608	29 632	23 170	77.0	33.3	29.2	2.1	13.8	12.8	0.5	10.8	12.6
Calhoun County	26 575	32 848	37 828	22 143	14 167	13 932	27 396	22 416	12 379	73.4	18.4	35.9	5.1	15.1	3.2	-9.1	21.0	20.0
Charlotte County	36 379	42 653	50 481	25 450	22 363	21 627	31 451	23 625	21 806	55.9	48.2	54.4	1.5	36.9	7.3	-5.0	8.1	10.9
Citrus County	31 001	36 711	46 418	23 433	17 728	18 783	29 882	22 321	18 585	55.3	43.0	52.5	2.3	35.2	5.4	-6.9	11.3	16.4
Clay County	48 854	53 814	59 015	31 995	23 866	26 928	38 565	26 375	20 868	84.8	35.4	21.8	1.7	22.9	11.4	-0.9	6.1	7.2
Collier County	48 289	54 816	54 962	26 447	23 862	31 931	35 118	27 420	31 195	68.2	50.2	41.1	1.5	26.1	18.1	5.8	7.8	13.1
Columbia County	30 881	35 927	41 756	24 492	18 685	18 153	28 052	22 336	14 598	74.4	23.9	33.6	4.0	21.2	4.3	-8.0	15.3	16.2
DeSoto County	30 714	34 726	38 036	21 958	15 932	18 937	24 184	20 574	14 000	68.7	32.1	40.3	3.8	24.8	4.1	-8.2	16.3	26.2
Dixie County	26 082	31 157	34 487	20 625	15 391	12 590	27 452	18 532	13 559	64.8	19.5	39.7	5.3	22.1	3.8	-8.5	20.0	21.9
Duval County	40 703	47 689	57 216	29 730	20 997	26 592	35 112	26 707	20 753	83.6	29.1	22.2	2.6	16.2	9.7	-2.6	11.6	13.5
Escambia County	35 234	41 708	49 464	24 536	16 033	22 574	32 281	22 808	18 641	77.2	32.4	28.1	3.5	24.6	7.0	-5.3	14.6	19.4
Flagler County	40 214	45 502	50 359	28 450	19 444	25 357	32 512	26 088	21 879	61.6	46.2	49.5	1.5	38.6	8.8	-3.5	7.7	13.3
Franklin County	26 756	31 157	39 875	20 227	14 561	16 250	25 684	20 905	16 140	68.9	26.6	35.9	3.0	21.0	4.8	-7.5	18.1	16.8
Gadsden County	31 248	36 238	46 045	26 810	15 276	18 252	27 957	22 199	14 499	76.5	21.3	29.5	4.0	18.2	4.0	-8.3	19.1	23.3
Gilchrist County	30 328	34 485	41 588	20 000	16 316	17 344	28 393	22 273	13 985	74.5	22.3	33.4	3.9	18.8	3.9	-8.4	15.2	15.5
Glades County	30 774	34 223	46 840	31 012	15 769	16 265	29 731	21 514	15 338	65.9	33.9	41.2	3.1	23.4	6.0	-6.3	14.2	17.3
Gulf County	30 276	36 289	43 081	26 250	12 444	16 206	29 003	21 485	14 449	68.8	26.0	37.4	3.4	26.1	3.8	-8.5	17.9	19.4
Hamilton County	25 638	30 677	40 667	13 125	13 839	12 486	27 283	21 288	10 562	71.8	16.8	32.0	4.8	19.0	2.4	-9.9	25.7	33.1
Hardee County	30 183	32 487	38 832	24 479	16 175	16 239	24 194	19 412	12 445	74.1	22.7	35.1	4.8	14.8	4.7	-7.6	20.3	25.5
Hendry County	33 592	34 902	40 929	24 177	16 740	18 902	26 083	20 995	13 663	79.7	22.1	26.4	4.3	14.4	5.0	-7.3	19.3	24.3
Hernando County	32 572	37 509	48 621	26 703	17 871	20 131	31 377	22 414	18 321	56.7	43.0	52.7	2.3	35.6	4.8	-7.5	9.8	13.4
Highlands County	30 160	35 647	43 735	23 409	15 725	17 644	27 904	21 764	17 222	54.8	42.2	53.9	2.7	32.6	4.8	-7.5	13.5	21.5
Hillsborough County	40 663	48 223	59 632	27 345	20 959	26 730	35 589	27 781	21 812	82.3	31.8	24.9	3.0	15.7	11.3	-1.0	11.5	13.7
Holmes County	27 923	34 286	40 313	12 917	12 604	13 569	26 627	21 305	14 135	71.8	21.8	36.4	5.6	19.4	3.5	-8.8	20.7	22.6
Indian River County	39 635	46 385	51 609	29 904	20 939	23 974	31 887	24 972	27 227	63.0	46.5	46.8	2.2	28.2	12.4	0.1	8.5	11.8
Jackson County	29 744	36 404	44 481	24 400	16 543	15 615	28 008	21 892	13 905	71.7	24.4	34.7	3.4	20.6	4.6	-7.7	17.8	18.9
Jefferson County	32 998	40 407	45 741	21 429	14 722	16 648	27 026	26 723	17 006	76.3	23.7	30.5	3.3	16.8	7.1	-5.2	18.1	18.6
Lafayette County	30 651	35 020	39 773	25 313	14 405	20 000	25 567	22 188	13 087	73.9	19.9	32.7	3.7	22.2	4.1	-8.2	14.9	21.5
Lake County	36 903	42 577	51 167	23 982	17 607	21 385	32 233	24 621	20 199	64.1	41.4	45.3	2.1	30.5	7.1	-5.2	9.1	13.0
Lee County	40 319	46 430	55 006	27 390	20 672	25 827	32 284	25 307	24 542	66.9	43.0	42.4	1.8	27.5	10.6	-1.7	8.6	12.3
Leon County	37 517	52 962	65 138	30 553	21 079	21 526	36 701	29 129	21 024	86.0	34.2	16.6	2.2	13.1	10.4	-1.9	18.8	13.1
Levy County	26 959	30 899	38 975	20 682	15 720	16 549	27 033	20 708	14 746	66.5	25.5	37.8	3.0	23.4	4.0	-8.3	18.0	24.9
Liberty County	28 840	34 244	42 292	21 827	11 364	18 183	22 397	22 732	17 225	71.8	18.7	31.9	5.4	17.9	5.0	-7.3	19.1	21.0
Madison County	26 533	31 753	47 557	20 921	12 181	12 683	25 919	20 303	12 511	68.6	20.2	36.6	5.4	17.8	3.8	-8.5	24.9	25.2
Manatee County	38 673	46 576	57 660	27 798	21 225	23 911	32 541	25 921	22 388	67.0	43.3	42.3	1.9	26.6	9.3	-3.0	9.1	12.8
Marion County	31 944	37 473	46 867	22 982	17 975	18 951	30 041	22 684	17 848	64.5	35.4	45.0	2.7	28.0	5.5	-6.8	12.2	16.6
Martin County	43 083	53 244	62 289	27 109	24 760	26 136	37 306	28 656	29 584	63.8	50.7	45.1	1.3	26.8	15.3	3.0	7.6	10.5
Miami-Dade County	35 966	40 260	49 720	24 492	19 802	21 807	30 806	25 408	18 497	80.8	23.5	25.2	6.0	11.1	10.8	-1.5	18.1	19.3
Monroe County	42 283	50 734	56 627	28 826	21 312	31 104	32 406	26 347	26 102	78.9	32.9	25.0	1.9	16.2	12.3	0.0	10.1	9.9
Nassau County	46 022	52 477	58 595	29 811	20 711	25 237	38 491	25 973	22 836	81.4	33.6	28.2	1.6	20.7	11.4	-0.9	9.2	9.4
Okaloosa County	41 474	47 711	50 820	25 013	19 149	27 232	33 634	23 239	20 918	81.4	38.6	24.7	2.4	27.8	9.1	-3.2	8.5	10.8
Okeechobee County	30 456	35 163	42 900	25 273	18 112	18 675	26 674	20 990	14 553	70.2	25.5	37.9	3.9	20.2	5.3	-7.0	15.1	17.2
Orange County	41 311	47 159	56 870	30 206	21 224	28 985	33 192	26 046	20 916	85.9	30.1	21.2	2.5	13.9	10.7	-1.6	10.9	13.0
Osceola County	38 214	42 061	48 351	27 153	19 958	24 088	30 073	22 217	17 022	82.8	25.1	26.2	2.8	16.8	6.3	-6.0	10.6	13.2
Palm Beach County	45 062	53 701	64 662	31 867	23 220	29 035	38 585	29 992	28 801	69.8	44.8	38.5	1.8	19.3	16.2	3.9	9.0	11.5
Pasco County	32 969	39 568	51 661	25 195	19 070	20 110	31 869	24 827	18 439	62.1	39.2	46.7	2.2	29.2	5.6	-6.7	10.4	12.8
Pinellas County	37 111	46 925	60 294	28 753	21 828	24 466	34 205	27 117	23 497	70.6	40.0	37.1	2.3	22.0	9.5	-2.8	9.5	11.2
Polk County	36 036	41 442	50 992	28 644	18 913	21 676	32 067	23 291	18 302	73.4	32.3	36.6	3.3	21.9	6.6	-5.7	11.9	15.5
Putnam County	28 180	34 499	42 645	21 328	13 164	16 227	30 787	21 883	15 603	66.2	26.3	39.7	4.5	21.6	4.6	-7.7	19.3	26.6
St. Johns County	50 099	59 153	71 314	26 932	24 909	28 940	43 338	28 309	28 674	78.5	43.6	29.7	1.5	21.4	18.3	6.0	8.2	8.4
St. Lucie County	36 363	41 381	50 242	26 302	17 047	23 241	30 786	23 857	18 790	67.7	36.7	41.4	2.9	26.0	6.8	-5.5	11.5	16.4
Santa Rosa County	41 881	46 929	52 099	26 558	16 396	24 455	36 685	23 348	20 089	80.1	36.4	25.6	2.8	24.2	9.4	-2.9	10.0	11.6

STATE/ County code	MSA/PMSA/ NECMA code[1]	STATE County	High school graduates			College graduates		College graduates (percent)				
			Total population 25 years and over	Percent with a high school diploma or less	Percent with a high school diploma or more	Percent with a bachelor's degree or more	+/- U.S. percent with bachelor's degree or more	Non-Hispanic White	Black or African American	American Indian and Alaska Native	Asian, Hawaiian, and Pacific Islander	Hispanic or Latino[2]
			1	2	3	4	5	6	7	8	9	10
		FLORIDA—Cont'd										
12 115	7510	Sarasota County	256 802	43.0	87.1	27.4	3.0	28.2	10.5	24.4	35.0	19.5
12 117	5960	Seminole County..........	243 216	35.7	88.7	31.0	6.6	32.8	18.5	26.6	47.6	23.3
12 119	...	Sumter County	41 509	61.6	77.3	12.2	-12.2	12.9	5.1	13.8	56.4	13.5
12 121	...	Suwannee County........	23 492	65.6	73.2	10.5	-13.9	10.9	6.5	25.2	56.1	7.7
12 123	...	Taylor County	12 914	70.9	70.0	8.9	-15.5	10.0	3.1	0.0	57.6	5.0
12 125	...	Union County	9 363	66.4	72.5	7.5	-16.9	9.3	2.1	4.0	15.8	5.8
12 127	2020	Volusia County	317 225	50.2	82.0	17.6	-6.8	18.1	14.7	16.9	35.8	11.7
12 129	...	Wakulla County	15 211	56.6	78.4	15.7	-8.7	17.4	4.5	0.0	10.0	16.1
12 131	...	Walton County..............	28 838	56.4	76.0	16.2	-8.2	17.4	2.6	12.6	25.8	12.6
12 133	...	Washington County.......	14 338	67.6	71.2	9.2	-15.2	9.5	6.1	8.6	0.0	8.0
13 000		GEORGIA	5 185 965	50.1	78.6	24.3	-0.1	27.7	15.5	18.1	43.8	13.6
13 001	...	Appling County.............	11 004	69.9	67.3	8.4	-16.0	9.6	3.8	0.0	32.7	0.0
13 003	...	Atkinson County	4 503	79.6	56.3	6.9	-17.5	9.0	3.4	0.0	20.0	0.5
13 005	...	Bacon County...............	6 525	76.3	67.7	6.6	-17.8	7.3	1.1	0.0	52.8	4.4
13 007	...	Baker County	2 543	74.4	66.0	10.7	-13.7	16.3	3.9	X	100.0	4.3
13 009	...	Baldwin County	28 445	62.8	72.6	16.2	-8.2	21.7	7.4	0.0	45.1	29.8
13 011	...	Banks County...............	9 401	72.9	65.4	8.6	-15.8	8.8	11.0	6.3	0.0	9.8
13 013	0520	Barrow County	29 317	62.7	73.3	10.9	-13.5	11.6	5.8	21.5	16.6	2.0
13 015	0520	Bartow County	48 709	62.4	71.8	14.1	-10.3	14.5	10.3	22.3	29.0	6.3
13 017	...	Ben Hill County	10 990	71.4	65.8	9.5	-14.9	12.8	2.6	19.4	0.0	0.0
13 019	...	Berrien County	10 451	68.6	66.0	9.4	-15.0	10.0	4.0	24.6	17.8	8.6
13 021	4680	Bibb County..................	97 463	54.5	77.2	21.3	-3.1	29.1	10.1	19.2	47.3	25.8
13 023	...	Bleckley County	7 268	64.0	71.7	12.5	-11.9	14.5	5.6	X	0.0	0.0
13 025	...	Brantley County	9 282	74.9	72.5	6.2	-18.2	6.4	2.8	100.0	11.1	0.0
13 027	...	Brooks County	10 455	69.6	67.5	11.3	-13.1	15.1	4.3	0.0	0.0	4.4
13 029	7520	Bryan County	14 333	53.8	79.0	19.3	-5.1	20.2	7.4	0.0	49.3	39.3
13 031	...	Bulloch County	28 740	51.7	77.9	25.4	1.0	29.6	11.5	0.0	70.4	15.8
13 033	...	Burke County	13 338	72.1	64.9	9.5	-14.9	14.0	4.5	0.0	60.0	0.0
13 035	...	Butts County.................	13 055	70.1	69.8	8.6	-15.8	9.5	5.6	0.0	43.8	25.0
13 037	...	Calhoun County	4 277	80.0	65.5	11.7	-12.7	18.6	6.4	X	X	8.3
13 039	...	Camden County	24 073	49.9	83.3	16.0	-8.4	17.1	10.0	30.5	22.7	16.2
13 043	...	Candler County	6 166	72.3	56.9	10.2	-14.2	13.6	3.0	0.0	X	3.6
13 045	0520	Carroll County	53 464	63.2	71.1	16.5	-7.9	17.7	8.6	23.5	49.3	15.8
13 047	1560	Catoosa County	35 231	58.8	76.0	13.8	-10.6	13.8	14.1	12.6	23.3	6.8
13 049	...	Charlton County	6 404	77.0	65.1	6.4	-18.0	8.0	1.7	5.9	28.3	0.0
13 051	7520	Chatham County	147 049	46.7	80.2	25.0	0.6	32.1	12.6	12.9	36.2	23.4
13 053	1800	Chattahoochee County .	6 417	34.3	88.8	25.0	0.6	32.5	11.2	25.0	21.3	29.4
13 055	...	Chattooga County	17 054	74.2	60.4	7.7	-16.7	8.0	3.9	40.9	33.3	6.6
13 057	0520	Cherokee County	91 141	42.9	84.4	27.0	2.6	27.6	21.7	22.7	39.9	14.5
13 059	0500	Clarke County...............	51 845	40.6	81.0	39.8	15.4	52.9	11.3	14.8	76.4	21.3
13 061	...	Clay County..................	2 215	71.2	64.3	10.1	-14.3	15.8	4.3	85.7	0.0	60.0
13 063	0520	Clayton County	141 554	51.8	80.1	16.6	-7.8	13.9	20.2	21.3	15.9	6.1
13 065	...	Clinch County...............	4 380	73.6	58.9	10.4	-14.0	12.8	3.0	0.0	61.5	41.7
13 067	0520	Cobb County.................	395 349	32.0	88.8	39.8	15.4	42.7	31.9	32.0	54.0	19.3
13 069	...	Coffee County	22 798	68.1	64.8	10.0	-14.4	11.9	4.1	22.7	55.8	5.3
13 071	...	Colquitt County	26 127	70.9	64.9	11.4	-13.0	14.5	3.6	7.0	36.8	1.4
13 073	0600	Columbia County...........	56 562	37.9	87.9	32.0	7.6	32.2	24.4	19.4	53.0	31.2
13 075	...	Cook County	9 876	71.4	64.6	8.1	-16.3	10.1	3.0	0.0	4.2	3.2
13 077	0520	Coweta County	56 821	51.2	81.6	20.6	-3.8	22.7	11.1	11.3	44.2	12.2
13 079	...	Crawford County	8 050	72.4	67.3	6.8	-17.6	7.5	5.0	0.0	X	0.0
13 081	...	Crisp County.................	13 709	68.6	65.9	12.8	-11.6	17.7	3.9	0.0	48.8	7.9
13 083	1560	Dade County.................	9 728	63.3	67.0	10.9	-13.5	10.8	0.0	0.0	36.1	12.5
13 085	...	Dawson County	10 752	53.7	79.5	18.1	-6.3	18.3	83.3	0.0	0.0	4.5
13 087	...	Decatur County	17 633	63.9	69.7	12.1	-12.3	14.0	8.2	14.1	37.1	13.0
13 089	0520	DeKalb County	429 981	35.3	85.1	36.3	11.9	55.7	22.8	24.5	46.6	14.8
13 091	...	Dodge County	12 501	70.3	66.3	11.6	-12.8	13.7	5.5	0.0	49.3	0.9
13 093	...	Dooly County	7 309	69.4	68.5	9.6	-14.8	13.6	5.1	0.0	51.3	1.2
13 095	0120	Dougherty County..........	58 024	54.6	73.7	17.8	-6.6	23.1	13.4	16.4	15.4	15.4
13 097	0520	Douglas County	58 687	53.5	81.1	19.2	-5.2	17.6	25.6	18.3	50.2	16.9
13 099	...	Early County	7 872	65.0	68.4	12.6	-11.8	16.4	7.1	X	100.0	10.1
13 101	...	Echols County	2 167	75.2	60.5	8.4	-16.0	10.3	0.0	X	50.0	2.0
13 103	7520	Effingham County..........	23 129	61.6	78.9	13.6	-10.8	13.8	11.0	14.3	28.3	16.5
13 105	...	Elbert County	13 617	72.0	67.2	9.8	-14.6	12.3	3.1	100.0	42.9	13.7
13 107	...	Emanuel County	13 465	73.7	61.4	10.1	-14.3	11.8	5.3	30.4	58.8	4.0
13 109	...	Evans County	6 540	73.5	65.7	9.0	-15.4	11.7	2.7	0.0	57.4	0.0

[1]MSA = Metropolitan Statistical Area. PMSA = Primary MSA. NECMA = New England County Metropolitan Area. See the Appendix A for explanation of these concepts. See Appendix B for list of metropolitan areas identified by type, with component counties.
[2]Hispanic or Latino persons may be of any race.

STATE County	School enrollment			Population 16 to 19 years				Employment status, 2000			Work status in 1999 of the population 16 years and over (percent)		
											Worked in 1999		
	Grades kindergarten through 12	College or graduate school	Percent private	Number	Percent in armed forces	Percent high school graduates	Percent not enrolled, not grads, not in armed forces, not employed	Total population 16 years and over	Percent in labor force	Unemployment rate	Full-time	Part-time	Did not work in 1999
	11	12	13	14	15	16	17	18	19	20	21	22	23
FLORIDA—Cont'd													
Sarasota County	40 983	10 210	15.1	10 743	0.0	11.3	4.1	278 756	50.5	3.7	42.2	13.0	44.8
Seminole County	69 909	22 095	14.8	18 797	0.0	8.9	4.1	283 100	70.1	3.7	60.3	14.3	25.3
Sumter County	7 121	1 221	10.7	2 078	0.0	9.8	13.4	45 812	34.7	4.8	33.3	10.3	56.4
Suwannee County........	6 459	953	11.6	1 987	0.0	10.9	9.5	27 577	54.5	7.3	48.1	10.8	41.1
Taylor County	3 760	585	6.4	1 093	0.0	6.0	11.2	15 108	51.9	5.5	47.9	9.6	42.4
Union County	2 297	429	6.8	665	0.3	10.2	16.1	10 884	38.5	4.0	43.6	7.0	49.4
Volusia County	68 193	26 362	19.1	22 260	0.1	9.9	6.0	364 534	55.4	6.3	46.3	13.5	40.1
Wakulla County	4 542	794	3.4	1 281	0.5	11.5	8.3	17 671	62.4	3.9	57.6	11.3	31.2
Walton County	6 868	1 108	5.8	1 863	0.5	10.6	4.5	32 813	55.0	4.4	48.8	11.9	39.4
Washington County	3 819	566	4.1	935	0.0	15.2	8.3	16 579	51.5	5.5	46.3	10.1	43.6
GEORGIA..................	1 598 291	436 555	12.1	471 799	1.7	11.2	7.3	6 250 687	66.1	5.4	59.0	12.5	28.5
Appling County............	3 615	394	6.5	1 130	0.0	11.3	8.3	13 261	61.3	4.8	56.0	10.3	33.8
Atkinson County	1 561	100	3.7	502	0.0	18.1	16.9	5 521	61.0	5.2	55.6	8.5	35.9
Bacon County	1 788	317	4.0	523	0.0	17.4	6.1	7 795	57.6	4.5	52.0	9.3	38.8
Baker County	913	103	8.8	249	0.0	3.2	5.6	3 081	56.5	8.3	52.7	9.2	38.1
Baldwin County	8 038	4 231	19.5	3 752	0.0	6.6	6.7	36 503	51.1	6.2	46.3	11.9	41.8
Banks County	2 631	328	6.6	815	0.0	13.5	6.4	11 136	65.7	3.0	60.4	9.7	29.9
Barrow County	9 130	1 143	8.0	2 225	0.0	11.4	8.2	34 376	69.5	4.2	63.4	10.2	26.4
Bartow County	15 176	2 093	7.0	3 768	0.0	13.6	12.2	56 847	67.2	4.0	61.0	11.0	27.9
Ben Hill County	3 554	591	6.8	1 111	0.0	9.2	9.0	13 216	59.7	6.3	54.0	10.5	35.4
Berrien County	3 090	604	3.8	857	0.0	15.4	8.5	12 287	63.4	4.4	57.2	9.0	33.8
Bibb County	30 324	8 815	19.9	8 916	0.1	9.5	9.5	117 052	59.7	7.5	51.9	13.1	35.0
Bleckley County	2 406	867	4.5	984	0.0	12.2	4.5	8 948	57.0	6.0	52.0	11.5	36.5
Brantley County...........	3 109	379	4.8	812	0.0	12.8	4.7	10 940	59.6	4.9	53.9	10.2	35.9
Brooks County	3 509	518	5.8	1 120	2.0	12.4	10.4	12 531	57.9	5.2	51.1	10.0	38.9
Bryan County	5 370	825	6.5	1 355	0.0	9.8	8.3	16 912	68.0	2.9	59.8	11.2	29.0
Bulloch County	9 391	12 889	5.3	6 536	0.1	4.9	2.7	44 892	61.7	10.2	50.5	20.9	28.6
Burke County	5 529	613	8.6	1 541	0.8	8.0	10.6	16 117	56.5	9.2	50.1	9.4	40.5
Butts County................	3 567	511	5.8	1 027	0.0	13.0	13.5	15 349	55.1	3.8	57.6	9.3	33.1
Calhoun County	1 132	228	20.9	333	0.0	10.8	6.0	5 091	43.9	5.6	44.9	10.7	44.4
Camden County	10 149	2 121	5.6	2 816	11.7	20.7	5.0	31 244	72.7	4.5	65.8	11.6	22.6
Candler County	1 917	240	5.2	491	0.0	5.7	8.8	7 250	54.1	7.1	49.0	10.8	40.2
Carroll County	16 383	6 435	5.5	5 999	0.0	8.7	8.0	67 034	63.6	4.8	56.4	13.3	30.3
Catoosa County	10 040	2 014	7.3	2 754	0.0	10.1	5.7	41 047	68.4	3.3	59.7	12.6	27.7
Charlton County	2 221	250	5.9	675	0.0	15.7	12.7	7 834	48.1	5.2	50.8	9.1	40.1
Chatham County	44 375	15 613	20.8	13 182	2.8	13.4	6.0	180 093	62.8	5.8	53.9	14.4	31.7
Chattahoochee County .	3 027	837	7.9	1 303	67.8	71.1	3.1	10 887	83.0	2.0	69.1	14.6	16.2
Chattooga County	4 234	619	7.2	1 417	0.4	17.7	10.6	20 307	56.0	5.6	52.9	8.4	38.7
Cherokee County	27 510	5 781	11.3	7 243	0.1	9.8	5.6	105 713	73.3	2.7	64.1	14.1	21.9
Clarke County	13 088	29 695	7.2	10 245	1.1	5.6	4.7	85 219	64.8	10.1	49.2	27.6	23.2
Clay County................	675	114	7.6	232	0.0	10.8	6.5	2 618	49.8	6.8	43.7	10.3	46.1
Clayton County	51 453	11 042	9.1	13 381	0.3	12.7	7.4	172 507	71.0	5.5	66.7	10.9	22.4
Clinch County	1 477	162	1.2	395	0.0	6.3	3.3	5 212	52.3	4.2	52.2	9.5	38.3
Cobb County	114 905	35 713	13.6	31 156	0.0	9.9	5.3	466 947	73.6	3.8	65.5	13.3	21.2
Coffee County	7 661	1 299	5.3	2 275	0.0	7.6	9.0	27 942	59.9	6.4	56.0	11.3	32.7
Colquitt County............	8 422	1 159	3.8	2 754	2.9	10.8	10.7	31 889	60.8	6.1	55.1	9.6	35.2
Columbia County..........	20 242	3 983	9.7	5 336	0.0	8.8	3.3	65 831	69.6	3.6	59.9	13.9	26.2
Cook County	3 266	530	2.5	915	0.0	15.2	7.2	11 774	60.5	5.3	53.6	12.1	34.3
Coweta County............	18 412	2 735	11.3	4 522	0.0	9.9	7.4	66 056	69.7	3.9	62.0	12.5	25.5
Crawford County	2 663	410	9.1	578	0.0	12.6	6.7	9 341	60.7	4.6	55.3	9.4	35.3
Crisp County	4 751	606	6.8	1 270	0.0	9.8	15.1	16 272	58.7	7.0	51.3	11.4	37.3
Dade County	2 698	1 047	23.5	1 042	0.0	8.1	8.5	11 960	62.5	5.4	52.5	14.5	33.0
Dawson County	2 804	358	6.0	752	0.0	19.4	10.0	12 330	68.6	3.4	61.1	13.3	25.6
Decatur County	6 026	1 019	5.3	1 605	0.0	8.8	9.3	21 071	57.6	6.5	51.2	10.2	38.6
DeKalb County	119 724	47 609	20.1	35 836	0.1	9.0	6.8	519 626	70.8	5.5	64.6	12.6	22.8
Dodge County	3 963	555	3.5	1 113	0.0	4.5	11.3	14 776	54.7	5.4	50.2	9.2	40.6
Dooly County...............	2 513	384	13.9	681	1.0	6.9	9.5	8 924	51.2	6.4	48.9	8.3	42.8
Dougherty County	19 974	6 215	10.5	6 697	10.6	12.7	7.0	72 632	59.4	9.8	50.7	12.4	36.9
Douglas County............	19 159	4 171	13.2	4 929	0.0	11.8	4.3	69 334	70.6	3.8	64.0	12.6	23.4
Early County	2 617	393	5.4	679	0.0	17.4	9.4	9 190	57.4	8.1	51.4	9.1	39.5
Echols County	831	97	1.5	235	0.0	3.0	5.5	2 745	63.9	3.7	53.2	7.6	39.3
Effingham County.........	8 498	1 184	4.4	2 334	0.0	12.1	6.8	27 608	66.0	4.2	59.5	11.9	28.6
Elbert County	4 043	492	4.4	1 142	0.0	14.7	9.8	15 861	58.6	5.8	51.5	12.5	36.0
Emanuel County...........	4 745	658	5.6	1 569	0.0	9.4	10.5	16 619	56.0	4.4	49.2	8.8	41.9
Evans County	2 265	205	8.3	629	0.0	6.4	14.8	7 970	58.1	8.1	52.4	10.6	37.0

Table B-3. States and Counties — **Education, Labor Force, and Income**

STATE County	Full-year full-time employed (percent)								Children under 18 years in families						Total employed by class of worker (percent)			
										With two parents (percent)		With one parent who is in labor force (percent)	+/− U.S. percent of children with no stay-at-home parent (percent)	+/− U.S. percent two-income couples				
	Total	Men	Women	Non-Hispanic White	Black or African American	American Indian and Alaska Native	Asian, Hawaiian, and Pacific Islander	Hispanic or Latino[1]	Number	Both in labor force	Father only in labor force				Private	Government	Self-employed	Unpaid family worker
	24	25	26	27	28	29	30	31	32	33	34	35	36	37	38	39	40	41
FLORIDA—Cont'd																		
Sarasota County	32.3	39.7	25.7	31.6	36.7	42.9	40.6	39.2	49 828	44.3	20.9	24.0	3.7	-15.1	73.1	10.0	16.6	0.3
Seminole County	47.3	57.8	37.4	48.8	39.9	46.2	46.3	42.2	87 823	46.6	25.1	19.6	1.6	4.5	77.0	11.4	11.3	0.2
Sumter County	22.4	25.4	19.0	23.0	20.7	25.1	9.6	17.6	7 949	36.5	19.1	27.1	-1.0	-25.8	69.0	19.7	11.0	0.4
Suwannee County	35.4	44.4	27.0	35.1	36.4	28.5	33.7	42.5	7 695	40.2	21.2	22.9	-1.5	-8.8	67.1	20.2	11.8	0.9
Taylor County	34.3	42.7	25.6	35.9	25.5	18.8	35.3	44.8	4 284	36.4	20.5	25.8	-2.4	-10.2	69.8	19.6	10.1	0.6
Union County	29.9	28.5	32.6	35.2	18.1	18.2	42.2	10.2	2 717	42.0	23.0	24.3	1.7	1.5	48.4	42.6	8.5	0.5
Volusia County	34.6	41.9	27.9	34.9	31.4	37.9	31.4	35.0	82 832	40.5	20.8	25.2	1.1	-10.6	74.4	13.3	12.0	0.3
Wakulla County	45.1	50.6	39.1	47.2	31.5	40.4	7.3	40.2	5 483	48.2	14.8	23.3	6.9	4.1	54.6	33.9	11.4	0.1
Walton County	34.4	40.7	27.8	35.3	21.7	37.7	41.5	29.5	8 446	38.4	22.3	21.6	-4.6	-9.7	66.9	16.7	16.0	0.4
Washington County	33.4	37.5	29.0	34.6	26.4	23.1	22.5	30.7	4 583	41.2	17.9	22.0	-1.4	-7.5	62.5	24.5	12.3	0.7
GEORGIA	44.3	54.0	35.1	46.7	39.4	41.2	41.5	39.9	2 015 574	41.2	21.3	24.1	0.7	2.3	75.3	14.9	9.5	0.3
Appling County	41.3	52.3	30.9	43.3	32.7	0.0	15.6	45.3	4 259	44.8	20.6	19.6	-0.2	-0.6	71.7	16.9	10.6	0.8
Atkinson County	38.3	48.4	28.3	40.9	34.4	66.7	59.3	30.8	2 096	37.8	22.5	21.1	-5.7	-1.5	73.5	14.3	11.7	0.5
Bacon County	39.3	52.6	27.0	41.5	23.7	0.0	52.8	51.3	2 315	38.3	22.9	24.4	-1.9	-6.5	70.2	15.8	13.4	0.6
Baker County	37.3	47.8	28.1	47.8	26.2	X	55.6	32.4	1 026	30.1	16.0	29.0	-5.5	-2.3	69.7	21.5	8.6	0.2
Baldwin County	33.3	34.3	32.1	37.0	28.4	17.7	35.7	31.8	8 570	36.1	12.1	34.0	5.5	-1.1	62.7	28.6	8.4	0.2
Banks County	47.3	55.9	38.5	47.1	46.7	56.8	76.5	59.2	3 516	49.6	24.9	13.9	-1.1	4.0	72.2	14.5	13.1	0.1
Barrow County	49.9	61.8	38.6	50.7	46.5	32.3	44.7	43.8	12 293	49.2	26.1	16.3	0.9	5.2	78.0	11.7	10.0	0.3
Bartow County	47.3	59.9	35.3	48.1	39.7	73.8	48.5	38.2	20 034	46.5	24.3	18.0	-0.1	2.5	76.8	13.5	9.5	0.2
Ben Hill County	38.5	49.6	28.7	40.8	32.9	33.3	31.0	40.8	4 460	35.7	14.8	29.6	0.7	-3.0	73.7	17.4	8.7	0.3
Berrien County	44.5	57.5	32.4	45.3	37.4	43.5	35.6	44.6	4 061	43.0	19.3	25.9	4.3	-1.8	74.5	14.7	10.4	0.4
Bibb County	38.6	48.1	30.9	42.7	33.2	42.3	39.8	46.8	37 655	33.6	13.1	34.7	3.7	-0.8	74.9	17.2	7.7	0.2
Bleckley County	39.4	48.3	31.5	42.3	31.8	X	19.1	9.1	2 774	41.0	16.0	24.4	0.8	-2.8	62.5	25.0	12.3	0.2
Brantley County	41.2	51.6	30.9	41.6	25.7	0.0	15.6	52.7	3 832	38.5	26.5	18.8	-7.3	-9.1	73.1	16.9	9.5	0.4
Brooks County	37.0	46.6	28.7	42.4	27.5	46.7	58.5	37.0	4 160	37.1	14.0	34.0	7.4	-0.6	72.2	17.5	9.4	0.9
Bryan County	46.5	59.0	34.8	48.5	36.8	64.2	41.7	32.6	6 958	48.4	21.1	20.7	4.5	7.3	74.3	17.0	8.7	0.0
Bulloch County	32.7	41.5	24.6	34.9	27.5	42.9	32.5	28.3	11 586	40.7	21.5	25.8	1.9	0.4	66.5	24.0	9.2	0.4
Burke County	31.2	41.2	26.0	20.5	29.0	0.0	0.0	47.8	6 166	29.7	13.5	33.3	-1.6	-3.5	71.5	20.9	7.3	0.3
Butts County	42.0	45.4	38.0	45.3	34.7	26.3	16.7	30.2	4 382	42.7	17.9	22.5	0.6	-2.1	77.0	14.8	7.8	0.4
Calhoun County	31.3	30.8	32.0	35.9	27.7	X	0.0	59.1	1 221	29.2	10.6	33.2	-2.2	2.2	64.7	24.6	10.4	0.3
Camden County	50.9	64.9	35.8	53.5	43.4	58.7	38.4	43.7	13 145	45.8	27.3	17.3	-1.5	4.1	66.3	26.4	7.1	0.1
Candler County	36.3	47.4	26.0	40.5	28.7	39.1	X	27.9	2 331	34.9	13.6	25.0	-4.7	-7.9	72.6	13.3	13.7	0.3
Carroll County	42.1	53.5	31.8	44.0	33.9	53.3	31.3	35.3	20 765	43.9	22.8	20.4	-0.3	0.8	75.4	14.6	9.7	0.3
Catoosa County	48.0	58.9	38.0	48.1	55.4	31.4	42.8	58.3	13 087	49.2	22.1	20.5	5.1	5.2	79.5	12.2	8.0	0.3
Charlton County	38.5	47.1	28.8	42.0	30.0	42.1	80.4	20.0	2 510	35.7	21.8	22.5	-6.4	-9.6	68.1	22.5	9.1	0.4
Chatham County	40.0	48.2	32.6	43.1	35.4	29.1	35.1	40.3	53 329	37.5	15.1	31.3	4.2	-0.5	74.8	15.4	9.6	0.2
Chattahoochee County	49.6	58.5	30.2	51.6	48.7	63.0	39.1	39.8	4 131	38.6	37.5	13.4	-12.6	-5.4	66.9	26.9	5.7	0.5
Chattooga County	39.6	45.2	33.7	41.5	24.8	0.0	12.0	51.0	5 457	46.8	14.4	24.8	7.0	-1.6	76.9	13.7	8.6	0.8
Cherokee County	51.7	65.3	38.2	52.3	48.7	57.0	51.3	44.9	38 299	47.7	30.9	14.8	-2.1	7.5	78.2	10.3	11.3	0.2
Clarke County	29.7	36.0	23.8	27.6	35.8	30.2	21.1	34.9	16 844	35.7	16.1	32.6	3.7	2.0	64.5	28.7	6.6	0.2
Clay County	30.9	38.1	25.2	39.1	24.5	85.7	83.3	0.0	695	25.6	6.8	49.8	10.8	-9.1	56.0	30.4	13.6	0.0
Clayton County	48.8	55.9	42.4	47.3	52.6	44.0	41.6	38.0	65 473	38.3	13.9	32.6	6.3	5.3	77.5	16.1	6.2	0.2
Clinch County	38.3	50.1	27.4	39.9	34.6	32.7	22.7	16.7	1 685	32.8	20.5	26.6	-5.2	-9.0	76.2	15.7	8.1	0.0
Cobb County	51.2	62.0	41.0	51.5	54.5	52.2	46.3	43.3	150 396	45.3	28.3	18.4	-0.9	6.2	80.7	9.9	9.3	0.2
Coffee County	40.5	49.2	32.1	42.4	34.6	45.5	57.7	41.6	9 636	38.6	20.5	23.0	-3.0	-2.5	75.4	13.2	11.1	0.2
Colquitt County	39.5	49.5	29.9	43.4	29.6	32.8	3.4	35.6	10 306	37.9	21.6	25.7	-1.0	-5.1	70.9	16.3	12.4	0.4
Columbia County	48.2	63.4	34.2	49.4	43.3	49.0	41.0	41.7	25 542	49.5	28.7	15.0	-0.1	5.7	68.3	21.6	9.9	0.2
Cook County	39.7	52.8	28.0	41.3	35.5	33.3	21.4	36.4	4 114	35.1	18.4	28.2	-1.3	-3.3	75.5	15.6	8.9	0.2
Coweta County	48.9	61.7	36.7	51.5	39.9	51.1	44.9	36.8	24 236	48.8	22.1	20.0	4.2	6.6	78.8	12.7	8.2	0.0
Crawford County	44.7	53.5	35.9	47.8	36.5	0.0	100.0	30.4	3 152	41.1	23.6	19.7	-3.8	-3.7	73.4	17.0	9.4	0.2
Crisp County	37.6	46.3	30.1	44.0	29.4	0.0	24.8	15.0	5 885	31.1	13.9	29.9	-3.6	0.8	67.6	21.0	11.0	0.3
Dade County	38.2	51.8	25.8	38.8	9.9	21.1	30.6	32.8	3 434	46.4	26.3	17.1	-1.1	-3.4	76.0	12.4	11.1	0.5
Dawson County	47.5	58.3	36.6	47.5	100.0	45.1	50.0	32.8	3 778	46.6	25.7	19.5	1.5	2.1	72.4	11.6	15.2	0.7
Decatur County	38.7	47.1	31.4	41.9	33.5	51.4	39.6	36.7	7 402	32.7	17.0	32.0	0.1	-3.9	69.7	19.4	10.4	0.4
DeKalb County	46.3	52.2	40.9	47.5	47.6	45.2	38.6	37.9	148 639	38.9	14.8	31.5	5.8	6.4	77.1	14.5	8.2	0.2
Dodge County	38.0	41.6	34.3	41.0	30.9	61.5	20.5	25.1	4 436	44.9	11.2	31.0	11.3	3.5	62.8	25.8	11.2	0.2
Dooly County	35.0	37.8	31.9	40.4	29.2	20.0	7.3	55.3	2 735	37.1	14.7	28.0	0.5	-0.9	69.1	19.3	10.9	0.6
Dougherty County	36.0	43.3	29.9	41.6	31.7	15.1	31.5	53.7	23 475	30.9	11.6	36.2	2.5	-1.3	69.2	21.8	8.5	0.5
Douglas County	50.0	60.6	39.9	50.0	50.0	50.8	54.0	46.0	24 071	47.6	21.7	20.0	3.0	5.3	77.7	12.8	9.2	0.3
Early County	37.4	47.5	29.4	42.4	31.4	X	0.0	26.7	3 218	32.4	9.7	38.6	6.4	1.8	69.6	18.3	11.6	0.5
Echols County	41.1	49.6	32.0	43.4	38.0	X	0.0	34.9	1 027	33.8	18.0	29.5	-1.3	-4.8	80.6	12.6	6.8	0.0
Effingham County	47.2	61.4	33.5	49.6	33.8	27.3	46.0	32.6	10 691	42.3	27.3	16.3	-6.0	0.6	75.1	15.8	9.0	0.1
Elbert County	38.3	48.0	29.7	40.3	33.1	0.0	49.1	47.4	4 861	39.6	17.9	25.1	0.1	-2.6	70.7	17.1	11.7	0.5
Emanuel County	35.1	44.5	26.6	37.8	30.4	42.7	25.0	25.4	5 426	37.3	18.5	25.9	-1.4	-0.4	67.3	21.0	11.5	0.1
Evans County	38.4	47.3	30.4	40.9	32.5	75.9	46.8	40.5	2 605	36.5	16.9	29.8	1.7	-2.4	68.4	18.1	13.4	0.1

[1] Hispanic or Latino persons may be of any race.

Table B-3. States and Counties — Education, Labor Force, and Income

STATE County	Percent who worked at home	Percent of the population 5 years and over with a disability	Veterans as a percent of the population 18 years and over	Occupation for employed population 16 years and over (percent)						Industry for employed population 16 years and over (percent)					
				Management, professional, and related occupations	Service occupations	Sales and office occupations	Farming, fishing, and forestry occupations	Construction, extraction, and maintenance occupations	Production, transportation and material moving occupations	Agriculture, forestry, fishing, and mining	Construction and manufacturing	Wholesale and retail trade	Transportation and warehousing, and utilities	Service industries	Public administration
	42	43	44	45	46	47	48	49	50	51	52	53	54	55	56
FLORIDA—Cont'd															
Sarasota County	4.7	22.2	19.7	31.7	19.1	29.7	0.3	10.2	8.9	0.5	15.5	18.6	3.0	59.0	3.5
Seminole County	3.8	17.2	14.5	38.7	12.9	31.6	0.2	8.6	8.1	0.3	16.0	18.0	4.4	57.5	3.8
Sumter County	3.1	27.9	21.7	21.2	20.3	27.1	2.0	14.4	14.9	4.6	16.2	17.2	7.5	46.5	7.9
Suwannee County	3.4	28.2	17.7	24.3	18.6	21.7	4.4	15.0	16.0	8.5	20.0	16.0	5.8	40.2	9.5
Taylor County	1.9	27.0	17.5	20.0	19.8	20.7	4.0	14.6	21.0	7.0	29.1	12.5	4.5	37.7	9.3
Union County	2.3	22.5	17.2	19.4	31.0	20.8	2.4	13.2	13.2	4.0	15.5	9.9	7.1	36.2	27.4
Volusia County	2.9	23.6	18.8	28.8	18.1	28.7	0.8	11.8	11.8	1.1	17.5	16.8	4.4	55.2	4.9
Wakulla County	3.5	19.9	16.1	28.6	15.7	28.6	2.0	13.9	11.2	2.0	16.9	13.1	4.6	44.0	19.3
Walton County	3.6	27.6	20.0	24.7	21.9	25.1	1.5	15.6	11.2	2.7	20.1	15.9	3.9	49.5	7.9
Washington County	2.6	26.8	17.3	25.6	17.5	24.0	1.7	16.6	14.5	3.4	25.0	13.0	4.7	42.5	11.4
GEORGIA	2.8	19.7	12.8	32.7	13.4	26.8	0.6	10.8	15.7	1.4	22.7	15.8	6.0	49.0	5.0
Appling County	1.5	23.4	10.8	21.1	10.9	22.7	3.9	16.6	24.7	7.3	30.2	13.6	9.3	34.6	5.0
Atkinson County	2.5	20.5	9.6	18.6	9.9	17.0	6.7	13.8	34.0	13.2	39.5	15.3	3.7	24.3	4.1
Bacon County	2.5	24.7	11.6	20.6	13.8	22.3	4.8	13.6	24.7	9.6	29.6	13.5	8.9	33.0	5.4
Baker County	1.9	24.9	11.6	26.5	16.8	18.9	6.5	6.2	25.1	16.8	21.0	14.9	6.2	31.5	9.5
Baldwin County	1.9	21.1	13.1	28.1	21.4	22.7	0.5	10.2	17.1	2.0	21.2	11.7	4.5	52.2	8.4
Banks County	3.6	22.7	10.8	21.1	12.3	22.7	1.7	16.7	25.5	4.5	35.8	17.3	4.2	32.3	6.0
Barrow County	2.4	19.4	12.3	22.5	11.3	28.1	0.4	16.3	21.4	0.8	32.6	18.8	6.1	37.6	4.1
Bartow County	2.3	18.5	13.4	24.8	12.7	25.6	0.4	15.3	21.3	1.1	34.9	16.2	5.6	38.0	4.2
Ben Hill County	1.2	25.1	11.5	23.0	11.6	19.5	1.4	12.4	32.0	4.3	38.4	12.7	5.9	33.5	5.2
Berrien County	2.9	25.0	13.7	22.2	13.0	24.4	2.2	12.6	25.6	5.1	29.3	19.8	4.7	36.7	4.5
Bibb County	1.9	22.8	13.4	32.3	16.0	28.7	0.2	8.8	14.0	0.8	17.0	15.9	4.8	54.6	7.0
Bleckley County	3.0	22.8	13.6	23.5	16.7	18.7	1.9	12.8	26.5	5.6	29.5	8.1	3.8	40.8	12.2
Brantley County	2.5	30.8	14.4	19.9	17.5	23.2	1.9	19.7	17.8	4.4	25.0	16.6	7.2	40.4	6.4
Brooks County	2.5	25.2	12.6	24.1	16.1	22.7	2.7	13.0	21.3	6.3	26.3	18.0	4.4	39.0	6.0
Bryan County	2.6	17.1	15.6	30.2	13.5	26.6	0.6	13.3	15.7	0.8	24.0	18.1	8.0	43.5	5.7
Bulloch County	2.2	17.4	10.3	31.5	17.2	24.1	0.8	11.0	15.4	1.9	20.7	16.8	3.3	52.4	4.9
Burke County	1.2	29.4	12.8	21.4	15.7	20.3	1.7	11.4	29.5	3.7	31.0	14.2	8.2	36.8	6.1
Butts County	2.3	22.8	13.6	17.7	13.8	26.2	0.3	15.0	27.1	0.7	32.1	15.8	10.0	34.8	6.6
Calhoun County	1.6	28.0	9.9	22.6	15.9	21.4	4.5	9.0	26.6	9.7	25.8	14.4	5.3	34.7	10.0
Camden County	1.4	18.1	17.5	27.9	19.6	24.6	0.3	13.5	14.1	0.6	21.2	12.8	4.2	49.3	12.0
Candler County	2.8	24.3	12.9	21.5	13.7	21.5	4.9	15.2	23.2	6.6	30.5	13.4	5.6	40.1	3.8
Carroll County	2.3	20.6	11.6	26.6	14.1	25.3	0.3	14.1	19.8	0.8	30.5	16.9	6.4	41.9	3.6
Catoosa County	1.4	20.5	13.2	25.0	12.0	30.0	0.1	11.5	21.4	0.5	29.0	17.4	7.0	42.5	3.4
Charlton County	2.3	23.1	13.5	14.5	19.2	20.0	2.6	15.5	28.2	5.0	26.5	12.1	7.3	39.0	10.1
Chatham County	2.5	22.0	15.6	32.3	16.8	27.2	0.2	10.5	13.0	0.3	18.4	15.8	6.0	54.5	4.9
Chattahoochee County	5.4	14.2	7.9	26.6	15.7	28.3	1.3	11.6	16.5	1.6	17.5	17.1	3.6	51.2	9.1
Chattooga County	2.2	25.1	12.2	17.9	11.9	18.5	1.0	11.9	38.8	1.7	50.2	12.0	3.5	27.9	4.7
Cherokee County	4.9	14.3	12.6	36.4	11.2	29.2	0.3	12.7	10.1	0.8	22.5	19.4	4.3	50.0	3.1
Clarke County	2.3	16.1	7.8	36.9	17.8	24.7	0.7	5.3	14.5	1.1	16.2	15.0	2.4	61.7	3.7
Clay County	3.3	28.3	12.8	23.8	16.7	24.2	5.3	11.3	18.8	9.5	24.6	17.8	6.4	33.1	8.6
Clayton County	1.5	18.3	14.5	24.1	15.4	30.6	0.1	11.7	18.0	0.2	17.2	14.9	14.9	46.7	6.0
Clinch County	0.2	26.8	12.0	20.7	13.1	19.5	5.8	10.2	30.8	8.0	31.0	15.5	7.6	32.9	5.0
Cobb County	4.1	14.8	12.4	42.4	10.6	30.0	0.1	8.7	8.1	0.2	17.6	17.8	5.6	55.5	3.2
Coffee County	1.6	23.1	10.3	20.2	11.2	24.2	2.8	12.5	29.1	5.4	35.6	20.0	5.0	29.6	4.4
Colquitt County	1.8	25.5	11.5	23.9	11.6	21.9	5.9	13.5	23.1	9.5	28.7	16.0	4.9	36.6	4.3
Columbia County	2.2	15.6	18.0	41.5	11.6	25.2	0.3	10.1	11.3	0.8	20.0	14.1	7.6	52.7	4.9
Cook County	2.5	23.4	12.9	23.0	13.5	23.4	2.0	11.7	26.5	4.7	34.0	16.1	5.0	35.9	4.3
Coweta County	2.9	16.5	14.3	29.6	13.3	26.9	0.1	13.5	16.6	0.5	25.4	15.1	13.7	40.7	4.6
Crawford County	1.4	19.4	12.6	21.1	12.1	24.8	1.2	19.0	21.8	3.4	32.3	16.8	5.3	34.5	7.7
Crisp County	2.5	26.9	11.4	25.2	16.7	26.0	1.6	10.6	19.9	3.7	23.8	17.4	5.0	43.1	7.0
Dade County	3.8	21.3	13.0	22.1	14.4	24.3	0.6	14.4	24.3	1.1	32.4	12.0	7.5	44.3	2.7
Dawson County	4.2	20.5	13.3	30.0	10.6	26.9	0.6	13.4	18.4	3.2	29.7	18.3	3.8	42.0	3.0
Decatur County	2.8	23.9	11.6	26.3	15.9	22.2	2.8	10.9	22.0	6.1	28.2	16.9	3.4	40.2	5.2
DeKalb County	3.0	17.3	10.5	39.6	13.1	28.0	0.1	8.3	10.9	0.2	14.4	13.4	6.1	60.3	5.7
Dodge County	1.6	27.1	12.2	24.4	16.5	21.8	1.3	11.7	24.3	4.6	28.6	11.8	5.9	36.3	12.8
Dooly County	1.1	25.4	11.5	23.8	15.4	20.5	3.5	13.8	22.9	9.8	29.1	13.3	4.4	36.5	6.8
Dougherty County	1.5	24.1	13.7	29.7	17.2	25.9	0.4	9.6	17.1	1.0	20.9	15.4	4.1	50.5	8.1
Douglas County	2.4	18.4	14.4	29.5	11.4	30.8	0.2	13.4	14.7	0.3	20.7	20.2	9.4	44.9	4.6
Early County	2.6	27.1	10.4	23.2	16.1	22.0	2.8	8.3	27.6	7.8	27.8	15.3	4.7	39.5	4.9
Echols County	0.5	22.4	9.7	14.7	9.5	22.6	20.1	16.3	16.8	23.2	24.4	20.4	3.0	25.1	3.9
Effingham County	1.3	18.0	16.5	25.5	13.5	24.4	0.6	17.6	18.3	1.3	32.9	14.9	8.0	37.8	5.2
Elbert County	2.4	24.9	12.1	20.4	11.5	23.4	1.1	11.3	32.3	3.7	37.0	16.8	4.0	33.6	5.0
Emanuel County	2.4	24.8	9.6	20.6	16.8	22.2	2.5	13.1	24.7	5.1	32.4	14.6	5.3	35.9	6.7
Evans County	1.5	23.7	11.1	19.6	17.7	19.9	4.0	13.7	25.1	5.5	31.4	14.5	4.5	37.3	6.8

Table B-3. States and Counties — Education, Labor Force, and Income

STATE County	Median house-hold income	Median family income — All families	Married-couple	Male house-holder	Female house-holder	Median nonfamily house-hold income	Men	Women	Per capita income	With earnings	With interest, dividend, or rental income	With Social Security income	With public assis-tance income	With retire-ment income	House-holds with income over $100,000 (percent)	+/− U.S. percent for income over $100,000 (percent)	House-holds with income below poverty (percent)	Families with children with income below poverty (percent)
	57	58	59	60	61	62	63	64	65	66	67	68	69	70	71	72	73	74
FLORIDA—Cont'd																		
Sarasota County	41 957	50 111	58 083	29 289	22 745	27 855	34 359	26 811	28 326	62.8	52.0	47.6	1.5	29.6	12.7	0.4	7.1	10.3
Seminole County	49 326	56 895	68 100	31 875	25 942	31 445	41 140	29 382	24 591	85.9	36.8	22.5	1.9	15.5	15.9	3.6	7.1	7.4
Sumter County	32 073	36 999	40 830	25 742	15 713	17 932	28 178	21 768	16 830	56.3	40.2	54.2	2.9	37.1	4.2	-8.1	12.5	21.3
Suwannee County	29 963	34 032	39 162	25 368	17 542	15 656	27 084	21 698	14 678	70.3	24.1	36.5	4.1	22.2	3.9	-8.4	18.6	20.4
Taylor County	30 032	35 061	40 711	26 250	13 176	13 887	30 407	20 028	15 281	71.9	22.2	33.0	6.8	17.0	5.0	-7.3	19.1	18.5
Union County	34 563	37 516	48 072	24 336	20 337	16 486	29 138	22 430	12 333	78.8	15.9	22.8	4.8	16.3	3.6	-8.7	15.2	13.0
Volusia County	35 219	41 767	51 519	25 771	18 891	22 095	31 487	23 567	19 664	69.2	38.3	39.9	2.1	25.7	7.1	-5.2	11.0	14.0
Wakulla County	37 149	42 222	50 949	27 007	20 313	23 514	30 388	22 031	17 678	82.9	26.4	25.8	2.7	15.9	6.6	-5.7	12.0	13.8
Walton County	32 407	37 663	40 878	20 909	14 462	20 895	27 689	22 031	18 198	74.3	27.7	33.6	3.3	22.2	6.4	-5.9	14.1	18.9
Washington County	27 922	33 057	40 291	19 732	13 288	15 816	27 296	20 729	14 980	71.7	22.5	37.4	4.6	20.2	5.0	-7.3	19.6	22.5
GEORGIA	42 433	49 280	59 178	29 371	20 011	26 509	36 710	27 336	21 154	83.8	28.8	21.9	2.9	14.4	12.3	0.0	12.6	13.9
Appling County	30 266	34 890	40 675	18 571	15 227	14 430	28 671	18 544	15 044	76.9	17.9	29.0	3.6	14.1	5.4	-6.9	19.6	21.1
Atkinson County	26 470	32 688	37 672	26 667	14 375	11 375	25 164	18 692	12 178	75.9	13.6	25.0	3.6	9.4	3.4	-8.9	23.7	21.7
Bacon County	26 910	32 579	45 120	31 848	13 073	13 030	27 910	20 104	14 289	75.9	14.7	27.3	2.7	10.9	4.7	-7.6	23.6	25.5
Baker County	30 338	36 438	38 333	15 250	11 500	16 818	26 250	17 306	16 969	75.1	16.0	31.6	5.8	12.6	5.2	-7.1	22.1	28.2
Baldwin County	35 159	42 736	53 450	27 566	18 011	20 574	31 774	23 481	16 271	79.5	24.4	24.4	3.1	18.8	7.5	-4.8	16.8	16.9
Banks County	38 523	43 136	44 325	24 500	17 500	19 648	30 476	21 882	17 424	81.7	24.6	26.7	1.7	14.2	6.5	-5.8	13.2	12.7
Barrow County	45 019	49 722	54 597	32 288	22 145	26 291	35 291	24 337	18 350	85.8	24.2	22.6	2.0	13.6	7.5	-4.8	8.9	8.0
Bartow County	43 660	49 198	53 246	29 872	20 761	24 994	35 807	25 438	18 989	84.0	25.2	22.7	2.2	14.9	8.1	-4.2	9.0	8.3
Ben Hill County	27 100	33 023	46 667	24 259	11 649	14 876	27 165	20 168	14 093	77.5	18.2	28.5	4.6	11.8	5.0	-7.3	20.3	28.6
Berrien County	30 044	34 643	41 808	21 583	14 710	18 933	26 281	20 356	16 375	78.0	20.4	28.4	4.2	15.6	4.0	-8.3	17.0	21.0
Bibb County	34 532	43 479	60 614	28 974	15 110	20 274	35 699	26 203	19 058	77.1	26.3	26.9	4.7	17.9	8.8	-3.5	18.5	23.4
Bleckley County	33 448	41 095	50 938	27 679	20 500	17 386	32 965	23 649	15 934	76.1	23.1	28.4	5.4	20.2	5.9	-6.4	15.4	19.1
Brantley County	30 361	35 534	38 731	26 667	14 674	14 008	29 911	20 975	13 713	77.4	19.6	31.1	3.2	13.0	2.4	-9.9	15.8	17.1
Brooks County	26 911	32 382	42 615	21 364	13 646	14 600	26 672	20 182	13 977	70.4	19.6	30.2	5.1	14.0	3.7	-8.6	22.9	27.6
Bryan County	48 345	53 680	63 180	38 015	16 481	22 727	40 872	26 485	19 794	83.7	27.8	19.8	1.8	16.5	12.6	0.3	12.4	13.9
Bulloch County	29 499	42 199	51 426	29 196	15 729	14 215	31 357	23 443	16 080	82.2	24.1	21.9	2.8	13.4	6.9	-5.4	25.2	16.9
Burke County	27 877	31 660	42 449	19 097	12 405	12 155	30 590	19 007	10 100	76.1	17.1	27.0	5.7	16.0	4.4	-7.9	27.8	29.8
Butts County	39 979	44 937	52 119	29 667	20 147	24 375	34 490	22 211	17 016	80.5	20.3	27.3	3.6	17.3	7.2	-5.1	12.5	10.5
Calhoun County	24 588	31 019	41 250	18 750	11 036	13 000	26 053	17 044	11 839	73.3	16.4	30.5	6.2	12.9	2.9	-9.4	27.5	**33.7**
Camden County	41 056	45 005	48 316	25 147	17 167	24 794	32 482	22 610	16 445	88.2	24.9	15.7	3.1	14.8	5.5	-6.8	10.9	10.8
Candler County	25 022	30 705	38 194	12 470	12 788	12 622	24 639	19 350	12 958	76.5	19.0	30.4	6.4	13.9	3.6	-8.7	24.0	31.7
Carroll County	38 799	44 642	51 406	32 424	17 939	19 164	34 507	23 439	17 656	81.1	24.5	24.9	3.3	14.4	7.4	-4.9	14.6	13.5
Catoosa County	39 998	45 710	51 899	27 101	19 515	18 357	32 423	24 684	18 009	83.1	27.2	25.6	2.2	14.2	6.1	-6.2	10.3	9.9
Charlton County	27 869	33 364	42 572	21 466	12 215	13 224	26 890	18 484	12 920	75.9	18.3	30.4	3.6	14.3	4.2	-8.1	21.5	24.9
Chatham County	37 752	46 125	57 237	30 336	16 954	22 551	36 198	25 507	21 152	79.0	28.4	27.6	3.2	17.8	10.4	-1.9	15.1	18.5
Chattahoochee County	37 106	38 313	42 174	27 083	17 454	20 000	22 377	20 869	14 049	91.6	22.2	8.9	2.6	8.3	3.6	-8.7	11.0	9.7
Chattooga County	30 664	36 230	45 277	24 609	19 055	17 368	26 765	21 379	14 508	74.9	22.1	32.1	2.4	16.0	3.5	-8.8	14.6	15.4
Cherokee County	60 896	66 419	71 903	36 591	32 061	36 674	46 279	31 800	24 871	90.1	37.5	16.7	1.0	13.1	19.9	7.6	5.4	4.2
Clarke County	28 403	41 607	54 500	26 994	15 161	17 310	31 301	23 680	17 123	85.1	31.4	17.1	2.7	10.7	8.2	-4.1	27.5	21.8
Clay County	21 448	27 037	52 115	20 000	11 010	10 515	28 548	17 679	16 819	66.1	19.9	40.0	5.3	15.1	4.2	-8.1	32.8	42.5
Clayton County	42 697	46 782	55 222	30 591	25 244	30 699	32 924	27 480	18 079	90.4	18.8	15.3	2.9	13.4	7.3	-5.0	8.9	10.9
Clinch County	26 755	31 755	41 083	17 188	14 136	12 792	27 768	19 713	13 023	74.1	13.1	32.4	7.2	9.1	4.1	-8.2	26.1	23.7
Cobb County	58 289	67 649	78 277	35 818	30 392	39 145	46 702	34 685	27 863	90.7	38.2	14.8	1.2	12.3	21.3	9.0	5.9	6.1
Coffee County	30 710	35 936	41 611	23 924	16 058	17 293	27 255	21 040	15 530	80.6	18.9	24.7	2.7	11.7	5.5	-6.8	19.6	20.6
Colquitt County	28 539	34 792	43 740	26 680	14 132	14 286	27 310	20 811	14 457	76.0	23.9	29.5	5.9	13.4	4.5	-7.8	20.1	21.8
Columbia County	55 682	61 232	67 217	33 750	25 091	30 540	46 686	29 085	23 496	87.3	39.4	18.2	2.0	18.8	16.1	3.8	5.4	5.2
Cook County	27 582	31 820	40 238	30 583	15 253	16 964	26 644	20 613	13 465	77.5	17.2	31.2	5.9	11.3	3.5	-8.8	21.1	23.1
Coweta County	52 706	58 750	66 782	35 000	23 063	30 123	42 228	28 241	21 949	87.3	30.3	20.0	2.2	15.2	14.1	1.8	8.2	8.1
Crawford County	37 848	41 799	45 417	29 453	20 208	10 668	31 491	21 848	15 768	78.3	17.5	20.8	2.7	13.6	5.6	-6.7	16.7	13.6
Crisp County	26 547	32 747	45 110	19 712	11 018	12 523	29 698	20 374	14 695	75.8	20.6	28.2	7.7	13.0	5.5	-6.8	28.3	35.4
Dade County	35 259	39 481	46 691	28 047	20 032	16 114	31 933	21 981	16 127	76.0	22.8	29.5	1.3	16.6	4.1	-8.2	11.6	8.4
Dawson County	47 486	52 320	55 550	26 250	23 092	29 591	38 809	26 847	22 520	86.1	32.5	22.4	1.0	13.9	11.6	-0.7	7.8	8.1
Decatur County	28 820	32 635	45 064	21 686	12 378	15 779	28 067	21 284	15 063	76.4	19.3	30.7	5.7	16.9	5.3	-7.0	21.0	28.4
DeKalb County	49 117	54 018	65 744	32 172	27 959	37 532	37 057	32 336	23 968	89.1	31.8	17.0	2.2	12.3	15.5	3.2	9.1	11.1
Dodge County	27 607	34 718	44 732	21 295	18 443	13 765	27 839	21 175	14 468	73.6	18.9	30.8	3.1	18.6	4.4	-7.9	19.1	17.9
Dooly County	27 980	35 337	45 250	14 659	16 157	15 000	27 245	19 495	13 628	75.6	20.4	27.7	5.6	14.3	4.5	-7.8	22.3	23.4
Dougherty County	30 934	36 655	52 067	23 260	13 892	18 990	31 651	23 166	16 645	76.1	23.1	26.9	6.5	16.7	7.4	-4.9	22.2	28.5
Douglas County	50 108	54 082	61 432	35 994	26 132	32 782	39 610	29 240	21 172	88.8	26.6	18.5	2.0	13.7	11.7	0.6	7.4	8.0
Early County	25 629	31 215	40 991	26 111	11 292	13 145	27 046	18 104	14 936	70.9	18.8	35.7	5.1	15.4	5.9	-6.4	26.1	32.0
Echols County	25 851	27 700	30 288	23 750	17 500	15 089	25 102	17 679	15 727	76.9	14.9	30.1	2.1	9.5	5.3	-7.0	23.7	29.7
Effingham County	46 505	50 351	56 910	42 900	20 750	25 492	40 412	25 219	18 873	85.5	27.0	22.2	2.4	16.8	8.8	-3.5	9.3	8.6
Elbert County	28 724	34 276	41 906	22 596	15 192	14 616	27 933	20 150	14 535	75.5	21.2	32.7	3.4	14.0	3.8	-8.5	18.2	20.3
Emanuel County	24 383	31 113	40 060	21 676	11 185	12 087	27 202	19 157	13 627	69.8	15.7	29.6	6.0	13.9	4.4	-7.9	25.7	31.2
Evans County	25 447	31 074	37 109	20 139	10 875	12 352	27 407	18 125	12 758	77.0	15.5	27.8	6.0	14.4	2.9	-9.4	27.0	33.9

STATE/ County code	MSA/PMSA/ NECMA code[1]	STATE County	High school graduates			College graduates		College graduates (percent)				
			Total population 25 years and over	Percent with a high school diploma or less	Percent with a high school diploma or more	Percent with a bachelor's degree or more	+/− U.S. percent with bachelor's degree or more	Non-Hispanic White	Black or African American	American Indian and Alaska Native	Asian, Hawaiian, and Pacific Islander	Hispanic or Latino[2]
			1	2	3	4	5	6	7	8	9	10
		GEORGIA—Cont'd										
13 111	...	Fannin County	14 291	68.0	70.9	10.4	−14.0	10.4	66.7	14.3	20.5	8.0
13 113	0520	Fayette County	59 016	31.6	92.4	36.2	11.8	35.5	42.5	25.5	46.0	26.5
13 115	...	Floyd County	58 651	61.8	71.5	15.8	−8.6	17.8	4.5	17.2	28.6	5.7
13 117	0520	Forsyth County	65 027	37.8	85.7	34.6	10.2	35.0	25.3	27.9	64.0	18.1
13 119	...	Franklin County	13 448	70.4	67.0	10.3	−14.1	11.2	0.8	0.0	37.5	0.0
13 121	0520	Fulton County	527 738	35.4	84.0	41.4	17.0	60.6	18.3	28.1	60.3	20.1
13 123	...	Gilmer County	15 718	67.3	66.0	12.9	−11.5	13.2	0.0	0.0	16.9	7.6
13 125	...	Glascock County	1 764	74.2	66.1	6.5	−17.9	7.2	0.0	0.0	X	0.0
13 127	...	Glynn County	44 806	47.0	82.2	23.8	−0.6	28.5	8.2	25.6	21.0	20.6
13 129	...	Gordon County	28 490	68.2	65.9	10.6	−13.8	11.1	3.5	12.3	30.1	4.5
13 131	...	Grady County	14 988	70.3	69.4	10.6	−13.8	13.3	3.7	16.9	84.6	6.0
13 133	...	Greene County	9 508	63.2	70.1	17.6	−6.8	26.8	3.0	0.0	27.7	6.0
13 135	0520	Gwinnett County	372 628	34.7	87.3	34.1	9.7	36.2	31.4	17.1	42.2	14.7
13 137	...	Habersham County	23 501	62.9	70.9	15.8	−8.6	16.8	11.7	23.7	9.0	3.7
13 139	...	Hall County	86 821	59.1	70.5	18.7	−5.7	22.3	11.1	3.8	14.8	3.3
13 141	...	Hancock County	6 618	72.2	62.2	9.8	−14.6	12.1	8.6	38.1	X	0.0
13 143	...	Haralson County	16 814	73.1	63.0	9.0	−15.4	9.3	3.9	0.0	0.0	25.0
13 145	1800	Harris County	16 231	50.5	79.0	21.1	−3.3	24.5	6.1	0.0	37.8	50.0
13 147	...	Hart County	15 838	65.8	71.1	13.5	−10.9	15.6	2.8	31.8	30.9	28.1
13 149	...	Heard County	7 020	75.7	66.0	7.3	−17.1	7.8	3.2	0.0	12.8	2.9
13 151	0520	Henry County	75 501	50.1	84.2	19.5	−4.9	18.0	24.5	22.2	42.9	26.3
13 153	4680	Houston County	69 038	48.1	84.3	19.8	−4.6	21.2	13.9	9.6	31.1	17.6
13 155	...	Irwin County	6 196	70.8	67.7	9.9	−14.5	10.8	5.8	0.0	71.4	15.6
13 157	...	Jackson County	26 849	67.5	68.1	11.7	−12.7	12.4	5.3	14.6	18.3	4.8
13 159	...	Jasper County	7 531	67.4	69.7	11.5	−12.9	13.4	6.0	0.0	16.3	17.7
13 161	...	Jeff Davis County	8 036	72.1	63.3	9.4	−15.0	9.7	4.9	0.0	69.4	1.6
13 163	...	Jefferson County	10 799	75.4	58.5	9.1	−15.3	13.8	4.9	0.0	0.0	10.7
13 165	...	Jenkins County	5 335	70.8	62.0	10.8	−13.6	15.2	2.5	0.0	100.0	0.0
13 167	...	Johnson County	5 206	77.0	62.4	7.8	−16.6	9.3	3.5	X	100.0	12.7
13 169	4680	Jones County	15 383	63.2	77.9	15.0	−9.4	15.1	14.1	0.0	35.1	37.6
13 171	...	Lamar County	10 227	65.7	71.3	11.3	−13.1	12.6	8.2	5.6	36.4	0.0
13 173	...	Lanier County	4 487	67.2	67.0	8.8	−15.6	10.4	4.2	14.0	0.0	0.0
13 175	...	Laurens County	28 875	66.8	70.3	14.4	−10.0	17.6	6.7	28.0	53.3	9.4
13 177	0120	Lee County	15 036	54.6	81.3	17.0	−7.4	18.1	9.2	38.1	56.4	9.8
13 179	...	Liberty County	30 797	47.5	86.8	14.5	−9.9	18.2	10.4	10.2	19.5	12.1
13 181	...	Lincoln County	5 701	65.3	71.0	10.1	−14.3	13.2	3.6	0.0	0.0	8.0
13 183	...	Long County	5 527	67.3	74.3	5.8	−18.6	6.5	4.1	16.7	12.9	3.6
13 185	...	Lowndes County	54 237	52.9	77.7	19.7	−4.7	24.2	10.3	12.4	16.9	17.3
13 187	...	Lumpkin County	12 665	58.4	72.0	17.6	−6.8	18.4	13.8	10.2	0.0	7.5
13 189	0600	McDuffie County	13 442	68.5	66.7	11.7	−12.7	15.2	4.3	36.1	35.7	2.1
13 191	...	McIntosh County	6 978	66.7	71.2	11.1	−13.3	13.9	5.8	0.0	25.0	0.0
13 193	...	Macon County	8 844	72.0	63.2	10.0	−14.4	14.0	6.8	10.3	33.3	9.2
13 195	0500	Madison County	16 881	70.0	70.8	10.9	−13.5	11.3	6.3	8.3	18.7	8.2
13 197	...	Marion County	4 437	70.7	65.4	8.9	−15.5	11.6	3.9	47.1	0.0	0.0
13 199	...	Meriwether County	14 434	69.9	65.8	10.8	−13.6	14.4	5.2	0.0	35.0	15.8
13 201	...	Miller County	4 281	66.9	69.0	11.3	−13.1	14.4	1.3	X	54.5	0.0
13 205	...	Mitchell County	14 972	70.1	65.3	9.1	−15.3	12.6	4.5	0.0	41.9	13.9
13 207	...	Monroe County	14 185	61.0	77.7	17.1	−7.3	20.9	6.4	39.4	71.2	0.0
13 209	...	Montgomery County	5 108	68.0	71.4	13.5	−10.9	16.2	5.4	X	48.8	0.0
13 211	...	Morgan County	10 125	63.1	74.0	18.7	−5.7	22.8	6.9	39.1	66.7	33.3
13 213	...	Murray County	22 803	74.3	61.1	7.2	−17.2	7.4	4.8	34.0	0.0	1.0
13 215	1800	Muscogee County	114 045	49.3	78.9	20.3	−4.1	26.4	12.0	21.4	33.7	15.8
13 217	0520	Newton County	39 144	60.0	74.7	14.5	−9.9	16.0	8.5	5.2	45.3	11.5
13 219	0500	Oconee County	16 470	36.7	86.7	39.8	15.4	42.0	12.0	9.8	63.1	17.7
13 221	...	Oglethorpe County	8 436	65.4	72.1	15.6	−8.8	19.0	1.4	9.1	0.0	19.1
13 223	0520	Paulding County	50 422	58.3	80.8	15.2	−9.2	14.3	24.4	13.9	27.9	26.2
13 225	4680	Peach County	14 055	59.8	73.4	16.8	−7.6	18.0	15.7	32.0	38.5	3.9
13 227	0520	Pickens County	15 868	62.9	70.2	15.6	−8.8	15.8	4.8	0.0	62.5	6.8
13 229	...	Pierce County	10 131	71.4	69.8	10.1	−14.3	10.5	4.0	0.0	X	22.2
13 231	...	Pike County	8 833	64.8	75.3	14.0	−10.4	15.5	6.2	25.0	0.0	4.8
13 233	...	Polk County	24 703	71.8	63.3	8.0	−16.4	8.3	8.4	0.0	0.0	1.5
13 235	...	Pulaski County	6 445	62.8	73.4	12.9	−11.5	16.0	5.4	0.0	86.4	8.6
13 237	...	Putnam County	12 931	65.1	75.5	14.4	−10.0	18.8	2.5	0.0	0.0	6.6
13 239	...	Quitman County	1 773	76.3	57.8	6.1	−18.3	9.0	2.1	0.0	X	0.0
13 241	...	Rabun County	10 675	59.6	75.4	17.6	−6.8	18.3	7.4	2.9	0.0	4.2
13 243	...	Randolph County	4 783	70.1	62.4	9.5	−14.9	15.7	4.2	X	X	21.9

[1]MSA = Metropolitan Statistical Area. PMSA = Primary MSA. NECMA = New England County Metropolitan Area. See the Appendix A for explanation of these concepts. See Appendix B for list of metropolitan areas identified by type, with component counties.
[2]Hispanic or Latino persons may be of any race.

Table B-3. States and Counties — Education, Labor Force, and Income

STATE County	School enrollment			Population 16 to 19 years				Employment status, 2000			Work status in 1999 of the population 16 years and over (percent)		
											Worked in 1999		
	Grades kindergarten through 12	College or graduate school	Percent private	Number	Percent in armed forces	Percent high school graduates	Percent not enrolled, not grads, not in armed forces, not employed	Total population 16 years and over	Percent in labor force	Unemployment rate	Full-time	Part-time	Did not work in 1999
	11	12	13	14	15	16	17	18	19	20	21	22	23
GEORGIA—Cont'd													
Fannin County	3 128	474	5.0	848	0.0	13.7	4.7	16 115	53.9	3.9	47.6	11.5	41.0
Fayette County	21 549	3 663	11.7	5 421	0.2	6.1	2.0	68 129	69.1	2.6	59.3	15.0	25.7
Floyd County	16 375	4 971	16.9	5 395	0.1	11.7	9.5	70 785	61.2	6.7	53.2	13.1	33.7
Forsyth County	17 633	2 978	11.0	3 849	0.0	7.3	4.3	73 145	72.3	2.1	63.6	13.6	22.8
Franklin County	3 659	1 013	15.1	1 120	0.0	11.3	5.1	15 930	59.0	4.2	52.4	11.9	35.6
Fulton County	145 409	55 078	20.7	44 610	0.2	7.9	8.0	637 017	67.7	8.9	60.3	12.4	27.2
Gilmer County	3 934	471	7.8	1 144	0.0	7.2	13.0	18 366	59.4	4.2	53.7	10.7	35.6
Glascock County	474	71	8.1	140	0.0	9.3	12.1	2 033	60.8	12.3	49.7	11.2	39.1
Glynn County	12 887	2 300	9.3	3 714	0.0	13.8	7.5	52 510	64.5	5.5	55.1	12.6	32.3
Gordon County	8 291	1 266	5.8	2 497	0.0	14.3	5.8	33 869	68.7	3.4	63.3	10.5	26.3
Grady County	4 966	764	6.3	1 473	0.0	12.5	9.0	17 995	60.6	7.4	53.2	10.9	35.9
Greene County	2 090	300	14.0	021	0.0	10.0	14.1	11 230	51.5	6.7	50.1	11.4	38.5
Gwinnett County	119 551	27 694	10.4	31 269	0.0	9.8	5.0	439 929	74.0	3.3	67.0	12.8	20.2
Habersham County	6 134	1 506	12.9	2 244	0.4	11.8	16.5	28 532	61.5	4.2	53.6	13.0	33.4
Hall County	26 158	4 668	7.7	8 005	0.0	8.5	12.8	105 772	65.5	3.8	59.8	11.8	28.3
Hancock County	2 155	330	8.2	587	0.0	11.6	8.9	7 905	43.1	13.7	38.7	9.0	52.2
Haralson County	4 784	635	5.1	1 523	0.0	10.2	7.6	19 803	59.3	4.1	52.9	10.2	36.9
Harris County	4 797	879	12.2	1 150	0.0	5.9	2.1	18 353	67.4	3.4	59.3	12.6	28.1
Hart County	3 969	613	6.2	1 096	0.3	12.9	7.8	18 128	60.7	5.3	52.8	11.4	35.8
Heard County	2 286	252	5.9	534	0.0	9.2	14.2	8 134	60.3	5.7	56.3	9.2	34.5
Henry County	25 449	4 652	11.7	6 124	0.0	11.9	4.6	88 036	71.7	2.7	65.6	11.2	23.1
Houston County	24 077	5 898	8.7	6 690	5.7	15.1	4.7	82 966	68.2	4.4	60.0	12.7	27.3
Irwin County	2 266	268	3.9	743	0.0	10.5	5.2	7 487	58.3	6.0	54.0	10.5	35.6
Jackson County	8 057	1 032	6.3	2 284	0.0	11.9	10.2	31 608	64.0	3.4	57.9	11.8	30.3
Jasper County	2 373	236	12.0	680	0.0	19.1	6.5	8 718	63.3	4.7	56.4	11.4	32.2
Jeff Davis County	2 328	289	6.2	739	0.0	17.3	6.0	9 603	58.2	5.6	54.4	8.6	37.0
Jefferson County	3 911	366	11.1	1 085	0.0	10.2	7.6	12 925	52.2	11.8	48.3	8.7	42.9
Jenkins County	1 969	267	4.3	516	0.0	8.9	10.1	6 404	58.2	10.7	46.8	10.4	42.8
Johnson County	1 060	007	1.0	701	0.0	5.6	26.2	6 471	49.4	5.4	44.5	8.5	47.0
Jones County	5 160	824	9.2	1 553	0.0	13.8	1.9	18 013	63.0	4.5	55.2	11.7	33.1
Lamar County	2 824	1 151	7.8	1 065	0.0	7.0	6.6	12 389	61.9	5.5	55.8	11.5	32.8
Lanier County	1 530	208	5.8	424	0.0	12.3	7.1	5 476	60.2	6.0	56.6	9.6	33.9
Laurens County	9 240	1 517	5.8	2 591	0.3	10.7	6.8	34 226	59.5	5.1	54.5	10.8	34.8
Lee County	6 043	1 136	7.9	1 666	0.0	6.7	2.1	18 151	68.8	3.4	62.3	12.9	24.8
Liberty County	13 082	2 604	6.7	4 433	26.0	35.6	5.8	43 765	71.1	5.2	62.9	12.7	24.4
Lincoln County	1 648	191	3.4	450	4.0	4.7	9.3	6 665	55.4	5.9	51.2	10.9	38.0
Long County	2 211	286	6.0	617	2.4	8.6	11.3	7 265	67.3	7.6	61.0	11.3	27.7
Lowndes County	18 445	9 466	6.8	6 030	2.5	9.9	6.0	70 577	63.2	5.4	57.4	15.4	27.2
Lumpkin County	3 764	2 321	6.2	1 663	1.1	10.8	4.8	16 458	65.5	3.9	55.8	17.7	26.5
McDuffie County	4 565	614	8.4	1 224	0.0	10.5	9.6	15 899	61.1	7.6	53.7	10.7	35.6
McIntosh County	2 355	231	10.2	641	0.0	11.4	8.9	8 139	57.8	5.6	50.1	14.2	35.6
Macon County	3 040	542	12.2	929	0.0	9.3	11.9	10 707	49.5	9.1	47.9	9.0	43.1
Madison County	4 759	669	8.9	1 342	0.0	15.9	7.0	19 715	65.2	2.7	57.6	11.1	31.2
Marion County	1 526	166	5.6	386	0.0	17.4	4.4	5 348	58.8	3.6	55.3	7.6	37.2
Meriwether County	4 659	473	11.5	1 359	0.0	17.3	9.8	17 109	57.5	7.0	53.5	9.5	37.0
Miller County	1 328	195	9.1	413	0.0	16.0	4.8	4 940	60.4	4.0	51.4	11.6	37.0
Mitchell County	5 285	825	11.1	1 467	0.0	11.4	11.7	18 085	52.5	6.2	49.7	9.7	40.6
Monroe County	4 410	1 012	15.6	1 241	0.0	15.0	5.6	16 715	64.6	3.4	59.5	10.9	29.6
Montgomery County	1 594	729	22.5	526	0.0	5.3	6.1	6 415	57.7	3.9	51.7	13.5	34.8
Morgan County	3 111	397	9.5	820	0.0	11.5	11.1	11 771	66.4	5.1	56.6	13.6	29.9
Murray County	7 119	779	3.9	1 995	0.3	13.3	12.5	27 358	67.8	4.0	63.8	9.2	27.0
Muscogee County	36 797	10 058	9.1	12 458	14.4	23.2	6.9	142 185	63.7	6.3	54.6	13.3	32.2
Newton County	12 419	2 259	14.0	3 508	0.0	10.2	8.2	46 554	66.0	5.2	59.8	12.5	27.8
Oconee County	6 034	1 045	13.1	1 493	0.0	10.6	2.5	19 129	71.1	3.7	60.1	15.4	24.5
Oglethorpe County	2 396	441	9.4	671	0.0	13.6	8.5	9 774	63.3	3.0	56.6	11.2	32.2
Paulding County	16 957	2 407	8.0	3 607	0.0	13.4	6.2	58 625	72.9	2.5	65.9	12.6	21.6
Peach County	4 930	2 274	14.9	1 796	0.0	6.5	9.6	18 242	61.9	12.9	52.1	15.3	32.6
Pickens County	3 842	504	5.7	1 029	0.0	10.2	10.0	18 101	63.8	2.3	57.9	11.5	30.6
Pierce County	3 108	593	2.6	760	0.0	18.7	11.2	11 933	60.9	4.0	54.4	10.1	35.5
Pike County	2 842	501	12.2	717	0.0	6.4	9.2	10 296	63.6	3.4	56.8	12.4	30.8
Polk County	7 361	1 270	6.5	2 229	0.0	9.2	15.2	29 364	57.7	6.0	51.8	11.0	37.2
Pulaski County	1 688	311	10.8	587	0.0	9.5	10.6	7 602	55.4	5.5	52.3	9.2	38.5
Putnam County	3 332	549	18.2	952	0.0	9.7	10.5	14 936	57.5	3.8	52.7	11.0	36.4
Quitman County	535	34	8.3	144	0.0	6.9	11.1	2 048	47.9	5.8	46.6	7.2	46.2
Rabun County	2 450	270	12.9	715	0.0	15.0	4.8	12 157	57.0	4.9	51.6	12.4	36.0
Randolph County	1 647	428	20.0	653	0.0	2.3	11.3	5 942	49.3	7.9	45.0	10.5	44.5

STATE County	Full-year full-time employed (percent)							Children under 18 years in families						Total employed by class of worker (percent)			
									With two parents (percent)		With one parent who is in labor force (percent)	+/− U.S. percent of children with no stay-at-home parent (percent)	+/− U.S. percent two-income couples				
	Total	Men	Women	Non-Hispanic White	Black or African American	American Indian and Alaska Native	Asian, Hawaiian, and Pacific Islander	Hispanic or Latino[1]	Number	Both in labor force	Father only in labor force				Private	Government	Self-employed	Unpaid family worker
	24	25	26	27	28	29	30	31	32	33	34	35	36	37	38	39	40	41
GEORGIA—Cont'd																		
Fannin County	33.9	43.6	25.2	33.8	100.0	42.9	-13.6	35.1	3 956	45.7	26.9	14.9	-4.0	-11.2	69.2	15.3	15.3	0.2
Fayette County	47.1	62.2	33.2	46.9	50.2	57.4	46.3	41.2	25 824	50.4	31.9	12.9	-1.3	3.6	74.9	16.2	8.7	0.2
Floyd County	37.9	47.3	29.5	38.7	34.0	29.6	44.8	33.3	20 661	44.9	19.7	23.1	3.4	-2.2	76.8	14.1	8.9	0.2
Forsyth County	52.3	67.1	37.2	52.8	24.9	36.4	49.1	44.9	26 681	51.3	33.6	10.0	-3.3	6.2	78.5	8.8	12.5	0.2
Franklin County	39.2	50.3	29.2	40.2	32.4	24.0	24.2	21.8	4 548	49.1	18.1	18.9	3.4	-3.5	73.3	13.7	12.4	0.6
Fulton County	43.4	52.3	35.0	50.1	36.1	43.6	42.1	41.5	182 700	30.5	23.2	29.1	-5.0	-0.2	78.8	10.9	10.1	0.2
Gilmer County	39.8	51.2	28.3	39.8	0.0	42.2	28.4	42.4	5 324	40.5	28.9	17.9	-6.2	-9.0	74.7	10.2	14.7	0.4
Glascock County	37.8	52.6	24.8	39.1	26.3	0.0	X	15.4	553	46.5	22.6	19.0	0.9	-0.8	77.2	14.4	8.1	0.2
Glynn County	42.0	51.5	33.6	43.6	37.3	33.7	30.3	39.8	15 350	43.4	16.2	29.5	8.3	0.8	68.8	17.9	12.9	0.4
Gordon County	48.5	58.2	39.1	49.1	44.9	27.6	53.4	44.5	10 847	47.9	23.2	19.4	2.7	4.2	80.1	10.1	9.4	0.4
Grady County	38.9	48.8	30.2	44.0	30.2	17.7	23.1	26.6	5 843	39.8	14.0	27.3	2.5	0.1	68.7	17.8	12.9	0.6
Greene County	36.0	45.6	27.5	38.8	32.0	0.0	12.5	50.2	3 248	29.2	11.7	34.7	-0.7	-7.3	73.1	11.7	14.7	0.5
Gwinnett County	52.4	63.5	41.2	54.3	56.0	35.8	44.6	41.2	158 129	48.7	27.0	15.2	-0.7	8.9	80.1	9.7	10.0	0.2
Habersham County	41.1	49.0	32.8	42.5	21.4	41.9	48.8	34.3	7 864	46.4	22.0	19.5	1.3	-0.4	74.3	13.2	12.1	0.4
Hall County	45.8	57.1	34.3	48.0	38.4	43.2	38.3	40.3	34 346	44.1	24.1	16.6	-3.9	1.7	78.1	11.9	9.8	0.3
Hancock County	23.0	22.2	24.0	30.1	21.0	12.5	X	0.0	2 168	30.1	6.0	36.5	2.0	-8.0	61.9	31.4	6.2	0.5
Haralson County	39.1	50.3	28.9	39.4	35.5	0.0	32.3	66.1	6 225	41.3	25.5	19.3	-2.4	-4.0	72.4	14.8	12.5	0.3
Harris County	47.4	58.0	37.5	50.1	36.9	84.3	41.4	49.6	5 726	47.7	24.3	18.9	2.0	7.0	71.2	18.3	10.2	0.3
Hart County	38.1	45.6	31.1	39.1	32.9	68.2	25.3	68.2	4 999	48.7	15.8	21.7	5.8	-2.4	72.8	12.8	14.0	0.4
Heard County	42.2	51.9	33.1	42.4	41.5	21.1	46.3	41.7	3 026	40.1	26.7	22.1	-2.4	-7.6	72.3	14.5	12.8	0.3
Henry County	52.9	64.8	41.8	54.1	47.2	47.6	45.3	48.6	33 258	52.1	22.1	17.3	4.8	9.3	75.7	15.4	8.6	0.2
Houston County	47.2	59.4	35.8	49.2	43.2	32.9	37.2	42.0	29 877	43.7	21.2	24.8	3.9	2.7	62.0	30.9	6.9	0.2
Irwin County	41.6	50.8	33.2	46.0	30.9	0.0	28.6	12.1	2 443	38.9	17.1	23.3	-2.4	-2.7	68.2	18.3	12.6	0.9
Jackson County	43.8	54.8	33.2	44.3	37.8	30.9	33.7	50.3	10 355	46.4	24.9	16.8	-1.4	1.9	72.8	14.3	12.5	0.4
Jasper County	41.0	51.8	31.0	43.3	33.6	60.0	61.2	47.3	2 904	41.9	20.6	23.6	0.9	-2.7	73.6	16.3	9.9	0.2
Jeff Davis County	37.1	48.1	26.7	38.3	26.8	100.0	53.2	44.5	3 059	45.4	19.1	18.2	-1.0	-5.9	74.9	15.2	8.9	0.9
Jefferson County	34.9	44.8	26.5	39.3	31.3	15.0	48.3	38.6	4 481	29.0	12.5	32.5	-3.1	-6.1	72.8	17.7	9.2	0.3
Jenkins County	34.4	44.4	25.9	41.3	23.7	0.0	100.0	32.3	2 241	26.6	12.5	39.5	1.5	-4.2	71.7	18.3	9.7	0.2
Johnson County	33.0	41.8	25.1	38.8	21.8	X	0.0	50.9	1 989	33.6	17.9	24.9	-6.1	-5.7	66.4	24.6	8.5	0.6
Jones County	43.2	53.5	33.7	46.1	34.7	13.8	31.5	37.9	6 061	43.6	20.5	20.6	-0.4	0.3	74.0	15.9	9.9	0.2
Lamar County	42.1	51.8	33.3	45.3	34.3	56.3	39.4	31.6	3 665	41.3	17.1	27.4	4.1	0.0	72.2	16.2	10.9	0.6
Lanier County	42.5	54.4	30.6	45.2	35.1	40.3	0.0	43.2	1 823	43.8	22.1	18.3	-2.5	1.1	69.5	19.5	10.1	1.0
Laurens County	40.9	49.5	33.2	44.5	32.8	46.7	54.2	50.0	11 138	39.5	13.5	29.6	4.5	2.4	68.8	21.5	9.6	0.1
Lee County	49.2	58.2	40.5	53.1	29.8	73.9	71.1	36.0	7 169	56.1	16.7	16.9	8.4	11.1	71.3	20.5	7.9	0.2
Liberty County	46.9	61.4	30.4	51.3	44.1	51.9	42.1	38.7	18 714	36.4	29.4	20.5	-7.7	-3.2	62.9	29.1	7.6	0.4
Lincoln County	37.1	46.7	27.9	39.3	33.0	0.0	47.1	26.4	1 896	47.0	17.7	21.3	3.7	-6.3	67.1	17.0	15.6	0.3
Long County	45.8	59.7	31.7	49.0	42.2	56.4	17.9	33.3	3 091	37.8	25.0	26.1	-0.7	-4.8	64.3	25.5	9.8	0.4
Lowndes County	42.9	54.1	32.1	47.1	35.1	45.1	40.4	38.8	22 250	40.1	16.7	27.6	3.1	5.8	70.8	20.1	8.7	0.3
Lumpkin County	41.8	53.7	30.4	41.8	36.5	48.3	38.8	42.5	4 705	52.0	22.1	17.8	5.2	2.2	70.4	15.2	13.9	0.5
McDuffie County	40.2	51.5	30.6	44.6	32.1	28.9	66.7	53.4	5 438	37.8	16.5	31.6	4.8	2.1	74.9	16.7	8.2	0.2
McIntosh County	36.5	43.0	30.2	38.9	32.9	25.4	0.0	91.3	2 568	40.1	18.0	25.4	0.9	-9.3	71.1	17.9	10.8	0.2
Macon County	31.0	38.1	24.1	36.3	27.7	6.0	57.1	30.2	3 454	35.1	12.4	26.1	-3.4	-6.3	64.3	23.1	11.4	1.1
Madison County	46.0	56.5	36.2	46.8	43.1	30.0	34.9	27.4	6 315	50.5	21.0	16.7	2.6	4.1	70.4	16.2	13.0	0.4
Marion County	40.0	50.4	30.4	44.4	30.7	0.0	80.0	50.8	1 823	43.6	16.1	23.2	2.2	-2.8	77.8	13.9	8.1	0.2
Meriwether County	38.0	45.4	31.5	41.7	32.1	8.3	68.2	19.3	5 402	35.0	14.8	31.5	1.9	-4.2	72.3	19.3	8.2	0.2
Miller County	40.0	49.6	32.0	41.7	34.3	X	100.0	100.0	1 560	46.5	15.2	27.8	9.7	3.5	67.1	20.7	11.9	0.2
Mitchell County	35.9	39.8	31.9	43.5	27.5	76.9	23.1	26.2	5 807	29.6	16.1	31.7	-3.3	-2.5	68.6	20.9	10.0	0.4
Monroe County	46.1	56.1	36.3	50.4	34.7	39.4	75.0	51.3	5 278	48.9	19.6	22.8	7.1	6.2	71.6	18.9	9.1	0.4
Montgomery County	36.5	42.8	30.1	40.4	27.8	40.0	29.5	20.9	1 878	42.1	19.1	24.7	2.2	-1.6	65.5	23.2	11.1	0.2
Morgan County	43.5	55.4	33.0	46.0	37.2	100.0	33.3	55.1	3 798	44.3	20.2	23.8	3.5	4.6	68.3	16.7	14.6	0.3
Murray County	49.5	59.5	39.6	49.9	43.6	12.5	39.3	45.2	9 472	44.5	21.0	20.8	0.7	3.0	82.6	9.9	7.3	0.1
Muscogee County	39.5	47.8	31.9	42.4	36.3	36.3	38.4	36.8	45 997	35.6	17.0	31.7	2.7	-0.6	72.8	19.1	7.9	0.3
Newton County	44.7	56.1	34.5	47.4	35.5	28.5	42.9	40.2	16 053	40.1	23.5	22.9	-1.6	1.5	75.5	14.0	10.3	0.1
Oconee County	46.8	59.6	34.7	47.6	40.4	45.7	45.8	36.9	7 777	54.7	24.2	13.6	3.7	9.4	61.6	26.3	11.6	0.5
Oglethorpe County	44.0	54.7	34.0	46.5	34.3	77.3	0.0	29.4	3 010	41.4	19.4	24.5	1.3	4.4	68.6	20.8	10.0	0.6
Paulding County	54.2	68.0	40.9	54.5	53.7	47.8	52.5	52.3	24 047	51.1	27.6	14.2	0.7	9.0	76.5	13.5	9.9	0.2
Peach County	36.9	45.6	29.2	48.7	23.2	74.1	33.0	45.4	5 760	36.8	13.9	34.1	6.3	0.4	68.6	24.7	6.4	0.3
Pickens County	44.6	55.0	34.9	44.5	32.1	24.4	45.0	47.3	5 157	46.7	24.0	17.5	-0.4	-1.7	70.6	16.1	12.7	0.5
Pierce County	41.3	53.2	30.4	43.1	32.6	21.4	X	18.8	3 832	49.6	15.4	16.8	1.8	0.6	69.5	19.1	10.6	0.7
Pike County	43.5	52.4	34.8	45.9	30.1	70.8	4.3	60.7	3 560	47.1	26.3	15.7	-1.8	1.6	69.2	17.4	13.1	0.2
Polk County	37.7	47.4	28.4	39.6	27.6	0.0	54.1	34.5	8 905	40.7	20.2	23.6	-0.3	-4.8	77.1	13.3	9.5	0.1
Pulaski County	38.4	51.6	29.6	44.8	28.0	0.0	0.0	21.7	2 122	47.9	11.1	28.7	12.0	7.0	65.2	22.5	11.6	0.7
Putnam County	38.7	47.5	30.2	40.1	35.3	76.9	55.9	42.9	4 054	39.7	17.9	25.1	0.2	-9.1	69.9	19.2	10.2	0.6
Quitman County	33.7	40.4	27.8	33.1	34.2	50.0	X	75.0	566	27.7	12.7	28.8	-2.1	-15.1	71.5	16.2	12.2	0.0
Rabun County	36.8	45.4	28.7	36.8	34.2	20.0	38.2	41.7	3 087	47.3	25.8	16.1	-1.2	-6.8	68.4	13.4	17.6	0.6
Randolph County	30.7	42.4	21.5	41.9	22.1	X	X	57.4	1 895	24.0	13.7	35.3	-5.3	-8.1	67.0	21.0	12.0	0.1

[1] Hispanic or Latino persons may be of any race.

STATE County	Percent who worked at home	Percent of the population 5 years and over with a disability	Veterans as a percent of the population 18 years and over	Occupation for employed population 16 years and over (percent)						Industry for employed population 16 years and over (percent)					
				Management, professional, and related occupations	Service occupations	Sales and office occupations	Farming, fishing, and forestry occupations	Construction, extraction, and maintenance occupations	Production, transportation and material moving occupations	Agriculture, forestry, fishing, and mining	Construction and manufacturing	Wholesale and retail trade	Transportation and warehousing, and utilities	Service industries	Public administration
	42	43	44	45	46	47	48	49	50	51	52	53	54	55	56
GEORGIA—Cont'd															
Fannin County	3.2	27.5	14.0	22.4	12.2	21.9	0.9	17.4	25.3	2.3	35.5	14.4	4.9	37.7	5.3
Fayette County	3.7	11.9	17.7	40.9	11.4	27.5	0.0	8.5	11.8	0.3	15.1	13.6	18.5	46.6	5.9
Floyd County	2.0	24.5	12.6	27.1	15.1	23.7	0.4	11.0	22.7	0.8	30.7	14.4	4.2	46.3	3.5
Forsyth County	5.4	14.0	12.2	41.1	9.3	29.1	0.5	11.0	9.1	0.8	24.3	18.1	4.5	49.8	2.5
Franklin County	3.1	25.9	13.0	24.0	15.1	22.6	1.7	11.6	25.1	4.9	33.3	15.1	4.7	38.1	3.8
Fulton County	4.4	18.3	10.0	43.6	13.5	27.7	0.2	6.0	9.1	0.3	13.7	14.7	5.9	61.7	3.8
Gilmer County	3.3	23.9	15.1	22.9	10.0	20.4	1.7	15.5	29.5	3.8	41.5	13.2	3.9	33.6	4.0
Glascock County	2.4	25.7	9.0	18.6	13.9	22.4	1.2	17.9	26.0	9.5	29.8	9.1	8.5	38.2	4.8
Glynn County	2.5	20.8	16.4	31.3	18.9	25.2	0.5	10.7	13.3	1.1	17.9	15.7	3.9	54.0	7.4
Gordon County	1.7	21.0	11.8	20.9	9.6	24.8	0.9	12.2	31.6	2.0	47.1	15.6	4.7	28.1	2.6
Grady County	3.9	22.4	11.5	24.1	15.7	22.1	5.1	11.2	21.9	8.4	25.1	15.8	4.4	39.6	6.6
Greene County	4.4	24.9	13.6	25.9	14.9	22.2	2.8	10.6	23.6	5.5	31.0	15.1	4.1	40.0	3.6
Gwinnett County	3.8	14.3	10.9	39.7	10.4	30.1	0.1	10.1	9.6	0.2	20.9	19.5	3.9	52.4	3.1
Habersham County	2.3	23.4	13.0	25.0	12.7	23.9	1.7	13.1	23.6	3.6	35.9	14.5	3.9	37.5	4.7
Hall County	2.2	21.4	11.4	26.3	12.1	23.9	0.9	12.8	24.0	1.6	35.3	15.8	4.1	40.3	2.9
Hancock County	0.9	32.2	9.9	18.4	26.6	12.3	3.0	8.3	31.5	3.9	31.3	6.7	5.7	40.0	12.5
Haralson County	3.1	24.7	12.1	20.3	13.9	22.4	0.6	18.5	24.4	0.9	36.2	16.8	5.6	36.0	4.5
Harris County	2.0	20.2	18.1	33.6	13.8	25.5	0.7	10.8	15.6	0.8	23.8	13.6	3.9	51.3	6.5
Hart County	3.5	24.0	13.0	24.6	13.2	23.2	1.1	14.0	23.9	4.4	38.6	12.7	1.6	36.3	3.4
Heard County	2.9	22.1	10.3	18.3	12.0	19.4	1.0	22.8	26.5	2.3	39.0	13.2	7.9	33.2	4.3
Henry County	2.3	16.3	14.8	30.3	10.4	31.0	0.1	13.5	14.6	0.5	18.9	16.9	16.1	41.5	6.2
Houston County	1.6	18.5	20.7	31.7	15.4	26.3	0.2	13.9	12.6	0.6	17.2	14.5	4.2	44.6	19.0
Irwin County	2.7	21.7	11.0	23.6	13.8	24.0	2.4	11.7	24.6	7.8	28.7	14.0	5.9	37.9	5.7
Jackson County	3.4	22.6	11.5	22.5	14.1	25.1	1.1	14.6	22.6	2.9	32.3	16.7	5.3	38.7	4.0
Jasper County	2.7	22.3	13.2	19.4	13.4	22.6	1.3	17.5	25.7	3.6	37.5	14.8	4.8	34.4	4.9
Jeff Davis County	2.2	25.8	9.9	20.5	11.4	20.9	3.3	14.6	29.2	5.8	34.9	15.9	8.6	30.4	4.3
Jefferson County	4.1	28.2	10.4	22.8	15.6	17.9	2.7	10.6	30.4	5.2	34.9	11.5	5.0	36.8	6.6
Jenkins County	1.1	25.4	12.7	23.5	13.7	17.9	2.9	13.6	28.4	7.0	33.8	14.5	6.6	33.1	4.9
Johnson County	2.0	28.1	9.9	20.2	13.4	22.3	2.4	14.8	20.9	0.1	02.4	10.1	6.0	21.5	8.7
Jones County	2.2	19.5	12.4	30.5	12.5	26.5	0.8	15.3	14.4	3.7	22.9	15.5	5.5	45.2	7.1
Lamar County	1.4	23.1	14.8	21.3	15.3	23.5	0.7	13.7	25.5	2.3	30.4	15.6	6.0	38.0	7.7
Lanier County	1.8	23.8	15.8	22.1	15.2	20.3	2.6	16.2	23.6	5.2	29.7	13.7	6.6	36.6	8.2
Laurens County	1.4	22.9	13.1	26.5	15.9	21.6	0.8	11.8	23.4	2.7	30.2	14.4	3.9	42.0	6.7
Lee County	1.2	16.7	14.5	29.5	12.0	32.6	1.1	10.9	13.8	1.7	21.0	18.3	6.3	42.8	9.9
Liberty County	1.5	17.0	18.2	24.4	20.2	27.0	0.7	11.9	15.8	1.3	16.7	15.8	5.1	49.3	11.9
Lincoln County	2.5	22.6	14.6	23.8	12.6	22.5	1.7	15.0	24.3	4.1	33.4	15.3	5.4	36.2	5.5
Long County	2.1	17.5	17.0	18.8	16.5	27.4	2.8	17.2	17.3	4.0	22.7	15.8	5.6	38.9	13.0
Lowndes County	1.8	20.3	17.5	26.9	17.5	28.7	0.6	10.3	16.0	1.5	18.4	19.4	5.4	49.7	5.6
Lumpkin County	2.0	21.2	11.5	25.3	14.0	25.4	1.1	15.2	19.0	2.8	30.4	16.6	2.4	44.7	3.1
McDuffie County	1.4	24.5	13.2	24.7	14.3	23.6	1.2	13.7	22.4	3.3	30.1	16.3	4.4	40.5	5.4
McIntosh County	2.5	26.3	16.3	21.5	17.7	26.1	4.2	13.5	17.0	4.6	23.6	19.8	3.5	42.1	6.5
Macon County	2.3	27.0	12.3	21.9	16.8	16.9	4.4	13.3	26.7	9.8	32.5	11.2	4.1	32.7	9.7
Madison County	3.2	22.4	13.2	21.9	11.7	25.5	0.8	17.3	22.7	3.1	31.1	16.8	4.9	40.2	4.0
Marion County	2.2	27.4	16.7	20.7	13.1	17.7	3.5	14.1	30.8	6.8	36.1	15.4	6.0	31.7	4.0
Meriwether County	2.6	27.0	11.7	20.3	15.7	20.6	1.4	13.7	28.3	2.3	34.8	12.3	6.7	39.3	4.6
Miller County	2.9	27.2	11.1	26.3	14.9	22.0	2.6	10.3	24.0	8.1	23.5	17.4	6.0	39.0	5.9
Mitchell County	1.7	25.5	10.5	24.2	15.6	21.4	4.5	11.1	23.2	9.5	25.1	14.5	6.3	37.2	7.5
Monroe County	1.2	23.6	12.6	28.3	15.8	22.3	1.0	13.2	19.5	3.0	24.0	15.7	5.9	44.2	7.2
Montgomery County	1.7	22.8	10.3	26.7	17.2	22.6	1.9	13.5	18.1	4.9	24.5	13.6	7.4	40.2	9.4
Morgan County	3.8	20.8	10.8	26.4	12.9	25.6	1.3	14.4	19.5	3.8	31.6	14.6	5.4	39.3	5.2
Murray County	1.4	24.9	10.4	16.6	9.1	22.4	0.4	12.6	38.8	1.4	54.4	12.2	4.1	25.1	2.7
Muscogee County	1.8	23.2	18.3	30.7	16.8	26.7	0.2	9.1	16.5	0.4	20.9	13.6	3.6	55.4	6.0
Newton County	2.0	20.7	12.6	26.2	12.5	26.0	0.3	15.9	19.1	0.7	34.5	14.2	5.8	39.4	5.4
Oconee County	3.0	14.9	12.7	44.2	9.7	25.6	1.0	8.7	10.7	1.7	17.3	15.8	3.1	57.7	4.4
Oglethorpe County	2.2	25.5	12.0	26.8	13.3	23.2	0.9	13.1	22.8	5.1	27.9	16.3	4.4	41.4	4.9
Paulding County	2.6	15.8	12.9	28.2	11.7	29.2	0.1	16.2	14.6	0.5	26.2	19.1	8.1	41.5	4.6
Peach County	1.4	21.8	13.4	26.1	16.3	24.6	1.0	14.9	17.1	2.1	24.6	14.8	4.5	42.0	12.0
Pickens County	2.0	22.6	13.9	24.1	11.9	24.7	1.0	18.5	19.9	3.1	33.3	15.8	6.0	36.6	5.3
Pierce County	2.2	28.8	11.7	22.2	14.5	25.0	3.7	14.9	19.7	7.3	20.8	18.4	8.7	37.7	7.0
Pike County	2.4	19.6	13.9	24.5	14.9	24.1	0.6	16.0	20.0	1.6	31.1	13.2	6.7	40.7	6.6
Polk County	1.9	26.0	11.6	19.5	12.9	21.8	1.0	16.0	28.7	1.4	39.1	13.6	5.3	36.3	4.3
Pulaski County	1.5	23.8	12.2	25.4	14.7	25.8	1.8	10.9	21.4	5.6	25.7	12.3	3.1	43.1	10.3
Putnam County	1.8	23.6	17.3	21.4	15.2	22.1	2.4	13.7	25.3	3.8	29.9	16.0	8.5	35.8	6.0
Quitman County	2.1	31.5	14.6	13.7	17.1	21.3	4.0	10.0	33.9	7.4	31.1	18.1	7.1	32.0	4.3
Rabun County	3.6	24.6	15.2	22.2	13.6	20.8	0.5	20.2	22.8	1.0	38.8	13.5	3.1	39.1	4.4
Randolph County	1.3	27.3	9.8	26.2	17.1	17.0	5.1	9.3	25.3	10.3	23.7	11.4	5.8	42.4	6.3

STATE County	Median house-hold income	Median family income All families	Married-couple	Male house-holder	Female house-holder	Median nonfamily house-hold income	Men	Women	Per capita income	With earnings	With interest, dividend, or rental income	With Social Security income	With public assis-tance income	With retire-ment income	House-holds with income over $100,000 (percent)	+/− U.S. percent for income over $100,000	House-holds with income below poverty (percent)	Families with children with income below poverty (percent)
	57	58	59	60	61	62	63	64	65	66	67	68	69	70	71	72	73	74
GEORGIA—Cont'd																		
Fannin County	30 612	35 258	40 365	19 375	18 125	16 418	29 675	21 497	16 269	69.8	30.9	37.6	1.9	23.3	4.1	−8.2	13.9	14.0
Fayette County	71 227	78 853	87 887	47 297	35 221	34 940	57 265	35 065	29 464	88.0	48.7	19.8	0.8	19.3	28.8	16.5	2.8	2.7
Floyd County	35 615	42 302	50 407	26 250	16 919	19 088	32 314	24 087	17 808	77.1	27.9	30.7	3.0	18.2	7.3	−5.0	14.3	16.1
Forsyth County	68 890	74 003	81 588	41 791	30 875	36 611	51 663	32 926	29 114	89.9	42.4	16.9	0.9	13.4	27.2	14.9	5.6	4.6
Franklin County	32 134	38 463	46 671	21 410	15 755	16 475	29 949	21 718	15 767	74.0	25.3	34.1	2.6	16.1	4.2	−8.1	15.7	13.8
Fulton County	47 321	58 143	91 618	29 286	18 464	34 750	45 412	33 082	30 003	84.8	33.3	17.6	3.6	11.4	21.5	9.2	13.9	18.2
Gilmer County	35 140	38 863	40 000	24 714	19 545	18 962	30 027	21 555	17 147	76.9	26.3	31.7	1.5	16.4	5.7	−6.6	13.4	12.1
Glascock County	29 743	36 629	45 000	21 458	22 500	10 809	33 914	23 810	14 185	72.9	18.3	31.8	2.7	14.0	3.8	−8.5	17.0	11.6
Glynn County	38 765	46 984	57 344	21 974	16 288	23 905	35 984	24 700	21 707	78.4	32.5	28.8	2.5	18.1	11.1	−1.2	13.9	18.6
Gordon County	38 831	43 184	48 231	30 531	17 225	18 133	30 332	22 522	17 586	84.4	24.8	24.6	1.6	12.3	6.3	−6.0	10.6	11.2
Grady County	28 656	34 253	39 804	21 667	14 040	14 227	27 646	20 873	14 278	76.2	22.0	33.3	3.9	12.7	4.3	−8.0	21.0	23.3
Greene County	33 479	39 794	47 204	26 354	14 955	15 818	31 819	20 993	23 389	75.2	27.8	31.8	3.5	17.6	13.3	1.0	19.3	27.1
Gwinnett County	60 537	66 693	71 617	41 023	33 958	39 325	43 888	32 355	25 006	93.0	35.2	12.3	1.1	10.1	19.8	7.5	4.8	5.0
Habersham County	36 321	42 235	47 302	28 311	19 813	17 419	30 037	23 725	17 706	78.7	29.8	30.8	1.4	16.9	6.5	−5.8	12.9	12.6
Hall County	44 908	50 100	53 027	32 323	20 630	25 558	32 350	25 364	19 690	84.9	30.0	22.6	1.9	12.9	11.0	−1.3	11.0	11.9
Hancock County	22 003	27 232	38 480	23 889	15 104	11 973	26 573	20 380	10 916	68.7	16.2	32.6	8.2	16.7	2.6	−9.7	28.7	36.8
Haralson County	31 656	38 373	46 439	34 375	19 291	14 627	32 362	21 380	15 823	76.1	21.6	30.8	2.3	16.9	4.8	−7.5	16.2	16.1
Harris County	47 763	54 834	59 916	40 956	21 632	23 135	40 259	27 404	21 680	82.9	33.4	26.2	1.5	19.4	14.1	1.8	9.2	8.8
Hart County	32 833	39 600	48 103	30 195	15 357	19 160	31 303	21 594	16 714	73.8	27.4	32.8	3.0	20.9	4.9	−7.4	15.1	18.6
Heard County	33 038	39 306	43 884	32 500	16 915	16 314	32 222	23 383	15 132	80.2	16.9	26.9	3.9	13.1	4.0	−8.3	14.4	13.8
Henry County	57 309	61 607	66 376	40 179	27 940	36 707	42 372	29 975	22 945	89.3	31.6	18.3	1.8	16.1	14.4	2.1	4.9	4.8
Houston County	43 638	50 384	57 811	33 063	19 043	26 750	37 593	26 333	19 515	84.3	30.8	19.8	2.5	23.6	8.5	−3.8	9.8	12.3
Irwin County	30 257	35 234	42 188	19 250	15 265	12 755	29 476	21 553	14 867	77.5	20.2	28.9	4.1	11.5	4.9	−7.4	18.7	18.1
Jackson County	40 349	46 211	52 321	27 083	15 035	20 250	35 260	23 518	17 808	83.7	24.2	24.8	2.9	13.0	7.9	−4.4	13.2	13.1
Jasper County	39 890	43 271	48 300	35 909	17 083	23 147	34 853	22 315	19 249	81.0	26.6	26.5	2.6	18.3	6.3	−6.0	13.7	15.3
Jeff Davis County	27 310	30 930	41 631	21 750	13 299	12 292	26 914	20 584	13 780	75.1	18.4	31.0	4.0	11.8	4.9	−7.4	20.6	19.2
Jefferson County	26 120	31 380	44 375	27 414	12 722	12 382	28 336	19 656	13 491	70.6	16.8	29.6	6.9	15.2	3.9	−8.4	24.0	25.5
Jenkins County	24 025	29 539	49 583	11 583	14 643	11 826	29 130	20 872	13 400	71.2	20.2	32.1	6.4	15.2	4.9	−7.4	26.4	31.9
Johnson County	23 848	29 663	45 273	32 188	9 083	11 264	29 659	19 063	12 384	69.5	16.5	34.4	5.9	14.3	3.2	−9.1	25.1	27.5
Jones County	43 301	48 966	55 829	34 079	22 121	21 536	37 010	27 669	19 126	82.0	25.6	25.4	2.1	19.3	8.7	−3.6	10.6	10.3
Lamar County	37 087	43 481	47 895	17 266	17 741	17 725	30 454	22 299	16 666	80.0	22.1	29.2	2.8	20.6	6.1	−6.2	13.1	13.6
Lanier County	29 171	34 512	40 466	23 333	14 167	15 036	26 618	20 295	13 690	81.6	13.0	23.2	6.1	12.6	2.8	−9.5	19.7	18.4
Laurens County	32 010	38 586	48 333	22 153	14 537	16 368	29 854	22 315	16 763	76.9	21.5	28.4	3.4	15.7	6.2	−6.1	18.3	21.0
Lee County	48 600	53 132	62 972	45 982	21 382	26 756	40 764	26 231	19 897	89.2	30.4	18.1	1.7	12.1	12.4	0.1	8.5	8.8
Liberty County	33 477	35 031	38 769	27 793	12 400	25 115	26 245	21 347	13 855	88.4	17.1	12.0	4.2	14.6	4.3	−8.0	14.9	17.4
Lincoln County	31 952	36 657	46 944	14 375	19 000	16 648	27 859	21 626	15 351	74.9	25.1	36.3	4.3	19.6	5.1	−7.2	17.5	16.7
Long County	30 640	32 473	38 585	20 464	12 731	20 243	27 097	19 018	12 586	86.0	12.8	16.5	4.0	13.8	2.3	−10.0	18.4	22.0
Lowndes County	32 132	41 580	50 495	25 181	14 552	18 064	29 837	21 418	16 683	82.3	24.9	22.0	3.8	14.4	6.6	−5.7	18.5	19.4
Lumpkin County	39 167	46 368	49 419	21 250	17 989	20 768	31 885	24 869	18 062	82.2	27.7	24.4	2.1	12.9	7.8	−4.5	13.8	11.8
McDuffie County	31 920	38 235	49 453	24 125	14 909	15 682	31 146	21 141	18 005	77.2	20.3	27.9	4.1	16.2	6.6	−5.7	18.5	19.1
McIntosh County	30 102	34 363	37 741	23 214	14 388	18 053	30 533	19 860	14 253	78.6	19.7	29.2	4.1	19.0	3.5	−8.8	18.9	21.9
Macon County	24 224	29 402	43 979	16 964	11 406	12 333	27 729	19 037	11 820	72.5	16.1	28.8	8.6	16.0	2.9	−9.4	25.8	33.4
Madison County	36 347	42 189	48 735	29 861	19 556	19 696	31 866	23 095	16 998	80.5	24.5	26.5	3.1	16.7	4.4	−7.9	12.6	12.5
Marion County	29 145	31 928	44 519	21 111	16 736	12 963	28 024	21 618	14 044	75.9	14.6	27.3	3.8	15.3	3.9	−8.4	22.4	23.4
Meriwether County	31 870	37 931	47 147	26 750	16 334	14 779	30 593	21 879	15 708	76.9	21.8	32.1	5.2	17.6	5.0	−7.3	17.6	19.4
Miller County	27 335	31 866	40 786	25 625	15 417	14 470	26 364	21 353	15 435	75.1	24.4	32.4	3.9	11.9	5.4	−6.9	20.4	25.4
Mitchell County	26 581	31 262	46 250	30 052	12 646	14 120	25 960	19 922	13 042	76.1	19.0	27.7	5.7	12.8	4.7	−7.6	25.4	32.1
Monroe County	44 195	51 093	61 522	24 531	15 932	20 625	35 740	23 209	19 580	82.7	24.9	24.0	2.4	18.1	10.4	−1.9	11.3	10.9
Montgomery County	30 240	38 418	46 750	19 306	14 000	13 601	28 049	21 667	14 182	76.7	20.6	28.9	1.8	12.6	5.8	−6.5	20.8	18.6
Morgan County	40 249	46 146	52 196	26 739	18 408	20 625	35 437	22 463	18 823	83.4	28.2	28.1	2.3	16.5	9.8	−2.5	11.1	12.9
Murray County	36 996	42 155	47 258	24 511	21 107	20 065	30 217	23 443	16 230	85.1	18.3	21.3	2.5	9.6	4.5	−7.8	13.1	12.8
Muscogee County	34 798	41 244	51 089	28 343	15 372	21 860	31 635	25 267	18 262	80.1	24.9	26.1	4.3	20.5	8.0	−4.3	15.1	18.6
Newton County	44 875	49 748	56 327	32 344	22 385	27 008	37 455	26 829	19 317	84.1	24.8	24.0	2.9	16.4	9.2	−3.1	9.3	10.4
Oconee County	55 211	61 502	66 738	32 727	20 789	28 691	43 007	28 119	24 153	87.3	43.2	19.8	2.1	15.3	18.8	6.5	6.2	6.5
Oglethorpe County	35 578	41 443	51 297	20 217	19 063	17 184	31 343	23 228	17 089	78.8	27.0	28.2	3.2	15.7	5.9	−6.4	14.2	13.3
Paulding County	52 161	56 039	59 493	34 830	25 931	29 902	39 861	27 881	19 974	90.0	25.3	15.6	1.4	12.2	8.8	−3.5	5.8	5.0
Peach County	34 453	41 570	54 458	26 719	17 123	17 442	35 213	25 204	16 031	80.0	23.3	27.0	5.4	21.0	6.8	−5.5	19.8	21.9
Pickens County	41 387	47 123	50 000	28 977	22 762	22 588	33 488	23 823	19 774	81.3	30.3	27.3	2.3	16.9	8.4	−3.9	9.2	10.3
Pierce County	29 895	35 903	40 925	17 768	11 304	12 169	28 891	20 025	14 230	75.8	17.2	31.2	4.0	11.0	3.7	−8.6	19.7	21.9
Pike County	44 370	49 798	54 492	37 813	24 167	20 542	34 912	24 409	17 661	82.4	27.5	25.3	1.9	17.7	8.8	−3.5	10.1	9.3
Polk County	32 328	37 847	44 658	23 000	17 938	14 725	30 617	22 045	15 617	76.0	22.6	33.7	2.5	17.8	4.7	−7.6	15.4	16.6
Pulaski County	31 895	38 924	52 961	28 125	16 944	15 869	31 195	20 884	16 435	77.0	24.9	30.6	3.2	19.4	6.1	−6.2	17.8	17.4
Putnam County	36 956	43 262	51 075	20 357	14 519	20 619	31 618	22 906	20 161	75.9	29.6	30.7	3.3	20.4	9.5	−2.8	13.8	18.8
Quitman County	25 875	30 691	33 491	17 321	14 375	15 491	24 318	19 331	14 301	72.3	16.9	37.6	3.0	18.8	3.7	−8.6	21.6	24.2
Rabun County	33 899	39 992	42 125	27 500	17 159	20 711	29 404	21 593	20 608	75.3	32.3	36.2	2.5	19.4	7.0	−5.3	11.7	10.3
Randolph County	22 004	30 278	45 357	26 528	10 824	9 615	29 457	20 900	11 809	66.5	17.7	36.4	7.4	13.0	3.1	−9.2	28.3	30.7

Table B-3. States and Counties — Education, Labor Force, and Income

STATE/ County code	MSA/PMSA/ NECMA code[1]	STATE County	High school graduates			College graduates		College graduates (percent)				
			Total population 25 years and over	Percent with a high school diploma or less	Percent with a high school diploma or more	Percent with a bachelor's degree or more	+/- U.S. percent with bachelor's degree or more	Non-Hispanic White	Black or African American	American Indian and Alaska Native	Asian, Hawaiian, and Pacific Islander	Hispanic or Latino[2]
			1	2	3	4	5	6	7	8	9	10
		GEORGIA—Cont'd										
13 245	0600	Richmond County	122 592	51.7	78.0	18.7	-5.7	24.2	12.5	8.9	27.8	16.6
13 247	0520	Rockdale County	44 794	47.0	82.4	23.4	-1.0	24.0	21.9	0.0	41.8	12.1
13 249	...	Schley County	2 364	70.1	70.0	13.7	-10.7	16.2	8.1	0.0	X	11.1
13 251	...	Screven County	9 685	71.7	66.9	10.2	-14.2	15.4	2.2	30.0	22.9	20.7
13 253	...	Seminole County	6 114	68.9	67.9	8.6	-15.8	9.9	6.1	0.0	50.0	0.0
13 255	0520	Spalding County	37 110	67.0	67.8	12.5	-11.9	14.9	5.3	12.0	44.0	7.5
13 257	...	Stephens County	16 771	64.7	71.1	14.1	-10.3	15.0	6.3	29.6	12.9	0.0
13 259	...	Stewart County	3 495	73.9	63.2	9.3	-15.1	15.4	4.2	0.0	65.5	0.0
13 261	...	Sumter County	20 040	60.3	69.9	19.3	-5.1	28.1	8.4	39.5	55.6	5.6
13 263	...	Talbot County	4 403	75.5	64.8	7.9	-16.5	15.6	2.4	0.0	X	0.0
13 265	...	Taliaferro County	1 434	76.4	56.2	8.4	-16.0	13.0	5.1	X	X	0.0
13 267	...	Tattnall County	14 688	72.9	66.3	7.9	-16.5	11.0	2.7	0.0	20.0	0.0
13 269	...	Taylor County	5 594	75.4	63.6	8.5	-15.9	10.5	5.0	0.0	100.0	0.0
13 271	...	Telfair County	7 906	76.5	63.6	8.3	-16.1	11.0	4.0	X	X	0.0
13 273	...	Terrell County	6 741	68.3	64.5	10.7	-13.7	16.3	5.7	0.0	0.0	25.7
13 275	...	Thomas County	27 697	60.0	73.5	16.8	-7.6	22.0	7.1	11.7	33.3	8.4
13 277	...	Tift County	23 433	62.4	67.9	15.6	-8.8	19.8	5.6	13.1	37.6	5.2
13 279	...	Toombs County	16 212	67.6	67.3	12.7	-11.7	15.8	4.8	0.0	17.0	2.8
13 281	...	Towns County	6 935	58.3	75.1	17.4	-7.0	17.5	X	0.0	16.7	14.3
13 283	...	Treutlen County	4 292	77.8	61.8	8.5	-15.9	9.7	5.3	0.0	8.2	0.0
13 285	...	Troup County	36 815	60.7	73.0	18.0	-6.4	22.5	6.5	5.7	37.8	15.5
13 287	...	Turner County	5 707	71.0	67.7	10.5	-13.9	14.5	3.5	0.0	9.1	1.5
13 289	4680	Twiggs County	6 702	77.6	63.2	5.4	-19.0	6.9	2.5	0.0	34.0	19.6
13 291	...	Union County	12 730	60.9	74.2	12.5	-11.9	12.7	0.0	26.2	0.0	0.0
13 293	...	Upson County	18 325	70.5	66.7	11.5	-12.9	14.7	2.1	7.0	15.0	0.0
13 295	1560	Walker County	40 837	68.2	66.8	10.2	-14.2	10.3	4.1	0.0	46.1	12.0
13 297	0520	Walton County	38 527	62.1	73.5	13.0	-11.4	14.1	5.2	8.5	36.0	11.2
13 299	...	Ware County	23 380	68.4	70.3	11.4	-13.0	13.0	6.6	31.0	13.6	4.6
13 301	...	Warren County	4 061	77.6	57.1	8.0	-16.4	13.7	2.9	0.0	71.4	20.0
13 303	...	Washington County	13 626	70.5	68.3	10.5	-13.9	16.7	4.3	0.0	0.0	0.0
13 305	...	Wayne County	17 531	66.9	70.1	11.6	-12.8	13.1	7.2	0.0	1.3	3.4
13 307	...	Webster County	1 588	72.7	61.3	9.1	-15.3	15.0	2.7	X	X	0.0
13 309	...	Wheeler County	4 144	74.0	67.9	7.1	-17.3	9.2	3.2	0.0	0.0	2.6
13 311	...	White County	13 473	59.2	76.0	15.4	-9.0	15.5	2.0	11.8	29.8	15.5
13 313	...	Whitfield County	52 570	66.0	63.0	12.8	-11.6	15.1	6.5	5.8	29.8	2.2
13 315	...	Wilcox County	5 761	75.5	68.2	7.0	-17.4	8.4	4.1	33.3	25.0	4.2
13 317	...	Wilkes County	7 265	70.9	65.0	12.0	-12.4	17.4	5.1	16.0	0.0	0.0
13 319	...	Wilkinson County	6 509	71.0	70.4	9.6	-14.8	12.5	4.9	0.0	0.0	4.7
13 321	...	Worth County	13 979	69.8	68.3	8.6	-15.8	8.7	8.6	0.0	0.0	0.0
15 000	...	HAWAII	802 477	43.9	84.6	26.2	1.8	37.3	21.0	21.5	24.5	13.3
15 001	...	Hawaii County	97 708	46.8	84.6	22.1	-2.3	32.4	14.3	17.4	19.4	9.4
15 003	3320	Honolulu County	579 998	43.0	84.8	27.9	3.5	40.4	20.9	22.8	26.3	15.1
15 005	...	Kalawao County	147	80.3	39.5	10.2	-14.2	0.0	X	0.0	12.7	X
15 007	...	Kauai County	38 872	46.4	83.3	19.4	-5.0	30.9	23.0	19.3	14.9	7.7
15 009	...	Maui County	85 752	46.1	83.4	22.4	-2.0	33.1	31.8	24.0	17.8	11.2
16 000	...	IDAHO	787 505	43.8	84.7	21.7	-2.7	22.6	22.4	9.5	36.8	6.6
16 001	1080	Ada County	188 662	32.3	90.8	31.2	6.8	31.7	27.3	16.0	41.0	16.2
16 003	...	Adams County	2 468	56.6	80.8	14.9	-9.5	14.6	0.0	18.9	X	6.7
16 005	6340	Bannock County	43 285	38.4	87.5	24.9	0.5	25.5	23.1	8.8	41.8	14.3
16 007	...	Bear Lake County	3 837	56.7	85.5	11.7	-12.7	11.9	0.0	0.0	100.0	2.6
16 009	...	Benewah County	6 051	61.3	79.8	11.4	-13.0	11.9	0.0	6.1	0.0	3.5
16 011	...	Bingham County	23 155	50.5	80.6	14.4	-10.0	16.7	0.0	4.2	20.3	1.8
16 013	...	Blaine County	13 021	25.7	90.2	43.1	18.7	46.3	11.1	25.0	29.7	8.1
16 015	...	Boise County	4 547	46.2	86.3	19.9	-4.5	20.2	X	6.8	22.2	12.5
16 017	...	Bonner County	25 043	47.9	85.6	16.9	-7.5	17.1	0.0	13.1	29.8	9.1
16 019	...	Bonneville County	48 502	38.7	87.8	26.1	1.7	27.1	40.7	6.6	35.1	10.4
16 021	...	Boundary County	6 314	55.9	80.0	14.7	-9.7	15.0	X	15.8	20.0	4.8
16 023	...	Butte County	1 873	50.4	82.6	13.0	-11.4	13.8	0.0	0.0	X	4.0
16 025	...	Camas County	675	43.0	88.4	22.2	-2.2	22.7	0.0	0.0	X	0.0
16 027	1080	Canyon County	76 619	54.3	76.0	14.9	-9.5	16.6	21.0	5.5	20.4	4.4
16 029	...	Caribou County	4 391	47.6	86.6	15.9	-8.5	16.2	0.0	18.2	0.0	7.8
16 031	...	Cassia County	12 206	52.9	76.9	13.9	-10.5	15.9	0.0	16.0	15.1	1.1
16 033	...	Clark County	580	60.5	64.0	12.6	-11.8	16.0	100.0	66.7	X	0.0
16 035	...	Clearwater County	6 352	57.2	80.1	13.4	-11.0	13.5	X	4.6	50.0	11.0

[1] MSA = Metropolitan Statistical Area. PMSA = Primary MSA. NECMA = New England County Metropolitan Area. See the Appendix A for explanation of these concepts. See Appendix B for list of metropolitan areas identified by type, with component counties.
[2] Hispanic or Latino persons may be of any race.

Table B-3. States and Counties — Education, Labor Force, and Income

STATE County	School enrollment			Population 16 to 19 years				Employment status, 2000			Work status in 1999 of the population 16 years and over (percent)		
											Worked in 1999		
	Grades kindergarten through 12	College or graduate school	Percent private	Number	Percent in armed forces	Percent high school graduates	Percent not enrolled, not grads, not in armed forces, not employed	Total population 16 years and over	Percent in labor force	Unemployment rate	Full-time	Part-time	Did not work in 1999
	11	12	13	14	15	16	17	18	19	20	21	22	23
GEORGIA—Cont'd													
Richmond County..........	41 134	11 630	10.4	13 139	12.5	20.5	5.7	152 037	62.3	8.4	53.8	13.2	32.9
Rockdale County..........	14 818	2 578	8.6	4 315	0.0	12.4	5.8	53 119	66.2	4.2	60.4	12.6	27.0
Schley County............	851	102	8.9	203	0.0	2.5	5.4	2 788	60.7	5.7	57.5	8.4	34.0
Screven County..........	3 439	580	4.6	899	0.0	9.8	2.3	11 570	56.8	9.4	49.9	10.2	39.9
Seminole County..........	1 800	387	7.9	525	6.1	14.7	8.2	7 204	55.7	6.8	50.9	8.2	40.9
Spalding County..........	11 806	1 678	9.8	3 477	0.0	8.9	15.4	44 206	61.4	6.2	55.7	10.9	33.4
Stephens County..........	4 381	1 500	22.4	1 448	0.0	11.3	6.8	20 117	62.3	4.2	53.9	12.9	33.2
Stewart County..........	991	152	13.8	335	0.0	10.4	14.9	4 104	51.6	10.1	44.8	10.6	44.6
Sumter County............	6 896	2 219	12.9	2 313	0.0	8.6	8.6	24 934	61.0	6.8	52.8	12.5	34.7
Talbot County............	1 236	178	14.8	310	0.0	17.1	4.5	5 076	54.6	8.7	52.0	9.2	38.9
Taliaferro County..........	379	46	12.7	109	0.0	14.7	18.3	1 636	51.3	9.8	45.7	10.5	43.8
Tattnall County..........	3 912	568	15.6	1 224	0.4	13.0	15.5	17 751	48.7	6.8	50.2	7.8	41.9
Taylor County............	1 805	256	4.3	538	0.0	5.2	20.3	6 730	49.6	8.0	47.9	8.1	44.0
Telfair County..........	2 006	247	4.7	654	0.0	7.0	12.5	9 489	46.8	6.4	48.1	7.3	44.6
Terrell County..........	2 402	336	13.0	719	0.0	2.4	13.4	8 180	55.9	8.5	48.9	9.4	41.7
Thomas County..........	9 084	1 646	12.4	2 440	0.0	11.7	6.9	32 492	59.4	6.5	52.5	11.1	36.4
Tift County..................	7 675	2 390	6.7	2 630	0.0	7.6	9.4	29 007	63.5	6.7	55.8	12.9	31.3
Toombs County............	5 445	731	5.9	1 484	0.0	9.7	10.8	19 419	60.0	5.7	54.3	9.1	36.6
Towns County	1 156	582	24.9	557	0.0	5.9	2.3	7 972	48.3	3.8	41.1	14.8	44.2
Treutlen County..........	1 385	216	7.4	489	0.0	9.0	19.8	5 309	47.9	9.4	48.2	9.3	42.6
Troup County..............	12 477	2 079	12.2	3 493	0.0	8.7	8.4	44 259	63.6	5.2	57.2	11.2	31.6
Turner County	2 117	299	2.8	605	0.0	15.5	4.5	6 997	61.1	8.0	55.3	9.1	35.6
Twiggs County	2 237	243	18.3	624	0.0	14.6	14.6	8 018	57.6	8.3	51.7	10.1	38.2
Union County	2 681	552	8.7	737	0.0	20.1	4.1	14 281	52.1	3.2	45.2	12.9	41.9
Upson County	5 366	952	7.8	1 272	0.0	14.9	6.0	21 243	58.4	7.0	54.7	9.7	35.6
Walker County	11 006	1 683	9.0	3 095	0.3	10.7	11.7	47 800	60.7	4.3	55.5	10.4	34.0
Walton County..............	12 393	1 606	11.0	3 385	0.0	12.8	7.8	45 185	67.3	3.4	59.5	12.6	27.9
Ware County	6 982	1 061	5.2	1 782	0.0	14.3	7.2	27 645	53.4	6.3	49.3	10.9	39.8
Warren County	1 329	165	6.8	401	0.0	10.7	16.2	4 879	52.9	9.4	47.4	10.0	42.6
Washington County.......	4 679	615	9.2	1 209	0.0	8.4	9.1	16 073	53.7	9.5	49.5	10.5	40.0
Wayne County..............	5 194	711	6.0	1 463	0.0	8.5	6.4	20 590	52.5	5.0	50.1	9.1	40.8
Webster County	469	47	12.2	110	0.0	12.7	4.5	1 847	57.7	7.5	52.5	10.8	36.7
Wheeler County	1 071	146	5.8	334	0.0	2.7	16.8	4 967	44.1	5.0	39.7	7.4	52.8
White County	3 284	970	15.3	1 070	0.0	9.9	5.6	15 824	62.9	2.8	55.4	13.1	31.5
Whitfield County............	16 101	2 007	5.5	4 452	0.0	11.2	15.7	63 043	65.2	3.6	61.8	9.3	28.9
Wilcox County	1 519	200	8.2	449	0.0	10.0	6.7	6 837	45.6	4.9	47.8	7.4	44.8
Wilkes County	1 976	289	4.9	628	0.0	10.2	7.5	8 440	56.3	4.4	49.6	10.2	40.2
Wilkinson County	2 089	391	14.8	603	0.0	7.3	6.3	7 776	57.1	6.7	53.1	8.2	38.7
Worth County	5 000	692	6.2	1 355	0.0	7.3	2.4	16 444	61.4	7.2	54.8	9.1	36.1
HAWAII......................	223 185	79 748	18.2	64 343	4.1	17.1	3.6	950 055	64.5	5.9	53.4	15.2	31.4
Hawaii County..............	30 747	7 220	10.0	8 798	0.0	13.6	5.0	114 647	61.7	7.9	48.2	17.3	34.5
Honolulu County..........	155 556	65 507	21.2	45 427	5.9	17.8	3.2	691 015	64.7	5.7	54.1	14.6	31.3
Kalawao County	0	0	X	0	X	X	X	147	39.5	0.0	29.9	19.7	50.3
Kauai County	12 272	1 736	8.0	3 275	0.0	16.1	2.5	44 920	63.1	5.3	51.1	16.9	32.1
Maui County	24 610	5 285	12.0	6 843	0.0	17.5	5.1	99 326	66.8	5.0	56.2	15.9	27.9
IDAHO......................	270 423	77 392	10.1	87 734	0.3	14.0	4.0	969 872	66.1	5.7	55.2	17.9	26.8
Ada County	58 736	17 989	9.2	17 019	0.1	17.3	2.5	227 917	71.9	3.9	61.0	17.2	21.8
Adams County..............	688	57	9.0	207	0.0	13.0	3.9	2 767	54.9	7.7	45.8	16.9	37.3
Bannock County..........	15 052	9 013	4.9	5 556	0.2	15.8	3.2	56 815	67.5	6.9	52.1	22.4	25.5
Bear Lake County	1 724	101	0.8	510	0.0	15.3	1.0	4 628	57.8	7.2	42.6	22.6	34.8
Benewah County..........	1 868	156	9.7	524	0.0	10.7	7.1	7 017	57.5	13.9	48.9	15.2	35.9
Bingham County..........	11 100	1 423	2.8	3 155	0.4	12.3	4.3	28 926	65.6	5.8	55.0	18.5	26.5
Blaine County..............	3 440	648	15.0	889	0.0	8.3	4.0	15 000	75.4	4.2	61.8	19.8	18.4
Boise County..................	1 327	165	10.6	332	0.0	11.7	4.8	5 096	65.9	7.2	55.7	16.7	27.6
Bonner County	7 188	761	16.2	2 159	0.4	14.8	6.3	28 747	59.7	7.3	49.1	17.2	33.6
Bonneville County	19 682	3 547	4.3	5 848	0.0	13.8	3.3	59 636	67.7	5.0	55.1	19.2	25.8
Boundary County	1 996	151	16.4	595	0.0	19.0	8.6	7 340	58.9	10.0	48.5	17.4	34.0
Butte County	651	74	4.3	183	0.0	14.2	0.0	2 178	59.8	5.8	49.5	16.4	34.1
Camas County	210	34	2.9	59	0.0	5.1	8.5	781	66.6	4.0	54.3	21.3	24.5
Canyon County	28 095	5 511	12.8	8 576	0.0	13.7	8.4	95 344	66.6	5.8	57.2	14.5	28.3
Caribou County	1 795	214	2.1	542	0.0	6.8	2.6	5 315	58.9	4.8	49.6	18.5	31.9
Cassia County	5 641	596	4.9	1 547	0.0	13.8	5.6	15 040	62.7	5.2	51.5	17.8	30.7
Clark County	243	6	2.8	86	0.0	14.0	5.8	721	66.2	6.1	61.0	12.5	26.5
Clearwater County	1 720	244	10.1	453	0.0	15.7	2.4	7 151	51.7	11.5	46.0	14.9	39.1

Table B-3. States and Counties — Education, Labor Force, and Income

STATE County	Full-year full-time employed (percent)								Children under 18 years in families						Total employed by class of worker (percent)			
										With two parents (percent)		With one parent who is in labor force (percent)	+/− U.S. percent of children with no stay-at-home parent (percent)					
	Total	Men	Women	Non-Hispanic White	Black or African American	American Indian and Alaska Native	Asian, Hawaiian, and Pacific Islander	Hispanic or Latino[1]	Number	Both in labor force	Father only in labor force			+/− U.S. percent two-income couples	Private	Government	Self-employed	Unpaid family worker
	24	25	26	27	28	29	30	31	32	33	34	35	36	37	38	39	40	41
GEORGIA—Cont'd																		
Richmond County	38.3	45.2	32.0	40.2	36.8	38.2	33.2	34.3	48 741	29.9	16.9	33.8	-0.9	-4.3	68.6	24.5	6.8	0.2
Rockdale County	46.3	56.8	36.0	47.7	45.1	64.6	44.8	33.0	18 205	46.2	23.5	21.5	3.1	2.6	73.9	16.0	9.9	0.2
Schley County	42.0	52.0	33.1	47.5	29.7	0.0	X	39.2	1 038	44.1	17.8	26.6	6.1	-0.2	73.8	14.0	12.1	0.1
Screven County	36.7	44.1	30.1	39.2	33.9	30.0	0.0	17.6	3 976	39.5	15.9	27.1	2.0	-0.7	73.4	19.1	7.2	0.3
Seminole County	37.9	46.3	30.4	41.3	30.9	100.0	40.0	36.1	2 136	34.2	14.3	32.6	2.2	-4.0	71.9	16.1	11.3	0.6
Spalding County	40.9	50.4	32.5	44.4	33.1	6.1	33.2	38.0	14 365	35.2	18.3	31.6	2.2	-2.8	76.3	14.6	8.8	0.3
Stephens County	41.2	52.4	31.3	41.0	42.7	70.4	34.6	48.8	5 600	50.0	17.0	21.1	6.5	1.2	78.3	12.8	8.7	0.2
Stewart County	31.1	35.0	27.6	38.0	26.3	28.6	45.7	0.0	1 141	35.1	6.8	30.1	0.6	-6.1	66.2	24.1	9.6	0.1
Sumter County	39.1	48.0	31.5	43.0	34.5	39.5	38.2	43.8	8 729	34.0	11.9	32.7	2.1	4.0	66.2	23.4	9.8	0.6
Talbot County	36.2	41.0	32.1	44.8	31.2	0.0	X	20.7	1 460	31.3	7.5	38.2	4.9	-1.3	71.8	20.2	8.0	0.1
Taliaferro County	36.1	43.5	29.6	33.2	38.2	X	X	60.0	449	32.5	10.0	36.5	4.4	-11.4	73.4	16.8	9.0	0.8
Tattnall County	35.7	38.8	31.3	42.5	24.0	47.4	10.7	01.0	4 002	00.0	21.2	21.1	5.2	3.6	61.6	26.1	10.0	0.4
Taylor County	33.2	37.9	28.9	40.7	23.0	0.0	50.0	21.2	2 176	29.9	13.6	25.4	-9.3	-6.9	68.7	20.5	9.7	1.1
Telfair County	32.5	37.7	26.6	36.6	26.3	X	0.0	32.8	2 410	37.3	18.7	25.4	-1.9	-7.8	68.7	20.0	11.1	0.1
Terrell County	33.6	39.6	28.6	43.1	27.4	0.0	13.0	15.4	2 759	26.7	14.3	37.8	-0.1	-7.0	69.3	19.9	10.6	0.1
Thomas County	40.1	48.7	32.9	44.3	31.6	32.9	48.2	34.2	10 557	40.7	15.5	29.8	5.9	0.7	70.6	19.3	9.8	0.4
Tift County	42.9	53.3	33.3	45.2	37.4	40.9	26.7	43.9	9 647	35.2	20.4	28.7	-0.7	0.1	72.3	17.0	10.5	0.1
Toombs County	41.1	52.6	31.1	42.2	36.3	18.3	45.8	44.8	6 756	34.4	18.0	29.1	-1.1	-5.3	70.0	19.5	10.3	0.1
Towns County	30.1	36.5	24.5	30.0	0.0	0.0	64.3	23.7	1 472	51.3	19.9	14.1	0.8	-17.1	68.7	15.3	15.7	0.4
Treutlen County	32.7	39.2	26.3	37.2	23.1	0.0	14.3	37.3	1 659	36.7	19.1	24.6	-3.3	-12.5	66.6	25.7	7.5	0.3
Troup County	42.8	52.6	34.2	45.6	36.6	47.0	37.4	40.4	14 996	39.4	14.9	30.8	5.6	3.1	77.0	13.7	9.0	0.3
Turner County	41.2	51.2	32.4	46.8	33.3	0.0	0.0	33.9	2 541	34.1	15.6	35.3	4.8	-2.1	65.7	23.2	11.0	0.1
Twiggs County	37.9	46.3	30.5	43.5	31.1	0.0	51.7	44.7	2 638	32.5	17.9	29.9	-2.2	-2.7	78.5	14.0	7.3	0.2
Union County	33.0	40.7	25.6	33.0	28.4	64.3	32.3	18.1	3 278	57.0	18.0	16.1	8.5	-9.2	68.3	13.8	17.2	0.7
Upson County	39.9	50.1	31.1	42.6	32.8	36.8	35.7	30.7	6 560	33.5	18.1	30.5	-0.6	-4.8	76.0	15.9	7.7	0.3
Walker County	42.0	54.4	30.6	42.5	34.8	30.8	42.5	37.7	14 162	41.2	27.1	20.9	-2.5	-3.8	79.5	11.3	8.9	0.3
Walton County	46.9	59.5	35.1	48.8	37.0	29.9	42.4	46.3	16 347	47.0	21.5	20.1	2.5	4.5	74.1	12.8	12.9	0.3
Ware County	34.9	43.1	27.1	37.8	28.0	33.3	30.7	23.0	7 037	38.4	16.2	27.3	1.1	7.6	68.4	21.3	9.9	0.5
Warren County	33.8	42.9	26.4	38.8	30.0	18.8	28.6	50.0	1 428	29.9	10.1	31.2	-3.5	-8.9	74.9	15.6	9.4	0.1
Washington County	35.3	47.3	26.1	43.7	27.6	100.0	11.8	37.0	5 209	32.4	14.3	30.4	-1.8	-4.4	70.1	22.4	7.0	0.4
Wayne County	36.8	45.5	27.2	38.8	29.6	34.2	41.2	34.0	6 329	44.4	21.9	17.9	-2.3	-5.9	67.5	21.7	10.2	0.7
Webster County	39.4	49.7	29.6	42.7	34.0	X	X	57.1	556	43.0	16.5	24.6	3.0	-6.2	68.5	19.7	10.5	1.3
Wheeler County	27.2	29.0	24.6	33.2	16.9	100.0	0.0	16.1	1 279	43.4	12.9	27.8	6.6	-4.0	64.2	21.7	13.7	0.3
White County	42.2	51.9	33.1	42.3	41.4	42.4	48.5	40.4	4 402	47.3	28.0	16.1	-1.2	0.6	70.2	13.7	15.4	0.7
Whitfield County	45.9	57.0	35.0	48.2	48.8	33.6	38.7	36.8	21 241	44.5	24.6	16.9	-3.2	0.1	81.5	9.6	8.6	0.3
Wilcox County	34.4	38.6	28.8	40.7	22.6	66.7	0.0	57.7	1 839	36.7	22.7	23.3	-4.6	-1.9	63.4	25.4	11.2	0.0
Wilkes County	37.6	48.5	27.9	44.5	28.4	100.0	0.0	31.9	2 442	38.2	11.9	37.0	10.6	-0.4	72.8	16.9	9.9	0.4
Wilkinson County	38.7	48.8	30.0	43.1	32.4	0.0	0.0	24.2	2 509	35.0	15.7	34.8	5.2	-7.1	66.7	25.8	7.0	0.4
Worth County	42.5	52.7	33.7	46.9	31.4	0.0	22.0	30.1	5 801	40.5	19.2	23.8	-0.3	-1.3	67.6	20.9	11.3	0.2
HAWAII	39.6	46.1	33.2	43.2	54.4	41.8	38.0	37.3	271 881	46.8	17.5	21.3	3.5	0.2	67.8	21.0	10.8	0.4
Hawaii County	34.1	38.6	29.6	33.5	39.0	28.0	34.9	31.5	35 528	44.2	13.4	24.6	4.2	-1.5	63.9	19.7	15.6	0.8
Honolulu County	40.8	47.7	33.8	47.2	55.0	44.8	38.3	39.4	192 025	47.1	19.0	20.1	2.6	0.1	67.8	22.5	9.3	0.3
Kalawao County	19.7	15.9	25.4	100.0	X	0.0	12.7	X	0	X	X	X	X	-49.8	24.1	75.9	0.0	0.0
Kauai County	36.4	41.2	31.7	36.4	54.8	29.8	36.0	32.6	14 413	47.0	13.7	23.9	6.3	0.2	68.5	17.2	13.9	0.4
Maui County	39.6	45.4	33.8	39.2	51.3	52.5	39.3	34.7	29 915	47.9	14.0	23.3	6.6	2.6	71.0	14.6	14.0	0.4
IDAHO	38.0	48.3	27.8	38.5	40.9	33.1	36.3	32.7	352 685	48.7	26.9	16.7	0.8	1.6	70.0	16.4	13.2	0.5
Ada County	45.9	56.4	35.6	46.3	39.7	37.0	44.0	43.2	78 956	49.3	26.8	18.1	2.8	8.4	73.8	14.7	11.4	0.2
Adams County	25.3	30.7	19.8	25.2	100.0	20.9	0.0	6.3	781	45.7	25.5	16.6	-2.3	-13.8	56.2	19.7	22.7	1.4
Bannock County	36.0	46.3	26.3	36.3	38.8	30.1	32.0	33.8	20 476	49.9	25.4	17.8	3.1	3.8	69.0	21.1	9.7	0.2
Bear Lake County	28.7	43.8	14.3	29.0	60.0	0.0	0.0	25.0	2 059	53.3	27.4	12.0	0.7	-5.6	64.2	18.0	17.0	0.8
Benewah County	29.6	36.8	22.3	29.1	57.1	35.9	15.8	37.5	2 321	45.2	25.2	15.3	-4.1	-13.9	65.9	20.7	12.9	0.5
Bingham County	36.7	48.5	25.0	38.0	0.0	32.8	45.3	29.5	14 018	49.8	25.3	16.3	1.5	1.7	64.6	21.2	13.5	0.7
Blaine County	39.4	47.2	31.0	41.3	11.4	34.6	34.6	23.2	4 435	51.7	23.7	17.1	4.2	8.7	65.0	10.0	24.6	0.5
Boise County	37.1	44.4	29.5	37.4	X	36.4	57.1	31.1	1 676	46.5	23.6	18.7	0.6	-1.1	58.2	23.9	17.0	0.8
Bonner County	30.4	38.4	22.4	30.3	12.5	23.3	29.8	35.9	8 828	43.1	24.6	20.3	-1.2	-9.3	67.9	14.3	17.5	0.4
Bonneville County	39.2	52.0	26.9	39.8	42.3	36.5	38.1	30.6	25 478	47.6	30.5	15.5	-1.5	2.6	70.2	17.5	11.9	0.4
Boundary County	31.3	41.1	21.4	31.0	X	27.5	42.0	43.8	2 711	39.5	34.9	15.0	-10.1	-12.5	63.2	16.9	17.7	2.1
Butte County	32.3	42.3	22.4	33.3	0.0	0.0	0.0	22.2	799	54.1	28.3	11.0	0.5	-2.7	55.4	22.0	21.3	0.5
Camas County	35.1	43.5	26.1	35.8	16.7	0.0	X	11.8	230	63.9	19.1	13.9	13.2	4.3	56.3	23.2	20.0	0.4
Canyon County	39.8	50.2	29.9	40.7	38.5	39.0	42.9	35.1	38 555	47.4	26.1	18.1	0.9	1.3	75.5	13.4	10.6	0.4
Caribou County	31.6	47.1	16.0	31.8	100.0	90.9	100.0	24.6	2 260	50.0	35.2	10.2	-4.4	-7.9	66.4	17.3	15.1	1.3
Cassia County	32.3	45.9	18.6	33.5	0.0	34.0	34.1	26.1	7 048	47.8	29.9	13.5	-3.3	-1.7	67.5	14.1	17.5	0.9
Clark County	32.9	41.4	23.4	43.1	0.0	33.3	X	12.4	336	36.0	40.5	13.1	-15.5	-6.9	58.7	27.5	12.3	1.6
Clearwater County	28.8	34.9	21.8	29.0	0.0	27.7	16.7	26.4	1 946	46.7	23.1	19.6	1.7	-13.3	55.7	30.6	13.2	0.5

[1] Hispanic or Latino persons may be of any race.

Table B-3. States and Counties — Education, Labor Force, and Income

STATE County	Percent who worked at home	Percent of the population 5 years and over with a disability	Veterans as a percent of the population 18 years and over	Occupation for employed population 16 years and over (percent)						Industry for employed population 16 years and over (percent)					
				Management, professional, and related occupations	Service occupations	Sales and office occupations	Farming, fishing, and forestry occupations	Construction, extraction, and maintenance occupations	Production, transportation and material moving occupations	Agriculture, forestry, fishing, and mining	Construction and manufacturing	Wholesale and retail trade	Transportation and warehousing, and utilities	Service industries	Public administration
	42	43	44	45	46	47	48	49	50	51	52	53	54	55	56
GEORGIA—Cont'd															
Richmond County..............	1.4	24.4	16.9	30.5	18.4	25.3	0.2	9.7	16.0	0.4	18.4	15.4	5.5	54.6	5.8
Rockdale County..........	2.7	18.2	15.9	33.6	11.6	26.0	0.1	14.1	14.6	0.3	25.9	14.5	6.3	47.0	6.0
Schley County..............	1.6	23.3	12.5	26.0	9.3	19.9	2.4	14.2	28.1	5.7	34.1	14.9	9.4	31.0	4.9
Screven County.............	2.9	27.2	12.1	21.7	15.4	20.1	2.7	11.3	28.8	5.3	34.9	12.8	7.1	34.3	5.6
Seminole County...........	1.4	25.9	13.2	22.0	14.2	24.6	2.0	12.9	24.2	6.4	30.2	17.1	5.2	36.5	4.6
Spalding County............	1.3	25.0	12.6	22.5	12.6	24.9	0.4	15.1	24.6	0.5	32.7	17.3	6.9	37.6	5.0
Stephens County..........	1.7	23.8	12.3	23.2	12.5	24.1	0.9	12.2	27.2	1.4	40.7	12.7	3.4	38.7	3.1
Stewart County..............	1.3	32.0	9.4	24.8	14.7	18.8	3.3	12.6	25.8	5.3	29.6	10.9	4.8	43.6	5.8
Sumter County	1.5	22.9	10.6	29.9	16.3	21.9	2.0	9.8	20.0	4.5	25.6	14.0	4.2	45.8	6.0
Talbot County...............	1.5	28.6	12.3	21.2	14.9	16.9	1.5	11.3	34.2	4.1	35.3	11.9	5.8	38.6	4.3
Taliaferro County...........	2.2	28.3	9.0	17.6	16.8	14.3	2.4	12.9	36.1	5.4	42.5	12.3	4.5	29.2	6.1
Tattnall County..............	2.7	22.5	12.9	23.3	16.3	20.3	9.5	14.0	16.7	14.4	20.1	13.0	5.0	34.4	13.1
Taylor County................	2.2	25.9	10.7	22.5	13.8	21.6	2.8	15.0	24.3	5.7	28.6	14.3	6.1	38.4	6.9
Telfair County................	1.5	29.8	10.7	22.2	14.6	17.7	4.0	10.0	31.5	8.1	29.4	14.3	8.6	31.2	8.4
Terrell County................	3.0	26.7	11.8	23.6	15.4	20.3	1.7	10.4	28.4	5.6	30.4	15.1	4.4	35.4	9.2
Thomas County.............	2.0	25.8	13.2	32.0	15.7	23.9	1.3	9.4	17.7	3.4	24.1	15.4	4.0	47.0	6.1
Tift County....................	1.6	22.9	11.2	26.5	14.8	24.6	3.1	11.2	19.8	5.4	23.5	18.1	4.3	43.8	4.9
Toombs County.............	1.1	24.1	11.1	27.0	16.2	21.7	5.7	11.8	17.6	8.2	22.9	14.2	7.7	38.1	8.9
Towns County	4.5	24.0	17.4	27.7	16.9	26.0	0.5	18.0	11.0	3.2	25.5	14.4	5.0	47.9	4.0
Treutlen County.............	1.3	28.6	10.2	25.5	17.3	20.3	1.8	18.3	16.7	2.0	33.6	11.9	3.9	40.5	8.0
Troup County	1.3	23.3	12.9	27.6	13.7	24.0	0.3	10.9	23.4	0.8	35.5	14.7	3.5	42.0	3.6
Turner County................	3.1	24.8	11.2	23.7	14.3	24.3	2.7	9.1	25.8	8.8	27.3	15.1	5.6	34.6	8.6
Twiggs County	2.8	23.3	9.6	15.4	14.6	25.8	1.3	19.1	23.7	7.3	31.3	13.7	5.0	35.5	7.2
Union County	3.6	24.2	18.4	22.4	15.6	24.2	2.2	17.0	18.6	4.3	26.6	17.0	5.3	43.5	3.3
Upson County	2.0	25.3	13.3	23.0	12.9	22.2	0.9	11.5	29.5	1.6	40.9	13.4	5.0	34.3	4.9
Walker County...............	1.6	25.7	13.1	20.9	13.9	24.0	0.6	13.6	27.1	1.1	36.3	15.7	5.1	38.4	3.5
Walton County...............	3.4	19.2	11.8	25.2	11.9	27.5	0.4	18.3	16.6	1.1	32.4	16.4	5.4	40.3	4.3
Ware County..................	2.3	28.9	15.2	24.5	17.0	25.5	1.5	12.7	18.9	2.8	21.1	17.2	8.1	43.1	7.7
Warren County	3.0	28.7	9.4	20.4	13.4	17.0	1.7	11.6	36.0	6.7	36.3	11.3	8.0	33.6	4.1
Washington County.......	1.3	24.6	10.3	22.8	20.1	19.4	1.5	13.4	22.8	10.8	20.1	12.2	9.8	38.8	8.4
Wayne County...............	2.4	22.6	14.8	24.3	14.6	23.8	1.1	16.0	20.2	2.3	27.6	16.5	6.7	39.2	7.8
Webster County	1.3	28.6	11.1	23.2	13.2	18.2	5.8	9.1	30.5	9.0	31.8	11.7	8.2	31.3	8.0
Wheeler County	2.8	29.6	11.4	23.4	18.0	13.6	5.1	13.1	26.8	10.3	26.0	11.6	9.3	34.5	8.3
White County................	3.7	22.0	15.5	25.4	14.0	27.4	1.3	15.7	16.2	3.4	29.1	17.3	4.2	41.8	4.2
Whitfield County............	1.7	22.0	10.5	21.9	9.6	25.0	0.9	8.5	34.1	1.2	49.4	13.7	3.8	29.7	2.1
Wilcox County	3.1	25.4	13.0	24.9	18.7	18.5	3.5	11.9	22.5	9.3	22.5	14.1	5.8	35.3	13.0
Wilkes County	3.4	26.7	13.2	20.9	13.1	22.1	1.6	14.2	28.2	4.4	38.0	15.8	4.2	32.2	5.3
Wilkinson County	1.4	25.8	11.0	22.0	17.6	20.9	0.9	18.5	20.3	11.5	22.6	9.4	5.8	42.1	8.5
Worth County	2.0	24.5	13.4	22.8	13.9	24.8	2.2	13.3	22.9	4.9	27.0	15.6	5.3	39.4	7.9
HAWAII.....................	3.6	18.4	13.1	32.2	20.9	28.1	1.3	8.6	8.9	2.3	9.5	15.4	6.2	58.5	8.1
Hawaii County..............	6.1	18.9	14.5	30.2	22.2	25.1	3.8	9.9	8.9	7.1	10.4	14.8	5.5	56.6	5.7
Honolulu County...........	2.9	17.9	13.2	33.8	19.6	29.1	0.7	8.1	8.8	1.1	9.2	15.7	6.5	58.2	9.3
Kalawao County...........	0.0	60.5	0.0	0.0	0.0	50.0	0.0	24.1	25.9	0.0	24.1	25.9	0.0	50.0	0.0
Kauai County................	5.4	19.6	13.2	29.0	24.2	25.6	2.3	9.9	9.1	4.6	10.2	14.2	5.6	59.5	6.0
Maui County.................	4.9	20.0	11.3	26.3	26.4	26.2	2.1	9.6	9.4	3.6	10.4	14.8	5.8	61.4	4.1
IDAHO.......................	4.7	17.1	14.8	31.4	15.6	25.3	2.7	10.8	14.2	5.8	21.2	16.2	4.7	47.1	5.1
Ada County	4.3	15.0	14.3	38.2	14.2	28.2	0.5	8.8	10.2	1.1	21.9	16.9	4.1	49.7	6.3
Adams County..............	13.0	20.3	19.8	27.7	18.1	21.7	5.3	14.3	12.9	18.4	18.0	14.8	3.7	38.8	6.4
Bannock County...........	2.9	16.9	13.0	32.3	16.3	27.8	0.6	9.9	13.1	1.5	17.8	15.3	6.0	54.9	4.5
Bear Lake County	5.1	17.2	14.6	25.9	17.2	22.0	3.1	13.9	17.8	12.9	23.4	17.3	4.6	38.3	3.7
Benewah County..........	4.3	21.0	18.0	21.4	18.1	23.2	4.5	10.0	22.8	9.9	20.7	14.7	5.2	42.3	7.1
Bingham County...........	5.6	17.0	12.5	28.7	15.5	21.3	4.7	11.5	18.2	8.8	23.3	15.2	4.1	42.7	5.9
Blaine County...............	8.5	10.2	11.5	35.6	17.9	25.0	2.0	13.7	5.9	4.0	18.4	14.4	3.1	57.6	2.6
Boise County................	5.0	19.4	19.3	33.1	14.2	22.8	3.2	14.6	12.2	6.6	26.3	12.8	5.3	39.0	10.0
Bonner County	6.7	19.7	18.5	26.8	16.7	23.2	2.9	13.4	17.0	5.5	23.4	17.1	5.1	45.4	3.5
Bonneville County	4.4	15.8	13.8	36.0	15.0	27.4	1.7	8.8	11.1	3.0	15.0	18.8	3.7	54.4	5.1
Boundary County	5.3	17.9	19.0	25.1	16.3	22.3	5.8	9.8	20.8	11.1	21.7	14.7	6.2	41.5	4.7
Butte County	7.3	17.6	14.6	36.7	16.2	20.1	4.3	10.8	12.0	17.5	11.8	11.2	8.5	43.6	7.3
Camas County	8.7	14.3	17.2	29.5	14.8	18.8	3.2	19.8	13.8	15.4	18.2	11.8	5.8	41.9	6.8
Canyon County.............	3.8	18.2	12.9	26.1	15.2	23.6	2.8	13.1	19.1	4.7	29.0	15.5	5.3	41.0	4.5
Caribou County	6.1	18.7	14.3	27.9	16.3	18.0	4.5	15.6	17.6	17.4	28.0	10.2	4.4	36.4	3.7
Cassia County	4.9	18.0	11.4	26.2	13.8	23.6	6.8	10.2	19.4	16.0	20.0	17.0	6.4	36.9	3.8
Clark County	7.7	19.7	9.8	21.7	13.8	13.8	20.1	11.6	19.0	34.4	23.4	8.7	3.3	22.8	7.4
Clearwater County	5.0	24.8	19.1	25.0	20.0	20.6	5.2	11.4	17.8	13.9	20.6	9.5	4.7	41.9	9.4

STATE County	Median house-hold income	Median family income				Median nonfamily house-hold income	Median income for full-year, full-time workers		Per capita income	Households by source of income (percent)					House-holds with income over $100,000 (percent)	+/- U.S. percent for income over $100,000 (percent)	House-holds with income below poverty (percent)	Families with children with income below poverty (percent)
		All families	Married-couple	Male house-holder	Female house-holder		Men	Women		With earnings	With interest, dividend, or rental income	With Social Security income	With public assis-tance income	With retire-ment income				
	57	58	59	60	61	62	63	64	65	66	67	68	69	70	71	72	73	74
GEORGIA—Cont'd																		
Richmond County	33 086	38 509	47 995	22 947	15 839	21 903	31 110	23 765	17 088	80.0	23.2	25.0	5.2	19.4	6.4	-5.9	17.9	23.1
Rockdale County	53 599	60 065	67 226	36 131	26 688	31 690	41 871	30 099	22 300	86.8	34.1	21.3	1.3	16.7	16.7	4.4	7.0	8.0
Schley County	32 035	36 215	50 625	20 625	16 750	15 563	29 688	20 802	14 981	77.1	17.7	26.3	4.3	15.2	3.7	-8.6	19.5	21.3
Screven County	29 312	34 753	45 679	26 250	15 000	13 372	30 874	20 648	13 894	74.8	19.8	32.4	4.8	15.4	2.9	-9.4	21.7	20.6
Seminole County	27 094	33 221	45 321	20 441	14 800	13 116	26 692	20 938	14 635	72.6	23.1	36.7	8.3	15.5	4.9	-7.4	20.1	25.6
Spalding County	36 221	41 631	53 216	21 776	18 502	20 982	33 898	22 652	16 791	79.7	23.0	28.1	3.6	17.4	6.8	-5.5	15.5	18.7
Stephens County	29 466	35 660	41 701	21 818	17 289	16 450	28 600	21 474	15 529	76.4	25.6	31.8	3.1	15.9	4.9	-7.4	16.3	15.0
Stewart County	24 789	29 611	44 306	12 361	15 304	13 750	28 373	19 643	16 071	73.4	15.7	33.4	7.1	16.9	4.1	-8.2	22.2	26.9
Sumter County	30 904	35 379	46 863	21 875	12 839	18 615	28 848	21 145	15 083	79.0	21.9	25.7	6.4	14.1	5.7	-6.6	21.2	25.5
Talbot County	26 611	35 208	46 750	38 125	12 196	12 068	30 000	19 820	14 539	71.5	15.3	35.5	4.6	17.1	4.4	-7.9	24.8	31.2
Taliaferro County	23 750	27 800	48 750	22 083	12 917	14 417	26 616	21 646	15 498	67.4	20.3	41.2	4.5	12.8	6.2	-6.1	25.2	30.8
Tattnall County	28 664	35 951	42 294	14 375	12 273	14 136	29 390	20 720	13 439	76.2	17.8	28.9	5.2	17.1	4.4	-7.9	22.5	26.3
Taylor County	25 148	30 000	43 636	16 442	12 464	11 343	30 574	21 073	13 432	71.9	16.4	31.9	7.2	16.6	4.0	-8.3	27.1	29.0
Telfair County	26 097	32 513	44 375	18 750	11 649	11 435	26 744	20 313	14 197	69.5	16.0	33.6	4.2	13.3	4.7	-7.6	23.4	22.2
Terrell County	26 969	31 693	47 037	20 066	13 237	13 327	28 538	20 585	13 894	73.8	20.6	31.7	10.5	14.6	5.0	-7.3	27.2	32.6
Thomas County	31 115	39 239	49 167	16 426	16 045	16 045	29 659	21 962	16 211	74.9	25.7	30.2	4.1	16.1	6.0	-6.3	18.6	19.3
Tift County	32 616	39 083	47 354	23 750	12 463	17 869	28 830	21 527	16 833	80.7	24.8	26.4	3.5	13.4	7.4	-4.9	18.7	22.9
Toombs County	26 811	34 478	41 627	22 104	14 383	12 935	27 336	19 140	14 252	75.9	20.8	28.4	4.9	12.3	5.3	-7.0	22.4	26.9
Towns County	31 950	37 295	42 852	17 656	17 125	15 571	30 175	22 882	18 221	63.6	38.8	48.0	1.7	27.7	7.1	-5.2	13.4	13.0
Treutlen County	24 644	32 762	37 314	26 042	15 536	8 929	27 068	20 772	13 122	71.1	14.3	32.9	6.3	13.6	3.4	-8.9	27.8	27.8
Troup County	35 469	41 891	55 160	28 818	17 829	19 732	32 829	23 194	17 626	80.1	24.5	27.8	3.6	13.8	8.0	-4.3	15.2	17.3
Turner County	25 676	31 445	36 731	30 469	13 910	13 155	26 217	20 594	13 454	77.5	21.4	32.2	6.5	10.2	4.7	-7.6	23.0	28.1
Twiggs County	31 608	38 715	52 600	28 690	16 705	12 288	31 683	22 402	14 259	74.2	15.1	29.2	4.9	18.6	5.4	-6.9	20.3	20.8
Union County	31 893	39 776	45 929	19 583	19 289	16 722	30 428	21 365	18 845	68.2	38.0	40.3	1.1	27.3	5.2	-7.1	14.1	9.9
Upson County	31 201	37 418	47 209	21 919	17 327	14 767	31 238	21 089	17 053	74.6	24.0	32.8	3.6	18.6	4.7	-7.6	14.7	17.2
Walker County	32 406	39 034	45 006	24 087	17 071	15 210	30 094	22 013	15 867	77.8	23.6	29.7	2.5	14.1	3.9	-8.4	13.5	15.7
Walton County	46 479	52 386	59 124	31 582	19 357	24 897	38 318	26 322	19 470	85.6	26.5	23.1	2.0	13.2	10.7	-1.6	9.9	10.9
Ware County	28 360	34 372	41 314	22 292	13 660	15 950	27 487	21 114	14 384	73.5	20.7	35.2	4.1	16.1	3.8	-8.5	20.1	24.8
Warren County	27 366	32 868	45 250	13 929	11 198	15 151	28 654	20 302	14 022	71.4	16.5	32.9	7.0	15.1	3.7	-8.6	26.4	32.9
Washington County	29 910	36 325	53 354	14 706	12 708	15 258	35 067	21 914	15 565	76.0	19.4	29.8	6.2	13.6	6.1	-6.2	22.1	25.3
Wayne County	32 766	39 442	49 866	21 012	14 464	14 936	33 283	20 105	15 628	76.4	21.7	29.6	3.7	15.8	6.4	-5.9	17.3	19.1
Webster County	27 992	32 462	43 889	24 583	15 714	14 773	26 722	19 760	14 772	73.4	21.3	33.6	3.9	12.1	3.7	-8.6	19.3	22.9
Wheeler County	24 053	29 696	39 615	25 893	16 615	11 380	27 659	23 293	13 005	70.8	11.2	32.9	5.0	14.0	4.3	-8.0	28.1	29.1
White County	36 084	40 704	43 107	21 964	18 571	21 250	30 410	22 905	17 193	78.2	31.1	31.0	1.9	17.5	4.8	-7.5	11.9	10.4
Whitfield County	39 377	44 652	46 750	28 971	21 939	21 424	30 802	24 574	18 515	84.3	27.1	25.1	2.4	9.5	8.9	-3.4	11.4	11.6
Wilcox County	27 483	34 968	42 571	21 667	11 174	12 369	27 725	20 960	14 014	73.0	18.5	32.5	5.1	16.2	5.1	-7.2	21.7	24.5
Wilkes County	27 644	36 219	47 148	26 500	14 089	13 175	28 583	21 867	15 020	70.0	22.6	34.0	5.1	16.4	4.1	-8.2	18.8	17.9
Wilkinson County	32 723	39 349	47 585	30 625	16 622	14 753	32 310	22 185	14 658	74.3	18.6	33.1	4.8	19.6	3.2	-9.1	18.3	21.8
Worth County	32 304	30 007	49 005	21 250	14 091	15 519	32 451	21 657	15 856	76.4	21.5	20.2	5.1	14.6	5.4	6.0	17.0	20.6
HAWAII	49 820	56 961	61 332	30 830	21 954	30 272	36 808	29 831	21 525	82.9	45.5	27.8	7.2	21.2	16.6	4.3	10.5	11.3
Hawaii County	39 805	46 480	53 128	24 060	18 076	22 359	34 158	27 171	18 791	78.5	41.2	29.9	9.7	20.5	10.5	-1.8	14.8	17.1
Honolulu County	51 914	60 118	62 676	33 020	22 711	31 440	37 423	30 444	21 998	83.6	46.9	27.5	6.8	21.9	18.2	5.9	9.7	10.3
Kalawao County	9 333	26 250	0	0	0	8 750	38 750	18 750	13 756	55.3	22.0	33.3	0.0	22.0	0.0	-12.3	44.7	X
Kauai County	45 020	51 384	59 384	27 444	23 931	26 033	35 117	27 797	20 301	80.9	44.6	30.0	7.8	21.0	12.2	-0.1	10.6	12.3
Maui County	49 489	55 277	62 086	32 393	21 284	31 089	35 453	28 176	22 033	84.4	42.0	26.6	6.3	15.5	15.5	3.2	10.1	10.6
IDAHO	37 572	43 490	49 381	27 714	18 494	21 861	34 323	23 991	17 841	82.2	36.4	25.2	3.4	15.6	7.3	-5.0	11.2	12.2
Ada County	46 140	54 416	62 064	31 167	21 959	28 429	39 887	27 202	22 519	86.5	40.6	18.9	2.7	13.9	12.0	-0.3	7.4	7.9
Adams County	28 423	32 335	36 938	25 000	20 083	17 083	31 587	16 339	14 908	74.4	32.7	33.7	3.1	22.4	3.6	-8.7	14.5	16.0
Bannock County	36 683	44 192	50 588	28 404	16 026	20 113	37 191	24 678	17 148	82.8	37.7	24.4	4.5	14.3	7.2	-5.1	14.1	14.5
Bear Lake County	32 162	38 351	48 616	24 107	14 000	16 250	34 375	18 403	13 592	72.9	33.4	36.8	3.6	19.6	2.0	-10.3	10.3	10.4
Benewah County	31 517	36 000	42 286	30 370	11 643	18 782	35 795	21 493	15 285	75.4	31.2	33.1	5.8	18.6	3.9	-8.4	13.3	16.4
Bingham County	36 423	40 312	46 884	25 156	17 380	17 742	32 798	22 310	14 365	84.2	32.0	26.3	4.0	15.3	5.3	-7.0	11.5	14.2
Blaine County	50 496	60 037	60 841	43 036	23 292	35 087	36 871	30 058	31 346	88.7	49.7	14.8	1.1	10.3	18.3	6.0	7.3	8.6
Boise County	38 651	43 138	48 203	19 167	17 955	22 155	36 892	27 599	18 787	81.3	36.4	25.9	3.0	19.2	8.2	-4.1	12.5	14.5
Bonner County	32 803	37 930	43 231	27 202	14 321	18 923	33 927	21 508	17 263	76.0	33.9	29.2	3.4	19.7	4.9	-7.4	14.6	17.7
Bonneville County	41 805	48 216	54 755	29 630	19 344	21 624	40 398	23 464	18 326	83.5	39.6	24.5	3.5	16.7	8.9	-3.4	10.0	11.2
Boundary County	31 250	36 440	44 548	26 250	13 281	16 182	31 537	19 048	14 636	76.8	33.0	27.7	2.4	16.7	3.3	-9.0	15.1	17.5
Butte County	30 473	36 950	45 208	21 875	10 179	17 434	39 375	22 308	14 948	74.9	35.8	34.0	3.2	20.8	4.4	-7.9	15.9	26.0
Camas County	34 167	40 156	47 083	21 667	14 375	21 806	31 522	21 786	19 550	84.2	33.4	32.2	0.8	20.4	6.0	-6.3	9.0	8.0
Canyon County	35 884	40 377	44 640	25 985	19 084	20 060	30 205	22 775	15 155	82.5	29.4	26.1	4.1	13.7	5.0	-7.3	11.3	12.9
Caribou County	37 609	42 630	48 438	28 750	16 979	16 535	39 750	20 972	15 179	78.2	34.9	30.7	3.9	17.6	5.6	-6.7	10.7	10.1
Cassia County	33 322	38 162	42 248	26 042	15 028	15 975	29 984	20 324	14 087	81.6	31.1	28.5	3.3	15.3	4.3	-8.0	13.0	16.6
Clark County	31 576	31 534	32 000	23 750	15 000	21 875	26 094	20 385	11 141	86.7	27.7	21.2	3.2	14.5	0.9	-11.4	18.9	25.3
Clearwater County	32 071	37 259	42 593	25 714	15 750	17 483	32 385	22 308	15 463	74.0	30.3	36.7	3.6	21.4	3.0	-9.3	12.1	16.4

Table B-3. States and Counties — Education, Labor Force, and Income

STATE/ County code	MSA/PMSA/ NECMA code[1]	STATE County	High school graduates			College graduates		College graduates (percent)				
			Total population 25 years and over	Percent with a high school diploma or less	Percent with a high school diploma or more	Percent with a bachelor's degree or more	+/− U.S. percent with bachelor's degree or more	Non-Hispanic White	Black or African American	American Indian and Alaska Native	Asian, Hawaiian, and Pacific Islander	Hispanic or Latino[2]
			1	2	3	4	5	6	7	8	9	10
		IDAHO—Cont'd										
16 037	...	Custer County	3 012	53.0	84.5	17.4	-7.0	17.6	X	28.6	X	12.4
16 039	...	Elmore County	17 034	37.8	87.2	17.3	-7.1	18.6	13.2	2.4	26.7	8.5
16 041	...	Franklin County	6 069	51.8	88.2	13.6	-10.8	14.0	X	12.5	33.3	0.0
16 043	...	Fremont County	6 790	54.2	80.4	12.0	-12.4	13.1	X	0.0	0.0	0.8
16 045	...	Gem County	9 663	55.6	79.4	11.4	-13.0	11.6	X	5.7	32.2	3.5
16 047	...	Gooding County	8 761	62.1	72.6	12.0	-12.4	13.7	X	0.0	6.7	0.6
16 049	...	Idaho County	10 638	55.4	82.9	14.4	-10.0	14.7	X	6.7	27.3	13.4
16 051	...	Jefferson County	10 335	45.0	84.4	15.2	-9.2	16.3	0.0	6.8	50.0	1.2
16 053	...	Jerome County	10 946	51.7	75.1	14.0	-10.4	15.7	0.0	14.3	29.1	3.5
16 055	...	Kootenai County	69 872	43.0	87.3	19.1	-5.3	19.3	10.8	8.1	33.2	13.3
16 057	...	Latah County	19 493	31.6	91.0	41.0	16.6	40.1	48.3	37.1	78.8	32.0
16 059	...	Lemhi County	5 373	48.8	82.5	17.9	-6.5	17.9	X	0.0	100.0	11.6
16 061	...	Lewis County	2 596	50.5	84.2	14.8	-9.6	14.7	22.2	7.4	20.0	7.4
16 063	...	Lincoln County	2 458	55.5	77.4	13.0	-11.4	14.2	0.0	7.1	14.3	1.3
16 065	...	Madison County	9 320	33.8	88.5	24.4	0.0	25.3	X	12.5	33.7	4.1
16 067	...	Minidoka County	11 940	59.1	73.7	10.1	-14.3	12.2	0.0	0.0	20.0	1.8
16 069	...	Nez Perce County	24 759	46.3	85.5	18.9	-5.5	19.2	20.0	11.7	37.4	5.8
16 071	...	Oneida County	2 493	45.3	86.4	15.0	-9.4	15.1	X	0.0	100.0	0.0
16 073	...	Owyhee County	6 372	67.0	67.6	10.2	-14.2	12.1	28.6	4.5	22.8	1.6
16 075	...	Payette County	12 761	57.5	74.5	10.6	-13.8	11.6	0.0	14.8	20.5	0.2
16 077	...	Power County	4 344	58.1	74.7	14.3	-10.1	17.4	X	2.7	0.0	0.9
16 079	...	Shoshone County	9 670	62.4	77.9	10.2	-14.2	10.3	62.5	5.1	23.8	9.0
16 081	...	Teton County	3 614	35.3	87.3	28.1	3.7	30.4	0.0	0.0	100.0	2.8
16 083	...	Twin Falls County	39 544	49.1	81.3	16.0	-8.4	16.9	0.0	8.7	9.8	4.7
16 085	...	Valley County	5 525	40.2	88.9	26.3	1.9	26.8	X	0.0	23.8	16.1
16 087	...	Washington County	6 542	58.9	76.6	12.7	-11.7	13.7	0.0	28.6	44.4	0.0
17 000	...	**ILLINOIS**..................	7 973 671	46.3	81.4	26.1	1.7	28.8	14.7	13.3	57.4	9.1
17 001	...	Adams County	45 101	53.8	83.7	17.6	-6.8	17.8	6.3	0.0	45.5	24.4
17 003	...	Alexander County	6 395	67.7	67.0	6.9	-17.5	8.6	3.6	0.0	8.3	0.0
17 005	...	Bond County	11 731	61.4	72.8	15.0	-9.4	16.4	2.1	4.2	23.1	9.6
17 007	6880	Boone County	26 061	57.5	80.8	14.5	-9.9	15.4	15.4	1.6	42.0	4.6
17 009	...	Brown County	4 844	65.6	63.3	9.2	-15.2	11.7	0.0	0.0	10.0	5.5
17 011	...	Bureau County	24 085	54.9	84.1	15.7	-8.7	15.8	24.0	9.1	52.2	6.1
17 013	...	Calhoun County	3 528	64.7	79.9	9.4	-15.0	9.3	X	27.8	0.0	14.3
17 015	...	Carroll County	11 516	60.7	83.3	13.1	-11.3	13.1	7.1	0.0	57.1	1.7
17 017	...	Cass County	9 056	64.3	80.0	12.6	-11.8	13.1	0.0	13.3	77.3	2.1
17 019	1400	Champaign County	100 559	33.3	91.0	38.0	13.6	37.7	16.6	11.1	79.4	41.4
17 021	...	Christian County	24 202	62.6	81.0	10.5	-13.9	10.7	2.0	9.8	23.0	7.0
17 023	...	Clark County	11 569	59.3	80.0	13.6	-10.8	13.6	0.0	0.0	0.0	35.0
17 025	...	Clay County	9 898	62.3	75.9	9.7	-14.7	9.7	X	0.0	23.9	0.0
17 027	7040	Clinton County	23 463	57.6	77.4	13.0	-11.4	13.6	1.2	0.0	11.9	10.6
17 029	...	Coles County	30 326	49.7	82.9	20.8	-3.6	20.3	21.5	7.7	66.4	31.4
17 031	1600	Cook County	3 454 738	46.5	77.7	28.0	1.9	36.7	15.0	15.3	54.5	8.8
17 033	...	Crawford County	13 995	57.6	79.3	10.3	-14.1	10.7	1.7	0.0	32.0	8.0
17 035	...	Cumberland County	7 352	62.8	80.2	10.1	-14.3	10.1	0.0	15.4	66.7	3.7
17 037	1600	DeKalb County	48 912	42.4	87.5	26.8	2.4	26.8	30.4	23.3	58.6	14.6
17 039	...	De Witt County	11 354	60.1	83.5	13.4	-11.0	13.3	0.0	0.0	89.3	0.0
17 041	...	Douglas County	12 923	60.3	79.3	13.8	-10.6	13.9	0.0	0.0	48.8	3.8
17 043	1600	DuPage County	589 120	30.6	90.0	41.7	17.3	41.8	33.5	14.3	66.4	14.8
17 045	...	Edgar County	13 395	60.5	81.4	13.3	-11.1	13.5	0.0	2.4	100.0	8.2
17 047	...	Edwards County	4 815	56.6	82.3	9.8	-14.6	9.5	0.0	36.4	45.5	X
17 049	...	Effingham County	21 635	54.7	83.4	15.1	-9.3	15.1	45.5	14.3	33.8	12.7
17 051	...	Fayette County	14 611	68.7	72.2	9.0	-15.4	9.7	0.0	0.0	0.0	0.0
17 053	...	Ford County	9 557	56.0	86.0	13.9	-10.5	13.8	15.8	100.0	55.6	4.7
17 055	...	Franklin County	26 965	57.7	76.7	11.3	-13.1	11.2	0.0	33.8	50.0	2.8
17 057	...	Fulton County	26 529	59.7	78.3	11.4	-13.0	11.8	2.0	0.0	13.9	1.7
17 059	...	Gallatin County	4 481	63.3	73.6	7.7	-16.7	7.7	37.5	0.0	40.0	4.3
17 061	...	Greene County	9 688	64.9	78.9	10.1	-14.3	10.2	0.0	0.0	23.1	14.8
17 063	1600	Grundy County	24 297	52.0	86.9	15.2	-9.2	15.3	0.0	0.0	55.8	12.5
17 065	...	Hamilton County	5 866	57.6	74.3	10.5	-13.9	10.4	0.0	0.0	100.0	0.0
17 067	...	Hancock County	13 724	55.8	85.7	15.6	-8.8	15.7	0.0	0.0	0.0	16.4
17 069	...	Hardin County	3 442	60.9	68.1	9.6	-14.8	9.7	0.0	X	61.1	0.0
17 071	...	Henderson County	5 680	63.9	82.4	10.0	-14.4	10.1	0.0	0.0	100.0	0.0
17 073	1960	Henry County	34 183	52.7	84.5	15.7	-8.7	16.0	14.0	16.7	34.9	3.0
17 075	...	Iroquois County	21 111	60.3	80.3	11.8	-12.6	11.8	8.7	31.6	78.2	5.0

[1]MSA = Metropolitan Statistical Area. PMSA = Primary MSA. NECMA = New England County Metropolitan Area. See the Appendix A for explanation of these concepts. See Appendix B for list of metropolitan areas identified by type, with component counties.
[2]Hispanic or Latino persons may be of any race.

Table B-3. States and Counties — **Education, Labor Force, and Income**

STATE County	School enrollment			Population 16 to 19 years				Employment status, 2000			Work status in 1999 of the population 16 years and over (percent)		
											Worked in 1999		
	Grades kindergarten through 12	College or graduate school	Percent private	Number	Percent in armed forces	Percent high school graduates	Percent not enrolled, not grads, not in armed forces, not employed	Total population 16 years and over	Percent in labor force	Unemployment rate	Full-time	Part-time	Did not work in 1999
	11	12	13	14	15	16	17	18	19	20	21	22	23
IDAHO—Cont'd													
Custer County	909	69	2.4	202	0.0	13.4	5.0	3 346	61.9	6.2	52.1	16.7	31.1
Elmore County	5 757	1 494	6.2	1 564	9.2	30.0	4.2	21 768	61.2	5.0	66.7	13.9	19.5
Franklin County	3 142	187	1.9	834	0.0	14.0	1.8	7 610	68.2	5.3	51.4	21.7	26.9
Fremont County	3 039	327	4.7	1 036	0.2	11.6	5.2	8 538	63.2	5.3	52.3	19.3	28.4
Gem County	3 180	417	6.8	950	0.0	19.6	6.4	11 449	59.0	5.0	49.0	15.8	35.2
Gooding County	2 944	363	5.2	1 005	0.0	12.3	7.1	10 585	61.2	3.4	51.1	14.6	34.3
Idaho County	3 080	284	11.9	1 023	0.0	10.7	7.1	12 255	53.8	10.2	46.5	15.6	37.9
Jefferson County	5 235	602	3.5	1 528	0.1	15.6	5.4	13 058	66.5	4.4	54.2	18.2	27.6
Jerome County	4 311	570	7.4	1 189	0.0	10.9	7.1	13 194	65.2	5.9	55.5	16.4	28.1
Kootenai County	21 760	5 072	11.1	6 362	0.1	16.1	3.6	82 674	65.9	7.7	53.6	17.6	28.8
Latah County	5 152	9 171	7.2	3 480	0.5	7.4	0.2	28 729	65.2	7.6	51.1	27.9	21.0
Lemhi County	1 580	66	7.0	473	0.0	16.9	3.2	6 132	57.0	0.0	48.8	16.4	34.8
Lewis County	753	92	7.6	208	0.0	8.7	1.9	2 947	56.2	8.6	49.2	13.4	37.5
Lincoln County	946	120	1.9	244	0.0	9.8	5.7	2 940	63.7	3.9	55.4	18.0	26.6
Madison County	5 209	9 416	57.9	6 308	0.0	4.0	0.4	21 245	59.3	7.3	49.5	31.8	18.7
Minidoka County	4 896	670	5.1	1 525	0.0	15.7	7.3	14 599	64.4	6.5	54.6	15.6	29.7
Nez Perce County	6 565	2 459	7.6	2 165	0.0	15.5	3.0	29 676	63.2	4.6	50.8	17.2	32.0
Oneida County	1 053	113	2.5	287	0.0	17.1	3.8	2 970	61.9	4.2	50.3	16.6	33.1
Owyhee County	2 532	207	7.1	698	0.0	12.3	9.3	7 705	61.2	6.8	55.0	13.3	31.7
Payette County	4 757	536	5.8	1 340	0.0	12.1	4.1	15 112	61.9	6.2	51.9	15.9	32.3
Power County	1 898	275	3.5	508	0.0	13.4	1.8	5 279	66.1	4.7	57.9	16.8	25.3
Shoshone County	2 463	285	2.9	678	0.0	12.8	4.9	10 982	55.6	11.8	46.4	15.0	38.6
Teton County	1 375	170	12.1	366	0.0	15.6	4.4	4 303	72.8	3.3	61.5	18.4	20.1
Twin Falls County	13 204	3 482	7.4	4 434	0.0	13.5	4.4	48 581	65.6	5.9	53.9	17.5	28.6
Valley County	1 474	91	3.8	447	1.1	13.0	1.1	6 166	62.2	6.1	50.4	19.7	29.9
Washington County	2 062	164	3.4	640	0.0	14.2	6.9	7 610	60.5	7.8	50.7	14.6	34.6
ILLINOIS	2 387 464	810 038	17.5	704 632	0.8	10.6	5.7	9 530 946	65.4	6.0	56.0	15.2	28.9
Adams County	13 042	3 338	23.2	4 153	0.0	10.8	2.9	53 348	65.8	5.0	52.1	17.8	30.1
Alexander County	1 937	275	6.1	490	0.0	9.6	2.9	7 383	49.3	10.6	45.4	12.2	42.4
Bond County	2 917	1 371	25.1	1 053	0.0	7.6	5.0	14 217	57.4	5.3	55.2	16.9	27.9
Boone County	9 317	1 392	15.1	2 341	0.0	11.0	4.6	30 671	68.7	4.4	59.9	14.8	25.3
Brown County	1 086	142	9.4	329	0.6	8.8	16.7	5 868	44.7	3.5	51.0	15.1	33.9
Bureau County	6 738	1 147	8.9	2 049	0.0	9.3	4.3	27 818	65.5	4.4	54.7	15.7	29.6
Calhoun County	919	179	16.1	269	0.0	6.7	4.8	4 063	60.3	4.9	50.6	13.5	35.9
Carroll County	3 177	503	3.9	915	0.0	12.9	3.0	13 162	63.0	6.9	52.8	14.5	32.7
Cass County	2 571	410	9.2	772	0.0	9.1	8.2	10 709	64.5	5.8	55.7	13.7	30.6
Champaign County	27 413	42 713	5.6	17 484	0.1	5.6	1.4	145 926	67.7	5.5	53.4	26.1	20.5
Christian County	6 481	1 063	10.1	1 722	0.5	13.1	7.5	27 791	60.4	4.0	63.7	14.2	32.1
Clark County	3 248	554	2.4	928	0.0	5.6	4.0	13 331	62.2	4.8	53.4	14.4	32.1
Clay County	2 665	452	1.2	773	0.0	10.6	4.3	11 493	60.2	5.6	50.6	13.5	35.9
Clinton County	6 852	1 666	15.8	2 018	0.0	12.0	4.5	27 757	64.5	3.3	57.0	15.2	27.8
Coles County	7 503	10 787	3.1	4 817	0.0	7.2	2.0	43 986	63.5	5.5	51.7	22.7	25.6
Cook County	1 025 425	359 786	22.5	287 976	0.1	10.3	7.4	4 129 256	63.5	7.5	55.0	13.6	31.3
Crawford County	4 035	1 063	3.3	1 127	0.0	11.1	1.8	16 348	55.6	5.4	53.5	12.0	34.5
Cumberland County	2 274	436	6.5	682	0.0	11.6	3.2	8 621	66.3	5.4	56.1	15.0	28.9
DeKalb County	14 995	18 467	5.1	8 241	0.0	6.8	1.4	70 542	69.3	6.1	54.6	25.2	20.2
De Witt County	3 168	542	6.0	915	0.0	7.4	3.5	13 172	67.2	5.3	58.0	14.9	27.1
Douglas County	3 988	581	11.8	1 293	0.0	10.2	4.1	15 284	64.4	2.8	54.4	15.4	30.1
DuPage County	175 369	57 695	20.0	47 205	0.0	7.7	2.8	688 428	71.5	3.3	61.4	16.0	22.6
Edgar County	3 580	477	6.7	1 068	0.0	13.7	7.2	15 606	60.2	4.8	52.4	14.1	33.6
Edwards County	1 220	297	4.3	398	0.0	11.6	0.8	5 599	61.6	3.9	54.3	12.3	33.4
Effingham County	7 337	1 366	13.8	1 943	0.0	13.6	2.2	25 498	70.8	4.5	58.3	17.0	24.7
Fayette County	3 925	646	7.1	1 268	0.0	16.4	8.3	17 266	57.5	5.8	52.9	15.2	31.9
Ford County	2 677	456	5.6	666	0.3	7.8	5.7	10 990	64.8	3.3	54.8	14.8	30.4
Franklin County	6 783	1 697	4.0	1 948	0.2	10.0	6.1	31 035	55.4	6.8	45.1	14.1	40.7
Fulton County	6 491	1 358	4.2	1 980	0.1	11.6	7.1	30 863	56.1	6.7	48.9	14.5	36.7
Gallatin County	1 113	294	3.1	393	0.0	10.7	3.6	5 202	53.7	6.9	45.5	14.4	40.0
Greene County	2 830	436	8.7	854	0.0	14.8	7.3	11 446	58.4	5.6	49.3	14.4	36.3
Grundy County	7 006	1 710	8.2	2 354	0.0	13.3	3.2	28 772	67.7	4.6	55.4	17.2	27.3
Hamilton County	1 530	324	7.7	490	0.0	9.8	3.3	6 821	56.8	4.6	48.2	14.9	36.0
Hancock County	3 940	731	5.6	1 156	0.6	9.9	3.3	15 805	66.6	4.8	54.9	16.1	29.0
Hardin County	708	214	4.2	297	0.0	12.8	8.1	3 971	47.9	5.9	46.8	10.5	42.8
Henderson County	1 461	278	6.9	470	0.0	10.9	3.4	6 567	64.3	5.2	57.3	12.5	30.3
Henry County	9 918	2 008	7.1	2 885	0.0	12.8	2.0	39 691	66.0	4.4	53.3	17.1	29.6
Iroquois County	6 120	1 007	7.5	1 832	0.0	10.9	5.9	24 372	63.9	3.8	53.2	15.6	31.2

Table B-3. States and Counties — Education, Labor Force, and Income

STATE County	___ Full-year full-time employed (percent) ___ Total	Men	Women	Non-Hispanic White	Black or African American	American Indian and Alaska Native	Asian, Hawaiian, and Pacific Islander	Hispanic or Latino[1]	___ Children under 18 years in families ___ Number	With two parents (percent) Both in labor force	Father only in labor force	With one parent who is in labor force (percent)	+/− U.S. percent of children with no stay-at-home parent (percent)	+/− U.S. percent two-income couples	___ Total employed by class of worker (percent) ___ Private	Government	Self-employed	Unpaid family worker
	24	25	26	27	28	29	30	31	32	33	34	35	36	37	38	39	40	41
IDAHO—Cont'd																		
Custer County	33.8	42.6	24.3	34.0	X	43.8	X	27.7	1 093	59.7	20.1	16.0	11.1	0.9	57.2	20.7	21.1	1.0
Elmore County	49.1	63.0	31.2	50.3	63.9	39.5	33.3	37.8	7 803	49.5	28.6	16.2	1.1	3.8	62.5	26.0	10.9	0.6
Franklin County	37.1	53.4	21.5	37.5	X	48.0	22.2	31.9	4 164	54.8	32.3	9.1	-0.7	3.1	69.1	14.1	15.7	1.0
Fremont County	31.1	41.7	19.6	32.2	X	30.0	32.0	20.7	3 694	54.4	29.1	11.3	1.1	-1.8	64.6	17.7	16.7	1.0
Gem County	33.9	45.4	22.7	34.6	X	40.9	61.9	19.1	4 016	49.1	30.8	12.0	-3.5	-2.9	68.5	15.5	15.3	0.6
Gooding County	34.8	46.3	23.2	34.0	X	28.1	12.5	39.4	3 852	45.0	30.9	16.0	-3.6	-5.1	68.7	13.9	16.4	1.1
Idaho County	27.8	35.2	20.0	28.1	X	30.1	14.3	15.0	3 621	45.9	23.9	15.9	-2.8	-11.7	55.8	21.9	21.1	1.2
Jefferson County	36.5	50.0	23.0	37.4	57.7	48.1	88.9	25.5	6 769	50.7	35.5	7.7	-6.2	-0.1	64.1	18.4	16.7	0.8
Jerome County	36.3	47.0	24.9	37.7	0.0	48.0	16.7	27.8	5 581	43.5	31.4	14.1	-7.0	-1.9	68.2	14.2	16.8	0.8
Kootenai County	36.2	45.8	27.1	36.5	30.8	30.9	31.8	29.2	27 942	45.5	26.9	19.3	0.2	-1.2	72.8	13.2	13.6	0.4
Latah County	29.6	34.7	24.0	30.4	19.7	19.0	12.5	20.8	6 885	51.4	28.8	13.0	-0.2	2.8	52.2	36.4	10.8	0.6
Lemhi County	31.3	40.7	21.9	31.4	X	80.0	0.0	27.8	1 869	52.8	24.2	15.2	3.4	-7.4	56.3	19.6	23.3	0.7
Lewis County	32.4	43.0	22.1	31.6	0.0	32.5	28.6	55.6	905	55.5	20.7	17.7	8.6	-5.6	58.6	21.8	19.4	0.3
Lincoln County	34.2	44.1	23.8	34.7	19.0	21.1	71.4	30.1	1 179	51.7	25.8	13.2	0.3	0.5	62.1	21.2	15.8	0.8
Madison County	21.5	31.5	13.1	21.5	25.0	23.6	6.5	22.3	6 974	52.7	33.8	8.9	-3.0	4.6	77.5	11.3	10.4	0.8
Minidoka County	32.9	44.3	21.8	36.1	30.0	34.8	24.5	22.8	6 066	48.1	27.4	13.4	-3.1	-0.8	70.8	10.7	17.6	0.9
Nez Perce County	37.1	45.4	29.2	37.5	27.5	36.8	22.1	31.8	8 284	52.6	16.6	22.1	10.1	1.1	72.6	17.4	9.8	0.2
Oneida County	34.2	49.0	19.3	34.1	X	55.6	50.0	30.3	1 287	52.1	35.5	7.0	-5.5	3.0	58.8	17.3	22.0	1.9
Owyhee County	34.5	44.7	23.4	35.9	43.8	32.6	10.2	31.6	3 184	43.6	31.1	13.9	-7.1	-7.0	67.8	14.5	16.8	0.9
Payette County	34.4	43.6	25.4	34.9	66.7	31.1	9.9	31.7	6 046	43.0	27.6	18.1	-3.5	-4.5	71.2	15.5	12.7	0.6
Power County	36.1	49.8	22.4	38.7	X	20.4	0.0	27.2	2 429	55.1	25.6	12.4	2.9	4.6	63.7	18.4	16.1	1.9
Shoshone County	29.1	36.9	21.6	29.1	75.0	23.9	70.6	16.5	3 021	44.4	17.6	25.9	5.7	-10.2	71.2	17.6	10.8	0.4
Teton County	37.5	44.3	29.4	38.9	0.0	64.7	0.0	25.5	1 861	51.2	22.9	13.4	0.0	12.3	64.1	12.1	23.2	0.7
Twin Falls County	37.1	47.5	27.3	37.7	10.0	26.4	32.6	32.1	16 970	49.8	22.5	19.5	4.7	2.7	71.5	13.2	15.0	0.3
Valley County	31.9	39.5	24.0	31.8	X	27.9	25.9	31.7	1 699	60.5	19.8	13.9	9.8	-2.1	56.0	23.6	19.6	0.8
Washington County	34.1	44.4	24.7	34.2	0.0	9.1	26.0	37.3	2 578	57.1	20.4	11.9	4.4	-1.2	63.0	17.8	18.3	1.0
ILLINOIS	41.6	51.1	32.7	43.8	32.9	37.9	41.8	38.1	3 046 677	44.1	22.1	20.8	0.3	1.8	78.6	12.7	8.4	0.3
Adams County	40.9	51.9	31.0	41.4	30.4	39.8	37.7	28.7	16 287	60.9	14.3	17.8	14.1	6.8	77.8	12.0	9.9	0.3
Alexander County	30.0	39.5	21.1	32.6	25.0	46.2	33.3	27.2	2 215	27.5	16.3	29.5	-7.6	-10.8	69.5	21.6	8.7	0.2
Bond County	39.6	48.5	29.0	40.4	36.0	29.3	18.8	21.7	3 662	49.4	22.0	19.7	4.5	2.6	73.7	13.8	12.1	0.3
Boone County	46.8	59.6	34.2	46.6	51.2	56.7	55.1	47.5	11 870	52.4	20.8	17.3	5.1	3.2	82.5	8.5	8.9	0.1
Brown County	37.9	40.5	33.1	42.0	26.3	100.0	50.0	21.8	1 170	60.7	12.2	18.6	14.7	8.7	66.3	18.5	13.1	2.1
Bureau County	42.3	53.9	31.6	42.4	26.2	36.7	45.2	41.3	8 432	54.8	20.2	18.8	9.0	4.0	78.2	10.1	11.2	0.5
Calhoun County	35.2	43.0	27.2	35.3	X	11.1	0.0	18.8	1 138	62.0	20.7	12.6	10.0	-1.3	70.2	14.4	14.3	0.8
Carroll County	38.6	48.0	29.6	38.6	31.9	21.7	46.2	35.4	3 853	58.1	13.8	19.6	13.1	1.0	73.3	11.0	15.1	0.6
Cass County	40.5	50.7	30.6	41.2	0.0	60.0	57.1	29.6	3 208	56.5	18.0	17.9	9.8	3.2	72.9	14.9	11.5	0.7
Champaign County	35.6	42.0	29.4	38.6	29.5	34.8	17.4	23.1	35 714	52.1	16.6	23.8	11.3	8.4	64.3	28.4	7.0	0.3
Christian County	39.7	49.6	30.1	40.2	29.7	43.9	40.9	16.7	8 014	50.4	19.2	21.4	7.2	0.9	72.7	16.5	10.4	0.4
Clark County	40.1	48.0	32.8	40.0	0.0	38.9	85.2	64.0	4 058	53.5	18.3	19.5	8.4	0.6	77.2	12.5	9.9	0.4
Clay County	36.7	47.0	27.6	36.9	X	25.0	44.2	76.7	3 341	50.3	18.8	20.5	6.2	1.1	73.6	12.0	13.8	0.6
Clinton County	44.2	51.4	36.5	45.7	20.7	52.3	41.5	26.7	8 503	64.1	14.3	16.2	15.7	10.1	73.9	15.0	10.4	0.7
Coles County	34.1	42.6	26.6	34.7	21.7	22.9	17.5	24.1	10 054	52.7	17.5	22.2	10.3	3.6	72.1	19.5	8.1	0.3
Cook County	39.7	47.8	32.4	44.1	32.3	35.7	40.9	36.7	1 281 548	36.0	20.9	24.4	-4.2	-2.4	79.7	12.4	7.7	0.2
Crawford County	37.6	43.5	31.3	37.9	36.2	100.0	25.3	32.7	4 438	54.8	17.2	21.0	11.2	-0.6	75.0	13.8	10.5	0.7
Cumberland County	42.6	52.8	33.1	42.6	58.3	69.2	26.7	51.4	2 879	58.2	14.2	17.3	10.9	4.9	78.0	9.9	11.3	0.8
DeKalb County	38.0	47.0	29.4	39.6	21.2	67.8	13.1	39.9	19 866	53.8	22.2	18.0	7.2	9.3	71.6	20.0	8.2	0.3
De Witt County	44.8	54.5	35.5	44.8	5.0	38.5	85.7	42.3	3 964	54.1	19.0	21.1	10.6	2.9	76.7	11.8	11.2	0.3
Douglas County	42.7	53.8	32.3	42.6	18.5	60.0	55.6	42.2	5 227	44.2	33.0	16.3	-4.1	1.6	73.2	12.6	13.8	0.4
DuPage County	48.8	61.8	36.7	49.1	53.6	46.7	47.8	45.6	235 724	50.9	30.8	11.4	-2.3	6.6	81.7	9.3	8.8	0.2
Edgar County	39.1	49.5	29.6	39.5	22.6	55.8	0.0	33.3	4 506	48.0	19.8	19.4	2.8	-1.5	74.4	13.7	11.4	0.5
Edwards County	41.4	51.4	32.3	41.6	71.4	0.0	38.5	0.0	1 561	57.1	18.6	15.6	8.1	0.3	77.5	10.0	11.7	0.8
Effingham County	44.9	56.4	34.1	45.0	23.8	38.6	30.2	44.5	9 499	59.8	17.9	18.2	13.4	10.2	78.2	9.4	11.9	0.5
Fayette County	37.3	44.8	28.9	38.0	31.6	0.0	0.0	20.3	4 926	50.2	21.1	19.5	5.1	-0.6	72.9	15.1	11.5	0.6
Ford County	42.9	56.2	31.2	43.2	28.3	0.0	35.6	34.1	3 442	56.9	18.8	19.2	11.5	4.7	72.7	11.2	15.5	0.6
Franklin County	33.1	42.9	24.5	33.1	20.8	30.8	0.0	37.1	8 508	45.0	22.0	17.8	-1.8	-8.7	74.6	15.2	9.7	0.5
Fulton County	35.4	43.4	27.1	36.2	24.9	44.8	19.4	18.2	7 965	49.6	20.2	20.1	5.1	-3.6	74.0	15.0	10.5	0.6
Gallatin County	31.9	41.1	23.5	31.9	37.5	0.0	38.5	25.0	1 374	39.7	24.4	18.1	-6.8	-10.7	71.8	12.7	14.9	0.6
Greene County	36.5	43.8	29.5	37.0	0.0	9.3	0.0	23.7	3 563	49.5	19.8	20.2	5.1	-4.4	70.8	14.8	13.8	0.7
Grundy County	41.8	53.6	30.2	41.6	43.6	41.8	34.8	47.4	9 677	48.8	26.3	17.9	2.1	1.0	80.9	10.4	8.1	0.6
Hamilton County	32.0	42.4	22.4	32.3	0.0	23.7	0.0	25.0	1 915	54.6	17.7	14.4	4.4	-2.3	67.7	20.4	11.0	0.8
Hancock County	41.6	52.6	31.7	41.7	0.0	20.0	53.3	36.2	4 795	65.2	15.0	14.6	15.2	7.6	73.5	11.1	14.4	1.0
Hardin County	30.7	40.0	21.5	30.1	42.6	X	52.4	24.2	941	34.9	25.3	15.9	-13.8	-12.6	69.4	20.0	10.5	0.2
Henderson County	41.9	51.2	32.7	42.2	56.3	60.0	40.0	5.6	1 777	54.4	16.4	18.4	8.2	0.8	75.6	11.4	12.3	0.8
Henry County	41.0	51.9	30.7	41.0	46.3	33.3	29.5	45.6	12 530	56.6	17.6	18.1	10.1	4.9	76.9	11.2	11.2	0.8
Iroquois County	40.4	52.2	29.5	40.6	11.3	65.0	46.2	37.1	7 601	54.9	21.0	16.9	7.2	4.8	72.6	11.2	15.2	1.0

[1] Hispanic or Latino persons may be of any race.

				Occupation for employed population 16 years and over (percent)						Industry for employed population 16 years and over (percent)					
STATE County Percent who worked at home	Percent of the population 5 years and over with a disability	Veterans as a percent of the population 18 years and over	Management, professional, and related occupations	Service occupa- tions	Sales and office occupa- tions	Farming, fishing, and forestry occupa- tions	Con- struction, extraction, and main- tenance occupa- tions	Production, transporta- tion and material moving occupa- tions	Agricul- ture, forestry, fishing, and mining	Construc- tion and manufac- turing	Whole- sale and retail trade	Trans- porta- tion and ware- housing, and utilities	Service industries	Public adminis- tration
42	43	44	45	46	47	48	49	50	51	52	53	54	55	56
IDAHO—Cont'd														
Custer County	10.0	18.6	18.4	35.1	13.1	20.4	5.2	17.2	9.1	29.2	11.4	11.4	8.0	35.5	4.4
Elmore County	2.6	15.9	33.2	27.1	18.9	24.6	4.5	10.6	14.2	7.7	17.8	15.2	5.5	44.2	9.7
Franklin County	7.3	13.9	10.3	25.1	14.7	20.3	5.1	12.7	22.1	11.4	29.5	15.6	2.5	38.7	2.2
Fremont County	5.0	16.3	15.4	22.7	14.8	23.0	6.9	12.0	20.7	10.5	20.6	17.6	6.3	37.9	7.1
Gem County	6.2	21.3	17.0	21.9	16.8	24.3	3.1	12.8	21.0	7.5	28.9	13.6	5.4	39.5	5.2
Gooding County	6.8	19.4	14.6	24.1	15.1	17.6	15.4	12.7	15.1	24.4	16.4	13.1	8.1	35.0	3.0
Idaho County	9.0	21.1	19.0	28.9	17.9	21.7	3.9	11.6	16.0	14.5	19.3	15.8	5.2	38.9	6.3
Jefferson County	7.0	15.6	11.5	30.4	13.2	23.7	5.1	11.0	16.6	12.1	19.1	17.1	5.7	41.5	4.5
Jerome County..............	6.3	17.2	15.0	27.6	15.5	21.4	9.2	10.2	16.1	16.6	19.5	16.5	7.7	34.5	5.3
Kootenai County	4.3	18.1	16.9	27.8	16.7	27.5	1.1	13.4	13.5	2.7	22.5	18.3	3.7	48.8	4.0
Latah County	3.6	12.2	11.2	39.5	16.4	24.2	2.4	8.3	9.1	5.6	10.1	13.1	2.5	65.3	3.3
Lemhi County	10.8	21.8	19.4	33.6	17.4	21.0	4.8	11.6	11.5	16.7	14.0	16.5	3.8	43.1	5.9
Lewis County	7.3	23.9	19.0	28.9	18.8	18.0	5.4	10.2	18.8	15.5	19.0	15.2	4.7	38.4	7.2
Lincoln County	7.3	17.1	14.0	27.7	13.6	16.3	10.8	16.6	14.9	18.5	21.6	12.5	5.2	36.3	5.9
Madison County	5.7	9.7	5.1	31.6	16.7	29.2	2.6	7.6	12.4	5.3	15.1	14.9	3.1	59.2	2.4
Minidoka County	5.3	20.1	11.6	24.8	13.2	19.6	8.6	10.7	23.0	16.6	22.1	15.5	6.6	36.1	3.0
Nez Perce County........	2.5	19.9	16.9	27.3	17.5	26.2	1.3	10.2	17.6	3.2	21.9	14.3	4.0	50.2	6.4
Oneida County	8.0	17.9	12.3	28.6	14.6	15.4	3.9	11.4	26.1	13.4	36.0	10.0	3.8	33.5	3.3
Owyhee County	7.3	21.0	13.8	24.8	13.3	15.7	14.0	12.2	20.0	25.5	24.7	10.2	5.1	29.7	4.8
Payette County.............	5.0	19.0	16.6	23.8	16.4	21.5	6.4	12.0	19.9	10.6	24.2	17.6	5.6	35.4	6.6
Power County	5.6	19.4	12.3	27.8	12.8	19.8	9.1	9.5	21.0	18.4	24.6	11.4	5.8	36.1	3.8
Shoshone County	3.0	24.5	20.2	24.7	20.3	21.3	0.9	18.6	14.2	14.9	13.7	14.7	3.9	48.4	4.4
Teton County................	9.5	10.3	8.7	29.3	18.7	19.0	4.6	19.3	9.1	10.2	20.8	14.3	3.9	48.3	2.4
Twin Falls County	4.6	20.5	14.0	27.4	16.6	25.3	4.4	9.8	16.4	8.6	18.6	18.4	5.6	45.1	3.7
Valley County	4.5	16.0	18.5	29.7	18.8	23.4	2.0	16.1	9.9	7.0	20.0	14.8	5.2	44.3	8.7
Washington County.......	9.3	19.7	15.7	26.5	15.5	20.9	5.7	9.5	21.8	13.7	23.4	14.5	5.5	35.4	7.6
ILLINOIS.................	3.1	17.6	10.9	34.2	13.9	27.6	0.3	8.2	15.7	1.1	21.7	14.9	6.0	52.3	4.0
Adams County..............	2.2	17.0	15.2	27.7	16.7	27.4	0.7	8.7	18.8	3.2	22.3	18.2	4.5	48.6	3.2
Alexander County..........	1.7	28.2	14.8	24.6	22.3	18.9	0.6	12.0	21.6	3.2	22.8	12.9	7.0	43.4	10.7
Bond County	5.0	17.8	13.5	26.8	16.8	24.7	1.3	9.7	20.7	4.9	24.6	14.4	6.1	43.1	6.9
Boone County	3.3	15.3	12.4	25.3	12.8	24.1	0.0	10.9	20.0	1.0	37.8	13.7	6.2	28.2	2.4
Brown County	4.6	18.2	10.8	24.7	18.0	26.5	2.7	6.4	21.7	9.2	14.8	24.5	6.6	33.9	11.1
Bureau County	4.5	18.1	14.5	26.2	15.8	22.7	1.8	9.6	24.0	6.0	26.5	17.6	6.3	41.1	2.5
Calhoun County	6.2	19.6	16.1	26.1	16.9	18.8	2.2	20.4	15.7	8.9	24.5	11.4	7.1	42.4	5.7
Carroll County	5.6	17.1	15.4	25.8	14.7	18.8	1.7	11.2	27.9	6.5	33.8	12.2	6.6	37.3	3.6
Cass County.................	4.5	18.5	14.3	25.3	15.1	21.3	2.4	9.0	26.4	5.8	27.3	13.2	8.2	37.9	7.6
Champaign County	3.7	13.1	9.5	42.2	14.9	25.3	0.4	6.0	11.1	1.4	12.7	14.0	4.0	64.4	3.6
Christian County	3.5	19.4	14.6	25.0	16.4	25.6	1.5	11.9	19.5	5.1	20.2	13.9	6.8	45.8	8.2
Clark County	3.6	21.2	14.9	26.1	14.1	22.1	1.2	12.2	24.3	4.5	34.3	13.3	5.3	39.2	3.4
Clay County	3.8	21.9	13.4	23.4	15.6	21.8	0.9	10.8	27.6	6.6	32.1	14.3	5.8	37.6	3.6
Clinton County	4.5	16.4	14.6	28.7	15.0	22.3	1.4	11.7	21.0	4.9	24.9	14.1	5.4	43.9	6.9
Coles County	2.8	17.6	11.0	27.2	18.4	25.4	0.5	8.6	19.8	2.0	23.4	13.2	3.7	54.7	3.1
Cook County	2.6	19.7	8.9	35.2	14.0	28.5	0.1	7.1	15.1	0.1	19.1	13.9	6.7	56.3	3.9
Crawford County	4.0	19.6	15.2	24.3	15.9	20.0	0.7	11.1	28.0	5.2	35.1	10.7	5.4	38.4	5.2
Cumberland County	4.0	18.4	14.0	21.2	12.7	23.8	0.5	12.4	29.4	4.5	36.6	14.9	4.4	37.1	2.5
DeKalb County	3.3	14.0	10.5	32.7	15.1	26.6	0.5	9.5	15.5	2.9	23.4	14.4	4.2	52.3	2.9
De Witt County.............	3.7	18.0	15.9	26.1	15.5	27.1	0.7	10.8	19.9	4.7	23.1	13.8	10.4	44.8	3.2
Douglas County	5.8	15.8	12.8	25.3	15.1	24.7	1.1	9.7	24.1	5.4	29.9	17.4	5.8	39.1	2.4
DuPage County.............	3.5	12.2	9.5	43.7	9.4	30.2	0.1	6.5	10.1	0.2	20.3	16.9	5.5	54.7	2.3
Edgar County	3.0	23.7	12.7	25.7	15.2	20.8	1.6	9.0	27.7	5.9	32.4	13.6	4.6	38.8	4.8
Edwards County	5.3	20.6	14.3	23.6	12.6	20.9	2.4	10.9	29.7	8.8	37.0	13.7	5.3	31.4	3.8
Effingham County	4.1	15.8	13.3	25.1	15.5	25.6	0.9	9.8	23.1	3.3	27.2	18.2	5.9	42.3	3.1
Fayette County	4.4	19.6	13.2	19.9	19.7	21.3	2.6	9.5	27.0	6.8	26.9	16.0	5.9	37.0	7.4
Ford County	6.0	16.7	15.4	26.9	14.4	23.3	1.6	11.5	22.3	6.8	26.8	14.0	7.5	41.4	3.6
Franklin County	3.3	24.3	16.2	24.6	18.2	25.3	0.4	11.5	20.0	4.6	21.2	16.3	6.0	46.4	5.4
Fulton County	3.8	19.9	14.4	27.6	18.1	22.9	0.9	10.9	19.6	5.0	23.3	14.7	5.6	46.1	5.3
Gallatin County	4.0	25.8	15.2	27.1	17.9	19.8	2.4	11.5	21.3	13.8	16.1	13.4	9.2	42.8	4.7
Greene County	5.9	21.7	15.6	27.5	17.9	19.8	2.1	10.1	22.5	8.0	23.7	13.7	6.4	43.6	4.6
Grundy County	3.1	13.9	13.3	25.2	14.7	24.8	0.4	15.5	19.4	2.2	27.9	13.4	10.5	42.7	3.2
Hamilton County...........	3.9	21.6	13.9	26.7	16.9	22.6	2.0	11.7	20.0	8.5	18.7	16.2	6.3	45.3	4.9
Hancock County	5.5	16.4	14.7	26.0	14.9	21.0	2.3	10.2	25.6	7.4	30.5	14.4	6.6	38.0	3.1
Hardin County	3.4	27.7	13.6	27.8	18.7	17.7	0.1	16.6	19.1	19.5	11.0	10.6	7.4	42.1	9.3
Henderson County	5.3	19.2	16.8	22.7	14.3	20.0	2.8	13.2	27.0	8.4	30.5	13.6	9.6	34.7	3.2
Henry County	4.4	15.3	14.6	28.4	14.9	26.1	1.0	10.6	19.0	4.8	26.1	16.5	5.7	43.2	3.6
Iroquois County............	6.1	18.4	14.1	26.4	16.0	22.4	2.0	10.6	22.5	7.9	24.3	14.9	7.5	42.2	3.3

STATE County	Median household income	Median family income: All families	Median family income: Families with children: Married-couple	Median family income: Families with children: Male householder	Median family income: Families with children: Female householder	Median nonfamily household income	Median income for full-year, full-time workers: Men	Median income for full-year, full-time workers: Women	Per capita income	Households by source of income (percent): With earnings	Households by source of income (percent): With interest, dividend, or rental income	Households by source of income (percent): With Social Security income	Households by source of income (percent): With public assistance income	Households by source of income (percent): With retirement income	Households with income over $100,000 (percent)	+/– U.S. percent for income over $100,000	Households with income below poverty (percent)	Families with children with income below poverty (percent)
	57	58	59	60	61	62	63	64	65	66	67	68	69	70	71	72	73	74
IDAHO—Cont'd																		
Custer County	32 174	39 551	45 822	29 766	17 813	18 214	33 707	21 909	15 783	76.5	37.8	28.9	2.0	16.4	3.6	-8.7	14.3	14.0
Elmore County	35 256	37 823	38 370	26 905	17 321	22 970	27 140	21 953	16 773	87.6	34.1	18.0	3.4	19.2	4.0	-8.3	10.0	13.2
Franklin County	36 061	40 185	41 339	26 250	30 313	18 406	30 853	21 596	13 702	84.6	32.2	27.9	2.4	15.5	4.8	-7.5	6.8	7.1
Fremont County	33 424	36 715	38 538	35 833	19 231	18 894	26 850	20 071	13 965	82.2	36.3	30.1	3.1	16.7	3.8	-8.5	12.9	14.4
Gem County	34 460	40 195	46 392	17 353	12 955	16 959	31 744	21 526	15 340	74.1	36.2	31.5	3.8	18.6	5.0	-7.3	13.7	15.4
Gooding County	31 888	36 290	41 276	25 250	20 484	16 537	26 467	18 413	14 612	75.9	32.2	32.9	2.2	15.3	4.0	-8.3	14.0	16.7
Idaho County	29 515	33 919	40 768	23 942	13 920	17 342	30 104	19 028	14 411	71.5	37.6	35.4	5.2	18.1	2.6	-9.7	15.7	18.5
Jefferson County	37 737	41 530	44 792	22 917	19 141	16 406	32 017	20 426	13 838	83.4	33.5	26.6	2.4	15.7	5.4	-6.9	9.7	11.4
Jerome County	34 696	39 083	41 506	24 395	12 054	19 418	29 229	21 129	15 530	82.5	32.9	28.9	2.7	13.9	4.8	-7.5	11.3	16.4
Kootenai County	37 754	42 905	48 855	26 510	18 311	22 453	35 461	23 241	18 430	80.8	36.0	26.6	3.2	17.7	6.6	-5.7	10.2	11.7
Latah County	32 524	46 303	50 270	26 974	16 952	18 311	35 573	25 506	16 690	85.5	44.2	19.3	2.6	13.6	5.9	-6.4	18.4	9.8
Lemhi County	30 185	35 261	39 960	29 615	15 625	15 077	31 625	18 971	16 037	74.0	39.0	36.7	3.2	21.1	4.7	-7.6	15.0	17.2
Lewis County	31 413	37 336	43 977	30 833	15 139	15 549	31 607	22 893	15 942	71.5	30.0	39.5	3.8	21.3	3.4	-8.9	12.1	14.0
Lincoln County	32 484	36 792	39 231	24 444	12 273	19 013	27 563	20 179	14 257	83.3	28.6	27.3	2.6	17.7	3.7	-8.6	11.8	14.9
Madison County	32 607	40 880	45 225	32 083	17 333	18 709	29 824	19 227	10 956	88.6	40.0	18.4	2.9	10.7	4.5	-7.8	24.8	11.2
Minidoka County	32 021	36 500	37 619	23 400	17 167	16 102	30 272	20 148	13 813	80.3	32.0	29.6	3.9	14.8	3.6	-8.7	13.8	18.0
Nez Perce County	36 282	44 212	55 823	27 070	14 724	20 271	35 605	23 980	18 544	75.4	38.1	32.6	5.5	19.4	5.6	-6.7	12.5	14.3
Oneida County	34 309	38 341	41 477	14 583	13 750	17 679	30 439	20 446	13 829	75.8	34.0	34.6	2.2	18.2	3.1	-9.2	10.9	11.7
Owyhee County	28 339	32 856	34 116	21 696	17 500	14 742	25 457	21 583	13 405	80.4	27.1	28.9	3.3	13.4	4.7	-7.6	16.0	19.3
Payette County	33 046	37 430	41 437	23 750	18 032	17 635	31 740	22 261	14 924	79.8	31.1	31.4	4.9	16.5	5.0	-7.3	12.7	13.6
Power County	32 226	36 685	39 635	24 545	16 964	15 333	30 151	21 967	14 007	86.9	32.8	25.3	5.0	13.0	5.4	-6.9	14.9	15.7
Shoshone County	28 535	35 694	45 141	24 625	12 287	15 404	31 291	19 604	15 934	70.0	29.3	37.0	5.8	22.6	3.2	-9.1	15.9	20.4
Teton County	41 968	45 848	48 922	25 909	17 321	31 795	33 243	23 125	17 778	89.4	36.2	18.7	1.2	9.8	5.7	-6.6	9.6	10.5
Twin Falls County	34 506	39 886	44 722	26 250	17 777	19 700	30 981	21 720	16 678	79.9	34.2	28.6	3.3	15.0	5.7	-6.6	11.9	13.9
Valley County	36 927	42 283	50 000	25 417	22 639	22 275	32 122	22 546	19 246	77.5	41.0	29.2	3.0	21.9	6.0	-6.3	9.4	8.8
Washington County	30 625	35 542	36 996	26 375	12 857	15 712	29 137	20 365	15 464	74.3	31.7	36.8	3.9	19.0	4.6	-7.7	12.6	15.7
ILLINOIS	46 590	55 545	65 628	32 231	22 200	28 368	41 870	30 081	23 104	81.7	39.7	24.7	3.3	15.4	14.4	2.1	10.1	11.6
Adams County	34 784	44 133	51 948	24 232	16 199	19 519	31 925	21 944	17 894	77.4	43.1	31.7	3.0	16.2	5.7	-6.6	10.8	11.6
Alexander County	26 042	31 824	35 437	31 406	13 924	12 965	30 237	19 153	16 084	66.0	25.2	38.1	8.2	17.7	3.8	-8.5	24.8	32.7
Bond County	37 680	45 413	51 250	31 000	16 477	19 330	32 433	21 827	17 947	77.9	39.9	32.9	3.0	17.0	5.3	-7.0	10.3	9.4
Boone County	52 397	59 305	63 388	45 000	21 198	25 739	43 536	26 217	21 590	84.1	40.5	23.7	1.3	14.1	13.0	0.7	6.8	7.2
Brown County	35 445	43 207	48 167	26 458	25 000	17 273	25 337	21 691	14 629	76.1	40.3	32.9	3.3	12.9	3.4	-8.9	10.7	7.2
Bureau County	40 233	48 488	54 688	30 455	19 430	23 238	36 374	22 122	19 542	77.2	43.8	32.5	1.9	18.0	6.1	-6.2	7.1	8.2
Calhoun County	34 375	43 107	51 536	28 542	16 667	17 695	33 480	21 750	16 785	72.4	42.9	36.2	2.1	19.2	2.9	-9.4	10.7	9.7
Carroll County	37 148	43 685	51 349	27 500	19 313	21 500	32 379	22 343	18 688	75.4	44.9	35.0	2.5	18.8	5.3	-7.0	8.7	12.0
Cass County	35 243	41 653	46 813	27 159	12 336	20 771	28 899	22 136	16 532	77.6	34.1	32.4	2.5	17.9	3.8	-8.5	10.9	14.6
Champaign County	37 780	52 591	60 786	32 403	20 729	21 555	38 119	27 258	19 708	85.6	41.9	18.8	2.3	14.4	9.0	-3.3	16.0	10.3
Christian County	36 561	43 342	49 536	30 938	19 688	19 380	33 952	23 938	17 937	75.2	36.7	34.0	2.0	20.4	5.5	-6.8	9.9	10.2
Clark County	35 967	43 213	51 853	31 250	18 662	19 468	33 157	21 612	17 655	74.9	39.6	34.8	1.9	17.4	4.9	-7.4	10.3	10.6
Clay County	30 599	36 675	41 320	30 694	17 264	16 399	29 636	21 158	15 771	72.6	36.3	36.5	2.5	17.7	3.7	-8.6	12.2	12.3
Clinton County	44 618	52 580	62 597	35 345	21 622	20 979	36 958	24 602	19 109	77.8	45.6	30.6	1.4	21.0	7.2	-5.1	6.8	6.6
Coles County	32 286	45 708	55 629	27 784	19 817	16 931	34 660	22 597	17 370	80.2	37.6	27.5	2.5	16.3	6.2	-6.1	18.4	10.2
Cook County	45 922	53 784	64 387	32 155	22 923	31 719	41 540	31 978	23 227	81.3	36.5	23.7	4.7	14.1	15.1	2.8	12.2	15.4
Crawford County	32 531	40 418	48 870	29 135	17 552	17 870	30 926	22 464	16 869	73.0	40.1	34.1	2.4	19.5	5.0	-7.3	11.3	13.0
Cumberland County	36 149	42 704	46 964	22 083	18 000	20 566	31 199	21 205	16 953	77.9	38.1	33.4	2.8	18.4	3.2	-9.1	9.9	11.6
DeKalb County	45 828	58 194	65 419	32 829	22 352	24 050	41 827	27 472	19 462	86.3	41.9	20.2	1.7	13.4	10.1	-2.2	12.5	7.3
De Witt County	41 256	50 429	57 027	34 107	20 408	21 883	36 777	25 008	20 488	80.1	39.4	31.7	2.0	17.8	9.6	-2.7	8.3	9.5
Douglas County	39 439	46 117	53 734	29 464	21 231	22 500	34 841	22 175	18 474	79.2	42.1	31.0	2.0	17.2	5.8	-6.5	7.0	6.6
DuPage County	67 887	79 314	86 708	48 026	35 894	40 665	54 918	36 285	31 315	88.6	51.0	18.9	1.1	12.9	27.5	15.2	3.5	3.5
Edgar County	35 203	41 245	46 045	23 047	18 684	19 651	31 388	21 674	17 857	74.4	39.4	36.5	2.4	17.3	4.3	-8.0	11.3	11.7
Edwards County	31 816	38 750	44 821	25 781	15 625	16 615	28 734	20 162	16 187	73.7	41.4	35.0	2.8	16.7	3.6	-8.7	10.3	10.6
Effingham County	39 379	46 895	52 454	27 386	19 909	20 394	32 250	21 935	18 301	80.8	45.9	28.8	2.1	15.1	6.2	-6.1	8.7	8.9
Fayette County	31 873	39 044	46 984	25 000	15 719	16 568	30 223	21 033	15 357	75.9	34.4	33.8	3.5	17.3	3.5	-8.8	13.0	12.8
Ford County	38 073	44 947	51 766	31 207	21 750	23 047	33 165	23 503	18 860	77.5	46.9	32.9	1.3	17.0	5.3	-7.0	7.2	8.6
Franklin County	28 411	36 294	43 816	19 783	12 257	15 607	32 192	20 449	15 407	68.0	29.4	37.4	3.5	22.3	3.4	-8.9	16.0	19.9
Fulton County	33 952	41 193	48 097	26 836	18 765	17 346	32 596	21 900	17 373	71.4	36.8	35.3	2.7	25.6	4.7	-7.6	9.8	11.4
Gallatin County	26 118	34 539	40 326	23 125	13 478	12 237	31 181	20 405	15 575	67.8	32.9	39.2	3.2	16.9	3.4	-8.9	20.8	24.7
Greene County	31 754	37 057	43 385	28 438	17 717	17 566	30 859	21 044	15 246	72.5	34.5	36.6	2.6	18.7	3.2	-9.1	13.2	13.5
Grundy County	51 719	60 862	68 497	41 296	28 729	29 198	47 909	27 427	22 591	81.7	42.8	25.5	1.7	17.7	12.5	0.2	5.8	4.4
Hamilton County	30 496	37 651	41 088	26 364	13 313	15 160	32 401	18 809	16 262	71.6	37.6	37.5	3.8	20.6	4.4	-7.9	13.3	14.5
Hancock County	36 654	44 457	50 775	27 426	18 194	19 868	31 764	21 671	17 478	78.8	43.7	33.2	1.9	17.1	4.3	-8.0	8.3	8.4
Hardin County	27 693	31 625	39 821	12 222	10 938	17 162	33 710	17 560	15 984	64.9	30.3	39.2	2.6	23.1	3.4	-8.9	17.6	24.1
Henderson County	36 405	42 400	49 271	27 500	19 211	20 625	32 002	21 510	17 456	77.2	35.1	33.8	2.3	18.3	4.3	-8.0	8.6	9.6
Henry County	39 854	48 413	57 123	29 583	17 482	20 940	36 205	22 363	18 716	76.9	47.5	32.2	1.8	21.2	6.6	-5.7	8.2	8.8
Iroquois County	38 071	45 417	51 583	25 227	16 081	21 293	32 426	21 508	18 435	77.2	43.3	34.8	2.4	17.0	5.7	-6.6	8.5	10.9

STATE/ County code	MSA/PMSA/ NECMA code[1]	STATE County	High school graduates			College graduates		College graduates (percent)				
			Total population 25 years and over	Percent with a high school diploma or less	Percent with a high school diploma or more	Percent with a bachelor's degree or more	+/− U.S. percent with bachelor's degree or more	Non-Hispanic White	Black or African American	American Indian and Alaska Native	Asian, Hawaiian, and Pacific Islander	Hispanic or Latino[2]
			1	2	3	4	5	6	7	8	9	10
		ILLINOIS—Cont'd										
17 077	...	Jackson County............	32 659	39.7	85.2	32.0	7.6	30.9	24.9	30.6	77.8	27.1
17 079	...	Jasper County.............	6 579	58.0	82.6	11.2	−13.2	11.1	X	0.0	0.0	0.0
17 081	...	Jefferson County..........	26 841	56.0	77.0	13.7	−10.7	14.2	7.0	10.9	44.1	5.1
17 083	7040	Jersey County.............	13 982	56.8	82.5	15.2	−11.8	12.4	28.0	14.6	29.5	53.1
17 085	...	Jo Daviess County........	15 625	58.0	83.6	15.2	−9.2	15.4	0.0	9.4	20.0	1.6
17 087	...	Johnson County...........	9 057	60.7	67.1	11.7	−12.7	13.9	0.0	0.0	53.8	4.1
17 089	1600	Kane County...............	245 486	44.8	80.2	27.7	3.3	33.6	15.2	4.5	46.6	4.9
17 091	3740	Kankakee County.........	65 844	56.0	79.8	15.0	−9.4	16.3	7.1	17.7	38.6	7.2
17 093	1600	Kendall County............	34 362	40.2	89.9	25.3	0.9	26.1	24.0	30.8	41.4	8.5
17 095	...	Knox County...............	38 049	54.9	81.8	14.6	−9.8	15.2	4.7	0.0	47.0	6.0
17 097	1600	Lake County...............	398 265	34.8	86.6	38.6	14.2	43.1	17.3	14.1	64.6	8.4
17 099	...	La Salle County............	74 431	57.2	81.4	13.3	−11.1	13.5	3.0	5.7	57.2	6.7
17 101	...	Lawrence County..........	10 752	60.6	81.3	9.7	−14.7	9.7	14.3	0.0	0.0	0.0
17 103	...	Lee County.................	24 540	56.5	80.2	13.2	−11.2	13.9	2.0	0.0	32.0	4.0
17 105	...	Livingston County.........	26 496	63.2	78.1	12.6	−11.8	13.5	0.4	28.3	13.0	0.8
17 107	...	Logan County.............	20 714	60.0	80.4	14.2	−10.2	15.2	1.7	0.0	46.6	4.5
17 109	...	McDonough County......	17 944	46.5	86.9	26.9	2.5	25.6	33.1	0.0	85.1	44.9
17 111	1600	McHenry County..........	163 780	39.1	89.2	27.7	3.3	28.4	46.6	17.4	55.4	9.3
17 113	1040	McLean County............	87 220	37.5	90.7	36.2	11.8	35.8	30.7	7.3	73.1	23.9
17 115	2040	Macon County.............	75 195	54.9	83.2	16.9	−7.5	18.3	5.2	14.5	53.6	11.0
17 117	...	Macoupin County.........	32 878	59.5	82.1	11.8	−12.6	11.8	5.2	12.5	35.9	18.0
17 119	7040	Madison County...........	170 432	49.7	84.3	19.2	−5.2	19.6	11.1	16.4	48.9	18.3
17 121	...	Marion County.............	27 710	56.8	79.1	12.1	−12.3	12.1	7.6	16.7	55.2	20.3
17 123	...	Marshall County...........	9 135	55.2	85.0	14.5	−9.9	14.7	0.0	0.0	0.0	0.0
17 125	...	Mason County..............	10 890	62.2	79.9	11.2	−13.2	11.3	0.0	0.0	0.0	0.0
17 127	...	Massac County............	10 471	58.3	76.5	10.7	−13.7	10.9	6.7	0.0	33.3	4.1
17 129	7880	Menard County............	8 298	50.0	88.3	20.5	−3.9	20.7	7.1	10.5	7.1	34.1
17 131	...	Mercer County.............	11 529	58.7	84.9	12.6	−11.8	12.6	0.0	0.0	35.5	30.6
17 133	7040	Monroe County............	19 277	45.4	87.2	20.4	−4.0	20.3	0.0	26.5	60.4	10.4
17 135	...	Montgomery County......	20 874	63.9	77.1	11.2	−13.2	11.7	1.8	10.0	17.2	8.1
17 137	...	Morgan County............	24 276	57.2	79.9	19.9	−4.5	20.8	4.0	11.9	63.5	6.7
17 139	...	Moultrie County...........	9 515	59.1	78.8	14.7	−9.7	14.6	0.0	0.0	53.8	33.8
17 141	6880	Ogle County................	33 317	53.3	83.1	17.0	−7.4	17.5	18.5	9.7	64.9	4.5
17 143	6120	Peoria County.............	110 498	46.6	83.8	23.3	−1.1	24.4	10.1	6.0	68.7	19.3
17 145	...	Perry County...............	15 727	61.9	72.3	10.1	−14.3	10.9	1.1	0.0	28.6	5.5
17 147	...	Piatt County................	11 118	48.5	88.7	21.0	−3.4	21.0	0.0	0.0	57.1	5.0
17 149	...	Pike County................	11 864	64.2	79.6	9.9	−14.5	9.7	0.0	0.0	55.6	31.1
17 151	...	Pope County................	2 989	57.3	75.8	10.5	−13.9	10.6	6.1	0.0	X	X
17 153	...	Pulaski County............	4 704	60.9	70.7	7.1	−17.3	6.7	8.8	0.0	0.0	0.0
17 155	...	Putnam County............	4 136	54.2	83.8	12.1	−12.3	12.2	0.0	25.0	0.0	4.1
17 157	...	Randolph County..........	23 141	65.9	71.3	8.6	−15.8	9.3	2.9	0.0	21.4	2.4
17 159	...	Richland County...........	10 827	49.4	83.4	15.2	−9.2	15.2	X	0.0	61.8	0.0
17 161	1960	Rock Island County.......	98 865	51.5	82.6	17.1	−7.3	18.0	7.7	4.8	56.0	7.3
17 163	7040	St. Clair County............	162 715	48.2	80.9	19.3	−5.1	21.8	11.4	16.0	32.1	17.3
17 165	...	Saline County..............	18 111	54.1	76.1	12.1	−12.3	12.2	11.4	16.3	21.6	0.0
17 167	7880	Sangamon County.........	126 620	43.0	88.1	28.6	4.2	29.3	15.8	24.4	63.6	29.9
17 169	...	Schuyler County...........	5 022	62.6	83.6	11.7	−12.7	11.7	66.7	0.0	0.0	0.0
17 171	...	Scott County...............	3 718	63.5	83.1	12.1	−12.3	12.1	100.0	0.0	0.0	0.0
17 173	...	Shelby County.............	15 448	61.0	82.9	11.5	−12.9	11.4	0.0	18.2	45.1	0.0
17 175	...	Stark County...............	4 312	55.7	83.4	13.4	−11.0	13.5	0.0	0.0	0.0	0.0
17 177	...	Stephenson County.......	32 851	54.2	84.1	15.6	−8.8	16.1	7.0	22.9	70.5	10.7
17 179	6120	Tazewell County...........	86 666	49.4	85.0	18.1	−6.3	18.4	0.5	7.5	30.6	14.2
17 181	...	Union County...............	12 695	56.2	74.8	15.8	−8.6	16.0	2.2	19.6	55.2	4.5
17 183	...	Vermilion County..........	55 778	59.6	78.7	12.5	−11.9	12.8	5.9	12.1	58.9	7.6
17 185	...	Wabash County............	8 627	48.7	82.2	12.5	−11.9	12.3	70.6	0.0	57.1	26.0
17 187	...	Warren County.............	12 131	57.3	82.3	15.8	−8.6	15.8	15.6	10.0	73.8	3.7
17 189	...	Washington County.......	10 168	55.8	79.1	13.4	−11.0	13.3	0.0	0.0	29.4	39.3
17 191	...	Wayne County..............	11 723	59.5	75.2	10.0	−14.4	9.8	0.0	0.0	38.0	7.8
17 193	...	White County...............	10 863	61.0	74.6	10.4	−14.0	10.3	18.2	13.3	0.0	20.0
17 195	...	Whiteside County.........	40 585	58.0	79.8	11.3	−13.1	11.8	15.1	19.8	30.4	3.9
17 197	1600	Will County.................	310 910	42.2	86.9	25.5	1.1	26.7	19.1	9.5	58.2	9.5
17 199	...	Williamson County........	41 973	52.6	79.8	17.2	−7.2	17.2	9.6	27.1	50.9	10.6
17 201	6880	Winnebago County........	181 803	51.4	81.4	19.4	−5.0	20.8	9.0	3.9	36.4	7.6
17 203	6120	Woodford County..........	22 945	47.5	87.8	21.1	−3.3	21.1	0.0	0.0	42.7	14.2

[1]MSA = Metropolitan Statistical Area. PMSA = Primary MSA. NECMA = New England County Metropolitan Area. See the Appendix A for explanation of these concepts. See Appendix B for list of metropolitan areas identified by type, with component counties.
[2]Hispanic or Latino persons may be of any race.

STATE County	School enrollment			Population 16 to 19 years				Employment status, 2000			Work status in 1999 of the population 16 years and over (percent)		
											Worked in 1999		
	Grades kindergarten through 12	College or graduate school	Percent private	Number	Percent in armed forces	Percent high school graduates	Percent not enrolled, not grads, not in armed forces, not employed	Total population 16 years and over	Percent in labor force	Unemploy-ment rate	Full-time	Part-time	Did not work in 1999
	11	12	13	14	15	16	17	18	19	20	21	22	23
ILLINOIS—Cont'd													
Jackson County............	8 336	16 882	4.0	5 741	0.1	6.8	4.1	49 687	61.8	7.9	46.0	27.2	26.8
Jasper County..............	2 078	459	7.1	752	0.0	12.4	1.3	7 904	64.7	3.5	54.9	15.0	30.1
Jefferson County..........	7 349	1 631	5.8	2 131	0.0	12.3	7.0	31 470	59.3	5.5	50.7	13.4	35.9
Jersey County	4 232	1 427	19.6	1 480	0.0	10.9	4.0	16 895	65.1	5.9	51.7	18.2	30.2
Jo Daviess County	3 967	725	14.2	1 150	0.0	9.7	2.7	17 779	67.5	4.0	54.4	19.1	26.5
Johnson County	2 159	501	4.1	705	0.0	7.8	14.6	10 801	44.1	7.5	53.4	12.6	34.0
Kane County.................	85 895	19 754	15.4	23 853	0.1	10.3	7.7	294 732	69.9	4.7	61.6	14.9	23.5
Kankakee County.........	20 874	5 437	17.5	6 115	0.0	14.0	5.7	78 807	65.4	6.4	54.5	15.2	30.3
Kendall County.............	11 607	2 555	12.9	3 225	0.0	6.8	3.6	40 187	73.9	2.9	62.2	16.4	21.4
Knox County.................	9 142	3 207	17.4	3 154	0.0	9.2	7.4	45 051	60.6	6.5	51.7	16.2	32.1
Lake County.................	135 526	32 659	15.4	38 104	12.6	20.6	3.7	474 018	71.1	4.1	61.9	14.7	23.4
La Salle County...........	21 364	3 807	12.0	6 275	0.1	13.0	5.1	86 868	62.1	5.4	51.8	16.1	32.0
Lawrence County	2 703	537	4.4	721	0.0	12.9	4.7	12 327	60.9	6.2	50.6	15.1	34.3
Lee County..................	6 980	1 434	12.4	1 955	0.0	12.0	4.3	28 407	60.7	5.3	54.8	15.0	30.2
Livingston County.........	7 786	1 009	8.8	2 204	0.0	11.7	9.8	30 984	61.2	5.2	54.0	15.6	30.4
Logan County..............	5 382	1 933	24.7	2 055	0.6	9.2	4.1	25 214	59.0	6.2	54.7	16.2	29.1
McDonough County	4 459	8 722	3.9	3 482	0.0	3.0	1.9	27 819	64.5	11.1	49.9	26.1	24.0
McHenry County	57 221	12 583	10.7	13 662	0.1	8.8	2.5	189 410	74.0	3.5	61.7	17.3	21.0
McLean County............	25 605	24 570	11.3	11 738	0.0	6.8	2.1	118 896	72.4	6.1	57.9	22.5	19.5
Macon County..............	20 713	6 495	19.0	6 574	0.0	11.9	7.5	89 625	63.3	7.1	52.7	15.6	31.7
Macoupin County	9 305	2 312	9.7	2 969	0.1	11.2	4.2	38 524	62.1	5.1	51.1	15.6	33.4
Madison County	48 026	17 380	13.2	14 923	0.0	10.1	4.7	201 929	64.8	5.3	53.5	16.2	30.4
Marion County..............	8 022	1 491	7.5	2 234	0.2	13.8	6.8	32 231	63.0	6.9	53.9	13.7	32.4
Marshall County	2 381	468	6.4	715	0.0	11.7	4.1	10 481	65.2	3.7	51.9	17.9	30.2
Mason County	2 923	476	2.1	914	0.0	9.2	7.8	12 621	60.0	6.1	50.3	15.3	34.5
Massac County	2 595	597	2.7	817	0.0	12.4	6.6	12 095	59.1	5.9	51.8	11.8	36.4
Menard County.............	2 558	445	7.6	717	0.0	8.5	1.4	9 588	70.6	3.9	59.8	15.3	24.9
Mercer County..............	3 312	605	4.1	1 074	0.0	14.9	2.0	13 344	64.0	5.9	54.2	16.2	29.6
Monroe County.............	5 685	1 344	18.3	1 704	0.0	13.0	1.3	21 247	70.1	2.5	60.2	14.5	25.3
Montgomery County	5 680	899	6.7	1 646	0.2	11.8	5.7	24 304	56.5	5.6	53.1	13.1	33.8
Morgan County.............	6 607	2 407	23.8	2 557	0.3	8.7	5.5	29 418	63.1	6.1	54.3	16.8	28.8
Moultrie County	2 739	357	11.8	816	0.0	11.9	4.4	11 086	64.8	3.3	54.7	14.7	30.6
Ogle County	10 898	1 842	5.4	2 985	0.0	11.3	2.8	38 694	67.3	4.6	56.9	15.3	27.8
Peoria County..............	33 553	12 443	24.7	10 361	0.1	9.4	5.0	142 375	63.7	5.8	52.9	16.9	30.2
Perry County................	4 020	977	7.9	1 378	0.0	10.4	12.0	18 678	53.5	8.0	51.8	14.8	33.4
Piatt County.................	3 156	728	2.7	972	0.0	11.9	0.5	12 743	68.8	2.9	56.7	17.2	26.1
Pike County	3 443	473	6.8	922	0.0	10.5	6.7	13 675	60.2	6.2	51.9	14.1	34.0
Pope County	731	186	5.9	264	0.0	18.9	17.8	3 609	58.8	11.2	48.1	14.3	37.6
Pulaski County	1 572	326	3.4	472	0.0	8.7	16.3	5 555	56.7	9.6	48.7	13.7	37.6
Putnam County	1 164	210	9.0	334	0.0	8.1	1.8	4 739	63.3	4.9	53.5	16.3	30.2
Randolph County	5 795	1 095	15.5	1 757	0.0	14.3	9.0	27 304	54.4	5.7	52.7	13.9	33.4
Richland County	2 941	898	7.8	938	0.0	9.3	6.8	12 660	62.0	7.3	51.0	15.2	33.8
Rock Island County......	26 365	8 734	16.3	9 001	0.1	10.2	5.0	118 209	64.5	6.3	53.5	16.7	29.8
St. Clair County............	54 017	14 400	13.7	15 449	1.1	12.4	6.0	193 330	63.8	6.5	53.4	15.3	31.3
Saline County...............	4 663	1 248	2.6	1 971	0.0	7.6	24.6	21 427	54.0	7.8	45.5	12.6	41.9
Sangamon County	34 965	9 460	16.3	9 836	0.3	12.6	4.5	147 423	69.2	4.1	59.9	14.4	25.7
Schuyler County	1 282	186	4.1	353	1.4	4.2	2.8	5 768	66.8	5.7	54.5	15.8	29.6
Scott County................	1 031	165	10.1	323	0.0	17.3	2.5	4 321	66.4	4.6	56.2	16.0	27.8
Shelby County	4 273	772	6.3	1 271	1.1	10.4	4.9	17 866	62.2	3.6	53.1	14.9	32.0
Stark County	1 200	151	10.7	352	0.0	6.0	6.8	4 950	57.9	6.9	50.2	14.5	35.2
Stephenson County.......	9 402	2 375	12.1	2 799	0.0	11.4	5.0	38 103	65.9	6.2	55.8	15.9	28.2
Tazewell County...........	23 416	5 906	10.2	6 903	0.0	12.6	2.4	100 938	65.1	4.0	54.9	16.2	28.9
Union County	3 292	717	4.7	1 033	0.0	12.6	4.2	14 599	58.2	10.7	48.7	13.1	38.3
Vermilion County..........	15 297	3 097	8.2	4 512	0.2	13.6	7.9	65 332	59.2	7.6	51.9	13.6	34.5
Wabash County............	2 379	730	7.2	840	0.0	11.5	2.0	10 204	65.7	6.5	54.1	15.2	30.7
Warren County	3 344	1 492	23.1	1 374	0.0	7.2	4.7	14 954	65.9	6.5	54.6	17.4	28.0
Washington County.......	2 962	689	12.8	854	0.0	10.8	4.1	11 790	67.3	3.2	56.8	15.0	28.1
Wayne County..............	3 053	676	2.7	904	0.0	14.6	6.1	13 563	60.4	6.6	52.9	11.9	35.2
White County	2 567	499	3.2	811	0.0	14.1	9.4	12 524	57.3	5.6	48.5	14.2	37.3
Whiteside County	11 644	2 286	10.2	3 411	0.0	12.7	4.6	47 198	63.2	4.9	54.0	15.3	30.7
Will County..................	107 495	26 437	14.9	28 159	0.0	10.7	5.3	367 606	70.3	4.4	59.7	16.1	24.2
Williamson County	10 550	3 462	7.7	3 199	0.0	12.3	5.7	48 921	59.8	6.7	48.7	15.9	35.4
Winnebago County.......	54 037	12 464	19.5	14 919	0.2	10.5	6.6	212 913	67.4	5.8	56.9	15.6	27.5
Woodford County	7 307	1 945	13.3	2 259	0.0	9.1	1.1	27 089	67.1	2.7	53.6	19.8	26.6

Table B-3. States and Counties — Education, Labor Force, and Income

STATE County	Full-year full-time employed (percent)								Children under 18 years in families						Total employed by class of worker (percent)			
						American Indian and Alaska Native	Asian, Hawaiian, and Pacific Islander			With two parents (percent)		With one parent who is in labor force (percent)	+/− U.S. percent of children with no stay-at-home parent (percent)	+/− U.S. percent two-income couples				Unpaid family worker
	Total	Men	Women	Non-Hispanic White	Black or African American			Hispanic or Latino[1]	Number	Both in labor force	Father only in labor force				Private	Government	Self-employed	
	24	25	26	27	28	29	30	31	32	33	34	35	36	37	38	39	40	41
ILLINOIS—Cont'd																		
Jackson County	28.2	32.0	24.2	30.5	20.3	19.2	15.0	10.7	10 576	45.5	18.6	22.3	3.2	3.1	59.0	33.7	6.8	0.5
Jasper County	41.5	52.0	31.4	41.5	X	0.0	10.0	0.0	2 539	59.8	19.4	12.8	8.0	5.6	70.7	14.9	14.0	0.4
Jefferson County	36.9	44.3	29.1	38.7	17.7	26.2	48.1	26.3	9 040	49.9	20.1	22.4	7.7	1.2	76.0	12.4	11.2	0.5
Jersey County	40.2	49.9	31.1	40.3	7.7	44.0	53.0	28.8	5 312	56.3	21.0	14.6	6.3	2.4	81.0	9.6	9.2	0.3
Jo Daviess County	42.4	50.9	34.2	42.6	15.8	63.6	42.9	29.3	4 921	61.7	14.7	16.0	13.1	5.6	71.6	9.7	18.0	0.8
Johnson County	33.7	38.2	26.7	33.7	36.0	33.3	0.0	26.7	2 276	56.2	22.6	14.9	6.5	−4.9	60.3	27.9	10.9	0.9
Kane County	46.2	57.8	34.8	48.3	41.1	43.1	49.2	40.1	115 637	46.6	25.2	15.8	−2.2	5.1	82.3	9.8	7.7	0.2
Kankakee County	40.8	49.6	32.7	42.0	32.2	25.7	37.2	47.8	26 338	46.3	19.3	23.4	5.1	3.7	79.2	12.9	7.6	0.3
Kendall County	50.7	64.7	36.9	50.4	68.8	32.5	56.2	52.3	15 738	56.6	27.1	11.4	3.4	10.9	79.9	10.9	9.0	0.2
Knox County	37.5	46.0	29.4	38.9	19.9	24.4	22.3	39.9	11 631	50.1	16.5	23.7	9.2	1.1	78.2	12.6	9.0	0.2
Lake County	47.6	59.7	35.6	48.9	42.6	41.6	49.7	42.1	182 023	47.8	29.0	14.3	−2.5	5.4	78.8	10.3	10.7	0.3
La Salle County	39.1	49.8	28.7	39.4	23.3	45.1	34.8	38.1	26 809	50.6	21.2	18.6	4.6	−0.6	79.0	11.3	9.3	0.4
Lawrence County	37.4	46.8	29.1	37.4	35.3	100.0	31.0	35.2	3 090	44.2	23.5	22.0	1.6	2.4	77.0	11.0	11.7	0.4
Lee County	40.8	49.5	31.6	42.5	14.9	24.5	45.7	40.0	8 207	51.9	21.4	18.6	5.9	2.9	74.6	14.6	10.3	0.5
Livingston County	39.7	49.8	30.0	41.7	12.4	27.9	42.9	34.1	9 442	51.3	21.7	21.0	7.7	5.9	73.7	14.3	11.5	0.4
Logan County	39.4	46.3	32.5	41.3	15.9	45.5	44.1	34.4	6 494	57.5	16.1	20.6	13.5	6.3	71.7	17.9	10.1	0.3
McDonough County	30.2	38.1	22.8	31.1	15.5	0.0	13.4	22.8	5 635	56.3	17.0	19.6	11.3	5.2	61.3	26.9	11.0	0.7
McHenry County	49.4	64.4	34.7	49.5	63.3	44.2	53.8	46.2	76 662	54.3	28.7	11.3	1.0	8.0	81.9	8.6	9.2	0.2
McLean County	42.7	52.0	34.3	43.2	39.9	42.7	32.3	39.0	33 769	56.1	19.3	19.7	11.2	11.6	78.5	13.8	7.4	0.3
Macon County	40.0	50.0	31.1	41.1	32.7	33.7	39.0	38.4	26 612	42.5	17.8	28.1	6.0	−0.4	81.3	11.1	7.4	0.3
Macoupin County	38.8	49.1	29.3	39.0	23.5	30.0	20.2	28.8	11 551	53.3	18.7	20.2	8.9	1.2	76.3	12.5	10.8	0.4
Madison County	40.7	50.9	31.6	41.4	31.7	46.5	32.3	40.7	61 314	47.7	18.4	22.9	6.0	2.0	79.7	12.7	7.3	0.3
Marion County	39.0	49.0	30.0	39.5	25.3	41.3	44.8	31.8	10 000	49.9	14.0	25.7	11.0	0.9	76.3	14.7	8.5	0.5
Marshall County	39.2	51.3	27.7	39.3	40.7	37.5	18.5	36.5	2 994	59.0	19.9	15.1	9.5	−0.2	75.9	11.5	12.4	0.2
Mason County	36.0	47.6	25.1	36.1	12.0	27.3	20.0	42.9	3 725	51.1	20.8	18.9	5.4	−4.4	71.8	16.5	11.3	0.5
Massac County	37.5	46.3	29.7	38.0	30.8	16.7	16.2	40.0	3 251	48.4	20.5	19.8	3.6	−4.1	78.9	11.3	9.6	0.1
Menard County	47.1	56.5	38.4	47.4	4.4	23.8	85.7	40.0	3 228	60.2	14.0	19.8	15.4	13.5	58.3	28.1	13.1	0.4
Mercer County	38.4	45.5	31.8	38.5	0.0	33.3	45.2	65.5	3 956	61.3	16.0	15.0	11.7	1.8	73.3	13.7	12.2	0.7
Monroe County	49.4	59.3	40.0	49.3	0.0	51.4	75.4	57.1	7 123	63.1	18.4	13.0	11.5	9.0	81.1	10.3	8.0	0.6
Montgomery County	38.3	48.3	31.1	38.5	80.0	45.7	56.4	16.0	6 006	51.4	16.7	21.4	8.2	1.1	71.2	15.7	12.8	0.2
Morgan County	39.2	46.9	31.7	39.8	30.3	54.7	48.1	25.9	7 691	55.9	15.8	21.2	12.5	5.9	73.8	16.0	9.8	0.3
Moultrie County	42.5	56.2	30.4	42.5	65.0	12.0	61.5	44.6	3 538	52.9	28.7	15.5	3.8	3.6	78.2	9.0	12.5	0.3
Ogle County	44.1	55.4	33.2	43.9	47.1	64.4	48.4	47.3	13 244	54.4	22.6	16.4	6.2	3.7	76.9	12.7	10.0	0.4
Peoria County	39.1	48.4	30.6	40.5	31.3	21.2	45.4	32.0	42 919	41.6	19.3	27.5	4.5	0.3	81.3	10.7	7.8	0.2
Perry County	35.7	42.6	27.7	36.6	28.7	62.5	38.6	28.0	4 779	48.4	20.2	22.0	6.6	−4.7	74.8	15.3	9.5	0.4
Piatt County	44.8	56.2	34.3	44.9	0.0	0.0	40.9	56.4	3 927	60.0	21.2	14.4	9.8	7.2	70.8	18.5	10.6	0.2
Pike County	37.6	48.5	27.2	37.8	29.5	33.3	31.9	30.1	4 047	60.3	15.2	17.1	12.8	2.1	67.1	15.9	16.1	0.8
Pope County	31.9	40.7	23.1	33.7	4.0	0.0	X	0.0	906	40.3	26.0	22.5	−1.8	−7.8	66.6	19.7	13.4	0.3
Pulaski County	32.9	40.1	26.4	34.4	27.9	0.0	16.9	72.6	1 832	40.3	14.3	28.3	4.0	−3.6	65.9	23.0	10.4	0.6
Putnam County	40.8	51.0	31.1	41.3	35.0	12.5	0.0	61.1	1 465	53.2	22.2	16.0	4.6	−1.9	78.5	10.5	10.4	0.7
Randolph County	37.8	44.7	29.4	38.8	31.1	26.3	37.1	19.1	7 176	55.1	17.6	17.2	7.7	0.9	72.2	17.7	9.5	0.6
Richland County	38.0	47.7	29.2	38.2	0.0	0.0	59.0	6.5	3 783	52.9	17.5	21.5	9.8	−1.5	73.9	12.5	13.2	0.3
Rock Island County	39.6	47.1	32.8	40.3	31.1	34.3	39.0	39.9	33 512	46.4	17.4	27.2	9.0	0.5	80.7	12.4	6.6	0.3
St. Clair County	40.5	49.1	33.1	44.2	30.2	46.1	45.6	39.4	66 437	41.9	14.5	28.4	5.7	3.5	77.7	14.5	7.6	0.2
Saline County	32.3	39.2	26.1	32.7	24.7	23.3	17.8	23.5	5 783	47.8	18.5	19.0	2.2	−5.7	69.9	19.7	10.0	0.4
Sangamon County	48.1	56.5	40.7	49.4	35.3	45.5	40.6	48.5	44 785	50.9	15.0	26.0	12.3	9.9	62.2	29.7	7.9	0.2
Schuyler County	41.5	50.7	32.7	41.5	50.0	45.5	0.0	50.0	1 548	62.7	23.5	8.1	6.2	4.4	67.6	15.9	15.3	1.2
Scott County	42.6	51.7	34.4	42.7	100.0	25.0	50.0	0.0	1 355	60.5	16.5	18.4	14.3	6.8	71.9	15.0	12.8	0.2
Shelby County	38.8	50.7	27.6	38.8	57.1	25.0	50.0	53.4	5 453	54.0	21.1	16.2	5.6	1.3	77.7	9.1	12.6	0.6
Stark County	37.7	50.0	26.5	37.9	0.0	60.0	33.3	25.6	1 530	51.4	24.2	12.2	−1.0	−5.6	71.8	10.8	16.4	1.0
Stephenson County	43.1	51.6	35.5	43.6	36.6	61.5	56.7	36.8	11 926	54.6	15.2	22.5	12.5	4.5	78.4	9.6	11.6	0.4
Tazewell County	42.1	52.7	32.1	42.2	26.5	47.1	44.3	47.0	29 821	55.3	20.7	18.0	8.7	1.8	81.3	10.1	8.3	0.3
Union County	33.9	39.5	28.6	34.3	2.1	51.4	47.9	18.1	4 091	47.4	19.0	19.2	2.0	−5.9	61.5	28.3	9.8	0.4
Vermilion County	37.7	45.9	29.9	39.3	25.6	37.5	37.2	33.7	19 669	41.9	18.1	26.6	3.9	−1.8	75.8	14.8	8.8	0.5
Wabash County	38.2	49.3	27.9	38.6	81.0	0.0	0.0	13.6	2 976	53.7	21.7	16.3	5.4	4.6	75.8	12.3	11.6	0.3
Warren County	40.1	49.9	31.3	40.6	26.5	90.9	16.5	31.9	4 118	57.1	16.1	19.9	12.4	7.0	75.4	11.9	12.3	0.5
Washington County	44.9	56.2	33.9	45.1	26.7	19.2	41.2	59.4	3 659	64.1	16.0	14.6	14.1	7.2	72.0	12.5	14.5	0.9
Wayne County	38.1	47.9	29.2	38.1	100.0	9.7	28.4	40.4	3 854	53.6	18.6	19.5	8.5	−3.6	75.3	11.6	12.3	0.8
White County	35.3	47.5	24.5	35.4	36.4	60.0	0.0	0.0	3 096	45.3	25.6	18.6	−0.7	−6.3	73.3	13.6	12.7	0.5
Whiteside County	40.9	51.1	31.3	41.4	25.4	32.0	29.5	38.4	14 412	49.8	18.5	23.2	8.4	−0.7	80.7	10.3	8.6	0.4
Will County	46.0	59.4	34.5	47.9	42.7	41.1	46.9	41.4	144 841	49.7	27.9	14.6	−0.3	6.3	81.8	10.7	7.3	0.2
Williamson County	35.8	43.9	28.4	36.3	25.7	15.6	33.5	26.1	13 307	48.3	19.1	21.1	4.8	−3.2	70.2	19.9	9.4	0.4
Winnebago County	43.8	53.9	34.4	45.0	36.3	34.1	43.1	39.5	69 171	46.4	18.5	24.9	6.7	3.4	82.8	9.2	7.8	0.2
Woodford County	41.0	55.6	27.4	41.1	17.5	16.0	37.0	33.3	9 159	59.2	26.4	10.0	4.6	5.2	77.7	10.3	11.3	0.6

[1]Hispanic or Latino persons may be of any race.

STATE County	Percent who worked at home	Percent of the population 5 years and over with a disability	Veterans as a percent of the population 18 years and over	Occupation for employed population 16 years and over (percent)						Industry for employed population 16 years and over (percent)					
				Management, professional, and related occupations	Service occupations	Sales and office occupations	Farming, fishing, and forestry occupations	Construction, extraction, and maintenance occupations	Production, transportation and material moving occupations	Agriculture, forestry, fishing, and mining	Construction and manufacturing	Wholesale and retail trade	Transportation and warehousing, and utilities	Service industries	Public administration
	42	43	44	45	46	47	48	49	50	51	52	53	54	55	56
ILLINOIS—Cont'd															
Jackson County	2.5	15.7	12.2	35.8	19.0	26.8	0.7	7.3	10.5	1.9	11.0	13.3	4.0	63.6	6.2
Jasper County	5.7	18.6	13.6	24.2	14.1	24.6	1.4	12.2	23.6	8.3	26.5	15.1	10.3	35.0	4.8
Jefferson County	3.1	20.8	14.0	26.2	16.3	26.9	0.6	10.0	20.0	3.0	21.5	20.3	5.5	45.2	4.3
Jersey County	3.8	15.5	15.7	26.8	15.8	25.9	0.6	12.9	18.0	3.5	23.5	15.7	5.3	49.4	2.7
Jo Daviess County	7.9	17.3	15.0	27.8	17.9	21.1	2.3	11.4	19.5	6.9	26.1	13.4	4.7	46.5	2.4
Johnson County	3.0	22.0	14.1	29.7	22.6	22.5	1.0	10.3	13.9	6.0	14.1	12.5	7.1	46.8	13.5
Kane County	3.4	15.3	9.8	32.4	12.4	27.8	0.3	8.9	18.3	0.6	28.2	16.3	4.9	47.4	2.6
Kankakee County	2.5	19.5	13.1	26.1	15.6	26.5	0.6	10.5	20.7	1.6	23.0	18.2	6.9	46.6	3.6
Kendall County	4.8	12.2	12.3	34.0	11.2	28.8	0.2	10.4	15.4	1.3	27.5	16.0	5.7	46.1	3.5
Knox County	3.0	18.3	14.1	26.7	17.4	23.2	0.9	8.6	23.2	3.2	22.5	16.0	8.0	45.9	4.4
Lake County	4.2	13.4	10.6	41.1	11.3	28.3	0.1	7.6	11.6	0.3	25.9	16.4	3.6	50.9	2.9
La Salle County	3.1	17.5	14.4	25.0	15.8	25.1	0.7	11.8	21.7	3.2	26.5	17.1	7.1	42.2	3.7
Lawrence County	3.6	22.2	14.8	25.6	16.5	23.8	0.8	12.1	21.2	6.4	21.4	15.9	5.6	46.4	4.1
Lee County	3.9	14.8	12.5	26.1	15.9	23.0	0.6	10.6	23.7	3.4	28.3	14.7	6.9	40.8	5.9
Livingston County	4.6	17.2	12.4	25.1	18.4	22.0	1.2	9.5	23.9	5.8	26.7	13.2	5.6	41.6	7.2
Logan County	4.0	18.4	12.5	27.5	20.4	23.7	1.0	9.6	17.7	5.4	20.4	13.2	5.0	46.8	9.2
McDonough County	4.2	17.0	10.9	33.3	19.8	24.8	1.3	7.8	13.0	5.0	15.9	13.7	3.0	59.1	3.2
McHenry County	3.8	11.4	11.4	34.6	10.9	28.3	0.3	10.7	15.2	1.0	30.2	16.5	5.1	44.9	2.3
McLean County	3.2	12.6	10.5	37.3	15.3	28.9	0.3	7.3	10.8	1.4	13.7	13.0	3.6	65.3	2.9
Macon County	2.5	19.2	15.0	28.4	15.7	26.2	0.4	9.7	19.6	1.9	25.4	15.2	7.8	46.0	3.6
Macoupin County	4.0	18.8	15.7	25.9	16.0	24.8	0.8	13.2	19.3	5.8	21.0	15.7	7.1	44.5	5.9
Madison County	2.4	19.3	15.5	30.9	16.1	26.8	0.2	9.4	16.6	0.9	21.9	14.9	6.4	52.4	3.6
Marion County	3.1	21.7	15.3	24.8	17.6	20.4	0.7	8.4	28.1	2.6	29.8	13.2	6.6	43.6	4.1
Marshall County	4.9	14.8	15.0	25.5	18.6	21.7	0.5	11.1	22.5	5.2	29.9	13.4	6.6	41.7	3.1
Mason County	4.6	18.3	16.3	24.9	17.6	23.4	2.8	10.2	21.0	7.5	22.4	15.2	5.8	40.9	8.3
Massac County	3.4	24.5	14.4	24.6	19.7	24.8	0.7	12.1	18.1	3.9	18.0	16.9	9.6	47.3	4.4
Menard County	4.5	14.1	13.7	34.9	16.4	26.2	1.2	11.0	10.3	5.8	13.0	11.5	4.9	46.0	18.8
Mercer County	4.3	16.7	15.3	26.9	15.1	22.7	1.6	11.9	21.8	5.9	26.5	15.2	7.5	40.3	4.6
Monroe County	3.5	13.6	14.0	33.4	13.4	27.0	1.0	11.9	13.3	3.3	21.4	14.2	6.6	51.0	3.5
Montgomery County	5.1	19.6	13.7	26.0	18.6	24.8	0.8	11.7	18.1	5.9	20.3	15.6	6.2	43.9	8.1
Morgan County	3.8	19.6	14.1	30.8	17.3	24.9	1.0	8.0	18.0	3.8	20.2	13.5	5.0	50.2	7.2
Moultrie County	4.4	17.1	13.5	26.2	14.0	22.0	1.2	9.5	27.2	5.3	34.4	13.2	6.8	37.5	2.7
Ogle County	4.1	16.7	13.9	28.3	13.3	23.4	0.8	11.0	23.1	3.1	29.8	15.1	7.8	40.8	3.4
Peoria County	2.3	17.6	13.4	35.2	16.2	26.6	0.1	7.7	14.1	0.7	23.0	14.3	4.1	54.3	3.5
Perry County	3.4	20.1	12.2	23.6	18.7	21.9	1.0	11.0	23.9	4.7	29.1	13.0	4.9	41.5	6.7
Piatt County	4.8	14.6	15.2	32.3	14.5	23.7	1.3	10.2	18.0	5.7	21.1	14.9	7.5	47.3	3.6
Pike County	4.9	21.2	13.5	25.8	18.7	21.9	2.7	9.9	21.0	10.4	19.4	17.3	6.9	39.8	6.3
Pope County	4.7	24.0	17.0	26.4	22.3	19.8	1.5	11.6	18.4	9.6	17.8	14.2	8.3	40.4	9.7
Pulaski County	4.1	27.7	14.1	23.1	22.6	20.9	1.4	10.5	21.6	5.1	20.8	12.2	8.6	42.4	11.0
Putnam County	4.4	17.9	16.8	23.4	13.1	23.8	2.1	13.7	23.9	5.2	31.5	17.4	6.5	36.4	3.0
Randolph County	3.9	20.0	14.1	24.1	19.1	20.4	0.8	12.2	23.4	4.0	26.6	13.2	7.9	40.0	8.2
Richland County	4.1	19.0	14.0	30.1	16.0	24.7	1.2	9.3	18.7	6.8	20.5	18.4	5.7	45.0	3.5
Rock Island County	2.2	17.7	14.5	27.2	17.3	27.3	0.2	8.8	19.1	0.6	24.2	15.6	5.9	48.7	4.9
St. Clair County	2.6	20.3	16.4	30.1	17.8	28.3	0.2	8.8	14.7	0.9	16.9	14.8	6.9	54.7	5.7
Saline County	3.0	25.0	15.0	27.5	20.7	22.9	0.7	14.2	14.0	7.6	14.8	16.0	5.9	48.0	7.8
Sangamon County	2.6	17.3	14.1	39.3	14.5	29.9	0.3	7.8	8.2	1.2	9.8	12.5	4.4	52.8	19.4
Schuyler County	4.7	18.3	14.4	27.9	20.5	20.6	1.6	8.6	20.8	10.4	19.4	14.8	6.7	43.1	5.7
Scott County	4.8	16.0	14.4	26.1	14.8	26.1	2.0	13.0	18.0	8.1	24.6	15.3	6.0	38.9	7.2
Shelby County	4.9	17.4	15.8	24.4	14.6	21.4	1.6	11.9	26.1	6.0	33.2	13.6	5.4	39.1	2.9
Stark County	6.2	17.2	13.9	28.1	13.9	25.2	2.7	10.2	20.0	9.3	28.3	14.4	5.8	39.7	2.4
Stephenson County	4.8	18.2	13.8	28.5	13.6	24.8	1.3	9.3	22.5	5.0	33.0	12.6	3.7	43.2	2.6
Tazewell County	2.5	17.4	15.2	29.3	15.0	28.1	0.3	9.7	17.7	1.3	26.7	15.6	5.1	48.2	3.1
Union County	4.4	26.2	15.1	31.2	22.4	20.5	1.4	11.0	13.5	4.8	14.6	13.0	5.9	52.9	8.8
Vermilion County	2.9	20.8	14.6	24.3	16.5	25.4	0.7	10.1	23.1	2.4	26.6	17.4	5.4	44.0	4.2
Wabash County	4.0	19.1	15.9	22.9	18.5	22.2	0.7	12.5	23.1	7.0	25.8	15.1	6.9	40.8	4.4
Warren County	4.8	19.0	12.7	27.5	16.6	23.5	1.5	7.6	23.2	6.1	22.3	14.4	7.1	46.4	3.7
Washington County	7.0	15.9	15.1	28.2	15.3	21.3	2.3	11.8	21.1	8.4	23.4	14.5	8.6	39.9	5.2
Wayne County	3.7	19.9	12.9	24.2	13.7	21.2	1.7	10.4	28.9	8.4	34.0	14.4	5.3	35.5	2.5
White County	3.7	21.7	15.5	24.2	18.1	20.7	1.4	12.7	22.8	10.5	19.3	15.8	7.8	42.5	4.1
Whiteside County	3.1	17.9	14.3	24.7	15.2	22.6	0.8	9.8	27.0	2.8	34.9	14.2	5.5	39.4	3.2
Will County	2.9	12.8	11.2	33.9	12.0	28.4	0.1	11.2	14.4	0.4	23.6	16.2	7.5	48.8	3.4
Williamson County	2.3	22.1	14.7	28.4	17.8	27.8	0.3	9.6	16.0	2.1	16.7	17.5	5.9	50.9	7.0
Winnebago County	2.5	18.2	13.1	29.7	12.9	26.7	0.2	8.6	22.0	0.5	32.9	14.7	5.1	44.4	2.4
Woodford County	4.7	13.4	13.4	33.6	14.2	24.9	0.8	9.7	16.7	4.4	26.2	13.9	5.2	47.5	2.8

Table B-3. States and Counties — Education, Labor Force, and Income

	Median family income				Median income for full-year, full-time workers				Households by source of income (percent)								
STATE County	Median house-hold income	All families	Married-couple	Male house-holder	Female house-holder	Median nonfamily house-hold income	Men	Women	Per capita income	With earnings	With interest, dividend, or rental income	With Social Security income	With public assis-tance income	With retire-ment income	House-holds with income over $100,000 (percent)	+/- U.S. percent for income over $100,000	House-holds with income below poverty (percent)	Families with children with income below poverty (percent)
	57	58	59	60	61	62	63	64	65	66	67	68	69	70	71	72	73	74

STATE County	57	58	59	60	61	62	63	64	65	66	67	68	69	70	71	72	73	74
ILLINOIS—Cont'd																		
Jackson County	24 946	40 950	48 029	20 450	12 059	13 641	33 084	23 516	15 755	79.3	32.8	21.4	3.3	14.2	5.4	-6.9	27.3	20.7
Jasper County	34 721	43 547	48 589	20 625	13 796	19 037	30 867	18 186	16 649	77.5	42.1	31.2	1.8	13.5	4.0	-8.3	10.0	13.2
Jefferson County	33 555	41 141	48 706	28 750	19 014	16 552	35 279	21 627	16 644	74.6	34.8	32.1	3.2	17.8	5.2	-7.1	13.7	12.6
Jersey County	42 065	49 666	56 357	32 917	19 958	19 322	40 120	23 382	19 581	77.3	42.1	31.0	1.8	20.9	7.8	-4.5	7.6	8.0
Jo Daviess County	40 411	48 335	54 882	35 417	21 979	22 256	34 298	23 037	21 497	78.5	49.4	34.5	1.9	20.4	7.3	-5.0	7.4	6.2
Johnson County	33 326	40 275	47 476	30 750	15 833	15 337	29 864	23 856	17 990	69.9	37.0	35.7	3.1	25.0	5.1	-7.2	13.0	11.3
Kane County	59 351	66 558	72 814	36 008	27 350	34 506	46 829	30 673	24 315	87.9	41.2	18.9	1.9	12.7	20.4	8.1	5.8	7.1
Kankakee County	41 532	48 975	59 052	32 422	19 989	23 408	38 904	26 020	19 055	79.6	36.2	27.7	3.6	17.0	7.9	-4.4	10.5	13.3
Kendall County	64 625	69 383	72 019	45 194	34 700	34 901	50 748	31 224	25 188	88.2	46.2	18.5	1.1	14.4	18.5	6.2	3.2	2.6
Knox County	35 407	44 010	51 393	25 136	17 436	21 084	33 613	22 199	17 985	75.0	42.6	35.0	3.0	20.8	5.3	-7.0	10.2	14.0
Lake County	66 973	76 424	85 483	40 339	29 865	37 328	51 788	34 986	32 102	88.4	47.2	18.3	1.6	12.8	29.1	16.8	5.3	5.7
La Salle County	40 308	49 533	57 572	31 461	16 544	21 657	40 141	22 798	19 185	77.1	42.4	31.8	2.0	19.3	6.7	-5.6	8.9	11.3
Lawrence County	30 001	07 050	40 056	26 750	16 833	16 399	29 745	19 939	17 070	73.2	33.6	35.6	2.7	17.9	4.1	-8.2	13.7	18.8
Lee County	40 967	48 730	55 195	27 174	21 946	23 803	36 533	23 358	18 650	79.6	40.1	28.7	2.2	18.4	6.8	-5.5	7.3	7.0
Livingston County	41 342	47 958	56 387	30 260	21 356	23 279	37 284	25 352	18 347	80.2	43.0	29.1	1.6	14.3	6.8	-5.5	8.4	8.5
Logan County	39 389	48 655	54 637	30 761	20 833	21 444	34 914	24 485	17 953	77.6	39.0	30.7	2.2	20.6	6.2	-6.1	8.1	9.4
McDonough County	32 141	43 385	47 185	23 657	13 207	17 209	30 503	21 509	15 890	78.3	40.3	27.6	2.5	16.7	5.0	-7.3	19.9	16.8
McHenry County	64 826	71 553	76 419	47 924	29 556	36 382	51 046	31 842	26 476	89.1	45.4	18.5	1.0	12.2	21.8	9.5	3.5	3.7
McLean County	47 021	61 073	70 676	32 743	24 231	26 416	42 375	29 547	22 227	86.1	44.1	20.1	1.7	13.9	13.5	1.2	10.1	6.3
Macon County	37 859	47 493	59 373	29 034	16 254	21 781	40 138	23 766	20 067	77.0	37.9	29.6	3.6	19.2	7.8	-4.5	12.1	15.9
Macoupin County	36 190	43 021	49 928	23 625	17 903	19 759	35 475	23 365	17 298	75.0	40.4	34.3	1.9	20.2	5.1	-7.2	9.9	11.5
Madison County	41 541	50 862	61 022	35 250	20 235	23 324	40 715	26 769	20 509	77.8	40.2	28.9	2.8	21.3	8.9	-3.4	9.9	11.1
Marion County	35 227	41 427	50 041	28 365	17 219	18 128	31 988	22 372	17 235	75.2	37.3	33.8	3.1	17.3	5.1	-7.2	11.4	15.0
Marshall County	41 576	48 061	55 549	31 250	20 526	22 451	37 048	22 408	19 065	79.4	48.0	33.5	2.0	21.4	5.4	-6.9	5.7	7.0
Mason County	35 985	42 239	49 578	26 534	14 712	21 226	35 469	21 299	17 357	76.0	38.8	32.4	2.6	19.9	4.4	-7.9	10.0	13.3
Massac County	31 498	39 068	54 333	21 667	15 500	13 066	33 981	20 847	16 334	71.8	29.8	34.2	3.8	18.6	3.6	-8.7	15.1	16.0
Menard County	40 590	52 995	60 543	29 107	21 477	26 260	37 792	28 778	21 584	81.9	44.5	27.2	2.0	15.7	8.7	-3.6	7.8	10.4
Mercer County	40 893	47 192	54 432	26 375	19 519	20 698	35 731	23 309	18 645	78.8	41.1	32.3	2.1	22.9	5.6	-6.7	7.7	8.5
Monroe County	55 320	62 397	69 927	40 243	29 406	27 807	42 293	27 834	22 954	82.8	52.6	25.6	0.7	19.5	12.1	-0.2	4.0	2.8
Montgomery County	33 123	39 923	47 331	23 147	15 802	17 572	31 504	21 340	16 272	73.9	39.1	34.4	2.0	19.0	4.5	-7.8	13.7	16.0
Morgan County	36 933	46 040	55 100	27 500	18 750	21 321	32 001	23 808	18 205	77.4	38.7	30.4	2.8	19.3	5.7	-6.6	10.2	9.2
Moultrie County	40 084	46 655	53 641	37 778	19 955	21 589	36 357	21 825	18 562	79.7	42.4	30.5	1.9	17.8	5.9	-6.4	8.1	8.5
Ogle County	45 448	53 028	61 056	30 341	18 421	26 526	40 537	24 791	20 515	82.7	42.2	26.0	1.9	14.8	10.0	-2.3	7.4	8.0
Peoria County	39 978	50 592	61 809	28 720	16 571	24 519	41 713	26 104	21 219	78.9	39.7	26.7	4.3	19.3	9.8	-2.5	12.2	16.7
Perry County	33 281	41 064	47 705	26 958	14 919	17 247	30 331	21 206	15 935	74.4	38.2	34.8	2.3	19.7	3.5	-8.8	13.9	14.5
Piatt County	45 752	52 218	61 263	30 481	24 563	23 309	38 760	24 700	21 075	81.1	45.1	28.7	1.1	20.5	7.7	-4.6	5.7	5.3
Pike County	31 127	38 583	45 103	21 750	18 194	16 481	29 043	19 295	15 946	74.4	37.4	36.8	3.1	16.0	2.6	-9.7	13.4	13.3
Pope County	30 048	37 860	50 573	39 219	14 861	13 779	34 628	20 421	16 440	71.0	33.3	32.6	2.8	24.3	3.3	-9.0	14.9	16.8
Pulaski County	25 361	33 193	39 412	19 000	13 088	11 855	29 650	20 453	13 325	68.3	23.7	37.1	6.1	19.4	2.2	-10.1	24.4	29.0
Putnam County	45 492	50 700	54 135	20 063	23 611	26 053	41 808	22 212	19 792	77.1	48.7	33.3	1.8	19.2	7.0	-5.3	5.0	7.7
Randolph County	37 013	44 766	50 059	26 136	18 561	20 136	31 490	22 246	17 696	74.9	42.0	33.8	2.6	23.4	5.2	-7.1	10.0	11.4
Richland County	31 185	40 000	48 887	22 266	14 961	16 117	30 260	20 377	16 847	73.8	44.7	35.1	3.3	18.0	4.6	-7.7	13.1	15.0
Rock Island County	38 608	47 956	56 137	33 342	16 920	23 204	37 053	25 256	20 164	76.9	39.6	29.5	3.1	22.9	7.6	-4.7	10.4	13.8
St. Clair County	39 148	47 409	60 765	29 171	17 088	23 162	37 744	26 472	18 932	78.2	35.2	27.7	4.7	19.8	8.5	-3.8	13.4	17.5
Saline County	28 768	37 295	43 542	24 659	14 762	14 641	31 819	19 885	15 590	68.5	32.3	36.8	4.2	20.7	3.8	-8.5	15.2	16.2
Sangamon County	42 957	53 900	64 721	28 942	21 877	27 164	39 186	29 860	23 173	81.6	40.8	25.7	2.6	18.8	10.5	-1.8	8.5	10.4
Schuyler County	35 233	41 489	45 481	25 357	17 917	17 909	29 964	21 696	17 158	77.2	41.4	33.5	1.2	16.1	4.4	-7.9	11.2	9.6
Scott County	36 566	42 924	49 605	22 361	23 333	17 500	30 457	21 884	16 998	79.0	35.0	32.2	1.7	13.8	4.1	-8.2	10.7	9.6
Shelby County	37 313	44 372	49 574	32 500	18 171	20 415	33 157	21 865	17 313	75.9	40.1	35.5	1.6	17.8	4.4	-7.9	9.9	9.6
Stark County	35 826	43 410	48 229	23 750	20 013	31 518	23 114	16 767	74.7	42.1	33.9	1.4	18.4	4.1	-8.2	9.5	9.0	
Stephenson County	40 366	48 510	57 127	27 417	21 132	22 548	36 991	25 246	19 794	78.1	45.9	30.4	2.0	17.9	6.5	-5.8	9.1	10.3
Tazewell County	45 250	53 412	61 125	31 079	20 245	23 885	41 981	25 598	21 511	79.1	43.1	29.3	2.0	21.9	9.2	-3.1	6.6	6.8
Union County	30 994	37 710	46 023	20 781	15 625	16 924	30 849	22 982	16 450	70.3	35.8	34.9	4.9	22.5	4.2	-8.1	15.0	18.1
Vermilion County	34 071	41 553	50 629	25 093	16 198	19 645	33 875	23 075	16 787	73.6	34.1	34.1	3.7	20.6	4.3	-8.0	12.9	15.2
Wabash County	34 473	42 142	44 101	21 667	13 969	16 776	32 116	18 645	16 747	77.9	36.6	32.9	3.1	16.7	5.3	-7.0	14.8	16.8
Warren County	36 224	42 437	47 978	28 672	17 500	19 981	31 132	21 207	16 946	78.6	39.8	33.5	2.1	16.6	4.7	-7.6	9.1	10.5
Washington County	40 932	48 433	53 674	31 875	22 647	20 439	34 096	23 099	19 108	78.7	47.3	33.2	1.0	17.2	6.4	-5.9	6.6	5.2
Wayne County	30 481	37 729	44 612	20 556	16 295	17 401	30 069	21 332	15 793	72.6	36.8	34.8	1.9	17.6	3.1	-9.2	13.4	14.4
White County	29 601	36 580	40 278	29 063	15 484	15 865	31 152	18 112	16 412	71.7	37.6	38.1	2.3	16.5	3.6	-8.7	12.7	13.6
Whiteside County	40 354	46 653	54 981	28 576	20 606	22 448	36 139	22 908	19 296	77.1	40.6	31.8	1.7	22.0	6.1	-6.2	7.9	9.9
Will County	62 238	69 608	76 576	40 362	30 943	32 858	50 690	32 066	24 613	87.7	40.7	19.4	1.8	13.5	21.0	8.7	4.6	4.6
Williamson County	31 991	40 692	47 151	25 227	14 273	17 944	33 855	22 433	17 779	73.0	33.4	32.5	4.2	21.6	5.8	-6.5	15.2	18.1
Winnebago County	43 886	52 456	62 197	32 104	20 239	26 193	41 119	26 700	21 194	81.7	37.9	25.5	3.3	15.3	10.0	-2.3	9.3	10.7
Woodford County	51 394	58 305	62 026	45 625	20 500	25 891	44 856	25 998	21 956	82.4	52.0	27.7	1.7	19.7	12.1	-0.2	4.4	4.7

Table B-3. States and Counties — **Education, Labor Force, and Income**

STATE/County code	MSA/PMSA/NECMA code[1]	STATE County	High school graduates			College graduates		College graduates (percent)				
			Total population 25 years and over	Percent with a high school diploma or less	Percent with a high school diploma or more	Percent with a bachelor's degree or more	+/− U.S. percent with bachelor's degree or more	Non-Hispanic White	Black or African American	American Indian and Alaska Native	Asian, Hawaiian, and Pacific Islander	Hispanic or Latino[2]
			1	2	3	4	5	6	7	8	9	10
18 000	...	INDIANA	3 893 278	55.1	82.1	19.4	-5.0	19.9	12.1	10.3	57.0	11.3
18 001	2760	Adams County	20 158	65.1	80.0	10.7	-13.7	10.7	0.0	40.0	89.1	1.4
18 003	2760	Allen County	208 769	46.3	85.7	22.7	-1.7	24.4	9.6	8.0	39.1	7.8
18 005	...	Bartholomew County	47 109	52.4	83.8	22.0	-2.4	21.4	16.3	11.4	72.4	12.8
18 007	...	Benton County	6 158	61.9	86.3	13.0	-11.4	13.4	0.0	50.0	11.1	0.0
18 009	...	Blackford County	9 550	68.2	81.3	10.3	-14.1	10.1	X	44.4	55.6	11.4
18 011	3480	Boone County	30 048	49.6	88.3	27.6	3.2	27.7	0.0	0.0	51.1	4.4
18 013	...	Brown County	10 530	55.2	83.6	18.5	-5.9	18.5	19.6	29.0	100.0	0.0
18 015	...	Carroll County	13 299	64.5	83.2	12.9	-11.5	13.1	0.0	0.0	100.0	6.8
18 017	...	Cass County	26 747	63.7	81.8	12.0	-12.4	12.3	0.0	10.4	46.9	7.4
18 019	4520	Clark County	64 389	56.6	79.9	14.3	-10.1	14.5	10.0	4.6	45.7	13.5
18 021	8320	Clay County	17 304	63.3	82.3	12.8	-11.6	12.8	15.4	0.0	40.6	13.2
18 023	3920	Clinton County	21 744	70.2	80.1	10.1	-14.3	10.2	0.0	0.0	37.9	5.0
18 025	...	Crawford County	7 088	74.5	70.6	8.4	-16.0	8.3	0.0	31.6	0.0	10.0
18 027	...	Daviess County	18 655	68.1	71.8	9.7	-14.7	9.6	0.0	14.1	65.8	0.7
18 029	1640	Dearborn County	29 712	59.2	82.0	15.4	-9.0	15.3	13.4	56.0	16.9	25.3
18 031	...	Decatur County	15 948	68.4	79.1	11.5	-12.9	11.1	0.0	0.0	51.8	6.7
18 033	2760	DeKalb County	25 500	61.2	84.7	12.4	-12.0	12.3	14.3	0.0	12.1	18.0
18 035	5280	Delaware County	72 444	55.6	81.6	20.4	-4.0	20.7	11.1	3.3	68.8	26.1
18 037	...	Dubois County	25 733	64.3	80.2	14.5	-9.9	14.6	0.0	0.0	78.6	9.4
18 039	2330	Elkhart County	112 908	61.3	75.7	15.5	-8.9	16.6	5.9	1.6	36.3	5.4
18 041	...	Fayette County	17 125	72.8	73.7	7.8	-16.6	7.9	0.0	18.2	0.0	9.8
18 043	4520	Floyd County	46 609	50.7	82.4	20.4	-4.0	20.6	13.4	2.9	53.0	13.0
18 045	...	Fountain County	11 914	66.8	80.7	10.1	-14.3	10.2	0.0	9.1	0.0	0.0
18 047	...	Franklin County	14 218	68.1	76.1	12.5	-11.9	12.6	0.0	0.0	10.3	13.9
18 049	...	Fulton County	13 613	69.0	80.2	10.3	-14.1	10.5	0.0	30.2	38.9	3.8
18 051	...	Gibson County	21 694	60.1	80.9	12.4	-12.0	12.3	2.2	0.0	63.2	11.9
18 053	...	Grant County	47 408	62.7	79.2	14.1	-10.3	14.4	7.4	22.7	53.2	5.7
18 055	...	Greene County	22 396	64.3	79.2	10.5	-13.9	10.5	0.0	0.0	31.3	8.9
18 057	3480	Hamilton County	116 457	25.6	94.2	48.9	24.5	48.6	48.8	13.7	69.5	43.9
18 059	3480	Hancock County	37 073	49.7	87.8	22.2	-2.2	22.1	29.2	20.9	38.6	39.0
18 061	4520	Harrison County	22 457	60.8	80.3	13.1	-11.3	13.1	0.0	2.1	42.5	7.7
18 063	3480	Hendricks County	67 683	48.7	88.5	23.1	-1.3	23.1	13.5	11.2	55.0	19.8
18 065	...	Henry County	33 198	64.8	79.6	11.7	-12.7	11.7	8.1	0.0	40.4	4.0
18 067	3850	Howard County	56 222	54.7	83.3	18.1	-6.3	18.0	13.3	41.8	57.5	14.2
18 069	2760	Huntington County	24 386	61.7	85.0	14.2	-10.2	14.1	74.1	6.6	39.1	16.6
18 071	...	Jackson County	27 131	66.9	79.8	11.5	-12.9	11.3	7.8	16.3	35.2	11.1
18 073	...	Jasper County	18 751	64.0	82.4	13.0	-11.4	13.2	47.6	0.0	27.8	4.4
18 075	...	Jay County	14 280	71.0	78.5	9.9	-14.5	9.8	0.0	25.0	22.2	5.3
18 077	...	Jefferson County	20 605	59.1	81.0	16.4	-8.0	16.5	7.8	0.0	42.9	20.9
18 079	...	Jennings County	17 709	70.8	76.2	8.4	-16.0	8.0	17.1	16.9	73.3	9.3
18 081	3480	Johnson County	73 966	50.5	85.7	23.1	-1.3	22.9	22.1	1.5	56.3	17.5
18 083	...	Knox County	24 865	55.6	81.7	14.4	-10.0	14.2	26.9	0.0	27.7	25.5
18 085	...	Kosciusko County	47 103	60.5	81.6	14.9	-9.5	15.1	15.0	13.1	18.4	8.1
18 087	...	LaGrange County	19 519	73.7	60.2	8.9	-15.5	8.9	0.0	0.0	35.9	3.2
18 089	2960	Lake County	310 220	56.6	80.7	16.2	-8.2	18.7	10.8	3.2	58.6	8.5
18 091	...	LaPorte County	73 723	60.4	80.6	14.0	-10.4	14.9	6.3	13.0	30.1	7.3
18 093	...	Lawrence County	31 175	69.0	77.4	10.7	-13.7	10.6	10.5	0.0	61.3	20.2
18 095	3480	Madison County	89 458	59.9	80.1	14.4	-10.0	15.0	8.4	4.9	13.9	11.7
18 097	3480	Marion County	553 459	48.0	81.6	25.4	1.0	28.7	13.6	12.2	55.8	14.2
18 099	...	Marshall County	28 555	61.3	79.8	14.9	-9.5	15.4	40.9	15.4	16.9	4.8
18 101	...	Martin County	7 066	68.1	74.2	8.8	-15.6	8.9	0.0	0.0	0.0	0.0
18 103	...	Miami County	23 741	64.3	81.9	10.4	-14.0	10.7	5.2	3.4	60.0	0.6
18 105	1020	Monroe County	65 489	37.7	88.5	39.6	15.2	38.0	36.8	37.4	81.4	59.7
18 107	...	Montgomery County	24 501	61.2	85.7	14.7	-9.7	14.5	25.4	30.3	0.0	18.1
18 109	3480	Morgan County	43 397	64.3	80.7	12.6	-11.8	12.4	72.0	1.6	30.5	30.9
18 111	...	Newton County	9 576	71.1	78.7	9.6	-14.8	9.7	0.0	0.0	28.6	3.5
18 113	...	Noble County	28 554	66.3	77.3	11.1	-13.3	11.4	17.0	0.0	7.5	4.6
18 115	1640	Ohio County	3 780	66.3	78.4	11.6	-12.8	11.7	0.0	X	X	23.5
18 117	...	Orange County	12 818	71.4	73.8	10.2	-14.2	10.2	0.0	0.0	0.0	32.6
18 119	...	Owen County	14 384	68.6	74.9	9.2	-15.2	9.0	0.0	0.0	29.2	14.5
18 121	...	Parke County	11 891	65.1	80.5	11.6	-12.8	11.7	4.2	24.6	22.7	9.4
18 123	...	Perry County	12 734	70.7	74.8	9.6	-14.8	9.5	7.2	0.0	0.0	24.4
18 125	...	Pike County	8 753	69.9	75.6	8.4	-16.0	8.5	0.0	0.0	0.0	13.2
18 127	2960	Porter County	94 462	49.8	88.3	22.6	-1.8	22.7	38.1	20.7	45.7	12.7
18 129	2440	Posey County	17 671	57.4	84.4	14.8	-9.6	14.9	9.7	7.3	33.3	14.1
18 131	2440	Pulaski County	9 038	65.3	79.8	10.3	-14.1	10.4	10.6	0.0	0.0	5.1

[1] MSA = Metropolitan Statistical Area. PMSA = Primary MSA. NECMA = New England County Metropolitan Area. See the Appendix A for explanation of these concepts. See Appendix B for list of metropolitan areas identified by type, with component counties.
[2] Hispanic or Latino persons may be of any race.

Table B-3. States and Counties — **Education, Labor Force, and Income**

STATE County	School enrollment			Population 16 to 19 years				Employment status, 2000			Work status in 1999 of the population 16 years and over (percent)		
											Worked in 1999		
	Grades kindergarten through 12	College or graduate school	Percent private	Number	Percent in armed forces	Percent high school graduates	Percent not enrolled, not grads, not in armed forces, not employed	Total population 16 years and over	Percent in labor force	Unemployment rate	Full-time	Part-time	Did not work in 1999
	11	12	13	14	15	16	17	18	19	20	21	22	23
INDIANA	1 142 156	352 687	14.2	360 606	0.0	10.6	5.1	4 683 717	66.6	4.9	57.0	15.8	27.2
Adams County	7 246	1 145	18.1	2 229	0.0	7.9	7.9	24 405	67.4	2.9	53.7	17.9	28.4
Allen County	65 971	18 136	22.0	19 231	0.1	10.4	4.1	250 040	70.2	4.7	58.5	17.0	24.6
Bartholomew County	13 359	2 882	12.0	3 330	0.0	9.8	4.4	54 521	68.2	3.7	58.8	14.8	26.4
Benton County	1 963	247	10.7	557	0.0	16.5	4.8	7 155	67.5	3.3	59.7	14.7	25.7
Blackford County	2 579	369	7.8	702	0.0	11.3	4.1	10 976	64.3	4.4	55.7	13.7	30.6
Boone County	9 369	1 276	8.5	2 357	0.0	12.6	4.2	34 387	69.3	3.0	61.3	12.1	26.6
Brown County	2 724	496	8.3	772	0.0	14.2	4.3	11 938	64.9	3.6	55.2	15.4	29.4
Carroll County	3 813	485	8.7	1 051	0.0	14.5	5.9	15 441	68.0	3.9	58.2	15.3	26.5
Cass County	7 749	1 161	7.3	2 406	0.0	11.4	7.8	31 818	63.8	4.0	56.1	14.8	29.1
Clark County	16 552	3 884	12.3	5 178	0.1	13.4	6.1	75 843	68.2	4.5	59.9	13.4	26.8
Clay County	5 323	872	7.4	1 574	0.3	10.3	7.1	20 428	62.8	5.1	52.8	14.7	32.6
Clinton County	6 832	726	6.7	2 077	0.0	11.0	5.7	25 829	62.9	5.4	56.8	12.0	31.2
Crawford County	2 049	224	8.8	582	0.0	17.0	4.0	8 290	59.5	5.3	52.6	12.1	35.3
Daviess County	5 947	653	16.2	1 704	0.0	9.5	9.7	22 111	62.9	4.3	52.7	14.8	32.5
Dearborn County	9 685	1 518	14.2	2 819	0.0	11.2	6.1	34 833	68.6	3.3	58.1	15.8	26.0
Decatur County	4 608	647	8.3	1 235	0.0	17.3	3.1	18 765	69.8	3.8	60.6	14.5	24.9
DeKalb County	8 065	1 537	8.7	2 225	0.0	12.5	2.5	30 196	71.4	4.2	62.2	15.0	22.8
Delaware County	19 279	16 227	4.2	8 631	0.1	6.1	2.4	95 328	63.1	7.1	49.8	21.2	29.0
Dubois County	8 012	1 112	8.7	2 132	0.0	13.2	2.0	29 974	71.5	2.5	61.7	14.3	24.0
Elkhart County	36 607	5 271	12.1	10 334	0.1	12.1	7.8	135 426	71.3	3.6	61.8	15.2	23.0
Fayette County	4 439	734	8.5	1 192	0.0	17.4	8.6	20 028	62.7	6.4	54.9	13.3	31.7
Floyd County	13 808	3 412	14.8	3 882	0.0	8.8	5.1	54 508	68.6	3.9	57.9	16.1	26.0
Fountain County	3 520	415	5.9	1 060	0.0	13.0	2.8	13 872	62.1	4.8	53.8	13.8	32.4
Franklin County	4 611	684	19.7	1 322	0.4	13.5	6.5	16 637	66.9	4.0	57.7	15.2	27.1
Fulton County	4 084	503	5.8	1 120	0.0	12.1	1.8	15 795	66.9	4.7	58.7	14.1	27.2
Gibson County	6 100	1 215	15.5	1 772	0.0	9.3	3.5	25 274	65.9	5.0	54.9	15.6	29.5
Grant County	12 773	5 296	26.0	4 635	0.1	10.8	4.1	57 902	61.8	7.3	53.1	16.2	30.7
Greene County	5 980	1 162	5.6	1 729	0.0	11.6	7.6	25 967	62.1	5.4	51.9	14.6	33.5
Hamilton County	38 330	7 048	14.7	8 026	0.1	6.3	1.7	131 532	74.6	2.3	64.5	15.8	19.7
Hancock County	10 799	2 262	11.9	2 726	0.0	9.2	1.0	42 302	70.5	3.0	60.4	15.7	23.9
Harrison County	6 637	1 159	13.2	2 153	0.0	17.7	2.8	26 515	69.2	4.0	58.6	14.8	26.7
Hendricks County	21 421	3 665	10.4	5 661	0.0	0.7	1.1	78 300	70.8	3.1	61.7	14.0	24.3
Henry County	8 779	1 428	6.7	2 528	0.0	10.5	7.6	38 230	60.9	4.9	52.3	13.8	34.0
Howard County	15 619	2 932	9.3	4 479	0.5	11.9	5.4	65 669	63.2	4.8	55.0	14.2	30.8
Huntington County	7 419	1 885	16.8	2 324	0.0	11.0	3.1	29 320	69.9	3.8	59.0	16.4	24.6
Jackson County	7 554	1 091	12.7	2 036	0.0	16.6	3.2	31 943	66.0	3.3	59.8	12.0	28.2
Jasper County	6 113	1 392	20.1	2 000	0.0	14.0	1.7	22 750	65.0	6.0	54.9	17.2	27.9
Jay County	4 202	526	5.6	1 169	0.0	15.0	2.5	16 556	65.7	4.2	55.8	14.5	29.7
Jefferson County	5 619	2 077	22.1	2 024	0.3	13.4	5.9	24 801	65.6	5.6	58.6	14.1	27.3
Jennings County	5 392	734	12.1	1 389	0.2	19.7	7.5	20 669	69.1	7.3	61.5	12.6	25.9
Johnson County	22 205	4 952	15.0	6 470	0.2	11.0	4.2	87 631	71.0	3.4	60.6	15.5	23.9
Knox County	6 828	3 756	6.0	3 422	0.0	6.3	4.4	31 531	63.5	8.7	51.1	17.6	31.4
Kosciusko County	14 606	2 247	12.6	4 018	0.0	11.4	5.2	55 714	69.5	3.3	59.5	15.1	25.4
LaGrange County	7 099	568	21.9	2 399	0.2	5.4	13.3	24 455	67.0	2.5	55.5	16.8	27.8
Lake County	96 754	24 644	13.3	28 733	0.1	11.5	5.1	369 963	62.4	7.5	51.5	15.7	32.8
LaPorte County	20 758	4 525	12.0	5 774	0.0	11.5	6.6	86 339	61.9	4.3	54.3	14.9	30.8
Lawrence County	8 125	979	6.1	2 320	0.0	12.3	6.6	36 026	63.8	5.7	54.6	13.5	31.9
Madison County	23 306	5 680	14.1	7 413	0.0	13.0	4.8	105 337	60.7	5.7	53.0	14.0	33.0
Marion County	156 431	45 864	19.5	45 632	0.0	12.6	8.0	661 929	69.1	5.4	60.7	14.1	25.3
Marshall County	9 285	1 346	12.2	2 884	0.0	13.1	4.3	34 135	67.6	4.2	58.2	15.6	26.3
Martin County	1 942	199	10.1	598	0.0	9.2	2.3	8 115	62.8	5.8	54.1	14.0	31.9
Miami County	6 949	1 208	8.3	2 034	0.0	12.2	7.8	27 815	62.1	3.7	55.8	13.9	30.3
Monroe County	15 547	34 916	5.2	12 966	0.0	5.5	1.7	101 432	63.9	4.1	51.3	28.4	20.3
Montgomery County	7 207	1 508	12.8	2 146	0.0	11.5	5.0	28 944	66.5	3.9	57.5	15.6	26.9
Morgan County	13 108	1 800	8.8	3 889	0.0	10.7	5.6	50 748	68.6	2.9	58.8	13.3	27.9
Newton County	2 961	243	7.1	924	0.0	15.8	8.9	11 217	64.7	4.4	56.3	14.3	29.5
Noble County	9 512	1 061	10.6	2 693	0.0	10.7	8.6	34 315	69.4	3.3	61.9	12.5	25.6
Ohio County	1 082	169	7.0	294	0.0	16.3	3.1	4 407	67.3	4.8	55.8	14.9	29.3
Orange County	3 605	471	6.6	985	0.0	15.9	7.2	14 832	62.3	5.1	55.3	11.6	33.1
Owen County	4 296	495	6.7	1 327	0.0	16.4	6.5	16 742	64.8	4.5	57.0	12.6	30.4
Parke County	3 225	488	6.7	909	0.0	8.3	5.3	13 616	57.0	4.0	52.4	13.9	33.7
Perry County	3 477	608	6.6	1 074	0.0	13.9	11.1	15 069	61.0	4.9	54.4	12.3	33.4
Pike County	2 279	333	4.4	693	0.0	8.7	3.9	10 139	61.7	5.4	52.0	14.9	33.1
Porter County	28 392	8 959	16.6	9 342	0.0	9.8	2.6	113 927	67.6	4.0	56.2	17.9	25.9
Posey County	5 659	1 022	14.5	1 495	0.0	10.1	3.0	20 569	66.7	4.1	57.8	14.6	27.6
Pulaski County	2 877	403	6.5	821	0.6	10.2	2.4	10 534	62.1	4.3	54.8	14.3	30.9

Table B-3. States and Counties — Education, Labor Force, and Income

STATE County	Full-year full-time employed (percent)								Children under 18 years in families					Total employed by class of worker (percent)			
										With two parents (percent)		With one parent who is in labor force (percent)	+/− U.S. percent of children with no stay-at-home parent (percent)	+/− U.S. percent two-income couples				
	Total	Men	Women	Non-Hispanic White	Black or African American	American Indian and Alaska Native	Asian, Hawaiian, and Pacific Islander	Hispanic or Latino[1]	Number	Both in labor force	Father only in labor force				Private	Government	Self-employed	Unpaid family worker
	24	25	26	27	28	29	30	31	32	33	34	35	36	37	38	39	40	41
INDIANA	43.4	54.1	33.3	44.2	37.0	39.5	37.1	38.6	1 493 290	47.6	21.7	21.3	4.3	3.6	80.6	10.9	8.2	0.3
Adams County	43.5	57.6	30.2	43.1	14.3	40.0	75.0	50.9	10 158	46.2	34.9	13.3	-5.1	3.1	80.9	7.0	12.0	0.1
Allen County	45.6	57.7	34.3	46.8	38.0	45.1	41.2	42.6	87 698	46.3	22.3	22.1	3.8	6.5	83.6	8.5	7.7	0.2
Bartholomew County	46.3	60.1	33.3	46.3	55.8	39.5	42.2	48.6	17 968	49.1	25.4	17.5	2.0	3.5	82.7	9.0	8.1	0.3
Benton County	46.9	58.2	36.2	47.2	58.3	50.0	0.0	47.6	2 458	62.9	12.1	16.6	14.9	9.5	73.2	12.1	14.4	0.2
Blackford County	42.1	52.2	32.7	41.9	100.0	29.0	55.6	52.7	3 353	51.9	19.1	18.6	5.9	0.1	83.3	9.5	6.7	0.4
Boone County	51.9	67.1	38.2	52.0	30.5	30.8	58.2	47.3	12 522	53.8	28.9	13.8	3.0	7.1	77.6	10.2	12.0	0.2
Brown County	42.7	51.4	34.1	42.7	61.4	32.3	25.9	38.3	3 346	50.2	24.0	16.4	2.0	0.4	74.1	11.6	14.2	0.1
Carroll County	44.8	58.1	31.9	44.6	100.0	41.7	50.0	48.5	5 054	55.5	23.3	14.3	5.2	3.8	78.3	9.7	11.9	0.1
Cass County	42.9	53.4	32.7	44.1	30.6	23.9	41.7	29.9	9 866	50.5	18.3	19.0	4.9	3.3	76.8	14.4	8.3	0.4
Clark County	47.2	56.8	38.3	47.5	42.8	50.5	40.2	43.6	22 088	48.9	15.7	24.7	9.0	5.8	80.2	12.2	7.4	0.2
Clay County	40.7	52.3	30.0	40.6	39.0	30.1	30.4	51.1	6 492	52.8	22.9	17.7	5.9	1.6	77.0	13.8	8.8	0.4
Clinton County	45.2	56.8	34.2	45.8	42.2	29.4	22.6	39.5	8 852	47.8	22.9	19.5	2.7	-0.2	83.2	8.7	7.9	0.2
Crawford County	36.4	44.8	28.3	36.6	0.0	32.0	0.0	59.1	2 603	38.6	27.6	18.9	-7.1	-5.8	73.3	14.5	11.2	0.9
Daviess County	40.0	53.4	27.5	40.1	25.0	17.2	57.5	39.0	8 242	42.3	36.1	15.1	-7.2	-1.2	71.6	14.6	13.4	0.5
Dearborn County	46.9	59.7	34.8	47.0	41.3	33.3	38.6	44.1	12 293	52.6	22.8	17.2	5.2	7.6	82.9	9.6	7.1	0.4
Decatur County	46.8	57.8	36.3	46.9	0.0	100.0	33.8	34.4	6 169	50.1	22.8	17.2	2.7	4.9	79.3	8.6	11.8	0.3
DeKalb County	48.0	60.0	36.4	48.2	36.6	38.0	47.1	53.7	10 850	54.4	20.4	19.3	9.1	10.1	84.3	7.5	8.0	0.2
Delaware County	35.0	44.6	26.3	35.6	30.5	37.8	20.4	21.7	24 734	45.1	19.4	24.0	4.5	-1.8	76.5	15.9	7.3	0.3
Dubois County	51.3	63.4	39.7	51.5	71.4	26.1	46.7	44.9	10 674	65.2	16.8	12.3	12.9	13.3	83.3	7.1	9.2	0.3
Elkhart County	46.9	59.4	34.9	47.7	41.9	32.8	39.1	43.2	49 708	47.5	23.2	20.9	3.8	7.1	84.7	6.6	8.5	0.2
Fayette County	41.1	53.4	30.0	41.4	31.0	36.4	70.0	27.5	5 849	48.0	21.8	20.6	4.0	-0.9	83.2	8.6	7.9	0.3
Floyd County	45.7	56.7	35.6	45.7	45.1	39.4	54.9	48.5	17 711	50.2	18.8	21.6	7.2	6.6	79.6	11.7	8.5	0.2
Fountain County	41.8	54.5	29.7	42.0	0.0	19.7	68.6	38.5	4 447	47.3	22.4	22.0	4.7	-1.3	78.3	10.6	10.6	0.4
Franklin County	43.7	56.8	30.8	44.0	0.0	53.8	35.0	13.8	6 048	49.6	26.7	16.0	1.0	2.4	80.3	7.8	11.5	0.4
Fulton County	44.8	56.4	33.9	44.8	36.9	37.7	88.9	46.7	5 017	48.9	22.3	20.0	4.3	3.3	80.6	9.3	9.4	0.7
Gibson County	41.3	52.4	31.0	41.6	29.9	45.8	38.3	43.8	7 817	56.3	20.1	18.4	10.1	4.6	83.3	8.4	8.1	0.2
Grant County	37.8	47.2	29.6	38.0	39.5	29.6	26.9	35.0	16 358	46.3	18.1	25.9	7.6	-1.3	81.8	11.0	7.0	0.3
Greene County	38.1	49.6	27.2	38.2	0.0	43.2	53.1	30.4	7 788	51.1	21.7	16.2	2.7	-0.8	69.4	19.2	10.9	0.5
Hamilton County	53.0	69.1	37.9	53.1	60.0	60.7	48.6	49.2	55 286	54.4	31.1	10.8	0.6	10.4	79.8	9.4	10.6	0.1
Hancock County	49.6	61.7	38.1	49.7	29.2	38.6	49.7	31.5	14 174	59.0	22.9	13.6	8.0	8.2	79.8	10.6	9.4	0.1
Harrison County	45.5	55.7	35.6	45.5	25.8	38.7	66.2	47.4	8 572	56.5	19.0	18.7	10.6	6.6	79.3	10.5	9.7	0.5
Hendricks County	51.3	62.9	39.7	51.7	21.8	59.8	58.7	50.5	27 943	59.3	21.1	14.8	9.5	11.5	82.4	10.7	6.9	0.1
Henry County	39.0	52.0	27.3	39.1	35.7	14.1	46.8	34.2	10 987	51.8	20.1	18.4	5.6	-3.0	78.1	13.0	8.4	0.5
Howard County	41.7	53.7	30.8	42.0	37.6	52.1	32.9	40.8	20 636	44.4	23.2	23.4	3.2	-3.9	83.5	9.2	7.0	0.3
Huntington County	46.8	58.5	35.9	46.9	69.0	65.7	15.3	38.0	9 458	57.4	17.2	18.7	11.5	7.0	84.1	7.5	8.1	0.3
Jackson County	47.1	60.1	34.7	47.0	34.1	78.2	51.0	48.5	9 941	48.3	21.7	18.8	2.5	0.9	82.7	8.3	8.3	0.7
Jasper County	39.1	53.5	25.2	39.2	34.3	13.5	0.0	35.3	7 944	48.0	30.2	15.3	-1.3	-2.6	77.3	10.6	11.5	0.6
Jay County	42.5	54.8	31.1	42.6	25.0	100.0	42.6	36.1	5 607	56.0	22.8	16.1	7.5	2.4	81.3	8.8	9.6	0.3
Jefferson County	42.2	50.8	33.9	42.4	36.3	45.5	33.9	40.6	7 294	49.2	19.4	22.6	7.2	4.5	77.4	12.6	9.6	0.4
Jennings County	47.5	57.2	38.0	47.6	43.9	35.1	43.1	44.0	7 192	50.7	21.1	17.3	3.4	1.9	79.2	13.0	7.7	0.1
Johnson County	48.0	60.6	36.1	48.3	24.4	51.3	48.8	44.7	30 130	54.4	23.6	16.9	6.7	8.8	83.6	9.9	6.4	0.1
Knox County	36.8	43.9	30.0	37.5	13.3	16.9	22.2	29.6	8 523	50.5	17.6	20.7	6.6	2.5	75.0	13.5	11.1	0.4
Kosciusko County	46.4	59.5	33.6	46.4	34.6	39.4	58.6	47.7	19 678	50.7	26.1	16.5	2.6	5.4	84.4	6.0	9.2	0.4
LaGrange County	40.9	55.9	26.1	41.2	32.8	8.9	43.5	35.5	11 424	32.6	50.8	11.1	-20.9	-4.5	78.3	7.2	13.7	0.8
Lake County	38.1	48.8	28.5	40.8	32.2	35.1	38.4	35.4	121 002	37.5	21.6	25.9	-1.2	-4.1	81.8	11.7	6.3	0.2
LaPorte County	41.5	49.3	33.3	42.9	31.5	38.1	37.4	37.9	25 404	46.4	21.1	24.1	5.9	1.7	79.9	11.3	8.4	0.4
Lawrence County	41.1	51.5	31.6	41.0	59.9	38.2	39.5	48.6	10 557	51.8	21.1	18.5	5.7	-0.4	78.5	13.7	7.4	0.4
Madison County	40.2	48.9	31.9	41.1	29.8	28.2	37.2	44.9	30 220	45.0	18.0	25.3	5.7	-1.9	81.7	10.6	7.4	0.3
Marion County	46.4	54.7	39.0	48.4	41.1	36.7	47.5	40.2	206 481	40.8	16.4	30.0	6.2	5.6	81.7	10.7	7.5	0.1
Marshall County	44.1	58.0	30.8	44.4	25.9	38.4	57.1	40.6	12 176	50.5	25.4	16.0	1.9	4.3	80.6	9.7	9.2	0.4
Martin County	40.9	52.4	29.1	41.1	0.0	25.0	100.0	66.7	2 535	58.4	18.1	15.5	9.3	-1.5	69.2	16.9	13.5	0.3
Miami County	43.4	52.7	33.9	44.3	26.2	48.7	30.0	29.8	8 861	49.8	21.8	19.2	4.4	1.2	78.1	12.4	9.2	0.3
Monroe County	32.4	37.8	27.3	33.7	23.9	35.8	13.5	27.0	20 388	47.8	20.7	21.8	5.0	6.5	68.4	23.4	7.9	0.3
Montgomery County	43.3	54.9	32.0	43.6	35.0	12.1	14.3	40.1	9 406	54.5	19.4	16.6	6.5	5.6	80.9	8.9	9.7	0.4
Morgan County	49.2	61.8	37.1	49.2	89.3	53.2	49.4	44.3	17 294	48.4	25.6	18.3	2.1	3.5	81.7	10.8	7.3	0.2
Newton County	41.7	54.8	29.0	42.0	20.0	44.1	34.8	31.7	3 720	49.1	28.0	17.0	1.5	-0.8	80.4	9.2	10.1	0.3
Noble County	47.6	58.3	36.8	48.4	22.0	60.0	36.9	38.4	12 870	49.6	24.9	15.9	0.9	6.2	84.8	7.4	7.5	0.3
Ohio County	44.1	55.5	33.2	44.2	80.0	X	X	53.6	1 372	55.7	22.7	12.5	3.6	4.4	78.3	10.8	10.6	0.3
Orange County	41.6	51.5	32.3	41.7	51.3	15.9	85.7	62.6	4 787	48.7	21.6	20.7	4.8	-0.8	77.7	10.1	11.6	0.6
Owen County	42.6	50.6	34.8	43.1	0.0	34.9	41.9	12.6	5 491	45.8	24.8	21.7	2.9	-0.7	76.5	11.9	11.0	0.6
Parke County	37.8	47.9	29.0	38.5	14.4	24.6	0.0	30.9	3 975	45.7	24.8	16.2	-2.7	-2.7	72.0	13.7	13.7	0.6
Perry County	40.4	47.1	33.2	41.2	1.9	0.0	25.0	48.4	4 124	55.3	15.0	20.3	11.0	3.1	79.6	12.1	7.9	0.4
Pike County	38.1	49.3	27.0	38.1	22.2	33.3	27.6	62.3	2 954	52.8	22.9	17.6	5.8	-3.8	81.0	10.9	7.8	0.3
Porter County	42.8	56.4	29.9	42.9	40.6	36.1	36.1	42.6	36 006	45.7	30.1	17.5	-1.4	1.0	80.8	10.7	8.3	0.2
Posey County	45.9	59.2	33.0	45.9	41.1	80.5	0.0	46.3	7 215	57.6	21.8	12.9	5.9	4.8	78.8	11.0	9.9	0.3
Pulaski County	41.2	54.4	27.9	41.2	52.1	16.0	0.0	44.8	3 602	48.9	21.6	19.5	3.8	-2.9	73.3	11.6	14.3	0.8

[1]Hispanic or Latino persons may be of any race.

STATE County	Percent who worked at home	Percent of the population 5 years and over with a disability	Veterans as a percent of the population 18 years and over	Occupation for employed population 16 years and over (percent)						Industry for employed population 16 years and over (percent)					
				Management, professional, and related occupations	Service occupations	Sales and office occupations	Farming, fishing, and forestry occupations	Construction, extraction, and maintenance occupations	Production, transportation and material moving occupations	Agriculture, forestry, fishing, and mining	Construction and manufacturing	Wholesale and retail trade	Transportation and warehousing, and utilities	Service industries	Public administration
	42	43	44	45	46	47	48	49	50	51	52	53	54	55	56
INDIANA	2.9	19.0	13.1	28.7	14.2	25.3	0.4	10.0	21.4	1.4	29.5	15.2	5.2	45.4	3.3
Adams County	3.6	16.4	10.4	22.6	14.3	21.4	1.0	13.1	27.5	3.4	39.1	16.1	3.3	36.2	2.0
Allen County	2.5	16.6	12.3	31.9	12.8	27.3	0.1	8.5	19.4	0.5	28.4	16.4	4.7	47.8	2.2
Bartholomew County	2.7	18.1	13.1	31.6	12.3	23.2	0.4	7.7	24.8	1.2	39.6	13.7	4.1	38.6	2.9
Benton County	4.7	19.6	12.7	25.0	12.9	23.9	1.1	12.8	24.2	7.0	32.5	13.3	5.1	40.2	1.9
Blackford County	3.9	20.2	14.5	19.8	11.8	20.8	0.5	10.6	36.5	2.1	41.0	16.3	4.2	33.2	3.2
Boone County	5.0	20.6	12.4	34.5	13.4	25.7	0.4	10.7	15.3	2.1	26.3	15.1	5.5	47.6	3.3
Brown County	4.3	19.0	16.4	28.4	14.3	24.5	0.6	14.0	18.2	1.6	31.3	15.1	4.0	45.0	3.0
Carroll County	4.6	18.5	13.0	23.3	14.3	20.1	1.3	11.3	29.7	5.0	37.4	13.1	4.9	37.7	1.9
Cass County	3.0	19.2	15.2	22.6	15.0	20.8	0.8	9.9	30.9	2.9	39.0	13.3	3.7	36.8	4.3
Clark County	2.1	20.6	14.4	26.0	14.5	28.1	0.2	10.2	21.0	0.6	26.4	14.4	6.9	45.7	6.0
Clay County	2.9	20.6	13.7	22.9	15.8	22.6	1.0	10.1	27.6	2.6	31.4	16.8	5.8	37.7	5.8
Clinton County	2.6	25.4	13.3	18.6	12.5	21.8	1.5	12.1	33.6	3.2	42.9	13.5	4.4	33.3	2.7
Crawford County	4.1	26.0	14.5	18.2	14.2	22.4	2.2	14.3	28.7	5.3	34.4	14.7	5.7	34.0	5.9
Daviess County	4.9	20.8	12.6	25.4	13.5	20.9	0.9	15.2	24.1	6.6	31.7	14.6	6.3	34.7	6.1
Dearborn County	2.4	17.9	13.6	26.2	14.4	25.5	0.3	13.0	20.6	0.7	29.7	14.5	8.6	44.2	2.3
Decatur County	3.1	17.4	13.8	21.7	13.4	20.6	0.9	9.9	33.4	3.6	42.4	14.7	3.9	32.9	2.5
DeKalb County	2.4	17.7	11.8	21.5	11.1	20.8	0.5	10.2	35.9	1.6	49.8	11.7	3.4	31.3	2.2
Delaware County	2.7	18.5	12.5	30.1	17.5	26.4	0.3	8.1	17.6	0.7	23.0	15.7	3.6	54.1	2.9
Dubois County	3.0	16.3	12.2	24.3	10.7	23.5	1.3	10.4	29.8	4.2	43.8	14.8	4.2	31.0	2.0
Elkhart County	3.3	18.6	11.1	23.8	11.0	23.4	0.4	8.7	32.7	1.4	47.8	13.1	3.1	33.0	1.7
Fayette County	2.3	25.0	14.3	20.3	14.8	18.3	0.3	10.1	36.2	1.8	41.9	11.3	3.0	39.7	2.4
Floyd County	2.6	17.9	14.9	29.8	13.4	27.8	0.2	9.7	19.1	0.4	26.7	14.0	6.6	48.0	4.2
Fountain County	4.0	21.3	14.0	20.7	14.8	19.7	1.5	9.1	34.2	4.6	40.2	13.9	4.6	34.4	2.3
Franklin County	3.3	18.0	12.7	23.9	13.4	21.7	0.7	12.4	27.9	2.7	39.5	13.1	5.4	36.9	2.3
Fulton County	4.7	21.5	14.2	20.8	13.2	20.8	1.3	10.0	34.0	2.8	40.8	14.1	4.8	34.7	2.8
Gibson County	2.2	21.4	13.4	21.4	16.8	22.3	0.8	11.8	26.9	4.2	30.3	15.3	8.7	39.0	2.5
Grant County	3.0	20.7	14.3	24.9	16.7	22.9	0.4	8.5	26.7	1.3	33.1	14.1	3.6	45.5	2.4
Greene County	3.3	22.5	15.9	25.0	15.4	21.2	0.8	16.0	21.5	5.4	25.9	13.0	6.1	41.1	8.5
Hamilton County	4.8	11.7	10.7	49.1	9.2	20.5	0.2	5.6	7.4	0.5	21.1	16.7	2.8	56.2	2.9
Hancock County	3.4	17.0	13.7	32.4	11.8	28.8	0.3	11.7	15.1	1.4	27.6	17.2	4.7	45.4	0.7
Harrison County	4.0	18.9	13.9	25.3	13.8	21.8	1.2	13.4	24.4	3.3	32.1	12.7	6.8	41.6	3.5
Hendricks County	3.3	17.0	14.5	32.8	11.2	29.1	0.3	11.9	14.7	0.9	22.8	16.1	11.0	45.5	3.7
Henry County	3.0	21.3	14.9	23.5	15.4	23.1	0.8	11.9	25.3	1.9	33.8	14.8	3.8	41.9	3.8
Howard County	2.2	19.5	14.8	26.6	15.6	20.4	0.2	10.0	27.2	0.7	39.1	13.4	3.1	40.2	3.5
Huntington County	3.7	17.6	12.7	22.9	15.3	21.6	0.6	9.7	30.0	2.1	36.9	15.0	4.3	39.3	2.3
Jackson County	2.9	21.2	12.3	22.1	10.5	22.1	1.2	11.4	32.7	3.4	41.1	18.1	4.0	30.7	2.6
Jasper County	3.6	17.6	12.9	25.5	13.9	20.7	1.9	14.5	23.5	5.4	31.0	15.0	7.7	38.5	2.4
Jay County	3.3	21.0	14.2	18.2	12.8	19.1	0.7	12.5	36.7	3.4	44.8	12.7	4.0	32.0	3.0
Jefferson County	2.6	21.3	14.0	25.8	15.6	21.5	0.5	11.4	25.1	1.9	34.8	13.3	5.3	41.8	2.8
Jennings County	2.2	22.0	13.6	21.0	14.2	19.4	0.6	13.0	31.9	2.4	42.1	15.5	3.5	34.1	2.4
Johnson County	2.4	18.0	13.2	33.9	11.6	27.4	0.2	10.3	16.4	0.8	26.0	16.9	6.7	46.5	3.0
Knox County	2.3	22.3	13.5	27.2	18.8	26.1	1.5	9.6	16.7	5.7	16.7	16.7	5.6	50.3	5.0
Kosciusko County	3.5	17.4	12.4	23.1	11.1	22.1	0.8	9.7	33.1	2.2	47.9	11.9	2.8	33.4	1.8
LaGrange County	6.7	17.3	9.0	18.5	12.2	16.3	2.0	12.5	38.5	5.0	50.7	12.6	2.8	27.4	1.6
Lake County	2.0	19.9	13.3	26.1	16.0	27.4	0.1	11.3	19.1	0.3	25.4	15.3	6.6	49.0	3.6
LaPorte County	2.6	19.4	15.7	24.5	15.8	24.2	0.4	11.7	23.4	1.5	33.1	14.7	5.5	41.3	3.9
Lawrence County	2.4	22.2	14.0	21.9	15.1	21.4	0.6	11.0	29.9	2.7	34.7	12.8	3.9	40.7	5.2
Madison County	2.5	22.4	14.8	25.2	15.9	26.5	0.2	9.9	22.3	0.9	28.7	16.6	3.5	46.1	4.2
Marion County	2.5	20.1	12.7	32.9	14.7	28.5	0.1	8.7	15.1	0.2	19.9	16.4	6.3	52.8	4.3
Marshall County	3.4	17.8	12.3	22.5	12.7	21.7	0.7	10.9	31.4	2.0	41.8	13.1	5.1	35.3	2.8
Martin County	3.7	23.8	17.0	26.2	13.1	18.0	0.7	14.0	28.0	3.9	36.1	12.0	6.1	34.8	7.1
Miami County	3.7	18.5	17.5	21.2	14.4	22.6	0.9	11.5	29.4	3.0	36.8	14.5	5.1	34.8	5.8
Monroe County	3.5	13.0	8.9	39.4	17.1	25.4	0.2	7.1	10.7	0.9	15.6	12.8	2.9	64.1	3.7
Montgomery County	3.0	20.2	13.5	23.7	12.4	23.9	0.6	9.5	30.0	2.4	37.6	13.2	4.3	39.9	2.5
Morgan County	2.7	20.0	14.8	23.4	14.1	24.1	0.3	16.6	21.5	1.5	29.8	15.1	11.0	38.7	3.9
Newton County	2.9	19.9	14.7	19.2	14.6	19.9	1.4	16.4	28.5	4.0	35.3	14.0	7.4	36.2	3.2
Noble County	2.6	17.3	12.1	19.7	10.7	19.0	0.8	9.9	39.9	2.0	53.6	10.8	3.3	28.5	1.9
Ohio County	3.3	19.5	15.3	23.9	17.4	22.0	0.4	13.6	22.8	1.2	28.8	12.5	9.8	44.7	3.0
Orange County	3.4	22.6	14.0	20.6	15.3	19.4	0.8	12.1	31.7	3.4	39.3	13.5	5.2	36.2	2.5
Owen County	3.6	23.2	16.6	19.7	14.3	20.6	0.6	16.4	28.4	3.0	38.1	12.3	6.4	36.3	3.9
Parke County	4.6	20.7	14.7	24.4	16.1	21.1	1.4	11.5	25.5	4.8	31.3	15.9	4.9	36.7	6.5
Perry County	3.8	18.7	14.4	18.4	14.4	20.1	0.5	12.9	33.7	3.8	44.6	11.3	4.2	30.5	5.5
Pike County	4.3	21.6	14.0	19.9	14.4	20.2	1.5	14.1	29.9	7.0	31.7	12.7	10.8	35.0	2.8
Porter County	2.5	15.8	14.0	30.5	14.0	24.7	0.1	13.3	17.3	0.4	29.2	14.6	5.9	47.1	2.9
Posey County	3.2	17.9	13.5	29.9	12.9	23.1	0.7	12.2	21.2	4.4	32.8	13.5	6.6	40.4	2.4
Pulaski County	5.6	21.9	13.2	23.3	13.5	20.1	2.8	11.1	29.1	9.0	33.5	13.4	5.4	34.4	4.4

STATE County	Median household income	Median family income: All families	Median family income: Families with children: Married-couple	Median family income: Families with children: Male householder	Median family income: Families with children: Female householder	Median nonfamily household income	Median income for full-year, full-time workers: Men	Median income for full-year, full-time workers: Women	Per capita income	Households by source of income (percent): With earnings	Households by source of income (percent): With interest, dividend, or rental income	Households by source of income (percent): With Social Security income	Households by source of income (percent): With public assistance income	Households by source of income (percent): With retirement income	Households with income over $100,000 (percent)	+/– U.S. percent for income over $100,000	Households with income below poverty (percent)	Families with children with income below poverty (percent)
	57	58	59	60	61	62	63	64	65	66	67	68	69	70	71	72	73	74
INDIANA	41 567	50 261	59 025	30 623	20 793	23 689	38 138	26 046	20 397	81.8	35.6	26.0	2.6	17.0	9.2	-3.1	9.5	10.2
Adams County	40 625	46 749	51 863	35 365	22 426	21 323	33 327	23 920	16 704	80.3	44.0	28.7	2.2	16.9	5.9	-6.4	7.7	9.0
Allen County	42 671	52 708	61 722	30 469	20 804	25 830	40 287	26 683	21 544	84.1	39.3	23.5	2.3	15.3	10.2	-2.1	8.6	10.3
Bartholomew County	44 184	52 097	58 974	30 885	20 313	24 740	40 015	25 704	21 536	82.9	39.7	25.7	2.1	17.8	9.9	-2.4	7.9	8.7
Benton County	39 813	46 869	55 445	28 958	20 938	22 386	31 411	23 275	17 220	81.7	41.7	30.3	1.9	15.0	4.3	-8.0	5.6	5.2
Blackford County	34 760	41 758	49 781	30 694	19 402	20 337	30 858	22 033	16 543	77.7	36.3	29.7	2.9	19.0	2.8	-9.5	9.2	9.6
Boone County	49 632	58 879	69 889	38 550	25 673	24 438	40 793	27 220	24 182	84.2	26.8	23.8	1.3	12.6	16.3	4.0	5.6	4.3
Brown County	43 708	49 252	58 114	30 977	21 324	26 613	37 329	24 943	20 548	82.9	32.3	27.6	1.8	22.2	9.1	-3.2	9.3	8.1
Carroll County	42 677	50 216	53 041	40 000	19 306	22 889	36 455	22 109	19 436	83.1	36.4	27.7	1.2	16.3	7.3	-5.0	5.8	6.6
Cass County	39 193	46 506	53 281	30 040	21 167	21 449	34 445	22 718	18 892	80.0	37.7	31.2	2.5	20.2	6.7	-5.6	7.2	7.6
Clark County	40 111	47 412	54 767	27 489	21 431	22 760	33 428	25 099	19 936	82.1	32.2	25.9	2.1	17.9	7.2	-5.1	8.7	8.9
Clay County	36 865	41 863	48 696	31 823	16 865	20 188	32 063	22 222	16 364	76.1	33.0	32.1	2.5	19.1	4.6	-7.7	8.8	9.8
Clinton County	40 759	48 864	57 411	30 875	24 934	21 236	37 110	25 422	17 862	78.0	25.1	28.1	2.3	15.6	6.3	-6.0	8.7	9.1
Crawford County	32 646	37 869	44 291	21 771	11 591	15 317	31 135	21 516	15 926	76.0	29.6	31.1	2.8	15.9	3.4	-8.9	16.6	18.5
Daviess County	34 064	41 818	47 444	26 250	16 100	16 623	31 290	20 920	16 015	77.6	34.1	30.5	3.1	15.2	5.0	-7.3	12.6	13.9
Dearborn County	48 899	54 806	60 051	32 500	22 194	25 476	40 224	26 883	20 431	82.6	39.9	24.8	1.8	17.0	10.0	-2.3	6.7	6.8
Decatur County	40 401	46 453	52 469	29 375	20 987	23 602	32 377	25 417	18 582	83.9	35.3	27.7	2.3	14.9	5.7	-6.6	8.8	10.2
DeKalb County	44 909	51 676	56 434	31 941	25 338	24 481	38 174	25 304	19 448	84.5	38.5	23.7	1.8	14.6	7.4	-4.9	6.2	5.3
Delaware County	34 659	45 394	53 184	28 784	18 385	20 373	37 092	24 434	19 233	78.3	35.2	28.3	3.3	19.7	7.3	-5.0	15.4	13.7
Dubois County	44 169	52 342	60 266	31 081	24 554	22 169	34 641	24 347	20 225	83.8	48.2	26.2	1.4	11.5	7.6	-4.7	6.1	4.9
Elkhart County	44 478	50 438	57 127	30 446	21 556	25 286	36 659	25 145	20 250	85.8	36.8	23.6	2.8	11.9	9.0	-3.3	7.3	8.8
Fayette County	38 840	46 111	51 051	28 750	20 066	20 150	35 969	24 420	18 624	77.0	33.9	30.6	2.8	21.3	7.0	-5.3	8.9	9.3
Floyd County	44 022	52 401	65 302	25 323	18 423	24 312	38 833	27 504	21 852	82.8	39.4	24.7	3.0	17.4	10.8	-1.5	9.1	11.4
Fountain County	38 119	43 330	50 000	33 281	21 379	20 522	34 965	22 616	17 779	76.5	33.6	32.6	1.8	17.3	4.1	-8.2	8.7	8.6
Franklin County	43 530	50 171	56 559	35 833	20 898	20 898	35 139	25 413	18 624	83.0	40.4	28.0	2.2	15.4	8.1	-4.2	6.9	7.2
Fulton County	38 290	44 865	53 189	27 321	20 046	21 351	33 922	22 684	17 950	79.4	37.8	31.0	1.8	15.9	4.7	-7.6	7.5	7.9
Gibson County	37 515	44 839	53 155	24 076	20 078	17 967	36 221	21 826	18 169	77.1	38.2	31.9	2.0	20.0	5.5	-6.8	9.5	10.5
Grant County	36 162	44 304	51 411	29 643	17 484	19 554	35 320	24 844	18 003	76.2	35.3	32.6	3.0	22.1	6.0	-6.3	11.4	13.8
Greene County	33 998	41 523	47 559	24 375	14 698	17 307	33 728	22 453	16 834	75.5	33.1	31.6	3.4	23.1	4.2	-8.1	11.1	13.4
Hamilton County	71 026	80 239	88 456	42 016	30 990	37 266	59 149	35 954	33 109	90.5	51.0	15.6	0.7	11.8	28.8	16.5	3.1	2.6
Hancock County	56 416	63 083	72 137	40 227	24 488	26 843	46 026	29 588	24 966	84.8	42.9	24.2	1.1	21.5	16.8	4.5	3.3	2.8
Harrison County	43 423	48 542	54 170	26 993	21 842	25 365	35 032	25 450	19 643	83.0	37.1	26.4	2.2	18.7	7.6	-4.7	6.8	6.2
Hendricks County	55 208	61 689	70 330	36 595	31 858	29 758	45 407	30 425	23 129	85.9	29.0	20.7	1.1	15.7	14.8	2.5	4.5	3.1
Henry County	38 150	45 470	52 876	24 779	18 518	20 403	37 148	24 009	19 355	76.3	34.7	32.2	3.4	25.8	7.8	-4.5	8.0	9.3
Howard County	43 487	53 051	64 453	35 859	20 383	24 491	45 523	27 584	22 049	78.7	36.0	27.7	3.0	23.7	10.3	-2.0	9.1	11.1
Huntington County	41 620	49 031	56 302	27 455	22 702	23 110	35 815	22 329	19 480	83.7	36.9	26.3	1.3	15.6	6.7	-5.6	5.6	5.5
Jackson County	39 401	45 210	52 325	27 500	20 294	21 648	32 072	23 070	18 400	81.0	32.7	28.0	2.2	17.6	5.8	-6.5	8.9	9.2
Jasper County	43 369	50 132	54 864	27 500	20 739	22 719	40 009	22 920	19 012	82.2	38.9	28.1	1.9	14.2	7.6	-4.7	7.7	6.9
Jay County	35 700	41 850	45 864	32 679	16 855	19 349	31 549	21 678	16 686	76.9	35.7	31.8	1.6	17.7	3.3	-9.0	9.4	10.3
Jefferson County	38 189	45 712	52 009	28 958	21 237	22 278	32 425	22 822	17 412	80.8	34.9	29.8	2.9	20.2	5.1	-7.2	9.5	11.0
Jennings County	39 402	42 519	45 948	27 500	18 958	20 880	31 058	21 477	17 059	82.9	30.0	24.8	2.3	19.5	5.7	-6.6	9.0	9.2
Johnson County	52 693	60 571	67 820	41 568	28 441	27 144	43 834	29 244	22 976	85.8	33.1	21.6	1.4	15.3	14.2	1.9	5.3	4.7
Knox County	31 362	41 273	47 363	21 908	14 329	15 863	31 167	21 494	16 085	74.8	33.9	31.3	4.6	17.0	5.3	-7.0	17.0	18.7
Kosciusko County	43 939	49 532	55 251	33 367	23 210	25 617	36 879	24 952	19 806	84.9	36.9	25.2	1.3	13.5	8.4	-3.9	6.3	6.2
LaGrange County	42 848	46 885	50 338	31 962	28 000	22 304	35 288	24 323	16 481	86.4	40.0	22.6	1.9	13.0	6.2	-6.1	7.6	7.0
Lake County	41 829	50 131	61 223	32 003	18 457	23 712	43 375	27 213	19 639	78.4	34.2	29.2	4.6	19.9	9.4	-2.9	11.9	15.1
LaPorte County	41 430	49 872	57 203	31 607	20 492	23 303	37 440	24 923	18 913	80.6	37.4	28.7	2.9	17.6	7.1	-5.2	8.7	9.7
Lawrence County	36 280	43 109	50 236	28 625	18 712	19 763	35 243	22 311	17 653	77.6	32.7	30.4	2.9	20.8	4.9	-7.4	10.7	11.5
Madison County	38 925	46 663	55 900	28 500	20 445	22 417	36 434	24 704	20 090	75.6	31.9	31.2	2.8	25.8	7.6	-4.7	9.3	11.3
Marion County	40 421	49 387	62 041	30 225	21 289	27 880	37 271	28 800	21 789	83.8	29.8	22.5	3.0	15.5	9.9	-2.4	10.6	13.1
Marshall County	42 581	48 527	52 557	35 313	22 440	22 558	35 133	23 450	18 427	83.1	40.5	27.0	1.6	14.6	6.8	-5.5	6.2	6.7
Martin County	36 411	43 550	50 359	27 321	16 250	20 854	31 904	22 106	17 054	78.6	35.1	28.7	2.8	20.7	4.3	-8.0	11.4	11.0
Miami County	39 184	45 816	50 792	27 344	19 601	20 570	35 878	21 834	17 726	79.5	35.5	28.0	1.6	18.6	5.5	-6.8	8.0	9.8
Monroe County	33 311	51 058	59 656	29 936	21 430	19 127	35 558	26 939	18 534	85.1	41.2	19.3	2.2	13.8	8.6	-3.7	18.9	10.0
Montgomery County	41 297	48 779	55 322	29 464	20 542	21 701	37 561	24 584	18 938	80.5	35.6	28.6	2.7	17.8	6.2	-6.1	8.3	9.9
Morgan County	47 739	52 851	60 740	33 750	20 946	23 007	40 367	26 692	20 657	84.4	21.1	23.8	2.8	15.3	9.4	-2.9	7.1	6.9
Newton County	40 944	46 741	51 644	21 094	18 348	20 983	37 259	21 077	17 755	82.2	33.1	28.2	2.1	15.0	5.0	-7.3	8.5	5.3
Noble County	42 700	49 037	53 105	31 629	24 236	24 263	35 908	24 817	17 896	84.5	34.2	24.3	1.7	14.0	6.4	-5.9	7.3	7.9
Ohio County	41 348	48 801	59 688	50 625	23 875	22 045	38 816	26 250	19 627	80.3	38.7	27.1	2.1	19.2	4.6	-7.7	8.5	6.1
Orange County	31 564	38 505	43 939	27 279	16 875	15 516	29 900	20 639	16 717	76.4	27.6	32.1	2.9	17.7	4.4	-7.9	13.1	11.9
Owen County	36 529	41 282	45 320	28 000	21 453	20 939	32 813	22 467	16 884	82.2	28.0	25.8	2.8	19.2	5.0	-7.3	9.0	10.3
Parke County	35 724	40 656	49 563	21 875	15 096	20 730	34 103	21 923	16 986	78.1	33.5	32.6	2.6	17.9	5.5	-6.8	10.5	15.9
Perry County	36 246	43 743	53 667	30 521	15 078	17 969	32 342	22 901	16 673	76.0	36.7	31.8	2.2	19.2	4.4	-7.9	10.1	11.4
Pike County	34 759	41 420	47 992	21 875	20 833	17 857	32 667	21 455	16 217	76.5	34.7	34.0	2.9	20.2	2.9	-9.4	8.9	7.7
Porter County	53 100	61 880	67 826	35 449	26 360	27 300	50 684	27 371	23 957	84.5	41.8	23.6	1.6	17.1	12.9	0.6	6.2	6.2
Posey County	44 209	53 737	60 394	31 875	17 318	21 412	40 872	25 292	19 516	80.8	40.8	27.3	2.4	15.5	7.9	-4.4	9.0	9.3
Pulaski County	35 422	41 028	49 332	27 813	21 575	21 637	31 479	21 839	16 835	79.2	39.9	32.1	2.3	17.8	5.8	-6.5	8.5	8.9

Table B-3. States and Counties — Education, Labor Force, and Income

STATE/ County code	MSA/PMSA/ NECMA code[1]	STATE County	High school graduates			College graduates		College graduates (percent)				
			Total population 25 years and over	Percent with a high school diploma or less	Percent with a high school diploma or more	Percent with a bachelor's degree or more	+/- U.S. percent with bachelor's degree or more	Non-Hispanic White	Black or African American	American Indian and Alaska Native	Asian, Hawaiian, and Pacific Islander	Hispanic or Latino[2]
			1	2	3	4	5	6	7	8	9	10
		INDIANA—Cont'd										
18 133	...	Putnam County	22 740	67.0	81.2	13.1	-11.3	13.4	2.3	0.0	42.7	8.9
18 135	...	Randolph County	18 310	67.9	79.6	9.9	-14.5	9.9	0.0	48.3	57.7	0.0
18 137	...	Ripley County	17 027	67.9	78.9	11.5	-12.9	11.3	X	36.5	51.4	14.3
18 139	...	Rush County	12 020	71.3	79.6	10.3	-14.1	10.1	0.0	0.0	100.0	26.1
18 141	7800	St. Joseph County........	166 060	50.1	82.4	23.6	-0.8	25.0	10.8	8.6	59.0	12.1
18 143	4520	Scott County.................	14 760	71.1	71.4	8.8	-15.6	8.7	0.0	21.7	100.0	14.3
18 145	3480	Shelby County	28 351	64.9	79.8	12.7	-11.7	12.6	13.3	72.1	28.2	0.0
18 147	...	Spencer County	13 491	61.6	81.2	13.0	-11.4	13.0	4.6	0.0	91.7	1.9
18 149	...	Starke County	15 290	71.5	72.0	8.4	-16.0	8.2	0.0	0.0	58.1	1.8
18 151	...	Steuben County	21 170	58.7	84.3	15.5	-8.9	15.5	10.7	0.0	63.2	19.4
18 153	...	Sullivan County	14 782	63.6	80.8	9.4	-15.0	10.0	0.0	0.0	0.0	7.6
18 155	...	Switzerland County	5 889	73.1	71.4	7.6	-16.8	7.3	X	0.0	90.5	0.0
18 157	3920	Tippecanoe County.......	79 911	42.7	87.8	33.2	8.8	31.6	29.4	12.4	81.7	18.8
18 159	3850	Tipton County	11 247	64.7	83.7	12.4	-12.0	12.4	X	0.0	5.1	1.3
18 161	...	Union County	4 784	65.7	79.9	11.1	-13.3	11.0	0.0	0.0	63.6	X
18 163	2440	Vanderburgh County	112 178	52.6	83.1	19.3	-5.1	19.9	7.0	7.1	54.8	16.6
18 165	8320	Vermillion County	11 410	64.0	81.2	11.2	-13.2	11.3	0.0	0.0	26.9	9.5
18 167	8320	Vigo County.................	66 714	53.8	81.0	21.4	-3.0	21.4	15.2	8.0	66.0	15.0
18 169	...	Wabash County	22 744	64.3	81.7	13.7	-10.7	13.8	23.5	5.1	32.8	0.0
18 171	...	Warren County	5 648	61.7	85.0	14.0	-10.4	14.2	X	0.0	0.0	0.0
18 173	2440	Warrick County	34 571	47.3	86.3	21.8	-2.6	21.6	30.0	22.7	54.9	10.7
18 175	...	Washington County	17 648	68.9	75.2	10.2	-14.2	10.1	0.0	0.0	25.0	21.0
18 177	...	Wayne County	47 322	61.4	78.1	13.7	-10.7	13.9	8.4	0.0	33.5	13.1
18 179	2760	Wells County	17 767	59.2	87.3	14.3	-10.1	14.4	13.3	15.0	47.6	2.9
18 181	...	White County	16 029	65.6	82.1	10.5	-13.9	10.5	55.6	12.1	56.2	4.7
18 183	2760	Whitley County	19 995	59.2	86.2	13.3	-11.1	13.2	21.4	26.3	5.3	13.5
19 000	...	IOWA....................	1 895 856	50.0	86.1	21.2	-3.2	21.3	14.7	9.9	42.4	11.0
19 001	...	Adair County	5 695	60.6	87.8	11.2	-13.2	11.2	0.0	0.0	100.0	5.3
19 003	...	Adams County	3 131	56.9	84.5	12.0	-12.4	12.1	X	0.0	0.0	0.0
19 005	...	Allamakee County	9 946	62.8	81.4	14.4	-10.0	14.6	0.0	9.1	31.3	0.0
19 007	...	Appanoose County	9 401	59.7	81.4	12.2	-12.2	12.1	13.8	0.0	52.9	3.9
19 009	...	Audubon County	4 704	62.2	82.5	12.3	-12.1	12.3	0.0	0.0	100.0	0.0
19 011	...	Benton County	16 567	55.5	87.8	13.9	-10.5	14.0	0.0	0.0	0.0	0.0
19 013	8920	Black Hawk County.......	78 401	48.7	86.5	23.0	-1.4	23.7	9.9	22.7	60.0	15.4
19 015	...	Boone County	17 529	49.2	89.0	18.8	-5.6	18.8	6.1	15.2	42.9	17.5
19 017	...	Bremer County	14 835	50.0	87.7	21.5	-2.9	21.4	0.0	0.0	34.5	38.5
19 019	...	Buchanan County	13 383	59.0	84.6	12.7	-11.7	12.5	17.6	0.0	30.6	22.9
19 021	...	Buena Vista County	12 736	54.8	81.3	18.7	-5.7	21.1	0.0	33.3	14.3	1.1
19 023	...	Butler County	10 563	59.3	82.2	12.4	-12.0	12.4	X	0.0	30.0	0.7
19 025	...	Calhoun County	7 877	52.7	85.4	15.4	-9.0	15.5	13.3	0.0	0.0	6.1
19 027	...	Carroll County	14 074	56.1	83.7	16.0	-8.4	16.0	33.3	X	5.7	5.8
19 029	...	Cass County	10 296	54.5	85.9	16.6	-7.8	16.6	0.0	0.0	54.3	12.3
19 031	...	Cedar County	12 291	54.2	87.7	16.3	-8.1	16.2	0.0	0.0	33.3	20.0
19 033	...	Cerro Gordo County......	31 215	46.0	87.3	20.3	-4.1	20.7	0.0	0.0	17.8	7.8
19 035	...	Cherokee County	8 918	55.2	87.5	15.2	-9.2	15.3	0.0	X	7.7	0.0
19 037	...	Chickasaw County	8 797	61.8	83.4	12.2	-12.2	12.2	0.0	0.0	0.0	35.3
19 039	...	Clarke County	6 070	58.6	84.4	12.1	-12.3	12.3	X	0.0	16.7	8.7
19 041	...	Clay County..................	11 692	48.8	88.0	16.3	-8.1	16.3	29.4	0.0	7.3	14.6
19 043	...	Clayton County	12 743	63.0	82.6	12.8	-11.6	12.7	19.2	0.0	38.9	16.0
19 045	...	Clinton County	33 158	55.9	85.6	14.4	-10.0	14.4	7.1	4.5	44.6	11.8
19 047	...	Crawford County	11 068	64.3	78.5	12.4	-12.0	13.1	0.0	0.0	36.4	2.5
19 049	2120	Dallas County	26 483	43.2	89.5	26.8	2.4	27.5	14.9	0.0	45.8	10.2
19 051	...	Davis County	5 578	62.5	78.9	11.4	-13.0	11.6	0.0	0.0	X	0.0
19 053	...	Decatur County	5 283	59.8	81.7	15.1	-9.3	15.0	0.0	0.0	45.5	20.4
19 055	...	Delaware County..........	11 784	62.1	85.1	13.0	-11.4	12.9	X	0.0	61.5	10.8
19 057	...	Des Moines County.......	28 425	53.5	85.8	16.0	-8.4	16.4	5.2	10.4	31.8	6.6
19 059	...	Dickinson County	11 730	46.1	89.2	21.3	-3.1	21.4	0.0	0.0	21.4	7.5
19 061	2200	Dubuque County	57 236	55.0	85.2	21.3	-3.1	21.3	22.7	24.4	50.4	17.3
19 063	...	Emmet County	7 265	53.8	82.2	13.0	-11.4	13.3	0.0	0.0	100.0	2.1
19 065	...	Fayette County	14 632	59.0	84.8	13.8	-10.6	13.8	40.6	0.0	23.2	8.6
19 067	...	Floyd County	11 451	55.0	85.9	14.8	-9.6	14.8	0.0	0.0	75.0	0.0
19 069	...	Franklin County	7 362	54.6	84.0	14.5	-9.9	15.0	X	37.5	5.0	1.7
19 071	...	Fremont County	5 557	57.4	85.0	14.0	-10.4	14.1	100.0	36.4	0.0	2.5
19 073	...	Greene County	7 048	56.7	85.6	14.6	-9.8	14.9	0.0	0.0	0.0	0.0
19 075	...	Grundy County	8 465	51.7	86.5	17.2	-7.2	17.1	100.0	0.0	31.3	25.0

[1] MSA = Metropolitan Statistical Area. PMSA = Primary MSA. NECMA = New England County Metropolitan Area. See the Appendix A for explanation of these concepts. See Appendix B for list of metropolitan areas identified by type, with component counties.
[2] Hispanic or Latino persons may be of any race.

Table B-3. States and Counties — **Education, Labor Force, and Income**

STATE County	School enrollment			Population 16 to 19 years				Employment status, 2000			Work status in 1999 of the population 16 years and over (percent)		
											Worked in 1999		
	Grades kindergarten through 12	College or graduate school	Percent private	Number	Percent in armed forces	Percent high school graduates	Percent not enrolled, not grads, not in armed forces, not employed	Total population 16 years and over	Percent in labor force	Unemployment rate	Full-time	Part-time	Did not work in 1999
	11	12	13	14	15	16	17	18	19	20	21	22	23
INDIANA—Cont'd													
Putnam County	6 440	2 674	25.9	2 567	0.0	6.7	7.3	28 554	59.6	4.8	55.7	15.9	28.5
Randolph County	5 132	660	3.8	1 419	0.0	13.3	4.2	21 247	62.9	5.5	54.2	14.4	31.5
Ripley County	5 318	770	12.9	1 414	0.0	15.8	3.7	19 892	66.8	3.3	57.0	14.5	28.5
Rush County	3 477	450	9.9	965	0.0	8.4	8.2	13 939	65.5	3.7	56.4	13.5	30.1
St. Joseph County	49 543	22 170	31.4	17 831	0.1	8.2	4.6	204 964	66.0	5.6	55.0	18.0	26.9
Scott County	4 284	582	6.7	1 222	0.0	12.5	9.1	17 612	62.9	4.5	55.7	11.5	32.8
Shelby County	8 496	1 443	7.7	2 308	0.0	16.2	5.6	33 198	69.8	3.7	61.6	12.8	25.6
Spencer County	4 199	573	8.0	1 102	0.0	12.3	1.8	15 611	67.6	4.6	58.6	14.1	27.4
Starke County	4 739	616	8.2	1 364	0.0	10.8	9.7	18 015	59.3	6.2	51.9	13.4	34.7
Steuben County	6 285	1 935	16.8	2 035	0.4	9.9	1.4	25 641	71.3	4.5	61.9	16.2	21.9
Sullivan County	4 013	825	5.8	1 130	0.0	12.7	3.1	17 432	53.0	6.9	50.1	14.3	35.6
Switzerland County	1 752	184	5.9	517	0.0	14.1	5.8	6 955	64.4	7.7	58.0	11.0	31.0
Tippecanoe County	22 061	36 162	5.8	14 890	0.0	5.0	2.0	121 214	66.5	6.9	55.4	24.5	20.2
Tipton County	3 108	490	8.6	887	0.0	10.5	1.9	12 982	65.6	2.6	57.6	14.2	28.2
Union County	1 492	227	4.8	361	0.0	17.2	4.2	5 523	66.9	5.2	57.1	16.2	26.7
Vanderburgh County	29 035	12 739	20.2	10 788	0.0	8.9	6.2	136 737	66.0	5.6	55.1	16.7	28.2
Vermillion County	3 044	618	5.5	967	0.0	11.3	4.4	13 306	60.7	5.4	52.0	15.0	33.0
Vigo County	17 768	11 618	10.8	7 380	0.0	7.5	3.7	84 432	61.3	7.0	50.8	18.1	31.1
Wabash County	6 638	1 794	16.9	2 283	0.0	8.7	2.5	27 429	65.4	4.5	57.5	15.2	27.3
Warren County	1 663	239	4.9	422	0.0	6.4	2.8	6 460	67.3	2.9	59.6	13.5	26.9
Warrick County	10 431	2 181	10.9	2 868	0.0	12.5	3.8	39 992	69.7	3.8	59.1	16.0	24.9
Washington County	5 241	809	6.5	1 488	0.0	14.9	4.9	20 874	66.2	4.4	58.6	12.1	29.3
Wayne County	12 838	3 686	11.3	4 143	0.0	11.7	7.9	55 938	64.7	6.5	53.6	16.1	30.3
Wells County	5 604	904	9.1	1 633	0.0	12.2	2.8	20 990	69.9	3.0	58.6	16.8	24.6
White County	4 895	511	2.6	1 331	0.0	11.8	3.8	19 525	67.1	3.4	59.2	13.8	27.0
Whitley County	6 205	905	9.4	1 684	0.2	16.9	2.1	23 410	71.4	2.5	60.6	16.5	22.9
IOWA	552 637	187 306	13.8	178 931	0.1	9.2	2.8	2 281 274	68.2	4.2	56.1	18.2	25.7
Adair County	1 524	206	4.2	427	0.0	6.3	3.3	6 520	66.2	3.4	54.9	16.1	29.0
Adams County	802	132	3.1	202	0.0	7.9	2.0	3 534	66.4	4.9	55.0	14.1	30.9
Allamakee County	2 922	334	11.4	797	0.0	8.4	1.0	11 438	66.1	3.8	54.0	17.1	28.9
Appanoose County	2 593	527	6.7	786	0.0	9.0	4.6	10 898	57.6	5.9	48.2	13.9	37.9
Audubon County	1 384	121	2.5	338	0.0	9.8	0.6	5 288	63.4	4.1	51.4	17.4	31.1
Benton County	5 344	868	6.6	1 402	0.0	12.6	1.2	19 193	68.7	2.9	57.5	16.5	26.0
Black Hawk County	22 272	15 933	11.3	8 922	0.2	7.8	2.3	101 854	66.2	4.8	51.2	22.1	26.7
Boone County	4 980	994	6.8	1 533	0.0	10.2	1.5	20 587	68.2	2.6	56.7	17.6	25.7
Bremer County	4 434	2 064	23.3	1 796	0.2	7.2	0.4	18 454	69.1	5.8	53.9	20.5	25.7
Buchanan County	4 565	546	10.8	1 202	0.0	6.7	7.8	15 784	65.8	4.3	54.6	16.5	28.9
Buena Vista County	4 165	1 449	28.5	1 487	0.3	5.0	4.2	15 811	64.6	3.8	54.0	19.2	26.8
Butler County	2 989	420	4.7	854	0.0	7.1	0.5	12 063	63.2	3.1	50.5	18.8	30.7
Calhoun County	2 081	284	4.3	604	0.0	7.1	1.2	8 950	57.7	3.3	50.6	15.8	33.6
Carroll County	4 556	772	28.5	1 344	0.0	8.5	1.1	16 470	68.4	2.4	55.6	18.0	26.4
Cass County	2 815	381	3.8	821	0.0	12.4	3.0	11 650	66.5	5.0	52.3	17.7	30.0
Cedar County	3 549	686	3.8	1 128	0.3	11.1	0.8	14 262	70.1	2.3	59.1	16.6	24.3
Cerro Gordo County	8 435	2 055	11.4	2 655	0.0	8.4	1.7	36 628	67.6	4.7	54.1	18.6	27.2
Cherokee County	2 556	209	3.5	796	0.0	9.2	0.9	10 304	65.8	3.6	53.6	17.5	28.9
Chickasaw County	2 675	446	12.8	726	0.0	7.9	2.5	10 124	65.5	6.4	55.0	15.7	29.3
Clarke County	1 843	179	4.5	464	0.0	14.2	5.8	7 009	68.8	5.9	57.7	15.7	26.7
Clay County	3 230	502	7.8	993	0.0	11.5	1.2	13 694	69.5	3.8	57.2	17.7	25.1
Clayton County	3 812	382	8.2	1 085	0.0	9.2	1.4	14 599	67.1	3.7	54.4	16.6	29.1
Clinton County	9 837	2 145	11.5	2 828	0.0	7.8	4.4	38 848	65.7	5.0	54.8	16.1	29.1
Crawford County	3 525	422	10.8	1 054	0.0	5.9	7.6	13 087	65.5	3.6	54.5	16.7	28.8
Dallas County	8 120	1 400	10.9	2 066	0.0	8.5	3.1	30 525	74.2	2.6	64.6	14.2	21.2
Davis County	1 670	263	15.8	511	0.0	4.5	5.9	6 523	62.6	3.6	52.2	14.6	33.2
Decatur County	1 531	1 075	36.3	735	0.0	9.9	3.4	6 907	64.1	7.5	50.7	19.1	30.2
Delaware County	4 200	557	15.2	1 122	0.0	7.3	2.2	13 750	70.0	3.4	56.8	16.9	26.2
Des Moines County	7 642	1 820	11.8	2 397	0.0	11.3	3.3	33 280	66.6	5.5	52.9	18.1	29.0
Dickinson County	2 760	599	5.0	772	0.3	5.1	1.8	13 290	65.6	2.8	55.8	17.3	26.9
Dubuque County	17 029	5 714	37.7	5 357	0.1	8.3	1.2	68 921	69.6	4.5	54.7	19.5	25.7
Emmet County	2 159	613	5.5	834	0.0	6.5	0.8	8 815	65.8	4.7	53.4	17.5	29.0
Fayette County	4 351	1 055	13.4	1 379	0.0	5.7	2.2	17 263	63.3	4.6	51.0	16.7	32.2
Floyd County	3 255	515	9.8	920	0.0	12.7	3.8	13 211	62.3	4.5	50.5	17.9	31.6
Franklin County	2 067	303	4.7	643	0.0	5.3	2.5	8 483	65.4	4.1	53.3	16.4	30.3
Fremont County	1 588	213	2.6	430	1.2	10.0	4.0	6 257	64.2	2.8	56.0	14.2	29.8
Greene County	2 143	235	6.7	585	0.0	3.8	5.0	8 064	60.4	4.8	50.7	16.3	33.0
Grundy County	2 530	441	5.6	661	0.0	8.3	1.1	9 642	66.0	3.6	53.7	18.4	28.0

Table B-3. States and Counties — Education, Labor Force, and Income

STATE County	Full-year full-time employed (percent)								Children under 18 years in families						Total employed by class of worker (percent)			
										With two parents (percent)		With one parent who is in labor force (percent)	+/- U.S. percent of children with no stay-at-home parent (percent)	+/- U.S. percent two-income couples				Unpaid family worker
	Total	Men	Women	Non-Hispanic White	Black or African American	American Indian and Alaska Native	Asian, Hawaiian, and Pacific Islander	Hispanic or Latino[1]	Number	Both in labor force	Father only in labor force				Private	Government	Self-employed	
	24	25	26	27	28	29	30	31	32	33	34	35	36	37	38	39	40	41
INDIANA—Cont'd																		
Putnam County	41.5	50.8	31.4	42.2	40.1	18.7	18.9	28.9	8 197	52.4	24.7	13.6	1.4	1.6	77.9	12.8	9.2	0.1
Randolph County	39.9	53.0	27.6	39.9	51.2	41.9	38.5	31.0	6 578	49.2	22.3	16.8	1.4	-1.4	77.4	11.8	10.2	0.6
Ripley County	44.4	56.1	33.4	44.4	0.0	55.4	45.7	42.3	7 213	52.4	23.1	17.3	5.1	4.2	80.6	9.5	9.5	0.4
Rush County	44.5	59.9	30.3	44.7	49.0	7.3	21.1	40.0	4 646	52.5	23.7	18.6	6.5	1.7	79.1	8.8	11.8	0.3
St. Joseph County	40.9	52.3	30.6	42.0	35.9	40.4	40.0	35.4	64 248	45.5	21.5	23.2	4.1	3.9	83.1	9.4	7.3	0.2
Scott County	41.5	50.2	33.0	41.8	0.0	8.9	0.0	30.4	5 723	45.2	19.9	18.5	-0.9	-2.2	81.4	10.4	7.6	0.6
Shelby County	49.2	60.8	38.1	49.3	56.1	35.2	47.1	43.6	10 951	54.6	20.0	20.5	10.5	8.0	82.2	9.1	8.5	0.2
Spencer County	44.3	54.7	34.0	44.6	35.7	25.4	75.0	34.9	5 259	64.1	15.7	14.2	13.7	5.8	79.2	10.2	9.8	0.8
Starke County	37.7	49.9	25.8	37.8	70.8	31.0	31.1	33.2	6 070	41.1	28.4	17.8	-5.7	-5.8	78.3	11.0	10.4	0.3
Steuben County	46.9	56.9	36.7	47.0	12.2	61.3	46.2	49.1	8 058	57.5	14.5	22.4	15.3	10.3	81.8	8.5	9.4	0.3
Sullivan County	34.8	41.0	27.7	35.9	17.4	32.9	40.0	19.2	4 674	48.6	24.6	15.4	-0.6	-4.4	74.3	15.5	9.8	0.3
Switzerland County	42.1	60.0	33.2	42.1	X	0.0	41.7	42.3	2 243	45.2	24.2	20.2	0.8	-5.8	77.2	10.3	11.6	0.9
Tippecanoe County	35.8	42.7	28.6	37.3	31.2	50.0	17.8	29.0	29 714	48.9	22.3	19.5	3.8	5.5	72.8	20.4	6.4	0.4
Tipton County	46.9	60.2	34.9	46.9	X	0.0	43.7	77.1	3 999	58.9	22.6	13.7	8.0	4.3	81.1	9.8	8.9	0.1
Union County	44.1	55.9	33.3	44.4	27.8	0.0	0.0	X	1 880	54.3	17.8	19.8	9.5	5.2	76.3	11.1	12.2	0.4
Vanderburgh County	42.1	51.8	33.7	42.7	33.9	60.7	44.3	41.9	37 730	49.9	15.5	24.5	9.8	5.3	83.1	9.4	7.3	0.2
Vermillion County	39.4	50.8	28.8	39.6	33.3	0.0	84.6	30.0	3 857	48.5	20.9	18.1	2.0	-2.5	80.8	11.1	8.0	0.1
Vigo County	36.5	45.0	28.3	37.2	29.8	27.0	24.1	29.9	22 699	41.9	21.5	24.3	1.6	-0.9	77.3	15.2	7.1	0.4
Wabash County	43.1	53.9	33.2	43.2	36.2	39.6	36.6	34.4	7 967	57.2	16.4	18.9	11.5	7.0	81.6	9.0	8.9	0.4
Warren County	47.1	59.7	35.0	47.3	X	100.0	25.0	39.1	2 110	58.7	23.3	14.6	8.7	7.1	73.1	14.9	11.6	0.4
Warrick County	48.2	60.7	36.5	48.4	23.2	47.4	52.5	30.5	13 572	56.3	23.5	13.8	5.5	7.4	80.3	10.1	9.2	0.4
Washington County	44.5	54.7	34.5	44.6	27.0	46.2	62.5	26.8	6 914	51.5	22.9	17.0	3.9	3.6	79.8	9.4	10.2	0.6
Wayne County	39.5	50.0	30.1	39.8	35.7	50.3	30.8	36.2	16 172	51.5	16.5	22.5	9.4	3.2	80.3	11.2	8.0	0.5
Wells County	46.7	59.8	34.5	46.4	40.0	80.0	52.9	37.7	7 262	57.2	18.5	19.1	11.7	8.4	81.9	8.0	9.6	0.4
White County	46.1	56.9	35.9	45.8	0.0	18.8	38.0	55.4	6 181	56.3	17.5	20.0	11.7	7.8	78.7	10.8	10.2	0.3
Whitley County	49.6	62.4	37.3	49.4	28.8	58.7	51.6	80.6	7 981	58.1	20.5	16.2	9.7	10.6	83.7	7.5	8.5	0.3
IOWA	43.3	52.9	34.3	43.8	33.0	30.3	38.5	38.1	703 382	59.1	15.3	17.9	12.4	9.1	74.8	13.6	11.1	0.4
Adair County	44.6	55.6	34.6	44.8	0.0	80.0	0.0	35.6	1 891	68.1	10.4	14.5	19.0	8.5	67.3	13.5	18.7	0.5
Adams County	42.6	52.6	33.3	42.8	53.8	0.0	0.0	0.0	1 049	69.3	9.9	13.3	18.0	9.4	66.7	13.4	18.3	1.6
Allamakee County	41.4	50.8	32.1	41.4	66.7	30.8	22.9	48.8	3 579	70.9	10.6	11.4	17.7	9.3	67.9	10.0	20.9	1.3
Appanoose County	35.2	44.4	27.0	35.3	42.6	11.1	25.5	34.4	3 124	46.9	21.6	19.8	2.1	-4.3	71.3	12.5	15.4	0.8
Audubon County	39.2	50.8	28.6	39.2	0.0	62.5	0.0	45.5	1 728	65.9	12.3	17.2	18.5	5.6	63.2	14.2	22.0	0.6
Benton County	46.0	55.3	36.9	46.1	37.1	57.1	27.8	46.9	6 735	68.6	11.4	13.7	17.7	12.1	76.1	10.7	12.5	0.7
Black Hawk County	37.4	45.8	29.9	38.2	28.3	12.3	36.9	33.7	28 362	50.7	15.3	22.2	8.3	4.4	76.9	14.8	8.1	0.2
Boone County	45.5	56.6	35.1	45.6	33.0	0.0	78.3	39.0	6 112	61.7	13.3	18.9	16.0	12.6	68.4	20.0	11.0	0.5
Bremer County	40.1	50.4	30.9	40.2	25.0	0.0	33.9	42.9	5 400	67.0	11.0	15.0	18.5	11.7	74.1	12.1	12.9	0.8
Buchanan County	42.2	53.0	31.9	42.3	70.0	0.0	52.7	26.3	5 728	60.5	20.0	11.6	7.5	7.0	71.8	14.4	13.4	0.4
Buena Vista County	38.6	48.6	28.7	38.4	19.6	0.0	30.7	43.2	4 959	57.4	16.2	15.3	8.1	6.2	73.5	11.4	14.3	0.8
Butler County	38.4	50.5	27.0	38.4	0.0	0.0	76.5	26.2	3 672	65.3	13.3	14.7	15.4	7.1	71.2	11.9	16.3	0.7
Calhoun County	37.9	46.9	29.1	38.1	34.7	10.0	100.0	32.5	2 473	64.5	12.3	16.8	16.7	4.4	63.9	17.1	18.6	0.3
Carroll County	45.1	56.6	34.4	45.1	33.3	0.0	70.0	36.8	5 628	71.1	10.0	13.5	20.0	14.1	74.1	8.6	16.6	0.8
Cass County	40.9	53.8	29.0	40.9	100.0	0.0	47.8	45.2	3 326	58.3	17.0	21.2	14.9	7.5	70.1	12.6	16.5	0.8
Cedar County	47.1	56.0	38.6	47.2	0.0	30.8	41.0	47.5	4 471	68.0	12.2	13.8	17.2	12.3	71.2	15.5	12.2	1.0
Cerro Gordo County	41.8	51.6	33.1	42.0	27.2	41.3	66.2	30.5	10 632	61.9	11.7	20.2	17.5	7.5	78.3	10.0	11.3	0.4
Cherokee County	42.1	52.4	32.3	41.7	87.0	X	89.7	60.0	3 065	70.9	9.5	15.2	21.5	10.0	69.2	14.2	16.1	0.5
Chickasaw County	42.6	51.9	33.4	42.7	60.0	100.0	60.0	0.0	3 316	68.2	12.1	14.4	18.0	5.1	69.9	10.2	19.3	0.6
Clarke County	44.7	50.9	39.0	44.9	X	7.1	83.3	41.2	2 275	63.4	9.9	20.6	19.4	10.0	73.9	12.4	13.0	0.8
Clay County	44.6	57.1	33.1	44.8	31.6	0.0	19.2	42.7	4 156	59.1	15.2	20.3	14.8	11.3	75.0	11.3	13.3	0.4
Clayton County	41.4	50.2	33.1	41.5	21.2	20.0	63.6	61.3	4 519	66.0	9.8	19.0	20.4	9.6	68.2	11.0	20.0	0.8
Clinton County	41.5	51.6	32.3	41.9	30.0	8.8	49.1	35.2	12 332	57.7	14.4	19.2	12.3	2.9	78.1	10.4	11.1	0.4
Crawford County	39.5	50.9	28.3	41.3	18.1	5.4	36.4	23.4	4 078	66.1	15.2	12.8	14.3	6.8	69.0	15.0	15.1	0.8
Dallas County	53.3	62.3	44.7	53.9	31.3	22.9	65.6	46.7	11 148	60.0	17.3	15.5	10.9	15.7	76.2	13.8	9.7	0.3
Davis County	39.2	51.0	28.0	39.4	0.0	25.0	X	20.5	2 205	48.6	36.2	11.1	-4.9	1.0	61.6	14.7	19.6	4.0
Decatur County	34.3	44.1	25.2	34.6	13.6	0.0	26.8	31.3	1 900	55.1	16.7	13.8	4.3	4.1	68.9	13.3	16.3	1.5
Delaware County	44.6	55.2	34.2	44.5	X	0.0	96.2	52.7	5 210	73.0	11.3	10.9	19.3	14.6	68.0	10.3	20.7	0.9
Des Moines County	41.1	52.5	30.6	41.7	28.7	20.4	34.8	29.0	9 902	53.9	14.0	22.7	12.0	4.7	80.0	11.2	8.5	0.3
Dickinson County	42.2	52.3	32.9	42.2	26.1	20.0	13.6	57.6	3 542	62.5	15.6	15.5	13.4	5.5	70.7	11.3	17.6	0.3
Dubuque County	42.9	53.3	33.4	43.2	34.2	22.7	31.2	33.5	22 167	62.2	14.9	15.0	12.6	10.4	82.1	8.4	9.1	0.4
Emmet County	40.1	48.8	31.8	40.0	23.8	33.3	100.0	45.0	2 413	63.3	12.2	19.2	17.9	7.9	75.6	11.0	12.5	0.9
Fayette County	38.3	47.3	29.7	38.9	8.2	33.3	16.2	22.7	5 303	62.6	11.3	19.2	17.2	5.6	70.2	10.9	17.3	1.6
Floyd County	39.6	50.7	29.6	39.6	95.0	60.0	42.9	21.2	4 138	59.8	15.7	17.9	13.1	4.6	72.5	11.3	15.7	0.5
Franklin County	40.9	52.9	29.7	40.4	X	38.9	90.9	46.6	2 459	58.1	18.3	15.7	9.2	7.7	68.1	13.1	18.0	0.8
Fremont County	43.2	52.7	34.3	43.3	100.0	9.1	50.0	45.1	1 925	57.2	16.8	18.4	11.0	7.8	69.1	14.9	15.1	0.9
Greene County	38.5	48.1	29.9	38.5	100.0	21.4	50.0	23.1	2 580	59.8	11.9	20.0	15.2	6.2	63.5	17.1	18.7	0.8
Grundy County	41.7	54.5	30.0	41.9	100.0	75.0	29.4	10.8	3 061	70.0	11.4	12.3	17.7	8.6	70.4	13.9	15.0	0.7

[1] Hispanic or Latino persons may be of any race.

STATE County	Percent who worked at home	Percent of the population 5 years and over with a disability	Veterans as a percent of the population 18 years and over	Occupation for employed population 16 years and over (percent)							Industry for employed population 16 years and over (percent)					
				Management, professional, and related occupations	Service occupations	Sales and office occupations	Farming, fishing, and forestry occupations	Construction, extraction, and maintenance occupations	Production, transportation and material moving occupations	Agriculture, forestry, fishing, and mining	Construction and manufacturing	Wholesale and retail trade	Transportation and warehousing, and utilities	Service industries	Public administration
	42	43	44	45	46	47	48	49	50	51	52	53	54	55	56

INDIANA—Cont'd

STATE County	42	43	44	45	46	47	48	49	50	51	52	53	54	55	56
Putnam County	3.2	22.1	12.6	24.2	15.2	22.9	0.3	12.9	24.5	2.2	28.9	16.5	8.2	39.3	4.8
Randolph County	3.7	21.8	12.6	22.4	15.3	20.9	0.7	10.3	30.4	3.0	38.3	13.9	3.8	37.8	3.2
Ripley County	4.2	22.0	13.2	23.2	13.2	20.8	0.5	10.9	31.5	3.2	40.7	12.9	5.3	35.6	2.3
Rush County	5.7	19.4	14.9	22.2	12.7	20.9	1.0	11.4	31.6	7.0	37.8	15.7	4.4	31.5	3.6
St. Joseph County	2.6	18.3	12.8	32.1	14.5	27.2	0.1	8.0	18.2	0.3	25.7	16.6	4.3	50.5	2.6
Scott County	2.2	23.6	12.7	20.1	15.2	20.0	0.8	9.7	34.3	1.8	41.1	14.7	4.6	34.5	3.3
Shelby County	2.6	21.4	14.3	25.6	13.7	22.4	0.7	12.0	25.6	2.2	36.9	14.2	5.0	37.9	3.8
Spencer County	3.8	17.9	14.1	23.1	13.2	22.6	1.1	11.8	28.2	5.2	35.2	15.8	7.1	33.9	2.7
Starke County	2.7	21.9	13.4	20.9	13.2	19.7	1.0	12.6	32.6	2.4	41.5	13.5	5.4	33.6	3.5
Steuben County	2.8	15.7	12.7	24.1	11.9	23.1	0.4	10.2	30.3	1.8	44.2	14.4	3.3	33.8	2.5
Sullivan County	2.4	24.5	15.1	23.6	17.8	22.8	1.2	12.6	22.1	4.1	24.2	15.0	6.6	42.7	7.4
Switzerland County	4.5	20.1	14.2	20.5	18.4	15.6	1.1	15.3	29.1	5.8	35.8	9.7	7.3	37.8	3.7
Tippecanoe County	2.8	14.5	10.1	36.7	16.0	23.2	0.5	6.9	16.6	1.2	23.9	13.2	2.6	56.9	2.2
Tipton County	2.6	19.0	14.1	23.0	15.8	21.3	1.6	13.3	25.1	5.7	36.6	14.0	4.4	36.6	2.6
Union County	4.8	21.8	12.3	24.7	13.7	23.5	0.7	12.7	24.6	4.9	28.2	16.6	5.1	41.9	3.4
Vanderburgh County	2.1	20.7	13.6	27.9	15.5	28.9	0.2	9.5	18.1	0.7	23.6	17.2	5.7	50.2	2.7
Vermillion County	2.3	21.3	15.9	22.6	17.3	21.0	0.3	14.4	24.3	2.3	33.3	19.2	5.6	36.4	3.3
Vigo County	2.1	20.7	13.0	29.4	17.9	28.0	0.2	8.9	15.7	0.8	20.7	18.6	3.6	52.5	3.8
Wabash County	3.3	19.8	13.1	23.3	13.9	22.0	1.1	8.4	31.2	3.4	41.0	12.3	2.7	38.3	2.3
Warren County	3.3	18.5	14.2	26.0	12.9	19.4	1.6	11.7	28.3	4.6	36.4	11.4	4.6	39.8	3.2
Warrick County	2.8	17.7	14.3	31.1	13.0	27.3	0.2	11.8	16.5	1.3	27.5	17.0	5.4	45.9	3.0
Washington County	3.9	20.0	13.6	20.8	13.1	19.1	1.4	11.7	34.0	3.7	41.5	13.2	5.1	33.0	3.5
Wayne County	2.7	21.7	14.6	24.8	15.3	24.8	0.4	9.4	25.2	1.4	31.4	15.7	4.1	44.7	2.6
Wells County	4.5	15.9	12.8	24.2	13.9	24.9	0.9	10.1	26.0	3.7	31.6	19.4	5.6	38.4	1.3
White County	4.5	22.4	14.6	22.8	13.5	22.2	1.1	10.4	29.9	4.4	36.6	15.0	4.5	36.9	2.6
Whitley County	3.3	16.8	13.9	24.6	12.2	23.7	0.6	10.7	28.1	2.1	39.0	15.1	5.0	36.5	2.4
IOWA	4.7	16.6	13.3	31.3	14.8	25.9	1.1	8.9	18.1	4.4	23.2	15.6	4.9	48.4	3.4
Adair County	7.2	16.7	15.6	27.9	14.1	23.5	2.1	12.0	20.4	14.1	25.9	12.4	5.2	38.8	3.6
Adams County	8.7	18.6	13.9	32.6	15.4	19.9	2.9	9.7	19.5	12.9	19.0	15.6	7.2	42.5	2.8
Allamakee County	9.9	15.5	14.2	28.6	13.4	20.0	4.6	10.6	22.9	14.4	28.4	14.3	5.1	35.3	2.5
Appanoose County	4.7	20.9	13.0	25.2	12.8	24.7	1.3	10.4	25.6	6.4	30.3	16.6	6.6	36.2	3.8
Audubon County	11.5	16.0	14.6	34.6	17.1	19.6	2.0	9.3	17.4	15.7	17.7	15.7	5.5	42.6	2.8
Benton County	6.3	17.1	13.6	27.7	14.3	24.9	1.4	10.9	20.8	7.4	27.2	15.4	6.0	41.8	2.2
Black Hawk County	2.9	18.2	13.3	30.3	16.0	27.5	0.3	8.0	17.8	1.3	23.1	16.4	3.9	52.4	2.9
Boone County	5.1	15.5	13.7	27.3	17.4	25.8	1.6	11.6	16.2	4.7	18.4	17.0	6.1	49.1	4.7
Bremer County	6.7	14.0	13.0	32.4	13.2	25.6	1.4	9.8	17.6	5.5	24.9	13.9	2.8	50.6	2.4
Buchanan County	7.0	17.0	14.0	28.1	14.0	22.7	1.5	11.3	22.3	7.3	30.8	15.3	4.5	38.4	3.7
Buena Vista County	6.6	16.3	12.1	27.8	14.4	24.2	2.5	7.5	23.7	8.2	26.5	15.6	4.2	42.6	3.0
Butler County	9.0	16.8	13.4	27.8	15.2	23.3	2.4	10.7	20.6	9.4	25.6	14.4	5.1	42.8	2.6
Calhoun County	5.8	19.3	15.5	32.8	17.4	22.7	1.7	10.9	14.6	9.2	17.1	15.8	6.6	46.0	5.3
Carroll County	7.4	15.1	13.0	28.3	14.5	28.0	1.9	10.9	16.4	8.1	18.9	20.8	4.2	45.8	2.2
Cass County	7.2	18.3	13.9	28.6	14.1	24.4	1.7	10.1	21.1	8.7	26.4	15.7	4.7	41.6	2.9
Cedar County	4.8	15.4	14.3	28.3	13.2	24.8	2.0	11.7	20.0	7.0	24.3	16.1	6.7	42.6	3.3
Cerro Gordo County	3.8	17.8	13.8	28.3	16.4	27.1	0.5	8.5	19.3	2.5	23.4	18.0	4.5	49.1	2.5
Cherokee County	6.4	15.9	14.4	29.2	15.3	21.7	2.3	10.4	21.2	10.1	25.0	18.2	4.0	39.3	3.4
Chickasaw County	10.6	14.4	13.4	28.4	12.2	20.7	2.5	10.6	25.6	11.6	32.3	14.8	4.8	34.3	2.3
Clarke County	6.8	18.8	13.2	26.7	14.3	21.6	2.1	11.2	24.1	6.8	29.4	13.3	4.8	43.4	2.4
Clay County	4.7	16.9	14.1	26.0	13.7	25.8	1.3	9.6	23.6	5.5	25.0	18.6	6.0	42.2	2.7
Clayton County	11.4	16.8	14.5	28.1	14.9	19.4	2.7	11.0	24.0	12.3	27.9	14.6	3.8	38.8	2.6
Clinton County	4.4	20.0	15.2	25.1	15.3	24.8	0.6	9.6	24.6	4.1	29.2	14.7	5.7	43.8	2.5
Crawford County	7.0	18.5	13.3	24.5	15.9	20.1	2.0	8.9	28.6	8.7	29.5	14.0	6.2	39.0	2.7
Dallas County	4.0	12.8	12.7	35.9	13.5	27.6	1.3	9.1	12.6	4.1	17.5	16.5	5.1	52.6	4.3
Davis County	11.8	16.8	12.6	28.2	9.7	19.6	4.6	12.5	25.3	12.5	29.4	12.6	6.6	36.5	2.5
Decatur County	7.8	19.2	11.6	29.3	17.4	23.5	2.6	10.5	16.7	9.7	20.8	10.9	6.2	50.9	1.6
Delaware County	12.1	15.6	11.6	29.2	12.3	21.2	1.6	11.0	24.7	12.9	29.1	16.3	3.8	35.2	2.7
Des Moines County	3.3	17.7	15.5	24.9	15.1	24.5	0.7	10.5	24.3	2.3	30.7	17.5	6.7	39.5	3.4
Dickinson County	5.1	15.8	15.4	29.9	13.9	25.9	0.9	10.3	19.2	4.5	28.7	15.2	4.5	44.0	3.1
Dubuque County	4.1	16.0	13.2	29.7	15.7	26.5	0.8	7.6	19.7	3.1	24.2	17.0	4.0	49.7	1.9
Emmet County	5.1	16.9	13.4	24.3	15.0	23.9	1.7	8.6	26.5	7.2	30.0	13.9	5.2	41.1	2.6
Fayette County	9.4	18.4	13.1	29.3	13.6	23.0	2.7	9.0	22.4	12.3	23.9	15.7	4.5	40.6	3.0
Floyd County	7.2	18.3	14.1	32.0	18.4	21.6	1.2	9.0	17.8	8.3	25.8	13.9	3.3	45.5	3.2
Franklin County	10.2	15.3	13.5	31.4	16.0	19.0	3.5	8.8	21.3	14.2	24.0	13.3	4.8	41.1	2.6
Fremont County	5.3	20.3	15.7	29.6	14.9	21.5	1.6	10.4	22.0	9.4	24.6	15.0	5.6	41.3	4.1
Greene County	6.0	18.3	13.4	31.7	15.1	20.1	1.7	10.7	20.7	9.0	23.9	14.0	4.7	45.2	3.3
Grundy County	7.6	14.4	13.6	30.8	14.2	24.7	1.5	8.7	20.1	8.3	23.1	17.7	5.7	41.3	4.0

Table B-3. States and Counties — **Education, Labor Force, and Income**

STATE County	Median household income	Median family income: All families	Median family income: Families with children: Married-couple	Median family income: Families with children: Male householder	Median family income: Families with children: Female householder	Median nonfamily household income	Median income for full-year, full-time workers: Men	Median income for full-year, full-time workers: Women	Per capita income	Households by source of income (percent): With earnings	Households by source of income (percent): With interest, dividend, or rental income	Households by source of income (percent): With Social Security income	Households by source of income (percent): With public assistance income	Households by source of income (percent): With retirement income	Households with income over $100,000 (percent)	+/− U.S. percent for income over $100,000	Households with income below poverty (percent)	Families with children with income below poverty (percent)
	57	58	59	60	61	62	63	64	65	66	67	68	69	70	71	72	73	74
INDIANA—Cont'd																		
Putnam County	38 882	45 916	51 804	27 450	21 141	20 398	33 211	22 886	17 163	79.2	25.0	27.5	2.0	19.5	6.7	-5.6	8.7	8.5
Randolph County	34 544	40 855	45 551	26 585	14 813	19 143	31 667	21 517	16 954	77.7	35.9	32.5	3.2	21.1	3.6	-8.7	11.1	13.0
Ripley County	41 426	47 019	53 075	28 333	22 770	21 996	35 085	24 612	17 559	80.5	37.2	29.6	2.0	18.0	5.7	-6.6	8.3	8.3
Rush County	38 152	42 633	52 104	35 781	23 227	19 564	34 209	23 448	17 997	79.6	25.7	29.6	3.1	16.3	6.0	-6.3	9.0	7.8
St. Joseph County	40 420	49 653	61 004	31 283	18 951	24 132	38 118	26 109	19 756	81.2	39.0	27.1	3.2	16.7	8.9	-3.4	9.7	12.3
Scott County	34 656	39 475	43 300	29 219	17 695	19 090	31 390	23 059	16 065	77.3	26.2	29.4	4.2	18.8	5.1	-7.2	12.7	16.5
Shelby County	43 649	51 271	60 083	30 294	25 689	23 944	38 288	25 689	20 324	84.0	26.0	26.0	1.7	14.1	9.1	-3.2	7.1	7.4
Spencer County	42 451	49 123	56 581	39 000	22 031	19 865	35 970	23 671	18 000	81.2	40.4	27.7	2.1	16.5	6.5	-5.8	6.9	6.6
Starke County	37 243	42 355	46 623	31 632	18 047	19 530	34 658	21 491	16 466	77.0	33.6	32.2	2.6	17.7	5.2	-7.1	10.9	13.4
Steuben County	44 089	50 567	58 043	31 250	22 961	26 953	36 164	24 909	20 647	84.7	38.5	25.6	1.9	16.3	7.4	-4.9	7.3	6.0
Sullivan County	32 976	39 290	47 836	26 000	16 382	17 845	31 064	21 522	16 234	76.4	32.5	34.4	3.3	23.1	5.0	-7.3	11.3	13.3
Switzerland County	37 002	41 306	46 351	29 479	17 440	21 433	30 748	21 886	17 466	79.9	26.9	30.2	1.7	20.1	4.3	-8.0	12.2	15.3
Tippecanoe County	38 652	51 791	58 505	28 333	21 511	22 170	39 148	26 198	19 375	86.1	41.6	18.8	2.0	13.4	9.5	-2.8	15.5	10.7
Tipton County	48 546	56 080	63 168	46 500	22 802	23 401	43 683	25 884	21 926	80.9	34.0	26.1	1.9	20.4	10.2	-2.1	6.2	4.1
Union County	36 672	41 752	45 875	19 500	21 719	22 139	32 452	22 261	19 549	81.6	40.1	27.8	2.1	17.2	5.7	-6.6	8.2	12.1
Vanderburgh County	36 823	47 416	58 043	26 650	18 000	21 389	35 228	24 225	20 655	78.4	39.3	29.5	3.5	17.3	7.7	-4.6	11.0	12.9
Vermillion County	34 837	41 809	47 451	25 750	17 981	16 675	33 897	23 328	18 579	75.6	31.2	31.7	1.7	18.3	5.7	-6.6	10.7	8.2
Vigo County	33 184	42 957	51 598	23 333	16 040	19 317	35 050	23 423	17 620	77.0	34.1	29.5	3.4	19.0	6.3	-6.0	14.6	15.8
Wabash County	40 413	47 067	54 743	33 375	19 837	22 202	35 356	22 525	18 192	80.8	42.3	30.9	1.5	18.9	5.1	-7.2	7.0	7.6
Warren County	41 825	48 647	51 496	27 292	23 194	20 212	36 130	21 712	18 070	81.8	35.4	27.7	1.2	15.2	7.0	-5.3	6.1	6.3
Warrick County	48 814	55 497	63 919	27 273	23 529	23 758	41 201	25 192	21 893	84.9	42.6	23.5	2.1	16.0	11.7	-0.6	5.1	5.5
Washington County	36 630	42 618	49 068	26 071	21 037	17 705	30 741	22 580	16 748	79.2	33.5	28.4	2.7	16.0	4.7	-7.6	11.0	10.7
Wayne County	34 885	42 811	50 245	25 527	16 881	19 898	33 633	22 552	17 727	77.1	35.9	32.0	3.2	18.6	5.4	-6.9	11.5	14.1
Wells County	43 934	51 517	55 945	35 685	22 386	22 652	36 563	23 813	19 158	83.2	40.7	27.3	1.8	16.7	6.9	-5.4	6.1	6.8
White County	40 707	46 436	52 143	30 223	23 724	21 882	34 306	22 448	18 323	82.3	35.9	30.1	1.4	16.9	5.4	-6.9	6.1	5.5
Whitley County	45 503	52 872	59 339	39 531	25 714	24 674	38 202	24 544	20 519	84.1	42.1	26.1	1.9	16.4	8.2	-4.1	5.8	4.9
IOWA	39 469	48 005	55 946	28 788	20 453	22 454	34 320	24 987	19 674	80.4	43.5	28.6	2.9	14.6	7.3	-5.0	9.3	9.3
Adair County	35 170	42 984	46 312	31 389	16 250	19 627	30 373	22 256	17 262	77.0	46.2	36.9	3.2	11.5	3.6	-8.7	8.8	8.6
Adams County	30 453	40 030	48 281	23 750	14 554	17 679	26 875	21 138	15 550	74.3	43.4	39.7	2.0	11.3	3.1	-9.2	9.5	8.2
Allamakee County	33 967	40 589	46 525	22 396	15 927	18 613	26 767	20 048	16 599	77.9	47.7	34.1	2.0	13.2	3.9	-8.4	9.5	10.7
Appanoose County	28 612	35 980	44 557	20 625	17 255	14 638	29 314	21 034	14 644	71.3	35.9	35.5	4.4	16.3	2.5	-9.8	16.5	13.7
Audubon County	32 215	37 288	44 764	31 500	17 045	17 960	30 337	18 560	17 489	75.2	45.5	37.7	3.4	12.8	5.0	-7.3	9.3	9.0
Benton County	42 427	49 701	55 808	31 842	19 079	22 855	35 983	24 857	18 891	78.9	42.7	29.5	1.7	13.7	4.8	-7.5	7.0	6.6
Black Hawk County	37 266	47 398	56 104	27 125	19 572	21 255	34 678	24 344	18 885	78.4	43.6	28.2	3.7	18.7	7.1	-5.2	12.8	12.7
Boone County	40 763	49 346	55 193	30 385	19 714	22 243	33 600	24 524	19 943	80.4	41.6	29.5	2.0	14.6	6.0	-6.3	7.7	6.5
Bremer County	40 826	50 299	59 490	27 321	22 308	21 031	35 044	20 215	19 100	78.3	56.6	32.0	2.4	17.3	6.8	-5.5	5.6	4.6
Buchanan County	38 036	45 421	51 634	25 875	17 031	20 000	31 202	22 797	18 405	77.7	44.8	31.3	3.2	17.3	5.5	-6.8	9.2	10.3
Buena Vista County	35 300	41 549	48 125	25 250	16 992	20 934	30 388	21 119	16 042	79.5	46.4	32.3	2.5	13.2	5.0	-7.3	10.9	12.0
Butler County	35 883	42 209	48 769	26 944	17 228	19 722	31 187	21 727	17 036	75.2	48.8	35.3	2.8	14.3	4.0	-8.3	8.7	9.4
Calhoun County	33 286	41 583	49 667	21 786	19 333	16 981	30 006	21 612	17 498	71.9	44.7	38.6	3.3	14.1	4.9	-7.4	10.5	10.7
Carroll County	37 275	47 040	55 754	23 684	19 848	19 800	30 711	22 297	18 595	78.0	50.7	34.2	2.3	12.1	5.8	-6.5	8.6	6.4
Cass County	32 922	40 564	44 880	20 795	18 393	19 393	30 291	20 988	17 067	77.1	44.3	35.8	3.7	13.2	4.5	-7.8	10.8	10.8
Cedar County	42 198	48 850	56 250	30 595	24 167	23 544	34 019	24 033	19 200	80.5	48.6	30.4	2.6	13.7	5.1	-7.2	6.4	5.0
Cerro Gordo County	35 867	46 099	54 349	23 333	19 587	20 415	32 658	22 431	19 184	77.5	44.3	32.0	2.7	14.8	5.9	-6.4	9.5	9.7
Cherokee County	35 142	42 897	47 542	22 167	19 821	20 131	30 629	21 840	17 934	75.8	51.1	35.4	2.5	13.4	4.0	-8.3	7.3	8.8
Chickasaw County	37 649	44 306	48 417	29 643	21 063	21 293	30 813	21 870	18 237	77.0	52.6	33.9	2.5	15.7	3.9	-8.4	8.0	7.9
Clarke County	34 474	42 171	48 005	24 750	20 516	19 750	30 248	21 261	16 409	81.1	37.5	32.3	4.4	14.9	4.4	-7.9	8.1	10.4
Clay County	35 799	42 769	49 522	27 500	15 530	20 026	31 230	21 940	19 451	79.0	44.5	29.8	3.0	10.3	5.7	-6.6	9.1	10.7
Clayton County	34 068	40 199	46 587	25 682	21 161	20 025	28 705	20 385	16 930	78.0	46.7	33.9	2.0	13.2	3.9	-8.4	9.1	8.3
Clinton County	37 423	46 450	54 232	29 886	18 526	20 264	36 147	22 024	17 724	76.9	42.7	32.1	3.3	17.7	4.1	-8.2	10.1	12.4
Crawford County	33 922	40 231	44 416	25 515	16 806	18 319	29 638	20 597	15 851	78.4	43.5	34.8	2.2	11.7	3.1	-9.2	9.6	10.0
Dallas County	48 528	58 293	65 949	32 454	24 358	26 210	38 480	27 614	22 970	85.8	42.8	22.1	2.1	12.1	13.1	0.8	5.8	5.6
Davis County	32 864	40 982	46 301	22 188	19 779	18 027	27 298	22 204	15 127	75.0	40.6	35.9	2.8	17.8	3.3	-9.0	11.8	12.5
Decatur County	27 343	34 831	38 885	20 417	18 529	14 503	26 854	19 880	14 209	74.6	35.1	34.0	5.6	13.7	3.5	-8.8	18.6	15.2
Delaware County	37 168	43 607	50 833	29 167	18 269	20 394	32 304	20 319	17 327	80.6	47.0	30.6	3.5	11.5	5.5	-6.8	9.2	8.1
Des Moines County	36 790	45 089	54 326	27 734	16 210	21 522	35 699	23 726	19 701	78.3	42.3	31.3	3.7	17.3	5.4	-6.9	9.8	14.6
Dickinson County	39 020	47 739	53 262	28 750	21 250	22 184	31 696	22 992	21 929	77.9	47.6	34.3	2.4	15.5	7.6	-4.7	7.2	6.1
Dubuque County	39 582	48 742	55 640	30 500	19 275	21 818	33 330	23 203	19 600	80.7	48.7	28.1	2.7	17.4	7.2	-5.1	7.9	7.4
Emmet County	33 305	41 296	49 214	24 375	19 583	21 068	28 750	21 192	16 619	75.8	44.1	34.0	3.1	14.2	4.5	-7.8	9.1	8.7
Fayette County	32 453	39 900	40 515	29 688	16 032	18 243	29 094	20 807	17 271	74.1	46.7	35.2	4.4	12.9	3.8	-8.5	11.5	10.7
Floyd County	35 237	41 133	49 731	32 500	18 925	20 126	30 952	21 523	17 091	75.0	47.5	34.9	3.7	17.5	3.7	-8.6	8.9	10.3
Franklin County	36 042	45 184	49 328	27 813	17 315	20 490	30 663	21 688	18 767	75.8	45.9	35.0	2.3	13.2	5.1	-7.2	7.8	8.2
Fremont County	38 345	46 547	51 480	26 875	22 059	17 432	31 606	24 341	18 081	76.7	37.9	37.1	3.4	14.1	4.7	-7.6	10.6	9.9
Greene County	33 883	41 230	48 899	27 105	17 431	17 446	30 074	22 325	16 866	72.6	42.5	38.7	4.0	15.6	3.3	-9.0	9.3	8.6
Grundy County	39 396	46 627	51 750	30 833	20 625	22 065	32 913	22 879	19 142	77.5	51.2	35.0	2.0	14.8	5.4	-6.9	5.5	4.1

Table B-3. States and Counties — Education, Labor Force, and Income

STATE/ County code	MSA/PMSA/ NECMA code[1]	STATE County	High school graduates			College graduates		College graduates (percent)				
			Total population 25 years and over	Percent with a high school diploma or less	Percent with a high school diploma or more	Percent with a bachelor's degree or more	+/− U.S. percent with bachelor's degree or more	Non-Hispanic White	Black or African American	American Indian and Alaska Native	Asian, Hawaiian, and Pacific Islander	Hispanic or Latino[2]
			1	2	3	4	5	6	7	8	9	10
		IOWA—Cont'd										
19 077	...	Guthrie County............	7 976	59.5	85.4	14.9	−9.5	15.0	0.0	0.0	100.0	8.1
19 079	...	Hamilton County...........	11 094	53.1	87.3	17.5	−6.9	17.6	0.0	0.0	20.4	16.1
19 081	...	Hancock County...........	8 084	52.8	85.8	15.4	−9.0	15.6	X	33.3	77.8	4.0
19 083	...	Hardin County	12 615	51.3	85.7	17.1	−7.3	17.4	0.0	X	22.2	0.6
19 085	...	Harrison County	10 487	59.1	85.0	12.7	−11.7	12.5	61.5	33.3	40.0	7.7
19 087	...	Henry County	13 509	53.5	86.1	16.2	−8.2	16.5	3.0	5.9	19.3	8.8
19 089	...	Howard County	6 645	63.7	79.3	12.6	−11.8	12.6	100.0	X	66.7	0.0
19 091	...	Humboldt County	7 078	52.0	86.3	15.4	−9.0	15.3	0.0	0.0	50.0	14.7
19 093	...	Ida County	5 349	58.3	85.0	13.6	−10.8	13.6	X	0.0	50.0	25.0
19 095	...	Iowa County	10 565	55.1	87.0	15.8	−8.6	15.6	25.0	0.0	23.5	35.2
19 097	...	Jackson County	13 596	63.2	81.5	12.1	−12.3	11.9	0.0	28.6	66.7	28.6
19 099	...	Jasper County	25 291	58.0	86.8	15.9	−8.5	15.9	4.8	8.2	40.2	7.2
19 101	...	Jefferson County	10 893	43.3	88.1	31.2	6.8	31.0	31.0	31.4	50.0	52.4
19 103	3500	Johnson County	62 859	26.1	93.7	47.6	23.2	47.0	34.9	41.1	76.5	34.5
19 105	...	Jones County	13 776	57.0	85.3	12.7	−11.7	13.0	3.1	16.1	17.2	3.7
19 107	...	Keokuk County	7 667	62.3	84.0	11.6	−12.8	11.5	0.0	0.0	64.7	11.8
19 109	...	Kossuth County............	11 694	53.4	85.6	13.6	−10.8	13.6	0.0	0.0	7.7	2.5
19 111	...	Lee County..................	25 828	59.1	83.6	12.5	−11.9	12.6	4.7	0.0	42.1	10.2
19 113	1360	Linn County.................	123 896	39.8	90.6	27.7	3.3	27.7	13.2	20.3	55.1	22.7
19 115	...	Louisa County	7 828	61.3	79.7	12.7	−11.7	13.5	27.3	0.0	32.5	2.8
19 117	...	Lucas County	6 336	65.4	79.1	11.1	−13.3	11.0	0.0	0.0	33.3	60.0
19 119	...	Lyon County	7 539	59.6	78.7	14.2	−10.2	14.1	20.0	0.0	100.0	52.6
19 121	...	Madison County	9 254	53.4	87.6	14.4	−10.0	14.4	0.0	0.0	35.3	12.5
19 123	...	Mahaska County	14 504	58.6	82.6	16.5	−7.9	16.5	0.0	0.0	29.9	4.8
19 125	...	Marion County	20 684	56.6	84.0	18.9	−5.5	18.9	19.1	12.9	18.4	9.8
19 127	...	Marshall County	26 179	54.9	82.3	17.0	−7.4	18.1	8.1	0.0	15.3	1.7
19 129	...	Mills County.................	9 662	53.5	83.2	16.3	−8.1	16.4	0.0	32.1	9.7	12.5
19 131	...	Mitchell County	7 320	60.0	84.4	12.8	−11.6	12.9	0.0	0.0	X	0.0
19 133	...	Monona County	7 072	61.2	81.7	13.4	−11.0	13.6	0.0	12.5	0.0	0.0
19 135	...	Monroe County	5 400	62.1	82.2	12.6	−11.8	12.7	0.0	0.0	X	0.0
19 137	...	Montgomery County	8 124	58.8	81.8	12.9	−11.5	13.0	X	X	27.3	0.0
19 139	...	Muscatine County	26 877	54.2	80.3	17.2	−7.2	18.0	10.8	4.7	27.6	7.9
19 141	...	O'Brien County	10 174	58.3	80.7	14.7	−9.7	14.8	25.0	0.0	25.0	1.6
19 143	...	Osceola County............	4 647	56.5	81.1	13.4	−11.0	13.5	0.0	33.3	0.0	8.7
19 145	...	Page County	11 655	53.8	85.5	16.6	−7.8	17.0	0.0	6.8	20.0	5.2
19 147	...	Palo Alto County	6 692	51.3	83.7	13.9	−10.5	14.0	X	0.0	0.0	0.0
19 149	...	Plymouth County	15 994	51.7	87.4	19.3	−5.1	19.4	57.9	0.0	8.7	5.2
19 151	...	Pocahontas County.......	6 002	53.2	86.6	15.0	−9.4	15.1	0.0	0.0	0.0	0.0
19 153	2120	Polk County..................	243 458	41.1	88.3	29.7	5.3	31.2	16.3	13.3	28.0	11.6
19 155	5920	Pottawattamie County ...	57 013	55.3	84.0	15.0	−9.4	15.1	5.5	15.0	35.3	12.1
19 157	...	Poweshiek County	12 176	55.8	86.7	18.5	−5.9	18.3	46.2	20.0	34.4	17.1
19 159	...	Ringgold County............	3 781	61.6	82.8	13.4	−11.0	13.3	X	0.0	88.9	66.7
19 161	...	Sac County..................	7 946	58.8	84.2	13.6	−10.8	13.6	0.0	0.0	16.7	13.3
19 163	1960	Scott County................	102 149	44.4	86.3	24.9	0.5	25.8	12.2	10.3	35.9	14.2
19 165	...	Shelby County	8 957	59.3	86.6	15.3	−9.1	15.1	0.0	0.0	72.0	8.6
19 167	...	Sioux County	18 172	53.3	80.4	19.8	−4.6	19.9	4.9	0.0	47.4	7.3
19 169	...	Story County	42 148	27.8	93.5	44.5	20.1	42.5	62.9	7.3	80.0	43.4
19 171	...	Tama County................	12 011	56.6	84.2	12.9	−11.5	13.3	0.0	5.2	48.2	3.1
19 173	...	Taylor County	4 766	63.3	83.3	12.0	−12.4	12.2	X	18.2	0.0	2.9
19 175	...	Union County	8 342	55.9	87.3	14.7	−9.7	14.7	X	0.0	0.0	41.2
19 177	...	Van Buren County.........	5 322	63.5	82.7	11.8	−12.6	11.9	X	33.3	0.0	8.3
19 179	...	Wapello County	24 120	58.4	81.5	14.6	−9.8	14.6	24.6	33.3	23.0	10.6
19 181	2120	Warren County	25 756	47.8	90.0	21.2	−3.2	21.3	20.3	0.0	26.4	20.2
19 183	...	Washington County.......	13 876	56.6	82.5	16.4	−8.0	16.5	10.9	13.3	100.0	9.7
19 185	...	Wayne County	4 722	62.0	83.9	12.1	−12.3	12.1	0.0	0.0	58.8	0.0
19 187	...	Webster County	25 981	52.6	84.2	16.9	−7.5	17.1	8.5	14.8	38.3	5.6
19 189	...	Winnebago County........	7 772	50.8	87.3	16.5	−7.9	16.5	0.0	0.0	0.0	20.8
19 191	...	Winneshiek County	12 864	53.2	84.1	20.5	−3.9	20.7	15.4	0.0	2.4	0.0
19 193	7720	Woodbury County	64 932	53.6	81.4	18.9	−5.5	20.6	10.9	2.1	11.8	3.0
19 195	...	Worth County	5 476	53.6	86.0	12.7	−11.7	13.0	0.0	0.0	0.0	0.0
19 197	...	Wright County	9 882	54.7	84.4	13.5	−10.9	13.9	0.0	0.0	0.0	3.9
20 000	...	KANSAS...................	1 701 207	43.8	86.0	25.8	1.4	27.2	14.9	14.9	40.0	9.7
20 001	...	Allen County................	9 292	52.7	83.1	15.2	−9.2	15.5	10.8	8.6	22.2	5.9
20 003	...	Anderson County..........	5 459	60.4	81.9	11.7	−12.7	11.7	0.0	0.0	0.0	11.8
20 005	...	Atchison County............	10 375	56.9	84.7	18.0	−6.4	17.8	19.5	0.0	44.4	29.6

[1] MSA = Metropolitan Statistical Area. PMSA = Primary MSA. NECMA = New England County Metropolitan Area. See the Appendix A for explanation of these concepts. See Appendix B for list of metropolitan areas identified by type, with component counties.
[2] Hispanic or Latino persons may be of any race.

Table B-3. States and Counties — Education, Labor Force, and Income

Items 11—23

STATE County	School enrollment			Population 16 to 19 years				Employment status, 2000			Work status in 1999 of the population 16 years and over (percent)		
											Worked in 1999		
	Grades kindergarten through 12	College or graduate school	Percent private	Number	Percent in armed forces	Percent high school graduates	Percent not enrolled, not grads, not in armed forces, not employed	Total population 16 years and over	Percent in labor force	Unemploy-ment rate	Full-time	Part-time	Did not work in 1999
	11	12	13	14	15	16	17	18	19	20	21	22	23
IOWA—Cont'd													
Guthrie County	2 110	239	4.3	568	0.0	10.2	1.1	9 039	65.1	3.8	54.5	15.7	29.7
Hamilton County	3 100	539	8.7	859	0.0	7.2	0.8	12 760	68.2	2.5	56.7	16.9	26.4
Hancock County	2 584	342	7.7	746	0.0	8.2	0.4	9 313	66.6	2.7	56.8	15.8	27.4
Hardin County	3 602	877	2.9	1 236	0.0	9.0	1.9	14 833	63.1	4.4	52.6	17.1	30.3
Harrison County	3 208	459	5.4	902	0.0	9.9	2.4	12 089	64.8	4.3	56.0	14.3	29.7
Henry County	3 950	974	15.7	1 126	0.0	8.1	2.6	15 903	65.1	4.4	57.2	16.2	26.6
Howard County	1 961	234	14.5	546	0.0	9.5	5.3	7 649	64.5	3.4	52.9	17.4	29.7
Humboldt County	2 040	325	9.0	603	0.0	7.1	0.0	8 126	62.6	3.5	52.6	16.1	31.3
Ida County	1 640	157	3.6	456	0.0	10.1	0.4	6 109	63.7	3.9	51.8	18.2	30.0
Iowa County	3 199	490	9.9	840	0.0	10.6	0.8	12 028	70.5	2.3	60.4	15.7	23.9
Jackson County	4 218	523	13.6	1 134	0.0	8.6	1.7	15 702	68.2	3.7	55.1	16.5	28.4
Jasper County	6 798	1 015	7.9	1 872	0.0	10.7	1.2	29 196	65.8	3.1	57.8	15.1	27.0
Jefferson County	3 191	875	28.2	942	0.0	6.8	4.8	12 746	68.8	4.1	52.8	21.0	26.2
Johnson County	16 189	26 885	6.1	9 749	0.2	5.4	0.9	91 234	73.4	3.9	55.1	29.0	15.9
Jones County	3 906	736	8.5	1 058	0.0	8.4	3.0	15 968	63.4	3.9	56.2	16.3	27.5
Keokuk County	2 307	298	2.2	596	0.0	12.2	1.8	8 805	63.1	3.9	54.5	13.7	31.8
Kossuth County	3 502	475	19.9	1 072	0.9	8.1	1.7	13 459	63.7	3.8	50.3	19.3	30.3
Lee County	7 169	1 153	13.7	1 967	0.0	10.8	2.7	29 915	61.6	5.8	52.9	14.8	32.4
Linn County	35 536	11 547	17.0	11 277	0.0	10.4	2.2	148 669	72.4	3.5	60.6	17.4	22.0
Louisa County	2 529	405	3.7	704	0.0	6.3	8.7	9 216	66.1	4.3	57.1	14.5	28.4
Lucas County	1 852	225	8.0	591	0.0	9.5	7.4	7 346	62.8	4.9	49.3	16.9	33.8
Lyon County	2 574	298	13.6	763	0.0	10.6	1.0	8 897	68.3	2.4	52.0	20.3	27.6
Madison County	2 823	408	5.6	758	0.7	13.5	3.4	10 648	69.4	4.2	59.5	15.4	25.1
Mahaska County	4 223	1 000	17.6	1 416	0.0	10.2	4.7	17 355	64.9	4.5	52.8	17.2	30.0
Marion County	6 153	1 856	24.4	2 152	0.0	7.6	0.4	24 960	67.5	3.4	53.8	19.2	27.0
Marshall County	7 783	1 316	8.0	2 313	0.0	10.1	5.5	30 622	65.4	4.4	55.7	15.2	29.0
Mills County	3 041	541	7.8	778	0.0	8.6	1.8	11 093	70.1	4.8	59.3	13.5	27.2
Mitchell County	2 183	268	10.9	563	0.0	8.5	2.0	8 309	63.4	3.1	50.0	18.6	31.3
Monona County	1 850	197	4.7	534	0.0	8.6	4.9	8 015	60.6	3.8	49.4	16.2	34.4
Monroe County	1 540	263	4.9	477	0.0	13.0	1.0	6 247	60.2	3.7	51.0	15.4	33.6
Montgomery County	2 186	278	5.6	664	0.0	5.6	6.5	9 224	62.8	5.0	53.3	14.7	32.0
Muscatine County	8 391	1 688	6.3	2 300	0.0	9.7	6.5	31 789	68.0	3.9	56.9	16.7	26.4
O'Brien County	2 939	385	15.6	933	0.0	8.9	2.6	11 903	64.0	3.0	50.1	21.5	28.3
Osceola County	1 466	172	10.5	366	0.0	7.1	4.4	5 353	65.2	3.3	54.9	17.5	27.6
Page County	3 201	502	7.9	939	0.4	13.5	3.4	13 579	60.2	6.0	51.1	16.2	32.7
Palo Alto County	1 937	591	11.2	707	0.0	5.4	1.3	8 051	62.4	2.1	53.4	17.7	28.8
Plymouth County	5 500	816	18.8	1 610	0.0	9.2	0.9	10 740	60.0	1.9	55.0	10.7	20.0
Pocahontas County	1 826	209	9.8	473	0.0	7.4	0.8	6 759	60.0	3.3	50.9	17.2	31.9
Polk County	68 002	21 022	17.7	19 619	0.1	12.6	3.9	288 558	73.1	4.7	62.6	15.8	21.6
Pottawattamie County	16 929	3 618	9.1	5 187	0.0	11.7	5.0	67 784	68.9	4.1	59.3	14.9	25.8
Poweshiek County	3 304	1 742	26.1	1 369	0.0	8.0	0.7	15 071	68.2	5.0	53.1	20.6	26.2
Ringgold County	996	196	10.2	340	0.0	5.6	8.2	4 361	57.2	4.1	47.5	16.7	35.7
Sac County	2 218	295	5.0	618	0.0	6.3	0.6	9 085	63.3	3.1	51.2	17.5	31.3
Scott County	30 835	10 824	17.8	8 960	0.0	11.8	4.0	121 570	69.0	5.2	56.6	18.1	25.3
Shelby County	2 779	252	9.7	762	0.0	9.7	2.0	10 173	66.6	2.6	53.6	18.2	28.2
Sioux County	6 808	2 920	48.9	2 865	0.0	7.2	0.6	24 040	71.3	1.8	51.6	26.6	21.8
Story County	11 147	23 057	3.1	8 266	0.0	4.3	0.6	66 647	70.1	4.4	51.8	30.7	17.5
Tama County	3 602	561	5.3	941	0.0	9.6	4.3	13 868	63.8	4.0	53.8	16.0	30.2
Taylor County	1 332	194	2.8	402	0.0	10.0	3.2	5 510	61.6	3.9	51.8	14.5	33.7
Union County	2 186	597	6.7	809	0.0	9.6	3.3	9 791	65.6	3.9	56.1	15.8	28.1
Van Buren County	1 477	171	11.9	418	0.0	13.2	7.9	6 118	63.9	3.7	52.5	15.0	32.4
Wapello County	6 430	1 607	6.9	2 061	0.0	10.8	6.0	28 604	61.9	6.7	48.7	17.4	33.9
Warren County	8 312	2 431	15.8	2 609	0.0	11.2	2.3	30 984	73.7	3.5	61.9	16.9	21.2
Washington County	4 083	584	10.5	1 020	0.0	10.7	2.8	15 872	69.7	2.6	57.7	15.9	26.4
Wayne County	1 276	191	5.3	355	0.0	8.5	3.4	5 341	59.7	4.0	48.8	15.8	35.4
Webster County	7 580	1 918	12.7	2 648	0.0	11.6	4.8	31 612	61.9	4.3	52.5	17.1	30.3
Winnebago County	2 287	567	14.0	938	0.0	6.4	2.9	9 340	66.7	3.0	54.2	19.2	26.6
Winneshiek County	3 900	2 830	43.5	1 974	0.0	4.1	1.4	17 166	71.7	4.5	53.1	24.6	22.3
Woodbury County	20 752	4 797	17.2	6 334	0.1	11.1	4.6	78 641	69.0	4.1	57.9	16.9	25.2
Worth County	1 493	241	2.4	412	0.0	7.0	0.5	6 248	67.6	3.8	54.8	17.3	27.9
Wright County	2 679	270	4.0	778	0.0	16.3	4.9	11 253	64.0	3.7	54.1	16.4	29.5
KANSAS	520 202	176 453	11.5	166 014	0.7	10.0	4.0	2 059 160	67.5	4.2	57.5	10.2	26.2
Allen County	2 790	647	2.9	1 114	0.0	11.1	3.5	11 279	63.5	4.3	53.3	14.6	32.0
Anderson County	1 660	173	10.3	496	0.0	2.4	1.8	6 306	62.0	3.7	53.3	13.0	33.8
Atchison County	3 549	1 058	33.2	1 171	0.0	9.3	0.1	12 823	64.8	6.2	56.2	14.5	29.3

Table B-3. States and Counties — **Education, Labor Force, and Income**

STATE County	Full-year full-time employed (percent)								Children under 18 years in families						Total employed by class of worker (percent)			
										With two parents (percent)								
	Total	Men	Women	Non-Hispanic White	Black or African American	American Indian and Alaska Native	Asian, Hawaiian, and Pacific Islander	Hispanic or Latino[1]	Number	Both in labor force	Father only in labor force	With one parent who is in labor force (percent)	+/− U.S. percent of children with no stay-at-home parent (percent)	+/− U.S. percent two-income couples	Private	Government	Self-employed	Unpaid family worker
	24	25	26	27	28	29	30	31	32	33	34	35	36	37	38	39	40	41
IOWA—Cont'd																		
Guthrie County	41.2	50.7	32.2	41.3	100.0	12.5	100.0	37.0	2 582	62.4	13.2	18.5	16.3	9.3	65.5	15.1	19.0	0.4
Hamilton County	45.4	56.9	34.5	45.6	100.0	50.0	31.6	45.2	4 077	70.3	8.8	16.3	22.0	10.9	72.2	14.3	13.3	0.3
Hancock County	44.1	55.3	33.3	44.3	X	33.3	37.5	38.8	3 163	70.6	10.9	13.7	19.7	11.5	73.0	10.8	15.6	0.6
Hardin County	39.4	51.0	28.5	39.7	3.2	X	47.2	27.8	4 342	60.8	14.9	18.9	15.1	6.8	71.1	15.1	13.5	0.3
Harrison County	43.7	55.2	33.1	43.8	23.1	29.4	29.5	46.9	3 935	57.6	20.1	14.6	7.6	6.5	71.4	13.1	15.2	0.3
Henry County	43.9	53.0	34.8	44.3	21.1	51.4	50.2	32.9	4 868	64.1	11.4	18.5	18.0	12.8	74.9	14.2	10.4	0.4
Howard County	41.7	53.8	30.2	41.8	100.0	X	14.3	40.0	2 553	66.5	14.8	14.1	16.0	7.6	71.7	10.0	17.0	1.3
Humboldt County	41.1	55.2	28.3	41.5	0.0	0.0	30.0	22.1	2 516	64.5	12.9	14.3	14.2	5.7	70.9	12.8	16.1	0.3
Ida County	40.8	53.1	29.5	40.8	60.0	84.6	0.0	50.0	1 923	66.9	12.0	12.0	14.3	6.4	71.8	9.7	17.4	1.1
Iowa County	50.1	59.7	41.0	50.1	72.7	0.0	27.3	38.7	4 044	69.6	12.3	13.5	18.5	15.4	73.2	12.9	13.3	0.6
Jackson County	42.9	52.9	33.6	42.9	77.8	35.0	57.1	38.8	5 070	65.9	9.6	17.3	18.6	11.3	73.0	10.5	15.7	0.8
Jasper County	45.2	54.1	36.2	45.5	18.1	24.1	21.6	43.0	8 853	61.9	13.2	18.9	16.2	9.1	77.2	12.4	10.1	0.3
Jefferson County	39.0	51.1	27.5	39.6	22.1	0.0	16.1	38.5	3 838	52.0	20.0	21.8	9.2	5.7	72.7	10.7	16.0	0.6
Johnson County	40.3	46.8	33.9	41.4	31.4	42.9	27.9	36.2	21 634	59.2	18.8	15.2	9.8	14.3	60.6	31.7	7.4	0.2
Jones County	43.0	50.2	35.3	43.9	14.8	35.7	41.7	24.7	4 560	67.0	10.3	17.9	20.3	10.7	72.1	13.9	13.4	0.6
Keokuk County	40.1	50.3	30.8	40.1	37.5	0.0	37.5	63.4	2 813	61.2	17.9	15.4	12.0	3.6	66.8	15.2	17.2	0.8
Kossuth County	38.1	49.9	26.9	38.1	0.0	0.0	24.1	49.5	4 328	66.8	14.7	13.1	15.3	6.6	68.7	10.5	19.7	1.0
Lee County	40.5	50.6	30.7	40.9	33.9	34.1	44.7	43.5	8 814	54.6	17.0	19.8	9.8	2.1	77.4	11.5	10.6	0.5
Linn County	48.6	58.7	39.2	49.1	37.2	45.6	51.5	42.2	46 414	58.1	16.5	18.3	11.8	11.7	82.6	9.9	7.4	0.1
Louisa County	43.3	55.4	31.4	43.2	15.4	0.0	29.5	45.4	3 160	56.7	16.3	13.7	5.8	6.1	75.4	11.9	11.8	0.9
Lucas County	38.2	50.0	27.4	38.1	100.0	100.0	0.0	71.4	2 275	49.6	19.5	18.5	3.5	0.3	72.3	13.5	13.0	1.2
Lyon County	41.4	53.9	29.5	41.7	10.0	50.0	0.0	8.7	3 254	73.6	13.1	7.3	16.3	10.5	69.1	8.3	21.8	0.8
Madison County	46.9	56.7	37.6	47.0	80.0	66.7	10.8	37.5	3 637	60.5	17.7	16.3	12.2	9.8	69.7	15.1	14.8	0.5
Mahaska County	41.1	53.9	28.8	41.3	0.0	36.9	57.0	23.8	5 543	53.1	19.5	16.8	5.3	5.4	76.1	9.8	13.9	0.3
Marion County	42.0	51.8	32.5	42.0	32.0	67.6	52.6	37.0	7 953	61.3	16.1	16.4	13.1	10.0	75.9	13.2	10.5	0.3
Marshall County	42.1	51.8	32.5	42.8	39.6	20.6	35.0	34.0	9 414	50.7	17.7	22.5	8.6	6.4	75.1	14.7	10.0	0.1
Mills County	46.3	53.7	39.1	46.4	52.0	47.5	39.4	47.5	3 706	60.0	17.1	18.3	13.7	12.0	65.9	21.2	12.4	0.4
Mitchell County	38.5	50.2	27.6	38.5	100.0	0.0	X	0.0	2 843	65.7	16.3	13.7	14.8	8.9	66.4	11.2	21.6	0.7
Monona County	37.3	48.4	27.2	37.5	0.0	20.8	16.7	3.7	2 220	59.0	16.3	17.5	11.9	0.7	66.7	14.6	18.0	0.8
Monroe County	41.6	56.4	32.3	41.8	100.0	29.4	X	0.0	1 925	54.5	17.0	15.6	5.5	-0.4	74.7	12.9	11.5	0.9
Montgomery County	41.6	50.1	34.2	41.6	X	X	91.7	33.0	2 810	55.7	12.1	20.8	11.9	5.0	72.9	12.5	14.0	0.7
Muscatine County	43.4	55.9	31.8	44.3	42.4	46.1	48.3	36.1	10 637	52.7	19.1	19.6	7.7	6.0	77.0	13.2	9.5	0.4
O'Brien County	37.9	49.9	26.7	38.2	40.6	15.4	30.8	23.8	3 676	68.6	16.7	10.1	14.3	7.5	70.4	12.8	16.2	0.6
Osceola County	43.8	56.9	31.7	44.0	33.3	22.2	0.0	42.0	1 780	72.5	11.1	9.3	17.2	10.7	68.6	10.9	19.7	0.8
Page County	38.1	45.2	30.8	39.2	0.0	24.2	9.7	7.5	3 589	61.2	11.1	17.9	14.5	5.3	70.1	15.7	13.5	0.6
Palo Alto County	38.9	51.8	27.2	39.3	X	16.7	0.0	12.5	2 421	63.9	12.7	15.1	14.4	7.4	66.4	14.0	18.8	0.8
Plymouth County	44.4	57.3	32.2	44.6	60.7	0.0	60.0	20.1	6 869	69.7	13.6	10.4	15.5	13.4	73.3	9.6	16.4	0.7
Pocahontas County	37.2	52.7	22.9	37.2	0.0	0.0	75.0	41.3	2 158	65.2	14.2	11.0	11.6	4.1	64.7	15.4	18.9	1.0
Polk County	50.1	58.7	42.4	51.3	38.8	38.5	46.1	41.3	91 459	54.2	17.4	19.7	9.3	11.6	79.8	12.6	7.5	0.2
Pottawattamie County	46.8	55.0	39.2	47.1	30.6	40.4	43.3	44.9	21 342	52.5	12.9	23.5	11.4	8.9	79.0	11.5	9.3	0.2
Poweshiek County	40.1	51.3	30.0	41.0	12.1	21.3	6.0	22.0	4 157	60.8	10.6	18.3	14.5	9.4	77.2	9.6	12.4	0.9
Ringgold County	35.2	44.7	26.6	35.4	0.0	31.3	7.7	0.0	1 277	54.7	17.0	19.5	9.6	-2.0	61.1	17.1	21.4	0.4
Sac County	39.5	50.8	28.9	39.7	45.5	0.0	12.5	25.0	2 731	69.0	6.3	16.9	21.3	9.6	67.8	11.2	20.0	1.1
Scott County	43.8	53.8	34.5	44.8	31.7	36.9	41.0	38.3	39 756	51.8	17.0	22.1	9.3	6.2	79.8	11.5	8.5	0.2
Shelby County	41.9	53.5	30.9	42.1	0.0	0.0	34.2	14.0	3 397	71.4	14.8	10.9	17.7	9.7	68.8	11.9	18.7	0.6
Sioux County	38.0	51.9	24.8	38.1	37.0	90.9	18.0	40.4	8 451	71.9	17.3	7.4	14.7	14.7	74.4	9.4	15.3	0.9
Story County	35.6	41.6	29.3	37.1	19.8	20.5	17.4	28.5	14 800	63.5	16.8	13.8	12.7	12.7	59.4	32.9	7.4	0.3
Tama County	40.7	50.7	31.3	41.7	57.1	23.2	46.6	37.4	4 471	59.0	14.6	16.8	11.2	6.8	68.8	14.9	15.4	0.9
Taylor County	39.3	50.7	28.7	39.3	X	50.0	33.3	40.4	1 575	64.1	12.4	16.8	16.3	5.0	64.3	16.5	18.3	0.8
Union County	43.4	53.1	34.7	43.6	0.0	0.0	48.6	32.3	2 800	57.6	13.7	19.9	12.9	9.2	67.7	16.9	14.5	0.9
Van Buren County	39.6	48.9	30.3	39.7	X	25.0	0.0	18.8	1 857	56.9	18.1	16.6	8.9	6.2	69.1	12.0	18.0	0.9
Wapello County	36.6	44.9	29.0	36.7	45.4	16.7	36.4	32.0	8 025	50.9	14.6	22.4	8.7	-0.9	77.2	12.7	9.3	0.8
Warren County	49.9	58.1	42.3	50.0	61.3	64.5	46.0	41.1	10 706	64.5	13.1	16.6	16.5	17.7	75.0	14.9	9.7	0.4
Washington County	46.0	56.9	36.2	46.2	22.6	23.8	37.5	39.6	5 155	65.9	14.9	15.5	16.8	14.0	64.0	17.1	18.2	0.7
Wayne County	37.9	46.4	30.0	38.2	0.0	0.0	15.0	39.3	1 527	55.7	17.7	15.6	6.7	2.9	63.0	15.4	20.1	1.6
Webster County	39.3	46.4	32.4	40.3	27.7	16.5	31.4	24.9	9 410	55.6	14.4	20.7	11.7	6.1	77.8	12.0	9.7	0.5
Winnebago County	43.3	53.6	33.6	43.8	75.0	41.7	3.3	27.3	2 720	68.1	11.6	14.8	18.3	11.9	75.7	8.8	14.9	0.6
Winneshiek County	39.3	48.4	30.7	39.7	12.2	0.0	17.9	32.8	4 774	78.2	10.0	8.8	22.4	15.0	73.4	10.8	15.0	0.7
Woodbury County	44.0	53.2	35.4	44.6	36.4	24.6	53.5	38.8	26 918	53.3	14.8	21.3	10.0	9.8	80.8	10.3	8.6	0.3
Worth County	43.1	53.2	33.5	43.2	20.0	86.7	65.0	41.5	1 858	68.5	8.6	16.8	20.7	10.9	74.5	10.3	14.5	0.7
Wright County	41.7	54.0	30.2	41.5	62.1	35.7	47.6	48.3	3 396	64.3	14.2	15.6	15.3	5.9	74.2	12.1	12.9	0.7
KANSAS	43.9	54.5	33.8	44.7	38.4	40.4	40.0	40.1	680 064	51.6	20.8	18.9	5.9	6.3	73.3	15.5	10.8	0.4
Allen County	38.9	48.4	30.2	39.4	22.6	27.1	22.2	41.2	3 435	53.7	11.9	24.8	13.9	7.3	70.3	15.8	13.3	0.5
Anderson County	37.9	48.2	28.4	38.2	22.2	27.3	0.0	37.5	2 015	62.8	14.1	15.1	13.3	3.7	65.5	16.7	17.1	0.7
Atchison County	40.5	47.9	33.7	41.3	34.9	28.9	45.5	24.1	4 044	52.6	17.8	22.4	10.4	5.6	74.4	15.7	9.8	0.1

[1] Hispanic or Latino persons may be of any race.

Table B-3. States and Counties — Education, Labor Force, and Income

STATE County	Percent who worked at home	Percent of the population 5 years and over with a disability	Veterans as a percent of the population 18 years and over	Occupation for employed population 16 years and over (percent)						Industry for employed population 16 years and over (percent)					
				Management, professional, and related occupations	Service occupations	Sales and office occupations	Farming, fishing, and forestry occupations	Construction, extraction, and maintenance occupations	Production, transportation and material moving occupations	Agriculture, forestry, fishing, and mining	Construction and manufacturing	Wholesale and retail trade	Transportation and warehousing, and utilities	Service industries	Public administration
	42	43	44	45	46	47	48	49	50	51	52	53	54	55	56
IOWA—Cont'd															
Guthrie County	7.0	17.8	15.1	31.5	16.0	22.7	2.5	10.5	16.8	10.2	20.0	15.4	5.7	44.8	3.9
Hamilton County	5.1	16.9	13.1	30.2	13.8	21.0	2.3	9.4	23.2	8.8	29.5	12.4	5.4	40.6	3.4
Hancock County	8.3	14.7	14.3	28.3	11.5	20.4	3.0	8.3	28.4	11.0	33.7	14.2	5.2	33.4	2.5
Hardin County	6.5	19.8	14.1	29.8	14.3	22.8	2.6	9.6	21.0	10.5	23.5	16.9	4.1	41.7	3.3
Harrison County	5.8	16.4	14.3	29.2	14.8	24.6	1.2	12.6	17.7	7.0	22.8	15.2	7.0	45.3	2.7
Henry County	3.3	19.4	12.4	25.6	15.4	22.1	0.9	8.6	27.3	3.8	31.1	16.8	4.8	38.9	4.6
Howard County	10.6	16.9	12.8	27.0	13.9	19.4	4.1	9.5	26.1	13.1	32.6	12.4	3.9	35.4	2.6
Humboldt County	5.5	17.9	14.6	29.5	12.2	24.6	2.1	10.6	20.9	9.1	27.4	15.9	7.0	36.2	4.5
Ida County	7.8	18.8	14.9	29.7	14.9	23.0	2.8	8.1	21.6	11.3	28.2	13.4	6.2	38.9	2.0
Iowa County	7.3	13.9	13.3	28.0	13.9	23.0	1.3	9.0	24.7	8.7	32.9	14.3	3.5	38.0	2.6
Jackson County	7.2	18.2	14.6	25.3	13.9	23.0	1.6	11.2	25.0	8.0	31.5	15.3	4.4	38.2	2.7
Jasper County	5.1	15.4	13.4	28.8	13.0	26.1	0.6	7.9	23.7	4.3	31.4	14.7	4.4	41.3	3.9
Jefferson County	8.1	14.3	11.8	35.0	13.3	26.1	0.8	8.0	16.8	5.1	22.7	16.4	2.9	50.5	2.5
Johnson County	3.1	12.0	8.5	43.3	15.5	26.1	0.3	6.0	8.9	1.4	12.1	13.3	2.8	68.1	2.4
Jones County	7.4	16.8	15.1	29.0	14.7	23.7	1.7	10.1	20.9	8.2	25.9	16.3	4.4	40.2	5.1
Keokuk County	5.8	18.1	13.1	27.5	16.0	20.4	2.5	11.2	22.4	10.9	26.0	14.6	6.0	39.5	2.9
Kossuth County	9.3	15.8	14.2	32.2	15.8	21.2	2.5	8.8	19.5	12.7	23.7	14.6	4.6	41.4	2.8
Lee County	3.8	21.0	15.5	23.2	16.2	20.7	1.5	10.5	27.9	3.9	33.5	13.2	5.4	39.3	4.7
Linn County	2.9	15.1	14.4	34.8	12.4	29.6	0.3	8.1	14.7	1.0	24.4	16.0	4.4	51.6	2.6
Louisa County	4.6	16.9	12.9	22.5	13.3	19.6	1.7	11.2	31.6	6.1	39.1	12.9	5.6	32.9	3.3
Lucas County	6.2	19.6	12.8	22.2	16.6	25.2	2.3	10.7	23.0	6.3	17.0	29.9	6.2	36.6	4.0
Lyon County	10.4	14.2	10.9	29.9	14.2	22.8	2.9	10.6	19.6	12.8	25.1	14.0	5.2	40.8	2.1
Madison County	5.8	14.8	14.4	32.4	11.5	28.0	1.3	12.5	14.3	6.5	19.0	16.4	6.1	47.8	4.3
Mahaska County	5.9	19.0	12.5	27.7	13.2	22.3	1.5	9.7	25.7	6.1	36.6	14.3	4.5	36.3	2.3
Marion County	4.4	16.7	13.7	30.5	14.5	24.3	0.6	7.6	22.6	3.5	34.1	11.6	3.0	45.1	2.6
Marshall County	3.4	17.4	15.2	27.6	16.8	22.7	0.8	8.9	23.1	3.6	31.4	13.6	4.1	44.0	3.2
Mills County	5.4	17.3	15.7	30.1	20.1	24.1	0.9	11.1	13.7	5.0	17.0	13.5	6.2	53.7	4.6
Mitchell County	11.6	16.4	14.6	31.9	14.2	19.5	2.6	11.1	20.7	14.0	28.5	13.9	3.6	38.2	1.8
Monona County	6.4	19.8	16.5	28.6	17.1	24.9	1.9	12.4	15.2	10.9	17.7	15.0	5.4	46.8	4.2
Monroe County	3.2	24.6	13.8	27.1	11.8	23.2	1.4	8.3	28.2	5.8	35.8	14.9	4.8	34.4	4.3
Montgomery County	5.2	21.5	13.4	24.4	15.9	23.7	3.1	11.3	21.6	7.5	27.5	17.1	5.1	39.2	3.6
Muscatine County	3.7	19.2	12.6	26.1	15.7	21.4	0.6	9.1	27.2	2.8	37.2	13.0	6.1	38.2	2.8
O'Brien County	6.2	16.1	13.3	28.3	15.0	19.8	2.5	10.5	23.9	10.3	24.9	14.2	6.5	41.3	2.7
Osceola County	9.1	14.8	13.7	28.9	13.9	18.2	3.6	11.5	23.8	12.7	31.5	9.5	6.8	36.5	3.0
Page County	5.3	21.4	14.3	28.0	16.9	20.5	1.7	7.6	25.3	5.8	29.0	15.3	3.6	41.7	4.6
Palo Alto County	8.3	15.8	14.3	31.6	16.6	20.8	2.0	10.0	19.0	10.3	20.8	12.0	6.5	47.8	2.6
Plymouth County	7.4	13.7	13.8	31.2	14.6	24.1	2.2	9.3	18.6	8.0	26.0	16.0	6.2	41.0	2.8
Pocahontas County	10.3	16.6	17.8	35.5	15.2	21.2	2.5	7.9	17.8	15.4	20.9	12.9	5.2	42.0	3.6
Polk County	3.1	16.5	12.3	36.1	13.6	31.0	0.2	7.7	11.4	0.6	14.8	16.3	5.1	58.4	4.8
Pottawattamie County	3.2	19.5	15.3	26.5	15.6	30.0	0.4	10.3	17.3	2.5	18.2	17.1	8.4	50.5	3.3
Poweshiek County	5.5	18.9	12.5	29.7	17.0	21.7	1.4	8.2	22.1	5.8	26.2	12.0	5.2	48.9	1.9
Ringgold County	8.2	19.3	14.5	33.3	16.4	17.7	3.4	13.0	16.2	14.0	19.5	11.9	5.3	45.4	3.9
Sac County	8.2	17.3	15.1	28.2	16.1	23.8	3.0	9.8	19.0	12.3	19.8	15.4	6.2	42.6	3.6
Scott County	3.1	16.3	14.2	31.7	15.4	27.7	0.3	8.1	16.9	0.9	23.1	17.5	5.5	48.6	4.3
Shelby County	8.5	16.0	15.1	29.0	14.5	27.1	2.3	10.4	16.7	10.4	16.4	22.6	6.9	41.2	2.5
Sioux County	7.3	11.2	9.9	31.0	16.6	21.9	3.6	8.6	18.4	9.7	24.6	15.0	3.7	45.6	1.4
Story County	3.5	10.5	9.2	43.0	15.1	25.2	1.0	6.5	9.1	2.1	13.7	13.6	2.8	62.6	5.2
Tama County	6.8	17.5	15.2	26.0	18.2	23.3	1.7	10.3	20.5	9.1	23.1	13.0	5.1	46.0	3.7
Taylor County	8.1	20.9	14.7	25.3	17.0	18.5	2.9	9.0	27.4	10.5	28.2	12.8	5.4	36.0	6.9
Union County	4.6	18.4	14.7	26.3	15.4	22.5	1.2	10.6	24.0	5.1	26.1	16.0	5.7	43.0	4.2
Van Buren County	9.3	20.6	14.4	27.2	14.3	18.1	1.7	10.2	28.5	10.4	31.4	12.8	5.0	36.9	3.5
Wapello County	2.9	23.4	16.0	24.5	17.6	22.4	0.9	10.1	24.7	2.5	28.9	17.0	5.3	42.8	3.5
Warren County	4.5	13.7	12.9	31.3	13.5	30.3	0.5	11.2	13.3	2.0	18.3	15.6	6.2	52.2	5.7
Washington County	9.0	17.9	12.4	31.5	14.0	24.0	1.7	10.8	18.1	9.0	23.6	15.8	3.9	44.8	2.8
Wayne County	10.1	21.7	13.7	30.2	13.8	22.7	2.6	9.7	21.0	12.6	24.9	14.0	5.6	40.3	2.5
Webster County	3.0	18.2	14.2	28.0	16.5	25.2	1.2	9.4	19.8	4.2	22.8	17.9	6.0	45.0	4.2
Winnebago County	6.5	15.6	12.5	27.3	13.6	19.0	1.5	10.0	28.6	7.1	38.6	11.5	4.4	36.3	2.1
Winneshiek County	7.7	13.9	10.2	33.4	15.4	22.6	2.7	8.5	17.4	10.4	22.0	14.7	2.8	47.4	2.7
Woodbury County	3.0	17.9	13.8	27.9	15.9	27.5	0.6	8.7	19.3	1.9	27.5	15.9	4.9	46.5	3.2
Worth County	6.2	18.2	16.1	22.7	13.3	23.6	2.2	11.2	27.0	9.1	33.0	17.1	4.1	34.1	2.5
Wright County	4.8	17.7	12.9	28.2	14.8	19.9	2.6	8.9	25.6	10.2	25.9	13.0	7.7	41.2	2.0
KANSAS	4.0	17.6	13.5	33.9	14.4	25.8	1.0	9.9	15.0	3.8	21.5	14.8	5.2	50.1	4.4
Allen County	4.6	21.0	14.5	24.9	16.1	21.5	1.1	10.3	26.1	5.4	33.4	14.0	5.0	38.7	3.5
Anderson County	4.8	22.6	13.6	28.0	13.4	22.3	1.7	14.4	20.1	10.5	23.5	16.1	8.2	38.0	3.7
Atchison County	3.6	17.7	13.6	30.7	18.1	20.4	0.7	10.9	19.1	4.2	24.9	13.1	5.2	46.8	5.8

STATE County	Median house-hold income	Median family income				Median nonfamily house-hold income	Median income for full-year, full-time workers		Per capita income	Households by source of income (percent)					House-holds with income over $100,000 (percent)	+/- U.S. percent for income over $100,000 (percent)	House-holds with income below poverty (percent)	Families with children with income below poverty (percent)
		All families	Married-couple	Male house-holder	Female house-holder		Men	Women		With earnings	With interest, dividend, or rental income	With Social Security income	With public assis-tance income	With retire-ment income				
	57	58	59	60	61	62	63	64	65	66	67	68	69	70	71	72	73	74

IOWA—Cont'd																		
Guthrie County	36 495	43 601	50 127	35 234	20 882	20 441	31 554	22 778	19 726	77.4	44.7	36.0	2.9	13.3	6.6	-5.7	8.7	7.3
Hamilton County	38 658	45 771	56 557	27 350	23 125	21 439	31 059	24 383	18 801	79.1	43.6	33.3	2.4	13.9	4.9	-7.4	6.4	7.2
Hancock County	37 703	44 248	50 102	23 669	19 297	22 250	30 231	21 076	17 957	78.7	45.9	32.3	1.9	11.9	4.5	-7.8	6.9	7.3
Hardin County	35 429	41 891	47 269	30 000	17 222	20 788	31 378	21 950	17 537	76.2	46.1	35.8	3.1	13.8	4.2	-8.1	7.9	8.5
Harrison County	38 141	44 586	51 544	27 308	17 431	20 102	31 068	22 305	17 662	77.5	38.5	34.4	2.2	11.8	4.6	-7.7	7.5	8.0
Henry County	39 087	46 985	53 667	23 241	19 844	18 891	32 604	24 070	18 192	78.7	38.2	29.6	2.6	14.6	5.7	-6.6	10.1	10.2
Howard County	34 641	43 284	49 395	30 938	23 661	18 597	29 618	22 339	17 842	77.0	53.1	35.4	3.0	11.0	4.7	-7.6	9.1	6.3
Humboldt County	38 201	46 510	53 531	27 404	15 667	20 547	31 767	23 153	18 300	74.3	49.8	38.1	2.1	15.1	5.7	-6.6	8.2	9.9
Ida County	34 805	43 179	46 705	27 750	18 036	18 373	30 310	20 547	18 675	77.1	48.6	39.8	2.4	10.1	4.6	-7.7	9.4	8.6
Iowa County	41 222	48 946	54 740	28 000	22 656	23 586	31 620	25 315	18 884	81.4	46.6	30.4	1.8	13.7	4.1	-8.2	6.9	4.9
Jackson County	34 529	42 526	49 183	26 250	15 862	19 375	30 590	21 226	17 329	77.3	45.3	33.0	2.6	15.9	3.7	-8.6	9.9	12.0
Jasper County	41 683	50 071	59 912	31 250	19 494	23 052	37 119	25 295	19 622	79.2	43.6	30.8	2.1	18.0	6.3	-6.0	7.2	6.5
Jefferson County	33 851	43 819	51 843	30 815	22 944	21 235	33 695	24 232	19 579	81.6	42.4	25.9	3.2	12.3	8.2	-4.1	12.0	12.3
Johnson County	40 060	60 112	69 133	33 629	22 431	24 174	37 358	30 638	22 220	89.3	46.9	15.5	1.8	10.7	11.9	-0.4	15.5	7.7
Jones County	37 449	44 269	49 407	25 313	19 519	22 163	31 826	23 312	17 816	78.8	44.4	32.0	2.9	13.1	4.6	-7.7	8.7	9.5
Keokuk County	34 025	41 818	45 000	26 250	16 750	18 654	29 423	22 950	17 120	74.7	45.7	38.1	2.6	13.1	4.1	-8.2	10.3	11.0
Kossuth County	34 562	41 159	47 778	24 318	15 069	19 935	30 719	21 004	16 598	75.9	49.0	37.1	2.5	10.2	4.7	-7.6	10.1	10.3
Lee County	36 193	42 658	50 364	31 250	17 602	20 631	33 967	22 728	18 430	75.9	38.7	32.0	3.4	17.2	5.4	-6.9	10.4	12.2
Linn County	46 206	56 494	66 360	34 736	23 508	27 321	39 761	27 192	22 977	83.5	46.2	24.3	2.5	16.4	10.2	-2.1	6.7	6.9
Louisa County	39 086	43 972	49 167	30 395	18 281	22 222	31 660	22 911	17 644	79.9	36.4	27.9	2.9	14.4	4.7	-7.6	8.9	10.7
Lucas County	30 876	38 352	49 074	17 153	17 727	15 321	31 849	21 539	15 341	73.6	35.9	36.5	4.3	15.8	2.8	-9.5	13.6	13.9
Lyon County	36 878	45 144	49 692	25 962	21 364	19 427	30 496	20 140	16 081	78.3	48.6	33.8	2.8	9.8	4.4	-7.9	8.4	6.7
Madison County	41 845	48 289	55 137	31 000	21 333	20 153	32 070	25 519	19 357	81.2	41.3	30.0	2.3	12.8	7.7	-4.6	8.1	5.3
Mahaska County	37 314	43 557	49 304	28 125	22 773	21 716	34 209	24 082	18 232	77.6	41.4	30.8	3.2	12.2	4.7	-7.6	10.3	10.7
Marion County	42 401	50 052	57 392	30 833	21 333	20 299	37 255	26 059	18 717	80.0	42.8	31.2	2.6	15.3	6.4	-5.9	7.9	8.5
Marshall County	38 268	46 627	53 315	31 818	18 750	22 266	35 056	25 095	19 176	79.3	40.2	29.6	3.5	15.4	5.5	-6.8	9.7	11.7
Mills County	42 428	49 592	55 625	25 250	18 555	22 244	32 707	25 518	18 736	81.8	38.9	27.3	2.7	13.6	8.0	-4.3	7.8	9.6
Mitchell County	34 843	41 233	47 757	26 635	20 132	20 148	31 078	22 800	16 809	73.8	53.7	39.9	2.2	14.5	3.5	-8.8	9.9	10.8
Monona County	33 235	41 172	47 308	21 500	20 595	16 731	28 990	20 650	17 477	72.5	42.1	40.6	2.4	14.1	4.0	-8.3	10.9	8.4
Monroe County	34 877	41 611	49 554	27 019	24 375	16 074	32 371	22 116	17 155	72.2	38.0	39.4	4.8	21.4	4.3	-8.0	8.6	9.6
Montgomery County	33 214	40 129	45 734	24 830	16 955	18 074	29 610	21 631	16 373	74.9	42.9	35.1	3.7	15.6	4.0	-8.3	10.4	11.3
Muscatine County	41 803	48 373	54 950	30 032	20 016	22 978	37 364	25 667	19 625	82.0	41.2	26.6	3.7	15.5	7.3	-5.0	8.4	9.1
O'Brien County	35 758	42 959	50 456	28 393	20 000	20 752	31 339	20 948	17 281	77.5	49.5	36.6	1.6	11.9	3.7	-8.6	8.4	6.4
Osceola County	34 274	41 977	51 287	25 893	22 768	16 798	30 193	20 887	16 463	76.6	47.6	34.4	2.6	11.2	4.8	-7.5	7.8	6.4
Page County	35 466	42 446	50 446	16 618	16 250	19 502	33 872	22 367	16 670	75.7	41.0	36.2	3.8	14.2	4.5	-7.8	12.2	14.9
Palo Alto County	32 409	41 808	46 781	27 143	15 682	19 119	30 251	20 202	17 733	77.7	44.5	37.2	3.3	10.6	4.8	-7.5	10.8	10.7
Plymouth County	41 638	50 009	56 240	32 083	22 708	21 650	35 319	24 117	19 442	80.4	48.7	30.6	1.9	9.7	7.7	-4.6	6.3	6.5
Pocahontas County	33 362	40 568	46 380	26 500	19 306	17 421	29 033	21 294	17 006	74.1	48.1	37.5	3.3	12.9	4.7	-7.6	9.8	12.3
Polk County	46 116	56 560	65 424	31 798	23 682	28 841	38 349	29 042	23 654	85.0	40.4	22.1	2.7	13.6	11.7	-0.6	7.6	8.3
Pottawattamie County	40 089	47 105	56 484	28 448	20 348	22 759	32 243	25 075	19 275	81.4	36.2	29.0	3.4	15.3	6.8	-5.5	8.5	10.3
Poweshiek County	37 836	46 599	55 182	26 725	21 986	22 489	32 489	23 677	18 629	78.0	43.3	31.8	2.8	14.7	6.3	-6.0	9.9	10.5
Ringgold County	29 110	34 472	40 500	20 714	19 583	14 478	25 788	21 293	15 023	70.3	41.6	42.7	4.7	16.2	3.3	-9.0	14.8	14.8
Sac County	32 874	40 504	45 117	25 500	16 118	17 076	27 145	20 804	16 902	74.4	47.9	38.6	3.3	11.6	3.7	-8.6	10.2	12.1
Scott County	42 701	52 045	62 332	30 763	19 175	24 610	40 424	26 367	21 310	82.3	42.1	23.4	3.6	17.7	9.5	-2.8	10.0	12.1
Shelby County	37 442	44 681	50 631	22 750	17 697	20 967	30 806	20 980	16 969	77.6	47.7	35.1	1.8	10.3	4.7	-7.6	7.7	6.1
Sioux County	40 536	45 846	49 648	33 281	21 250	20 056	32 420	20 628	16 532	82.2	51.0	29.5	2.0	8.6	5.4	-6.9	6.8	6.8
Story County	40 442	55 472	62 123	31 172	21 310	23 411	37 570	27 873	19 944	86.4	49.3	19.2	1.5	12.6	9.5	-2.8	14.5	7.2
Tama County	37 419	43 646	47 736	25 667	19 531	22 133	31 584	23 660	17 097	77.2	43.5	33.7	2.8	12.9	4.3	-8.0	9.8	11.9
Taylor County	31 297	37 194	44 750	33 750	20 156	16 037	27 174	19 583	15 082	73.8	41.8	38.6	4.4	13.1	2.4	-9.9	12.6	11.5
Union County	31 905	41 453	47 727	27 946	21 094	18 472	28 527	21 255	16 690	76.2	40.5	33.2	2.2	14.5	3.7	-8.6	12.0	12.1
Van Buren County	31 094	36 420	42 297	25 938	21 563	16 699	28 447	21 826	15 748	74.7	39.4	37.0	2.5	17.1	2.9	-9.4	13.3	11.1
Wapello County	32 188	39 224	50 179	26 759	16 234	18 092	31 885	22 014	16 500	73.4	33.9	34.2	5.0	20.0	3.8	-8.5	13.7	16.6
Warren County	50 349	56 344	65 179	34 732	25 054	24 662	37 880	27 367	20 558	85.6	41.6	24.7	2.6	15.6	9.3	-3.0	5.3	6.0
Washington County	39 103	45 636	51 738	31 125	21 063	21 850	30 348	23 898	18 221	80.4	45.8	31.7	2.8	14.3	4.5	-7.8	7.7	8.0
Wayne County	29 380	35 534	42 204	23 125	18 393	17 309	26 599	19 410	15 613	72.4	39.2	40.9	4.4	15.4	4.1	-8.2	15.1	14.9
Webster County	35 334	43 772	51 811	25 208	21 464	20 802	31 818	23 865	17 857	77.7	40.6	32.8	4.1	14.8	4.7	-7.6	10.2	10.7
Winnebago County	38 381	47 306	52 332	29 844	19 607	22 309	31 633	23 481	18 494	77.3	47.1	33.5	2.3	12.4	4.3	-8.0	8.2	8.7
Winneshiek County	38 908	45 966	53 132	25 729	21 964	22 208	30 568	21 865	17 047	80.7	53.9	31.0	1.9	11.8	5.6	-6.7	10.3	6.6
Woodbury County	38 509	46 499	55 556	25 768	18 438	21 995	32 360	23 809	18 771	81.2	36.3	28.1	3.0	14.2	7.1	-5.2	9.7	11.0
Worth County	36 444	41 763	45 946	25 000	21 161	22 204	29 151	21 596	16 952	76.8	46.5	33.4	2.6	13.0	2.9	-9.4	9.0	9.2
Wright County	36 197	44 043	49 949	28 750	18 088	20 134	30 328	22 242	18 247	75.7	43.9	36.8	2.6	13.0	4.4	-7.9	7.6	6.8
KANSAS	40 624	49 624	56 918	29 587	21 194	23 002	36 188	25 978	20 506	81.8	39.1	26.2	2.4	14.8	9.3	-3.0	10.1	10.0
Allen County	31 481	39 117	44 514	25 766	14 281	17 443	28 109	20 087	15 640	75.7	38.0	35.8	4.3	16.3	3.3	-9.0	13.8	17.1
Anderson County	33 244	39 101	46 071	28 750	22 009	19 289	30 414	21 259	16 458	73.5	43.0	38.6	2.9	17.0	3.3	-9.0	12.4	14.9
Atchison County	34 355	40 614	48 221	28 250	20 670	18 956	31 380	21 098	15 207	77.5	34.3	31.7	3.4	15.9	3.9	-8.4	13.5	10.9

Table B-3. States and Counties — Education, Labor Force, and Income

STATE/County code	MSA/PMSA/NECMA code[1]	STATE County	High school graduates			College graduates		College graduates (percent)				
			Total population 25 years and over	Percent with a high school diploma or less	Percent with a high school diploma or more	Percent with a bachelor's degree or more	+/− U.S. percent with bachelor's degree or more	Non-Hispanic White	Black or African American	American Indian and Alaska Native	Asian, Hawaiian, and Pacific Islander	Hispanic or Latino[2]
			1	2	3	4	5	6	7	8	9	10
		KANSAS—Cont'd										
20 007	...	Barber County	3 646	47.0	85.8	21.0	−3.4	21.2	0.0	0.0	0.0	22.2
20 009	...	Barton County	18 265	49.1	82.3	16.6	−7.8	17.5	4.4	26.8	53.5	1.3
20 011	...	Bourbon County	9 965	47.5	84.2	17.8	−6.6	18.2	6.7	23.5	X	15.6
20 013	...	Brown County	7 080	54.5	84.6	19.0	−5.4	18.8	39.8	15.0	54.8	15.2
20 015	9040	Butler County	37 560	45.0	87.3	20.4	−4.0	20.8	7.6	13.3	33.6	8.5
20 017	...	Chase County	2 081	52.6	87.1	19.6	−4.8	20.1	17.6	0.0	0.0	0.0
20 019	...	Chautauqua County	3 058	59.7	81.0	12.3	−12.1	12.1	X	18.2	37.5	13.6
20 021	...	Cherokee County	14 704	58.5	80.3	11.3	−13.1	11.2	5.4	17.9	19.4	5.4
20 023	...	Cheyenne County	2 257	50.2	85.5	16.0	−8.4	16.1	X	0.0	0.0	0.0
20 025	...	Clark County	1 640	40.1	87.4	22.1	−2.3	22.3	0.0	27.3	0.0	15.2
20 027	...	Clay County	6 026	52.5	87.0	16.5	−7.9	16.6	15.4	0.0	36.4	5.0
20 029	...	Cloud County	6 909	52.6	85.5	18.0	−6.4	17.8	0.0	29.4	46.2	50.0
20 031	...	Coffey County	5 932	53.7	86.9	20.1	−4.3	19.9	0.0	21.6	66.7	20.8
20 033	...	Comanche County	1 440	45.8	91.3	15.1	−9.3	15.0	X	X	100.0	18.2
20 035	...	Cowley County	22 982	45.6	85.4	18.3	−6.1	19.1	17.2	10.8	3.1	8.4
20 037	...	Crawford County	23 395	46.2	84.5	23.9	−0.5	24.2	9.5	16.5	53.5	11.3
20 039	...	Decatur County	2 479	53.6	86.4	15.4	−9.0	15.2	0.0	0.0	50.0	25.0
20 041	...	Dickinson County	13 156	52.9	86.4	15.2	−9.2	15.3	0.0	7.1	33.3	6.4
20 043	...	Doniphan County	5 176	56.6	80.2	14.8	−9.6	15.0	9.1	0.0	23.1	10.5
20 045	4150	Douglas County	53 257	29.9	92.4	42.7	18.3	42.8	33.2	25.9	71.3	33.0
20 047	...	Edwards County	2 378	51.1	81.2	16.3	−8.1	17.3	37.5	33.3	54.5	0.0
20 049	...	Elk County	2 354	61.6	80.0	10.6	−13.8	10.8	X	0.0	X	0.0
20 051	...	Ellis County	16 278	42.7	87.2	29.2	4.8	29.2	60.0	0.0	56.9	12.1
20 053	...	Ellsworth County	4 660	50.7	84.8	16.4	−8.0	17.6	0.0	13.0	0.0	2.4
20 055	...	Finney County	22 196	57.5	67.4	14.3	−10.1	20.9	0.0	14.2	18.0	2.8
20 057	...	Ford County	18 632	53.2	69.9	16.4	−8.0	22.7	9.4	5.3	0.0	3.7
20 059	...	Franklin County	15 753	54.2	85.3	16.5	−7.9	16.8	12.7	8.6	46.5	6.3
20 061	...	Geary County	15 744	44.0	86.0	17.1	−7.3	19.4	10.3	21.3	14.6	12.8
20 063	...	Gove County	2 120	50.7	84.5	18.4	−6.0	18.7	0.0	0.0	X	0.0
20 065	...	Graham County	2 125	50.4	83.6	17.4	−7.0	17.0	20.6	22.2	66.7	37.5
20 067	...	Grant County................	4 712	56.5	71.5	15.2	−9.2	19.6	X	18.2	X	3.7
20 069	...	Gray County	3 536	52.1	73.6	16.3	−8.1	17.2	0.0	0.0	X	5.8
20 071	...	Greeley County	983	45.6	83.7	17.4	−7.0	18.6	X	0.0	X	1.5
20 073	...	Greenwood County	5 343	57.7	80.9	14.5	−9.9	14.8	X	0.0	6.9	0.0
20 075	...	Hamilton County...........	1 727	53.7	76.7	17.4	−7.0	20.0	0.0	0.0	25.0	2.2
20 077	...	Harper County	4 462	55.3	83.8	14.0	−10.4	13.9	44.0	0.0	33.3	11.8
20 079	9040	Harvey County	21 278	44.9	85.3	23.0	−1.4	24.3	19.8	2.1	12.7	5.3
20 081	...	Haskell County	2 505	50.6	74.8	17.5	−6.9	20.7	0.0	0.0	70.4	0.9
20 083	...	Hodgeman County	1 376	43.8	86.9	19.7	−4.7	20.3	0.0	0.0	X	0.0
20 085	...	Jackson County............	8 228	58.2	87.7	15.4	−9.0	15.8	11.4	11.9	63.6	10.2
20 087	...	Jefferson County	12 127	53.7	88.9	17.9	−6.5	17.9	17.4	30.4	20.0	19.8
20 089	...	Jewell County...............	2 798	51.9	87.6	13.8	−10.6	13.4	0.0	0.0	100.0	18.8
20 091	3760	Johnson County	295 829	22.6	94.9	47.7	23.3	48.5	41.1	26.6	59.4	25.3
20 093	...	Kearny County	2 592	51.9	75.8	15.0	−9.4	17.8	0.0	25.0	100.0	3.7
20 095	...	Kingman County...........	5 809	49.0	84.7	17.8	−6.6	17.5	100.0	40.0	85.7	20.0
20 097	...	Kiowa County	2 227	44.8	85.2	18.9	−5.5	19.2	X	0.0	33.3	0.0
20 099	...	Labette County	15 007	48.9	83.0	15.9	−8.5	16.1	5.1	11.4	80.0	19.3
20 101	...	Lane County................	1 491	45.6	88.5	18.5	−5.9	18.7	0.0	X	50.0	16.7
20 103	3760	Leavenworth County	44 792	47.4	86.5	23.1	−1.3	24.1	16.4	11.1	22.6	15.1
20 105	...	Lincoln County	2 548	50.6	85.0	17.4	−7.0	17.6	0.0	0.0	33.3	17.6
20 107	...	Linn County	6 538	58.6	80.9	12.7	−11.7	12.7	7.7	0.0	100.0	12.5
20 109	...	Logan County	2 058	52.0	86.7	17.5	−6.9	17.5	0.0	100.0	100.0	6.9
20 111	...	Lyon County................	20 559	50.0	81.8	23.0	−1.4	25.9	9.9	11.7	14.2	5.3
20 113	...	McPherson County.......	19 078	46.2	85.9	22.2	−2.2	22.0	20.6	30.8	42.9	18.4
20 115	...	Marion County	9 000	54.2	84.4	17.9	−6.5	18.3	0.0	0.0	0.0	6.8
20 117	...	Marshall County	7 460	60.6	85.1	13.2	−11.2	13.4	0.0	0.0	3.3	0.0
20 119	...	Meade County	2 946	48.2	80.3	19.6	−4.8	20.8	0.0	20.0	11.1	5.3
20 121	3760	Miami County	18 444	49.2	87.5	19.4	−5.0	19.7	7.1	17.9	36.2	4.7
20 123	...	Mitchell County............	4 645	48.1	88.1	16.9	−7.5	16.8	X	0.0	77.8	0.0
20 125	...	Montgomery County	24 090	49.0	81.2	16.0	−8.4	17.1	5.1	8.9	20.2	6.0
20 127	...	Morris County	4 224	56.1	84.7	16.0	−8.4	16.2	0.0	0.0	0.0	13.7
20 129	...	Morton County.............	2 165	52.7	81.9	17.6	−6.8	18.1	0.0	14.7	70.2	1.0
20 131	...	Nemaha County	7 038	62.5	83.7	14.6	−9.8	14.7	10.5	0.0	62.5	0.0
20 133	...	Neosho County	11 113	51.7	83.5	15.0	−9.4	15.1	12.9	29.9	0.0	2.7
20 135	...	Ness County................	2 498	52.1	84.4	17.9	−6.5	18.1	0.0	X	50.0	0.0
20 137	...	Norton County.............	4 178	52.8	84.8	15.4	−9.0	16.5	0.0	0.0	58.3	0.0

[1]MSA = Metropolitan Statistical Area. PMSA = Primary MSA. NECMA = New England County Metropolitan Area. See the Appendix A for explanation of these concepts. See Appendix B for list of metropolitan areas identified by type, with component counties.
[2]Hispanic or Latino persons may be of any race.

Table B-3. States and Counties — Education, Labor Force, and Income

STATE County	School enrollment			Population 16 to 19 years				Employment status, 2000			Work status in 1999 of the population 16 years and over (percent)		
											Worked in 1999		
	Grades kindergarten through 12	College or graduate school	Percent private	Number	Percent in armed forces	Percent high school graduates	Percent not enrolled, not grads, not in armed forces, not employed	Total population 16 years and over	Percent in labor force	Unemploy- ment rate	Full-time	Part-time	Did not work in 1999
	11	12	13	14	15	16	17	18	19	20	21	22	23
KANSAS—Cont'd													
Barber County	1 108	112	5.7	332	0.0	3.6	1.8	4 177	62.4	2.0	52.1	16.7	31.2
Barton County	5 651	1 206	9.7	1 968	0.6	5.9	4.4	21 773	65.9	5.3	55.0	15.6	29.4
Bourbon County	3 162	684	11.3	991	0.0	11.2	1.5	11 894	64.6	3.8	53.1	15.0	31.9
Brown County	2 160	349	5.0	648	0.0	10.2	6.2	8 269	63.5	5.8	53.9	14.1	32.0
Butler County	12 933	3 044	10.2	3 806	0.3	11.0	4.1	44 424	65.9	3.6	57.8	14.9	27.3
Chase County	599	86	4.7	186	0.0	5.9	5.9	2 405	65.5	2.7	57.8	14.5	27.7
Chautauqua County	874	124	6.8	262	0.0	4.6	2.3	3 499	52.1	4.8	44.6	14.1	41.3
Cherokee County	4 460	781	4.7	1 334	0.0	10.6	7.3	17 343	62.5	5.5	52.0	14.4	33.6
Cheyenne County	619	71	2.3	177	0.0	9.6	0.0	2 518	61.6	2.8	49.1	17.6	33.4
Clark County	499	56	1.8	157	0.0	8.3	1.9	1 863	62.5	2.6	54.6	15.1	30.3
Clay County	1 746	244	1.7	416	0.0	12.5	7.0	6 890	65.0	3.4	51.5	15.9	32.6
Cloud County	1 847	710	4.2	805	0.0	6.2	1.0	8 311	62.1	4.3	48.0	19.4	32.6
Coffey County	1 880	280	3.5	489	0.0	6.1	2.9	6 823	68.0	4.4	57.4	14.3	28.3
Comanche County	337	31	2.4	71	0.0	5.6	0.0	1 575	61.7	0.2	53.8	13.8	32.3
Cowley County	7 205	2 584	15.3	2 626	0.0	8.7	4.5	28 031	63.6	7.8	52.6	15.2	32.1
Crawford County	6 338	5 069	6.6	2 708	1.0	9.7	2.4	30 561	63.2	4.9	49.6	20.1	30.3
Decatur County	675	106	2.4	190	0.0	10.5	0.0	2 775	58.2	1.1	50.5	15.1	34.5
Dickinson County	3 963	663	5.5	1 057	0.6	7.4	4.4	14 977	67.3	3.2	56.9	16.2	26.9
Doniphan County	1 599	643	3.3	711	0.0	5.9	1.3	6 424	65.0	7.0	54.8	16.2	29.0
Douglas County	15 063	25 640	7.2	9 344	0.1	5.4	1.3	81 876	70.9	4.6	52.9	28.4	18.7
Edwards County	676	118	8.8	196	0.0	9.7	3.1	2 709	60.4	2.7	52.3	15.5	32.2
Elk County	603	92	3.6	137	0.0	12.4	2.9	2 612	52.5	4.7	45.7	12.7	41.6
Ellis County	4 663	4 298	8.0	2 324	0.0	10.5	1.9	22 244	69.9	4.1	53.8	23.2	23.0
Ellsworth County	1 085	177	3.6	349	0.6	10.9	0.9	5 380	57.5	3.5	52.9	15.4	31.7
Finney County	9 588	1 747	5.7	2 803	0.0	7.3	10.0	28 042	69.8	4.9	62.6	14.0	23.4
Ford County	7 038	1 285	6.4	2 167	0.0	9.6	8.8	23 513	68.3	4.9	60.1	13.1	26.7
Franklin County	5 217	1 069	12.9	1 428	0.0	8.3	2.5	18 763	68.2	3.5	59.5	14.6	25.9
Geary County	5 664	1 899	7.6	1 724	9.2	22.4	3.8	20 511	70.0	5.1	61.4	14.5	24.2
Gove County	640	61	2.3	179	0.0	6.1	2.2	2 384	63.4	1.9	50.3	19.6	30.1
Graham County	560	81	2.7	168	0.0	4.8	2.4	2 399	60.9	2.7	50.5	16.5	33.0
Grant County	1 954	199	6.7	510	0.0	11.8	6.7	5 602	65.6	4.7	60.7	13.5	25.8
Gray County	1 343	133	15.9	371	0.0	7.8	10.2	4 244	68.8	3.2	58.9	16.2	24.9
Greeley County	359	19	5.0	98	0.0	7.1	5.1	1 153	62.4	2.5	56.2	15.4	28.4
Greenwood County	1 418	168	2.0	455	0.0	11.0	11.4	6 103	58.9	4.3	48.8	14.8	36.4
Hamilton County............	584	63	6.8	158	0.0	4.4	3.8	2 008	60.8	2.0	51.5	17.6	30.9
Harper County	1 337	144	4.5	378	0.0	9.0	1.9	5 144	60.4	3.8	50.3	15.6	34.1
Harvey County	6 503	1 711	19.3	2 099	0.0	8.9	2.0	25 408	66.6	3.7	54.9	17.7	27.4
Haskell County	1 071	128	8.8	288	0.0	11.1	3.1	3 047	65.8	2.9	59.4	14.2	26.4
Hodgeman County	519	64	4.1	143	0.0	9.1	1.4	1 573	64.1	1.4	51.7	16.8	31.5
Jackson County.............	2 712	305	8.2	743	0.0	12.5	2.4	9 515	67.0	3.4	58.5	14.3	27.2
Jefferson County	3 942	491	5.8	1 081	0.0	11.3	2.1	14 016	66.9	3.4	59.3	13.1	27.6
Jewell County...............	656	73	1.8	175	0.0	5.7	1.7	3 073	60.3	2.3	49.1	16.8	34.1
Johnson County	88 153	24 951	17.1	23 106	0.0	8.0	1.7	342 691	73.9	2.3	62.9	16.6	20.5
Kearny County	1 147	134	5.5	309	0.0	8.7	7.1	3 155	63.9	2.9	58.3	13.7	28.0
Kingman County............	1 916	248	7.8	516	0.0	4.3	0.8	6 628	61.7	1.4	52.5	15.0	32.5
Kiowa County	621	150	16.7	217	0.0	8.3	0.9	2 619	62.5	3.4	49.6	18.4	32.1
Labette County.............	4 570	1 066	2.9	1 454	0.0	10.6	2.6	17 770	63.2	3.6	53.4	15.3	31.3
Lane County.................	440	28	1.5	112	0.0	1.8	2.7	1 686	64.8	1.9	54.5	17.8	27.7
Leavenworth County	13 771	3 720	13.7	3 602	1.1	12.5	3.1	52 378	62.3	3.1	59.1	14.3	26.7
Lincoln County	657	101	4.7	178	0.0	9.0	3.9	2 862	65.5	2.4	54.2	16.4	29.5
Linn County	1 788	183	9.3	531	0.0	18.3	3.8	7 516	61.7	5.5	50.7	14.8	34.5
Logan County	576	86	8.0	184	0.0	14.7	0.5	2 373	66.2	3.8	56.7	16.1	27.1
Lyon County	6 992	4 142	3.5	2 942	0.0	10.5	3.9	27 774	69.4	6.0	55.0	19.8	25.2
McPherson County........	5 809	1 897	12.9	2 018	0.1	6.4	2.6	23 046	68.2	4.1	54.6	19.5	25.9
Marion County	2 604	680	18.3	823	0.0	6.0	2.9	10 469	62.2	2.9	50.5	18.9	30.6
Marshall County	2 317	153	12.0	685	0.0	7.7	1.9	8 630	63.3	3.5	51.6	16.6	31.7
Meade County	1 027	146	7.2	270	0.0	7.8	2.2	3 420	61.4	2.9	54.7	13.6	31.7
Miami County...............	6 086	838	9.2	1 588	0.2	8.8	2.3	21 369	69.2	2.5	59.4	15.9	24.7
Mitchell County.............	1 424	374	13.6	579	0.0	2.1	2.1	5 494	64.3	4.2	54.2	17.5	28.3
Montgomery County	7 003	1 733	8.2	2 291	0.0	7.4	3.9	28 355	60.9	4.7	51.6	14.7	33.7
Morris County	1 202	133	2.5	352	0.0	15.6	2.6	4 788	64.3	2.9	53.3	13.3	33.4
Morton County..............	812	108	3.6	233	0.0	5.6	2.6	2 577	65.9	3.8	60.2	13.5	26.3
Nemaha County	2 303	234	7.9	620	0.0	9.5	1.3	8 067	62.6	1.9	51.2	17.3	31.5
Neosho County	3 440	751	6.1	1 126	0.0	7.4	2.2	13 218	63.4	4.9	54.5	15.3	30.2
Ness County................	625	92	7.8	164	0.0	4.3	0.0	2 771	62.1	1.8	54.1	16.1	29.8
Norton County	1 120	138	10.0	278	0.0	10.4	6.1	4 795	54.7	4.0	50.6	12.9	36.5

Table B-3. States and Counties — Education, Labor Force, and Income

| STATE County | Full-year full-time employed (percent) | | | | | | | | Children under 18 years in families | | | With two parents (percent) | | | Total employed by class of worker (percent) | | | |
	Total	Men	Women	Non-Hispanic White	Black or African American	American Indian and Alaska Native	Asian, Hawaiian, and Pacific Islander	Hispanic or Latino[1]	Number	Both in labor force	Father only in labor force	With one parent who is in labor force (percent)	+/− U.S. percent of children with no stay-at-home parent (percent)	+/− U.S. percent two-income couples	Private	Government	Self-employed	Unpaid family worker
	24	25	26	27	28	29	30	31	32	33	34	35	36	37	38	39	40	41
KANSAS—Cont'd																		
Barber County	39.6	53.5	27.1	39.8	35.7	47.1	0.0	43.8	1 284	64.4	20.2	11.2	11.0	4.3	60.9	16.4	21.5	1.3
Barton County	40.6	51.9	30.6	41.0	31.5	43.4	73.2	34.8	6 984	53.7	20.3	19.8	8.9	6.5	72.0	13.9	13.6	0.6
Bourbon County	39.0	48.0	30.8	39.1	31.0	32.4	44.4	50.6	3 774	54.5	18.4	18.7	8.6	4.8	75.8	13.0	10.5	0.6
Brown County	41.6	50.3	33.6	41.6	44.4	43.6	25.8	34.1	2 729	55.1	13.1	24.7	15.2	4.3	67.7	16.5	15.3	0.5
Butler County	45.2	57.1	33.5	45.7	24.1	37.4	23.9	52.7	16 289	53.3	23.8	15.1	3.8	6.7	75.4	13.7	10.6	0.3
Chase County	44.6	53.2	36.0	45.1	15.0	100.0	100.0	6.5	697	56.1	19.9	18.5	10.0	9.0	62.4	19.9	16.6	1.2
Chautauqua County	29.6	36.8	23.2	30.3	X	14.0	0.0	25.9	965	49.1	18.2	15.3	-0.2	-10.0	65.2	18.0	16.2	0.7
Cherokee County	39.5	50.5	29.4	39.8	34.7	31.1	15.0	40.0	5 527	52.9	17.0	21.1	9.4	2.8	76.3	12.1	11.5	0.0
Cheyenne County	36.2	46.8	26.1	36.2	X	0.0	50.0	44.4	722	58.3	17.5	18.4	12.1	3.3	51.6	14.9	33.0	0.5
Clark County	40.0	52.1	29.6	40.0	33.3	63.6	11.1	42.2	601	59.6	19.1	12.0	7.0	5.0	59.3	19.2	20.8	0.7
Clay County	38.4	50.4	26.9	38.4	30.8	0.0	0.0	68.0	2 055	63.1	10.3	20.2	18.7	6.6	60.8	19.4	19.2	0.5
Cloud County	36.1	47.8	26.3	36.4	0.0	23.8	22.2	50.0	2 196	66.8	11.1	15.5	17.7	8.8	66.1	16.3	17.2	0.5
Coffey County	42.0	54.2	30.6	42.0	12.5	52.1	40.0	43.1	2 266	65.8	14.4	15.7	16.9	8.9	63.4	20.4	15.0	1.2
Comanche County	42.3	55.5	30.4	42.5	X	X	40.0	6.7	395	65.1	16.7	17.2	17.7	8.6	49.8	17.3	30.8	2.1
Cowley County	39.9	51.0	29.5	40.4	19.2	43.2	48.6	34.0	8 883	48.5	23.3	19.0	2.9	1.9	72.0	16.6	11.0	0.4
Crawford County	36.0	45.1	27.5	36.3	27.2	35.6	8.1	40.2	8 386	50.6	15.2	24.2	10.2	4.3	69.5	19.4	10.6	0.5
Decatur County	37.6	49.0	27.0	37.8	0.0	46.7	0.0	40.0	742	60.4	20.5	15.5	11.3	2.3	57.7	17.4	23.8	1.1
Dickinson County	43.1	55.3	31.9	43.4	55.0	63.8	57.7	35.4	4 789	65.0	13.8	16.6	17.0	8.8	70.5	15.1	14.0	0.4
Doniphan County	39.4	48.9	30.2	39.4	34.7	30.6	50.0	29.3	1 975	57.5	15.4	17.7	10.6	5.3	67.7	18.2	13.6	0.5
Douglas County	36.8	44.2	29.6	38.1	36.1	30.1	22.6	27.7	19 785	54.3	19.6	19.6	9.3	12.0	67.9	23.4	8.5	0.2
Edwards County	37.7	48.0	27.8	38.3	62.5	60.0	18.2	32.9	822	55.5	24.2	12.7	3.6	-0.5	58.4	18.0	22.9	0.7
Elk County	33.7	47.7	20.7	33.9	X	0.0	X	44.4	686	55.0	16.6	16.2	6.6	-12.0	55.5	20.8	22.6	1.1
Ellis County	41.1	51.8	31.0	41.2	18.4	100.0	25.8	45.4	5 889	61.2	13.2	18.5	15.1	11.0	65.9	21.4	12.3	0.5
Ellsworth County	38.5	46.2	29.5	40.5	9.8	13.2	28.6	32.2	1 264	67.9	12.7	17.1	20.4	10.8	60.4	20.4	18.4	0.8
Finney County	45.0	55.0	34.8	49.2	29.2	42.5	50.7	38.8	13 012	44.2	22.2	15.9	-4.5	4.7	74.5	14.0	11.0	0.4
Ford County	44.2	54.6	33.0	47.0	34.8	26.9	30.6	39.5	9 411	50.9	18.8	17.2	3.5	8.1	75.6	14.4	9.7	0.3
Franklin County	46.0	55.2	37.3	46.3	39.3	52.8	20.3	43.0	6 522	58.4	13.6	22.0	15.8	9.0	75.5	13.1	10.6	0.8
Geary County	45.5	58.9	33.0	47.5	43.3	39.9	37.1	41.6	7 856	45.2	21.6	22.4	3.0	4.0	65.2	26.6	7.6	0.6
Gove County	38.1	53.7	23.7	38.3	28.6	0.0	X	55.0	770	65.4	21.1	12.1	12.9	5.3	52.1	18.6	28.4	0.9
Graham County	39.0	50.0	28.7	40.0	12.3	0.0	50.0	58.8	647	67.5	9.3	12.5	15.4	4.4	52.8	22.5	23.7	1.0
Grant County	43.6	58.5	29.0	46.0	X	42.4	X	37.5	2 468	43.1	27.8	16.7	-4.8	-2.1	70.2	14.1	14.2	1.5
Gray County	44.0	59.1	29.4	45.3	0.0	61.1	X	28.6	1 820	50.5	32.6	12.2	-1.9	4.4	65.1	12.9	21.5	0.6
Greeley County	40.4	54.6	26.9	41.0	X	0.0	X	35.5	428	51.9	31.3	8.9	-3.8	1.6	52.8	22.8	24.4	0.0
Greenwood County	35.6	46.6	25.3	35.9	0.0	20.0	13.8	26.6	1 679	59.8	13.6	17.5	12.7	0.8	62.6	17.5	19.3	0.6
Hamilton County	38.2	53.0	24.1	36.3	0.0	100.0	50.0	45.0	731	41.2	30.5	17.9	-5.5	-4.8	52.6	21.9	24.4	1.1
Harper County	37.4	50.6	25.0	37.1	72.0	64.5	0.0	35.3	1 563	59.9	19.3	17.3	12.0	3.9	61.9	16.5	19.7	1.8
Harvey County	40.5	51.5	30.3	41.4	31.2	34.5	28.3	35.3	8 051	56.9	19.8	15.8	8.1	7.7	76.6	11.9	11.2	0.3
Haskell County	41.1	57.2	25.3	44.3	50.0	26.7	82.8	30.9	1 373	43.6	34.7	10.5	-10.5	1.7	62.9	16.3	20.0	0.8
Hodgeman County	41.3	66.5	26.7	41.7	50.0	0.0	X	26.8	589	72.2	12.4	11.5	19.1	9.7	53.2	20.3	25.4	1.1
Jackson County	45.3	55.0	36.1	44.7	49.2	55.7	61.1	50.4	3 422	60.1	16.7	17.2	12.7	10.6	66.1	21.0	12.4	0.5
Jefferson County	46.1	55.5	36.8	46.6	4.3	24.8	48.1	25.7	4 818	60.6	16.2	15.3	11.3	6.7	68.3	19.4	12.1	0.3
Jewell County	36.7	51.9	22.2	36.6	100.0	42.9	16.7	50.0	781	72.5	11.0	11.1	19.0	0.4	51.2	18.6	28.5	1.7
Johnson County	51.2	64.4	39.1	51.5	51.2	49.8	46.9	48.4	119 141	54.0	27.2	13.6	3.0	10.0	79.1	10.6	10.2	0.1
Kearny County	40.4	53.6	27.2	41.9	66.7	38.9	0.0	35.4	1 496	47.0	29.5	13.2	-4.4	-0.8	61.0	20.0	16.7	0.9
Kingman County	39.6	52.2	27.7	39.2	0.0	55.0	92.9	51.7	2 278	56.9	19.4	15.8	8.1	5.3	65.1	16.2	17.9	0.9
Kiowa County	37.5	49.6	26.0	37.5	X	35.0	20.0	45.7	763	53.5	26.1	15.5	4.4	4.4	60.9	19.5	18.5	1.1
Labette County	40.7	48.9	33.0	40.8	40.3	39.2	58.8	32.8	5 503	53.4	14.6	23.2	12.0	6.0	70.0	18.3	11.1	0.6
Lane County	40.9	55.2	26.7	41.1	0.0	X	28.6	37.5	515	66.8	17.3	13.4	15.6	5.5	54.4	19.4	25.8	0.4
Leavenworth County	43.4	49.5	36.3	45.5	30.7	27.6	40.4	34.9	17 648	49.3	25.7	18.4	3.1	7.3	67.8	23.6	8.2	0.4
Lincoln County	41.1	52.9	29.8	41.1	100.0	22.2	33.3	35.0	776	58.9	17.9	16.4	10.7	8.8	54.2	21.7	23.3	0.8
Linn County	36.5	46.0	27.2	37.0	0.0	20.5	0.0	21.2	2 254	56.9	24.6	11.4	3.7	0.0	70.4	16.5	12.2	0.9
Logan County	42.2	56.1	29.6	42.8	0.0	100.0	0.0	21.9	760	57.2	25.0	9.6	2.2	6.8	58.5	17.7	22.4	1.4
Lyon County	40.8	52.2	30.0	40.7	40.8	54.5	42.2	41.0	8 894	50.9	17.0	21.5	7.8	6.9	73.0	18.4	8.0	0.5
McPherson County	42.5	56.3	29.7	42.7	35.4	75.6	14.3	27.4	7 300	62.3	20.9	12.8	10.5	9.6	73.7	12.3	13.6	0.5
Marion County	38.2	52.3	25.3	38.4	19.6	51.4	64.7	32.0	3 186	61.6	20.2	13.1	10.1	5.0	68.1	14.6	16.3	1.0
Marshall County	40.0	53.1	27.9	40.1	0.0	34.8	26.9	46.2	2 674	70.0	16.3	11.1	16.5	6.0	66.6	14.2	18.3	0.9
Meade County	40.1	53.5	27.2	40.0	27.3	50.0	44.4	39.5	1 335	53.2	30.3	7.9	-3.5	2.9	60.3	17.5	20.9	1.3
Miami County	47.0	58.9	35.6	47.7	25.3	27.5	72.5	37.9	7 563	57.5	21.1	15.6	8.5	9.9	73.7	13.6	12.2	0.5
Mitchell County	42.3	53.9	31.2	42.7	0.0	50.0	69.2	25.0	1 598	66.5	10.8	16.1	18.0	7.8	60.1	18.0	20.5	1.4
Montgomery County	39.5	49.3	30.8	40.2	29.1	43.1	31.4	38.2	8 586	50.3	18.8	21.3	7.0	0.0	77.1	12.6	9.7	0.6
Morris County	41.4	49.9	33.7	41.5	33.3	60.6	0.0	43.1	1 514	55.6	17.4	18.3	9.3	2.9	62.5	18.2	18.0	1.3
Morton County	42.7	56.2	30.2	44.0	25.0	47.7	44.7	30.9	1 003	60.3	18.8	15.3	11.0	5.7	58.3	27.5	13.5	0.7
Nemaha County	40.9	53.0	29.3	41.0	39.1	30.8	75.0	33.3	2 972	70.7	16.4	8.4	14.5	10.6	65.3	13.5	19.7	1.5
Neosho County	42.0	52.2	32.6	42.2	37.9	54.4	12.2	42.2	4 203	53.6	18.4	19.2	8.2	2.8	70.0	16.4	12.9	0.6
Ness County	40.9	54.3	28.2	41.3	100.0	X	0.0	22.7	773	62.0	17.7	14.9	12.3	5.0	53.7	18.6	26.5	1.2
Norton County	38.7	42.8	33.6	40.3	17.3	9.7	52.2	27.4	1 265	64.7	12.8	12.6	12.7	7.6	53.5	26.4	19.2	0.9

[1] Hispanic or Latino persons may be of any race.

STATE County	Percent who worked at home	Percent of the population 5 years and over with a disability	Veterans as a percent of the population 18 years and over	Occupation for employed population 16 years and over (percent)						Industry for employed population 16 years and over (percent)					
				Management, professional, and related occupations	Service occupations	Sales and office occupations	Farming, fishing, and forestry occupations	Construction, extraction, and maintenance occupations	Production, transportation and material moving occupations	Agriculture, forestry, fishing, and mining	Construction and manufacturing	Wholesale and retail trade	Transportation and warehousing, and utilities	Service industries	Public administration
	42	43	44	45	46	47	48	49	50	51	52	53	54	55	56
KANSAS—Cont'd															
Barber County	5.2	19.6	14.2	34.3	15.6	17.6	2.7	13.0	16.9	16.3	14.9	13.0	7.4	45.4	2.9
Barton County	3.3	18.0	13.4	27.6	17.2	26.0	2.4	10.6	16.3	9.8	17.6	17.3	5.3	46.2	3.8
Bourbon County	4.1	24.1	15.0	26.5	15.9	24.8	1.2	9.1	22.5	4.2	25.9	15.9	4.2	45.9	3.8
Brown County	6.1	22.9	14.9	31.5	20.6	21.4	3.1	10.5	13.0	8.4	17.3	11.5	5.6	51.1	6.1
Butler County	3.4	17.2	14.6	31.7	13.7	24.6	0.7	12.9	16.5	2.9	32.8	12.1	4.3	44.1	3.8
Chase County	7.1	18.3	16.3	32.4	17.2	19.8	2.8	9.1	18.6	12.1	20.5	12.3	5.8	41.9	7.4
Chautauqua County	5.9	26.0	16.1	33.0	15.5	17.0	4.5	13.5	16.5	18.2	18.1	7.7	6.3	46.8	2.9
Cherokee County	3.7	22.9	13.5	24.5	15.5	20.9	1.1	11.5	26.6	3.8	34.0	13.2	5.5	39.9	3.5
Cheyenne County	11.9	22.0	13.9	33.8	16.8	22.8	6.8	9.6	10.2	24.5	7.6	18.4	6.2	38.5	4.8
Clark County	5.9	18.4	14.8	37.3	12.5	21.7	8.3	8.8	11.4	20.8	9.1	11.3	7.0	45.7	6.2
Clay County	7.5	19.3	17.1	31.4	14.2	22.1	1.9	14.4	16.0	11.3	21.8	13.4	4.8	44.7	4.0
Cloud County	5.9	19.5	14.7	27.3	18.1	24.2	1.6	9.0	19.8	8.3	17.0	18.2	7.1	45.9	3.6
Coffey County	6.6	17.9	14.8	31.4	17.4	20.5	1.9	12.8	15.9	8.8	18.2	11.6	17.2	39.2	5.0
Comanche County	6.5	19.9	16.5	40.2	15.3	17.6	3.1	10.1	13.7	20.0	13.5	10.6	6.9	46.2	2.8
Cowley County	3.6	20.7	13.2	28.7	16.4	20.4	1.0	12.1	21.4	4.1	29.8	10.7	5.4	45.2	4.7
Crawford County	3.5	20.4	12.7	30.9	18.3	21.6	0.8	9.2	19.1	2.2	23.0	12.4	3.8	54.9	3.7
Decatur County	9.6	20.1	15.4	34.4	18.0	20.0	5.4	10.4	11.7	22.3	9.1	14.4	6.4	41.6	6.2
Dickinson County	4.8	19.7	17.5	25.9	15.4	24.7	1.8	13.2	18.9	7.8	20.6	19.0	7.7	39.9	5.0
Doniphan County	5.1	16.5	13.1	29.0	15.4	22.8	1.8	10.3	20.6	8.1	21.6	14.0	6.0	45.9	4.4
Douglas County	3.7	13.1	8.7	40.4	16.6	25.0	0.2	7.7	10.1	1.0	15.4	13.6	3.1	62.8	3.9
Edwards County	5.0	20.2	13.6	34.3	13.4	20.6	5.9	10.4	15.5	20.3	19.1	12.8	5.1	37.1	5.6
Elk County	8.6	23.7	15.8	33.4	14.8	12.5	1.8	18.7	18.8	18.4	24.6	8.7	7.0	38.3	3.0
Ellis County	2.5	15.0	10.8	33.2	18.1	28.0	1.0	8.9	10.7	5.5	11.0	15.7	4.6	58.5	4.7
Ellsworth County	6.1	20.6	15.2	32.9	20.0	20.2	1.7	10.4	14.9	12.2	16.4	13.1	5.3	44.2	8.8
Finney County	3.1	15.3	8.3	24.5	14.0	22.5	3.1	10.0	25.9	7.6	29.6	15.9	5.3	37.6	4.0
Ford County	2.3	18.7	9.5	24.5	14.3	22.6	2.4	10.2	26.0	5.7	30.8	14.9	5.0	40.0	3.6
Franklin County	3.8	19.1	13.4	25.2	14.4	24.8	0.7	14.6	20.4	4.1	24.4	17.3	6.1	44.5	3.5
Geary County	2.2	19.3	21.9	25.4	19.3	27.7	0.7	10.2	16.7	2.0	16.3	18.6	4.8	48.4	9.9
Gove County	13.5	16.4	13.0	37.5	11.5	21.8	6.0	10.4	12.7	24.5	10.5	12.3	5.7	44.1	2.8
Graham County	7.6	20.4	13.8	35.0	18.1	20.5	4.1	11.2	11.1	17.1	10.1	12.2	6.1	49.2	5.2
Grant County	5.6	14.2	8.2	25.8	12.9	23.7	5.1	17.1	15.3	19.9	14.8	10.9	11.9	40.2	2.3
Gray County	7.7	13.4	8.0	33.9	13.0	20.4	8.6	11.2	13.0	23.6	15.0	14.3	6.6	35.8	4.6
Greeley County	8.7	17.6	11.8	35.2	10.4	20.7	9.5	10.7	13.5	30.8	10.0	13.7	7.0	33.5	5.1
Greenwood County	5.5	25.9	16.3	29.7	18.7	18.6	1.5	14.2	17.3	9.7	22.4	12.4	4.2	45.1	6.1
Hamilton County	4.8	24.5	12.1	32.0	15.9	21.1	10.9	9.9	10.2	29.3	7.6	10.5	6.9	39.8	5.8
Harper County	6.3	21.6	13.8	30.0	17.4	20.4	2.9	11.3	18.1	12.9	21.9	11.4	5.0	45.1	3.7
Harvey County	4.5	17.4	12.1	31.6	16.4	22.7	0.6	10.8	17.9	2.8	27.4	13.3	4.2	49.2	3.1
Haskell County	7.9	14.7	7.9	32.8	11.9	18.0	11.2	10.7	15.5	27.6	10.0	13.9	8.6	37.3	2.6
Hodgeman County	12.1	18.0	12.4	38.5	14.4	21.9	4.5	9.9	10.8	22.9	10.7	13.9	7.0	40.3	5.1
Jackson County	4.8	17.0	15.1	28.3	16.3	24.5	1.5	13.1	16.4	6.2	20.1	12.7	6.8	47.1	7.1
Jefferson County	4.4	16.4	15.6	28.5	15.0	25.3	0.7	14.9	15.6	3.8	23.1	13.2	6.8	46.6	6.5
Jewell County	11.3	21.2	15.9	35.0	14.4	17.9	5.3	15.0	12.3	22.3	14.9	11.7	7.1	39.2	4.8
Johnson County	4.7	11.8	12.3	47.5	10.0	29.6	0.1	5.7	7.1	0.4	15.1	16.8	4.4	60.3	3.1
Kearny County	5.6	14.9	11.4	31.0	15.6	16.6	8.6	11.6	16.7	22.5	15.0	11.7	8.3	38.3	4.1
Kingman County	5.9	18.4	15.2	31.6	14.3	22.0	2.3	12.2	17.6	11.6	24.9	12.8	6.6	40.8	3.4
Kiowa County	6.7	21.1	13.9	35.3	15.9	20.4	6.4	10.3	11.7	18.5	9.0	12.3	10.1	46.0	4.1
Labette County	4.1	22.9	13.6	30.8	16.1	20.1	1.2	9.0	22.8	4.1	26.6	12.6	5.5	47.0	4.2
Lane County	8.6	16.4	16.1	33.1	13.7	21.1	8.1	10.6	13.4	26.4	7.2	13.6	10.5	36.0	6.3
Leavenworth County	3.4	19.9	20.5	31.0	17.0	26.6	0.4	11.7	13.3	1.3	17.2	13.8	6.7	51.1	9.9
Lincoln County	9.5	17.5	17.3	36.7	13.1	19.6	3.4	10.4	16.7	19.2	18.2	11.6	6.7	38.9	5.4
Linn County	4.2	22.0	15.1	25.3	12.7	23.1	1.4	17.3	20.2	5.3	23.3	13.8	9.9	43.3	4.4
Logan County	7.1	18.1	14.9	30.8	14.3	25.3	4.9	11.9	12.8	19.0	6.6	17.5	7.7	45.4	3.8
Lyon County	3.1	17.3	11.0	25.7	17.3	23.2	1.4	9.2	23.3	2.7	27.6	14.1	4.5	47.1	4.0
McPherson County	5.5	16.0	12.2	29.7	16.1	20.6	0.8	10.7	22.1	5.4	31.8	10.9	4.0	45.8	2.1
Marion County	6.9	20.1	10.7	32.1	16.9	18.5	2.2	11.1	19.3	10.3	23.1	12.6	5.5	46.0	2.5
Marshall County	7.0	20.4	16.0	30.3	16.2	20.0	2.3	9.9	21.3	11.8	20.4	13.0	9.6	42.2	2.9
Meade County	7.1	16.1	12.1	35.2	15.8	17.9	6.9	11.7	12.5	21.8	11.4	12.1	8.5	41.9	4.4
Miami County	4.0	17.3	13.7	29.6	11.8	26.4	0.7	15.9	15.6	3.6	26.6	14.6	6.2	45.2	3.8
Mitchell County	6.5	17.5	12.6	33.4	16.6	23.0	3.3	9.4	14.2	12.2	14.9	18.6	5.2	42.2	6.8
Montgomery County	2.8	22.7	15.9	26.9	16.8	23.3	0.7	9.6	22.6	3.6	30.6	14.2	4.8	43.5	3.3
Morris County	9.9	17.7	17.0	29.2	12.5	24.2	3.3	12.5	18.2	11.8	21.5	12.4	7.4	41.5	5.4
Morton County	3.4	15.3	9.8	33.4	17.1	19.3	7.3	9.9	13.0	25.0	7.2	10.8	6.5	45.9	4.6
Nemaha County	8.9	17.6	14.6	31.3	16.8	21.1	2.4	11.0	17.3	11.6	22.0	13.3	7.2	42.9	3.1
Neosho County	4.4	22.0	13.3	27.0	15.5	20.3	0.9	11.6	24.7	4.6	31.5	13.8	5.0	41.3	3.8
Ness County	7.7	19.1	15.3	39.3	11.3	21.7	3.4	11.9	12.4	26.0	9.0	11.1	5.6	44.9	3.4
Norton County	5.2	19.7	15.0	33.4	20.1	26.8	3.6	7.5	8.6	12.7	9.6	16.4	6.2	43.9	11.1

Table B-3. States and Counties — Education, Labor Force, and Income

STATE County	Median house-hold income	Median family income				Median nonfamily house-hold income	Median income for full-year, full-time workers		Per capita income	Households by source of income (percent)					House-holds with income over $100,000 (percent)	+/- U.S. percent for income over $100,000 (percent)	House-holds with income below poverty (percent)	Families with children with income below poverty (percent)
		All families	Married-couple	Male house-holder	Female house-holder		Men	Women		With earnings	With interest, dividend, or rental income	With Social Security income	With public assis-tance income	With retire-ment income				
	57	58	59	60	61	62	63	64	65	66	67	68	69	70	71	72	73	74

KANSAS—Cont'd

STATE County	57	58	59	60	61	62	63	64	65	66	67	68	69	70	71	72	73	74
Barber County	33 407	40 234	44 583	32 917	20 694	19 306	30 720	21 324	16 627	74.3	46.1	38.2	1.2	13.0	4.7	-7.6	10.2	10.5
Barton County	32 176	39 929	47 190	23 281	18 386	18 372	29 933	20 999	16 695	76.5	39.4	31.9	2.8	11.3	4.7	-7.6	12.4	15.0
Bourbon County	31 199	39 239	47 619	24 904	16 948	15 508	27 621	21 462	16 393	74.1	33.1	36.6	4.1	14.4	3.7	-8.6	13.8	15.1
Brown County	31 971	39 525	45 313	24 643	18 147	16 581	30 660	20 367	15 163	74.5	38.0	36.0	2.4	13.2	2.5	-9.8	14.1	15.6
Butler County	45 474	53 632	59 864	37 625	21 519	22 443	40 133	26 863	20 150	82.2	37.3	26.4	2.3	16.3	9.6	-2.7	7.5	8.1
Chase County	32 656	39 848	42 917	30 833	16 111	18 750	29 773	22 143	17 422	81.0	37.8	31.2	2.1	13.9	4.2	-8.1	10.0	7.0
Chautauqua County	28 717	33 871	40 500	26 042	16 071	14 965	26 348	23 200	16 280	69.7	37.7	46.5	4.8	18.0	3.9	-8.4	13.1	13.7
Cherokee County	30 505	37 284	44 682	29 286	14 393	15 124	30 096	20 228	14 710	74.1	28.3	32.8	3.6	16.5	3.0	-9.3	14.3	16.2
Cheyenne County	30 599	34 816	39 453	21 750	23 750	17 292	26 117	20 250	17 862	74.2	50.0	39.9	0.8	16.0	4.4	-7.9	10.1	11.1
Clark County	33 857	40 521	44 773	25 417	14 583	21 250	28 894	22 000	17 795	77.1	44.9	38.1	2.7	14.1	6.3	-6.0	10.8	15.8
Clay County	33 965	41 103	46 688	31 161	15 188	17 103	30 347	18 669	17 939	73.2	47.0	37.4	2.2	20.0	4.4	-7.9	10.5	12.2
Cloud County	31 758	39 745	48 798	19 896	14 737	18 096	29 321	20 873	17 536	75.2	44.0	37.0	3.3	17.3	4.6	-7.7	10.7	11.3
Coffey County	37 839	44 912	53 370	23 750	26 023	19 759	32 383	21 365	18 337	79.0	42.3	32.2	2.5	14.2	5.4	-6.9	8.7	4.9
Comanche County	29 415	36 790	37 167	40 417	21 875	19 940	27 269	18 438	17 037	77.1	42.4	40.4	1.7	13.2	3.3	-9.0	10.7	12.9
Cowley County	34 406	43 636	48 772	25 781	15 408	18 328	32 837	22 018	17 509	75.8	34.7	31.3	3.2	17.3	4.8	-7.5	11.9	14.4
Crawford County	29 409	40 582	48 616	26 591	17 226	15 325	29 063	22 057	16 245	75.5	33.9	30.2	3.1	14.3	4.6	-7.7	17.3	14.8
Decatur County	30 257	34 982	39 554	26 563	18 333	18 750	26 618	20 297	16 348	76.3	46.5	39.4	1.2	15.6	2.7	-9.6	10.3	14.6
Dickinson County	35 975	43 952	51 918	25 750	16 767	17 568	32 416	19 533	17 780	79.0	40.2	33.5	2.1	17.5	3.9	-8.4	8.7	7.7
Doniphan County	32 537	39 357	44 917	25 000	14 286	16 810	28 834	20 333	14 849	77.6	32.9	32.3	3.0	15.0	2.8	-9.5	13.7	12.9
Douglas County	37 547	53 991	60 835	28 427	22 133	21 780	36 559	28 097	19 952	87.5	39.0	16.7	1.8	10.9	9.0	-3.3	17.1	8.9
Edwards County	30 530	38 250	42 321	23 750	18 250	16 923	27 892	20 786	17 586	74.0	39.1	38.6	3.1	14.8	4.2	-8.1	11.1	11.8
Elk County	27 267	34 148	35 000	43 750	16 339	15 188	30 189	16 802	16 066	69.3	38.6	45.8	2.7	18.1	3.2	-9.1	15.4	17.0
Ellis County	32 339	44 498	54 450	21 800	18 603	17 500	30 621	22 053	18 259	81.6	41.9	25.2	1.7	9.5	6.4	-5.9	15.3	9.2
Ellsworth County	35 772	44 360	52 981	31 875	18 333	17 398	30 840	21 055	16 569	73.5	41.0	38.0	1.0	16.4	4.2	-8.1	8.5	6.2
Finney County	38 474	42 839	45 111	25 705	20 392	21 861	30 466	21 835	15 377	89.5	28.8	17.9	2.0	7.7	5.9	-6.4	11.8	14.0
Ford County	37 860	42 734	46 400	21 806	19 877	21 809	27 442	22 688	15 721	84.2	31.5	22.9	3.3	10.1	6.1	-6.2	11.1	14.2
Franklin County	39 052	45 197	54 931	26 993	22 414	20 739	31 882	23 994	17 311	80.5	35.8	28.8	3.0	13.8	4.3	-8.0	8.6	7.5
Geary County	31 917	36 372	40 191	24 306	15 521	21 630	27 449	22 284	16 199	85.5	30.0	21.1	3.4	20.4	5.1	-7.2	11.7	14.3
Gove County	33 510	40 400	45 902	30 750	18 500	19 356	28 438	23 126	17 862	76.8	52.7	39.0	1.0	11.5	4.5	-7.8	10.0	11.9
Graham County	31 286	38 634	41 136	21 250	19 375	16 250	27 703	19 013	18 050	74.5	42.0	41.4	1.4	14.1	5.1	-7.2	11.6	12.1
Grant County	39 854	44 914	44 020	49 554	26 625	22 467	35 725	22 888	17 072	86.1	36.8	21.7	2.8	10.2	7.3	-5.0	8.7	10.6
Gray County	40 000	44 299	48 170	25 833	18 542	22 708	32 383	21 895	18 632	86.9	37.1	24.7	1.3	7.7	7.7	-4.6	7.4	10.1
Greeley County	34 605	45 625	43 750	31 875	26 563	20 650	30 114	19 712	19 974	83.3	43.9	31.8	3.7	11.5	9.3	-3.0	10.8	13.9
Greenwood County	30 169	38 140	43 984	20 469	15 714	14 918	28 545	20 726	15 976	69.7	38.1	40.5	3.3	17.3	3.8	-8.5	14.1	13.1
Hamilton County	32 033	38 550	42 045	23 571	19 167	22 054	27 558	22 885	16 484	80.2	40.6	34.8	2.3	10.0	5.4	-6.9	13.4	19.0
Harper County	29 776	39 866	46 167	37 656	14 375	16 525	29 649	21 119	16 368	72.3	38.2	39.4	2.4	15.2	3.4	-8.9	12.3	13.3
Harvey County	40 907	48 793	54 552	31 771	19 959	21 174	36 369	23 734	18 715	79.9	44.8	30.8	2.4	15.4	6.0	-6.3	7.6	6.3
Haskell County	38 634	43 354	42 026	30 833	27 750	23 077	31 807	25 063	17 349	86.7	36.9	23.0	1.4	9.1	7.3	-5.0	9.5	10.8
Hodgeman County	35 994	39 358	46 125	26 458	18 750	20 556	28 750	22 431	15 599	76.4	46.4	34.4	1.7	16.6	5.1	-7.2	12.5	16.1
Jackson County	40 451	46 520	49 552	26 696	22 500	20 729	33 562	23 563	18 606	80.0	41.5	29.8	2.9	17.2	4.9	-7.4	8.9	9.7
Jefferson County	45 535	50 557	54 724	31 923	22 895	22 348	36 985	26 282	19 373	82.8	39.0	28.4	1.6	18.5	6.1	-6.2	7.8	6.4
Jewell County	30 538	36 953	38 221	35 625	24 250	16 213	26 483	19 844	16 644	72.5	46.9	41.6	2.5	18.4	3.9	-8.4	13.0	11.9
Johnson County	61 455	72 987	81 397	40 967	33 346	36 588	50 962	33 199	30 919	88.2	44.9	18.8	0.9	13.3	22.7	10.4	3.6	3.0
Kearny County	40 149	43 703	42 195	27 031	20 833	21 397	30 982	20 388	15 708	84.6	34.7	25.4	2.5	11.2	7.1	-5.2	10.3	12.1
Kingman County	37 790	44 547	52 000	25 972	21 827	19 740	33 605	25 718	18 533	77.1	44.5	34.8	2.8	15.4	6.0	-6.3	9.7	13.2
Kiowa County	31 576	40 950	45 114	24 750	13 750	19 135	30 738	22 378	17 207	75.3	45.9	36.5	2.6	14.5	4.1	-8.2	11.2	11.2
Labette County	30 875	37 519	45 783	27 414	16 535	16 668	30 242	22 307	15 525	75.5	34.5	34.7	3.1	15.3	2.8	-9.5	12.5	13.3
Lane County	36 047	41 892	45 833	27 250	19 375	20 057	30 313	21 912	18 606	77.3	49.6	35.8	0.9	14.5	6.0	-6.3	8.6	9.0
Leavenworth County	48 114	54 805	61 309	28 385	23 478	26 213	41 481	26 742	20 292	83.5	41.2	23.7	2.6	23.1	9.0	-3.3	6.8	7.2
Lincoln County	30 893	36 538	41 509	26 563	17 604	18 060	26 821	21 071	15 788	76.2	45.2	39.8	2.3	12.7	3.4	-8.9	10.3	10.1
Linn County	35 906	42 571	47 299	34 545	18 214	18 521	32 486	23 465	17 009	74.5	33.9	35.9	3.1	20.6	3.9	-8.4	11.3	12.9
Logan County	32 131	40 104	42 426	35 481	21 786	19 167	30 168	21 250	17 294	78.7	44.7	35.6	1.5	12.3	5.9	-6.4	9.0	6.7
Lyon County	32 819	43 112	47 795	31 062	16 250	18 410	29 718	21 645	15 724	81.9	34.3	24.5	3.4	12.3	4.3	-8.0	15.4	14.4
McPherson County	41 138	48 243	52 961	32 917	19 022	21 931	35 130	22 136	18 921	81.4	43.9	30.4	1.8	14.4	6.1	-6.2	8.1	5.4
Marion County	34 500	41 386	48 103	25 875	19 135	17 623	31 092	21 919	16 100	79.3	44.1	36.4	2.1	13.2	3.5	-8.8	8.0	7.8
Marshall County	32 089	39 705	48 603	21 250	13 281	17 921	29 329	19 835	17 090	74.4	45.2	40.1	1.1	14.8	4.9	-7.4	10.5	9.1
Meade County	36 761	44 593	44 342	29 063	15 250	19 063	30 720	20 765	16 824	77.9	42.2	33.9	1.2	11.8	6.3	-6.0	8.9	9.9
Miami County	46 665	55 830	64 004	31 350	21 055	21 728	39 299	28 230	21 408	84.1	38.8	26.2	1.6	14.3	10.8	-1.5	6.9	5.2
Mitchell County	33 385	41 899	45 964	27 292	16 897	18 908	27 068	21 132	17 653	76.1	46.4	36.2	1.8	15.1	5.1	-7.2	9.8	12.1
Montgomery County	30 997	38 516	46 937	21 691	16 449	16 278	30 560	20 830	16 421	74.1	31.3	35.1	3.2	18.0	4.0	-8.3	13.0	14.2
Morris County	32 163	39 717	45 417	28 750	20 104	17 326	30 786	21 691	18 491	74.6	39.4	35.5	1.8	17.6	5.0	-7.3	10.0	8.2
Morton County	37 232	43 494	46 136	30 000	15 208	22 313	32 798	20 484	17 076	81.7	38.6	28.6	2.3	12.2	5.1	-7.2	9.7	12.4
Nemaha County	34 296	41 838	46 382	23 250	20 833	16 923	29 785	20 431	17 121	75.3	49.7	37.6	0.9	12.1	4.1	-8.2	10.0	8.2
Neosho County	32 167	38 532	43 622	23 229	14 464	17 777	27 958	19 919	16 539	77.8	32.2	33.3	4.0	15.9	4.8	-7.5	13.3	16.7
Ness County	32 340	39 775	48 750	24 750	17 292	18 068	29 303	21 354	17 787	77.2	48.6	39.1	2.0	12.6	4.7	-7.6	9.7	8.0
Norton County	31 050	37 036	42 132	26 250	18 393	20 702	26 915	20 817	16 835	73.3	38.0	39.1	1.9	18.5	4.0	-8.3	10.0	10.3

Table B-3. States and Counties — Education, Labor Force, and Income

STATE/ County code	MSA/PMSA/ NECMA code[1]	STATE County	High school graduates			College graduates		College graduates (percent)				
			Total population 25 years and over	Percent with a high school diploma or less	Percent with a high school diploma or more	Percent with a bachelor's degree or more	+/− U.S. percent with bachelor's degree or more	Non-Hispanic White	Black or African American	American Indian and Alaska Native	Asian, Hawaiian, and Pacific Islander	Hispanic or Latino[2]
			1	2	3	4	5	6	7	8	9	10
		KANSAS—Cont'd										
20 139	...	Osage County	11 117	56.8	85.5	14.3	−10.1	14.5	0.0	10.0	29.7	7.6
20 141	...	Osborne County	3 115	55.5	84.8	15.5	−8.9	15.4	X	60.0	30.0	0.0
20 143	...	Ottawa County	4 228	51.7	86.2	16.3	−8.1	16.5	0.0	0.0	37.5	13.3
20 145	...	Pawnee County	4 875	45.0	84.8	21.8	−2.6	22.2	15.3	7.0	100.0	4.9
20 147	...	Phillips County	4 182	52.5	84.4	16.1	−8.3	16.2	0.0	0.0	30.8	11.1
20 149	...	Pottawatomie County	11 441	48.2	89.2	22.7	−1.7	22.8	3.2	16.0	0.0	21.7
20 151	...	Pratt County	6 365	41.4	86.3	21.0	−3.4	21.5	29.3	0.0	0.0	5.1
20 153	...	Rawlins County	2 152	49.9	84.7	15.9	−8.5	16.1	0.0	0.0	0.0	0.0
20 155	...	Reno County	43 082	47.8	82.7	17.3	−7.1	18.1	8.6	7.4	23.6	6.0
20 157	...	Republic County	4 256	52.7	88.6	14.9	−9.5	14.9	0.0	18.2	0.0	0.0
20 159	...	Rice County	6 701	50.2	83.4	17.5	−6.9	18.1	8.3	18.2	33.3	4.9
20 161	...	Riley County	29 358	28.6	93.8	40.5	16.1	41.5	18.8	36.7	69.1	23.1
20 163	...	Rooks County	3 901	54.3	87.1	15.4	−9.0	15.8	0.0	28.6	0.0	0.0
20 165	...	Rush County	2 568	49.6	82.8	16.4	−8.0	16.4	X	0.0	50.0	0.0
20 167	...	Russell County	5 323	52.7	83.1	16.7	−7.7	17.0	X	0.0	0.0	0.0
20 169	...	Saline County	34 680	47.5	87.0	20.4	−4.0	21.2	17.0	15.0	12.6	8.5
20 171	...	Scott County	3 376	44.3	84.5	23.0	−1.4	23.5	100.0	100.0	0.0	0.0
20 173	9040	Sedgwick County	282 585	44.2	85.1	25.4	1.0	28.0	13.1	13.9	23.8	10.0
20 175	...	Seward County	12 690	63.1	63.7	13.6	−10.8	19.8	9.3	7.4	22.6	2.5
20 177	8440	Shawnee County	111 709	45.5	88.1	26.0	1.6	28.0	12.2	15.5	48.7	13.9
20 179	...	Sheridan County	1 905	48.8	87.8	15.9	−8.5	15.6	X	0.0	100.0	33.3
20 181	...	Sherman County	4 319	49.3	86.6	15.0	−9.4	16.2	0.0	0.0	X	0.0
20 183	...	Smith County	3 338	53.4	84.6	16.7	−7.7	16.6	0.0	0.0	45.0	0.0
20 185	...	Stafford County	3 254	46.2	82.9	18.4	−6.0	19.1	0.0	9.5	17.6	1.7
20 187	...	Stanton County	1 468	53.0	78.0	16.9	−7.5	19.6	0.0	12.5	100.0	4.6
20 189	...	Stevens County	3 287	51.5	80.5	17.5	−6.9	19.7	X	26.5	50.0	3.3
20 191	...	Sumner County	16 662	51.4	86.3	15.7	−8.7	16.1	12.6	4.9	22.7	3.6
20 193	...	Thomas County	4 978	37.5	92.7	25.0	0.6	25.0	0.0	X	56.0	7.1
20 195	...	Trego County	2 342	53.3	84.3	14.0	−10.4	14.1	X	0.0	0.0	0.0
20 197	...	Wabaunsee County	4 623	55.6	89.9	17.3	−7.1	17.4	0.0	0.0	55.6	28.2
20 199	...	Wallace County	1 133	52.7	84.0	17.2	−7.2	17.9	0.0	0.0	X	4.2
20 201	...	Washington County	4 572	56.9	81.2	15.2	−9.2	15.3	0.0	16.7	X	0.0
20 203	...	Wichita County	1 625	55.1	77.7	15.5	−8.9	17.2	X	33.3	0.0	5.1
20 205	...	Wilson County	6 944	56.1	81.1	10.9	−13.5	10.7	0.0	2.2	27.8	22.2
20 207	...	Woodson County	2 667	56.8	83.4	11.4	−13.0	11.1	0.0	0.0	55.0	20.0
20 209	3760	Wyandotte County........	96 608	60.3	74.0	12.0	−12.4	13.8	10.6	3.7	21.0	5.6
21 000	...	KENTUCKY................	2 646 397	59.4	74.1	17.1	−7.3	17.4	10.7	13.9	52.0	13.0
21 001	...	Adair County	11 270	71.1	60.1	10.9	−13.5	10.9	12.7	0.0	27.8	0.0
21 003	...	Allen County	11 643	74.7	64.5	9.1	−15.3	8.9	5.5	0.0	28.6	12.4
21 005	...	Anderson County	12 600	62.6	80.4	12.0	−12.4	12.3	3.8	0.0	0.0	12.3
21 007	...	Ballard County	5 766	64.1	76.3	10.6	−13.8	10.8	0.0	100.0	70.0	0.0
21 009	...	Barren County	25 751	70.9	69.5	11.1	−13.3	11.1	8.1	0.0	43.9	7.0
21 011	...	Bath County	7 451	75.5	59.0	10.1	−14.3	10.0	0.0	0.0	46.7	47.6
21 013	...	Bell County	20 042	76.5	56.6	9.0	−15.4	8.9	13.2	22.2	30.4	0.0
21 015	1640	Boone County	54 166	47.7	85.1	22.8	−1.6	22.5	20.2	16.1	61.8	14.6
21 017	4280	Bourbon County	13 015	63.3	75.4	13.5	−10.9	14.0	5.8	0.0	0.0	6.5
21 019	3400	Boyd County	34 697	57.3	78.0	14.1	−10.3	14.3	9.8	29.8	38.5	2.3
21 021	...	Boyle County	18 491	57.7	76.6	19.3	−5.1	20.6	8.0	0.0	63.7	5.7
21 023	...	Bracken County	5 460	71.0	69.6	9.5	−14.9	9.4	17.1	0.0	X	X
21 025	...	Breathitt County	10 393	73.6	57.5	10.0	−14.4	9.8	X	0.0	90.5	0.0
21 027	...	Breckinridge County	12 501	75.3	68.9	7.4	−17.0	7.4	4.4	0.0	60.0	11.6
21 029	4520	Bullitt County	39 307	65.1	76.0	9.2	−15.2	9.2	16.9	6.1	34.6	11.8
21 031	...	Butler County	8 489	79.7	60.7	6.4	−18.0	6.2	0.0	X	9.8	15.3
21 033	...	Caldwell County	9 265	68.1	73.1	10.0	−14.4	10.4	3.0	0.0	31.3	10.2
21 035	...	Calloway County	21 032	52.4	77.9	24.0	−0.4	23.6	23.7	12.5	60.4	23.1
21 037	1640	Campbell County	57 184	53.9	80.8	20.5	−3.9	20.5	10.2	0.0	55.0	23.4
21 039	...	Carlisle County	3 690	66.1	73.4	10.6	−13.8	10.6	9.5	0.0	X	0.0
21 041	...	Carroll County	6 690	69.4	68.1	8.3	−16.1	7.9	0.0	34.1	55.6	0.0
21 043	3400	Carter County	17 394	72.9	64.4	8.9	−15.5	8.9	0.0	0.0	18.0	13.6
21 045	...	Casey County	10 423	79.3	57.4	7.4	−17.0	7.4	0.0	0.0	0.0	0.0
21 047	1660	Christian County	40 344	56.1	77.2	12.5	−11.9	14.3	5.6	6.9	33.7	11.3
21 049	4280	Clark County	22 187	61.2	75.0	15.6	−8.8	16.0	7.5	0.0	29.7	5.0
21 051	...	Clay County	16 083	79.5	49.4	8.0	−16.4	8.2	5.5	12.5	46.7	7.9
21 053	...	Clinton County	6 594	78.1	53.5	8.0	−16.4	8.1	0.0	X	0.0	7.4
21 055	...	Crittenden County	6 460	73.2	67.0	7.3	−17.1	7.2	0.0	0.0	100.0	17.2

[1]MSA = Metropolitan Statistical Area. PMSA = Primary MSA. NECMA = New England County Metropolitan Area. See the Appendix A for explanation of these concepts. See Appendix B for list of metropolitan areas identified by type, with component counties.
[2]Hispanic or Latino persons may be of any race.

Table B-3. States and Counties — Education, Labor Force, and Income

STATE County	School enrollment			Population 16 to 19 years				Employment status, 2000			Work status in 1999 of the population 16 years and over (percent)		
											Worked in 1999		
	Grades kindergarten through 12	College or graduate school	Percent private	Number	Percent in armed forces	Percent high school graduates	Percent not enrolled, not grads, not in armed forces, not employed	Total population 16 years and over	Percent in labor force	Unemployment rate	Full-time	Part-time	Did not work in 1999
	11	12	13	14	15	16	17	18	19	20	21	22	23
KANSAS—Cont'd													
Osage County	3 378	581	4.1	944	1.0	13.2	2.0	12 793	66.1	3.5	57.0	14.2	28.8
Osborne County	925	72	3.9	240	0.0	5.0	0.8	3 527	62.2	3.7	50.0	16.5	33.5
Ottawa County	1 244	149	6.7	387	0.0	4.4	2.6	4 826	67.4	4.4	57.9	14.1	28.0
Pawnee County	1 420	177	7.3	594	0.0	11.1	15.0	5 809	64.1	12.0	57.2	11.2	31.6
Phillips County	1 170	124	0.6	316	0.0	7.0	2.2	4 701	62.5	2.1	52.2	15.1	32.8
Pottawatomie County	4 131	822	12.2	1 181	0.0	11.7	1.5	13 553	69.5	3.1	60.1	15.6	24.3
Pratt County	1 874	533	8.6	697	0.0	9.3	0.9	7 630	65.8	4.6	51.7	18.4	29.9
Rawlins County	593	36	2.9	181	0.0	7.2	1.7	2 392	58.2	2.0	46.8	20.4	32.7
Reno County	11 953	2 673	10.4	3 815	0.0	10.5	4.0	50 915	62.6	4.6	55.7	14.6	29.7
Republic County	1 109	110	2.1	275	0.0	4.4	0.0	4 700	61.1	2.4	49.9	16.5	33.5
Rice County	2 089	989	10.7	894	0.0	4.0	2.9	8 477	62.5	5.8	49.0	21.7	29.3
Riley County	8 195	19 026	4.1	6 991	9.5	15.9	1.9	52 359	72.2	6.0	51.7	28.3	17.0
Rooks County	1 122	100	6.8	314	0.0	13.4	3.2	4 440	61.4	4.1	53.6	13.4	32.9
Rush County	644	104	3.3	145	0.0	13.1	0.0	2 839	59.8	2.7	50.7	14.5	34.8
Russell County	1 340	135	3.3	431	0.0	6.5	0.2	6 002	58.9	4.2	47.3	15.8	37.0
Saline County	10 731	2 260	13.2	3 217	0.0	8.4	3.9	41 234	69.6	3.4	59.4	16.1	24.5
Scott County	1 033	130	5.3	297	0.0	6.1	5.7	3 921	71.7	2.2	64.9	14.8	20.3
Sedgwick County	92 478	27 503	15.3	25 400	0.6	11.2	5.4	338 935	68.7	4.8	60.1	14.3	25.6
Seward County	5 207	766	3.3	1 483	0.0	6.3	12.1	15 957	64.1	4.9	59.7	11.7	28.6
Shawnee County	31 221	8 815	14.9	9 610	0.0	13.8	5.9	132 070	67.1	4.0	58.0	14.6	27.3
Sheridan County	630	63	0.9	175	0.0	1.7	0.0	2 179	64.1	0.6	53.3	17.8	28.9
Sherman County	1 203	484	2.7	548	0.0	12.4	9.9	5 328	65.7	3.1	55.6	17.9	26.5
Smith County	817	69	1.8	253	0.0	2.8	3.2	3 707	57.3	2.3	47.0	16.9	36.1
Stafford County	1 020	108	3.0	272	0.0	6.6	7.4	3 681	61.4	3.5	52.7	14.8	32.5
Stanton County	538	50	5.8	138	0.0	8.0	8.0	1 761	67.8	2.8	60.0	13.3	26.6
Stevens County	1 292	184	3.5	420	0.0	6.2	2.4	4 005	63.0	3.8	55.5	14.6	30.0
Sumner County	5 745	997	7.4	1 637	0.0	11.6	2.1	19 485	63.6	5.0	54.4	15.1	30.5
Thomas County	1 622	745	8.1	632	0.0	4.1	0.8	6 277	68.0	5.8	54.6	19.7	25.7
Trego County	631	131	3.9	181	0.0	0.0	3.9	2 643	59.9	1.8	50.8	16.0	33.1
Wabaunsee County	1 407	195	5.0	374	0.0	8.3	3.7	5 275	68.2	2.7	60.5	13.9	25.6
Wallace County	415	31	9.6	133	0.0	12.8	1.5	1 325	66.8	1.5	55.8	17.4	26.9
Washington County	1 161	139	11.3	329	0.0	8.8	0.9	5 159	63.3	2.2	50.2	16.9	32.9
Wichita County	546	37	7.2	149	0.0	4.7	4.0	1 909	62.2	3.0	55.6	15.9	28.5
Wilson County	2 047	264	1.9	554	0.0	12.5	4.5	8 001	61.7	4.2	51.2	14.9	33.9
Woodson County	680	120	0.9	212	0.0	6.6	0.0	3 064	54.7	3.6	47.8	13.8	38.4
Wyandotte County	32 339	6 959	11.8	9 384	0.0	14.5	10.6	117 571	63.2	8.2	57.2	12.3	30.6
KENTUCKY	738 747	206 367	13.3	228 979	0.8	11.9	7.1	3 161 542	60.9	5.7	52.4	13.6	34.0
Adair County	2 934	1 122	23.0	1 172	0.0	8.2	9.4	13 665	60.2	10.8	47.6	13.8	38.6
Allen County	3 357	430	8.4	1 015	0.0	15.5	9.4	13 776	59.5	4.9	53.0	9.9	37.1
Anderson County	3 715	539	6.6	900	0.0	11.7	4.2	14 463	68.5	4.0	61.0	13.4	25.6
Ballard County	1 417	222	3.4	380	0.0	9.2	3.7	6 609	60.8	4.2	51.4	13.4	35.2
Barren County	6 748	983	7.5	2 012	0.0	14.4	7.9	29 918	62.0	5.4	55.0	11.9	33.1
Bath County	1 962	232	5.5	621	0.8	8.2	11.4	8 743	54.0	6.6	49.2	9.9	40.9
Bell County	5 616	912	7.7	1 676	0.0	10.1	10.6	23 636	42.6	11.1	37.2	9.1	53.8
Boone County	17 525	3 592	19.0	4 691	0.0	13.2	6.0	64 033	73.1	3.1	61.3	17.0	21.7
Bourbon County	3 554	558	7.9	932	0.0	7.9	7.1	15 011	64.2	3.8	57.6	11.2	31.2
Boyd County	8 720	2 318	8.9	2 790	0.0	10.4	4.5	40 349	53.0	8.5	46.5	12.8	40.7
Boyle County	4 994	1 614	19.8	1 635	0.0	10.9	7.3	22 143	58.9	4.3	53.1	14.1	32.8
Bracken County	1 606	263	6.6	410	0.0	7.3	4.6	6 395	63.9	4.9	55.7	13.0	31.3
Breathitt County	3 269	677	10.1	1 033	0.0	13.7	8.9	12 553	43.2	10.1	37.1	8.5	54.5
Breckinridge County	3 621	364	10.9	1 038	0.0	10.0	4.1	14 536	57.9	6.0	50.8	12.4	36.8
Bullitt County	12 247	1 964	12.7	3 475	0.4	12.5	3.2	46 491	69.1	3.1	59.5	14.4	26.1
Butler County	2 482	324	3.6	824	0.0	12.6	3.2	10 180	61.2	4.8	53.0	12.1	34.9
Caldwell County	2 182	456	5.1	722	0.0	10.2	4.3	10 602	57.0	5.5	47.3	12.3	40.4
Calloway County	5 013	6 520	4.1	2 686	0.0	9.1	1.7	28 491	62.1	9.6	47.6	20.8	31.6
Campbell County	16 747	5 232	22.2	5 010	0.0	11.6	5.9	68 338	66.1	3.9	55.1	16.7	28.2
Carlisle County	956	180	10.3	275	0.0	12.0	6.2	4 253	55.7	6.2	49.2	12.4	38.4
Carroll County	1 768	281	9.4	532	0.0	15.0	11.8	7 929	62.0	6.7	57.2	11.7	31.1
Carter County	4 789	1 317	12.7	1 586	0.0	12.2	5.9	21 021	54.2	8.1	47.1	12.0	40.9
Casey County	2 740	259	9.0	807	0.0	13.8	12.4	12 116	55.0	5.9	47.9	8.5	43.6
Christian County	13 514	3 364	10.4	4 276	21.3	31.5	8.2	53 581	66.6	5.0	59.5	12.0	28.5
Clark County	6 084	951	11.3	1 844	0.0	11.9	10.5	26 011	63.3	4.6	57.2	12.0	30.8
Clay County	4 815	518	10.7	1 504	0.0	13.3	16.8	19 171	37.6	10.7	37.4	6.8	55.8
Clinton County	1 570	293	5.1	470	0.0	14.0	11.1	7 683	55.7	6.1	49.2	11.4	39.4
Crittenden County	1 663	266	10.0	534	0.9	12.7	20.0	7 487	55.8	6.7	48.5	10.7	40.9

STATE County	Full-year full-time employed (percent)								Children under 18 years in families						Total employed by class of worker (percent)			
							Asian, Hawaiian,			With two parents (percent)								
	Total	Men	Women	Non-Hispanic White	Black or African American	American Indian and Alaska Native	and Pacific Islander	Hispanic or Latino[1]	Number	Both in labor force	Father only in labor force	With one parent who is in labor force (percent)	+/- U.S. percent of children with no stay-at-home parent (percent)	+/- U.S. percent two-income couples	Private	Government	Self-employed	Unpaid family worker
	24	25	26	27	28	29	30	31	32	33	34	35	36	37	38	39	40	41
KANSAS—Cont'd																		
Osage County	44.4	53.4	36.0	44.5	14.3	51.1	23.1	52.0	4 298	57.4	15.5	18.6	11.4	5.9	68.1	20.1	11.5	0.3
Osborne County	39.7	51.6	28.4	39.7	X	33.3	30.0	23.5	1 037	61.5	19.2	15.1	12.0	4.3	58.7	15.5	24.5	1.3
Ottawa County	45.7	55.6	36.3	46.3	0.0	8.3	0.0	42.4	1 523	64.7	10.2	21.9	22.0	14.3	69.1	12.6	17.8	0.5
Pawnee County	41.0	47.1	34.3	41.2	16.2	100.0	83.3	55.9	1 439	63.8	7.4	17.9	17.1	11.3	47.2	36.0	16.1	0.8
Phillips County	40.0	53.2	28.0	40.0	0.0	33.3	60.0	35.7	1 439	75.2	10.2	10.6	21.2	6.8	60.4	18.0	20.3	1.4
Pottawatomie County	46.5	58.3	34.9	46.9	69.0	28.2	62.5	42.2	5 185	57.5	15.1	15.1	8.0	10.1	65.0	22.1	11.9	1.1
Pratt County	39.6	50.5	29.9	39.9	40.0	100.0	0.0	35.7	2 285	53.7	17.9	17.9	7.0	7.3	64.7	17.1	17.4	0.9
Rawlins County	34.7	45.8	23.8	34.9	22.2	0.0	33.3	26.7	692	56.4	23.0	15.3	7.1	1.2	48.0	18.5	31.1	2.4
Reno County	41.5	51.3	31.9	42.3	32.4	34.2	37.6	36.8	15 183	50.0	20.2	22.1	7.5	2.4	75.6	13.2	10.7	0.5
Republic County	40.9	53.2	29.7	40.9	0.0	57.1	5.0	51.4	1 246	66.4	12.0	12.6	14.4	5.7	57.8	16.9	24.7	0.6
Rice County	34.9	47.4	23.7	35.1	40.0	44.2	34.0	25.1	2 504	53.2	19.7	15.5	4.1	0.8	68.1	18.6	12.6	0.8
Riley County	34.9	42.6	26.0	34.5	45.9	41.1	27.3	35.4	11 405	52.1	22.4	17.2	4.7	8.7	57.8	34.1	7.8	0.3
Rooks County	41.2	52.5	30.6	41.9	10.7	44.4	0.0	17.2	1 412	64.7	13.3	15.4	15.5	7.6	58.0	20.5	20.7	0.8
Rush County	38.7	47.8	30.4	38.7	X	0.0	50.0	25.0	781	62.5	15.2	15.2	13.1	3.6	57.3	19.7	21.5	1.5
Russell County	36.6	44.7	29.2	36.3	X	54.3	0.0	40.0	1 586	57.9	9.0	21.9	15.2	-1.5	63.5	12.5	23.1	0.9
Saline County	46.7	56.6	37.2	47.1	44.3	61.8	53.1	39.0	13 353	54.4	15.2	20.3	10.1	10.0	77.9	11.7	10.1	0.3
Scott County	47.6	60.8	34.5	47.9	100.0	100.0	0.0	42.9	1 354	59.1	17.4	19.4	13.9	14.2	64.9	13.7	20.8	0.6
Sedgwick County	46.6	57.8	35.8	48.0	39.5	44.0	41.5	41.9	121 066	47.0	22.4	21.1	3.5	4.6	80.2	11.7	8.0	0.2
Seward County	42.1	52.9	31.3	46.2	38.8	48.6	37.1	36.6	6 777	41.6	24.1	15.1	-7.9	-0.1	75.2	13.1	10.8	0.9
Shawnee County	45.4	53.2	38.3	46.3	40.1	37.1	36.7	42.6	40 485	50.8	16.1	24.2	10.4	8.6	71.1	20.8	7.9	0.2
Sheridan County	42.6	60.5	25.3	42.7	X	0.0	0.0	100.0	724	62.6	25.4	7.9	5.9	4.3	49.0	13.7	35.9	1.4
Sherman County	42.2	53.2	30.9	41.6	100.0	27.3	X	44.8	1 597	47.5	27.6	13.3	-3.8	3.3	65.3	15.4	18.0	1.2
Smith County	35.7	47.7	24.8	35.8	0.0	100.0	25.0	0.0	964	67.6	11.0	12.1	15.1	4.9	53.4	19.1	26.1	1.4
Stafford County	40.1	53.5	27.6	40.1	15.4	14.3	36.0	48.0	1 243	57.1	17.0	18.0	10.5	3.7	55.6	23.1	20.9	0.3
Stanton County	44.3	58.6	29.6	46.4	0.0	40.0	57.1	37.5	706	56.7	21.5	14.6	6.7	8.0	55.7	21.5	21.5	1.6
Stevens County	40.3	56.8	24.8	42.1	X	70.0	25.7	32.2	1 639	44.5	29.1	14.5	-5.6	-1.8	55.3	22.8	20.8	1.0
Sumner County	41.9	56.0	28.5	42.2	43.1	44.4	31.0	29.4	7 026	52.1	23.9	17.7	5.2	1.0	70.3	16.4	12.7	0.6
Thomas County	40.5	54.6	27.8	41.0	0.0	X	0.0	19.6	2 086	66.8	19.6	7.3	9.5	8.3	65.6	15.9	17.5	1.0
Trego County	39.3	52.9	27.5	39.3	X	0.0	0.0	54.5	743	75.9	6.7	9.4	20.7	8.5	57.8	13.9	26.0	2.2
Wabaunsee County	48.2	58.4	38.2	48.6	25.0	0.0	16.7	33.3	1 748	57.7	14.7	17.1	10.2	11.5	61.4	21.7	16.5	0.4
Wallace County	42.1	58.9	25.2	42.0	60.0	100.0	0.0	50.8	471	63.7	25.9	8.9	8.0	7.6	57.2	15.4	26.6	0.8
Washington County	39.2	52.2	26.4	39.2	66.7	50.0	X	34.4	1 479	65.7	18.5	10.9	12.0	8.2	61.3	14.6	23.1	0.9
Wichita County	40.2	56.4	24.0	41.6	X	41.7	0.0	34.0	701	51.5	23.5	12.8	-0.3	-4.0	58.1	15.9	23.5	2.5
Wilson County	39.3	48.4	31.0	39.5	19.2	46.8	27.8	48.0	2 519	56.4	17.0	16.0	7.8	4.5	68.8	15.5	14.9	0.8
Woodson County	35.8	43.0	28.9	36.0	31.6	12.0	65.0	31.0	807	61.3	11.0	23.0	19.7	-2.5	61.8	17.9	19.2	1.0
Wyandotte County	40.8	48.0	34.1	43.0	36.5	39.1	44.6	39.6	41 355	32.9	15.6	32.5	0.8	-2.8	79.1	15.0	5.7	0.2
KENTUCKY	38.7	48.1	30.0	39.0	35.9	34.5	39.7	37.3	939 639	43.1	21.8	19.7	-1.8	-2.9	75.5	14.4	9.6	0.4
Adair County	32.5	41.2	24.4	33.2	8.0	0.0	0.0	33.8	3 799	45.9	22.0	17.8	-0.9	-2.6	66.7	15.4	16.8	1.1
Allen County	39.0	47.4	31.0	39.4	25.6	40.0	50.0	20.2	4 372	43.5	24.8	18.5	-2.6	-2.3	75.9	12.9	10.8	0.4
Anderson County	49.2	60.2	38.8	49.6	33.4	45.5	38.2	41.6	4 878	55.8	21.1	16.5	7.7	5.9	71.1	19.1	9.3	0.5
Ballard County	38.9	49.6	28.8	38.9	47.3	0.0	31.8	25.8	1 817	54.4	17.8	14.9	4.7	0.3	73.2	15.1	11.6	0.0
Barren County	41.2	52.3	31.3	41.3	40.1	63.6	52.2	41.2	8 842	48.4	22.1	15.7	-0.5	-0.8	74.9	12.5	11.9	0.7
Bath County	33.5	39.8	27.6	33.5	32.3	0.0	100.0	31.4	2 537	45.2	23.7	11.8	-7.6	-8.9	68.8	17.1	12.9	1.3
Bell County	25.8	32.9	19.6	25.7	29.0	16.7	36.7	34.3	6 996	24.5	24.2	16.9	-23.2	-22.6	73.3	18.0	8.1	0.7
Boone County	49.4	63.2	36.2	49.5	44.4	59.0	47.0	48.7	23 665	54.2	23.9	14.9	4.5	8.9	82.4	10.2	7.1	0.2
Bourbon County	43.6	53.9	34.1	44.5	30.8	0.0	54.2	41.6	4 596	43.5	22.6	21.5	0.4	0.2	72.2	12.0	14.6	1.2
Boyd County	32.9	43.3	23.2	33.3	29.0	31.5	34.5	21.3	10 185	38.8	24.1	20.7	-5.1	-11.6	78.4	13.3	8.2	0.1
Boyle County	36.9	43.7	30.2	38.0	27.7	32.7	38.9	34.8	5 850	47.0	18.6	21.7	4.1	2.0	74.2	13.6	11.8	0.3
Bracken County	40.5	50.9	30.7	40.4	69.2	0.0	X	0.0	2 019	47.5	20.8	21.1	4.0	0.3	73.1	14.0	12.7	0.3
Breathitt County	24.7	28.5	21.1	24.7	0.0	7.4	55.6	10.2	3 690	27.6	21.2	14.7	-22.3	-20.3	66.3	25.1	7.4	1.2
Breckinridge County	34.3	43.7	25.5	34.8	26.5	14.3	10.5	17.9	4 364	43.1	28.5	16.9	-4.6	-7.0	70.7	14.4	14.4	0.6
Bullitt County	47.4	59.1	36.1	47.7	26.5	35.0	48.1	38.4	15 848	49.4	21.5	20.0	4.8	5.4	82.4	9.5	7.8	0.3
Butler County	37.2	48.1	26.7	37.0	15.4	X	64.2	45.6	3 123	49.8	20.3	14.9	0.1	-2.2	72.7	13.7	13.2	0.3
Caldwell County	33.7	44.4	24.1	33.4	35.2	0.0	68.8	45.8	2 733	46.7	20.2	18.8	0.9	-7.0	73.5	15.0	10.9	0.6
Calloway County	31.7	39.4	24.7	32.0	30.7	27.3	16.7	34.6	6 048	47.4	24.0	16.0	-1.2	-4.7	68.3	21.6	9.6	0.5
Campbell County	43.5	54.5	33.6	43.7	29.8	55.2	54.4	41.2	21 827	47.4	20.4	20.5	3.3	2.8	81.3	11.1	7.3	0.3
Carlisle County	33.9	46.4	22.2	33.8	23.5	100.0	X	75.0	1 191	40.1	33.5	16.3	-8.2	-12.0	73.3	11.5	14.1	1.1
Carroll County	41.5	51.6	31.8	42.2	24.4	0.0	55.6	52.9	2 343	43.1	17.1	18.4	-3.1	-2.5	76.9	15.1	7.7	0.4
Carter County	28.8	35.4	22.6	28.9	0.0	24.1	22.2	35.3	6 266	35.4	31.0	16.3	-12.9	-13.9	72.5	15.3	11.8	0.4
Casey County	32.4	41.1	24.3	32.3	50.0	32.5	0.0	40.7	3 595	36.7	30.7	15.1	-12.8	-9.4	70.4	12.3	16.1	1.2
Christian County	43.8	56.4	30.2	44.3	40.2	50.2	42.1	52.4	19 463	39.9	27.5	20.6	-4.1	-4.0	71.9	17.2	10.4	0.5
Clark County	43.0	53.5	33.5	43.6	28.5	54.1	48.3	31.7	7 646	51.0	17.9	19.3	5.7	1.1	75.5	15.2	8.9	0.4
Clay County	23.7	26.4	20.6	24.4	15.9	0.0	20.6	17.5	5 549	25.5	23.3	12.2	-26.9	-24.8	69.6	21.0	9.1	0.2
Clinton County	35.1	44.0	27.1	34.7	0.0	X	100.0	74.6	2 084	45.8	20.5	19.4	0.6	-7.4	69.6	16.6	13.6	0.1
Crittenden County	35.2	45.1	26.0	35.2	34.0	57.1	60.0	17.2	2 084	36.4	32.6	16.8	-11.4	-8.8	70.8	14.6	14.3	0.3

[1]Hispanic or Latino persons may be of any race.

Table B-3. States and Counties — Education, Labor Force, and Income

STATE County	Percent who worked at home	Percent of the population 5 years and over with a disability	Veterans as a percent of the population 18 years and over	Occupation for employed population 16 years and over (percent)						Industry for employed population 16 years and over (percent)					
				Management, professional, and related occupations	Service occupations	Sales and office occupations	Farming, fishing, and forestry occupations	Construction, extraction, and maintenance occupations	Production, transportation and material moving occupations	Agriculture, forestry, fishing, and mining	Construction and manufacturing	Wholesale and retail trade	Transportation and warehousing, and utilities	Service industries	Public administration
	42	43	44	45	46	47	48	49	50	51	52	53	54	55	56
KANSAS—Cont'd															
Osage County	4.3	20.0	16.6	27.4	14.0	24.5	1.2	15.8	17.0	4.9	21.0	17.1	8.0	40.7	8.3
Osborne County	9.6	21.7	15.4	35.1	14.4	18.8	2.2	10.9	18.6	17.0	18.5	14.8	6.1	39.3	4.3
Ottawa County	5.4	17.9	14.8	28.4	15.5	23.8	2.4	13.0	16.9	9.7	22.5	14.5	7.3	42.1	4.1
Pawnee County............	3.4	26.0	13.3	34.6	19.3	24.9	4.1	8.5	8.5	13.6	9.1	12.5	5.4	50.7	8.6
Phillips County	8.1	19.4	15.2	33.1	16.4	22.1	3.6	10.2	14.6	15.5	17.3	11.2	8.3	43.6	4.1
Pottawatomie County	5.3	15.1	15.3	32.8	13.7	22.5	2.0	15.0	14.0	6.1	19.9	13.0	6.8	48.3	5.9
Pratt County	6.5	18.6	13.5	32.3	15.3	27.5	2.6	9.8	12.5	13.1	9.7	17.2	7.6	46.8	5.6
Rawlins County	10.5	19.9	15.7	40.8	16.5	21.2	5.9	7.6	7.9	25.8	9.2	12.7	5.9	42.2	4.3
Reno County	3.9	21.0	14.3	27.9	17.6	25.7	0.9	9.3	18.5	3.8	23.0	17.3	4.6	47.2	4.2
Republic County...........	10.8	20.0	15.5	35.1	10.9	22.9	3.9	10.2	17.1	19.4	17.1	16.5	7.5	35.7	3.8
Rice County.................	4.4	19.9	13.8	28.2	16.4	22.0	2.8	11.0	18.8	10.8	18.0	13.1	7.5	47.6	3.0
Riley County................	3.5	10.7	10.3	38.4	18.4	27.1	0.7	8.0	7.4	2.1	9.4	14.7	2.2	66.0	5.5
Rooks County	4.8	28.4	13.7	32.3	15.5	22.8	2.8	12.1	14.5	17.6	17.3	12.7	7.3	39.5	5.6
Rush County................	6.8	20.7	17.2	33.0	17.0	18.9	1.9	11.8	17.4	14.8	19.2	9.6	6.8	44.5	5.1
Russell County	7.9	24.8	16.6	30.6	19.7	21.5	1.9	12.4	13.9	13.8	15.6	11.1	4.0	52.2	3.3
Saline County	4.0	17.9	15.0	28.0	16.1	26.3	0.5	10.6	18.6	2.1	24.6	15.8	4.4	49.8	3.3
Scott County................	5.8	17.2	12.7	34.7	15.7	19.5	9.1	12.0	9.0	24.9	10.7	13.9	5.6	43.0	2.0
Sedgwick County	2.5	17.9	13.9	32.1	13.6	27.0	0.3	11.1	16.0	0.8	30.5	14.7	3.9	46.8	3.3
Seward County	2.1	16.8	8.6	21.0	15.0	22.5	3.3	12.0	26.2	11.5	27.3	14.0	6.1	37.6	3.4
Shawnee County	2.6	20.0	15.9	34.2	14.4	29.8	0.2	8.9	12.4	0.7	15.4	14.6	6.7	52.7	10.0
Sheridan County	12.6	13.9	15.7	39.0	15.2	20.8	5.0	9.7	10.2	26.8	6.4	15.8	7.3	40.3	3.5
Sherman County	7.4	19.9	13.7	25.9	19.0	27.0	3.9	12.6	11.6	12.5	10.9	20.8	5.2	45.5	5.1
Smith County................	9.1	20.6	14.7	35.5	16.2	23.1	3.9	7.3	14.0	17.2	13.4	14.6	8.5	41.7	4.6
Stafford County	5.4	18.5	12.9	37.6	15.2	17.7	4.5	9.3	15.7	20.9	11.1	10.7	6.6	45.8	4.9
Stanton County	3.2	15.5	8.8	28.7	12.5	22.2	13.8	10.9	12.0	29.7	11.9	14.0	6.5	33.2	4.6
Stevens County............	5.4	14.8	11.4	31.4	14.4	20.7	6.8	13.6	13.1	23.7	11.0	14.5	10.3	38.4	2.1
Sumner County	5.2	18.8	14.3	31.9	13.9	20.7	1.2	11.6	20.6	5.9	30.6	11.7	6.8	41.9	3.1
Thomas County	6.9	16.8	10.8	35.6	16.8	22.5	3.4	11.5	10.2	13.2	9.5	17.3	5.6	50.6	3.7
Trego County	7.7	21.5	15.1	33.0	17.0	20.5	4.4	11.7	10.3	18.4	8.9	13.6	9.6	46.0	3.5
Wabaunsee County.......	4.6	15.1	15.5	33.3	13.2	22.8	1.7	13.2	15.9	8.4	21.6	12.8	7.8	43.0	6.3
Wallace County	11.8	13.2	13.4	33.4	14.4	21.9	6.9	12.6	10.8	24.2	9.4	14.9	8.0	37.3	6.2
Washington County.......	9.3	20.7	14.9	33.0	14.3	20.6	3.7	11.9	16.5	18.7	19.2	13.2	4.9	40.1	3.8
Wichita County	8.3	18.0	12.2	31.5	12.0	19.5	14.3	8.9	13.7	34.5	10.2	10.7	8.9	31.9	3.7
Wilson County	5.0	21.9	15.6	25.1	16.8	19.9	1.4	11.0	25.7	7.4	33.0	10.5	7.0	38.4	3.8
Woodson County..........	6.7	24.3	17.3	26.4	14.0	21.3	1.8	12.1	24.3	10.7	26.1	11.3	7.5	37.9	6.4
Wyandotte County.........	2.0	24.6	13.2	22.0	17.0	27.8	0.3	11.7	21.2	0.4	22.0	15.6	8.5	48.6	4.9
KENTUCKY	2.7	23.7	12.5	28.7	14.3	25.4	0.9	11.0	19.7	3.3	24.8	15.5	6.0	46.1	4.3
Adair County	5.1	27.1	9.6	26.3	13.0	23.1	3.3	11.6	22.8	8.5	27.7	12.8	4.5	42.9	3.5
Allen County	3.4	26.7	12.0	22.1	11.0	18.0	1.6	13.8	33.5	4.5	41.4	14.6	4.4	31.9	3.2
Anderson County	2.2	20.6	11.8	25.9	9.6	25.3	1.0	11.6	26.6	3.3	36.3	12.9	3.4	33.6	10.4
Ballard County.............	2.4	22.4	14.9	21.7	14.2	24.6	2.5	16.8	20.2	3.7	30.2	16.1	5.5	40.9	3.7
Barren County	3.4	24.9	11.5	23.9	15.1	24.5	1.8	9.1	25.5	4.5	32.8	16.4	4.1	39.2	2.9
Bath County	2.7	29.3	11.1	25.7	12.2	19.9	1.7	14.4	26.1	5.9	31.5	13.4	5.7	38.0	5.4
Bell County.................	1.5	36.3	11.1	24.2	17.5	23.7	1.1	13.5	20.0	6.6	19.9	16.4	5.4	46.0	5.7
Boone County	2.6	16.1	13.0	32.0	11.8	30.1	0.3	8.9	16.9	0.8	23.7	16.4	11.4	44.1	3.6
Bourbon County	3.5	22.8	13.5	25.2	15.9	22.3	3.7	10.2	22.7	10.9	30.2	11.9	4.0	39.3	3.7
Boyd County	1.8	26.4	15.5	28.3	16.4	27.5	0.1	12.9	14.8	1.6	20.2	17.3	6.7	49.5	4.7
Boyle County...............	3.7	21.7	13.4	29.6	14.8	24.5	1.0	8.4	21.6	2.9	28.8	13.4	3.8	47.2	3.3
Bracken County	3.7	26.4	13.2	23.1	11.1	19.5	1.0	17.5	27.8	7.0	32.9	16.0	6.9	34.4	2.8
Breathitt County	2.7	36.6	9.3	27.8	18.1	23.6	0.6	12.8	17.2	4.6	16.7	17.2	6.1	50.1	5.3
Breckinridge County......	3.6	23.8	13.1	21.9	15.0	17.5	2.0	14.2	29.3	5.5	35.1	14.6	6.4	34.5	3.9
Bullitt County	1.9	20.0	13.3	21.7	12.2	27.6	0.2	13.8	24.4	0.9	28.9	16.9	9.5	41.0	2.7
Butler County	2.7	23.5	11.4	16.5	13.9	18.4	2.3	16.7	32.2	5.7	39.5	13.0	6.1	32.5	3.3
Caldwell County	4.6	25.2	14.2	23.9	14.6	21.8	1.7	14.0	23.9	6.4	29.6	15.7	6.0	37.7	4.6
Calloway County	2.9	21.5	11.5	31.4	15.1	24.4	1.0	8.9	19.3	2.5	22.5	15.2	4.7	52.3	2.9
Campbell County	2.3	19.4	12.4	31.4	13.9	29.9	0.2	10.2	14.4	0.4	21.3	15.7	7.3	51.6	3.7
Carlisle County............	2.8	23.6	12.5	20.2	12.2	19.8	2.5	19.3	26.0	6.8	30.5	17.3	8.7	34.5	2.1
Carroll County	2.8	23.5	16.2	19.0	15.9	22.1	1.3	14.4	27.2	2.4	39.7	15.1	4.8	32.1	5.9
Carter County	4.0	20.7	10.1	22.7	14.7	20.1	1.6	20.3	20.6	4.3	24.8	14.2	5.8	47.7	3.1
Casey County...............	4.8	29.8	11.7	19.5	14.3	18.5	3.0	11.8	33.0	8.3	34.9	14.4	4.9	34.5	2.9
Christian County	2.5	24.0	13.6	25.2	16.8	24.1	1.2	10.0	22.8	3.8	27.3	14.9	4.6	44.3	5.2
Clark County	2.0	23.8	13.6	26.8	14.8	24.8	0.8	11.9	20.8	2.2	29.3	17.4	5.9	40.9	4.2
Clay County.................	1.8	35.6	8.0	23.1	13.1	25.9	0.6	12.4	24.9	7.3	25.1	15.5	6.3	40.3	5.5
Clinton County..............	2.2	33.3	11.1	21.6	17.1	18.3	2.0	12.6	28.4	6.2	33.8	12.1	5.1	39.0	3.7
Crittenden County	3.7	25.6	13.4	21.9	15.4	19.5	2.4	16.2	24.6	11.5	27.6	13.6	5.5	37.4	4.4

Table B-3. States and Counties — **Education, Labor Force, and Income**

STATE County	Median house-hold income	Median family income: All families	Median family income: Families with children: Married-couple	Median family income: Families with children: Male house-holder	Median family income: Families with children: Female house-holder	Median nonfamily house-hold income	Median income for full-year, full-time workers: Men	Median income for full-year, full-time workers: Women	Per capita income	Households by source of income (percent): With earnings	Households by source of income (percent): With interest, dividend, or rental income	Households by source of income (percent): With Social Security income	Households by source of income (percent): With public assis-tance income	Households by source of income (percent): With retire-ment income	House-holds with income over $100,000 (percent)	+/– U.S. percent for income over $100,000	House-holds with income below poverty (percent)	Families with children with income below poverty (percent)
	57	58	59	60	61	62	63	64	65	66	67	68	69	70	71	72	73	74
KANSAS—Cont'd																		
Osage County	37 928	44 581	52 697	31 125	18 750	19 878	31 380	23 971	17 691	78.4	37.6	32.5	2.9	17.4	4.0	-8.3	9.6	8.8
Osborne County	29 145	35 438	42 670	20 833	17 750	16 540	26 199	17 641	16 236	73.6	48.1	39.6	0.6	11.9	3.7	-8.6	11.7	11.8
Ottawa County	38 009	46 033	53 500	25 417	20 694	20 353	31 961	21 926	17 663	79.3	39.6	32.8	0.7	12.9	4.5	-7.8	9.2	8.7
Pawnee County	35 175	45 634	46 141	21 250	23 080	19 925	27 212	21 599	17 584	79.5	39.3	32.0	1.3	16.0	6.2	-6.1	7.7	6.6
Phillips County	35 013	41 638	50 201	29 167	14 583	19 755	30 745	18 770	17 121	73.3	46.1	37.8	1.8	15.5	4.0	-8.3	10.5	11.3
Pottawatomie County	40 176	47 261	51 617	35 938	16 696	19 795	32 500	24 627	17 785	83.7	41.8	26.5	1.3	16.5	6.1	-6.2	9.5	10.1
Pratt County	35 529	43 156	50 222	26 250	17 024	20 560	31 691	21 250	17 906	75.5	44.5	34.3	3.0	13.9	4.6	-7.7	10.3	11.8
Rawlins County	32 105	40 074	45 909	25 250	17 574	15 862	29 141	20 709	17 161	74.5	49.1	42.3	1.6	12.4	4.4	-7.9	12.9	14.4
Reno County	35 510	42 643	51 039	23 576	19 159	20 627	32 274	22 055	18 520	78.2	38.5	30.1	2.6	15.5	5.8	-6.5	11.3	12.4
Republic County	30 494	39 215	43 250	36 000	15 781	16 595	26 881	18 602	17 433	72.8	47.2	42.8	1.5	16.8	4.8	-7.5	9.7	11.2
Rice County	35 671	40 960	45 816	33 500	15 455	19 468	32 247	20 092	16 064	75.9	37.7	36.3	2.0	16.0	4.6	-7.7	10.7	13.5
Riley County	32 042	46 489	51 589	26 328	19 803	18 982	28 242	24 766	16 349	87.9	41.8	16.5	1.2	13.3	7.2	-5.1	20.8	10.9
Rooks County	30 457	36 931	43 413	29 821	18 125	17 717	27 596	19 290	15 588	73.2	37.8	37.6	1.9	13.7	2.3	-10.0	11.0	10.3
Rush County	31 268	38 821	40 938	22 500	18 125	18 203	27 054	20 975	18 033	72.6	47.9	40.6	2.8	14.9	4.0	-8.3	10.2	10.4
Russell County	29 284	40 355	44 583	17 404	15 776	15 850	26 747	19 118	17 073	69.6	44.2	41.7	2.9	15.1	5.8	-6.5	13.3	15.3
Saline County	37 308	46 362	53 088	28 214	21 875	22 215	32 458	23 118	19 073	81.8	38.5	26.8	2.1	13.6	5.9	-6.4	9.0	9.0
Scott County	40 534	50 549	55 074	19 583	20 000	19 232	33 278	21 875	20 443	84.9	43.6	29.4	0.4	7.8	8.7	-3.6	5.5	4.2
Sedgwick County	42 485	51 645	59 342	31 768	21 876	25 839	38 986	26 954	20 907	83.1	35.4	23.0	2.8	15.1	9.1	-3.2	9.4	10.5
Seward County	36 752	41 134	44 951	21 563	15 714	23 792	30 315	22 472	15 059	84.8	29.6	20.7	1.9	9.5	6.6	-5.7	14.6	19.3
Shawnee County	40 988	51 464	60 199	28 111	22 092	23 885	36 511	27 231	20 904	80.4	39.9	27.8	2.7	18.5	8.4	-3.9	9.6	10.2
Sheridan County	33 547	38 292	39 565	28 750	10 625	16 771	28 500	17 740	16 299	79.6	48.1	35.0	1.9	10.5	5.1	-7.2	12.4	21.2
Sherman County	32 684	38 824	46 991	8 500	23 451	20 655	28 779	22 586	16 761	80.1	42.5	31.6	2.6	11.1	3.7	-8.6	11.9	15.2
Smith County	28 486	36 951	42 583	31 250	17 857	15 997	26 754	20 141	14 983	72.7	50.6	43.0	1.5	12.7	2.6	-9.7	12.1	11.0
Stafford County	31 107	38 235	42 500	25 000	20 938	18 086	28 552	22 610	16 409	73.3	42.8	38.6	2.7	12.6	3.1	-9.2	11.7	11.7
Stanton County	40 172	46 300	47 721	30 781	12 188	22 344	31 932	21 993	18 043	87.2	36.7	25.8	0.8	10.0	7.7	-4.6	13.0	15.4
Stevens County	41 830	49 063	54 113	24 464	18 438	26 773	37 414	24 357	17 814	85.2	40.4	26.9	1.5	12.2	5.9	-6.4	8.0	13.2
Sumner County	39 415	46 739	52 555	38 269	20 529	19 468	37 893	24 178	18 305	77.8	36.2	31.2	3.1	16.0	5.6	-6.7	10.2	11.3
Thomas County	37 034	45 931	49 408	21 250	12 813	20 478	35 989	22 604	19 028	79.9	46.7	28.1	1.1	10.2	7.6	-4.7	12.9	9.5
Trego County	29 677	40 524	45 667	20 000	9 821	17 642	27 917	17 500	16 239	70.3	45.9	41.4	2.3	10.8	3.4	-8.9	13.1	14.2
Wabaunsee County	41 710	47 500	53 370	31 563	23 333	23 056	32 500	24 116	17 704	81.7	42.8	30.2	2.0	15.8	4.1	-8.2	7.5	8.4
Wallace County	33 000	42 022	42 188	27 500	10 417	15 774	26 585	18 625	17 016	81.1	45.3	33.2	1.0	8.3	7.9	-4.4	13.2	15.8
Washington County	29 363	37 260	41 411	28 500	19 375	15 723	26 508	18 371	15 515	74.2	47.1	41.2	1.3	12.6	3.3	-9.0	10.9	9.8
Wichita County	33 462	41 034	40 724	21 719	15 469	18 661	29 077	19 550	16 720	82.5	41.6	27.8	2.7	9.4	6.3	-6.0	11.4	18.2
Wilson County	29 747	36 990	41 658	26 250	17 900	14 485	27 500	19 297	14 910	72.4	32.5	37.1	3.7	15.1	2.8	-9.5	12.8	12.1
Woodson County	25 335	31 369	45 625	22 500	11 458	15 469	25 087	16 725	14 283	67.0	35.7	43.5	2.3	17.7	2.6	-9.7	17.0	18.4
Wyandotte County	33 784	40 333	49 222	28 403	19 534	20 895	31 907	25 454	16 005	79.1	23.5	26.9	4.5	15.9	4.7	-7.6	15.7	18.5
KENTUCKY	33 672	40 939	49 851	24 350	15 713	18 972	33 836	24 194	18 093	76.5	29.0	28.5	3.8	17.5	7.2	-5.1	16.2	18.1
Adair County	24 055	29 779	38 873	20 139	14 688	11 327	24 346	17 540	14 931	70.9	23.8	31.3	4.2	14.4	4.7	-7.6	24.8	22.8
Allen County	31 238	36 815	44 361	26 058	19 063	13 380	28 580	22 928	14 506	73.9	24.0	31.8	3.2	16.3	3.2	-9.1	18.0	17.8
Anderson County	45 433	50 837	56 648	35 694	24 432	22 355	34 620	25 589	18 621	83.3	30.9	23.9	2.0	16.5	5.4	-6.9	9.1	7.3
Ballard County	32 130	41 386	48 255	21 667	13 750	17 169	33 987	21 523	19 035	74.3	29.9	33.8	1.8	16.7	4.7	-7.6	14.0	15.6
Barren County	31 240	37 231	44 216	30 699	15 453	15 669	30 818	21 606	16 816	75.8	29.4	30.7	3.2	15.9	4.3	-8.0	16.6	16.4
Bath County	26 018	31 758	38 250	23 750	12 313	10 742	29 105	21 777	15 326	70.2	23.1	33.5	7.7	16.6	3.9	-8.4	23.6	24.8
Bell County	19 057	23 818	29 172	14 697	8 802	9 356	25 288	20 520	11 526	60.1	13.7	37.3	7.6	16.8	2.4	-9.9	32.1	38.6
Boone County	53 593	61 114	68 598	33 375	22 468	29 288	43 553	28 674	23 535	87.8	35.6	20.1	1.6	14.3	14.9	2.6	6.2	6.4
Bourbon County	35 038	42 294	53 217	26 042	13 725	17 948	31 879	24 592	18 335	78.4	26.1	27.4	3.5	18.9	7.2	-5.1	15.2	19.6
Boyd County	32 749	41 125	50 538	17 135	15 173	16 674	37 065	24 144	18 212	70.5	33.4	35.9	4.1	24.4	6.4	-5.9	15.6	18.8
Boyle County	35 241	42 699	51 549	25 435	16 250	18 620	35 357	24 444	18 288	76.6	32.2	31.8	3.0	18.0	7.2	-5.1	13.4	14.6
Bracken County	34 823	40 469	47 636	32 391	15 000	16 220	32 101	21 378	16 478	78.3	27.4	30.1	2.8	16.5	3.9	-8.4	13.2	10.2
Breathitt County	19 155	23 721	29 076	13 382	9 201	8 696	26 529	20 683	11 044	60.3	14.3	37.3	8.6	15.1	2.1	-10.2	34.2	37.9
Breckinridge County	30 554	36 575	41 903	22 065	16 838	14 192	31 778	20 066	15 402	73.4	28.1	32.0	3.3	19.4	3.5	-8.8	17.1	16.0
Bullitt County	45 106	49 481	54 819	28 534	19 121	23 307	36 420	24 667	18 339	85.5	26.7	22.5	2.3	17.3	7.6	-4.7	8.0	9.5
Butler County	29 405	35 317	38 715	18 224	12 232	13 646	27 220	20 338	14 617	77.0	21.4	31.8	4.0	19.1	2.6	-9.7	18.5	18.5
Caldwell County	28 686	35 258	48 625	31 477	13 640	15 940	32 904	20 755	16 264	70.2	29.2	35.4	3.2	21.1	4.2	-8.1	16.7	17.7
Calloway County	30 134	39 914	49 643	22 261	15 804	16 582	32 332	22 682	16 566	76.6	36.1	31.0	3.3	20.0	5.4	-6.9	17.5	14.8
Campbell County	41 903	51 481	63 641	35 368	19 314	23 917	39 298	28 727	20 637	80.3	38.5	26.3	2.5	18.0	9.0	-3.3	9.7	11.5
Carlisle County	30 087	33 433	36 650	16 250	15 887	16 473	30 137	20 087	16 276	72.4	29.7	32.8	3.0	20.1	5.0	-7.3	14.0	17.5
Carroll County	35 925	44 037	51 843	20 781	11 220	14 884	35 139	21 483	17 057	80.1	24.9	31.1	3.8	17.0	3.4	-8.9	15.5	17.4
Carter County	26 427	31 278	36 513	21 042	13 989	13 297	30 183	20 799	13 442	71.6	19.5	32.6	4.4	18.4	2.6	-9.7	22.2	25.4
Casey County	21 580	27 044	31 617	13 846	16 944	11 156	22 464	18 515	12 867	68.3	19.0	33.1	4.7	16.1	3.0	-9.3	26.5	27.4
Christian County	31 177	35 240	38 618	25 980	16 446	18 742	25 564	21 408	14 611	81.6	23.3	23.9	3.9	16.2	4.2	-8.1	14.8	16.0
Clark County	39 946	45 647	53 310	30 380	16 272	20 552	36 736	25 112	19 170	79.6	29.9	26.9	4.0	20.0	7.2	-5.1	11.0	13.0
Clay County	16 271	18 925	23 364	13 977	8 801	8 462	24 633	18 243	9 716	58.6	11.1	32.9	10.6	12.1	1.5	-10.8	39.5	43.3
Clinton County	19 563	25 919	29 718	16 786	10 425	9 041	21 335	16 493	13 286	66.9	15.9	36.5	4.8	11.6	2.4	-9.9	29.3	28.2
Crittenden County	29 060	36 462	40 972	17 188	12 604	15 593	31 070	20 044	15 262	70.7	29.2	35.0	3.0	21.7	3.3	-9.0	17.8	23.2

STATE/ County code	MSA/PMSA/ NECMA code[1]	STATE County	High school graduates			College graduates		College graduates (percent)				
			Total population 25 years and over	Percent with a high school diploma or less	Percent with a high school diploma or more	Percent with a bachelor's degree or more	+/− U.S. percent with bachelor's degree or more	Non-Hispanic White	Black or African American	American Indian and Alaska Native	Asian, Hawaiian, and Pacific Islander	Hispanic or Latino[2]
			1	2	3	4	5	6	7	8	9	10
		KENTUCKY—Cont'd										
21 057	...	Cumberland County	4 972	80.4	56.0	7.1	-17.3	7.1	8.5	0.0	20.0	0.0
21 059	5990	Daviess County	59 745	56.9	80.7	17.0	-7.4	17.2	7.6	17.6	63.5	17.6
21 061	...	Edmonson County	7 865	78.4	61.7	4.9	-19.5	4.9	0.0	33.3	0.0	0.0
21 063	...	Elliott County	4 422	78.5	52.6	7.8	-16.6	7.8	X	X	X	X
21 065	...	Estill County	10 189	78.8	58.5	6.9	-17.5	6.7	0.0	0.0	35.7	41.2
21 067	4280	Fayette County	167 235	36.6	85.8	35.6	11.2	38.7	14.5	17.7	67.3	14.6
21 069	...	Fleming County	9 154	71.5	66.5	8.8	-15.6	9.0	5.0	0.0	X	0.0
21 071	...	Floyd County	28 370	68.6	61.3	9.7	-14.7	9.6	2.5	0.0	76.9	6.1
21 073	...	Franklin County	32 388	52.6	78.8	23.8	-0.6	23.7	24.9	20.0	74.2	14.3
21 075	...	Fulton County	5 111	69.4	69.5	11.5	-12.9	13.9	1.1	X	X	0.0
21 077	1640	Gallatin County	5 007	76.4	68.0	6.9	-17.5	6.7	12.5	0.0	0.0	11.5
21 079	...	Garrard County	9 951	66.3	69.4	10.5	-13.9	10.5	0.0	100.0	36.8	17.9
21 081	1640	Grant County	13 861	71.8	72.4	9.4	-15.0	9.3	0.0	65.5	13.4	0.0
21 083	...	Graves County	24 932	65.5	73.4	12.6	-11.8	12.7	7.7	20.0	56.9	1.5
21 085	...	Grayson County	15 940	74.3	62.8	7.7	-16.7	7.7	7.1	13.3	0.0	8.3
21 087	...	Green County	7 983	74.8	61.4	9.1	-15.3	8.9	6.1	0.0	40.0	0.0
21 089	3400	Greenup County	25 323	62.6	75.1	11.5	-12.9	11.2	14.2	0.0	65.7	26.4
21 091	...	Hancock County	5 427	68.5	77.2	8.1	-16.3	8.3	0.0	0.0	0.0	0.0
21 093	...	Hardin County	58 358	52.0	82.3	15.4	-9.0	15.7	11.5	13.1	30.9	10.8
21 095	...	Harlan County	22 041	75.6	58.7	8.9	-15.5	8.7	5.6	13.0	51.3	19.4
21 097	...	Harrison County	12 009	68.5	74.2	10.6	-13.8	10.6	5.7	7.9	0.0	9.4
21 099	...	Hart County	11 474	76.9	58.2	7.0	-17.4	7.3	0.9	34.0	100.0	2.4
21 101	2440	Henderson County	29 960	59.5	78.3	13.8	-10.6	13.9	6.7	15.8	63.2	32.4
21 103	...	Henry County	10 032	71.1	73.4	9.8	-14.6	9.8	9.3	0.0	35.0	9.4
21 105	...	Hickman County	3 734	74.7	64.4	8.8	-15.6	9.3	0.9	0.0	85.7	18.2
21 107	...	Hopkins County	31 464	67.0	71.3	10.6	-13.8	10.7	8.2	9.4	45.2	8.1
21 109	...	Jackson County	8 611	80.5	52.9	6.8	-17.6	6.8	X	0.0	0.0	0.0
21 111	4520	Jefferson County	464 284	47.2	81.8	24.8	0.4	27.2	11.9	19.1	50.6	18.4
21 113	4280	Jessamine County	24 182	53.3	79.1	21.5	-2.0	21.4	11.6	11.2	67.9	24.4
21 115	...	Johnson County	15 735	71.4	63.8	9.3	-15.1	9.0	22.2	0.0	61.7	9.1
21 117	1640	Kenton County	97 727	50.4	82.1	22.9	-1.5	23.4	9.4	18.9	43.0	13.5
21 119	...	Knott County	11 427	72.1	58.7	10.2	-14.2	10.2	0.0	70.6	7.7	0.0
21 121	...	Knox County	20 401	78.5	54.1	8.8	-15.6	8.8	5.7	15.0	44.4	11.4
21 123	...	Larue County	9 017	69.2	71.0	10.9	-13.5	10.7	6.1	32.1	0.0	49.1
21 125	...	Laurel County	34 431	71.0	63.9	10.6	-13.8	10.6	5.6	13.5	50.5	13.8
21 127	...	Lawrence County	10 256	74.8	58.2	6.6	-17.8	6.5	0.0	50.0	X	0.0
21 129	...	Lee County	5 381	79.9	50.9	6.3	-18.1	6.5	0.0	0.0	0.0	0.0
21 131	...	Leslie County	8 214	77.6	52.5	6.3	-18.1	6.2	0.0	0.0	100.0	15.4
21 133	...	Letcher County	16 930	74.4	58.5	7.7	-16.7	7.5	11.7	0.0	68.0	0.0
21 135	...	Lewis County	9 256	77.3	57.4	6.4	-18.0	6.4	0.0	6.5	X	0.0
21 137	...	Lincoln County	15 440	76.1	64.6	8.4	-16.0	8.3	3.6	0.0	91.7	23.6
21 139	...	Livingston County	6 851	66.4	74.3	8.4	-16.0	8.3	0.0	8.7	0.0	0.0
21 141	...	Logan County	17 471	71.0	68.5	9.6	-14.8	9.9	4.8	0.0	69.7	5.7
21 143	...	Lyon County	6 185	68.5	68.0	10.1	-14.3	10.5	0.0	0.0	76.7	6.5
21 145	...	McCracken County	45 038	53.1	80.3	18.1	-6.3	19.2	6.9	9.7	46.4	16.9
21 147	...	McCreary County	10 668	78.4	52.6	6.7	-17.7	6.4	0.0	0.0	52.2	49.1
21 149	...	McLean County	6 737	67.8	70.8	8.7	-15.7	8.9	0.0	0.0	0.0	0.0
21 151	4280	Madison County	42 125	54.5	75.2	21.8	-2.6	22.0	10.5	16.2	67.4	13.0
21 153	...	Magoffin County	8 410	78.1	50.1	6.3	-18.1	6.3	0.0	0.0	20.0	0.0
21 155	...	Marion County	11 772	73.4	70.5	9.1	-15.3	9.2	3.7	0.0	47.2	19.7
21 157	...	Marshall County	21 278	61.1	76.9	13.7	-10.7	13.8	0.0	11.8	27.0	13.2
21 159	...	Martin County	7 835	75.6	54.0	9.0	-15.4	9.2	0.0	0.0	X	0.0
21 161	...	Mason County	11 372	62.5	73.3	14.4	-10.0	15.0	6.6	0.0	27.3	0.0
21 163	...	Meade County	16 131	62.0	77.9	11.3	-13.1	11.0	16.6	0.0	33.0	14.8
21 165	...	Menifee County	4 213	81.7	57.6	8.4	-16.0	8.6	0.0	0.0	X	0.0
21 167	...	Mercer County	14 158	65.8	75.8	13.5	-10.9	13.9	8.3	0.0	19.1	0.0
21 169	...	Metcalfe County	6 729	79.6	58.0	6.6	-17.8	6.7	13.0	0.0	X	0.0
21 171	...	Monroe County	7 896	76.8	57.8	8.4	-16.0	8.6	0.0	0.0	100.0	0.0
21 173	...	Montgomery County	15 033	68.8	70.5	13.4	-11.0	13.5	9.3	0.0	85.7	18.9
21 175	...	Morgan County	9 321	76.4	56.4	7.7	-16.7	7.9	2.5	0.0	15.4	2.0
21 177	...	Muhlenberg County	21 676	74.9	65.8	8.1	-16.3	8.3	5.2	0.0	0.0	0.0
21 179	...	Nelson County	23 785	64.1	79.0	13.4	-11.0	13.4	9.4	0.0	52.5	15.6
21 181	...	Nicholas County	4 636	74.7	62.9	7.5	-16.9	7.2	21.7	0.0	X	0.0
21 183	...	Ohio County	15 237	74.5	67.0	7.4	-17.0	7.4	15.0	0.0	100.0	0.0
21 185	4520	Oldham County	30 366	40.0	86.5	30.6	6.2	31.7	9.8	50.8	43.7	16.1
21 187	...	Owen County	6 999	73.3	67.9	9.1	-15.3	9.0	18.4	0.0	28.6	3.5

[1]MSA = Metropolitan Statistical Area. PMSA = Primary MSA. NECMA = New England County Metropolitan Area. See the Appendix A for explanation of these concepts. See Appendix B for list of metropolitan areas identified by type, with component counties.
[2]Hispanic or Latino persons may be of any race.

STATE County	School enrollment			Population 16 to 19 years				Employment status, 2000			Work status in 1999 of the population 16 years and over (percent)		
											Worked in 1999		
	Grades kindergarten through 12	College or graduate school	Percent private	Number	Percent in armed forces	Percent high school graduates	Percent not enrolled, not grads, not in armed forces, not employed	Total population 16 years and over	Percent in labor force	Unemployment rate	Full-time	Part-time	Did not work in 1999
	11	12	13	14	15	16	17	18	19	20	21	22	23
KENTUCKY—Cont'd													
Cumberland County	1 375	140	4.3	372	0.0	6.7	9.9	5 704	53.4	6.5	49.7	8.6	41.7
Daviess County	17 533	3 889	20.0	5 545	0.0	10.5	3.1	70 915	64.4	5.8	54.4	15.2	30.4
Edmonson County........	2 170	282	1.6	675	0.0	11.6	5.9	9 259	53.8	6.9	49.3	11.2	39.5
Elliott County	1 251	176	1.3	400	0.0	17.3	11.3	5 252	45.9	10.5	41.5	8.6	49.9
Estill County	2 847	385	4.1	873	0.0	7.3	14.4	12 067	49.1	7.4	41.2	10.6	48.2
Fayette County	40 156	31 508	12.7	15 177	0.2	8.0	4.9	210 783	69.8	5.4	58.2	18.2	23.6
Fleming County	2 635	412	6.4	806	0.0	10.8	10.5	10 730	59.6	6.7	52.9	10.8	36.3
Floyd County	7 480	1 534	7.1	2 405	0.0	11.2	13.7	33 750	41.4	10.0	37.7	8.1	54.3
Franklin County	8 273	2 644	14.6	2 671	0.0	10.1	6.4	38 206	66.4	6.2	60.0	12.2	27.8
Fulton County	1 546	133	4.9	443	0.0	17.6	7.0	6 048	51.6	8.6	45.3	11.9	42.8
Gallatin County............	1 630	155	7.1	445	0.0	12.8	13.5	5 856	64.2	3.5	58.5	10.5	31.0
Garrard County	2 688	476	6.7	836	0.0	19.1	8.5	11 586	63.0	5.1	55.4	13.1	31.6
Grant County................	4 684	503	6.9	1 275	0.0	17.5	5.3	16 629	67.6	5.4	59.7	13.3	27.0
Graves County	6 694	1 251	10.7	1 907	0.0	12.0	8.5	28 979	58.1	5.5	48.8	13.0	38.2
Grayson County	4 304	684	5.0	1 296	0.0	14.4	8.2	18 829	57.1	5.7	51.0	11.8	37.2
Green County	2 001	377	8.2	557	0.0	9.3	3.1	9 210	55.2	5.1	48.9	11.3	39.8
Greenup County............	6 591	1 152	5.6	1 879	0.0	11.4	4.5	29 201	53.1	7.3	46.0	12.1	41.9
Hancock County	1 641	253	7.7	434	0.0	6.2	2.8	6 402	62.6	5.1	54.4	12.4	33.1
Hardin County	19 560	4 879	9.1	6 193	12.9	25.3	3.3	71 243	67.6	5.0	57.6	14.1	28.3
Harlan County	6 320	1 004	5.4	1 960	0.0	9.3	15.5	25 978	39.7	13.2	31.7	8.8	59.5
Harrison County	3 420	518	6.1	978	0.0	8.4	2.6	14 019	62.8	3.6	54.7	13.2	32.0
Hart County	3 178	420	8.3	847	0.0	16.9	9.8	13 463	55.8	6.6	47.5	11.6	40.9
Henderson County	8 367	1 374	9.7	2 613	0.0	14.8	6.9	35 161	63.8	5.4	55.8	12.8	31.4
Henry County	2 770	331	10.3	774	0.0	15.8	7.8	11 611	64.6	3.7	55.8	13.9	30.3
Hickman County	923	113	2.9	261	0.0	4.2	6.1	4 265	55.0	6.5	52.2	7.2	40.6
Hopkins County	8 418	1 433	7.2	2 442	0.0	14.4	8.1	36 580	57.5	7.0	48.7	12.4	38.9
Jackson County............	2 680	189	6.1	768	0.0	15.2	16.0	10 333	48.8	8.8	43.2	9.5	47.3
Jefferson County	123 874	37 969	22.6	35 085	0.1	10.6	6.7	543 567	65.0	5.0	55.1	15.1	29.8
Jessamine County	7 372	3 131	27.6	2 362	0.0	9.7	3.9	29 867	67.2	4.3	56.0	17.8	26.1
Johnson County	4 333	778	3.7	1 332	0.0	8.2	9.9	18 543	48.4	8.4	41.1	10.3	48.6
Kenton County	28 640	6 815	26.2	7 870	0.0	12.7	5.4	115 879	69.1	3.5	58.4	16.3	25.3
Knott County	3 352	1 107	11.2	1 250	0.0	6.0	11.1	13 933	43.8	15.6	36.4	8.5	55.0
Knox County	6 176	987	9.7	1 734	0.0	10.0	16.5	24 321	45.7	8.9	39.3	9.8	50.9
Larue County................	2 527	400	7.7	663	0.0	8.6	2.7	10 433	59.8	4.8	53.4	11.6	35.1
Laurel County...............	9 704	1 465	7.7	2 800	0.0	16.6	10.4	40 701	56.3	5.4	50.3	10.4	39.2
Lawrence County	3 083	401	3.0	978	0.0	8.0	10.7	12 187	46.4	11.5	38.2	10.3	51.5
Lee County..................	1 513	163	14.6	431	0.0	16.9	16.0	6 358	39.4	9.4	36.8	9.2	54.1
Leslie County	2 347	342	6.5	682	0.0	8.7	7.5	9 733	39.8	10.2	34.6	7.5	57.9
Letcher County.............	4 656	858	4.9	1 577	0.0	11.0	10.3	20 112	43.4	11.0	37.8	8.0	54.2
Lewis County................	2 737	374	5.0	838	0.0	19.1	6.4	10 981	50.8	11.7	43.3	11.1	45.6
Lincoln County	4 377	603	5.2	1 166	0.0	14.9	6.4	18 026	58.0	5.0	51.8	10.3	37.9
Livingston County	1 758	306	5.4	527	0.0	13.7	2.8	7 894	60.1	4.7	51.4	12.9	35.8
Logan County	4 992	521	7.4	1 479	0.0	12.6	5.3	20 533	63.1	4.2	55.0	12.0	33.0
Lyon County	1 240	160	16.1	214	0.0	24.3	0.0	6 941	43.3	5.5	44.1	10.5	45.4
McCracken County........	11 690	2 443	11.4	3 145	0.2	8.5	5.7	51 952	60.2	6.0	51.6	13.2	35.2
McCreary County	3 653	433	6.4	1 091	0.0	9.0	20.2	12 975	47.5	11.3	41.0	10.4	48.5
McLean County	1 740	327	6.5	501	0.0	12.4	7.8	7 782	59.1	6.1	52.2	11.8	36.0
Madison County	11 078	10 200	10.9	5 219	0.0	9.1	4.1	56 904	64.8	5.0	53.5	19.3	27.2
Magoffin County	2 717	410	3.3	852	0.0	14.1	13.6	10 212	43.4	12.8	37.7	7.3	55.0
Marion County	3 538	462	13.5	1 008	0.0	13.7	9.3	14 134	58.3	5.9	50.1	13.1	36.9
Marshall County	5 122	1 056	7.8	1 377	0.0	12.6	4.1	24 280	57.5	4.2	50.4	12.7	37.0
Martin County	2 630	435	1.9	828	0.0	14.9	15.2	9 522	37.4	12.8	32.6	7.9	59.5
Mason County	3 002	598	9.1	958	0.3	17.0	3.1	13 198	61.6	5.4	53.2	12.4	34.4
Meade County	5 499	976	6.7	1 551	0.6	17.4	7.6	19 395	64.6	6.7	57.2	12.3	30.6
Menifee County	1 264	177	3.5	496	0.0	11.3	20.0	5 153	48.8	8.3	43.7	8.4	47.9
Mercer County	3 691	529	6.0	949	0.0	14.9	7.4	16 275	62.8	3.6	55.8	12.2	32.0
Metcalfe County	1 807	258	8.1	540	0.0	13.3	13.1	7 836	57.3	6.5	50.3	12.0	37.7
Monroe County	2 077	438	3.8	701	0.0	10.4	8.0	9 318	57.6	10.0	47.6	12.1	40.3
Montgomery County......	4 032	574	5.8	1 145	0.0	14.5	10.3	17 618	61.1	5.9	55.8	11.5	32.8
Morgan County.............	2 506	420	9.3	809	0.0	17.3	11.6	11 243	42.4	8.4	38.8	10.9	50.3
Muhlenberg County.......	5 522	919	6.5	1 809	0.0	12.5	13.7	25 569	50.8	7.6	45.6	11.1	43.3
Nelson County..............	7 711	1 030	17.1	2 121	0.0	11.3	5.6	28 270	66.1	3.7	57.5	14.1	28.4
Nicholas County	1 178	158	0.7	364	0.0	18.7	4.4	5 402	61.1	9.6	53.4	10.1	36.5
Ohio County	4 398	646	4.9	1 317	0.0	9.3	5.4	17 960	56.2	5.3	49.9	11.4	38.7
Oldham County	10 171	1 972	17.1	2 389	0.0	6.4	3.9	35 002	64.6	2.5	56.8	15.4	27.9
Owen County	2 076	227	5.7	622	0.0	15.0	6.3	8 215	59.6	5.3	53.9	11.0	35.1

Table B-3. States and Counties — **Education, Labor Force, and Income**

STATE County	Full-year full-time employed (percent)								Children under 18 years in families					+/− U.S. percent two-income couples	Total employed by class of worker (percent)			
										With two parents (percent)		With one parent who is in labor force (percent)	+/− U.S. percent of children with no stay-at-home parent (percent)					
	Total	Men	Women	Non-Hispanic White	Black or African American	American Indian and Alaska Native	Asian, Hawaiian, and Pacific Islander	Hispanic or Latino[1]	Number	Both in labor force	Father only in labor force				Private	Government	Self-employed	Unpaid family worker
	24	25	26	27	28	29	30	31	32	33	34	35	36	37	38	39	40	41
KENTUCKY—Cont'd																		
Cumberland County	31.4	34.8	28.3	31.4	34.4	0.0	20.0	10.0	1 557	44.7	17.3	18.5	-1.4	-3.9	69.3	14.7	15.8	0.2
Daviess County	41.4	53.0	31.0	41.8	36.5	31.9	33.8	33.6	22 366	50.4	21.8	18.0	3.8	0.8	79.5	11.4	8.5	0.6
Edmonson County........	32.5	42.9	22.7	32.9	18.2	33.3	27.3	0.0	2 616	42.7	23.0	12.6	-9.3	-9.9	72.2	14.6	12.8	0.4
Elliott County	22.3	27.4	17.3	22.3	X	X	X	X	1 585	38.0	23.8	13.9	-12.7	-20.3	68.4	19.4	10.9	1.4
Estill County	30.1	38.9	22.2	30.1	0.0	53.8	35.7	20.4	3 520	31.9	27.4	17.0	-15.7	-16.1	75.3	14.4	10.1	0.1
Fayette County	43.4	51.4	35.8	44.9	39.0	39.0	35.4	30.9	52 507	45.9	19.9	24.4	5.7	7.2	74.4	17.3	8.0	0.3
Fleming County	37.5	45.2	30.3	37.5	38.6	33.3	X	29.0	3 354	43.2	24.1	15.4	-6.0	-4.0	69.4	12.9	16.8	1.0
Floyd County	24.9	30.2	19.8	25.2	8.6	0.0	41.7	8.1	9 340	26.9	25.0	12.9	-24.8	-23.7	69.8	18.9	11.1	0.2
Franklin County	46.6	53.8	40.1	48.4	33.7	44.9	15.4	33.1	10 343	53.1	13.9	22.7	11.2	8.1	53.8	38.0	8.0	0.2
Fulton County	31.7	41.4	23.8	32.2	29.4	X	X	100.0	1 754	33.2	17.3	27.7	-3.7	-9.8	70.3	17.1	12.0	0.6
Gallatin County	43.4	53.5	33.5	43.6	37.3	0.0	0.0	17.2	2 130	38.3	29.3	16.8	-9.5	-0.1	78.4	11.6	9.0	1.0
Garrard County	42.6	51.1	34.6	42.7	55.2	0.0	100.0	17.2	3 460	49.8	19.1	17.7	2.9	1.1	70.6	15.1	13.6	0.6
Grant County	44.6	53.5	36.1	44.6	36.8	63.9	47.0	37.1	5 954	49.1	16.8	18.5	3.0	3.6	77.9	11.7	9.6	0.7
Graves County	36.3	49.2	24.7	36.9	26.2	13.8	36.3	32.2	8 335	45.2	24.3	18.4	-1.0	-5.7	74.8	12.4	12.3	0.6
Grayson County	35.1	44.6	26.1	35.1	11.3	13.3	0.0	63.4	5 491	43.7	25.2	16.7	-4.2	-5.1	77.8	11.2	10.4	0.6
Green County	34.5	44.7	25.0	34.7	38.5	0.0	12.5	26.9	2 428	50.4	18.1	15.8	1.6	-6.6	67.6	14.5	17.3	0.6
Greenup County...........	32.9	42.9	23.9	32.9	25.7	44.7	43.3	37.6	8 254	42.3	28.4	14.6	-7.7	-14.6	78.3	13.2	8.0	0.5
Hancock County	39.6	52.2	27.4	39.6	43.1	53.8	0.0	38.7	2 144	50.9	22.9	17.3	3.6	-3.4	81.9	11.4	6.2	0.5
Hardin County	44.3	55.4	33.0	44.1	47.9	43.2	36.2	40.9	24 727	44.7	25.0	19.9	0.0	0.7	70.8	18.9	9.9	0.4
Harlan County	21.5	26.1	17.4	21.6	19.5	16.9	27.9	22.3	7 814	25.7	25.2	14.7	-24.2	-25.4	70.2	21.3	7.9	0.5
Harrison County	40.4	50.5	30.9	40.5	50.2	25.4	0.0	40.3	4 305	45.5	23.2	19.0	-0.1	1.2	72.7	13.0	13.1	1.2
Hart County	33.8	42.3	25.8	33.6	34.5	70.2	X	27.6	4 311	41.9	25.7	16.9	-5.8	-7.4	67.9	12.4	18.0	1.7
Henderson County	42.6	52.9	33.2	42.9	39.8	15.8	37.5	45.7	10 518	47.3	19.2	19.8	2.5	2.3	80.6	10.6	8.4	0.4
Henry County	42.2	51.9	33.0	42.6	38.3	33.3	59.5	40.2	3 605	49.0	20.8	21.0	5.4	-0.2	71.6	17.8	10.2	0.4
Hickman County	39.2	49.2	30.4	39.7	32.9	0.0	28.6	47.1	1 107	37.7	16.4	24.4	-2.5	-4.7	71.1	13.7	14.1	1.0
Hopkins County	36.2	47.7	26.2	36.4	34.5	18.8	30.7	39.0	10 489	41.3	25.2	19.8	-3.5	-7.8	76.4	13.9	9.4	0.2
Jackson County	28.2	34.8	21.9	28.2	X	6.7	0.0	16.7	3 292	32.8	26.5	13.7	-18.1	-15.5	71.2	16.6	11.9	0.3
Jefferson County	42.3	51.6	34.1	43.7	36.5	37.0	42.7	39.4	158 200	41.7	16.6	27.3	4.4	1.8	80.1	11.6	8.2	0.2
Jessamine County	42.8	54.2	32.3	43.0	43.1	48.1	17.3	42.3	9 883	44.4	26.1	17.1	-3.1	3.8	74.3	14.2	11.4	0.1
Johnson County	28.8	36.6	21.8	28.8	0.0	0.0	40.4	55.1	5 321	32.7	27.0	13.2	-18.7	-17.7	73.7	17.0	8.9	0.4
Kenton County	46.1	57.0	35.9	46.6	36.0	45.4	41.9	42.4	37 959	46.8	22.4	20.2	2.4	5.5	82.3	10.9	6.6	0.3
Knott County	23.5	29.6	17.8	23.6	16.4	35.3	42.3	13.1	4 073	29.2	25.8	12.0	-23.4	-23.0	64.6	25.2	9.7	0.5
Knox County	26.0	32.1	20.5	25.9	23.3	13.6	0.0	31.5	7 647	34.0	21.7	14.8	-15.8	-17.3	71.4	17.1	11.2	0.3
Larue County	38.5	48.7	29.1	39.2	17.4	71.4	61.1	46.7	3 214	49.3	19.4	15.9	0.6	-3.9	71.2	14.4	13.2	1.2
Laurel County	36.2	46.2	26.9	36.3	34.0	41.9	30.9	40.8	12 606	40.6	22.5	16.4	-7.6	-7.5	73.8	14.3	11.6	0.3
Lawrence County	24.3	32.9	16.3	24.2	0.0	15.4	X	27.8	3 696	25.6	30.2	11.1	-27.9	-23.6	73.0	15.8	10.4	0.8
Lee County	23.3	27.2	10.9	24.0	4.6	0.0	0.0	0.0	1 660	31.6	23.7	16.0	-17.0	-20.4	64.2	24.8	10.7	0.3
Leslie County	22.4	29.0	16.3	22.7	23.5	0.0	83.3	2.9	2 865	23.5	29.3	8.0	-33.1	-28.0	67.7	24.6	6.7	0.9
Letcher County	25.1	32.6	18.1	25.1	28.3	9.1	21.7	38.8	5 644	28.6	28.3	12.0	-24.0	-22.4	72.3	17.7	9.7	0.3
Lewis County	25.6	31.9	19.5	25.7	25.9	0.0	X	32.6	3 335	38.7	23.6	15.8	-10.1	-15.1	71.0	13.2	14.7	0.5
Lincoln County	36.1	44.7	28.0	36.4	24.2	0.0	91.7	38.2	5 682	42.7	21.5	17.9	-4.0	-4.1	76.2	11.0	12.2	0.6
Livingston County	35.9	45.3	26.9	36.1	100.0	20.7	0.0	7.7	2 111	45.5	29.9	15.3	-3.8	-5.8	76.3	11.8	11.3	0.6
Logan County	42.1	53.9	31.4	42.5	37.6	35.7	51.4	52.3	6 333	45.6	20.6	22.5	3.5	2.0	75.3	11.5	12.9	0.3
Lyon County	31.5	34.9	26.8	32.4	21.7	0.0	54.1	12.5	1 204	53.1	20.5	19.6	8.1	-8.3	67.2	20.4	12.3	0.2
McCracken County.......	38.9	50.4	29.0	39.9	32.2	19.5	52.6	29.5	14 576	41.4	21.4	24.9	1.7	-3.1	76.5	12.3	11.0	0.2
McCreary County	25.4	31.2	19.9	25.4	6.7	34.6	100.0	18.6	4 381	30.3	20.9	17.0	-17.3	-18.4	73.0	18.1	8.7	0.2
McLean County	37.6	46.1	29.6	37.7	20.5	0.0	0.0	38.0	2 232	46.9	21.7	17.6	-0.1	-6.5	70.8	16.2	12.3	0.7
Madison County	37.2	47.4	28.0	37.6	28.9	34.4	44.7	40.8	14 715	45.4	23.8	20.0	0.8	0.6	73.0	17.7	8.8	0.4
Magoffin County	21.4	29.3	13.9	21.2	100.0	0.0	11.1	100.0	3 311	24.4	29.2	12.4	-27.8	-21.9	66.4	20.9	12.7	0.0
Marion County	34.9	41.6	27.9	36.9	19.1	0.0	26.4	15.1	4 422	50.3	13.3	21.1	6.8	0.7	75.0	11.8	12.4	0.8
Marshall County	37.8	48.7	27.4	37.8	46.3	0.0	48.6	37.7	6 257	49.0	25.7	15.8	0.2	-6.5	74.9	13.9	10.4	0.7
Martin County	19.5	25.7	13.8	19.7	100.0	0.0	X	0.0	3 376	19.7	24.7	9.6	-35.3	-28.3	67.3	23.2	8.6	0.9
Mason County	37.8	47.4	29.1	38.1	32.5	0.0	41.7	40.1	3 909	47.0	17.9	22.2	4.6	-0.1	73.7	12.8	12.7	0.8
Meade County	41.7	54.0	29.5	41.6	47.7	48.8	25.0	39.6	7 445	45.3	25.5	16.0	-3.3	-2.3	72.0	19.0	8.6	0.5
Menifee County	30.4	35.7	25.3	31.2	0.0	100.0	X	5.9	1 475	33.3	22.6	11.5	-19.8	-18.0	64.1	23.6	11.9	0.5
Mercer County.............	42.0	51.9	33.0	42.6	41.0	43.8	39.3	15.2	4 806	53.4	17.4	17.4	6.2	2.6	74.6	13.9	11.1	0.4
Metcalfe County	34.4	42.2	27.1	34.9	44.6	0.0	X	13.0	2 329	51.9	20.0	12.2	-0.5	-7.9	69.6	13.9	15.6	0.9
Monroe County	32.8	45.3	21.2	33.0	17.9	0.0	0.0	55.7	2 627	44.7	20.8	17.2	-2.7	-4.5	67.5	15.1	16.5	0.9
Montgomery County	40.3	50.8	30.9	40.2	41.4	40.9	50.0	40.9	5 281	41.7	24.8	16.7	-6.2	-2.9	72.3	15.9	11.4	0.4
Morgan County	24.7	27.9	20.7	26.0	6.7	20.6	84.6	9.0	2 888	36.4	26.5	11.0	-17.2	-14.9	60.7	27.0	11.8	0.5
Muhlenberg County	32.3	41.1	23.9	32.9	24.5	100.0	10.0	21.7	6 702	36.9	28.4	15.5	-12.2	-13.2	73.1	16.7	9.8	0.4
Nelson County	44.1	54.9	33.8	44.3	40.4	54.3	46.1	39.5	9 869	48.8	16.9	22.4	6.6	3.8	78.2	10.3	11.3	0.3
Nicholas County	40.3	46.0	35.2	40.6	31.9	0.0	X	46.7	1 545	49.7	17.5	21.6	6.7	-2.7	75.4	13.0	11.5	1.1
Ohio County	34.4	43.7	25.7	34.5	47.7	24.4	44.4	32.4	5 403	40.9	28.0	17.2	-6.5	-9.6	75.5	15.0	9.1	0.3
Oldham County	45.6	53.9	35.8	46.9	22.7	51.9	40.6	39.1	12 282	53.7	28.5	12.2	1.3	8.0	75.3	13.1	11.4	0.2
Owen County	39.4	45.7	33.2	39.5	26.6	57.5	57.1	41.7	2 564	45.5	18.0	14.7	-4.4	-3.8	65.8	19.0	14.6	0.7

[1] Hispanic or Latino persons may be of any race.

STATE County	Percent who worked at home	Percent of the population 5 years and over with a disability	Veterans as a percent of the population 18 years and over	Occupation for employed population 16 years and over (percent)						Industry for employed population 16 years and over (percent)					
				Management, professional, and related occupations	Service occupations	Sales and office occupations	Farming, fishing, and forestry occupations	Construction, extraction, and maintenance occupations	Production, transportation and material moving occupations	Agriculture, forestry, fishing, and mining	Construction and manufacturing	Wholesale and retail trade	Transportation and warehousing, and utilities	Service industries	Public administration
	42	43	44	45	46	47	48	49	50	51	52	53	54	55	56
KENTUCKY—Cont'd															
Cumberland County	2.6	30.9	10.6	25.0	14.4	15.0	3.3	11.3	30.9	7.7	34.2	11.8	3.2	41.0	2.2
Daviess County	2.0	21.6	14.5	28.1	15.4	23.6	0.6	12.0	20.3	2.2	28.6	15.7	5.7	45.0	2.8
Edmonson County	5.4	29.2	11.1	17.9	16.0	20.8	1.3	17.0	27.1	4.1	35.6	12.6	5.4	40.0	2.3
Elliott County	4.2	34.2	7.0	19.7	16.5	14.0	3.1	24.2	22.5	6.4	29.9	9.6	5.6	43.5	5.0
Estill County	1.5	32.1	10.6	19.3	13.1	19.4	1.1	16.7	30.4	3.0	38.5	14.8	4.4	35.5	3.8
Fayette County	2.5	17.7	11.4	40.4	14.6	26.1	1.0	6.7	11.2	2.1	17.4	15.3	3.5	58.1	3.6
Fleming County	4.5	27.4	11.3	25.8	12.3	19.8	2.0	15.6	24.5	8.0	32.3	15.2	6.6	35.1	2.7
Floyd County	2.3	34.8	8.7	29.2	15.9	23.8	0.6	16.1	14.3	10.5	10.8	18.6	6.2	48.5	5.4
Franklin County	2.5	23.0	13.5	35.1	12.8	28.1	0.4	9.4	14.2	1.6	19.8	10.6	3.0	38.4	26.6
Fulton County	2.6	25.0	12.7	22.5	14.9	21.2	1.4	7.6	32.4	5.3	38.8	14.0	4.0	32.9	5.1
Gallatin County	3.3	25.2	13.3	17.4	16.1	22.0	0.4	15.8	28.3	2.4	34.2	16.0	8.5	34.3	4.6
Garrard County	4.2	25.3	11.9	27.0	12.3	21.7	1.4	15.5	22.1	5.0	31.5	15.1	3.7	40.3	4.3
Grant County	3.2	23.2	13.8	19.9	14.0	25.0	1.0	11.9	28.1	2.7	31.0	16.7	7.8	37.8	4.1
Graves County	3.4	24.0	12.9	24.9	14.0	24.3	1.5	11.6	23.7	5.0	29.3	16.4	5.4	40.8	3.1
Grayson County	3.5	28.2	12.2	18.5	11.9	19.2	2.0	16.4	32.1	4.2	42.2	16.5	4.0	30.7	2.3
Green County	4.7	25.6	12.6	23.5	13.5	19.0	2.6	12.8	28.7	8.3	36.0	11.3	4.0	36.3	4.1
Greenup County	2.0	27.7	14.4	26.1	14.6	27.5	0.6	13.1	18.1	1.3	19.3	17.4	9.8	48.3	3.9
Hancock County	2.5	16.5	12.8	19.0	15.9	19.6	0.9	13.0	31.6	2.8	45.5	10.5	5.6	31.5	4.0
Hardin County	3.3	20.5	19.9	26.2	15.6	26.6	0.5	10.1	21.0	2.0	23.4	15.9	6.5	45.3	6.8
Harlan County	1.4	37.4	10.2	27.8	17.4	24.4	1.1	17.3	12.0	14.1	10.2	15.9	4.3	50.0	5.5
Harrison County	4.4	22.0	12.3	22.3	13.5	20.8	2.2	12.6	28.8	6.6	38.5	10.6	4.3	36.3	3.7
Hart County	8.5	26.7	10.6	24.1	13.5	18.3	3.5	12.1	28.5	9.7	35.9	11.5	4.3	35.6	3.0
Henderson County	2.0	22.6	12.7	25.4	13.6	24.5	0.5	10.8	25.2	2.8	31.7	14.0	5.8	42.7	3.0
Henry County	3.7	24.5	13.0	22.5	13.9	23.2	1.4	13.1	25.9	4.7	31.9	13.8	5.9	35.5	8.2
Hickman County	2.5	25.7	13.0	21.5	15.7	15.9	2.6	13.1	31.2	9.4	34.7	12.2	8.0	31.8	3.9
Hopkins County	1.6	25.5	12.8	23.8	15.7	23.3	0.8	14.5	22.0	6.1	25.7	15.1	5.4	43.7	4.0
Jackson County	3.7	32.6	6.9	19.5	11.4	20.6	1.1	15.6	31.9	3.5	39.4	12.6	5.3	36.0	3.2
Jefferson County	2.2	20.4	13.7	33.0	14.1	28.6	0.2	8.4	15.7	0.4	19.5	15.5	7.1	53.9	3.6
Jessamine County	3.7	18.9	11.2	31.0	14.7	25.5	0.8	11.5	16.5	2.1	22.7	16.6	4.3	51.2	3.1
Johnson County	1.9	33.6	11.2	25.2	16.4	25.0	1.2	17.0	15.1	8.5	14.3	18.1	5.3	48.5	5.3
Kenton County	2.1	19.3	13.4	31.9	13.9	30.4	0.1	9.0	14.8	0.3	20.1	16.1	8.6	50.6	4.3
Knott County	2.5	33.9	7.6	29.3	14.7	20.4	0.3	19.5	15.8	12.8	12.6	12.6	5.8	49.4	6.8
Knox County	1.8	34.7	10.4	22.8	15.2	25.8	1.4	13.8	21.0	3.6	22.2	18.5	6.5	44.8	4.4
Larue County	5.0	25.5	14.6	24.2	14.3	22.1	2.1	12.3	25.0	5.9	31.8	14.9	5.9	37.6	3.9
Laurel County	2.5	27.9	10.7	22.9	13.8	28.0	0.7	12.0	22.6	2.5	24.6	19.9	7.2	41.7	4.1
Lawrence County	2.7	30.8	10.9	20.3	16.9	23.5	0.7	18.5	20.1	8.9	18.2	18.1	8.3	42.2	4.3
Lee County	0.9	33.5	10.6	24.3	14.4	19.7	2.2	14.5	24.9	5.0	24.7	16.6	7.6	38.1	7.9
Leslie County	0.9	37.0	6.3	24.1	15.0	20.5	2.9	19.1	18.3	19.4	13.1	10.3	7.0	43.6	6.6
Letcher County	1.7	34.6	9.1	23.9	15.0	23.8	1.0	21.2	15.1	17.4	11.2	18.5	5.6	42.5	4.7
Lewis County	3.5	30.4	9.4	19.7	12.4	18.5	3.1	15.1	31.2	9.8	33.8	12.6	7.3	33.7	2.8
Lincoln County	4.1	28.7	11.8	22.0	13.4	21.5	1.7	12.2	29.3	5.5	35.0	15.6	5.5	35.6	2.9
Livingston County	2.7	21.5	14.3	23.2	15.3	24.9	2.3	15.7	18.6	9.3	19.7	16.7	10.4	41.1	2.7
Logan County	3.6	22.8	11.9	21.6	13.9	18.6	1.7	11.1	33.1	5.6	42.1	13.0	4.9	31.2	3.2
Lyon County	1.8	32.7	14.5	26.3	18.2	22.5	1.4	12.4	19.2	4.9	27.4	11.6	5.2	42.5	8.5
McCracken County	2.7	22.7	14.6	29.0	16.3	28.2	0.4	10.9	15.3	1.1	20.3	19.5	6.8	48.6	3.6
McCreary County	2.7	35.0	11.2	20.5	16.6	15.7	1.6	12.4	33.3	4.2	36.9	12.2	4.8	39.3	2.5
McLean County	2.4	26.2	14.0	23.7	14.1	21.2	2.8	14.4	23.9	7.6	29.2	13.6	7.2	37.5	4.9
Madison County	2.7	21.0	9.8	29.0	16.0	27.2	0.8	10.0	17.1	1.9	25.1	16.1	3.7	49.4	3.7
Magoffin County	2.4	31.8	5.7	23.2	14.6	19.2	0.9	20.3	21.9	9.3	24.0	12.7	5.6	43.8	4.5
Marion County	4.1	26.0	10.0	24.3	13.8	18.2	1.9	11.6	30.1	6.7	40.9	12.5	2.8	33.7	3.4
Marshall County	2.8	23.4	16.0	25.2	13.8	24.1	0.7	15.1	21.2	2.1	27.8	15.9	7.6	42.9	3.7
Martin County	1.8	37.7	8.2	27.1	13.5	21.9	0.5	20.6	16.3	19.5	6.8	16.1	7.8	46.6	3.2
Mason County	4.1	24.5	12.4	25.8	16.1	21.3	1.1	10.7	25.0	6.6	27.8	16.7	8.0	37.2	3.7
Meade County	2.5	20.4	17.6	20.9	13.1	24.6	0.9	17.0	23.5	2.4	27.3	13.7	9.9	39.8	7.0
Menifee County	3.3	30.4	10.8	23.3	12.3	15.1	3.1	16.1	30.1	6.5	34.3	11.5	4.6	36.2	6.8
Mercer County	3.3	23.3	12.1	24.7	13.4	23.5	1.5	12.5	24.4	4.0	34.7	12.1	5.7	38.6	4.9
Metcalfe County	5.9	27.4	10.3	20.3	13.3	18.2	2.8	11.2	34.1	9.5	38.7	13.0	5.4	30.9	2.5
Monroe County	4.6	29.5	8.4	24.8	11.5	18.5	2.1	11.9	31.2	8.0	38.3	11.5	4.1	34.8	3.2
Montgomery County	1.7	25.5	12.2	24.7	12.8	25.3	0.7	11.1	25.4	3.1	31.9	17.8	4.4	38.0	4.9
Morgan County	2.7	29.8	9.9	23.0	16.4	20.2	2.7	19.5	18.2	6.6	23.6	12.4	4.1	41.1	12.2
Muhlenberg County	2.3	26.3	11.3	20.4	15.3	21.2	1.3	14.5	27.3	5.3	26.3	16.9	9.1	38.8	3.6
Nelson County	3.3	21.1	12.5	22.6	12.5	22.2	0.8	13.2	28.7	2.7	38.1	13.5	5.1	38.1	2.5
Nicholas County	3.5	25.2	12.4	23.1	11.5	19.0	4.0	13.7	28.7	10.2	37.3	12.4	4.8	31.6	3.7
Ohio County	3.0	26.8	13.5	19.6	14.9	20.6	1.4	17.2	26.3	6.3	32.3	14.9	5.5	37.0	4.0
Oldham County	3.9	13.0	13.6	40.1	11.9	26.0	1.0	8.1	13.0	2.0	22.2	15.7	6.5	49.0	4.7
Owen County	4.7	25.8	12.4	25.4	14.4	21.7	1.9	14.0	22.5	6.3	30.6	13.3	6.5	34.6	8.7

Table B-3. States and Counties — Education, Labor Force, and Income

STATE County	Median house-hold income	Median family income - All families	Median family income - Married-couple	Median family income - Male house-holder	Median family income - Female house-holder	Median nonfamily house-hold income	Median income for full-year, full-time workers - Men	Women	Per capita income	With earnings	With interest, dividend, or rental income	With Social Security income	With public assis-tance income	With retire-ment income	House-holds with income over $100,000 (percent)	+/- U.S. percent for income over $100,000	House-holds with income below poverty (percent)	Families with children with income below poverty (percent)
	57	58	59	60	61	62	63	64	65	66	67	68	69	70	71	72	73	74

KENTUCKY—Cont'd

STATE County	57	58	59	60	61	62	63	64	65	66	67	68	69	70	71	72	73	74
Cumberland County	21 572	28 701	33 945	23 958	15 602	8 864	21 890	17 126	12 643	67.8	20.7	38.1	5.5	13.3	2.3	-10.0	26.8	24.8
Daviess County	36 813	45 404	54 830	28 136	15 775	18 992	36 096	23 178	18 739	78.5	34.6	28.9	3.2	18.6	6.2	-6.1	12.7	14.6
Edmonson County	25 413	31 843	34 804	23 611	11 346	12 191	27 150	17 917	14 480	71.8	19.5	33.5	4.3	17.9	2.8	-9.5	20.1	22.8
Elliott County	21 014	27 125	31 750	30 208	11 250	10 101	30 539	20 589	12 067	65.2	18.8	33.2	6.5	14.6	3.7	-8.6	26.0	27.1
Estill County	23 318	27 284	32 028	8 594	12 500	11 774	30 332	19 233	12 285	65.9	20.4	32.7	6.4	17.7	2.4	-9.9	27.4	31.7
Fayette County	39 813	53 264	65 931	25 614	19 535	24 770	37 114	27 830	23 109	85.4	35.4	19.6	2.1	14.7	11.5	-0.8	12.9	12.6
Fleming County	27 990	33 300	39 397	25 250	16 211	13 701	27 019	20 331	14 214	74.8	23.9	31.4	4.1	14.6	3.5	-8.8	19.8	18.2
Floyd County	21 168	25 717	30 766	14 741	8 347	10 916	30 803	21 004	12 442	60.0	17.2	34.5	8.9	17.7	3.2	-9.1	30.7	35.2
Franklin County	40 011	51 052	59 765	26 319	17 120	24 078	34 676	26 711	21 229	79.3	36.3	26.5	1.9	22.3	8.9	-3.4	11.6	11.6
Fulton County	24 382	30 788	39 500	19 306	11 146	12 267	27 398	19 856	14 309	68.2	24.0	37.9	4.9	16.5	3.1	-9.2	24.6	30.7
Gallatin County	36 422	41 136	46 932	15 000	14 167	16 761	32 339	22 776	16 416	82.8	17.4	23.8	3.4	11.9	6.0	-6.3	15.0	16.1
Garrard County	34 284	41 250	45 600	32 321	15 233	10 400	01 504	22 021	16 015	80.1	28.5	28.6	2.4	18.5	4.1	-8.2	15.0	17.3
Grant County	38 438	42 605	53 159	30 500	17 463	22 821	32 551	24 143	16 776	83.0	27.0	24.2	3.1	15.1	5.6	-6.7	11.3	13.0
Graves County	30 874	38 054	47 332	18 542	11 663	14 605	33 230	20 902	16 834	72.2	33.5	34.7	3.0	18.6	5.8	-6.5	17.6	20.5
Grayson County	27 639	33 080	39 877	20 524	11 605	13 869	28 484	19 652	14 759	72.7	24.1	32.3	4.6	18.2	3.5	-8.8	19.4	21.4
Green County	25 463	31 852	36 943	20 446	10 536	12 002	26 722	18 073	16 107	71.9	27.9	36.5	4.5	16.4	4.5	-7.8	19.5	19.9
Greenup County	32 142	38 928	45 246	27 813	14 462	15 275	36 388	21 975	17 137	71.7	28.7	36.7	3.3	19.5	5.8	-6.5	15.0	17.8
Hancock County	36 914	42 994	49 327	29 934	15 000	18 560	35 958	24 544	16 623	79.0	29.0	25.7	2.9	18.5	5.1	-7.2	14.0	15.0
Hardin County	37 744	43 610	49 476	26 536	17 361	22 186	32 032	23 926	17 487	83.1	29.5	23.0	2.6	22.9	5.7	-6.6	9.9	11.5
Harlan County	18 665	23 536	28 432	12 468	10 894	10 826	30 182	20 248	11 585	54.8	15.7	41.6	7.0	21.1	2.3	-10.0	31.9	36.0
Harrison County	36 210	42 065	49 695	25 156	15 563	18 540	31 769	24 500	17 478	78.5	30.2	30.4	2.8	19.1	6.4	-5.9	12.8	13.4
Hart County	25 378	31 746	36 431	28 333	15 216	12 344	27 814	20 212	13 495	71.3	25.7	31.3	4.0	16.3	3.1	-9.2	23.1	24.2
Henderson County	35 892	44 703	52 341	16 899	15 534	19 334	35 350	23 320	18 470	77.6	30.2	27.3	3.4	17.7	6.3	-6.0	12.9	15.8
Henry County	37 263	45 009	49 994	24 861	15 909	19 040	32 173	22 431	17 846	80.0	29.8	30.4	3.5	18.1	7.6	-4.7	14.9	14.3
Hickman County	31 615	37 049	43 173	31 250	12 895	14 341	30 060	19 500	17 279	73.8	28.4	33.7	2.8	14.7	4.7	7.6	16.3	24.1
Hopkins County	30 868	36 794	44 192	20 230	13 570	16 487	31 880	20 616	17 382	74.0	27.1	32.9	3.5	20.3	5.1	-7.2	16.2	21.1
Jackson County	20 177	23 638	29 313	13 571	10 000	9 650	25 474	16 467	10 711	66.0	14.8	31.7	7.8	13.9	1.1	-11.2	30.5	33.1
Jefferson County	39 457	49 161	63 254	27 194	18 307	24 528	37 382	26 988	22 352	78.9	34.1	27.1	3.1	18.8	10.7	-1.6	12.2	15.3
Jessamine County	40 096	48 152	52 255	31 000	17 750	21 053	34 300	24 414	18 842	85.3	30.9	22.1	2.3	16.5	10.1	-2.2	11.2	11.9
Johnson County	24 911	29 142	32 237	21 667	11 101	11 344	30 698	20 605	14 051	67.1	17.1	33.2	7.4	16.4	3.9	-8.4	26.1	30.5
Kenton County	43 906	52 953	62 539	30 527	20 555	26 492	39 478	28 203	22 085	83.0	37.9	24.0	3.1	15.2	11.1	-1.2	9.0	10.8
Knott County	20 373	24 930	29 000	22 000	7 015	10 029	30 165	21 575	11 297	60.8	16.2	33.7	7.5	17.2	2.6	-9.7	31.0	35.6
Knox County	18 294	23 136	28 679	13 750	9 183	8 890	25 704	19 136	10 660	61.0	15.6	34.2	9.4	15.4	2.2	-10.1	35.1	36.9
Larue County	32 056	37 786	45 933	25 313	13 917	17 334	30 157	20 070	15 865	77.1	30.6	30.8	3.7	18.6	4.8	-7.5	16.6	17.5
Laurel County	27 015	31 318	35 650	17 125	12 675	13 690	29 039	20 268	14 165	72.8	21.2	30.6	4.7	15.1	4.1	-8.2	21.3	24.7
Lawrence County	21 610	26 113	29 326	20 341	10 363	10 517	31 000	19 920	12 008	64.6	18.7	34.8	8.6	16.8	3.1	-9.2	29.6	34.1
Lee County	18 544	24 918	27 563	20 250	8 466	9 764	26 726	19 688	13 325	55.4	10.7	37.5	7.5	17.0	3.6	-8.7	30.8	34.6
Leslie County	18 546	22 225	31 250	9 545	6 329	9 191	29 342	18 408	10 429	56.5	11.4	37.1	9.1	15.7	1.3	-11.0	33.8	36.5
Letcher County	21 110	24 869	30 516	15 083	9 050	11 001	31 120	18 158	11 984	60.4	14.3	36.5	8.2	17.8	2.1	-10.2	27.9	32.0
Lewis County	22 208	26 109	30 000	12 500	10 652	11 156	26 055	20 008	12 031	67.4	19.8	33.4	5.6	17.3	2.1	-10.2	27.8	33.0
Lincoln County	26 542	32 284	38 315	24 375	16 685	12 921	26 805	20 759	13 602	73.2	20.2	32.0	4.0	16.9	3.3	-9.0	21.4	22.0
Livingston County	31 776	39 486	47 478	23 750	13 841	18 869	33 912	20 052	17 072	76.3	25.6	34.3	2.2	19.4	4.4	-7.9	11.8	9.5
Logan County	32 474	39 307	45 350	30 909	18 469	14 917	30 157	20 864	15 962	76.4	27.7	29.6	2.8	15.1	4.1	-8.2	15.7	16.3
Lyon County	31 694	39 940	45 714	25 417	12 500	17 448	39 343	22 853	16 016	70.1	26.4	38.3	4.2	23.7	5.7	-6.6	14.0	16.4
McCracken County	33 865	42 513	55 408	23 456	13 355	17 726	37 999	23 463	19 533	73.2	33.4	32.4	3.4	19.2	7.3	-5.0	15.5	18.9
McCreary County	19 348	22 261	23 566	10 667	9 044	9 043	20 944	16 510	9 896	65.1	11.1	29.6	11.6	13.1	1.1	-11.2	32.6	36.7
McLean County	29 675	35 322	40 799	23 438	13 929	16 813	29 519	20 174	16 046	74.6	24.7	30.9	2.4	19.9	3.3	-9.0	16.7	20.4
Madison County	32 861	41 383	48 744	23 833	15 176	17 256	32 824	23 111	16 790	81.3	24.1	23.1	3.4	15.0	5.7	-6.6	18.3	17.6
Magoffin County	19 421	24 031	30 993	16 319	7 964	7 738	27 958	18 764	10 685	61.1	13.3	27.4	10.2	10.5	2.4	-9.9	35.7	37.1
Marion County	30 387	35 648	48 314	23 977	12 819	15 744	29 007	21 265	14 472	76.9	26.7	30.4	4.8	17.6	3.9	-8.4	19.2	20.8
Marshall County	35 553	43 670	53 027	26 842	16 917	16 948	37 364	22 919	18 069	73.1	34.0	35.9	2.3	23.3	5.7	-6.6	10.7	9.8
Martin County	18 279	21 574	26 961	20 625	7 454	9 527	32 024	19 250	10 650	54.0	12.2	34.4	12.6	19.0	1.8	-10.5	36.3	40.6
Mason County	30 195	37 257	45 918	21 087	14 583	16 951	31 311	21 565	16 589	76.0	28.4	31.7	3.2	14.0	5.8	-6.5	16.5	19.3
Meade County	36 966	40 592	44 553	24 375	16 434	21 362	31 697	22 633	16 000	82.9	26.9	22.7	1.9	18.9	5.0	-7.3	11.4	11.0
Menifee County	22 064	26 325	29 167	11 250	8 462	11 446	25 938	17 164	11 399	65.2	12.1	32.9	7.9	19.1	1.7	-10.6	28.5	35.3
Mercer County	35 555	43 121	50 022	35 547	17 554	19 195	35 236	23 562	17 972	77.5	31.8	32.5	3.4	19.7	4.8	-7.5	12.7	14.7
Metcalfe County	23 540	29 178	37 195	12 171	12 407	10 545	23 300	18 941	13 236	74.0	20.9	33.8	4.2	15.6	2.9	-9.4	25.9	25.9
Monroe County	22 356	27 112	32 073	16 083	13 036	11 222	22 215	18 867	14 365	70.3	22.7	35.4	4.8	13.1	2.9	-9.4	25.6	24.4
Montgomery County	31 746	36 939	45 712	30 365	16 250	18 089	32 039	21 423	16 701	77.4	23.4	30.3	2.8	16.4	5.1	-7.2	17.4	17.1
Morgan County	21 869	26 135	28 048	19 750	11 290	10 533	24 646	18 960	12 657	66.5	19.7	31.4	6.9	14.2	3.1	-9.2	28.4	31.8
Muhlenberg County	28 566	33 513	38 695	18 077	11 727	13 222	30 848	19 308	14 798	68.5	25.8	35.2	3.4	21.5	3.8	-8.5	19.8	22.4
Nelson County	39 010	44 600	52 114	24 095	15 474	20 263	32 425	22 861	18 120	82.0	27.6	24.8	3.1	15.3	6.9	-5.4	12.8	14.5
Nicholas County	29 886	35 491	39 856	24 500	19 500	14 449	27 221	21 597	15 880	73.9	25.6	36.5	4.1	18.9	4.1	-8.2	15.7	12.8
Ohio County	29 557	34 970	38 346	29 000	14 408	13 761	30 275	20 165	15 317	73.1	24.9	33.7	3.5	20.6	3.5	-8.8	17.9	18.5
Oldham County	63 229	70 495	79 971	34 375	28 845	28 151	49 760	30 383	25 374	89.6	44.5	17.9	1.1	16.0	23.5	11.2	4.7	4.1
Owen County	33 310	38 844	43 654	20 000	21 875	15 909	30 264	21 756	15 521	76.4	28.3	30.8	2.4	19.3	4.5	-7.8	17.6	14.7

STATE/ County code	MSA/PMSA/ NECMA code[1]	STATE County	High school graduates			College graduates		College graduates (percent)				
			Total population 25 years and over	Percent with a high school diploma or less	Percent with a high school diploma or more	Percent with a bachelor's degree or more	+/− U.S. percent with bachelor's degree or more	Non-Hispanic White	Black or African American	American Indian and Alaska Native	Asian, Hawaiian, and Pacific Islander	Hispanic or Latino[2]
			1	2	3	4	5	6	7	8	9	10
		KENTUCKY—Cont'd										
21 189	...	Owsley County	3 242	78.7	49.2	7.7	-16.7	7.8	X	0.0	X	0.0
21 191	1640	Pendleton County	9 081	74.1	72.8	9.7	-14.7	9.8	6.9	0.0	33.3	0.0
21 193	...	Perry County	19 596	73.0	58.3	8.9	-15.5	8.6	7.4	0.0	78.6	0.0
21 195	...	Pike County	46 153	72.6	61.8	9.9	-14.5	9.9	0.0	0.0	35.2	13.0
21 197	...	Powell County	8 485	80.4	56.1	6.5	-17.9	6.5	0.0	13.3	X	10.4
21 199	...	Pulaski County	38 430	69.2	65.6	10.5	-13.9	10.4	5.7	8.6	40.2	0.7
21 201	...	Robertson County	1 566	75.5	60.9	8.7	-15.7	8.8	0.0	X	0.0	0.0
21 203	...	Rockcastle County	11 109	79.3	57.7	8.3	-16.1	8.3	0.0	0.0	X	2.9
21 205	...	Rowan County	12 455	58.1	70.9	21.9	-2.5	21.7	47.3	0.0	92.4	0.0
21 207	...	Russell County	11 437	72.6	61.8	9.6	-14.8	9.6	5.3	33.3	12.1	0.0
21 209	4280	Scott County	20 459	52.8	80.5	20.3	-4.1	20.6	11.8	0.0	66.1	19.5
21 211	...	Shelby County	22 096	55.4	79.1	18.7	-5.7	20.4	7.5	0.0	0.0	5.7
21 213	...	Simpson County	10 680	67.4	73.6	11.9	-12.5	12.9	3.6	0.0	22.2	0.0
21 215	...	Spencer County	7 672	65.0	75.4	11.1	-13.3	11.2	0.0	0.0	0.0	0.0
21 217	...	Taylor County	15 253	68.1	68.0	12.2	-12.2	12.4	11.7	0.0	0.0	0.0
21 219	...	Todd County	7 758	73.2	63.5	9.2	-15.2	10.2	0.6	0.0	0.0	5.6
21 221	...	Trigg County	8 897	64.6	72.1	12.0	-12.4	12.7	4.6	0.0	41.7	5.0
21 223	...	Trimble County	5 340	70.2	70.7	7.6	-16.8	7.7	18.2	0.0	X	0.0
21 225	...	Union County	9 524	66.0	76.9	10.9	-13.5	11.4	6.0	0.0	21.6	0.0
21 227	...	Warren County	56 069	51.0	80.3	24.7	0.3	25.8	10.6	17.1	50.1	9.5
21 229	...	Washington County	7 144	69.7	68.8	13.3	-11.1	14.1	2.7	39.1	18.2	0.0
21 231	...	Wayne County	13 153	78.0	57.8	7.2	-17.2	7.4	0.0	13.5	0.0	0.0
21 233	...	Webster County	9 424	72.6	70.9	7.1	-17.3	7.3	4.5	X	0.0	0.0
21 235	...	Whitley County	22 708	70.1	61.3	13.4	-11.0	13.3	0.0	28.0	53.2	13.0
21 237	...	Wolfe County	4 571	77.1	53.6	10.6	-13.8	10.2	0.0	X	84.6	61.5
21 239	4280	Woodford County	15 546	46.9	82.6	25.9	1.5	27.1	11.8	100.0	90.0	3.7
22 000	...	LOUISIANA	2 775 468	57.6	74.8	18.7	-5.7	21.7	10.9	9.2	35.2	19.5
22 001	3880	Acadia Parish	35 573	73.4	64.7	9.4	-15.0	10.2	5.0	0.0	19.0	14.5
22 003	...	Allen Parish	16 817	74.8	63.2	9.3	-15.1	11.3	4.2	0.7	6.4	10.3
22 005	0760	Ascension Parish	46 258	62.1	79.6	14.5	-9.9	15.9	7.8	6.6	26.1	15.0
22 007	...	Assumption Parish	14 411	77.5	59.4	7.4	-17.0	7.9	6.4	0.0	8.8	0.0
22 009	...	Avoyelles Parish	26 606	77.3	59.8	8.3	-16.1	9.4	4.4	4.8	28.7	17.2
22 011	...	Beauregard Parish	21 036	64.5	75.0	13.8	-10.6	14.2	8.6	20.2	14.3	28.4
22 013	...	Bienville Parish	10 172	69.4	71.9	11.5	-12.9	13.6	8.5	7.7	0.0	8.3
22 015	7680	Bossier Parish	61 237	49.5	83.0	18.1	-6.3	20.5	8.5	12.7	23.8	13.1
22 017	7680	Caddo Parish	159 011	53.5	78.7	20.6	-3.8	27.1	10.6	11.6	43.8	17.8
22 019	3960	Calcasieu Parish	114 563	57.5	77.0	16.9	-7.5	19.0	8.3	6.3	37.0	19.5
22 021	...	Caldwell Parish	6 922	73.2	65.4	8.8	-15.6	9.8	4.2	0.0	22.2	6.3
22 023	...	Cameron Parish	6 257	74.7	68.1	7.9	-16.5	8.3	4.2	0.0	0.0	6.8
22 025	...	Catahoula Parish	6 904	75.3	61.4	9.4	-15.0	10.4	6.0	0.0	X	12.5
22 027	...	Claiborne Parish	11 169	69.5	65.7	12.4	-12.0	17.4	6.0	25.0	0.0	14.9
22 029	...	Concordia Parish	12 814	69.9	64.6	9.6	-14.8	10.9	6.6	3.8	41.9	7.4
22 031	...	De Soto Parish	16 118	70.3	70.3	10.2	-14.2	12.6	6.7	0.8	40.0	7.3
22 033	0760	East Baton Rouge Parish	245 296	42.5	83.9	30.8	6.4	37.4	17.8	27.3	51.6	35.8
22 035	...	East Carroll Parish	5 542	73.3	57.9	12.3	-12.1	18.1	8.4	100.0	70.6	0.0
22 037	...	East Feliciana Parish	13 877	68.8	70.7	11.3	-13.1	16.4	4.8	0.0	18.6	8.5
22 039	...	Evangeline Parish	21 511	75.2	55.5	9.5	-14.9	11.4	3.6	0.0	22.1	2.0
22 041	...	Franklin Parish	13 423	75.1	61.4	9.8	-14.6	10.6	7.1	0.0	25.0	0.0
22 043	...	Grant Parish	11 921	68.5	73.1	9.8	-14.6	10.1	5.6	18.3	22.9	15.4
22 045	...	Iberia Parish	43 965	71.6	66.9	11.2	-13.2	13.1	6.4	20.5	7.9	12.0
22 047	...	Iberville Parish	21 101	73.2	65.7	9.6	-14.8	11.9	6.6	0.0	11.1	13.1
22 049	...	Jackson Parish	10 062	66.1	73.6	12.9	-11.5	12.9	13.1	0.0	29.4	0.0
22 051	5560	Jefferson Parish	298 761	50.7	79.3	21.5	-2.9	23.6	12.2	10.9	35.4	18.6
22 053	...	Jefferson Davis Parish ..	19 352	71.8	69.4	9.9	-14.5	10.8	6.2	4.5	15.2	0.0
22 055	3880	Lafayette Parish	116 183	49.2	79.8	25.5	1.1	29.1	11.1	17.5	46.2	20.5
22 057	3350	Lafourche Parish	55 891	71.7	66.3	12.4	-12.0	13.1	5.1	3.7	42.4	13.9
22 059	...	La Salle Parish	9 219	70.0	68.5	11.2	-13.2	12.2	4.3	0.0	3.4	3.1
22 061	...	Lincoln Parish	22 059	44.3	80.4	31.8	7.4	35.1	22.9	27.1	84.5	22.0
22 063	0760	Livingston Parish	56 528	66.0	77.2	11.4	-13.0	11.6	6.5	9.6	26.5	11.7
22 065	...	Madison Parish	7 670	70.3	63.4	11.0	-13.4	14.8	8.0	0.0	28.6	6.9
22 067	...	Morehouse Parish	19 446	72.2	66.6	9.7	-14.7	11.6	6.7	14.7	0.0	6.8
22 069	...	Natchitoches Parish	22 033	59.4	72.7	18.4	-6.0	23.8	8.6	12.3	50.7	26.7
22 071	5560	Orleans Parish	300 568	48.8	74.7	25.8	1.4	47.6	13.4	17.1	31.5	27.1
22 073	5200	Ouachita Parish	88 430	51.4	78.6	22.7	-1.7	26.6	13.1	9.1	48.0	12.2
22 075	5560	Plaquemines Parish	16 448	65.5	68.7	10.8	-13.6	13.4	3.3	1.6	10.3	7.7

[1]MSA = Metropolitan Statistical Area. PMSA = Primary MSA. NECMA = New England County Metropolitan Area. See the Appendix A for explanation of these concepts. See Appendix B for list of metropolitan areas identified by type, with component counties.
[2]Hispanic or Latino persons may be of any race.

Table B-3. States and Counties — Education, Labor Force, and Income

STATE County	School enrollment			Population 16 to 19 years				Employment status, 2000			Work status in 1999 of the population 16 years and over (percent)		
											Worked in 1999		
	Grades kindergarten through 12	College or graduate school	Percent private	Number	Percent in armed forces	Percent high school graduates	Percent not enrolled, not grads, not in armed forces, not employed	Total population 16 years and over	Percent in labor force	Unemployment rate	Full-time	Part-time	Did not work in 1999
	11	12	13	14	15	16	17	18	19	20	21	22	23
KENTUCKY—Cont'd													
Owsley County	936	154	8.2	292	0.0	12.0	18.8	3 830	39.3	8.8	32.7	10.8	56.4
Pendleton County.........	3 053	345	5.7	885	0.0	12.5	5.2	10 827	64.2	5.0	55.9	12.9	31.2
Perry County	5 444	1 179	4.4	1 843	0.0	10.1	12.6	23 172	43.8	11.6	37.4	8.6	54.0
Pike County	12 398	2 322	7.9	3 840	0.0	10.6	9.0	54 578	44.8	8.9	39.3	8.4	52.2
Powell County	2 704	196	4.4	871	0.0	11.7	6.4	10 226	54.7	5.6	50.6	9.4	40.0
Pulaski County	10 027	1 781	6.1	3 108	0.0	9.7	6.7	44 762	55.0	5.1	48.1	11.3	40.6
Robertson County	425	81	5.3	130	0.0	13.8	6.2	1 789	55.3	5.7	50.9	13.0	36.2
Rockcastle County	2 971	366	2.8	832	0.0	13.6	8.2	13 054	54.5	6.7	48.6	9.9	41.5
Rowan County...............	3 346	4 503	5.1	2 245	0.0	5.1	2.6	18 193	58.3	8.1	47.6	20.1	32.3
Russell County	2 771	541	5.7	867	0.0	11.0	11.3	13 135	53.5	6.5	46.0	10.9	43.1
Scott County	6 358	2 150	22.5	2 233	0.0	7.5	3.0	25 372	69.2	3.8	61.0	14.4	24.6
Shelby County	6 228	820	14.7	1 923	1.0	9.6	8.4	25 886	68.3	3.9	60.4	13.4	26.1
Simpson County	3 074	394	8.0	708	0.0	18.9	3.2	12 504	65.0	3.2	58.3	11.6	30.2
Spencer County	2 321	307	12.2	631	0.0	11.7	4.3	8 913	69.8	4.1	61.0	13.7	25.3
Taylor County	4 009	1 403	21.7	1 385	0.0	12.9	7.1	18 165	59.1	7.3	48.2	14.6	37.2
Todd County................	2 208	237	9.2	623	0.0	17.2	3.2	9 103	62.9	4.4	54.7	11.9	33.4
Trigg County................	2 101	399	3.5	492	0.0	11.2	5.7	10 000	58.5	4.8	52.9	10.9	36.2
Trimble County.............	1 683	215	6.7	407	0.0	17.9	4.7	6 182	64.0	5.2	56.0	11.9	32.1
Union County	3 197	530	12.2	1 607	0.0	13.8	16.9	12 451	63.2	12.8	53.6	13.0	33.4
Warren County.............	15 725	10 926	5.7	6 961	0.0	8.4	4.6	73 674	67.5	5.8	55.0	18.8	26.3
Washington County.......	2 182	369	20.5	684	0.0	14.0	8.0	8 476	60.0	4.6	53.1	12.6	34.4
Wayne County..............	3 808	423	2.5	1 151	0.0	13.7	12.4	15 485	51.6	7.9	46.9	9.5	43.6
Webster County	2 617	543	6.9	853	0.0	9.4	7.9	11 185	58.2	4.7	51.3	12.0	36.7
Whitley County	6 860	1 972	15.4	2 382	0.0	9.4	9.2	27 760	50.3	6.7	43.7	11.5	44.8
Wolfe County...............	1 333	217	6.6	413	0.0	10.4	19.6	5 469	45.6	9.1	40.2	8.8	51.0
Woodford County	4 442	960	20.9	1 151	0.0	14.5	5.2	17 924	71.7	2.6	64.4	13.6	22.0
LOUISIANA	923 702	258 000	17.2	289 111	0.4	10.4	8.0	3 394 546	59.4	7.3	51.2	13.0	35.8
Acadia Parish	12 993	1 884	21.0	3 945	0.2	10.3	10.3	43 387	53.4	7.1	46.9	10.6	42.6
Allen Parish	5 056	646	10.7	1 453	0.0	13.8	11.2	19 897	43.4	7.3	41.2	8.0	50.8
Ascension Parish	17 104	3 105	13.7	4 719	0.2	10.8	4.9	56 116	66.3	5.4	58.5	11.6	29.8
Assumption Parish	5 203	666	10.8	1 438	0.0	5.6	12.7	17 517	55.8	9.3	48.7	10.4	40.9
Avoyelles Parish	8 525	1 013	11.9	2 560	0.0	10.2	18.3	31 782	48.5	8.1	43.6	9.1	47.3
Beauregard Parish	6 966	853	9.0	2 068	0.2	13.9	8.0	25 050	55.4	7.2	49.4	10.9	39.7
Bienville Parish	3 377	514	10.2	979	0.3	11.5	6.8	12 010	49.6	9.9	43.9	8.9	47.2
Bossier Parish	20 323	5 161	7.0	5 796	4.4	13.7	6.1	73 905	66.3	5.2	58.7	12.1	29.3
Caddo Parish	50 825	10 004	9.6	15 746	0.3	11.3	9.5	192 786	60.5	9.2	52.7	11.8	35.5
Calcasieu Parish	37 247	9 274	11.5	11 513	0.1	12.7	5.8	139 391	61.3	6.9	52.8	12.9	34.3
Caldwell Parish	2 067	311	3.5	512	0.0	11.3	18.8	8 201	51.4	7.3	47.3	9.8	43.0
Cameron Parish	2 165	230	4.8	612	0.0	12.6	7.4	7 551	58.1	4.6	54.4	12.3	33.3
Catahoula Parish	2 161	325	5.9	843	0.0	14.9	16.6	8 497	47.2	8.6	42.7	10.3	47.1
Claiborne Parish...........	3 463	455	13.7	1 032	0.0	11.2	12.8	13 046	48.3	9.4	43.3	9.5	47.3
Concordia Parish	4 294	406	8.9	1 161	0.6	9.8	14.3	15 217	50.1	9.9	43.0	10.4	46.6
De Soto Parish.............	5 510	782	6.6	1 533	0.0	14.6	10.8	19 135	55.2	8.1	48.3	10.8	40.9
East Baton Rouge Parish	79 781	45 355	19.3	30 936	0.0	8.2	6.0	318 021	64.7	6.3	53.9	17.0	29.2
East Carroll Parish	2 518	218	12.2	622	0.0	10.6	10.3	6 871	45.8	15.0	42.9	9.6	47.5
East Feliciana Parish	4 186	530	24.3	1 273	0.0	11.9	8.4	16 604	51.5	11.2	49.6	9.6	40.8
Evangeline Parish	7 763	1 127	9.9	2 313	0.0	8.7	13.7	26 147	46.0	7.3	39.7	9.9	50.4
Franklin Parish	4 430	464	13.1	1 346	0.0	15.1	13.4	15 978	49.6	8.3	46.4	9.4	44.2
Grant Parish	3 868	436	6.1	1 052	0.0	13.4	9.2	14 002	54.9	6.9	49.7	9.0	41.3
Iberia Parish................	16 481	2 222	11.9	4 571	0.0	11.5	10.2	53 797	56.4	9.2	49.0	12.0	38.9
Iberville Parish.............	6 794	1 124	19.3	2 182	0.0	12.6	14.5	25 656	48.2	7.4	46.1	10.6	43.3
Jackson Parish	2 916	541	7.3	961	0.0	13.2	11.9	11 959	54.4	5.4	47.3	11.3	41.4
Jefferson Parish	86 794	25 389	35.0	25 239	0.1	9.7	6.5	354 056	63.9	5.6	55.5	13.6	30.9
Jefferson Davis Parish ..	6 879	903	11.3	2 076	0.0	16.3	9.7	23 294	54.2	7.9	46.6	11.9	41.5
Lafayette Parish	38 737	13 951	17.7	12 509	0.1	9.9	6.7	144 549	65.9	6.9	54.6	15.7	29.7
Lafourche Parish	18 800	4 683	14.3	6 126	0.0	12.7	5.4	68 385	57.9	5.9	49.7	13.0	37.3
La Salle Parish.............	2 811	371	4.5	1 078	0.0	9.1	18.8	11 204	50.7	5.5	46.1	9.4	44.5
Lincoln Parish..............	7 049	10 157	7.9	4 912	0.0	4.2	2.5	34 148	59.4	13.3	45.4	20.3	34.3
Livingston Parish..........	20 338	3 235	5.8	5 829	0.0	12.0	6.2	68 053	63.2	4.8	56.4	11.2	32.4
Madison Parish	3 448	325	11.7	1 402	0.0	6.8	20.3	10 030	48.7	12.5	46.5	9.6	43.9
Morehouse Parish	6 574	810	12.9	2 109	0.0	12.5	14.2	23 571	52.6	11.1	46.6	9.5	43.9
Natchitoches Parish	7 674	5 204	8.1	3 932	0.0	6.3	5.7	30 206	54.8	9.8	45.5	15.7	38.8
Orleans Parish	99 998	39 625	26.1	30 841	0.3	9.6	8.0	370 138	57.8	9.4	48.4	14.4	37.3
Ouachita Parish............	30 577	10 363	9.2	10 101	0.1	10.9	8.8	110 838	63.1	8.2	52.9	13.8	33.2
Plaquemines Parish	6 134	1 234	16.9	1 648	0.0	12.0	4.3	19 790	55.4	6.6	50.7	11.6	37.7

Table B-3. States and Counties — Education, Labor Force, and Income

STATE County	Full-year full-time employed (percent) Total	Men	Women	Non-Hispanic White	Black or African American	American Indian and Alaska Native	Asian, Hawaiian, and Pacific Islander	Hispanic or Latino[1]	Children under 18 years in families Number	With two parents (percent) Both in labor force	Father only in labor force	With one parent who is in labor force (percent)	+/- U.S. percent of children with no stay-at-home parent (percent)	+/- U.S. percent two-income couples	Total employed by class of worker (percent) Private	Government	Self-employed	Unpaid family worker
	24	25	26	27	28	29	30	31	32	33	34	35	36	37	38	39	40	41
KENTUCKY—Cont'd																		
Owsley County	21.0	24.0	18.1	21.1	X	0.0	X	27.8	1 069	30.3	16.0	8.4	-25.9	-18.5	55.6	34.7	9.3	0.4
Pendleton County........	41.5	53.2	30.0	41.7	11.4	100.0	100.0	27.8	3 863	46.2	24.9	17.1	-1.3	-2.6	74.1	15.1	10.6	0.2
Perry County	26.1	31.6	21.2	26.2	19.5	0.0	45.2	10.7	6 641	26.9	23.7	15.3	-22.4	-23.3	73.7	16.9	8.9	0.5
Pike County	27.3	34.4	20.7	27.3	18.7	14.5	45.5	30.6	15 498	28.6	26.2	13.4	-22.6	-21.0	74.4	15.8	9.4	0.3
Powell County	33.6	42.7	24.8	33.5	59.2	55.3	X	22.9	3 296	34.1	24.7	18.3	-12.2	-8.1	74.9	16.6	8.2	0.3
Pulaski County	35.2	43.9	27.1	35.4	30.4	35.1	33.1	23.4	12 410	38.7	25.8	17.2	-8.7	-9.2	73.5	13.9	12.0	0.6
Robertson County	32.4	39.3	26.2	32.4	0.0	X	72.7	20.0	499	38.7	18.8	17.6	-8.3	-7.8	63.8	18.9	16.1	1.3
Rockcastle County	33.8	41.2	26.9	34.0	0.0	10.4	X	31.5	3 745	40.9	21.7	16.8	-6.9	-9.6	72.8	14.6	12.3	0.3
Rowan County..............	28.5	34.5	23.0	29.2	18.1	9.7	23.2	9.9	4 160	46.5	24.0	14.4	-3.7	-6.1	64.9	26.4	8.1	0.6
Russell County	30.5	40.4	21.5	30.6	28.1	0.0	21.3	19.8	3 446	46.4	19.4	16.0	-2.2	-8.3	67.5	16.5	15.4	0.7
Scott County	48.0	59.9	37.0	48.5	41.3	43.5	38.7	45.6	8 372	48.5	24.0	17.2	1.1	6.7	75.4	14.3	9.8	0.5
Shelby County	47.4	59.1	36.6	48.2	38.4	41.7	35.2	53.2	7 986	53.2	18.5	21.3	9.9	9.4	71.7	14.8	12.9	0.6
Simpson County	46.4	58.3	35.3	46.4	44.6	63.2	67.6	100.0	3 980	44.9	24.7	21.7	2.0	3.9	78.2	9.2	11.2	1.3
Spencer County	46.3	57.4	35.5	46.8	2.4	0.0	0.0	64.4	3 066	57.4	21.1	12.3	5.1	7.1	77.6	13.3	8.6	0.5
Taylor County	33.2	43.8	23.7	33.4	27.7	100.0	31.0	43.5	5 101	45.9	20.4	19.8	1.1	-2.0	74.6	12.5	12.3	0.7
Todd County	41.5	52.7	31.3	41.8	39.2	0.0	0.0	56.1	2 985	45.5	23.9	19.7	0.6	-0.2	68.7	11.8	18.4	1.1
Trigg County	39.6	47.5	32.0	40.2	37.3	0.0	79.2	29.2	2 754	52.8	17.1	20.9	9.1	-2.5	68.9	17.1	13.5	0.5
Trimble County	43.3	54.3	32.8	43.3	18.2	0.0	X	59.3	2 046	43.0	27.8	18.2	-3.4	-0.5	75.7	12.9	11.0	0.4
Union County	36.9	46.0	27.6	41.0	18.1	0.0	62.2	5.1	3 429	46.8	18.0	23.2	5.4	-0.2	78.3	12.4	9.3	0.1
Warren County..............	40.6	50.5	31.4	41.0	37.8	25.8	42.3	36.6	20 079	46.7	20.8	20.4	2.5	5.5	74.2	15.9	9.2	0.6
Washington County.......	39.5	51.0	28.8	40.4	27.1	64.2	58.6	33.8	2 616	48.2	22.8	22.2	5.8	0.1	70.9	14.2	14.6	0.2
Wayne County	31.9	40.7	23.4	32.4	17.8	24.4	100.0	16.3	4 813	39.5	20.2	15.3	-9.8	-11.6	74.5	13.1	11.6	0.8
Webster County	37.4	49.6	25.8	37.1	38.9	X	27.8	49.4	3 211	38.3	29.8	17.9	-8.4	-7.4	78.5	11.7	9.4	0.5
Whitley County	29.5	34.7	24.8	29.6	2.1	0.0	33.8	44.6	8 718	34.9	22.5	17.6	-12.1	-14.1	75.3	16.1	7.9	0.7
Wolfe County	26.7	32.3	21.2	26.6	100.0	X	10.5	61.5	1 697	29.1	23.3	13.0	-22.5	-19.5	68.5	21.7	9.7	0.1
Woodford County	50.2	60.7	40.3	51.4	39.4	70.0	4.5	41.8	5 615	57.7	20.4	14.5	7.6	11.1	70.4	17.1	11.8	0.7
LOUISIANA	36.4	45.0	28.6	39.7	29.5	32.1	34.3	35.5	1 126 561	36.3	19.8	26.7	-1.6	-4.3	72.8	17.4	9.4	0.3
Acadia Parish	32.1	41.7	23.6	33.3	26.0	27.6	49.0	34.3	16 702	33.5	25.6	20.8	-10.3	-12.3	74.9	13.9	10.8	0.4
Allen Parish	27.8	29.5	25.5	31.4	19.0	43.2	37.9	14.1	5 826	38.6	23.2	19.2	-6.8	-12.2	64.7	24.8	10.0	0.5
Ascension Parish	44.4	56.2	33.3	47.9	30.9	30.2	38.6	40.2	21 562	43.3	25.1	20.5	-0.8	1.5	80.0	12.7	7.1	0.2
Assumption Parish	32.2	42.7	22.7	36.1	23.8	36.4	21.1	25.7	6 137	36.5	22.0	21.3	-6.8	-8.4	78.3	14.4	7.0	0.3
Avoyelles Parish	28.6	34.7	22.9	33.3	16.9	34.7	14.0	22.7	10 373	34.3	18.9	25.1	-5.2	-10.0	67.1	21.7	10.9	0.3
Beauregard Parish	33.5	42.8	24.2	34.2	28.1	52.0	24.0	34.3	8 377	38.8	28.9	19.9	-5.9	-10.2	69.1	19.7	10.8	0.5
Bienville Parish............	31.0	38.7	24.3	33.4	27.8	21.6	38.5	25.3	3 886	33.9	17.9	26.6	-4.1	-11.0	71.3	19.2	9.2	0.3
Bossier Parish	44.5	55.2	34.5	47.1	35.4	30.4	38.2	42.3	25 959	43.9	20.1	25.6	4.9	2.5	72.6	18.8	8.3	0.3
Caddo Parish	38.3	46.2	31.5	41.6	33.8	38.1	39.7	37.8	61 296	33.1	14.4	35.6	4.1	-2.2	74.1	17.4	8.3	0.3
Calcasieu Parish	38.3	48.7	28.8	39.8	33.8	22.4	31.8	39.2	46 964	40.2	22.6	23.2	-1.2	-4.2	77.3	14.3	8.2	0.3
Caldwell Parish	28.9	33.6	24.2	30.7	20.6	0.0	44.4	36.2	2 417	41.1	26.4	19.3	-4.2	-8.0	67.4	22.8	9.6	0.2
Cameron Parish	33.0	41.7	24.6	33.3	21.8	52.8	23.1	34.0	2 653	41.8	29.7	14.4	-8.4	-9.7	67.3	16.8	15.5	0.3
Catahoula Parish	25.1	31.5	18.8	28.1	16.4	42.1	X	31.6	2 512	29.2	22.4	25.1	-10.3	-15.7	63.2	21.9	14.1	0.9
Claiborne Parish...........	30.0	36.3	23.8	35.1	23.8	100.0	0.0	20.2	3 877	33.2	15.0	31.2	-0.2	-9.6	67.9	22.0	9.9	0.2
Concordia Parish	28.1	33.4	23.2	33.8	18.9	16.9	13.3	13.6	5 086	28.5	18.6	28.9	-7.2	-14.2	70.6	19.2	10.0	0.3
De Soto Parish..............	34.6	41.7	28.2	39.7	27.3	26.5	56.3	26.2	6 552	34.1	16.1	29.1	-1.4	-6.6	74.2	17.0	8.5	0.3
East Baton Rouge Parish	39.0	47.0	32.0	42.7	33.8	41.1	32.5	35.9	100 200	36.9	18.9	29.1	1.4	0.9	70.0	21.4	8.4	0.2
East Carroll Parish	22.9	27.4	18.1	31.2	18.4	0.0	26.1	15.2	2 572	22.6	13.5	35.4	-6.6	-15.5	57.8	32.0	10.0	0.1
East Feliciana Parish	32.3	33.2	31.3	39.7	23.7	50.0	55.7	23.3	4 936	39.3	16.9	26.6	1.3	-0.8	59.5	31.7	8.3	0.5
Evangeline Parish	25.0	29.1	20.8	28.9	14.7	12.3	13.2	12.8	9 739	38.0	14.5	18.1	-8.5	-11.4	66.8	20.1	12.5	0.6
Franklin Parish	26.9	34.6	20.5	30.0	19.5	22.1	38.4	25.9	5 471	29.8	24.9	21.9	-12.9	-13.3	69.9	16.6	12.8	0.7
Grant Parish	33.1	41.4	25.2	34.5	21.5	19.8	20.7	25.8	4 770	40.1	20.6	20.9	-3.6	-8.4	65.6	24.5	9.6	0.2
Iberia Parish	33.0	42.7	24.3	36.5	25.4	28.9	31.4	22.5	20 315	33.5	20.7	23.8	-7.3	-9.0	77.2	12.0	10.4	0.4
Iberville Parish..............	31.3	35.5	27.3	37.0	25.2	25.0	25.9	31.5	7 842	35.7	13.5	26.9	-2.0	-7.1	73.9	18.8	6.9	0.4
Jackson Parish..............	35.1	46.7	24.8	38.8	25.9	9.5	7.3	9.1	3 585	41.0	23.4	22.1	-1.5	-6.2	75.4	15.9	8.4	0.3
Jefferson Parish	41.7	51.3	33.0	43.7	35.6	42.1	40.7	39.3	106 949	38.8	19.0	27.2	1.4	-1.4	76.4	13.4	10.0	0.2
Jefferson Davis Parish ..	31.0	38.9	23.9	32.0	26.2	47.9	23.7	20.0	8 805	39.0	21.7	19.3	-6.3	-10.9	71.4	16.3	11.7	0.6
Lafayette Parish	39.3	49.5	30.1	42.1	30.9	37.6	34.0	30.0	49 302	39.1	22.8	24.8	-0.7	-1.3	75.5	13.3	10.9	0.3
Lafourche Parish	33.2	45.3	22.2	34.8	24.7	22.5	19.4	26.3	23 116	36.2	25.8	20.2	-8.2	-10.4	73.8	15.6	10.3	0.3
La Salle Parish..............	28.9	35.2	22.5	30.4	17.5	35.7	25.7	31.8	3 223	44.3	22.5	14.3	-6.0	-6.1	66.7	20.9	11.8	0.7
Lincoln Parish..............	29.3	37.5	22.0	35.0	21.2	40.0	21.9	12.1	8 808	40.5	18.0	26.4	2.3	0.9	65.3	25.2	9.0	0.5
Livingston Parish	42.0	53.4	31.2	42.7	33.1	40.7	38.9	28.7	25 720	44.9	27.2	16.9	-2.8	-4.0	74.7	15.9	9.0	0.3
Madison Parish	26.3	28.3	24.4	37.5	18.1	27.8	28.6	37.4	3 667	21.7	11.6	40.5	-2.4	-12.0	67.2	24.8	7.4	0.7
Morehouse Parish	31.3	39.4	24.3	35.3	25.4	14.7	27.7	26.6	7 722	33.3	16.2	31.1	-0.2	-9.7	75.4	15.1	9.3	0.2
Natchitoches Parish	29.6	38.6	21.9	33.7	23.4	20.3	27.3	22.9	9 325	35.3	19.9	26.2	-3.1	-6.6	64.6	25.7	9.3	0.4
Orleans Parish	33.1	38.5	28.5	39.4	30.0	35.9	29.4	33.7	114 871	24.7	10.4	39.9	0.0	-2.6	70.5	20.4	8.8	0.3
Ouachita Parish............	38.5	47.3	30.9	42.6	29.6	35.9	41.5	31.4	37 411	38.0	15.2	31.5	4.9	2.2	72.7	18.0	9.1	0.2
Plaquemines Parish	34.6	42.9	26.3	38.6	22.6	29.8	26.1	34.2	7 360	39.1	26.3	17.2	-8.3	-7.0	68.2	19.5	11.6	0.7

[1] Hispanic or Latino persons may be of any race.

Table B-3. States and Counties — Education, Labor Force, and Income

STATE County	42 Percent who worked at home	43 Percent of the population 5 years and over with a disability	44 Veterans as a percent of the population 18 years and over	Occupation for employed population 16 years and over (percent)						Industry for employed population 16 years and over (percent)					
				45 Management, professional, and related occupations	46 Service occupations	47 Sales and office occupations	48 Farming, fishing, and forestry occupations	49 Construction, extraction, and maintenance occupations	50 Production, transportation and material moving occupations	51 Agriculture, forestry, fishing, and mining	52 Construction and manufacturing	53 Wholesale and retail trade	54 Transportation and warehousing, and utilities	55 Service industries	56 Public administration
KENTUCKY—Cont'd															
Owsley County	3.9	37.4	9.0	29.4	17.0	16.0	1.4	15.1	21.0	5.2	21.3	11.0	3.5	52.4	6.5
Pendleton County	3.0	22.8	13.0	20.5	12.6	24.6	1.0	16.2	25.1	3.1	30.0	14.2	7.0	40.7	5.1
Perry County	1.9	31.6	9.6	24.1	16.2	25.7	0.9	17.4	15.8	10.7	14.0	18.3	5.4	45.9	5.7
Pike County	1.9	33.0	9.3	25.0	13.8	26.5	0.3	19.2	15.1	14.7	10.1	17.8	7.3	46.0	4.1
Powell County	2.2	32.3	11.2	15.8	14.6	20.6	0.6	14.7	33.7	2.1	39.7	12.1	7.0	35.2	3.9
Pulaski County	3.4	29.7	13.4	24.3	15.6	24.9	1.0	10.4	23.7	3.8	26.7	19.0	5.3	41.7	3.4
Robertson County	4.9	22.7	12.0	27.0	15.6	18.3	3.8	10.6	24.7	11.0	34.4	10.1	2.6	36.9	5.0
Rockcastle County	3.8	28.5	9.4	19.6	15.3	20.3	1.6	14.9	28.4	5.2	34.8	12.2	4.3	40.3	3.2
Rowan County	2.3	21.9	9.7	29.1	16.7	26.0	1.5	11.2	15.5	2.1	20.4	16.0	3.0	53.0	5.4
Russell County	4.1	29.9	13.2	23.6	15.0	21.8	1.3	13.5	24.9	4.1	32.8	15.6	4.2	38.8	4.5
Scott County	3.1	18.5	11.7	26.9	14.8	22.9	1.4	9.7	24.2	4.4	32.9	12.6	4.3	41.0	4.9
Shelby County	4.4	17.4	11.6	30.4	12.2	23.9	1.7	8.9	22.8	4.7	29.8	14.8	4.6	39.1	6.9
Simpson County	2.7	21.4	13.1	21.2	11.4	21.7	1.6	10.6	33.5	5.2	41.8	14.5	5.1	31.8	1.8
Spencer County	2.7	20.3	12.6	22.2	12.1	26.9	1.3	14.2	23.3	2.6	30.5	15.4	6.5	40.8	4.3
Taylor County	3.3	27.2	10.6	25.5	13.3	24.1	1.1	11.2	24.8	4.4	29.1	18.5	4.4	41.1	2.5
Todd County	6.5	24.5	11.6	21.4	10.8	17.3	4.1	11.7	34.6	13.6	39.8	12.1	4.7	27.3	2.5
Trigg County	3.2	27.5	16.5	24.0	15.2	21.1	1.6	12.6	25.5	5.8	35.8	11.4	5.2	37.6	4.3
Trimble County	3.0	23.5	12.3	19.8	16.9	20.2	1.2	15.1	26.8	4.5	33.8	13.8	7.3	36.1	4.6
Union County	2.4	24.0	12.0	24.9	12.6	18.6	2.7	17.9	23.2	13.8	28.5	11.7	5.3	37.8	3.0
Warren County	2.3	19.0	11.9	30.0	14.8	28.5	0.7	8.0	18.0	1.8	24.9	18.2	4.5	47.4	3.2
Washington County	4.7	22.2	8.7	26.5	12.5	18.4	2.8	11.6	28.5	8.4	34.2	11.9	3.5	37.9	4.0
Wayne County	2.7	35.5	11.9	19.9	13.6	20.9	3.6	12.9	29.0	6.7	36.4	11.5	2.9	39.6	3.0
Webster County	2.5	25.8	11.8	18.9	14.2	18.0	2.0	17.1	29.9	11.0	34.5	12.5	5.6	34.1	2.3
Whitley County	2.4	30.3	11.4	26.3	14.6	23.4	0.9	12.3	22.5	2.9	24.1	17.1	6.3	45.8	3.8
Wolfe County	3.1	35.3	9.4	24.3	12.6	16.9	1.2	13.4	31.6	3.8	29.2	14.3	7.5	38.7	6.5
Woodford County	3.5	20.0	12.4	36.0	12.3	24.4	3.5	8.3	15.6	8.7	25.7	11.9	4.2	41.8	7.6
LOUISIANA	2.1	21.8	12.1	29.9	16.7	26.8	0.8	11.7	14.1	4.2	18.0	15.4	5.3	51.3	5.8
Acadia Parish	1.7	24.3	10.7	24.0	15.4	24.6	1.1	15.3	19.7	12.2	17.6	18.6	5.1	42.5	3.9
Allen Parish	1.9	26.1	12.0	23.2	24.9	21.4	1.9	13.0	15.6	5.8	16.9	11.3	4.9	49.8	11.4
Ascension Parish	1.9	17.4	10.8	26.3	12.5	27.9	0.3	16.2	16.8	1.0	31.5	15.9	5.3	42.0	4.4
Assumption Parish	1.8	22.1	9.3	22.5	14.5	22.5	2.3	16.0	22.1	8.0	31.2	14.7	5.0	37.4	3.7
Avoyelles Parish	1.8	27.0	11.1	23.6	25.2	21.1	2.0	14.2	13.9	6.0	16.9	13.3	4.3	49.2	10.3
Beauregard Parish	2.5	21.3	15.8	25.5	15.9	22.1	1.8	17.6	17.1	6.7	24.1	15.0	5.6	40.2	8.4
Bienville Parish	1.9	25.4	12.5	22.6	15.1	20.1	2.7	13.0	26.5	7.5	29.5	11.8	5.8	40.5	5.0
Bossier Parish	1.6	20.0	18.0	29.1	17.6	28.3	0.4	11.6	13.1	2.3	15.6	15.9	5.6	54.1	6.6
Caddo Parish	1.0	22.6	14.0	29.3	16.3	26.5	0.3	9.6	14.9	1.8	17.1	15.6	5.1	56.0	4.4
Calcasieu Parish	1.7	21.1	13.9	27.2	18.2	25.6	0.3	13.9	14.8	2.1	24.2	14.4	4.9	50.3	4.2
Caldwell Parish	1.2	24.4	12.5	23.8	16.9	21.7	4.0	14.3	19.3	11.2	19.2	11.5	4.8	45.7	7.6
Cameron Parish	3.0	19.0	10.4	18.5	17.2	22.8	4.8	14.2	22.6	16.6	18.3	13.6	9.5	37.6	4.4
Catahoula Parish	1.6	28.0	10.8	24.2	14.8	22.4	4.9	15.3	18.4	18.2	14.2	14.4	6.2	38.8	8.2
Claiborne Parish	2.0	26.5	12.8	23.2	19.4	20.5	2.3	13.4	21.3	9.1	23.6	12.5	5.3	41.6	7.8
Concordia Parish	2.4	25.8	11.8	23.9	18.4	25.3	2.2	14.6	15.7	9.5	18.7	15.8	5.3	43.4	7.3
De Soto Parish	1.3	24.4	11.9	21.1	16.2	22.7	1.8	15.7	22.5	6.0	28.9	14.5	5.9	40.2	4.4
East Baton Rouge Parish	2.3	19.2	11.1	36.7	14.8	29.0	0.2	8.4	10.9	0.8	16.5	14.7	4.2	56.2	7.8
East Carroll Parish	0.8	24.6	9.5	30.0	21.9	18.4	5.9	6.1	17.6	15.1	13.7	10.3	4.5	43.1	13.3
East Feliciana Parish	2.1	22.9	12.5	24.7	22.0	22.5	1.1	13.5	16.1	3.5	23.6	11.1	6.2	44.8	10.7
Evangeline Parish	1.9	27.6	10.1	25.9	18.0	22.3	2.4	15.4	16.0	11.1	16.7	15.1	3.7	46.6	6.8
Franklin Parish	2.0	20.9	11.4	27.3	15.4	20.7	3.9	16.5	16.3	12.7	19.3	15.2	5.9	41.1	5.7
Grant Parish	2.5	25.0	16.1	25.2	17.0	22.5	1.9	15.5	18.1	7.8	23.6	13.8	5.8	40.6	8.3
Iberia Parish	2.2	22.3	11.0	23.6	15.8	25.0	1.4	16.0	18.2	14.2	18.7	16.6	4.4	42.6	3.5
Iberville Parish	0.9	23.8	9.6	23.5	17.3	24.8	1.1	14.4	18.9	3.1	27.4	12.2	5.8	43.4	8.1
Jackson Parish	1.4	25.0	13.4	23.8	14.8	23.3	2.2	12.2	23.7	4.6	29.8	13.7	6.3	40.8	4.7
Jefferson Parish	2.0	21.0	12.1	32.4	15.3	29.9	0.4	10.6	11.3	1.9	16.0	16.8	5.9	54.4	5.0
Jefferson Davis Parish	2.4	22.8	12.0	24.9	17.8	22.6	1.6	17.6	15.5	12.3	18.0	15.3	3.8	46.3	4.3
Lafayette Parish	2.6	18.1	11.0	34.7	14.6	28.8	0.2	10.5	11.2	10.0	11.0	17.1	5.0	52.9	3.9
Lafourche Parish	2.1	22.2	9.4	25.4	13.1	25.9	1.7	13.7	20.2	8.2	21.2	17.4	7.4	41.9	3.9
La Salle Parish	2.6	23.6	12.1	23.8	18.4	19.8	1.8	15.4	20.7	17.3	15.5	13.3	4.2	41.1	8.6
Lincoln Parish	1.8	16.2	8.7	33.3	16.6	28.1	0.8	8.1	13.1	2.8	15.7	15.5	4.1	58.5	3.4
Livingston Parish	1.8	20.6	12.1	24.8	12.6	27.5	0.4	20.6	14.2	1.2	29.0	16.9	4.3	41.7	6.8
Madison Parish	1.6	21.9	9.6	23.6	24.5	23.6	3.6	7.7	17.0	7.0	16.1	13.0	4.9	48.6	10.4
Morehouse Parish	1.7	24.4	12.1	21.9	17.3	23.6	2.7	13.0	21.3	6.7	28.4	13.3	4.4	42.2	5.0
Natchitoches Parish	2.6	21.4	11.3	27.3	16.3	26.3	1.6	11.9	16.6	5.2	21.2	13.7	4.2	49.3	6.3
Orleans Parish	2.7	23.2	10.8	34.7	22.1	25.8	0.2	6.8	10.4	1.0	10.1	12.4	5.9	64.1	6.4
Ouachita Parish	1.7	21.1	12.2	30.8	16.6	29.6	0.2	10.2	12.6	1.1	17.4	15.9	3.9	56.4	5.4
Plaquemines Parish	2.3	19.1	11.1	24.7	13.3	24.9	4.6	13.6	18.9	12.2	16.2	14.2	8.7	40.7	7.9

Table B-3. States and Counties — Education, Labor Force, and Income

STATE County	Median household income	Median family income — All families	Married-couple	Male householder	Female householder	Median nonfamily household income	Median income for full-year, full-time workers — Men	Women	Per capita income	With earnings	With interest, dividend, or rental income	With Social Security income	With public assistance income	With retirement income	Households with income over $100,000 (percent)	+/- U.S. percent for income over $100,000 (percent)	Households with income below poverty (percent)	Families with children with income below poverty (percent)
	57	58	59	60	61	62	63	64	65	66	67	68	69	70	71	72	73	74
KENTUCKY—Cont'd																		
Owsley County	15 805	18 034	23 750	2 499	9 514	9 458	25 700	20 865	10 742	58.7	12.4	35.2	16.5	16.5	1.9	-10.4	43.9	53.0
Pendleton County	38 125	42 589	48 983	17 639	18 627	20 508	32 660	23 641	16 551	81.9	28.4	25.9	3.8	14.7	3.9	-8.4	11.6	13.3
Perry County	22 089	26 718	31 884	13 644	10 158	10 674	32 639	20 918	12 224	62.3	15.1	35.9	9.2	16.4	3.0	-9.3	29.3	33.0
Pike County	23 930	29 302	35 961	16 125	8 642	12 768	33 475	20 002	14 005	62.5	18.2	38.3	6.4	20.3	3.7	-8.6	24.4	27.8
Powell County	25 515	30 483	33 792	14 850	8 971	12 478	27 500	19 128	13 060	72.8	15.4	29.1	4.7	17.3	3.1	-9.2	24.2	27.0
Pulaski County	27 370	32 350	37 300	19 943	13 324	13 221	28 755	19 696	15 352	71.7	26.4	34.6	3.7	17.7	4.2	-8.1	20.2	23.0
Robertson County	30 581	35 521	44 188	11 250	15 375	18 571	27 500	20 952	13 404	76.9	27.9	32.2	2.7	18.8	2.3	-10.0	20.2	25.3
Rockcastle County	23 475	30 278	36 523	17 250	13 030	9 807	27 252	18 953	12 337	70.1	19.1	30.6	4.2	14.0	2.4	-9.9	25.3	25.6
Rowan County	28 055	34 338	41 637	21 354	12 478	14 288	28 045	21 004	13 888	75.9	26.3	30.3	4.5	15.7	4.8	-7.5	22.7	20.1
Russell County	22 042	27 803	33 207	17 083	11 213	10 886	24 855	19 449	13 183	65.6	21.8	38.1	4.6	17.3	3.4	-8.9	26.3	27.3
Scott County	47 081	54 117	65 710	26 875	20 556	24 876	41 676	27 006	21 490	86.1	31.3	20.4	2.3	15.2	12.6	0.3	9.3	10.0
Shelby County	45 534	52 764	60 640	30 625	18 729	22 145	36 370	26 384	20 195	85.6	33.5	24.3	2.8	15.7	10.3	-2.0	9.6	10.1
Simpson County	36 432	42 525	51 696	31 339	20 959	18 147	32 833	23 724	17 150	77.1	26.3	27.9	1.6	16.8	4.2	-8.1	12.9	11.2
Spencer County	47 042	52 038	57 083	31 786	12 000	17 415	37 364	25 102	19 848	85.4	28.8	21.9	3.2	18.1	8.5	-3.8	10.8	10.9
Taylor County	28 089	33 854	42 072	17 955	12 938	13 861	27 664	21 130	15 162	71.8	30.2	35.9	4.3	17.5	4.1	-8.2	19.1	20.6
Todd County	29 718	36 043	43 141	21 250	17 574	13 653	29 568	21 586	15 462	77.5	25.6	28.6	4.8	14.8	3.4	-8.9	18.6	20.1
Trigg County	33 002	40 886	50 231	40 536	15 357	14 063	31 839	22 557	17 184	71.3	28.2	34.3	3.0	21.3	4.4	-7.9	14.7	12.1
Trimble County	36 192	41 925	49 286	22 115	20 750	19 193	31 379	21 806	16 354	79.3	25.7	26.4	3.4	20.5	5.2	-7.1	14.9	13.1
Union County	35 018	43 103	46 510	21 534	12 554	17 390	30 714	21 333	17 465	76.8	29.2	31.8	3.4	19.5	5.8	-6.5	12.7	14.4
Warren County	36 151	45 142	54 627	25 485	13 801	20 326	33 425	23 734	18 847	81.9	31.4	23.6	2.7	15.0	8.0	-4.3	16.0	15.9
Washington County	33 136	39 240	44 390	22 344	16 250	16 339	29 040	22 176	15 722	75.6	32.1	31.8	3.0	17.7	5.0	-7.3	14.8	13.8
Wayne County	20 863	24 869	30 126	12 589	10 129	10 079	24 675	18 875	12 601	67.7	17.4	32.2	7.3	11.2	3.0	-9.3	30.0	30.6
Webster County	31 529	38 208	46 454	27 083	19 457	14 870	32 008	21 355	15 657	75.2	27.9	31.9	3.7	19.8	3.4	-8.9	15.7	16.3
Whitley County	22 075	27 871	35 929	22 063	11 012	10 067	26 792	17 478	12 777	65.6	19.4	34.9	6.2	15.5	3.5	-8.8	27.7	30.7
Wolfe County	19 310	23 333	23 934	14 408	8 355	9 375	24 674	19 211	10 321	62.7	15.0	33.2	6.4	14.9	1.4	-10.9	34.3	45.0
Woodford County	49 491	58 218	70 309	24 531	26 298	24 361	40 616	30 112	22 839	87.7	34.4	22.2	1.1	16.4	12.2	-0.1	8.1	7.5
LOUISIANA	32 566	39 774	51 507	25 613	14 101	18 393	35 108	22 778	16 912	78.1	25.9	25.2	3.3	14.8	7.4	-4.9	19.1	22.1
Acadia Parish	26 684	31 812	41 758	21 182	11 278	12 032	29 956	17 797	13 424	73.0	22.9	28.2	4.1	10.7	4.6	-7.7	25.6	27.0
Allen Parish	27 777	33 920	42 246	22 321	14 151	12 995	34 391	17 809	13 101	73.3	18.9	32.2	2.7	16.7	4.5	-7.8	21.3	21.9
Ascension Parish	44 288	50 626	59 472	32 447	17 225	22 213	41 715	23 767	17 858	84.6	26.7	17.1	2.2	12.6	8.3	-4.0	12.6	13.7
Assumption Parish	31 168	36 052	51 233	31 518	9 909	14 763	37 039	18 673	14 008	75.3	21.3	27.4	3.4	13.0	4.8	-7.5	21.2	24.7
Avoyelles Parish	23 851	29 389	39 946	20 846	10 819	10 703	27 889	18 826	12 146	69.5	17.7	29.8	4.9	14.2	3.6	-8.7	26.8	27.7
Beauregard Parish	32 582	37 886	44 319	28 500	14 158	15 930	36 549	20 542	15 514	76.7	23.8	27.8	2.0	17.9	5.6	-6.7	15.8	17.6
Bienville Parish	23 663	30 241	41 305	20 625	11 424	10 851	28 961	19 745	12 471	66.2	18.0	33.9	4.2	18.5	2.6	-9.7	26.4	29.1
Bossier Parish	39 203	45 542	53 713	27 283	17 124	22 116	35 187	24 134	18 119	82.9	28.6	23.2	2.5	18.7	7.3	-5.0	13.6	15.8
Caddo Parish	31 467	38 872	52 164	24 988	14 322	19 762	32 756	22 800	17 839	77.2	25.1	26.6	3.6	16.5	7.8	-4.5	19.5	25.5
Calcasieu Parish	35 372	41 903	54 100	28 701	14 514	19 050	37 961	21 967	17 710	78.8	26.9	26.0	2.6	15.5	7.6	-4.7	15.8	17.7
Caldwell Parish	26 972	33 653	42 315	17 333	13 009	12 817	30 526	19 928	13 884	72.4	19.3	29.5	2.8	17.6	3.8	-8.5	21.1	23.5
Cameron Parish	34 232	39 663	46 603	34 167	20 096	16 781	31 921	19 788	15 348	80.6	24.9	25.5	1.5	13.2	4.4	-7.9	13.4	9.3
Catahoula Parish	22 528	27 206	32 267	17 778	10 244	11 333	27 181	19 049	12 608	70.9	15.7	30.0	3.2	16.7	3.8	-8.5	26.7	35.3
Claiborne Parish	25 344	32 225	44 195	30 952	12 160	12 036	30 035	20 818	13 825	68.0	21.2	35.0	3.1	18.0	4.2	-8.1	26.1	28.8
Concordia Parish	22 742	28 629	40 725	19 063	10 734	13 449	28 345	19 870	11 966	69.6	19.3	30.8	4.1	14.5	3.0	-9.3	27.2	33.2
De Soto Parish	28 252	33 196	44 579	24 524	11 323	12 886	31 308	20 833	13 606	72.7	19.3	30.8	4.6	15.7	3.4	-8.9	24.9	29.1
East Baton Rouge Parish	37 224	47 480	61 916	28 681	16 872	22 215	39 943	25 776	19 790	83.4	31.4	20.2	2.5	14.7	10.9	-1.4	17.3	19.0
East Carroll Parish	20 723	24 554	32 107	19 423	9 354	10 390	24 189	18 778	9 629	72.0	13.7	30.9	7.4	10.9	2.7	-9.6	36.0	47.0
East Feliciana Parish	31 631	37 278	50 909	14 741	14 009	15 699	32 459	20 983	15 428	77.1	21.2	23.0	3.2	18.0	6.0	-6.3	20.8	26.5
Evangeline Parish	20 532	27 243	37 610	20 813	8 321	8 132	30 826	17 274	11 432	63.8	15.0	32.0	5.0	13.4	3.0	-9.3	33.9	35.1
Franklin Parish	22 964	27 440	33 013	16 944	9 659	10 473	27 194	17 317	12 675	71.7	16.2	29.2	4.9	14.4	3.1	-9.2	27.8	35.0
Grant Parish	29 622	34 878	41 455	19 364	13 092	14 396	31 902	20 888	14 410	73.0	19.2	27.7	3.5	19.4	4.4	-7.9	20.8	24.1
Iberia Parish	31 204	36 017	47 035	21 952	9 559	15 767	33 229	18 929	14 145	77.4	24.6	27.1	4.1	13.9	5.6	-6.7	22.7	27.1
Iberville Parish	29 039	34 100	47 868	26 611	13 236	15 136	32 767	20 544	13 272	73.8	21.8	27.5	4.6	13.8	5.8	-6.5	23.1	25.7
Jackson Parish	28 352	36 317	43 613	22 188	10 884	11 817	32 344	20 686	15 354	69.7	20.4	33.1	3.1	19.6	4.6	-7.7	21.1	23.9
Jefferson Parish	38 435	45 834	58 094	30 038	18 028	24 594	35 924	25 588	19 953	82.0	32.4	25.1	2.6	15.1	9.2	-3.1	12.6	16.6
Jefferson Davis Parish	27 736	33 129	43 870	20 880	11 529	12 137	30 134	19 435	13 398	72.3	24.4	30.4	3.5	13.3	3.9	-8.4	21.9	22.3
Lafayette Parish	36 518	45 158	57 299	31 006	16 507	21 248	37 757	23 854	19 371	83.6	30.6	20.1	1.8	11.2	9.5	-2.8	15.9	15.8
Lafourche Parish	34 910	40 504	48 996	28 917	12 136	16 257	35 685	19 962	15 809	78.7	28.5	27.0	2.8	11.4	5.6	-6.7	16.8	18.3
La Salle Parish	28 189	36 197	42 609	13 750	10 174	11 176	28 601	20 410	14 033	70.5	21.4	31.9	4.5	16.1	4.2	-8.1	20.9	21.4
Lincoln Parish	26 977	38 972	52 995	22 120	10 650	12 592	34 197	21 380	14 313	77.1	25.4	22.1	3.0	15.4	5.1	-7.2	27.9	26.9
Livingston Parish	38 887	44 071	50 138	30 255	20 629	18 674	37 029	23 219	16 282	82.1	21.9	21.0	2.0	15.0	5.8	-6.5	12.5	11.1
Madison Parish	20 509	23 589	35 746	16 827	11 592	13 284	26 940	16 504	10 114	76.1	12.7	24.3	4.1	11.1	2.1	-10.2	32.0	41.0
Morehouse Parish	25 124	31 358	42 847	14 792	11 299	11 344	31 831	18 941	13 197	71.8	18.8	30.7	5.1	15.9	4.0	-8.3	26.1	31.5
Natchitoches Parish	25 722	32 816	42 625	19 861	11 280	12 449	30 308	20 350	13 743	73.8	21.3	27.1	3.2	16.1	4.9	-7.4	27.0	28.9
Orleans Parish	27 133	32 338	51 346	19 879	13 166	19 453	31 675	24 777	17 258	75.8	23.7	24.7	5.4	13.4	7.8	-4.5	25.6	33.5
Ouachita Parish	32 047	40 206	51 703	21 820	14 211	17 242	32 332	23 860	17 084	78.7	24.8	24.8	3.2	14.6	7.6	-4.7	19.5	25.0
Plaquemines Parish	38 173	42 610	52 112	21 484	14 902	17 490	38 828	22 257	15 937	79.4	25.1	21.7	2.7	14.4	7.7	-4.6	17.0	18.3

Table B-3. States and Counties — **Education, Labor Force, and Income**

STATE/ County code	MSA/PMSA/ NECMA code[1]	STATE County	High school graduates			College graduates		College graduates (percent)				
			Total population 25 years and over	Percent with a high school diploma or less	Percent with a high school diploma or more	Percent with a bachelor's degree or more	+/− U.S. percent with bachelor's degree or more	Non-Hispanic White	Black or African American	American Indian and Alaska Native	Asian, Hawaiian, and Pacific Islander	Hispanic or Latino[2]
			1	2	3	4	5	6	7	8	9	10
		LOUISIANA—Cont'd										
22 077	...	Pointe Coupee Parish...	14 577	70.0	69.1	12.8	-11.6	14.7	9.0	0.0	3.0	12.3
22 079	0220	Rapides Parish	79 811	59.1	74.6	16.5	-7.9	19.5	8.5	9.0	37.3	14.9
22 081	...	Red River Parish	5 792	74.4	67.4	8.7	-15.7	11.0	4.7	0.0	0.0	0.0
22 083	...	Richland Parish	13 060	70.3	61.9	12.8	-11.6	16.9	3.9	0.0	100.0	19.0
22 085	...	Sabine Parish	15 388	70.1	70.8	11.1	-13.3	12.6	4.7	7.2	39.1	6.0
22 087	5560	St. Bernard Parish	44 127	64.8	73.1	8.9	-15.5	9.1	5.6	7.9	20.3	7.4
22 089	5560	St. Charles Parish	29 551	56.1	80.0	17.5	-6.9	19.5	9.7	0.0	42.3	19.3
22 091	...	St. Helena Parish	6 489	72.0	67.5	11.2	-13.2	13.6	8.9	0.0	0.0	14.6
22 093	5560	St. James Parish	12 840	71.2	73.9	10.1	-14.3	11.1	8.7	0.0	13.3	18.4
22 095	5560	St. John the Baptist Parish	25 377	62.1	76.9	12.9	-11.5	14.5	10.0	9.6	44.5	13.5
22 097	3880	St. Landry Parish	53 592	71.2	62.0	10.7	-13.7	12.7	7.4	4.7	24.6	9.7
22 099	3880	St. Martin Parish	29 617	74.9	62.9	8.5	-15.9	10.6	3.4	9.6	5.5	14.4
22 101	...	St. Mary Parish	33 158	72.3	65.9	9.4	-15.0	10.8	6.1	3.9	9.5	11.5
22 103	5560	St. Tammany Parish	122 959	42.6	83.9	28.3	3.9	29.7	15.0	20.7	38.0	28.9
22 105	...	Tangipahoa Parish	59 909	62.8	71.5	16.3	-8.1	19.2	7.2	11.1	30.4	17.9
22 107	...	Tensas Parish	4 208	68.3	63.2	14.8	-9.6	23.3	6.7	0.0	0.0	9.6
22 109	3350	Terrebonne Parish	63 271	68.7	67.1	12.3	-12.1	13.6	7.0	2.0	32.0	15.7
22 111	...	Union Parish	14 819	68.4	71.7	11.8	-12.6	13.5	6.5	17.0	0.0	10.5
22 113	...	Vermilion Parish	33 616	72.4	65.6	10.7	-13.7	11.4	6.9	14.6	4.0	5.9
22 115	...	Vernon Parish	29 329	56.3	80.1	13.5	-10.9	14.3	8.9	9.1	22.7	15.2
22 117	...	Washington Parish	27 954	71.9	68.2	10.9	-13.5	12.7	6.6	10.6	0.0	10.2
22 119	7680	Webster Parish	27 687	65.1	70.8	12.6	-11.8	14.3	8.4	8.1	27.7	4.7
22 121	0760	West Baton Rouge Parish	13 347	67.2	73.4	11.1	-13.3	12.2	9.2	17.6	0.0	15.5
22 123	...	West Carroll Parish	7 994	75.3	59.5	9.5	-14.9	10.9	2.8	0.0	0.0	0.0
22 125	...	West Feliciana Parish ...	10 749	70.8	53.3	10.6	-13.8	19.1	2.7	0.0	11.8	8.8
22 127	...	Winn Parish	11 093	74.6	65.4	9.4	-15.0	11.8	4.1	0.0	11.8	0.0
23 000	...	MAINE	869 893	50.8	85.4	22.9	-1.5	22.9	22.5	12.1	31.7	21.0
23 001	4243	Androscoggin County	69 560	60.3	79.8	14.4	-10.0	14.3	14.9	19.8	29.7	14.5
23 003	...	Aroostook County	51 439	61.6	76.9	14.6	-9.8	14.6	33.9	2.5	41.1	12.1
23 005	6403	Cumberland County	181 276	38.1	90.1	34.2	9.8	34.6	26.3	16.4	28.0	30.3
23 007	...	Franklin County	19 260	55.8	85.2	20.9	-3.5	20.8	0.0	27.3	25.6	46.3
23 009	...	Hancock County	36 416	46.7	87.8	27.1	2.7	27.1	41.7	10.9	42.6	10.6
23 011	...	Kennebec County	79 362	52.4	85.2	20.7	-3.7	20.7	20.4	6.2	28.8	16.4
23 013	...	Knox County	28 303	40.9	87.5	26.2	1.8	26.3	0.0	30.4	36.5	18.6
23 015	...	Lincoln County	24 094	47.2	87.9	26.6	2.2	26.6	0.0	17.0	57.8	19.6
23 017	...	Oxford County	37 929	60.7	82.4	15.7	-8.7	15.8	37.9	6.2	29.4	9.4
23 019	0733	Penobscot County	95 505	52.7	85.7	20.3	-4.1	20.2	15.0	11.0	47.0	20.1
23 021	...	Piscataquis County	12 240	63.4	80.3	13.3	-11.1	13.5	16.7	3.3	0.0	8.3
23 023	...	Sagadahoc County	23 862	47.8	88.0	25.0	0.6	25.0	26.0	50.0	36.2	26.4
23 025	...	Somerset County	34 750	64.5	80.8	11.8	-12.6	11.9	16.7	8.6	2.6	9.6
23 027	...	Waldo County	24 818	54.2	84.6	22.3	2.1	22.4	21.4	11.1	35.6	24.7
23 029	...	Washington County	23 488	62.0	79.9	14.7	-9.7	14.6	12.1	6.5	38.2	20.0
23 031	...	York County	127 591	48.5	86.5	22.9	-1.5	22.9	22.6	20.2	25.1	17.3
24 000	...	MARYLAND	3 495 595	42.9	83.8	31.4	7.0	34.9	20.3	21.2	54.7	21.4
24 001	1900	Allegany County	51 205	62.5	79.9	14.1	-10.3	14.0	9.3	7.9	58.7	17.3
24 003	0720	Anne Arundel County....	326 999	41.5	86.4	30.6	6.2	32.1	19.4	22.8	40.7	28.2
24 005	0720	Baltimore County	511 434	43.2	84.3	30.6	6.2	30.9	24.6	17.9	54.8	29.1
24 009	8840	Calvert County	47 768	47.5	86.9	22.5	-1.9	24.4	8.4	9.9	56.1	28.2
24 011	...	Caroline County	19 550	67.0	75.0	12.1	-12.3	13.3	4.2	35.9	50.0	3.4
24 013	0720	Carroll County	98 684	48.0	85.3	24.8	0.4	24.8	16.4	38.2	39.9	28.3
24 015	9160	Cecil County	55 809	56.7	81.2	16.4	-8.0	16.3	11.1	29.9	50.1	22.9
24 017	8840	Charles County	76 987	47.5	85.8	20.0	-4.4	21.2	15.9	7.6	31.5	26.4
24 019	...	Dorchester County	21 435	67.8	74.2	12.0	-12.4	14.0	5.6	0.0	37.0	11.9
24 021	8840	Frederick County	127 256	43.0	87.1	30.0	5.6	30.8	11.5	20.9	54.4	27.1
24 023	...	Garrett County	20 004	64.4	79.2	13.8	-10.6	13.8	0.0	25.0	100.0	15.8
24 025	0720	Harford County	143 056	41.5	86.7	27.3	2.9	27.8	20.3	38.7	36.6	23.3
24 027	0720	Howard County	163 308	23.1	93.1	52.9	28.5	54.5	42.9	35.1	62.0	37.5
24 029	...	Kent County	13 103	57.1	78.8	21.7	-2.7	25.3	5.6	21.4	96.3	5.9
24 031	8840	Montgomery County	594 034	24.2	90.3	54.6	30.2	62.1	39.6	32.2	59.7	22.1
24 033	8840	Prince George's County	503 698	42.4	84.9	27.2	2.8	34.4	23.9	17.6	46.6	12.8
24 035	0720	Queen Anne's County...	28 018	46.0	84.2	25.4	1.0	27.2	6.7	23.5	25.9	27.2
24 037	...	St. Mary's County	54 552	49.6	85.3	22.6	-1.8	23.9	8.6	11.7	50.6	31.5
24 039	...	Somerset County	16 321	67.2	69.5	11.6	-12.8	13.7	7.3	0.0	52.7	6.5
24 041	0720	Talbot County	24 809	46.3	84.4	27.8	3.4	31.4	6.6	22.2	34.5	22.3

[1]MSA = Metropolitan Statistical Area. PMSA = Primary MSA. NECMA = New England County Metropolitan Area. See the Appendix A for explanation of these concepts. See Appendix B for list of metropolitan areas identified by type, with component counties.
[2]Hispanic or Latino persons may be of any race.

STATE County	School enrollment			Population 16 to 19 years				Employment status, 2000			Work status in 1999 of the population 16 years and over (percent)		
											Worked in 1999		
	Grades kindergarten through 12	College or graduate school	Percent private	Number	Percent in armed forces	Percent high school graduates	Percent not enrolled, not grads, not in armed forces, not employed	Total population 16 years and over	Percent in labor force	Unemployment rate	Full-time	Part-time	Did not work in 1999
	11	12	13	14	15	16	17	18	19	20	21	22	23
LOUISIANA—Cont'd													
Pointe Coupee Parish ...	4 852	683	26.4	1 517	0.5	12.3	8.0	17 378	55.4	7.2	48.6	11.4	40.1
Rapides Parish............	26 221	4 620	12.4	8 535	0.2	11.7	9.8	96 383	56.7	7.0	49.4	11.3	39.2
Red River Parish..........	2 257	285	10.1	689	0.0	8.9	10.2	7 132	50.0	11.9	43.5	9.3	47.2
Richland Parish............	4 427	647	12.8	1 283	0.0	12.2	13.4	15 834	52.2	6.9	47.5	10.7	41.8
Sabine Parish.............	4 685	705	5.3	1 334	0.0	8.5	8.0	18 025	51.2	8.2	44.4	11.0	44.6
St. Bernard Parish........	12 950	3 378	27.1	3 813	0.2	11.6	5.8	52 363	59.7	5.7	51.4	12.5	36.1
St. Charles Parish........	11 466	2 134	14.8	3 070	0.0	7.0	6.6	35 295	64.6	5.2	56.9	12.4	30.7
St. Helena Parish.........	2 370	453	18.7	740	0.0	13.4	9.3	7 873	52.5	9.5	45.1	10.3	44.6
St. James Parish..........	4 953	712	19.2	1 450	0.0	10.8	9.2	15 660	54.6	10.2	48.5	9.6	41.9
St. John the Baptist Parish ...	10 116	1 978	30.9	2 839	0.3	7.2	9.5	31 212	61.6	6.9	54.5	11.1	34.4
St. Landry Parish	19 809	3 169	12.7	5 787	0.0	9.0	9.8	64 913	50.5	10.4	42.7	10.6	46.8
St. Martin Parish	10 914	1 475	15.3	3 133	0.0	9.2	10.2	36 011	58.1	8.6	50.9	11.1	38.0
St. Mary Parish	12 006	1 563	12.1	3 311	0.0	10.9	9.5	39 534	55.9	8.5	48.7	11.1	40.3
St. Tammany Parish	41 459	8 143	19.6	10 690	0.1	8.3	5.1	142 988	64.6	3.8	55.9	14.0	30.1
Tangipahoa Parish........	20 980	7 455	12.0	7 310	0.1	9.8	10.0	76 019	58.7	8.6	48.6	13.9	37.5
Tensas Parish	1 428	179	14.4	456	0.0	9.6	14.5	5 090	48.1	11.6	43.0	9.9	47.1
Terrebonne Parish	23 114	3 785	14.1	7 026	0.0	8.5	8.6	77 851	56.6	5.9	50.1	12.5	37.4
Union Parish.................	4 340	670	7.7	1 297	0.0	8.9	7.2	17 616	56.6	7.0	50.9	9.5	39.6
Vermilion Parish	11 657	1 667	10.7	3 486	0.3	8.8	10.4	40 504	56.1	7.0	47.5	12.2	40.3
Vernon Parish	10 708	2 577	5.2	3 387	18.1	30.5	4.2	38 624	64.7	6.2	56.2	12.2	31.6
Washington Parish........	9 038	1 262	8.8	2 637	0.3	13.7	11.4	33 505	48.9	8.1	43.7	9.2	47.1
Webster Parish.............	8 397	1 480	6.3	2 383	0.0	9.9	9.7	32 388	56.0	8.0	48.3	11.5	40.2
West Baton Rouge Parish ...	4 728	838	15.7	1 482	0.0	14.2	6.3	16 262	61.3	5.6	54.3	11.5	34.2
West Carroll Parish	2 498	305	2.4	773	0.0	14.4	7.6	9 594	49.1	12.2	45.7	10.1	44.2
West Feliciana Parish ...	3 181	447	19.1	749	0.0	11.3	8.9	12 504	37.0	5.6	48.9	10.2	40.9
Winn Parish.................	3 319	494	3.7	966	0.0	6.3	10.1	13 203	45.0	7.7	41.5	8.6	49.9
MAINE	236 267	67 216	12.4	69 770	0.3	10.0	3.4	1 010 318	65.3	4.7	53.7	17.4	28.9
Androscoggin County....	18 993	5 688	18.9	5 914	0.1	12.6	3.9	81 987	66.5	5.0	55.6	16.0	28.4
Aroostook County	13 414	3 541	4.3	4 324	0.0	9.4	4.5	59 545	58.6	6.5	48.1	16.3	35.6
Cumberland County	47 766	16 414	14.7	13 901	0.6	8.9	2.2	210 662	69.0	3.6	56.5	18.2	25.2
Franklin County	5 706	2 382	6.8	2 046	0.0	5.5	4.3	23 382	63.4	7.3	51.1	19.3	29.6
Hancock County	9 173	2 559	12.4	2 771	0.8	8.8	4.8	41 733	64.3	5.3	54.9	17.6	27.4
Kennebec County.........	22 240	6 428	14.5	6 528	0.0	8.6	3.2	92 545	64.8	4.7	54.0	16.2	29.8
Knox County	6 908	1 146	12.2	1 781	0.4	14.6	4.0	31 782	63.0	3.4	50.3	20.3	29.4
Lincoln County	6 137	976	15.3	1 605	0.2	12.3	5.1	26 954	63.0	4.2	51.7	18.0	30.3
Oxford County	10 674	1 405	10.2	2 969	0.1	12.4	3.9	43 285	62.7	5.3	50.9	16.6	32.5
Penobscot County........	26 268	12 276	10.4	9 564	0.1	8.9	2.8	116 139	64.0	5.6	51.0	18.7	30.4
Piscataquis County	3 221	432	8.2	971	0.0	12.3	5.0	13 811	57.4	8.0	48.0	14.4	37.6
Sagadahoc County........	7 054	1 396	9.8	1 848	0.6	10.3	3.2	27 216	69.6	3.2	57.4	18.2	24.5
Somerset County	9 920	1 445	8.6	2 737	0.1	9.7	4.4	39 982	62.0	6.2	51.5	14.9	33.6
Waldo County	6 873	1 306	10.3	1 860	0.3	10.1	3.2	28 551	64.5	5.6	53.6	17.5	28.9
Washington County.......	6 122	1 543	7.2	1 912	0.8	11.7	6.0	27 214	57.0	8.5	47.4	16.2	36.4
York County	35 798	8 279	13.6	9 039	0.5	11.4	3.2	145 530	68.1	3.5	56.7	17.3	26.0
MARYLAND	1 024 955	354 477	18.1	277 834	0.7	11.6	4.8	4 085 942	67.8	4.7	59.6	13.8	26.6
Allegany County...........	11 666	5 521	6.8	4 583	0.0	13.3	3.9	61 607	53.6	8.9	44.2	15.0	40.8
Anne Arundel County....	93 322	29 356	17.7	24 457	5.6	15.8	4.1	379 394	71.1	3.0	63.2	13.7	23.0
Baltimore County..........	135 001	53 162	21.2	39 091	0.0	11.5	3.9	595 770	66.6	4.2	57.4	14.6	28.0
Calvert County.............	17 349	3 148	10.1	4 209	0.0	14.0	1.8	54 988	71.5	3.0	63.0	13.2	23.8
Caroline County	6 178	836	8.8	1 692	0.1	17.8	5.3	22 743	66.2	4.8	58.6	12.2	29.3
Carroll County	31 629	7 232	15.1	8 043	0.0	12.4	2.5	113 461	71.2	2.7	60.2	15.2	24.6
Cecil County...............	17 589	3 383	13.0	4 586	0.2	19.6	6.0	64 715	69.3	4.1	60.9	12.7	26.5
Charles County	26 224	6 299	15.1	6 551	0.3	15.2	3.7	89 512	72.6	3.3	64.7	12.5	22.8
Dorchester County	5 525	1 012	10.2	1 435	0.0	16.6	7.6	24 351	62.2	5.8	54.5	12.8	32.7
Frederick County..........	39 734	10 587	12.9	10 177	0.1	11.5	1.9	147 144	72.8	3.1	63.4	14.3	22.3
Garrett County.............	5 660	1 015	7.5	1 783	0.0	11.0	6.1	23 299	59.5	5.6	49.0	15.3	35.8
Harford County	45 281	11 837	14.9	10 922	0.5	13.0	2.2	164 126	71.3	3.0	60.9	15.2	24.0
Howard County	51 631	16 025	15.6	11 305	0.1	8.4	1.8	185 381	75.5	2.4	65.9	14.5	19.7
Kent County	3 114	1 568	31.4	1 140	0.0	11.8	2.5	15 657	62.2	4.4	50.5	16.5	33.0
Montgomery County......	164 578	57 291	21.5	38 934	0.2	7.1	3.3	675 119	70.7	3.1	62.1	14.2	23.7
Prince George's County	162 830	72 662	17.5	46 313	0.4	10.0	4.1	608 651	70.8	5.8	64.9	12.7	22.5
Queen Anne's County...	7 714	1 540	11.1	1 952	0.6	11.6	5.1	31 417	69.5	2.8	60.6	13.9	25.5
St. Mary's County.........	17 963	5 548	16.4	5 076	2.5	14.8	4.7	64 673	71.2	4.3	62.1	13.4	24.5
Somerset County	3 949	2 785	10.9	1 704	0.2	12.3	2.1	20 646	50.3	9.7	51.6	17.6	30.9
Talbot County..............	5 584	1 167	20.2	1 267	0.0	13.5	9.2	27 193	61.7	3.4	52.1	15.6	32.3

Table B-3. States and Counties — Education, Labor Force, and Income

STATE County	Full-year full-time employed (percent)								Children under 18 years in families			With one parent who is in labor force (percent)	+/− U.S. percent of children with no stay-at-home parent (percent)	+/− U.S. percent two-income couples	Total employed by class of worker (percent)			
	Total	Men	Women	Non-Hispanic White	Black or African American	American Indian and Alaska Native	Asian, Hawaiian, and Pacific Islander	Hispanic or Latino[1]	Number	Both in labor force	Father only in labor force				Private	Government	Self-employed	Unpaid family worker
	24	25	26	27	28	29	30	31	32	33	34	35	36	37	38	39	40	41
LOUISIANA—Cont'd																		
Pointe Coupee Parish ...	33.8	42.8	25.5	39.1	23.7	18.9	45.5	43.2	5 744	40.2	16.7	24.5	0.1	-5.1	72.1	18.1	9.1	0.7
Rapides Parish..............	35.5	42.7	29.1	37.8	29.8	37.3	35.7	35.3	31 479	39.0	17.3	26.7	1.1	-4.0	67.2	23.3	9.1	0.4
Red River Parish..........	29.2	36.9	22.5	34.1	21.6	100.0	28.6	22.0	2 539	30.6	21.8	28.4	-5.6	-16.5	70.6	18.5	10.5	0.4
Richland Parish...........	30.8	39.0	24.3	35.8	21.4	70.0	34.2	35.3	5 285	37.8	16.9	25.1	-1.7	-5.2	69.1	19.7	10.7	0.5
Sabine Parish..............	29.7	37.4	22.4	30.6	23.9	29.4	39.2	26.2	5 751	31.9	29.1	22.0	-10.7	-15.4	68.5	19.0	12.0	0.5
St. Bernard Parish........	40.0	49.1	32.0	40.9	31.8	47.2	37.1	36.1	15 926	41.3	19.7	24.0	0.7	-5.2	78.0	13.3	8.5	0.2
St. Charles Parish........	42.4	53.9	31.9	45.8	33.2	17.9	31.9	35.6	13 771	43.4	22.0	23.8	2.6	1.1	77.8	14.8	7.1	0.2
St. Helena Parish	29.8	35.8	24.5	34.4	25.3	0.0	40.0	21.9	2 775	30.2	16.9	28.7	-5.7	-10.9	63.8	26.8	8.5	0.9
St. James Parish...........	32.2	41.3	23.9	38.8	24.9	42.9	25.0	31.9	5 765	42.5	15.4	23.0	0.9	-7.9	78.3	17.1	4.5	0.2
St. John the Baptist Parish	40.0	50.0	31.0	44.7	33.6	50.6	33.5	46.5	12 477	39.8	15.7	27.7	2.9	-0.4	81.2	11.9	6.8	0.1
St. Landry Parish	29.6	37.3	22.8	33.6	23.5	30.2	54.5	26.7	23 823	31.7	19.8	23.9	-9.0	-12.5	72.8	17.2	9.6	0.4
St. Martin Parish	34.3	43.2	26.0	37.9	26.6	23.9	24.7	28.8	13 582	30.8	19.7	27.4	-0.4	-12.8	76.6	12.8	10.4	0.2
St. Mary Parish............	34.3	44.4	25.1	37.4	27.9	26.2	31.6	35.6	14 742	31.4	24.6	23.9	-9.3	-11.7	77.3	14.3	8.3	0.1
St. Tammany Parish	42.5	55.9	30.1	43.1	39.1	40.3	38.7	38.6	51 792	43.7	28.7	18.2	-2.7	-0.7	71.8	15.0	13.0	0.2
Tangipahoa Parish	34.2	44.0	25.4	37.3	25.7	27.4	37.2	33.6	25 582	36.3	21.1	24.2	-4.1	-4.7	70.6	19.1	9.9	0.4
Tensas Parish..............	24.7	30.0	19.7	33.3	17.2	0.0	100.0	24.7	1 583	30.1	18.3	32.0	-2.5	-4.6	61.8	21.9	15.7	0.6
Terrebonne Parish	34.2	44.8	24.2	35.7	30.6	24.1	38.3	27.0	28 092	31.8	25.9	20.1	-12.7	-12.0	75.8	13.9	10.0	0.4
Union Parish................	37.1	45.7	29.3	39.3	30.7	20.7	50.0	45.4	5 415	41.3	19.9	23.1	-0.2	-6.2	75.1	14.6	10.1	0.2
Vermilion Parish..........	30.2	39.3	22.2	31.7	22.4	11.8	24.6	23.3	14 312	35.7	25.8	20.9	-8.0	-10.2	72.8	14.3	12.4	0.5
Vernon Parish..............	39.0	51.5	25.4	38.7	41.9	46.4	26.9	40.9	14 587	36.4	34.2	16.2	-12.0	-10.2	60.0	31.2	8.6	0.2
Washington Parish........	28.1	35.5	21.3	31.7	19.9	37.9	60.0	14.1	10 697	30.9	19.9	28.3	-5.4	-14.7	69.9	19.4	10.4	0.3
Webster Parish............	35.2	45.1	26.5	38.5	27.4	37.7	47.1	47.0	9 817	37.4	18.2	30.2	3.0	-7.7	75.3	15.1	9.3	0.3
West Baton Rouge Parish	40.3	47.4	33.5	47.2	28.0	29.3	100.0	31.3	5 582	40.9	16.7	27.6	3.9	-1.3	74.3	18.0	7.1	0.6
West Carroll Parish	25.7	31.8	19.4	28.5	13.3	0.0	0.0	19.6	2 938	39.1	26.2	21.3	-4.2	-15.4	68.3	17.5	13.5	0.7
West Feliciana Parish ...	26.2	23.0	33.2	39.6	14.0	100.0	88.2	13.9	2 818	46.3	16.7	26.9	8.6	4.7	58.3	29.9	11.4	0.4
Winn Parish.................	28.6	33.4	23.2	33.3	18.6	29.0	0.0	21.4	3 799	34.1	22.4	25.1	-5.4	-11.0	60.0	20.1	0.7	0.3
MAINE	40.6	50.4	31.6	40.8	38.3	34.1	36.8	35.4	287 045	51.4	10.0	20.0	7.1	4.2	72.8	14.5	12.4	0.3
Androscoggin County	43.1	52.7	34.3	43.5	33.7	41.6	32.6	23.0	23 491	53.0	12.2	24.4	12.8	7.9	80.0	11.2	8.7	0.2
Aroostook County..........	33.8	43.3	25.0	34.0	19.2	26.8	36.1	26.3	15 890	49.4	19.1	18.3	3.1	-4.1	71.0	17.7	11.1	0.2
Cumberland County	43.9	54.4	34.3	44.2	43.9	37.5	32.5	39.6	59 565	53.6	19.3	18.7	7.7	8.7	75.8	11.8	12.1	0.2
Franklin County	35.5	45.3	26.5	35.5	40.0	33.8	36.9	46.2	6 626	48.8	19.4	19.0	3.2	1.1	72.5	14.9	12.1	0.5
Hancock County...........	38.2	47.2	29.8	38.2	48.1	42.1	40.7	30.2	10 970	50.8	18.1	20.3	6.5	1.8	65.5	14.0	20.2	0.3
Kennebec County..........	41.6	50.4	33.6	41.7	36.5	40.2	47.1	33.3	26 805	51.2	15.2	23.2	9.8	5.3	67.8	21.4	10.5	0.3
Knox County................	37.4	46.9	28.6	37.6	27.7	37.6	32.4	25.8	8 471	46.7	20.2	24.7	6.8	2.0	66.1	13.0	20.6	0.3
Lincoln County	38.2	47.8	29.4	38.2	15.0	43.5	47.3	61.3	7 158	54.3	17.0	19.3	9.0	2.2	61.0	16.0	22.4	0.5
Oxford County	37.9	47.8	28.6	37.9	32.4	31.9	42.6	29.0	12 551	50.8	17.9	20.2	6.4	0.5	74.1	12.7	12.8	0.3
Penobscot County	37.9	47.6	28.9	38.1	26.1	31.7	32.6	35.1	30 909	49.3	18.9	19.7	4.4	3.1	73.5	16.6	9.7	0.2
Piscataquis County	34.8	42.3	27.7	34.8	11.5	34.2	33.3	34.1	3 864	44.8	20.8	20.3	0.5	-5.1	73.1	15.0	11.6	0.3
Sagadahoc County........	46.1	57.3	35.8	46.3	47.4	23.5	45.2	33.8	8 786	52.7	18.5	21.3	9.4	7.9	73.3	13.6	12.8	0.3
Somerset County	38.6	48.2	29.6	38.7	23.5	35.7	18.1	40.0	11 749	47.8	17.6	21.3	4.5	0.0	75.3	12.2	12.2	0.3
Waldo County..............	39.6	47.5	32.2	39.7	39.3	24.2	35.1	33.9	8 456	46.7	19.7	21.6	3.7	0.6	68.3	14.2	17.0	0.4
Washington County	31.2	38.7	24.2	31.3	20.2	29.7	39.7	29.6	7 249	44.1	19.9	22.1	1.6	-7.7	63.1	20.5	16.1	0.3
York County	44.3	55.0	34.5	44.3	47.4	44.4	49.1	42.1	44 425	54.7	18.4	18.5	8.6	7.2	74.4	13.7	11.6	0.2
MARYLAND	46.5	55.3	38.6	47.4	45.2	47.3	44.5	42.5	1 267 484	46.3	18.7	24.2	5.9	6.5	68.9	22.3	8.5	0.2
Allegany County	31.0	37.7	24.4	32.5	9.3	20.7	43.7	17.1	14 334	47.7	20.7	20.3	3.4	-5.6	71.4	21.8	6.6	0.3
Anne Arundel County....	51.3	61.5	41.3	51.9	49.0	60.3	44.1	50.3	117 074	51.1	21.2	19.7	6.2	8.8	69.4	21.7	8.6	0.2
Baltimore County..........	45.6	55.2	37.3	44.3	51.9	52.8	42.7	41.1	168 108	46.9	20.2	23.9	6.2	3.3	73.1	18.4	8.3	0.2
Calvert County	51.5	62.0	41.4	52.4	46.3	61.9	52.9	45.5	21 468	55.0	20.0	17.9	8.3	11.1	63.6	26.5	9.6	0.3
Caroline County	45.0	55.1	35.7	45.4	44.3	49.4	34.7	41.2	7 446	43.9	17.9	29.5	8.8	3.9	70.7	16.4	12.2	0.7
Carroll County.............	50.8	63.3	39.0	51.3	34.5	49.5	43.3	43.6	40 413	56.1	24.7	14.4	5.9	11.2	72.6	17.9	9.3	0.3
Cecil County	48.5	58.7	38.7	48.9	43.0	51.6	44.1	46.5	22 564	48.9	21.8	21.4	5.7	5.3	75.6	15.1	9.0	0.2
Charles County	53.3	63.7	43.8	53.6	53.0	57.4	46.3	50.1	32 888	50.4	16.8	23.5	9.3	11.3	63.2	29.2	7.3	0.3
Dorchester County	40.9	49.9	33.1	42.1	37.7	34.4	38.0	32.8	6 526	42.6	13.3	32.6	10.6	0.7	69.7	17.0	13.1	0.2
Frederick County..........	52.0	64.6	40.1	52.3	49.8	66.0	43.4	51.5	51 821	53.3	24.1	16.7	5.4	10.6	70.9	19.7	9.2	0.2
Garrett County	37.4	48.3	27.0	37.6	0.0	0.0	75.0	28.8	7 121	48.6	24.8	16.4	0.4	-5.5	68.4	18.0	13.0	0.6
Harford County	50.2	63.0	38.4	50.2	51.7	57.8	46.9	51.0	58 511	53.2	22.9	16.9	5.5	8.5	73.2	18.8	7.9	0.2
Howard County	53.7	65.8	42.5	54.7	52.6	47.2	48.3	52.8	67 368	55.4	24.2	15.3	6.1	14.6	68.4	22.0	9.3	0.3
Kent County	36.2	43.7	29.6	36.7	34.4	80.0	21.0	30.3	3 724	48.1	13.9	30.3	13.8	0.2	69.4	15.0	15.0	0.6
Montgomery County......	48.4	59.1	39.1	49.2	50.1	49.4	47.7	42.9	212 352	51.4	23.3	16.7	3.5	8.4	67.4	21.7	10.7	0.2
Prince George's County .	49.3	53.7	45.4	45.3	52.8	42.2	40.3	40.2	196 658	41.9	11.2	32.7	10.0	9.0	63.0	31.0	5.9	0.1
Queen Anne's County ...	48.1	58.1	38.2	49.2	38.3	54.8	29.5	40.6	9 757	53.5	21.8	18.1	7.0	9.6	65.1	20.3	14.4	0.2
St. Mary's County.........	50.7	61.7	39.7	51.8	46.3	35.7	46.3	46.4	23 026	50.9	21.7	19.9	6.2	7.5	61.7	28.8	9.1	0.3
Somerset County	33.0	37.6	27.6	40.0	24.3	26.0	15.7	10.4	4 214	34.1	18.9	34.6	4.1	-3.0	58.8	27.8	12.5	0.9
Talbot County..............	40.9	50.3	32.6	41.4	36.7	61.1	61.3	34.8	6 930	52.1	17.9	21.2	8.7	1.5	66.4	14.2	19.2	0.1

[1] Hispanic or Latino persons may be of any race.

STATE County	Percent who worked at home	Percent of the population 5 years and over with a disability	Veterans as a percent of the population 18 years and over	Occupation for employed population 16 years and over (percent)						Industry for employed population 16 years and over (percent)					
				Management, professional, and related occupations	Service occupations	Sales and office occupations	Farming, fishing, and forestry occupations	Construction, extraction, and maintenance occupations	Production, transportation and material moving occupations	Agriculture, forestry, fishing, and mining	Construction and manufacturing	Wholesale and retail trade	Transportation and warehousing, and utilities	Service industries	Public administration
	42	43	44	45	46	47	48	49	50	51	52	53	54	55	56
LOUISIANA—Cont'd															
Pointe Coupee Parish ...	1.5	24.1	11.3	25.2	14.8	25.9	2.0	12.5	19.5	6.9	22.1	16.5	7.0	40.2	7.2
Rapides Parish	2.4	25.3	14.7	31.4	18.6	26.5	1.2	11.1	11.3	3.5	13.5	16.4	5.1	54.4	7.1
Red River Parish	2.0	22.0	10.6	22.2	16.7	19.1	2.0	18.2	21.8	10.9	28.8	10.1	4.4	41.0	4.7
Richland Parish	1.6	25.0	9.8	26.8	16.7	23.8	3.0	12.4	17.2	8.1	18.4	16.0	5.6	45.9	6.0
Sabine Parish	3.1	25.0	14.7	24.2	14.3	21.3	4.2	14.4	21.6	12.9	19.3	15.0	5.2	42.0	5.6
St. Bernard Parish	1.3	23.4	12.7	24.4	13.6	31.4	1.1	14.7	14.8	1.9	20.0	17.0	7.0	48.1	6.0
St. Charles Parish	1.3	17.1	11.9	30.0	12.8	26.6	0.5	14.2	15.9	1.6	27.8	15.2	8.1	42.7	4.6
St. Helena Parish	2.8	26.3	11.1	23.7	19.2	21.5	2.8	11.9	20.9	7.1	23.8	12.2	7.5	41.9	7.5
St. James Parish	1.2	19.5	9.8	23.7	16.1	22.1	1.5	12.1	24.6	2.6	34.2	11.8	7.6	38.7	5.2
St. John the Baptist Parish	1.5	17.1	11.6	24.1	15.4	28.2	0.4	14.6	17.2	1.2	25.5	16.8	7.6	44.4	4.6
St. Landry Parish	1.8	25.9	10.7	26.2	18.3	23.6	0.7	14.5	16.7	6.8	16.8	17.4	5.3	48.3	5.3
St. Martin Parish	2.4	23.6	9.6	20.2	15.8	25.0	1.2	15.0	22.8	10.9	24.8	17.0	4.0	39.3	4.0
St. Mary Parish	2.0	24.0	11.1	22.1	16.9	25.8	1.5	12.9	20.9	8.8	20.9	14.4	6.7	44.6	4.5
St. Tammany Parish	3.7	17.6	14.7	37.0	14.8	27.9	0.2	11.2	8.9	2.6	16.9	17.0	4.9	53.0	5.6
Tangipahoa Parish	2.6	22.5	11.6	27.5	16.5	25.9	1.1	13.5	15.5	3.7	19.8	17.9	4.5	49.0	5.0
Tensas Parish	3.4	26.5	12.0	28.3	18.3	20.2	8.0	10.5	14.7	22.6	10.5	13.0	3.9	41.9	8.0
Terrebonne Parish	2.0	24.1	10.7	25.0	14.4	26.4	1.7	14.7	17.8	11.9	16.1	17.0	6.7	44.5	3.8
Union Parish	2.2	23.3	12.2	24.7	13.1	22.8	2.7	14.3	22.5	7.1	27.3	14.6	5.5	41.4	4.1
Vermilion Parish	2.0	24.3	10.8	23.5	14.7	25.8	1.7	14.5	19.8	16.3	14.5	16.9	6.1	41.7	4.5
Vernon Parish	1.3	20.8	17.9	26.1	17.4	24.6	1.8	16.7	13.4	5.8	15.9	15.3	5.0	45.8	12.2
Washington Parish	2.0	28.2	13.1	23.5	19.6	21.7	1.4	14.3	19.5	7.3	23.4	14.1	5.0	43.8	6.3
Webster Parish	1.8	22.8	13.8	22.9	15.9	24.2	0.7	15.1	21.2	4.0	28.3	15.6	5.6	41.7	4.8
West Baton Rouge Parish	1.7	22.2	9.8	22.5	18.4	27.7	0.4	13.5	17.5	1.2	25.9	15.4	6.5	43.1	8.0
West Carroll Parish	1.9	23.6	11.0	25.9	14.0	21.8	4.4	13.4	20.5	12.6	23.9	14.5	7.8	35.4	5.8
West Feliciana Parish ...	2.8	19.1	13.1	31.7	22.1	20.2	0.6	9.4	16.0	4.7	22.2	8.9	8.7	39.2	16.3
Winn Parish	1.8	24.9	13.3	21.1	19.4	18.6	5.3	13.5	22.1	12.7	24.3	12.5	4.2	38.9	7.4
MAINE	4.4	20.0	15.9	31.5	15.3	25.9	1.7	10.3	15.3	2.6	21.1	17.0	4.3	50.6	4.5
Androscoggin County....	2.6	22.4	15.8	26.0	14.5	28.8	0.7	10.9	19.0	1.2	25.6	18.7	3.7	47.1	3.6
Aroostook County	3.6	25.2	15.8	27.4	17.2	23.8	3.5	10.0	18.1	6.2	17.5	16.3	6.4	48.6	5.0
Cumberland County	4.6	17.1	14.2	38.8	14.2	28.2	0.6	7.2	11.1	1.0	15.2	18.5	3.9	57.8	3.5
Franklin County	4.9	19.8	15.8	27.6	17.1	24.2	2.0	11.0	18.0	3.2	24.6	14.9	3.3	50.7	3.3
Hancock County	6.3	19.1	16.8	30.7	17.1	23.1	4.1	13.2	11.9	5.3	19.5	14.5	3.5	53.2	4.0
Kennebec County	4.2	21.0	16.1	33.2	14.8	26.7	0.8	10.8	13.7	1.5	18.2	17.3	5.0	48.4	9.6
Knox County	7.1	17.4	17.3	29.7	15.4	25.3	5.0	11.1	13.4	6.0	18.4	17.1	3.2	50.7	4.5
Lincoln County	6.2	19.8	18.3	31.7	15.4	21.7	5.1	12.8	13.2	6.4	21.7	15.0	3.2	48.1	5.5
Oxford County	4.6	21.8	16.9	26.6	17.6	21.3	1.6	12.9	20.1	3.0	29.3	14.3	3.6	46.4	3.3
Penobscot County	3.8	19.5	14.8	30.3	16.7	26.8	1.3	9.8	15.1	2.3	17.7	17.8	5.6	52.4	4.2
Piscataquis County	3.9	26.3	18.9	25.1	14.7	21.8	2.3	12.5	23.5	4.5	31.0	14.7	5.9	38.9	5.0
Sagadahoc County	4.5	18.3	19.1	33.1	15.4	23.9	1.3	12.2	14.0	1.9	26.6	16.6	3.4	46.9	4.6
Somerset County	4.6	22.3	16.0	23.9	15.5	22.0	2.5	12.0	24.1	4.6	32.5	15.2	4.2	39.9	3.6
Waldo County	6.0	19.8	15.9	30.3	14.8	24.0	2.4	12.0	16.5	3.6	23.2	14.9	4.0	49.7	4.5
Washington County	5.0	27.0	18.3	25.4	17.8	20.6	8.2	10.9	17.1	10.9	20.7	13.6	4.1	43.7	7.0
York County	3.9	18.9	16.5	31.0	14.4	26.2	0.7	11.0	16.7	1.0	26.1	16.7	4.2	48.6	3.4
MARYLAND	3.3	17.6	13.3	41.3	13.9	26.4	0.3	8.6	9.5	0.6	14.2	13.3	4.9	56.5	10.5
Allegany County	1.5	21.2	16.1	27.1	19.2	25.6	0.3	10.3	17.5	0.9	18.9	15.1	6.5	51.3	7.3
Anne Arundel County....	3.4	15.5	16.8	40.5	12.5	28.0	0.1	9.9	9.1	0.2	15.5	15.5	5.7	51.3	11.9
Baltimore County	2.8	18.2	13.4	39.5	13.2	29.0	0.1	8.0	10.2	0.2	14.9	14.7	4.9	57.6	7.6
Calvert County	3.6	15.9	16.8	36.8	14.7	24.4	0.2	15.0	8.8	0.7	18.3	12.8	7.6	45.7	14.9
Caroline County	5.0	20.5	14.1	24.8	14.5	24.6	2.2	15.6	18.3	4.4	25.9	15.8	5.1	42.8	6.1
Carroll County	3.9	14.7	14.2	37.1	13.2	25.8	0.6	12.9	10.4	1.4	20.3	14.9	4.4	51.0	7.9
Cecil County	3.0	18.3	15.2	28.1	13.3	26.4	0.6	14.3	17.2	2.4	26.3	15.5	5.6	44.5	5.7
Charles County	2.7	16.7	16.8	35.7	13.9	28.3	0.2	12.7	9.2	0.8	14.6	14.2	6.2	46.2	18.0
Dorchester County	3.8	22.9	14.4	23.3	16.0	23.8	2.5	13.0	21.5	4.1	29.0	15.5	5.0	40.6	5.7
Frederick County	4.0	14.6	14.2	40.5	12.9	25.7	0.4	11.2	9.3	1.4	18.6	14.3	3.7	54.2	7.9
Garrett County	5.2	20.0	13.3	25.7	17.8	22.9	1.9	14.1	17.6	6.5	22.9	13.6	5.7	45.6	5.7
Harford County	3.0	15.8	15.7	38.0	13.0	27.4	0.1	10.2	11.2	0.5	19.3	16.7	5.0	49.5	9.0
Howard County	4.5	11.7	12.1	57.0	9.4	23.6	0.1	4.9	4.9	0.3	12.0	13.0	3.6	60.4	10.6
Kent County	4.7	20.5	15.7	31.6	18.0	22.7	4.0	11.0	12.7	6.3	22.0	12.2	3.3	50.7	5.6
Montgomery County	4.8	13.4	9.9	56.6	11.5	22.0	0.1	5.2	4.6	0.2	9.3	10.5	2.5	67.4	10.1
Prince George's County	2.0	17.7	13.3	38.9	14.8	29.0	0.1	8.2	9.0	0.2	9.3	11.4	6.7	56.5	15.9
Queen Anne's County ...	5.5	17.2	15.4	36.3	13.8	25.8	1.5	12.0	10.6	3.4	18.5	15.7	5.1	48.0	9.3
St. Mary's County	3.1	15.3	18.3	39.1	13.1	23.5	0.7	14.3	9.3	1.1	18.7	12.9	6.2	44.7	16.4
Somerset County	2.8	24.7	13.8	24.8	21.2	23.5	3.8	11.7	15.1	5.5	18.6	16.0	4.8	44.3	10.7
Talbot County	5.4	19.3	16.9	34.9	16.6	24.9	1.7	10.3	11.5	3.5	19.5	14.6	3.3	53.7	5.4

Table B-3. States and Counties — **Education, Labor Force, and Income**

STATE County	Median house-hold income	Median family income — All families	Married-couple	Male house-holder	Female house-holder	Median nonfamily house-hold income	Men	Women	Per capita income	With earnings	With interest, dividend, or rental income	With Social Security income	With public assis-tance income	With retire-ment income	House-holds with income over $100,000 (percent)	+/- U.S. percent for income over $100,000	House-holds with income below poverty (percent)	Families with children with income below poverty (percent)
	57	58	59	60	61	62	63	64	65	66	67	68	69	70	71	72	73	74
LOUISIANA—Cont'd																		
Pointe Coupee Parish ...	30 618	36 625	47 697	20 000	12 336	15 113	35 565	21 047	15 387	74.5	25.7	28.9	3.8	16.3	5.8	-6.5	22.5	24.8
Rapides Parish............	29 856	36 671	49 623	21 671	14 009	16 571	30 764	21 156	16 088	75.3	23.4	27.8	3.6	18.1	6.5	-5.8	19.5	22.5
Red River Parish..........	23 153	27 870	38 281	12 222	10 459	12 326	27 958	18 822	12 119	70.5	16.5	33.5	5.2	18.0	2.9	-9.4	27.3	35.1
Richland Parish...........	23 668	29 075	39 617	15 556	9 565	11 803	29 005	19 241	12 479	73.7	19.2	30.7	4.3	13.3	4.2	-8.1	26.4	32.9
Sabine Parish.............	26 655	32 470	39 653	23 264	11 601	11 907	30 824	20 135	15 199	69.2	22.3	33.8	2.6	19.0	4.6	-7.7	21.7	25.9
St. Bernard Parish........	35 939	42 785	52 201	30 231	19 031	17 525	35 610	24 559	16 718	77.1	27.8	29.8	2.9	17.8	5.3	-7.0	13.7	14.7
St. Charles Parish........	45 139	50 562	63 994	35 402	21 814	21 482	41 202	25 419	19 054	84.7	30.5	21.5	1.7	15.0	11.1	-1.2	11.7	12.1
St. Helena Parish.........	24 970	29 950	45 606	14 167	12 220	14 413	30 617	17 097	12 318	71.8	18.2	24.4	2.8	17.0	4.0	-8.3	26.4	29.8
St. James Parish..........	35 277	41 751	56 250	31 111	11 362	15 762	38 420	22 067	14 381	75.7	23.0	26.8	2.5	17.0	6.5	-5.8	20.5	25.0
St. John the Baptist Parish...............	39 456	43 925	56 290	31 318	16 647	20 095	38 128	22 901	15 445	82.0	22.3	19.5	3.0	14.6	6.8	-5.5	15.8	17.7
St. Landry Parish	22 855	28 908	40 990	19 590	9 489	10 287	30 246	19 410	12 042	67.2	16.9	30.2	5.5	12.9	3.5	-8.8	29.5	32.7
St. Martin Parish	30 701	36 316	46 331	23 000	12 450	13 914	31 106	18 926	13 619	77.3	20.2	25.3	3.1	12.1	3.8	-8.5	21.8	24.2
St. Mary Parish	28 072	33 064	45 392	26 313	10 431	14 832	32 338	18 997	13 399	75.2	17.5	27.1	3.7	12.5	3.9	-8.4	23.2	27.5
St. Tammany Parish	47 883	55 346	65 989	29 040	19 796	23 520	44 246	26 771	22 514	83.3	35.8	22.8	1.9	15.1	15.6	3.3	10.2	10.6
Tangipahoa Parish	29 412	36 731	47 400	27 534	11 503	13 909	32 049	20 649	14 461	76.0	21.0	24.1	3.7	13.7	5.2	-7.1	23.2	24.0
Tensas Parish	19 799	25 739	31 250	19 583	11 435	10 934	27 717	17 464	12 622	70.8	20.0	32.6	4.1	14.3	5.9	-6.4	33.7	41.8
Terrebonne Parish	35 235	39 912	50 401	24 115	13 508	19 875	35 453	21 253	16 051	78.2	26.1	26.4	3.0	12.2	6.5	-5.8	17.6	20.9
Union Parish................	29 061	36 035	43 242	22 891	15 375	14 130	31 080	21 769	14 819	74.1	20.3	30.8	2.6	16.8	4.0	-8.3	18.7	19.9
Vermilion Parish	29 500	36 093	44 473	28 750	11 369	14 686	31 711	19 569	14 201	74.6	25.9	29.2	3.4	12.2	4.7	-7.6	21.8	24.5
Vernon Parish	31 216	34 680	37 068	28 382	14 024	18 209	27 402	20 922	14 036	82.5	22.2	18.9	2.7	18.5	3.3	-9.0	15.1	15.9
Washington Parish	24 264	29 480	36 644	25 784	11 650	12 183	28 827	18 451	12 915	68.3	17.9	33.1	4.0	16.7	3.4	-8.9	24.8	26.6
Webster Parish............	28 408	35 119	44 574	27 083	12 393	15 123	30 812	21 708	15 203	72.8	22.9	32.2	3.1	19.7	4.6	-7.7	19.4	24.2
West Baton Rouge Parish...............	37 117	43 204	56 691	29 018	17 051	20 867	36 356	23 768	15 773	81.7	23.0	23.1	3.5	17.5	7.4	-4.9	16.1	18.2
West Carroll Parish	24 637	31 806	38 255	21 818	12 986	11 320	29 015	19 022	12 302	71.5	18.7	32.7	4.0	14.1	3.2	-9.1	22.5	25.2
West Feliciana Parish ...	39 667	47 239	58 136	32 969	18 963	19 073	35 736	24 559	16 201	80.1	24.0	20.4	2.3	14.8	10.0	-2.3	19.0	19.3
Winn Parish.................	25 462	31 513	40 230	17 216	11 106	9 946	30 104	19 175	11 794	69.4	16.2	32.4	5.2	16.8	3.6	-8.7	23.3	22.0
MAINE	37 240	45 179	53 839	27 407	17 632	21 715	34 180	25 151	19 533	78.5	37.8	28.9	4.8	17.4	7.1	-5.2	11.5	11.9
Androscoggin County....	35 793	44 082	53 997	26 126	17 794	20 146	32 327	23 205	18 734	78.1	34.4	29.2	5.9	15.7	5.4	-6.9	12.1	12.3
Aroostook County.........	28 837	36 044	43 628	24 677	14 432	14 110	30 690	20 787	15 033	72.4	27.1	34.9	6.9	16.4	3.1	-9.2	16.1	14.9
Cumberland County	44 048	54 485	64 808	35 173	21 877	27 149	37 034	29 441	23 949	81.3	45.3	26.1	3.8	17.7	11.7	-0.6	8.0	8.4
Franklin County	31 459	37 863	45 503	21 875	14 068	18 021	30 885	21 073	15 796	77.7	32.2	30.0	6.1	17.7	3.8	-8.5	15.1	17.2
Hancock County...........	35 811	43 216	48 970	24 940	19 375	20 966	31 441	23 521	19 809	78.9	38.9	30.4	3.7	18.3	7.0	-5.3	10.8	10.7
Kennebec County.........	36 498	43 814	53 021	26 490	19 026	21 075	33 492	25 003	18 520	77.7	37.7	28.4	5.2	18.3	5.8	-6.5	12.0	12.5
Knox County	36 774	43 819	50 457	26 393	20 633	22 325	31 642	23 612	19 981	78.3	42.3	30.3	3.4	17.5	7.4	-4.9	10.2	10.1
Lincoln County	38 686	45 427	50 069	23 850	21 000	22 634	32 542	24 139	20 760	77.1	45.1	32.7	3.3	20.9	7.8	-4.5	10.0	10.9
Oxford County	33 435	39 794	47 920	27 424	15 201	19 754	31 367	21 694	16 945	75.8	35.0	32.8	6.0	18.7	4.2	-8.1	12.0	13.2
Penobscot County........	34 274	42 206	51 170	27 126	14 424	19 982	34 314	24 111	17 801	77.7	34.0	27.8	5.8	18.3	5.8	-0.5	14.4	14.0
Piscataquis County......	28 250	34 852	42 598	22 500	15 351	14 880	29 554	20 808	14 374	70.2	22.0	35.6	5.2	17.7	2.4	-9.9	15.7	16.8
Sagadahoc County.......	41 908	49 714	54 038	27 337	15 422	25 788	36 064	26 084	20 378	82.9	47.0	25.2	4.1	19.5	7.5	-4.8	8.2	11.6
Somerset County	30 731	36 464	43 908	23 846	14 530	17 796	30 154	21 224	15 474	76.9	29.5	30.7	5.9	15.1	3.7	-8.6	14.9	16.8
Waldo County	33 986	40 402	47 401	25 958	14 588	20 441	30 013	24 883	17 438	79.6	35.5	27.9	4.6	16.4	5.1	-7.2	14.2	16.1
Washington County	25 869	31 657	40 135	23 047	12 921	13 233	29 884	20 571	14 119	72.0	18.6	34.0	6.4	16.9	3.1	-9.2	20.9	20.3
York County	43 630	51 419	60 079	32 402	20 355	25 286	37 514	26 738	21 225	80.8	41.3	27.3	3.7	18.3	8.8	-3.5	8.7	8.9
MARYLAND	52 868	61 876	74 531	36 405	27 166	32 654	42 857	33 301	25 614	83.8	39.2	22.5	2.4	18.7	18.1	5.8	8.3	8.7
Allegany County	30 821	39 886	47 779	22 330	16 329	15 590	32 381	21 846	16 780	68.3	35.2	37.4	2.6	23.4	4.3	-8.0	15.3	16.2
Anne Arundel County....	61 768	69 019	76 745	40 964	29 257	39 866	45 762	33 584	27 578	86.8	44.2	20.6	1.2	20.3	21.8	9.5	4.9	5.1
Baltimore County.........	50 667	59 998	72 021	35 621	29 844	31 669	41 927	32 180	26 167	81.1	42.6	27.1	1.7	20.5	15.3	3.0	6.4	6.5
Calvert County	65 945	71 545	78 534	48 711	30 981	39 669	50 575	33 205	25 410	87.4	41.1	19.4	1.4	21.1	22.0	9.7	4.1	4.4
Caroline County...........	38 832	44 825	54 589	30 486	18 342	21 935	31 661	22 619	17 275	81.1	29.6	29.1	3.1	16.9	5.9	-6.4	11.9	12.6
Carroll County	60 021	66 430	73 527	48 306	28 777	30 093	45 700	31 281	23 829	85.4	46.3	23.9	1.2	17.9	18.0	5.7	3.9	3.7
Cecil County................	50 510	56 469	64 161	38 017	26 186	28 664	41 203	29 622	21 384	84.6	33.2	23.6	2.1	19.2	11.8	-0.5	6.9	7.9
Charles County	62 199	67 602	76 262	40 892	32 117	38 226	45 451	35 389	24 285	88.2	35.5	18.0	1.8	20.7	20.2	7.9	5.2	5.3
Dorchester County	34 077	41 917	51 882	22 929	17 090	18 911	29 639	23 210	18 929	76.1	28.6	32.8	3.6	20.1	5.9	-6.4	13.7	15.9
Frederick County	60 276	67 879	75 301	40 116	27 208	34 599	44 234	31 259	25 404	87.5	42.7	20.3	1.4	16.6	19.0	6.7	4.6	4.1
Garrett County.............	32 238	37 811	43 508	30 000	14 367	15 955	30 592	21 217	16 219	75.9	33.6	31.4	3.1	18.6	5.5	-6.8	14.5	14.2
Harford County............	57 234	63 868	72 032	40 690	27 859	32 616	45 710	31 537	24 232	85.9	43.8	21.7	1.5	20.6	16.3	4.0	5.2	5.1
Howard County............	74 167	85 422	95 422	51 703	36 072	45 966	60 268	41 340	32 402	91.4	51.6	14.4	1.0	14.0	31.9	19.6	3.6	3.5
Kent County................	39 869	46 708	54 615	32 000	17 719	23 548	33 652	25 587	21 573	74.7	36.5	37.0	1.9	24.2	9.2	-3.1	11.6	14.5
Montgomery County......	71 551	84 035	94 232	44 227	36 263	47 365	56 554	41 843	35 684	87.2	53.6	18.7	1.3	17.3	32.4	20.1	4.9	5.0
Prince George's County	55 256	62 467	74 323	37 146	32 809	37 429	40 287	36 518	23 360	89.1	28.6	16.5	2.0	18.8	17.0	4.7	7.0	7.2
Queen Anne's County ...	57 037	63 713	67 445	44 196	26 438	31 177	46 330	31 110	26 364	84.5	40.7	25.8	1.5	20.3	17.4	5.1	6.5	6.6
St. Mary's County	54 706	61 397	67 094	33 750	27 524	34 190	43 688	30 911	22 662	86.9	37.8	18.5	2.2	21.5	14.5	2.2	6.7	7.3
Somerset County	29 903	37 643	45 313	22 311	16 184	16 841	29 449	23 710	15 965	76.4	23.4	33.7	3.0	17.4	5.7	-6.6	20.6	22.8
Talbot County..............	43 532	53 214	60 050	26 414	22 692	23 543	35 817	27 659	28 164	75.4	46.3	36.0	2.7	20.6	14.8	2.5	8.4	9.2

STATE/ County code	MSA/PMSA/ NECMA code[1]	STATE County	High school graduates			College graduates		College graduates (percent)				
			Total population 25 years and over	Percent with a high school diploma or less	Percent with a high school diploma or more	Percent with a bachelor's degree or more	+/− U.S. percent with bachelor's degree or more	Non-Hispanic White	Black or African American	American Indian and Alaska Native	Asian, Hawaiian, and Pacific Islander	Hispanic or Latino[2]
			1	2	3	4	5	6	7	8	9	10
		MARYLAND—Cont'd										
24 043	3180	Washington County.......	90 371	61.1	77.8	14.6	−9.8	15.2	4.1	8.5	32.3	15.3
24 045	...	Wicomico County	53 521	53.7	80.7	21.9	−2.5	24.9	9.9	22.9	32.5	25.7
24 047	...	Worcester County	34 092	52.5	81.7	21.6	−2.8	24.1	6.9	0.0	35.4	10.4
24 510	0720	Baltimore city...............	419 581	59.8	68.4	19.1	−5.3	32.9	10.0	16.7	51.8	24.6
25 000	...	MASSACHUSETTS ...	4 273 275	42.5	84.8	33.2	8.8	34.6	19.7	19.2	49.6	14.1
25 001	0743	Barnstable County........	165 115	35.4	91.8	33.6	9.2	34.4	20.0	15.5	42.4	21.3
25 003	6323	Berkshire County..........	93 339	49.1	85.1	26.0	1.6	26.2	12.3	4.3	53.4	19.9
25 005	1123	Bristol County..............	357 829	56.4	73.2	19.9	−4.5	20.1	16.9	16.6	39.6	9.5
25 007	...	Dukes County	10 693	32.8	90.4	38.4	14.0	39.4	32.0	14.7	42.6	40.6
25 009	1123	Essex County	487 103	43.5	84.6	31.3	6.9	33.4	16.6	20.1	40.3	9.1
25 011	...	Franklin County	49 121	43.3	88.0	29.1	4.7	29.2	31.5	14.5	43.3	17.2
25 013	8003	Hampden County	295 837	53.4	79.2	20.5	−3.9	22.7	14.4	10.2	31.5	6.2
25 015	8003	Hampshire County	93 193	36.4	89.4	37.9	13.5	37.0	55.6	49.4	67.8	36.7
25 017	1123	Middlesex County..........	1 006 497	34.9	88.5	43.6	19.2	43.9	30.3	34.1	61.2	24.1
25 019	...	Nantucket County..........	6 976	36.1	91.6	38.4	14.0	42.4	7.5	X	43.1	7.1
25 021	1123	Norfolk County.............	452 517	33.0	91.3	42.9	18.5	42.8	37.3	19.4	52.0	37.3
25 023	1123	Plymouth County	312 683	43.1	87.6	27.8	3.4	29.1	16.0	12.6	36.4	14.3
25 025	1123	Suffolk County..............	446 504	47.6	78.1	32.5	8.1	42.7	15.7	12.9	35.7	13.2
25 027	1123	Worcester County	495 868	46.7	83.5	26.9	2.5	27.6	19.3	17.3	42.7	11.5
26 000	...	MICHIGAN	6 415 941	47.9	83.4	21.8	−2.6	22.7	12.8	10.3	60.5	12.9
26 001	...	Alcona County..............	8 958	62.1	79.7	10.9	−13.5	10.8	0.0	0.0	46.7	0.0
26 003	...	Alger County................	7 169	60.8	81.5	14.7	−9.7	15.8	0.0	9.3	33.3	13.6
26 005	3000	Allegan County.............	66 925	56.8	82.3	15.8	−8.6	16.3	7.8	8.5	31.6	6.2
26 007	...	Alpena County	21 399	52.6	83.1	13.2	−11.2	13.1	24.1	1.5	48.7	14.0
26 009	...	Antrim County	16 025	52.5	84.6	19.4	−5.0	19.5	20.8	4.3	50.0	23.7
26 011	...	Arenac County..............	11 868	65.4	76.8	9.1	−15.3	9.1	3.9	7.7	57.5	1.9
26 013	...	Baraga County..............	6 097	58.4	80.6	10.9	−13.5	12.1	0.0	6.7	30.8	0.0
26 015	...	Barry County................	37 132	52.5	86.8	14.7	−9.7	14.7	13.6	12.0	47.6	19.7
26 017	6960	Bay County..................	74 146	54.5	82.4	14.2	−10.2	14.3	7.0	8.8	42.0	6.3
26 019	...	Benzie County	11 283	51.0	85.4	20.0	−4.4	20.4	0.0	5.5	28.6	11.1
26 021	0870	Berrien County	106 690	49.9	81.9	19.6	−4.8	20.5	10.9	11.1	61.0	18.2
26 023	...	Branch County..............	30 300	60.8	80.0	10.6	−13.8	11.0	2.8	1.5	49.2	4.0
26 025	3720	Calhoun County	90 137	52.4	83.2	16.0	−8.4	16.6	9.7	7.7	41.7	11.2
26 027	...	Cass County	34 286	57.2	80.4	12.1	−12.3	12.6	7.2	6.2	24.2	5.2
26 029	...	Charlevoix County	17 528	49.1	86.0	19.8	−4.6	20.1	29.2	10.8	34.4	11.4
26 031	...	Cheboygan County	18 562	58.7	81.9	13.9	−10.5	14.3	0.0	4.4	31.5	0.0
26 033	...	Chippewa County..........	25 683	53.6	82.4	15.0	−9.4	16.7	4.2	10.4	25.4	10.5
26 035	...	Clare County	21 333	64.3	76.1	8.8	−15.6	8.8	0.0	5.9	36.4	8.8
26 037	4040	Clinton County..............	41 864	43.7	89.2	21.2	−3.2	21.3	34.1	14.2	38.3	12.8
26 039	...	Crawford County	9 871	56.8	80.8	12.9	−11.5	13.2	0.0	3.2	29.2	27.7
26 041	...	Delta County	26 362	49.7	86.1	17.1	−7.3	17.3	46.2	4.1	36.2	10.3
26 043	...	Dickinson County	18 831	55.6	88.8	16.7	−7.7	16.5	53.1	1.6	42.3	14.5
26 045	4040	Eaton County	67 044	40.8	89.5	21.7	−2.7	21.2	29.1	18.9	48.2	14.8
26 047	...	Emmet County	21 258	42.4	89.0	26.2	1.8	26.9	0.0	8.2	41.7	11.0
26 049	2640	Genesee County	277 660	50.2	83.1	16.2	−8.2	17.3	10.3	9.1	58.1	10.1
26 051	...	Gladwin County............	18 308	63.3	78.3	9.2	−15.2	9.1	8.3	7.3	32.4	16.2
26 053	...	Gogebic County	12 311	53.0	85.5	15.8	−8.6	16.2	0.0	0.0	33.3	4.0
26 055	...	Grand Traverse County	51 801	38.6	89.3	26.1	1.7	26.5	12.9	15.2	31.1	6.2
26 057	...	Gratiot County	27 322	58.6	83.5	12.9	−11.5	13.5	4.2	3.5	49.1	6.5
26 059	...	Hillsdale County	29 595	59.8	83.1	12.0	−12.4	12.0	31.0	2.4	43.7	1.0
26 061	...	Houghton County	21 233	51.4	84.6	23.0	−1.4	22.4	21.1	16.2	71.3	9.3
26 063	...	Huron County	24 954	64.7	78.3	10.9	−13.5	10.8	12.5	5.3	56.6	3.2
26 065	4040	Ingham County.............	162 909	35.3	88.1	33.0	8.6	34.0	22.8	16.8	63.3	15.4
26 067	...	Ionia County	37 835	57.0	83.4	10.8	−13.6	11.1	3.9	11.2	25.2	6.5
26 069	...	Iosco County	19 764	62.3	77.9	11.3	−13.1	11.3	0.0	18.2	38.5	6.1
26 071	...	Iron County..................	9 670	60.8	84.8	13.7	−10.7	13.9	0.0	13.5	23.8	9.3
26 073	...	Isabella County	31 677	47.8	86.1	23.9	−0.5	23.9	21.9	6.3	70.9	12.8
26 075	3520	Jackson County............	104 880	48.6	84.2	16.3	−8.1	17.2	5.2	7.6	56.1	9.2
26 077	3720	Kalamazoo County........	144 995	37.2	88.8	31.2	6.8	32.1	16.3	19.1	69.9	18.0
26 079	...	Kalkaska County	11 073	64.7	80.0	9.7	−14.7	9.8	8.0	7.1	33.3	0.0
26 081	3000	Kent County	351 875	43.6	84.6	25.8	1.4	28.1	11.7	8.2	32.9	9.1
26 083	...	Keweenaw County	1 634	53.5	83.7	19.1	−5.3	18.9	X	X	0.0	50.0
26 085	...	Lake County	7 964	67.5	72.2	7.8	−16.6	8.1	7.5	0.0	0.0	5.8
26 087	2160	Lapeer County.............	56 454	54.0	84.5	12.7	−11.7	12.9	2.8	9.4	42.1	6.5

[1]MSA = Metropolitan Statistical Area. PMSA = Primary MSA. NECMA = New England County Metropolitan Area. See the Appendix A for explanation of these concepts. See Appendix B for list of metropolitan areas identified by type, with component counties.
[2]Hispanic or Latino persons may be of any race.

Table B-3. States and Counties — **Education, Labor Force, and Income**

STATE County	School enrollment			Population 16 to 19 years				Employment status, 2000			Work status in 1999 of the population 16 years and over (percent)		
											Worked in 1999		
	Grades kindergarten through 12	College or graduate school	Percent private	Number	Percent in armed forces	Percent high school graduates	Percent not enrolled, not grads, not in armed forces, not employed	Total population 16 years and over	Percent in labor force	Unemployment rate	Full-time	Part-time	Did not work in 1999
	11	12	13	14	15	16	17	18	19	20	21	22	23
MARYLAND—Cont'd													
Washington County.......	23 374	4 852	12.1	6 116	0.1	16.4	8.0	104 251	61.1	3.3	53.7	12.9	33.3
Wicomico County	16 004	7 234	10.2	5 618	0.0	11.5	4.5	66 207	67.7	5.5	56.8	16.6	26.6
Worcester County	7 510	1 681	8.7	1 930	0.0	14.4	4.1	38 103	60.7	6.8	52.4	15.4	32.2
Baltimore city...............	125 546	48 736	22.6	38 950	0.0	12.0	11.6	507 534	56.6	10.7	49.8	12.4	37.8
MASSACHUSETTS ...	1 129 778	473 403	23.9	330 827	0.1	8.2	3.7	5 010 241	66.2	4.6	54.4	17.4	28.1
Barnstable County........	35 283	8 492	10.9	8 984	0.5	10.1	2.9	181 996	58.9	5.1	46.3	18.7	35.0
Berkshire County..........	23 446	8 313	17.3	7 721	0.0	10.2	3.0	108 466	63.4	5.1	49.0	20.1	30.9
Bristol County...............	99 120	28 891	15.6	28 560	0.1	9.7	5.0	417 857	65.8	5.8	53.5	16.8	29.7
Dukes County...............	2 622	409	7.5	693	0.0	11.8	6.3	11 949	68.2	2.7	56.8	19.3	23.9
Essex County................	138 179	41 131	18.5	35 775	0.1	7.8	3.4	560 484	65.5	4.6	53.8	17.1	29.1
Franklin County	13 222	4 171	11.0	3 862	0.1	7.8	5.7	56 950	69.2	4.5	54.0	19.8	26.2
Hampden County	90 633	28 292	16.7	26 293	0.1	8.2	6.8	350 913	62.4	5.6	50.7	17.4	32.0
Hampshire County	23 193	29 423	21.0	14 283	0.0	4.0	1.0	126 209	69.3	5.1	51.2	26.6	22.2
Middlesex County.........	239 751	121 081	29.5	70 607	0.0	7.8	2.5	1 170 483	68.8	3.4	57.6	17.2	25.2
Nantucket County.........	1 412	250	19.0	263	0.0	11.8	1.9	7 825	74.0	4.2	66.5	15.7	17.9
Norfolk County	112 513	42 232	27.2	28 590	0.0	6.7	1.9	513 198	68.0	3.2	56.1	17.1	26.8
Plymouth County	95 640	23 274	13.5	24 590	0.0	9.3	3.3	360 063	68.4	4.1	55.0	18.5	26.6
Suffolk County..............	110 369	91 260	42.2	41 057	0.1	7.4	4.9	565 141	62.8	7.0	54.2	15.1	30.7
Worcester County	144 395	46 184	19.4	39 549	0.1	10.2	4.2	578 707	66.3	4.3	54.3	17.3	28.4
MICHIGAN	1 971 459	635 836	12.3	566 976	0.0	9.1	4.9	7 630 645	64.6	5.8	53.9	16.5	29.6
Alcona County..............	1 764	211	5.3	516	0.6	8.7	5.0	9 768	44.3	9.9	37.2	13.7	49.1
Alger County	1 715	190	3.9	400	0.0	13.0	4.1	8 102	51.0	8.6	42.7	16.0	41.3
Allegan County............	23 175	3 319	13.3	6 337	0.0	12.4	4.8	78 789	69.0	4.2	57.1	17.5	25.4
Alpena County..............	5 933	1 635	9.6	1 803	0.0	7.0	3.8	24 804	60.4	7.2	47.7	17.4	34.9
Antrim County	4 437	565	4.5	1 093	0.0	9.0	3.8	18 125	59.1	6.4	48.5	17.1	34.4
Arenac County	3 230	567	4.5	927	0.0	13.1	6.8	13 758	52.3	8.4	43.7	15.1	41.1
Baraga County	1 668	224	7.1	449	0.0	11.1	4.7	7 013	54.2	7.9	44.7	16.3	39.0
Barry County	11 597	2 195	9.3	3 145	0.1	9.9	4.4	43 070	67.1	4.6	57.4	15.8	26.9
Bay County...................	20 593	5 444	13.8	5 860	0.3	7.9	4.3	86 542	62.8	6.3	50.1	17.5	32.5
Benzie County..............	2 795	435	8.3	767	0.0	14.1	2.9	12 704	61.0	6.2	51.4	16.8	31.8
Berrien County	32 070	8 218	19.0	9 364	0.0	7.8	6.8	125 198	64.8	5.5	52.8	16.7	30.4
Branch County	9 109	1 547	8.8	2 534	0.0	9.6	5.4	35 421	62.7	4.8	56.0	14.3	29.7
Calhoun County	27 015	7 216	12.7	7 887	0.0	9.3	7.7	106 437	62.9	5.8	53.6	15.1	31.3
Cass County.................	10 025	1 816	8.0	2 834	0.0	9.1	7.2	39 611	65.9	5.0	56.0	15.1	28.9
Charlevoix County........	5 162	701	7.0	1 057	0.0	12.7	3.2	20 097	64.0	6.0	54.7	16.4	28.8
Cheboygan County	4 839	587	10.1	1 358	0.0	10.7	4.1	20 994	57.5	14.2	48.7	15.9	35.4
Chippewa County.........	6 715	3 124	6.0	2 214	0.0	11.2	4.0	31 353	53.6	10.0	47.8	17.8	34.4
Clare County	5 985	953	5.8	1 582	0.0	12.4	5.5	24 435	52.3	8.6	43.2	14.8	42.0
Clinton County..............	13 925	3 148	10.4	3 817	0.0	7.2	2.0	48 847	69.6	3.0	57.4	16.9	25.8
Crawford County	2 843	400	5.0	745	0.0	10.5	3.6	11 214	56.7	7.5	45.0	18.0	37.0
Delta County	7 366	1 968	7.5	2 386	0.0	12.0	1.8	30 828	61.0	7.5	45.8	19.3	35.0
Dickinson County	5 563	775	5.8	1 513	0.0	11.0	3.7	21 445	61.1	5.6	47.1	19.0	33.8
Eaton County	21 041	5 893	11.8	6 355	0.0	11.8	4.0	79 886	70.0	4.3	59.0	16.2	24.8
Emmet County	6 103	1 372	8.5	1 778	0.0	9.4	2.6	24 511	67.0	7.3	56.3	17.1	26.5
Genesee County	90 051	22 250	10.4	24 358	0.0	10.6	6.8	329 331	63.1	7.1	52.6	15.9	31.5
Gladwin County............	4 696	660	8.9	1 282	0.2	9.5	8.1	20 737	51.3	8.4	41.0	14.8	44.2
Gogebic County	2 933	725	9.7	1 080	0.0	10.5	6.4	14 346	51.6	9.4	43.5	16.1	40.3
Grand Traverse County	15 076	3 729	13.8	4 385	0.0	8.1	2.2	60 352	69.6	4.6	57.2	18.5	24.4
Gratiot County	7 956	2 560	17.5	2 718	0.0	9.4	4.7	33 445	56.5	5.7	49.4	16.6	34.0
Hillsdale County	9 235	2 261	15.3	3 098	0.0	8.5	6.9	35 801	65.0	5.3	55.6	14.6	29.7
Houghton County	6 172	6 142	5.8	3 162	0.3	5.7	2.9	29 160	56.8	7.9	45.6	22.9	31.5
Huron County	6 984	888	10.4	1 908	0.6	9.6	3.0	28 498	58.2	5.9	48.5	14.7	36.7
Ingham County	49 177	49 242	7.6	22 172	0.0	5.2	3.2	221 109	68.5	5.7	53.8	23.2	23.0
Ionia County	13 143	1 877	10.8	3 880	0.0	12.9	9.8	46 964	60.4	4.6	53.8	15.0	31.2
Iosco County	4 899	569	6.7	1 337	0.3	10.9	8.4	22 045	50.7	9.0	42.6	13.6	43.7
Iron County...................	2 246	253	2.8	629	0.2	7.8	2.1	10 802	51.1	9.4	41.5	15.9	42.5
Isabella County	9 886	17 635	5.8	7 903	0.0	3.5	1.7	51 955	65.8	7.2	49.6	28.5	22.0
Jackson County............	31 331	7 379	14.4	8 107	0.0	8.6	7.0	122 154	62.1	5.5	55.0	14.9	30.2
Kalamazoo County........	42 746	31 709	11.2	16 967	0.1	6.9	2.9	187 445	69.0	6.6	54.7	20.9	24.4
Kalkaska County	3 169	399	5.5	868	0.0	14.9	7.4	12 783	62.0	6.4	52.5	15.7	31.8
Kent County	120 383	34 031	19.8	34 941	0.0	9.8	5.2	429 573	70.5	4.4	57.8	18.1	24.0
Keweenaw County	423	57	13.8	171	0.0	4.1	5.3	1 898	54.3	11.1	42.3	21.2	36.5
Lake County.................	1 939	237	8.1	824	0.0	16.5	23.1	9 225	46.4	8.4	39.9	13.2	47.0
Lapeer County..............	19 201	3 526	10.7	5 230	0.0	10.4	3.4	66 033	65.7	5.5	54.8	15.8	29.4

STATE County	Full-year full-time employed (percent)								Children under 18 years in families						Total employed by class of worker (percent)			
										With two parents (percent)		With one parent who is in labor force (percent)	+/− U.S. percent of children with no stay-at-home parent (percent)	+/− U.S. percent two-income couples				
	Total	Men	Women	Non-Hispanic White	Black or African American	American Indian and Alaska Native	Asian, Hawaiian, and Pacific Islander	Hispanic or Latino[1]	Number	Both in labor force	Father only in labor force				Private	Government	Self-employed	Unpaid family worker
	24	25	26	27	28	29	30	31	32	33	34	35	36	37	38	39	40	41
MARYLAND—Cont'd																		
Washington County........	42.8	50.3	35.1	45.1	17.5	61.5	40.7	37.6	29 335	49.5	19.6	21.2	6.1	2.6	75.1	16.4	8.1	0.4
Wicomico County	42.7	50.6	35.7	44.1	40.0	37.4	31.8	28.3	19 635	43.9	15.8	32.0	11.3	5.6	72.4	18.1	9.1	0.3
Worcester County	38.0	45.5	30.9	38.6	35.3	12.8	33.6	34.8	8 876	47.3	15.8	26.1	8.8	−5.6	67.1	16.2	16.4	0.3
Baltimore city................	34.7	38.5	31.4	38.7	32.6	27.8	29.6	33.5	137 315	22.3	9.7	42.6	0.3	−6.3	71.6	22.3	5.9	0.2
MASSACHUSETTS ...	42.3	53.2	32.5	43.3	38.7	33.9	39.3	34.0	1 434 842	48.2	20.1	19.1	2.7	4.9	77.3	13.5	9.0	0.2
Barnstable County.........	34.1	44.4	25.2	33.9	39.1	37.1	41.4	39.0	43 430	48.8	21.7	19.5	3.7	−6.4	68.9	14.5	16.3	0.2
Berkshire County..........	37.4	47.5	28.4	37.7	32.0	28.6	35.9	34.9	28 605	51.3	15.7	23.8	10.5	2.4	75.3	13.1	11.3	0.2
Bristol County	42.3	53.1	32.6	43.1	38.0	36.1	40.4	29.6	125 838	50.1	16.1	20.9	6.4	4.9	79.1	13.3	7.4	0.2
Dukes County	39.3	48.7	30.7	39.6	33.2	58.7	17.2	51.9	3 326	44.8	20.4	25.7	5.9	6.6	59.1	11.7	28.6	0.6
Essex County	42.5	54.7	31.8	43.4	42.7	26.1	41.7	35.1	174 311	46.5	20.8	19.5	1.4	4.7	77.0	13.0	9.8	0.2
Franklin County	41.5	51.4	32.7	42.2	29.4	29.2	26.6	30.0	16 047	54.4	13.4	22.9	12.7	10.6	68.6	19.3	11.8	0.3
Hampden County...........	39.1	50.1	29.5	41.3	36.1	36.8	39.6	26.1	111 408	40.0	15.7	24.7	0.1	3.1	75.5	17.0	7.3	0.2
Hampshire County.........	36.8	46.6	28.6	38.1	29.0	23.3	21.0	25.3	28 482	56.9	15.5	19.8	12.1	10.7	67.4	22.9	9.6	0.1
Middlesex County..........	45.1	56.8	34.6	45.8	41.9	35.6	42.7	39.9	318 373	52.0	23.6	14.7	2.1	6.5	78.8	11.6	9.3	0.2
Nantucket County..........	46.5	55.1	37.6	47.2	45.4	X	22.5	28.7	1 778	56.5	23.2	16.6	8.5	13.8	54.9	12.4	32.7	0.0
Norfolk County	45.0	57.4	34.1	45.2	46.1	39.3	45.1	40.1	149 157	55.6	24.6	12.3	3.5	6.7	77.6	12.5	9.7	0.2
Plymouth County	44.4	56.4	33.4	45.0	42.1	32.2	46.6	37.5	121 858	50.6	22.7	17.1	3.1	7.4	77.0	13.9	8.9	0.2
Suffolk County	38.3	43.8	33.3	41.0	36.9	28.6	28.3	34.0	127 895	30.0	12.9	30.1	−4.5	−2.4	80.1	13.4	6.4	0.1
Worcester County	43.1	55.2	31.9	43.9	37.5	38.3	43.2	33.9	184 328	49.4	20.3	19.1	3.9	6.0	78.2	13.5	8.0	0.2
MICHIGAN	40.1	50.5	30.5	41.6	32.8	37.1	39.3	36.6	2 456 837	44.2	21.9	22.8	2.4	0.1	79.9	11.4	8.4	0.3
Alcona County..............	25.3	30.6	20.0	25.3	0.0	21.1	41.2	25.0	2 138	47.2	20.1	20.1	2.7	−21.2	68.1	14.3	16.8	0.8
Alger County	29.4	33.8	24.1	30.7	4.0	45.3	32.3	16.1	1 924	55.4	18.7	15.5	6.3	−8.2	65.5	22.1	11.7	0.7
Allegan County.............	44.8	57.2	32.8	45.4	41.3	38.3	38.8	38.6	28 817	52.9	21.8	17.1	5.4	5.0	82.2	8.0	9.5	0.3
Alpena County	34.0	43.4	25.3	34.0	30.1	29.1	48.4	44.9	7 131	54.0	17.6	18.5	7.9	−2.1	75.2	13.0	11.1	0.7
Antrim County	35.1	43.8	26.6	35.2	26.7	35.2	32.1	29.2	5 365	50.4	20.2	20.9	6.7	−7.8	70.8	12.6	15.9	0.7
Arenac County	30.2	36.3	23.9	31.1	0.0	35.2	47.6	16.2	3 780	47.3	20.1	19.1	1.8	−10.6	75.3	12.2	12.3	0.2
Baraga County	30.9	36.3	24.7	33.0	1.3	34.6	14.8	20.5	1 924	52.8	10.7	22.1	10.3	−1.4	62.1	27.5	9.9	0.5
Barry County	44.2	55.9	32.6	43.9	48.8	72.7	75.0	48.7	14 764	53.2	22.9	17.2	5.8	2.3	78.9	10.7	10.0	0.4
Bay County.................	38.6	49.5	28.7	38.9	28.6	40.2	35.7	35.3	25 741	50.8	18.1	20.6	6.8	−2.2	80.3	10.9	8.4	0.4
Benzie County	37.2	44.8	29.9	37.3	0.0	31.5	21.7	29.0	3 532	54.0	19.1	19.6	9.0	−3.4	72.9	13.1	13.7	0.3
Berrien County	40.0	50.5	30.5	41.7	31.7	37.0	37.6	33.5	39 264	42.6	18.5	27.3	5.3	1.2	80.4	9.2	10.0	0.3
Branch County	42.1	50.8	33.4	43.0	17.8	41.8	28.9	41.0	11 103	49.1	20.2	23.1	7.6	5.0	77.0	11.9	10.7	0.4
Calhoun County	39.5	47.4	32.2	40.3	33.0	25.6	37.9	42.1	33 302	44.6	17.2	26.7	6.7	0.1	78.9	13.0	7.7	0.4
Cass County	42.6	53.5	31.9	43.6	31.1	47.2	46.2	30.7	12 129	47.6	20.7	22.7	5.7	2.1	81.0	8.7	9.8	0.5
Charlevoix County.........	40.0	50.0	30.4	40.1	8.3	39.9	20.9	25.8	6 525	53.6	16.8	21.8	10.8	−1.1	74.6	12.2	12.9	0.3
Cheboygan County	30.1	36.6	23.8	30.1	41.4	31.5	33.9	25.5	5 980	48.1	17.5	22.1	5.6	−13.2	73.0	12.6	13.9	0.5
Chippewa County..........	31.6	34.0	28.4	32.6	7.6	42.2	16.5	16.0	7 925	51.2	13.4	25.9	12.5	−3.1	60.9	30.8	8.0	0.3
Clare County	29.8	36.9	22.9	29.8	15.8	29.6	36.6	37.4	7 163	42.8	18.6	25.2	3.4	−14.5	75.0	11.9	12.1	1.0
Clinton County	46.8	58.5	35.5	46.9	54.7	48.8	29.5	42.5	17 667	58.6	21.5	15.1	9.1	7.5	70.9	18.9	9.8	0.4
Crawford County	32.1	38.8	25.2	32.5	14.9	11.6	38.3	35.0	3 278	46.9	15.5	26.5	2.8	−8.4	72.3	16.9	10.4	0.4
Delta County	34.0	45.5	23.0	33.9	19.4	33.3	27.4	28.7	8 875	56.1	19.2	17.5	9.0	−4.1	76.3	12.8	10.6	0.4
Dickinson County	35.5	47.3	24.6	35.4	38.6	40.8	45.4	36.6	6 764	51.9	20.7	19.6	6.9	−0.9	74.8	15.8	9.1	0.3
Eaton County	46.1	56.3	36.8	46.6	44.6	40.5	31.0	44.7	26 020	55.2	18.4	20.3	10.9	7.7	72.7	18.4	8.7	0.2
Emmet County	39.5	48.9	30.6	39.7	41.9	34.0	43.5	25.0	7 656	55.6	18.4	20.5	11.5	3.3	71.6	12.2	15.9	0.3
Genesee County	37.9	47.6	29.3	40.0	29.9	35.2	45.1	34.8	111 999	37.8	18.8	30.4	3.6	−3.5	82.5	9.7	7.6	0.3
Gladwin County	29.3	37.5	21.5	29.5	21.4	27.0	34.9	23.0	5 774	46.9	21.9	18.4	0.7	−14.4	74.4	11.7	13.2	0.7
Gogebic County	28.1	35.0	21.2	28.9	1.7	28.0	29.2	10.3	3 368	53.2	13.1	22.8	11.4	−9.8	69.6	19.9	10.0	0.5
Grand Traverse County	42.4	53.3	32.3	42.5	22.3	50.2	20.4	44.5	18 985	55.1	19.7	20.1	10.6	6.2	77.0	9.8	12.9	0.3
Gratiot County	34.5	41.7	26.7	36.2	8.4	22.2	26.2	35.0	9 710	52.4	18.5	20.8	8.6	0.4	75.6	13.4	10.6	0.5
Hillsdale County	42.1	52.9	31.7	42.4	30.5	13.1	37.4	37.2	11 514	51.2	22.0	17.9	4.5	0.8	79.1	10.0	10.5	0.4
Houghton County	27.6	32.2	22.2	28.0	4.8	42.4	21.1	5.5	7 741	48.1	25.0	18.6	2.1	−4.2	66.0	25.1	8.5	0.3
Huron County	36.6	47.5	26.1	36.8	37.1	40.4	26.1	29.0	8 475	55.4	20.0	16.6	7.4	−3.8	74.9	10.7	13.8	0.6
Ingham County	38.9	46.2	32.3	40.3	35.2	39.2	23.7	37.2	62 200	45.2	17.7	25.6	6.2	6.1	71.3	21.6	6.9	0.2
Ionia County	40.8	46.3	34.4	43.7	4.1	15.7	22.2	36.4	15 723	50.4	19.8	21.0	6.8	5.8	75.7	15.2	8.7	0.4
Iosco County	28.9	36.0	22.3	28.7	44.4	28.1	61.0	27.7	5 699	47.8	15.3	25.5	8.7	−14.7	75.0	12.1	12.4	0.5
Iron County.................	28.7	34.4	23.3	28.7	17.1	35.8	4.8	43.7	2 597	51.9	16.9	22.9	10.2	−10.2	67.0	19.3	13.5	0.3
Isabella County	30.2	37.3	24.0	30.8	13.1	30.7	23.4	27.7	12 342	52.7	16.0	23.2	11.3	4.5	71.7	19.8	8.0	0.5
Jackson County............	40.3	47.9	32.4	42.0	21.5	29.2	33.1	39.1	38 545	47.8	18.4	24.1	7.3	3.5	79.5	11.9	8.4	0.2
Kalamazoo County........	39.9	49.8	30.8	40.6	35.8	39.3	29.7	38.2	54 644	48.3	19.4	24.0	7.7	6.0	79.3	12.1	8.3	0.3
Kalkaska County	36.9	45.7	28.1	36.9	24.0	43.4	31.8	43.2	3 996	51.8	19.2	19.1	6.3	−5.1	78.5	11.1	10.0	0.4
Kent County	44.9	56.9	33.6	45.9	38.6	36.1	45.0	39.3	155 096	48.0	22.5	20.2	3.6	6.4	84.5	7.5	7.8	0.2
Keweenaw County	28.5	35.0	21.2	29.5	0.0	X	0.0	38.5	395	57.0	19.0	19.5	11.9	−9.0	58.7	27.5	13.1	0.7
Lake County	26.1	29.3	22.6	26.9	22.7	24.1	30.0	20.7	2 170	40.7	16.1	23.8	−0.1	−16.4	70.5	15.8	12.8	0.9
Lapeer County.............	41.4	53.9	28.9	42.0	9.1	38.0	45.0	33.1	23 903	48.8	29.5	15.5	−0.3	−2.0	79.5	10.1	9.9	0.5

[1] Hispanic or Latino persons may be of any race.

Table B-3. States and Counties — Education, Labor Force, and Income

STATE County	Percent who worked at home	Percent of the population 5 years and over with a disability	Veterans as a percent of the population 18 years and over	Occupation for employed population 16 years and over (percent)						Industry for employed population 16 years and over (percent)					
				Management, professional, and related occupations	Service occupations	Sales and office occupations	Farming, fishing, and forestry occupations	Construction, extraction, and maintenance occupations	Production, transportation and material moving occupations	Agriculture, forestry, fishing, and mining	Construction and manufacturing	Wholesale and retail trade	Transportation and warehousing, and utilities	Service industries	Public administration
	42	43	44	45	46	47	48	49	50	51	52	53	54	55	56
MARYLAND—Cont'd															
Washington County......	3.3	19.7	14.5	26.6	15.5	27.9	0.4	11.9	17.7	1.6	23.7	16.6	5.6	45.0	7.5
Wicomico County	3.5	18.5	14.1	30.8	17.2	26.7	0.9	10.0	14.3	2.2	21.7	16.2	4.3	50.0	5.6
Worcester County	4.9	21.0	18.2	29.3	21.2	27.8	0.9	11.6	9.2	2.2	15.9	16.8	3.0	55.9	6.3
Baltimore city...............	2.3	27.2	11.2	32.4	20.0	27.1	0.1	7.0	13.4	0.1	12.9	11.6	5.6	60.5	9.3
MASSACHUSETTS ...	3.1	18.5	11.5	41.1	14.1	25.9	0.2	7.5	11.3	0.4	18.3	14.4	4.2	58.4	4.3
Barnstable County........	5.2	20.3	18.4	35.1	18.2	27.5	0.7	11.0	7.5	0.9	14.5	17.1	4.3	58.2	5.0
Berkshire County..........	3.6	19.0	14.3	35.1	18.7	25.0	0.4	8.8	11.9	1.1	19.5	15.0	2.8	58.1	3.5
Bristol County..............	2.1	20.2	12.0	30.7	15.4	26.3	0.4	9.5	17.8	0.5	25.4	17.1	4.2	48.3	4.4
Dukes County..............	10.0	18.1	13.1	31.8	16.0	25.2	0.6	18.9	7.5	1.4	21.2	17.6	3.9	50.9	5.0
Essex County	3.3	18.8	12.0	39.4	13.6	27.0	0.3	7.3	12.4	0.5	21.2	14.9	4.5	54.8	4.1
Franklin County	5.1	18.4	11.6	35.3	16.5	23.2	0.7	9.8	15.6	1.8	21.1	13.8	4.2	54.7	4.4
Hampden County	2.1	22.4	13.5	31.0	16.7	26.8	0.2	8.0	17.3	0.4	21.0	16.2	6.0	51.5	4.9
Hampshire County	4.1	15.7	11.2	42.9	15.4	23.7	0.4	6.6	10.9	0.8	14.6	12.3	3.7	64.4	4.3
Middlesex County.........	3.6	16.0	10.0	49.7	11.5	24.2	0.1	6.1	8.4	0.2	17.0	12.8	3.4	62.9	3.8
Nantucket County.........	6.5	20.2	12.0	30.0	16.9	23.8	0.6	22.3	6.3	1.2	24.9	12.6	6.0	51.5	3.8
Norfolk County.............	3.6	15.0	11.6	48.1	11.2	26.8	0.1	6.8	6.9	0.2	14.1	14.5	3.8	63.4	4.1
Plymouth County..........	2.6	18.3	13.6	35.8	14.2	28.5	0.3	9.5	11.7	0.6	17.4	17.8	5.0	54.8	4.4
Suffolk County.............	2.3	22.7	7.0	41.0	18.0	26.2	0.1	5.4	9.2	0.1	10.6	10.9	4.8	68.4	5.2
Worcester County	2.7	18.8	12.7	37.6	13.9	25.5	0.2	8.1	14.7	0.5	24.6	15.2	4.0	51.6	4.0
MICHIGAN	2.8	18.7	12.4	31.5	14.8	25.6	0.5	9.2	18.5	1.1	28.5	15.1	4.1	47.5	3.6
Alcona County.............	6.9	25.7	22.2	23.8	18.6	23.2	1.6	13.6	19.2	4.7	28.1	14.8	5.4	42.0	4.9
Alger County	4.1	19.5	17.4	26.0	22.6	21.8	2.1	10.5	17.0	4.3	27.0	10.4	3.3	43.7	11.4
Allegan County	4.1	17.2	12.3	24.0	13.2	22.1	1.7	11.3	27.7	2.9	39.9	15.1	4.1	35.8	2.0
Alpena County	4.2	22.5	16.1	27.2	18.2	25.1	1.1	10.1	18.4	3.6	23.4	17.1	3.6	48.3	4.1
Antrim County	5.4	21.2	16.7	24.9	17.2	22.6	0.9	12.8	21.6	3.4	31.0	13.2	2.9	46.0	3.4
Arenac County	4.2	22.6	16.7	22.3	18.7	23.8	1.7	12.5	21.1	3.7	27.7	16.4	4.6	43.3	4.3
Baraga County	4.2	22.7	16.1	21.4	20.8	22.6	2.1	9.4	19.7	4.8	22.0	13.2	4.0	45.1	11.1
Barry County	4.4	17.5	14.2	27.4	11.2	23.7	0.8	11.3	25.6	2.5	37.5	13.8	3.6	39.6	3.0
Bay County..................	2.7	19.7	14.2	26.9	16.8	27.1	0.4	10.9	18.0	1.1	25.5	18.0	4.6	47.5	3.3
Benzie County.............	4.3	20.0	17.4	24.2	19.3	24.2	0.8	13.9	17.6	1.5	27.1	17.1	3.0	46.4	4.9
Berrien County	3.3	20.2	13.6	29.3	15.3	24.1	1.0	8.9	21.3	1.9	30.6	13.7	6.5	44.6	2.7
Branch County	4.5	19.5	13.3	22.7	13.6	21.9	1.4	9.1	31.3	3.7	36.3	16.7	4.2	34.3	4.8
Calhoun County	2.8	21.1	14.9	26.9	16.3	24.2	0.4	8.4	23.8	1.0	30.7	13.7	4.3	44.6	5.6
Cass County	3.7	20.9	15.2	22.6	12.9	23.4	1.0	11.6	28.5	2.7	40.5	13.7	4.3	36.5	2.3
Charlevoix County........	4.2	18.8	15.9	27.2	17.0	22.9	0.7	13.8	18.3	1.5	31.8	13.8	4.0	45.5	3.5
Cheboygan County	4.5	21.6	16.6	23.4	20.3	25.6	0.8	13.0	16.9	1.7	23.9	17.5	3.8	48.2	5.0
Chippewa County.........	3.6	10.1	16.9	26.2	28.3	25.0	0.6	9.1	10.8	1.9	11.8	13.6	4.1	55.2	13.4
Clare County	3.9	26.4	17.8	22.6	19.1	23.1	1.1	12.4	21.6	3.4	26.5	16.3	4.2	45.4	4.2
Clinton County.............	4.3	15.5	12.2	31.0	13.4	27.0	1.1	10.6	16.9	2.5	24.3	14.0	3.9	44.7	10.6
Crawford County	3.6	23.3	18.5	24.3	21.0	24.7	1.0	11.4	17.6	1.8	20.5	17.7	3.9	48.6	7.5
Delta County	2.6	19.7	18.0	25.3	18.3	23.6	1.4	10.5	21.0	3.0	24.8	15.7	6.1	46.2	4.1
Dickinson County	2.4	19.2	17.6	28.0	16.7	26.6	0.8	10.4	17.5	1.7	26.4	17.1	5.9	45.1	3.8
Eaton County...............	3.2	17.4	12.9	30.5	13.4	27.8	0.3	9.7	18.3	1.0	24.3	14.5	4.3	45.5	10.4
Emmet County.............	4.7	17.0	14.1	30.7	18.5	26.7	0.5	12.0	11.7	1.2	20.3	17.7	2.6	54.4	3.7
Genesee County	2.0	20.6	13.2	27.0	16.5	24.3	0.1	10.6	21.4	0.3	30.3	15.7	3.5	47.5	2.7
Gladwin County............	5.4	23.0	17.0	24.1	15.8	23.9	1.3	13.6	21.2	3.9	31.9	14.4	4.2	41.7	4.0
Gogebic County	3.4	24.5	19.5	26.1	21.4	22.0	1.4	11.3	17.8	2.4	20.9	15.6	4.1	49.9	7.1
Grand Traverse County	4.3	16.5	13.7	31.4	16.8	28.0	0.4	10.6	12.8	1.7	21.1	18.5	3.2	52.5	3.0
Gratiot County	4.1	18.3	11.9	25.1	18.9	22.4	1.6	9.3	22.7	4.3	27.6	13.1	4.5	44.2	6.2
Hillsdale County	4.3	20.5	13.2	23.2	13.4	20.2	1.3	9.4	32.5	3.6	40.7	12.6	3.6	36.5	3.0
Houghton County	3.8	16.3	14.1	34.4	21.3	25.3	0.7	8.3	10.0	1.4	13.0	14.8	2.0	65.1	3.7
Huron County	5.4	20.2	13.4	26.2	14.1	21.4	2.3	9.8	26.3	7.9	33.9	12.8	3.9	37.9	3.4
Ingham County	3.0	16.7	9.9	36.9	16.5	27.1	0.3	7.0	12.2	0.7	15.3	13.6	3.1	58.5	8.7
Ionia County	3.9	17.3	12.4	22.4	15.6	23.3	1.1	11.6	25.9	3.2	34.3	14.6	3.4	36.3	8.2
Iosco County	3.5	24.9	21.4	22.3	18.1	24.5	0.5	13.1	21.7	1.8	25.8	16.6	6.9	44.5	4.5
Iron County..................	3.3	22.8	19.4	24.8	23.7	23.5	2.4	11.1	14.5	4.3	17.4	15.5	4.6	51.5	6.8
Isabella County............	3.2	14.5	9.1	28.4	23.6	27.8	0.7	7.7	11.8	2.5	15.6	15.1	2.5	61.0	3.3
Jackson County............	2.8	19.7	13.8	27.5	16.5	24.6	0.4	9.4	21.7	1.1	29.2	15.5	5.9	43.2	5.1
Kalamazoo County........	3.1	16.5	11.1	34.7	15.5	26.0	0.7	7.7	15.4	1.1	26.0	14.8	3.2	52.3	2.6
Kalkaska County	3.6	21.0	17.5	19.7	17.2	24.1	0.8	14.8	23.4	6.5	28.9	15.5	4.0	41.7	3.5
Kent County	3.0	16.3	11.1	31.1	13.3	26.8	0.4	7.7	20.7	0.6	29.3	18.6	3.4	46.1	2.0
Keweenaw County	6.6	18.8	21.3	32.6	21.8	20.2	1.7	9.1	14.5	2.4	19.3	10.9	2.3	52.6	12.4
Lake County................	3.8	31.2	19.2	19.8	17.0	22.7	1.8	12.9	25.7	3.6	32.1	14.7	5.1	36.1	8.3
Lapeer County.............	2.9	17.0	13.1	26.9	13.7	20.9	0.4	13.9	24.2	1.5	39.0	12.8	3.5	40.1	3.1

Table B-3. States and Counties — **Education, Labor Force, and Income**

STATE County	Median household income	Median family income: All families	Median family income: Families with children: Married-couple	Median family income: Families with children: Male householder	Median family income: Families with children: Female householder	Median nonfamily household income	Median income for full-year, full-time workers: Men	Median income for full-year, full-time workers: Women	Per capita income	Households by source of income (percent): With earnings	Households by source of income (percent): With interest, dividend, or rental income	Households by source of income (percent): With Social Security income	Households by source of income (percent): With public assistance income	Households by source of income (percent): With retirement income	Households with income over $100,000 (percent)	+/− U.S. percent for income over $100,000	Households with income below poverty (percent)	Families with children with income below poverty (percent)
	57	58	59	60	61	62	63	64	65	66	67	68	69	70	71	72	73	74
MARYLAND—Cont'd																		
Washington County	40 617	48 962	56 912	30 773	17 904	22 622	35 754	25 211	20 062	78.3	33.1	28.4	2.3	18.7	7.5	-4.8	9.7	10.5
Wicomico County	39 035	47 129	58 921	31 038	19 079	22 741	34 485	24 590	19 171	81.7	32.1	26.6	2.9	16.6	8.4	-3.9	12.0	13.3
Worcester County	40 650	47 293	56 505	26 653	17 762	25 683	33 851	25 105	22 505	76.4	41.4	35.4	2.5	25.7	8.8	-3.5	9.1	13.6
Baltimore city	30 078	35 438	54 653	25 800	18 281	20 884	32 401	27 478	16 978	74.0	22.2	27.7	7.3	16.9	6.3	-6.0	21.8	26.2
MASSACHUSETTS	50 502	61 664	74 589	34 532	22 138	29 774	45 130	33 281	25 952	80.1	42.1	26.2	2.9	16.5	17.7	5.4	9.8	10.1
Barnstable County	45 933	54 728	65 306	36 439	24 439	28 339	42 207	31 071	25 318	72.0	46.7	39.0	1.8	26.3	12.4	0.1	7.0	8.1
Berkshire County	39 047	50 162	59 662	30 424	19 963	21 483	38 170	27 469	21 807	75.0	45.6	32.9	2.7	20.9	9.7	-2.6	10.2	11.6
Bristol County	43 496	53 733	66 334	31 175	17 935	21 213	40 497	28 548	20 978	77.7	37.3	28.0	3.9	16.9	11.0	-1.3	11.3	11.5
Dukes County	45 559	55 018	61 556	30 357	28 750	31 088	40 543	31 557	26 472	83.8	43.9	26.4	1.0	15.1	13.0	0.7	7.2	8.5
Essex County	51 576	63 746	77 645	32 775	22 557	27 953	46 109	33 761	26 358	79.7	41.9	27.3	3.1	17.1	19.0	6.7	9.5	10.1
Franklin County	40 768	50 915	61 665	29 420	18 253	22 279	37 257	28 422	20 672	79.6	43.6	27.6	3.3	17.0	8.0	-4.3	10.4	10.5
Hampden County	39 718	49 257	61 560	31 537	16 940	22 345	39 021	28 896	19 541	75.6	35.0	30.0	5.4	18.0	8.8	-3.5	14.1	18.7
Hampshire County	46 098	57 480	66 662	36 550	24 068	28 576	40 676	31 238	21 685	82.5	46.8	24.9	2.4	16.8	12.4	0.1	9.7	7.7
Middlesex County	60 821	74 194	86 960	40 020	28 238	36 954	50 801	37 421	31 199	83.5	49.1	24.0	1.9	15.4	24.9	12.6	7.0	6.3
Nantucket County	55 522	66 786	73 438	44 444	41 429	40 323	42 246	32 282	31 314	87.3	44.4	20.3	0.6	12.2	22.6	10.3	5.3	2.0
Norfolk County	63 432	77 847	90 476	47 045	34 542	36 024	52 535	38 456	32 484	82.1	50.3	26.8	1.3	17.9	26.3	14.0	5.5	4.1
Plymouth County	55 615	65 554	75 418	39 907	24 051	28 348	46 702	32 154	24 789	83.0	38.7	25.5	2.5	16.7	18.8	6.5	7.4	7.2
Suffolk County	39 355	44 361	55 926	28 982	20 085	31 767	38 306	33 216	22 766	78.3	31.2	20.1	4.1	11.7	12.4	0.1	18.4	21.6
Worcester County	47 874	58 394	71 783	33 354	21 628	25 577	43 710	31 275	22 983	80.1	38.4	26.4	3.3	16.3	14.8	2.5	9.6	9.9
MICHIGAN	44 667	53 457	65 021	32 208	21 208	26 194	42 962	29 256	22 168	80.2	38.0	26.2	3.6	19.2	12.7	0.4	10.1	11.3
Alcona County	31 362	35 669	40 625	27 500	15 294	19 356	30 956	21 498	17 653	57.9	44.7	46.7	3.4	37.0	4.1	-8.2	12.5	15.2
Alger County	35 892	42 017	49 769	29 250	17 885	20 568	38 878	25 559	18 210	72.3	41.9	35.6	2.2	27.9	4.5	-7.8	10.7	11.3
Allegan County	45 813	51 908	60 002	31 997	24 963	26 608	39 654	27 767	19 918	83.5	38.5	24.2	2.1	16.4	8.6	-3.7	7.5	7.0
Alpena County	34 177	42 366	51 620	28 162	15 500	17 898	35 506	22 376	17 566	72.7	43.0	34.9	3.8	24.2	4.1	-8.2	11.3	11.8
Antrim County	38 107	43 488	49 203	25 573	19 710	21 554	34 394	22 426	19 485	74.8	39.4	35.1	2.5	26.4	6.8	-5.5	8.6	10.3
Arenac County	32 805	39 033	46 675	23 250	13 431	18 003	32 204	20 894	16 300	68.7	36.7	36.3	4.3	26.5	4.9	-7.4	13.3	19.1
Baraga County	33 673	42 500	50 884	27 500	16 917	18 083	33 810	22 467	15 860	72.9	38.7	35.3	4.1	23.4	3.8	-8.5	9.8	12.2
Barry County	46 820	51 794	58 529	30 351	24 486	26 694	40 220	27 200	20 636	81.7	37.5	26.0	2.4	20.5	9.9	-2.4	5.3	6.1
Bay County	38 646	48 111	57 500	25 401	18 584	20 598	39 611	24 939	19 698	75.7	40.8	30.5	3.9	22.6	8.7	-3.6	10.1	10.9
Benzie County	37 350	42 716	47 956	27 232	22 216	21 736	31 051	22 386	18 524	74.6	41.4	34.6	2.0	25.7	5.6	-6.7	7.4	7.7
Berrien County	38 567	46 548	57 724	29 815	17 022	21 249	37 538	24 870	19 952	78.5	36.4	29.6	3.9	17.3	8.7	-3.6	11.6	14.4
Branch County	38 760	44 777	52 381	27 228	21 086	22 796	32 918	23 284	17 552	80.4	34.7	29.8	2.8	19.9	5.7	-6.6	8.0	9.3
Calhoun County	38 918	47 167	56 663	30 972	20 967	23 494	38 092	27 215	19 230	77.9	35.7	28.9	4.3	21.0	7.7	-4.6	10.9	12.5
Cass County	41 264	46 901	53 601	30 160	21 482	23 533	36 357	25 623	19 474	80.1	34.5	30.2	3.1	17.7	7.7	-4.6	9.6	11.1
Charlevoix County	39 788	46 260	54 473	33 456	19 099	23 730	34 622	24 006	20 130	79.2	39.7	30.6	2.0	21.3	7.9	-4.4	8.2	8.7
Cheboygan County	33 417	38 390	44 769	22 009	18 125	19 077	30 828	21 278	18 088	72.5	38.0	36.4	3.1	25.6	5.7	-6.6	12.1	15.1
Chippewa County	34 464	41 450	49 964	29 397	15 769	18 813	32 497	23 021	15 858	76.3	34.2	29.7	3.9	22.5	3.9	-8.4	13.6	14.7
Clare County	28 845	33 934	42 589	23 343	15 365	16 752	30 998	21 282	15 922	67.3	29.5	38.2	5.0	27.3	4.5	-7.8	15.5	18.0
Clinton County	52 806	60 491	68 570	40 982	25 730	30 447	43 973	31 786	22 913	83.5	45.3	23.3	1.9	21.2	13.0	0.7	5.1	5.0
Crawford County	33 364	37 056	48 665	27 000	17 443	22 585	32 344	22 018	16 903	72.7	36.3	35.6	4.0	28.5	5.2	-7.1	11.5	16.0
Delta County	35 511	45 079	55 227	34 412	16 964	19 057	38 899	23 094	18 667	73.0	42.6	34.0	2.5	21.7	5.9	-6.4	10.8	9.9
Dickinson County	34 825	43 021	52 049	28 750	19 276	18 981	37 451	23 898	18 516	72.3	42.8	34.5	2.9	22.7	5.7	-6.6	9.6	10.5
Eaton County	49 588	57 898	65 553	32 483	24 833	28 507	43 024	30 515	22 411	83.4	41.7	24.0	2.4	20.6	11.1	-1.2	6.2	6.6
Emmet County	40 222	48 140	55 113	21 413	24 102	22 483	34 827	25 289	21 070	80.9	39.9	28.2	1.9	17.8	9.5	-2.8	8.2	6.5
Genesee County	41 951	50 090	63 308	31 998	17 496	25 549	45 476	28 608	20 883	78.6	32.5	26.1	5.3	23.4	10.7	-1.6	12.2	16.2
Gladwin County	32 019	37 090	46 852	23 889	15 189	17 367	35 293	22 976	16 614	65.5	34.5	38.9	3.5	32.7	5.3	-7.0	12.9	17.9
Gogebic County	27 405	35 738	46 473	21 875	11 856	16 106	30 094	21 927	16 169	65.1	39.1	41.6	4.1	26.0	3.9	-8.4	14.3	17.6
Grand Traverse County	43 169	51 211	59 118	30 746	21 846	27 287	35 996	25 458	22 111	82.6	42.7	25.3	2.0	18.7	10.4	-1.9	6.2	5.5
Gratiot County	37 262	43 954	52 908	29 032	20 718	20 347	34 048	23 214	17 118	77.5	37.0	30.1	2.4	19.0	5.8	-6.5	9.8	10.1
Hillsdale County	40 396	45 895	53 139	29 792	22 417	21 537	35 924	24 559	18 255	79.3	35.1	29.0	2.9	18.9	6.8	-5.5	8.2	7.3
Houghton County	28 817	38 635	46 765	21 726	19 648	15 704	31 039	23 413	15 078	72.6	41.4	33.1	3.7	20.6	4.4	-7.9	18.2	14.9
Huron County	35 315	42 436	50 412	27 045	17 843	18 897	32 575	21 939	17 851	71.0	44.9	36.7	2.9	20.7	5.0	-7.3	10.4	10.6
Ingham County	40 774	53 063	63 788	31 813	21 385	25 642	41 039	30 805	21 079	83.7	38.6	20.8	3.4	16.4	10.8	-1.5	14.2	12.8
Ionia County	43 074	49 797	57 500	26 425	21 232	23 264	38 026	26 072	17 451	82.0	35.3	24.8	3.3	18.6	6.8	-5.5	8.7	9.9
Iosco County	31 321	37 452	44 196	26 129	18 029	18 788	31 555	22 329	17 115	64.1	38.1	41.7	4.1	33.0	4.2	-8.1	12.4	15.3
Iron County	28 560	37 038	46 835	22 778	16 250	15 779	30 377	21 750	16 506	64.1	45.2	44.4	4.0	28.6	2.8	-9.5	11.8	14.7
Isabella County	34 262	45 953	56 161	26 397	20 967	19 921	33 478	24 986	16 242	84.1	36.2	21.0	2.4	15.5	6.8	-5.5	19.8	10.4
Jackson County	43 171	50 970	60 851	31 301	19 540	23 489	39 905	27 117	20 171	79.0	36.9	28.5	3.5	20.7	8.9	-3.4	8.7	10.5
Kalamazoo County	42 022	53 953	64 866	35 009	20 260	24 936	40 510	28 945	21 739	82.6	39.5	23.1	2.9	15.6	11.4	-0.9	11.6	10.7
Kalkaska County	36 072	39 932	45 933	26 510	14 654	21 994	32 416	20 927	16 309	77.3	30.7	30.4	3.4	24.0	4.3	-8.0	10.7	13.5
Kent County	45 980	54 770	63 819	32 955	22 501	27 662	40 614	28 276	21 629	84.8	38.4	21.8	2.8	13.5	11.4	-0.9	8.4	9.2
Keweenaw County	28 140	36 758	37 917	25 000	20 750	16 895	28 224	22 241	16 769	66.9	44.6	40.6	3.7	28.2	4.7	-7.6	13.8	14.9
Lake County	26 622	32 086	39 632	22 188	12 227	15 288	30 474	22 328	14 457	63.5	25.9	41.3	6.3	26.0	3.6	-8.7	18.6	25.5
Lapeer County	51 717	57 817	65 866	36 667	24 083	27 443	48 517	27 249	21 462	84.0	36.9	22.9	1.9	20.2	13.8	1.5	5.5	5.0

STATE/ County code	MSA/PMSA/ NECMA code[1]	STATE County	High school graduates			College graduates		College graduates (percent)				
			Total population 25 years and over	Percent with a high school diploma or less	Percent with a high school diploma or more	Percent with a bachelor's degree or more	+/− U.S. percent with bachelor's degree or more	Non-Hispanic White	Black or African American	American Indian and Alaska Native	Asian, Hawaiian, and Pacific Islander	Hispanic or Latino[2]
			1	2	3	4	5	6	7	8	9	10
		MICHIGAN—Cont'd										
26 089	...	Leelanau County	14 785	35.7	90.7	31.4	7.0	32.5	0.0	7.3	33.3	10.9
26 091	0440	Lenawee County	64 311	55.1	83.4	16.3	-8.1	16.6	13.1	5.2	59.7	8.0
26 093	0440	Livingston County.........	101 381	36.9	91.4	28.2	3.8	28.2	15.1	10.8	52.4	26.5
26 095	...	Luce County	4 927	61.9	75.5	11.8	-12.6	13.4	0.0	10.4	100.0	0.0
26 097	...	Mackinac County..........	8 588	58.8	82.5	14.9	-9.5	16.9	0.0	3.6	33.3	9.5
26 099	2160	Macomb County	535 836	49.8	82.9	17.6	-6.8	17.1	15.2	11.5	44.2	17.9
26 101	...	Manistee County	17 298	58.0	81.4	14.2	-10.2	14.7	0.0	2.8	8.7	6.1
26 103	...	Marquette County.........	41 934	46.9	88.5	23.7	-0.7	24.2	6.3	8.3	21.0	14.7
26 105	...	Mason County	19 449	52.8	82.7	15.9	-8.5	16.4	5.0	5.3	30.6	3.2
26 107	...	Mecosta County	23 314	52.7	83.8	19.1	-5.3	19.0	14.3	11.2	82.4	15.5
26 109	...	Menominee County	17 342	62.9	83.5	11.0	-13.4	11.1	0.0	6.3	0.0	16.7
26 111	6960	Midland County	53 497	41.0	89.0	29.3	4.9	28.4	54.5	6.0	75.1	41.7
26 113	...	Missaukee County........	9 466	64.0	78.6	10.2	-14.2	10.2	0.0	0.0	30.8	5.4
26 115	2160	Monroe County	94 281	54.2	83.1	14.3	-10.1	14.4	6.6	3.9	40.2	11.1
26 117	...	Montcalm County	39 560	58.8	81.2	10.8	-13.6	11.0	6.3	4.0	23.6	4.6
26 119	...	Montmorency County	7 604	66.9	74.8	8.2	-16.2	8.3	0.0	9.5	0.0	5.7
26 121	3000	Muskegon County	108 661	52.4	83.1	13.9	-10.5	15.5	5.5	8.2	26.9	5.4
26 123	...	Newaygo County	30 329	61.7	78.7	11.4	-13.0	11.7	7.2	4.2	28.9	3.5
26 125	2160	Oakland County	007 910	32.8	80.3	38.2	13.8	37.9	30.2	17.2	72.6	25.8
26 127	...	Oceana County	17 134	59.6	79.8	12.6	-11.8	13.5	6.5	11.1	27.3	1.5
26 129	...	Ogemaw County	15 191	64.9	75.0	9.6	-14.8	9.5	0.0	4.3	60.7	3.4
26 131	...	Ontonagon County	5 899	59.7	83.8	13.0	-11.4	12.9	X	3.2	33.3	38.2
26 133	...	Osceola County	15 033	63.3	80.5	11.3	-13.1	11.2	14.3	17.9	36.0	7.9
26 135	...	Oscoda County	6 716	66.8	73.7	8.0	-16.4	8.0	42.9	0.0	100.0	0.0
26 137	...	Otsego County	15 468	50.9	85.5	17.4	-7.0	17.5	0.0	9.6	31.6	14.0
26 139	3000	Ottawa County	141 870	44.5	86.6	26.0	1.6	27.1	12.2	18.1	26.5	8.3
26 141	...	Presque Isle County......	10 463	61.3	77.0	11.5	-12.9	11.6	33.3	0.0	0.0	6.5
26 143	...	Roscommon County......	18 930	59.8	79.5	10.9	-13.5	10.9	20.0	9.9	25.4	7.1
26 145	6900	Saginaw County	105 190	54.0	81.0	16.0	-9.6	17.6	9.6	10.5	57.4	7.7
26 147	2160	St. Clair County	107 583	54.4	82.8	12.6	-11.8	12.7	8.3	8.6	39.1	5.3
26 149	...	St. Joseph County	39 807	59.7	78.6	12.7	-11.7	13.1	2.6	3.8	30.7	6.4
26 151	...	Sanilac County	29 197	64.2	79.7	10.0	-14.4	10.0	0.0	9.3	42.6	1.5
26 153	...	Schoolcraft County	6 272	64.5	79.4	11.3	-13.1	12.1	0.0	1.9	18.2	4.8
26 155	...	Shiawassee County	46 557	54.1	84.4	13.7	-10.7	13.8	22.6	5.2	51.4	8.2
26 157	...	Tuscola County	37 898	60.6	81.2	10.6	-13.8	10.7	8.9	0.6	43.0	3.3
26 159	3720	Van Buren County........	48 920	57.0	78.9	14.3	-10.1	15.6	4.3	5.8	26.2	4.1
26 161	0440	Washtenaw County.......	197 414	25.6	91.5	48.1	23.7	49.1	25.0	27.2	82.3	44.1
26 163	2160	Wayne County..............	1 305 288	53.7	77.0	17.2	-7.2	21.4	10.3	12.9	57.3	10.6
26 165	...	Wexford County	19 905	50.7	82.0	15.3	0.1	16.2	25.0	18.2	52.8	14.2
27 000	...	MINNESOTA	3 164 345	40.9	87.9	27.4	3.0	28.0	18.7	8.8	36.1	14.0
27 001	...	Aitkin County	11 263	59.2	80.4	11.3	-13.1	11.5	37.5	3.6	0.0	0.0
27 003	5120	Anoka County	187 122	41.4	91.0	21.3	-3.1	21.3	20.4	8.8	31.3	13.3
27 005	...	Becker County..............	19 834	51.7	82.9	16.7	-7.7	17.5	29.2	4.6	17.5	19.2
27 007	...	Beltrami County............	22 748	45.2	83.4	23.5	-0.9	26.4	45.6	4.5	31.4	11.5
27 009	6980	Benton County	20 789	49.9	84.9	17.2	-7.2	17.2	27.1	23.7	14.0	11.0
27 011	...	Big Stone County	4 050	61.1	79.0	11.4	-13.0	11.3	0.0	18.2	X	0.0
27 013	...	Blue Earth County.........	31 684	40.4	87.7	26.6	2.2	26.6	26.0	15.1	44.1	20.1
27 015	...	Brown County...............	17 485	56.8	81.7	16.5	-7.9	16.7	0.0	3.7	43.5	4.6
27 017	...	Carlton County	21 238	53.1	84.3	14.9	-9.5	15.3	1.0	12.4	11.9	7.6
27 019	5120	Carver County	43 218	35.3	91.4	34.3	9.9	34.8	37.0	14.1	40.1	9.7
27 021	...	Cass County................	18 721	52.5	83.9	16.6	-7.8	17.4	100.0	6.4	14.0	11.3
27 023	...	Chippewa County	8 819	56.0	81.6	13.7	-10.7	13.8	50.0	3.2	14.3	11.0
27 025	5120	Chisago County............	25 859	48.4	88.7	15.3	-9.1	15.4	7.8	9.4	19.8	11.3
27 027	2520	Clay County.................	29 580	41.5	86.7	24.7	0.3	25.5	29.3	4.4	23.3	6.6
27 029	...	Clearwater County	5 576	59.0	76.4	14.7	-9.7	15.4	X	6.5	38.5	0.0
27 031	...	Cook County	3 864	39.9	88.7	28.8	4.4	30.8	0.0	6.4	0.0	66.7
27 033	...	Cottonwood County.......	8 344	56.8	80.4	14.2	-10.2	14.1	0.0	100.0	32.9	7.7
27 035	...	Crow Wing County	37 092	47.2	86.3	18.4	-6.0	18.4	13.9	10.2	54.5	24.8
27 037	5120	Dakota County	224 313	30.3	93.2	34.9	10.5	35.4	30.9	11.2	42.0	13.7
27 039	...	Dodge County	10 989	49.2	86.7	17.1	-7.3	17.2	0.0	20.0	38.1	7.1
27 041	...	Douglas County............	21 961	47.5	85.6	17.3	-7.1	17.4	0.0	28.1	17.5	23.6
27 043	...	Faribault County	11 128	57.2	83.6	13.8	-10.6	14.0	66.7	0.0	3.6	4.8
27 045	...	Fillmore County	14 116	55.2	81.7	15.1	-9.3	15.0	0.0	0.0	42.1	17.4
27 047	...	Freeborn County	22 363	56.5	81.2	12.8	-11.6	13.2	4.9	0.0	23.9	3.7
27 049	...	Goodhue County	29 127	49.8	86.7	19.1	-5.3	19.3	19.4	5.6	22.5	7.7

[1]MSA = Metropolitan Statistical Area. PMSA = Primary MSA. NECMA = New England County Metropolitan Area. See the Appendix A for explanation of these concepts. See Appendix B for list of metropolitan areas identified by type, with component counties.
[2]Hispanic or Latino persons may be of any race.

Table B-3. States and Counties — Education, Labor Force, and Income

STATE County	School enrollment			Population 16 to 19 years				Employment status, 2000			Work status in 1999 of the population 16 years and over (percent)		
											Worked in 1999		
	Grades kindergarten through 12	College or graduate school	Percent private	Number	Percent in armed forces	Percent high school graduates	Percent not enrolled, not grads, not in armed forces, not employed	Total population 16 years and over	Percent in labor force	Unemployment rate	Full-time	Part-time	Did not work in 1999
	11	12	13	14	15	16	17	18	19	20	21	22	23
MICHIGAN—Cont'd													
Leelanau County	4 165	769	13.1	1 082	0.0	6.7	1.2	16 599	63.1	5.0	52.6	18.8	28.6
Lenawee County	20 161	4 573	14.3	5 962	0.0	10.0	2.9	76 323	64.5	4.7	56.0	15.2	28.8
Livingston County	34 074	7 127	9.7	8 764	0.0	8.1	4.5	116 890	71.7	3.3	59.4	17.7	22.9
Luce County	1 391	147	10.6	377	0.0	8.5	16.7	5 745	45.3	8.7	41.3	13.2	45.6
Mackinac County	2 148	246	3.4	592	0.5	9.6	7.6	9 626	58.1	14.7	50.7	14.0	35.3
Macomb County	141 959	45 059	12.4	37 980	0.1	9.5	3.5	618 864	66.0	4.1	55.8	15.4	28.8
Manistee County	4 633	651	11.5	1 350	0.0	9.2	5.9	19 713	56.0	6.5	46.3	16.2	37.5
Marquette County	11 017	6 988	4.7	4 651	0.0	8.8	2.0	52 694	62.1	6.2	47.2	22.7	30.0
Mason County	5 450	965	7.5	1 587	0.3	8.1	4.2	22 278	61.4	7.3	49.9	17.0	33.1
Mecosta County	6 865	7 024	5.3	3 794	0.2	5.3	2.7	32 489	60.9	11.6	47.6	21.9	30.6
Menominee County	4 709	831	6.9	1 422	0.1	12.1	3.0	20 023	62.3	5.1	49.7	17.3	33.0
Midland County	17 269	5 050	12.4	4 905	0.0	7.7	2.4	63 149	64.8	5.1	51.5	18.7	29.8
Missaukee County	3 056	369	11.5	866	0.0	9.4	3.6	11 027	61.1	6.5	49.4	17.1	33.5
Monroe County	30 708	6 669	12.2	8 547	0.0	10.3	4.0	110 933	65.8	3.5	55.0	15.9	29.1
Montcalm County	12 865	1 937	8.7	3 461	0.0	8.4	7.7	46 659	60.3	5.5	52.0	15.3	32.7
Montmorency County	1 700	186	5.6	491	0.0	11.4	3.9	8 505	45.3	12.4	37.9	13.1	49.0
Muskegon County	36 265	7 581	8.9	9 731	0.0	9.6	5.5	128 751	63.1	5.4	52.0	16.5	31.5
Newaygo County	10 726	1 354	9.0	2 708	0.0	13.0	5.6	35 458	61.6	5.8	52.0	15.1	32.9
Oakland County	225 089	76 393	15.0	57 371	0.0	7.1	2.6	926 468	68.9	3.7	58.8	15.8	25.5
Oceana County	5 974	734	7.0	1 736	1.2	9.6	7.0	20 318	60.9	7.9	52.1	15.9	32.0
Ogemaw County	4 137	611	8.2	1 151	0.0	7.5	5.2	17 212	52.2	8.5	42.1	15.0	42.9
Ontonagon County	1 281	186	2.8	347	0.3	5.2	4.3	6 469	54.2	9.6	44.9	15.4	39.6
Osceola County	4 933	652	8.8	1 443	0.0	12.8	4.3	17 711	60.5	6.6	50.9	14.4	34.7
Oscoda County	1 704	221	9.2	485	0.0	5.2	6.8	7 528	48.0	8.8	38.5	13.8	47.7
Otsego County	4 899	534	15.1	1 223	0.0	8.9	1.6	17 800	64.9	5.6	55.1	16.4	28.5
Ottawa County	51 323	18 166	20.7	16 429	0.0	8.9	1.9	177 134	72.5	4.0	56.3	22.1	21.6
Presque Isle County	2 388	443	11.8	806	0.0	8.8	4.7	11 840	51.3	10.9	42.1	14.6	43.3
Roscommon County	4 212	763	7.9	1 180	0.0	9.2	4.2	21 040	46.9	8.8	38.2	14.0	47.7
Saginaw County	43 311	11 612	10.8	11 932	0.1	7.7	6.4	160 074	61.6	7.6	49.1	17.6	33.3
St. Clair County	33 310	6 578	9.2	9 089	0.0	10.4	5.2	125 544	65.6	5.2	54.6	16.5	28.9
St. Joseph County	12 532	1 819	9.1	3 779	0.4	9.9	7.2	47 426	66.0	4.6	57.5	14.3	28.2
Sanilac County	9 257	1 231	6.4	2 566	0.2	9.4	3.4	34 067	61.1	6.0	51.6	15.0	33.4
Schoolcraft County	1 618	144	11.0	386	0.0	13.2	7.8	7 089	52.9	12.4	44.5	16.8	38.7
Shiawassee County	14 847	2 940	10.2	4 146	0.0	8.9	3.6	54 666	66.2	5.4	54.5	16.5	29.0
Tuscola County	12 490	2 369	11.2	3 616	0.0	6.4	5.8	44 638	61.7	6.2	51.8	15.6	32.6
Van Buren County	16 500	2 430	7.4	4 696	0.0	9.5	5.8	57 485	65.8	5.8	55.3	15.1	29.6
Washtenaw County	51 410	60 032	8.2	23 697	0.0	5.2	2.0	259 162	69.2	3.8	56.8	22.1	21.1
Wayne County	438 464	110 846	13.0	108 591	0.0	11.4	7.6	1 541 459	60.4	8.5	51.6	13.5	34.9
Wexford County	6 305	914	8.7	1 908	0.1	10.5	5.6	23 381	64.0	6.9	52.1	16.7	31.2
MINNESOTA	975 733	296 258	14.3	293 223	0.1	8.5	2.8	3 781 756	71.2	4.1	57.9	19.2	22.9
Aitkin County	2 584	349	3.1	789	0.0	8.7	2.2	12 551	53.9	7.7	43.0	17.6	39.4
Anoka County	64 379	13 340	10.6	16 477	0.0	9.6	3.4	221 006	77.3	3.3	64.9	17.9	17.1
Becker County	6 313	784	4.5	1 887	0.0	9.2	4.9	23 078	64.0	6.3	52.2	18.3	29.5
Beltrami County	8 628	3 916	6.7	3 157	0.0	5.9	5.8	29 650	65.9	7.5	51.3	20.8	27.9
Benton County	7 027	2 068	11.9	2 105	0.8	15.5	1.3	26 071	75.2	3.4	60.6	19.6	19.8
Big Stone County	1 200	113	4.6	364	0.0	1.6	9.3	4 612	57.6	5.3	44.1	19.9	36.0
Blue Earth County	9 039	10 105	9.9	5 277	0.0	5.7	0.7	45 506	72.6	4.6	52.9	27.5	19.6
Brown County	5 538	1 418	37.0	1 820	0.0	7.3	0.4	21 055	69.5	5.4	54.6	21.0	24.4
Carlton County	6 397	1 582	8.0	1 856	0.0	8.6	2.5	24 710	61.8	5.8	49.4	19.3	31.3
Carver County	16 043	2 867	21.4	3 635	0.0	9.3	0.6	50 082	78.0	3.2	64.5	18.9	16.6
Cass County	5 583	582	4.3	1 495	0.0	9.7	3.9	21 223	59.0	6.8	49.2	16.0	34.8
Chippewa County	2 643	263	5.0	777	0.0	9.1	3.0	10 219	65.6	5.5	52.7	18.8	28.5
Chisago County	9 221	1 228	7.2	2 258	0.0	8.4	3.7	30 084	72.6	3.4	59.2	19.3	21.5
Clay County	9 873	7 152	19.2	4 649	0.0	5.2	2.0	39 877	68.5	5.2	54.1	23.2	22.8
Clearwater County	1 734	202	4.0	565	0.0	10.4	4.6	6 539	61.0	10.3	50.7	16.7	32.7
Cook County	826	71	5.5	210	0.0	14.8	0.0	4 252	66.9	6.2	56.1	19.1	24.8
Cottonwood County	2 391	287	9.0	686	0.0	8.6	2.8	9 521	64.1	3.8	49.4	19.3	31.2
Crow Wing County	10 486	1 951	6.0	3 131	0.0	11.3	3.6	43 106	63.3	5.5	50.0	18.9	31.0
Dakota County	76 682	17 197	13.4	19 283	0.2	8.8	1.8	263 505	78.4	2.6	64.9	18.5	16.6
Dodge County	4 102	525	5.1	1 207	0.0	7.7	2.9	13 073	74.3	3.5	60.4	18.7	20.9
Douglas County	6 271	1 348	8.6	2 089	0.0	7.5	1.5	25 976	66.1	3.9	51.1	20.8	28.1
Faribault County	3 224	369	7.6	973	0.0	7.6	2.0	12 798	63.4	4.6	50.9	18.7	30.4
Fillmore County	4 306	493	8.6	1 294	0.0	6.6	4.7	16 361	68.4	3.5	53.9	19.0	27.2
Freeborn County	6 153	789	6.4	1 850	0.0	9.0	5.9	25 812	64.9	4.3	53.4	17.4	29.3
Goodhue County	9 219	1 302	7.9	2 867	0.0	10.6	2.8	34 075	70.8	3.1	56.8	19.2	24.0

Table B-3. States and Counties — Education, Labor Force, and Income

STATE County	Full-year full-time employed (percent)								Children under 18 years in families						Total employed by class of worker (percent)			
										With two parents (percent)		With one parent who is in labor force (percent)	+/– U.S. percent of children with no stay-at-home parent (percent)	+/– U.S. percent two-income couples				
	Total	Men	Women	Non-Hispanic White	Black or African American	American Indian and Alaska Native	Asian, Hawaiian, and Pacific Islander	Hispanic or Latino[1]	Number	Both in labor force	Father only in labor force				Private	Government	Self-employed	Unpaid family worker
	24	25	26	27	28	29	30	31	32	33	34	35	36	37	38	39	40	41
MICHIGAN—Cont'd																		
Leelanau County	38.3	47.1	29.7	38.1	33.3	50.5	32.7	25.8	4 954	58.1	19.5	16.1	9.6	-0.4	68.6	12.9	18.1	0.3
Lenawee County	41.9	52.4	31.5	42.7	21.7	33.3	28.9	39.1	24 284	51.3	21.3	20.1	6.8	2.5	80.2	10.6	9.0	0.2
Livingston County	47.5	61.8	33.3	47.8	21.8	51.4	42.4	45.9	43 762	52.7	29.7	11.9	0.0	6.1	79.5	9.7	10.5	0.3
Luce County	27.9	30.0	25.0	30.5	9.2	30.7	0.0	18.4	1 426	47.3	18.8	19.6	2.3	-11.1	59.8	28.1	11.7	0.3
Mackinac County	29.3	36.4	22.3	29.1	66.7	28.7	35.7	35.4	2 572	51.6	18.3	21.3	8.3	-12.7	58.6	24.7	15.9	0.7
Macomb County	43.9	57.1	31.5	43.9	44.5	43.7	43.3	44.0	183 996	47.1	28.3	16.7	-0.8	-0.9	84.6	8.2	7.0	0.2
Manistee County	33.7	40.8	26.5	34.1	7.5	38.6	12.7	45.1	5 181	52.6	17.3	22.1	10.1	-5.9	72.1	14.0	13.5	0.4
Marquette County	32.7	40.0	25.4	33.2	10.4	28.7	32.9	23.2	13 295	53.5	18.4	20.7	9.6	1.0	73.6	18.0	8.2	0.2
Mason County	35.2	44.7	26.1	35.2	31.2	41.5	51.1	30.1	6 552	49.6	18.0	23.8	8.8	-2.9	73.8	14.0	11.7	0.5
Mecosta County	29.6	34.3	24.8	30.8	11.8	23.0	10.0	22.8	8 652	45.6	20.2	21.7	2.7	-7.3	69.5	19.8	10.0	0.7
Menominee County	37.2	47.2	27.3	37.2	29.4	38.2	42.1	29.6	5 885	52.1	17.1	23.1	10.6	1.2	78.4	11.2	9.9	0.6
Midland County	40.1	51.6	29.4	40.2	37.1	35.0	46.9	34.0	21 580	50.3	27.4	16.5	2.2	-0.9	81.2	10.2	8.4	0.3
Missaukee County	35.3	46.2	24.5	35.2	40.0	47.5	51.5	24.7	3 732	53.2	21.2	16.8	5.4	-4.2	73.6	10.0	15.9	0.5
Monroe County	43.4	56.8	30.5	43.8	37.9	24.0	31.7	38.4	38 168	49.4	25.6	17.1	1.9	0.9	83.7	8.9	7.2	0.3
Montcalm County	38.0	46.7	28.8	39.1	7.9	35.1	43.5	29.3	15 769	48.7	22.5	20.5	4.6	-1.6	78.8	10.4	10.5	0.3
Montmorency County	24.4	30.5	18.7	24.4	22.2	19.2	33.3	25.0	2 001	40.0	25.1	19.8	-4.8	-21.6	68.9	16.7	13.7	0.7
Muskegon County	39.3	48.5	30.5	41.2	28.9	37.7	36.8	34.7	44 296	46.0	15.6	27.9	9.3	2.8	82.4	9.7	7.7	0.2
Newaygo County	37.4	47.2	27.7	37.7	20.6	34.4	29.6	33.6	13 184	47.6	22.7	18.8	1.8	-3.6	77.4	11.4	10.7	0.5
Oakland County	46.0	59.4	33.6	46.2	46.0	46.8	46.1	42.1	290 073	46.2	29.9	16.1	-2.3	2.2	81.1	8.7	9.9	0.2
Oceana County	34.0	42.5	25.4	34.9	12.1	30.6	20.7	27.2	6 981	48.0	18.2	20.0	3.4	-4.8	74.2	13.1	12.2	0.4
Ogemaw County	29.9	36.9	23.2	30.0	50.0	48.0	26.2	23.4	4 855	50.9	17.8	20.2	6.5	-13.8	72.5	13.0	13.5	1.0
Ontonagon County	29.9	35.0	24.7	30.1	X	35.3	22.2	20.0	1 492	55.9	14.7	17.9	9.2	-9.0	68.4	19.0	11.8	0.9
Osceola County	37.2	46.2	28.6	37.3	34.9	37.9	21.3	35.0	5 845	47.7	21.5	21.3	4.4	-4.1	75.0	12.2	12.2	0.6
Oscoda County	26.5	35.4	18.2	26.4	57.1	33.3	100.0	34.4	2 113	40.7	26.6	20.1	-3.8	-20.6	70.7	12.9	15.3	1.2
Otsego County	41.1	51.2	31.2	41.2	31.0	48.2	25.7	50.0	6 055	54.3	21.2	16.5	6.2	-0.6	75.7	11.0	12.9	0.4
Ottawa County	43.7	59.1	29.2	43.8	34.3	47.1	47.1	43.5	66 227	57.2	24.8	12.6	5.2	9.9	83.3	8.1	8.3	0.3
Presque Isle County	27.9	34.5	21.5	28.1	0.0	8.5	40.0	30.0	2 886	52.4	20.9	16.4	4.2	-13.0	73.6	11.0	14.8	0.6
Roscommon County	25.7	30.7	20.9	25.7	4.3	9.3	37.3	43.4	4 742	47.4	16.2	25.0	7.8	-20.4	69.9	15.8	13.8	0.5
Saginaw County	38.5	45.8	28.2	38.7	27.2	30.2	33.0	35.7	52 850	41.5	18.4	29.1	0.0	-2.7	80.5	11.0	7.0	0.3
St. Clair County	41.3	53.9	29.3	41.5	33.2	39.3	32.9	39.6	41 711	45.2	27.6	19.6	0.2	-1.4	81.7	9.4	8.5	0.4
St. Joseph County	42.8	53.4	32.5	43.4	27.3	37.9	47.2	34.8	16 036	43.4	21.9	24.8	3.6	2.8	81.4	8.6	9.5	0.4
Sanilac County	37.6	47.4	28.3	37.8	7.0	25.9	36.0	34.2	11 421	50.1	24.4	16.8	2.3	-3.5	73.9	10.4	15.0	0.7
Schoolcraft County	31.0	40.2	22.0	30.4	50.4	33.8	45.5	44.2	1 922	49.7	18.7	22.8	7.9	-14.8	64.9	21.3	13.5	0.3
Shiawassee County	40.7	52.3	29.7	40.6	53.6	40.8	33.7	45.8	18 496	49.9	21.6	21.6	6.9	0.5	78.5	11.6	9.5	0.4
Tuscola County	37.5	46.6	28.6	38.1	10.2	35.9	43.4	29.5	14 747	51.8	21.0	19.0	6.2	-2.7	77.8	11.8	10.0	0.4
Van Buren County	41.1	51.4	31.2	42.4	30.5	26.4	31.3	34.1	19 666	49.7	18.5	21.6	6.7	2.0	80.2	10.6	8.7	0.4
Washtenaw County	40.7	49.8	31.9	42.5	37.4	37.5	29.0	32.2	67 995	48.8	23.4	19.4	3.0	7.3	70.0	10.0	0.0	0.3
Wayne County	36.7	45.0	29.4	41.1	31.3	35.2	39.6	31.8	530 026	30.7	18.3	32.2	-1.7	-5.4	81.8	12.2	5.8	0.2
Wexford County	38.6	48.3	29.6	38.7	50.0	26.4	43.0	44.5	7 760	48.6	20.3	23.7	7.7	-1.7	77.6	11.2	10.9	0.3
MINNESOTA	44.7	54.6	35.2	45.5	37.1	34.1	38.5	37.8	1 239 179	57.3	16.9	17.7	10.4	11.0	77.1	12.4	10.2	0.3
Aitkin County	29.8	36.3	23.3	29.6	21.4	38.0	51.4	35.2	3 025	54.6	17.6	16.9	6.9	-10.8	64.9	15.1	19.5	0.5
Anoka County	53.1	64.1	42.2	53.6	42.8	46.2	48.3	42.3	83 339	60.0	16.3	17.0	12.4	17.3	80.9	11.1	7.8	0.2
Becker County	36.5	45.6	27.5	37.0	16.7	31.7	21.2	46.9	7 666	57.2	16.1	18.0	10.6	3.2	66.1	16.9	16.4	0.6
Beltrami County	33.3	40.7	26.2	33.9	42.6	31.8	21.4	25.5	10 290	46.7	15.2	24.8	6.9	4.6	63.2	24.8	11.5	0.5
Benton County	47.4	56.4	38.7	47.7	39.8	23.9	43.1	38.9	8 961	64.9	11.9	17.6	17.9	16.0	78.5	12.0	9.0	0.5
Big Stone County	32.0	43.0	22.0	32.2	0.0	8.7	X	0.0	1 427	60.9	16.3	13.5	9.8	1.0	57.9	16.9	24.6	0.6
Blue Earth County	38.4	46.4	30.5	39.1	19.1	36.5	11.1	48.6	11 560	60.9	12.7	18.8	15.1	12.7	76.3	14.0	9.3	0.4
Brown County	41.4	52.3	31.0	41.5	59.6	23.2	50.0	29.6	6 636	70.1	10.4	13.7	19.2	11.9	76.3	9.5	13.7	0.5
Carlton County	36.1	44.9	27.2	36.5	6.4	39.9	30.7	10.8	7 689	59.6	15.1	18.4	13.4	4.0	71.8	19.4	8.4	0.3
Carver County	53.9	68.8	39.2	54.0	53.2	43.9	60.7	44.6	21 755	61.3	23.1	11.2	7.9	16.3	79.3	9.2	11.2	0.3
Cass County	33.9	39.9	27.9	34.1	26.3	32.2	33.3	52.1	6 334	49.9	15.7	22.0	7.3	-4.2	61.2	19.8	18.5	0.5
Chippewa County	38.0	48.2	28.6	38.2	50.0	38.9	14.3	28.0	3 216	68.4	10.8	15.5	19.3	10.1	67.4	15.4	16.4	0.8
Chisago County	46.5	58.4	34.3	46.9	33.1	24.5	29.6	32.9	11 844	59.7	16.6	17.7	12.8	12.0	76.4	13.2	10.1	0.3
Clay County	37.3	46.2	29.3	38.0	20.2	25.6	24.4	29.7	12 420	60.1	13.7	20.2	15.7	11.4	73.4	16.4	9.9	0.3
Clearwater County	31.6	38.3	24.9	31.9	X	27.2	26.3	16.0	2 091	52.6	19.6	18.6	6.6	-3.1	60.5	22.1	16.9	0.5
Cook County	38.5	45.6	31.4	37.7	40.0	45.6	41.7	5.6	1 000	57.9	16.7	20.2	13.5	0.2	54.7	24.3	20.5	0.5
Cottonwood County	34.5	46.2	23.8	34.6	0.0		40.9	27.1	2 943	63.7	16.3	15.1	14.2	6.4	69.1	12.2	17.9	0.8
Crow Wing County	37.3	46.7	28.3	37.3	23.7	30.0	46.6	48.2	13 031	56.6	15.9	20.9	12.9	1.7	71.2	15.2	13.2	0.4
Dakota County	53.3	65.2	42.0	53.0	50.8	41.1	48.0	46.5	101 073	60.6	18.6	16.6	11.5	17.3	81.1	11.4	7.4	0.2
Dodge County	47.6	58.0	37.5	48.1	29.4	23.5	43.3	34.3	5 179	69.4	11.2	15.5	20.3	17.0	76.9	10.0	12.4	0.7
Douglas County	38.4	49.0	28.1	38.6	6.1	23.1	35.8	29.7	7 662	64.7	15.4	14.1	14.2	4.9	70.0	12.8	16.7	0.6
Faribault County	37.7	47.6	28.2	38.2	28.6	6.3	28.6	29.6	3 756	65.7	13.8	14.1	15.2	7.1	70.6	10.1	18.7	0.6
Fillmore County	41.4	50.6	32.7	41.5	10.5	35.7	26.3	34.9	5 370	66.0	15.3	13.9	15.3	12.8	68.3	11.1	19.4	1.2
Freeborn County	41.5	51.6	31.9	41.8	19.6	15.0	34.0	37.3	7 421	60.3	11.9	19.1	14.8	6.8	77.9	9.3	12.2	0.6
Goodhue County	45.0	56.4	34.2	45.3	40.3	21.8	57.8	42.6	11 211	65.8	14.6	15.4	16.6	14.0	75.8	10.6	13.1	0.4

[1] Hispanic or Latino persons may be of any race.

STATE County	Percent who worked at home	Percent of the population 5 years and over with a disability	Veterans as a percent of the population 18 years and over	Occupation for employed population 16 years and over (percent)						Industry for employed population 16 years and over (percent)					
				Management, professional, and related occupations	Service occupations	Sales and office occupations	Farming, fishing, and forestry occupations	Construction, extraction, and maintenance occupations	Production, transportation and material moving occupations	Agriculture, forestry, fishing, and mining	Construction and manufacturing	Wholesale and retail trade	Transportation and warehousing, and utilities	Service industries	Public administration
	42	43	44	45	46	47	48	49	50	51	52	53	54	55	56
MICHIGAN—Cont'd															
Leelanau County	7.0	15.6	16.4	35.1	15.7	24.6	1.4	12.2	11.0	3.3	21.4	13.7	2.7	54.7	4.3
Lenawee County	3.1	18.9	13.3	25.3	14.8	24.4	0.5	10.1	24.8	1.7	35.0	14.3	3.4	41.8	3.7
Livingston County	3.4	12.9	12.0	36.8	11.8	26.0	0.2	11.3	13.9	0.6	32.5	16.2	3.1	44.7	2.9
Luce County	6.3	24.1	16.6	24.5	29.3	22.7	2.4	9.8	11.4	3.9	14.2	13.4	4.2	49.3	15.0
Mackinac County	5.1	22.8	16.6	26.0	22.6	23.6	1.8	15.4	10.6	3.4	16.5	13.4	6.0	49.8	10.9
Macomb County	1.7	17.4	12.6	30.9	13.1	28.3	0.1	9.9	17.7	0.2	32.8	16.3	3.2	44.5	3.0
Manistee County	5.2	21.4	17.2	23.5	22.2	22.1	1.1	12.3	18.7	3.0	26.9	13.8	3.7	46.7	5.8
Marquette County	2.3	15.6	16.3	29.3	20.6	26.6	0.3	11.8	11.3	5.3	11.9	15.8	5.2	55.7	6.1
Mason County	4.6	20.2	16.9	28.5	16.5	22.4	1.5	10.8	20.2	3.0	30.3	14.2	4.2	43.8	4.6
Mecosta County	4.9	18.3	13.1	27.3	17.9	24.1	0.9	9.7	20.0	2.5	23.4	14.8	4.2	52.3	2.9
Menominee County	3.3	19.0	16.8	21.3	16.1	19.8	1.9	9.7	31.3	3.6	38.6	12.6	5.3	36.3	3.5
Midland County	3.2	15.1	12.8	37.4	15.9	23.3	0.2	10.0	13.2	0.6	33.4	12.7	2.9	47.8	2.5
Missaukee County	5.6	20.7	15.1	22.5	14.9	22.3	3.6	12.5	24.2	7.9	30.9	16.3	4.4	37.8	2.8
Monroe County	1.8	17.8	13.6	24.8	13.9	23.6	0.6	12.9	24.1	1.3	33.4	15.3	7.3	40.5	2.3
Montcalm County	4.1	20.1	13.6	22.0	14.5	22.1	1.3	11.8	28.2	3.3	37.3	14.9	3.4	37.4	3.8
Montmorency County	5.2	26.7	18.7	21.5	19.9	23.2	1.7	13.2	20.6	5.3	24.7	13.9	4.2	44.7	7.1
Muskegon County	2.7	22.3	14.3	24.3	15.6	25.0	0.5	8.8	25.8	0.7	36.3	15.9	2.9	40.6	3.6
Newaygo County	3.9	20.3	15.0	22.7	14.5	21.9	1.7	13.3	25.9	3.7	36.0	14.3	4.1	38.6	3.2
Oakland County	2.9	14.8	10.7	44.6	10.7	26.8	0.1	6.9	10.9	0.1	27.1	15.8	2.7	51.8	2.5
Oceana County	4.9	21.4	15.6	23.8	15.3	18.9	3.8	11.7	26.6	6.7	35.8	12.1	3.3	38.0	4.2
Ogemaw County	4.9	25.1	17.7	24.0	20.3	23.6	1.6	11.7	18.9	4.4	21.5	19.0	4.5	45.8	4.8
Ontonagon County	5.3	21.6	21.5	23.8	23.3	21.0	2.2	11.7	18.0	6.9	22.1	12.3	4.5	48.8	5.4
Osceola County	4.8	21.8	15.8	23.0	14.3	19.5	1.6	10.7	30.8	3.8	37.8	13.6	4.2	36.9	3.6
Oscoda County	5.2	26.1	19.4	21.3	19.2	21.5	2.0	12.2	23.9	3.7	29.5	15.3	3.5	43.9	4.1
Otsego County	4.6	17.0	15.3	27.5	16.5	26.6	0.4	11.6	17.4	4.8	23.9	18.3	4.8	44.2	4.0
Ottawa County	3.1	13.3	10.5	31.8	12.8	24.7	1.0	8.0	21.7	1.6	35.2	16.2	3.3	41.6	2.1
Presque Isle County	5.3	22.0	18.5	25.7	17.6	23.4	2.4	14.0	17.1	9.7	19.6	15.8	5.6	45.1	4.1
Roscommon County	3.5	25.2	19.5	27.3	19.5	27.3	0.4	11.8	13.8	1.1	19.0	21.1	3.6	48.8	6.5
Saginaw County	2.9	20.3	12.8	27.3	17.9	27.1	0.4	9.3	18.0	0.9	26.1	17.2	3.4	49.1	3.2
St. Clair County	2.6	18.3	13.9	24.0	14.6	23.4	0.3	12.9	24.8	0.9	36.3	14.5	5.5	39.4	3.4
St. Joseph County	3.8	18.8	13.4	22.1	12.4	20.3	0.9	10.1	34.3	2.5	47.5	12.3	2.7	32.9	2.1
Sanilac County	6.2	19.9	13.0	24.8	13.7	20.5	2.2	11.9	26.9	7.9	35.4	14.7	3.6	35.2	3.2
Schoolcraft County	5.2	21.0	18.0	24.3	23.1	20.3	2.5	14.1	15.6	7.6	18.5	13.2	4.1	48.7	7.9
Shiawassee County	3.7	17.7	13.6	25.2	14.9	22.5	0.9	12.1	24.5	2.3	33.6	14.3	3.9	41.7	4.1
Tuscola County	3.5	18.9	13.5	23.1	15.8	21.2	0.9	13.1	25.7	3.1	33.9	15.6	4.1	40.3	3.1
Van Buren County	2.5	21.5	14.3	25.4	15.1	21.7	1.9	11.4	24.6	3.8	34.1	14.2	5.5	40.0	2.5
Washtenaw County	3.5	13.4	8.6	48.3	13.4	22.6	0.3	5.6	9.7	0.6	19.4	12.0	3.4	62.1	2.5
Wayne County	1.8	23.0	11.6	28.1	16.7	26.8	0.1	8.7	19.6	0.1	26.5	13.8	6.4	49.2	4.0
Wexford County	3.7	20.4	14.9	25.5	15.7	23.5	0.7	9.1	25.5	2.2	32.4	16.7	4.2	41.1	3.3
MINNESOTA	4.6	15.0	12.8	35.8	13.7	26.5	0.7	8.4	14.9	2.6	22.2	15.5	5.1	51.2	3.4
Aitkin County	8.0	21.7	20.3	26.1	19.2	23.2	1.7	12.4	17.4	5.2	23.4	12.8	4.8	48.8	4.9
Anoka County	3.2	13.6	13.4	32.2	11.9	28.3	0.1	10.4	17.1	0.3	28.6	16.7	5.7	45.4	3.3
Becker County	7.1	17.4	16.4	29.3	16.8	22.1	2.3	12.2	17.4	6.6	22.6	15.5	6.2	44.8	4.4
Beltrami County	5.1	17.6	14.2	32.5	18.9	23.6	1.6	9.7	13.7	3.8	16.4	14.7	3.7	55.5	5.9
Benton County	4.4	15.7	12.8	25.8	13.4	27.3	0.9	10.6	22.0	3.5	27.3	20.4	5.0	40.6	3.2
Big Stone County	9.5	18.8	13.6	33.8	17.6	20.8	2.1	11.3	14.4	13.4	13.1	15.7	6.2	47.0	4.6
Blue Earth County	4.4	13.7	11.3	29.8	16.5	27.2	0.8	7.8	17.8	3.6	23.6	16.8	3.7	49.8	2.4
Brown County	7.2	14.9	13.3	28.4	15.1	22.1	1.9	9.1	23.4	7.5	29.2	13.4	4.9	42.3	2.8
Carlton County	3.7	16.9	15.7	27.1	19.2	22.3	1.3	11.5	18.7	2.3	22.9	13.1	6.1	49.3	6.3
Carver County	5.5	11.0	10.3	40.7	11.3	26.6	0.4	7.9	13.0	1.7	27.1	16.7	4.1	47.9	2.5
Cass County	6.8	20.4	20.2	27.8	18.3	25.2	1.6	12.7	14.5	4.2	19.3	16.4	4.0	50.1	6.0
Chippewa County	8.1	16.4	12.5	30.5	16.4	21.7	1.9	10.9	18.5	8.8	26.0	13.9	4.8	42.9	3.7
Chisago County	4.2	14.4	14.6	28.9	13.8	25.1	0.5	12.7	19.0	1.7	29.1	15.8	5.4	43.0	5.0
Clay County	3.8	15.3	12.3	31.9	17.4	27.9	0.7	9.5	12.7	3.1	15.4	17.3	4.1	56.8	3.3
Clearwater County	6.3	19.0	16.7	31.1	17.5	18.3	3.5	14.4	15.2	8.3	21.6	13.2	6.0	45.6	5.3
Cook County	7.5	13.9	17.0	32.7	21.0	21.1	1.8	13.3	10.0	3.8	17.2	13.8	6.0	51.8	7.4
Cottonwood County	9.0	15.5	12.3	30.6	17.2	21.1	2.1	8.4	20.6	11.6	24.2	15.4	4.5	41.4	2.9
Crow Wing County	4.5	18.4	16.7	29.4	17.6	26.3	0.4	10.8	15.5	1.1	21.5	17.1	3.7	52.3	4.3
Dakota County	3.6	12.7	12.6	39.5	11.6	29.8	0.2	7.9	11.0	0.6	19.2	15.9	8.8	51.9	3.5
Dodge County	6.3	12.4	12.9	32.2	13.4	23.8	2.1	11.0	17.5	7.7	26.6	14.1	3.9	45.0	2.7
Douglas County	7.6	18.4	14.9	29.6	14.8	25.2	1.1	9.9	19.5	5.0	25.7	17.8	4.2	44.9	2.5
Faribault County	8.2	18.2	14.2	29.7	14.4	21.8	2.8	10.8	20.6	11.6	26.7	13.4	5.2	40.3	2.8
Fillmore County	11.3	17.2	13.0	32.1	15.1	21.6	3.5	10.5	17.1	13.0	22.3	13.1	4.8	43.5	3.3
Freeborn County	5.3	18.9	14.9	25.8	16.1	22.7	1.4	8.4	25.5	5.2	31.4	15.4	4.1	40.5	3.3
Goodhue County	5.5	15.0	13.8	29.5	14.9	23.6	1.7	10.4	19.8	5.5	26.2	14.3	6.3	44.6	3.2

STATE County	Median house-hold income	Median family income				Median nonfamily house-hold income	Median income for full-year, full-time workers		Per capita income	Households by source of income (percent)					House-holds with income over $100,000 (percent)	+/- U.S. percent for income over $100,000	House-holds with income below poverty (percent)	Families with children with income below poverty (percent)
		All families	Families with children				Men	Women		With earnings	With interest, dividend, or rental income	With Social Security income	With public assis-tance income	With retire-ment income				
			Married-couple	Male house-holder	Female house-holder													
	57	58	59	60	61	62	63	64	65	66	67	68	69	70	71	72	73	74

MICHIGAN—Cont'd

STATE County	57	58	59	60	61	62	63	64	65	66	67	68	69	70	71	72	73	74
Leelanau County	47 062	53 228	57 740	36 429	26 103	26 782	37 981	26 743	24 686	78.3	52.9	32.8	1.5	23.4	11.9	-0.4	5.5	5.9
Lenawee County	45 739	53 661	60 733	35 438	22 603	23 908	39 956	26 465	20 186	80.7	36.8	28.5	2.6	21.0	9.8	-2.5	6.9	6.4
Livingston County	67 400	75 284	80 168	44 355	28 626	36 733	55 879	32 983	28 069	88.8	45.3	19.3	1.3	17.2	25.5	13.2	3.4	3.5
Luce County	32 031	36 359	45 515	19 583	15 114	19 135	32 137	21 716	16 828	69.9	36.3	36.2	4.0	28.5	3.0	-9.3	13.2	17.1
Mackinac County	33 356	39 929	47 973	23 750	18 472	20 240	32 258	23 870	17 777	73.2	38.5	35.5	2.8	25.0	4.5	-7.8	10.7	12.5
Macomb County	52 102	62 816	71 472	40 636	26 257	30 213	49 969	30 918	24 446	80.8	41.9	27.1	2.0	20.4	15.3	3.0	5.9	6.3
Manistee County	34 208	41 664	51 260	24 489	18 396	18 742	34 618	21 477	17 204	71.9	40.2	36.8	3.5	23.0	4.6	-7.7	10.7	10.9
Marquette County	35 548	46 281	55 978	27 287	19 096	19 570	37 817	24 511	18 070	77.2	41.7	27.8	2.8	23.0	5.1	-7.2	12.3	10.5
Mason County	34 704	41 654	50 745	26 875	16 681	19 602	35 325	23 537	17 713	74.6	38.5	33.2	3.6	20.0	5.9	-6.4	10.7	14.1
Mecosta County	33 849	40 465	50 345	25 875	17 157	19 167	32 958	23 404	16 372	75.2	35.7	30.4	3.6	22.1	6.2	-6.1	16.3	14.6
Menominee County	32 888	40 268	49 852	24 740	16 292	19 750	32 813	22 388	16 909	74.7	39.6	32.2	3.3	18.1	3.3	-9.0	12.0	13.1
Midland County	45 674	55 483	70 257	27 596	20 893	23 550	46 834	28 777	23 383	80.3	49.0	25.1	2.7	21.3	15.5	3.2	8.6	8.2
Missaukee County	35 224	39 057	45 485	25 625	19 688	20 323	31 121	21 533	16 072	74.7	33.9	32.6	4.3	20.8	4.3	-8.0	10.7	11.5
Monroe County	51 743	59 659	67 846	41 037	24 132	25 772	47 515	28 801	22 458	81.4	40.0	25.9	2.4	19.1	13.7	1.4	7.3	6.7
Montcalm County	37 218	42 823	50 542	30 477	19 736	20 390	33 832	24 467	16 183	77.6	32.0	29.2	3.5	20.4	4.3	-8.0	10.5	11.2
Montmorency County	30 005	34 784	43 148	28 125	12 188	17 836	31 875	20 193	16 493	60.2	40.0	45.3	3.6	35.2	3.6	-8.7	12.2	17.3
Muskegon County	38 008	45 710	56 237	29 063	17 718	21 175	36 575	26 041	17 967	77.7	32.6	30.0	4.7	20.2	6.6	-5.7	11.1	13.8
Newaygo County	37 130	42 498	49 835	29 527	19 005	20 189	36 218	23 754	16 976	77.2	33.5	30.5	3.8	19.8	4.7	-7.6	11.0	13.0
Oakland County	61 907	75 540	87 012	41 469	29 535	37 615	57 323	36 922	32 534	85.2	46.4	21.8	1.8	16.6	25.3	13.0	5.4	5.5
Oceana County	35 307	40 602	46 734	25 391	16 794	20 188	32 310	22 796	15 878	76.9	35.4	32.7	4.9	21.0	4.3	-8.0	12.3	17.8
Ogemaw County	30 474	34 988	46 183	17 813	16 458	18 185	32 066	21 354	15 768	66.3	33.2	38.3	4.0	27.0	3.8	-8.5	13.4	16.1
Ontonagon County	29 552	36 690	46 705	27 222	16 591	16 602	32 713	21 773	16 695	66.9	39.3	39.6	3.6	29.4	3.7	-8.6	11.8	11.8
Osceola County	34 102	39 205	46 779	27 778	18 406	19 333	30 630	22 930	15 632	74.8	31.8	32.2	3.8	21.4	3.9	-8.4	12.3	13.2
Oscoda County	28 228	32 225	41 696	23 333	16 053	16 018	31 396	21 096	15 697	62.7	37.7	42.1	4.6	31.4	3.3	-9.0	13.8	16.6
Otsego County	40 876	46 628	55 429	27 596	19 208	23 079	35 521	22 160	19 810	78.9	40.6	30.1	3.4	22.8	8.0	-4.3	7.0	6.7
Ottawa County	52 347	59 896	65 328	35 368	25 627	28 493	43 319	28 688	21 676	86.1	45.2	21.6	1.4	14.3	12.8	0.5	5.3	4.4
Presque Isle County	31 656	37 426	44 345	27 396	16 250	17 611	32 135	21 028	17 363	64.0	46.7	41.1	3.0	28.7	3.9	-8.4	10.9	11.3
Roscommon County	30 029	35 757	46 706	21 761	15 021	19 003	33 253	21 062	17 837	60.3	38.5	44.4	3.4	35.8	4.3	-8.0	11.8	17.6
Saginaw County	00 007	4C 101	61 030	26 715	16 996	22 404	41 373	26 155	19 438	76.5	37.2	28.4	5.6	22.6	9.3	-3.0	13.1	17.4
St. Clair County	46 313	54 450	62 048	33 750	21 377	24 638	44 048	26 673	21 582	81.1	38.1	26.6	3.1	18.5	11.0	-1.3	8.2	8.3
St. Joseph County	40 355	46 391	54 542	31 364	19 725	22 986	35 639	24 648	18 247	81.1	32.3	28.3	3.9	16.5	6.5	-5.8	10.2	13.2
Sanilac County	36 870	42 306	50 379	27 440	17 339	20 199	33 406	21 915	17 089	76.6	36.7	32.6	2.7	19.1	4.8	-7.5	10.0	11.3
Schoolcraft County	31 140	36 810	47 857	17 500	18 100	17 308	34 187	22 468	17 137	69.2	37.2	38.3	3.7	26.1	4.5	-7.8	11.8	14.9
Shiawassee County	42 553	49 329	58 122	31 710	21 900	22 188	39 907	25 990	19 229	80.7	36.5	27.4	2.8	21.6	7.8	-4.5	8.2	8.3
Tuscola County	40 174	46 729	53 199	30 326	21 529	21 485	36 675	25 164	17 985	78.2	40.1	28.6	2.5	23.1	6.9	-5.4	7.8	8.0
Van Buren County	39 365	45 824	56 495	30 332	19 832	22 053	35 964	26 053	17 878	80.2	32.2	28.1	4.1	16.3	6.6	-5.7	10.7	11.1
Washtenaw County	51 990	70 393	80 529	37 560	25 720	31 467	50 597	35 181	27 173	87.7	45.9	16.7	2.0	13.3	19.8	7.5	10.8	7.4
Wayne County	40 776	48 805	65 365	33 228	20 581	24 881	43 947	30 085	20 058	77.2	30.0	27.5	6.5	19.8	11.5	-0.8	14.9	18.5
Wexford County	35 000	39 915	40 750	27 434	18 813	20 467	31 846	22 538	17 144	76.7	33.5	30.6	4.2	21.2	6.1	-6.2	11.1	11.2
MINNESOTA	47 111	56 874	66 428	32 454	24 335	27 913	40 408	29 670	23 198	83.4	44.0	23.9	3.4	13.7	12.6	0.3	7.9	7.6
Aitkin County	31 139	37 290	44 972	20 781	16 875	19 170	32 839	21 386	17 848	67.1	41.0	42.4	4.8	23.5	4.6	-7.7	12.1	14.1
Anoka County	57 754	64 261	71 093	37 927	28 474	34 287	42 080	31 089	23 297	89.9	39.1	17.1	2.8	12.5	13.9	1.6	4.1	4.3
Becker County	34 797	41 807	48 341	24 595	16 755	17 600	30 615	21 199	17 085	77.3	38.7	33.8	4.8	15.8	5.3	-7.0	12.9	14.0
Beltrami County	33 392	40 345	49 470	20 758	16 231	20 017	31 304	22 995	15 497	79.1	32.0	26.6	8.0	15.0	5.5	6.8	16.8	19.1
Benton County	41 968	51 277	57 312	31 995	22 377	24 399	34 099	23 282	19 008	85.3	35.8	21.5	2.4	10.3	5.9	-6.4	8.5	5.3
Big Stone County	30 721	37 354	45 417	30 625	19 097	17 373	29 324	20 769	15 708	69.8	45.0	41.2	4.7	12.4	3.0	-9.3	11.8	12.2
Blue Earth County	38 940	50 257	56 798	30 250	20 473	24 076	33 122	23 425	18 712	83.9	41.8	23.7	3.1	11.2	6.8	-5.5	12.4	8.7
Brown County	39 800	49 811	57 152	31 477	21 378	20 840	33 641	25 019	19 535	77.6	54.6	33.2	2.2	12.1	5.8	-6.5	7.7	7.2
Carlton County	40 021	48 406	58 057	29 219	21 089	19 380	39 722	26 363	18 073	75.6	39.9	32.3	3.2	19.4	5.5	-6.8	8.9	8.1
Carver County	65 540	73 577	82 663	41 685	33 504	33 703	48 631	33 107	28 486	90.1	48.0	16.3	1.2	9.3	24.1	11.8	3.8	3.1
Cass County	34 332	40 156	46 968	20 395	18 214	18 384	31 064	22 227	17 189	72.6	37.5	36.5	3.8	21.5	5.4	-6.9	12.9	15.8
Chippewa County	35 582	45 160	51 567	26 518	19 375	19 218	31 757	20 946	18 039	76.3	47.0	35.1	2.2	11.5	4.0	-8.3	8.8	8.0
Chisago County	52 012	57 335	64 081	41 000	24 483	26 575	41 265	28 595	21 013	85.3	39.0	22.8	2.6	13.3	10.9	-1.4	5.1	4.6
Clay County	37 889	49 192	57 869	27 356	18 582	18 946	35 266	24 398	17 557	81.1	40.6	26.5	4.8	13.4	6.4	-5.9	13.4	11.5
Clearwater County	30 517	39 698	48 352	18 500	15 667	15 014	30 453	21 100	15 694	74.6	32.5	34.5	6.3	15.2	4.2	-8.1	16.9	15.3
Cook County	36 640	47 132	52 750	28 571	12 500	23 384	31 622	24 228	21 775	81.7	45.9	29.1	3.2	21.1	6.4	-5.9	10.7	14.3
Cottonwood County	31 943	40 237	45 554	22 344	17 229	18 036	30 367	20 876	16 647	76.6	47.6	35.4	3.5	11.0	4.0	-8.3	10.3	12.7
Crow Wing County	37 589	44 847	54 183	28 452	18 297	19 450	35 135	23 649	19 174	75.0	39.1	33.7	3.8	19.3	5.9	-6.4	10.2	10.4
Dakota County	61 863	71 062	79 205	41 357	30 838	37 284	47 950	33 252	27 008	90.0	45.2	16.1	1.9	11.8	20.1	7.8	3.8	3.3
Dodge County	47 437	54 261	61 222	31 375	22 727	24 784	35 324	26 595	19 259	84.4	42.5	25.2	1.9	12.4	7.8	-4.5	6.7	5.8
Douglas County	37 703	46 250	55 367	27 006	16 615	19 205	31 658	21 666	18 850	77.0	44.8	32.5	2.7	17.1	6.3	-6.0	10.2	8.7
Faribault County	34 440	41 793	47 437	25 000	19 485	19 917	30 135	20 914	17 193	74.6	46.5	37.9	3.2	12.4	4.1	-8.2	9.8	8.7
Fillmore County	36 651	44 883	52 752	25 625	21 176	19 804	30 635	22 371	17 067	79.0	46.0	33.7	2.6	14.2	4.6	-7.7	9.9	9.9
Freeborn County	36 964	45 142	54 152	31 080	20 694	19 700	32 205	22 800	18 325	75.3	44.7	34.9	3.5	17.5	4.8	-7.5	8.8	8.7
Goodhue County	46 972	55 689	63 326	33 804	22 068	24 961	37 651	26 100	21 934	81.6	46.9	28.1	2.2	14.8	9.7	-2.6	6.7	5.2

STATE/ County code	MSA/PMSA/ NECMA code[1]	STATE County	High school graduates			College graduates		College graduates (percent)				
			Total population 25 years and over	Percent with a high school diploma or less	Percent with a high school diploma or more	Percent with a bachelor's degree or more	+/− U.S. percent with bachelor's degree or more	Non-Hispanic White	Black or African American	American Indian and Alaska Native	Asian, Hawaiian, and Pacific Islander	Hispanic or Latino[2]
			1	2	3	4	5	6	7	8	9	10
		MINNESOTA—Cont'd										
27 051	...	Grant County..............	4 370	51.8	83.5	15.7	−8.7	15.8	X	0.0	0.0	0.0
27 053	5120	Hennepin County	740 444	30.5	90.6	39.1	14.7	42.0	17.8	10.1	38.6	18.0
27 055	3870	Houston County	13 063	49.2	85.5	20.5	−3.9	20.2	55.6	0.0	49.2	33.8
27 057	...	Hubbard County	12 694	48.3	86.1	20.2	−4.2	20.5	0.0	9.3	27.6	0.0
27 059	5120	Isanti County	19 915	51.8	86.6	14.5	−9.9	14.5	19.7	17.7	32.6	11.4
27 061	...	Itasca County	29 931	47.7	85.6	17.6	−6.8	18.0	27.0	8.0	4.5	5.1
27 063	...	Jackson County............	7 768	53.9	84.1	14.2	−10.2	14.2	0.0	13.3	20.7	9.7
27 065	...	Kanabec County...........	9 797	61.6	80.6	10.5	−13.9	10.4	22.2	4.7	25.9	4.3
27 067	...	Kandiyohi County	26 419	47.7	83.5	18.3	−6.1	19.1	3.4	6.7	61.3	2.3
27 069	...	Kittson County	3 661	54.8	79.7	14.8	−9.6	14.7	42.9	0.0	0.0	6.7
27 071	...	Koochiching County	9 999	55.5	81.9	15.1	−9.3	15.4	0.0	4.4	40.0	0.0
27 073	...	Lac qui Parle County	5 644	56.9	80.8	13.0	−11.4	12.8	0.0	50.0	38.9	14.3
27 075	...	Lake County................	7 847	51.1	86.4	19.5	−4.9	19.5	0.0	28.1	X	6.3
27 077	...	Lake of the Woods County	3 155	52.8	84.6	17.2	−7.2	17.3	0.0	0.0	0.0	60.0
27 079	...	Le Sueur County	16 499	53.7	84.6	16.9	−7.5	17.2	3.6	5.2	25.0	3.6
27 081	...	Lincoln County	4 516	58.7	79.8	14.1	−10.3	14.0	X	X	100.0	0.0
27 083	...	Lyon County	15 355	49.8	82.6	21.4	−3.0	21.7	20.0	26.8	44.1	3.2
27 085	...	McLeod County	22 495	52.6	84.7	15.4	−9.0	15.5	3.6	20.0	44.6	3.4
27 087	...	Mahnomen County	3 292	59.0	75.0	12.4	−12.0	14.8	0.0	6.8	17.1	0.0
27 089	...	Marshall County	6 914	57.9	79.1	12.0	−12.4	12.1	40.0	8.3	20.0	1.8
27 091	...	Martin County	14 935	54.2	83.7	16.1	−8.3	16.2	0.0	0.0	25.8	2.6
27 093	...	Meeker County	14 841	56.8	81.5	13.9	−10.5	14.0	0.0	4.4	0.0	5.8
27 095	...	Mille Lacs County.........	14 622	59.0	81.3	12.2	−12.2	12.3	20.0	3.8	53.1	7.4
27 097	...	Morrison County	20 347	59.0	79.7	12.6	−11.8	12.6	37.5	10.0	36.6	6.1
27 099	...	Mower County	25 749	53.0	82.3	14.7	−9.7	15.0	7.4	8.1	30.6	3.6
27 101	...	Murray County	6 320	58.7	79.1	11.9	−12.5	11.9	28.6	18.2	13.3	1.5
27 103	...	Nicollet County	17 496	37.6	90.1	29.3	4.9	29.9	7.8	50.0	22.8	7.0
27 105	...	Nobles County	13 654	58.5	75.8	13.5	−10.9	14.3	12.5	12.9	13.2	4.7
27 107	...	Norman County	5 105	54.8	80.0	13.1	−11.3	13.4	0.0	0.0	54.5	3.8
27 109	6820	Olmsted County	80 277	32.9	91.1	34.7	10.3	34.7	16.8	21.2	54.1	14.5
27 111	...	Otter Tail County..........	38 739	51.7	81.4	17.2	−7.2	17.4	10.5	2.9	23.8	4.7
27 113	...	Pennington County	8 848	49.8	81.3	14.9	−9.5	14.8	33.3	0.0	35.8	9.5
27 115	...	Pine County	17 714	61.9	79.0	10.3	−14.1	10.7	2.2	5.8	20.4	3.7
27 117	...	Pipestone County	6 671	58.5	77.6	13.9	−10.5	14.2	0.0	3.0	0.0	11.5
27 119	2985	Polk County.................	20 203	49.8	82.0	17.6	−6.8	18.0	15.4	7.8	27.8	6.6
27 121	...	Pope County	7 719	51.7	81.8	14.7	−9.7	14.7	50.0	0.0	0.0	0.0
27 123	5120	Ramsey County............	323 214	37.7	87.6	34.3	9.9	37.0	18.6	16.2	29.6	16.1
27 125	...	Red Lake County	2 879	59.4	78.8	10.7	−13.7	10.9	X	0.0	50.0	0.0
27 127	...	Redwood County	11 269	56.8	80.2	13.4	−11.0	13.8	0.0	1.7	6.7	11.9
27 129	...	Renville County	11 464	57.1	80.9	12.6	−11.8	13.0	0.0	0.0	20.0	2.6
27 131	...	Rice County.................	33 400	47.8	85.2	22.4	−2.0	23.2	11.8	3.4	27.7	8.0
27 133	...	Rock County................	6 485	54.2	81.5	15.4	−9.0	15.2	27.5	58.3	38.9	6.1
27 135	...	Roseau County	10 366	55.3	82.5	14.9	−9.5	15.1	44.4	0.0	14.5	0.0
27 137	2240	St. Louis County...........	132 801	44.6	87.2	21.9	−2.5	22.1	21.0	9.0	28.8	13.8
27 139	5120	Scott County................	55 564	37.4	91.0	29.4	5.0	30.1	15.7	7.5	30.6	7.6
27 141	5120	Sherburne County........	38 349	42.6	89.9	19.4	−5.0	19.5	12.5	10.2	33.1	16.7
27 143	...	Sibley County..............	9 970	60.9	79.2	11.6	−12.8	11.8	0.0	0.0	56.3	2.9
27 145	6980	Stearns County	77 519	47.1	86.2	22.0	−2.4	21.9	13.9	8.7	31.1	18.7
27 147	...	Steele County..............	21 550	49.4	86.6	20.1	−4.3	20.4	3.4	0.0	28.8	9.7
27 149	...	Stevens County	5 790	49.7	84.4	20.6	−3.8	20.2	42.1	0.0	55.6	47.2
27 151	...	Swift County	8 336	54.8	80.4	14.0	−10.4	15.0	0.6	7.7	9.3	2.3
27 153	...	Todd County................	15 758	62.0	79.3	10.0	−14.4	10.1	0.0	2.9	4.4	6.4
27 155	...	Traverse County...........	2 850	57.4	82.2	10.7	−13.7	10.8	X	0.0	20.0	20.0
27 157	...	Wabasha County..........	14 189	51.8	85.6	16.9	−7.5	16.9	40.0	52.6	19.7	15.0
27 159	...	Wadena County	9 047	57.4	79.5	13.4	−11.0	13.2	6.5	7.5	82.9	0.0
27 161	...	Waseca County............	12 818	53.7	84.8	16.2	−8.2	16.8	0.3	2.0	93.3	8.9
27 163	5120	Washington County.......	128 215	32.0	94.0	33.9	9.5	33.9	28.9	11.3	52.2	26.0
27 165	...	Watonwan County	7 745	63.1	75.9	13.7	−10.7	15.1	0.0	26.7	17.0	2.2
27 167	...	Wilkin County	4 673	48.0	84.5	14.0	−10.4	14.3	0.0	0.0	42.9	0.0
27 169	...	Winona County	29 165	46.2	84.0	23.2	−1.2	23.3	5.8	13.5	39.1	11.9
27 171	5120	Wright County	55 234	48.7	88.1	17.9	−6.5	18.0	12.4	9.0	36.4	3.6
27 173	...	Yellow Medicine County	7 394	53.4	81.9	14.4	−10.0	14.4	0.0	14.7	71.4	0.0

[1]MSA = Metropolitan Statistical Area. PMSA = Primary MSA. NECMA = New England County Metropolitan Area. See the Appendix A for explanation of these concepts. See Appendix B for list of metropolitan areas identified by type, with component counties.
[2]Hispanic or Latino persons may be of any race.

STATE County	School enrollment			Population 16 to 19 years				Employment status, 2000			Work status in 1999 of the population 16 years and over (percent)		
											Worked in 1999		
	Grades kindergarten through 12	College or graduate school	Percent private	Number	Percent in armed forces	Percent high school graduates	Percent not enrolled, not grads, not in armed forces, not employed	Total population 16 years and over	Percent in labor force	Unemployment rate	Full-time	Part-time	Did not work in 1999
	11	12	13	14	15	16	17	18	19	20	21	22	23
MINNESOTA—Cont'd													
Grant County	1 215	165	4.0	376	0.0	8.5	3.2	5 009	63.0	4.8	48.5	19.8	31.7
Hennepin County	197 828	78 624	15.6	56 930	0.0	8.6	3.7	876 731	73.2	3.8	60.3	18.4	21.3
Houston County	4 268	645	13.1	1 148	0.0	12.5	1.7	15 011	70.1	3.9	56.5	19.0	24.5
Hubbard County	3 538	467	5.4	1 044	0.0	10.5	5.7	14 459	59.3	6.6	50.0	17.9	32.1
Isanti County	7 169	959	6.9	2 105	0.0	9.4	3.9	23 535	72.7	4.3	57.1	20.8	22.1
Itasca County	8 676	1 681	6.8	2 789	0.0	8.1	3.4	34 794	59.2	6.7	47.5	18.3	34.2
Jackson County	2 261	350	7.6	679	0.0	4.6	1.3	8 895	66.0	3.5	53.2	17.9	28.9
Kanabec County	3 324	269	3.7	940	0.0	10.0	4.3	11 424	67.0	6.2	53.4	19.1	27.5
Kandiyohi County	8 630	1 628	7.7	2 842	0.0	10.2	2.7	31 704	69.2	3.6	54.0	20.8	25.1
Kittson County	1 093	101	8.8	252	0.0	7.5	0.0	4 101	58.9	5.0	51.8	15.7	32.5
Koochiching County	2 770	475	9.0	829	0.0	10.5	3.4	11 366	60.5	5.5	49.8	16.0	34.3
Lac qui Parle County	1 588	128	4.8	466	0.0	8.6	3.0	6 354	62.6	3.3	49.0	19.5	31.5
Lake County	1 956	322	7.2	573	0.0	18.8	1.7	8 873	62.0	5.3	48.3	19.5	32.1
Lake of the Woods County	940	85	3.0	195	0.0	8.2	0.5	3 549	64.5	4.8	55.0	14.8	30.2
Le Sueur County	5 495	729	10.1	1 640	0.0	8.4	2.3	19 331	72.2	3.8	59.2	18.3	22.5
Lincoln County	1 187	169	5.5	318	0.0	3.1	0.0	5 114	62.9	3.5	49.4	19.0	31.5
Lyon County	5 024	2 194	12.1	1 885	0.0	7.6	2.3	19 644	72.0	5.1	54.3	22.4	23.2
McLeod County	7 328	1 188	13.8	1 949	0.0	8.4	1.4	26 377	72.8	3.8	60.7	17.0	22.3
Mahnomen County	1 161	149	5.7	370	0.0	7.3	5.9	3 888	61.2	6.7	54.1	14.2	31.8
Marshall County	2 029	248	3.9	600	0.0	5.7	3.0	7 942	62.4	8.7	54.5	15.7	29.8
Martin County	4 421	492	11.5	1 363	0.0	10.8	0.2	17 183	65.3	4.1	52.1	18.3	29.7
Meeker County	4 762	570	4.3	1 431	0.0	10.6	3.7	17 337	67.7	4.8	55.3	19.3	25.4
Mille Lacs County	4 771	536	10.1	1 375	0.0	9.3	4.9	17 118	65.8	5.4	51.9	19.6	28.5
Morrison County	6 879	850	9.3	2 052	0.1	13.0	1.7	23 986	66.9	5.6	53.0	18.5	28.4
Mower County	7 306	1 309	10.2	2 263	0.0	9.1	6.5	30 132	64.3	3.9	50.0	18.4	31.6
Murray County	1 812	211	10.1	523	0.0	8.0	3.6	7 205	65.8	3.6	52.3	18.8	28.9
Nicollet County	5 666	3 662	34.7	2 757	0.0	5.1	1.6	23 431	74.9	4.5	56.4	25.7	18.0
Nobles County	4 207	593	7.5	1 283	0.0	5.0	3.1	16 026	66.2	3.9	53.7	18.0	28.3
Norman County	1 479	147	2.8	418	0.0	6.9	1.0	5 808	62.0	6.1	51.5	18.9	29.7
Olmsted County	25 301	6 285	14.6	6 769	0.0	7.5	1.9	94 560	73.5	3.7	59.4	19.5	21.1
Otter Tail County	11 462	1 858	7.5	3 746	0.0	8.2	2.3	44 908	62.2	5.2	49.3	19.5	31.2
Pennington County	2 556	795	6.5	949	0.0	7.2	1.8	10 748	67.4	7.6	55.4	19.2	25.3
Pine County	5 447	600	8.2	1 564	0.0	10.5	6.2	20 637	61.9	6.8	51.7	17.4	30.9
Pipestone County	2 079	256	11.3	599	0.0	8.0	0.8	7 701	65.9	2.5	49.8	21.2	29.0
Polk County	6 352	2 029	7.8	2 145	0.4	9.0	2.7	24 291	62.9	5.9	52.5	18.8	28.7
Pope County	2 357	247	5.5	707	0.0	3.4	1.8	8 859	62.5	3.0	49.0	19.2	31.2
Ramsey County	98 122	41 484	23.9	30 219	0.1	9.0	3.9	394 501	70.2	4.3	57.0	19.1	23.9
Red Lake County	871	122	8.3	311	0.0	10.6	1.9	3 381	62.8	9.1	53.6	15.6	30.8
Redwood County	3 504	303	11.2	1 004	0.0	6.7	2.4	12 977	65.1	3.1	51.4	19.5	29.1
Renville County	3 651	367	10.0	1 024	0.0	7.2	2.8	13 194	65.5	3.8	54.1	17.5	28.4
Rice County	11 284	6 359	36.9	4 870	0.0	6.6	1.6	44 154	70.2	6.3	55.6	23.3	21.1
Rock County	2 019	276	7.7	583	0.0	4.8	1.4	7 501	66.7	1.7	51.6	20.4	28.0
Roseau County	3 729	303	3.2	1 001	0.0	8.9	2.1	12 078	72.7	3.3	63.9	14.4	21.7
St. Louis County	35 402	16 743	9.9	13 530	0.1	8.4	2.4	161 520	62.7	6.8	47.6	21.3	31.1
Scott County	19 902	3 500	14.9	4 375	0.0	10.9	1.9	64 042	79.4	2.6	67.9	17.5	14.6
Sherburne County	14 644	3 410	10.0	3 971	0.1	13.2	2.9	46 642	76.0	2.6	63.8	19.2	17.0
Sibley County	3 274	370	13.1	888	0.0	9.5	0.5	11 644	70.4	2.7	57.9	17.6	24.5
Stearns County	26 236	15 315	19.3	11 213	0.0	6.5	1.3	103 463	72.8	3.7	55.7	23.9	20.4
Steele County	7 229	1 184	12.0	2 056	0.0	6.9	1.3	25 559	73.0	3.4	59.8	18.4	21.8
Stevens County	1 680	1 713	4.2	1 126	0.0	3.5	1.1	8 232	67.5	5.3	50.0	27.2	22.8
Swift County	2 212	347	5.5	617	0.0	4.2	0.6	9 586	56.7	4.3	50.5	18.1	31.4
Todd County	5 498	663	10.8	1 777	0.0	7.3	3.9	18 687	63.3	5.2	51.3	17.9	30.8
Traverse County	825	122	2.5	243	0.0	5.3	0.8	3 241	54.4	5.2	43.2	18.5	38.4
Wabasha County	4 651	654	8.7	1 296	0.0	9.4	1.8	16 509	70.8	2.9	56.8	18.4	24.8
Wadena County	2 792	569	5.0	757	0.0	6.6	1.8	10 565	59.6	5.6	47.0	19.0	34.0
Waseca County	3 883	582	9.7	1 133	0.0	7.4	3.3	15 112	66.3	2.5	59.6	17.6	22.8
Washington County	44 185	9 321	13.6	10 958	0.0	7.6	1.7	148 385	75.4	2.6	62.8	18.9	18.3
Watonwan County	2 536	261	9.8	706	0.0	6.5	1.6	9 028	64.3	3.5	54.5	17.8	27.7
Wilkin County	1 530	175	11.6	417	0.0	2.6	2.6	5 421	65.8	3.7	53.8	19.1	27.1
Winona County	8 791	7 565	19.2	4 572	0.0	6.7	1.0	39 976	70.5	5.3	54.8	23.8	21.4
Wright County	20 802	2 738	9.5	5 251	0.0	9.8	2.2	64 943	76.3	3.0	63.4	18.4	18.2
Yellow Medicine County	2 282	405	4.5	750	0.0	6.5	1.3	8 642	63.9	5.5	51.1	18.4	30.5

	Full-year full-time employed (percent)								Children under 18 years in families						Total employed by class of worker (percent)			
STATE County										With two parents (percent)		With one parent who is in labor force (percent)	+/- U.S. percent of children with no stay-at-home parent (percent)	+/- U.S. percent two-income couples				
	Total	Men	Women	Non-Hispanic White	Black or African American	American Indian and Alaska Native	Asian, Hawaiian, and Pacific Islander	Hispanic or Latino[1]	Number	Both in labor force	Father only in labor force				Private	Government	Self-employed	Unpaid family worker
	24	25	26	27	28	29	30	31	32	33	34	35	36	37	38	39	40	41
MINNESOTA—Cont'd																		
Grant County	33.3	42.8	24.6	33.3	0.0	80.0	0.0	34.6	1 461	68.4	11.7	14.0	17.8	6.3	64.3	12.8	21.7	1.1
Hennepin County	46.9	56.1	38.2	48.8	38.0	34.5	39.9	37.8	255 571	49.7	19.5	20.4	5.5	10.8	80.4	10.6	8.8	0.2
Houston County	44.2	54.5	34.4	44.2	59.1	25.0	48.6	46.5	5 237	66.9	11.8	17.0	19.3	13.1	74.5	9.8	15.0	0.8
Hubbard County	33.6	41.4	26.0	33.7	30.0	23.4	43.8	25.4	4 279	57.6	15.6	18.4	11.4	-3.2	64.2	18.4	17.1	0.4
Isanti County	44.6	56.4	33.0	44.9	24.3	42.4	28.9	30.7	8 602	59.0	15.5	19.8	14.2	10.8	76.1	13.4	10.2	0.3
Itasca County	32.6	41.4	23.9	32.8	44.3	27.2	13.8	30.2	10 109	51.8	21.1	16.9	4.1	-3.8	71.5	16.5	11.6	0.4
Jackson County	40.7	50.6	30.5	40.5	0.0	73.3	46.8	45.8	2 698	69.7	10.5	14.4	19.5	9.3	66.1	12.0	20.7	1.1
Kanabec County	37.1	45.1	29.0	37.2	38.5	31.3	18.4	38.1	3 941	55.0	16.6	19.2	9.6	2.3	72.7	12.8	13.9	0.6
Kandiyohi County	40.7	51.2	30.5	41.3	25.6	25.6	46.2	33.5	10 505	60.2	13.5	17.1	12.7	10.2	71.0	15.1	13.5	0.4
Kittson County	35.9	46.2	25.8	36.1	0.0	28.6	0.0	44.1	1 282	62.6	15.6	14.7	12.7	0.4	63.6	15.8	19.4	1.2
Koochiching County	35.1	44.2	26.3	35.5	0.0	28.8	41.2	17.2	3 288	46.9	22.1	24.1	6.4	-1.7	71.7	15.7	12.1	0.5
Lac qui Parle County	37.4	48.5	26.8	37.3	0.0	50.0	32.0	50.0	1 911	69.3	14.0	11.7	16.4	5.1	63.8	13.5	21.6	1.1
Lake County	33.7	43.7	23.7	33.8	100.0	46.3	0.0	6.3	2 416	54.9	17.1	20.8	11.1	-0.9	67.3	20.2	12.3	0.2
Lake of the Woods County	40.1	49.4	30.7	40.2	50.0	23.1	60.0	72.7	1 065	65.5	15.8	14.6	15.5	7.6	66.2	13.6	19.4	0.7
Le Sueur County	44.4	54.2	34.7	45.0	38.5	41.2	34.4	30.9	6 729	68.2	11.4	15.2	18.8	14.5	73.7	12.9	12.7	0.6
Lincoln County	37.2	48.2	26.9	37.2	X	0.0	46.2	26.1	1 492	71.6	13.6	9.9	16.9	7.9	62.7	13.0	22.8	1.4
Lyon County	41.0	50.2	32.4	41.6	34.3	22.6	26.1	36.9	6 518	62.9	16.1	14.0	12.3	15.3	72.9	13.7	13.0	0.4
McLeod County	48.8	59.5	38.5	49.0	53.7	37.8	62.8	38.4	9 416	67.0	13.3	14.5	16.9	15.0	78.5	10.0	10.9	0.5
Mahnomen County	36.2	43.5	28.9	37.2	0.0	32.6	22.5	44.8	1 377	47.1	11.2	26.6	9.1	4.5	56.1	25.6	18.0	0.3
Marshall County	36.2	45.6	26.6	36.7	33.3	38.9	38.5	12.9	2 485	66.4	13.6	12.1	13.9	1.5	65.0	15.2	18.8	1.0
Martin County	40.8	53.2	29.3	41.3	52.9	5.7	25.7	8.6	5 254	60.6	14.4	19.0	15.0	8.3	73.8	10.1	15.6	0.5
Meeker County	41.3	51.0	31.7	41.4	49.1	32.9	12.2	39.4	6 001	62.9	14.8	16.0	14.3	8.8	71.9	12.6	14.9	0.6
Mille Lacs County	38.3	47.4	29.5	38.4	55.6	29.5	46.3	46.9	5 722	57.9	13.7	20.9	14.2	6.3	75.0	11.6	12.9	0.5
Morrison County	38.0	46.8	29.0	38.0	19.4	28.8	54.7	23.6	8 645	61.8	14.3	17.7	14.9	7.7	69.6	13.7	16.0	0.7
Mower County	39.1	49.2	29.4	39.4	13.9	61.3	43.3	31.9	9 222	58.3	12.5	22.2	15.9	6.0	78.4	9.8	11.2	0.6
Murray County	38.3	49.7	27.3	38.1	50.0	18.2	36.4	52.5	2 223	73.8	10.4	12.1	21.3	7.7	62.9	13.0	23.2	0.9
Nicollet County	42.2	51.2	33.5	43.0	19.7	0.0	12.4	34.8	7 195	69.3	9.6	15.1	19.8	20.1	76.2	13.0	10.4	0.3
Nobles County	41.3	52.4	30.6	41.2	55.2	45.8	45.8	39.1	5 333	61.1	13.6	17.0	13.5	7.8	71.6	10.8	16.9	0.8
Norman County	34.2	43.8	24.9	34.3	0.0	40.4	69.2	20.2	1 858	65.6	15.0	12.4	13.4	5.2	66.7	14.6	18.0	0.7
Olmsted County	47.4	58.2	37.3	48.6	26.5	48.4	41.8	34.5	32 620	59.4	18.6	15.3	10.1	13.4	82.5	9.3	8.0	0.2
Otter Tail County	36.0	44.8	27.2	35.9	10.0	32.5	40.2	38.1	13 767	62.5	14.8	15.8	13.7	3.3	68.7	13.5	17.1	0.7
Pennington County	38.6	48.3	31.1	39.0	52.9	26.4	30.9	13.2	3 202	63.6	9.5	17.8	16.8	5.9	73.8	14.7	11.0	0.4
Pine County	36.9	42.9	30.4	37.0	31.2	37.1	31.5	37.1	6 350	51.5	16.4	22.8	9.7	1.2	69.2	16.6	13.4	0.8
Pipestone County	37.6	50.2	26.3	37.9	0.0	17.5	37.2	36.4	2 508	62.9	9.6	17.3	15.6	10.2	66.1	13.9	19.4	0.7
Polk County	35.1	44.1	26.6	35.7	12.8	25.9	27.7	25.6	7 830	62.0	12.2	18.0	15.4	5.0	68.2	17.1	14.2	0.5
Pope County	37.8	50.2	26.4	37.7	62.5	40.0	23.5	52.2	2 708	66.6	16.1	10.6	12.6	4.4	65.4	12.5	20.6	1.6
Ramsey County	43.5	52.4	35.5	45.4	35.8	38.2	33.1	37.5	124 815	47.5	16.2	21.6	4.5	8.9	77.6	14.8	7.4	0.2
Red Lake County	35.3	42.3	28.3	36.0	X	10.1	50.0	33.3	1 053	64.8	11.2	15.8	16.0	6.0	70.7	14.7	14.4	0.2
Redwood County	39.5	50.5	28.8	39.9	0.0	28.5	51.4	37.1	4 313	63.9	13.3	15.2	14.5	8.9	68.3	11.3	19.6	0.8
Renville County	39.0	50.5	27.6	39.4	0.0	19.4	34.8	33.2	4 450	64.6	15.6	13.1	13.1	7.3	67.9	12.6	18.7	0.8
Rice County	40.4	50.5	30.3	41.2	23.9	47.6	26.0	38.1	13 633	62.6	14.1	17.0	15.0	13.2	76.8	12.9	9.8	0.4
Rock County	40.2	50.4	30.2	40.4	26.9	6.7	61.1	30.2	2 482	74.0	10.6	11.1	20.5	11.6	67.9	12.7	18.5	0.9
Roseau County	49.2	58.4	39.6	49.1	55.6	55.8	55.4	28.6	4 740	67.5	9.9	15.9	18.8	16.4	78.0	8.9	12.4	0.7
St. Louis County	34.6	44.1	25.7	34.8	24.7	30.2	28.0	35.4	42 744	52.1	17.2	22.0	9.5	2.1	74.6	16.3	8.8	0.3
Scott County	55.8	68.4	43.4	56.6	39.8	41.0	57.7	38.9	27 365	63.0	18.4	13.9	12.3	21.0	81.0	9.1	9.7	0.2
Sherburne County	50.3	61.0	39.2	50.9	23.7	31.1	38.0	36.3	19 170	63.5	17.8	13.3	12.2	17.2	77.2	12.2	10.4	0.2
Sibley County	44.5	53.8	35.3	45.0	17.6	47.4	25.0	35.3	4 039	64.8	12.5	14.9	15.1	13.7	72.9	10.4	16.1	0.6
Stearns County	42.3	51.2	33.4	42.8	25.4	32.3	25.0	39.0	33 376	65.1	14.7	14.2	14.7	14.2	77.1	11.3	11.2	0.4
Steele County	47.8	58.5	37.7	48.6	29.1	11.1	28.3	36.5	9 071	63.4	14.6	16.0	14.8	15.5	80.1	9.7	9.9	0.3
Stevens County	31.6	41.2	22.9	32.5	13.7	3.9	0.0	22.7	2 099	70.1	15.7	9.9	15.4	10.2	60.6	23.3	15.6	0.6
Swift County	36.6	43.0	28.5	39.0	8.4	7.1	20.9	9.6	2 632	69.4	12.5	13.1	17.9	12.4	63.8	16.2	19.3	0.8
Todd County	37.6	46.9	28.2	37.9	0.0	17.3	45.2	29.2	6 469	61.4	17.7	13.3	10.1	5.8	69.3	11.8	18.1	0.8
Traverse County	28.6	39.8	17.9	28.8	X	19.4	0.0	8.3	1 042	59.1	21.6	13.4	7.9	-4.5	54.2	16.0	28.5	1.3
Wabasha County	45.3	54.6	36.2	45.5	4.5	19.0	28.2	41.3	5 713	67.4	13.8	14.9	17.7	11.7	73.1	9.9	16.2	0.8
Wadena County	32.1	40.6	23.9	32.2	12.1	28.8	28.6	21.9	3 440	55.5	18.4	17.5	8.4	-1.7	68.4	14.8	16.0	0.9
Waseca County	43.8	52.3	34.2	44.6	36.7	14.3	30.2	29.9	4 800	63.1	14.9	17.6	16.1	14.0	75.0	11.4	13.0	0.6
Washington County	51.6	63.0	40.6	52.1	34.7	36.7	52.3	48.2	57 924	60.4	20.2	14.3	10.1	15.3	77.5	13.7	8.6	0.1
Watonwan County	38.2	49.2	27.6	38.6	18.8	0.0	32.8	36.9	3 195	55.4	14.8	19.2	10.0	3.3	73.7	11.3	14.0	1.0
Wilkin County	39.0	51.2	27.3	39.1	0.0	53.3	14.3	23.7	1 944	65.4	14.4	13.1	13.9	7.6	69.3	12.7	17.4	0.5
Winona County	40.7	49.9	32.3	41.3	27.1	14.0	28.0	20.6	11 028	62.2	15.7	15.8	13.4	13.5	77.1	11.4	10.7	0.7
Wright County	50.0	61.6	38.5	50.1	54.7	66.3	42.3	44.4	27 124	64.2	17.6	13.4	13.0	16.1	78.4	9.9	11.4	0.4
Yellow Medicine County	37.9	47.5	28.6	38.3	14.3	22.5	68.0	26.5	2 799	67.6	11.7	15.0	18.0	7.8	66.5	13.6	18.9	1.0

[1] Hispanic or Latino persons may be of any race.

STATE County	Percent who worked at home	Percent of the population 5 years and over with a disability	Veterans as a percent of the population 18 years and over	Occupation for employed population 16 years and over (percent)						Industry for employed population 16 years and over (percent)					
				Management, professional, and related occupations	Service occupations	Sales and office occupations	Farming, fishing, and forestry occupations	Construction, extraction, and maintenance occupations	Production, transportation and material moving occupations	Agriculture, forestry, fishing, and mining	Construction and manufacturing	Wholesale and retail trade	Transportation and warehousing, and utilities	Service industries	Public administration
	42	43	44	45	46	47	48	49	50	51	52	53	54	55	56
MINNESOTA—Cont'd															
Grant County	10.6	17.2	13.8	33.3	14.6	23.3	3.0	10.1	15.7	14.1	17.5	16.1	5.1	44.1	3.1
Hennepin County	3.9	14.3	11.3	42.5	12.4	28.6	0.1	5.6	10.8	0.2	18.0	16.2	4.4	58.8	2.5
Houston County	8.5	15.6	14.3	33.6	14.5	22.6	2.3	10.4	16.7	7.9	21.6	16.7	4.2	47.0	2.6
Hubbard County	6.1	19.0	19.3	30.2	16.0	23.8	1.9	13.2	14.9	5.0	21.6	15.4	3.6	49.6	4.8
Isanti County	3.9	15.5	14.5	27.2	12.9	23.3	0.8	14.1	21.7	2.0	33.0	13.9	4.9	42.4	3.8
Itasca County	4.1	19.3	18.4	26.2	16.0	24.5	1.1	12.9	19.3	4.6	21.3	15.2	6.5	48.0	4.5
Jackson County	9.8	15.0	13.9	31.5	15.1	23.7	2.5	9.3	17.9	13.3	24.2	14.8	5.0	39.9	2.8
Kanabec County	5.5	18.3	16.5	23.5	16.1	22.2	1.2	14.0	23.0	5.0	31.3	15.2	3.8	41.2	3.6
Kandiyohi County	5.1	17.0	12.3	30.8	14.8	24.7	1.8	9.3	18.7	5.8	21.0	16.6	5.3	48.2	3.1
Kittson County	8.3	18.0	14.0	32.5	15.4	20.1	3.8	9.4	18.8	14.2	20.3	14.8	5.6	40.5	4.6
Koochiching County	4.4	19.6	15.8	24.0	16.6	23.1	2.0	11.1	23.1	4.4	28.9	13.5	4.7	43.4	5.1
Lac qui Parle County	11.2	17.6	13.7	32.9	15.2	22.6	2.3	9.1	10.0	14.4	10.4	15.0	5.6	41.6	1.1
Lake County	5.1	16.3	19.4	29.7	19.7	19.4	1.7	13.2	16.4	10.6	15.7	10.3	6.4	53.0	4.1
Lake of the Woods County	9.6	18.1	18.4	27.2	20.7	17.5	1.2	10.4	22.9	5.6	30.5	9.9	4.2	44.0	5.8
Le Sueur County	5.4	15.2	12.9	27.9	13.9	21.9	1.2	11.1	24.0	5.1	33.6	12.5	3.7	41.9	3.1
Lincoln County	12.7	18.1	13.7	33.3	17.3	18.9	3.5	10.5	16.5	16.7	18.3	13.1	6.3	42.4	3.3
Lyon County	5.2	14.9	11.6	31.6	14.9	25.6	1.0	8.4	18.6	6.4	27.7	16.8	3.5	42.3	3.3
McLeod County	5.9	14.1	13.2	27.7	11.9	21.8	1.2	11.0	26.4	4.3	40.1	13.2	3.6	36.8	2.0
Mahnomen County	10.6	30.6	14.7	32.1	23.6	19.6	3.0	11.6	10.2	11.9	11.7	8.7	6.1	55.3	6.3
Marshall County	7.9	17.5	13.0	31.2	14.4	20.5	2.4	10.9	20.6	11.6	24.4	13.8	7.4	37.9	4.8
Martin County	6.5	17.8	14.3	30.1	16.2	21.9	2.7	8.1	20.9	9.7	24.5	15.3	5.6	41.9	3.0
Meeker County	6.3	16.7	14.2	27.6	13.7	21.4	1.9	10.1	25.3	7.6	35.7	12.7	4.2	37.4	2.3
Mille Lacs County	5.8	19.5	16.3	24.1	16.1	22.7	1.0	11.4	24.6	4.0	30.6	14.4	5.0	43.1	2.9
Morrison County	8.8	19.9	14.6	29.2	14.3	20.7	2.4	11.5	21.8	9.2	26.2	14.3	4.0	41.7	4.6
Mower County	4.5	17.8	15.1	26.9	16.8	23.9	1.4	9.2	21.7	5.0	27.8	14.4	3.9	45.9	3.1
Murray County	11.0	17.6	14.1	32.0	16.4	21.1	2.5	10.0	17.9	15.2	19.1	15.0	6.1	41.1	3.5
Nicollet County	5.0	12.8	11.4	35.7	14.0	24.6	1.0	6.9	17.7	4.9	25.8	12.2	3.7	50.5	2.9
Nobles County	7.5	17.4	12.6	25.6	16.3	22.9	1.7	9.2	24.4	8.7	26.4	17.2	4.7	40.7	2.3
Norman County	8.6	18.7	14.8	30.1	18.3	23.6	4.3	11.6	12.1	13.9	11.3	16.1	6.4	48.7	3.6
Olmsted County	3.7	13.7	12.2	44.5	14.1	23.4	0.3	7.5	10.2	1.3	21.3	13.1	2.7	58.9	2.8
Otter Tail County	7.3	18.8	15.9	31.2	15.6	23.1	2.3	10.3	17.5	7.9	20.9	16.4	6.1	45.0	3.7
Pennington County	4.7	18.3	13.2	28.6	16.0	25.5	1.5	8.3	20.1	4.8	23.1	20.9	5.1	42.3	3.8
Pine County	6.3	19.1	16.7	24.4	22.5	20.5	1.7	12.3	18.6	5.2	22.6	12.7	5.0	47.3	7.3
Pipestone County	7.9	16.0	12.5	30.1	18.2	20.4	3.9	8.7	18.7	13.7	19.5	14.3	5.7	45.0	1.9
Polk County	5.4	17.5	13.9	30.3	17.3	24.0	2.4	11.1	14.8	7.9	16.5	14.9	5.5	51.0	4.2
Pope County	11.4	17.3	14.5	33.8	15.5	22.4	3.0	8.6	16.6	12.3	20.7	15.6	5.1	43.6	2.7
Ramsey County	3.1	15.8	11.5	39.9	13.7	27.3	0.1	6.3	12.8	0.3	18.5	13.7	5.0	58.0	4.5
Red Lake County	8.4	17.1	15.2	30.2	15.3	22.1	2.3	9.9	20.2	9.9	21.7	18.4	6.4	38.4	6.2
Redwood County	9.2	16.8	13.5	29.6	16.1	23.5	1.9	10.7	18.2	11.1	23.9	15.4	5.8	40.9	2.9
Renville County	9.0	16.5	13.6	30.9	15.1	19.8	2.5	9.3	22.4	13.1	25.3	13.1	5.9	39.1	3.5
Rice County	4.9	14.5	11.5	30.6	15.4	23.8	1.0	10.1	19.1	3.1	25.8	12.7	4.3	50.4	3.8
Rock County	9.9	16.1	13.1	33.2	17.1	22.9	2.5	10.0	14.4	13.0	18.6	13.4	4.4	48.2	2.5
Roseau County	5.4	16.3	12.3	26.0	11.2	19.2	1.1	6.9	35.5	5.5	47.2	10.5	3.1	31.5	2.2
St. Louis County	3.5	18.0	15.0	30.5	18.2	26.2	0.5	11.9	12.8	5.7	13.7	16.1	6.5	53.3	4.6
Scott County	4.6	11.4	11.5	36.1	12.3	27.3	0.2	10.4	13.7	0.9	26.3	16.2	6.3	47.8	2.5
Sherburne County	4.3	13.4	12.3	29.0	12.6	26.1	0.5	12.7	19.2	1.1	30.8	16.9	6.1	41.7	3.3
Sibley County	8.2	16.3	13.3	26.7	11.8	20.4	1.8	11.1	28.2	9.5	34.7	12.5	4.3	36.4	2.6
Stearns County	5.8	13.6	12.2	30.2	14.6	26.6	1.1	8.8	18.6	4.4	23.3	19.8	3.7	46.6	2.3
Steele County	5.2	13.9	13.0	29.6	12.5	27.8	1.0	8.6	20.4	3.4	34.1	14.6	3.1	42.0	2.8
Stevens County	7.8	14.4	9.6	37.3	17.6	24.1	2.1	6.3	12.6	11.0	14.4	13.0	4.0	54.2	3.4
Swift County	8.3	18.2	13.6	33.3	13.4	24.2	2.0	9.2	17.9	11.9	22.7	17.0	5.3	37.0	6.2
Todd County	10.3	20.6	14.9	25.0	14.8	19.7	3.4	10.2	26.8	10.3	30.5	12.7	4.9	38.7	2.9
Traverse County	14.4	18.4	14.0	35.2	18.5	19.8	3.5	8.9	14.2	20.1	12.2	15.5	5.9	42.9	3.5
Wabasha County	8.5	14.7	14.2	32.1	14.8	21.4	2.8	10.6	18.4	9.1	27.2	12.7	4.0	44.0	3.0
Wadena County	8.1	21.4	14.7	29.3	15.1	21.2	2.6	10.2	21.5	7.6	23.2	17.4	4.6	44.1	3.1
Waseca County	5.7	15.0	14.2	26.8	12.4	24.9	1.4	9.9	24.6	5.2	33.9	13.8	4.0	39.6	3.4
Washington County	3.8	11.1	12.4	41.0	11.6	28.2	0.1	7.8	11.2	0.4	23.2	15.1	5.8	50.4	5.1
Watonwan County	6.3	17.1	13.7	26.3	14.5	18.8	1.7	8.8	29.8	7.9	33.6	12.1	6.5	37.4	2.5
Wilkin County	8.2	17.2	12.3	32.8	16.0	19.0	3.0	11.2	17.9	12.4	25.5	13.1	4.0	42.0	2.9
Winona County	5.6	14.6	11.9	30.0	15.7	24.9	1.6	6.9	20.9	4.8	28.9	14.5	3.7	45.8	2.2
Wright County	4.9	13.8	12.4	29.2	12.5	26.1	0.6	12.5	19.1	2.1	30.7	17.0	4.9	43.0	2.4
Yellow Medicine County	8.9	16.1	14.0	33.4	13.8	19.4	2.1	10.4	20.9	11.6	24.4	12.4	5.9	43.0	2.7

STATE County	Median house-hold income	Median family income All families	Married-couple	Male house-holder	Female house-holder	Median nonfamily house-hold income	Median income for full-year, full-time workers Men	Women	Per capita income	With earnings	With interest, dividend, or rental income	With Social Security income	With public assis-tance income	With retire-ment income	House-holds with income over $100,000 (percent)	+/- U.S. percent for income over $100,000 (percent)	House-holds with income below poverty (percent)	Families with children with income below poverty (percent)
	57	58	59	60	61	62	63	64	65	66	67	68	69	70	71	72	73	74
MINNESOTA—Cont'd																		
Grant County	33 775	42 214	48 810	27 917	16 635	17 712	30 015	20 744	17 131	74.6	48.7	39.3	4.2	14.1	4.4	-7.9	9.5	9.6
Hennepin County	51 711	65 985	79 378	36 295	27 657	33 518	44 302	33 844	28 789	85.7	45.7	20.1	3.8	12.7	17.9	5.6	7.4	8.0
Houston County	40 680	49 196	57 998	29 417	22 344	21 433	34 055	22 775	18 826	81.2	47.9	30.7	2.3	13.9	6.0	-6.3	7.6	5.6
Hubbard County	35 321	41 177	48 232	24 464	17 361	19 269	31 325	22 696	18 115	73.7	42.0	35.9	4.1	22.1	5.5	-6.8	10.3	11.4
Isanti County	50 127	55 996	61 849	33 750	22 561	27 109	40 259	27 226	20 348	84.9	38.9	23.6	3.3	14.1	9.1	-3.2	6.0	5.8
Itasca County	36 234	44 025	52 739	25 179	16 830	19 012	38 216	23 151	17 717	73.6	37.1	34.0	3.5	22.5	4.9	-7.4	10.6	13.0
Jackson County	36 746	43 426	48 179	27 279	25 469	20 457	30 530	21 305	17 499	79.5	50.0	32.4	2.3	10.5	3.8	-8.5	8.6	8.9
Kanabec County	38 520	43 603	50 961	33 750	21 250	20 488	33 564	23 281	17 741	79.4	40.2	30.3	3.5	16.6	5.1	-7.2	10.0	9.8
Kandiyohi County	39 772	48 016	56 837	25 507	20 257	21 254	33 994	22 671	19 627	81.2	42.3	29.1	4.1	11.8	7.2	-5.1	9.7	9.2
Kittson County	32 515	40 072	47 600	29 000	13 750	18 932	31 021	21 793	16 525	74.4	44.4	37.8	3.7	13.2	3.2	-9.1	11.2	11.2
Koochiching County	36 262	43 608	59 056	23 750	15 664	19 415	41 232	22 899	19 167	72.9	38.1	35.2	4.2	20.6	4.8	-7.5	13.1	14.7
Lac qui Parle County	32 626	41 556	48 500	29 286	18 889	16 860	29 669	20 554	17 399	74.6	49.0	38.2	3.2	11.7	4.4	-7.9	10.2	8.3
Lake County	40 402	46 980	54 521	32 292	19 479	21 354	40 934	27 327	19 761	75.6	46.5	35.1	2.0	25.6	5.0	-7.3	7.7	9.5
Lake of the Woods County	32 861	38 936	43 333	27 917	24 583	21 700	30 938	25 211	16 976	75.7	37.9	34.6	2.3	15.3	4.3	-8.0	11.7	8.6
Le Sueur County	45 933	53 000	59 939	27 448	21 250	23 936	35 553	24 907	20 151	82.5	45.5	27.6	2.3	12.4	7.8	-4.5	7.5	5.8
Lincoln County	31 607	38 605	44 848	32 500	19 318	15 913	27 353	20 737	16 009	73.4	48.8	39.7	2.4	12.5	2.6	-9.7	11.5	7.8
Lyon County	38 996	48 512	56 409	31 250	17 938	20 825	33 716	21 937	18 013	80.5	45.2	28.3	2.8	11.3	5.5	-6.8	10.9	8.4
McLeod County	45 953	55 003	60 755	32 679	23 725	24 508	36 497	25 890	20 137	82.6	48.9	26.9	2.4	11.9	6.8	-5.5	5.2	4.2
Mahnomen County	30 053	35 500	43 750	25 893	13 844	16 354	25 188	21 699	13 438	76.3	29.9	37.1	5.9	13.7	2.1	-10.2	14.9	19.2
Marshall County	34 804	41 908	48 111	31 250	21 528	18 607	30 741	21 447	16 317	75.6	45.1	34.2	2.6	10.7	3.4	-8.9	11.0	8.8
Martin County	34 810	44 541	50 530	25 385	14 590	19 228	31 469	22 467	18 529	75.5	47.8	34.8	4.0	13.2	4.3	-8.0	10.8	12.3
Meeker County	40 908	47 923	53 916	29 311	22 628	20 798	34 419	23 609	18 628	79.8	43.2	30.2	2.8	11.5	7.1	-5.2	9.1	6.4
Mille Lacs County	36 977	44 054	51 408	27 969	22 027	18 652	33 499	22 496	17 666	76.7	37.4	32.3	4.8	16.2	5.9	-6.4	10.5	9.8
Morrison County	37 047	44 175	50 916	24 881	19 583	17 095	31 763	22 853	16 566	76.9	41.3	31.4	3.3	15.1	4.9	-7.4	12.2	10.3
Mower County	36 654	45 154	56 648	25 755	19 612	20 329	32 438	24 467	19 795	73.6	45.1	35.6	3.8	18.6	6.2	-6.1	8.7	10.2
Murray County	34 966	40 893	45 705	23 929	18 750	19 929	28 638	20 047	17 930	75.6	50.6	36.0	2.7	13.0	4.1	-8.2	9.4	8.4
Nicollet County	46 170	55 694	62 830	33 006	21 483	26 454	37 304	26 220	20 517	85.7	49.6	22.0	2.8	10.2	9.2	-3.1	7.6	6.5
Nobles County	35 684	43 076	47 756	22 031	19 130	19 090	29 230	20 864	16 987	76.5	46.6	33.0	4.1	12.3	5.0	-7.3	11.4	10.7
Norman County	32 535	41 280	46 306	24 375	17 813	16 099	29 985	21 383	15 895	76.5	47.1	38.7	3.8	13.2	3.7	-8.6	12.4	9.0
Olmsted County	51 316	61 610	71 708	33 036	26 186	29 456	41 322	30 650	24 939	85.8	49.5	20.8	2.9	14.9	15.1	2.8	6.2	5.9
Otter Tail County	35 395	42 740	50 649	27 938	19 620	18 298	31 145	21 587	18 014	74.7	44.6	35.8	3.7	17.4	5.5	-6.8	11.0	9.7
Pennington County	34 216	43 936	52 578	21 875	16 833	18 863	31 436	22 361	17 346	81.0	39.1	29.5	4.6	12.1	4.1	-8.2	12.5	9.6
Pine County	37 379	44 058	53 679	30 391	18 446	20 311	32 348	23 632	17 445	77.7	37.0	32.5	4.2	19.0	5.2	-7.1	11.4	11.7
Pipestone County	31 909	40 133	49 024	20 956	18 347	18 504	28 863	21 556	16 450	75.6	47.0	36.1	3.1	12.2	3.5	-8.8	11.3	11.3
Polk County	35 105	44 310	52 323	24 444	17 439	18 189	32 992	22 246	17 279	76.7	42.9	32.7	5.3	13.8	5.5	-6.8	11.5	11.5
Pope County	35 633	42 818	48 929	26 094	17 500	18 343	31 319	21 333	19 032	74.9	47.2	37.6	2.3	13.9	5.2	-7.1	10.4	7.8
Ramsey County	45 722	57 747	68 711	33 810	23 461	30 542	40 612	31 508	23 536	82.7	43.6	22.7	5.4	14.5	13.1	0.8	9.2	11.9
Red Lake County	32 052	40 275	47 784	28 750	18 125	17 928	30 313	21 125	15 372	76.4	44.6	32.8	3.6	10.4	2.7	-9.6	12.2	10.1
Redwood County	37 352	46 250	52 131	23 295	24 545	21 490	31 064	22 329	18 903	75.8	51.1	35.4	2.1	11.4	5.0	-7.3	8.5	7.6
Renville County	37 652	45 065	50 013	26 063	18 250	23 130	31 746	22 727	17 770	78.1	44.7	34.5	2.6	10.9	4.5	-7.8	8.4	9.2
Rice County	48 651	56 407	61 976	33 472	25 761	27 064	37 508	26 914	19 695	84.4	44.4	24.9	2.4	13.5	9.8	-2.5	6.8	5.3
Rock County	38 102	44 996	50 450	30 000	22 045	18 003	30 475	22 940	17 411	75.3	46.9	36.0	3.5	12.6	4.4	-7.9	9.5	7.2
Roseau County	39 852	46 185	52 157	28 333	23 205	22 920	30 256	24 107	17 053	84.3	41.5	24.2	1.9	9.9	4.3	-8.0	7.8	5.6
St. Louis County	36 306	47 134	57 181	27 689	18 132	20 185	39 253	25 291	18 982	74.3	41.3	30.9	5.1	20.2	6.1	-6.2	12.3	11.7
Scott County	66 612	72 212	79 053	39 188	30 513	36 050	47 572	33 206	26 418	92.1	44.5	13.9	1.4	8.4	21.2	8.9	3.7	2.8
Sherburne County	57 014	61 790	66 475	45 199	25 929	32 032	42 041	28 434	21 322	90.4	36.9	16.9	1.5	10.8	11.6	-0.7	4.4	3.1
Sibley County	41 458	48 923	54 408	27 500	25 341	20 593	31 702	23 466	18 004	80.1	49.5	32.0	2.9	10.8	5.5	-6.8	7.7	7.9
Stearns County	42 426	51 553	60 060	30 818	22 113	23 646	35 376	24 045	19 211	84.1	44.3	23.6	2.6	12.3	8.7	-3.6	9.0	6.1
Steele County	46 106	53 981	60 754	30 531	22 829	26 733	37 168	25 701	20 328	82.6	45.5	25.2	2.9	11.9	8.0	-4.3	6.5	6.2
Stevens County	37 267	47 518	54 620	36 250	19 231	15 652	33 984	22 923	17 569	78.7	50.0	31.3	2.2	9.6	5.9	-6.4	15.4	7.2
Swift County	34 820	44 208	50 813	25 833	20 000	18 347	30 336	22 368	16 360	75.3	44.5	37.8	3.0	12.2	3.8	-8.5	10.4	6.5
Todd County	32 281	39 920	46 327	25 357	16 756	16 414	29 469	20 835	15 658	75.7	39.9	33.7	4.6	13.8	4.3	-8.0	13.7	13.1
Traverse County	30 617	39 655	46 917	27 813	14 107	17 784	31 136	21 296	16 378	68.4	47.8	42.5	4.4	15.6	5.3	-7.0	13.8	14.9
Wabasha County	42 117	50 480	59 982	31 607	21 731	24 652	35 025	25 120	19 664	81.8	45.4	28.5	1.7	15.7	6.7	-5.6	6.9	5.6
Wadena County	30 651	38 618	47 351	19 821	15 636	14 025	29 781	21 583	15 146	72.8	40.4	38.3	5.3	15.7	3.3	-9.0	15.0	14.2
Waseca County	42 440	50 081	56 820	29 792	24 031	24 823	35 004	23 339	18 631	83.1	44.8	25.9	3.7	10.9	5.9	-6.4	6.0	5.6
Washington County	66 305	74 576	81 851	45 905	31 320	36 400	50 580	34 962	28 148	89.2	49.5	17.2	1.5	10.8	23.1	10.8	2.8	2.9
Watonwan County	35 441	42 321	49 760	27 563	18 409	21 719	30 324	20 553	16 413	77.0	46.5	34.8	2.9	12.5	3.5	-8.8	9.5	11.3
Wilkin County	38 093	46 220	55 134	24 792	12 250	19 651	31 790	21 642	16 873	79.5	45.8	32.0	3.7	12.1	4.6	-7.7	10.0	8.5
Winona County	38 700	49 845	56 808	27 813	20 745	21 362	33 095	24 269	18 077	82.5	44.4	26.6	2.7	13.6	6.3	-6.0	12.3	8.0
Wright County	53 945	60 940	66 624	32 316	27 062	30 490	41 220	28 945	21 844	88.4	40.2	19.9	2.2	11.3	12.7	0.4	5.0	4.8
Yellow Medicine County	34 393	42 002	48 393	23 214	16 761	17 995	29 031	21 349	17 120	75.7	48.2	34.8	3.2	13.5	3.8	-8.5	12.1	10.1

Table B-3. States and Counties — Education, Labor Force, and Income

STATE/ County code	MSA/PMSA/ NECMA code[1]	STATE County	High school graduates			College graduates		College graduates (percent)				
			Total population 25 years and over	Percent with a high school diploma or less	Percent with a high school diploma or more	Percent with a bachelor's degree or more	+/− U.S. percent with bachelor's degree or more	Non-Hispanic White	Black or African American	American Indian and Alaska Native	Asian, Hawaiian, and Pacific Islander	Hispanic or Latino[2]
			1	2	3	4	5	6	7	8	9	10
28 000	...	MISSISSIPPI............	1 757 517	56.5	72.9	16.9	-7.5	20.1	10.1	9.1	35.2	12.1
28 001	...	Adams County............	22 211	58.3	73.4	17.5	-6.9	24.0	10.7	14.3	9.4	16.6
28 003	...	Alcorn County..............	23 159	66.8	68.1	11.7	-12.7	12.1	7.5	21.7	43.6	9.9
28 005	...	Amite County................	8 981	68.4	67.2	9.4	-15.0	11.7	6.0	0.0	0.0	9.8
28 007	...	Attala County.............	12 674	66.4	63.4	11.6	-12.8	14.9	5.9	0.0	0.0	14.0
28 009	...	Benton County..............	5 073	73.3	58.8	7.8	-16.6	7.7	8.2	0.0	X	0.0
28 011	...	Bolivar County..............	22 956	59.1	65.3	18.8	-5.6	33.3	9.4	6.9	50.6	9.0
28 013	...	Calhoun County............	10 021	70.2	64.4	10.2	-14.2	11.8	4.7	0.0	50.0	21.9
28 015	...	Carroll County..............	7 121	68.1	66.6	10.9	-13.5	12.6	6.7	X	44.4	5.7
28 017	...	Chickasaw County	12 159	71.0	59.4	9.5	-14.9	11.1	7.1	0.0	0.0	0.6
28 019	...	Choctaw County..........	6 171	67.6	65.1	11.2	-13.2	14.1	3.6	27.3	X	0.0
28 021	...	Claiborne County	5 954	53.7	71.6	18.9	-5.5	28.6	15.9	0.0	X	16.7
28 023	...	Clarke County..............	11 541	68.0	68.8	9.6	-14.8	12.1	4.0	0.0	52.4	7.0
28 025	...	Clay County...................	13 441	63.1	68.6	14.6	-9.8	19.8	9.3	21.9	31.8	8.1
28 027	...	Coahoma County	17 403	59.3	62.2	16.2	-8.2	25.1	10.5	0.0	61.8	6.6
28 029	...	Copiah County	17 405	60.9	69.3	11.6	-12.8	15.0	7.6	31.3	24.0	0.0
28 031	...	Covington County..........	11 923	64.7	67.2	11.4	-13.0	13.7	6.4	0.0	0.0	12.5
28 033	4920	DeSoto County..............	68 302	52.5	81.6	14.3	-10.1	14.9	9.0	10.4	27.2	9.3
28 035	3285	Forrest County	41 526	48.6	79.3	22.8	-1.6	28.2	10.2	0.0	39.0	12.5
28 037	...	Franklin County	5 377	66.3	67.5	10.5	-13.9	12.4	6.8	3.0	0.0	0.0
28 039	...	George County	11 838	68.9	69.8	9.1	-15.3	9.8	2.9	0.0	0.0	6.8
28 041	...	Greene County	8 352	70.6	67.4	8.0	-16.4	9.2	4.0	0.0	60.0	13.1
28 043	...	Grenada County	14 675	63.8	63.8	13.5	-10.9	17.0	7.1	24.1	23.2	8.8
28 045	0920	Hancock County	28 840	51.4	77.9	17.3	-7.1	17.9	8.7	13.9	37.5	16.3
28 047	0920	Harrison County	119 169	48.1	80.3	18.4	-6.0	20.3	10.8	12.9	16.7	15.8
28 049	3560	Hinds County.................	150 287	41.5	80.4	27.2	2.8	37.7	18.5	13.9	58.0	24.5
28 051	...	Holmes County..............	12 071	67.0	59.7	11.2	-13.2	20.0	7.9	50.0	22.2	8.6
28 053	...	Humphreys County	6 379	67.9	53.7	11.6	-12.8	16.9	8.9	12.5	0.0	14.5
28 055	...	Issaquena County	1 380	72.4	58.8	7.1	-17.3	10.6	4.6	X	X	0.0
28 057	...	Itawamba County	14 833	66.6	65.0	8.0	-15.0	0.0	0.5	0.0	38.5	16.5
28 059	0920	Jackson County..............	82 818	51.1	81.0	16.5	-7.9	18.1	9.1	12.0	21.4	11.8
28 061	...	Jasper County	11 263	67.8	66.7	9.8	-14.6	13.8	5.3	0.0	25.0	5.7
28 063	...	Jefferson County	5 785	68.5	59.7	10.6	-13.8	16.9	9.4	0.0	100.0	0.0
28 065	...	Jefferson Davis County.	8 613	68.4	66.4	10.4	-14.0	13.6	7.6	0.0	0.0	0.0
28 067	...	Jones County	41 403	58.4	73.9	14.0	-10.4	16.1	6.9	7.4	44.9	7.4
28 069	...	Kemper County	6 498	67.8	60.5	10.3	-14.1	16.1	5.5	0.0	0.0	0.0
28 071	...	Lafayette County	20 628	44.2	78.5	31.1	6.7	36.8	11.9	8.6	70.7	30.5
28 073	3285	Lamar County................	23 855	44.0	83.0	26.8	2.4	28.1	15.7	15.0	49.5	33.1
28 075	...	Lauderdale County........	49 511	53.2	74.9	16.2	-8.2	19.7	8.7	3.6	51.1	16.7
28 077	...	Lawrence County	8 394	61.2	72.9	12.0	-12.4	12.2	11.1	77.8	9.1	12.0
28 079	...	Leake County	13 160	67.7	64.1	11.6	-12.8	14.2	6.9	7.6	20.8	12.7
28 081	...	Lee County	48 382	53.5	74.7	18.1	-6.3	20.7	8.8	16.7	47.5	4.5
28 083	...	Leflore County	21 581	63.7	61.9	15.9	-8.5	23.2	10.9	28.6	52.0	13.2
28 085	...	Lincoln County	21 074	59.6	72.0	12.4	-12.0	13.5	9.3	0.0	57.8	0.0
28 087	...	Lowndes County	37 520	54.3	75.5	20.5	-3.9	27.2	9.2	31.0	32.2	12.1
28 089	3560	Madison County.............	46 773	35.3	83.0	37.9	13.5	48.7	16.3	0.0	48.1	16.0
28 091	...	Marion County..............	16 025	66.9	66.5	11.5	-12.9	12.7	8.1	0.0	18.2	15.2
28 093	...	Marshall County	21 519	71.5	61.0	9.0	-15.4	8.1	10.0	0.0	30.8	2.5
28 095	...	Monroe County	24 288	66.9	65.5	10.9	-13.5	12.6	6.1	15.0	50.0	4.3
28 097	...	Montgomery County......	7 830	69.9	62.1	11.0	-13.4	15.1	4.9	0.0	0.0	4.5
28 099	...	Neshoba County	17 780	64.0	67.7	11.4	-13.0	13.0	8.7	3.3	20.0	0.0
28 101	...	Newton County..............	13 663	60.5	72.9	12.1	-12.3	15.8	3.0	0.0	21.4	5.5
28 103	...	Noxubee County	7 456	72.2	58.4	10.9	-13.5	19.8	6.2	0.0	0.0	5.3
28 105	...	Oktibbeha County	21 250	41.8	80.0	34.8	10.4	45.9	12.6	65.9	80.7	39.5
28 107	...	Panola County..............	20 668	66.1	63.5	10.8	-13.6	15.7	3.7	0.0	35.7	1.1
28 109	...	Pearl River County........	30 940	56.6	74.6	13.9	-10.5	14.6	7.7	6.3	26.8	18.8
28 111	...	Perry County	7 400	66.1	72.0	7.7	-16.7	8.0	6.5	12.0	3.4	0.0
28 113	...	Pike County...................	24 139	61.7	70.3	12.5	-11.9	17.1	5.8	20.8	34.8	5.9
28 115	...	Pontotoc County	17 082	67.1	66.7	11.4	-13.0	11.8	8.1	6.1	31.8	8.3
28 117	...	Prentiss County	16 114	66.4	64.9	9.9	-14.5	10.8	2.9	44.4	0.0	11.2
28 119	...	Quitman County	5 906	69.9	55.1	10.6	-13.8	15.8	7.2	28.6	58.3	0.0
28 121	3560	Rankin County...............	74 885	45.6	81.8	23.8	-0.6	26.0	11.7	23.0	42.3	16.0
28 123	...	Scott County.................	17 496	70.0	62.0	8.6	-15.8	11.4	4.1	0.0	90.9	2.8
28 125	...	Sharkey County.............	3 704	68.2	60.6	12.6	-11.8	21.5	7.4	X	29.4	0.0
28 127	...	Simpson County	17 269	66.5	68.8	10.9	-13.5	12.7	5.9	0.0	68.3	7.6
28 129	...	Smith County.................	10 274	67.5	70.8	9.1	-15.3	11.0	1.8	0.0	0.0	0.0
28 131	...	Stone County................	8 258	55.4	74.8	12.4	-12.0	13.5	4.3	0.0	0.0	26.5

[1]MSA = Metropolitan Statistical Area. PMSA = Primary MSA. NECMA = New England County Metropolitan Area. See the Appendix A for explanation of these concepts. See Appendix B for list of metropolitan areas identified by type, with component counties.
[2]Hispanic or Latino persons may be of any race.

STATE County	School enrollment			Population 16 to 19 years				Employment status, 2000			Work status in 1999 of the population 16 years and over (percent)		
											Worked in 1999		
	Grades kindergarten through 12	College or graduate school	Percent private	Number	Percent in armed forces	Percent high school graduates	Percent not enrolled, not grads, not in armed forces, not employed	Total population 16 years and over	Percent in labor force	Unemploy-ment rate	Full-time	Part-time	Did not work in 1999
	11	12	13	14	15	16	17	18	19	20	21	22	23
MISSISSIPPI	582 848	152 997	11.1	184 029	1.2	9.9	7.8	2 158 941	59.4	7.3	52.4	11.9	35.7
Adams County	7 561	1 538	18.7	2 125	0.0	8.3	6.4	26 313	53.8	9.1	45.1	12.1	42.8
Alcorn County	5 928	1 016	5.4	1 759	0.0	13.5	6.9	27 164	57.4	4.7	51.2	9.5	39.3
Amite County	2 697	392	22.4	854	0.0	11.6	8.3	10 571	51.9	8.9	45.8	11.0	43.2
Attala County	4 109	576	10.4	1 173	0.0	6.5	8.1	15 123	52.2	7.0	46.9	10.2	42.8
Benton County	1 627	210	10.1	483	0.0	8.3	10.6	6 136	50.5	7.1	48.2	10.0	41.8
Bolivar County	9 559	3 752	7.2	3 414	0.1	7.2	6.6	30 283	55.1	15.1	44.8	12.5	42.7
Calhoun County	2 950	338	8.7	935	0.0	14.1	6.3	11 759	57.2	6.5	52.3	10.7	36.9
Carroll County	2 175	335	24.5	633	0.0	5.7	13.6	8 452	56.4	7.4	49.8	10.3	39.9
Chickasaw County	4 121	487	7.6	1 159	0.0	8.6	7.9	14 507	58.3	5.2	53.7	8.5	37.9
Choctaw County	2 091	276	12.4	670	0.0	7.3	6.6	7 409	54.1	11.7	48.0	8.2	43.7
Claiborne County	2 350	2 118	4.8	1 275	0.0	7.1	6.4	9 098	50.8	18.0	41.3	15.4	43.2
Clarke County	3 627	488	5.6	1 063	0.5	9.0	7.8	13 677	53.5	8.5	48.5	8.2	43.3
Clay County	4 843	1 013	14.7	1 445	0.3	7.1	12.6	16 435	57.9	8.0	50.8	10.9	38.2
Coahoma County	7 404	1 099	10.1	2 163	0.0	8.2	14.2	21 642	52.1	10.1	46.7	10.1	43.2
Copiah County	6 183	1 605	16.0	2 235	7.7	10.6	2.1	22 047	56.0	10.9	47.5	11.4	41.1
Covington County	4 337	648	6.2	1 244	0.0	9.6	8.1	14 442	56.0	7.7	49.6	11.3	39.1
DeSoto County	21 613	4 155	13.4	5 314	0.0	9.7	8.8	79 900	69.9	3.6	62.5	12.1	25.5
Forrest County	12 986	10 506	10.1	5 766	1.6	9.4	6.4	56 912	61.5	7.8	49.0	18.5	32.5
Franklin County	1 809	235	5.8	566	0.0	7.4	12.4	6 452	51.9	8.7	44.3	9.8	45.9
George County	4 096	452	3.9	1 128	0.0	12.2	6.1	14 269	56.9	9.1	50.9	9.9	39.2
Greene County	2 292	311	4.5	813	0.2	14.1	17.7	10 469	44.6	10.4	42.6	8.1	49.3
Grenada County	4 888	740	9.5	1 257	0.0	9.1	14.4	17 575	56.4	6.0	50.9	9.5	39.7
Hancock County	8 068	1 463	15.4	2 214	0.0	8.4	5.2	33 333	56.7	6.9	49.1	12.5	38.4
Harrison County	35 754	8 867	11.9	11 619	11.9	22.2	7.4	145 662	65.1	5.6	58.3	12.2	29.5
Hinds County	53 035	19 813	17.7	17 271	0.1	6.8	6.5	188 911	63.1	7.9	54.4	14.4	31.1
Holmes County	5 799	1 087	9.0	1 697	0.0	7.0	7.7	15 536	49.0	17.3	41.7	10.0	48.3
Humphreys County	3 076	337	13.2	904	0.0	2.9	8.5	7 978	51.7	11.4	45.3	10.2	44.5
Issaquena County	560	63	9.3	158	0.0	3.2	11.4	1 724	47.2	13.5	43.2	9.5	47.3
Itawamba County	4 215	1 268	3.1	1 538	0.0	7.0	5.9	17 826	60.5	7.2	54.1	11.1	34.8
Jackson County	27 188	5 397	5.9	7 461	1.4	12.4	6.4	99 044	63.8	6.4	57.3	11.8	30.9
Jasper County	3 964	576	9.3	1 226	0.0	10.9	6.5	13 684	52.8	8.3	49.4	8.5	42.1
Jefferson County	2 133	419	6.7	705	0.0	11.6	9.6	7 320	42.3	14.2	40.2	8.2	51.6
Jefferson Davis County	2 991	445	14.2	951	0.0	10.3	10.3	10 505	51.5	12.9	46.0	9.2	44.7
Jones County	12 363	3 040	6.1	4 375	0.0	6.8	6.4	50 320	57.0	5.7	49.3	12.2	38.5
Kemper County	2 011	729	13.5	832	0.0	8.7	4.1	8 143	54.2	12.6	47.2	10.5	42.3
Lafayette County	5 569	9 856	4.3	3 715	0.1	3.5	2.8	31 921	59.6	6.6	51.0	20.7	28.4
Lamar County	8 107	2 681	9.1	2 298	0.3	11.7	5.0	29 242	65.8	4.2	56.2	14.0	29.9
Lauderdale County	15 416	3 921	7.6	5 091	4.3	12.9	6.1	59 788	58.4	7.2	50.2	11.7	38.2
Lawrence County	2 808	458	6.6	898	0.0	8.7	7.5	10 115	54.0	6.3	47.7	11.0	41.3
Leake County	4 251	436	19.2	1 227	0.0	9.0	10.4	15 904	52.5	7.1	49.3	8.7	41.9
Lee County	15 438	2 574	5.6	4 086	0.0	10.2	7.2	56 996	66.8	4.8	61.5	10.3	28.1
Leflore County	8 537	2 418	12.2	2 781	0.0	6.9	12.8	27 964	52.9	15.9	44.2	11.0	44.9
Lincoln County	6 673	1 149	9.7	1 912	0.0	14.6	4.6	25 293	56.0	7.1	48.8	11.8	39.5
Lowndes County	13 298	3 480	12.3	3 766	1.1	8.4	5.9	45 932	61.1	7.6	53.1	13.0	33.9
Madison County	15 931	3 713	23.8	4 043	0.3	7.6	5.8	55 470	67.1	5.0	59.5	12.4	28.1
Marion County	5 432	726	9.3	1 605	0.0	10.6	9.3	19 407	53.3	7.0	47.4	10.7	41.9
Marshall County	7 008	1 444	21.2	2 362	0.0	9.1	13.9	26 751	56.7	8.8	50.4	9.8	39.8
Monroe County	7 890	889	6.4	2 347	0.0	9.6	6.1	28 981	57.8	6.7	53.1	10.3	36.6
Montgomery County	2 600	363	7.0	779	0.0	7.2	7.6	9 301	54.8	6.9	49.7	8.6	41.7
Neshoba County	6 084	891	16.5	1 808	0.0	13.4	8.8	21 486	60.3	7.4	53.3	10.8	35.9
Newton County	4 247	1 443	9.2	1 523	0.3	7.4	2.9	16 736	56.9	5.1	51.3	10.7	38.0
Noxubee County	2 955	387	18.3	881	0.2	9.1	7.9	9 147	48.9	9.4	45.0	9.4	45.6
Oktibbeha County	6 653	12 335	8.0	4 337	0.1	4.0	2.8	34 965	61.2	11.7	46.8	23.2	29.9
Panola County	7 843	1 070	8.5	2 449	0.0	8.3	10.1	25 451	55.1	7.7	50.6	9.2	40.2
Pearl River County	9 827	2 015	8.0	2 788	0.0	8.1	6.2	36 884	56.4	7.3	48.4	12.4	39.2
Perry County	2 470	326	6.3	878	0.8	9.8	8.9	9 188	54.4	7.1	50.3	9.5	40.2
Pike County	7 868	1 453	10.4	2 711	0.3	15.0	8.3	29 434	53.6	9.4	47.0	10.6	42.4
Pontotoc County	5 267	787	4.4	1 509	0.0	13.3	11.2	20 157	65.1	5.5	58.9	9.6	31.4
Prentiss County	4 658	1 586	2.6	1 819	0.3	6.1	5.9	19 915	58.5	5.6	52.2	11.5	36.3
Quitman County	2 433	237	13.4	655	0.0	11.5	13.9	7 253	52.5	8.4	48.4	8.5	43.0
Rankin County	21 903	4 647	11.1	6 799	0.0	11.3	9.6	89 056	66.9	3.8	60.8	11.9	27.3
Scott County	6 012	669	7.9	1 756	0.2	9.5	10.0	21 221	57.5	6.0	53.7	9.1	37.2
Sharkey County	1 716	156	11.3	500	0.0	2.8	16.8	4 696	54.8	14.5	45.3	11.0	43.7
Simpson County	5 802	777	10.0	1 566	0.6	7.1	11.2	20 766	54.8	6.3	50.3	9.9	39.9
Smith County	3 404	444	5.6	883	0.0	11.3	5.4	12 219	57.0	5.9	53.0	10.2	36.8
Stone County	2 687	970	3.6	1 060	0.0	7.4	4.2	10 398	60.7	6.7	52.7	12.7	34.6

Table B-3. States and Counties — Education, Labor Force, and Income

STATE County	Full-year full-time employed (percent)								Children under 18 years in families						Total employed by class of worker (percent)			
										With two parents (percent)		With one parent who is in labor force (percent)	+/− U.S. percent of children with no stay-at-home parent (percent)	+/− U.S. percent two-income couples				Unpaid family worker
	Total	Men	Women	Non-Hispanic White	Black or African American	American Indian and Alaska Native	Asian, Hawaiian, and Pacific Islander	Hispanic or Latino[1]	Number	Both in labor force	Father only in labor force				Private	Government	Self-employed	
	24	25	26	27	28	29	30	31	32	33	34	35	36	37	38	39	40	41
MISSISSIPPI	36.9	45.4	29.3	40.8	29.8	36.7	36.7	35.6	711 441	37.3	17.2	27.7	0.4	−2.5	72.7	17.6	9.3	0.4
Adams County	29.4	37.5	22.7	35.9	22.2	26.2	43.9	51.1	8 380	31.1	12.8	36.2	2.7	−9.1	70.6	18.9	10.1	0.4
Alcorn County	38.7	49.2	29.3	39.3	35.2	31.0	51.3	29.0	7 745	43.3	21.5	21.1	−0.2	−5.6	77.1	11.7	10.8	0.4
Amite County	31.4	40.4	23.3	36.1	24.6	0.0	57.1	20.6	3 162	34.4	18.9	21.3	−8.9	−10.1	66.7	18.3	14.1	0.9
Attala County	31.5	38.9	25.0	34.4	26.3	0.0	36.4	44.7	4 654	37.0	19.7	27.2	−0.4	−7.7	73.7	16.2	9.1	1.0
Benton County	30.7	37.0	25.0	35.4	22.1	22.2	X	26.9	2 037	31.0	17.9	30.3	−3.3	−10.7	78.5	12.5	8.6	0.3
Bolivar County	27.5	32.5	23.3	36.6	22.0	25.8	40.4	16.7	10 415	26.9	8.2	38.4	0.7	−0.5	64.0	26.1	8.9	1.0
Calhoun County	37.5	45.2	30.7	39.2	32.1	40.0	0.0	46.5	3 516	41.3	10.9	30.6	7.3	−0.2	74.6	14.0	11.1	0.3
Carroll County	35.1	43.3	27.0	39.2	27.1	X	53.3	24.7	2 456	46.7	19.0	21.7	3.8	−3.8	71.9	15.4	12.3	0.4
Chickasaw County	39.1	46.9	32.1	40.7	36.4	100.0	36.8	45.5	5 187	39.2	12.5	32.7	7.3	0.0	77.7	11.8	10.2	0.3
Choctaw County	32.3	42.8	22.9	35.5	24.7	18.2	X	18.4	2 384	36.6	16.8	22.0	−6.0	−9.9	68.6	19.5	11.3	0.7
Claiborne County	23.1	27.6	19.5	40.1	19.6	0.0	0.0	40.0	2 708	24.9	14.1	27.9	−11.8	−7.8	66.2	26.4	6.9	0.4
Clarke County	33.0	40.8	26.2	35.8	27.8	4.3	0.0	32.5	4 480	33.7	17.5	23.0	−7.9	−10.5	75.2	15.8	8.6	0.4
Clay County	34.9	42.9	28.0	39.9	30.6	0.0	59.1	27.0	5 905	30.3	13.7	37.8	3.5	−1.6	74.8	14.9	9.7	0.5
Coahoma County	29.9	35.6	25.4	42.5	23.5	60.0	7.8	26.9	8 817	20.1	10.6	38.3	−6.2	−4.9	70.8	19.6	9.2	0.5
Copiah County	30.6	37.6	24.3	35.7	25.3	80.0	24.0	37.4	7 027	34.3	16.8	26.7	−3.6	−9.3	72.5	18.4	8.8	0.3
Covington County	33.5	43.6	24.2	37.1	26.5	0.0	0.0	27.8	5 056	33.2	18.7	26.9	−4.5	−5.5	70.5	17.8	10.9	0.8
DeSoto County	50.0	61.7	38.9	51.4	41.7	34.2	47.0	40.8	28 670	47.9	24.3	20.2	3.5	4.2	82.2	9.5	8.1	0.2
Forrest County	33.8	42.4	26.5	35.9	30.5	29.2	6.9	29.1	15 913	34.9	16.9	32.3	2.6	−2.6	71.2	19.0	9.4	0.4
Franklin County	29.0	35.0	23.7	31.3	23.5	44.7	100.0	40.6	2 145	39.1	19.3	18.7	−6.8	−10.4	71.7	18.0	9.8	0.5
George County	33.6	47.2	20.1	34.5	25.2	44.4	0.0	39.7	5 126	38.5	36.1	12.4	−13.7	−11.0	75.9	14.4	9.4	0.3
Greene County	24.4	27.0	20.9	28.6	13.3	25.0	20.0	34.7	3 008	35.9	28.1	20.2	−8.5	−14.1	67.7	21.4	10.3	0.6
Grenada County	37.3	48.7	27.6	42.4	29.2	100.0	48.1	48.1	5 621	37.4	16.3	31.6	4.4	−5.6	75.3	14.9	9.6	0.2
Hancock County	33.8	41.4	26.4	33.9	35.1	44.5	27.3	27.5	10 205	41.6	23.1	22.4	−0.6	−12.4	72.2	15.5	11.6	0.7
Harrison County	41.6	49.7	33.8	40.3	37.1	39.7	37.6	43.1	45 706	40.4	17.9	26.9	2.7	−1.0	72.3	17.8	9.5	0.3
Hinds County	37.9	43.9	32.8	42.1	35.0	41.3	35.9	32.5	63 522	34.1	11.4	35.1	4.6	2.9	68.5	22.8	8.4	0.3
Holmes County	23.9	26.6	21.7	32.3	21.3	28.6	38.9	16.3	6 087	21.1	6.9	36.1	−7.4	−11.4	66.3	23.5	9.9	0.3
Humphreys County	26.5	32.8	21.5	39.8	20.8	0.0	20.0	13.7	3 125	22.0	14.2	42.0	−0.6	−8.5	71.6	19.3	8.6	0.5
Issaquena County	25.3	30.0	19.4	37.2	17.3	X	X	0.0	584	29.3	13.2	39.4	4.1	−4.6	64.6	20.6	14.6	0.1
Itawamba County	40.0	50.7	30.1	40.5	31.7	71.4	52.4	46.0	5 230	46.7	17.7	20.7	2.0	−4.3	78.4	12.5	8.6	0.5
Jackson County	41.4	52.3	30.9	42.3	37.3	36.7	45.1	41.4	34 182	40.9	22.0	23.5	−0.2	−3.3	75.3	16.7	7.7	0.4
Jasper County	33.0	41.6	25.4	37.2	28.4	0.0	80.0	46.8	4 646	31.9	19.0	25.5	−7.2	−11.3	76.2	14.9	8.7	0.2
Jefferson County	24.4	27.2	21.5	31.2	23.3	0.0	0.0	0.0	2 477	17.8	6.7	38.5	−8.3	−19.0	65.3	29.8	4.6	0.3
Jefferson Davis County	27.1	33.8	21.4	30.0	24.2	33.3	54.2	52.2	3 567	27.2	14.7	32.5	−4.9	−17.4	70.4	20.4	8.8	0.4
Jones County	34.8	43.9	26.6	37.1	29.8	26.6	27.2	14.5	15 316	36.5	21.7	25.9	−2.2	−8.1	73.1	16.5	10.1	0.4
Kemper County	29.4	37.9	22.0	36.5	23.9	28.4	0.0	20.0	2 368	38.7	11.1	26.1	0.2	−7.7	68.0	19.7	11.3	1.0
Lafayette County	32.5	38.9	26.4	32.0	35.4	22.7	16.4	24.3	7 187	46.5	18.1	24.5	6.4	3.4	62.0	28.7	9.0	0.4
Lamar County	41.5	53.1	31.0	41.5	40.1	51.9	63.6	49.6	10 450	44.1	28.9	16.7	−3.8	0.8	72.1	16.5	10.9	0.5
Lauderdale County	37.4	48.0	28.3	42.2	28.6	43.8	46.2	53.0	19 611	35.7	17.1	28.6	−0.3	−1.2	73.1	18.1	8.5	0.3
Lawrence County	31.6	42.1	22.3	34.1	26.2	100.0	37.8	27.2	3 388	38.3	21.3	20.4	−5.9	−5.4	72.6	17.2	9.2	0.9
Leake County	34.3	40.1	28.9	38.4	26.9	39.1	22.0	45.1	5 275	39.1	16.8	24.0	−1.5	−3.6	74.5	15.5	9.7	0.3
Lee County	46.4	56.5	37.6	48.0	41.2	52.7	31.5	55.4	19 630	45.1	18.1	25.5	6.0	4.5	80.4	10.1	9.3	0.3
Leflore County	29.2	34.6	24.5	40.8	23.3	0.0	21.3	25.3	10 069	21.7	8.5	42.4	−0.5	−3.2	70.0	20.8	8.6	0.5
Lincoln County	32.3	41.3	24.5	33.7	28.5	55.1	43.9	28.8	8 227	38.6	26.7	21.3	−4.7	−7.3	73.5	14.7	11.2	0.6
Lowndes County	38.0	50.2	27.6	42.5	30.0	51.4	40.3	55.9	16 169	36.5	16.9	28.5	0.4	−1.6	73.3	17.0	9.4	0.3
Madison County	45.8	55.9	37.1	53.4	33.1	30.6	45.5	39.0	19 921	43.2	17.9	23.6	2.2	8.0	60.6	18.8	11.3	0.2
Marion County	29.4	38.5	21.3	31.9	22.4	29.2	47.0	47.5	6 293	33.4	22.9	23.9	−7.3	−10.7	71.2	15.7	12.5	0.6
Marshall County	34.7	40.3	29.2	39.9	29.1	57.6	44.2	27.5	8 470	32.5	15.9	31.7	−0.4	−5.6	77.9	13.5	8.3	0.3
Monroe County	37.5	49.7	27.2	40.0	31.5	20.0	29.3	34.8	9 672	39.2	18.7	24.1	−1.3	−4.3	79.6	11.4	8.6	0.5
Montgomery County	36.5	44.1	30.4	38.4	34.0	0.0	0.0	39.3	2 942	32.8	11.8	33.2	1.4	−4.0	74.9	16.0	8.8	0.4
Neshoba County	37.8	47.0	29.9	40.7	26.9	38.0	50.9	12.1	7 261	41.8	13.5	28.0	5.2	−0.2	70.5	19.0	9.7	0.7
Newton County	36.1	44.4	28.7	38.8	29.8	29.2	54.5	40.9	5 322	46.8	15.0	23.1	5.3	−1.3	71.3	18.5	9.8	0.4
Noxubee County	29.4	35.1	24.4	37.1	25.7	12.5	0.0	25.0	3 459	19.5	17.5	30.4	−14.7	−14.6	70.7	16.9	12.0	0.4
Oktibbeha County	28.6	32.8	24.3	30.6	25.5	73.2	21.6	18.6	8 625	35.8	16.1	30.8	2.0	1.7	57.9	36.1	5.7	0.4
Panola County	36.2	43.4	29.9	40.1	31.1	20.7	44.0	47.8	9 103	32.3	12.9	28.2	−4.1	−6.1	74.5	17.0	8.1	0.4
Pearl River County	34.2	43.2	26.0	34.8	30.7	13.6	18.5	23.8	12 206	38.4	24.0	20.7	−5.5	−11.1	69.7	18.0	11.6	0.7
Perry County	33.1	42.6	24.4	35.2	25.6	0.0	28.3	31.3	3 171	36.0	27.3	14.5	−14.1	−10.0	71.3	19.9	8.6	0.1
Pike County	31.0	37.9	25.2	34.6	26.4	26.1	27.6	30.0	9 825	29.2	16.5	32.7	−2.7	−8.6	74.8	14.8	10.0	0.4
Pontotoc County	44.4	55.5	34.3	45.4	38.9	37.3	40.9	42.7	6 880	48.2	20.9	21.2	4.8	1.8	81.3	9.8	8.4	0.5
Prentiss County	38.0	47.1	29.7	38.3	35.6	50.0	47.2	44.6	6 047	43.6	21.8	20.2	−0.8	−4.0	78.0	12.9	8.9	0.2
Quitman County	32.3	38.5	27.2	37.8	29.3	37.5	75.0	38.5	2 790	27.0	8.7	37.1	−0.5	−4.9	72.1	18.6	9.1	0.2
Rankin County	47.7	56.8	39.1	50.6	33.5	65.3	42.2	46.0	28 111	49.5	18.2	21.3	6.2	8.2	72.5	17.7	9.6	0.2
Scott County	38.5	46.5	31.2	42.8	32.0	11.1	22.0	38.5	7 334	32.5	16.1	31.6	−0.5	−5.4	74.6	14.5	10.2	0.7
Sharkey County	26.7	33.8	20.5	41.7	18.8	X	47.1	32.5	1 883	30.0	7.7	34.3	−0.3	3.8	69.1	20.5	10.4	0.0
Simpson County	35.5	43.3	28.4	38.3	29.5	64.0	16.7	54.5	6 912	38.9	20.2	18.7	−7.0	−5.6	70.1	19.5	9.9	0.5
Smith County	36.9	47.4	27.1	38.2	31.8	92.9	57.6	16.2	4 274	42.9	23.1	15.7	−6.0	−4.9	71.7	16.7	11.5	0.2
Stone County	36.2	46.2	26.5	38.8	24.4	0.0	16.7	28.1	3 410	42.4	19.1	20.0	−2.2	−3.0	67.4	19.0	12.6	1.0

[1] Hispanic or Latino persons may be of any race.

				Occupation for employed population 16 years and over (percent)						Industry for employed population 16 years and over (percent)					
STATE County	Percent who worked at home	Percent of the population 5 years and over with a disability	Veterans as a percent of the population 18 years and over	Management, professional, and related occupations	Service occupations	Sales and office occupations	Farming, fishing, and forestry occupations	Construction, extraction, and maintenance occupations	Production, transportation and material moving occupations	Agriculture, forestry, fishing, and mining	Construction and manufacturing	Wholesale and retail trade	Transportation and warehousing, and utilities	Service industries	Public administration
	42	43	44	45	46	47	48	49	50	51	52	53	54	55	56
MISSISSIPPI	1.9	23.6	12.0	27.4	14.9	24.9	1.2	11.2	20.4	3.4	25.9	15.2	5.4	45.0	5.1
Adams County	2.2	27.3	13.3	27.8	18.5	26.4	0.7	10.7	15.9	4.3	17.7	16.1	4.4	50.9	6.6
Alcorn County	2.1	25.9	10.2	22.4	11.9	23.2	0.8	11.2	30.5	1.7	39.6	16.0	4.6	35.3	2.7
Amite County	4.0	31.2	12.6	20.9	12.7	22.9	3.8	13.4	26.3	10.5	28.4	16.6	6.2	33.5	4.9
Attala County	1.8	27.5	11.9	23.6	13.9	23.5	3.2	11.2	24.6	6.5	29.0	15.9	5.5	38.5	4.6
Benton County	1.2	27.8	10.1	17.8	11.1	22.7	1.1	12.7	34.6	3.2	42.2	15.0	6.4	30.0	3.2
Bolivar County	1.5	23.9	8.6	31.2	15.6	21.4	2.9	8.7	20.2	7.1	23.3	13.9	3.8	44.8	7.0
Calhoun County	1.5	26.9	10.2	20.1	10.5	19.1	2.6	8.6	39.0	5.5	45.5	11.9	4.8	29.0	3.2
Carroll County	1.4	27.6	11.6	24.4	11.4	24.6	2.6	15.4	21.6	5.8	30.6	15.0	6.3	36.1	6.2
Chickasaw County	1.6	28.0	9.1	17.6	9.2	17.2	2.1	9.7	44.1	3.8	54.1	10.6	3.3	24.9	3.3
Choctaw County	3.0	28.0	12.3	24.0	11.1	16.6	3.9	15.4	29.0	9.7	37.9	11.2	3.8	33.0	4.3
Claiborne County	1.1	21.3	6.8	25.1	16.9	24.0	2.2	7.5	24.3	4.2	23.5	10.8	7.5	47.0	7.0
Clarke County	1.3	24.0	12.7	20.8	9.9	23.0	2.2	14.3	29.9	8.3	35.4	13.7	4.6	33.6	4.4
Clay County	1.2	23.7	10.6	22.6	13.4	21.1	1.0	8.5	33.2	3.2	41.4	11.2	5.2	35.6	3.4
Coahoma County	1.5	26.4	8.7	24.2	25.1	27.4	2.4	9.0	11.8	6.2	14.7	13.4	4.2	56.4	5.2
Copiah County	1.1	26.6	11.5	22.3	12.7	26.0	2.0	12.1	24.8	3.8	28.7	15.6	6.4	40.5	5.0
Covington County	3.1	24.2	11.0	23.8	13.2	20.4	2.6	14.6	25.5	6.6	28.7	14.5	7.0	39.8	3.4
DeSoto County	2.1	16.7	13.7	26.5	13.4	29.9	0.3	13.1	16.7	0.7	22.2	17.9	14.0	41.9	3.3
Forrest County	2.1	22.0	11.8	30.1	17.8	27.9	0.5	9.3	14.4	1.9	17.1	17.1	4.2	55.6	4.0
Franklin County	1.2	26.4	11.5	23.3	12.9	24.2	4.5	14.8	20.3	11.8	22.7	15.3	5.7	40.1	4.5
George County	1.4	21.6	12.6	22.2	12.0	20.1	2.0	20.8	23.0	4.8	36.8	14.9	5.5	34.0	4.1
Greene County	2.3	25.1	10.7	21.3	15.2	17.4	4.0	19.7	22.4	9.9	32.7	10.1	5.5	33.3	8.6
Grenada County	0.7	29.5	11.2	23.8	12.8	25.7	0.9	9.2	27.5	2.3	34.5	17.9	4.4	36.6	4.3
Hancock County	3.3	27.1	18.1	27.9	19.2	24.2	0.7	15.3	12.7	2.6	21.0	14.0	4.9	51.1	6.5
Harrison County	1.6	24.4	18.6	27.5	21.8	26.6	0.7	11.8	11.6	1.2	16.3	15.1	4.7	56.1	6.6
Hinds County	1.6	22.0	11.3	32.7	16.9	28.8	0.3	8.4	12.9	0.7	14.3	15.4	5.1	57.0	7.4
Holmes County	0.9	29.8	7.7	23.5	15.0	20.7	2.1	9.9	28.8	5.5	30.5	13.6	5.2	39.5	5.8
Humphreys County	1.1	27.6	7.0	26.1	15.1	18.0	6.5	8.1	26.3	16.6	27.0	12.1	2.4	38.3	3.6
Issaquena County	2.9	22.6	8.0	26.0	20.6	18.8	7.4	9.2	18.0	19.9	15.5	13.8	8.2	31.8	10.8
Itawamba County	1.8	25.6	11.3	19.6	10.7	21.5	1.1	13.2	33.9	2.4	47.7	12.2	4.7	30.4	2.7
Jackson County	2.3	21.3	16.7	27.9	17.8	23.6	0.4	14.7	15.6	1.5	29.3	13.8	3.5	46.4	5.6
Jasper County	1.9	27.9	11.1	19.4	11.8	20.6	2.2	13.2	32.8	7.5	39.9	11.9	5.7	31.9	3.1
Jefferson County	1.9	28.4	7.6	21.9	19.4	21.6	3.2	9.7	24.1	5.0	25.3	13.5	6.2	42.1	7.8
Jefferson Davis County	1.8	30.3	10.8	22.9	14.7	17.0	2.7	14.1	28.6	8.8	31.9	12.6	4.2	38.2	4.3
Jones County	1.7	27.4	12.1	24.0	14.8	23.4	1.3	12.8	23.6	6.0	30.8	14.7	4.1	41.5	3.0
Kemper County	2.7	25.6	9.3	20.6	15.7	19.5	3.7	11.7	28.8	8.3	30.5	12.3	5.3	38.9	4.7
Lafayette County	2.5	17.4	9.1	36.9	15.5	26.5	0.4	7.9	12.9	1.2	18.6	12.6	2.5	59.8	5.4
Lamar County	2.6	19.6	11.9	32.9	13.7	28.6	0.9	10.9	13.1	3.9	17.1	17.8	5.7	51.4	4.0
Lauderdale County	1.5	22.5	13.0	29.6	15.7	27.0	0.8	9.9	16.9	1.8	20.7	17.0	5.7	49.6	5.2
Lawrence County	1.8	26.0	12.2	22.5	12.2	23.5	2.2	15.5	24.1	9.0	28.4	17.5	4.9	35.6	4.6
Leake County	2.1	26.9	8.6	25.1	13.1	21.6	2.5	12.8	25.0	9.5	31.8	13.8	6.2	35.0	3.6
Lee County	1.8	21.4	11.3	26.8	10.7	26.9	0.5	7.6	27.4	0.9	35.6	17.1	4.2	39.5	2.7
Leflore County	1.6	25.9	8.3	28.1	16.1	23.5	3.1	7.9	21.3	6.8	23.7	13.8	4.0	44.8	6.9
Lincoln County	1.9	23.5	10.7	24.2	14.0	22.5	2.3	15.4	21.6	8.2	22.7	17.6	5.7	42.0	3.7
Lowndes County	1.6	20.4	13.5	27.8	13.3	25.4	0.4	12.0	21.1	1.3	30.7	14.9	5.7	43.1	4.3
Madison County	3.1	16.1	10.0	43.1	11.0	28.9	0.4	6.0	10.7	1.2	14.7	16.7	4.7	56.2	6.5
Marion County	1.8	27.2	11.9	23.5	13.4	21.8	1.8	15.7	23.8	10.4	25.3	17.0	5.7	37.5	4.1
Marshall County	1.7	23.7	9.3	18.9	13.5	23.5	0.9	15.7	27.7	2.4	34.6	17.0	8.3	34.0	3.8
Monroe County	1.8	24.1	10.8	21.8	10.2	22.4	0.5	10.9	34.2	2.1	44.5	14.0	4.5	32.0	2.8
Montgomery County	1.4	28.8	10.7	23.5	11.3	24.1	1.1	11.3	28.6	3.7	35.7	16.0	5.8	34.2	4.5
Neshoba County	1.9	24.2	11.4	25.7	16.2	23.2	2.5	12.0	20.4	5.1	29.9	14.3	3.2	43.0	4.6
Newton County	2.6	24.8	12.9	25.1	13.9	18.3	2.5	9.9	30.2	5.6	34.8	13.4	4.7	36.6	4.8
Noxubee County	2.3	27.7	7.3	20.1	12.0	19.2	4.8	9.0	34.9	8.2	40.7	12.3	4.3	29.0	5.4
Oktibbeha County	1.9	18.8	7.7	39.6	14.4	24.2	1.3	7.5	12.9	1.9	17.9	12.8	2.7	61.0	3.7
Panola County	1.1	28.1	9.5	20.8	13.8	24.9	1.8	12.7	26.0	3.8	32.0	17.4	5.5	36.5	4.8
Pearl River County	2.4	27.3	14.9	27.6	14.3	24.9	0.8	15.7	16.8	4.9	23.3	15.9	5.9	44.1	5.9
Perry County	2.5	27.7	13.1	23.0	13.9	18.2	2.8	15.6	26.4	7.1	33.8	10.6	4.4	38.0	6.1
Pike County	1.8	26.7	12.5	24.3	14.8	24.0	0.9	11.5	24.5	4.5	26.1	18.7	6.2	40.0	4.4
Pontotoc County	1.5	21.6	11.7	18.7	9.8	21.5	0.6	8.3	41.1	1.3	48.3	13.3	5.0	29.7	2.4
Prentiss County	1.6	25.2	10.4	20.2	11.6	20.7	1.0	11.5	34.9	2.4	44.5	12.7	4.4	32.4	3.6
Quitman County	1.8	27.8	8.7	21.0	20.2	21.6	2.9	9.7	24.5	9.1	24.6	11.8	3.9	44.9	5.8
Rankin County	2.6	18.4	12.6	34.8	11.1	29.8	0.5	11.6	12.2	1.1	18.2	18.1	6.0	50.5	6.3
Scott County	2.1	27.1	9.2	18.1	13.6	20.2	3.6	13.2	31.4	6.2	40.1	13.6	5.0	30.0	5.1
Sharkey County	1.9	24.9	8.0	27.4	17.5	19.9	6.7	9.3	19.2	15.2	17.8	13.6	7.0	41.4	5.1
Simpson County	2.6	26.1	11.8	25.8	15.0	23.8	1.6	15.1	18.7	5.1	23.6	17.4	5.7	43.1	5.1
Smith County	4.8	30.4	10.8	25.8	8.3	19.2	2.5	12.9	31.3	8.9	37.9	11.3	8.1	30.4	3.5
Stone County	4.0	24.2	15.5	24.3	15.4	23.2	4.2	14.7	18.2	7.9	24.3	13.1	6.5	44.1	4.1

STATE County	Median house-hold income (57)	All families (58)	Families with children Married-couple (59)	Male house-holder (60)	Female house-holder (61)	Median nonfamily house-hold income (62)	Men (63)	Women (64)	Per capita income (65)	With earnings (66)	With interest, dividend, or rental income (67)	With Social Security income (68)	With public assis-tance income (69)	With retire-ment income (70)	House-holds with income over $100,000 (percent) (71)	+/- U.S. percent for income over $100,000 (72)	House-holds with income below poverty (percent) (73)	Families with children with income below poverty (percent) (74)
MISSISSIPPI	31 330	37 406	47 589	23 153	14 655	16 616	31 246	22 109	15 853	77.2	22.6	27.9	3.5	15.6	6.0	-6.3	19.7	22.2
Adams County	25 234	29 591	42 336	19 079	12 744	14 432	31 179	21 152	15 778	70.0	19.4	32.9	5.1	17.0	5.0	-7.3	25.6	32.9
Alcorn County	29 041	36 899	46 243	17 917	16 691	13 054	30 449	20 910	15 418	71.7	19.7	32.8	3.4	16.2	4.1	-8.2	19.6	17.2
Amite County	26 033	31 256	36 972	19 286	12 358	12 868	29 073	16 702	14 048	71.1	19.4	34.2	3.6	17.7	3.5	-8.8	23.0	27.1
Attala County	24 794	30 796	41 204	21 250	13 231	13 949	26 760	18 045	13 782	69.7	19.8	36.8	3.7	19.0	4.4	-7.9	22.1	24.9
Benton County	24 149	29 907	38 625	23 824	13 125	11 657	26 997	20 050	12 212	71.9	15.9	34.5	3.9	16.4	3.0	-9.3	24.0	24.1
Bolivar County	23 428	27 301	42 400	15 370	12 129	12 138	28 514	21 187	12 088	73.5	17.1	27.5	6.4	12.1	4.3	-8.0	31.5	37.3
Calhoun County	27 113	34 407	45 637	21 161	14 831	12 165	26 940	19 864	15 106	72.0	18.7	35.8	4.2	13.3	3.8	-8.5	20.5	21.0
Carroll County	28 878	35 711	43 429	24 773	14 669	11 892	30 042	20 304	15 744	74.9	21.4	33.3	3.0	13.6	5.4	-6.9	19.1	19.8
Chickasaw County	26 364	33 819	43 500	33 292	14 268	11 912	25 705	20 492	13 279	73.6	15.8	30.8	3.3	13.6	2.7	-9.6	22.2	20.1
Choctaw County	27 020	31 095	37 583	28 750	11 717	13 262	27 334	18 151	13 474	70.9	21.6	34.2	5.3	17.0	4.4	-7.9	23.2	27.6
Claiborne County	22 615	29 867	40 417	10 417	11 484	11 250	29 271	20 618	11 244	67.9	14.2	29.7	5.2	18.9	5.1	-7.2	31.9	34.8
Clarke County	26 610	33 396	41 739	21 705	11 680	12 933	28 229	20 033	14 288	69.2	19.6	31.8	2.4	16.1	3.1	-9.2	23.5	26.4
Clay County	27 372	35 461	48 258	18 750	14 079	12 818	30 821	20 223	14 512	74.0	20.4	28.9	3.7	17.3	6.0	-6.3	23.7	28.0
Coahoma County	22 338	26 640	45 121	22 850	13 652	11 675	27 149	20 176	12 558	71.8	16.8	29.6	5.8	13.3	5.1	-7.2	32.6	37.9
Copiah County	26 358	31 079	40 554	22 083	13 346	13 534	29 519	20 616	12 408	72.9	16.8	32.7	5.1	14.9	3.6	-8.7	24.7	29.6
Covington County	26 669	31 264	39 511	16 607	12 160	12 395	27 216	19 202	14 506	74.4	18.5	32.7	3.7	15.8	4.6	-7.7	22.7	27.2
DeSoto County	48 206	53 590	60 058	35 048	24 058	28 250	39 205	27 064	20 468	86.2	26.4	21.1	1.7	14.4	9.0	-3.3	7.3	7.1
Forrest County	27 420	35 791	46 553	19 211	14 674	15 894	29 737	21 265	15 160	78.6	21.7	25.5	3.7	13.9	5.3	-7.0	22.3	24.2
Franklin County	24 885	31 114	38 571	22 125	10 801	11 732	27 717	20 533	13 643	67.8	22.0	37.4	2.8	18.1	2.9	-9.4	25.2	27.0
George County	34 730	39 386	41 173	24 674	11 196	12 535	34 926	20 769	14 337	76.0	18.2	28.8	2.8	14.9	4.1	-8.2	17.4	17.8
Greene County	28 336	33 037	39 133	21 771	12 700	12 104	30 217	18 475	11 868	75.9	16.4	30.6	3.5	14.9	3.2	-9.1	20.1	21.0
Grenada County	27 385	33 115	44 474	25 054	14 606	13 379	30 072	22 019	13 786	74.8	19.7	30.7	2.9	14.0	4.1	-8.2	22.3	24.5
Hancock County	35 202	40 307	45 788	24 007	16 116	19 534	33 804	22 991	17 748	75.1	28.6	31.8	3.3	21.8	5.9	-6.4	15.1	15.7
Harrison County	35 624	41 445	48 432	25 329	17 247	22 604	30 766	22 772	18 024	80.8	26.8	25.8	2.5	20.0	6.5	-5.8	14.0	17.0
Hinds County	33 991	40 525	54 490	24 231	16 524	21 304	31 511	25 338	17 785	81.0	23.6	24.7	4.1	15.6	7.7	-4.6	18.4	22.4
Holmes County	17 235	21 757	37 475	17 969	10 318	8 404	24 366	18 218	10 683	65.4	12.3	31.1	9.6	12.6	3.3	-9.0	40.6	45.1
Humphreys County	20 566	23 719	36 192	13 352	13 085	10 527	26 680	19 525	10 920	73.8	12.8	31.2	6.8	11.5	2.6	-9.7	35.6	42.5
Issaquena County	19 936	23 913	38 036	14 792	7 019	10 707	24 205	17 115	10 581	70.9	16.4	30.0	5.3	10.2	3.1	-9.2	31.9	36.4
Itawamba County	31 156	36 793	43 933	30 000	18 449	11 974	29 754	21 159	14 956	75.4	21.4	31.5	1.7	15.2	4.1	-8.2	17.0	12.7
Jackson County	39 110	45 091	51 305	27 157	16 593	22 285	36 190	22 781	17 760	81.2	25.0	25.0	2.5	20.3	7.4	-4.9	12.9	15.5
Jasper County	24 441	29 951	40 132	15 469	14 885	10 319	27 520	17 439	12 889	71.1	18.0	32.9	4.3	13.9	3.4	-8.9	24.6	25.3
Jefferson County	18 447	23 188	35 484	20 469	12 237	9 940	26 700	20 133	9 709	67.3	9.3	30.6	6.7	15.2	1.7	-10.6	35.9	39.7
Jefferson Davis County	21 834	27 594	36 850	13 636	13 564	10 615	24 844	16 827	11 974	68.9	15.3	33.9	4.9	18.4	3.2	-9.1	28.2	31.6
Jones County	28 786	34 465	41 833	21 569	15 149	14 851	29 086	20 123	14 820	74.9	22.8	32.2	2.4	16.5	4.8	-7.5	18.5	21.3
Kemper County	23 998	30 248	40 463	10 441	10 833	11 105	25 245	18 750	11 985	68.8	15.1	34.5	4.5	17.0	3.8	-8.5	27.5	30.9
Lafayette County	28 517	42 910	51 215	21 848	18 511	14 269	31 841	21 582	16 406	82.5	25.7	20.1	1.5	13.6	6.1	-6.2	23.0	13.6
Lamar County	37 628	44 611	50 462	30 000	16 573	20 196	34 555	22 910	18 849	82.7	29.4	22.3	2.4	14.2	9.4	-2.9	12.9	12.5
Lauderdale County	30 768	37 581	50 991	26 098	13 196	16 461	32 062	21 780	16 026	74.0	25.2	29.9	3.4	15.8	5.9	-6.4	21.0	24.2
Lawrence County	28 495	37 899	47 593	26 094	11 525	12 179	29 973	19 440	14 469	72.6	19.4	32.7	3.8	15.7	3.2	-9.1	20.7	21.0
Leake County	27 055	32 147	40 064	27 157	12 022	11 804	27 478	19 120	13 365	72.0	19.2	32.3	3.6	12.5	4.1	-8.2	23.4	25.1
Lee County	36 165	43 149	53 147	25 192	16 591	20 498	31 732	22 988	18 956	82.4	24.1	23.0	2.4	13.6	7.0	-5.3	14.4	15.1
Leflore County	21 518	26 059	44 180	14 135	12 189	12 251	26 663	19 317	12 553	70.7	17.9	27.6	6.2	12.8	5.3	-7.0	31.7	39.8
Lincoln County	27 279	33 552	42 230	16 964	13 262	14 442	30 008	19 519	13 961	74.8	19.6	30.0	4.4	16.5	5.2	-7.1	19.7	21.8
Lowndes County	32 123	38 248	48 514	30 086	10 625	18 266	33 201	21 270	16 514	78.5	25.2	25.6	4.3	15.3	6.5	-5.8	20.7	27.0
Madison County	46 970	58 172	73 029	24 722	20 678	28 173	43 441	30 145	23 469	85.3	33.2	19.6	2.2	11.7	16.4	4.1	12.2	14.7
Marion County	24 555	29 894	36 655	21 309	10 798	11 758	27 317	18 000	12 301	70.9	17.5	32.4	4.2	15.2	3.3	-9.0	25.5	28.3
Marshall County	28 756	33 125	44 781	21 133	15 588	14 029	29 634	21 780	14 028	77.9	14.4	26.0	3.4	13.6	4.7	-7.6	22.3	24.4
Monroe County	30 307	36 749	46 616	27 837	13 642	12 231	30 896	20 793	14 072	74.9	21.8	31.6	2.9	14.8	3.3	-9.0	19.7	18.8
Montgomery County	25 270	31 602	37 112	18 077	12 201	11 828	27 033	18 063	14 040	68.7	20.4	35.0	2.7	15.7	4.6	-7.7	25.6	30.2
Neshoba County	28 300	33 439	42 462	21 875	14 405	12 886	28 755	20 181	14 964	75.0	22.4	32.9	3.1	15.6	4.7	-7.6	21.9	24.4
Newton County	28 735	34 606	42 585	19 531	12 649	13 477	28 393	21 326	14 008	74.2	21.6	32.5	3.5	18.9	3.4	-8.9	20.7	24.0
Noxubee County	22 330	27 312	40 240	14 911	12 542	12 148	25 725	18 281	12 018	69.2	17.1	32.6	5.7	14.4	4.8	-7.5	31.9	37.9
Oktibbeha County	24 899	36 914	50 721	19 700	11 559	13 957	34 838	21 562	14 998	81.1	26.3	19.5	2.9	12.7	7.1	-5.2	28.5	26.3
Panola County	26 785	32 675	43 313	23 094	14 286	13 132	28 428	19 698	13 075	73.9	17.8	28.7	4.5	14.3	4.7	-7.6	24.3	27.3
Pearl River County	30 912	35 924	41 892	19 871	12 565	16 136	31 172	22 178	15 160	75.8	23.8	30.6	3.5	18.9	5.4	-6.9	18.0	22.7
Perry County	27 189	32 791	36 342	16 964	9 688	12 301	29 552	19 355	12 837	75.6	16.4	27.5	5.1	13.8	2.7	-9.6	22.7	24.9
Pike County	24 562	29 415	40 713	18 500	11 768	13 477	28 644	17 961	14 040	70.9	19.9	30.9	4.5	14.4	4.7	-7.6	24.5	29.9
Pontotoc County	32 055	39 845	46 890	27 045	20 072	14 109	29 865	21 658	15 658	78.5	17.4	29.2	2.0	13.1	4.3	-8.0	16.4	12.9
Prentiss County	28 446	35 125	40 064	26 424	16 280	12 788	27 042	20 132	14 131	73.8	20.7	34.0	1.9	14.9	4.1	-8.2	19.3	16.7
Quitman County	20 636	25 394	38 966	16 667	12 614	10 224	24 321	17 640	10 817	70.5	11.9	32.6	5.0	13.0	2.5	-9.8	33.3	37.3
Rankin County	44 946	51 707	60 113	26 711	22 085	26 873	36 949	26 778	20 412	85.9	29.6	21.6	1.7	14.7	10.4	-1.9	9.5	10.2
Scott County	26 686	31 487	42 096	17 072	14 005	13 006	20 975	19 174	14 013	75.5	17.2	29.0	5.1	13.4	3.8	-8.5	21.4	22.1
Sharkey County	22 285	26 786	36 250	16 250	11 176	11 632	27 241	19 394	11 396	74.1	16.7	29.9	6.8	11.8	3.4	-8.9	32.7	43.2
Simpson County	28 343	32 797	39 823	18 750	13 349	13 207	27 394	20 302	13 344	73.4	16.6	30.6	4.1	16.4	3.6	-8.7	22.1	24.1
Smith County	30 840	36 780	43 355	20 909	14 214	12 794	29 258	20 365	14 752	75.6	21.4	34.5	3.0	13.9	4.2	-8.1	17.6	18.1
Stone County	30 495	36 856	44 032	27 917	13 875	14 912	27 311	21 518	14 693	76.5	25.4	29.7	3.7	18.8	5.7	-6.6	17.4	19.9

			High school graduates			College graduates		College graduates (percent)				
STATE/ County code	MSA/PMSA/ NECMA code[1]	STATE County	Total population 25 years and over	Percent with a high school diploma or less	Percent with a high school diploma or more	Percent with a bachelor's degree or more	+/− U.S. percent with bachelor's degree or more	Non-Hispanic White	Black or African American	American Indian and Alaska Native	Asian, Hawaiian, and Pacific Islander	Hispanic or Latino[2]
			1	2	3	4	5	6	7	8	9	10
		MISSISSIPPI—Cont'd										
28 133	...	Sunflower County..........	19 976	66.3	59.3	12.0	−12.4	18.8	8.3	18.2	21.1	9.9
28 135	...	Tallahatchie County	8 979	69.8	54.4	10.9	−13.5	16.3	5.8	100.0	31.8	0.0
28 137	...	Tate County.................	15 460	60.8	71.7	12.3	−12.1	14.6	6.2	0.0	33.3	0.0
28 139	...	Tippah County.............	13 557	70.3	65.5	9.0	−15.4	10.1	2.9	0.0	0.0	11.5
28 141	...	Tishomingo County	13 276	71.3	64.6	8.7	−15.7	8.9	3.5	6.1	18.2	6.5
28 143	...	Tunica County..............	5 263	69.6	60.5	9.1	−15.3	19.2	3.5	14.3	0.0	5.2
28 145	...	Union County................	16 499	65.3	68.5	13.2	−11.2	13.8	8.5	0.0	67.2	5.4
28 147	...	Walthall County	9 366	67.1	67.0	10.4	−14.0	12.8	5.9	0.0	74.3	12.2
28 149	...	Warren County	30 955	49.5	77.0	20.8	−3.6	26.8	10.5	14.3	53.0	26.8
28 151	...	Washington County	36 852	62.2	66.5	16.4	−8.0	23.8	10.7	17.6	46.3	13.4
28 153	...	Wayne County..............	12 933	70.1	64.7	9.5	−14.9	10.9	5.9	0.0	100.0	0.0
28 155	...	Webster County	6 717	66.3	67.7	13.0	−11.4	13.8	8.1	0.0	0.0	32.5
28 157	...	Wilkinson County	6 515	75.0	58.1	10.0	−14.4	15.9	6.8	0.0	X	23.7
28 159	...	Winston County	12 896	65.1	68.2	13.8	−10.6	18.4	6.8	0.0	46.2	6.3
28 161	...	Yalobusha County.........	8 539	68.6	69.0	9.6	−14.8	12.4	3.5	23.3	0.0	21.4
28 163	...	Yazoo County...............	17 308	66.0	65.0	11.8	−12.6	16.8	7.4	0.0	31.7	5.3
29 000	...	MISSOURI................	3 634 906	51.4	81.3	21.6	−2.8	22.3	13.2	12.9	50.1	16.1
29 001	...	Adair County................	13 316	48.9	84.6	28.5	4.1	28.0	32.6	7.7	79.8	11.9
29 003	7000	Andrew County.............	10 847	56.8	84.7	18.8	−5.6	18.7	18.4	13.3	61.8	14.6
29 005	...	Atchison County	4 500	59.2	80.0	16.6	−7.8	16.8	0.0	0.0	30.8	11.1
29 007	...	Audrain County	17 476	67.8	75.1	12.7	−11.7	13.4	2.7	11.3	30.0	5.0
29 009	...	Barry County................	22 381	65.4	75.7	10.7	−13.7	10.9	13.8	0.0	52.3	4.5
29 011	...	Barton County..............	8 070	65.7	77.3	10.6	−13.8	10.6	12.5	22.7	3.1	10.2
29 013	...	Bates County................	10 977	68.4	76.9	10.1	−14.3	10.1	0.0	8.3	31.8	0.0
29 015	...	Benton County..............	12 669	66.8	71.8	8.8	−15.6	8.7	0.0	9.5	0.0	6.1
29 017	...	Bollinger County	7 956	75.8	70.7	6.9	−17.5	7.0	0.0	4.7	0.0	9.1
29 019	1740	Boone County..............	77 919	34.1	89.2	41.7	17.3	42.6	22.3	28.7	71.2	38.9
29 021	7000	Buchanan County..........	55 583	56.5	81.5	16.9	−7.5	17.2	9.6	28.7	35.3	8.9
29 023	...	Butler County...............	27 596	63.8	70.5	11.6	−12.8	11.5	3.5	5.1	47.7	32.2
29 025	...	Caldwell County	5 890	64.7	81.5	11.7	−12.7	11.8	28.6	18.2	22.2	0.0
29 027	...	Callaway County	25 848	58.2	78.9	16.5	−7.9	17.1	7.6	1.4	42.0	12.6
29 029	...	Camden County	27 303	54.4	82.9	17.7	−6.7	17.8	42.2	8.6	46.7	3.2
29 031	...	Cape Girardeau County	43 440	52.2	81.1	24.2	−0.2	24.4	17.2	14.6	61.6	14.5
29 033	...	Carroll County	6 945	67.3	79.1	14.0	−10.4	14.3	5.6	12.8	0.0	5.6
29 035	...	Carter County	3 959	68.7	66.6	10.8	−13.6	10.4	X	0.0	0.0	16.7
29 037	3760	Cass County.................	52 767	51.0	86.7	17.7	−6.7	17.7	22.9	14.6	26.7	17.3
29 039	...	Cedar County...............	9 473	69.8	74.0	10.0	−14.4	9.9	0.0	4.8	23.9	16.7
29 041	...	Chariton County	5 900	68.6	79.6	11.4	−13.0	11.6	4.9	0.0	0.0	25.0
29 043	7920	Christian County	34 790	48.3	85.9	20.9	−3.5	21.1	57.4	9.8	22.6	8.1
29 045	...	Clark County................	4 976	65.7	79.6	10.7	−13.7	10.6	X	100.0	100.0	0.0
29 047	3760	Clay County.................	120 500	43.3	88.7	24.9	0.5	25.2	21.4	15.9	39.2	15.8
29 049	3760	Clinton County..............	12 496	56.4	86.1	14.5	−9.9	14.7	9.1	11.0	8.1	14.0
29 051	...	Cole County	47 339	46.7	85.3	27.4	3.0	28.1	18.2	11.5	65.0	24.5
29 053	...	Cooper County	10 545	63.5	80.3	13.7	−10.7	14.5	2.3	0.0	11.1	35.9
29 055	...	Crawford County	15 057	69.8	69.4	8.4	−16.0	8.5	0.0	2.0	13.3	0.9
29 057	...	Dade County................	5 451	66.9	78.5	9.9	−14.5	9.7	0.0	19.4	0.0	32.0
29 059	...	Dallas County	10 251	68.7	72.8	9.5	−14.9	9.6	0.0	10.2	21.4	0.0
29 061	...	Daviess County	5 213	63.2	79.1	12.0	−12.4	12.0	50.0	0.0	0.0	0.0
29 063	...	DeKalb County.............	8 252	64.2	77.0	10.7	−13.7	11.6	2.5	6.7	67.6	0.0
29 065	...	Dent County.................	10 098	69.5	66.3	10.1	−14.3	10.1	0.0	6.7	0.0	21.6
29 067	...	Douglas County............	8 774	69.1	69.7	9.9	−14.5	10.0	X	4.9	50.0	1.8
29 069	...	Dunklin County.............	21 890	73.7	63.7	9.1	−15.3	9.6	2.1	5.7	49.3	1.0
29 071	7040	Franklin County	60 467	57.9	77.7	12.8	−11.6	12.9	8.0	3.2	19.9	12.2
29 073	...	Gasconade County	10 530	66.2	74.0	10.4	−14.0	10.4	20.0	0.0	0.0	17.1
29 075	...	Gentry County..............	4 599	63.8	81.8	14.5	−9.9	14.6	0.0	0.0	66.7	0.0
29 077	7920	Greene County	153 930	46.1	84.7	24.2	−0.2	24.5	14.0	11.3	41.6	17.3
29 079	...	Grundy County	7 149	60.4	79.0	12.5	−11.9	12.6	0.0	23.1	21.7	5.0
29 081	...	Harrison County	6 101	67.8	80.1	9.3	−15.1	9.2	0.0	0.0	63.6	7.7
29 083	...	Henry County	15 050	66.6	77.3	11.7	−12.7	11.6	8.2	11.1	25.6	12.1
29 085	...	Hickory County	6 712	68.8	73.4	7.7	−16.7	7.6	0.0	0.0	28.6	22.0
29 087	...	Holt County	3 736	67.6	81.9	11.7	−12.7	11.7	X	0.0	0.0	0.0
29 089	...	Howard County	6 420	61.7	81.3	17.9	−6.5	18.6	7.0	64.0	0.0	3.8
29 091	...	Howell County	24 600	65.5	73.4	10.9	−13.5	10.9	5.6	4.7	33.8	2.9
29 093	...	Iron County..................	7 204	69.9	65.2	8.4	−16.0	8.2	6.6	2.3	30.0	10.7
29 095	3760	Jackson County............	427 077	46.6	83.4	23.4	−1.0	26.9	13.2	15.3	34.9	11.0

[1] MSA = Metropolitan Statistical Area. PMSA = Primary MSA. NECMA = New England County Metropolitan Area. See the Appendix A for explanation of these concepts. See Appendix B for list of metropolitan areas identified by type, with component counties.
[2] Hispanic or Latino persons may be of any race.

Table B-3. States and Counties — Education, Labor Force, and Income

STATE County	School enrollment			Population 16 to 19 years				Employment status, 2000			Work status in 1999 of the population 16 years and over (percent)		
											Worked in 1999		
	Grades kindergarten through 12	College or graduate school	Percent private	Number	Percent in armed forces	Percent high school graduates	Percent not enrolled, not grads, not in armed forces, not employed	Total population 16 years and over	Percent in labor force	Unemployment rate	Full-time	Part-time	Did not work in 1999
	11	12	13	14	15	16	17	18	19	20	21	22	23
MISSISSIPPI—Cont'd													
Sunflower County..........	7 690	1 673	12.5	2 833	0.1	9.5	18.1	26 041	45.8	12.8	44.4	9.1	46.5
Tallahatchie County	3 664	519	8.3	975	0.0	5.5	13.5	10 955	51.3	9.6	44.7	10.1	45.2
Tate County..................	5 059	1 708	11.0	1 923	0.0	10.5	6.8	19 262	61.9	10.3	54.0	13.2	32.9
Tippah County	3 900	607	8.5	1 213	0.0	11.8	8.4	16 221	56.8	5.3	51.9	9.4	38.7
Tishomingo County	3 228	375	2.1	901	0.0	11.3	6.7	15 265	55.5	5.7	49.7	9.4	40.9
Tunica County	2 166	132	10.1	591	1.0	10.0	14.2	6 636	60.3	9.3	54.4	8.7	36.9
Union County	4 833	819	4.8	1 405	0.0	4.3	10.5	19 566	60.9	4.8	55.9	9.9	34.2
Walthall County	3 329	493	3.4	1 099	0.0	17.0	6.8	11 413	55.0	9.8	47.7	11.0	41.3
Warren County	10 568	1 814	11.6	3 021	0.0	9.6	9.5	37 221	63.1	6.6	56.3	12.0	31.8
Washington County.......	15 260	2 144	13.2	4 186	0.0	6.7	8.9	45 466	56.7	11.9	48.1	11.3	40.6
Wayne County	4 731	453	6.7	1 424	0.0	12.3	7.4	15 781	53.6	7.8	47.3	10.1	42.6
Webster County	1 992	309	9.3	677	0.0	8.1	10.3	7 989	56.4	6.7	49.1	10.5	40.4
Wilkinson County	2 241	251	21.4	683	0.0	17.0	10.8	7 947	42.3	10.4	37.4	7.5	55.1
Winston County	4 234	534	14.8	1 230	0.0	8.3	13.9	15 375	54.8	7.4	50.3	10.0	39.7
Yalobusha County.........	2 646	453	8.0	828	0.0	8.8	8.9	10 086	54.1	7.0	49.8	9.3	40.9
Yazoo County...............	6 117	618	19.3	1 783	0.0	8.9	11.8	21 059	49.6	10.6	42.6	10.1	47.3
MISSOURI................	1 057 556	319 515	16.7	323 992	0.7	11.2	5.6	4 331 369	65.2	5.3	55.7	15.0	29.3
Adair County	3 520	6 226	8.8	2 820	0.0	4.7	0.6	20 733	61.4	4.8	49.7	26.9	23.4
Andrew County	3 290	597	7.2	925	0.0	10.7	1.8	12 699	66.5	3.0	56.1	15.3	28.6
Atchison County	1 144	163	4.0	376	0.0	8.0	13.3	5 133	61.3	3.7	52.0	14.8	33.2
Audrain County	4 572	636	12.4	1 323	0.0	12.9	9.8	20 262	58.9	4.0	54.3	11.7	34.0
Barry County	6 700	710	5.0	1 877	0.0	12.3	7.7	26 088	59.8	4.8	51.7	12.5	35.8
Barton County	2 446	289	4.7	701	0.0	8.7	6.0	9 481	64.1	3.0	55.3	14.1	30.6
Bates County................	3 379	323	8.5	967	0.0	15.0	5.4	12 804	60.7	5.0	50.4	14.4	35.1
Benton County	2 727	293	5.4	790	0.0	10.9	2.7	14 116	49.9	6.1	42.1	12.0	45.9
Bollinger County............	2 402	220	9.7	699	0.0	14.0	8.0	9 200	61.3	6.1	52.7	14.0	32.5
Boone County	22 625	24 827	8.7	11 018	0.0	7.0	2.1	107 690	71.7	5.3	56.3	23.7	20.0
Buchanan County.........	15 543	4 905	10.0	5 210	0.0	11.5	7.3	67 462	61.7	5.9	54.4	14.5	31.1
Butler County	7 004	1 067	7.1	2 111	0.0	10.7	10.5	32 100	56.1	6.6	50.0	11.6	38.2
Caldwell County	1 840	199	3.5	488	0.4	15.6	3.1	6 822	61.4	3.1	54.1	12.5	33.4
Callaway County	7 820	2 025	18.8	2 679	0.0	14.6	7.4	31 604	65.1	3.9	59.3	15.1	25.7
Camden County	5 598	952	7.4	1 571	0.0	13.7	3.9	30 460	56.3	4.6	50.3	12.8	36.9
Cape Girardeau County	12 003	6 507	12.5	4 820	0.1	9.4	4.9	54 508	67.4	5.0	54.4	18.4	27.2
Carroll County	1 921	173	4.2	527	0.0	14.8	10.6	7 987	60.7	4.1	53.6	13.3	33.1
Carter County	1 168	186	3.0	317	3.2	7.6	5.0	4 623	52.3	8.0	43.0	13.9	43.1
Cass County.................	16 705	2 813	12.0	4 374	0.2	13.3	4.8	61 394	69.4	3.1	61.2	13.1	25.7
Cedar County	2 529	376	9.6	737	0.0	9.4	13.3	10 849	51.3	4.3	43.1	12.4	44.5
Chariton County	1 604	179	9.9	509	0.0	10.4	3.5	6 719	59.6	4.0	50.4	14.9	34.7
Christian County...........	10 704	2 010	9.5	3 004	0.0	12.0	4.7	40 067	70.4	3.2	60.1	14.4	25.5
Clark County	1 383	284	7.4	438	0.0	13.0	4.1	5 807	63.0	5.3	53.9	13.3	32.8
Clay County..................	33 951	9 442	14.3	9 711	0.2	10.0	4.1	141 769	71.7	3.3	63.3	14.2	22.5
Clinton County..............	3 836	582	5.6	1 150	0.0	11.0	4.2	14 549	65.5	4.4	56.8	13.8	29.3
Cole County..................	12 875	4 429	24.5	3 815	0.0	11.2	3.3	55 957	67.4	3.7	60.8	13.6	25.5
Cooper County	3 264	738	14.9	1 103	0.0	14.1	9.4	13 347	57.6	3.4	54.3	13.8	31.9
Crawford County	4 525	480	8.9	1 325	0.0	11.0	6.9	17 604	58.6	6.0	50.9	12.8	36.3
Dade County	1 528	134	8.4	467	0.0	13.5	4.7	6 231	58.0	5.2	50.2	13.4	36.4
Dallas County	3 218	446	9.8	859	0.0	7.2	6.5	11 919	57.2	4.9	50.4	12.6	37.0
Daviess County	1 560	179	9.6	419	0.0	11.5	8.8	6 076	61.6	4.3	52.0	14.6	33.3
DeKalb County	2 096	280	8.3	569	0.0	13.5	6.7	9 496	44.1	3.8	47.2	12.7	40.1
Dent County	2 739	402	7.7	776	0.0	12.9	9.0	11 677	56.3	7.1	48.3	12.5	39.2
Douglas County............	2 584	387	9.1	736	0.0	19.6	5.3	10 107	56.2	4.7	47.2	11.9	40.9
Dunklin County.............	6 185	817	3.8	1 923	0.0	10.3	10.5	25 623	54.9	6.2	49.3	10.0	40.7
Franklin County	19 146	3 167	15.3	5 360	0.1	13.0	4.5	70 986	67.2	3.5	58.3	14.6	27.1
Gasconade County	2 906	322	7.9	833	0.0	12.5	5.9	12 033	61.4	4.1	54.3	12.5	33.3
Gentry County	1 402	129	6.9	404	0.0	8.4	3.2	5 298	59.2	5.3	50.0	14.3	35.8
Greene County	38 501	25 481	15.8	15 093	0.1	10.9	4.3	193 048	66.5	5.5	53.9	18.7	27.4
Grundy County	1 766	450	3.6	639	0.0	6.6	10.2	8 305	59.8	4.8	50.5	13.9	35.6
Harrison County	1 565	171	7.2	458	0.0	18.8	3.7	6 976	62.3	3.7	52.4	14.5	33.1
Henry County	4 055	486	5.6	1 033	0.0	15.5	9.0	17 301	60.6	5.0	51.8	12.7	35.4
Hickory County	1 371	107	4.1	379	0.0	12.1	6.6	7 379	42.9	8.1	37.7	10.0	52.3
Holt County	1 062	128	3.3	272	0.0	7.7	2.2	4 234	60.1	2.2	51.0	15.5	33.5
Howard County	1 894	974	33.4	813	0.0	6.2	1.2	8 106	64.4	5.2	56.3	16.1	27.6
Howell County	7 057	1 369	6.0	2 134	0.0	12.2	6.1	28 747	58.7	6.3	49.7	13.0	37.2
Iron County..................	2 038	293	3.0	638	0.0	13.5	5.2	8 393	53.2	6.7	45.1	12.5	42.4
Jackson County............	123 402	34 768	15.8	34 885	0.0	12.5	7.1	504 285	66.5	5.7	58.6	13.7	27.7

STATE County	Full-year full-time employed (percent)							Children under 18 years in families						Total employed by class of worker (percent)			
									With two parents (percent)		With one parent who is in labor force (percent)	+/- U.S. percent of children with no stay-at-home parent (percent)	+/- U.S. percent two-income couples				
	Total	Men	Women	Non-Hispanic White	Black or African American	American Indian and Alaska Native	Asian, Hawaiian, and Pacific Islander	Hispanic or Latino[1]	Number	Both in labor force	Father only in labor force				Private	Government	Self-employed	Unpaid family worker
	24	25	26	27	28	29	30	31	32	33	34	35	36	37	38	39	40	41
MISSISSIPPI—Cont'd																		
Sunflower County	27.3	29.2	25.1	36.4	23.2	18.2	59.3	15.9	8 084	25.3	10.9	38.9	-0.4	-2.5	66.7	24.2	8.8	0.3
Tallahatchie County	28.6	36.3	22.1	35.8	23.0	60.0	31.9	33.8	3 870	27.4	10.2	32.7	-4.5	-6.0	67.9	22.1	9.4	0.5
Tate County	38.2	47.5	29.7	41.1	31.6	0.0	29.8	39.1	6 363	42.1	21.7	24.3	1.8	-3.6	75.6	13.6	10.7	0.2
Tippah County	38.4	47.7	30.1	37.9	42.5	18.0	27.3	36.0	4 820	41.1	20.3	19.2	-4.3	-7.6	79.9	10.9	8.9	0.3
Tishomingo County	35.2	46.5	25.0	35.7	20.0	27.3	60.6	40.5	4 130	48.6	22.6	15.7	-0.3	-7.2	77.6	10.9	10.7	0.8
Tunica County	35.0	38.8	31.7	39.8	32.2	64.3	76.0	31.0	2 373	29.3	7.0	40.8	5.5	2.5	75.5	16.8	7.1	0.7
Union County	42.3	53.0	32.6	42.7	41.0	61.1	32.8	36.0	6 326	45.9	20.5	21.9	3.2	-2.8	79.2	12.3	8.4	0.1
Walthall County	30.0	37.9	23.0	33.4	24.9	100.0	51.4	23.8	3 944	37.0	14.3	24.6	-3.0	-7.3	68.7	19.8	11.1	0.5
Warren County	41.4	52.3	32.2	45.1	35.9	15.1	47.2	44.1	13 088	38.7	13.1	33.1	7.2	2.3	68.1	22.4	9.3	0.2
Washington County	32.1	41.0	25.0	40.7	26.6	39.4	55.0	32.7	17 377	29.4	9.9	37.4	2.2	-3.9	72.8	18.5	8.7	0.1
Wayne County	32.1	42.4	23.1	34.4	28.0	62.5	35.9	0.0	5 654	33.3	23.6	22.0	-9.3	-9.4	73.9	14.5	11.1	0.4
Webster County	34.5	42.8	26.9	36.9	25.0	0.0	12.5	34.7	2 509	47.1	16.8	20.0	2.5	-3.6	76.5	14.4	8.4	0.7
Wilkinson County	22.2	24.7	19.7	31.8	17.3	36.0	X	2.5	2 341	25.7	14.2	28.4	-10.5	-12.5	58.4	30.2	10.7	0.7
Winston County	36.1	43.9	29.2	40.5	29.2	38.1	30.8	42.1	4 885	35.4	13.1	32.7	3.5	-3.9	71.3	17.0	11.1	0.6
Yalobusha County	32.9	42.3	24.8	34.6	29.6	40.0	12.5	28.8	3 079	34.5	15.8	30.2	0.1	-7.9	74.9	16.3	8.7	0.2
Yazoo County	27.8	31.9	23.6	37.0	21.7	45.2	28.1	8.0	7 245	25.7	10.9	38.5	-0.4	-4.9	73.5	17.6	8.8	0.1
MISSOURI	42.1	51.3	33.7	43.0	36.0	38.4	40.0	40.1	1 350 334	47.2	19.4	22.5	5.1	2.7	77.2	12.8	9.7	0.4
Adair County	31.5	39.0	25.2	32.1	22.6	40.5	13.8	15.9	4 592	56.5	18.1	15.8	7.7	4.2	66.6	22.0	10.9	0.5
Andrew County	44.5	55.5	34.2	44.6	21.7	0.0	11.4	61.5	4 184	53.7	20.9	19.3	8.4	6.7	72.8	12.6	14.1	0.6
Atchison County	39.2	51.6	27.4	39.6	4.0	71.4	0.0	90.0	1 355	58.2	13.8	17.7	11.3	3.5	63.3	16.5	19.7	0.4
Audrain County	40.1	51.0	31.5	41.8	19.8	28.0	68.4	30.4	6 073	51.0	19.4	19.5	5.9	3.9	71.6	13.5	13.8	1.1
Barry County	37.0	46.1	28.3	37.2	35.7	20.8	18.2	39.0	8 384	46.7	20.2	20.2	2.3	-3.9	73.5	9.3	16.5	0.8
Barton County	42.2	52.1	32.9	42.1	76.9	41.8	45.7	35.6	3 296	55.5	20.5	16.0	6.9	4.7	71.4	12.1	15.3	1.2
Bates County	36.5	47.9	26.0	36.9	24.0	11.5	25.0	22.3	4 253	51.0	22.5	16.6	3.0	-2.8	71.2	11.5	16.1	1.2
Benton County	30.1	36.4	23.9	30.1	36.0	17.9	0.0	49.3	3 305	43.4	21.8	19.0	-2.2	-15.2	63.0	14.5	21.3	1.1
Bollinger County	39.0	48.9	29.4	39.1	0.0	14.3	100.0	46.4	3 035	49.1	26.3	15.5	0.0	-1.9	75.1	10.1	14.0	0.9
Boone County	42.0	48.8	35.7	43.1	35.6	30.4	31.4	37.5	29 420	53.6	15.5	22.4	11.4	12.9	65.5	26.2	8.2	0.2
Buchanan County	40.4	48.8	32.6	40.8	31.3	47.7	51.0	45.3	19 559	44.9	19.4	25.6	5.9	1.1	78.4	13.5	7.9	0.2
Butler County	37.0	43.7	31.1	37.5	26.3	27.2	36.9	29.9	9 282	41.7	19.5	22.0	-0.9	-5.5	72.2	17.1	10.3	0.4
Caldwell County	40.8	53.3	29.0	40.8	42.9	46.2	33.3	50.0	2 343	46.3	23.6	21.3	3.0	-1.3	64.5	19.3	15.5	0.7
Callaway County	44.2	48.2	39.9	45.7	26.3	36.0	21.9	36.2	9 720	59.5	11.6	21.1	16.0	13.0	63.7	26.5	9.1	0.6
Camden County	35.4	42.2	29.0	35.6	29.2	17.0	32.3	43.3	6 976	45.5	23.7	19.8	0.7	-8.8	69.3	12.7	17.5	0.5
Cape Girardeau County	41.6	51.8	32.4	42.5	32.6	38.2	21.5	28.3	15 302	51.8	17.9	20.6	7.8	5.7	75.7	14.0	10.0	0.4
Carroll County	39.3	50.3	29.4	39.7	30.8	31.7	0.0	26.5	2 497	58.4	17.2	16.1	9.9	1.7	66.4	14.2	18.8	0.6
Carter County	27.7	35.1	20.6	28.3	0.0	6.7	0.0	32.3	1 432	37.7	24.4	20.7	-6.2	-11.9	64.8	19.7	15.0	0.5
Cass County	48.0	57.9	38.6	47.9	53.1	45.8	41.6	48.5	22 276	54.4	21.0	17.1	6.9	7.9	77.2	12.0	10.5	0.4
Cedar County	30.7	37.5	24.5	31.0	34.8	14.6	24.0	37.0	3 095	45.7	25.4	12.8	-6.1	-8.4	68.7	12.7	18.2	0.4
Chariton County	36.9	46.5	28.2	37.7	12.4	0.0	0.0	50.0	1 934	71.4	7.6	14.5	21.3	5.5	66.8	13.1	19.3	0.9
Christian County	47.0	58.2	36.8	47.0	82.3	35.9	50.7	51.9	14 636	51.9	23.3	18.3	5.6	7.7	75.1	11.6	12.8	0.5
Clark County	39.8	49.7	30.4	40.2	X	0.0	0.0	11.1	1 758	53.2	17.6	16.7	5.3	2.6	72.6	11.6	14.6	1.2
Clay County	50.8	61.4	41.0	51.0	49.7	50.3	50.3	48.2	45 565	52.0	21.2	20.6	8.0	8.2	81.4	10.9	7.5	0.2
Clinton County	44.5	56.7	33.3	44.8	36.9	40.0	8.1	34.1	4 796	53.8	20.2	16.8	6.0	1.8	74.7	13.6	11.1	0.6
Cole County	48.3	50.9	45.5	51.7	24.2	30.9	42.3	35.1	16 665	62.6	10.9	18.8	16.8	16.1	58.3	33.6	7.9	0.3
Cooper County	39.6	43.1	35.5	42.1	21.5	10.8	0.0	43.5	3 638	59.4	13.5	17.8	12.6	8.4	67.5	17.9	13.9	0.6
Crawford County	37.3	46.4	28.5	37.1	60.0	44.8	33.3	45.7	5 632	44.4	23.2	18.1	-2.1	-8.6	77.2	10.5	11.5	0.3
Dade County	37.7	48.8	27.3	37.8	100.0	63.9	40.0	25.8	1 865	49.2	22.8	18.0	2.6	-4.4	69.5	11.6	17.8	1.1
Dallas County	36.2	46.7	26.0	35.8	75.0	34.7	21.4	70.3	3 974	43.2	27.5	16.1	-5.3	-7.8	70.3	12.5	16.7	0.4
Daviess County	38.6	50.9	27.3	38.7	100.0	50.0	14.3	50.0	2 110	49.4	31.4	11.7	-3.5	-4.3	61.2	16.4	20.8	1.5
DeKalb County	29.2	29.9	28.0	32.8	2.4	12.5	26.7	33.3	2 316	50.0	29.1	14.6	0.0	0.6	65.8	17.8	15.9	0.5
Dent County	34.6	44.2	25.8	34.5	31.1	37.1	53.3	48.2	3 543	49.3	21.8	16.5	1.2	-8.0	70.9	14.6	13.9	0.6
Douglas County	31.9	42.1	22.3	32.1	X	29.5	100.0	0.0	3 225	47.4	22.5	15.7	-1.5	-4.3	65.6	12.8	20.3	1.3
Dunklin County	34.9	44.4	26.8	35.5	26.9	40.4	33.3	37.3	7 998	38.2	19.8	22.7	-3.7	-5.5	74.2	13.0	12.2	0.5
Franklin County	44.9	55.9	34.4	45.1	40.0	43.3	44.2	51.0	24 524	50.6	20.4	19.6	5.6	3.0	82.8	8.6	8.4	0.2
Gasconade County	42.0	51.8	32.9	41.9	0.0	25.0	14.3	71.7	3 664	56.6	16.6	18.9	10.9	2.1	77.2	9.4	12.3	1.1
Gentry County	36.1	46.8	26.2	36.3	0.0	18.2	0.0	14.3	1 755	62.7	14.0	16.5	14.6	4.1	64.3	15.5	19.7	0.6
Greene County	40.4	50.0	31.7	41.0	28.6	29.2	33.8	34.8	50 731	46.9	21.6	22.8	5.1	2.0	78.8	10.9	10.0	0.3
Grundy County	37.2	47.5	28.1	37.5	0.0	50.0	0.0	15.0	2 206	49.5	17.5	19.9	4.8	0.3	71.2	12.1	15.9	0.8
Harrison County	39.0	48.6	30.3	38.9	38.9	63.6	72.7	50.0	2 039	60.9	11.5	20.3	16.6	5.1	66.0	14.5	18.7	0.8
Henry County	39.4	49.0	30.4	39.3	55.3	29.2	52.3	47.3	4 986	47.9	16.5	23.4	6.7	-1.3	75.9	11.4	12.3	0.4
Hickory County	25.0	30.7	19.7	24.8	0.0	52.0	14.3	9.3	1 665	39.2	26.7	15.5	-9.9	-24.1	65.2	11.6	21.5	1.6
Holt County	37.7	48.5	27.5	37.7	X	21.4	0.0	50.0	1 214	52.7	23.6	19.4	7.5	0.0	64.8	15.2	19.0	1.0
Howard County	40.1	47.3	33.5	40.9	35.5	66.7	9.7	20.7	2 338	55.0	17.8	16.8	7.2	5.3	67.2	17.8	13.8	1.2
Howell County	36.2	45.2	28.2	36.4	0.0	29.1	39.5	30.0	9 057	46.3	24.6	18.6	0.3	-5.6	72.0	13.2	14.1	0.7
Iron County	31.6	40.7	23.2	31.7	34.7	26.3	20.0	26.5	2 501	39.3	22.6	17.7	-7.6	-11.0	74.6	14.9	10.2	0.3
Jackson County	44.3	52.4	37.1	46.7	38.2	41.8	40.0	39.3	157 472	40.3	16.4	28.8	4.5	3.1	79.4	12.7	7.8	0.2

[1] Hispanic or Latino persons may be of any race.

Table B-3. States and Counties — Education, Labor Force, and Income

STATE County	Percent who worked at home	Percent of the population 5 years and over with a disability	Veterans as a percent of the population 18 years and over	Occupation for employed population 16 years and over (percent)						Industry for employed population 16 years and over (percent)					
				Management, professional, and related occupations	Service occupations	Sales and office occupations	Farming, fishing, and forestry occupations	Construction, extraction, and maintenance occupations	Production, transportation and material moving occupations	Agriculture, forestry, fishing, and mining	Construction and manufacturing	Wholesale and retail trade	Transportation and warehousing, and utilities	Service industries	Public administration
	42	43	44	45	46	47	48	49	50	51	52	53	54	55	56
MISSISSIPPI—Cont'd															
Sunflower County	1.7	25.7	8.7	25.5	16.9	21.6	2.5	8.3	25.1	8.7	25.1	15.4	3.3	38.5	9.1
Tallahatchie County	0.9	31.5	9.0	24.9	16.1	17.1	4.5	9.6	27.6	9.2	29.3	13.2	3.9	36.3	8.1
Tate County	2.5	21.7	11.4	23.1	14.3	23.9	1.0	14.8	22.9	3.4	29.7	16.6	6.2	40.9	3.3
Tippah County	2.0	26.5	10.5	20.5	10.6	20.1	1.0	9.7	38.1	1.8	46.0	12.7	5.8	31.4	2.2
Tishomingo County	1.0	26.1	12.3	19.6	11.5	21.2	1.3	13.6	32.8	2.1	44.6	14.6	4.7	31.7	2.4
Tunica County	0.8	25.9	9.2	18.7	30.9	22.1	4.3	10.4	13.7	10.7	15.6	7.7	3.0	57.7	5.5
Union County	1.2	23.6	11.7	21.3	7.9	23.8	0.2	9.6	37.3	0.9	44.8	15.7	6.1	29.6	2.9
Walthall County	2.7	26.9	10.0	23.1	14.1	21.1	2.0	13.1	26.6	7.8	28.5	15.1	7.3	37.2	4.1
Warren County	1.8	22.4	12.3	31.5	17.1	23.0	1.1	9.8	17.6	2.7	21.4	13.5	6.2	47.3	8.8
Washington County	1.1	23.1	9.8	27.2	14.9	25.2	2.2	9.4	21.2	5.7	23.9	15.2	5.0	44.4	5.7
Wayne County	2.8	26.0	10.9	19.9	11.5	20.5	2.9	16.6	28.6	12.3	31.6	16.7	4.6	31.0	3.8
Webster County	1.6	25.0	13.1	23.1	12.9	20.1	3.0	10.2	30.7	5.6	38.2	11.2	6.0	35.6	3.4
Wilkinson County	2.4	30.0	7.4	22.1	22.8	21.5	2.6	9.8	21.2	7.0	25.5	14.1	5.0	34.9	13.5
Winston County	2.0	23.5	11.6	23.7	15.0	21.9	1.9	10.1	27.3	3.9	35.1	12.1	5.0	40.4	3.5
Yalobusha County	1.5	28.5	11.7	18.3	12.0	20.3	1.4	12.6	35.3	2.9	42.9	11.6	6.0	32.2	4.4
Yazoo County	1.4	26.0	10.8	23.9	16.1	22.0	2.7	11.3	24.1	7.1	27.1	14.3	4.8	41.2	5.6
MISSOURI	3.5	19.0	14.2	31.5	15.0	26.9	0.6	9.8	16.3	2.2	21.7	15.5	5.7	50.3	4.6
Adair County	3.3	15.2	9.0	35.2	18.3	23.5	0.8	7.7	14.5	3.4	16.2	13.5	2.7	60.9	3.3
Andrew County	4.8	18.1	14.5	30.0	15.3	23.3	1.1	12.3	18.0	4.7	26.0	11.8	7.4	45.2	4.8
Atchison County	5.3	23.1	15.9	32.1	15.5	21.2	2.8	9.6	18.9	11.7	17.9	14.2	10.0	41.3	4.9
Audrain County	8.0	21.2	14.2	28.3	13.3	23.7	1.2	9.2	24.3	6.9	28.2	15.1	4.9	38.9	6.0
Barry County	4.6	21.4	14.9	22.3	13.7	21.6	2.5	10.8	29.2	6.7	36.8	13.7	5.0	35.3	2.5
Barton County	7.0	19.3	13.8	24.5	14.4	21.6	1.6	10.9	27.0	8.5	36.7	12.3	5.0	34.1	3.4
Bates County	6.1	21.1	15.1	23.6	15.7	21.7	2.6	16.8	19.6	9.9	24.2	14.4	8.2	41.0	2.3
Benton County	8.2	29.4	22.4	23.0	15.9	22.8	2.1	16.5	19.8	8.0	27.6	15.4	3.9	40.4	4.6
Bollinger County	4.6	24.1	16.0	18.3	11.0	21.1	2.2	16.7	30.6	5.0	37.8	15.2	5.8	32.4	3.7
Boone County	3.2	14.5	10.5	41.8	14.8	27.0	0.5	6.6	9.4	1.1	11.9	14.4	2.9	65.4	4.4
Buchanan County	2.4	20.8	14.7	27.4	17.3	27.0	0.3	10.0	18.1	1.1	23.7	15.3	6.1	48.6	5.2
Butler County	2.4	26.7	16.4	26.8	15.7	24.5	0.9	9.4	22.7	3.3	24.5	14.7	5.9	47.0	4.7
Caldwell County	6.8	20.0	16.9	24.4	15.1	22.9	2.4	15.4	19.8	7.8	25.1	15.3	6.0	38.0	7.8
Callaway County	2.8	18.7	14.7	27.8	16.2	26.9	0.7	12.5	16.0	2.6	19.4	13.9	5.7	46.1	12.2
Camden County	5.4	20.9	19.2	27.4	16.3	29.3	0.6	13.7	12.7	1.8	21.7	19.3	3.4	48.4	5.3
Cape Girardeau County	2.7	16.2	13.2	30.9	15.7	27.5	0.5	9.4	16.0	2.1	21.0	18.5	4.2	50.8	3.6
Carroll County	6.4	21.6	14.3	30.0	13.1	19.0	3.1	11.3	23.6	12.9	24.5	12.5	7.3	38.6	4.3
Carter County	4.4	27.8	16.6	24.6	15.2	20.1	3.4	13.3	23.3	6.3	29.6	11.7	6.5	39.1	6.9
Cass County	3.8	15.8	16.1	30.2	12.8	27.4	0.5	14.3	14.8	1.9	25.3	15.6	6.0	45.9	5.4
Cedar County	6.8	26.5	18.0	25.3	16.3	21.8	2.1	12.9	21.7	8.5	26.1	14.2	4.6	42.9	3.8
Chariton County	7.7	21.6	15.7	29.4	12.7	20.0	2.9	12.0	23.0	12.0	23.9	12.2	7.0	40.3	4.5
Christian County	4.5	16.3	14.6	30.7	13.2	28.2	0.6	12.0	15.2	2.2	22.0	19.2	5.9	47.7	3.1
Clark County	5.5	22.4	14.0	22.3	14.1	19.4	2.5	11.0	30.7	9.3	32.2	13.5	7.3	34.1	3.6
Clay County	2.7	15.7	14.9	32.5	13.7	30.6	0.1	9.2	13.8	0.6	18.2	17.4	8.0	51.2	4.5
Clinton County	4.4	16.5	15.9	25.3	17.0	24.8	1.0	13.5	18.5	3.4	22.8	15.7	8.6	43.8	5.7
Cole County	2.9	16.6	14.6	35.6	13.3	30.6	0.3	8.6	11.5	1.1	15.0	12.7	3.5	43.3	24.4
Cooper County	3.8	17.4	12.6	26.3	18.1	23.6	1.4	12.7	17.9	5.7	22.9	13.9	4.7	44.7	8.2
Crawford County	3.3	22.4	17.2	19.2	15.7	20.3	1.1	16.0	27.7	4.0	35.9	16.2	4.1	36.0	3.8
Dade County	7.2	21.1	16.2	24.9	14.9	19.5	2.7	11.3	26.6	10.4	30.5	15.2	5.7	34.9	3.2
Dallas County	6.0	22.0	17.0	21.3	15.3	23.5	1.1	14.2	24.6	5.4	26.6	17.8	8.0	38.6	3.6
Daviess County	8.4	18.0	16.8	25.2	16.3	20.9	4.5	14.0	19.1	12.3	21.7	14.5	6.0	37.1	8.4
DeKalb County	7.1	22.1	18.0	29.3	17.8	21.8	0.8	12.7	17.5	7.0	21.1	12.5	7.4	42.4	9.5
Dent County	4.0	26.8	15.7	22.4	16.4	21.7	1.7	13.5	24.3	8.7	22.3	19.1	4.9	40.2	4.7
Douglas County	8.2	25.0	14.9	24.5	11.6	20.5	3.7	10.5	29.3	13.1	30.3	14.3	6.1	32.6	3.6
Dunklin County	3.2	26.2	12.5	21.9	14.9	22.5	2.6	10.9	27.1	6.0	29.5	15.7	6.1	38.7	4.1
Franklin County	3.3	17.7	13.6	23.8	14.4	22.4	0.5	14.8	24.1	2.0	35.0	14.1	4.8	41.5	2.6
Gasconade County	4.1	23.5	16.1	21.6	12.3	20.5	1.2	12.0	32.5	4.1	40.5	11.3	5.0	36.0	3.2
Gentry County	4.9	22.9	14.6	30.2	15.6	21.3	2.8	10.5	19.6	10.5	17.6	16.1	5.2	44.4	6.2
Greene County	3.2	18.4	13.9	29.8	16.2	30.1	0.3	8.2	15.4	0.9	17.2	19.2	5.7	54.1	2.8
Grundy County	6.3	24.3	14.5	24.5	18.4	19.3	3.7	10.9	23.1	7.9	27.3	15.0	4.1	41.4	4.4
Harrison County	6.9	20.2	14.9	26.8	19.6	21.3	4.0	11.4	16.9	14.2	14.2	18.1	6.5	41.9	5.1
Henry County	4.1	22.6	17.1	24.4	14.8	24.2	1.6	12.4	22.6	5.6	27.4	16.9	5.5	41.1	3.6
Hickory County	8.2	29.0	22.3	22.1	16.8	22.2	2.2	14.4	22.3	7.8	24.9	15.4	8.2	39.8	3.8
Holt County	6.2	20.5	15.4	30.7	18.4	19.0	2.3	11.6	18.0	12.9	20.5	15.9	5.3	40.1	5.1
Howard County	6.0	18.5	13.7	27.9	16.6	23.5	2.3	11.4	18.2	7.4	22.0	13.3	5.5	45.7	6.1
Howell County	4.5	23.2	16.3	24.0	15.7	23.3	1.9	10.1	25.0	4.3	27.1	16.1	5.9	42.8	3.7
Iron County	4.2	27.3	17.6	23.7	20.1	20.5	2.0	12.8	20.8	8.7	24.3	14.6	4.0	43.1	5.2
Jackson County	2.7	20.0	13.7	33.0	15.1	29.1	0.1	9.2	13.5	0.3	17.6	15.2	5.4	56.2	5.3

STATE County	Median house-hold income	Median family income All families	Married-couple	Male house-holder	Female house-holder	Median nonfamily house-hold income	Median income for full-year, full-time workers Men	Women	Per capita income	With earnings	With interest, dividend, or rental income	With Social Security income	With public assis-tance income	With retire-ment income	House-holds with income over $100,000 (percent)	+/- U.S. percent for income over $100,000	House-holds with income below poverty (percent)	Families with children with income below poverty (percent)
	57	58	59	60	61	62	63	64	65	66	67	68	69	70	71	72	73	74
MISSISSIPPI—Cont'd																		
Sunflower County	24 970	29 144	44 500	18 785	13 750	12 462	26 995	19 873	11 365	78.0	15.9	28.4	5.9	12.6	4.2	-8.1	27.6	32.7
Tallahatchie County	22 229	26 509	36 573	16 534	11 429	10 649	24 897	19 389	10 749	70.0	14.2	30.8	6.3	15.4	2.4	-9.9	30.8	36.8
Tate County	35 836	41 423	50 687	29 138	20 875	16 011	33 658	21 437	16 154	80.5	21.0	26.5	2.2	16.2	6.0	-6.3	15.5	12.5
Tippah County	29 300	34 547	41 262	21 161	12 925	13 657	28 133	20 765	14 041	72.9	19.9	31.6	4.3	15.4	3.1	-9.2	19.6	18.6
Tishomingo County	28 315	34 378	41 343	26 500	15 293	12 175	29 701	20 316	15 395	69.5	22.2	37.5	2.8	18.8	4.3	-8.0	16.2	14.2
Tunica County	23 270	25 443	36 705	19 417	15 369	13 648	25 785	18 822	11 978	76.7	12.8	22.2	6.7	9.9	3.6	-8.7	31.0	35.1
Union County	32 682	39 666	47 832	20 197	20 260	13 911	29 857	21 915	15 700	76.6	22.9	30.3	3.4	15.6	3.4	-8.9	15.5	11.4
Walthall County	22 945	29 169	34 730	18 571	10 485	10 486	27 372	18 214	12 563	70.9	19.3	31.7	3.4	16.0	3.3	-9.0	25.9	32.1
Warren County	35 056	41 706	53 043	25 938	15 491	20 333	35 338	22 330	17 527	80.4	26.2	26.0	4.2	16.0	8.1	-4.2	16.8	22.2
Washington County	25 757	30 324	43 406	18 424	12 204	13 177	29 586	20 775	13 430	75.1	17.7	27.8	5.1	13.8	5.2	-7.1	27.9	33.1
Wayne County	25 918	30 513	36 008	26 875	10 180	11 901	27 795	17 013	12 757	72.5	15.2	30.5	4.8	12.3	4.5	-7.8	25.6	28.2
Webster County	28 834	34 969	40 727	26 786	12 966	12 353	27 962	20 300	14 109	70.8	19.4	38.0	4.1	15.7	3.0	-9.3	20.0	22.0
Wilkinson County	18 929	23 447	35 150	15 000	9 458	9 754	25 371	16 576	10 868	65.1	13.9	32.9	5.1	15.4	3.6	-8.7	36.2	43.1
Winston County	28 256	33 602	45 128	30 114	13 254	15 213	29 329	19 211	14 548	73.9	21.1	33.6	4.1	15.7	4.0	-8.3	23.0	26.4
Yalobusha County	26 315	31 801	43 458	17 500	12 377	14 812	27 606	20 607	14 953	69.1	22.1	35.7	2.9	21.4	3.9	-8.4	22.1	28.2
Yazoo County	24 795	29 395	42 194	20 625	12 629	12 259	29 319	20 370	12 062	71.4	19.5	31.9	5.4	15.6	3.6	-8.7	29.0	35.8
MISSOURI	37 934	46 044	55 854	26 864	19 614	22 293	35 604	25 552	19 936	79.5	36.2	27.6	3.4	17.0	8.8	-3.5	11.8	12.8
Adair County	26 677	38 085	46 821	18 393	14 429	14 373	27 527	22 652	15 484	80.3	39.8	24.4	3.3	12.7	5.5	-6.8	24.4	17.7
Andrew County	40 688	46 067	52 397	26 346	21 875	22 939	33 750	23 971	19 375	79.3	40.8	28.7	1.9	16.6	8.2	-4.1	9.0	9.2
Atchison County	30 959	38 279	44 449	21 875	15 461	18 636	29 745	19 638	16 956	73.9	39.3	37.0	2.7	12.4	4.5	-7.8	12.0	12.4
Audrain County	32 057	40 448	45 830	26 875	18 233	19 332	30 064	21 538	16 441	75.2	40.6	33.6	2.9	16.5	4.6	-7.7	12.9	17.0
Barry County	28 906	34 043	39 245	20 313	16 356	16 297	26 080	19 365	14 980	73.5	29.1	34.2	4.2	16.4	3.7	-8.6	15.4	17.7
Barton County	29 275	35 638	42 878	22 132	15 987	15 320	25 736	20 269	13 987	75.4	35.7	34.4	3.3	12.7	2.7	-9.6	14.6	13.3
Bates County	30 731	36 470	45 176	21 250	15 938	16 943	31 115	21 123	15 477	74.6	31.5	35.2	2.6	18.3	4.0	-8.3	14.7	15.3
Benton County	26 646	32 459	40 506	17 557	14 890	14 604	27 895	19 729	15 457	62.8	34.2	44.5	5.0	28.0	3.1	-9.2	15.7	20.2
Bollinger County	30 462	35 741	38 188	20 625	13 462	13 284	26 748	18 521	13 641	75.6	28.0	32.2	3.4	16.9	2.4	-9.9	15.8	14.5
Boone County	37 485	51 210	59 668	26 145	21 288	22 040	34 952	26 583	19 844	86.4	40.2	17.6	2.5	13.0	9.2	-3.1	15.2	10.9
Buchanan County	34 704	42 408	51 706	28 217	17 161	19 803	32 403	22 450	17 882	76.4	35.3	30.8	4.1	17.9	5.4	-6.9	12.7	13.3
Butler County	27 228	33 371	40 969	16 818	13 961	14 324	28 540	19 177	15 721	70.9	26.8	36.0	5.4	16.8	4.7	-7.6	18.9	21.7
Caldwell County	31 240	37 087	46 219	25 000	15 278	17 460	30 210	20 190	15 343	77.0	34.6	32.7	3.6	15.2	4.0	-8.3	12.9	13.1
Callaway County	39 110	44 474	50 625	27 022	20 359	22 192	30 448	23 047	17 005	81.9	35.3	26.0	2.8	17.3	5.6	-6.7	8.4	8.7
Camden County	35 840	40 695	44 779	21 515	16 233	22 465	30 420	21 969	20 197	71.8	40.6	37.3	2.0	26.0	6.6	-5.7	9.9	14.9
Cape Girardeau County	36 458	45 518	53 061	23 913	20 252	19 904	33 810	21 393	18 593	80.5	38.0	26.6	2.8	14.2	7.0	-5.3	12.5	9.8
Carroll County	30 643	36 773	40 986	21 484	19 250	15 792	26 722	19 634	15 522	74.5	37.4	35.9	3.4	14.0	4.5	-7.8	14.2	12.7
Carter County	22 863	28 506	30 750	16 563	12 875	12 250	27 056	17 043	13 349	67.7	27.5	38.6	5.1	17.9	4.0	-8.3	23.2	28.1
Cass County	49 562	55 258	60 644	35 161	24 561	25 731	40 385	26 857	21 073	83.6	38.0	24.3	2.0	19.5	9.8	-2.5	6.1	6.3
Cedar County	26 694	32 710	38 938	16 550	16 136	12 574	25 798	18 682	14 356	65.9	33.1	42.6	4.3	24.8	2.7	-9.6	18.6	20.4
Chariton County	32 285	39 176	45 049	27 788	17 500	15 649	26 475	20 085	15 515	71.2	43.3	39.4	3.3	13.7	2.7	-9.6	13.5	9.2
Christian County	38 085	44 428	50 941	29 241	16 250	20 368	32 667	22 683	18 422	84.8	34.8	22.4	2.2	13.8	6.4	-5.9	8.8	11.2
Clark County	29 457	36 270	43 393	22 292	19 375	16 875	27 710	20 275	15 988	76.7	35.1	34.3	2.4	12.4	3.3	-9.0	12.9	15.7
Clay County	48 347	56 772	65 540	32 227	26 621	29 782	40 893	28 777	23 144	86.2	39.3	21.4	1.6	15.7	10.7	-1.6	5.4	5.5
Clinton County	41 629	48 244	55 375	26 875	22 250	21 138	37 141	23 924	19 056	80.1	34.8	28.6	1.9	18.7	8.3	-4.0	9.3	9.5
Cole County	42 924	53 416	61 847	26 573	20 199	24 555	35 246	26 040	20 739	84.1	44.5	23.7	2.7	16.8	8.1	-4.2	8.7	8.7
Cooper County	35 313	41 526	48 432	20 341	20 833	19 146	29 835	21 425	15 648	76.9	41.1	32.9	2.4	18.0	3.4	-8.9	11.6	12.3
Crawford County	30 860	36 558	41 178	22 031	11 957	15 824	29 589	19 232	14 825	73.9	28.0	33.4	3.9	18.9	3.6	-8.7	15.9	19.4
Dade County	29 097	33 651	39 796	17 308	19 000	14 789	26 923	19 455	14 254	72.6	38.5	38.0	2.7	17.3	2.4	-9.9	14.2	16.4
Dallas County	27 346	33 500	39 583	32 500	12 664	13 771	26 956	17 738	15 106	72.2	28.0	33.1	3.9	15.6	3.4	-8.9	17.9	19.8
Daviess County	30 855	35 585	40 969	21 563	11 563	17 250	26 364	19 362	15 953	76.0	36.0	35.1	2.7	17.1	4.5	-7.8	15.2	18.1
DeKalb County	31 654	37 329	42 418	23 603	20 739	14 122	30 202	20 814	12 687	75.0	35.8	34.7	3.3	15.5	3.2	-9.1	13.4	9.9
Dent County	27 193	33 061	38 306	20 833	15 172	14 230	27 576	18 227	14 463	71.0	28.9	36.6	4.7	20.4	2.8	-9.5	16.4	19.4
Douglas County	25 918	30 269	34 768	21 917	11 116	11 722	24 842	17 583	13 785	69.6	32.0	36.0	5.1	17.4	3.0	-9.3	19.6	17.0
Dunklin County	24 878	30 779	38 952	18 000	11 068	11 898	27 791	18 871	13 561	69.2	21.8	35.0	6.8	14.9	2.9	-9.4	25.0	27.7
Franklin County	43 474	50 122	57 877	29 276	22 738	22 246	36 626	24 195	19 705	82.5	36.3	26.9	2.2	17.7	7.4	-4.9	7.4	6.3
Gasconade County	35 047	41 518	47 222	26 964	17 457	18 761	30 696	21 525	17 319	73.7	39.6	35.7	2.0	22.6	4.4	-7.9	10.6	10.2
Gentry County	28 750	35 933	41 714	20 809	17 946	16 476	27 200	20 471	15 879	70.2	39.2	37.9	2.5	15.7	3.6	-8.7	12.8	13.3
Greene County	34 157	42 613	51 177	23 661	18 907	20 447	31 445	22 844	19 185	80.5	36.0	26.1	3.3	15.5	7.1	-5.2	12.5	11.8
Grundy County	27 333	34 583	41 703	17 596	13 144	16 474	27 372	20 006	15 432	70.9	35.6	37.2	3.2	16.2	4.2	-8.1	16.0	20.4
Harrison County	28 707	34 298	37 527	26 000	17 232	13 996	25 040	18 182	14 192	72.7	38.3	37.7	3.0	13.6	2.6	-9.7	14.7	13.4
Henry County	30 949	36 328	43 301	19 808	15 706	18 019	29 139	20 061	16 468	72.7	33.9	35.1	3.4	17.3	4.2	-8.1	15.0	17.2
Hickory County	25 346	28 779	32 188	19 219	11 726	14 912	23 941	18 454	13 536	58.0	38.8	50.1	4.5	28.1	2.3	-10.0	18.1	25.1
Holt County	29 461	35 685	41 048	25 833	17 656	16 595	28 194	19 068	15 876	72.9	38.1	37.7	3.1	13.8	3.3	-9.0	13.7	15.2
Howard County	31 614	40 167	46 021	22 813	16 464	16 404	27 206	20 503	15 198	78.8	37.1	32.1	3.3	13.9	3.0	-9.3	11.6	12.0
Howell County	25 628	30 534	35 551	16 310	13 385	12 339	24 078	17 533	13 959	73.5	31.5	35.0	4.6	16.1	3.1	-9.2	17.9	22.0
Iron County	26 080	31 731	37 625	20 417	13 272	14 661	29 744	17 272	14 227	70.1	27.4	36.3	4.7	21.9	2.7	-9.6	18.7	22.8
Jackson County	39 277	48 435	60 882	28 897	21 161	25 529	36 765	28 416	20 788	80.6	32.7	25.1	3.5	16.6	8.8	-3.5	11.5	13.9

Table B-3. States and Counties — Education, Labor Force, and Income

STATE/ County code	MSA/PMSA/ NECMA code[1]	STATE County	High school graduates			College graduates		College graduates (percent)				
			Total population 25 years and over	Percent with a high school diploma or less	Percent with a high school diploma or more	Percent with a bachelor's degree or more	+/− U.S. percent with bachelor's degree or more	Non-Hispanic White	Black or African American	American Indian and Alaska Native	Asian, Hawaiian, and Pacific Islander	Hispanic or Latino[2]
			1	2	3	4	5	6	7	8	9	10
		MISSOURI—Cont'd										
29 097	3710	Jasper County	66 206	55.9	79.5	16.5	-7.9	16.7	12.9	11.5	34.2	7.9
29 099	7040	Jefferson County	125 956	57.0	79.4	12.1	-12.3	12.1	8.2	10.1	34.5	14.8
29 101	...	Johnson County	26 558	46.5	86.0	23.2	-1.2	23.3	18.5	24.2	39.4	13.1
29 103	...	Knox County	2 990	66.6	80.0	12.8	-11.6	13.0	X	0.0	0.0	0.0
29 105	...	Laclede County	21 120	68.2	72.9	11.3	-13.1	11.5	4.9	0.0	7.0	5.3
29 107	3760	Lafayette County	21 863	62.3	79.9	13.8	-10.6	13.8	12.1	2.3	29.7	26.1
29 109	...	Lawrence County	22 882	64.1	77.4	12.1	-12.3	12.2	0.0	10.0	14.3	13.4
29 111	...	Lewis County	6 533	65.0	79.5	13.0	-11.4	13.1	3.7	55.6	X	0.0
29 113	7040	Lincoln County	24 092	66.5	76.4	9.7	-14.7	9.5	10.7	7.1	22.2	24.9
29 115	...	Linn County	9 279	69.0	80.0	10.8	-13.6	10.8	0.0	30.0	0.0	13.5
29 117	...	Livingston County	9 954	65.1	80.6	13.1	-11.3	13.3	8.8	8.0	13.3	35.1
29 119	...	McDonald County	13 418	69.1	69.4	7.0	-17.4	7.4	18.2	10.0	3.8	1.9
29 121	...	Macon County	10 718	67.0	77.8	13.0	-11.4	13.2	4.3	25.6	0.0	0.0
29 123	...	Madison County	7 964	70.4	68.6	7.8	-16.6	7.3	0.0	15.8	69.6	0.0
29 125	...	Maries County	5 969	67.7	74.5	11.0	-13.4	10.9	0.0	0.0	X	45.5
29 127	...	Marion County	18 322	61.4	79.4	15.6	-8.8	16.1	7.4	0.0	25.0	5.8
29 129	...	Mercer County	2 647	64.0	82.5	12.2	-12.2	12.3	X	0.0	0.0	0.0
29 131	...	Miller County	15 369	66.3	73.9	11.4	-13.0	11.6	0.0	0.0	11.9	0.0
29 133	...	Mississippi County	8 702	76.6	61.1	9.6	-14.8	9.9	8.0	0.0	18.8	0.0
29 135	...	Moniteau County	9 751	66.3	77.6	13.0	-11.4	13.9	3.9	0.0	24.5	0.0
29 137	...	Monroe County	6 212	67.9	78.7	9.5	-14.9	9.7	3.5	8.6	0.0	20.0
29 139	...	Montgomery County	8 182	70.4	71.1	9.9	-14.5	9.8	0.0	0.0	41.7	0.0
29 141	...	Morgan County	13 466	66.1	74.5	10.7	-13.7	10.8	4.5	9.4	57.1	6.6
29 143	...	New Madrid County	12 868	76.0	63.6	9.6	-14.8	10.5	2.8	31.8	100.0	0.0
29 145	3710	Newton County	34 211	54.6	79.8	16.1	-8.3	16.3	4.8	17.2	22.3	12.1
29 147	...	Nodaway County	12 169	54.1	87.1	23.6	-0.8	23.4	12.5	0.0	75.8	0.0
29 149	...	Oregon County	7 134	72.3	72.0	9.1	-15.3	9.0	0.0	2.2	43.8	28.6
29 151	...	Osage County	8 375	68.9	75.2	10.4	-14.0	10.3	X	6.9	85.7	0.0
29 153	...	Ozark County	6 795	70.0	73.0	8.3	-16.1	8.2	0.0	35.0	13.3	17.2
29 155	...	Pemiscot County	12 228	75.6	58.2	8.4	-16.0	9.8	2.8	0.0	57.1	0.0
29 157	...	Perry County	11 865	73.2	71.2	9.9	-14.5	10.0	0.0	0.0	13.0	0.0
29 159	...	Pettis County	25 355	55.5	78.3	15.0	-9.4	15.0	12.3	10.8	71.3	4.0
29 161	...	Phelps County	24 665	53.9	79.0	21.1	-3.3	19.9	15.2	7.3	74.9	22.0
29 163	...	Pike County	12 242	68.2	76.0	10.2	-14.2	10.6	5.4	41.4	41.9	2.2
29 165	3760	Platte County	48 721	34.8	91.8	33.3	8.9	33.7	26.9	22.6	45.7	19.6
29 167	...	Polk County	16 645	62.2	77.5	14.6	-9.8	14.3	40.5	28.9	70.3	27.4
29 169	...	Pulaski County	23 062	48.5	85.1	18.8	-5.6	18.5	21.2	12.9	26.8	16.0
29 171	...	Putnam County	3 649	64.8	80.0	11.2	-13.2	11.2	0.0	0.0	100.0	0.0
29 173	...	Ralls County	6 506	67.8	78.7	12.3	-12.1	12.3	4.9	0.0	53.3	34.8
29 175	...	Randolph County	16 452	61.2	77.1	11.7	-12.7	12.3	3.5	10.8	47.7	16.2
29 177	3760	Ray County	15 165	66.6	79.3	10.8	-13.6	11.0	0.0	0.0	23.8	3.7
29 179	...	Reynolds County	4 639	74.5	65.2	7.5	-16.9	7.7	0.0	0.0	55.6	0.0
29 181	...	Ripley County	9 092	71.0	62.1	7.8	-16.6	7.8	0.0	4.3	36.2	0.0
29 183	7040	St. Charles County	178 498	40.5	89.1	26.3	1.9	26.3	22.7	16.4	51.9	26.7
29 185	...	St. Clair County	6 876	72.6	73.1	9.0	-15.4	8.9	0.0	3.3	70.8	11.4
29 186	...	Ste. Genevieve County	11 743	69.0	73.8	8.1	-16.3	8.0	25.5	0.0	100.0	11.4
29 187	...	St. Francois County	37 236	62.3	72.4	10.2	-14.2	10.2	4.3	23.6	24.8	19.6
29 189	7040	St. Louis County	677 027	36.0	88.0	35.4	11.0	38.4	17.4	16.4	65.7	32.7
29 195	...	Saline County	15 185	64.2	74.0	15.8	-8.6	16.0	12.3	6.0	38.2	11.6
29 197	...	Schuyler County	2 870	65.2	81.4	11.6	-12.8	11.7	X	0.0	0.0	0.0
29 199	...	Scotland County	3 172	67.8	76.8	11.2	-13.2	11.3	X	0.0	0.0	6.7
29 201	...	Scott County	25 749	69.8	72.9	10.6	-13.8	11.3	2.6	14.3	28.6	2.9
29 203	...	Shannon County	5 552	75.6	67.6	7.6	-16.8	7.5	0.0	11.5	0.0	3.4
29 205	...	Shelby County	4 589	66.4	81.0	12.5	-11.9	12.6	0.0	0.0	0.0	27.8
29 207	...	Stoddard County	20 121	72.0	66.9	10.1	-14.3	10.0	0.6	8.3	48.2	18.4
29 209	...	Stone County	20 799	58.5	80.4	14.2	-10.2	14.1	0.0	14.6	0.0	37.0
29 211	...	Sullivan County	4 870	72.4	72.4	8.4	-16.0	8.8	0.0	0.0	0.0	3.2
29 213	...	Taney County	26 814	56.4	81.4	14.9	-9.5	15.1	19.3	8.1	11.0	16.8
29 215	...	Texas County	15 641	68.3	71.4	10.8	-13.6	10.8	22.2	4.3	23.1	9.6
29 217	...	Vernon County	13 169	63.3	76.6	14.2	-10.2	14.1	7.1	18.2	33.3	0.0
29 219	7040	Warren County	16 137	60.8	79.5	11.1	-13.3	11.3	5.5	0.0	0.0	19.2
29 221	...	Washington County	14 706	72.9	62.5	7.5	-16.9	7.6	0.0	15.2	47.6	4.1
29 223	...	Wayne County	9 301	74.6	59.7	6.8	-17.6	6.7	0.0	3.1	53.8	28.6
29 225	7920	Webster County	19 515	65.0	74.8	11.0	-13.4	11.2	1.5	9.3	43.1	2.1
29 227	...	Worth County	1 644	65.5	80.2	11.3	-13.1	11.3	X	18.2	X	0.0
29 229	...	Wright County	11 638	69.6	71.1	9.8	-14.6	10.0	14.8	15.5	0.0	3.0

[1]MSA = Metropolitan Statistical Area. PMSA = Primary MSA. NECMA = New England County Metropolitan Area. See the Appendix A for explanation of these concepts. See Appendix B for list of metropolitan areas identified by type, with component counties.
[2]Hispanic or Latino persons may be of any race.

Table B-3. States and Counties — Education, Labor Force, and Income

STATE County	School enrollment			Population 16 to 19 years				Employment status, 2000			Work status in 1999 of the population 16 years and over (percent)		
											Worked in 1999		
	Grades kindergarten through 12	College or graduate school	Percent private	Number	Percent in armed forces	Percent high school graduates	Percent not enrolled, not grads, not in armed forces, not employed	Total population 16 years and over	Percent in labor force	Unemployment rate	Full-time	Part-time	Did not work in 1999
	11	12	13	14	15	16	17	18	19	20	21	22	23
MISSOURI—Cont'd													
Jasper County	19 008	5 495	10.2	6 416	0.2	12.4	7.3	80 723	65.2	6.6	53.9	16.1	30.0
Jefferson County	40 986	7 775	12.1	11 789	0.0	11.5	6.0	149 213	70.2	4.6	59.6	15.3	25.1
Johnson County	8 573	7 687	4.6	4 128	4.6	14.2	3.3	37 455	68.7	5.5	56.8	18.9	24.3
Knox County	780	90	12.3	202	0.0	23.3	0.0	3 370	59.3	4.7	47.7	15.5	36.8
Laclede County	6 408	1 016	7.3	1 948	0.0	13.7	7.0	24 967	62.7	4.8	54.0	13.2	32.8
Lafayette County	6 574	947	9.7	1 906	0.0	11.9	3.9	25 465	65.4	3.7	56.7	13.8	29.4
Lawrence County	6 744	852	9.1	1 799	0.0	13.6	9.9	26 664	62.7	4.4	55.0	13.0	32.0
Lewis County	1 904	776	29.7	702	0.0	7.4	3.7	8 131	65.6	4.8	53.5	18.8	27.7
Lincoln County	8 749	1 230	13.7	2 353	0.0	12.0	5.4	28 581	68.5	4.8	58.5	14.7	26.8
Linn County	2 630	298	5.8	776	0.0	8.9	4.3	10 743	60.5	3.4	54.4	12.2	33.4
Livingston County	2 700	452	6.6	856	0.0	8.5	5.1	11 501	59.5	3.2	51.4	15.3	33.4
McDonald County	4 447	382	7.7	1 275	0.0	13.6	6.3	16 134	63.2	4.2	55.7	12.0	32.3
Macon County	2 833	339	6.6	913	0.8	13.9	5.4	12 442	62.5	3.9	54.1	12.8	33.1
Madison County	2 177	261	3.4	635	0.0	16.4	4.7	9 261	56.3	6.8	47.7	12.5	39.8
Maries County	1 704	212	14.0	470	0.0	12.3	7.4	6 892	62.2	3.6	54.3	13.3	32.4
Marion County	5 474	1 080	18.8	1 823	0.4	11.2	6.1	21 912	63.1	6.7	53.6	15.1	31.4
Mercer County	671	83	6.5	209	0.0	14.8	1.4	3 020	60.5	3.8	52.2	11.8	36.0
Miller County	4 555	659	6.9	1 341	0.0	11.9	8.2	18 105	63.9	5.3	56.4	12.2	31.4
Mississippi County	2 592	311	3.5	824	0.0	9.5	13.8	10 355	57.2	8.8	50.2	10.1	39.7
Moniteau County	2 923	406	14.1	768	0.0	12.0	3.6	11 440	60.9	3.0	57.2	15.6	27.2
Monroe County	1 817	170	10.5	565	0.0	18.2	2.7	7 214	62.3	4.5	53.9	12.7	33.4
Montgomery County	2 364	269	8.7	730	0.0	14.1	8.5	9 463	62.1	6.1	53.7	14.0	32.3
Morgan County	3 290	385	13.4	898	0.0	9.4	5.3	15 230	56.6	4.8	50.0	12.5	37.5
New Madrid County	3 895	499	3.6	1 160	0.0	11.6	8.9	15 176	57.1	6.0	51.1	11.1	37.8
Newton County	9 905	1 910	11.6	3 040	0.1	12.9	8.3	40 408	64.7	4.6	55.7	14.0	30.3
Nodaway County	3 338	4 747	6.0	2 357	0.2	4.0	1.7	18 292	64.3	5.6	50.8	24.3	25.0
Oregon County	1 838	240	4.4	574	0.0	13.1	10.6	8 169	50.9	7.3	41.3	13.3	45.4
Osage County	2 661	531	22.4	770	0.0	9.1	2.6	9 999	68.1	2.7	60.3	13.0	26.7
Ozark County	1 584	196	7.8	505	0.4	18.2	6.7	7 743	53.0	5.9	44.7	12.4	42.9
Pemiscot County	4 356	499	1.2	1 248	0.0	11.7	12.8	14 688	54.1	8.6	48.3	9.1	42.6
Perry County	3 386	497	25.4	992	0.0	14.6	4.6	13 973	66.6	3.0	56.0	14.3	29.8
Pettis County	7 583	1 572	10.7	2 403	0.0	11.3	8.9	30 238	64.6	5.1	54.7	14.3	31.0
Phelps County	7 081	4 814	8.0	2 892	0.3	9.4	4.2	31 553	60.1	6.4	50.5	16.6	32.8
Pike County	3 415	429	12.2	1 082	0.0	9.3	14.1	14 641	55.0	4.8	50.1	12.8	37.1
Platte County	14 016	3 735	12.0	3 765	0.0	12.3	1.1	56 807	74.9	2.6	66.5	13.8	19.8
Polk County	4 889	2 320	28.8	1 976	0.1	10.3	2.0	20 947	59.9	4.6	50.4	15.2	34.4
Pulaski County	8 183	2 825	9.9	3 777	48.4	55.2	1.9	31 025	71.7	4.3	61.1	12.9	26.0
Putnam County	924	174	4.6	265	0.0	3.0	5.7	4 120	55.6	4.6	48.8	13.5	37.7
Ralls County	1 817	221	7.0	524	0.0	13.2	4.4	7 516	68.4	4.9	59.1	14.6	26.3
Randolph County	4 618	944	10.6	1 322	0.0	12.2	6.7	19 455	57.8	4.6	52.1	13.1	34.8
Ray County	4 916	554	6.8	1 424	0.0	16.3	3.9	17 726	65.6	5.5	58.0	13.2	28.7
Reynolds County	1 250	175	4.6	379	0.0	6.1	7.9	5 313	51.3	10.2	44.9	12.4	42.7
Ripley County	2 501	272	7.0	718	0.0	18.1	11.0	10 533	51.3	8.4	45.1	10.2	44.7
St. Charles County	60 232	15 745	20.6	15 689	0.0	8.6	3.0	210 479	74.6	3.8	62.3	16.9	20.8
St. Clair County	1 738	140	4.0	426	0.0	11.0	7.0	7 687	53.7	6.3	47.6	10.8	41.6
Ste. Genevieve County	3 636	496	22.0	1 046	0.0	10.3	4.3	13 681	64.3	3.2	55.4	14.2	30.4
St. Francois County	10 223	1 941	7.3	3 248	0.0	10.3	12.4	43 996	54.8	7.4	48.9	12.4	38.7
St. Louis County	193 194	64 556	29.0	55 360	0.1	7.7	3.2	789 909	67.1	4.6	56.2	16.3	27.5
Saline County	4 267	1 643	20.7	1 637	0.0	10.8	5.1	18 619	64.1	4.5	55.4	15.6	29.0
Schuyler County	783	76	2.9	231	0.0	6.1	1.3	3 290	61.7	4.8	50.8	14.8	34.4
Scotland County	976	79	18.0	269	0.0	12.6	9.7	3 720	65.2	4.6	51.7	13.6	34.7
Scott County	8 074	1 166	9.1	2 275	0.0	10.4	9.5	30 552	63.7	6.3	54.9	13.1	32.0
Shannon County	1 680	220	4.8	483	0.0	20.1	14.5	6 389	52.9	6.7	44.6	12.6	42.8
Shelby County	1 324	185	8.7	406	0.0	16.5	6.9	5 315	62.8	4.8	51.7	14.8	33.5
Stoddard County	5 455	811	4.0	1 820	0.0	11.8	8.0	23 653	58.6	6.0	51.0	12.5	36.5
Stone County	4 560	517	6.0	1 443	0.0	15.5	7.6	23 324	56.1	9.6	49.1	13.5	37.4
Sullivan County	1 302	107	3.0	317	0.0	16.7	1.9	5 590	62.1	5.2	53.5	12.1	34.4
Taney County	6 354	2 123	19.1	2 329	0.0	13.1	4.6	31 862	65.7	10.1	56.0	15.8	28.2
Texas County	4 354	712	8.3	1 358	0.0	12.6	9.6	18 034	54.7	6.4	46.0	13.6	40.4
Vernon County	4 047	704	13.1	1 402	0.1	8.2	4.5	15 726	61.4	4.4	51.9	14.2	33.9
Warren County	4 928	664	17.1	1 369	0.0	12.3	6.4	18 716	68.0	4.3	56.8	15.6	27.5
Washington County	4 737	634	6.4	1 522	0.0	18.7	12.1	17 957	52.7	7.7	48.4	10.3	41.3
Wayne County	2 401	222	5.3	727	0.0	10.3	8.1	10 602	48.3	9.3	42.0	11.5	46.5
Webster County	6 524	825	9.9	1 745	0.0	11.6	8.9	23 057	61.9	4.0	54.6	12.8	32.7
Worth County	469	42	1.6	152	0.0	4.6	2.6	1 897	60.4	5.9	48.0	18.2	33.8
Wright County	3 515	549	7.2	1 128	0.0	15.4	9.1	13 726	57.1	5.9	48.4	12.8	38.8

Table B-3. States and Counties — Education, Labor Force, and Income

STATE County	Full-year full-time employed (percent) Total	Men	Women	Non-Hispanic White	Black or African American	American Indian and Alaska Native	Asian, Hawaiian, and Pacific Islander	Hispanic or Latino[1]	Children under 18 years in families Number	With two parents (percent) Both in labor force	Father only in labor force	With one parent who is in labor force (percent)	+/- U.S. percent of children with no stay-at-home parent (percent)	+/- U.S. percent two-income couples	Total employed by class of worker (percent) Private	Government	Self-employed	Unpaid family worker
	24	25	26	27	28	29	30	31	32	33	34	35	36	37	38	39	40	41
MISSOURI—Cont'd																		
Jasper County	41.0	52.4	30.7	41.0	40.0	36.9	34.8	47.8	25 325	44.1	23.2	22.3	1.8	-0.1	80.6	9.6	9.6	0.2
Jefferson County	47.7	58.3	37.5	47.9	34.4	54.5	44.7	41.2	52 579	49.8	22.3	20.1	5.3	5.3	84.4	8.5	7.0	0.2
Johnson County	39.5	50.0	29.0	39.6	36.1	56.0	27.9	44.7	11 679	50.3	22.2	17.2	2.9	4.4	66.2	23.2	9.9	0.7
Knox County	35.3	45.6	25.6	35.4	X	0.0	0.0	0.0	1 044	60.5	17.3	12.0	7.9	0.8	56.4	16.4	26.1	1.2
Laclede County	40.0	50.8	30.0	40.1	32.2	66.7	44.8	41.6	8 269	51.7	20.8	17.4	4.5	-1.3	75.3	10.2	13.6	1.0
Lafayette County	43.3	53.7	33.7	43.4	36.2	73.1	47.2	37.4	8 233	54.1	19.1	18.5	8.0	4.9	73.9	13.2	12.3	1.0
Lawrence County	40.7	51.4	30.8	40.9	0.0	49.1	16.7	40.0	9 139	50.0	21.7	18.4	3.8	0.8	75.1	11.4	12.9	0.6
Lewis County	39.3	48.2	31.1	39.9	32.2	23.5	0.0	20.7	2 499	52.4	16.4	24.0	11.8	3.8	75.9	10.8	12.1	1.2
Lincoln County	44.8	55.6	34.3	45.3	33.7	19.1	75.0	35.4	11 110	52.0	22.9	18.2	5.6	5.1	80.4	7.9	11.2	0.5
Linn County	39.0	50.1	29.3	39.1	35.4	34.8	21.7	41.9	3 275	50.3	17.3	22.0	7.7	3.0	73.8	11.7	13.5	1.0
Livingston County	38.4	52.3	27.3	39.0	17.1	43.6	46.7	57.1	3 343	50.0	18.2	19.9	5.3	6.9	67.1	17.0	14.4	0.5
McDonald County	41.3	51.9	30.8	41.5	46.2	36.1	48.1	44.0	5 853	40.6	20.7	24.7	0.7	-2.0	74.5	8.2	16.4	0.9
Macon County	39.6	48.7	31.3	39.4	51.8	62.8	52.4	22.9	3 572	54.0	15.6	22.8	12.2	1.1	71.3	14.3	10.5	0.9
Madison County	32.4	41.4	24.3	32.4	0.0	61.9	33.9	37.9	2 737	49.0	16.3	23.1	7.5	-2.6	72.8	14.8	11.9	0.6
Maries County	41.1	50.3	32.2	41.0	41.7	54.2	X	51.4	2 188	50.0	22.6	14.9	0.3	0.5	63.1	21.8	13.9	1.1
Marion County	41.5	51.2	33.1	42.2	27.5	14.3	21.4	45.9	6 914	52.8	16.6	20.5	8.7	1.5	78.0	12.8	8.9	0.3
Mercer County	38.1	49.0	27.9	38.3	X	0.0	60.0	20.0	840	58.3	14.5	17.5	11.2	2.0	66.5	14.8	18.0	0.6
Miller County	40.3	49.8	31.4	40.4	10.0	68.6	6.9	26.9	5 901	54.9	15.5	20.0	10.3	3.9	68.9	16.2	14.4	0.5
Mississippi County	34.5	44.5	26.2	36.9	24.6	41.2	0.0	35.3	3 167	33.8	10.0	39.6	8.8	-0.8	71.6	13.7	13.8	0.9
Moniteau County	43.9	48.2	39.0	45.6	8.3	62.7	13.6	43.3	3 707	57.1	16.5	19.7	12.2	10.6	64.6	22.1	12.6	0.6
Monroe County	39.0	50.0	28.7	39.2	30.8	31.7	50.0	63.6	2 302	52.8	22.9	15.5	3.7	0.5	67.0	15.6	16.0	1.4
Montgomery County	39.2	48.7	30.1	39.5	39.2	9.5	31.3	31.5	2 851	54.5	15.2	21.2	11.1	-0.6	73.3	14.2	12.2	0.2
Morgan County	35.8	42.4	29.4	35.8	30.0	18.2	57.1	43.5	4 392	44.8	25.6	14.3	-5.5	-8.4	65.5	13.7	20.3	0.6
New Madrid County	36.0	45.4	27.8	37.3	28.8	31.8	66.7	22.9	4 759	40.9	15.5	24.7	1.0	-3.5	72.4	15.5	11.4	0.7
Newton County	41.7	54.1	30.2	42.2	49.5	38.7	31.2	33.3	13 012	51.0	23.4	17.3	3.7	0.2	77.6	9.1	12.7	0.6
Nodaway County	34.1	43.2	25.3	34.9	10.9	20.5	8.1	16.9	4 143	65.5	12.0	16.2	17.1	11.1	65.9	21.3	12.2	0.6
Oregon County	28.9	37.7	20.7	28.9	0.0	34.9	0.0	20.6	2 267	38.9	25.9	16.9	-8.8	-10.5	65.9	14.8	17.1	2.1
Osage County	48.9	54.3	43.2	49.0	0.0	51.1	0.0	65.2	3 321	66.1	14.8	13.6	15.1	10.0	60.9	25.3	12.8	1.0
Ozark County	31.0	36.8	25.4	31.2	100.0	26.8	26.7	35.6	2 000	47.6	20.5	18.1	1.1	-7.8	65.3	11.7	21.9	1.1
Pemiscot County	33.3	43.0	25.2	36.3	22.7	64.0	42.5	37.3	5 551	26.6	14.5	36.1	-1.9	-9.5	73.7	16.0	9.7	0.6
Perry County	45.7	55.7	35.9	45.8	0.0	39.5	35.1	54.3	4 600	57.2	16.3	15.3	7.9	7.1	77.6	10.2	11.7	0.5
Pettis County	40.6	52.8	29.4	41.0	43.6	53.9	23.5	27.2	9 814	48.6	21.5	22.4	6.4	0.8	76.4	12.4	11.0	0.3
Phelps County	34.6	39.8	29.2	35.0	25.6	31.8	23.7	40.8	8 843	47.5	21.0	19.8	2.7	-2.1	64.3	24.7	10.3	0.7
Pike County	36.8	39.9	32.8	39.4	16.1	0.0	43.2	26.2	4 002	52.0	15.9	21.5	2.8	2.9	69.6	16.8	13.2	0.4
Platte County	53.7	63.6	44.2	54.0	50.4	48.6	52.6	46.5	18 286	55.7	18.8	19.0	10.1	12.3	79.4	12.1	8.2	0.2
Polk County	34.9	44.3	26.5	35.2	24.6	30.1	10.2	37.0	6 612	49.1	24.4	16.7	1.2	-0.3	75.5	10.2	13.4	0.9
Pulaski County	41.7	51.5	30.4	41.6	48.1	41.1	28.3	39.3	10 726	46.3	28.1	15.1	-3.2	0.0	58.5	32.2	8.6	0.7
Putnam County	34.5	44.8	24.9	34.5	0.0	0.0	100.0	53.3	1 189	52.9	21.5	13.1	1.4	-7.0	64.5	13.1	21.0	1.4
Ralls County	46.4	56.8	36.2	46.7	38.6	20.0	11.8	51.7	2 329	63.3	14.6	9.9	8.6	6.1	70.2	16.5	12.8	0.4
Randolph County	37.8	42.6	32.5	39.5	20.1	16.2	35.3	32.4	5 400	47.6	15.6	24.8	7.0	2.3	75.4	14.1	10.2	0.3
Ray County	44.1	55.1	33.5	44.3	32.1	59.4	66.7	38.9	6 170	52.2	23.2	17.0	4.6	-0.1	77.2	11.0	11.0	0.8
Reynolds County	29.2	39.9	18.2	28.9	15.4	23.1	77.8	22.2	1 388	39.6	23.6	15.6	-9.4	-19.4	72.0	16.6	10.9	0.5
Ripley County	31.0	37.5	24.7	31.1	33.3	24.8	36.5	28.6	3 192	44.3	20.8	16.8	-3.5	-10.9	67.6	17.2	14.4	0.8
St. Charles County	51.1	63.4	39.4	51.3	47.4	38.2	49.5	48.8	79 584	57.0	22.0	15.9	8.3	11.2	84.6	8.5	6.7	0.2
St. Clair County	34.3	39.4	29.3	34.7	55.6	12.1	48.1	7.9	2 073	46.0	13.4	21.9	3.3	-7.6	66.6	13.0	19.9	0.6
Ste. Genevieve County	43.0	50.6	35.3	43.2	15.5	62.5	100.0	37.5	4 516	55.2	14.6	19.0	9.6	3.4	79.0	10.2	10.1	0.6
St. Francois County	35.0	41.6	28.2	35.9	11.9	29.2	23.5	28.2	12 605	44.4	17.8	20.3	0.1	-4.1	76.2	15.5	8.1	0.3
St. Louis County	44.0	54.7	34.9	44.4	42.6	48.2	45.1	42.3	244 982	47.1	21.6	22.2	4.7	3.4	81.6	9.7	8.5	0.2
Saline County	39.9	48.0	32.3	40.4	35.5	51.4	26.3	36.8	5 314	51.7	13.8	23.9	11.0	8.2	68.4	18.9	12.3	0.4
Schuyler County	38.1	46.1	30.9	38.3	X	15.4	100.0	20.0	979	60.6	15.8	15.2	11.2	2.3	67.1	13.8	18.1	1.0
Scotland County	39.5	48.0	31.9	39.6	X	0.0	27.3	37.0	1 346	49.6	33.9	11.7	-3.3	6.7	62.2	14.9	22.4	0.5
Scott County	40.9	50.6	32.3	41.8	32.2	41.7	42.9	27.2	10 385	47.5	14.8	25.0	7.9	1.6	77.4	11.6	10.5	0.5
Shannon County	29.2	38.5	20.6	29.5	0.0	27.3	53.8	0.0	2 034	42.2	21.8	18.1	-4.3	-13.2	64.7	15.8	17.4	2.1
Shelby County	38.3	48.5	29.2	38.7	17.1	37.5	0.0	27.8	1 640	55.5	18.9	16.3	7.2	4.0	67.9	14.3	17.1	0.8
Stoddard County	35.8	46.4	26.2	36.0	22.6	36.0	60.6	19.0	6 476	43.6	21.1	22.5	1.5	-5.4	74.6	12.2	12.9	0.4
Stone County	31.8	39.4	24.7	31.9	11.1	33.8	16.7	36.8	5 765	50.0	20.9	17.6	3.0	-11.5	71.1	10.0	18.4	0.6
Sullivan County	39.1	48.0	30.5	39.0	42.9	26.1	36.4	40.7	1 731	54.9	17.4	21.5	11.8	3.1	75.2	9.3	14.3	1.2
Taney County	35.4	41.8	29.5	35.3	27.2	39.4	47.7	29.4	8 325	48.7	20.3	22.3	6.4	-2.1	79.0	8.3	11.9	0.8
Texas County	31.5	40.4	23.6	31.5	63.6	31.2	51.6	24.7	5 411	42.6	23.9	18.4	-3.6	-9.2	63.6	18.0	17.3	1.2
Vernon County	39.4	48.2	31.4	39.4	4.3	59.6	56.2	20.2	5 042	51.8	19.1	19.2	6.4	3.6	70.7	14.2	14.6	0.5
Warren County	43.5	54.9	32.3	43.4	42.6	54.7	0.0	48.5	6 313	52.8	19.0	18.7	6.9	4.4	79.6	9.0	10.9	0.5
Washington County	32.8	38.8	26.5	33.3	8.5	45.9	57.1	36.5	5 727	38.0	25.8	19.5	-7.1	-12.7	76.1	13.6	9.6	0.7
Wayne County	29.6	35.8	23.7	29.5	0.0	28.8	15.4	28.6	2 865	36.7	20.7	24.1	-3.8	-16.8	66.6	17.7	15.2	0.5
Webster County	40.6	49.5	31.6	41.2	5.3	35.3	24.1	40.9	8 648	42.7	28.2	14.9	-7.0	-0.4	74.7	11.0	13.3	0.9
Worth County	34.3	45.5	23.7	34.3	X	27.3	X	0.0	562	60.0	16.2	15.8	11.2	1.7	56.9	18.0	23.7	1.4
Wright County	33.2	43.7	23.7	33.5	4.4	10.7	0.0	26.2	4 542	43.9	22.9	20.9	0.2	-5.6	66.9	12.9	19.2	1.0

[1]Hispanic or Latino persons may be of any race.

				Occupation for employed population 16 years and over (percent)						Industry for employed population 16 years and over (percent)					
STATE County	Percent who worked at home	Percent of the population 5 years and over with a disability	Veterans as a percent of the population 18 years and over	Management, professional, and related occupations	Service occupations	Sales and office occupations	Farming, fishing, and forestry occupations	Construction, extraction, and maintenance occupations	Production, transportation and material moving occupations	Agriculture, forestry, fishing, and mining	Construction and manufacturing	Wholesale and retail trade	Transportation and warehousing, and utilities	Service industries	Public administration
	42	43	44	45	46	47	48	49	50	51	52	53	54	55	56
MISSOURI—Cont'd															
Jasper County	2.7	20.5	13.9	25.9	15.2	26.0	0.5	9.8	22.6	1.8	27.7	16.4	6.7	44.8	2.6
Jefferson County	2.1	17.9	14.7	23.8	14.7	28.0	0.1	14.8	18.6	0.6	27.0	16.8	5.9	47.0	2.8
Johnson County	3.8	15.2	15.6	28.2	18.0	23.6	1.0	10.9	18.2	2.9	22.7	13.8	3.9	50.6	6.1
Knox County	10.0	21.8	13.6	29.1	14.1	23.3	2.8	13.8	17.0	17.0	18.4	13.5	7.1	38.8	5.2
Laclede County	5.0	21.7	15.8	21.6	13.7	22.4	1.1	10.0	31.3	3.9	37.2	16.0	5.2	34.8	2.9
Lafayette County	4.0	19.5	15.3	23.8	16.6	25.7	0.9	13.3	19.8	3.9	25.0	16.6	6.5	43.2	4.9
Lawrence County	5.1	21.6	14.8	26.2	15.0	21.8	1.8	10.5	24.7	6.3	31.3	13.7	6.0	39.7	3.0
Lewis County	6.9	16.0	12.7	25.4	15.2	22.0	2.0	9.3	26.2	8.4	27.0	14.0	6.0	41.5	3.0
Lincoln County	3.7	18.2	14.7	21.1	13.7	23.6	0.7	17.7	23.2	3.6	34.5	15.7	4.8	38.8	2.7
Linn County	5.9	26.5	14.7	25.9	12.6	23.0	1.9	10.5	26.1	5.9	30.9	12.2	8.1	39.4	3.6
Livingston County	5.2	20.1	14.9	27.5	18.7	24.4	1.1	10.3	18.0	5.8	20.2	17.8	7.6	40.2	8.5
McDonald County	6.2	20.8	13.8	19.7	14.2	21.1	3.4	12.1	29.5	10.1	35.7	19.5	4.6	27.3	2.8
Macon County	5.9	22.6	14.1	23.8	18.3	21.7	1.9	12.3	21.9	5.3	26.2	15.2	7.1	41.1	5.2
Madison County	2.9	27.5	16.4	18.1	17.9	22.0	2.7	13.5	25.9	5.6	27.2	17.1	7.9	35.6	6.6
Maries County	6.1	22.4	16.9	24.1	14.2	22.4	1.3	14.3	23.8	5.8	31.0	13.3	4.5	34.2	11.2
Marion County	2.6	18.3	15.3	24.7	15.8	24.3	0.8	10.5	23.9	3.4	30.4	14.4	5.7	41.8	4.4
Mercer County	9.6	22.0	16.2	32.8	16.1	17.0	8.6	9.6	15.9	28.4	16.2	9.6	7.5	33.0	. 5.4
Miller County	4.8	22.2	15.6	23.2	18.0	23.6	0.9	14.3	20.0	4.4	24.7	13.9	5.3	43.2	8.5
Mississippi County	3.0	28.3	10.5	21.7	17.1	22.3	3.4	9.8	25.7	8.8	21.2	16.3	10.0	39.3	4.4
Moniteau County	5.0	19.0	14.4	26.2	15.9	24.3	1.4	13.5	18.7	5.8	25.9	13.2	4.7	36.4	14.1
Monroe County	8.6	19.9	14.9	24.5	18.5	18.1	2.0	10.7	26.2	9.2	30.0	13.9	6.4	34.6	5.9
Montgomery County	4.9	21.3	15.9	21.6	15.5	21.6	1.3	12.9	27.2	5.5	31.7	14.2	6.7	36.4	5.6
Morgan County	8.6	27.5	18.6	23.0	16.2	24.3	2.0	13.6	21.0	6.9	28.9	15.2	4.1	39.1	5.9
New Madrid County	2.2	24.5	13.4	22.1	17.4	21.2	3.1	9.2	27.1	8.1	30.7	14.3	6.1	36.2	4.7
Newton County	3.5	19.4	15.1	26.1	12.9	23.8	1.2	10.1	25.9	3.1	31.5	15.7	6.9	40.0	2.8
Nodaway County	4.0	15.5	10.1	32.9	17.5	21.6	1.3	8.6	18.1	7.1	23.7	12.6	2.2	50.5	3.8
Oregon County	6.6	28.9	17.2	23.3	13.8	20.6	4.1	10.8	27.4	8.3	24.4	16.6	7.1	40.7	3.0
Osage County	5.7	17.4	13.2	26.1	11.1	27.4	1.4	11.9	22.0	6.5	28.7	12.5	4.4	30.8	17.1
Ozark County	7.6	26.8	18.7	25.2	14.8	19.1	3.5	13.5	23.9	8.9	31.3	14.3	5.2	37.0	3.3
Pemiscot County	1.8	27.1	11.9	21.4	18.5	21.7	2.6	9.7	26.0	5.5	27.8	13.3	6.1	42.7	4.7
Perry County	3.8	19.6	14.4	21.3	15.1	22.0	1.3	12.8	27.5	5.8	35.0	14.5	6.2	34.8	3.6
Pettis County	3.6	20.3	14.9	26.4	15.3	21.0	1.1	11.0	25.3	3.6	30.7	15.8	4.6	41.4	4.0
Phelps County	3.9	20.8	16.3	33.6	17.0	24.1	0.5	10.6	14.3	2.3	17.2	14.2	4.8	55.1	6.4
Pike County	4.2	20.2	15.6	23.5	18.4	19.5	2.6	13.3	22.6	6.4	27.6	16.5	5.1	35.8	8.7
Platte County	3.5	14.3	14.3	38.8	12.1	28.9	0.2	9.3	10.6	1.1	15.5	16.1	10.3	51.9	5.0
Polk County	5.7	20.8	14.6	27.9	15.8	24.5	1.8	10.7	19.3	6.1	20.8	15.2	6.8	48.8	2.2
Pulaski County	2.6	20.8	19.2	28.5	21.1	23.3	1.2	10.6	15.3	2.1	15.5	14.3	4.8	48.2	15.2
Putnam County	6.9	24.5	14.6	31.7	12.6	15.2	5.2	12.6	22.7	17.9	27.6	9.9	7.6	35.3	1.6
Ralls County	4.0	17.6	14.3	25.7	16.2	20.7	2.3	12.0	23.2	8.4	29.1	12.0	5.4	38.7	6.4
Randolph County	2.9	21.5	15.1	25.4	17.0	23.8	0.8	9.8	23.2	2.6	24.6	16.2	7.2	43.0	6.4
Ray County	3.7	19.5	14.4	22.5	14.8	23.4	0.8	14.0	24.5	4.0	27.7	15.5	7.5	41.8	3.4
Reynolds County	3.9	28.0	16.0	21.0	15.3	14.8	4.3	16.8	27.8	17.3	27.5	9.6	3.1	38.2	4.3
Ripley County	2.6	28.0	16.8	23.0	14.4	19.2	2.8	10.4	30.2	6.3	30.5	14.5	5.7	39.3	3.7
St. Charles County	3.0	12.7	14.0	34.6	12.8	29.7	0.1	10.4	12.5	0.4	23.9	17.3	6.0	49.2	3.2
St. Clair County	10.3	25.1	18.7	26.6	16.7	21.7	1.7	13.6	19.7	10.3	25.5	15.0	4.2	40.3	4.6
Ste. Genevieve County	3.9	18.7	15.5	21.8	14.5	21.4	1.0	15.5	25.8	5.9	35.0	12.5	5.3	37.0	4.2
St. Francois County	2.8	24.1	15.9	23.6	18.8	23.9	0.7	13.1	19.8	3.0	25.6	15.3	4.4	45.7	6.0
St. Louis County	3.2	15.6	13.6	41.6	12.5	29.4	0.1	6.4	10.0	0.2	17.6	15.5	5.4	58.0	3.3
Saline County	3.2	21.9	12.2	27.0	18.9	19.9	1.8	9.5	22.9	6.4	25.4	13.3	5.2	44.9	4.7
Schuyler County	7.9	26.7	12.8	27.4	15.0	23.1	3.6	12.6	18.2	12.7	22.4	13.8	9.4	38.4	3.4
Scotland County	12.0	19.8	13.0	32.9	14.0	16.6	3.8	11.4	21.3	15.5	21.0	12.7	5.7	40.6	4.5
Scott County	2.8	21.0	13.8	22.7	15.3	26.2	1.3	11.2	23.4	3.7	25.5	18.7	7.2	41.3	3.6
Shannon County	5.9	27.0	15.9	18.5	12.4	18.0	3.8	12.8	34.4	9.7	35.8	11.1	7.5	31.1	4.8
Shelby County	8.8	19.3	14.2	27.5	14.5	19.3	3.3	10.0	25.5	13.7	27.6	12.4	5.9	36.0	4.3
Stoddard County	3.1	25.2	14.8	21.5	14.7	20.8	3.0	12.4	27.7	7.0	30.1	15.2	7.0	37.7	3.0
Stone County	6.0	21.1	18.5	23.5	19.5	27.7	0.7	14.9	13.8	3.1	21.5	16.4	4.4	51.9	2.7
Sullivan County	6.8	25.4	12.2	23.7	15.0	17.0	4.2	10.4	29.8	13.5	36.8	10.7	3.8	32.7	2.6
Taney County	4.5	21.5	16.0	25.9	23.1	30.0	0.4	10.4	10.1	1.2	13.8	18.0	3.3	61.3	2.4
Texas County	7.1	25.8	17.8	26.3	15.6	21.0	3.2	10.3	23.7	8.6	24.5	14.6	7.9	37.5	6.9
Vernon County	5.1	21.8	13.4	28.2	16.5	21.7	2.1	10.2	21.3	7.3	25.1	12.8	4.6	46.8	3.4
Warren County	3.4	17.8	15.6	23.5	14.8	23.2	0.3	16.7	21.3	2.0	33.1	16.0	5.8	40.7	2.3
Washington County	2.3	24.8	13.1	17.9	19.2	20.2	1.1	16.0	25.6	4.5	30.7	12.7	5.6	40.6	5.9
Wayne County	5.2	29.0	17.9	22.7	15.4	19.3	2.8	11.0	28.8	5.4	31.3	12.8	6.3	36.9	7.3
Webster County	4.7	19.1	16.1	23.2	14.1	22.3	1.5	14.2	24.7	5.2	29.9	17.7	6.9	37.3	3.0
Worth County	6.4	23.6	15.5	30.0	15.4	20.4	4.0	11.1	19.1	17.1	22.3	12.6	7.1	34.3	6.6
Wright County	9.4	23.7	14.7	27.9	13.7	18.5	2.7	12.1	25.1	10.0	26.7	14.9	7.2	38.2	3.0

Table B-3. States and Counties — Education, Labor Force, and Income

STATE County	Median household income	Median family income — All families	Median family income — Families with children Married-couple	Median family income — Families with children Male householder	Median family income — Families with children Female householder	Median nonfamily household income	Median income for full-year, full-time workers Men	Median income for full-year, full-time workers Women	Per capita income	With earnings	With interest, dividend, or rental income	With Social Security income	With public assistance income	With retirement income	Households with income over $100,000 (percent)	+/− U.S. percent for income over $100,000 (percent)	Households with income below poverty (percent)	Families with children with income below poverty (percent)
	57	58	59	60	61	62	63	64	65	66	67	68	69	70	71	72	73	74
MISSOURI—Cont'd																		
Jasper County	31 323	37 611	45 192	23 431	16 105	18 189	29 524	21 120	16 227	78.8	31.5	29.2	3.9	15.1	4.5	−7.8	14.1	16.1
Jefferson County	46 338	51 787	59 776	31 913	24 812	25 087	38 741	26 019	19 435	85.7	31.9	22.5	2.4	16.6	8.1	−4.2	6.7	7.1
Johnson County	35 391	43 050	46 121	25 208	15 823	20 557	30 197	21 913	16 037	84.2	32.8	21.8	2.2	17.4	5.4	−6.9	15.3	13.0
Knox County	27 124	31 741	34 542	23 750	13 125	15 030	24 857	20 197	13 075	72.8	41.3	41.0	2.8	13.3	1.2	−11.1	17.6	18.5
Laclede County	29 562	35 962	40 818	21 488	13 750	15 678	27 855	18 991	15 572	76.6	29.3	30.6	3.4	15.0	4.5	−7.8	15.4	16.3
Lafayette County	38 235	45 717	52 726	27 721	17 396	20 867	33 891	23 920	18 493	79.4	36.8	31.4	2.6	18.3	6.3	−6.0	10.0	10.9
Lawrence County	31 239	36 846	41 450	25 000	14 497	16 217	28 381	19 541	15 399	77.2	32.5	32.2	3.6	16.0	3.5	−8.8	14.3	16.2
Lewis County	30 651	35 740	45 123	21 741	15 972	17 143	28 411	20 376	14 746	78.6	37.6	31.4	3.2	15.4	3.9	−8.4	14.3	18.8
Lincoln County	42 592	47 747	56 237	30 494	20 974	21 563	36 533	24 299	17 149	83.0	30.5	25.1	2.8	15.7	6.1	−6.2	8.1	8.1
Linn County	28 242	36 134	44 730	21 563	16 434	15 897	26 403	19 918	15 378	72.3	36.6	38.7	2.9	16.5	3.2	−9.1	14.8	16.5
Livingston County	32 290	40 902	45 000	26 250	14 167	15 347	30 767	20 333	16 685	74.9	39.1	34.0	3.6	15.1	5.7	−6.6	13.7	13.8
McDonald County	27 010	31 530	36 352	18 611	12 237	15 148	24 488	18 694	13 175	79.8	23.4	26.6	4.7	12.1	3.0	−9.3	20.5	23.6
Macon County	30 195	36 370	43 373	26 726	17 109	15 846	27 433	19 448	16 189	74.0	38.3	35.6	2.6	19.1	3.7	−8.6	13.7	12.2
Madison County	25 601	31 145	39 042	16 250	12 578	13 503	28 621	16 464	13 215	67.3	28.4	37.4	5.3	19.0	2.3	−10.0	18.1	19.1
Maries County	31 925	39 187	46 891	22 083	19 792	16 127	30 000	21 373	15 662	77.9	38.0	33.3	2.8	20.6	2.8	−9.5	13.4	15.7
Marion County	31 774	41 290	47 254	20 104	15 625	17 319	31 415	21 363	16 964	77.3	35.2	32.5	4.1	14.0	4.6	−7.7	12.8	14.5
Mercer County	29 640	35 313	41 184	29 250	14 519	15 776	27 440	20 775	15 140	72.0	39.0	40.3	3.2	17.6	3.4	−8.9	14.3	13.8
Miller County	30 977	36 770	43 763	25 769	14 107	16 778	27 096	19 525	15 144	76.1	29.7	33.6	4.6	16.5	3.7	−8.6	14.3	15.9
Mississippi County	23 012	28 833	40 929	18 750	9 922	10 614	26 564	18 121	13 038	69.2	19.3	35.2	9.4	13.5	3.6	−8.7	25.0	27.7
Moniteau County	37 168	42 487	48 994	22 176	20 516	19 816	27 476	21 283	16 609	77.3	38.7	29.3	2.1	16.9	4.3	−8.0	10.2	10.2
Monroe County	30 871	36 895	45 600	30 714	20 833	16 036	27 481	20 975	14 695	76.0	33.7	35.0	2.2	16.5	2.8	−9.5	12.3	12.4
Montgomery County	32 772	38 632	44 440	24 940	14 179	18 088	29 284	20 381	15 092	76.4	37.2	35.0	2.6	14.6	2.8	−9.5	12.5	14.0
Morgan County	30 659	35 908	40 208	21 106	11 836	16 124	27 427	20 155	15 950	72.2	35.7	38.2	3.6	21.7	5.0	−7.3	14.6	20.6
New Madrid County	26 826	32 462	40 856	20 368	11 775	14 357	29 436	19 987	14 204	72.2	20.9	32.1	6.5	13.9	3.2	−9.1	22.2	27.6
Newton County	35 041	40 616	45 736	21 716	20 372	18 293	30 743	21 981	17 502	80.6	32.7	29.1	3.1	16.0	5.8	−6.5	12.0	12.0
Nodaway County	31 781	42 203	48 196	25 096	16 797	16 570	29 820	21 744	15 384	79.9	41.3	26.9	2.1	12.1	4.4	−7.9	18.7	9.8
Oregon County	22 359	26 727	31 453	16 364	13 214	10 910	23 285	16 745	12 812	65.3	26.7	39.7	5.5	15.5	2.9	−9.4	23.0	24.2
Osage County	39 565	46 503	51 630	25 250	19 231	18 787	30 620	23 232	17 245	80.6	43.8	29.6	2.4	16.0	4.1	−8.2	9.7	8.4
Ozark County	25 861	30 100	32 192	16 544	14 250	12 840	22 355	17 577	14 133	67.2	31.5	39.6	4.7	21.8	2.9	−9.4	21.1	24.7
Pemiscot County	21 911	27 553	36 220	17 870	10 869	11 393	28 326	18 586	12 968	68.5	15.8	32.4	8.0	10.8	3.5	−8.8	29.2	36.3
Perry County	36 632	43 240	48 149	22 308	20 186	17 303	29 505	20 366	16 554	77.1	39.9	29.9	4.0	18.2	3.7	−8.6	11.0	6.7
Pettis County	31 822	38 073	46 069	25 820	17 485	19 878	30 505	20 406	16 251	78.1	34.0	31.0	3.3	16.3	4.2	−8.1	12.4	14.4
Phelps County	29 378	38 693	46 062	18 077	15 127	16 222	30 928	20 677	16 084	74.5	32.4	28.7	3.4	19.5	5.0	−7.3	17.7	17.9
Pike County	32 373	39 959	45 638	23 077	15 913	18 396	29 169	19 905	14 442	75.8	34.9	32.9	4.3	15.3	3.9	−8.4	15.2	16.3
Platte County	55 849	65 236	72 036	33 804	29 317	35 054	45 665	31 707	26 356	87.9	41.7	17.8	1.6	13.8	16.4	4.1	4.8	4.9
Polk County	29 656	35 843	39 122	22 545	14 435	13 891	26 600	19 783	13 645	74.0	34.5	31.8	3.7	16.1	3.5	−8.8	16.2	17.4
Pulaski County	34 247	37 786	40 457	26 161	16 973	21 042	27 887	21 380	14 586	83.4	27.2	20.7	3.8	20.7	3.5	−8.8	11.1	10.5
Putnam County	26 282	32 031	35 898	19 318	12 813	15 318	23 639	19 182	14 647	70.2	36.5	42.3	3.4	17.3	2.2	−10.1	16.1	21.9
Ralls County	37 094	41 955	45 250	56 250	15 000	19 682	29 296	20 691	16 456	82.9	39.7	28.8	2.2	12.0	3.4	−8.9	9.7	9.9
Randolph County	31 464	39 468	46 060	18 654	16 964	17 194	27 462	21 141	15 010	76.1	32.9	33.3	3.4	14.7	3.7	−8.6	12.4	13.9
Ray County	41 886	49 192	55 978	32 500	20 393	21 366	37 778	22 473	18 685	80.8	30.3	27.2	2.9	17.9	6.5	−5.8	8.0	7.8
Reynolds County	25 867	31 383	35 804	20 938	9 800	12 127	28 750	19 177	13 065	68.3	29.2	39.0	4.9	16.6	1.8	−10.5	20.3	23.6
Ripley County	22 761	27 799	31 757	17 917	11 667	10 769	22 223	18 523	12 889	64.6	25.5	38.3	5.0	18.5	2.6	−9.7	23.5	25.6
St. Charles County	57 258	64 415	71 208	36 200	28 369	32 379	45 801	30 243	23 592	87.7	42.5	19.8	1.4	16.9	15.1	2.8	3.9	4.2
St. Clair County	25 321	31 448	37 466	21 078	11 447	13 910	24 045	19 167	14 025	65.7	30.7	41.5	4.1	22.2	2.2	−10.1	20.3	23.4
Ste. Genevieve County	39 200	44 484	53 273	34 022	19 574	21 914	34 681	19 750	17 283	78.9	42.0	31.2	3.3	19.4	4.8	−7.5	7.5	8.7
St. Francois County	31 199	37 266	45 368	21 683	14 929	16 020	30 673	20 247	15 273	72.8	28.0	33.0	4.1	20.6	4.1	−8.2	14.9	17.5
St. Louis County	50 532	61 680	76 464	33 649	26 275	30 691	47 199	31 218	27 595	81.7	47.0	26.7	2.2	18.6	17.5	5.2	6.7	7.9
Saline County	32 743	39 234	45 901	20 978	16 289	19 814	28 047	20 193	16 132	78.6	34.5	33.0	4.0	15.9	4.9	−7.4	12.9	17.1
Schuyler County	27 385	34 564	39 500	32 083	20 250	14 199	26 301	19 412	15 850	70.8	35.0	38.7	3.0	14.4	2.6	−9.7	18.8	19.0
Scotland County	27 409	33 529	38 214	24 000	15 714	14 487	25 441	18 016	14 474	74.0	41.1	36.6	3.0	11.1	4.4	−7.9	17.6	16.5
Scott County	31 352	38 090	45 939	24 833	12 479	14 608	30 743	20 122	15 620	76.8	28.4	30.9	5.6	14.6	3.9	−8.4	16.0	19.7
Shannon County	20 878	25 379	30 273	15 278	12 132	11 399	22 432	16 911	11 492	67.9	25.2	37.8	5.2	19.7	1.9	−10.4	26.1	31.3
Shelby County	29 448	35 944	39 258	11 806	17 634	17 188	26 821	20 175	15 632	75.5	40.9	35.8	2.8	12.7	3.3	−9.0	14.6	17.8
Stoddard County	26 987	33 330	40 123	21 333	14 214	13 720	27 055	18 758	14 656	72.6	26.4	35.4	4.7	15.1	3.4	−8.9	17.4	18.6
Stone County	32 637	36 844	40 900	21 071	14 461	18 704	27 489	19 779	18 036	73.2	38.2	38.5	3.1	25.3	5.2	−7.1	12.6	16.9
Sullivan County	26 107	33 590	40 313	22 125	14 514	13 450	24 699	19 789	13 392	72.6	29.4	35.7	3.7	15.6	2.5	−9.8	17.9	16.1
Taney County	30 898	36 757	40 355	17 847	16 641	19 796	26 676	20 199	17 267	79.2	31.7	32.1	3.0	19.9	4.5	−7.8	11.9	14.7
Texas County	24 545	29 039	34 451	19 000	12 037	13 410	26 276	17 951	13 799	69.7	29.2	37.2	4.4	21.1	3.3	−9.0	21.3	24.4
Vernon County	30 021	37 714	44 489	19 688	15 071	15 772	29 873	19 763	15 047	75.5	33.2	32.9	3.7	18.2	3.8	−8.5	15.1	15.1
Warren County	41 016	46 863	55 763	28 750	16 899	22 019	36 958	24 499	19 690	80.8	36.5	27.4	3.5	19.1	7.7	−4.6	9.6	10.0
Washington County	27 112	31 634	38 142	25 085	10 610	12 987	29 103	18 951	12 934	71.5	20.3	28.6	7.3	18.2	2.6	−9.7	20.9	23.9
Wayne County	24 007	28 046	39 205	12 206	13 110	12 191	27 102	17 818	13 434	62.7	25.3	44.9	5.6	23.5	2.5	−9.8	21.8	27.3
Webster County	31 929	36 934	39 978	26 107	21 049	17 149	29 652	21 355	14 502	79.8	31.1	27.3	3.2	16.2	4.2	−8.1	13.3	14.6
Worth County	27 471	34 044	36 563	19 375	15 833	15 104	25 809	18 125	14 367	75.4	38.6	37.9	3.5	15.7	2.6	−9.7	16.0	15.5
Wright County	24 691	29 923	34 870	14 712	12 582	12 063	26 202	18 408	13 135	70.8	28.5	34.7	4.8	16.7	3.4	−8.9	22.1	25.7

Table B-3. States and Counties — Education, Labor Force, and Income

STATE/ County code	MSA/PMSA/ NECMA code[1]	STATE County	High school graduates			College graduates		College graduates (percent)				
			Total population 25 years and over	Percent with a high school diploma or less	Percent with a high school diploma or more	Percent with a bachelor's degree or more	+/− U.S. percent with bachelor's degree or more	Non-Hispanic White	Black or African American	American Indian and Alaska Native	Asian, Hawaiian, and Pacific Islander	Hispanic or Latino[2]
			1	2	3	4	5	6	7	8	9	10
		MISSOURI—Cont'd										
29 510	7040	St. Louis city................	221 951	56.2	71.3	19.1	−5.3	28.2	8.8	11.3	33.0	16.6
30 000	...	MONTANA	586 621	44.1	87.2	24.4	0.0	25.2	33.2	10.5	38.9	15.4
30 001	...	Beaverhead County	5 825	39.8	89.3	26.4	2.0	27.0	0.0	3.4	X	5.2
30 003	...	Big Horn County...........	7 051	53.8	76.4	14.3	−10.1	20.3	X	9.3	36.7	0.0
30 005	...	Blaine County.............	4 144	49.3	78.7	17.4	−7.0	22.1	0.0	9.6	0.0	10.3
30 007	...	Broadwater County	3 061	54.5	85.2	15.0	−9.4	15.3	0.0	0.0	100.0	0.0
30 009	...	Carbon County............	6 701	48.0	88.1	23.3	−1.1	23.4	66.7	21.4	14.3	15.6
30 011	...	Carter County.............	946	52.5	83.3	13.6	−10.8	13.9	0.0	0.0	0.0	X
30 013	3040	Cascade County...........	52 333	46.2	87.1	21.5	−2.9	22.1	27.2	7.2	25.4	17.1
30 015	...	Chouteau County	3 837	43.3	87.1	20.5	−3.9	21.6	0.0	9.7	55.6	23.5
30 017	...	Custer County	7 819	44.9	84.9	18.8	−5.6	19.2	X	3.5	37.0	1.1
30 019	...	Daniels County	1 467	51.0	85.3	14.1	−10.3	14.3	X	0.0	33.3	0.0
30 021	...	Dawson County	6 161	47.8	82.7	15.1	−9.3	15.2	0.0	0.0	0.0	25.7
30 023	...	Deer Lodge County	6 584	58.4	84.5	14.7	−9.7	14.9	X	5.5	44.0	0.0
30 025	...	Fallon County	1 935	57.7	85.7	14.4	−10.0	14.3	50.0	0.0	100.0	20.0
30 027	...	Fergus County	8 290	50.4	86.3	19.1	−5.3	19.4	100.0	6.6	50.0	0.0
30 029	...	Flathead County	49 648	43.2	87.4	22.4	−2.0	22.5	64.0	15.5	31.9	20.8
30 031	...	Gallatin County	40 461	27.9	93.3	41.0	16.6	41.1	45.9	29.4	64.6	25.7
30 033	...	Garfield County	871	54.1	84.7	16.8	−7.6	16.8	X	X	X	0.0
30 035	...	Glacier County	7 383	48.7	78.6	16.5	−7.9	26.0	0.0	8.6	0.0	0.0
30 037	...	Golden Valley County ...	704	58.4	70.5	16.2	−8.2	16.4	X	0.0	X	0.0
30 039	...	Granite County	1 988	47.1	87.8	22.1	−2.3	22.5	X	0.0	0.0	13.3
30 041	...	Hill County.................	10 031	45.3	86.8	20.0	−4.4	20.9	0.0	12.3	32.1	22.4
30 043	...	Jefferson County	6 717	41.0	90.2	27.7	3.3	28.0	0.0	10.5	23.5	18.8
30 045	...	Judith Basin County	1 595	42.8	87.6	23.6	−0.8	23.9	X	0.0	0.0	0.0
30 047	...	Lake County	16 971	47.5	84.2	22.2	−2.2	24.6	8.3	11.1	35.5	24.9
30 049	...	Lewis and Clark County ...	36 690	37.9	91.4	31.6	7.2	32.1	34.8	11.4	52.3	25.8
30 051	...	Liberty County	1 470	50.0	75.0	17.6	−6.8	17.5	X	X	0.0	100.0
30 053	...	Lincoln County	13 008	57.8	80.2	13.7	−10.7	13.8	100.0	6.9	0.0	0.0
30 055	...	McCone County	1 374	52.1	86.1	16.4	−8.0	16.4	0.0	0.0	100.0	25.0
30 057	...	Madison County	4 945	42.8	89.8	25.5	1.1	25.8	X	12.5	0.0	22.9
30 059	...	Meagher County	1 334	53.8	83.4	18.7	−5.7	18.9	X	27.3	X	0.0
30 061	...	Mineral County	2 691	60.5	83.2	12.3	−12.1	12.5	X	6.7	20.0	21.4
30 063	5140	Missoula County...........	59 298	35.5	91.0	32.8	8.4	33.1	50.7	19.3	39.9	29.4
30 065	...	Musselshell County	3 181	55.5	82.6	16.7	−7.7	16.8	X	0.0	50.0	3.0
30 067	...	Park County	11 013	44.7	87.6	23.1	−1.3	23.4	0.0	21.6	42.4	15.5
30 069	...	Petroleum County	333	52.9	82.9	17.4	−7.0	17.7	X	X	X	0.0
30 071	...	Phillips County	3 102	53.1	82.4	17.1	−7.3	17.6	X	11.9	22.6	0.0
30 073	...	Pondera County	4 108	53.4	81.6	19.8	−4.6	21.1	0.0	9.8	12.5	0.0
30 075	...	Powder River County	1 272	48.0	83.4	16.0	−8.4	16.0	X	16.7	0.0	0.0
30 077	...	Powell County	5 098	56.9	81.9	13.1	−11.3	13.3	68.2	1.1	44.0	0.0
30 079	...	Prairie County	913	53.6	78.8	14.8	−9.6	14.8	X	22.2	0.0	0.0
30 081	...	Ravalli County	24 565	44.1	87.4	22.5	−1.9	22.7	87.5	13.8	33.3	17.4
30 083	...	Richland County	6 398	51.9	83.5	17.2	−7.2	17.8	X	0.0	X	2.4
30 085	...	Roosevelt County	6 107	51.8	80.6	15.6	−8.8	20.9	X	8.9	29.8	38.2
30 087	...	Rosebud County	5 543	51.5	84.4	17.6	−6.8	20.2	X	10.2	23.1	8.9
30 089	...	Sanders County	7 242	56.0	81.2	15.5	−8.9	16.0	0.0	7.3	15.6	25.6
30 091	...	Sheridan County	2 931	50.3	81.2	18.4	−6.0	18.8	X	0.0	25.0	10.5
30 093	...	Silver Bow County	23 097	49.2	85.1	21.7	−2.7	22.2	18.2	8.4	45.6	9.8
30 095	...	Stillwater County	5 632	51.6	87.5	17.8	−6.6	17.8	50.0	28.6	42.9	18.3
30 097	...	Sweet Grass County	2 487	46.5	88.9	23.6	−0.8	24.1	X	0.0	0.0	0.0
30 099	...	Teton County	4 295	48.4	83.4	20.8	−3.6	21.3	X	9.6	42.9	17.2
30 101	...	Toole County...............	3 570	54.1	81.0	16.8	−7.6	17.7	0.0	3.4	0.0	0.0
30 103	...	Treasure County	577	54.8	86.3	18.2	−6.2	18.1	X	0.0	100.0	0.0
30 105	...	Valley County	5 345	55.8	83.9	15.7	−8.7	16.8	40.0	4.6	0.0	0.0
30 107	...	Wheatland County........	1 508	61.8	69.0	13.5	−10.9	13.7	X	15.4	X	0.0
30 109	...	Wibaux County.............	738	58.0	76.8	16.0	−8.4	16.0	X	0.0	X	0.0
30 111	0880	Yellowstone County	84 233	42.6	88.5	26.4	2.0	27.0	38.9	15.4	48.1	10.3
31 000	...	NEBRASKA...............	1 087 241	44.7	86.6	23.7	−0.7	24.6	14.1	8.8	41.6	8.5
31 001	...	Adams County.............	19 814	46.8	86.3	19.9	−4.5	20.3	21.6	14.8	18.2	5.6
31 003	...	Antelope County...........	4 939	54.3	85.5	14.3	−10.1	14.3	0.0	11.1	X	40.0
31 005	...	Arthur County	306	42.5	89.5	15.7	−8.7	16.1	X	0.0	X	0.0
31 007	...	Banner County.............	551	38.8	94.2	19.6	−4.8	19.7	0.0	X	X	28.6

[1]MSA = Metropolitan Statistical Area. PMSA = Primary MSA. NECMA = New England County Metropolitan Area. See the Appendix A for explanation of these concepts. See Appendix B for list of metropolitan areas identified by type, with component counties.
[2]Hispanic or Latino persons may be of any race.

STATE County	School enrollment			Population 16 to 19 years				Employment status, 2000			Work status in 1999 of the population 16 years and over (percent)		
											Worked in 1999		
	Grades kindergarten through 12	College or graduate school	Percent private	Number	Percent in armed forces	Percent high school graduates	Percent not enrolled, not grads, not in armed forces, not employed	Total population 16 years and over	Percent in labor force	Unemploy-ment rate	Full-time	Part-time	Did not work in 1999
	11	12	13	14	15	16	17	18	19	20	21	22	23
MISSOURI—Cont'd													
St. Louis city................	67 241	24 410	27.0	19 036	0.0	10.4	10.3	268 036	60.5	11.3	51.0	13.8	35.2
MONTANA	176 805	51 255	8.3	55 369	0.6	11.0	4.4	701 168	65.4	6.3	53.1	18.6	28.2
Beaverhead County	1 587	1 117	6.2	835	0.0	4.6	1.6	7 338	63.6	3.8	52.8	21.6	25.6
Big Horn County...........	3 455	420	10.9	908	0.0	8.9	12.4	8 680	62.6	13.9	55.7	11.5	32.8
Blaine County	1 724	213	7.2	506	0.0	9.9	8.5	5 018	62.5	10.9	52.2	14.6	33.2
Broadwater County	869	112	7.8	226	0.0	10.6	8.8	3 415	62.5	4.5	51.9	17.1	31.0
Carbon County	1 854	215	5.4	520	0.0	8.3	5.2	7 590	63.1	4.7	52.4	18.1	29.5
Carter County	306	15	10.3	86	0.0	0.0	0.0	1 066	70.1	0.5	56.4	18.0	25.6
Cascade County............	15 730	3 154	11.4	4 335	7.0	21.6	3.9	61 744	65.0	5.8	53.6	16.6	29.8
Chouteau County	1 369	174	4.5	369	0.0	5.1	7.9	4 469	62.0	5.7	51.7	17.5	30.8
Custer County	2 237	514	6.7	756	0.0	11.9	0.7	9 203	63.8	5.4	50.6	19.2	30.2
Daniels County	365	30	2.3	114	0.0	2.6	0.0	1 642	56.8	3.1	45.4	18.8	35.7
Dawson County	1 678	445	6.0	605	0.0	9.6	0.2	7 253	62.9	4.4	50.5	17.8	31.7
Deer Lodge County	1 811	330	5.3	591	0.0	17.4	5.9	7 627	55.6	10.2	45.2	17.4	37.4
Fallon County	608	16	1.3	166	0.0	4.8	0.0	2 222	66.5	3.0	53.3	19.5	27.2
Fergus County	2 340	187	3.1	680	0.0	9.6	4.3	9 408	62.8	5.3	49.8	18.7	31.4
Flathead County	14 879	2 223	9.7	4 238	0.0	10.1	4.8	57 687	64.3	6.4	52.3	18.6	29.1
Gallatin County	10 879	10 816	6.8	5 008	0.0	8.2	1.5	54 704	73.3	6.1	58.4	23.5	18.0
Garfield County	250	14	6.8	81	0.0	13.6	3.7	1 008	67.0	3.1	56.5	15.0	28.5
Glacier County	3 548	469	4.2	913	0.0	11.1	9.2	9 110	61.6	15.4	53.9	11.5	34.6
Golden Valley County ...	227	13	8.8	50	0.0	4.0	6.0	786	66.4	1.9	54.3	16.8	28.9
Granite County	556	39	8.9	129	0.0	11.6	9.3	2 219	60.6	5.4	48.4	18.8	32.8
Hill County...................	3 528	1 378	5.8	1 207	0.0	8.8	5.0	12 565	65.6	9.9	52.3	18.8	29.0
Jefferson County	2 312	210	7.1	658	0.0	9.7	4.1	7 665	67.6	5.1	57.3	17.0	25.7
Judith Basin County......	487	23	6.5	140	0.0	8.6	9.3	1 800	60.8	2.5	49.9	17.1	33.0
Lake County	5 485	1 057	5.8	1 805	0.0	9.4	14.0	20 151	59.7	8.0	50.5	16.3	33.2
Lewis and Clark County	10 836	2 691	13.4	3 520	0.4	11.3	1.2	43 363	70.0	5.1	56.9	18.0	25.1
Liberty County..............	456	34	6.1	149	0.0	2.7	14.8	1 688	54.8	3.5	46.8	19.3	33.9
Lincoln County	3 918	428	6.8	1 144	0.0	11.8	3.5	14 798	53.5	13.8	41.7	16.8	41.5
McCone County	397	24	1.7	114	0.0	5.3	7.9	1 553	66.6	2.2	55.9	16.7	27.4
Madison County	1 251	138	3.2	355	0.0	9.0	3.1	5 516	60.8	5.2	50.8	18.1	31.1
Meagher County	384	10	4.8	123	0.0	10.6	13.0	1 516	63.1	5.4	50.8	17.3	31.9
Mineral County	784	68	5.9	221	0.0	9.5	5.0	3 074	59.0	7.4	49.7	17.2	33.1
Missoula County...........	16 769	11 985	6.9	6 412	0.1	10.4	2.2	76 484	70.4	6.1	54.8	22.7	22.5
Musselshell County	847	120	6.3	274	0.0	6.6	4.4	3 595	58.1	7.6	47.7	16.8	35.5
Park County	2 678	376	11.3	742	0.0	20.1	4.0	12 472	66.4	5.0	56.0	16.7	27.3
Petroleum County	97	12	0.0	22	0.0	0.0	0.0	377	62.9	2.1	53.1	17.5	29.4
Phillips County	1 043	55	2.8	291	0.0	10.3	1.0	3 548	63.5	4.2	50.5	18.3	31.2
Pondera County	1 534	159	6.0	409	0.0	5.9	7.8	4 779	60.8	6.8	50.2	17.4	32.5
Powder River County	388	14	2.2	101	0.0	15.8	0.0	1 424	67.5	3.6	56.8	17.3	25.9
Powell County	1 245	155	10.5	336	1.5	5.1	12.5	5 832	47.6	5.5	48.2	14.8	37.1
Prairie County	187	25	2.4	47	0.0	0.0	4.3	997	60.2	3.8	51.5	14.4	34.1
Ravalli County	7 168	798	12.7	2 087	0.1	12.2	8.2	28 076	59.6	5.9	47.7	17.9	34.4
Richland County	2 129	162	3.0	587	0.0	11.2	2.7	7 362	64.6	6.1	53.2	17.2	29.6
Roosevelt County..........	2 891	492	4.9	766	0.4	7.3	12.4	7 393	62.1	15.7	50.9	14.2	34.9
Rosebud County	2 426	291	9.2	661	0.0	7.9	9.4	6 611	64.9	8.4	57.0	15.7	27.3
Sanders County	1 967	229	8.2	628	0.0	7.6	4.6	8 178	53.6	9.7	44.2	16.6	39.2
Sheridan County	750	70	5.7	212	0.0	6.1	0.0	3 307	58.9	3.5	46.8	19.7	33.5
Silver Bow County	6 390	2 458	11.7	1 981	0.0	9.7	4.0	27 369	62.0	6.8	49.1	18.4	32.5
Stillwater County	1 657	138	4.8	423	0.0	8.5	0.5	6 399	65.5	6.8	54.9	16.8	28.3
Sweet Grass County	713	53	5.6	175	0.0	8.0	1.1	2 784	65.1	2.3	55.0	17.5	27.5
Teton County	1 398	106	8.4	368	0.5	13.9	5.2	4 888	58.0	3.7	48.8	17.3	33.9
Toole County................	1 135	104	9.2	348	0.0	7.5	8.3	4 141	57.8	4.3	51.4	19.8	28.8
Treasure County	199	9	2.4	53	0.0	11.3	1.9	655	68.4	4.2	54.5	21.2	24.3
Valley County	1 596	129	5.4	460	0.0	7.4	4.3	6 055	61.3	5.4	52.1	16.6	31.2
Wheatland County........	393	40	3.9	124	0.0	9.7	4.8	1 734	62.5	5.9	53.4	16.7	29.9
Wibaux County.............	228	17	0.8	64	0.0	3.1	3.1	832	63.6	4.9	49.4	17.2	33.4
Yellowstone County	24 867	6 681	9.1	7 246	0.1	12.2	3.4	99 998	68.7	4.5	55.4	19.0	25.6
NEBRASKA...............	338 004	112 315	15.4	107 180	0.3	9.0	3.4	1 315 715	69.7	3.5	58.2	17.7	24.2
Adams County.............	5 519	2 565	25.7	2 035	0.6	5.7	1.7	24 416	68.2	3.5	56.2	19.2	24.6
Antelope County...........	1 636	163	11.0	496	0.0	9.3	0.2	5 709	66.1	2.2	50.2	19.7	30.2
Arthur County	105	11	2.6	26	0.0	0.0	0.0	350	72.6	1.2	65.4	14.9	19.7
Banner County	187	13	2.5	51	0.0	11.8	3.9	619	65.1	1.7	54.3	16.5	29.2

Table B-3. States and Counties — **Education, Labor Force, and Income**

STATE County	\multicolumn{8}{Full-year full-time employed (percent)}								Children under 18 years in families						Total employed by class of worker (percent)			
										With two parents (percent)									
	Total	Men	Women	Non-Hispanic White	Black or African American	American Indian and Alaska Native	Asian, Hawaiian, and Pacific Islander	Hispanic or Latino[1]	Number	Both in labor force	Father only in labor force	With one parent who is in labor force (percent)	+/− U.S. percent of children with no stay-at-home parent (percent)	+/− U.S. percent two-income couples	Private	Government	Self-employed	Unpaid family worker
	24	25	26	27	28	29	30	31	32	33	34	35	36	37	38	39	40	41
MISSOURI—Cont'd																		
St. Louis city	35.7	40.8	31.3	42.0	29.3	32.9	36.4	35.0	80 760	25.5	9.2	42.1	3.0	−2.1	79.7	14.5	5.5	0.2
MONTANA	36.4	45.0	28.1	37.2	34.6	25.7	28.5	33.1	218 232	51.2	18.9	20.4	7.0	3.1	64.3	18.3	16.7	0.7
Beaverhead County	34.9	43.8	25.8	35.3	0.0	10.3	X	30.8	2 091	55.7	24.6	11.1	2.2	3.1	56.9	25.4	16.6	1.1
Big Horn County	34.4	40.7	28.6	42.3	X	28.7	24.5	39.7	3 978	45.0	7.7	28.9	9.3	−3.4	47.9	38.7	12.9	0.5
Blaine County	32.9	38.7	27.1	38.8	66.7	24.4	0.0	27.3	2 018	44.5	13.7	22.8	2.7	0.8	37.7	36.0	25.2	1.2
Broadwater County	35.6	45.6	25.0	35.5	100.0	26.5	100.0	47.1	1 073	54.4	24.4	15.6	5.4	1.3	55.2	20.8	22.4	1.6
Carbon County	35.2	45.1	25.4	35.3	40.0	21.7	28.6	37.3	2 213	55.8	18.8	17.9	9.1	0.4	58.6	15.2	25.3	0.9
Carter County	48.0	61.8	34.5	48.3	0.0	0.0	0.0	X	348	60.6	22.1	13.5	9.5	18.2	27.5	13.5	54.2	4.8
Cascade County	39.0	49.0	29.4	39.6	44.9	22.8	32.8	41.7	20 018	49.9	19.0	22.9	8.2	2.3	69.6	17.1	12.8	0.5
Chouteau County	34.2	45.1	23.4	35.4	0.0	26.2	55.6	21.9	1 645	55.7	15.3	15.7	6.8	4.4	43.8	20.5	34.2	1.5
Custer County	37.1	45.4	29.4	37.7	X	19.9	51.9	17.0	2 697	55.6	12.6	25.3	16.3	4.3	59.2	23.5	16.7	0.5
Daniels County	34.0	44.0	23.9	34.0	X	33.3	66.7	23.8	426	51.2	23.0	14.3	0.9	−1.8	44.1	19.8	34.6	1.6
Dawson County	33.9	44.4	23.6	34.3	0.0	18.8	0.0	27.3	2 050	56.4	17.7	19.0	10.8	1.9	61.7	20.1	17.5	0.7
Deer Lodge County	30.3	33.8	26.9	30.7	0.0	34.5	0.0	16.9	2 014	57.8	12.0	16.6	9.8	−4.3	59.0	26.4	13.7	0.9
Fallon County	38.2	53.3	23.4	38.5	50.0	0.0	0.0	13.3	703	64.0	19.3	13.7	13.1	8.7	52.3	21.3	26.0	0.4
Fergus County	33.9	45.2	23.5	34.1	75.0	32.7	20.0	17.3	2 682	60.2	16.7	17.3	12.9	6.4	53.2	19.0	25.4	2.4
Flathead County	34.2	42.9	25.7	34.3	29.7	24.5	34.4	33.1	18 482	46.4	23.7	21.0	2.8	−1.8	70.2	11.5	17.8	0.4
Gallatin County	37.3	45.6	28.2	37.6	28.0	29.4	22.3	41.2	14 407	54.9	22.3	15.7	6.0	10.3	64.8	17.9	16.7	0.5
Garfield County	44.4	60.2	27.9	44.3	X	X	X	100.0	315	61.3	13.3	16.2	12.9	11.8	32.0	20.9	44.6	2.4
Glacier County	30.5	34.1	27.2	36.9	0.0	26.1	40.7	1.7	4 169	43.6	14.5	26.1	5.1	−6.0	42.8	44.6	10.7	2.0
Golden Valley County	41.7	54.8	28.5	41.6	X	60.0	X	50.0	225	62.2	19.1	9.8	7.4	−2.0	40.0	18.8	30.5	10.7
Granite County	30.6	40.9	19.7	31.8	X	2.1	0.0	10.0	666	46.4	26.0	21.9	3.7	−6.7	52.0	20.9	24.9	2.1
Hill County	34.4	44.4	25.0	36.5	0.0	24.3	22.0	20.5	4 403	52.3	14.3	21.5	9.2	1.8	65.6	20.0	13.4	1.0
Jefferson County	41.4	50.0	32.7	41.8	25.0	28.0	15.8	30.7	2 636	56.5	23.1	13.1	5.0	6.8	52.0	31.2	16.5	0.3
Judith Basin County	36.2	50.2	21.1	36.5	X	0.0	0.0	0.0	612	53.6	24.3	6.4	−4.6	−0.7	36.0	16.8	41.3	5.9
Lake County	32.3	38.5	26.5	33.1	25.0	29.0	18.3	40.7	6 860	44.3	17.9	24.9	4.6	−4.1	56.6	21.6	21.0	0.7
Lewis and Clark County	38.5	50.0	36.4	43.5	31.5	28.7	29.4	24.2	13 602	57.1	14.4	20.2	12.7	10.0	59.2	28.2	12.4	0.3
Liberty County	34.3	46.8	22.6	34.3	X	X	100.0	0.0	542	47.0	25.6	10.1	−7.5	−5.4	44.2	15.3	37.3	3.1
Lincoln County	24.3	31.2	17.3	24.0	28.6	28.6	25.0	26.8	4 512	41.6	21.4	19.8	−3.2	−15.4	60.7	21.5	16.5	1.2
McCone County	43.0	55.2	30.4	42.6	75.0	50.0	100.0	66.7	472	65.7	18.2	11.2	12.3	7.2	41.9	15.9	39.9	2.3
Madison County	33.2	41.6	24.4	33.5	0.0	54.2	0.0	16.4	1 527	59.0	20.7	12.6	7.0	−0.1	51.4	18.1	29.1	1.3
Meagher County	35.4	47.0	23.8	35.5	X	36.4	0.0	60.0	475	49.1	16.0	21.3	5.8	5.0	51.9	18.7	27.7	1.8
Mineral County	30.4	37.0	23.3	30.6	X	45.9	46.2	9.1	877	49.6	16.9	20.0	5.0	−5.4	63.1	17.0	18.6	1.3
Missoula County	37.0	44.5	29.6	37.6	17.9	21.6	27.8	34.9	20 918	50.5	20.7	20.5	6.4	7.7	69.6	17.1	13.0	0.3
Musselshell County	30.5	39.4	22.1	30.7	X	20.8	0.0	35.1	982	54.0	18.8	14.2	3.6	−4.3	54.6	16.9	28.6	1.9
Park County	37.5	48.4	27.1	37.9	9.4	18.1	12.1	23.3	3 523	51.7	21.6	19.9	7.0	2.2	65.4	13.2	20.7	0.8
Petroleum County	39.3	54.9	22.5	38.3	X	X	X	100.0	123	48.8	28.5	11.4	−4.4	4.4	24.1	26.7	49.1	0.0
Phillips County	35.3	48.8	22.4	35.6	100.0	25.5	58.8	33.3	1 157	57.7	20.0	16.0	9.1	5.4	48.0	22.5	27.1	2.4
Pondera County	32.5	43.6	21.9	35.1	0.0	16.7	42.1	15.0	1 824	56.9	11.3	14.2	6.5	2.5	46.5	23.0	28.4	2.1
Powder River County	44.3	58.1	30.7	44.0	0.0	70.8	0.0	50.0	483	59.2	22.6	16.8	11.4	4.4	30.3	25.8	40.9	3.0
Powell County	31.6	32.4	30.3	33.1	31.8	8.5	20.0	14.0	1 396	51.0	17.9	22.1	8.5	−2.1	50.2	29.7	19.1	0.9
Prairie County	41.1	54.2	27.1	41.8	X	0.0	0.0	50.0	223	63.7	14.8	16.1	15.2	3.9	40.7	23.1	35.4	0.9
Ravalli County	31.0	37.1	25.1	30.9	25.0	32.6	28.6	40.6	8 810	47.0	25.8	17.1	−0.5	−4.8	61.3	14.3	23.6	0.8
Richland County	36.4	48.3	24.8	37.0	100.0	12.0	X	20.3	2 567	56.0	17.1	18.0	9.4	5.3	62.8	15.7	20.2	1.4
Roosevelt County	31.8	38.7	25.4	38.8	X	24.5	31.0	28.8	3 187	35.1	9.8	36.5	7.0	5.2	42.7	37.5	18.5	1.2
Rosebud County	37.2	47.3	26.8	41.6	X	25.7	34.5	38.8	2 834	41.4	16.6	23.5	0.3	2.2	61.5	25.1	12.8	0.7
Sanders County	25.1	31.9	18.2	25.4	71.4	18.4	21.9	16.5	2 301	42.5	25.7	19.9	−2.2	−12.5	58.1	18.5	22.3	1.1
Sheridan County	32.5	42.5	22.9	31.7	0.0	56.6	66.7	51.6	886	74.4	9.0	10.7	20.5	4.4	48.2	15.6	34.2	2.0
Silver Bow County	35.8	42.9	29.0	36.4	44.4	11.5	5.0	31.0	7 799	51.2	15.1	24.8	11.4	3.9	72.7	16.4	10.3	0.6
Stillwater County	37.4	50.2	24.3	37.5	0.0	25.5	42.9	38.1	2 006	55.8	25.7	11.1	2.3	−0.4	67.9	12.2	18.9	1.0
Sweet Grass County	37.8	50.7	25.4	38.2	X	0.0	41.7	20.7	890	62.4	22.4	9.0	6.8	9.2	50.7	17.8	29.3	2.1
Teton County	33.4	44.7	22.4	33.5	X	31.0	37.5	21.7	1 724	48.5	27.2	12.8	−3.3	−5.7	53.6	18.0	26.8	1.6
Toole County	34.0	42.3	25.4	35.1	0.0	15.2	0.0	10.3	1 322	58.3	17.1	15.6	9.3	6.3	54.6	24.3	19.4	1.7
Treasure County	38.0	50.8	25.2	38.2	X	0.0	0.0	37.5	214	62.6	14.0	12.6	10.6	9.9	48.5	21.4	27.7	2.3
Valley County	39.9	50.4	29.9	41.2	0.0	27.3	0.0	53.7	1 848	63.6	12.9	17.3	16.3	4.3	58.7	19.6	20.5	1.3
Wheatland County	40.7	52.3	28.8	41.6	0.0	23.1	X	50.0	503	51.3	22.5	15.5	2.2	−3.3	46.2	17.1	26.7	10.1
Wibaux County	35.6	45.3	26.3	35.5	X	66.7	0.0	0.0	265	61.9	16.2	12.1	9.4	13.9	46.5	21.7	28.4	3.4
Yellowstone County	40.6	50.8	31.3	41.3	32.4	27.6	35.7	32.2	31 709	52.2	17.8	22.2	9.8	8.1	75.5	11.9	12.3	0.3
NEBRASKA	45.2	55.8	35.2	46.0	38.2	32.6	40.4	40.2	430 210	56.7	16.7	18.3	10.4	10.5	73.7	13.7	12.1	0.5
Adams County	42.5	53.4	32.1	42.7	40.7	13.5	42.2	39.5	7 269	62.2	14.1	17.7	15.3	12.3	74.5	13.3	11.6	0.5
Antelope County	39.0	52.1	26.5	39.0	0.0	43.5	0.0	61.1	1 976	66.5	13.1	13.6	15.5	10.5	56.4	14.2	27.2	2.2
Arthur County	49.7	70.2	28.5	49.4	X	0.0	X	100.0	104	72.1	7.7	20.2	27.7	23.8	46.6	16.7	31.9	4.8
Banner County	39.1	56.8	21.5	38.9	0.0	X	X	28.6	219	60.7	26.0	5.5	1.6	0.9	46.7	21.5	29.5	2.3

[1] Hispanic or Latino persons may be of any race.

STATE County	Percent who worked at home	Percent of the population 5 years and over with a disability	Veterans as a percent of the population 18 years and over	Occupation for employed population 16 years and over (percent)						Industry for employed population 16 years and over (percent)					
				Management, professional, and related occupations	Service occupations	Sales and office occupations	Farming, fishing, and forestry occupations	Construction, extraction, and maintenance occupations	Production, transportation and material moving occupations	Agriculture, forestry, fishing, and mining	Construction and manufacturing	Wholesale and retail trade	Transportation and warehousing, and utilities	Service industries	Public administration
	42	43	44	45	46	47	48	49	50	51	52	53	54	55	56
MISSOURI—Cont'd															
St. Louis city................	1.7	24.8	11.6	29.7	22.1	26.5	0.1	6.2	15.4	0.3	15.9	12.5	5.8	59.3	6.1
MONTANA	6.4	17.5	16.1	33.1	17.2	25.5	2.2	10.7	11.2	7.9	13.4	15.8	5.4	51.5	5.9
Beaverhead County	7.2	16.2	16.3	34.6	20.0	17.5	6.8	10.1	11.0	19.3	11.5	11.4	4.5	48.2	5.1
Big Horn County...........	4.9	23.0	13.7	33.5	23.1	21.4	3.4	11.4	7.3	14.6	7.5	10.1	3.2	49.6	15.0
Blaine County.............	10.6	16.7	14.0	41.4	16.9	18.0	5.7	11.1	6.8	22.4	7.7	10.1	4.1	44.6	11.0
Broadwater County	9.7	19.7	16.5	32.5	15.4	18.8	4.4	15.5	13.5	17.9	19.2	10.5	5.9	38.8	7.7
Carbon County.............	11.5	17.1	14.9	35.4	16.7	21.4	2.9	13.8	9.8	15.4	13.6	12.4	6.3	48.6	3.7
Carter County.............	43.9	21.7	10.6	59.5	8.9	11.6	8.6	8.3	3.1	56.7	5.2	4.3	2.2	28.9	2.7
Cascade County...........	3.8	19.7	19.6	30.5	18.4	29.7	1.0	10.0	10.4	3.0	11.1	17.9	5.6	55.5	7.0
Chouteau County	15.1	16.0	16.2	45.3	15.1	17.0	6.5	8.0	8.0	32.7	7.9	10.2	2.8	41.0	5.4
Custer County.............	5.9	19.3	17.5	32.1	22.1	25.5	2.7	9.8	7.7	10.6	7.5	16.3	4.7	52.3	8.6
Daniels County	16.6	16.9	16.0	43.3	13.6	23.5	5.6	7.9	6.1	28.5	5.0	12.1	5.0	44.3	5.2
Dawson County	7.6	16.7	16.0	32.7	20.1	20.9	2.1	13.1	11.0	13.1	4.4	12.3	13.2	51.7	5.3
Deer Lodge County.......	3.7	23.8	18.3	27.7	31.9	19.2	1.2	10.5	9.5	4.5	11.6	9.5	4.1	63.0	7.3
Fallon County..............	9.7	15.1	12.8	34.5	18.1	18.5	3.1	12.0	13.7	23.2	8.4	12.2	10.6	40.7	4.8
Fergus County.............	11.8	18.6	17.3	37.0	18.1	20.3	3.5	11.1	10.0	16.9	14.7	13.7	4.2	45.4	5.2
Flathead County...........	5.1	16.6	17.1	28.2	15.7	26.0	1.9	12.8	15.3	4.2	21.2	17.4	5.0	49.5	2.7
Gallatin County	7.3	11.7	11.6	35.4	15.4	25.6	1.4	11.3	10.8	3.8	18.4	16.1	3.1	55.3	3.2
Garfield County	13.9	19.7	14.7	48.9	12.1	13.3	9.3	8.3	8.1	43.4	6.4	6.6	5.7	29.2	8.7
Glacier County	5.3	17.3	12.9	37.8	20.0	21.1	3.3	9.7	8.1	9.3	7.2	10.7	5.5	52.1	15.2
Golden Valley County ...	31.3	21.8	15.0	43.9	15.2	12.9	8.6	9.4	10.0	41.8	10.7	8.4	3.9	32.4	2.7
Granite County	10.5	21.7	19.3	31.2	17.2	17.9	9.1	14.0	10.5	21.1	18.6	9.6	4.5	39.2	7.0
Hill County.................	4.2	17.1	14.3	33.1	18.9	22.3	2.8	12.7	10.2	9.5	6.3	14.6	10.0	53.8	5.8
Jefferson County	6.1	15.5	18.6	39.3	16.3	23.1	1.6	11.9	7.8	8.4	12.2	11.1	4.8	48.1	15.4
Judith Basin County	21.8	17.2	16.6	50.0	14.2	14.2	9.1	5.0	7.5	42.0	7.4	6.5	3.6	35.9	4.7
Lake County	8.6	19.3	17.9	31.4	15.8	22.8	4.1	11.8	14.1	9.7	20.3	13.2	4.4	45.4	7.0
Lewis and Clark County	4.8	17.2	17.0	39.6	14.7	27.5	1.0	8.2	8.9	3.0	10.3	13.1	3.5	52.9	17.2
Liberty County.............	19.0	16.2	10.8	40.9	15.0	21.5	7.3	8.7	6.6	33.7	9.7	10.5	2.6	37.8	5.6
Lincoln County	7.3	22.7	20.1	27.1	18.2	22.3	4.4	10.6	17.4	10.8	18.7	14.5	5.2	47.0	3.8
McCone County	16.3	16.0	14.6	43.1	11.3	23.7	6.0	9.0	6.8	35.7	7.1	12.9	5.0	33.2	6.0
Madison County	11.9	15.8	18.5	32.4	14.8	19.6	6.5	15.1	11.6	20.7	18.4	11.1	4.3	40.6	5.0
Meagher County	13.6	16.4	17.9	34.4	16.8	17.9	14.6	11.2	5.1	30.6	10.7	10.5	2.5	39.0	6.5
Mineral County	6.8	21.4	21.4	24.2	18.7	21.9	4.1	15.1	16.0	8.7	21.3	14.3	6.1	45.1	4.5
Missoula County...........	4.5	15.6	13.9	32.3	17.9	28.3	0.9	9.7	10.9	2.8	13.6	17.5	5.3	67.5	3.2
Musselshell County	8.5	19.5	18.6	30.6	15.1	20.8	6.3	15.6	11.6	20.6	15.2	15.2	4.4	41.4	5.2
Park County	9.2	18.8	16.2	31.1	19.2	20.9	1.9	15.7	11.2	7.3	15.8	13.2	4.2	54.7	4.9
Petroleum County	24.1	16.6	15.8	51.7	10.8	11.2	10.8	12.9	2.6	58.2	3.4	1.7	3.9	25.4	7.3
Phillips County	10.4	19.2	13.2	36.1	17.3	21.9	6.7	7.5	10.4	26.1	5.8	11.2	7.3	43.2	6.3
Pondera County	9.8	20.5	14.7	41.6	15.6	21.3	3.5	8.1	10.0	20.2	6.4	16.6	4.8	45.6	6.4
Powder River County	20.0	18.0	12.1	44.8	16.0	13.5	12.3	6.5	6.8	43.0	5.6	7.8	3.8	34.0	5.8
Powell County	9.9	21.7	20.8	32.5	21.9	18.4	5.2	7.6	14.3	15.8	14.6	10.6	2.8	38.5	17.6
Prairie County	8.6	16.1	19.1	48.0	14.4	16.6	4.7	7.8	8.5	36.0	5.9	7.6	4.3	39.9	6.2
Ravalli County.............	9.8	18.5	19.6	32.2	15.5	24.0	2.4	14.1	11.9	7.1	19.9	16.2	4.3	49.3	3.3
Richland County...........	8.0	16.5	12.5	32.7	15.8	22.0	4.4	11.8	13.3	19.6	10.2	16.6	5.5	41.9	6.2
Roosevelt County	7.2	16.7	15.4	38.8	20.2	21.5	2.3	9.1	8.1	13.3	8.3	11.2	4.8	51.3	11.1
Rosebud County	3.5	17.1	15.8	34.0	18.4	16.7	3.9	14.0	12.9	19.6	6.4	7.2	11.6	48.4	6.9
Sanders County	9.5	24.4	21.8	30.1	15.8	16.9	5.3	14.5	17.5	12.8	20.0	11.9	6.9	43.7	4.7
Sheridan County	12.2	16.2	12.5	37.8	17.7	19.6	3.4	8.4	13.1	24.9	6.9	12.7	7.1	43.3	5.1
Silver Bow County	2.7	18.8	16.7	32.4	19.4	27.0	0.7	9.4	11.1	4.1	9.4	17.8	9.3	54.3	5.1
Stillwater County	9.0	18.4	15.9	27.9	13.5	19.2	3.3	21.1	14.9	27.0	16.3	12.2	4.6	36.5	3.3
Sweet Grass County	14.7	15.5	17.1	35.2	18.2	19.0	6.8	12.4	8.4	23.9	16.5	11.2	2.8	41.5	4.0
Teton County...............	14.2	17.6	15.8	39.4	15.6	20.2	5.4	9.8	9.7	20.6	8.0	13.0	6.1	48.3	4.1
Toole County...............	8.5	19.3	16.1	30.4	24.3	23.7	3.1	9.0	9.5	15.4	6.1	13.4	7.5	48.0	9.6
Treasure County	13.8	16.1	17.0	34.3	16.3	17.5	16.6	9.3	6.1	37.1	4.4	7.0	5.4	35.9	10.3
Valley County	7.9	19.0	17.1	35.2	19.5	23.9	3.2	10.5	7.7	17.1	7.5	15.7	7.1	44.2	8.3
Wheatland County........	27.1	19.3	15.1	37.5	20.6	14.4	13.7	8.4	5.4	41.0	6.5	6.8	4.4	36.1	5.3
Wibaux County............	18.3	26.1	12.8	41.0	14.9	15.1	5.4	10.9	12.7	27.2	5.4	11.1	7.2	41.9	7.2
Yellowstone County	4.1	17.6	15.4	31.0	16.7	30.8	0.7	9.1	11.8	3.0	11.9	20.7	6.7	53.6	4.0
NEBRASKA...............	4.6	16.0	13.7	33.0	14.6	26.4	1.6	9.3	15.1	5.6	18.7	16.5	6.1	50.0	3.9
Adams County.............	3.7	17.4	12.8	30.4	16.7	24.0	1.2	9.1	18.6	4.5	22.5	16.5	4.4	48.3	3.8
Antelope County...........	12.7	16.3	15.5	35.4	14.7	20.7	7.2	10.2	11.8	24.5	13.6	15.7	4.7	38.3	3.3
Arthur County	22.3	12.4	14.6	42.2	6.4	10.4	27.1	7.6	6.4	54.2	8.0	4.8	3.2	23.1	6.8
Banner County	17.3	13.3	9.0	41.9	9.1	21.0	11.4	8.3	8.3	35.6	9.1	9.6	5.1	33.3	7.3

STATE County	Median house-hold income	Median family income				Median income for full-year, full-time workers			Households by source of income (percent)									
		All families	Families with children			Median nonfamily house-hold income			Per capita income	With earnings	With interest, dividend, or rental income	With Social Security income	With public assis-tance income	With retire-ment income	House-holds with income over $100,000 (percent)	+/− U.S. percent for income over $100,000	House-holds with income below poverty (percent)	Families with children with income below poverty (percent)
			Married-couple	Male house-holder	Female house-holder		Men	Women										
	57	58	59	60	61	62	63	64	65	66	67	68	69	70	71	72	73	74
MISSOURI—Cont'd																		
St. Louis city	27 156	32 585	48 632	24 251	15 108	20 560	30 657	25 665	16 108	73.6	23.9	27.7	8.1	15.7	4.6	−7.7	22.1	29.8
MONTANA	33 024	40 487	46 202	25 095	16 203	19 484	31 591	21 679	17 151	79.6	40.0	27.7	3.3	16.3	5.6	−6.7	14.1	16.4
Beaverhead County	28 962	38 971	42 750	16 500	13 750	15 997	27 328	19 259	15 621	80.2	38.4	29.9	2.9	15.8	4.0	−8.3	19.2	18.2
Big Horn County	27 684	31 095	35 026	16 719	14 336	15 449	25 500	20 081	10 792	84.6	25.9	22.6	8.7	10.1	2.1	−10.2	24.5	31.2
Blaine County	25 247	30 616	36 625	21 563	12 647	16 838	25 119	21 250	12 101	77.8	30.4	27.5	8.9	11.8	3.7	−8.6	24.8	32.4
Broadwater County	32 689	36 524	40 078	29 375	13 750	17 161	29 651	21 667	16 237	78.2	38.1	35.2	2.7	20.6	4.9	−7.4	11.9	13.4
Carbon County	32 139	38 405	45 788	24 583	20 568	20 041	31 215	21 234	17 204	78.0	45.1	31.9	1.7	16.0	3.7	−8.6	11.7	12.8
Carter County	26 313	32 262	35 385	23 750	16 563	15 078	24 342	15 234	13 280	82.8	42.0	34.4	2.6	9.1	2.4	−9.9	18.6	13.9
Cascade County	32 971	39 949	45 215	23 682	16 056	19 671	30 683	21 695	17 566	78.0	39.9	28.6	3.4	19.6	5.4	−6.9	13.4	17.1
Chouteau County	29 150	32 399	33 500	23 750	14 750	20 536	24 760	20 392	14 851	81.5	42.0	32.6	3.9	10.9	4.2	−8.1	16.4	23.3
Custer County	30 000	38 779	45 729	23 125	15 477	17 308	29 543	18 861	15 876	77.6	38.7	33.3	2.2	16.1	4.6	−7.7	14.6	16.7
Daniels County	27 306	35 722	35 893	11 875	19 375	16 576	26 532	18 690	16 055	73.9	50.3	39.5	1.6	12.7	4.0	−8.3	17.4	22.2
Dawson County	31 393	38 455	43 074	22 308	16 250	15 723	30 998	20 702	15 368	78.1	44.6	32.5	2.4	14.6	3.0	−9.3	15.6	17.2
Deer Lodge County	26 305	36 158	41 250	11 042	16 250	17 679	28 696	19 601	15 580	67.8	37.2	40.0	4.1	24.6	2.4	−9.9	16.7	19.7
Fallon County	29 944	38 636	41 842	31 000	16 250	17 125	29 394	18 846	16 014	80.8	41.2	36.5	2.1	10.7	3.1	−9.2	11.5	14.7
Fergus County	30 409	36 609	42 254	16 875	16 875	16 614	29 167	19 362	15 862	75.8	41.0	34.0	1.7	16.9	4.2	−8.1	14.4	15.8
Flathead County	34 466	40 702	45 631	28 059	17 253	20 149	33 380	21 602	18 112	80.2	39.2	26.3	2.3	16.6	6.0	−6.3	12.7	14.9
Gallatin County	38 120	46 639	50 357	30 000	18 675	24 514	31 899	21 932	19 074	88.2	45.7	17.1	1.2	12.0	8.0	−4.3	12.3	9.6
Garfield County	25 917	31 111	29 904	11 250	11 964	14 432	22 305	15 855	13 930	77.7	37.1	37.3	1.9	11.3	2.4	−9.9	20.1	26.5
Glacier County	27 921	31 193	35 909	25 517	14 813	13 664	28 135	23 450	11 597	79.6	25.2	24.2	13.4	14.1	3.1	−9.2	24.9	29.2
Golden Valley County	27 308	35 000	37 917	0	10 417	16 136	16 625	20 096	13 573	77.2	44.7	36.9	2.8	9.7	3.9	−8.4	17.2	23.2
Granite County	27 813	33 485	37 813	26 250	15 000	17 679	27 917	18 681	16 636	75.4	37.1	32.4	3.2	21.5	4.9	−7.4	14.8	21.9
Hill County	30 781	38 179	44 720	19 063	13 832	17 399	31 542	20 544	14 935	78.7	37.4	27.5	4.2	12.4	4.6	−7.7	17.7	22.9
Jefferson County	41 506	48 912	55 318	31 250	23 942	19 441	36 048	25 345	18 250	83.1	40.7	24.2	2.4	18.6	7.0	−5.3	10.0	9.9
Judith Basin County	29 241	34 243	34 500	22 083	20 833	17 826	23 565	17 143	14 291	77.4	43.3	34.6	1.8	15.5	5.0	−7.3	16.3	24.7
Lake County	28 740	34 033	37 321	21 875	15 368	16 389	28 650	19 774	15 173	76.5	32.0	31.7	4.6	17.3	4.7	−7.6	17.2	23.1
Lewis and Clark County	37 360	46 766	54 617	24 240	18 850	22 814	34 956	24 708	18 763	81.1	45.1	25.2	3.0	19.2	6.0	−6.3	11.4	11.5
Liberty County	30 284	37 361	37 778	21 250	14 375	19 957	25 000	17 100	14 882	76.0	48.3	33.9	2.3	12.8	4.5	−7.8	15.8	27.6
Lincoln County	26 754	31 784	36 068	25 000	11 000	14 315	31 266	21 295	13 923	68.5	33.7	35.8	5.3	22.1	2.1	−10.2	18.5	22.6
McCone County	29 718	35 887	37 375	38 125	16 042	15 852	25 846	16 250	15 162	81.1	45.0	35.2	2.5	12.7	3.5	−8.8	16.9	16.9
Madison County	30 233	35 536	39 900	30 625	16 094	19 268	28 294	19 133	16 944	77.6	43.4	31.0	1.4	18.6	4.8	−7.5	12.7	13.0
Meagher County	29 375	33 879	36 458	18 333	10 000	15 625	23 945	16 667	15 019	76.8	41.8	35.6	1.4	16.0	2.9	−9.4	18.3	25.9
Mineral County	27 143	32 096	36 974	24 375	17 031	15 545	28 516	19 079	15 166	75.7	30.5	31.3	5.2	18.9	4.9	−7.4	15.4	17.1
Missoula County	34 454	44 865	51 448	28 375	17 352	20 347	32 510	22 802	17 808	84.2	41.3	21.0	3.0	13.6	6.2	−6.1	15.5	13.4
Musselshell County	25 527	32 298	33 039	15 938	11 477	16 384	25 950	18 494	15 389	71.7	40.3	36.4	2.3	17.1	2.7	−9.6	18.0	23.5
Park County	31 739	40 561	44 678	26 875	17 188	16 899	29 768	20 575	17 704	78.8	39.8	28.7	2.6	13.9	5.4	−6.9	13.0	9.8
Petroleum County	24 107	32 667	33 056	9 583	13 333	11 641	22 083	18 250	15 986	70.8	26.8	35.4	2.9	8.1	5.7	−6.6	23.4	28.8
Phillips County	28 702	37 529	43 348	26 250	21 250	16 713	29 122	20 956	15 058	77.2	39.4	31.5	3.2	10.2	2.9	−9.4	17.0	20.6
Pondera County	30 464	36 484	43 500	23 500	14 375	16 944	29 362	19 902	14 276	76.0	42.8	34.3	5.7	14.8	4.2	−8.1	17.3	21.2
Powder River County	28 398	34 671	39 500	24 375	19 500	16 406	26 522	20 083	15 351	85.7	33.3	31.3	1.1	10.6	3.4	−8.9	13.8	11.6
Powell County	30 625	35 836	42 295	24 375	15 163	19 342	26 702	20 975	13 816	73.3	40.3	34.6	4.3	21.6	3.5	−8.8	12.5	15.9
Prairie County	25 451	32 292	35 139	42 500	7 083	18 125	25 000	19 667	14 422	71.3	39.1	38.2	0.7	14.2	1.9	−10.4	15.6	23.4
Ravalli County	31 992	38 397	41 596	25 136	14 103	19 539	31 848	20 574	17 935	75.8	39.4	32.4	2.4	20.9	6.7	−5.6	12.1	17.2
Richland County	32 110	39 348	44 297	24 000	16 842	18 265	30 253	19 834	16 006	78.4	38.4	30.4	2.7	12.6	3.3	−9.0	12.5	12.4
Roosevelt County	24 834	27 833	38 494	20 368	12 432	14 750	26 133	20 650	11 347	77.7	30.2	27.1	15.3	10.7	3.6	−8.7	27.7	35.9
Rosebud County	35 898	41 631	45 688	21 364	15 819	20 684	40 691	21 185	15 052	83.9	35.4	23.3	5.3	12.4	5.0	−7.3	17.8	26.0
Sanders County	26 852	31 340	36 463	23 125	14 868	14 564	29 979	18 736	14 593	70.7	35.2	35.6	3.5	20.2	4.0	−8.3	16.8	22.2
Sheridan County	29 518	35 345	37 500	16 250	15 577	20 147	25 072	20 699	16 038	73.6	51.8	39.6	0.6	13.4	4.6	−7.7	13.1	16.1
Silver Bow County	30 402	40 018	49 842	23 510	14 525	18 237	32 341	22 449	17 009	74.8	38.2	31.9	4.3	20.9	4.9	−7.4	14.3	17.9
Stillwater County	39 205	45 238	49 023	30 500	21 354	20 205	34 125	20 369	18 468	80.9	43.9	29.3	2.0	15.6	5.3	−7.0	9.2	9.2
Sweet Grass County	32 422	38 750	42 105	26 875	16 750	19 167	30 423	18 600	17 880	79.4	53.8	33.4	1.0	16.2	6.0	−6.3	10.0	13.5
Teton County	30 197	36 662	38 750	22 813	14 464	18 365	27 447	19 514	14 635	74.6	45.9	36.2	2.3	17.4	3.3	−9.0	14.1	20.4
Toole County	30 169	39 600	42 422	34 643	18 646	16 232	28 716	20 425	14 731	77.8	39.5	33.2	3.6	13.6	3.3	−9.0	11.2	14.1
Treasure County	29 830	34 219	31 806	14 688	13 750	15 625	24 196	16 875	14 392	82.9	37.5	35.5	1.4	11.6	3.9	−8.4	13.5	15.4
Valley County	30 979	39 044	47 281	21 429	14 215	16 651	29 413	19 712	16 246	78.0	41.5	37.5	3.9	16.1	4.2	−8.1	14.3	15.3
Wheatland County	24 492	32 500	34 063	28 750	17 917	14 744	14 948	16 250	11 954	68.3	38.3	44.2	3.1	15.7	1.8	−10.5	14.7	15.7
Wibaux County	28 224	34 265	35 417	14 167	17 500	13 229	23 125	18 462	16 121	76.7	39.1	35.3	3.5	13.6	3.8	−8.5	15.3	14.6
Yellowstone County	36 727	45 277	52 661	26 799	16 440	20 855	34 975	22 268	19 303	80.7	40.4	26.8	3.0	15.8	7.3	−5.0	11.1	13.6
NEBRASKA	39 250	48 032	55 343	27 526	20 480	22 985	33 399	24 635	19 613	82.5	41.6	26.4	2.8	12.8	8.1	−4.2	9.7	10.2
Adams County	37 160	45 620	51 533	28 056	17 244	20 981	30 779	21 956	18 308	80.1	43.4	31.0	2.5	13.2	6.0	−6.3	9.9	9.6
Antelope County	30 114	36 240	40 104	27 500	15 809	15 577	27 223	17 342	14 601	74.0	45.0	37.4	2.7	9.0	3.6	−8.7	14.1	15.9
Arthur County	27 375	31 979	30 500	25 417	15 625	15 833	22 171	15 781	15 810	90.3	42.2	35.1	2.2	12.4	4.9	−7.4	14.6	20.0
Banner County	31 339	41 538	43 438	0	7 500	17 031	25 417	18 750	17 149	81.0	42.5	32.4	0.0	13.3	4.8	−7.5	12.7	16.3

Table B-3. States and Counties — Education, Labor Force, and Income

STATE/ County code	MSA/PMSA/ NECMA code[1]	STATE County	High school graduates			College graduates		College graduates (percent)				
			Total population 25 years and over	Percent with a high school diploma or less	Percent with a high school diploma or more	Percent with a bachelor's degree or more	+/− U.S. percent with bachelor's degree or more	Non-Hispanic White	Black or African American	American Indian and Alaska Native	Asian, Hawaiian, and Pacific Islander	Hispanic or Latino[2]
			1	2	3	4	5	6	7	8	9	10
		NEBRASKA—Cont'd										
31 009	...	Blaine County	407	45.2	93.4	12.3	-12.1	11.9	X	X	X	X
31 011	...	Boone County	4 134	57.4	84.4	13.1	-11.3	13.1	X	0.0	50.0	0.0
31 013	...	Box Butte County	7 864	49.4	88.1	15.3	-9.1	16.4	0.0	6.7	0.0	4.1
31 015	...	Boyd County	1 698	59.9	83.0	12.8	-11.6	12.8	X	X	33.3	X
31 017	...	Brown County	2 478	54.0	83.3	17.2	-7.2	17.0	X	0.0	0.0	50.0
31 019	...	Buffalo County	24 177	37.5	89.2	30.2	5.8	30.8	52.9	9.0	61.3	11.0
31 021	...	Burt County	5 382	56.5	84.1	14.2	-10.2	14.4	0.0	0.0	0.0	4.0
31 023	...	Butler County	5 741	58.2	83.4	13.6	-10.8	13.6	0.0	0.0	71.4	0.0
31 025	5920	Cass County	15 887	47.6	89.4	18.7	-5.7	18.8	33.3	11.8	20.0	6.7
31 027	...	Cedar County	6 208	56.7	83.5	13.0	-11.4	13.0	X	0.0	X	0.0
31 029	...	Chase County	2 791	53.2	86.4	16.6	-7.8	16.8	X	0.0	X	0.0
31 031	...	Cherry County	4 115	46.1	85.2	19.4	-5.0	19.7	X	11.5	0.0	22.2
31 033	...	Cheyenne County	6 543	48.5	86.7	16.8	-7.6	17.2	X	2.5	52.6	0.0
31 035	...	Clay County	4 685	50.7	86.7	16.2	-8.2	16.2	66.7	20.0	42.9	2.2
31 037	...	Colfax County	6 562	65.0	72.0	11.5	-12.9	13.2	X	0.0	0.0	3.8
31 039	...	Cuming County	6 755	61.8	78.7	12.3	-12.1	12.7	X	0.0	100.0	0.0
31 041	...	Custer County	8 026	51.3	87.5	16.1	-8.3	16.2	X	0.0	0.0	8.6
31 043	7720	Dakota County	12 103	62.8	73.5	12.4	-12.0	14.1	32.7	8.0	8.6	4.8
31 045	...	Dawes County	5 018	39.2	86.9	28.4	4.0	29.0	0.0	21.1	0.0	6.6
31 047	...	Dawson County	15 175	61.9	73.6	14.4	-10.0	17.4	0.0	6.9	8.0	2.1
31 049	...	Deuel County	1 515	50.6	85.3	17.4	-7.0	17.1	X	0.0	81.8	0.0
31 051	...	Dixon County	4 147	57.4	82.1	14.1	-10.3	14.5	X	22.7	0.0	2.4
31 053	...	Dodge County	23 787	56.7	83.5	15.0	-9.4	15.4	32.6	0.0	22.5	4.7
31 055	5920	Douglas County	293 076	38.9	87.3	30.6	6.2	33.6	12.0	7.6	57.0	11.1
31 057	...	Dundy County	1 630	48.5	82.4	16.7	-7.7	17.1	X	0.0	25.0	0.0
31 059	...	Fillmore County	4 561	54.5	88.2	15.7	-8.7	15.8	0.0	0.0	25.0	0.0
31 061	...	Franklin County	2 533	53.6	85.7	15.8	-8.6	15.9	X	0.0	0.0	0.0
31 063	...	Frontier County	1 941	46.4	88.3	17.9	-6.5	18.1	66.7	0.0	0.0	21.1
31 065	...	Furnas County	3 764	55.6	84.2	16.1	-8.3	16.3	X	0.0	0.0	9.5
31 067	...	Gage County	15 689	56.9	82.0	15.4	-9.0	15.4	11.1	0.0	81.6	10.6
31 069	...	Garden County	1 685	55.1	85.2	14.2	-10.2	14.5	X	0.0	0.0	0.0
31 071	...	Garfield County	1 374	55.5	81.1	13.4	-11.0	13.3	X	0.0	0.0	28.6
31 073	...	Gosper County	1 517	50.1	88.9	17.6	-6.8	17.6	X	X	100.0	10.0
31 075	...	Grant County	493	41.0	90.3	24.7	0.3	24.9	X	X	X	0.0
31 077	...	Greeley County	1 813	56.1	83.2	13.5	-10.9	13.5	0.0	X	X	0.0
31 079	...	Hall County	34 369	53.3	82.2	15.9	-8.5	17.4	4.7	10.3	24.7	2.9
31 081	...	Hamilton County	6 126	45.5	89.6	18.6	-5.8	18.6	0.0	X	X	29.0
31 083	...	Harlan County	2 675	52.1	85.8	15.3	-9.1	15.4	25.0	0.0	X	0.0
31 085	...	Hayes County	727	61.4	89.1	11.6	-12.8	11.8	X	X	X	0.0
31 087	...	Hitchcock County	2 180	52.0	85.6	13.8	-10.6	13.8	0.0	0.0	100.0	0.0
31 089	...	Holt County	7 748	56.6	84.5	14.5	-9.9	14.6	X	0.0	28.6	0.0
31 091	...	Hooker County	562	51.4	89.7	15.7	-8.7	15.4	X	0.0	0.0	40.0
31 093	...	Howard County	4 327	56.0	87.2	14.2	-10.2	14.4	0.0	0.0	0.0	0.0
31 095	...	Jefferson County	5 878	56.4	84.2	14.4	-10.0	14.0	0.0	64.7	0.0	22.2
31 097	...	Johnson County	3 143	63.0	80.4	14.7	-9.7	15.0	X	0.0	19.7	3.2
31 099	...	Kearney County	4 594	47.0	88.5	21.3	-3.1	21.4	100.0	0.0	0.0	19.0
31 101	...	Keith County	6 103	50.3	86.6	16.8	-7.6	17.0	X	19.0	14.7	6.2
31 103	...	Keya Paha County	681	53.9	82.2	15.7	-8.7	16.0	X	X	X	0.0
31 105	...	Kimball County	2 849	52.5	84.6	13.5	-10.9	13.6	0.0	12.0	60.0	5.7
31 107	...	Knox County	6 462	57.6	82.0	14.4	-10.0	14.8	0.0	5.1	26.7	0.0
31 109	4360	Lancaster County	152 747	34.7	90.5	32.6	8.2	33.4	17.7	17.6	36.3	19.3
31 111	...	Lincoln County	22 736	47.0	86.3	16.2	-8.2	16.6	28.6	12.2	38.7	3.8
31 113	...	Logan County	524	47.1	90.8	10.5	-13.9	10.8	X	0.0	X	0.0
31 115	...	Loup County	487	50.9	91.8	13.3	-11.1	13.0	X	X	X	66.7
31 117	...	McPherson County	360	51.1	88.6	22.2	-2.2	22.5	X	0.0	X	X
31 119	...	Madison County	21 724	51.2	82.6	17.0	-7.4	18.1	5.0	6.0	29.8	2.8
31 121	...	Merrick County	5 432	56.3	85.3	14.9	-9.5	15.1	0.0	0.0	0.0	7.9
31 123	...	Morrill County	3 575	55.7	79.4	14.3	-10.1	15.2	0.0	22.2	0.0	3.7
31 125	...	Nance County	2 651	58.2	80.6	11.4	-13.0	11.4	X	0.0	33.3	0.0
31 127	...	Nemaha County	4 907	47.6	85.5	22.9	-1.5	23.0	0.0	0.0	43.6	8.0
31 129	...	Nuckolls County	3 567	55.5	84.5	13.1	-11.3	12.8	100.0	0.0	100.0	6.7
31 131	...	Otoe County	10 373	53.9	85.6	18.1	-6.3	18.2	30.8	13.3	26.5	11.3
31 133	...	Pawnee County	2 228	61.4	83.7	14.4	-10.0	14.4	X	12.5	0.0	40.0
31 135	...	Perkins County	2 159	47.7	87.1	17.6	-6.8	17.8	X	X	0.0	0.0
31 137	...	Phelps County	6 565	46.8	89.1	20.4	-4.0	20.8	X	9.1	100.0	0.0
31 139	...	Pierce County	5 019	57.6	84.6	13.3	-11.1	13.3	100.0	0.0	15.4	0.0

[1]MSA = Metropolitan Statistical Area. PMSA = Primary MSA. NECMA = New England County Metropolitan Area. See the Appendix A for explanation of these concepts. See Appendix B for list of metropolitan areas identified by type, with component counties.
[2]Hispanic or Latino persons may be of any race.

STATE County	Grades kindergarten through 12	College or graduate school	Percent private	Number	Percent in armed forces	Percent high school graduates	Percent not enrolled, not grads, not in armed forces, not employed	Total population 16 years and over	Percent in labor force	Unemployment rate	Full-time	Part-time	Did not work in 1999
	11	12	13	14	15	16	17	18	19	20	21	22	23
NEBRASKA—Cont'd													
Blaine County	125	10	0.0	38	0.0	15.8	0.0	453	62.3	1.4	56.7	15.7	27.6
Boone County	1 459	131	10.3	362	0.0	7.2	0.8	4 686	64.5	1.5	51.8	17.7	30.5
Box Butte County	2 779	394	5.0	824	0.0	13.2	1.9	9 224	66.7	5.1	57.2	17.1	25.7
Boyd County	509	33	1.1	166	0.0	3.0	3.0	1 941	61.2	2.0	47.8	17.0	35.2
Brown County	699	44	2.8	179	0.0	7.8	0.6	2 780	63.7	1.6	52.8	17.0	30.2
Buffalo County	7 775	5 852	6.9	3 642	0.0	6.7	2.5	33 080	72.7	2.7	57.3	23.1	19.6
Burt County	1 632	172	3.9	443	0.0	4.7	2.3	6 072	63.4	2.8	53.4	15.9	30.7
Butler County	1 942	195	28.5	499	0.0	5.4	1.6	6 631	68.0	4.0	55.3	17.1	27.6
Cass County................	5 203	1 018	10.5	1 461	0.0	9.7	3.7	18 392	71.2	2.6	62.7	14.6	22.7
Cedar County	2 293	215	25.5	615	0.0	7.3	0.7	7 160	66.2	2.6	52.9	17.4	29.7
Chase County	822	57	3.2	241	0.0	3.7	5.0	3 197	62.2	1.4	51.0	19.1	30.0
Cherry County	1 291	127	7.1	326	0.0	8.9	3.1	4 720	68.8	1.8	61.4	14.7	23.9
Cheyenne County	2 060	256	3.2	608	0.0	15.8	0.3	7 560	68.1	2.1	58.3	14.6	27.1
Clay County................	1 568	193	7.4	468	0.0	6.2	1.9	5 405	64.4	2.8	54.9	16.5	28.6
Colfax County..............	2 336	296	8.5	720	0.0	9.7	9.3	7 845	69.7	3.5	58.3	13.9	27.8
Cuming County	2 182	200	32.3	598	0.0	8.0	3.7	7 792	68.3	2.0	54.9	18.7	26.4
Custer County	2 520	168	5.5	599	0.5	4.8	0.7	9 079	64.7	2.5	52.1	18.5	29.4
Dakota County	4 479	647	10.3	1 218	0.0	11.2	5.5	14 773	71.2	3.9	65.3	12.4	22.4
Dawes County	1 535	1 769	3.2	1 088	1.6	7.4	4.6	7 469	66.8	4.0	54.0	23.6	22.4
Dawson County	5 288	530	3.0	1 522	0.0	6.2	8.3	18 034	65.6	3.8	58.7	14.7	26.6
Deuel County	421	22	5.9	132	0.0	8.3	2.3	1 683	64.6	2.2	56.4	17.5	26.0
Dixon County	1 411	179	4.6	368	0.0	6.5	4.1	4 803	67.6	3.1	57.6	15.1	27.3
Dodge County	6 752	1 741	18.7	2 296	0.0	8.4	3.3	28 369	67.0	3.3	55.4	17.3	27.3
Douglas County	89 728	33 759	22.3	26 622	0.0	9.2	5.4	354 155	70.6	3.9	59.6	16.7	23.7
Dundy County	421	59	2.3	118	0.0	5.1	2.5	1 823	62.4	1.5	53.3	15.7	31.0
Fillmore County	1 361	133	6.3	399	0.0	10.0	2.8	5 160	63.9	2.2	52.3	17.7	30.0
Franklin County	689	83	0.6	170	0.0	6.5	1.8	2 805	60.2	2.5	49.7	17.0	33.3
Frontier County	664	240	1.4	290	0.0	4.5	0.7	2 421	68.1	2.0	54.8	18.8	26.4
Furnas County	1 020	104	3.9	317	0.0	5.7	1.3	4 248	58.9	3.6	50.2	17.3	32.5
Gage County................	4 267	800	8.3	1 333	0.0	9.8	3.4	18 158	66.6	2.8	54.8	17.1	28.1
Garden County	427	23	3.8	118	0.0	12.7	3.4	1 867	62.1	1.9	50.3	18.1	31.7
Garfield County	385	31	1.9	100	0.0	4.0	0.0	1 510	61.5	1.8	44.4	20.7	35.0
Gosper County	427	42	3.4	112	0.0	1.8	2.7	1 703	62.6	0.8	54.4	16.2	29.4
Grant County	193	12	7.3	55	0.0	0.0	0.0	566	73.1	1.0	68.0	18.0	14.0
Greeley County	593	101	17.4	184	0.0	0.0	0.0	2 092	62.4	2.1	50.6	16.6	32.8
Hall County.................	10 391	1 645	8.7	3 014	0.0	13.7	6.4	40 723	69.3	4.5	58.7	16.3	25.0
Hamilton County	2 143	264	5.9	581	0.0	6.0	2.8	7 033	69.5	2.5	57.0	18.6	24.4
Harlan County	782	62	6.3	224	0.0	6.7	0.0	2 994	60.6	2.6	49.7	18.0	32.2
Hayes County	259	27	2.8	62	0.0	9.7	4.8	822	65.0	2.1	49.9	21.2	29.0
Hitchcock County	628	101	2.1	206	0.0	5.8	0.5	2 495	59.2	2.6	49.9	18.9	31.3
Holt County	2 558	216	12.7	722	0.0	5.0	0.7	8 873	65.9	2.2	52.6	18.0	29.4
Hooker County	160	7	0.0	52	0.0	5.8	0.0	625	60.3	1.3	53.1	15.4	31.5
Howard County	1 495	161	4.3	331	0.0	9.4	2.1	4 943	69.4	2.9	56.0	17.2	26.8
Jefferson County	1 528	184	10.3	464	0.0	12.1	5.6	6 668	63.5	3.6	51.7	15.9	32.4
Johnson County	878	95	6.9	240	0.0	7.5	2.1	3 545	63.5	4.6	52.6	16.8	30.6
Kearney County	1 467	205	3.8	413	0.0	2.9	3.4	5 312	69.4	4.1	58.1	17.6	24.2
Keith County	1 814	145	5.6	549	0.0	9.8	1.5	6 958	66.0	3.3	53.7	18.2	28.1
Keya Paha County	182	12	2.6	54	0.0	13.0	0.0	770	61.8	1.7	50.6	16.8	32.6
Kimball County	778	84	3.4	193	0.0	4.7	2.1	3 198	64.3	2.0	52.4	17.9	29.7
Knox County	1 957	197	7.9	490	0.0	5.1	1.2	7 278	62.4	3.7	50.6	16.7	32.6
Lancaster County	42 543	29 849	14.9	17 077	0.0	9.0	2.0	198 307	73.3	3.6	60.4	20.6	19.1
Lincoln County	6 868	1 332	8.1	2 168	0.0	11.5	3.6	26 776	66.0	4.0	55.1	16.4	28.5
Logan County...............	171	13	1.1	44	0.0	0.0	0.0	599	66.3	1.8	56.4	15.5	28.0
Loup County................	150	8	11.4	28	0.0	17.9	7.1	534	61.2	0.9	45.3	18.4	36.3
McPherson County........	117	14	8.4	30	0.0	0.0	0.0	405	63.2	0.0	65.7	7.7	26.7
Madison County	7 256	1 964	19.8	2 661	0.1	10.0	2.1	26 979	69.3	4.7	56.1	17.2	26.7
Merrick County	1 682	197	12.5	456	0.0	15.6	3.1	6 227	66.5	3.0	54.9	16.8	28.2
Morrill County	1 161	114	2.6	344	0.0	7.3	6.7	4 171	64.3	5.1	54.1	16.7	29.2
Nance County	865	83	3.4	228	0.0	8.8	2.2	3 083	63.2	2.8	53.2	15.0	31.8
Nemaha County	1 481	679	4.6	607	0.0	8.9	0.0	6 087	64.6	6.2	50.8	19.3	29.9
Nuckolls County	981	119	6.8	296	0.0	7.4	0.0	4 024	61.7	2.4	48.3	19.3	32.3
Otoe County	3 134	496	11.7	840	0.2	6.4	3.3	11 849	68.0	4.0	55.9	16.2	27.9
Pawnee County............	579	49	3.2	160	0.0	6.9	2.5	2 480	61.7	3.4	48.4	17.5	34.2
Perkins County.............	694	53	10.3	211	0.0	7.6	1.4	2 483	63.3	2.5	52.8	18.3	28.9
Phelps County	1 987	227	4.3	544	0.0	8.3	1.7	7 499	68.0	3.0	56.0	17.5	26.5
Pierce County..............	1 865	282	11.8	548	0.0	5.3	3.8	5 893	68.0	2.3	54.1	18.2	27.7

Table B-3. States and Counties — Education, Labor Force, and Income

STATE County	Full-year full-time employed (percent)								Children under 18 years in families						Total employed by class of worker (percent)			
										With two parents (percent)		With one parent who is in labor force (percent)	+/- U.S. percent of children with no stay-at-home parent (percent)	+/- U.S. percent two-income couples				
	Total	Men	Women	Non-Hispanic White	Black or African American	American Indian and Alaska Native	Asian, Hawaiian, and Pacific Islander	Hispanic or Latino[1]	Number	Both in labor force	Father only in labor force				Private	Government	Self-employed	Unpaid family worker
	24	25	26	27	28	29	30	31	32	33	34	35	36	37	38	39	40	41
NEBRASKA—Cont'd																		
Blaine County	36.6	54.3	18.1	36.8	X	X	X	X	155	63.2	20.0	3.2	1.8	-0.4	39.2	19.8	38.8	2.2
Boone County	40.3	53.6	27.3	40.6	X	20.0	0.0	34.6	1 790	69.8	14.6	9.8	15.0	10.6	59.3	11.3	27.4	1.9
Box Butte County	42.6	59.1	27.0	44.0	46.8	44.9	54.3	23.3	3 263	51.1	20.5	18.3	4.8	4.7	73.2	12.3	13.9	0.6
Boyd County	36.2	49.7	23.5	36.2	X	X	33.3	X	575	71.1	11.7	11.5	18.0	7.9	50.4	15.0	30.7	3.9
Brown County	39.5	53.9	26.5	39.5	X	0.0	0.0	42.9	838	67.4	13.7	16.3	19.1	4.3	52.2	19.2	26.7	1.8
Buffalo County	43.4	54.7	32.9	43.8	25.7	38.8	39.8	40.5	9 896	64.1	12.3	16.9	16.4	17.1	74.0	13.9	11.6	0.4
Burt County	39.6	51.6	28.4	39.8	0.0	38.6	60.0	19.1	1 950	63.6	13.8	16.3	15.3	6.5	63.7	13.9	21.7	0.7
Butler County	44.3	54.9	33.5	44.5	0.0	22.2	28.6	31.1	2 370	66.5	18.1	9.3	11.2	9.9	67.7	11.9	18.8	1.6
Cass County	50.4	61.1	40.1	50.2	61.3	62.1	38.0	54.7	6 550	58.5	18.0	16.9	10.8	11.1	73.3	14.6	11.8	0.3
Cedar County	42.3	56.5	28.3	42.2	X	44.4	0.0	87.5	2 783	75.0	12.1	9.0	19.4	10.8	64.1	10.4	23.9	1.6
Chase County	39.0	53.5	24.9	38.9	X	0.0	0.0	52.2	1 023	59.2	22.0	11.3	5.9	3.7	58.6	14.0	26.5	1.0
Cherry County	46.8	60.1	33.9	47.2	X	32.8	40.9	0.0	1 559	60.7	14.0	18.5	14.6	9.7	54.8	18.5	25.5	1.2
Cheyenne County	45.2	57.8	33.5	45.2	X	50.0	33.3	43.7	2 524	61.5	15.5	15.4	12.3	12.0	68.4	12.5	18.2	0.9
Clay County	40.9	55.3	27.1	41.1	66.7	20.0	52.4	35.3	1 868	65.4	16.8	13.4	14.2	9.6	58.1	17.9	22.8	1.2
Colfax County	43.2	56.2	29.9	43.5	X	94.1	60.9	41.5	2 934	64.8	15.6	11.5	11.7	12.2	73.2	8.8	17.4	0.6
Cuming County	44.7	58.4	31.1	44.9	100.0	57.6	0.0	39.6	2 691	72.6	11.6	11.9	19.9	12.6	68.6	8.7	21.3	1.4
Custer County	40.1	53.4	27.8	40.2	0.0	38.1	0.0	38.9	2 947	64.8	16.7	12.4	12.6	8.5	60.3	12.1	26.0	1.6
Dakota County	48.4	55.4	41.5	50.0	67.7	35.4	58.1	42.1	5 816	51.2	10.7	22.2	8.8	9.5	82.0	9.2	8.2	0.5
Dawes County	33.6	41.6	26.2	34.5	0.0	32.3	47.4	22.8	1 719	57.2	15.7	16.1	8.7	9.7	55.7	26.8	16.0	1.5
Dawson County	43.6	54.3	32.9	44.0	30.4	23.5	43.5	42.3	6 813	50.6	21.6	16.5	2.5	6.4	74.6	10.1	14.8	0.5
Deuel County	39.8	51.6	28.4	40.1	X	0.0	36.4	31.4	484	67.1	10.7	17.4	19.9	8.6	60.6	14.4	24.4	0.6
Dixon County	44.3	56.0	33.4	44.6	X	40.4	23.1	44.8	1 665	62.0	16.3	13.5	10.9	10.3	68.5	14.1	16.4	1.0
Dodge County	43.9	55.4	33.6	44.0	58.3	26.3	60.2	42.5	8 605	57.9	14.9	19.8	13.1	7.8	79.2	9.9	10.4	0.5
Douglas County	47.2	57.2	38.0	49.3	36.9	31.5	38.4	42.1	115 725	49.0	17.3	22.7	7.1	9.8	81.6	10.3	7.9	0.2
Dundy County	41.1	59.0	24.6	39.7	X	100.0	55.6	95.7	512	66.8	21.7	7.4	9.6	5.0	58.4	11.7	27.1	2.8
Fillmore County	40.6	54.3	28.5	40.8	0.0	30.8	37.5	19.1	1 608	65.0	17.5	12.9	13.3	11.3	58.9	13.4	26.4	1.3
Franklin County	38.5	53.7	24.9	38.6	X	0.0	0.0	50.0	852	66.8	14.4	13.8	16.0	3.0	57.2	15.8	25.7	1.3
Frontier County	40.1	51.7	28.3	40.1	33.3	83.3	28.6	42.9	778	69.3	13.8	11.1	15.8	10.9	53.7	18.9	26.4	1.0
Furnas County	38.6	51.7	27.0	38.9	X	14.3	0.0	19.0	1 238	61.4	13.7	17.0	13.8	5.9	64.1	13.0	21.0	0.8
Gage County	43.7	52.7	35.5	43.8	22.2	29.8	55.1	47.5	5 404	68.4	10.1	16.2	20.0	12.4	69.4	15.8	14.1	0.7
Garden County	38.1	50.4	27.0	37.7	X	0.0	70.0	60.0	476	62.4	14.3	16.6	14.4	7.9	53.7	18.7	26.1	1.4
Garfield County	32.9	45.6	22.0	32.6	X	X	100.0	71.4	438	71.5	15.5	8.2	15.1	10.3	53.9	18.0	26.7	1.4
Gosper County	41.6	52.5	30.2	41.7	X	X	100.0	40.9	495	61.8	20.8	7.7	4.9	6.3	60.2	14.7	23.8	1.3
Grant County	49.5	61.5	35.5	49.7	X	0.0	X	50.0	212	61.3	21.7	16.0	12.7	12.8	55.1	17.1	26.6	1.2
Greeley County	36.0	49.7	23.4	35.7	66.7	X	X	60.0	717	62.1	16.6	14.8	12.3	6.6	53.1	14.6	29.9	2.4
Hall County	44.1	53.9	34.8	45.1	19.1	39.8	56.3	36.8	13 846	55.0	14.4	19.9	10.3	9.4	76.8	11.8	11.1	0.3
Hamilton County	43.9	57.1	31.1	43.9	100.0	X	X	46.3	2 635	66.1	16.1	13.2	14.7	13.3	68.0	12.3	19.4	0.3
Harlan County	39.1	48.5	29.8	39.0	55.0	100.0	X	11.8	867	61.8	16.8	12.6	9.8	1.6	56.4	17.9	24.4	1.3
Hayes County	38.0	53.6	21.5	38.6	X	X	X	23.8	279	71.0	20.8	0.0	6.4	3.3	48.2	13.2	36.3	2.3
Hitchcock County	35.8	47.3	24.6	36.0	100.0	0.0	50.0	25.0	719	55.4	22.5	15.6	6.4	3.1	54.0	17.2	27.1	1.7
Holt County	41.4	54.8	28.9	41.4	100.0	47.1	28.6	45.0	3 052	65.0	17.9	10.2	10.6	9.1	59.0	11.3	27.5	2.2
Hooker County	38.9	54.8	25.1	38.5	X	0.0	X	42.9	180	66.7	22.8	3.9	6.0	5.3	53.8	18.5	27.7	0.0
Howard County	45.8	56.6	34.9	46.1	0.0	23.5	18.2	26.0	1 769	68.6	13.3	14.9	18.9	12.2	64.1	14.1	21.0	0.8
Jefferson County	40.7	50.3	31.8	41.0	0.0	0.0	0.0	46.4	1 903	62.6	16.0	14.9	12.9	9.5	69.2	12.3	17.8	0.7
Johnson County	42.0	55.5	29.7	41.9	X	63.6	50.0	37.4	1 058	68.8	10.2	15.0	19.2	8.1	59.1	19.8	19.7	1.4
Kearney County	45.1	54.9	35.8	45.3	0.0	0.0	0.0	50.8	1 783	64.5	14.1	17.4	17.3	11.3	66.9	13.1	19.2	0.9
Keith County	41.0	52.5	30.2	40.8	X	47.1	34.2	50.0	2 113	63.7	10.7	19.1	18.2	8.0	68.6	13.1	17.7	0.7
Keya Paha County	37.9	54.8	20.2	37.8	X	X	X	41.2	229	55.5	27.5	9.6	0.5	1.3	37.8	11.5	45.9	4.7
Kimball County	39.6	46.5	33.2	39.4	0.0	19.2	33.3	44.8	928	69.6	10.1	12.2	17.2	4.3	62.2	17.3	19.9	0.6
Knox County	38.0	47.8	28.7	38.3	0.0	30.1	55.0	46.7	2 307	69.2	12.5	10.7	15.3	6.0	56.9	16.5	24.8	1.8
Lancaster County	46.7	54.8	38.7	47.7	38.5	32.5	38.6	36.4	56 480	55.4	17.0	20.2	11.0	13.8	71.7	19.9	8.2	0.2
Lincoln County	41.7	55.6	28.9	42.3	19.3	22.9	32.9	35.4	8 613	51.5	23.3	16.9	3.8	4.1	74.3	12.9	12.4	0.5
Logan County	44.6	60.5	28.5	44.0	X	100.0	X	66.7	207	49.3	33.8	15.5	0.2	11.1	52.3	14.1	30.0	3.6
Loup County	36.3	51.1	21.9	36.4	X	X	0.0	66.7	181	74.0	16.6	7.7	17.1	-1.2	54.6	14.8	29.0	1.5
McPherson County	49.6	67.6	30.3	49.9	X	0.0	X	X	143	59.4	26.6	11.2	6.0	6.3	35.2	16.4	47.7	0.8
Madison County	43.2	53.6	33.3	44.0	30.8	36.7	41.9	36.2	9 077	61.3	13.5	17.8	14.5	11.9	76.3	12.5	11.0	0.2
Merrick County	41.7	56.1	28.0	41.9	28.6	0.0	0.0	33.9	2 146	61.7	17.3	16.8	13.9	7.8	67.6	10.6	20.8	0.9
Morrill County	38.2	52.2	24.8	39.0	50.0	0.0	40.0	32.7	1 394	58.1	23.1	12.8	6.3	4.1	60.1	17.3	21.6	1.1
Nance County	40.4	50.0	29.7	40.5	X	33.3	33.3	53.1	1 075	64.0	18.0	12.3	11.7	7.6	63.8	12.1	22.6	1.5
Nemaha County	37.0	47.3	27.4	37.0	0.0	36.4	35.4	50.0	1 727	53.5	23.3	15.2	4.1	1.2	62.1	21.2	14.6	2.1
Nuckolls County	36.9	49.3	25.5	36.9	0.0	0.0	33.3	52.9	1 150	71.7	12.0	12.2	19.3	6.7	58.4	14.1	26.3	1.2
Otoe County	43.8	54.8	33.7	43.5	52.9	51.0	73.5	47.4	3 872	61.0	19.7	15.3	11.7	9.7	67.8	14.7	16.8	0.7
Pawnee County	38.8	53.1	25.8	38.9	X	60.0	0.0	0.0	666	69.2	10.5	14.1	18.7	8.1	54.1	18.6	26.3	1.1
Perkins County	39.2	54.1	24.5	39.3	0.0	X	33.3	31.6	831	51.3	32.4	13.8	0.5	5.8	55.7	14.6	28.2	1.5
Phelps County	44.0	57.1	31.7	44.5	X	27.5	75.0	26.5	2 502	63.3	15.8	13.1	11.8	11.1	67.6	13.0	18.9	0.4
Pierce County	42.8	56.2	29.7	42.7	50.0	32.0	47.1	39.5	2 203	70.2	13.1	10.3	15.9	15.0	66.9	12.5	19.4	1.2

[1] Hispanic or Latino persons may be of any race.

STATE County	Percent who worked at home	Percent of the population 5 years and over with a disability	Veterans as a percent of the population 18 years and over	Occupation for employed population 16 years and over (percent)						Industry for employed population 16 years and over (percent)					
				Management, professional, and related occupations	Service occupations	Sales and office occupations	Farming, fishing, and forestry occupations	Construction, extraction, and maintenance occupations	Production, transportation and material moving occupations	Agriculture, forestry, fishing, and mining	Construction and manufacturing	Wholesale and retail trade	Transportation and warehousing, and utilities	Service industries	Public administration
	42	43	44	45	46	47	48	49	50	51	52	53	54	55	56
NEBRASKA—Cont'd															
Blaine County	22.9	10.4	10.1	42.4	14.7	9.0	14.4	10.8	8.6	46.0	9.7	2.9	6.1	32.4	2.9
Boone County	10.5	15.0	16.2	36.5	14.7	19.8	6.5	8.7	13.9	23.0	15.5	14.0	4.7	40.3	2.5
Box Butte County	5.5	15.8	14.4	23.6	14.6	19.8	4.2	14.0	23.9	10.4	11.5	12.1	26.0	36.3	3.6
Boyd County	14.7	18.6	15.7	41.2	16.7	16.9	6.7	7.7	10.8	26.9	10.1	9.7	8.5	40.9	4.0
Brown County	10.4	20.0	14.5	34.6	15.8	20.6	6.0	11.8	11.2	19.6	12.7	14.9	6.4	41.8	4.7
Buffalo County	3.7	14.5	10.6	30.2	16.4	27.8	1.3	9.3	14.9	4.4	20.6	18.3	2.9	50.6	3.2
Burt County	8.7	15.1	16.5	29.3	17.2	23.1	2.9	13.3	14.3	14.5	17.4	14.1	6.3	43.5	4.2
Butler County	8.5	17.3	15.0	29.3	13.6	19.5	3.2	9.6	24.8	14.3	28.2	11.8	6.4	36.2	3.2
Cass County	3.7	16.1	17.5	29.0	14.4	27.0	0.4	14.1	15.1	4.5	21.6	14.9	8.2	45.9	4.9
Cedar County	12.3	13.5	14.4	32.2	13.4	22.8	4.4	10.7	16.4	18.4	20.5	12.3	5.9	40.3	2.5
Chase County	7.2	17.1	14.2	32.9	14.0	24.2	7.4	9.9	11.6	20.8	11.8	17.5	5.8	40.8	3.3
Cherry County	13.6	17.2	12.5	37.6	13.9	20.1	12.7	8.2	7.6	28.8	8.3	12.8	5.3	40.6	4.2
Cheyenne County	5.6	18.3	13.0	27.9	14.7	31.7	1.9	8.7	15.1	10.4	12.4	29.8	7.7	36.4	3.3
Clay County	7.7	17.2	15.0	33.2	15.7	18.9	3.8	10.5	17.9	15.7	18.4	11.7	7.8	41.1	5.4
Colfax County	7.6	17.4	11.9	22.3	13.3	16.0	3.6	9.1	35.7	11.3	38.8	12.6	5.0	30.5	1.7
Cuming County	11.2	14.2	13.4	29.7	14.3	21.2	5.3	8.7	20.8	18.2	22.9	13.6	5.6	38.0	1.8
Custer County	12.7	18.0	14.9	34.8	13.7	17.8	6.7	10.3	16.6	23.3	16.4	12.4	6.0	39.0	2.9
Dakota County	2.7	16.1	11.9	22.6	12.9	24.6	1.3	9.2	29.5	2.6	35.0	13.8	6.1	39.2	3.2
Dawes County	5.8	14.8	13.1	32.4	19.3	25.8	4.4	9.6	8.6	13.1	7.0	17.9	5.2	52.0	4.8
Dawson County	4.1	17.9	12.4	22.2	14.1	19.8	3.9	9.6	30.4	9.9	35.9	12.7	5.3	33.1	3.1
Deuel County	5.8	16.8	17.4	31.1	17.5	23.2	4.3	9.8	14.1	16.1	7.9	21.2	10.5	40.7	3.6
Dixon County	7.9	13.6	14.3	27.9	12.7	22.5	4.3	11.7	20.9	12.5	29.6	13.1	5.5	35.5	3.9
Dodge County	3.4	17.9	15.2	23.9	15.9	27.8	1.1	9.7	21.5	4.3	26.4	18.6	5.2	42.4	3.1
Douglas County	2.8	15.9	13.3	36.5	13.5	30.1	0.2	7.8	11.9	0.4	16.0	16.8	5.9	58.5	2.4
Dundy County	8.5	17.8	14.6	38.2	11.0	19.9	11.3	9.9	9.7	33.3	7.8	14.4	4.3	38.1	2.2
Fillmore County	9.8	16.3	14.4	34.6	14.8	19.4	4.4	12.4	14.4	19.3	19.1	12.5	6.5	38.9	3.6
Franklin County	8.0	22.2	16.6	35.9	15.0	19.9	5.8	10.0	13.4	21.5	14.3	12.9	5.1	42.2	4.0
Frontier County	13.8	16.2	14.3	33.8	17.5	19.1	7.9	9.0	12.7	25.1	11.6	11.6	6.0	42.7	3.0
Furnas County	5.8	19.8	15.6	33.9	16.0	18.8	4.8	9.0	17.4	16.3	13.6	15.1	7.6	44.0	3.4
Gage County	5.8	19.1	12.4	29.3	17.8	22.7	1.6	8.5	19.9	6.7	24.2	15.7	6.0	43.1	4.3
Garden County	9.9	18.9	13.9	36.2	14.7	17.9	10.0	10.6	10.6	29.3	7.9	16.4	7.3	34.0	5.0
Garfield County	12.4	18.1	14.8	36.3	14.3	19.6	7.0	13.1	9.7	21.3	13.1	13.4	5.3	42.0	4.9
Gosper County	6.8	19.3	15.0	34.4	13.0	24.1	4.8	9.8	13.8	19.8	19.2	11.9	5.2	39.4	4.5
Grant County	23.3	9.3	12.1	31.7	10.0	17.8	22.2	11.2	7.1	41.0	7.6	11.2	8.3	29.3	2.7
Greeley County	15.3	16.2	15.6	43.5	13.0	19.2	8.1	8.0	8.3	29.7	9.2	12.6	4.2	40.2	4.1
Hall County	3.0	18.7	14.0	25.1	15.2	27.7	1.3	10.3	20.5	3.7	24.4	19.2	5.3	44.6	2.8
Hamilton County	7.4	13.1	14.4	32.5	14.1	23.7	3.1	10.4	16.2	12.1	19.9	13.3	7.0	43.9	3.7
Harlan County	8.5	20.3	15.8	32.0	16.5	22.2	4.4	9.3	15.6	18.7	17.5	15.3	4.6	39.5	4.4
Hayes County	18.6	16.0	15.2	43.4	9.8	17.0	13.6	6.1	10.1	47.0	7.6	8.4	4.8	28.3	3.8
Hitchcock County	11.7	17.0	15.2	32.2	19.6	19.8	4.6	9.7	14.2	20.5	12.1	11.7	9.5	41.2	5.0
Holt County	11.6	16.8	13.7	32.7	15.7	21.8	8.5	9.3	12.0	24.8	9.3	18.7	6.1	37.7	3.4
Hooker County	10.9	16.3	16.4	26.9	15.6	23.1	10.5	9.9	14.0	23.9	10.2	14.0	7.3	39.8	4.8
Howard County	8.9	17.5	14.3	29.5	13.9	24.7	5.1	11.0	15.7	15.9	18.2	16.5	6.9	39.4	3.1
Jefferson County	7.5	20.1	15.6	28.5	15.6	20.1	3.5	9.5	22.8	14.4	28.3	12.0	5.2	36.9	3.2
Johnson County	7.3	16.8	14.7	34.3	14.8	19.1	2.6	12.4	16.9	12.5	20.7	13.3	6.1	42.2	5.2
Kearney County	6.0	15.4	13.7	31.8	16.3	22.2	3.9	10.8	15.0	14.9	20.7	13.7	4.2	44.1	2.4
Keith County	5.5	18.5	15.2	28.9	15.7	26.7	3.6	11.0	14.1	10.6	15.0	19.6	7.6	43.6	3.5
Keya Paha County	25.0	16.8	13.8	51.1	7.3	15.6	12.0	8.5	5.6	50.6	5.8	8.8	1.7	29.1	4.1
Kimball County	6.8	17.4	17.6	28.0	15.7	23.3	3.5	10.5	18.9	15.4	16.3	16.2	8.5	38.1	5.4
Knox County	12.3	18.1	15.5	36.4	16.5	18.3	5.6	12.0	11.2	19.8	12.7	14.6	4.0	44.2	4.7
Lancaster County	3.2	14.6	11.4	36.0	15.0	26.8	0.3	8.4	13.4	1.0	18.4	14.0	4.3	55.6	6.8
Lincoln County	4.0	19.9	14.9	24.7	15.7	26.0	2.4	13.1	18.1	6.5	10.2	16.7	18.9	44.1	3.6
Logan County	20.1	23.2	15.2	36.7	12.3	18.5	11.5	10.3	10.8	31.8	6.7	12.6	14.1	28.7	6.2
Loup County	23.1	17.1	13.5	40.1	16.7	10.8	13.0	6.5	13.0	36.7	9.0	8.0	5.6	37.0	3.7
McPherson County	42.6	21.9	11.9	65.2	2.0	10.5	9.8	10.2	2.3	53.5	3.1	7.8	6.6	25.8	3.1
Madison County	4.5	16.1	12.7	25.7	15.6	25.7	1.4	9.8	21.9	4.6	26.3	18.7	4.5	43.1	2.9
Merrick County	6.2	18.4	15.0	30.0	16.1	21.3	2.6	12.2	17.9	12.1	23.6	15.6	5.3	40.0	3.3
Morrill County	9.8	18.2	14.1	31.8	16.3	20.4	5.7	11.2	14.7	19.7	12.1	14.6	10.3	39.3	4.0
Nance County	8.9	18.6	15.0	30.6	15.4	17.8	6.3	13.2	16.7	19.7	20.9	12.8	5.8	37.9	3.0
Nemaha County	7.8	18.6	14.4	33.5	16.6	22.0	2.1	9.3	16.6	8.5	14.9	11.4	17.2	44.6	3.5
Nuckolls County	9.1	19.8	15.7	31.9	16.1	23.9	4.3	9.9	13.9	18.3	12.3	15.7	7.0	42.5	4.3
Otoe County	6.7	17.7	15.2	30.2	16.0	21.9	1.4	11.2	19.3	8.3	22.9	14.2	7.7	42.6	4.3
Pawnee County	9.8	21.4	15.7	36.2	16.9	17.7	3.5	11.3	14.3	19.4	17.8	11.4	5.3	41.5	4.6
Perkins County	11.9	16.4	13.9	39.8	14.0	20.3	5.4	10.4	10.1	23.5	9.7	14.7	9.7	38.6	3.9
Phelps County	5.5	15.2	13.9	30.5	14.9	23.8	4.6	11.2	15.1	14.1	19.8	13.2	6.9	42.3	3.8
Pierce County	9.3	16.9	13.0	29.5	14.0	22.9	3.1	10.6	20.0	14.3	22.0	16.6	5.7	38.3	3.1

Table B-3. States and Counties — Education, Labor Force, and Income

STATE County	Median household income	Median family income				Median nonfamily household income	Median income for full-year, full-time workers		Per capita income	Households by source of income (percent)					Households with income over $100,000 (percent)	+/− U.S. percent for income over $100,000	Households with income below poverty (percent)	Families with children with income below poverty (percent)
		All families	Married-couple	Families with children														
				Male householder	Female householder		Men	Women		With earnings	With interest, dividend, or rental income	With Social Security income	With public assistance income	With retirement income				
	57	58	59	60	61	62	63	64	65	66	67	68	69	70	71	72	73	74

NEBRASKA—Cont'd

STATE County	57	58	59	60	61	62	63	64	65	66	67	68	69	70	71	72	73	74
Blaine County	25 278	28 472	29 583	0	11 875	19 464	19 375	21 875	12 323	82.2	33.9	30.2	3.7	14.5	1.7	-10.6	18.6	25.7
Boone County	31 444	38 226	43 958	26 667	16 667	17 978	27 949	19 167	15 831	76.0	44.0	36.5	2.5	8.8	4.3	-8.0	11.7	11.0
Box Butte County	39 366	46 670	52 089	30 455	15 000	21 432	38 540	23 608	18 407	82.8	40.4	30.1	3.8	10.6	6.0	-6.3	11.6	15.1
Boyd County	26 075	32 000	33 182	24 250	30 000	16 192	22 838	18 092	13 840	72.3	46.9	40.8	2.6	10.9	2.8	-9.5	15.1	18.8
Brown County	28 356	35 029	41 400	20 625	15 313	16 607	25 753	17 500	15 924	76.2	45.3	37.6	1.9	11.7	3.0	-9.3	11.2	14.3
Buffalo County	36 782	46 247	53 056	25 081	17 639	21 425	31 051	22 826	17 510	84.9	40.0	23.2	2.4	9.7	5.7	-6.6	11.7	9.8
Burt County	33 954	40 515	48 917	21 944	20 000	17 099	30 503	21 550	16 654	76.6	43.1	37.1	3.1	10.1	3.4	-8.9	9.2	10.9
Butler County	36 331	44 441	50 617	25 000	23 036	19 250	30 531	21 461	16 394	77.3	48.0	34.5	1.8	12.2	3.7	-8.6	8.5	7.2
Cass County	46 515	52 196	58 321	30 341	21 330	28 015	38 495	25 211	20 156	84.9	40.8	26.2	2.0	16.7	8.4	-3.9	5.4	7.0
Cedar County	33 435	39 422	44 583	27 250	19 306	18 305	27 719	19 128	15 514	77.3	49.5	35.4	1.0	9.7	3.5	-8.8	9.6	8.6
Chase County	32 351	39 225	45 865	24 688	18 125	19 032	29 323	18 155	17 490	77.3	43.2	35.0	2.0	10.2	6.1	-6.2	10.5	11.0
Cherry County	29 268	36 500	39 896	20 893	21 458	18 084	25 246	18 867	15 943	81.9	35.7	30.9	3.9	7.9	4.6	-7.7	12.9	13.3
Cheyenne County	33 438	41 024	51 425	33 375	17 778	20 845	31 066	21 023	17 437	78.7	42.2	31.1	3.3	12.7	5.4	-6.9	10.0	11.0
Clay County	34 259	39 541	46 066	26 125	17 750	20 440	29 985	20 609	16 870	78.2	44.3	32.6	2.6	12.5	4.8	-7.5	9.8	11.9
Colfax County	35 849	40 936	45 579	27 813	19 167	20 278	26 426	20 933	15 148	80.7	44.4	31.0	1.7	7.7	4.5	-7.8	9.9	11.2
Cuming County	33 186	39 369	38 369	22 500	18 235	21 268	27 458	19 828	16 443	81.4	47.9	32.8	1.5	7.3	3.5	-8.8	9.2	9.1
Custer County	30 677	37 063	40 946	20 714	15 000	18 185	26 334	20 404	16 171	77.3	49.4	36.9	2.5	12.1	3.5	-8.8	11.6	14.5
Dakota County	38 834	43 702	49 047	33 438	18 867	21 864	29 030	22 468	16 125	85.8	28.7	23.9	3.5	9.9	6.0	-6.3	10.9	13.0
Dawes County	29 476	41 092	46 652	24 688	18 088	16 292	30 240	18 792	16 353	81.1	38.1	29.4	2.3	11.0	5.9	-6.4	20.0	13.1
Dawson County	36 132	42 224	47 234	21 940	18 571	20 959	27 780	21 117	15 973	80.6	34.6	29.5	3.5	10.4	5.4	-6.9	10.0	12.4
Deuel County	32 981	41 550	47 292	25 417	21 458	20 993	26 944	19 922	17 891	79.9	44.3	39.3	2.3	12.4	4.4	-7.9	8.5	11.2
Dixon County	34 201	41 122	45 969	25 208	19 722	18 902	29 088	20 945	15 350	79.5	42.6	33.5	1.6	6.8	3.0	-9.3	10.9	10.2
Dodge County	37 188	44 790	51 957	26 429	21 611	20 176	31 919	21 581	17 757	78.5	41.2	31.5	2.3	14.3	4.8	-7.5	8.8	8.9
Douglas County	43 209	54 651	66 950	31 014	21 874	26 792	37 588	28 242	22 879	83.9	38.8	22.3	3.2	13.4	11.9	-0.4	9.3	10.3
Dundy County	27 010	35 862	40 750	4 583	18 500	16 250	25 082	19 417	15 786	75.7	43.7	37.1	2.8	11.2	4.5	-7.8	14.2	16.7
Fillmore County	35 162	41 725	46 058	31 250	16 488	20 908	30 656	19 433	17 465	76.1	48.3	34.6	2.2	10.0	3.8	-8.5	8.8	7.1
Franklin County	29 304	34 958	44 150	20 208	17 708	16 219	27 471	19 063	15 390	75.6	45.0	38.4	3.0	10.5	3.6	-8.7	12.9	16.0
Frontier County	33 038	38 664	39 896	32 500	22 778	18 309	26 853	19 125	16 648	83.1	41.5	30.5	3.6	11.6	4.9	-7.4	13.8	11.7
Furnas County	30 498	37 000	40 671	24 375	18 636	17 220	27 470	20 583	17 223	72.3	41.6	40.4	1.9	12.9	4.7	-7.6	11.0	10.5
Gage County	34 908	43 072	50 417	22 344	20 265	20 569	30 727	21 954	17 190	77.9	44.1	34.3	2.1	13.4	4.2	-8.1	9.3	10.2
Garden County	26 458	32 546	33 250	21 875	11 250	17 757	22 316	17 444	15 414	74.1	40.9	37.2	2.7	13.8	3.3	-9.0	13.7	21.9
Garfield County	27 407	34 762	40 313	23 750	19 107	14 118	26 193	16 957	14 368	69.9	46.1	45.2	2.0	11.9	2.9	-9.4	15.3	10.9
Gosper County	36 827	42 702	40 875	31 250	18 750	16 250	30 729	21 979	17 957	80.3	43.8	33.6	2.5	14.2	5.7	-6.6	7.4	8.5
Grant County	34 821	37 011	36 250	55 417	14 375	16 607	29 375	15 268	14 815	92.6	29.5	26.8	0.7	8.4	2.0	-10.3	7.4	13.8
Greeley County	28 375	34 159	37 500	21 667	14 500	16 515	23 476	17 813	13 731	75.2	46.6	41.6	1.8	7.5	2.8	-9.5	13.4	17.3
Hall County	36 972	43 963	49 088	22 209	17 419	20 852	30 416	21 241	17 386	82.8	40.2	26.3	3.9	12.6	6.0	-6.3	11.5	14.5
Hamilton County	40 277	45 659	50 161	25 515	21 250	21 088	30 935	20 871	17 590	82.5	43.0	28.1	2.8	10.6	6.3	-6.0	7.1	8.8
Harlan County	30 679	36 875	40 000	35 313	18 125	18 348	29 622	19 173	15 618	73.1	45.3	39.5	1.5	14.9	3.5	-8.8	10.5	11.7
Hayes County	26 667	31 125	28 194	0	0	15 278	21 000	17 321	14 099	78.9	46.6	38.8	2.5	9.4	3.2	-9.1	16.1	21.6
Hitchcock County	28 287	34 490	34 844	23 750	16 176	15 855	27 151	19 194	14 804	76.9	44.0	37.9	2.7	14.6	3.8	-8.5	13.9	17.7
Holt County	30 738	37 463	41 391	30 625	20 804	16 750	26 735	19 518	15 256	78.1	41.2	34.7	2.3	9.3	3.7	-8.6	14.0	12.6
Hooker County	27 868	35 114	41 528	0	27 917	16 333	27 375	16 389	15 513	73.9	41.8	40.9	1.2	10.7	3.3	-9.0	10.1	7.0
Howard County	33 305	40 259	47 562	11 917	17 917	20 434	28 453	20 417	15 535	77.9	44.6	33.1	1.9	12.7	3.5	-8.8	11.8	10.6
Jefferson County	32 629	40 747	49 095	14 643	18 409	16 908	27 801	19 488	18 380	72.4	45.3	39.8	2.7	13.4	4.4	-7.9	10.3	12.8
Johnson County	32 460	41 000	47 784	25 000	19 375	19 158	27 099	21 433	16 437	73.8	48.3	37.9	2.0	13.1	4.2	-8.1	10.2	10.1
Kearney County	39 247	44 877	47 936	24 375	20 694	22 338	30 975	21 073	18 118	81.2	45.8	29.9	1.9	10.3	4.2	-8.1	8.0	9.0
Keith County	32 325	39 118	42 344	18 917	21 200	27 384	20 047	17 421	76.7	38.5	35.0	3.4	14.6	3.9	-8.4	9.2	9.7	
Keya Paha County	24 911	28 287	28 611	20 000	5 625	13 750	20 536	19 545	11 860	73.8	44.8	36.6	2.9	12.6	2.2	-10.1	24.7	35.1
Kimball County	30 586	35 880	45 250	25 313	13 250	20 042	30 037	17 487	17 525	77.8	45.9	39.3	1.7	14.3	4.7	-7.6	11.3	13.7
Knox County	27 564	34 073	39 012	22 083	14 922	15 579	24 484	19 555	13 971	73.3	45.7	40.0	3.5	9.6	2.5	-9.8	14.8	18.1
Lancaster County	41 850	53 676	61 495	27 988	20 912	25 574	35 690	26 321	21 265	86.1	43.7	20.3	2.9	13.1	9.4	-2.9	9.7	8.7
Lincoln County	36 568	45 185	51 953	23 828	15 704	19 979	37 145	20 970	18 696	78.5	38.6	30.7	4.1	11.1	6.5	-5.8	9.8	11.4
Logan County	33 125	38 958	32 222	28 750	16 250	22 778	28 000	21 250	14 937	82.5	41.6	33.3	2.2	7.3	3.8	-8.5	11.1	12.9
Loup County	26 250	27 788	27 813	2 499	21 250	18 750	21 250	21 250	12 427	77.0	40.1	37.2	1.4	10.3	2.1	-10.2	16.0	23.3
McPherson County	25 750	31 250	36 250	20 000	12 375	25 625	14 375	13 055	77.9	40.4	37.6	1.9	5.6	3.3	-9.0	13.1	13.6	
Madison County	35 807	45 073	52 124	28 148	16 742	20 506	31 524	21 892	16 804	80.9	41.5	28.4	3.5	10.7	4.7	-7.6	11.5	11.9
Merrick County	34 961	39 729	48 988	22 500	18 466	20 114	28 445	20 512	15 958	80.8	40.4	32.4	1.8	11.3	2.9	-9.4	9.6	10.2
Morrill County	30 235	36 673	38 021	23 750	15 000	16 477	28 056	20 192	14 725	80.8	37.3	32.9	2.4	11.7	2.9	-9.4	13.7	15.5
Nance County	31 267	38 717	39 609	23 750	15 972	18 686	26 282	20 123	16 886	77.4	43.6	35.0	2.5	8.6	4.1	-8.2	12.5	15.8
Nemaha County	32 588	43 780	51 958	21 250	19 286	20 130	32 351	20 231	17 004	75.8	44.9	35.6	3.2	13.6	4.4	-7.9	13.6	12.1
Nuckolls County	28 958	35 018	40 368	24 375	18 750	17 955	25 750	19 243	15 608	71.9	49.2	41.6	2.1	16.3	3.0	-9.3	11.1	11.9
Otoe County	37 302	45 295	54 707	25 625	19 728	19 911	31 957	22 140	17 752	78.2	45.7	32.5	2.1	13.5	5.6	-6.7	8.7	8.5
Pawnee County	29 000	36 326	40 375	28 250	21 563	16 094	25 797	18 787	16 687	71.2	48.7	45.5	2.6	14.9	3.9	-8.4	12.9	9.1
Perkins County	34 205	42 112	43 958	20 625	17 083	19 000	30 211	20 625	17 830	79.1	44.0	34.2	1.6	7.9	6.3	-6.0	12.4	14.3
Phelps County	37 319	44 943	47 411	23 056	19 135	19 930	30 133	22 466	19 044	80.8	43.9	32.3	1.7	10.9	7.1	-5.2	9.6	9.6
Pierce County	32 239	40 500	46 149	25 625	13 906	17 784	27 712	21 199	15 980	78.4	42.6	31.2	2.3	8.6	4.8	-7.5	12.1	11.5

STATE/ County code	MSA/PMSA/ NECMA code[1]	STATE County	High school graduates			College graduates		College graduates (percent)				
			Total population 25 years and over	Percent with a high school diploma or less	Percent with a high school diploma or more	Percent with a bachelor's degree or more	+/− U.S. percent with bachelor's degree or more	Non-Hispanic White	Black or African American	American Indian and Alaska Native	Asian, Hawaiian, and Pacific Islander	Hispanic or Latino[2]
			1	2	3	4	5	6	7	8	9	10
		NEBRASKA—Cont'd										
31 141	...	Platte County................	19 988	51.5	84.7	17.2	-7.2	17.8	0.0	11.4	53.0	2.0
31 143	...	Polk County..................	3 886	53.4	86.6	13.5	-10.9	13.4	X	0.0	X	21.1
31 145	...	Red Willow County........	7 490	47.0	87.9	15.2	-9.2	15.3	X	45.5	X	5.8
31 147	...	Richardson County........	6 543	60.1	81.8	13.6	-10.8	13.6	0.0	13.3	26.4	0.0
31 149	...	Rock County.................	1 242	54.6	87.4	12.2	-12.2	12.2	X	0.0	40.0	0.0
31 151	...	Saline County...............	8 691	58.2	81.2	14.0	-10.4	15.1	0.0	0.0	12.0	0.0
31 153	5920	Sarpy County................	73 804	31.4	93.3	30.2	5.8	30.9	28.2	13.6	33.6	14.8
31 155	...	Saunders County	13 047	51.6	86.8	16.9	-7.5	16.9	0.0	0.0	44.4	15.9
31 157	...	Scotts Bluff County	24 314	50.0	79.6	17.3	-7.1	19.2	0.0	0.8	50.9	5.2
31 159	...	Seward County.............	10 009	44.4	87.5	22.6	-1.8	22.4	0.0	10.5	56.8	28.0
31 161	...	Sheridan County	4 232	50.3	86.1	17.2	-7.2	17.9	0.0	5.2	10.0	21.6
31 163	...	Sherman County	2 355	58.8	82.0	10.8	-13.6	11.0	0.0	X	0.0	0.0
31 165	...	Sioux County................	1 009	45.5	86.4	21.5	-2.9	22.0	X	50.0	0.0	0.0
31 167	...	Stanton County.............	4 065	51.8	86.2	13.7	-10.7	14.0	X	0.0	0.0	8.3
31 169	...	Thayer County..............	4 301	56.4	80.9	15.0	-9.4	15.0	X	0.0	X	16.0
31 171	...	Thomas County.............	528	48.5	83.7	17.2	-7.2	17.9	X	0.0	X	0.0
31 173	...	Thurston County............	3 953	56.7	80.4	12.0	-12.4	14.9	14.3	6.7	33.3	0.0
31 175	...	Valley County	3 285	53.4	84.7	16.4	-8.0	16.5	X	0.0	0.0	0.0
31 177	5920	Washington County........	11 956	45.9	89.7	22.7	-1.7	22.7	45.2	34.2	24.2	10.0
31 179	...	Wayne County...............	5 115	44.1	87.0	28.0	3.6	28.2	100.0	0.0	35.7	3.3
31 181	...	Webster County	2 910	55.9	83.6	13.7	-10.7	13.7	0.0	0.0	24.0	0.0
31 183	...	Wheeler County	577	46.4	90.8	14.9	-9.5	15.1	X	X	X	0.0
31 185	...	York County	9 579	50.4	87.2	17.0	-7.4	17.3	0.0	12.5	100.0	3.5
32 000	...	NEVADA...................	1 310 176	48.7	80.7	18.2	-6.2	20.7	12.0	8.6	27.1	6.4
32 001	...	Churchill County	15 167	45.4	85.1	16.7	-7.7	17.6	21.4	7.1	21.8	7.4
32 003	4120	Clark County	900 400	50.4	79.5	17.3	-7.1	20.0	11.9	10.1	26.2	6.4
32 005	...	Douglas County............	29 279	35.0	91.6	23.2	-1.2	24.0	35.1	6.8	25.7	12.2
32 007	...	Elko County..................	26 798	51.3	79.1	14.8	-9.6	17.4	8.4	6.1	19.7	4.0
32 009	...	Esmeralda County.........	711	65.4	78.9	9.6	-14.8	9.9	X	0.0	0.0	0.0
32 011	...	Eureka County	1 104	55.0	76.7	13.6	-10.8	14.4	0.0	0.0	30.0	0.0
32 013	...	Humboldt County	9 846	53.0	78.3	14.2	-10.2	17.1	0.0	0.5	12.5	4.2
32 015	...	Lander County...............	3 581	57.6	79.2	10.8	-13.6	11.9	X	6.6	0.0	4.9
32 017	...	Lincoln County	2 654	54.7	83.0	15.1	-9.3	15.1	0.0	0.0	93.8	3.4
32 019	...	Lyon County.................	22 863	51.4	81.5	11.3	-13.1	12.0	24.6	5.0	17.8	3.3
32 021	...	Mineral County	3 527	59.1	77.1	10.1	-14.3	11.9	0.0	6.8	64.3	3.4
32 023	4120	Nye County	23 234	62.0	79.2	10.1	-14.3	10.5	7.2	2.9	7.2	6.9
32 027	...	Pershing County............	4 498	60.7	75.9	8.7	-15.7	11.1	0.8	4.2	4.3	3.1
32 029	...	Storey County	2 540	43.0	86.7	18.0	-6.4	16.8	X	30.5	36.7	32.5
32 031	6720	Washoe County.............	221 837	41.2	83.9	23.7	-0.7	26.4	16.7	8.8	32.4	6.9
32 033	...	White Pine County	6 184	52.8	82.0	11.8	-12.6	13.5	2.1	6.0	9.5	4.8
32 510	...	Carson City	35 953	45.4	82.5	18.5	-5.9	20.1	3.6	13.4	40.3	4.8
33 000	...	NEW HAMPSHIRE.....	823 987	42.7	87.4	28.7	4.3	28.5	27.8	17.0	54.2	22.7
33 001	...	Belknap County............	39 260	46.9	85.7	23.3	-1.1	23.4	37.0	10.4	24.9	26.9
33 003	...	Carroll County	31 534	44.0	88.2	26.5	2.1	26.5	31.0	17.8	25.6	31.9
33 005	...	Cheshire County	48 032	48.2	86.2	26.6	2.2	26.5	36.0	17.3	46.2	28.0
33 007	...	Coos County	23 490	64.7	76.9	11.9	-12.5	11.9	11.1	3.8	20.4	23.9
33 009	...	Grafton County.............	52 795	43.3	87.7	32.7	8.3	32.4	40.7	16.8	68.4	42.7
33 011	1123	Hillsborough County......	251 908	40.5	87.0	30.1	5.7	29.9	24.3	21.0	58.1	18.3
33 013	...	Merrimack County	91 278	41.5	88.2	29.1	4.7	29.0	26.4	1.5	59.1	28.7
33 015	1123	Rockingham County.......	187 172	38.1	90.5	31.7	7.3	31.5	32.3	26.0	52.3	26.0
33 017	1123	Strafford County	70 319	44.1	86.4	26.4	2.0	26.2	29.3	19.5	43.9	29.7
33 019	...	Sullivan County	28 199	55.5	83.0	19.7	-4.7	19.6	64.9	4.8	26.1	24.0
34 000	...	NEW JERSEY............	5 657 799	47.3	82.1	29.8	5.4	32.3	16.2	16.4	61.9	12.5
34 001	0560	Atlantic County	168 546	56.5	78.2	18.7	-5.7	21.0	10.8	21.1	30.7	7.2
34 003	0875	Bergen County	623 469	39.6	86.6	38.2	13.8	38.1	27.3	19.3	60.8	20.8
34 005	6160	Burlington County	285 553	44.0	87.2	28.4	4.0	29.7	19.8	22.5	48.0	18.8
34 007	6160	Camden County	331 765	51.9	80.3	24.0	-0.4	26.5	13.9	12.0	47.6	8.6
34 009	0560	Cape May County	72 878	54.5	81.9	22.0	-2.4	22.6	7.8	28.0	54.3	13.5
34 011	8760	Cumberland County	96 899	67.8	68.5	11.7	-12.7	14.4	6.0	7.5	46.4	5.6
34 013	5640	Essex County	513 570	51.6	75.6	27.5	3.1	41.5	14.6	12.7	62.9	10.7
34 015	6160	Gloucester County	164 801	52.6	84.3	22.0	-2.4	21.9	17.1	17.7	54.2	19.0
34 017	3640	Hudson County	408 799	56.3	70.5	25.3	0.9	31.8	16.5	19.2	56.4	12.1
34 019	5015	Hunterdon County	83 548	34.0	91.5	41.8	17.4	42.0	14.4	30.3	70.9	29.6

[1]MSA = Metropolitan Statistical Area. PMSA = Primary MSA. NECMA = New England County Metropolitan Area. See the Appendix A for explanation of these concepts. See Appendix B for list of metropolitan areas identified by type, with component counties.
[2]Hispanic or Latino persons may be of any race.

STATE County	School enrollment			Population 16 to 19 years				Employment status, 2000			Work status in 1999 of the population 16 years and over (percent)		
											Worked in 1999		
	Grades kindergarten through 12	College or graduate school	Percent private	Number	Percent in armed forces	Percent high school graduates	Percent not enrolled, not grads, not in armed forces, not employed	Total population 16 years and over	Percent in labor force	Unemploy- ment rate	Full-time	Part-time	Did not work in 1999
	11	12	13	14	15	16	17	18	19	20	21	22	23
NEBRASKA—Cont'd													
Platte County..............	6 970	1 155	27.5	2 076	0.0	7.9	2.2	23 680	70.4	2.5	59.0	16.2	24.8
Polk County.................	1 140	152	3.7	333	0.0	5.4	4.8	4 426	64.6	1.8	53.7	16.9	29.4
Red Willow County.......	2 257	454	4.8	737	0.0	9.5	1.4	8 967	66.2	2.8	53.7	18.4	27.9
Richardson County.......	1 927	209	7.3	600	0.0	14.7	3.5	7 493	60.9	4.9	51.1	15.4	33.5
Rock County................	333	22	7.3	109	0.0	3.7	1.8	1 423	64.8	2.3	51.6	18.7	29.7
Saline County..............	2 680	1 012	22.6	1 086	0.7	9.2	3.1	10 887	66.6	2.5	57.4	16.1	26.5
Sarpy County...............	27 289	8 803	14.2	7 065	3.6	13.9	1.6	89 129	77.5	2.6	66.2	17.2	16.6
Saunders County	4 334	585	18.8	1 094	0.0	7.9	4.7	14 952	70.6	2.3	58.6	16.4	24.9
Scotts Bluff County	7 191	1 541	8.8	2 264	0.3	10.7	6.8	28 624	64.1	5.8	54.1	15.5	30.4
Seward County............	3 218	1 915	31.7	1 521	0.0	6.5	1.0	12 951	69.3	3.0	56.1	20.7	23.2
Sheridan County	1 254	106	3.5	378	0.0	5.6	2.1	4 857	63.6	2.7	53.6	15.8	30.6
Sherman County	676	67	2.6	194	0.0	7.7	0.0	2 640	63.8	2.9	49.7	17.8	32.6
Sioux County................	306	36	8.8	86	0.0	3.5	2.3	1 157	64.7	4.1	56.4	17.6	25.9
Stanton County............	1 498	193	11.8	418	0.0	4.5	3.3	4 763	71.1	2.7	61.6	15.8	22.6
Thayer County.............	1 178	99	8.6	327	0.0	4.0	0.6	4 808	61.3	2.2	50.6	18.6	30.7
Thomas County............	141	19	0.0	45	0.0	0.0	0.0	588	66.5	2.0	56.0	15.1	28.9
Thurston County...........	1 970	217	7.5	465	0.0	9.9	15.7	4 796	60.8	12.6	53.4	11.3	35.2
Valley County	898	100	8.2	207	0.0	6.3	2.9	3 648	63.5	3.2	51.1	16.4	32.5
Washington County.......	3 954	993	16.1	1 189	0.0	6.9	0.4	14 323	73.3	3.3	58.9	19.3	21.8
Wayne County..............	1 673	2 296	3.5	1 133	0.0	5.5	1.1	7 981	70.2	2.9	53.4	26.5	20.1
Webster County	795	82	6.6	201	0.0	6.0	0.0	3 215	59.8	5.9	49.7	14.5	35.8
Wheeler County	205	17	5.4	57	0.0	7.0	3.5	663	71.0	3.2	56.1	19.6	24.3
York County	2 860	890	22.5	919	0.0	6.0	1.6	11 361	66.2	3.5	53.7	20.6	25.6
NEVADA....................	366 909	98 631	7.0	90 513	0.3	12.7	8.3	1 538 516	65.2	6.2	59.9	12.0	28.1
Churchill County...........	5 258	1 101	3.8	1 249	1.8	15.1	3.0	17 727	66.4	5.4	57.4	13.4	29.2
Clark County	246 960	64 457	7.3	65 482	0.5	13.6	9.5	1 058 120	65.1	6.5	60.5	11.1	28.3
Douglas County............	7 885	1 924	6.5	2 027	0.0	9.5	4.2	32 544	63.3	5.9	53.9	15.2	30.9
Elko County..................	10 760	1 917	5.1	3 053	0.0	8.1	6.8	32 399	70.8	5.7	64.4	13.2	22.5
Esmeralda County........	185	39	8.5	68	0.0	5.8	0.0	812	56.4	3.3	50.9	11.9	37.2
Eureka County	379	39	4.1	93	0.0	5.4	8.6	1 242	60.4	4.0	53.9	15.5	30.6
Humboldt County	3 024	402	2.0	1 050	0.0	11.7	5.0	11 680	66.6	8.3	60.6	13.8	26.2
Lander County..............	1 456	210	3.0	327	0.0	5.2	0.0	4 129	66.4	7.8	58.0	14.2	27.8
Lincoln County.............	1 007	116	2.1	328	0.0	11.6	2.1	3 139	49.0	5.2	45.3	15.8	38.9
Lyon County	7 280	1 086	7.3	2 086	0.0	12.7	4.5	26 423	62.7	6.9	54.8	13.0	32.2
Mineral County	973	142	6.9	269	0.0	9.7	3.7	4 024	58.9	12.9	49.7	13.4	36.9
Nye County	5 747	601	7.0	1 235	0.0	11.2	5.9	25 663	51.7	7.1	47.2	10.0	42.8
Pershing County...........	1 537	230	5.1	355	0.0	8.5	6.8	5 178	47.9	7.5	58.9	8.6	32.5
Storey County..............	513	144	6.2	161	0.0	34.2	0.0	2 816	66.8	5.2	62.7	11.5	25.8
Washoe County............	62 229	22 839	7.2	17 960	0.1	11.1	6.6	263 862	68.6	4.9	60.7	14.7	24.6
White Pine County	1 810	359	4.9	471	0.0	9.3	2.5	7 238	49.6	7.6	56.7	13.2	30.1
Carson City	9 106	2 995	5.9	2 290	0.0	10.5	7.0	41 517	59.8	4.6	56.1	13.0	30.9
NEW HAMPSHIRE.....	237 188	74 832	17.9	67 668	0.0	8.9	3.1	960 498	70.5	3.8	58.6	17.7	23.7
Belknap County............	10 516	2 006	11.9	2 705	0.0	9.9	4.1	44 614	67.0	3.4	56.9	16.3	26.8
Carroll County	8 026	1 231	9.9	2 073	0.0	11.4	2.3	35 009	63.6	3.8	51.0	18.6	30.5
Cheshire County	13 485	6 717	17.6	5 241	0.0	6.8	3.1	58 826	69.6	6.9	56.6	19.3	24.1
Coos County	6 106	932	7.3	1 721	0.0	8.7	5.1	26 513	62.6	5.4	51.4	16.4	32.3
Grafton County	13 924	9 172	27.5	6 267	0.0	6.7	2.9	66 228	67.2	4.8	56.4	20.0	23.6
Hillsborough County......	75 632	20 594	20.8	19 010	0.1	9.0	3.3	290 803	72.1	3.4	60.6	16.6	22.9
Merrimack County	26 380	8 216	19.7	7 363	0.0	8.7	3.1	106 078	69.9	4.3	59.0	16.7	24.2
Rockingham County......	55 638	12 255	16.9	13 218	0.1	9.2	2.8	211 780	73.5	2.7	60.1	18.1	21.8
Strafford County	20 046	12 656	11.5	8 166	0.0	9.9	2.6	88 752	70.2	4.1	57.6	20.3	22.1
Sullivan County............	7 435	1 053	9.4	1 904	0.0	11.1	3.2	31 895	66.4	3.3	56.6	15.0	28.4
NEW JERSEY...........	1 566 107	470 302	18.5	408 187	0.2	8.9	4.3	6 546 155	64.2	5.8	55.7	13.7	30.5
Atlantic County.............	48 899	12 659	12.6	12 559	0.0	10.2	5.5	195 002	64.5	7.5	55.3	14.8	29.9
Bergen County	150 192	50 740	22.9	37 929	0.0	6.7	1.7	702 617	64.6	4.1	55.9	13.5	30.6
Burlington County..........	82 014	20 140	15.1	21 045	1.2	9.8	3.9	328 907	66.8	3.8	58.7	14.3	27.0
Camden County	104 979	25 699	15.9	27 751	0.0	8.2	6.2	388 191	64.6	6.0	54.3	15.2	30.5
Cape May County	18 054	3 466	14.1	4 563	3.3	11.6	4.0	81 988	60.0	8.1	50.7	15.1	34.1
Cumberland County	29 889	5 087	11.8	7 976	0.0	11.4	6.0	113 545	57.8	9.9	51.0	12.5	36.5
Essex County	155 379	47 684	20.5	41 257	0.1	10.3	6.9	608 592	61.0	9.3	53.2	12.3	34.5
Gloucester County	51 446	17 149	15.1	14 528	0.0	9.4	2.8	194 905	68.1	6.0	56.1	16.6	27.3
Hudson County	106 450	41 431	24.7	29 361	0.1	10.0	7.7	486 268	61.2	8.7	56.6	10.5	32.9
Hunterdon County........	23 496	4 876	12.0	5 282	0.0	5.9	2.2	93 861	69.4	2.5	59.9	16.0	24.2

STATE County	Full-year full-time employed (percent)								Children under 18 years in families						Total employed by class of worker (percent)			
	Total	Men	Women	Non-Hispanic White	Black or African American	American Indian and Alaska Native	Asian, Hawaiian, and Pacific Islander	Hispanic or Latino[1]	Number	With two parents (percent) Both in labor force	Father only in labor force	With one parent who is in labor force (percent)	+/- U.S. percent of children with no stay-at-home parent (percent)	+/- U.S. percent two-income couples	Private	Government	Self-employed	Unpaid family worker
	24	25	26	27	28	29	30	31	32	33	34	35	36	37	38	39	40	41
NEBRASKA—Cont'd																		
Platte County	46.9	58.9	35.3	47.0	52.5	62.2	44.9	43.3	8 963	66.6	13.9	13.2	15.2	11.0	77.5	9.3	12.5	0.7
Polk County	40.7	53.5	28.5	40.7	0.0	50.0	X	36.4	1 373	63.2	20.1	10.9	9.5	9.3	65.9	11.3	21.5	1.4
Red Willow County	42.0	52.9	31.9	41.8	0.0	15.4	0.0	57.4	2 772	64.0	11.6	16.1	15.5	8.7	68.5	14.1	15.9	1.5
Richardson County	38.8	50.3	28.6	38.1	37.5	54.3	60.0	51.9	2 327	58.1	14.9	20.8	14.3	4.3	66.4	14.7	17.7	1.2
Rock County	40.0	56.4	26.2	40.6	X	0.0	60.0	0.0	386	60.4	16.3	16.3	12.1	7.9	46.5	14.9	36.5	2.1
Saline County	41.8	51.1	32.9	42.2	7.0	50.0	42.6	37.9	3 323	62.2	13.3	18.4	16.0	13.8	73.2	13.3	12.9	0.6
Sarpy County	54.3	66.1	43.0	55.2	53.5	49.9	45.3	45.9	36 435	57.1	21.4	16.3	8.8	14.7	77.1	15.2	7.5	0.2
Saunders County	47.4	58.9	36.2	47.5	37.5	40.5	19.7	55.5	5 370	64.5	16.5	13.6	13.5	13.1	70.2	13.9	15.3	0.6
Scotts Bluff County	39.7	49.4	31.2	40.9	55.7	13.8	28.4	34.7	9 106	48.0	14.7	23.1	6.5	2.2	72.3	13.6	13.6	0.5
Seward County	42.7	52.8	32.3	42.6	42.9	7.4	38.2	67.0	4 022	69.5	13.1	12.3	17.2	15.2	70.8	14.4	14.1	0.8
Sheridan County	38.5	49.6	28.1	39.1	100.0	29.3	70.0	33.3	1 515	62.7	13.2	16.9	15.0	6.9	54.5	18.1	25.9	1.6
Sherman County	38.4	48.4	29.0	38.6	100.0	0.0	0.0	31.3	742	65.5	18.1	11.5	12.4	7.9	57.3	12.4	27.7	2.6
Sioux County	39.8	55.0	23.9	40.0	X	0.0	42.9	36.8	356	67.7	17.4	7.0	10.1	-1.1	46.2	17.7	34.0	2.1
Stanton County	48.8	60.4	37.8	49.1	X	30.0	60.0	47.9	1 859	63.3	16.7	12.0	10.7	16.4	65.7	13.9	18.3	2.1
Thayer County	37.9	48.0	28.6	38.1	X	10.0	X	22.2	1 405	67.3	7.9	15.1	17.8	8.9	62.8	13.7	22.3	1.1
Thomas County	40.6	57.6	24.9	41.3	X	0.0	X	33.3	174	66.1	18.4	11.5	13.0	10.5	49.9	15.9	30.0	4.2
Thurston County	35.9	40.9	31.2	41.1	9.5	29.7	40.0	22.2	2 359	40.4	10.0	29.4	5.2	-0.5	60.7	26.8	12.0	0.5
Valley County	38.2	51.4	26.3	38.3	X	0.0	0.0	27.3	1 127	61.0	19.4	13.8	10.2	3.6	55.5	17.4	26.0	1.2
Washington County	47.7	59.5	36.5	47.9	33.3	78.9	47.2	38.8	4 972	59.3	20.8	14.9	9.6	15.9	78.6	10.3	10.7	0.3
Wayne County	35.6	46.2	25.8	35.7	0.0	27.5	7.1	40.7	2 109	70.7	12.3	11.9	18.0	12.9	65.5	19.1	13.6	1.8
Webster County	36.7	46.3	27.8	36.7	100.0	0.0	24.1	53.8	949	62.0	21.1	12.8	10.2	2.1	57.6	15.7	25.4	1.3
Wheeler County	40.9	58.8	22.6	40.9	X	X	X	50.0	242	73.1	14.0	12.0	20.5	8.8	44.3	16.4	37.1	2.2
York County	41.2	55.1	28.6	41.6	12.2	27.8	7.9	32.0	3 548	66.6	13.2	13.9	15.9	10.4	72.1	11.2	15.7	1.1
NEVADA	42.4	49.7	34.9	43.7	40.3	40.2	43.4	37.7	475 371	39.6	21.8	23.9	-1.1	-3.1	79.6	12.5	7.7	0.3
Churchill County	42.1	54.8	29.7	42.7	55.4	38.0	43.1	35.2	6 634	50.2	22.8	19.7	5.3	1.0	67.6	22.2	9.9	0.3
Clark County	42.5	49.4	35.5	44.2	40.5	43.9	43.7	37.2	325 756	37.0	22.1	24.7	-2.9	-4.6	82.2	10.7	6.9	0.2
Douglas County	39.5	47.9	31.0	39.9	52.3	29.6	44.7	34.3	9 497	51.1	20.2	21.1	7.6	-3.5	66.4	17.1	16.2	0.4
Elko County	46.5	58.3	33.6	47.6	22.3	37.2	47.7	45.2	13 838	45.7	29.0	17.3	-1.6	3.0	76.9	15.7	6.9	0.5
Esmeralda County	35.7	45.7	23.4	38.2	X	12.5	100.0	33.3	179	45.8	22.9	18.4	-0.4	-11.2	56.0	30.0	13.5	0.5
Eureka County	38.0	49.8	25.0	38.7	0.0	16.7	30.0	39.2	443	47.6	31.6	10.6	-6.4	-6.6	56.4	28.9	14.0	0.7
Humboldt County	38.7	49.3	26.9	41.3	32.0	27.2	9.4	32.9	4 750	46.8	23.6	18.4	0.6	-1.4	72.2	18.2	9.3	0.3
Lander County	40.0	56.3	23.1	42.3	X	24.6	23.5	33.1	1 783	38.4	31.6	18.3	-7.9	-6.3	67.9	25.5	6.3	0.3
Lincoln County	30.3	39.1	20.9	29.6	45.3	7.1	43.5	40.0	1 048	49.2	28.4	15.6	0.2	-8.7	49.5	38.5	10.4	1.7
Lyon County	38.1	44.9	31.2	37.8	42.7	40.4	49.1	37.5	8 384	51.6	19.1	19.9	6.9	-0.8	71.0	17.8	10.6	0.7
Mineral County	34.3	40.4	28.1	36.8	22.4	25.8	28.6	34.5	1 083	46.6	10.0	28.4	10.4	-9.3	59.8	30.3	8.9	0.9
Nye County	33.3	42.7	23.5	33.0	38.8	29.1	35.2	36.6	7 126	38.7	30.2	19.6	-6.3	-16.6	72.1	18.3	9.3	0.3
Pershing County	39.2	46.1	27.0	43.8	0.6	39.9	8.5	32.7	1 595	42.8	19.3	25.8	4.0	-1.3	63.6	28.0	7.9	0.5
Storey County	43.9	52.6	35.0	43.9	X	33.9	40.8	46.7	599	56.1	20.5	17.7	9.2	-0.6	68.3	16.6	13.7	1.5
Washoe County	44.0	51.5	36.4	45.0	41.5	40.9	42.4	39.1	78 967	44.6	19.7	23.1	3.1	2.8	77.6	13.4	8.8	0.3
White Pine County	36.1	42.8	27.1	35.6	40.5	31.4	40.3	39.0	2 060	42.8	19.0	23.1	1.3	-7.0	56.7	36.4	6.3	0.6
Carson City	41.3	48.5	33.6	41.4	33.4	44.3	41.3	41.3	11 629	42.7	16.3	28.9	7.0	0.3	66.1	23.1	10.5	0.2
NEW HAMPSHIRE	46.5	58.0	35.7	46.7	44.3	37.9	44.3	43.7	297 516	53.7	20.7	18.4	7.5	9.3	76.5	12.8	10.5	0.2
Belknap County	44.4	53.2	36.0	44.5	40.6	42.7	49.6	39.5	12 918	54.5	17.1	19.9	9.8	6.3	70.6	15.3	13.6	0.5
Carroll County	38.3	47.4	29.7	38.3	58.6	50.8	27.0	37.4	9 427	52.6	17.5	21.6	9.6	-0.7	68.5	12.5	18.6	0.4
Cheshire County	42.2	51.2	33.8	42.4	17.0	22.9	45.0	37.9	16 417	54.0	17.6	20.3	9.7	10.0	76.2	12.4	11.2	0.2
Coos County	39.8	51.2	29.1	39.9	0.0	34.5	50.0	54.2	7 100	52.7	14.6	23.9	12.0	3.0	74.7	16.3	8.9	0.2
Grafton County	40.5	48.4	33.1	41.2	32.1	30.4	28.2	24.0	17 090	57.6	16.0	19.5	12.5	9.0	74.1	13.8	11.9	0.2
Hillsborough County	49.1	62.1	36.6	49.4	50.0	38.2	47.1	44.9	96 668	52.8	21.5	17.7	5.9	10.0	80.4	10.7	8.8	0.1
Merrimack County	47.4	56.9	38.4	47.7	27.1	32.2	33.9	39.8	32 490	55.9	17.4	19.5	10.8	11.9	71.9	17.1	10.6	0.3
Rockingham County	49.5	63.0	36.5	49.5	48.1	44.3	49.6	47.8	71 073	53.6	25.8	15.1	4.1	10.5	76.9	11.7	11.2	0.2
Strafford County	44.3	54.9	34.6	44.4	42.7	44.8	43.2	44.6	25 259	51.9	18.0	22.6	9.9	9.6	76.7	15.1	8.0	0.2
Sullivan County	44.9	54.7	35.7	45.1	16.4	25.5	47.8	38.7	9 074	52.6	15.6	21.5	9.5	6.5	74.3	12.9	12.4	0.4
NEW JERSEY	42.4	53.0	32.6	43.0	39.5	36.6	46.1	39.7	1 981 051	44.4	24.6	18.6	-1.6	0.3	77.1	13.9	8.8	0.2
Atlantic County	40.4	48.6	33.0	40.3	39.0	48.2	45.5	40.6	59 692	42.5	16.6	25.6	3.5	1.1	77.6	14.4	7.9	0.2
Bergen County	43.7	56.0	32.7	42.9	47.4	36.5	44.5	47.3	197 234	47.8	31.3	12.0	-4.8	-0.9	76.6	11.2	11.9	0.3
Burlington County	46.2	56.6	36.2	46.8	44.6	49.3	45.2	40.2	101 981	50.3	23.8	17.5	3.2	4.8	74.4	17.4	8.0	0.2
Camden County	41.7	51.9	32.6	43.5	37.9	26.4	41.7	33.4	127 678	43.1	19.7	23.9	2.4	2.8	78.0	14.1	7.7	0.2
Cape May County	35.8	46.1	26.7	35.8	33.7	50.5	55.0	33.5	21 766	49.3	21.3	22.3	7.0	-6.1	66.4	19.7	13.3	0.5
Cumberland County	36.7	41.2	32.0	39.7	28.2	41.3	41.3	34.2	33 995	37.4	14.7	31.0	3.8	-1.3	71.9	20.5	7.4	0.2
Essex County	38.6	46.1	32.2	41.3	36.4	32.2	45.8	35.2	187 832	34.2	17.3	28.8	-1.6	-2.1	76.5	15.3	8.1	0.2
Gloucester County	43.5	56.4	32.0	43.9	41.1	47.9	44.6	41.5	64 514	51.7	22.4	17.2	4.3	4.4	77.7	15.0	7.1	0.2
Hudson County	39.6	47.6	32.0	42.7	36.3	33.6	42.9	36.5	127 471	30.8	18.7	26.5	-7.3	-8.6	81.0	12.5	6.3	0.2
Hunterdon County	47.9	62.6	33.8	49.0	12.0	33.2	50.9	38.0	30 755	53.7	33.3	8.8	-2.1	8.0	74.0	12.1	13.7	0.2

[1] Hispanic or Latino persons may be of any race.

STATE County	Percent who worked at home	Percent of the population 5 years and over with a disability	Veterans as a percent of the population 18 years and over	Occupation for employed population 16 years and over (percent)						Industry for employed population 16 years and over (percent)					
				Management, professional, and related occupations	Service occupations	Sales and office occupations	Farming, fishing, and forestry occupations	Construction, extraction, and maintenance occupations	Production, transportation and material moving occupations	Agriculture, forestry, fishing, and mining	Construction and manufacturing	Wholesale and retail trade	Transportation and warehousing, and utilities	Service industries	Public administration
	42	43	44	45	46	47	48	49	50	51	52	53	54	55	56
NEBRASKA—Cont'd															
Platte County	6.2	15.1	12.9	28.5	12.4	22.2	1.9	8.4	26.5	6.7	37.6	12.9	7.3	34.0	1.7
Polk County	8.4	16.1	14.0	31.6	14.9	19.3	5.2	12.7	16.2	18.1	20.2	12.9	6.0	39.6	3.2
Red Willow County	5.0	20.4	14.4	28.5	16.8	24.3	3.1	10.9	16.4	8.9	15.8	19.6	6.0	46.0	3.6
Richardson County	5.3	18.7	16.1	28.6	16.0	21.2	2.5	13.0	18.6	10.3	20.1	12.1	9.9	43.5	4.1
Rock County	17.7	17.0	14.3	39.2	11.8	20.6	8.0	10.7	9.8	31.4	10.3	13.3	8.0	33.4	3.6
Saline County	5.8	15.3	14.2	29.1	13.8	18.1	1.4	9.3	28.3	8.2	31.4	12.7	4.4	40.4	2.8
Sarpy County	3.1	12.5	19.0	36.8	13.1	31.3	0.2	8.6	10.1	0.5	14.0	16.8	6.9	56.3	5.4
Saunders County	5.9	14.5	14.7	28.5	14.6	24.9	1.0	12.5	18.6	7.1	25.4	15.9	6.3	41.1	4.1
Scotts Bluff County	3.8	19.6	13.4	31.1	15.4	26.8	1.6	11.5	13.7	5.5	15.3	16.4	8.4	50.8	3.6
Seward County	5.4	11.6	11.9	31.4	15.6	22.3	1.4	12.4	16.9	7.8	19.6	12.8	5.9	48.8	5.2
Sheridan County	14.0	19.5	15.7	36.9	15.8	22.5	6.8	9.9	8.0	22.4	7.3	15.3	5.7	44.1	5.4
Sherman County	11.8	19.4	17.2	33.4	13.9	22.0	4.0	11.3	15.5	20.8	18.4	12.9	5.4	39.0	3.5
Sioux County	23.3	16.1	12.9	50.3	9.7	15.3	10.4	5.8	8.4	40.5	6.4	7.8	6.7	34.1	4.5
Stanton County	10.5	15.4	13.8	30.2	15.1	20.2	4.2	11.0	19.3	14.0	23.2	14.4	5.4	40.5	2.6
Thayer County	8.6	19.2	14.8	34.3	15.9	20.2	3.4	10.2	16.0	15.7	19.7	12.5	6.0	43.1	2.9
Thomas County	8.1	17.5	15.7	34.7	13.1	14.6	13.8	11.0	12.8	30.0	17.5	11.2	5.7	33.7	1.8
Thurston County	6.1	20.1	14.4	31.1	20.6	22.9	2.5	8.4	14.5	10.0	16.0	10.2	4.4	47.9	11.5
Valley County	10.9	20.9	15.4	33.2	17.0	20.9	6.9	10.3	11.8	20.4	9.2	16.2	7.1	42.6	4.6
Washington County	4.4	14.6	13.8	32.6	13.0	28.8	0.7	12.9	12.0	4.5	19.9	14.3	7.3	51.1	2.9
Wayne County	7.2	12.5	11.1	30.0	16.9	26.0	4.6	8.2	14.3	10.8	18.2	16.1	3.1	48.9	2.9
Webster County	9.5	19.7	15.6	34.2	17.4	20.0	4.2	9.6	14.6	19.7	14.7	14.1	6.4	41.2	3.8
Wheeler County	21.9	11.2	16.3	42.8	12.5	13.4	14.9	6.8	9.6	46.1	6.1	7.5	5.9	28.9	5.5
York County	5.8	16.2	13.5	29.2	17.8	23.2	1.8	11.1	16.9	9.1	18.6	14.4	7.3	46.8	3.8
NEVADA	2.6	20.6	16.0	25.7	24.6	27.6	0.3	11.4	10.4	1.6	14.2	14.0	5.2	60.6	4.5
Churchill County	3.8	19.4	23.0	26.4	17.5	24.3	2.2	15.1	14.4	6.1	17.6	15.2	5.6	45.1	10.5
Clark County	2.3	21.1	15.5	24.4	26.9	27.9	0.1	11.2	9.5	0.3	13.4	13.5	5.1	64.0	3.6
Douglas County	6.1	17.0	18.5	33.4	20.2	25.4	0.5	11.8	8.7	2.2	18.9	11.2	3.5	57.0	7.2
Elko County	2.5	10.0	14.0	23.6	22.3	21.2	1.3	20.7	10.0	22.1	9.4	12.1	3.4	48.0	4.9
Esmeralda County	6.1	26.9	23.2	24.2	19.2	16.3	3.8	23.0	13.5	22.6	15.3	11.1	6.5	28.7	15.8
Eureka County	7.6	22.2	17.1	31.7	17.9	17.1	7.1	21.5	4.7	36.3	5.4	8.9	4.4	33.3	11.7
Humboldt County	1.9	15.7	13.9	25.7	15.5	21.7	2.4	20.5	14.2	24.6	11.6	13.7	6.0	38.1	6.1
Lander County	3.5	20.9	14.5	24.4	16.1	16.9	1.9	21.7	19.1	28.5	11.6	9.3	6.3	34.4	10.0
Lincoln County	3.4	24.6	19.6	25.2	20.2	25.4	3.4	16.7	9.0	7.3	13.2	16.5	7.3	43.2	12.4
Lyon County	3.7	22.3	20.3	25.4	16.4	26.1	1.7	12.8	17.5	5.0	21.8	17.0	5.6	42.8	7.8
Mineral County	4.2	29.8	23.6	26.4	22.1	23.0	0.5	16.6	11.3	5.3	12.4	13.0	1.6	56.5	11.2
Nye County	3.5	20.0	20.0	21.6	21.6	24.5	0.7	10.0	12.6	10.1	16.6	11.2	5.0	49.3	7.8
Pershing County	3.2	20.4	16.2	22.7	19.9	18.9	2.8	18.6	17.1	22.8	12.0	9.6	6.7	34.5	14.4
Storey County	3.1	25.9	22.1	25.9	16.1	27.2	0.0	18.0	12.8	1.3	22.3	17.4	7.8	43.7	7.5
Washoe County	2.9	18.8	15.8	29.5	19.9	28.9	0.2	9.5	12.1	0.8	15.1	16.1	6.0	57.7	4.3
White Pine County	4.9	22.9	19.4	26.1	25.7	23.1	2.1	13.6	9.4	11.1	7.4	16.3	5.2	41.2	18.8
Carson City	3.4	20.8	18.0	30.2	18.2	28.2	0.3	9.3	13.8	0.6	21.7	13.9	2.7	47.8	13.3
NEW HAMPSHIRE	4.0	16.9	15.0	35.8	13.0	26.6	0.4	9.4	14.8	0.9	24.9	17.3	4.1	49.0	3.8
Belknap County	3.0	18.2	16.6	30.7	15.5	25.6	0.4	11.7	16.1	1.1	26.1	17.4	3.2	47.2	5.0
Carroll County	5.7	20.8	18.7	30.0	18.0	27.3	0.9	13.4	10.5	1.6	19.5	19.1	3.4	52.8	3.6
Cheshire County	4.5	17.8	15.4	32.4	13.0	26.4	0.6	9.9	17.7	1.4	25.8	18.3	3.8	48.1	2.5
Coos County	3.8	26.0	16.8	24.3	17.0	23.2	1.9	11.6	22.0	3.1	27.6	16.8	4.4	43.0	5.0
Grafton County	5.3	16.1	14.5	36.6	16.0	23.6	1.0	9.4	13.4	1.8	19.5	14.9	3.6	57.4	2.9
Hillsborough County	3.5	16.9	14.4	37.8	11.9	26.9	0.2	8.4	14.8	0.4	26.7	17.1	4.5	48.4	2.9
Merrimack County	4.0	17.0	15.2	36.0	12.7	27.9	0.4	10.0	13.1	0.8	20.9	16.9	3.3	50.9	7.2
Rockingham County	4.1	14.7	14.4	38.4	11.5	27.4	0.4	9.3	13.1	0.7	25.2	18.1	4.8	47.6	3.6
Strafford County	3.0	16.7	15.0	34.0	14.7	26.6	0.5	8.3	16.0	1.0	24.4	17.2	4.0	49.5	4.0
Sullivan County	4.6	19.3	16.5	27.9	13.4	24.0	0.8	10.6	23.3	1.8	31.4	16.2	3.2	43.8	3.5
NEW JERSEY	2.7	18.0	10.6	38.0	13.6	28.5	0.2	7.8	12.0	0.3	17.6	15.7	5.9	55.9	4.5
Atlantic County	1.9	20.9	12.3	25.6	30.3	26.0	0.4	8.6	9.1	0.7	10.8	13.0	4.2	65.9	5.5
Bergen County	3.1	15.7	9.8	43.1	10.9	30.2	0.0	6.6	9.1	0.1	16.4	17.6	5.3	57.6	3.0
Burlington County	2.8	15.9	14.7	38.7	12.7	29.4	0.2	7.6	11.3	0.4	16.6	16.4	5.6	53.5	7.5
Camden County	2.3	18.9	12.1	35.5	14.4	29.3	0.1	8.4	12.3	0.1	16.2	17.0	5.6	56.4	4.7
Cape May County	2.9	20.5	15.9	31.5	21.1	27.3	0.8	11.2	8.0	1.1	12.7	15.3	4.3	59.1	7.6
Cumberland County	2.2	23.1	11.2	24.8	19.0	23.8	1.8	9.8	20.9	2.5	24.0	14.6	5.4	46.1	7.4
Essex County	2.8	21.9	8.1	35.6	15.8	28.9	0.1	6.8	12.9	0.1	15.4	13.5	7.5	59.2	4.3
Gloucester County	2.6	16.6	13.1	33.3	13.3	29.2	0.3	10.4	13.6	0.5	19.5	17.4	6.9	51.1	4.5
Hudson County	1.8	23.8	6.0	32.3	15.1	29.2	0.1	6.3	17.0	0.1	15.7	15.8	9.2	55.8	3.5
Hunterdon County	5.9	10.9	11.3	49.0	9.7	25.2	0.4	8.2	7.5	1.3	22.5	14.1	3.6	55.0	3.6

Table B-3. States and Counties — Education, Labor Force, and Income

STATE County	Median house-hold income (57)	All families (58)	Married-couple (59)	Male house-holder (60)	Female house-holder (61)	Median nonfamily house-hold income (62)	Men (63)	Women (64)	Per capita income (65)	With earnings (66)	With interest, dividend, or rental income (67)	With Social Security income (68)	With public assis-tance income (69)	With retire-ment income (70)	House-holds with income over $100,000 (percent) (71)	+/- U.S. percent for income over $100,000 (percent) (72)	House-holds with income below poverty (percent) (73)	Families with children with income below poverty (percent) (74)
NEBRASKA—Cont'd																		
Platte County	39 359	47 776	52 300	27 014	21 182	20 840	31 649	22 466	18 064	81.4	45.2	27.4	2.3	11.3	6.0	-6.3	8.1	7.7
Polk County	37 819	45 081	49 946	27 500	16 625	20 924	31 682	20 859	17 934	78.1	51.2	34.5	2.2	11.8	4.2	-8.1	6.3	5.4
Red Willow County	32 293	40 279	45 127	15 938	16 012	16 963	28 842	19 409	16 303	77.6	41.4	34.3	2.2	11.7	4.0	-8.3	11.3	12.4
Richardson County	29 884	39 779	44 787	24 375	20 854	16 458	27 928	20 169	16 460	72.5	40.6	39.0	2.4	11.9	3.1	-9.2	11.1	9.8
Rock County	25 795	29 917	28 906	23 750	15 625	16 779	25 722	17 321	14 350	78.1	44.4	36.4	2.9	8.1	3.6	-8.7	19.5	30.7
Saline County	35 914	44 199	50 268	26 513	20 298	18 966	31 108	23 507	16 287	77.0	43.8	32.7	2.9	12.4	3.9	-8.4	10.5	9.6
Sarpy County	53 804	59 723	63 154	37 603	27 538	30 735	39 823	27 780	21 985	91.4	42.6	15.7	1.7	18.1	12.3	0.0	4.0	4.6
Saunders County	42 173	49 443	56 089	29 583	25 036	21 987	35 159	24 111	18 392	82.9	46.9	30.1	1.3	13.7	6.0	-6.3	7.1	7.1
Scotts Bluff County	32 016	38 932	48 825	20 208	17 500	18 967	31 178	21 481	17 355	76.8	37.6	32.0	4.7	14.0	5.9	-6.4	13.2	17.9
Seward County	42 700	51 813	55 552	35 357	25 125	20 650	34 511	23 403	18 379	80.5	49.4	28.4	1.1	12.4	7.6	-4.7	8.4	6.5
Sheridan County	29 484	35 167	37 471	25 000	13 229	16 642	24 736	19 609	14 844	76.8	43.7	38.7	2.9	11.1	3.1	-9.2	11.9	17.3
Sherman County	28 646	34 821	35 365	23 000	17 083	15 600	24 033	18 977	14 064	73.0	44.9	42.7	1.9	13.7	2.3	-10.0	13.5	15.6
Sioux County	29 851	31 406	31 875	11 250	13 750	24 167	25 556	22 163	15 999	87.2	44.4	30.9	1.7	16.0	5.7	-6.6	11.5	18.7
Stanton County	36 676	41 040	47 375	25 313	18 194	20 789	29 702	20 313	15 511	86.1	41.3	24.5	1.7	9.1	4.2	-8.1	8.1	6.6
Thayer County	30 740	38 346	46 827	22 813	21 964	16 223	28 448	19 039	17 043	75.8	49.2	40.0	2.3	9.8	3.9	-8.4	10.8	10.2
Thomas County	27 292	36 618	36 607	27 500	19 167	17 917	27 212	20 577	15 335	71.6	35.8	38.6	0.0	10.5	1.9	-10.4	13.3	15.1
Thurston County	28 170	30 893	40 759	21 875	15 909	17 083	25 539	21 250	10 951	79.0	28.7	31.7	11.1	7.6	1.8	-10.5	20.1	27.0
Valley County	27 926	35 571	41 103	26 375	13 750	15 858	26 475	17 895	14 996	73.6	45.9	38.7	2.9	9.6	3.3	-9.0	13.5	15.2
Washington County	48 500	56 429	65 000	30 813	25 075	24 012	38 513	26 483	21 055	83.7	45.1	27.9	1.5	13.2	11.5	-0.8	6.2	6.3
Wayne County	32 366	43 840	50 265	27 321	19 500	18 487	29 342	20 876	14 644	83.1	46.0	26.9	1.8	10.0	4.7	-7.6	14.1	10.5
Webster County	30 026	36 513	38 836	30 313	16 250	16 863	27 454	19 833	16 802	73.5	46.9	41.6	2.5	14.0	3.3	-9.0	11.8	13.2
Wheeler County	26 771	33 750	35 500	26 250	12 250	17 188	21 902	17 917	14 355	82.4	36.0	31.3	4.2	7.0	4.7	-7.6	19.3	21.0
York County	37 093	44 741	50 801	29 083	17 072	21 849	31 785	20 499	17 670	79.0	47.3	33.7	2.3	11.7	4.6	-7.7	7.9	9.0
NEVADA	44 581	50 849	57 707	32 114	24 148	30 088	36 812	28 019	21 989	83.5	29.6	23.6	2.3	17.4	11.3	-1.0	9.4	11.4
Churchill County	40 808	46 624	51 982	38 906	16 424	24 684	38 651	26 146	19 264	81.0	32.5	25.6	3.2	24.1	6.8	-5.5	8.6	10.3
Clark County	44 616	50 485	57 286	32 015	24 380	30 541	36 312	27 910	21 785	83.9	27.9	23.2	2.4	17.4	11.5	-0.8	9.5	11.8
Douglas County	51 849	57 092	62 791	48 750	22 051	32 310	41 655	30 270	27 288	79.1	45.3	27.5	1.9	22.7	14.6	2.3	7.3	9.4
Elko County	48 383	52 206	56 663	38 553	22 319	31 132	41 927	25 365	18 482	90.1	24.1	16.3	1.8	9.8	8.6	-3.7	8.5	8.8
Esmeralda County	33 203	40 917	44 292	49 375	11 875	22 273	41 458	25 469	18 971	75.7	24.3	35.1	4.6	25.8	5.5	-6.8	18.1	7.9
Eureka County	41 417	49 438	52 206	50 625	14 375	17 045	45 625	27 250	18 629	81.9	30.5	28.4	2.4	13.1	6.9	-5.4	14.2	10.1
Humboldt County	47 147	52 156	58 620	45 473	21 310	28 889	45 500	26 279	19 539	89.4	28.2	18.6	1.6	11.6	8.0	-4.3	8.8	9.6
Lander County	46 067	51 538	60 000	40 724	18 333	25 771	46 136	24 886	16 998	88.9	18.3	16.3	1.4	13.9	4.0	-8.3	10.8	12.2
Lincoln County	31 979	45 588	50 625	27 143	18 654	13 235	40 580	24 167	17 326	67.9	27.8	39.6	5.0	26.0	3.7	-8.6	17.9	15.3
Lyon County	40 699	44 887	49 359	24 557	18 167	23 946	35 429	26 701	18 543	79.5	31.0	30.7	2.4	23.0	5.8	-6.5	9.6	11.2
Mineral County	32 891	39 477	46 339	17 604	17 202	18 125	32 254	26 024	16 952	71.9	27.7	35.3	4.3	27.6	3.6	-8.7	15.9	19.9
Nye County	36 024	41 642	51 646	27 188	19 028	21 590	38 750	23 652	17 962	68.6	23.3	40.4	3.5	27.9	5.6	-6.7	10.7	12.1
Pershing County	40 670	46 268	49 458	30 714	16 688	22 171	35 323	25 313	16 589	83.2	27.5	22.7	2.0	14.7	4.9	-7.4	11.1	14.5
Storey County	45 490	57 095	67 500	44 844	30 938	29 643	40 758	28 278	23 642	82.6	39.7	24.5	4.1	19.8	7.1	-5.2	5.8	5.3
Washoe County	45 815	54 283	61 367	31 638	25 527	30 235	37 190	29 348	24 277	85.0	34.1	21.9	2.1	15.0	12.9	0.6	9.1	10.3
White Pine County	36 688	44 136	51 747	63 409	12 479	22 995	36 398	26 783	18 309	77.4	26.5	32.0	2.7	21.2	4.8	-7.5	12.0	16.0
Carson City	41 809	49 570	58 101	26 607	24 026	27 162	36 035	28 617	20 943	78.2	37.2	29.3	2.7	21.3	9.3	-3.0	9.2	11.7
NEW HAMPSHIRE	49 467	57 575	67 028	35 036	24 774	28 945	40 819	28 669	23 844	83.8	41.9	24.7	3.0	16.4	13.8	1.5	6.9	6.5
Belknap County	43 605	50 510	57 238	30 737	23 180	25 651	35 917	26 320	22 758	81.1	41.1	29.5	3.0	19.0	9.3	-3.0	6.5	7.6
Carroll County	39 990	46 922	52 716	28 438	21 723	24 076	33 292	25 022	21 931	77.5	38.1	32.6	3.2	20.3	9.4	-2.9	7.9	8.9
Cheshire County	42 382	51 043	57 848	37 535	23 054	25 245	35 135	26 298	20 685	82.3	42.8	27.2	3.1	17.6	8.6	-3.7	8.2	6.8
Coos County	33 593	40 654	49 935	31 250	18 587	17 283	33 154	21 641	17 218	73.1	28.4	35.7	6.0	18.5	4.1	-8.2	11.7	10.6
Grafton County	41 962	50 424	57 201	31 594	22 402	25 251	33 172	26 146	22 227	82.3	42.3	27.1	2.9	16.3	10.1	-2.2	8.4	7.7
Hillsborough County	53 384	62 363	72 118	38 546	24 961	31 154	43 693	30 304	25 198	85.3	43.0	22.5	3.3	14.8	16.6	4.3	6.4	6.3
Merrimack County	48 522	56 842	66 316	30 975	25 086	28 268	39 197	28 324	23 208	83.3	43.9	25.7	2.9	17.0	12.0	-0.3	6.6	6.3
Rockingham County	58 150	66 345	74 879	37 637	29 739	34 969	47 218	31 449	26 656	86.9	43.2	21.4	1.6	15.6	19.0	6.7	4.8	4.5
Strafford County	44 803	53 075	64 681	32 247	22 734	27 602	37 760	26 850	20 479	83.8	38.5	23.9	3.9	17.3	9.3	-3.0	8.8	8.2
Sullivan County	40 938	48 516	54 699	29 622	18 407	24 720	33 626	25 639	21 319	78.4	40.5	30.8	4.6	20.1	7.7	-4.6	8.9	8.6
NEW JERSEY	55 146	65 370	77 760	35 172	25 473	31 298	48 027	34 636	27 006	81.4	42.4	26.9	2.8	17.1	21.3	9.0	8.3	9.2
Atlantic County	43 933	51 710	62 181	31 404	23 017	26 478	37 311	29 155	21 034	80.5	32.2	28.4	3.0	17.0	10.6	-1.7	10.1	10.9
Bergen County	65 241	78 079	89 696	42 316	34 969	36 337	52 836	38 990	33 638	82.5	50.3	28.2	1.5	16.3	28.6	16.3	5.3	4.6
Burlington County	58 608	67 481	77 066	37 535	32 319	34 506	48 250	33 434	26 339	84.7	43.5	25.6	1.8	19.5	20.1	7.8	4.7	4.6
Camden County	48 097	57 429	70 416	35 131	21 642	27 124	42 429	31 148	22 354	81.1	36.5	26.9	3.9	17.0	14.7	2.4	10.0	12.0
Cape May County	41 591	51 402	62 740	28 988	23 167	24 456	40 807	30 003	24 172	74.2	43.9	37.6	2.4	23.7	12.3	0.0	8.3	10.1
Cumberland County	39 150	45 403	57 440	25 938	18 211	21 844	36 064	26 069	17 376	78.2	28.1	29.9	5.3	18.3	8.2	-4.1	13.7	16.7
Essex County	44 944	54 818	74 881	30 995	20 462	26 017	42 341	33 133	24 943	78.8	32.1	25.2	6.5	14.0	18.5	6.2	15.4	17.9
Gloucester County	54 273	62 482	72 184	37 563	26 099	28 880	45 433	31 772	22 708	83.5	38.8	26.2	1.5	18.2	15.5	3.2	6.7	6.2
Hudson County	40 293	44 053	51 219	27 134	19 915	30 029	36 932	31 682	21 154	80.5	28.2	23.0	4.8	12.0	12.8	0.5	15.3	18.9
Hunterdon County	79 888	91 050	100 268	48 333	43 125	41 993	64 976	42 328	36 370	88.1	57.8	20.8	1.2	15.0	37.0	24.7	2.8	2.1

STATE/ County code	MSA/PMSA/ NECMA code[1]	STATE County	High school graduates			College graduates		College graduates (percent)				
			Total population 25 years and over	Percent with a high school diploma or less	Percent with a high school diploma or more	Percent with a bachelor's degree or more	+/− U.S. percent with bachelor's degree or more	Non-Hispanic White	Black or African American	American Indian and Alaska Native	Asian, Hawaiian, and Pacific Islander	Hispanic or Latino[2]
			1	2	3	4	5	6	7	8	9	10
		NEW JERSEY— Cont'd										
34 021	8480	Mercer County..............	231 139	43.8	81.8	34.0	9.6	39.5	12.8	17.3	71.1	11.6
34 023	5015	Middlesex County..........	501 552	44.7	84.4	33.0	8.6	29.7	26.1	22.5	70.4	11.4
34 025	5190	Monmouth County........	413 058	39.5	87.9	34.6	10.2	36.0	14.8	18.1	63.5	16.6
34 027	5640	Morris County..............	323 881	33.4	90.6	44.1	19.7	44.8	26.8	27.9	69.9	18.5
34 029	5190	Ocean County..............	358 354	54.7	83.0	19.5	-4.9	19.5	15.3	11.3	47.1	12.2
34 031	0875	Passaic County	316 401	57.9	73.3	21.2	-3.2	27.9	8.7	4.7	48.1	7.8
34 033	6160	Salem County..............	42 789	59.8	79.4	15.2	-9.2	16.5	7.2	3.2	48.6	8.9
34 035	5015	Somerset County	204 343	31.9	89.6	46.5	22.1	47.4	31.5	29.9	76.0	18.5
34 037	5640	Sussex County	95 094	43.6	89.8	27.2	2.8	27.1	24.5	18.8	56.8	22.5
34 039	5640	Union County	351 903	50.4	79.3	28.5	4.1	35.0	16.6	16.9	61.0	12.7
34 041	5640	Warren County	69 457	50.5	84.9	24.4	0.0	24.4	24.7	12.6	61.0	18.6
35 000	...	NEW MEXICO............	1 134 801	47.7	78.9	23.5	-0.9	34.3	18.8	7.7	43.0	10.8
35 001	0200	Bernalillo County	358 680	40.3	84.4	30.5	6.1	42.2	22.9	15.0	38.8	13.8
35 003	...	Catron County	2 657	50.6	78.4	18.4	-6.0	20.7	100.0	9.4	100.0	8.3
35 005	...	Chaves County............	37 811	53.9	72.6	16.2	-8.2	22.6	5.9	10.6	54.9	5.1
35 006	...	Cibola County	15 273	61.5	75.0	12.0	-12.4	23.4	11.8	7.4	29.7	6.0
35 007	...	Colfax County	9 518	53.4	80.8	18.5	-5.9	28.4	0.0	7.2	0.0	5.4
35 009	...	Curry County	26 403	49.5	78.4	15.3	-9.1	19.6	11.0	5.9	27.7	4.2
35 011	...	De Baca County	1 584	57.6	72.3	16.2	-8.2	23.2	X	0.0	0.0	2.2
35 013	4100	Dona Ana County........	99 893	52.4	70.0	22.3	-2.1	39.3	25.0	14.7	64.2	9.6
35 015	...	Eddy County	32 572	59.4	75.0	13.5	-10.9	17.3	13.7	8.4	51.4	4.8
35 017	...	Grant County...............	20 350	49.7	79.4	20.5	-3.9	28.5	40.0	10.0	28.2	9.8
35 019	...	Guadalupe County	3 099	69.2	68.3	10.3	-14.1	18.5	6.4	11.3	100.0	8.5
35 021	...	Harding County	609	59.6	72.2	18.1	-6.3	26.2	X	0.0	X	0.0
35 023	...	Hidalgo County	3 506	68.1	68.8	9.9	-14.5	17.4	0.0	3.6	0.0	2.9
35 025	...	Lea County..................	33 291	60.8	67.1	11.6	-12.8	15.7	5.3	4.4	37.5	4.1
35 027	...	Lincoln County	13 849	43.6	84.5	22.8	-1.6	26.5	12.5	16.6	40.1	9.9
35 028	7490	Los Alamos County......	12 822	15.7	96.3	60.5	36.1	63.4	0.0	61.7	76.1	31.7
35 029	...	Luna County................	15 777	70.1	59.8	10.4	-14.0	15.6	8.1	21.3	26.1	3.7
35 031	...	McKinley County	38 988	62.7	65.2	12.0	-12.4	42.9	17.0	4.6	58.3	7.2
35 033	...	Mora County................	3 348	61.9	69.8	15.5	8.0	34.0	X	6.9	X	10.7
35 035	...	Otero County...............	38 061	48.1	81.0	15.4	-9.0	20.2	11.5	8.3	25.2	5.2
35 037	...	Quay County................	6 970	62.9	73.8	13.7	-10.7	17.1	21.3	0.0	31.9	6.6
35 039	...	Rio Arriba County	25 930	58.3	73.0	15.4	-9.0	34.6	7.2	9.7	32.5	11.1
35 041	...	Roosevelt County..........	10 245	48.5	75.2	22.6	-1.8	28.0	7.6	25.8	77.4	9.2
35 043	0200	Sandoval County...........	56 479	42.6	86.0	24.8	0.4	33.4	23.2	5.8	37.6	14.2
35 045	...	San Juan County...........	65 262	53.7	76.8	13.5	-10.9	19.8	27.5	5.4	25.2	6.5
35 047	...	San Miguel County........	18 531	51.1	74.5	21.2	-3.2	37.5	10.4	25.7	68.1	15.4
35 049	7490	Santa Fe County..........	87 870	35.2	84.5	36.9	12.5	56.2	30.2	16.8	56.6	14.0
35 051	...	Sierra County	9 906	55.3	76.1	13.1	-11.3	14.6	27.8	18.9	44.4	6.7
35 053	...	Socorro County	10 642	56.9	72.1	19.4	-5.0	31.6	13.5	11.2	73.3	7.6
35 055	...	Taos County................	20 526	47.5	79.1	25.9	1.5	46.7	50.5	10.9	42.4	11.1
35 057	...	Torrance County	10 556	55.9	77.1	14.4	-10.0	19.1	1.1	18.1	31.7	4.9
35 059	...	Union County	2 786	64.0	79.9	13.0	-11.4	17.2	X	50.0	100.0	2.2
35 061	0200	Valencia County	40 917	56.2	76.1	14.8	-9.6	20.6	15.7	9.4	27.3	8.9
36 000	...	NEW YORK...............	12 542 536	48.7	79.1	27.4	3.0	31.8	15.8	14.4	41.2	11.5
36 001	0160	Albany County..............	195 381	40.7	86.3	33.3	8.9	34.3	15.7	27.8	66.5	30.6
36 003	...	Allegany County	30 019	56.4	83.2	17.2	-7.2	16.8	8.8	21.5	67.7	20.2
36 005	5600	Bronx County	794 792	63.5	62.3	14.6	-9.8	26.0	14.1	9.4	35.4	8.2
36 007	0960	Broome County............	132 541	48.9	83.8	22.7	-1.7	22.3	20.5	2.7	50.4	26.6
36 009	...	Cattaraugus County	54 154	60.0	81.2	14.9	-9.5	14.9	9.3	10.3	48.5	15.6
36 011	8160	Cayuga County	54 649	56.9	79.1	15.5	-8.9	16.2	3.0	13.7	16.8	7.9
36 013	3610	Chautauqua County	91 261	55.3	81.2	16.9	-7.5	17.5	5.7	6.6	47.0	5.2
36 015	2335	Chemung County	60 796	54.0	82.1	18.6	-5.8	19.0	9.9	3.2	51.7	10.4
36 017	...	Chenango County	34 363	59.3	80.6	14.4	-10.0	14.4	4.9	11.7	51.9	19.6
36 019	...	Clinton County.............	51 598	57.1	76.4	17.8	-6.6	18.5	3.1	10.4	36.4	6.6
36 021	...	Columbia County	43 990	51.7	81.0	22.6	-1.8	23.3	6.4	13.2	34.7	13.1
36 023	...	Cortland County	29 527	53.0	82.8	18.8	-5.6	18.8	14.0	9.4	88.5	13.1
36 025	...	Delaware County	33 070	57.5	79.9	16.6	-7.8	16.5	23.2	13.9	65.9	10.7
36 027	2281	Dutchess County..........	183 725	44.1	84.0	27.6	3.2	28.9	12.2	16.2	62.4	16.7
36 029	1280	Erie County.................	637 676	47.0	82.9	24.5	0.1	26.0	11.5	13.1	64.0	15.3
36 031	...	Essex County	27 337	57.7	80.4	18.3	-6.1	19.0	2.3	17.2	28.0	4.0
36 033	...	Franklin County	34 482	64.1	69.7	13.0	-11.4	14.8	1.8	7.3	38.5	1.7
36 035	...	Fulton County	37 483	60.8	77.8	13.5	-10.9	13.6	6.9	0.0	46.0	8.7

[1]MSA = Metropolitan Statistical Area. PMSA = Primary MSA. NECMA = New England County Metropolitan Area. See the Appendix A for explanation of these concepts. See Appendix B for list of metropolitan areas identified by type, with component counties.
[2]Hispanic or Latino persons may be of any race.

STATE County	School enrollment			Population 16 to 19 years				Employment status, 2000			Work status in 1999 of the population 16 years and over (percent)		
											Worked in 1999		
	Grades kindergarten through 12	College or graduate school	Percent private	Number	Percent in armed forces	Percent high school graduates	Percent not enrolled, not grads, not in armed forces, not employed	Total population 16 years and over	Percent in labor force	Unemployment rate	Full-time	Part-time	Did not work in 1999
	11	12	13	14	15	16	17	18	19	20	21	22	23
NEW JERSEY— Cont'd													
Mercer County	62 905	28 687	23.8	19 442	0.1	7.0	4.0	275 489	65.4	7.5	56.2	15.2	28.6
Middlesex County	130 731	54 877	15.3	37 947	0.0	8.1	3.6	591 453	66.1	5.2	57.8	14.0	28.2
Monmouth County	120 378	30 358	18.3	29 062	1.0	8.1	2.6	471 156	66.1	4.6	55.7	15.3	29.1
Morris County	84 319	25 292	20.0	20 713	0.0	6.3	1.8	365 030	69.3	3.5	60.1	14.2	25.8
Ocean County	88 689	20 490	18.9	21 495	0.2	10.7	2.8	403 883	55.9	5.1	45.9	14.9	39.3
Passaic County	94 172	25 785	19.3	25 693	0.0	10.8	7.1	374 502	62.1	7.3	55.7	12.5	31.9
Salem County	13 039	2 436	11.2	3 614	0.0	10.2	3.7	49 884	63.1	6.6	53.4	14.2	32.3
Somerset County	54 020	14 627	17.8	11 724	0.0	7.4	2.0	228 283	69.6	3.1	62.1	12.7	25.2
Sussex County	30 665	6 368	11.7	7 179	0.0	8.9	1.5	108 225	70.9	3.5	59.7	15.9	24.4
Union County	96 772	28 216	18.8	24 207	0.0	9.8	3.9	405 859	63.7	5.6	56.5	12.5	31.0
Warren County	19 619	4 235	13.4	4 860	0.0	11.6	2.3	78 515	67.9	3.8	57.7	14.5	27.8
NEW MEXICO	384 924	120 265	9.5	113 028	0.4	11.2	7.5	1 369 176	61.0	7.2	52.2	14.7	33.0
Bernalillo County	102 911	44 365	12.5	31 866	0.5	12.3	7.0	431 799	65.5	5.7	55.5	15.9	28.6
Catron County	583	92	9.3	188	0.0	8.5	13.3	2 921	47.8	8.9	36.7	16.4	46.9
Chaves County	13 835	3 290	8.0	4 460	0.3	10.1	8.2	45 882	55.3	9.0	47.5	13.2	39.3
Cibola County	5 833	1 259	13.9	1 603	0.1	17.2	7.4	18 579	53.0	11.5	48.6	12.8	38.6
Colfax County	2 885	324	6.8	952	0.2	10.8	10.5	11 135	58.1	6.4	48.7	14.2	37.2
Curry County	9 807	3 355	4.1	2 839	7.6	19.2	5.5	32 829	63.1	6.1	53.5	13.5	33.0
De Baca County	439	42	0.4	131	0.0	7.6	3.8	1 786	52.9	5.4	43.0	13.9	43.1
Dona Ana County	39 730	17 779	5.1	12 338	0.1	8.2	6.6	128 197	58.5	9.2	49.7	16.5	33.8
Eddy County	11 526	1 944	7.2	3 339	0.0	11.7	7.7	38 653	57.2	6.8	49.2	13.3	37.5
Grant County	6 107	2 049	6.2	1 799	0.0	13.3	7.1	23 840	52.1	8.0	43.5	13.8	42.7
Guadalupe County	1 017	218	7.9	279	0.0	20.1	5.0	3 676	47.1	7.7	48.0	13.4	38.6
Harding County	151	20	10.5	44	0.0	0.0	6.8	678	55.5	3.2	45.7	13.7	40.6
Hidalgo County	1 499	116	2.7	389	0.0	10.5	6.4	4 280	54.9	9.7	47.3	13.9	38.7
Lea County	13 004	2 754	5.9	4 063	0.1	9.1	7.1	40 893	54.5	9.1	48.9	12.8	38.3
Lincoln County	3 497	746	7.3	950	0.8	13.5	3.9	15 541	57.3	3.9	50.9	15.4	33.7
Los Alamos County	3 656	997	7.1	963	0.0	5.1	3.0	14 191	69.4	2.0	58.3	16.7	25.0
Luna County	5 600	539	1.8	1 570	0.0	10.3	13.1	18 423	46.9	17.1	42.3	11.6	46.1
McKinley County	22 597	3 502	8.5	5 677	0.0	9.0	9.0	49 620	53.4	17.2	48.3	10.0	41.7
Mora County	1 112	212	9.7	348	0.0	12.4	5.7	3 967	49.2	13.1	39.6	13.8	46.6
Otero County	13 944	3 323	6.0	3 602	2.3	14.4	8.9	45 925	59.8	7.1	51.8	12.7	35.5
Quay County	2 062	413	2.2	600	0.0	4.5	9.3	8 005	53.4	5.2	46.1	13.2	40.6
Rio Arriba County	8 918	2 050	11.9	2 409	0.0	8.2	11.7	30 735	58.8	8.2	52.7	11.1	36.2
Roosevelt County	3 739	2 589	4.5	1 397	0.0	9.6	6.2	13 526	61.0	7.8	48.4	18.8	32.7
Sandoval County	20 360	4 415	11.6	5 178	0.0	13.1	7.3	66 064	63.0	6.2	55.4	13.9	30.7
San Juan County	28 682	6 004	5.6	8 335	0.0	10.9	7.7	81 251	60.3	9.1	52.4	13.2	34.4
San Miguel County	6 438	2 723	9.2	2 274	0.0	5.0	3.8	22 856	54.6	8.7	46.0	14.0	39.9
Santa Fe County	23 538	8 294	19.0	6 863	0.0	11.6	8.3	101 952	66.9	4.7	56.8	16.6	26.6
Sierra County	2 156	352	9.2	602	0.0	5.6	8.8	10 983	43.6	6.6	38.3	11.0	50.8
Socorro County	3 840	1 715	5.0	1 361	0.5	11.1	8.1	13 565	57.8	9.1	46.6	16.2	37.3
Taos County	5 752	1 330	12.8	1 664	0.0	17.3	8.2	23 536	63.4	8.9	49.8	18.7	31.5
Torrance County	3 946	569	6.2	968	0.0	10.5	12.1	12 351	58.5	6.0	50.1	14.0	35.9
Union County	977	50	8.0	230	0.0	6.1	0.0	3 161	61.2	1.9	51.6	16.0	32.4
Valencia County	14 783	2 835	8.8	3 747	0.0	10.3	9.3	48 376	60.0	6.3	52.2	13.1	34.7
NEW YORK	3 584 279	1 301 375	21.8	1 017 375	0.3	8.1	5.6	14 805 912	61.1	7.1	51.7	14.1	34.2
Albany County	50 548	28 317	21.0	17 925	0.0	6.4	3.0	235 932	65.8	6.7	54.5	16.5	29.0
Allegany County	9 624	6 015	23.4	4 482	0.0	5.5	2.3	39 335	60.1	9.0	47.6	19.5	32.9
Bronx County	310 307	86 014	21.0	80 832	0.0	7.7	11.1	975 755	51.3	14.3	44.8	10.9	44.3
Broome County	35 644	17 211	8.5	12 657	0.0	7.7	3.0	159 704	60.5	5.4	49.3	17.5	33.2
Cattaraugus County	16 729	4 328	16.7	5 430	0.0	10.3	6.4	64 739	63.1	7.4	50.7	17.0	32.3
Cayuga County	15 927	3 240	10.0	4 806	0.0	10.7	6.1	64 008	61.9	5.1	52.8	15.6	31.6
Chautauqua County	26 607	8 752	6.4	9 278	2.4	8.2	5.8	109 945	61.4	6.3	48.8	18.5	32.7
Chemung County	17 140	4 239	18.3	5 057	0.0	10.2	7.3	71 569	59.5	7.8	50.7	15.5	33.9
Chenango County	10 767	1 583	5.3	2 771	0.0	9.7	5.2	39 535	60.9	5.6	52.5	13.1	34.4
Clinton County	14 676	6 653	7.8	5 362	0.0	7.4	5.4	63 792	58.8	6.2	53.0	16.6	30.4
Columbia County	12 255	2 000	12.9	3 355	0.1	6.4	3.6	49 953	62.0	4.3	52.2	15.5	32.3
Cortland County	8 751	5 898	6.1	3 836	0.1	6.6	2.8	38 421	64.5	8.5	54.9	17.6	27.5
Delaware County	8 884	2 388	5.3	3 127	0.0	7.8	3.1	38 528	57.7	6.2	47.7	15.7	36.6
Dutchess County	53 680	20 086	20.6	16 633	0.1	7.0	5.3	218 021	63.7	5.7	52.9	16.3	30.8
Erie County	176 728	63 289	19.3	50 513	0.0	8.3	4.4	745 814	62.4	7.3	49.0	17.9	33.1
Essex County	7 210	1 200	9.1	1 895	0.0	9.8	4.2	31 099	57.2	6.8	52.6	14.4	33.0
Franklin County	9 270	2 202	11.1	2 877	0.0	8.9	5.0	41 040	54.9	10.6	52.8	12.9	34.3
Fulton County	10 748	1 822	5.2	2 993	0.2	7.4	6.3	43 251	59.9	6.3	51.2	13.5	35.3

STATE County	Full-year full-time employed (percent)								Children under 18 years in families						Total employed by class of worker (percent)			
										With two parents (percent)		With one parent who is in labor force (percent)	+/- U.S. percent of children with no stay-at-home parent (percent)	+/- U.S. percent two-income couples				
	Total	Men	Women	Non-Hispanic White	Black or African American	American Indian and Alaska Native	Asian, Hawaiian, and Pacific Islander	Hispanic or Latino[1]	Number	Both in labor force	Father only in labor force				Private	Government	Self-employed	Unpaid family worker
	24	25	26	27	28	29	30	31	32	33	34	35	36	37	38	39	40	41
NEW JERSEY— Cont'd																		
Mercer County	41.9	50.0	34.5	43.3	38.2	36.2	44.1	38.6	79 045	45.7	21.1	21.2	2.3	4.5	71.8	20.6	7.5	0.2
Middlesex County	44.0	54.5	34.2	43.0	47.5	34.5	46.8	43.9	169 683	48.6	24.7	15.7	-0.3	1.1	79.5	13.6	6.7	0.2
Monmouth County	43.5	57.5	30.8	43.8	38.8	51.8	50.7	41.9	154 636	46.3	31.8	13.3	-5.0	1.1	74.4	14.6	10.7	0.3
Morris County	47.9	61.4	35.4	47.8	50.0	38.2	51.1	46.0	113 808	50.2	33.3	10.5	-3.9	4.4	78.3	10.8	10.7	0.2
Ocean County	35.0	46.8	24.8	34.6	41.1	37.6	41.5	38.6	115 138	45.8	28.7	14.5	-4.3	-8.9	74.5	15.9	9.3	0.3
Passaic County	41.2	51.1	32.2	42.5	38.4	28.8	45.1	39.6	119 380	38.0	21.1	22.1	-4.5	-2.4	79.9	12.1	7.7	0.3
Salem County	40.1	50.6	30.5	41.7	32.0	21.3	45.7	31.0	15 352	45.1	19.4	24.8	5.3	0.4	78.0	14.5	7.2	0.3
Somerset County	49.6	61.7	38.3	49.1	52.5	29.6	53.9	47.8	73 616	50.9	30.5	11.7	-2.0	6.1	79.7	10.6	9.6	0.2
Sussex County	48.0	62.5	34.0	47.8	46.6	34.8	55.5	51.5	39 332	53.1	29.9	10.8	-0.7	7.8	75.8	14.2	9.7	0.3
Union County	42.4	52.2	33.6	42.0	43.2	36.2	47.6	40.8	122 287	43.9	22.4	20.2	-0.5	-0.3	79.2	12.8	7.8	0.2
Warren County	45.9	60.2	32.8	46.1	41.2	13.5	42.6	44.8	25 856	50.4	28.0	15.3	1.1	5.1	76.5	13.7	9.5	0.3
NEW MEXICO	36.4	45.1	28.2	39.1	38.2	28.0	39.7	34.5	475 039	36.6	21.7	24.4	-3.6	-5.8	65.1	22.7	11.8	0.4
Bernalillo County	40.8	50.0	32.3	42.8	43.1	34.9	40.2	38.6	132 101	38.5	20.9	26.1	0.0	-1.2	70.4	18.8	10.5	0.3
Catron County	24.0	30.9	16.8	24.7	0.0	13.7	28.6	20.6	689	35.1	29.0	22.6	-6.9	-20.6	45.4	27.7	25.3	1.7
Chaves County	32.7	43.4	22.9	34.1	26.7	29.3	40.9	30.7	16 462	30.7	26.5	23.1	-10.8	-12.2	68.5	18.0	12.8	0.7
Cibola County	30.6	37.2	24.5	32.9	23.7	28.1	55.8	31.1	7 007	35.4	12.2	26.2	-3.0	-9.3	55.8	34.5	8.8	0.9
Colfax County	32.6	40.9	24.3	34.3	8.1	28.8	42.1	30.9	3 254	45.7	17.4	26.2	7.3	-5.9	58.3	24.1	16.8	0.7
Curry County	39.2	52.6	26.5	40.9	39.0	32.1	40.7	34.8	12 862	37.7	25.3	22.5	-4.4	-5.1	63.0	21.9	14.0	0.4
De Baca County	32.1	43.0	22.2	35.7	X	44.0	100.0	24.4	498	67.3	5.8	15.5	18.2	-5.5	47.6	27.2	24.4	0.8
Dona Ana County	31.6	39.4	24.3	34.0	32.4	31.0	32.3	30.3	48 651	32.2	24.0	23.5	-8.9	-10.7	63.8	25.4	10.4	0.4
Eddy County	34.2	45.7	23.6	35.2	24.9	38.0	49.0	32.5	14 032	36.1	27.0	23.1	-5.4	-10.1	72.0	16.9	10.6	0.5
Grant County	29.2	36.4	22.5	29.8	22.0	31.1	25.5	28.8	7 684	32.4	22.9	26.7	5.5	-15.0	59.9	26.3	13.4	0.5
Guadalupe County	27.7	30.6	24.0	34.3	6.4	24.4	100.0	26.5	1 085	38.1	18.1	20.1	-6.4	-9.8	58.0	32.8	8.9	0.3
Harding County	30.5	38.6	22.4	39.7	X	66.7	X	19.5	160	36.9	21.9	24.4	-3.3	-9.6	32.4	37.4	25.3	4.9
Hidalgo County	29.1	39.1	19.2	30.3	33.3	21.4	0.0	28.1	1 781	32.2	22.0	24.6	-7.8	-13.6	65.5	22.4	11.4	0.8
Lea County	31.6	42.4	21.1	35.7	22.9	23.8	35.7	25.8	15 643	31.5	27.1	19.7	-13.4	-10.8	71.1	16.4	11.8	0.7
Lincoln County	35.1	42.9	27.8	35.7	44.0	51.6	21.3	32.1	4 116	39.1	20.8	24.0	-1.5	-12.1	59.3	17.4	22.2	1.1
Los Alamos County	49.6	64.5	34.5	49.4	32.6	16.5	50.0	51.2	4 692	49.5	35.5	13.1	-2.0	2.8	32.4	58.8	8.7	0.2
Luna County	22.7	29.7	16.3	22.5	17.5	16.0	24.1	23.0	6 858	28.4	20.4	24.7	-11.5	-22.6	63.0	24.6	11.5	0.9
McKinley County	28.3	32.0	24.9	42.7	27.2	23.4	51.5	37.0	25 837	29.4	14.0	26.9	-8.3	-14.0	53.2	37.2	9.2	0.4
Mora County	21.9	27.9	15.8	26.3	0.0	3.1	X	21.0	1 278	33.4	12.8	30.1	-1.1	-21.2	48.1	36.2	12.5	3.2
Otero County	36.1	48.1	24.6	37.6	46.4	32.8	34.0	32.9	17 285	36.1	26.6	22.7	-5.8	-9.8	58.1	29.3	12.0	0.5
Quay County	32.8	41.4	25.2	33.8	57.4	26.8	37.2	30.5	2 338	44.6	14.9	22.5	2.5	-5.9	54.6	24.2	19.8	1.4
Rio Arriba County	37.2	41.7	32.7	39.5	39.0	38.7	46.8	36.3	11 011	35.1	15.4	27.9	-1.6	-7.1	53.3	37.0	9.4	0.4
Roosevelt County	31.9	43.3	21.5	32.9	53.8	17.3	35.2	28.6	4 767	40.5	23.4	19.0	-5.1	-5.6	58.9	27.3	13.3	0.5
Sandoval County	42.1	52.0	33.0	45.2	43.9	27.2	44.3	43.8	25 258	40.4	22.0	21.2	-3.0	-1.6	70.5	19.2	10.1	0.2
San Juan County	35.1	44.5	26.1	39.9	38.9	27.3	50.5	37.1	34 565	37.2	23.9	22.8	-4.6	-7.1	70.2	20.1	9.3	0.4
San Miguel County	28.8	32.8	25.0	30.2	19.0	16.1	24.6	28.8	7 562	36.5	15.4	27.6	-0.5	-5.0	50.3	35.8	13.2	0.6
Santa Fe County	39.9	47.6	32.7	42.0	46.4	34.6	42.6	37.5	29 294	42.6	17.2	24.5	2.5	2.2	58.8	23.4	17.3	0.5
Sierra County	25.2	29.2	21.3	22.9	27.8	35.4	33.3	33.0	2 381	45.0	17.1	22.3	2.7	-19.4	56.6	24.2	18.0	1.2
Socorro County	31.4	37.8	24.9	35.3	9.1	11.2	26.8	32.9	4 698	28.0	18.9	31.1	-5.5	-7.8	52.8	35.0	11.8	0.4
Taos County	30.0	34.8	25.6	31.4	9.1	28.1	22.9	29.4	6 927	37.5	14.4	31.3	4.2	-3.1	59.9	19.2	20.3	0.6
Torrance County	32.5	40.6	23.8	35.3	5.3	18.7	20.8	29.5	4 789	37.8	28.7	21.7	-5.1	-8.5	61.6	21.4	16.1	0.9
Union County	37.3	50.3	24.8	39.8	X	81.3	0.0	32.1	1 125	44.1	23.1	21.3	0.8	-0.3	55.1	23.0	21.0	1.0
Valencia County	36.8	45.0	28.6	38.6	36.5	42.5	31.0	35.2	18 349	37.9	24.8	22.6	-4.1	-7.7	68.7	20.9	9.9	0.4
NEW YORK	38.2	47.1	30.1	40.3	34.5	33.0	36.9	32.6	4 383 249	38.9	22.1	21.7	-4.0	-2.8	73.4	17.0	9.4	0.2
Albany County	42.1	50.7	34.5	43.4	36.0	23.6	34.8	35.9	62 851	48.3	16.5	24.4	8.1	5.6	64.7	27.9	7.3	0.1
Allegany County	31.0	39.3	22.8	31.5	12.1	24.0	17.0	16.0	11 563	49.4	21.6	18.6	3.4	-3.4	70.8	18.4	10.2	0.6
Bronx County	29.7	35.9	24.7	30.6	32.0	23.0	33.7	27.2	356 320	18.6	12.3	32.2	-13.8	-14.8	74.0	20.3	5.5	0.2
Broome County	37.0	46.0	28.9	37.9	33.7	22.4	22.4	24.7	43 833	47.9	18.5	23.1	6.4	-0.1	73.5	18.9	7.4	0.2
Cattaraugus County	37.1	46.3	28.7	37.5	24.7	32.4	38.7	32.2	20 665	48.6	19.1	21.4	5.4	-0.1	72.9	17.3	9.1	0.7
Cayuga County	38.7	47.1	30.3	40.5	15.1	18.7	27.4	19.4	19 496	49.7	17.3	24.0	9.1	3.9	71.8	17.9	9.9	0.3
Chautauqua County	35.4	45.7	26.0	36.1	20.6	39.4	26.0	25.4	32 259	47.8	18.4	22.0	5.2	0.4	73.7	16.1	9.9	0.4
Chemung County	37.7	45.6	30.1	39.3	20.8	16.1	35.4	20.6	20 884	45.2	16.2	27.3	7.9	0.5	74.4	18.0	7.3	0.3
Chenango County	39.5	47.7	31.7	39.9	15.7	22.5	51.0	29.8	12 764	47.9	17.8	22.7	6.0	-0.1	70.8	17.2	11.5	0.5
Clinton County	38.1	46.8	29.1	38.7	33.2	30.7	30.5	32.6	17 392	49.5	17.4	23.2	8.1	0.7	65.3	25.0	9.2	0.5
Columbia County	39.9	48.7	31.4	40.8	29.9	39.6	38.8	26.4	14 056	49.6	18.7	20.6	5.6	2.2	65.5	19.3	14.8	0.4
Cortland County	37.7	46.0	30.2	38.1	25.1	20.0	22.1	28.2	10 820	48.8	15.5	25.7	9.9	4.0	70.3	20.2	8.9	0.5
Delaware County	34.2	42.9	25.9	34.4	19.7	46.9	29.9	32.5	10 382	48.9	17.5	20.4	4.7	-4.3	60.6	22.9	15.7	0.7
Dutchess County	40.7	50.7	30.8	41.5	35.4	27.1	42.6	38.0	66 386	48.3	25.6	17.0	0.7	2.2	72.6	17.9	9.3	0.3
Erie County	37.4	47.5	28.5	39.1	28.7	34.3	30.2	27.9	220 824	46.4	17.8	23.1	4.9	0.6	75.4	17.4	6.9	0.2
Essex County	37.0	44.7	28.5	37.3	33.1	28.4	42.1	30.9	8 377	54.0	16.5	21.0	10.4	-1.1	63.7	24.2	12.0	0.2
Franklin County	36.9	42.8	29.5	37.2	35.5	37.6	20.0	31.6	11 018	47.4	16.3	25.2	8.0	0.1	58.9	30.0	10.7	0.3
Fulton County	38.8	46.7	31.4	39.0	32.8	43.8	52.8	25.4	12 584	45.9	16.0	26.9	8.2	-2.9	74.5	16.1	9.2	0.2

[1] Hispanic or Latino persons may be of any race.

				Occupation for employed population 16 years and over (percent)						Industry for employed population 16 years and over (percent)					
STATE County	Percent who worked at home	Percent of the population 5 years and over with a disability	Veterans as a percent of the population 18 years and over	Management, professional, and related occupations	Service occupa- tions	Sales and office occupa- tions	Farming, fishing, and forestry occupa- tions	Con- struction, extraction, and main- tenance occupa- tions	Production, transporta- tion and material moving occupa- tions	Agricul- ture, forestry, fishing, and mining	Construc- tion and manufac- turing	Whole- sale and retail trade	Trans- porta- tion and ware- housing, and utilities	Service industries	Public adminis- tration
	42	43	44	45	46	47	48	49	50	51	52	53	54	55	56
NEW JERSEY— Cont'd															
Mercer County............	3.2	17.1	10.4	43.2	14.3	26.5	0.2	6.1	9.7	0.3	14.2	12.0	3.8	59.2	10.4
Middlesex County........	2.1	16.2	9.7	40.6	11.0	28.4	0.1	7.1	12.8	0.1	18.2	15.9	6.7	55.6	3.5
Monmouth County........	3.3	14.9	11.9	41.8	12.4	29.4	0.2	7.7	8.4	0.4	14.7	15.8	5.4	58.4	5.4
Morris County............	3.7	13.6	10.3	47.7	10.1	27.4	0.1	6.6	8.1	0.2	20.2	14.4	4.2	57.9	3.0
Ocean County	2.5	20.1	16.3	31.6	16.0	29.2	0.2	11.8	11.1	0.4	16.6	17.9	6.2	53.1	5.8
Passaic County	2.1	21.7	8.1	30.0	14.5	28.6	0.1	8.3	18.4	0.2	23.3	17.8	5.4	50.1	3.3
Salem County	2.2	20.2	14.7	28.4	15.0	24.8	0.8	11.4	19.7	1.9	22.8	16.5	10.0	44.2	4.6
Somerset County	3.6	12.6	9.6	50.3	9.3	25.4	0.2	6.1	8.7	0.4	20.7	13.6	3.8	58.8	2.8
Sussex County	3.4	13.5	11.9	37.0	12.0	28.6	0.2	10.7	11.4	0.9	21.6	17.3	5.5	50.2	4.5
Union County	2.4	18.1	9.5	35.4	13.3	28.4	0.1	7.6	15.3	0.1	20.0	14.9	7.5	53.8	3.8
Warren County	3.3	16.4	13.4	34.8	13.8	27.1	0.4	10.9	13.1	1.2	23.4	16.3	5.4	49.0	4.7
NEW MEXICO........	4.2	20.4	14.5	34.0	17.0	25.9	1.0	11.4	10.7	4.0	14.5	14.9	4.7	53.9	8.0
Bernalillo County	3.8	19.7	15.1	37.9	15.6	28.3	0.1	8.8	9.2	0.4	14.8	15.4	4.1	59.4	5.9
Catron County	14.4	21.2	21.1	31.0	15.8	22.0	5.2	15.5	10.4	19.8	19.9	10.9	3.9	38.5	6.9
Chaves County	3.4	22.4	14.5	27.6	16.2	24.9	4.4	11.1	15.8	9.9	16.5	15.8	5.3	47.8	4.7
Cibola County	3.8	21.3	14.8	29.6	23.8	21.2	1.1	12.6	11.7	5.1	15.2	12.1	4.5	50.8	12.3
Colfax County	5.5	19.3	17.9	29.6	19.3	22.4	2.8	14.3	11.6	8.5	14.7	12.1	4.6	51.2	8.7
Curry County	3.1	21.0	15.8	27.4	18.2	27.3	2.3	11.5	13.2	5.9	11.7	18.1	7.5	48.8	8.0
De Baca County	5.5	24.9	16.5	32.7	17.1	19.3	6.8	12.8	11.3	19.6	11.1	12.2	8.7	40.2	8.2
Dona Ana County........	3.5	19.8	12.5	32.3	18.3	25.1	1.8	11.0	11.6	3.7	15.0	14.2	4.5	54.2	8.4
Eddy County	2.8	22.3	13.4	25.1	17.1	24.9	2.1	16.4	14.4	14.3	13.1	15.9	5.3	46.2	5.3
Grant County..............	5.4	21.5	17.3	29.9	19.7	21.8	0.6	16.4	11.6	14.2	10.8	12.1	4.6	53.4	5.0
Guadalupe County	2.5	25.2	14.4	26.3	30.1	19.3	1.0	13.1	10.1	5.3	12.3	11.1	5.1	55.3	10.8
Harding County	13.9	25.3	18.1	39.6	14.6	15.7	13.2	11.8	5.2	32.1	9.9	4.9	3.8	35.2	14.0
Hidalgo County	2.0	24.4	13.6	20.5	22.5	20.8	4.6	17.4	14.2	14.7	13.4	14.6	6.1	42.5	8.7
Lea County	2.7	21.5	11.7	25.1	16.2	23.1	1.6	18.4	15.7	20.7	9.8	15.2	6.7	42.6	5.1
Lincoln County	6.2	21.1	18.8	27.9	19.6	27.8	1.8	13.8	9.1	4.5	14.3	17.1	4.3	54.4	5.5
Los Alamos County......	4.0	11.3	15.8	68.4	9.2	14.8	0.1	4.2	3.4	0.1	4.1	5.5	0.8	46.9	42.6
Luna County	2.7	24.7	15.9	22.7	23.5	20.9	3.1	13.8	16.0	6.9	17.9	13.4	5.3	47.2	9.3
McKinley County	5.8	20.6	9.4	32.4	16.6	24.8	0.7	12.0	13.5	2.3	13.6	16.8	4.3	53.5	9.5
Mora County................	4.2	23.1	15.0	28.2	22.5	18.1	6.5	16.8	7.9	12.9	12.6	8.0	6.3	51.7	8.4
Otero County	3.2	20.2	20.6	28.3	18.8	22.4	1.1	16.3	13.1	3.1	16.8	13.9	5.5	48.4	12.3
Quay County	5.4	27.5	17.3	29.7	18.7	26.4	3.0	13.4	8.9	11.7	8.7	18.2	6.6	47.5	7.3
Rio Arriba County	4.6	24.5	12.6	29.9	21.1	24.7	1.5	13.4	9.4	4.2	14.2	11.2	3.7	50.3	16.4
Roosevelt County..........	4.2	19.7	12.2	34.6	14.3	23.6	5.4	9.1	12.9	11.3	10.5	14.7	4.8	52.4	6.3
Sandoval County	4.3	18.7	15.9	36.0	14.8	27.8	0.3	10.4	10.8	0.8	21.3	15.3	4.7	50.4	7.4
San Juan County	3.0	20.3	12.8	25.2	16.6	25.7	0.7	17.3	14.5	10.8	12.8	16.8	8.3	46.0	5.3
San Miguel County........	3.5	23.9	12.9	34.1	21.6	25.3	0.8	11.1	7.1	2.8	10.9	14.7	3.3	57.9	10.3
Santa Fe County	7.4	17.6	12.6	41.7	16.4	25.5	0.2	9.7	6.4	0.9	12.6	13.7	2.3	57.6	12.9
Sierra County	6.6	32.2	24.1	26.8	22.7	21.7	3.2	16.3	9.4	8.3	14.3	13.3	4.0	53.0	7.0
Socorro County	4.1	21.4	14.8	36.6	17.8	20.1	2.8	14.0	8.8	6.3	13.6	10.2	3.9	57.4	8.6
Taos County	7.0	21.1	14.1	31.5	22.4	24.9	1.2	12.8	7.2	4.4	13.3	14.4	3.0	58.4	6.5
Torrance County	5.0	24.5	17.4	30.3	17.3	21.6	1.7	15.0	14.2	5.8	17.8	16.7	7.9	43.9	7.9
Union County	8.6	19.0	12.7	32.3	16.3	20.9	10.0	9.6	11.0	25.7	8.9	14.1	7.8	37.5	6.1
Valencia County	3.9	21.0	16.0	26.9	17.3	25.7	0.6	14.3	15.1	1.2	18.9	16.2	7.7	48.4	7.6
NEW YORK..............	3.0	20.6	9.5	36.7	16.6	27.1	0.3	7.6	11.7	0.6	15.2	13.8	5.5	59.7	5.2
Albany County	2.6	17.9	12.2	42.3	13.9	28.9	0.1	6.2	8.6	0.3	10.1	13.0	4.3	56.9	15.3
Allegany County	4.1	19.3	14.3	31.3	17.6	21.4	1.9	9.8	18.0	3.8	23.0	12.5	4.0	53.1	3.6
Bronx County	1.9	28.4	5.8	26.6	24.5	28.9	0.1	7.7	12.3	0.1	10.7	12.8	6.8	64.4	5.2
Broome County	2.5	19.0	13.8	34.6	16.2	27.1	0.3	7.0	14.9	0.6	22.4	15.7	4.8	52.2	4.3
Cattaraugus County	3.4	19.7	15.6	27.4	17.5	23.3	1.3	9.5	21.1	2.9	24.8	15.3	4.8	47.3	4.7
Cayuga County	3.4	19.6	14.3	27.8	17.9	23.1	1.6	9.9	19.6	3.9	24.7	15.3	5.1	43.7	7.2
Chautauqua County	3.3	20.3	14.7	27.2	18.2	23.4	1.2	8.6	21.5	2.7	26.6	14.5	4.8	47.7	3.7
Chemung County	2.3	21.1	15.6	32.0	19.2	25.2	0.3	7.4	15.9	0.6	24.0	15.6	4.2	48.8	6.7
Chenango County	4.5	22.2	15.6	29.5	15.0	22.8	1.8	11.0	19.9	3.9	27.7	13.2	4.2	46.6	4.4
Clinton County	3.2	19.5	13.6	28.9	21.6	24.3	1.0	8.4	15.8	2.4	19.3	14.8	5.9	45.9	11.6
Columbia County..........	5.1	18.8	15.1	33.6	16.8	23.5	1.5	10.8	13.8	3.1	19.2	13.4	4.6	51.9	7.8
Cortland County	4.5	17.8	12.5	31.6	17.6	23.4	1.6	8.9	16.9	3.5	22.9	13.6	2.9	52.8	4.4
Delaware County..........	5.7	22.4	15.0	31.6	16.9	20.4	2.4	10.9	17.9	6.2	22.2	12.7	3.7	49.4	5.9
Dutchess County..........	3.2	16.3	12.6	38.4	15.6	25.3	0.4	10.1	10.2	1.0	19.1	13.9	4.9	55.6	5.5
Erie County	2.1	19.2	13.4	34.7	15.6	28.1	0.2	6.8	14.6	0.3	18.9	16.1	5.2	54.7	4.8
Essex County	4.8	21.8	16.9	29.1	23.1	21.1	1.2	11.9	13.7	2.4	19.5	12.6	3.1	53.2	9.1
Franklin County	4.4	23.9	12.8	29.1	23.8	21.7	1.8	10.4	13.1	4.4	16.1	13.1	3.6	50.3	12.5
Fulton County	2.8	21.0	15.1	26.5	16.0	24.5	0.5	10.5	22.1	1.6	27.7	14.7	4.2	46.9	4.9

STATE County	Median house-hold income	Median family income				Median nonfamily house-hold income	Median income for full-year, full-time workers		Per capita income	Households by source of income (percent)					House-holds with income over $100,000 (percent)	+/- U.S. percent for income over $100,000 (percent)	House-holds with income below poverty (percent)	Families with children with income below poverty (percent)
		All families	Families with children				Men	Women		With earnings	With interest, dividend, or rental income	With Social Security income	With public assis-tance income	With retire-ment income				
			Married-couple	Male house-holder	Female house-holder													
	57	58	59	60	61	62	63	64	65	66	67	68	69	70	71	72	73	74
NEW JERSEY— Cont'd																		
Mercer County	56 613	68 494	83 836	35 625	26 746	31 972	49 699	35 667	27 914	81.5	44.5	25.7	2.7	18.1	23.0	10.7	8.6	8.9
Middlesex County	61 446	70 749	79 453	39 430	31 342	35 748	50 592	35 879	26 535	84.0	45.1	25.2	1.9	17.0	22.9	10.6	6.1	6.0
Monmouth County	64 271	76 823	89 172	40 768	26 993	34 117	57 650	36 475	31 149	82.9	47.7	25.8	1.8	17.7	27.9	15.6	6.3	6.6
Morris County	77 340	89 773	99 460	46 012	38 837	42 476	61 463	41 244	36 964	87.2	55.2	22.7	1.0	16.1	35.8	23.5	3.6	3.3
Ocean County	46 443	56 420	67 280	36 752	26 302	24 997	46 221	31 564	23 054	68.0	47.3	41.4	1.9	27.1	13.2	0.9	6.5	7.9
Passaic County	49 210	56 054	65 562	30 801	21 633	28 203	40 188	30 621	21 370	81.4	36.7	26.6	4.0	14.3	17.3	5.0	11.0	14.1
Salem County	45 573	54 890	66 384	32 708	20 457	23 878	42 790	28 096	20 874	78.0	37.7	30.4	3.0	22.8	10.7	-1.6	9.1	10.9
Somerset County	76 933	90 605	104 295	51 182	41 667	45 110	61 721	43 690	37 970	87.5	55.4	21.3	1.2	15.7	35.9	23.6	3.5	3.3
Sussex County	65 266	73 335	77 836	42 358	29 529	35 248	51 174	34 888	26 992	87.8	44.3	21.1	1.7	14.0	23.5	11.2	4.4	3.9
Union County	55 339	65 234	79 268	32 363	27 296	29 662	46 183	34 053	26 992	81.0	42.6	27.7	3.1	17.5	22.1	9.8	8.3	9.2
Warren County	56 100	66 223	75 047	38 676	26 458	29 867	49 068	32 438	25 728	82.8	44.6	26.5	2.2	17.4	18.3	6.0	6.0	5.3
NEW MEXICO	34 133	39 425	46 011	23 054	16 453	21 791	32 232	24 532	17 261	79.5	30.2	25.5	4.7	17.4	7.6	-4.7	16.8	20.8
Bernalillo County	38 788	46 613	56 270	25 849	19 237	25 712	35 531	27 050	20 790	82.5	35.9	23.0	3.9	17.6	10.3	-2.0	12.7	15.4
Catron County	23 892	30 742	33 400	25 000	10 278	12 632	27 071	18 594	13 951	65.8	29.7	38.9	4.4	22.8	2.6	-9.7	22.2	32.7
Chaves County	28 513	32 532	37 091	22 500	14 386	17 370	27 971	21 855	14 990	74.5	28.2	32.9	6.2	17.1	4.9	-7.4	19.1	26.1
Cibola County	27 774	30 714	37 632	13 775	17 787	15 880	28 750	20 769	11 731	77.4	16.5	26.5	5.9	16.5	2.8	-9.5	23.4	28.5
Colfax County	30 744	36 827	43 667	20 227	14 808	19 235	28 750	20 908	16 418	73.2	30.8	35.3	4.2	23.1	4.9	-7.4	14.1	19.7
Curry County	28 917	33 900	37 708	22 917	15 890	16 330	26 300	20 237	15 049	79.3	23.6	25.8	5.8	15.2	4.6	-7.7	17.9	22.3
De Baca County	25 441	32 870	39 464	21 250	11 667	14 205	29 333	18 958	14 065	67.2	30.2	43.6	2.3	20.5	2.6	-9.7	19.2	25.1
Dona Ana County	29 808	33 576	37 345	18 377	13 900	18 022	28 098	21 639	13 999	80.5	26.6	24.1	6.0	17.6	5.3	-7.0	22.3	28.9
Eddy County	31 998	36 789	42 980	20 453	16 422	16 818	32 917	20 563	15 823	75.6	26.1	30.3	4.5	16.1	5.0	-7.3	16.7	19.0
Grant County	29 134	34 231	40 867	23 516	12 775	16 336	31 890	20 327	14 597	71.4	28.1	34.9	6.0	23.3	4.1	-8.2	17.3	24.0
Guadalupe County	24 783	28 279	40 893	13 958	13 929	9 826	23 966	18 696	11 241	71.3	17.3	32.6	5.9	16.6	1.2	-11.1	25.2	23.5
Harding County	26 111	36 667	34 375	22 500	8 750	16 786	28 875	16 154	16 240	67.2	35.0	54.1	4.1	21.6	4.1	-8.2	16.9	30.7
Hidalgo County	24 819	31 552	36 917	15 179	13 317	13 640	26 729	19 770	12 431	74.1	18.6	30.9	7.1	15.9	3.8	-8.5	25.4	31.5
Lea County	29 799	34 665	39 230	23 160	11 613	15 613	32 834	21 839	14 184	75.7	23.2	29.9	6.1	13.4	4.5	-7.8	19.9	24.1
Lincoln County	33 886	40 035	42 428	22 159	15 852	20 250	30 122	21 085	19 338	76.2	36.9	34.3	3.2	22.8	7.8	-4.5	12.8	20.2
Los Alamos County	70 933	90 052	85 526	38 542	38 938	44 375	72 204	41 512	34 646	87.1	65.6	19.1	0.5	22.5	34.1	21.8	3.9	2.0
Luna County	20 784	24 252	26 862	15 625	10 456	12 408	26 008	17 594	11 218	64.9	22.7	40.4	7.4	19.8	2.2	-10.1	28.9	39.9
McKinley County	25 005	26 806	35 628	15 965	15 073	13 271	27 329	21 501	9 872	78.0	11.9	18.4	9.9	10.1	3.6	-8.7	33.1	36.7
Mora County	24 518	27 648	35 948	25 673	13 984	11 417	25 116	19 451	12 340	66.7	22.5	36.9	7.4	15.9	3.7	-8.6	27.4	27.5
Otero County	30 861	34 781	38 933	24 141	12 293	20 231	29 308	19 270	14 345	77.1	28.8	26.2	4.4	22.8	3.3	-9.0	17.1	22.7
Quay County	24 894	30 362	36 723	18 021	15 326	12 433	25 884	18 303	14 938	69.4	29.0	39.9	4.2	17.4	3.0	-9.3	20.9	22.5
Rio Arriba County	29 429	32 901	42 987	21 503	17 715	17 063	27 365	22 816	14 263	76.5	15.3	27.4	3.5	17.2	4.5	-7.8	20.7	20.3
Roosevelt County	26 586	31 813	37 750	27 667	14 632	13 528	27 085	21 196	14 185	77.5	25.5	27.5	4.2	15.2	4.3	-8.0	23.8	22.1
Sandoval County	44 949	48 984	55 986	31 603	22 534	28 362	38 266	27 200	19 174	82.0	33.0	23.1	3.9	19.9	9.2	-3.1	10.2	12.4
San Juan County	33 762	37 382	42 560	22 512	14 472	19 671	35 616	21 822	14 282	81.5	20.6	22.5	4.3	13.6	5.5	-6.8	19.9	23.1
San Miguel County	26 524	31 250	40 472	15 455	16 283	15 583	29 236	23 197	13 268	74.7	20.5	27.8	8.0	18.0	3.9	-8.4	24.2	25.4
Santa Fe County	42 207	50 000	55 100	25 349	21 926	31 197	35 683	29 122	23 594	82.8	38.8	22.3	2.6	16.9	13.0	0.7	11.5	13.4
Sierra County	24 152	29 787	36 482	23 750	11 184	13 588	25 645	20 818	15 023	57.1	32.7	47.2	5.0	25.6	3.1	-9.2	20.2	25.0
Socorro County	23 439	29 544	43 472	18 447	10 089	12 557	30 133	23 684	12 026	74.8	25.1	25.3	9.0	15.0	4.5	-7.8	29.3	35.3
Taos County	26 762	33 995	42 859	21 422	15 883	15 987	29 151	21 812	16 103	78.3	24.9	26.5	3.8	14.5	5.1	-7.2	22.3	21.2
Torrance County	30 446	34 461	39 330	21 736	13 700	16 224	30 075	23 002	14 134	79.4	25.2	28.4	6.2	17.1	4.1	-8.2	18.1	21.6
Union County	28 080	35 313	39 023	21 250	11 719	18 500	28 913	18 750	14 700	75.9	33.9	32.8	3.8	15.5	2.8	-9.5	15.8	24.1
Valencia County	34 099	37 157	41 801	26 331	16 773	20 860	31 041	23 992	14 747	80.2	23.9	25.6	4.7	17.8	4.5	-7.8	15.0	18.7
NEW YORK	43 393	51 691	63 281	30 373	18 992	27 073	41 188	31 800	23 389	78.1	36.5	26.0	4.9	16.9	15.3	3.0	13.9	16.9
Albany County	42 935	56 724	70 705	29 943	20 443	26 924	40 866	30 959	23 345	78.8	45.4	27.3	3.3	20.1	12.6	0.3	10.7	11.7
Allegany County	32 106	38 580	43 889	25 063	14 867	17 262	31 197	22 277	14 975	75.1	35.3	32.9	4.4	22.1	4.2	-8.1	15.3	17.2
Bronx County	27 611	30 682	44 125	25 762	12 471	18 481	31 580	30 075	13 959	70.5	16.4	22.3	14.6	12.1	6.1	-6.2	29.0	36.5
Broome County	35 347	45 424	55 479	26 891	17 863	20 050	35 662	25 513	19 168	74.8	43.5	31.7	3.6	23.7	7.8	-4.5	12.8	14.4
Cattaraugus County	33 404	39 318	47 327	23 258	16 023	19 056	31 563	22 882	15 959	76.5	36.5	31.4	3.4	20.4	4.6	-7.7	12.3	16.0
Cayuga County	37 487	44 973	54 651	28 872	18 197	20 057	35 358	24 894	18 003	76.7	35.9	31.3	2.4	21.4	6.1	-6.2	10.8	12.5
Chautauqua County	33 458	41 054	48 644	25 487	15 030	18 661	33 111	22 967	16 840	75.8	40.6	32.2	3.9	20.7	5.6	-6.7	12.8	16.9
Chemung County	36 415	43 994	54 236	24 572	17 369	20 398	35 700	25 512	18 264	75.1	38.0	32.2	3.4	23.2	6.6	-5.7	12.9	15.5
Chenango County	33 679	39 711	46 457	21 466	16 064	20 388	31 204	23 271	16 427	76.9	37.2	31.7	2.4	21.5	5.1	-7.2	12.9	17.4
Clinton County	37 028	45 732	55 709	24 577	17 423	19 973	35 551	26 230	17 946	78.4	33.9	27.7	2.8	21.3	6.1	-6.2	14.3	13.8
Columbia County	41 915	49 357	57 025	30 339	20 382	25 444	36 325	27 124	22 265	78.1	44.7	32.4	2.2	22.1	10.5	-1.8	8.9	10.6
Cortland County	34 364	42 204	50 028	25 506	17 098	19 513	31 583	22 952	16 622	80.4	34.6	27.2	3.5	17.5	5.6	-6.7	15.3	14.1
Delaware County	32 461	39 695	46 425	21 987	15 521	19 927	29 519	23 164	17 357	73.0	41.7	37.6	2.4	24.0	5.6	-6.7	12.5	15.2
Dutchess County	53 086	63 254	73 948	35 745	24 280	29 105	46 929	31 523	23 940	81.7	44.8	26.9	2.1	22.0	17.2	4.9	7.5	7.6
Erie County	38 567	49 490	62 283	30 056	16 904	21 464	40 059	27 333	20 357	74.7	42.7	30.8	4.5	21.2	9.4	-2.9	12.3	15.2
Essex County	34 823	41 927	50 203	28 935	15 669	20 120	31 916	22 987	18 194	76.6	30.9	33.6	3.1	24.3	5.2	-7.1	11.4	12.6
Franklin County	31 517	38 472	46 755	25 179	20 506	17 494	30 117	22 982	15 888	76.3	26.9	30.4	3.5	20.6	4.4	-7.9	14.2	14.7
Fulton County	33 663	39 801	47 063	27 330	17 014	19 236	30 558	23 191	16 844	74.2	37.1	34.6	3.6	22.0	4.7	-7.6	11.6	14.8

STATE/ County code	MSA/PMSA/ NECMA code[1]	STATE County	Total population 25 years and over	Percent with a high school diploma or less	Percent with a high school diploma or more	Percent with a bachelor's degree or more	+/− U.S. percent with bachelor's degree or more	Non-Hispanic White	Black or African American	American Indian and Alaska Native	Asian, Hawaiian, and Pacific Islander	Hispanic or Latino[2]
			1	2	3	4	5	6	7	8	9	10
		NEW YORK—Cont'd										
36 037	6840	Genesee County	40 125	53.7	84.4	16.3	−8.1	16.6	2.8	7.8	39.3	8.6
36 039	...	Greene County	32 570	57.9	78.6	16.4	−8.0	17.1	5.7	1.9	27.8	5.0
36 041	...	Hamilton County	4 022	53.9	83.4	18.4	−6.0	18.7	0.0	10.0	0.0	0.0
36 043	8680	Herkimer County	43 455	56.0	79.4	15.7	−8.7	15.5	7.7	11.9	48.6	23.2
36 045	...	Jefferson County	68 965	53.4	82.9	16.0	−8.4	16.5	6.5	9.1	23.9	13.0
36 047	5600	Kings County	1 552 870	57.9	68.8	21.8	−2.6	33.7	14.4	13.5	23.5	8.5
36 049	...	Lewis County	17 367	67.1	81.0	11.7	−12.7	11.7	10.6	11.7	35.3	11.1
36 051	6840	Livingston County	40 081	51.5	82.3	19.2	−5.2	20.0	3.8	12.9	36.0	4.7
36 053	8160	Madison County	43 762	49.8	83.3	21.6	−2.8	21.7	9.9	10.0	46.5	18.2
36 055	6840	Monroe County	477 957	41.3	84.9	31.2	6.8	34.2	11.4	15.7	53.7	13.3
36 057	0160	Montgomery County	33 900	61.1	78.1	13.6	−10.8	13.8	4.1	26.9	52.8	4.4
36 059	5380	Nassau County	908 693	40.1	86.7	35.4	11.0	37.7	23.7	13.9	57.4	15.4
36 061	5600	New York County	1 125 987	34.8	78.7	49.4	25.0	73.9	18.9	19.2	45.3	14.0
36 063	1280	Niagara County	147 153	53.7	83.3	17.4	−7.0	17.8	8.0	14.7	46.7	19.2
36 065	8680	Oneida County	158 846	53.5	79.0	18.3	−6.1	19.3	5.9	4.3	27.9	6.5
36 067	8160	Onondaga County	296 914	43.4	85.7	28.5	4.1	29.5	10.5	19.7	55.8	23.3
36 069	6840	Ontario County	66 539	44.2	87.4	24.7	0.3	25.0	10.5	13.1	51.7	13.3
36 071	5660	Orange County	212 816	49.2	81.8	22.5	−1.9	24.1	13.4	11.2	50.3	11.6
36 073	6840	Orleans County	29 043	63.2	76.4	13.0	−11.4	14.1	2.5	4.6	20.7	5.5
36 075	8160	Oswego County	76 165	60.8	80.4	14.4	−10.0	14.2	28.3	18.9	46.5	14.0
36 077	...	Otsego County	38 808	51.7	83.0	22.0	−2.4	21.8	30.0	23.3	57.2	22.5
36 079	5600	Putnam County	64 624	37.9	90.2	33.9	9.5	34.3	33.1	36.9	64.3	22.6
36 081	5600	Queens County	1 509 502	53.4	74.4	24.3	−0.1	29.2	17.8	14.1	37.6	11.6
36 083	0160	Rensselaer County	100 233	47.6	84.9	23.7	−0.7	23.5	17.1	24.6	71.3	21.2
36 085	5600	Richmond County	293 795	51.1	82.6	23.2	−1.2	23.2	18.7	8.9	46.8	13.0
36 087	5600	Rockland County	184 012	37.2	85.3	37.5	13.1	40.5	22.2	18.2	58.5	16.8
36 089	...	St. Lawrence County	70 201	58.5	79.2	16.4	−8.0	16.7	4.2	15.5	60.6	4.5
36 091	0160	Saratoga County	135 015	40.8	88.2	30.9	6.5	30.6	20.9	16.4	63.0	38.8
36 093	0160	Schenectady County	99 568	46.1	84.8	26.3	1.9	26.8	12.8	16.4	62.0	13.2
36 095	0160	Schoharie County	20 695	56.4	81.7	17.3	−7.1	17.5	8.5	0.0	20.0	21.2
36 097	...	Schuyler County	12 842	57.5	82.4	15.5	−8.9	15.5	9.6	28.3	29.4	19.1
36 099	...	Seneca County	22 585	56.6	79.1	17.5	−6.9	17.8	7.5	23.4	31.6	6.7
36 101	...	Steuben County	65 765	54.5	82.8	17.9	−6.5	17.3	28.2	11.7	67.0	29.8
36 103	5380	Suffolk County	942 401	45.1	86.2	27.5	3.1	29.1	16.5	23.0	56.7	12.0
36 105	...	Sullivan County	50 228	57.7	76.2	16.7	−7.7	18.1	6.6	4.1	38.1	8.7
36 107	0960	Tioga County	34 223	52.6	84.8	19.7	−4.7	19.5	26.7	19.3	42.6	21.6
36 109	...	Tompkins County	53 075	30.9	91.4	47.5	23.1	45.0	37.7	45.4	87.9	61.2
36 111	...	Ulster County	120 670	48.3	81.7	25.0	0.6	26.3	11.5	16.7	51.6	12.1
36 113	2975	Warren County	43 364	49.0	84.6	23.2	−1.2	23.2	26.3	8.8	45.2	17.4
36 115	2975	Washington County	40 957	61.1	79.2	14.3	−10.1	14.8	2.0	22.3	14.5	3.5
36 117	6840	Wayne County	61 731	53.9	82.3	17.0	−7.4	17.7	3.1	7.4	20.0	5.7
36 119	5600	Westchester County	628 941	38.5	83.6	40.9	16.5	47.5	22.6	17.1	65.7	16.3
36 121	...	Wyoming County	29 522	63.4	75.6	11.5	−12.9	12.6	0.3	24.4	43.8	1.9
36 123	...	Yates County	15 714	56.2	80.0	18.2	−6.2	18.4	3.4	36.7	60.0	1.3
37 000	...	**NORTH CAROLINA ...**	5 282 994	50.3	78.1	22.5	−1.9	25.2	13.1	10.4	43.0	10.5
37 001	3120	Alamance County	86 635	54.6	76.5	19.2	−5.2	22.1	9.3	24.7	37.6	5.0
37 003	3290	Alexander County	22 729	66.9	68.7	9.3	−15.1	9.6	2.9	0.0	14.1	2.2
37 005	...	Alleghany County	7 829	63.8	68.0	11.7	−12.7	12.0	0.0	27.3	26.7	2.3
37 007	...	Anson County	16 824	68.2	70.2	9.2	−15.2	12.7	4.9	0.0	52.6	22.6
37 009	...	Ashe County	17 722	64.7	68.6	12.1	−12.3	12.3	2.3	7.7	11.8	7.4
37 011	...	Avery County	12 058	61.2	70.6	14.5	−9.9	14.7	5.1	7.7	44.9	17.2
37 013	...	Beaufort County	30 868	58.7	75.0	16.0	−8.4	20.2	5.1	0.0	0.0	10.2
37 015	...	Bertie County	13 135	72.9	63.8	8.8	−15.6	11.4	6.7	44.1	45.8	15.2
37 017	...	Bladen County	21 409	63.2	70.6	11.3	−13.1	14.1	6.8	6.0	66.7	11.2
37 019	9200	Brunswick County	52 605	55.0	78.3	16.1	−8.3	17.3	9.2	5.8	29.2	6.6
37 021	0480	Buncombe County	143 649	46.4	81.9	25.3	0.9	26.5	9.9	14.3	41.3	13.7
37 023	3290	Burke County	59 922	62.8	67.6	12.8	−11.6	13.6	6.6	12.0	7.9	3.0
37 025	1520	Cabarrus County	86 732	51.9	78.2	19.1	−5.3	20.4	12.7	15.7	34.0	3.6
37 027	3290	Caldwell County	53 539	65.9	66.2	10.4	−14.0	10.7	6.3	7.6	22.5	1.6
37 029	...	Camden County	4 770	51.9	82.1	16.2	−8.2	16.1	15.4	0.0	0.0	51.0
37 031	...	Carteret County	43 457	47.6	82.1	19.8	−4.6	20.7	6.4	14.8	5.5	26.9
37 033	...	Caswell County	16 212	67.5	69.2	8.3	−16.1	10.4	4.2	4.2	42.4	10.1
37 035	3290	Catawba County	94 747	56.5	74.8	17.0	−7.4	18.6	7.8	3.9	13.5	4.3
37 037	6640	Chatham County	34 920	48.8	77.9	27.6	3.2	33.2	10.8	30.8	62.0	3.7
37 039	...	Cherokee County	17 709	61.5	73.3	11.0	−13.4	11.1	12.6	7.0	0.0	12.1

[1] MSA = Metropolitan Statistical Area. PMSA = Primary MSA. NECMA = New England County Metropolitan Area. See the Appendix A for explanation of these concepts. See Appendix B for list of metropolitan areas identified by type, with component counties.
[2] Hispanic or Latino persons may be of any race.

STATE County	School enrollment			Population 16 to 19 years				Employment status, 2000			Work status in 1999 of the population 16 years and over (percent)		
											Worked in 1999		
	Grades kindergarten through 12	College or graduate school	Percent private	Number	Percent in armed forces	Percent high school graduates	Percent not enrolled, not grads, not in armed forces, not employed	Total population 16 years and over	Percent in labor force	Unemployment rate	Full-time	Part-time	Did not work in 1999
	11	12	13	14	15	16	17	18	19	20	21	22	23
NEW YORK—Cont'd													
Genesee County	12 183	2 893	10.9	3 500	1.0	11.7	3.2	46 639	66.6	4.3	53.9	17.7	28.4
Greene County	8 504	1 577	8.5	2 717	0.0	10.8	27.3	38 448	56.6	6.1	50.1	15.3	34.5
Hamilton County	868	131	7.5	272	0.0	9.9	5.5	4 470	57.7	9.7	48.9	15.9	35.2
Herkimer County	12 567	3 133	5.9	3 633	0.0	7.0	3.6	50 728	61.8	6.7	51.1	15.2	33.7
Jefferson County	21 771	4 962	8.5	6 514	12.1	21.0	4.7	85 441	63.9	7.5	55.1	14.6	30.3
Kings County	512 325	174 210	25.2	140 351	0.1	8.9	8.0	1 877 751	55.4	10.7	46.7	11.3	42.0
Lewis County	6 031	617	6.4	1 663	0.5	12.7	2.4	20 443	63.0	7.7	51.6	14.9	33.6
Livingston County	11 944	6 866	9.7	5 183	0.0	6.0	3.1	51 247	63.5	6.1	54.8	19.9	25.3
Madison County	13 451	6 099	19.4	5 586	0.0	4.9	2.6	54 306	64.8	7.1	54.0	17.5	28.5
Monroe County	145 226	56 430	21.9	41 721	0.0	7.5	3.8	567 731	66.0	6.0	54.0	16.9	29.1
Montgomery County	9 532	1 456	8.8	2 523	0.0	9.0	5.9	39 030	59.2	5.8	50.7	13.3	36.0
Nassau County	246 184	81 375	23.0	64 413	0.0	6.0	2.3	1 041 416	63.0	3.7	52.4	15.2	32.3
New York County	195 948	141 083	38.9	61 349	0.0	6.1	7.0	1 307 423	64.4	8.5	56.0	12.6	31.4
Niagara County	41 852	12 165	15.4	12 334	0.1	10.3	3.9	171 806	62.6	6.1	50.3	17.0	32.7
Oneida County	44 252	12 772	14.3	13 254	0.0	7.6	3.4	186 008	58.9	5.9	50.1	15.3	34.6
Onondaga County	89 450	35 188	22.9	26 156	0.0	7.7	4.5	353 100	64.7	5.4	53.7	16.6	29.7
Ontario County	19 305	5 865	16.8	5 640	0.3	7.8	3.5	77 820	68.4	4.5	56.5	17.6	25.9
Orange County	75 204	18 607	17.9	19 867	5.0	12.9	4.7	252 668	65.2	5.0	54.8	15.1	30.1
Orleans County	8 851	1 208	6.1	2 641	0.2	13.3	12.4	34 090	59.0	6.9	51.7	15.4	32.9
Oswego County	25 412	8 876	5.1	7 967	0.0	10.2	5.4	93 393	64.0	9.2	52.8	16.6	30.6
Otsego County	11 317	7 215	8.2	5 220	0.1	5.8	5.1	49 668	63.8	12.8	50.0	18.4	31.7
Putnam County	18 867	4 700	17.2	4 536	0.0	7.5	2.5	73 278	69.2	3.5	58.4	16.0	25.6
Queens County	389 860	164 114	23.6	108 616	0.0	9.0	6.2	1 775 449	58.4	7.7	51.7	10.9	37.4
Rensselaer County	27 840	12 107	25.2	9 232	0.0	6.9	5.3	119 772	66.9	6.1	55.8	16.2	28.0
Richmond County	85 662	28 243	28.9	22 953	0.1	7.9	4.2	343 053	60.6	5.9	51.5	12.5	35.9
Rockland County	60 015	17 843	35.2	15 172	0.1	5.2	3.9	214 669	65.5	3.7	54.9	15.5	29.6
St. Lawrence County	20 580	11 100	19.3	8 623	0.0	5.3	4.0	88 953	56.0	8.5	48.3	16.8	34.9
Saratoga County	37 384	10 297	15.1	10 398	1.2	7.9	3.0	156 118	69.4	3.9	59.0	16.1	24.9
Schenectady County	26 871	8 381	17.1	7 012	0.0	7.7	4.1	114 671	62.3	5.1	51.6	15.6	32.8
Schoharie County	5 836	2 354	9.7	2 544	0.1	6.8	3.7	25 051	60.4	7.2	51.1	15.7	33.3
Schuyler County	3 770	610	8.6	1 235	0.0	11.7	14.5	15 021	61.8	7.4	51.6	16.1	32.3
Seneca County	6 410	1 543	15.7	1 580	0.0	6.5	7.3	25 982	60.2	6.0	52.6	14.8	32.5
Steuben County	19 977	3 253	8.2	5 585	0.0	10.2	6.4	76 162	62.4	7.0	51.6	14.9	33.5
Suffolk County	273 741	82 092	13.6	68 844	0.0	8.9	3.3	1 086 848	65.5	3.9	54.2	15.6	30.1
Sullivan County	14 622	2 730	11.0	4 092	0.0	9.0	7.1	57 901	57.6	9.2	50.6	14.0	35.4
Tioga County	10 850	1 571	8.3	2 719	0.0	12.1	4.4	39 294	66.2	5.1	55.2	15.6	29.1
Tompkins County	14 395	27 205	52.5	10 977	0.2	3.9	1.3	80 460	63.6	5.8	51.7	25.8	22.4
Ulster County	32 223	11 682	10.2	9 585	0.3	9.0	5.1	141 015	63.5	6.3	52.6	17.2	30.1
Warren County	11 896	2 944	9.5	3 419	0.3	6.8	4.7	49 974	63.6	5.3	53.7	16.0	30.3
Washington County	12 040	1 750	6.1	3 107	0.0	7.5	11.5	47 692	60.4	4.9	55.0	14.1	30.9
Wayne County	19 792	3 271	8.3	4 896	0.0	10.8	5.0	70 924	67.7	5.1	57.6	15.4	27.0
Westchester County	170 768	52 847	25.3	41 585	0.0	6.7	4.9	716 252	63.2	4.4	54.4	13.8	31.8
Wyoming County	8 372	1 414	7.8	2 444	0.2	10.4	4.3	34 376	58.7	6.0	56.0	14.6	29.3
Yates County	4 836	1 279	24.6	1 798	0.0	12.8	5.3	18 930	63.2	6.4	50.4	19.0	30.6
NORTH CAROLINA	1 445 635	462 275	11.3	428 384	1.8	11.8	6.4	6 290 618	65.7	5.2	58.1	13.0	28.9
Alamance County	23 114	7 545	18.3	7 316	0.0	10.1	7.3	102 847	66.5	5.1	59.6	12.6	27.8
Alexander County	5 825	979	5.9	1 582	0.0	11.2	4.9	26 309	71.1	2.5	62.6	13.1	24.3
Alleghany County	1 524	392	4.2	526	0.0	17.7	9.7	8 900	60.6	4.6	53.2	12.5	34.3
Anson County	5 003	1 107	5.1	1 194	0.0	14.2	6.2	19 582	54.9	6.0	51.6	9.7	38.7
Ashe County	3 566	795	4.8	1 108	0.0	16.8	4.9	20 137	59.3	4.6	52.6	10.7	36.7
Avery County	2 609	1 024	19.3	825	0.0	12.2	4.8	14 186	54.7	7.0	48.2	14.0	37.8
Beaufort County	8 251	1 728	7.3	2 219	0.0	14.8	6.4	35 529	56.9	6.4	50.3	11.4	38.3
Bertie County	4 164	481	10.7	1 092	0.0	4.6	9.3	15 220	53.4	7.0	48.7	9.6	41.7
Bladen County	5 739	1 484	6.0	1 877	0.0	11.7	12.7	25 181	55.2	5.6	50.7	10.3	39.0
Brunswick County	11 662	2 062	8.8	3 253	5.6	18.1	5.6	59 310	57.7	4.6	48.8	14.0	37.2
Buncombe County	33 328	10 777	12.1	9 782	0.1	13.1	6.7	166 200	63.8	4.8	54.2	15.1	30.7
Burke County	16 382	3 109	5.7	4 896	0.0	12.6	17.4	70 064	64.4	4.2	58.3	10.5	31.2
Cabarrus County	24 893	5 028	9.6	6 202	0.1	9.2	6.0	100 501	69.7	4.2	61.9	12.5	25.6
Caldwell County	13 418	2 403	6.0	3 415	0.0	13.1	8.0	61 167	67.4	3.4	61.1	11.1	27.9
Camden County	1 353	264	4.5	404	0.0	4.0	5.2	5 419	61.1	3.6	54.9	11.8	33.3
Carteret County	9 458	2 223	10.8	2 592	0.7	8.9	6.4	48 683	60.0	4.9	51.4	13.9	34.8
Caswell County	4 358	786	6.8	1 071	0.0	13.4	6.8	18 580	58.5	6.5	55.2	10.7	34.1
Catawba County	25 244	5 405	9.3	6 953	0.0	13.2	7.1	110 788	70.3	3.3	62.5	12.0	25.4
Chatham County	8 127	1 797	8.3	2 021	0.0	12.3	5.8	39 391	65.7	2.9	58.0	11.8	30.1
Cherokee County	3 761	835	5.5	1 110	0.0	6.2	6.9	19 952	54.1	5.5	47.1	12.2	40.7

Items 11—23

Table B-3. States and Counties — **Education, Labor Force, and Income**

STATE County	Full-year full-time employed (percent)								Children under 18 years in families						Total employed by class of worker (percent)			
										With two parents (percent)		With one parent who is in labor force (percent)	+/− U.S. percent of children with no stay-at-home parent (percent)	+/− U.S. percent two-income couples				
	Total	Men	Women	Non-Hispanic White	Black or African American	American Indian and Alaska Native	Asian, Hawaiian, and Pacific Islander	Hispanic or Latino¹	Number	Both in labor force	Father only in labor force				Private	Government	Self-employed	Unpaid family worker
	24	25	26	27	28	29	30	31	32	33	34	35	36	37	38	39	40	41
NEW YORK—Cont'd																		
Genesee County	40.8	52.4	29.7	41.3	27.5	38.7	35.4	21.1	15 052	55.1	17.8	20.5	11.0	6.2	74.6	17.0	8.2	0.1
Greene County	35.6	41.9	28.7	36.8	22.8	31.9	36.5	30.4	10 341	46.2	18.1	23.7	5.3	-1.6	64.4	22.6	12.5	0.4
Hamilton County	32.9	41.0	24.7	33.3	0.0	0.0	0.0	13.3	1 009	57.1	17.9	18.2	10.7	-7.8	48.8	36.7	14.0	0.4
Herkimer County	39.4	47.6	31.9	39.5	43.8	36.0	43.6	31.9	14 834	48.5	15.8	24.3	8.2	0.5	72.6	17.3	9.8	0.4
Jefferson County	40.3	51.7	28.0	40.0	43.2	44.4	44.6	40.0	28 282	47.3	23.6	19.0	1.7	-2.3	65.2	23.9	10.3	0.6
Kings County	32.4	38.7	27.2	32.8	33.6	27.8	33.2	29.1	603 669	25.2	22.3	25.9	-13.5	-12.9	73.8	18.5	7.5	0.2
Lewis County	37.0	48.5	25.8	37.1	38.9	40.2	50.0	24.4	7 156	53.2	22.2	16.0	4.6	-0.7	63.3	21.8	14.2	0.7
Livingston County	37.1	44.8	29.4	38.3	14.9	42.1	23.7	26.5	14 496	54.4	16.4	21.4	11.2	6.9	70.7	20.1	8.9	0.3
Madison County	39.1	48.5	30.1	39.9	14.0	39.3	25.3	23.1	16 590	52.0	20.8	20.6	8.0	3.4	74.0	14.9	10.6	0.5
Monroe County	41.2	50.7	32.6	42.5	35.7	36.2	37.6	33.9	178 732	46.1	17.5	24.7	6.2	4.7	80.7	11.7	7.5	0.2
Montgomery County	38.8	48.2	30.6	39.0	47.5	13.0	58.0	33.0	11 549	47.3	17.1	21.5	4.2	-2.1	72.4	17.4	9.8	0.5
Nassau County	41.7	54.0	30.6	41.0	43.9	47.2	45.6	42.8	314 526	47.7	30.5	12.3	-4.6	-1.3	71.2	17.1	11.5	0.2
New York County	39.0	45.7	33.2	48.7	28.0	31.1	35.6	27.6	231 051	26.6	17.7	27.3	-10.7	-3.1	76.0	10.1	13.6	0.2
Niagara County	38.1	48.5	28.9	38.8	29.9	36.8	27.8	32.9	52 311	48.3	17.4	22.1	5.8	-0.9	79.6	13.8	6.4	0.2
Oneida County	37.2	45.3	29.5	38.4	24.9	38.7	33.9	26.7	53 411	48.0	16.0	22.6	6.0	0.6	72.5	19.3	8.0	0.2
Onondaga County	40.5	50.2	31.8	41.6	32.9	40.0	36.5	29.9	112 845	45.2	18.6	25.2	5.8	3.7	76.3	15.7	7.8	0.2
Ontario County	43.6	54.2	33.8	44.1	32.4	19.5	38.6	30.3	24 616	53.6	19.1	20.7	9.7	7.0	74.2	15.1	10.3	0.4
Orange County	42.9	54.1	32.0	43.3	38.6	41.2	43.9	42.6	93 869	42.3	29.1	16.9	-5.4	1.2	70.4	20.9	8.4	0.3
Orleans County	36.3	45.9	27.2	39.0	14.3	29.7	41.8	20.7	10 950	46.5	17.9	24.8	6.7	0.4	74.2	17.5	8.1	0.3
Oswego County	37.9	47.6	28.7	38.1	27.7	34.8	30.0	27.1	30 987	43.9	21.7	23.2	2.5	-2.1	73.4	18.7	7.6	0.3
Otsego County	34.1	40.8	28.1	34.8	12.8	18.2	16.9	26.8	13 052	50.9	17.7	22.4	8.7	0.2	67.6	18.8	13.3	0.4
Putnam County	46.4	58.8	34.3	46.6	39.0	27.8	49.4	45.0	24 499	53.2	29.0	10.5	-0.9	4.9	70.7	17.9	11.2	0.2
Queens County	37.0	44.7	30.2	35.6	39.1	36.1	37.1	36.8	467 949	33.5	23.7	21.2	-9.9	-10.5	76.0	15.5	8.3	0.2
Rensselaer County	43.5	51.3	36.2	44.5	39.1	46.1	19.8	35.1	35 418	48.6	16.4	24.2	8.2	6.3	69.0	23.5	7.2	0.3
Richmond County	40.9	52.0	30.9	41.1	37.6	33.5	43.7	41.1	108 278	37.8	31.3	16.1	-10.7	-6.4	70.0	22.3	7.5	0.2
Rockland County	43.2	53.5	33.8	42.4	46.1	39.2	48.1	44.2	77 228	45.1	32.0	12.1	-7.4	3.0	71.1	17.9	10.8	0.3
St. Lawrence County	32.5	39.9	25.0	32.9	28.2	33.9	22.2	25.9	25 085	45.2	18.2	23.6	4.2	-5.1	66.8	22.4	10.2	0.5
Saratoga County	46.0	57.3	35.2	46.0	41.3	41.5	44.3	52.7	48 690	54.5	21.9	17.1	7.0	7.3	72.0	19.0	8.7	0.3
Schenectady County	39.6	49.2	31.0	40.2	34.1	29.8	38.1	30.7	33 860	48.9	16.8	23.9	8.2	2.6	71.7	20.3	7.8	0.3
Schoharie County	36.9	44.8	29.1	37.3	18.9	17.5	30.1	33.4	7 170	48.6	19.9	21.6	5.6	-1.1	64.0	24.7	10.9	0.4
Schuyler County	38.0	46.0	30.1	38.7	8.0	48.0	33.3	15.7	4 476	48.0	16.2	23.8	7.2	0.6	69.4	17.4	12.4	0.8
Seneca County	39.3	46.3	32.4	40.1	21.6	31.3	36.4	28.9	7 875	48.2	18.8	22.3	5.9	-0.6	70.7	17.7	10.9	0.7
Steuben County	38.7	47.5	30.4	38.8	37.5	37.3	35.5	34.2	24 271	48.1	17.8	24.4	7.9	0.2	72.4	17.0	10.0	0.6
Suffolk County	43.1	54.5	31.7	43.3	42.7	35.9	39.8	43.4	352 325	46.3	28.9	14.5	-3.8	0.4	71.5	18.0	10.3	0.2
Sullivan County	34.9	41.1	28.4	36.4	25.0	34.0	38.3	28.0	16 955	39.9	21.9	23.8	-0.9	-6.7	66.2	22.1	11.4	0.3
Tioga County	43.6	53.8	33.9	43.8	34.5	23.8	35.5	43.6	13 078	53.8	19.1	19.6	8.8	4.4	77.1	14.5	8.0	0.5
Tompkins County	32.4	37.7	27.3	34.8	26.1	31.3	16.2	18.1	17 314	49.9	16.6	23.1	8.4	7.5	76.0	14.7	9.1	0.2
Ulster County	38.4	47.2	29.8	39.6	28.1	29.8	29.7	32.7	39 028	46.4	20.8	21.6	3.4	1.6	66.7	20.1	12.9	0.3
Warren County	39.1	49.5	29.7	39.3	35.0	30.4	35.3	28.0	14 601	48.4	19.0	23.0	6.8	-0.3	71.4	16.7	11.6	0.4
Washington County	39.8	47.9	31.2	40.9	21.3	29.7	42.8	21.4	14 283	50.5	18.5	22.5	8.4	1.7	69.6	17.9	12.0	0.5
Wayne County	44.7	54.4	35.4	45.2	32.9	49.6	39.9	35.5	24 473	51.8	16.3	23.4	10.6	6.9	76.8	14.0	8.9	0.3
Westchester County	41.6	52.4	32.1	42.6	39.4	37.5	44.3	38.2	218 447	42.6	29.0	16.3	-5.7	-0.8	72.9	14.2	12.7	0.2
Wyoming County	38.8	44.7	31.6	42.0	12.1	22.0	24.8	14.8	10 063	53.5	20.7	18.6	7.5	2.6	67.0	21.2	11.3	0.4
Yates County	36.4	46.9	26.6	36.6	35.0	10.0	20.5	25.3	6 081	44.9	22.7	21.8	2.1	-0.4	69.4	15.7	13.9	1.0
NORTH CAROLINA	43.8	53.6	34.7	45.4	39.0	38.3	42.7	40.8	1 837 327	44.2	20.5	23.1	2.7	2.2	75.6	14.5	9.6	0.3
Alamance County	45.6	54.5	37.6	46.1	44.4	32.3	42.3	42.9	29 578	47.0	17.2	25.2	7.6	5.0	79.3	12.2	8.3	0.2
Alexander County	49.4	61.0	38.0	49.7	44.4	68.4	57.8	59.4	7 686	52.2	16.9	19.7	7.3	8.0	79.8	10.0	10.0	0.3
Alleghany County	37.6	46.1	29.6	38.0	29.8	44.4	13.3	37.0	1 947	57.8	18.3	16.2	9.4	-0.4	70.3	13.1	16.2	0.4
Anson County	37.2	44.6	30.1	42.0	32.1	21.2	47.6	45.4	5 753	35.7	13.3	30.9	2.0	-1.5	75.0	16.8	8.0	0.2
Ashe County	36.0	44.3	28.1	36.4	30.5	10.2	15.0	25.0	4 684	53.5	20.2	15.4	4.3	-2.6	71.5	13.3	14.6	0.6
Avery County	32.6	36.0	28.9	33.9	4.4	36.1	53.3	31.3	3 167	48.9	24.0	16.5	0.8	-3.1	65.6	16.9	17.4	0.2
Beaufort County	36.7	46.1	28.5	40.2	27.7	15.4	27.0	42.8	9 901	39.9	16.1	24.3	-0.4	-6.3	69.6	16.5	13.6	0.3
Bertie County	34.5	41.8	28.6	43.1	29.1	38.1	29.4	17.1	4 680	37.8	9.6	26.3	-0.5	-6.0	72.5	17.6	9.6	0.3
Bladen County	36.0	44.4	28.7	39.5	30.6	30.3	85.7	39.0	7 102	31.8	15.0	29.4	-3.4	-6.3	70.3	19.6	9.6	0.5
Brunswick County	34.9	43.2	27.0	34.7	35.2	47.1	33.3	36.3	14 260	40.7	21.2	26.0	2.1	-10.8	72.0	12.7	14.9	0.5
Buncombe County	40.2	49.8	31.8	40.7	34.1	29.1	41.0	45.4	42 073	45.5	20.8	22.6	3.5	0.0	74.7	13.5	11.6	0.2
Burke County	45.4	52.9	38.0	46.2	35.0	30.5	50.0	42.0	19 870	50.4	17.2	22.4	8.2	4.0	74.5	17.4	7.9	0.2
Cabarrus County	49.3	60.5	38.7	50.0	46.9	43.6	52.7	42.2	31 991	50.1	22.6	19.6	5.1	7.9	80.5	11.2	8.2	0.1
Caldwell County	47.9	56.8	39.4	48.3	38.7	52.5	36.4	53.4	16 770	47.7	17.8	24.5	7.6	6.1	82.5	9.3	8.0	0.2
Camden County	42.5	57.0	28.7	43.4	35.7	0.0	58.8	69.0	1 557	50.9	22.5	18.6	4.9	-3.0	60.8	27.0	12.2	0.0
Carteret County	38.1	47.5	29.2	38.2	34.6	42.4	25.0	45.0	11 453	45.4	21.2	23.1	3.9	-4.7	59.5	22.3	17.8	0.4
Caswell County	41.3	46.2	36.3	46.2	33.0	61.3	51.5	40.8	5 078	45.2	16.4	20.7	1.3	2.5	74.7	15.3	9.6	0.5
Catawba County	49.4	60.2	39.1	50.2	43.1	40.0	47.9	46.5	32 624	50.7	17.7	22.7	8.8	8.2	82.8	9.3	7.6	0.3
Chatham County	45.5	55.7	35.9	46.8	39.2	47.9	47.8	45.8	10 213	52.5	17.7	17.8	5.7	4.5	68.3	18.8	12.8	0.1
Cherokee County	32.4	39.9	25.5	32.1	38.6	41.5	15.5	35.4	4 687	50.7	20.7	16.4	2.5	-10.7	71.8	14.9	12.3	0.9

¹Hispanic or Latino persons may be of any race.

STATE County	Percent who worked at home	Percent of the population 5 years and over with a disability	Veterans as a percent of the population 18 years and over	Occupation for employed population 16 years and over (percent)						Industry for employed population 16 years and over (percent)					
				Management, professional, and related occupations	Service occupations	Sales and office occupations	Farming, fishing, and forestry occupations	Construction, extraction, and maintenance occupations	Production, transportation and material moving occupations	Agriculture, forestry, fishing, and mining	Construction and manufacturing	Wholesale and retail trade	Transportation and warehousing, and utilities	Service industries	Public administration
	42	43	44	45	46	47	48	49	50	51	52	53	54	55	56
NEW YORK—Cont'd															
Genesee County	2.6	17.0	13.8	28.6	16.8	23.8	1.6	9.6	19.6	3.6	26.4	15.2	4.5	45.1	5.2
Greene County	4.2	23.2	14.4	30.5	17.8	25.4	1.4	11.6	13.3	2.5	17.1	13.3	6.8	49.7	10.5
Hamilton County	4.0	22.6	19.1	30.2	19.5	22.9	1.8	14.5	11.1	2.4	19.9	10.7	4.0	48.3	14.7
Herkimer County	3.4	19.4	15.7	28.1	17.7	26.7	0.9	8.8	17.8	2.9	22.2	14.7	3.5	51.3	5.3
Jefferson County	4.1	19.1	15.3	29.9	19.3	25.6	1.3	10.0	13.9	3.4	15.4	16.9	4.5	49.3	10.4
Kings County	2.3	26.6	5.0	32.5	20.2	27.7	0.1	7.2	12.3	0.1	12.2	12.2	7.2	63.7	4.7
Lewis County	6.2	19.7	14.7	26.3	16.9	19.8	4.3	11.4	21.3	10.3	25.6	12.4	4.0	40.5	7.2
Livingston County	3.5	17.2	12.3	32.0	15.7	24.3	1.3	10.3	16.5	3.1	23.6	15.2	4.6	49.4	4.1
Madison County	4.0	17.5	12.7	31.9	15.4	25.5	1.5	9.5	16.2	3.7	22.8	14.1	3.9	51.5	4.2
Monroe County	2.7	17.6	11.5	40.0	14.4	26.2	0.1	5.9	13.7	0.3	24.9	14.4	3.3	54.3	2.8
Montgomery County	3.5	20.6	14.6	28.1	15.5	25.2	1.4	9.3	20.5	3.5	24.6	14.7	4.5	46.4	6.2
Nassau County	3.0	15.8	10.6	41.0	13.7	30.4	0.1	7.0	7.8	0.1	11.6	15.0	6.0	62.0	5.2
New York County	5.8	20.9	5.4	55.8	12.4	23.5	0.0	2.3	6.0	0.1	6.9	9.7	2.7	77.4	3.2
Niagara County	2.0	18.8	14.4	28.6	16.1	26.7	0.4	9.0	19.1	0.9	25.9	16.2	5.4	47.8	3.8
Oneida County	2.4	20.9	14.6	31.8	18.1	26.7	0.6	7.5	15.3	1.4	18.1	15.2	3.9	54.7	6.8
Onondaga County	2.8	17.6	12.5	37.5	14.6	28.5	0.3	6.4	12.6	0.6	17.2	16.1	5.3	57.1	3.8
Ontario County	3.6	16.6	14.1	35.0	15.2	24.8	0.7	8.9	15.5	1.9	25.4	15.4	3.3	50.7	3.4
Orange County	2.7	18.6	12.2	33.2	16.5	27.6	0.4	10.2	12.1	1.0	16.9	17.5	6.0	51.0	7.6
Orleans County	3.2	19.8	13.0	25.9	16.5	21.5	1.3	11.7	23.2	3.1	28.5	14.5	5.0	42.4	6.5
Oswego County	2.5	18.9	14.5	25.1	16.1	24.5	0.6	12.8	21.0	1.3	24.1	16.2	8.8	45.9	3.8
Otsego County	5.4	19.2	13.0	35.3	17.0	24.0	1.5	9.3	12.9	4.4	17.1	13.8	3.3	57.2	4.3
Putnam County	3.3	14.5	11.2	41.1	13.9	26.1	0.2	11.9	6.9	0.4	16.9	14.4	5.0	57.4	5.9
Queens County	1.8	23.7	5.9	30.5	19.5	28.8	0.0	7.9	13.2	0.1	13.3	13.7	8.3	60.3	4.3
Rensselaer County	2.6	18.1	13.5	35.9	14.0	28.1	0.2	9.0	12.7	0.8	14.7	13.5	4.9	54.4	11.6
Richmond County	1.7	18.9	9.8	35.0	17.2	30.3	0.0	8.6	8.8	0.0	9.1	11.8	7.8	63.4	7.9
Rockland County	3.5	16.3	9.3	44.2	15.1	25.9	0.1	7.0	7.7	0.2	14.3	13.9	4.3	62.5	4.8
St. Lawrence County	4.4	20.2	13.2	29.8	21.0	23.1	1.8	10.1	14.2	4.2	18.3	13.5	4.0	53.3	6.7
Saratoga County	3.6	14.7	13.7	39.9	13.4	26.9	0.4	8.0	11.4	0.7	16.9	15.6	4.1	54.3	8.4
Schenectady County	2.9	19.1	13.6	36.5	15.7	28.9	0.1	7.5	11.2	0.3	14.1	15.4	4.0	56.7	9.5
Schoharie County	4.3	19.1	14.7	30.0	15.3	24.5	1.5	11.5	17.2	4.1	10.0	17.4	5.0	40.1	0.5
Schuyler County	5.1	20.9	16.1	29.8	18.1	22.2	2.2	10.1	17.5	5.4	25.7	13.4	4.3	45.1	6.1
Seneca County	4.0	19.2	14.4	30.4	17.3	24.2	1.0	8.6	18.6	2.9	24.8	15.9	3.8	46.6	5.9
Steuben County	3.9	20.8	16.0	32.5	16.0	21.0	1.4	10.4	18.7	3.6	30.4	11.7	3.8	46.1	4.4
Suffolk County	2.7	16.4	11.4	35.7	14.4	28.8	0.3	10.2	10.7	0.3	17.0	16.4	5.9	54.7	5.6
Sullivan County	3.7	23.2	14.0	31.0	20.6	24.4	0.9	11.1	12.0	1.7	13.8	14.9	5.4	56.0	8.3
Tioga County	3.2	17.1	15.3	34.2	13.9	23.3	1.1	8.9	18.6	2.3	30.1	14.3	3.7	45.8	3.7
Tompkins County	5.1	13.1	8.1	50.2	14.6	21.5	0.7	5.4	7.5	1.9	10.2	9.3	2.4	73.5	2.6
Ulster County	4.8	18.9	12.7	35.4	16.6	25.4	0.6	9.9	12.1	1.4	16.7	15.2	4.9	55.2	6.6
Warren County	3.1	18.6	16.3	32.1	17.5	27.6	0.5	9.6	12.7	1.1	18.9	15.8	3.9	54.3	6.0
Washington County	4.6	19.8	14.9	25.1	17.3	24.0	1.9	10.8	21.0	5.0	26.3	16.1	3.3	42.4	7.0
Wayne County	3.0	16.6	13.4	30.7	13.4	23.1	1.0	9.9	21.9	2.8	32.5	15.0	3.8	42.8	3.2
Westchester County	3.8	17.4	9.2	45.6	14.3	26.2	0.1	7.2	6.6	0.2	12.4	12.7	4.0	66.6	4.0
Wyoming County	4.4	17.9	13.3	26.1	17.8	22.0	4.0	11.6	18.5	8.6	24.1	14.0	4.2	40.9	8.1
Yates County	6.6	19.6	15.2	28.5	18.4	22.1	2.8	10.5	17.7	6.5	22.8	13.9	3.9	49.1	3.8
NORTH CAROLINA	2.7	21.1	13.0	31.2	13.5	24.8	0.8	11.0	18.7	1.6	27.9	14.9	4.6	46.9	4.1
Alamance County	1.9	22.2	12.5	28.2	12.3	25.3	0.3	10.8	23.0	0.9	34.9	14.4	3.6	43.5	2.7
Alexander County	2.5	21.6	12.0	19.6	13.0	19.8	1.0	9.8	39.5	2.7	48.9	12.2	5.5	28.4	2.4
Alleghany County	3.0	24.0	13.4	25.1	14.5	18.2	2.5	12.9	26.7	6.2	37.6	12.4	4.1	36.2	3.5
Anson County	2.2	30.4	11.4	19.4	14.6	19.8	2.4	11.5	32.4	5.7	38.6	12.8	4.6	33.3	5.0
Ashe County	5.2	26.5	13.0	22.4	14.0	20.5	2.3	15.3	25.5	5.2	37.6	12.5	3.5	37.4	3.9
Avery County	3.8	25.6	11.2	25.7	20.7	20.1	2.1	15.1	16.3	5.3	27.4	11.1	3.3	47.5	5.2
Beaufort County	3.3	24.7	14.7	28.1	14.0	22.8	2.4	13.4	19.3	5.8	27.3	14.2	4.1	44.4	4.3
Bertie County	1.7	28.7	9.3	22.7	17.7	16.3	2.8	10.9	29.7	6.6	34.4	11.6	3.3	38.6	5.4
Bladen County	2.1	27.9	11.7	24.0	14.9	21.3	3.8	13.2	22.8	6.9	32.4	11.1	5.4	38.6	5.5
Brunswick County	3.4	24.7	19.0	23.5	18.0	25.0	1.0	19.0	13.5	1.3	24.8	15.8	6.3	47.2	4.7
Buncombe County	3.8	20.8	15.0	32.0	15.6	25.5	0.3	10.0	16.6	0.9	24.4	16.5	3.7	51.3	3.2
Burke County	1.7	25.2	12.9	22.3	15.6	20.0	0.6	9.2	32.3	0.9	41.8	12.5	3.5	36.9	4.5
Cabarrus County	2.3	19.9	13.1	29.0	12.0	27.9	0.7	12.8	17.7	0.9	27.3	17.5	6.2	45.3	2.8
Caldwell County	1.7	24.3	12.6	20.1	10.1	21.2	0.2	10.2	38.1	0.5	49.5	13.9	5.1	28.9	2.1
Camden County	3.0	20.6	17.6	29.1	15.1	23.0	1.3	16.4	15.1	3.7	18.8	14.6	7.7	43.2	12.0
Carteret County	3.2	23.7	20.7	29.3	15.9	24.4	2.4	16.5	11.4	3.0	18.8	15.6	4.0	48.3	10.4
Caswell County	1.9	27.1	12.2	20.0	13.5	22.2	0.8	12.3	31.1	2.9	41.4	10.9	4.7	34.4	5.7
Catawba County	1.7	20.3	12.8	23.8	10.9	24.0	0.4	8.8	32.0	0.5	43.7	15.6	4.6	33.5	2.0
Chatham County	4.5	18.4	12.7	35.1	10.8	21.1	1.1	11.4	20.4	2.7	31.2	11.9	3.3	47.7	3.2
Cherokee County	3.1	26.2	16.2	22.6	15.6	20.2	1.6	17.2	22.8	2.9	34.8	15.2	3.9	40.3	3.0

Table B-3. States and Counties — Education, Labor Force, and Income

STATE County	Median house-hold income	Median family income — All families	Married-couple	Male house-holder	Female house-holder	Median nonfamily house-hold income	Median income for full-year, full-time workers — Men	Women	Per capita income	With earnings	With interest, dividend, or rental income	With Social Security income	With public assis-tance income	With retire-ment income	House-holds with income over $100,000 (percent)	+/- U.S. percent for income over $100,000	House-holds with income below poverty (percent)	Families with children with income below poverty (percent)
	57	58	59	60	61	62	63	64	65	66	67	68	69	70	71	72	73	74
NEW YORK—Cont'd																		
Genesee County	40 542	47 771	55 151	31 028	21 102	23 100	35 401	24 708	18 498	81.2	41.4	29.1	2.1	21.3	6.0	-6.3	7.8	8.9
Greene County	36 493	43 854	52 618	25 389	17 338	21 430	36 376	26 101	18 931	75.8	36.1	33.9	2.8	22.1	7.7	-4.6	12.2	13.3
Hamilton County	32 287	39 676	46 467	23 646	20 694	18 468	30 175	22 448	18 643	73.1	33.6	39.8	2.4	27.3	6.3	-6.0	10.6	10.6
Herkimer County	32 924	40 570	48 835	21 625	17 269	16 343	30 899	22 159	16 141	73.6	35.4	34.1	3.1	23.5	3.7	-8.6	12.9	14.2
Jefferson County	34 006	39 296	44 542	22 260	15 208	19 024	29 879	22 315	16 202	78.7	34.7	27.2	3.9	19.1	4.9	-7.4	13.3	14.9
Kings County	32 135	36 188	46 085	27 389	16 603	22 340	35 374	31 099	16 775	73.8	23.8	21.7	9.2	11.7	9.4	-2.9	24.0	29.1
Lewis County	34 361	39 287	45 171	27 500	14 063	17 629	31 237	21 532	14 971	77.0	27.4	30.3	3.1	19.2	3.7	-8.6	13.5	14.5
Livingston County	42 066	50 513	60 411	30 047	19 619	22 834	37 522	26 123	18 062	81.7	39.2	27.3	2.8	20.7	7.3	-5.0	9.8	9.0
Madison County	40 184	47 889	56 954	30 275	21 782	23 495	34 643	25 585	19 105	80.0	39.6	28.8	2.0	19.3	9.1	-3.2	10.1	9.8
Monroe County	44 891	55 900	70 156	34 417	19 541	26 564	42 256	30 504	22 821	78.7	43.5	26.0	5.4	19.8	13.1	0.8	10.8	13.1
Montgomery County	32 128	40 688	50 673	25 104	17 699	18 398	31 522	24 017	17 005	72.5	37.8	36.3	2.7	20.8	5.2	-7.1	11.8	13.9
Nassau County	72 030	81 246	90 665	47 221	36 254	35 442	55 644	39 126	32 151	82.3	49.5	31.1	1.3	20.3	32.3	20.0	5.3	4.9
New York County	47 030	50 229	75 128	29 013	16 350	43 825	54 974	47 508	42 922	79.1	39.0	19.3	5.5	9.8	23.9	11.6	16.6	26.8
Niagara County	38 136	47 817	57 740	27 120	17 252	20 721	38 408	25 503	19 219	75.3	41.1	31.7	4.0	23.2	7.8	-4.5	11.1	13.5
Oneida County	35 909	45 341	54 200	26 649	16 177	20 750	33 695	25 250	18 516	73.4	40.4	33.1	4.1	23.8	6.9	-5.4	12.8	16.5
Onondaga County	40 847	51 876	64 860	31 042	19 090	22 801	40 233	28 181	21 336	78.2	39.9	27.8	3.4	19.8	11.0	-1.3	12.3	13.3
Ontario County	44 579	52 698	61 941	32 309	21 118	25 313	37 864	26 859	21 533	81.8	42.5	27.9	2.3	19.8	10.3	-2.0	7.4	7.8
Orange County	52 058	60 355	68 004	34 407	23 531	28 862	44 834	31 677	21 597	83.4	36.7	25.0	3.1	19.3	16.1	3.8	9.1	11.1
Orleans County	37 972	42 830	49 577	30 596	17 587	22 927	33 638	23 406	16 457	78.1	37.9	29.6	3.8	25.4	5.2	-7.1	9.1	12.4
Oswego County	36 598	43 821	52 937	25 139	16 676	20 011	35 760	24 926	16 853	78.9	30.4	26.7	2.8	18.8	6.2	-6.1	13.4	14.6
Otsego County	33 444	41 110	48 274	20 817	18 615	19 457	30 988	23 619	16 806	76.9	40.9	32.0	1.9	22.3	6.0	-6.3	14.2	14.3
Putnam County	72 279	82 197	86 850	50 385	35 966	41 292	55 569	39 931	30 127	87.8	46.7	23.3	1.0	18.6	31.4	19.1	4.0	3.6
Queens County	42 439	48 608	52 172	31 919	24 383	28 283	36 348	32 103	19 222	78.9	30.7	25.0	4.3	14.6	12.2	-0.1	14.1	16.5
Rensselaer County	42 905	52 864	63 586	29 443	19 812	24 446	37 657	29 231	21 095	80.0	42.6	27.5	2.7	20.9	10.0	-2.3	9.9	10.4
Richmond County	55 039	64 333	71 227	38 471	23 583	30 552	50 831	36 616	23 905	80.6	35.8	25.3	3.3	18.8	19.3	7.0	10.1	11.4
Rockland County	67 971	78 806	84 457	37 585	34 818	35 862	52 244	38 299	28 082	85.2	43.4	24.7	1.8	18.5	30.8	18.5	7.5	9.5
St. Lawrence County	32 356	38 510	46 992	24 593	14 655	18 804	34 391	23 197	15 728	74.4	33.4	30.4	3.8	22.8	4.6	-7.7	16.0	18.9
Saratoga County	49 460	58 213	67 193	30 487	24 278	29 886	42 002	30 412	23 945	83.7	45.1	24.4	1.1	19.1	13.3	1.0	6.0	6.0
Schenectady County	41 739	53 670	65 212	31 298	18 092	24 963	40 265	28 582	21 992	75.1	45.2	30.9	2.8	22.8	10.5	-1.8	10.4	12.8
Schoharie County	36 585	43 118	49 154	25 625	18 775	21 261	33 047	25 212	17 778	75.9	39.8	32.6	2.2	24.1	6.5	-5.8	11.2	12.2
Schuyler County	36 010	41 441	47 228	25 486	17 064	21 440	32 334	22 135	17 039	77.8	38.0	31.9	2.8	24.7	5.2	-7.1	10.6	14.4
Seneca County	37 140	45 445	52 480	27 708	16 423	21 551	34 420	25 000	17 630	77.4	39.1	32.6	2.5	25.0	5.9	-6.4	10.3	12.5
Steuben County	35 479	41 940	49 776	25 446	17 301	20 344	33 433	24 984	18 197	75.7	38.7	31.6	3.1	22.7	6.8	-5.5	12.0	15.8
Suffolk County	65 288	72 112	78 969	44 007	29 988	34 445	50 835	34 793	26 577	83.9	41.4	27.5	1.5	19.5	25.5	13.2	5.6	5.7
Sullivan County	36 998	43 458	52 331	21 943	18 629	22 462	37 131	26 445	18 892	75.7	35.2	32.9	3.0	20.0	8.7	-3.6	13.7	18.6
Tioga County	40 266	46 509	54 031	24 206	20 521	21 493	33 508	24 738	18 673	79.8	44.8	28.6	2.9	23.0	7.9	-4.4	8.0	8.8
Tompkins County	37 272	53 041	61 819	35 956	22 013	21 748	36 540	28 822	19 659	83.4	48.8	20.1	1.9	15.5	10.8	-1.5	17.1	10.6
Ulster County	42 551	51 708	60 916	30 269	20 408	25 240	38 108	28 189	20 846	79.5	40.3	28.7	2.5	20.0	10.8	-1.5	10.5	11.2
Warren County	39 198	46 793	54 906	25 643	19 644	24 088	34 900	23 349	20 727	78.9	39.9	30.3	2.3	22.2	8.6	-3.7	9.3	11.9
Washington County	37 668	43 500	49 660	29 259	19 854	21 890	32 105	22 969	17 958	78.3	38.9	30.9	3.1	20.7	6.1	-6.2	9.3	10.3
Wayne County	44 157	51 495	58 944	28 942	21 946	22 950	38 022	27 275	19 258	81.7	39.6	27.2	2.5	18.9	8.1	-4.2	8.5	9.2
Westchester County	63 582	79 881	100 516	40 667	26 055	35 234	56 850	41 052	36 726	81.5	45.8	26.2	2.7	17.2	31.0	18.7	8.5	9.4
Wyoming County	39 895	45 088	51 143	30 256	18 526	21 821	34 008	23 194	17 248	81.3	39.0	28.8	2.3	19.8	4.9	-7.4	8.0	9.7
Yates County	34 640	40 681	48 081	27 115	17 575	20 077	30 484	22 213	16 781	77.6	39.9	32.6	2.9	21.9	4.9	-7.4	10.7	15.4
NORTH CAROLINA	39 184	46 335	55 255	27 115	19 250	23 240	33 398	25 631	20 307	81.5	30.5	25.3	2.8	16.4	9.4	-2.9	12.4	13.3
Alamance County	39 168	46 479	57 002	24 519	20 627	21 907	32 522	24 590	19 391	81.4	29.3	27.3	1.5	16.5	7.4	-4.9	11.2	10.8
Alexander County	38 684	45 691	56 277	27 750	19 779	20 093	30 394	22 163	18 507	85.4	28.0	25.0	2.7	10.3	5.3	-7.0	9.8	8.5
Alleghany County	29 244	38 473	42 817	28 000	17 308	13 438	26 158	19 660	17 691	73.3	31.7	36.5	2.6	15.3	5.1	-7.2	18.5	15.0
Anson County	29 849	35 870	46 923	20 673	15 789	16 265	28 118	21 197	14 853	75.0	21.1	32.0	4.0	17.0	4.0	-8.3	19.0	20.8
Ashe County	28 824	36 052	38 410	20 417	14 934	14 090	26 664	20 343	16 429	72.9	30.8	34.0	2.2	19.2	4.3	-8.0	14.9	15.2
Avery County	30 627	37 454	40 179	18 250	17 283	14 609	26 672	22 157	15 176	74.9	24.9	33.2	3.4	14.8	4.6	-7.7	17.1	15.7
Beaufort County	31 066	37 893	44 741	22 188	13 270	16 191	31 426	21 680	16 722	73.0	27.3	32.0	3.7	19.6	5.6	-6.7	19.8	23.7
Bertie County	25 177	30 186	42 776	17 500	16 084	11 738	27 411	18 850	14 096	70.0	19.1	35.7	5.4	18.7	4.3	-8.0	24.7	26.0
Bladen County	26 877	33 974	41 592	24 207	15 130	13 438	28 881	22 479	14 735	71.9	17.8	32.4	5.6	17.7	4.0	-8.3	21.6	23.2
Brunswick County	35 888	42 037	48 041	23 315	14 335	20 211	30 884	22 883	19 857	73.4	33.1	35.2	2.6	26.4	7.3	-5.0	12.3	16.0
Buncombe County	36 666	45 011	52 048	25 788	17 806	22 429	31 369	24 719	20 384	78.5	34.5	29.7	2.8	19.1	7.8	-4.5	11.5	12.7
Burke County	35 629	42 114	48 697	22 118	19 519	20 394	28 736	22 526	17 397	80.4	25.8	28.0	2.5	15.7	4.9	-7.4	11.2	12.3
Cabarrus County	46 140	53 692	63 078	28 685	25 333	24 167	37 454	26 681	21 121	85.1	31.7	24.0	1.5	15.9	11.4	-0.9	7.0	7.4
Caldwell County	35 739	41 665	50 551	26 781	18 676	19 121	29 527	22 322	17 353	82.0	25.1	28.2	2.9	12.8	5.1	-7.2	11.1	11.5
Camden County	39 493	45 387	53 267	38 611	13 889	20 438	38 719	25 640	18 681	81.6	33.2	27.6	2.0	22.9	8.9	-3.4	11.1	11.1
Carteret County	38 344	45 499	50 642	24 550	16 064	21 104	33 573	23 095	21 260	75.3	36.4	33.5	2.3	26.7	8.1	-4.2	11.0	14.0
Caswell County	35 018	41 905	49 498	30 338	18 792	16 301	30 178	22 965	16 470	78.5	23.4	30.7	4.0	17.7	3.9	-8.4	15.1	14.8
Catawba County	40 536	47 474	53 994	28 714	19 823	24 320	31 391	24 230	20 358	83.6	30.8	25.5	2.1	14.2	8.3	-4.0	9.0	10.4
Chatham County	42 851	50 909	58 143	26 250	18 133	24 518	34 484	26 649	23 355	79.3	34.2	28.0	1.9	17.3	11.2	-1.1	10.1	11.8
Cherokee County	27 992	33 768	40 821	21 591	14 792	13 916	26 838	19 377	15 814	69.3	29.2	40.2	3.0	20.4	3.9	-8.4	16.8	16.7

Table B-3. States and Counties — Education, Labor Force, and Income

STATE/ County code	MSA/PMSA/ NECMA code[1]	STATE County	High school graduates			College graduates		College graduates (percent)				
			Total population 25 years and over	Percent with a high school diploma or less	Percent with a high school diploma or more	Percent with a bachelor's degree or more	+/− U.S. percent with bachelor's degree or more	Non-Hispanic White	Black or African American	American Indian and Alaska Native	Asian, Hawaiian, and Pacific Islander	Hispanic or Latino[2]
			1	2	3	4	5	6	7	8	9	10
		NORTH CAROLINA—Cont'd										
37 041	...	Chowan County............	9 583	60.5	73.1	16.4	-8.0	19.7	10.0	0.0	0.0	20.7
37 043	...	Clay County.................	6 578	57.3	76.5	15.4	-9.0	15.5	0.0	15.8	0.0	0.0
37 045	...	Cleveland County.........	63 396	61.9	72.2	13.3	-11.1	14.9	6.3	6.2	30.4	10.4
37 047	...	Columbus County.........	35 921	65.1	68.6	10.1	-14.3	12.0	6.1	5.8	36.6	3.5
37 049	...	Craven County.............	57 027	47.9	82.1	19.3	-5.1	23.4	7.0	16.7	23.2	10.6
37 051	2560	Cumberland County......	176 714	43.4	85.0	19.1	-5.3	22.5	14.6	10.9	19.6	13.6
37 053	5720	Currituck County	12 361	56.9	77.6	13.3	-11.1	13.4	8.9	8.5	32.3	14.5
37 055	...	Dare County.................	21 713	39.0	88.6	27.7	3.3	28.2	6.6	19.4	28.6	18.0
37 057	3120	Davidson County..........	100 128	61.2	72.0	12.8	-11.6	13.3	7.9	7.4	18.5	4.8
37 059	3120	Davie County...............	23 840	56.6	78.1	17.6	-6.8	18.6	9.2	0.0	100.0	2.5
37 061	...	Duplin County..............	31 700	65.8	65.8	10.5	-13.9	12.9	7.4	0.0	12.9	5.1
37 063	6640	Durham County............	143 804	36.2	83.0	40.1	15.7	49.5	26.6	35.3	77.8	14.5
37 065	6895	Edgecombe County......	35 748	71.3	65.6	8.5	-15.9	12.0	5.8	0.0	8.6	4.3
37 067	3120	Forsyth County............	204 081	45.0	82.0	28.7	4.3	32.8	18.0	20.0	52.8	8.9
37 069	6640	Franklin County............	31 467	60.9	73.6	13.2	-11.2	16.1	6.4	5.7	48.1	6.0
37 071	1520	Gaston County.............	127 748	58.2	71.4	14.2	-10.2	14.8	9.8	7.4	22.5	10.4
37 073	...	Gates County...............	7 095	63.9	71.4	10.5	-13.9	10.3	9.7	32.4	46.8	0.0
37 075	...	Graham County............	5 622	67.6	68.4	11.2	-13.2	11.8	X	0.0	0.0	0.0
37 077	...	Granville County...........	32 641	61.1	73.0	13.0	-11.4	16.8	6.3	4.1	26.7	7.9
37 079	...	Greene County.............	12 380	69.3	65.4	8.2	-16.2	11.4	3.9	0.0	0.0	4.8
37 081	3120	Guilford County	275 494	42.2	83.0	30.3	5.9	35.1	19.7	12.3	30.8	13.3
37 083	...	Halifax County.............	37 719	67.7	65.4	11.1	-13.3	15.6	7.0	2.8	32.7	10.1
37 085	...	Harnett County............	57 138	57.6	75.0	12.8	-11.6	14.9	6.4	8.0	20.9	6.2
37 087	...	Haywood County..........	39 552	54.4	77.7	16.0	-8.4	16.0	7.0	27.3	64.7	5.9
37 089	...	Henderson County	65 039	46.0	83.2	24.1	-0.3	25.4	8.2	3.0	26.3	5.6
37 091	...	Hertford County...........	14 976	65.3	65.6	11.1	-13.3	14.2	8.8	12.1	17.0	7.3
37 093	...	Hoke County	19 934	58.9	73.5	10.9	-13.5	16.3	4.6	7.1	23.0	9.8
37 095	...	Hyde County	4 190	67.9	68.4	10.6	-13.8	12.7	6.4	0.0	X	0.0
37 097	...	Iredell County..............	82 036	53.7	78.4	17.4	-7.0	19.4	5.4	11.8	26.8	7.9
37 099	...	Jackson County	20 881	46.9	78.8	25.5	1.1	27.2	36.7	8.9	19.5	14.9
37 101	6640	Johnston County	80 268	55.9	75.9	15.9	-8.5	17.5	9.5	20.7	25.8	6.9
37 103	...	Jones County	6 998	64.2	72.2	9.5	-14.9	10.8	7.1	0.0	37.5	1.6
37 105	...	Lee County.................	32 043	53.6	76.3	17.2	-7.2	21.2	6.7	13.0	40.8	5.6
37 107	...	Lenoir County.............	39 833	59.4	71.9	13.3	-11.1	17.1	7.4	8.1	39.7	0.9
37 109	1520	Lincoln County.............	43 259	60.1	71.7	13.0	-11.4	13.6	4.8	12.8	15.2	11.1
37 111	...	McDowell County	29 157	65.9	70.2	9.0	-15.4	9.0	5.4	10.1	30.5	1.2
37 113	...	Macon County..............	21 908	54.9	77.0	10.2	-8.2	16.2	12.4	0.0	34.7	5.3
37 115	0480	Madison County	13 409	62.5	69.3	16.1	-8.3	16.1	5.0	66.7	10.5	18.9
37 117	...	Martin County..............	17 014	63.9	70.7	11.6	-12.8	15.9	6.0	0.0	35.7	3.3
37 119	1520	Mecklenburg County	455 163	33.7	86.2	37.1	12.7	45.2	20.3	20.7	39.7	14.3
37 121	...	Mitchell County............	11 315	64.3	68.6	12.2	-12.2	12.0	0.0	0.0	56.7	13.0
37 123	...	Montgomery County	17 713	67.9	64.2	10.0	-14.4	12.3	4.6	8.1	14.4	1.7
37 125	...	Moore County..............	53 347	43.3	82.6	26.8	2.4	30.7	6.7	11.0	38.5	8.3
37 127	6895	Nash County...............	57 522	58.3	75.6	17.2	-7.2	21.6	8.3	19.9	45.6	7.7
37 129	9200	New Hanover County....	107 671	38.2	86.3	31.0	6.6	34.4	13.2	21.5	49.9	17.0
37 131	...	Northampton County	15 199	69.0	62.5	10.8	-13.6	15.2	7.3	24.2	20.0	6.4
37 133	3605	Onslow County............	75 286	48.5	84.3	14.8	-9.6	16.1	10.0	14.3	11.6	12.7
37 135	6640	Orange County............	69 530	28.3	87.6	51.5	27.1	57.2	19.5	15.7	80.6	27.6
37 137	...	Pamlico County............	9 332	56.1	75.2	14.7	-9.7	18.1	4.8	0.0	3.8	1.7
37 139	...	Pasquotank County.......	22 223	53.5	76.8	16.4	-8.0	16.1	16.2	32.5	29.3	20.8
37 141	...	Pender County.............	28 566	56.7	76.8	13.6	-10.8	15.8	6.8	0.0	27.5	6.3
37 143	...	Perquimans County.......	7 970	61.1	71.9	12.3	-12.1	13.3	9.6	0.0	X	19.1
37 145	...	Person County.............	24 473	63.2	74.9	10.3	-14.1	11.4	7.3	0.0	30.1	18.5
37 147	3150	Pitt County.................	79 040	45.3	79.9	26.4	2.0	34.0	11.0	30.6	53.7	13.6
37 149	...	Polk County.................	13 653	47.6	80.6	25.7	1.3	26.7	6.4	49.1	74.1	14.0
37 151	3120	Randolph County..........	87 450	65.7	70.0	11.1	-13.3	11.5	6.9	6.7	25.4	5.6
37 153	...	Richmond County..........	29 870	66.5	69.2	10.1	-14.3	11.6	6.6	7.6	14.0	6.1
37 155	...	Robeson County...........	74 458	65.8	64.9	11.4	-13.0	16.4	8.3	8.5	27.7	5.0
37 157	...	Rockingham County	63 470	64.4	68.9	10.8	-13.6	12.0	6.5	8.2	17.7	2.6
37 159	1520	Rowan County..............	86 345	59.3	74.2	14.2	-10.2	14.8	12.2	10.6	15.9	4.4
37 161	...	Rutherford County........	42 880	62.9	70.4	12.5	-11.9	13.3	5.0	4.8	29.5	11.8
37 163	...	Sampson County..........	38 796	66.1	69.1	11.1	-13.3	13.5	6.9	9.8	10.4	6.6
37 165	...	Scotland County...........	22 563	58.1	71.4	15.9	-8.5	20.7	10.3	2.8	48.9	42.0
37 167	...	Stanly County..............	38 702	62.5	73.4	12.7	-11.7	13.4	6.5	4.9	30.0	9.2
37 169	3120	Stokes County.............	30 598	66.9	73.2	9.3	-15.1	9.6	4.8	0.0	32.5	6.2
37 171	...	Surry County	49 018	62.5	67.0	12.0	-12.4	12.8	6.7	4.6	15.1	1.3

[1]MSA = Metropolitan Statistical Area. PMSA = Primary MSA. NECMA = New England County Metropolitan Area. See the Appendix A for explanation of these concepts. See Appendix B for list of metropolitan areas identified by type, with component counties.
[2]Hispanic or Latino persons may be of any race.

Items 1—10

STATE County	School enrollment			Population 16 to 19 years				Employment status, 2000			Work status in 1999 of the population 16 years and over (percent)		
											Worked in 1999		
	Grades kindergarten through 12	College or graduate school	Percent private	Number	Percent in armed forces	Percent high school graduates	Percent not enrolled, not grads, not in armed forces, not employed	Total population 16 years and over	Percent in labor force	Unemploy- ment rate	Full-time	Part-time	Did not work in 1999
	11	12	13	14	15	16	17	18	19	20	21	22	23
NORTH CAROLINA—Cont'd													
Chowan County.............	2 579	899	15.9	940	0.0	12.2	1.3	11 473	56.4	6.7	47.4	14.6	38.0
Clay County.................	1 279	426	3.5	340	0.0	12.1	7.6	7 355	53.5	4.0	47.9	10.9	41.2
Cleveland County........	17 800	4 276	11.4	4 941	0.0	11.2	8.0	74 360	64.0	5.4	56.8	11.7	31.5
Columbus County.........	10 826	2 284	5.5	3 173	0.2	10.6	7.8	42 319	53.8	7.7	47.9	10.8	41.3
Craven County.............	15 939	4 413	8.9	4 794	11.5	22.9	6.3	71 338	62.8	4.5	56.2	13.0	30.8
Cumberland County	61 841	20 830	11.2	18 240	13.2	21.5	4.6	226 671	69.4	6.6	61.1	12.9	25.9
Currituck County	3 441	555	9.1	831	1.0	15.8	5.4	14 102	64.3	3.6	56.1	13.7	30.2
Dare County	4 960	682	7.1	1 337	1.0	19.4	2.5	24 314	68.3	4.9	59.2	15.4	25.5
Davidson County..........	26 183	4 371	7.6	6 866	0.0	10.4	7.7	115 466	67.0	4.1	60.7	11.3	28.0
Davie County...............	6 395	1 180	9.1	1 620	0.0	9.3	6.2	27 262	64.6	3.7	57.3	12.0	30.7
Duplin County..............	9 674	1 402	5.8	2 630	0.1	10.0	9.8	37 640	62.2	7.4	54.9	10.1	34.9
Durham County............	36 078	23 187	27.0	12 343	0.1	6.5	7.0	177 253	68.1	5.1	61.5	13.8	24.7
Edgecombe County......	11 844	1 822	5.4	3 223	0.0	10.8	9.3	42 327	59.4	9.6	54.9	10.7	34.5
Forsyth County............	53 625	18 750	18.9	15 448	0.0	9.7	6.1	240 086	65.9	4.6	58.6	13.2	28.2
Franklin County	8 663	1 802	13.5	2 375	0.0	10.9	6.8	36 469	65.4	4.7	59.9	11.2	28.9
Gaston County.............	34 448	7 020	11.9	9 162	0.0	11.1	9.2	148 421	65.3	5.7	59.3	11.4	29.3
Gates County	2 281	324	4.0	526	0.0	5.7	8.2	8 012	56.8	4.4	51.1	11.7	37.2
Graham County	1 173	220	6.8	368	0.0	13.9	12.2	6 475	54.1	5.9	50.6	8.7	40.7
Granville County...........	8 670	1 852	7.4	2 273	0.0	9.6	20.1	38 032	57.5	4.4	55.9	9.6	34.5
Greene County	3 749	628	7.7	982	0.0	5.6	5.3	14 779	57.7	7.3	54.9	10.7	34.3
Guilford County	74 078	32 524	13.3	24 144	0.0	8.4	3.3	331 721	69.3	5.5	60.0	15.2	24.7
Halifax County	11 856	1 959	7.8	2 911	0.0	15.5	7.9	43 840	51.8	8.1	47.2	10.0	42.8
Harnett County	17 716	6 071	14.4	4 959	1.1	12.7	8.8	68 919	65.4	7.8	58.8	11.0	30.2
Haywood County	8 354	2 173	7.0	2 318	0.0	14.7	4.2	44 172	57.2	4.6	49.5	12.8	37.7
Henderson County	13 934	2 843	9.8	3 764	0.0	12.1	7.1	72 583	57.1	4.6	49.2	12.8	38.0
Hertford County	4 586	781	11.2	1 408	0.0	7.7	7.0	17 625	54.1	8.7	48.6	11.6	39.7
Hoke County	7 050	1 723	7.7	1 896	0.5	19.6	10.4	24 586	63.4	6.4	57.8	10.2	32.0
Hyde County	1 124	72	12.1	265	0.0	7.5	17.4	4 798	49.2	5.3	46.1	11.0	42.9
Iredell County	22 667	4 050	8.1	5 937	0.0	13.7	7.9	94 615	67.4	4.0	60.2	12.2	27.6
Jackson County............	4 647	5 086	4.8	2 707	0.1	6.1	2.5	27 591	63.4	10.2	51.3	18.7	29.9
Johnston County	22 380	4 186	6.1	5 837	0.0	12.0	7.7	93 069	66.9	3.9	61.2	10.7	28.2
Jones County...............	2 091	379	12.7	593	0.0	7.9	5.9	8 052	57.0	5.0	51.3	10.9	37.9
Lee County..................	9 442	1 780	9.4	2 655	0.0	8.7	9.6	37 817	64.3	4.6	58.9	10.3	30.8
Lenoir County	11 328	2 379	7.5	3 200	0.5	8.1	12.2	46 289	60.1	8.0	53.6	11.9	34.5
Lincoln County	11 777	2 024	7.5	2 958	0.0	9.4	5.5	49 625	67.8	3.9	62.1	10.2	27.6
McDowell County	7 313	1 318	6.4	1 966	0.0	13.7	7.3	33 547	61.2	4.5	56.1	10.1	33.8
Macon County	4 626	1 062	7.6	1 421	0.7	17.9	8.2	24 541	55.1	4.8	46.4	13.7	39.9
Madison County	3 000	1 267	25.2	1 162	0.3	11.5	5.0	15 909	58.0	5.2	52.8	11.9	35.3
Martin County	5 229	930	5.8	1 359	0.0	9.6	4.2	19 815	58.5	8.0	51.7	10.9	37.5
Mecklenburg County	125 015	42 462	17.0	34 198	0.0	8.6	5.7	538 229	72.4	5.2	64.4	13.3	22.3
Mitchell County	2 508	452	8.1	740	0.0	21.4	5.7	12 786	57.5	4.1	52.5	10.8	36.7
Montgomery County	4 965	844	5.4	1 425	0.1	8.8	11.8	20 900	59.7	5.1	54.5	10.7	34.8
Moore County...............	12 571	2 803	5.9	3 374	0.0	13.6	6.0	59 996	57.5	5.5	48.5	12.6	38.9
Nash County................	16 862	3 925	11.3	4 745	0.0	11.9	6.8	67 663	62.1	5.5	56.9	11.7	31.4
New Hanover County	24 410	14 962	9.2	8 624	0.6	8.5	3.6	130 292	66.5	5.7	54.1	17.6	28.3
Northampton County	4 343	733	9.5	1 148	0.0	12.8	9.1	17 334	50.3	8.6	45.4	9.9	44.7
Onslow County	26 211	8 820	7.0	11 465	36.1	48.3	3.4	114 643	74.2	4.3	64.0	13.7	22.3
Orange County	18 131	24 674	7.5	10 630	0.0	4.0	1.8	96 919	67.1	3.7	55.2	23.2	21.5
Pamlico County	2 171	457	5.3	615	0.0	15.0	11.4	10 534	50.8	5.6	46.6	12.4	41.1
Pasquotank County.......	6 789	2 936	8.5	2 189	0.0	6.4	2.0	27 224	60.4	9.5	49.8	14.5	35.8
Pender County	7 385	1 339	6.8	2 057	0.0	10.7	8.5	32 642	58.5	5.6	51.9	12.1	36.0
Perquimans County.......	2 100	343	7.1	622	0.0	8.4	13.0	9 069	52.5	5.9	46.0	12.3	41.8
Person County	6 460	1 268	7.0	1 605	0.0	12.1	4.6	27 933	63.2	4.7	59.3	10.1	30.6
Pitt County..................	23 462	20 154	6.7	10 156	0.1	6.0	4.2	105 514	65.8	6.8	54.5	18.0	27.5
Polk County.................	2 662	582	13.4	637	0.0	10.4	6.6	15 023	55.0	4.1	46.7	11.8	41.5
Randolph County..........	23 613	3 898	7.7	6 383	0.0	10.3	8.9	101 238	68.5	3.1	62.6	11.3	26.1
Richmond County.........	9 150	1 641	4.8	2 850	2.7	15.5	13.4	35 948	58.0	6.7	51.9	10.2	37.9
Robeson County...........	26 723	5 683	4.8	7 841	0.0	10.3	11.6	91 573	58.4	9.6	54.0	9.0	36.9
Rockingham County......	15 761	2 722	7.5	4 393	0.3	13.7	8.4	72 900	61.8	5.8	56.1	10.7	33.2
Rowan County..............	24 024	5 618	13.2	6 535	0.0	12.3	6.2	101 606	64.8	6.3	58.4	11.2	30.4
Rutherford County	11 037	2 368	7.5	3 047	0.3	11.9	10.1	49 499	60.7	6.0	54.2	11.3	34.5
Sampson County..........	11 235	2 078	4.5	3 314	0.1	10.6	9.8	46 344	61.5	6.9	55.7	10.2	34.2
Scotland County...........	7 652	1 881	8.2	2 083	0.0	10.6	5.8	26 939	59.0	9.9	53.1	11.1	35.7
Stanly County..............	11 004	2 196	9.9	3 090	0.2	10.9	6.6	45 294	64.7	4.5	57.5	12.3	30.2
Stokes County.............	8 106	1 163	9.4	2 042	0.0	13.4	6.2	34 938	67.6	5.9	60.2	11.8	28.0
Surry County	12 328	2 652	5.2	3 178	0.0	11.4	6.6	56 188	63.0	3.4	57.9	10.5	31.6

Table B-3. States and Counties — **Education, Labor Force, and Income**

STATE County	Full-year full-time employed (percent)								Children under 18 years in families						Total employed by class of worker (percent)			
										With two parents (percent)		With one parent who is in labor force (percent)	+/− U.S. percent of children with no stay-at-home parent (percent)	+/− U.S. percent two-income couples				Unpaid family worker
	Total	Men	Women	Non-Hispanic White	Black or African American	American Indian and Alaska Native	Asian, Hawaiian, and Pacific Islander	Hispanic or Latino[1]	Number	Both in labor force	Father only in labor force				Private	Government	Self-employed	
	24	25	26	27	28	29	30	31	32	33	34	35	36	37	38	39	40	41
NORTH CAROLINA—Cont'd																		
Chowan County	35.6	43.9	28.5	36.9	33.3	0.0	20.6	34.7	3 147	38.8	15.6	30.9	5.1	−6.9	66.2	21.8	11.3	0.7
Clay County	34.7	43.4	26.8	34.6	100.0	57.1	50.0	35.4	1 567	52.1	24.4	12.5	0.0	−7.3	67.8	16.1	15.1	1.0
Cleveland County	43.1	54.1	33.3	44.2	38.9	46.2	46.3	38.1	22 540	43.7	18.3	26.5	5.6	1.8	79.2	11.7	8.8	0.2
Columbus County	34.0	43.4	25.6	37.2	26.4	33.2	20.8	40.7	12 868	33.4	20.6	24.7	−6.5	−8.9	71.4	17.1	11.0	0.4
Craven County	43.7	56.0	31.2	45.1	38.5	47.9	38.3	51.6	20 934	42.4	23.5	23.1	0.9	−3.9	66.2	23.4	10.0	0.4
Cumberland County	45.5	57.9	32.8	48.9	40.4	45.7	37.8	46.1	78 687	38.8	23.1	24.9	−0.9	0.8	66.8	24.1	8.9	0.2
Currituck County	43.2	55.6	31.2	44.3	37.0	50.8	25.2	13.7	4 336	44.1	22.4	20.3	−0.2	0.9	65.3	20.9	13.6	0.3
Dare County	41.6	50.7	32.5	41.8	43.6	11.1	65.5	29.2	6 173	52.9	21.7	19.2	7.5	2.0	59.8	16.9	22.9	0.4
Davidson County	47.4	57.4	38.1	48.0	42.2	47.1	43.8	47.2	33 584	51.4	16.5	21.1	7.9	5.4	81.5	9.5	8.8	0.2
Davie County	44.9	56.0	34.5	45.5	41.9	68.6	0.0	37.4	8 010	47.8	24.2	18.7	1.9	2.3	77.6	10.4	11.3	0.8
Duplin County	38.9	48.3	29.9	42.5	29.4	11.1	42.9	42.8	11 805	41.1	20.7	22.0	−1.5	−3.6	71.7	14.8	12.7	0.8
Durham County	44.8	51.1	39.2	47.5	43.7	46.4	38.3	34.4	47 013	42.7	16.1	25.4	6.5	7.3	75.5	16.8	7.4	0.3
Edgecombe County	39.3	46.4	33.5	45.3	34.7	39.5	36.7	38.0	13 464	35.1	8.5	34.0	4.5	0.4	78.1	14.4	7.3	0.3
Forsyth County	44.5	53.7	36.4	45.9	41.7	45.9	44.1	38.6	68 353	44.5	18.6	25.1	5.0	4.1	81.0	10.7	8.1	0.2
Franklin County	45.7	54.0	37.8	50.0	37.6	35.9	40.4	33.9	11 132	43.7	22.3	21.1	0.2	4.5	75.0	14.8	9.9	0.3
Gaston County	46.1	56.9	36.2	47.0	40.7	48.6	56.3	37.2	43 311	45.0	18.6	23.3	3.7	2.6	81.4	10.7	7.7	0.2
Gates County	36.2	46.2	26.8	39.9	30.4	25.0	61.1	0.0	2 682	45.9	19.5	18.5	−0.2	−4.5	69.3	21.5	8.9	0.2
Graham County	31.7	38.8	25.3	31.2	X	35.4	42.3	70.5	1 604	40.6	25.4	12.7	−11.3	−12.0	69.5	20.6	9.7	0.2
Granville County	42.2	44.8	39.4	48.0	33.8	31.6	18.9	32.5	10 466	41.6	14.3	26.8	3.8	3.1	69.3	22.0	8.5	0.3
Groene County	38.3	46.4	29.8	43.1	31.7	41.6	41.2	38.9	4 423	34.1	16.8	32.9	2.4	2.1	70.8	19.2	9.3	0.6
Guilford County	45.0	54.6	36.5	46.3	42.7	49.5	41.6	40.3	94 187	45.1	18.2	26.1	6.6	6.2	78.4	12.6	8.8	0.2
Halifax County	33.6	39.7	28.2	38.8	29.2	25.5	40.1	24.2	13 568	33.4	12.2	29.4	−1.8	−5.2	71.7	19.9	8.3	0.2
Harnett County	43.8	53.7	34.4	45.3	39.0	46.8	35.5	42.5	22 793	41.3	20.0	25.5	2.2	1.3	73.6	16.8	9.4	0.3
Haywood County	36.2	46.4	27.1	36.3	25.4	35.7	40.0	32.7	10 635	45.8	22.7	20.3	1.5	−7.5	71.5	15.2	13.0	0.3
Henderson County	37.5	47.8	28.1	37.2	32.7	43.5	46.8	43.8	17 717	46.4	24.2	19.6	1.4	−7.2	75.3	11.6	12.7	0.4
Hertford County	34.3	42.4	27.8	40.0	30.5	10.2	20.3	41.2	5 181	37.4	8.0	31.9	4.7	−6.4	71.4	19.1	9.5	0.1
Hoke County	40.4	48.8	32.1	47.6	31.7	36.8	36.0	44.5	9 004	37.6	20.0	28.6	1.6	1.2	75.0	17.3	7.6	0.1
Hyde County	31.6	37.1	25.4	37.3	20.4	0.0	0.0	34.9	1 086	47.1	19.0	19.8	2.3	−0.9	56.0	26.6	17.4	0.0
Iredell County	46.7	56.8	36.5	47.7	41.7	37.0	40.1	38.0	28 041	48.1	22.3	20.0	4.1	4.1	79.2	10.2	10.2	0.0
Jackson County	33.2	40.3	26.7	33.0	22.9	37.4	26.1	40.1	5 839	47.1	19.6	22.0	4.5	−1.7	60.1	25.6	13.5	0.7
Johnston County	48.7	58.2	39.7	51.3	40.1	57.5	40.8	37.8	30 301	45.7	22.5	19.3	0.4	5.6	71.9	18.2	9.7	0.3
Jones County	37.6	45.4	30.3	39.6	33.5	22.2	66.0	37.1	2 494	41.3	19.3	24.3	1.0	−5.0	67.0	20.1	11.9	1.0
Lee County	43.8	53.9	34.3	44.5	38.2	21.4	61.3	44.3	11 613	45.3	18.4	24.1	4.8	3.2	76.5	13.6	9.7	0.1
Lenoir County	38.9	47.3	31.7	43.3	32.4	35.5	35.0	35.8	13 818	37.8	14.8	30.4	3.6	−1.7	69.0	20.0	10.5	0.4
Lincoln County	47.9	58.9	37.3	49.0	41.3	20.8	43.5	38.6	15 074	48.9	23.1	17.9	2.2	6.3	80.6	10.9	8.2	0.3
McDowell County	43.5	53.0	34.3	44.0	35.4	40.2	63.2	39.0	8 989	48.5	19.7	20.1	4.0	0.4	79.0	13.3	7.5	0.2
Macon County	33.8	42.4	26.2	33.9	14.1	57.9	35.2	38.7	5 612	43.1	24.6	22.4	0.9	−10.7	67.0	14.8	17.8	0.3
Madison County	38.2	48.2	28.9	38.6	16.3	0.0	20.9	47.7	3 980	46.9	23.1	16.8	−0.9	−2.2	70.6	16.1	12.8	0.4
Martin County	36.8	47.4	28.1	42.4	29.4	66.7	37.8	41.9	6 083	39.0	11.5	28.7	3.1	−4.2	72.5	16.0	10.7	0.3
Mecklenburg County	49.6	60.1	39.8	51.7	47.6	42.5	47.4	39.3	163 182	41.8	24.7	23.7	0.9	5.8	81.8	9.4	8.6	0.2
Mitchell County	39.7	50.5	29.7	39.6	80.6	19.4	56.7	45.5	3 160	51.7	22.8	14.0	1.1	−4.7	75.1	13.8	11.2	0.0
Montgomery County	39.3	45.2	33.3	42.6	28.4	32.3	49.4	36.9	6 127	43.0	16.5	25.3	3.7	1.0	74.2	14.7	10.8	0.3
Moore County	37.7	48.1	28.3	37.7	36.5	35.0	34.1	44.9	15 438	44.2	20.7	22.8	2.4	−7.9	72.1	13.9	13.4	0.5
Nash County	42.9	52.2	34.6	45.7	38.0	61.8	44.6	36.0	20 788	42.7	19.8	21.8	−0.1	−0.8	76.2	15.1	8.4	0.2
New Hanover County	40.2	50.3	31.0	41.5	33.3	56.0	39.4	39.8	31 559	44.0	21.2	23.2	2.6	0.1	72.6	14.2	12.8	0.4
Northampton County	32.3	39.0	25.5	37.5	28.5	28.6	43.3	16.9	4 813	31.1	12.9	29.0	−1.5	−8.0	69.3	21.0	9.5	0.3
Onslow County	47.4	61.2	29.6	48.9	42.1	51.3	38.0	46.7	37 575	43.4	29.0	17.9	−3.3	0.3	63.4	25.5	10.7	0.5
Orange County	37.9	46.1	30.9	38.7	37.4	38.0	28.0	38.6	23 000	48.3	19.8	21.4	5.1	7.7	60.8	29.6	9.2	0.3
Pamlico County	32.6	39.8	25.4	34.6	26.0	44.4	40.7	32.9	2 456	39.5	21.3	23.5	−1.6	−7.8	63.7	21.1	14.8	0.4
Pasquotank County	35.2	42.6	28.4	41.8	25.1	15.1	29.6	56.7	8 102	39.8	14.0	33.9	9.1	−0.2	63.1	26.9	9.5	0.6
Pender County	38.3	46.1	30.6	40.7	31.1	24.4	32.7	40.7	8 867	46.1	20.8	19.3	0.8	−4.4	69.9	15.8	13.6	0.7
Perquimans County	33.1	43.6	23.8	35.6	26.3	42.3	X	16.4	2 352	40.1	18.6	24.0	−0.5	−10.5	59.0	25.9	14.7	0.4
Person County	45.0	52.9	37.8	46.9	40.5	40.8	63.5	25.4	8 163	46.2	16.6	23.0	4.6	1.8	76.1	13.8	9.8	0.2
Pitt County	39.2	48.6	31.0	42.2	33.4	47.0	38.3	38.1	29 261	38.7	18.8	28.0	2.1	3.6	71.9	19.9	8.0	0.2
Polk County	34.6	44.1	26.2	34.9	31.7	27.9	74.1	34.1	3 437	46.1	27.3	14.2	−4.3	−10.8	69.6	13.9	16.1	0.4
Randolph County	48.3	58.7	38.4	49.0	42.2	45.7	45.6	42.6	31 100	50.2	20.9	18.7	4.3	5.8	80.4	10.0	9.4	0.2
Richmond County	38.0	44.6	31.8	41.3	30.4	41.0	45.0	33.4	10 835	39.0	11.8	30.5	4.9	−2.3	76.7	14.6	8.3	0.5
Robeson County	36.2	43.4	29.7	41.3	29.6	36.1	43.4	34.7	32 158	31.5	16.3	30.1	−3.0	−4.1	75.4	16.1	8.1	0.4
Rockingham County	42.3	51.1	34.4	43.9	36.8	23.1	44.3	37.3	19 847	44.2	18.3	23.4	3.0	−0.7	79.6	11.4	8.6	0.3
Rowan County	44.0	54.0	34.5	45.2	37.7	48.4	35.3	46.1	30 014	46.1	17.5	24.9	6.4	2.4	79.5	12.6	7.6	0.3
Rutherford County	38.9	49.3	29.5	39.6	31.7	42.1	28.7	42.8	13 762	45.4	22.1	21.7	2.5	−3.6	76.7	12.1	10.8	0.3
Sampson County	41.5	50.7	32.7	46.1	33.7	32.3	28.8	38.9	14 285	42.7	15.9	24.5	2.6	−0.4	74.4	14.3	11.1	0.2
Scotland County	37.6	47.2	29.4	42.5	29.9	36.5	37.4	56.4	9 364	35.4	15.7	29.1	−0.1	−2.1	76.8	16.1	6.8	0.2
Stanly County	44.0	53.3	35.2	45.7	33.3	32.3	32.3	41.9	13 569	50.8	20.1	20.0	6.2	3.3	76.6	13.2	9.7	0.4
Stokes County	46.8	56.8	37.4	47.0	41.4	31.8	62.3	46.8	10 441	52.0	21.2	18.7	6.1	2.7	77.8	11.0	10.7	0.4
Surry County	43.7	53.9	34.1	44.1	36.4	33.6	34.5	44.3	15 943	50.4	22.3	17.2	3.0	1.5	78.2	11.4	10.1	0.3

[1] Hispanic or Latino persons may be of any race.

				Occupation for employed population 16 years and over (percent)						Industry for employed population 16 years and over (percent)					
STATE County	Percent who worked at home	Percent of the population 5 years and over with a disability	Veterans as a percent of the population 18 years and over	Management, professional, and related occupations	Service occupa- tions	Sales and office occupa- tions	Farming, fishing, and forestry occupa- tions	Con- struction, extraction, and main- tenance occupa- tions	Production, transporta- tion and material moving occupa- tions	Agricul- ture, forestry, fishing, and mining	Construc- tion and manufac- turing	Whole- sale and retail trade	Trans- porta- tion and ware- housing, and utilities	Service industries	Public adminis- tration
	42	43	44	45	46	47	48	49	50	51	52	53	54	55	56
NORTH CARO-LINA—Cont'd															
Chowan County	3.7	23.9	14.2	24.3	18.1	20.8	3.3	12.7	20.7	5.1	26.6	12.7	4.5	44.3	6.8
Clay County	2.7	26.7	18.2	24.0	16.0	24.2	1.4	19.8	14.7	2.3	28.9	15.5	3.7	44.8	4.7
Cleveland County	2.0	24.1	12.8	22.8	12.3	21.8	0.5	11.2	31.4	1.2	40.4	14.2	4.3	36.9	3.0
Columbus County	2.0	31.0	11.5	24.1	17.1	21.2	2.3	15.2	20.2	4.8	27.0	15.1	4.6	43.5	4.9
Craven County	2.2	21.9	18.9	28.7	17.1	23.4	0.9	13.9	16.1	2.2	21.1	14.4	4.0	48.1	10.2
Cumberland County	2.2	22.0	19.5	28.8	16.7	27.0	0.4	10.5	16.6	0.7	19.3	17.1	5.3	50.4	7.1
Currituck County	2.2	24.0	18.3	26.1	16.4	24.0	1.4	20.3	11.9	2.9	23.6	18.0	4.7	42.7	8.2
Dare County	4.7	15.4	16.9	29.8	17.0	25.9	3.5	16.3	7.6	3.4	18.5	17.3	3.3	50.4	7.1
Davidson County	1.7	21.6	12.7	22.8	11.5	24.4	0.2	11.9	29.2	0.7	39.0	15.3	5.1	37.2	2.7
Davie County	2.5	21.6	13.2	29.7	10.5	24.6	0.6	11.1	23.5	1.5	35.9	13.8	5.1	40.9	2.7
Duplin County	2.5	26.6	11.2	23.7	13.4	18.4	6.3	13.5	24.8	14.0	31.9	12.9	3.8	33.0	4.3
Durham County	2.7	18.0	10.1	45.8	13.4	23.3	0.2	8.3	9.0	0.3	17.3	10.2	3.4	64.6	4.2
Edgecombe County	1.9	26.5	10.6	19.4	15.8	23.9	1.1	11.5	28.4	2.9	34.6	14.2	4.4	39.0	5.0
Forsyth County	2.5	17.8	12.4	35.6	13.9	25.9	0.1	8.6	15.9	0.3	23.1	14.1	5.3	54.4	2.9
Franklin County	2.1	22.2	11.3	25.3	13.6	23.7	0.8	15.9	20.7	2.1	32.1	15.2	4.5	40.2	5.8
Gaston County	1.6	23.6	13.5	24.6	11.9	25.6	0.2	11.9	25.7	0.4	35.7	15.3	7.2	38.2	3.2
Gates County	2.4	26.6	13.4	25.5	14.1	21.4	3.1	12.7	23.2	6.1	30.7	13.3	6.3	39.7	4.0
Graham County	1.0	27.3	12.8	19.9	16.3	19.3	1.6	19.4	23.6	4.5	39.5	11.4	2.9	38.4	3.3
Granville County	1.9	24.3	11.1	29.8	15.1	20.8	1.5	12.4	20.5	2.7	30.6	11.2	3.4	46.2	6.0
Greene County	1.3	24.6	9.7	22.6	16.4	19.0	4.9	12.3	25.0	7.3	33.2	12.9	4.2	36.3	6.1
Guilford County	2.8	19.1	12.1	34.7	12.6	28.8	0.2	8.2	15.5	0.3	25.0	16.1	5.3	50.5	2.8
Halifax County	1.8	30.2	11.0	21.5	18.5	23.5	1.8	11.0	23.7	3.6	29.2	14.6	4.4	40.3	7.8
Harnett County	1.9	22.5	14.7	24.9	14.3	23.3	1.1	15.5	21.0	2.2	32.5	15.2	3.9	40.1	6.2
Haywood County	2.7	23.8	16.5	27.3	17.0	22.7	1.0	13.8	18.2	2.2	26.9	14.9	3.5	48.4	4.1
Henderson County	3.2	21.9	17.6	28.6	15.0	24.6	1.2	12.0	18.6	2.1	31.0	15.5	3.8	44.7	3.0
Hertford County	1.8	31.9	10.6	26.2	15.7	21.1	2.4	11.1	23.5	4.0	29.7	13.8	3.3	42.6	6.6
Hoke County	2.0	25.5	14.2	23.5	16.6	20.4	1.6	12.8	25.1	3.2	36.0	12.8	4.5	39.1	4.4
Hyde County	3.2	31.4	11.9	19.1	24.6	23.6	9.2	10.1	13.5	15.9	15.5	13.8	6.1	36.1	12.7
Iredell County	2.9	20.2	13.0	27.6	11.4	24.1	0.5	10.9	25.6	1.8	35.8	16.5	5.1	38.3	2.4
Jackson County	2.7	21.6	13.3	31.3	19.8	23.4	0.9	13.1	11.6	1.8	18.6	13.6	3.0	59.4	3.6
Johnston County	2.3	22.0	12.4	30.5	11.7	25.2	0.7	15.5	16.4	1.9	27.9	17.0	4.4	41.2	7.5
Jones County	1.9	29.4	15.2	21.7	17.1	20.3	3.1	18.6	19.3	6.9	23.7	14.7	5.7	43.7	5.4
Lee County	1.8	20.4	14.2	27.3	12.1	21.2	0.6	13.6	25.3	1.3	38.8	15.0	3.5	38.2	3.1
Lenoir County	2.0	25.6	13.1	25.8	16.4	22.3	1.4	13.1	21.0	3.6	29.4	14.1	3.7	43.9	5.5
Lincoln County	2.1	21.5	12.4	22.3	10.8	22.3	0.3	13.9	30.4	0.9	40.8	13.6	8.2	33.9	2.5
McDowell County	2.0	26.1	13.7	19.4	14.1	18.1	0.7	12.6	35.0	1.2	48.2	12.1	2.9	31.8	3.9
Macon County	4.6	24.7	17.8	26.7	15.5	26.0	1.1	17.1	13.5	2.6	26.1	16.2	2.9	48.5	3.6
Madison County	3.7	21.4	12.3	27.9	14.1	21.0	1.5	14.1	21.3	3.6	29.6	14.4	5.1	42.4	4.9
Martin County	2.1	26.6	11.1	22.7	14.8	22.3	2.8	12.4	25.0	5.1	30.7	14.8	3.8	40.8	4.7
Mecklenburg County	3.4	16.3	11.0	39.5	12.0	29.2	0.1	8.0	11.1	0.2	18.0	15.8	6.0	57.8	2.2
Mitchell County	1.5	26.5	13.1	21.0	15.8	19.6	1.6	11.7	30.2	5.8	37.4	13.0	3.2	35.3	5.3
Montgomery County	2.6	25.4	12.2	23.2	11.7	18.5	1.6	12.4	32.7	3.6	48.1	10.8	2.8	30.2	4.5
Moore County	4.1	20.6	18.0	31.2	16.8	23.1	1.3	12.2	15.5	3.2	25.6	14.1	3.1	49.8	4.2
Nash County	1.9	23.4	12.7	29.2	12.3	26.4	0.9	10.9	20.3	2.0	29.0	17.2	4.3	43.2	4.2
New Hanover County	2.9	19.3	14.7	34.5	16.5	27.0	0.2	10.7	11.1	0.5	19.9	17.1	4.1	54.3	4.1
Northampton County	1.4	32.0	10.8	22.3	19.3	20.6	2.8	12.3	22.6	5.8	30.6	14.3	4.0	37.0	8.4
Onslow County	2.4	20.2	16.9	26.1	19.2	28.0	1.2	14.1	11.4	2.0	15.7	17.2	4.6	51.1	9.3
Orange County	4.4	12.9	8.4	49.8	13.2	22.5	0.3	7.3	7.0	0.7	13.5	10.1	1.9	70.6	3.3
Pamlico County	3.5	25.0	17.0	25.4	13.6	22.7	4.1	16.2	18.1	10.1	21.8	15.8	4.4	39.2	8.7
Pasquotank County	1.5	25.2	14.8	28.0	19.9	23.9	1.7	14.2	12.3	3.1	17.3	16.8	3.9	49.4	9.5
Pender County	3.3	24.9	17.0	23.7	15.6	24.3	1.7	16.3	18.3	3.5	28.5	16.8	5.5	39.5	6.2
Perquimans County	4.4	26.4	17.5	23.6	19.3	22.5	2.2	15.2	17.2	5.5	19.8	16.2	6.3	43.1	9.2
Person County	2.5	22.5	12.2	24.6	14.2	22.0	0.8	15.0	23.3	2.4	35.6	12.5	5.0	40.4	4.1
Pitt County	2.1	19.6	10.2	33.7	15.5	26.1	0.8	9.4	14.5	1.7	22.3	15.5	3.3	53.3	3.9
Polk County	4.7	24.1	17.8	28.9	14.2	23.6	1.2	12.8	19.3	2.0	33.1	12.5	4.0	45.2	3.3
Randolph County	2.1	22.1	12.4	21.5	10.9	23.3	0.5	12.5	31.4	1.2	42.9	15.1	5.3	32.9	2.6
Richmond County	1.5	27.9	13.3	22.4	14.9	20.5	1.5	13.2	27.5	2.8	35.0	15.2	4.8	38.1	4.1
Robeson County	1.5	27.0	10.1	20.3	14.7	19.5	1.9	16.3	27.3	3.1	38.3	12.8	4.2	37.3	4.3
Rockingham County	2.1	24.3	13.2	22.3	12.7	22.4	0.5	13.6	28.5	1.1	39.0	13.5	5.9	37.8	2.6
Rowan County	2.1	23.4	14.2	23.2	13.5	22.2	0.4	13.8	27.0	0.8	36.7	14.9	5.4	38.9	3.3
Rutherford County	2.6	25.5	14.0	21.7	13.6	21.1	0.8	13.4	29.5	1.5	42.5	14.5	4.2	34.5	2.8
Sampson County	2.0	29.0	10.7	23.9	13.3	20.2	5.9	11.4	25.3	12.2	28.5	16.1	3.3	35.9	4.1
Scotland County	1.8	25.7	12.7	28.8	13.4	19.8	1.5	10.2	26.3	2.9	39.0	11.9	3.6	37.9	4.7
Stanly County	2.4	22.4	12.6	23.4	14.7	21.0	0.6	14.8	25.5	1.4	37.6	15.0	3.7	38.3	3.9
Stokes County	2.9	22.7	11.8	22.4	10.7	24.0	0.7	15.8	26.4	2.2	37.0	13.7	5.9	38.6	2.7
Surry County	2.5	23.3	11.4	24.0	12.0	21.9	1.0	13.8	27.3	2.9	40.4	14.7	4.7	34.4	2.9

STATE County	Median house-hold income	Median family income		Families with children			Median nonfamily house-hold income	Median income for full-year, full-time workers		Per capita income	Households by source of income (percent)					House-holds with income over $100,000 (percent)	+/− U.S. percent for income over $100,000	House-holds with income below poverty (percent)	Families with children with income below poverty (percent)
		All families	Married-couple	Male house-holder	Female house-holder			Men	Women		With earnings	With interest, dividend, or rental income	With Social Security income	With public assis-tance income	With retire-ment income				
	57	58	59	60	61	62	63	64	65	66	67	68	69	70	71	72	73	74

NORTH CAROLINA—Cont'd

STATE County	57	58	59	60	61	62	63	64	65	66	67	68	69	70	71	72	73	74
Chowan County	30 928	36 986	50 337	18 359	15 471	16 341	30 404	19 845	15 027	72.1	29.0	35.5	5.7	21.0	3.2	-9.1	17.8	19.9
Clay County	31 397	38 264	38 083	35 556	10 875	15 100	30 644	20 366	18 221	68.5	35.8	41.3	3.3	23.4	5.3	-7.0	13.6	13.6
Cleveland County	35 283	41 733	50 876	25 313	18 744	17 877	31 420	22 725	17 395	79.2	25.6	29.1	3.3	15.9	5.9	-6.4	13.4	14.8
Columbus County	26 805	33 849	42 033	20 405	14 252	12 575	29 614	20 469	14 415	71.9	20.0	32.4	5.1	17.0	3.9	-8.4	22.3	24.8
Craven County	35 966	42 574	48 025	26 736	15 996	20 713	29 740	21 889	18 423	78.3	30.9	27.8	3.3	22.5	6.3	-6.0	13.1	15.6
Cumberland County	37 466	41 459	46 971	27 710	17 712	24 743	30 131	23 432	17 376	84.6	24.3	19.5	3.6	19.6	6.3	-6.0	12.6	14.2
Currituck County	40 822	46 382	51 229	35 185	16 520	22 150	35 186	24 137	19 908	82.4	29.3	25.9	2.8	21.7	7.0	-5.3	9.4	14.4
Dare County	42 411	49 302	51 786	30 189	21 674	29 828	32 287	25 563	23 614	82.1	41.7	27.0	1.3	22.6	10.3	-2.0	8.1	8.5
Davidson County	38 640	46 241	53 041	25 724	19 391	20 588	31 872	24 408	18 703	82.0	29.8	26.0	2.6	15.7	6.1	-6.2	10.3	10.8
Davie County	40 174	47 699	55 261	34 605	23 182	20 595	34 289	25 735	21 359	80.8	35.6	28.4	1.8	19.3	10.1	-2.2	9.7	9.1
Duplin County	29 890	34 760	40 332	19 238	17 052	14 858	26 957	20 668	14 499	77.3	20.4	29.1	4.1	15.7	4.4	-7.9	19.8	21.3
Durham County	43 337	53 223	65 613	27 087	21 655	29 689	36 753	31 362	23 156	84.9	33.5	19.2	2.7	14.5	12.9	0.6	12.8	14.8
Edgecombe County	30 983	35 902	50 066	21 598	15 880	17 059	28 430	22 180	14 435	77.4	17.7	30.3	7.0	17.9	4.2	-8.1	19.4	22.5
Forsyth County	42 097	52 032	63 706	30 488	20 456	25 460	37 034	28 162	23 023	80.9	35.9	25.3	2.5	17.6	11.5	-0.8	10.8	12.3
Franklin County	38 968	44 540	52 060	26 810	17 331	21 927	32 111	25 251	17 562	82.7	21.7	25.1	3.3	15.2	5.6	-6.7	13.1	14.0
Gaston County	39 482	46 271	54 993	31 681	20 070	21 661	34 786	24 668	19 225	81.8	26.3	26.7	2.5	15.6	7.7	-4.6	10.9	12.5
Gates County	35 647	41 511	50 243	23 750	16 591	15 960	34 006	21 768	15 963	73.8	25.6	34.0	2.6	20.6	4.8	-7.5	18.0	15.5
Graham County	26 645	32 750	37 859	28 889	11 343	11 261	25 013	20 081	14 237	68.6	28.1	40.1	2.5	16.2	3.4	-8.9	20.7	21.4
Granville County	39 965	46 013	56 179	30 469	19 468	21 221	30 881	25 505	17 118	81.4	25.6	27.2	2.7	17.0	7.3	-5.0	12.2	13.0
Greene County	32 074	36 419	45 347	17 125	14 155	15 140	27 883	21 557	15 452	76.4	19.7	28.2	5.9	16.6	3.4	-8.9	21.0	23.1
Guilford County	42 618	52 638	64 835	30 945	20 970	27 146	36 769	27 832	23 340	84.7	33.5	22.5	2.4	14.8	12.6	0.3	10.3	11.7
Halifax County	26 459	33 515	46 335	18 667	13 141	13 961	29 198	20 976	13 810	69.8	20.1	33.7	6.7	18.7	4.3	-8.0	23.7	27.6
Harnett County	35 105	41 176	48 659	25 582	16 504	18 797	30 973	22 964	16 775	81.5	21.1	24.1	3.1	15.5	5.4	-6.9	15.7	15.6
Haywood County	33 922	40 438	44 348	29 688	16 509	17 697	31 611	22 288	18 554	72.6	34.0	37.0	2.8	25.5	4.9	-7.4	11.6	14.1
Henderson County	38 109	44 974	50 077	26 919	17 917	22 206	32 683	24 705	21 110	70.9	41.9	38.1	2.0	25.9	7.7	-4.6	9.6	12.4
Hertford County	26 422	32 002	44 397	30 104	16 717	15 520	27 173	20 958	15 641	72.7	16.7	32.4	5.8	22.2	4.4	-7.9	19.9	19.7
Hoke County	33 230	36 110	42 348	21 974	17 395	18 489	30 059	21 714	13 635	83.2	18.6	21.3	4.8	14.3	4.0	-8.3	17.5	18.0
Hyde County	28 444	35 558	38 288	24 411	16 250	13 135	25 990	20 042	13 164	74.7	22.7	35.0	6.0	20.4	3.8	-8.5	16.0	14.6
Iredell County	41 920	49 078	57 155	27 483	20 243	22 688	35 836	24 741	21 148	82.9	31.3	25.3	1.3	15.4	9.2	-3.1	9.9	9.1
Jackson County	32 552	40 876	47 196	21 447	18 505	18 343	28 743	22 711	17 582	78.4	30.7	30.3	2.8	19.4	5.9	-6.4	17.1	15.1
Johnston County	40 872	48 599	54 579	26 840	22 160	20 602	34 220	26 197	18 788	82.2	24.7	24.0	2.8	15.3	7.0	-5.3	12.8	11.9
Jones County	30 882	35 180	41 667	15 375	16 141	16 659	30 032	19 901	15 916	76.1	20.5	31.2	4.0	21.4	4.0	-8.3	17.8	19.4
Lee County	38 900	44 953	55 974	22 167	16 303	21 892	34 352	24 172	19 147	80.5	28.2	27.2	2.4	16.2	8.6	-3.7	12.5	14.3
Lenoir County	31 191	38 815	47 452	21 121	16 303	16 884	30 144	22 240	16 744	76.7	23.8	30.6	4.2	17.9	5.0	-7.3	17.0	18.6
Lincoln County	41 421	47 752	52 051	27 672	17 904	21 750	33 364	23 093	18 877	82.4	28.9	25.9	1.9	13.6	7.6	-4.7	10.1	9.9
McDowell County	32 396	37 789	42 586	25 331	17 260	18 127	27 296	22 109	16 109	77.5	22.7	30.6	2.6	16.7	4.4	-7.9	12.6	13.2
Macon County	32 139	37 381	45 092	19 559	14 750	18 095	29 800	20 042	18 642	69.2	30.9	41.8	2.0	21.5	5.7	-6.6	12.6	14.2
Madison County	30 985	37 383	40 764	25 801	16 452	13 664	28 952	23 153	16 076	73.5	26.8	31.9	3.4	17.9	4.5	-7.8	17.6	16.0
Martin County	28 793	35 428	46 506	22 991	14 361	13 601	30 445	19 953	15 102	73.8	23.0	34.0	4.6	17.6	4.4	-7.9	20.8	22.4
Mecklenburg County	50 579	60 608	72 721	31 933	25 339	34 020	41 792	30 780	27 352	88.6	35.4	17.3	2.3	12.0	17.2	4.9	8.2	9.3
Mitchell County	30 508	36 367	40 951	29 706	13 875	15 397	26 950	21 189	15 933	74.2	25.2	35.3	2.2	17.7	4.0	-8.3	15.0	14.6
Montgomery County	32 903	39 616	44 917	22 426	17 095	13 841	29 028	21 253	16 504	78.0	23.2	31.5	3.2	14.2	5.7	-6.6	15.8	15.9
Moore County	41 240	48 492	52 579	26 020	17 729	23 950	31 984	24 614	23 377	71.5	39.6	37.3	1.9	25.5	10.9	-1.4	10.8	14.2
Nash County	37 147	44 769	56 014	25 064	18 068	19 678	33 879	25 170	18 863	79.4	28.0	27.5	3.1	16.4	8.2	-4.1	13.8	15.2
New Hanover County	40 172	50 861	60 661	31 551	16 545	25 652	36 936	26 157	23 123	80.5	35.9	25.2	2.6	18.3	10.7	-1.6	13.3	13.6
Northampton County	26 652	34 648	47 357	29 659	12 723	12 754	28 892	21 756	15 413	68.9	20.0	36.5	6.0	21.1	4.7	-7.6	22.2	25.7
Onslow County	33 756	35 428	40 141	23 772	15 762	21 965	22 754	20 638	14 853	86.3	23.7	17.2	3.5	18.4	4.1	-8.2	12.2	14.8
Orange County	42 372	59 874	75 125	32 634	24 705	24 908	40 713	32 016	24 873	86.8	43.8	17.0	1.5	13.1	17.4	5.1	14.8	8.4
Pamlico County	34 084	41 659	49 923	19 643	12 935	18 327	33 242	21 706	18 005	71.4	31.4	36.2	4.0	26.4	6.0	-6.3	15.2	20.1
Pasquotank County	30 444	36 402	47 553	24 167	15 000	17 826	30 870	22 350	14 815	75.1	25.8	30.5	5.5	21.2	4.7	-7.6	18.1	23.2
Pender County	35 902	41 633	47 032	25 724	17 160	17 795	32 183	21 981	17 882	75.6	25.3	30.9	3.4	21.4	6.7	-5.6	13.7	14.6
Perquimans County	29 538	35 212	42 007	15 441	14 955		28 844	19 542	15 728	68.2	30.3	37.5	5.0	25.8	3.2	-9.1	18.5	23.5
Person County	37 159	44 598	53 313	26 250	22 500	18 497	31 517	24 035	18 709	80.2	26.8	28.4	2.7	16.5	5.0	-7.3	13.0	11.8
Pitt County	32 868	43 971	57 289	23 821	17 909	19 125	32 684	25 969	18 243	82.1	25.1	21.6	3.5	13.8	7.5	-4.8	20.8	18.7
Polk County	36 259	45 096	46 382	25 750	24 120	21 186	30 658	24 264	19 804	70.0	40.5	40.5	2.1	25.6	7.2	-5.1	11.7	10.2
Randolph County	38 348	44 369	50 708	27 242	19 123	21 239	31 042	23 085	18 236	84.5	28.1	24.4	1.9	13.3	5.8	-6.5	9.7	10.4
Richmond County	28 830	35 226	46 039	19 063	14 923	13 568	27 843	20 992	14 485	73.6	20.0	30.8	4.4	16.4	4.3	-8.0	19.9	23.2
Robeson County	28 202	32 514	41 833	21 358	13 726	14 237	27 153	21 082	13 224	77.0	15.5	26.2	6.1	14.4	4.1	-8.2	23.7	26.4
Rockingham County	33 784	40 821	48 155	25 250	18 235	18 083	31 052	23 133	17 120	77.1	26.6	30.1	3.0	18.8	5.3	-7.0	13.9	14.1
Rowan County	37 494	44 242	52 216	27 450	18 903	20 503	32 154	24 521	18 071	80.0	26.9	27.3	2.7	17.1	5.8	-6.5	11.1	12.1
Rutherford County	31 122	37 787	44 322	25 833	17 459	15 700	30 102	22 061	16 270	76.3	24.4	31.9	3.7	16.6	4.6	-7.7	15.1	16.7
Sampson County	31 793	38 072	45 950	26 683	16 153	15 213	27 269	21 031	14 976	77.4	20.7	30.3	3.1	16.5	5.4	-6.9	18.0	19.0
Scotland County	31 010	39 178	48 163	21 898	13 403	17 726	31 806	24 172	15 693	76.7	20.8	26.5	5.2	18.2	5.4	-6.9	20.7	25.8
Stanly County	36 898	43 956	51 344	26 667	17 097	18 001	32 057	22 203	17 825	79.1	30.6	30.3	2.8	17.3	5.8	-6.5	11.0	12.6
Stokes County	38 808	44 615	49 441	35 231	22 903	20 214	31 478	24 864	18 130	81.8	27.9	25.4	1.8	15.1	5.2	-7.1	10.5	8.6
Surry County	33 046	38 902	43 027	23 542	18 970	16 680	29 011	21 140	17 722	78.3	27.9	30.8	2.0	14.0	5.5	-6.8	13.4	12.4

Table B-3. States and Counties — Education, Labor Force, and Income

STATE/ County code	MSA/PMSA/ NECMA code[1]	STATE County	High school graduates			College graduates		College graduates (percent)				
			Total population 25 years and over	Percent with a high school diploma or less	Percent with a high school diploma or more	Percent with a bachelor's degree or more	+/− U.S. percent with bachelor's degree or more	Non-Hispanic White	Black or African American	American Indian and Alaska Native	Asian, Hawaiian, and Pacific Islander	Hispanic or Latino[2]
			1	2	3	4	5	6	7	8	9	10
		NORTH CAROLINA—Cont'd										
37 173	...	Swain County	8 739	59.6	70.5	13.9	-10.5	14.8	24.4	9.8	59.1	9.3
37 175	...	Transylvania County	20 973	47.5	82.5	23.7	-0.7	24.0	14.3	19.7	50.0	16.1
37 177	...	Tyrrell County	2 828	67.5	66.3	10.6	-13.8	13.9	5.0	0.0	0.0	15.7
37 179	1520	Union County	78 878	50.6	80.2	21.3	-3.1	23.6	9.1	23.8	41.8	6.6
37 181	...	Vance County	27 360	66.2	68.1	10.7	-13.7	14.0	6.6	11.1	68.5	5.4
37 183	6640	Wake County	403 481	28.4	89.3	43.9	19.5	49.2	24.3	29.8	65.6	17.8
37 185	...	Warren County	13 599	64.5	67.5	11.6	-12.8	16.8	7.2	2.0	17.0	20.5
37 187	...	Washington County.......	9 091	67.5	69.9	11.6	-12.8	15.9	5.9	X	63.3	3.9
37 189	...	Watauga County	23 939	42.2	81.6	33.2	8.8	33.5	27.0	28.3	56.1	33.6
37 191	2980	Wayne County	72 894	55.3	77.2	15.0	-9.4	17.9	9.5	2.5	31.9	6.1
37 193	...	Wilkes County	45 498	65.5	66.0	11.3	-13.1	11.7	4.7	0.0	20.1	4.1
37 195	...	Wilson County	48 061	62.3	69.4	15.1	-9.3	21.4	5.5	31.0	38.9	3.1
37 197	3120	Yadkin County	24 916	64.8	72.0	10.3	-14.1	10.5	4.4	0.0	82.9	6.5
37 199	...	Yancey County	12 709	65.7	71.1	13.1	-11.3	13.2	0.0	19.2	8.3	6.6
38 000	...	NORTH DAKOTA......	408 585	44.0	83.9	22.0	-2.4	22.4	20.5	9.7	47.4	16.3
38 001	...	Adams County...............	1 885	52.3	83.1	16.6	-7.8	16.5	11.1	8.7	X	60.0
38 003	...	Barnes County	7 792	47.5	85.0	22.1	-2.3	22.1	13.3	14.9	38.9	56.3
38 005	...	Benson County..............	3 902	56.4	73.8	10.9	-13.5	14.1	X	4.4	0.0	8.0
38 007	...	Billings County	644	54.2	77.8	18.8	-5.6	18.9	X	X	X	X
38 009	...	Bottineau County...........	4 973	48.4	81.3	14.9	-9.5	14.8	X	20.0	100.0	0.0
38 011	...	Bowman County............	2 290	49.9	82.2	17.9	-6.5	17.8	0.0	50.0	X	100.0
38 013	...	Burke County................	1 687	56.1	78.8	12.0	-12.4	11.8	100.0	0.0	0.0	X
38 015	1010	Burleigh County.............	44 636	35.8	87.9	28.7	4.3	29.2	6.7	6.8	38.1	26.6
38 017	2520	Cass County.................	74 668	32.0	90.9	31.3	6.9	31.5	22.6	8.5	59.8	16.6
38 019	...	Cavalier County.............	3 462	51.6	78.8	13.1	-11.3	13.1	X	25.0	0.0	0.0
38 021	...	Dickey County	3 815	52.3	79.6	16.6	-7.8	16.4	0.0	26.3	100.0	15.6
38 023	...	Divide County	1 741	54.5	80.4	13.3	-11.1	13.2	X	0.0	50.0	0.0
38 025	...	Dunn County	2 393	54.7	77.5	16.3	-8.1	16.5	0.0	13.1	66.7	0.0
38 027	...	Eddy County.................	1 933	52.5	75.5	15.9	-8.5	15.8	X	17.4	100.0	X
38 029	...	Emmons County............	3 125	64.1	65.9	12.3	-12.1	12.2	0.0	50.0	0.0	10.0
38 031	...	Foster County...............	2 569	51.9	78.0	19.8	-4.6	19.9	X	X	60.0	0.0
38 033	...	Golden Valley County ...	1 278	46.6	87.4	19.8	-4.6	19.9	X	X	X	0.0
38 035	2985	Grand Forks County......	37 366	35.2	89.2	27.8	3.4	28.3	16.6	17.0	40.2	16.9
38 037	...	Grant County................	2 044	59.7	73.4	11.2	-13.2	10.9	X	18.2	100.0	0.0
38 039	...	Griggs County	1 993	53.9	78.7	15.7	-8.7	15.6	X	50.0	0.0	X
38 041	...	Hettinger County	1 978	57.8	74.8	14.4	-10.0	14.3	X	22.2	0.0	0.0
38 043	...	Kidder County	1 982	63.0	72.0	11.0	-13.4	11.1	X	0.0	X	0.0
38 045	...	LaMoure County	3 297	58.5	75.3	13.9	-10.5	13.8	X	22.2	X	18.2
38 047	...	Logan County...............	1 693	63.7	66.0	12.9	-11.5	12.7	X	X	25.0	54.5
38 049	...	McHenry County	4 192	57.9	76.9	13.2	-11.2	13.1	33.3	25.0	60.0	20.0
38 051	...	McIntosh County	2 580	66.6	59.3	9.9	-14.5	9.6	X	0.0	60.0	16.7
38 053	...	McKenzie County	3 644	53.5	79.1	15.7	-8.7	16.4	33.3	10.5	31.6	12.5
38 055	...	McLean County	6 620	51.8	79.0	15.1	-9.3	15.2	X	12.4	60.0	11.8
38 057	...	Mercer County	5 780	52.0	79.0	14.4	-10.0	14.1	X	15.7	84.6	42.9
38 059	1010	Morton County...............	16 520	51.7	80.2	17.0	-7.4	17.0	75.0	11.1	0.0	11.3
38 061	...	Mountrail County	4 309	51.7	77.9	15.6	-8.8	16.0	X	10.6	78.1	0.0
38 063	...	Nelson County	2 753	49.5	81.4	17.5	-6.9	17.2	100.0	12.5	88.9	X
38 065	...	Oliver County	1 402	55.4	79.9	12.0	-12.4	12.2	X	0.0	X	50.0
38 067	...	Pembina County............	5 908	52.1	79.8	16.4	-8.0	16.7	50.0	5.6	80.0	9.4
38 069	...	Pierce County	3 300	53.3	76.7	14.7	-9.7	14.8	X	21.1	0.0	X
38 071	...	Ramsey County.............	8 123	45.1	80.1	18.8	-5.6	19.4	X	7.6	66.7	28.9
38 073	...	Ransom County	4 065	54.4	81.3	15.8	-8.6	15.7	0.0	0.0	80.0	23.5
38 075	...	Renville County	1 872	48.8	84.1	16.1	-8.3	15.6	X	18.2	57.1	0.0
38 077	...	Richland County............	10 991	44.2	83.2	15.2	-9.2	15.3	X	5.1	23.3	3.5
38 079	...	Rolette County	7 406	52.9	73.7	14.7	-9.7	21.8	0.0	10.3	73.4	0.0
38 081	...	Sargent County	2 989	54.0	81.1	12.7	-11.7	12.6	100.0	28.6	X	0.0
38 083	...	Sheridan County	1 280	63.4	67.8	9.7	-14.7	9.8	X	0.0	X	0.0
38 085	...	Sioux County	1 919	53.5	78.5	11.2	-13.2	17.5	X	8.5	12.5	9.1
38 087	...	Slope County................	538	53.9	82.5	16.0	-8.4	16.0	X	X	X	X
38 089	...	Stark County	14 252	47.9	79.9	22.3	-2.1	22.2	84.6	31.0	74.1	2.4
38 091	...	Steele County...............	1 529	42.2	86.1	19.8	-4.6	19.8	0.0	16.7	X	66.7
38 093	...	Stutsman County...........	14 618	52.9	81.1	19.7	-4.7	19.6	0.0	13.0	64.7	31.6
38 095	...	Towner County..............	2 057	51.9	81.9	16.1	-8.3	16.6	0.0	0.0	X	0.0
38 097	...	Traill County	5 542	42.2	83.7	21.8	-2.6	22.2	0.0	5.3	0.0	0.0
38 099	...	Walsh County................	8 530	55.5	76.6	13.3	-11.1	13.8	0.0	0.0	0.0	0.7

[1]MSA = Metropolitan Statistical Area. PMSA = Primary MSA. NECMA = New England County Metropolitan Area. See the Appendix A for explanation of these concepts. See Appendix B for list of metropolitan areas identified by type, with component counties.
[2]Hispanic or Latino persons may be of any race.

STATE County	School enrollment			Population 16 to 19 years				Employment status, 2000			Work status in 1999 of the population 16 years and over (percent)		
											Worked in 1999		
	Grades kindergarten through 12	College or graduate school	Percent private	Number	Percent in armed forces	Percent high school graduates	Percent not enrolled, not grads, not in armed forces, not employed	Total population 16 years and over	Percent in labor force	Unemployment rate	Full-time	Part-time	Did not work in 1999
	11	12	13	14	15	16	17	18	19	20	21	22	23
NORTH CAROLINA—Cont'd													
Swain County	2 409	438	5.7	813	0.0	24.8	7.3	10 207	58.5	10.1	54.0	9.8	36.2
Transylvania County	4 469	1 462	15.7	1 557	0.0	11.1	6.5	24 193	54.8	4.9	47.3	14.3	38.4
Tyrrell County	803	156	5.3	198	0.0	7.6	3.5	3 323	50.3	6.0	44.2	13.0	42.8
Union County	24 979	4 781	13.3	6 438	0.0	12.3	4.6	92 443	70.4	4.3	61.9	13.2	24.8
Vance County	8 523	1 332	6.3	2 354	0.1	14.1	18.8	32 491	61.2	8.3	55.4	9.8	34.8
Wake County	112 881	51 713	13.9	32 322	0.0	7.9	3.9	485 147	73.8	3.9	64.5	14.9	20.6
Warren County	3 818	618	12.1	1 056	0.0	11.0	10.4	15 826	50.3	8.3	47.3	10.6	42.2
Washington County	2 797	377	7.9	796	0.0	9.3	8.3	10 591	55.1	7.1	48.2	11.1	40.7
Watauga County	5 355	10 952	7.0	4 685	0.0	3.6	0.8	36 673	63.4	8.2	49.3	26.1	24.6
Wayne County	22 655	5 211	10.7	6 104	1.8	10.8	6.9	86 989	61.8	5.9	56.0	12.5	31.5
Wilkes County	10 722	2 024	4.0	3 082	0.0	10.3	6.0	52 377	62.8	3.8	57.0	10.9	32.1
Wilson County	13 997	3 210	11.9	4 250	0.0	8.7	11.3	57 083	63.4	7.2	56.3	12.2	31.5
Yadkin County	6 360	1 149	8.9	1 581	0.0	8.9	5.8	28 439	64.3	3.1	57.9	11.2	30.9
Yancey County	2 764	444	8.4	852	0.0	21.4	8.7	14 454	56.4	4.5	49.2	11.7	39.1
NORTH DAKOTA	123 939	47 003	7.9	43 073	1.0	8.6	2.6	502 306	67.5	4.5	55.7	18.7	25.5
Adams County	526	35	1.6	142	0.0	6.3	1.4	2 083	60.1	1.8	50.6	17.5	31.9
Barnes County	2 060	912	4.5	860	0.1	6.9	2.9	9 541	62.3	4.7	52.2	18.0	29.7
Benson County	1 927	169	2.1	490	0.0	5.3	10.2	4 746	57.5	12.9	53.3	10.4	36.3
Billings County	183	23	3.4	59	0.0	6.8	0.0	718	64.1	2.8	56.8	12.5	30.6
Bottineau County	1 324	406	0.8	538	0.0	3.7	0.4	5 830	57.3	4.7	48.6	17.9	33.6
Bowman County	665	61	1.8	165	0.0	2.4	0.0	2 571	66.1	2.1	51.7	18.6	29.8
Burke County	408	21	5.1	120	0.0	2.5	1.7	1 850	56.5	2.6	44.3	18.1	37.7
Burleigh County	12 849	4 801	19.7	4 638	0.0	7.7	1.6	54 456	71.6	3.5	59.6	18.2	22.3
Cass County	20 881	14 297	6.4	7 786	0.1	8.6	2.1	97 405	75.5	3.9	61.3	20.8	17.9
Cavalier County	1 031	28	9.1	246	0.0	1.6	0.0	3 809	58.3	3.8	51.0	16.1	32.9
Dickey County	1 047	410	21.6	355	0.0	8.5	0.8	4 578	64.9	3.8	50.7	20.6	28.7
Divide County	407	24	0.5	122	0.0	2.5	4.1	1 902	54.1	4.4	44.7	16.7	38.6
Dunn County	862	71	4.0	203	0.0	8.4	2.5	2 735	63.2	6.4	51.1	15.7	33.2
Eddy County	522	48	1.9	140	0.0	7.1	2.1	2 184	58.7	4.7	50.2	16.0	33.8
Emmons County	840	60	2.2	215	0.0	2.8	0.0	3 419	56.6	3.3	45.5	14.7	39.8
Foster County	818	77	4.7	208	0.0	5.8	0.0	2 907	64.1	3.3	53.4	16.2	30.4
Golden Valley County	445	49	5.1	155	0.0	7.1	2.6	1 491	59.0	3.9	52.6	17.2	30.2
Grand Forks County	11 757	11 022	4.0	5 458	2.0	8.7	1.7	52 229	71.2	4.1	57.0	24.4	18.6
Grant County	552	41	3.0	175	0.0	5.7	2.3	2 293	56.1	2.3	44.5	17.5	38.0
Griggs County	545	40	1.4	171	0.0	2.3	0.6	2 229	59.4	3.2	47.6	19.2	33.2
Hettinger County	540	37	1.8	145	0.0	7.6	1.4	2 181	55.0	4.8	45.8	15.5	38.7
Kidder County	507	26	2.6	178	0.0	10.7	7.9	2 236	55.2	4.9	45.4	16.7	37.8
LaMoure County	977	65	4.9	319	0.0	5.1	2.8	3 757	57.6	2.8	49.1	16.9	34.0
Logan County	421	42	4.8	98	0.0	5.1	2.0	1 846	53.8	2.9	42.8	16.6	40.5
McHenry County	1 183	108	0.5	355	0.0	6.8	0.8	4 768	57.7	5.1	47.9	16.8	35.4
McIntosh County	569	63	5.4	166	0.0	3.0	0.0	2 812	52.1	2.5	43.0	14.5	42.5
McKenzie County	1 454	116	5.2	400	0.0	5.0	2.3	4 220	62.0	6.6	51.1	16.3	32.6
McLean County	1 858	159	1.6	570	0.2	7.0	1.4	7 458	57.9	5.6	47.6	16.9	35.5
Mercer County	2 108	151	4.0	597	0.0	6.9	0.8	6 536	66.8	5.4	52.3	20.6	27.1
Morton County	5 190	716	10.5	1 511	0.2	9.7	5.6	19 403	69.0	3.7	56.7	17.6	25.8
Mountrail County	1 464	235	4.8	400	0.3	4.8	5.3	5 005	58.3	5.9	50.0	14.6	35.4
Nelson County	730	61	5.7	205	0.0	1.0	0.0	3 034	56.3	3.3	48.8	16.6	34.5
Oliver County	500	39	9.3	135	0.0	1.5	1.5	1 585	65.8	5.0	53.5	17.3	29.2
Pembina County	1 734	101	1.7	555	0.0	8.5	3.6	6 810	62.1	4.8	55.6	15.8	28.6
Pierce County	894	101	6.1	249	0.0	8.0	0.0	3 715	58.5	4.1	50.1	16.2	33.6
Ramsey County	2 346	518	6.5	844	0.0	11.7	6.0	9 488	64.8	6.9	55.4	16.1	28.5
Ransom County	1 181	75	3.2	329	0.0	4.6	2.7	4 620	64.2	3.2	51.2	18.8	30.0
Renville County	521	50	1.9	165	1.2	11.5	0.0	2 101	61.3	1.8	51.2	16.9	31.9
Richland County	3 497	2 039	5.6	1 655	0.0	5.5	0.3	14 181	66.0	6.1	56.0	20.1	23.9
Rolette County	3 857	719	2.9	1 027	0.0	6.3	11.9	9 251	57.4	14.3	51.9	10.4	37.8
Sargent County	874	56	2.8	194	0.0	7.2	0.0	3 349	65.2	1.9	56.3	15.2	28.5
Sheridan County	322	11	0.9	75	0.0	4.0	5.3	1 395	51.8	7.5	42.4	17.5	40.1
Sioux County	1 258	196	9.1	348	0.0	6.6	12.9	2 583	58.7	23.3	52.8	6.3	40.9
Slope County	157	8	0.0	52	0.0	7.7	0.0	610	67.4	2.9	55.2	20.5	24.3
Stark County	4 586	1 509	17.2	1 687	0.2	10.8	3.2	17 663	66.6	4.8	53.0	19.2	27.8
Steele County	500	59	1.6	139	0.2	2.9	2.2	1 733	63.0	2.9	53.7	17.4	29.0
Stutsman County	3 983	1 215	23.0	1 471	0.2	9.2	3.3	17 621	64.7	3.4	55.0	17.6	27.5
Towner County	595	49	1.1	165	0.0	2.4	2.4	2 287	60.1	2.3	54.0	14.4	31.5
Traill County	1 606	670	1.4	544	0.0	4.2	1.3	6 626	61.7	3.2	54.0	18.6	27.4
Walsh County	2 438	194	3.5	789	0.0	11.9	2.4	9 778	63.6	6.2	54.0	16.1	29.8

Table B-3. States and Counties — Education, Labor Force, and Income

STATE County	Full-year full-time employed (percent)								Children under 18 years in families					Total employed by class of worker (percent)				
						American Indian and Alaska Native	Asian, Hawaiian, and Pacific Islander			With two parents (percent)		With one parent who is in labor force (percent)	+/- U.S. percent of children with no stay-at-home parent (percent)	+/- U.S. percent two-income couples				Unpaid family worker
	Total	Men	Women	Non-Hispanic White	Black or African American			Hispanic or Latino[1]	Number	Both in labor force	Father only in labor force				Private	Government	Self-employed	
	24	25	26	27	28	29	30	31	32	33	34	35	36	37	38	39	40	41
NORTH CAROLINA—Cont'd																		
Swain County	34.8	41.5	28.8	34.7	23.7	36.8	59.1	9.4	2 822	40.3	18.6	26.6	2.3	-5.9	64.2	22.5	12.9	0.3
Transylvania County	35.6	45.6	26.7	35.5	34.9	38.8	44.3	24.1	5 565	43.6	26.7	21.0	0.0	-10.6	74.9	11.8	12.9	0.4
Tyrrell County	29.1	33.4	24.2	36.3	20.1	60.0	0.0	15.5	875	36.9	13.7	34.4	6.7	-3.8	60.3	23.0	15.1	1.5
Union County	49.0	60.7	37.6	50.7	42.9	42.5	50.0	38.2	33 370	47.5	26.6	16.3	-0.8	6.4	79.0	9.8	10.9	0.3
Vance County	40.3	47.6	34.1	45.2	35.0	45.1	53.1	38.0	10 579	32.8	13.4	29.1	-2.7	0.2	75.4	16.5	7.8	0.3
Wake County	50.4	61.3	40.0	51.9	48.2	43.6	46.6	41.9	150 757	47.4	26.4	18.4	1.2	8.9	75.1	15.8	8.9	0.2
Warren County	32.5	38.4	26.9	36.9	29.2	26.0	54.5	24.3	4 260	35.4	13.8	27.1	-2.1	-10.3	66.6	21.5	11.4	0.5
Washington County	37.0	46.7	28.6	41.7	31.3	X	29.0	48.0	3 194	34.9	11.5	30.4	0.7	-7.2	69.8	17.8	11.5	0.9
Watauga County	32.0	38.2	26.0	32.4	22.2	46.6	13.8	19.4	6 750	52.5	24.9	16.8	4.7	2.4	63.1	23.4	13.0	0.5
Wayne County	41.9	51.8	32.5	45.6	34.8	31.1	42.4	42.4	27 438	41.4	18.4	25.0	1.8	-0.3	69.1	21.4	8.9	0.5
Wilkes County	44.3	53.7	35.2	44.8	40.1	32.3	40.6	39.3	14 171	50.5	22.0	16.2	2.1	-0.1	76.7	11.6	11.4	0.4
Wilson County	41.5	51.2	33.0	45.9	35.6	41.0	30.1	38.5	17 153	37.2	15.9	30.8	3.4	2.4	77.0	14.4	8.3	0.2
Yadkin County	44.9	54.2	36.1	45.2	37.3	36.2	32.6	45.2	8 312	53.5	16.7	17.3	6.2	1.9	79.8	10.4	9.5	0.3
Yancey County	36.2	45.9	27.2	36.4	37.9	12.2	45.8	32.0	3 603	45.6	24.3	15.8	-3.2	-7.7	70.5	15.1	14.5	0.0
NORTH DAKOTA	40.4	49.6	31.4	40.9	40.9	30.8	30.9	39.1	155 201	60.2	14.9	17.0	12.6	8.8	69.1	16.5	13.9	0.6
Adams County	39.7	51.7	29.1	39.1	50.0	80.0	X	0.0	601	61.7	11.6	17.6	14.7	2.5	61.4	11.8	25.5	1.4
Barnes County	34.5	44.8	24.9	34.6	11.1	42.4	77.8	15.8	2 575	62.6	13.7	17.1	15.1	3.4	64.6	16.5	18.2	0.7
Benson County	33.4	38.8	28.0	35.7	X	29.7	100.0	23.1	2 253	33.4	13.1	36.4	5.2	-4.7	53.5	25.8	19.1	1.5
Billings County	39.0	49.1	28.0	38.7	X	X	X	X	202	66.8	23.8	5.4	7.6	1.6	40.5	21.9	33.6	4.0
Bottineau County	32.1	41.9	22.5	32.5	X	11.9	0.0	0.0	1 521	70.3	12.0	10.7	16.4	1.7	58.2	20.0	21.2	0.7
Bowman County	39.4	54.5	24.9	39.6	0.0	50.0	X	0.0	769	76.1	6.8	12.1	23.6	14.4	60.9	11.0	27.2	1.0
Burke County	31.0	41.6	20.1	31.1	100.0	28.6	0.0	X	449	67.5	9.6	14.0	16.9	-2.2	50.7	18.4	28.8	2.2
Burleigh County	46.6	55.2	38.5	47.4	15.9	28.6	21.5	19.7	16 708	65.2	13.7	15.3	15.9	14.8	70.4	19.0	10.3	0.4
Cass County	45.8	54.3	37.4	46.4	35.1	31.7	31.3	43.6	28 063	60.0	15.4	18.0	13.4	15.1	78.3	12.9	8.6	0.2
Cavalier County	35.8	47.3	24.7	35.7	X	20.0	100.0	45.5	1 170	58.7	19.8	12.4	6.5	-1.6	59.2	15.2	25.1	0.6
Dickey County	36.6	46.9	27.1	36.8	28.6	33.3	10.0	41.3	1 322	69.3	12.5	15.8	20.5	11.4	64.9	10.7	23.4	1.0
Divide County	31.3	42.4	20.8	31.1	X	100.0	25.0	71.4	454	70.3	8.4	14.1	19.8	2.5	54.9	15.3	29.4	0.4
Dunn County	36.9	44.1	29.5	38.4	100.0	20.8	75.0	75.0	955	60.2	11.2	14.5	10.1	5.6	53.9	17.3	27.4	1.4
Eddy County	34.4	42.6	26.8	34.1	X	56.0	100.0	0.0	649	67.8	16.0	8.5	11.7	-1.3	62.6	13.3	23.4	0.7
Emmons County	33.1	40.2	25.9	32.8	100.0	50.0	100.0	60.0	1 061	67.6	9.6	12.3	15.3	0.2	52.8	10.0	33.8	3.4
Foster County	39.0	50.9	27.8	39.0	X	X	70.0	20.0	948	68.1	11.9	11.3	14.8	7.6	65.9	12.5	20.1	1.5
Golden Valley County	35.3	46.9	24.8	35.7	X	X	0.0	20.0	480	62.5	16.0	13.3	11.2	2.9	49.4	17.8	31.8	0.9
Grand Forks County	40.3	49.5	30.9	40.7	43.8	34.1	26.7	36.6	15 383	56.8	17.7	17.4	9.6	12.3	70.1	21.4	8.2	0.2
Grant County	33.4	43.0	23.6	33.6	X	17.6	100.0	100.0	615	55.6	19.0	14.0	5.0	2.5	46.1	11.6	39.9	2.4
Griggs County	33.3	45.3	21.3	33.1	X	75.0	100.0	X	614	72.1	13.5	6.7	14.2	3.9	61.4	13.1	23.9	1.6
Hettinger County	32.5	47.7	17.1	32.4	X	30.0	0.0	33.3	622	59.2	22.8	8.0	2.6	-5.0	49.0	12.3	34.3	4.4
Kidder County	30.3	38.8	21.6	30.2	X	0.0	X	64.3	625	62.7	17.1	10.7	8.8	-4.0	49.4	15.4	32.9	2.2
LaMoure County	34.9	45.2	24.7	34.9	X	22.2	X	28.6	1 103	60.8	16.8	12.4	8.6	-1.2	57.2	12.4	28.5	1.9
Logan County	30.8	41.6	20.3	30.8	X	X	50.0	18.2	525	72.2	14.3	3.4	11.0	-4.9	47.5	12.6	36.7	3.2
McHenry County	31.3	40.1	22.2	31.4	25.0	15.4	0.0	40.0	1 408	60.7	18.0	12.4	8.5	-0.2	57.6	16.2	24.7	1.5
McIntosh County	31.3	39.9	23.4	31.2	X	0.0	60.0	47.4	647	75.0	9.6	7.4	17.8	2.2	58.2	11.8	27.3	2.7
McKenzie County	35.8	48.1	23.8	36.8	33.3	31.7	34.5	52.2	1 612	55.1	14.9	18.4	8.9	4.3	50.8	23.0	25.3	0.8
McLean County	32.7	43.0	22.4	32.8	X	31.6	20.0	47.1	2 113	58.3	20.6	15.0	8.7	-2.7	65.4	14.8	18.6	1.2
Mercer County	40.4	57.9	23.0	40.4	X	26.0	25.0	57.1	2 397	65.0	20.7	9.9	10.3	6.2	73.0	14.5	12.0	0.5
Morton County	42.2	51.2	33.5	42.4	94.3	25.7	0.0	67.4	6 582	63.4	12.2	16.9	15.7	9.8	71.8	15.4	12.2	0.7
Mountrail County	33.2	41.2	25.6	31.9	0.0	35.1	3.1	43.5	1 760	49.1	14.7	21.9	6.4	1.4	56.8	23.1	19.2	0.9
Nelson County	33.3	43.3	23.9	33.3	100.0	31.6	45.5	X	792	66.7	12.0	14.1	16.2	3.9	59.0	13.0	26.8	1.2
Oliver County	37.5	51.0	23.1	37.8	X	44.0	X	28.6	562	64.8	21.4	11.9	12.1	6.2	63.7	12.1	23.1	1.1
Pembina County	38.3	48.7	27.9	38.7	50.0	29.5	40.0	25.2	2 066	62.5	18.2	13.3	11.2	1.5	68.1	12.7	18.4	0.8
Pierce County	33.8	42.3	26.0	33.5	0.0	73.7	100.0	0.0	1 083	61.3	14.4	17.5	14.2	0.7	61.5	12.2	23.3	3.0
Ramsey County	38.7	47.2	30.7	39.6	X	29.5	28.0	35.9	2 896	58.1	8.2	24.6	18.1	5.9	65.5	18.4	15.5	0.5
Ransom County	38.6	48.8	27.8	38.6	33.3	35.7	20.0	42.1	1 430	66.3	15.2	12.9	14.6	8.9	67.4	11.2	20.6	0.8
Renville County	35.7	45.2	26.3	35.1	83.3	50.0	100.0	25.0	598	68.9	11.2	13.4	17.7	3.9	54.5	15.1	28.3	2.0
Richland County	36.8	45.3	27.7	37.0	0.0	41.6	23.1	22.2	4 259	66.4	13.2	12.9	14.7	8.9	70.0	14.0	15.0	1.0
Rolette County	32.3	35.5	29.4	37.5	0.0	30.4	28.1	42.3	4 664	37.3	8.5	27.9	0.6	-0.6	50.6	38.1	10.5	0.8
Sargent County	41.9	55.2	27.3	41.7	100.0	57.9	X	16.7	1 122	71.5	12.8	11.4	18.3	6.2	66.6	10.8	22.0	0.7
Sheridan County	27.5	37.8	16.7	27.8	X	0.0	X	0.0	356	51.7	30.1	8.7	-4.2	-10.7	43.8	15.7	35.0	5.5
Sioux County	31.6	31.9	31.2	40.8	X	28.7	35.0	30.0	1 396	24.4	9.2	45.8	5.6	-2.7	40.9	47.2	11.3	0.5
Slope County	43.3	58.7	24.6	43.3	X	X	X	X	193	64.8	19.2	4.7	4.9	3.2	33.1	14.8	49.6	2.5
Stark County	37.1	45.7	29.1	37.3	15.0	40.4	36.1	19.9	5 604	67.7	14.9	12.7	15.8	12.6	69.4	14.5	15.2	0.9
Steele County	35.9	45.7	25.3	36.1	100.0	33.3	X	33.3	597	66.8	16.1	11.1	13.3	7.3	57.1	12.2	28.8	1.9
Stutsman County	40.4	47.6	33.7	40.9	0.0	28.3	0.0	21.2	4 779	62.3	12.8	19.4	17.1	11.0	70.8	15.2	13.8	0.3
Towner County	37.1	45.2	29.2	37.1	0.0	43.8	X	0.0	679	67.0	9.6	12.8	15.2	6.7	59.4	13.6	25.9	1.2
Traill County	35.3	46.9	23.8	35.5	25.0	27.9	0.0	28.6	2 076	62.0	15.4	16.6	14.0	5.2	67.0	16.6	15.3	1.1
Walsh County	38.6	46.6	31.0	38.4	100.0	30.4	71.4	41.2	2 995	63.3	11.0	15.3	14.0	5.5	62.1	19.8	17.4	0.7

[1] Hispanic or Latino persons may be of any race.

Table B-3. States and Counties — Education, Labor Force, and Income

STATE County	Percent who worked at home	Percent of the population 5 years and over with a disability	Veterans as a percent of the population 18 years and over	Occupation for employed population 16 years and over (percent)						Industry for employed population 16 years and over (percent)					
				Management, professional, and related occupations	Service occupations	Sales and office occupations	Farming, fishing, and forestry occupations	Construction, extraction, and maintenance occupations	Production, transportation and material moving occupations	Agriculture, forestry, fishing, and mining	Construction and manufacturing	Wholesale and retail trade	Transportation and warehousing, and utilities	Service industries	Public administration
	42	43	44	45	46	47	48	49	50	51	52	53	54	55	56
NORTH CAROLINA—Cont'd															
Swain County	3.5	26.9	14.5	25.5	22.7	24.1	0.3	13.3	14.1	1.8	20.1	12.3	4.0	55.2	6.6
Transylvania County	2.7	20.5	18.2	27.3	17.1	22.6	0.7	13.7	18.6	1.8	31.7	13.5	2.7	47.0	3.3
Tyrrell County	4.4	30.5	12.7	20.0	18.0	21.3	9.8	12.2	18.8	16.8	16.4	13.6	3.8	40.8	8.6
Union County	3.5	18.1	11.7	30.7	11.8	28.1	0.5	12.5	16.5	1.5	30.1	18.5	4.5	42.8	2.6
Vance County	1.3	26.2	10.5	23.1	14.4	25.5	0.6	11.4	25.0	1.7	34.7	17.7	3.4	37.0	5.4
Wake County	3.8	13.5	10.9	47.0	11.0	26.0	0.2	7.8	7.9	0.5	20.0	14.1	4.1	55.7	5.7
Warren County	3.2	27.1	11.6	25.2	17.1	20.5	2.6	11.0	23.7	5.4	28.5	13.3	5.3	40.2	7.3
Washington County	2.1	25.5	11.7	22.5	18.2	21.3	1.3	14.1	22.4	5.2	33.6	12.4	3.9	39.3	5.6
Watauga County	4.1	15.5	10.4	34.3	18.6	26.6	1.0	11.0	8.6	1.0	15.6	15.6	2.6	62.5	2.7
Wayne County	1.9	23.9	16.0	28.1	15.1	24.3	2.1	11.6	18.8	3.9	24.2	18.2	4.3	43.1	6.3
Wilkes County	2.5	24.7	11.1	22.4	12.3	23.2	1.6	11.4	29.1	3.5	36.1	19.7	3.7	34.5	2.5
Wilson County	1.6	27.1	11.3	25.3	15.0	22.8	1.5	12.1	23.3	2.6	32.3	15.0	3.8	42.9	3.6
Yadkin County	2.2	22.7	11.4	23.9	12.3	22.0	0.9	14.0	26.9	2.4	39.2	14.4	4.0	37.4	2.6
Yancey County	2.9	27.0	13.9	22.8	16.6	17.0	2.3	14.0	27.4	5.0	38.0	11.1	4.5	37.6	3.9
NORTH DAKOTA	6.0	16.7	12.7	33.3	16.7	26.1	1.7	9.8	12.4	8.2	13.3	16.4	5.7	51.6	4.8
Adams County	13.8	19.9	12.6	38.3	16.8	22.4	2.5	9.9	10.0	17.3	6.9	16.1	4.4	51.4	3.9
Barnes County	6.9	16.2	13.4	32.3	19.5	21.0	2.3	9.9	15.0	10.7	17.1	15.2	4.1	48.5	4.3
Benson County	9.8	19.1	11.8	34.9	18.9	20.8	2.7	8.4	14.3	15.8	14.8	9.0	4.5	49.5	6.5
Billings County	29.1	13.3	18.7	38.7	13.4	22.8	5.4	11.2	8.5	37.1	11.0	9.4	2.7	31.3	8.5
Bottineau County	7.9	18.3	13.5	30.3	16.4	26.7	3.2	11.9	11.5	16.1	10.6	14.3	7.5	46.2	5.4
Bowman County	11.3	14.6	10.3	37.3	14.1	20.9	2.8	10.3	14.6	22.5	8.9	18.1	3.4	44.4	2.8
Burke County	13.9	15.9	14.8	36.1	16.8	19.3	2.9	9.8	15.1	23.5	7.9	11.5	9.1	40.7	7.4
Burleigh County	4.0	16.2	12.7	36.5	16.0	28.8	0.4	8.5	9.7	2.6	10.9	16.3	6.6	54.4	9.2
Cass County	3.4	14.8	11.1	33.4	14.6	30.8	0.6	8.2	12.4	1.8	15.3	20.0	4.9	55.2	2.7
Cavalier County	7.6	14.4	13.0	34.6	18.2	24.7	1.4	9.9	11.2	16.2	7.4	16.3	7.7	47.6	4.9
Dickey County	11.1	18.2	12.2	33.0	15.6	24.2	4.4	8.1	14.7	17.3	12.4	15.7	4.8	47.6	2.3
Divide County	7.9	15.0	15.2	40.9	18.0	19.6	4.0	7.5	10.1	25.2	4.6	12.8	4.6	47.0	5.9
Dunn County	20.9	16.3	13.8	37.9	14.8	17.5	3.6	11.9	14.3	26.4	17.8	11.9	4.8	32.4	0.7
Eddy County	13.2	17.6	13.0	39.1	17.9	16.5	3.5	9.0	14.1	19.6	13.5	9.9	4.3	48.9	3.8
Emmons County	22.4	21.6	12.4	40.9	15.3	20.7	5.0	9.1	9.0	28.0	8.4	10.6	5.0	44.6	3.4
Foster County	9.1	16.1	11.2	35.6	14.9	21.2	1.7	8.9	17.7	13.5	17.7	15.4	6.7	42.4	4.2
Golden Valley County	12.2	20.5	14.8	43.6	17.8	15.6	3.7	9.2	10.0	26.0	6.5	11.8	5.6	43.6	6.5
Grand Forks County	3.2	14.4	12.7	32.2	20.1	25.4	0.7	10.5	11.1	2.4	13.6	16.6	5.0	58.0	4.5
Grant County	25.8	19.3	12.9	46.7	15.3	15.6	4.1	8.8	9.5	33.5	6.1	11.8	4.9	38.3	5.3
Griggs County	13.5	16.2	13.3	35.1	16.7	20.4	3.0	10.3	14.5	16.0	16.4	16.7	5.7	41.2	4.1
Hettinger County	17.3	18.2	15.9	41.8	13.6	15.3	7.7	10.3	11.3	32.9	9.2	12.3	5.5	37.2	2.8
Kidder County	22.3	18.7	13.0	40.9	13.7	18.5	6.3	8.4	12.1	30.1	8.2	8.3	7.8	42.7	3.0
LaMoure County	16.0	17.1	12.1	36.4	12.8	19.8	5.6	9.8	15.6	23.3	13.0	15.3	7.2	37.3	3.9
Logan County	18.1	23.0	11.4	39.9	16.0	17.4	4.9	10.2	11.6	27.1	10.2	11.5	5.5	42.9	2.8
McHenry County	13.8	21.0	15.0	33.2	15.3	21.6	4.2	14.2	11.4	20.5	14.5	11.3	8.2	40.6	4.8
McIntosh County	16.2	23.8	11.0	37.2	19.7	18.7	4.5	8.0	11.9	21.3	7.7	13.1	6.1	49.0	2.9
McKenzie County	14.1	15.8	15.0	37.5	16.2	19.8	2.9	11.6	11.9	24.4	8.3	12.4	6.6	42.3	6.0
McLean County	9.5	19.4	14.7	31.8	16.5	22.1	2.0	15.8	11.8	16.7	10.8	11.9	11.5	44.2	4.9
Mercer County	6.6	16.7	14.0	27.2	17.1	19.2	0.6	17.9	17.9	16.6	10.5	11.2	18.4	39.5	3.9
Morton County	6.4	17.3	12.8	30.5	17.9	25.9	1.6	11.9	12.2	6.4	13.6	15.3	8.0	51.2	5.6
Mountrail County	10.4	17.9	14.5	36.8	18.6	22.9	1.9	11.4	8.4	17.5	8.6	11.3	4.5	49.9	8.3
Nelson County	7.2	21.0	16.2	36.7	14.8	20.5	3.5	11.5	13.0	16.3	13.0	14.2	6.5	45.7	4.2
Oliver County	16.5	15.0	11.7	35.2	12.8	15.8	4.9	15.4	15.7	34.1	10.5	7.2	12.5	30.9	4.8
Pembina County	4.7	16.8	14.7	28.7	13.6	23.3	6.1	10.2	18.2	15.9	21.6	15.6	6.0	35.3	5.6
Pierce County	17.0	18.1	13.7	37.0	16.6	24.8	3.6	7.3	10.6	16.5	9.0	15.2	5.3	50.9	3.2
Ramsey County	4.2	20.4	11.6	32.4	19.9	27.2	1.0	10.0	9.5	5.7	11.0	18.8	4.0	54.5	6.0
Ransom County	8.0	15.8	15.2	31.4	15.5	18.3	3.6	9.1	22.0	15.7	24.7	14.5	5.6	37.6	1.8
Renville County	14.6	16.4	16.5	38.6	16.3	19.1	3.6	9.9	12.4	23.5	9.0	12.0	3.9	45.5	6.1
Richland County	7.2	16.0	10.6	28.9	17.2	21.3	3.4	10.6	18.6	11.6	23.5	13.3	5.5	43.2	3.0
Rolette County	4.8	18.7	11.1	36.0	18.5	25.0	1.0	8.5	11.1	6.4	10.1	10.8	2.7	61.7	8.3
Sargent County	11.2	15.9	13.0	29.3	12.5	16.3	4.4	7.3	30.3	17.5	35.3	9.9	4.8	29.3	3.3
Sheridan County	24.8	21.7	14.3	43.0	12.9	18.7	6.0	9.3	10.2	35.0	9.1	11.8	4.6	32.3	7.2
Sioux County	5.6	18.9	13.8	33.3	30.9	18.6	1.6	8.3	7.3	10.0	6.6	4.3	1.6	60.8	16.6
Slope County	32.6	28.1	9.1	56.1	5.5	9.8	10.5	9.0	9.0	56.4	8.0	7.0	4.8	19.5	4.3
Stark County	5.8	18.6	12.3	32.2	14.3	27.0	1.5	10.4	14.6	10.0	14.9	16.5	4.6	50.2	3.8
Steele County	12.8	12.8	14.8	38.8	11.8	19.5	7.3	12.4	10.1	24.7	11.4	13.8	8.6	37.3	4.2
Stutsman County	5.8	18.0	12.9	31.8	19.3	24.7	1.6	9.5	13.1	7.9	16.7	14.0	5.1	52.8	3.5
Towner County	12.6	15.1	13.2	38.8	16.3	18.9	3.4	9.8	12.9	20.7	13.5	12.0	8.2	40.9	4.8
Traill County	4.8	16.3	14.0	30.3	18.0	22.3	2.9	10.9	15.7	9.4	16.0	15.5	6.1	49.9	3.2
Walsh County	4.4	20.4	14.4	29.1	16.8	20.3	6.7	11.5	15.6	15.1	15.2	13.2	5.8	45.4	5.3

Table B-3. States and Counties — Education, Labor Force, and Income

STATE County	Median family income					Median income for full-year, full-time workers			Households by source of income (percent)								
			Families with children														Families with children with income below poverty (percent)
	Median house-hold income	All families	Married-couple	Male house-holder	Female house-holder	Median nonfamily house-hold income	Men	Women	Per capita income	With earnings	With interest, dividend, or rental income	With Social Security income	With public assis-tance income	With retire-ment income	House-holds with income over $100,000 (percent)	+/− U.S. percent for income over $100,000	House-holds with income below poverty (percent)	
	57	58	59	60	61	62	63	64	65	66	67	68	69	70	71	72	73	74
NORTH CAROLINA—Cont'd																		
Swain County	28 608	33 786	41 641	24 152	17 107	15 793	27 283	21 216	14 647	76.5	29.5	32.7	2.3	15.3	3.8	−8.5	17.2	19.9
Transylvania County	38 587	45 579	50 269	21 591	16 932	21 110	33 307	21 623	20 767	69.3	43.1	39.1	2.2	28.8	6.9	−5.4	10.2	11.5
Tyrrell County	25 684	32 468	42 411	14 583	9 545	12 222	26 915	18 977	13 326	73.1	19.6	40.2	4.7	19.4	3.3	−9.0	24.0	27.3
Union County	50 638	56 197	62 599	32 143	23 323	25 565	38 431	27 074	21 978	87.0	32.6	20.8	1.7	14.1	13.7	1.4	7.9	8.0
Vance County	31 301	36 389	45 345	23 750	15 641	16 674	29 664	22 134	15 897	77.7	21.5	29.3	5.2	15.2	5.7	−6.6	19.3	22.9
Wake County	54 988	67 149	78 385	35 909	25 300	35 263	46 002	32 291	27 004	89.9	40.7	15.3	1.6	12.6	19.6	7.3	7.4	7.2
Warren County	28 351	33 602	43 438	25 208	15 057	13 958	28 244	21 458	14 716	71.9	21.1	34.4	4.4	22.0	4.3	−8.0	20.7	21.7
Washington County	28 865	34 888	41 646	19 464	11 175	13 955	27 448	20 435	14 994	71.3	25.0	35.2	4.9	20.3	5.3	−7.0	21.1	27.7
Watauga County	32 611	45 508	51 481	22 500	21 577	17 830	30 585	22 471	17 258	81.8	38.3	22.5	1.2	14.1	6.1	−6.2	18.8	9.9
Wayne County	33 942	40 492	48 316	25 495	16 854	20 023	29 721	22 355	17 010	79.9	25.9	26.4	2.9	19.9	5.4	−6.9	13.8	15.2
Wilkes County	34 258	40 607	44 859	21 445	19 176	15 907	28 298	21 543	17 516	78.4	28.8	29.4	2.1	13.1	5.1	−7.2	13.7	12.5
Wilson County	33 116	41 551	51 193	26 066	15 991	16 523	31 025	22 475	17 102	78.3	23.8	27.9	4.4	17.4	6.4	−5.9	18.5	20.1
Yadkin County	36 660	43 758	49 774	22 177	19 426	17 878	30 519	23 756	18 576	77.9	30.4	30.1	1.4	16.9	5.9	−6.4	11.9	10.3
Yancey County	29 674	35 879	39 055	37 857	15 726	15 127	27 506	21 319	16 335	70.2	27.7	35.2	2.8	18.7	3.7	−8.6	16.7	17.7
NORTH DAKOTA	34 604	43 654	51 447	26 194	16 538	20 296	31 410	21 552	17 769	80.7	42.4	27.5	2.9	10.8	5.7	−6.6	12.5	12.0
Adams County	29 079	34 306	41 591	25 417	16 944	16 792	25 302	19 236	18 425	75.4	44.1	40.8	1.7	9.3	5.2	−7.1	12.1	10.3
Barnes County	31 166	42 149	48 389	18 109	16 453	30 703	19 655	16 566	16 566	74.6	49.0	35.8	4.1	11.2	4.2	−8.1	12.8	9.6
Benson County	26 688	31 558	40 982	19 583	13 125	15 988	25 556	18 512	11 509	77.4	35.0	32.0	9.9	6.9	2.6	−9.7	24.2	33.1
Billings County	32 667	35 750	44 688	0	11 667	22 321	35 000	22 778	16 186	83.1	43.1	29.6	0.8	2.8	5.0	−7.3	13.0	8.4
Bottineau County	29 853	37 701	45 068	19 250	16 563	17 928	28 333	19 637	16 227	72.0	49.2	38.6	4.2	11.8	4.1	−8.2	12.2	9.7
Bowman County	31 906	39 485	46 389	21 875	20 625	18 636	30 168	19 688	17 662	76.5	45.8	36.1	1.0	10.0	4.2	−8.1	9.3	8.8
Burke County	25 330	31 384	41 667	36 667	15 000	13 405	29 957	17 228	14 026	72.4	39.6	44.3	1.4	6.9	1.6	−10.7	17.2	12.9
Burleigh County	41 309	52 085	59 897	26 908	17 403	22 576	35 717	23 249	20 436	83.6	44.4	23.7	2.5	13.0	7.5	−4.8	9.1	8.8
Cass County	38 147	51 469	59 523	30 342	19 221	23 403	33 388	23 162	20 889	87.0	39.8	18.3	2.3	9.7	8.2	−4.1	10.8	8.3
Cavalier County	31 868	39 601	47 697	26 250	21 042	20 303	30 040	20 208	15 817	73.9	46.9	39.9	1.8	7.3	3.8	−8.5	11.1	11.9
Dickey County	29 231	36 682	39 865	31 250	12 500	16 098	28 221	16 545	15 846	75.1	51.2	36.6	2.4	11.5	4.7	−7.6	14.5	17.7
Divide County	30 089	39 292	40 000	16 875	14 375	14 133	29 537	17 177	16 225	68.2	51.0	45.6	1.9	8.5	3.4	−8.9	17.1	16.1
Dunn County	30 015	34 405	40 250	20 417	15 313	16 250	27 060	18 581	14 624	79.1	45.4	31.2	2.4	9.8	4.4	−7.9	17.4	19.4
Eddy County	28 642	37 625	46 563	19 167	23 750	16 920	25 388	21 174	15 941	73.2	51.4	41.5	1.8	8.7	5.8	−6.5	10.9	9.3
Emmons County	26 119	31 857	36 313	21 071	20 875	12 404	25 896	16 477	14 604	68.7	46.0	42.8	3.2	7.8	4.2	−8.1	22.0	19.6
Foster County	32 019	40 469	52 609	32 083	12 885	20 263	31 951	20 592	17 928	77.4	44.2	34.0	2.4	10.4	5.0	−7.3	10.7	11.1
Golden Valley County	29 967	37 105	40 703	17 188	21 250	16 528	26 920	19 000	14 173	79.1	46.9	37.4	0.4	11.1	3.2	−9.1	15.0	17.3
Grand Forks County	35 785	46 620	53 860	28 646	16 314	22 202	31 026	22 030	17 868	85.8	39.6	19.7	2.5	11.3	5.7	−6.6	13.0	11.9
Grant County	23 165	30 625	36 406	14 750	14 750	11 903	22 740	17 973	14 616	68.8	47.9	42.3	4.3	10.8	2.8	−9.5	20.2	20.5
Griggs County	29 572	38 611	43 750	16 250	20 179	17 107	27 500	20 571	16 131	72.6	51.8	38.6	1.9	11.6	4.0	−8.3	11.0	6.8
Hettinger County	29 209	34 668	35 000	21 250	16 250	16 818	24 375	17 257	15 555	70.7	53.4	42.5	2.2	8.6	4.2	−8.1	14.5	19.0
Kidder County	25 389	30 469	35 170	23 333	22 500	14 537	26 200	19 063	14 270	71.2	49.1	42.1	0.8	8.7	3.4	−8.9	20.4	19.2
LaMoure County	29 707	36 495	45 729	30 000	22 750	18 889	27 610	18 261	17 059	74.8	48.3	40.4	1.4	9.8	5.1	−7.2	14.4	17.0
Logan County	27 986	33 125	36 250	26 250	26 250	16 359	26 118	18 500	16 947	70.3	49.9	43.1	2.2	7.4	5.7	−6.6	15.4	18.7
McHenry County	27 274	35 676	42 026	28 750	15 000	15 026	26 715	20 176	15 140	72.0	46.6	40.4	2.2	12.1	3.5	−8.8	16.7	17.0
McIntosh County	26 389	31 771	42 826	30 625	17 500	12 370	23 359	18 063	15 018	66.1	53.3	48.4	2.2	9.3	4.3	−8.0	17.8	13.1
McKenzie County	29 342	34 091	42 083	22 188	14 427	18 262	27 905	20 912	14 732	77.5	44.0	31.8	5.6	12.1	4.3	−8.0	15.7	18.9
McLean County	32 337	39 604	49 948	30 139	15 515	16 250	35 316	19 104	16 220	73.4	47.0	35.8	2.5	12.4	3.2	−9.1	14.6	16.3
Mercer County	42 269	51 983	59 323	36 875	20 000	18 319	49 102	22 095	18 256	80.1	37.7	27.3	1.7	10.5	5.4	−6.9	10.3	5.7
Morton County	37 028	44 592	50 987	25 303	17 039	17 841	31 343	21 733	17 202	81.2	40.8	30.0	2.6	10.5	5.8	−6.5	10.9	9.3
Mountrail County	27 098	31 864	39 435	22 083	15 833	15 938	25 853	21 234	13 422	76.3	35.2	33.2	4.8	8.6	2.9	−9.4	19.4	20.2
Nelson County	28 892	37 406	44 403	28 542	15 714	17 389	28 151	19 755	16 320	70.1	51.0	43.2	0.9	13.3	2.9	−9.4	12.1	9.2
Oliver County	36 650	45 430	51 912	21 250	18 333	18 333	41 818	19 537	16 271	81.2	50.4	30.7	1.2	11.0	3.8	−8.5	13.7	16.1
Pembina County	36 430	45 338	51 818	28 438	17 344	22 813	31 991	22 302	18 692	77.5	48.4	33.9	1.6	10.5	5.5	−6.8	9.8	9.2
Pierce County	26 524	34 412	41 364	18 250	17 115	15 365	25 670	19 275	14 055	74.5	45.9	40.2	2.9	8.3	3.4	−8.9	14.3	12.7
Ramsey County	35 600	42 439	49 665	26 932	13 160	19 308	30 860	19 547	18 060	77.5	42.9	32.8	3.9	13.9	5.6	−6.7	12.3	14.2
Ransom County	37 672	44 865	52 107	30 938	15 156	20 329	35 929	20 047	18 219	77.5	48.6	34.3	2.5	9.9	4.0	−8.3	9.6	8.0
Renville County	30 746	36 023	41 458	26 458	20 469	18 750	27 083	17 194	16 478	75.5	53.8	36.5	4.0	11.7	2.9	−9.4	11.7	11.1
Richland County	36 098	45 484	52 229	24 792	20 385	19 741	31 443	21 262	16 339	81.6	42.2	28.1	1.9	9.7	4.5	−7.8	12.9	8.6
Rolette County	26 232	29 744	40 631	15 345	10 679	13 033	24 910	21 385	10 873	74.9	19.2	25.7	13.3	9.9	3.0	−9.3	30.1	35.5
Sargent County	37 213	44 063	51 129	31 042	21 250	21 250	35 588	20 638	18 689	78.5	46.0	32.4	2.2	10.9	5.3	−7.0	9.6	8.0
Sheridan County	24 450	30 156	31 563	28 750	11 875	14 167	23 618	16 719	13 283	69.9	48.0	44.8	4.5	9.6	2.2	−10.1	20.6	23.4
Sioux County	22 483	24 000	35 625	20 625	12 386	11 691	22 385	19 625	7 731	80.4	12.6	16.8	18.6	7.7	1.4	−10.9	34.7	38.9
Slope County	24 667	26 058	24 479	20 714	6 563	14 219	21 100	13 750	14 513	85.6	29.5	37.5	1.9	10.6	4.5	−7.8	20.8	19.2
Stark County	32 526	41 527	47 938	30 221	16 638	16 222	31 346	20 697	15 929	77.0	43.9	27.4	2.6	8.7	4.5	−7.8	15.2	10.6
Steele County	35 757	43 914	46 389	13 125	19 750	21 818	31 667	21 528	17 601	77.6	54.6	34.4	2.4	11.4	5.5	−6.8	7.9	8.3
Stutsman County	33 848	42 853	50 673	22 750	18 223	17 850	30 054	21 125	17 706	77.2	45.9	34.4	3.0	11.8	4.4	−7.9	11.0	9.7
Towner County	32 740	39 286	44 444	26 875	17 679	17 891	27 368	17 564	17 605	75.6	49.8	37.7	2.2	8.9	5.4	−6.9	10.5	9.2
Traill County	37 445	45 852	50 030	32 031	17 768	20 422	31 269	21 534	18 014	75.7	46.3	34.4	1.7	11.9	5.0	−7.3	10.3	9.3
Walsh County	33 845	41 619	47 175	25 714	15 602	18 985	29 399	20 541	16 496	77.0	45.2	35.8	2.6	10.2	3.9	−8.4	11.6	11.8

Table B-3. States and Counties — **Education, Labor Force, and Income**

STATE/ County code	MSA/PMSA/ NECMA code[1]	STATE County	High school graduates			College graduates		College graduates (percent)				
			Total population 25 years and over	Percent with a high school diploma or less	Percent with a high school diploma or more	Percent with a bachelor's degree or more	+/− U.S. percent with bachelor's degree or more	Non-Hispanic White	Black or African American	American Indian and Alaska Native	Asian, Hawaiian, and Pacific Islander	Hispanic or Latino[2]
			1	2	3	4	5	6	7	8	9	10
		NORTH DAKOTA— Cont'd										
38 101	...	Ward County	35 957	41.6	87.4	22.1	-2.3	22.4	21.1	8.5	20.0	25.6
38 103	...	Wells County	3 715	58.3	72.6	13.7	-10.7	13.8	0.0	0.0	X	0.0
38 105	...	Williams County	13 048	49.2	82.5	16.5	-7.9	17.1	X	8.5	23.8	2.4
39 000	...	OHIO	7 411 740	53.1	83.0	21.1	-3.3	21.8	11.9	12.4	58.0	15.2
39 001	...	Adams County	17 775	75.8	68.6	7.2	-17.2	7.2	X	15.2	22.2	0.0
39 003	4320	Allen County	69 669	60.1	82.5	13.4	-11.0	14.1	7.4	14.3	46.4	9.1
39 005	...	Ashland County	33 339	63.7	83.3	15.9	-8.5	15.7	12.3	0.0	56.3	11.8
39 007	1680	Ashtabula County	67 994	65.9	79.9	11.1	-13.3	11.3	6.6	2.4	25.6	4.1
39 009	...	Athens County	31 563	51.2	82.9	25.7	1.3	24.3	31.5	19.1	76.6	49.4
39 011	4320	Auglaize County	30 093	61.9	85.7	13.4	-11.0	13.4	8.7	0.0	53.6	11.9
39 013	9000	Belmont County	49 616	65.5	80.9	11.1	-13.3	11.2	1.9	10.2	69.1	27.1
39 015	1640	Brown County	27 209	70.5	74.8	8.8	-15.6	8.8	11.0	0.0	22.4	23.8
39 017	3200	Butler County	207 213	50.3	83.3	23.5	-0.9	23.3	18.2	17.8	56.4	22.2
39 019	1320	Carroll County	19 460	72.9	80.1	9.1	-15.3	9.1	11.8	24.4	27.8	13.7
39 021	...	Champaign County	25 644	65.8	82.3	10.6	-13.8	10.4	12.2	17.3	26.0	6.9
39 023	2000	Clark County	95 298	58.4	81.2	14.9	-9.5	15.2	10.5	10.0	50.8	12.5
39 025	1640	Clermont County	113 513	53.3	82.0	20.8	-3.6	20.4	28.7	16.9	55.4	22.9
39 027	...	Clinton County	25 720	59.0	83.1	14.1	-10.3	14.1	12.0	10.9	68.2	7.9
39 029	9320	Columbiana County	76 022	67.1	80.6	10.8	-13.6	11.0	3.8	13.6	40.7	2.9
39 031	...	Coshocton County	24 172	72.4	78.7	9.8	-14.6	9.8	3.3	0.0	21.2	0.0
39 033	4800	Crawford County	31 379	69.2	80.2	9.7	-14.7	9.5	9.0	10.1	57.1	6.9
39 035	1680	Cuyahoga County	936 148	48.4	81.6	25.1	0.7	29.5	10.9	14.3	60.1	13.8
39 037	...	Darke County	35 206	67.6	82.8	10.1	-14.3	10.0	7.9	0.0	40.2	13.0
39 039	...	Defiance County	25 426	61.1	84.7	14.3	-10.1	14.9	10.2	0.0	8.3	6.9
39 041	1840	Delaware County	70 617	32.1	92.9	41.0	16.6	40.7	36.5	33.3	71.1	38.5
39 043	...	Erie County	54 232	57.0	84.0	16.6	-7.8	17.6	6.5	0.0	40.1	8.0
39 045	1840	Fairfield County	79 948	50.8	87.6	20.8	-3.6	20.5	29.8	7.3	44.6	21.2
39 047	...	Fayette County	18 954	68.9	78.7	10.7	-13.7	10.8	10.1	0.0	22.6	0.0
39 049	1840	Franklin County	676 318	41.4	85.7	31.8	7.4	34.5	15.2	15.7	59.8	21.1
39 051	8400	Fulton County	26 887	58.8	85.3	13.2	-11.2	13.6	4.0	0.0	25.7	4.4
39 053	...	Gallia County	20 207	67.9	73.7	11.6	-12.8	11.5	8.0	0.0	67.8	5.1
39 055	1680	Geauga County	59 216	41.8	86.3	31.7	7.3	31.8	16.0	17.4	59.1	35.6
39 057	2000	Greene County	92 414	41.1	87.8	31.1	6.7	30.2	35.9	27.2	56.0	40.4
39 059	...	Guernsey County	26 839	67.8	78.4	10.0	-14.4	9.9	6.6	0.0	50.0	22.0
39 061	1640	Hamilton County	540 040	45.0	82.7	29.2	4.8	32.9	12.4	14.9	66.7	36.2
39 063	...	Hancock County	45 871	52.2	88.4	21.7	-2.7	21.5	17.5	19.5	62.7	10.7
39 065	...	Hardin County	19 220	69.9	80.6	11.4	-13.0	11.3	10.1	16.0	8.4	19.3
39 067	...	Harrison County	11 097	70.1	79.6	9.0	-15.4	9.1	0.0	0.0	X	30.0
39 069	...	Henry County	18 833	66.4	83.5	11.1	-13.3	11.3	0.0	14.1	52.8	0.9
39 071	...	Highland County	26 372	68.5	76.3	9.7	-14.7	9.6	0.0	18.0	68.5	8.1
39 073	...	Hocking County	18 720	68.2	78.0	9.8	-14.6	9.9	3.7	0.0	55.0	29.3
39 075	...	Holmes County	21 016	80.6	51.5	8.3	-16.1	8.3	0.0	0.0	21.6	1.9
39 077	...	Huron County	37 576	67.7	81.0	10.9	-13.5	11.1	7.6	7.7	24.1	6.9
39 079	...	Jackson County	21 306	69.6	73.5	11.0	-13.4	11.0	9.0	0.0	23.4	27.5
39 081	8080	Jefferson County	51 819	64.8	81.7	11.8	-12.6	11.8	9.8	26.3	41.7	24.4
39 083	...	Knox County	34 485	60.3	81.8	16.7	-7.7	16.6	25.2	7.3	52.4	3.6
39 085	1680	Lake County	156 177	48.0	86.4	21.5	-2.9	21.5	13.3	13.3	54.7	14.2
39 087	3400	Lawrence County	41 685	67.8	75.6	10.3	-14.1	10.0	10.3	26.8	66.0	28.8
39 089	1840	Licking County	95 009	56.0	84.7	18.4	-6.0	18.3	21.4	8.7	38.1	21.0
39 091	...	Logan County	29 962	68.2	83.6	11.5	-12.9	11.5	12.4	12.7	24.9	2.3
39 093	1680	Lorain County	185 491	54.0	82.8	16.6	-7.8	17.8	7.7	10.6	48.9	6.2
39 095	8400	Lucas County	291 022	49.4	82.9	21.3	-3.1	23.2	10.2	13.0	60.8	10.1
39 097	1840	Madison County	26 615	62.7	79.0	13.0	-11.4	13.3	4.8	36.6	45.3	16.0
39 099	9320	Mahoning County	174 803	57.7	82.4	17.5	-6.9	19.3	6.8	7.2	45.2	11.8
39 101	...	Marion County	44 466	64.7	80.3	11.1	-13.3	11.3	6.4	9.7	34.8	6.0
39 103	1680	Medina County	99 005	47.6	88.8	24.8	0.4	24.7	13.5	13.8	55.1	27.4
39 105	...	Meigs County	15 602	73.4	73.2	7.4	-17.0	7.4	14.9	0.0	26.7	0.0
39 107	...	Mercer County	26 614	65.8	84.0	12.7	-11.7	12.5	0.0	0.0	62.0	21.0
39 109	2000	Miami County	65 765	57.1	82.7	16.3	-8.1	16.2	6.3	0.0	43.3	14.9
39 111	...	Monroe County	10 544	71.3	78.8	8.4	-16.0	8.4	0.0	0.0	45.0	0.0
39 113	2000	Montgomery County	367 099	46.9	83.5	22.8	-1.6	24.0	14.9	17.2	53.6	29.1
39 115	...	Morgan County	9 934	69.9	80.6	9.1	-15.3	9.4	0.9	0.0	73.9	0.0
39 117	...	Morrow County	20 591	68.7	78.6	9.5	-14.9	9.4	10.3	6.7	0.0	2.2
39 119	...	Muskingum County	54 616	63.7	80.6	12.6	-11.8	12.6	13.3	14.3	29.8	28.8
39 121	...	Noble County	9 210	69.3	78.6	8.1	-16.3	8.2	3.8	14.6	68.2	1.3

[1]MSA = Metropolitan Statistical Area. PMSA = Primary MSA. NECMA = New England County Metropolitan Area. See the Appendix A for explanation of these concepts. See Appendix B for list of metropolitan areas identified by type, with component counties.
[2]Hispanic or Latino persons may be of any race.

STATE County	School enrollment			Population 16 to 19 years				Employment status, 2000			Work status in 1999 of the population 16 years and over (percent)		
											Worked in 1999		
	Grades kindergarten through 12	College or graduate school	Percent private	Number	Percent in armed forces	Percent high school graduates	Percent not enrolled, not grads, not in armed forces, not employed	Total population 16 years and over	Percent in labor force	Unemployment rate	Full-time	Part-time	Did not work in 1999
	11	12	13	14	15	16	17	18	19	20	21	22	23
NORTH DAKOTA— Cont'd													
Ward County	11 203	4 170	7.0	3 782	7.7	17.8	2.7	45 224	69.4	4.0	57.7	17.7	24.6
Wells County	998	95	3.3	278	0.0	4.0	4.0	4 106	55.9	6.0	46.4	18.9	34.7
Williams County	4 161	747	7.8	1 400	0.1	6.6	2.0	15 348	66.4	5.7	52.9	18.9	28.2
OHIO	2 157 981	652 393	16.0	639 825	0.1	10.5	4.6	8 788 494	64.8	5.0	54.5	15.9	29.6
Adams County..............	5 423	550	6.3	1 538	0.0	16.2	6.2	21 010	58.2	7.6	48.9	12.5	38.6
Allen County................	21 705	5 414	18.3	6 965	0.1	9.2	4.9	83 540	60.9	5.7	50.2	16.6	33.2
Ashland County............	10 029	3 166	22.2	3 732	0.0	10.5	5.6	40 668	64.7	4.3	54.9	16.4	28.7
Ashtabula County..........	20 225	2 903	8.3	5 742	0.2	16.9	5.9	78 993	62.4	5.1	52.1	14.6	33.4
Athens County..............	8 535	18 795	3.3	7 591	0.0	4.0	1.1	52 238	56.9	11.1	48.9	25.0	26.1
Auglaize County............	9 877	1 549	8.0	2 790	0.0	9.7	0.2	35 348	69.0	3.2	55.5	17.5	27.0
Belmont County............	12 369	2 477	13.2	3 577	0.0	10.2	3.2	57 010	53.7	7.1	44.3	15.3	40.4
Brown County...............	8 815	1 164	7.1	2 323	0.2	12.6	4.4	31 808	63.3	5.3	55.3	13.4	31.3
Butler County	63 221	26 012	11.8	21 825	0.1	10.6	3.1	256 128	66.6	4.0	57.4	17.1	25.6
Carroll County	5 595	679	7.6	1 449	0.0	13.8	2.1	22 370	61.7	4.3	50.9	15.4	33.7
Champaign County	7 597	1 085	11.1	2 230	0.0	14.4	3.5	29 904	67.4	4.2	58.1	14.6	27.4
Clark County	27 318	7 419	14.3	8 403	0.2	9.6	6.8	112 527	63.7	5.9	54.2	15.1	30.7
Clermont County	36 411	6 609	15.1	9 787	0.0	11.1	5.1	133 724	69.8	3.5	59.9	15.7	24.5
Clinton County	7 852	2 142	15.3	2 584	0.0	12.9	1.2	31 118	68.7	4.4	57.1	16.5	26.4
Columbiana County.......	21 122	3 521	7.2	6 022	0.0	12.4	3.5	88 084	60.1	4.9	50.8	14.3	34.9
Coshocton County........	7 235	758	10.3	2 168	0.0	10.7	5.2	28 313	63.1	5.7	54.5	13.9	31.5
Crawford County	8 889	1 143	11.5	2 618	0.0	14.2	3.3	36 617	62.8	5.2	54.1	14.1	31.8
Cuyahoga County	263 086	75 981	22.8	70 120	0.1	9.6	5.9	1 083 541	62.5	6.2	52.6	14.8	32.6
Darke County	10 595	1 540	8.3	2 868	0.0	10.5	2.8	41 002	65.7	4.2	55.6	14.4	30.0
Defiance County	7 970	1 478	12.9	2 452	0.0	10.6	3.4	30 382	68.2	3.7	57.1	15.4	27.5
Delaware County..........	22 024	6 126	21.5	5 872	0.0	9.6	2.3	82 043	74.3	3.8	62.9	16.5	20.6
Erie County	15 363	2 641	12.4	3 995	0.0	10.0	3.1	62 321	63.4	4.4	53.7	15.6	30.6
Fairfield County	24 594	4 719	11.5	6 316	0.2	10.5	3.6	93 414	68.2	3.3	58.3	15.7	26.0
Fayette County	5 355	718	4.1	1 575	0.0	16.1	4.5	22 104	65.1	4.9	55.7	14.6	29.7
Franklin County	191 642	95 799	14.8	59 036	0.0	10.1	4.6	827 131	70.7	4.2	60.3	16.3	23.4
Fulton County...............	8 815	1 611	8.0	2 467	0.0	11.2	1.9	31 621	69.5	3.3	57.7	16.6	25.7
Gallia County...............	5 887	1 494	15.6	2 026	0.4	10.6	6.5	24 289	55.2	9.5	47.3	12.4	40.3
Geauga County	19 058	3 361	24.1	5 057	0.0	7.5	7.8	68 113	66.2	2.8	56.4	16.7	26.9
Greene County	26 857	16 907	20.1	11 371	0.9	6.1	2.9	116 856	66.8	5.0	54.2	19.6	26.2
Guernsey County	8 153	1 105	8.6	2 326	0.0	11.3	4.5	31 389	58.2	6.8	50.0	13.2	36.9
Hamilton County	163 773	53 200	24.5	48 268	0.0	9.0	6.0	651 898	65.5	5.0	54.4	17.1	28.6
Hancock County...........	13 404	4 538	19.7	4 131	0.3	9.6	2.5	54 951	68.3	3.0	58.2	16.1	25.8
Hardin County	5 458	3 395	32.1	2 406	0.0	8.1	4.5	25 009	61.3	4.1	53.0	16.7	30.3
Harrison County	2 750	392	7.3	808	0.0	12.0	3.7	12 703	55.2	4.7	44.9	14.5	40.6
Henry County	6 173	852	12.5	1 818	0.0	8.9	9.5	22 152	66.5	4.3	57.4	14.8	27.9
Highland County...........	8 190	1 221	5.8	2 293	0.0	13.4	6.3	31 046	61.7	6.1	52.2	14.2	33.6
Hocking County............	5 370	979	8.3	1 598	0.0	13.7	1.9	21 968	58.5	5.7	50.1	14.0	35.9
Holmes County.............	8 145	372	35.0	2 701	0.0	7.7	19.7	26 511	64.4	2.3	52.0	14.9	33.1
Huron County	12 304	1 801	15.8	3 327	0.0	12.5	6.2	44 534	66.5	5.1	57.6	14.2	28.2
Jackson County............	6 429	917	8.3	1 734	0.0	16.4	3.4	25 105	57.4	7.7	49.0	11.9	39.1
Jefferson County	12 315	4 123	20.9	4 010	0.0	12.0	2.9	59 973	53.1	7.6	42.9	14.8	42.2
Knox County	10 108	3 824	25.8	3 711	0.0	7.8	2.7	42 469	64.2	6.1	53.9	16.6	29.5
Lake County	41 818	10 082	17.1	11 692	0.0	11.0	2.6	178 996	68.8	3.5	57.3	16.0	26.7
Lawrence County	11 614	2 743	5.0	3 417	0.1	10.1	7.2	48 874	53.2	8.5	45.1	11.8	43.1
Licking County	28 214	7 135	16.1	8 478	0.0	11.5	4.1	111 782	67.5	3.8	57.2	16.5	26.4
Logan County...............	9 184	1 230	7.5	2 484	0.0	11.3	3.1	35 139	66.6	3.7	57.1	14.8	28.1
Lorain County...............	55 489	13 711	18.3	15 543	0.0	11.5	4.5	218 114	65.0	4.3	55.0	16.2	28.8
Lucas County	88 948	31 806	18.3	25 237	0.0	10.1	5.9	348 524	65.0	6.3	52.5	17.4	30.0
Madison County............	7 663	1 584	15.9	2 427	0.0	14.3	6.3	31 563	59.6	3.1	56.2	14.7	29.1
Mahoning County..........	47 024	12 736	13.1	13 145	0.0	10.7	4.5	203 419	58.5	6.3	47.3	15.9	36.7
Marion County..............	12 999	2 291	8.8	3 280	0.0	11.3	6.0	51 814	60.2	4.5	54.1	13.5	32.4
Medina County	31 234	5 804	13.5	7 814	0.0	9.6	2.0	114 163	70.6	3.3	58.5	17.1	24.4
Meigs County	4 275	688	5.4	1 308	0.0	13.9	7.6	18 242	54.6	10.0	45.5	12.6	41.9
Mercer County..............	9 147	1 275	5.3	2 664	0.0	12.0	2.1	30 301	68.2	3.2	54.3	18.3	27.4
Miami County	19 342	3 450	11.3	5 406	0.0	12.9	3.4	76 287	68.7	3.1	57.7	16.4	26.0
Monroe County.............	2 778	493	11.3	841	0.0	13.4	6.9	12 070	52.4	6.8	43.5	13.2	43.3
Montgomery County......	101 609	38 583	20.4	30 764	0.2	11.2	6.0	436 241	64.1	5.3	54.6	15.4	30.0
Morgan County.............	2 863	504	6.2	873	0.0	12.0	4.7	11 599	56.1	8.4	47.2	13.0	39.8
Morrow County.............	6 556	871	8.6	1 811	0.0	15.0	2.9	23 951	66.9	4.3	58.6	13.4	28.1
Muskingum County	16 340	3 766	14.9	4 856	0.1	12.8	4.4	65 022	63.0	5.8	53.6	14.8	31.6
Noble County	2 613	798	10.1	762	0.0	16.0	3.3	11 251	48.3	6.0	45.8	15.6	38.5

Table B-3. States and Counties — Education, Labor Force, and Income

STATE County	Full-year full-time employed (percent)								Children under 18 years in families						Total employed by class of worker (percent)			
	Total	Men	Women	Non-Hispanic White	Black or African American	American Indian and Alaska Native	Asian, Hawaiian, and Pacific Islander	Hispanic or Latino[1]	Number	With two parents (percent) Both in labor force	Father only in labor force	With one parent who is in labor force (percent)	+/- U.S. percent of children with no stay-at-home parent (percent)	+/- U.S. percent two-income couples	Private	Government	Self-employed	Unpaid family worker
	24	25	26	27	28	29	30	31	32	33	34	35	36	37	38	39	40	41
NORTH DAKOTA— Cont'd																		
Ward County	43.1	54.0	32.5	43.2	50.1	26.7	49.8	55.1	14 822	57.9	17.9	16.5	9.8	7.7	71.1	18.0	10.5	0.3
Wells County	30.3	39.5	21.6	30.6	0.0	0.0	X	0.0	1 130	65.5	13.2	11.0	11.9	-2.3	62.5	10.3	24.8	2.4
Williams County	37.9	47.8	28.6	38.2	0.0	34.8	8.7	38.8	4 916	57.8	16.3	20.9	14.1	6.8	69.6	13.7	15.9	0.8
OHIO	42.0	52.4	32.5	42.9	35.5	36.4	40.8	38.6	2 744 090	45.8	21.2	22.3	3.5	1.8	79.5	12.2	8.0	0.3
Adams County	33.9	41.0	27.1	33.8	28.6	24.0	77.8	42.7	6 769	40.3	25.0	20.3	-4.0	-7.8	73.7	13.2	12.1	1.0
Allen County	38.3	47.8	29.1	39.8	29.8	27.2	44.8	26.5	26 753	45.4	17.6	25.6	6.4	-0.7	80.9	11.5	7.3	0.3
Ashland County	40.8	52.8	29.7	41.2	18.2	14.6	26.9	39.8	12 911	47.3	28.4	16.5	-0.8	1.3	78.5	10.8	10.2	0.5
Ashtabula County	39.2	49.6	29.6	39.4	35.4	43.4	33.1	39.1	25 550	42.1	23.2	23.2	0.7	-2.2	80.2	11.2	8.3	0.3
Athens County	26.5	31.9	21.4	27.0	20.9	35.0	13.4	26.4	10 732	43.1	20.8	19.2	-2.3	-4.3	58.5	33.1	8.1	0.3
Auglaize County	44.7	58.8	31.6	44.7	66.7	32.6	54.3	33.2	12 395	61.8	17.3	15.8	13.0	9.3	80.0	10.8	8.8	0.5
Belmont County	33.3	42.6	24.7	33.8	22.4	22.0	28.3	50.6	14 559	46.5	20.5	19.7	1.6	-5.6	76.4	15.0	8.1	0.5
Brown County	42.0	52.8	31.7	42.1	40.5	37.5	62.7	52.9	11 110	44.9	23.6	17.7	-2.0	-1.6	77.7	11.5	10.0	0.7
Butler County	43.5	55.0	33.0	43.8	40.6	38.6	45.0	39.3	82 769	48.3	23.9	18.8	2.5	4.2	81.5	11.5	6.9	0.2
Carroll County	39.1	51.5	27.3	39.3	19.4	42.0	8.3	29.0	6 900	51.0	23.5	15.9	2.3	-4.6	79.3	10.1	10.4	0.2
Champaign County	45.7	58.0	34.1	45.9	37.1	39.0	44.0	36.8	9 765	52.9	21.7	17.9	6.2	4.3	80.4	9.5	9.6	0.5
Clark County	42.0	52.0	33.1	42.5	37.6	35.0	52.0	37.5	34 228	46.0	17.7	25.5	6.9	0.4	79.7	13.7	6.4	0.2
Clermont County	47.4	59.5	36.1	47.4	40.4	59.1	52.6	52.4	47 603	50.0	25.9	16.4	1.8	5.3	83.1	8.2	8.5	0.3
Clinton County	44.3	54.7	34.7	44.5	36.9	53.5	74.0	32.7	10 220	50.1	20.0	20.9	6.4	5.4	81.8	9.9	8.0	0.3
Columbiana County	38.9	50.2	27.8	39.5	22.5	36.3	32.6	27.8	25 942	46.8	24.1	20.0	2.2	-2.0	82.3	8.7	8.5	0.4
Coshocton County	41.4	52.2	31.2	41.6	41.4	20.7	33.3	36.8	9 336	47.2	30.0	15.8	-1.6	-2.6	79.5	10.0	10.0	0.5
Crawford County	42.0	51.6	33.2	42.1	37.3	50.7	54.7	42.1	11 147	47.1	18.1	22.4	4.9	-1.2	82.4	9.8	7.6	0.1
Cuyahoga County	40.2	49.6	32.1	42.3	35.0	33.8	40.8	35.9	326 340	38.3	18.7	28.1	1.8	-1.0	79.5	12.8	7.5	0.2
Darke County	43.6	55.7	32.3	43.6	66.1	25.5	54.2	36.9	13 323	53.4	21.8	16.5	5.3	2.7	79.6	8.8	11.5	0.2
Defiance County	44.4	67.4	31.8	44.4	50.5	71.4	60.2	40.0	9 993	57.8	15.6	21.5	14.7	6.2	83.5	8.7	7.7	0.1
Delaware County	51.8	65.4	38.8	52.0	47.1	61.0	55.4	45.2	30 027	53.9	29.6	12.0	1.3	10.6	77.4	12.2	10.1	0.3
Erie County	42.2	52.4	32.8	42.5	37.6	16.9	51.2	47.5	18 596	49.7	17.8	23.9	9.0	1.0	79.1	12.2	8.4	0.4
Fairfield County	46.9	58.1	36.1	47.1	40.6	30.0	54.2	45.8	31 797	54.5	22.8	15.9	5.8	6.7	77.2	13.7	8.9	0.2
Fayette County	43.5	53.9	33.7	43.3	52.0	54.5	52.7	43.6	6 724	48.5	17.4	22.4	6.3	5.0	75.9	12.8	10.8	0.4
Franklin County	47.0	55.6	39.0	48.6	42.0	38.6	39.7	44.4	253 506	42.9	19.1	26.4	4.7	7.3	77.4	15.5	6.9	0.2
Fulton County	45.9	59.0	33.4	46.2	39.4	45.3	47.2	40.3	11 544	59.1	16.6	15.6	10.1	7.9	79.3	9.8	10.5	0.3
Gallia County	33.5	41.1	26.5	33.6	29.7	53.3	22.0	22.2	7 380	43.3	23.6	15.4	-5.9	-8.6	75.4	15.3	9.2	0.2
Geauga County	45.6	60.8	31.2	45.7	34.4	60.7	55.1	43.4	25 251	46.6	37.0	10.9	-7.1	2.3	73.7	10.1	15.8	0.4
Greene County	41.2	53.3	30.1	42.3	28.9	50.6	37.6	40.2	34 037	49.7	23.5	18.7	3.8	2.4	72.3	19.4	8.1	0.2
Guernsey County	37.7	48.6	27.8	38.0	26.4	30.7	38.7	41.8	10 179	42.2	25.0	22.0	-0.4	-6.6	75.4	14.2	9.8	0.6
Hamilton County	41.8	51.8	33.1	43.4	36.4	35.1	41.2	42.5	208 388	41.4	20.2	25.7	2.5	2.9	80.0	11.5	7.7	0.2
Hancock County	45.4	57.8	34.0	45.5	53.3	47.6	28.9	47.1	17 668	53.4	20.4	19.8	8.6	6.1	83.7	8.8	7.3	0.2
Hardin County	37.7	49.5	26.8	37.9	30.7	63.0	27.2	26.3	7 345	47.5	22.7	19.5	2.4	-0.1	78.5	11.1	9.7	0.8
Harrison County	34.0	46.5	22.6	34.1	29.0	0.0	X	29.4	3 517	40.9	29.8	15.6	-8.1	-10.0	76.5	13.3	10.0	0.1
Henry County	43.5	53.9	33.7	44.3	13.5	16.9	36.4	31.6	7 669	59.2	16.1	16.6	11.2	6.0	79.8	10.5	9.5	0.2
Highland County	39.4	48.1	31.3	39.6	27.9	32.4	37.5	50.0	10 327	46.0	22.1	20.3	1.7	-4.0	78.0	10.3	11.3	0.4
Hocking County	36.7	45.6	28.0	37.0	18.9	33.3	42.9	22.4	6 843	43.8	23.4	17.7	-3.1	-6.9	74.6	15.8	9.3	0.3
Holmes County	40.4	58.2	23.2	40.5	7.5	33.3	28.3	35.2	13 654	28.9	57.8	7.4	-28.3	-9.7	67.6	8.4	22.4	1.6
Huron County	44.2	55.9	33.2	44.4	42.4	77.0	38.8	30.3	10 008	49.5	20.4	20.0	5.7	0.1	82.8	9.2	7.8	0.3
Jackson County	35.8	46.8	25.9	36.0	36.4	29.0	0.0	28.3	7 989	41.4	23.0	20.2	-3.0	-8.5	77.6	13.2	8.8	0.4
Jefferson County	31.3	41.9	22.0	31.6	30.3	10.4	41.7	14.4	15 117	39.6	26.1	20.1	-4.9	-12.3	83.0	10.8	6.0	0.2
Knox County	39.8	51.1	29.4	40.0	31.7	27.8	27.2	34.0	12 969	49.6	27.3	16.0	1.0	2.6	75.3	12.1	11.7	0.8
Lake County	46.4	57.4	36.2	46.5	43.2	35.0	49.2	39.4	53 336	54.0	21.0	18.0	7.4	4.7	82.7	9.7	7.4	0.2
Lawrence County	32.9	41.7	25.1	32.9	34.6	40.0	33.1	33.7	14 493	37.6	20.9	20.9	-6.1	-12.8	77.4	15.6	6.7	0.3
Licking County	45.0	55.3	35.6	45.2	41.9	40.4	35.7	47.4	36 189	52.1	19.7	19.9	7.4	5.0	78.9	12.5	8.3	0.2
Logan County	45.1	57.0	33.9	45.3	41.8	42.6	50.5	40.7	11 723	49.2	20.7	21.6	6.2	3.2	81.2	9.6	8.9	0.3
Lorain County	42.4	53.1	32.3	43.5	34.0	36.4	45.2	38.6	71 063	46.0	20.4	23.2	4.6	2.0	82.0	10.7	7.0	0.3
Lucas County	40.1	50.1	31.1	42.2	31.2	38.4	34.1	36.2	112 860	42.3	16.9	27.6	5.3	1.8	80.9	11.9	7.0	0.2
Madison County	43.5	48.0	38.0	45.8	16.0	33.7	43.4	34.5	9 394	53.6	18.9	18.7	7.7	6.3	73.6	15.7	10.5	0.2
Mahoning County	35.6	46.2	26.2	37.2	27.2	38.3	40.4	32.9	57 075	42.2	19.3	25.5	3.1	-4.9	80.4	11.5	7.8	0.3
Marion County	42.1	48.6	35.2	43.5	24.6	15.5	52.0	32.3	15 391	49.4	15.6	23.5	8.3	4.6	80.2	11.9	7.7	0.3
Medina County	47.1	61.4	33.6	47.2	40.5	39.7	49.5	51.0	40 360	55.3	26.2	12.1	2.8	6.8	80.1	10.4	9.2	0.3
Meigs County	30.2	38.1	22.8	30.4	48.3	3.3	0.0	29.7	5 135	40.4	25.8	17.6	-6.6	-14.2	72.7	16.8	10.0	0.5
Mercer County	43.5	57.4	30.0	43.5	22.2	35.9	60.5	34.3	11 877	65.1	10.1	10.2	10.7	8.6	78.6	10.0	10.9	0.5
Miami County	46.2	58.3	35.0	46.4	40.5	43.4	41.4	44.6	24 484	51.2	19.8	21.4	8.0	5.7	81.6	9.8	8.5	0.2
Monroe County	31.6	43.0	20.6	31.8	100.0	14.8	25.0	19.4	3 433	40.9	31.1	12.0	-11.7	-14.6	73.2	15.3	10.6	0.9
Montgomery County	41.8	50.8	33.8	43.1	36.3	38.6	41.8	42.5	129 666	41.9	18.5	27.5	4.8	0.6	79.5	13.6	6.7	0.2
Morgan County	33.4	41.6	25.4	33.6	30.5	41.5	60.9	0.0	3 565	41.2	22.6	20.0	-3.4	-13.0	72.5	15.5	11.2	0.8
Morrow County	45.3	55.8	34.9	45.3	3.4	36.2	39.1	50.4	8 247	50.6	22.7	17.2	3.2	2.3	77.7	11.6	10.0	0.6
Muskingum County	40.6	50.4	31.8	41.0	32.5	60.8	47.2	45.5	20 915	47.9	17.4	22.3	5.6	0.6	79.6	11.9	8.2	0.3
Noble County	31.8	36.3	25.6	34.0	10.4	0.0	64.3	7.3	3 059	56.1	21.6	14.8	6.3	-6.5	71.8	17.2	10.6	0.4

[1] Hispanic or Latino persons may be of any race.

Table B-3. States and Counties — Education, Labor Force, and Income

				Occupation for employed population 16 years and over (percent)						Industry for employed population 16 years and over (percent)					
STATE County	Percent who worked at home	Percent of the population 5 years and over with a disability	Veterans as a percent of the population 18 years and over	Management, professional, and related occupations	Service occupa-tions	Sales and office occupa-tions	Farming, fishing, and forestry occupa-tions	Con-struction, extraction, and main-tenance occupa-tions	Production, transporta-tion and material moving occupa-tions	Agricul-ture, forestry, fishing, and mining	Construc-tion and manufac-turing	Whole-sale and retail trade	Transpor-tation and ware-housing, and utilities	Service industries	Public adminis-tration
	42	43	44	45	46	47	48	49	50	51	52	53	54	55	56
NORTH DAKOTA— Cont'd															
Ward County	4.1	16.8	14.2	32.0	17.5	30.3	0.7	9.1	10.3	4.4	8.3	19.2	5.6	57.5	4.9
Wells County	12.1	19.8	13.0	33.6	18.2	21.4	4.6	8.6	13.6	18.2	8.1	16.6	8.5	45.8	2.8
Williams County	4.6	18.1	14.2	27.4	19.0	26.5	1.4	12.7	13.0	12.8	9.7	18.4	4.8	49.7	4.6
OHIO	2.8	18.3	13.5	31.0	14.6	26.4	0.3	8.7	19.0	1.1	26.0	15.5	4.9	48.4	4.1
Adams County..............	4.6	25.8	13.4	20.4	16.1	18.8	1.5	15.5	27.6	5.4	34.3	13.1	6.2	38.6	2.4
Allen County.................	2.1	18.7	14.1	25.0	16.8	23.1	0.3	9.2	25.6	1.0	29.7	16.7	4.4	43.6	4.6
Ashland County............	3.9	16.1	12.6	24.8	14.5	21.8	1.3	9.5	28.1	3.6	35.2	14.0	4.0	40.1	3.1
Ashtabula County.........	2.3	20.6	14.9	22.1	16.8	21.0	1.0	11.4	27.7	2.1	36.4	13.5	5.5	39.2	3.2
Athens County..............	4.0	16.7	10.0	34.6	20.9	24.0	0.4	9.0	11.1	1.9	13.1	12.1	3.3	65.3	4.4
Auglaize County...........	3.5	15.7	14.0	26.4	14.4	21.3	0.9	9.2	27.8	3.1	38.2	13.7	3.9	38.2	2.9
Belmont County............	2.7	23.4	15.0	24.5	18.6	26.2	0.3	11.8	18.6	3.5	19.1	18.7	5.4	47.6	5.8
Brown County...............	3.3	21.8	13.7	21.6	14.1	22.6	0.7	15.2	25.8	3.0	33.4	16.0	5.4	38.5	3.7
Butler County	2.5	16.4	12.9	33.4	13.2	27.5	0.1	9.0	16.7	0.4	28.6	15.5	4.7	47.7	3.1
Carroll County	3.5	18.4	14.8	20.6	15.1	20.3	0.9	12.8	30.3	4.2	36.2	14.2	4.9	37.8	2.6
Champaign County	2.6	19.1	13.3	23.0	13.5	21.5	0.9	9.4	31.6	3.9	41.1	13.2	4.3	34.4	3.1
Clark County	2.0	21.1	16.4	27.0	15.2	25.2	0.4	9.4	22.8	0.9	27.1	15.5	5.1	45.6	5.8
Clermont County	2.8	17.2	13.4	30.5	13.2	28.2	0.2	11.9	16.0	0.3	27.6	17.7	4.8	46.9	2.6
Clinton County	3.5	18.8	14.2	24.2	13.5	24.5	0.6	11.4	25.9	2.8	26.6	13.6	16.5	37.2	3.3
Columbiana County......	3.1	19.4	15.0	21.3	15.8	23.3	0.7	11.3	27.7	2.4	32.8	15.9	5.8	40.4	2.7
Coshocton County........	3.7	20.7	14.5	22.0	13.5	21.0	1.1	9.2	33.3	4.1	41.2	10.4	6.1	35.7	2.5
Crawford County	2.4	19.6	14.5	21.9	13.2	21.9	0.6	10.1	32.3	2.0	39.0	13.9	4.5	37.3	3.4
Cuyahoga County	2.6	19.8	12.5	34.8	14.9	28.7	0.1	6.7	14.9	0.1	20.7	14.7	4.9	55.4	4.2
Darke County	4.0	19.0	13.3	23.6	13.1	22.1	1.4	11.1	28.7	4.6	37.4	14.5	5.1	35.6	2.8
Defiance County...........	2.3	17.7	13.5	22.2	12.6	20.8	0.2	10.0	34.2	1.7	45.1	13.7	3.4	33.4	2.7
Delaware County..........	4.6	12.2	12.2	45.6	10.7	27.4	0.3	6.6	9.4	0.9	19.7	15.7	3.7	55.4	4.6
Erie County	2.3	17.8	16.3	26.9	16.1	24.4	0.3	8.7	23.5	1.5	29.7	14.7	4.4	46.0	3.8
Fairfield County	3.3	15.6	15.1	32.2	13.4	28.7	0.3	10.2	15.3	1.0	22.6	19.0	5.5	45.8	6.1
Fayette County.............	3.2	19.7	13.8	22.1	14.4	25.0	1.1	8.8	28.6	3.4	29.6	19.6	8.0	33.9	5.4
Franklin County	2.7	17.0	11.8	37.5	14.0	29.9	0.1	6.5	11.9	0.2	14.4	17.1	5.3	57.1	5.8
Fulton County	3.1	17.7	11.8	23.2	13.0	23.5	0.8	12.0	27.4	2.8	38.6	12.9	6.2	36.7	2.6
Gallia County................	2.0	25.5	13.2	25.8	16.0	24.3	0.9	12.6	20.3	3.7	18.9	16.2	9.6	48.0	3.5
Geauga County	5.4	13.6	12.7	38.8	11.4	25.6	0.7	10.6	12.8	1.5	29.4	15.0	3.5	48.0	2.6
Greene County	2.9	15.0	15.7	38.7	14.5	25.9	0.3	7.4	13.1	0.7	19.3	14.9	3.9	52.3	8.9
Guernsey County	3.3	21.1	15.0	22.6	18.1	21.2	0.7	11.9	25.5	3.4	28.7	13.8	5.6	43.8	4.7
Hamilton County...........	2.8	17.9	12.3	36.9	15.1	28.1	0.1	7.0	12.8	0.1	20.1	15.2	4.7	56.0	4.0
Hancock County	3.1	14.5	13.3	29.3	13.5	22.4	0.3	8.9	25.6	2.1	34.4	14.9	5.3	41.0	2.3
Hardin County	4.3	19.2	11.4	23.2	15.0	20.7	1.0	9.0	31.1	4.4	36.7	12.0	3.8	39.7	3.4
Harrison County	3.2	20.2	16.2	21.7	16.1	21.9	0.7	13.8	25.8	5.3	29.4	14.9	6.4	40.7	3.3
Henry County	3.1	16.7	13.3	21.6	12.7	20.8	0.7	12.1	32.1	2.6	41.3	11.5	5.7	35.7	3.2
Highland County...........	4.3	24.6	14.0	21.5	12.0	21.7	0.7	13.1	30.9	3.2	31.1	13.4	12.9	36.8	2.7
Hocking County............	2.5	22.5	15.7	22.4	15.8	21.1	0.7	15.0	24.9	1.7	32.1	14.7	5.0	41.5	5.0
Holmes County.............	12.5	16.9	7.5	20.9	12.5	18.3	2.1	14.2	32.0	9.0	41.8	14.4	4.0	29.3	1.6
Huron County...............	2.7	17.7	13.7	21.2	13.5	20.3	1.0	10.7	33.4	2.5	41.1	12.5	6.5	34.8	2.6
Jackson County............	2.9	25.1	15.0	24.1	14.9	20.9	1.5	12.8	25.9	4.4	31.1	16.1	5.4	38.7	4.4
Jefferson County..........	2.2	20.4	16.2	22.3	17.4	27.7	0.4	12.1	20.1	1.3	24.7	15.8	7.3	47.3	3.7
Knox County.................	4.6	18.8	13.4	27.6	15.6	23.5	0.8	10.4	22.1	3.2	30.7	13.0	3.9	45.4	3.7
Lake County.................	2.2	15.9	14.3	32.1	13.0	28.2	0.3	8.7	17.7	0.6	30.5	16.0	3.9	46.0	3.1
Lawrence County	1.8	27.5	14.6	24.3	18.2	28.0	0.3	11.4	17.9	0.7	20.8	17.8	6.1	50.1	4.5
Licking County..............	3.3	17.7	15.4	29.2	14.5	27.7	0.4	10.5	17.7	1.3	25.0	15.6	5.0	47.3	5.7
Logan County...............	3.9	18.8	14.8	22.6	13.5	21.1	0.4	10.2	32.2	2.0	38.8	15.4	4.4	36.8	2.5
Lorain County...............	2.2	17.5	14.8	27.4	14.5	25.7	0.4	10.5	21.6	0.8	31.0	14.5	4.9	45.0	3.7
Lucas County................	1.9	20.4	12.8	30.0	15.8	26.4	0.2	8.4	19.1	0.4	24.1	16.2	5.5	50.5	3.4
Madison County	3.3	20.4	14.8	25.9	14.9	25.7	0.4	11.3	21.7	2.4	24.7	17.1	6.6	41.1	8.0
Mahoning County	2.0	20.2	15.0	26.9	16.3	27.9	0.2	8.4	20.2	0.7	24.3	17.6	4.7	48.9	3.8
Marion County..............	2.2	21.8	14.5	22.7	15.8	25.0	0.5	8.4	27.7	1.9	33.1	13.5	4.0	42.0	5.5
Medina County	3.6	14.0	13.1	33.0	13.0	27.2	0.3	11.0	15.5	0.9	27.9	16.9	5.2	46.1	3.1
Meigs County	3.7	25.6	15.5	22.0	17.5	20.7	2.5	16.8	20.6	8.6	20.6	16.3	8.9	41.6	3.9
Mercer County..............	4.5	14.9	12.4	25.2	13.7	21.3	1.5	9.2	29.0	5.2	38.9	13.4	3.8	36.4	2.3
Miami County	2.7	16.4	14.2	29.1	12.8	25.5	0.6	8.0	24.1	1.2	35.3	15.4	5.2	39.2	3.8
Monroe County	4.4	22.1	17.3	21.4	15.0	20.9	1.1	14.5	27.1	5.7	32.5	14.5	5.7	36.5	5.1
Montgomery County......	2.2	19.6	14.9	33.5	14.8	26.8	0.1	7.7	17.1	0.3	23.3	15.2	4.8	50.8	5.6
Morgan County.............	6.9	22.4	14.4	23.8	16.6	18.8	2.9	14.0	23.9	7.2	28.8	13.2	6.2	40.0	4.6
Morrow County.............	3.7	19.4	14.5	22.1	15.1	22.4	0.9	14.0	25.5	2.7	34.3	15.5	3.9	39.0	4.6
Muskingum County	2.5	20.0	13.6	25.7	15.5	23.1	0.5	9.8	25.4	1.9	30.7	15.2	4.3	44.0	3.9
Noble County	4.1	21.1	13.7	23.4	15.5	18.4	0.9	12.7	29.1	5.4	32.0	12.4	5.6	39.0	5.6

STATE County	Median household income	Median family income — All families	Median family income — Married-couple	Families with children — Male householder	Families with children — Female householder	Median nonfamily household income	Median income for full-year, full-time workers — Men	Median income for full-year, full-time workers — Women	Per capita income	Households by source of income (percent) — With earnings	With interest, dividend, or rental income	With Social Security income	With public assistance income	With retirement income	Households with income over $100,000 (percent)	+/− U.S. percent for income over $100,000 (percent)	Households with income below poverty (percent)	Families with children with income below poverty (percent)
	57	58	59	60	61	62	63	64	65	66	67	68	69	70	71	72	73	74
NORTH DAKOTA— Cont'd																		
Ward County	33 670	41 342	47 500	27 353	14 483	20 210	29 587	20 666	16 926	81.9	39.8	24.6	2.9	12.5	4.9	-7.4	11.5	11.5
Wells County	31 894	39 284	43 682	18 750	17 604	16 581	28 776	18 267	17 932	70.8	50.2	42.3	1.7	8.9	4.6	-7.7	16.0	9.8
Williams County	31 491	39 065	45 945	22 019	13 323	18 098	31 166	20 249	16 763	79.0	41.9	31.1	2.6	12.2	4.8	-7.5	12.0	16.0
OHIO	40 956	50 037	60 491	30 270	19 627	24 005	38 977	27 152	21 003	79.6	36.6	26.4	3.2	18.9	9.8	-2.5	10.7	12.2
Adams County	29 315	34 714	41 250	22 417	14 238	13 693	30 436	20 873	14 515	72.2	25.1	30.6	4.4	18.4	3.6	-8.7	18.0	19.8
Allen County	37 048	44 723	55 408	27 585	17 391	20 426	36 411	24 786	17 511	76.5	34.3	28.3	3.1	20.6	6.7	-5.6	12.5	14.9
Ashland County	39 179	46 306	52 440	27 016	20 042	20 946	34 314	23 324	17 308	79.5	39.9	28.4	1.5	19.8	6.2	-6.1	9.1	10.7
Ashtabula County	35 607	42 449	49 522	32 467	17 370	19 979	34 873	23 479	16 814	77.1	33.3	30.6	3.5	19.9	4.9	-7.4	11.6	14.5
Athens County	27 322	39 785	45 114	21 648	13 261	14 279	31 430	24 621	14 171	79.1	32.1	20.6	4.8	17.1	5.8	-6.5	27.7	19.7
Auglaize County	43 367	50 024	60 140	30 707	20 700	22 070	37 605	25 131	19 503	79.6	44.0	28.3	1.6	21.2	7.8	-4.5	6.2	6.9
Belmont County	29 714	37 538	45 922	23 021	12 316	15 408	31 725	20 541	16 221	69.6	33.5	35.8	4.6	24.9	3.7	-8.6	15.3	18.4
Brown County	38 303	43 040	49 291	26 800	20 724	21 045	33 718	23 392	17 100	80.0	28.4	27.6	2.2	18.0	5.1	-7.2	11.4	13.0
Butler County	47 885	57 513	66 942	34 089	22 234	25 747	43 135	28 597	22 076	83.7	38.6	23.6	2.3	18.2	12.9	0.6	8.9	7.9
Carroll County	35 509	41 114	46 896	20 625	14 591	20 362	32 268	22 508	16 701	77.0	34.0	29.4	3.5	20.6	4.3	-8.0	11.4	14.0
Champaign County	43 139	50 430	56 866	30 568	22 143	23 343	39 033	26 904	19 542	82.4	34.5	26.6	2.0	19.4	6.8	-5.5	7.5	8.6
Clark County	40 340	48 259	57 330	27 667	18 317	22 820	38 435	25 528	19 501	78.1	33.5	28.9	3.6	23.5	7.9	-4.4	10.1	12.9
Clermont County	49 386	57 032	64 370	31 960	22 255	27 793	41 417	28 807	22 370	85.4	36.8	21.3	1.7	15.5	13.1	0.8	7.6	7.8
Clinton County	40 467	48 158	52 772	31 613	18 688	22 912	35 482	24 720	18 462	81.5	32.3	25.8	1.9	17.2	5.8	-6.5	9.3	8.7
Columbiana County	34 226	40 486	48 445	25 361	15 520	18 266	33 248	20 999	16 655	76.2	32.7	31.5	2.9	20.4	4.3	-8.0	11.3	14.5
Coshocton County	34 701	41 676	46 440	27 875	18 801	18 920	32 156	22 193	16 364	76.6	33.9	31.4	2.1	21.9	4.3	-8.0	9.6	8.9
Crawford County	36 227	43 169	49 086	25 599	19 279	20 493	34 478	22 060	17 466	77.4	34.4	31.3	2.8	19.3	4.3	-8.0	10.5	12.0
Cuyahoga County	39 168	49 559	64 867	30 415	19 420	25 009	40 594	29 462	22 272	76.5	37.2	28.3	5.3	18.3	10.7	-1.6	12.7	16.2
Darke County	39 307	45 735	53 290	32 201	20 176	20 378	34 164	24 431	18 670	79.4	40.6	30.0	2.5	18.9	6.1	-6.2	7.8	9.3
Defiance County	44 938	50 876	60 644	33 750	21 544	25 935	30 305	24 268	19 667	82.0	41.6	26.5	1.8	18.7	6.9	-5.4	6.3	6.8
Delaware County	67 258	76 453	85 192	36 815	29 046	34 421	52 798	34 529	31 600	89.6	48.6	17.6	1.4	14.5	27.4	15.1	3.9	4.1
Erie County	42 746	51 756	62 258	32 574	20 559	24 236	40 408	24 923	21 530	78.4	39.0	28.5	2.0	21.6	9.1	-3.2	8.3	9.7
Fairfield County	47 302	55 509	60 404	06 011	06 001	06 018	19 700	29 403	21 671	83.5	39.1	24.7	2.2	19.2	12.9	0.6	6.5	6.9
Fayette County	36 735	43 692	50 224	27 414	16 692	21 939	32 454	23 745	18 063	79.0	27.1	27.7	3.2	17.0	5.0	-7.3	10.9	11.1
Franklin County	42 734	53 905	66 734	30 416	22 223	29 027	38 999	30 585	23 059	84.8	33.6	18.9	3.0	14.6	11.5	-0.8	11.3	12.1
Fulton County	44 074	50 952	55 892	28 491	27 961	22 886	36 845	25 753	18 999	82.0	41.5	25.6	1.8	17.2	7.0	-5.3	5.8	5.7
Gallia County	30 191	35 938	41 694	19 464	12 818	15 477	32 883	23 565	15 183	71.4	25.4	31.4	5.7	20.6	4.9	-7.4	17.4	20.6
Geauga County	60 200	67 427	76 239	43 750	30 247	30 066	50 272	31 578	27 944	85.7	52.4	24.2	1.2	16.6	22.7	10.4	4.1	4.3
Greene County	48 656	57 954	66 174	31 434	22 971	26 722	44 706	29 795	23 057	83.1	42.9	22.0	2.0	23.4	13.7	1.4	9.3	8.0
Guernsey County	30 110	35 660	43 069	23 250	14 123	17 651	30 944	21 550	15 542	74.4	28.6	31.4	3.5	22.1	3.7	-8.6	15.8	18.6
Hamilton County	40 964	54 449	68 590	31 642	19 619	25 259	40 748	29 657	24 053	79.4	39.4	25.3	3.0	17.0	12.8	0.5	12.0	13.8
Hancock County	43 856	51 490	59 757	27 927	21 906	25 002	38 577	25 380	20 991	82.5	40.3	25.5	1.8	17.3	9.0	-3.3	7.7	8.3
Hardin County	34 440	42 395	48 779	27 057	10 750	10 016	34 471	22 364	16 200	76.6	30.8	28.6	1.9	19.3	4.4	-7.9	14.6	13.3
Harrison County	30 318	36 646	41 617	23 304	13 750	16 656	31 230	20 056	16 479	70.8	32.2	34.2	2.7	24.1	4.1	-8.2	13.9	15.5
Henry County	42 657	49 881	55 730	33 068	17 694	23 507	36 517	24 772	18 667	81.5	42.9	27.7	1.0	17.7	5.9	-6.4	6.7	8.9
Highland County	35 313	41 091	50 085	26 195	16 908	17 500	33 725	23 413	16 521	76.5	29.8	31.1	3.0	18.4	4.7	-7.6	12.5	13.2
Hocking County	34 261	40 888	49 118	25 455	13 295	18 451	32 337	24 822	16 095	76.1	29.3	28.3	3.2	20.9	4.6	-7.7	15.2	14.6
Holmes County	36 944	40 230	41 958	25 625	17 072	22 463	29 359	20 927	14 197	85.3	41.4	20.7	2.2	13.3	7.0	-5.3	11.6	13.5
Huron County	40 558	46 911	54 728	31 083	22 500	22 662	36 392	23 790	18 133	81.6	35.5	27.7	1.8	17.1	5.7	-6.6	8.3	9.5
Jackson County	30 661	36 022	43 417	23 125	13 872	13 876	31 056	22 035	14 789	72.6	25.3	30.8	4.4	18.0	2.7	-9.6	17.8	18.6
Jefferson County	30 853	38 807	46 564	24 565	12 242	16 820	36 492	21 108	16 476	68.1	32.7	36.2	4.5	27.6	4.3	-8.0	15.3	19.2
Knox County	38 877	45 119	51 062	26 311	16 214	20 164	35 339	25 124	17 695	80.0	38.6	28.8	3.1	19.5	6.5	-5.8	9.6	10.9
Lake County	48 763	57 134	65 860	37 554	27 021	28 897	41 679	29 349	23 160	81.8	42.7	27.3	1.8	19.7	11.5	-0.8	5.3	6.0
Lawrence County	29 127	35 308	40 659	21 900	13 526	14 701	31 321	21 923	14 678	69.5	25.0	34.3	5.9	23.2	3.7	-8.6	18.5	23.7
Licking County	44 124	51 969	61 551	30 330	21 193	23 959	39 058	27 699	20 581	82.2	36.7	26.1	2.2	19.9	9.4	-2.9	8.0	8.3
Logan County	41 479	47 516	57 022	31 648	19 854	23 102	38 209	25 517	18 984	81.2	34.4	27.1	2.3	17.9	7.2	-5.1	9.3	10.3
Lorain County	45 042	52 856	62 716	31 754	18 592	24 720	40 632	26 752	21 054	80.9	36.9	26.8	2.9	20.9	10.7	-1.6	8.8	10.9
Lucas County	38 004	48 190	61 669	28 836	16 593	23 020	40 384	27 189	20 518	78.5	34.2	26.2	4.4	17.9	9.3	-3.0	13.6	17.0
Madison County	44 212	50 520	59 866	31 101	20 773	24 036	35 963	26 753	18 721	82.4	33.1	25.1	3.1	18.5	8.3	-4.0	8.4	9.9
Mahoning County	35 248	44 185	56 003	26 976	16 375	19 130	37 077	24 120	18 818	73.4	35.9	34.0	4.1	22.9	7.1	-5.2	12.5	16.1
Marion County	38 709	45 297	53 669	29 728	21 799	21 304	34 633	24 646	18 255	78.8	32.0	29.8	2.9	19.3	5.5	-6.8	9.7	11.3
Medina County	55 811	62 489	69 010	40 968	23 387	29 939	45 943	28 547	24 251	86.1	44.5	22.5	1.4	17.1	15.0	2.7	4.3	5.2
Meigs County	27 287	33 071	38 140	16 786	12 073	13 236	31 193	20 042	13 848	70.8	26.0	31.4	7.3	19.8	2.7	-9.6	19.9	22.7
Mercer County	42 742	50 157	56 486	27 204	17 284	22 020	36 400	23 024	19 531	80.8	46.8	29.0	2.6	19.1	6.7	-5.6	7.3	6.7
Miami County	44 109	51 169	59 830	32 384	20 901	24 684	38 805	26 464	21 669	82.6	39.2	26.8	1.7	20.6	9.5	-2.8	7.1	8.4
Monroe County	30 467	36 297	41 196	22 125	12 083	15 265	34 163	20 515	15 096	69.3	35.8	34.6	3.5	25.6	2.3	-10.0	14.5	16.4
Montgomery County	40 156	50 071	62 530	30 795	20 201	25 266	40 002	28 434	21 743	78.6	34.0	26.2	3.0	22.0	9.8	-2.5	11.2	13.2
Morgan County	28 868	34 973	39 500	24 500	11 875	16 735	30 894	21 794	13 967	71.9	29.6	32.8	4.3	22.4	2.5	-9.8	18.7	24.1
Morrow County	40 882	45 747	50 244	28 179	19 950	21 667	34 733	23 259	17 830	82.8	33.8	27.0	2.9	21.1	5.6	-6.7	8.8	9.6
Muskingum County	35 185	41 938	50 204	26 284	15 033	19 533	32 178	22 945	17 533	77.4	31.4	30.5	4.7	20.6	5.0	-7.3	12.3	15.4
Noble County	32 940	38 939	43 750	29 265	21 304	15 612	31 574	21 250	14 100	76.3	31.6	33.5	3.4	22.4	2.8	-9.5	12.6	11.4

Table B-3. States and Counties — Education, Labor Force, and Income

STATE/ County code	MSA/PMSA/ NECMA code[1]	STATE County	High school graduates			College graduates		College graduates (percent)				
			Total population 25 years and over	Percent with a high school diploma or less	Percent with a high school diploma or more	Percent with a bachelor's degree or more	+/− U.S. percent with bachelor's degree or more	Non-Hispanic White	Black or African American	American Indian and Alaska Native	Asian, Hawaiian, and Pacific Islander	Hispanic or Latino[2]
			1	2	3	4	5	6	7	8	9	10
		OHIO—Cont'd										
39 123	...	Ottawa County	28 829	56.3	84.2	16.0	−8.4	16.5	0.0	9.9	17.9	4.7
39 125	...	Paulding County	13 108	70.9	81.6	7.8	−16.6	7.9	7.5	7.4	40.0	3.7
39 127	...	Perry County	21 626	72.2	78.9	6.9	−17.5	6.8	1.6	0.0	44.6	12.5
39 129	1840	Pickaway County	35 258	65.5	77.2	11.4	−13.0	12.2	2.2	0.0	27.1	14.8
39 131	...	Pike County	17 710	71.4	70.1	9.7	−14.7	9.5	4.3	5.2	79.7	9.3
39 133	0080	Portage County	94 073	54.0	85.9	21.0	−3.4	20.7	16.2	6.8	76.1	20.1
39 135	...	Preble County	28 079	67.8	81.7	10.1	−14.3	10.0	3.7	3.8	44.6	16.3
39 137	...	Putnam County	21 524	61.6	86.1	12.9	−11.5	13.3	35.0	11.9	8.3	2.8
39 139	4800	Richland County	86 184	62.8	80.2	12.6	−11.8	13.2	6.5	7.3	32.5	4.6
39 141	...	Ross County	49 443	66.1	76.1	11.3	−13.1	11.6	6.7	2.2	39.8	9.3
39 143	...	Sandusky County	40 565	61.6	82.1	11.9	−12.5	12.5	6.4	5.0	16.3	2.4
39 145	...	Scioto County	52 236	65.8	74.1	10.1	−14.3	10.2	4.5	6.5	50.3	2.0
39 147	...	Seneca County	37 271	63.2	83.1	12.5	−11.9	12.6	7.3	5.1	27.3	6.3
39 149	...	Shelby County	30 280	63.8	81.5	12.8	−11.6	12.4	16.2	15.6	49.0	17.1
39 151	1320	Stark County	252 971	57.8	83.4	17.9	−6.5	18.6	7.0	11.6	48.0	19.4
39 153	0080	Summit County	362 645	47.9	85.7	25.1	0.7	26.5	10.6	10.9	61.1	26.7
39 155	9320	Trumbull County	153 044	61.8	82.5	14.5	−9.9	14.9	6.9	8.1	48.3	12.3
39 157	...	Tuscarawas County	60 653	67.9	80.3	12.2	−12.2	12.1	5.2	14.1	41.3	15.1
39 159	...	Union County	26 534	57.9	86.0	15.9	−8.5	16.2	2.5	0.0	53.0	18.6
39 161	...	Van Wert County	19 453	65.0	86.6	12.0	−12.4	12.0	20.0	0.0	15.2	4.3
39 163	...	Vinton County	8 223	76.9	70.7	6.0	−18.4	6.0	0.0	11.4	X	9.1
39 165	1640	Warren County	103 306	45.0	86.2	28.4	4.0	28.3	13.9	12.3	66.1	29.3
39 167	6020	Washington County	42 770	58.5	84.5	15.0	−9.4	15.0	14.7	0.0	57.7	10.2
39 169	...	Wayne County	69 953	62.0	80.0	17.2	−7.2	17.0	17.9	7.8	53.5	23.9
39 171	...	Williams County	25 690	65.6	83.1	10.7	−13.7	10.8	0.0	14.9	0.0	8.2
39 173	8400	Wood County	71 551	46.2	88.6	26.2	1.8	26.1	34.6	28.3	59.3	11.0
39 175	...	Wyandot County	15 097	66.5	82.5	9.8	−14.6	9.8	0.0	0.0	25.9	7.5
40 000	...	OKLAHOMA	2 203 173	50.9	80.6	20.3	−4.1	21.7	13.7	13.2	36.7	9.6
40 001	...	Adair County	12 764	71.4	66.7	9.8	−14.6	11.3	0.0	7.1	27.3	3.9
40 003	...	Alfalfa County	4 543	59.4	81.4	14.9	−9.5	16.5	4.5	2.0	X	2.6
40 005	...	Atoka County	9 377	70.5	69.4	10.1	−14.3	10.7	1.6	10.3	0.0	0.0
40 007	...	Beaver County	3 898	55.1	81.2	17.6	−6.8	18.6	0.0	22.0	71.4	6.4
40 009	...	Beckham County	12 968	58.8	75.9	15.5	−8.9	16.7	0.0	15.7	76.7	5.4
40 011	...	Blaine County	8 118	65.7	75.5	14.0	−10.4	16.7	10.9	3.2	11.4	3.3
40 013	...	Bryan County	23 175	56.9	74.9	17.9	−6.5	17.6	13.9	16.9	53.5	11.7
40 015	...	Caddo County	19 020	64.6	75.9	14.2	−10.2	15.2	5.9	13.2	7.7	5.0
40 017	5880	Canadian County	56 207	44.7	87.3	20.9	−3.5	21.4	13.5	16.2	32.1	9.8
40 019	...	Carter County	30 195	59.8	77.0	15.1	−9.3	15.8	9.7	8.6	53.1	18.8
40 021	...	Cherokee County	25 237	53.5	76.7	22.1	−2.3	23.8	26.2	18.1	22.7	9.9
40 023	...	Choctaw County	10 210	67.7	69.0	9.9	−14.5	9.6	5.2	13.2	22.7	28.2
40 025	...	Cimarron County	2 077	55.0	76.6	17.7	−6.7	19.7	0.0	16.7	0.0	1.3
40 027	5880	Cleveland County	126 569	38.6	88.1	28.0	3.6	28.1	27.1	21.8	48.6	17.9
40 029	...	Coal County	3 964	68.4	68.6	12.4	−12.0	12.2	0.0	14.8	35.7	10.6
40 031	4200	Comanche County	67 220	46.3	85.2	19.1	−5.3	21.8	11.6	13.0	21.5	11.2
40 033	...	Cotton County	4 436	62.2	77.0	14.0	−10.4	14.8	1.4	11.8	33.3	7.5
40 035	...	Craig County	10 197	63.8	76.9	10.5	−13.9	10.5	8.8	9.5	0.0	21.6
40 037	8560	Creek County	43 523	62.4	77.6	11.7	−12.7	12.1	9.8	8.0	20.5	7.6
40 039	...	Custer County	15 156	50.2	81.2	22.8	−1.6	25.2	3.1	12.0	29.0	4.6
40 041	...	Delaware County	25 549	61.7	75.4	13.3	−11.1	14.0	15.4	11.2	24.0	5.8
40 043	...	Dewey County	3 310	61.0	79.8	16.6	−7.8	17.3	0.0	3.7	100.0	1.6
40 045	...	Ellis County	2 918	57.1	81.2	19.2	−5.2	19.5	X	16.7	X	8.9
40 047	2340	Garfield County	38 067	53.4	82.2	19.6	−4.8	20.2	5.6	10.5	25.9	12.6
40 049	...	Garvin County	18 263	67.4	73.0	12.0	−12.4	12.2	14.7	9.3	26.0	5.6
40 051	...	Grady County	29 172	58.8	79.5	14.4	−10.0	14.7	7.0	17.4	29.9	4.3
40 053	...	Grant County	3 500	53.3	85.7	16.2	−8.2	16.0	0.0	22.9	22.2	34.5
40 055	...	Greer County	4 302	59.6	76.7	12.6	−11.8	14.6	4.1	2.7	58.8	0.0
40 057	...	Harmon County	2 192	69.0	63.2	12.1	−12.3	15.6	0.0	0.0	50.0	1.7
40 059	...	Harper County	2 507	54.2	82.1	19.2	−5.2	19.3	X	22.7	0.0	14.5
40 061	...	Haskell County	7 762	65.7	66.9	10.3	−14.1	10.6	10.5	8.1	0.0	2.5
40 063	...	Hughes County	9 762	68.3	70.8	9.7	−14.7	10.8	2.2	5.4	0.0	6.5
40 065	...	Jackson County	17 270	47.8	79.1	18.5	−5.9	20.5	10.6	21.3	35.1	5.6
40 067	...	Jefferson County	4 710	68.1	69.3	10.6	−13.8	10.8	0.0	13.3	5.9	8.5
40 069	...	Johnston County	6 759	61.4	69.1	13.3	−11.1	13.8	0.0	11.1	36.8	15.3
40 071	...	Kay County	31 106	52.3	80.9	18.3	−6.1	19.4	4.2	8.7	35.3	8.9
40 073	...	Kingfisher County	8 984	57.6	81.2	16.1	−8.3	17.5	4.8	11.3	0.0	1.8

[1]MSA = Metropolitan Statistical Area. PMSA = Primary MSA. NECMA = New England County Metropolitan Area. See the Appendix A for explanation of these concepts. See Appendix B for list of metropolitan areas identified by type, with component counties.
[2]Hispanic or Latino persons may be of any race.

STATE County	School enrollment			Population 16 to 19 years				Employment status, 2000			Work status in 1999 of the population 16 years and over (percent)		
											Worked in 1999		
	Grades kindergarten through 12	College or graduate school	Percent private	Number	Percent in armed forces	Percent high school graduates	Percent not enrolled, not grads, not in armed forces, not employed	Total population 16 years and over	Percent in labor force	Unemployment rate	Full-time	Part-time	Did not work in 1999
	11	12	13	14	15	16	17	18	19	20	21	22	23
OHIO—Cont'd													
Ottawa County	7 672	1 503	7.5	2 130	0.7	12.4	1.4	32 648	63.4	4.1	55.2	14.6	30.2
Paulding County	4 243	601	8.9	1 258	0.0	11.8	2.0	15 583	65.4	3.3	54.7	16.3	29.1
Perry County	7 113	1 068	7.9	2 012	0.0	13.0	5.7	25 562	61.0	5.9	53.5	12.3	34.1
Pickaway County	9 880	1 905	8.8	2 688	0.0	14.2	8.1	41 529	56.0	4.1	52.8	13.8	33.4
Pike County	5 690	774	6.6	1 664	0.0	14.2	7.4	21 094	54.3	9.5	47.9	11.5	40.6
Portage County	26 926	17 050	8.9	10 892	0.1	8.2	1.8	120 208	69.5	4.5	56.1	20.3	23.6
Preble County	8 465	1 356	6.8	2 336	0.0	12.8	2.5	32 607	65.9	4.3	56.3	14.9	28.9
Putnam County	7 856	1 215	11.6	2 204	0.0	8.7	1.9	25 640	68.7	2.9	57.2	17.4	25.5
Richland County	24 217	4 997	11.9	6 751	0.3	11.3	4.0	100 548	61.0	4.8	52.7	15.0	32.3
Ross County	13 531	2 809	6.6	3 851	0.1	12.0	4.7	57 818	56.7	5.4	50.6	14.1	35.2
Sandusky County	12 206	2 609	12.1	3 570	0.1	10.9	4.3	47 628	66.9	4.3	56.6	14.3	29.1
Scioto County	14 844	3 208	6.2	4 630	0.0	13.6	6.2	62 385	51.1	9.1	43.2	12.2	44.6
Seneca County	11 688	3 270	21.5	3 819	0.0	11.4	2.4	45 390	66.9	5.1	55.5	16.1	28.4
Shelby County	10 196	1 321	9.9	2 734	0.3	9.3	2.4	35 730	69.3	3.2	60.5	14.2	25.3
Stark County	71 024	16 696	15.7	20 471	0.0	10.3	4.0	295 090	64.1	4.5	52.9	16.1	31.0
Summit County	101 486	29 977	13.2	28 072	0.1	11.6	3.3	421 407	65.8	5.0	54.3	16.0	29.7
Trumbull County	41 257	8 496	11.5	11 881	0.0	12.0	5.6	176 895	59.7	5.7	50.4	14.5	35.2
Tuscarawas County	17 119	2 663	9.1	4 984	0.0	13.9	2.9	70 453	63.5	4.1	52.9	14.8	32.3
Union County	8 259	1 275	10.1	2 015	0.0	14.0	4.6	30 747	69.4	2.3	61.7	14.8	23.5
Van Wert County	5 933	875	12.1	1 888	0.0	12.6	4.3	22 945	66.9	4.9	55.4	14.9	29.7
Vinton County	2 646	296	4.7	662	0.0	8.6	4.7	9 665	55.7	9.0	49.0	12.3	38.7
Warren County	32 241	5 886	14.9	7 779	0.1	11.5	2.9	118 933	67.5	3.0	58.8	15.8	25.4
Washington County	11 269	3 317	14.6	3 646	0.0	11.4	3.3	50 225	61.6	7.4	51.4	14.8	33.9
Wayne County	22 085	5 283	18.7	7 222	0.0	10.0	4.8	84 608	67.8	3.2	55.2	17.5	27.3
Williams County	7 807	983	7.4	2 325	0.0	15.4	6.2	30 122	68.9	3.4	60.0	14.5	25.6
Wood County	22 026	18 158	7.8	10 651	0.1	6.3	1.7	96 086	69.4	6.2	54.9	22.2	22.8
Wyandot County	4 476	772	13.8	1 258	0.0	12.7	2.8	17 671	67.0	2.9	56.4	15.3	28.3
OKLAHOMA	667 503	203 262	9.2	213 273	1.1	11.3	5.6	2 666 724	62.1	5.2	54.2	13.8	32.0
Adair County	4 761	511	6.1	1 263	0.0	13.9	6.5	15 364	59.1	7.1	51.9	10.9	37.3
Alfalfa County	982	170	4.0	276	0.0	7.6	1.1	5 087	47.9	2.8	48.6	12.7	38.7
Atoka County	2 646	383	3.7	751	0.0	9.9	3.3	11 006	47.2	6.6	49.4	8.9	41.6
Beaver County	1 254	119	1.4	365	0.8	11.8	4.7	4 508	62.0	2.6	55.2	11.8	32.9
Beckham County	3 766	566	3.9	1 033	0.0	5.1	5.4	15 542	54.2	6.3	48.1	14.3	37.5
Blaine County	2 336	266	2.6	684	0.0	7.5	7.3	9 465	50.5	5.3	46.7	12.9	40.4
Bryan County	6 831	2 495	5.1	2 337	0.0	10.0	6.2	28 409	58.7	6.4	49.3	14.0	36.6
Caddo County	6 832	1 024	4.1	2 150	0.0	11.7	8.5	22 792	54.3	8.0	47.9	11.2	40.9
Canadian County	18 887	3 883	7.3	5 547	0.1	8.0	2.6	66 346	68.5	3.4	60.8	13.5	25.7
Carter County	9 131	1 212	5.4	2 472	0.2	10.2	5.6	35 081	58.4	5.6	50.2	13.1	36.6
Cherokee County	8 375	4 448	5.0	3 278	0.1	9.0	6.3	32 794	59.4	8.2	49.4	16.6	34.0
Choctaw County	2 962	495	2.6	847	0.0	9.7	11.6	11 850	51.7	7.1	46.4	10.9	42.6
Cimarron County	685	66	4.0	165	0.0	3.0	4.2	2 391	60.6	2.0	53.2	13.6	33.2
Cleveland County	37 689	26 884	7.1	14 804	0.3	7.6	2.8	163 651	67.9	4.1	57.7	18.3	24.0
Coal County	1 241	172	4.5	341	0.0	12.0	8.2	4 608	53.0	6.9	48.0	10.5	41.5
Comanche County	23 102	7 129	5.7	8 397	21.3	32.6	5.7	86 873	65.0	5.9	55.4	14.2	30.4
Cotton County	1 301	155	1.3	397	0.8	12.3	4.0	5 141	55.2	4.8	48.6	12.1	39.3
Craig County	2 777	386	3.0	862	0.0	8.7	5.3	11 853	55.9	3.9	51.7	11.9	36.4
Creek County	14 067	2 269	6.7	4 151	0.0	11.3	3.7	51 175	60.6	4.8	54.5	11.9	33.6
Custer County	5 064	3 431	2.8	2 358	0.0	6.2	3.4	20 773	62.7	4.7	52.1	19.2	28.8
Delaware County	6 721	796	5.0	1 901	0.0	13.5	7.8	29 090	54.3	6.6	47.9	11.5	40.6
Dewey County	956	107	2.4	329	0.0	7.3	1.5	3 837	57.2	3.3	47.8	14.6	37.6
Ellis County	729	63	4.3	236	0.0	4.2	5.5	3 302	60.4	2.3	51.7	13.0	35.3
Garfield County	10 951	2 079	8.6	3 212	0.0	8.3	6.4	45 196	63.3	4.9	54.5	14.1	31.4
Garvin County	5 211	572	3.3	1 646	0.0	10.9	5.0	21 357	57.7	5.6	49.8	12.0	38.2
Grady County	9 242	2 073	4.8	3 000	0.0	10.4	4.4	34 986	62.0	4.8	54.1	13.0	32.9
Grant County	1 115	113	4.0	301	0.0	8.3	0.7	3 991	60.4	2.7	51.2	13.3	35.5
Greer County	971	261	4.8	344	0.0	14.5	2.9	5 050	43.8	6.9	43.2	12.1	44.7
Harmon County	728	43	2.3	219	0.0	8.7	7.8	2 557	53.8	6.9	46.5	10.8	42.6
Harper County	713	74	2.0	212	0.0	7.1	2.4	2 862	60.8	1.4	52.9	13.3	33.8
Haskell County	2 301	281	0.9	710	0.0	18.5	3.7	9 102	53.1	4.7	45.9	11.2	42.9
Hughes County	2 591	434	5.9	643	0.0	10.6	6.8	11 291	47.8	7.6	43.1	10.8	46.1
Jackson County	5 965	1 543	2.6	1 801	6.6	16.0	6.9	21 081	63.4	4.6	55.1	13.7	31.3
Jefferson County	1 255	149	1.7	334	0.0	9.9	4.5	5 375	51.3	5.5	45.1	12.1	42.8
Johnston County	2 038	536	3.1	743	0.0	9.0	6.7	8 161	54.4	6.1	47.1	11.8	41.1
Kay County	9 483	1 774	6.7	2 970	0.0	9.6	6.7	36 926	59.8	7.7	51.3	13.2	35.5
Kingfisher County	3 003	316	7.7	877	0.0	8.9	2.9	10 674	64.5	3.5	56.0	13.8	30.2

Table B-3. States and Counties — Education, Labor Force, and Income

STATE County	Full-year full-time employed (percent)								Children under 18 years in families			With two parents (percent)			Total employed by class of worker (percent)			
	Total	Men	Women	Non-Hispanic White	Black or African American	American Indian and Alaska Native	Asian, Hawaiian, and Pacific Islander	Hispanic or Latino[1]	Number	Both in labor force	Father only in labor force	With one parent who is in labor force (percent)	+/− U.S. percent of children with no stay-at-home parent (percent)	+/− U.S. percent two-income couples	Private	Government	Self-employed	Unpaid family worker
	24	25	26	27	28	29	30	31	32	33	34	35	36	37	38	39	40	41
OHIO—Cont'd																		
Ottawa County	42.0	51.7	32.7	42.0	32.4	63.4	29.9	40.6	9 157	51.7	19.6	20.2	7.3	-0.3	77.3	11.5	10.7	0.5
Paulding County	42.7	56.9	29.2	43.0	35.2	25.8	0.0	37.5	5 174	52.6	21.7	16.0	4.0	1.2	83.2	8.5	8.2	0.1
Perry County	40.1	50.4	30.1	40.3	6.6	30.0	33.8	13.7	9 166	45.4	24.4	18.6	-0.6	-4.2	76.8	13.7	8.5	1.0
Pickaway County	39.1	42.4	35.0	41.9	7.8	37.7	38.9	15.9	12 071	49.3	19.0	18.1	2.8	1.2	75.4	14.9	9.4	0.2
Pike County	34.6	42.8	27.1	35.0	24.3	24.2	34.1	23.1	7 046	34.7	23.1	22.4	-7.5	-11.4	75.8	15.3	8.0	0.9
Portage County	42.5	53.1	32.6	43.1	33.5	22.3	20.3	33.5	34 625	50.9	21.6	19.9	6.2	4.1	78.6	13.2	7.9	0.3
Preble County	44.7	56.4	33.4	45.0	20.3	34.8	27.2	18.6	10 550	56.0	21.8	15.0	6.4	3.5	78.4	12.1	9.1	0.4
Putnam County	46.3	58.1	35.0	46.5	25.9	61.4	66.0	41.6	10 106	68.2	13.3	11.5	15.1	11.7	81.2	9.4	9.0	0.4
Richland County	40.0	48.9	31.1	41.3	29.0	34.2	39.2	31.5	29 984	44.7	22.4	22.6	2.7	0.7	80.1	11.8	7.8	0.4
Ross County	38.4	45.7	30.4	39.6	24.1	33.7	37.5	50.3	16 621	44.2	25.0	18.2	-2.2	-3.2	76.2	16.3	7.3	0.2
Sandusky County	43.6	55.9	32.3	44.3	36.6	23.2	23.8	37.6	15 338	53.6	16.4	23.1	12.1	5.4	81.8	10.4	7.5	0.3
Scioto County	31.4	39.0	24.4	32.1	14.1	25.8	26.7	30.2	17 965	35.8	24.6	18.9	-9.9	-12.6	74.2	17.0	8.5	0.3
Seneca County	42.6	52.8	32.9	43.2	31.4	20.2	33.5	35.6	14 542	54.4	15.9	23.2	13.0	5.8	81.4	10.5	7.8	0.3
Shelby County	48.3	61.0	36.0	48.7	33.7	22.8	59.5	26.9	13 145	56.1	19.3	17.8	9.3	7.9	82.9	9.2	7.7	0.3
Stark County	41.1	52.9	30.6	41.6	35.3	32.7	36.6	38.3	88 610	47.6	22.2	21.2	4.2	0.8	81.9	9.7	8.1	0.3
Summit County	42.3	53.4	32.3	43.3	35.8	39.3	41.9	38.0	129 271	45.0	22.0	22.7	3.1	1.4	80.4	11.4	8.0	0.2
Trumbull County	38.4	49.6	28.1	38.9	32.6	25.1	41.9	32.4	52 495	43.6	22.7	23.5	2.5	-4.5	81.3	10.4	8.0	0.2
Tuscarawas County	42.0	55.7	29.4	42.0	37.5	28.2	43.5	52.4	22 143	47.5	25.7	19.7	2.6	-0.5	81.6	10.1	8.2	0.2
Union County	49.3	63.3	37.1	50.8	8.3	21.4	58.2	40.9	10 797	62.0	18.8	14.3	11.7	14.1	79.6	10.7	9.2	0.4
Van Wert County	44.0	56.3	32.7	43.8	50.4	63.2	53.8	44.2	7 459	62.9	14.8	16.9	15.2	6.0	81.9	8.9	9.0	0.2
Vinton County	32.8	41.9	24.0	32.7	100.0	48.8	X	28.2	3 201	30.7	28.0	24.6	-9.3	-14.5	76.5	15.9	7.2	0.3
Warren County	47.3	58.3	36.1	48.1	25.1	34.7	57.7	36.6	42 634	54.3	25.7	14.0	3.7	7.0	82.1	9.5	8.1	0.3
Washington County	38.5	49.7	28.5	38.6	48.5	33.6	34.1	35.2	14 228	47.4	23.3	18.6	1.4	-2.5	79.0	12.1	8.4	0.5
Wayne County	43.4	56.3	31.2	43.4	38.7	27.6	42.0	29.5	29 568	50.6	29.1	14.2	0.2	4.4	77.9	10.3	11.2	0.7
Williams County	46.7	57.0	36.8	47.1	19.1	42.4	51.3	42.1	9 836	59.4	14.6	21.1	15.9	11.1	82.9	8.6	8.2	0.3
Wood County	41.2	52.7	30.7	41.4	28.7	40.3	30.5	44.6	27 552	52.8	21.3	19.7	7.9	7.9	76.8	15.8	7.2	0.2
Wyandot County	45.5	57.8	34.1	45.6	37.5	58.3	65.1	40.0	5 724	57.0	17.1	19.1	11.5	7.2	81.2	9.5	8.8	0.4
OKLAHOMA	39.6	49.2	30.5	40.5	34.6	36.7	36.9	38.1	832 936	42.9	23.1	21.9	0.2	-1.7	71.3	16.8	11.4	0.5
Adair County	34.5	43.9	25.7	36.0	0.0	31.8	17.6	43.6	5 704	41.1	20.9	22.5	-1.0	-4.2	71.6	16.8	11.0	0.6
Alfalfa County	33.8	38.4	27.4	36.1	5.6	20.0	0.0	24.6	1 160	55.8	23.5	15.9	7.1	2.8	52.3	22.0	24.5	1.2
Atoka County	31.8	36.2	26.6	32.8	19.0	31.5	75.0	28.0	2 968	39.9	25.4	19.4	-5.3	-9.0	58.0	25.6	15.1	1.3
Beaver County	40.1	53.1	26.8	40.0	31.3	46.5	20.0	36.5	1 500	51.8	24.2	14.4	1.6	-0.3	57.8	19.4	21.3	1.5
Beckham County	32.6	40.0	24.4	33.6	17.0	30.0	73.3	37.3	4 596	44.9	23.2	20.8	1.1	-2.7	65.5	17.0	16.3	1.2
Blaine County	31.7	35.7	26.6	34.8	19.8	20.6	16.7	31.0	2 697	48.2	22.8	17.2	0.8	-1.4	60.8	20.0	17.7	1.5
Bryan County	34.6	43.0	26.7	34.6	23.4	35.9	17.1	29.6	8 339	44.3	21.8	20.4	0.1	-6.5	69.8	18.4	11.2	0.6
Caddo County	33.2	39.5	27.0	35.3	23.5	27.4	18.8	33.4	7 553	41.3	20.6	20.8	-2.5	-4.5	61.2	22.3	15.5	1.0
Canadian County	47.4	57.5	37.4	48.9	19.4	41.5	42.6	38.6	23 310	52.1	22.1	18.3	5.8	8.6	72.7	15.8	11.1	0.4
Carter County	36.6	47.1	27.2	37.7	31.1	32.3	32.1	29.9	11 026	45.1	21.1	21.5	2.0	-3.5	72.7	13.3	13.1	0.9
Cherokee County	32.3	39.3	25.6	31.4	12.3	34.2	11.7	34.4	10 177	40.5	22.3	20.9	-3.2	-7.4	59.9	27.7	11.9	0.4
Choctaw County	31.1	37.9	25.3	31.5	23.1	35.6	31.3	29.5	3 666	37.4	17.5	22.6	-4.6	-11.6	66.7	18.1	14.3	0.9
Cimarron County	40.1	53.1	27.8	40.0	60.0	44.4	100.0	39.5	824	48.7	26.2	14.4	-1.5	0.1	48.6	22.7	27.5	1.1
Cleveland County	43.7	52.4	35.1	44.7	36.7	40.9	37.8	39.9	48 535	49.2	23.4	18.4	3.0	6.1	66.4	23.8	9.5	0.3
Coal County	32.3	39.2	25.9	33.1	52.9	31.7	0.0	20.7	1 469	47.0	19.6	18.7	1.1	-12.5	61.9	23.5	13.1	1.5
Comanche County	39.1	49.8	27.6	40.0	39.7	34.9	33.4	35.5	29 277	39.7	25.6	22.5	-2.4	-2.9	64.0	26.0	9.6	0.4
Cotton County	34.9	45.0	25.3	35.9	14.9	32.7	36.4	38.0	1 570	43.9	22.9	21.1	0.4	-5.3	61.4	20.6	16.6	1.3
Craig County	39.8	48.8	30.9	38.1	42.3	46.4	37.5	50.7	3 387	48.7	19.6	20.1	4.2	-2.3	69.6	17.6	12.3	0.5
Creek County	39.9	49.4	30.9	40.8	34.8	35.3	42.3	36.7	17 172	42.5	24.6	20.0	-2.1	-4.2	76.5	13.2	10.2	0.2
Custer County	35.0	44.8	25.8	35.5	34.8	29.4	18.8	32.8	5 912	46.9	19.9	21.5	3.8	2.1	66.3	19.6	13.4	0.7
Delaware County	33.9	41.7	26.4	33.1	45.5	35.5	52.0	45.6	8 297	41.1	21.3	21.7	-1.8	-11.3	71.0	13.3	15.1	0.6
Dewey County	34.7	50.2	20.4	35.1	33.3	19.7	100.0	35.1	1 024	53.3	27.1	9.7	-1.6	-5.0	54.4	18.8	26.0	0.8
Ellis County	40.1	50.7	29.9	39.8	X	57.7	X	48.5	863	54.2	16.5	19.6	9.2	2.6	59.0	18.3	21.5	1.2
Garfield County	40.9	53.0	30.0	41.2	40.4	39.8	40.1	38.0	13 469	45.6	24.7	20.6	1.6	-0.3	70.8	14.8	13.6	0.7
Garvin County	35.3	45.8	26.2	35.2	34.0	33.9	34.6	46.0	6 239	44.5	26.9	20.6	0.5	-7.1	67.2	18.0	13.6	1.2
Grady County	40.1	51.3	29.9	40.4	30.8	39.7	21.6	46.0	11 346	44.7	25.8	17.7	-2.2	-1.3	70.6	15.8	12.8	0.8
Grant County	38.0	49.9	26.6	38.3	100.0	25.8	55.6	30.8	1 256	56.8	16.5	16.2	8.4	4.2	58.3	16.9	23.8	1.0
Greer County	30.2	33.8	25.7	32.5	12.6	7.5	88.2	36.4	1 096	42.6	19.3	25.0	3.0	-8.1	50.5	28.7	18.8	2.0
Harmon County	33.3	42.4	25.3	35.6	12.3	0.0	100.0	31.5	746	43.0	20.9	18.9	-2.7	-3.6	58.8	24.3	15.1	1.9
Harper County	41.8	51.7	32.0	41.9	X	24.0	0.0	41.1	800	49.0	22.8	15.1	-0.5	2.7	64.2	24.3	20.3	1.3
Haskell County	31.3	42.8	20.8	30.5	24.6	36.6	50.0	40.7	2 795	40.9	27.6	17.5	-6.2	-8.6	64.7	17.5	17.4	0.4
Hughes County	28.1	32.3	23.6	28.8	19.8	26.2	30.0	23.7	3 016	42.0	23.0	18.0	-4.6	-10.4	62.4	21.8	15.2	0.7
Jackson County	41.6	55.3	28.7	43.6	36.2	34.5	32.1	35.9	7 882	41.4	27.4	19.9	-3.3	-1.0	59.0	28.6	12.0	0.4
Jefferson County	32.1	40.8	23.9	32.9	69.4	39.1	4.5	27.2	1 544	45.9	28.5	14.3	-4.4	-12.0	61.6	19.7	18.0	0.7
Johnston County	31.3	39.9	23.0	31.5	42.4	30.6	10.5	31.5	2 484	40.6	25.0	16.9	-7.1	-8.8	64.3	23.1	11.9	0.6
Kay County	37.1	47.3	28.0	37.4	38.0	34.8	47.3	33.9	11 874	46.6	22.3	21.7	3.7	-5.1	74.4	13.5	11.4	0.7
Kingfisher County	43.2	57.1	30.3	44.1	30.8	44.7	33.3	39.8	3 682	50.2	22.8	15.7	1.3	3.6	70.6	12.4	16.2	0.9

[1] Hispanic or Latino persons may be of any race.

Table B-3. States and Counties — Education, Labor Force, and Income

STATE County	Percent who worked at home	Percent of the population 5 years and over with a disability	Veterans as a percent of the population 18 years and over	Occupation for employed population 16 years and over (percent)						Industry for employed population 16 years and over (percent)					
				Management, professional, and related occupations	Service occupations	Sales and office occupations	Farming, fishing, and forestry occupations	Construction, extraction, and maintenance occupations	Production, transportation and material moving occupations	Agriculture, forestry, fishing, and mining	Construction and manufacturing	Wholesale and retail trade	Transportation and warehousing, and utilities	Service industries	Public administration
	42	43	44	45	46	47	48	49	50	51	52	53	54	55	56
OHIO—Cont'd															
Ottawa County	3.1	18.9	15.3	26.2	14.9	24.1	0.6	12.4	21.7	2.1	28.6	14.1	8.2	43.4	3.7
Paulding County	2.5	19.2	13.7	20.7	12.7	19.6	1.2	10.4	35.5	3.8	42.7	13.7	4.4	32.7	2.7
Perry County	2.6	21.7	13.7	20.2	13.5	21.3	0.7	15.2	29.2	3.5	36.7	12.3	4.8	37.7	5.0
Pickaway County	2.5	18.8	15.2	26.2	14.2	25.7	0.5	11.9	21.4	2.3	25.0	18.1	6.8	41.9	5.8
Pike County	1.9	25.8	14.8	21.0	15.3	23.1	1.4	12.4	26.8	4.1	32.4	14.3	5.1	38.3	5.8
Portage County	2.6	15.5	12.5	28.4	15.1	25.7	0.3	9.5	20.9	0.8	30.2	15.7	3.9	46.4	2.9
Preble County	3.2	18.7	14.3	24.2	13.1	22.6	0.9	12.0	27.1	2.8	36.3	14.5	5.8	37.3	3.3
Putnam County	2.7	14.7	10.5	24.3	12.8	20.2	0.9	11.3	30.6	3.2	40.1	13.1	4.3	36.3	3.0
Richland County	2.8	18.7	15.0	23.9	15.9	24.3	0.4	9.4	26.0	1.1	33.3	15.0	4.3	41.5	4.8
Ross County	1.8	21.8	15.6	23.9	17.5	21.9	0.6	10.8	25.3	1.5	29.5	15.0	5.3	42.3	6.3
Sandusky County	2.1	17.7	13.2	22.9	13.1	19.7	0.6	10.8	32.9	2.5	41.1	11.6	4.5	37.8	2.5
Scioto County	2.3	26.0	14.5	26.1	20.6	22.1	0.6	11.9	18.7	2.8	21.7	14.7	6.0	48.1	6.7
Seneca County	2.6	17.3	13.6	21.7	15.1	20.6	0.7	10.3	31.7	2.3	38.6	13.1	4.7	38.0	3.2
Shelby County	2.9	17.5	13.0	25.0	12.7	20.4	0.7	9.0	32.2	2.4	47.3	10.9	3.7	32.9	2.9
Stark County	2.3	17.7	14.2	28.7	14.6	26.6	0.3	8.4	21.5	0.9	29.5	16.4	4.3	46.0	2.9
Summit County	2.6	17.8	13.6	33.1	14.4	28.4	0.1	7.9	16.1	0.2	25.2	16.4	5.0	49.8	3.4
Trumbull County	2.0	19.2	16.0	24.5	15.0	24.6	0.3	9.4	26.2	0.6	33.7	15.4	4.4	42.5	3.4
Tuscarawas County	2.5	18.1	14.0	22.7	15.5	23.1	0.7	9.9	28.2	2.2	34.1	16.8	4.5	39.3	3.1
Union County	3.3	16.3	13.0	27.1	13.8	26.3	0.8	8.7	23.4	3.2	31.7	15.0	4.7	41.5	3.9
Van Wert County	2.7	17.8	14.1	22.4	13.4	21.4	0.2	9.5	33.0	2.5	40.7	13.1	4.0	36.9	2.9
Vinton County	2.3	24.3	13.9	16.6	12.0	19.6	1.4	17.5	33.0	6.2	35.0	13.0	6.4	33.8	5.6
Warren County	3.4	14.3	13.1	37.7	11.2	26.6	0.2	8.8	15.6	0.6	30.1	16.1	3.9	46.2	3.1
Washington County	2.7	18.9	15.5	27.5	15.4	26.7	0.7	9.6	20.1	2.3	26.0	17.0	5.4	45.5	3.8
Wayne County	5.1	15.9	12.2	26.4	14.2	22.5	1.4	9.8	25.6	4.1	33.6	14.2	4.7	40.7	2.7
Williams County	2.9	17.4	13.5	20.6	12.2	18.8	0.6	9.0	38.8	1.7	52.3	10.6	3.8	29.1	2.5
Wood County	2.2	14.5	11.3	32.9	14.5	24.0	0.4	8.1	20.1	1.1	26.4	14.0	5.6	50.1	2.8
Wyandot County	3.1	17.7	12.3	20.7	14.3	18.8	0.8	11.6	33.8	4.8	41.8	11.9	4.4	33.9	3.2
OKLAHOMA	3.1	21.6	14.7	30.3	15.5	26.6	0.9	11.3	15.4	4.1	19.5	15.4	5.6	49.5	5.9
Adair County	3.6	24.4	11.6	22.1	13.5	17.3	3.8	11.5	31.8	8.6	36.8	12.0	4.5	34.6	3.6
Alfalfa County	5.3	21.2	18.6	33.8	19.0	21.0	4.1	9.8	12.3	19.3	10.4	13.0	10.1	37.9	9.3
Atoka County	3.8	27.0	15.6	24.9	18.4	19.4	1.9	12.5	22.9	7.0	24.8	12.5	6.7	37.0	12.0
Beaver County	4.4	17.3	11.4	31.2	11.7	22.3	4.5	14.0	16.3	21.0	15.0	13.0	8.9	37.7	4.3
Beckham County	2.9	23.7	13.1	27.2	19.8	22.9	2.2	15.5	12.4	15.5	11.1	16.7	4.8	44.9	7.1
Blaine County	3.2	22.2	12.3	29.9	15.9	20.8	2.8	13.5	17.1	14.2	19.0	11.5	6.9	41.4	7.1
Bryan County	2.1	26.0	14.4	27.8	15.7	25.3	1.3	10.1	19.8	3.8	21.7	16.6	4.3	48.6	4.9
Caddo County	3.8	22.6	13.4	29.1	16.3	22.7	2.4	12.8	16.7	10.9	17.3	14.1	7.7	42.2	7.8
Canadian County	2.8	16.2	14.3	31.6	13.3	28.9	0.5	10.5	15.2	3.9	19.9	16.8	6.0	45.6	7.8
Carter County	3.0	24.8	15.3	25.6	17.9	25.2	0.8	10.9	19.6	7.9	18.0	18.3	5.5	47.1	3.2
Cherokee County	3.4	22.6	14.3	29.7	16.2	25.2	2.4	11.9	14.6	3.7	17.1	14.7	3.9	53.1	7.5
Choctaw County	3.6	27.6	14.7	26.6	16.6	23.6	2.1	13.3	17.8	6.5	18.2	15.2	8.8	45.3	5.9
Cimarron County	5.0	18.3	10.8	35.3	13.1	20.3	9.7	8.6	13.0	27.2	9.8	11.4	7.4	38.2	5.9
Cleveland County	2.6	16.2	14.3	35.3	14.8	28.8	0.2	10.0	10.8	1.4	15.7	15.6	4.7	53.7	8.9
Coal County	4.9	29.9	13.5	28.1	18.9	16.3	3.1	12.2	21.4	10.1	24.1	11.3	3.9	42.5	8.0
Comanche County	2.3	19.6	19.5	29.5	19.5	25.6	0.6	10.5	14.3	2.2	16.5	15.1	4.2	53.5	8.5
Cotton County	2.8	22.5	14.8	29.0	13.0	23.6	3.5	12.3	18.7	11.2	20.6	13.9	8.4	38.7	7.2
Craig County	4.6	23.9	14.0	24.0	18.8	22.8	1.8	9.3	23.4	6.2	20.8	15.2	9.2	43.4	5.1
Creek County	2.9	23.1	15.7	23.6	14.2	26.4	0.3	13.5	21.8	2.7	26.3	15.2	7.2	45.1	3.5
Custer County	2.6	17.6	11.5	29.5	16.2	26.8	1.9	11.8	13.9	9.3	17.8	16.8	3.6	48.3	4.2
Delaware County	4.3	27.2	17.7	23.4	15.9	23.4	1.8	12.2	23.4	5.0	31.2	14.5	5.2	40.8	3.4
Dewey County	5.7	22.2	11.7	32.9	15.4	21.1	4.7	11.6	14.3	24.3	10.8	15.0	7.9	37.8	4.3
Ellis County	6.9	23.7	16.2	33.7	14.1	20.7	4.5	13.8	13.2	20.1	11.2	12.9	7.1	42.7	5.9
Garfield County	3.0	21.6	15.3	27.2	19.1	25.6	0.9	12.3	14.8	6.4	18.2	16.7	5.8	47.4	5.5
Garvin County	3.8	25.6	12.9	23.1	18.4	23.6	1.7	12.4	20.8	11.3	18.4	16.7	6.9	41.5	5.1
Grady County	3.3	22.7	13.2	26.2	13.8	24.6	1.6	14.3	19.5	7.4	24.4	14.6	6.1	41.5	5.9
Grant County	9.0	20.0	14.2	34.3	13.4	24.1	4.7	11.7	11.8	22.9	14.0	12.4	8.5	35.9	6.3
Greer County	2.7	27.0	15.0	31.8	19.4	20.1	3.8	12.1	12.7	12.3	14.0	10.9	6.2	44.3	12.3
Harmon County	2.9	25.4	13.0	30.6	16.9	21.8	4.1	13.1	13.5	16.5	18.4	12.2	4.7	39.9	8.3
Harper County	4.8	20.5	14.7	33.5	16.3	17.0	8.9	13.0	11.2	26.4	11.5	9.6	5.8	38.7	7.9
Haskell County	6.5	29.1	14.5	26.5	14.3	19.0	2.1	17.4	20.8	13.4	21.3	15.0	7.7	36.8	5.8
Hughes County	2.9	28.7	14.6	26.1	16.1	22.9	3.0	14.7	17.2	11.4	19.1	15.2	5.9	39.2	9.2
Jackson County	1.7	17.8	18.5	28.5	20.2	23.1	1.6	13.3	13.2	4.6	13.7	13.6	5.4	48.9	13.8
Jefferson County	4.1	27.1	16.1	26.6	17.6	19.4	5.0	12.1	19.3	14.5	18.3	12.9	5.5	41.7	7.1
Johnston County	2.6	29.5	14.2	25.7	16.1	21.4	1.7	12.6	22.5	7.3	26.1	15.0	4.4	40.8	6.4
Kay County	3.2	22.5	15.3	29.3	16.8	24.0	0.8	10.8	18.2	3.9	27.6	17.2	4.2	43.2	3.9
Kingfisher County	3.7	18.9	11.2	27.8	12.2	25.7	2.0	14.6	17.8	15.9	15.2	16.3	6.2	42.0	4.4

Table B-3. States and Counties — **Education, Labor Force, and Income**

STATE County	Median household income	Median family income: All families	Median family income: Families with children: Married-couple	Median family income: Families with children: Male householder	Median family income: Families with children: Female householder	Median nonfamily household income	Median income for full-year, full-time workers: Men	Median income for full-year, full-time workers: Women	Per capita income	Households by source of income (percent): With earnings	Households by source of income (percent): With interest, dividend, or rental income	Households by source of income (percent): With Social Security income	Households by source of income (percent): With public assistance income	Households by source of income (percent): With retirement income	Households with income over $100,000 (percent)	+/– U.S. percent for income over $100,000	Households with income below poverty (percent)	Families with children with income below poverty (percent)
	57	58	59	60	61	62	63	64	65	66	67	68	69	70	71	72	73	74
OHIO—Cont'd																		
Ottawa County	44 224	51 919	63 478	31 691	23 902	24 793	40 829	26 071	21 973	78.2	44.0	31.5	1.6	24.4	9.1	-3.2	6.3	6.9
Paulding County	40 327	45 481	51 053	26 736	24 659	21 796	36 672	22 500	18 062	79.5	36.4	28.7	2.5	20.0	5.0	-7.3	7.7	7.8
Perry County	34 383	40 294	44 668	22 984	15 978	16 714	32 396	21 668	15 674	76.5	25.9	28.8	3.4	20.1	3.2	-9.1	12.8	13.6
Pickaway County	42 832	49 259	55 913	32 132	19 309	22 127	37 046	26 852	17 478	80.8	32.4	26.0	2.9	20.4	7.6	-4.7	9.6	11.9
Pike County	31 649	35 934	43 685	25 104	16 875	17 137	35 026	21 040	16 093	72.0	25.1	28.9	7.0	20.8	4.8	-7.5	18.7	21.7
Portage County	44 347	52 820	59 878	32 535	19 596	24 636	38 673	26 836	20 428	84.7	35.7	22.8	2.0	17.9	9.8	-2.5	9.9	9.5
Preble County	42 093	47 547	55 463	31 116	21 420	23 655	36 418	24 584	18 444	80.8	37.6	27.8	1.9	21.9	5.7	-6.6	6.1	6.6
Putnam County	46 426	52 859	61 851	27 578	24 635	21 601	37 221	24 920	18 680	81.2	46.2	27.5	1.5	16.6	7.2	-5.1	5.9	4.9
Richland County	37 397	45 036	53 019	29 005	18 988	20 942	36 088	23 951	18 582	78.0	35.1	28.9	3.0	20.0	6.9	-5.4	10.3	13.7
Ross County	37 117	43 241	50 437	27 279	17 195	19 646	36 452	24 554	17 569	77.2	33.9	27.2	4.2	19.4	5.8	-6.5	12.0	13.4
Sandusky County	40 584	47 675	57 421	28 272	20 205	24 117	36 375	24 843	19 239	79.4	38.2	29.1	1.7	19.1	6.7	-5.6	7.6	8.6
Scioto County	28 008	34 691	42 308	26 054	12 670	14 482	32 937	22 313	15 408	67.9	24.4	34.0	5.5	21.0	4.2	-8.1	19.9	23.2
Seneca County	38 037	44 600	53 427	26 250	20 473	21 026	34 188	23 119	17 027	79.6	37.9	28.7	2.4	19.6	4.1	-8.2	8.9	9.2
Shelby County	44 507	51 331	60 950	29 750	22 900	25 719	36 959	25 339	20 255	82.6	39.2	26.0	1.5	16.9	8.0	-4.3	6.9	7.7
Stark County	39 824	47 747	57 785	29 583	18 287	22 056	38 098	24 911	20 417	78.0	37.4	29.1	3.0	20.7	8.6	-3.7	9.3	11.3
Summit County	42 304	52 200	65 650	31 902	18 004	25 119	40 891	27 589	22 842	79.2	36.6	26.7	3.7	19.3	11.3	-1.0	9.9	12.2
Trumbull County	38 298	46 203	53 838	27 351	17 555	21 312	37 571	25 323	19 188	75.3	37.0	31.8	3.4	24.8	7.3	-5.0	10.4	13.4
Tuscarawas County	35 489	41 677	49 118	24 348	18 091	20 558	32 759	21 165	17 276	77.1	36.0	29.6	2.4	19.7	4.9	-7.4	9.8	10.3
Union County	51 743	58 384	66 289	35 221	24 279	27 243	41 708	28 088	20 577	86.0	38.8	20.6	1.7	17.5	10.8	-1.5	5.8	4.6
Van Wert County	39 497	46 503	53 635	29 010	21 277	22 727	33 058	24 475	18 293	79.3	37.5	29.5	1.9	20.5	4.5	-7.8	6.0	5.5
Vinton County	29 465	34 371	42 394	18 000	12 568	13 095	31 333	21 643	13 731	73.6	22.3	27.5	7.1	17.0	3.0	-9.3	18.9	21.3
Warren County	57 952	64 692	75 596	35 191	28 300	31 437	48 491	31 559	25 517	85.4	43.8	21.0	1.0	17.9	19.3	7.0	4.6	4.4
Washington County	34 275	41 605	48 148	24 053	14 812	19 393	33 570	21 885	18 082	75.9	36.7	29.8	2.5	21.8	5.8	-6.5	11.6	14.6
Wayne County	41 538	48 294	53 639	28 848	19 861	23 031	35 022	24 188	18 330	82.4	40.8	25.7	2.4	16.8	7.3	-5.0	8.0	8.4
Williams County	40 735	47 398	53 848	31 183	23 102	21 943	34 746	22 610	18 441	81.6	36.5	27.7	1.6	16.1	4.7	-7.6	6.5	5.3
Wood County	44 442	56 468	65 859	32 114	22 157	23 556	41 281	27 339	21 284	83.9	40.1	22.2	1.4	15.8	11.1	-1.2	10.1	7.2
Wyandot County	38 839	45 173	51 439	26 450	24 583	22 219	32 336	23 110	17 170	79.1	37.9	30.1	0.9	19.1	3.6	-8.7	6.0	5.2
OKLAHOMA	33 400	40 709	47 652	24 745	16 657	19 331	31 973	23 450	17 646	78.6	30.5	27.2	5.1	16.4	6.6	-5.7	14.6	16.5
Adair County	24 881	29 525	32 799	21 250	13 780	10 619	24 299	20 000	11 185	75.5	16.5	29.5	9.4	12.6	2.0	-10.3	24.3	26.9
Alfalfa County	30 259	35 000	36 914	20 208	11 161	17 210	25 472	18 750	14 704	73.1	38.8	39.9	2.4	18.1	4.2	-8.1	14.1	17.0
Atoka County	24 752	29 409	34 276	18 125	13 667	11 832	26 779	19 622	12 919	69.2	17.7	35.4	10.2	14.3	3.1	-9.2	20.9	21.4
Beaver County	36 715	41 542	47 833	23 750	17 708	20 536	34 267	20 993	17 905	78.3	41.0	32.2	2.5	14.3	5.5	-6.8	10.9	13.8
Beckham County	27 402	34 315	39 645	22 721	13 500	14 850	26 940	19 701	14 488	73.8	29.7	31.8	6.7	12.6	4.5	-7.8	17.8	22.1
Blaine County	28 356	34 565	40 417	16 786	14 091	16 415	27 418	19 358	13 546	74.9	35.9	34.3	5.6	16.6	3.2	-9.1	16.6	19.4
Bryan County	27 888	33 984	40 683	21 019	14 159	13 404	27 374	20 734	14 217	73.0	23.4	33.0	7.5	16.4	3.5	-8.8	20.5	19.4
Caddo County	27 347	32 118	37 143	21 953	13 641	14 382	27 187	19 223	13 298	73.3	27.9	32.4	7.7	15.5	2.9	-9.4	20.1	23.5
Canadian County	45 439	51 180	55 859	31 318	23 050	24 619	36 930	25 378	19 691	85.8	35.2	21.1	2.4	15.7	9.0	-3.3	8.1	8.3
Carter County	29 405	36 729	43 499	21 034	13 491	14 350	30 972	21 492	15 511	74.6	27.6	32.2	7.1	16.4	4.2	-8.1	17.0	19.3
Cherokee County	26 536	32 369	37 732	22 679	13 713	13 427	26 565	21 652	13 436	76.4	22.5	28.3	6.5	15.5	3.2	-9.1	22.2	24.4
Choctaw County	22 743	28 331	37 337	19 265	11 661	11 554	26 508	19 688	12 296	69.2	18.0	35.8	12.2	14.5	1.8	-10.5	25.2	30.5
Cimarron County	30 625	36 250	38 750	25 000	16 667	16 667	25 670	18 598	15 744	76.6	36.0	33.6	2.3	15.5	4.4	-7.9	16.5	19.8
Cleveland County	41 846	51 257	56 813	31 780	21 777	22 212	36 709	26 805	20 114	86.0	35.5	18.4	2.9	15.7	9.3	-3.0	11.5	9.0
Coal County	23 705	28 333	35 458	10 938	14 211	11 881	23 906	18 924	12 013	69.3	20.6	38.2	9.9	17.1	2.5	-9.8	22.9	23.7
Comanche County	33 867	39 214	44 377	25 725	13 364	20 071	30 503	22 904	15 728	81.0	26.3	22.5	5.8	21.1	5.2	-7.1	15.4	18.6
Cotton County	27 210	35 129	44 167	17 917	13 214	14 103	29 661	20 339	14 626	71.2	26.7	34.5	6.2	17.8	3.8	-8.5	19.1	21.8
Craig County	30 997	36 499	43 813	21 016	12 474	17 155	27 619	20 610	16 539	73.7	29.1	35.6	4.6	19.9	3.7	-8.6	14.2	15.3
Creek County	33 168	38 470	44 090	26 922	18 408	16 001	31 747	22 197	16 191	78.8	24.5	28.0	4.6	14.6	4.8	-7.5	13.7	14.6
Custer County	28 524	37 247	44 981	22 500	14 038	16 217	28 653	20 346	15 584	80.7	34.3	26.9	4.9	14.6	4.8	-7.5	19.8	18.8
Delaware County	27 996	33 093	37 830	17 875	13 349	15 810	26 532	20 412	15 424	70.4	27.5	36.6	5.6	19.9	4.6	-7.7	17.1	22.4
Dewey County	28 172	36 114	38 516	26 250	18 750	14 490	28 934	20 343	15 806	72.3	38.9	36.8	4.5	11.9	4.3	-8.0	16.6	15.4
Ellis County	27 951	33 750	39 167	23 750	14 028	17 567	28 977	19 188	16 472	72.8	38.6	40.3	3.7	15.0	4.0	-8.3	12.8	18.3
Garfield County	33 006	39 872	46 118	23 894	15 463	19 249	31 240	21 234	17 457	78.8	36.3	29.3	4.6	16.4	5.1	-7.2	13.1	16.7
Garvin County	28 070	34 774	39 786	27 639	18 517	14 829	29 422	19 607	14 856	72.3	29.0	35.5	7.4	16.8	3.7	-8.6	16.0	15.9
Grady County	32 625	39 636	44 219	20 962	17 027	17 155	31 218	21 758	15 846	77.9	28.3	28.2	6.7	15.7	4.4	-7.9	15.1	15.1
Grant County	28 977	35 833	42 315	19 688	16 731	17 713	30 000	19 762	15 709	75.9	38.2	38.1	3.1	16.4	3.7	-8.6	12.7	15.2
Greer County	25 793	30 702	35 972	17 857	15 804	13 370	25 610	20 229	14 053	67.8	34.2	41.4	5.9	18.1	3.5	-8.8	19.3	25.4
Harmon County	22 365	29 063	31 793	18 750	7 188	10 972	23 244	17 226	13 464	71.6	22.1	37.8	9.1	14.1	3.1	-9.2	26.9	33.3
Harper County	33 705	40 907	44 231	30 781	21 250	18 250	29 917	21 585	18 011	74.1	43.7	38.8	2.4	18.6	5.4	-6.9	9.2	12.7
Haskell County	24 553	29 872	33 539	17 303	15 789	9 913	25 931	18 239	13 775	66.9	25.9	38.6	8.7	17.5	3.8	-8.5	22.0	22.1
Hughes County	22 621	29 153	35 104	19 479	11 307	11 950	23 750	18 592	12 687	67.1	24.7	39.9	7.9	16.9	2.8	-9.5	21.4	23.8
Jackson County	30 737	38 265	42 003	17 417	14 282	17 019	29 539	19 897	15 454	80.1	28.0	25.0	5.4	18.5	4.6	-7.7	15.6	19.8
Jefferson County	23 674	30 563	33 600	20 000	14 766	12 136	25 833	17 037	12 899	70.4	23.2	38.1	9.5	16.4	2.8	-9.5	20.6	23.2
Johnston County	24 592	30 292	35 718	22 232	11 761	12 457	25 630	20 427	13 747	69.4	21.1	35.8	10.5	17.8	3.3	-9.0	21.8	22.4
Kay County	30 762	38 144	45 204	21 615	14 750	18 363	31 079	20 479	16 643	73.1	35.4	33.4	5.0	16.6	5.7	-6.6	14.8	18.8
Kingfisher County	36 676	43 242	45 182	27 500	15 759	20 015	31 557	20 989	18 167	80.6	38.2	29.6	3.8	14.6	7.5	-4.8	10.4	13.5

Table B-3. States and Counties — Education, Labor Force, and Income

STATE/ County code	MSA/PMSA/ NECMA code[1]	STATE County	High school graduates			College graduates		College graduates (percent)				
			Total population 25 years and over	Percent with a high school diploma or less	Percent with a high school diploma or more	Percent with a bachelor's degree or more	+/- U.S. percent with bachelor's degree or more	Non-Hispanic White	Black or African American	American Indian and Alaska Native	Asian, Hawaiian, and Pacific Islander	Hispanic or Latino[2]
			1	2	3	4	5	6	7	8	9	10
		OKLAHOMA—Cont'd										
40 075	...	Kiowa County	6 963	58.9	77.4	14.8	-9.6	16.1	2.0	5.3	X	11.1
40 077	...	Latimer County	6 716	61.1	73.8	12.0	-12.4	11.6	25.0	14.4	25.0	26.7
40 079	...	Le Flore County	30 966	64.7	70.4	11.3	-13.1	11.7	10.4	10.4	29.1	4.1
40 081	...	Lincoln County	20 746	64.5	77.5	11.1	-13.3	11.4	11.4	8.6	11.4	2.4
40 083	5880	Logan County	21 195	53.1	81.5	19.1	-5.3	18.9	23.1	15.2	43.4	17.1
40 085	...	Love County	5 931	67.8	73.6	10.8	-13.6	11.1	1.8	19.7	0.0	3.2
40 087	5880	McClain County	18 069	57.4	79.3	15.7	-8.7	16.1	8.8	18.8	28.6	4.6
40 089	...	McCurtain County	21 875	66.9	69.2	10.8	-13.6	11.7	7.3	9.0	8.0	1.9
40 091	...	McIntosh County	13 787	62.6	71.6	13.1	-11.3	12.5	9.1	16.1	20.0	15.1
40 093	...	Major County	5 191	61.8	78.6	14.4	-10.0	14.9	14.3	6.4	X	0.0
40 095	...	Marshall County	9 078	63.3	71.0	11.4	-13.0	12.1	0.7	10.8	0.0	4.1
40 097	...	Mayes County	24 840	62.0	76.1	12.1	-12.3	12.8	3.0	9.2	50.9	6.5
40 099	...	Murray County	8 566	61.5	74.3	14.9	-9.5	15.1	30.4	12.0	18.2	6.7
40 101	...	Muskogee County	44 890	56.8	75.1	15.4	-9.0	16.5	12.3	12.0	40.4	11.9
40 103	...	Noble County	7 635	58.6	81.5	15.8	-8.6	16.3	3.9	10.9	36.5	0.0
40 105	...	Nowata County	7 092	66.5	76.2	9.5	-14.9	9.9	11.6	10.6	X	12.7
40 107	...	Okfuskee County	7 904	70.2	69.4	9.2	-15.2	9.8	7.9	7.9	0.0	10.4
40 109	5880	Oklahoma County	420 823	43.5	82.5	25.4	1.0	28.8	14.8	14.6	34.4	8.5
40 111	...	Okmulgee County	25 225	60.5	74.7	11.4	-13.0	11.8	9.3	11.1	9.7	13.5
40 113	8560	Osage County	29 417	56.2	80.2	14.6	-9.8	14.1	22.3	11.5	35.9	9.6
40 115	...	Ottawa County	21 510	58.9	75.7	12.2	-12.2	12.5	13.3	11.9	19.7	2.7
40 117	...	Pawnee County	10 997	61.4	78.8	12.1	-12.3	12.5	8.6	10.4	18.2	2.7
40 119	...	Payne County	37 237	40.0	86.7	34.2	9.8	33.8	22.5	23.8	80.6	36.6
40 121	...	Pittsburg County	30 162	60.3	76.2	12.9	-11.5	13.3	7.7	12.4	35.7	7.0
40 123	...	Pontotoc County	22 031	53.5	78.2	21.8	-2.6	22.6	11.9	18.0	77.8	10.3
40 125	5880	Pottawatomie County	41 142	56.4	79.3	15.5	-8.9	16.3	9.2	10.3	24.0	7.6
40 127	...	Pushmataha County	7 861	66.3	69.0	12.4	-12.0	12.1	4.4	11.5	64.7	14.5
40 129	...	Roger Mills County	2 396	59.3	79.3	15.8	-8.6	16.6	X	3.7	0.0	10.3
40 131	0500	Rogers County	45 162	49.4	83.4	16.9	-7.5	17.4	12.0	13.1	30.9	23.2
40 133	...	Seminole County	15 988	61.6	73.2	12.1	-12.3	12.9	10.9	6.9	50.0	4.4
40 135	2720	Sequoyah County	24 980	64.7	70.2	10.9	-13.5	10.3	12.9	13.6	42.9	6.3
40 137	...	Stephens County	29 111	60.3	77.0	16.6	-7.8	16.9	8.9	13.2	65.6	10.1
40 139	...	Texas County	11 776	56.7	71.9	17.7	-6.7	21.9	0.0	17.8	43.9	3.6
40 141	...	Tillman County	6 141	67.0	67.4	12.5	-11.9	15.4	5.0	2.8	27.6	1.3
40 143	8560	Tulsa County	359 386	41.5	85.1	26.9	2.5	29.7	14.3	17.8	38.6	11.8
40 145	8560	Wagoner County	36 895	54.5	81.3	15.4	-9.0	16.0	16.0	11.9	13.6	6.6
40 147	...	Washington County	32 905	46.9	85.2	25.8	1.4	26.0	12.1	10.2	19.4	16.8
40 149	...	Washita County	7 613	59.3	79.7	15.1	-9.3	15.5	0.0	10.3	0.0	8.3
40 151	...	Woods County	5 993	49.2	82.7	23.7	-0.7	24.9	8.0	27.6	84.6	13.9
40 153	...	Woodward County	11 992	58.2	79.9	15.2	-9.2	15.8	7.6	11.6	26.3	5.0
41 000	...	OREGON	2 250 998	41.1	85.1	25.1	0.7	26.0	17.8	12.2	37.2	9.6
41 001	...	Baker County	11 712	51.0	80.3	16.4	-8.0	16.8	0.0	0.0	2.7	7.7
41 003	1890	Benton County	45 758	22.2	93.1	47.4	23.0	47.6	49.0	30.7	67.2	28.0
41 005	6440	Clackamas County	223 211	35.2	88.9	20.4	4.0	28.5	27.4	20.5	44.2	14.5
41 007	...	Clatsop County	24 069	43.5	85.6	19.1	-5.3	19.6	16.3	9.1	22.7	7.0
41 009	6440	Columbia County	28 725	49.6	85.6	14.0	-10.4	14.1	20.0	9.3	32.1	11.1
41 011	...	Coos County	44 667	49.2	81.6	15.0	-9.4	15.3	23.5	8.5	26.9	10.9
41 013	...	Crook County	12 692	58.4	80.5	12.6	-11.8	13.1	X	12.1	14.7	1.6
41 015	...	Curry County	16 168	50.4	81.7	16.4	-8.0	17.1	28.0	6.4	2.4	7.4
41 017	...	Deschutes County	77 981	38.8	88.4	25.0	0.6	25.6	0.0	13.2	31.3	8.2
41 019	...	Douglas County	68 783	53.7	81.0	13.3	-11.1	13.3	8.9	9.9	22.6	13.8
41 021	...	Gilliam County	1 368	45.8	89.3	13.4	-11.0	13.5	0.0	20.0	0.0	0.0
41 023	...	Grant County	5 428	52.8	84.5	15.7	-8.7	16.0	X	9.1	85.7	4.5
41 025	...	Harney County	5 130	57.1	81.2	11.9	-12.5	11.9	X	15.1	19.3	9.7
41 027	...	Hood River County	12 972	48.5	78.2	23.1	-1.3	26.7	20.7	1.0	34.6	5.2
41 029	4890	Jackson County	121 155	45.1	85.0	22.3	-2.1	23.0	16.1	14.2	26.0	10.4
41 031	...	Jefferson County	11 972	55.2	76.5	13.7	-10.7	17.1	30.0	4.4	14.4	1.6
41 033	...	Josephine County	53 427	49.3	81.8	14.1	-10.3	14.5	32.1	6.5	18.9	4.6
41 035	...	Klamath County	41 833	52.6	81.5	15.0	-8.5	16.8	15.5	10.2	24.5	5.3
41 037	...	Lake County	5 199	53.7	79.6	15.5	-8.9	16.0	X	10.0	16.7	7.8
41 039	2400	Lane County	210 601	38.3	87.5	25.5	1.1	25.7	29.2	15.6	47.0	15.8
41 041	...	Lincoln County	32 000	44.1	84.9	20.8	-3.6	21.3	3.5	11.2	40.3	6.0
41 043	...	Linn County	67 605	51.1	81.9	13.4	-11.0	13.8	9.0	3.4	16.2	5.4
41 045	...	Malheur County	19 587	59.5	71.0	11.1	-13.3	13.2	3.0	3.9	22.2	1.7
41 047	7080	Marion County	177 683	47.0	79.3	19.8	-4.6	22.1	10.9	10.2	24.8	5.0

[1]MSA = Metropolitan Statistical Area. PMSA = Primary MSA. NECMA = New England County Metropolitan Area. See the Appendix A for explanation of these concepts. See Appendix B for list of metropolitan areas identified by type, with component counties.
[2]Hispanic or Latino persons may be of any race.

Table B-3. States and Counties — Education, Labor Force, and Income

STATE County	School enrollment			Population 16 to 19 years				Employment status, 2000			Work status in 1999 of the population 16 years and over (percent)		
											Worked in 1999		
	Grades kindergarten through 12	College or graduate school	Percent private	Number	Percent in armed forces	Percent high school graduates	Percent not enrolled, not grads, not in armed forces, not employed	Total population 16 years and over	Percent in labor force	Unemployment rate	Full-time	Part-time	Did not work in 1999
	11	12	13	14	15	16	17	18	19	20	21	22	23
OKLAHOMA—Cont'd													
Kiowa County	1 934	314	1.9	623	0.0	13.6	7.2	8 102	54.9	5.9	48.3	12.2	39.5
Latimer County	2 020	754	3.0	810	0.0	3.7	7.8	8 291	51.8	7.8	44.5	11.0	44.4
Le Flore County	9 487	1 658	3.2	3 001	0.0	13.9	6.4	37 061	55.4	6.3	50.5	10.9	38.6
Lincoln County	6 765	883	6.7	1 954	0.0	11.7	4.1	24 422	60.2	4.9	52.3	12.5	35.3
Logan County	6 700	2 817	8.7	2 637	0.0	8.6	4.1	26 515	64.0	5.6	54.2	16.3	29.4
Love County	1 740	248	4.0	521	0.0	5.2	6.1	6 884	59.9	5.2	53.2	11.2	35.6
McClain County	5 761	1 154	6.8	1 782	0.0	13.0	3.3	21 271	63.6	3.7	56.8	12.4	30.9
McCurtain County	7 167	908	2.3	2 022	0.0	12.6	8.5	25 836	55.3	7.4	48.2	11.6	40.3
McIntosh County	3 409	557	5.3	1 016	0.0	11.6	10.1	15 604	50.0	6.6	42.7	10.9	46.4
Major County	1 470	136	8.5	421	0.0	2.4	5.2	5 935	63.1	3.3	53.4	13.5	33.1
Marshall County	2 290	332	2.9	729	0.0	10.3	8.2	10 482	52.7	4.2	46.3	11.0	42.8
Mayes County	7 797	1 062	4.4	2 327	0.0	10.4	6.1	29 411	59.4	5.4	52.0	11.9	36.1
Murray County	2 273	325	2.7	765	0.0	14.2	0.4	10 041	59.0	5.7	50.5	13.2	36.3
Muskogee County	13 298	2 819	4.5	4 261	0.0	10.9	6.7	53 730	54.8	7.3	49.2	11.5	39.3
Noble County	2 256	371	2.3	622	0.0	9.0	2.1	8 864	62.7	3.7	56.7	11.2	32.1
Nowata County	2 114	270	2.4	576	0.0	10.2	3.8	8 132	57.9	3.9	50.1	12.7	37.2
Okfuskee County	2 224	288	4.5	703	0.0	13.1	10.8	9 264	51.1	12.5	44.4	10.4	45.2
Oklahoma County	122 501	43 237	13.8	38 506	0.7	11.9	6.7	510 717	64.2	5.1	56.8	13.6	29.6
Okmulgee County	8 238	1 790	4.1	2 682	0.1	9.3	8.7	30 353	56.1	7.8	48.0	12.3	39.7
Osage County	9 312	1 282	6.9	2 643	0.1	11.3	3.7	34 270	59.6	5.6	54.5	12.1	33.4
Ottawa County	6 198	1 586	3.2	2 180	0.0	8.5	6.8	25 692	58.8	6.0	49.6	13.3	37.1
Pawnee County	3 437	460	3.6	986	0.0	13.4	4.9	12 750	60.1	5.1	52.8	11.9	35.4
Payne County	9 937	17 412	2.4	6 044	0.5	6.9	1.9	56 615	64.1	4.8	49.4	24.5	26.1
Pittsburg County	8 296	1 301	3.9	2 398	0.0	11.0	5.6	34 922	51.4	7.2	47.4	11.1	41.5
Pontotoc County	6 720	2 957	4.0	2 380	0.0	9.6	4.3	27 562	61.1	6.8	52.3	14.5	33.2
Pottawatomie County	12 422	4 315	14.0	4 293	0.0	13.3	6.7	50 594	59.4	5.6	51.0	14.5	34.5
Pushmataha County	2 361	277	1.9	665	0.0	12.5	6.9	9 014	50.7	6.7	43.1	11.0	45.9
Roger Mills County	641	59	3.1	218	0.0	5.5	0.9	2 752	60.9	2.4	51.5	15.6	33.0
Rogers County	15 430	2 378	7.6	4 198	0.0	12.5	4.4	52 662	65.7	3.7	58.6	12.4	28.9
Seminole County	5 073	1 022	4.5	1 728	0.0	6.9	9.0	19 243	54.6	8.6	47.9	11.3	40.7
Sequoyah County	7 874	1 007	3.2	2 354	0.0	15.2	8.4	29 501	57.6	6.1	49.7	11.4	38.8
Stephens County	8 339	1 230	4.5	2 537	0.0	8.2	3.1	33 969	56.1	6.5	47.7	12.6	39.7
Texas County	4 143	1 065	4.9	1 478	0.0	7.2	7.8	15 019	67.2	4.9	59.9	14.1	26.0
Tillman County	2 032	160	3.1	542	0.9	8.1	2.0	7 114	51.6	4.3	46.2	10.5	43.4
Tulsa County	107 559	34 049	18.2	31 914	0.0	10.4	6.3	432 088	67.1	4.8	58.5	14.0	27.5
Wagoner County	12 342	1 948	8.5	3 573	0.0	9.7	5.1	43 308	65.7	3.7	57.1	14.2	28.7
Washington County	9 627	1 783	10.6	2 723	0.1	11.6	4.9	38 255	58.7	4.9	50.4	13.0	36.6
Washita County	2 476	378	5.2	729	0.0	6.4	1.5	8 921	59.1	4.0	51.4	14.1	34.5
Woods County	1 454	995	1.1	623	0.0	3.4	1.8	7 598	58.5	4.1	50.1	17.9	32.1
Woodward County	3 724	397	2.4	1 153	0.0	12.1	7.6	14 333	62.8	6.1	55.4	14.2	30.3
OREGON	621 408	204 811	11.7	191 546	0.1	12.3	5.4	2 673 782	65.2	6.5	53.7	17.2	29.1
Baker County	3 141	284	5.8	875	0.0	12.1	7.7	13 197	55.6	8.3	46.0	16.4	37.6
Benton County	12 857	16 823	5.5	6 792	0.1	5.5	0.7	63 608	63.6	4.9	51.0	24.6	24.4
Clackamas County	66 117	15 812	12.6	18 703	0.0	11.9	4.4	260 423	68.6	5.0	56.8	17.2	26.0
Clatsop County	6 425	1 633	8.8	2 291	1.0	12.7	8.7	28 474	63.6	6.4	49.3	19.4	31.3
Columbia County	8 920	1 210	6.5	2 267	1.0	15.1	4.1	33 035	64.8	6.3	53.4	15.4	31.1
Coos County	10 859	2 558	4.3	3 549	0.7	13.2	5.8	51 025	54.3	8.4	43.3	15.5	41.2
Crook County	3 743	485	6.3	1 073	0.0	14.7	10.1	14 753	59.4	7.7	51.1	14.1	34.8
Curry County	3 197	463	5.2	884	0.0	10.9	4.6	17 625	49.3	7.3	38.2	16.4	45.4
Deschutes County	21 359	4 761	9.1	5 855	0.0	14.4	2.8	90 114	65.3	5.2	53.1	18.2	28.7
Douglas County	18 784	3 038	8.6	5 456	0.2	12.0	5.6	79 431	56.9	7.6	45.8	15.4	38.8
Gilliam County	381	37	3.6	94	0.0	5.3	2.1	1 532	65.9	6.8	52.0	17.2	30.9
Grant County	1 612	145	10.1	466	0.0	9.7	3.0	6 178	61.4	11.9	50.6	16.4	32.9
Harney County	1 535	72	4.9	453	0.0	14.3	8.6	5 903	63.8	9.4	56.3	12.3	31.4
Hood River County	4 269	562	10.1	1 147	0.0	12.3	6.8	15 339	66.5	6.6	55.2	17.9	26.9
Jackson County	32 724	9 304	8.7	10 013	0.1	12.6	5.8	142 297	61.3	7.3	48.3	18.5	33.2
Jefferson County	4 137	388	3.7	921	0.0	11.2	9.6	13 967	63.9	8.6	55.8	15.2	29.0
Josephine County	13 426	2 498	11.2	3 650	0.0	14.5	7.6	60 251	52.1	9.8	40.8	14.7	44.5
Klamath County	12 484	2 970	7.6	3 556	0.0	13.4	4.3	49 102	59.7	10.0	48.3	16.5	35.3
Lake County	1 497	101	4.7	365	0.0	11.5	2.5	5 829	57.8	8.5	48.2	15.2	36.5
Lane County	54 942	30 647	7.1	19 632	0.0	12.9	3.6	258 327	64.3	6.4	50.1	20.5	29.4
Lincoln County	7 409	1 053	5.8	2 274	1.0	18.1	7.7	36 161	58.3	8.3	46.1	17.4	36.4
Linn County	19 774	4 574	11.7	6 161	0.0	12.1	6.9	79 582	63.0	7.8	51.1	16.2	32.6
Malheur County	6 489	1 349	8.4	1 807	0.0	11.8	5.9	23 863	53.3	11.1	51.5	13.8	34.6
Marion County	55 606	14 424	12.9	17 704	0.0	13.9	8.5	215 834	63.7	7.7	54.6	15.7	29.7

Table B-3. States and Counties — Education, Labor Force, and Income

STATE County	Full-year full-time employed (percent)								Children under 18 years in families					+/− U.S. percent two-income couples	Total employed by class of worker (percent)			
										With two parents (percent)		With one parent who is in labor force (percent)	+/− U.S. percent of children with no stay-at-home parent (percent)					
	Total	Men	Women	Non-Hispanic White	Black or African American	American Indian and Alaska Native	Asian, Hawaiian, and Pacific Islander	Hispanic or Latino[1]	Number	Both in labor force	Father only in labor force				Private	Government	Self-employed	Unpaid family worker
	24	25	26	27	28	29	30	31	32	33	34	35	36	37	38	39	40	41
OKLAHOMA—Cont'd																		
Kiowa County	34.1	43.5	25.3	34.6	31.7	30.3	X	31.4	2 264	46.2	17.1	22.1	3.7	−4.2	56.9	25.1	17.1	1.0
Latimer County	27.9	34.7	21.3	27.6	15.0	28.3	13.6	19.3	2 458	33.6	25.8	23.8	−7.2	−11.5	54.0	30.3	14.7	1.0
Le Flore County	34.5	42.6	26.5	34.0	25.1	37.6	33.0	47.9	11 554	43.4	22.9	18.5	−2.7	−8.0	70.2	17.6	11.6	0.6
Lincoln County	38.8	49.1	29.0	38.9	35.0	35.8	37.1	34.4	8 201	45.8	24.4	18.8	0.0	−5.0	67.9	18.5	12.7	0.9
Logan County	39.1	48.3	30.6	42.4	18.3	43.8	34.9	29.4	8 116	47.2	26.3	18.1	0.7	1.5	66.7	18.8	13.6	0.9
Love County	40.0	50.7	29.7	39.5	38.5	48.1	31.0	41.1	2 119	43.1	22.5	20.7	−0.8	−2.5	71.9	14.6	12.8	0.6
McClain County	43.6	53.3	34.1	44.3	44.1	42.8	44.2	31.8	6 991	48.3	25.2	17.2	0.9	0.4	65.7	18.9	14.8	0.6
McCurtain County	33.8	44.3	24.5	34.8	25.1	33.9	33.3	30.6	8 844	35.3	22.9	24.7	−4.6	−9.8	67.1	18.0	14.1	0.8
McIntosh County	30.1	36.1	24.7	30.1	21.1	31.8	50.0	44.2	3 982	41.7	22.8	20.5	−2.4	−15.1	62.0	19.0	18.2	0.8
Major County	41.3	54.8	29.1	41.2	100.0	58.7	X	37.6	1 782	51.6	28.6	13.9	0.9	0.9	64.0	13.8	20.3	2.0
Marshall County	32.4	40.3	24.8	32.2	8.4	35.3	30.8	39.1	2 856	42.6	22.1	23.7	1.7	−11.3	72.8	12.6	13.9	0.8
Mayes County	37.7	48.6	27.3	37.5	10.3	39.2	54.4	39.5	9 544	45.0	25.0	17.5	1.6	6.2	72.0	14.8	12.3	0.9
Murray County	35.2	44.8	26.4	34.4	20.6	40.2	9.1	39.4	2 854	49.3	22.8	17.0	1.7	−5.2	62.0	21.6	15.9	0.5
Muskogee County	34.1	42.4	26.6	35.0	27.1	35.4	31.8	41.3	16 245	37.1	22.7	23.7	−3.8	−8.9	71.2	18.2	10.1	0.4
Noble County	42.3	52.9	32.0	43.1	42.9	33.9	40.4	39.7	2 758	47.7	24.1	21.4	4.5	2.2	71.5	16.6	11.2	0.7
Nowata County	36.6	44.9	28.5	36.8	19.1	40.8	X	18.2	2 584	44.2	24.4	20.0	−0.4	−4.5	75.9	10.7	12.4	1.0
Okfuskee County	30.4	36.2	24.3	31.8	18.2	34.3	0.0	22.2	2 657	35.3	27.0	22.3	−7.0	−10.6	62.7	22.0	14.1	1.3
Oklahoma County	41.9	51.2	33.4	43.5	37.5	40.0	39.3	37.5	157 239	37.8	20.8	27.3	0.5	−0.2	73.2	16.3	10.2	0.3
Okmulgee County	34.0	42.9	25.9	34.9	24.3	37.7	51.5	32.2	9 778	38.7	23.3	21.2	−4.7	−8.5	70.1	18.3	10.9	0.7
Osage County	39.7	48.7	30.6	40.0	38.8	37.6	35.0	39.4	10 866	47.6	21.1	18.8	1.8	−3.4	71.2	16.5	11.7	0.6
Ottawa County	34.6	42.9	27.2	34.3	9.7	36.1	15.7	38.8	7 918	44.0	20.8	22.8	2.2	−4.1	72.2	16.2	10.8	0.8
Pawnee County	38.4	48.7	28.6	38.9	28.6	34.3	20.0	35.5	4 186	44.5	28.1	16.4	−3.7	−3.5	68.4	16.9	13.7	0.9
Payne County	32.4	39.3	25.4	33.8	25.8	31.4	16.1	26.2	12 697	47.6	23.1	21.0	4.0	3.5	58.4	31.9	9.1	0.6
Pittsburg County	33.5	40.3	26.8	34.0	24.6	35.9	40.0	28.8	9 327	42.9	20.4	22.9	1.2	−8.5	61.6	25.6	12.2	0.6
Pontotoc County	37.0	43.8	30.7	37.5	29.8	36.2	27.9	34.1	8 149	44.1	19.3	22.7	2.2	−2.0	66.8	19.8	12.7	0.7
Pottawatomie County	36.3	46.0	27.6	37.3	25.0	31.9	29.4	38.5	15 696	43.1	21.8	22.1	0.6	−3.7	67.8	21.5	10.3	0.4
Pushmataha County	29.7	36.8	23.2	30.2	17.2	27.7	26.3	38.7	2 798	40.5	21.3	19.0	−5.1	−11.8	58.4	24.4	16.4	0.8
Roger Mills County	37.1	48.8	25.7	38.1	X	19.1	0.0	32.6	772	56.0	19.6	15.0	6.4	2.1	53.1	21.1	23.5	2.3
Rogers County	45.7	57.5	34.6	46.5	39.3	43.5	46.1	45.8	19 331	49.8	27.4	16.5	1.7	2.6	74.7	14.0	11.0	0.4
Seminole County	32.4	40.6	25.3	33.2	28.3	29.5	30.6	24.6	5 956	37.5	18.8	24.3	−2.8	−9.4	65.5	22.2	11.6	0.8
Sequoyah County	35.9	45.8	26.6	35.7	37.2	35.9	39.7	37.9	9 886	43.1	22.5	19.3	−2.2	−8.5	71.0	16.7	11.9	0.5
Stephens County	33.8	45.1	23.6	33.7	25.4	32.5	87.0	39.5	10 047	44.9	23.7	19.3	−0.4	−8.1	71.2	14.8	13.5	0.5
Texas County	44.0	55.9	31.5	45.7	25.2	45.8	34.9	40.9	5 549	45.8	25.2	15.2	−3.6	3.3	70.6	14.5	14.3	0.6
Tillman County	33.8	43.3	25.1	36.3	14.3	33.3	9.0	33.6	2 241	42.5	24.8	15.1	−7.0	−7.6	60.5	21.2	17.3	1.0
Tulsa County	43.9	55.0	33.6	45.2	36.9	42.5	38.5	41.9	139 413	41.6	24.1	23.5	0.5	1.5	80.3	9.4	10.0	0.3
Wagoner County	44.5	57.1	32.6	45.5	40.5	38.1	49.2	48.4	15 324	45.0	25.9	18.1	−1.5	0.5	76.9	11.9	10.9	0.3
Washington County	37.7	46.9	29.5	37.5	33.8	42.5	30.2	42.8	11 632	47.0	25.5	19.1	1.5	−7.8	78.8	9.6	11.1	0.5
Washita County	35.4	46.2	25.6	35.6	12.5	28.8	30.0	37.1	2 871	48.6	24.1	14.8	−1.2	−2.0	59.4	20.6	18.9	1.0
Woods County	34.4	42.1	26.5	34.9	13.0	23.1	100.0	40.0	1 608	56.6	20.3	20.7	11.7	3.7	55.0	24.9	19.2	0.9
Woodward County	41.8	51.5	32.1	42.7	20.1	31.9	16.7	34.2	4 558	47.8	22.1	19.1	2.3	2.2	67.4	15.1	16.8	0.7
OREGON	37.3	46.7	28.2	37.6	34.0	34.5	38.5	34.5	796 563	45.7	23.8	20.7	1.8	−0.1	72.5	14.4	12.7	0.4
Baker County	29.8	37.9	22.1	30.1	0.0	31.8	26.6	35.6	3 871	49.0	21.7	18.5	2.9	−8.7	56.9	19.5	22.5	1.1
Benton County	31.9	41.7	22.4	32.9	29.5	24.6	21.7	27.2	16 053	50.6	25.5	15.7	1.7	2.3	64.1	25.4	10.4	0.2
Clackamas County	42.2	54.1	30.9	42.3	46.7	41.0	43.0	40.5	84 615	47.1	28.1	17.4	−0.1	3.3	73.4	12.4	13.8	0.4
Clatsop County	33.5	42.2	25.1	34.3	23.4	39.4	21.3	23.3	7 851	47.6	19.6	25.0	8.0	1.2	68.8	15.4	15.3	0.4
Columbia County	39.5	51.2	28.0	39.5	33.3	45.0	37.4	44.7	11 240	48.4	25.1	18.9	2.7	−0.4	75.3	13.3	11.0	0.4
Coos County	29.4	36.3	23.0	29.6	22.9	26.4	27.7	27.6	12 813	42.5	15.8	24.8	2.7	−10.4	66.7	17.3	15.4	0.7
Crook County	34.5	45.1	24.2	35.0	X	34.2	35.9	22.4	4 630	50.1	22.4	19.7	5.2	−5.7	67.3	16.8	15.1	0.8
Curry County	24.8	30.0	19.8	24.7	12.0	23.6	42.6	24.6	3 739	47.5	21.4	21.1	4.0	−13.7	59.6	19.2	20.3	0.9
Deschutes County	36.1	46.1	26.5	36.3	30.9	29.9	37.7	36.2	27 255	49.0	22.3	19.9	4.3	−1.0	69.5	12.4	17.7	0.4
Douglas County	31.5	40.4	23.1	31.4	19.1	26.6	25.1	37.2	22 545	44.8	21.6	22.0	2.2	−7.9	69.6	17.0	12.8	0.6
Gilliam County	37.8	48.6	27.0	37.5	0.0	47.1	33.3	50.0	420	57.6	20.2	17.1	10.1	7.7	59.9	21.3	18.3	0.5
Grant County	31.1	38.3	24.1	31.6	X	12.3	0.0	15.4	1 951	49.2	21.7	21.9	6.5	−6.8	52.3	27.6	19.2	0.8
Harney County	36.8	46.5	27.1	37.7	0.0	18.1	31.7	42.5	1 877	50.9	15.5	21.7	8.0	−3.4	55.9	26.4	17.1	0.6
Hood River County	31.6	41.1	21.9	33.3	33.3	15.3	24.7	24.9	5 218	53.2	22.3	16.0	4.6	0.2	68.2	15.2	16.2	0.4
Jackson County	32.4	42.0	23.7	32.7	32.8	34.8	31.2	29.1	41 548	44.0	23.3	23.0	2.4	−5.3	69.5	13.7	16.3	0.5
Jefferson County	34.4	43.1	25.5	34.7	66.7	29.4	32.4	38.3	5 090	43.0	21.6	23.4	1.8	−2.4	63.2	22.3	13.8	0.7
Josephine County	27.7	36.0	20.1	27.8	22.9	25.6	26.1	28.3	16 293	37.4	28.3	22.4	−4.8	−15.6	66.5	14.6	18.1	0.8
Klamath County	31.0	38.8	23.5	32.0	28.0	27.0	36.8	19.8	15 335	44.3	20.4	22.9	2.0	−7.0	67.4	18.2	13.5	0.8
Lake County	30.1	39.6	21.1	29.9	X	34.5	31.3	35.4	1 730	49.0	19.7	24.1	8.5	−6.5	50.2	28.1	20.2	1.5
Lane County	34.3	43.6	25.5	34.7	30.7	33.7	26.5	33.7	69 351	45.5	21.2	23.1	4.0	0.2	70.2	16.1	13.3	0.5
Lincoln County	30.0	36.4	24.3	29.7	42.0	43.4	33.4	25.9	8 714	41.8	17.0	28.1	5.3	−8.4	63.6	17.0	18.7	0.7
Linn County	35.7	46.8	25.1	36.0	34.6	29.3	35.0	30.6	25 207	45.6	25.1	18.9	−0.1	−2.5	73.9	13.9	11.6	0.7
Malheur County	29.0	34.7	22.0	29.8	22.8	21.8	21.4	27.9	8 196	43.5	26.4	18.8	−2.3	−6.9	62.0	20.4	16.8	0.7
Marion County	36.5	44.4	28.7	37.5	28.6	38.2	35.2	31.4	72 870	44.2	21.6	22.4	2.0	−0.6	69.0	19.6	10.9	0.4

[1] Hispanic or Latino persons may be of any race.

STATE County	Percent who worked at home	Percent of the population 5 years and over with a disability	Veterans as a percent of the population 18 years and over	Occupation for employed population 16 years and over (percent)						Industry for employed population 16 years and over (percent)					
				Management, professional, and related occupations	Service occupa-tions	Sales and office occupa-tions	Farming, fishing, and forestry occupa-tions	Con-struction, extraction, and main-tenance occupa-tions	Production, transporta-tion and material moving occupa-tions	Agricul-ture, forestry, fishing, and mining	Construc-tion and manufac-turing	Whole-sale and retail trade	Transporta-tion and ware-housing, and utilities	Service industries	Public adminis-tration
	42	43	44	45	46	47	48	49	50	51	52	53	54	55	56
OKLAHOMA—Cont'd															
Kiowa County	3.0	24.1	15.8	30.3	20.0	19.6	3.4	10.1	16.6	12.2	17.4	12.7	4.7	42.7	10.4
Latimer County	4.1	27.5	14.7	26.9	17.9	19.2	2.3	16.1	17.6	11.8	19.1	11.0	5.6	46.9	5.7
Le Flore County	3.1	25.3	14.3	24.3	15.0	19.9	2.2	11.4	27.2	7.1	29.9	13.8	5.9	39.0	4.3
Lincoln County	3.8	23.7	15.9	22.9	14.9	25.0	1.0	15.5	20.6	4.7	23.5	14.8	7.0	41.6	8.5
Logan County	4.6	21.3	14.8	29.7	17.8	25.3	1.0	13.7	12.6	4.3	17.6	15.0	4.6	52.7	5.8
Love County	2.3	23.4	13.7	23.7	16.2	20.6	1.6	10.7	27.2	7.3	31.6	12.6	6.6	38.2	3.7
McClain County	4.4	20.4	13.9	27.4	14.0	26.3	1.4	15.8	15.2	6.3	20.8	17.2	6.2	42.0	7.5
McCurtain County	3.4	26.6	13.1	21.9	16.1	21.3	5.2	12.4	23.1	9.3	29.2	15.5	4.4	36.9	4.6
McIntosh County	5.6	30.6	19.3	27.9	16.9	22.9	1.5	13.3	17.6	4.9	20.5	16.2	6.7	46.3	5.4
Major County	6.6	19.6	12.5	29.0	13.8	21.3	4.3	15.3	16.4	22.6	15.7	13.9	6.3	36.8	4.8
Marshall County	3.5	27.8	16.7	22.2	17.0	21.5	2.1	11.5	25.7	3.9	28.8	18.4	4.3	40.3	4.3
Mayes County	3.5	23.4	15.0	22.8	14.3	22.5	1.7	14.4	24.4	3.9	33.6	14.4	7.2	37.6	3.4
Murray County	3.7	25.7	16.2	26.5	18.6	21.0	1.2	13.4	19.3	8.2	18.8	15.8	5.0	46.5	5.6
Muskogee County	2.7	27.1	15.3	26.4	17.8	23.6	1.2	11.4	19.5	2.3	24.6	15.5	6.1	45.6	5.9
Noble County	2.7	21.3	12.8	26.0	17.9	22.1	1.2	11.5	21.3	5.3	33.8	11.7	5.3	38.9	4.9
Nowata County	6.2	26.2	15.3	23.1	15.6	22.4	2.3	14.3	22.4	8.3	27.6	17.0	5.5	39.3	2.4
Okfuskee County	4.9	25.2	14.3	25.8	19.5	17.3	2.5	12.0	22.9	8.3	25.5	10.6	4.4	42.4	8.9
Oklahoma County	2.8	21.5	14.6	32.2	15.3	29.4	0.2	10.1	12.7	1.4	16.5	15.8	4.0	54.3	7.9
Okmulgee County	4.0	24.5	15.3	22.9	19.6	24.3	0.8	13.6	18.7	4.0	23.2	14.0	6.1	47.6	5.1
Osage County	3.0	22.5	15.8	28.4	14.9	25.0	0.8	13.9	17.0	6.0	21.0	13.8	7.9	45.3	6.1
Ottawa County	3.3	26.4	16.5	25.8	21.1	20.2	2.0	10.0	20.9	4.9	24.0	13.0	5.0	48.8	4.3
Pawnee County	3.2	23.0	15.7	25.7	14.6	24.5	0.9	13.9	20.4	5.8	24.4	14.2	7.3	42.5	5.8
Payne County	3.3	16.1	10.4	37.5	16.2	25.6	0.7	7.8	12.2	2.8	14.2	13.5	3.1	62.4	4.0
Pittsburg County	2.8	28.0	17.3	27.9	20.6	23.3	1.1	11.7	15.4	4.3	18.3	15.0	5.0	46.8	10.7
Pontotoc County	2.2	23.0	12.9	29.1	16.8	24.9	0.8	11.7	16.6	4.1	20.6	14.4	3.7	51.7	5.5
Pottawatomie County	2.1	23.1	15.5	27.8	15.8	25.6	0.4	12.9	17.5	2.4	21.2	14.8	4.6	47.3	9.8
Pushmataha County	4.2	30.9	16.8	26.4	19.5	21.0	3.3	11.9	17.9	8.9	17.6	13.6	6.0	47.3	6.5
Roger Mills County	8.4	22.5	13.4	34.6	16.5	19.6	5.6	13.6	10.1	27.4	9.7	10.9	6.3	39.3	6.4
Rogers County	3.3	18.6	17.2	29.7	12.2	26.5	0.3	14.2	17.0	2.5	23.7	14.5	10.9	44.2	4.2
Seminole County	3.4	27.9	14.9	25.4	16.6	22.4	1.8	12.3	21.4	7.8	23.0	13.4	4.8	42.9	8.2
Sequoyah County	2.5	26.7	15.5	22.1	14.3	23.7	0.7	13.7	22.4	2.6	27.3	15.5	5.2	44.8	4.6
Stephens County	2.3	23.8	16.0	29.2	15.1	24.4	0.8	13.4	17.1	11.7	21.0	15.1	4.2	43.3	4.6
Texas County	2.9	16.7	10.2	27.4	13.9	20.9	6.2	11.9	19.7	17.0	23.1	14.5	5.3	36.5	3.6
Tillman County	2.7	26.5	13.1	27.4	16.0	19.1	4.0	13.8	19.7	11.8	22.3	12.5	6.6	39.9	7.0
Tulsa County	3.2	19.4	13.6	34.3	13.8	29.8	0.1	9.9	12.2	1.4	17.7	16.1	6.9	55.0	2.8
Wagoner County	3.0	20.9	16.1	26.2	14.0	28.6	0.4	14.2	16.5	1.8	24.6	16.6	8.0	45.5	3.5
Washington County	2.8	22.4	15.9	33.9	15.3	26.1	0.3	10.3	14.1	4.5	24.2	17.4	3.2	47.6	3.0
Washita County	4.7	20.6	14.1	30.2	16.3	20.4	3.0	13.3	16.8	17.8	14.7	12.7	5.2	43.1	6.4
Woods County	3.5	18.4	11.4	30.9	20.6	23.7	3.6	10.6	10.5	13.5	8.9	15.3	5.7	49.8	6.8
Woodward County	3.9	19.1	13.5	26.6	15.1	26.8	1.7	13.6	16.3	13.4	13.0	16.9	7.8	43.7	5.2
OREGON	5.0	18.8	15.1	33.1	15.3	26.1	1.7	9.1	14.7	3.2	21.3	16.5	4.7	49.9	4.4
Baker County	10.6	24.1	18.3	30.5	18.3	22.4	3.4	9.3	16.1	14.4	16.6	12.6	6.5	43.7	6.4
Benton County	4.4	12.9	11.5	46.9	14.8	20.7	1.7	6.3	9.7	3.7	21.1	11.1	2.0	58.6	3.4
Clackamas County	5.4	16.0	15.0	34.8	12.6	28.9	0.7	9.9	13.1	1.6	21.7	18.9	5.4	48.5	3.9
Clatsop County	5.0	20.7	18.1	26.6	21.4	24.8	3.0	10.9	13.3	4.6	17.4	17.7	4.1	51.2	5.1
Columbia County	4.6	19.4	19.4	26.4	13.4	23.0	1.4	13.8	22.0	3.6	30.6	13.9	9.5	38.5	3.8
Coos County	5.2	26.4	19.8	28.5	19.6	23.9	3.4	10.5	14.1	6.3	14.9	15.6	5.6	51.7	5.9
Crook County	5.3	23.0	17.1	24.5	15.6	21.0	3.7	11.7	23.4	10.3	29.9	15.2	4.0	37.0	3.6
Curry County	7.4	28.0	23.0	26.9	20.1	24.8	3.5	10.6	14.0	6.8	14.8	16.5	4.2	50.6	7.1
Deschutes County	6.5	17.2	16.7	31.3	15.0	26.8	1.0	13.2	12.8	2.5	22.5	17.7	3.7	50.2	3.4
Douglas County	4.8	23.0	20.2	25.5	18.2	23.2	2.8	9.8	20.5	5.4	23.9	15.6	4.8	45.6	4.7
Gilliam County	6.6	19.8	17.7	27.8	14.3	22.7	5.1	12.5	17.4	18.1	8.6	10.3	8.4	45.8	8.8
Grant County	8.2	18.0	15.8	32.5	16.9	20.7	5.1	9.3	15.5	17.3	16.5	11.2	5.1	43.1	6.9
Harney County	8.7	20.9	19.1	32.6	16.3	18.9	7.3	8.7	16.3	19.4	19.8	11.2	2.7	36.5	10.3
Hood River County	7.5	16.8	12.6	32.5	17.0	20.2	8.7	9.5	12.2	14.0	16.1	17.8	3.5	44.7	3.8
Jackson County	5.6	20.2	18.3	30.6	17.4	26.6	1.5	9.5	14.4	2.8	18.2	18.9	4.3	52.1	3.7
Jefferson County	5.7	20.0	16.1	25.0	16.9	21.1	5.1	8.3	23.6	10.3	25.6	11.4	3.0	42.2	7.5
Josephine County	6.8	23.5	20.5	26.5	18.2	26.4	1.5	12.1	15.2	3.7	20.4	17.5	4.5	49.3	4.5
Klamath County	5.0	22.4	18.8	28.3	18.0	24.4	2.6	10.4	16.3	6.1	19.1	16.1	5.6	48.6	4.6
Lake County	6.1	21.7	19.8	30.2	20.2	18.8	6.2	10.2	14.4	20.4	15.2	10.5	4.3	40.2	9.4
Lane County	5.1	19.0	15.1	31.9	15.7	26.3	1.3	9.3	15.5	2.3	20.8	17.3	4.2	52.0	3.3
Lincoln County	6.1	23.2	19.5	27.3	21.9	27.5	2.9	10.4	9.9	4.3	14.4	17.0	4.3	54.6	5.4
Linn County	4.5	22.1	17.2	25.1	15.9	23.7	2.3	11.0	21.9	5.5	29.3	15.0	4.4	41.7	4.0
Malheur County	7.5	20.4	13.8	26.7	18.1	21.5	7.4	9.8	16.5	14.7	16.5	16.6	4.5	40.2	7.5
Marion County	4.5	19.7	14.5	29.1	16.3	25.8	3.8	9.6	15.4	4.7	20.5	15.6	3.7	45.9	9.6

STATE County	Median house-hold income	Median family income — All families	Families with children — Married-couple	Male house-holder	Female house-holder	Median nonfamily house-hold income	Median income for full-year, full-time workers — Men	Women	Per capita income	Households by source of income (percent) — With earnings	With interest, dividend, or rental income	With Social Security income	With public assis-tance income	With retire-ment income	House-holds with income over $100,000 (percent)	+/- U.S. percent for income over $100,000	House-holds with income below poverty (percent)	Families with children with income below poverty (percent)
	57	58	59	60	61	62	63	64	65	66	67	68	69	70	71	72	73	74
OKLAHOMA—Cont'd																		
Kiowa County	26 053	34 654	39 279	25 208	11 786	12 492	26 730	19 987	14 231	71.6	28.8	37.7	7.9	18.8	3.5	-8.8	20.6	23.2
Latimer County	23 962	29 661	35 613	18 889	13 512	12 793	28 294	20 310	12 842	69.7	23.9	35.1	8.4	18.8	3.3	-9.0	22.4	26.9
Le Flore County	27 278	32 603	38 715	21 957	14 540	13 583	26 874	20 429	13 737	73.8	20.1	33.2	8.3	16.8	3.4	-8.9	19.0	21.7
Lincoln County	31 187	36 310	41 217	23 194	18 341	16 084	29 876	20 990	14 890	76.8	26.9	30.3	4.9	17.1	4.0	-8.3	14.3	15.1
Logan County	36 784	44 340	50 015	23 529	16 861	18 939	32 267	23 535	17 872	80.8	31.1	27.3	4.1	16.4	7.1	-5.2	12.4	13.0
Love County	32 558	38 212	44 063	30 000	20 855	14 930	31 005	21 261	16 648	75.2	29.7	34.1	5.1	16.6	4.9	-7.4	12.9	10.9
McClain County	37 275	42 487	47 206	28 250	19 683	20 095	32 029	21 877	18 158	81.4	29.8	26.3	3.9	18.8	7.5	-4.8	10.4	11.8
McCurtain County	24 162	29 933	35 811	18 646	11 750	12 091	27 898	18 519	13 693	72.4	18.4	32.6	9.9	14.1	3.5	-8.8	24.8	29.8
McIntosh County	25 964	31 990	39 702	19 583	12 847	13 516	29 647	19 744	16 410	64.6	28.1	43.2	5.7	23.2	5.4	-6.9	18.2	21.7
Major County	30 949	36 888	42 740	26 500	16 034	16 814	29 602	18 533	17 272	75.7	38.4	33.4	2.5	13.9	4.5	-7.8	12.7	12.7
Marshall County	26 437	31 025	36 037	22 891	13 750	13 667	25 901	20 187	14 982	66.6	27.9	40.1	6.2	19.8	3.6	-8.7	18.1	20.4
Mayes County	31 125	37 542	42 284	20 938	17 255	17 214	32 197	21 096	15 350	74.2	26.2	31.3	5.3	17.6	4.0	-8.3	14.3	16.9
Murray County	30 294	37 303	41 786	20 313	20 250	16 042	29 500	20 711	16 084	74.3	26.1	35.0	6.6	18.4	3.8	-8.5	14.7	13.9
Muskogee County	28 438	34 793	43 025	19 762	14 938	15 941	29 753	21 377	14 828	72.8	24.8	33.6	6.8	19.4	4.4	-7.9	17.6	20.5
Noble County	33 968	40 180	47 176	21 111	17 667	19 643	33 618	22 105	17 022	79.5	34.3	29.8	5.3	13.6	5.4	-6.9	13.2	14.8
Nowata County	29 470	36 354	43 113	24 028	17 115	12 451	27 937	19 900	14 244	73.1	28.4	35.8	5.7	18.0	3.2	-9.1	15.1	13.7
Okfuskee County	24 324	30 325	34 787	23 750	13 920	11 895	25 569	18 458	12 746	69.2	22.8	36.3	8.0	19.4	3.1	-9.2	22.0	25.5
Oklahoma County	35 063	42 797	51 331	25 046	17 007	22 988	32 513	25 175	19 551	80.7	32.1	23.3	5.0	16.8	8.0	-4.3	14.1	18.1
Okmulgee County	27 652	33 987	42 615	19 671	13 992	13 341	30 712	21 444	14 065	72.2	23.8	33.0	7.7	17.3	3.5	-8.8	19.7	22.1
Osage County	34 477	40 784	47 137	23 750	20 401	18 020	31 942	24 171	17 014	77.1	27.3	29.3	4.8	16.2	5.8	-6.5	13.6	15.0
Ottawa County	27 507	32 368	38 484	22 167	13 707	15 499	26 729	20 025	14 478	72.6	27.2	35.7	6.4	19.3	3.0	0.3	16.0	20.1
Pawnee County	31 661	37 274	41 985	24 500	19 471	16 119	29 500	21 795	15 261	75.8	27.5	32.7	4.7	16.4	4.0	-8.3	13.5	13.7
Payne County	28 733	40 823	50 014	25 370	16 479	14 780	31 784	22 022	15 983	82.4	33.3	20.8	3.1	13.3	6.4	-5.9	22.8	14.6
Pittsburg County	28 679	35 190	41 510	25 000	15 045	13 182	29 951	20 163	15 494	69.6	30.2	35.6	6.7	21.8	4.0	-8.3	17.7	20.4
Pontotoc County	26 955	35 400	43 333	20 125	14 566	13 943	27 608	19 498	14 664	75.6	27.5	31.7	5.5	16.1	4.3	-8.0	17.7	17.4
Pottawatomie County	31 573	38 162	42 092	24 507	16 375	16 958	31 958	22 230	15 972	76.4	28.4	29.8	6.1	19.5	4.8	-7.5	14.8	17.0
Pushmataha County	22 127	27 808	34 474	13 125	12 308	11 205	26 278	19 105	12 864	65.8	21.4	40.0	10.2	19.5	2.8	-9.5	24.8	26.9
Roger Mills County	30 078	35 921	41 339	29 375	15 469	16 154	26 094	21 701	16 821	75.1	44.4	38.0	4.1	14.1	5.1	-7.2	16.5	18.2
Rogers County	44 471	50 707	57 684	30 341	18 576	20 512	38 810	25 578	19 073	83.1	33.6	24.5	2.9	16.3	8.3	-4.0	9.4	10.0
Seminole County	25 568	30 791	37 991	17 045	13 724	12 357	26 697	19 375	13 956	69.7	23.7	37.7	9.3	19.1	3.0	-9.3	20.3	24.3
Sequoyah County	27 615	32 673	38 686	20 946	13 547	12 323	27 337	20 134	13 405	72.1	19.6	31.7	6.6	15.7	3.3	-9.0	20.3	22.0
Stephens County	30 709	36 371	44 350	23 636	11 766	15 708	31 453	20 631	16 357	71.0	32.3	34.9	4.8	18.4	4.6	-7.7	15.2	17.1
Texas County	35 872	42 226	42 996	20 313	16 979	18 730	28 142	20 826	15 692	85.1	28.5	22.2	2.3	10.3	5.5	-6.8	13.1	15.4
Tillman County	24 828	30 854	37 337	19 688	10 650	12 708	24 508	19 803	14 270	69.8	24.8	38.5	6.5	17.9	4.4	-7.9	21.6	24.5
Tulsa County	38 213	47 489	57 049	27 770	18 735	23 930	36 414	26 398	21 115	82.2	33.2	23.2	3.8	13.8	9.8	-2.5	11.3	13.4
Wagoner County	41 744	47 062	52 066	24 012	21 235	18 548	36 784	24 292	18 272	83.3	29.2	25.3	3.8	14.7	7.4	-4.9	9.3	10.1
Washington County	35 010	40 514	51 118	23 020	17 636	18 611	36 466	23 406	20 250	72.5	39.8	34.5	3.7	21.2	9.7	-2.6	12.5	14.3
Washita County	29 563	35 598	40 889	23 750	12 500	16 784	26 740	18 725	15 528	76.3	32.9	33.8	4.0	16.4	4.6	-7.7	15.1	19.7
Woods County	28 927	39 143	45 741	22 125	15 893	14 685	28 225	20 203	17 487	78.8	36.9	32.4	2.6	15.3	5.5	-6.8	15.5	13.4
Woodward County	33 581	39 916	45 554	27 391	17 096	17 457	30 550	20 639	16 734	79.9	33.7	28.6	3.8	13.6	4.8	-7.5	12.1	11.8
OREGON	40 916	48 680	56 294	29 546	19 921	25 761	37 680	27 915	20 940	80.2	39.6	25.8	3.6	17.2	10.0	-2.3	10.8	12.4
Baker County	30 367	36 106	39 063	25 366	15 625	17 230	28 804	21 402	15 612	71.8	38.9	36.0	4.1	20.1	3.7	-8.6	14.1	16.6
Benton County	41 897	56 319	64 005	32 313	20 863	22 685	44 708	30 485	21 868	84.3	50.4	20.1	2.0	15.1	12.5	0.2	14.6	9.9
Clackamas County	52 080	60 791	69 579	34 593	27 089	31 625	45 359	31 673	25 973	84.3	44.0	22.8	2.2	17.0	17.5	5.2	6.1	7.1
Clatsop County	36 301	44 575	51 906	32 625	16 136	21 815	35 096	24 383	19 515	76.8	39.5	30.5	3.6	19.8	6.4	-5.9	11.7	14.6
Columbia County	45 797	51 381	58 144	30 444	20 221	23 972	43 862	28 135	20 078	80.7	37.1	27.3	3.4	19.4	8.7	-3.6	9.0	10.4
Coos County	31 542	38 040	44 670	21 289	16 500	17 739	34 226	23 080	17 547	68.2	35.4	36.4	5.3	23.3	4.8	-7.5	14.8	17.8
Crook County	35 186	40 746	43 877	25 000	17 043	18 134	33 042	23 267	16 899	76.5	33.3	31.4	4.6	17.7	4.7	-7.6	11.0	14.4
Curry County	30 117	35 627	42 772	22 250	16 183	17 719	35 170	23 613	18 138	62.0	39.0	45.8	3.8	28.3	4.9	-7.4	13.2	13.6
Deschutes County	41 847	48 403	54 945	27 953	19 985	25 727	35 441	25 926	21 767	79.9	39.8	26.2	2.8	19.2	10.3	-2.0	8.9	9.3
Douglas County	33 223	39 364	48 151	25 052	15 760	18 295	33 944	23 385	16 581	72.1	32.7	35.5	4.3	21.8	4.6	-7.7	12.8	15.5
Gilliam County	33 611	41 477	43 500	31 250	20 179	17 563	31 648	21 875	17 659	76.7	35.1	34.1	2.3	16.0	5.2	-7.1	9.9	10.2
Grant County	32 560	37 159	43 500	32 500	18 571	21 074	33 250	23 933	16 794	77.4	37.3	31.1	3.0	18.7	4.9	-7.4	12.4	16.3
Harney County	30 957	36 917	42 802	22 083	22 116	19 511	29 417	22 253	16 166	78.3	36.6	30.8	3.2	22.7	5.0	-7.3	12.4	11.0
Hood River County	38 326	41 422	41 930	30 598	21 080	26 563	33 434	25 632	17 877	81.5	39.9	27.2	3.2	17.5	7.4	-4.9	10.7	14.1
Jackson County	36 461	43 675	50 770	24 054	17 040	21 717	34 731	24 639	19 498	75.8	39.0	32.1	3.8	20.3	8.0	-4.3	11.9	14.7
Jefferson County	35 853	39 151	44 028	25 625	16 417	22 371	31 812	22 821	15 675	80.9	31.6	27.9	5.5	18.6	5.9	-6.4	12.1	17.4
Josephine County	31 229	36 894	41 572	29 013	14 159	18 034	31 999	23 772	17 234	66.5	38.8	39.1	5.2	24.4	5.4	-6.9	14.3	19.7
Klamath County	31 537	38 171	44 636	25 127	15 425	18 919	33 547	23 682	16 719	75.0	35.1	31.8	4.7	19.8	5.0	-7.3	15.1	19.9
Lake County	29 506	36 182	41 986	16 071	19 107	16 445	30 568	23 913	16 136	72.6	34.0	34.8	3.7	18.4	3.3	-9.0	15.7	19.9
Lane County	36 942	45 111	53 353	28 498	16 404	22 297	35 454	26 197	19 681	79.2	40.9	25.9	3.5	17.2	7.9	-4.4	14.1	14.8
Lincoln County	32 769	39 403	50 342	25 238	16 369	21 507	34 642	23 975	18 692	71.3	39.5	36.4	4.2	23.2	5.5	-6.8	12.1	17.9
Linn County	37 518	44 188	50 611	30 295	17 110	21 347	36 580	25 064	17 633	77.1	35.8	29.8	3.9	18.7	6.0	-6.3	10.6	13.4
Malheur County	30 241	35 672	38 904	29 091	14 459	17 978	26 992	22 381	13 895	76.5	31.5	32.8	4.9	17.0	4.9	-7.4	16.7	22.1
Marion County	40 314	46 202	51 486	28 951	18 997	25 685	35 282	27 050	18 408	79.9	36.8	26.7	4.3	18.3	7.8	-4.5	11.4	15.1

STATE/ County code	MSA/PMSA/ NECMA code[1]	STATE County	High school graduates			College graduates		College graduates (percent)				
			Total population 25 years and over	Percent with a high school diploma or less	Percent with a high school diploma or more	Percent with a bachelor's degree or more	+/− U.S. percent with bachelor's degree or more	Non-Hispanic White	Black or African American	American Indian and Alaska Native	Asian, Hawaiian, and Pacific Islander	Hispanic or Latino[2]
			1	2	3	4	5	6	7	8	9	10
		OREGON—Cont'd										
41 049	...	Morrow County..............	6 627	57.9	74.1	11.0	-13.4	12.9	14.3	2.2	34.1	1.9
41 051	6440	Multnomah County.......	446 322	37.4	85.6	30.7	6.3	33.3	15.2	13.5	27.2	12.7
41 053	7080	Polk County..............	39 357	40.4	85.5	25.3	0.9	26.9	6.3	10.3	25.2	8.5
41 055	...	Sherman County	1 316	48.6	84.3	19.0	-5.4	18.9	100.0	31.6	0.0	20.0
41 057	...	Tillamook County	17 145	52.9	84.1	17.6	-6.8	18.1	0.0	2.8	14.5	6.6
41 059	...	Umatilla County	44 515	51.9	77.8	16.0	-8.4	17.6	15.4	9.9	17.2	5.9
41 061	...	Union County	15 562	45.3	85.6	21.8	-2.6	22.1	14.3	21.1	15.6	14.1
41 063	...	Wallowa County	5 099	49.2	87.5	20.3	-4.1	20.6	X	0.0	0.0	13.0
41 065	...	Wasco County............	16 023	51.9	82.1	15.7	-8.7	16.5	15.9	5.6	34.8	6.3
41 067	6440	Washington County.......	285 518	31.2	88.9	34.5	10.1	35.7	32.0	21.0	50.2	11.3
41 069	...	Wheeler County	1 143	57.8	79.4	14.3	-10.1	13.9	0.0	0.0	X	26.9
41 071	6440	Yamhill County	52 645	48.1	82.8	20.6	-3.8	22.1	9.8	15.8	22.6	6.6
42 000	...	**PENNSYLVANIA**........	8 266 284	56.2	81.9	22.4	-2.0	23.2	12.0	13.2	48.8	12.0
42 001	...	Adams County..............	60 173	64.1	79.7	16.7	-7.7	16.7	15.4	21.3	55.5	6.7
42 003	6280	Allegheny County	891 171	47.5	86.3	28.3	3.9	29.3	13.4	19.1	72.5	37.9
42 005	...	Armstrong County	50 638	71.1	80.0	10.4	-14.0	10.5	3.9	4.8	15.4	24.2
42 007	6280	Beaver County	126 933	58.8	83.6	15.8	-8.6	16.2	7.1	3.1	48.1	18.1
42 009	...	Bedford County	34 582	72.4	78.3	10.2	-14.2	10.2	10.3	19.2	8.5	12.9
42 011	6680	Berks County	248 864	61.3	78.0	18.5	-5.9	19.6	8.4	9.0	38.6	4.7
42 013	0280	Blair County..................	88 366	66.2	83.8	13.9	-10.5	13.8	9.9	3.6	55.1	14.1
42 015	...	Bradford County	42 428	65.4	81.7	14.8	-9.6	14.7	6.7	15.4	67.8	24.1
42 017	6160	Bucks County	402 575	43.6	88.6	31.2	6.8	31.1	22.4	26.2	57.0	16.2
42 019	6280	Butler County	116 072	52.2	86.8	23.5	-0.9	23.2	23.6	3.7	65.4	28.7
42 021	3680	Cambria County	106 780	67.3	80.0	13.7	-10.7	13.9	5.1	5.4	41.4	8.7
42 023	...	Cameron County	4 150	70.2	79.8	12.1	-12.3	12.1	0.0	X	100.0	0.0
42 025	0240	Carbon County	41 690	68.9	79.0	11.0	-13.4	10.9	31.5	62.9	19.0	8.6
42 027	8050	Centre County	74 785	45.6	88.2	36.3	11.9	34.5	20.0	24.8	84.4	48.8
42 029	6160	Chester County	285 816	36.7	89.3	42.5	18.1	44.2	17.5	21.0	70.0	16.6
42 031	...	Clarion County	26 334	68.7	81.8	15.3	-9.1	15.0	60.5	0.0	44.2	18.5
42 033	...	Clearfield County	58 138	71.9	79.1	11.1	-13.3	11.1	2.3	7.7	66.2	7.7
42 035	...	Clinton County..............	24 701	67.6	80.4	13.4	-11.0	13.4	2.4	5.9	27.0	7.0
42 037	7560	Columbia County..........	41 658	65.8	80.6	15.8	-8.6	15.5	41.1	0.0	49.8	11.7
42 039	...	Crawford County	59 684	66.6	81.6	14.7	-9.7	14.7	8.3	9.3	37.7	8.0
42 041	3240	Cumberland County	144 215	49.7	86.1	27.9	3.5	28.0	13.3	26.5	46.4	15.9
42 043	3240	Dauphin County	171 783	54.0	83.4	23.5	-0.9	25.6	12.8	18.8	39.3	9.0
42 045	6160	Delaware County	365 174	46.5	86.5	30.0	5.6	31.4	15.4	12.9	50.9	30.0
42 047	...	Elk County....................	24 337	66.8	82.7	12.3	-12.1	12.2	0.0	0.0	40.5	30.0
42 049	2360	Erie County..................	180 106	57.1	84.6	20.9	-3.5	21.5	8.7	10.8	51.0	11.0
42 051	6280	Fayette County..............	103 227	71.8	76.0	11.5	-12.9	11.5	10.1	0.0	27.0	7.1
42 053	...	Forest County	3 540	73.8	79.4	8.9	-15.5	9.0	0.0	6.3	50.0	0.0
42 055	...	Franklin County	87 959	66.0	78.9	14.8	-9.6	14.7	8.5	5.3	52.8	12.7
42 057	...	Fulton County................	9 687	75.1	73.2	9.3	-15.1	9.3	0.0	33.3	30.0	0.0
42 059	...	Greene County	27 758	71.8	75.7	12.2	-12.2	12.7	2.2	0.0	46.9	2.7
42 061	...	Huntingdon County	31 152	72.7	74.6	11.9	-12.5	12.5	1.2	38.9	19.4	2.7
42 063	...	Indiana County	55 995	65.4	81.0	17.0	-7.4	16.6	27.3	8.5	60.5	21.4
42 065	...	Jefferson County	31 583	70.4	81.0	11.7	-12.7	11.5	9.5	0.0	58.5	24.4
42 067	...	Juniata County	15 225	77.2	74.5	8.8	-15.6	8.7	33.3	0.0	12.5	11.9
42 069	7560	Lackawanna County......	148 116	58.5	82.0	19.6	-4.8	19.6	8.6	8.4	46.6	11.0
42 071	4000	Lancaster County	302 503	61.5	77.4	20.5	-3.9	21.2	11.8	9.6	24.6	7.4
42 073	...	Lawrence County	64 767	64.1	81.6	15.1	-9.3	15.3	3.8	2.5	54.0	29.9
42 075	3240	Lebanon County............	82 008	68.0	78.6	15.4	-9.0	15.7	12.7	31.4	35.1	3.8
42 077	0240	Lehigh County	212 665	53.8	81.1	23.3	-1.1	24.3	10.4	5.4	52.8	7.0
42 079	7560	Luzerne County............	226 374	60.4	81.1	16.4	-8.0	16.4	5.8	10.3	50.3	10.4
42 081	9140	Lycoming County	80 500	61.3	80.6	15.1	-9.3	15.2	6.9	12.1	38.6	13.8
42 083	...	McKean County..............	31 529	65.7	82.2	14.0	-10.4	14.5	1.3	10.0	29.8	3.5
42 085	7610	Mercer County..............	81 499	62.2	82.9	17.3	-7.1	17.7	6.2	12.5	44.9	21.1
42 087	...	Mifflin County................	31 722	74.8	77.2	10.9	-13.5	10.8	35.6	0.0	35.2	7.8
42 089	...	Monroe County..............	89 793	54.8	83.8	20.5	-3.9	20.6	21.5	27.2	47.1	13.9
42 091	6160	Montgomery County......	515 871	38.8	88.5	38.7	14.3	39.4	22.4	21.6	57.4	28.6
42 093	...	Montour County............	12 573	59.8	82.3	22.1	-2.3	21.3	23.3	78.9	86.0	30.3
42 095	0240	Northampton County	180 018	55.8	80.7	21.2	-3.2	21.5	15.7	16.3	55.7	10.1
42 097	...	Northumberland County	67 112	72.3	77.8	11.1	-13.3	11.0	9.3	8.2	35.2	17.6
42 099	3240	Perry County................	29 250	69.7	79.9	11.3	-13.1	11.2	6.3	14.3	53.6	21.1
42 101	6160	Philadelphia County	966 197	62.1	71.2	17.9	-6.5	24.1	10.3	9.9	32.6	9.2
42 103	5660	Pike County..................	31 525	54.5	86.8	19.0	-5.4	18.8	29.0	6.9	31.4	18.0

[1]MSA = Metropolitan Statistical Area. PMSA = Primary MSA. NECMA = New England County Metropolitan Area. See the Appendix A for explanation of these concepts. See Appendix B for list of metropolitan areas identified by type, with component counties.
[2]Hispanic or Latino persons may be of any race.

STATE County	School enrollment			Population 16 to 19 years				Employment status, 2000			Work status in 1999 of the population 16 years and over (percent)		
											Worked in 1999		
	Grades kindergarten through 12	College or graduate school	Percent private	Number	Percent in armed forces	Percent high school graduates	Percent not enrolled, not grads, not in armed forces, not employed	Total population 16 years and over	Percent in labor force	Unemployment rate	Full-time	Part-time	Did not work in 1999
	11	12	13	14	15	16	17	18	19	20	21	22	23
OREGON—Cont'd													
Morrow County	2 526	209	2.5	710	0.0	9.3	7.2	7 995	65.1	10.7	59.0	12.7	28.3
Multnomah County	104 972	47 924	17.1	33 149	0.0	12.7	5.7	529 051	69.0	6.4	57.3	16.8	25.9
Polk County	11 511	5 087	10.7	4 256	0.0	10.7	3.4	48 612	64.1	6.2	51.6	18.2	30.2
Sherman County	411	16	5.6	103	0.0	13.6	5.8	1 490	59.9	7.3	50.1	15.9	34.0
Tillamook County	4 214	547	7.4	1 322	0.7	14.7	4.8	19 585	58.7	4.4	46.0	18.2	35.8
Umatilla County	14 484	2 743	6.0	4 001	0.0	8.8	6.8	53 222	63.2	7.5	56.8	14.3	28.9
Union County	4 662	2 077	5.2	1 748	0.5	7.9	2.7	19 302	61.4	7.9	48.9	19.4	31.8
Wallowa County	1 450	161	9.0	341	0.0	10.3	2.1	5 683	60.7	11.8	48.8	18.5	32.7
Wasco County	4 426	777	11.4	1 182	0.0	8.6	5.6	18 501	60.5	7.9	50.3	16.8	33.0
Washington County	83 868	24 771	14.3	23 102	0.0	12.1	5.3	338 288	72.3	4.6	61.1	16.0	22.9
Wheeler County	296	31	15.0	99	0.0	12.1	0.0	1 262	52.5	7.3	42.1	15.7	42.2
Yamhill County	16 901	5 277	21.3	5 545	0.0	10.2	5.0	64 941	64.5	6.4	54.2	18.0	27.8
PENNSYLVANIA	2 228 837	703 163	21.4	672 849	0.1	9.3	4.0	9 693 040	61.9	5.7	51.9	15.2	32.9
Adams County	17 333	4 694	21.3	5 427	0.1	11.0	3.2	71 242	67.8	4.2	57.5	16.0	26.5
Allegheny County	212 715	87 059	22.1	64 811	0.0	8.6	3.1	1 032 364	61.1	6.1	50.5	15.2	34.3
Armstrong County	12 826	2 012	6.2	3 837	0.0	11.6	4.1	57 954	55.8	6.2	46.1	13.0	40.9
Beaver County	31 636	6 954	13.9	9 127	0.0	10.2	3.6	145 097	60.1	5.3	49.2	14.7	36.1
Bedford County	8 761	1 066	7.1	2 431	0.0	14.7	4.2	39 528	60.3	5.7	50.9	13.4	35.7
Berks County	69 719	18 185	14.7	20 694	0.0	10.0	4.9	291 683	65.4	5.1	55.2	15.2	29.6
Blair County	22 369	5 251	11.9	7 576	0.1	13.1	3.4	103 079	59.6	6.2	48.6	15.4	36.0
Bradford County	12 501	1 436	10.2	3 428	0.0	12.0	5.1	48 686	60.9	5.5	51.4	13.5	35.1
Bucks County	115 596	28 682	23.6	29 976	0.1	9.1	2.2	461 356	69.4	3.5	57.8	16.0	26.2
Butler County	32 159	10 254	9.5	9 699	0.1	8.2	2.1	135 890	63.6	4.4	52.3	16.0	31.6
Cambria County	24 953	7 614	17.1	8 601	0.1	10.1	3.8	124 713	53.8	8.8	44.9	14.1	40.9
Cameron County	1 192	95	7.8	313	0.0	8.9	3.2	4 690	57.8	6.3	49.6	13.7	36.7
Carbon County	10 303	1 770	12.0	2 820	0.0	12.1	5.2	47 244	59.3	5.5	50.0	13.3	36.6
Centre County	18 306	36 356	5.2	11 929	0.1	4.8	1.6	114 077	60.1	5.5	51.5	24.6	23.9
Chester County	84 718	25 130	23.2	23 454	0.0	6.7	2.9	332 513	69.1	3.6	57.9	16.4	25.7
Clarion County	6 868	4 650	6.2	3 245	0.0	5.7	2.6	33 781	57.0	6.6	47.8	17.2	34.9
Clearfield County	14 719	2 156	9.0	4 163	0.2	11.4	7.4	66 758	57.4	6.9	49.0	14.8	36.2
Clinton County	6 141	3 407	8.9	2 646	0.4	7.6	5.3	30 705	58.5	5.8	49.5	15.7	34.8
Columbia County	10 468	6 640	5.7	4 862	0.2	5.7	2.8	52 499	61.7	7.3	51.3	18.1	30.7
Crawford County	16 917	4 041	18.7	5 741	0.1	9.7	4.8	70 845	59.3	6.0	50.2	15.5	34.3
Cumberland County	35 816	15 608	20.2	13 107	0.1	7.2	2.7	172 209	64.5	3.2	56.2	16.0	27.8
Dauphin County	46 556	9 782	14.3	12 418	0.0	10.4	4.6	197 683	65.2	4.5	58.3	12.8	28.9
Delaware County	103 230	39 070	34.7	32 263	0.0	6.7	3.2	429 983	63.3	4.9	52.7	16.2	31.1
Elk County	6 516	882	20.3	1 785	0.0	14.8	2.2	27 692	63.3	4.5	54.1	13.7	32.2
Erie County	53 964	18 832	23.9	18 122	0.0	8.2	3.5	218 948	62.8	5.8	51.3	17.2	31.5
Fayette County	25 608	4 864	10.3	7 221	0.1	13.3	5.1	118 862	54.2	8.3	43.6	13.2	43.1
Forest County	993	61	25.0	322	0.0	11.5	1.9	4 015	49.2	7.0	43.5	12.8	43.7
Franklin County	22 600	4 467	14.1	6 695	0.0	12.7	4.4	101 768	64.2	3.7	55.5	14.1	30.4
Fulton County	2 580	285	5.8	681	0.0	19.1	4.0	11 132	62.8	3.9	56.1	11.6	32.3
Greene County	7 221	1 857	12.0	2 254	0.2	12.7	3.3	32 829	51.0	9.2	44.7	13.0	42.3
Huntingdon County	8 043	2 034	15.7	2 532	0.0	9.9	4.7	36 941	54.2	5.6	49.9	13.8	36.3
Indiana County	14 434	11 981	6.2	7 091	0.0	6.4	3.2	73 288	56.1	8.1	44.5	19.3	36.2
Jefferson County	8 348	1 283	8.9	2 512	0.0	10.7	4.1	36 466	58.4	6.7	47.0	14.9	37.2
Juniata County	4 117	433	12.3	1 166	0.0	17.2	5.7	17 730	62.0	3.5	52.6	13.8	33.5
Lackawanna County	36 314	12 508	29.9	11 494	0.0	8.0	2.9	172 253	59.1	5.3	48.2	15.9	36.0
Lancaster County	89 947	18 811	21.7	26 608	0.1	10.2	5.3	358 317	67.9	3.0	55.3	17.6	27.0
Lawrence County	16 641	3 916	12.1	4 946	0.3	9.8	5.6	75 345	58.1	6.1	46.5	15.5	38.0
Lebanon County	21 104	4 081	18.4	6 325	0.0	11.1	4.6	95 090	65.7	4.0	55.8	15.0	29.2
Lehigh County	57 231	15 378	20.8	15 872	0.1	10.3	5.1	245 633	64.1	4.4	54.1	15.2	30.7
Luzerne County	53 178	15 918	24.2	16 639	0.0	8.5	3.9	260 412	58.3	5.4	48.9	15.0	36.1
Lycoming County	21 522	6 190	13.6	7 224	0.2	10.3	3.8	95 468	61.4	6.3	51.6	15.5	32.9
McKean County	8 417	1 656	9.7	2 437	0.0	9.2	3.2	36 362	58.8	6.0	50.3	13.4	36.3
Mercer County	21 881	5 921	20.0	7 085	0.0	7.1	3.7	95 664	58.1	6.0	48.5	15.5	36.0
Mifflin County	8 244	722	15.9	2 298	0.1	14.8	8.6	36 280	58.8	4.1	49.2	13.2	37.6
Monroe County	28 869	8 213	10.5	8 287	0.2	9.4	2.8	105 937	64.3	6.6	53.9	15.1	31.0
Montgomery County	134 756	43 510	30.0	35 196	0.1	8.0	1.7	589 000	68.5	4.5	57.4	16.0	26.6
Montour County	3 479	498	14.6	1 002	0.0	11.8	3.9	14 373	61.6	7.2	51.1	13.8	35.1
Northampton County	48 206	17 800	26.6	15 697	0.0	7.1	3.0	212 133	63.2	4.6	53.6	15.6	30.8
Northumberland County	16 362	2 148	13.8	4 801	0.0	11.4	4.5	76 577	57.6	5.2	49.5	14.3	36.2
Perry County	8 317	982	8.7	2 341	0.1	12.9	6.8	33 808	66.9	3.7	58.3	13.7	28.0
Philadelphia County	298 504	115 671	32.4	88 916	0.0	10.1	7.4	1 174 798	55.9	10.9	46.7	13.3	40.0
Pike County	9 714	1 412	8.8	2 212	0.0	9.2	2.3	35 354	58.8	5.4	49.1	15.1	35.8

STATE County	Full-year full-time employed (percent)								Children under 18 years in families					+/- U.S. percent two-income couples	Total employed by class of worker (percent)			
										With two parents (percent)		With one parent who is in labor force (percent)	+/- U.S. percent of children with no stay-at-home parent (percent)					
	Total	Men	Women	Non-Hispanic White	Black or African American	American Indian and Alaska Native	Asian, Hawaiian, and Pacific Islander	Hispanic or Latino[1]	Number	Both in labor force	Father only in labor force				Private	Government	Self-employed	Unpaid family worker
	24	25	26	27	28	29	30	31	32	33	34	35	36	37	38	39	40	41
OREGON—Cont'd																		
Morrow County	35.7	46.2	24.6	39.2	28.6	31.2	25.0	21.3	3 198	45.7	22.5	20.9	2.0	-1.7	66.8	19.4	13.5	0.3
Multnomah County	40.1	48.1	32.5	41.0	33.1	35.6	39.2	37.5	136 851	43.1	21.8	23.5	2.0	3.8	77.1	11.9	10.7	0.3
Polk County	35.0	44.4	26.5	35.1	27.0	36.9	33.7	33.7	15 003	49.1	26.5	15.9	0.4	1.5	63.3	23.8	12.5	0.4
Sherman County	30.7	43.4	17.1	30.6	0.0	46.7	42.9	22.6	493	41.4	29.0	17.4	-5.8	-6.5	49.1	26.7	24.2	0.0
Tillamook County	32.9	43.6	22.4	32.3	0.0	28.2	68.3	41.6	4 989	50.0	21.8	20.0	5.4	-4.0	65.4	14.5	19.6	0.5
Umatilla County	37.5	46.2	28.4	38.0	18.8	39.1	45.5	35.7	18 182	49.3	18.0	23.0	7.7	2.1	66.7	20.2	12.5	0.6
Union County	32.0	41.7	22.9	31.9	12.9	44.7	22.8	45.2	5 566	51.0	20.6	16.9	3.3	-0.1	63.8	21.6	14.1	0.5
Wallowa County	31.2	39.9	22.9	31.2	X	43.5	33.3	16.7	1 661	48.9	21.0	19.4	3.7	-5.1	51.6	20.8	26.2	1.3
Wasco County	33.2	41.8	25.0	33.8	27.9	36.1	23.3	28.2	5 742	44.9	18.3	22.6	2.9	-2.1	69.9	17.5	12.3	0.3
Washington County	45.2	56.9	33.8	46.0	50.3	43.9	44.5	39.3	114 748	47.0	28.7	17.2	-0.4	5.3	80.4	9.3	10.1	0.2
Wheeler County	23.5	32.8	14.6	22.8	100.0	0.0	X	28.6	323	65.6	13.6	10.2	11.2	-14.3	49.3	22.3	25.1	3.3
Yamhill County	37.3	46.9	27.5	37.9	13.8	44.1	30.5	35.6	21 395	50.4	24.1	17.9	3.7	2.5	74.6	13.3	11.6	0.4
PENNSYLVANIA	40.0	50.4	30.6	41.0	33.4	34.9	36.7	33.2	2 774 571	45.4	22.7	20.7	1.5	-0.3	80.0	11.3	8.4	0.3
Adams County	45.0	56.3	34.3	45.4	38.9	50.4	33.5	39.9	21 601	54.1	20.2	18.7	8.2	5.7	80.2	10.5	9.0	0.4
Allegheny County	39.0	48.7	30.6	40.0	32.9	30.5	34.4	35.0	269 860	43.4	23.0	22.9	1.7	-2.4	82.2	10.0	7.6	0.2
Armstrong County	35.3	47.2	24.3	35.4	27.7	4.5	32.5	44.6	15 939	43.7	28.1	18.1	-2.8	-9.0	81.0	10.0	8.7	0.3
Beaver County	38.3	48.6	29.1	38.8	30.7	13.5	36.6	41.0	39 405	47.2	22.7	20.1	2.7	-3.0	84.0	9.0	6.8	0.2
Bedford County	38.8	51.0	27.2	38.8	36.8	51.7	17.3	38.5	11 350	47.0	28.1	16.1	-1.5	-5.2	76.5	11.1	11.7	0.7
Berks County	43.5	54.8	33.0	44.7	37.0	48.6	39.1	32.0	87 043	47.5	22.1	18.8	1.7	3.0	82.6	9.0	8.1	0.3
Blair County	38.1	50.1	27.4	38.3	31.0	13.7	29.5	39.4	28 038	45.2	21.8	22.3	2.9	-2.4	80.5	11.4	7.7	0.3
Bradford County	40.1	51.2	30.0	40.2	48.6	35.4	31.7	38.9	15 286	50.6	20.5	18.9	4.9	-1.0	75.4	11.0	12.7	0.9
Bucks County	47.1	59.9	35.2	47.2	47.0	50.1	47.3	45.1	148 964	53.5	25.8	14.0	2.9	5.9	81.0	9.2	9.6	0.2
Butler County	41.3	54.9	28.7	41.4	22.6	37.7	39.1	39.2	41 389	48.4	30.1	15.1	-1.1	-0.4	82.3	9.7	7.7	0.3
Cambria County	33.2	42.4	24.7	33.6	18.9	44.9	49.5	27.9	30 476	48.0	22.6	18.5	1.9	-7.0	77.3	14.9	7.4	0.4
Cameron County	38.1	47.7	28.9	38.3	0.0	X	0.0	0.0	1 403	54.9	12.8	24.4	14.7	-4.7	80.5	10.7	8.2	0.6
Carbon County	39.0	50.9	27.9	38.9	28.0	61.9	59.5	49.0	12 385	49.7	18.7	19.1	4.2	-3.9	81.2	11.2	7.2	0.4
Centre County	32.5	39.6	25.2	33.9	21.6	57.1	18.1	17.8	23 404	52.1	25.1	15.4	2.9	3.6	70.4	21.5	7.7	0.4
Chester County	46.7	60.0	34.3	47.6	37.6	31.4	48.3	42.3	109 529	50.0	31.2	13.1	-1.5	4.8	80.7	8.5	10.5	0.3
Clarion County	33.4	44.0	23.7	33.5	22.1	13.3	28.5	23.5	8 709	46.4	26.9	16.2	-2.0	-6.6	74.4	15.3	9.9	0.5
Clearfield County	35.9	46.2	25.7	36.2	19.3	11.5	44.2	24.6	18 118	47.3	25.5	17.5	0.2	-4.2	79.0	11.0	9.7	0.2
Clinton County	35.5	45.4	26.6	35.8	19.4	15.4	15.0	28.1	7 754	46.2	21.4	21.1	2.7	-3.3	75.6	15.5	8.5	0.4
Columbia County	36.5	47.2	27.1	36.8	17.7	41.6	47.5	22.7	12 807	50.7	20.0	20.5	6.6	-0.4	78.5	12.6	8.5	0.4
Crawford County	36.5	47.9	26.1	36.8	24.5	24.7	29.2	16.4	21 096	44.8	26.8	18.9	-0.9	-2.5	76.0	11.6	11.9	0.5
Cumberland County	44.4	54.9	34.5	44.9	28.5	50.0	47.7	33.9	45 343	50.7	24.2	18.0	4.1	4.3	73.9	17.5	8.3	0.3
Dauphin County	46.0	54.5	38.3	47.2	41.9	40.4	47.2	34.3	57 762	43.8	18.1	27.0	6.2	3.2	73.5	19.6	6.6	0.2
Delaware County	41.1	51.1	32.4	41.5	40.1	34.6	40.2	34.4	130 079	47.1	23.3	20.0	2.5	1.4	81.2	9.8	8.7	0.3
Elk County	42.7	54.5	31.4	42.8	44.4	27.6	21.3	33.3	8 143	54.6	20.6	17.5	7.5	2.4	84.3	8.0	7.2	0.5
Erie County	38.9	49.0	29.6	39.6	32.0	27.4	34.7	25.6	67 225	46.1	20.4	23.1	4.6	0.8	82.4	10.0	7.2	0.3
Fayette County	32.0	42.1	23.1	32.3	24.3	40.0	22.9	21.1	31 805	38.9	23.4	20.1	-5.6	-10.7	81.5	10.5	7.6	0.4
Forest County	31.2	41.5	20.6	31.5	31.4	21.9	0.0	33.3	867	46.6	21.8	14.1	-3.9	-15.3	72.0	19.0	8.5	0.5
Franklin County	44.0	55.6	33.2	44.3	40.7	37.1	32.5	40.1	29 590	51.1	24.5	16.6	3.1	1.1	77.9	12.4	9.4	0.4
Fulton County	43.3	53.3	33.3	43.6	18.3	52.6	20.0	17.4	3 306	50.5	19.4	19.1	5.0	-1.0	77.6	11.6	10.3	0.5
Greene County	31.1	38.8	23.1	32.0	16.0	37.5	20.2	27.4	8 574	41.5	26.3	16.1	-7.0	-10.6	75.4	15.9	8.0	0.7
Huntingdon County	34.5	41.7	26.7	35.8	19.2	38.9	25.0	18.5	9 343	50.4	22.3	17.3	3.1	-2.4	73.1	16.1	10.2	0.5
Indiana County	30.3	40.9	20.6	30.8	11.2	42.3	13.6	15.9	18 254	43.5	29.4	14.8	-6.3	-8.7	74.2	16.8	8.4	0.6
Jefferson County	35.7	49.2	23.1	35.8	65.2	58.5	23.7	19.7	10 453	47.7	26.3	17.5	0.6	-6.4	78.4	10.3	10.8	0.5
Juniata County	40.6	53.2	28.6	40.8	25.0	50.0	33.8	36.5	5 505	47.8	31.1	13.4	-3.4	-2.6	74.1	13.1	12.1	0.7
Lackawanna County	37.6	48.5	28.2	37.7	30.3	50.3	43.4	34.3	44 555	48.8	21.7	17.3	1.5	-1.9	79.5	12.0	8.2	0.4
Lancaster County	45.1	59.2	32.1	45.4	40.9	34.2	48.3	40.1	120 405	47.0	30.0	15.9	-1.7	4.6	82.0	7.2	10.2	0.5
Lawrence County	35.4	46.8	25.5	35.6	30.2	49.0	33.9	36.2	20 952	44.5	24.5	19.6	-0.5	-5.7	79.5	11.0	9.1	0.4
Lebanon County	44.9	57.0	33.7	45.3	42.9	62.7	39.2	38.2	27 354	50.2	24.0	18.5	4.1	3.8	79.5	11.0	9.0	0.5
Lehigh County	42.9	54.3	32.8	43.4	45.1	41.5	44.3	37.2	70 976	48.2	20.6	20.7	4.3	2.6	83.8	8.3	7.7	0.2
Luzerne County	37.4	48.1	27.8	37.8	23.0	21.1	39.7	32.0	64 310	47.1	21.5	20.1	2.6	-2.0	79.8	12.1	7.9	0.3
Lycoming County	39.5	48.5	31.1	39.9	30.9	31.3	33.2	37.5	26 519	48.0	20.4	22.6	6.0	0.0	80.0	11.2	8.4	0.4
McKean County	38.3	45.8	30.8	39.4	7.7	25.8	18.5	19.5	10 313	48.1	18.2	22.4	5.9	-1.0	78.7	12.4	8.5	0.3
Mercer County	35.6	45.2	26.8	36.3	23.5	20.0	36.1	26.4	26 456	45.3	22.9	20.4	1.1	-3.9	79.7	11.1	8.8	0.5
Mifflin County	38.3	51.1	26.7	38.3	47.5	26.7	70.4	40.1	10 976	46.9	26.5	15.7	-2.0	-2.4	79.0	10.4	9.9	0.7
Monroe County	40.4	51.3	30.0	39.9	42.7	49.1	50.8	44.7	35 167	44.3	28.0	17.3	-3.0	-2.3	77.4	12.9	9.4	0.3
Montgomery County	46.5	58.8	35.4	46.7	44.7	54.1	45.4	47.3	174 926	54.7	25.5	14.3	4.4	6.2	81.4	8.1	10.3	0.2
Montour County	40.5	50.3	31.9	40.7	41.3	10.5	38.7	30.6	4 211	47.4	25.8	17.1	-0.1	-1.2	79.1	11.4	8.9	0.6
Northampton County	42.1	52.9	32.1	42.6	41.4	31.3	33.9	35.4	59 704	49.6	23.4	18.3	3.3	2.4	82.0	10.5	7.2	0.2
Northumberland County	38.8	49.7	28.6	39.2	21.5	26.7	42.0	30.6	19 540	48.4	21.1	19.4	3.2	-2.2	77.6	14.3	7.7	0.4
Perry County	47.0	57.8	36.3	47.2	10.0	27.5	44.2	30.9	10 528	50.6	24.4	16.6	2.6	4.7	74.6	16.1	8.9	0.5
Philadelphia County	33.2	38.7	28.6	36.5	31.1	25.7	27.3	26.0	343 503	25.3	12.1	37.0	-2.3	-8.4	77.8	16.5	5.5	0.2
Pike County	37.9	49.3	26.8	37.4	46.4	37.1	36.3	42.5	11 933	45.7	29.8	15.0	-3.9	-8.7	73.7	14.6	11.3	0.3

[1] Hispanic or Latino persons may be of any race.

STATE County	Percent who worked at home	Percent of the population 5 years and over with a disability	Veterans as a percent of the population 18 years and over	Occupation for employed population 16 years and over (percent)						Industry for employed population 16 years and over (percent)					
				Management, professional, and related occupations	Service occupations	Sales and office occupations	Farming, fishing, and forestry occupations	Construction, extraction, and maintenance occupations	Production, transportation and material moving occupations	Agriculture, forestry, fishing, and mining	Construction and manufacturing	Wholesale and retail trade	Transportation and warehousing, and utilities	Service industries	Public administration
	42	43	44	45	46	47	48	49	50	51	52	53	54	55	56
OREGON—Cont'd															
Morrow County	5.1	18.4	15.4	24.9	15.0	17.9	6.7	12.1	23.5	17.8	22.0	14.3	9.7	31.4	4.7
Multnomah County	4.3	18.7	12.3	35.7	15.1	27.1	0.4	7.6	14.1	0.6	18.5	16.5	5.8	55.2	3.5
Polk County	5.2	19.0	15.5	33.8	17.4	23.9	2.9	7.7	14.3	5.4	17.8	12.7	3.3	50.5	10.4
Sherman County	9.5	16.8	21.7	34.1	14.9	20.3	4.0	10.8	16.0	19.8	13.7	14.8	9.1	37.2	5.4
Tillamook County	6.5	24.3	18.0	27.3	17.4	21.8	6.5	9.8	17.2	11.0	21.3	15.1	4.9	42.9	4.8
Umatilla County	3.6	19.6	15.1	25.4	17.4	23.3	3.5	11.1	19.3	7.6	19.6	16.9	6.8	40.8	8.3
Union County	6.6	20.0	15.9	30.7	17.3	24.3	2.5	8.3	17.0	7.3	18.3	15.8	5.3	47.2	6.1
Wallowa County	9.6	19.4	18.4	32.9	14.2	24.2	4.7	10.0	14.1	16.8	17.5	13.9	3.3	43.5	5.0
Wasco County	4.8	19.6	18.9	27.1	19.0	24.4	3.4	10.1	16.0	6.6	17.3	18.7	5.6	47.5	4.3
Washington County	4.5	14.8	12.4	40.0	12.0	27.4	1.0	7.4	12.3	1.2	26.6	16.2	4.0	49.6	2.4
Wheeler County	18.9	19.1	21.7	34.7	16.6	13.5	10.6	11.7	12.9	20.4	12.5	10.3	4.6	47.6	4.7
Yamhill County	4.7	18.7	15.3	27.6	16.3	23.9	2.8	10.7	18.7	4.5	26.8	15.8	4.5	43.6	4.9
PENNSYLVANIA	3.0	18.6	13.7	32.6	14.8	27.0	0.5	8.9	16.3	1.3	22.0	15.7	5.4	51.5	4.2
Adams County	3.3	17.1	14.1	24.9	14.9	23.8	1.7	11.8	23.0	3.5	30.7	15.5	4.2	41.8	4.3
Allegheny County	2.5	18.0	14.3	37.8	15.8	28.7	0.5	7.5	10.1	0.2	14.5	15.4	6.0	60.6	3.3
Armstrong County	3.0	20.1	15.6	22.1	16.6	21.9	1.3	12.9	25.2	4.2	28.8	15.5	6.8	41.6	3.0
Beaver County	1.9	18.5	16.1	26.2	17.1	27.9	0.2	10.4	18.1	0.5	21.6	16.2	11.5	47.4	2.8
Bedford County	4.7	20.2	14.0	23.0	14.0	21.3	1.6	13.3	26.8	4.9	31.4	15.9	6.6	37.4	3.8
Berks County	2.9	17.5	13.4	29.3	13.3	26.1	0.9	9.1	21.3	1.8	30.0	15.9	4.9	45.2	2.3
Blair County	2.4	21.1	15.9	25.6	16.4	26.7	0.8	11.0	19.5	1.6	22.0	19.0	7.1	46.5	3.8
Bradford County	5.0	20.0	15.6	27.6	13.8	20.5	2.3	10.0	25.9	6.3	31.6	13.4	4.8	41.1	2.7
Bucks County	3.6	15.3	12.9	38.4	10.7	29.7	0.2	9.0	12.0	0.5	22.7	17.9	3.9	51.7	3.3
Butler County	3.1	15.3	14.0	32.0	14.7	25.9	0.4	10.0	17.0	1.3	25.1	18.3	6.1	46.6	2.6
Cambria County	2.3	20.4	15.7	27.9	18.6	25.4	0.5	10.3	17.2	1.7	17.8	18.0	6.4	52.7	5.4
Cameron County	2.2	22.4	17.8	20.0	13.5	18.7	0.4	9.4	38.0	1.0	45.2	15.3	4.7	29.7	4.1
Carbon County	1.7	22.6	17.3	22.0	14.9	24.6	0.2	12.9	24.5	1.2	30.6	15.2	6.7	42.6	3.8
Centre County	4.0	11.2	9.9	41.6	16.5	23.5	0.6	6.7	11.1	1.7	15.4	11.8	3.1	64.6	3.5
Chester County	4.9	13.3	11.9	45.2	10.9	26.3	1.0	6.9	9.7	2.0	20.4	15.2	4.1	56.1	2.3
Clarion County	3.6	17.9	13.6	25.8	16.6	23.7	1.4	11.8	20.7	3.5	23.9	16.7	6.4	46.4	3.1
Clearfield County	2.8	20.3	15.1	23.1	15.3	24.9	0.9	11.7	24.1	3.3	25.4	19.1	7.2	40.8	4.3
Clinton County	3.1	20.8	15.1	23.6	15.8	23.5	1.1	11.1	24.9	2.7	30.8	14.8	4.5	42.9	4.2
Columbia County	2.6	17.9	14.3	23.7	16.2	25.4	0.9	9.5	24.4	1.9	29.5	14.7	5.2	45.4	3.3
Crawford County	4.3	19.2	15.6	26.4	15.7	21.5	1.4	9.2	25.9	3.5	32.2	13.3	4.3	42.7	4.0
Cumberland County	3.1	15.4	14.8	34.6	13.3	29.7	0.5	7.3	14.5	1.3	15.6	16.1	6.8	50.1	10.0
Dauphin County	2.6	17.6	14.5	34.9	14.0	28.8	0.4	7.7	14.2	0.7	16.2	14.2	6.8	50.1	12.0
Delaware County	2.7	17.2	12.9	39.3	13.3	29.3	0.1	8.4	9.7	0.2	15.6	14.4	5.7	60.7	3.5
Elk County	2.1	18.9	15.8	22.5	13.3	18.6	0.7	8.7	36.2	1.3	48.1	11.4	3.8	32.9	2.5
Erie County	2.3	17.1	13.9	29.2	16.3	25.6	0.5	7.8	20.5	1.0	28.5	14.7	3.5	49.4	2.9
Fayette County	2.0	24.9	14.7	23.0	16.7	25.2	0.7	12.8	20.7	3.2	22.5	18.4	7.2	45.2	3.5
Forest County	3.5	23.3	21.2	23.6	16.4	19.0	1.7	12.5	26.8	4.9	28.1	13.7	6.9	39.0	7.3
Franklin County	4.0	18.2	15.0	27.5	15.4	24.1	1.1	10.3	21.6	3.0	28.0	14.9	4.2	44.0	5.8
Fulton County	3.9	20.6	13.8	21.3	13.5	21.4	1.5	15.4	26.8	5.2	37.8	12.6	4.6	34.8	5.0
Greene County	3.3	22.4	14.7	24.9	17.4	21.9	0.8	18.7	16.4	8.1	18.3	14.2	8.1	44.9	6.3
Huntingdon County	3.8	19.5	14.7	24.8	17.2	19.8	1.4	12.5	24.2	3.9	30.8	12.0	4.2	41.7	7.5
Indiana County	3.1	18.4	12.5	26.0	17.7	25.8	1.5	11.7	17.3	5.1	16.8	16.0	7.0	52.4	2.7
Jefferson County	3.3	19.1	14.8	21.9	15.1	22.1	1.3	11.4	28.2	3.6	30.1	15.9	7.6	39.4	3.6
Juniata County	5.0	18.4	12.3	23.1	13.7	20.8	2.5	13.1	26.8	5.5	32.9	12.8	6.6	36.0	6.2
Lackawanna County	2.0	21.6	14.6	29.6	15.6	29.1	0.2	8.2	17.4	0.5	20.9	17.0	5.5	51.6	4.5
Lancaster County	4.8	16.0	12.0	28.1	13.9	24.9	1.1	10.0	22.0	2.9	30.2	17.5	4.3	43.1	2.0
Lawrence County	2.9	19.4	14.9	26.6	15.2	26.6	0.4	10.5	20.7	1.3	24.3	17.3	7.2	45.8	4.1
Lebanon County	4.0	17.1	14.7	25.4	16.0	23.9	1.1	10.4	23.2	2.8	28.4	16.2	4.6	44.2	3.8
Lehigh County	2.7	17.6	13.5	33.5	14.0	27.3	0.2	8.1	16.9	0.5	25.6	15.7	5.2	50.7	2.4
Luzerne County	2.1	22.3	15.9	27.7	15.2	28.1	0.2	9.8	19.0	0.7	22.5	17.2	5.8	48.4	5.4
Lycoming County	2.4	19.4	15.1	24.4	15.8	26.7	0.7	9.7	22.6	1.7	29.1	16.5	4.0	44.3	4.5
McKean County	2.4	19.9	16.7	25.9	16.1	20.9	0.8	8.9	27.5	2.5	33.5	12.0	5.0	42.6	4.4
Mercer County	3.2	19.0	15.0	27.6	17.3	25.3	0.6	8.2	21.0	1.6	25.2	17.2	5.0	46.8	4.2
Mifflin County	4.6	20.2	15.2	21.8	13.9	21.6	1.7	9.8	31.2	4.3	35.9	16.6	4.5	35.1	3.7
Monroe County	3.3	19.8	14.9	29.5	15.6	27.4	0.2	11.2	16.1	0.5	21.0	17.6	6.5	50.3	4.1
Montgomery County	3.6	13.8	12.3	44.5	10.5	28.2	0.1	6.9	9.9	0.3	20.7	15.2	3.2	57.9	2.7
Montour County	4.1	18.6	14.1	34.3	15.4	20.6	1.4	9.1	19.2	3.5	21.7	11.8	5.6	53.0	4.3
Northampton County	2.3	15.9	13.7	31.4	14.0	27.0	0.2	9.2	18.1	0.6	26.8	14.8	5.4	49.3	3.0
Northumberland County	2.6	21.2	16.0	22.9	17.1	22.8	0.9	9.9	26.5	2.1	27.5	16.2	6.0	41.5	6.7
Perry County	3.6	16.9	14.6	23.9	12.9	27.8	1.2	12.8	21.4	2.9	20.9	16.8	9.9	40.6	8.9
Philadelphia County	1.9	25.3	10.9	31.5	19.7	29.6	0.1	6.5	12.5	0.1	12.7	13.4	5.9	60.4	7.4
Pike County	3.4	19.4	17.4	28.6	17.6	26.6	0.4	12.6	14.3	0.7	19.0	17.2	6.5	51.9	4.7

Table B-3. States and Counties — **Education, Labor Force, and Income**

STATE County	Median household income	Median family income: All families	Families with children: Married-couple	Families with children: Male householder	Families with children: Female householder	Median nonfamily household income	Median income for full-year, full-time workers: Men	Median income for full-year, full-time workers: Women	Per capita income	Households by source of income (percent): With earnings	With interest, dividend, or rental income	With Social Security income	With public assistance income	With retirement income	Households with income over $100,000 (percent)	+/– U.S. percent for income over $100,000	Households with income below poverty (percent)	Families with children with income below poverty (percent)
	57	58	59	60	61	62	63	64	65	66	67	68	69	70	71	72	73	74
OREGON—Cont'd																		
Morrow County	37 521	40 731	43 427	24 500	16 800	25 318	34 182	24 332	15 802	84.5	31.4	24.7	5.4	14.7	5.3	-7.0	11.3	17.2
Multnomah County	41 278	51 118	59 751	30 578	21 483	29 100	36 830	30 250	22 606	82.6	39.2	21.5	4.2	14.1	10.5	-1.8	11.4	12.9
Polk County	42 311	50 483	55 815	32 500	20 558	22 402	37 616	26 803	19 282	78.5	40.2	29.3	3.1	20.2	8.4	-3.9	10.9	11.2
Sherman County	35 142	42 563	49 107	23 750	12 321	21 477	33 611	21 667	17 448	74.3	42.2	36.2	1.5	19.2	5.6	-6.7	14.5	17.6
Tillamook County	34 269	40 197	46 010	36 776	15 764	21 694	32 479	22 604	19 052	71.4	39.4	37.6	3.2	22.6	5.4	-6.9	10.9	14.1
Umatilla County	36 249	41 850	49 194	25 784	16 598	21 008	32 213	22 924	16 410	80.9	31.9	27.4	3.4	15.9	5.5	-6.8	11.6	14.1
Union County	33 738	40 520	47 246	31 786	16 359	16 894	35 149	22 160	16 907	75.8	37.0	30.0	4.2	17.2	5.3	-7.0	15.0	12.3
Wallowa County	32 129	38 682	46 283	21 875	14 375	16 463	30 604	22 150	17 276	73.9	42.8	35.9	2.7	19.6	5.9	-6.4	14.5	17.2
Wasco County	35 959	42 412	50 324	28 167	13 962	20 561	37 075	22 267	17 195	75.6	36.3	32.5	4.2	20.9	5.8	-6.5	12.0	15.9
Washington County	52 122	61 499	68 678	34 035	26 063	33 432	45 056	31 721	24 969	87.7	43.2	17.8	2.3	12.9	16.1	3.8	6.4	7.4
Wheeler County	28 750	34 048	34 375	23 750	13 750	20 568	34 028	25 139	15 884	70.9	39.9	44.1	2.8	27.9	4.2	-8.1	13.9	22.7
Yamhill County	44 111	50 336	55 470	32 045	19 627	24 652	36 727	26 123	18 951	81.4	37.5	25.4	3.0	17.1	8.9	-3.4	9.0	8.9
PENNSYLVANIA	40 106	49 184	60 167	29 595	19 585	22 205	38 176	27 365	20 880	76.7	40.4	30.4	3.1	19.7	10.3	-2.0	11.0	12.1
Adams County	42 704	48 810	54 304	30 411	21 816	23 736	34 625	24 152	18 577	82.1	43.8	27.4	1.8	18.8	7.0	-5.3	7.1	7.5
Allegheny County	38 329	49 815	63 537	30 822	18 749	22 106	40 118	28 532	22 491	74.9	41.7	31.9	3.1	20.1	10.5	-1.8	11.5	13.1
Armstrong County	31 557	38 271	45 003	26 643	16 134	16 335	31 502	21 478	15 709	70.0	36.9	35.8	3.3	24.3	4.1	-8.2	12.0	14.0
Beaver County	36 995	45 495	56 329	26 327	18 266	19 027	36 829	24 959	18 402	73.1	38.9	35.4	2.9	24.6	6.1	-6.2	9.7	12.1
Bedford County	32 731	37 741	42 311	22 288	16 885	17 465	29 364	20 500	16 316	74.8	34.9	33.1	2.0	19.4	3.9	-8.4	11.1	10.7
Berks County	44 714	52 997	62 633	31 522	20 696	24 751	39 693	26 669	21 232	79.7	44.7	29.2	2.4	19.1	10.2	-2.1	8.8	10.3
Blair County	32 861	40 160	46 941	25 382	14 456	17 302	31 586	22 318	16 743	73.8	35.3	33.7	3.0	17.9	4.6	-7.7	12.8	14.8
Bradford County	35 038	40 664	47 955	23 750	19 442	19 929	31 776	23 048	17 148	75.3	38.4	32.8	3.0	20.7	5.5	-6.8	11.7	13.5
Bucks County	59 727	68 727	78 404	40 397	29 976	32 722	48 095	32 902	27 430	84.6	47.8	24.7	1.4	17.1	21.6	9.3	4.8	4.2
Butler County	42 308	51 215	60 004	26 845	19 750	21 311	40 826	26 153	20 794	78.7	42.5	27.6	1.8	19.9	10.5	-1.8	9.4	8.4
Cambria County	30 179	37 797	46 399	23 094	13 403	15 954	30 683	21 763	16 058	68.0	38.6	38.9	3.1	27.1	4.1	-8.2	13.2	15.7
Cameron County	32 212	39 479	49 052	31 667	22 778	17 500	31 264	24 235	15 968	73.1	32.7	37.4	2.2	23.1	3.0	-9.3	10.3	9.8
Carbon County	35 113	42 118	50 394	31 094	18 232	18 047	32 882	22 431	17 064	72.3	36.6	36.2	1.9	23.2	4.2	-8.1	9.8	11.7
Centre County	36 165	50 557	57 568	25 471	22 024	20 041	35 016	25 739	18 020	83.4	43.1	22.0	1.2	16.1	8.5	-3.8	17.7	8.7
Chester County	65 295	76 916	88 591	39 104	30 968	36 196	52 361	35 885	31 627	85.6	51.6	23.2	1.2	16.8	27.4	15.1	5.0	4.4
Clarion County	30 770	37 964	45 395	21 319	11 725	16 872	30 685	20 237	15 243	74.0	37.7	32.5	2.8	19.9	3.9	-8.4	16.1	16.2
Clearfield County	31 357	38 004	42 294	25 321	13 596	16 681	29 949	20 840	16 010	72.8	36.6	33.9	3.0	20.0	4.0	-8.3	12.7	15.4
Clinton County	31 064	38 177	44 705	26 250	15 286	16 415	30 550	20 757	15 750	72.1	35.1	34.8	2.7	19.7	4.4	-7.9	13.5	15.5
Columbia County	34 094	41 398	49 083	25 931	19 151	18 418	30 939	22 222	16 973	76.2	40.5	31.8	1.7	18.6	5.3	-7.0	12.4	11.1
Crawford County	33 560	40 755	46 763	24 647	16 801	18 633	33 338	22 183	16 870	74.8	39.0	32.6	3.5	19.0	5.5	-6.8	12.2	14.0
Cumberland County	46 707	56 406	63 682	31 327	26 378	27 289	40 297	28 735	23 610	81.1	49.2	26.7	1.2	22.1	12.0	-0.3	6.6	6.2
Dauphin County	41 507	50 974	63 796	29 568	21 221	26 686	37 566	28 725	22 134	80.1	39.6	26.0	2.6	20.5	9.8	-2.5	9.4	12.0
Delaware County	50 092	61 590	73 904	35 789	25 387	28 168	45 950	32 693	25 040	79.2	43.8	30.0	2.6	20.2	16.8	4.5	7.9	8.6
Elk County	37 550	46 402	54 013	30 616	17 807	19 421	34 900	23 232	18 174	75.7	42.8	33.4	2.1	21.8	3.9	-8.4	7.4	8.3
Erie County	36 627	44 829	53 258	26 968	16 891	20 308	36 226	24 646	17 932	78.0	41.0	28.8	3.6	18.1	6.4	-5.9	11.7	13.5
Fayette County	27 451	34 881	42 032	21 070	12 105	13 943	31 075	21 384	15 274	67.8	29.5	36.9	4.9	21.8	4.2	-8.1	18.2	22.6
Forest County	27 581	34 257	41 950	25 000	19 028	16 179	28 537	21 563	14 341	66.5	28.2	41.7	2.3	29.4	2.8	-9.5	12.7	12.4
Franklin County	40 476	47 075	54 004	29 107	18 033	22 364	34 017	24 391	19 339	77.7	41.0	29.2	1.7	23.1	6.5	-5.8	7.9	8.3
Fulton County	34 882	40 341	44 683	27 450	14 271	19 288	30 334	20 918	16 409	76.7	35.0	29.5	2.0	19.2	3.6	-8.7	11.3	12.9
Greene County	30 352	37 435	45 567	25 395	12 068	16 233	33 048	21 997	14 959	70.1	31.6	34.0	4.9	22.3	4.4	-7.9	15.9	19.6
Huntingdon County	33 313	40 388	45 406	28 952	15 432	17 197	30 572	22 313	15 379	73.6	33.8	33.0	2.5	22.1	4.1	-8.2	11.7	12.1
Indiana County	30 233	38 386	42 710	25 556	15 695	15 218	31 172	21 391	15 312	74.2	35.9	31.5	2.3	20.3	4.8	-7.5	16.8	14.9
Jefferson County	31 722	37 364	42 507	27 866	14 259	16 953	30 993	20 795	16 186	72.7	39.7	34.7	2.9	20.2	3.9	-8.4	11.8	13.9
Juniata County	34 698	39 757	43 365	27 035	19 044	19 459	30 451	21 654	16 142	77.3	41.3	30.5	1.5	17.4	4.0	-8.3	9.5	9.7
Lackawanna County	34 438	44 949	55 005	27 068	16 767	17 301	34 752	24 386	18 710	71.4	41.1	37.9	2.6	20.9	7.0	-5.3	11.6	11.4
Lancaster County	45 507	52 513	59 032	31 875	21 376	26 348	37 964	25 832	20 398	82.7	44.3	26.5	1.8	16.9	9.7	-2.6	7.0	8.0
Lawrence County	33 152	41 463	49 523	25 417	13 958	15 934	33 984	22 178	16 835	72.0	37.8	37.7	3.7	22.3	5.6	-6.7	12.2	15.4
Lebanon County	40 838	48 906	55 682	26 000	19 339	22 691	34 802	24 855	19 773	78.8	41.8	30.4	1.8	20.6	7.7	-4.6	7.4	8.9
Lehigh County	43 449	53 147	64 278	30 677	20 552	25 579	39 869	27 651	21 897	78.0	45.9	29.9	2.5	20.2	11.9	-0.4	8.6	10.9
Luzerne County	33 771	43 335	53 255	26 213	16 115	17 782	33 621	24 164	18 228	71.9	39.6	36.8	2.7	21.6	6.1	-6.2	11.9	12.9
Lycoming County	34 016	41 040	49 105	24 006	16 508	18 389	31 486	21 944	17 224	75.9	39.5	32.3	2.5	20.0	5.7	-6.6	11.9	13.0
McKean County	33 040	40 924	47 051	23 074	15 339	18 711	32 224	22 475	16 777	74.3	37.5	33.1	3.2	21.2	4.1	-8.2	12.5	16.9
Mercer County	34 666	41 776	50 629	28 099	14 686	19 975	34 956	22 470	17 636	73.7	41.0	34.8	3.2	24.2	5.4	-6.9	11.0	14.9
Mifflin County	32 175	38 486	45 103	24 292	13 795	15 364	31 143	20 713	15 553	72.5	37.3	34.0	3.1	18.6	3.8	-8.5	13.8	12.7
Monroe County	46 257	51 995	61 374	36 707	23 100	25 828	41 037	26 723	20 011	80.8	36.4	28.7	2.0	19.2	10.9	-1.4	8.7	8.5
Montgomery County	60 829	72 183	83 635	40 414	32 458	35 360	50 440	36 023	30 898	83.1	51.9	26.8	1.2	17.0	23.5	11.2	4.7	4.1
Montour County	38 075	45 224	55 473	30 893	19 188	21 273	33 944	24 900	19 302	77.6	41.4	30.8	1.9	21.9	8.9	-3.4	7.5	7.5
Northampton County	45 234	53 955	63 646	32 691	21 656	24 157	40 503	27 466	21 399	77.9	44.9	31.0	1.9	21.0	11.1	-1.2	8.1	8.6
Northumberland County	31 314	39 551	47 180	25 878	15 591	16 092	30 928	21 506	16 489	71.4	37.7	36.4	2.2	21.6	3.5	-8.8	12.7	13.9
Perry County	41 909	47 997	54 337	28 646	20 906	21 856	35 017	25 417	18 551	81.4	39.7	25.4	1.9	17.8	6.2	-6.1	7.5	8.2
Philadelphia County	30 746	37 036	52 612	27 170	17 875	20 323	35 342	29 239	16 509	71.8	24.3	28.5	8.7	17.4	6.3	-6.0	21.8	26.0
Pike County	44 608	49 340	54 854	36 492	22 454	25 071	40 627	26 837	20 315	76.1	35.9	32.0	1.6	24.1	9.2	-3.1	6.9	7.6

Table B-3. States and Counties — Education, Labor Force, and Income

STATE/ County code	MSA/PMSA/ NECMA code[1]	STATE County	High school graduates			College graduates		College graduates (percent)				
			Total population 25 years and over	Percent with a high school diploma or less	Percent with a high school diploma or more	Percent with a bachelor's degree or more	+/- U.S. percent with bachelor's degree or more	Non-Hispanic White	Black or African American	American Indian and Alaska Native	Asian, Hawaiian, and Pacific Islander	Hispanic or Latino[2]
			1	2	3	4	5	6	7	8	9	10
		PENNSYLVANIA— Cont'd										
42 105	...	Potter County	12 144	66.7	80.6	12.3	-12.1	12.2	0.0	0.0	41.1	12.8
42 107	...	Schuylkill County..........	108 010	71.1	77.2	10.7	-13.7	10.9	1.8	1.5	41.1	3.7
42 109	...	Snyder County	24 217	73.2	73.2	12.5	-11.9	12.6	4.6	0.0	0.0	6.2
42 111	3680	Somerset County	55 956	72.9	77.5	10.8	-13.6	11.0	1.6	0.0	6.7	5.2
42 113	...	Sullivan County	4 659	67.6	78.0	12.8	-11.6	12.9	0.0	0.0	0.0	0.0
42 115	...	Susquehanna County....	28 581	64.7	82.5	13.2	-11.2	13.2	8.1	11.1	36.6	25.8
42 117	...	Tioga County................	27 176	64.2	80.5	14.2	-10.2	14.1	23.9	9.8	51.0	23.3
42 119	...	Union County	27 521	65.9	73.1	18.0	-6.4	20.5	1.8	8.0	18.0	2.9
42 121	...	Venango County	39 366	68.4	81.0	13.1	-11.3	13.2	7.2	0.0	14.7	4.9
42 123	...	Warren County	30 535	63.7	84.8	14.2	-10.2	14.2	17.2	20.4	41.0	13.8
42 125	6280	Washington County.......	142 118	60.0	82.6	18.8	-5.6	19.0	10.2	6.1	45.2	13.2
42 127	...	Wayne County	33 326	62.8	80.7	14.6	-9.8	14.7	6.8	10.5	24.0	9.1
42 129	6280	Westmoreland County...	263 593	55.6	85.6	20.2	-4.2	20.2	12.3	13.2	59.9	20.1
42 131	7560	Wyoming County	18 741	61.6	83.7	15.4	-9.0	15.3	16.0	27.6	26.0	45.1
42 133	9280	York County	259 040	60.9	80.7	18.4	-6.0	18.7	9.8	7.3	36.3	10.8
44 000	...	RHODE ISLAND	694 573	49.8	78.0	25.6	1.2	27.3	16.7	14.1	35.9	8.6
44 001	6483	Bristol County	34 218	42.7	80.7	34.3	9.9	34.1	32.4	32.3	75.8	37.3
44 003	6483	Kent County	116 628	47.2	83.9	24.8	0.4	24.5	34.0	7.0	46.8	23.8
44 005	...	Newport County	59 084	36.4	87.7	38.3	13.9	39.3	17.8	22.3	48.3	26.1
44 007	6483	Providence County.......	403 779	55.6	72.5	21.3	-3.1	23.4	15.6	12.4	31.2	7.0
44 009	6483	Washington County.......	80 864	37.4	88.6	35.5	11.1	35.7	20.6	17.5	49.3	31.2
45 000	...	SOUTH CAROLINA ...	2 596 010	53.6	76.3	20.4	-4.0	24.3	9.9	11.2	39.8	14.1
45 001	...	Abbeville County	17 068	65.8	70.1	12.8	-11.6	15.9	4.2	0.0	46.5	37.3
45 003	0600	Aiken County................	92 922	54.0	77.7	19.9	-4.5	23.4	9.0	12.1	40.7	10.0
45 005	...	Allendale County	7 094	71.3	60.0	9.3	-15.1	19.2	4.7	0.0	0.0	0.0
45 007	3160	Anderson County	111 037	59.3	73.4	15.9	-8.5	17.3	7.4	8.1	42.8	17.9
45 009	...	Bamberg County	10 213	63.6	64.7	15.4	-9.0	19.7	11.6	100.0	0.0	37.5
45 011	...	Barnwell County	14 770	67.2	67.5	11.6	-12.8	14.8	6.4	6.7	65.2	13.2
45 013	...	Beaufort County	78 502	36.3	87.8	33.2	8.8	40.7	10.8	10.7	31.9	13.1
45 015	1440	Berkeley County............	86 015	54.1	80.2	14.4	-10.0	15.4	10.0	12.8	28.4	14.8
45 017	...	Calhoun County	10 266	62.5	72.8	14.2	-10.2	20.4	6.5	22.6	9.4	0.0
45 019	1440	Charleston County	199 361	41.4	81.5	30.7	6.3	40.4	10.7	19.6	41.2	18.9
45 021	3160	Cherokee County	34 283	69.9	66.7	11.8	-12.6	13.1	6.0	0.0	28.6	14.5
45 023	...	Chester County	22 043	69.0	67.1	9.6	-14.8	11.9	5.0	0.0	22.7	21.2
45 025	...	Chesterfield County.......	27 760	60.4	65.2	9.7	-14.7	11.7	4.2	12.8	52.7	20.0
45 027	...	Clarendon County	20 698	69.2	65.3	11.4	-13.0	17.7	5.0	36.5	0.0	5.9
45 029	...	Colleton County	24 716	67.3	69.6	11.5	-12.9	14.7	6.6	0.0	33.3	7.7
45 031	...	Darlington County	43 512	63.2	69.3	13.5	-10.9	17.4	6.7	10.2	30.1	18.4
45 033	...	Dillon County	18 867	72.9	60.7	9.2	-15.2	12.1	5.1	2.7	8.9	5.7
45 035	1440	Dorchester County	61 334	47.5	82.2	21.4	-3.0	24.4	11.7	14.3	46.9	9.6
45 037	0600	Edgefield County	16 227	64.0	71.4	12.5	-11.9	17.7	5.0	17.2	34.2	0.0
45 039	...	Fairfield County	15 244	68.7	67.0	11.7	-12.7	20.5	4.5	0.0	100.0	2.1
45 041	2655	Florence County	80 904	57.8	73.1	18.7	-5.7	23.6	9.0	17.3	58.6	13.2
45 043	...	Georgetown County	37 340	55.0	75.2	20.0	-4.4	26.0	7.7	47.6	53.8	10.5
45 045	3160	Greenville County	250 258	46.8	79.5	26.2	1.8	29.6	11.1	7.4	43.5	14.6
45 047	...	Greenwood County	42 412	56.6	73.1	18.9	-5.5	24.0	7.1	9.0	37.6	5.0
45 049	...	Hampton County	13 668	70.8	66.9	10.1	-14.3	14.5	6.3	18.4	22.5	2.9
45 051	5330	Horry County	136 551	51.0	81.1	18.7	-5.7	20.4	8.0	12.4	28.4	10.8
45 053	...	Jasper County	13 112	70.8	65.2	8.7	-15.7	11.5	5.9	6.0	32.2	6.3
45 055	...	Kershaw County	34 863	60.1	75.4	16.3	-8.1	18.5	9.9	7.0	8.3	11.8
45 057	...	Lancaster County	40 520	65.8	69.8	10.2	-14.2	11.6	5.5	10.5	26.5	14.4
45 059	...	Laurens County	45 470	67.3	67.7	11.7	-12.7	13.7	5.2	14.2	39.6	7.2
45 061	...	Lee County	12 918	73.7	61.4	9.2	-15.2	14.3	5.7	0.0	0.0	5.8
45 063	1760	Lexington County	142 083	46.5	83.0	24.6	0.2	26.0	13.2	8.6	46.9	17.8
45 065	...	McCormick County........	7 192	64.4	66.1	16.0	-8.4	26.9	4.3	X	100.0	6.9
45 067	...	Marion County	22 224	70.5	68.0	10.2	-14.2	14.2	6.5	0.0	73.7	0.3
45 069	...	Marlboro County	18 482	74.1	60.9	8.3	-16.1	10.4	5.8	5.6	58.0	19.8
45 071	...	Newberry County	23 881	64.4	69.1	14.8	-9.6	19.8	4.2	27.5	52.6	5.2
45 073	...	Oconee County	45 896	59.3	73.9	18.2	-6.2	18.9	7.3	14.4	67.4	12.5
45 075	...	Orangeburg County.......	57 037	60.1	71.5	16.3	-8.1	18.1	15.0	7.8	25.6	4.1
45 077	3160	Pickens County	66 787	57.1	73.7	19.1	-5.3	19.2	9.5	5.6	68.6	12.8
45 079	1760	Richland County	198 703	37.7	85.2	32.5	8.1	43.5	18.0	21.9	50.1	23.0
45 081	...	Saluda County..............	12 654	69.3	69.3	11.9	-12.5	15.6	3.9	0.0	25.7	1.3
45 083	3160	Spartanburg County.......	167 802	56.8	73.1	18.2	-6.2	20.6	8.0	10.0	26.1	14.2

[1]MSA = Metropolitan Statistical Area. PMSA = Primary MSA. NECMA = New England County Metropolitan Area. See the Appendix A for explanation of these concepts. See Appendix B for list of metropolitan areas identified by type, with component counties.
[2]Hispanic or Latino persons may be of any race.

Table B-3. States and Counties — Education, Labor Force, and Income

STATE County	School enrollment			Population 16 to 19 years				Employment status, 2000			Work status in 1999 of the population 16 years and over (percent)		
											Worked in 1999		
	Grades kindergarten through 12	College or graduate school	Percent private	Number	Percent in armed forces	Percent high school graduates	Percent not enrolled, not grads, not in armed forces, not employed	Total population 16 years and over	Percent in labor force	Unemployment rate	Full-time	Part-time	Did not work in 1999
	11	12	13	14	15	16	17	18	19	20	21	22	23
PENNSYLVANIA— Cont'd													
Potter County	3 590	301	6.5	947	0.0	17.7	3.7	13 916	59.8	6.2	50.5	13.4	36.1
Schuylkill County	24 600	4 303	14.0	6 825	0.1	11.1	5.2	122 842	55.3	5.9	48.8	13.8	37.4
Snyder County	6 727	2 379	29.6	2 487	0.0	9.2	3.7	29 592	62.6	3.8	52.2	16.9	30.8
Somerset County	14 074	1 978	8.0	4 227	0.0	11.8	3.5	64 519	56.8	5.7	48.3	13.9	37.8
Sullivan County	1 140	165	8.7	535	0.0	11.0	11.8	5 476	54.8	8.9	44.1	14.1	41.8
Susquehanna County	8 458	1 028	9.0	2 370	0.0	10.8	4.6	32 843	60.7	4.3	51.0	14.3	34.7
Tioga County	7 667	2 767	7.0	2 805	0.0	9.6	1.8	32 893	59.3	6.0	49.8	15.1	35.1
Union County	6 646	3 717	37.8	3 014	0.0	6.7	3.8	34 270	49.5	3.9	51.9	19.4	28.7
Venango County	11 097	1 398	10.9	3 341	0.0	9.2	3.6	45 521	58.1	7.2	47.6	15.0	37.4
Warren County	8 301	1 060	9.8	2 277	0.1	11.0	4.7	34 582	62.2	5.1	52.5	13.5	34.0
Washington County	34 487	8 902	12.3	10 346	0.0	9.2	3.1	163 159	58.9	5.2	48.4	14.6	36.9
Wayne County	8 953	1 318	10.5	2 409	0.0	12.5	4.3	37 677	57.0	5.7	49.6	14.0	36.5
Westmoreland County	63 187	14 834	13.8	17 603	0.1	9.3	2.4	298 300	59.4	5.1	49.0	14.6	36.5
Wyoming County	5 615	1 011	13.3	1 662	0.0	9.3	1.6	21 870	61.6	4.9	51.0	15.8	33.2
York County	71 383	13 146	15.2	19 672	0.1	12.0	4.0	298 226	68.2	3.6	58.4	14.8	26.7
RHODE ISLAND	190 389	84 009	22.7	61 409	0.3	8.7	4.6	827 797	64.6	5.6	52.6	17.4	30.0
Bristol County	9 004	4 188	33.0	3 024	0.0	6.8	2.2	40 300	65.0	4.8	51.2	18.9	29.9
Kent County	29 276	8 945	17.2	7 752	0.0	11.1	3.3	132 876	67.7	4.3	54.5	17.3	28.1
Newport County	14 785	6 086	24.1	4 400	3.6	11.1	3.9	68 299	68.4	4.9	55.9	17.6	26.5
Providence County	115 371	51 819	25.4	38 449	0.0	8.9	5.9	488 469	62.2	6.2	51.4	16.5	32.1
Washington County	21 953	12 971	10.9	7 784	0.0	4.6	0.8	97 853	69.1	5.1	54.0	21.2	24.8
SOUTH CAROLINA	767 586	216 839	12.0	235 984	3.0	13.2	6.4	3 114 016	63.4	5.7	55.8	12.8	31.5
Abbeville County	5 041	1 241	16.5	1 566	0.0	8.0	4.9	20 254	60.2	5.1	53.7	11.5	34.8
Aiken County	28 650	6 691	10.6	8 068	0.1	10.1	5.9	109 551	62.0	5.9	54.3	12.0	33.7
Allendale County	2 505	439	5.0	699	0.0	8.0	14.6	8 595	44.5	10.1	38.4	9.3	52.4
Anderson County	29 839	6 724	10.8	8 498	0.0	13.2	8.0	129 319	62.9	4.3	55.8	11.9	32.4
Bamberg County	3 485	1 135	16.1	1 424	1.3	12.8	3.4	13 013	51.8	11.6	44.5	11.3	44.2
Barnwell County	5 287	669	5.2	1 439	0.0	11.0	5.0	17 631	57.9	7.7	52.5	10.3	37.2
Beaufort County	20 802	4 807	15.0	7 076	30.5	39.5	3.0	95 640	61.8	3.6	53.6	13.4	33.0
Berkeley County	30 440	6 897	11.0	10 369	18.0	31.1	4.1	107 155	65.7	4.6	60.4	11.6	28.1
Calhoun County	2 971	462	15.7	791	0.0	9.9	5.9	11 846	58.9	5.9	53.9	9.9	36.3
Charleston County	55 508	25 683	17.6	18 939	1.1	9.1	4.8	244 381	63.7	5.8	55.2	14.5	30.3
Cherokee County	9 811	1 664	8.3	2 788	0.0	15.7	10.5	40 344	62.2	6.2	57.1	11.2	31.7
Chester County	6 922	800	5.5	1 880	0.0	15.3	13.1	25 880	61.3	6.8	56.7	9.2	34.1
Chesterfield County	8 840	1 026	8.4	2 324	0.1	11.8	9.5	32 642	59.5	8.9	53.8	9.4	36.8
Clarendon County	7 083	883	9.3	2 077	0.0	10.2	9.1	25 114	51.2	6.7	47.1	9.3	43.7
Colleton County	7 878	1 129	10.8	2 146	0.0	10.1	11.4	29 001	56.2	6.4	50.0	10.4	39.7
Darlington County	14 074	2 538	12.2	3 497	0.0	9.7	7.1	51 476	60.8	8.0	53.0	11.2	35.9
Dillon County	6 996	835	6.9	1 941	0.3	11.3	9.6	22 828	59.7	8.7	54.3	9.1	36.6
Dorchester County	21 791	4 471	13.3	5 397	0.0	11.3	5.0	71 831	65.8	4.7	58.3	12.3	29.4
Edgefield County	4 936	829	9.0	1 542	0.0	10.6	14.7	19 342	53.0	6.4	46.4	10.6	43.0
Fairfield County	4 946	646	10.5	1 271	0.0	14.1	4.1	17 969	60.3	6.9	54.3	8.9	36.8
Florence County	25 584	6 166	11.0	7 754	0.1	10.5	6.1	97 016	62.4	7.9	53.7	12.7	33.6
Georgetown County	10 912	1 500	5.8	2 997	0.0	11.2	6.5	43 417	58.2	6.2	51.0	11.8	37.2
Greenville County	69 888	20 732	21.3	20 669	0.0	9.5	5.4	296 250	66.8	4.6	58.1	13.9	28.0
Greenwood County	12 478	4 024	8.8	3 786	0.3	9.6	10.7	51 171	63.1	6.3	54.6	13.1	32.3
Hampton County	4 917	633	11.0	1 292	0.2	11.7	5.7	16 228	51.4	6.1	46.0	10.3	43.8
Horry County	31 435	8 531	8.3	10 024	0.0	12.3	7.6	159 541	64.2	4.6	55.9	14.0	30.2
Jasper County	4 429	578	20.3	1 233	0.0	11.4	10.0	15 694	57.4	3.9	51.5	10.3	38.3
Kershaw County	10 443	1 348	6.7	2 747	0.0	15.4	6.6	40 442	65.6	5.3	57.4	11.8	30.8
Lancaster County	12 038	1 936	6.3	3 320	0.0	13.1	10.1	47 434	63.3	6.4	57.6	10.6	31.8
Laurens County	13 504	2 822	14.9	4 189	0.0	10.9	8.1	53 977	62.4	7.1	55.5	10.9	33.6
Lee County	4 312	465	16.1	1 109	0.0	14.4	7.6	15 494	53.8	10.0	49.9	9.8	40.3
Lexington County	41 574	10 063	7.0	10 975	0.2	12.6	3.8	165 705	69.5	3.7	61.5	12.7	25.8
McCormick County	1 737	255	11.4	521	0.0	9.0	13.8	8 281	43.5	5.8	38.7	10.1	51.2
Marion County	7 824	1 234	6.5	2 204	0.2	10.8	5.9	26 835	58.4	9.8	54.9	9.3	35.8
Marlboro County	5 872	698	7.3	1 682	0.0	12.5	11.4	22 143	54.4	8.2	52.0	8.6	39.4
Newberry County	6 688	1 525	15.3	2 200	0.0	8.5	9.5	28 403	60.7	7.8	54.2	11.1	34.7
Oconee County	11 032	2 461	8.1	3 211	0.4	13.9	6.7	52 823	59.7	4.3	53.3	11.4	35.3
Orangeburg County	18 826	6 858	13.7	6 474	0.0	9.2	5.8	70 658	57.0	8.5	49.8	12.0	38.2
Pickens County	17 757	15 364	7.5	8 600	0.0	6.3	4.4	88 523	63.6	5.4	54.6	17.4	28.0
Richland County	59 220	31 645	12.2	23 297	11.5	17.6	5.6	252 390	67.6	6.3	57.9	15.7	26.4
Saluda County	3 701	509	4.8	1 109	0.0	9.0	9.7	14 908	61.7	5.0	55.9	9.9	34.2
Spartanburg County	46 790	11 226	11.8	13 520	0.1	11.4	7.6	197 290	64.3	5.5	56.9	12.3	30.9

	Full-year full-time employed (percent)								Children under 18 years in families					+/− U.S. percent two-income couples	Total employed by class of worker (percent)			
											With two parents (percent)								
STATE County	Total	Men	Women	Non-Hispanic White	Black or African American	American Indian and Alaska Native	Asian, Hawaiian, and Pacific Islander	Hispanic or Latino[1]	Number	Both in labor force	Father only in labor force	With one parent who is in labor force (percent)	+/− U.S. percent of children with no stay-at-home parent (percent)		Private	Government	Self-employed	Unpaid family worker
	24	25	26	27	28	29	30	31	32	33	34	35	36	37	38	39	40	41
PENNSYLVANIA— Cont'd																		
Potter County	37.0	48.3	26.3	37.1	75.0	25.0	35.4	41.5	4 434	48.8	25.3	16.4	0.6	-4.4	73.8	12.1	13.4	0.8
Schuylkill County	37.5	48.0	27.2	37.8	26.8	18.8	36.7	29.8	29 881	48.8	20.2	20.3	4.5	-4.4	79.8	11.4	8.4	0.4
Snyder County	39.2	52.8	26.4	39.7	11.2	9.1	3.1	23.3	8 714	47.6	30.5	14.5	-2.5	-0.8	74.8	13.1	11.3	0.7
Somerset County	35.2	44.6	26.0	35.9	8.7	31.9	43.7	11.9	17 282	53.4	23.5	14.7	3.5	-3.2	77.1	11.2	11.0	0.7
Sullivan County	31.4	39.1	23.5	32.7	7.3	7.1	0.0	0.0	1 165	54.1	15.1	20.3	9.8	-8.0	66.2	19.6	13.7	0.4
Susquehanna County	38.9	48.9	29.2	39.0	44.6	40.0	31.4	43.8	10 226	48.5	22.7	19.5	3.4	-1.6	74.2	11.2	14.1	0.5
Tioga County	36.1	45.8	27.0	36.3	13.2	36.8	13.0	16.8	9 132	49.5	21.6	20.3	5.2	-3.1	72.6	14.3	12.3	0.7
Union County	33.3	39.8	25.0	35.7	21.0	11.5	9.3	17.2	8 018	48.9	29.8	12.2	-3.5	-1.3	76.4	11.9	11.1	0.6
Venango County	35.9	46.2	26.4	36.2	18.5	25.0	37.5	16.1	13 025	45.9	21.7	22.0	3.3	-4.0	74.8	15.6	9.2	0.4
Warren County	41.4	52.2	31.3	41.5	35.5	37.9	35.3	28.9	10 067	49.9	21.6	19.4	4.7	0.3	77.3	13.2	9.1	0.3
Washington County	37.4	48.6	27.4	37.5	33.3	50.0	42.3	37.6	43 517	47.2	26.3	16.6	-0.8	-4.5	81.5	9.9	8.2	0.3
Wayne County	36.3	45.2	27.5	00.5	02.4	20.6	37.8	20.0	11 026	48.8	20.8	17.4	1.6	-4.8	73.0	12.7	13.8	0.6
Westmoreland County	37.9	49.6	27.3	38.0	32.2	41.1	45.1	36.7	78 604	48.6	26.7	15.8	-0.2	-4.6	81.8	9.7	8.2	0.3
Wyoming County	38.9	50.9	27.5	39.0	18.2	24.1	50.0	28.8	6 735	44.6	26.8	17.7	-2.3	-5.4	78.6	9.8	11.1	0.5
York County	47.2	59.1	36.0	47.8	39.2	38.3	43.6	36.5	89 612	51.7	21.6	19.9	7.0	6.1	82.5	9.4	7.8	0.3
RHODE ISLAND	40.0	50.2	31.0	41.0	33.8	34.7	34.0	33.0	237 201	46.6	17.0	21.0	3.0	3.3	77.3	13.8	8.7	0.2
Bristol County	39.7	50.6	29.9	39.8	17.9	37.2	47.7	30.8	11 347	56.2	22.1	15.8	7.4	4.0	75.9	12.7	11.2	0.2
Kent County	44.2	56.1	33.6	44.2	43.8	47.2	36.1	47.9	37 559	54.8	18.4	17.8	8.0	5.4	78.3	13.4	8.2	0.1
Newport County	42.8	54.7	31.9	42.9	40.2	38.9	49.2	36.9	18 673	51.5	21.2	19.7	6.6	4.1	70.4	17.6	11.8	0.2
Providence County	38.3	47.5	30.2	39.7	33.1	32.6	33.0	32.3	141 923	41.4	15.1	23.0	-0.2	1.3	79.8	12.4	7.5	0.2
Washington County	41.0	52.3	30.7	41.5	30.0	35.3	29.4	34.8	27 699	55.0	20.1	18.0	8.4	7.7	69.5	18.6	11.7	0.3
SOUTH CAROLINA	41.7	51.0	33.2	44.2	35.8	42.5	40.3	39.8	937 333	41.4	18.6	25.8	2.6	0.1	75.0	15.9	8.8	0.3
Abbeville County	39.6	50.8	29.7	40.3	38.0	0.0	48.0	35.6	6 022	41.7	18.7	25.2	2.3	-3.3	76.6	14.8	8.3	0.2
Aiken County	41.8	52.4	32.3	42.8	00.5	53.3	35.8	41.6	34 725	41.9	19.7	25.4	2.7	-2.4	73.6	18.7	7.5	0.2
Allendale County	28.3	30.1	26.4	37.5	24.7	0.0	0.0	24.6	2 609	21.0	14.9	34.8	-8.8	-8.0	65.8	24.1	9.2	0.9
Anderson County	43.2	53.7	33.7	43.8	40.7	19.1	37.3	41.6	38 043	42.7	21.1	23.7	1.8	0.5	78.9	12.2	8.7	0.2
Bamberg County	31.0	00.5	00.0	00.0	05.4	11.8	100.0	24.5	3 753	29.5	14.2	31.7	-0.4	-0.9	66.2	23.0	10.6	0.2
Barnwell County	38.0	46.7	30.4	41.2	33.7	46.5	19.6	24.7	6 202	33.3	14.5	32.7	1.4	-1.9	68.8	23.5	7.3	0.4
Beaufort County	38.9	48.8	28.9	39.4	36.2	40.9	36.7	42.5	26 377	41.9	23.2	21.8	-0.9	-8.8	67.8	16.8	15.1	0.4
Berkeley County	45.0	53.9	35.8	48.5	35.6	47.1	42.4	43.9	37 114	40.9	21.1	24.5	0.8	0.2	72.9	19.5	7.3	0.3
Calhoun County	39.8	48.3	32.3	45.8	33.3	30.8	27.0	36.7	3 413	40.2	14.0	27.7	3.3	-2.0	71.1	18.9	9.8	0.2
Charleston County	40.4	48.8	32.7	43.8	33.2	50.0	39.5	39.6	68 438	35.7	19.0	28.4	-0.5	-0.7	69.1	20.1	10.4	0.3
Cherokee County	41.5	51.9	32.1	41.6	41.2	28.0	38.3	37.9	12 615	40.2	14.4	28.0	3.6	-1.8	81.9	10.9	7.0	0.2
Chester County	40.5	49.1	32.9	42.5	36.8	19.2	68.2	43.7	8 543	35.9	12.2	36.6	7.9	0.0	81.8	12.3	5.8	0.1
Chesterfield County	39.1	49.5	29.8	42.9	31.3	23.0	37.3	41.4	10 313	42.2	14.4	24.5	2.1	-2.9	78.4	12.8	8.5	0.3
Clarendon County	32.1	37.5	27.0	38.2	27.1	14.6	11.5	24.6	7 548	33.9	14.7	30.8	0.1	-7.3	69.8	19.3	10.3	0.6
Colleton County	36.8	46.4	20.1	41.5	00.6	8.6	27.7	38.2	9 498	34.2	15.5	23.0	-7.4	-7.6	69.9	18.4	11.4	0.3
Darlington County	40.3	48.8	33.2	43.6	35.6	32.8	41.4	34.8	16 042	34.9	15.6	30.1	0.4	-2.2	78.7	12.9	7.9	0.5
Dillon County	38.3	47.3	31.0	42.1	34.3	31.9	24.5	30.7	8 112	32.7	14.3	31.6	-0.3	-1.4	75.8	15.0	8.6	0.6
Dorchester County	45.2	56.1	35.1	48.2	36.6	45.0	47.6	46.7	26 200	45.8	20.0	21.6	2.8	3.8	71.7	19.9	8.2	0.2
Edgefield County	35.9	39.9	31.4	41.8	28.0	25.0	42.6	24.8	5 568	35.1	20.9	24.6	-4.9	-3.6	70.1	19.6	10.1	0.2
Fairfield County	41.0	47.9	34.8	44.3	38.6	83.0	100.0	20.7	5 693	34.9	11.7	35.6	5.9	-2.7	75.7	17.6	6.6	0.1
Florence County	40.4	50.0	32.4	44.8	33.2	28.4	44.2	39.8	30 345	38.6	16.1	27.5	1.5	0.4	75.3	15.6	8.9	0.2
Georgetown County	36.5	44.6	29.4	38.5	32.7	45.2	45.2	36.9	12 838	41.3	14.2	29.0	5.7	-6.6	73.0	14.8	11.8	0.4
Greenville County	44.3	55.9	33.7	45.5	40.7	51.7	45.9	36.3	88 319	42.8	25.0	21.6	-0.2	1.4	82.4	8.5	9.0	0.2
Greenwood County	40.2	49.6	32.2	41.5	38.2	49.2	47.2	25.9	15 588	43.6	14.4	29.3	8.3	3.5	77.7	14.0	8.1	0.1
Hampton County	33.6	38.3	28.6	40.1	28.8	34.2	27.9	14.6	5 348	37.2	14.0	27.0	-0.4	-2.4	68.7	21.7	9.2	0.5
Horry County	41.3	49.1	34.0	42.2	36.1	34.3	42.4	43.0	39 278	43.2	17.4	25.5	4.1	-2.3	75.9	11.6	12.2	0.3
Jasper County	37.7	43.1	31.6	46.4	29.5	80.0	41.1	43.0	5 066	33.8	21.6	27.2	-3.6	-1.7	75.8	15.4	8.5	0.3
Kershaw County	43.5	53.5	34.5	45.6	37.9	54.0	57.7	30.9	12 959	47.6	17.6	24.7	7.7	3.4	76.2	15.0	8.5	0.3
Lancaster County	43.4	51.0	36.2	45.7	37.8	53.2	26.6	29.1	14 327	42.9	14.8	30.4	8.7	2.8	81.2	11.7	6.9	0.2
Laurens County	41.9	50.9	33.8	43.1	38.6	41.7	59.8	39.5	16 204	41.0	16.9	28.1	4.5	-1.2	79.2	14.1	6.4	0.3
Lee County	35.4	39.6	31.1	39.8	32.6	0.0	0.0	37.5	4 549	35.8	11.8	34.4	5.8	-1.9	76.7	17.0	5.9	0.4
Lexington County	49.0	60.8	38.1	49.8	44.9	50.1	41.4	43.7	53 684	47.8	21.9	20.5	3.7	6.4	71.2	18.9	9.6	0.2
McCormick County	26.6	29.4	23.4	28.9	24.7	X	40.0	19.0	1 769	37.7	8.4	35.5	8.6	-10.1	68.3	23.9	7.6	0.1
Marion County	38.4	45.7	32.5	45.4	32.1	31.4	76.3	52.7	8 707	30.5	11.4	37.9	3.8	-3.6	75.6	16.2	7.8	0.5
Marlboro County	35.5	41.0	30.5	40.9	30.5	32.9	20.1	54.2	6 677	37.8	10.8	29.9	3.1	-2.6	77.1	16.3	6.4	0.3
Newberry County	41.0	49.5	33.4	42.9	39.2	59.3	23.3	23.8	7 917	41.8	13.1	30.6	7.8	-0.5	72.7	19.6	7.5	0.2
Oconee County	39.8	50.5	29.8	39.9	40.5	32.9	37.2	37.5	14 047	45.7	21.4	20.8	1.9	-6.0	74.1	15.5	10.1	0.2
Orangeburg County	34.8	43.3	27.7	41.3	30.4	32.4	58.2	36.4	21 309	36.1	13.7	30.2	1.7	-4.1	71.7	20.0	8.0	0.3
Pickens County	38.9	47.3	30.6	39.3	35.0	47.1	26.4	44.7	23 506	47.6	24.7	18.9	1.9	1.4	76.0	15.7	8.0	0.3
Richland County	42.6	49.3	36.6	44.7	40.5	47.0	34.7	41.5	70 903	41.0	15.9	29.9	6.3	4.3	66.9	25.6	7.3	0.1
Saluda County	43.7	54.3	33.6	47.1	33.7	73.8	42.9	49.7	4 321	42.7	16.1	24.3	2.4	0.7	73.9	14.1	11.5	0.4
Spartanburg County	43.4	54.1	33.7	45.2	36.8	44.4	39.5	43.5	58 970	44.8	19.1	23.9	4.1	1.9	81.0	10.9	7.8	0.3

[1] Hispanic or Latino persons may be of any race.

STATE County	Percent who worked at home	Percent of the population 5 years and over with a disability	Veterans as a percent of the population 18 years and over	Occupation for employed population 16 years and over (percent)						Industry for employed population 16 years and over (percent)					
				Management, professional, and related occupations	Service occupations	Sales and office occupations	Farming, fishing, and forestry occupations	Construction, extraction, and maintenance occupations	Production, transportation and material moving occupations	Agriculture, forestry, fishing, and mining	Construction and manufacturing	Wholesale and retail trade	Transportation and warehousing, and utilities	Service industries	Public administration
	42	43	44	45	46	47	48	49	50	51	52	53	54	55	56
PENNSYLVANIA— Cont'd															
Potter County	4.8	22.9	16.7	26.3	12.2	21.4	3.1	11.4	25.6	6.4	28.7	11.5	5.8	43.5	4.2
Schuylkill County	2.6	21.3	15.8	23.7	14.4	22.8	0.5	11.7	26.9	2.1	32.5	15.9	4.9	39.8	4.7
Snyder County	4.6	18.8	14.8	22.8	14.5	22.8	1.5	10.9	27.5	4.2	33.8	15.3	3.9	38.5	4.3
Somerset County	4.4	21.0	14.1	24.7	16.6	22.5	1.3	12.6	22.2	5.1	24.8	15.0	5.6	44.5	5.0
Sullivan County	4.5	22.2	18.2	23.2	16.9	20.1	2.1	14.7	23.0	5.1	31.2	11.5	4.4	41.7	6.1
Susquehanna County....	4.4	19.8	16.3	26.3	14.0	22.5	1.7	12.4	23.2	7.5	27.9	15.6	5.4	40.5	3.1
Tioga County	5.2	19.8	16.4	25.9	15.5	21.6	1.7	10.0	25.2	4.7	29.9	14.2	5.5	42.0	3.8
Union County	3.7	17.4	11.8	31.0	16.6	20.2	1.0	8.6	22.5	3.1	27.9	11.4	4.0	48.3	5.3
Venango County	2.8	21.3	16.5	25.5	16.7	24.0	0.7	9.4	23.7	1.8	25.0	16.6	5.9	46.0	4.8
Warren County	3.0	19.4	16.8	26.0	15.0	23.7	1.1	8.8	25.4	3.1	30.7	20.6	4.6	37.5	3.5
Washington County.......	2.5	19.8	15.2	29.3	16.4	26.5	0.3	11.6	15.9	2.0	23.0	17.1	5.9	48.8	3.3
Wayne County	4.2	20.2	16.6	26.8	17.4	24.7	1.1	13.3	16.8	3.4	19.9	17.9	5.4	48.5	5.0
Westmoreland County...	2.2	18.2	15.7	30.8	15.4	26.7	0.3	9.7	17.1	0.9	23.6	17.0	6.4	49.1	3.0
Wyoming County	3.6	18.9	14.5	25.9	15.5	23.2	1.1	13.4	20.9	3.7	27.1	15.3	6.5	43.8	3.6
York County	2.7	17.0	14.2	28.4	12.5	26.2	0.4	9.9	22.7	1.1	31.1	16.7	5.2	41.9	4.0
RHODE ISLAND	2.2	20.2	12.8	33.9	15.7	27.1	0.3	7.7	15.2	0.5	21.9	15.5	3.9	53.8	4.5
Bristol County	2.8	17.7	13.2	41.6	13.9	24.9	0.4	8.3	10.9	0.5	20.7	13.6	2.6	59.1	3.5
Kent County	1.8	18.8	15.1	33.4	15.1	29.6	0.2	7.8	14.0	0.3	21.7	16.9	5.2	51.2	4.7
Newport County	3.8	17.5	15.8	41.2	16.9	25.4	0.7	7.7	8.1	0.9	14.9	13.7	3.9	61.0	5.6
Providence County........	1.9	22.2	11.4	31.2	15.8	27.3	0.1	7.5	18.1	0.2	23.5	15.7	3.8	52.5	4.3
Washington County.......	3.2	15.5	14.4	39.4	16.1	24.8	1.1	8.3	10.4	1.5	19.9	14.1	3.1	56.4	5.0
SOUTH CAROLINA ...	2.1	22.2	14.0	29.1	14.7	25.2	0.6	11.5	19.0	1.1	27.7	15.2	5.0	46.2	4.7
Abbeville County	1.7	24.4	12.6	21.8	11.9	19.0	0.3	11.6	35.3	1.5	45.5	11.1	4.5	33.9	3.6
Aiken County	1.8	21.5	14.8	30.8	14.6	22.7	0.7	12.4	18.7	1.6	25.8	13.4	11.5	43.5	4.1
Allendale County	1.8	27.1	9.7	22.2	18.0	20.8	1.5	8.1	29.3	4.8	32.3	15.2	5.1	34.8	7.9
Anderson County	1.6	23.6	14.2	26.2	13.3	23.4	0.4	12.5	24.2	0.6	36.1	14.9	4.2	41.2	2.9
Bamberg County	2.0	32.5	12.0	28.0	15.8	20.8	1.3	11.0	23.0	2.8	28.9	13.2	5.3	44.1	5.7
Barnwell County	1.8	29.1	11.8	22.2	14.2	22.8	1.0	10.9	29.0	1.7	33.9	11.8	11.0	36.4	5.3
Beaufort County	4.7	17.6	18.2	32.3	19.0	26.6	0.7	13.4	8.1	0.9	18.1	15.9	3.5	55.8	5.7
Berkeley County	1.3	23.0	19.0	25.2	14.6	26.3	0.4	15.4	18.0	0.7	26.3	15.5	7.8	43.2	6.5
Calhoun County	1.8	25.4	12.5	24.2	13.5	23.0	1.0	12.3	26.1	3.5	30.1	14.2	6.9	39.8	5.6
Charleston County	2.7	21.1	15.1	35.9	17.9	26.2	0.5	9.5	9.9	0.6	15.1	15.5	4.9	58.2	5.6
Cherokee County	1.1	27.1	12.8	18.3	13.5	21.8	0.4	13.8	32.3	0.8	44.2	14.9	4.9	32.6	2.6
Chester County	0.9	26.8	12.1	19.8	13.1	21.5	0.9	13.4	31.3	1.3	40.0	14.5	5.2	35.8	3.1
Chesterfield County.......	1.6	24.5	11.0	20.3	12.4	22.0	1.3	12.0	31.9	2.8	40.7	14.6	5.3	33.2	3.3
Clarendon County	1.8	28.6	11.5	22.5	15.4	22.7	1.9	11.9	25.7	3.7	32.8	14.4	4.2	38.6	6.2
Colleton County	2.0	26.6	14.2	22.1	17.0	23.2	1.7	16.0	19.9	3.0	26.5	15.0	4.5	44.7	6.4
Darlington County	1.7	26.1	12.0	24.6	14.8	24.4	0.9	10.7	24.6	2.3	31.4	15.5	5.5	41.6	3.7
Dillon County................	1.6	28.4	10.4	18.8	15.0	23.5	1.8	11.7	29.2	3.6	36.7	14.6	4.8	36.4	4.0
Dorchester County	2.1	20.1	19.4	31.5	13.0	26.4	0.5	12.2	16.4	1.0	24.4	16.3	5.9	45.2	7.3
Edgefield County	2.0	22.0	10.6	24.3	15.8	21.2	1.9	11.3	25.4	2.7	29.9	13.5	9.9	38.7	5.4
Fairfield County	1.0	24.8	12.0	19.8	16.4	20.2	1.2	12.7	29.8	3.0	34.3	12.9	6.1	37.8	5.9
Florence County	1.6	23.8	12.1	30.2	14.9	24.8	0.6	11.0	18.4	1.3	24.6	16.1	4.7	49.1	4.3
Georgetown County	2.1	21.8	14.5	25.4	18.6	23.2	1.8	12.9	18.0	2.7	26.7	15.1	3.9	48.0	3.5
Greenville County.........	2.4	18.8	12.9	33.2	13.1	26.7	0.3	9.5	17.1	0.4	29.2	16.8	4.2	47.2	2.2
Greenwood County	1.0	22.4	12.0	27.5	15.1	20.4	0.3	10.9	25.8	0.8	38.1	12.8	3.6	41.2	3.5
Hampton County	1.6	24.2	11.6	21.3	18.6	21.5	1.5	11.9	25.1	3.4	30.5	13.2	5.0	39.6	8.2
Horry County	2.7	23.2	16.2	26.2	20.1	29.8	0.5	13.2	10.1	1.1	18.5	17.9	3.2	56.0	3.2
Jasper County	2.1	28.4	12.1	17.1	23.2	24.5	0.8	20.0	14.4	1.5	27.3	15.4	4.0	45.7	6.0
Kershaw County	1.4	23.3	15.3	26.8	13.6	24.8	1.2	12.3	21.3	2.4	32.7	13.9	4.5	41.5	5.1
Lancaster County	1.2	23.1	13.1	19.6	10.7	24.7	0.4	15.6	28.9	1.1	41.9	16.9	3.7	33.5	3.0
Laurens County	1.5	27.2	12.2	21.1	14.1	20.5	0.4	12.5	31.3	1.0	40.7	15.1	4.3	34.9	4.1
Lee County...................	1.4	23.0	10.8	19.3	16.1	18.5	2.4	11.8	32.0	4.9	34.5	12.1	4.7	38.0	5.8
Lexington County	2.8	18.4	14.7	35.1	12.0	28.7	0.3	11.8	12.0	0.8	20.6	16.0	6.2	48.8	7.7
McCormick County........	1.8	29.9	14.5	22.6	16.2	18.6	0.8	13.4	28.3	1.8	37.9	12.3	5.3	37.4	5.4
Marion County	1.8	26.4	10.9	21.8	14.7	21.6	1.6	10.5	29.8	2.6	36.6	13.7	4.0	39.3	3.8
Marlboro County	1.3	26.7	10.5	17.7	13.6	19.6	1.1	10.0	38.0	3.2	43.4	11.9	3.9	32.1	5.5
Newberry County	1.4	26.1	11.8	23.7	13.2	24.3	2.1	12.0	24.6	3.9	32.4	14.2	6.0	37.0	6.6
Oconee County	2.1	24.2	15.4	25.1	11.9	21.3	0.7	14.1	26.9	1.5	40.1	12.9	5.9	37.0	2.6
Orangeburg County.......	1.8	25.3	11.5	25.3	15.2	25.0	1.0	10.9	22.7	2.4	29.8	14.2	4.8	44.0	4.8
Pickens County	2.1	19.9	12.2	28.2	14.4	22.8	0.4	13.4	20.8	0.7	33.8	13.1	4.4	45.4	2.6
Richland County	2.2	19.2	14.7	38.9	15.6	27.6	0.2	7.1	10.5	0.4	14.0	13.6	4.1	58.2	9.7
Saluda County..............	2.2	22.2	11.3	21.0	12.3	20.9	2.2	14.1	29.6	4.9	38.6	13.4	5.4	31.9	5.6
Spartanburg County	2.0	23.0	12.9	26.6	12.6	25.1	0.3	11.0	24.5	0.5	35.4	16.2	4.5	41.1	2.3

STATE County	Median house-hold income	Median family income				Median nonfamily house-hold income	Median income for full-year, full-time workers		Per capita income	Households by source of income (percent)					House-holds with income over $100,000 (percent)	+/− U.S. percent for income over $100,000	House-holds with income below poverty (percent)	Families with children with income below poverty (percent)
		All families	Married-couple	Male house-holder	Female house-holder		Men	Women		With earnings	With interest, dividend, or rental income	With Social Security income	With public assis-tance income	With retire-ment income				
	57	58	59	60	61	62	63	64	65	66	67	68	69	70	71	72	73	74
PENNSYLVANIA— Cont'd																		
Potter County	32 253	38 066	45 750	23 472	16 518	18 570	31 822	21 606	16 070	74.8	33.4	33.9	3.0	20.7	4.0	-8.3	11.9	15.7
Schuylkill County	32 699	41 279	50 754	28 194	17 523	16 427	32 043	22 107	17 230	69.8	38.4	38.7	1.9	23.0	4.4	-7.9	10.7	10.4
Snyder County	35 981	41 682	47 469	25 761	16 473	19 294	31 022	21 541	16 756	78.1	41.2	30.1	2.0	17.2	5.3	-7.0	9.8	9.7
Somerset County	30 911	36 822	41 361	23 194	13 714	16 399	28 874	20 786	15 178	72.2	37.0	35.9	2.5	21.8	3.3	-9.0	12.1	13.7
Sullivan County	30 279	37 196	47 222	23 068	16 563	18 364	28 947	21 747	16 438	67.7	37.5	41.1	2.0	25.4	4.9	-7.4	12.8	12.1
Susquehanna County	33 622	39 564	46 758	24 767	17 676	18 016	30 927	21 632	16 435	75.5	34.7	32.2	2.9	20.5	4.8	-7.5	11.9	13.7
Tioga County	32 020	37 907	44 246	25 786	17 122	17 697	30 179	21 256	15 549	74.0	36.5	33.1	2.4	21.2	4.0	-8.3	13.2	14.0
Union County	40 336	47 538	52 750	35 625	17 218	19 556	31 985	22 661	17 918	75.0	44.7	30.5	3.0	20.6	8.1	-4.2	9.6	7.5
Venango County	32 257	39 405	46 510	21 750	13 430	16 626	32 404	22 265	16 252	71.8	37.6	34.2	3.1	23.8	4.5	-7.8	13.2	17.3
Warren County	36 083	42 658	50 410	29 700	19 250	20 713	34 121	22 816	17 862	76.0	42.2	32.4	1.8	21.3	4.9	-7.4	8.8	10.7
Washington County	37 607	47 287	56 147	27 383	17 113	18 928	38 600	25 405	19 935	73.2	40.3	34.9	2.4	23.6	8.4	-3.9	10.6	11.6
Wayne County	34 082	40 589	46 650	23 056	16 882	17 852	31 142	21 424	16 977	73.1	39.9	36.2	2.6	20.8	5.4	-6.9	11.5	12.9
Westmoreland County	37 106	45 996	55 364	26 655	17 414	18 949	37 348	25 416	19 674	73.3	41.9	35.1	2.1	22.7	7.8	-4.5	9.4	10.3
Wyoming County	36 365	42 824	47 161	31 196	19 500	19 270	33 577	22 093	17 452	77.9	39.7	28.5	3.0	19.6	6.4	-5.9	10.5	12.0
York County	45 268	52 278	60 321	31 803	22 032	25 982	37 833	25 874	21 086	82.1	45.5	26.3	1.5	18.0	8.8	-3.5	6.7	7.1
RHODE ISLAND	42 090	52 781	63 706	29 776	17 252	23 561	39 202	28 472	21 688	77.4	37.0	27.9	4.6	17.4	11.5	-0.8	12.4	14.2
Bristol County	50 737	63 114	75 637	33 523	24 667	24 293	44 220	30 441	26 503	78.8	43.2	29.1	2.6	18.4	19.0	6.7	7.8	5.9
Kent County	47 617	57 491	67 250	37 042	22 410	26 832	40 815	30 191	23 833	79.1	39.1	29.0	2.5	19.2	11.8	-0.5	7.5	7.2
Newport County	50 448	60 610	67 665	32 273	19 919	30 452	44 547	30 503	26 779	79.9	45.9	26.8	3.1	21.5	16.0	3.7	7.9	9.0
Providence County	36 950	46 694	59 098	26 204	15 517	21 021	36 227	27 033	19 255	75.5	33.2	28.2	6.0	15.8	9.2	-3.1	15.7	19.0
Washington County	53 103	64 112	72 563	32 447	25 865	29 319	46 111	31 484	25 530	82.2	44.0	25.1	2.0	19.5	16.7	4.4	7.5	6.7
SOUTH CAROLINA	37 082	44 227	53 649	27 291	17 982	21 508	33 279	24 187	18 795	79.9	27.2	26.5	2.5	17.9	8.1	-4.2	14.1	15.7
Abbeville County	32 635	38 847	47 418	29 274	18 414	14 327	30 811	21 697	15 370	73.7	25.7	32.5	2.6	18.3	3.4	-8.9	14.8	15.2
Aiken County	37 889	45 769	56 419	29 167	17 631	20 922	37 683	24 920	18 772	78.1	28.5	27.7	2.9	18.8	8.6	-3.7	14.0	16.1
Allendale County	20 898	27 348	40 329	25 192	9 984	10 513	26 758	20 784	11 293	67.1	13.4	32.3	6.3	14.2	3.9	-0.4	33.6	40.0
Anderson County	36 807	44 229	52 879	28 603	19 399	18 148	33 403	24 705	18 365	78.1	25.9	28.9	1.8	18.5	6.9	-5.4	13.0	13.1
Bamberg County	24 007	29 360	40 689	20 990	13 547	14 171	26 332	19 617	12 584	70.2	16.1	34.0	4.8	17.5	3.5	-8.8	26.9	30.8
Barnwell County	28 591	35 866	50 781	22 109	15 616	13 707	31 648	22 193	15 870	72.5	17.6	28.2	4.1	15.4	5.5	-6.8	22.5	23.6
Beaufort County	46 992	52 704	53 163	28 525	19 958	31 409	32 033	26 041	25 377	76.8	41.1	30.4	1.9	25.4	15.6	3.3	9.5	13.9
Berkeley County	39 908	44 242	50 103	30 697	19 974	23 643	33 137	23 160	16 879	83.5	24.5	21.4	2.1	21.4	6.3	-6.0	11.8	13.5
Calhoun County	32 736	39 823	48 644	26 023	16 926	17 331	32 191	22 578	17 446	74.0	22.2	20.5	3.2	18.2	6.6	-5.7	17.0	17.8
Charleston County	37 810	47 139	60 795	30 030	15 789	25 812	35 108	26 387	21 393	80.4	31.7	24.0	2.2	19.1	11.0	-1.3	15.5	18.7
Cherokee County	33 787	39 393	48 145	24 938	19 688	18 245	31 408	21 843	16 421	79.4	20.9	28.2	2.4	15.5	4.8	-7.5	14.8	15.0
Chester County	32 425	38 087	48 950	28 438	17 941	16 426	30 971	21 926	14 709	77.5	19.7	29.4	2.8	16.4	3.9	-8.4	16.8	17.3
Chesterfield County	29 483	36 200	47 012	22 625	13 993	14 990	30 807	21 312	14 233	75.3	17.2	27.6	3.6	13.8	3.5	-8.8	21.0	21.4
Clarendon County	27 131	33 951	45 586	21 190	16 085	11 853	29 934	20 402	13 998	70.5	18.9	33.5	3.7	17.0	4.5	-7.8	23.8	24.7
Colleton County	29 733	34 169	42 371	26 597	14 161	15 694	29 345	19 626	14 831	74.7	18.8	29.7	2.6	19.7	4.2	-8.1	20.9	24.5
Darlington County	31 087	37 662	49 515	28 712	15 934	16 431	32 112	21 398	16 283	77.1	21.3	26.6	4.0	16.0	5.9	-6.4	20.4	22.9
Dillon County	26 630	32 690	41 851	17 969	13 960	12 322	27 058	18 475	13 272	76.9	14.0	27.7	4.5	13.4	3.5	-8.8	24.5	26.8
Dorchester County	43 316	50 177	58 660	31 417	20 339	24 014	37 567	25 009	18 840	83.9	28.6	22.1	2.3	21.8	8.7	-3.6	10.0	9.8
Edgefield County	35 146	41 810	50 217	23 553	16 667	16 796	33 745	23 774	15 415	77.1	24.9	28.4	3.5	17.6	6.5	-5.8	16.1	17.4
Fairfield County	30 376	35 943	48 449	27 188	16 237	15 857	29 187	21 534	14 911	76.4	18.4	27.8	3.9	17.6	5.2	-7.1	21.0	23.4
Florence County	35 144	41 274	52 405	26 955	16 319	19 763	32 849	22 587	17 876	80.6	24.0	25.9	3.3	15.2	7.3	-5.0	16.3	18.4
Georgetown County	35 312	41 554	48 925	26 313	16 353	19 191	31 625	21 347	19 805	74.8	29.3	31.7	2.9	23.7	8.7	-3.6	15.9	21.6
Greenville County	41 149	50 332	61 418	30 816	19 973	24 822	38 659	26 656	22 081	82.5	31.4	24.5	1.8	14.6	11.7	-0.6	10.6	11.7
Greenwood County	34 702	42 022	50 874	24 963	20 152	18 341	31 341	24 257	17 446	77.7	25.2	28.9	2.3	19.0	6.1	-6.2	14.1	14.2
Hampton County	28 771	34 559	44 873	23 250	14 232	12 773	30 253	20 913	13 129	73.8	15.5	31.0	2.9	17.5	4.0	-8.3	22.4	24.4
Horry County	36 470	42 676	50 855	23 053	18 635	25 193	29 272	22 320	19 949	79.2	32.5	30.2	2.4	21.5	7.1	-5.2	11.2	14.4
Jasper County	30 727	36 793	43 551	23 784	15 182	15 903	30 069	22 110	14 161	78.4	14.8	27.1	2.5	15.3	5.5	-6.8	19.9	21.6
Kershaw County	38 804	44 836	53 531	29 083	17 553	21 387	33 865	23 495	18 360	80.3	26.8	27.2	2.1	20.3	5.9	-6.4	13.0	13.5
Lancaster County	34 688	40 955	50 559	22 267	19 113	18 688	30 620	22 938	16 276	79.4	23.0	29.0	2.6	16.3	4.9	-7.4	13.0	14.0
Laurens County	33 933	39 739	48 093	25 199	17 576	18 954	30 746	22 227	15 761	78.8	19.9	30.4	3.3	18.9	4.4	-7.9	13.8	17.1
Lee County	26 907	34 209	44 398	30 234	14 978	11 169	26 808	19 669	13 896	73.0	15.9	30.3	3.2	17.4	4.3	-8.0	25.3	22.5
Lexington County	44 659	50 332	61 359	26 844	22 314	25 605	37 329	27 066	21 063	84.9	31.5	21.8	1.8	15.6	9.9	-2.4	8.9	9.4
McCormick County	31 577	38 822	42 566	25 714	15 428	13 895	29 848	21 789	14 770	67.3	26.1	35.7	2.1	25.4	5.1	-7.2	19.3	24.0
Marion County	26 526	32 932	43 933	22 614	13 632	13 208	26 702	19 311	13 878	76.8	15.4	29.4	4.3	15.7	3.9	-8.4	23.1	26.4
Marlboro County	26 598	32 019	40 350	21 250	15 601	12 417	26 218	20 914	13 385	74.8	12.7	29.8	5.0	15.7	3.0	-9.3	22.9	23.9
Newberry County	32 867	40 580	48 160	28 162	17 278	17 233	30 460	21 040	16 045	74.8	26.1	31.5	2.6	20.3	5.1	-7.2	17.0	20.7
Oconee County	36 666	43 047	48 432	29 967	17 927	18 686	31 572	22 663	18 965	75.0	30.0	33.0	2.1	21.4	6.7	-5.6	12.0	12.6
Orangeburg County	29 567	36 165	47 825	22 939	16 877	15 403	30 147	21 443	15 057	74.3	19.4	29.7	3.8	17.8	4.7	-7.6	21.9	22.9
Pickens County	36 214	44 507	50 236	28 397	18 695	18 424	32 410	23 307	17 434	81.4	28.8	25.7	1.6	15.9	6.5	-5.8	14.4	10.6
Richland County	39 961	49 466	62 063	27 991	19 968	26 448	35 851	26 588	20 794	84.9	29.8	21.0	2.1	17.0	10.8	-1.5	13.1	14.5
Saluda County	35 774	41 603	52 371	23 646	18 197	16 698	30 099	21 769	16 328	77.4	23.9	32.2	3.0	17.9	4.8	-7.5	15.4	18.3
Spartanburg County	37 579	45 349	53 514	26 960	18 969	20 512	34 327	24 613	18 738	80.4	25.7	28.0	2.1	16.3	7.5	-4.8	12.8	13.4

Table B-3. States and Counties — Education, Labor Force, and Income

STATE/ County code	MSA/PMSA/ NECMA code[1]	STATE County	High school graduates			College graduates		College graduates (percent)				
			Total population 25 years and over	Percent with a high school diploma or less	Percent with a high school diploma or more	Percent with a bachelor's degree or more	+/− U.S. percent with bachelor's degree or more	Non-Hispanic White	Black or African American	American Indian and Alaska Native	Asian, Hawaiian, and Pacific Islander	Hispanic or Latino[2]
			1	2	3	4	5	6	7	8	9	10
		SOUTH CAROLINA—Cont'd										
45 085	8140	Sumter County	64 144	55.4	74.3	15.8	-8.6	19.9	10.5	13.8	22.4	14.1
45 087	...	Union County	20 222	69.5	66.9	9.8	-14.6	11.3	5.8	0.0	26.8	0.0
45 089	...	Williamsburg County	23 189	69.6	65.5	11.5	-12.9	15.1	9.2	12.8	46.2	2.4
45 091	1520	York County	105 757	51.2	77.2	20.9	-3.5	23.7	8.8	5.6	28.6	16.0
46 000	...	**SOUTH DAKOTA.......**	474 359	48.3	84.6	21.5	-2.9	22.3	19.3	8.5	39.2	11.7
46 003	...	Aurora County	2 020	56.5	79.5	12.7	-11.7	12.9	X	0.0	0.0	8.0
46 005	...	Beadle County	11 368	51.9	83.0	18.3	-6.1	18.0	13.8	46.9	9.3	0.0
46 007	...	Bennett County	1 972	56.4	71.3	12.7	-11.7	16.4	23.1	5.9	X	14.3
46 009	...	Bon Homme County......	5 026	57.1	79.0	15.3	-9.1	15.7	0.0	4.0	X	14.3
46 011	...	Brookings County	14 819	38.0	90.2	32.2	7.8	31.8	78.1	5.2	68.7	20.6
46 013	...	Brown County	22 959	45.8	85.8	23.6	-0.8	23.8	37.9	14.0	63.0	16.4
46 015	...	Brule County	3 371	50.5	81.1	20.6	-3.8	20.7	X	21.5	0.0	30.8
46 017	...	Buffalo County..............	948	69.7	63.9	5.4	-19.0	13.8	0.0	2.9	0.0	0.0
46 019	...	Butte County	5 859	57.2	79.8	12.2	-12.2	12.3	X	2.9	0.0	13.3
46 021	...	Campbell County	1 251	54.1	79.2	14.8	-9.6	14.9	X	0.0	X	X
46 023	...	Charles Mix County.......	5 676	59.9	74.7	14.1	-10.3	16.2	0.0	6.1	25.0	8.2
46 025	...	Clark County	2 781	63.3	76.6	11.4	-13.0	11.3	X	0.0	33.3	0.0
46 027	...	Clay County.................	6 719	33.6	89.5	38.7	14.3	38.0	59.5	23.8	77.5	53.6
46 029	...	Codington County	16 377	52.8	85.3	18.8	-5.6	19.1	0.0	1.5	7.5	15.7
46 031	...	Corson County	2 238	61.9	76.0	11.3	-13.1	15.4	0.0	7.1	50.0	0.0
46 033	...	Custer County	5 099	44.4	88.9	24.4	0.0	24.7	X	19.4	0.0	36.0
46 035	...	Davison County	11 719	50.0	83.9	20.2	-4.2	20.2	56.4	6.0	37.0	0.0
46 037	...	Day County	4 354	58.3	80.0	15.4	-9.0	15.7	X	6.9	30.8	0.0
46 039	...	Deuel County	3 094	60.3	81.9	13.3	-11.1	13.3	0.0	0.0	X	22.2
46 041	...	Dewey County	3 107	54.8	77.4	12.2	-12.2	20.4	100.0	7.5	14.8	28.6
46 043	...	Douglas County............	2 332	59.8	68.8	14.5	-9.9	14.5	X	14.3	X	0.0
46 045	...	Edmunds County...........	2 975	59.7	73.6	15.5	-8.9	15.6	X	X	0.0	0.0
46 047	...	Fall River County	5 313	51.9	82.5	19.2	-5.2	19.9	0.0	6.2	25.0	24.1
46 049	...	Faulk County	1 803	60.4	73.7	13.1	-11.3	13.3	X	0.0	0.0	0.0
46 051	...	Grant County	5 303	63.1	79.5	14.8	-9.6	14.8	X	0.0	0.0	80.0
46 053	...	Gregory County	3 367	61.3	77.7	12.0	-12.4	12.4	0.0	0.7	0.0	0.0
46 055	...	Haakon County	1 477	54.4	86.3	15.4	-9.0	15.1	X	14.8	0.0	100.0
46 057	...	Hamlin County..............	3 507	62.9	79.9	12.8	-11.6	12.7	0.0	26.3	50.0	18.8
46 059	...	Hand County	2 627	58.1	80.1	15.6	-8.8	15.6	0.0	0.0	0.0	0.0
46 061	...	Hanson County	1 962	61.1	75.1	14.0	-10.4	13.8	X	X	60.0	50.0
46 063	...	Harding County	850	46.6	87.8	17.8	-6.6	17.5	X	50.0	X	X
46 065	...	Hughes County	10 853	38.1	89.5	32.0	7.6	33.3	13.0	8.4	72.7	12.2
46 067	...	Hutchinson County.......	5 629	57.6	71.7	14.1	-10.3	14.1	100.0	18.8	X	25.0
46 069	...	Hyde County	1 147	56.2	80.5	16.0	-8.4	16.0	X	12.1	X	X
46 071	...	Jackson County.............	1 662	51.6	82.7	16.2	-8.2	21.7	X	5.9	0.0	100.0
46 073	...	Jerauld County	1 661	61.0	79.6	12.3	-12.1	12.2	X	50.0	X	0.0
46 075	...	Jones County	811	53.3	86.2	17.8	-6.6	18.2	X	12.5	X	X
46 077	...	Kingsbury County	4 015	59.6	82.3	16.2	-8.2	16.2	X	12.5	25.0	0.0
46 079	...	Lake County	6 917	50.9	85.7	21.1	-3.3	20.6	0.0	19.0	86.5	22.0
46 081	...	Lawrence County	13 746	44.2	87.5	24.0	-0.4	24.1	0.0	18.4	44.8	15.1
46 083	7760	Lincoln County	15 093	41.4	89.4	25.5	1.1	25.5	27.3	17.1	36.5	25.6
46 085	...	Lyman County	2 344	59.7	81.1	15.9	-8.5	17.9	0.0	8.7	37.5	0.0
46 087	...	McCook County	3 827	55.8	82.9	16.3	-8.1	16.3	X	0.0	100.0	8.7
46 089	...	McPherson County.......	2 128	68.7	58.8	10.7	-13.7	10.7	X	X	X	0.0
46 091	...	Marshall County	3 111	57.8	75.6	16.2	-8.2	16.7	X	8.3	X	0.0
46 093	...	Meade County	14 816	46.1	87.7	16.8	-7.6	17.0	19.7	5.8	23.5	20.6
46 095	...	Mellette County	1 199	56.3	78.1	16.6	-7.8	25.3	X	4.6	66.7	0.0
46 097	...	Miner County	1 982	60.8	79.6	13.5	-10.9	13.4	0.0	40.0	0.0	0.0
46 099	7760	Minnehaha County	93 400	42.3	88.5	26.0	1.6	26.8	20.0	7.7	28.7	7.6
46 101	...	Moody County	4 193	51.8	84.7	17.4	-7.0	17.9	23.1	9.5	37.1	33.3
46 103	6660	Pennington County	55 535	41.5	87.8	25.0	0.6	26.5	10.5	9.7	29.9	8.8
46 105	...	Perkins County.............	2 367	56.9	80.3	14.6	-9.8	14.9	0.0	0.0	33.3	0.0
46 107	...	Potter County	1 969	56.6	80.8	16.2	-8.2	16.1	X	22.2	50.0	X
46 109	...	Roberts County	6 301	61.4	75.8	13.4	-11.0	14.4	0.0	8.4	77.8	0.0
46 111	...	Sanborn County	1 788	56.2	82.7	14.8	-9.6	15.1	X	0.0	0.0	5.6
46 113	...	Shannon County	5 524	56.4	70.0	12.1	-12.3	41.3	0.0	9.3	64.0	9.5
46 115	...	Spink County	5 024	57.5	81.4	14.4	-10.0	14.4	0.0	17.7	0.0	0.0
46 117	...	Stanley County.............	1 823	47.3	87.7	22.1	-2.3	22.3	0.0	11.3	100.0	0.0
46 119	...	Sully County	1 065	53.2	84.9	16.4	-8.0	16.6	X	0.0	X	0.0
46 121	...	Todd County	4 173	57.2	74.1	12.1	-12.3	22.2	X	8.4	73.3	0.0

[1]MSA = Metropolitan Statistical Area. PMSA = Primary MSA. NECMA = New England County Metropolitan Area. See the Appendix A for explanation of these concepts. See Appendix B for list of metropolitan areas identified by type, with component counties.
[2]Hispanic or Latino persons may be of any race.

Table B-3. States and Counties — Education, Labor Force, and Income

STATE County	School enrollment			Population 16 to 19 years				Employment status, 2000			Work status in 1999 of the population 16 years and over (percent)		
											Worked in 1999		
	Grades kindergarten through 12	College or graduate school	Percent private	Number	Percent in armed forces	Percent high school graduates	Percent not enrolled, not grads, not in armed forces, not employed	Total population 16 years and over	Percent in labor force	Unemploy- ment rate	Full-time	Part-time	Did not work in 1999
	11	12	13	14	15	16	17	18	19	20	21	22	23
SOUTH CAROLINA—Cont'd													
Sumter County	22 355	5 724	14.0	6 376	2.5	13.2	6.6	78 457	62.1	7.0	55.2	11.9	32.8
Union County	5 463	967	4.3	1 531	0.0	11.7	9.6	23 482	59.5	7.2	55.1	9.4	35.5
Williamsburg County	8 584	1 289	7.2	2 407	0.5	9.5	6.6	27 913	53.9	9.1	47.5	11.2	41.3
York County	32 418	8 717	8.1	9 025	0.0	10.5	5.8	125 729	69.1	6.1	60.1	13.9	26.0
SOUTH DAKOTA	152 642	42 894	9.7	49 305	0.3	10.2	4.7	577 129	68.4	4.4	57.0	17.4	25.5
Aurora County	664	75	5.4	230	0.0	4.8	11.7	2 379	62.0	1.8	50.4	18.2	31.4
Beadle County	3 358	517	16.6	987	0.0	14.1	2.8	13 338	65.2	3.2	54.5	16.3	29.2
Bennett County	983	170	5.1	245	0.0	6.5	15.1	2 440	56.7	10.5	47.5	12.2	40.3
Bon Homme County	1 341	96	5.6	432	0.0	12.5	5.1	5 850	53.9	2.1	48.1	14.0	37.9
Brookings County	4 361	6 622	2.0	2 817	0.1	6.1	0.2	23 109	74.7	4.9	57.9	25.5	16.6
Brown County	6 207	2 787	12.8	2 384	0.0	9.2	1.4	28 141	69.7	3.5	56.3	19.1	24.6
Brule County	1 315	78	3.3	372	0.0	5.1	7.5	3 940	68.4	6.9	56.5	16.9	26.6
Buffalo County	662	49	10.7	200	1.5	10.5	14.5	1 282	43.4	21.6	35.3	8.0	56.8
Butte County	2 000	258	7.8	583	0.0	16.8	1.5	6 861	68.3	5.7	56.1	16.1	27.8
Campbell County	380	16	1.8	96	0.0	5.2	0.0	1 382	61.6	1.5	48.0	17.9	34.1
Charles Mix County	2 178	160	12.4	580	0.0	5.9	13.8	6 705	59.6	8.5	46.7	15.5	37.8
Clark County	880	53	3.0	268	0.0	9.0	4.9	3 203	60.6	3.0	52.4	16.3	31.3
Clay County	1 853	4 397	2.8	1 472	0.0	2.4	0.7	11 214	67.0	7.9	49.8	31.3	18.9
Codington County	5 198	1 100	9.7	1 741	0.0	12.2	2.3	19 878	73.2	3.9	59.3	18.3	22.4
Corson County	1 181	116	3.5	290	0.0	6.9	13.1	2 798	51.4	13.2	45.9	10.7	43.4
Custer County	1 476	185	9.7	609	0.0	9.4	1.8	5 929	59.6	3.3	53.6	17.7	28.7
Davison County	3 642	1 283	20.4	1 338	0.0	6.7	3.3	14 557	67.9	2.9	53.9	19.9	26.2
Day County	1 284	102	3.5	351	0.0	10.3	2.8	4 913	57.9	4.6	48.7	17.2	34.1
Deuel County	922	89	3.9	248	0.0	9.3	2.0	3 493	64.6	1.3	55.3	16.4	28.3
Dewey County	1 745	262	2.8	467	0.0	13.3	13.7	3 911	59.0	14.3	51.5	11.4	37.1
Douglas County	761	41	21.1	208	0.0	7.2	2.4	2 638	61.4	1.4	46.5	20.2	33.2
Edmunds County	919	59	11.6	239	0.0	3.8	7.1	3 349	60.5	2.4	50.4	15.7	33.9
Fall River County	1 209	125	9.5	347	0.0	7.8	2.6	5 988	56.9	6.9	48.2	16.4	35.4
Faulk County	539	27	14.0	167	0.0	4.2	10.8	2 042	58.0	1.8	47.2	14.5	38.2
Grant County	1 591	119	7.4	442	0.0	9.5	6.1	6 041	64.5	3.3	51.2	18.0	30.8
Gregory County	957	43	2.3	257	0.0	8.9	1.2	3 782	60.1	3.8	47.6	16.2	36.2
Haakon County	461	32	2.0	156	0.0	8.3	0.0	1 727	68.3	3.5	58.2	16.4	25.4
Hamlin County	1 267	123	6.5	380	0.0	8.4	5.3	4 132	62.1	2.6	52.3	15.3	32.5
Hand County	723	33	1.9	222	0.0	2.7	0.9	2 944	63.7	1.2	50.7	16.4	32.8
Hanson County	685	61	4.2	188	0.0	8.5	6.9	2 308	64.9	2.1	57.3	14.0	28.7
Harding County	365	28	8.1	128	0.0	0.0	10.4	1 012	60.4	1.0	54.1	15.5	30.4
Hughes County	3 589	183	6.2	992	0.0	13.0	3.9	12 460	73.3	2.7	64.2	15.6	20.2
Hutchinson County	1 538	139	8.5	453	0.0	2.9	10.2	6 367	58.0	1.9	49.5	15.3	35.1
Hyde County	305	20	2.5	86	0.0	5.8	0.0	1 294	61.8	1.5	51.5	16.5	31.9
Jackson County	803	137	2.1	211	0.0	15.6	2.4	1 998	56.7	15.7	48.7	11.6	39.7
Jerauld County	402	49	3.3	122	0.0	2.5	2.5	1 881	60.5	2.5	49.5	19.5	31.0
Jones County	281	12	1.4	83	0.0	0.0	0.0	938	70.6	3.0	62.8	16.4	20.8
Kingsbury County	1 177	97	4.4	351	0.0	6.6	2.3	4 588	60.9	3.0	51.4	15.3	33.2
Lake County	2 085	1 213	4.2	1 065	0.4	6.0	2.7	9 011	68.2	3.4	55.0	20.4	23.7
Lawrence County	4 091	2 245	4.7	1 900	0.0	11.9	4.6	17 551	65.8	9.1	53.0	19.5	27.5
Lincoln County	5 286	994	10.0	1 421	0.5	7.4	0.6	17 844	76.5	1.8	64.8	16.8	18.4
Lyman County	934	101	2.4	213	0.0	4.7	4.7	2 774	67.6	9.4	57.0	17.0	26.1
McCook County	1 281	140	9.9	326	0.0	9.2	4.9	4 365	65.1	1.8	54.4	17.3	28.3
McPherson County	497	23	4.6	118	0.0	6.8	12.7	2 337	52.1	2.2	41.3	15.3	43.4
Marshall County	925	99	3.0	271	0.0	7.4	14.0	3 518	59.0	4.4	50.8	15.5	33.6
Meade County	5 047	1 061	9.8	1 376	8.0	21.7	4.8	18 138	72.5	3.4	60.8	17.6	21.6
Mellette County	533	66	2.2	136	0.0	14.7	5.9	1 419	61.2	11.5	52.3	13.8	33.9
Miner County	611	40	1.8	175	0.0	5.1	1.1	2 267	62.4	1.3	50.2	17.9	32.0
Minnehaha County	27 965	7 981	17.7	8 653	0.0	12.3	3.7	113 748	75.3	3.0	63.8	16.8	19.4
Moody County	1 535	191	4.5	466	0.0	5.4	5.6	4 968	70.2	3.0	59.8	15.9	24.3
Pennington County	17 352	5 409	9.8	5 548	0.3	13.7	4.5	67 712	70.5	4.4	59.4	17.9	22.8
Perkins County	652	27	4.4	186	0.0	10.2	3.8	2 656	63.1	3.9	52.3	14.8	33.0
Potter County	535	26	7.1	137	0.0	2.2	0.0	2 150	60.9	1.4	51.9	16.6	31.5
Roberts County	2 294	210	2.0	627	0.0	6.9	10.7	7 407	61.5	7.2	52.0	16.4	31.6
Sanborn County	570	67	4.1	174	0.0	7.5	6.9	2 080	66.1	2.3	54.9	17.0	28.2
Shannon County	4 036	537	5.9	1 015	0.0	12.2	27.6	7 416	52.4	33.0	42.6	7.7	49.7
Spink County	1 483	90	5.5	462	0.6	5.6	8.9	5 791	56.9	3.3	50.6	15.3	34.1
Stanley County	603	42	5.7	178	0.0	6.2	2.2	2 130	81.3	1.4	68.8	16.5	14.7
Sully County	330	13	2.9	92	0.0	13.0	0.0	1 214	66.1	2.0	57.4	16.1	26.5
Todd County	2 824	504	1.2	754	0.0	10.1	12.9	5 507	58.1	18.4	51.6	9.4	39.0

Table B-3. States and Counties — **Education, Labor Force, and Income**

STATE County	Full-year full-time employed (percent)								Children under 18 years in families						Total employed by class of worker (percent)			
						American Indian and Alaska Native	Asian, Hawaiian, and Pacific Islander			With two parents (percent)		With one parent who is in labor force (percent)	+/− U.S. percent of children with no stay-at-home parent (percent)	+/− U.S. percent two-income couples				Unpaid family worker
	Total	Men	Women	Non-Hispanic White	Black or African American			Hispanic or Latino[1]	Number	Both in labor force	Father only in labor force				Private	Government	Self-employed	
	24	25	26	27	28	29	30	31	32	33	34	35	36	37	38	39	40	41
SOUTH CAROLINA—Cont'd																		
Sumter County	40.8	50.4	32.1	45.4	35.5	44.7	43.4	40.9	26 899	38.7	17.4	28.7	2.8	−1.0	72.4	18.5	8.7	0.3
Union County	41.3	50.2	33.7	41.9	39.5	90.9	54.9	43.2	6 532	38.1	12.8	31.5	5.0	−2.6	78.0	15.1	6.7	0.2
Williamsburg County	32.9	40.2	26.8	40.1	28.8	20.4	72.3	38.7	9 839	34.1	11.3	28.0	−2.5	−7.4	73.0	17.3	9.4	0.4
York County	46.0	57.6	35.5	47.7	39.0	50.8	45.5	41.3	40 604	49.0	19.8	21.7	6.1	5.6	80.8	11.2	7.7	0.3
SOUTH DAKOTA	42.8	51.7	34.2	44.3	33.4	24.6	39.4	38.4	191 501	57.8	13.4	19.5	12.7	10.7	69.2	15.3	14.7	0.8
Aurora County	38.5	47.4	29.3	39.8	0.0	0.0	50.0	30.0	710	70.1	6.5	12.3	17.8	8.3	57.4	15.1	26.7	0.9
Beadle County	42.4	52.0	33.3	42.8	40.6	18.8	38.5	12.5	4 100	61.1	14.3	18.6	15.1	7.7	69.8	14.2	15.4	0.6
Bennett County	30.9	37.1	25.3	45.3	23.1	16.1	X	16.1	1 142	33.0	10.8	26.0	−5.6	3.2	41.4	31.7	25.8	1.0
Bon Homme County	36.1	39.6	31.7	37.2	14.6	11.5	X	24.1	1 548	69.1	14.0	10.1	14.6	8.1	56.7	18.1	23.6	1.6
Brookings County	39.7	46.1	33.2	40.2	14.6	32.8	26.0	26.3	5 717	68.9	12.1	15.0	19.3	16.3	66.4	23.5	8.8	1.3
Brown County	44.8	54.9	35.6	44.8	16.7	49.0	46.8	30.5	8 114	62.2	12.2	19.7	17.3	11.1	70.9	15.5	13.3	0.2
Brule County	40.0	50.0	30.7	40.5	X	36.7	41.7	38.5	1 404	61.8	12.9	17.2	14.4	10.0	60.1	14.2	25.1	0.7
Buffalo County	23.6	28.2	18.9	37.2	0.0	19.8	50.0	33.3	705	27.4	6.7	24.1	−13.1	−13.4	30.5	54.0	13.2	2.3
Butte County	38.9	47.6	30.8	38.8	X	41.7	34.6	35.9	2 461	57.9	14.2	21.2	14.5	6.6	62.7	14.4	22.4	0.5
Campbell County	35.1	48.6	22.3	35.0	X	0.0	X	X	466	82.8	10.3	1.9	20.1	7.7	48.9	14.7	33.2	3.2
Charles Mix County	34.0	44.2	24.5	36.9	40.0	24.7	57.1	23.7	2 762	47.4	8.5	22.2	5.0	4.3	55.2	19.4	24.0	1.4
Clark County	36.2	48.8	24.2	36.2	X	100.0	0.0	18.2	1 094	63.3	21.3	9.5	8.2	3.0	51.1	12.1	29.9	6.9
Clay County	28.6	35.1	22.5	28.9	23.3	20.6	18.9	32.3	2 515	52.3	18.4	20.8	8.5	9.4	58.1	29.6	11.8	0.5
Codington County	46.1	57.3	35.3	46.0	100.0	48.7	76.2	59.2	6 707	68.5	8.9	16.3	20.2	13.5	75.5	10.2	13.4	0.9
Corson County	25.8	31.7	20.0	32.8	0.0	20.0	33.3	32.4	1 281	29.6	12.6	25.2	−9.8	−7.9	41.3	36.9	20.2	1.7
Custer County	33.8	39.3	28.0	33.8	0.0	33.9	100.0	37.5	1 499	59.6	13.2	16.1	11.1	1.9	53.9	24.7	20.6	0.8
Davison County	40.8	51.8	30.8	41.2	33.0	29.8	37.0	4.5	4 554	62.7	11.6	17.6	15.7	12.6	76.4	8.7	14.0	0.8
Day County	34.8	44.9	24.9	35.9	X	21.0	0.0	50.0	1 480	54.0	17.8	13.0	2.4	−0.1	58.6	13.7	25.8	1.9
Deuel County	43.5	52.1	34.9	43.7	0.0	38.5	0.0	48.0	1 110	69.8	13.6	11.8	17.0	8.9	63.7	12.6	22.8	0.9
Dewey County	30.9	33.1	28.8	36.9	100.0	28.1	37.0	0.0	1 993	33.1	10.0	31.9	0.4	−5.4	40.4	47.6	11.2	0.9
Douglas County	36.6	53.4	21.2	36.6	X	29.4	X	33.3	931	68.9	14.3	8.4	12.7	5.9	58.6	10.7	29.3	1.5
Edmunds County	39.1	50.0	29.1	39.2	X	50.0	0.0	36.4	1 144	62.2	17.7	9.4	7.0	5.8	56.8	14.8	25.5	2.9
Fall River County	32.4	37.4	27.2	33.1	0.0	21.0	33.3	47.1	1 475	51.9	14.9	24.6	11.9	−1.7	53.6	26.2	19.5	0.7
Faulk County	37.0	48.4	25.9	36.9	X	15.4	100.0	60.0	680	60.0	19.7	7.8	3.2	0.0	45.4	15.5	33.4	5.6
Grant County	41.4	53.9	29.2	41.3	X	44.7	50.0	11.8	2 062	68.0	14.2	10.7	14.1	10.0	70.3	8.5	20.0	1.2
Gregory County	36.8	50.3	24.3	37.7	28.6	19.1	85.7	38.1	1 113	68.6	11.4	12.0	16.0	5.9	54.0	11.3	33.3	1.4
Haakon County	44.1	57.9	30.9	44.2	X	36.7	75.0	0.0	542	63.8	12.4	13.5	12.7	14.3	56.4	12.4	29.9	1.3
Hamlin County	38.9	50.6	27.7	39.2	16.7	25.7	25.0	60.0	1 617	52.2	29.2	11.5	−0.9	6.6	65.0	11.6	22.1	1.3
Hand County	38.6	51.6	26.0	38.5	0.0	28.6	28.6	44.4	913	80.1	7.0	10.6	26.1	11.2	53.6	14.0	30.8	1.6
Hanson County	43.1	53.2	32.9	43.2	X	X	60.0	0.0	920	65.4	9.5	6.5	7.3	7.1	64.7	11.9	20.6	2.8
Harding County	42.4	54.5	29.1	43.1	X	7.7	X	0.0	398	71.1	20.1	6.8	13.3	16.5	29.7	17.9	47.7	4.7
Hughes County	50.9	58.7	43.9	52.6	52.2	26.5	29.5	37.7	4 205	64.5	11.6	17.7	17.6	18.9	52.4	36.4	11.0	0.2
Hutchinson County	38.4	51.9	26.1	38.3	100.0	37.5	X	50.0	1 941	62.3	11.4	12.1	9.8	2.9	61.9	9.1	25.7	3.4
Hyde County	39.0	52.0	26.0	39.1	X	35.8	X	X	424	62.3	14.6	19.3	17.0	6.9	46.7	21.1	30.1	2.2
Jackson County	27.8	33.9	21.9	37.4	X	14.2	40.0	100.0	888	31.6	18.9	28.8	−4.2	−9.6	47.3	30.9	20.5	1.3
Jerauld County	40.0	52.0	28.5	39.8	X	100.0	X	71.4	478	48.3	22.8	19.2	2.9	−1.2	58.3	10.2	28.9	2.5
Jones County	45.4	60.5	29.9	45.5	0.0	30.0	X	X	302	52.6	16.6	28.8	16.8	9.5	52.2	15.6	31.6	0.6
Kingsbury County	39.1	52.6	26.1	39.2	X	25.0	12.5	66.7	1 372	64.7	12.6	16.5	16.6	4.5	62.5	12.5	23.6	1.5
Lake County	41.7	48.9	34.5	41.6	0.0	55.1	29.5	44.0	2 631	69.9	12.8	12.0	17.3	8.7	73.2	14.1	11.5	1.2
Lawrence County	35.2	43.3	27.6	35.4	42.9	33.6	21.6	33.4	4 678	58.2	14.6	19.9	13.5	4.5	71.3	14.4	13.7	0.6
Lincoln County	52.9	64.5	41.6	53.4	9.4	20.3	47.8	24.0	7 006	67.3	15.4	12.7	15.4	20.7	77.3	9.2	13.2	0.3
Lyman County	40.0	51.1	28.6	45.6	100.0	26.1	0.0	0.0	1 166	47.6	11.0	28.0	11.0	11.3	47.5	24.3	27.4	0.8
McCook County	42.6	54.9	30.9	42.8	X	63.6	100.0	11.8	1 622	69.9	12.6	11.8	17.1	10.9	65.0	10.1	23.8	1.1
McPherson County	32.1	42.1	22.8	32.0	X	100.0	X	100.0	625	60.2	17.0	7.0	2.6	−5.0	51.1	12.8	30.8	5.4
Marshall County	37.9	50.4	25.9	39.1	X	21.4	0.0	0.0	1 194	53.4	15.9	17.3	6.1	0.7	56.8	15.0	27.7	0.5
Meade County	45.9	57.2	34.5	46.3	38.9	27.9	48.4	37.7	6 700	56.2	19.8	15.6	7.2	10.9	63.7	18.6	16.8	1.0
Mellette County	34.5	43.6	25.2	49.5	X	16.9	0.0	14.3	651	33.8	9.2	35.8	5.0	−1.3	41.9	31.8	25.4	0.9
Miner County	37.9	46.5	29.6	37.8	0.0	60.0	100.0	55.6	726	70.7	11.0	12.7	18.8	5.1	60.5	12.5	25.0	1.9
Minnehaha County	50.6	58.3	43.2	51.6	36.3	23.6	46.5	41.0	37 015	62.1	12.9	19.0	16.5	17.8	82.5	8.8	8.4	0.3
Moody County	46.6	55.3	38.0	48.0	23.1	37.7	50.0	38.9	1 847	63.9	11.6	18.1	17.4	14.5	66.0	16.4	16.5	1.0
Pennington County	43.6	52.8	34.8	45.2	37.8	23.7	36.4	43.9	22 403	50.8	15.1	24.0	10.2	9.7	74.5	14.7	10.5	0.3
Perkins County	40.5	49.7	31.6	41.0	0.0	42.4	15.4	0.0	792	61.6	15.0	15.4	12.4	6.8	51.7	11.6	35.4	1.3
Potter County	36.8	49.3	24.8	37.0	X	22.2	25.0	X	618	57.9	23.8	13.6	6.9	2.9	55.2	15.7	26.8	2.2
Roberts County	35.3	45.1	25.8	36.4	40.0	32.1	48.5	27.8	2 775	42.3	15.0	29.3	7.0	1.7	57.9	20.9	19.7	1.5
Sanborn County	42.9	52.5	33.0	42.9	X	0.0	60.0	60.0	641	56.0	15.3	17.5	8.9	5.8	63.3	10.7	23.6	2.3
Shannon County	20.6	21.4	19.7	31.0	0.0	19.6	0.0	22.4	4 591	18.1	11.7	44.2	−2.3	−19.9	38.1	55.4	6.0	0.6
Spink County	37.5	44.5	30.0	37.9	50.0	11.8	0.0	60.0	1 843	65.9	12.5	12.6	13.9	3.5	46.7	24.5	26.8	2.0
Stanley County	56.6	63.5	49.6	56.8	100.0	55.3	50.0	100.0	708	63.7	8.2	24.6	23.7	22.7	50.6	30.0	19.0	0.5
Sully County	43.9	56.2	30.4	44.5	X	0.0	X	0.0	364	67.0	20.9	8.5	10.9	5.0	52.1	17.5	30.1	0.3
Todd County	30.4	31.8	29.1	47.1	X	26.9	13.3	31.4	3 387	18.0	5.3	46.2	−0.4	−9.2	48.0	43.2	8.7	0.0

[1] Hispanic or Latino persons may be of any race.

Table B-3. States and Counties — Education, Labor Force, and Income

STATE County	Percent who worked at home	Percent of the population 5 years and over with a disability	Veterans as a percent of the population 18 years and over	Occupation for employed population 16 years and over (percent)						Industry for employed population 16 years and over (percent)					
				Management, professional, and related occupations	Service occupations	Sales and office occupations	Farming, fishing, and forestry occupations	Construction, extraction, and maintenance occupations	Production, transportation and material moving occupations	Agriculture, forestry, fishing, and mining	Construction and manufacturing	Wholesale and retail trade	Transportation and warehousing, and utilities	Service industries	Public administration
	42	43	44	45	46	47	48	49	50	51	52	53	54	55	56
SOUTH CAROLINA—Cont'd															
Sumter County	1.6	23.3	16.0	24.9	15.5	24.5	0.6	11.4	23.1	1.4	31.4	14.7	3.8	42.6	6.1
Union County	0.7	26.6	11.4	19.3	13.0	21.1	0.8	12.9	32.9	1.4	44.4	11.8	4.2	33.7	4.5
Williamsburg County	1.4	29.3	9.2	22.6	17.5	18.7	1.6	13.0	26.6	3.9	34.1	11.7	3.6	42.5	4.1
York County	2.1	19.8	13.8	29.6	12.4	26.3	0.4	11.7	19.6	0.6	29.3	17.4	6.2	43.8	2.6
SOUTH DAKOTA	6.5	16.7	14.4	32.6	15.6	26.5	1.9	9.1	14.2	8.1	17.3	15.3	4.7	49.8	4.8
Aurora County	14.8	16.9	14.7	39.7	17.2	17.7	4.0	7.7	13.7	24.0	11.5	14.2	3.6	39.4	7.3
Beadle County	6.6	20.6	16.3	32.0	16.9	20.3	2.6	8.1	20.1	8.9	18.6	13.7	7.0	46.9	5.0
Bennett County	6.7	20.9	10.9	40.5	15.7	19.9	5.3	10.9	7.7	19.3	8.6	15.9	4.6	43.0	8.6
Bon Homme County	13.6	17.5	15.5	38.5	19.7	14.9	3.0	8.4	15.5	17.4	18.0	11.9	3.9	39.5	9.2
Brookings County	4.8	13.2	10.4	32.1	15.7	24.6	2.3	6.8	18.6	5.9	24.8	11.6	3.3	51.5	3.0
Brown County	4.2	10.9	12.0	30.1	15.7	30.3	1.6	8.7	13.7	5.7	17.3	17.1	3.3	51.4	5.2
Brule County	11.7	18.4	13.4	40.5	18.2	22.0	2.8	9.0	7.4	16.0	9.1	15.9	4.2	50.5	4.3
Buffalo County	10.8	33.8	12.9	31.6	23.6	21.2	7.9	8.5	7.2	20.1	9.7	6.5	1.2	49.9	12.7
Butte County	8.9	22.2	15.2	27.0	19.5	21.1	4.9	11.8	15.7	19.4	15.2	14.5	5.2	41.4	4.3
Campbell County	21.1	16.0	12.7	42.6	13.1	20.4	5.7	7.6	10.5	29.8	12.6	9.8	5.6	38.3	3.8
Charles Mix County	12.7	17.0	14.1	37.7	21.4	21.0	3.5	7.7	8.8	19.1	6.9	13.9	4.1	49.2	6.7
Clark County	19.4	19.1	12.1	36.3	16.3	17.3	7.7	9.4	13.1	27.8	16.7	10.3	5.8	35.4	3.8
Clay County	5.4	12.1	9.6	35.1	20.6	30.2	0.5	5.5	8.1	4.9	12.5	13.8	4.0	61.8	3.0
Codington County	5.1	16.0	13.2	26.4	14.3	25.3	1.8	8.2	24.0	4.9	27.0	17.7	4.7	43.1	2.5
Corson County	10.4	19.8	15.1	41.4	19.0	18.7	5.3	7.9	7.7	21.6	7.5	6.5	2.7	51.3	10.4
Custer County	8.1	18.6	21.7	34.6	16.8	23.9	2.2	9.6	12.9	12.2	14.0	11.3	6.5	50.1	5.8
Davison County	6.2	15.9	12.1	29.9	16.8	25.3	1.5	9.9	16.7	5.9	22.6	17.5	3.0	48.5	2.5
Day County	13.4	20.6	15.2	35.6	16.4	19.2	4.4	10.5	13.9	18.9	19.0	11.1	5.3	42.2	3.6
Deuel County	11.8	18.8	16.4	33.0	15.0	18.1	4.1	10.5	19.4	17.1	25.7	10.0	6.2	37.7	3.2
Dewey County	8.2	21.4	15.4	35.4	10.6	24.8	2.5	7.3	10.3	9.8	8.8	11.7	3.6	49.6	16.5
Douglas County	19.4	14.4	14.6	41.9	15.7	15.0	5.5	9.3	12.6	27.0	13.7	12.0	4.4	39.7	3.1
Edmunds County	13.9	17.6	13.4	37.8	16.1	21.1	4.0	9.5	11.5	19.7	10.7	14.4	7.1	44.0	4.0
Fall River County	7.6	25.8	26.8	24.7	19.0	19.9	2.7	10.4	13.2	10.8	11.3	11.2	9.1	52.9	4.7
Faulk County	18.4	17.5	15.4	40.6	15.2	18.7	8.0	8.8	8.7	31.4	8.6	12.0	6.2	38.1	3.6
Grant County	9.5	16.6	15.1	31.1	14.7	25.6	3.1	10.0	15.5	15.5	14.1	17.6	7.5	42.0	3.3
Gregory County	20.1	22.1	14.5	39.2	15.3	20.0	4.4	12.0	9.1	24.0	10.8	15.0	6.1	40.9	3.3
Haakon County	14.1	15.1	12.4	37.4	10.5	21.8	6.6	9.0	14.7	24.2	12.4	16.3	5.8	37.0	4.3
Hamlin County	9.5	18.4	13.0	30.9	14.3	20.4	3.1	10.6	20.8	14.6	25.7	15.0	5.8	36.5	2.4
Hand County	19.3	16.9	15.5	40.9	15.3	18.6	8.5	8.9	7.9	29.1	8.6	13.4	5.2	39.9	3.7
Hanson County	12.0	12.9	13.4	33.0	13.6	22.6	4.5	9.0	17.3	19.6	18.8	12.6	4.1	41.4	3.5
Harding County	31.4	13.0	10.9	54.3	8.2	13.4	11.5	8.2	4.4	54.3	5.6	7.8	4.7	22.2	5.4
Hughes County	3.8	16.0	15.0	40.7	14.0	28.4	1.2	8.9	6.8	4.0	9.6	14.2	4.2	44.7	23.3
Hutchinson County	10.1	10.0	12.1	37.0	16.6	19.2	4.1	9.5	13.6	19.8	16.9	15.6	3.0	41.8	2.8
Hyde County	20.4	18.7	13.6	47.0	15.0	16.8	7.6	8.0	5.7	28.8	6.5	9.5	3.0	46.8	5.3
Jackson County	16.6	21.1	15.2	42.7	18.6	18.0	5.0	7.0	8.6	19.5	6.0	10.2	4.7	50.3	9.4
Jerauld County	16.5	18.1	14.3	35.4	15.0	19.8	4.8	10.0	15.0	22.8	16.3	16.3	5.6	35.1	3.9
Jones County	12.7	15.5	15.3	37.7	10.9	26.2	6.5	10.0	8.7	26.3	7.6	18.5	8.1	35.5	3.9
Kingsbury County	11.4	16.0	15.1	34.9	13.5	18.4	3.4	7.6	22.2	17.5	24.7	10.8	5.7	38.4	2.9
Lake County	5.6	14.6	12.3	29.5	14.9	25.8	1.9	10.9	17.0	6.4	24.6	17.3	4.5	45.1	2.2
Lawrence County	3.9	16.6	15.0	28.8	23.0	22.9	1.7	12.1	11.5	9.0	12.1	14.1	3.0	58.8	3.0
Lincoln County	4.8	11.5	13.4	33.8	11.3	30.8	0.5	9.5	14.0	3.5	19.9	17.9	4.8	51.1	2.8
Lyman County	14.3	16.4	15.5	42.7	15.8	19.7	6.0	8.0	7.7	26.4	7.2	12.2	5.3	38.7	10.3
McCook County	10.9	16.5	13.2	34.5	15.3	22.4	2.7	9.8	15.2	15.6	16.8	14.6	4.9	45.2	2.9
McPherson County	22.4	25.4	14.1	38.9	14.3	20.5	7.6	8.0	10.7	30.3	10.8	10.7	3.5	40.3	4.4
Marshall County	13.1	17.5	13.4	36.5	13.9	18.5	5.0	8.8	17.3	23.6	19.5	11.6	4.2	37.1	4.0
Meade County	5.9	15.4	18.9	27.4	17.1	27.5	1.8	11.4	14.8	7.7	14.5	16.4	7.1	47.5	6.8
Mellette County	20.8	19.6	15.1	43.8	16.4	13.4	9.4	10.8	6.3	29.6	9.5	8.2	4.4	42.4	5.9
Miner County	15.2	19.8	15.6	36.5	14.5	14.6	4.2	8.2	22.0	19.8	20.3	10.1	4.1	42.3	3.4
Minnehaha County	3.2	15.8	13.1	30.7	13.1	32.4	0.4	8.7	14.7	1.5	18.2	16.8	5.0	55.4	3.1
Moody County	10.3	15.4	16.6	30.8	18.9	21.2	2.5	9.9	16.6	11.8	20.9	10.5	4.3	48.6	3.9
Pennington County	3.1	17.2	17.5	31.8	16.8	28.6	0.9	9.9	12.1	2.3	16.6	17.4	4.2	54.5	5.1
Perkins County	21.7	17.2	13.2	43.8	10.9	20.0	4.5	7.9	13.0	29.6	14.3	10.5	7.3	34.6	3.8
Potter County	10.1	21.3	16.5	37.3	15.7	21.1	5.0	11.3	9.6	21.2	11.9	17.1	4.8	39.7	5.2
Roberts County	9.2	18.4	14.3	34.0	10.2	22.7	3.6	8.8	12.0	14.4	11.0	13.5	4.1	51.0	6.1
Sanborn County	11.9	16.6	16.8	35.9	14.3	16.7	4.6	10.8	17.6	20.1	19.3	13.9	3.1	40.3	3.2
Shannon County	2.5	18.5	11.8	37.8	20.5	24.5	0.5	7.7	9.0	2.0	6.7	6.0	3.3	61.7	20.3
Spink County	13.7	20.7	14.9	34.0	23.1	19.8	3.3	9.1	10.7	20.7	9.9	13.3	4.7	43.3	8.1
Stanley County	8.9	16.5	13.3	34.8	13.0	28.7	3.0	9.0	11.5	13.1	10.3	14.8	5.4	37.9	18.5
Sully County	15.6	13.4	13.4	41.7	12.7	19.4	7.5	9.3	9.4	29.7	10.3	13.9	4.7	33.3	8.1
Todd County	4.2	15.1	14.4	36.9	19.9	21.2	2.0	10.5	9.4	8.3	7.6	7.4	2.9	62.5	11.3

Table B-3. States and Counties — Education, Labor Force, and Income

STATE County	Median family income					Median income for full-year, full-time workers			Households by source of income (percent)									
	Median house-hold income	All families	Married-couple	Male house-holder	Female house-holder	Median nonfamily house-hold income	Men	Women	Per capita income	With earnings	With interest, dividend, or rental income	With Social Security income	With public assis-tance income	With retire-ment income	House-holds with income over $100,000 (percent)	+/- U.S. percent for income over $100,000	House-holds with income below poverty (percent)	Families with children with income below poverty (percent)
	57	58	59	60	61	62	63	64	65	66	67	68	69	70	71	72	73	74
SOUTH CAROLINA—Cont'd																		
Sumter County	33 278	38 970	47 383	26 206	18 107	17 619	29 772	21 930	15 657	78.9	23.5	27.0	3.4	19.8	5.3	-7.0	16.3	18.2
Union County	31 441	37 661	46 023	23 813	16 686	15 341	30 133	21 331	15 877	75.5	19.3	33.0	2.8	18.7	3.7	-8.6	16.0	17.3
Williamsburg County	24 214	30 379	40 061	21 667	12 494	10 770	27 213	18 578	12 794	71.2	13.1	29.5	4.8	16.6	3.4	-8.9	29.0	32.4
York County	44 539	51 815	60 387	30 406	21 269	25 237	37 599	25 512	20 536	84.6	30.2	23.6	2.1	15.5	10.2	-2.1	10.1	10.6
SOUTH DAKOTA	35 282	43 237	50 872	24 255	17 977	20 672	30 723	22 172	17 562	81.4	41.0	28.0	3.0	12.7	5.9	-6.4	12.5	13.9
Aurora County	29 783	37 227	40 469	23 125	19 500	16 289	26 210	21 360	13 887	78.1	49.5	35.4	2.9	12.5	2.3	-10.0	12.3	10.5
Beadle County	30 510	40 596	46 644	22 500	18 264	17 627	28 570	20 835	17 832	76.7	42.6	35.2	2.7	15.2	3.4	-8.9	14.3	13.7
Bennett County	25 313	28 363	32 500	18 125	11 667	18 594	27 689	18 281	10 106	77.6	31.3	29.2	9.9	10.8	2.0	-10.3	29.2	39.4
Bon Homme County	30 644	36 924	41 992	24 821	20 000	16 781	25 497	20 923	13 892	74.3	49.1	39.5	2.1	13.2	2.4	-9.9	13.6	13.8
Brookings County	35 438	48 052	56 932	23 958	17 778	19 925	31 530	22 856	17 586	86.1	43.9	20.9	1.3	10.7	5.5	-6.8	15.1	9.5
Brown County	35 017	44 788	52 135	27 120	16 813	19 976	30 429	21 117	18 464	80.5	42.0	28.7	2.0	12.9	5.3	-7.0	11.3	10.6
Brule County	32 370	37 361	47 102	25 000	25 000	20 233	27 833	20 757	14 874	80.5	41.2	31.7	1.3	10.9	3.8	-8.5	10.9	9.8
Buffalo County	12 692	14 167	29 688	15 000	6 719	6 618	19 219	20 592	5 213	57.7	13.1	17.5	10.8	3.8	1.3	-11.0	56.2	61.2
Butte County	29 040	34 173	41 518	26 016	15 726	15 515	27 348	17 123	13 997	80.3	36.9	34.3	4.4	13.8	3.2	-9.1	13.4	14.6
Campbell County	28 793	35 938	40 455	0	24 375	12 583	24 097	17 500	14 117	74.7	48.9	41.1	2.2	10.9	2.6	-9.7	18.4	9.3
Charles Mix County	26 060	30 688	39 261	16 125	13 603	14 830	25 830	20 320	11 502	72.2	34.0	35.4	6.2	12.3	1.9	-10.4	23.4	29.3
Clark County	30 208	35 559	42 798	30 000	20 250	15 938	25 546	20 405	15 597	75.7	43.3	39.9	2.3	10.8	3.2	-9.1	13.0	14.4
Clay County	27 535	41 391	51 250	21 304	12 000	16 214	27 940	22 289	14 452	84.3	42.0	19.6	3.1	11.4	5.4	-6.9	21.6	17.2
Codington County	36 257	45 153	51 333	25 476	15 982	18 347	30 869	20 313	18 761	81.9	41.5	27.6	2.5	12.1	6.2	-6.1	10.7	8.4
Corson County	20 654	23 889	30 417	10 938	14 000	11 600	24 474	20 690	8 615	73.8	24.4	27.7	15.0	7.7	1.3	-11.0	34.5	41.2
Custer County	36 303	43 628	48 165	16 600	20 714	18 040	32 267	21 673	17 945	78.4	46.6	34.9	2.5	23.0	4.9	-7.4	9.3	12.2
Davison County	33 476	44 357	52 407	26 827	17 500	18 599	31 518	21 667	17 879	78.5	42.8	29.9	2.5	12.6	5.1	-7.2	13.6	12.1
Day County	30 227	38 011	41 654	19 688	14 375	17 263	28 478	19 012	15 856	73.9	46.3	41.2	3.5	12.6	3.0	-9.3	15.4	17.0
Deuel County	31 788	39 511	46 161	28 750	16 932	17 820	27 331	19 823	15 977	77.0	46.4	37.5	2.9	13.1	3.1	-9.2	11.8	9.3
Dewey County	23 272	24 917	35 978	19 167	14 291	12 989	21 854	19 559	9 251	78.4	19.5	22.9	13.3	9.5	1.8	-10.5	31.5	36.9
Douglas County	28 478	33 935	39 837	25 313	15 250	16 067	26 707	18 583	13 827	76.7	46.2	38.1	1.2	7.7	2.7	-9.6	15.4	14.6
Edmunds County	32 205	37 174	40 850	26 250	19 000	16 875	28 576	20 063	16 149	74.1	46.2	38.6	2.0	11.3	4.4	-7.9	14.4	14.2
Fall River County	29 631	37 827	44 115	22 986	18 393	16 638	32 314	21 414	17 048	73.2	38.1	39.0	2.7	21.0	4.5	-7.8	13.2	14.3
Faulk County	30 237	34 508	37 386	23 125	17 813	19 655	26 250	16 636	14 660	72.5	47.9	40.9	2.7	16.4	3.3	-9.0	14.3	18.9
Grant County	33 088	40 407	47 396	36 719	16 719	17 003	30 075	20 652	16 543	76.1	46.6	33.8	3.7	12.6	4.5	-7.8	11.3	8.6
Gregory County	22 732	30 833	34 712	19 286	16 125	13 322	22 101	17 500	13 656	70.6	41.5	43.2	2.8	13.1	2.1	-10.2	20.6	22.3
Haakon County	29 894	35 958	43 036	11 875	14 688	19 934	25 784	19 659	16 780	81.8	47.0	30.5	1.6	9.0	6.7	-5.6	14.2	16.0
Hamlin County	33 851	41 511	44 962	19 792	20 000	18 664	29 710	21 629	16 982	77.4	43.7	33.8	2.4	12.2	4.7	-7.6	9.9	10.2
Hand County	32 377	38 017	44 545	18 500	18 500	16 328	27 607	17 083	18 735	74.8	45.2	41.3	1.9	10.8	5.8	-6.5	12.2	8.7
Hanson County	33 049	39 500	45 968	41 250	22 500	19 100	28 443	20 878	14 778	80.0	44.7	29.6	1.5	10.1	5.1	-7.2	13.5	16.7
Harding County	25 000	31 667	39 219	30 833	24 375	12 417	27 250	17 404	12 794	75.7	38.7	30.5	1.5	5.7	3.4	-8.9	21.8	23.5
Hughes County	42 970	51 235	56 974	25 057	21 250	24 400	33 602	24 514	20 689	85.4	45.5	25.3	2.0	13.0	7.3	-5.0	9.1	7.6
Hutchinson County	30 026	37 715	43 044	28 125	20 417	17 012	26 521	18 908	15 922	74.3	50.6	40.9	3.0	10.2	3.0	-9.3	12.2	12.4
Hyde County	31 103	40 700	45 000	20 000	26 875	18 571	26 125	19 600	16 356	78.2	47.5	40.7	2.5	11.2	4.3	-8.0	14.3	10.7
Jackson County	23 945	25 161	28 194	13 281	13 261	15 156	25 313	18 382	9 981	76.1	32.2	29.9	6.6	11.3	2.2	-10.1	29.9	40.8
Jerauld County	30 690	36 076	39 821	28 500	13 750	16 118	25 966	18 553	16 856	75.4	48.8	41.6	2.2	10.2	4.0	-8.3	16.8	25.1
Jones County	30 288	37 500	48 750	21 875	15 694	17 143	25 625	17 727	15 896	84.1	42.2	34.7	1.8	7.8	4.2	-8.1	12.7	21.1
Kingsbury County	31 262	41 057	47 411	33 438	21 023	17 011	28 605	20 247	16 522	73.9	51.1	41.0	1.6	12.2	4.5	-7.8	10.1	10.2
Lake County	34 087	43 750	51 400	19 375	19 688	20 779	29 964	21 616	16 446	81.6	44.0	30.6	2.7	12.9	4.2	-8.1	10.4	8.0
Lawrence County	31 755	40 501	48 311	21 667	16 739	17 062	31 100	20 798	17 195	77.7	40.4	28.7	2.9	18.6	5.5	-6.8	14.3	15.1
Lincoln County	48 338	55 401	61 019	31 920	21 658	25 958	35 474	24 867	22 304	86.9	45.1	20.5	1.4	9.7	11.6	-0.7	5.3	4.0
Lyman County	28 509	32 028	44 400	20 000	13 472	16 563	24 861	19 448	13 862	82.5	32.6	31.1	4.5	8.2	3.8	-8.5	20.5	26.9
McCook County	35 396	42 609	46 181	34 167	19 625	18 500	29 963	21 611	16 374	78.7	50.1	36.5	1.8	10.7	4.2	-8.1	8.4	7.2
McPherson County	22 380	29 811	32 396	34 375	23 125	11 987	25 230	17 717	12 748	66.3	44.1	46.1	2.4	9.3	3.0	-9.3	22.8	22.5
Marshall County	30 567	36 295	41 607	26 875	16 094	16 250	29 301	18 861	15 462	74.7	44.8	37.9	2.6	11.8	3.3	-9.0	14.0	14.8
Meade County	36 992	40 537	43 613	22 315	19 107	20 989	28 205	21 354	17 680	85.2	37.8	23.4	2.5	14.6	5.0	-7.3	9.6	11.1
Mellette County	23 219	25 221	37 500	15 000	9 444	17 935	25 170	19 009	10 362	78.1	32.7	27.9	14.6	7.3	2.2	-10.1	33.7	40.5
Miner County	29 519	36 667	44 643	9 500	20 750	15 227	26 053	20 938	15 155	73.4	47.5	40.4	3.1	11.9	2.9	-9.4	13.1	12.9
Minnehaha County	42 566	52 031	59 620	29 301	22 010	25 038	33 519	25 401	20 713	86.4	40.1	22.0	2.2	11.9	8.4	-3.9	7.5	7.8
Moody County	35 467	41 623	49 375	27 500	20 179	20 179	28 964	21 650	16 541	82.2	44.3	28.5	2.3	10.2	4.9	-7.4	9.7	10.7
Pennington County	37 485	44 796	53 057	22 767	17 447	23 002	31 991	22 272	18 938	83.7	39.2	25.0	3.2	16.1	7.1	-5.2	10.8	14.3
Perkins County	27 750	33 537	39 250	22 000	26 667	17 772	24 925	17 383	15 734	73.9	46.6	39.3	2.6	12.5	4.5	-7.8	16.3	18.7
Potter County	30 086	37 827	38 833	25 000	15 179	17 383	26 763	18 008	17 417	76.3	48.0	40.5	1.1	11.3	4.5	-7.8	12.6	15.4
Roberts County	28 322	33 361	39 797	20 804	15 606	16 497	26 315	20 428	13 428	78.7	37.2	34.5	5.0	10.5	3.3	-9.0	19.6	24.6
Sanborn County	33 375	38 256	41 591	25 000	20 781	20 313	27 083	18 878	18 301	79.1	46.2	32.9	1.6	12.5	5.5	-6.8	14.5	14.2
Shannon County	20 916	20 897	28 148	30 278	13 390	9 213	26 187	23 634	6 286	77.2	10.6	20.4	17.0	7.0	2.3	-10.0	45.5	51.8
Spink County	31 717	37 114	42 381	31 667	15 000	19 232	26 630	20 729	15 728	74.6	45.1	37.9	3.4	15.2	5.1	-7.2	12.2	16.4
Stanley County	41 170	47 197	56 750	17 292	25 179	26 618	30 784	21 617	20 300	89.9	33.5	23.4	2.2	9.3	6.8	-5.5	9.2	9.8
Sully County	32 500	38 304	41 667	28 750	12 250	22 059	26 008	20 938	17 407	82.0	44.1	31.4	2.4	11.3	5.1	-7.2	11.6	15.3
Todd County	20 035	19 533	35 096	14 250	14 022	14 293	21 379	21 815	7 714	79.6	12.4	15.6	17.7	7.7	2.8	-9.5	42.7	49.9

Table B-3. States and Counties — **Education, Labor Force, and Income**

STATE/ County code	MSA/PMSA/ NECMA code[1]	STATE County	High school graduates			College graduates		College graduates (percent)				
			Total population 25 years and over	Percent with a high school diploma or less	Percent with a high school diploma or more	Percent with a bachelor's degree or more	+/− U.S. percent with bachelor's degree or more	Non-Hispanic White	Black or African American	American Indian and Alaska Native	Asian, Hawaiian, and Pacific Islander	Hispanic or Latino[2]
			1	2	3	4	5	6	7	8	9	10
		SOUTH DAKOTA— Cont'd										
46 123	...	Tripp County	4 218	58.7	80.2	13.5	-10.9	14.0	X	2.6	0.0	9.1
46 125	..:	Turner County	6 019	54.1	83.2	17.0	-7.4	17.0	0.0	0.0	0.0	0.0
46 127	...	Union County	8 262	45.6	87.2	26.3	1.9	25.5	19.0	24.3	74.6	30.8
46 129	...	Walworth County	4 083	58.7	78.1	15.8	-8.6	15.8	X	9.6	0.0	0.0
46 135	...	Yankton County	14 178	47.9	86.1	23.0	-1.4	23.9	9.4	2.5	0.0	10.5
46 137	...	Ziebach County	1 223	64.3	71.4	12.0	-12.4	17.1	X	8.4	22.2	X
47 000	...	TENNESSEE	3 744 928	55.7	75.9	19.6	-4.8	20.5	12.9	14.8	46.7	14.1
47 001	3840	Anderson County	49 499	54.0	78.9	20.8	-3.6	20.7	14.6	19.4	67.8	20.8
47 003	...	Bedford County	24 232	60.3	69.7	11.1	-13.3	12.3	4.3	0.0	16.4	4.5
47 005	...	Benton County	11 798	76.6	65.8	6.3	-18.1	6.1	12.7	0.0	14.6	30.2
47 007	...	Bledsoe County	8 455	75.1	66.0	7.1	-17.3	7.5	0.0	0.0	0.0	3.3
47 009	3840	Blount County	72 938	56.0	78.4	17.9	-6.5	18.1	9.6	7.0	47.7	19.4
47 011	...	Bradley County	57 163	56.0	73.3	15.9	-8.5	15.8	10.3	11.2	39.0	28.4
47 013	...	Campbell County	27 359	76.8	58.7	7.0	-17.4	6.9	7.5	0.0	40.4	19.5
47 015	...	Cannon County	8 486	76.0	67.2	8.4	-16.0	8.4	12.5	0.0	0.0	0.0
47 017	...	Carroll County	20 238	70.5	67.9	11.1	-13.3	11.6	7.2	22.2	17.4	11.7
47 019	3660	Carter County	39 450	64.4	69.1	12.8	-11.6	12.8	11.7	16.7	14.7	10.6
47 021	5360	Cheatham County	23 341	61.7	75.4	15.1	-9.3	15.1	10.0	22.5	32.7	20.4
47 023	3580	Chester County	9 531	65.3	67.8	11.2	-13.2	11.6	7.1	X	85.7	0.0
47 025	...	Claiborne County	20 200	74.2	60.3	8.9	-15.5	9.0	3.8	0.0	68.8	0.0
47 027	...	Clay County	5 623	80.2	58.4	6.8	-17.6	6.4	0.0	0.0	72.7	0.0
47 029	...	Cocke County	23 070	76.9	61.2	6.2	-18.2	6.2	1.8	0.0	35.5	0.0
47 031	...	Coffee County	32 079	59.2	73.7	17.5	-6.9	17.3	13.3	19.8	46.7	15.6
47 033	...	Crockett County	9 690	72.1	65.1	9.1	-15.3	10.3	2.8	0.0	60.0	3.4
47 035	...	Cumberland County	33 595	63.1	72.5	13.7	-10.7	13.6	37.7	13.6	25.5	13.4
47 037	5360	Davidson County	377 734	43.1	81.5	30.5	6.1	34.1	20.2	15.9	50.0	14.4
47 039	...	Decatur County	8 247	76.3	63.6	7.3	-17.1	7.4	2.7	0.0	50.0	0.0
47 041	...	DeKalb County	11 870	72.9	64.6	11.3	-13.1	11.0	21.1	88.9	45.5	6.7
47 043	5360	Dickson County	28 108	67.1	72.6	11.3	-13.1	11.6	4.0	13.5	31.0	15.1
47 045	...	Dyer County	24 356	67.3	66.3	12.0	-12.4	12.6	5.7	0.0	37.0	10.2
47 047	4920	Fayette County	18 991	64.3	70.6	12.8	-11.6	15.4	7.5	8.6	33.3	5.1
47 049	...	Fentress County	11 275	79.9	57.3	8.3	-16.1	8.3	0.0	X	0.0	19.6
47 051	...	Franklin County	25 963	61.7	73.8	15.3	-9.1	15.8	6.6	3.4	31.8	15.4
47 053	...	Gibson County	32 751	68.4	70.9	10.1	-14.3	10.8	6.8	0.0	13.0	10.7
47 055	...	Giles County	19 829	70.1	72.5	10.6	-13.8	11.2	4.1	39.6	51.3	3.4
47 057	...	Grainger County	14 210	77.1	60.1	7.8	-16.6	7.8	0.0	47.4	0.0	1.3
47 059	...	Greene County	43 752	67.8	69.6	12.8	-11.6	12.8	8.7	0.0	40.4	6.9
47 061	...	Grundy County	9 441	80.3	55.2	7.1	-17.3	7.1	0.0	10.5	50.0	6.6
47 063	...	Hamblen County	39 340	63.7	69.3	13.3	-11.1	13.5	8.6	5.8	35.7	9.8
47 065	1560	Hamilton County	207 180	46.5	80.7	23.9	-0.5	26.6	10.6	22.1	48.9	19.4
47 067	...	Hancock County	4 617	76.0	55.9	10.2	-14.2	10.1	0.0	0.0	46.2	16.7
47 069	...	Hardeman County	18 595	71.3	66.7	7.8	-16.6	9.4	5.1	2.7	16.2	0.0
47 071	...	Hardin County	17 644	72.1	66.9	9.8	-14.6	10.0	4.4	0.0	17.0	7.6
47 073	3660	Hawkins County	37 146	69.3	70.4	10.0	-14.4	9.7	13.4	0.0	60.6	19.4
47 075	...	Haywood County	12 421	71.8	65.6	11.1	-13.3	15.9	5.7	25.0	52.2	0.0
47 077	...	Henderson County	17 140	70.5	69.3	9.3	-15.1	9.3	8.8	15.9	0.0	16.4
47 079	...	Henry County	21 791	69.6	70.5	12.1	-12.3	12.5	7.4	0.0	61.1	11.5
47 081	...	Hickman County	14 899	73.1	64.3	6.7	-17.7	6.9	2.4	0.0	0.0	5.9
47 083	...	Houston County	5 539	71.0	70.1	10.3	-14.1	10.0	2.4	0.0	87.5	19.6
47 085	...	Humphreys County	12 270	71.2	72.0	9.3	-15.1	9.1	2.7	4.8	47.8	8.3
47 087	...	Jackson County	7 671	77.2	61.6	8.4	-16.0	7.8	0.0	21.9	71.4	0.0
47 089	...	Jefferson County	29 455	64.6	71.0	12.8	-11.6	12.8	14.5	0.0	50.8	6.3
47 091	...	Johnson County	12 755	76.1	58.4	6.9	-17.5	6.9	2.1	0.0	40.7	6.4
47 093	3840	Knox County	252 530	44.6	82.5	29.0	4.6	29.7	16.4	19.4	63.3	30.0
47 095	...	Lake County	5 492	79.3	56.0	5.4	-19.0	7.3	0.9	0.0	X	0.0
47 097	...	Lauderdale County	17 507	75.9	62.3	7.7	-16.7	9.3	4.1	24.4	6.0	18.1
47 099	...	Lawrence County	26 145	72.8	65.5	8.7	-15.7	8.8	9.7	0.0	13.8	4.8
47 101	...	Lewis County	7 466	70.7	69.5	8.5	-15.9	8.3	7.7	46.2	50.0	0.0
47 103	...	Lincoln County	21 361	67.1	69.6	11.9	-12.5	12.5	4.3	0.0	0.0	13.2
47 105	3840	Loudon County	27 899	57.6	75.6	17.0	-7.4	17.3	4.1	42.4	31.8	8.4
47 107	...	McMinn County	33 110	66.9	69.3	10.8	-13.6	10.7	10.4	5.1	69.7	6.5
47 109	...	McNairy County	16 787	71.7	68.5	8.8	-15.6	8.8	6.2	0.0	67.9	0.0
47 111	...	Macon County	13 331	78.8	60.2	5.6	-18.8	5.6	0.0	0.0	51.9	1.3
47 113	3580	Madison County	58 038	52.1	78.8	21.5	-2.9	25.6	11.4	16.8	50.8	15.1
47 115	1560	Marion County	18 815	69.8	64.6	9.5	-14.9	9.8	3.7	0.0	16.7	8.3

[1]MSA = Metropolitan Statistical Area. PMSA = Primary MSA. NECMA = New England County Metropolitan Area. See the Appendix A for explanation of these concepts. See Appendix B for list of metropolitan areas identified by type, with component counties.
[2]Hispanic or Latino persons may be of any race.

STATE County	School enrollment			Population 16 to 19 years				Employment status, 2000			Work status in 1999 of the population 16 years and over (percent)		
											Worked in 1999		
	Grades kindergarten through 12	College or graduate school	Percent private	Number	Percent in armed forces	Percent high school graduates	Percent not enrolled, not grads, not in armed forces, not employed	Total population 16 years and over	Percent in labor force	Unemployment rate	Full-time	Part-time	Did not work in 1999
	11	12	13	14	15	16	17	18	19	20	21	22	23
SOUTH DAKOTA— Cont'd													
Tripp County...............	1 421	65	3.5	391	0.0	8.4	9.7	4 861	64.7	4.2	54.0	15.7	30.3
Turner County..............	1 860	203	7.0	490	0.4	9.6	1.0	6 860	66.3	1.7	56.2	16.9	27.0
Union County	2 602	477	10.6	721	0.0	11.0	1.4	9 596	71.9	1.9	61.4	14.8	23.7
Walworth County...........	1 134	113	7.4	320	0.0	10.0	9.7	4 705	59.8	6.1	49.7	17.0	33.3
Yankton County............	4 219	1 130	15.9	1 157	0.0	7.8	3.0	16 692	66.5	2.4	56.8	17.2	25.9
Ziebach County............	735	84	7.1	201	0.0	9.5	23.4	1 600	51.4	17.4	43.4	9.3	47.3
TENNESSEE.............	1 037 539	287 550	13.0	312 760	0.2	12.4	5.2	4 445 909	63.5	5.4	55.9	13.0	31.1
Anderson County	12 729	2 453	5.9	3 567	0.0	15.7	2.1	56 756	58.3	5.2	50.5	12.5	37.0
Bedford County............	7 088	966	7.0	2 189	0.0	9.5	8.3	29 024	66.8	4.4	60.3	11.3	28.4
Benton County	2 861	246	6.9	759	0.0	14.2	5.1	13 321	54.2	7.3	47.4	11.5	41.1
Bledsoe County	2 178	228	8.1	615	0.0	13.5	10.1	9 864	53.8	6.6	48.5	8.3	43.2
Blount County..............	18 075	4 291	10.5	5 248	0.1	12.1	3.3	84 333	62.5	4.5	54.1	12.9	33.0
Bradley County.............	15 197	5 736	19.1	5 067	0.0	14.6	3.7	69 244	64.6	5.0	56.3	14.2	29.6
Campbell County...........	6 799	809	5.0	1 994	0.3	15.9	11.7	31 804	49.3	6.7	44.6	9.4	46.0
Cannon County	2 358	323	9.0	641	0.0	14.0	5.5	9 922	62.7	4.6	55.6	11.2	33.3
Carroll County	5 136	1 042	9.0	1 578	0.0	15.2	4.6	23 448	59.5	8.3	52.6	11.2	36.1
Carter County	9 100	2 710	8.2	2 857	0.0	14.9	4.3	46 053	59.2	5.9	51.7	13.2	35.2
Cheatham County	7 369	989	10.2	1 771	0.0	12.6	3.6	27 008	70.1	2.8	61.8	13.3	24.9
Chester County	2 770	1 525	31.9	1 147	0.0	8.7	4.4	12 112	62.9	6.8	54.5	13.6	31.9
Claiborne County	5 431	1 005	11.6	1 589	0.0	15.1	6.2	23 690	53.5	7.3	47.1	10.4	42.5
Clay County	1 388	245	0.8	419	2.1	27.9	2.9	6 418	58.2	7.6	52.3	9.5	38.2
Cocke County	5 823	713	4.0	1 631	0.0	12.4	7.4	26 755	57.6	8.8	51.3	11.6	37.1
Coffee County	8 906	1 738	6.7	2 636	0.3	10.5	4.7	37 439	62.7	6.0	53.6	12.8	33.6
Crockett County	2 787	302	8.2	794	0.0	10.7	7.6	11 297	59.1	5.1	53.5	9.0	37.5
Cumberland County	7 599	1 259	6.9	2 124	0.0	18.3	3.2	37 933	52.4	5.2	45.8	11.8	42.4
Davidson County	90 547	41 321	27.6	32 378	0.0	10.0	6.6	456 655	67.4	5.2	60.6	13.9	25.5
Decatur County	1 897	280	4.9	572	0.0	16.4	2.8	9 502	57.4	5.2	51.7	11.0	37.3
DeKalb County	3 071	389	5.3	940	0.0	17.6	5.3	13 851	60.8	5.2	54.4	10.1	35.5
Dickson County	8 621	1 006	8.5	2 410	0.0	13.4	4.1	33 022	65.6	4.4	59.4	11.0	29.7
Dyer County	7 032	1 232	6.7	1 898	0.0	14.3	7.1	28 737	62.7	7.5	56.7	9.9	33.4
Fayette County	5 551	775	24.6	1 663	0.0	15.6	4.9	22 326	60.6	5.4	54.5	11.5	34.0
Fentress County...........	3 084	341	4.0	818	0.0	10.6	6.5	13 023	52.4	7.3	48.3	9.3	42.4
Franklin County............	6 782	2 292	20.7	2 411	0.0	10.0	4.8	31 281	59.2	5.0	51.9	13.3	34.7
Gibson County	8 732	1 395	5.7	2 453	0.0	16.3	4.6	37 889	60.0	5.7	55.8	9.3	34.9
Giles County................	5 637	1 011	10.2	1 705	0.0	18.2	2.9	23 077	62.5	4.3	56.5	10.4	33.1
Grainger County	3 564	523	4.5	985	0.0	13.2	5.2	16 431	57.2	4.9	51.9	9.7	38.4
Greene County	10 392	2 118	9.6	2 947	0.5	19.2	3.8	50 370	60.9	5.6	55.9	10.3	33.8
Grundy County	2 654	244	5.5	802	0.0	12.5	10.8	11 171	51.5	6.4	45.2	10.5	44.3
Hamblen County	9 572	1 719	5.5	3 083	0.2	20.1	4.4	46 240	62.0	4.2	55.9	11.0	33.2
Hamilton County...........	53 191	18 563	19.5	16 060	0.0	10.6	5.2	244 332	64.6	5.4	55.4	14.4	30.1
Hancock County	1 218	116	6.2	428	0.0	13.3	4.4	5 456	48.4	5.7	43.3	9.5	47.2
Hardeman County	5 433	607	10.5	1 500	0.0	9.0	9.4	22 173	49.1	6.6	46.4	10.1	43.5
Hardin County	4 457	588	9.3	1 275	0.0	14.7	5.8	20 358	56.1	5.3	50.0	10.9	39.1
Hawkins County	9 175	1 552	7.2	2 464	0.0	15.7	5.7	42 473	56.5	5.1	51.7	10.5	37.9
Haywood County	4 095	451	5.8	1 174	0.0	14.1	7.3	14 982	60.8	6.8	55.2	10.2	34.6
Henderson County	4 547	577	7.9	1 211	0.0	18.8	7.2	19 944	61.5	4.5	57.2	9.3	33.5
Henry County	5 384	716	4.0	1 608	0.0	15.5	7.0	25 099	58.0	6.1	51.5	11.2	37.3
Hickman County	4 174	457	11.9	1 114	0.0	20.6	5.2	17 348	54.9	4.6	52.2	12.4	35.4
Houston County	1 490	138	4.6	366	1.1	21.3	0.5	6 333	54.3	3.7	49.2	9.9	41.0
Humphreys County	3 242	424	7.7	956	0.0	15.6	2.6	14 210	60.1	4.6	55.3	9.6	35.1
Jackson County............	1 807	212	4.7	604	0.0	12.3	4.6	8 893	55.6	6.3	50.8	10.9	38.4
Jefferson County	7 627	2 593	18.6	2 513	0.0	10.3	5.1	35 276	62.0	5.4	54.1	13.4	32.5
Johnson County............	2 768	392	5.0	747	0.0	7.1	9.9	14 447	47.0	7.0	44.6	10.1	45.3
Knox County................	62 407	33 984	12.0	22 203	0.0	9.8	3.7	306 264	64.4	4.8	54.5	16.4	29.1
Lake County	1 167	205	4.9	429	0.0	6.5	20.3	6 756	37.8	8.6	37.3	10.6	52.1
Lauderdale County........	5 096	702	7.0	1 509	0.0	15.4	8.0	21 187	51.9	6.9	51.7	7.8	40.4
Lawrence County	7 663	1 058	7.4	2 081	0.0	10.3	6.6	30 692	60.5	7.6	54.0	9.9	36.1
Lewis County	2 176	346	10.7	708	0.0	13.3	8.8	8 817	59.7	7.9	52.8	10.1	37.1
Lincoln County	5 671	943	5.5	1 543	0.0	14.4	5.3	24 738	63.3	5.6	55.0	11.7	33.3
Loudon County.............	6 232	1 118	6.0	1 748	0.0	14.7	3.4	31 500	59.5	3.6	52.6	12.6	34.9
McMinn County	8 587	1 433	9.1	2 446	0.0	14.6	6.5	38 553	60.2	5.3	54.1	11.3	34.5
McNairy County	4 393	592	9.1	1 289	0.0	16.4	3.1	19 533	58.3	5.2	51.6	10.9	37.4
Macon County	3 926	378	2.2	1 135	0.1	13.4	4.3	15 664	63.9	5.0	56.6	12.0	31.3
Madison County	17 759	5 342	26.6	5 751	0.0	10.9	4.3	70 711	66.2	6.9	57.0	14.0	29.0
Marion County..............	5 111	763	5.9	1 481	0.0	11.3	7.6	21 961	58.0	5.4	53.0	9.9	37.1

Table B-3. States and Counties — Education, Labor Force, and Income

STATE County	Full-year full-time employed (percent) Total	Men	Women	Non-Hispanic White	Black or African American	American Indian and Alaska Native	Asian, Hawaiian, and Pacific Islander	Hispanic or Latino[1]	Children under 18 years in families Number	Both in labor force	Father only in labor force	With one parent who is in labor force (percent)	+/- U.S. percent of children with no stay-at-home parent (percent)	+/- U.S. percent two-income couples	Total employed by class of worker (percent) Private	Government	Self-employed	Unpaid family worker
	24	25	26	27	28	29	30	31	32	33	34	35	36	37	38	39	40	41
SOUTH DAKOTA— Cont'd																		
Tripp County	42.2	54.6	30.8	43.3	X	30.2	100.0	9.1	1 664	62.6	13.6	18.8	16.8	9.7	53.7	14.8	29.5	1.9
Turner County	43.5	54.1	33.4	43.5	0.0	62.5	100.0	60.0	2 214	71.8	13.0	11.2	18.4	11.6	67.3	10.1	21.8	0.8
Union County	49.8	61.1	38.6	49.7	55.6	60.9	43.6	61.1	3 287	63.0	17.1	15.6	14.0	12.0	74.3	10.6	14.2	0.8
Walworth County	36.2	45.7	27.7	38.2	X	18.2	100.0	4.0	1 390	51.7	8.5	31.5	18.6	1.3	59.2	17.6	21.5	1.6
Yankton County	45.2	53.1	37.2	45.8	24.8	35.8	60.7	40.5	5 273	66.5	11.2	16.4	18.3	15.2	70.9	14.4	13.9	0.7
Ziebach County	23.5	30.4	16.9	32.8	X	18.5	0.0	0.0	923	23.4	5.4	30.8	-10.4	-14.0	34.5	42.7	21.4	1.5
TENNESSEE	41.8	51.6	32.7	42.6	38.1	42.2	40.5	40.0	1 308 599	42.6	21.4	22.9	0.9	-0.4	76.2	13.9	9.6	0.3
Anderson County	38.6	49.7	28.8	38.5	38.9	44.2	31.9	52.7	15 618	42.5	20.9	22.9	0.8	-4.8	74.2	17.2	8.4	0.2
Bedford County	44.3	53.7	35.1	44.4	38.9	34.7	39.2	50.6	8 812	47.3	20.3	20.3	3.0	3.7	76.2	12.3	10.7	0.8
Benton County	32.5	43.7	22.3	32.3	37.1	11.1	29.3	44.1	3 343	46.7	20.4	15.0	-2.9	-10.9	71.2	15.6	12.1	1.1
Bledsoe County	30.8	37.5	20.3	35.3	6.3	12.5	0.0	28.0	2 621	46.3	10.8	10.1	0.8	1.1	70.8	16.7	12.2	1.3
Blount County	41.8	52.6	32.0	42.1	35.2	34.2	32.2	39.7	22 677	51.1	21.3	16.4	2.9	-0.8	75.8	13.9	10.0	0.3
Bradley County	42.5	53.9	32.1	42.7	40.6	38.8	41.5	35.3	19 740	46.3	24.7	18.5	0.2	0.0	79.7	10.1	9.9	0.3
Campbell County	31.7	40.6	23.6	31.7	39.7	49.6	55.6	45.0	8 584	34.0	25.5	14.8	-15.8	-15.7	74.9	14.8	10.2	0.1
Cannon County	43.0	53.9	33.0	42.8	52.6	43.5	55.6	62.3	3 083	52.4	22.8	14.8	2.6	0.3	72.3	13.8	13.1	0.7
Carroll County	36.6	46.6	27.8	37.3	33.1	11.1	31.4	33.8	6 485	48.3	17.3	23.1	6.8	-5.2	76.6	13.7	9.1	0.6
Carter County	36.4	45.6	27.8	36.5	29.9	28.8	30.1	34.8	11 606	42.3	22.3	21.2	-1.1	-5.3	75.1	15.0	9.7	0.3
Cheatham County	49.1	60.8	37.8	49.6	30.3	53.2	32.2	40.7	9 467	52.2	21.2	19.2	6.8	7.8	74.3	14.4	11.0	0.3
Chester County	38.8	49.8	29.0	39.6	31.1	X	0.0	69.7	3 563	50.1	23.2	19.7	5.2	3.0	76.1	14.0	9.2	0.6
Claiborne County	33.7	42.2	25.7	33.8	41.2	9.3	25.4	37.9	6 615	40.4	25.0	15.4	-8.8	-10.9	75.1	13.8	10.5	0.6
Clay County	34.1	42.2	26.5	34.2	15.4	60.0	57.6	71.0	1 613	48.2	22.1	14.8	-1.6	-4.6	69.9	15.2	14.0	0.9
Cocke County	35.1	44.3	26.7	35.3	34.0	16.5	39.7	34.5	7 166	40.4	18.4	20.1	-4.1	-8.9	76.9	11.3	10.9	0.9
Coffee County	40.2	51.8	29.4	40.3	38.1	40.2	49.3	38.0	11 219	44.5	25.6	19.5	-0.6	-2.9	73.7	15.1	10.5	0.8
Crockett County	39.8	50.4	30.1	40.5	35.8	71.4	45.0	39.2	3 433	48.2	22.6	16.4	0.0	-3.2	76.1	10.7	12.6	0.5
Cumberland County	32.3	39.4	25.7	32.3	37.0	33.3	30.0	30.3	9 471	45.3	10.0	20.4	1.1	13.0	73.1	13.8	12.5	0.6
Davidson County	45.0	53.0	37.8	47.1	40.4	46.5	39.4	41.7	117 003	38.3	18.1	30.0	3.7	3.8	78.2	12.2	9.4	0.2
Decatur County	38.3	48.7	28.5	38.0	26.1	58.1	45.7	74.7	2 356	48.9	18.9	16.7	1.0	-8.1	75.5	12.9	11.2	0.3
DeKalb County	40.1	47.0	22.6	40.2	50.0	44.0	26.7	76.4	3 440	46.7	17.0	19.0	0.6	-3.7	72.7	11.2	12.6	0.6
Dickson County	44.4	55.0	34.6	44.7	36.0	57.8	82.6	55.4	11 000	44.6	20.2	23.4	3.4	1.5	73.8	14.4	11.4	0.4
Dyer County	42.6	54.6	31.9	43.8	34.2	25.9	46.1	30.9	8 908	46.0	17.0	24.9	6.3	0.1	75.4	15.3	8.8	0.5
Fayette County	41.1	50.8	32.2	45.8	32.1	32.7	59.6	54.6	6 637	40.5	22.3	20.7	-3.4	-2.5	72.3	15.8	11.7	0.2
Fentress County	33.0	42.3	24.2	33.0	57.1	X	0.0	24.6	3 841	37.4	28.1	17.7	-9.5	-12.9	69.2	16.4	14.0	0.4
Franklin County	37.9	47.5	28.9	38.1	36.8	63.3	42.6	33.5	8 440	47.0	21.5	19.5	1.9	-4.0	73.9	13.8	11.7	0.3
Gibson County	41.8	52.7	32.6	42.8	37.8	51.4	45.5	39.8	10 707	46.8	17.0	25.5	7.7	-1.6	80.1	11.2	8.5	0.2
Giles County	43.2	53.2	34.0	43.9	39.0	28.4	35.0	42.5	6 950	50.2	19.8	17.5	3.1	1.1	76.9	11.4	11.0	0.7
Grainger County	38.7	49.1	28.7	38.7	31.4	47.4	33.3	52.7	4 394	41.0	24.4	17.9	-5.7	-6.7	75.3	11.9	12.1	0.7
Greene County	39.8	48.9	31.4	39.9	36.3	17.9	41.1	43.0	13 118	48.0	20.7	18.7	2.1	-3.0	75.7	13.7	10.1	0.4
Grundy County	30.3	11.8	10.4	30.4	0.0	7.1	0.0	36.4	3 348	36.0	20.8	14.3	11.3	13.4	70.7	11.6	-11.1	0.6
Hamblen County	40.9	52.6	29.8	41.9	37.0	51.0	50.8	30.1	12 482	42.1	25.1	20.7	-1.8	-3.1	80.8	9.9	9.0	0.4
Hamilton County	42.0	52.5	32.8	43.4	36.6	41.0	42.8	42.6	66 493	41.5	21.6	25.1	2.0	0.8	77.2	13.9	8.7	0.2
Hancock County	28.9	38.5	19.9	29.3	21.7	0.0	23.1	6.7	1 456	35.0	26.7	13.3	-16.3	-12.8	65.6	19.7	13.2	1.5
Hardeman County	33.1	35.3	30.4	36.5	28.7	39.5	5.7	7.9	6 027	37.8	18.2	28.4	1.6	-1.3	68.4	21.7	9.3	0.6
Hardin County	35.3	45.1	26.2	35.4	36.5	43.4	64.8	31.6	5 564	39.3	23.9	18.1	-7.2	-7.2	69.4	15.0	15.1	0.5
Hawkins County	38.7	50.5	27.8	39.0	31.8	16.7	35.4	27.4	11 756	38.6	27.0	16.9	-9.1	-8.4	79.1	11.8	8.7	0.4
Haywood County	38.4	44.9	33.1	41.8	35.7	20.0	47.8	29.2	4 896	38.2	12.4	32.5	6.1	2.4	74.9	14.8	10.1	0.2
Henderson County	42.3	53.2	32.5	41.9	48.0	15.9	65.2	37.4	5 774	47.0	20.0	21.9	4.3	-1.0	76.3	13.3	10.2	0.2
Henry County	37.4	47.1	28.6	37.2	36.7	59.5	83.3	50.3	6 455	48.9	20.0	18.9	3.2	-4.6	72.3	14.8	12.6	0.4
Hickman County	36.0	45.9	25.0	36.9	20.8	37.0	100.0	40.4	5 265	38.6	35.6	14.4	-11.6	-8.9	74.6	12.5	12.2	0.4
Houston County	34.2	45.5	23.3	34.2	42.9	0.0	3.4	47.6	1 879	42.6	24.7	18.2	-3.8	-7.1	71.4	18.3	9.6	0.6
Humphreys County	40.3	51.8	29.4	40.5	32.4	56.3	48.1	40.2	4 047	49.9	20.8	19.8	5.1	-5.6	74.8	14.9	10.0	0.4
Jackson County	33.8	41.1	27.0	33.8	100.0	43.8	22.9	65.0	2 267	46.3	19.5	19.3	1.0	-7.9	71.9	14.9	12.7	0.5
Jefferson County	39.3	49.4	29.7	39.8	29.6	15.6	27.4	26.6	9 384	46.5	23.2	19.8	1.7	-4.0	76.2	12.7	10.7	0.4
Johnson County	28.4	32.7	23.5	29.1	0.0	19.6	35.5	44.7	3 198	36.7	24.3	22.3	-5.6	-12.4	71.1	15.8	12.7	0.4
Knox County	41.2	51.6	31.8	41.9	34.8	43.6	35.6	33.9	80 630	43.7	24.9	18.8	-2.1	0.3	73.7	16.4	9.6	0.3
Lake County	25.5	23.3	28.9	32.5	12.1	0.0	X	58.8	1 240	38.8	17.2	27.1	1.3	-3.7	64.3	27.1	8.5	0.0
Lauderdale County	37.1	41.7	32.0	41.7	27.9	35.8	37.2	27.1	6 110	39.3	17.0	25.9	0.6	-1.5	72.2	18.8	8.6	0.3
Lawrence County	36.8	47.3	27.2	36.9	28.6	48.6	31.4	37.4	9 892	44.3	25.0	17.1	-3.2	-5.2	76.0	12.4	11.0	0.5
Lewis County	36.9	47.5	27.1	37.4	13.8	0.0	0.0	50.5	2 711	45.4	26.7	16.3	-2.9	-7.4	75.3	13.0	11.3	0.4
Lincoln County	41.2	52.8	30.7	41.6	33.7	46.3	22.5	50.2	7 062	48.1	22.1	19.3	2.8	-0.4	72.3	14.7	12.7	0.3
Loudon County	40.5	50.5	31.3	40.5	45.7	27.2	31.7	41.2	8 213	48.0	24.0	17.9	1.3	-4.1	78.3	12.1	9.2	0.5
McMinn County	40.2	50.7	30.8	40.2	38.7	45.8	44.1	40.6	10 900	44.2	25.4	19.8	-0.6	-4.9	78.9	10.4	10.3	0.3
McNairy County	38.5	49.5	28.3	38.4	44.3	11.6	60.7	37.4	5 394	43.1	25.0	18.7	-2.8	-6.0	74.1	13.6	11.6	0.6
Macon County	41.4	50.2	32.9	41.4	54.5	43.1	14.8	43.2	5 073	50.2	21.0	15.7	1.3	1.1	76.3	10.2	13.1	0.5
Madison County	42.5	51.6	34.5	45.2	36.7	29.1	43.6	34.6	22 079	44.4	14.9	26.4	6.2	4.4	78.0	14.4	7.4	0.3
Marion County	38.8	51.0	27.5	38.9	34.7	70.6	32.3	42.5	6 023	37.7	24.3	20.6	-6.3	-9.4	77.4	12.2	10.1	0.3

[1] Hispanic or Latino persons may be of any race.

Table B-3. States and Counties — Education, Labor Force, and Income

STATE County	Percent who worked at home	Percent of the population 5 years and over with a disability	Veterans as a percent of the population 18 years and over	Occupation for employed population 16 years and over (percent)						Industry for employed population 16 years and over (percent)					
				Management, professional, and related occupations	Service occupations	Sales and office occupations	Farming, fishing, and forestry occupations	Construction, extraction, and maintenance occupations	Production, transportation and material moving occupations	Agriculture, forestry, fishing, and mining	Construction and manufacturing	Wholesale and retail trade	Transportation and warehousing, and utilities	Service industries	Public administration
	42	43	44	45	46	47	48	49	50	51	52	53	54	55	56
SOUTH DAKOTA—Cont'd															
Tripp County	12.8	19.2	14.1	39.5	14.1	22.5	5.7	8.9	9.3	23.6	6.7	15.2	6.3	44.2	4.1
Turner County	11.7	16.3	14.2	34.1	13.9	22.3	2.7	11.8	15.3	14.9	17.2	14.5	6.0	44.7	2.8
Union County	6.6	13.5	13.7	37.7	13.0	24.0	2.4	7.8	15.1	6.5	31.2	13.0	4.6	42.1	2.6
Walworth County	7.4	19.8	15.7	34.5	19.2	24.8	2.7	10.0	8.7	14.1	9.1	14.9	5.9	50.6	5.5
Yankton County	5.4	15.6	14.7	29.0	17.2	27.3	0.7	7.3	18.5	4.9	23.4	16.9	3.4	46.6	4.7
Ziebach County	19.1	25.4	12.3	49.3	12.4	19.9	4.0	7.8	6.6	19.6	4.9	11.0	4.1	47.0	13.4
TENNESSEE	2.6	22.0	13.1	29.5	13.7	26.1	0.6	10.3	19.9	1.4	26.2	15.6	6.3	46.5	4.0
Anderson County	2.0	23.5	15.3	31.6	15.1	25.5	0.2	11.7	15.9	0.7	24.0	14.0	4.9	52.2	4.1
Bedford County	3.4	23.2	12.6	21.2	12.5	21.8	2.0	12.2	30.3	4.5	41.0	13.8	4.2	33.3	3.3
Benton County	3.1	32.0	15.1	20.7	15.5	19.0	1.4	14.9	28.5	3.4	32.6	13.2	10.2	37.4	3.3
Bledsoe County	2.3	26.6	10.5	18.2	12.6	18.3	3.2	14.0	33.6	6.4	42.6	9.2	5.0	31.0	5.9
Blount County	2.5	21.5	14.4	28.9	14.4	25.5	0.5	11.6	19.1	1.0	26.5	16.3	5.4	46.8	3.9
Bradley County	2.2	21.7	13.1	25.4	11.8	25.0	0.6	11.0	26.2	1.4	36.4	15.1	3.9	40.7	2.5
Campbell County	1.8	31.9	12.4	19.2	15.7	21.4	0.4	15.1	28.1	2.4	33.1	14.9	6.2	39.3	4.2
Cannon County	3.5	24.0	11.6	18.2	14.0	23.0	2.1	13.2	29.4	4.4	37.7	15.5	5.5	33.6	3.3
Carroll County	1.8	25.2	12.9	22.8	13.1	19.2	0.7	12.5	31.6	2.1	42.0	11.4	6.4	34.8	3.3
Carter County	1.6	25.4	15.1	23.9	16.2	24.5	0.6	13.2	21.5	1.0	28.9	15.3	4.2	46.7	3.8
Cheatham County	2.3	21.0	12.2	27.4	13.4	24.9	0.6	16.8	17.0	1.1	27.5	14.8	5.9	45.5	5.3
Chester County	2.2	24.0	12.3	22.8	12.3	26.1	0.6	15.1	23.0	2.1	32.8	16.1	5.2	40.1	3.6
Claiborne County	2.9	30.3	10.7	22.1	12.7	20.4	1.0	13.2	30.6	5.5	36.6	11.6	6.6	36.6	3.1
Clay County	2.8	29.0	10.6	19.1	10.9	18.8	2.4	13.7	35.0	4.6	41.3	13.4	5.3	31.8	3.7
Cocke County	2.5	27.8	12.4	18.1	20.2	19.9	0.3	13.5	28.0	1.5	36.7	12.3	4.5	42.2	2.8
Coffee County	2.4	22.1	14.7	27.9	12.5	22.5	1.3	12.2	23.7	2.5	32.3	14.2	4.0	43.1	3.9
Crockett County	3.0	27.3	10.8	21.0	11.5	20.8	2.5	13.3	30.8	6.0	36.6	15.1	6.9	32.3	3.0
Cumberland County	2.2	24.5	17.7	23.8	15.1	24.7	1.6	12.6	22.2	4.0	29.2	16.3	3.4	41.6	5.5
Davidson County	3.1	20.1	11.5	37.2	13.8	28.5	0.1	8.4	11.9	0.2	15.9	14.9	4.6	59.6	4.7
Decatur County	2.2	25.9	13.1	19.7	15.0	17.7	0.8	14.9	31.8	4.4	39.6	13.5	6.2	32.8	3.6
DeKalb County	3.5	26.0	10.7	25.4	10.2	19.6	2.1	11.9	30.7	4.7	39.0	13.6	5.4	34.5	2.8
Dickson County	3.0	21.9	14.9	23.0	13.8	26.1	0.8	15.6	20.7	1.8	31.9	16.6	5.3	39.9	4.5
Dyer County	1.7	26.9	12.1	24.6	13.5	23.4	0.3	10.3	27.8	1.8	36.4	13.5	4.6	39.5	4.2
Fayette County	3.0	22.9	13.0	26.4	14.0	24.8	0.8	14.6	19.3	2.7	27.9	16.1	8.5	40.1	4.7
Fentress County	3.0	29.4	10.3	21.2	11.7	20.4	2.7	13.9	30.2	5.3	36.1	14.2	5.8	34.6	4.0
Franklin County	3.0	23.3	14.4	26.4	11.9	23.2	1.1	11.2	26.1	2.2	33.5	14.7	4.0	42.0	3.6
Gibson County	1.5	25.4	13.1	22.0	12.5	21.1	0.7	10.3	33.3	2.1	42.1	14.0	5.9	32.9	3.1
Giles County	3.0	21.9	12.9	21.5	11.0	21.6	1.5	9.9	34.4	3.8	43.3	14.8	3.4	32.0	2.6
Grainger County	3.0	26.8	11.6	18.0	11.1	20.4	2.2	14.7	33.7	5.9	39.9	14.4	7.0	31.1	1.6
Greene County	2.9	26.3	13.3	23.8	14.1	20.2	1.3	10.6	30.0	3.3	39.2	12.8	4.3	37.3	2.9
Grundy County	4.5	27.6	9.7	17.6	16.6	15.4	1.9	14.2	34.3	5.4	40.3	12.7	4.8	33.7	3.2
Hamblen County	1.1	22.3	13.3	22.3	12.2	22.9	0.6	9.6	32.6	1.2	41.8	15.8	4.4	34.3	2.6
Hamilton County	2.3	21.1	13.9	33.5	13.8	27.2	0.1	8.3	17.1	0.3	22.9	14.6	7.0	52.0	3.3
Hancock County	6.5	32.2	9.8	23.2	13.1	15.5	1.2	14.4	32.7	5.4	41.3	10.7	4.5	33.3	4.7
Hardeman County	2.2	24.7	13.0	21.7	16.4	21.4	1.9	9.9	28.8	3.7	34.4	10.9	6.6	38.3	6.2
Hardin County	2.0	26.5	14.1	20.0	15.7	19.4	1.8	14.4	28.7	3.0	38.2	13.8	5.2	35.3	4.5
Hawkins County	2.0	24.3	13.3	21.1	12.7	20.7	0.7	11.7	33.0	1.7	42.8	12.9	5.0	34.6	3.0
Haywood County	0.9	28.3	8.8	21.4	16.8	17.8	1.9	9.5	32.6	4.6	37.5	11.5	4.1	37.3	4.9
Henderson County	2.3	24.0	11.6	21.5	11.2	22.3	0.5	11.0	33.7	1.6	41.1	15.5	7.0	30.6	4.3
Henry County	2.4	24.8	15.6	23.2	12.8	24.0	1.3	11.2	27.4	3.7	33.5	16.3	6.0	37.1	3.2
Hickman County	3.7	26.3	12.9	19.4	13.2	21.0	0.8	19.3	26.2	2.2	37.2	14.8	5.0	36.5	4.2
Houston County	2.5	26.3	16.1	21.7	11.3	16.2	2.0	18.2	30.7	3.4	40.1	9.4	10.2	32.7	4.2
Humphreys County	2.3	22.9	15.5	20.3	13.7	20.3	0.5	17.4	27.7	2.0	41.4	14.3	7.2	31.1	4.0
Jackson County	2.9	29.1	11.0	19.1	13.3	18.6	2.3	14.1	32.6	4.0	41.9	11.6	5.0	34.4	3.0
Jefferson County	3.0	23.7	13.5	22.9	16.3	23.6	0.4	12.6	24.2	2.8	31.6	14.9	6.2	41.0	3.5
Johnson County	3.0	32.2	14.2	20.6	16.8	18.5	1.4	17.0	25.7	3.9	37.3	12.2	4.5	35.3	6.8
Knox County	2.7	20.2	13.3	36.7	14.5	29.0	0.2	7.9	11.7	0.4	16.4	18.3	5.2	56.0	3.7
Lake County	1.7	32.6	9.8	17.0	25.3	19.5	2.5	9.6	26.1	7.7	26.6	13.4	4.1	34.9	13.3
Lauderdale County	1.6	27.9	11.8	21.4	13.3	19.5	1.0	10.2	34.7	3.2	43.6	11.6	5.0	28.6	8.0
Lawrence County	3.2	23.7	11.3	21.4	11.7	20.9	0.8	13.4	31.9	2.5	39.5	16.5	5.1	33.3	3.0
Lewis County	2.1	23.2	12.0	20.9	16.2	18.8	2.3	13.6	28.3	2.5	37.3	12.0	5.3	39.3	3.6
Lincoln County	2.7	22.7	13.1	25.6	10.7	23.6	1.2	12.2	26.7	3.8	35.4	16.6	4.4	35.4	4.4
Loudon County	3.3	23.0	15.4	25.6	13.3	25.3	0.9	12.2	22.7	2.1	30.4	16.4	6.6	42.0	2.5
McMinn County	2.4	24.4	13.0	21.8	12.4	20.6	0.7	11.3	33.1	2.3	42.8	13.0	5.7	34.0	2.2
McNairy County	3.1	26.2	14.5	21.8	11.3	20.9	1.0	12.5	32.5	1.9	44.9	13.4	6.1	31.0	2.6
Macon County	3.0	27.4	10.2	17.0	10.8	20.5	2.0	15.5	34.1	5.0	44.6	15.3	4.4	27.8	2.9
Madison County	1.9	21.5	12.1	30.9	14.2	26.1	0.3	8.8	19.7	0.5	27.2	16.1	4.4	47.8	3.9
Marion County	2.1	27.5	12.2	21.6	11.8	22.6	0.5	13.2	30.3	1.2	38.7	14.2	7.3	35.4	3.2

Table B-3. States and Counties — **Education, Labor Force, and Income**

STATE County	Median household income	Median family income — All families	Families with children — Married-couple	Male householder	Female householder	Median nonfamily household income	Median income for full-year, full-time workers — Men	Women	Per capita income	With earnings	With interest, dividend, or rental income	With Social Security income	With public assistance income	With retirement income	Households with income over $100,000 (percent)	+/− U.S. percent for income over $100,000 (percent)	Households with income below poverty (percent)	Families with children with income below poverty (percent)
	57	58	59	60	61	62	63	64	65	66	67	68	69	70	71	72	73	74
SOUTH DAKOTA—Cont'd																		
Tripp County	28 333	36 219	41 595	22 250	15 300	14 022	24 321	18 646	13 776	76.4	37.1	35.6	2.2	7.9	3.4	-8.9	21.3	17.6
Turner County	36 059	42 704	48 689	25 625	25 313	18 908	30 199	20 618	17 343	79.1	47.0	35.1	0.9	12.9	4.9	-7.4	8.7	5.9
Union County	44 790	51 227	57 482	32 375	24 583	23 073	36 503	24 789	24 355	84.0	42.2	25.2	1.3	10.0	11.6	-0.7	6.5	4.9
Walworth County	27 834	33 654	40 887	23 906	14 732	17 646	25 648	19 024	15 492	74.2	41.9	36.5	4.2	12.5	3.3	-9.0	17.2	23.2
Yankton County	35 374	43 600	49 591	23 125	16 107	20 496	29 811	21 103	17 312	80.1	44.9	27.8	2.6	12.9	5.1	-7.2	9.6	10.1
Ziebach County	18 063	18 672	26 458	7 708	7 132	11 500	20 385	22 045	7 463	71.0	20.7	18.1	18.3	7.2	2.0	-10.3	45.1	55.0
TENNESSEE	36 360	43 517	52 047	26 932	17 912	21 032	33 643	24 832	19 393	79.7	29.4	26.5	3.5	16.2	8.3	-4.0	14.0	15.0
Anderson County	35 483	42 584	51 113	26 719	17 688	20 380	34 987	24 455	19 009	72.8	36.1	33.5	3.6	23.0	7.4	-4.9	13.4	15.9
Bedford County	36 729	40 691	46 305	25 139	20 359	19 231	29 664	21 445	16 698	80.7	28.2	27.9	2.4	14.4	6.0	-6.3	13.6	13.8
Benton County	28 679	32 727	40 216	20 278	11 293	15 703	29 983	19 704	14 646	70.7	28.6	38.6	4.4	21.9	2.6	-9.7	15.4	19.4
Bledsoe County	28 982	34 593	40 513	18 750	12 500	13 485	27 233	20 704	13 559	75.0	22.0	29.8	3.3	18.2	3.8	-8.5	19.7	18.0
Blount County	37 862	45 038	50 240	28 563	18 213	20 600	33 060	23 997	19 416	77.1	34.9	30.0	2.6	21.1	7.3	-5.0	10.9	11.4
Bradley County	35 034	41 779	47 128	22 091	15 930	17 770	31 234	21 827	18 108	81.2	27.2	25.6	3.0	15.7	6.2	-6.1	13.3	14.2
Campbell County	25 285	30 197	33 868	19 115	17 340	11 766	27 049	19 599	13 301	64.9	19.3	39.2	5.2	18.4	2.9	-9.4	23.5	27.6
Cannon County	32 809	38 424	49 670	23 333	17 340	15 054	29 786	22 419	16 405	77.5	24.5	29.7	3.8	17.5	3.8	-8.5	15.1	13.6
Carroll County	30 463	36 880	44 316	25 776	15 085	16 491	30 477	20 655	16 251	73.6	27.0	34.1	3.4	19.0	4.3	-8.0	15.1	16.4
Carter County	27 931	33 825	37 484	25 464	14 101	13 701	26 931	20 227	14 678	74.5	25.1	30.8	3.9	16.4	3.0	-9.3	18.1	19.8
Cheatham County	45 836	49 143	53 448	35 772	25 021	25 495	35 191	25 842	18 882	87.7	29.1	20.4	1.7	13.4	7.7	-4.6	7.7	7.4
Chester County	34 349	41 127	47 500	16 250	17 893	15 496	32 288	22 403	15 756	77.6	26.1	31.2	2.9	15.3	3.7	-8.6	15.6	16.0
Claiborne County	25 782	31 234	35 610	18 889	10 680	10 878	26 629	20 441	13 032	69.9	21.3	33.6	5.5	15.6	2.6	-9.7	24.5	23.9
Clay County	23 958	29 784	33 017	13 864	11 979	11 887	24 142	17 015	13 320	70.5	23.6	35.4	4.7	13.7	3.3	-9.0	20.8	21.0
Cocke County	25 553	30 418	34 939	14 167	12 307	12 604	26 527	19 414	13 881	73.4	23.5	30.7	4.7	16.3	3.2	-9.1	23.6	28.7
Coffee County	34 898	40 228	48 369	32 228	15 130	18 856	34 459	21 504	18 137	77.9	33.5	29.0	2.7	15.0	6.0	-6.3	15.2	16.0
Crockett County	30 015	36 713	42 949	23 571	16 141	14 638	28 044	21 507	14 600	74.7	23.6	31.6	3.4	13.8	3.6	-8.7	18.3	17.6
Cumberland County	30 901	35 928	41 018	22 593	14 237	16 125	27 534	21 068	16 808	67.7	33.9	41.4	3.1	27.1	4.6	-7.7	14.9	19.1
Davidson County	39 797	49 317	59 548	29 829	20 075	28 553	35 187	28 679	23 069	84.0	31.5	21.5	3.6	14.1	10.6	-1.7	11.9	15.7
Decatur County	28 741	34 919	39 415	22 917	13 229	13 864	26 469	20 691	17 285	71.5	24.5	35.4	4.1	18.9	4.0	-8.3	18.9	18.5
DeKalb County	30 059	40 705	40 250	18 250	10 022	12 103	30 043	21 313	17 217	74.4	27.2	32.5	3.0	13.5	4.5	-7.4	15.0	16.7
Dickson County	39 056	45 575	52 767	26 346	18 363	20 076	33 048	24 599	18 043	80.6	28.7	25.9	3.1	16.2	6.0	-6.3	11.1	11.7
Dyer County	32 788	39 848	48 730	28 837	14 901	17 673	30 575	22 038	16 451	76.4	24.7	28.2	4.3	13.6	4.9	-7.4	17.0	18.4
Fayette County	40 279	46 283	53 041	26 500	17 799	18 211	34 882	25 251	17 969	79.9	23.8	30.4	2.9	17.5	9.5	-2.8	15.9	15.8
Fentress County	23 238	28 856	32 770	20 139	13 810	10 319	24 541	18 911	12 999	67.5	18.0	35.4	5.5	16.9	3.0	-9.3	25.4	23.6
Franklin County	36 044	42 279	47 548	23 906	18 722	15 576	32 876	21 916	17 987	74.9	33.8	33.4	2.2	19.9	6.1	-6.2	14.5	14.9
Gibson County	31 105	39 318	50 266	23 793	17 551	16 695	31 028	21 811	16 320	75.1	26.5	32.2	3.4	17.6	4.1	-8.2	14.6	14.6
Giles County	34 824	41 714	50 951	26 823	16 667	18 994	31 803	22 929	17 543	77.9	28.2	30.1	2.3	18.3	5.4	-6.9	12.8	12.7
Grainger County	27 997	33 347	37 755	22 443	14 387	12 247	26 335	19 848	14 505	73.9	21.7	31.1	4.2	15.7	3.8	-8.5	20.3	18.6
Greene County	30 382	36 889	42 755	21 750	15 344	15 929	26 974	20 704	15 746	76.7	29.0	30.7	3.4	18.3	3.7	-8.6	15.9	17.0
Grundy County	22 959	27 091	32 133	10 140	9 779	11 008	27 888	18 405	12 039	69.0	16.4	32.4	5.3	16.0	2.5	-9.8	25.9	29.5
Hamblen County	32 350	39 138	47 549	22 800	15 489	17 673	30 575	21 917	17 743	77.8	26.8	30.2	3.6	16.7	5.9	-6.4	15.1	15.7
Hamilton County	38 930	48 037	57 631	26 703	18 979	22 143	36 239	25 397	21 593	79.5	32.8	27.5	3.3	17.4	9.9	-2.4	12.3	14.1
Hancock County	19 760	25 372	28 314	9 583	13 409	9 415	24 189	19 139	11 986	65.3	16.9	33.9	4.3	11.2	1.9	-10.4	31.2	32.9
Hardeman County	29 111	34 746	42 108	25 357	16 176	14 349	28 584	21 126	13 349	74.2	19.7	31.1	5.0	14.9	2.9	-9.4	20.4	22.7
Hardin County	27 819	34 157	39 903	24 688	14 099	14 468	29 157	19 299	15 598	72.2	24.8	33.9	4.2	16.7	4.5	-7.8	19.3	20.8
Hawkins County	31 300	37 557	41 975	21 754	13 217	15 857	31 344	22 475	16 073	73.8	27.8	30.5	3.0	16.1	3.7	-8.6	17.3	18.8
Haywood County	27 671	32 447	43 093	29 643	17 135	14 722	28 191	21 754	14 669	75.9	20.4	30.9	4.2	14.9	4.5	-7.8	21.7	21.7
Henderson County	32 057	38 475	45 943	27 479	17 253	15 986	29 505	22 178	17 019	76.7	25.5	30.7	3.0	16.6	4.0	-8.3	13.8	12.3
Henry County	30 169	35 836	43 333	24 625	16 163	16 830	28 642	21 019	15 855	72.3	30.4	36.3	4.6	20.1	3.9	-8.4	14.1	17.1
Hickman County	31 013	36 342	43 734	16 655	18 315	14 988	30 150	21 977	14 446	76.8	22.7	31.8	4.6	18.3	3.6	-8.7	16.0	15.0
Houston County	29 968	35 396	40 673	24 050	11 292	12 663	30 025	20 827	15 614	70.1	28.0	35.4	3.4	20.8	3.7	-8.6	19.5	18.9
Humphreys County	35 786	42 129	47 093	21 688	20 046	18 279	32 166	21 407	17 757	74.8	29.4	31.9	2.9	20.5	4.5	-7.8	12.6	12.0
Jackson County	26 502	32 088	37 515	25 875	14 474	13 974	25 394	20 092	15 020	73.4	25.0	34.7	2.4	16.5	3.8	-8.5	21.2	15.3
Jefferson County	32 824	38 537	42 455	24 884	16 357	16 391	30 002	20 783	16 841	78.2	26.7	28.9	3.8	17.3	5.1	-7.2	14.3	14.5
Johnson County	23 067	28 400	33 833	21 071	11 296	11 610	24 661	19 974	13 388	68.4	24.3	36.9	5.1	17.8	2.6	-9.7	24.2	25.7
Knox County	37 454	49 182	59 548	29 368	16 975	21 418	36 671	25 962	21 875	80.3	35.4	25.5	3.1	16.6	10.4	-1.9	13.7	12.9
Lake County	21 995	30 339	40 673	18 250	11 875	13 141	25 690	19 418	10 794	71.3	19.9	36.7	7.2	16.4	1.9	-10.4	23.6	29.5
Lauderdale County	29 751	36 841	45 682	21 833	13 317	12 463	29 237	21 622	13 682	73.6	16.9	31.1	5.3	13.6	3.4	-8.9	21.0	21.4
Lawrence County	30 498	35 326	40 263	26 224	18 627	14 355	28 475	21 548	15 848	73.9	27.4	32.4	3.6	18.4	3.6	-8.7	15.1	15.3
Lewis County	30 444	35 972	42 614	32 292	17 830	15 227	27 860	20 983	14 664	76.1	24.0	31.6	4.5	17.1	2.9	-9.4	14.3	14.8
Lincoln County	33 434	41 211	46 040	30 833	16 875	15 123	31 825	22 727	18 837	77.5	30.1	32.7	3.6	18.5	7.7	-4.6	15.6	14.8
Loudon County	40 401	46 517	50 449	30 781	21 563	19 229	35 259	23 809	21 061	76.2	36.8	32.5	2.4	23.3	9.0	-3.3	10.5	10.4
McMinn County	31 919	38 992	44 872	30 194	15 444	14 684	31 627	21 058	16 725	76.3	26.7	31.5	3.0	15.9	4.6	-7.7	16.0	15.7
McNairy County	30 154	36 045	41 769	22 348	17 930	11 968	30 608	21 794	16 385	73.7	22.5	35.8	3.5	15.7	3.7	-8.6	17.8	16.1
Macon County	29 867	37 577	44 277	23 500	16 719	12 767	28 919	20 490	15 286	78.6	23.7	27.9	4.5	13.0	3.3	-9.0	17.5	14.0
Madison County	36 982	44 595	57 348	27 917	17 436	22 457	35 436	24 768	19 389	81.3	29.0	25.7	3.4	15.2	8.7	-3.6	14.2	15.4
Marion County	31 419	36 351	44 058	23 500	17 207	15 363	31 103	22 197	16 419	75.5	25.5	30.8	4.0	17.0	5.3	-7.0	14.7	16.6

STATE/ County code	MSA/PMSA/ NECMA code[1]	STATE County	High school graduates			College graduates		College graduates (percent)				
			Total population 25 years and over	Percent with a high school diploma or less	Percent with a high school diploma or more	Percent with a bachelor's degree or more	+/– U.S. percent with bachelor's degree or more	Non- Hispanic White	Black or African American	American Indian and Alaska Native	Asian, Hawaiian, and Pacific Islander	Hispanic or Latino[2]
			1	2	3	4	5	6	7	8	9	10
		TENNESSEE— Cont'd										
47 117	...	Marshall County	17 615	67.6	73.6	10.6	-13.8	11.2	4.7	0.0	50.0	6.3
47 119	...	Maury County	45 288	58.4	77.9	13.6	-10.8	14.9	6.0	4.3	65.5	7.1
47 121	...	Meigs County	7 405	73.2	63.5	7.0	-17.4	7.1	0.0	0.0	100.0	0.0
47 123	...	Monroe County	25 955	70.5	66.7	10.1	-14.3	10.1	7.3	8.2	24.5	9.4
47 125	1660	Montgomery County	79 823	46.1	84.3	19.3	-5.1	21.6	10.6	6.5	18.1	16.0
47 127	...	Moore County	3 939	63.4	76.6	11.8	-12.6	12.1	6.6	0.0	0.0	X
47 129	...	Morgan County	13 371	77.1	63.8	6.0	-18.4	6.2	0.0	61.1	0.0	0.0
47 131	...	Obion County	22 119	70.3	71.0	10.3	-14.1	10.8	3.7	0.0	60.0	11.5
47 133	...	Overton County	13 751	78.9	59.0	8.3	-16.1	8.2	0.0	14.0	57.1	10.1
47 135	...	Perry County	5 209	74.6	63.8	7.1	-17.3	7.2	3.8	0.0	X	0.0
47 137	...	Pickett County	3 466	76.5	62.9	9.1	-15.3	8.7	0.0	37.5	X	68.8
47 139	...	Polk County	11 113	75.4	62.2	7.5	-16.9	7.5	100.0	0.0	0.0	10.0
47 141	...	Putnam County	39 403	59.5	72.6	20.2	-4.2	20.1	25.1	6.5	60.1	9.7
47 143	...	Rhea County	18 894	68.9	65.3	9.1	-15.3	9.3	1.4	8.0	21.9	4.9
47 145	...	Roane County	36 455	61.3	74.8	14.8	-9.6	14.7	6.9	22.6	53.9	10.2
47 147	5360	Robertson County	35 252	64.2	74.8	11.9	-12.5	12.7	4.4	4.9	17.6	3.3
47 149	5360	Rutherford County	109 913	50.0	81.8	22.9	-1.5	23.5	18.8	17.5	31.1	11.8
47 151	...	Scott County...............	13 480	77.4	60.7	7.5	-16.9	7.5	0.0	14.3	0.0	0.0
47 153	...	Sequatchie County........	7 610	71.8	66.7	10.2	-14.2	9.6	0.0	X	63.8	20.8
47 155	3840	Sevier County..............	48 843	61.8	74.6	13.5	-10.9	13.4	16.5	24.2	35.5	8.4
47 157	4920	Shelby County	558 056	45.4	80.8	25.3	0.9	35.1	12.8	16.2	48.6	15.2
47 159	...	Smith County	11 798	73.0	67.5	9.3	-15.1	9.1	6.9	23.2	58.5	1.2
47 161	...	Stewart County	8 486	67.7	74.3	10.2	-14.2	9.9	8.0	0.0	31.4	82.6
47 163	3660	Sullivan County	108 605	57.2	75.8	18.1	-6.3	18.2	13.2	2.4	41.7	12.2
47 165	5360	Sumner County	85 651	52.4	79.7	18.6	-5.8	18.8	11.8	17.3	38.2	13.2
47 167	4920	Tipton County	31 856	62.1	74.6	10.8	-13.6	11.5	6.7	14.0	37.1	6.9
47 169	...	Trousdale County	4 852	73.8	61.4	8.9	-15.5	9.5	5.3	36.4	0.0	0.0
47 171	3660	Unicoi County	12 744	68.3	67.7	10.6	-13.8	10.6	X	0.0	100.0	4.1
47 173	3840	Union County	11 632	79.2	56.3	5.8	-18.6	5.8	0.0	0.0	0.0	0.0
47 175	...	Van Buren County........	3 738	80.4	62.0	7.8	-16.6	7.9	0.0	0.0	X	0.0
47 177	...	Warren County	25 691	72.0	67.2	9.1	-15.3	9.4	1.8	0.0	60.4	5.5
47 179	3660	Washington County	72 947	51.8	77.2	22.9	-1.5	22.7	17.2	46.6	71.1	21.3
47 181	...	Wayne County..............	11 733	76.7	61.3	8.0	-16.4	7.5	14.1	0.0	23.1	4.9
47 183	...	Weakley County	21 908	65.6	70.3	15.3	-9.1	15.0	12.3	6.0	58.8	19.1
47 185	...	White County...............	15 806	74.3	64.8	7.9	-16.5	8.0	2.8	0.0	33.3	0.0
47 187	5360	Williamson County	81 620	29.8	90.1	44.4	20.0	46.2	20.9	26.7	56.5	17.6
47 189	5360	Wilson County	58 683	53.0	80.9	19.6	-4.8	20.1	10.9	38.3	41.1	20.5
48 000	...	TEXAS......................	12 790 893	49.2	75.7	23.2	-1.2	30.0	15.3	15.7	47.2	8.9
48 001	...	Anderson County	38 506	63.8	64.4	11.1	-13.3	14.9	4.3	17.9	27.3	2.3
48 003	...	Andrews County	7 815	64.6	68.0	12.4	-12.0	16.9	6.3	16.3	0.0	3.8
48 005	...	Angelina County	50 290	58.1	71.2	14.7	-9.7	17.5	5.9	7.3	26.0	5.0
48 007	...	Aransas County	15 728	54.5	74.6	16.7	-7.7	19.7	1.8	1.1	7.1	4.9
48 009	9080	Archer County	5 729	54.9	81.1	15.9	-8.5	15.9	0.0	32.1	85.7	7.9
48 011	...	Armstrong County	1 458	45.4	82.4	20.5	-3.9	20.9	X	50.0	X	0.0
48 013	...	Atascosa County	22 751	66.8	65.2	10.5	-13.9	17.3	0.0	19.2	28.1	4.3
48 015	...	Austin County..............	15 280	57.8	74.5	17.3	-7.1	21.0	3.5	20.0	72.0	3.0
48 017	...	Bailey County	3 960	70.0	61.5	9.3	-15.1	14.5	0.0	0.0	X	1.3
48 019	...	Bandera County	12 287	47.1	84.8	19.4	-5.0	20.8	0.0	14.7	8.3	9.0
48 021	0640	Bastrop County	37 249	54.8	76.9	17.0	-7.4	21.0	6.6	4.4	14.6	6.5
48 023	...	Baylor County	2 939	62.6	70.1	12.1	-12.3	13.4	0.0	15.8	0.0	2.8
48 025	...	Bee County	20 568	61.1	73.7	12.2	-12.2	20.4	3.7	0.0	25.9	7.5
48 027	3810	Bell County	137 430	42.8	84.7	19.8	-4.6	24.5	11.1	17.0	22.3	9.5
48 029	7240	Bexar County	849 004	47.4	76.9	22.7	-1.7	36.6	17.8	13.3	38.0	10.8
48 031	...	Blanco County	5 895	49.9	80.6	22.2	-2.2	24.8	23.2	26.2	0.0	3.0
48 033	...	Borden County	490	49.0	83.9	21.4	-3.0	23.2	X	0.0	100.0	0.0
48 035	...	Bosque County.............	11 910	56.2	75.9	15.4	-9.0	16.7	5.1	9.0	64.3	2.5
48 037	8360	Bowie County	58 767	54.6	77.3	16.1	-8.3	19.1	7.5	18.2	48.1	3.7
48 039	1145	Brazoria County	152 244	47.7	79.5	19.6	-4.8	22.3	17.2	11.8	51.2	7.6
48 041	1260	Brazos County	70 708	38.8	81.3	37.0	12.6	43.7	10.4	24.4	80.6	14.9
48 043	...	Brewster County	5 519	42.5	78.6	27.7	3.3	36.9	44.0	0.0	38.1	12.7
48 045	...	Briscoe County.............	1 181	55.6	74.8	17.5	-6.9	20.9	6.7	X	X	1.1
48 047	...	Brooks County	4 717	73.5	49.9	6.8	-17.6	9.7	0.0	21.8	X	6.3
48 049	...	Brown County..............	24 016	60.4	74.6	15.0	-9.4	16.7	10.1	11.9	35.3	2.6
48 051	...	Burleson County	10 787	66.4	71.1	13.2	-11.2	16.4	4.5	19.5	85.7	2.7
48 053	...	Burnet County	23 436	54.7	77.8	17.4	-7.0	19.2	2.4	10.8	12.9	3.5

[1]MSA = Metropolitan Statistical Area. PMSA = Primary MSA. NECMA = New England County Metropolitan Area. See the Appendix A for explanation of these concepts. See Appendix B for list of metropolitan areas identified by type, with component counties.

[2]Hispanic or Latino persons may be of any race.

STATE County	School enrollment			Population 16 to 19 years				Employment status, 2000			Work status in 1999 of the population 16 years and over (percent)		
											Worked in 1999		
	Grades kindergarten through 12	College or graduate school	Percent private	Number	Percent in armed forces	Percent high school graduates	Percent not enrolled, not grads, not in armed forces, not employed	Total population 16 years and over	Percent in labor force	Unemployment rate	Full-time	Part-time	Did not work in 1999
	11	12	13	14	15	16	17	18	19	20	21	22	23
TENNESSEE— Cont'd													
Marshall County	5 294	784	4.8	1 554	0.0	13.4	6.4	20 773	65.8	4.3	60.3	9.9	29.8
Maury County	13 184	2 338	13.8	4 198	0.0	16.7	4.7	53 524	66.7	4.2	58.2	13.3	28.5
Meigs County	2 017	223	11.0	520	0.0	12.7	7.7	8 573	55.5	6.3	50.9	10.5	38.6
Monroe County	7 117	1 196	9.1	2 095	0.0	15.6	7.0	30 389	57.9	7.4	52.3	11.2	36.4
Montgomery County	27 284	8 526	7.3	7 580	7.2	19.2	3.0	100 126	70.6	5.2	61.3	13.7	25.0
Moore County	1 015	245	7.0	254	0.0	6.3	5.1	4 542	64.0	4.9	55.0	13.8	31.2
Morgan County	3 480	556	5.0	1 042	0.0	17.6	3.4	15 735	50.7	7.0	51.6	9.5	38.9
Obion County	5 636	980	2.6	1 554	0.0	14.7	4.2	25 643	60.9	5.3	54.1	12.2	33.6
Overton County	3 473	661	3.4	1 142	0.0	14.3	3.1	16 053	58.5	5.5	51.7	11.1	37.2
Perry County	1 392	146	6.2	350	0.0	13.1	2.6	5 986	57.1	5.4	50.2	9.9	39.9
Pickett County	825	162	3.3	261	0.0	17.2	4.6	4 003	55.4	4.0	48.1	12.2	39.7
Polk County	2 577	304	8.2	660	0.0	16.1	8.0	12 799	57.1	4.9	52.6	9.4	38.1
Putnam County	9 895	6 958	5.1	4 098	0.0	12.6	4.1	50 089	62.5	5.0	53.1	15.9	31.0
Rhea County	5 023	1 202	7.2	1 649	0.0	15.3	2.9	22 466	59.4	6.4	52.2	10.6	37.1
Roane County	8 612	1 573	6.7	2 421	0.0	15.1	4.7	41 688	57.9	5.6	51.4	10.4	38.3
Robertson County	10 877	1 227	10.9	3 183	0.0	20.7	3.7	41 507	68.9	3.4	61.3	12.4	26.3
Rutherford County	34 723	16 117	7.6	11 646	0.0	11.3	3.0	139 055	72.8	5.0	62.2	16.0	21.8
Scott County	4 182	608	2.2	1 185	0.0	13.2	6.6	16 270	52.5	7.3	48.3	7.5	44.2
Sequatchie County	1 943	316	8.1	490	0.0	22.2	1.2	8 811	59.1	5.1	53.5	11.6	34.9
Sevier County	12 154	2 101	7.5	3 433	0.0	14.3	4.2	56 576	66.6	6.5	58.9	12.9	28.2
Shelby County	189 061	50 931	14.4	51 491	0.1	9.5	7.1	671 029	65.6	6.8	57.6	13.1	29.3
Smith County	3 366	391	4.7	1 003	0.0	14.6	5.3	13 784	62.6	4.4	58.1	10.8	31.1
Stewart County	2 300	329	4.2	672	0.0	25.9	1.5	9 763	57.2	7.3	51.5	10.0	38.5
Sullivan County	25 279	4 970	9.1	7 230	0.1	12.0	5.3	123 608	57.8	4.6	50.4	12.9	36.7
Sumner County	25 901	4 410	12.2	7 587	0.0	13.4	4.0	100 360	68.3	3.7	60.1	13.5	26.4
Tipton County	11 411	1 769	7.7	3 060	0.0	15.0	5.8	37 961	65.3	4.8	59.1	12.0	29.0
Trousdale County	1 398	154	8.4	436	0.0	16.1	5.7	5 722	59.8	3.4	56.6	8.3	35.1
Unicoi County	2 692	495	3.2	824	1.6	19.2	5.3	14 494	55.9	6.8	51.6	9.2	39.2
Union County	3 345	379	3.5	1 041	0.0	25.8	4.3	13 759	57.3	5.2	51.7	11.0	37.4
Van Buren County	1 016	149	3.3	287	0.0	17.8	5.9	4 384	61.7	6.7	55.7	9.6	34.7
Warren County	6 653	864	4.3	1 748	0.0	18.1	3.1	30 067	62.3	4.7	56.0	11.0	32.9
Washington County	16 544	8 627	6.7	5 817	0.1	10.0	3.3	87 072	62.5	5.4	52.8	15.7	31.5
Wayne County	2 826	553	3.6	758	0.0	12.9	7.5	13 668	47.5	7.4	47.7	9.1	43.2
Weakley County	5 595	4 274	4.0	2 710	0.0	10.8	2.8	28 284	59.6	6.1	52.4	15.2	32.4
White County	4 215	477	4.8	1 244	0.0	16.9	5.3	18 249	60.6	6.2	53.3	11.1	35.7
Williamson County	28 159	4 118	18.3	6 880	0.0	7.4	1.5	93 553	72.0	2.6	61.5	16.1	22.4
Wilson County	17 549	2 961	16.5	4 623	0.0	14.1	2.8	67 848	71.6	3.9	63.2	13.6	23.2
TEXAS	4 355 276	1 202 890	9.2	1 289 185	0.9	11.0	7.1	15 617 373	63.6	6.0	57.3	12.5	30.3
Anderson County	9 247	1 438	6.9	2 368	0.0	18.1	7.3	44 971	41.0	7.5	52.0	7.0	41.0
Andrews County	3 345	334	3.2	1 054	0.0	8.8	8.9	9 503	58.0	8.1	50.9	11.5	37.6
Angelina County	16 317	3 308	5.7	4 890	0.0	11.5	5.4	60 704	59.4	6.0	53.5	12.4	34.1
Aransas County	4 278	498	7.6	1 352	0.4	16.3	4.7	17 930	52.1	7.3	45.3	12.8	41.9
Archer County	1 914	316	2.9	542	0.0	12.5	1.8	6 706	67.1	3.2	55.9	15.9	28.2
Armstrong County	441	81	2.3	120	0.0	9.2	5.0	1 666	60.6	3.4	53.0	13.8	33.2
Atascosa County	9 568	1 183	4.9	2 596	0.0	13.4	5.3	27 732	59.3	6.0	54.5	10.9	34.6
Austin County	4 954	647	6.3	1 567	0.0	9.3	2.9	18 100	62.3	4.4	55.2	12.1	32.8
Bailey County	1 520	139	1.7	412	0.5	6.6	2.2	4 843	61.6	8.7	55.6	12.0	32.4
Bandera County	3 514	423	8.1	907	0.0	6.5	2.0	13 814	59.8	4.8	52.5	12.5	35.1
Bastrop County	12 022	1 514	7.2	3 217	0.0	16.1	6.6	43 462	63.6	3.9	59.8	10.7	29.5
Baylor County	725	99	3.4	182	0.0	8.8	8.8	3 267	50.5	4.8	46.3	10.0	43.6
Bee County	6 038	1 373	7.4	2 204	0.0	6.9	12.6	25 782	42.0	8.0	43.3	8.8	47.9
Bell County	47 400	13 867	9.7	14 633	8.5	21.9	5.4	176 000	68.9	5.4	61.5	12.5	26.0
Bexar County	293 733	88 075	12.3	87 106	4.4	14.3	6.8	1 039 178	63.4	5.6	56.5	13.2	30.3
Blanco County	1 529	196	8.5	427	0.0	8.9	7.3	6 616	61.3	2.9	55.2	12.4	32.4
Borden County	169	29	5.6	48	0.0	0.0	8.3	573	62.1	3.7	49.0	16.4	34.6
Bosque County	3 183	456	2.9	938	0.0	10.8	4.4	13 559	55.3	5.2	49.1	12.0	38.9
Bowie County	17 634	3 226	4.5	4 819	0.0	13.7	4.8	69 563	55.6	6.9	52.6	10.8	36.6
Brazoria County	51 867	11 894	8.7	13 901	0.1	10.6	6.3	180 217	62.6	5.4	57.1	10.8	32.1
Brazos County	23 599	47 039	3.7	17 536	0.1	5.0	1.8	123 410	64.1	8.5	50.2	26.9	22.9
Brewster County	1 557	1 330	3.5	601	0.0	9.2	2.5	7 093	64.0	10.7	51.0	19.2	29.8
Briscoe County	391	26	4.8	110	0.0	5.5	6.4	1 364	59.5	3.4	53.3	13.6	33.1
Brooks County	1 946	280	1.1	597	0.0	9.2	16.2	5 794	46.3	8.5	39.4	10.6	50.0
Brown County	7 533	1 805	14.0	2 771	0.0	12.6	7.1	29 437	56.9	7.0	50.9	12.3	36.8
Burleson County	3 357	413	6.3	980	0.0	12.0	5.1	12 631	58.3	4.6	52.5	10.9	36.7
Burnet County	6 182	599	6.5	1 721	0.0	16.8	4.6	26 747	57.8	2.9	52.1	11.4	36.5

Table B-3. States and Counties — Education, Labor Force, and Income

STATE County	Full-year full-time employed (percent)								Children under 18 years in families						Total employed by class of worker (percent)			
				Non-Hispanic White	Black or African American	American Indian and Alaska Native	Asian, Hawaiian, and Pacific Islander	Hispanic or Latino[1]		With two parents (percent)		With one parent who is in labor force (percent)	+/− U.S. percent of children with no stay-at-home parent (percent)	+/− U.S. percent two-income couples				Unpaid family worker
	Total	Men	Women						Number	Both in labor force	Father only in labor force				Private	Government	Self-employed	
	24	25	26	27	28	29	30	31	32	33	34	35	36	37	38	39	40	41
TENNESSEE— Cont'd																		
Marshall County	46.7	58.1	36.0	47.3	40.4	31.3	50.0	46.8	6 459	47.1	23.4	20.7	3.2	4.4	78.3	10.9	10.3	0.4
Maury County	45.0	57.2	34.0	45.8	40.2	41.5	61.5	45.0	16 761	43.8	23.7	23.1	2.3	2.7	79.8	10.9	9.0	0.3
Meigs County	36.0	44.9	27.2	36.0	28.5	47.2	0.0	52.9	2 623	36.8	35.3	13.5	-14.3	-11.1	75.1	12.1	12.3	0.4
Monroe County	37.7	46.4	29.3	37.8	33.4	43.6	16.2	37.0	9 120	40.7	25.3	19.2	-4.7	-10.1	78.7	11.6	9.3	0.3
Montgomery County	46.4	60.8	32.3	47.6	45.4	43.4	30.8	43.3	36 608	44.6	25.5	19.1	-0.9	2.8	68.8	21.9	9.1	0.3
Moore County	43.5	54.2	33.6	43.7	38.1	100.0	100.0	X	1 249	59.0	13.9	23.1	17.5	3.1	71.0	16.2	12.4	0.4
Morgan County	36.1	44.4	26.4	36.2	45.2	0.0	0.0	28.8	4 197	38.9	27.5	17.0	-8.7	-13.3	70.9	14.2	9.6	0.3
Obion County	39.9	53.8	27.3	40.8	32.4	10.7	36.7	37.5	7 137	42.5	22.7	20.7	-1.4	-4.6	76.8	14.4	8.7	0.2
Overton County	37.2	46.2	28.7	37.1	50.0	31.7	25.5	46.0	4 392	41.6	27.0	17.4	-5.6	-8.0	73.6	14.6	11.0	0.8
Perry County	38.0	46.4	30.0	38.2	45.7	0.0	X	29.3	1 740	47.0	24.3	14.3	-3.3	-8.4	72.4	13.3	13.9	0.5
Pickett County	33.5	39.2	28.2	33.7	0.0	0.0	X	11.8	1 029	47.2	22.4	14.0	-3.4	-5.6	68.8	16.2	14.1	0.8
Polk County	39.0	50.2	28.3	39.1	45.0	40.9	0.0	67.8	3 411	43.8	30.2	11.5	-9.3	-6.8	76.1	13.1	9.7	1.1
Putnam County	37.2	44.8	29.8	37.5	30.6	14.4	33.9	35.9	13 021	48.0	19.6	19.3	2.7	-0.3	71.3	18.3	9.9	0.5
Rhea County	38.1	48.7	28.4	38.2	27.1	17.2	68.2	51.5	6 393	44.3	21.3	18.6	-1.7	-2.8	77.9	14.4	7.4	0.3
Roane County	38.8	48.8	29.9	38.8	44.4	38.0	28.9	41.4	10 863	43.5	25.3	20.0	-1.1	-5.6	72.5	19.3	8.0	0.1
Robertson County	47.9	58.9	37.3	49.6	33.7	84.3	68.0	30.5	13 659	51.6	20.2	18.0	5.0	6.6	76.8	11.5	11.2	0.5
Rutherford County	48.3	58.3	38.5	49.2	42.8	49.8	49.7	42.4	45 675	50.9	21.5	20.1	6.4	9.4	78.7	13.2	7.9	0.2
Scott County	33.5	43.6	23.8	33.5	0.0	46.5	29.4	47.5	5 281	36.5	28.4	14.9	-13.2	-13.2	75.5	14.5	9.7	0.3
Sequatchie County	39.7	48.1	31.4	39.9	0.0	X	24.1	25.0	2 639	33.5	28.5	25.6	-5.5	-8.4	75.5	13.0	11.1	0.4
Sevier County	42.3	51.6	33.7	42.2	27.0	66.0	40.9	50.8	15 495	48.2	21.4	21.0	4.6	-1.7	75.2	11.3	13.2	0.4
Shelby County	43.0	51.6	35.5	47.3	38.5	47.0	43.1	38.5	232 947	33.9	16.4	33.1	2.4	3.2	77.0	15.4	7.5	0.1
Smith County	43.1	54.3	32.6	42.9	45.7	47.7	69.1	46.9	4 314	50.2	24.3	17.3	2.9	-0.2	74.2	11.4	13.9	0.5
Stewart County	36.7	47.2	26.8	37.9	15.9	40.4	1.3	9.3	2 746	41.6	32.3	15.5	-7.5	-10.1	66.0	23.5	10.0	0.4
Sullivan County	38.1	48.4	28.8	38.3	35.1	21.3	41.8	40.0	31 556	42.5	25.3	18.1	-4.0	-6.9	79.8	10.4	9.4	0.4
Sumner County	47.2	59.5	35.8	47.7	41.4	64.3	52.4	38.8	32 400	49.1	23.3	17.1	1.6	4.0	76.8	11.6	11.3	0.3
Tipton County	44.6	54.1	35.7	47.1	35.1	42.1	39.7	34.8	13 996	46.8	16.4	22.0	4.2	5.8	76.5	14.9	8.4	0.2
Trousdale County	43.1	53.2	33.9	44.2	32.0	41.2	22.2	69.8	1 594	46.2	28.0	15.4	-3.0	4.4	75.5	12.5	10.9	1.1
Unicoi County	37.8	48.7	27.9	38.0	X	53.3	54.5	24.2	3 404	40.2	29.3	16.7	-7.7	-11.2	76.7	16.0	7.0	0.2
Union County	39.8	49.3	30.8	40.0	0.0	72.7	20.0	39.7	4 317	42.6	23.9	14.6	-7.4	-8.3	76.0	13.7	10.0	0.2
Van Buren County.........	40.7	48.0	33.7	40.5	23.1	66.7	X	70.0	1 176	47.1	14.8	19.9	2.4	-1.1	68.5	21.9	8.9	0.7
Warren County	40.8	52.5	29.7	41.1	43.3	27.5	13.9	37.4	8 701	43.4	23.1	19.0	-2.2	-2.1	75.7	10.8	12.8	0.7
Washington County	39.3	49.0	30.3	39.5	33.7	46.9	35.5	38.2	21 547	43.6	24.7	19.5	-1.5	-4.0	75.1	15.1	9.4	0.4
Wayne County	31.2	37.4	23.6	32.4	19.4	48.6	20.7	19.1	3 345	45.5	22.2	15.8	-3.3	-10.0	69.8	19.1	10.4	0.6
Weakley County	35.9	45.8	26.9	37.1	26.6	25.0	17.1	37.2	7 102	47.8	20.6	20.4	3.6	-1.0	71.7	17.0	10.9	0.4
White County	39.1	48.8	30.1	39.4	30.5	3.0	52.4	44.0	5 127	52.1	15.7	20.2	7.7	-1.9	75.4	12.1	12.2	0.3
Williamson County	49.4	65.8	34.0	49.9	45.1	45.7	45.8	44.8	36 542	49.3	34.5	11.1	-4.2	5.6	76.5	9.7	13.5	0.4
Wilson County	51.1	61.9	40.8	51.7	41.0	46.6	46.8	45.2	22 096	55.0	20.5	18.7	9.1	8.9	78.7	11.0	10.0	0.3
TEXAS....................	41.0	50.4	31.9	44.6	38.1	39.4	41.6	35.0	5 503 509	39.0	25.2	20.6	-5.0	-2.5	75.3	14.6	9.8	0.3
Anderson County	29.8	30.3	29.1	34.6	19.0	37.3	47.6	26.0	10 596	41.5	18.4	27.8	4.7	-2.4	63.1	26.2	10.2	0.5
Andrews County	34.6	44.5	25.5	37.2	45.1	37.0	25.7	29.8	3 888	40.0	29.2	13.4	-11.2	-12.2	65.6	21.3	12.0	1.1
Angelina County	38.5	48.4	29.2	39.5	32.2	30.5	34.6	41.7	20 564	41.0	22.9	21.5	-2.1	-4.0	74.8	15.5	9.3	0.3
Aransas County	29.7	38.1	21.7	30.0	35.2	34.0	19.1	30.1	4 994	35.2	27.4	22.2	-7.2	-15.1	65.2	14.9	19.4	0.4
Archer County	43.7	54.7	33.0	43.7	25.0	31.7	42.9	45.2	2 370	62.9	19.1	11.9	10.2	5.4	63.1	19.1	16.6	1.3
Armstrong County	40.9	55.0	27.8	41.1	X	0.0	X	37.2	529	58.4	24.0	9.8	3.6	1.3	57.2	20.3	21.2	1.2
Atascosa County	38.1	49.2	27.8	41.2	18.8	23.6	40.6	36.1	11 436	39.6	23.7	18.7	-6.3	-3.9	69.8	17.7	12.0	0.5
Austin County	40.2	52.3	28.9	41.4	33.1	20.0	44.0	39.3	6 114	45.6	28.4	16.8	-2.2	-1.8	70.2	15.7	13.4	0.8
Bailey County	38.0	53.6	22.8	39.1	33.3	25.0	X	36.0	1 878	43.8	34.8	12.0	-8.8	-12.5	71.1	13.1	14.8	0.9
Bandera County	38.0	47.2	29.1	38.7	47.6	26.5	44.7	33.3	4 032	41.9	30.5	19.7	-3.0	-8.0	67.8	15.4	16.4	0.5
Bastrop County	45.5	53.6	37.1	48.2	33.4	41.1	42.8	42.0	15 025	40.5	28.0	19.9	-4.2	1.4	66.9	21.3	11.1	0.7
Baylor County	32.7	35.9	29.8	35.1	30.9	0.0	0.0	16.6	885	44.3	11.2	15.7	-4.6	-13.2	56.9	23.0	19.0	1.1
Bee County	24.7	24.6	24.7	30.5	3.8	16.4	34.3	25.0	6 907	35.0	20.8	26.4	-3.2	-8.3	59.7	30.5	9.1	0.7
Bell County	45.4	58.1	32.9	46.0	48.0	46.3	36.7	42.3	65 133	43.2	24.4	21.7	0.3	1.2	69.8	21.9	8.0	0.3
Bexar County	40.7	49.9	32.3	44.3	41.0	38.0	41.4	37.8	371 547	36.3	22.1	24.0	-4.3	-3.5	74.8	16.3	8.6	0.3
Blanco County	41.6	51.3	32.3	42.0	31.7	31.0	11.1	41.4	1 929	46.7	26.1	19.9	2.0	-1.7	64.5	15.6	19.2	0.7
Borden County	36.0	44.5	27.0	36.2	X	100.0	44.4	30.7	178	41.6	39.9	15.7	-7.3	-4.3	48.7	24.2	24.8	2.3
Bosque County.............	34.5	43.8	25.8	34.5	21.2	37.0	21.4	35.9	3 974	49.5	24.3	13.4	-1.7	-5.7	71.5	13.3	14.8	0.4
Bowie County	36.9	44.0	29.8	40.2	27.6	47.4	43.8	25.1	20 678	38.9	19.4	26.4	0.7	-3.0	68.9	20.1	10.7	0.3
Brazoria County	42.8	51.7	33.3	45.6	32.7	33.5	45.8	37.6	65 395	43.3	28.1	18.0	-3.3	-1.1	76.8	14.6	8.3	0.3
Brazos County	30.9	36.8	25.0	31.6	30.1	25.1	20.5	31.2	30 383	44.2	21.9	20.0	-0.4	4.0	60.9	31.4	7.2	0.4
Brewster County	33.2	41.8	24.5	34.1	13.4	26.8	100.0	31.7	1 837	41.2	24.9	21.1	-2.3	-2.8	53.8	34.7	11.0	0.6
Briscoe County.............	39.3	57.6	22.3	40.0	26.3	X	X	38.7	444	46.6	24.3	22.1	4.1	0.5	48.6	24.7	25.4	1.3
Brooks County	23.8	34.4	14.2	20.9	0.0	23.6	X	23.9	2 343	28.4	21.2	27.1	-9.1	-18.2	66.8	22.5	9.8	0.9
Brown County	35.5	44.2	27.4	35.8	27.8	39.3	35.2	36.2	8 781	44.6	20.1	22.8	2.8	-4.3	70.6	16.3	12.4	0.7
Burleson County	37.8	48.7	27.9	39.5	30.7	22.6	0.0	36.9	4 135	45.0	20.0	17.7	-1.9	-5.0	61.0	23.6	15.0	0.5
Burnet County	37.6	48.2	28.0	37.2	31.2	29.0	31.2	41.4	7 962	42.8	27.3	18.9	-2.9	-6.6	67.2	16.1	15.8	1.0

[1] Hispanic or Latino persons may be of any race.

				Occupation for employed population 16 years and over (percent)						Industry for employed population 16 years and over (percent)					
STATE County	Percent who worked at home	Percent of the population 5 years and over with a disability	Veterans as a percent of the population 18 years and over	Management, professional, and related occupations	Service occupations	Sales and office occupations	Farming, fishing, and forestry occupations	Construction, extraction, and maintenance occupations	Production, transportation and material moving occupations	Agriculture, forestry, fishing, and mining	Construction and manufacturing	Wholesale and retail trade	Transportation and warehousing, and utilities	Service industries	Public administration
	42	43	44	45	46	47	48	49	50	51	52	53	54	55	56
TENNESSEE— Cont'd															
Marshall County	3.0	22.4	11.8	21.5	11.5	20.2	1.2	10.5	35.2	3.8	46.7	12.5	4.7	29.6	2.8
Maury County	1.9	19.6	13.0	24.8	13.4	24.1	0.7	11.9	25.1	1.5	34.6	14.8	4.3	41.5	3.3
Meigs County	2.0	25.3	13.9	16.6	12.9	19.4	1.7	15.2	34.2	2.8	43.0	12.2	6.4	32.2	3.4
Monroe County	2.5	25.8	11.9	19.0	11.6	19.9	1.6	13.6	34.3	3.8	45.4	11.9	4.6	31.6	2.8
Montgomery County	1.9	20.2	20.3	27.3	16.6	25.8	0.4	11.0	18.9	0.9	23.7	15.2	5.5	48.0	6.7
Moore County	3.4	24.4	13.8	24.7	14.0	23.3	0.3	12.6	25.1	4.3	35.1	12.1	5.6	38.2	4.7
Morgan County	2.2	29.0	13.6	17.7	17.6	17.3	2.0	17.3	28.1	3.7	36.2	11.6	5.3	34.3	8.8
Obion County	2.1	24.1	13.2	19.3	14.9	22.9	1.2	9.0	32.7	2.6	37.3	16.7	4.3	33.8	5.3
Overton County	1.7	27.2	11.9	20.1	13.0	19.7	1.8	13.0	32.4	3.7	38.2	14.9	5.1	34.3	3.8
Perry County	4.7	24.5	13.3	21.4	13.7	16.7	1.1	10.3	37.0	3.9	43.4	11.5	4.6	31.6	5.0
Pickett County	4.9	27.3	13.3	20.1	13.2	24.2	1.7	11.8	29.0	4.6	36.1	16.7	2.9	36.9	2.8
Polk County	0.0	26.7	12.0	10.5	11.0	17.9	2.0	10.1	35.8	4.8	45.5	13.7	4.6	27.7	3.6
Putnam County	2.6	22.1	12.1	28.7	14.4	25.4	0.7	8.6	22.1	1.4	29.5	15.0	4.7	45.3	4.1
Rhea County	2.6	26.7	13.7	18.5	13.3	20.4	1.1	11.9	34.8	1.9	44.0	11.9	6.8	32.3	3.1
Roane County	1.7	26.3	15.8	26.7	14.4	22.4	0.5	13.3	22.7	1.5	28.0	13.9	6.1	46.4	4.1
Robertson County	2.8	21.4	12.9	24.7	12.3	27.6	1.1	13.1	21.1	2.9	31.1	16.8	5.9	39.1	4.3
Rutherford County	2.5	16.4	12.5	30.5	12.6	28.0	0.2	10.3	18.4	0.8	26.5	17.9	5.8	45.6	3.5
Scott County	1.0	31.0	10.3	21.0	11.2	19.4	0.8	13.9	33.6	2.5	42.3	14.2	5.7	31.9	3.4
Sequatchie County	0.8	23.9	13.4	21.9	11.7	20.4	1.3	15.3	29.3	2.7	40.2	14.8	5.9	31.1	5.3
Sevier County	3.3	22.3	13.5	23.0	18.8	30.1	0.3	13.2	14.6	1.0	22.2	17.8	3.8	52.3	2.9
Shelby County	2.2	20.7	12.1	33.4	14.3	30.1	0.1	7.6	14.6	0.2	15.7	16.2	11.9	51.1	4.9
Smith County	3.3	21.3	11.6	22.3	11.1	21.0	1.6	14.3	29.6	5.9	37.3	12.9	8.1	32.0	3.9
Stewart County	1.7	27.0	20.8	23.1	15.0	20.3	1.6	15.2	24.7	2.9	29.1	11.3	11.0	38.5	7.2
Sullivan County	2.4	24.0	15.1	28.6	13.8	27.3	0.3	11.2	18.9	0.9	29.1	18.3	4.5	44.6	2.5
Sumner County	3.2	18.5	12.9	30.2	11.4	29.5	0.4	10.8	17.7	0.9	25.5	18.9	5.5	45.6	3.6
Tipton County	2.2	19.8	15.1	23.6	12.3	27.0	0.5	15.7	20.9	1.5	28.7	17.1	7.6	39.3	5.7
Trousdale County	3.0	26.3	12.0	18.7	9.6	24.8	3.5	14.1	29.3	6.9	34.8	17.2	6.5	31.4	3.2
Unicoi County	1.7	27.7	16.6	22.3	13.5	21.3	0.7	14.9	27.2	0.9	37.9	10.9	7.0	39.9	3.5
Union County	1.0	27.6	10.1	16.0	11.7	22.1	0.0	10.5	27.0	2.2	37.2	14.8	5.5	37.3	3.0
Van Buren County	3.4	27.3	13.3	15.5	15.0	17.1	2.3	9.1	41.0	4.1	45.8	9.3	3.6	29.6	7.6
Warren County	3.3	26.3	11.6	20.2	12.7	21.0	4.2	11.2	30.8	5.2	37.7	17.3	4.4	32.9	2.6
Washington County	2.2	23.5	14.6	31.3	15.1	27.6	0.4	9.2	16.6	1.3	24.3	17.6	4.1	49.9	2.8
Wayne County	1.7	28.1	10.9	19.5	14.7	16.6	2.7	11.4	35.2	3.9	35.6	14.3	6.8	32.7	6.6
Weakley County	2.9	22.1	11.6	22.9	15.7	22.1	1.2	10.1	28.0	3.4	35.8	14.2	3.6	39.3	3.7
White County	3.1	26.9	13.2	18.8	10.9	22.2	1.2	12.0	34.9	3.7	42.3	15.9	7.2	28.0	2.9
Williamson County	5.4	11.4	10.4	46.0	9.7	27.9	0.3	6.8	9.3	1.0	18.4	16.0	3.1	58.5	3.0
Wilson County	3.2	18.5	13.3	31.7	11.2	29.5	0.2	10.4	17.0	0.8	24.5	16.9	7.2	46.6	3.9
TEXAS	2.8	19.2	11.7	33.3	14.6	27.2	0.7	10.9	13.2	2.7	19.9	15.9	5.8	51.2	4.5
Anderson County	2.3	24.6	12.8	24.9	23.1	24.9	1.1	11.2	14.9	5.9	11.7	18.3	7.2	41.7	15.1
Andrews County	2.3	18.0	10.5	25.5	16.4	20.9	1.3	16.2	19.6	21.0	13.6	13.9	4.1	44.1	3.2
Angelina County	2.5	22.2	12.7	26.8	16.4	23.2	1.3	11.6	20.7	3.3	26.7	17.3	4.1	45.1	3.6
Aransas County	3.4	23.3	20.6	25.9	19.3	24.3	2.6	17.1	10.8	6.4	19.9	13.0	5.0	50.3	5.4
Archer County	4.4	18.9	14.4	30.4	14.0	22.1	3.0	13.8	16.7	12.4	17.0	14.1	4.7	45.2	6.5
Armstrong County	6.0	19.4	15.9	33.7	16.1	23.0	2.7	10.7	13.8	10.7	17.0	14.6	9.8	40.9	7.0
Atascosa County	2.3	23.4	12.1	23.8	16.8	23.5	1.3	18.2	16.3	6.2	22.3	15.2	6.9	43.6	5.8
Austin County	4.1	19.1	12.8	30.0	13.2	27.1	1.4	11.2	17.0	7.1	23.9	18.4	6.5	40.4	3.7
Bailey County	2.3	27.3	9.8	24.0	16.6	18.0	11.9	9.9	19.7	18.8	12.8	14.7	10.9	39.3	3.6
Bandera County	5.2	20.7	20.8	35.0	14.3	24.0	1.9	15.6	9.1	6.4	18.8	13.7	5.0	51.9	4.2
Bastrop County	2.7	19.4	15.0	30.5	12.7	24.6	0.8	16.6	14.8	2.7	25.2	13.1	5.8	43.8	9.4
Baylor County	4.2	27.1	14.4	36.3	17.4	21.5	4.6	11.6	8.5	13.0	10.4	11.4	5.5	51.8	8.0
Bee County	3.3	23.4	12.5	25.3	25.2	22.1	3.0	12.4	12.0	8.5	12.2	12.6	4.0	44.9	17.7
Bell County	1.7	18.8	20.5	30.7	17.2	27.1	0.4	10.4	14.3	1.0	16.5	16.3	5.0	53.5	7.8
Bexar County	2.5	21.0	15.4	32.9	16.0	29.9	0.2	10.3	10.6	0.5	14.3	16.1	4.9	58.6	5.6
Blanco County	7.2	18.2	17.1	30.9	13.8	27.2	3.0	15.1	9.9	9.5	18.5	15.0	6.6	44.5	5.8
Borden County	2.9	11.5	14.4	49.6	10.2	12.0	12.0	7.3	9.0	39.4	6.4	4.7	6.4	32.7	10.5
Bosque County	3.9	21.2	17.2	29.5	14.5	22.7	2.7	14.0	16.6	7.8	23.6	14.4	7.1	44.0	3.1
Bowie County	2.3	23.7	14.9	27.6	16.4	27.8	0.6	10.9	16.7	1.7	18.2	19.0	4.9	45.7	10.5
Brazoria County	2.2	17.6	13.4	32.7	12.8	24.4	0.4	14.8	15.0	2.2	29.5	13.7	5.6	43.7	5.3
Brazos County	2.6	12.6	7.3	39.3	16.4	25.3	0.6	8.9	9.5	2.3	13.0	13.4	2.8	64.6	4.0
Brewster County	4.6	23.2	14.0	31.9	21.6	25.0	2.7	11.2	7.6	5.4	11.4	13.9	3.8	58.3	7.3
Briscoe County	4.2	23.0	13.7	34.9	17.0	20.9	8.9	9.7	8.5	24.7	9.8	12.1	6.5	35.6	11.2
Brooks County	2.8	26.7	10.9	22.6	27.9	20.0	5.7	10.3	13.5	15.5	10.4	12.6	5.6	48.6	7.3
Brown County	2.3	23.1	13.6	25.8	18.9	24.6	0.7	10.8	19.1	3.6	25.5	14.8	3.9	46.1	6.2
Burleson County	3.2	24.9	14.3	26.6	16.3	23.3	0.9	15.2	17.6	9.7	19.2	15.3	5.8	45.0	5.0
Burnet County	3.9	22.5	16.6	28.2	17.0	23.7	1.4	16.9	12.7	4.6	23.7	15.8	5.9	45.6	4.4

Table B-3. States and Counties — Education, Labor Force, and Income

STATE County	Median household income	Median family income — All families	Families with children — Married-couple	Families with children — Male householder	Families with children — Female householder	Median nonfamily household income	Median income for full-year, full-time workers — Men	Median income for full-year, full-time workers — Women	Per capita income	With earnings	With interest, dividend, or rental income	With Social Security income	With public assistance income	With retirement income	House-holds with income over $100,000 (percent)	+/- U.S. percent for income over $100,000 (percent)	House-holds with income below poverty (percent)	Families with children with income below poverty (percent)
	57	58	59	60	61	62	63	64	65	66	67	68	69	70	71	72	73	74
TENNESSEE— Cont'd																		
Marshall County	38 457	45 731	51 902	30 202	20 450	19 164	32 463	22 965	17 749	81.2	26.9	26.6	2.7	15.1	6.3	-6.0	11.5	10.8
Maury County	41 591	48 010	58 344	28 929	17 842	22 821	39 106	23 930	19 365	83.0	29.7	24.5	2.3	15.4	9.1	-3.2	11.1	12.2
Meigs County	29 354	34 114	39 150	16 818	12 563	15 813	30 282	20 873	14 551	75.3	22.3	29.3	5.3	15.8	2.8	-9.5	18.5	22.6
Monroe County	30 337	34 902	40 253	21 313	17 254	15 509	30 208	21 623	14 951	76.9	22.9	31.4	3.9	15.6	4.1	-8.2	16.4	16.5
Montgomery County	38 981	43 023	47 448	26 523	19 175	24 798	31 890	23 341	17 265	86.1	25.9	18.8	3.2	18.9	6.3	-6.0	10.5	11.2
Moore County	36 591	41 484	44 792	39 531	14 236	17 955	33 894	21 500	19 040	80.0	35.4	32.9	3.0	18.4	7.6	-4.7	11.3	10.2
Morgan County	27 712	31 901	37 487	23 000	16 250	14 471	26 169	19 570	12 925	74.3	22.3	33.1	3.4	17.2	2.6	-9.7	17.7	15.5
Obion County	32 764	40 533	46 027	24 891	12 969	16 227	34 383	20 538	17 409	76.1	28.0	32.6	3.0	15.7	5.3	-7.0	13.7	15.6
Overton County	26 915	32 156	38 713	23 571	14 309	12 306	26 091	20 243	13 910	74.9	22.9	33.3	4.3	13.6	2.0	-10.3	17.9	17.5
Perry County	28 061	34 792	40 204	22 344	18 646	12 433	27 086	21 353	16 969	71.6	22.9	32.9	2.1	23.1	4.2	-8.1	17.8	14.9
Pickett County	24 673	31 355	38 456	21 161	18 750	13 608	24 632	17 985	14 681	68.4	27.1	40.8	3.0	18.1	3.6	-8.7	16.8	20.2
Polk County	29 643	36 370	40 281	26 250	17 404	14 892	28 962	21 215	16 025	74.1	22.9	33.8	2.6	18.8	5.0	-7.3	15.3	10.9
Putnam County	30 914	39 553	45 410	25 061	16 793	16 621	30 249	21 519	16 927	77.6	28.4	27.9	2.8	15.8	5.6	-6.7	17.7	14.7
Rhea County	30 418	35 580	42 358	29 479	13 016	14 770	30 621	21 660	15 672	73.7	24.6	29.8	4.1	18.8	4.9	-7.4	16.5	16.6
Roane County	33 226	41 399	47 760	29 375	15 885	15 618	33 114	23 389	18 456	73.0	31.0	34.0	4.1	21.3	6.5	-5.8	15.3	16.0
Robertson County	43 174	49 412	55 658	27 847	20 313	20 596	35 865	24 964	19 054	84.5	28.0	25.1	2.8	15.0	7.6	-4.7	9.6	9.4
Rutherford County	46 312	53 553	60 454	31 577	23 104	25 584	37 421	27 044	19 938	88.8	28.3	17.2	2.1	12.4	9.2	-3.1	10.0	7.6
Scott County	24 093	28 595	32 614	21 458	13 466	11 766	25 306	19 743	12 927	68.9	16.4	34.9	4.7	13.4	2.5	-9.8	22.0	22.2
Sequatchie County	30 959	36 435	41 563	19 464	14 957	14 632	28 911	21 236	16 468	78.2	23.9	27.0	4.3	15.7	4.9	-7.4	17.3	19.7
Sevier County	34 719	40 474	44 678	24 882	17 714	19 408	28 101	21 237	18 064	82.1	29.2	27.2	3.3	16.4	5.5	-6.8	11.8	11.5
Shelby County	39 593	47 386	64 000	28 680	19 460	25 542	37 948	27 443	20 856	82.8	26.8	21.4	4.5	14.0	11.6	-0.7	14.9	18.3
Smith County	35 625	41 645	46 119	30 313	17 463	17 767	31 332	23 004	17 473	79.7	29.2	27.9	3.5	16.8	5.2	-7.1	13.7	13.2
Stewart County	32 316	38 655	42 708	28 125	15 660	15 660	31 813	22 574	16 302	74.3	24.3	31.5	2.9	24.0	3.8	-8.5	14.9	11.5
Sullivan County	33 529	41 025	45 707	26 000	15 339	16 891	31 895	22 218	19 202	74.3	34.5	33.4	3.5	19.9	6.7	-5.6	13.9	15.4
Sumner County	46 030	52 125	58 941	30 156	21 556	24 220	37 663	26 563	21 164	84.6	31.8	23.6	2.3	15.6	10.8	-1.5	8.5	9.1
Tipton County	41 856	46 807	53 255	31 856	17 849	19 372	36 880	24 596	17 952	82.9	25.4	24.1	3.4	17.5	7.4	-4.9	13.0	14.0
Trousdale County	32 212	37 401	43 700	29 583	13 750	17 056	28 063	21 540	15 838	75.6	25.4	30.7	3.9	15.4	3.9	-8.4	14.5	12.5
Unicoi County	29 863	36 871	41 393	28 393	17 784	14 069	30 975	21 014	15 612	70.9	30.0	35.6	2.7	18.1	3.7	-8.6	14.2	14.6
Union County	27 335	31 843	37 353	20 875	12 806	12 394	26 833	18 951	13 375	75.1	17.3	28.9	4.2	15.4	4.0	-8.3	20.2	22.9
Van Buren County	28 165	34 949	45 357	25 625	16 250	14 453	26 573	21 287	17 497	75.7	19.8	29.9	2.9	15.3	3.2	-9.1	16.5	17.3
Warren County	30 920	37 835	42 351	29 011	13 478	15 405	29 450	21 354	15 759	77.1	25.7	29.8	3.6	14.9	4.5	-7.8	17.4	19.9
Washington County	33 116	41 162	47 788	21 566	16 136	18 480	31 614	22 011	19 085	78.3	32.7	28.7	3.2	17.7	7.0	-5.3	15.2	15.5
Wayne County	26 576	30 973	36 381	21 534	15 259	14 963	28 812	19 612	14 472	71.9	22.5	34.0	4.2	18.9	2.8	-9.5	17.5	17.9
Weakley County	30 008	38 658	46 684	25 260	14 437	13 786	29 646	21 330	15 408	76.4	29.2	29.9	2.6	14.5	3.8	-8.5	18.5	15.9
White County	29 383	34 854	41 660	19 076	16 197	14 877	27 164	20 914	14 791	74.4	26.4	34.0	2.4	17.5	3.5	-8.8	15.5	15.2
Williamson County	69 104	78 315	89 361	39 667	30 585	34 942	59 387	33 381	32 496	90.5	48.0	16.6	1.1	11.6	30.2	17.9	4.9	4.5
Wilson County	50 140	56 650	63 900	36 672	24 026	24 023	40 496	27 333	22 739	86.6	33.1	22.0	2.0	15.0	12.4	0.1	7.3	6.4
TEXAS	39 927	45 861	52 372	27 667	19 769	25 623	35 893	26 827	19 617	83.9	29.2	21.6	3.2	13.2	11.5	-0.8	14.0	16.6
Anderson County	31 957	37 513	45 269	21 719	15 377	15 829	27 739	22 009	13 838	73.6	24.1	32.8	3.2	15.9	4.4	-7.9	16.8	18.2
Andrews County	34 036	37 017	39 733	25 250	14 924	18 514	33 793	22 731	15 916	77.6	24.1	27.3	3.7	13.2	4.7	-7.6	16.7	17.8
Angelina County	33 806	39 505	46 302	25 058	14 691	16 968	31 014	21 074	15 876	78.8	26.2	28.7	3.6	15.3	6.0	-6.3	15.2	18.5
Aransas County	30 702	34 915	38 634	18 182	12 361	18 401	32 627	21 079	18 560	70.5	35.4	38.5	4.2	22.4	7.5	-4.8	17.5	26.0
Archer County	38 514	45 984	50 949	26 667	15 556	18 851	32 381	23 433	19 300	81.1	36.0	29.5	2.4	15.4	7.0	-5.3	10.0	9.3
Armstrong County	38 194	43 894	47 440	41 250	15 625	18 571	33 583	22 109	17 151	77.4	38.9	33.4	1.1	15.8	6.3	-6.0	10.0	10.4
Atascosa County	33 081	37 705	41 607	31 510	14 505	14 603	28 825	19 348	14 276	80.0	20.5	26.0	4.3	13.8	5.6	-6.7	19.3	21.3
Austin County	38 615	46 342	52 250	25 260	23 235	19 845	33 717	22 872	18 140	78.3	37.4	30.6	1.5	14.4	8.4	-3.9	12.5	12.7
Bailey County	27 901	32 898	32 207	34 318	13 466	13 821	25 812	19 609	12 979	80.2	22.5	30.8	2.4	8.0	3.7	-8.6	16.5	16.9
Bandera County	39 013	45 906	48 465	30 458	17 833	20 774	35 780	25 931	19 635	76.6	37.0	31.2	2.2	24.3	7.9	-4.4	11.3	11.3
Bastrop County	43 578	49 456	53 295	40 068	19 388	23 826	34 825	26 227	18 146	83.9	30.2	23.3	2.7	15.3	8.9	-3.4	11.3	12.5
Baylor County	24 627	34 583	41 528	15 750	10 833	14 412	22 335	21 573	16 384	65.2	35.5	45.3	3.4	19.7	3.1	-9.2	15.7	20.8
Bee County	28 392	32 967	45 108	22 216	16 659	16 659	27 688	21 412	10 625	76.8	20.5	29.8	3.8	14.5	3.2	-9.1	21.6	27.5
Bell County	36 872	41 455	45 290	29 055	17 519	24 036	29 721	23 075	17 219	85.4	26.5	18.9	2.8	18.5	6.5	-5.8	11.6	13.8
Bexar County	38 328	43 724	49 745	25 685	18 810	25 575	31 727	25 674	18 363	83.4	29.4	22.6	3.7	18.2	9.9	-2.4	14.3	18.0
Blanco County	39 369	45 382	46 875	30 000	16 154	18 594	34 698	22 563	19 721	78.8	39.5	27.6	1.9	18.1	9.5	-2.8	11.4	13.3
Borden County	29 205	36 458	47 500	26 250	26 250	20 500	27 955	21 719	18 364	82.6	38.9	34.8	1.4	17.7	9.6	-2.7	13.7	13.1
Bosque County	34 181	40 763	42 246	22 833	16 736	16 702	32 442	22 343	17 455	72.1	32.5	38.5	2.6	18.7	6.2	-6.1	14.0	14.4
Bowie County	33 001	41 108	51 713	20 367	12 934	17 003	33 160	22 325	17 357	75.3	28.1	28.4	3.5	20.4	6.5	-5.8	17.1	21.7
Brazoria County	48 632	55 282	63 468	31 559	21 350	26 436	43 385	28 634	20 021	85.5	33.4	20.1	2.0	14.1	13.6	1.3	9.7	11.1
Brazos County	29 104	46 530	53 915	29 214	14 356	15 154	34 783	25 215	16 212	87.2	33.6	14.1	2.3	9.8	8.3	-4.0	27.7	18.1
Brewster County	27 386	33 962	44 489	27 778	14 489	17 574	27 785	22 513	15 183	76.3	28.6	28.2	1.7	16.7	4.2	-8.1	19.9	19.2
Briscoe County	29 917	35 326	41 250	30 357	10 000	14 306	27 073	17 955	14 218	77.9	28.7	35.5	2.6	11.5	3.6	-8.7	16.0	16.8
Brooks County	18 622	22 473	34 063	9 459	4 670	10 560	23 306	16 341	10 234	69.3	14.3	33.2	9.8	10.6	3.1	-9.2	37.7	42.9
Brown County	30 974	37 725	42 979	25 036	12 797	16 029	31 302	20 503	15 624	74.4	28.2	33.2	3.8	17.2	4.9	-7.4	17.5	21.2
Burleson County	33 026	39 385	44 583	20 500	15 042	17 044	30 251	20 677	16 616	73.9	32.7	35.1	2.4	18.0	5.5	-6.8	16.2	18.9
Burnet County	37 921	43 871	48 781	26 442	17 073	19 774	31 800	21 818	18 850	75.4	35.2	34.6	2.3	21.4	8.4	-3.9	10.3	12.8

Table B-3. States and Counties — Education, Labor Force, and Income

STATE/ County code	MSA/PMSA/ NECMA code[1]	STATE County	High school graduates			College graduates		College graduates (percent)				
			Total population 25 years and over	Percent with a high school diploma or less	Percent with a high school diploma or more	Percent with a bachelor's degree or more	+/− U.S. percent with bachelor's degree or more	Non-Hispanic White	Black or African American	American Indian and Alaska Native	Asian, Hawaiian, and Pacific Islander	Hispanic or Latino[2]
			1	2	3	4	5	6	7	8	9	10
		TEXAS—Cont'd										
48 055	0640	Caldwell County	20 337	63.5	71.3	13.3	−11.1	19.9	3.9	7.3	35.2	4.7
48 057	...	Calhoun County	13 012	64.1	69.0	12.1	−12.3	15.0	3.0	0.0	65.0	3.1
48 059	...	Callahan County	8 658	58.8	79.3	12.8	−12.1	12.8	7.4	4.2	62.5	1.1
48 061	1240	Cameron County	187 064	64.9	55.2	13.4	−11.0	28.9	28.0	10.4	56.6	8.9
48 063	...	Camp County	7 474	63.1	69.5	12.2	−12.2	15.2	5.4	0.0	50.9	1.1
48 065	...	Carson County	4 305	48.4	82.6	15.5	−8.9	16.1	0.0	0.0	50.0	5.9
48 067	...	Cass County	20 546	63.2	75.0	12.0	−12.4	13.6	4.8	8.5	4.3	6.0
48 069	...	Castro County	4 871	64.3	65.4	14.7	−9.7	24.7	7.7	0.0	0.0	2.4
48 071	3360	Chambers County	16 348	55.5	76.9	12.1	−12.3	13.0	8.3	18.0	21.4	6.1
48 073	...	Cherokee County	30 008	63.6	68.4	11.4	−13.0	13.4	5.7	16.7	43.5	3.3
48 075	...	Childress County	5 173	66.0	65.0	8.6	−15.8	10.9	6.0	0.0	50.0	0.0
48 077	...	Clay County................	7 549	59.2	80.4	13.9	−10.5	14.1	0.0	0.0	0.0	8.0
48 079	...	Cochran County	2 236	65.6	62.7	10.2	−14.2	15.1	9.5	0.0	X	2.5
48 081	...	Coke County	2 620	59.8	74.2	14.7	−9.7	15.7	0.0	40.0	100.0	5.4
48 083	...	Coleman County	6 373	67.2	71.0	11.7	−12.7	12.7	2.3	19.6	0.0	4.1
48 085	1920	Collin County	315 665	23.2	91.8	47.3	22.9	48.2	42.9	28.7	72.0	22.4
48 087	...	Collingsworth County	2 159	54.2	71.3	15.3	−9.1	18.0	9.7	0.0	100.0	1.9
48 089	...	Colorado County	13 383	64.3	69.1	14.4	−10.0	18.6	5.0	38.9	0.0	3.1
48 091	7240	Comal County	52 549	44.6	83.9	26.2	1.8	30.0	26.3	20.7	46.6	9.0
48 093	...	Comanche County	9 411	64.4	70.2	13.0	−11.4	14.8	0.0	0.0	9.1	2.6
48 095	...	Concho County	2 921	67.9	59.3	14.1	−10.3	19.8	15.2	50.0	0.0	5.9
48 097	...	Cooke County	23 148	52.3	79.2	15.7	−8.7	16.6	10.8	11.6	57.5	3.5
48 099	3810	Coryell County	41 764	51.0	81.1	12.4	−12.0	14.8	7.4	7.6	17.8	6.6
48 101	...	Cottle County	1 342	64.5	66.1	15.3	−9.1	19.0	0.0	X	X	2.1
48 103	...	Crane County	2 394	64.2	68.7	12.8	−11.6	17.6	0.0	0.0	80.5	2.1
48 105	...	Crockett County	2 659	66.8	62.1	10.4	−14.0	19.4	0.0	31.8	0.0	1.9
48 107	...	Crosby County	4 299	68.8	61.8	10.5	−13.9	17.8	2.9	0.0	0.0	1.4
48 109	...	Culberson County	1 781	71.5	56.1	13.9	−10.5	31.0	66.7	0.0	80.0	4.5
48 111	...	Dallam County..............	3 703	67.1	65.0	9.6	−14.8	12.7	0.0	17.3	X	0.1
48 113	1920	Dallas County	1 365 848	46.7	75.0	27.0	2.6	38.0	17.0	16.2	45.2	7.0
48 115	...	Dawson County	9 949	69.6	65.2	10.5	−13.9	20.2	1.3	54.5	15.4	1.4
48 117	...	Deaf Smith County........	10 539	65.6	60.9	11.8	−12.6	20.7	2.4	0.0	21.8	2.2
48 119	...	Delta County	3 618	60.6	75.5	13.9	−10.5	15.1	3.1	14.8	0.0	0.0
48 121	1920	Denton County	265 220	30.5	89.4	36.6	12.2	38.7	33.8	24.1	47.1	17.9
48 123	...	DeWitt County	13 969	65.0	67.9	11.8	−12.6	17.1	2.3	0.0	53.8	2.4
48 125	...	Dickens County	1 940	67.9	70.6	8.4	−16.0	10.8	0.0	44.4	25.0	0.8
48 127	...	Dimmit County	5 982	72.0	54.3	10.1	−14.3	19.1	27.2	42.1	45.5	7.5
48 129	...	Donley County	2 586	48.3	78.2	15.8	−8.6	16.6	0.0	6.4	0.0	7.2
48 131	...	Duval County...............	8 042	70.0	59.7	8.9	−15.5	13.7	0.0	0.0	0.0	8.3
48 133	...	Eastland County...........	12 171	60.9	72.6	12.7	−11.7	13.6	18.4	4.5	100.0	2.4
48 135	5800	Ector County	71 756	58.8	68.0	12.0	−12.4	16.2	7.7	8.3	56.4	4.5
48 137	...	Edwards County	1 418	62.3	67.1	17.3	−7.1	26.1	0.0	0.0	0.0	3.5
48 139	1920	Ellis County	67 470	53.0	77.8	17.1	−7.3	19.8	11.6	16.0	62.9	4.2
48 141	2320	El Paso County	391 540	56.8	65.8	16.6	−7.8	35.1	21.1	13.6	40.8	10.6
48 143	...	Erath County	19 350	49.5	77.1	25.0	0.6	27.4	50.9	0.0	50.6	4.2
48 145	...	Falls County	12 013	67.9	66.2	9.6	−14.8	12.8	5.3	0.0	37.5	1.8
48 147	...	Fannin County	21 120	63.2	72.5	12.6	−11.8	13.9	3.0	10.0	31.7	3.2
48 149	...	Fayette County	15 183	64.5	71.3	14.6	−9.8	16.7	1.5	37.9	77.3	2.8
48 151	...	Fisher County	3 036	65.1	73.3	12.4	−12.0	15.1	0.0	0.0	100.0	0.8
48 153	...	Floyd County	4 773	67.5	63.5	12.3	−12.1	18.9	0.0	0.0	0.0	2.6
48 155	...	Foard County	1 116	65.1	70.0	10.5	−13.9	12.1	8.3	0.0	0.0	1.5
48 157	3360	Fort Bend County	214 461	35.1	84.3	36.9	12.5	44.1	30.0	18.0	56.1	11.9
48 159	...	Franklin County	6 421	58.2	77.4	16.2	−8.2	17.5	5.0	4.5	16.7	2.1
48 161	...	Freestone County........	12 085	60.9	76.8	10.9	−13.5	11.6	10.3	22.9	32.0	2.8
48 163	...	Frio County	9 807	70.7	57.7	8.4	−16.0	20.8	14.0	14.3	30.0	3.1
48 165	...	Gaines County	8 006	70.2	56.2	10.5	−13.9	15.2	0.0	0.0	100.0	2.0
48 167	2920	Galveston County........	161 503	45.5	80.9	22.7	−1.7	27.0	10.7	22.4	47.9	10.1
48 169	...	Garza County	3 131	68.3	70.1	10.0	−14.4	14.8	4.3	X	X	1.2
48 171	...	Gillespie County	15 255	49.4	80.1	22.9	−1.5	25.3	0.0	22.2	13.0	4.4
48 173	...	Glasscock County	836	54.3	69.9	18.7	−5.7	24.7	100.0	0.0	X	1.4
48 175	...	Goliad County	4 603	57.2	72.4	12.3	−12.1	16.5	10.9	20.0	0.0	3.2
48 177	...	Gonzales County..........	11 797	71.8	62.0	10.7	−13.7	17.1	2.0	6.7	35.3	1.4
48 179	...	Gray County	15 420	58.3	75.3	11.9	−12.5	12.9	8.0	9.7	66.0	3.8
48 181	7640	Grayson County............	72 382	49.8	80.2	17.2	−7.2	17.9	10.5	12.7	46.6	8.0
48 183	4420	Gregg County...............	70 006	48.6	79.1	19.5	−4.9	22.8	10.3	17.7	33.9	6.5
48 185	...	Grimes County	16 080	65.5	67.3	10.3	−14.1	13.7	3.4	9.8	25.6	2.7

[1]MSA = Metropolitan Statistical Area. PMSA = Primary MSA. NECMA = New England County Metropolitan Area. See the Appendix A for explanation of these concepts. See Appendix B for list of metropolitan areas identified by type, with component counties.
[2]Hispanic or Latino persons may be of any race.

STATE County	School enrollment			Population 16 to 19 years				Employment status, 2000			Work status in 1999 of the population 16 years and over (percent)		
											Worked in 1999		
	Grades kindergarten through 12	College or graduate school	Percent private	Number	Percent in armed forces	Percent high school graduates	Percent not enrolled, not grads, not in armed forces, not employed	Total population 16 years and over	Percent in labor force	Unemploy-ment rate	Full-time	Part-time	Did not work in 1999
	11	12	13	14	15	16	17	18	19	20	21	22	23

TEXAS—Cont'd

Caldwell County	6 758	948	5.5	1 963	0.0	16.1	7.5	24 081	59.0	5.5	56.0	11.0	33.1
Calhoun County	4 555	541	7.3	1 206	0.0	12.7	6.6	15 374	58.0	7.4	51.9	10.9	37.1
Callahan County	2 652	308	3.1	731	0.0	11.9	3.4	9 968	59.4	5.0	52.0	11.8	36.2
Cameron County	85 966	16 722	5.4	23 139	0.1	8.2	8.1	234 211	52.6	11.4	46.0	11.4	42.6
Camp County	2 441	333	6.7	723	0.0	16.5	3.7	8 814	55.7	6.0	49.1	10.6	40.3
Carson County	1 445	264	4.0	394	0.0	13.5	1.0	4 942	63.2	2.8	56.3	12.1	31.6
Cass County	5 920	817	5.1	1 700	0.0	14.1	6.1	23 727	53.1	5.7	46.5	10.9	42.6
Castro County	2 104	140	1.6	561	0.0	8.9	6.2	5 864	60.7	5.8	54.8	12.4	32.8
Chambers County	5 800	942	4.0	1 623	0.0	9.1	5.5	19 393	63.7	5.0	58.0	10.7	31.3
Cherokee County	9 174	1 712	10.1	2 826	0.0	14.6	6.0	35 695	55.5	5.6	50.4	10.7	38.9
Childress County	1 356	237	6.8	424	0.0	9.4	18.2	6 258	43.5	5.7	39.9	10.8	49.3
Clay County	2 156	372	3.1	607	0.0	9.1	7.4	8 592	64.5	3.4	56.0	13.9	30.2
Cochran County	945	85	1.7	310	0.0	9.7	3.5	2 723	55.1	11.1	49.6	12.9	37.5
Coke County	803	80	2.6	411	0.0	5.4	21.7	3 162	48.0	4.4	42.3	13.6	44.1
Coleman County	1 748	180	4.4	473	0.0	14.0	2.3	7 313	53.4	6.4	44.6	10.9	44.5
Collin County	96 997	25 951	11.1	23 575	0.0	10.8	3.5	363 924	75.7	3.0	68.7	12.0	19.3
Collingsworth County	671	81	1.7	203	0.0	10.3	3.9	2 477	54.0	4.3	48.1	12.8	39.1
Colorado County	4 002	821	11.2	1 417	0.0	10.3	4.0	15 910	57.8	5.1	50.1	13.8	36.1
Comal County	15 339	2 441	10.0	4 523	0.0	15.8	5.1	60 463	62.8	3.8	55.3	13.0	31.7
Comanche County	2 762	291	3.2	814	0.0	5.7	4.5	10 917	56.4	4.4	49.7	11.7	38.5
Concho County	544	144	6.7	210	0.0	7.1	18.1	3 423	35.9	3.6	49.0	8.5	42.4
Cooke County	7 465	1 538	9.2	2 350	0.1	10.3	5.8	27 742	62.2	4.6	55.2	12.6	32.2
Coryell County	13 801	4 134	8.4	4 827	31.6	41.0	4.3	57 064	63.5	4.2	65.1	10.9	24.0
Cottle County	365	17	1.3	92	0.0	6.5	5.4	1 509	56.9	5.8	49.3	13.7	37.0
Crane County	1 055	127	2.9	341	0.0	10.3	6.5	2 875	55.0	8.3	47.9	11.0	41.1
Crockett County	1 026	42	0.6	203	0.0	0.0	0.0	3 018	63.6	6.6	51.8	12.1	36.2
Crosby County	1 671	184	3.3	456	0.0	11.2	6.8	5 155	56.0	8.2	49.3	13.7	37.1
Culberson County	741	111	3.8	257	0.0	9.3	5.1	2 183	63.1	6.1	55.9	10.4	33.7
Dallam County	1 394	138	6.1	397	0.0	14.6	7.8	4 462	65.3	4.7	58.4	13.9	27.8
Dallas County..............	441 372	108 942	13.0	126 851	0.0	10.6	9.6	1 664 195	67.5	5.6	63.2	10.9	25.9
Dawson County	3 057	579	4.4	880	0.0	11.8	9.5	11 709	46.1	8.2	47.4	10.7	41.9
Deaf Smith County	4 821	553	6.9	1 254	0.0	16.8	6.4	12 961	60.1	8.6	53.8	12.2	34.0
Delta County	1 091	186	6.5	317	0.0	12.0	7.9	4 176	57.5	5.6	47.2	13.4	39.4
Denton County	82 738	37 656	8.7	24 095	0.1	10.6	3.0	325 232	76.5	3.8	66.9	15.0	18.1
DeWitt County	3 894	578	6.0	1 062	0.0	9.8	9.2	15 874	52.8	5.8	46.2	10.8	43.1
Dickens County	443	63	4.0	120	0.0	8.3	10.8	2 333	44.2	5.1	38.7	10.0	51.3
Dimmit County	2 679	419	3.7	637	0.0	7.5	6.8	7 208	54.1	14.2	45.3	14.1	40.6
Donley County.............	716	282	3.2	300	0.0	6.3	0.7	3 079	59.4	9.5	47.4	16.0	36.6
Duval County	2 972	583	3.2	867	0.0	11.3	4.0	9 767	48.5	9.5	43.2	11.4	45.3
Eastland County..........	3 255	1 000	4.3	1 262	0.0	5.5	5.9	14 496	57.1	7.9	47.6	13.9	38.4
Ector County	27 951	5 731	4.2	8 435	0.1	10.4	5.9	88 658	61.1	7.7	53.4	13.2	33.4
Edwards County	510	44	2.0	120	0.0	1.7	0.0	1 627	52.3	4.9	44.9	11.9	43.2
Ellis County	25 302	4 799	9.5	7 342	0.0	11.7	4.2	81 597	69.2	5.2	61.5	12.3	26.2
El Paso County	167 423	46 798	7.3	45 857	1.3	9.9	6.6	486 398	56.5	9.2	50.4	12.6	37.0
Erath County	5 998	4 587	4.9	2 435	0.0	7.2	3.8	25 734	64.9	10.7	52.1	17.8	30.1
Falls County	4 202	539	7.0	1 445	0.1	11.7	12.5	14 314	48.0	7.4	44.4	12.8	42.7
Fannin County	5 730	945	7.3	1 694	0.0	17.0	9.4	24 794	52.5	5.2	48.4	10.9	40.7
Fayette County	4 067	585	11.2	1 245	0.0	7.9	5.4	17 466	59.5	3.4	49.8	14.1	36.1
Fisher County.............	832	77	1.4	269	0.0	13.0	1.9	3 443	56.1	4.4	48.4	13.3	38.3
Floyd County	1 888	122	2.6	509	0.0	3.7	15.3	5 624	56.1	6.7	52.1	12.6	35.4
Foard County	336	40	1.9	90	0.0	4.4	0.0	1 260	55.0	2.2	51.3	13.1	35.6
Fort Bend County.........	87 855	18 037	10.3	22 536	0.0	10.6	4.6	253 911	68.8	4.9	62.6	11.6	25.8
Franklin County	1 781	308	3.3	545	0.0	10.6	5.0	7 449	54.5	4.5	45.5	13.0	41.5
Freestone County........	3 443	826	6.2	984	0.7	10.9	6.0	14 228	51.1	4.2	51.0	9.9	39.1
Frio County..................	3 752	584	3.8	978	0.0	11.7	7.5	12 073	47.1	7.3	44.4	10.0	45.6
Gaines County	3 831	268	11.4	1 139	0.0	7.1	15.0	10 062	57.4	5.5	52.1	12.3	35.6
Galveston County.........	50 267	14 654	8.4	14 462	0.1	9.2	5.6	190 919	64.4	6.7	57.5	11.7	30.8
Garza County	1 104	164	3.2	294	0.0	18.4	3.7	3 640	53.4	5.7	47.8	16.2	36.0
Gillespie County	3 474	397	12.8	936	0.0	13.0	4.3	16 933	57.1	3.7	48.5	13.5	38.0
Glasscock County	389	40	0.7	124	0.0	1.6	6.5	1 003	61.9	3.5	58.0	9.7	32.3
Goliad County	1 429	159	6.7	417	0.0	8.9	5.3	5 360	56.8	3.2	49.6	12.3	38.2
Gonzales County..........	3 989	312	4.1	1 060	0.0	11.1	10.8	14 064	59.1	4.8	52.9	10.8	36.2
Gray County................	4 460	920	7.0	1 261	0.0	19.2	4.0	18 008	51.3	5.4	45.3	12.3	42.4
Grayson County	20 779	5 331	9.7	6 426	0.0	11.5	7.2	85 902	62.1	4.7	54.5	13.1	32.4
Gregg County	22 659	5 017	9.5	7 360	0.0	10.5	9.5	85 238	61.8	6.9	54.1	13.0	32.9
Grimes County	4 727	787	3.9	1 213	0.0	13.7	6.7	18 370	51.7	6.2	48.6	9.2	42.3

STATE County	Full-year full-time employed (percent)								Children under 18 years in families					+/- U.S. percent two-income couples	Total employed by class of worker (percent)			
										With two parents (percent)		With one parent who is in labor force (percent)	+/- U.S. percent of children with no stay-at-home parent (percent)						
	Total	Men	Women	Non-Hispanic White	Black or African American	American Indian and Alaska Native	Asian, Hawaiian, and Pacific Islander	Hispanic or Latino¹	Number	Both in labor force	Father only in labor force				Private	Government	Self-employed	Unpaid family worker
	24	25	26	27	28	29	30	31	32	33	34	35	36	37	38	39	40	41
TEXAS—Cont'd																		
Caldwell County	41.7	49.7	34.2	44.4	25.6	28.5	21.9	41.8	8 340	42.6	21.0	22.6	0.6	-2.2	70.3	19.4	10.0	0.3
Calhoun County	33.9	44.6	23.6	36.2	21.7	36.9	29.0	32.1	5 462	37.7	28.0	20.1	-6.8	-9.6	73.2	15.3	10.8	0.6
Callahan County	40.2	48.5	32.7	40.5	7.4	28.8	25.0	38.9	3 210	49.1	23.1	16.0	0.5	-1.8	63.8	18.5	17.1	0.5
Cameron County	28.3	36.7	21.1	28.2	33.8	28.0	40.2	28.2	104 916	31.0	25.8	18.4	-15.2	-17.1	69.5	19.9	10.2	0.4
Camp County	33.6	44.6	23.7	35.9	25.3	36.0	32.8	35.6	2 835	37.8	21.6	21.0	-5.8	-9.0	73.9	14.3	11.6	0.2
Carson County	44.6	59.2	31.2	45.1	0.0	35.5	28.0	38.8	1 730	54.4	29.1	11.4	1.2	2.0	62.9	24.6	14.6	0.9
Cass County	33.0	43.3	23.9	34.1	27.3	25.4	26.9	44.8	7 111	36.9	24.2	20.9	-6.8	-11.6	71.7	16.7	11.4	0.2
Castro County	36.1	51.8	20.3	42.0	36.7	58.5	0.0	29.7	2 523	39.9	32.4	15.7	-9.0	-4.4	62.5	17.7	19.1	0.7
Chambers County	43.3	55.7	30.8	44.1	38.1	32.3	40.6	43.1	7 118	45.8	28.9	14.5	-4.3	-1.5	77.9	14.1	7.6	0.4
Cherokee County	35.2	41.6	28.9	36.7	26.8	28.3	6.9	38.2	11 407	37.8	24.1	22.8	-4.0	-6.8	69.5	18.9	10.9	0.7
Childress County	28.2	27.1	29.8	35.4	7.5	33.3	25.0	18.8	1 463	51.3	13.3	18.1	4.8	-2.6	53.0	28.8	17.5	0.7
Clay County	41.6	51.7	32.2	41.8	68.4	31.3	33.3	38.1	2 577	56.7	19.7	16.6	8.7	4.0	63.6	18.6	16.7	1.1
Cochran County	32.6	43.9	22.1	35.4	21.4	48.6	X	29.8	1 051	37.9	22.9	17.3	-9.4	-11.0	60.1	22.2	17.2	0.4
Coke County	31.0	38.0	23.9	31.1	0.0	46.7	100.0	32.2	799	58.9	17.3	13.8	8.1	-6.5	61.2	22.0	15.7	1.0
Coleman County	33.6	42.6	25.6	33.6	28.9	39.7	0.0	34.8	2 009	50.1	20.8	18.3	3.8	-6.5	59.2	22.2	17.8	0.9
Collin County	54.9	68.3	41.7	56.5	57.0	50.2	50.1	45.3	136 347	46.9	34.9	12.7	-5.0	7.3	81.6	8.2	10.0	0.2
Collingsworth County	35.4	47.0	25.2	36.3	28.8	21.2	45.5	31.5	780	36.9	28.1	18.8	-8.9	-4.7	49.6	24.5	24.6	1.3
Colorado County	35.5	45.1	26.7	37.4	31.0	69.4	20.5	32.3	4 786	50.2	19.4	15.2	0.8	-4.1	70.4	12.6	16.0	1.0
Comal County	41.7	52.5	31.8	41.8	49.9	47.2	31.5	41.1	19 169	48.1	23.7	19.8	3.3	-2.0	71.1	15.0	13.3	0.6
Comanche County	35.6	46.6	25.4	35.9	13.4	54.2	6.8	36.2	3 352	46.2	22.9	17.3	-1.1	-7.4	64.1	16.1	18.9	0.9
Concho County	27.5	28.9	24.9	32.0	27.3	14.3	50.0	21.3	611	56.6	15.4	15.9	7.9	1.4	50.3	27.0	20.8	1.9
Cooke County	41.0	51.3	31.2	43.0	31.0	25.8	28.2	27.2	9 236	49.4	23.9	16.0	0.8	-0.4	71.0	13.7	14.6	0.7
Coryell County	43.7	56.1	30.5	46.2	40.2	47.9	41.5	37.2	18 775	46.1	25.8	19.1	0.6	2.0	58.5	31.3	9.4	0.7
Cottle County	33.7	46.3	23.3	34.3	19.6	X	X	37.0	403	54.8	16.9	17.4	7.6	-0.6	51.2	30.3	17.8	0.6
Crane County	32.3	42.9	22.4	35.5	10.8	16.0	44.7	20.7	1 186	35.1	33.8	18.0	-11.5	-8.7	73.4	17.0	8.4	1.2
Crockett County	35.3	47.9	23.0	42.4	0.0	48.3	100.0	27.7	1 124	44.2	24.6	23.8	3.4	-4.0	68.7	17.8	12.0	1.5
Crosby County	34.4	46.0	24.0	39.0	15.4	30.0	22.2	30.8	1 971	45.0	17.2	19.2	-0.4	-5.5	65.5	18.3	16.0	0.2
Culberson County	41.1	50.7	31.6	47.0	100.0	50.0	61.1	38.5	885	49.3	21.1	17.4	2.1	-0.7	66.9	26.6	6.0	0.5
Dallam County	41.1	66.6	26.7	42.6	43.5	35.2	0.0	37.9	1 075	33.1	21.4	21.4	-10.1	-2.1	68.0	14.7	16.0	1.3
Dallas County	45.5	53.9	37.4	50.0	43.4	44.1	45.0	39.0	571 616	36.0	22.7	23.7	-4.9	-0.4	81.4	9.7	8.7	0.2
Dawson County	27.6	33.5	20.0	35.8	8.7	45.5	28.8	23.6	3 594	40.1	24.7	19.5	-5.0	-8.1	60.7	21.2	17.7	0.4
Deaf Smith County	37.1	51.6	23.4	40.7	17.0	19.3	15.2	34.5	5 758	38.6	24.5	19.5	-6.5	-6.8	70.4	14.6	14.0	0.9
Delta County	31.9	39.0	25.2	32.2	34.8	16.1	0.0	25.6	1 265	54.9	22.9	15.3	5.6	-2.1	67.5	19.6	12.5	0.3
Denton County	52.6	64.2	41.4	54.1	51.5	48.9	43.2	46.5	115 028	48.6	28.5	16.2	0.2	10.7	79.9	11.5	8.3	0.2
DeWitt County	32.4	38.8	25.6	35.0	21.2	38.0	0.0	30.6	4 404	41.0	21.2	26.3	2.7	-2.4	66.8	17.8	14.7	0.7
Dickens County	27.4	27.5	27.3	33.7	3.9	36.4	20.0	15.4	476	55.0	19.3	15.5	5.9	0.5	53.1	29.4	16.5	0.9
Dimmit County	22.8	29.6	16.6	32.5	25.9	0.0	50.0	21.0	3 180	37.0	26.0	19.0	-8.6	-15.1	62.8	27.9	9.1	0.2
Donley County	33.7	42.1	25.8	34.2	25.0	28.0	0.0	31.2	815	47.7	13.6	27.5	10.6	-0.2	55.0	23.9	19.9	1.1
Duval County	25.4	33.8	16.5	28.7	41.2	13.8	75.0	24.8	3 531	32.5	24.6	19.2	-12.9	-16.8	62.3	26.0	11.1	0.6
Eastland County	33.5	42.7	25.1	34.2	3.2	27.8	75.0	35.2	3 989	43.2	26.4	18.8	-2.6	-8.9	65.5	17.2	16.6	0.6
Ector County	36.5	47.3	26.6	40.8	28.4	31.8	39.6	31.0	34 478	35.2	26.4	23.8	-5.6	-7.0	75.9	14.2	9.6	0.4
Edwards County	28.9	38.3	19.2	32.1	0.0	0.0	37.5	24.1	571	32.0	33.3	18.4	-14.2	-13.1	49.9	24.4	24.1	1.6
Ellis County	47.4	58.5	36.9	49.8	33.7	57.6	49.1	43.3	31 577	47.2	23.7	18.6	1.2	6.2	77.3	12.0	10.3	0.4
El Paso County	33.2	43.4	24.1	39.4	39.8	30.6	37.2	31.2	202 841	29.9	27.4	21.1	-13.6	-14.1	71.4	20.0	8.2	0.3
Erath County	36.4	46.8	26.7	36.6	36.8	32.0	33.2	35.7	7 667	49.0	26.7	11.6	-4.0	-1.1	64.6	18.7	16.1	0.6
Falls County	31.6	43.2	22.5	35.4	24.5	57.4	0.0	28.3	4 264	34.0	20.4	27.9	-2.7	-9.8	60.6	23.7	15.0	0.7
Fannin County	34.3	38.8	29.1	36.8	14.9	24.8	22.5	27.2	6 824	45.2	21.1	20.0	0.6	-3.4	69.9	17.6	12.0	0.6
Fayette County	38.7	51.0	27.5	39.9	29.2	41.2	15.4	35.8	4 718	59.3	14.6	14.6	9.3	1.3	68.3	13.2	18.0	0.5
Fisher County	33.9	45.7	23.3	36.0	17.2	61.1	40.0	27.6	993	45.1	22.4	17.0	-2.5	-5.1	58.7	22.1	18.3	0.9
Floyd County	36.0	49.7	23.8	37.8	26.2	25.8	100.0	34.4	2 211	44.5	22.0	14.9	-5.2	-3.8	58.2	23.3	18.2	0.3
Foard County	37.1	50.8	25.5	38.5	13.3	0.0	60.0	32.2	395	58.7	13.2	12.9	7.0	4.9	58.1	22.1	18.7	1.0
Fort Bend County	48.2	59.0	37.7	50.8	50.7	43.7	46.5	40.6	108 537	45.9	27.7	16.1	-2.6	5.9	75.8	13.7	10.2	0.3
Franklin County	32.6	41.9	24.0	32.8	28.7	32.1	37.5	33.9	2 190	43.5	29.2	17.5	-3.6	-10.9	69.2	14.5	15.9	0.3
Freestone County	33.3	39.4	26.5	35.8	26.1	21.4	51.9	28.7	3 832	44.4	24.4	17.2	-3.0	-6.9	64.4	21.1	13.7	0.7
Frio County	28.1	33.5	21.1	35.0	15.1	26.5	11.7	27.0	4 327	37.2	23.5	22.8	-4.6	-11.3	64.8	24.5	10.3	0.4
Gaines County	35.6	51.7	20.4	37.8	27.6	60.7	0.0	31.7	4 799	33.2	42.8	12.5	-18.9	-11.3	63.6	18.0	17.3	1.1
Galveston County	42.1	51.0	33.8	45.3	32.5	37.1	39.2	38.9	62 793	39.9	23.4	24.3	-0.4	-1.9	69.8	20.9	8.9	0.4
Garza County	31.0	44.6	16.1	35.1	20.9	X	X	25.5	1 207	41.8	18.1	25.6	2.8	-8.7	55.3	25.2	19.3	0.2
Gillespie County	36.8	47.3	27.6	36.4	0.0	28.6	47.4	39.7	4 282	55.1	16.1	14.7	5.2	-5.1	62.0	14.0	22.3	1.6
Glasscock County	44.0	60.3	26.1	45.9	100.0	100.0	X	39.0	464	43.1	39.4	8.6	-12.9	-3.8	51.8	21.7	25.2	1.3
Goliad County	35.6	42.7	28.8	37.0	33.5	81.8	0.0	33.6	1 750	48.1	20.2	16.7	0.2	-4.5	60.2	22.6	16.3	0.9
Gonzales County	37.3	49.2	26.3	37.0	32.0	11.8	47.8	39.2	4 923	40.6	23.9	21.1	-2.9	-3.9	69.2	16.6	13.4	0.7
Gray County	32.9	41.5	23.8	34.3	14.8	43.5	31.3	30.9	4 999	45.6	27.0	15.3	-3.3	-9.0	72.4	16.1	11.0	0.6
Grayson County	39.9	50.4	30.4	40.4	36.4	43.4	39.0	35.3	26 029	44.8	23.5	21.5	1.7	-1.3	77.4	11.0	10.4	0.5
Gregg County	38.8	48.5	30.0	40.9	33.5	24.3	39.6	34.9	27 676	40.3	22.1	24.5	0.2	-1.4	77.9	11.5	10.2	0.4
Grimes County	33.6	36.6	29.9	38.4	21.0	28.8	15.7	30.5	5 453	44.4	22.3	21.2	1.0	-2.8	62.5	23.3	13.3	0.9

¹Hispanic or Latino persons may be of any race.

STATE County	Percent who worked at home	Percent of the population 5 years and over with a disability	Veterans as a percent of the population 18 years and over	Management, professional, and related occupations	Service occupations	Sales and office occupations	Farming, fishing, and forestry occupations	Construction, extraction, and maintenance occupations	Production, transportation and material moving occupations	Agriculture, forestry, fishing, and mining	Construction and manufacturing	Wholesale and retail trade	Transportation and warehousing, and utilities	Service industries	Public administration
	42	43	44	45	46	47	48	49	50	51	52	53	54	55	56
TEXAS—Cont'd															
Caldwell County	2.4	21.6	13.2	24.1	15.9	27.2	1.2	14.9	16.6	3.3	24.4	14.7	5.1	44.2	8.4
Calhoun County	1.9	20.3	15.1	25.6	14.9	18.3	3.2	17.4	20.7	6.3	38.0	11.0	4.0	36.1	4.5
Callahan County..........	3.6	21.7	16.5	27.0	16.1	25.2	1.2	14.7	15.8	5.4	18.3	15.8	7.2	47.1	6.2
Cameron County	2.5	21.8	8.7	27.7	19.8	24.9	1.4	10.4	15.8	2.1	17.6	16.1	5.5	53.3	5.3
Camp County	2.9	23.2	14.5	23.7	16.6	22.6	3.4	15.6	18.1	7.7	25.5	19.2	4.7	39.3	3.6
Carson County	2.4	17.8	14.8	29.9	15.2	19.9	3.1	13.0	18.9	11.5	24.5	10.6	6.5	39.2	7.7
Cass County.................	2.1	25.5	15.3	23.5	16.7	21.6	1.8	14.4	22.0	5.4	27.0	14.1	6.9	41.5	5.0
Castro County	3.3	17.3	8.7	31.4	12.4	17.8	11.9	8.5	18.0	25.0	15.7	12.0	6.3	37.2	3.8
Chambers County	1.8	17.4	12.3	26.9	12.5	23.1	1.8	13.6	22.0	3.9	31.7	14.5	6.0	39.3	4.6
Cherokee County	2.9	24.5	13.4	23.3	17.7	22.8	4.0	12.9	19.3	8.3	24.0	15.6	4.8	40.7	6.6
Childress County..........	4.2	23.7	11.3	28.8	20.8	25.0	3.9	12.9	8.6	12.0	11.1	16.8	5.4	41.6	13.2
Clay County.................	4.0	21.2	16.8	28.7	13.3	25.5	3.8	11.5	17.3	9.5	20.1	14.2	7.1	42.8	6.4
Cochran County	3.7	21.0	9.2	31.3	18.9	17.8	12.1	8.1	11.8	27.1	4.9	14.0	7.4	40.2	6.4
Coke County.................	3.4	23.2	16.3	30.8	18.4	20.9	2.6	12.3	15.0	12.4	11.2	14.1	6.1	48.5	7.7
Coleman County	2.6	24.5	16.2	28.1	16.6	21.7	1.9	12.7	18.9	12.1	19.3	12.0	7.1	44.4	5.1
Collin County...............	4.4	11.6	10.4	51.8	8.7	27.6	0.2	5.9	5.8	0.9	19.6	17.0	3.1	57.2	2.3
Collingsworth County	3.0	22.5	12.5	34.5	20.5	20.5	6.7	8.8	8.9	20.3	7.8	12.4	5.0	47.4	7.1
Colorado County	3.6	20.0	12.0	26.6	17.2	21.4	2.8	12.3	19.8	10.4	21.9	16.9	5.7	41.8	3.3
Comal County	3.7	18.0	17.2	35.4	13.4	27.2	0.5	11.2	12.4	1.5	20.9	16.3	5.3	51.6	4.3
Comanche County	7.9	27.1	14.0	26.4	15.9	22.7	6.6	11.1	17.3	14.6	20.2	14.8	6.1	40.6	3.7
Concho County	7.1	21.6	10.0	40.7	17.5	16.5	4.1	12.7	8.5	19.2	10.9	9.5	5.3	44.4	10.6
Cooke County	3.7	20.4	13.9	25.2	14.3	24.1	1.4	12.3	22.8	5.4	29.2	16.5	5.7	39.4	3.8
Coryell County	1.9	17.8	17.1	27.8	21.0	26.6	1.1	11.7	11.8	2.6	14.8	13.3	4.9	48.6	15.9
Cottle County	3.5	24.9	11.9	30.2	20.5	20.7	7.1	13.0	8.5	17.5	11.1	11.3	7.4	40.5	12.3
Crane County	2.3	22.1	11.6	25.5	15.1	21.7	1.8	17.5	18.3	29.1	7.7	15.9	4.1	38.7	4.6
Crockett County	4.5	20.9	11.2	21.7	23.4	18.2	3.3	20.1	13.3	25.6	9.2	12.9	5.0	40.1	7.2
Crosby County	3.1	24.0	9.7	30.7	15.7	21.2	7.7	10.6	14.1	20.0	13.8	14.5	5.1	39.8	6.8
Culberson County	3.6	18.3	9.5	23.6	26.8	18.9	6.5	12.7	11.5	12.1	9.7	15.4	4.7	48.4	9.6
Dallam County.............	3.8	21.4	12.8	26.9	20.6	19.3	7.4	11.5	14.4	24.0	12.9	11.6	8.1	36.0	7.3
Dallas County..............	2.7	19.5	9.4	33.8	13.3	28.9	0.1	10.8	13.1	0.4	20.4	16.0	5.8	54.8	2.5
Dawson County	2.7	23.0	8.9	23.7	22.3	26.6	4.7	12.1	10.7	16.1	8.6	18.3	5.0	42.7	9.2
Deaf Smith County........	2.8	22.3	7.8	26.5	16.6	20.0	5.4	10.1	21.4	14.1	20.7	13.7	5.8	42.8	2.9
Delta County................	4.3	25.9	15.9	25.2	17.1	21.8	1.8	14.2	20.0	4.8	28.3	13.2	6.0	44.7	2.9
Denton County	3.7	12.1	10.9	41.3	11.1	30.5	0.2	7.7	9.2	0.8	17.2	18.6	6.2	54.5	2.7
DeWitt County	4.5	25.3	14.2	27.7	19.4	19.8	2.0	12.4	18.7	9.0	23.4	13.6	3.9	43.7	6.4
Dickens County	3.6	27.1	11.9	30.1	24.9	18.0	6.9	12.2	7.9	18.9	8.3	11.2	6.5	36.9	18.2
Dimmit County..............	2.2	25.6	8.0	22.6	21.6	22.3	4.4	11.9	17.3	12.0	8.4	13.4	10.0	46.8	9.3
Donley County..............	3.3	23.2	14.5	33.8	20.9	20.1	5.7	9.2	10.2	17.1	8.2	14.7	5.6	47.4	7.0
Duval County	3.2	24.9	10.4	23.4	20.9	19.8	1.5	16.1	18.2	18.7	13.1	10.0	4.6	44.5	9.2
Eastland County...........	2.5	26.7	14.8	27.7	16.7	22.4	1.8	12.4	19.1	7.9	21.8	15.2	6.3	44.0	4.8
Ector County	2.4	18.7	10.9	23.8	16.2	29.1	0.3	14.3	16.4	7.9	18.3	18.7	4.3	47.7	3.0
Edwards County	6.4	21.0	10.5	38.4	16.3	15.9	10.3	11.4	7.7	27.9	11.2	8.9	5.1	39.6	7.3
Ellis County	2.2	17.8	12.4	29.1	12.5	26.7	0.4	13.1	18.1	1.3	28.5	15.8	6.4	44.2	3.8
El Paso County	2.1	20.3	11.4	29.1	16.9	28.1	0.4	8.7	16.8	0.6	19.8	15.7	6.8	51.1	6.0
Erath County	4.3	17.8	10.5	32.9	14.9	22.1	4.6	9.9	15.6	10.3	19.5	13.3	5.5	48.0	3.5
Falls County................	3.4	26.7	12.4	26.3	16.9	22.1	2.3	13.7	18.7	7.5	22.1	13.5	5.5	43.6	7.7
Fannin County..............	4.0	24.4	14.4	26.7	15.3	23.2	1.4	13.5	19.9	4.4	27.5	13.5	5.4	43.8	5.4
Fayette County.............	5.0	21.8	14.5	28.5	16.0	23.2	1.9	13.3	17.0	9.9	21.2	15.6	7.6	41.7	3.9
Fisher County	3.5	24.2	15.4	30.4	17.5	20.6	3.7	12.9	14.9	15.7	14.9	12.6	6.8	41.1	8.9
Floyd County	1.9	21.2	8.2	30.2	17.4	20.1	8.6	10.2	13.6	17.9	12.8	15.3	7.5	40.1	6.5
Foard County	3.1	33.3	10.6	32.6	18.7	16.5	4.9	10.6	16.7	19.8	17.0	10.0	5.5	42.3	5.5
Fort Bend County........	2.9	14.5	9.1	44.4	11.2	27.7	0.3	7.6	8.9	3.9	17.1	16.2	5.6	53.5	3.7
Franklin County	4.8	24.1	15.4	28.4	13.7	23.0	2.3	15.8	16.9	9.5	22.8	18.1	5.7	40.0	3.8
Freestone County.........	3.7	22.8	13.8	25.3	20.5	21.2	2.1	15.1	15.7	10.5	15.7	12.6	11.2	43.6	6.4
Frio County..................	1.9	22.6	7.6	21.3	22.6	21.6	7.7	14.0	12.8	14.0	14.6	14.4	5.4	40.5	11.2
Gaines County	2.2	17.2	7.4	27.2	12.3	21.2	6.7	16.5	16.1	25.0	12.5	14.4	7.4	37.9	2.7
Galveston County.........	2.5	18.6	13.8	35.9	15.8	25.4	0.4	11.2	11.3	1.5	20.3	13.3	5.4	54.0	5.5
Garza County	3.1	26.1	10.1	28.0	22.8	19.1	1.4	17.7	11.0	17.7	13.0	9.4	6.8	43.8	9.3
Gillespie County	7.5	23.4	18.0	33.9	16.9	26.1	2.2	11.9	9.0	7.9	17.3	17.3	3.3	50.8	3.4
Glasscock County	9.9	15.3	9.9	40.7	8.3	15.5	12.5	10.5	12.4	42.9	7.7	8.8	4.8	32.2	3.5
Goliad County	6.1	19.0	14.3	27.5	16.3	24.1	2.8	15.7	13.6	11.3	18.4	14.2	4.8	42.3	9.1
Gonzales County..........	3.7	22.8	12.9	25.3	17.4	20.5	6.7	12.3	17.8	14.8	21.9	15.6	4.7	38.6	4.4
Gray County	1.7	20.1	13.9	24.0	21.7	22.3	1.7	13.0	17.3	10.4	19.3	16.1	5.0	41.9	7.3
Grayson County	2.9	22.1	15.4	29.6	14.4	26.5	0.5	11.5	17.5	1.9	26.4	15.9	4.5	48.0	3.4
Gregg County	2.2	21.8	13.6	29.2	14.8	27.3	0.3	10.7	17.7	4.4	21.9	17.8	4.3	48.3	3.3
Grimes County	4.8	23.5	13.1	23.8	18.0	23.2	2.1	13.7	19.1	6.8	24.4	13.7	7.8	37.9	9.4

Table B-3. States and Counties — **Education, Labor Force, and Income**

STATE County	Median house-hold income	Median family income — All families	Married-couple	Male house-holder	Female house-holder	Median nonfamily house-hold income	Men	Women	Per capita income	With earnings	With interest, dividend, or rental income	With Social Security income	With public assis-tance income	With retire-ment income	House-holds with income over $100,000 (percent)	+/- U.S. percent for income over $100,000 (percent)	House-holds with income below poverty (percent)	Families with children with income below poverty (percent)
	57	58	59	60	61	62	63	64	65	66	67	68	69	70	71	72	73	74
TEXAS—Cont'd																		
Caldwell County	36 573	41 300	48 448	27 609	20 815	22 727	30 468	22 108	15 099	81.7	28.4	26.7	3.6	15.7	5.6	-6.7	12.4	12.5
Calhoun County	35 849	39 900	50 908	25 962	15 000	19 952	36 756	20 757	17 125	77.4	25.6	30.0	3.5	17.8	6.3	-6.0	15.1	17.5
Callahan County	32 463	37 165	41 232	40 000	18 654	15 000	28 818	20 459	15 204	74.5	29.8	35.1	3.3	18.9	3.9	-8.4	12.9	13.7
Cameron County	26 155	27 853	30 047	19 167	11 889	14 551	23 445	18 875	10 960	76.9	19.6	28.4	9.9	12.5	4.8	-7.5	29.3	36.5
Camp County	31 164	36 142	42 253	21 917	16 116	16 495	32 957	19 550	16 500	71.9	23.0	34.1	4.2	18.1	7.0	-5.3	17.7	25.5
Carson County	40 285	47 147	52 400	38 906	22 813	21 484	36 004	24 114	19 368	79.5	38.9	31.0	1.5	17.3	6.4	-5.9	7.7	7.0
Cass County	28 441	35 623	42 909	27 888	11 667	13 577	32 388	20 544	15 777	69.9	24.8	36.0	3.6	18.9	4.0	-8.3	18.8	20.3
Castro County	30 619	35 422	37 470	18 500	12 596	19 205	26 051	20 719	14 457	84.6	26.3	27.6	3.8	9.0	6.6	-5.7	17.2	21.7
Chambers County	47 964	52 986	64 556	36 154	15 337	23 538	45 480	26 570	19 863	83.0	26.1	22.2	2.1	12.9	12.8	0.5	10.6	11.3
Cherokee County	29 313	34 750	40 191	21 270	17 552	15 447	27 265	20 606	13 980	74.7	24.8	33.8	3.4	17.4	4.4	-7.9	17.6	19.8
Childress County	27 457	35 543	46 250	9 667	10 313	16 526	25 932	21 030	12 452	74.7	33.2	37.7	4.4	14.2	2.6	-9.7	16.5	24.5
Clay County	35 738	41 514	49 744	25 893	25 000	18 444	29 678	21 771	16 361	78.9	34.8	33.1	2.3	17.8	4.8	-7.5	10.8	10.3
Cochran County	27 525	31 163	30 905	11 750	11 000	17 969	26 250	18 529	13 125	77.9	22.3	31.5	7.2	13.6	5.4	-6.9	21.7	31.3
Coke County	29 085	36 724	43 235	29 167	13 750	13 750	31 568	20 344	16 734	62.9	34.5	45.3	2.3	22.5	6.0	-6.3	14.2	15.5
Coleman County	25 658	31 168	34 186	27 578	15 982	13 943	26 888	17 925	14 911	64.8	28.3	42.0	4.2	16.9	5.0	-7.3	20.6	24.4
Collin County	70 835	81 856	91 063	42 037	34 906	42 419	60 086	37 377	33 345	93.7	42.8	10.7	0.8	8.3	30.4	18.1	4.2	4.3
Collingsworth County	25 438	33 323	35 000	15 625	11 667	13 654	26 842	20 435	15 318	73.7	27.2	38.3	6.0	14.7	5.7	-6.6	17.9	21.8
Colorado County	32 425	41 388	51 641	34 375	12 939	15 611	31 169	20 653	16 910	73.2	35.3	35.4	3.2	13.9	6.4	-5.9	16.5	17.2
Comal County	46 147	52 455	58 803	27 019	21 908	25 729	37 265	26 901	21 914	79.4	40.2	29.8	1.8	22.2	12.3	0.0	8.1	10.4
Comanche County	28 422	34 810	42 766	18 250	14 191	14 199	27 062	19 350	14 677	71.9	27.6	38.3	2.4	15.0	3.9	-8.4	18.5	21.4
Concho County	31 313	36 094	44 318	22 083	20 750	15 806	22 344	23 239	15 727	75.8	32.2	39.1	3.2	18.2	6.1	-6.2	12.9	11.1
Cooke County	37 649	44 869	49 923	28 750	16 938	19 558	35 280	22 632	17 889	78.5	33.5	30.8	2.6	17.3	7.3	-5.0	13.6	18.4
Coryell County	35 999	38 307	39 455	28 431	21 208	22 264	25 289	21 809	14 410	88.4	23.0	17.7	2.3	20.2	4.5	-7.8	9.2	10.6
Cottle County	25 446	33 036	35 729	28 750	21 094	12 902	25 966	17 632	16 212	68.8	30.4	44.1	2.8	13.7	3.7	-8.6	18.0	23.8
Crane County	32 194	36 820	41 944	17 143	12 596	14 539	34 762	17 083	15 374	74.0	28.3	29.4	2.2	13.3	7.3	-5.0	14.4	15.2
Crockett County	29 355	34 653	40 365	32 500	13 864	16 667	31 771	16 316	14 414	78.1	22.0	25.6	3.7	13.1	3.8	-8.5	18.9	21.8
Crosby County	25 769	29 891	32 234	20 000	12 917	13 050	24 896	18 475	14 445	76.4	25.5	33.2	6.0	10.2	5.4	-6.9	24.9	29.0
Culberson County	25 882	28 547	33 750	26 875	13 365	10 664	24 234	15 242	11 493	81.7	10.8	25.2	4.2	10.0	1.7	-10.6	25.5	27.5
Dallam County	27 946	33 558	33 650	14 773	17 500	14 347	27 727	19 426	13 653	85.0	16.5	21.9	6.1	7.8	4.0	-8.3	16.5	14.4
Dallas County	43 324	49 062	55 144	29 676	23 750	32 308	35 623	30 256	22 603	87.7	27.5	16.8	2.4	10.1	13.7	1.4	11.0	14.0
Dawson County	28 211	32 745	31 489	15 370	15 727	14 881	28 367	17 722	15 011	75.5	27.7	35.6	2.9	15.6	5.7	-6.6	17.0	26.1
Deaf Smith County	29 601	32 391	36 028	24 348	13 300	17 524	26 632	20 200	13 119	81.0	21.0	28.3	6.2	8.8	4.5	-7.8	19.9	24.3
Delta County	29 094	37 925	44 485	15 250	16 250	15 685	32 359	21 023	15 080	71.6	28.4	36.7	4.1	19.5	3.9	-8.4	18.3	19.2
Denton County	58 216	69 292	76 809	41 230	31 150	32 514	46 706	32 203	26 895	93.2	33.9	11.1	1.1	8.5	21.7	9.4	7.1	5.4
DeWitt County	28 714	33 513	47 026	22 422	15 345	15 053	28 675	19 364	14 780	72.3	32.6	37.9	3.1	15.4	5.1	-7.2	19.1	20.3
Dickens County	25 898	32 500	38 438	35 000	11 719	14 784	26 944	19 038	13 156	69.6	29.6	41.8	4.3	14.2	3.0	-9.3	17.1	21.6
Dimmit County	21 917	24 579	33 836	7 857	11 641	9 899	25 380	15 844	9 765	75.3	11.2	33.0	9.6	9.6	0.5	-11.8	32.6	38.1
Donley County	29 006	37 287	45 438	29 375	13 375	16 364	26 849	19 483	15 593	69.3	32.5	44.0	3.9	20.9	4.6	-7.7	16.8	18.9
Duval County	22 416	26 014	34 925	20 156	13 156	11 129	26 225	16 937	11 324	71.5	14.0	33.5	7.0	12.8	3.5	-8.8	27.1	28.3
Eastland County	26 832	33 562	36 817	13 864	12 908	11 630	26 906	18 013	14 870	69.7	28.2	40.0	3.4	17.8	4.3	-8.0	18.1	20.3
Ector County	31 152	36 369	40 604	23 492	15 236	18 162	31 290	22 055	15 031	80.5	23.2	24.6	4.5	11.1	5.2	-7.1	18.4	21.8
Edwards County	25 298	27 083	25 662	10 833	14 500	16 250	26 310	17 667	12 691	73.8	31.3	37.1	3.1	17.2	3.5	-8.8	24.5	38.7
Ellis County	50 350	55 358	60 503	30 202	23 711	24 251	38 953	27 246	20 212	86.8	29.5	21.4	2.1	14.9	12.4	0.1	8.3	9.6
El Paso County	31 051	33 410	36 193	22 427	15 479	19 437	27 822	21 389	13 421	82.5	21.3	23.9	6.9	14.8	6.3	-6.0	21.6	26.6
Erath County	30 708	39 491	47 722	28 793	18 451	16 348	29 277	21 369	16 655	79.5	29.8	24.8	1.5	12.7	7.0	-5.3	17.6	14.7
Falls County	26 589	32 666	41 047	16 154	12 372	13 736	28 740	20 869	14 311	73.5	27.2	35.7	4.4	14.8	4.1	-8.2	22.6	25.9
Fannin County	34 501	42 193	50 446	23 958	18 548	14 838	31 979	24 117	16 066	74.4	28.5	34.1	2.6	16.9	5.2	-7.1	15.3	15.6
Fayette County	34 526	43 156	49 660	35 417	17 132	17 434	31 339	21 502	18 888	73.1	44.0	38.2	2.2	16.9	7.1	-5.2	13.4	12.0
Fisher County	27 659	34 907	44 545	11 000	11 000	14 053	27 050	21 184	15 123	70.3	26.8	43.7	4.1	17.1	3.4	-8.9	15.8	22.6
Floyd County	26 851	32 123	36 010	17 250	8 971	14 923	26 305	20 051	14 206	77.4	22.6	30.2	4.0	9.2	6.3	-6.0	20.4	26.4
Foard County	25 813	34 211	36 250	21 250	20 556	12 557	23 523	18 417	14 799	73.8	28.7	42.5	3.9	16.7	3.1	-9.2	17.3	12.4
Fort Bend County	63 831	69 781	77 501	40 474	31 494	35 390	49 684	34 149	24 985	92.1	37.9	13.2	1.4	9.3	25.5	13.2	6.4	6.8
Franklin County	31 955	37 064	37 938	22 917	17 727	17 479	30 201	20 083	17 563	71.3	29.2	34.3	3.0	19.1	8.0	-4.3	15.0	20.4
Freestone County	31 283	39 586	50 745	21 250	15 076	14 760	33 775	19 820	16 338	72.4	27.7	35.0	3.3	19.2	4.9	-7.4	14.9	15.1
Frio County	24 504	26 578	34 028	19 219	10 380	11 710	24 544	17 540	14 069	76.6	16.9	33.0	4.7	12.3	3.3	-9.0	27.6	31.5
Gaines County	30 432	34 046	35 733	23 365	11 250	15 525	30 152	18 079	13 088	82.1	20.7	26.7	4.1	10.8	5.3	-7.0	19.1	23.7
Galveston County	42 419	51 435	63 307	33 065	19 588	24 694	42 482	29 692	21 568	82.2	32.1	23.0	3.0	16.3	13.0	0.7	12.7	15.0
Garza County	27 206	31 173	37 581	12 500	11 500	11 816	27 358	19 129	12 704	78.9	29.9	29.1	5.2	8.5	5.2	-7.1	23.5	25.9
Gillespie County	38 109	45 315	46 074	24 659	22 292	21 197	28 832	22 320	20 423	73.1	49.8	40.8	1.8	24.2	7.8	-4.5	10.5	9.9
Glasscock County	35 655	43 000	41 667	3 750	19 688		30 435	27 292	18 279	88.2	32.3	19.2	2.3	8.9	9.9	-2.4	11.2	13.0
Gollad County	34 201	40 446	44 293	35 313	16 012	16 593	32 279	20 737	17 126	74.1	35.6	33.1	3.7	20.8	5.8	-6.5	15.0	22.5
Gonzales County	28 368	35 218	38 432	20 273	15 208	13 532	24 990	17 527	14 269	75.1	26.4	33.9	3.5	16.3	4.6	-7.7	19.6	19.9
Gray County	31 368	40 019	46 387	14 792	12 361	15 618	33 955	21 179	16 702	70.6	34.1	36.1	3.1	18.2	6.1	-6.2	14.9	16.2
Grayson County	37 178	45 048	52 351	27 583	21 378	19 829	34 587	24 347	18 862	77.6	31.0	30.2	2.8	17.7	7.5	-4.8	12.1	13.2
Gregg County	35 006	42 617	52 076	24 383	16 371	20 800	34 804	22 089	18 449	78.0	30.9	29.1	3.3	15.9	7.9	-4.4	14.7	17.7
Grimes County	32 280	38 008	45 809	29 659	16 895	18 333	30 737	22 247	14 368	77.8	24.9	27.7	3.5	14.0	5.8	-6.5	17.3	18.7

Table B-3. States and Counties — Education, Labor Force, and Income

STATE/ County code	MSA/PMSA/ NECMA code[1]	STATE County	High school graduates			College graduates		College graduates (percent)				
			Total population 25 years and over	Percent with a high school diploma or less	Percent with a high school diploma or more	Percent with a bachelor's degree or more	+/− U.S. percent with bachelor's degree or more	Non-Hispanic White	Black or African American	American Indian and Alaska Native	Asian, Hawaiian, and Pacific Islander	Hispanic or Latino[2]
			1	2	3	4	5	6	7	8	9	10
		TEXAS—Cont'd										
48 187	7240	Guadalupe County	55 679	52.0	78.1	19.1	-5.3	24.2	21.1	28.2	16.9	6.3
48 189	...	Hale County	21 498	62.8	65.9	14.4	-10.0	21.7	4.2	6.3	78.1	4.3
48 191	...	Hall County	2 527	71.1	61.7	10.3	-14.1	13.6	0.0	0.0	0.0	1.3
48 193	...	Hamilton County............	5 792	59.2	73.8	16.8	-7.6	17.6	X	0.0	X	2.8
48 195	...	Hansford County	3 420	59.9	69.9	18.6	-5.8	24.3	X	6.8	X	0.5
48 197	...	Hardeman County	3 135	62.6	70.7	12.8	-11.6	14.3	2.4	26.7	70.6	1.4
48 199	0840	Hardin County	30 747	60.8	79.5	13.0	-11.4	13.5	5.7	4.5	29.8	10.1
48 201	3360	Harris County	2 067 399	47.0	74.6	26.9	2.5	38.5	17.4	18.1	45.6	8.2
48 203	4420	Harrison County	39 130	55.8	78.3	15.4	-9.0	16.6	11.7	3.0	31.4	10.0
48 205	...	Hartley County	4 136	56.6	77.3	17.6	-6.8	21.3	8.3	0.0	0.0	5.5
48 207	...	Haskell County	4 314	65.4	71.1	14.4	-10.0	17.4	9.8	0.0	0.0	0.3
48 209	0640	Hays County	53 635	38.2	84.7	31.3	6.9	39.6	11.0	23.3	48.5	10.8
48 211	...	Hemphill County	2 190	49.3	79.9	17.9	-6.5	20.0	0.0	0.0	X	2.7
48 213	1920	Henderson County	49 886	58.9	73.5	12.1	-12.3	12.7	7.6	27.3	26.5	3.4
48 215	4880	Hidalgo County.............	304 670	69.8	50.5	12.9	-11.5	27.8	16.7	7.4	65.1	9.6
48 217	...	Hill County	21 209	61.5	71.8	12.5	-11.9	14.4	3.0	17.8	51.3	1.6
48 219	...	Hockley County	13 466	58.0	68.2	13.6	-10.8	19.0	3.1	7.4	83.8	2.4
48 221	2800	Hood County	28 621	46.1	83.5	20.5	-3.9	21.1	70.0	23.9	44.6	7.5
48 223	...	Hopkins County	21 003	62.1	73.6	15.1	-9.3	16.6	5.3	2.7	80.3	4.0
48 225	...	Houston County	16 244	64.7	70.0	12.2	-12.2	15.0	7.8	6.1	7.1	1.1
48 227	...	Howard County	22 544	60.7	70.6	11.1	-13.3	15.7	12.6	0.0	39.6	2.8
48 229	...	Hudspeth County	1 910	74.5	46.1	9.7	-14.7	26.5	0.0	25.0	0.0	2.5
48 231	1920	Hunt County	48 548	57.4	76.9	16.8	-7.6	18.1	7.7	12.3	56.6	7.1
48 233	...	Hutchinson County	15 282	54.5	79.6	14.3	-10.1	15.4	4.8	16.9	58.6	7.1
48 235	...	Irion County	1 217	52.2	78.8	21.5	-2.9	26.9	0.0	0.0	X	3.8
48 237	...	Jack County	5 830	60.8	75.8	12.8	-11.6	13.5	8.6	0.0	58.6	3.5
48 239	...	Jackson County.............	9 278	61.6	72.7	12.8	-11.6	16.9	3.3	0.0	69.2	2.0
48 241	...	Jasper County	23 420	66.6	73.0	10.5	-13.9	12.0	3.4	11.6	31.5	5.3
48 243	...	Jeff Davis County.........	1 560	44.3	74.7	35.1	10.7	46.0	X	X	X	12.0
48 245	0840	Jefferson County	161 261	54.7	78.5	16.3	-8.1	21.2	8.2	7.5	32.5	7.9
48 247	...	Jim Hogg County	3 203	70.3	58.0	9.5	-14.9	11.8	0.0	0.0	0.0	9.3
48 249	...	Jim Wells County	23 525	67.5	64.8	10.9	-13.5	17.3	10.6	13.6	64.9	8.2
48 251	2800	Johnson County	79 417	55.7	77.6	13.8	-10.6	14.7	8.9	13.0	27.7	4.6
48 253	...	Jones County	13 780	70.3	64.3	8.2	-16.2	11.3	1.3	0.0	5.1	1.1
48 255	...	Karnes County	10 352	73.2	59.1	9.4	-15.0	17.2	1.6	6.6	50.0	2.7
48 257	1920	Kaufman County	44 859	59.3	74.5	12.3	-12.1	13.4	8.1	8.5	38.5	4.3
48 259	...	Kendall County	15 827	37.6	85.4	31.4	7.0	34.5	0.0	24.3	69.7	11.8
48 261	...	Kenedy County	261	64.0	57.9	20.3	-4.1	45.7	0.0	X	X	14.9
48 263	...	Kent County	643	58.9	78.1	15.1	-9.3	16.1	0.0	0.0	X	7.5
48 265	...	Kerr County	31 006	48.0	81.2	23.3	-1.1	26.9	2.6	11.0	19.7	4.9
48 267	...	Kimble County	3 146	62.1	72.1	17.3	-7.1	20.3	0.0	0.0	50.0	2.3
48 269	...	King County..................	228	47.8	78.1	24.6	0.2	26.0	X	X	X	0.0
48 271	...	Kinney County	2 335	60.4	66.9	17.7	-6.7	28.4	0.0	0.0	63.6	3.7
48 273	...	Kleberg County	17 896	54.8	68.2	20.4	-4.0	32.8	8.8	21.9	48.5	13.5
48 275	...	Knox County.................	2 819	66.9	66.8	11.8	-12.6	14.6	1.2	33.3	53.3	2.7
48 277	...	Lamar County...............	31 612	56.9	76.3	14.5	-9.9	15.9	5.7	13.1	34.2	7.9
48 279	...	Lamb County................	9 202	64.7	63.7	11.1	-13.3	16.7	2.0	0.0	0.0	2.9
48 281	...	Lampasas County	11 491	51.7	78.8	16.2	-8.2	18.0	9.2	0.0	13.1	6.5
48 283	...	La Salle County............	3 602	75.6	50.1	6.4	-18.0	20.7	0.0	0.0	10.0	2.2
48 285	...	Lavaca County	13 214	68.1	68.6	11.4	-13.0	12.6	7.1	4.8	30.8	3.4
48 287	...	Lee County	9 804	65.0	71.7	13.1	-11.3	15.5	6.9	0.0	0.0	4.2
48 289	...	Leon County	10 652	64.1	73.8	12.1	-12.3	13.6	6.7	0.0	0.0	0.7
48 291	3360	Liberty County	44 206	66.6	69.6	8.1	-16.3	9.3	4.5	11.4	11.3	2.0
48 293	...	Limestone County	14 564	62.6	67.4	11.1	-13.3	14.3	3.2	10.7	0.0	1.1
48 295	...	Lipscomb County	2 047	54.8	74.5	18.9	-5.5	21.3	37.5	0.0	X	5.6
48 297	...	Live Oak County	8 399	61.2	67.1	12.0	-12.4	17.3	1.8	9.4	20.0	3.0
48 299	...	Llano County	13 571	49.1	83.5	21.0	-3.4	21.9	0.0	0.0	0.0	2.8
48 301	...	Loving County	51	51.0	86.3	5.9	-18.5	6.3	X	X	X	0.0
48 303	4600	Lubbock County	141 363	46.9	78.4	24.4	0.0	31.1	10.0	14.6	64.2	7.2
48 305	...	Lynn County	4 037	66.1	61.9	13.4	-11.0	21.7	2.7	38.5	33.3	0.4
48 307	...	McCulloch County	5 550	64.5	70.5	14.0	-10.4	16.4	15.9	0.0	X	5.0
48 309	8800	McLennan County	125 961	51.3	76.6	19.1	-5.3	23.2	9.1	9.0	47.7	6.8
48 311	...	McMullen County	613	60.5	74.7	16.2	-8.2	20.8	0.0	100.0	X	3.9
48 313	...	Madison County	8 907	71.1	72.8	11.5	-12.9	16.2	1.5	27.3	82.8	3.8
48 315	...	Marion County..............	7 792	65.7	67.5	8.5	-15.9	9.4	5.4	9.9	X	0.0
48 317	...	Martin County...............	2 785	65.6	65.8	11.8	-12.6	16.4	0.0	0.0	45.5	3.1

[1]MSA = Metropolitan Statistical Area. PMSA = Primary MSA. NECMA = New England County Metropolitan Area. See the Appendix A for explanation of these concepts. See Appendix B for list of metropolitan areas identified by type, with component counties.
[2]Hispanic or Latino persons may be of any race.

STATE County	School enrollment			Population 16 to 19 years				Employment status, 2000			Work status in 1999 of the population 16 years and over (percent)		
											Worked in 1999		
	Grades kindergarten through 12	College or graduate school	Percent private	Number	Percent in armed forces	Percent high school graduates	Percent not enrolled, not grads, not in armed forces, not employed	Total population 16 years and over	Percent in labor force	Unemployment rate	Full-time	Part-time	Did not work in 1999
	11	12	13	14	15	16	17	18	19	20	21	22	23
TEXAS—Cont'd													
Guadalupe County	19 460	4 172	12.0	5 454	0.7	13.0	4.0	66 557	66.4	5.3	59.7	12.7	27.7
Hale County	8 463	1 730	10.8	2 597	0.0	11.4	6.8	26 854	58.5	6.7	53.5	12.5	34.1
Hall County	767	54	2.9	204	0.0	5.4	6.4	2 883	54.2	9.0	46.2	12.1	41.8
Hamilton County	1 544	196	2.4	385	0.0	5.7	4.7	6 496	54.1	2.6	46.7	12.8	40.5
Hansford County	1 193	94	1.4	357	0.0	3.9	5.6	4 051	62.2	4.0	55.8	12.9	31.3
Hardeman County	928	99	0.5	306	0.0	14.1	5.6	3 706	59.7	4.2	50.5	12.3	37.3
Hardin County	10 212	1 418	3.8	3 021	0.0	11.0	3.3	36 547	59.9	5.7	53.2	11.3	35.5
Harris County	722 117	186 214	9.6	199 589	0.0	9.4	8.4	2 519 937	65.6	6.4	60.1	11.4	28.5
Harrison County	12 987	3 252	14.5	4 405	0.1	10.6	5.0	47 610	59.8	7.4	52.3	12.3	35.4
Hartley County	942	174	17.6	179	0.0	6.1	2.2	4 487	46.3	1.2	54.6	9.0	36.4
Haskell County	1 172	90	2.4	349	0.0	11.7	2.0	4 862	52.4	5.2	45.2	12.8	42.0
Hays County	17 740	16 274	5.9	8 049	0.1	8.9	5.3	76 853	70.2	6.3	55.9	22.0	22.0
Hemphill County	784	59	1.1	263	0.0	6.8	3.0	2 573	63.0	3.1	54.0	16.2	29.7
Henderson County	13 310	2 412	6.4	3 964	0.0	12.9	4.8	57 674	54.9	6.5	48.2	11.3	40.5
Hidalgo County	148 929	27 046	3.3	40 746	0.0	7.2	11.1	389 868	52.6	12.0	46.8	11.1	42.1
Hill County	6 183	1 100	5.2	2 009	0.0	7.5	8.9	25 057	56.2	4.9	50.1	11.6	38.3
Hockley County	5 043	1 511	3.6	1 843	0.0	10.6	4.5	16 921	60.7	6.9	52.1	13.5	34.5
Hood County	7 446	1 234	6.6	2 183	0.0	11.5	4.2	32 501	58.9	4.8	52.1	12.5	35.4
Hopkins County	6 452	1 000	5.0	1 918	0.2	13.7	3.8	24 584	61.8	4.8	53.3	11.7	35.0
Houston County	4 723	487	11.7	1 282	0.0	13.4	10.1	18 471	45.9	6.1	48.4	9.6	42.0
Howard County	6 459	1 702	5.5	2 044	0.0	15.0	10.7	26 513	48.9	6.7	52.2	9.5	38.3
Hudspeth County	857	69	4.3	233	0.0	9.9	6.9	2 331	52.7	8.2	51.3	7.1	41.6
Hunt County	15 431	4 348	7.1	4 659	0.0	12.3	4.9	58 747	62.5	5.8	55.2	12.1	32.7
Hutchinson County	4 939	1 034	4.6	1 654	0.0	11.3	5.0	18 194	57.3	5.6	49.9	13.0	37.1
Irion County	392	54	4.0	96	0.0	5.2	0.0	1 362	64.0	2.6	56.3	11.9	31.8
Jack County	1 705	315	9.6	513	0.0	15.2	7.6	6 965	49.8	4.0	48.4	11.8	39.8
Jackson County	3 043	397	1.6	912	0.0	12.8	3.1	10 932	58.1	5.0	50.7	12.3	37.0
Jasper County	7 329	751	5.7	2 086	0.4	9.7	5.7	27 330	52.6	7.2	46.2	11.2	42.5
Jeff Davis County	486	54	10.4	116	0.0	4.3	1.7	1 739	62.9	5.8	55.8	13.4	30.8
Jefferson County	51 343	11 596	7.9	15 411	0.1	10.8	7.1	194 853	55.8	8.1	48.9	12.3	38.8
Jim Hogg County	1 255	168	2.4	344	0.0	10.8	1.2	3 831	53.3	8.1	43.5	14.6	41.9
Jim Wells County	9 350	1 531	3.3	2 643	0.0	8.5	9.1	28 492	53.9	6.6	45.8	13.5	40.6
Johnson County	27 610	4 806	11.5	8 065	0.2	12.1	6.7	94 457	66.0	4.6	59.2	11.8	29.0
Jones County	4 722	438	8.7	1 529	0.0	8.2	23.9	16 915	43.3	6.1	55.1	8.7	36.2
Karnes County	2 936	336	4.0	817	0.0	12.0	8.0	12 508	40.2	6.5	38.0	9.6	52.3
Kaufman County	15 607	2 336	9.1	4 403	0.0	10.2	8.5	53 214	65.5	4.5	58.8	11.1	30.1
Kendall County	5 062	820	8.2	1 296	0.0	7.9	3.2	18 061	62.7	3.3	54.4	12.3	33.3
Kenedy County	94	6	3.0	27	0.0	7.4	11.1	304	65.8	6.5	56.3	14.8	28.9
Kent County	165	12	1.1	42	0.0	0.0	0.0	705	56.3	3.8	48.1	13.2	38.7
Kerr County	7 821	1 142	13.7	2 204	0.0	10.7	3.5	35 019	51.9	4.6	44.8	11.9	43.3
Kimble County	908	42	2.3	249	0.0	10.0	9.2	3 504	57.5	3.0	50.2	12.6	37.2
King County	82	2	2.4	9	0.0	0.0	0.0	241	61.8	0.0	60.2	8.7	31.1
Kinney County	699	57	2.1	180	0.0	6.7	2.8	2 631	42.4	9.3	38.8	9.8	51.4
Kleberg County	6 437	4 469	6.6	2 384	0.2	6.4	4.5	23 922	60.1	10.2	47.8	16.0	36.2
Knox County	985	78	3.1	249	0.0	8.0	0.8	3 226	52.5	6.4	45.5	10.7	43.9
Lamar County	9 355	1 847	6.4	2 750	0.0	9.5	5.6	37 185	58.4	5.6	51.2	12.6	36.1
Lamb County	3 310	284	2.7	992	0.0	9.2	7.0	10 985	55.4	5.8	49.0	13.6	37.4
Lampasas County	3 831	605	5.8	1 187	0.8	7.1	3.4	13 575	62.2	4.5	54.5	13.0	32.5
La Salle County	1 318	157	2.4	367	0.0	10.1	16.9	4 349	45.7	7.9	42.2	9.2	48.6
Lavaca County	3 668	546	14.0	1 116	0.0	9.8	6.2	15 206	58.5	2.5	50.0	12.8	37.2
Lee County	3 331	323	10.7	1 236	0.0	10.4	19.0	11 861	63.3	2.6	57.1	12.4	30.5
Leon County	2 957	338	3.6	896	0.0	8.6	3.7	12 176	52.2	5.4	45.4	10.7	43.9
Liberty County	15 097	1 634	5.3	4 116	0.0	12.9	7.9	53 126	53.7	6.9	51.8	9.6	38.7
Limestone County	4 356	785	4.0	1 204	0.0	12.1	5.2	17 127	52.7	5.5	48.4	10.5	41.1
Lipscomb County	664	37	1.4	193	0.0	8.3	2.6	2 349	57.2	4.2	53.3	12.0	34.7
Live Oak County	2 360	284	6.8	741	0.0	13.5	5.7	9 942	45.3	5.8	42.3	11.0	46.8
Llano County	2 070	182	6.6	527	0.0	16.5	5.1	14 659	46.1	2.9	40.2	11.2	48.6
Loving County	16	11	14.8	5	0.0	0.0	0.0	56	75.0	0.0	64.3	16.1	19.6
Lubbock County	46 144	30 844	7.4	17 939	0.1	10.6	3.8	187 461	65.0	5.8	54.7	18.1	27.2
Lynn County	1 625	168	4.4	449	0.0	11.1	5.6	4 761	56.6	6.1	52.9	11.8	35.3
McCulloch County	1 587	84	2.2	374	0.0	12.8	8.3	6 258	55.0	6.9	47.8	10.9	41.4
McLennan County	41 749	22 657	23.4	16 641	0.1	8.6	5.5	163 207	62.5	7.6	53.7	14.9	31.4
McMullen County	172	19	5.2	46	0.0	17.4	0.0	681	51.8	1.7	46.4	11.2	42.4
Madison County	2 184	542	3.9	496	0.0	11.5	5.4	10 482	42.4	5.8	53.2	7.3	39.5
Marion County	1 872	238	9.1	554	0.0	14.1	6.0	8 832	50.4	8.2	41.9	13.2	44.9
Martin County	1 176	103	2.7	334	0.0	6.3	9.9	3 342	56.7	4.9	51.5	11.7	36.8

Table B-3. States and Counties — Education, Labor Force, and Income

STATE County	Full-year full-time employed (percent)								Children under 18 years in families						Total employed by class of worker (percent)			
										With two parents (percent)								
	Total	Men	Women	Non-Hispanic White	Black or African American	American Indian and Alaska Native	Asian, Hawaiian, and Pacific Islander	Hispanic or Latino[1]	Number	Both in labor force	Father only in labor force	With one parent who is in labor force (percent)	+/− U.S. percent of children with no stay-at-home parent (percent)	+/− U.S. percent two-income couples	Private	Government	Self-employed	Unpaid family worker
	24	25	26	27	28	29	30	31	32	33	34	35	36	37	38	39	40	41
TEXAS—Cont'd																		
Guadalupe County	44.6	54.8	34.9	45.7	44.4	36.6	30.5	43.0	23 731	47.2	21.6	19.8	2.4	2.7	71.8	17.8	9.9	0.4
Hale County	36.1	46.1	26.0	37.2	23.8	28.7	45.8	36.1	10 431	45.8	22.9	19.8	1.0	-2.8	70.0	16.6	13.0	0.4
Hall County	30.5	45.7	17.8	31.6	23.9	80.0	0.0	28.9	965	33.4	29.4	15.5	-15.7	-10.2	58.7	20.3	20.7	0.4
Hamilton County	35.5	47.1	25.3	34.6	X	30.8	X	49.0	1 833	48.2	20.5	19.0	2.6	-4.8	62.0	19.4	17.8	0.9
Hansford County	40.8	56.5	25.8	42.3	X	37.0	X	36.9	1 486	45.0	31.6	11.4	-8.2	0.8	69.0	12.9	17.7	0.5
Hardeman County	38.0	51.3	26.7	39.2	12.6	45.5	77.3	40.4	1 103	47.0	21.8	21.9	4.3	-1.7	61.2	23.0	14.2	1.6
Hardin County	40.1	53.1	27.9	40.9	29.1	38.1	32.1	45.4	12 741	41.0	30.3	18.2	-5.4	-5.8	74.6	15.3	9.7	0.4
Harris County	42.6	51.9	33.5	48.7	38.9	41.2	40.7	35.8	919 971	35.0	26.1	21.4	-8.2	-3.6	79.7	11.2	8.9	0.2
Harrison County	37.6	47.4	28.8	40.8	29.1	15.0	18.3	35.7	15 536	38.6	23.4	23.4	-2.6	-4.7	76.2	12.8	10.5	0.5
Hartley County	37.3	41.0	30.8	42.5	13.1	0.0	0.0	26.3	1 127	52.9	32.6	9.6	-2.1	7.1	63.8	17.2	18.9	0.0
Haskell County	30.5	40.7	21.4	29.7	34.2	0.0	71.4	33.7	1 372	45.0	21.0	17.5	-2.1	-7.0	59.1	19.9	20.4	0.6
Hays County	39.5	47.8	31.2	40.4	23.1	29.2	23.7	40.1	22 104	51.4	21.2	17.2	4.0	6.9	67.5	22.0	10.3	0.2
Hemphill County	40.3	54.3	27.1	42.1	21.4	22.9	0.0	30.1	816	54.5	25.0	13.7	3.6	1.2	60.9	20.4	17.3	1.3
Henderson County	34.6	43.5	26.3	34.6	30.1	35.9	56.6	38.3	16 469	39.7	25.9	21.7	-3.2	-11.5	72.7	13.3	13.5	0.6
Hidalgo County	25.9	33.4	19.2	24.8	24.5	23.6	36.6	26.0	187 365	30.6	31.1	15.5	-18.5	-18.9	68.9	19.2	11.6	0.4
Hill County	36.2	45.2	27.7	37.0	28.4	44.0	22.7	36.2	7 557	37.8	25.6	21.0	-5.8	-7.5	72.3	14.2	12.8	0.6
Hockley County	35.2	48.4	23.4	38.6	15.4	27.7	0.0	30.9	6 242	41.5	24.4	19.3	-3.8	-3.5	69.4	17.9	12.1	0.6
Hood County	37.3	48.5	26.8	37.9	70.0	38.8	40.3	29.1	9 135	48.6	26.8	17.8	1.8	-8.4	73.1	11.8	14.3	0.7
Hopkins County	39.6	50.7	29.3	39.6	33.2	42.9	75.0	41.0	7 680	47.9	26.7	16.3	-0.4	-4.4	72.4	13.1	13.8	0.7
Houston County	32.1	38.7	24.4	34.3	26.1	48.5	66.7	33.4	4 821	38.0	23.8	23.8	-2.8	-8.2	61.3	24.9	13.1	0.7
Howard County	33.2	37.4	28.1	37.4	27.2	47.4	17.1	26.5	7 478	40.4	21.2	26.5	2.3	-5.2	65.1	24.7	9.9	0.3
Hudspeth County	29.9	41.2	19.2	40.8	16.7	20.5	0.0	25.8	1 034	31.5	31.4	15.0	-18.1	-16.2	61.2	30.8	6.7	1.2
Hunt County	41.0	51.3	31.2	42.5	32.5	34.4	22.0	39.5	18 701	42.5	24.1	22.4	0.3	-3.3	74.3	15.3	9.9	0.4
Hutchinson County	36.5	49.7	24.3	37.1	28.3	47.5	15.8	32.5	6 152	44.1	29.7	14.3	-6.2	-7.3	75.8	14.4	9.2	0.6
Irion County	43.2	52.1	34.4	46.4	50.0	30.0	X	32.3	430	60.0	17.0	16.7	12.1	4.3	60.5	19.2	20.0	0.3
Jack County	34.1	41.3	24.9	36.4	11.7	15.8	31.0	31.5	1 900	47.8	23.3	18.5	1.7	-4.9	61.8	19.8	18.1	0.3
Jackson County	36.3	48.3	24.8	38.1	25.8	55.0	51.4	34.1	3 617	44.6	21.5	20.1	0.1	-2.5	71.5	14.7	12.9	0.8
Jasper County	31.0	40.0	22.7	31.0	30.9	49.3	20.2	30.7	8 816	37.2	28.6	21.5	-5.9	-13.1	71.2	17.6	10.5	0.7
Jeff Davis County	42.2	52.4	31.4	43.7	0.0	X	X	38.3	447	61.5	19.5	12.3	9.2	-0.9	54.3	26.0	19.5	0.2
Jefferson County	34.0	39.8	28.2	38.6	28.4	36.7	31.5	27.0	60 658	35.3	20.3	26.8	-2.5	-6.3	74.6	17.1	8.0	0.3
Jim Hogg County	27.0	37.3	17.2	30.5	55.6	0.0	27.3	26.6	1 542	35.8	31.9	11.5	-17.3	-14.8	63.2	25.7	10.5	0.6
Jim Wells County	29.9	39.8	20.8	33.3	16.4	30.2	21.0	28.8	11 524	34.1	22.2	20.7	-9.8	-10.3	71.2	17.9	10.1	0.8
Johnson County	45.0	56.6	33.8	46.1	28.3	47.9	29.3	40.1	34 306	48.0	26.1	15.8	-0.8	2.6	78.7	11.4	9.6	0.4
Jones County	28.2	26.9	30.2	34.6	5.8	25.5	61.5	20.2	4 091	48.6	24.2	17.9	1.9	-1.2	65.1	17.6	16.3	0.9
Karnes County	24.7	25.1	24.0	32.8	4.2	4.7	0.0	22.8	3 097	46.2	15.8	21.9	3.5	-5.0	61.1	26.5	11.5	1.0
Kaufman County	45.5	56.3	35.3	47.1	31.1	44.4	55.0	47.6	19 294	47.5	23.4	17.9	0.8	3.9	75.3	13.7	10.5	0.4
Kendall County	40.7	53.1	29.1	40.9	37.5	64.9	13.6	40.0	6 223	46.5	31.1	13.5	-4.6	-1.0	66.6	15.3	17.3	0.8
Kenedy County	46.4	70.1	22.0	56.3	100.0	X	X	44.5	107	39.3	14.0	33.6	8.3	0.9	64.2	21.9	13.9	0.0
Kent County	32.9	48.5	18.9	32.2	40.0	0.0	X	38.4	174	50.6	23.6	20.1	6.1	1.6	47.6	29.3	23.0	0.0
Kerr County	32.6	41.0	25.3	31.4	37.3	27.9	35.6	38.6	8 910	46.3	22.5	21.8	3.5	-10.9	63.9	17.4	18.1	0.6
Kimble County	38.2	49.9	27.6	40.0	0.0	58.8	0.0	31.3	987	53.1	13.8	21.7	10.2	-5.8	64.2	15.5	19.0	1.2
King County	47.3	63.3	31.4	49.3	X	X	X	26.7	85	40.0	55.3	0.0	-24.6	-8.7	41.6	37.6	20.8	0.0
Kinney County	22.4	31.3	13.5	24.3	2.9	30.8	21.4	21.0	817	34.0	29.1	15.4	-15.2	-19.6	55.9	30.2	12.5	1.3
Kleberg County	31.4	40.2	23.0	37.5	25.3	36.1	18.2	29.2	8 035	37.4	21.5	18.6	-8.6	-7.0	64.3	26.7	8.4	0.6
Knox County	31.1	43.6	20.1	33.7	18.3	25.9	11.1	26.1	1 094	41.6	30.9	15.3	-7.7	-12.7	56.6	20.0	21.9	1.5
Lamar County	36.9	47.0	28.2	37.9	32.4	45.0	30.9	34.6	11 870	40.0	21.8	26.0	1.4	-4.4	73.6	13.7	12.4	0.4
Lamb County	31.6	44.6	20.1	34.6	23.9	24.5	0.0	28.0	4 032	40.6	23.9	18.7	-5.3	-5.8	66.3	17.7	14.6	1.4
Lampasas County	39.2	49.3	29.8	40.6	44.8	58.7	41.1	27.8	4 554	49.8	18.7	18.0	3.2	-0.9	58.8	23.2	17.2	0.9
La Salle County	23.9	27.8	19.2	32.6	0.0	0.0	25.0	23.0	1 513	39.2	15.3	17.8	-7.6	-9.7	64.5	22.3	12.3	0.9
Lavaca County	37.9	46.8	29.8	37.4	29.4	28.3	23.1	48.9	4 410	56.9	15.7	16.3	8.6	0.6	70.2	13.7	15.4	0.7
Lee County	41.1	49.9	32.3	44.4	29.7	45.0	14.3	35.5	4 018	53.7	23.2	15.7	4.8	4.3	65.2	19.1	15.1	0.5
Leon County	33.1	43.1	23.8	33.8	26.4	46.7	26.7	37.8	3 504	39.4	28.8	18.4	-6.8	-15.0	66.7	16.9	15.6	0.9
Liberty County	35.3	46.9	24.7	38.7	25.7	23.4	28.7	23.0	17 949	37.2	30.3	18.1	-9.3	-9.7	76.8	13.6	9.0	0.6
Limestone County	33.6	37.5	29.8	37.0	23.2	50.0	0.0	31.6	5 133	43.5	18.3	26.0	4.9	-5.2	60.7	26.9	12.0	0.4
Lipscomb County	35.6	46.8	25.1	36.6	25.0	60.7	X	29.0	795	49.2	27.0	10.4	-5.0	-4.6	55.2	19.9	23.5	1.5
Live Oak County	28.1	32.5	22.1	32.0	5.6	7.1	6.7	23.8	2 592	37.5	31.9	17.0	-10.1	-13.9	63.2	22.2	13.9	0.6
Llano County	30.0	38.0	22.7	30.3	0.0	24.0	27.8	25.5	2 520	44.0	26.9	17.5	-3.1	-18.4	60.2	14.4	24.5	0.9
Loving County	14.3	32.0	0.0	14.3	X	X	X	14.3	14	21.4	57.1	0.0	-43.2	3.1	28.6	47.6	23.8	0.0
Lubbock County	39.2	47.4	31.6	39.6	33.2	40.7	30.7	40.6	57 522	43.7	18.1	24.1	3.2	2.5	69.7	19.9	10.0	0.4
Lynn County	37.0	50.6	24.0	41.8	34.4	27.3	100.0	30.6	1 878	39.3	29.8	16.1	-9.2	-9.1	59.1	22.6	18.0	0.4
McCulloch County	32.6	44.4	22.4	34.0	0.0	37.0	X	29.5	1 942	35.0	30.6	20.5	-9.1	-13.8	67.2	16.0	15.4	1.5
McLennan County	38.6	47.3	30.7	40.4	32.2	38.9	23.9	37.9	52 008	41.2	20.8	24.0	0.6	-0.8	76.4	14.6	8.6	0.4
McMullen County	34.4	46.3	21.6	31.8	50.0	100.0	X	38.8	192	28.6	38.0	19.3	-16.7	-16.9	49.6	29.1	21.3	0.0
Madison County	33.4	35.8	29.6	37.1	22.9	27.3	31.0	33.9	2 522	43.0	18.1	23.0	1.4	-7.7	57.9	27.1	13.6	1.4
Marion County	28.4	34.6	22.6	30.1	21.7	36.5	X	43.3	2 230	40.7	18.5	24.7	0.8	-15.4	74.4	14.0	11.3	0.3
Martin County	36.4	50.5	23.0	38.7	32.0	33.3	0.0	32.9	1 499	36.6	33.6	17.2	-10.8	-9.8	61.8	21.0	16.7	0.5

[1] Hispanic or Latino persons may be of any race.

Table B-3. States and Counties — Education, Labor Force, and Income

STATE County	Percent who worked at home	Percent of the population 5 years and over with a disability	Veterans as a percent of the population 18 years and over	Occupation for employed population 16 years and over (percent)						Industry for employed population 16 years and over (percent)					
				Management, professional, and related occupations	Service occupations	Sales and office occupations	Farming, fishing, and forestry occupations	Construction, extraction, and maintenance occupations	Production, transportation and material moving occupations	Agriculture, forestry, fishing, and mining	Construction and manufacturing	Wholesale and retail trade	Transportation and warehousing, and utilities	Service industries	Public administration
	42	43	44	45	46	47	48	49	50	51	52	53	54	55	56
TEXAS—Cont'd															
Guadalupe County	2.6	19.0	18.2	28.8	14.4	26.9	0.6	13.0	16.5	2.2	25.0	16.4	4.9	44.3	7.2
Hale County	1.9	19.6	9.1	28.0	16.5	23.2	3.7	8.8	19.8	8.8	18.6	18.9	4.9	42.5	6.4
Hall County	2.4	26.8	11.2	29.4	23.2	17.8	7.7	10.3	11.7	21.7	10.7	10.6	8.0	40.5	8.4
Hamilton County	6.0	24.6	15.6	30.5	15.8	21.4	5.4	11.5	15.4	13.0	16.1	14.7	6.5	41.8	7.8
Hansford County	3.3	18.0	10.6	29.8	13.4	19.9	8.4	12.2	16.2	26.9	11.1	15.2	8.2	36.0	2.6
Hardeman County	1.3	26.0	11.9	27.2	21.0	17.4	3.9	12.6	18.0	9.9	19.6	11.5	5.8	46.2	7.1
Hardin County	1.8	19.6	14.8	25.1	14.4	25.6	0.9	15.3	18.7	3.8	25.4	16.0	6.2	42.9	5.6
Harris County	2.4	18.5	9.1	34.8	13.8	27.7	0.1	10.9	12.6	2.2	20.5	16.0	6.8	51.6	2.9
Harrison County	2.4	22.2	13.0	26.1	13.4	26.6	0.5	12.7	20.8	4.4	24.7	15.6	6.3	45.0	4.0
Hartley County	3.4	13.5	12.9	34.9	11.5	24.9	7.4	9.1	12.2	20.9	7.5	14.2	7.8	42.1	7.6
Haskell County	3.0	24.4	12.9	34.7	17.8	19.8	4.5	9.0	14.1	17.4	8.1	16.2	6.8	46.3	5.2
Hays County	3.6	14.6	11.3	36.0	15.3	28.7	0.4	10.0	10.0	1.1	18.6	11.6	3.6	55.3	7.0
Hemphill County	5.2	13.5	11.9	30.7	14.7	22.0	4.8	14.8	13.0	27.1	8.3	12.6	5.6	40.7	5.7
Henderson County	3.0	25.8	17.2	24.5	15.9	25.4	0.9	16.7	16.6	3.3	24.2	16.7	6.5	45.0	4.4
Hidalgo County	2.2	20.9	6.8	26.3	18.5	25.4	2.9	12.4	14.4	4.1	16.9	18.4	5.0	51.0	4.4
Hill County	3.3	24.7	15.8	24.5	15.3	25.4	2.1	13.3	19.4	5.9	23.6	17.1	6.9	43.2	4.6
Hockley County	2.3	20.2	10.2	27.5	16.0	24.2	3.7	14.6	14.0	19.7	9.8	14.2	4.8	47.5	4.0
Hood County	3.8	21.2	19.3	30.9	14.7	27.1	0.6	14.3	12.4	2.4	19.3	17.7	10.1	47.0	3.5
Hopkins County	3.6	22.4	13.2	25.5	13.9	24.4	3.2	12.2	20.7	7.7	22.0	20.2	7.2	39.6	3.3
Houston County	3.4	22.9	15.7	25.2	22.8	22.0	2.5	11.0	16.4	7.6	18.8	14.3	4.3	43.8	11.3
Howard County	1.8	22.6	13.0	30.8	21.4	20.4	1.7	11.6	14.1	8.2	16.1	11.0	4.5	52.2	7.9
Hudspeth County	1.4	20.6	8.1	20.3	20.7	19.7	10.1	9.7	19.5	18.0	16.8	11.9	6.6	31.2	15.5
Hunt County	3.0	23.1	15.9	28.3	14.2	26.4	0.8	13.5	16.8	2.0	29.2	14.9	6.4	43.8	3.5
Hutchinson County	2.2	21.5	15.1	24.8	16.2	22.2	1.1	17.2	18.3	8.4	30.6	13.4	5.2	38.1	4.3
Irion County	3.1	20.1	14.5	29.9	11.9	23.2	6.1	11.0	17.9	22.4	9.5	12.2	8.5	41.0	6.4
Jack County	5.2	23.4	11.9	25.4	19.5	22.3	2.2	15.7	15.0	16.1	13.1	14.7	7.2	40.5	8.4
Jackson County	2.8	24.3	14.1	27.0	15.4	19.6	2.7	15.1	20.1	13.7	25.3	12.2	4.5	40.8	3.6
Jasper County	2.1	23.9	13.4	22.4	16.3	23.9	1.8	16.4	19.3	5.5	26.8	16.0	5.1	40.9	5.7
Jeff Davis County	6.3	24.5	16.7	39.0	19.1	21.3	6.7	8.0	6.9	14.4	7.6	12.7	1.9	55.2	6.0
Jefferson County	1.6	21.9	13.3	28.8	17.6	26.8	0.4	11.4	14.9	1.5	22.0	15.7	5.3	48.9	6.5
Jim Hogg County	1.5	23.8	9.9	22.7	21.0	23.4	1.6	18.4	12.8	14.3	11.5	15.1	6.7	44.0	8.5
Jim Wells County	2.6	22.9	11.2	24.2	20.6	24.2	1.8	15.1	14.1	15.7	12.7	12.9	4.4	47.8	6.6
Johnson County	2.6	20.0	13.7	26.2	12.6	27.5	0.4	14.5	18.8	1.4	29.8	17.1	6.2	41.6	4.0
Jones County	2.8	23.4	11.7	27.7	20.0	21.0	1.8	13.7	14.9	10.5	14.2	14.0	6.8	46.9	6.8
Karnes County	4.0	20.7	9.8	28.7	20.0	20.9	2.4	14.0	14.0	9.5	16.7	14.2	6.2	43.4	10.0
Kaufman County	2.7	19.6	12.6	26.9	13.0	27.0	0.8	15.3	17.1	1.7	26.0	16.0	6.9	44.8	4.6
Kendall County	4.9	16.4	16.1	39.9	14.5	24.6	0.9	12.6	7.4	4.3	17.8	13.9	3.7	56.0	4.3
Kenedy County	9.6	28.3	9.3	38.0	19.3	15.5	20.3	4.8	2.1	48.7	2.1	4.3	2.7	31.0	11.2
Kent County	3.5	22.2	14.9	41.6	12.8	16.0	6.0	14.1	9.4	28.0	11.3	7.3	3.4	41.4	8.6
Kerr County	4.5	25.2	19.2	31.5	19.8	23.8	0.9	13.5	10.5	3.5	18.5	13.8	3.0	57.1	4.0
Kimble County	6.4	25.2	15.0	28.8	17.1	23.1	4.1	13.4	13.6	11.9	21.5	16.5	4.5	40.5	5.0
King County	0.0	17.5	7.6	32.9	14.1	20.1	18.1	8.7	6.0	45.6	8.1	8.1	0.7	17.4	20.1
Kinney County	5.0	22.9	21.1	34.7	20.5	17.6	5.7	13.2	8.3	12.6	10.3	9.2	11.8	45.3	10.7
Kleberg County	1.4	19.9	11.4	31.3	20.0	23.4	2.1	11.7	11.5	7.4	14.3	12.1	5.7	53.4	7.1
Knox County	4.4	21.3	11.2	31.1	18.5	18.5	8.8	13.5	9.6	25.9	9.1	10.6	6.0	42.6	5.7
Lamar County	2.3	24.4	15.1	27.0	17.0	25.0	0.8	11.2	19.1	2.4	25.3	15.4	5.9	46.7	4.2
Lamb County	3.0	23.4	10.2	28.2	14.1	22.5	6.4	11.0	17.9	17.0	18.2	15.2	7.1	38.9	3.6
Lampasas County	3.0	23.8	23.0	30.3	17.9	23.6	1.8	14.5	11.9	5.6	18.4	15.4	3.3	47.5	9.8
La Salle County	3.2	26.9	7.8	19.6	28.3	15.4	6.3	16.9	13.5	15.1	12.9	12.4	3.7	45.7	10.2
Lavaca County	4.9	24.0	13.4	26.3	14.4	21.6	1.6	13.0	23.2	8.1	32.3	12.7	3.7	39.0	4.1
Lee County	5.1	17.9	12.4	27.0	15.7	21.6	1.9	17.5	16.3	11.6	22.7	13.1	7.0	37.4	8.1
Leon County	6.7	23.8	16.0	24.5	19.3	22.9	2.4	14.8	16.1	11.8	21.4	15.4	7.2	37.3	7.0
Liberty County	2.2	22.4	12.8	20.4	15.5	23.5	1.0	18.7	20.9	4.2	28.7	16.3	8.0	38.1	4.7
Limestone County	2.5	25.1	13.2	29.0	21.5	19.4	1.1	12.0	17.1	6.8	17.8	12.6	6.5	49.2	7.2
Lipscomb County	3.9	17.3	11.8	31.7	17.1	19.5	5.2	12.2	14.3	21.6	13.9	11.5	7.5	39.9	5.5
Live Oak County	2.9	24.7	14.7	29.0	18.9	20.2	3.0	14.2	14.7	12.5	17.5	11.6	6.7	41.0	10.6
Llano County	5.3	26.9	22.0	30.3	13.9	26.5	0.6	18.7	9.9	5.7	22.8	14.3	5.9	46.4	4.9
Loving County	0.0	32.8	9.4	26.2	14.3	23.8	0.0	21.4	14.3	28.6	7.1	0.0	16.7	16.7	31.0
Lubbock County	2.4	19.4	10.7	33.2	16.7	29.3	0.6	9.4	10.8	1.9	18.1	14.2	6.6	59.4	4.4
Lynn County	4.1	19.8	8.6	33.5	17.9	21.2	8.8	8.4	10.1	23.0	7.6	10.6	6.6	44.6	7.5
McCulloch County	2.3	22.6	14.8	29.2	17.0	20.1	3.2	10.0	17.0	10.5	10.9	17.9	6.8	42.4	5.6
McLennan County	2.5	20.9	13.3	30.0	16.0	27.6	0.4	10.4	15.5	1.1	21.6	15.6	4.1	53.3	4.3
McMullen County	6.5	25.3	15.3	34.0	9.5	15.9	6.3	17.9	16.4	26.8	16.4	12.1	5.2	28.5	11.0
Madison County	4.6	24.4	12.4	21.4	24.9	22.0	5.9	12.8	13.0	13.4	11.2	15.0	5.5	39.9	14.9
Marion County	2.3	30.9	19.2	23.6	19.7	20.1	1.9	13.8	20.9	4.1	24.1	13.9	6.4	47.0	4.5
Martin County	3.3	14.2	10.2	31.8	16.9	21.9	5.8	11.5	12.1	25.2	8.6	13.5	6.0	40.7	6.0

Table B-3. States and Counties — Education, Labor Force, and Income

STATE County	Median house-hold income	Median family income				Median nonfamily house-hold income	Median income for full-year, full-time workers		Per capita income	Households by source of income (percent)					House-holds with income over $100,000 (percent)	+/- U.S. percent for income over $100,000	House-holds with income below poverty (percent)	Families with children with income below poverty (percent)
		All families	Married-couple	Male house-holder	Female house-holder		Men	Women		With earnings	With interest, dividend, or rental income	With Social Security income	With public assis-tance income	With retire-ment income				
	57	58	59	60	61	62	63	64	65	66	67	68	69	70	71	72	73	74
TEXAS—Cont'd																		
Guadalupe County	43 949	49 645	52 707	25 466	21 530	23 712	35 006	24 760	18 430	83.5	35.3	25.6	2.2	20.6	9.1	-3.2	9.3	10.4
Hale County	31 280	35 250	39 014	24 107	14 459	16 638	26 598	20 647	13 655	81.6	23.2	28.3	4.8	10.9	5.0	-7.3	17.1	19.0
Hall County	23 016	27 325	29 053	9 167	9 135	14 726	23 583	21 307	13 210	69.7	24.7	40.5	2.8	10.2	1.6	-10.7	23.7	36.0
Hamilton County	31 150	39 494	42 500	23 864	15 789	15 600	28 028	20 971	16 800	68.2	34.4	41.9	2.7	19.8	5.8	-6.5	13.9	17.5
Hansford County	35 438	40 281	44 018	23 125	16 429	21 188	30 475	18 203	17 408	79.6	33.7	29.5	1.7	13.3	6.3	-6.0	14.9	18.4
Hardeman County	28 312	33 325	34 327	33 750	12 841	16 741	28 536	19 508	16 824	73.0	33.8	38.0	4.0	17.3	5.2	-7.1	16.6	23.3
Hardin County	37 612	42 890	51 342	29 417	18 619	18 081	36 920	24 224	17 962	78.4	27.7	26.9	2.3	16.8	7.1	-5.2	12.2	11.7
Harris County	42 598	49 004	55 668	29 190	21 552	30 634	38 431	29 795	21 435	87.4	28.0	16.1	2.5	9.6	14.4	2.1	13.1	16.3
Harrison County	33 520	41 112	48 647	24 267	17 626	16 580	33 966	21 577	16 702	76.6	26.9	27.8	3.1	16.0	5.3	-7.0	16.4	17.9
Hartley County	46 327	53 004	51 311	26 667	16 964	25 095	30 887	22 394	18 067	81.6	44.5	28.2	0.4	12.1	11.4	-0.9	6.3	6.7
Haskell County	23 690	29 506	33 750	21 250	15 893	12 188	25 172	17 528	14 918	68.9	29.6	40.6	5.1	14.3	4.4	-7.9	21.4	29.0
Hays County	45 006	56 287	62 740	36 104	28 214	21 885	36 570	28 479	19 931	88.7	33.1	17.5	1.4	12.9	12.9	0.6	14.4	8.3
Hemphill County	35 456	42 036	43 875	28 750	11 250	22 616	32 500	21 207	16 929	82.1	37.3	29.1	2.9	10.4	5.1	-7.2	12.3	15.0
Henderson County	32 533	38 255	43 383	23 904	16 024	17 024	32 425	22 613	17 772	71.6	27.3	37.0	2.3	21.3	6.9	-5.4	15.4	17.3
Hidalgo County	24 863	26 009	26 950	15 198	12 156	14 445	21 805	18 972	9 899	79.0	16.0	25.8	10.8	10.7	4.7	-7.6	31.9	39.1
Hill County	31 600	37 791	44 947	20 000	17 140	14 776	30 409	21 487	15 514	72.9	26.5	35.3	3.3	16.4	4.8	-7.5	15.5	16.9
Hockley County	31 085	35 288	39 651	22 045	15 074	16 627	30 813	21 737	15 022	79.6	24.5	27.0	4.9	12.0	4.9	-7.4	17.1	20.3
Hood County	43 668	50 111	54 400	29 688	20 556	26 331	39 603	25 130	22 261	75.7	37.1	34.5	2.2	23.2	11.5	-0.8	9.0	9.3
Hopkins County	32 136	38 580	44 337	21 815	16 726	14 800	31 038	21 230	17 182	76.9	25.7	30.3	3.1	15.6	6.5	-5.8	15.4	16.0
Houston County	28 119	35 033	45 293	26 667	12 500	14 705	30 991	20 751	14 525	69.3	26.3	37.1	3.7	20.1	4.2	-8.1	20.9	23.3
Howard County	30 805	37 262	43 875	22 813	16 235	16 231	30 477	22 157	15 027	73.0	26.7	34.2	4.0	17.7	5.7	-6.6	18.2	20.2
Hudspeth County	21 045	22 314	26 458	2 499	15 089	13 631	23 454	19 702	9 549	77.4	12.6	26.0	9.5	10.6	3.1	-9.2	32.9	36.9
Hunt County	36 752	44 388	50 855	32 903	17 572	18 176	35 032	24 061	17 554	79.0	27.0	27.4	3.6	16.5	6.8	-5.5	13.0	12.9
Hutchinson County	36 588	42 500	50 310	20 938	13 158	18 785	40 622	21 242	17 317	75.5	34.5	30.7	2.6	16.5	6.1	-6.2	11.4	12.9
Irion County	37 500	45 458	48 750	47 500	23 125	18 438	36 914	21 250	20 515	78.5	34.8	30.1	1.4	13.9	9.4	-2.9	10.0	8.2
Jack County	32 500	37 323	45 143	23 542	19 135	16 731	30 363	20 223	15 210	75.4	28.0	33.0	2.1	13.8	4.5	-7.8	13.5	12.2
Jackson County	35 254	42 066	50 909	21 667	14 154	16 191	34 494	21 250	16 693	74.8	29.6	33.4	2.7	16.6	5.6	-6.7	15.9	16.0
Jasper County	30 902	35 709	43 800	25 500	12 617	13 103	32 069	20 088	15 636	70.7	23.3	34.3	4.3	17.6	4.3	-8.0	18.6	20.5
Jeff Davis County	32 212	39 083	41 761	27 917	13 750	20 625	27 763	21 940	18 846	78.8	33.3	32.3	1.8	16.5	6.3	-6.0	15.2	16.1
Jefferson County	34 706	42 290	53 645	28 851	14 586	20 050	37 794	24 925	17 571	75.2	28.9	28.9	4.2	16.5	8.3	-4.0	16.9	21.3
Jim Hogg County	25 883	29 844	33 447	28 295	5 313	18 750	29 034	20 121	12 185	73.5	15.7	32.9	5.6	11.3	3.7	-8.6	28.5	27.5
Jim Wells County	28 843	32 616	39 282	21 213	11 893	13 105	30 623	17 870	12 252	77.5	18.3	28.7	4.7	13.0	4.3	-8.0	23.1	27.3
Johnson County	44 621	49 963	54 406	32 250	24 316	22 319	37 594	25 997	18 400	83.7	25.6	23.5	2.1	14.3	8.8	-3.5	9.3	9.2
Jones County	29 572	35 391	37 571	22 813	12 898	13 114	28 314	18 699	13 656	74.5	25.3	35.6	3.9	14.8	5.4	-6.9	17.5	18.8
Karnes County	26 526	30 565	43 640	16 442	12 470	15 199	28 594	20 201	13 603	73.1	26.8	36.3	4.5	17.6	4.1	-8.2	21.0	25.2
Kaufman County	44 783	50 354	57 766	27 344	21 480	21 574	36 178	26 923	18 827	83.8	25.0	23.9	3.0	14.8	10.4	-1.9	10.5	10.8
Kendall County	49 521	58 081	62 303	20 729	25 703	24 453	41 902	30 311	24 619	80.3	42.1	26.1	1.4	21.2	17.0	4.7	9.6	11.1
Kenedy County	25 000	26 719	27 500	23 750	19 688	15 417	20 000	15 417	17 959	92.0	14.5	31.2	3.6	19.6	3.6	-8.7	13.8	11.0
Kent County	30 433	35 568	37 625	50 417	4 750	18 750	24 700	21 875	17 626	74.1	29.3	41.3	0.6	17.9	5.4	-6.9	10.8	11.1
Kerr County	34 283	40 713	44 975	20 043	17 232	20 133	28 977	22 015	19 767	65.7	41.9	42.1	2.4	27.3	7.8	-4.5	13.2	17.6
Kimble County	29 396	34 966	36 776	25 938	11 042	16 576	26 667	21 127	17 127	72.3	37.4	39.3	2.3	20.0	5.1	-7.2	18.0	21.3
King County	35 625	36 875	38 958	0		13 750	21 389	31 023	12 321	90.1	14.4	22.5	0.0	8.1	0.0	-12.3	17.1	21.3
Kinney County	28 320	32 045	35 938	17 500	16 667	14 583	27 386	16 397	15 350	59.7	30.2	48.3	4.7	29.2	4.9	-7.4	21.8	26.9
Kleberg County	29 313	33 055	41 783	16 736	10 289	14 156	31 787	20 070	13 542	77.8	22.0	25.1	7.3	14.1	5.8	-6.5	25.5	30.1
Knox County	25 453	30 602	31 724	18 333	14 583	14 009	26 974	21 577	13 443	68.6	28.3	39.1	3.7	12.0	3.2	-9.1	20.8	28.2
Lamar County	31 609	38 359	46 349	22 371	14 437	15 620	31 210	21 622	17 000	74.4	27.6	31.9	3.8	18.0	5.1	-7.2	16.4	18.8
Lamb County	27 898	31 833	35 381	20 833	12 895	17 184	27 093	20 905	15 169	75.7	25.9	34.3	3.3	11.2	4.9	-7.4	18.6	23.2
Lampasas County	36 176	41 395	42 059	21 750	14 352	20 742	32 627	21 492	17 184	79.6	30.2	29.3	3.4	25.1	7.1	-5.2	13.8	15.0
La Salle County	21 857	25 494	31 132	22 500	7 356	13 967	22 652	18 438	9 692	69.4	11.8	35.2	7.0	10.8	2.1	-10.2	30.2	34.6
Lavaca County	29 132	36 760	48 385	16 850	14 591	15 755	27 804	18 805	16 398	71.6	38.1	38.9	2.9	16.3	5.1	-7.2	15.4	14.5
Lee County	36 280	42 073	48 428	19 712	19 330	18 571	31 407	22 446	17 163	79.3	33.0	28.5	1.5	15.3	6.2	-6.1	13.6	12.0
Leon County	30 981	38 029	46 289	28 750	13 661	14 944	34 614	20 392	17 599	68.4	28.0	40.1	2.9	20.0	6.4	-5.9	16.2	18.3
Liberty County	38 361	43 744	49 626	31 685	14 903	16 059	38 811	23 367	15 539	79.1	20.7	27.1	4.1	12.0	6.4	-5.9	14.3	14.9
Limestone County	29 366	36 924	45 190	21 528	14 718	15 680	29 382	19 366	14 352	72.3	23.2	34.4	3.9	19.4	4.1	-8.2	18.0	20.0
Lipscomb County	31 964	39 375	41 417	23 750	11 071	19 798	30 288	21 031	16 328	76.3	36.0	33.9	2.7	13.1	5.8	-6.5	13.9	17.7
Live Oak County	32 057	38 235	46 359	16 827	11 950	19 728	32 355	20 092	15 886	74.4	30.1	35.1	3.3	17.6	5.4	-6.9	15.6	18.9
Llano County	34 830	40 597	39 246	28 056	19 363	22 662	31 859	22 088	23 547	62.0	44.2	48.0	0.9	28.6	9.1	-3.2	9.2	13.8
Loving County	40 000	53 750	33 125	0	0	22 188	45 000		24 084	90.0	46.7	20.0	0.0	30.0	13.3	1.0	0.0	0.0
Lubbock County	32 198	41 067	48 177	21 763	17 220	18 022	30 775	22 185	17 323	83.4	28.2	22.5	3.1	12.4	7.0	-5.3	18.1	17.9
Lynn County	26 694	33 146	39 405	16 563	11 625	13 568	29 505	20 179	14 090	77.9	23.9	30.1	2.8	10.7	6.1	-6.2	23.0	24.5
McCulloch County	25 705	30 783	31 484	14 118	15 743	12 464	26 377	19 306	14 579	69.3	23.6	39.1	3.9	15.2	2.8	-9.5	23.2	26.5
McLennan County	33 560	41 414	49 626	25 351	16 138	17 800	31 732	22 739	17 174	80.8	29.4	26.1	3.0	15.4	7.5	-4.8	17.6	17.6
McMullen County	32 500	35 417	37 500	41 250	21 250	21 364	29 688	21 953	22 258	72.9	36.9	33.2	0.6	16.2	8.4	-3.9	17.9	21.6
Madison County	29 418	35 779	43 514	11 500	19 271	17 750	26 112	20 386	14 056	70.5	26.4	36.8	4.0	17.9	5.9	-6.4	16.1	17.8
Marion County	25 347	32 039	41 290	28 000	10 722	12 382	31 204	18 662	14 535	68.3	22.6	39.9	4.2	23.3	4.0	-8.3	22.3	28.4
Martin County	31 836	35 965	36 619	25 625	11 875	15 560	30 352	19 770	15 647	77.1	25.7	28.9	3.5	12.3	6.3	-6.0	18.7	21.1

Table B-3. States and Counties — **Education, Labor Force, and Income**

			High school graduates			College graduates		College graduates (percent)				
STATE/ County code	MSA/PMSA/ NECMA code[1]	STATE County	Total population 25 years and over	Percent with a high school diploma or less	Percent with a high school diploma or more	Percent with a bachelor's degree or more	+/− U.S. percent with bachelor's degree or more	Non-Hispanic White	Black or African American	American Indian and Alaska Native	Asian, Hawaiian, and Pacific Islander	Hispanic or Latino[2]
			1	2	3	4	5	6	7	8	9	10
		TEXAS—Cont'd										
48 319	...	Mason County	2 701	49.7	78.1	18.7	-5.7	21.4	0.0	35.1	X	2.9
48 321	...	Matagorda County	23 509	60.9	70.3	12.5	-11.9	17.6	8.1	15.4	14.3	2.1
48 323	...	Maverick County	25 468	76.7	42.1	9.1	-15.3	33.0	17.1	2.9	25.2	8.0
48 325	...	Medina County	24 629	61.2	72.2	13.3	-11.1	19.5	0.4	23.1	29.6	5.3
48 327	...	Menard County	1 660	61.6	69.4	17.2	-7.2	23.0	42.9	0.0	100.0	1.1
48 329	5800	Midland County	71 008	43.8	79.2	24.8	0.4	32.1	10.4	21.9	50.0	6.0
48 331	...	Milam County	15 641	66.1	70.9	11.6	-12.8	14.1	3.4	16.5	0.0	2.4
48 333	...	Mills County	3 582	59.2	76.7	20.2	-4.2	21.6	50.0	80.0	X	2.5
48 335	...	Mitchell County	6 634	69.3	71.7	10.4	-14.0	16.6	0.4	5.0	0.0	2.7
48 337	...	Montague County	13 208	62.4	73.0	11.3	-13.1	11.4	0.0	4.4	43.5	5.5
48 339	3360	Montgomery County	183 743	45.8	81.6	25.3	0.9	27.1	15.4	14.5	50.0	11.3
48 341	...	Moore County	11 460	66.4	62.1	11.0	-13.4	16.7	0.0	0.0	34.8	1.2
48 343	...	Morris County	8 776	60.7	73.7	11.2	-13.2	13.6	4.1	11.5	21.7	4.5
48 345	...	Motley County	987	60.2	73.5	14.7	-9.7	16.1	0.0	100.0	X	3.9
48 347	...	Nacogdoches County	33 175	53.6	73.7	22.8	-1.6	27.3	8.6	10.5	61.1	5.3
48 349	...	Navarro County	28 324	61.0	71.7	12.2	-12.2	15.0	4.2	31.3	26.0	3.6
48 351	...	Newton County	9 738	76.7	68.7	5.5	-18.9	5.5	4.8	0.0	68.0	5.1
48 353	...	Nolan County	10 203	62.2	69.9	13.2	-11.2	17.2	4.8	0.0	10.6	1.7
48 355	1880	Nueces County	191 848	50.7	74.4	18.8	-5.6	29.3	13.8	11.5	43.2	9.4
48 357	...	Ochiltree County	5 441	58.2	69.2	16.1	-8.3	19.9	X	26.2	0.0	3.7
48 359	...	Oldham County	1 250	46.6	80.5	19.4	-5.0	19.4	80.0	0.0	X	17.1
48 361	0840	Orange County	54 229	59.7	79.0	11.0	-13.4	11.3	7.3	3.4	19.4	6.4
48 363	...	Palo Pinto County	17 764	60.5	71.2	12.1	-12.3	13.4	4.2	2.9	9.0	1.9
48 365	...	Panola County	14 848	58.9	75.9	13.4	-11.0	15.7	4.6	0.0	0.0	0.5
48 367	2800	Parker County	57 072	49.9	80.5	18.6	-5.8	19.7	4.9	16.4	18.1	4.9
48 369	...	Parmer County	5 868	64.7	60.7	13.4	-11.0	22.0	0.0	15.6	27.3	1.4
48 371	...	Pecos County	9 870	66.9	62.5	12.9	-11.5	22.9	9.3	25.0	8.6	6.2
48 373	...	Polk County	28 453	66.5	70.0	10.4	-14.0	12.1	2.2	2.3	44.8	5.3
48 375	0320	Potter County	69 427	58.2	71.1	13.5	-10.9	17.8	5.6	10.0	16.5	3.6
48 377	...	Presidio County	4 303	75.2	44.7	11.7	-12.7	34.5	28.6	60.0	44.0	6.0
48 379	...	Rains County	6 298	64.5	73.0	11.5	-12.9	11.7	7.6	12.1	47.6	2.7
48 381	0320	Randall County	65 628	33.8	89.5	28.9	4.5	30.3	14.5	26.5	16.7	12.8
48 383	...	Reagan County	1 955	66.9	63.0	9.2	-15.2	15.1	0.0	31.6	0.0	0.5
48 385	...	Real County	2 150	55.3	73.0	17.3	-7.1	19.7	0.0	0.0	0.0	6.3
48 387	...	Red River County	9 801	68.0	65.7	9.0	-15.4	10.2	4.2	1.5	88.9	0.9
48 389	...	Reeves County	7 692	78.2	46.6	8.0	-16.4	22.0	5.6	5.4	68.6	2.2
48 391	...	Refugio County	5 178	64.4	68.1	11.6	-12.8	19.1	0.6	16.7	0.0	3.4
48 393	...	Roberts County	623	38.5	90.0	25.4	1.0	25.4	X	X	0.0	0.0
48 395	...	Robertson County	10 218	67.8	68.1	12.7	-11.7	16.5	6.4	0.0	0.0	1.7
48 397	1920	Rockwall County	27 113	36.2	86.7	32.7	8.3	34.8	27.4	37.1	41.4	10.0
48 399	...	Runnels County	7 723	66.3	68.9	13.1	-11.3	15.9	0.0	25.4	12.5	3.1
48 401	...	Rusk County	31 843	58.9	74.1	12.8	-11.6	15.8	3.8	28.4	24.3	1.5
48 403	...	Sabine County	7 676	65.2	72.5	10.6	-13.8	10.9	7.6	18.8	50.0	4.5
48 405	...	San Augustine County ..	6 221	68.7	69.9	11.8	-12.6	14.0	5.3	27.8	0.0	6.8
48 407	...	San Jacinto County	15 040	66.0	72.6	9.6	-14.8	10.4	4.9	50.0	0.0	1.9
48 409	1880	San Patricio County	39 551	58.4	71.4	13.0	-11.4	19.2	13.1	13.0	22.2	5.7
48 411	...	San Saba County	3 997	61.2	70.0	15.8	-8.6	18.2	0.0	15.4	33.3	3.4
48 413	...	Schleicher County	1 913	60.2	60.4	17.6	-6.8	26.3	0.0	0.0	80.0	2.3
48 415	...	Scurry County	10 632	59.6	72.3	11.8	-12.6	15.3	5.6	0.0	43.3	1.6
48 417	...	Shackelford County	2 221	53.4	79.2	20.8	-3.6	21.8	0.0	0.0	66.7	5.1
48 419	...	Shelby County	16 266	66.6	68.9	12.2	-12.2	14.8	4.2	8.3	24.5	3.7
48 421	...	Sherman County	1 968	53.8	73.1	20.4	-4.0	25.6	25.0	0.0	0.0	2.8
48 423	8640	Smith County	111 020	44.6	80.2	22.5	-1.9	26.9	11.2	17.9	47.6	3.4
48 425	...	Somervell County	4 372	54.4	78.0	17.2	-7.2	18.9	0.0	28.0	14.3	0.9
48 427	...	Starr County	27 716	82.2	34.7	6.9	-17.5	26.0	34.6	0.0	79.8	6.2
48 429	...	Stephens County	6 471	57.0	72.3	13.4	-11.0	14.2	17.7	0.0	46.9	0.0
48 431	...	Sterling County	916	57.5	70.4	17.1	-7.3	23.0	X	0.0	X	2.0
48 433	...	Stonewall County	1 211	66.9	71.0	12.6	-11.8	14.1	5.7	0.0	X	2.8
48 435	...	Sutton County	2 632	65.4	64.4	13.0	-11.4	21.4	X	0.0	82.4	3.0
48 437	...	Swisher County	5 200	61.3	69.7	16.2	-8.2	23.6	0.0	13.6	0.0	1.5
48 439	2800	Tarrant County	898 850	42.2	81.3	26.6	2.2	31.7	17.1	18.5	35.9	9.6
48 441	0040	Taylor County	75 496	47.2	81.2	22.5	-1.9	25.9	15.3	13.4	27.2	6.5
48 443	...	Terrell County	736	56.5	70.9	19.0	-5.4	31.9	X	0.0	X	4.7
48 445	...	Terry County	8 008	69.3	62.5	9.5	-14.9	15.0	2.1	0.0	100.0	0.6
48 447	...	Throckmorton County	1 272	56.1	77.4	18.2	-6.2	19.4	X	0.0	X	1.4
48 449	...	Titus County	16 899	63.9	65.5	13.2	-11.2	16.9	8.8	17.9	40.0	2.1

[1] MSA = Metropolitan Statistical Area. PMSA = Primary MSA. NECMA = New England County Metropolitan Area. See the Appendix A for explanation of these concepts. See Appendix B for list of metropolitan areas identified by type, with component counties.
[2] Hispanic or Latino persons may be of any race.

Items 1—10

Table B-3. States and Counties — Education, Labor Force, and Income

STATE County	School enrollment			Population 16 to 19 years				Employment status, 2000			Work status in 1999 of the population 16 years and over (percent)	
											Worked in 1999	
	Grades kindergarten through 12	College or graduate school	Percent private	Number	Percent in armed forces	Percent high school graduates	Percent not enrolled, not grads, not in armed forces, not employed	Total population 16 years and over	Percent in labor force	Unemployment rate	Full-time	Part-time	Did not work in 1999
	11	12	13	14	15	16	17	18	19	20	21	22	23
TEXAS—Cont'd													
Mason County	666	44	4.9	182	0.0	7.7	8.8	3 005	57.5	1.6	47.6	13.7	38.7
Matagorda County	8 924	932	6.2	2 573	0.0	12.5	8.0	28 036	58.6	8.4	51.7	12.2	36.1
Maverick County	13 100	1 552	2.8	3 350	0.0	7.0	13.9	31 546	50.7	17.6	46.2	11.1	42.7
Medina County	8 698	1 529	5.6	2 431	0.0	10.8	4.9	29 296	58.6	5.2	55.6	11.5	32.9
Menard County	482	33	1.6	150	0.0	9.3	4.0	1 887	54.8	3.5	45.7	13.0	41.3
Midland County	26 914	5 824	11.0	7 590	0.0	9.4	5.4	85 018	64.3	5.4	55.3	14.0	30.8
Milam County	5 256	647	4.2	1 463	0.0	13.3	2.6	18 489	58.5	4.7	50.8	11.5	37.7
Mills County	1 050	57	2.7	284	0.0	8.1	7.4	4 009	55.1	2.6	47.4	11.6	41.0
Mitchell County	1 662	248	4.2	723	0.0	15.6	19.4	8 075	37.8	3.8	51.8	8.3	39.9
Montague County	3 510	446	2.8	1 067	0.0	15.1	9.0	15 100	56.8	5.6	49.7	11.7	38.6
Montgomery County	63 588	11 460	8.7	17 271	0.1	10.0	6.3	217 285	65.9	4.5	59.0	12.2	28.8
Moore County	4 854	612	1.8	1 300	0.0	18.0	6.4	14 089	63.8	4.3	56.9	13.3	29.9
Morris County	2 607	419	3.3	741	0.0	14.2	6.2	10 107	54.2	6.5	48.1	9.9	42.0
Motley County	241	28	13.0	80	0.0	13.8	2.5	1 135	56.5	2.2	48.0	15.1	36.9
Nacogdoches County	10 692	9 575	4.7	5 187	0.0	6.0	3.2	46 592	61.7	10.7	49.1	18.6	32.3
Navarro County	9 301	2 132	5.5	3 172	0.0	6.7	8.0	34 222	58.6	7.8	52.5	11.6	35.8
Newton County	3 083	214	6.3	1 053	0.0	16.2	11.5	11 657	50.1	10.5	45.6	9.6	44.8
Nolan County	3 396	559	2.0	999	0.0	14.3	3.9	12 020	57.1	6.4	50.0	11.6	38.4
Nueces County	67 291	18 244	6.6	20 381	0.6	10.6	7.3	234 965	61.9	7.5	53.2	13.7	33.0
Ochiltree County	2 020	178	3.5	477	0.0	6.7	6.1	6 519	66.7	4.6	59.3	13.0	27.7
Oldham County	641	57	3.3	195	0.0	5.6	3.6	1 551	67.8	6.9	56.4	14.0	29.6
Orange County	17 626	2 925	6.2	5 240	0.0	12.0	4.4	64 730	59.9	7.9	51.4	12.1	36.5
Palo Pinto County	5 296	610	3.6	1 644	0.0	10.0	11.4	20 936	60.4	5.1	52.8	11.2	36.0
Panola County	4 667	831	5.1	1 545	0.0	8.9	2.7	17 727	54.7	6.4	47.4	11.8	40.8
Parker County	18 732	3 105	7.7	5 353	0.0	10.8	6.1	66 893	65.0	4.2	59.5	11.6	28.9
Parmer County	2 689	280	3.3	677	0.0	9.3	5.5	7 063	57.6	5.3	54.3	11.2	34.5
Pecos County	3 906	787	4.8	1 395	0.0	18.6	10.7	12 793	50.5	5.7	50.0	11.1	38.9
Polk County	7 149	1 496	5.3	1 972	0.1	9.8	9.0	32 924	45.6	6.7	46.2	10.0	43.8
Potter County	22 798	5 877	6.5	7 166	0.0	14.0	15.2	85 201	59.1	7.0	53.6	12.5	33.9
Presidio County	1 869	164	1.3	512	0.0	8.4	12.1	5 181	53.3	13.0	47.3	10.5	42.2
Rains County	1 696	216	4.5	548	0.0	16.4	4.4	7 243	57.7	6.1	51.3	10.2	38.5
Randall County	19 793	9 190	7.7	6 773	0.1	11.7	2.3	80 508	71.0	4.2	59.9	16.1	24.0
Reagan County	910	40	0.0	251	0.0	5.6	0.0	2 356	61.7	3.3	53.1	12.2	34.7
Real County	596	95	2.7	172	0.0	11.0	4.1	2 415	50.3	3.6	44.3	9.8	46.0
Red River County	2 610	306	4.0	860	0.0	12.3	8.8	11 329	55.8	5.9	47.4	12.3	40.2
Reeves County	3 116	297	1.1	825	0.0	9.9	7.0	9 675	49.9	12.4	46.3	12.4	41.3
Refugio County	1 640	166	2.2	492	0.0	12.0	4.5	6 045	56.4	4.9	49.4	11.9	38.7
Roberts County	184	25	3.8	54	0.0	0.0	3.7	701	66.5	1.3	61.3	9.7	29.0
Robertson County	3 339	368	4.9	925	0.0	16.5	12.3	11 951	56.4	6.2	50.8	10.0	39.2
Rockwall County	9 821	1 854	9.6	2 275	0.0	9.5	3.9	31 459	69.9	1.8	63.1	12.2	24.8
Runnels County	2 481	227	3.7	681	0.0	8.4	5.0	8 849	55.2	5.7	49.9	10.7	39.5
Rusk County	9 081	1 715	7.2	2 579	0.0	11.4	6.9	36 919	53.9	5.5	49.5	10.5	39.9
Sabine County	1 747	188	5.6	471	0.0	5.5	4.7	8 568	41.9	9.2	37.9	8.4	53.7
San Augustine County	1 657	178	2.4	421	1.2	10.7	1.7	7 084	48.8	6.9	42.3	10.1	47.5
San Jacinto County	4 384	386	6.8	1 249	0.0	11.4	7.7	17 290	52.2	7.5	47.5	10.4	42.1
San Patricio County	15 739	2 740	4.4	4 600	3.3	15.5	7.7	48 789	59.0	6.6	53.2	12.4	34.4
San Saba County	1 329	136	3.3	640	0.0	12.7	28.1	4 840	52.0	3.7	47.5	11.9	40.6
Schleicher County	669	75	0.0	180	0.0	9.4	3.3	2 222	58.6	1.8	50.6	14.8	34.6
Scurry County	3 247	704	1.7	1 306	0.0	10.4	15.0	12 796	53.5	6.0	50.6	12.7	36.7
Shackelford County	732	82	3.9	182	0.0	9.9	1.1	2 529	58.2	1.8	51.6	14.6	33.8
Shelby County	5 129	653	4.2	1 477	0.0	11.0	9.6	19 314	53.5	5.2	46.9	10.0	43.0
Sherman County	774	95	5.1	193	0.0	8.3	5.7	2 308	62.3	4.5	57.3	12.3	30.4
Smith County	34 152	9 012	9.7	11 093	0.0	11.7	5.8	133 774	62.0	6.5	53.8	12.8	33.4
Somervell County	1 502	263	5.3	385	0.0	8.8	2.3	5 099	64.1	4.7	56.9	12.3	30.8
Starr County	14 828	2 009	2.1	4 069	0.0	7.0	13.0	35 749	47.3	20.9	40.4	12.9	46.7
Stephens County	1 944	346	5.2	599	0.0	6.3	12.5	7 619	53.5	3.7	50.4	13.0	36.5
Sterling County	336	42	5.8	84	0.0	11.9	0.0	1 047	61.8	2.0	52.8	13.2	34.0
Stonewall County	312	23	8.1	115	0.0	13.9	0.0	1 386	53.3	3.0	47.1	11.7	41.2
Sutton County	937	63	2.4	241	0.0	6.6	3.3	3 054	62.9	3.5	53.6	12.9	33.5
Swisher County	1 823	193	5.2	499	0.0	13.4	8.6	6 322	55.9	5.8	53.1	12.7	34.2
Tarrant County	291 485	78 661	12.9	81 998	0.1	11.4	6.9	1 082 374	69.5	4.5	62.7	12.7	24.6
Taylor County	25 143	10 826	24.3	9 283	3.0	14.0	4.9	96 805	66.7	7.7	55.1	16.3	28.6
Terrell County	249	17	9.4	70	0.0	8.6	2.9	832	59.1	5.3	47.8	14.9	37.3
Terry County	2 833	304	2.5	874	0.0	15.1	5.1	9 616	52.5	5.7	51.3	11.6	37.1
Throckmorton County	386	38	0.9	122	0.0	6.6	1.6	1 455	61.0	4.4	51.7	14.2	34.1
Titus County	6 333	929	3.1	1 766	0.0	10.8	7.2	20 526	58.3	5.8	52.8	9.8	37.4

Table B-3. States and Counties — Education, Labor Force, and Income

STATE County	Full-year full-time employed (percent)								Children under 18 years in families						Total employed by class of worker (percent)			
										With two parents (percent)		With one parent who is in labor force (percent)	+/- U.S. percent of children with no stay-at-home parent (percent)	+/- U.S. percent two-income couples				
	Total	Men	Women	Non-Hispanic White	Black or African American	American Indian and Alaska Native	Asian, Hawaiian, and Pacific Islander	Hispanic or Latino[1]	Number	Both in labor force	Father only in labor force				Private	Government	Self-employed	Unpaid family worker
	24	25	26	27	28	29	30	31	32	33	34	35	36	37	38	39	40	41
TEXAS—Cont'd																		
Mason County	32.9	43.3	23.5	33.7	50.0	24.5	X	29.5	803	59.7	20.8	11.2	6.3	-4.6	50.6	19.4	27.7	2.3
Matagorda County	34.1	43.2	25.5	37.3	25.0	40.0	26.3	32.3	10 634	39.7	27.8	17.5	-7.4	-10.3	72.9	16.1	10.5	0.5
Maverick County	22.5	31.3	15.0	39.7	29.3	11.3	42.4	21.8	16 662	30.3	30.5	14.4	-19.9	-23.2	67.1	23.2	9.4	0.4
Medina County	39.5	47.6	30.9	41.1	32.2	32.8	36.1	38.0	10 792	45.8	21.0	17.5	-1.3	-1.9	68.4	19.1	12.1	0.4
Menard County	29.3	36.3	22.7	31.3	0.0	37.5	50.0	24.4	545	37.4	17.2	24.8	-2.4	-7.0	58.5	22.3	18.1	1.1
Midland County	40.7	52.4	30.2	43.4	34.9	37.9	35.0	35.2	33 187	41.4	28.6	18.9	-4.3	-2.7	72.9	13.9	12.8	0.4
Milam County	37.1	49.3	26.1	38.1	26.9	21.6	60.0	38.1	6 152	44.7	20.1	20.2	0.3	-4.6	70.3	14.3	14.3	1.1
Mills County	35.6	45.3	25.8	35.9	21.4	0.0	X	32.9	1 107	43.4	26.3	18.5	-2.7	-5.6	56.6	18.7	23.5	1.3
Mitchell County	24.2	23.1	26.0	28.3	7.2	30.0	10.7	25.0	1 736	32.9	31.0	21.8	-9.9	-9.2	57.1	31.3	10.6	1.0
Montague County	35.4	47.6	24.5	35.6	9.6	25.9	62.5	34.8	4 293	45.7	25.3	18.2	-0.7	-7.6	67.4	15.7	15.9	0.9
Montgomery County	44.5	58.5	31.3	45.6	36.4	41.6	44.8	39.7	82 129	41.9	33.4	14.8	-7.9	-2.5	77.5	11.3	10.8	0.4
Moore County	40.6	55.3	26.3	42.2	27.5	42.7	64.1	38.0	6 396	44.0	23.7	17.3	-3.3	-1.0	76.2	12.9	10.3	0.5
Morris County	33.5	42.6	25.5	35.0	28.6	42.3	52.2	35.1	2 976	39.9	19.3	27.5	2.8	-9.1	74.0	14.4	11.1	0.5
Motley County	34.4	45.8	24.2	35.6	28.6	0.0	X	31.1	303	50.2	22.8	15.2	0.8	-3.5	50.2	22.8	24.9	2.1
Nacogdoches County	32.3	40.6	25.1	33.7	26.5	37.1	32.6	29.4	13 078	41.3	19.8	22.5	-0.8	-1.1	66.7	22.0	10.8	0.5
Navarro County	37.3	45.0	30.0	39.8	28.4	35.8	23.2	35.3	11 487	37.3	21.6	21.9	-5.4	-4.4	73.9	15.6	9.8	0.7
Newton County	28.7	36.9	20.1	30.1	25.0	31.1	20.0	22.3	3 627	35.4	28.4	20.6	-8.6	-19.0	70.3	18.8	10.3	0.5
Nolan County	35.8	46.9	25.7	37.8	26.6	0.0	20.8	32.5	4 027	41.9	20.3	21.0	-1.7	-3.0	66.8	19.4	13.0	0.7
Nueces County	37.5	47.2	28.4	40.9	32.6	40.0	43.9	35.1	82 197	35.7	22.3	24.6	-4.3	-4.9	71.2	18.3	10.1	0.4
Ochiltree County	43.7	58.0	29.8	45.3	X	36.1	73.9	39.0	2 688	44.9	29.6	14.7	-5.0	1.4	71.3	9.8	18.4	0.4
Oldham County	42.3	52.9	32.0	43.1	50.0	54.5	X	33.9	508	55.7	29.7	11.4	2.5	-0.1	65.0	19.0	15.1	0.8
Orange County	36.6	47.3	26.6	37.1	29.7	39.3	34.8	41.4	21 674	40.8	26.9	20.8	-3.0	-9.4	79.7	11.3	8.5	0.4
Palo Pinto County	39.4	48.1	31.2	39.8	29.4	43.0	46.4	37.8	6 285	45.4	18.1	23.4	4.2	-3.0	71.9	14.8	12.9	0.4
Panola County	32.4	45.0	21.3	32.9	29.5	27.3	54.5	32.6	5 559	37.6	32.8	15.7	-11.3	-10.9	71.9	16.0	11.4	0.7
Parker County	45.0	55.5	34.3	45.9	19.4	51.7	46.2	39.1	23 149	48.6	26.7	18.4	2.4	2.3	73.4	12.5	13.6	0.5
Parmer County	34.2	40.6	19.9	37.0	23.6	20.0	13.6	30.4	3 179	41.9	28.6	11.5	-11.2	-7.5	68.3	15.6	15.8	0.3
Pecos County	33.0	38.6	25.7	39.6	18.4	54.8	54.3	30.2	4 206	38.8	27.0	16.5	-9.3	-7.1	63.3	27.7	8.5	0.5
Polk County	28.3	32.7	23.5	29.0	22.1	33.1	57.7	28.6	8 442	39.6	24.8	19.1	-5.9	-16.3	66.6	21.2	11.6	0.6
Potter County	36.8	44.2	29.6	38.3	29.0	36.7	43.1	35.0	29 670	35.5	22.1	28.1	-1.0	-4.2	76.6	13.0	10.0	0.4
Presidio County	26.1	34.9	18.3	40.5	0.0	0.0	16.0	23.4	2 205	32.4	30.6	18.3	-13.9	-16.9	58.7	32.7	8.4	0.3
Rains County	36.8	45.8	27.7	37.0	34.7	51.5	48.0	32.8	2 057	42.7	26.9	15.1	-6.8	-8.6	65.1	15.5	19.1	0.3
Randall County	46.5	57.9	36.0	46.4	51.7	42.7	32.8	50.1	25 590	52.6	23.6	17.9	5.9	7.0	70.8	17.6	11.2	0.4
Reagan County	38.4	52.3	23.9	41.7	16.9	26.3	100.0	35.1	1 077	49.0	29.6	9.7	-5.9	-3.3	61.1	21.8	15.9	1.2
Real County	29.2	35.1	23.5	28.2	100.0	33.3	100.0	32.1	674	44.1	23.3	21.4	0.9	-12.1	54.6	20.8	23.5	1.1
Red River County	34.9	46.2	24.7	34.5	33.9	53.5	0.0	44.5	3 096	42.7	20.2	22.5	0.6	-8.0	70.2	15.5	13.3	0.9
Reeves County	28.0	34.4	20.8	31.9	19.0	22.7	51.4	26.4	3 654	28.2	26.6	24.2	-12.2	-14.9	69.6	22.2	8.0	0.2
Refugio County	35.6	46.7	25.3	37.5	25.4	50.0	28.6	34.9	1 856	43.9	19.9	19.1	-1.6	-5.7	71.4	18.5	9.7	0.4
Roberts County	49.6	62.6	36.2	49.5	X	X	0.0	66.7	209	70.8	23.4	5.7	11.9	10.2	54.6	23.3	20.4	1.7
Robertson County	35.9	45.3	27.6	39.3	25.7	33.3	44.0	38.1	4 189	38.3	17.1	23.3	-3.0	-3.9	65.1	22.2	11.6	1.0
Rockwall County	51.2	65.7	37.2	51.4	50.9	79.2	46.1	49.7	12 491	48.1	31.7	15.1	-1.4	5.0	72.9	12.3	14.3	0.5
Runnels County	34.2	46.5	23.5	35.4	42.2	21.5	53.8	29.7	2 909	46.0	20.0	20.1	1.5	-1.9	63.6	18.8	16.8	0.8
Rusk County	34.1	41.2	26.9	36.2	26.1	35.2	32.2	32.4	11 009	42.3	27.1	19.5	-2.8	-6.8	74.8	13.1	11.6	0.4
Sabine County	23.1	29.5	17.2	23.3	21.0	23.8	100.0	28.5	2 048	40.5	24.1	15.4	-8.7	-23.7	67.8	16.8	14.9	0.6
San Augustine County	28.7	36.5	21.7	26.2	32.7	27.8	100.0	45.5	1 901	31.6	27.9	20.8	-12.2	-16.4	67.6	17.4	14.5	0.5
San Jacinto County	32.2	41.3	23.5	32.7	27.7	8.9	39.7	32.6	5 248	39.9	27.6	16.5	-8.2	-16.6	64.1	21.1	14.2	0.6
San Patricio County	36.5	47.5	25.7	40.9	36.9	32.2	22.4	32.3	19 589	37.8	25.5	19.4	-7.4	-7.9	70.7	18.5	10.1	0.6
San Saba County	31.4	40.6	21.7	32.3	1.9	18.2	33.3	31.9	1 322	47.0	27.6	14.3	-3.3	-3.3	52.9	26.4	19.4	1.2
Schleicher County	35.6	47.0	24.7	40.9	34.6	33.3	0.0	28.7	781	46.4	20.1	17.7	-0.5	2.5	58.1	21.3	18.4	2.2
Scurry County	34.2	40.2	27.8	36.7	21.2	36.7	12.8	30.0	3 879	44.5	24.3	24.3	4.2	-2.2	64.3	22.8	12.5	0.4
Shackelford County	38.6	52.7	26.6	38.8	0.0	18.2	66.7	35.0	845	53.8	22.0	16.2	5.4	1.5	60.5	21.1	17.7	0.8
Shelby County	33.0	43.8	23.3	32.7	32.2	27.7	43.5	38.1	5 911	33.1	28.8	21.7	-9.8	-9.3	70.4	14.2	14.6	0.9
Sherman County	41.9	56.8	27.2	44.2	50.0	50.0	0.0	34.7	935	40.3	31.7	14.2	-10.1	-4.7	60.9	17.7	20.3	1.1
Smith County	39.4	50.3	29.7	40.1	36.0	47.9	49.0	40.4	43 457	41.3	24.0	22.3	-1.0	-3.5	75.9	12.2	11.5	0.4
Somervell County	42.1	55.7	29.2	42.2	0.0	30.0	33.3	42.0	1 803	50.9	26.8	15.9	2.2	1.9	70.1	16.8	12.2	0.8
Starr County	13.4	18.0	9.3	25.8	20.9	6.5	28.8	13.1	18 759	26.4	29.1	14.5	-23.7	-26.8	61.1	27.9	10.0	1.0
Stephens County	36.0	44.5	27.4	36.9	12.2	66.7	55.1	34.9	2 201	45.9	19.9	19.8	1.1	-5.5	67.0	17.5	14.8	0.7
Sterling County	40.6	57.6	24.1	40.1	X	0.0	X	42.1	380	45.0	35.8	12.6	-7.0	0.3	54.3	22.1	22.2	1.4
Stonewall County	33.8	47.0	21.6	35.8	15.2	0.0	X	29.7	343	42.9	25.1	14.3	-7.4	-8.9	61.9	19.8	18.0	0.3
Sutton County	36.8	49.0	24.5	43.1	0.0	100.0	66.7	30.0	1 131	47.2	26.4	14.8	-2.6	-2.8	66.9	15.2	17.1	0.8
Swisher County	37.1	48.4	24.6	39.7	20.8	86.4	33.3	35.2	2 214	50.4	24.7	17.6	3.4	-2.7	61.9	19.5	17.6	1.1
Tarrant County	47.3	57.9	37.2	49.8	43.9	44.6	42.5	41.3	382 076	41.4	24.8	20.9	-2.3	3.2	80.5	11.1	8.2	0.2
Taylor County	39.4	49.7	30.1	39.8	38.4	38.1	43.6	38.6	31 493	47.6	20.0	21.9	4.9	1.8	72.0	17.7	9.9	0.4
Terrell County	37.4	52.2	22.7	40.0	X	100.0	X	34.3	265	49.1	24.5	23.4	7.9	-8.3	46.4	29.6	23.2	0.9
Terry County	32.6	42.5	21.8	37.0	12.3	53.7	57.7	28.9	3 306	41.0	28.3	13.4	-10.2	-5.8	65.7	19.5	13.9	0.9
Throckmorton County	36.7	50.1	24.1	35.7	X	0.0	X	53.4	459	61.4	12.2	15.3	12.1	-0.4	53.2	27.2	18.3	1.3
Titus County	38.0	48.5	28.1	38.1	28.4	25.6	49.1	42.1	7 907	36.8	23.7	20.3	-7.5	-5.8	75.5	13.3	11.0	0.3

[1]Hispanic or Latino persons may be of any race.

Table B-3. States and Counties — Education, Labor Force, and Income

STATE County	Percent who worked at home	Percent of the population 5 years and over with a disability	Veterans as a percent of the population 18 years and over	Occupation for employed population 16 years and over (percent)						Industry for employed population 16 years and over (percent)					
				Management, professional, and related occupations	Service occupations	Sales and office occupations	Farming, fishing, and forestry occupations	Construction, extraction, and maintenance occupations	Production, transportation and material moving occupations	Agriculture, forestry, fishing, and mining	Construction and manufacturing	Wholesale and retail trade	Transportation and warehousing, and utilities	Service industries	Public administration
	42	43	44	45	46	47	48	49	50	51	52	53	54	55	56
TEXAS—Cont'd															
Mason County	11.7	25.1	13.9	35.6	15.3	19.3	4.8	16.0	8.9	17.8	13.9	12.0	5.3	47.1	4.0
Matagorda County	1.8	20.3	12.8	26.5	16.6	21.1	3.9	16.7	15.2	8.1	22.8	13.8	11.5	38.9	5.0
Maverick County	2.1	20.7	5.0	21.5	21.4	23.7	2.2	10.7	20.5	3.8	16.9	16.7	9.6	45.4	7.6
Medina County	3.0	19.9	15.5	27.2	17.0	24.8	1.9	15.9	13.2	5.6	18.3	15.1	5.6	48.3	7.1
Menard County	5.4	25.5	16.5	31.0	19.0	18.6	4.2	11.4	15.7	17.3	16.3	11.8	3.9	42.0	8.6
Midland County	2.4	16.4	11.9	34.9	15.4	28.2	0.2	11.0	10.4	13.6	11.3	15.6	4.8	50.8	3.8
Milam County	3.2	20.6	15.5	23.3	16.3	23.1	2.0	16.2	19.0	7.6	27.5	15.0	5.1	39.7	5.2
Mills County	6.5	23.5	14.7	32.1	15.9	19.0	6.9	13.2	13.0	17.5	15.5	13.0	4.2	43.8	6.0
Mitchell County	1.9	22.6	13.0	26.0	26.5	19.6	1.5	12.6	13.6	12.5	9.9	8.8	7.4	46.8	14.6
Montague County	4.0	22.1	15.8	25.7	16.8	21.4	1.5	14.1	20.4	10.6	23.1	13.4	7.3	41.6	3.9
Montgomery County	3.3	17.6	13.1	33.9	12.7	28.1	0.3	12.5	12.4	3.5	21.6	17.6	7.9	45.8	3.6
Moore County	1.8	16.4	9.3	19.6	17.6	17.6	3.4	12.2	29.5	8.5	35.3	11.7	7.0	33.8	3.6
Morris County	2.1	24.6	15.3	23.4	16.4	22.9	1.8	11.0	24.5	4.7	29.9	13.9	7.5	40.4	3.5
Motley County	5.3	22.7	15.4	34.0	16.1	20.7	8.5	10.7	10.0	21.4	15.5	14.5	5.6	36.4	6.7
Nacogdoches County	2.9	20.0	10.7	29.7	17.8	25.9	2.1	9.3	15.2	5.1	19.6	16.0	3.7	51.4	4.3
Navarro County	2.0	24.5	13.0	24.7	15.4	24.4	0.9	11.7	22.9	3.4	26.4	16.5	7.2	42.7	3.9
Newton County	2.6	26.0	13.0	17.2	17.6	22.4	2.9	20.0	19.8	7.2	29.9	14.8	5.7	34.8	7.5
Nolan County	2.3	23.5	12.8	29.7	18.8	21.3	1.5	10.0	18.7	6.0	18.8	13.0	7.4	49.5	5.2
Nueces County	2.3	21.1	14.2	30.0	17.6	27.8	0.4	12.5	11.7	2.1	15.7	15.5	4.7	55.6	6.4
Ochiltree County	2.5	17.7	9.3	24.3	12.8	23.7	6.0	16.2	17.1	35.1	7.9	14.8	5.4	33.4	3.4
Oldham County	6.3	18.9	13.8	29.9	24.5	18.0	10.2	7.8	9.6	20.1	7.4	12.0	3.0	48.4	9.2
Orange County	1.7	22.2	13.9	25.1	14.2	24.6	0.4	17.8	18.0	1.6	32.2	14.6	5.1	42.4	4.1
Palo Pinto County	2.7	23.9	15.9	24.8	15.1	23.7	1.5	13.3	21.6	5.2	26.9	15.9	7.1	39.5	5.4
Panola County	2.6	23.0	13.1	24.9	14.3	21.8	2.0	16.6	20.4	11.6	22.7	12.6	8.3	41.0	3.8
Parker County	3.2	18.4	15.6	31.0	13.2	26.4	0.6	14.1	14.7	3.0	25.0	17.2	6.5	43.9	4.3
Parmer County	3.0	17.2	8.3	28.4	12.6	20.2	8.5	6.9	23.4	18.7	25.2	12.5	6.2	33.9	3.4
Pecos County	1.6	27.4	10.1	23.5	23.5	19.7	4.3	15.5	13.5	15.5	12.4	14.0	5.3	41.3	11.5
Polk County	3.1	26.0	16.4	24.7	18.6	22.4	2.5	15.0	16.7	5.0	20.9	14.2	6.7	43.6	9.6
Potter County	2.0	22.7	12.2	22.4	21.2	25.5	0.5	12.6	17.8	1.1	20.7	17.4	5.4	50.7	4.7
Presidio County	2.4	28.5	9.4	23.0	23.0	21.9	7.3	15.6	9.3	11.4	13.5	14.1	5.5	43.3	12.3
Rains County	5.0	25.6	16.8	24.1	16.0	26.7	1.5	14.8	16.9	6.3	27.0	19.0	5.4	37.6	4.8
Randall County	2.9	15.6	13.6	35.7	14.8	29.5	0.6	9.0	10.5	2.0	14.0	19.4	6.0	53.1	5.5
Reagan County	2.6	14.5	8.6	24.2	16.1	20.1	4.4	15.6	19.6	38.9	6.4	11.5	3.8	32.7	6.8
Real County	6.8	26.8	17.3	31.1	18.9	18.5	5.7	16.5	9.3	14.4	16.6	10.0	3.6	50.6	4.7
Red River County	3.8	26.9	13.5	20.4	16.1	19.9	3.6	11.4	28.7	8.7	32.6	13.1	4.3	35.2	6.2
Reeves County	1.3	21.5	7.5	19.2	22.1	21.7	2.0	12.6	22.4	11.2	19.9	13.5	6.4	41.0	8.0
Refugio County	2.6	22.9	13.9	24.4	22.0	18.9	4.3	14.7	15.7	18.9	17.7	11.1	3.6	42.1	6.6
Roberts County	3.5	14.7	12.9	39.6	11.3	20.2	6.5	10.2	12.2	26.1	7.6	8.0	6.5	41.5	10.2
Robertson County	3.5	25.7	14.2	24.5	17.4	23.6	2.6	13.8	18.2	7.7	20.4	13.0	7.3	43.8	7.8
Rockwall County	4.2	14.3	12.3	43.0	10.6	27.7	0.3	9.5	8.8	0.9	22.1	16.3	4.4	52.1	4.3
Runnels County	5.1	24.4	13.8	28.7	15.0	22.3	2.7	9.5	21.9	12.4	24.3	12.6	5.1	39.9	5.8
Rusk County	2.3	22.9	13.9	23.2	14.4	25.2	2.0	15.0	20.1	8.9	21.7	16.6	7.4	41.4	3.9
Sabine County	2.0	26.5	18.4	24.1	16.5	21.7	3.3	15.4	19.0	9.1	21.9	12.6	7.6	43.5	5.3
San Augustine County	2.2	26.5	14.8	25.4	16.3	17.3	5.1	14.7	21.2	11.1	25.3	11.7	7.0	40.0	4.9
San Jacinto County	3.8	25.5	17.7	25.2	16.6	22.8	1.6	15.8	17.9	5.2	23.1	14.3	9.0	39.9	8.6
San Patricio County	2.8	21.5	13.7	27.4	18.0	24.2	1.5	14.2	14.6	5.7	20.3	13.7	5.0	48.3	7.0
San Saba County	2.8	21.5	13.5	30.5	19.8	21.4	4.4	10.9	13.0	12.2	14.1	14.6	5.2	43.1	10.8
Schleicher County	4.4	24.2	9.0	35.5	15.5	17.3	5.1	18.2	8.5	27.2	9.6	8.3	5.4	45.2	4.3
Scurry County	2.4	20.0	11.6	28.3	17.5	22.3	1.7	13.8	16.5	18.4	11.0	13.4	3.9	45.4	7.8
Shackelford County	3.8	18.9	11.6	29.8	17.3	25.1	2.7	11.1	14.0	16.7	12.1	14.2	5.4	43.2	8.3
Shelby County	3.8	25.4	11.2	24.8	13.1	22.2	4.6	11.8	23.4	12.9	25.5	15.8	4.7	38.1	3.0
Sherman County	1.9	11.7	10.0	36.3	12.3	19.0	12.2	8.2	12.1	32.0	11.1	12.6	5.1	34.7	4.4
Smith County	2.6	21.9	13.5	30.3	15.3	27.1	0.6	10.7	16.1	2.6	20.5	18.4	3.9	51.5	3.2
Somervell County	2.3	14.3	13.7	29.1	18.1	21.1	1.4	14.7	15.8	4.9	21.0	11.4	12.5	45.1	5.1
Starr County	2.5	28.4	3.3	22.7	22.7	20.1	7.0	14.2	13.2	11.5	13.7	16.3	4.0	50.5	4.0
Stephens County	2.2	25.3	15.1	25.8	19.0	22.8	2.3	14.0	16.2	11.6	21.2	10.8	5.4	44.2	6.8
Sterling County	8.6	18.6	9.5	30.4	18.1	17.0	9.3	9.3	15.8	27.8	6.9	12.9	9.6	37.2	5.5
Stonewall County	2.4	21.8	13.6	30.5	16.3	18.3	4.6	17.9	12.4	22.2	13.4	10.3	5.2	41.0	7.9
Sutton County	2.9	20.6	10.3	26.0	18.5	19.0	3.8	14.8	17.8	27.5	8.4	10.7	4.5	46.0	3.0
Swisher County	1.9	25.8	12.1	33.9	15.2	19.4	6.2	8.4	17.0	19.4	12.9	13.9	7.1	39.9	6.8
Tarrant County	2.6	17.6	12.3	34.5	12.8	29.7	0.1	9.7	13.3	0.5	21.1	16.9	8.5	49.6	3.4
Taylor County	2.0	20.1	14.5	32.1	19.5	26.9	0.4	10.0	11.1	2.2	12.1	14.9	5.5	59.3	6.0
Terrell County	4.1	27.3	15.2	33.0	20.0	20.4	5.2	12.9	8.6	19.1	11.4	9.2	7.9	43.6	8.8
Terry County	2.2	18.3	10.2	24.8	15.4	23.5	9.1	12.9	14.4	22.8	10.4	18.2	3.9	38.1	6.5
Throckmorton County	5.2	20.3	14.6	34.9	12.5	19.5	9.2	10.0	13.9	25.0	13.2	10.1	5.8	37.9	8.0
Titus County	2.1	22.2	11.9	23.5	17.2	21.5	2.2	12.7	23.0	5.3	31.4	15.1	4.9	40.2	3.2

Table B-3. States and Counties — Education, Labor Force, and Income

STATE County	Median house-hold income	All families	Married-couple	Male house-holder	Female house-holder	Median nonfamily house-hold income	Men	Women	Per capita income	With earnings	With interest, dividend, or rental income	With Social Security income	With public assis-tance income	With retire-ment income	House-holds with income over $100,000 (percent)	+/- U.S. percent for income over $100,000 (percent)	House-holds with income below poverty (percent)	Families with children with income below poverty (percent)
	57	58	59	60	61	62	63	64	65	66	67	68	69	70	71	72	73	74
TEXAS—Cont'd																		
Mason County	30 921	39 360	41 563	23 750	6 875	16 250	30 814	20 987	20 931	71.6	43.8	43.7	2.2	18.8	6.7	-5.6	13.8	20.4
Matagorda County	32 174	40 586	49 271	25 833	15 861	16 785	38 805	22 595	15 709	78.3	26.0	28.3	3.0	14.8	7.7	-4.6	18.3	21.3
Maverick County	21 232	23 614	26 653	16 026	9 403	7 469	21 552	16 114	8 758	79.3	10.6	29.0	9.1	8.3	3.4	-8.9	35.4	35.4
Medina County	36 063	40 288	42 298	24 219	18 036	18 282	28 217	22 315	15 210	81.2	28.6	28.9	3.4	17.7	6.5	-5.8	15.0	16.1
Menard County	24 762	30 872	33 542	24 375	11 518	14 091	24 083	22 875	15 987	71.2	26.0	38.1	3.6	16.5	4.2	-8.1	23.1	31.7
Midland County	39 082	47 269	53 461	26 301	19 401	21 715	38 247	25 609	20 369	84.2	33.1	23.9	2.7	12.3	11.9	-0.4	12.1	14.6
Milam County	33 186	40 431	45 384	27 155	16 806	15 989	31 347	21 176	16 920	75.2	28.3	34.1	3.0	19.5	5.3	-7.0	16.4	17.3
Mills County	30 579	37 519	42 292	20 417	21 406	12 621	27 891	21 987	15 915	70.9	36.9	39.5	3.0	17.8	5.9	-6.4	18.3	16.9
Mitchell County	25 399	31 481	38 487	19 063	14 423	11 658	24 142	21 062	14 043	71.0	26.8	38.3	4.7	17.3	3.1	-9.2	20.5	22.4
Montague County	31 048	38 226	44 950	22 240	15 469	14 109	32 612	20 444	17 115	72.6	31.0	37.1	2.6	16.7	5.3	-7.0	14.5	15.1
Montgomery County	50 864	58 983	66 542	36 442	21 500	27 214	44 454	29 257	24 544	85.3	33.8	20.6	2.1	12.7	19.0	6.7	9.4	9.5
Moore County	34 852	37 985	40 561	25 833	16 897	18 866	30 588	20 006	15 214	83.7	22.5	22.5	2.9	10.6	4.9	-7.4	12.4	14.3
Morris County	29 011	35 326	43 396	30 313	13 125	14 820	31 450	20 825	15 612	70.1	24.8	37.3	3.2	20.4	4.4	-7.9	18.3	22.7
Motley County	28 348	33 977	38 864	13 750	10 938	18 056	26 413	16 029	16 584	72.7	34.7	38.6	2.9	11.5	5.2	-7.1	18.4	23.4
Nacogdoches County	28 301	38 347	45 397	30 030	11 521	12 994	30 608	21 976	15 437	78.9	27.2	24.4	3.3	13.7	6.8	-5.5	23.8	23.0
Navarro County	31 268	38 130	44 767	24 500	16 162	14 899	30 744	21 424	15 266	74.6	22.2	32.8	3.7	14.9	5.7	-6.6	17.8	19.5
Newton County	28 500	34 345	39 174	21 458	12 462	13 359	33 095	18 720	13 381	71.7	20.0	33.5	5.0	16.2	3.0	-9.3	19.8	22.0
Nolan County	26 209	32 004	41 250	16 471	11 792	13 920	29 946	19 635	14 077	73.6	25.4	32.3	5.8	13.9	3.9	-8.4	22.2	26.8
Nueces County	35 959	41 066	49 253	23 388	16 542	22 309	32 334	23 245	17 036	81.6	25.9	24.4	4.8	15.2	7.8	-4.5	16.8	20.2
Ochiltree County	38 013	45 565	45 291	25 156	15 580	20 608	33 204	20 204	16 707	85.5	29.3	24.6	1.9	9.1	6.7	-5.6	11.1	14.5
Oldham County	33 713	39 091	36 786	28 750	18 906	15 625	27 143	20 463	14 806	85.7	26.0	27.3	3.1	10.0	5.9	-6.4	13.2	19.1
Orange County	37 586	44 152	51 800	30 461	15 273	17 802	41 015	22 396	17 554	77.4	27.6	27.0	4.0	18.1	7.7	-4.6	14.1	15.6
Palo Pinto County	31 203	36 977	40 306	26 389	16 154	16 959	29 551	19 747	15 454	74.4	24.6	35.1	3.5	17.6	3.7	-8.6	15.7	18.0
Panola County	31 909	37 595	41 852	18 715	19 044	13 516	32 489	19 511	15 439	71.8	30.5	33.6	3.3	16.4	5.4	-6.9	16.5	15.3
Parker County	45 497	51 530	60 832	28 116	24 278	23 162	38 915	26 315	20 305	84.8	31.1	24.6	1.5	15.8	11.2	-1.1	8.9	8.1
Parmer County	30 813	34 149	34 844	23 000	11 842	15 167	28 151	19 918	14 184	81.6	25.1	26.2	2.3	0.3	5.5	-6.8	16.8	18.7
Pecos County	28 033	31 122	36 233	26 042	13 563	19 284	26 607	19 183	12 212	78.6	21.1	30.0	4.8	12.7	3.5	-8.8	19.9	24.9
Polk County	30 495	35 957	40 476	21 389	16 431	16 058	31 521	21 669	15 834	67.4	26.9	39.8	4.0	23.4	5.1	-7.2	16.7	20.1
Potter County	29 492	35 321	39 600	20 649	16 204	17 378	26 743	20 775	14 947	80.2	23.4	25.6	4.3	12.7	5.1	-7.2	18.3	22.1
Presidio County	19 880	22 314	20 847	25 000	9 457	10 900	24 075	16 452	9 550	79.8	10.0	30.1	10.0	9.9	2.3	10.1	35.0	38.2
Rains County	33 712	40 329	46 797	33 125	20 313	18 175	34 083	22 277	16 442	73.6	26.6	35.6	3.5	20.7	4.8	-7.5	13.7	14.6
Randall County	42 712	52 420	60 187	35 568	21 990	23 849	37 552	26 257	21 840	84.3	37.2	23.4	1.4	14.8	9.9	-2.4	9.2	8.2
Reagan County	33 231	36 806	37 281	26 042	11 806	17 112	31 271	19 250	13 174	82.6	22.4	23.0	3.6	12.4	3.0	-9.3	12.7	9.2
Real County	25 118	29 839	31 875	23 750	12 500	14 904	23 831	18 984	14 321	65.9	31.4	40.7	2.5	20.1	2.5	-9.8	19.3	24.6
Red River County	27 558	33 436	37 571	22 212	13 382	13 561	25 276	18 723	15 058	71.4	26.5	35.2	3.4	18.9	4.1	-8.2	17.7	20.2
Reeves County	23 306	24 856	30 318	17 115	13 125	11 141	24 816	13 954	10 811	77.8	13.6	30.7	7.5	11.6	2.6	-9.7	27.5	30.5
Refugio County	29 986	36 162	43 929	26 364	13 485	16 786	30 357	16 978	15 481	76.4	26.3	32.6	3.4	15.4	5.0	-7.3	18.0	21.7
Roberts County	44 792	50 400	52 344	0	15 025	21 750	00 170	24 420	20 020	79.7	37.0	27.4	1.1	15.3	8.6	3.8	7.9	3.9
Robertson County	28 886	35 590	47 679	24 236	8 851	13 584	31 689	22 446	14 714	71.6	24.2	32.8	3.9	15.2	5.0	-7.3	21.4	25.4
Rockwall County	65 164	71 448	77 069	40 074	31 820	33 462	50 929	33 892	28 573	89.9	40.8	17.2	0.9	12.6	25.1	12.8	4.2	4.9
Runnels County	27 806	32 917	40 615	15 313	13 289	12 307	26 670	20 117	13 577	70.8	31.5	37.7	3.4	13.6	2.8	-9.5	19.3	21.3
Rusk County	32 898	39 185	44 917	21 736	16 684	16 422	31 601	20 354	16 674	73.9	29.1	31.9	3.3	16.4	5.7	-6.6	14.7	17.6
Sabine County	27 198	32 554	40 250	21 250	9 844	13 212	29 142	22 183	15 821	57.3	27.4	46.5	2.6	28.5	3.7	-8.6	17.2	21.2
San Augustine County	27 025	32 772	34 767	30 625	12 188	12 347	28 943	19 214	15 548	65.2	22.9	39.1	4.6	23.7	4.6	-7.7	21.8	25.8
San Jacinto County	32 220	37 781	44 599	23 239	17 125	15 074	35 600	23 116	16 144	72.0	24.2	33.0	3.7	16.2	4.8	-7.5	19.5	19.2
San Patricio County	34 006	40 002	44 766	27 034	14 541	16 070	32 065	21 365	16 426	80.1	24.6	26.8	3.9	14.4	6.5	-5.8	17.1	19.8
San Saba County	30 104	35 255	35 804	22 500	13 088	16 250	26 683	20 373	15 309	70.9	29.8	38.3	2.8	18.3	5.2	-7.1	15.3	21.0
Schleicher County	29 746	37 813	43 333	20 750	11 000	13 938	29 911	22 543	15 969	78.0	31.5	33.8	3.9	13.8	5.6	-6.7	20.0	24.9
Scurry County	31 646	38 467	44 151	17 375	14 336	17 489	31 904	19 192	15 871	75.5	27.5	30.6	2.9	13.2	5.5	-6.8	16.0	18.6
Shackelford County	30 479	38 447	41 719	15 625	16 250	13 105	28 950	20 833	16 341	76.8	31.9	32.3	2.3	12.5	4.2	-8.1	15.3	14.9
Shelby County	29 112	34 347	37 791	26 000	16 056	14 339	27 311	21 244	15 186	71.2	23.5	34.6	5.8	17.6	5.1	-7.2	19.7	20.5
Sherman County	33 179	38 821	41 058	24 750	17 917	19 333	29 199	21 360	17 210	83.7	33.5	24.5	2.7	10.1	6.3	-6.0	12.8	17.2
Smith County	37 148	44 534	51 122	28 377	17 840	21 000	33 778	23 461	19 072	79.1	31.8	28.0	2.4	16.5	9.1	-3.2	13.2	15.0
Somervell County	39 404	46 458	53 405	27 188	17 273	19 153	33 425	23 940	18 367	80.8	31.1	26.5	2.1	12.6	8.4	-3.9	9.0	8.9
Starr County	16 504	17 556	19 673	10 324	7 454	7 146	18 432	14 216	7 069	76.6	9.7	23.8	16.1	8.8	2.2	-10.1	48.5	53.8
Stephens County	29 583	35 293	40 788	21 429	14 783	18 661	27 493	21 791	15 475	74.9	30.2	34.0	3.8	13.7	5.8	-6.5	14.4	20.0
Sterling County	35 129	37 813	39 375	36 250	12 143	17 222	30 592	20 417	16 972	80.0	29.1	25.6	1.0	11.5	6.4	-5.9	16.7	21.4
Stonewall County	27 935	35 571	38 281	17 917	12 188	15 000	29 167	16 176	16 094	73.5	30.7	39.3	6.1	15.9	4.4	-7.9	19.4	25.1
Sutton County	34 385	38 143	41 786	28 125	11 250	17 752	32 023	20 198	17 105	83.4	23.7	26.4	4.2	8.8	8.7	-3.6	16.9	20.4
Swisher County	29 846	34 444	38 646	12 083	16 250	19 750	25 617	21 575	14 326	76.7	30.5	34.1	6.1	10.8	4.0	-8.3	16.5	22.3
Tarrant County	46 179	54 068	62 045	32 316	23 395	30 134	39 694	29 602	22 548	87.6	30.8	17.5	2.1	12.2	13.9	1.6	9.6	11.3
Taylor County	34 035	40 850	45 499	22 389	17 174	20 088	30 632	21 753	17 176	82.0	31.3	25.3	3.1	16.5	6.1	-6.2	14.2	15.3
Terrell County	24 219	28 906	35 833	48 125	14 375	15 000	22 875	15 938	13 721	71.9	24.3	36.1	7.0	16.1	4.3	-8.0	25.6	23.1
Terry County	28 090	33 339	37 652	16 500	10 227	14 199	25 262	20 545	13 860	78.4	23.1	30.0	5.4	13.6	4.7	-7.6	20.5	27.4
Throckmorton County	28 277	34 563	40 673	13 750	16 875	17 222	24 464	20 074	17 719	73.4	33.3	36.6	4.2	17.7	4.3	-8.0	12.7	16.5
Titus County	32 452	37 390	41 278	19 830	17 881	16 140	27 146	19 046	15 501	76.9	24.8	28.2	3.8	15.8	6.3	-6.0	16.4	20.6

STATE/ County code	MSA/PMSA/ NECMA code[1]	STATE County	High school graduates			College graduates		College graduates (percent)				
			Total population 25 years and over	Percent with a high school diploma or less	Percent with a high school diploma or more	Percent with a bachelor's degree or more	+/– U.S. percent with bachelor's degree or more	Non-Hispanic White	Black or African American	American Indian and Alaska Native	Asian, Hawaiian, and Pacific Islander	Hispanic or Latino[2]
			1	2	3	4	5	6	7	8	9	10
		TEXAS—Cont'd										
48 451	7200	Tom Green County	63 430	52.3	76.2	19.5	-4.9	24.7	12.4	17.0	27.3	6.1
48 453	0640	Travis County	501 361	32.7	84.7	40.6	16.2	51.0	20.5	24.9	63.3	15.8
48 455	...	Trinity County	9 623	66.4	73.1	9.4	-15.0	9.9	5.7	0.0	50.0	10.4
48 457	...	Tyler County	14 433	69.6	71.9	9.7	-14.7	10.9	2.6	3.6	66.7	4.0
48 459	4420	Upshur County	22 977	60.0	76.3	11.1	-13.3	11.6	7.5	8.5	24.6	6.6
48 461	...	Upton County	2 165	67.1	67.1	11.8	-12.6	17.6	0.0	17.4	X	2.7
48 463	...	Uvalde County..............	15 280	62.8	59.6	13.8	-10.6	25.6	0.0	6.0	30.1	5.4
48 465	...	Val Verde County.........	26 281	66.1	58.7	14.1	-10.3	27.0	25.2	15.2	42.5	9.0
48 467	...	Van Zandt County	32 427	62.4	72.0	11.6	-12.8	12.3	3.3	10.3	19.0	2.8
48 469	8750	Victoria County	51 985	52.8	76.2	16.2	-8.2	22.3	9.4	6.8	50.3	6.0
48 471	...	Walker County	36 678	58.6	73.1	18.3	-6.1	25.3	6.4	7.4	45.5	4.3
48 473	3360	Waller County	18 395	57.6	73.9	16.8	-7.6	18.2	21.4	13.7	19.7	4.9
48 475	...	Ward County	6 765	64.4	70.1	12.4	-12.0	17.9	0.0	3.9	100.0	4.5
48 477	...	Washington County	19 451	56.5	72.1	19.0	-5.4	23.0	5.9	0.0	21.4	2.8
48 479	4080	Webb County	101 182	65.0	53.0	13.9	-10.5	36.7	23.4	6.1	43.9	12.3
48 481	...	Wharton County	25 567	59.5	69.8	14.3	-10.1	20.2	9.2	8.3	47.1	2.6
48 483	...	Wheeler County	3 601	58.6	72.0	13.0	-11.4	13.8	0.0	0.0	62.5	7.0
48 485	9080	Wichita County	80 740	49.9	79.9	20.0	-4.4	22.5	10.5	16.1	21.0	8.6
48 487	...	Wilbarger County	9 313	57.3	72.2	17.1	-7.3	20.2	4.8	77.1	41.9	2.8
48 489	...	Willacy County	11 332	75.6	48.7	7.5	-16.9	23.3	0.7	0.0	0.0	4.7
48 491	0640	Williamson County	155 565	33.4	88.8	33.6	9.2	36.3	29.0	24.1	55.3	16.7
48 493	7240	Wilson County	20 590	60.3	73.8	12.8	-11.6	15.8	7.8	16.2	28.7	6.5
48 495	...	Winkler County	4 380	67.0	60.3	10.5	-13.9	16.0	0.0	25.0	0.0	1.6
48 497	...	Wise County	31 130	58.7	76.1	13.0	-11.4	13.8	5.8	7.7	34.5	4.1
48 499	...	Wood County	25 895	56.5	76.3	14.5	-9.9	15.4	8.2	6.7	29.0	3.8
48 501	...	Yoakum County.............	4 322	67.1	59.4	10.2	-14.2	14.9	19.4	0.0	100.0	2.3
48 503	...	Young County	12 265	60.0	72.1	14.4	-10.0	15.1	20.1	9.8	75.9	4.2
48 505	...	Zapata County	6 945	74.6	53.1	8.7	-15.7	12.2	X	X	0.0	7.6
48 507	...	Zavala County	6 371	76.9	43.4	7.6	-16.8	26.3	0.0	0.0	100.0	5.4
49 000	...	UTAH................	1 197 892	36.9	87.7	26.1	1.7	27.7	19.8	9.1	31.1	9.8
49 001	...	Beaver County	3 442	55.2	83.2	12.1	-12.3	12.5	0.0	0.0	35.7	1.1
49 003	...	Box Elder County	22 766	43.6	87.8	19.5	-4.9	20.4	0.0	20.6	22.5	4.0
49 005	...	Cache County	42 544	32.2	90.4	31.9	7.5	32.9	38.1	6.5	51.7	7.7
49 007	...	Carbon County	12 090	50.3	81.1	12.3	-12.1	13.4	0.0	3.7	26.1	2.9
49 009	...	Daggett County	632	51.6	83.7	11.9	-12.5	13.0	X	X	0.0	0.0
49 011	7160	Davis County	125 532	31.1	92.2	28.8	4.4	29.9	19.2	11.3	24.9	10.9
49 013	...	Duchesne County	7 752	56.7	81.0	12.7	-11.7	13.2	X	7.1	30.8	8.4
49 015	...	Emery County	5 980	51.1	84.2	11.6	-12.8	12.1	0.0	11.5	0.0	2.3
49 017	...	Garfield County	2 829	46.7	85.8	20.3	-4.1	20.8	0.0	0.0	0.0	18.5
49 019	...	Grand County	5 486	44.3	82.5	22.9	-1.5	23.7	0.0	0.0	25.0	15.7
49 021	...	Iron County...................	16 318	35.5	88.6	23.8	-0.6	24.5	0.0	11.1	39.0	7.2
49 023	...	Juab County	4 290	52.4	82.9	12.2	-12.2	12.3	X	0.0	X	0.0
49 025	2620	Kane County	3 842	39.8	86.4	21.1	-3.3	21.4	0.0	0.0	0.0	12.5
49 027	...	Millard County	6 769	43.9	86.7	16.8	-7.6	17.4	X	22.5	17.9	2.6
49 029	...	Morgan County	3 805	37.0	92.6	23.3	-1.1	23.6	X	0.0	33.3	4.8
49 031	...	Piute County	893	51.1	85.7	14.4	-10.0	14.8	X	0.0	0.0	0.0
49 033	...	Rich County.................	1 144	42.5	91.5	22.0	-2.4	22.4	X	0.0	X	0.0
49 035	7160	Salt Lake County..........	509 453	37.2	86.8	27.4	3.0	29.5	22.5	11.4	30.0	10.0
49 037	...	San Juan County	7 290	54.0	69.6	13.9	-10.5	26.2	0.0	3.5	20.0	5.7
49 039	...	Sanpete County	11 522	44.3	84.6	17.3	-7.1	17.9	22.6	5.6	14.0	7.3
49 041	...	Sevier County	10 480	48.5	85.8	15.2	-9.2	15.7	0.0	0.0	11.1	7.8
49 043	...	Summit County	18 366	24.6	92.5	45.5	21.1	48.1	22.2	58.5	60.5	9.9
49 045	...	Tooele County	21 752	47.4	85.6	15.9	-8.5	17.1	8.7	11.0	20.8	5.1
49 047	...	Uintah County	13 736	56.2	79.8	13.2	-11.2	13.9	0.0	4.0	41.3	9.1
49 049	6520	Utah County	166 240	28.3	90.9	31.5	7.1	32.5	25.7	20.6	41.6	16.2
49 051	...	Wasatch County	8 448	35.7	89.3	26.3	1.9	27.0	X	11.1	47.4	8.1
49 053	...	Washington County	51 842	39.1	87.6	21.0	-3.4	21.7	17.0	9.1	19.0	5.2
49 055	...	Wayne County	1 493	37.8	88.5	20.9	-3.5	20.9	100.0	10.0	0.0	0.0
49 057	7160	Weber County	111 156	42.6	85.0	19.9	-4.5	21.7	10.1	13.7	27.9	5.9
50 000	...	VERMONT	404 223	45.9	86.4	29.4	5.0	29.4	34.8	18.1	46.1	36.8
50 001	...	Addison County............	22 468	47.4	86.4	29.8	5.4	29.9	45.5	14.5	57.7	32.6
50 003	...	Bennington County........	25 311	48.2	84.9	27.1	2.7	27.2	34.4	0.0	45.6	25.1
50 005	...	Caledonia County........	19 596	55.0	82.6	22.5	-1.9	22.6	15.4	6.3	42.5	28.7

[1]MSA = Metropolitan Statistical Area. PMSA = Primary MSA. NECMA = New England County Metropolitan Area. See the Appendix A for explanation of these concepts. See Appendix B for list of metropolitan areas identified by type, with component counties.
[2]Hispanic or Latino persons may be of any race.

STATE County	School enrollment			Population 16 to 19 years				Employment status, 2000			Work status in 1999 of the population 16 years and over (percent)		
											Worked in 1999		
	Grades kindergarten through 12	College or graduate school	Percent private	Number	Percent in armed forces	Percent high school graduates	Percent not enrolled, not grads, not in armed forces, not employed	Total population 16 years and over	Percent in labor force	Unemploy-ment rate	Full-time	Part-time	Did not work in 1999
	11	12	13	14	15	16	17	18	19	20	21	22	23
TEXAS—Cont'd													
Tom Green County	20 707	7 281	4.3	7 663	6.7	17.7	4.1	80 282	64.5	7.0	54.0	15.1	31.0
Travis County	133 691	87 661	8.6	48 677	0.1	9.7	6.5	639 474	72.0	4.1	63.4	15.4	21.2
Trinity County	2 369	256	2.9	721	0.0	15.3	9.0	11 005	48.9	6.7	44.0	9.2	46.9
Tyler County	3 784	491	5.8	1 026	0.7	12.8	6.2	16 635	43.9	6.4	44.8	10.5	44.7
Upshur County	7 267	1 046	6.3	2 166	0.0	10.5	6.9	26 999	57.5	5.2	50.6	11.3	38.1
Upton County	868	57	0.8	274	0.0	5.8	2.6	2 570	53.7	5.5	49.6	11.1	39.3
Uvalde County	6 142	1 099	5.6	1 758	0.0	8.0	7.1	18 699	56.8	6.6	50.0	12.6	37.4
Val Verde County	10 622	1 443	6.0	2 750	1.1	10.0	10.2	32 115	56.8	10.5	50.6	10.7	38.7
Van Zandt County	9 289	1 205	7.0	2 568	0.0	11.3	4.2	37 323	56.8	5.9	49.6	10.6	39.7
Victoria County	18 552	3 966	9.7	5 069	0.0	11.8	4.8	62 238	64.8	4.7	57.2	12.8	30.0
Walker County	10 092	9 404	8.6	5 932	0.2	14.3	13.4	52 241	47.4	8.8	50.9	15.4	33.7
Waller County	6 445	4 267	4.7	3 146	0.0	8.0	3.5	25 272	62.9	13.8	53.7	15.2	31.1
Ward County	2 640	253	4.0	873	0.0	13.5	9.3	8 121	53.3	8.4	47.6	11.9	40.6
Washington County	5 844	1 938	9.6	2 541	0.0	7.9	3.6	23 826	59.3	4.3	50.8	13.8	35.4
Webb County	51 488	11 089	5.6	13 908	0.0	10.3	10.3	130 196	53.0	9.3	49.0	11.5	39.5
Wharton County	9 347	1 417	5.6	2 943	0.0	11.1	6.8	30 818	60.6	6.0	53.5	11.4	35.1
Wheeler County	1 098	82	5.8	333	0.0	9.6	2.7	4 146	59.1	1.8	51.3	13.7	35.0
Wichita County	24 628	8 736	7.3	10 345	24.1	35.5	5.8	102 528	64.2	5.1	56.0	14.7	29.3
Wilbarger County	2 881	665	3.8	1 235	0.0	14.3	14.8	11 304	59.5	3.8	52.8	11.8	35.3
Willacy County	5 013	620	1.9	1 527	0.0	11.3	13.2	14 531	48.1	13.8	43.2	10.6	46.1
Williamson County	53 372	11 436	9.8	13 778	0.0	11.0	2.4	182 974	72.8	2.8	66.6	12.4	21.0
Wilson County	7 296	1 099	6.3	1 950	0.0	7.5	7.4	24 131	61.2	4.8	55.9	9.9	34.2
Winkler County	1 698	135	0.5	506	0.0	9.9	5.3	5 338	52.3	8.2	47.1	11.3	41.6
Wise County	10 784	1 230	6.3	2 800	0.0	15.1	5.2	36 548	64.8	4.2	57.6	12.6	29.8
Wood County	6 157	1 175	9.2	2 096	0.0	14.7	6.9	29 824	52.9	8.4	45.4	13.3	41.4
Yoakum County	I 972	182	1.0	588	0.0	5.8	3.7	5 320	59.2	9.2	52.7	11.5	35.8
Young County	3 556	443	4.9	1 041	0.0	7.5	5.3	14 097	59.0	5.2	51.0	12.2	36.8
Zapata County	3 093	359	3.1	938	0.0	13.1	13.6	8 666	43.9	11.1	40.2	9.8	50.1
Zavala County	3 147	460	2.7	901	0.0	6.7	11.1	8 130	44.9	16.7	40.6	11.2	48.1
UTAH......................	508 724	186 743	10.6	173 747	0.1	13.8	3.9	1 600 279	69.0	4.9	54.5	20.9	24.5
Beaver County	1 488	127	1.0	384	0.5	14.1	1.6	4 218	60.7	2.2	48.5	10.9	31.6
Box Elder County	11 538	1 685	2.9	3 425	0.0	15.0	4.9	29 257	66.1	5.2	52.3	20.3	27.4
Cache County	19 663	16 337	2.2	8 606	0.0	12.9	2.4	66 216	70.8	5.1	50.2	28.4	21.4
Carbon County	4 291	1 565	3.2	1 724	0.0	8.5	3.0	15 434	61.4	8.9	46.1	19.6	34.3
Daggett County	165	11	0.0	59	0.0	10.2	3.4	743	55.6	7.7	47.2	20.1	32.7
Davis County	60 679	14 267	5.0	18 896	0.7	15.9	2.9	165 082	72.4	4.3	56.5	21.4	22.1
Duchesne County	4 002	445	2.8	1 158	0.0	15.4	7.8	9 753	60.8	7.8	47.0	18.9	34.1
Emery County	3 042	283	1.4	943	0.0	9.1	3.0	7 609	61.2	6.4	46.1	20.1	33.7
Garfield County	1 119	82	1.2	344	0.0	17.4	0.9	3 425	63.6	8.1	52.5	19.6	27.9
Grand County	1 649	248	5.7	539	0.0	13.5	6.9	6 532	68.8	8.8	54.7	19.1	26.2
Iron County.................	7 356	5 249	2.6	3 214	0.0	8.3	1.9	24 402	67.1	5.3	48.5	26.9	24.6
Juab County	2 251	186	5.4	643	0.0	9.5	1.9	5 453	65.0	3.6	50.1	20.9	29.0
Kane County	1 371	243	4.8	425	0.0	9.2	3.5	4 541	62.0	5.3	50.5	18.0	31.4
Millard County	3 704	216	2.9	1 107	0.0	8.8	3.6	8 470	61.3	5.8	44.8	21.6	33.6
Morgan County	2 103	377	2.3	726	0.0	9.6	1.5	4 919	67.2	3.8	52.7	20.6	26.8
Piute County...............	313	35	2.9	105	0.0	12.4	1.9	1 066	54.2	6.4	43.2	18.9	37.9
Rich County................	544	51	2.0	152	0.0	10.5	2.6	1 366	61.4	4.2	52.0	18.1	29.9
Salt Lake County..........	193 851	63 514	8.5	62 241	0.0	13.9	4.6	657 612	71.1	4.5	58.5	18.7	22.9
San Juan County	4 410	725	1.5	1 122	0.0	10.8	4.1	9 340	53.4	15.1	45.3	15.2	39.5
Sanpete County	5 588	2 563	3.9	2 615	0.3	6.8	2.3	16 181	57.3	6.8	46.5	22.4	31.1
Sevier County	4 876	661	3.3	1 548	0.0	8.6	5.6	13 305	60.5	6.3	45.8	20.2	33.9
Summit County	6 661	1 350	9.0	1 752	0.0	10.4	5.7	21 940	77.7	2.8	62.9	20.1	17.1
Tooele County	9 805	1 318	4.4	3 169	0.1	15.1	9.1	28 052	68.5	5.5	59.5	15.2	25.3
Uintah County	6 634	773	2.9	2 151	0.4	15.9	4.9	17 694	63.0	7.7	48.5	19.9	31.6
Utah County	83 763	57 002	28.0	34 454	0.0	14.1	2.5	256 863	68.0	4.8	49.2	27.5	23.3
Wasatch County	3 926	620	5.7	1 040	0.0	10.7	2.4	10 604	68.9	4.3	55.1	20.7	24.2
Washington County	19 539	5 019	5.8	6 967	0.0	14.5	3.3	65 505	57.6	5.5	43.6	19.3	37.1
Wayne County	590	76	1.8	164	0.0	12.8	0.0	1 802	63.8	3.3	50.2	21.5	28.3
Weber County	43 794	11 715	4.8	14 074	0.1	14.7	5.4	142 895	69.0	6.0	56.2	17.9	25.8
VERMONT	114 318	40 318	16.5	36 432	0.1	10.2	2.5	479 140	69.3	4.2	56.8	18.8	24.4
Addison County............	6 890	3 126	30.2	2 868	0.0	8.7	5.0	28 251	70.1	4.5	57.5	20.5	22.0
Bennington County........	6 897	1 816	20.8	2 015	0.0	11.7	1.6	29 302	66.8	4.6	52.5	19.6	27.9
Caledonia County..........	5 971	1 584	19.6	1 941	0.0	12.1	4.8	23 128	67.1	6.2	54.1	18.7	27.2

Table B-3. States and Counties — Education, Labor Force, and Income

STATE County	Full-year full-time employed (percent)								Children under 18 years in families					+/− U.S. percent two-income couples	Total employed by class of worker (percent)			
	Total	Men	Women	Non-Hispanic White	Black or African American	American Indian and Alaska Native	Asian, Hawaiian, and Pacific Islander	Hispanic or Latino[1]	Number	With two parents (percent) Both in labor force	Father only in labor force	With one parent who is in labor force (percent)	+/− U.S. percent of children with no stay-at-home parent (percent)		Private	Government	Self-employed	Unpaid family worker
	24	25	26	27	28	29	30	31	32	33	34	35	36	37	38	39	40	41
TEXAS—Cont'd																		
Tom Green County	39.5	48.3	31.6	40.2	35.6	47.0	33.4	38.6	25 530	44.6	18.1	23.9	3.9	-1.7	71.3	17.8	10.5	0.3
Travis County	46.0	54.2	37.5	48.2	43.6	43.3	37.9	43.4	180 304	40.7	24.2	22.6	-1.3	5.6	72.0	18.5	9.3	0.2
Trinity County	30.5	37.6	23.9	30.7	29.7	32.5	47.4	29.2	2 890	44.5	16.7	27.2	7.1	-16.6	60.5	27.6	11.7	0.2
Tyler County	27.1	34.0	19.8	28.6	19.7	6.6	58.3	21.7	4 492	37.2	31.5	13.2	-14.2	-19.9	66.4	21.7	11.8	0.1
Upshur County	36.1	47.7	25.5	36.8	32.6	36.8	28.8	29.5	8 556	42.3	27.7	17.1	-5.2	-7.5	75.6	11.8	12.0	0.5
Upton County	34.4	45.2	24.6	38.9	27.7	5.7	X	29.0	912	43.2	26.9	16.1	-5.3	-8.9	58.1	26.8	14.6	0.5
Uvalde County	32.0	41.9	23.2	34.1	32.1	8.4	42.9	30.7	7 728	40.6	23.9	17.1	-6.9	-8.6	67.3	19.6	12.6	0.5
Val Verde County	32.1	43.2	21.7	42.7	59.8	33.3	41.6	27.9	13 564	36.8	26.5	15.9	-11.9	-14.3	63.4	25.6	10.1	0.9
Van Zandt County	36.7	47.5	26.4	36.8	29.2	40.3	26.8	36.8	11 405	43.9	27.2	17.3	-3.4	-8.6	70.1	15.2	13.9	0.8
Victoria County	42.4	54.3	31.5	43.9	39.0	30.0	41.9	40.9	22 853	46.5	19.7	22.4	4.3	0.9	77.6	13.3	8.8	0.2
Walker County	29.4	28.1	31.6	34.0	20.1	63.0	24.5	23.9	9 985	44.0	19.5	23.5	2.9	0.4	54.5	36.0	9.0	0.5
Waller County	36.5	44.5	28.8	45.0	22.2	25.0	20.6	37.9	7 739	36.9	25.6	22.3	-5.4	-2.2	69.7	17.9	11.8	0.7
Ward County	31.7	42.1	21.5	34.8	20.2	13.2	0.0	28.5	2 959	39.6	26.6	18.2	-6.8	-13.5	67.2	22.2	10.3	0.3
Washington County	37.7	48.1	28.1	39.3	32.1	46.5	38.8	33.2	7 127	47.1	21.8	21.5	4.0	1.1	71.0	16.0	12.5	0.5
Webb County	30.6	41.7	20.9	35.8	27.7	23.0	34.0	30.3	65 096	28.0	29.3	15.6	-21.0	-16.7	68.0	19.8	11.8	0.4
Wharton County	38.7	49.4	28.7	41.7	29.7	32.9	43.6	37.2	11 053	44.7	22.1	19.6	-0.3	-2.7	71.8	16.1	11.7	0.4
Wheeler County	37.0	48.3	27.3	37.9	16.7	28.9	0.0	36.4	1 257	49.6	27.4	17.3	2.3	-2.4	62.8	18.6	17.6	1.0
Wichita County	40.2	49.1	31.2	41.7	34.1	31.4	36.3	38.3	30 944	45.2	20.2	23.4	4.0	0.2	70.0	19.3	10.2	0.4
Wilbarger County	41.3	50.2	33.1	42.7	20.1	35.1	42.8	46.8	3 591	52.1	15.7	24.6	12.1	3.4	58.5	29.0	11.7	0.8
Willacy County	24.7	29.4	19.8	23.5	12.5	2.0	9.1	25.4	6 003	30.5	24.8	17.9	-16.2	-19.5	65.8	24.7	9.1	0.5
Williamson County	52.4	63.8	41.4	52.8	54.3	62.4	47.7	50.7	72 085	51.6	26.7	14.7	1.7	9.5	75.4	15.3	9.0	0.2
Wilson County	42.7	51.9	33.7	44.2	46.2	22.6	43.8	39.4	8 874	49.2	22.1	17.2	1.8	-1.6	68.4	19.8	11.5	0.4
Winkler County	28.6	36.1	21.5	35.5	28.4	25.0	50.0	18.4	1 982	38.5	27.9	16.2	-9.9	-12.0	65.0	26.4	7.9	0.7
Wise County	43.8	55.9	31.5	44.7	30.9	38.4	30.8	37.4	13 217	51.3	26.5	13.6	0.3	0.2	72.8	13.0	13.9	0.3
Wood County	31.7	40.3	23.6	32.4	20.6	27.5	38.0	36.0	7 551	43.8	21.7	22.4	1.6	-11.9	69.6	12.5	16.8	1.1
Yoakum County	35.0	49.4	21.5	38.6	27.3	10.0	100.0	29.8	2 277	41.9	33.1	14.0	-8.7	-11.7	69.9	18.9	10.5	0.6
Young County	36.5	49.2	25.2	36.7	32.2	50.0	100.0	33.9	4 308	46.0	22.7	17.5	-1.1	-2.1	69.4	12.9	17.1	0.6
Zapata County	20.4	24.9	16.2	14.0	X	X	53.3	21.9	3 719	27.8	33.2	15.8	-21.0	-23.0	61.0	24.8	13.2	0.9
Zavala County	20.0	27.0	13.3	27.2	6.7	15.6	17.6	19.4	3 603	26.6	21.7	26.3	-11.7	-23.9	66.2	26.3	7.3	0.2
UTAH	39.3	51.4	27.4	39.6	40.8	28.5	39.0	37.8	689 581	46.5	32.9	13.2	-4.9	2.2	74.3	15.7	9.7	0.3
Beaver County	34.8	49.2	19.5	35.0	0.0	25.9	50.0	31.1	1 917	53.4	30.1	12.5	1.3	3.0	66.1	20.4	12.2	1.3
Box Elder County	39.1	53.7	24.4	39.1	0.0	31.4	37.2	41.5	14 954	50.6	33.5	10.1	-3.9	-0.2	74.1	14.0	11.5	0.4
Cache County	33.7	47.3	20.9	34.0	34.1	31.0	25.1	34.8	27 921	52.0	33.2	9.9	-2.7	6.4	69.6	20.3	9.7	0.4
Carbon County	33.8	47.7	20.9	34.5	14.8	40.4	34.3	29.0	5 471	44.6	29.0	15.8	-4.2	-4.1	71.7	20.0	8.2	0.1
Daggett County	30.4	36.9	21.7	32.3	0.0	X	0.0	8.6	204	59.8	20.1	18.1	13.3	0.7	40.7	39.9	18.6	0.8
Davis County	43.4	58.5	28.5	43.6	49.3	32.4	41.2	41.3	81 556	49.0	34.4	11.4	-4.2	4.9	71.4	19.1	9.2	0.2
Duchesne County	30.8	45.9	15.5	31.5	X	25.0	21.9	26.9	5 002	45.7	32.7	14.5	-4.4	-6.7	59.8	24.8	14.8	0.6
Emery County	33.0	49.2	17.1	33.0	0.0	28.6	21.9	38.8	3 707	49.5	32.2	10.3	-4.8	-3.7	70.1	20.0	9.1	0.8
Garfield County	32.1	42.6	21.4	32.8	0.0	19.6	0.0	26.2	1 478	62.3	22.2	10.6	8.3	-1.8	58.4	27.1	13.9	0.6
Grand County	33.6	39.6	27.8	33.7	100.0	25.1	50.0	39.6	2 159	47.4	15.7	25.2	8.0	1.2	64.2	20.0	15.8	0.0
Iron County	31.2	43.7	19.4	31.3	0.0	29.2	17.0	34.3	10 247	44.7	37.4	10.1	-9.8	-1.8	68.7	20.0	10.8	0.5
Juab County	37.6	52.3	23.2	38.6	0.0	5.7	0.0	13.1	3 042	46.2	30.5	13.9	-4.5	-0.1	76.9	13.8	9.2	0.1
Kane County	34.4	44.8	24.4	33.8	40.0	46.7	0.0	38.5	1 682	55.1	24.3	10.9	1.4	-4.5	59.3	21.2	17.8	1.7
Millard County	31.1	46.3	15.6	31.2	X	49.6	38.5	27.0	4 496	46.6	37.9	8.8	-9.2	-3.0	62.7	19.8	15.3	2.2
Morgan County	37.0	51.6	22.5	36.8	X	100.0	0.0	32.4	2 588	49.3	38.8	7.0	-8.3	1.6	62.3	21.0	15.3	1.3
Piute County	26.8	40.6	12.5	27.1	X	0.0	0.0	26.7	412	50.2	29.6	14.1	-0.3	-12.0	40.7	32.0	24.0	3.3
Rich County	35.9	53.1	18.5	36.1	X	0.0	0.0	33.3	659	48.0	41.7	7.0	-9.6	-3.9	51.0	20.6	25.7	2.6
Salt Lake County	43.2	53.7	32.6	43.8	42.2	38.9	42.7	39.4	260 425	46.5	29.4	15.7	-2.4	5.0	77.4	13.5	8.8	0.2
San Juan County	25.2	33.1	17.7	33.9	50.0	17.9	0.0	28.9	5 335	37.2	20.9	16.2	-11.2	-11.0	54.0	34.1	11.4	0.5
Sanpete County	28.2	40.9	15.4	28.5	31.6	23.8	8.3	25.9	7 259	45.3	37.6	8.9	-10.4	-7.3	61.9	23.3	14.2	0.6
Sevier County	32.3	47.4	17.6	32.8	5.0	19.5	22.2	27.6	6 142	50.3	31.7	11.8	-2.5	-4.1	64.5	20.1	14.6	0.9
Summit County	46.9	59.2	33.7	47.4	55.8	49.3	57.1	41.3	8 557	53.7	30.3	11.4	0.5	12.2	71.9	11.3	16.5	0.3
Tooele County	45.3	61.0	30.7	46.5	23.0	21.5	26.5	45.7	13 469	48.1	32.9	13.5	-3.0	3.1	71.5	20.9	7.3	0.3
Uintah County	31.6	44.1	19.6	33.1	0.0	16.1	55.6	40.2	8 275	39.4	34.5	15.9	-9.3	-7.3	66.3	19.7	13.3	0.6
Utah County	32.7	45.6	20.5	32.9	36.9	32.1	24.4	32.0	121 354	41.7	42.7	8.9	-14.0	-1.2	77.8	12.1	9.8	0.3
Wasatch County	38.9	54.2	23.2	39.4	X	28.2	13.5	29.7	5 092	46.7	36.0	10.9	-7.0	-0.3	68.2	15.8	15.3	0.7
Washington County	30.2	41.6	19.4	29.8	10.7	32.0	27.3	36.4	27 255	45.1	37.2	11.8	-7.7	-11.1	72.3	13.5	13.6	0.6
Wayne County	34.5	46.4	22.2	34.6	0.0	50.0	0.0	18.8	797	56.6	24.0	13.4	5.4	0.0	52.6	25.9	21.2	0.3
Weber County	41.2	52.2	30.3	41.8	37.2	32.1	44.4	37.3	58 126	49.5	24.5	17.7	2.6	3.8	70.2	21.7	7.8	0.3
VERMONT	42.7	52.6	33.3	42.9	34.4	41.6	35.1	32.7	141 993	55.5	16.1	19.9	10.8	10.2	71.5	14.2	14.1	0.3
Addison County	42.3	52.0	32.9	43.1	7.3	45.6	7.2	16.0	8 465	57.3	17.3	17.4	10.1	13.3	70.9	11.6	17.2	0.2
Bennington County	40.1	49.7	31.6	40.3	29.2	34.8	44.1	36.1	8 500	54.5	14.0	20.3	10.2	7.5	71.6	12.2	16.0	0.2
Caledonia County	39.5	48.6	30.7	39.6	15.4	45.8	29.3	37.8	7 192	54.2	14.2	21.3	10.9	8.8	68.4	15.5	15.6	0.5

[1] Hispanic or Latino persons may be of any race.

STATE County	Percent who worked at home	Percent of the population 5 years and over with a disability	Veterans as a percent of the population 18 years and over	Occupation for employed population 16 years and over (percent) Management, professional, and related occupations	Service occupa- tions	Sales and office occupa- tions	Farming, fishing, and forestry occupa- tions	Con- struction, extraction, and main- tenance occupa- tions	Production, transporta- tion and material moving occupa- tions	Industry for employed population 16 years and over (percent) Agricul- ture, forestry, fishing, and mining	Construc- tion and manufac- turing	Whole- sale and retail trade	Trans- porta- tion and ware- housing, and utilities	Service industries	Public adminis- tration
	42	43	44	45	46	47	48	49	50	51	52	53	54	55	56
TEXAS—Cont'd															
Tom Green County	2.2	20.8	14.6	27.9	18.9	28.5	0.9	10.7	13.2	3.5	15.0	16.0	3.2	56.1	6.1
Travis County	3.6	14.9	9.9	43.7	12.6	26.1	0.2	8.9	8.6	0.5	20.9	13.1	2.8	55.1	7.6
Trinity County	3.0	27.3	19.1	24.7	21.1	22.7	3.4	12.3	15.7	7.0	17.5	14.8	3.5	40.5	16.7
Tyler County	3.2	27.0	16.8	22.5	16.8	22.9	3.0	17.1	17.7	6.9	26.4	14.1	5.3	39.6	7.8
Upshur County	3.3	22.8	15.2	23.5	14.2	24.6	1.1	16.4	20.2	3.9	27.0	18.1	6.2	41.6	3.2
Upton County	2.9	24.4	12.1	28.8	17.2	17.8	4.4	13.5	18.2	23.4	6.1	10.0	12.6	41.2	6.7
Uvalde County	3.2	22.9	10.9	25.9	20.2	20.2	4.2	13.1	16.4	7.7	16.6	15.4	6.7	47.6	6.0
Val Verde County	1.9	20.9	12.1	25.2	20.9	24.5	1.2	13.4	14.8	2.8	18.2	15.9	6.0	45.2	11.9
Van Zandt County	4.3	24.5	15.3	25.0	14.7	26.6	2.2	14.5	17.0	5.5	22.0	16.2	7.9	43.5	4.9
Victoria County	2.1	19.4	12.9	28.5	15.1	27.4	0.4	13.4	15.1	4.5	22.4	18.2	4.2	47.0	3.8
Walker County	1.7	18.2	10.8	29.8	23.1	25.8	1.6	8.8	10.9	3.6	12.6	13.3	3.1	47.2	20.2
Waller County..............	3.4	19.7	10.8	28.6	15.5	26.1	1.6	13.3	14.9	5.7	24.0	15.6	5.8	44.4	4.6
Ward County	1.6	20.7	12.0	20.0	16.8	21.1	1.0	13.7	18.4	14.4	10.1	15.5	9.8	42.2	7.7
Washington County	4.5	19.5	12.3	27.3	16.4	25.6	1.5	10.9	18.4	6.0	25.2	17.9	3.2	44.7	3.0
Webb County	2.9	20.2	5.5	26.7	17.8	29.0	0.6	11.4	14.6	2.5	12.2	18.1	13.9	46.7	6.6
Wharton County	2.9	19.7	10.9	27.3	16.6	21.3	3.3	10.3	21.1	11.5	20.5	15.2	5.2	43.6	4.0
Wheeler County	1.7	28.2	13.3	27.9	24.0	21.5	3.7	10.8	12.1	17.7	7.4	13.4	5.1	48.9	7.6
Wichita County	1.9	20.9	15.5	28.9	18.8	26.4	0.4	10.0	15.6	2.1	18.8	16.2	4.0	51.2	7.9
Wilbarger County	1.3	21.4	11.8	28.3	22.8	22.0	1.7	8.4	16.8	7.2	15.9	13.9	5.8	49.8	7.4
Willacy County	2.2	20.8	7.8	24.1	23.6	22.1	4.5	11.8	14.0	10.9	11.7	16.7	5.0	47.1	8.7
Williamson County	3.7	13.3	13.5	42.4	10.0	28.2	0.2	9.4	9.8	1.1	26.3	15.3	3.2	47.5	6.7
Wilson County	2.5	19.3	15.3	27.6	14.3	27.0	0.8	15.4	14.9	4.0	19.9	16.2	9.5	43.2	7.3
Winkler County	0.5	21.2	11.8	21.3	21.0	16.8	0.7	19.3	20.9	18.7	10.4	10.2	10.8	43.7	6.2
Wise County	3.4	17.8	14.7	26.2	14.2	25.4	1.1	14.1	19.0	7.3	22.8	16.6	9.3	40.0	4.1
Wood County	5.0	23.9	18.1	26.6	15.5	25.6	2.5	12.7	17.0	6.5	19.9	16.2	7.0	46.4	4.0
Yoakum County............	1.9	20.4	10.2	25.9	13.6	21.0	6.3	15.4	17.7	34.9	7.6	11.7	4.1	36.5	5.2
Young County	3.1	23.7	13.0	26.3	16.2	24.2	1.6	13.3	18.3	12.7	21.5	14.0	4.9	43.1	3.8
Zapata County..............	2.5	26.4	9.6	22.2	25.0	17.1	2.2	15.5	18.1	18.9	8.2	10.4	6.9	48.4	7.2
Zavala County..............	2.5	27.1	4.7	24.3	23.8	17.9	4.8	11.8	17.4	10.7	16.7	12.2	6.2	48.6	5.6
UTAH......................	4.2	14.9	10.6	32.5	14.0	28.9	0.5	10.6	13.5	1.9	20.3	16.3	4.9	51.1	5.5
Beaver County	3.5	18.5	12.9	26.2	18.9	18.8	10.1	10.8	15.2	20.6	11.9	13.6	9.9	37.8	6.1
Box Elder County	4.8	15.3	11.3	27.9	14.7	21.4	1.9	10.7	23.5	5.0	38.5	13.5	2.9	33.9	6.0
Cache County	4.6	11.0	7.5	32.7	14.6	24.2	1.6	8.1	18.9	2.8	28.5	13.5	2.3	50.3	2.7
Carbon County	3.0	22.6	14.6	24.1	17.3	25.7	0.2	17.3	15.5	12.0	9.7	16.4	9.1	47.0	5.8
Daggett County	12.5	17.8	16.4	26.8	26.0	19.9	3.9	15.5	7.9	19.9	12.9	6.6	7.6	36.7	16.3
Davis County................	4.1	12.8	12.6	34.5	12.4	30.9	0.2	10.0	11.9	0.7	18.4	18.5	5.1	48.2	9.1
Duchesne County..........	6.2	18.9	11.8	27.5	15.8	21.3	3.0	14.5	17.9	16.8	13.2	14.4	7.9	41.5	6.1
Emery County	4.2	16.7	12.0	23.0	15.1	21.6	1.6	22.7	15.9	17.5	11.2	15.0	10.8	39.6	5.9
Garfield County	5.3	15.0	15.1	32.0	22.8	21.0	3.2	12.5	8.6	9.7	10.3	11.4	4.7	56.3	7.6
Grand County	6.3	19.0	14.0	30.0	23.9	22.8	1.2	13.2	9.0	5.1	11.9	15.5	3.4	57.4	6.7
Iron County	2.9	13.6	10.0	27.5	16.2	28.5	1.7	13.0	13.1	4.3	21.4	14.8	3.9	51.3	4.4
Juab County.................	2.2	18.2	12.7	22.5	19.6	20.4	1.1	15.9	20.4	4.8	28.8	15.2	5.2	41.5	4.5
Kane County	10.5	17.0	17.9	29.2	18.0	24.4	1.2	15.3	11.8	5.6	14.4	12.3	8.0	51.9	7.9
Millard County	5.4	16.7	11.8	29.1	17.0	18.7	7.1	12.9	15.2	17.1	12.3	13.3	14.1	38.4	4.8
Morgan County	4.9	11.9	13.4	32.9	12.5	26.1	2.0	12.9	13.5	6.2	22.9	12.4	6.0	43.5	9.0
Piute County	6.3	20.4	15.4	33.5	15.2	20.1	7.6	10.9	12.8	15.5	13.7	10.9	9.4	40.5	10.0
Rich County.................	8.6	13.8	10.9	38.8	14.2	17.5	6.3	13.6	9.6	27.5	13.2	10.8	4.7	39.2	4.6
Salt Lake County..........	3.9	16.2	10.2	32.8	13.0	31.4	0.1	9.7	13.0	0.7	19.2	16.7	5.9	53.3	4.2
San Juan County	4.9	21.3	8.4	32.9	19.6	19.9	1.3	12.6	13.7	7.3	15.2	12.2	3.7	52.4	9.1
Sanpete County	5.2	16.7	11.7	28.3	16.1	20.8	3.9	14.5	16.3	10.2	22.9	12.9	3.7	44.4	5.9
Sevier County..............	5.0	17.0	13.7	24.1	18.7	24.4	2.5	13.5	16.8	8.3	15.7	17.6	8.0	43.6	6.9
Summit County	7.4	8.7	10.0	39.4	16.7	25.3	0.6	9.9	8.1	2.5	16.6	13.9	5.6	58.0	3.4
Tooele County	3.8	14.9	13.9	25.7	16.1	26.1	0.9	14.0	17.2	3.0	23.0	13.9	6.4	43.2	10.5
Uintah County	3.6	18.9	12.9	24.9	16.1	24.4	1.5	17.7	15.4	18.0	11.1	15.1	7.7	42.0	6.0
Utah County	5.0	11.8	7.0	36.5	14.0	27.7	0.3	10.1	11.4	1.0	20.0	16.1	2.6	57.1	3.1
Wasatch County	5.3	13.8	10.9	30.9	17.8	23.8	0.7	14.7	12.1	2.1	21.7	14.3	5.1	52.9	3.9
Washington County.......	5.0	16.8	15.1	26.9	18.3	27.5	0.4	13.8	13.2	1.1	20.0	19.8	4.5	51.1	3.5
Wayne County..............	5.1	16.8	13.7	34.2	20.0	15.9	6.1	13.8	10.0	16.0	15.4	9.2	4.0	48.1	7.4
Weber County	3.0	16.7	13.7	29.8	13.9	27.6	0.4	11.7	16.6	1.2	25.6	15.2	3.6	42.1	12.3
VERMONT	5.7	17.1	13.6	36.3	14.6	24.5	1.3	9.3	14.0	3.0	21.7	15.1	3.7	51.8	4.6
Addison County............	7.9	14.4	12.4	36.6	14.7	21.8	2.8	10.4	13.6	6.9	21.9	13.6	3.2	51.6	2.7
Bennington County.......	5.4	19.3	16.8	32.4	16.2	23.6	0.7	10.5	16.6	1.6	24.4	16.8	2.4	51.9	2.9
Caledonia County..........	6.6	18.5	15.4	31.0	15.1	24.2	2.6	10.1	17.0	5.0	22.4	16.0	4.3	47.2	5.0

Table B-3. States and Counties — **Education, Labor Force, and Income**

STATE County	Median house-hold income	Median family income — All families	Median family income — Married-couple	Families with children — Male house-holder	Families with children — Female house-holder	Median nonfamily house-hold income	Median income for full-year, full-time workers — Men	Median income for full-year, full-time workers — Women	Per capita income	With earnings	With interest, dividend, or rental income	With Social Security income	With public assis-tance income	With retire-ment income	House-holds with income over $100,000 (percent)	+/− U.S. percent for income over $100,000	House-holds with income below poverty (percent)	Families with children with income below poverty (percent)
	57	58	59	60	61	62	63	64	65	66	67	68	69	70	71	72	73	74
TEXAS—Cont'd																		
Tom Green County	33 148	39 482	46 069	21 845	16 244	19 007	29 409	21 428	17 325	79.1	30.8	27.7	4.1	18.5	5.8	-6.5	14.9	16.5
Travis County	46 761	58 555	68 286	31 526	25 017	32 200	38 992	31 131	25 883	89.9	37.1	13.2	1.7	10.7	16.1	3.8	11.3	11.0
Trinity County	27 070	32 304	40 135	25 446	19 890	12 420	28 601	22 293	15 472	64.9	24.2	41.8	4.8	23.0	3.7	-8.6	18.2	20.0
Tyler County.................	29 808	35 195	44 567	31 667	11 827	16 154	32 310	20 402	15 367	68.7	26.1	41.4	3.7	20.4	4.9	-7.4	15.5	19.0
Upshur County.............	33 347	38 857	42 417	29 219	16 406	16 068	31 754	21 253	16 358	75.2	27.2	32.1	3.4	17.5	5.0	-7.3	15.2	16.6
Upton County................	28 977	37 083	38 813	15 625	12 708	17 550	31 523	19 153	14 274	76.9	26.8	31.3	3.1	14.0	3.8	-8.5	17.5	24.2
Uvalde County..............	27 164	30 671	35 094	20 000	12 292	13 296	25 817	16 983	12 557	76.8	22.5	29.9	5.8	14.4	4.7	-7.6	23.3	26.8
Val Verde County.........	28 376	31 434	33 161	15 486	13 977	13 736	28 031	18 812	12 096	79.7	20.5	25.8	5.7	13.3	4.8	-7.5	24.5	28.9
Van Zandt County........	35 029	41 175	47 781	28 393	16 652	15 747	32 727	22 074	16 930	72.3	28.6	35.2	2.6	19.6	6.0	-6.3	13.8	14.9
Victoria County............	38 732	44 443	53 387	23 021	16 829	22 174	36 263	21 760	18 379	82.2	29.9	25.7	2.9	13.4	8.7	-3.6	12.7	15.0
Walker County..............	31 468	42 589	42 977	23 088	19 935	17 115	28 614	23 311	14 508	80.7	25.7	22.8	2.6	15.1	6.7	-5.6	19.6	15.7
Waller County...............	38 136	45 868	50 813	21 607	20 147	19 904	35 765	26 061	16 338	82.8	23.4	24.0	2.7	13.7	10.9	-1.4	15.5	16.2
Ward County.................	29 386	36 014	42 456	26 964	12 798	12 170	31 907	19 229	14 393	74.9	22.0	31.1	4.5	15.3	4.8	-7.5	19.2	21.5
Washington County.......	36 760	43 982	52 532	26 500	18 520	16 855	32 428	22 510	17 384	74.2	40.4	32.0	2.4	15.3	7.2	-5.1	14.6	13.2
Webb County	28 100	29 394	32 211	17 137	12 081	14 288	24 267	19 543	10 759	85.2	14.3	21.6	7.9	9.0	6.2	-6.1	28.1	32.8
Wharton County	32 208	39 919	47 559	24 375	19 771	16 242	31 348	20 949	15 388	78.0	26.9	29.5	2.7	11.9	6.4	-5.9	17.5	17.1
Wheeler County............	31 029	36 989	37 813	25 938	13 036	16 378	29 302	20 046	16 083	76.6	32.4	36.4	2.1	13.2	4.0	-8.3	16.0	15.2
Wichita County	33 780	40 937	45 341	26 481	17 015	20 478	30 186	22 774	16 965	80.5	31.8	26.9	3.2	17.5	5.8	-6.5	13.3	14.9
Wilbarger County.........	29 500	38 685	44 417	24 609	19 628	14 815	26 996	20 410	16 520	76.1	29.0	32.7	3.0	17.6	6.5	-5.8	14.0	14.2
Willacy County	22 114	25 076	28 252	19 792	12 250	8 970	20 248	16 413	9 421	72.2	13.3	33.9	9.8	11.5	2.5	-9.8	32.9	36.2
Williamson County	60 642	66 208	71 907	40 110	31 280	36 301	45 525	31 344	24 547	90.1	39.0	15.4	1.2	13.3	18.6	6.3	4.6	4.6
Wilson County	40 006	45 681	53 646	30 529	21 746	19 608	32 259	24 345	17 253	81.1	27.2	27.7	1.9	17.6	7.9	-4.4	12.2	10.7
Winkler County.............	30 591	34 021	39 475	15 547	14 875	14 487	33 611	19 223	13 725	73.7	25.5	28.2	5.8	15.3	3.0	-9.3	18.6	21.0
Wise County.................	41 933	47 909	53 429	31 576	19 571	20 573	36 981	24 225	17 729	83.5	27.9	24.3	2.0	14.2	8.0	-4.3	10.1	9.9
Wood County................	32 885	38 219	42 429	25 996	17 750	16 844	31 745	21 049	17 702	69.7	34.5	40.3	3.2	23.6	5.7	-6.6	14.1	16.9
Yoakum County............	32 672	36 772	36 939	28 214	10 972	15 443	33 672	21 115	14 504	81.3	23.4	26.2	3.4	11.1	6.2	-6.1	18.2	21.8
Young County	30 499	36 698	42 175	26 389	15 045	16 230	30 989	20 360	16 710	74.8	32.5	35.3	3.6	13.6	5.9	-6.4	15.3	19.2
Zapata County..............	24 635	24 722	29 505	11 563	8 214	13 689	27 279	17 333	10 486	68.2	26.7	37.6	9.6	15.6	3.3	-9.0	29.6	40.7
Zavala County..............	16 844	19 418	25 728	9 583	9 913	7 392	23 779	15 012	10 034	70.8	10.5	33.8	15.5	10.9	1.6	-10.7	41.5	42.3
UTAH......................	45 726	51 022	56 556	32 364	22 090	26 405	38 046	25 579	18 185	86.1	37.5	20.6	3.1	15.7	11.2	-1.1	8.9	8.7
Beaver County	34 544	39 253	41 442	35 000	16 806	14 438	32 133	18 333	14 957	76.5	29.0	31.7	4.0	15.3	3.6	-8.7	10.7	8.5
Box Elder County	44 630	49 421	52 765	32 670	20 189	21 546	40 100	23 258	15 625	83.6	38.9	26.0	2.7	20.4	6.4	-5.9	7.3	7.6
Cache County	39 730	44 453	49 926	36 500	22 460	23 897	33 631	21 588	15 094	88.2	40.0	17.2	2.5	12.1	7.7	-4.6	13.1	9.4
Carbon County	34 036	40 900	52 960	31 528	14 333	16 290	40 128	22 091	15 325	73.7	24.5	31.3	4.7	20.1	4.8	-7.5	14.0	12.4
Daggett County	30 833	41 484	46 563	10 417	16 875	19 750	38 906	21 583	15 511	78.2	34.0	29.1	4.4	24.7	4.7	-7.6	7.6	5.1
Davis County	53 726	58 329	63 078	36 530	23 231	29 225	42 019	26 613	19 506	89.4	41.2	17.7	2.9	18.2	14.1	1.8	5.1	5.5
Duchesne County.........	31 298	35 350	39 931	27 250	13 274	14 107	33 020	20 489	12 326	80.0	23.3	26.4	7.6	13.5	3.3	-9.0	17.4	18.7
Emery County	39 850	44 086	48 868	30 750	13 854	17 045	40 039	20 049	14 243	79.5	29.3	27.5	4.8	20.6	4.3	-8.0	10.9	11.9
Garfield County	35 180	40 192	45 350	14 375	21 806	16 795	31 021	20 969	13 439	79.5	32.0	32.4	2.0	21.5	2.3	-10.0	8.8	8.2
Grand County	32 387	39 095	45 255	18 542	17 500	21 018	31 758	23 480	17 356	81.8	34.5	24.8	6.1	14.0	5.7	-6.6	13.0	19.3
Iron County..................	33 114	37 171	40 301	20 438	14 853	20 463	31 438	20 299	13 568	85.7	35.3	21.3	3.9	15.9	5.3	-7.0	16.8	18.0
Juab County	38 139	42 655	47 278	29 375	20 417	15 781	34 782	22 208	12 790	78.0	20.2	24.8	6.6	16.6	4.5	-7.8	11.2	9.5
Kane County	34 247	40 030	44 330	35 000	20 833	19 069	31 863	21 387	15 455	79.4	33.6	34.0	2.7	23.2	3.3	-9.0	8.5	7.3
Millard County	36 178	41 797	47 456	28 750	17 500	16 385	37 730	20 914	13 408	79.0	33.7	29.9	5.1	20.1	3.5	-8.8	11.5	13.2
Morgan County	50 273	53 365	61 123	28 125	30 357	21 313	45 458	23 625	17 684	87.6	43.8	23.5	2.4	23.3	13.4	1.1	5.3	4.8
Piute County................	29 625	35 147	40 909	2 499	16 875	11 719	28 583	20 125	12 697	73.4	24.3	40.6	6.2	23.3	3.0	-9.3	15.1	19.1
Rich County.................	39 766	44 783	43 906	26 250	16 250	19 792	35 655	22 422	16 267	83.9	38.0	31.5	4.3	21.6	7.2	-5.1	9.5	8.2
Salt Lake County.........	48 373	54 470	60 645	35 180	24 040	29 099	37 854	26 742	20 190	87.3	37.9	19.2	3.0	13.9	13.0	0.7	7.7	8.0
San Juan County	28 137	31 673	37 125	16 875	13 750	13 492	33 299	20 014	10 229	78.9	20.6	20.4	10.6	11.1	3.4	-8.9	29.1	30.3
Sanpete County	33 042	37 796	42 658	25 893	16 701	16 689	31 113	20 788	12 442	78.6	30.6	30.3	4.3	18.2	4.1	-8.2	15.1	13.2
Sevier County	35 822	40 110	45 321	32 292	14 280	15 948	34 593	19 927	14 180	77.7	34.3	31.7	4.5	21.2	3.9	-8.4	11.1	11.9
Summit County	64 962	72 510	80 212	40 417	31 250	42 231	50 691	30 120	33 767	92.6	47.2	11.6	1.4	9.7	28.7	16.4	4.6	4.3
Tooele County	45 773	50 438	52 935	32 386	18 977	24 870	39 132	24 930	16 321	86.8	27.9	17.2	3.0	20.5	6.6	-5.7	7.2	7.0
Uintah County	34 518	38 877	46 129	25 250	12 455	19 488	35 495	22 117	13 571	82.0	28.4	23.4	5.3	12.9	4.5	-7.8	13.6	16.2
Utah County	45 833	50 196	55 408	35 577	23 389	26 794	39 601	23 551	15 557	89.4	38.7	17.9	2.4	13.4	11.1	-1.2	10.7	7.8
Wasatch County...........	49 612	52 102	58 275	40 625	20 880	26 518	40 236	24 762	19 869	87.0	36.6	21.2	2.5	15.1	11.3	-1.0	5.3	5.7
Washington County......	37 212	41 845	46 499	20 179	18 046	20 209	32 221	21 795	15 873	72.7	38.1	35.9	3.0	25.1	6.9	-5.4	9.7	13.0
Wayne County..............	32 000	36 940	40 909	24 583	13 281	17 232	26 938	20 156	15 392	75.7	37.4	30.8	1.7	20.9	4.1	-8.2	14.4	20.4
Weber County	44 014	49 724	55 904	30 580	20 090	24 976	37 140	25 544	18 246	83.8	36.5	22.8	3.8	19.6	9.2	-3.1	9.1	10.3
VERMONT	40 856	48 625	56 642	28 817	19 973	24 557	34 148	26 223	20 625	82.2	45.0	26.5	4.8	15.5	8.7	-3.6	9.7	9.7
Addison County............	43 142	49 351	53 992	31 429	22 173	24 018	33 094	25 713	19 539	84.0	48.1	26.3	3.8	13.8	8.3	-4.0	8.4	7.5
Bennington County.......	39 926	46 565	55 114	29 833	17 517	22 190	33 483	24 917	21 193	79.2	44.4	31.4	4.9	17.8	9.6	-2.7	10.2	11.6
Caledonia County.........	34 800	42 215	48 813	26 250	16 667	19 210	31 247	23 281	16 976	78.6	40.4	30.3	7.5	16.6	5.1	-7.2	12.4	14.5

STATE/ County code	MSA/PMSA/ NECMA code[1]	STATE County	High school graduates		College graduates		College graduates (percent)				
			Total population 25 years and over	Percent with a high school diploma or less	Percent with a high school diploma or more	Percent with a bachelor's degree or more	+/− U.S. percent with bachelor's degree or more	Non-Hispanic White	Black or African American	American Indian and Alaska Native	Asian, Hawaiian, and Pacific Islander	Hispanic or Latino[2]
			1	2	3	4	5	6	7	8	9	10
		VERMONT—Cont'd										
50 007	1303	Chittenden County	92 651	32.9	90.6	41.2	16.8	41.1	38.3	33.2	46.3	47.1
50 009	...	Essex County	4 384	71.0	75.0	10.8	-13.6	10.4	0.0	5.4	18.2	62.5
50 011	1303	Franklin County	29 485	58.5	82.6	16.6	-7.8	16.8	30.0	8.1	36.1	4.9
50 013	1303	Grand Isle County	4 796	49.6	84.2	25.0	0.6	25.2	50.0	0.0	30.0	20.0
50 015	...	Lamoille County	15 281	43.6	87.0	31.2	6.8	31.5	31.3	26.6	37.5	42.3
50 017	...	Orange County	18 821	53.4	84.1	23.9	-0.5	23.8	29.6	10.7	55.0	32.3
50 019	...	Orleans County	17 814	62.5	78.2	16.1	-8.3	16.1	38.1	8.7	31.8	17.1
50 021	...	Rutland County	43 289	51.5	84.3	23.2	-1.2	23.2	12.7	14.4	45.7	37.5
50 023	...	Washington County..........	39 167	43.1	88.4	32.2	7.8	32.3	29.7	33.6	39.1	38.0
50 025	...	Windham County..........	30 542	45.4	87.3	30.5	6.1	30.3	47.5	14.3	51.1	44.6
50 027	...	Windsor County..........	40 618	44.2	88.1	30.2	5.8	30.1	33.3	33.8	53.4	24.5
51 000	...	VIRGINIA................	4 000 574	44.5	81.5	20.5	5.1	32.4	15.1	19.6	48.5	20.7
51 001	...	Accomack County	25 894	66.2	67.9	13.5	-10.9	17.8	4.7	0.0	44.2	2.3
51 003	1540	Albemarle County	53 847	30.4	87.4	47.7	23.3	49.8	20.7	27.7	77.5	32.0
51 005	...	Alleghany County	9 168	61.7	77.5	13.6	-10.8	13.3	10.0	X	74.5	0.0
51 007	...	Amelia County	7 789	67.9	68.3	9.8	-14.6	10.9	7.1	0.0	0.0	100.0
51 009	4640	Amherst County	21 293	62.8	70.6	13.1	-11.3	15.0	4.7	9.8	43.1	9.7
51 011	...	Appomattox County	9 421	67.6	70.7	10.5	-13.9	12.4	2.6	0.0	50.0	59.0
51 013	8840	Arlington County	138 844	23.9	87.8	60.2	35.8	73.8	29.9	31.7	59.8	20.6
51 015	...	Augusta County..........	45 609	62.1	78.2	15.4	-9.0	15.7	8.2	0.0	32.1	17.3
51 017	...	Bath County	3 705	65.1	74.0	11.1	-13.3	11.5	0.0	X	0.0	33.9
51 019	4640	Bedford County	42 413	52.6	80.1	20.9	-3.5	21.8	3.6	27.8	42.7	17.8
51 021	...	Bland County..............	4 989	67.2	70.9	9.2	-15.2	9.3	0.0	X	X	57.1
51 023	6800	Botetourt County	21 621	52.5	81.4	19.6	-4.8	19.9	12.3	4.0	36.4	25.7
51 025	...	Brunswick County	12 777	67.8	63.2	10.8	-13.6	10.9	10.9	22.2	0.0	7.6
51 027	...	Buchanan County	18 051	74.7	52.0	8.0	-16.1	7.9	11.7	X	29.8	3.0
51 029	...	Buckingham County	10 893	75.3	62.8	8.5	-15.9	10.1	6.1	X	100.0	13.7
51 031	4640	Campbell County..........	35 018	59.9	73.4	14.6	-9.8	15.9	4.6	7.3	59.4	24.1
51 033	...	Caroline County	16 099	44.7	71.7	13.1	-12.3	15.3	5.8	6.0	21.1	14.4
51 035	...	Carroll County	21 006	69.6	64.3	9.5	-14.9	9.5	0.0	0.0	20.0	15.9
51 036	6760	Charles City County	4 845	68.9	65.7	10.5	-13.9	19.1	5.3	1.2	0.0	0.0
51 037	...	Charlotte County	8 570	71.6	63.2	10.3	-14.1	12.2	5.9	X	0.0	17.9
51 041	6760	Chesterfield County	167 037	36.7	88.1	32.6	8.2	33.0	26.4	21.0	45.0	20.8
51 043	8840	Clarke County	9 015	50.8	82.1	23.9	-0.5	24.9	10.5	32.4	37.2	14.9
51 045	...	Craig County	3 561	64.2	76.6	10.8	-13.6	10.9	0.0	0.0	18.2	X
51 047	8840	Culpeper County	22 628	62.0	73.7	15.7	-8.7	17.4	5.0	22.9	46.0	18.5
51 049	...	Cumberland County	6 183	69.8	63.8	11.8	-12.6	14.0	7.8	0.0	100.0	12.4
51 051	...	Dickenson County	11 308	76.0	58.9	6.7	-17.7	6.7	0.0	0.0	15.4	0.0
51 053	6760	Dinwiddie County	17 199	68.0	70.0	11.0	-13.4	12.5	7.8	9.3	54.0	5.8
51 057	...	Essex County	7 052	61.3	73.5	17.4	-7.0	21.4	9.7	75.0	55.9	37.5
51 059	8840	Fairfax County	653 237	23.1	90.7	54.8	30.4	62.0	37.5	38.2	51.6	23.3
51 061	8840	Fauquier County............	36 792	43.4	84.5	27.1	2.7	29.1	6.3	26.4	35.0	25.7
51 063	...	Floyd County	9 836	68.2	70.1	12.5	-11.9	12.6	9.0	X	52.4	0.0
51 065	1540	Fluvanna County	14 125	52.5	80.0	24.5	0.1	28.1	9.0	0.0	37.8	24.1
51 067	...	Franklin County	33 037	60.4	72.2	14.8	-9.6	15.3	8.1	25.6	23.5	14.5
51 069	...	Frederick County	39 271	57.1	78.6	18.6	-5.8	18.6	13.9	28.3	38.4	10.7
51 071	...	Giles County................	11 856	64.9	75.9	12.4	-12.0	12.3	12.0	100.0	61.1	10.8
51 073	5720	Gloucester County	23 273	49.9	81.7	17.6	-6.8	18.4	11.1	34.9	32.1	8.2
51 075	6760	Goochland County	12 248	50.6	78.8	29.4	5.0	36.0	8.4	0.0	71.3	35.0
51 077	...	Grayson County	13 086	73.6	64.1	8.0	-16.4	8.1	6.9	0.0	11.1	10.6
51 079	1540	Greene County	10 120	56.3	78.4	19.8	-4.6	21.1	2.5	0.0	32.0	0.0
51 081	...	Greensville County	8 610	77.1	62.1	11.0	-13.4	7.9	12.9	0.0	100.0	13.0
51 083	...	Halifax County..............	26 073	69.9	63.9	9.5	-14.9	11.6	5.2	5.3	31.8	20.1
51 085	6760	Hanover County............	56 892	42.2	86.6	28.7	4.3	29.8	17.5	14.1	41.3	26.4
51 087	6760	Henrico County	177 191	37.1	86.6	34.9	10.5	39.2	20.1	9.1	50.3	21.4
51 089	...	Henry County	40 518	67.8	64.9	9.4	-15.0	10.4	6.0	10.9	23.1	4.5
51 091	...	Highland County...........	1 929	65.4	72.8	13.2	-11.2	13.3	0.0	0.0	X	0.0
51 093	5720	Isle of Wight County......	20 121	54.3	76.2	17.5	-6.9	21.1	6.7	5.9	28.6	37.6
51 095	5720	James City County.......	34 042	31.6	89.3	41.5	17.1	46.5	10.8	8.7	60.2	32.8
51 097	...	King and Queen County	4 663	69.0	68.2	10.3	-14.1	13.4	4.6	25.6	X	12.1
51 099	8840	King George County	10 803	52.0	80.4	23.6	-0.8	26.3	9.5	11.5	50.0	48.2
51 101	...	King William County	8 960	59.1	79.1	14.8	-9.6	16.2	9.5	7.1	32.4	8.8
51 103	...	Lancaster County	8 841	53.5	74.4	24.5	0.1	31.7	1.6	100.0	68.9	47.8
51 105	...	Lee County	16 314	71.2	60.6	9.5	-14.9	9.3	0.0	25.0	67.2	0.0
51 107	8840	Loudoun County	109 567	25.1	92.5	47.2	22.8	49.6	32.0	23.9	53.0	24.7

[1]MSA = Metropolitan Statistical Area. PMSA = Primary MSA. NECMA = New England County Metropolitan Area. See the Appendix A for explanation of these concepts. See Appendix B for list of metropolitan areas identified by type, with component counties.
[2]Hispanic or Latino persons may be of any race.

STATE County	School enrollment			Population 16 to 19 years				Employment status, 2000			Work status in 1999 of the population 16 years and over (percent)		
											Worked in 1999		
	Grades kindergarten through 12	College or graduate school	Percent private	Number	Percent in armed forces	Percent high school graduates	Percent not enrolled, not grads, not in armed forces, not employed	Total population 16 years and over	Percent in labor force	Unemployment rate	Full-time	Part-time	Did not work in 1999
	11	12	13	14	15	16	17	18	19	20	21	22	23
VERMONT—Cont'd													
Chittenden County	25 849	17 217	18.2	9 953	0.0	5.9	1.5	116 010	72.9	4.0	60.2	20.3	19.5
Essex County	1 322	121	7.6	342	0.0	18.1	6.4	5 004	63.2	6.2	53.1	14.3	32.6
Franklin County	9 512	1 223	5.2	2 438	0.1	18.9	3.2	34 081	70.4	3.7	59.7	15.0	25.4
Grand Isle County	1 327	192	8.0	321	0.0	5.9	2.2	5 388	67.8	3.4	58.3	15.4	26.3
Lamoille County	4 237	1 637	9.3	1 316	0.0	9.8	2.4	18 222	71.4	4.6	58.3	20.7	21.0
Orange County	5 634	1 232	12.4	1 679	0.0	11.4	1.9	21 891	70.5	4.4	57.9	18.3	23.8
Orleans County	5 214	811	10.1	1 408	0.0	14.3	4.3	20 562	62.7	6.7	52.1	15.9	31.9
Rutland County	11 748	3 396	12.2	3 623	0.2	11.5	2.7	50 474	65.8	4.7	53.0	18.7	28.3
Washington County	10 728	3 593	19.9	3 245	0.3	11.0	1.1	46 016	70.5	3.2	58.2	18.6	23.2
Windham County	8 180	2 145	21.2	2 438	0.0	9.1	3.2	35 119	69.1	4.0	55.5	19.7	24.8
Windsor County	10 809	2 225	13.4	2 845	0.0	12.1	2.1	45 692	66.4	3.2	54.5	18.1	27.3
VIRGINIA	1 291 600	450 800	13.2	382 918	2.0	12.2	4.0	5 529 980	66.8	4.1	59.6	13.6	26.8
Accomack County	7 110	881	8.5	1 972	0.0	13.8	8.2	30 048	60.3	7.5	51.0	14.0	35.1
Albemarle County	14 705	5 379	13.3	3 371	0.0	9.1	3.9	61 615	66.6	3.1	59.2	14.7	26.1
Alleghany County	2 198	382	4.4	599	0.0	13.2	1.5	10 322	57.1	5.3	51.5	10.8	37.7
Amelia County	2 238	219	12.3	533	0.0	10.7	2.1	8 794	65.2	2.9	57.4	13.4	29.2
Amherst County	5 609	1 757	23.4	2 053	0.0	14.7	6.3	25 315	61.0	5.0	52.9	13.5	33.6
Appomattox County	2 628	350	10.0	667	0.0	6.9	1.6	10 712	61.5	2.9	53.2	13.1	33.7
Arlington County	21 548	16 371	30.9	5 912	3.9	12.1	3.7	161 333	74.9	2.7	69.6	10.7	19.8
Augusta County	12 054	1 580	11.2	3 215	0.0	15.2	2.9	51 860	65.2	2.5	59.1	12.6	28.3
Bath County	836	135	6.6	181	0.0	4.4	0.0	4 124	63.5	4.2	56.2	11.3	32.5
Bedford County	10 747	1 752	13.5	2 735	0.0	16.6	3.7	47 464	66.0	2.9	58.1	13.1	28.8
Bland County	1 104	258	9.8	325	0.0	7.4	4.9	5 723	49.3	4.5	51.1	10.8	38.1
Botetourt County	5 518	937	11.6	1 502	0.0	13.3	1.3	24 204	66.8	2.7	60.1	11.9	28.0
Brunswick County	3 224	908	18.2	990	0.7	12.0	9.0	15 074	46.4	7.2	51.3	10.0	38.7
Buchanan County	4 398	905	4.8	1 585	0.0	13.3	12.6	22 008	39.8	8.3	36.7	8.5	54.8
Buckingham County	2 914	336	7.6	672	0.0	19.2	10.3	12 484	49.2	5.5	51.5	10.3	38.2
Campbell County	9 357	1 918	13.5	2 394	0.0	14.3	1.5	40 079	64.7	3.0	58.1	11.8	30.1
Caroline County	4 191	459	6.7	1 117	0.0	19.3	6.4	17 267	63.9	4.3	60.3	11.3	28.4
Carroll County	4 542	935	4.6	1 200	0.0	13.8	5.0	23 758	61.4	6.1	55.2	10.4	34.4
Charles City County	1 216	240	12.9	353	0.0	14.7	1.1	5 587	64.0	3.7	60.0	9.5	30.5
Charlotte County	2 414	284	6.8	671	0.0	15.6	8.5	9 777	56.1	5.6	49.7	10.0	40.3
Chesterfield County	56 777	13 958	9.3	15 826	0.2	8.9	3.1	195 326	72.1	3.1	63.2	15.0	21.9
Clarke County	2 349	385	14.4	535	0.0	8.6	3.7	10 002	67.1	2.1	59.7	12.6	27.7
Craig County	883	110	10.8	206	0.0	21.4	11.2	3 998	61.1	2.8	57.5	9.1	33.4
Culpeper County	6 702	919	10.4	2 106	0.0	10.6	13.2	26 543	63.4	3.2	57.2	13.2	29.6
Cumberland County	1 712	193	20.3	453	0.0	20.5	4.6	7 023	59.6	3.5	52.3	11.3	36.4
Dickenson County	2 829	668	2.1	969	0.0	16.1	4.3	13 259	41.7	7.2	37.7	7.9	54.4
Dinwiddie County	4 508	686	7.2	1 075	0.0	12.7	4.4	19 258	62.2	3.7	56.7	11.1	32.2
Essex County	1 912	311	10.6	421	0.0	9.0	1.0	7 936	63.0	3.2	55.6	12.3	32.1
Fairfax County	181 731	62 896	16.7	45 985	0.2	7.0	3.3	750 436	73.1	2.5	65.7	13.2	21.1
Fauquier County	11 091	2 217	16.1	2 883	0.5	16.6	1.7	42 007	70.1	2.5	60.8	14.3	24.9
Floyd County	2 169	405	8.6	651	0.0	17.5	2.3	11 161	61.4	3.6	53.3	13.1	33.6
Fluvanna County	3 538	827	11.2	868	0.0	9.3	0.6	15 856	63.9	2.9	58.3	13.5	28.2
Franklin County	7 814	2 126	14.3	2 227	0.0	14.1	3.1	37 923	63.0	3.8	57.3	12.1	30.6
Frederick County	11 715	1 918	7.8	3 070	0.1	14.4	3.7	45 387	70.0	2.5	61.7	13.9	24.4
Giles County	2 747	504	4.8	745	0.0	18.7	2.7	13 406	58.1	5.4	53.2	10.7	36.1
Gloucester County	7 144	1 627	7.6	1 902	0.0	11.5	2.6	26 749	66.8	3.9	57.1	14.4	28.5
Goochland County	2 779	587	26.8	691	0.0	10.9	1.3	13 717	63.1	1.7	59.0	14.1	26.9
Grayson County	2 667	439	7.4	769	0.0	20.5	5.6	14 819	55.3	3.6	53.8	10.1	36.1
Greene County	3 014	492	12.4	805	0.0	15.8	4.8	11 493	72.3	2.7	62.3	13.7	23.9
Greensville County	2 063	445	14.1	459	0.0	13.1	3.5	9 736	40.8	4.4	56.8	7.1	36.1
Halifax County	6 553	1 112	6.6	1 799	0.0	18.6	5.1	29 648	54.9	7.4	51.6	9.6	38.8
Hanover County	17 536	4 301	11.3	4 777	0.0	7.4	2.7	65 561	70.6	2.2	61.9	15.0	23.1
Henrico County	46 900	13 581	11.9	11 991	0.1	10.4	3.1	204 487	70.0	2.9	62.3	13.4	24.3
Henry County	9 981	2 200	7.4	2 787	0.5	15.5	6.6	46 420	61.2	5.4	56.5	10.2	33.3
Highland County	412	43	6.6	113	0.0	20.4	0.0	2 101	57.3	6.7	48.0	14.9	37.1
Isle of Wight County	5 731	969	15.2	1 477	0.0	8.3	4.8	23 081	64.3	4.1	57.2	12.6	30.2
James City County	8 630	2 277	11.0	2 111	0.0	12.2	3.8	38 248	60.5	3.5	53.4	15.1	31.5
King and Queen County	1 132	136	10.4	337	0.0	20.8	5.0	5 316	59.2	4.1	53.6	11.8	34.7
King George County	3 444	735	9.1	940	6.5	24.5	1.1	12 632	69.1	4.0	61.3	12.8	25.8
King William County	2 537	348	7.2	567	0.0	10.8	1.2	10 096	68.6	3.1	65.4	11.2	23.5
Lancaster County	1 805	197	10.8	437	0.0	10.5	3.4	9 616	48.7	6.4	41.1	14.3	44.6
Lee County	3 985	833	6.7	1 185	0.0	12.9	8.8	18 905	48.0	8.0	40.6	11.0	48.4
Loudoun County	33 317	8 012	14.1	6 931	0.1	8.3	3.1	123 421	77.5	2.0	69.7	13.5	16.8

Table B-3. States and Counties — Education, Labor Force, and Income

STATE County	Full-year full-time employed (percent)								Children under 18 years in families						Total employed by class of worker (percent)			
										With two parents (percent)		With one parent who is in labor force (percent)	+/− U.S. percent of children with no stay-at-home parent (percent)	+/− U.S. percent two-income couples				
	Total	Men	Women	Non-Hispanic White	Black or African American	American Indian and Alaska Native	Asian, Hawaiian, and Pacific Islander	Hispanic or Latino[1]	Number	Both in labor force	Father only in labor force				Private	Government	Self-employed	Unpaid family worker
	24	25	26	27	28	29	30	31	32	33	34	35	36	37	38	39	40	41
VERMONT—Cont'd																		
Chittenden County	45.2	56.4	34.9	45.5	38.7	47.7	38.6	30.2	33 440	55.9	19.2	17.7	9.0	13.4	76.9	12.5	10.4	0.2
Essex County	37.9	45.8	30.0	37.9	0.0	43.6	30.8	66.7	1 571	51.0	15.6	19.9	6.3	1.5	70.3	17.0	12.8	0.0
Franklin County	46.9	57.7	36.6	47.2	37.0	43.1	41.0	34.4	12 285	58.1	15.2	18.7	12.2	12.6	71.0	15.1	13.4	0.5
Grand Isle County	44.5	53.5	35.6	44.9	0.0	13.8	8.3	21.4	1 646	53.4	18.1	19.6	8.4	3.4	68.5	14.9	16.2	0.4
Lamoille County	41.6	51.6	31.8	41.9	60.7	48.9	18.5	42.7	5 422	52.6	15.9	23.5	11.5	7.9	67.1	15.5	17.0	0.4
Orange County	43.2	51.9	34.8	43.3	34.1	41.4	32.7	40.4	6 979	52.8	16.9	20.0	8.2	9.7	68.1	16.0	15.7	0.2
Orleans County	37.6	48.2	27.5	37.9	47.6	37.2	30.2	27.2	6 310	50.6	15.8	21.4	7.4	3.1	65.8	15.7	18.0	0.5
Rutland County	40.8	51.9	30.5	41.0	33.8	27.8	28.8	42.4	14 098	53.5	14.8	21.8	10.7	7.2	73.2	13.4	13.1	0.3
Washington County	43.9	51.7	36.6	44.2	29.9	46.4	32.3	43.8	13 202	58.4	14.1	20.7	14.5	13.8	66.5	20.0	13.2	0.2
Windham County	40.6	50.2	31.7	40.9	44.8	31.0	35.6	25.5	10 048	54.3	15.5	22.0	11.7	10.0	70.4	12.4	16.8	0.3
Windsor County	41.7	50.9	33.2	41.9	35.6	32.2	34.2	29.8	12 835	57.8	13.8	20.1	13.3	7.2	69.2	14.0	16.5	0.3
VIRGINIA	45.6	55.6	36.2	46.9	41.4	45.8	44.3	43.5	1 639 504	46.4	21.4	21.5	3.3	4.3	71.6	19.6	8.6	0.2
Accomack County	36.9	45.4	29.3	38.8	34.5	41.9	47.9	25.7	8 160	37.9	16.1	30.4	3.7	-4.1	68.2	18.2	13.3	0.3
Albemarle County	44.6	54.1	36.1	44.7	45.4	44.4	40.0	41.3	18 892	49.6	23.3	19.9	4.9	4.0	59.9	27.6	12.1	0.4
Alleghany County	39.2	51.2	27.4	39.4	34.4	X	34.0	0.0	2 753	49.1	27.2	13.4	-2.1	-10.4	81.0	12.8	5.8	0.4
Amelia County	43.0	52.6	33.8	45.1	38.4	0.0	0.0	100.0	2 749	48.2	23.0	19.7	3.3	0.9	68.6	18.3	12.7	0.3
Amherst County	42.1	53.1	32.6	43.4	38.3	28.7	30.5	42.5	6 906	51.5	14.2	22.4	9.3	-0.1	77.2	15.5	7.0	0.3
Appomattox County	42.2	52.5	33.0	43.3	39.6	16.2	43.3	20.5	3 181	44.2	18.3	25.2	4.8	-1.6	77.3	15.0	7.5	0.2
Arlington County	52.4	59.3	45.5	57.9	44.3	49.1	44.1	41.5	29 107	48.2	21.6	17.6	1.2	9.1	69.1	24.0	6.7	0.2
Augusta County	47.2	57.1	37.4	47.8	33.4	72.2	37.0	50.8	14 689	54.3	21.3	16.3	6.0	4.4	74.9	14.8	9.9	0.4
Bath County	42.1	55.1	29.6	43.3	35.3	X	0.0	22.9	1 003	52.7	33.2	11.2	-0.7	-6.5	68.0	20.2	11.1	0.6
Bedford County	46.2	57.5	35.1	46.7	40.0	41.1	49.6	35.8	13 891	53.4	23.4	14.6	3.4	3.0	77.9	11.2	10.6	0.3
Bland County	35.5	42.5	26.9	36.4	20.6	X	X	35.7	1 246	47.8	25.4	8.7	-8.1	-8.1	66.7	19.9	12.8	0.6
Botetourt County	48.8	60.0	37.8	49.6	37.6	47.4	20.4	38.5	6 756	57.1	25.1	12.6	5.1	5.0	76.0	13.3	10.5	0.3
Brunswick County	34.8	38.1	31.0	40.0	30.7	8.3	30.3	54.3	3 420	36.6	10.6	32.1	4.1	-3.5	63.6	25.2	10.9	0.2
Buchanan County	24.1	30.1	17.9	24.5	8.2	X	32.7	16.1	5 203	30.7	23.9	7.7	-20.2	-24.2	71.2	19.5	8.7	0.6
Buckingham County	35.3	38.6	31.1	38.4	30.4	X	0.0	12.7	3 090	43.0	13.3	29.4	7.8	-4.3	61.0	26.6	11.1	1.3
Campbell County	46.4	57.1	36.6	47.7	40.3	45.8	42.0	27.8	11 504	45.9	20.6	22.0	3.3	1.8	78.2	12.6	8.9	0.3
Caroline County	45.9	54.2	37.8	48.9	40.8	29.4	43.1	45.9	5 114	42.3	21.6	26.0	3.7	0.3	72.9	18.6	8.3	0.2
Carroll County	41.8	52.2	31.9	42.0	27.7	0.0	60.0	40.1	5 908	49.1	22.2	18.3	2.8	-2.1	74.8	14.5	10.2	0.5
Charles City County	46.4	54.4	39.1	47.0	45.0	58.1	100.0	41.7	1 337	40.3	11.1	31.4	7.1	5.9	75.2	16.6	8.0	0.2
Charlotte County	36.2	45.0	28.4	37.4	34.1	X	66.7	30.5	2 762	48.1	15.9	17.7	1.2	-6.3	68.5	17.0	13.9	0.6
Chesterfield County	50.8	62.2	40.4	50.9	52.0	46.9	46.8	46.2	69 951	52.9	22.2	17.2	5.5	9.6	74.0	17.7	8.2	0.2
Clarke County	47.1	58.4	36.5	48.2	36.5	41.2	80.4	25.9	2 862	51.2	22.9	20.3	6.9	4.5	66.7	18.0	14.7	0.6
Craig County	47.0	56.7	37.1	47.1	100.0	0.0	45.5	X	1 153	39.1	35.3	16.3	-9.2	-7.4	72.5	19.7	7.8	0.0
Culpeper County	44.6	54.0	34.8	45.0	40.2	33.0	62.3	59.3	8 092	48.9	22.6	20.3	4.6	3.4	68.4	17.8	13.3	0.5
Cumberland County	37.4	45.2	30.5	39.3	34.3	0.0	0.0	41.5	2 121	40.5	17.9	28.8	4.7	-2.7	67.1	23.4	9.3	0.2
Dickenson County	26.4	34.9	18.5	26.6	23.7	42.9	46.2	5.5	3 389	27.1	27.0	14.8	-22.7	-24.3	68.6	21.4	9.7	0.3
Dinwiddie County	43.9	49.7	38.4	47.4	37.7	22.2	46.0	34.1	5 505	45.9	12.4	25.2	6.5	5.7	70.8	20.0	8.9	0.3
Essex County	42.0	51.3	33.7	43.0	40.4	0.0	34.9	60.0	2 066	50.5	12.6	25.0	10.9	6.2	68.5	19.9	11.4	0.1
Fairfax County	52.1	63.0	41.6	54.5	53.8	56.2	47.2	43.4	237 868	51.1	27.3	13.6	0.1	9.2	69.2	21.6	9.0	0.2
Fauquier County	49.9	63.2	37.2	50.3	46.1	40.9	43.6	49.1	14 078	50.0	29.0	15.1	0.5	6.0	70.7	16.8	12.1	0.5
Floyd County	39.4	51.0	28.0	40.1	32.8	X	19.0	16.5	2 956	47.9	25.5	16.4	-0.3	-6.8	73.3	13.1	12.8	0.7
Fluvanna County	45.6	55.2	37.7	46.7	42.0	44.0	41.0	38.1	4 500	52.8	18.7	22.9	11.1	3.9	68.0	19.4	12.4	0.2
Franklin County	42.3	52.0	32.8	43.2	34.6	45.3	39.6	41.1	9 904	49.1	22.0	18.0	2.5	0.0	75.3	12.2	12.1	0.4
Frederick County	49.6	61.5	38.0	49.8	50.9	23.9	46.2	34.5	14 985	51.7	24.1	16.9	4.0	7.1	75.5	13.6	10.6	0.3
Giles County	39.1	49.8	29.2	39.2	37.1	100.0	11.1	43.4	3 498	47.9	23.4	16.1	-0.6	-6.4	69.4	22.0	8.2	0.4
Gloucester County	44.0	55.7	33.0	45.2	33.8	36.8	29.4	54.2	8 785	54.7	21.6	16.5	6.6	4.4	66.3	22.8	10.5	0.3
Goochland County	45.5	55.5	35.7	50.1	33.4	0.0	52.7	21.3	3 343	50.8	24.8	15.9	2.1	6.9	69.0	14.6	16.0	0.3
Grayson County	37.1	43.0	30.7	38.1	24.7	37.5	58.1	40.9	3 317	49.1	20.2	17.1	1.6	-3.1	77.3	11.7	10.6	0.4
Greene County	50.9	62.1	40.0	51.3	52.6	23.5	18.0	43.9	3 941	54.0	19.2	17.2	6.6	13.4	70.4	18.4	10.9	0.3
Greensville County	36.6	35.9	38.0	40.7	33.8	0.0	100.0	13.0	1 844	42.6	9.7	28.6	6.6	-1.2	70.8	19.9	8.9	0.4
Halifax County	36.9	46.5	28.6	38.7	34.2	36.6	26.4	37.8	8 068	38.0	15.0	26.8	0.2	-6.9	74.7	15.2	9.5	0.5
Hanover County	51.4	63.3	40.3	52.3	43.0	50.0	59.1	42.2	22 473	58.9	20.3	15.1	9.4	11.9	74.2	16.0	9.6	0.2
Henrico County	49.6	60.2	40.7	49.1	52.4	48.2	45.5	46.0	61 646	46.3	21.0	23.6	5.3	7.3	76.8	15.4	7.6	0.2
Henry County	41.8	49.9	34.2	42.4	40.3	44.2	43.8	39.4	12 126	43.4	17.2	24.9	3.7	-2.0	80.8	10.9	8.1	0.2
Highland County	36.0	48.7	23.5	36.1	0.0	33.3	X	0.0	491	44.6	38.3	13.8	-6.2	-7.7	58.4	17.8	23.4	0.4
Isle of Wight County	44.4	55.7	34.0	47.5	35.2	40.5	22.2	63.7	7 191	48.4	21.1	20.4	4.2	2.9	73.7	16.2	9.7	0.3
James City County	41.0	51.9	30.9	40.8	40.5	41.2	44.5	40.0	10 707	46.2	26.2	19.5	1.1	-2.9	67.2	22.6	10.0	0.3
King and Queen County	39.4	50.7	29.2	44.8	30.4	39.6	X	10.6	1 317	42.9	23.8	23.2	1.5	-3.1	71.9	14.7	13.1	0.3
King George County	50.4	61.6	39.0	51.3	46.1	32.8	52.8	53.9	4 397	50.3	23.6	18.0	3.7	5.4	60.6	30.7	8.5	0.2
King William County	51.7	61.0	42.9	54.7	41.2	56.2	79.4	33.9	3 229	52.6	17.8	22.1	10.1	7.5	73.2	17.1	9.4	0.3
Lancaster County	30.5	36.2	25.9	30.6	30.5	100.0	6.7	35.4	2 027	36.9	20.4	24.1	-3.6	-14.2	66.2	15.4	18.2	0.2
Lee County	29.0	36.7	21.8	29.1	29.2	27.1	32.8	21.6	4 912	34.8	24.4	15.2	-14.6	-14.1	69.4	19.1	10.9	0.6
Loudoun County	57.4	71.5	44.0	58.1	54.5	44.4	55.7	52.5	48 887	52.1	30.6	12.5	0.0	13.7	74.7	16.8	8.4	0.2

[1] Hispanic or Latino persons may be of any race.

STATE County	Percent who worked at home	Percent of the population 5 years and over with a disability	Veterans as a percent of the population 18 years and over	Occupation for employed population 16 years and over (percent)						Industry for employed population 16 years and over (percent)					
				Management, professional, and related occupations	Service occupations	Sales and office occupations	Farming, fishing, and forestry occupations	Construction, extraction, and maintenance occupations	Production, transportation and material moving occupations	Agriculture, forestry, fishing, and mining	Construction and manufacturing	Whole-sale and retail trade	Transportation and warehousing, and utilities	Service industries	Public administration
	42	43	44	45	46	47	48	49	50	51	52	53	54	55	56
VERMONT—Cont'd															
Chittenden County	4.2	13.4	10.9	43.8	12.9	25.8	0.3	6.7	10.5	0.8	20.8	15.0	3.3	56.4	3.7
Essex County	4.5	20.4	17.3	22.9	14.9	18.3	3.8	10.5	29.7	6.2	35.2	12.0	4.8	36.2	5.6
Franklin County	5.6	18.7	13.6	30.6	12.7	24.1	2.2	10.7	19.6	5.9	30.2	14.6	4.4	38.2	6.7
Grand Isle County	5.9	16.5	14.7	33.9	12.0	25.4	1.8	13.4	13.4	4.5	26.5	12.7	4.7	45.9	5.8
Lamoille County	6.9	15.5	12.4	35.0	18.2	22.9	1.8	10.7	11.5	3.5	19.3	14.6	4.0	54.0	4.6
Orange County	7.1	20.1	14.5	33.2	14.5	23.0	2.1	12.0	15.1	4.8	23.1	14.6	3.6	49.5	4.3
Orleans County	7.4	21.3	14.8	28.9	14.9	21.4	4.2	10.6	20.0	8.3	25.4	14.1	4.7	41.8	5.8
Rutland County	4.8	19.1	14.5	30.6	15.9	25.9	1.1	9.9	16.6	2.7	21.4	17.1	4.6	50.6	3.6
Washington County......	5.9	18.3	13.9	39.2	14.8	26.6	0.6	8.5	10.3	2.1	16.7	14.3	2.7	54.1	10.1
Windham County..........	6.8	19.0	14.5	34.1	16.3	23.1	1.3	10.7	14.4	2.6	19.0	16.7	4.6	53.9	3.3
Windsor County............	6.1	16.9	15.4	36.8	15.3	24.1	1.0	9.5	13.3	2.5	20.4	14.2	3.9	55.8	3.2
VIRGINIA.................	3.2	18.1	14.7	38.2	13.7	25.5	0.5	9.6	12.5	1.3	18.7	14.2	4.6	53.0	8.3
Accomack County	2.8	21.4	14.8	24.2	16.7	22.1	5.9	11.0	20.0	6.3	25.9	16.0	3.5	41.2	7.1
Albemarle County	5.1	13.4	12.3	51.9	11.2	22.4	0.6	7.7	6.2	2.2	14.8	11.3	2.6	65.8	3.3
Alleghany County	2.3	21.3	16.4	23.4	12.9	20.4	1.4	13.5	28.4	2.8	40.5	12.7	4.9	36.1	3.0
Amelia County	2.9	24.3	14.4	20.8	15.6	24.7	1.8	18.8	18.2	4.8	26.9	15.7	5.8	40.4	6.4
Amherst County	2.5	22.3	13.6	24.9	15.2	25.7	1.5	12.0	20.7	1.7	29.8	15.7	5.5	43.7	3.6
Appomattox County	1.9	23.9	14.3	21.9	13.8	22.4	0.9	15.1	25.8	2.9	36.9	13.5	5.0	37.3	4.3
Arlington County	3.4	15.5	9.8	61.3	11.3	18.1	0.1	5.8	3.4	0.2	7.9	6.5	2.5	66.3	16.7
Augusta County............	3.6	18.5	14.4	25.6	13.0	24.8	1.3	12.3	23.1	3.4	31.4	15.1	6.8	38.7	4.6
Bath County	2.6	24.5	12.3	24.4	21.6	20.3	4.3	14.8	14.6	5.7	21.7	5.5	8.4	50.9	7.8
Bedford County	3.0	18.6	15.6	29.3	11.9	28.1	0.7	12.0	18.0	1.7	30.0	17.9	5.7	41.4	3.2
Bland County...............	2.5	28.9	16.7	25.9	15.4	20.2	1.8	11.4	25.2	6.7	26.9	14.5	6.9	34.8	10.2
Botetourt County	3.1	18.2	15.6	30.3	11.9	28.9	0.6	12.6	15.6	2.5	22.2	18.0	8.8	44.1	4.4
Brunswick County	3.2	28.0	13.1	24.3	17.8	21.7	2.5	12.2	21.5	7.8	23.1	13.7	4.9	38.4	12.1
Buchanan County.........	1.3	35.9	7.6	24.8	14.1	23.0	0.3	19.9	17.9	15.6	14.0	14.0	7.7	43.1	5.7
Buckingham County	3.5	24.9	12.6	20.9	21.5	20.9	2.5	13.3	20.9	8.0	21.7	11.9	6.0	38.2	14.2
Campbell County	2.8	20.2	14.6	25.8	11.7	26.4	0.6	12.3	23.2	1.4	34.5	15.5	5.3	40.0	3.2
Caroline County	2.5	21.9	14.6	23.8	15.5	27.6	0.7	13.7	18.7	2.6	20.3	18.2	8.6	41.9	8.5
Carroll County	1.8	25.6	12.4	19.9	14.2	18.9	1.2	14.0	31.9	2.8	40.4	13.9	4.9	34.0	4.2
Charles City County	3.0	25.3	13.4	20.8	14.4	24.3	2.1	9.9	28.6	4.9	30.4	13.4	6.2	39.2	5.9
Charlotte County	3.3	25.0	12.2	23.1	12.6	20.0	1.8	13.5	29.0	6.7	36.6	13.1	5.7	33.1	4.7
Chesterfield County......	3.1	14.0	14.5	39.5	10.9	29.1	0.1	9.5	11.0	0.3	20.5	17.2	5.4	49.2	7.5
Clarke County	5.8	17.8	15.9	34.3	13.0	24.0	2.2	14.8	11.7	5.1	22.3	13.9	4.5	47.2	6.9
Craig County	2.4	21.3	14.7	24.4	13.6	25.2	0.0	18.1	18.7	2.9	35.6	11.3	2.9	43.2	4.0
Culpeper County	3.6	17.7	13.9	27.7	17.2	24.0	1.4	15.4	14.3	3.0	22.9	15.0	4.2	47.0	7.9
Cumberland County	1.6	28.4	11.4	21.9	16.7	24.8	3.4	16.4	16.8	6.0	21.2	13.7	5.7	44.9	8.5
Dickenson County	1.1	34.9	10.4	16.6	20.3	23.4	1.0	21.0	17.7	17.4	13.4	15.7	7.3	37.4	8.7
Dinwiddie County	2.0	24.2	14.2	25.3	13.5	24.7	0.5	14.5	21.6	2.1	28.5	17.1	6.2	38.2	7.8
Essex County	1.9	22.4	13.3	27.5	13.9	25.1	1.1	13.0	19.4	2.3	25.7	16.4	3.0	44.4	8.0
Fairfax County.............	4.2	12.3	13.3	55.7	11.3	22.9	0.1	5.4	4.6	0.2	9.0	10.7	3.7	63.8	12.6
Fauquier County	5.1	14.0	16.8	39.5	13.0	25.4	1.3	12.6	8.3	4.0	17.8	14.5	4.9	51.2	7.6
Floyd County	6.3	22.2	12.5	23.3	14.7	22.0	2.9	14.2	22.9	4.7	33.1	15.7	5.2	38.3	2.9
Fluvanna County	4.2	16.7	15.5	33.3	15.3	28.0	1.1	11.9	10.3	2.3	17.6	15.0	4.4	56.6	4.2
Franklin County	3.4	20.2	14.2	24.4	12.5	25.1	1.3	14.2	22.5	2.7	34.9	14.9	5.2	38.3	3.9
Frederick County	2.8	17.1	15.2	29.9	11.5	26.0	0.4	13.7	18.5	2.1	28.8	17.6	5.0	41.8	4.7
Giles County................	2.4	24.8	14.0	24.7	14.7	21.9	0.4	13.9	24.4	1.6	36.4	12.9	3.9	40.9	4.4
Gloucester County	3.5	18.6	18.8	31.3	15.2	23.6	1.5	15.9	12.6	2.3	22.0	14.4	4.3	47.7	9.4
Goochland County	3.8	15.4	11.1	35.9	13.5	27.6	0.5	12.7	9.8	2.4	18.4	15.2	4.5	52.4	7.0
Grayson County	4.3	26.4	12.3	19.4	13.5	19.1	2.0	10.8	35.3	4.8	41.4	12.3	4.3	34.3	3.0
Greene County.............	3.2	16.4	14.1	31.5	14.9	26.1	0.6	13.7	13.2	1.9	23.6	17.1	4.0	49.5	3.9
Greensville County	2.8	26.4	14.5	20.8	18.9	21.8	2.3	11.1	25.1	5.7	26.7	12.3	5.3	40.1	9.9
Halifax County.............	2.3	25.0	12.4	23.4	13.1	20.6	0.5	12.9	29.5	2.1	39.3	14.1	5.0	36.0	3.6
Hanover County	3.3	14.4	14.0	38.5	10.8	30.3	0.2	10.2	9.9	0.8	19.7	18.1	4.9	50.1	6.4
Henrico County	2.6	15.4	12.8	40.2	11.3	30.9	0.1	7.5	9.9	0.3	15.3	16.6	4.6	57.0	6.1
Henry County	1.4	24.8	13.0	18.9	11.5	23.7	0.5	10.7	34.5	0.6	47.1	13.8	4.1	31.7	2.8
Highland County...........	7.9	21.9	18.9	29.4	11.7	19.1	5.8	19.2	14.9	15.4	27.2	6.3	6.6	37.7	6.8
Isle of Wight County......	3.1	20.0	14.9	31.3	12.1	23.7	0.9	13.1	18.9	2.8	33.6	12.7	5.7	39.6	5.7
James City County.......	4.7	16.2	19.8	41.1	15.7	25.3	0.2	8.8	8.8	0.4	17.1	13.1	3.2	59.5	6.7
King and Queen County	3.3	24.6	12.8	22.3	16.2	19.3	2.8	16.5	23.0	4.5	32.3	13.3	3.2	41.4	5.4
King George County	2.8	18.1	19.2	38.0	12.3	24.3	0.9	11.3	13.1	2.0	17.2	14.2	5.1	40.3	21.3
King William County	2.7	16.8	13.6	28.1	11.6	28.8	1.5	13.9	16.1	3.0	28.7	15.4	4.2	42.2	6.5
Lancaster County	3.8	21.6	19.2	27.6	20.6	25.1	1.9	11.2	13.7	3.0	16.8	15.0	4.5	55.5	5.1
Lee County..................	2.9	32.7	12.8	26.3	16.0	20.1	1.2	16.9	19.4	9.5	21.6	13.2	6.3	43.9	5.6
Loudoun County	5.1	10.4	13.3	52.7	10.6	24.7	0.3	6.1	5.8	0.9	12.1	12.3	5.7	60.6	8.3

Table B-3. States and Counties — Education, Labor Force, and Income

STATE County	Median house-hold income	Median family income — All families	Married-couple	Male house-holder	Female house-holder	Median nonfamily house-hold income	Median income for full-year, full-time workers — Men	Women	Per capita income	With earnings	With interest, dividend, or rental income	With Social Security income	With public assis-tance income	With retire-ment income	House-holds with income over $100,000 (percent)	+/- U.S. percent for income over $100,000 (percent)	House-holds with income below poverty (percent)	Families with children with income below poverty (percent)
	57	58	59	60	61	62	63	64	65	66	67	68	69	70	71	72	73	74
VERMONT—Cont'd																		
Chittenden County	47 673	59 460	68 231	32 414	23 784	30 477	40 195	28 995	23 501	86.8	50.1	19.8	3.8	14.1	13.1	0.8	8.9	7.3
Essex County	30 490	34 984	45 909	23 750	16 250	16 579	28 695	21 192	14 388	75.9	23.7	33.5	7.4	15.6	2.3	-10.0	13.9	15.2
Franklin County	41 659	46 733	55 357	25 792	17 826	24 328	32 537	25 143	17 816	82.8	36.6	24.4	5.1	13.2	5.7	-6.6	8.9	9.8
Grand Isle County	43 033	48 878	56 298	36 667	27 188	26 144	36 938	26 989	22 207	81.6	45.0	28.5	3.7	17.8	9.8	-2.5	8.1	8.6
Lamoille County	39 356	44 620	51 076	27 212	20 357	26 070	31 872	25 432	20 972	85.9	42.6	24.4	4.5	12.6	8.8	-3.5	9.4	9.6
Orange County	39 855	45 771	52 984	26 810	20 823	23 640	31 533	25 105	18 784	83.0	39.8	28.4	4.4	15.0	6.1	-6.2	8.9	9.9
Orleans County	31 084	36 630	43 049	22 037	15 211	17 536	29 077	21 342	16 518	77.5	32.7	31.6	7.0	15.4	4.2	-8.1	14.2	16.5
Rutland County	36 743	44 742	51 534	27 596	17 969	21 071	31 953	24 864	18 874	79.1	42.5	30.6	5.6	17.2	6.1	-6.2	11.2	11.9
Washington County	40 972	51 075	58 719	30 214	21 433	23 940	34 977	27 109	21 113	81.6	47.9	26.5	5.3	16.9	8.5	-3.8	8.9	8.7
Windham County	38 204	46 989	55 175	26 875	19 397	23 310	31 903	26 063	20 533	80.9	46.2	28.2	5.2	14.9	7.7	-4.6	9.5	10.2
Windsor County	40 688	49 002	56 899	29 554	21 059	24 299	34 128	26 663	22 369	79.6	49.5	29.6	3.9	18.1	9.5	-2.8	8.9	7.8
VIRGINIA	46 677	54 169	63 157	31 274	21 602	29 642	39 613	29 164	23 975	83.4	38.2	23.4	2.5	18.8	15.1	2.8	9.6	10.2
Accomack County	30 250	34 821	42 112	25 313	15 512	17 683	27 740	20 398	16 309	75.4	28.7	34.8	3.3	19.8	4.7	-7.6	16.6	19.8
Albemarle County	50 749	63 407	71 273	35 847	28 542	31 937	41 641	31 690	28 852	84.3	51.4	22.9	1.3	17.0	17.3	5.0	7.0	5.9
Alleghany County	38 545	45 843	54 223	21 333	13 667	18 452	36 592	21 660	19 635	75.2	37.6	35.4	3.6	22.4	5.8	-6.5	8.0	7.5
Amelia County	40 252	47 157	52 283	30 658	23 092	25 812	34 413	23 819	18 858	82.2	32.2	27.7	1.2	19.3	7.5	-4.8	9.1	8.5
Amherst County	37 393	42 876	51 997	22 434	15 808	21 104	29 189	22 900	16 952	78.4	29.7	30.5	2.8	18.9	5.3	-7.0	11.0	12.3
Appomattox County	36 507	41 563	51 319	22 452	20 962	17 405	32 063	22 157	18 086	79.0	29.0	34.0	3.2	18.1	5.0	-7.3	13.3	12.3
Arlington County	63 001	78 877	81 850	36 992	30 293	52 423	52 255	42 577	37 706	88.1	53.5	13.7	1.7	15.1	26.7	14.4	6.4	7.5
Augusta County	43 045	48 579	56 128	30 226	22 681	22 793	32 397	25 007	19 744	83.1	37.1	27.6	1.7	20.5	8.0	-4.3	6.2	5.8
Bath County	35 013	41 276	44 318	22 656	16 944	21 912	31 137	22 325	23 092	80.8	33.3	31.4	1.2	22.7	6.4	-5.9	9.0	6.6
Bedford County	43 136	49 303	55 124	32 434	19 380	24 801	35 986	24 421	21 582	81.9	37.7	27.6	1.1	18.1	9.6	-2.7	7.7	7.3
Bland County	30 397	35 765	46 442	25 000	30 417	17 201	31 224	23 575	17 744	76.7	20.7	38.1	2.7	19.7	5.9	-6.4	13.9	9.5
Botetourt County	48 731	55 125	60 601	27 411	24 444	22 481	38 641	26 284	22 218	83.0	38.9	28.5	1.4	17.5	10.8	-1.5	5.8	5.1
Brunswick County	31 288	38 354	47 903	21 625	16 921	14 422	27 817	20 993	14 890	73.0	24.2	35.9	3.8	19.6	3.8	-8.5	18.5	19.4
Buchanan County	22 213	27 328	32 675	15 167	9 219	11 208	30 488	18 695	12 788	59.3	18.4	47.7	6.0	20.1	2.4	-9.9	23.9	26.4
Buckingham County	29 882	37 465	47 212	24 226	17 723	17 008	27 236	20 873	13 669	76.2	24.4	36.3	4.7	18.6	4.4	-7.9	18.2	23.2
Campbell County	37 280	42 901	50 027	29 018	18 181	21 128	33 130	22 818	18 134	80.9	30.5	28.4	2.6	16.6	5.7	-6.6	11.1	11.5
Caroline County	39 845	43 533	50 769	31 217	24 470	24 803	32 253	23 244	18 342	82.5	28.3	29.5	2.6	19.1	7.1	-5.2	9.9	9.0
Carroll County	30 507	36 755	41 837	20 393	14 329	14 259	26 629	20 161	16 475	74.2	27.6	36.2	4.2	16.8	3.5	-8.8	14.3	13.3
Charles City County	42 745	49 361	60 819	28 438	19 125	20 521	32 990	26 305	19 182	79.7	23.8	30.6	2.7	22.8	7.1	-5.2	11.7	12.2
Charlotte County	28 929	34 830	45 596	21 875	14 730	15 581	27 477	20 756	14 717	71.6	27.6	37.1	3.1	16.8	3.4	-8.9	18.5	16.6
Chesterfield County	58 537	65 058	71 914	37 944	29 165	35 495	45 126	31 167	25 286	89.1	41.1	18.2	1.4	17.3	17.8	5.5	4.2	4.8
Clarke County	51 601	59 750	62 620	40 114	34 688	28 678	41 398	30 791	24 844	82.8	40.8	28.5	1.5	19.8	15.1	2.8	6.8	6.1
Craig County	37 314	41 750	43 958	31 250	16 667	19 316	27 455	21 574	17 322	70.1	37.3	28.0	1.6	17.8	5.0	-7.3	9.1	10.3
Culpeper County	45 290	51 475	61 987	25 917	20 648	24 935	37 794	26 464	20 162	82.9	35.5	25.9	2.9	21.0	10.4	-1.9	8.9	9.8
Cumberland County	31 816	37 965	48 958	14 663	17 569	20 273	30 147	23 422	15 103	78.4	24.9	32.8	2.0	16.6	3.6	-8.7	16.1	16.9
Dickenson County	23 431	27 986	31 788	20 855	12 450	11 526	27 973	17 856	12 822	59.9	19.6	45.1	7.5	23.7	2.1	-10.2	22.4	24.2
Dinwiddie County	41 582	47 961	56 696	26 250	20 564	22 253	34 003	25 325	19 122	82.2	25.8	27.7	2.6	23.7	7.3	-5.0	10.1	9.3
Essex County	37 395	43 588	55 286	26 429	17 411	21 471	30 468	23 222	17 994	76.1	29.9	33.2	3.0	19.2	6.2	-6.1	11.5	11.1
Fairfax County	81 050	92 146	96 355	49 368	39 762	55 774	42 477	43 538	36 888	91.0	54.8	14.2	1.1	18.6	37.6	25.3	3.6	4.3
Fauquier County	61 999	69 507	73 432	41 029	30 343	35 605	47 214	32 300	28 757	87.6	43.4	20.8	1.7	19.9	23.8	11.5	5.9	4.6
Floyd County	31 585	38 128	40 530	25 000	15 197	17 115	31 343	20 756	16 345	77.0	33.5	32.2	2.9	15.4	3.3	-9.0	14.8	11.6
Fluvanna County	46 372	51 141	55 412	27 344	25 326	26 733	33 836	25 629	20 338	82.9	40.8	30.7	2.1	22.2	9.1	-3.2	6.8	4.5
Franklin County	38 056	45 163	49 080	26 071	18 153	19 134	30 995	22 955	19 605	78.4	34.1	30.6	2.0	19.3	7.8	-4.5	10.4	10.7
Frederick County	46 941	52 281	61 202	30 341	24 420	29 049	36 744	25 698	21 080	85.3	36.8	23.9	1.8	18.1	9.4	-2.9	6.4	5.8
Giles County	34 927	42 089	48 412	27 574	17 542	17 428	32 828	23 558	18 396	73.5	31.6	36.2	3.5	24.1	4.6	-7.7	10.7	11.3
Gloucester County	45 421	51 426	54 020	28 672	19 306	26 162	37 298	25 483	19 990	82.4	38.1	26.8	2.2	23.1	7.7	-4.6	8.1	9.8
Goochland County	56 307	64 685	68 241	51 161	29 750	31 445	42 706	30 244	29 105	86.4	45.9	25.2	1.9	17.1	22.8	10.5	7.1	6.2
Grayson County	28 676	35 076	37 143	16 176	16 600	13 023	24 585	18 414	16 768	73.8	26.5	36.9	3.5	15.3	3.5	-8.8	15.1	16.0
Greene County	45 931	48 548	54 092	28 750	21 343	32 161	32 572	27 219	19 478	89.1	33.4	20.6	1.9	15.7	7.8	-4.5	5.8	6.1
Greensville County	32 002	38 810	48 063	23 661	20 703	16 642	25 193	20 759	14 632	77.6	21.3	35.4	3.2	16.6	3.9	-8.4	17.2	15.0
Halifax County	29 929	37 845	46 543	27 462	17 593	14 525	28 323	21 198	16 353	72.2	26.8	36.3	3.7	16.9	4.0	-8.3	17.3	15.8
Hanover County	59 223	65 809	73 128	37 404	26 223	30 631	44 233	31 644	25 120	86.2	45.9	23.0	1.1	17.4	17.8	5.5	4.1	3.3
Henrico County	49 185	59 298	71 252	35 464	26 223	32 304	40 952	30 538	26 410	85.0	40.0	22.6	1.6	16.8	14.5	2.2	6.1	6.9
Henry County	31 816	38 649	45 762	23 447	19 446	17 234	27 473	21 219	17 110	76.0	27.1	32.0	3.1	19.4	4.4	-7.9	12.5	13.3
Highland County	29 732	37 530	42 981	27 500	21 000	14 795	27 278	19 734	15 976	70.9	36.1	42.0	2.4	20.5	3.4	-8.9	14.7	10.3
Isle of Wight County	45 387	52 597	60 930	33 000	19 705	20 347	40 164	23 885	20 235	81.6	35.2	26.5	3.8	21.7	10.1	-2.2	9.7	9.0
James City County	55 594	66 171	70 752	30 938	24 453	30 907	46 551	28 226	29 256	78.5	51.6	30.1	1.8	29.1	20.6	8.3	6.5	6.9
King and Queen County	35 941	40 563	52 981	25 125	18 250	17 455	34 182	22 311	17 236	76.5	27.8	34.4	3.6	20.5	5.7	-6.6	12.6	7.0
King George County	49 882	55 160	61 378	26 458	24 036	29 634	39 697	26 607	21 562	87.1	34.9	22.2	2.6	21.5	12.0	-0.3	5.6	5.3
King William County	49 876	54 037	59 016	38 750	28 875	26 455	35 329	26 121	21 928	86.3	35.6	23.4	2.0	16.8	10.0	-2.3	6.1	5.9
Lancaster County	33 239	42 957	42 750	31 458	17 560	20 411	32 009	23 624	24 663	64.6	44.2	44.8	2.9	26.7	11.8	-0.5	13.4	16.1
Lee County	22 972	28 525	35 558	22 419	9 648	11 491	28 702	19 912	13 625	63.6	22.6	42.2	8.7	19.2	3.7	-8.6	25.4	26.8
Loudoun County	80 648	88 387	94 232	51 391	40 596	52 021	60 831	41 015	33 530	93.8	49.3	12.0	0.8	13.4	35.3	23.0	2.6	2.3

Table B-3. States and Counties — Education, Labor Force, and Income

STATE/ County code	MSA/PMSA/ NECMA code[1]	STATE County	Total population 25 years and over	High school graduates — Percent with a high school diploma or less	Percent with a high school diploma or more	College graduates — Percent with a bachelor's degree or more	+/- U.S. percent with bachelor's degree or more	College graduates (percent) — Non-Hispanic White	Black or African American	American Indian and Alaska Native	Asian, Hawaiian, and Pacific Islander	Hispanic or Latino[2]
			1	2	3	4	5	6	7	8	9	10
		VIRGINIA—Cont'd										
51 109	...	Louisa County	17 697	63.1	71.7	14.0	-10.4	16.0	6.4	8.1	32.2	0.0
51 111	...	Lunenburg County........	9 305	68.2	63.4	9.2	-15.2	12.7	3.4	0.0	14.3	7.8
51 113	...	Madison County	8 644	61.2	75.0	19.4	-5.0	20.7	5.1	0.0	47.4	32.8
51 115	5720	Mathews County	6 926	53.0	80.8	19.2	-5.2	20.8	5.0	61.5	X	19.1
51 117	...	Mecklenburg County	22 981	66.3	67.8	12.1	-12.3	15.3	5.6	13.3	68.3	18.1
51 119	...	Middlesex County	7 436	56.2	73.7	18.9	-5.5	22.1	5.5	0.0	0.0	0.0
51 121	...	Montgomery County......	43 106	41.0	82.8	35.9	11.5	34.2	29.6	7.4	85.6	37.8
51 125	...	Nelson County	10 403	57.6	69.0	20.8	-3.6	22.9	7.9	X	27.3	24.4
51 127	6760	New Kent County	9 285	54.1	80.6	16.3	-8.1	18.6	6.9	6.6	40.0	6.5
51 131	...	Northampton County	9 133	61.8	67.4	15.7	-8.7	23.3	5.6	0.0	85.7	3.5
51 133	...	Northumberland County	9 476	55.0	75.9	21.7	-2.7	25.8	6.4	63.9	55.6	0.0
51 135	...	Nottoway County	10 841	67.4	64.4	11.1	-13.3	15.0	5.7	0.0	19.6	0.0
51 137	...	Orange County	18 202	58.8	75.2	18.5	-5.9	20.1	6.7	0.0	21.4	28.3
51 139	...	Page County	16 085	74.9	64.8	9.8	-14.6	9.8	9.3	0.0	18.4	9.9
51 141	...	Patrick County	13 815	72.2	62.2	8.6	-15.8	8.3	3.3	47.4	94.9	19.5
51 143	1950	Pittsylvania County	43 120	67.9	67.3	9.3	-15.1	10.6	4.4	22.6	0.0	20.9
51 145	6760	Powhatan County..........	15 411	53.3	78.9	19.1	-5.3	21.2	8.9	38.9	0.0	45.1
51 147	...	Prince Edward County ..	11 089	58.5	69.9	19.2	-5.2	27.2	6.0	0.0	60.6	46.2
51 149	6760	Prince George County ..	20 272	50.1	81.6	19.4	-5.0	21.5	14.6	8.8	30.1	15.5
51 153	8840	Prince William County...	171 058	36.1	88.8	31.5	7.1	34.5	24.9	30.8	40.5	15.2
51 155	...	Pulaski County	25 362	59.6	74.2	12.5	-11.9	12.9	7.2	7.1	0.0	0.0
51 157	...	Rappahannock County..	5 059	54.1	76.0	22.9	-1.5	23.6	7.0	0.0	46.7	8.3
51 159	...	Richmond County	6 552	71.3	60.0	9.9	-14.5	13.5	3.0	0.0	8.3	8.5
51 161	6800	Roanoke County	60 771	42.1	85.8	28.2	3.8	28.1	22.7	9.8	50.8	34.7
51 163	...	Rockbridge County........	14 556	61.4	71.0	18.7	-5.7	19.2	8.9	0.0	17.9	4.6
51 165	...	Rockingham County	45 123	63.0	72.4	17.6	-6.8	18.0	7.2	6.9	16.4	7.9
51 167	...	Russell County	21 362	69.9	62.5	9.4	-15.0	9.7	1.8	0.0	0.0	4.1
51 169	3660	Scott County	16 846	71.9	64.4	8.3	-16.1	8.3	5.1	62.1	41.2	2.7
51 171	...	Shenandoah County	24 926	63.1	75.3	14.7	-9.7	14.9	10.5	0.0	14.9	12.2
51 173	...	Smyth County	23 255	66.9	67.5	10.6	-13.8	10.5	13.1	0.0	34.4	12.9
51 175	...	Southampton County	12 070	63.3	63.2	11.7	-12.7	15.6	6.3	16.7	X	0.0
51 177	8840	Spotsylvania County	56 633	47.8	83.8	22.8	-1.6	23.7	15.4	19.1	26.8	23.1
51 179	8840	Stafford County	56 029	39.3	88.6	29.6	5.2	29.9	25.9	29.7	33.5	31.5
51 181	...	Surry County	4 569	62.6	70.4	12.8	-11.6	16.0	9.8	16.7	0.0	15.6
51 183	...	Sussex County	8 899	75.6	57.6	10.0	-14.4	16.6	6.1	0.0	0.0	0.0
51 185	...	Tazewell County	31 291	65.0	67.5	11.0	-13.4	10.5	15.2	0.0	71.4	37.9
51 187	8840	Warren County	21 127	62.2	75.5	15.0	-9.4	15.2	8.6	0.0	49.2	5.1
51 191	3660	Washington County.......	35 958	58.9	72.3	16.1	-8.3	16.1	14.7	0.0	27.0	40.6
51 193	...	Westmoreland County...	11 808	64.1	69.3	13.3	-11.1	17.3	3.3	33.3	42.9	9.1
51 195	...	Wise County..................	26 731	67.4	62.5	10.8	-13.6	10.6	12.1	0.0	65.6	3.5
51 197	...	Wythe County	19 528	62.2	70.2	12.1	-12.3	12.0	9.2	0.0	65.8	9.8
51 199	5720	York County	36 168	29.5	91.7	37.4	13.0	39.2	23.5	45.4	44.7	41.3
		Independent Cities										
51 510	8840	Alexandria city..............	95 730	25.8	86.8	54.3	29.9	70.0	28.3	55.6	55.4	21.3
51 515	4640	Bedford city	4 494	61.5	70.9	15.2	-9.2	17.6	5.4	0.0	45.0	52.6
51 520	3660	Bristol city....................	12 366	56.9	72.4	17.0	-7.4	17.3	5.9	21.7	34.1	34.1
51 530	...	Buena Vista city	4 250	65.0	69.0	10.5	-13.9	10.4	7.8	X	100.0	X
51 540	1540	Charlottesville city	22 868	40.6	80.8	40.8	16.4	49.1	8.6	41.9	75.2	47.8
51 550	5720	Chesapeake city...........	125 498	42.6	85.1	24.7	0.3	25.5	20.3	12.3	49.8	32.2
51 560	...	Clifton Forge city	3 110	61.4	75.0	9.6	-14.8	9.4	9.1	X	100.0	0.0
51 570	6760	Colonial Heights city	11 675	50.8	83.7	19.0	-5.4	18.5	28.5	0.0	22.4	19.2
51 580	...	Covington city...............	4 485	68.4	71.4	6.4	-18.0	7.0	3.8	X	0.0	0.0
51 590	1950	Danville city	33 196	62.2	68.5	13.9	-10.5	18.0	6.7	14.6	45.4	27.8
51 595	...	Emporia city	3 775	70.3	58.5	14.2	-10.2	22.1	7.2	X	28.6	0.0
51 600	8840	Fairfax city...................	15 222	30.9	88.6	45.7	21.3	48.3	34.5	52.1	52.8	24.4
51 610	8840	Falls Church city	7 464	16.7	95.9	63.7	39.3	68.0	37.6	40.0	55.5	31.9
51 620	...	Franklin city	5 642	56.6	71.0	16.4	-8.0	25.1	7.3	0.0	X	15.6
51 630	8840	Fredericksburg city........	11 211	47.3	80.2	30.5	6.1	37.5	9.9	32.5	8.3	13.7
51 640	...	Galax city	4 782	68.2	60.4	11.1	-13.3	12.4	0.0	0.0	0.0	3.4
51 650	5720	Hampton city	92 477	42.5	85.5	21.8	-2.6	24.1	18.7	18.3	24.4	17.4
51 660	...	Harrisonburg city	17 448	46.7	76.8	31.2	6.8	34.6	18.5	0.0	29.4	7.2
51 670	6760	Hopewell city	14 323	64.1	71.8	10.2	-14.2	11.1	7.5	14.0	21.4	6.6
51 678	...	Lexington city	3 285	40.2	77.1	42.6	18.2	47.4	15.9	0.0	0.0	78.9
51 680	4640	Lynchburg city	40 806	49.7	78.0	25.2	0.8	31.3	8.3	10.1	58.0	26.2

[1] MSA = Metropolitan Statistical Area. PMSA = Primary MSA. NECMA = New England County Metropolitan Area. See the Appendix A for explanation of these concepts. See Appendix B for list of metropolitan areas identified by type, with component counties.
[2] Hispanic or Latino persons may be of any race.

Table B-3. States and Counties — Education, Labor Force, and Income

| | School enrollment | | | Population 16 to 19 years | | | | Employment status, 2000 | | | Work status in 1999 of the population 16 years and over (percent) | | |
| | | | | | | | | | | | Worked in 1999 | | |
STATE County	Grades kindergarten through 12	College or graduate school	Percent private	Number	Percent in armed forces	Percent high school graduates	Percent not enrolled, not grads, not in armed forces, not employed	Total population 16 years and over	Percent in labor force	Unemployment rate	Full-time	Part-time	Did not work in 1999
	11	12	13	14	15	16	17	18	19	20	21	22	23
VIRGINIA—Cont'd													
Louisa County	4 854	677	9.4	1 131	0.0	14.4	5.0	19 953	63.4	3.4	56.7	12.2	31.1
Lunenburg County	2 160	281	8.7	610	0.0	11.8	8.9	10 652	50.9	5.2	49.9	10.7	39.4
Madison County	2 212	374	17.7	649	0.0	28.8	4.3	9 875	64.6	3.2	54.6	15.8	29.6
Mathews County	1 390	261	6.1	284	1.1	14.8	0.0	7 569	56.0	3.2	50.1	14.0	35.8
Mecklenburg County	5 325	1 027	5.4	1 577	0.0	13.8	3.7	26 267	55.3	6.6	51.6	10.7	37.7
Middlesex County	1 552	310	7.9	401	0.0	11.0	6.7	8 216	54.5	3.9	47.8	14.4	37.9
Montgomery County	10 341	26 224	3.9	9 640	0.1	3.9	0.7	70 742	59.0	5.4	53.3	23.7	23.0
Nelson County	2 353	393	8.8	714	1.0	15.1	4.8	11 783	60.6	4.8	55.3	11.5	33.2
New Kent County	2 549	319	5.0	662	0.0	15.3	5.3	10 461	69.6	3.8	63.9	12.3	23.8
Northampton County	2 566	486	12.0	780	0.0	8.2	4.7	10 412	53.6	7.0	46.2	13.6	40.3
Northumberland County	1 753	211	9.7	421	0.0	10.9	0.7	10 238	49.8	3.9	44.8	14.0	41.2
Nottoway County	2 965	226	7.1	737	0.0	7.6	6.5	12 518	51.0	5.9	51.0	8.8	40.2
Orange County	4 492	720	10.6	1 159	0.0	15.0	5.9	20 562	60.7	2.9	53.8	12.5	33.7
Page County	4 080	373	5.3	1 196	0.0	16.5	4.3	18 497	62.3	3.9	53.9	12.7	33.5
Patrick County	2 997	543	4.4	838	0.0	23.2	4.2	15 657	60.0	4.0	55.1	9.5	35.3
Pittsylvania County	11 025	1 891	9.4	3 202	0.0	10.6	2.7	49 255	62.8	4.3	57.0	11.0	31.9
Powhatan County	4 188	807	10.8	1 094	0.0	14.4	4.8	17 611	61.5	1.8	64.4	13.2	22.4
Prince Edward County	3 130	3 885	18.8	2 403	0.0	3.7	4.2	16 218	54.7	13.3	48.4	19.8	31.8
Prince George County	6 578	1 738	9.7	2 557	33.9	42.3	4.0	25 735	65.9	3.2	61.3	13.0	25.7
Prince William County	61 279	16 310	12.7	15 375	1.5	11.9	3.6	204 002	77.1	2.8	69.0	13.3	17.7
Pulaski County	5 145	1 296	2.4	1 341	0.0	24.7	7.8	28 671	60.7	5.5	54.8	11.3	33.9
Rappahannock County	1 166	216	16.8	258	0.0	8.1	4.3	5 569	65.9	2.2	55.6	16.5	27.9
Richmond County	1 374	298	9.4	359	0.0	9.2	17.5	7 400	45.8	5.0	49.0	14.1	36.9
Roanoke County	15 132	3 952	14.3	4 242	0.0	8.4	1.6	68 544	65.7	2.1	56.8	14.1	29.0
Rockbridge County	3 550	779	13.6	1 027	0.0	17.4	4.9	16 794	62.7	3.6	55.8	13.5	30.6
Rockingham County	12 333	2 824	16.5	3 724	0.0	14.6	4.9	52 819	67.9	3.4	57.6	15.1	27.4
Russell County	4 934	1 011	5.4	1 583	0.4	12.6	3.8	24 782	47.2	6.9	44.3	9.6	46.1
Scott County	3 654	634	2.1	1 015	0.0	16.1	3.6	19 082	51.5	5.9	44.7	10.0	45.3
Shenandoah County	5 774	824	11.5	1 614	0.0	18.4	3.7	28 092	65.0	2.7	56.0	14.0	30.0
Smyth County	5 448	1 040	4.2	1 645	0.4	14.3	3.7	26 793	58.4	4.7	54.0	9.9	36.2
Southampton County	3 189	565	13.5	910	0.0	10.2	7.3	13 983	53.6	4.7	52.5	10.8	36.7
Spotsylvania County	20 291	3 690	10.6	4 902	0.0	13.0	2.9	66 138	72.2	3.1	63.4	13.7	22.9
Stafford County	22 283	4 879	8.8	5 363	0.5	12.8	0.9	66 359	76.0	2.8	66.3	14.3	19.4
Surry County	1 443	211	16.8	375	0.0	6.4	0.5	5 289	63.8	5.3	55.3	14.2	30.4
Sussex County	2 200	442	16.2	451	0.0	16.2	3.8	10 317	43.7	5.3	54.2	7.1	38.8
Tazewell County	7 262	1 954	8.3	2 341	0.0	11.9	5.6	36 235	53.4	9.1	45.7	10.1	44.2
Warren County	5 905	1 085	17.7	1 522	0.0	12.4	3.4	24 361	66.7	3.4	58.4	12.7	28.9
Washington County	7 994	2 539	13.9	2 728	0.2	13.5	3.4	41 848	59.4	4.2	52.4	12.0	35.6
Westmoreland County	3 019	428	8.2	768	0.0	13.9	1.6	13 301	56.2	4.1	49.6	11.8	38.7
Wise County	7 019	2 059	4.5	2 621	0.0	11.5	5.5	32 114	50.0	7.2	42.3	11.8	45.9
Wythe County	4 471	1 024	4.5	1 421	0.0	21.5	2.1	22 381	61.9	4.3	55.3	12.2	32.5
York County	12 874	3 066	10.8	3 212	3.1	8.5	3.4	41 855	70.9	2.5	60.1	15.7	24.2
Independent Cities													
Alexandria city	14 135	10 296	24.8	3 819	0.2	11.8	5.3	108 764	74.4	3.1	70.1	10.3	19.6
Bedford city	1 022	232	10.0	244	0.0	7.4	11.9	5 070	56.5	13.2	47.2	11.4	41.4
Bristol city	2 616	792	18.1	792	0.0	13.0	4.2	14 279	53.8	6.5	47.4	11.3	41.4
Buena Vista city	1 018	419	18.1	377	0.0	4.5	0.0	5 099	62.3	3.9	54.0	14.4	31.6
Charlottesville city	4 959	15 501	5.2	5 798	0.2	3.8	1.5	38 906	56.3	4.3	52.8	24.3	22.9
Chesapeake city	43 542	10 785	11.6	11 484	1.8	12.3	4.0	148 512	69.0	3.8	60.7	14.1	25.2
Clifton Forge city	708	120	5.7	221	0.0	14.0	1.8	3 510	52.2	7.3	45.5	11.1	43.3
Colonial Heights city	2 991	690	6.7	841	0.0	14.0	2.1	13 537	62.8	2.3	53.1	14.3	32.6
Covington city	937	164	1.5	264	0.0	25.8	3.4	5 088	55.6	4.8	49.8	10.5	39.7
Danville city	8 649	1 709	10.3	2 475	0.0	11.6	9.5	38 388	57.0	10.0	48.7	12.0	39.3
Emporia city	1 113	106	7.1	265	0.0	19.6	13.6	4 353	55.5	6.7	51.8	8.3	39.9
Fairfax city	3 157	1 693	15.8	983	0.0	7.8	4.9	17 690	69.9	2.3	60.9	13.6	25.5
Falls Church city	1 828	636	21.4	426	0.0	4.2	0.0	8 262	73.5	2.9	64.0	14.0	22.0
Franklin city	1 709	356	10.0	477	0.0	8.4	6.7	6 565	55.9	7.0	47.7	14.9	37.4
Fredericksburg city	2 329	3 503	8.5	1 904	0.8	14.4	2.8	16 157	67.5	9.5	56.1	19.4	24.5
Galax city	1 171	195	1.9	302	0.0	14.9	2.0	5 421	58.2	2.7	52.1	11.2	36.7
Hampton city	27 044	12 830	21.1	9 310	1.3	13.3	3.0	115 091	62.4	6.0	61.1	14.1	24.8
Harrisonburg city	4 247	14 822	8.2	6 261	0.0	2.8	2.5	35 052	59.4	9.3	49.8	29.2	21.0
Hopewell city	4 204	859	8.7	1 112	0.0	17.0	6.7	16 905	60.0	6.6	55.7	10.2	34.1
Lexington city	533	2 876	46.0	1 238	0.0	1.5	0.6	6 202	38.3	9.8	46.0	25.6	28.4
Lynchburg city	10 830	7 622	37.3	4 792	0.3	6.9	4.2	52 279	59.8	6.7	50.1	17.2	32.7

Table B-3. States and Counties — Education, Labor Force, and Income

STATE County	Full-year full-time employed (percent)								Children under 18 years in families						Total employed by class of worker (percent)			
	Total	Men	Women	Non-Hispanic White	Black or African American	American Indian and Alaska Native	Asian, Hawaiian, and Pacific Islander	Hispanic or Latino[1]	Number	Both in labor force	Father only in labor force	With one parent who is in labor force (percent)	+/- U.S. percent of children with no stay-at-home parent (percent)	+/- U.S. percent two-income couples	Private	Government	Self-employed	Unpaid family worker
	24	25	26	27	28	29	30	31	32	33	34	35	36	37	38	39	40	41
VIRGINIA—Cont'd																		
Louisa County	44.6	54.3	35.5	46.3	38.2	13.5	47.5	59.5	5 949	44.4	17.7	24.3	4.1	-0.5	70.8	16.8	12.0	0.4
Lunenburg County	33.7	38.7	27.9	37.8	27.3	10.3	42.9	43.2	2 509	34.8	16.5	29.2	-0.6	-5.7	63.5	23.7	12.6	0.3
Madison County	44.7	52.8	37.1	44.5	42.9	0.0	32.1	69.6	2 899	44.2	30.9	13.6	-6.8	-0.8	70.2	15.4	14.0	0.4
Mathews County	37.6	47.2	28.7	38.8	25.8	36.4	X	56.0	1 751	57.0	15.5	18.1	10.5	-5.7	64.4	19.4	16.2	0.0
Mecklenburg County	36.5	43.7	29.4	39.8	30.6	80.0	35.1	50.5	6 513	42.6	14.5	28.8	6.8	-4.1	71.7	16.9	11.0	0.4
Middlesex County	35.5	43.3	28.4	37.4	27.7	0.0	73.9	29.6	1 693	38.6	22.4	27.9	1.9	-8.2	60.2	21.6	17.8	0.4
Montgomery County	31.5	36.7	25.8	33.0	30.3	27.9	9.4	23.9	13 953	47.4	22.6	19.3	2.1	3.9	61.9	31.7	6.2	0.2
Nelson County	39.7	48.0	32.2	40.9	32.9	X	77.3	35.0	2 951	46.0	18.1	20.6	2.0	-4.3	66.9	20.8	11.9	0.4
New Kent County	50.0	56.3	43.7	52.9	36.7	46.7	44.0	56.5	3 071	58.4	17.0	16.5	10.3	8.9	72.4	16.5	10.7	0.4
Northampton County	31.1	37.5	25.6	36.7	25.1	0.0	64.3	14.1	2 649	30.7	20.6	33.3	-0.6	-12.4	66.7	20.0	12.6	0.7
Northumberland County	32.0	38.3	26.6	31.2	34.7	45.1	15.6	35.7	2 148	49.1	18.6	20.3	4.8	-14.3	61.3	19.3	18.9	0.6
Nottoway County	35.9	41.2	30.3	41.6	28.2	39.0	28.3	26.7	3 321	46.0	14.0	25.6	7.0	-3.2	63.3	25.1	11.1	0.5
Orange County	41.4	51.8	31.8	41.2	41.4	21.1	45.3	45.6	5 643	42.7	20.5	27.7	5.8	-3.6	71.8	16.1	11.6	0.5
Page County	40.5	49.2	32.2	40.6	35.6	61.5	47.5	43.0	4 940	53.1	13.2	23.7	12.2	-1.2	76.7	12.3	10.7	0.3
Patrick County	39.8	48.7	31.4	40.1	38.9	42.1	16.4	31.6	3 977	47.1	17.9	21.9	4.4	-1.9	78.4	10.9	10.3	0.5
Pittsylvania County	43.9	54.3	34.3	45.8	37.8	50.0	24.0	48.9	13 187	50.0	18.3	19.5	4.9	0.9	78.6	11.6	9.6	0.2
Powhatan County	46.2	52.0	39.0	48.5	35.9	81.8	25.9	14.0	5 057	58.7	21.5	12.1	6.2	9.7	72.1	15.4	12.2	0.2
Prince Edward County	26.8	31.4	22.4	27.2	27.0	0.0	24.4	7.1	3 698	47.2	10.5	29.0	11.6	-1.8	65.9	22.9	10.5	0.7
Prince George County	43.2	49.4	35.7	47.9	36.7	40.9	21.0	39.1	7 930	50.2	20.6	18.7	4.3	6.7	67.2	24.3	8.3	0.2
Prince William County	56.4	68.2	44.9	57.4	59.4	61.1	48.1	48.3	81 586	49.5	23.5	19.0	3.9	13.0	69.1	23.9	6.8	0.2
Pulaski County	42.7	53.1	32.9	43.4	30.5	50.0	30.4	37.9	6 795	47.8	14.4	22.0	5.2	-0.3	77.7	16.2	5.5	0.6
Rappahannock County	43.2	56.2	30.6	43.7	27.8	67.7	0.0	53.7	1 517	51.4	24.4	17.5	4.3	0.2	59.7	17.3	22.9	0.1
Richmond County	33.7	34.2	33.0	39.1	25.1	0.0	9.7	14.8	1 462	49.9	11.4	24.7	10.0	-0.9	65.8	21.6	12.5	0.2
Roanoke County	45.4	58.1	34.6	45.2	54.1	11.0	50.4	42.7	18 869	53.4	23.2	17.0	5.8	3.4	76.7	14.0	9.2	0.2
Rockbridge County	41.2	48.9	33.4	41.6	31.2	55.6	24.5	21.0	4 391	56.8	12.5	22.5	14.7	1.0	70.2	16.2	12.8	0.7
Rockingham County	44.8	57.3	33.1	45.3	37.0	44.6	46.3	31.1	15 785	54.7	22.0	17.3	7.4	6.1	74.5	12.8	12.3	0.3
Russell County	30.0	37.9	21.9	30.4	22.4	32.6	0.0	13.4	6 174	36.6	25.9	11.9	-16.1	-15.2	74.0	17.4	7.9	0.7
Scott County	32.3	41.7	23.6	32.3	34.3	58.6	17.6	0.0	4 644	44.9	23.5	14.7	-5.0	-13.0	76.7	13.7	8.7	0.8
Shenandoah County	43.9	55.4	33.2	43.9	53.3	76.3	33.6	39.2	7 403	50.9	19.8	21.8	8.1	1.0	74.9	12.4	12.2	0.4
Smyth County	41.1	51.6	31.5	41.3	33.7	46.3	23.7	49.7	6 664	48.2	19.6	21.2	4.8	-3.1	73.3	17.2	9.1	0.4
Southampton County	38.0	44.5	30.7	43.7	30.9	13.9	0.0	50.0	3 584	37.2	23.2	27.4	0.0	-2.7	71.4	19.5	8.6	0.5
Spotsylvania County	52.0	65.3	39.5	52.1	51.7	51.0	44.8	51.5	25 754	53.1	25.4	15.1	3.6	8.7	70.3	21.8	7.8	0.1
Stafford County	53.7	66.5	40.8	53.9	55.9	49.0	46.5	48.4	28 022	55.4	24.9	15.1	5.9	13.1	64.7	27.7	7.3	0.2
Surry County	39.8	47.9	32.3	42.1	38.4	0.0	77.8	13.3	1 560	46.1	14.4	26.0	7.5	-0.7	68.2	21.8	9.4	0.5
Sussex County	33.9	35.7	31.3	43.9	27.9	33.3	40.7	68.5	2 252	38.7	12.1	28.6	2.7	-2.2	71.8	20.5	7.5	0.2
Tazewell County	32.7	41.9	24.7	32.7	28.4	12.9	31.0	58.3	9 120	38.6	24.7	17.0	-9.0	-12.7	73.5	16.0	10.0	0.5
Warren County	45.1	58.0	33.1	45.2	41.0	60.8	40.8	57.1	7 554	42.3	23.3	26.0	3.7	2.9	74.6	16.8	8.3	0.3
Washington County	40.2	49.6	31.5	40.3	34.9	45.5	29.1	57.9	10 123	44.7	28.6	14.5	-5.4	-5.7	76.4	12.7	10.3	0.5
Westmoreland County	36.6	42.9	31.0	35.4	39.4	33.3	53.6	33.4	3 521	41.8	18.3	26.4	3.6	-11.0	65.5	22.9	11.7	0.0
Wise County	30.6	41.2	20.8	30.7	20.4	22.0	27.2	26.9	8 680	35.1	24.4	16.3	-13.2	-15.6	71.9	20.7	7.3	0.1
Wythe County	42.2	52.1	33.5	42.4	39.8	21.9	61.5	25.5	5 675	47.9	19.4	22.4	5.7	-1.5	76.8	14.0	8.9	0.4
York County	47.8	61.6	35.2	49.0	43.5	47.7	41.8	42.1	15 914	55.4	25.9	13.5	4.3	7.1	64.7	25.9	9.2	0.2
Independent Cities																		
Alexandria city	53.5	59.9	47.6	59.0	47.9	59.6	43.1	42.7	19 982	36.6	20.7	26.6	-1.4	7.9	70.3	21.8	7.7	0.2
Bedford city	34.0	38.5	30.2	34.3	32.4	0.0	28.1	47.4	1 286	36.7	11.3	39.8	11.9	-3.7	77.0	14.8	8.2	0.0
Bristol city	35.6	47.0	26.8	35.8	29.2	34.8	36.1	41.5	3 276	40.3	21.2	24.0	-0.3	-8.2	80.9	11.3	7.7	0.1
Buena Vista city	41.7	49.1	35.6	41.5	45.7	100.0	69.2	0.0	1 352	51.4	15.8	22.3	9.1	6.8	80.5	14.3	5.0	0.2
Charlottesville city	29.0	33.7	25.1	28.2	36.9	41.9	15.5	29.6	6 313	36.2	11.2	37.4	9.0	3.8	58.9	33.2	7.7	0.1
Chesapeake city	47.7	59.3	37.1	50.5	41.0	48.8	48.0	49.2	53 826	48.5	20.7	21.5	5.4	7.3	67.0	25.3	7.5	0.3
Clifton Forge city	30.6	38.7	24.5	31.3	27.1	X	45.5	0.0	828	31.5	17.1	37.2	4.1	-3.8	74.6	18.7	6.4	0.3
Colonial Heights city	41.7	54.0	31.5	41.3	48.3	23.3	40.4	57.0	3 606	45.4	19.3	26.8	7.6	-3.4	71.2	19.4	8.8	0.5
Covington city	35.1	44.9	26.6	36.0	30.8	X	34.8	29.7	1 197	41.2	13.4	27.7	4.3	-9.1	79.2	14.0	6.8	0.0
Danville city	35.1	43.9	28.2	35.3	34.6	37.8	49.5	32.7	10 339	31.6	10.3	41.5	8.5	-4.2	80.0	13.2	6.6	0.2
Emporia city	38.8	45.7	33.3	38.8	38.0	X	0.0	59.8	1 258	40.7	6.4	32.0	8.1	6.2	72.3	21.7	6.0	0.0
Fairfax city	47.8	57.0	39.0	48.8	53.6	51.7	41.2	46.5	4 107	47.1	28.8	16.9	-0.6	6.6	71.1	20.1	8.6	0.2
Falls Church city	52.0	62.3	42.6	52.4	52.6	60.0	55.9	43.9	2 366	54.8	21.8	18.6	8.8	15.3	62.2	27.5	10.1	0.1
Franklin city	35.4	49.3	25.1	39.5	31.4	0.0	0.0	74.4	1 935	34.3	11.0	38.0	7.7	-4.6	71.4	21.6	6.4	0.6
Fredericksburg city	38.3	50.2	28.8	36.7	44.9	73.2	16.1	44.3	3 113	34.8	18.5	37.4	7.6	0.2	69.4	22.2	8.3	0.1
Galax city	38.6	49.6	29.3	37.8	50.5	0.0	0.0	42.7	1 478	41.2	23.5	18.5	-4.9	-4.9	82.7	10.6	6.2	0.5
Hampton city	46.6	57.2	36.4	50.8	41.6	54.4	38.2	46.4	32 785	38.5	17.0	32.5	6.4	3.2	71.3	22.8	5.8	0.1
Harrisonburg city	25.7	33.1	19.1	26.0	27.3	0.0	19.3	25.5	5 870	46.7	20.4	22.8	4.9	5.3	74.0	19.9	6.0	0.2
Hopewell city	39.6	46.4	34.0	41.0	36.2	14.0	15.0	42.2	5 619	32.1	15.2	34.9	2.4	-8.9	74.1	19.5	6.0	0.4
Lexington city	18.6	20.9	15.6	18.4	25.2	0.0	13.3	7.6	705	47.9	21.3	24.3	7.6	-7.7	67.3	25.2	7.1	0.3
Lynchburg city	35.8	45.2	28.3	34.9	38.6	28.7	33.3	33.8	13 485	35.3	17.1	32.9	3.6	-1.2	80.5	12.1	7.2	0.1

[1] Hispanic or Latino persons may be of any race.

Table B-3. States and Counties — Education, Labor Force, and Income

STATE County	Percent who worked at home	Percent of the population 5 years and over with a disability	Veterans as a percent of the population 18 years and over	Occupation for employed population 16 years and over (percent)						Industry for employed population 16 years and over (percent)					
				Management, professional, and related occupations	Service occupations	Sales and office occupations	Farming, fishing, and forestry occupations	Construction, extraction, and maintenance occupations	Production, transportation and material moving occupations	Agriculture, forestry, fishing, and mining	Construction and manufacturing	Wholesale and retail trade	Transportation and warehousing, and utilities	Service industries	Public administration
	42	43	44	45	46	47	48	49	50	51	52	53	54	55	56
VIRGINIA—Cont'd															
Louisa County	4.3	22.2	14.3	24.1	13.8	24.8	1.2	18.2	18.0	2.9	27.4	15.2	6.7	41.0	6.8
Lunenburg County	2.4	27.8	15.8	23.2	16.8	21.1	1.5	13.4	23.9	2.8	29.9	13.4	5.6	38.1	10.1
Madison County	5.9	21.9	12.7	31.6	12.1	21.7	2.1	14.8	17.8	5.3	29.4	13.3	5.0	42.7	4.2
Mathews County	4.4	19.3	19.3	27.3	17.1	22.9	1.6	15.4	15.7	1.9	23.4	14.3	8.3	45.1	7.1
Mecklenburg County	2.9	26.3	13.9	21.8	14.7	24.3	1.4	14.1	23.6	3.5	32.0	17.2	5.0	34.7	7.6
Middlesex County	1.7	23.1	18.7	30.1	14.0	23.3	2.1	15.4	14.9	2.9	23.7	15.3	5.3	46.4	6.5
Montgomery County	3.0	14.5	8.8	40.2	16.4	22.2	0.4	8.2	12.7	0.9	18.8	12.7	2.7	62.2	2.6
Nelson County	5.2	24.6	13.8	28.0	15.0	21.9	2.9	16.0	16.3	4.2	24.7	11.0	6.1	50.5	3.5
New Kent County	2.0	17.2	15.4	30.7	13.8	27.2	0.8	13.8	13.9	1.6	26.3	13.8	6.4	45.4	6.6
Northampton County	4.7	25.8	14.3	27.1	20.0	19.9	6.6	10.0	16.4	7.9	19.2	13.2	6.4	47.5	5.7
Northumberland County	4.7	23.7	18.3	30.0	16.4	23.3	3.8	12.4	14.0	5.9	19.8	16.6	2.8	48.3	6.6
Nottoway County	3.5	22.0	14.4	23.5	19.0	24.4	1.3	10.5	21.2	3.5	19.5	18.8	7.8	39.8	10.5
Orange County	3.3	24.1	17.0	27.3	16.0	25.1	1.6	15.1	14.9	4.0	23.9	18.4	5.1	40.0	5.0
Page County	4.4	21.0	14.0	18.7	15.8	19.9	1.1	17.2	27.3	4.0	40.3	12.9	3.3	36.3	3.1
Patrick County	2.9	25.7	12.3	19.4	10.3	17.1	2.7	14.6	35.9	4.6	46.2	12.9	4.7	29.0	2.5
Pittsylvania County	2.3	23.3	12.8	19.9	12.2	23.2	1.0	13.3	30.4	2.4	41.5	14.9	4.0	33.3	3.9
Powhatan County	3.0	14.1	14.1	33.0	12.7	26.4	0.8	16.7	10.4	1.8	22.7	16.1	5.4	47.6	6.4
Prince Edward County	3.0	21.1	10.2	31.4	19.5	24.4	2.1	7.6	15.1	3.9	18.4	13.0	3.7	52.7	8.3
Prince George County	2.1	18.1	17.4	29.8	15.9	27.5	0.5	11.4	14.9	1.0	24.7	14.0	5.4	43.0	11.9
Prince William County	2.9	12.7	17.7	41.1	13.5	27.8	0.1	10.2	7.2	0.3	13.6	14.2	5.6	53.1	13.2
Pulaski County	1.5	23.6	14.6	24.0	14.1	22.7	1.0	10.7	27.4	1.5	39.0	13.5	5.2	37.0	3.9
Rappahannock County	9.1	17.8	13.9	35.8	15.4	20.2	2.1	16.9	9.6	8.0	20.6	9.2	3.9	50.4	7.8
Richmond County	3.0	22.4	13.8	23.1	16.7	29.1	2.9	11.2	17.0	4.6	17.3	19.4	7.4	43.6	7.8
Roanoke County	2.7	16.8	15.0	38.3	10.8	30.5	0.1	8.3	12.1	0.4	18.1	18.9	7.1	51.9	3.7
Rockbridge County	4.6	22.4	14.0	24.1	15.9	20.8	2.4	12.7	24.1	4.7	30.0	12.2	4.3	45.7	3.1
Rockingham County	5.2	18.3	11.9	26.6	12.8	21.7	2.1	12.9	23.9	6.2	33.3	16.0	4.0	38.0	2.6
Russell County	2.6	31.5	10.1	24.4	12.3	20.4	1.1	13.8	28.0	9.5	26.1	13.8	7.5	38.0	5.1
Scott County	2.9	29.1	12.9	21.3	14.1	24.5	1.4	15.4	23.4	4.2	30.1	16.9	4.6	40.3	4.0
Shenandoah County	4.2	17.9	15.3	22.5	14.1	24.9	1.5	13.2	23.8	3.9	31.9	16.0	4.5	39.0	4.8
Smyth County	1.7	24.9	13.1	21.8	15.1	20.7	0.8	10.4	31.1	2.2	39.5	14.2	0.0	36.2	6.1
Southampton County	2.5	23.3	13.6	23.2	14.8	22.3	2.4	13.0	24.3	5.6	29.3	15.8	5.3	35.6	8.5
Spotsylvania County	3.1	16.3	17.2	34.9	13.3	27.5	0.2	11.9	12.2	0.7	15.3	16.9	6.6	48.7	11.8
Stafford County	2.9	12.6	20.1	41.1	13.3	25.7	0.1	11.7	8.0	0.3	14.6	14.0	5.0	50.6	15.5
Surry County	3.1	24.5	14.5	22.2	18.0	22.1	1.8	18.7	17.1	5.0	29.9	11.3	8.1	39.2	6.6
Sussex County	1.9	22.8	12.4	21.7	17.1	22.2	3.4	11.7	24.0	6.9	25.5	16.3	6.8	36.5	8.0
Tazewell County	1.9	29.8	12.1	25.5	15.1	25.6	0.7	15.5	17.7	6.8	18.8	19.5	6.7	43.5	4.8
Warren County	2.6	10.6	16.1	26.9	15.3	23.8	0.4	19.9	13.7	1.1	26.2	15.1	4.7	45.8	7.1
Washington County	3.1	23.2	13.0	27.6	12.0	25.8	1.0	10.5	23.0	4.0	29.3	17.7	4.3	41.2	3.3
Westmoreland County	2.0	24.2	16.3	26.5	16.3	25.8	1.9	13.4	16.1	2.9	21.9	15.3	4.3	44.4	11.2
Wise County	1.6	28.7	11.6	26.8	15.5	24.3	0.8	17.3	15.4	10.7	13.4	16.9	5.7	40.0	6.6
Wythe County	3.8	24.0	13.1	20.9	17.2	22.3	0.9	10.7	28.0	3.3	31.2	16.6	4.4	40.2	4.2
York County	2.5	13.3	19.1	45.9	13.1	24.3	0.3	7.3	9.1	0.2	16.4	13.3	3.5	55.7	10.9
Independent Cities															
Alexandria city	3.5	15.0	11.1	56.2	11.9	21.2	0.1	5.4	5.2	0.2	7.9	8.7	4.1	64.9	14.2
Bedford city	2.8	30.8	13.8	22.7	17.0	26.6	0.0	8.1	25.6	0.3	30.3	17.4	3.0	45.7	3.2
Bristol city	1.7	25.8	13.1	26.6	13.0	31.5	0.3	7.3	21.2	1.3	28.4	19.4	3.8	44.1	3.0
Buena Vista city	1.7	23.6	13.4	17.4	20.4	20.0	0.6	12.1	29.5	1.1	38.3	12.3	2.7	39.8	5.7
Charlottesville city	5.4	13.7	7.4	44.0	19.5	23.3	0.2	5.7	7.4	0.4	8.7	11.4	2.5	73.6	3.2
Chesapeake city	2.4	18.4	18.1	35.6	13.7	27.5	0.3	11.5	11.5	0.5	18.7	14.7	5.9	51.4	8.9
Clifton Forge city	2.6	27.5	15.9	21.9	19.9	21.1	0.3	12.2	24.6	0.3	27.5	12.4	8.6	47.1	4.0
Colonial Heights city	1.3	20.9	17.2	31.9	11.7	31.4	0.1	11.5	13.3	0.3	22.3	18.6	4.4	46.1	8.3
Covington city	4.1	28.0	16.4	14.2	20.7	22.4	0.3	14.2	28.2	1.1	35.1	19.2	5.1	35.0	4.5
Danville city	1.4	25.8	14.9	23.9	17.0	25.0	0.2	7.9	26.0	0.1	31.6	16.5	3.0	45.7	3.1
Emporia city	1.0	27.3	10.2	26.1	17.4	20.1	1.2	8.6	26.6	0.5	30.9	17.4	3.9	35.8	11.4
Fairfax city	2.9	15.0	13.0	50.0	14.6	22.9	0.1	6.9	5.5	0.4	10.9	10.1	3.4	64.9	10.3
Falls Church city	5.0	12.1	14.7	65.5	10.2	18.0	0.0	2.9	3.4	0.2	5.2	8.6	2.9	65.2	18.0
Franklin city	3.0	22.6	14.6	27.2	18.6	22.1	0.5	12.2	19.4	1.3	30.1	14.7	2.4	44.2	7.2
Fredericksburg city	3.4	19.7	11.3	37.4	17.5	26.8	0.1	8.8	9.5	0.3	11.2	16.4	2.6	61.2	8.4
Galax city	1.5	28.3	11.3	18.3	12.2	21.0	0.4	8.8	39.3	0.7	43.9	17.3	3.6	30.4	4.2
Hampton city	1.5	19.5	25.5	32.1	15.1	27.8	0.3	11.0	13.7	0.3	21.9	15.0	4.1	49.6	8.9
Harrisonburg city	3.7	13.5	6.3	31.2	19.9	26.2	0.7	5.6	16.4	1.3	17.8	15.7	2.0	60.4	2.7
Hopewell city	2.1	25.5	19.0	19.6	18.5	25.8	0.3	13.2	22.5	0.5	27.8	16.8	6.7	39.9	8.4
Lexington city	5.1	13.9	10.4	45.8	18.6	21.6	0.0	7.0	7.0	0.9	11.3	10.7	1.8	70.4	4.9
Lynchburg city	2.4	22.8	12.5	33.3	17.1	26.3	0.2	6.9	16.1	0.4	23.9	15.3	3.8	54.2	2.4

STATE County	Median house-hold income	Median family income: All families	Married-couple	Male house-holder	Female house-holder	Median nonfamily house-hold income	Median income for full-year, full-time workers: Men	Women	Per capita income	With earnings	With interest, dividend, or rental income	With Social Security income	With public assis-tance income	With retire-ment income	House-holds with income over $100,000 (percent)	+/- U.S. percent for income over $100,000 (percent)	House-holds with income below poverty (percent)	Families with children with income below poverty (percent)
	57	58	59	60	61	62	63	64	65	66	67	68	69	70	71	72	73	74
VIRGINIA—Cont'd																		
Louisa County	39 402	44 722	49 786	23 897	20 500	22 533	32 346	25 426	19 479	79.1	31.1	28.1	2.2	17.7	7.6	-4.7	11.2	10.7
Lunenburg County........	27 899	34 302	40 455	18 500	17 900	13 554	27 719	21 031	14 951	70.9	28.3	39.9	4.4	17.5	2.8	-9.5	19.0	23.0
Madison County	39 856	44 857	47 792	26 250	21 136	22 285	31 830	25 394	18 636	82.2	38.5	31.3	1.3	22.5	7.4	-4.9	8.8	10.6
Mathews County	43 222	50 653	56 378	35 357	21 080	23 250	37 143	24 103	23 610	71.5	44.4	39.1	1.5	32.8	7.1	-5.2	6.8	7.4
Mecklenburg County	31 380	37 752	43 480	25 938	17 767	16 787	27 747	20 151	17 171	71.7	30.3	37.7	3.7	21.1	5.6	-6.7	16.1	16.4
Middlesex County	36 875	43 440	45 645	24 519	17 607	25 463	31 430	24 356	22 708	71.6	42.1	40.9	3.0	29.8	8.4	-3.9	12.1	14.4
Montgomery County	32 330	47 239	52 801	29 813	18 378	18 610	34 622	24 544	17 077	84.0	38.7	19.8	2.4	14.3	7.3	-5.0	22.1	12.8
Nelson County..............	36 769	42 917	50 455	22 857	25 582	21 385	30 494	24 861	22 230	79.0	36.3	31.1	2.3	22.7	9.4	-2.9	12.5	12.3
New Kent County	53 595	60 678	66 813	35 982	25 714	29 787	41 001	29 576	22 893	85.2	36.4	22.6	1.9	22.2	12.7	0.4	4.8	5.3
Northampton County	28 276	35 034	44 205	23 750	14 479	15 747	27 334	22 057	16 591	69.6	30.1	41.6	5.4	23.1	5.9	-6.4	19.5	24.2
Northumberland County .	38 129	49 047	49 196	33 929	17 118	17 714	30 887	25 066	22 917	67.8	43.4	44.6	2.9	33.6	10.3	-2.0	14.2	15.5
Nottoway County	30 866	39 625	45 734	25 139	17 663	16 571	30 233	20 273	15 552	71.9	30.1	38.1	6.2	21.4	4.5	-7.8	18.1	21.9
Orange County	42 889	48 197	52 280	33 672	20 967	25 979	32 721	24 977	21 107	76.3	35.2	32.8	2.7	22.5	9.5	-2.8	10.2	11.2
Page County	33 359	39 005	43 981	23 472	18 218	18 460	28 243	20 499	16 321	76.2	31.0	33.0	2.6	17.8	4.4	-7.9	13.4	14.2
Patrick County.............	28 705	36 232	41 089	26 810	15 048	15 869	25 777	19 788	15 574	76.3	28.0	33.0	4.7	17.3	3.1	-9.2	15.2	12.5
Pittsylvania County.......	35 153	41 175	48 525	27 425	17 208	17 208	30 739	21 885	16 991	79.0	28.8	30.3	2.7	16.4	4.0	-8.3	13.6	13.1
Powhatan County	53 992	58 142	60 462	37 024	25 682	31 209	39 456	29 010	24 104	87.6	37.4	21.7	1.0	19.9	15.4	3.1	5.7	8.0
Prince Edward County ..	31 301	38 509	49 341	22 266	12 188	19 327	29 669	22 493	14 510	73.2	31.4	35.2	3.7	17.9	5.8	-6.5	18.1	21.6
Prince George County ..	49 877	53 750	57 631	35 000	24 321	26 310	39 841	27 268	20 196	84.7	32.1	21.5	2.6	23.3	11.3	-1.0	8.0	8.6
Prince William County...	65 960	71 622	75 228	40 723	33 499	43 938	47 507	35 328	25 641	93.7	38.0	11.8	1.6	17.3	23.6	11.3	3.9	4.6
Pulaski County	33 873	42 251	49 078	23 900	14 946	18 726	31 363	22 343	18 973	75.0	27.9	32.0	3.8	19.2	4.7	-7.6	13.7	15.9
Rappahannock County..	45 943	51 848	56 531	28 214	21 771	26 491	34 814	25 181	23 863	85.3	42.5	29.1	2.3	23.7	12.8	0.5	6.9	7.4
Richmond County	33 026	42 143	56 389	22 083	16 065	16 538	31 770	22 271	16 675	72.7	35.7	36.8	3.1	21.1	6.0	-6.3	17.0	17.3
Roanoke County	47 689	56 450	65 873	35 104	29 961	26 660	40 428	27 451	24 637	80.8	46.0	29.9	1.1	19.6	12.1	-0.2	4.8	3.9
Rockbridge County	36 035	41 324	46 901	30 769	21 944	19 292	28 911	20 999	18 356	78.8	35.3	33.8	2.9	18.1	5.9	-6.4	10.9	9.5
Rockingham County......	40 748	46 262	52 390	25 720	21 667	21 872	31 437	22 538	18 795	83.3	38.8	27.9	1.8	14.9	6.9	-5.4	8.4	8.0
Russell County	26 834	31 491	36 211	22 159	15 423	12 667	27 705	20 380	14 863	66.5	21.9	41.2	5.8	19.4	3.7	-8.6	17.6	18.1
Scott County	27 339	33 163	39 696	26 250	14 020	12 563	29 161	21 205	15 073	66.4	27.1	38.2	4.5	20.7	2.9	-9.4	19.3	16.5
Shenandoah County	39 173	45 080	50 380	28 750	19 458	23 675	31 237	23 676	19 755	79.4	38.8	32.9	2.3	20.6	6.6	-5.7	8.7	10.9
Smyth County	30 083	36 392	42 260	28 350	15 833	16 797	27 191	20 525	16 105	74.8	26.5	35.6	2.7	18.0	4.0	-8.3	14.3	14.1
Southampton County	33 995	41 324	53 608	21 484	16 231	16 588	34 514	21 295	16 930	77.0	28.5	32.9	3.0	18.4	4.4	-7.9	15.1	18.1
Spotsylvania County	57 525	62 422	69 233	38 942	23 583	32 960	42 061	28 991	22 558	88.6	36.5	18.7	1.3	18.2	15.1	2.8	4.4	5.0
Stafford County	66 809	71 575	74 926	40 054	33 032	39 123	49 671	32 300	24 762	92.7	41.0	14.3	1.6	19.6	20.9	8.6	3.4	3.0
Surry County	37 558	41 234	44 917	22 344	17 135	19 375	31 774	21 433	16 682	80.4	29.9	33.7	4.3	19.7	3.9	-8.4	12.8	12.7
Sussex County	31 007	36 739	48 661	27 500	15 885	18 012	30 644	22 273	14 670	74.2	26.5	33.8	3.9	19.4	5.0	-7.3	17.9	20.2
Tazewell County	27 304	33 732	40 012	21 400	16 397	14 354	29 801	20 273	15 282	68.2	25.2	40.2	5.0	21.1	4.2	-8.1	16.2	16.7
Warren County	42 422	50 487	56 508	42 039	22 196	26 398	37 711	26 125	19 841	82.0	31.3	25.8	1.5	19.3	8.0	-4.3	9.0	8.1
Washington County.......	32 742	40 162	43 065	22 756	16 684	17 231	30 799	21 645	18 350	76.4	29.9	32.7	2.7	17.8	5.8	-6.5	12.5	12.6
Westmoreland County...	35 797	41 357	47 381	26 953	15 740	21 151	32 160	24 171	19 473	71.9	31.2	36.9	5.1	26.8	5.7	-6.6	15.3	19.0
Wise County.................	26 149	32 898	37 815	22 162	10 744	13 412	29 624	21 639	14 271	67.2	22.0	38.3	6.3	18.7	3.3	-9.0	19.9	24.5
Wythe County	32 235	40 188	44 781	24 375	16 797	15 957	30 017	20 970	17 639	75.7	28.5	33.7	3.9	16.7	4.9	-7.4	13.9	12.6
York County	57 956	64 892	70 063	35 901	29 462	32 400	47 742	29 933	24 560	87.3	54.3	20.8	0.9	27.3	18.5	6.2	3.6	3.8
Independent Cities																		
Alexandria city..............	56 054	67 023	70 000	34 455	25 261	49 338	49 365	42 159	37 645	88.9	43.7	13.0	1.4	13.5	22.0	9.7	6.8	11.2
Bedford city	28 792	35 023	40 739	19 327	11 055	18 635	29 755	18 740	15 423	68.7	27.2	36.2	6.1	19.8	5.2	-7.1	19.4	28.0
Bristol city	27 389	34 266	42 439	21 125	13 480	16 460	29 275	21 543	17 311	66.1	33.0	41.4	5.7	20.8	3.9	-8.4	16.4	22.8
Buena Vista city	32 410	39 449	48 548	25 114	18 125	18 636	29 121	21 966	16 377	77.8	28.9	35.6	1.8	14.8	4.2	-8.1	12.5	14.4
Charlottesville city	31 007	45 110	58 750	28 026	16 606	21 431	32 118	27 432	16 973	83.7	40.1	20.9	2.4	14.2	7.6	-4.7	22.7	19.2
Chesapeake city...........	50 743	56 302	64 604	35 775	22 530	30 378	40 944	27 273	20 949	86.9	35.5	20.8	2.2	20.9	11.9	-0.4	7.4	8.7
Clifton Forge city	26 090	31 509	42 941	16 667	15 625	16 808	28 636	21 445	15 182	67.5	28.6	41.7	6.3	16.6	4.5	-7.8	17.5	28.2
Colonial Heights city	43 224	51 806	62 193	32 727	26 713	27 685	38 962	27 532	23 659	76.9	42.2	33.6	1.9	31.0	9.7	-2.6	5.6	5.2
Covington city...............	30 325	36 640	37 813	19 875	18 145	20 351	31 193	21 567	16 758	68.7	26.1	38.2	3.6	22.4	2.2	-10.1	12.0	17.1
Danville city	26 900	36 024	51 017	21 696	15 063	16 957	30 788	22 083	17 151	71.0	27.1	37.1	5.3	20.9	5.2	-7.1	18.6	27.1
Emporia city	30 333	35 743	55 946	22 279	17 241	17 557	28 102	21 966	15 377	71.5	25.6	35.2	2.3	18.1	4.1	-8.2	14.4	16.9
Fairfax city	67 642	78 921	77 946	56 094	33 594	46 230	51 494	40 092	31 247	87.6	53.8	20.5	1.9	24.0	26.5	14.2	4.6	3.6
Falls Church city	74 924	97 225	108 621	40 313	42 115	50 359	67 688	48 032	41 051	84.8	62.6	20.2	1.3	20.3	35.9	23.6	3.9	4.5
Franklin city	31 687	40 299	62 452	32 250	9 661	17 797	34 236	22 560	18 573	73.9	27.6	33.3	4.0	22.3	9.4	-2.9	18.9	29.7
Fredericksburg city	34 585	47 148	57 045	25 898	18 750	26 817	35 417	25 651	21 527	79.7	34.3	26.1	3.4	16.4	10.1	-2.2	13.1	16.7
Galax city	28 236	36 832	48 098	32 593	14 896	14 178	24 669	18 650	17 447	71.1	26.9	35.2	5.9	12.4	4.4	-7.9	20.4	22.3
Hampton city	39 532	46 110	52 498	32 527	19 345	25 882	33 092	25 455	19 774	83.8	30.0	23.1	2.9	23.6	6.9	-5.4	10.8	13.4
Harrisonburg city	29 949	45 159	52 413	26 563	20 152	19 204	30 337	23 933	14 898	84.9	35.3	20.3	3.2	10.4	7.0	-5.3	26.5	17.7
Hopewell city	33 196	38 024	51 017	21 696	17 011	22 163	31 746	24 202	16 338	75.1	26.4	28.8	6.1	24.8	4.6	-7.7	14.3	19.6
Lexington city	28 982	58 529	75 158	100 470	33 571	15 850	40 282	27 755	16 497	74.2	45.3	32.6	1.8	20.2	11.6	-0.7	22.5	13.0
Lynchburg city..............	32 234	40 844	55 751	22 250	17 452	20 013	32 089	23 689	18 263	75.2	32.8	31.7	3.9	19.0	7.3	-5.0	15.6	19.5

Table B-3. States and Counties — Education, Labor Force, and Income

STATE/ County code	MSA/PMSA/ NECMA code[1]	STATE County	High school graduates			College graduates		College graduates (percent)				
			Total population 25 years and over	Percent with a high school diploma or less	Percent with a high school diploma or more	Percent with a bachelor's degree or more	+/− U.S. percent with bachelor's degree or more	Non-Hispanic White	Black or African American	American Indian and Alaska Native	Asian, Hawaiian, and Pacific Islander	Hispanic or Latino[2]
			1	2	3	4	5	6	7	8	9	10
		VIRGINIA—Cont'd										
51 683	8840	Manassas city	21 188	42.7	81.3	28.1	3.7	33.7	17.2	0.0	31.2	9.9
51 685	8840	Manassas Park city	6 224	51.0	76.4	20.3	-4.1	18.6	26.7	65.4	68.0	6.2
51 690	...	Martinsville city	10 843	60.8	68.5	16.6	-7.8	23.4	5.6	100.0	50.0	10.1
51 700	5720	Newport News city	110 083	45.6	84.5	19.9	-4.5	25.0	11.7	18.4	25.2	13.7
51 710	5720	Norfolk city	135 258	51.2	78.4	19.6	-4.8	26.3	9.7	9.3	34.3	16.5
51 720	...	Norton city	2 665	60.3	66.5	14.0	-10.4	15.0	4.2	0.0	0.0	0.0
51 730	6760	Petersburg city	22 289	61.7	68.6	14.8	-9.6	21.1	12.4	23.9	34.9	17.0
51 735	5720	Poquoson city	7 759	38.5	88.5	31.6	7.2	30.7	40.0	0.0	76.6	39.7
51 740	5720	Portsmouth city	63 685	54.2	75.2	13.8	-10.6	17.0	10.0	18.2	23.1	18.6
51 750	...	Radford city	6 766	36.3	83.4	34.1	9.7	35.6	11.0	0.0	90.2	29.4
51 760	6760	Richmond city	128 555	48.4	75.2	29.5	5.1	51.4	11.2	22.4	49.0	20.3
51 770	6800	Roanoke city	65 593	54.4	76.0	18.7	-5.7	22.2	7.8	20.9	37.4	19.4
51 775	6800	Salem city	16 657	50.2	82.0	19.8	-4.6	20.5	0.5	0.0	29.7	15.0
51 790	...	Staunton city	16 703	55.5	75.6	20.4	-4.0	22.3	6.2	0.0	0.0	33.3
51 800	5720	Suffolk city	41 662	52.8	76.8	17.3	-7.1	21.5	10.8	17.0	40.6	17.0
51 810	5720	Virginia Beach city	266 627	35.5	90.4	28.1	3.7	30.6	18.1	12.7	33.3	19.1
51 820	...	Waynesboro city	13 303	56.0	77.9	20.6	-3.8	22.4	7.2	18.4	42.9	12.5
51 830	5720	Williamsburg city	5 360	31.2	89.6	45.0	20.6	54.1	10.3	X	38.9	23.8
51 840	...	Winchester city	15 316	51.3	75.4	23.7	-0.7	26.6	7.4	0.0	34.2	7.4
53 000	...	WASHINGTON..........	3 827 507	37.8	87.1	27.7	3.3	28.9	19.4	12.4	35.5	11.1
53 001	...	Adams County..............	9 242	62.9	63.3	12.2	-12.2	17.3	0.0	8.6	27.9	3.0
53 003	...	Asotin County..............	13 619	46.9	85.8	18.0	-6.4	17.9	62.5	29.2	57.1	11.6
53 005	6740	Benton County	88 217	38.9	85.1	26.3	1.9	27.6	23.7	10.3	50.1	6.9
53 007	...	Chelan County	42 425	46.7	79.1	21.9	-2.5	24.9	24.6	6.8	19.0	3.7
53 009	...	Clallam County	45 711	42.3	85.5	20.8	-3.6	21.5	7.7	11.3	24.1	5.3
53 011	6440	Clark County	217 293	39.2	87.8	22.1	-2.3	22.4	22.5	11.1	29.9	10.1
53 013	...	Columbia County..........	2 827	47.8	82.7	17.5	-6.9	18.3	0.0	28.6	35.7	3.8
53 015	...	Cowlitz County..............	60 355	49.6	83.2	13.3	-11.1	13.6	17.7	4.7	12.2	0.0
53 017	...	Douglas County..............	20 435	51.0	78.4	16.2	-8.2	18.3	19.3	11.4	16.2	3.5
53 019	...	Ferry County	4 748	51.7	82.7	13.5	-10.9	15.4	0.0	4.7	7.7	26.8
53 021	6740	Franklin County	26 779	60.3	63.5	13.6	-10.8	19.4	12.2	5.3	23.1	2.9
53 023	...	Garfield County	1 655	45.1	84.4	17.0	-7.4	17.1	X	0.0	50.0	25.0
53 025	...	Grant County	43 309	55.6	72.2	13.7	-10.7	16.9	9.5	14.1	28.2	2.5
53 027	...	Grays Harbor County	44 588	53.2	81.1	12.7	-11.7	12.9	0.0	9.4	24.0	7.0
53 029	7600	Island County..............	47 112	32.2	92.1	27.0	2.6	28.0	24.2	15.2	21.1	13.2
53 031	...	Jefferson County	19 551	35.6	91.6	28.4	4.0	29.5	12.3	9.9	24.9	4.9
53 033	7600	King County..............	1 188 740	28.9	90.3	40.0	15.6	42.5	21.1	18.2	40.9	20.4
53 035	1150	Kitsap County..............	148 704	34.7	90.8	25.3	0.9	20.4	17.7	15.9	24.0	14.1
53 037	...	Kittitas County..............	19 303	43.8	87.2	26.2	1.8	26.6	23.5	21.8	39.0	12.7
53 039	...	Klickitat County	12 806	52.6	81.7	16.4	-8.0	17.4	0.0	2.9	20.0	4.1
53 041	...	Lewis County..............	44 857	52.4	80.5	12.9	-11.5	13.2	30.1	8.8	24.7	4.2
53 043	...	Lincoln County	7 117	44.7	86.5	18.8	-5.6	19.0	11.1	15.9	31.3	16.4
53 045	...	Mason County..............	33 936	48.7	83.7	15.6	-8.8	16.0	4.2	8.2	28.4	8.7
53 047	...	Okanogan County..........	25 826	54.1	76.6	15.9	-8.5	17.9	0.0	11.2	25.0	3.9
53 049	...	Pacific County	15 298	52.6	78.9	15.2	-9.2	15.7	0.0	13.3	8.1	10.4
53 051	...	Pend Oreille County	7 995	52.4	81.0	12.3	-12.1	12.7	27.3	0.0	1.2	6.6
53 053	8200	Pierce County	442 665	42.9	86.9	20.6	-3.8	21.8	15.0	13.0	19.5	11.8
53 055	...	San Juan County	10 691	24.3	94.4	40.2	15.8	41.3	X	0.0	8.2	7.4
53 057	...	Skagit County	66 959	42.4	84.0	20.8	-3.6	22.2	20.7	3.7	33.2	3.7
53 059	...	Skamania County	6 557	47.6	85.9	16.8	-7.6	17.4	20.0	3.1	51.6	3.6
53 061	7600	Snohomish County........	388 997	36.7	89.2	24.4	0.0	24.3	21.1	10.9	36.6	14.6
53 063	7840	Spokane County..........	266 829	37.7	89.1	25.0	0.6	25.5	14.8	13.3	27.0	17.3
53 065	...	Stevens County	25 984	50.1	85.4	15.3	-9.1	15.7	17.8	6.9	19.2	12.3
53 067	5910	Thurston County	135 686	34.3	89.5	29.8	5.4	30.8	28.7	16.4	24.9	18.9
53 069	...	Wahkiakum County	2 715	48.0	84.2	14.8	-9.6	14.7	X	23.6	100.0	0.0
53 071	...	Walla Walla County.......	34 372	43.0	81.1	23.3	-1.1	25.9	19.1	7.7	30.2	4.8
53 073	0860	Whatcom County..........	102 787	40.1	87.5	27.2	2.8	28.3	26.7	7.1	31.0	12.5
53 075	...	Whitman County	20 070	26.4	92.8	44.0	19.6	41.5	58.3	10.8	73.0	66.7
53 077	9260	Yakima County..............	130 747	58.7	68.7	15.3	-9.1	19.8	16.6	11.7	27.2	3.9
54 000	...	WEST VIRGINIA	1 233 581	64.2	75.2	14.8	-9.6	14.6	11.5	12.8	62.1	19.7
54 001	...	Barbour County..............	10 510	73.4	72.7	11.8	-12.6	11.7	39.3	7.5	20.0	0.0
54 003	8840	Berkeley County............	50 092	62.8	77.6	15.1	-9.3	15.2	11.3	4.2	42.3	10.6
54 005	...	Boone County	17 282	77.0	64.0	7.2	-17.2	7.0	14.6	20.0	100.0	11.0

[1]MSA = Metropolitan Statistical Area. PMSA = Primary MSA. NECMA = New England County Metropolitan Area. See the Appendix A for explanation of these concepts. See Appendix B for list of metropolitan areas identified by type, with component counties.
[2]Hispanic or Latino persons may be of any race.

STATE County	School enrollment			Population 16 to 19 years				Employment status, 2000			Work status in 1999 of the population 16 years and over (percent)		
											Worked in 1999		
	Grades kindergarten through 12	College or graduate school	Percent private	Number	Percent in armed forces	Percent high school graduates	Percent not enrolled, not grads, not in armed forces, not employed	Total population 16 years and over	Percent in labor force	Unemploy-ment rate	Full-time	Part-time	Did not work in 1999
	11	12	13	14	15	16	17	18	19	20	21	22	23
VIRGINIA—Cont'd													
Manassas city	7 433	1 916	15.4	1 923	0.0	8.6	5.6	25 719	74.3	3.7	66.5	14.1	19.4
Manassas Park city	2 118	477	10.9	499	0.0	11.4	5.2	7 348	77.2	2.2	70.5	12.0	17.5
Martinsville city	2 630	661	5.1	703	0.0	7.7	4.6	12 351	54.1	8.7	48.7	11.3	39.9
Newport News city	35 994	10 611	10.6	10 506	7.7	19.2	4.0	135 532	68.3	5.0	59.9	14.2	25.9
Norfolk city	40 850	19 085	13.0	16 165	19.0	27.0	5.6	183 922	67.1	7.0	56.9	15.2	27.9
Norton city	699	180	3.9	218	0.0	18.8	3.2	3 164	49.6	7.3	40.2	14.0	45.7
Petersburg city	6 381	1 388	8.7	1 704	0.3	13.3	11.2	26 200	56.5	8.7	52.6	11.0	36.3
Poquoson city	2 524	527	7.8	651	0.0	5.5	3.8	8 838	66.8	3.1	57.8	15.1	27.1
Portsmouth city	19 171	5 211	12.2	5 791	9.8	19.7	7.4	77 524	62.1	7.0	53.0	13.5	33.5
Radford city	1 435	6 952	3.5	2 507	0.0	2.4	0.0	13 998	54.8	6.4	47.3	28.3	24.4
Richmond city	31 524	19 116	18.1	11 559	0.1	9.9	6.2	158 612	62.4	8.0	55.1	14.8	30.1
Roanoke city	15 292	3 590	9.3	4 030	0.0	18.1	12.8	75 372	62.7	5.8	55.1	12.8	32.1
Salem city	4 103	2 195	25.6	1 715	0.0	5.4	0.5	20 185	64.0	3.8	54.8	16.5	28.6
Staunton city	3 528	1 387	27.3	1 364	0.0	9.7	2.3	19 711	58.7	3.9	52.5	15.2	32.3
Suffolk city	13 372	3 129	13.3	3 204	0.0	8.7	6.6	47 731	63.6	4.7	55.6	13.0	31.5
Virginia Beach city	86 963	26 275	12.1	23 384	5.4	15.8	3.7	321 282	72.9	3.5	63.8	14.3	21.9
Waynesboro city	3 412	488	5.5	845	0.0	12.3	6.2	15 293	60.9	6.5	51.8	14.0	34.3
Williamsburg city	832	5 403	9.5	2 080	0.0	1.6	0.0	10 951	67.5	41.4	47.7	27.2	25.1
Winchester city	3 690	1 688	21.9	1 688	0.0	10.5	9.5	19 052	67.1	4.6	57.6	15.6	26.8
WASHINGTON	1 127 448	358 414	11.1	335 082	0.9	11.3	4.6	4 553 591	66.5	6.1	55.5	16.5	27.9
Adams County	4 249	466	5.5	1 110	0.0	6.8	9.8	11 406	62.3	8.7	56.1	13.5	30.5
Asotin County	3 900	853	5.4	1 155	0.0	10.8	3.7	15 985	61.7	6.4	50.8	15.6	33.7
Benton County	31 831	5 789	7.2	8 530	0.0	8.6	6.1	105 052	67.2	6.1	56.3	16.2	27.6
Chelan County	14 315	2 623	8.5	4 091	0.0	11.4	8.9	50 075	63.6	10.4	53.2	16.4	30.3
Clallam County	11 058	2 425	9.2	3 460	0.0	12.5	7.1	52 214	51.2	7.6	40.3	17.4	42.3
Clark County	70 778	15 495	9.1	18 895	0.1	11.3	5.9	256 455	68.0	5.9	57.1	15.7	27.2
Columbia County	759	96	7.3	251	1.6	15.5	6.4	3 227	58.7	9.0	49.3	14.7	36.0
Cowlitz County	18 394	3 602	6.5	5 382	0.3	12.0	6.5	70 982	61.0	7.7	49.1	16.7	34.2
Douglas County	7 284	1 088	4.3	1 883	0.0	7.5	5.1	24 049	64.7	9.0	56.4	15.1	28.5
Ferry County	1 554	230	7.9	587	0.0	16.2	11.8	5 655	57.8	18.8	47.3	15.2	37.5
Franklin County	12 379	1 654	4.8	3 692	0.0	8.5	12.5	34 262	63.8	10.8	56.9	13.8	29.3
Garfield County	496	54	2.4	153	0.0	8.5	1.3	1 879	54.8	4.9	49.6	13.3	37.1
Grant County	17 754	2 622	3.7	5 232	0.0	10.6	7.9	53 387	62.3	11.7	54.2	14.8	31.0
Grays Harbor County	13 316	2 347	4.5	3 943	0.2	8.7	6.0	52 065	57.9	8.3	45.9	16.4	37.7
Island County	13 317	3 165	8.7	3 514	7.8	16.8	3.2	55 267	63.1	4.7	51.4	16.5	32.1
Jefferson County	3 934	678	8.9	1 118	0.0	13.8	5.3	21 502	54.5	6.7	41.7	19.0	39.3
King County	287 823	125 584	14.8	85 185	0.1	10.3	3.2	1 389 714	70.1	4.5	59.4	16.3	24.3
Kitsap County	46 929	11 528	9.8	13 475	4.6	14.7	4.4	177 191	64.9	5.5	54.0	16.1	29.9
Kittitas County	5 204	6 679	3.7	2 752	0.0	7.9	2.9	27 431	62.3	9.1	48.0	25.8	26.2
Klickitat County	4 081	441	7.8	1 038	0.0	13.8	3.9	14 573	60.1	10.4	50.4	15.0	34.5
Lewis County	13 805	2 619	8.2	4 210	0.1	11.0	7.7	52 750	56.1	9.0	45.7	15.5	38.8
Lincoln County	1 980	227	9.0	549	0.0	8.7	1.8	7 983	55.8	6.1	48.6	15.9	35.4
Mason County	9 123	1 522	6.5	2 739	0.0	14.2	9.3	39 301	54.0	8.2	45.9	14.1	40.0
Okanogan County	8 692	1 047	5.6	2 277	0.0	9.2	6.0	29 898	58.4	12.0	49.4	15.9	34.7
Pacific County	3 735	606	5.4	1 017	0.7	8.8	4.2	17 073	51.1	7.7	39.6	17.1	43.4
Pend Oreille County	2 413	365	10.3	715	0.0	11.3	9.2	9 081	49.7	10.4	40.2	15.9	43.9
Pierce County	142 171	37 999	12.5	40 956	3.4	13.8	5.2	531 215	66.4	6.1	56.1	15.5	28.5
San Juan County	2 184	348	10.8	567	0.0	13.1	4.8	11 611	58.8	3.2	45.7	21.0	33.2
Skagit County	20 524	4 095	6.9	6 523	0.2	12.1	7.3	79 422	62.6	6.8	51.0	17.5	31.5
Skamania County	1 955	283	7.4	614	0.0	12.1	5.7	7 602	64.3	11.1	51.5	16.5	32.0
Snohomish County	122 466	29 961	9.7	33 396	1.2	11.8	3.9	458 108	70.4	4.9	59.9	15.6	24.5
Spokane County	80 540	30 682	13.3	26 628	0.7	12.1	3.1	323 980	65.1	7.9	51.4	18.5	30.1
Stevens County	8 901	955	8.3	2 621	0.0	12.1	5.3	30 146	57.4	9.9	45.3	17.1	37.6
Thurston County	40 428	13 181	10.3	12 447	0.0	11.4	2.8	161 642	67.3	5.8	55.5	16.4	28.1
Wahkiakum County	690	127	6.2	202	0.0	6.4	3.5	3 063	55.2	8.1	42.9	18.3	38.7
Walla Walla County	10 530	5 541	28.1	4 044	0.0	3.7	3.3	43 253	59.3	8.2	50.5	18.9	30.6
Whatcom County	29 602	19 135	9.2	11 267	0.1	9.6	2.7	131 195	66.6	7.4	50.3	23.2	26.5
Whitman County	5 320	15 058	3.5	4 413	0.0	2.9	0.8	34 252	61.1	9.6	46.9	31.9	21.2
Yakima County	53 034	7 244	7.2	14 451	0.0	11.8	8.7	159 645	62.2	11.1	54.8	13.8	31.5
WEST VIRGINIA	304 216	92 329	7.7	99 445	0.1	11.8	6.4	1 455 101	54.5	7.3	46.8	12.3	40.9
Barbour County	2 726	827	15.1	931	0.0	11.4	9.8	12 413	53.6	8.7	43.9	12.3	43.8
Berkeley County	14 127	2 424	7.5	4 037	0.0	19.3	8.1	58 653	64.9	4.3	58.2	12.2	29.5
Boone County	4 458	808	4.1	1 266	0.0	13.1	2.6	20 278	47.4	8.5	42.1	9.9	48.0

Table B-3. States and Counties — Education, Labor Force, and Income

STATE County	Full-year full-time employed (percent)								Children under 18 years in families						Total employed by class of worker (percent)			
										With two parents (percent)		With one parent who is in labor force (percent)	+/- U.S. percent of children with no stay-at-home parent (percent)	+/- U.S. percent two-income couples				
	Total	Men	Women	Non-Hispanic White	Black or African American	American Indian and Alaska Native	Asian, Hawaiian, and Pacific Islander	Hispanic or Latino¹	Number	Both in labor force	Father only in labor force				Private	Government	Self-employed	Unpaid family worker
	24	25	26	27	28	29	30	31	32	33	34	35	36	37	38	39	40	41
VIRGINIA—Cont'd																		
Manassas city	53.1	63.5	42.6	54.6	55.3	51.1	50.6	46.5	9 744	49.4	24.0	17.0	1.8	13.4	75.5	17.9	6.5	0.1
Manassas Park city	54.4	66.2	42.4	59.5	51.3	84.6	41.2	37.1	2 998	48.3	20.2	23.8	7.5	11.5	76.3	17.4	5.9	0.4
Martinsville city	33.1	41.7	26.3	33.4	31.8	30.0	69.6	39.8	3 141	32.0	13.9	36.8	4.2	-8.3	79.9	12.5	7.6	0.0
Newport News city	44.3	54.7	34.9	47.0	40.9	37.3	37.5	45.2	46 235	39.2	16.5	31.9	6.5	4.6	72.6	21.0	6.2	0.2
Norfolk city	41.3	51.3	30.8	46.5	34.9	37.4	38.5	45.9	51 472	30.5	15.8	34.6	0.5	-1.8	73.0	20.6	6.2	0.2
Norton city	30.4	39.6	23.2	30.5	31.6	0.0	40.0	0.0	813	22.8	14.5	38.4	-3.4	-11.9	75.3	18.0	6.3	0.4
Petersburg city	37.4	42.3	33.4	31.3	38.9	0.0	38.4	44.6	7 368	26.4	6.5	46.9	8.7	-4.9	67.9	27.3	4.6	0.3
Poquoson city	44.9	61.0	29.5	44.7	12.5	23.3	43.1	49.4	2 998	54.6	26.5	11.5	1.5	4.0	62.9	25.3	11.2	0.6
Portsmouth city	38.9	48.0	30.6	43.1	33.8	39.8	48.4	49.1	22 726	30.7	14.2	40.0	6.1	-1.7	67.3	26.4	6.3	0.1
Radford city	23.6	31.4	17.2	24.3	17.6	100.0	9.3	9.5	1 964	57.5	12.0	22.1	15.0	7.9	62.2	32.9	4.7	0.2
Richmond city	38.2	44.0	33.3	41.9	35.7	33.4	23.3	35.1	38 128	25.0	9.6	43.0	3.4	0.2	74.0	19.1	6.9	0.1
Roanoke city	42.1	50.1	35.3	43.4	38.2	41.6	40.6	41.7	19 747	34.2	15.3	35.6	5.2	0.1	81.7	11.8	6.4	0.1
Salem city	42.0	50.9	34.4	42.2	39.1	46.7	27.5	53.7	4 876	55.2	15.0	22.3	12.9	4.4	80.4	12.3	7.3	0.0
Staunton city	38.5	47.6	30.6	39.4	34.5	18.6	0.0	26.5	4 325	46.2	14.8	30.7	12.3	2.4	72.2	20.6	7.1	0.0
Suffolk city	44.0	55.5	34.0	49.1	37.3	54.7	49.2	39.4	16 510	44.0	15.9	26.6	6.0	4.9	70.1	22.0	7.5	0.4
Virginia Beach city	49.5	61.6	38.0	50.3	49.0	48.5	42.1	48.1	111 408	48.3	21.6	21.4	5.1	7.3	71.2	19.4	9.2	0.2
Waynesboro city	40.3	49.9	32.1	40.4	39.5	61.4	33.3	34.1	4 310	40.8	11.2	30.8	7.0	-3.4	77.5	14.9	7.2	0.4
Williamsburg city	22.9	30.5	16.7	21.3	34.2	0.0	21.6	22.6	1 095	19.9	23.7	33.3	-11.4	-10.6	70.2	22.8	7.0	0.0
Winchester city	42.4	52.1	33.5	41.9	42.5	64.3	44.2	48.8	4 732	43.9	20.2	25.8	5.1	1.7	80.5	11.7	7.5	0.3
WASHINGTON	39.4	49.3	29.8	40.2	40.8	33.3	37.4	32.6	1 433 592	45.0	24.2	20.1	0.5	0.6	72.8	16.5	10.4	0.3
Adams County	29.9	39.3	20.2	36.2	16.7	13.0	20.8	21.9	5 275	45.7	26.3	15.3	-3.6	-3.1	70.4	16.4	12.7	0.5
Asotin County	34.2	43.1	26.6	34.4	0.0	36.1	24.7	25.1	4 956	44.2	15.5	28.6	8.2	0.5	70.5	16.1	12.8	0.6
Benton County	40.9	52.8	29.5	42.0	37.6	34.9	40.8	31.3	40 297	45.5	25.4	19.7	0.6	1.1	72.8	18.0	8.8	0.4
Chelan County	32.0	40.1	24.0	34.3	21.8	32.5	28.6	19.7	17 618	54.4	18.3	16.4	6.2	-2.0	66.9	18.0	14.6	0.5
Clallam County	26.7	33.4	20.1	26.7	29.0	27.5	18.7	27.4	13 292	42.5	22.3	22.1	0.0	-13.0	60.9	22.1	16.6	0.4
Clark County	41.4	53.1	30.3	41.8	44.1	34.8	39.9	37.4	94 617	42.8	28.5	19.6	-2.2	0.7	77.6	12.5	9.6	0.3
Columbia County	31.1	41.7	21.0	30.8	0.0	9.7	57.1	39.6	937	42.0	29.2	19.5	-3.1	-2.4	58.2	25.1	16.2	0.5
Cowlitz County	33.8	45.1	23.0	34.1	43.4	18.9	30.5	33.7	23 484	39.2	24.8	24.3	-1.1	-6.5	76.7	13.8	9.2	0.3
Douglas County	34.7	44.5	25.5	37.1	44.5	39.3	22.6	22.2	9 052	46.8	20.9	17.7	-0.1	-3.1	69.1	18.0	12.3	0.6
Ferry County	25.3	29.2	21.1	26.4	17.6	22.6	11.1	12.7	1 775	40.2	19.8	24.3	-0.1	-13.5	44.3	38.7	16.7	0.3
Franklin County	31.7	39.4	23.3	37.2	22.6	27.6	32.6	24.8	15 911	38.6	25.3	17.9	-8.1	-4.7	74.8	15.4	9.4	0.4
Garfield County	32.6	41.7	24.1	32.4	X	0.0	50.0	53.3	598	45.8	19.2	25.1	6.3	-5.8	44.1	31.3	24.0	0.7
Grant County	30.7	40.7	20.5	33.4	21.3	29.8	33.1	24.0	22 559	46.6	21.8	18.8	0.8	-6.2	68.1	19.0	12.3	0.6
Grays Harbor County	30.5	38.4	22.7	30.7	29.8	30.2	38.4	26.7	16 008	36.5	21.7	25.7	-2.4	-8.7	67.2	19.7	12.6	0.5
Island County	37.1	49.2	25.1	36.6	51.1	35.0	36.3	43.0	17 528	46.0	31.8	14.1	-4.5	-5.2	63.6	20.3	15.6	0.5
Jefferson County	26.8	33.8	20.2	26.3	21.6	37.0	36.2	37.8	4 815	38.2	25.9	26.6	0.2	-13.0	57.1	19.1	23.2	0.7
King County	43.7	53.3	34.5	45.1	40.4	37.4	39.3	40.4	371 386	46.2	24.8	19.0	0.6	4.2	77.1	12.9	9.7	0.2
Kitsap County	40.1	52.3	27.8	40.5	46.5	34.0	36.3	43.0	59 023	44.3	27.3	19.2	-1.1	-1.5	60.6	27.6	11.5	0.3
Kittitas County	27.2	34.8	19.7	27.9	17.8	26.7	14.8	23.2	6 526	51.0	21.9	17.2	3.6	-1.7	60.0	27.3	12.2	0.4
Klickitat County	31.5	40.5	22.6	32.2	17.9	24.5	39.0	24.5	4 874	45.2	24.3	18.7	-0.7	-7.6	60.8	23.3	15.6	0.3
Lewis County	29.6	38.7	20.7	29.3	23.2	39.4	34.7	32.2	17 020	40.4	25.9	19.6	-4.6	-10.1	69.0	18.5	12.1	0.4
Lincoln County	32.8	44.4	21.7	33.0	33.3	28.2	36.4	30.5	2 430	50.9	24.4	17.1	3.4	-4.4	51.3	25.4	22.1	1.3
Mason County	32.0	38.0	25.5	32.8	20.7	28.3	31.5	21.9	10 682	42.4	21.0	22.6	0.4	-10.7	60.2	27.1	12.2	0.5
Okanogan County	28.6	34.6	22.6	28.3	42.9	34.3	37.2	25.9	10 095	42.5	17.6	25.0	2.9	-10.5	58.3	26.0	14.8	0.9
Pacific County	26.1	31.6	20.8	26.0	0.0	25.7	28.9	27.5	4 069	46.0	19.2	21.4	2.8	-13.3	60.3	22.7	16.1	0.9
Pend Oreille County	25.0	34.4	15.6	25.4	0.0	28.0	9.0	22.9	2 858	34.7	23.0	21.7	-8.2	-18.1	58.2	24.0	17.0	0.8
Pierce County	40.9	51.7	30.5	41.5	43.3	38.7	32.3	40.6	180 254	43.3	22.9	22.9	1.6	1.1	73.2	17.7	8.8	0.3
San Juan County	30.6	39.2	22.3	30.5	X	26.1	23.0	29.9	2 618	48.4	20.0	21.5	5.3	-4.2	55.3	13.2	30.3	1.2
Skagit County	33.9	43.7	24.6	35.0	30.9	29.6	28.0	26.9	25 094	47.7	21.7	19.7	2.8	-2.6	70.6	15.8	13.2	0.5
Skamania County	34.4	44.9	24.0	34.7	61.9	29.3	18.9	26.7	2 469	42.9	27.5	23.0	1.3	-8.4	64.6	22.5	12.5	0.4
Snohomish County	44.5	56.0	33.2	45.1	44.6	37.7	40.4	42.5	158 827	47.2	26.2	18.6	1.2	5.0	76.8	13.3	9.7	0.3
Spokane County	36.7	45.8	28.1	37.2	31.8	31.9	27.9	34.0	101 799	45.3	22.9	22.1	2.8	0.4	74.2	15.7	9.8	0.3
Stevens County	29.5	38.1	21.2	29.5	13.7	31.9	24.2	29.8	10 854	41.7	27.3	17.8	-5.1	-10.1	63.9	20.5	14.5	1.1
Thurston County	40.6	49.3	32.6	41.1	46.6	36.0	35.7	39.6	49 299	48.4	20.9	21.0	4.8	3.4	57.9	32.3	9.3	0.5
Wahkiakum County	24.3	29.4	19.3	24.4	X	18.7	60.0	27.3	846	49.1	14.2	20.4	4.9	-8.5	57.1	25.8	16.9	0.1
Walla Walla County	30.0	36.2	23.5	30.9	17.0	37.2	24.1	27.0	12 450	48.3	19.2	20.7	4.4	-1.5	67.5	20.9	11.2	0.5
Whatcom County	33.2	42.9	24.0	33.4	35.5	28.8	31.9	33.4	38 565	45.5	26.0	18.7	-0.4	0.5	70.9	15.2	13.4	0.5
Whitman County	24.7	30.9	18.4	26.0	22.3	19.0	12.9	18.1	7 091	52.8	21.7	16.2	4.4	4.2	43.6	45.6	10.4	0.4
Yakima County	31.7	39.8	24.0	36.7	26.4	26.4	29.4	22.1	65 761	41.2	19.1	21.3	-2.1	-3.4	72.7	16.7	10.2	0.4
WEST VIRGINIA	33.2	42.0	25.1	33.4	28.6	26.9	31.6	34.3	380 926	39.5	25.1	18.6	-6.5	-10.5	73.5	17.9	8.2	0.4
Barbour County	30.1	39.0	21.7	30.4	18.6	19.8	0.0	26.5	3 480	44.4	24.5	17.0	-3.2	-12.5	71.8	17.9	9.6	0.7
Berkeley County	44.5	53.6	35.6	44.8	41.0	32.2	44.4	49.3	18 241	43.9	21.6	22.0	1.3	-0.1	75.6	16.8	7.3	0.3
Boone County	26.9	36.6	17.9	26.8	33.6	14.3	31.6	33.6	5 595	30.7	28.5	14.8	-19.1	-20.6	74.0	19.0	6.7	0.2

¹Hispanic or Latino persons may be of any race.

Table B-3. States and Counties — Education, Labor Force, and Income

				Occupation for employed population 16 years and over (percent)						Industry for employed population 16 years and over (percent)					
STATE County	Percent who worked at home	Percent of the population 5 years and over with a disability	Veterans as a percent of the population 18 years and over	Management, professional, and related occupations	Service occupations	Sales and office occupations	Farming, fishing, and forestry occupations	Construction, extraction, and maintenance occupations	Production, transportation and material moving occupations	Agriculture, forestry, fishing, and mining	Construction and manufacturing	Wholesale and retail trade	Transportation and warehousing, and utilities	Service industries	Public administration
	42	43	44	45	46	47	48	49	50	51	52	53	54	55	56
VIRGINIA—Cont'd															
Manassas city	2.4	14.2	14.1	38.5	13.9	27.1	0.1	12.1	8.3	0.2	17.9	14.4	5.4	53.5	8.6
Manassas Park city	3.0	16.1	12.6	30.5	14.3	25.5	0.0	18.8	10.9	0.2	21.0	16.5	6.4	50.1	5.8
Martinsville city	1.9	26.1	12.9	26.0	13.9	22.3	0.0	6.9	30.8	0.4	39.3	12.4	3.5	41.8	2.6
Newport News city	1.6	19.1	18.4	30.5	17.6	27.6	0.3	10.4	13.6	0.3	22.3	15.1	3.8	50.6	7.9
Norfolk city	3.8	23.2	16.9	29.1	19.1	27.7	0.2	10.7	13.2	0.2	14.4	15.9	5.7	56.2	7.6
Norton city	2.3	34.5	12.0	27.0	20.6	27.6	0.7	9.7	14.4	5.7	13.8	15.3	4.4	56.1	4.7
Petersburg city	1.1	28.2	17.6	24.9	22.0	21.8	0.2	6.8	24.4	0.6	21.6	13.9	5.3	50.0	8.6
Poquoson city	3.1	14.6	17.3	44.1	13.5	20.8	1.5	10.3	9.9	1.3	21.6	13.7	2.8	48.6	12.0
Portsmouth city	2.7	25.3	17.3	27.7	16.7	27.8	0.2	12.8	14.7	0.4	22.1	14.9	5.1	49.9	7.6
Radford city	2.4	16.0	8.1	35.5	20.3	26.0	0.1	5.5	12.6	0.2	19.1	11.0	1.9	63.5	4.1
Richmond city	2.3	24.3	11.6	35.5	18.7	26.9	0.1	6.4	12.5	0.2	13.7	13.2	4.6	61.6	6.7
Roanoke city	1.9	25.5	15.0	26.7	16.9	30.3	0.1	8.7	17.2	0.3	19.3	19.9	5.9	51.8	2.9
Salem city	1.6	19.0	15.8	29.5	15.5	31.8	0.2	8.8	14.2	0.5	19.6	18.3	5.6	52.2	3.7
Staunton city	2.6	20.8	14.9	27.4	18.9	26.1	0.3	8.4	18.9	0.3	19.7	17.2	3.5	53.0	6.2
Suffolk city	1.7	23.1	16.4	30.9	13.8	25.3	0.4	11.3	18.5	0.9	25.9	15.0	6.3	43.8	8.2
Virginia Beach city	2.8	15.8	19.5	35.9	14.9	30.1	0.1	10.0	9.0	0.2	13.9	16.7	4.4	57.6	7.1
Waynesboro city	1.8	25.6	16.2	26.4	15.4	26.7	1.0	9.8	20.7	0.5	31.2	17.7	4.6	42.2	3.8
Williamsburg city	4.1	14.5	8.8	41.7	18.0	28.1	0.2	6.5	5.5	0.2	11.5	13.9	1.7	68.9	3.8
Winchester city	3.1	20.8	13.4	29.2	13.7	26.6	0.8	9.7	20.0	1.4	26.7	16.4	3.9	48.3	3.3
WASHINGTON	4.3	18.2	15.3	35.6	14.9	25.9	1.6	9.4	12.7	2.5	19.5	16.2	5.4	51.4	5.0
Adams County	5.5	20.4	10.0	25.2	13.3	17.7	16.1	9.6	18.1	25.6	17.3	15.3	4.8	33.9	3.1
Asotin County	4.9	22.7	16.3	28.4	19.2	24.8	1.4	10.6	15.7	3.3	19.4	16.6	5.1	51.9	3.8
Benton County	3.6	18.1	14.9	37.9	14.1	23.9	2.5	10.1	11.5	4.1	14.8	14.7	6.2	55.5	4.6
Chelan County	5.4	19.1	14.6	30.5	17.9	23.3	7.4	9.4	11.5	8.9	13.5	18.2	6.3	49.7	3.5
Clallam County	5.6	23.2	20.9	28.7	20.0	24.0	3.6	10.8	13.0	6.0	14.7	15.4	5.1	50.1	4.4
Clark County	4.4	17.6	15.2	30.9	13.6	27.3	0.5	11.0	16.6	1.1	24.7	17.1	7.9	45.5	3.7
Columbia County	4.8	24.6	15.8	31.6	18.2	21.6	5.0	10.9	12.7	13.3	15.1	10.5	5.8	46.1	9.3
Cowlitz County	2.9	21.7	16.5	23.6	17.6	23.5	1.9	12.4	21.1	3.5	28.6	14.9	5.2	43.7	4.0
Douglas County	4.5	18.3	14.3	28.2	16.3	23.7	8.3	9.6	13.9	12.2	15.0	21.4	5.5	41.4	4.6
Ferry County	8.0	23.1	20.7	33.1	16.8	21.7	3.5	12.0	13.0	12.8	14.2	9.6	4.1	44.9	14.4
Franklin County	4.4	20.8	10.9	24.7	15.9	20.1	12.5	9.2	17.5	17.0	17.9	14.9	6.4	39.8	3.9
Garfield County	5.4	20.1	15.1	39.5	12.8	24.4	3.6	7.9	11.8	18.6	8.0	20.4	3.7	39.7	9.6
Grant County	4.7	19.7	13.5	26.1	14.7	20.8	12.5	9.7	16.2	18.8	17.7	15.3	6.0	37.9	4.3
Grays Harbor County	4.2	24.1	16.9	24.3	19.7	22.8	4.7	11.6	16.9	7.3	20.2	15.6	4.8	45.1	7.2
Island County	5.5	17.4	22.0	33.8	17.6	23.1	0.9	11.7	12.9	1.7	19.7	13.5	4.8	53.4	6.9
Jefferson County	9.7	19.1	21.1	33.3	18.3	21.7	1.5	13.1	12.1	3.7	20.9	13.2	5.4	50.2	6.6
King County	4.4	16.1	12.2	43.4	12.9	26.4	0.3	6.9	10.1	0.4	18.2	16.1	5.3	56.6	3.3
Kitsap County	4.6	18.3	22.3	34.9	17.4	24.8	0.5	12.0	10.4	0.9	18.7	14.6	4.3	52.1	9.5
Kittitas County	5.7	18.3	12.8	30.7	20.4	26.1	2.9	8.9	11.1	5.2	12.7	16.5	5.4	55.5	4.7
Klickitat County	6.2	21.4	16.4	29.8	14.5	20.3	7.0	10.5	17.8	13.1	19.8	13.2	5.5	42.9	5.4
Lewis County	4.7	23.9	17.7	23.9	17.8	24.3	4.4	12.1	17.5	8.0	19.1	16.6	7.2	45.3	5.6
Lincoln County	10.0	22.0	19.6	37.0	15.9	22.8	4.3	11.2	8.8	17.6	9.9	14.7	5.7	44.3	7.7
Mason County	4.2	22.5	21.9	25.9	18.4	24.0	3.1	13.5	15.1	4.6	21.1	14.5	5.3	42.2	12.3
Okanogan County	8.2	20.7	16.3	29.8	18.3	22.1	9.5	8.2	12.0	16.0	10.5	15.8	4.6	45.8	7.3
Pacific County	5.7	27.4	21.3	26.6	21.5	20.5	5.8	10.3	15.3	8.3	16.7	11.9	4.5	51.7	6.9
Pend Oreille County	6.8	26.0	21.7	26.8	17.5	20.7	2.5	13.3	19.2	5.6	22.3	10.9	9.3	47.0	5.0
Pierce County	3.6	19.7	18.9	30.1	16.3	26.8	0.5	11.2	15.1	1.0	20.3	17.0	6.9	49.0	15.8
San Juan County	13.7	17.1	18.8	33.4	16.3	23.9	1.5	15.0	9.7	3.3	22.3	13.2	5.0	52.7	3.7
Skagit County	4.6	19.4	17.2	28.5	15.7	24.8	4.0	11.5	15.5	5.9	22.5	17.1	4.6	45.7	4.3
Skamania County	5.7	17.5	18.2	28.2	18.8	20.0	1.8	12.9	18.3	5.0	26.8	11.9	6.3	43.8	6.1
Snohomish County	4.0	16.8	15.0	33.7	13.5	26.8	0.5	12.3	13.2	0.9	26.7	16.5	4.8	47.1	3.9
Spokane County	4.1	19.1	16.8	33.0	16.9	28.4	0.4	8.6	12.7	0.9	16.5	17.3	4.6	55.9	4.7
Stevens County	6.6	20.2	19.5	29.9	16.9	21.8	3.0	11.6	16.8	7.5	21.7	14.1	5.5	45.6	5.6
Thurston County	3.8	18.8	18.3	37.4	15.4	27.1	1.1	9.0	10.0	2.1	13.5	13.4	3.7	48.2	19.1
Wahkiakum County	3.6	23.2	18.6	29.5	15.2	22.1	8.3	10.8	14.2	14.6	18.0	8.6	6.2	46.1	6.5
Walla Walla County	3.6	21.0	13.1	35.4	18.9	23.4	3.9	8.8	9.6	6.8	13.8	11.6	3.8	57.1	6.9
Whatcom County	5.0	15.5	13.3	31.5	16.5	26.3	2.0	10.1	13.5	3.3	20.5	17.8	4.0	50.9	3.6
Whitman County	5.0	12.5	9.1	45.5	17.4	24.1	1.8	4.9	6.3	6.4	5.9	10.3	2.6	70.6	4.3
Yakima County	3.5	22.2	12.2	27.4	16.1	22.5	9.3	8.3	16.5	10.7	16.9	19.0	4.6	43.7	5.2
WEST VIRGINIA	2.4	24.4	14.3	27.9	16.6	26.1	0.7	12.3	16.4	4.1	18.9	15.9	6.0	49.3	5.8
Barbour County	3.3	24.3	12.5	24.6	17.4	22.7	1.2	16.9	17.2	7.5	19.9	15.4	5.7	45.2	6.3
Berkeley County	1.7	21.6	16.5	25.9	13.7	25.1	0.4	12.7	22.4	1.5	27.3	15.4	5.3	43.8	6.7
Boone County	1.1	31.1	12.5	21.7	15.8	26.3	0.4	19.7	16.0	16.0	10.6	17.1	6.4	43.3	6.7

STATE County	Median household income	Median family income — All families	Median family income — Married-couple	Median family income — Families with children, Male householder	Median family income — Families with children, Female householder	Median nonfamily household income	Median income for full-year, full-time workers — Men	Median income for full-year, full-time workers — Women	Per capita income	With earnings	With interest, dividend, or rental income	With Social Security income	With public assistance income	With retirement income	Households with income over $100,000 (percent)	+/− U.S. percent for income over $100,000	Households with income below poverty (percent)	Families with children with income below poverty (percent)
	57	58	59	60	61	62	63	64	65	66	67	68	69	70	71	72	73	74
VIRGINIA—Cont'd																		
Manassas city	60 409	70 141	77 545	38 250	33 191	38 919	44 695	31 403	24 453	91.7	37.2	12.3	1.3	13.8	19.5	7.2	4.8	5.0
Manassas Park city	60 794	61 075	69 119	32 137	28 173	47 739	38 719	31 475	21 048	93.8	26.6	12.5	2.1	12.2	13.8	1.5	4.8	5.3
Martinsville city	27 441	35 321	51 563	19 375	18 542	16 732	29 252	22 398	17 251	71.0	28.3	34.8	5.8	18.4	5.9	-6.4	19.8	23.7
Newport News city	36 597	42 520	50 126	25 576	16 378	25 293	32 375	23 289	17 843	83.0	28.3	21.1	3.8	19.9	5.9	-6.4	13.0	17.0
Norfolk city	31 815	36 891	45 417	27 517	15 247	23 548	26 695	22 506	17 372	80.1	25.8	23.6	4.6	19.5	6.3	-6.0	18.1	23.2
Norton city	22 788	30 889	45 385	18 750	10 750	13 816	30 926	24 074	16 024	63.2	23.9	37.6	6.0	17.1	5.3	-7.0	23.3	32.0
Petersburg city	28 851	33 955	49 309	18 651	17 904	20 896	29 192	22 784	15 989	74.9	19.7	31.9	4.9	24.6	4.4	-7.9	19.1	24.4
Poquoson city	60 920	65 460	71 156	35 909	30 625	30 670	49 810	30 306	25 336	84.3	54.0	23.4	0.5	30.8	18.7	6.4	4.3	4.9
Portsmouth city	33 742	39 577	50 989	28 814	17 238	22 239	30 792	24 423	16 507	77.2	25.2	28.2	4.6	23.7	4.8	-7.5	14.9	20.6
Radford city	24 654	46 332	61 050	25 833	19 154	12 966	33 365	22 938	14 289	79.5	32.0	21.2	1.7	14.6	5.3	-7.0	30.6	9.8
Richmond city	31 121	38 348	58 193	24 494	16 735	24 224	31 589	26 580	20 337	77.9	28.3	25.9	4.7	16.4	8.3	-4.0	19.3	26.9
Roanoke city	30 719	37 826	48 056	25 455	16 665	20 472	29 680	22 302	18 468	76.4	27.8	30.3	4.3	16.6	5.0	-7.3	15.3	21.7
Salem city	38 997	47 174	55 000	34 226	20 436	23 026	33 835	24 350	20 091	78.2	38.0	32.9	1.7	20.0	0.5	0.0	7.5	6.6
Staunton city	32 941	44 422	52 088	25 913	19 355	20 142	31 086	22 613	19 161	75.8	37.1	33.8	2.2	22.1	6.6	-5.7	13.2	13.1
Suffolk city	41 115	47 342	55 714	33 060	16 514	22 011	37 408	24 767	18 836	80.9	31.0	26.2	3.5	20.7	9.0	-3.3	13.4	15.6
Virginia Beach city	48 705	53 242	56 781	32 008	24 722	33 184	35 860	26 963	22 365	88.6	37.9	17.7	1.6	20.5	12.1	-0.2	6.3	7.4
Waynesboro city	32 686	40 772	48 036	27 813	14 754	20 017	31 572	22 721	17 932	74.1	35.5	31.7	4.5	21.2	5.4	-6.9	12.4	19.7
Williamsburg city	37 093	52 358	74 250	21 875	11 794	23 116	30 179	28 182	18 483	78.1	49.6	26.3	2.0	26.1	13.2	0.9	15.7	22.5
Winchester city	34 335	44 675	57 844	23 162	21 087	23 933	30 593	25 757	20 500	81.3	32.5	28.1	2.1	16.2	8.4	-3.9	12.9	12.5
WASHINGTON	45 776	53 760	61 575	32 356	21 832	29 394	41 774	30 787	22 973	81.9	40.0	22.9	3.8	17.1	12.6	0.3	9.8	11.2
Adams County	33 888	37 075	38 700	25 515	15 765	21 370	29 914	22 086	13 534	81.4	29.0	26.0	5.2	13.4	3.8	-8.5	14.5	19.5
Asotin County	33 524	40 592	48 476	26 667	13 556	20 920	36 915	23 343	17 748	76.0	37.9	32.6	6.6	17.8	6.4	-5.9	13.4	19.5
Benton County	47 044	54 146	60 855	31 405	20 905	27 638	46 992	28 211	21 301	83.4	40.9	23.1	4.5	18.1	11.3	-1.0	9.1	11.7
Chelan County	37 316	46 293	51 546	28 304	17 134	21 113	36 542	26 636	19 273	77.3	37.7	29.6	3.9	18.3	9.4	-2.9	11.3	13.4
Clallam County	36 449	44 381	50 384	28 482	16 180	21 600	36 755	25 796	19 517	65.6	44.4	39.6	4.4	27.5	5.9	-6.4	12.2	16.0
Clark County	48 376	54 016	60 963	35 078	21 323	31 332	42 223	29 676	21 448	84.7	38.3	21.2	4.4	10.1	11.0	-0.5	8.2	10.3
Columbia County	33 500	44 038	45 568	21 786	14 844	18 108	35 591	21 761	17 374	73.8	41.5	35.5	4.7	20.6	5.1	-7.2	12.0	13.6
Cowlitz County	39 797	46 532	53 145	26 949	17 235	21 861	41 121	26 569	18 583	76.4	37.9	28.4	5.5	18.9	7.3	-5.0	12.7	16.5
Douglas County	38 464	43 777	49 087	30 417	14 125	21 753	37 608	25 670	17 148	80.8	36.3	26.4	4.2	16.9	5.9	-6.4	12.1	17.8
Ferry County	30 388	35 691	40 119	27 813	12 054	14 911	33 097	23 969	15 019	74.3	28.4	29.9	7.6	18.1	3.4	-8.9	18.1	21.3
Franklin County	38 991	41 967	43 985	25 060	13 531	21 366	33 790	25 078	15 459	84.2	30.2	21.9	6.4	13.1	9.0	-3.3	16.8	22.3
Garfield County	33 398	41 645	50 441	29 375	14 286	20 083	35 388	22 434	16 992	72.1	45.0	36.8	4.0	16.2	4.7	-7.6	12.9	15.4
Grant County	35 276	38 938	42 660	27 885	16 213	20 960	34 035	24 972	15 037	79.2	32.5	27.1	5.7	16.0	6.1	-6.2	15.2	19.3
Grays Harbor County	34 160	39 709	49 220	26 997	15 497	19 527	36 750	25 081	16 799	72.3	32.5	33.5	6.2	20.2	5.1	-7.2	15.1	19.0
Island County	46 513	51 363	52 195	35 694	19 973	26 679	37 095	26 604	21 472	77.2	45.5	28.4	2.6	27.4	9.9	-2.4	7.1	8.4
Jefferson County	37 869	45 415	52 325	35 347	17 372	22 238	39 603	26 916	22 211	68.5	50.2	36.5	3.6	29.3	8.3	-4.0	11.3	15.4
King County	53 157	66 035	76 229	37 689	27 593	36 073	47 257	35 471	29 521	84.9	45.4	19.1	2.8	14.3	18.7	6.4	7.8	8.0
Kitsap County	46 840	53 878	58 563	32 725	20 535	28 732	41 375	29 933	22 317	81.0	41.0	21.7	0.0	24.2	11.6	0.7	8.2	0.4
Kittitas County	32 546	46 057	53 630	20 357	14 482	15 300	37 616	26 776	18 928	79.9	36.1	24.1	3.2	16.2	7.2	-5.1	21.5	15.9
Klickitat County	34 267	40 414	46 955	20 804	14 028	17 616	36 660	22 459	16 502	75.5	35.6	29.2	5.7	16.3	4.7	-7.6	15.7	19.2
Lewis County	35 511	41 105	47 747	27 042	16 010	19 911	36 851	24 321	17 082	71.8	34.8	33.9	4.8	22.1	5.2	-7.1	13.2	16.5
Lincoln County	35 255	41 260	45 451	33 000	18 400	20 794	32 319	23 864	17 888	72.5	46.3	35.8	3.8	20.4	5.6	-6.7	11.8	14.4
Mason County	39 586	44 246	50 695	28 702	17 941	23 886	38 694	26 582	18 056	71.8	35.4	34.0	4.9	27.2	6.1	-6.2	11.7	15.3
Okanogan County	29 726	35 012	40 423	19 583	14 117	16 644	30 689	22 429	14 900	75.8	30.7	30.4	6.3	19.5	4.1	-8.2	19.3	24.3
Pacific County	31 209	39 302	45 577	21 466	15 000	17 144	36 040	23 644	17 322	64.2	38.0	43.4	5.4	26.6	4.4	-7.9	14.0	16.4
Pend Oreille County	31 677	36 977	44 942	30 132	9 970	17 295	38 896	22 044	15 731	68.3	31.4	34.7	7.9	23.6	5.2	-7.1	16.8	25.7
Pierce County	45 204	52 098	60 093	34 106	21 837	28 539	40 307	29 615	20 948	82.4	33.2	21.9	4.7	18.8	10.4	-1.9	9.6	11.3
San Juan County	43 491	51 835	51 735	30 515	22 500	30 471	37 389	29 250	30 603	74.7	53.6	32.0	2.2	25.3	13.7	1.4	9.6	11.1
Skagit County	42 381	48 347	56 667	36 761	19 914	26 565	38 692	26 984	21 256	77.6	39.5	30.6	3.8	20.9	9.5	-2.8	9.5	11.6
Skamania County	39 317	44 586	52 195	16 667	10 987	23 750	37 633	26 039	18 002	80.8	36.7	24.5	4.4	16.6	6.3	-6.0	12.2	16.5
Snohomish County	53 060	60 726	68 238	40 537	27 382	33 382	45 287	32 098	23 417	85.8	39.6	19.7	2.7	15.1	14.3	2.0	6.5	6.7
Spokane County	37 308	46 463	54 527	27 868	18 335	21 649	36 358	26 352	19 233	79.1	36.6	25.6	4.9	16.6	7.9	-4.4	12.2	12.9
Stevens County	34 673	40 250	44 940	25 000	16 779	17 445	36 406	24 507	15 895	75.4	34.4	29.4	5.3	19.5	4.3	-8.0	15.2	16.5
Thurston County	46 975	55 027	61 523	35 192	23 070	28 596	41 953	31 341	22 415	82.0	42.4	23.5	3.3	21.6	10.8	-1.5	8.8	9.4
Wahkiakum County	39 444	47 604	60 324	13 438	20 536	27 303	40 174	30 324	19 063	72.1	44.4	35.0	4.8	28.4	4.7	-7.6	7.5	11.5
Walla Walla County	35 900	44 962	51 628	26 250	16 113	20 060	35 910	25 796	16 509	75.5	40.4	32.5	3.9	19.1	6.5	-5.8	13.7	16.6
Whatcom County	40 005	49 325	55 124	31 199	20 859	22 904	38 997	27 011	20 025	81.2	42.1	23.8	3.1	16.0	8.9	-3.4	13.6	11.9
Whitman County	28 584	44 830	50 261	26 786	18 199	15 407	35 743	27 905	15 298	85.2	45.3	18.8	2.2	11.7	6.3	-6.0	25.4	15.8
Yakima County	34 828	39 746	44 118	23 007	16 109	20 218	32 411	25 298	15 606	79.8	30.0	26.3	6.3	14.9	7.0	-5.3	16.4	21.9
WEST VIRGINIA	29 696	36 484	42 228	21 310	12 861	16 007	32 044	21 767	16 477	70.6	28.7	33.9	4.0	22.0	5.0	-7.3	18.0	21.4
Barbour County	24 729	29 722	33 241	15 375	10 710	13 208	25 841	18 159	12 440	67.8	27.1	34.7	4.8	20.7	2.3	-10.0	22.2	27.1
Berkeley County	38 763	44 302	51 803	29 944	17 724	23 911	33 033	24 159	17 982	81.3	28.5	24.8	2.5	19.3	6.0	-6.3	11.4	13.1
Boone County	25 669	31 999	37 279	18 906	13 590	13 451	35 836	20 097	14 453	64.9	19.6	35.3	7.4	23.5	2.8	-9.5	21.9	25.7

Table B-3. States and Counties — **Education, Labor Force, and Income**

STATE/ County code	MSA/PMSA/ NECMA code[1]	STATE County	High school graduates			College graduates		College graduates (percent)				
			Total population 25 years and over	Percent with a high school diploma or less	Percent with a high school diploma or more	Percent with a bachelor's degree or more	+/– U.S. percent with bachelor's degree or more	Non-Hispanic White	Black or African American	American Indian and Alaska Native	Asian, Hawaiian, and Pacific Islander	Hispanic or Latino[2]
			1	2	3	4	5	6	7	8	9	10
		WEST VIRGINIA— Cont'd										
54 007	...	Braxton County	10 273	75.0	67.3	9.2	-15.2	9.2	0.0	33.3	100.0	0.0
54 009	8080	Brooke County	17 855	63.9	79.7	13.4	-11.0	13.5	13.4	100.0	0.0	21.9
54 011	3400	Cabell County	64 444	54.0	80.0	20.9	-3.5	21.1	10.6	20.3	48.9	16.4
54 013	...	Calhoun County	5 283	77.4	62.4	9.3	-15.1	8.9	X	0.0	100.0	41.7
54 015	...	Clay County	6 766	80.8	63.7	7.3	-17.1	7.4	0.0	0.0	0.0	0.0
54 017	...	Doddridge County	4 897	71.9	69.4	10.2	-14.2	10.3	X	0.0	50.0	0.0
54 019	...	Fayette County	32 721	71.2	68.6	10.7	-13.7	10.8	4.9	8.7	69.2	20.9
54 021	...	Gilmer County	4 515	66.9	70.0	17.1	-7.3	17.1	0.0	50.0	9.5	0.0
54 023	...	Grant County	7 859	72.3	70.8	11.4	-13.0	11.4	0.0	0.0	X	23.5
54 025	...	Greenbrier County	24 373	67.8	73.4	13.6	-10.8	13.9	4.6	10.1	62.5	7.5
54 027	...	Hampshire County	13 690	72.9	71.3	11.3	-13.1	11.3	5.8	50.0	42.5	0.0
54 029	8080	Hancock County	23 502	64.7	82.9	11.5	-12.9	11.6	9.8	0.0	12.2	27.5
54 031	...	Hardy County	8 759	74.3	70.3	9.4	-15.0	9.7	3.3	28.6	X	0.0
54 033	...	Harrison County	46 870	62.0	78.4	16.3	-8.1	16.2	9.5	11.9	52.8	18.4
54 035	...	Jackson County	19 074	62.3	77.4	12.4	-12.0	12.1	100.0	20.6	72.7	14.7
54 037	8840	Jefferson County	27 920	55.6	79.0	21.6	-2.8	22.3	9.5	20.5	35.0	9.5
54 039	1480	Kanawha County	140 588	56.2	80.0	20.6	-3.8	20.4	15.5	24.0	70.3	21.9
54 041	...	Lewis County	11 872	70.4	73.7	11.2	-13.2	10.9	100.0	0.0	74.2	71.8
54 043	...	Lincoln County	14 864	79.5	62.7	5.9	-18.5	5.9	X	0.0	16.7	2.9
54 045	...	Logan County	25 824	71.7	63.1	8.8	-15.6	8.2	16.2	0.0	81.3	32.6
54 047	...	McDowell County	18 802	83.1	50.0	5.6	-18.8	5.1	9.5	0.0	44.0	2.8
54 049	...	Marion County	38 957	60.1	79.5	16.0	-8.4	16.1	9.6	0.0	55.6	25.5
54 051	9000	Marshall County	24 707	66.8	79.7	10.7	-13.7	10.5	11.1	26.5	70.2	11.7
54 053	...	Mason County	17 947	73.8	72.4	8.8	-15.6	8.5	7.5	57.9	80.8	0.0
54 055	...	Mercer County	43 673	64.5	72.1	13.8	-10.6	13.5	13.4	28.1	72.6	8.5
54 057	1900	Mineral County	18 443	66.1	80.3	11.7	-12.7	11.8	5.9	X	34.3	4.8
54 059	...	Mingo County	18 793	76.1	59.6	7.3	-17.1	6.9	12.1	0.0	71.8	4.8
54 061	...	Monongalia County	47 943	46.9	83.6	32.4	8.0	31.4	23.5	12.6	80.8	36.1
54 063	...	Monroe County	10 474	73.1	73.7	8.2	-16.2	8.8	1.1	30.0	25.0	0.0
54 065	...	Morgan County	10 591	70.2	75.8	11.2	-13.2	11.2	2.7	23.7	0.0	5.8
54 067	...	Nicholas County	18 149	73.6	70.0	9.8	-14.6	9.4	X	23.1	75.0	59.5
54 069	9000	Ohio County	32 263	53.1	83.0	23.1	-1.3	23.2	10.2	0.0	69.0	29.7
54 071	...	Pendleton County	5 813	70.6	72.0	10.8	-13.6	10.9	0.7	0.0	100.0	0.0
54 073	...	Pleasants County	5 121	69.6	79.4	9.7	-14.7	9.5	12.5	23.8	40.0	46.2
54 075	...	Pocahontas County	6 556	71.7	70.9	11.8	-12.6	11.7	6.5	9.1	87.5	40.0
54 077	...	Preston County	20 050	73.1	74.0	10.8	-13.6	10.6	19.2	X	68.4	35.4
54 079	1480	Putnam County	34 854	55.0	83.8	19.7	-4.7	19.2	56.3	0.0	48.9	38.0
54 081	...	Raleigh County	55 201	64.3	72.0	12.7	-11.7	12.6	5.9	0.0	64.5	12.8
54 083	...	Randolph County	19 498	69.4	73.5	13.6	-10.8	13.5	16.6	0.0	32.6	43.4
54 085	...	Ritchie County	7 177	70.3	73.4	7.1	-17.3	7.1	31.3	31.8	0.0	4.0
54 087	...	Roane County	10 442	74.9	66.8	9.0	-15.4	9.0	0.0	0.0	60.0	25.8
54 089	...	Summers County	9 302	74.9	65.4	10.1	-14.3	10.2	3.8	0.0	0.0	0.0
54 091	...	Taylor County	11 146	69.4	74.7	11.3	-13.1	11.2	15.2	6.5	31.3	11.3
54 093	...	Tucker County	5 301	73.0	75.5	10.6	-13.8	10.3	X	0.0	0.0	0.0
54 095	...	Tyler County	6 749	69.4	75.4	8.5	-15.9	8.4	100.0	0.0	71.4	0.0
54 097	...	Upshur County	15 222	69.8	74.6	13.8	-10.6	13.7	0.0	0.0	40.0	33.0
54 099	3400	Wayne County	29 223	67.9	70.5	11.9	-12.5	11.7	37.5	3.6	43.8	35.6
54 101	...	Webster County	6 701	78.2	58.2	8.7	-15.7	8.7	X	0.0	100.0	X
54 103	...	Wetzel County	12 287	69.9	77.6	10.4	-14.0	10.3	0.0	19.2	100.0	0.0
54 105	...	Wirt County	3 944	72.6	72.4	9.9	-14.5	9.9	X	0.0	0.0	0.0
54 107	6020	Wood County	60 697	56.9	81.4	15.2	-9.2	15.0	18.6	17.9	51.5	25.4
54 109	...	Wyoming County	17 722	77.5	64.3	7.1	-17.3	7.1	18.9	0.0	0.0	0.0
55 000	...	WISCONSIN	3 475 878	49.5	85.1	22.4	-2.0	23.1	10.5	10.4	42.5	11.4
55 001	...	Adams County	13 730	65.2	76.7	10.0	-14.4	9.9	7.1	3.9	49.1	5.9
55 003	...	Ashland County	10 668	56.4	84.1	16.5	-7.9	17.1	0.0	9.2	12.9	23.1
55 005	...	Barron County	29 942	57.1	82.4	14.9	-9.5	14.9	0.0	1.2	50.0	11.9
55 007	...	Bayfield County	10 526	47.2	86.9	21.6	-2.8	22.5	0.0	9.5	30.4	0.0
55 009	3080	Brown County	144 172	48.6	86.3	22.5	-1.9	23.3	7.7	11.1	21.3	7.3
55 011	...	Buffalo County	9 384	59.7	84.1	14.0	-10.4	13.9	40.0	9.1	18.2	21.9
55 013	...	Burnett County	11 273	59.9	82.8	14.0	-10.4	14.4	0.0	3.3	12.5	0.0
55 015	0460	Calumet County	26 068	53.2	87.3	20.8	-3.6	20.5	60.0	12.9	43.2	32.0
55 017	2290	Chippewa County	36 330	56.7	84.3	14.7	-9.7	14.6	10.0	9.8	29.1	29.1
55 019	...	Clark County	20 991	67.3	75.4	10.3	-14.1	10.2	5.4	10.3	51.1	11.8
55 021	...	Columbia County	35 529	53.5	86.2	16.7	-7.7	16.8	7.6	1.6	42.5	12.5
55 023	...	Crawford County	11 301	61.2	81.3	13.2	-11.2	13.2	0.0	4.8	22.9	0.0

[1] MSA = Metropolitan Statistical Area. PMSA = Primary MSA. NECMA = New England County Metropolitan Area. See the Appendix A for explanation of these concepts. See Appendix B for list of metropolitan areas identified by type, with component counties.
[2] Hispanic or Latino persons may be of any race.

STATE County	Grades kindergarten through 12	College or graduate school	Percent private	Number	Percent in armed forces	Percent high school graduates	Percent not enrolled, not grads, not in armed forces, not employed	Total population 16 years and over	Percent in labor force	Unemployment rate	Full-time	Part-time	Did not work in 1999
	11	12	13	14	15	16	17	18	19	20	21	22	23
WEST VIRGINIA— Cont'd													
Braxton County	2 532	320	3.6	683	0.0	12.7	13.5	11 774	47.7	8.6	40.9	10.8	48.2
Brooke County	3 926	1 611	17.4	1 370	0.2	9.6	5.5	20 889	55.2	5.1	45.5	14.9	39.5
Cabell County	14 222	9 752	6.8	6 110	0.2	9.5	4.9	79 729	56.3	7.8	46.0	15.9	38.1
Calhoun County	1 335	204	7.1	445	0.0	12.1	11.2	6 141	47.1	12.1	39.9	8.3	51.8
Clay County	2 016	258	2.9	631	0.0	14.4	10.3	8 022	45.1	11.5	41.8	7.6	50.6
Doddridge County	1 497	155	5.4	519	0.0	15.4	3.3	5 825	49.2	8.9	42.5	10.1	47.5
Fayette County	7 779	2 079	7.1	2 559	0.1	15.4	7.2	38 561	47.6	11.9	40.7	10.7	48.7
Gilmer County	1 154	953	1.2	667	0.0	5.5	7.0	5 970	48.6	14.9	39.7	14.1	46.2
Grant County	1 877	323	5.4	427	0.0	15.9	4.0	8 988	59.2	5.7	53.8	10.2	36.0
Greenbrier County	5 733	1 108	7.2	1 691	0.0	13.2	5.2	27 914	52.9	8.5	45.9	11.5	42.5
Hampshire County	3 862	474	5.4	1 039	0.0	11.1	6.4	15 759	57.5	5.0	52.5	9.9	37.6
Hancock County	5 263	927	11.2	1 548	0.0	11.0	7.4	26 657	57.6	5.5	48.7	13.2	00.1
Hardy County	2 286	345	3.2	574	0.0	13.9	4.4	10 001	63.5	3.5	57.1	10.5	32.4
Harrison County	12 116	2 738	8.8	3 828	0.0	11.5	6.1	54 808	55.7	7.6	46.6	12.7	40.7
Jackson County	5 170	867	3.9	1 353	0.0	8.2	5.6	22 064	55.4	5.9	48.4	11.4	40.2
Jefferson County	7 404	2 359	8.7	2 565	0.4	12.9	4.0	33 354	68.0	4.5	58.4	14.3	27.4
Kanawha County	31 608	8 345	9.7	9 522	0.1	12.3	8.5	162 379	58.3	5.7	51.4	11.7	36.9
Lewis County	2 923	459	7.0	843	1.8	10.6	2.0	13 647	53.7	7.5	44.8	11.9	43.4
Lincoln County	3 861	541	2.9	1 319	0.0	13.4	11.2	17 607	45.7	10.1	39.1	10.3	50.6
Logan County	6 299	1 181	5.1	2 087	0.0	12.2	9.8	30 527	45.0	10.5	39.2	8.5	52.3
McDowell County	4 949	473	3.3	1 595	0.0	15.0	19.7	21 801	32.4	14.4	28.5	5.9	65.6
Marion County	9 024	3 891	5.5	3 165	0.0	11.4	3.8	46 377	55.8	7.9	45.8	13.3	40.8
Marshall County	6 370	1 228	7.5	1 707	0.0	10.3	4.7	28 301	55.2	7.5	46.6	13.3	40.1
Mason County	4 444	752	3.2	1 373	0.0	13.6	6.3	20 813	50.1	10.1	44.7	9.6	45.7
Mercer County	9 810	3 223	5.2	3 199	0.1	11.5	6.5	51 202	50.9	9.8	44.2	10.7	45.1
Mineral County	4 814	1 189	4.2	1 576	0.0	11.7	3.4	21 460	58.4	5.8	48.6	14.0	37.3
Mingo County	5 274	765	3.3	1 663	0.0	13.1	13.2	22 279	40.5	10.8	35.4	7.3	57.3
Monongalia County	10 864	18 429	5.0	7 414	0.1	6.6	2.7	68 722	59.0	7.2	49.2	21.2	29.6
Monroe County	2 379	482	3.3	633	0.0	14.1	7.6	11 978	46.5	5.2	45.4	10.2	44.4
Morgan County	2 480	238	6.4	568	0.0	10.7	5.5	11 962	58.1	4.1	52.0	10.6	37.3
Nicholas County	4 007	707	4.5	1 307	0.0	13.3	7.9	21 114	50.7	7.7	44.1	11.6	44.4
Ohio County	7 815	3 900	23.4	2 803	0.0	6.0	4.5	38 581	58.7	8.7	45.9	16.5	37.7
Pendleton County	1 384	177	8.4	338	2.1	18.3	2.7	6 619	59.6	6.7	53.6	11.8	34.6
Pleasants County	1 379	215	5.5	373	0.0	9.7	4.3	5 930	53.9	6.6	49.0	10.5	40.4
Pocahontas County	1 457	234	7.9	368	0.0	13.0	2.7	7 445	52.2	6.3	45.8	11.5	42.7
Preston County	5 368	691	3.5	1 729	0.0	15.4	4.4	23 413	55.3	6.8	48.2	11.1	40.7
Putnam County	9 541	2 105	8.2	2 514	0.1	10.5	1.7	40 124	62.6	4.5	54.8	12.7	32.4
Raleigh County	13 215	3 688	12.5	4 028	0.5	16.1	5.3	64 225	49.8	7.6	42.6	10.6	46.8
Randolph County	4 723	998	12.0	1 367	0.0	13.7	8.6	22 690	54.8	8.9	48.7	11.0	39.4
Ritchie County	1 804	294	3.1	601	0.0	15.3	5.7	8 315	52.1	7.5	46.6	11.1	42.2
Roane County	2 820	278	3.1	906	1.2	13.2	7.4	12 314	51.0	12.6	43.1	10.7	46.1
Summers County	2 026	415	8.7	715	0.0	9.7	16.2	10 719	45.0	12.5	37.6	10.6	51.9
Taylor County	2 944	444	5.2	794	0.0	8.9	6.8	12 853	52.8	7.3	44.3	12.3	43.4
Tucker County	1 212	192	6.8	393	0.0	14.0	7.6	6 021	54.0	7.7	47.5	11.7	40.8
Tyler County	1 721	245	3.2	478	0.0	10.0	4.0	7 654	50.6	10.1	42.0	11.6	46.4
Upshur County	4 079	1 781	25.6	1 641	0.2	7.1	4.5	18 775	53.1	7.0	44.5	14.6	41.0
Wayne County	7 637	1 433	3.7	2 342	0.0	14.1	9.3	34 105	50.8	6.6	43.1	10.5	46.4
Webster County	1 752	152	3.1	556	0.0	9.9	5.4	7 816	43.6	14.5	37.9	7.7	54.4
Wetzel County	3 238	464	2.6	945	0.0	8.6	5.4	14 018	49.8	10.1	42.1	10.9	47.1
Wirt County	1 249	140	1.7	373	0.0	6.7	4.6	4 585	52.6	6.2	50.3	9.3	40.4
Wood County	14 998	3 348	8.1	4 561	0.1	12.1	6.6	70 231	58.4	6.4	49.2	13.7	37.1
Wyoming County	4 385	610	3.2	1 316	0.0	11.7	9.3	20 699	40.6	9.5	35.9	8.1	56.0
WISCONSIN	1 049 456	328 537	15.7	319 738	0.0	10.6	3.4	4 157 030	69.1	4.7	57.1	18.1	24.8
Adams County	3 073	371	6.2	805	0.0	16.8	2.6	15 220	56.0	7.8	48.5	14.3	37.3
Ashland County	3 243	1 192	20.7	1 212	0.0	12.0	3.9	13 138	64.7	8.1	50.6	20.8	28.6
Barron County	8 961	1 371	7.0	2 697	0.0	10.8	3.3	35 130	67.5	4.7	54.9	17.3	27.9
Bayfield County	2 996	453	8.8	824	0.0	8.6	0.8	11 813	62.5	8.5	49.8	18.6	31.5
Brown County	43 878	13 385	18.4	13 524	0.1	10.3	4.4	174 305	72.0	3.8	60.9	17.9	21.2
Buffalo County	2 687	374	8.9	755	0.0	12.7	0.3	10 793	69.5	3.8	58.1	16.0	26.0
Burnett County	2 733	248	7.5	812	0.0	13.3	3.9	12 670	57.8	5.8	47.5	17.0	35.5
Calumet County	8 975	1 476	15.8	2 233	0.0	11.2	1.4	30 294	75.1	2.2	62.4	17.8	19.8
Chippewa County	11 414	1 800	15.0	3 310	0.1	13.5	2.4	42 499	68.2	4.7	56.0	17.5	26.5
Clark County	7 381	711	18.1	2 251	0.1	10.8	6.8	24 853	66.7	4.1	54.3	16.5	29.1
Columbia County	10 054	1 668	9.5	2 849	0.0	13.2	2.9	40 848	69.5	3.5	60.9	16.6	22.5
Crawford County	3 496	432	13.4	1 216	0.0	18.8	5.8	13 385	64.9	4.8	55.2	17.6	27.2

Table B-3. States and Counties — Education, Labor Force, and Income

STATE County	Full-year full-time employed (percent) Total	Men	Women	Non-Hispanic White	Black or African American	American Indian and Alaska Native	Asian, Hawaiian, and Pacific Islander	Hispanic or Latino[1]	Children under 18 years in families Number	With two parents (percent) Both in labor force	Father only in labor force	With one parent who is in labor force (percent)	+/− U.S. percent of children with no stay-at-home parent (percent)	+/− U.S. percent two-income couples	Total employed by class of worker (percent) Private	Government	Self-employed	Unpaid family worker
	24	25	26	27	28	29	30	31	32	33	34	35	36	37	38	39	40	41
WEST VIRGINIA— Cont'd																		
Braxton County	27.9	37.1	18.2	27.8	34.2	42.9	60.0	31.0	3 139	27.3	40.8	16.1	-21.2	-23.6	69.3	20.0	10.4	0.3
Brooke County	33.1	43.5	23.8	33.2	28.3	100.0	13.6	26.7	5 000	47.2	19.8	19.8	2.4	-8.7	82.7	11.9	5.1	0.3
Cabell County	32.0	39.9	24.9	32.4	25.0	27.4	27.1	32.5	18 222	38.7	23.3	21.1	-4.8	-8.5	73.4	18.3	7.8	0.5
Calhoun County	24.0	31.0	17.1	24.2	X	0.0	0.0	14.7	1 525	42.6	22.7	12.9	-9.1	-14.3	68.4	20.4	10.2	1.0
Clay County	24.6	32.5	16.8	24.6	0.0	14.8	0.0	0.0	2 499	27.7	25.6	17.5	-19.4	-23.1	72.7	19.5	7.1	0.7
Doddridge County	29.2	37.4	21.2	29.5	0.0	0.0	21.7	0.0	1 695	34.2	28.7	17.6	-12.8	-15.2	73.5	17.4	7.8	1.3
Fayette County	27.0	34.5	19.9	27.4	19.2	34.4	20.3	50.0	9 596	29.4	25.7	21.5	-13.7	-17.0	72.1	19.3	8.2	0.5
Gilmer County	22.4	25.8	19.0	22.8	0.0	20.0	36.2	0.0	1 368	39.0	20.2	19.2	-6.4	-18.3	59.8	29.2	9.9	1.1
Grant County	38.8	49.3	28.8	38.8	57.4	22.2	X	23.5	2 468	46.6	26.8	16.9	-1.1	-4.5	70.4	15.3	13.4	0.9
Greenbrier County	31.4	41.2	22.6	31.8	21.2	20.7	41.7	47.6	7 060	39.6	24.5	20.0	-5.0	-11.1	71.1	16.8	11.5	0.7
Hampshire County	37.7	48.5	27.4	38.1	18.8	0.0	22.5	44.4	4 674	39.2	27.5	19.3	-6.1	-7.8	71.7	17.5	10.6	0.3
Hancock County	34.7	46.4	24.1	34.9	36.1	16.9	12.2	46.0	6 498	47.3	23.1	20.5	3.2	-5.7	85.1	8.6	5.9	0.4
Hardy County	43.7	53.8	34.1	44.2	40.9	28.6	X	30.9	2 784	55.2	18.9	19.9	10.5	3.0	75.6	12.6	11.5	0.3
Harrison County	34.3	42.8	26.7	34.4	37.5	42.9	18.9	35.1	15 114	43.4	22.1	20.6	-0.6	-8.3	71.1	20.3	8.2	0.4
Jackson County	34.8	45.6	24.9	35.0	50.0	0.0	36.4	0.0	6 446	41.8	27.7	17.7	-5.1	-8.7	71.5	18.9	8.9	0.7
Jefferson County	45.1	56.2	34.3	45.4	41.8	56.1	41.7	38.7	9 397	45.6	24.5	22.1	3.1	1.2	69.8	21.1	8.9	0.3
Kanawha County	39.1	47.5	31.7	39.5	34.2	30.5	44.2	36.0	40 418	39.8	23.7	23.3	-1.5	-6.6	72.8	19.2	7.7	0.3
Lewis County	32.6	40.8	25.0	32.7	0.0	76.9	0.0	17.9	3 487	43.6	21.5	19.3	-1.7	-9.4	65.9	23.5	10.1	0.5
Lincoln County	24.2	31.4	17.3	24.4	X	0.0	0.0	11.8	4 904	27.6	27.1	14.5	-22.5	-23.0	75.7	16.9	6.8	0.6
Logan County	25.8	32.9	19.3	26.1	15.2	6.8	39.5	34.6	7 751	28.9	27.2	15.6	-20.1	-21.2	75.1	16.0	8.3	0.6
McDowell County	18.0	22.7	13.9	18.3	15.8	0.0	40.0	22.6	5 766	15.0	21.2	14.9	-34.7	-34.7	69.6	25.1	5.2	0.1
Marion County	32.2	40.5	24.9	32.5	30.3	14.1	32.1	26.2	11 153	44.9	23.0	18.4	-1.3	-8.2	72.4	20.2	7.0	0.4
Marshall County	34.5	44.8	25.0	34.4	59.5	21.3	53.2	27.9	7 766	42.5	25.0	19.1	-3.0	-8.5	79.9	13.4	6.3	0.4
Mason County	30.0	39.1	21.6	30.3	21.2	17.4	7.9	4.7	5 656	32.6	33.0	15.9	-16.1	-19.2	75.9	15.0	8.7	0.4
Mercer County	31.1	39.5	23.7	31.4	26.6	19.0	29.2	39.5	12 482	34.0	24.1	19.1	-11.5	-14.7	75.2	16.3	8.4	0.1
Mineral County	35.3	47.1	24.5	35.6	32.5	100.0	26.9	25.0	6 046	43.6	26.3	16.3	-4.7	-9.3	74.8	17.5	7.3	0.4
Mingo County	22.3	29.5	15.7	22.4	18.5	0.0	36.2	26.3	6 486	23.6	28.4	11.5	-29.5	-26.8	76.2	16.7	6.9	0.2
Monongalia County	31.5	36.9	26.1	32.0	26.2	30.2	22.7	32.5	14 325	46.5	26.9	15.1	-3.0	-2.6	64.0	28.5	7.2	0.3
Monroe County	31.1	45.3	20.5	32.6	11.4	40.0	52.6	0.0	2 794	47.7	26.1	13.4	-3.5	-11.8	76.9	12.6	9.9	0.6
Morgan County	39.8	49.8	30.1	39.9	25.3	21.1	60.0	57.1	3 225	46.4	25.5	18.0	-0.2	-7.1	75.3	15.8	8.6	0.4
Nicholas County	29.6	37.8	22.0	29.6	X	23.1	18.4	44.0	5 927	38.9	29.7	13.5	-12.2	-14.5	71.1	17.8	10.3	0.8
Ohio County	34.1	44.4	25.3	34.0	35.0	34.5	22.4	46.2	9 603	45.1	21.4	22.8	3.3	-2.0	78.3	13.0	8.4	0.3
Pendleton County	38.0	47.4	28.6	37.9	48.8	40.0	36.0	55.6	1 740	49.6	21.1	17.4	2.4	-6.4	68.6	17.8	13.1	0.5
Pleasants County	35.4	45.7	25.4	35.9	9.7	10.3	0.0	66.7	1 747	40.4	31.5	16.8	-7.4	-8.9	78.4	14.2	7.3	0.1
Pocahontas County	30.6	37.9	22.9	30.9	16.7	13.6	75.0	0.0	1 802	40.0	28.7	12.6	-12.0	-11.5	65.2	20.3	13.1	1.3
Preston County	33.2	42.9	23.7	33.1	44.2	X	60.7	63.7	6 504	42.7	28.6	16.0	-5.9	-12.0	73.4	16.6	9.4	0.6
Putnam County	41.7	53.6	30.7	41.7	54.7	51.3	43.1	29.0	12 477	48.4	26.9	14.2	-2.0	-3.5	76.4	15.2	8.2	0.2
Raleigh County	30.1	37.9	22.6	31.1	20.5	13.1	38.0	13.2	16 272	34.1	25.7	19.0	-11.5	-13.8	73.6	17.5	8.6	0.3
Randolph County	34.1	42.9	25.4	34.1	30.6	63.5	35.3	43.4	5 974	45.7	22.1	17.1	-1.8	-5.7	73.0	17.3	9.4	0.3
Ritchie County	31.6	41.4	22.3	31.7	43.8	60.0	66.7	18.5	2 267	41.3	30.0	14.5	-8.8	-11.6	74.9	16.5	8.0	0.6
Roane County	27.4	32.0	22.8	27.6	0.0	12.7	61.5	17.7	3 401	36.2	24.6	15.8	-12.6	-17.3	71.1	17.0	10.8	1.1
Summers County	23.2	29.6	17.3	23.4	21.1	0.0	0.0	32.4	2 529	28.9	23.4	21.0	-14.7	-22.5	64.9	21.0	13.1	0.9
Taylor County	31.7	40.1	23.9	31.9	24.7	12.9	0.0	53.2	3 536	44.1	23.2	16.0	-4.5	-7.1	72.9	17.9	8.6	0.6
Tucker County	33.1	41.7	24.8	32.9	X	0.0	100.0	40.0	1 457	45.1	21.2	15.0	-4.5	-9.2	69.6	20.6	9.0	0.8
Tyler County	28.8	41.4	16.8	28.9	0.0	0.0	42.9	45.0	2 094	37.5	33.6	20.5	-6.6	-17.8	72.3	15.3	11.0	1.4
Upshur County	29.8	38.3	22.0	29.8	26.3	73.9	7.2	43.7	5 096	38.6	27.3	17.3	-8.7	-13.0	72.2	18.2	8.8	0.8
Wayne County	30.6	38.9	22.9	30.8	34.4	7.2	17.4	7.1	9 512	40.3	23.6	14.7	-9.6	-13.5	75.4	17.9	6.5	0.3
Webster County	24.0	31.3	17.0	24.1	X	0.0	0.0	X	2 137	30.7	24.2	15.7	-18.2	-25.8	69.4	21.6	8.8	0.1
Wetzel County	29.0	41.5	17.6	29.1	100.0	0.0	0.0	0.0	4 019	35.4	32.9	15.8	-13.4	-18.3	77.4	13.9	8.5	0.2
Wirt County	32.1	39.4	25.1	32.2	X	0.0	0.0	100.0	1 369	47.3	24.5	12.8	-4.5	-9.0	76.6	15.7	5.9	1.9
Wood County	36.5	47.5	26.6	36.5	33.8	53.6	47.1	32.8	19 021	42.5	24.3	21.1	-1.0	-6.7	78.7	13.7	7.3	0.3
Wyoming County	23.1	33.0	13.9	23.1	41.5	0.0	0.0	10.7	5 382	23.1	29.8	12.6	-28.9	-25.4	70.7	20.1	8.6	0.6
WISCONSIN	43.8	53.6	34.6	44.9	32.8	38.5	35.1	37.0	1 308 767	55.0	16.5	19.4	9.8	8.6	78.2	12.5	9.0	0.3
Adams County	33.1	39.0	27.1	33.2	40.5	32.3	27.4	21.9	3 606	48.3	15.8	22.8	6.5	-10.2	74.0	13.0	12.3	0.7
Ashland County	34.5	44.2	25.5	34.2	10.0	37.3	32.7	24.6	4 104	53.5	16.0	21.8	10.7	5.2	71.2	17.7	10.4	0.7
Barron County	41.8	51.5	32.4	42.0	32.7	30.2	51.5	34.3	10 937	61.4	13.5	17.1	13.9	7.6	74.6	10.5	14.2	0.7
Bayfield County	33.9	40.9	26.9	34.3	0.0	29.0	47.8	29.5	3 559	50.2	17.5	22.9	8.5	-2.5	61.5	22.0	16.0	0.5
Brown County	47.7	58.0	37.6	48.5	34.1	43.7	34.6	37.9	57 050	58.3	16.0	18.2	11.9	11.4	82.7	9.8	7.3	0.2
Buffalo County	45.3	53.8	36.7	45.4	80.0	47.8	30.0	36.0	3 368	67.6	10.5	14.7	17.7	11.9	70.3	10.8	18.0	1.0
Burnett County	34.1	41.7	26.4	34.1	0.0	32.7	39.0	44.4	3 280	53.0	16.8	20.8	9.2	-6.5	70.1	13.5	15.8	0.6
Calumet County	51.2	63.0	39.3	51.6	70.2	16.7	32.5	33.5	11 430	63.0	18.2	13.3	11.7	15.1	82.9	7.7	8.9	0.5
Chippewa County	43.2	52.9	33.9	43.4	58.3	39.4	28.1	46.4	14 114	58.7	15.2	18.0	12.1	7.5	76.1	11.2	12.2	0.6
Clark County	41.6	52.2	31.0	41.7	28.6	26.1	39.2	31.1	9 676	59.0	20.8	12.6	7.0	6.1	67.3	11.0	19.9	1.8
Columbia County	47.2	55.9	38.3	47.6	20.1	33.8	57.0	37.7	12 746	62.7	16.1	16.2	14.3	11.8	74.3	14.3	10.8	0.6
Crawford County	40.7	47.2	34.1	41.4	2.1	50.0	54.8	37.8	4 294	61.2	15.4	16.6	13.2	5.7	69.6	13.0	16.6	0.9

[1] Hispanic or Latino persons may be of any race.

STATE County	Percent who worked at home	Percent of the population 5 years and over with a disability	Veterans as a percent of the population 18 years and over	Occupation for employed population 16 years and over (percent)						Industry for employed population 16 years and over (percent)					
				Management, professional, and related occupations	Service occupations	Sales and office occupations	Farming, fishing, and forestry occupations	Construction, extraction, and maintenance occupations	Production, transportation and material moving occupations	Agriculture, forestry, fishing, and mining	Construction and manufacturing	Wholesale and retail trade	Transportation and warehousing, and utilities	Service industries	Public administration
	42	43	44	45	46	47	48	49	50	51	52	53	54	55	56

WEST VIRGINIA— Cont'd

STATE County	42	43	44	45	46	47	48	49	50	51	52	53	54	55	56
Braxton County	3.8	29.4	14.8	19.6	17.7	21.5	2.4	18.1	20.7	6.5	20.9	16.5	9.7	39.9	6.5
Brooke County	1.5	20.5	15.8	24.4	16.3	25.1	0.1	11.7	22.4	1.4	28.4	13.2	6.3	48.2	2.5
Cabell County	2.2	24.4	14.6	30.8	17.8	30.8	0.2	8.1	12.2	0.8	15.2	17.4	4.6	57.3	4.7
Calhoun County	6.4	29.9	14.2	25.9	16.3	17.8	2.0	14.3	23.7	6.2	24.3	13.9	5.5	45.7	4.3
Clay County	1.5	30.7	11.9	19.1	18.7	22.5	1.7	18.2	19.9	6.8	24.3	11.7	7.4	44.2	5.6
Doddridge County	3.1	25.2	13.9	22.0	16.7	20.7	2.0	19.4	19.3	7.3	21.7	12.0	7.4	48.3	3.5
Fayette County	2.0	28.7	15.2	23.3	19.3	26.9	0.8	15.5	14.3	5.7	14.7	18.3	6.4	48.5	6.3
Gilmer County	3.8	22.5	11.8	28.4	21.6	22.1	1.8	11.9	14.2	10.8	13.1	12.1	4.7	55.7	3.6
Grant County	3.4	19.4	13.7	21.4	13.2	19.3	2.9	12.9	30.2	7.0	35.3	11.0	7.7	34.8	4.2
Greenbrier County	3.0	24.6	14.6	26.0	20.9	24.4	2.2	12.0	14.4	5.6	18.2	15.3	4.8	50.3	5.9
Hampshire County	3.1	25.1	16.0	21.4	14.6	19.7	1.8	16.1	26.4	3.0	33.5	13.7	6.6	38.5	4.7
Hancock County	1.8	20.2	16.3	21.4	18.9	25.4	0.2	10.9	23.1	0.9	30.2	10.5	0.7	40.4	2.4
Hardy County	4.5	24.1	14.8	19.4	14.6	19.8	1.9	11.5	32.9	5.0	39.8	11.1	5.6	34.7	3.8
Harrison County	2.5	23.0	15.7	29.6	17.9	27.2	0.4	11.5	13.4	2.6	15.5	16.2	7.5	49.8	8.5
Jackson County	3.0	21.7	14.3	28.5	14.6	23.8	0.3	12.6	20.1	2.6	25.4	14.8	6.8	44.2	6.3
Jefferson County	3.4	17.4	15.2	33.4	17.1	22.3	0.8	12.9	13.4	2.6	21.8	14.0	3.8	49.4	8.5
Kanawha County	2.2	23.5	14.5	33.6	14.9	30.5	0.2	9.3	11.5	1.6	13.8	16.0	5.8	53.9	8.9
Lewis County	4.6	27.3	14.8	24.6	19.7	24.1	0.8	13.5	17.3	6.8	18.3	16.1	6.4	46.3	6.0
Lincoln County	1.8	34.6	10.4	19.2	19.3	24.1	0.9	17.0	19.6	5.9	18.0	18.7	8.9	42.7	5.8
Logan County	2.0	31.3	11.5	23.9	16.4	27.1	0.5	16.7	15.4	11.9	9.0	18.7	5.8	49.1	5.5
McDowell County	0.6	39.7	10.2	22.4	18.8	23.6	0.4	15.7	19.1	14.3	8.5	16.4	8.2	46.2	6.4
Marion County	2.2	22.7	15.7	30.1	15.9	28.0	0.3	12.9	12.7	4.4	13.8	16.5	6.6	52.3	6.3
Marshall County	2.5	21.4	15.9	22.7	17.4	24.7	0.3	15.3	19.6	4.9	21.0	16.3	5.9	47.1	4.8
Mason County	2.4	24.8	13.7	22.3	16.9	22.8	1.5	13.9	22.6	4.8	21.3	16.8	11.1	42.6	3.5
Mercer County	1.8	28.6	14.7	28.0	18.4	26.4	0.4	11.4	15.5	2.9	16.3	19.4	5.7	51.9	3.8
Mineral County	1.8	21.1	17.4	22.2	17.4	23.5	0.6	13.4	22.9	1.1	26.6	13.3	8.4	45.8	4.9
Mingo County	0.9	33.8	10.2	23.8	17.1	22.8	0.7	20.6	15.0	18.6	7.9	16.6	8.2	44.7	4.0
Monongalia County	3.1	16.4	10.5	39.1	16.6	25.7	0.4	8.6	9.6	2.7	11.6	13.4	2.9	65.0	4.4
Monroe County	3.6	24.2	12.9	21.6	16.4	21.7	3.3	13.2	23.0	0.9	20.7	10.0	5.0	41.3	7.1
Morgan County	2.0	23.1	16.1	21.4	17.1	20.6	0.3	16.2	24.4	2.8	30.8	11.2	4.7	45.7	4.9
Nicholas County	2.6	28.5	13.2	23.8	17.1	24.3	1.9	15.4	17.5	10.4	16.0	15.9	6.9	46.7	4.2
Ohio County	2.8	19.7	15.3	33.7	18.6	27.3	0.2	8.2	12.0	1.4	13.0	15.3	5.1	61.3	3.9
Pendleton County	5.8	23.8	15.1	24.8	14.7	19.1	3.3	14.2	23.9	11.7	32.9	10.7	4.4	34.3	6.0
Pleasants County	1.2	19.1	14.2	21.6	19.4	25.2	0.8	12.1	20.9	2.2	27.7	15.7	6.4	42.6	5.5
Pocahontas County	4.8	27.1	15.3	25.1	20.9	20.9	4.4	14.3	14.4	8.1	19.1	10.6	4.2	51.0	7.0
Preston County	3.2	23.3	14.2	21.6	17.6	22.2	1.6	15.9	21.1	7.1	21.6	15.6	6.5	44.1	5.2
Putnam County	2.9	18.1	13.8	32.8	13.3	28.7	0.5	10.8	13.8	1.9	20.6	16.8	7.5	47.1	6.1
Raleigh County	1.9	26.6	14.0	26.8	17.1	29.0	0.4	14.5	12.2	6.2	13.2	17.7	5.5	51.7	5.6
Randolph County	2.3	24.6	15.0	26.1	18.8	22.6	1.7	11.7	19.1	4.3	21.7	14.5	4.4	48.6	6.6
Ritchie County	3.0	25.1	15.1	17.5	14.5	23.2	1.4	13.2	30.1	4.9	34.0	16.1	6.0	33.6	5.3
Roane County	3.6	26.6	14.4	23.9	14.4	23.4	1.4	17.1	19.7	7.3	23.8	17.3	5.2	41.8	4.6
Summers County	3.6	32.4	15.7	23.3	21.1	19.2	2.1	14.7	19.5	5.3	14.7	15.8	10.2	47.7	6.3
Taylor County	1.3	25.1	15.5	25.1	17.7	24.0	0.7	14.0	18.5	2.7	18.0	17.6	9.9	44.8	7.1
Tucker County	2.1	25.2	14.7	25.8	22.1	18.3	0.9	16.4	16.5	6.0	23.7	9.7	4.2	50.4	6.0
Tyler County	3.0	23.7	16.2	21.9	19.3	19.6	1.6	15.0	22.5	5.5	32.6	13.6	4.5	39.9	4.0
Upshur County	3.1	23.8	14.2	27.9	16.9	22.6	2.1	12.9	17.6	7.0	18.9	15.3	5.8	47.5	5.6
Wayne County	2.1	30.6	13.8	25.0	14.4	28.5	0.4	12.1	19.6	2.7	19.7	17.5	9.5	46.2	4.2
Webster County	3.5	34.2	13.8	22.2	16.0	18.8	5.5	17.8	19.8	17.4	18.7	14.7	4.7	39.5	4.9
Wetzel County	2.6	24.7	14.5	22.8	18.6	20.4	1.1	16.2	20.8	4.3	32.3	12.8	6.4	39.7	4.4
Wirt County	1.9	22.7	14.5	21.9	9.5	27.0	3.9	13.4	24.2	5.1	26.3	19.7	6.8	37.1	5.0
Wood County	1.9	21.1	15.9	28.8	14.3	28.8	0.3	9.5	18.4	0.7	24.5	18.4	5.2	46.2	5.1
Wyoming County	2.0	32.7	11.9	24.6	15.7	22.1	1.6	20.5	15.6	20.6	9.4	14.1	8.6	43.3	4.1
WISCONSIN	3.9	16.0	12.9	31.3	14.0	25.2	0.9	8.7	19.8	2.8	28.1	14.8	4.5	46.3	3.5
Adams County	5.2	23.0	18.8	21.7	19.6	21.6	2.1	12.0	23.0	5.2	25.8	13.6	6.6	43.1	5.6
Ashland County	4.1	18.7	14.8	26.2	20.8	21.9	2.7	8.8	19.6	4.5	23.2	11.8	4.3	50.6	5.5
Barron County	6.8	17.9	14.4	26.4	15.8	22.4	2.6	9.7	23.0	7.5	31.9	14.7	4.1	39.4	2.4
Bayfield County	6.7	20.3	18.8	31.5	16.9	23.0	3.1	12.8	12.7	6.0	19.4	12.7	4.7	49.5	7.7
Brown County	2.5	14.9	12.3	30.6	12.6	28.5	0.5	9.2	18.7	1.2	27.3	16.6	6.2	45.8	2.9
Buffalo County	10.2	17.6	14.7	29.9	13.2	20.9	4.5	9.4	22.1	14.2	27.3	12.5	7.4	35.4	3.2
Burnett County	6.1	21.5	18.7	25.6	17.9	20.4	1.8	12.3	22.0	4.4	29.8	13.8	4.1	42.8	5.2
Calumet County	4.2	13.2	11.8	29.1	10.8	23.7	1.4	9.4	25.7	4.5	39.1	13.8	4.0	36.7	2.0
Chippewa County	5.7	16.8	14.4	26.8	15.2	23.8	1.6	9.9	22.6	5.8	30.8	16.1	4.5	39.7	3.2
Clark County	13.7	16.4	12.2	28.1	14.6	16.7	4.6	9.9	26.0	16.1	30.2	12.0	4.6	34.7	2.4
Columbia County	5.4	16.0	14.3	28.2	13.3	24.9	1.1	11.6	20.8	4.7	29.7	14.9	4.9	40.4	5.4
Crawford County	8.9	17.4	13.7	23.5	18.1	21.0	2.7	9.1	25.5	9.9	28.8	14.5	4.3	37.8	4.7

STATE County	Median household income	Median family income: All families	Families with children: Married-couple	Families with children: Male householder	Families with children: Female householder	Median nonfamily household income	Median income for full-year, full-time workers: Men	Median income for full-year, full-time workers: Women	Per capita income	Households by source of income (percent): With earnings	With interest, dividend, or rental income	With Social Security income	With public assistance income	With retirement income	Households with income over $100,000 (percent)	+/– U.S. percent for income over $100,000	Households with income below poverty (percent)	Families with children with income below poverty (percent)
	57	58	59	60	61	62	63	64	65	66	67	68	69	70	71	72	73	74
WEST VIRGINIA—Cont'd																		
Braxton County	24 412	29 133	29 682	15 625	14 412	12 180	28 202	18 333	13 349	66.8	25.3	36.6	6.6	18.1	3.0	-9.3	21.5	26.6
Brooke County	32 981	39 948	45 882	22 917	12 470	18 171	35 397	20 500	17 131	69.7	33.5	36.5	2.0	26.8	4.8	-7.5	11.5	15.2
Cabell County	28 479	37 691	44 060	16 579	12 348	15 465	32 560	23 081	17 638	71.2	30.3	33.3	3.9	19.6	5.6	-6.7	20.0	22.1
Calhoun County	21 578	26 701	30 893	23 646	9 000	9 267	26 662	14 899	11 491	61.4	22.4	36.9	5.3	19.9	1.5	-10.8	27.1	28.2
Clay County	22 120	27 137	30 352	19 375	10 606	11 006	31 356	17 233	12 021	63.7	17.5	33.9	5.9	20.8	2.3	-10.0	28.2	33.3
Doddridge County	26 744	30 502	33 224	20 714	15 391	14 592	27 778	20 524	13 507	66.3	28.8	38.0	4.3	27.2	2.4	-9.9	20.6	22.8
Fayette County	24 788	30 243	34 703	17 745	10 261	13 843	29 712	18 771	13 809	64.0	20.8	39.2	6.3	24.8	3.0	-9.3	21.7	27.7
Gilmer County	22 857	28 685	40 216	19 107	8 333	13 703	26 023	16 832	12 498	66.4	27.6	34.5	5.1	24.4	2.9	-9.4	26.1	27.3
Grant County	28 916	33 813	36 972	17 500	17 566	15 276	26 260	19 142	15 696	75.7	30.9	32.0	3.1	17.3	2.9	-9.4	16.8	17.5
Greenbrier County	26 927	33 292	38 739	24 167	13 934	13 478	26 591	20 392	16 247	69.4	27.7	35.7	3.0	20.9	4.6	-7.7	19.6	22.4
Hampshire County	31 666	37 616	41 964	25 000	14 438	17 474	29 840	20 271	14 851	74.9	25.4	33.4	4.3	21.9	2.7	-9.6	16.1	19.6
Hancock County	33 759	40 719	46 892	24 028	12 269	19 160	35 910	19 839	17 724	71.5	34.5	35.1	2.3	27.3	4.6	-7.7	12.1	15.6
Hardy County	31 846	37 003	41 566	21 250	14 141	16 807	29 027	19 330	15 859	76.1	28.1	31.9	2.5	17.7	4.0	-8.3	15.1	13.8
Harrison County	30 562	36 870	43 629	18 867	14 790	16 697	31 297	22 701	16 810	70.7	32.0	34.4	3.8	22.4	5.0	-7.3	16.5	21.6
Jackson County	32 434	38 021	44 149	19 427	11 760	16 438	34 112	21 494	16 205	71.3	33.1	34.7	4.1	24.4	4.3	-8.0	15.3	20.2
Jefferson County	44 374	51 351	57 594	27 386	20 150	24 271	36 034	26 841	20 441	83.5	33.4	23.9	1.7	17.7	10.1	-2.2	10.7	10.9
Kanawha County	33 766	42 568	50 605	23 125	15 315	19 970	35 229	25 156	20 354	73.0	31.7	33.0	3.1	22.0	7.7	-4.6	14.3	18.2
Lewis County	27 066	32 431	35 370	16 429	12 021	13 720	28 833	19 709	13 933	67.3	28.5	38.2	3.7	23.4	2.7	-9.6	20.1	24.8
Lincoln County	22 662	28 297	32 668	14 750	9 844	9 968	31 132	19 075	13 073	64.1	20.7	33.5	6.7	19.7	2.6	-9.7	28.2	33.3
Logan County	24 603	29 072	35 775	23 917	9 683	14 604	32 357	20 588	14 102	63.3	18.1	39.2	5.7	26.0	3.7	-8.6	23.5	29.5
McDowell County	16 931	20 496	22 161	15 000	7 204	10 272	26 717	18 967	10 174	47.8	12.1	44.5	9.8	24.0	1.6	-10.7	35.9	47.5
Marion County	28 626	37 182	44 130	15 208	14 171	15 474	30 224	21 636	16 246	69.5	29.9	35.1	3.7	23.5	4.5	-7.8	16.5	19.5
Marshall County	30 989	39 053	45 643	23 125	11 416	15 131	32 327	20 035	16 472	71.8	30.7	33.5	3.2	23.5	4.5	-7.8	15.5	20.4
Mason County	27 134	32 953	37 830	21 250	11 705	13 607	33 781	18 609	14 804	68.5	26.2	32.6	4.9	20.6	3.7	-8.6	20.5	23.7
Mercer County	26 628	33 524	38 801	17 453	12 453	13 916	29 755	19 674	15 564	65.3	25.2	39.2	5.3	23.4	3.8	-8.5	19.2	24.4
Mineral County	31 149	37 866	41 988	26 750	13 199	16 207	33 584	20 696	15 384	73.8	32.1	32.5	3.1	20.2	3.3	-9.0	15.1	19.3
Mingo County	21 347	26 581	30 639	20 885	7 270	10 958	32 342	18 327	12 445	57.4	14.6	39.2	8.3	20.6	2.8	-9.5	29.8	36.5
Monongalia County	28 625	43 628	52 911	18 795	14 971	14 385	34 525	24 800	17 106	79.6	33.5	22.2	2.4	16.8	7.1	-5.2	24.1	16.9
Monroe County	27 575	35 299	36 910	22 750	14 615	14 293	26 481	22 776	17 435	69.5	27.2	36.6	3.5	25.5	4.0	-8.3	16.8	19.7
Morgan County	35 016	40 690	45 945	29 167	19 886	21 412	30 309	23 131	18 109	74.2	28.4	31.9	2.1	23.0	4.8	-7.5	10.9	11.0
Nicholas County	26 974	32 074	35 009	10 250	12 055	14 440	30 968	19 016	15 207	67.4	24.3	36.5	5.3	25.8	3.9	-8.4	19.9	22.2
Ohio County	30 836	41 261	50 421	22 212	11 673	15 960	32 233	22 698	17 734	69.7	39.6	35.7	3.1	21.6	5.9	-6.4	16.6	19.1
Pendleton County	30 429	34 860	38 654	28 750	14 125	16 747	26 056	17 078	15 805	76.6	35.6	35.9	2.6	21.0	3.6	-8.7	13.2	9.8
Pleasants County	32 736	37 795	42 031	22 000	13 304	16 923	31 850	19 087	16 920	72.3	32.6	33.5	3.0	26.1	5.2	-7.1	13.2	17.3
Pocahontas County	26 401	32 511	33 194	22 031	11 691	15 367	26 775	17 083	14 384	69.3	31.9	38.2	2.6	23.4	3.3	-9.0	18.4	19.0
Preston County	27 927	32 904	38 198	19 583	11 324	14 916	27 413	18 452	13 596	72.7	28.9	33.2	3.2	21.5	2.9	-9.4	18.1	21.0
Putnam County	41 892	48 674	57 063	35 625	20 224	20 660	41 847	24 365	20 471	80.2	33.7	26.9	2.1	20.1	10.1	-2.2	9.9	10.5
Raleigh County	28 181	35 315	41 919	15 648	12 102	15 493	34 625	21 150	16 233	67.0	24.5	36.6	4.3	24.7	5.0	-7.3	17.7	23.8
Randolph County	27 299	32 632	35 398	20 469	12 305	16 151	25 599	18 355	14 918	71.6	27.5	34.3	4.1	20.9	3.2	-9.1	18.0	20.7
Ritchie County	27 332	34 809	36 441	16 250	13 646	11 361	30 197	18 714	15 175	70.7	29.4	36.3	2.8	21.0	2.6	-9.7	20.0	22.0
Roane County	24 511	29 280	32 342	15 625	11 068	12 179	29 670	17 754	13 195	67.3	29.6	37.0	4.8	19.2	3.7	-8.6	22.3	27.5
Summers County	21 147	27 251	30 747	22 083	11 701	11 180	30 332	18 729	12 419	60.4	22.4	44.7	4.6	21.9	2.4	-9.9	24.2	32.2
Taylor County	27 124	32 222	36 274	23 958	12 679	15 445	30 430	20 488	13 681	69.0	27.7	36.1	3.6	19.2	3.0	-9.3	20.4	23.9
Tucker County	26 250	32 574	34 427	20 250	12 500	14 345	25 919	18 882	16 349	71.3	29.0	36.9	2.2	21.4	4.0	-8.3	17.6	22.9
Tyler County	29 290	35 320	38 254	26 875	16 467	16 269	35 143	19 330	15 216	69.5	33.8	35.0	4.0	26.4	4.0	-8.3	16.4	19.6
Upshur County	26 973	32 399	35 997	18 125	9 336	12 873	30 074	19 050	13 559	68.3	32.7	36.1	5.4	20.7	3.1	-9.2	20.9	25.5
Wayne County	27 352	32 458	40 148	21 944	12 944	13 076	31 958	21 257	14 906	66.3	22.8	35.3	5.6	19.8	3.7	-8.6	20.0	22.4
Webster County	21 055	25 049	26 538	11 765	8 750	11 322	26 047	16 604	12 284	61.0	18.8	39.7	7.1	20.3	1.9	-10.4	30.6	40.5
Wetzel County	30 935	36 793	42 180	18 906	9 468	16 497	39 030	20 168	16 818	67.9	34.4	36.5	4.2	27.9	4.4	-7.9	18.8	23.5
Wirt County	30 748	33 872	37 098	21 875	12 000	14 657	30 308	18 448	14 000	71.9	28.0	35.7	6.1	24.7	2.8	-9.5	17.8	22.0
Wood County	33 285	40 436	47 288	24 397	13 076	19 176	35 930	23 160	18 073	73.8	34.5	32.8	3.8	22.4	6.3	-6.0	13.6	18.2
Wyoming County	23 932	29 709	32 694	17 344	9 646	12 830	34 411	19 371	14 220	59.3	18.0	41.4	7.3	27.4	3.5	-8.8	24.0	31.1
WISCONSIN	43 791	52 911	61 834	31 599	22 057	25 837	38 180	26 644	21 271	81.8	47.2	26.4	1.7	15.7	9.4	-2.9	8.4	8.8
Adams County	33 408	39 164	47 366	32 426	18 958	20 141	33 141	22 464	17 777	71.1	39.7	42.0	1.7	24.8	4.1	-8.2	10.4	12.2
Ashland County	31 628	39 531	45 989	23 553	15 645	16 217	30 612	20 882	16 069	76.5	36.9	31.2	2.7	17.4	3.0	-9.3	14.3	12.5
Barron County	37 275	43 367	49 911	28 051	19 497	19 473	30 961	21 582	18 091	78.0	46.1	32.1	1.9	14.5	5.6	-6.7	9.4	9.5
Bayfield County	33 390	39 774	47 500	26 957	16 196	17 441	32 321	22 195	16 407	74.9	31.7	33.1	2.5	18.5	4.2	-8.1	13.3	14.1
Brown County	46 447	56 194	64 908	31 148	23 255	27 080	38 657	26 131	21 784	84.5	46.9	22.0	1.6	12.3	9.7	-2.6	7.0	7.1
Buffalo County	37 200	44 534	51 111	35 714	23 229	20 337	30 643	21 779	18 123	79.7	48.9	33.2	1.6	14.1	4.7	-7.6	8.7	6.2
Burnett County	34 218	40 372	48 250	29 271	17 132	21 208	32 366	22 440	17 712	72.7	42.5	39.0	1.6	22.1	4.7	-7.6	9.3	10.1
Calumet County	52 569	58 654	64 790	40 417	27 676	29 488	40 562	27 025	21 919	87.1	55.0	21.8	0.8	12.6	9.8	-2.5	3.8	3.7
Chippewa County	39 596	46 460	54 465	29 046	19 756	22 085	32 321	23 112	18 243	80.4	46.7	29.4	1.5	16.6	5.5	-6.8	8.4	9.1
Clark County	34 577	40 941	47 823	27 788	19 566	18 161	29 338	21 245	15 100	78.7	42.9	32.8	1.6	12.3	4.3	-8.0	11.3	12.2
Columbia County	45 064	52 540	58 881	30 938	26 447	25 015	36 327	25 749	21 014	82.2	48.4	28.7	1.4	16.5	7.5	-4.8	5.9	4.6
Crawford County	34 135	41 540	46 366	30 795	17 652	18 620	29 725	20 547	16 833	80.1	41.2	32.7	2.0	17.3	4.9	-7.4	10.5	11.3

Table B-3. States and Counties — **Education, Labor Force, and Income**

STATE/ County code	MSA/PMSA/ NECMA code[1]	STATE County	High school graduates			College graduates		College graduates (percent)				
			Total population 25 years and over	Percent with a high school diploma or less	Percent with a high school diploma or more	Percent with a bachelor's degree or more	+/− U.S. percent with bachelor's degree or more	Non-Hispanic White	Black or African American	American Indian and Alaska Native	Asian, Hawaiian, and Pacific Islander	Hispanic or Latino[2]
			1	2	3	4	5	6	7	8	9	10
		WISCONSIN—Cont'd										
55 025	4720	Dane County	269 998	30.1	92.2	40.6	16.2	41.1	19.2	23.1	65.0	27.2
55 027	...	Dodge County	57 453	61.2	82.3	13.2	−11.2	13.5	2.7	10.7	39.1	8.7
55 029	...	Door County.............	20 062	50.8	87.8	21.4	−3.0	21.5	11.8	8.4	38.9	13.0
55 031	2240	Douglas County............	28 653	50.3	85.9	18.3	−6.1	18.7	20.9	2.2	38.0	12.0
55 033	...	Dunn County	22 644	50.2	86.6	21.1	−3.3	21.2	13.6	29.3	16.0	18.1
55 035	2290	Eau Claire County........	55 290	42.2	88.9	27.0	2.6	27.1	29.9	8.6	26.5	25.7
55 037	...	Florence County	3 641	60.6	83.7	12.4	−12.0	12.6	0.0	0.0	0.0	0.0
55 039	...	Fond du Lac County	63 548	55.9	84.2	16.9	−7.5	17.0	8.0	10.5	38.8	8.3
55 041	...	Forest County.............	6 694	64.2	78.5	10.0	−14.4	10.1	0.0	6.0	66.7	5.0
55 043	...	Grant County	30 625	56.5	83.5	17.2	−7.2	17.1	5.2	6.6	63.3	21.0
55 045	...	Green County	22 523	56.2	84.1	16.7	−7.7	16.7	18.9	16.9	57.1	6.9
55 047	...	Green Lake County.......	13 229	60.0	81.9	14.5	−9.9	14.6	12.5	0.0	100.0	4.2
55 049	...	Iowa County	15 100	53.3	88.5	18.5	−5.9	18.4	0.0	16.2	15.4	3.0
55 051	...	Iron County	5 124	54.4	83.7	13.2	−11.2	13.1	0.0	0.0	16.7	0.0
55 053	...	Jackson County	12 779	62.8	79.0	11.3	−13.1	11.8	3.9	7.3	8.9	6.4
55 055	...	Jefferson County	49 057	53.8	84.7	17.4	−7.0	17.7	10.7	8.1	38.2	5.8
55 057	...	Juneau County	16 457	64.5	78.5	10.0	−14.4	10.0	5.6	4.3	30.6	7.6
55 059	3800	Kenosha County............	95 038	49.8	83.5	19.2	−5.2	19.7	11.3	16.2	51.1	9.5
55 061	...	Kewaunee County	13 336	63.5	84.0	11.4	−13.0	11.4	X	0.0	24.1	3.7
55 063	3870	La Crosse County	65 263	42.2	89.7	25.4	1.0	25.6	15.3	11.4	27.6	16.8
55 065	...	Lafayette County	10 528	61.1	85.5	13.3	−11.1	13.3	0.0	20.0	33.3	3.3
55 067	...	Langlade County	14 372	64.4	80.9	11.7	−12.7	11.7	15.4	4.6	20.9	8.3
55 069	...	Lincoln County	20 120	59.8	81.6	13.6	−10.8	13.6	0.0	0.0	12.9	7.0
55 071	...	Manitowoc County	55 452	58.5	84.6	15.5	−8.9	15.6	12.0	2.5	21.5	6.7
55 073	8940	Marathon County.............	81 925	54.2	83.8	18.3	−6.1	18.5	39.1	5.7	11.2	10.5
55 075	...	Marinette County	29 575	62.2	82.5	12.9	−11.5	12.9	0.0	3.8	32.8	4.5
55 077	...	Marquette County.........	11 428	62.6	78.8	10.1	−14.3	10.4	6.3	9.4	23.8	5.3
55 078	...	Menominee County	2 399	63.8	78.2	12.9	−11.5	27.8	60.0	8.8	7.9	0.0
55 079	5080	Milwaukee County.........	594 387	49.2	80.2	23.6	−0.8	28.3	9.9	11.2	39.9	9.6
55 081	...	Monroe County	26 323	60.1	81.1	13.2	−11.2	13.2	15.6	10.5	39.6	3.5
55 083	...	Oconto County	24 186	64.5	80.6	10.6	−13.8	10.6	0.0	10.4	4.3	12.8
55 085	...	Oneida County	26 449	51.4	85.1	20.0	−4.4	20.2	5.5	0.0	51.1	11.4
55 087	0460	Outagamie County	102 218	49.6	88.1	22.5	−1.9	22.7	21.5	14.3	28.2	12.3
55 089	5080	Ozaukee County	54 912	32.3	91.9	38.6	14.2	38.5	46.1	23.0	72.0	24.9
55 091	...	Pepin County	4 733	60.2	82.6	13.3	−11.1	13.5	X	0.0	0.0	0.0
55 003	5120	Pierce County................	21 542	45.3	89.6	24.6	0.2	24.5	18.2	44.9	34.6	46.6
55 095	...	Polk County................	27 725	55.2	85.9	15.6	−8.8	15.5	36.4	15.2	27.9	27.5
55 097	...	Portage County	40 143	50.8	86.5	23.4	−1.0	23.6	0.0	5.3	15.2	6.8
55 099	...	Price County	11 122	61.1	82.4	13.0	−11.4	13.0	0.0	6.1	9.1	5.7
55 101	6600	Racine County.............	122 350	49.0	82.9	20.0	−4.1	22.1	7.1	11.2	43.6	8.3
55 103	...	Richland County	11 896	58.7	82.1	14.1	−10.3	14.0	0.0	8.3	61.5	6.2
55 105	3620	Rock County	98 770	55.3	83.9	16.7	−7.7	17.3	6.0	16.7	39.0	5.2
55 107	...	Rusk County	10 296	64.3	79.1	11.2	−13.2	11.2	15.4	0.0	8.0	10.3
55 109	5120	St. Croix County.............	40 357	41.7	91.6	26.3	1.9	26.3	25.9	25.4	49.0	20.6
55 111	...	Sauk County	36 701	54.3	83.5	17.6	−6.8	17.6	12.6	14.0	45.8	8.2
55 113	...	Sawyer County	11 343	55.2	84.7	16.5	−7.9	17.6	7.0	7.8	19.6	31.7
55 115	...	Shawano County	27 503	64.3	81.5	12.6	−11.8	12.7	0.0	11.5	34.3	7.1
55 117	7620	Sheboygan County........	74 561	55.5	84.4	17.9	−6.5	18.3	6.8	3.0	15.2	9.2
55 119	...	Taylor County	12 872	66.1	78.3	11.0	−13.4	10.9	0.0	15.2	58.8	3.6
55 121	...	Trempealeau County.....	18 317	59.9	80.9	13.3	−11.1	13.2	12.5	13.3	25.0	18.5
55 123	...	Vernon County	18 473	59.6	78.9	14.0	−10.4	14.0	7.1	0.0	19.0	8.1
55 125	...	Vilas County	15 667	54.3	85.4	17.6	−6.8	18.1	0.0	6.7	34.6	10.4
55 127	...	Walworth County.............	58 153	49.3	84.2	21.8	−2.6	22.5	24.0	3.1	42.1	4.3
55 129	...	Washburn County	11 248	55.9	83.7	15.2	−9.2	15.5	0.0	9.5	11.8	0.0
55 131	5080	Washington County.........	77 709	46.4	88.8	21.9	−2.5	22.0	22.1	21.6	30.8	14.5
55 133	5080	Waukesha County	241 299	35.7	92.0	34.1	9.7	34.0	34.5	9.9	67.9	18.5
55 135	...	Waupaca County	34 726	61.0	82.7	14.8	−9.6	14.9	27.8	12.1	21.0	10.2
55 137	...	Waushara County	16 310	64.3	78.8	11.7	−12.7	11.8	0.0	3.7	45.2	5.5
55 139	0460	Winnebago County........	101 095	51.2	86.3	22.8	−1.6	22.9	7.8	10.7	38.3	16.3
55 141	...	Wood County	50 259	56.3	84.8	16.9	−7.5	16.6	31.5	10.8	39.9	19.3
56 000	...	**WYOMING**	315 663	43.1	87.9	21.9	−2.5	23.0	18.6	8.1	34.3	7.8
56 001	...	Albany County.............	17 016	28.4	93.5	44.1	19.7	46.2	37.8	30.2	64.2	13.5
56 003	...	Big Horn County.........	7 343	50.9	83.2	15.9	−8.5	16.6	100.0	0.0	18.8	2.8
56 005	...	Campbell County.............	20 107	47.0	88.3	15.7	−8.7	15.9	0.0	3.2	44.7	3.2
56 007	...	Carbon County	10 508	51.5	83.5	17.2	−7.2	19.0	13.2	7.5	51.5	4.3

[1]MSA = Metropolitan Statistical Area. PMSA = Primary MSA. NECMA = New England County Metropolitan Area. See the Appendix A for explanation of these concepts. See Appendix B for list of metropolitan areas identified by type, with component counties.
[2]Hispanic or Latino persons may be of any race.

STATE County	School enrollment			Population 16 to 19 years				Employment status, 2000			Work status in 1999 of the population 16 years and over (percent)		
											Worked in 1999		
	Grades kindergarten through 12	College or graduate school	Percent private	Number	Percent in armed forces	Percent high school graduates	Percent not enrolled, not grads, not in armed forces, not employed	Total population 16 years and over	Percent in labor force	Unemployment rate	Full-time	Part-time	Did not work in 1999
	11	12	13	14	15	16	17	18	19	20	21	22	23
WISCONSIN—Cont'd													
Dane County	71 417	53 744	8.7	27 257	0.0	8.2	2.4	341 422	75.0	3.8	60.8	21.7	17.4
Dodge County	16 963	2 735	18.8	4 863	0.0	12.2	3.4	67 223	66.5	3.3	59.7	16.4	23.9
Door County	4 918	636	10.1	1 455	0.0	8.0	2.1	22 710	64.8	5.4	53.8	18.9	27.3
Douglas County	7 878	2 719	9.5	2 480	0.3	9.4	3.3	34 376	64.8	7.1	50.4	20.0	29.7
Dunn County	7 115	6 457	6.3	3 635	0.1	8.8	1.5	31 773	70.6	7.2	56.3	22.8	20.9
Eau Claire County	16 477	12 337	9.3	7 422	0.0	7.0	2.1	74 048	70.2	4.7	53.4	24.4	22.2
Florence County	935	83	3.3	250	0.0	11.6	4.0	4 067	61.4	5.7	49.3	17.4	33.3
Fond du Lac County	19 140	4 722	20.6	6 311	0.2	13.2	2.8	76 009	70.7	4.3	58.2	18.2	23.6
Forest County	2 045	222	5.2	591	0.0	9.3	8.5	7 815	56.1	7.6	48.0	15.2	36.8
Grant County	9 319	5 323	8.8	4 046	0.2	6.9	2.0	39 475	66.8	4.7	53.9	20.9	25.2
Green County	6 905	933	5.7	1 822	0.0	10.8	3.0	25 846	72.8	3.2	60.8	17.2	22.0
Green Lake County	3 554	402	14.7	1 146	0.3	13.4	2.6	17 414	67.0	5.1	54.7	17.1	28.2
Iowa County	4 809	642	7.8	1 298	0.0	11.6	1.8	17 414	75.5	3.9	62.0	18.1	19.9
Iron County	1 104	189	3.2	365	0.5	7.4	1.6	5 743	55.0	8.8	45.2	16.6	38.2
Jackson County	3 728	493	6.2	1 038	0.0	12.6	6.8	15 053	64.5	8.3	57.7	15.5	26.8
Jefferson County	13 994	3 174	18.9	3 996	0.1	13.8	2.8	57 539	72.3	4.1	59.9	18.1	21.9
Juneau County	4 840	554	12.3	1 292	0.0	13.1	3.0	18 892	64.2	6.1	53.9	15.1	31.0
Kenosha County	30 494	9 631	15.4	8 661	0.2	11.5	3.9	113 533	68.7	5.7	57.7	16.7	25.6
Kewaunee County	4 139	602	16.3	1 142	0.0	11.5	0.6	15 591	70.5	2.6	59.3	16.0	24.7
La Crosse County	19 081	12 713	13.7	7 770	0.0	10.3	1.0	84 831	70.2	4.1	55.8	21.9	22.3
Lafayette County	3 525	479	5.5	1 063	0.4	6.3	0.8	12 383	70.6	2.6	57.5	18.1	24.4
Langlade County	3 948	446	12.3	1 131	0.0	14.3	2.7	16 386	62.8	5.8	50.6	17.7	31.7
Lincoln County	5 830	855	10.1	1 781	0.0	9.9	7.2	23 226	66.1	5.3	55.1	16.3	28.6
Manitowoc County	16 665	3 031	20.3	4 655	0.0	10.4	3.0	64 339	69.3	3.6	56.9	17.5	25.6
Marathon County	25 711	4 793	12.1	7 652	0.0	12.7	1.7	96 478	71.7	3.8	59.3	17.7	23.0
Marinette County	8 300	1 945	15.0	2 788	0.0	9.3	2.4	34 572	62.3	5.4	50.0	18.0	32.0
Marquette County	2 782	509	12.1	764	0.0	12.6	1.8	12 949	54.1	5.4	50.6	14.7	34.7
Menominee County	1 335	170	5.0	347	0.0	16.4	11.0	2 992	56.4	16.5	52.2	11.8	36.0
Milwaukee County	190 432	65 887	22.7	53 378	0.0	9.9	6.7	718 569	65.4	6.9	54.9	16.2	28.9
Monroe County	8 652	1 027	14.6	2 333	0.1	12.9	4.5	30 763	68.8	4.7	57.9	15.1	27.0
Oconto County	7 363	870	7.7	1 929	0.0	8.9	2.6	27 558	66.8	3.9	56.4	15.6	28.0
Oneida County	6 676	1 306	9.5	1 779	0.0	13.6	3.0	29 592	61.9	6.1	50.9	16.6	32.5
Outagamie County	33 537	7 729	19.4	9 485	0.1	12.2	2.3	121 728	72.7	3.2	60.0	18.4	21.6
Ozaukee County	16 931	4 454	25.3	4 502	0.0	8.2	1.6	62 858	72.0	2.2	57.3	20.2	22.5
Pepin County	1 498	247	14.9	457	0.0	9.4	1.3	5 567	67.3	4.4	55.0	17.1	27.9
Pierce County	7 033	4 736	8.6	3 203	0.3	8.3	1.4	28 905	76.7	4.6	59.9	22.9	17.2
Polk County	8 586	1 120	5.1	2 405	0.3	12.3	2.6	31 857	67.2	3.9	56.0	16.5	27.5
Portage County	12 280	8 526	7.1	5 331	0.0	8.9	1.3	53 135	71.4	5.9	58.1	21.4	20.5
Price County	3 111	388	8.8	858	0.0	11.1	1.6	12 574	62.7	5.7	51.9	16.4	31.8
Racine County	38 957	8 818	19.5	10 703	0.1	11.5	4.5	143 597	67.5	6.0	57.0	16.4	26.6
Richland County	3 620	626	13.1	1 151	0.0	9.5	2.4	13 992	66.7	4.8	54.1	17.7	28.2
Rock County	30 300	6 280	11.4	8 757	0.0	11.6	4.6	116 674	69.3	5.6	57.7	17.2	25.0
Rusk County	3 078	477	13.5	901	0.0	8.5	3.0	12 039	62.1	6.3	50.6	16.0	33.4
St. Croix County	13 251	2 913	11.0	3 525	0.0	10.2	1.8	47 535	75.5	2.6	62.6	18.2	19.2
Sauk County	10 922	1 768	11.0	3 029	0.0	15.1	3.8	42 480	71.6	4.2	59.5	17.7	22.8
Sawyer County	3 075	465	11.2	862	0.0	17.1	4.1	12 774	60.4	6.6	51.0	16.3	32.7
Shawano County	8 151	1 189	11.5	2 320	0.1	12.0	2.9	31 605	65.9	3.8	54.0	17.0	29.0
Sheboygan County	22 043	4 720	20.2	6 439	0.0	11.5	2.9	87 548	69.8	2.6	58.4	17.6	24.0
Taylor County	4 353	378	9.6	1 175	0.0	12.1	3.3	15 054	68.9	5.2	58.6	14.7	26.7
Trempealeau County	5 212	694	7.3	1 467	0.0	12.0	2.6	21 021	69.2	3.5	58.0	15.5	26.5
Vernon County	5 816	679	16.2	1 610	0.0	10.6	7.7	21 268	64.4	4.2	53.3	16.5	30.2
Vilas County	3 520	547	7.1	902	0.0	8.8	3.1	17 238	57.3	6.1	47.7	15.8	36.5
Walworth County	17 448	9 549	10.3	6 786	0.0	8.4	1.7	73 753	70.4	5.3	57.0	20.7	22.3
Washburn County	3 056	355	6.6	881	0.0	10.3	3.4	12 748	59.8	6.1	48.3	17.8	33.9
Washington County	23 736	4 500	19.6	6 175	0.0	14.5	1.5	89 668	74.2	2.7	61.5	18.0	20.5
Waukesha County	72 586	17 704	21.8	19 496	0.0	10.3	1.1	277 331	72.5	2.8	58.2	19.4	22.4
Waupaca County	10 414	1 145	12.3	2 753	0.0	13.4	3.6	39 961	65.9	3.6	54.7	16.9	28.4
Waushara County	4 340	437	7.9	1 232	0.0	12.5	2.6	18 398	61.3	6.6	50.9	16.5	32.6
Winnebago County	28 544	12 191	11.6	9 974	0.1	9.8	1.7	123 806	69.4	3.7	57.5	19.1	23.4
Wood County	15 093	2 792	13.6	4 431	0.0	11.7	3.3	58 610	67.1	5.0	55.4	17.0	27.6
WYOMING	98 562	29 697	5.4	32 130	0.6	11.4	3.8	381 912	67.5	5.2	58.0	16.9	25.1
Albany County	4 311	10 055	7.9	3 357	0.0	6.1	1.4	26 866	67.7	5.4	55.3	27.3	17.4
Big Horn County	2 557	302	3.3	757	0.3	9.5	4.5	8 602	59.7	6.3	49.0	17.1	33.9
Campbell County	7 977	1 160	3.5	2 180	0.0	11.1	4.9	24 560	76.6	4.4	66.2	15.7	18.0
Carbon County	2 969	389	3.2	933	0.0	11.9	4.1	12 392	62.5	5.3	58.4	15.3	26.2

Table B-3. States and Counties — Education, Labor Force, and Income

STATE County	Full-year full-time employed (percent)								Children under 18 years in families						Total employed by class of worker (percent)			
	Total	Men	Women	Non-Hispanic White	Black or African American	American Indian and Alaska Native	Asian, Hawaiian, and Pacific Islander	Hispanic or Latino[1]	Number	With two parents (percent) Both in labor force	With two parents (percent) Father only in labor force	With one parent who is in labor force (percent)	+/− U.S. percent of children with no stay-at-home parent (percent)	+/− U.S. percent two-income couples	Private	Government	Self-employed	Unpaid family worker
	24	25	26	27	28	29	30	31	32	33	34	35	36	37	38	39	40	41
WISCONSIN—Cont'd																		
Dane County	46.6	54.7	38.8	48.1	38.6	38.7	29.2	34.9	92 684	60.4	14.7	17.9	13.7	16.5	68.5	23.5	7.8	0.2
Dodge County	45.5	53.5	36.6	46.8	16.9	31.8	40.1	32.1	20 617	61.8	16.2	16.0	13.2	12.3	79.6	10.0	9.9	0.4
Door County	39.7	49.3	30.6	39.7	52.9	27.1	62.8	42.0	5 967	59.7	15.4	17.9	13.0	3.0	72.4	9.8	17.0	0.8
Douglas County	37.0	45.2	29.2	37.4	42.6	29.9	19.1	17.6	9 662	50.5	16.2	22.2	8.1	0.8	76.4	15.5	7.8	0.3
Dunn County	37.9	45.3	30.3	38.2	30.8	32.2	25.4	40.6	8 971	58.6	17.2	16.0	10.0	8.3	71.2	16.8	11.4	0.6
Eau Claire County	39.4	49.2	30.4	39.7	20.0	27.8	34.9	36.2	20 877	58.4	18.1	16.0	9.8	9.9	76.7	14.7	8.3	0.2
Florence County	34.9	43.5	26.2	35.1	0.0	27.3	0.0	0.0	1 140	64.3	12.6	14.1	13.8	1.2	65.4	18.2	15.5	0.9
Fond du Lac County	46.4	58.3	35.4	47.0	20.5	40.9	22.3	37.4	23 592	62.3	15.3	16.5	14.2	12.9	80.4	10.7	8.5	0.4
Forest County	33.2	38.0	28.5	33.4	34.6	31.1	50.0	15.6	2 372	47.2	13.2	23.7	6.3	-6.8	61.8	21.1	16.2	0.8
Grant County	38.2	45.7	30.5	38.5	20.7	33.7	18.9	29.8	11 460	63.2	14.1	15.7	14.3	9.5	68.8	15.1	15.1	1.0
Green County	47.9	57.8	38.6	47.9	48.9	46.7	46.4	51.9	8 589	64.2	11.0	19.5	19.1	15.7	74.2	11.1	14.0	0.7
Green Lake County	42.1	52.3	32.3	42.5	12.0	71.4	100.0	22.3	4 485	62.7	15.7	15.0	13.1	7.5	74.7	9.4	15.1	0.9
Iowa County	40.0	50.0	40.6	10.6	100.0	73.2	7.4	37.5	5 996	67.2	9.7	18.6	21.2	19.6	71.1	11.6	16.3	1.1
Iron County	31.0	37.4	24.7	30.9	0.0	9.1	50.0	30.0	1 263	51.4	18.4	20.5	7.3	-10.4	69.3	14.0	15.8	0.9
Jackson County	40.5	45.9	34.2	41.3	34.6	36.9	40.6	23.6	4 433	60.9	12.2	20.9	17.2	6.9	66.2	18.2	14.6	0.9
Jefferson County	47.8	57.9	38.0	47.8	59.1	53.8	38.4	47.6	18 018	61.2	16.0	16.9	13.5	12.7	81.4	9.7	8.6	0.3
Juneau County	39.4	48.1	30.9	39.3	53.5	44.0	41.7	38.5	5 907	52.6	18.3	22.2	10.2	0.6	75.8	11.6	11.8	0.8
Kenosha County	44.2	53.8	35.1	45.1	35.2	37.7	45.3	38.5	38 514	49.8	19.0	21.9	7.1	5.3	82.2	11.1	6.5	0.2
Kewaunee County	48.6	59.1	38.2	48.9	X	33.3	17.9	37.8	4 999	66.4	12.9	14.2	16.0	13.2	77.6	7.5	14.3	0.6
La Crosse County	41.4	51.0	32.6	41.9	23.0	34.0	31.8	31.2	24 320	60.3	15.1	18.2	13.9	10.9	79.3	13.5	7.0	0.2
Lafayette County	46.1	54.5	37.8	46.1	0.0	15.4	47.6	43.8	4 246	65.5	11.5	17.3	18.2	16.2	67.6	11.3	19.6	1.5
Langlade County	38.7	48.8	29.1	38.9	15.4	13.2	59.6	32.1	4 824	56.7	15.5	18.4	10.5	-0.3	75.7	10.6	13.1	0.6
Lincoln County	42.7	51.3	34.3	43.1	2.0	20.3	47.5	18.3	7 077	58.5	15.9	17.9	11.8	6.4	78.1	11.8	9.8	0.2
Manitowoc County	46.0	57.5	34.9	46.2	52.0	34.0	37.1	39.0	20 416	62.4	14.7	16.7	14.5	9.4	82.4	8.5	8.7	0.4
Marathon County	47.0	57.1	37.0	47.5	46.5	31.0	31.6	42.1	32 730	61.6	15.5	15.4	12.4	11.9	79.9	9.4	10.2	0.5
Marinette County	37.5	47.9	27.5	37.6	25.0	33.9	30.5	22.2	9 871	58.0	17.5	16.7	10.1	0.8	78.4	10.8	10.2	0.5
Marquette County	36.4	41.3	30.4	37.0	14.0	15.3	19.0	24.7	3 158	54.4	18.9	20.4	10.2	-3.3	73.4	12.8	12.9	1.0
Menominee County	32.9	35.6	30.5	17.8	60.0	35.6	31.8	30.2	1 538	28.4	8.6	43.0	6.8	-9.0	48.3	43.6	6.4	1.8
Milwaukee County	40.7	40.6	33.8	43.8	33.1	39.1	38.2	35.5	228 032	37.4	13.5	30.8	3.6	3.4	81.1	13.2	5.5	0.1
Monroe County	43.9	51.5	36.2	44.2	37.0	37.0	48.5	31.9	10 950	55.1	19.0	19.9	10.4	10.0	65.7	19.6	13.9	0.8
Oconto County	43.7	52.1	35.2	43.9	31.3	36.2	45.3	43.1	8 838	62.2	15.0	15.3	12.9	5.3	76.8	9.5	12.9	0.8
Oneida County	37.1	44.9	29.4	37.0	19.1	46.0	40.0	50.4	7 899	58.3	16.9	18.7	12.4	-1.3	74.5	15.1	10.3	0.1
Outagamie County	48.2	60.5	36.3	48.9	40.6	48.8	30.8	30.8	43 315	59.0	20.5	14.3	8.7	10.8	84.8	7.4	7.5	0.3
Ozaukee County	47.0	60.5	34.1	47.1	54.7	47.8	33.2	43.1	21 601	57.7	26.4	11.4	4.5	9.8	80.5	8.8	10.4	0.3
Pepin County	42.8	52.7	32.7	42.6	0.0	20.0	57.1	91.3	1 862	57.5	24.8	12.9	5.8	8.1	70.7	11.6	16.7	0.9
Pierce County	44.4	55.0	34.3	44.6	34.7	36.6	17.9	63.3	8 706	67.4	12.4	15.2	18.0	16.7	74.0	15.1	10.4	0.5
Polk County	42.9	52.0	33.9	43.0	16.7	31.4	47.5	43.5	10 458	59.5	15.3	18.7	13.6	6.5	74.4	11.4	13.6	0.6
Portage County	40.6	50.3	31.2	41.0	26.5	23.9	24.9	32.5	15 628	58.8	17.5	15.8	10.0	10.0	76.8	14.0	8.9	0.3
Price County	37.3	46.2	28.5	37.2	13.6	61.4	72.7	41.0	3 669	54.8	18.7	17.3	7.5	-1.2	73.9	12.1	13.1	0.9
Racine County	40.7	50.1	31.6	45.0	28.6	40.4	41.4	36.6	48 337	49.4	17.9	21.7	6.5	5.7	82.8	10.8	6.3	0.2
Richland County	40.8	49.0	32.8	40.9	37.5	46.3	38.1	33.7	4 364	57.2	14.7	20.0	12.6	5.5	71.0	11.6	16.4	0.9
Rock County	43.8	54.2	34.0	44.5	34.3	41.8	34.6	39.8	38 216	54.4	15.2	22.4	12.2	6.3	81.5	10.8	7.5	0.3
Rusk County	37.6	44.9	30.4	37.7	32.0	32.3	11.9	46.2	3 611	56.9	16.0	16.5	8.8	0.7	69.2	13.5	16.6	0.7
St. Croix County	50.6	62.3	38.9	50.8	31.5	53.3	43.9	35.2	17 219	65.1	15.7	14.6	15.1	17.1	77.0	11.6	10.9	0.5
Sauk County	46.1	56.8	36.0	46.3	44.9	39.2	41.8	38.8	13 843	61.2	14.8	17.9	14.5	12.4	75.6	10.9	13.0	0.6
Sawyer County	34.7	40.0	29.2	35.1	11.3	32.3	32.7	41.9	3 747	49.9	11.8	25.6	10.9	-1.8	67.6	15.6	16.5	0.3
Shawano County	42.4	52.0	33.0	42.6	7.7	42.8	14.4	29.4	9 865	60.2	14.2	20.0	15.6	6.6	75.1	10.7	13.4	0.7
Sheboygan County	46.5	57.8	35.1	47.5	19.2	30.9	31.8	39.4	27 818	60.5	16.6	15.9	11.8	11.1	83.6	8.8	7.3	0.3
Taylor County	44.5	51.8	37.1	44.4	64.3	55.6	45.8	47.9	5 165	62.1	14.6	15.8	13.3	8.2	73.5	8.4	17.5	0.6
Trempealeau County	46.3	55.0	37.7	46.4	45.0	19.6	45.0	48.2	6 570	61.0	14.3	18.1	14.5	12.3	73.5	10.9	14.7	0.9
Vernon County	40.3	49.1	32.0	40.5	0.0	37.9	14.3	33.3	7 435	56.6	20.2	13.1	5.1	5.7	67.6	12.4	18.7	1.3
Vilas County	34.1	39.4	29.0	33.5	87.5	41.6	35.7	33.1	4 163	57.9	12.1	22.7	16.0	-6.3	67.6	14.8	17.4	0.2
Walworth County	41.5	51.4	31.8	41.5	29.7	49.4	35.2	42.9	21 872	55.1	19.4	17.3	7.8	8.0	76.7	12.1	10.7	0.5
Washburn County	33.4	40.8	26.0	33.4	33.3	23.1	37.5	38.1	3 635	55.3	18.5	16.3	7.0	-3.7	66.8	14.6	18.0	0.7
Washington County	50.7	63.9	37.7	50.8	39.6	33.2	40.4	45.9	30 632	60.8	21.2	13.1	9.3	12.9	84.1	7.6	8.1	0.2
Waukesha County	48.2	62.0	35.0	48.3	39.0	53.3	45.7	48.3	92 585	59.9	23.4	12.0	7.3	10.5	82.7	8.6	8.6	0.2
Waupaca County	42.9	54.4	31.5	43.0	20.0	33.1	42.0	48.0	12 671	59.2	17.2	15.6	10.2	7.9	76.0	10.8	12.7	0.5
Waushara County	36.9	46.1	27.8	37.1	33.3	38.1	51.5	31.1	5 255	53.3	17.9	17.7	6.4	-2.3	72.3	14.0	13.1	0.6
Winnebago County	44.7	54.4	35.1	45.3	18.1	45.0	35.2	36.3	36 032	58.2	16.5	18.5	12.1	9.4	81.1	12.2	6.5	0.2
Wood County	42.1	53.9	31.2	42.3	34.2	43.1	35.1	33.0	18 884	62.6	14.9	15.1	13.1	6.5	80.4	10.1	9.1	0.4
WYOMING	40.6	51.1	30.2	41.1	39.2	28.2	34.3	37.8	121 984	51.3	21.3	20.1	6.8	4.8	66.1	20.4	13.0	0.5
Albany County	33.2	39.9	26.0	32.9	28.6	34.8	20.7	41.6	5 579	49.4	22.2	18.6	3.4	7.1	58.3	31.2	10.0	0.5
Big Horn County	32.0	43.2	21.2	32.4	50.0	16.1	0.0	31.7	3 132	54.7	20.9	16.7	6.8	-1.0	61.4	20.8	16.4	1.4
Campbell County	49.9	63.9	35.4	50.2	0.0	44.8	57.8	40.3	10 164	49.3	27.5	17.2	1.9	10.4	75.7	15.3	8.6	0.3
Carbon County	38.4	47.5	27.7	39.7	22.6	21.8	11.9	33.2	3 556	53.9	18.6	21.4	10.7	4.0	60.3	24.9	14.1	0.7

[1] Hispanic or Latino persons may be of any race.

STATE County	Percent who worked at home	Percent of the population 5 years and over with a disability	Veterans as a percent of the population 18 years and over	Occupation for employed population 16 years and over (percent)						Industry for employed population 16 years and over (percent)					
				Management, professional, and related occupations	Service occupations	Sales and office occupations	Farming, fishing, and forestry occupations	Construction, extraction, and maintenance occupations	Production, transportation and material moving occupations	Agriculture, forestry, fishing, and mining	Construction and manufacturing	Wholesale and retail trade	Transportation and warehousing, and utilities	Service industries	Public administration
	42	43	44	45	46	47	48	49	50	51	52	53	54	55	56
WISCONSIN—Cont'd															
Dane County	3.8	12.9	10.1	43.6	12.7	26.5	0.4	6.7	10.1	1.2	15.8	13.7	3.3	59.5	6.5
Dodge County	4.5	15.0	12.3	25.3	13.8	21.5	1.5	9.6	28.2	5.0	39.8	13.5	3.7	34.1	4.0
Door County	7.6	16.0	14.9	27.5	15.6	23.6	1.9	13.3	18.0	4.5	28.8	15.0	2.8	45.8	3.2
Douglas County	2.4	18.5	15.8	26.7	18.4	27.8	0.7	10.2	16.2	1.4	16.0	16.3	8.5	53.4	4.4
Dunn County	6.8	14.8	10.9	28.0	17.0	21.8	2.6	9.2	21.4	7.2	23.0	16.5	4.9	45.5	2.8
Eau Claire County	3.5	15.2	12.3	31.4	16.4	28.2	0.6	7.8	15.6	1.9	18.0	20.8	3.7	52.7	2.9
Florence County	2.8	18.6	19.9	24.8	18.3	19.5	1.9	13.0	22.5	4.8	31.6	11.8	4.8	42.3	4.8
Fond du Lac County	3.5	14.3	13.6	26.3	15.1	22.6	1.2	9.4	25.3	4.2	33.6	14.1	4.9	38.7	4.5
Forest County	5.8	22.0	17.4	20.5	21.1	19.8	4.4	11.7	22.5	7.5	24.0	11.4	6.3	43.4	7.4
Grant County	7.8	17.1	11.6	29.9	16.0	22.0	3.0	9.1	19.9	10.1	22.7	16.9	4.0	43.4	2.9
Green County	7.2	17.4	10.9	28.3	12.7	23.8	2.6	10.5	22.0	7.8	29.3	17.6	4.0	38.2	3.1
Green Lake County	6.7	16.9	13.6	24.1	14.4	23.2	2.0	11.3	24.9	6.6	33.8	14.1	3.6	37.3	4.5
Iowa County	8.4	14.0	11.0	30.9	12.8	25.5	2.5	10.9	17.4	10.4	22.8	26.1	3.3	34.6	2.7
Iron County	5.8	22.6	19.5	23.6	19.4	21.6	1.5	14.2	19.6	3.6	27.0	15.0	4.6	44.7	5.2
Jackson County	7.3	20.8	14.8	24.6	19.3	21.3	4.0	10.8	20.1	9.9	23.8	13.0	5.3	41.0	7.0
Jefferson County	3.6	15.1	13.1	26.1	14.0	23.4	1.0	9.2	26.4	2.8	36.1	14.7	3.9	39.8	2.7
Juneau County	5.0	20.3	16.8	22.2	17.9	22.0	1.6	9.8	26.5	5.3	31.3	14.8	5.5	38.1	4.9
Kenosha County	2.3	17.2	13.2	28.8	14.4	27.0	0.2	9.7	19.9	0.7	32.8	15.7	4.4	42.9	3.5
Kewaunee County	7.4	16.9	11.7	26.4	11.6	19.9	3.4	12.6	26.1	10.1	38.6	11.8	6.2	31.5	1.9
La Crosse County	2.9	14.6	13.3	30.8	16.8	27.4	0.3	7.6	17.0	1.3	21.4	18.6	4.2	51.3	3.2
Lafayette County	11.1	15.5	10.7	29.8	12.6	21.0	5.2	8.9	22.4	16.4	23.3	17.7	5.1	34.7	2.8
Langlade County	4.7	19.2	16.1	22.4	15.6	23.3	3.8	10.9	23.9	8.2	28.7	16.7	4.9	38.2	3.3
Lincoln County	4.4	17.9	15.4	23.5	13.7	25.2	1.2	9.4	27.1	3.6	36.0	15.3	4.1	37.2	3.9
Manitowoc County	3.9	14.5	14.4	24.3	13.5	20.7	1.9	9.9	29.7	4.2	41.2	12.4	4.4	35.3	2.4
Marathon County	5.1	14.7	13.0	29.7	12.2	26.2	1.4	8.7	21.8	4.3	30.4	16.2	4.8	42.4	1.8
Marinette County	4.5	17.8	16.8	24.5	16.3	21.8	1.8	10.4	25.3	3.9	35.2	13.9	4.2	40.0	2.8
Marquette County	6.4	20.9	17.4	22.1	18.3	18.8	2.3	12.5	26.0	6.1	34.5	11.7	4.8	36.9	6.0
Menominee County	2.2	20.8	17.7	24.5	31.1	19.3	1.4	9.4	14.2	2.1	18.2	6.1	1.5	56.2	15.9
Milwaukee County	2.1	19.7	11.7	32.3	15.5	27.2	0.2	6.4	18.4	0.3	22.5	13.6	5.3	54.4	3.9
Monroe County	7.2	19.2	17.1	27.2	16.9	21.2	2.1	9.4	23.3	7.7	26.1	13.3	5.6	39.2	8.0
Oconto County	6.1	17.0	15.5	23.9	14.2	20.2	2.4	11.8	27.4	6.3	36.6	11.2	7.1	35.8	3.0
Oneida County	3.7	22.2	18.1	29.8	16.0	26.0	1.6	11.6	15.1	3.1	20.6	18.8	4.0	48.5	5.0
Outagamie County	3.2	12.6	12.5	30.5	11.6	26.0	0.7	10.1	21.2	1.9	34.3	14.3	3.9	43.6	1.9
Ozaukee County	3.7	11.1	12.7	42.8	10.5	25.9	0.4	6.3	14.1	1.0	28.0	14.5	2.9	51.5	2.0
Pepin County	8.8	15.4	13.1	27.7	14.8	19.3	3.0	11.0	24.1	10.7	26.6	15.2	5.3	39.4	2.8
Pierce County	5.6	13.1	11.1	30.1	15.3	24.3	1.5	9.1	19.6	5.0	26.3	13.8	5.0	46.7	3.2
Polk County	6.3	17.9	15.0	26.4	13.8	21.7	1.6	10.4	26.1	4.8	35.5	12.7	4.3	39.6	3.1
Portage County	4.3	12.9	11.4	30.0	14.3	27.2	1.2	8.1	19.1	3.5	22.5	17.0	5.5	49.3	2.4
Price County	5.4	19.9	16.7	25.9	15.3	18.5	3.3	9.9	27.2	6.7	36.7	11.1	4.1	37.7	3.7
Racine County	2.2	16.4	13.0	30.7	13.2	25.6	0.2	9.0	21.3	0.8	34.3	14.7	4.8	41.8	3.7
Richland County	9.2	17.3	12.7	26.3	13.7	20.5	3.3	9.5	26.6	11.4	33.1	14.5	4.0	34.4	2.5
Rock County	2.7	17.3	14.2	25.4	14.0	23.7	0.5	9.7	26.8	1.7	35.5	15.5	4.6	40.0	2.7
Rusk County	9.7	20.8	15.4	26.0	14.5	18.9	2.2	9.8	28.7	9.1	35.4	11.7	4.2	35.7	3.9
St. Croix County	4.7	12.7	12.6	33.6	12.5	24.4	0.9	10.1	18.4	3.1	31.1	13.2	6.1	43.3	3.2
Sauk County	6.3	17.1	13.0	28.0	17.1	23.7	1.7	10.7	18.9	5.3	26.9	16.4	4.0	43.9	3.5
Sawyer County	6.1	23.5	19.4	26.6	20.1	24.4	2.3	12.6	13.9	4.0	21.9	14.8	3.8	50.0	5.6
Shawano County	7.6	17.7	14.4	26.4	15.3	21.0	2.6	10.9	23.7	8.7	29.3	13.2	5.1	40.3	3.3
Sheboygan County	3.0	14.6	13.1	25.9	13.6	21.6	0.9	8.2	29.8	1.9	43.8	12.1	2.8	37.3	2.0
Taylor County	10.8	16.4	12.5	24.4	12.3	19.0	3.8	10.4	30.1	11.4	35.7	12.6	4.5	33.4	2.3
Trempealeau County	7.1	17.8	12.4	27.5	14.1	18.9	2.9	9.2	27.4	8.5	34.8	12.3	4.6	36.9	2.8
Vernon County	11.0	17.0	13.0	29.9	15.2	20.7	3.1	10.2	20.9	11.6	23.9	15.3	4.9	40.8	3.5
Vilas County	4.5	24.8	20.6	25.2	20.5	28.1	1.4	14.4	10.4	2.5	18.9	18.6	3.5	50.9	5.6
Walworth County	4.1	14.9	12.3	28.6	15.5	24.1	1.0	9.6	21.3	2.5	32.3	14.1	4.4	44.1	2.6
Washburn County	7.6	20.8	17.2	24.7	17.2	23.6	2.2	11.6	20.6	5.4	25.7	16.3	5.6	41.2	5.8
Washington County	3.3	11.9	11.7	32.2	11.2	25.1	0.5	10.0	21.0	1.5	37.0	14.6	3.7	41.3	1.9
Waukesha County	3.2	11.7	12.5	40.4	10.0	28.4	0.1	7.9	13.2	0.4	27.5	16.6	4.1	49.3	2.1
Waupaca County	5.3	17.1	14.7	25.4	14.6	21.5	1.6	10.2	26.7	4.8	35.8	13.2	3.7	39.5	3.0
Waushara County	5.6	19.2	17.8	23.5	16.1	21.4	2.9	11.1	25.0	7.1	30.2	13.6	5.9	38.6	4.6
Winnebago County	2.6	14.3	13.5	29.4	14.6	25.6	0.4	7.6	22.4	1.0	32.4	15.2	4.3	43.8	3.4
Wood County	4.1	16.1	14.0	26.8	15.0	24.1	1.3	10.4	22.4	3.5	30.7	16.3	4.5	42.3	2.6
WYOMING	4.3	17.1	15.8	30.0	16.7	24.2	1.5	14.8	12.8	10.7	13.5	14.1	6.6	48.9	6.3
Albany County	3.8	13.4	10.7	40.4	18.9	23.2	1.4	7.6	8.5	3.5	9.8	11.4	3.3	67.9	4.2
Big Horn County	7.9	18.7	15.9	30.1	17.9	17.3	4.6	16.1	14.0	19.0	14.7	12.3	6.0	44.0	4.1
Campbell County	2.3	17.9	13.0	23.9	13.7	21.1	0.7	23.7	16.8	23.3	12.1	13.6	7.5	39.9	3.7
Carbon County	3.8	19.9	17.7	23.4	21.0	21.9	3.1	17.1	13.6	12.1	16.6	11.7	8.5	40.4	10.7

STATE County	Median household income	Median family income				Median income for full-year, full-time workers			Per capita income	Households by source of income (percent)								
		All families	Married-couple	Male house-holder	Female house-holder	Median nonfamily house-hold income	Men	Women		With earnings	With interest, dividend, or rental income	With Social Security income	With public assis-tance income	With retire-ment income	House-holds with income over $100,000 (percent)	+/- U.S. percent for income over $100,000 (percent)	House-holds with income below poverty (percent)	Families with children with income below poverty (percent)
	57	58	59	60	61	62	63	64	65	66	67	68	69	70	71	72	73	74
WISCONSIN—Cont'd																		
Dane County	49 223	62 964	70 858	34 071	25 982	30 980	40 348	30 917	24 985	87.8	53.2	18.0	1.3	12.6	13.0	0.7	9.2	6.1
Dodge County	45 190	52 205	58 151	35 204	25 698	25 994	36 250	25 435	19 574	81.9	47.8	28.2	1.2	15.4	6.9	-5.4	5.7	5.4
Door County	38 813	48 460	54 141	31 250	20 351	21 412	32 728	23 150	21 356	76.6	53.0	34.0	1.1	18.8	8.6	-3.7	6.7	6.9
Douglas County	35 226	43 813	51 609	26 719	18 551	20 598	35 545	23 179	17 638	76.8	41.1	29.9	2.3	17.1	4.3	-8.0	11.2	12.8
Dunn County	38 753	47 247	53 220	26 838	20 204	22 275	32 191	22 561	17 520	83.7	46.4	24.2	1.4	15.4	5.7	-6.6	12.3	9.0
Eau Claire County	39 219	50 737	60 606	27 358	22 492	23 346	34 825	24 454	19 250	82.3	49.7	25.6	1.7	15.4	7.4	-4.9	10.3	7.6
Florence County	34 750	40 840	50 536	23 750	15 865	18 750	31 738	21 058	18 328	72.5	39.7	34.7	1.9	21.3	4.7	-7.6	10.1	12.4
Fond du Lac County	45 578	53 325	59 378	34 474	21 417	24 008	37 352	24 185	20 022	82.6	50.7	27.8	1.1	14.9	6.9	-5.4	5.9	5.1
Forest County	32 023	38 978	45 975	25 000	23 661	17 411	30 356	21 045	16 451	71.0	35.9	37.8	2.4	20.5	4.1	-8.2	12.3	14.5
Grant County	36 268	43 428	50 457	26 579	20 188	20 303	30 274	21 469	16 764	79.4	48.3	31.1	1.4	15.4	4.7	-7.6	10.7	9.8
Green County	43 228	50 521	56 142	33 074	24 517	22 670	34 180	25 206	20 795	82.4	49.0	28.5	1.6	13.2	7.0	-5.3	5.8	4.5
Green Lake County	39 462	46 969	54 414	31 369	22 629	21 567	33 685	22 564	19 024	77.3	51.9	34.8	1.2	18.5	5.1	-7.2	7.1	6.2
Iowa County	42 518	49 872	57 100	30 227	20 010	22 020	32 337	24 716	19 197	85.4	46.6	25.1	1.7	12.6	6.8	-5.5	7.8	6.3
Iron County	29 580	36 482	41 492	25 000	17 917	17 217	29 840	21 319	17 371	67.1	39.8	42.1	2.0	22.9	4.1	-8.2	12.5	13.7
Jackson County	37 015	43 548	50 603	25 357	25 086	19 004	30 358	21 155	17 604	78.5	45.3	32.4	1.8	17.1	5.3	-7.0	9.8	7.7
Jefferson County	46 901	53 953	59 141	34 963	23 340	27 643	37 130	25 712	21 236	84.0	48.3	27.0	1.0	16.6	8.7	-3.6	5.2	6.2
Juneau County	35 335	41 421	51 183	25 776	19 922	21 091	31 786	22 300	17 892	77.2	40.6	33.9	2.1	18.1	4.2	-8.1	10.0	10.7
Kenosha County	46 970	56 525	66 582	29 798	23 628	27 287	41 880	28 371	21 207	82.3	41.9	25.2	1.7	17.4	10.8	-1.5	7.3	8.0
Kewaunee County	43 824	50 216	56 353	33 393	25 938	20 452	33 625	23 004	18 456	80.7	51.9	29.6	1.2	13.2	5.9	-6.4	6.5	5.5
La Crosse County	39 472	50 300	58 326	28 065	21 967	23 043	35 419	24 351	19 800	82.7	45.3	26.0	1.2	15.2	7.7	-4.6	10.4	8.4
Lafayette County	37 220	44 326	51 486	28 269	21 326	20 956	29 284	23 194	16 811	81.0	49.5	32.3	1.0	13.0	4.8	-7.5	9.3	8.9
Langlade County	33 168	41 512	48 569	23 125	15 726	17 086	30 497	21 029	16 960	73.7	45.7	37.3	2.1	18.6	3.7	-8.6	11.2	11.7
Lincoln County	39 120	47 469	55 411	30 326	19 229	18 735	33 311	22 362	17 940	77.3	42.9	32.1	1.3	17.4	4.8	-7.5	8.4	6.5
Manitowoc County	43 286	51 995	60 065	33 333	22 349	24 138	36 847	25 092	20 285	79.6	53.3	29.9	0.9	15.4	6.1	-6.2	5.8	5.7
Marathon County	45 165	52 632	59 518	30 998	23 834	24 675	35 628	25 436	20 703	83.2	51.0	26.4	1.5	14.9	8.3	-4.0	6.4	6.5
Marinette County	35 256	42 356	50 697	29 152	21 858	19 211	33 938	22 295	17 492	73.8	44.3	34.5	2.4	20.4	4.6	-7.7	8.6	8.4
Marquette County	35 746	40 918	49 903	31 042	24 259	19 447	31 260	22 065	16 924	73.3	39.6	37.9	1.4	21.6	3.7	-8.6	8.4	6.6
Menominee County	29 440	28 385	45 625	21 838	14 688	19 063	23 651	21 882	10 625	75.6	65.4	35.4	3.6	16.4	2.4	-9.9	25.0	32.7
Milwaukee County	38 100	47 175	61 308	30 107	18 786	26 463	37 740	28 466	19 939	79.3	40.0	25.9	3.2	16.3	7.9	-4.4	13.2	18.5
Monroe County	37 170	43 835	50 224	26 275	20 301	21 767	31 339	22 369	17 056	80.9	41.9	28.4	2.1	10.1	4.8	-7.5	10.5	12.4
Oconto County	41 201	46 846	54 591	31 189	24 025	21 100	35 162	23 627	19 016	78.1	45.5	32.0	1.7	16.1	5.9	-6.4	7.4	6.6
Oneida County	37 619	44 293	54 890	35 556	21 088	21 521	35 632	23 068	19 746	75.0	36.5	35.3	1.9	21.3	6.5	-5.8	8.2	8.0
Outagamie County	49 613	57 464	64 302	39 258	24 613	28 924	41 110	26 602	21 943	85.0	53.2	22.6	1.0	13.4	9.9	-2.4	4.9	4.2
Ozaukee County	62 745	72 547	83 550	40 625	32 020	32 704	51 243	31 733	31 947	85.7	59.2	24.6	1.0	15.7	23.9	11.6	2.9	2.3
Pepin County	37 609	45 391	50 625	34 875	19 688	19 028	31 353	22 600	18 288	78.1	48.0	33.7	1.5	11.9	4.9	-7.4	8.8	9.4
Pierce County	49 551	58 121	63 978	34 191	27 159	28 040	37 642	26 762	20 172	87.3	48.2	20.9	1.3	11.9	9.5	-2.8	7.4	4.7
Polk County	41 183	48 538	56 896	31 228	24 638	22 033	36 121	24 123	19 129	79.6	44.7	30.5	1.9	16.0	6.5	-5.8	8.0	6.8
Portage County	43 487	53 446	60 531	31 071	21 605	23 506	37 857	25 133	19 854	83.8	48.4	24.0	0.7	14.6	8.2	-4.1	10.0	6.8
Price County	35 249	42 837	50 677	25 870	17 083	19 561	33 452	22 247	17 837	75.1	47.0	36.4	1.7	18.5	4.9	-7.4	9.2	9.2
Racine County	48 059	50 001	55 005	01 005	21 308	26 702	11 776	27 935	21 772	82.0	45.8	26.0	1.7	18.3	10.8	-1.5	7.6	9.4
Richland County	33 998	41 705	49 075	26 429	20 583	19 094	29 870	21 587	17 042	78.6	46.9	33.9	2.3	16.0	4.4	-7.9	9.6	11.3
Rock County	45 517	53 830	60 763	32 069	23 858	26 266	39 638	26 532	20 895	81.9	43.5	26.4	1.7	17.3	9.1	-3.2	7.2	7.9
Rusk County	31 344	38 359	45 205	24 808	16 250	18 270	28 293	22 160	15 563	74.6	39.8	37.2	1.8	16.1	3.2	-9.1	12.3	12.3
St. Croix County	54 930	63 816	70 587	39 423	28 965	31 351	42 597	30 353	23 937	87.4	47.4	20.6	0.7	11.8	15.0	2.7	4.3	3.4
Sauk County	41 941	49 091	55 136	31 953	23 935	24 438	34 500	23 669	19 695	82.0	46.0	28.2	1.5	14.0	7.0	-5.3	7.4	7.3
Sawyer County	32 287	38 843	47 672	28 021	20 078	18 445	31 285	21 744	17 034	74.3	30.9	34.5	2.3	18.0	5.6	-6.7	13.0	14.2
Shawano County	38 069	43 940	52 449	29 826	20 387	20 611	32 345	22 163	17 991	77.3	48.2	34.1	1.5	15.7	5.2	-7.1	8.4	9.0
Sheboygan County	46 237	53 984	60 767	32 688	24 643	26 851	38 644	26 064	21 509	81.4	50.5	26.7	1.2	15.4	7.8	-4.5	5.2	5.4
Taylor County	38 502	46 176	53 448	28 214	23 900	20 919	30 787	23 702	17 570	79.4	47.5	30.2	1.4	13.0	5.2	-7.1	9.6	8.3
Trempealeau County	37 889	45 369	51 677	29 087	20 326	20 363	30 111	22 217	17 681	79.9	45.8	32.0	1.5	13.4	4.5	-7.8	8.9	6.7
Vernon County	33 178	40 466	46 633	26 912	18 689	18 943	30 120	21 280	15 859	78.4	46.8	33.5	2.4	15.0	4.1	-8.2	12.2	14.4
Vilas County	33 759	40 876	50 986	23 875	22 303	20 433	30 907	23 293	18 361	71.2	36.7	41.9	1.8	22.7	5.2	-7.1	7.9	9.9
Walworth County	46 274	55 310	60 732	31 458	23 505	26 536	38 637	26 034	21 229	84.3	45.9	26.2	1.1	14.9	9.9	-2.4	7.9	7.5
Washburn County	33 716	40 486	45 317	25 875	17 422	18 759	31 424	21 173	17 341	73.0	40.6	37.6	1.6	20.5	4.8	-7.5	10.8	11.3
Washington County	57 033	63 542	69 905	35 964	26 733	32 557	43 636	28 272	24 319	85.7	54.4	23.2	1.1	14.4	14.8	2.5	3.7	3.9
Waukesha County	62 839	71 773	79 840	46 190	32 367	33 675	50 645	32 771	29 164	85.3	58.4	24.0	0.7	16.6	21.5	9.2	2.9	2.5
Waupaca County	40 910	48 837	56 862	32 993	21 216	21 156	36 013	22 935	18 664	78.8	45.8	31.0	1.6	15.7	6.1	-6.2	7.1	7.0
Waushara County	37 000	42 416	50 297	28 516	21 056	20 458	32 357	22 133	18 144	75.7	44.5	37.6	1.4	21.6	4.8	-7.5	8.7	8.5
Winnebago County	44 445	51 505	61 505	33 347	21 147	26 540	38 431	26 266	21 706	82.6	49.1	25.1	1.2	16.9	8.0	-4.3	6.7	6.2
Wood County	41 595	50 798	58 944	31 610	21 306	22 509	37 241	24 839	20 203	78.6	50.4	29.8	1.4	17.0	7.4	-4.9	7.2	6.9
WYOMING	37 892	45 685	51 815	29 194	17 122	21 689	35 831	22 397	19 134	82.5	38.2	24.5	2.6	14.6	6.7	-5.6	11.2	12.4
Albany County	28 790	44 334	50 929	21 250	11 076	16 667	32 956	22 778	16 706	87.9	41.0	15.5	1.8	10.3	5.4	-6.9	22.2	16.6
Big Horn County	32 682	38 237	42 439	28 750	12 788	18 307	31 748	20 085	15 086	75.8	38.0	35.8	2.7	17.6	3.8	-8.5	12.6	16.5
Campbell County	49 536	53 927	59 819	38 092	18 295	28 813	43 351	22 292	20 063	91.6	30.6	12.8	1.5	8.0	8.6	-3.7	7.7	6.7
Carbon County	36 060	41 991	50 082	30 515	15 000	19 672	32 339	22 160	18 375	80.6	33.9	25.3	3.1	13.8	5.9	-6.4	13.1	14.1

STATE/ County code	MSA/PMSA/ NECMA code[1]	STATE County	High school graduates			College graduates		College graduates (percent)				
			Total population 25 years and over	Percent with a high school diploma or less	Percent with a high school diploma or more	Percent with a bachelor's degree or more	+/− U.S. percent with bachelor's degree or more	Non-Hispanic White	Black or African American	American Indian and Alaska Native	Asian, Hawaiian, and Pacific Islander	Hispanic or Latino[2]
			1	2	3	4	5	6	7	8	9	10
		WYOMING—Cont'd										
56 009	...	Converse County	7 818	49.0	86.4	14.7	-9.7	15.4	27.3	5.3	0.0	1.7
56 011	...	Crook County	3 888	52.3	85.8	17.5	-6.9	17.4	X	10.0	0.0	31.3
56 013	...	Fremont County	23 053	48.4	84.8	19.7	-4.7	22.7	37.5	6.4	9.1	10.4
56 015	...	Goshen County	8 406	48.7	84.7	18.6	-5.8	19.9	60.7	16.9	X	1.3
56 017	...	Hot Springs County	3 515	51.9	84.2	17.9	-6.5	18.4	100.0	6.1	0.0	0.0
56 019	...	Johnson County	4 981	40.8	90.1	22.2	-2.2	22.2	X	0.0	X	11.6
56 021	1580	Laramie County	53 041	37.4	89.1	23.4	-1.0	25.3	14.2	12.9	24.9	8.0
56 023	...	Lincoln County	9 049	46.9	87.9	17.2	-7.2	17.4	0.0	18.0	27.3	4.4
56 025	1350	Natrona County	42 656	42.3	88.3	20.0	-4.4	20.7	23.7	3.7	33.6	7.0
56 027	...	Niobrara County	1 731	51.6	87.3	15.3	-9.1	15.5	X	22.2	0.0	22.2
56 029	...	Park County	17 145	42.8	87.6	23.7	-0.7	23.9	0.0	19.6	26.0	18.0
56 031	...	Platte County................	6 034	53.6	84.9	15.2	-9.2	15.8	X	0.0	0.0	2.5
56 033	...	Sheridan County	17 980	40.4	88.4	22.4	-2.0	22.8	0.0	4.4	14.6	17.6
56 035	...	Sublette County	4 044	46.4	89.0	21.6	-2.8	21.8	0.0	7.7	0.0	15.6
56 037	...	Sweetwater County	23 053	47.3	87.4	17.0	-7.4	18.0	18.5	3.4	29.4	5.9
56 039	...	Teton County................	12 838	24.2	94.7	45.8	21.4	47.2	100.0	48.2	48.9	17.4
56 041	...	Uinta County	11 443	50.8	84.8	15.0	-9.4	15.5	0.0	10.6	56.3	5.7
56 043	...	Washakie County	5 460	48.2	85.6	18.7	-5.7	20.1	X	0.0	0.0	5.6
56 045	...	Weston County..............	4 554	55.0	85.2	14.5	-9.9	14.6	0.0	21.4	36.8	1.7

[1] MSA = Metropolitan Statistical Area. PMSA = Primary MSA. NECMA = New England County Metropolitan Area. See the Appendix A for explanation of these concepts. See Appendix B for list of metropolitan areas identified by type, with component counties.
[2] Hispanic or Latino persons may be of any race.

STATE County	School enrollment			Population 16 to 19 years				Employment status, 2000			Work status in 1999 of the population 16 years and over (percent)		
											Worked in 1999		
	Grades kindergarten through 12	College or graduate school	Percent private	Number	Percent in armed forces	Percent high school graduates	Percent not enrolled, not grads, not in armed forces, not employed	Total population 16 years and over	Percent in labor force	Unemploy-ment rate	Full-time	Part-time	Did not work in 1999
	11	12	13	14	15	16	17	18	19	20	21	22	23
WYOMING—Cont'd													
Converse County	2 604	350	3.2	731	0.7	11.4	4.8	9 099	68.6	4.6	58.9	16.4	24.7
Crook County	1 345	86	1.3	403	0.0	7.7	1.7	4 562	64.4	3.3	55.3	16.1	28.5
Fremont County	7 484	1 462	4.3	2 261	0.5	8.7	8.7	27 196	64.9	8.9	53.2	17.0	29.7
Goshen County	2 279	660	8.2	722	0.0	12.6	3.9	9 856	62.0	6.4	53.7	14.5	31.8
Hot Springs County	900	94	4.2	274	0.0	11.3	1.5	3 973	62.2	1.8	52.5	15.1	32.4
Johnson County	1 456	134	2.6	442	0.0	10.9	0.0	5 626	61.7	6.0	54.2	15.9	29.9
Laramie County	15 626	4 235	7.4	4 423	3.7	15.1	3.9	63 149	66.3	4.6	61.1	13.9	25.1
Lincoln County	3 620	328	4.4	1 019	0.5	12.2	3.2	10 687	63.3	3.8	54.6	17.7	27.7
Natrona County	12 864	3 904	3.8	4 204	0.0	12.7	4.5	51 397	68.3	5.2	57.0	16.7	26.2
Niobrara County	428	67	3.2	140	0.0	28.6	1.4	1 941	61.5	3.4	53.4	16.0	30.6
Park County	5 000	1 469	5.6	1 737	0.0	8.2	2.1	20 299	64.0	5.0	55.4	17.4	27.2
Platte County................	1 841	173	6.6	477	0.2	3.8	4.0	6 871	66.1	4.3	53.5	16.9	29.5
Sheridan County	5 051	1 071	0.0	1 500	0.0	6.7	3.2	21 015	66.1	4.4	55.3	16.8	27.9
Sublette County............	1 178	105	7.0	289	0.0	5.5	2.4	4 577	69.7	4.8	62.3	13.9	23.8
Sweetwater County	8 471	2 004	2.6	2 861	0.0	9.8	2.8	28 371	70.6	5.7	59.9	16.9	23.3
Teton County................	2 438	465	11.5	800	0.0	29.5	6.6	15 179	79.4	2.9	68.9	16.7	14.5
Uinta County	5 003	580	3.6	1 567	0.0	13.1	2.8	14 081	71.3	6.4	60.5	17.1	22.4
Washakie County	1 850	105	2.8	519	0.0	17.3	3.7	6 309	66.9	8.3	54.6	18.6	26.8
Weston County..............	1 310	199	2.3	444	0.0	17.1	5.6	5 304	60.0	5.6	52.5	16.3	31.2

STATE County	Full-year full-time employed (percent)								Children under 18 years in families						Total employed by class of worker (percent)			
										With two parents (percent)		With one parent who is in labor force (percent)	+/− U.S. percent of children with no stay-at-home parent (percent)	+/− U.S. percent two-income couples				
	Total	Men	Women	Non-Hispanic White	Black or African American	American Indian and Alaska Native	Asian, Hawaiian, and Pacific Islander	Hispanic or Latino[1]	Number	Both in labor force	Father only in labor force				Private	Government	Self-employed	Unpaid family worker
	24	25	26	27	28	29	30	31	32	33	34	35	36	37	38	39	40	41
WYOMING—Cont'd																		
Converse County	41.7	54.0	29.7	42.2	27.3	43.4	0.0	33.0	3 273	50.8	21.2	20.5	6.7	6.2	68.0	19.4	11.9	0.7
Crook County	39.4	51.5	27.0	39.4	X	30.8	0.0	34.8	1 533	50.3	24.8	18.5	4.2	2.9	56.2	23.2	19.6	1.0
Fremont County	35.4	42.9	28.3	37.5	25.0	24.5	33.7	41.3	9 045	47.6	14.1	26.1	9.1	1.3	59.1	25.2	15.2	0.5
Goshen County	37.9	51.7	25.1	38.0	46.4	35.6	0.0	36.5	2 820	53.7	20.3	16.4	5.5	-2.0	61.5	22.7	15.0	0.7
Hot Springs County	37.3	43.2	31.8	36.5	0.0	52.6	42.3	69.1	1 035	67.9	14.4	11.4	14.7	5.1	58.7	23.1	17.5	0.8
Johnson County	36.4	48.3	25.5	37.0	0.0	46.2	X	15.2	1 635	51.6	21.7	20.1	7.1	-2.6	56.6	20.3	20.6	2.5
Laramie County	45.7	55.8	35.7	46.6	47.0	25.4	43.3	40.8	19 683	50.7	19.6	22.4	8.5	6.5	63.1	26.1	10.5	0.3
Lincoln County	37.6	52.2	22.7	37.5	50.0	52.2	26.5	38.7	4 347	54.2	29.2	13.2	2.8	0.5	65.7	17.6	15.8	0.8
Natrona County	40.5	50.8	30.8	41.0	21.9	27.6	40.6	34.7	16 348	48.5	18.8	24.2	8.1	4.8	72.1	15.9	11.7	0.3
Niobrara County	39.9	53.8	27.2	40.1	X	33.3	0.0	23.8	522	58.2	13.4	20.9	14.5	2.5	42.0	29.4	28.0	0.6
Park County	36.0	44.3	28.3	36.3	0.0	22.2	25.8	37.0	6 073	51.3	22.2	20.3	7.0	0.6	65.4	16.1	17.7	0.8
Platte County	36.8	50.1	24.0	36.4	X	50.0	77.8	46.4	2 159	61.1	16.9	15.2	11.7	5.5	61.0	19.5	18.2	1.3
Sheridan County	39.0	46.3	32.0	39.2	8.3	32.7	17.0	36.0	5 938	55.5	18.2	19.0	9.9	5.2	66.8	18.0	15.0	0.2
Sublette County............	41.6	52.4	30.1	41.6	40.0	73.1	0.0	38.5	1 462	54.9	24.8	15.8	6.1	7.2	58.2	18.9	21.7	1.2
Sweetwater County	42.5	57.0	28.0	43.5	45.2	45.2	28.8	35.5	10 325	46.6	27.0	20.8	2.8	4.4	74.5	17.7	7.6	0.2
Teton County................	45.0	52.5	36.4	45.6	0.0	64.7	56.3	31.9	3 331	57.8	21.7	14.5	7.7	11.3	69.1	10.9	19.6	0.4
Uinta County	43.7	57.2	30.0	44.2	40.0	25.0	11.1	37.6	6 370	52.4	25.6	16.7	4.5	7.7	70.1	19.3	10.1	0.5
Washakie County	38.0	48.3	28.3	37.9	0.0	56.0	50.0	35.9	2 125	61.8	15.7	16.2	13.4	6.2	64.2	17.8	17.0	0.9
Weston County..............	37.4	51.2	22.9	37.8	0.0	23.9	26.3	21.1	1 529	56.9	20.5	13.1	5.4	-0.3	67.3	18.8	13.8	0.1

[1] Hispanic or Latino persons may be of any race.

Table B-3. States and Counties — Education, Labor Force, and Income

STATE County	Percent who worked at home	Percent of the population 5 years and over with a disability	Veterans as a percent of the population 18 years and over	Occupation for employed population 16 years and over (percent)						Industry for employed population 16 years and over (percent)					
				Management, professional, and related occupations	Service occupations	Sales and office occupations	Farming, fishing, and forestry occupations	Construction, extraction, and maintenance occupations	Production, transportation and material moving occupations	Agriculture, forestry, fishing, and mining	Construction and manufacturing	Wholesale and retail trade	Transportation and warehousing, and utilities	Service industries	Public administration
	42	43	44	45	46	47	48	49	50	51	52	53	54	55	56
WYOMING—Cont'd															
Converse County	3.8	16.9	16.9	23.2	17.7	21.4	2.6	17.9	17.1	20.1	11.3	10.6	11.3	40.6	6.0
Crook County	7.3	19.4	16.8	29.9	15.2	18.9	4.3	16.6	15.1	24.7	14.1	9.4	7.3	37.5	7.0
Fremont County	3.6	18.2	15.3	33.9	17.7	22.5	2.0	12.7	11.2	9.5	11.4	14.1	4.6	53.1	7.3
Goshen County	6.2	23.9	15.4	31.4	17.7	20.3	4.2	11.1	15.3	13.4	11.2	13.9	9.1	46.6	5.7
Hot Springs County.......	6.8	21.2	18.9	34.3	21.6	20.3	3.6	10.9	9.3	11.8	10.2	7.5	6.9	57.2	6.4
Johnson County	10.2	19.5	19.1	37.5	15.4	20.3	5.3	11.8	9.7	19.5	12.0	10.8	4.4	46.9	6.4
Laramie County	3.6	17.9	21.3	32.2	14.8	27.7	0.6	11.2	13.4	2.5	12.9	15.2	7.4	48.6	13.5
Lincoln County	5.6	14.1	14.4	26.8	14.2	21.8	1.7	20.8	14.8	12.4	20.8	12.7	9.1	40.4	4.7
Natrona County	3.3	18.9	14.5	28.5	15.8	29.9	0.4	13.5	12.0	6.7	14.2	18.8	4.9	50.1	5.2
Niobrara County	9.9	20.7	15.4	34.4	18.6	20.9	4.8	9.7	11.5	24.7	7.2	9.0	9.2	37.8	12.1
Park County	5.8	15.4	15.3	30.3	16.9	25.3	2.4	12.8	12.3	11.3	14.1	14.8	4.6	51.2	3.9
Platte County................	6.5	17.7	19.7	30.3	18.0	19.4	4.5	14.5	13.2	14.7	11.0	12.0	14.4	42.8	5.2
Sheridan County	5.1	17.9	18.1	32.3	17.0	24.1	1.8	14.5	10.2	9.0	13.3	14.0	4.9	54.2	3.7
Sublette County............	6.9	13.9	14.9	28.6	15.2	21.6	4.5	17.6	12.4	21.9	14.8	11.4	6.3	38.5	7.0
Sweetwater County	2.6	15.4	14.8	23.3	15.9	23.4	0.2	21.1	16.1	14.8	16.8	14.2	9.6	40.7	3.9
Teton County................	6.9	9.5	9.8	34.1	21.0	24.1	0.7	15.2	4.9	3.4	16.2	12.4	4.5	60.4	3.1
Uinta County	3.4	14.5	12.1	25.4	18.4	21.6	1.0	17.1	16.5	15.0	14.1	13.3	7.4	46.9	3.2
Washakie County	6.2	15.6	16.1	29.7	18.2	25.6	3.4	12.0	11.1	14.3	13.6	15.0	5.5	46.3	5.3
Weston County..............	5.1	20.6	16.8	24.3	16.4	18.5	2.9	18.2	19.8	22.4	13.7	11.1	7.5	38.6	6.8

Items 42—56

Table B-3. States and Counties — Education, Labor Force, and Income

| STATE County | Median house-hold income | Median family income | | | | Median nonfamily house-hold income | Median income for full-year, full-time workers | | Per capita income | Households by source of income (percent) | | | | | House-holds with income over $100,000 (percent) | +/− U.S. percent for income over $100,000 | House-holds with income below poverty (percent) | Families with children with income below poverty (percent) |
| | | All families | Married-couple | Male house-holder | Female house-holder | | Men | Women | | With earnings | With interest, dividend, or rental income | With Social Security income | With public assis-tance income | With retire-ment income | | | | |
	57	58	59	60	61	62	63	64	65	66	67	68	69	70	71	72	73	74
WYOMING—Cont'd																		
Converse County	39 603	45 905	50 828	24 667	13 424	17 222	38 688	20 551	18 744	82.8	31.0	24.5	3.5	12.1	6.1	-6.2	12.0	13.9
Crook County	35 601	43 105	53 594	25 313	21 750	20 617	36 012	20 242	17 379	78.1	34.5	30.2	1.7	12.4	6.2	-6.1	11.7	11.5
Fremont County	32 503	37 983	44 156	26 103	16 500	19 613	31 417	20 677	16 519	79.2	33.6	28.3	5.7	15.8	5.0	-7.3	15.3	20.4
Goshen County	32 228	40 297	42 009	29 167	13 036	14 865	30 068	18 735	15 965	75.1	33.4	35.0	4.8	16.5	3.6	-8.7	14.7	15.9
Hot Springs County	29 888	39 364	45 486	18 654	13 500	19 293	27 694	19 079	16 858	75.0	37.6	38.9	1.8	20.0	4.2	-8.1	11.8	13.6
Johnson County	34 012	42 299	49 342	50 417	15 694	20 156	31 029	20 994	19 030	75.4	44.7	36.9	0.6	20.4	5.8	-6.5	11.5	10.2
Laramie County	39 607	46 536	50 573	27 328	20 058	24 218	33 049	25 387	19 634	81.8	40.7	24.7	2.6	19.4	6.5	-5.8	9.1	10.2
Lincoln County	40 794	44 919	47 519	27 411	17 100	23 681	38 533	21 335	17 533	80.8	38.0	25.1	1.2	16.1	5.3	-7.0	8.1	9.9
Natrona County	36 619	45 575	51 904	28 281	17 072	22 044	35 180	21 944	18 913	81.5	38.7	26.0	3.0	14.3	6.3	-6.0	11.3	14.5
Niobrara County	29 701	33 714	44 375	26 875	19 375	16 654	26 944	18 462	15 757	76.1	28.9	38.2	3.7	11.4	4.0	-8.3	13.8	10.9
Park County	35 829	41 406	50 115	28 203	15 400	20 992	35 316	21 451	18 020	80.8	46.3	28.2	2.2	16.0	5.3	-7.0	11.7	14.5
Platte County	33 866	41 449	44 258	41 389	16 696	18 393	32 481	20 625	17 530	78.5	32.2	33.8	3.3	17.2	5.3	-7.0	11.1	13.0
Sheridan County	34 538	42 669	49 390	21 023	13 837	19 518	32 307	21 135	19 407	77.3	44.6	31.7	2.5	14.8	6.9	-5.4	10.7	14.6
Sublette County	39 044	45 000	49 479	25 313	17 500	23 720	36 066	21 936	20 056	85.3	42.5	22.3	2.2	13.4	7.2	-5.1	10.1	10.1
Sweetwater County	46 537	54 173	58 333	39 565	19 119	25 332	47 147	23 693	19 575	86.7	35.7	19.0	1.8	13.2	8.3	-4.0	7.3	8.4
Teton County	54 614	63 916	66 500	34 844	26 827	37 452	36 006	30 134	38 260	90.4	50.8	12.3	1.3	9.4	18.8	6.5	4.9	4.2
Uinta County	44 544	49 520	54 632	26 250	17 236	23 247	38 681	22 002	16 994	89.1	28.1	17.0	2.8	10.2	5.1	-7.2	9.5	10.3
Washakie County	34 943	42 584	48 500	40 481	11 275	16 918	31 917	21 742	17 780	80.4	40.2	31.7	2.2	16.0	7.3	-5.0	13.1	18.9
Weston County	32 348	40 472	50 236	35 417	15 119	14 824	35 061	19 656	17 366	76.3	27.6	32.1	2.0	14.7	5.5	-6.8	11.0	9.8

CMSA/MSA/PMSA/NECMA code[1]	Area name	High school graduates			College graduates		College graduates (percent)				
		Total population 25 years and over	Percent with a high school diploma or less	Percent with a high school diploma or more	Percent with a bachelor's degree or more	+/− U.S. percent with bachelor's degree or more	Non-Hispanic White	Black or African American	American Indian and Alaska Native	Asian, Hawaiian, and Pacific Islander	Hispanic or Latino[2]
		1	2	3	4	5	6	7	8	9	10
0040	Abilene, TX	75 496	47.2	81.2	22.5	-1.9	25.9	15.3	13.4	27.2	6.5
0120	Albany, GA	73 060	54.6	75.2	17.7	-6.7	21.5	13.1	24.3	21.2	13.9
0160	Albany-Schenectady-Troy, NY	584 792	44.6	85.6	28.2	3.8	28.4	15.5	21.7	65.3	23.6
0200	Albuquerque, NM	456 076	42.0	83.9	28.4	4.0	39.4	22.5	11.3	38.3	13.2
0220	Alexandria, LA	79 811	59.1	74.6	16.5	-7.9	19.5	8.5	9.0	37.3	14.9
0240	Allentown-Bethlehem-Easton, PA	434 373	56.1	80.8	21.2	-3.2	21.7	13.0	12.1	53.1	8.1
0280	Altoona, PA	88 366	66.2	83.8	13.9	-10.5	13.8	9.9	3.6	55.1	14.1
0320	Amarillo, TX	135 055	46.4	80.0	21.0	-3.4	24.8	6.5	16.5	26.1	5.9
0380	Anchorage, AK	159 931	33.9	90.3	28.9	4.5	33.0	15.5	10.6	23.1	16.3
0450	Anniston, AL	74 015	58.3	73.9	15.2	-9.2	16.4	8.9	13.2	31.7	9.5
0460	Appleton-Oshkosh-Neenah, WI	229 381	50.7	87.2	22.4	-2.0	22.5	13.4	13.4	33.5	15.3
0480	Asheville, NC	157 055	47.0	86.0	24.5	0.1	25.6	9.9	14.6	39.3	13.9
0500	Athens, GA	85 196	45.7	80.1	34.1	9.7	40.1	11.0	12.0	72.3	20.0
0520	Atlanta, GA	2 630 798	40.4	84.0	32.0	7.6	36.8	21.9	23.2	46.1	16.1
0580	Auburn-Opalika, AL	62 170	45.3	81.4	27.9	3.5	31.9	12.2	25.9	64.7	23.8
0600	Augusta-Aiken, GA-SC	301 745	51.2	78.9	20.9	-3.5	25.1	11.6	14.6	39.9	17.1
0640	Austin-San Marcos, TX	768 147	35.1	84.8	36.7	12.3	44.5	20.1	22.7	61.3	14.7
0680	Bakersfield, CA	383 667	56.9	68.5	13.5	-10.9	18.6	7.4	6.9	28.0	3.7
0733	Bangor, ME	95 505	52.7	85.7	20.3	-4.1	20.2	15.0	11.0	47.8	26.1
0743	Barnstable-Yarmouth, MA	165 115	35.4	91.8	33.6	9.2	34.4	20.0	15.5	42.4	21.3
0760	Baton Rouge, LA	361 429	49.6	81.9	24.9	0.5	27.8	16.4	21.3	49.7	30.0
0840	Beaumont-Port Arthur, TX	246 237	56.5	78.7	14.7	-9.7	17.1	8.0	6.3	31.1	7.8
0860	Bellingham, WA	102 787	40.1	87.5	27.2	2.8	28.3	26.7	7.1	31.0	12.5
0870	Benton Harbor, MI	106 690	49.9	81.9	10.6	-4.8	20.5	10.9	11.1	61.0	18.2
0880	Billings, MT	84 233	42.6	88.5	26.4	2.0	27.0	38.9	15.4	48.1	10.3
0920	Biloxi-Gulfport-Pascagoula, MS	230 827	49.6	80.2	17.6	-6.8	19.2	10.1	12.9	18.4	14.4
0960	Binghamton, NY	166 764	49.7	84.0	22.0	-2.4	21.7	20.9	6.2	49.7	26.0
1000	Birmingham, AL	605 146	47.5	80.6	24.7	0.3	28.4	14.6	19.6	64.6	17.3
1010	Bismarck, ND	61 156	40.1	85.8	25.5	1.1	25.8	19.7	7.9	35.0	22.9
1020	Bloomington, IN	65 489	37.7	88.5	39.6	15.2	38.0	36.8	37.4	81.4	59.7
1040	Bloomington-Normal, IL	87 220	37.5	90.7	36.2	11.8	35.8	30.7	7.3	73.1	23.9
1080	Boise City, ID	265 281	38.6	86.5	26.5	2.1	27.7	26.3	13.3	37.1	8.8
1123	Boston-Worcester-Lawrence-Lowell-Brockton, MA-NH	4 068 400	41.7	85.1	33.8	9.4	35.0	20.3	20.4	50.2	15.3
1240	Brownsville-Harlingen-San Benito, TX	187 064	64.9	55.2	13.4	-11.0	28.9	28.0	10.4	56.6	8.9
1260	Bryan-College Station, TX	70 708	38.8	81.3	37.0	12.6	43.7	10.4	24.4	80.6	14.9
1280	Buffalo-Niagara Falls, NY	784 829	48.2	83.0	23.2	-1.2	24.3	11.1	13.5	62.5	15.6
1303	Burlington, VT	126 932	39.5	88.5	34.8	10.4	34.8	37.7	19.3	45.8	42.9
1320	Canton-Massillon, OH	272 431	58.9	83.2	17.3	-7.1	17.8	7.0	12.7	47.7	19.2
1350	Casper, WY	42 656	42.3	88.3	20.0	-4.4	20.7	23.7	3.7	33.6	7.0
1360	Cedar Rapids, IA	123 896	39.8	90.6	27.7	3.3	27.7	13.2	20.3	55.1	22.7
1400	Champaign-Urbana, IL	100 559	33.3	91.0	38.0	13.6	37.7	16.6	11.1	79.4	41.4
1480	Charleston, WV	175 442	56.0	80.8	20.4	-4.0	20.2	16.4	21.9	67.3	25.3
1440	Charleston-North Charleston, SC	346 710	45.7	81.3	25.0	0.6	31.0	10.7	15.4	37.0	16.5
1520	Charlotte-Gastonia-Rock Hill, NC-SC	983 882	45.1	80.5	26.5	2.1	29.4	16.5	14.9	37.2	11.9
1540	Charlottesville, VA	100 960	38.4	84.0	40.1	15.7	43.5	12.8	20.7	75.2	33.5
1560	Chattanooga, TN-GA	311 791	52.6	77.0	19.7	-4.7	20.9	10.3	16.8	45.9	17.3
1580	Cheyenne, WY	53 041	37.4	89.1	23.4	-1.0	25.3	14.2	12.9	24.9	8.0
14	Chicago-Gary-Kenosha, IL-IN-WI	5 835 442	44.3	81.1	28.9	4.5	34.4	15.2	13.9	57.2	8.9
1600	Chicago, IL	5 269 878	43.2	81.0	30.1	5.7	36.3	15.6	14.3	57.3	8.9
2960	Gary, IN	404 682	55.0	82.5	17.7	-6.7	19.9	11.2	7.1	56.2	9.0
3740	Kankakee, IL	65 844	56.0	79.8	15.0	-9.4	16.3	7.1	17.7	38.6	7.2
3800	Kenosha, WI	95 038	49.8	83.5	19.2	-5.2	19.7	11.3	16.2	51.1	9.5
1620	Chico-Paradise, CA	126 736	42.1	82.3	21.8	-2.6	23.2	14.6	10.5	25.6	11.7
21	Cincinnati-Hamilton, OH-KY-IN	1 267 807	49.1	82.6	25.0	0.6	26.0	13.0	15.6	61.9	27.7
1640	Cincinnati, OH-KY-IN	1 060 594	48.9	82.4	25.3	0.9	26.5	12.6	15.1	63.3	29.0
3200	Hamilton-Middletown, OH	207 213	50.3	83.3	23.5	-0.9	23.3	18.2	17.8	56.4	22.2
1660	Clarksville-Hopkinsville, TN-KY	120 167	49.5	81.9	17.0	-7.4	19.2	8.7	6.6	20.9	14.8
28	Cleveland-Akron, OH	1 960 749	49.4	83.5	23.5	-0.9	25.5	10.8	12.0	59.5	13.0
0080	Akron, OH	456 718	49.1	85.7	24.3	-0.1	25.2	10.9	10.3	63.2	25.7
1680	Cleveland-Lorain-Elyria, OH	1 504 031	49.5	82.9	23.3	-1.1	25.6	10.8	12.7	58.6	12.1
1720	Colorado Springs, CO	320 420	31.6	91.3	31.8	7.4	34.9	19.0	13.3	33.7	14.1
1740	Columbia, MO	77 919	34.1	89.2	41.7	17.3	42.6	22.3	28.7	71.2	38.9

[1]MSA = Metropolitan Statistical Area. CMSA = Consolidated MSA. PMSA = Primary MSA. NECMA = New England County Metropolitan Area. See the Appendix A for explanation of these concepts. See Appendix B for list of metropolitan areas identified by type, with component counties.
[2]Hispanic or Latino persons may be of any race.

Items 1—10

Area name	School enrollment			Population 16 to 19 years				Employment status, 2000			Work status in 1999 of the population 16 years and over (percent)		
											Worked in 1999		
	Grades kindergarten through 12	College or graduate school	Percent private	Number	Percent in armed forces	Percent high school graduates	Percent not enrolled, not grads, not in armed forces, not employed	Total population 16 years and over	Percent in labor force	Unemploy- ment rate	Full-time	Part-time	Did not work in 1999
	11	12	13	14	15	16	17	18	19	20	21	22	23
Abilene, TX..................	25 143	10 826	24.3	9 283	3.0	14.0	4.9	96 805	66.7	7.7	55.1	16.3	28.6
Albany, GA..................	26 017	7 351	9.9	8 363	8.5	11.5	6.1	90 783	61.3	8.3	53.0	12.5	34.5
Albany-Schenectady- Troy, NY	158 011	62 912	18.8	49 634	0.3	7.1	3.8	690 574	65.7	5.6	54.9	16.0	29.1
Albuquerque, NM	138 054	51 615	12.1	40 791	0.4	12.2	7.2	546 239	64.7	5.8	55.2	15.4	29.4
Alexandria, LA..............	26 221	4 620	12.4	8 535	0.2	11.7	9.8	96 383	56.7	7.0	49.4	11.3	39.2
Allentown-Bethlehem- Easton, PA	115 740	34 948	22.7	34 389	0.0	9.0	4.2	505 010	63.3	4.6	53.5	15.2	31.3
Altoona, PA	22 369	5 251	11.9	7 576	0.1	13.1	3.4	103 379	59.6	6.2	48.6	15.4	36.0
Amarillo, TX.................	42 591	15 067	7.1	13 939	0.1	12.9	8.9	165 709	64.9	5.5	56.6	14.3	29.1
Anchorage, AK	55 296	15 169	10.2	15 210	3.1	16.6	4.7	192 782	74.4	6.4	66.0	14.7	19.3
Anniston, AL	19 267	7 129	7.7	6 252	0.2	8.9	7.2	88 878	57.8	6.6	51.2	12.2	36.6
Appleton-Oshkosh- Neenah, WI	71 056	21 396	15.6	21 692	0.1	11.0	1.9	275 828	71.5	3.3	59.1	18.6	22.2
Asheville, NC	36 328	12 044	13.2	10 944	0.1	12.9	6.5	182 109	63.3	4.8	54.1	14.8	31.1
Athens, GA..................	23 881	31 409	8.1	13 080	0.9	7.2	4.7	124 063	65.8	7.9	52.2	23.1	24.7
Atlanta, GA..................	793 678	221 819	14.4	219 653	0.1	9.6	6.6	3 130 486	70.6	5.0	63.5	12.6	23.9
Auburn-Opalika, AL........	19 485	24 433	7.1	10 016	0.0	5.0	2.9	91 203	62.0	5.7	53.8	20.1	26.1
Augusta-Aiken, GA-SC .	99 527	23 747	10.2	29 309	5.6	14.6	6.0	362 660	63.0	6.6	54.7	12.7	32.6
Austin-San Marcos, TX .	223 583	117 833	8.4	75 684	0.1	10.3	5.7	966 844	71.3	4.0	63.1	15.0	21.9
Bakersfield, CA	161 296	34 561	6.9	42 920	0.5	11.6	7.2	473 552	56.5	11.8	51.1	12.6	36.4
Bangor, ME	26 268	12 276	10.4	9 564	0.1	8.9	2.8	116 139	64.0	5.6	51.0	18.7	30.4
Barnstable-Yarmouth, MA	35 283	8 492	10.9	8 984	0.5	10.1	2.9	181 996	58.9	5.1	46.3	18.7	35.0
Baton Rouge, LA..........	121 951	52 533	16.7	42 966	0.0	9.2	5.9	458 452	64.6	5.9	54.8	15.3	29.9
Beaumont-Port Arthur, TX............................	79 181	15 939	7.0	23 672	0.1	11.1	6.0	296 130	57.2	7.7	50.0	12.1	37.9
Bellingham, WA.............	29 602	19 135	9.2	11 267	0.1	9.6	2.7	131 195	66.6	7.4	50.3	23.2	26.5
Benton Harbor, MI........	32 070	8 218	19.0	9 364	0.0	7.8	6.8	125 198	64.8	5.5	52.8	16.7	30.4
Billings, MT.................	24 867	6 681	9.1	7 246	0.1	12.2	3.4	99 998	68.7	4.5	55.4	19.0	25.6
Biloxi-Gulfport- Pascagoula, MS	71 010	15 727	10.0	21 294	7.0	17.3	6.8	278 039	63.6	6.0	56.8	12.1	31.1
Binghamton, NY	46 494	18 782	8.5	15 376	0.0	8.5	3.3	198 998	61.6	5.3	50.5	17.1	32.4
Birmingham, AL............	172 811	49 191	13.0	49 801	0.0	9.9	6.3	715 412	62.6	5.5	55.2	12.2	32.6
Bismarck, ND	18 039	5 517	17.4	6 149	0.0	8.2	2.5	73 859	70.9	3.6	58.8	18.0	23.2
Bloomington, IN............	15 547	34 916	5.2	12 966	0.0	5.5	1.7	101 432	63.9	4.1	51.3	28.4	20.3
Bloomington-Normal, IL	25 605	24 570	11.3	11 738	0.0	6.8	2.1	118 896	72.4	6.1	57.9	22.5	19.5
Boise City, ID	86 831	23 500	10.3	25 595	0.1	16.1	4.5	323 261	70.4	4.4	59.8	16.4	23.7
Boston-Worcester- Lawrence-Lowell- Brockton, MA-NH	1 091 283	439 558	24.5	309 122	0.1	8.4	3.4	4 757 268	67.5	4.3	55.9	17.1	27.0
Brownsville-Harlingen- San Benito, TX...........	85 966	16 722	5.4	23 139	0.1	8.2	8.1	234 211	52.6	11.4	46.0	11.4	42.6
Bryan-College Station, TX............................	23 599	47 039	3.7	17 536	0.1	5.0	1.8	123 410	64.1	8.5	50.2	26.9	22.9
Buffalo-Niagara Falls, NY	218 580	75 454	18.6	62 847	0.0	8.7	4.3	917 620	62.4	7.0	49.2	17.7	33.0
Burlington, VT..............	36 688	18 632	15.4	12 712	0.0	8.4	1.8	155 479	72.2	3.9	60.0	19.0	21.0
Canton-Massillon, OH ...	76 619	17 375	15.2	21 920	0.0	10.6	3.9	317 460	64.0	4.5	52.8	16.0	31.2
Casper, WY.................	12 864	3 904	3.8	4 204	0.0	12.7	4.5	51 397	68.3	5.2	57.0	16.7	26.2
Cedar Rapids, IA..........	35 536	11 547	17.0	11 277	0.0	10.4	2.2	148 669	72.4	3.5	60.6	17.4	22.0
Champaign-Urbana, IL..	27 413	42 713	5.6	17 484	0.1	5.6	1.4	145 926	67.7	5.5	53.4	26.1	20.5
Charleston, WV	41 149	10 450	9.3	12 036	0.1	11.9	7.1	202 503	59.1	5.5	52.1	11.9	36.0
Charleston-North Charleston, SC..........	107 739	37 051	15.1	34 705	6.0	16.0	4.7	423 367	64.5	5.3	57.1	13.4	29.6
Charlotte-Gastonia- Rock Hill, NC-SC	277 554	75 650	13.8	74 518	0.0	9.9	6.1	1 156 554	69.9	5.2	62.3	12.7	25.0
Charlottesville, VA........	26 216	22 199	9.7	10 842	0.1	6.8	2.4	127 870	63.7	3.4	57.4	17.4	25.2
Chattanooga, TN-GA	82 046	24 070	16.3	24 432	0.0	10.5	6.4	367 100	64.1	5.0	55.7	13.4	30.9
Cheyenne, WY	15 626	4 235	7.4	4 423	3.7	15.1	3.9	63 149	66.3	4.6	61.1	13.9	25.1
Chicago-Gary-Kenosha, IL-IN-WI	1 797 733	580 317	19.6	505 630	1.0	10.9	6.0	6 958 640	66.0	6.2	56.8	14.6	28.6
Chicago, IL..................	1 621 219	531 646	20.1	452 779	1.1	10.8	6.2	6 282 410	66.1	6.2	57.1	14.4	28.5
Gary, IN.....................	125 146	33 603	14.1	38 075	0.1	11.1	4.5	483 890	63.6	6.6	52.6	16.2	31.2
Kankakee, IL	20 874	5 437	17.5	6 115	0.0	14.0	5.7	78 807	65.4	6.4	54.5	15.2	30.3
Kenosha, WI...............	30 494	9 631	15.4	8 661	0.2	11.5	3.9	113 533	68.7	5.5	57.7	16.7	25.6
Chico-Paradise, CA.......	38 232	25 780	5.7	13 482	0.1	8.2	2.7	160 320	56.8	9.3	42.7	20.0	37.3
Cincinnati-Hamilton, OH-KY-IN	387 507	111 200	19.4	113 271	0.0	10.5	5.1	1 513 293	66.9	4.2	56.5	16.6	26.9
Cincinnati, OH-KY-IN .	324 286	85 188	21.1	91 446	0.0	10.5	5.6	1 257 165	66.9	4.3	56.4	16.4	27.2
Hamilton-Middletown, OH..........................	63 221	26 012	11.8	21 825	0.1	10.6	3.1	256 128	66.6	4.0	57.4	17.1	25.6
Clarksville-Hopkinsville, TN-KY........................	40 798	11 890	8.3	11 856	12.3	23.6	4.9	153 707	69.2	5.1	60.7	13.1	26.2
Cleveland-Akron, OH	559 322	158 869	18.5	154 932	0.1	10.4	4.6	2 283 535	64.8	5.2	54.1	15.7	30.2
Akron, OH	128 412	47 027	12.2	38 964	0.1	10.7	2.8	541 615	66.6	4.9	54.7	17.0	28.3
Cleveland-Lorain- Elyria, OH	430 910	111 842	20.5	115 968	0.1	10.3	5.2	1 741 920	64.2	5.3	53.9	15.3	30.8
Colorado Springs, CO ...	103 247	33 737	14.2	30 763	6.7	18.6	5.0	389 986	71.9	4.3	62.4	15.4	22.2
Columbia, MO	22 625	24 827	8.7	11 018	0.0	7.0	2.1	107 690	71.7	5.3	56.3	23.7	20.0

Table B-4. Metropolitan Areas — Education, Labor Force, and Income

Area name	Full-year full-time employed (percent)								Children under 18 years in families (percent, except where noted)					+/− U.S. percent two-income couples	Total employed by class of worker (percent)			
	Total	Men	Women	Non-Hispanic White	Black or African American	American Indian and Alaska Native	Asian, Hawaiian, and Pacific Islander	Hispanic or Latino[1]	Number	With two parents — Both in labor force	With two parents — Father only in labor force	With one parent who is in labor force	+/− U.S. percent of children with no stay-at-home parent		Private	Government	Self-employed	Unpaid family worker
	24	25	26	27	28	29	30	31	32	33	34	35	36	37	38	39	40	41
Abilene, TX..................	39.4	49.7	30.1	39.8	38.4	38.1	43.6	38.6	31 493	47.6	20.0	21.9	4.9	1.8	72.0	17.7	9.9	0.4
Albany, GA...................	38.6	46.5	31.9	45.4	31.6	31.5	36.3	49.4	30 644	36.8	12.8	31.7	3.9	2.1	69.7	21.5	8.4	0.4
Albany-Schenectady-Troy, NY.............	42.4	51.7	33.9	43.2	36.3	30.1	34.7	36.7	199 538	49.9	18.0	22.2	7.5	5.0	68.7	23.1	7.9	0.2
Albuquerque, NM	40.6	49.8	32.1	42.8	42.8	32.7	40.2	38.6	175 708	38.7	21.4	25.0	-0.8	-1.9	70.3	19.0	10.4	0.3
Alexandria, LA..............	35.5	42.7	29.1	37.8	29.8	37.3	35.7	35.3	31 479	39.0	17.3	26.7	1.1	-4.0	67.2	23.3	9.1	0.4
Allentown-Bethlehem-Easton, PA.............	42.2	53.3	32.0	42.6	43.2	39.3	40.9	36.7	143 065	49.0	21.6	19.6	3.9	1.9	82.8	9.5	7.5	0.2
Altoona, PA..................	38.1	50.1	27.4	38.3	31.0	13.7	29.5	39.4	28 038	45.2	21.8	22.3	3.0	-2.4	80.5	11.4	7.7	0.3
Amarillo, TX.................	41.5	50.7	32.8	42.9	31.4	39.2	40.0	38.9	55 260	43.4	22.8	23.4	2.2	1.9	73.5	15.5	10.7	0.4
Anchorage, AK..............	44.6	51.9	37.1	47.5	46.0	29.0	33.5	39.6	71 592	46.4	21.2	21.1	2.9	9.3	67.9	22.0	9.9	0.2
Anniston, AL................	38.3	49.4	28.3	39.1	33.8	28.4	31.3	45.9	24 403	38.2	22.3	23.2	-3.2	-8.0	73.4	18.0	8.3	0.4
Appleton-Oshkosh-Neenah, WI.............	46.9	58.0	36.1	47.6	26.6	46.6	32.7	33.8	90 777	59.2	18.6	15.8	10.4	10.7	83.0	9.6	7.2	0.3
Asheville, NC................	40.1	49.6	31.6	40.5	33.9	28.9	39.6	45.5	46 053	45.6	21.0	22.1	3.1	-0.2	74.4	13.7	11.7	0.2
Athens, GA..................	34.9	42.9	27.5	35.0	36.6	33.5	24.1	34.6	30 936	43.5	19.2	24.6	3.5	4.3	65.0	26.2	8.6	0.3
Atlanta, GA..................	48.1	58.1	38.7	50.6	45.0	45.1	43.1	40.9	1 024 972	42.5	23.5	22.4	0.4	5.2	78.3	12.1	9.4	0.2
Auburn-Opalika, AL......	37.2	45.4	29.4	37.8	35.3	33.2	30.4	39.2	25 210	44.5	21.3	23.9	3.8	5.0	69.8	20.6	8.9	0.7
Augusta-Aiken, GA-SC .	41.1	50.6	32.4	43.6	36.8	42.7	36.8	37.5	120 004	38.2	20.4	26.8	0.4	-1.0	70.4	21.5	7.9	0.2
Austin-San Marcos, TX..	46.6	55.3	37.7	48.5	43.1	44.5	38.9	43.9	297 858	44.2	24.7	20.2	-0.3	6.2	72.1	18.3	9.4	0.2
Bakersfield, CA	30.8	39.3	21.8	35.5	27.5	28.7	29.4	23.9	195 676	35.5	23.6	21.2	-7.9	-9.6	69.0	20.6	9.9	0.5
Bangor, ME	37.9	47.6	28.9	38.1	26.1	31.7	32.6	35.1	30 989	49.3	18.9	19.7	4.5	3.1	73.5	16.6	9.7	0.2
Barnstable-Yarmouth, MA...........................	34.1	44.4	25.2	33.9	39.1	37.1	41.4	39.0	43 430	48.8	21.7	19.5	3.6	-6.4	68.9	14.5	16.3	0.2
Baton Rouge, LA...........	40.2	49.1	32.1	43.6	33.3	39.2	32.9	36.0	153 064	39.3	21.1	25.8	0.4	0.0	72.1	19.4	8.2	0.2
Beaumont-Port Arthur, TX...........................	35.3	43.0	27.8	38.5	28.5	37.4	31.9	28.9	95 073	37.3	23.1	24.3	-3.0	-7.0	75.8	15.6	8.3	0.3
Bellingham, WA............	33.2	42.9	24.0	33.4	35.5	28.8	31.9	33.4	38 565	45.5	26.0	16.7	-0.4	0.5	70.9	15.2	13.4	0.5
Benton Harbor, MI........	40.0	50.5	30.5	41.7	31.7	37.0	37.6	33.5	39 264	42.6	18.5	27.3	5.3	1.2	80.4	9.4	10.0	0.3
Billings, MT.................	40.6	50.8	31.3	41.3	32.4	27.6	35.7	32.2	31 709	52.2	17.8	22.2	9.8	8.1	75.5	11.9	12.3	0.3
Biloxi-Gulfport-Pascagoula, MS	40.6	49.6	31.9	41.5	37.1	39.7	39.4	41.4	90 090	40.7	20.1	25.1	1.2	3.4	73.4	17.2	9.1	0.4
Binghamton, NY	38.3	47.6	29.8	39.1	33.8	22.7	23.3	26.4	56 911	49.2	18.6	22.3	6.9	0.9	74.3	18.0	7.5	0.3
Birmingham, AL............	42.6	52.7	33.7	45.4	36.0	45.8	42.1	38.5	216 657	40.7	22.5	22.9	-1.0	-0.4	77.6	13.5	8.6	0.3
Bismarck, ND...............	45.4	54.2	37.2	46.1	29.6	27.9	18.9	29.6	23 290	64.7	13.3	15.8	15.9	13.4	70.7	18.1	10.7	0.5
Bloomington, IN............	32.4	37.8	27.3	33.7	23.9	35.8	13.5	27.0	20 388	47.8	20.7	21.8	5.1	6.5	68.4	23.4	7.9	0.3
Bloomington-Normal, IL..	42.7	52.0	34.3	43.2	30.9	42.7	32.3	39.0	33 769	56.1	19.3	19.7	11.3	11.6	78.5	13.8	7.4	0.3
Boise City, ID	44.1	54.6	33.9	44.8	39.5	37.5	43.8	38.1	117 511	48.7	26.6	18.1	2.2	6.3	74.2	14.3	11.2	0.3
Boston-Worcester-Lawrence-Lowell-Brockton, MA-NH	43.9	55.1	33.7	44.9	39.4	34.1	40.1	36.0	1 394 766	49.2	21.0	18.2	2.8	6.1	78.4	12.6	8.8	0.2
Brownsville-Harlingen-San Benito, TX..........	28.3	36.7	21.1	28.2	33.8	28.0	40.2	28.2	104 916	31.0	25.8	18.4	-15.2	-17.1	69.5	19.9	10.2	0.4
Bryan-College Station, TX...........................	30.9	36.8	25.0	31.6	30.1	25.1	20.5	31.2	30 383	44.2	21.9	20.0	-0.3	4.0	60.9	31.4	7.2	0.4
Buffalo-Niagara Falls, NY...........................	37.5	47.7	28.6	39.1	28.8	34.9	30.0	28.4	273 135	46.8	17.7	22.9	5.1	0.3	76.2	16.8	6.8	0.2
Burlington, VT	45.6	56.5	35.3	45.9	38.5	44.3	38.5	30.6	47 371	56.4	18.1	18.0	9.9	12.8	75.4	13.1	11.2	0.2
Canton-Massillon, OH ...	41.0	52.8	30.4	41.5	35.2	33.4	36.2	37.9	95 510	47.8	22.3	20.8	4.1	0.3	81.7	9.7	8.3	0.3
Casper, WY.................	40.5	50.8	30.8	41.0	21.9	27.6	40.6	34.7	16 348	48.5	18.8	24.2	8.1	4.8	72.1	15.9	11.7	0.3
Cedar Rapids, IA..........	48.6	58.7	39.2	49.1	37.2	45.6	51.5	42.2	46 414	58.1	16.5	18.3	11.8	11.7	82.6	9.9	7.4	0.1
Champaign-Urbana, IL..	35.6	42.0	29.4	38.6	29.5	34.8	17.4	23.1	35 714	52.1	16.6	23.8	11.3	8.4	64.3	28.4	7.0	0.3
Charleston, WV	39.6	48.7	31.5	40.0	34.7	32.4	44.0	34.7	52 895	41.8	24.5	21.1	-1.6	-5.9	73.5	18.4	7.8	0.3
Charleston-North Charleston, SC	42.3	51.4	33.9	45.8	34.2	47.4	41.8	41.6	131 752	39.2	19.8	25.9	0.5	0.4	70.5	19.9	9.3	0.3
Charlotte-Gastonia-Rock Hill, NC-SC	48.1	58.9	38.0	49.5	45.1	44.8	47.6	39.7	357 546	44.9	22.7	22.2	2.6	5.3	81.1	10.3	8.4	0.2
Charlottesville, VA........	40.6	48.9	33.2	41.1	41.4	38.7	27.4	37.1	33 646	48.0	19.9	23.3	6.7	5.0	61.7	27.1	10.8	0.3
Chattanooga, TN-GA	42.4	53.3	32.6	43.4	36.6	38.7	42.5	43.5	103 199	42.4	22.7	23.4	1.2	-0.1	77.8	13.2	8.8	0.2
Cheyenne, WY	45.7	55.8	35.7	46.6	47.0	25.4	43.3	40.8	19 683	50.7	19.6	22.4	8.6	6.5	63.1	26.1	10.5	0.3
Chicago-Gary-Kenosha, IL-IN-WI.............	42.2	52.0	33.1	45.6	33.3	37.7	42.9	38.1	2 303 576	41.4	23.7	20.5	-2.7	1.0	80.3	11.5	8.0	0.2
Chicago, IL................	42.4	52.1	33.4	46.0	33.4	38.1	43.0	38.1	2 081 716	41.3	23.8	20.2	-3.1	1.2	80.2	11.5	8.1	0.2
Gary, IN	39.2	50.6	28.8	41.5	32.3	35.3	37.9	36.1	157 008	39.4	23.5	24.0	-1.2	-2.7	81.5	11.5	6.8	0.2
Kankakee, IL	40.8	49.6	32.7	42.0	32.2	25.7	37.2	47.8	26 338	46.3	19.3	23.4	5.1	3.7	79.2	12.9	7.6	0.3
Kenosha, WI.............	44.2	53.8	35.1	45.1	35.2	37.7	45.3	38.5	38 514	49.8	19.0	21.9	7.1	5.3	82.2	11.1	6.5	0.2
Chico-Paradise, CA.......	27.5	34.3	21.1	28.2	27.1	28.6	19.4	23.6	45 378	39.3	19.7	21.6	-3.7	-8.4	66.9	19.2	13.3	0.6
Cincinnati-Hamilton, OH-KY-IN.............	43.9	54.8	33.9	44.9	36.5	41.6	44.6	42.4	499 565	46.2	22.4	20.9	2.6	4.2	81.3	10.9	7.6	0.2
Cincinnati, OH-KY-IN .	44.0	54.8	34.1	45.2	36.2	42.3	44.5	43.2	416 796	45.8	22.0	21.3	2.6	4.2	81.2	10.8	7.8	0.3
Hamilton-Middletown, OH.........................	43.5	55.0	33.0	43.8	40.6	38.6	45.0	39.3	82 769	48.3	23.9	18.8	2.5	4.2	81.5	11.5	6.9	0.2
Clarksville-Hopkinsville, TN-KY........................	45.5	59.2	31.6	46.4	43.4	45.7	33.2	46.2	56 071	43.0	26.2	19.6	-2.0	0.6	69.7	20.4	9.5	0.3
Cleveland-Akron, OH	41.9	52.4	32.5	43.3	35.2	36.0	41.3	37.2	705 796	43.5	21.1	23.8	2.7	1.1	80.0	11.8	8.0	0.2
Akron, OH	42.3	53.3	32.3	43.2	35.7	36.6	38.7	37.1	163 896	46.2	21.9	22.1	3.8	2.0	80.0	11.8	8.0	0.2
Cleveland-Lorain-Elyria, OH	41.7	52.1	32.5	43.4	35.1	35.7	42.0	37.2	541 900	42.7	20.8	24.2	2.4	0.8	80.0	11.8	8.0	0.2
Colorado Springs, CO ...	47.3	59.4	35.3	47.6	50.9	44.9	42.4	44.9	136 188	47.0	25.5	19.5	1.9	5.8	74.6	14.5	10.6	0.3
Columbia, MO	42.0	48.8	35.7	43.1	35.6	30.4	31.4	37.5	29 420	53.6	15.5	22.4	11.4	12.9	65.5	26.2	8.2	0.2

[1] Hispanic or Latino persons may be of any race.

Area name	Percent who worked at home	Percent of the population 5 years and over with a disability	Veterans as a percent of the population 18 years and over	Occupation for employed population 16 years and over (percent)						Industry for employed population 16 years and over (percent)					
				Management, professional, and related occupations	Service occupations	Sales and office occupations	Farming, fishing, and forestry occupations	Construction, extraction, and maintenance occupations	Production, transportation and material moving occupations	Agriculture, forestry, fishing, and mining	Construction and manufacturing	Wholesale and retail trade	Transportation and warehousing, and utilities	Service industries	Public administration
	42	43	44	45	46	47	48	49	50	51	52	53	54	55	56
Abilene, TX...................	2.0	20.1	14.5	32.1	19.5	26.9	0.4	10.0	11.1	2.2	12.1	14.9	5.5	59.3	6.0
Albany, GA..................	1.5	22.6	13.8	29.7	16.0	27.6	0.5	9.9	16.3	1.2	20.9	16.1	4.6	48.7	8.6
Albany-Schenectady-Troy, NY.............	3.0	17.6	13.2	38.5	14.2	27.9	0.3	7.7	11.3	0.8	14.2	14.3	4.4	54.9	11.4
Albuquerque, NM........	3.9	19.7	15.3	36.8	15.7	28.1	0.2	9.4	9.9	0.5	15.9	15.4	4.5	57.4	6.2
Alexandria, LA..............	2.4	25.3	14.7	31.4	18.6	26.5	1.2	11.1	11.3	3.5	13.5	16.4	5.1	54.4	7.1
Allentown-Bethlehem-Easton, PA..............	2.5	17.3	13.9	31.7	14.1	27.0	0.2	9.0	18.0	0.6	26.5	15.3	5.4	49.4	2.8
Altoona, PA	2.4	21.1	15.9	25.6	16.4	26.7	0.8	11.0	19.5	1.6	22.0	19.0	7.1	46.5	3.8
Amarillo, TX................	2.5	19.1	12.9	29.6	17.7	27.7	0.5	10.6	13.8	1.6	17.1	18.5	5.7	52.0	5.1
Anchorage, AK.............	3.7	14.9	16.7	36.8	15.1	28.5	0.3	9.7	9.6	3.1	8.4	15.7	9.4	53.8	9.7
Anniston, AL.................	1.7	24.8	16.3	25.5	14.6	25.0	0.5	11.2	23.2	0.9	28.3	16.4	4.7	41.6	8.0
Appleton-Oshkosh-Neenah, WI	3.0	13.4	12.9	29.8	12.8	25.5	0.7	8.9	22.3	1.8	34.0	14.6	4.1	42.9	2.6
Asheville, NC...............	3.8	20.9	14.7	31.7	15.4	25.2	0.4	10.3	17.0	1.1	24.8	16.4	3.8	50.6	3.3
Athens, GA..................	2.6	16.9	9.4	35.7	15.4	25.0	0.8	7.9	15.2	1.5	18.9	15.5	2.9	57.4	3.8
Atlanta, GA..................	3.5	16.8	11.8	37.5	12.1	28.7	0.2	10.0	11.6	0.4	19.1	16.4	6.9	53.1	4.2
Auburn-Opalika, AL.......	1.8	17.7	11.0	33.9	15.2	25.8	0.6	9.2	15.4	1.1	21.7	14.7	3.3	55.2	4.1
Augusta-Aiken, GA-SC .	1.7	21.7	16.0	32.4	15.5	24.2	0.5	10.9	16.6	1.1	22.1	14.4	8.0	49.4	5.1
Austin-San Marcos, TX .	3.6	15.0	11.0	41.9	12.4	26.7	0.2	9.5	9.3	0.8	22.0	13.7	3.1	53.0	7.4
Bakersfield, CA	2.7	22.5	12.1	27.0	17.6	24.1	6.7	11.0	13.5	12.3	12.9	15.5	5.3	45.8	8.2
Bangor, ME..................	3.8	19.5	14.8	30.3	16.7	26.8	1.3	9.8	15.1	2.3	17.7	17.8	5.6	52.4	4.2
Barnstable-Yarmouth, MA..........	5.2	20.3	18.4	35.1	18.2	27.5	0.7	11.0	7.5	0.9	14.5	17.1	4.3	58.2	5.0
Baton Rouge, LA..........	2.2	19.3	11.1	33.2	14.3	28.6	0.2	11.4	12.4	0.9	20.5	15.2	4.4	51.8	7.2
Beaumont-Port Arthur, TX..................	1.7	21.7	13.6	27.5	16.4	26.2	0.5	13.4	16.1	1.8	24.8	15.5	5.4	46.6	5.8
Bellingham, WA.............	5.0	15.5	13.3	31.5	16.5	26.3	2.0	10.1	13.5	3.3	20.5	17.8	4.0	50.9	3.6
Benton Harbor, MI........	3.3	20.2	13.6	29.3	15.3	24.1	1.0	8.9	21.3	1.9	30.6	13.7	6.5	44.6	2.7
Billings, MT..................	4.1	17.6	15.4	31.0	16.7	30.8	0.7	9.1	11.8	3.0	11.9	20.7	6.7	53.6	4.0
Biloxi-Gulfport-Pascagoula, MS	2.0	23.6	17.9	27.7	20.1	25.3	0.6	13.2	13.1	1.5	21.5	14.5	4.3	52.0	6.3
Binghamton, NY	2.7	18.6	14.1	34.5	15.7	26.3	0.5	7.4	15.7	1.0	24.1	15.4	4.6	50.9	4.1
Birmingham, AL............	2.2	21.4	12.7	34.4	12.7	29.8	0.2	9.9	12.9	0.9	18.4	16.6	5.5	54.6	3.9
Bismarck, ND	4.6	16.5	12.8	35.0	16.5	28.1	0.7	9.4	10.3	3.6	11.6	16.1	7.0	53.6	8.3
Bloomington, IN............	3.5	13.0	8.9	39.4	17.1	25.4	0.2	7.1	10.7	0.9	15.6	12.8	2.9	64.1	3.7
Bloomington-Normal, IL .	3.2	12.6	10.5	37.3	15.3	28.9	0.3	7.3	10.8	1.4	13.7	13.0	3.6	65.3	2.9
Boise City, ID	4.1	16.0	13.9	34.9	14.5	26.9	1.1	10.0	12.6	2.1	23.9	16.5	4.5	47.3	5.8
Boston-Worcester-Lawrence-Lowell-Brockton, MA-NH	3.1	17.9	11.4	41.7	13.3	26.1	0.2	7.4	11.4	0.4	19.3	14.7	4.1	57.5	4.1
Brownsville-Harlingen-San Benito, TX...........	2.5	21.8	8.7	27.7	19.8	24.9	1.4	10.4	15.8	2.1	17.6	16.1	5.5	53.3	5.3
Bryan-College Station, TX..................	2.6	12.6	7.3	39.3	16.4	25.3	0.6	8.9	9.5	2.3	13.0	13.4	2.8	64.6	4.0
Buffalo-Niagara Falls, NY.................	2.1	19.2	13.6	33.6	15.7	27.9	0.2	7.2	15.4	0.5	20.2	16.2	5.2	53.4	4.6
Burlington, VT	4.5	14.7	11.6	40.6	12.8	25.4	0.8	7.8	12.5	2.0	23.0	14.8	3.6	52.2	4.4
Canton-Massillon, OH ...	2.4	17.8	14.2	28.1	14.6	26.2	0.3	8.7	22.1	1.1	29.9	16.3	4.4	45.5	2.9
Casper, WY	3.3	18.9	14.5	28.5	15.8	29.9	0.4	13.5	12.0	6.7	14.2	18.8	4.9	50.1	5.2
Cedar Rapids, IA..........	2.9	15.1	14.4	34.8	12.4	29.6	0.3	8.1	14.7	1.0	24.4	16.0	4.4	51.6	2.6
Champaign-Urbana, IL..	3.7	13.1	9.5	42.2	14.9	25.3	0.4	6.0	11.1	1.4	12.7	14.0	4.0	64.4	3.6
Charleston, WV	2.4	22.4	14.4	33.4	14.6	30.1	0.2	9.6	12.0	1.7	15.2	16.2	6.1	52.4	8.3
Charleston-North Charleston, SC...........	2.2	21.4	16.8	32.5	16.2	26.3	0.5	11.5	13.1	0.7	19.5	15.7	5.8	52.2	6.1
Charlotte-Gastonia-Rock Hill, NC-SC	2.8	18.9	12.2	33.0	12.1	27.4	0.3	10.4	16.9	0.5	25.6	16.1	6.1	49.1	2.5
Charlottesville, VA........	4.9	14.2	11.4	45.4	14.3	23.7	0.6	8.3	7.7	1.7	14.4	12.4	2.9	65.0	3.5
Chattanooga, TN-GA ...	2.1	22.0	13.6	29.9	13.5	26.8	0.2	9.8	19.8	0.5	26.4	15.0	6.8	48.0	3.3
Cheyenne, WY	3.6	17.9	21.3	32.2	14.8	27.7	0.6	11.2	13.4	2.5	12.9	15.2	7.4	48.6	13.5
Chicago-Gary-Kenosha, IL-IN-WI	2.9	17.5	9.8	35.5	13.1	28.4	0.1	8.0	14.8	0.3	21.6	14.9	6.2	53.5	3.4
Chicago, IL.................	3.0	17.4	9.4	36.4	12.9	28.6	0.1	7.6	14.4	0.2	21.1	14.9	6.2	54.2	3.4
Gary, IN..................	2.1	18.9	13.5	27.2	15.5	26.7	0.1	11.8	18.6	0.3	26.3	15.1	6.4	48.5	3.4
Kankakee, IL	2.5	19.5	13.1	26.1	15.6	26.5	0.6	10.5	20.7	1.6	23.0	18.2	6.9	46.6	3.6
Kenosha, WI	2.3	17.2	13.2	28.8	14.4	27.0	0.2	9.7	19.9	0.7	32.8	15.7	4.4	42.9	3.5
Chico-Paradise, CA......	4.3	21.5	14.9	31.7	18.7	26.7	2.0	9.3	11.6	3.7	13.7	16.0	4.1	57.9	4.6
Cincinnati-Hamilton, OH-KY-IN	2.7	17.6	12.8	33.9	13.9	28.0	0.2	8.8	15.2	0.4	24.0	15.7	5.6	50.7	3.6
Cincinnati, OH-KY-IN .	2.8	17.8	12.8	34.0	14.1	28.1	0.2	8.8	14.8	0.4	23.1	15.7	5.7	51.3	3.7
Hamilton-Middletown, OH	2.5	16.4	12.9	33.4	13.2	27.5	0.1	9.0	16.7	0.4	28.6	15.5	4.7	47.7	3.1
Clarksville-Hopkinsville, TN-KY..................	2.1	21.4	17.9	26.6	16.6	25.3	0.6	10.7	20.1	1.8	24.8	15.1	5.2	46.9	6.2
Cleveland-Akron, OH	2.7	18.2	13.2	32.8	14.5	27.7	0.2	8.1	16.7	0.4	25.1	15.3	4.7	50.7	3.7
Akron, OH	2.6	17.3	13.4	32.0	14.6	27.8	0.2	8.3	17.3	0.3	26.4	16.3	4.7	49.0	3.3
Cleveland-Lorain-Elyria, OH	2.7	18.5	13.2	33.0	14.4	27.7	0.2	8.1	16.6	0.5	24.7	14.9	4.7	51.3	3.8
Colorado Springs, CO ...	4.0	15.7	20.0	37.2	14.5	27.7	0.1	9.8	10.7	0.5	19.2	15.0	3.9	56.5	4.9
Columbia, MO	3.2	14.5	10.5	41.8	14.8	27.0	0.5	6.6	9.4	1.1	11.9	14.4	2.9	65.4	4.4

Area name	Median house-hold income	Median family income — All families	Median family income — Married-couple	Families with children — Male house-holder	Families with children — Female house-holder	Median nonfamily house-hold income	Median income full-year full-time workers — Men	Median income full-year full-time workers — Women	Per capita income	With earnings	With interest, dividend, or rental income	With Social Security income	With public assis-tance income	With retire-ment income	House-holds with income over $100,000 (percent)	+/- U.S. percent for income over $100,000	House-holds with income below poverty (percent)	Families with children with income below poverty (percent)
	57	58	59	60	61	62	63	64	65	66	67	68	69	70	71	72	73	74
Abilene, TX	34 035	40 859	45 499	22 389	17 174	20 088	30 632	21 753	17 176	82.0	31.3	25.3	3.1	16.5	6.1	-6.2	14.2	15.3
Albany, GA	34 829	40 636	55 719	24 747	14 785	19 842	34 519	23 961	17 312	78.6	24.5	25.2	5.6	15.9	8.3	-4.0	19.7	23.8
Albany-Schenectady-Troy, NY	43 250	54 304	65 420	29 585	20 472	25 917	40 012	29 748	22 303	79.0	44.2	28.0	2.5	20.6	11.3	-1.0	9.5	10.4
Albuquerque, NM	39 088	46 037	54 476	26 314	19 400	25 573	35 492	26 826	20 025	82.3	34.6	23.2	3.9	17.8	9.7	-2.6	12.6	15.3
Alexandria, LA	29 856	36 671	49 623	21 671	14 009	16 571	30 764	21 156	16 088	75.3	23.4	27.8	3.6	18.1	6.5	-5.8	19.5	22.5
Allentown-Bethlehem-Easton, PA	43 098	52 114	62 359	31 556	20 836	24 202	39 468	27 183	21 243	77.4	44.6	31.0	2.2	20.8	10.8	-1.5	8.5	10.0
Altoona, PA	32 861	40 160	46 941	25 382	14 456	17 302	31 586	22 318	16 743	73.8	35.3	33.7	3.0	17.9	4.6	-7.7	12.8	14.8
Amarillo, TX	35 679	43 514	49 955	24 789	18 263	20 602	32 118	23 686	18 247	82.3	30.4	24.5	2.9	13.7	7.5	-4.8	13.7	15.3
Anchorage, AK	55 546	63 682	69 621	38 140	26 325	37 503	43 971	33 606	25 287	90.8	69.6	12.4	7.0	14.4	18.8	6.5	6.4	7.4
Anniston, AL	31 768	39 908	45 553	24 425	13 440	16 629	31 839	21 641	17 367	74.8	26.2	29.6	2.3	22.9	5.9	-6.4	16.9	19.5
Appleton-Oshkosh-Neenah, WI	47 438	56 178	63 306	36 627	24 109	27 509	40 217	26 506	21 837	84.2	51.6	23.7	1.1	14.9	9.0	-3.3	5.6	5.0
Asheville, NC	36 179	43 999	51 271	25 791	17 623	21 958	31 143	24 559	20 010	70.0	00.0	00.8	2.0	10.0	7.6	-4.8	12.0	13.0
Athens, GA	33 416	45 675	57 127	29 172	16 515	18 225	33 067	24 729	18 303	84.6	32.1	19.1	2.7	12.4	9.2	-3.1	21.7	16.4
Atlanta, GA	51 948	59 313	69 911	33 217	25 459	35 365	41 585	31 425	25 033	88.4	32.7	17.0	2.1	12.6	17.5	5.2	8.7	9.6
Auburn-Opalika, AL	30 952	46 781	56 256	27 936	16 280	12 643	35 137	24 217	17 158	84.5	26.9	17.9	1.5	13.0	7.2	-5.1	25.2	14.1
Augusta-Aiken, GA-SC	38 103	45 079	55 369	25 949	17 054	21 880	36 358	24 956	18 744	80.4	27.7	25.0	3.8	18.9	8.8	-3.5	14.4	16.9
Austin-San Marcos, TX	48 950	59 426	67 438	33 247	25 688	31 696	39 892	30 643	24 516	89.4	36.6	14.6	1.7	11.7	15.8	3.5	10.3	9.4
Bakersfield, CA	35 446	39 403	45 817	23 835	14 858	21 286	39 696	26 599	15 760	78.9	25.0	24.8	7.5	15.9	8.3	-4.0	17.7	22.9
Bangor, ME	34 274	42 206	51 170	27 126	14 424	19 982	34 314	24 111	17 801	77.7	34.0	27.8	5.8	16.3	5.8	-6.5	14.4	14.6
Barnstable-Yarmouth, MA	45 933	54 728	65 306	36 439	24 439	28 339	42 207	31 071	25 318	72.0	46.7	39.0	1.8	26.3	12.4	0.1	7.0	8.1
Baton Rouge, LA	38 438	47 077	58 919	29 732	17 264	21 774	39 568	25 166	18 867	83.3	29.1	20.1	2.4	14.6	9.7	-2.6	16.0	16.9
Beaumont-Port Arthur, TX	35 669	42 788	52 584	29 453	14 955	19 437	38 561	24 234	17 616	76.1	28.4	28.3	3.9	16.9	8.0	-4.3	15.7	18.7
Bellingham, WA	40 005	49 325	55 124	31 199	20 859	22 904	38 997	27 011	20 025	81.2	42.1	23.8	3.1	16.0	8.9	-3.4	13.6	11.9
Benton Harbor, MI	38 567	46 548	57 724	29 815	17 022	21 249	37 538	24 870	19 952	78.5	30.4	29.6	3.0	17.3	8.7	-3.6	11.6	14.4
Billings, MT	36 727	45 277	52 661	26 799	16 440	20 855	34 975	22 268	19 303	80.7	40.4	26.8	3.0	15.8	7.3	-5.0	11.1	13.6
Biloxi-Gulfport-Pascagoula, MS	36 662	42 328	49 528	25 878	16 949	22 208	32 155	23 125	17 899	80.2	27.9	26.6	2.7	20.3	6.7	-5.6	13.8	16.3
Binghamton, NY	36 374	45 698	55 049	25 810	18 410	20 289	35 291	25 436	19 067	75.8	43.8	31.1	3.4	23.5	7.8	-4.5	11.9	13.1
Birmingham, AL	39 278	48 079	60 213	29 600	19 079	22 616	37 704	27 684	21 410	79.5	30.1	26.7	2.0	16.5	11.0	-1.3	13.3	14.7
Bismarck, ND	40 148	49 941	57 150	26 162	17 259	21 768	34 572	22 760	19 572	82.9	43.4	25.3	2.5	12.3	7.1	-5.2	9.6	8.9
Bloomington, IN	33 311	51 058	59 656	29 936	21 430	19 127	35 558	26 939	18 534	85.1	41.2	19.3	2.2	13.8	8.6	-3.7	18.9	10.0
Bloomington-Normal, IL	47 021	61 073	70 676	32 743	24 231	26 416	42 375	29 547	22 227	86.1	44.1	20.1	1.7	13.9	13.5	1.2	10.1	6.3
Boise City, ID	42 570	49 262	55 984	30 129	20 841	26 226	36 366	26 005	20 280	85.3	37.4	20.9	3.1	13.8	10.0	-2.3	8.5	9.5
Boston-Worcester-Lawrence-Lowell-Brockton, MA-NH	52 306	63 874	76 326	35 596	23 439	30 977	46 001	33 577	26 594	81.6	42.2	24.8	2.7	15.8	18.9	6.6	9.1	9.0
Brownsville-Harlingen-San Benito, TX	26 155	27 853	30 047	19 167	11 889	14 551	23 445	18 875	10 960	76.9	19.6	28.4	9.9	12.5	4.8	-7.5	29.3	36.5
Bryan-College Station, TX	29 104	46 530	53 915	29 214	14 354	15 154	34 783	25 215	16 212	87.2	33.6	14.1	2.3	9.8	8.3	-4.0	27.7	18.1
Buffalo-Niagara Falls, NY	38 488	49 146	61 422	29 411	16 967	21 324	39 777	26 987	20 143	74.8	42.4	31.0	4.4	21.6	9.1	-3.2	12.1	14.9
Burlington, VT	46 056	55 397	63 809	31 259	22 131	29 291	37 669	27 738	22 158	85.7	46.9	21.1	4.1	14.0	11.4	-0.9	8.9	8.0
Canton-Massillon, OH	39 457	47 169	56 755	28 895	18 108	21 927	37 640	24 701	20 154	77.9	37.1	29.1	3.0	20.6	8.3	-4.0	9.4	11.5
Casper, WY	36 619	45 575	51 904	28 281	17 072	22 044	35 180	21 944	18 913	81.5	38.7	26.0	3.0	14.3	6.3	-6.0	11.3	14.5
Cedar Rapids, IA	46 206	56 494	66 360	34 736	23 508	27 321	39 761	27 192	22 977	83.5	46.2	24.3	2.5	16.4	10.2	-2.1	6.7	6.9
Champaign-Urbana, IL	37 780	52 591	60 786	32 403	20 729	21 555	38 119	27 258	19 708	85.6	41.9	18.8	2.3	14.4	9.0	-3.3	16.0	10.3
Charleston, WV	35 418	43 991	51 769	25 583	16 012	20 051	36 618	25 027	20 378	74.4	32.1	31.8	2.9	21.6	8.2	-4.1	13.5	16.4
Charleston-North Charleston, SC	39 491	46 801	56 609	30 567	17 418	25 241	35 068	25 314	19 772	81.7	29.4	23.1	2.2	20.1	9.5	-2.8	13.7	15.5
Charlotte-Gastonia-Rock Hill, NC-SC	46 119	53 868	63 663	30 880	23 215	29 126	38 410	27 502	23 417	85.9	32.1	21.2	2.2	13.8	13.1	0.8	9.0	9.8
Charlottesville, VA	44 356	55 455	64 830	30 098	23 244	27 021	36 883	29 571	23 353	84.4	45.4	23.1	1.8	16.7	12.8	0.5	11.2	8.4
Chattanooga, TN-GA	37 411	45 084	53 259	26 240	18 722	20 815	34 164	24 558	19 944	79.3	30.2	27.8	3.0	16.6	8.3	-4.0	12.4	13.8
Cheyenne, WY	39 607	46 536	50 573	27 328	20 058	24 218	33 049	25 387	19 634	81.8	40.7	24.7	2.6	19.4	6.5	-5.8	9.1	10.2
Chicago-Gary-Kenosha, IL-IN-WI	51 046	60 367	70 644	35 401	24 488	32 085	45 502	31 936	24 581	83.3	39.5	22.7	3.6	14.2	17.4	5.1	9.7	11.4
Chicago, IL	51 680	61 182	71 492	35 726	25 140	32 095	45 657	32 339	25 011	83.6	39.7	22.1	3.6	13.7	18.2	5.9	9.7	11.4
Gary, IN	44 637	52 755	63 313	32 638	19 867	24 618	40 457	27 249	20 643	79.8	35.9	27.9	4.0	19.2	10.2	-2.1	10.6	13.0
Kankakee, IL	41 532	48 975	59 052	32 422	19 989	23 408	38 904	26 020	19 055	79.6	36.2	27.7	3.6	17.0	7.9	-4.4	10.5	13.3
Kenosha, WI	46 970	56 525	66 582	29 798	23 628	27 287	41 880	28 371	21 207	82.3	41.9	25.2	1.7	17.4	10.8	-1.5	7.3	8.0
Chico-Paradise, CA	31 924	41 010	49 906	24 981	16 684	19 339	35 675	26 211	17 517	72.5	33.8	31.3	6.5	20.8	6.7	-5.6	17.6	19.8
Cincinnati-Hamilton, OH-KY-IN	44 914	55 198	66 244	32 043	20 698	25 774	41 232	28 986	22 947	81.8	38.5	24.1	2.5	16.6	12.7	0.4	9.9	10.6
Cincinnati, OH-KY-IN	44 248	54 690	66 077	31 808	20 441	25 777	40 926	29 066	23 124	81.5	38.5	24.2	2.6	16.6	12.6	0.3	10.1	11.1
Hamilton-Middletown, OH	47 885	57 513	66 942	34 089	22 234	25 747	43 135	28 597	22 076	83.7	38.6	23.6	2.3	18.2	12.9	0.6	8.9	7.9
Clarksville-Hopkinsville, TN-KY	36 313	40 348	44 285	26 283	18 102	22 626	30 047	22 515	16 339	84.6	25.0	20.5	3.4	18.0	5.6	-6.7	12.0	12.8
Cleveland-Akron, OH	42 215	52 115	64 410	32 012	19 704	25 313	40 900	28 478	22 319	78.9	38.1	27.2	4.0	18.8	11.2	-1.1	10.5	12.8
Akron, OH	42 691	52 321	63 691	32 034	18 271	25 028	40 483	27 392	22 314	80.3	36.4	25.9	3.4	19.0	11.0	-1.3	9.9	11.6
Cleveland-Lorain-Elyria, OH	42 089	52 047	64 647	32 002	20 081	25 396	41 036	28 810	22 321	78.5	38.6	27.6	4.2	18.7	11.2	-1.1	10.6	13.1
Colorado Springs, CO	46 844	53 995	59 931	32 062	22 592	28 712	37 776	26 898	22 005	86.9	40.3	19.1	2.6	19.0	12.2	-0.1	7.9	8.6
Columbia, MO	37 485	51 210	59 668	26 145	21 288	22 040	34 952	26 583	19 844	86.4	40.2	17.6	2.5	13.0	9.2	-3.1	15.2	10.9

Table B-4. Metropolitan Areas — Education, Labor Force, and Income

CMSA/MSA/PMSA/NECMA code[1]	Area name	High school graduates — Total population 25 years and over	Percent with a high school diploma or less	Percent with a high school diploma or more	College graduates — Percent with a bachelor's degree or more	+/− U.S. percent with bachelor's degree or more	College graduates (percent) — Non-Hispanic White	Black or African American	American Indian and Alaska Native	Asian, Hawaiian, and Pacific Islander	Hispanic or Latino[2]
		1	2	3	4	5	6	7	8	9	10
1760	Columbia, SC	340 786	41.3	84.3	29.2	4.8	34.2	17.3	16.2	49.2	21.1
1800	Columbus, GA-AL	168 800	52.1	76.9	18.6	−5.8	23.3	10.6	20.7	33.6	17.6
1840	Columbus, OH	983 765	44.3	85.8	29.1	4.7	30.4	15.4	14.9	59.3	21.6
1880	Corpus Christi, TX	231 399	52.0	73.9	17.8	−6.6	27.3	13.7	11.8	41.1	8.8
1890	Corvallis, OR	45 758	22.2	93.1	47.4	23.0	47.6	49.0	30.7	67.2	28.0
1900	Cumberland, MD-WV	69 648	63.5	80.0	13.4	−11.0	13.4	8.9	7.9	53.7	15.0
31	Dallas-Fort Worth, TX	3 248 569	42.7	79.9	28.4	4.0	34.2	18.1	18.9	47.6	8.8
1920	Dallas, TX	2 184 609	42.2	79.4	30.0	5.6	37.2	18.5	19.3	51.9	8.7
2800	Fort Worth-Arlington, TX	1 063 960	43.7	81.0	25.1	0.7	28.9	16.8	18.2	35.8	9.2
1950	Danville, VA	76 316	65.4	67.8	11.3	−13.1	13.4	5.7	18.5	34.5	23.8
1960	Davenport-Moline-Rock Island, IA-IL	235 197	48.6	84.5	20.3	−4.1	21.1	9.8	8.1	43.7	9.1
2000	Dayton-Springfield, OH	620 576	48.9	83.7	22.1	−2.3	22.6	15.5	16.2	53.3	28.0
2020	Daytona Beach, FL	355 841	49.8	82.5	18.0	−6.4	18.4	15.2	17.7	36.0	12.2
2030	Decatur, AL	96 225	58.7	73.8	15.8	−8.6	16.9	6.8	15.3	50.8	11.4
2040	Decatur, IL	75 195	54.9	83.2	16.9	−7.5	18.3	5.2	14.5	53.6	11.0
34	Denver-Boulder-Greeley, CO	1 670 518	34.9	86.6	35.5	11.1	40.8	21.5	16.8	43.3	10.7
1125	Boulder-Longmont, CO	186 126	22.3	92.8	52.4	28.0	55.2	45.0	31.2	64.9	18.2
2080	Denver, CO	1 378 147	35.6	86.4	34.2	9.8	39.7	21.0	15.9	40.1	10.6
3060	Greeley, CO	106 245	47.2	79.6	21.6	−2.8	25.7	23.4	13.0	48.4	6.5
2120	Des Moines, IA	295 697	41.9	88.6	28.7	4.3	29.9	16.3	11.6	28.3	11.7
35	Detroit-Ann Arbor-Flint, MI	3 548 118	46.1	83.0	23.7	−0.7	25.5	13.1	13.1	64.9	16.0
0440	Ann Arbor, MI	363 106	34.0	90.1	36.9	12.5	36.5	24.1	18.1	80.0	28.9
2160	Detroit, MI	2 907 352	47.2	82.1	22.8	−1.6	24.7	12.8	13.0	62.2	14.7
2640	Flint, MI	277 660	50.2	83.1	16.2	−8.2	17.3	10.3	9.1	58.1	10.1
2180	Dothan, AL	90 061	53.0	77.0	16.9	−7.5	19.0	8.2	10.5	26.5	14.7
2190	Dover, DE	79 249	53.5	79.4	18.6	−5.8	19.4	15.6	9.4	33.9	11.8
2200	Dubuque, IA	57 236	55.0	85.2	21.3	−3.1	21.3	22.7	24.4	50.4	17.3
2240	Duluth-Superior, MN-WI	161 454	45.6	87.0	21.2	−3.2	21.5	21.0	7.6	29.9	13.5
2290	Eau Claire, WI	91 620	48.0	87.1	22.1	−2.3	22.1	27.7	9.0	27.0	26.8
2320	El Paso, TX	391 540	56.8	65.8	16.6	−7.8	35.1	21.1	13.6	40.8	10.6
2330	Elkhart-Goshen, IN	112 908	61.3	75.7	15.5	−8.9	16.6	5.9	1.6	36.3	5.4
2335	Elmira, NY	60 796	54.0	82.1	18.6	−5.8	19.0	9.9	3.2	51.7	10.4
2340	Enid, OK	38 067	53.4	82.2	19.6	−4.8	20.2	5.6	10.5	25.9	12.6
2360	Erie, PA	180 106	57.1	84.6	20.9	−3.5	21.5	8.7	10.8	51.0	11.0
2400	Eugene-Springfield, OR	210 601	38.3	87.5	25.5	1.1	25.7	29.2	15.6	47.0	15.8
2440	Evansville-Henderson, IN-KY	194 380	53.1	83.1	18.5	−5.9	18.8	7.4	9.9	55.6	17.9
2520	Fargo-Moorhead, ND-MN	104 248	34.7	89.7	29.4	5.0	29.8	23.8	7.4	52.9	11.3
2560	Fayetteville, NC	176 714	43.4	85.0	19.1	−5.3	22.5	14.6	10.9	19.6	13.6
2580	Fayetteville-Springdale-Rogers, AR	193 455	51.7	80.0	22.4	−2.0	23.2	25.5	12.2	44.9	6.1
2620	Flagstaff, AZ-UT	69 818	38.0	83.9	29.5	5.1	38.7	21.6	7.8	44.7	15.3
2650	Florence, AL	96 278	58.8	75.2	16.8	−7.6	17.7	8.5	14.2	45.3	16.2
2655	Florence, SC	80 904	57.8	73.1	18.7	−5.7	23.6	9.0	17.3	58.6	13.2
2670	Fort Collins-Loveland, CO	156 426	29.0	92.3	39.5	15.1	40.8	39.4	16.9	61.9	17.4
2700	Fort Myers-Cape Coral, FL	327 672	50.2	82.3	21.1	−3.3	22.6	8.9	11.4	40.7	8.9
2710	Fort Pierce-Port St. Lucie, FL	232 915	50.0	80.8	19.7	−4.7	21.3	8.6	6.5	34.1	12.5
2720	Fort Smith, AR-OK	133 346	59.0	74.1	13.8	−10.6	14.7	8.3	13.1	7.6	5.5
2750	Fort Walton Beach, FL	112 429	39.1	88.0	24.2	−0.2	26.1	11.9	15.4	14.8	19.6
2760	Fort Wayne, IN	316 575	51.4	85.3	19.4	−5.0	20.2	9.8	9.0	38.5	7.9
2840	Fresno, CA	530 370	54.5	67.2	16.8	−7.6	24.8	11.2	7.8	24.6	5.4
2880	Gadsden, AL	69 829	58.2	74.1	13.4	−11.0	14.3	7.4	8.0	33.8	7.8
2900	Gainesville, FL	123 524	32.2	88.1	38.7	14.3	42.2	14.3	35.3	78.6	47.0
2975	Glens Falls, NY	84 321	54.8	82.0	18.9	−5.5	19.2	5.3	18.2	36.1	7.0
2980	Goldsboro, NC	72 894	55.3	77.2	15.0	−9.4	17.9	9.5	2.5	31.9	6.1
2985	Grand Forks, ND-MN	57 569	40.3	86.6	24.2	−0.2	24.6	16.5	15.3	38.1	11.9
2995	Grand Junction, CO	76 358	45.3	85.0	22.0	−2.4	23.2	16.8	4.7	24.5	9.9
3000	Grand Rapids-Muskegon-Holland, MI	669 331	46.6	84.6	22.9	−1.5	24.6	9.7	9.5	30.9	8.3
3040	Great Falls, MT	52 333	46.2	87.1	21.5	−2.9	22.1	27.2	7.2	25.4	17.1
3080	Green Bay, WI	144 172	48.6	86.3	22.5	−1.9	23.3	7.7	11.1	21.3	7.3
3120	Greensboro—Winston-Salem—High Point, NC	833 142	50.9	78.6	22.9	−1.5	24.8	16.7	13.4	35.6	8.7
3150	Greenville, NC	79 040	45.3	79.9	26.4	2.0	34.0	11.0	30.6	53.7	13.6
3160	Greenville-Spartanburg-Anderson, SC	630 167	54.0	75.4	20.7	−3.7	22.9	9.1	7.9	40.0	14.6
3240	Harrisburg-Lebanon-Carlisle, PA	427 256	56.3	83.1	22.6	−1.8	23.4	12.8	22.2	41.4	8.8

[1]MSA = Metropolitan Statistical Area. CMSA = Consolidated MSA. PMSA = Primary MSA. NECMA = New England County Metropolitan Area. See the Appendix A for explanation of these concepts. See Appendix B for list of metropolitan areas identified by type, with component counties.
[2]Hispanic or Latino persons may be of any race.

Table B-4. Metropolitan Areas — Education, Labor Force, and Income

Area name	School enrollment			Population 16 to 19 years				Employment status, 2000			Work status in 1999 of the population 16 years and over (percent)		
											Worked in 1999		
	Grades kindergarten through 12	College or graduate school	Percent private	Number	Percent in armed forces	Percent high school graduates	Percent not enrolled, not grads, not in armed forces, not employed	Total population 16 years and over	Percent in labor force	Unemployment rate	Full-time	Part-time	Did not work in 1999
	11	12	13	14	15	16	17	18	19	20	21	22	23
Columbia, SC	100 794	41 708	10.3	34 272	7.8	16.0	5.0	418 095	68.4	5.3	59.3	14.5	26.2
Columbus, GA-AL	54 487	13 540	9.0	17 574	15.3	23.5	6.3	209 377	63.9	5.7	55.4	12.5	32.1
Columbus, OH	284 017	117 268	15.0	84 817	0.0	10.5	4.5	1 187 462	69.6	4.0	59.7	16.2	24.2
Corpus Christi, TX	83 030	20 984	6.2	24 981	1.1	11.5	7.4	283 754	61.4	7.3	53.2	13.5	33.3
Corvallis, OR	12 857	16 823	5.5	6 792	0.1	5.5	0.7	63 608	63.6	4.9	51.0	24.6	24.4
Cumberland, MD-WV	16 480	6 710	6.2	6 159	0.0	12.9	3.8	83 067	54.8	8.0	45.4	14.7	39.9
Dallas-Fort Worth, TX	1 045 851	276 104	11.9	294 763	0.1	10.9	7.3	3 912 267	69.2	4.8	63.2	12.0	24.9
Dallas, TX	700 578	188 298	11.7	197 164	0.0	10.7	7.6	2 636 042	69.4	4.9	63.7	11.7	24.6
Fort Worth-Arlington, TX	345 273	87 806	12.4	97 599	0.1	11.4	6.8	1 276 225	68.7	4.5	62.0	12.6	25.4
Danville, VA	19 674	3 600	9.8	5 677	0.0	11.1	5.7	87 643	60.3	6.7	53.4	11.5	35.2
Davenport-Moline-Rock Island, IA-IL	67 118	21 566	15.8	20 846	0.0	11.2	4.2	279 470	66.7	5.5	54.9	17.3	27.8
Dayton-Springfield, OH	175 126	66 359	18.6	55 944	0.3	10.1	5.2	741 911	64.9	5.1	54.8	16.1	29.1
Daytona Beach, FL	75 075	28 146	18.3	24 009	0.1	10.1	5.9	406 404	54.5	6.1	45.7	13.4	40.0
Decatur, AL	27 270	4 922	7.3	7 880	0.1	10.4	8.9	113 007	61.4	5.6	54.9	11.3	33.8
Decatur, IL	20 713	6 495	19.0	6 574	0.0	11.9	7.5	89 625	63.3	7.1	52.7	15.6	31.7
Denver-Boulder-Greeley, CO	478 405	172 487	12.8	140 405	0.1	11.7	6.4	1 991 053	71.7	4.1	62.5	15.6	21.9
Boulder-Longmont, CO	48 758	35 657	10.9	18 302	0.0	8.2	3.1	231 690	73.4	4.4	59.2	21.2	19.6
Denver, CO	392 521	121 299	13.8	109 190	0.1	12.6	7.0	1 624 055	71.8	3.9	63.2	14.6	22.1
Greeley, CO	37 126	15 531	6.9	12 913	0.0	9.0	6.2	135 308	68.6	5.4	59.0	17.5	23.6
Des Moines, IA	84 434	24 853	16.9	24 294	0.0	12.1	3.7	350 067	73.3	4.4	62.7	15.7	21.5
Detroit-Ann Arbor-Flint, MI	1 084 427	343 053	12.5	289 589	0.0	9.5	5.1	4 171 007	64.6	5.8	54.7	15.3	29.9
Ann Arbor, MI	105 645	71 732	9.4	38 423	0.0	6.6	2.7	452 375	69.1	3.8	57.3	19.8	22.9
Detroit, MI	888 731	249 071	13.2	226 808	0.0	9.9	5.3	3 389 301	64.2	5.9	54.6	14.7	30.7
Flint, MI	90 051	22 250	10.4	24 358	0.0	10.6	6.8	329 331	63.1	7.1	52.6	15.9	31.5
Dothan, AL	26 743	5 466	10.9	7 607	2.2	11.7	5.6	105 934	62.3	5.7	55.3	11.6	33.0
Dover, DE	25 303	8 588	11.5	7 812	1.3	11.1	5.1	95 895	67.1	5.0	50.0	14.2	27.6
Dubuque, IA	17 029	5 714	37.7	5 357	0.1	8.3	1.2	66 921	69.0	1.6	61.7	19.6	26.7
Duluth-Superior, MN-WI	43 280	19 462	9.8	16 010	0.2	8.6	2.6	195 896	63.1	6.8	48.1	21.0	30.9
Eau Claire, WI	27 891	14 137	11.1	10 732	0.0	9.0	2.2	116 547	69.5	4.7	54.4	21.9	23.7
El Paso, TX	167 423	46 798	7.3	45 857	1.3	9.9	6.6	486 398	56.5	9.2	50.4	12.6	37.0
Elkhart-Goshen, IN	36 607	5 271	12.1	10 334	0.1	12.1	7.8	135 426	71.3	3.6	61.8	15.2	23.0
Elmira, NY	17 140	4 239	18.3	5 057	0.0	10.2	7.3	71 569	59.5	7.8	50.7	15.5	33.9
Enid, OK	10 951	2 079	8.6	3 212	0.0	8.3	6.4	45 196	63.3	4.9	54.5	14.1	31.4
Erie, PA	53 064	18 832	23.9	18 122	0.0	8.2	3.5	218 948	62.8	5.8	51.3	17.2	31.5
Eugene-Springfield, OR	54 942	30 647	7.1	19 632	0.0	12.9	3.6	258 327	64.3	6.4	50.1	20.5	29.4
Evansville-Henderson, IN-KY	53 492	17 316	16.6	17 764	0.0	10.4	5.7	232 459	66.3	5.1	56.1	15.8	28.1
Fargo-Moorhead, ND-MN	30 754	21 449	10.6	12 435	0.0	7.3	2.1	137 282	73.5	4.3	59.2	21.5	19.3
Fayetteville, NC	61 841	20 830	11.2	18 240	13.2	21.5	4.6	226 671	69.4	6.6	61.1	12.9	25.9
Fayetteville-Springdale-Rogers, AR	56 693	22 080	8.6	19 064	0.0	12.6	4.5	239 465	66.1	5.7	57.4	14.2	28.3
Flagstaff, AZ-UT	26 588	15 085	5.5	8 617	0.0	8.0	6.5	91 518	68.3	6.9	56.2	19.1	24.7
Florence, AL	24 981	7 522	7.8	7 806	0.0	8.1	5.9	113 462	57.9	5.4	49.3	13.7	37.0
Florence, SC	25 584	6 166	11.0	7 754	0.1	10.5	6.1	97 016	62.4	7.9	53.7	12.7	33.6
Fort Collins-Loveland, CO	44 334	31 384	8.2	17 029	0.1	9.2	2.9	198 990	71.9	4.2	57.8	21.8	20.5
Fort Myers-Cape Coral, FL	62 918	12 539	12.7	17 053	0.4	14.5	7.2	363 694	53.3	3.7	46.5	11.9	41.6
Fort Pierce-Port St. Lucie, FL	51 617	11 432	12.1	13 567	0.0	8.5	9.3	259 731	52.2	4.8	44.4	12.3	43.3
Fort Smith, AR-OK	40 358	7 014	6.9	11 805	0.2	13.1	6.3	158 002	61.8	5.3	54.5	11.9	33.6
Fort Walton Beach, FL	31 577	9 816	7.8	9 554	5.7	17.8	3.0	133 583	65.1	4.1	56.3	13.9	29.8
Fort Wayne, IN	100 510	24 512	19.0	29 326	0.1	10.9	4.0	378 361	70.2	4.2	58.6	16.8	24.6
Fresno, CA	225 955	60 658	6.0	62 332	0.0	9.4	7.2	662 234	59.0	12.0	50.0	14.8	35.2
Gadsden, AL	17 868	4 130	8.9	5 786	0.0	10.1	10.5	81 735	56.6	6.0	49.4	11.8	38.8
Gainesville, FL	32 792	53 371	6.4	19 335	0.0	5.6	1.9	179 084	63.3	7.0	49.1	23.2	27.7
Glens Falls, NY	23 936	4 694	7.9	6 616	0.2	7.1	8.0	97 666	62.1	5.1	54.3	15.1	30.6
Goldsboro, NC	22 655	5 211	10.7	6 104	1.8	10.8	6.9	86 989	61.8	5.9	56.0	12.5	31.5
Grand Forks, ND-MN	18 109	13 051	5.1	7 603	1.6	8.8	2.0	76 520	68.6	4.6	55.5	22.6	21.8
Grand Junction, CO	21 719	5 836	8.8	7 200	0.0	13.8	6.9	90 939	64.2	5.7	51.4	18.1	30.5
Grand Rapids-Muskegon-Holland, MI	231 146	63 097	17.8	67 438	0.0	9.8	4.4	814 247	69.6	4.4	56.5	18.7	24.8
Great Falls, MT	15 730	3 154	11.4	4 335	7.0	21.6	3.9	61 744	65.0	5.8	53.6	16.6	29.8
Green Bay, WI	43 878	13 385	18.4	13 524	0.1	10.3	4.4	174 305	72.0	3.8	60.9	17.9	21.2
Greensboro—Winston-Salem—High Point, NC	221 474	70 580	13.7	65 400	0.0	9.5	5.6	981 997	67.5	4.7	59.9	13.3	26.9
Greenville, NC	23 462	20 154	6.7	10 156	0.1	6.0	4.2	105 514	65.8	6.8	54.5	18.0	27.5
Greenville-Spartanburg-Anderson, SC	174 085	55 710	14.6	54 075	0.0	10.3	6.5	751 726	64.9	5.0	56.9	13.4	29.7
Harrisburg-Lebanon-Carlisle, PA	111 793	30 453	16.8	34 191	0.1	9.5	4.0	498 790	65.2	3.9	57.1	14.4	28.5

Table B-4. Metropolitan Areas — Education, Labor Force, and Income

Area name	Full-year full-time employed (percent)								Children under 18 years in families (percent, except where noted)						Total employed by class of worker (percent)			
											With two parents								
	Total	Men	Women	Non-Hispanic White	Black or African American	American Indian and Alaska Native	Asian, Hawaiian, and Pacific Islander	Hispanic or Latino[1]	Number	Both in labor force	Father only in labor force	With one parent who is in labor force	+/– U.S. percent of children with no stay-at-home parent	+/– U.S. percent two-income couples	Private	Government	Self-employed	Unpaid family worker
	24	25	26	27	28	29	30	31	32	33	34	35	36	37	38	39	40	41
Columbia, SC	45.1	53.9	37.2	47.3	41.2	48.3	36.3	42.3	124 587	44.0	18.5	25.8	5.2	5.3	68.7	22.8	8.3	0.2
Columbus, GA-AL	40.6	49.6	32.1	43.7	36.5	42.2	39.3	37.5	67 953	36.7	18.8	28.6	0.7	-0.3	73.4	18.4	7.8	0.3
Columbus, OH	46.7	55.7	38.3	48.0	41.0	38.6	40.6	43.9	372 984	46.2	20.3	23.3	4.8	7.1	77.4	14.8	7.6	0.2
Corpus Christi, TX	37.3	47.3	28.0	40.9	33.1	38.3	41.3	34.7	101 786	36.1	22.9	23.6	-4.9	-5.4	71.1	18.3	10.1	0.4
Corvallis, OR	31.9	41.7	22.4	32.9	29.5	24.6	21.7	27.2	16 053	50.6	25.5	15.7	1.7	2.3	64.1	25.4	10.4	0.2
Cumberland, MD-WV	32.1	40.1	24.4	33.3	12.5	21.4	40.9	18.2	20 380	46.5	22.4	19.1	1.0	-6.7	72.3	20.6	6.8	0.3
Dallas-Fort Worth, TX	47.2	57.3	37.5	50.2	43.6	45.6	44.9	40.4	1 370 189	40.9	25.3	20.5	-3.2	2.6	80.3	10.4	9.0	0.3
Dallas, TX	47.5	57.2	38.0	51.0	43.7	45.9	45.9	40.2	921 523	40.1	25.5	20.6	-3.8	2.5	80.6	10.1	9.1	0.3
Fort Worth-Arlington, TX	46.8	57.4	36.5	48.8	43.4	45.0	42.3	41.1	448 666	42.4	25.0	20.3	-1.8	2.7	79.9	11.2	8.7	0.2
Danville, VA	40.1	50.0	31.5	41.8	36.0	43.5	43.1	41.8	23 526	41.9	14.8	29.2	6.5	-0.9	79.1	12.2	8.4	0.2
Davenport-Moline-Rock Island, IA-IL	41.6	50.7	33.2	42.4	31.7	35.6	39.9	39.8	85 798	50.4	17.2	23.5	9.3	3.8	79.8	11.8	8.1	0.3
Dayton-Springfield, OH	42.2	52.1	33.2	43.3	36.0	40.3	41.3	41.5	222 415	44.7	19.3	25.2	5.3	1.5	78.6	14.1	7.1	0.2
Daytona Beach, FL	34.0	41.2	27.4	34.3	30.5	38.8	31.2	34.5	91 258	41.2	20.5	24.8	1.5	-11.8	74.1	13.4	12.2	0.3
Decatur, AL	41.2	53.5	29.7	40.1	36.8	41.1	39.3	34.3	35 430	44.2	25.7	18.7	-1.7	-4.0	77.9	12.2	9.7	0.3
Decatur, IL	40.0	50.0	31.1	41.1	32.7	33.7	39.0	38.4	26 612	42.5	17.8	28.1	5.9	-0.4	81.3	11.1	7.4	0.3
Denver-Boulder-Greeley, CO	47.2	56.8	37.6	49.2	44.0	41.2	43.4	39.7	626 898	46.4	22.8	19.9	1.7	7.1	76.2	12.8	10.7	0.3
Boulder-Longmont, CO	43.1	53.4	32.7	43.9	43.0	31.3	41.9	38.3	63 936	48.5	26.2	18.1	2.0	7.5	72.0	15.0	12.8	0.3
Denver, CO	48.2	57.6	38.9	50.5	44.1	42.3	44.0	40.2	514 692	45.9	22.6	20.4	1.6	7.2	77.1	12.3	10.3	0.2
Greeley, CO	41.9	52.7	31.3	43.9	40.5	40.0	29.8	36.3	48 270	49.7	21.3	16.9	2.0	5.7	72.4	15.2	12.0	0.4
Des Moines, IA	50.4	59.0	42.6	51.4	38.8	40.3	46.5	41.9	113 313	55.7	17.0	19.0	10.1	12.6	79.0	12.9	7.9	0.2
Detroit-Ann Arbor-Flint, MI	41.0	51.9	30.9	43.3	33.3	38.8	40.8	35.7	1 355 917	40.1	23.5	23.9	-0.6	-0.9	81.5	10.6	7.6	0.2
Ann Arbor, MI	42.7	53.4	32.2	44.1	36.3	40.8	30.1	35.9	136 041	50.5	25.1	17.1	3.0	6.0	76.3	14.6	8.8	0.3
Detroit, MI	41.1	52.2	30.9	43.5	33.4	39.1	43.2	35.7	1 107 877	39.0	23.8	24.0	-1.5	-1.6	82.2	10.1	7.5	0.2
Flint, MI	37.9	47.6	29.3	40.0	29.9	35.2	45.1	34.8	111 999	37.8	18.8	30.4	3.5	-3.5	82.5	9.7	7.6	0.3
Dothan, AL	42.9	54.7	32.3	45.0	36.0	44.0	41.3	35.9	34 088	40.2	21.5	23.3	-1.1	-1.7	75.1	15.0	9.6	0.3
Dover, DE	44.8	54.9	35.8	46.4	39.8	42.7	39.9	44.6	32 338	44.0	19.1	26.2	5.6	3.7	68.3	22.4	9.0	0.3
Dubuque, IA	42.9	53.3	33.4	43.2	34.2	22.7	31.2	33.5	22 167	62.2	14.9	15.0	12.6	10.4	82.1	8.4	9.1	0.4
Duluth-Superior, MN-WI	35.0	44.3	26.3	35.2	26.4	30.2	26.7	32.9	52 406	51.8	17.0	22.1	9.3	1.8	74.9	16.2	8.6	0.3
Eau Claire, WI	40.8	50.6	31.7	41.1	22.6	30.6	33.7	38.7	34 991	58.5	17.0	16.8	10.8	8.9	76.5	13.4	9.7	0.3
El Paso, TX	33.2	43.4	24.1	39.4	39.8	30.6	37.2	31.2	202 841	29.9	27.4	21.1	-13.6	-14.1	71.4	20.0	8.2	0.3
Elkhart-Goshen, IN	46.9	59.4	34.9	47.7	41.9	32.8	39.1	43.2	49 708	47.5	23.2	20.9	3.8	7.1	84.7	6.6	8.5	0.2
Elmira, NY	37.7	45.6	30.1	39.3	20.8	16.1	35.4	20.6	20 884	45.2	16.2	27.3	8.0	0.5	74.4	18.0	7.3	0.3
Enid, OK	40.9	53.0	30.0	41.2	40.4	39.8	40.1	38.0	13 469	45.6	24.7	20.6	1.7	-0.3	70.8	14.8	13.6	0.7
Erie, PA	38.9	49.0	29.6	39.6	32.0	27.4	34.7	25.6	67 225	46.1	20.4	23.1	4.7	0.8	82.4	10.0	7.2	0.3
Eugene-Springfield, OR	34.3	43.6	25.5	34.7	30.7	33.7	26.5	33.7	69 351	45.5	21.2	23.1	4.0	0.2	70.2	16.1	13.3	0.5
Evansville-Henderson, IN-KY	43.6	54.2	34.1	44.1	35.0	56.7	44.4	41.3	69 035	51.6	18.3	20.5	7.4	5.2	81.8	9.9	8.0	0.3
Fargo-Moorhead, ND-MN	43.4	52.0	35.0	44.0	30.9	30.1	29.6	36.3	40 483	60.0	14.9	18.7	14.1	14.1	77.0	13.9	9.0	0.2
Fayetteville, NC	45.5	57.9	32.8	48.9	40.4	45.7	37.8	46.1	78 687	38.8	23.1	24.9	-0.9	0.8	66.8	24.1	8.9	0.2
Fayetteville-Springdale-Rogers, AR	42.2	51.6	33.1	42.4	40.4	44.3	40.3	40.5	76 475	46.7	24.3	17.8	-0.1	0.7	77.8	11.3	10.6	0.3
Flagstaff, AZ-UT	36.4	44.1	28.9	39.8	40.0	25.6	46.5	38.1	32 396	42.6	17.6	21.8	-0.1	3.1	61.2	27.7	10.7	0.4
Florence, AL	36.5	48.3	25.9	37.2	31.0	32.0	33.4	39.4	31 827	40.9	26.4	19.0	-4.7	-8.2	74.3	15.9	9.4	0.3
Florence, SC	40.4	50.0	32.4	44.8	33.2	28.4	44.2	39.8	30 345	38.6	16.1	27.5	1.6	0.4	75.3	15.6	8.9	0.2
Fort Collins-Loveland, CO	41.8	53.1	30.7	42.2	40.3	41.7	32.6	39.4	57 552	52.2	25.1	16.1	3.7	7.8	70.7	16.1	12.7	0.4
Fort Myers-Cape Coral, FL	34.9	41.9	28.4	34.1	38.3	38.9	45.7	40.3	80 672	44.2	18.8	26.0	5.5	-12.9	75.5	11.5	12.7	0.3
Fort Pierce-Port St. Lucie, FL	33.2	40.6	26.3	33.0	30.4	38.8	40.8	38.3	61 864	41.1	20.5	23.5	0.0	-13.4	74.5	12.4	12.7	0.3
Fort Smith, AR-OK	40.4	50.7	30.7	40.9	36.5	36.6	42.5	37.8	52 403	44.0	20.9	20.1	-0.5	-2.5	78.2	11.3	10.1	0.4
Fort Walton Beach, FL	43.8	55.3	32.0	44.0	44.9	49.4	39.3	41.9	39 540	43.8	26.4	20.3	-0.5	-2.4	69.7	20.0	10.2	0.2
Fort Wayne, IN	46.1	58.4	34.5	46.9	38.0	48.2	41.8	43.7	133 407	49.0	22.5	20.5	4.9	7.0	83.4	8.1	8.2	0.2
Fresno, CA	29.7	37.2	22.6	35.8	24.7	24.6	22.5	24.5	270 898	34.0	22.7	20.9	-9.7	-8.5	70.0	19.4	10.1	0.5
Gadsden, AL	35.7	46.6	26.2	36.7	30.5	31.6	42.9	24.9	22 854	37.9	23.7	22.2	-4.5	-8.0	77.6	12.7	9.4	0.3
Gainesville, FL	34.0	40.3	28.1	36.0	30.9	44.8	25.8	24.2	40 825	39.8	19.7	26.8	2.1	3.3	59.6	31.6	8.5	0.3
Glens Falls, NY	39.4	48.7	30.4	40.1	23.0	29.9	37.5	23.0	28 884	49.5	18.8	22.8	7.7	0.7	70.5	17.2	11.8	0.4
Goldsboro, NC	41.9	51.8	32.5	45.6	34.8	31.1	42.4	42.4	27 438	41.4	18.4	25.0	1.8	-0.3	69.1	21.4	8.9	0.5
Grand Forks, ND-MN	38.7	47.9	29.5	39.1	39.8	32.8	26.8	31.5	23 213	58.5	15.8	17.6	11.6	9.8	69.5	20.1	10.0	0.3
Grand Junction, CO	36.7	45.5	28.4	36.8	37.6	40.0	35.5	35.3	27 282	48.1	21.1	21.5	5.0	0.4	71.8	14.0	13.4	0.8
Grand Rapids-Muskegon-Holland, MI	43.7	56.1	32.1	44.7	35.5	38.1	45.0	39.9	294 436	50.2	21.9	19.3	5.0	6.6	83.7	8.0	8.1	0.2
Great Falls, MT	39.0	49.0	29.4	39.6	44.9	22.8	32.8	41.7	20 018	49.9	19.0	22.9	8.2	2.3	69.6	17.1	12.8	0.5
Green Bay, WI	47.7	58.0	37.6	48.5	34.1	43.7	34.6	37.9	57 050	58.3	16.0	18.2	11.9	11.4	82.7	9.8	7.3	0.2
Greensboro—Winston-Salem—High Point, NC	45.6	55.2	36.9	46.7	42.5	45.7	42.5	41.1	283 565	47.0	18.5	23.6	6.1	5.0	79.7	11.3	8.8	0.2
Greenville, NC	39.2	48.6	31.0	42.2	33.4	47.0	38.3	38.1	29 261	38.7	18.8	28.0	2.2	3.6	71.9	19.9	8.0	0.2
Greenville-Spartanburg-Anderson, SC	43.1	53.8	33.3	44.1	39.2	43.1	40.5	39.2	221 453	43.7	22.1	22.7	1.8	1.2	80.7	10.7	8.4	0.2
Harrisburg-Lebanon-Carlisle, PA	45.3	55.4	36.0	46.0	40.2	46.0	46.4	35.3	140 987	47.8	21.7	21.7	4.8	3.8	74.9	17.0	7.8	0.3

[1] Hispanic or Latino persons may be of any race.

Table B-4. Metropolitan Areas — **Education, Labor Force, and Income**

Area name	Percent who worked at home	Percent of the population 5 years and over with a disability	Veterans as a percent of the population 18 years and over	Occupation for employed population 16 years and over (percent)						Industry for employed population 16 years and over (percent)					
				Management, professional, and related occupations	Service occupations	Sales and office occupations	Farming, fishing, and forestry occupations	Construction, extraction, and maintenance occupations	Production, transportation and material moving occupations	Agriculture, forestry, fishing, and mining	Construction and manufacturing	Wholesale and retail trade	Transportation and warehousing, and utilities	Service industries	Public administration
	42	43	44	45	46	47	48	49	50	51	52	53	54	55	56
Columbia, SC	2.5	18.9	14.7	37.3	14.1	28.0	0.3	9.1	11.2	0.6	16.8	14.6	5.0	54.2	8.9
Columbus, GA-AL	1.9	23.2	17.1	29.4	16.0	26.5	0.4	10.1	17.5	0.7	22.9	13.7	3.8	52.9	6.0
Columbus, OH	3.0	16.7	12.6	36.4	13.7	29.2	0.2	7.4	13.0	0.5	16.9	17.1	5.2	54.4	5.8
Corpus Christi, TX	2.4	21.2	14.1	29.6	17.7	27.2	0.5	12.8	12.2	2.7	16.4	15.2	4.8	54.4	6.5
Corvallis, OR	4.4	12.9	11.5	46.9	14.8	20.7	1.7	6.3	9.7	3.7	21.1	11.1	2.0	58.6	3.4
Cumberland, MD-WV	1.6	21.2	16.4	25.7	18.7	25.0	0.4	11.2	19.0	1.0	21.1	14.6	7.0	49.8	6.6
Dallas-Fort Worth, TX	3.0	17.7	11.0	36.0	12.4	28.9	0.2	10.1	12.4	0.7	20.9	16.6	6.4	52.4	2.9
Dallas, TX	3.1	17.6	10.2	37.1	12.3	28.7	0.2	9.9	11.8	0.7	20.5	16.5	5.5	54.2	2.7
Fort Worth-Arlington, TX	2.7	17.9	12.7	33.6	12.8	29.3	0.1	10.3	13.8	0.7	21.9	17.0	8.3	48.7	3.5
Danville, VA	2.0	24.4	13.7	21.5	14.1	23.9	0.7	11.2	28.7	1.5	37.5	15.6	3.6	38.2	3.6
Davenport-Moline-Rock Island, IA-IL	2.9	16.7	14.4	29.4	16.1	27.3	0.4	8.7	18.1	1.4	24.0	16.6	5.7	47.9	4.5
Dayton-Springfield, OH	2.3	18.8	15.2	32.8	14.6	26.3	0.2	7.9	18.1	0.5	24.6	15.2	4.8	49.0	5.9
Daytona Beach, FL	3.0	23.4	19.2	28.9	18.2	28.7	0.8	11.7	11.7	1.1	17.7	17.0	4.4	54.8	4.9
Decatur, AL	1.9	22.9	12.4	25.1	13.0	22.9	0.7	12.8	25.5	1.7	37.7	14.6	4.5	37.9	3.6
Decatur, IL	2.5	19.2	15.0	28.4	15.7	26.2	0.4	9.7	19.6	1.9	25.4	15.2	7.8	46.0	3.6
Denver-Boulder-Greeley, CO	4.7	15.9	12.5	39.4	12.5	28.0	0.3	9.6	10.1	1.0	17.6	15.4	5.1	56.5	4.3
Boulder-Longmont, CO	6.4	11.8	10.0	50.2	12.1	23.7	0.2	6.3	7.6	0.7	20.0	13.8	2.7	59.6	3.2
Denver, CO	4.5	16.3	13.0	38.6	12.4	28.9	0.1	9.9	10.1	0.8	16.8	15.6	5.5	56.9	4.5
Greeley, CO	4.2	17.9	11.7	29.5	14.6	25.2	2.0	12.8	15.9	5.1	24.5	15.5	4.9	46.0	4.0
Des Moines, IA	3.3	15.9	12.3	35.6	13.6	30.6	0.3	8.1	11.7	1.0	15.3	16.3	5.2	57.3	4.9
Detroit-Ann Arbor-Flint, MI	2.3	18.9	11.7	33.8	14.1	26.2	0.2	8.8	16.9	0.3	28.5	14.8	4.4	48.9	3.2
Ann Arbor, MI	3.4	14.2	10.3	41.6	13.2	23.8	0.3	7.9	13.2	0.8	25.4	13.5	3.3	54.3	2.8
Detroit, MI	2.1	19.3	11.7	33.3	14.0	26.7	0.1	8.8	17.1	0.2	28.7	14.9	4.6	48.2	3.3
Flint, MI	2.0	20.6	13.2	27.0	16.5	24.3	0.1	10.6	21.4	0.3	30.3	15.7	3.5	47.5	2.7
Dothan, AL	1.7	22.7	16.5	27.7	15.7	26.5	0.6	12.1	17.3	1.4	21.2	18.2	9.0	45.0	5.1
Dover, DE	3.1	19.2	18.0	28.5	17.0	26.0	0.7	11.6	15.3	1.6	20.9	15.5	5.3	45.7	10.8
Dubuque, IA	4.1	16.0	13.2	29.7	15.7	26.5	0.8	7.6	19.7	3.1	24.2	17.0	4.0	49.7	1.0
Duluth-Superior, MN-WI	3.3	18.1	15.2	29.8	18.2	26.5	0.5	11.6	13.4	4.9	14.2	16.1	6.9	53.3	4.6
Eau Claire, WI	4.3	15.8	13.1	29.7	16.0	26.6	1.0	8.6	18.1	3.3	22.6	19.1	4.0	48.0	3.0
El Paso, TX	2.1	20.3	11.4	29.1	16.9	28.1	0.4	8.7	16.8	0.6	19.8	15.7	6.8	51.1	6.0
Elkhart-Goshen, IN	3.3	18.6	11.1	23.8	11.0	23.4	0.4	8.7	32.7	1.4	47.8	13.1	3.1	33.0	1.7
Elmira, NY	2.3	21.1	15.6	32.0	19.2	25.2	0.3	7.4	15.9	0.6	24.0	15.6	4.2	48.8	6.7
Enid, OK	3.0	21.6	15.3	27.2	19.1	25.6	0.9	12.3	14.8	6.4	18.2	16.7	5.8	47.4	5.5
Erie, PA	2.3	17.1	13.9	29.2	16.3	25.6	0.5	7.8	20.5	1.0	28.5	14.7	3.5	49.4	2.9
Eugene-Springfield, OR	5.1	19.0	15.1	31.9	15.7	26.3	1.3	9.3	15.5	2.3	20.8	17.3	4.2	52.0	3.3
Evansville-Henderson, IN-KY	2.3	20.2	13.6	28.3	14.5	27.4	0.3	10.3	19.1	1.4	26.3	16.3	5.7	47.4	2.7
Fargo-Moorhead, ND-MN	3.5	14.9	11.4	33.0	15.4	30.0	0.6	8.6	12.5	2.2	15.3	19.3	4.7	55.6	2.9
Fayetteville, NC	2.2	22.0	19.5	28.8	16.7	27.0	0.4	10.5	16.6	0.7	19.3	17.1	5.3	50.4	7.1
Fayetteville-Springdale-Rogers, AR	3.4	18.9	13.8	30.8	13.3	26.7	1.0	9.6	18.6	2.7	25.8	20.9	5.6	42.7	2.3
Flagstaff, AZ-UT	4.1	16.3	12.0	34.5	19.1	25.6	0.5	10.2	10.0	1.9	12.9	14.7	5.5	58.1	6.8
Florence, AL	1.7	24.1	13.1	25.4	13.9	25.9	0.6	12.1	22.1	1.5	29.6	17.4	6.6	41.3	3.6
Florence, SC	1.6	23.8	12.1	30.2	14.9	24.8	0.6	11.0	18.4	1.3	24.6	16.1	4.7	49.1	4.3
Fort Collins-Loveland, CO	5.1	13.3	12.1	39.6	13.9	24.8	0.5	9.6	11.5	1.5	23.8	15.4	3.4	52.5	3.4
Fort Myers-Cape Coral, FL	3.5	22.0	19.2	28.1	18.5	29.7	0.8	13.5	9.3	1.1	17.1	19.1	4.0	54.4	4.1
Fort Pierce-Port St. Lucie, FL	3.5	23.5	18.8	28.3	18.1	28.2	2.1	12.7	10.7	2.5	17.2	18.6	5.1	51.4	5.2
Fort Smith, AR-OK	2.1	23.8	14.7	25.0	14.4	24.3	0.7	10.2	25.4	2.0	31.3	15.6	5.4	42.6	3.2
Fort Walton Beach, FL	2.1	20.1	25.0	32.0	19.0	26.9	0.5	12.3	9.2	0.7	13.8	15.6	4.0	55.0	10.9
Fort Wayne, IN	2.8	16.7	12.3	28.9	13.0	25.6	0.3	9.2	23.0	1.2	32.3	16.0	4.5	43.8	2.2
Fresno, CA	3.2	21.5	10.4	28.9	16.2	25.7	6.9	8.7	13.5	9.1	14.3	16.0	4.6	49.4	6.7
Gadsden, AL	1.9	25.6	14.1	25.3	13.7	25.0	0.7	12.2	23.2	1.1	28.8	16.9	5.1	43.6	4.5
Gainesville, FL	3.2	16.1	11.2	44.0	16.2	26.3	0.6	6.2	6.7	1.1	9.1	12.7	2.8	68.8	5.5
Glens Falls, NY	3.0	16.2	16.6	28.8	17.4	25.9	1.1	10.2	16.6	2.9	22.4	15.9	3.6	48.6	6.5
Goldsboro, NC	1.9	23.9	16.0	28.1	15.1	24.3	2.1	11.6	18.8	3.9	24.2	18.2	4.3	43.1	6.3
Grand Forks, ND-MN	3.9	15.4	13.1	31.6	19.2	25.0	1.2	10.7	12.2	4.0	14.4	16.1	5.1	55.9	4.4
Grand Junction, CO	5.3	21.1	17.1	29.3	17.2	27.9	0.9	11.8	12.9	3.0	17.6	17.2	5.5	52.2	4.4
Grand Rapids-Muskegon-Holland, MI	3.1	16.6	11.6	29.6	13.5	25.6	0.7	8.3	22.3	1.1	32.7	17.3	3.4	43.3	2.2
Great Falls, MT	3.8	19.7	19.6	30.5	18.4	29.7	1.0	10.0	10.4	3.0	11.1	17.9	5.6	55.5	7.0
Green Bay, WI	2.5	14.9	12.3	30.6	12.6	28.5	0.5	9.2	18.7	1.2	27.3	16.6	6.2	45.8	2.9
Greensboro—Winston-Salem—High Point, NC	2.4	20.0	12.3	30.6	12.4	26.2	0.3	10.0	20.6	0.7	30.2	15.0	5.1	46.2	2.8
Greenville, NC	2.1	19.6	10.2	33.7	15.5	26.1	0.8	9.4	14.5	1.7	22.3	15.5	3.3	53.3	3.9
Greenville-Spartanburg-Anderson, SC	2.1	21.3	13.0	29.0	13.2	25.0	0.3	11.1	21.4	0.5	33.3	15.8	4.3	43.7	2.4
Harrisburg-Lebanon-Carlisle, PA	3.1	16.7	14.6	32.2	14.1	28.1	0.6	8.5	16.5	1.5	18.7	15.4	6.6	48.3	9.5

Area name	Median house-hold income	Median family income — All families	Median family income — Married-couple (Families with children)	Median family income — Male house-holder (Families with children)	Median family income — Female house-holder (Families with children)	Median nonfamily house-hold income	Median income for full-year, full-time workers — Men	Median income for full-year, full-time workers — Women	Per capita income	With earnings	With interest, dividend, or rental income	With Social Security income	With public assis-tance income	With retire-ment income	House-holds with income over $100,000 (percent)	+/- U.S. percent for income over $100,000	House-holds with income below poverty (percent)	Families with children with income below poverty (percent)
	57	58	59	60	61	62	63	64	65	66	67	68	69	70	71	72	73	74
Columbia, SC	41 677	50 956	61 729	27 371	20 879	26 173	36 514	26 783	20 902	84.9	30.5	21.3	1.9	16.4	10.4	-1.9	11.4	12.3
Columbus, GA-AL	34 512	41 106	50 140	27 894	17 327	20 756	31 012	24 539	17 559	79.4	23.9	26.3	3.9	19.3	7.3	-5.0	15.5	18.1
Columbus, OH	44 782	55 039	66 644	30 810	22 359	28 438	40 058	30 320	23 020	84.6	35.2	20.2	2.8	15.7	12.3	0.0	10.1	10.6
Corpus Christi, TX	35 773	40 856	48 087	24 122	16 270	21 720	32 283	22 888	16 752	81.4	25.7	24.8	4.6	15.1	7.6	-4.7	16.8	20.1
Corvallis, OR	41 897	56 319	64 005	32 313	20 863	22 685	44 708	30 485	21 868	84.3	50.4	20.1	2.0	15.1	12.5	0.2	14.6	9.9
Cumberland, MD-WV	30 916	39 242	46 210	23 651	14 993	15 701	32 557	21 550	16 409	69.8	34.4	36.1	2.7	22.5	4.0	-8.3	15.2	17.1
Dallas-Fort Worth, TX	47 418	55 016	62 928	31 587	24 644	31 605	40 073	30 487	23 616	88.0	30.8	17.0	2.1	11.1	15.6	3.3	9.7	11.4
Dallas, TX	48 364	55 854	64 154	31 348	25 177	32 567	40 289	31 047	24 342	88.6	30.9	16.2	2.0	10.3	16.8	4.5	9.7	11.6
Fort Worth-Arlington, TX	45 962	53 230	61 198	32 010	23 438	29 337	39 470	29 013	22 115	86.9	30.6	18.7	2.1	12.8	13.3	1.0	9.5	10.9
Danville, VA	31 201	39 183	49 250	26 204	15 622	17 063	30 756	21 961	17 061	75.3	28.0	33.4	3.9	18.5	4.5	-7.8	15.9	19.1
Davenport-Moline-Rock Island, IA-IL	40 621	50 055	59 305	31 522	17 924	23 443	38 350	25 429	20 464	79.2	41.8	27.2	3.1	20.4	8.3	-4.0	9.9	12.3
Dayton-Springfield, OH	41 550	50 965	61 900	30 966	20 251	25 054	40 334	27 670	21 598	79.6	35.7	26.1	2.8	22.3	10.0	-2.3	10.3	11.9
Daytona Beach, FL	35 722	42 127	51 415	25 971	18 948	22 287	31 562	23 810	19 888	68.4	39.1	40.9	2.1	27.0	7.3	-5.0	10.7	13.9
Decatur, AL	36 299	43 874	50 942	31 530	16 225	17 539	35 768	22 120	18 577	79.0	28.2	26.3	1.8	17.4	7.9	-4.4	14.1	14.5
Decatur, IL	37 859	47 493	59 373	29 034	16 254	21 781	40 138	23 766	20 067	77.0	37.9	29.6	3.6	19.2	7.8	-4.5	12.1	15.9
Denver-Boulder-Greeley, CO	51 088	61 088	69 768	36 504	26 948	33 410	41 830	31 968	26 011	87.2	41.3	18.0	2.1	13.3	16.7	4.4	7.9	8.4
Boulder-Longmont, CO	55 861	70 572	81 942	39 750	29 066	35 276	50 054	33 541	28 976	88.3	51.4	15.0	1.6	12.6	21.7	9.4	9.2	6.5
Denver, CO	51 191	61 185	70 025	36 876	27 227	33 860	41 767	32 158	26 206	87.1	40.3	18.2	2.1	13.5	16.5	4.2	7.4	8.3
Greeley, CO	42 321	49 569	54 465	27 656	19 943	23 967	35 886	26 415	18 957	85.9	36.5	21.2	2.9	12.6	9.5	-2.8	11.7	11.9
Des Moines, IA	46 651	56 674	65 469	32 128	23 868	28 281	38 317	28 790	23 316	85.1	40.7	22.3	2.7	13.6	11.7	-0.6	7.2	7.8
Detroit-Ann Arbor-Flint, MI	49 160	59 380	71 985	36 492	22 131	29 245	49 564	31 478	24 275	81.0	37.8	25.0	3.9	19.0	16.1	3.8	10.0	11.7
Ann Arbor, MI	55 016	67 765	76 628	39 803	25 634	31 143	50 564	32 451	26 222	86.8	44.3	19.3	1.9	15.6	19.6	7.3	8.3	6.0
Detroit, MI	49 175	59 205	72 187	36 707	22 486	29 384	49 751	31 537	24 354	80.5	37.5	25.7	4.0	18.9	16.1	3.8	10.0	12.0
Flint, MI	41 951	50 090	63 308	31 998	17 496	25 549	45 476	28 608	20 883	78.6	32.5	26.1	5.3	23.4	10.7	-1.6	12.2	16.2
Dothan, AL	33 455	40 898	50 056	24 671	13 607	17 792	32 345	21 552	17 780	77.4	26.7	26.8	2.1	17.8	6.6	-5.7	15.9	18.0
Dover, DE	40 950	46 504	53 856	30 731	20 443	24 698	35 197	25 429	18 662	82.1	33.0	25.7	3.3	21.9	8.1	-4.2	10.2	12.3
Dubuque, IA	39 582	48 742	55 640	30 586	19 275	21 818	33 330	23 203	19 600	80.7	48.7	28.1	2.7	17.4	7.2	-5.1	7.9	7.4
Duluth-Superior, MN-WI	36 081	46 478	56 344	27 479	18 222	20 360	38 301	24 937	18 743	74.8	41.3	30.8	4.6	19.6	5.8	-6.5	12.1	11.9
Eau Claire, WI	39 372	48 922	57 664	28 212	21 312	22 999	33 701	23 912	18 875	81.6	48.6	27.0	1.6	15.9	6.7	-5.6	9.6	8.2
El Paso, TX	31 051	33 410	36 193	22 427	15 479	19 437	27 822	21 389	13 421	82.5	21.3	23.9	6.9	14.8	6.3	-6.0	21.6	26.6
Elkhart-Goshen, IN	44 478	50 438	57 127	30 446	21 556	25 286	36 659	25 145	20 250	85.8	36.8	23.6	2.8	11.9	9.0	-3.3	7.3	8.8
Elmira, NY	36 415	43 994	54 236	24 572	17 369	20 398	35 700	25 512	18 264	75.1	38.0	32.2	3.4	23.2	6.6	-5.7	12.9	15.5
Enid, OK	33 006	39 872	46 118	23 894	15 463	19 249	31 240	21 234	17 457	78.8	36.3	29.3	4.6	16.4	5.1	-7.2	13.1	16.7
Erie, PA	36 627	44 829	53 258	26 968	16 891	20 308	36 226	24 646	17 932	78.0	41.0	28.8	3.6	18.1	6.4	-5.9	11.7	13.5
Eugene-Springfield, OR	36 942	45 111	53 353	28 498	16 404	22 297	35 454	26 197	19 681	79.2	40.9	25.9	3.5	17.2	7.9	-4.4	14.1	14.8
Evansville-Henderson, IN-KY	39 307	49 207	58 575	25 748	17 936	21 355	36 565	24 331	20 439	79.6	38.6	28.0	3.2	17.0	8.2	-4.1	10.2	11.6
Fargo-Moorhead, ND-MN	38 069	50 872	58 935	29 808	19 031	22 305	33 923	23 445	19 910	85.4	40.0	20.5	3.0	10.7	7.7	-4.6	11.5	9.2
Fayetteville, NC	37 466	41 459	46 971	27 710	17 712	24 743	30 131	23 432	17 376	84.6	24.3	19.5	3.6	19.6	6.3	-6.0	12.6	14.2
Fayetteville-Springdale-Rogers, AR	37 322	44 109	49 586	24 081	19 188	21 758	30 788	22 701	18 348	81.7	33.3	25.8	1.9	14.6	7.8	-4.5	12.1	12.7
Flagstaff, AZ-UT	37 971	45 375	52 477	26 341	17 399	25 151	33 538	25 618	17 056	86.4	30.6	18.1	3.8	13.2	8.2	-4.1	15.7	18.2
Florence, AL	32 704	40 653	47 387	24 570	14 927	16 475	34 575	21 105	18 205	74.0	31.3	31.2	1.8	21.7	6.6	-5.7	15.5	16.2
Florence, SC	35 144	41 274	52 405	26 955	16 319	19 763	32 849	22 587	17 876	80.6	24.0	25.9	3.3	15.2	7.3	-5.0	16.3	18.4
Fort Collins-Loveland, CO	48 655	58 866	66 937	35 453	25 385	28 303	41 792	28 958	23 689	86.8	47.8	19.1	1.8	13.8	13.9	1.6	9.1	6.1
Fort Myers-Cape Coral, FL	40 319	46 430	55 006	27 390	20 672	25 827	32 284	25 307	24 542	66.9	43.0	42.4	1.8	27.5	10.6	-1.7	8.6	12.3
Fort Pierce-Port St. Lucie, FL	38 724	45 529	53 508	26 690	19 259	24 669	32 227	25 569	23 072	66.1	42.6	43.0	2.2	26.3	10.3	-2.0	9.8	14.3
Fort Smith, AR-OK	32 399	38 128	44 545	21 786	15 684	18 202	30 233	21 964	16 604	77.6	27.5	29.0	3.8	15.1	5.8	-6.5	14.8	17.3
Fort Walton Beach, FL	41 474	47 711	50 820	25 013	19 149	27 232	33 634	23 239	20 918	81.4	38.6	24.7	2.4	27.8	9.1	-3.2	8.5	10.8
Fort Wayne, IN	42 817	51 830	59 699	31 218	21 750	25 078	38 755	25 795	20 701	83.8	39.6	24.4	2.2	15.5	9.1	-3.2	7.8	8.9
Fresno, CA	34 960	38 515	43 331	22 713	16 383	22 053	34 762	27 047	15 386	80.3	26.6	24.3	8.5	14.7	8.5	-3.8	18.0	24.6
Gadsden, AL	31 170	38 697	46 806	23 750	14 608	15 628	32 255	21 834	16 783	72.0	25.3	34.1	2.3	21.2	5.6	-6.7	16.2	18.9
Gainesville, FL	31 426	46 587	57 211	25 935	17 758	18 982	33 661	26 885	18 465	83.4	34.2	19.0	2.7	13.4	8.7	-3.6	23.2	16.9
Glens Falls, NY	38 526	45 159	52 393	27 182	19 735	23 205	33 142	23 156	19 368	78.6	39.4	30.6	2.7	21.5	7.4	-4.9	9.3	11.1
Goldsboro, NC	33 942	40 492	48 316	25 495	16 854	20 023	29 721	22 355	17 010	79.9	25.9	26.4	2.9	19.9	5.4	-6.9	13.8	15.2
Grand Forks, ND-MN	35 562	45 860	53 351	27 845	16 775	21 273	31 507	22 086	17 679	82.9	40.7	23.9	3.4	12.1	5.7	-6.6	12.5	11.8
Grand Junction, CO	35 864	43 009	51 210	27 134	18 513	20 687	34 001	23 352	18 715	78.0	38.3	30.0	3.5	17.9	7.1	-5.2	10.2	11.0
Grand Rapids-Muskegon-Holland, MI	46 116	54 118	62 491	32 414	22 057	26 736	40 605	27 877	20 901	83.8	38.9	23.3	2.7	15.0	10.7	-1.6	8.1	8.6
Great Falls, MT	32 971	39 949	45 215	23 682	16 056	19 671	30 683	21 695	17 566	78.0	39.9	28.6	3.4	19.6	5.4	-6.9	13.4	17.1
Green Bay, WI	46 447	56 194	64 908	31 148	23 255	27 080	38 657	26 131	21 784	84.5	46.9	22.0	1.6	12.3	9.7	-2.6	7.0	7.1
Greensboro—Winston-Salem—High Point, NC	40 913	49 327	58 302	28 994	20 525	24 441	34 758	26 331	21 392	82.7	32.5	24.8	2.2	15.8	9.8	-2.5	10.5	11.3
Greenville, NC	32 868	43 971	57 289	23 821	17 909	19 125	32 684	25 969	18 243	82.1	25.1	21.6	3.5	13.8	7.5	-4.8	20.8	18.7
Greenville-Spartanburg-Anderson, SC	38 458	46 365	55 485	28 696	19 426	21 281	35 644	25 176	19 716	80.9	28.1	26.5	1.9	15.9	8.8	-3.5	12.3	12.5
Harrisburg-Lebanon-Carlisle, PA	43 022	51 892	61 134	29 977	21 862	26 007	37 356	27 568	21 936	80.3	43.2	27.0	2.0	20.9	9.9	-2.4	8.0	9.3

Table B-4. Metropolitan Areas — **Education, Labor Force, and Income**

CMSA/MSA/ PMSA/NECMA code[1]	Area name	High school graduates — Total population 25 years and over	Percent with a high school diploma or less	Percent with a high school diploma or more	College graduates — Percent with a bachelor's degree or more	+/− U.S. percent with bachelor's degree or more	College graduates (percent) — Non-Hispanic White	Black or African American	American Indian and Alaska Native	Asian, Hawaiian, and Pacific Islander	Hispanic or Latino[2]
		1	2	3	4	5	6	7	8	9	10
3283	Hartford, CT	775 147	44.6	84.0	30.5	6.1	33.3	13.8	16.7	53.2	11.3
3285	Hattiesburg, MS	65 381	46.9	80.6	24.3	-0.1	28.1	11.2	4.7	43.5	18.6
3290	Hickory-Morganton-Lenoir, NC	230 937	61.3	70.3	13.6	-10.8	14.5	6.8	6.6	12.0	3.6
3320	Honolulu, HI	579 998	43.0	84.8	27.9	3.5	40.4	20.9	22.8	26.3	15.1
3350	Houma, LA	119 162	70.1	66.7	12.3	-12.1	13.3	6.3	2.4	36.5	14.9
42	Houston-Galveston-Brazoria, TX	2 858 299	46.4	76.4	26.5	2.1	34.8	18.0	17.5	47.5	8.5
1145	Brazoria, TX	152 244	47.7	79.5	19.6	-4.8	22.3	17.2	11.8	51.2	7.6
2920	Galveston-Texas City, TX	161 503	45.5	80.9	22.7	-1.7	27.0	10.7	22.4	47.9	10.1
3360	Houston, TX	2 544 552	46.4	75.9	27.2	2.8	36.5	18.4	17.6	47.4	8.5
3400	Huntington-Ashland, WV-KY-OH	212 766	61.7	75.6	14.4	-10.0	14.3	10.7	19.0	49.7	15.1
3440	Huntsville, AL	223 845	40.7	83.3	30.9	6.5	32.8	21.8	20.5	52.0	22.4
3480	Indianapolis, IN	1 039 892	48.0	84.0	25.8	1.4	27.4	13.8	11.6	56.6	16.7
3500	Iowa City, IA	62 859	26.1	93.7	47.6	23.2	47.0	34.9	41.1	76.5	34.5
3520	Jackson, MI	104 880	48.6	84.2	16.3	-8.1	17.2	5.2	7.6	56.1	9.2
3560	Jackson, MS	271 945	41.6	81.2	28.1	3.7	35.3	17.5	13.5	51.8	20.2
3580	Jackson, TN	67 569	53.9	77.2	20.1	-4.3	23.1	11.2	16.8	51.5	14.5
3600	Jacksonville, FL	715 155	45.5	83.6	22.9	-1.5	25.0	13.2	18.6	34.8	21.4
3605	Jacksonville, NC	75 286	48.5	84.3	14.8	-9.6	16.1	10.0	14.3	11.6	12.7
3610	Jamestown, NY	91 261	55.3	81.2	16.9	-7.5	17.5	5.7	6.6	47.0	5.2
3620	Janesville-Beloit, WI	98 770	55.3	83.9	16.7	-7.7	17.3	6.0	16.7	39.0	5.2
3660	Johnson City-Kingsport-Bristol, TN-VA	336 062	59.6	73.3	16.6	-7.8	16.5	13.9	21.1	51.9	17.2
3680	Johnstown, PA	162 736	69.2	79.2	12.7	-11.7	12.9	4.2	3.3	35.3	7.6
3700	Jonesboro, AR	50 725	55.5	77.3	20.9	-3.5	21.5	14.4	8.6	22.0	11.6
3710	Joplin, MO	100 417	55.4	79.6	16.4	-8.0	16.6	11.5	14.0	30.9	0.9
3720	Kalamazoo-Battle Creek, MI	284 052	45.4	85.3	23.5	-0.9	24.4	12.4	12.1	61.1	11.4
3760	Kansas City, MO-KS	1 154 262	41.7	86.7	28.5	4.1	31.0	14.6	15.8	45.3	13.3
3810	Killeen-Temple, TX	179 194	44.7	83.8	18.1	-6.3	22.2	10.2	15.1	21.5	9.0
3840	Knoxville, TN	463 341	50.9	79.0	23.6	-0.9	23.6	15.6	19.3	60.1	23.6
3850	Kokomo, IN	67 469	56.3	83.4	17.1	-7.3	17.0	13.3	37.7	52.0	13.1
3870	La Crosse, WI-MN	78 326	43.4	89.0	24.6	0.2	24.7	16.9	11.1	28.9	19.6
3920	Lafayette, IN	101 655	48.6	86.1	28.2	3.8	26.8	28.7	11.9	81.4	15.6
3880	Lafayette, LA	234 965	61.1	71.3	17.5	-6.9	20.5	8.1	12.2	38.6	18.2
3960	Lake Charles, LA	114 563	57.5	77.0	16.0	-7.5	19.0	8.3	6.3	37.0	19.5
3980	Lakeland-Winter Haven, FL	326 208	58.9	74.8	14.9	-9.5	16.0	8.9	13.0	40.0	8.6
4000	Lancaster, PA	302 503	61.5	77.4	20.5	-3.9	21.2	11.8	9.6	24.6	7.4
4040	Lansing-East Lansing, MI	271 817	37.9	88.6	28.4	4.0	28.4	23.9	16.8	61.0	15.1
4080	Laredo, TX	101 182	65.0	53.0	13.9	-10.5	36.7	23.4	6.1	43.9	12.3
4100	Las Cruces, NM	99 893	52.4	70.0	22.3	-2.1	39.3	25.0	14.7	64.2	9.6
4120	Las Vegas, NV-AZ	1 032 981	51.4	79.2	16.4	-8.0	18.4	11.9	8.9	26.1	6.4
4150	Lawrence, KS	53 257	29.9	92.4	42.7	18.3	42.8	33.2	25.9	71.3	33.0
4200	Lawton, OK	67 220	46.3	85.2	19.1	-5.3	21.8	11.6	13.0	21.5	11.2
4243	Lewiston-Auburn, ME	69 560	60.3	79.8	14.4	-10.0	14.3	14.9	19.8	29.7	14.5
4280	Lexington, KY	304 749	44.9	82.1	28.7	4.3	29.9	13.5	16.9	65.8	13.9
4320	Lima, OH	99 762	60.6	83.5	13.4	-11.0	13.8	7.5	11.9	48.5	9.5
4360	Lincoln, NE	152 747	34.7	90.5	32.6	8.2	33.4	17.7	17.6	36.3	19.3
4400	Little Rock-North Little Rock, AR	376 034	46.7	83.3	24.8	0.4	27.0	15.2	18.3	43.1	15.4
4420	Longview-Marshall, TX	132 113	52.7	78.4	16.8	-7.6	18.8	10.6	13.0	32.3	7.3
49	Los Angeles-Riverside-Orange County, CA	10 087 457	46.8	73.0	24.4	0.0	33.3	17.8	11.3	41.9	6.9
4480	Los Angeles-Long Beach, CA	5 882 948	48.9	69.9	24.9	0.5	37.7	17.8	11.6	42.4	6.8
5945	Orange County, CA	1 813 456	38.0	79.5	30.8	6.4	37.6	27.6	13.3	40.9	8.5
6780	Riverside-San Bernardino, CA	1 919 297	50.3	74.6	16.3	-8.1	20.0	14.9	9.2	39.8	6.1
8735	Ventura, CA	471 756	39.6	80.1	26.9	2.5	33.3	27.1	15.1	46.3	7.8
4520	Louisville, KY-IN	682 172	50.0	81.3	22.2	-2.2	23.4	11.8	15.9	50.2	17.2
4600	Lubbock, TX	141 363	46.9	78.4	24.4	0.0	31.1	10.0	14.6	64.2	7.2
4640	Lynchburg, VA	144 024	55.4	76.2	19.3	-5.1	21.5	6.3	12.7	52.6	22.4
4680	Macon, GA	202 641	54.1	78.9	19.5	-4.9	23.4	11.3	13.2	37.7	18.4
4720	Madison, WI	269 998	30.1	92.2	40.6	16.2	41.1	19.2	23.1	65.0	27.2
4800	Mansfield, OH	117 563	64.5	80.2	11.8	-12.6	12.1	6.6	7.9	35.8	5.1
4880	McAllen-Edinburg-Mission, TX	304 670	69.8	50.5	12.9	-11.5	27.8	16.7	7.4	65.1	9.6
4890	Medford-Ashland, OR	121 155	45.1	85.0	22.3	-2.1	23.0	16.1	14.2	26.0	10.4
4900	Melbourne-Titusville-Palm Bay, FL	339 738	42.5	86.3	23.6	-0.8	24.3	12.1	10.3	37.0	22.9
4920	Memphis, TN-AR-MS	707 456	48.1	79.8	22.7	-1.7	29.3	12.1	15.0	47.0	14.1

[1]MSA = Metropolitan Statistical Area. CMSA = Consolidated MSA. PMSA = Primary MSA. NECMA = New England County Metropolitan Area. See the Appendix A for explanation of these concepts. See Appendix B for list of metropolitan areas identified by type, with component counties.
[2]Hispanic or Latino persons may be of any race.

Table B-4. Metropolitan Areas — Education, Labor Force, and Income

Area name	School enrollment			Population 16 to 19 years				Employment status, 2000			Work status in 1999 of the population 16 years and over (percent)		
											Worked in 1999		
	Grades kindergarten through 12	College or graduate school	Percent private	Number	Percent in armed forces	Percent high school graduates	Percent not enrolled, not grads, not in armed forces, not employed	Total population 16 years and over	Percent in labor force	Unemployment rate	Full-time	Part-time	Did not work in 1999
	11	12	13	14	15	16	17	18	19	20	21	22	23
Hartford, CT	213 193	75 171	13.2	59 368	0.1	7.7	4.6	899 991	66.7	5.7	55.3	16.5	28.2
Hattiesburg, MS	21 093	13 187	9.8	8 064	1.2	10.1	6.0	86 154	63.0	6.5	51.4	17.0	31.6
Hickory-Morganton-Lenoir, NC	60 869	11 896	7.3	16 846	0.0	12.8	10.1	268 328	68.2	3.4	61.1	11.5	27.4
Honolulu, HI	155 556	65 507	21.2	45 427	5.9	17.8	3.2	691 015	64.7	5.7	54.1	14.6	31.3
Houma, LA	41 914	8 468	14.2	13 152	0.0	10.4	7.1	146 236	57.2	5.9	49.9	12.7	37.4
Houston-Galveston-Brazoria, TX	1 003 036	249 102	9.4	276 644	0.0	9.4	7.6	3 460 060	65.4	6.2	59.8	11.5	28.8
Brazoria, TX	51 867	11 894	8.7	13 901	0.1	10.6	6.3	180 217	62.6	5.4	57.1	10.8	32.1
Galveston-Texas City, TX	50 267	14 654	8.4	14 462	0.1	9.2	5.6	190 919	64.4	6.7	57.5	11.7	30.8
Houston, TX	900 902	222 554	9.5	248 281	0.0	9.3	7.8	3 088 924	65.7	6.2	60.0	11.5	28.5
Huntington-Ashland, WV-KY-OH	53 573	18 715	6.8	18 124	0.1	10.8	5.9	253 279	53.9	7.9	45.6	13.1	41.3
Huntsville, AL	63 791	24 110	12.8	18 865	1.1	9.1	6.1	264 733	66.3	5.4	58.0	13.2	28.8
Indianapolis, IN	303 474	73 980	16.2	84 481	0.0	11.6	6.1	1 225 454	69.3	4.4	60.4	14.3	25.3
Iowa City, IA	16 189	26 885	6.1	9 749	0.2	5.4	0.9	91 234	73.4	3.9	55.1	29.0	15.9
Jackson, MI	31 331	7 379	14.4	8 107	0.1	8.6	7.0	122 154	62.1	5.5	55.0	14.9	30.2
Jackson, MS	90 869	28 173	17.2	28 113	0.1	8.0	7.1	333 437	64.8	6.2	57.0	13.4	29.6
Jackson, TN	20 529	6 867	27.4	6 898	0.0	10.5	4.3	82 823	65.7	6.9	56.6	13.9	29.5
Jacksonville, FL	214 891	58 856	15.0	59 518	1.5	11.6	5.8	844 759	66.8	4.6	59.6	12.5	27.9
Jacksonville, NC	26 211	8 820	7.0	11 465	36.1	48.3	3.4	114 643	74.2	4.3	64.0	13.7	22.3
Jamestown, NY	26 607	8 752	6.4	9 278	2.4	8.2	5.8	109 945	61.4	6.3	48.8	18.5	32.7
Janesville-Beloit, WI	30 300	6 280	11.4	8 757	0.0	11.6	4.6	116 674	69.3	5.6	57.7	17.2	25.0
Johnson City-Kingsport-Bristol, TN-VA	77 054	22 319	8.5	23 727	0.1	12.9	4.4	388 909	58.5	5.2	51.1	12.9	36.1
Johnstown, PA	39 027	9 592	14.1	12 828	0.1	10.6	3.7	189 232	54.8	7.7	46.1	14.1	39.9
Jonesboro, AR	14 353	6 945	5.6	5 400	0.0	14.2	2.0	64 417	66.0	5.7	55.9	15.6	28.6
Joplin, MO	28 913	7 405	10.7	9 456	0.2	12.6	7.6	121 131	65.0	5.9	54.5	15.4	30.1
Kalamazoo-Battle Creek, MI	86 261	41 355	11.0	29 550	0.0	8.0	4.6	351 367	66.7	6.3	54.5	18.2	27.3
Kansas City, MO-KS	343 749	89 309	14.8	94 895	0.1	11.3	5.1	1 356 004	68.9	4.3	60.5	14.4	25.1
Killeen-Temple, TX	61 201	18 001	9.4	19 460	14.2	26.6	5.1	233 064	67.5	5.1	62.4	12.1	25.5
Knoxville, TN	114 942	44 326	10.3	37 240	0.0	11.8	3.6	549 188	63.3	4.9	54.3	14.7	30.9
Kokomo, IN	18 727	3 422	9.2	5 366	0.4	11.7	4.8	78 651	63.6	4.5	55.4	14.2	30.4
La Crosse, WI-MN	23 349	13 358	13.7	8 918	0.0	10.6	1.1	99 842	70.2	4.1	55.9	21.4	22.6
Lafayette, IN	28 893	36 888	5.9	16 967	0.0	5.8	2.5	147 043	65.9	6.7	55.6	22.3	22.1
Lafayette, LA	82 453	20 479	16.8	25 374	0.1	9.7	8.4	288 860	59.6	7.8	50.3	13.2	36.5
Lake Charles, LA	37 247	9 274	11.5	11 513	0.1	12.7	5.8	139 391	61.3	6.9	52.8	12.9	34.3
Lakeland-Winter Haven, FL	88 103	18 134	13.2	25 278	0.0	9.9	8.1	379 236	57.8	5.7	51.1	11.4	37.5
Lancaster, PA	89 947	18 811	21.7	26 608	0.1	10.2	5.3	358 317	67.9	3.0	55.3	17.6	27.0
Lansing-East Lansing, MI	84 143	58 283	8.8	32 344	0.0	6.7	3.2	349 842	69.0	5.0	55.5	20.7	23.8
Laredo, TX	51 488	11 089	5.6	13 908	0.0	8.0	10.3	130 196	53.0	9.3	49.0	11.5	39.5
Las Cruces, NM	39 730	17 779	5.1	12 338	0.1	8.2	6.6	128 197	58.5	9.2	49.7	16.5	33.8
Las Vegas, NV-AZ	278 436	70 317	7.2	73 755	0.4	13.6	9.6	1 207 040	63.6	6.5	58.7	11.2	30.1
Lawrence, KS	15 063	25 640	7.2	9 344	0.1	5.4	1.3	81 876	70.9	4.6	52.9	28.4	18.7
Lawton, OK	23 102	7 129	5.7	8 397	21.3	32.6	5.7	86 873	65.0	5.9	55.4	14.2	30.4
Lewiston-Auburn, ME	18 993	5 688	18.9	5 914	0.1	12.6	3.9	81 987	66.5	5.0	55.6	16.0	28.4
Lexington, KY	79 044	49 458	14.4	28 918	0.1	8.8	5.0	381 872	68.3	4.9	57.7	17.2	25.1
Lima, OH	31 582	6 963	15.2	9 755	0.0	9.3	3.6	118 888	63.3	4.9	51.8	16.8	31.4
Lincoln, NE	42 543	29 849	14.9	17 077	0.0	9.0	2.0	198 307	73.3	3.6	60.4	20.6	19.1
Little Rock-North Little Rock, AR	110 308	34 144	14.5	32 551	0.8	12.9	4.8	450 925	66.6	5.1	58.9	13.4	27.7
Longview-Marshall, TX	42 913	9 315	10.5	13 931	0.0	10.6	7.7	159 847	60.5	6.8	53.0	12.5	34.5
Los Angeles-Riverside-Orange County, CA	3 550 636	1 206 473	12.8	938 382	0.3	9.1	6.4	12 177 732	61.5	7.4	53.0	13.9	33.1
Los Angeles-Long Beach, CA	2 041 738	730 314	14.2	539 900	0.1	8.0	7.1	7 122 525	60.5	8.2	52.4	13.6	33.9
Orange County, CA	569 481	230 749	12.1	151 675	0.1	8.0	4.9	2 153 952	65.5	5.0	56.5	14.7	28.8
Riverside-San Bernardino, CA	776 897	196 965	9.5	203 148	1.0	12.6	6.4	2 339 175	59.4	7.8	50.7	13.7	35.6
Ventura, CA	162 520	48 445	11.7	43 659	0.8	9.5	4.6	562 080	66.2	5.1	56.3	14.9	28.7
Louisville, KY-IN	187 573	50 942	19.6	53 384	0.1	11.0	6.1	799 538	65.9	4.6	56.2	14.9	28.9
Lubbock, TX	46 144	30 844	7.4	17 939	0.1	10.6	3.8	187 461	65.0	5.8	54.7	18.1	27.2
Lynchburg, VA	37 565	13 281	23.5	12 218	0.1	11.9	4.1	170 207	62.8	4.6	54.6	14.1	31.4
Macon, GA	66 728	18 054	14.7	19 579	2.0	11.6	7.4	244 291	62.9	6.6	54.9	12.9	32.1
Madison, WI	71 417	53 744	8.7	27 257	0.0	8.2	2.4	341 422	75.0	3.8	60.8	21.7	17.4
Mansfield, OH	33 106	6 140	11.8	9 369	0.2	12.1	3.8	137 165	61.5	4.9	53.1	14.8	32.2
McAllen-Edinburg-Mission, TX	148 929	27 046	3.3	40 746	0.0	7.2	11.1	389 868	52.6	12.0	46.8	11.1	42.1
Medford-Ashland, OR	32 724	9 304	8.7	10 013	0.1	12.6	5.8	142 297	61.3	7.3	48.3	18.5	33.2
Melbourne-Titusville-Palm Bay, FL	80 722	23 877	15.6	22 865	0.2	9.1	6.1	384 076	57.4	4.9	48.7	13.2	38.1
Memphis, TN-AR-MS	239 228	59 558	13.9	64 758	0.1	9.9	7.2	848 002	65.6	6.4	57.9	12.8	29.3

Table B-4. Metropolitan Areas — Education, Labor Force, and Income

Area name	Full-year full-time employed (percent)								Children under 18 years in families (percent, except where noted)						Total employed by class of worker (percent)			
										With two parents		With one parent who is in labor force	+/- U.S. percent of children with no stay-at-home parent	+/- U.S. percent two-income couples				Unpaid family worker
	Total	Men	Women	Non-Hispanic White	Black or African American	American Indian and Alaska Native	Asian, Hawaiian, and Pacific Islander	Hispanic or Latino[1]	Number	Both in labor force	Father only in labor force				Private	Government	Self-employed	
	24	25	26	27	28	29	30	31	32	33	34	35	36	37	38	39	40	41
Hartford, CT	43.5	53.2	34.7	44.9	39.4	31.5	43.2	34.3	265 587	49.8	17.4	22.3	7.5	6.5	76.5	14.9	8.4	0.2
Hattiesburg, MS	36.5	46.1	28.0	38.1	32.1	34.5	23.9	34.3	26 363	38.6	21.7	26.1	0.1	-1.1	71.5	18.1	10.0	0.4
Hickory-Morganton-Lenoir, NC	48.0	57.6	38.8	48.6	40.2	40.6	48.5	47.1	76 950	50.1	17.5	22.7	8.3	6.6	80.4	11.3	8.0	0.2
Honolulu, HI	40.8	47.7	33.8	47.2	55.0	44.8	38.3	39.4	192 025	47.1	19.0	20.1	2.6	0.1	67.8	22.5	9.3	0.3
Houma, LA	33.7	45.0	23.3	35.3	28.3	23.7	30.8	26.7	51 208	33.8	25.9	20.2	-10.7	-11.2	74.8	14.7	10.1	0.4
Houston-Galveston-Brazoria, TX	42.9	52.7	33.5	47.8	39.0	40.1	41.7	36.3	1 271 631	37.1	26.7	20.4	-7.1	-2.5	78.5	12.2	9.1	0.3
Brazoria, TX	42.8	51.7	33.3	45.6	32.7	33.5	45.8	37.6	65 395	43.3	28.1	18.0	-3.3	-1.1	76.8	14.6	8.3	0.3
Galveston-Texas City, TX	42.1	51.0	33.8	45.3	32.5	37.1	39.2	38.9	62 793	39.9	23.4	24.3	-0.4	-1.9	69.8	20.9	8.9	0.4
Houston, TX	43.0	52.8	33.5	48.2	39.5	40.8	41.7	36.1	1 143 443	36.6	26.8	20.3	-7.7	-2.6	79.1	11.5	9.1	0.3
Huntington-Ashland, WV-KY-OH	32.0	40.6	24.1	32.2	27.8	29.1	29.4	28.0	66 932	38.8	24.3	18.8	-6.9	-11.8	75.7	16.1	7.8	0.3
Huntsville, AL	44.7	55.4	34.6	46.3	39.4	42.8	39.0	44.5	83 089	45.9	22.7	21.4	2.7	1.6	72.8	18.6	8.4	0.2
Indianapolis, IN	47.5	57.8	38.0	48.8	40.6	40.6	48.1	41.4	405 001	47.0	20.5	23.2	5.6	6.5	81.5	10.4	7.9	0.1
Iowa City, IA	40.3	46.8	33.9	41.4	31.4	42.9	27.9	36.2	21 634	59.2	18.8	15.2	9.8	14.3	60.6	31.7	7.4	0.2
Jackson, MI	40.3	47.9	32.4	42.0	21.5	29.2	33.1	39.1	38 545	47.8	18.4	24.1	7.4	3.5	79.5	11.9	8.4	0.2
Jackson, MS	41.8	49.5	35.2	47.5	34.6	44.7	39.7	38.8	111 554	39.6	14.3	29.6	4.6	5.6	69.9	20.7	9.3	0.2
Jackson, TN	41.9	51.3	33.7	44.2	36.4	29.1	42.7	35.6	25 642	45.2	16.0	25.4	6.0	4.2	77.7	14.3	7.6	0.3
Jacksonville, FL	45.9	55.8	36.9	47.3	41.3	43.9	47.1	44.2	268 710	41.4	20.4	25.4	2.2	1.3	77.2	13.6	8.9	0.2
Jacksonville, NC	47.4	61.2	29.6	48.9	42.1	51.3	38.0	46.7	37 575	43.4	29.0	17.9	-3.2	0.3	63.4	25.5	10.7	0.5
Jamestown, NY	35.4	45.7	26.0	36.1	20.6	39.4	26.0	25.4	32 259	47.8	18.4	22.0	5.2	0.4	73.7	16.1	9.9	0.4
Janesville-Beloit, WI	43.8	54.2	34.0	44.5	34.3	41.8	34.6	39.8	38 216	54.4	15.2	22.4	12.3	6.3	81.5	10.8	7.5	0.3
Johnson City-Kingsport-Bristol, TN-VA	38.1	48.2	28.8	38.2	33.4	33.5	36.5	36.6	97 912	42.4	25.3	18.2	-3.9	-6.7	77.5	12.8	9.3	0.4
Johnstown, PA	33.9	43.2	25.1	34.4	16.2	39.8	48.5	22.6	47 758	49.9	22.9	17.1	2.4	-5.6	77.2	13.6	8.7	0.5
Jonesboro, AR	40.8	51.6	31.1	42.0	32.3	33.3	27.6	22.6	18 911	46.4	21.3	21.0	2.8	2.6	74.5	14.0	11.2	0.2
Joplin, MO	41.2	52.9	30.6	41.4	41.5	37.6	33.7	44.9	38 337	46.4	23.3	20.0	2.4	0.0	70.6	9.4	10.6	0.3
Kalamazoo-Battle Creek, MI	39.9	49.4	31.3	40.8	34.2	31.6	31.6	37.9	107 612	47.4	18.5	24.4	7.2	3.4	70.3	12.1	8.2	0.3
Kansas City, MO-KS.....	47.0	56.8	37.9	48.6	38.7	43.5	44.7	42.0	448 511	47.0	20.6	22.2	4.6	6.2	78.8	12.4	8.6	0.2
Killeen-Temple, TX.......	45.0	57.6	32.3	46.1	45.9	46.7	37.6	41.2	83 908	43.8	24.7	21.2	0.4	1.3	67.7	23.6	8.3	0.4
Knoxville, TN	41.0	51.4	31.6	41.5	35.1	45.2	35.2	38.4	146 950	45.4	23.5	18.9	-0.3	-1.2	74.5	15.3	9.9	0.3
Kokomo, IN	42.5	54.8	31.5	42.9	37.6	47.1	34.1	43.4	24 635	46.7	23.1	21.8	4.0	-2.4	83.1	9.3	7.3	0.2
La Crosse, WI-MN	41.8	51.6	32.9	42.3	24.0	33.7	32.5	33.2	29 557	61.5	14.5	18.0	14.9	11.2	78.5	12.9	8.2	0.3
Lafayette, IN	37.5	45.1	29.7	38.9	31.4	49.2	17.8	31.3	38 566	48.6	22.4	19.5	0.5	4.2	74.6	18.4	6.6	0.3
Lafayette, LA	35.4	44.8	27.0	38.5	27.3	32.8	35.4	29.8	103 409	36.2	22.1	24.3	-4.1	-6.1	75.1	14.0	10.6	0.3
Lake Charles, LA	38.3	48.7	28.8	39.8	33.8	22.4	31.8	39.2	46 964	40.2	22.6	23.2	-1.2	-4.2	77.3	14.3	8.2	0.3
Lakeland-Winter Haven, FL	38.1	45.8	30.8	38.2	36.2	34.0	41.5	38.5	107 722	40.9	19.7	24.7	1.0	-7.7	77.9	13.0	8.9	0.3
Lancaster, PA...............	45.1	59.2	32.1	45.4	40.9	34.2	48.3	40.1	120 405	47.0	30.0	15.9	1.7	1.6	82.0	7.2	10.2	0.5
Lansing-East Lansing, MI	41.6	50.3	33.7	42.8	36.8	40.7	24.6	38.8	105 887	49.9	18.5	22.5	7.8	6.8	71.6	20.5	7.7	0.2
Laredo, TX	30.6	41.7	20.9	35.8	27.7	23.0	34.0	30.3	65 096	28.0	29.3	15.6	-21.0	-16.7	68.0	19.8	11.8	0.4
Las Cruces, NM	31.6	39.4	24.3	34.0	32.4	31.0	32.3	30.3	48 651	32.2	24.0	23.5	-8.9	-10.7	63.8	25.4	10.4	0.4
Las Vegas, NV-AZ	41.2	48.1	34.3	42.2	40.4	40.8	43.6	37.2	365 731	37.1	22.2	24.6	-2.8	-6.1	81.5	11.0	7.2	0.2
Lawrence, KS	36.8	44.2	29.6	38.1	36.1	30.1	22.6	27.7	19 785	54.3	19.6	19.6	9.2	12.0	67.9	23.4	8.5	0.2
Lawton, OK	39.1	49.8	27.6	40.0	39.7	34.9	33.4	35.5	29 277	39.7	25.6	22.5	-2.4	-2.9	64.0	26.0	9.6	0.4
Lewiston-Auburn, ME....	43.1	52.7	34.3	43.5	33.7	41.6	32.6	23.0	23 491	53.0	12.2	24.4	12.8	7.9	80.0	11.2	8.7	0.4
Lexington, KY	43.0	52.2	34.4	44.0	37.9	39.3	35.7	33.3	103 334	46.8	21.4	21.5	3.7	5.3	74.1	16.6	9.0	0.4
Lima, OH	40.2	51.0	29.8	41.4	30.0	28.4	47.5	27.5	39 148	50.6	17.5	22.5	8.5	2.6	80.6	11.2	7.8	0.4
Lincoln, NE.................	46.7	54.8	38.7	47.7	38.5	32.5	38.6	36.4	56 480	55.4	17.0	20.2	11.0	13.8	71.7	19.9	8.2	0.2
Little Rock-North Little Rock, AR	44.8	54.2	36.2	46.6	38.4	44.2	37.3	40.9	139 476	43.8	19.2	24.5	3.7	3.6	72.2	18.4	9.2	0.2
Longview-Marshall, TX..	38.0	48.0	28.9	40.1	31.7	25.3	33.7	34.6	51 768	40.1	23.4	23.0	-1.5	-3.5	77.0	11.9	10.6	0.4
Los Angeles-Riverside-Orange County, CA-	35.7	44.5	27.3	39.5	33.4	32.3	35.7	31.8	4 308 049	34.4	24.9	19.9	-10.2	-6.4	75.0	13.2	11.4	0.4
Los Angeles-Long Beach, CA	34.1	42.0	26.7	38.4	32.1	31.4	34.7	30.7	2 448 852	31.9	23.5	20.8	-11.9	-8.1	75.2	12.6	11.8	0.4
Orange County, CA....	40.9	51.5	30.7	44.0	46.7	36.3	37.9	36.0	714 668	39.4	28.1	16.9	-8.3	-2.1	77.0	11.1	11.6	0.4
Riverside-San Bernardino, CA.........	34.7	44.4	25.3	36.2	35.3	31.2	35.3	32.2	943 808	35.6	25.5	20.5	-8.4	-7.4	72.9	16.8	9.9	0.4
Ventura, CA...............	40.3	50.6	30.1	42.9	44.9	37.6	43.1	34.0	200 721	42.0	26.7	17.5	-5.1	-0.4	73.0	14.4	12.2	0.4
Louisville, KY-IN	43.5	53.1	34.8	44.7	36.7	38.2	43.1	40.3	240 424	44.7	17.8	24.8	5.0	3.2	80.0	11.5	8.3	0.2
Lubbock, TX	39.2	47.4	31.6	39.6	33.2	40.7	30.7	40.6	57 522	43.7	18.1	24.1	3.2	2.5	69.7	19.9	10.0	0.4
Lynchburg, VA	42.1	52.6	32.7	43.0	38.8	33.6	38.7	35.0	47 072	45.6	19.2	23.5	4.5	1.1	78.6	12.5	8.6	0.2
Macon, GA	41.7	52.3	32.6	46.0	34.4	36.1	38.1	43.6	81 991	38.2	16.8	29.8	3.5	0.7	69.9	22.4	7.5	0.2
Madison, WI	46.6	54.7	38.8	48.1	38.6	38.7	29.2	34.9	92 684	60.4	14.7	17.9	13.7	16.5	68.5	23.5	7.8	0.2
Mansfield, OH	40.6	49.6	31.7	41.5	29.2	37.3	42.1	34.0	41 131	45.3	21.2	22.5	3.3	0.2	80.7	11.2	7.7	0.3
McAllen-Edinburg-Mission, TX	25.9	33.4	19.2	24.8	24.5	23.6	36.6	26.0	187 365	30.6	31.1	15.5	-18.4	-18.9	68.9	19.2	11.6	0.4
Medford-Ashland, OR ...	32.4	42.0	23.7	32.7	32.8	34.8	31.2	29.1	41 548	44.0	23.3	23.0	2.4	-5.3	69.5	13.7	16.3	0.5
Melbourne-Titusville-Palm Bay,FL..............	37.4	46.3	28.9	37.5	35.3	41.1	35.8	39.4	97 602	42.2	23.2	24.0	1.7	-9.0	74.0	15.4	10.3	0.3
Memphis, TN-AR-MS	43.5	52.6	35.6	47.8	38.0	45.9	43.2	38.8	296 520	35.9	17.2	30.9	2.4	3.1	77.5	14.7	7.7	0.3

[1] Hispanic or Latino persons may be of any race.

Area name	Percent who worked at home	Percent of the population 5 years and over with a disability	Veterans as a percent of the population 18 years and over	Occupation for employed population 16 years and over (percent)						Industry for employed population 16 years and over (percent)					
				Management, professional, and related occupations	Service occupations	Sales and office occupations	Farming, fishing, and forestry occupations	Construction, extraction, and maintenance occupations	Production, transportation and material moving occupations	Agriculture, forestry, fishing, and mining	Construction and manufacturing	Wholesale and retail trade	Transportation and warehousing, and utilities	Service industries	Public administration
	42	43	44	45	46	47	48	49	50	51	52	53	54	55	56
Hartford, CT	2.6	17.5	12.2	39.6	13.7	27.1	0.2	7.3	12.1	0.4	19.9	14.1	4.1	56.7	4.8
Hattiesburg, MS	2.3	21.2	11.9	31.1	16.3	28.1	0.7	9.9	13.9	2.7	17.1	17.4	4.8	54.1	4.0
Hickory-Morganton-Lenoir, NC	1.8	22.6	12.7	22.2	11.8	21.9	0.5	9.3	34.3	0.8	45.1	14.1	4.6	32.8	2.7
Honolulu, HI	2.9	17.9	13.2	33.8	19.6	29.1	0.7	8.1	8.8	1.1	9.2	15.7	6.5	58.2	9.3
Houma, LA	2.1	23.3	10.1	25.2	13.8	26.1	1.7	14.3	18.9	10.2	18.6	17.2	7.0	43.3	3.8
Houston-Galveston-Brazoria, TX	2.5	18.2	9.9	35.2	13.6	27.3	0.2	11.1	12.5	2.5	20.9	15.8	6.6	50.8	3.3
Brazoria, TX	2.2	17.6	13.4	32.7	12.8	24.4	0.4	14.8	15.0	2.2	29.5	13.7	5.6	43.7	5.3
Galveston-Texas City, TX	2.5	18.6	13.8	35.9	15.8	25.4	0.4	11.2	11.3	1.5	20.3	13.3	5.4	54.0	5.5
Houston, TX	2.5	18.2	9.5	35.3	13.6	27.6	0.2	10.9	12.5	2.5	20.5	16.1	6.8	51.0	3.1
Huntington-Ashland, WV-KY-OH	2.2	26.5	14.3	27.2	16.6	28.2	0.4	11.6	16.0	1.5	18.9	17.2	6.5	51.5	4.4
Huntsville, AL	2.3	18.7	15.4	40.4	12.4	23.5	0.3	8.6	14.8	0.7	26.6	13.5	3.3	47.1	8.8
Indianapolis, IN	2.9	19.0	13.0	33.7	13.5	27.9	0.2	9.3	15.4	0.6	22.7	16.4	6.1	50.4	3.9
Iowa City, IA	3.1	12.0	8.5	43.3	15.5	26.1	0.3	6.0	8.9	1.4	12.1	13.3	2.8	68.1	2.4
Jackson, MI	2.8	19.7	13.8	27.5	16.5	24.6	0.4	9.4	21.7	1.1	29.2	15.5	5.9	43.2	5.1
Jackson, MS	2.2	20.1	11.4	35.1	14.2	29.1	0.4	8.9	12.3	0.9	15.4	16.4	5.3	55.0	6.9
Jackson, TN	2.0	21.9	12.2	29.8	13.9	26.1	0.4	9.7	20.1	0.8	28.0	16.1	4.5	46.7	3.9
Jacksonville, FL	2.3	20.6	18.0	32.0	14.4	31.4	0.3	10.1	11.8	0.5	15.2	16.6	7.5	55.0	5.3
Jacksonville, NC	2.4	20.2	16.9	26.1	19.2	28.0	1.2	14.1	11.4	2.0	15.7	17.2	4.6	51.1	9.3
Jamestown, NY	3.3	20.3	14.7	27.2	18.2	23.4	1.2	8.6	21.5	2.7	26.6	14.5	4.8	47.7	3.7
Janesville-Beloit, WI	2.7	17.3	14.2	25.4	14.0	23.7	0.5	9.7	26.8	1.7	35.5	15.5	4.6	40.0	2.7
Johnson City-Kingsport-Bristol, TN-VA	2.2	24.5	14.4	27.2	14.0	26.0	0.5	11.1	21.2	1.6	29.7	16.9	4.5	44.3	3.0
Johnstown, PA	3.0	20.6	15.1	26.8	17.9	24.4	0.8	11.1	19.0	2.9	20.3	15.6	6.1	49.8	5.3
Jonesboro, AR	2.6	22.7	12.1	28.5	14.4	26.0	1.0	9.8	20.5	2.6	24.7	17.7	4.7	47.3	3.0
Joplin, MO	3.0	20.1	14.3	25.9	14.4	25.3	0.7	9.9	23.8	2.2	29.0	16.1	6.8	43.2	2.7
Kalamazoo-Battle Creek, MI	2.9	18.7	12.8	31.0	15.7	24.8	0.8	8.5	19.3	1.5	28.7	14.4	3.9	48.1	3.5
Kansas City, MO-KS	3.4	17.3	13.9	35.8	13.5	28.9	0.2	9.0	12.6	0.7	18.0	15.9	6.0	54.7	4.7
Killeen-Temple, TX	1.8	18.6	19.7	30.1	17.9	27.0	0.5	10.7	13.8	1.3	16.2	15.7	4.9	52.5	9.3
Knoxville, TN	2.7	21.3	13.7	32.5	15.0	27.9	0.3	9.9	14.5	0.7	20.5	17.4	5.1	52.7	3.6
Kokomo, IN	2.3	19.4	14.7	25.9	15.7	20.6	0.5	10.6	26.8	1.6	38.7	13.5	3.3	39.5	3.4
La Crosse, WI-MN	3.8	14.7	13.4	31.2	16.4	26.7	0.6	8.0	17.0	2.3	21.4	18.3	4.2	50.6	3.1
Lafayette, IN	2.8	16.5	10.7	33.6	15.4	23.0	0.7	7.8	19.5	1.5	27.1	13.3	2.9	52.9	2.3
Lafayette, LA	2.3	21.5	10.7	29.9	15.6	26.8	0.5	12.4	14.8	9.8	14.7	17.4	4.9	49.0	4.2
Lake Charles, LA	1.7	21.1	13.9	27.2	18.2	25.6	0.3	13.9	14.8	2.1	24.2	14.4	4.9	50.3	4.2
Lakeland-Winter Haven, FL	2.1	24.6	17.0	26.2	16.7	27.1	2.0	11.8	16.1	3.4	17.7	19.8	6.1	48.3	4.8
Lancaster, PA	4.8	16.0	12.0	28.1	13.9	24.9	1.1	10.0	22.0	2.9	30.2	17.5	4.3	43.1	2.0
Lansing-East Lansing, MI	3.2	16.7	10.9	34.6	15.3	27.2	0.4	8.2	14.3	1.1	18.7	13.9	3.5	53.5	9.4
Laredo, TX	2.9	20.2	5.5	26.7	17.8	29.0	0.6	11.4	14.6	2.5	12.2	18.1	13.9	46.7	6.6
Las Cruces, NM	3.5	19.8	12.5	32.3	18.3	25.1	1.8	11.0	11.6	3.7	15.0	14.2	4.5	54.2	8.4
Las Vegas, NV-AZ	2.3	21.8	16.3	24.0	26.7	27.8	0.1	11.5	9.8	0.5	13.8	13.7	5.1	63.1	3.8
Lawrence, KS	3.7	13.1	8.7	40.4	16.6	25.0	0.2	7.7	10.1	1.0	15.4	13.6	3.1	62.8	3.9
Lawton, OK	2.3	19.6	19.5	29.5	19.5	25.6	0.6	10.5	14.3	2.2	16.5	15.1	4.2	53.5	8.5
Lewiston-Auburn, ME	2.6	22.4	15.8	26.0	14.5	28.8	0.7	10.9	19.0	1.2	25.6	18.7	3.7	47.1	3.6
Lexington, KY	2.7	19.1	11.5	35.5	14.8	25.7	1.2	8.3	14.6	2.9	21.6	15.2	3.8	52.6	3.9
Lima, OH	2.6	17.8	14.1	25.4	16.0	22.5	0.5	9.2	26.3	1.7	32.5	15.7	4.2	41.8	4.0
Lincoln, NE	3.2	14.6	11.4	36.0	15.0	26.8	0.3	8.4	13.4	1.0	18.4	14.0	4.3	55.6	6.8
Little Rock-North Little Rock, AR	2.3	21.2	14.7	33.7	13.6	29.2	0.4	9.8	13.4	0.9	17.4	16.4	6.1	52.9	6.2
Longview-Marshall, TX	2.5	22.1	13.7	27.4	14.3	26.6	0.5	12.2	19.0	4.3	23.5	17.2	5.2	46.3	3.5
Los Angeles-Riverside-Orange County, CA	3.6	19.5	9.0	34.0	14.7	27.7	0.5	8.4	14.8	0.7	20.7	15.7	4.9	54.4	3.6
Los Angeles-Long Beach, CA	3.5	20.4	7.4	34.3	14.7	27.6	0.2	7.8	15.5	0.3	20.0	15.2	5.0	56.4	3.2
Orange County, CA	3.7	16.6	9.3	38.1	13.2	28.7	0.3	7.3	12.5	0.4	23.1	16.3	3.6	53.7	2.9
Riverside-San Bernardino, CA	3.5	19.9	12.7	28.0	16.6	27.2	1.0	11.5	15.7	1.5	20.7	16.6	6.2	49.8	5.2
Ventura, CA	4.2	17.7	11.8	36.5	13.4	27.3	3.1	8.2	11.5	4.1	20.1	15.0	3.3	52.0	5.4
Louisville, KY-IN	2.4	20.0	13.8	31.2	13.9	27.9	0.3	9.2	17.6	0.6	22.3	15.3	7.1	50.8	3.8
Lubbock, TX	2.4	19.4	10.7	33.2	16.7	29.3	0.6	9.4	10.8	1.9	12.2	18.1	4.1	59.4	4.4
Lynchburg, VA	2.7	21.1	14.0	28.8	13.9	26.8	0.6	10.5	19.3	1.2	29.3	16.2	5.0	45.2	3.1
Macon, GA	1.8	21.0	15.7	31.0	15.5	27.3	0.3	11.8	14.1	1.2	18.5	15.2	4.6	48.9	11.6
Madison, WI	3.8	12.9	10.1	43.6	12.7	26.5	0.4	6.7	10.1	1.2	15.8	13.7	3.3	59.5	6.5
Mansfield, OH	2.7	19.0	14.9	23.3	15.2	23.7	0.5	9.6	27.7	1.3	34.9	14.7	4.4	40.3	4.4
McAllen-Edinburg-Mission, TX	2.2	20.9	6.8	26.3	18.5	25.4	2.9	12.4	14.4	4.1	16.9	18.4	5.0	51.0	4.6
Medford-Ashland, OR	5.6	20.2	18.3	30.6	17.4	26.6	1.5	9.5	14.4	2.8	18.2	18.9	4.3	52.1	3.7
Melbourne-Titusville-Palm Bay, FL	2.7	21.9	21.3	34.9	16.5	26.9	0.3	10.5	10.8	0.5	21.5	15.9	4.1	50.8	7.3
Memphis, TN-AR-MS	2.2	20.5	12.4	31.7	14.1	29.7	0.2	8.9	15.4	0.5	17.5	16.5	11.7	49.1	4.8

Area name	Median house-hold income	All families	Married-couple	Male house-holder	Female house-holder	Median nonfamily house-hold income	Men	Women	Per capita income	With earnings	With interest, dividend, or rental income	With Social Security income	With public assis-tance income	With retire-ment income	House-holds with income over $100,000 (percent)	+/− U.S. percent for income over $100,000	House-holds with income below poverty (percent)	Families with children with income below poverty (percent)
	57	58	59	60	61	62	63	64	65	66	67	68	69	70	71	72	73	74
Hartford, CT	52 603	64 784	77 752	36 252	24 341	31 078	46 548	35 012	26 277	80.6	44.6	26.9	4.0	18.8	17.9	5.6	8.2	9.1
Hattiesburg, MS	30 981	39 078	48 610	22 667	15 145	16 966	31 230	21 833	16 450	80.0	24.4	24.4	3.2	14.0	6.8	−5.5	19.0	19.7
Hickory-Morganton-Lenoir, NC	37 818	44 475	51 412	26 658	19 451	21 449	30 387	23 095	18 723	82.6	27.9	26.7	2.4	13.9	6.4	−5.9	10.1	10.9
Honolulu, HI	51 914	60 118	62 676	33 020	22 711	31 440	37 423	30 444	21 998	83.6	46.9	27.5	6.8	21.9	18.2	5.9	9.7	10.3
Houma, LA	35 089	40 225	49 653	25 696	12 843	18 143	35 579	20 636	15 939	78.5	27.2	26.7	2.9	11.8	6.1	−6.2	17.2	19.7
Houston-Galveston-Brazoria, TX	44 761	51 426	59 362	30 704	21 815	30 082	40 402	29 987	21 701	87.0	29.4	17.0	2.4	10.5	15.1	2.8	12.2	14.6
Brazoria, TX	48 632	55 282	63 468	31 559	21 350	26 436	43 385	28 634	20 021	85.5	33.4	20.1	2.0	14.1	13.6	1.3	9.7	11.1
Galveston-Texas City, TX	42 419	51 435	63 307	33 065	19 588	24 694	42 482	29 692	21 568	82.2	32.1	23.0	3.0	16.3	13.0	0.7	12.7	15.0
Houston, TX	44 655	51 212	58 739	30 483	21 967	30 442	40 124	30 053	21 806	87.4	29.0	16.5	2.4	9.9	15.4	3.1	12.3	14.8
Huntington-Ashland, WV-KY-OH	29 415	36 619	42 808	20 524	13 621	14 983	33 030	22 271	16 357	70.2	27.7	34.5	4.5	20.9	4.9	−7.4	18.6	21.7
Huntsville, AL	43 104	52 248	61 675	27 284	18 871	24 988	41 151	26 969	22 073	82.9	36.8	22.0	2.2	19.5	12.3	0.0	11.3	12.6
Indianapolis, IN	45 548	55 191	67 131	31 864	22 313	27 582	40 929	29 093	23 198	84.1	32.3	22.6	2.4	16.0	12.6	0.3	8.4	9.2
Iowa City, IA	40 060	60 112	69 133	33 629	22 431	24 174	37 358	30 638	22 220	89.3	46.9	15.5	1.8	10.7	11.9	−0.4	15.5	7.7
Jackson, MI	43 171	50 970	60 851	31 301	19 540	23 489	39 905	27 117	20 171	79.0	36.9	28.5	3.5	20.7	8.9	−3.4	8.7	10.5
Jackson, MS	38 887	46 355	59 988	25 151	17 821	23 579	35 421	26 468	19 435	83.0	26.8	23.0	3.1	14.7	9.9	−2.4	15.0	17.9
Jackson, TN	36 649	43 948	55 700	26 406	17 477	21 764	35 122	24 489	18 863	80.8	28.6	26.4	3.3	15.2	8.0	−4.3	14.4	15.5
Jacksonville, FL............	42 439	50 189	58 961	30 044	21 448	26 788	36 290	26 746	21 763	83.0	31.8	23.3	2.3	17.9	11.0	−1.3	10.4	11.9
Jacksonville, NC............	33 756	36 692	40 141	23 772	15 762	21 965	22 754	20 678	14 853	86.3	23.7	17.2	3.5	18.4	4.1	−8.2	12.2	14.8
Jamestown, NY	33 458	41 054	48 644	25 487	15 030	18 661	33 111	22 967	16 840	75.8	40.6	32.2	3.9	20.7	5.6	−6.7	12.8	16.9
Janesville-Beloit, WI	45 517	53 380	60 763	32 069	23 858	26 266	39 638	26 532	20 895	81.9	43.5	26.4	1.7	17.3	9.1	−3.2	7.2	7.9
Johnson City-Kingsport-Bristol, TN-VA	31 596	38 720	43 907	24 114	15 246	16 459	30 926	21 776	17 800	74.5	31.2	32.3	3.4	18.4	5.5	−6.8	15.3	16.3
Johnstown, PA	30 442	37 413	44 504	23 141	13 484	16 084	30 127	21 388	15 755	69.4	38.1	37.9	2.9	25.3	3.8	−8.5	12.8	15.0
Jonesboro, AR	32 425	40 688	47 290	26 495	13 902	17 774	31 134	21 716	17 091	81.7	27.2	25.3	2.8	13.3	6.2	−6.1	16.0	16.9
Joplin, MO	32 446	38 677	45 403	22 483	17 168	18 219	30 033	21 424	16 653	79.4	31.9	29.2	3.6	15.4	4.9	−7.4	13.4	14.8
Kalamazoo-Battle Creek, MI.................	42 710	50 494	60 441	32 271	20 425	24 137	38 772	27 735	20 324	80.8	37.1	25.7	3.5	17.4	9.5	−2.8	11.2	11.3
Kansas City, MO-KS....	46 193	55 779	66 581	31 226	23 618	28 111	40 824	29 432	23 326	83.5	37.9	23.1	2.5	15.9	12.5	0.2	8.4	9.2
Killeen-Temple, TX.......	36 669	40 882	43 412	28 736	18 284	23 753	28 328	22 707	16 546	86.0	25.8	18.6	2.7	18.8	6.1	−6.2	11.1	13.1
Knoxville, TN	36 874	45 697	53 734	27 869	17 242	20 744	34 506	24 601	20 538	78.9	34.5	27.7	3.1	18.3	8.9	−3.4	13.0	13.0
Kokomo, IN	44 531	53 509	64 155	37 422	20 771	24 343	45 202	27 150	22 209	79.1	35.7	27.5	2.9	23.2	10.3	−2.0	8.6	9.9
La Crosse, WI-MN	39 092	50 165	58 255	28 505	22 056	22 791	35 236	24 096	19 649	82.4	45.7	26.7	1.4	15.0	7.5	−4.8	10.0	7.9
Lafayette, IN................	39 072	51 134	58 233	29 190	22 119	22 066	38 566	26 018	19 095	84.6	38.5	20.5	2.1	13.8	8.9	−3.4	14.2	10.3
Lafayette, LA................	30 998	37 687	50 039	24 899	13 360	16 009	33 833	21 415	16 072	77.5	25.1	24.2	3.1	11.6	6.7	−5.6	21.1	22.5
Lake Charles, LA	35 372	41 903	54 100	28 701	14 514	19 050	37 961	21 967	17 710	78.8	26.9	26.0	2.6	15.5	7.6	−4.7	15.8	17.7
Lakeland-Winter Haven, FL..............	36 036	41 442	50 992	28 644	18 913	21 676	32 067	23 291	18 302	73.4	32.3	36.6	3.3	21.9	6.6	−5.7	11.9	15.5
Lancaster, PA...............	45 507	52 513	59 032	31 875	21 376	26 348	37 964	25 832	20 398	82.7	44.3	26.5	1.8	16.9	9.7	−2.6	7.0	8.0
Lansing-East Lansing, MI.....................	44 441	55 698	65 403	33 173	22 442	26 619	41 902	30 885	21 653	83.6	40.3	21.9	3.0	18.0	11.2	−1.1	11.1	10.0
Laredo, TX	28 100	29 394	32 211	17 137	12 081	14 288	24 267	19 543	10 759	85.2	14.3	21.6	7.9	9.0	6.2	−6.1	28.1	32.8
Las Cruces, NM	29 808	33 576	37 345	18 377	13 900	18 022	28 098	21 639	13 999	80.5	26.6	24.1	6.0	17.6	5.3	−7.0	22.3	28.9
Las Vegas, NV-AZ	42 468	48 420	56 019	31 303	23 492	28 933	35 876	27 297	21 210	81.9	28.2	25.5	2.5	18.6	10.6	−1.7	9.8	12.2
Lawrence, KS..............	37 547	53 991	60 835	28 427	22 133	21 780	36 559	28 097	19 952	87.5	39.0	16.7	1.8	10.9	9.0	−3.3	17.1	8.9
Lawton, OK	33 867	39 214	44 377	25 725	13 364	20 071	30 503	22 940	15 728	81.0	26.3	22.5	5.8	21.1	5.2	−7.1	15.4	18.6
Lewiston-Auburn, ME....	35 793	44 082	53 997	26 126	17 794	20 146	32 327	23 205	18 734	78.1	34.4	29.2	5.9	15.7	5.4	−6.9	12.1	12.3
Lexington, KY...............	39 357	49 876	60 251	26 382	18 545	23 150	36 540	26 712	21 237	84.3	32.4	21.3	2.4	15.5	10.2	−2.1	13.0	13.1
Lima, OH	39 284	46 642	56 751	28 750	18 215	21 132	36 884	24 915	18 137	77.4	37.2	28.3	2.6	20.8	7.0	−5.3	10.6	12.4
Lincoln, NE	41 850	53 676	61 495	27 988	20 912	25 574	35 690	26 321	21 265	86.1	43.7	20.3	2.9	13.1	9.4	−2.9	9.7	8.7
Little Rock-North Little Rock, AR	39 145	46 753	55 179	27 279	18 761	23 745	34 369	25 881	20 263	82.9	30.9	23.6	2.3	15.8	8.9	−3.4	11.8	13.9
Longview-Marshall, TX..	34 253	41 325	48 956	24 632	16 570	18 751	33 817	21 801	17 576	77.1	29.1	29.2	3.2	16.2	6.6	−5.7	15.3	17.6
Los Angeles-Riverside-Orange County, CA....	45 903	50 645	56 092	30 071	21 545	31 476	40 020	31 724	21 170	83.3	31.4	21.1	5.4	13.7	16.2	3.9	13.0	16.9
Los Angeles-Long Beach, CA	42 189	46 452	51 165	27 278	20 044	30 917	37 089	31 583	20 683	83.3	29.7	19.7	6.4	12.1	15.1	2.8	15.1	19.9
Orange County, CA.....	58 820	64 611	69 855	37 506	31 285	40 152	46 263	35 268	25 826	86.3	39.5	20.2	2.7	14.1	23.5	11.2	7.7	10.1
Riverside-San Bernardino, CA........	42 404	47 400	54 381	29 146	19 950	25 177	38 888	29 030	17 726	80.2	27.3	25.4	5.4	17.1	11.5	−0.8	12.8	16.0
Ventura, CA.............	59 666	65 285	71 930	40 902	29 864	36 651	46 937	33 737	24 600	85.2	40.2	23.2	2.9	17.5	22.8	10.5	7.2	9.1
Louisville, KY-IN............	40 821	49 774	61 635	27 367	18 986	24 288	37 100	26 643	21 756	80.3	34.1	26.2	2.9	18.4	10.5	−1.8	11.0	13.2
Lubbock, TX	32 198	41 067	48 177	21 763	17 220	18 022	30 775	22 185	17 323	83.4	28.2	22.5	3.1	12.4	7.0	−5.3	18.1	17.9
Lynchburg, VA..............	37 010	44 344	52 876	27 325	17 657	21 412	33 540	23 380	18 887	78.8	33.0	29.7	2.7	18.2	7.2	−5.1	11.7	13.1
Macon, GA	38 565	46 279	58 279	30 839	16 894	22 005	36 503	26 134	18 840	80.0	27.2	24.5	3.8	20.2	8.5	−3.8	15.1	18.2
Madison, WI	49 223	62 964	70 858	34 071	25 982	30 980	40 348	30 917	24 985	87.8	53.2	18.0	1.3	12.6	13.0	0.7	9.2	6.1
Mansfield, OH	37 060	44 409	51 898	27 549	19 063	20 809	35 710	23 339	18 284	77.9	34.9	29.6	2.9	19.8	6.2	−6.1	10.4	13.4
McAllen-Edinburg-Mission, TX	24 863	26 009	26 950	15 198	12 156	14 445	21 805	18 972	9 899	79.0	16.0	25.8	10.8	10.7	4.7	−7.6	31.9	39.1
Medford-Ashland, OR ...	36 461	43 675	50 770	24 054	17 040	21 717	34 731	24 639	19 498	75.8	39.0	32.1	3.8	20.3	8.0	−4.3	11.9	14.7
Melbourne-Titusville-Palm Bay, FL............	40 099	47 571	57 702	30 930	20 145	24 911	38 090	25 551	21 484	72.3	40.7	35.8	2.3	27.2	9.3	−3.0	9.1	11.2
Memphis, TN-AR-MS	40 201	47 440	61 592	28 965	19 356	25 244	37 558	27 051	20 327	82.9	26.2	21.8	4.2	14.2	10.8	−1.5	14.5	17.4

Table B-4. Metropolitan Areas — Education, Labor Force, and Income

CMSA/MSA/PMSA/NECMA code[1]	Area name	High school graduates			College graduates		College graduates (percent)				
		Total population 25 years and over	Percent with a high school diploma or less	Percent with a high school diploma or more	Percent with a bachelor's degree or more	+/− U.S. percent with bachelor's degree or more	Non-Hispanic White	Black or African American	American Indian and Alaska Native	Asian, Hawaiian, and Pacific Islander	Hispanic or Latino[2]
		1	2	3	4	5	6	7	8	9	10
4940	Merced, CA	116 725	60.1	63.8	11.0	−13.4	16.6	11.1	7.4	13.2	3.5
56	Miami-Fort Lauderdale, FL	2 618 291	51.0	73.9	22.9	−1.5	30.5	12.9	15.6	41.3	18.9
2680	Fort Lauderdale, FL	1 126 502	46.4	82.0	24.5	0.1	27.2	14.7	15.2	38.4	23.0
5000	Miami, FL	1 491 789	54.5	67.9	21.7	−2.7	38.0	11.5	15.8	44.7	18.1
63	Milwaukee-Racine, WI	1 090 663	45.2	84.3	26.2	1.8	29.1	10.1	11.7	46.0	10.4
5080	Milwaukee-Waukesha, WI	968 307	44.6	84.5	27.0	2.6	30.1	10.3	11.7	46.1	10.7
6600	Racine, WI	122 356	49.6	82.9	20.3	−4.1	22.1	7.1	11.2	43.6	8.3
5120	Minneapolis-St. Paul, MN-WI	1 903 346	34.8	90.6	33.3	8.9	34.5	19.1	11.5	36.2	16.7
5140	Missoula, MT	59 298	35.5	91.0	32.8	8.4	33.1	50.7	19.3	39.9	29.4
5160	Mobile, AL	346 132	53.1	78.2	19.9	−4.5	22.9	10.4	9.5	33.4	20.2
5170	Modesto, CA	264 578	55.7	70.4	14.1	−10.3	17.2	14.7	7.4	21.0	5.1
5200	Monroe, LA	88 430	51.4	78.6	22.7	−1.7	26.6	13.1	9.1	48.0	12.2
5240	Montgomery, AL	212 108	48.0	79.5	24.7	0.3	29.3	16.3	11.8	31.4	21.6
5280	Muncie, IN	72 444	55.6	81.6	20.4	−4.0	20.7	11.1	3.3	68.8	26.1
5330	Myrtle Beach, SC	136 551	51.0	81.1	18.7	−5.7	20.4	8.0	12.4	28.4	10.8
5345	Naples, FL	185 357	44.5	81.8	27.9	3.5	32.4	8.9	8.5	43.8	7.1
5360	Nashville, TN	800 302	46.7	81.4	26.9	2.5	28.3	18.9	17.9	45.7	14.2
5523	New London-Norwich, CT	173 910	46.0	86.0	26.2	1.8	27.5	12.5	10.9	42.8	11.9
5560	New Orleans, LA	850 631	50.7	77.7	22.6	−1.8	27.6	12.7	13.0	33.2	20.8
70	New York-Northern New Jersey-Long Island, NY-NJ-CT-PA	14 142 132	47.2	79.4	30.5	6.1	36.9	16.5	15.5	47.8	11.7
0875	Bergen-Passaic, NJ	939 870	45.8	82.1	32.5	8.1	35.2	17.1	11.4	58.8	13.1
2281	Dutchess County, NY	183 725	44.1	84.0	27.6	3.2	28.9	12.2	16.2	62.4	16.7
3640	Jersey City, NJ	408 799	56.3	70.5	25.3	0.9	31.8	16.5	19.2	56.4	12.1
5015	Middlesex-Somerset-Hunterdon, NJ	789 443	40.3	86.5	37.4	13.0	36.3	27.2	25.7	71.5	13.3
5190	Monmouth-Ocean, NJ	771 412	46.6	85.6	27.6	3.2	27.9	14.9	14.5	60.0	14.9
5380	Nassau-Suffolk, NY	1 851 094	42.6	86.4	31.3	6.9	33.2	20.8	20.0	57.2	13.6
5483	New Haven-Bridgeport-Stamford-Danbury-Waterbury, CT	1 148 013	43.3	83.7	34.0	9.6	38.0	13.8	18.3	61.8	11.0
5600	New York, NY	6 154 523	50.2	74.0	29.2	4.8	42.5	16.3	14.1	38.0	11.0
5640	Newark, NJ	1 353 905	46.3	81.6	31.5	7.1	38.2	15.5	16.4	64.8	12.8
5660	Newburgh, NY-PA	244 341	49.9	82.5	22.1	−2.3	23.3	14.3	11.1	49.2	11.9
8480	Trenton, NJ	231 139	43.8	81.8	34.0	9.6	39.5	12.8	17.3	71.1	11.6
5720	Norfolk-Virginia Beach-Newport News, VA-NC	981 300	43.1	84.7	23.8	−0.6	27.6	14.2	14.9	34.6	19.8
5790	Ocala, FL	187 187	57.7	78.2	13.7	−10.7	14.0	10.5	16.5	34.9	9.5
5800	Odessa-Midland, TX	142 764	51.3	73.5	18.4	−6.0	24.7	9.3	14.7	52.9	5.1
5880	Oklahoma City, OK	684 005	44.1	83.6	24.4	0.0	26.4	15.6	15.6	36.9	9.6
5920	Omaha, NE-IA	451 736	40.2	88.0	28.0	3.6	29.6	13.5	9.3	50.3	11.6
5960	Orlando, FL	1 083 496	44.7	82.8	24.8	0.4	27.4	14.6	15.5	41.7	17.0
5990	Owensboro, KY	59 745	56.9	80.7	17.0	−7.4	17.2	7.6	17.6	63.5	17.6
6015	Panama City, FL	99 771	49.6	81.0	17.7	−6.7	18.5	9.5	9.8	22.5	19.0
6020	Parkersburg-Marietta, WV-OH	103 467	57.6	82.7	15.2	−9.2	15.0	16.9	8.7	53.5	20.4
6080	Pensacola, FL	267 876	45.5	83.0	21.5	−2.9	23.8	9.5	9.9	24.5	23.1
6120	Peoria-Pekin, IL	228 109	47.2	84.7	21.1	−3.3	21.6	9.5	6.4	62.1	17.7
77	Philadelphia-Wilmington-Atlantic City, PA-NJ-DE-MD	4 079 483	49.9	81.9	26.9	2.5	30.2	12.8	15.9	46.9	11.8
0560	Atlantic-Cape May, NJ	241 424	55.9	79.3	19.7	−4.7	21.6	10.5	22.3	31.9	7.8
6160	Philadelphia, PA-NJ	3 360 541	49.4	82.2	27.7	3.3	31.4	12.8	15.3	46.4	12.8
8760	Vineland-Millville-Bridgeton, NJ	96 899	67.8	68.5	11.7	−12.7	14.4	6.0	7.5	46.4	5.6
9160	Wilmington-Newark, DE-MD	380 619	46.0	84.8	27.6	3.2	29.3	15.8	27.0	66.6	14.7
6200	Phoenix-Mesa, AZ	2 054 059	41.6	81.9	25.1	0.7	29.4	19.4	9.4	45.3	7.8
6240	Pine Bluff, AR	53 132	60.0	74.4	15.7	−8.7	15.6	15.7	8.6	49.5	5.2
6280	Pittsburgh, PA	1 643 114	52.6	85.1	23.8	−0.6	24.1	12.8	13.6	69.8	31.6
6323	Pittsfield, MA	93 339	49.1	85.1	26.0	1.6	26.2	12.3	4.3	53.4	19.9
6340	Pocatello, ID	43 285	38.4	87.5	24.9	0.5	25.5	23.1	8.8	41.8	14.3
6403	Portland, ME	181 276	38.1	90.1	34.2	9.8	34.6	26.3	16.4	28.0	30.3
79	Portland-Salem, OR-WA	1 470 754	38.0	86.2	27.7	3.3	29.0	17.7	14.2	36.2	10.1
6440	Portland-Vancouver, OR-WA	1 253 714	36.6	87.2	28.8	4.4	30.0	18.0	15.3	37.0	11.8
7080	Salem, OR	217 040	45.8	80.4	20.8	−3.6	23.0	10.6	10.2	24.9	5.3
6483	Providence-Warwick-Pawtucket, RI	635 489	51.1	77.1	24.4	0.0	26.0	16.6	13.5	35.3	8.2
6520	Provo-Orem, UT	166 240	28.3	90.9	31.5	7.1	32.5	25.7	20.6	41.6	16.2
6560	Pueblo, CO	92 080	49.7	81.3	18.3	−6.1	22.8	15.7	11.0	42.1	9.5
6580	Punta Gorda, FL	113 071	53.5	82.1	17.6	−6.8	17.6	14.0	8.8	42.7	17.3
6640	Raleigh-Durham-Chapel Hill, NC	763 470	35.0	85.4	38.9	14.5	44.2	22.2	26.2	69.3	15.3
6660	Rapid City, SD	55 535	41.5	87.8	25.0	0.6	26.5	10.5	9.7	29.9	8.8

[1] MSA = Metropolitan Statistical Area. CMSA = Consolidated MSA. PMSA = Primary MSA. NECMA = New England County Metropolitan Area. See the Appendix A for explanation of these concepts. See Appendix B for list of metropolitan areas identified by type, with component counties.
[2] Hispanic or Latino persons may be of any race.

Table B-4. Metropolitan Areas — **Education, Labor Force, and Income**

Area name	School enrollment			Population 16 to 19 years				Employment status, 2000			Work status in 1999 of the population 16 years and over (percent)		
											Worked in 1999		
	Grades kindergarten through 12	College or graduate school	Percent private	Number	Percent in armed forces	Percent high school graduates	Percent not enrolled, not grads, not in armed forces, not employed	Total population 16 years and over	Percent in labor force	Unemployment rate	Full-time	Part-time	Did not work in 1999
	11	12	13	14	15	16	17	18	19	20	21	22	23
Merced, CA	55 741	11 077	5.8	14 424	0.0	10.2	7.2	145 720	59.5	13.1	51.0	13.8	35.2
Miami-Fort Lauderdale, FL	734 202	248 971	17.2	196 536	0.0	8.3	6.3	3 039 852	59.7	7.2	54.0	11.6	34.5
Fort Lauderdale, FL ...	290 350	88 536	17.2	73 499	0.0	9.3	5.4	1 281 478	62.7	5.3	55.2	11.8	32.9
Miami, FL	443 852	160 435	17.2	123 037	0.1	7.7	6.8	1 758 374	57.5	8.7	53.0	11.4	35.6
Milwaukee-Racine, WI ..	342 642	101 363	22.1	94 254	0.0	10.4	4.7	1 292 023	68.1	5.3	56.4	17.2	26.3
Milwaukee-Waukesha, WI..........	303 685	92 545	22.4	83 551	0.0	10.2	4.8	1 148 426	68.1	5.2	56.3	17.4	26.3
Racine, WI................	38 957	8 818	19.5	10 703	0.1	11.5	4.5	143 597	67.5	6.0	57.0	16.4	26.6
Minneapolis-St. Paul, MN-WI	589 261	182 317	15.6	162 190	0.1	9.0	3.1	2 259 896	74.3	3.5	61.3	18.6	20.1
Missoula, MT................	16 769	11 985	6.9	6 412	0.1	10.4	2.2	76 484	70.4	6.1	54.8	22.7	22.5
Mobile, AL	107 953	25 417	17.7	30 996	0.1	9.4	6.9	412 114	59.5	6.7	52.0	12.7	35.3
Modesto, CA	106 277	24 120	7.8	28 694	0.0	12.5	6.4	322 469	61.2	11.6	51.3	14.6	34.1
Monroe, LA	30 577	10 363	9.2	10 101	0.1	10.9	8.8	110 838	62.1	8.2	52.9	13.8	33.2
Montgomery, AL............	65 987	20 819	16.6	18 922	0.2	10.1	8.1	255 390	61.4	5.9	56.0	12.2	31.7
Muncie, IN	19 279	16 227	4.2	8 631	0.1	6.1	2.4	95 328	63.1	7.1	49.8	21.2	29.0
Myrtle Beach, SC	31 435	8 531	8.3	10 024	0.0	12.3	7.6	159 541	64.2	4.6	55.9	14.0	30.2
Naples, FL	36 873	6 692	11.3	10 207	0.1	11.1	8.9	206 955	52.9	3.7	46.5	12.3	41.1
Nashville, TN................	223 746	72 149	19.0	70 478	0.0	11.3	4.7	959 008	69.1	4.5	61.1	14.1	24.8
New London-Norwich, CT................	48 220	14 440	15.1	13 209	6.6	17.1	3.4	202 798	67.8	3.9	56.4	17.0	26.6
New Orleans, LA	273 870	82 593	27.5	79 590	0.2	9.4	7.0	1 021 502	61.2	6.8	52.6	13.7	33.8
New York-Northern New Jersey-Long Island, NY-NJ-CT-PA..	3 961 237	1 360 880	22.6	1 050 174	0.2	8.3	5.5	16 507 958	61.9	6.7	53.1	13.3	33.6
Bergen-Passaic, NJ ...	244 364	76 525	21.6	63 622	0.0	8.4	3.9	1 077 119	63.7	5.1	55.8	13.1	31.1
Dutchess County, NY.	53 680	20 086	20.6	16 633	0.1	7.0	5.3	218 021	63.7	5.7	52.9	16.3	30.8
Jersey City, NJ...........	106 450	41 431	24.7	29 361	0.1	10.0	7.7	486 268	61.2	8.7	56.6	10.5	32.9
Middlesex-Somerset-Hunterdon, NJ	208 247	74 380	15.6	54 953	0.0	7.7	3.1	913 597	67.3	4.4	59.1	13.9	27.1
Monmouth-Ocean, NJ	209 067	50 848	18.6	50 557	0.6	9.3	2.7	875 039	61.4	4.8	51.1	15.1	33.8
Nassau-Suffolk, NY	519 925	163 467	18.1	133 257	0.0	7.5	2.8	2 128 264	64.3	6.0	60.4	16.1	31.2
New Haven-Bridgeport-Stamford-Danbury-Waterbury, CT.....	322 602	100 288	21.1	82 287	0.0	8.1	4.5	1 322 280	65.8	5.3	55.3	15.6	29.1
New York, NY	1 743 752	669 054	26.5	475 394	0.0	8.0	7.3	7 283 630	58.6	8.7	50.7	11.8	37.5
Newark, NJ	386 754	111 795	19.0	98 216	0.0	9.3	4.5	1 566 221	64.6	6.2	56.3	13.2	30.5
Newburgh, NY-PA......	84 918	20 019	17.0	22 079	4.5	12.6	4.4	288 022	64.5	5.0	54.1	15.1	30.8
Trenton, NJ	62 905	28 687	23.8	19 442	0.1	7.0	4.0	275 489	65.4	7.5	56.2	15.2	28.6
Norfolk-Virginia Beach-Newport News, VA-NC	309 502	102 611	12.7	92 392	6.6	16.5	4.3	1 200 987	67.9	5.0	59.5	14.4	26.0
Ocala, FL......................	42 621	8 078	12.3	11 281	0.1	10.9	7.5	209 732	49.8	5.8	43.0	11.5	45.5
Odessa-Midland, TX	54 865	11 555	7.6	16 025	0.0	9.9	5.7	173 676	62.7	6.6	54.3	13.6	32.1
Oklahoma City, OK	203 960	82 290	11.4	67 569	0.5	10.6	5.3	839 094	64.9	4.8	56.9	14.6	28.5
Omaha, NE-IA.............	143 103	48 191	18.8	41 524	0.6	10.3	4.5	543 783	71.6	3.7	60.7	16.6	22.7
Orlando, FL.................	304 600	98 846	14.0	85 654	0.1	9.9	5.8	1 280 077	65.7	4.6	58.1	13.2	28.7
Owensboro, KY	17 533	3 889	20.0	5 545	0.0	10.5	3.1	70 915	64.4	5.8	54.4	15.2	30.4
Panama City, FL	27 420	6 965	7.8	7 949	2.3	13.4	5.2	116 666	61.8	4.7	53.8	12.8	33.4
Parkersburg-Marietta, WV-OH	26 267	6 665	11.0	8 207	0.0	11.8	5.2	120 456	59.7	6.9	50.1	14.2	35.7
Pensacola, FL..............	76 879	26 405	15.1	26 155	11.4	20.1	4.2	323 123	60.4	5.8	52.6	13.8	33.6
Peoria-Pekin, IL.............	64 276	20 294	18.4	19 523	0.0	10.5	3.6	270 402	64.6	4.8	53.7	16.9	29.4
Philadelphia-Wilmington-Atlantic City, PA-NJ-DE-MD....	1 194 754	380 076	25.0	335 529	0.2	9.3	4.7	4 793 823	64.0	6.2	54.0	14.9	31.1
Atlantic-Cape May, NJ	66 953	16 125	13.0	17 122	0.9	10.6	5.1	276 990	63.1	7.7	53.9	14.9	31.2
Philadelphia, PA-NJ ...	988 282	318 117	26.4	276 743	0.1	8.8	4.6	3 949 537	63.7	6.2	53.5	15.0	31.5
Vineland-Millville-Bridgeton, NJ	29 889	5 087	11.8	7 976	0.0	11.4	6.0	113 545	57.8	9.9	51.0	12.5	36.5
Wilmington-Newark, DE-MD....................	109 630	40 747	22.5	33 688	0.1	12.5	5.5	453 751	67.9	5.0	59.4	14.7	25.9
Phoenix-Mesa, AZ........	617 740	204 753	9.5	178 173	0.2	11.3	8.8	2 467 211	63.7	4.9	56.2	12.8	31.0
Pine Bluff, AR..............	16 558	4 998	5.1	5 609	0.0	12.9	6.0	64 892	56.0	8.3	51.6	11.1	37.3
Pittsburgh, PA	399 792	132 867	17.8	118 807	0.0	9.1	3.1	1 893 672	60.3	5.8	49.7	15.0	35.4
Pittsfield, MA	23 446	8 313	17.3	7 721	0.0	10.2	3.0	108 466	63.4	5.1	49.0	20.1	30.9
Pocatello, ID...............	15 052	9 013	4.9	5 556	0.2	15.8	3.2	56 815	67.5	6.9	52.1	22.4	25.5
Portland, ME	47 766	16 414	14.7	13 901	0.6	8.9	2.2	210 662	69.0	3.6	56.5	18.2	25.2
Portland-Salem, OR-WA......................	418 673	130 000	13.8	123 621	0.0	12.3	5.7	1 746 639	68.4	5.9	57.2	16.5	26.3
Portland-Vancouver, OR-WA	351 556	110 489	14.1	101 661	0.0	12.1	5.4	1 482 193	69.2	5.6	57.8	16.5	25.7
Salem, OR................	67 117	19 511	12.5	21 960	0.0	13.3	7.5	264 446	63.8	7.5	54.0	16.2	29.8
Providence-Warwick-Pawtucket, RI	175 604	77 923	22.6	57 009	0.0	8.5	4.6	759 498	64.2	5.6	52.3	17.4	30.3
Provo-Orem, UT...........	83 763	57 002	28.0	34 454	0.0	14.1	2.5	256 863	68.0	4.8	49.2	27.5	23.3
Pueblo, CO.................	27 023	8 081	6.7	8 387	0.0	9.9	8.6	109 584	58.3	6.3	49.1	15.3	35.6
Punta Gorda, FL	17 899	3 279	9.5	4 880	0.0	13.7	4.9	122 061	43.0	3.5	35.8	12.4	51.8
Raleigh-Durham-Chapel Hill, NC	206 260	107 359	14.7	65 528	0.0	7.6	4.6	928 248	70.6	4.1	62.2	14.9	23.0
Rapid City, SD	17 352	5 409	9.8	5 548	0.3	13.7	4.5	67 712	70.5	4.4	59.4	17.9	22.8

Area name	Full-year full-time employed (percent)								Children under 18 years in families (percent, except where noted)						Total employed by class of worker (percent)			
												With two parents							
	Total	Men	Women	Non-Hispanic White	Black or African American	American Indian and Alaska Native	Asian, Hawaiian, and Pacific Islander	Hispanic or Latino[1]	Number	Both in labor force	Father only in labor force	With one parent who is in labor force	+/− U.S. percent of children with no stay-at-home parent	+/− U.S. percent two-income couples	Private	Government	Self-employed	Unpaid family worker
	24	25	26	27	28	29	30	31	32	33	34	35	36	37	38	39	40	41
Merced, CA	29.6	38.8	20.6	35.0	27.0	33.4	21.1	24.8	67 821	35.3	24.7	19.2	-10.1	-10.3	73.1	16.8	9.6	0.6
Miami-Fort Lauderdale, FL	39.0	47.3	31.6	40.6	37.9	35.3	42.0	37.8	870 763	37.7	18.3	25.1	-1.8	-5.4	75.9	12.3	11.5	0.3
Fort Lauderdale, FL	42.0	51.0	33.9	41.2	43.1	42.8	44.1	43.7	357 728	41.5	19.8	25.2	2.1	-2.1	76.7	11.7	11.3	0.2
Miami, FL	36.8	44.6	29.9	39.3	34.2	29.4	39.6	36.6	513 035	35.0	17.3	25.0	-4.6	-8.1	75.2	12.7	11.7	0.3
Milwaukee-Racine, WI	43.7	53.7	34.4	46.0	32.9	40.6	39.6	36.9	421 187	46.5	17.4	23.3	5.2	6.8	81.9	11.2	6.8	0.2
Milwaukee-Waukesha, WI	43.7	53.8	34.4	46.0	33.3	40.6	39.5	36.9	372 850	46.1	17.3	23.6	5.0	7.0	81.7	11.2	6.8	0.2
Racine, WI	43.7	53.1	34.6	45.9	28.6	40.4	41.4	36.6	48 337	49.4	17.9	21.7	6.5	5.7	82.8	10.8	6.3	0.2
Minneapolis-St. Paul, MN-WI	48.6	58.9	38.7	50.0	38.2	37.7	39.5	39.2	764 507	55.2	18.3	18.0	8.6	13.5	79.5	11.7	8.6	0.2
Missoula, MT	37.0	44.5	29.6	37.6	17.9	21.6	27.8	34.9	20 918	50.5	20.7	20.5	6.4	7.7	69.6	17.1	13.0	0.3
Mobile, AL	38.8	49.2	29.6	41.3	32.2	33.3	32.3	39.0	134 608	37.8	21.9	24.5	-2.3	-5.8	75.7	14.1	10.0	0.2
Modesto, CA	32.9	43.0	23.4	35.8	31.8	36.2	29.8	26.5	128 843	38.8	23.8	18.8	-7.0	-7.5	74.5	14.7	10.4	0.5
Monroe, LA	38.5	47.3	30.9	42.6	29.6	35.9	41.5	31.4	37 411	38.0	15.2	31.5	4.9	2.2	72.7	18.0	9.1	0.2
Montgomery, AL	43.4	52.1	35.5	48.4	35.3	37.9	50.2	48.3	81 555	40.2	17.7	25.9	1.5	1.7	68.6	22.5	8.6	0.3
Muncie, IN	35.0	44.6	26.3	35.6	30.5	37.8	20.4	21.7	24 734	45.1	19.4	24.0	4.5	-1.8	76.5	15.9	7.3	0.3
Myrtle Beach, SC	41.3	49.1	34.0	42.2	36.1	34.3	42.4	43.0	39 278	43.2	17.4	25.5	4.1	-2.3	75.9	11.6	12.2	0.3
Naples, FL	32.4	39.7	25.1	31.2	35.2	32.8	56.8	35.7	45 804	39.7	22.6	23.2	-1.7	-15.8	74.6	9.2	15.9	0.3
Nashville, TN	46.8	56.9	37.4	48.3	40.6	50.6	42.8	41.6	287 842	45.5	21.8	22.5	3.5	5.6	77.7	12.1	10.0	0.3
New London-Norwich, CT	44.4	55.9	33.3	45.1	37.8	39.3	49.4	41.0	60 353	51.7	18.6	21.9	9.0	6.1	76.1	15.2	8.5	0.2
New Orleans, LA	38.3	47.1	30.5	42.5	31.5	38.9	35.7	37.6	328 911	35.1	17.7	29.7	0.1	-1.9	73.9	16.1	9.7	0.3
New York-Northern New Jersey-Long Island, NY-NJ-CT-PA	39.7	49.4	31.0	41.8	36.4	33.2	40.2	34.9	4 913 721	38.5	24.6	19.8	-6.2	-2.9	75.1	15.1	9.6	0.2
Bergen-Passaic, NJ	42.9	54.3	32.5	42.8	42.3	32.4	44.6	42.7	316 614	44.1	27.5	15.8	-4.7	-1.4	77.7	11.5	10.5	0.3
Dutchess County, NY	40.7	50.7	30.8	41.5	35.4	27.1	42.6	38.0	66 386	48.3	25.6	17.0	0.7	2.2	72.6	17.9	9.3	0.3
Jersey City, NJ	39.6	47.6	32.0	42.7	36.3	33.6	42.9	36.5	127 471	30.8	18.7	26.5	-7.3	-8.6	81.0	12.5	6.3	0.2
Middlesex-Somerset-Hunterdon, NJ	45.8	57.1	35.2	45.5	47.6	33.1	48.2	44.6	274 054	49.8	27.2	13.9	-1.0	3.2	79.0	12.6	8.2	0.2
Monmouth-Ocean, NJ	39.6	52.6	28.0	39.3	39.3	44.6	48.7	40.6	269 774	46.1	30.5	13.8	-4.7	-3.6	74.5	15.2	10.1	0.3
Nassau-Suffolk, NY	42.4	54.7	31.2	42.2	43.4	39.4	43.4	43.1	666 851	47.0	29.7	13.4	-4.2	-0.5	71.4	17.6	10.9	0.2
New Haven-Bridgeport-Stamford-Danbury-Waterbury, CT	42.9	53.8	33.0	43.8	39.4	42.0	45.1	38.5	407 680	45.1	24.3	19.8	0.3	2.4	77.3	11.8	10.7	0.2
New York, NY	36.1	43.8	29.5	39.5	34.2	30.4	36.6	31.3	2 087 441	29.6	22.0	23.9	-11.1	-8.2	74.4	16.0	9.4	0.2
Newark, NJ	42.8	53.2	33.4	44.6	38.5	33.5	48.3	39.2	489 115	42.7	23.9	20.2	-1.6	1.5	77.6	13.3	8.9	0.2
Newburgh, NY-PA	42.3	53.5	31.3	42.5	39.0	41.1	43.5	42.6	105 802	42.7	29.2	16.7	-5.2	-0.2	70.8	20.2	8.7	0.3
Trenton, NJ	41.9	50.0	34.5	43.3	38.2	36.2	44.1	38.6	79 045	45.7	21.1	21.2	2.3	4.5	71.8	20.6	7.5	0.2
Norfolk-Virginia Beach-Newport News, VA-NC	45.3	56.4	34.7	47.9	39.9	44.6	41.1	46.7	387 739	43.2	19.3	26.1	4.7	4.2	70.1	21.8	7.9	0.2
Ocala, FL	31.1	38.2	24.7	31.1	30.7	33.2	34.2	33.1	50 719	40.0	20.8	24.9	0.3	-15.6	73.8	13.4	12.4	0.4
Odessa-Midland, TX	38.5	49.8	28.4	42.2	32.3	34.6	37.1	32.7	67 665	38.3	27.5	21.4	-4.9	-4.8	74.3	14.1	11.2	0.4
Oklahoma City, OK	42.3	51.6	33.6	43.8	36.1	39.2	39.0	37.7	259 887	42.1	21.7	23.9	1.4	1.7	71.1	18.3	10.3	0.4
Omaha, NE-IA	48.5	58.6	39.0	50.0	38.4	36.0	40.2	42.9	185 024	51.6	17.7	21.1	8.1	10.9	80.2	11.4	8.2	0.2
Orlando, FL	43.8	52.7	35.3	45.1	40.1	40.9	42.8	40.9	381 324	41.6	21.1	24.1	1.2	-0.3	79.4	10.9	9.5	0.2
Owensboro, KY	41.4	53.0	31.0	41.8	36.5	31.9	33.8	33.6	22 366	50.4	21.8	18.0	3.9	0.8	79.5	11.4	8.5	0.6
Panama City, FL	40.1	49.3	31.3	40.8	36.0	36.3	32.6	38.1	33 366	41.5	22.7	22.9	-0.2	-4.6	71.7	17.7	10.4	0.2
Parkersburg-Marietta, WV-OH	37.3	48.4	27.4	37.4	39.7	43.1	42.0	33.7	33 249	44.6	23.8	20.0	0.0	-5.0	78.8	13.0	7.8	0.3
Pensacola, FL	38.5	47.4	29.9	39.7	33.3	36.9	37.2	34.6	93 719	38.4	21.6	26.6	0.3	-5.8	71.5	18.0	10.2	0.2
Peoria-Pekin, IL	40.4	50.9	30.8	41.3	31.0	33.7	45.0	35.7	81 899	48.6	20.6	22.1	6.1	1.5	80.9	10.4	8.4	0.3
Philadelphia-Wilmington-Atlantic City, PA-NJ-DE-MD	41.5	51.3	32.8	43.7	35.4	37.8	38.8	34.2	1 471 318	43.5	20.5	23.2	2.1	2.0	78.9	12.7	8.1	0.2
Atlantic-Cape May, NJ	39.1	47.9	31.2	38.6	38.5	48.6	46.0	40.0	81 458	44.3	17.8	24.7	4.5	-1.2	74.5	15.9	9.4	0.3
Philadelphia, PA-NJ	41.3	51.4	32.4	43.8	34.7	35.1	37.7	32.6	1 216 526	43.2	21.0	22.7	1.3	1.9	79.2	12.4	8.2	0.2
Vineland-Millville-Bridgeton, NJ	36.7	41.2	32.0	39.7	28.2	41.3	41.3	34.2	33 995	37.4	14.7	31.0	3.8	-1.3	71.9	20.5	7.4	0.2
Wilmington-Newark, DE-MD	46.0	55.1	37.6	46.9	43.2	51.5	45.1	41.4	139 339	47.2	18.8	24.1	6.7	6.1	80.6	12.2	7.1	0.2
Phoenix-Mesa, AZ	41.5	50.5	32.6	43.1	41.6	36.1	41.8	36.6	812 503	38.2	25.7	21.7	-4.7	-3.9	77.9	12.5	9.4	0.2
Pine Bluff, AR	34.8	41.0	29.0	40.8	28.0	33.5	45.5	31.4	20 023	36.0	14.1	28.1	-0.5	-2.6	69.6	21.6	8.3	0.5
Pittsburgh, PA	38.4	48.9	29.1	39.0	32.5	33.7	35.4	35.6	504 580	45.0	24.4	20.2	0.6	-3.4	82.2	9.9	7.7	0.2
Pittsfield, MA	37.4	47.5	28.4	37.7	32.0	28.6	35.9	34.9	28 605	51.3	15.7	23.8	10.5	2.4	75.3	13.1	11.3	0.2
Pocatello, ID	36.0	46.3	26.3	36.3	38.8	30.1	32.0	33.8	20 476	49.9	25.4	17.8	3.1	3.8	69.0	21.1	9.7	0.2
Portland, ME	43.9	54.4	34.3	44.2	43.9	37.5	32.5	39.6	59 565	53.6	19.3	18.7	7.7	8.7	75.8	11.8	12.1	0.3
Portland-Salem, OR-WA	40.9	50.9	31.3	41.5	35.8	38.4	40.9	36.6	551 459	45.2	25.6	19.9	0.5	2.8	75.9	12.8	11.0	0.3
Portland-Vancouver, OR-WA	41.7	52.0	31.8	42.3	36.2	38.5	41.3	38.4	463 466	45.2	26.2	19.7	0.3	3.3	77.2	11.5	11.0	0.3
Salem, OR	36.2	44.4	28.3	37.0	28.5	37.9	35.0	31.6	87 873	45.0	22.4	21.3	1.7	-0.2	68.0	20.4	11.2	0.4
Providence-Warwick-Pawtucket, RI	39.7	49.8	30.9	40.8	33.3	34.3	33.3	32.9	218 528	46.2	16.6	21.1	2.7	3.2	77.9	13.5	8.4	0.2
Provo-Orem, UT	32.7	45.6	20.5	32.9	36.9	32.1	24.4	32.0	121 354	41.7	42.7	8.9	-13.9	-1.2	77.8	12.1	9.8	0.3
Pueblo, CO	35.6	42.0	29.5	37.0	29.3	37.3	36.2	33.3	33 775	41.8	15.0	26.8	4.0	-4.8	72.3	18.3	8.9	0.5
Punta Gorda, FL	26.5	31.3	22.2	26.0	28.5	32.5	41.5	35.6	20 879	46.1	19.1	23.2	4.8	-21.3	72.9	12.6	14.1	0.4
Raleigh-Durham-Chapel Hill, NC	47.5	57.1	38.5	49.4	44.7	44.2	41.9	39.4	272 418	46.5	23.1	20.6	2.5	7.7	73.2	17.7	8.9	0.2
Rapid City, SD	43.6	52.8	34.8	45.2	37.8	23.7	36.4	43.9	22 403	50.8	15.1	24.0	10.1	9.7	74.5	14.7	10.5	0.3

[1] Hispanic or Latino persons may be of any race.

Table B-4. Metropolitan Areas — Education, Labor Force, and Income

Area name	Percent who worked at home	Percent of the population 5 years and over with a disability	Veterans as a percent of the population 18 years and over	Occupation for employed population 16 years and over (percent)						Industry for employed population 16 years and over (percent)					
				Management, professional, and related occupations	Service occupations	Sales and office occupations	Farming, fishing, and forestry occupations	Construction, extraction, and maintenance occupations	Production, transportation and material moving occupations	Agriculture, forestry, fishing, and mining	Construction and manufacturing	Wholesale and retail trade	Transportation and warehousing, and utilities	Service industries	Public administration
	42	43	44	45	46	47	48	49	50	51	52	53	54	55	56
Merced, CA	3.2	20.9	11.1	25.6	15.8	22.0	8.7	10.5	17.4	12.5	19.7	15.2	4.8	43.6	4.2
Miami-Fort Lauderdale, FL	2.8	21.9	8.0	31.6	16.7	31.0	0.4	9.6	10.7	0.5	14.0	18.5	6.7	56.1	4.3
Fort Lauderdale, FL	2.9	20.6	11.5	33.3	16.3	31.0	0.2	9.8	9.3	0.3	14.1	18.6	5.7	56.8	4.5
Miami, FL	2.7	22.8	5.4	30.2	16.9	31.0	0.6	9.5	11.9	0.7	13.9	18.3	7.5	55.4	4.1
Milwaukee-Racine, WI	2.5	16.7	12.0	34.6	13.4	27.1	0.2	7.3	17.5	0.5	26.4	14.6	4.7	50.6	3.2
Milwaukee-Waukesha, WI	2.6	16.7	11.9	35.1	13.4	27.3	0.2	7.1	17.0	0.5	25.4	14.5	4.7	51.7	3.2
Racine, WI	2.2	16.4	13.0	30.7	13.2	25.6	0.2	9.0	21.3	0.8	34.3	14.7	4.8	41.8	3.7
Minneapolis-St. Paul, MN-WI	3.8	13.8	11.9	38.9	12.4	28.0	0.2	7.5	12.9	0.6	21.5	15.7	5.4	53.6	3.3
Missoula, MT	4.5	15.6	13.9	32.3	17.9	28.3	0.9	9.7	10.9	2.8	13.6	17.5	5.3	57.5	3.2
Mobile, AL	2.3	23.3	14.7	29.2	15.0	27.1	0.7	12.6	15.5	1.3	22.8	17.4	5.4	49.1	4.0
Modesto, CA	3.2	21.5	10.6	26.5	15.4	25.6	3.6	11.4	17.5	5.6	22.6	16.7	5.3	46.0	3.9
Monroe, LA	1.7	21.1	12.2	30.8	16.6	29.6	0.2	10.2	12.0	1.1	17.4	15.0	0.0	56.1	5.4
Montgomery, AL	1.8	21.7	15.0	33.8	14.8	28.7	0.4	8.8	13.5	1.0	17.0	15.4	4.4	50.9	11.2
Muncie, IN	2.7	18.5	12.5	30.1	17.5	26.4	0.3	8.1	17.6	0.7	23.0	15.7	3.6	54.1	2.9
Myrtle Beach, SC	2.7	23.2	16.2	26.2	20.1	29.8	0.5	13.2	10.1	1.1	18.5	17.9	3.2	56.0	3.2
Naples, FL	4.7	20.8	17.6	28.4	19.9	27.9	2.8	12.9	8.1	3.5	16.6	17.6	3.4	55.5	3.3
Nashville, TN	3.2	18.5	12.0	34.7	12.7	28.3	0.3	9.6	14.4	0.7	20.9	16.2	5.1	53.0	4.2
New London-Norwich, CT	2.6	17.9	16.3	35.6	19.9	24.4	0.4	8.9	10.8	0.8	20.5	13.8	4.7	54.5	5.6
New Orleans, LA	2.4	21.1	12.0	32.9	17.3	28.0	0.4	10.0	11.5	1.9	15.4	15.2	6.0	55.9	5.7
New York-Northern New Jersey-Long Island, NY-NJ-CT-PA	3.0	20.0	8.6	38.6	15.2	27.9	0.1	7.4	10.8	0.2	14.9	14.2	5.8	60.4	4.5
Bergen-Passaic, NJ	2.8	17.9	9.2	38.8	12.1	29.7	0.1	7.2	12.2	0.1	18.7	17.7	5.4	55.1	3.1
Dutchess County, NY	3.2	16.3	12.6	38.4	15.6	25.3	0.4	10.1	10.2	1.0	19.1	13.9	4.9	55.6	5.5
Jersey City, NJ	1.8	23.8	6.0	32.3	15.1	29.2	0.1	6.3	17.0	0.1	15.7	15.8	9.2	55.8	3.5
Middlesex-Somerset-Hunterdon, NJ	2.9	14.8	9.8	44.0	10.4	27.3	0.1	7.0	11.2	0.3	19.3	15.1	5.6	56.4	3.3
Monmouth-Ocean, NJ	3.0	17.3	13.9	37.6	13.9	29.3	0.2	9.4	9.5	0.4	15.5	16.7	5.7	56.1	5.6
Nassau-Suffolk, NY	2.8	16.1	11.0	38.2	14.0	29.6	0.2	8.7	9.3	0.2	14.4	15.8	6.0	55.2	5.4
New Haven-Bridgeport-Stamford-Danbury-Waterbury, CT	3.5	17.5	11.0	40.4	13.6	26.7	0.1	7.8	11.3	0.3	20.5	14.5	3.7	57.7	3.3
New York, NY	3.0	23.5	6.2	38.1	17.9	27.2	0.1	6.6	10.2	0.1	11.3	12.3	6.1	65.8	4.5
Newark, NJ	3.0	18.1	9.5	38.7	13.3	28.2	0.1	7.5	12.2	0.2	18.7	14.6	6.4	56.2	3.9
Newburgh, NY-PA	2.8	18.7	12.8	32.7	16.6	27.4	0.4	10.5	12.4	1.0	17.2	17.5	6.0	51.1	7.2
Trenton, NJ	3.2	17.1	10.4	43.2	14.3	26.5	0.2	6.1	9.7	0.3	14.2	12.0	3.8	59.2	10.4
Norfolk-Virginia Beach-Newport News, VA-NC	2.7	19.0	18.9	33.6	15.6	27.8	0.3	10.9	11.9	0.5	18.3	15.4	4.8	53.2	7.9
Ocala, FL	3.1	25.9	21.3	26.4	17.5	28.2	1.3	12.1	14.5	3.5	19.6	18.9	4.9	48.5	4.7
Odessa-Midland, TX	2.4	17.6	11.4	29.4	15.8	28.6	0.2	12.6	13.3	10.8	14.8	17.1	4.5	49.3	3.4
Oklahoma City, OK	2.8	20.1	14.6	32.4	15.1	28.8	0.3	10.5	12.9	1.9	17.0	15.8	4.4	52.7	8.1
Omaha, NE-IA	2.9	15.7	14.6	35.0	13.7	30.1	0.2	8.6	12.3	0.9	16.2	16.7	6.4	56.5	3.1
Orlando, FL	2.9	20.3	14.3	32.6	17.3	29.8	0.5	9.5	10.2	0.7	14.7	16.7	5.2	59.0	3.6
Owensboro, KY	2.0	21.6	14.5	28.1	15.4	23.6	0.6	12.0	20.3	2.2	28.6	15.7	5.7	45.0	2.8
Panama City, FL	2.3	22.0	20.1	28.5	19.7	28.1	0.6	12.3	10.8	0.9	15.6	16.8	4.7	54.2	7.7
Parkersburg-Marietta, WV-OH	2.3	20.2	15.8	28.2	14.8	27.9	0.4	9.5	19.1	1.4	25.1	17.8	5.3	45.9	4.5
Pensacola, FL	2.6	22.1	21.1	30.7	17.0	28.0	0.5	12.0	11.7	0.9	16.1	16.9	5.6	53.3	7.2
Peoria-Pekin, IL	2.6	17.1	14.1	32.8	15.5	27.0	0.3	8.6	15.7	1.3	24.8	14.8	4.6	51.3	3.3
Philadelphia-Wilmington-Atlantic City, PA-NJ-DE-MD	2.8	18.7	12.3	36.9	14.8	28.6	0.3	8.0	11.5	0.5	17.6	15.1	5.0	56.9	4.8
Atlantic-Cape May, NJ	2.2	20.8	13.4	27.2	27.7	26.4	0.6	9.3	8.8	0.8	11.3	13.6	4.2	64.0	6.1
Philadelphia, PA-NJ	2.9	18.6	12.2	37.8	13.9	28.9	0.2	7.7	11.5	0.4	17.5	15.4	5.1	56.8	4.7
Vineland-Millville-Bridgeton, NJ	2.2	23.1	11.2	24.8	19.0	23.8	1.8	9.8	20.9	2.5	24.0	14.6	5.4	46.1	7.4
Wilmington-Newark, DE-MD	2.7	17.1	12.9	37.5	13.4	28.1	0.3	9.0	11.6	0.8	20.3	13.4	4.9	56.5	4.2
Phoenix-Mesa, AZ	3.7	18.3	13.9	33.4	14.9	29.5	0.5	10.6	11.1	0.9	20.3	15.8	5.1	53.4	4.7
Pine Bluff, AR	1.8	25.0	14.0	27.2	15.6	25.3	0.7	9.3	21.8	1.7	26.3	15.0	6.1	41.9	8.9
Pittsburgh, PA	2.4	18.5	14.7	33.9	15.9	27.7	0.2	8.9	13.4	0.7	18.4	16.2	6.6	54.9	3.2
Pittsfield, MA	3.6	19.0	14.3	35.1	18.7	25.0	0.4	8.8	11.9	1.1	19.5	15.0	2.8	58.1	3.5
Pocatello, ID	2.9	16.9	13.0	32.3	16.3	27.8	0.6	9.9	13.1	1.5	17.8	15.3	6.0	54.9	4.5
Portland, ME	4.6	17.1	14.2	38.8	14.2	28.2	0.6	7.2	11.1	1.0	15.2	18.5	3.9	57.8	3.5
Portland-Salem, OR-WA	4.6	17.5	13.8	34.5	14.0	27.1	1.1	8.8	14.4	1.7	22.2	16.6	5.4	49.7	4.3
Portland-Vancouver, OR-WA	4.6	17.1	13.6	35.2	13.6	27.3	0.7	8.8	14.3	1.2	22.6	16.9	5.7	50.2	3.4
Salem, OR	4.6	19.6	14.7	30.0	16.5	25.5	3.6	9.2	15.2	4.9	20.0	15.1	3.6	46.8	9.7
Providence-Warwick-Pawtucket, RI	2.1	20.5	12.5	33.3	15.6	27.3	0.3	7.7	15.9	0.4	22.5	15.6	3.9	53.1	4.4
Provo-Orem, UT	5.0	11.8	7.0	36.5	14.0	27.7	0.3	10.1	11.4	1.0	20.0	16.1	2.6	57.1	3.1
Pueblo, CO	3.3	23.5	16.7	28.2	18.2	28.2	0.4	11.7	13.3	1.4	17.5	16.1	5.3	52.9	6.8
Punta Gorda, FL	3.2	24.9	22.8	27.2	20.9	29.6	0.5	12.6	9.3	0.7	14.5	19.9	3.8	56.3	4.9
Raleigh-Durham-Chapel Hill, NC	3.5	15.7	10.7	44.3	11.8	24.8	0.3	9.0	9.8	0.7	20.5	13.2	3.8	56.6	5.2
Rapid City, SD	3.1	17.2	17.5	31.8	16.8	28.6	0.9	9.9	12.1	2.3	16.6	17.4	4.2	54.5	5.1

Table B-4. Metropolitan Areas — **Education, Labor Force, and Income**

Area name	Median household income	Median family income: All families	Median family income, Families with children: Married-couple	Median family income, Families with children: Male householder	Median family income, Families with children: Female householder	Median nonfamily household income	Median income for full-year, full-time workers: Men	Median income for full-year, full-time workers: Women	Per capita income	Households by source of income (percent): With earnings	Households by source of income (percent): With interest, dividend, or rental income	Households by source of income (percent): With Social Security income	Households by source of income (percent): With public assistance income	Households by source of income (percent): With retirement income	Households with income over $100,000 (percent)	+/– U.S. percent for income over $100,000	Households with income below poverty (percent)	Families with children with income below poverty (percent)
	57	58	59	60	61	62	63	64	65	66	67	68	69	70	71	72	73	74
Merced, CA	35 532	38 009	42 519	23 691	15 129	21 465	32 540	24 994	14 257	81.2	24.7	24.0	9.1	16.4	6.9	-5.4	17.8	22.8
Miami-Fort Lauderdale, FL	38 632	44 365	55 509	26 861	21 387	25 065	33 886	27 087	20 454	79.1	28.0	27.0	4.2	12.3	11.7	-0.6	14.8	16.5
Fort Lauderdale, FL	41 691	50 531	63 460	30 181	24 093	27 417	37 608	29 632	23 170	77.0	33.3	29.2	2.1	13.8	12.8	0.5	10.8	12.6
Miami, FL	35 966	40 260	49 720	24 492	19 802	21 807	30 806	25 408	18 497	80.8	23.5	25.2	6.0	11.1	10.8	-1.5	18.1	19.3
Milwaukee-Racine, WI	46 132	56 739	68 726	32 991	20 934	28 001	42 033	29 607	23 003	81.6	46.3	25.3	2.3	16.4	12.2	-0.1	9.4	12.1
Milwaukee-Waukesha, WI	45 901	56 797	69 214	32 495	20 875	28 140	42 066	29 839	23 158	81.5	46.3	25.2	2.4	16.2	12.4	0.1	9.6	12.4
Racine, WI	48 059	56 331	65 812	35 995	21 398	26 702	41 775	27 835	21 772	82.0	45.8	26.0	1.7	18.3	10.8	-1.5	7.6	9.4
Minneapolis-St. Paul, MN-WI	54 304	65 450	75 045	37 217	27 477	32 944	43 974	32 255	26 219	86.7	44.5	19.4	3.3	12.7	16.9	4.6	6.3	6.5
Missoula, MT	34 454	44 865	51 448	28 375	17 352	20 347	32 510	22 802	17 808	84.2	41.3	21.0	3.0	13.6	6.2	-6.1	15.5	13.4
Mobile, AL	35 629	42 118	51 491	26 329	13 765	19 791	34 584	23 004	18 126	77.3	27.7	28.4	2.3	18.6	7.5	-4.8	16.1	20.0
Modesto, CA	40 101	44 703	51 669	28 810	18 160	23 262	37 795	27 315	16 913	80.6	27.7	25.1	6.3	16.3	9.1	-3.2	13.6	17.3
Monroe, LA	32 047	40 206	51 703	21 820	14 211	17 242	32 332	23 860	17 084	78.7	24.8	24.8	3.2	14.6	7.6	-4.7	19.5	23.2
Montgomery, AL	37 619	45 819	55 627	28 125	17 143	22 180	34 327	25 486	18 910	80.7	29.7	25.6	2.2	19.3	9.1	-3.2	14.2	17.1
Muncie, IN	34 659	45 394	53 184	28 784	18 385	20 373	37 092	24 434	19 233	78.3	35.2	28.3	3.3	19.7	7.3	-5.0	15.4	13.7
Myrtle Beach, SC	36 470	42 676	50 855	23 053	18 635	25 193	29 272	22 320	19 949	79.2	32.5	30.2	2.4	21.5	7.1	-5.2	11.2	14.4
Naples, FL	48 289	54 816	54 962	26 447	23 862	31 931	35 118	27 420	31 195	68.2	50.2	41.1	1.5	26.1	18.1	5.8	7.8	13.1
Nashville, TN	44 223	52 679	61 903	31 478	21 195	27 294	37 469	28 002	22 874	85.5	32.4	21.0	2.8	13.9	12.0	-0.3	10.1	10.9
New London-Norwich, CT	50 646	59 857	68 759	35 537	25 120	30 486	42 286	31 339	24 678	81.6	44.0	26.5	3.1	20.1	14.5	2.2	6.7	7.3
New Orleans, LA	35 317	42 626	57 669	26 191	15 505	21 565	36 339	25 241	18 834	79.6	28.8	24.6	3.5	14.6	9.3	-3.0	17.4	21.5
New York-Northern New Jersey-Long Island, NY-NJ-CT-PA	50 795	60 254	72 996	33 369	21 620	31 383	46 586	35 582	26 604	79.7	38.2	25.2	4.5	15.6	20.4	8.1	12.4	14.8
Bergen-Passaic, NJ	59 405	70 502	81 305	35 686	27 331	33 670	49 246	36 006	29 269	82.1	45.8	27.7	2.3	15.7	24.9	12.6	7.2	8.1
Dutchess County, NY	53 086	63 254	73 948	35 745	24 280	29 105	46 929	31 523	23 940	81.7	44.8	26.9	2.1	22.0	17.2	4.9	7.5	7.6
Jersey City, NJ	40 293	44 053	51 219	27 134	19 915	30 029	36 932	31 682	21 154	80.5	28.2	23.0	4.8	12.0	12.8	0.5	15.3	18.9
Middlesex-Somerset-Hunterdon, NJ	66 731	77 073	87 250	41 538	34 579	38 924	53 660	38 335	30 469	85.3	49.1	23.8	1.6	16.4	27.8	15.5	5.1	4.9
Monmouth-Ocean, NJ	54 865	65 994	78 478	38 419	26 669	29 276	51 550	34 363	27 477	75.9	47.5	33.2	1.8	22.2	20.9	8.6	6.4	7.1
Nassau-Suffolk, NY	68 351	76 430	84 063	45 242	32 100	35 009	52 102	36 631	29 278	83.1	45.4	29.2	1.4	19.9	28.8	16.5	5.5	5.3
New Haven-Bridgeport-Stamford-Danbury-Waterbury, CT	56 054	68 042	83 404	36 409	24 714	31 325	50 065	35 923	31 633	81.4	44.3	27.1	3.7	16.5	23.5	11.2	8.3	9.0
New York, NY	41 053	46 471	58 822	30 028	17 523	30 641	40 975	35 315	24 076	77.1	31.0	22.8	6.9	13.1	16.0	3.7	18.1	23.3
Newark, NJ	56 957	67 886	82 871	35 172	24 391	31 249	50 097	35 608	28 435	82.1	41.7	25.0	3.8	15.6	23.8	11.5	9.6	10.7
Newburgh, NY-PA	51 151	58 416	66 252	34 888	23 341	28 298	43 923	31 310	21 444	82.4	36.6	25.9	2.9	19.9	15.2	2.9	8.8	10.7
Trenton, NJ	56 613	68 494	83 836	35 625	26 746	31 972	49 699	35 667	27 914	81.5	44.5	25.7	2.7	18.1	23.0	10.7	8.6	8.9
Norfolk-Virginia Beach-Newport News, VA-NC	42 448	49 186	56 150	30 922	19 333	27 206	35 106	25 754	20 328	84.0	33.9	22.1	2.8	21.7	9.7	-2.6	10.4	12.5
Ocala, FL	31 944	37 473	46 867	22 982	17 975	18 951	30 041	22 684	17 848	64.5	35.4	45.0	2.7	28.0	5.5	-6.8	12.2	16.6
Odessa-Midland, TX	34 773	40 807	46 197	24 660	17 024	20 113	34 557	23 763	17 642	82.3	28.1	24.2	3.6	11.7	8.5	-3.8	15.3	18.3
Oklahoma City, OK	36 797	45 059	52 118	26 959	17 982	22 374	34 095	25 316	19 366	81.9	32.6	22.8	4.4	16.7	8.1	-4.2	13.1	15.1
Omaha, NE-IA	44 981	54 596	64 310	31 318	22 385	26 693	37 278	27 423	22 145	84.8	39.3	22.4	2.9	14.5	11.2	-1.1	8.2	9.0
Orlando, FL	41 871	47 760	57 403	29 724	21 488	27 833	34 684	26 153	21 232	82.5	32.7	25.4	2.3	16.9	10.9	-1.4	9.8	11.7
Owensboro, KY	36 813	45 404	54 830	28 136	15 775	18 992	36 096	23 178	18 739	78.5	34.6	28.9	3.2	18.6	6.2	-6.1	12.7	14.6
Panama City, FL	36 092	42 729	50 302	24 033	16 621	21 747	31 571	22 541	18 700	77.6	34.8	28.0	3.2	22.7	6.6	-5.7	12.7	15.9
Parkersburg-Marietta, WV-OH	33 696	40 938	47 692	24 272	13 926	19 272	35 187	22 434	18 076	74.6	35.4	31.6	3.3	22.2	6.1	-6.2	12.8	16.7
Pensacola, FL	36 975	43 231	50 571	25 267	16 162	22 983	33 730	22 935	19 054	78.0	33.5	27.4	3.3	24.5	7.7	-4.6	13.3	16.9
Peoria-Pekin, IL	42 986	52 361	61 480	30 745	17 614	24 445	42 040	25 906	21 402	79.3	42.1	27.8	3.2	20.3	9.8	-2.5	9.4	11.7
Philadelphia-Wilmington-Atlantic City, PA-NJ-DE-MD	47 528	57 868	71 852	32 705	22 627	27 576	43 293	31 768	23 699	79.8	38.7	27.1	3.8	18.0	15.5	3.2	10.7	11.7
Atlantic-Cape May, NJ	43 109	51 622	62 320	31 092	23 058	25 956	38 516	29 326	21 939	78.6	35.8	31.2	2.8	19.1	11.1	-1.2	9.5	10.7
Philadelphia, PA-NJ	47 536	58 395	72 662	33 160	22 332	27 363	44 166	32 005	23 874	79.5	39.1	27.1	4.0	17.8	15.9	3.6	11.0	12.0
Vineland-Millville-Bridgeton, NJ	39 150	45 403	57 440	25 938	18 211	21 844	36 064	26 069	17 376	78.2	28.1	29.9	5.3	18.3	8.2	-4.1	13.7	16.7
Wilmington-Newark, DE-MD	52 121	61 246	73 367	35 577	26 368	32 304	43 659	32 100	24 822	83.7	39.8	24.1	2.3	19.0	16.6	4.3	7.8	8.3
Phoenix-Mesa, AZ	44 752	51 126	58 888	30 398	24 392	30 161	37 467	29 575	21 907	81.1	35.1	24.9	2.3	16.8	12.9	0.6	9.9	12.7
Pine Bluff, AR	31 327	38 252	49 758	25 068	15 787	17 113	32 824	22 711	15 417	76.8	24.1	30.3	3.9	15.5	5.6	-6.7	19.5	24.1
Pittsburgh, PA	37 467	47 546	59 244	28 302	17 925	20 688	38 728	26 835	20 935	74.2	40.7	32.9	2.9	21.2	9.2	-3.1	11.3	12.7
Pittsfield, MA	39 047	50 162	59 662	30 424	19 963	21 483	38 170	27 469	21 807	75.0	45.6	32.9	2.7	20.9	9.7	-2.6	10.2	11.6
Pocatello, ID	36 683	44 192	50 588	28 404	16 026	20 113	37 191	24 678	17 148	82.8	37.7	24.4	4.5	14.3	7.2	-5.1	14.1	14.5
Portland, ME	44 048	54 485	64 808	35 173	21 877	27 149	37 034	29 441	23 949	81.3	45.3	26.1	3.8	17.2	11.7	-0.6	8.0	8.4
Portland-Salem, OR-WA	46 090	54 171	61 567	31 876	22 406	30 010	40 656	30 226	22 592	83.6	40.2	22.0	3.5	15.5	12.4	0.1	9.0	10.4
Portland-Vancouver, OR-WA	47 077	55 669	63 129	32 283	23 115	30 648	41 257	30 648	23 321	84.3	40.7	21.1	3.4	14.9	13.1	0.8	8.6	9.7
Salem, OR	40 665	47 009	52 190	29 286	19 189	25 166	35 743	26 992	18 565	79.6	37.4	27.2	4.1	18.7	7.9	-4.4	11.3	14.4
Providence-Warwick-Pawtucket, RI	41 462	51 981	63 301	29 592	17 045	22 840	38 622	28 281	21 236	77.1	36.1	28.0	4.7	17.0	11.1	-1.2	12.8	14.7
Provo-Orem, UT	45 833	50 196	55 408	35 577	23 389	26 794	39 601	23 551	15 557	89.4	38.7	17.9	2.4	13.4	11.1	-1.2	10.7	7.8
Pueblo, CO	32 775	40 130	48 940	26 533	17 133	19 254	32 344	23 823	17 163	74.0	31.9	31.9	4.9	22.5	5.8	-6.5	14.5	17.5
Punta Gorda, FL	36 379	42 653	50 481	25 450	22 363	21 627	31 451	23 625	21 806	55.9	48.2	54.4	1.5	36.9	7.3	-5.0	8.1	10.9
Raleigh-Durham-Chapel Hill, NC	48 845	59 405	70 518	31 463	23 670	30 733	40 948	31 061	24 698	87.1	37.0	18.0	2.0	13.6	15.9	3.6	10.0	9.7
Rapid City, SD	37 485	44 796	53 057	22 767	17 447	23 002	31 991	22 272	18 938	83.7	39.2	25.0	3.2	16.1	7.1	-5.2	10.8	14.3

CMSA/MSA/PMSA/NECMA code[1]	Area name	High school graduates			College graduates		College graduates (percent)				
		Total population 25 years and over	Percent with a high school diploma or less	Percent with a high school diploma or more	Percent with a bachelor's degree or more	+/− U.S. percent with bachelor's degree or more	Non-Hispanic White	Black or African American	American Indian and Alaska Native	Asian, Hawaiian, and Pacific Islander	Hispanic or Latino[2]
		1	2	3	4	5	6	7	8	9	10
6680	Reading, PA	248 864	61.3	78.0	18.5	−5.9	19.6	8.4	9.0	38.6	4.7
6690	Redding, CA	107 272	44.4	83.3	16.6	−7.8	17.2	12.7	5.4	17.3	10.8
6720	Reno, NV	221 837	41.2	83.9	23.7	−0.7	26.4	16.7	8.8	32.4	6.9
6740	Richland-Kennewick-Pasco, WA	114 996	43.9	80.1	23.3	−1.1	26.2	17.7	9.1	44.2	4.7
6760	Richmond-Petersburg, VA	657 222	43.6	82.6	29.2	4.8	34.6	15.4	12.9	46.7	20.2
6800	Roanoke, VA	164 642	49.2	80.9	22.5	−1.9	24.1	9.4	16.2	42.3	26.5
6820	Rochester, MN	80 277	32.9	91.1	34.7	10.3	34.7	16.8	21.2	54.1	14.5
6840	Rochester, NY	715 476	44.8	84.4	27.1	2.7	28.9	10.6	13.2	52.2	12.2
6880	Rockford, IL	241 181	52.3	81.6	18.5	−5.9	19.7	9.1	4.8	37.7	6.7
6895	Rocky Mount, NC	93 270	63.3	71.8	13.9	−10.5	18.8	7.0	17.5	38.4	6.5
82	Sacramento-Yolo, CA	1 138 839	37.8	84.6	26.5	2.1	29.6	16.3	14.2	32.4	11.9
6920	Sacramento, CA	1 043 416	37.5	85.0	25.9	1.5	28.7	16.2	14.2	30.7	12.3
9270	Yolo, CA	95 423	40.0	79.8	34.1	9.7	40.7	22.3	14.2	55.0	0.0
6960	Saginaw-Bay City-Midland, MI	262 841	51.8	83.3	18.1	−6.3	19.0	9.3	9.0	60.6	9.5
7120	Salinas, CA	244 128	50.1	68.4	22.5	−1.9	36.4	11.3	8.7	26.5	4.6
7160	Salt Lake City-Ogden, UT	746 141	37.0	87.5	26.5	2.1	28.4	19.5	11.8	29.2	9.4
7200	San Angelo, TX	63 430	52.3	76.2	19.5	−4.9	24.7	12.4	17.0	27.3	6.1
7240	San Antonio, TX	977 822	47.8	77.3	22.4	−2.0	34.3	18.0	14.3	37.3	10.6
7320	San Diego, CA	1 773 327	37.3	82.6	29.5	5.1	36.1	16.3	13.8	36.0	10.7
84	San Francisco-Oakland-San Jose, CA	4 764 188	33.7	83.9	37.3	12.9	44.1	19.2	16.9	44.4	12.4
5775	Oakland, CA	1 579 357	35.2	84.2	35.0	10.6	41.5	18.6	17.1	46.0	12.6
7360	San Francisco, CA	1 269 784	30.8	84.2	43.6	19.2	54.8	18.5	25.0	38.3	16.2
7400	San Jose, CA	1 113 058	32.5	83.4	40.5	16.1	47.1	29.7	16.3	50.9	11.0
7485	Santa Cruz-Watsonville, CA	164 999	33.3	83.2	34.2	9.8	41.0	22.7	18.1	40.7	9.3
7500	Santa Rosa, CA	306 564	35.5	84.9	28.5	4.1	31.7	21.6	10.6	35.3	9.6
8720	Vallejo-Fairfield-Napa, CA	330 426	40.6	82.9	22.7	−1.7	26.0	14.6	9.1	31.8	9.1
7460	San Luis Obispo-Atascadero-Paso Robles, CA	159 196	36.2	85.6	26.7	2.3	29.8	7.6	11.6	34.1	8.9
7480	Santa Barbara-Santa Maria-Lompoc, CA	246 729	30.8	79.2	29.4	5.0	38.9	16.9	12.3	37.1	7.0
7490	Santa Fe, NM	100 692	32.7	86.0	39.9	15.5	57.6	28.2	18.0	64.7	14.6
7610	Sarasota-Bradenton, FL	449 591	46.2	84.7	24.6	0.2	25.8	10.8	18.5	33.8	13.0
7520	Savannah, GA	185 311	49.1	79.9	23.2	−1.2	27.9	12.4	11.4	36.6	24.2
7560	Scranton—Wilkes-Barre—Hazleton, PA	434 889	60.3	81.5	17.4	−7.0	17.4	8.2	9.4	48.0	11.4
91	Seattle-Tacoma-Bremerton, WA	2 351 904	33.6	89.5	32.0	7.6	33.3	19.5	15.3	36.0	17.4
1150	Bremerton, WA	148 704	34.7	90.8	25.3	0.9	26.4	17.7	15.9	24.0	14.1
5910	Olympia, WA	135 686	34.3	89.5	29.8	5.4	30.8	28.7	16.4	24.9	18.9
7600	Seattle-Bellevue-Everett, WA	1 624 849	30.9	90.1	35.9	11.5	37.3	21.1	15.9	40.0	19.0
8200	Tacoma, WA	442 665	42.9	86.9	20.6	−3.8	21.8	15.0	13.0	19.5	11.8
7610	Sharon, PA	81 499	62.2	82.9	17.3	−7.1	17.7	6.2	12.5	44.9	21.1
7620	Sheboygan, WI	74 561	55.5	84.4	17.9	−6.5	18.3	6.8	3.0	15.2	9.2
7640	Sherman-Denison, TX	72 382	49.8	80.2	17.2	−7.2	17.9	10.5	12.7	46.6	8.0
7680	Shreveport-Bossier City, LA	247 935	53.8	78.9	19.1	−5.3	23.6	10.1	11.5	36.0	15.1
7720	Sioux City, IA-NE	77 035	55.0	80.2	17.9	−6.5	19.7	11.9	3.4	11.1	3.6
7760	Sioux Falls, SD	108 493	42.2	88.6	25.9	1.5	26.6	20.4	8.0	29.3	8.2
7800	South Bend, IN	166 060	50.1	82.4	23.6	−0.8	25.0	10.8	8.6	59.0	12.1
7840	Spokane, WA	266 829	37.7	89.1	25.0	0.6	25.5	14.8	13.3	27.0	17.3
7880	Springfield, IL	134 918	43.4	88.1	28.1	3.7	28.7	15.7	23.3	63.0	30.1
8003	Springfield, MA	389 030	49.3	81.7	24.7	0.3	26.5	17.0	18.6	44.5	8.3
7920	Springfield, MO	208 235	48.2	84.0	22.4	−2.0	22.7	13.9	11.0	40.0	15.1
6980	St. Cloud, MN	98 308	47.7	86.0	21.0	−3.4	20.9	16.6	12.5	27.4	17.2
7000	St. Joseph, MO	66 430	56.6	82.0	17.2	−7.2	17.4	9.8	28.0	38.7	9.4
7040	St. Louis, MO-IL	1 692 997	45.3	83.4	25.3	0.9	27.3	13.0	13.8	54.4	24.0
8050	State College, PA	74 785	45.6	88.2	36.3	11.9	34.5	20.0	24.8	84.4	48.8
8080	Steubenville-Weirton, OH-WV	93 176	64.6	81.6	12.1	−12.3	12.1	10.0	15.8	25.2	25.2
8120	Stockton-Lodi, CA	333 572	54.0	71.2	14.5	−9.9	18.2	9.7	6.4	20.7	5.3
8140	Sumter, SC	64 144	55.4	74.3	15.8	−8.6	19.9	10.5	13.8	22.4	14.1
8160	Syracuse, NY	471 490	48.4	83.8	24.1	−0.3	24.5	10.0	18.7	53.5	19.7
8240	Tallahassee, FL	166 469	35.9	85.9	36.7	12.3	43.2	20.9	27.3	64.8	29.5
8280	Tampa-St. Petersburg-Clearwater, FL	1 694 489	48.6	81.5	21.7	−2.7	22.7	13.0	17.3	38.8	16.2
8320	Terre Haute, IN	95 428	56.7	81.3	18.6	−5.8	18.4	15.2	5.5	63.5	14.4
8360	Texarkana, TX-Texarkana, AR	84 557	56.7	76.4	15.0	−9.4	17.5	7.1	13.0	48.8	4.5
8400	Toledo, OH	389 460	49.4	84.1	21.6	−2.8	23.1	10.5	13.7	59.7	9.8
8440	Topeka, KS	111 709	45.5	88.1	26.0	1.6	28.0	12.2	15.5	48.7	13.9

[1]MSA = Metropolitan Statistical Area. CMSA = Consolidated MSA. PMSA = Primary MSA. NECMA = New England County Metropolitan Area. See the Appendix A for explanation of these concepts. See Appendix B for list of metropolitan areas identified by type, with component counties.
[2]Hispanic or Latino persons may be of any race.

Items 1—10

Area name	School enrollment			Population 16 to 19 years				Employment status, 2000			Work status in 1999 of the population 16 years and over (percent)		
											Worked in 1999		
	Grades kindergarten through 12	College or graduate school	Percent private	Number	Percent in armed forces	Percent high school graduates	Percent not enrolled, not grads, not in armed forces, not employed	Total population 16 years and over	Percent in labor force	Unemployment rate	Full-time	Part-time	Did not work in 1999
	11	12	13	14	15	16	17	18	19	20	21	22	23
Reading, PA	69 719	18 185	14.7	20 694	0.0	10.0	4.9	291 683	65.4	5.1	55.2	15.2	29.6
Redding, CA	33 592	8 952	10.4	9 897	0.0	10.3	4.1	125 913	57.3	8.7	44.4	16.7	38.9
Reno, NV	62 229	22 839	7.2	17 960	0.1	11.1	6.6	263 862	68.6	4.9	60.7	14.7	24.6
Richland-Kennewick-Pasco, WA	44 210	7 443	6.5	12 222	0.0	8.6	8.0	139 314	66.4	7.2	56.4	15.6	28.0
Richmond-Petersburg, VA	188 131	58 270	12.1	54 242	1.7	11.6	4.1	772 997	65.4	4.1	60.2	14.0	25.8
Roanoke, VA	40 045	10 674	13.5	11 489	0.0	12.0	5.3	188 305	64.5	3.8	56.4	13.6	30.1
Rochester, MN	25 301	6 285	14.6	6 769	0.0	7.5	1.9	94 560	73.5	3.7	59.4	19.5	21.1
Rochester, NY	217 301	76 533	18.5	63 581	0.1	8.1	4.1	848 451	65.9	5.7	54.5	17.0	28.5
Rockford, IL	74 252	15 698	17.0	20 245	0.1	10.7	5.8	282 278	67.5	5.5	57.2	15.5	27.3
Rocky Mount, NC	28 706	5 747	8.9	7 968	0.0	11.4	7.8	109 990	61.1	7.0	56.1	11.3	32.6
Sacramento-Yolo, CA	368 825	147 392	9.7	103 513	0.2	10.8	4.6	1 363 173	64.0	6.2	53.5	15.9	30.6
Sacramento, CA	336 825	117 288	10.2	89 244	0.3	11.5	4.8	1 232 584	64.0	6.1	53.9	15.2	30.9
Yolo, CA	32 000	30 104	6.1	14 269	0.0	6.5	3.0	130 589	63.3	7.1	50.5	22.2	27.3
Saginaw-Bay City-Midland, MI	81 173	22 106	11.9	22 697	0.2	7.8	5.0	309 765	62.6	6.7	49.9	17.8	32.4
Salinas, CA	86 811	24 295	9.5	25 375	3.6	11.9	7.6	299 915	61.6	8.5	54.5	14.3	31.1
Salt Lake City-Ogden, UT	298 324	89 496	7.3	95 211	0.2	14.4	4.4	965 589	71.0	4.7	57.8	19.0	23.2
San Angelo, TX	20 707	7 281	4.3	7 663	6.7	17.7	4.1	80 282	64.5	7.0	54.0	15.1	31.0
San Antonio, TX	335 828	95 787	12.0	99 033	3.9	14.2	6.5	1 190 329	63.5	5.5	56.6	13.1	30.3
San Diego, CA	539 834	242 117	11.3	158 984	5.9	14.7	4.6	2 165 034	65.0	5.6	54.6	15.4	30.0
San Francisco-Oakland-San Jose, CA	1 248 596	573 152	16.2	344 802	0.2	8.9	4.4	5 553 473	66.1	4.5	57.0	14.9	28.1
Oakland, CA	454 193	188 896	14.2	120 917	0.1	8.9	4.6	1 849 418	65.4	5.2	56.1	14.9	29.0
San Francisco, CA	247 352	150 922	22.3	67 951	0.1	7.9	4.2	1 441 331	66.3	3.8	57.3	14.8	27.9
San Jose, CA	305 563	141 601	17.2	85 189	0.0	7.9	4.5	1 308 666	67.2	3.9	60.0	13.2	26.7
Santa Cruz-Watsonville, CA	46 143	27 005	11.1	15 913	0.0	8.1	4.6	201 874	68.2	6.1	53.6	20.8	25.5
Santa Rosa, CA	86 107	32 351	11.0	25 183	0.5	11.3	4.5	359 736	66.8	4.3	53.3	18.5	28.2
Vallejo-Fairfield-Napa, CA	109 238	32 377	12.3	29 649	1.4	12.0	4.1	392 448	64.1	5.5	54.9	14.9	30.2
San Luis Obispo-Atascadero-Paso Robles, CA	42 791	31 338	7.2	18 175	0.1	8.8	2.3	200 572	58.3	5.9	47.2	19.6	33.2
Santa Barbara-Santa Maria-Lompoc, CA	74 970	46 317	11.8	26 449	0.3	7.3	4.2	310 929	63.1	6.6	49.1	19.1	31.8
Santa Fe, NM	27 194	9 291	17.5	7 826	0.0	10.8	7.7	116 143	67.2	4.4	57.0	16.6	26.4
Sarasota-Bradenton, FL	81 208	18 393	13.3	21 267	0.3	11.5	5.4	493 837	52.2	3.6	44.7	12.4	42.9
Savannah, GA	58 243	17 622	17.5	16 871	2.2	12.9	6.3	224 613	63.6	5.4	55.0	13.8	31.1
Scranton—Wilkes-Barre—Hazleton, PA	105 575	36 077	23.4	34 657	0.1	8.0	3.3	507 034	59.1	5.6	49.0	15.6	35.4
Seattle-Tacoma-Bremerton, WA	653 134	221 418	12.7	188 973	1.5	11.8	3.8	2 773 137	68.8	5.0	58.1	16.0	25.9
Bremerton, WA	46 929	11 528	9.8	13 475	4.6	14.7	4.4	177 191	64.9	5.5	54.0	16.1	29.9
Olympia, WA	40 428	13 181	10.3	12 447	0.0	11.4	2.8	161 642	67.3	5.8	55.5	16.4	28.1
Seattle-Bellevue-Everett, WA	423 606	158 710	13.3	122 095	0.6	10.9	3.4	1 903 089	70.0	4.6	59.3	16.1	24.6
Tacoma, WA	142 171	37 999	12.5	40 956	3.4	13.8	5.2	531 215	66.4	6.1	56.1	15.5	28.5
Sharon, PA	21 881	5 921	20.0	7 085	0.0	7.1	3.7	95 664	58.1	6.0	48.5	15.5	36.0
Sheboygan, WI	22 043	4 720	20.2	6 439	0.0	11.5	2.9	87 548	69.8	2.6	58.4	17.6	24.0
Sherman-Denison, TX	20 779	5 331	9.7	6 426	0.0	11.5	7.2	85 902	62.1	4.7	54.5	13.1	32.4
Shreveport-Bossier City, LA	79 545	19 645	8.6	23 925	1.3	11.8	8.7	299 079	61.5	8.0	53.7	11.9	34.5
Sioux City, IA-NE	25 231	5 444	16.1	7 552	0.1	11.1	4.8	93 414	69.3	4.1	59.0	16.2	24.8
Sioux Falls, SD	33 251	8 975	16.6	10 074	0.1	11.6	3.3	131 592	75.4	2.8	63.9	16.8	19.3
South Bend, IN	49 543	22 170	31.4	17 831	0.1	8.2	4.6	204 964	66.0	5.6	55.0	18.0	26.9
Spokane, WA	80 540	30 682	13.3	26 628	0.7	12.1	3.1	323 980	65.1	7.9	51.4	18.5	30.1
Springfield, IL	37 523	9 905	15.7	10 553	0.2	12.4	4.3	157 011	69.3	4.0	59.9	14.4	25.6
Springfield, MA	113 826	57 715	18.0	40 576	0.0	6.7	4.8	477 122	64.2	5.5	50.8	19.8	29.4
Springfield, MO	55 729	28 624	14.3	19 842	0.1	11.2	4.8	256 972	66.7	5.0	55.0	17.5	27.5
St. Cloud, MN	33 263	17 383	18.0	13 318	0.1	7.9	1.3	129 534	73.3	3.6	56.7	23.1	20.3
St. Joseph, MO	18 833	5 502	9.5	6 135	0.0	11.4	6.5	80 161	62.5	5.4	54.7	14.6	30.7
St. Louis, MO-IL	513 208	153 764	22.3	146 530	0.1	9.6	4.9	1 997 084	66.7	5.5	56.0	15.7	28.3
State College, PA	18 306	36 356	5.2	11 929	0.1	4.8	1.6	114 077	60.1	5.5	51.5	24.6	23.9
Steubenville-Weirton, OH-WV	21 504	6 661	18.1	6 928	0.0	11.3	4.4	107 519	54.6	6.6	44.9	14.4	40.7
Stockton-Lodi, CA	133 856	33 087	11.1	37 229	0.0	10.7	7.0	408 554	59.8	10.3	51.3	13.7	35.0
Sumter, SC	22 355	5 724	14.0	6 376	2.5	13.2	6.6	78 457	62.1	7.0	55.2	11.9	32.8
Syracuse, NY	144 240	53 403	18.2	44 515	0.0	8.1	4.6	564 807	64.3	6.2	53.5	16.6	29.9
Tallahassee, FL	47 570	52 485	8.0	23 968	0.1	5.8	2.6	228 794	67.2	8.2	54.9	18.7	26.4
Tampa-St. Petersburg-Clearwater, FL	391 559	117 146	15.3	108 624	0.2	11.2	6.7	1 928 587	59.2	4.9	51.7	12.4	35.9
Terre Haute, IN	26 135	13 108	9.8	9 921	0.1	8.3	4.4	118 166	61.5	6.5	51.3	17.2	31.6
Texarkana, TX-Texarkana, AR	25 326	4 618	5.6	7 044	0.0	14.0	6.0	100 417	56.6	6.9	51.9	11.2	36.8
Toledo, OH	119 789	51 575	15.2	38 355	0.0	9.1	4.5	476 231	66.2	6.1	53.4	18.3	28.3
Topeka, KS	31 221	8 815	14.9	9 610	0.0	13.8	5.9	132 070	67.1	4.0	58.0	14.6	27.3

Table B-4. Metropolitan Areas — Education, Labor Force, and Income

Area name	Full-year full-time employed (percent)								Children under 18 years in families (percent, except where noted)						Total employed by class of worker (percent)			
					American Indian and Alaska Native	Asian, Hawaiian, and Pacific Islander				Both in labor force	Father only in labor force	With one parent who is in labor force	+/- U.S. percent of children with no stay-at-home parent	+/- U.S. percent two-income couples				Unpaid family worker
	Total	Men	Women	Non-Hispanic White	Black or African American			Hispanic or Latino[1]	Number						Private	Government	Self-employed	
	24	25	26	27	28	29	30	31	32	33	34	35	36	37	38	39	40	41
Reading, PA	43.5	54.8	33.0	44.7	37.0	48.6	39.1	32.0	87 043	47.5	22.1	18.8	1.7	3.0	82.6	9.0	8.1	0.3
Redding, CA	30.4	38.3	23.1	30.8	32.3	26.4	24.1	27.9	39 363	38.7	21.2	22.4	-3.5	-9.3	68.5	18.4	12.6	0.5
Reno, NV	44.0	51.5	36.4	45.0	41.5	40.9	42.4	39.1	78 967	44.6	19.7	23.1	3.1	2.8	77.6	13.4	8.8	0.3
Richland-Kennewick-Pasco, WA	38.7	49.4	28.0	41.2	29.7	33.2	38.9	27.6	56 208	43.6	25.4	19.2	-1.9	-0.2	73.3	17.4	8.9	0.4
Richmond-Petersburg, VA	46.4	55.7	38.2	48.5	42.4	44.9	41.8	42.3	235 034	45.6	18.6	24.6	5.6	6.9	74.2	17.6	8.0	0.2
Roanoke, VA	44.1	54.4	35.2	44.9	39.7	35.4	42.3	43.2	50 248	46.5	19.6	24.2	6.2	2.7	78.9	12.9	8.1	0.1
Rochester, MN	47.4	58.2	37.3	48.6	26.5	48.4	41.8	34.5	32 620	59.4	18.6	15.3	10.0	13.4	82.5	9.3	8.0	0.2
Rochester, NY	41.2	50.9	32.4	42.5	34.1	36.1	37.1	32.7	268 319	48.2	17.5	23.8	7.5	5.2	78.6	13.2	8.0	0.2
Rockford, IL	44.2	54.7	34.2	45.0	36.4	41.5	43.6	41.9	94 285	48.3	19.4	22.8	6.5	3.4	82.0	9.6	8.2	0.2
Rocky Mount, NC	41.5	50.0	34.2	45.6	36.3	58.2	42.6	36.7	34 252	39.7	15.3	26.6	1.7	-0.4	76.9	14.8	8.0	0.2
Sacramento-Yolo, CA	38.5	46.3	31.3	40.6	35.6	36.2	32.6	34.8	455 009	39.5	22.4	22.1	-2.9	-1.2	67.4	22.4	9.9	0.3
Sacramento, CA	39.1	46.8	31.9	40.9	35.9	36.5	34.2	35.7	414 999	39.2	22.5	22.3	3.0	-1.4	68.1	21.7	10.0	0.3
Yolo, CA	32.0	10.0	26.6	36.0	24.5	33.6	19.8	30.1	40 010	42.7	22.3	20.1	-1.7	0.9	61.2	29.7	8.7	0.3
Saginaw-Bay City-Midland, MI	37.9	48.1	28.6	39.1	27.5	34.5	38.1	35.5	100 177	45.8	19.2	24.2	5.4	-2.1	80.6	11.1	8.0	0.3
Salinas, CA	30.7	36.9	24.1	37.7	31.8	27.8	33.2	22.3	103 507	40.6	21.7	18.3	-5.7	-5.3	71.6	16.3	11.8	0.4
Salt Lake City-Ogden, UT	42.9	54.3	31.6	43.5	42.7	37.1	42.7	39.2	400 107	47.4	29.7	15.1	-2.1	4.8	75.4	15.6	8.8	0.2
San Angelo, TX	39.5	48.3	31.6	40.2	35.6	47.0	33.4	38.6	25 530	44.6	18.1	23.9	3.9	-1.7	71.3	17.8	10.5	0.3
San Antonio, TX	41.0	50.3	32.5	44.2	41.2	38.0	40.8	38.1	423 321	37.7	22.1	23.4	-3.5	-3.0	74.3	16.4	9.0	0.3
San Diego, CA	39.2	49.1	29.3	41.7	41.4	36.1	36.9	33.5	676 014	38.3	25.7	20.8	-5.5	-2.8	72.3	16.0	11.4	0.3
San Francisco-Oakland-San Jose, CA	41.0	49.8	32.4	43.2	36.6	37.7	40.9	36.0	1 549 416	42.6	23.9	19.1	-3.0	0.8	76.3	12.7	10.8	0.3
Oakland, CA	40.6	49.6	32.1	43.4	36.4	40.1	39.9	35.9	568 038	40.7	23.7	20.1	-3.8	0.5	75.2	14.6	9.9	0.3
San Francisco, CA	40.7	47.9	33.5	44.0	30.8	36.1	38.4	35.9	300 809	44.6	22.4	17.8	-2.2	0.9	75.5	11.3	12.9	0.3
San Jose, CA	43.8	54.0	33.5	46.1	47.2	36.9	44.6	37.8	387 650	42.6	26.4	17.2	-4.8	0.4	82.1	9.2	8.4	0.3
Santa Cruz-Watsonville, CA	35.4	44.8	26.2	38.0	36.6	30.2	32.0	28.0	56 258	42.2	23.1	21.7	-0.7	1.7	69.8	15.4	14.4	0.4
Santa Rosa, CA	38.8	48.6	29.6	39.0	35.8	40.3	41.6	37.1	104 433	46.0	23.1	20.2	1.6	2.2	71.4	13.6	14.5	0.4
Vallejo-Fairfield-Napa, CA	39.3	47.0	31.7	40.7	39.2	35.7	39.9	34.3	132 228	43.2	22.2	21.1	-0.3	0.9	71.7	18.7	9.3	0.3
San Luis Obispo-Atascadero-Paso Robles, CA	31.7	39.7	23.3	32.0	25.3	35.1	28.3	32.0	50 070	44.7	25.0	19.9	0.0	-4.1	63.2	20.6	15.7	0.5
Santa Barbara-Santa Maria-Lompoc, CA	33.5	42.2	25.0	34.2	36.6	30.1	31.6	32.5	91 811	43.1	24.1	18.2	-3.3	-3.5	69.8	16.3	13.6	0.3
Santa Fe, NM	41.0	49.7	32.9	43.4	45.7	34.1	45.5	38.0	33 986	43.5	19.7	22.9	1.9	2.3	55.4	28.0	16.2	0.4
Sarasota-Bradenton, FL	34.0	41.7	27.1	33.1	39.2	39.6	40.7	41.0	99 791	43.8	20.2	24.7	4.0	-13.2	74.4	11.1	14.3	0.3
Savannah, GA	41.4	50.7	32.9	44.7	35.4	32.5	36.2	39.4	70 978	39.3	17.5	28.0	2.7	0.4	74.8	15.6	9.4	0.2
Scranton-Wilkes-Barre—Hazleton, PA	37.4	48.3	27.9	37.7	24.5	32.2	42.4	32.1	128 407	47.9	21.7	19.0	2.4	-2.0	79.5	12.0	8.2	0.3
Seattle-Tacoma-Bremerton, WA	42.8	53.1	32.8	43.6	42.0	37.3	38.2	40.9	836 317	45.8	24.8	19.8	1.0	3.0	74.1	15.9	9.7	0.3
Bremerton, WA	40.1	52.3	27.8	40.5	46.5	34.0	36.3	43.0	59 023	44.3	27.3	19.2	-1.1	-1.5	60.6	27.6	11.5	0.3
Olympia, WA	40.6	49.3	32.6	41.1	46.6	36.0	35.7	39.6	49 299	48.4	20.9	21.0	4.8	3.4	57.9	32.3	9.3	0.5
Seattle-Bellevue-Everett, WA	43.7	53.8	33.9	44.8	41.0	37.4	39.4	40.9	547 741	46.5	25.5	18.8	0.7	4.1	76.7	13.2	9.9	0.2
Tacoma, WA	40.9	51.7	30.5	41.5	43.3	38.7	32.3	40.6	180 254	43.3	22.9	22.9	1.6	1.1	73.2	17.7	8.8	0.3
Sharon, PA	35.6	45.2	26.8	36.3	23.5	20.0	36.1	26.4	26 456	45.3	22.9	20.4	1.1	-3.9	79.7	11.1	8.8	0.5
Sheboygan, WI	46.5	57.8	35.1	47.5	19.2	30.9	31.8	39.4	27 818	60.5	16.6	15.9	11.8	11.1	83.6	8.8	7.3	0.3
Sherman-Denison, TX	39.9	50.4	30.4	40.4	36.4	43.4	39.0	35.3	26 029	44.8	23.5	21.5	1.7	-1.3	77.4	11.8	10.4	0.5
Shreveport-Bossier City, LA	39.5	48.4	31.7	42.9	33.4	35.9	39.4	40.2	97 072	36.4	16.3	32.4	4.2	-1.5	73.8	17.5	8.4	0.3
Sioux City, IA-NE	44.7	53.6	36.3	45.3	37.9	27.0	54.3	39.9	32 734	52.9	14.0	21.4	9.7	9.8	81.0	10.1	8.6	0.3
Sioux Falls, SD	50.9	59.2	43.0	51.9	34.9	23.5	46.6	40.2	44 021	62.9	13.3	18.0	16.3	18.3	81.8	8.8	9.1	0.3
South Bend, IN	40.9	52.3	30.6	42.0	35.9	40.4	40.0	35.4	64 248	45.5	21.5	23.2	4.1	3.9	83.1	9.4	7.3	0.2
Spokane, WA	36.7	45.8	28.1	37.2	31.8	31.9	27.9	34.0	101 779	45.3	22.9	22.1	2.7	0.4	74.2	15.7	9.8	0.3
Springfield, IL	48.0	56.5	40.5	49.3	35.2	44.1	41.1	48.0	48 013	51.5	15.0	25.6	12.5	10.1	61.9	29.6	8.2	0.2
Springfield, MA	38.5	49.2	29.2	40.4	35.4	33.7	30.7	26.0	139 890	43.5	15.6	23.7	2.6	5.0	73.2	18.7	7.9	0.2
Springfield, MO	41.5	51.3	32.5	42.0	27.9	30.7	34.8	37.2	74 015	47.4	22.7	21.0	3.8	2.8	77.8	11.1	10.7	0.4
St. Cloud, MN	43.3	52.2	34.5	43.8	28.2	29.9	28.2	39.0	42 337	65.1	14.2	15.0	15.5	14.6	77.4	11.5	10.7	0.4
St. Joseph, MO	41.1	49.8	32.9	41.4	31.1	45.7	46.8	46.7	23 743	46.5	19.7	24.4	6.3	2.1	77.4	13.3	9.0	0.3
St. Louis, MO-IL	43.3	53.2	34.5	45.1	35.3	43.8	43.3	41.0	648 541	46.1	18.9	24.0	5.5	4.2	81.3	10.7	7.7	0.2
State College, PA	32.5	39.6	25.2	33.9	21.6	57.1	18.1	17.8	23 404	52.1	25.1	15.4	2.9	3.6	70.4	21.5	7.7	0.4
Steubenville-Weirton, OH-WV	32.5	43.3	22.9	32.8	31.0	15.1	28.1	23.0	26 615	42.9	24.2	20.2	-1.5	-9.9	83.5	10.4	5.8	0.3
Stockton-Lodi, CA	33.2	41.4	25.3	37.7	30.1	29.5	27.2	27.9	161 571	35.6	23.6	20.4	-8.6	-6.7	75.4	15.8	8.4	0.3
Sumter, SC	40.8	50.4	32.1	45.4	35.5	44.7	43.4	40.9	26 899	38.7	17.4	28.7	2.8	-1.0	72.4	18.6	8.7	0.3
Syracuse, NY	39.7	49.2	31.0	40.6	30.9	38.0	35.3	27.6	179 918	46.1	19.2	24.3	5.8	2.7	75.1	16.3	8.3	0.2
Tallahassee, FL	39.8	46.1	34.3	43.9	32.8	48.2	39.8	32.0	58 674	42.8	15.9	28.3	6.5	8.3	55.5	36.1	8.0	0.3
Tampa-St. Petersburg-Clearwater, FL	39.1	47.2	31.8	39.1	38.6	46.8	41.8	38.5	489 023	41.2	19.6	25.6	2.2	-5.9	77.2	12.1	10.5	0.2
Terre Haute, IN	37.5	46.9	28.7	38.1	29.9	24.4	25.9	31.7	33 048	44.8	21.7	22.3	2.5	-0.6	77.7	14.5	7.5	0.4
Texarkana, TX-Texarkana, AR	37.0	45.0	29.2	40.2	27.6	47.9	46.0	25.9	30 530	37.8	19.9	27.0	0.2	-3.3	70.8	18.5	10.3	0.4
Toledo, OH	40.7	51.2	31.2	42.3	31.1	39.0	33.9	38.0	151 956	45.5	17.9	25.3	6.1	3.6	79.9	12.6	7.3	0.2
Topeka, KS	45.4	53.2	38.3	46.3	40.1	37.1	36.7	42.6	40 485	50.8	16.1	24.2	10.3	8.6	71.1	20.8	7.9	0.2

[1]Hispanic or Latino persons may be of any race.

Table B-4. Metropolitan Areas — **Education, Labor Force, and Income**

Area name	Percent who worked at home	Percent of the population 5 years and over with a disability	Veterans as a percent of the population 18 years and over	Occupation for employed population 16 years and over (percent)						Industry for employed population 16 years and over (percent)					
				Management, professional, and related occupations	Service occupations	Sales and office occupations	Farming, fishing, and forestry occupations	Construction, extraction, and maintenance occupations	Production, transportation and material moving occupations	Agriculture, forestry, fishing, and mining	Construction and manufacturing	Wholesale and retail trade	Transportation and warehousing, and utilities	Service industries	Public administration
	42	43	44	45	46	47	48	49	50	51	52	53	54	55	56
Reading, PA	2.9	17.5	13.4	29.3	13.3	26.1	0.9	9.1	21.3	1.8	30.0	15.9	4.9	45.2	2.3
Redding, CA	4.1	22.8	17.0	30.4	19.6	27.0	0.9	9.8	12.3	2.5	13.8	17.2	5.7	55.1	5.8
Reno, NV	2.9	18.8	15.8	29.5	19.9	28.9	0.2	9.5	12.1	0.8	15.1	16.1	6.0	57.7	4.3
Richland-Kennewick-Pasco, WA	3.8	18.8	13.9	34.9	14.5	23.1	4.7	9.9	12.9	7.1	15.5	14.7	6.3	51.9	4.5
Richmond-Petersburg, VA	2.6	17.9	13.7	37.0	13.2	28.8	0.2	8.9	11.9	0.5	18.4	16.1	5.0	53.0	7.0
Roanoke, VA	2.3	20.7	15.2	31.9	13.8	30.3	0.2	9.1	14.7	0.6	19.3	19.1	6.7	50.8	3.5
Rochester, MN	3.7	13.7	12.2	44.5	14.1	23.4	0.3	7.5	10.2	1.3	21.3	13.1	2.7	58.9	2.8
Rochester, NY	2.9	17.4	12.1	37.1	14.5	25.4	0.4	7.2	15.4	1.1	25.7	14.7	3.5	51.7	3.2
Rockford, IL	2.8	17.7	13.1	29.0	12.9	25.9	0.3	9.2	22.6	1.0	33.0	14.6	5.6	43.2	2.5
Rocky Mount, NC	1.9	24.6	11.9	25.6	13.6	25.4	1.0	11.1	23.2	2.3	31.1	16.1	4.3	41.7	4.5
Sacramento-Yolo, CA	4.0	19.0	13.7	37.3	14.7	28.6	0.6	8.9	9.8	1.1	14.7	14.9	4.6	54.0	10.8
Sacramento, CA	4.1	19.2	14.2	36.9	14.8	29.1	0.4	9.1	9.7	0.9	15.1	14.9	4.6	53.5	11.1
Yolo, CA	3.8	16.7	9.1	41.4	14.2	23.8	2.6	7.1	10.9	3.9	11.3	14.3	4.5	58.4	7.7
Saginaw-Bay City-Midland, MI	2.9	19.1	13.2	29.4	17.2	26.3	0.3	9.9	17.0	0.9	27.5	16.5	3.6	48.4	3.1
Salinas, CA	3.6	19.8	11.0	29.2	16.8	23.2	11.2	8.5	11.1	12.4	12.0	17.2	3.3	49.7	5.5
Salt Lake City-Ogden, UT	3.8	15.7	11.1	32.7	13.0	30.8	0.2	10.0	13.3	0.8	20.0	16.8	5.4	50.8	6.2
San Angelo, TX	2.2	20.8	14.6	27.9	18.9	28.5	0.9	10.7	13.2	3.5	15.0	16.0	3.2	56.1	6.1
San Antonio, TX	2.6	20.7	15.7	32.7	15.7	29.5	0.2	10.6	11.2	0.7	15.4	16.1	5.0	57.1	5.7
San Diego, CA	4.4	17.9	14.0	37.7	16.1	27.2	0.5	8.7	9.9	0.7	17.6	14.5	3.8	57.9	5.4
San Francisco-Oakland-San Jose, CA	4.1	17.6	9.8	43.6	12.9	25.6	0.5	7.4	10.0	0.8	20.6	14.2	4.7	56.2	3.6
Oakland, CA	3.8	17.9	10.1	41.8	12.5	27.0	0.2	8.1	10.5	0.4	18.4	15.0	5.6	56.7	3.9
San Francisco, CA	4.8	18.0	8.4	46.7	13.7	26.1	0.2	5.8	7.5	0.3	12.7	13.9	5.2	64.6	3.3
San Jose, CA	3.1	16.4	8.4	48.5	10.5	22.7	0.4	6.6	11.2	0.5	32.5	12.9	2.8	48.8	2.5
Santa Cruz-Watsonville, CA	5.3	15.9	9.8	40.3	14.8	23.4	3.7	8.9	8.9	4.4	20.3	14.8	2.8	54.3	3.4
Santa Rosa, CA	5.4	17.7	12.7	35.0	15.1	26.6	1.6	10.2	11.4	2.6	21.1	15.0	4.1	53.3	3.9
Vallejo-Fairfield-Napa, CA	3.6	19.1	15.5	31.9	16.8	26.9	1.2	10.6	12.6	1.9	18.9	14.9	6.1	51.3	6.8
San Luis Obispo-Atascadero-Paso Robles, CA	5.6	17.6	14.4	34.3	18.8	25.3	2.1	9.8	9.8	3.8	15.0	14.8	4.5	55.7	6.2
Santa Barbara-Santa Maria-Lompoc, CA	4.6	17.7	12.0	35.4	17.1	25.3	4.9	7.7	9.6	6.7	15.6	14.5	2.9	56.0	4.2
Santa Fe, NM	6.9	16.8	13.0	45.2	15.5	24.1	0.2	9.0	6.0	0.8	11.5	12.7	2.1	56.2	16.8
Sarasota-Bradenton, FL	4.1	22.7	19.2	30.5	18.1	29.0	0.8	10.7	10.9	1.0	18.0	18.3	3.3	55.5	4.0
Savannah, GA	2.4	21.1	15.7	31.2	16.1	26.8	0.3	11.7	13.9	0.4	20.8	15.9	6.4	51.4	5.0
Scranton—Wilkes-Barre—Hazleton, PA	2.2	21.4	15.2	27.9	15.4	27.9	0.3	9.4	19.1	0.9	22.9	16.8	5.7	49.0	4.8
Seattle-Tacoma-Bremerton, WA	4.2	17.2	15.1	38.4	14.0	26.4	0.4	9.1	11.6	0.8	19.8	16.1	5.4	52.8	5.1
Bremerton, WA	4.6	18.3	22.3	34.9	17.4	24.8	0.5	12.0	10.4	0.9	18.7	14.6	4.3	52.1	9.5
Olympia, WA	3.8	18.8	18.3	37.4	15.4	27.1	1.1	9.0	10.0	2.1	13.5	13.4	3.7	48.2	19.1
Seattle-Bellevue-Everett, WA	4.4	16.3	13.1	40.9	13.1	26.4	0.3	8.3	10.9	0.6	20.3	16.2	5.2	54.2	3.5
Tacoma, WA	3.6	19.7	18.9	30.1	16.3	26.8	0.5	11.2	15.1	1.0	20.3	17.0	6.9	49.0	5.8
Sharon, PA	3.2	19.0	15.0	27.6	17.3	25.3	0.6	8.2	21.0	1.6	25.2	17.2	5.0	46.8	4.2
Sheboygan, WI	3.0	14.6	13.1	25.9	13.6	21.6	0.9	8.2	29.8	1.9	43.8	12.1	2.8	37.3	2.0
Sherman-Denison, TX	2.9	22.1	15.4	29.6	14.4	26.5	0.5	11.5	17.5	1.9	26.4	15.9	4.5	48.0	3.4
Shreveport-Bossier City, LA	1.7	22.0	14.9	28.6	18.5	26.7	0.3	10.7	15.1	2.1	17.9	15.7	5.3	54.0	5.0
Sioux City, IA-NE	3.0	17.6	13.5	27.0	15.4	27.1	0.7	8.8	21.0	2.0	28.7	15.6	5.1	45.3	3.2
Sioux Falls, SD	3.4	15.2	13.2	31.1	12.9	32.2	0.4	8.8	14.6	1.8	18.5	17.0	5.0	54.8	3.1
South Bend, IN	2.6	18.3	12.8	32.1	14.5	27.2	0.1	8.0	18.2	0.3	25.7	16.6	4.3	50.5	2.6
Spokane, WA	4.1	19.1	16.8	33.0	16.9	28.4	0.4	8.6	12.7	0.9	16.5	17.3	4.6	55.9	4.7
Springfield, IL	2.7	17.1	14.1	39.0	14.6	29.7	0.3	8.0	8.4	1.4	10.0	12.4	4.5	52.4	19.4
Springfield, MA	2.7	20.7	12.9	34.4	16.4	25.9	0.3	7.6	15.4	0.5	19.2	15.1	5.3	55.2	4.7
Springfield, MO	3.6	18.1	14.2	29.4	15.5	29.1	0.5	9.4	16.2	1.5	19.1	19.1	5.8	51.6	2.9
St. Cloud, MN	5.5	14.0	12.3	29.3	14.4	26.8	1.1	9.2	19.3	4.2	24.1	19.9	4.0	45.3	2.5
St. Joseph, MO	2.8	20.4	14.7	27.8	16.9	26.3	0.4	10.4	18.1	1.7	24.1	14.7	6.3	48.0	5.1
St. Louis, MO-IL	2.8	17.6	14.0	34.4	14.8	28.1	0.2	8.8	13.7	0.7	20.5	15.3	5.8	54.0	3.8
State College, PA	4.0	11.2	9.9	41.6	16.5	23.5	0.6	6.7	11.1	1.7	15.4	11.8	3.1	64.6	3.5
Steubenville-Weirton, OH-WV	2.0	20.4	16.2	22.5	17.6	26.6	0.3	11.7	21.3	1.2	26.9	14.6	6.9	47.2	3.1
Stockton-Lodi, CA	2.9	21.4	11.4	27.1	14.6	27.1	4.1	10.2	16.8	5.4	19.6	16.6	6.2	42.6	5.3
Sumter, SC	1.6	23.3	16.0	24.9	15.5	24.5	0.6	11.4	23.1	1.4	31.4	14.7	3.8	42.6	6.1
Syracuse, NY	3.0	18.0	13.0	33.9	15.3	27.0	0.6	8.1	15.1	1.3	19.7	15.8	5.7	53.3	4.2
Tallahassee, FL	2.4	15.8	11.1	42.8	15.1	28.3	0.5	6.6	6.6	0.9	8.2	13.2	2.6	56.0	19.2
Tampa-St. Petersburg-Clearwater, FL	3.1	23.6	17.1	32.8	15.2	31.1	0.5	9.1	11.2	0.8	15.3	18.3	4.8	56.8	4.1
Terre Haute, IN	2.3	20.8	13.5	27.5	17.4	26.2	0.4	9.7	18.8	1.3	24.0	18.3	4.2	48.1	4.1
Texarkana, TX-Texarkana, AR	2.0	23.7	14.6	27.2	16.3	26.9	0.7	11.3	17.6	1.8	20.1	18.7	5.4	44.9	9.0
Toledo, OH	2.1	19.0	12.4	30.2	15.4	25.7	0.3	8.6	19.9	0.7	25.6	15.5	5.6	49.4	3.2
Topeka, KS	2.6	20.0	15.9	34.2	14.4	29.8	0.2	8.9	12.4	0.7	15.4	14.6	6.7	52.7	10.0

Table B-4. Metropolitan Areas — Education, Labor Force, and Income

Area name	Median house-hold income	Median family income				Median non-family house-hold income	Median income for full-year, full-time workers		Per capita income	Households by source of income (percent)					House-holds with income over $100,000 (percent)	+/- U.S. percent for income over $100,000	House-holds with income below poverty (percent)	Families with children with income below poverty (percent)
		All families	Families with children							With earnings	With interest, dividend, or rental income	With Social Security income	With public assis-tance income	With retire-ment income				
			Married-couple	Male house-holder	Female house-holder		Men	Women										
	57	58	59	60	61	62	63	64	65	66	67	68	69	70	71	72	73	74
Reading, PA	44 714	52 997	62 633	31 522	20 696	24 751	39 693	26 669	21 232	79.7	44.7	29.2	2.4	19.1	10.2	-2.1	8.8	10.3
Redding, CA	34 335	40 491	49 712	26 058	16 353	19 535	36 925	25 704	17 738	73.0	31.6	32.1	6.9	21.4	7.2	-5.1	13.9	18.1
Reno, NV	45 815	54 283	61 367	31 638	25 527	30 235	37 190	29 348	24 277	85.0	34.1	21.9	2.1	15.0	12.9	0.6	9.1	10.3
Richland-Kennewick-Pasco, WA	44 886	51 273	56 762	30 022	18 849	26 604	43 655	27 240	19 798	83.5	38.5	22.9	4.9	17.0	10.8	-1.5	10.8	14.3
Richmond-Petersburg, VA	46 800	56 309	67 912	32 476	22 481	29 115	40 354	29 493	23 685	83.8	36.5	23.1	2.5	18.1	13.3	1.0	9.2	10.3
Roanoke, VA	39 288	48 206	58 523	28 843	20 138	22 559	35 469	24 813	21 366	78.9	36.6	30.2	2.5	18.1	8.5	-3.8	9.7	11.3
Rochester, MN	51 316	61 610	71 708	33 036	26 186	29 456	41 322	30 650	24 939	85.8	49.5	20.8	2.9	14.9	15.1	2.8	6.2	5.9
Rochester, NY	43 955	53 609	65 342	31 830	19 897	25 716	40 704	28 959	21 627	79.5	42.5	26.6	4.5	20.0	11.4	-0.9	10.0	11.8
Rockford, IL	44 988	53 423	62 124	33 292	20 260	26 201	41 229	26 430	21 145	82.1	38.8	25.4	2.9	15.1	10.3	-2.0	8.8	9.9
Rocky Mount, NC	34 795	41 102	53 494	22 563	16 819	18 496	31 533	23 812	17 142	78.6	24.1	28.6	4.6	16.9	6.7	-5.6	15.9	18.2
Sacramento-Yolo, CA	46 106	53 795	63 457	33 119	24 100	30 245	42 007	32 346	22 302	81.5	35.9	23.0	5.5	18.6	14.0	1.7	10.7	13.1
Sacramento, CA	46 602	54 006	64 000	33 550	24 097	30 909	42 152	32 466	22 607	81.3	35.7	23.3	5.6	19.0	14.1	1.8	10.2	13.1
Yolo, CA	40 769	51 623	59 134	29 643	24 134	22 194	40 079	31 228	19 365	83.7	38.1	19.8	4.4	14.9	13.0	0.7	16.8	13.3
Saginaw-Bay City-Midland, MI	39 909	48 806	61 742	26 488	17 015	22 095	41 453	26 186	20 320	77.0	40.6	28.3	4.5	22.3	10.4	-1.9	11.3	13.8
Salinas, CA	48 305	51 169	52 342	30 832	23 662	33 014	40 169	30 775	20 165	83.7	36.3	24.6	4.0	17.7	15.2	2.9	10.3	14.0
Salt Lake City-Ogden, UT	48 594	54 470	60 492	34 498	23 292	28 316	38 741	26 557	19 781	87.1	38.3	19.5	3.1	15.5	12.6	0.3	7.5	7.8
San Angelo, TX	33 148	39 482	46 069	21 845	16 244	19 007	29 409	21 428	17 325	79.1	30.8	27.7	4.1	18.5	5.8	-6.5	14.9	16.5
San Antonio, TX	39 140	44 729	50 558	25 821	19 098	25 405	32 080	25 657	18 518	83.1	30.2	23.3	3.5	18.5	9.9	-2.4	13.7	17.1
San Diego, CA	47 067	53 438	60 332	31 338	23 092	32 044	38 612	31 095	22 926	82.6	37.5	22.5	3.6	17.7	15.7	3.4	10.3	13.3
San Francisco-Oakland-San Jose, CA	62 024	71 333	82 716	42 108	31 211	41 824	51 492	39 428	30 769	84.3	44.5	21.1	3.1	15.6	26.7	14.4	7.6	8.2
Oakland, CA	59 365	68 902	81 247	41 295	29 758	38 108	51 313	38 749	28 241	84.0	41.8	20.8	3.7	16.1	24.0	11.7	8.5	9.7
San Francisco, CA	63 297	75 219	87 715	45 066	35 019	46 624	51 723	41 589	36 651	82.8	49.2	22.3	2.7	14.7	29.0	16.7	7.6	7.6
San Jose, CA	74 335	81 717	93 371	47 972	35 375	51 732	58 224	41 379	32 795	87.7	45.9	18.2	2.7	13.6	34.6	22.3	6.1	6.8
Santa Cruz-Watsonville, CA	53 998	61 941	70 496	41 033	28 545	35 297	48 103	35 404	26 396	84.9	43.4	21.3	2.7	14.4	21.0	0.6	9.5	9.8
Santa Rosa, CA	53 076	61 921	70 829	41 567	29 530	33 047	44 038	33 500	25 724	81.2	44.1	25.5	2.3	18.1	18.1	5.8	7.0	6.9
Vallejo-Fairfield-Napa, CA	53 431	60 754	68 719	36 315	27 196	32 737	43 020	32 733	22 040	86.0	05.4	22.0	0.5	21.6	17.0	4.7	7.3	8.6
San Luis Obispo-Atascadero-Paso Robles, CA	42 428	52 447	60 919	33 832	23 185	25 261	41 857	28 975	21 864	76.9	43.2	29.2	2.3	20.3	12.0	-0.3	11.8	9.9
Santa Barbara-Santa Maria-Lompoc, CA	46 677	54 042	57 696	31 643	22 160	30 309	39 862	30 611	23 059	80.5	42.4	26.8	3.1	18.1	16.0	3.7	11.6	13.0
Santa Fe, NM	45 822	54 579	61 413	26 170	22 811	32 015	40 080	30 393	24 967	83.3	42.1	21.9	2.4	17.6	15.6	3.3	10.6	11.9
Sarasota-Bradenton, FL	40 649	48 623	57 894	28 557	21 829	26 144	33 515	26 399	25 669	64.6	48.3	45.4	1.7	28.3	11.2	-1.1	8.0	11.5
Savannah, GA	39 622	47 323	57 864	31 490	17 216	22 695	37 166	25 571	20 752	80.1	28.2	26.4	3.0	17.6	10.4	-1.9	14.3	16.6
Scranton—Wilkes-Barre—Hazleton, PA	34 161	43 606	52 927	26 549	16 681	17 709	33 568	23 931	18 229	72.4	40.2	36.0	2.6	21.0	6.4	-5.9	11.8	12.2
Seattle-Tacoma-Bremerton, WA	50 733	60 195	68 075	36 716	25 298	33 156	44 465	32 461	25 744	84.0	41.8	20.3	3.2	16.6	15.4	3.1	8.0	8.6
Bremerton, WA	46 840	53 878	58 563	32 725	20 535	28 732	41 375	29 933	22 317	81.0	41.8	21.7	3.8	24.2	11.6	-0.7	8.2	9.4
Olympia, WA	46 975	55 027	61 523	35 192	23 070	28 596	41 953	31 141	22 415	82.0	42.4	23.5	3.3	21.6	10.8	-1.5	8.8	9.4
Seattle-Bellevue-Everett, WA	52 804	63 758	72 329	38 658	27 315	35 493	46 408	34 437	27 751	84.9	44.0	19.5	2.8	14.9	17.4	5.1	7.5	7.6
Tacoma, WA	45 204	52 098	60 093	34 106	21 837	28 539	40 307	29 615	20 948	82.4	33.2	21.9	4.7	18.8	10.4	-1.9	9.6	11.3
Sharon, PA	34 666	41 776	50 029	29 199	14 686	19 975	34 956	22 470	17 636	73.7	41.0	34.8	3.2	24.2	5.4	-6.9	11.0	14.9
Sheboygan, WI	46 237	53 984	60 767	32 688	24 643	26 851	38 644	26 064	21 509	81.4	50.5	26.7	1.2	15.4	7.8	-4.5	5.2	5.4
Sherman-Denison, TX	37 178	45 048	52 351	27 583	21 378	19 829	34 587	24 347	18 862	77.6	31.0	30.2	2.8	17.7	7.5	-4.8	12.1	13.2
Shreveport-Bossier City, LA	32 558	40 216	51 920	25 659	14 719	19 712	32 858	23 070	17 628	78.1	25.7	26.4	3.3	17.3	7.4	-4.9	18.0	22.8
Sioux City, IA-NE	38 563	46 048	54 661	26 318	18 622	21 973	31 874	23 521	18 339	81.9	35.2	27.4	3.1	13.6	6.9	-5.4	9.9	11.4
Sioux Falls, SD	43 387	52 387	59 888	30 125	21 968	25 139	33 900	25 342	20 936	86.5	40.8	21.8	2.1	11.6	8.9	-3.4	7.2	7.2
South Bend, IN	40 420	49 653	61 004	31 283	18 951	24 132	38 118	26 109	19 756	81.2	39.0	27.1	3.2	16.7	8.9	-3.4	9.7	12.3
Spokane, WA	37 308	46 463	54 527	27 868	18 335	21 649	36 358	26 352	19 233	79.1	36.6	25.6	4.9	16.6	7.9	-4.4	12.2	12.9
Springfield, IL	43 180	53 834	64 235	28 958	21 863	27 135	39 103	29 808	23 074	81.6	41.0	25.8	2.5	18.6	10.4	-1.9	8.4	10.4
Springfield, MA	41 095	51 193	62 555	32 118	17 916	24 135	39 545	29 612	20 078	77.2	37.9	28.8	4.7	17.7	9.7	-2.6	13.1	16.4
Springfield, MO	34 661	42 262	49 879	25 565	18 581	20 232	31 510	22 597	18 611	81.1	35.4	25.6	3.1	15.3	6.8	-5.5	12.0	12.0
St. Cloud, MN	42 321	51 481	59 466	31 240	22 171	23 830	35 143	23 831	19 170	84.3	41.6	23.2	2.6	11.9	8.1	-4.2	8.9	6.0
St. Joseph, MO	35 675	43 152	51 829	27 944	17 417	20 086	32 668	22 672	18 123	76.9	36.2	30.5	3.7	17.7	5.8	-6.5	12.1	12.6
St. Louis, MO-IL	44 437	54 113	66 467	31 438	21 377	26 300	41 422	28 504	22 698	80.6	39.6	26.2	3.3	18.2	12.2	-0.1	9.7	11.2
State College, PA	36 165	50 557	57 568	25 471	22 024	20 041	36 016	25 739	18 020	83.4	43.1	22.0	1.2	16.1	8.5	-3.8	17.7	8.7
Steubenville-Weirton, OH-WV	31 982	39 548	46 518	24 006	12 310	17 642	36 166	20 614	16 911	69.3	33.3	36.0	3.4	27.4	4.5	-7.8	13.8	17.5
Stockton-Lodi, CA	41 282	46 919	54 871	29 061	18 286	23 873	40 324	28 677	17 365	79.9	28.1	24.6	7.2	17.1	10.6	-1.7	14.5	19.0
Sumter, SC	33 278	38 970	47 383	26 206	18 107	17 619	29 772	21 930	15 657	78.9	23.5	27.0	3.4	19.8	5.3	-7.0	16.3	18.2
Syracuse, NY	39 750	49 270	60 830	29 523	18 749	22 183	37 869	26 948	20 002	78.3	37.9	28.1	3.1	19.8	9.5	-2.8	12.1	13.1
Tallahassee, FL	36 441	50 086	61 825	29 208	20 074	21 254	35 408	27 971	19 990	84.6	32.4	18.4	2.5	13.8	9.5	-2.8	18.8	15.0
Tampa-St. Petersburg-Clearwater, FL	37 406	45 353	57 795	27 390	20 999	24 432	34 464	26 941	21 784	73.1	36.9	34.6	2.6	21.4	9.9	-2.9	10.4	12.7
Terre Haute, IN	34 222	42 502	50 289	25 042	16 344	19 142	33 958	23 166	17 504	76.7	33.5	30.2	3.1	19.0	6.0	-6.3	13.1	13.8
Texarkana, TX-Texarkana, AR	32 238	39 704	50 795	21 630	12 780	17 113	33 582	22 146	17 072	75.5	27.1	28.7	3.4	19.0	6.2	-6.1	17.4	22.0
Toledo, OH	39 902	50 286	61 911	29 644	17 784	23 114	40 346	27 089	20 565	79.7	35.7	25.4	3.7	17.5	9.5	-2.8	12.4	14.4
Topeka, KS	40 988	51 464	60 199	28 111	22 092	23 885	36 511	27 231	20 904	80.4	39.9	27.8	2.7	18.5	8.4	-3.9	9.6	10.2

Table B-4. Metropolitan Areas — Education, Labor Force, and Income

CMSA/MSA/PMSA/NECMA code[1]	Area name	High school graduates			College graduates		College graduates (percent)				
		Total population 25 years and over	Percent with a high school diploma or less	Percent with a high school diploma or more	Percent with a bachelor's degree or more	+/− U.S. percent with bachelor's degree or more	Non-Hispanic White	Black or African American	American Indian and Alaska Native	Asian, Hawaiian, and Pacific Islander	Hispanic or Latino[2]
		1	2	3	4	5	6	7	8	9	10
8520	Tucson, AZ..................	546 200	39.9	83.4	26.7	2.3	32.5	16.8	9.4	42.2	10.9
8560	Tulsa, OK....................	514 373	45.7	83.7	23.2	-1.2	25.1	14.8	14.9	37.0	11.8
8600	Tuscaloosa, AL	99 039	49.6	78.8	24.0	-0.4	27.9	12.1	15.7	65.6	22.7
8640	Tyler, TX.....................	111 020	44.6	80.2	22.5	-1.9	26.9	11.2	17.9	47.6	3.4
8680	Utica-Rome, NY	202 301	54.1	79.1	17.7	-6.7	18.4	6.0	5.1	29.9	7.4
8750	Victoria, TX.................	51 985	52.8	76.2	16.2	-8.2	22.3	9.4	6.8	50.3	6.0
8780	Visalia-Tulare-Porterville, CA	204 888	61.3	61.7	11.5	-12.9	17.5	6.7	4.6	18.4	3.6
8800	Waco, TX	125 961	51.3	76.6	19.1	-5.3	23.2	9.1	9.0	47.7	6.8
97	Washington-Baltimore, DC-MD-VA-WV	5 036 513	38.3	84.9	37.1	12.7	43.0	21.2	25.4	53.5	21.8
0720	Baltimore, MD	1 691 080	45.2	81.9	29.2	4.8	33.0	16.1	22.4	52.8	28.7
3180	Hagerstown, MD	90 371	61.1	77.8	14.6	-9.8	15.2	4.1	8.5	32.3	15.3
8840	Washington, DC-MD-VA-WV.......................	3 255 062	34.0	86.7	41.8	17.4	50.3	24.1	27.0	53.8	21.0
8920	Waterloo-Cedar Falls, IA	78 401	48.7	86.5	23.0	-1.4	23.7	9.9	22.7	60.0	15.4
8940	Wausau, WI.................	81 925	54.2	83.8	18.3	-6.1	18.5	39.1	5.7	11.2	10.5
8960	West Palm Beach-Boca Raton, FL	817 899	43.3	83.6	27.7	3.3	31.3	11.4	16.5	47.3	15.3
9000	Wheeling, WV-OH........	106 586	62.0	81.2	14.6	-9.8	14.7	5.2	11.9	69.2	24.2
9080	Wichita Falls, TX	86 469	50.3	80.0	19.7	-4.7	22.0	10.5	16.9	21.6	8.6
9040	Wichita, KS.................	341 423	44.3	85.3	24.7	0.3	26.8	13.0	13.5	23.8	9.6
9140	Williamsport, PA...........	80 500	61.3	80.6	15.1	-9.3	15.2	6.9	12.1	38.6	13.8
9200	Wilmington, NC	160 276	43.7	83.7	26.1	1.7	28.7	12.1	16.4	48.0	13.2
9260	Yakima, WA.................	130 747	58.7	68.7	15.3	-9.1	19.8	16.6	11.7	27.2	3.9
9280	York, PA......................	259 040	60.9	80.7	18.4	-6.0	18.7	9.8	7.3	36.3	10.8
9320	Youngstown-Warren, OH..............................	403 869	61.0	82.1	15.1	-9.3	15.9	6.7	8.6	45.9	10.5
9340	Yuba City, CA	84 289	52.6	72.5	13.2	-11.2	14.8	13.6	7.4	16.8	4.7
9360	Yuma, AZ.....................	97 680	59.9	65.8	11.8	-12.6	16.6	12.6	6.2	23.4	4.7

[1]MSA = Metropolitan Statistical Area. CMSA = Consolidated MSA. PMSA = Primary MSA. NECMA = New England County Metropolitan Area. See the Appendix A for explanation of these concepts. See Appendix B for list of metropolitan areas identified by type, with component counties.
[2]Hispanic or Latino persons may be of any race.

Area name	School enrollment			Population 16 to 19 years				Employment status, 2000			Work status in 1999 of the population 16 years and over (percent)		
											Worked in 1999		
	Grades kindergarten through 12	College or graduate school	Percent private	Number	Percent in armed forces	Percent high school graduates	Percent not enrolled, not grads, not in armed forces, not employed	Total population 16 years and over	Percent in labor force	Unemploy-ment rate	Full-time	Part-time	Did not work in 1999
	11	12	13	14	15	16	17	18	19	20	21	22	23
Tucson, AZ..................	153 693	69 727	8.9	49 172	0.7	10.0	6.8	658 638	60.3	5.3	51.0	15.9	33.1
Tulsa, OK	158 710	41 926	15.1	46 479	0.0	10.7	5.6	613 503	65.9	4.6	57.8	13.6	28.5
Tuscaloosa, AL	28 564	21 141	9.2	12 685	0.0	7.2	4.4	130 752	60.7	6.2	51.6	16.5	31.9
Tyler, TX......................	34 152	9 012	9.7	11 093	0.0	11.7	5.8	133 774	62.0	6.5	53.8	12.8	33.4
Utica-Rome, NY	56 819	15 905	12.4	16 887	0.0	7.5	3.4	236 736	59.5	6.0	50.3	15.3	34.4
Victoria, TX..................	18 552	3 966	9.7	5 069	0.0	11.8	4.8	62 238	64.8	4.7	57.2	12.8	30.0
Visalia-Tulare-Porterville, CA	94 339	17 959	5.6	25 935	0.0	10.0	7.5	257 320	59.8	12.7	50.7	13.3	36.0
Waco, TX	41 749	22 657	23.4	16 641	0.1	8.6	5.5	163 207	62.5	7.6	53.7	14.9	31.4
Washington-Baltimore, DC-MD-VA-WV	1 435 252	523 028	19.0	388 030	0.7	10.7	4.7	5 888 970	69.4	4.4	61.6	13.4	25.0
Baltimore, MD	490 124	167 888	19.3	134 720	1.1	12.3	5.8	1 977 083	66.4	4.9	57.9	13.9	28.2
Hagerstown, MD	23 374	4 852	12.1	6 116	0.1	16.4	8.0	104 251	61.1	3.3	53.7	12.9	33.3
Washington, DC-MD-VA-WV....................	921 754	350 288	18.9	247 194	0.5	9.6	4.0	3 807 636	71.2	4.2	63.7	13.2	23.1
Waterloo-Cedar Falls, IA	22 272	15 933	11.3	8 922	0.2	7.8	2.3	101 854	66.2	4.8	51.2	22.1	26.7
Wausau, WI..................	25 711	4 793	12.1	7 652	0.0	12.7	1.7	96 478	71.7	3.8	59.3	17.7	23.0
West Palm Beach-Boca Raton, FL	183 941	50 064	17.0	49 015	0.0	8.5	6.9	917 453	55.6	5.0	48.1	12.5	39.4
Wheeling, WV-OH........	26 554	7 605	15.4	8 087	0.0	8.8	4.0	123 892	55.6	7.7	45.3	15.2	39.5
Wichita Falls, TX	26 542	9 052	7.0	10 887	22.9	34.4	5.6	109 234	64.4	5.0	56.0	14.8	29.2
Wichita, KS...................	111 914	32 258	14.9	31 305	0.5	11.0	5.0	408 767	68.3	4.6	59.6	14.5	25.9
Williamsport, PA...........	21 522	6 190	13.6	7 224	0.2	10.3	3.8	95 468	61.4	6.3	51.6	15.5	32.9
Wilmington, NC	36 072	17 024	9.1	11 877	2.0	11.1	4.1	189 602	63.7	5.4	52.4	16.5	31.1
Yakima, WA	53 034	7 244	7.2	14 451	0.0	11.8	8.7	159 645	62.2	11.1	54.8	13.8	31.5
York, PA.......................	71 383	13 146	15.2	19 672	0.1	12.0	4.0	298 226	68.2	3.6	58.4	14.8	26.7
Youngstown-Warren, OH..............................	109 403	24 753	11.4	31 048	0.0	11.5	4.7	468 398	59.3	5.8	49.1	15.1	35.8
Yuba City, CA	31 706	7 804	6.2	8 652	1.6	12.3	6.2	102 436	59.2	11.1	51.5	13.0	35.5
Yuma, AZ	34 014	7 061	3.7	9 194	3.3	11.4	9.6	118 463	50.3	11.4	47.3	10.5	42.3

Area name	Full-year full-time employed (percent)								Children under 18 years in families (percent, except where noted)						Total employed by class of worker (percent)			
										With two parents		With one parent who is in labor force	+/− U.S. percent of children with no stay-at-home parent	+/− U.S. percent two-income couples				
	Total	Men	Women	Non-Hispanic White	Black or African American	American Indian and Alaska Native	Asian, Hawaiian, and Pacific Islander	Hispanic or Latino[1]	Number	Both in labor force	Father only in labor force				Private	Government	Self-employed	Unpaid family worker
	24	25	26	27	28	29	30	31	32	33	34	35	36	37	38	39	40	41
Tucson, AZ..............	36.3	45.2	28.1	36.9	36.5	30.1	32.3	35.8	194 133	37.8	22.5	24.1	-2.6	-6.2	71.0	18.7	10.0	0.3
Tulsa, OK	43.5	54.6	33.2	44.7	37.1	40.9	39.2	42.0	202 106	43.0	24.5	21.9	0.3	0.7	78.8	10.6	10.2	0.3
Tuscaloosa, AL	37.5	47.1	28.8	39.6	33.0	44.3	22.5	29.3	36 506	38.7	20.1	26.4	0.5	-2.1	72.3	20.0	7.3	0.4
Tyler, TX...................	39.4	50.3	29.7	40.1	36.0	47.9	49.0	40.4	43 457	41.3	24.0	22.3	-1.1	-3.5	75.9	12.2	11.5	0.4
Utica-Rome, NY	37.7	45.8	30.0	38.6	25.3	38.4	34.8	27.1	68 245	48.1	16.0	23.0	6.5	0.6	72.5	18.8	8.4	0.3
Victoria, TX..............	42.4	54.3	31.5	43.9	39.0	30.0	41.9	40.9	22 853	46.5	19.7	22.4	4.4	0.9	77.6	13.3	8.8	0.2
Visalia-Tulare-Porterville, CA	28.9	36.9	21.1	34.3	22.0	23.4	23.5	23.7	114 629	36.2	22.2	21.1	-7.3	-9.3	70.5	18.4	10.6	0.5
Waco, TX	38.6	47.3	30.7	40.4	32.2	38.9	23.9	37.9	52 008	41.2	20.8	24.0	0.6	-0.8	76.4	14.6	8.6	0.4
Washington-Baltimore, DC-MD-VA-WV	47.9	57.1	39.6	50.2	44.2	49.1	45.3	43.1	1 800 617	46.1	20.3	22.6	4.1	7.5	69.1	22.5	8.2	0.2
Baltimore, MD	45.4	54.6	37.1	47.6	39.8	46.6	42.4	44.2	598 566	44.4	19.0	25.0	4.8	5.6	71.4	20.3	8.1	0.2
Hagerstown, MD	42.8	50.3	35.1	45.1	17.5	61.5	40.7	37.6	29 335	49.5	19.6	21.2	6.2	2.6	75.1	16.4	8.1	0.4
Washington, DC-MD-VA-WV	49.4	58.6	41.0	52.0	46.8	50.0	46.0	43.0	1 172 716	46.8	21.0	21.4	3.6	8.7	67.8	23.7	8.3	0.2
Waterloo-Cedar Falls, IA.................	37.4	45.8	29.9	38.2	28.3	12.3	36.9	33.7	28 362	50.7	15.3	22.2	8.3	4.4	76.9	14.8	8.1	0.2
Wausau, WI.................	47.0	57.1	37.0	47.5	46.5	31.0	31.6	42.1	32 730	61.6	15.5	15.4	12.4	11.9	79.9	9.4	10.2	0.5
West Palm Beach-Boca Raton, FL	36.4	45.4	28.2	35.1	39.7	38.8	44.4	39.8	224 561	41.0	22.1	23.3	-0.3	-11.1	73.9	11.8	14.0	0.3
Wheeling, WV-OH	33.8	43.7	25.0	34.0	27.7	24.3	28.4	43.8	31 928	45.1	21.9	20.5	1.0	-5.3	77.8	14.0	7.8	0.4
Wichita Falls, TX	40.5	49.4	31.3	41.9	34.1	31.4	36.3	38.4	33 314	46.5	20.1	22.6	4.5	0.6	69.5	19.3	10.7	0.5
Wichita, KS.................	46.1	57.4	35.2	47.3	39.1	42.9	41.1	41.7	145 406	48.2	22.4	20.1	3.8	5.1	79.4	11.9	8.4	0.2
Williamsport, PA...........	39.5	48.5	31.1	39.9	30.9	31.3	33.2	37.5	26 519	48.0	20.4	22.6	6.0	0.0	80.0	11.2	8.4	0.4
Wilmington, NC	38.6	48.0	29.8	39.3	33.9	53.4	38.8	38.4	45 819	42.9	21.2	24.1	2.4	-3.8	72.4	13.7	13.4	0.4
Yakima, WA	31.7	39.8	24.0	36.7	26.4	26.4	29.4	22.1	65 761	41.2	19.1	21.3	-2.1	-3.4	72.7	16.7	10.2	0.4
York, PA	47.2	59.1	36.0	47.8	39.2	38.3	43.6	36.5	89 612	51.7	21.6	19.9	7.0	6.1	82.5	9.4	7.8	0.3
Youngstown-Warren, OH.................	37.3	48.3	27.2	38.3	28.5	33.5	40.0	32.1	135 512	43.6	21.5	23.7	2.7	-4.2	81.1	10.6	8.0	0.3
Yuba City, CA	32.4	41.5	23.5	35.3	37.4	28.7	25.8	25.1	38 717	39.0	23.3	19.2	-6.4	-8.9	69.0	18.5	11.8	0.7
Yuma, AZ	28.1	36.0	20.2	28.6	36.3	27.1	38.2	26.9	43 110	34.3	27.1	19.2	-11.0	-19.5	68.1	22.4	8.9	0.6

[1] Hispanic or Latino persons may be of any race.

Area name	Percent who worked at home	Percent of the population 5 years and over with a disability	Veterans as a percent of the population 18 years and over	Occupation for employed population 16 years and over (percent)						Industry for employed population 16 years and over (percent)						
				Management, professional, and related occupations	Service occupations	Sales and office occupations	Farming, fishing, and forestry occupations	Construction, extraction, and maintenance occupations	Production, transportation and material moving occupations	Agriculture, forestry, fishing, and mining	Construction and manufacturing	Wholesale and retail trade	Transportation and warehousing, and utilities	Service industries	Public administration
	42	43	44	45	46	47	48	49	50	51	52	53	54	55	56
Tucson, AZ...................	3.6	20.1	16.0	35.0	17.6	27.1	0.2	10.7	9.4	0.9	17.5	14.4	4.5	56.9	5.8
Tulsa, OK	3.1	19.9	14.4	32.2	13.7	28.9	0.2	11.0	13.9	1.9	19.5	15.8	7.4	52.2	3.2
Tuscaloosa, AL	2.0	20.9	12.1	32.0	14.1	27.1	0.4	9.7	16.7	2.1	21.5	16.7	3.5	52.7	3.6
Tyler, TX......................	2.6	21.9	13.5	30.3	15.3	27.1	0.6	10.7	16.1	2.6	20.5	18.4	3.9	51.5	3.2
Utica-Rome, NY	2.6	20.6	14.9	31.0	18.0	26.7	0.7	7.8	15.8	1.7	19.0	15.1	3.8	53.9	6.5
Victoria, TX..................	2.1	19.4	12.9	28.5	15.1	27.4	0.4	13.4	15.1	4.5	22.4	18.2	4.2	47.0	3.8
Visalia-Tulare-Porterville, CA	3.5	21.1	9.6	25.3	16.2	22.7	13.2	8.4	14.2	15.2	14.7	16.8	4.2	43.3	5.7
Waco, TX	2.5	20.9	13.3	30.0	16.0	27.6	0.4	10.4	15.5	1.1	21.6	15.6	4.1	53.3	4.3
Washington-Baltimore, DC-MD-VA-WV	3.5	16.7	13.1	45.4	13.4	25.3	0.2	7.8	8.0	0.4	12.3	12.2	4.6	58.9	11.6
Baltimore, MD	3.2	18.9	13.6	39.8	14.0	27.4	0.2	8.4	10.2	0.4	15.1	14.2	5.1	55.9	9.3
Hagerstown, MD	3.3	19.7	14.5	26.6	15.5	27.9	0.4	11.9	17.7	1.6	23.7	16.6	5.6	45.0	7.5
Washington, DC-MD-VA-WV.................	3.7	15.4	12.8	48.6	13.0	24.3	0.2	7.4	6.7	0.4	10.7	11.1	4.3	60.7	12.7
Waterloo-Cedar Falls, IA	2.9	18.2	13.3	30.3	16.0	27.5	0.3	8.0	17.8	1.3	23.1	16.4	3.9	52.4	2.9
Wausau, WI..................	5.1	14.7	13.0	29.7	12.2	26.2	1.4	8.7	21.8	4.3	30.4	16.2	4.8	42.4	1.8
West Palm Beach-Boca Raton, FL	4.1	21.2	15.1	34.4	17.7	29.0	0.8	9.7	8.4	1.1	14.6	16.8	4.5	58.5	4.4
Wheeling, WV-OH........	2.7	21.7	15.3	27.1	18.3	26.2	0.3	11.4	16.7	3.1	17.5	17.1	5.4	51.9	5.0
Wichita Falls, TX	2.1	20.7	15.4	29.0	18.4	26.1	0.6	10.3	15.7	2.8	18.6	16.0	4.0	50.7	7.8
Wichita, KS..................	2.7	17.8	13.9	32.0	13.7	26.5	0.3	11.3	16.2	1.1	30.6	14.3	4.0	46.7	3.4
Williamsport, PA...........	2.4	19.4	15.1	24.4	15.8	26.7	0.7	9.7	22.6	1.7	29.1	16.5	4.0	44.3	4.5
Wilmington, NC	3.0	21.0	16.0	31.3	16.9	26.5	0.5	13.0	11.8	0.7	21.3	16.7	4.7	52.3	4.3
Yakima, WA	3.5	22.2	12.2	27.4	16.1	22.5	9.3	8.3	16.5	10.7	16.9	19.0	4.6	43.7	5.2
York, PA	2.7	17.0	14.2	28.4	12.5	26.2	0.4	9.9	22.7	1.1	31.1	16.7	5.2	41.9	4.0
Youngstown-Warren, OH...............................	2.2	19.6	15.3	24.9	15.7	25.7	0.3	9.4	23.9	1.0	29.5	16.4	4.8	44.8	3.4
Yuba City, CA	3.4	22.8	15.1	26.3	16.3	24.5	5.3	11.6	15.9	8.3	18.3	16.5	5.5	45.7	5.6
Yuma, AZ	1.9	20.8	16.0	26.7	17.7	26.4	6.3	10.7	12.2	8.8	12.5	18.4	5.0	44.5	10.7

Table B-4. Metropolitan Areas — Education, Labor Force, and Income

Area name	Median house-hold income	Median family income — All families	Families with children — Married-couple	Families with children — Male house-holder	Families with children — Female house-holder	Median nonfamily house-hold income	Median income for full-year, full-time workers — Men	Median income for full-year, full-time workers — Women	Per capita income	With earnings	With interest, dividend, or rental income	With Social Security income	With public assis-tance income	With retire-ment income	House-holds with income over $100,000 (percent)	+/− U.S. percent for income over $100,000	House-holds with income below poverty (percent)	Families with children with income below poverty (percent)
	57	58	59	60	61	62	63	64	65	66	67	68	69	70	71	72	73	74
Tucson, AZ	36 758	44 446	50 767	26 241	18 917	23 936	33 839	25 789	19 785	77.7	37.8	28.0	3.1	19.7	9.0	-3.3	13.3	16.4
Tulsa, OK	38 261	46 479	54 945	27 086	18 897	22 660	36 094	25 771	20 092	81.8	31.9	24.0	3.8	14.2	8.9	-3.4	11.3	13.0
Tuscaloosa, AL	34 436	45 485	56 523	30 210	17 226	16 729	35 973	25 219	18 998	79.3	28.4	24.2	1.6	17.6	7.8	-4.5	18.8	16.2
Tyler, TX	37 148	44 534	51 122	28 377	17 840	21 000	33 778	23 461	19 072	79.1	31.8	28.0	2.4	16.5	9.1	-3.2	13.2	15.0
Utica-Rome, NY	35 292	44 174	52 891	24 858	16 404	19 859	32 705	24 495	18 006	73.5	39.3	33.4	3.9	23.7	6.2	-6.1	12.8	16.0
Victoria, TX	38 732	44 443	53 387	23 021	16 829	22 174	36 263	21 760	18 379	82.2	29.9	25.7	2.9	13.4	8.7	-3.6	12.7	15.0
Visalia-Tulare-Porterville, CA	33 983	36 297	38 960	22 143	15 092	20 526	31 524	25 445	14 006	80.6	23.6	25.3	8.6	14.6	7.6	-4.7	19.0	26.6
Waco, TX	33 560	41 414	49 626	25 351	16 138	17 800	31 732	22 739	17 174	80.8	29.4	26.1	3.0	15.4	7.5	-4.8	17.6	17.6
Washington-Baltimore, DC-MD-VA-WV	57 291	66 909	78 713	37 077	27 846	37 699	46 753	35 896	28 175	85.5	41.3	19.6	2.4	18.1	21.7	9.4	7.9	8.3
Baltimore, MD	49 938	59 324	73 556	35 979	24 513	30 393	42 523	31 861	24 398	81.9	38.6	24.3	3.0	18.8	15.9	3.6	9.7	10.3
Hagerstown, MD	40 617	48 962	56 912	30 773	17 904	22 622	35 754	25 211	20 062	78.3	33.1	28.4	2.3	18.7	7.5	-4.8	9.7	10.5
Washington, DC-MD-VA-WV	62 216	72 247	82 186	38 498	30 696	42 303	50 072	38 063	30 350	87.7	42.9	16.9	2.0	17.8	25.1	12.8	6.8	7.2
Waterloo-Cedar Falls, IA	37 266	47 398	56 104	27 125	19 572	21 255	34 678	24 344	18 885	78.4	43.6	28.2	3.7	18.7	7.1	-5.2	12.8	12.7
Wausau, WI	45 165	52 632	59 518	30 998	23 834	24 675	35 628	25 436	20 703	83.2	51.0	26.4	1.5	14.9	8.3	-4.0	6.4	6.5
West Palm Beach-Boca Raton, FL	45 062	53 701	64 662	31 867	23 220	29 035	38 585	29 992	28 801	69.8	44.8	38.5	1.8	19.3	16.2	3.9	9.0	11.5
Wheeling, WV-OH	30 335	38 936	47 183	22 828	11 855	15 499	32 017	21 143	16 748	70.1	34.8	35.3	3.8	23.6	4.6	-7.7	15.8	19.1
Wichita Falls, TX	34 098	41 231	45 734	26 494	16 965	20 412	30 354	22 816	17 113	80.5	32.1	27.1	3.2	17.4	5.9	-6.4	13.1	14.6
Wichita, KS	42 651	51 660	59 032	31 998	21 758	25 343	38 943	26 804	20 692	82.8	36.2	23.8	2.7	15.2	9.0	-3.3	9.1	10.0
Williamsport, PA	34 016	41 040	49 105	24 006	16 508	18 389	31 486	21 944	17 224	75.9	39.5	32.3	2.5	20.0	5.7	-6.6	11.9	13.0
Wilmington, NC	38 632	47 544	55 911	28 355	15 831	24 182	35 415	25 316	22 100	78.3	35.1	28.3	2.6	20.8	9.6	-2.7	13.0	14.3
Yakima, WA	34 828	39 746	44 118	23 007	16 109	20 218	32 411	25 298	15 606	79.8	30.0	26.3	6.3	14.9	7.0	-5.3	16.4	21.9
York, PA	45 268	52 278	60 321	31 803	22 032	25 982	37 833	25 874	21 086	82.1	45.5	26.3	1.5	18.0	8.8	-3.5	6.7	7.1
Youngstown-Warren, OH	36 255	44 111	53 142	26 691	16 745	19 845	36 572	23 867	18 551	74.6	35.7	32.7	3.6	23.2	6.7	-5.6	11.5	14.7
Yuba City, CA	34 658	39 479	44 334	26 667	15 476	20 157	33 075	24 775	15 998	79.0	26.6	26.3	7.0	18.4	7.2	-5.1	15.6	20.1
Yuma, AZ	32 182	34 659	36 340	23 426	16 228	21 736	29 143	23 379	14 802	70.3	31.0	35.8	3.5	25.1	6.0	-6.3	15.8	24.4

STATE Place code	City	High school graduates			College graduates		College graduates (percent)				
		Total population 25 years and over	Percent with a high school diploma or less	Percent with a high school diploma or more	Percent with a bachelor's degree or more	+/− U.S. percent with bachelor's degree or more	Non-Hispanic White	Black or African American	American Indian and Alaska Native	Asian, Hawaiian, and Pacific Islander	Hispanic or Latino[1]
		1	2	3	4	5	6	7	8	9	10
00 00000	UNITED STATES....	182 211 639	48.2	80.4	24.4	0.0	27.0	14.3	11.5	43.1	10.4
01 00000	ALABAMA	2 887 400	55.1	75.3	19.0	-5.4	21.2	11.5	13.0	47.2	14.6
01 03076	Auburn city	17 060	21.6	91.2	56.0	31.6	63.8	24.0	56.0	78.9	37.0
01 05980	Bessemer city	18 876	64.4	67.4	9.2	-15.2	8.7	9.2	24.1	39.1	0.0
01 07000	Birmingham city............	154 953	52.2	75.5	18.5	-5.9	30.9	12.8	28.5	64.6	15.7
01 20104	Decatur city	35 427	46.8	80.0	23.7	-0.7	27.3	7.4	25.9	58.2	10.9
01 21184	Dothan city	38 398	48.5	78.5	22.9	-1.5	27.8	9.1	10.0	37.1	12.5
01 26896	Florence city	23 416	49.3	78.3	25.0	0.6	28.1	9.8	10.3	50.4	11.7
01 28696	Gadsden city	26 229	58.4	70.3	14.4	-10.0	17.5	7.2	18.5	32.3	3.1
01 35800	Homewood city..............	15 327	20.8	93.4	54.2	29.8	58.0	36.8	15.8	66.7	21.0
01 35896	Hoover city	42 100	20.7	94.7	52.6	28.2	53.3	49.5	46.0	69.7	21.3
01 37000	Huntsville city	104 714	34.7	85.7	36.1	11.7	41.3	20.5	22.4	53.5	28.4
01 45784	Madison city	18 563	18.3	94.6	52.0	27.6	54.7	36.9	29.5	55.9	36.0
01 50000	Mobile city	124 672	46.8	80.5	24.9	0.5	34.1	12.1	12.2	38.1	23.8
01 51000	Montgomery city	126 671	43.0	80.7	29.4	5.0	38.0	18.7	9.9	32.7	24.2
01 59472	Phenix City city	18 160	62.4	69.0	12.6	-11.8	16.0	7.1	32.9	38.8	16.8
01 62496	Prichard city	16 399	70.5	65.0	6.7	-17.7	7.2	6.4	0.0	0.0	18.5
01 77256	Tuscaloosa city	43 501	44.8	78.8	30.9	6.5	43.3	12.1	18.1	74.8	25.0
02 00000	ALASKA	379 556	39.5	88.3	24.7	0.3	29.5	14.9	6.0	20.4	15.3
02 03000	Anchorage municipality .	159 931	33.9	90.3	28.9	4.5	33.0	15.5	10.6	23.1	16.3
02 24230	Fairbanks city	17 003	40.2	88.9	19.4	-5.0	23.2	11.1	3.8	19.2	9.2
02 36400	Juneau city and borough	19 899	28.8	93.2	36.0	11.6	41.5	23.0	7.9	32.1	19.9
04 00000	ARIZONA	3 256 184	43.3	81.0	23.5	-0.9	28.1	18.6	7.3	43.2	8.1
04 02830	Apache Junction city	22 690	58.2	77.9	9.0	-15.4	9.0	0.0	0.0	35.8	7.9
04 04720	Avondale city	29 221	52.0	71.2	18.2	-8.2	22.7	25.0	1.9	40.0	5.2
04 08220	Bullhead City city	23 800	62.4	72.4	8.6	-15.8	9.1	11.3	3.7	19.3	4.9
04 10530	Casa Grande city	14 996	54.0	73.6	17.8	-6.6	25.0	10.2	0.0	23.7	6.5
04 12000	Chandler city	108 790	30.7	87.8	32.5	8.1	34.8	33.3	26.9	58.4	14.4
04 23620	Flagstaff city	28 722	27.2	89.8	39.4	15.0	47.3	15.7	13.5	49.6	16.8
04 27400	Gilbert town	64 467	23.4	94.3	36.1	11.7	37.1	34.9	41.5	51.4	20.7
04 27820	Glendale city	129 927	43.2	82.4	21.0	-3.4	23.6	20.2	7.8	41.7	8.5
04 39370	Lake Havasu City city ...	31 347	48.8	83.8	13.1	-11.3	13.3	10.0	5.9	25.0	10.6
04 46000	Mesa city	245 104	41.0	84.7	21.6	-2.8	23.7	23.3	13.0	38.2	9.0
04 51600	Oro Valley town............	22 189	21.2	95.7	43.5	19.1	44.2	30.6	9.4	63.2	32.2
04 54050	Peoria city	70 583	39.7	88.3	21.7	-2.7	22.9	31.0	19.7	26.1	11.0
04 55000	Phoenix city.................	795 297	46.2	76.6	22.7	-1.7	29.4	15.2	8.9	40.8	6.1
04 57380	Prescott city	25 125	33.2	89.6	30.6	6.2	32.0	66.1	11.6	47.5	8.7
04 65000	Scottsdale city	150 662	22.9	93.5	44.1	19.7	45.3	41.6	14.3	56.8	21.3
04 66820	Sierra Vista city	22 854	31.3	91.5	25.7	1.3	29.1	22.8	10.9	15.7	12.7
04 71510	Surprise city	22 608	43.9	85.0	20.5	-3.9	23.2	25.7	24.6	41.1	3.7
04 73000	Tempe city	93 273	27.8	90.1	39.6	15.2	43.2	28.2	22.4	59.5	17.9
04 77000	Tucson city	301 036	43.6	80.4	22.9	-1.5	29.3	14.7	11.2	38.7	9.8
04 85540	Yuma city	45 137	51.9	73.3	16.2	-8.2	21.7	17.4	7.0	27.9	6.6
05 00000	ARKANSAS...............	1 731 200	58.8	75.3	16.7	-7.7	17.9	10.2	12.1	31.5	7.1
05 15190	Conway city.................	23 529	37.1	85.9	36.0	11.6	38.6	16.5	19.1	53.4	15.8
05 23290	Fayetteville city.............	31 508	33.7	86.9	41.2	16.8	41.9	26.5	14.2	71.1	17.3
05 24550	Fort Smith city	52 076	52.8	75.7	18.6	-5.8	21.6	8.0	15.4	5.7	3.4
05 33400	Hot Springs city............	25 484	57.5	74.0	16.6	-7.8	18.3	7.6	9.2	43.1	11.8
05 34750	Jacksonville city	17 417	47.5	85.2	15.4	-9.0	16.4	11.0	9.3	14.5	15.3
05 35710	Jonesboro city..............	33 549	48.4	80.3	26.6	2.2	28.0	14.4	10.3	22.3	14.6
05 41000	Little Rock city..............	120 093	36.2	85.9	35.5	11.1	45.2	17.8	15.9	58.3	18.5
05 50450	North Little Rock city.....	39 593	50.1	80.8	22.0	-2.4	26.7	9.6	17.5	22.7	11.9
05 55310	Pine Bluff city	33 011	58.8	73.3	17.6	-6.8	18.4	16.6	23.7	62.2	8.0
05 60410	Rogers city	23 954	52.6	76.1	21.1	-3.3	24.1	28.3	15.0	18.5	4.3
05 66000	Springdale city.............	27 641	57.1	73.6	17.7	-6.7	20.2	10.2	15.9	18.1	2.9
05 68810	Texarkana city..............	17 160	58.7	75.3	14.7	-9.7	17.7	6.6	0.0	47.1	11.3
05 74540	West Memphis city........	16 304	64.3	68.8	11.5	-12.9	17.2	5.6	27.3	9.1	0.0
06 00000	CALIFORNIA.............	21 298 900	43.3	76.8	26.6	2.2	33.8	17.2	11.4	40.9	7.7
06 00562	Alameda city................	51 952	28.1	88.4	42.2	17.8	45.9	28.6	23.9	41.5	30.0
06 00884	Alhambra city	58 579	46.6	73.0	27.5	3.1	32.6	27.3	16.4	32.9	15.5
06 02000	Anaheim city................	194 374	52.1	69.3	19.6	-4.8	24.9	22.5	10.8	40.3	5.5
06 02252	Antioch city.................	54 041	43.0	85.7	18.2	-6.2	18.1	22.5	15.3	35.2	8.7
06 02364	Apple Valley town	32 892	45.4	82.4	16.4	-8.0	16.8	13.6	8.3	48.7	9.3
06 02462	Arcadia city.................	36 799	27.1	89.7	44.4	20.0	39.2	34.0	31.1	55.3	21.7
06 03064	Atascadero city.............	17 412	37.4	88.4	20.3	-4.1	21.4	4.6	7.6	35.2	8.4

[1] Hispanic or Latino persons may be of any race.

City	School enrollment			Population 16 to 19 years				Employment status, 2000			Work status in 1999 of the population 16 years and over		
											Worked in 1999		
	Grades kindergarten through 12	College or graduate school	Percent private	Number	Percent in armed forces	Percent high school graduates	Percent not enrolled, not grads, not in armed forces, not employed	Total population 16 years and over	Percent in labor force	Unemploy-ment rate	Full-time	Part-time	Did not work in 1999
	11	12	13	14	15	16	17	18	19	20	21	22	23
UNITED STATES....	54 192 083	17 483 262	14.3	15 930 458	0.6	10.5	5.5	217 168 077	63.9	5.7	54.9	14.6	30.5
ALABAMA	837 350	243 275	11.5	255 315	0.2	9.6	7.1	3 450 542	59.7	6.2	52.9	12.1	35.1
Auburn city	4 922	20 033	4.9	6 006	0.0	2.1	0.7	36 842	56.1	7.4	43.6	32.5	23.8
Bessemer city	5 910	1 058	12.3	1 740	0.0	15.7	13.9	22 620	50.6	10.9	43.4	11.2	45.4
Birmingham city............	46 320	15 655	11.8	14 072	0.0	10.7	8.8	188 947	58.6	10.8	50.9	12.1	37.0
Decatur city	10 021	2 268	8.2	2 810	0.3	9.0	10.1	41 785	61.8	5.7	54.6	12.0	33.4
Dothan city	10 835	2 237	16.2	3 077	0.0	7.6	5.6	44 861	61.1	5.7	54.6	11.9	33.5
Florence city	6 010	3 739	8.9	2 367	0.0	5.4	7.6	29 383	56.2	7.6	44.6	17.2	38.2
Gadsden city	6 315	1 488	9.5	2 278	0.0	8.8	15.4	31 013	50.3	9.0	44.1	11.1	44.8
Homewood city..............	3 693	4 461	34.1	1 748	0.0	5.1	0.0	20 321	70.2	2.4	58.6	19.5	21.9
Hoover city	11 038	3 743	15.5	3 039	0.0	5.1	2.1	48 878	71.1	2.5	62.3	13.6	24.1
Huntsville city	26 756	14 598	14.7	9 224	0.0	6.9	7.1	125 708	64.7	6.9	55.9	14.5	29.6
Madison city	6 232	2 049	14.7	1 506	0.0	7.4	2.9	21 398	77.4	2.6	67.0	14.3	18.7
Mobile city	39 096	13 798	21.1	11 734	0.1	8.0	6.9	151 865	58.7	8.3	50.6	13.5	36.0
Montgomery city...........	39 207	16 052	17.8	11 617	0.2	9.4	7.8	154 806	62.0	6.7	55.9	13.1	31.0
Phenix City city	5 729	1 078	6.9	1 585	0.6	9.3	4.3	21 654	57.4	6.4	53.2	8.9	37.9
Prichard city	7 160	1 178	9.9	2 054	0.0	11.0	7.3	20 797	50.1	15.9	42.2	11.6	46.2
Tuscaloosa city	11 633	16 889	9.6	7 650	0.0	4.2	4.1	64 457	57.6	7.6	46.7	20.9	32.4
ALASKA	142 653	32 303	8.3	38 321	2.3	15.1	5.2	458 054	71.3	8.6	63.2	15.7	21.1
Anchorage municipality .	55 296	15 169	10.2	15 210	3.1	16.6	4.7	192 782	74.4	6.4	66.0	14.7	19.3
Fairbanks city	5 951	2 020	8.4	1 747	14.0	22.8	6.2	22 225	71.2	8.6	63.2	15.0	21.8
Juneau city and borough	6 210	1 890	6.9	1 692	0.4	13.2	1.2	23 342	75.5	5.3	67.2	15.2	17.6
ARIZONA	988 818	331 099	8.7	288 587	0.6	11.1	8.4	3 907 229	61.1	5.6	53.4	13.4	33.2
Apache Junction city	4 142	1 182	7.5	1 064	0.0	14.5	10.4	25 540	52.9	6.5	46.6	10.8	42.6
Avondale city	8 764	1 780	6.3	2 171	0.1	7.6	10.4	24 760	67.8	4.2	62.0	10.9	27.1
Bullhead City city	5 384	945	3.6	1 483	0.0	10.3	18.1	27 092	56.5	6.5	50.5	11.0	38.6
Casa Grande city	5 673	922	5.9	1 669	0.0	10.4	10.5	18 102	60.7	7.1	51.5	13.1	35.4
Chandler city	36 116	11 946	8.5	9 043	0.0	10.2	5.8	128 635	74.7	3.4	66.0	13.4	20.6
Flagstaff city	9 437	11 790	5.4	4 036	0.0	7.3	2.8	41 844	73.7	5.1	56.3	24.8	18.9
Gilbert town	25 556	7 799	9.0	5 766	0.0	7.8	1.3	75 611	76.9	2.5	66.9	15.0	18.1
Glendale city	46 942	15 059	10.8	13 400	1.7	14.7	6.5	159 700	69.4	5.0	60.9	13.3	25.8
Lake Havasu City city ...	6 050	1 717	4.4	1 769	0.0	17.8	4.6	34 720	50.4	5.5	42.5	13.3	44.2
Mesa city	76 153	27 318	7.8	22 540	0.1	14.2	6.0	299 777	64.8	4.2	56.3	13.5	30.3
Oro Valley town............	5 006	1 411	10.1	1 326	0.0	6.2	0.7	24 245	53.8	3.5	45.3	14.2	40.5
Peoria city	22 479	5 735	8.5	5 550	0.2	8.6	4.1	80 930	64.7	3.9	56.7	12.5	30.9
Phoenix city	267 407	73 315	10.1	77 080	0.0	11.2	11.8	976 578	66.4	5.6	59.8	12.2	28.1
Prescott city	4 446	3 569	23.7	1 873	0.0	5.6	2.3	29 556	48.1	5.0	38.0	17.5	44.6
Scottsdale city	28 547	13 251	14.1	7 597	0.0	10.2	3.6	167 939	64.5	3.5	55.5	14.2	30.3
Sierra Vista city	6 719	3 301	9.4	2 609	30.3	40.0	3.6	28 816	66.9	3.0	56.3	13.9	29.8
Surprise city	3 832	1 219	9.7	989	0.4	15.3	14.6	25 191	45.5	5.6	41.8	10.1	48.0
Tempe city...................	22 295	30 240	8.1	12 555	0.0	9.4	3.9	130 466	72.8	4.3	58.6	20.2	21.2
Tucson city..................	85 709	52 143	8.4	31 300	1.1	10.9	7.7	379 464	61.7	5.8	52.2	17.0	30.8
Yuma city	16 501	4 243	4.3	4 821	6.1	14.3	7.7	56 874	59.6	8.3	53.6	12.4	34.0
ARKANSAS...............	503 693	128 063	8.9	156 258	0.2	13.2	5.4	2 072 068	60.6	6.1	53.5	12.4	34.2
Conway city.................	7 219	7 611	16.8	3 866	0.0	7.3	1.4	34 107	70.0	9.2	56.4	20.3	23.3
Fayetteville city.............	7 261	13 166	6.5	5 140	0.0	10.6	2.3	47 554	71.4	13.9	56.4	21.4	22.1
Fort Smith city	14 354	3 056	11.1	4 411	0.5	11.9	8.6	62 233	62.4	5.1	55.3	11.9	32.8
Hot Springs city............	5 266	1 311	8.4	1 563	0.0	15.7	7.5	29 065	53.2	6.4	44.8	13.2	42.0
Jacksonville city	5 883	1 588	8.7	1 754	11.9	25.8	6.7	22 097	70.9	5.1	63.1	14.2	22.7
Jonesboro city	9 215	6 307	5.7	3 956	0.0	12.5	1.6	44 199	66.8	6.4	54.3	17.5	28.1
Little Rock city..............	33 455	11 871	20.5	9 551	0.3	11.1	6.3	143 404	66.0	6.0	58.8	13.3	27.9
North Little Rock city.....	11 465	2 935	13.2	3 157	0.0	10.9	5.6	46 704	64.3	4.5	55.8	13.5	30.7
Pine Bluff city	11 096	3 869	5.1	3 852	0.0	11.6	6.5	41 339	54.2	10.0	48.6	11.7	39.8
Rogers city	7 893	1 279	9.0	1 999	0.0	14.2	4.4	28 418	66.4	3.0	60.0	11.4	28.6
Springdale city..............	9 032	1 407	7.5	2 789	0.0	13.1	10.5	34 063	65.7	4.2	60.3	11.6	28.1
Texarkana city..............	4 938	981	8.8	1 406	0.0	15.4	9.4	20 559	59.0	7.9	49.9	12.8	37.3
West Memphis city........	6 481	1 088	5.2	1 667	0.0	9.2	8.1	19 866	58.6	8.1	53.7	11.0	35.3
CALIFORNIA..............	7 026 326	2 556 598	12.2	1 925 479	0.8	9.9	5.8	25 596 144	62.4	6.9	53.5	14.6	31.9
Alameda city.................	11 589	6 153	19.0	2 772	2.8	6.9	2.6	58 400	68.2	4.3	58.5	14.1	27.4
Alhambra city................	15 204	9 517	15.4	4 352	0.0	6.2	2.0	68 824	58.4	6.8	50.0	13.4	36.6
Anaheim city.................	70 742	21 688	10.6	18 121	0.1	9.3	7.5	237 298	64.2	6.2	57.7	13.1	29.3
Antioch city..................	21 961	5 337	9.9	5 367	0.0	8.5	2.9	64 459	68.2	5.2	57.4	15.6	27.1
Apple Valley town	13 567	2 751	7.7	3 381	0.3	12.1	4.1	38 982	55.8	8.9	44.7	13.9	41.4
Arcadia city..................	10 363	4 818	16.9	3 321	0.0	3.6	1.4	42 634	57.5	4.4	48.6	13.0	38.4
Atascadero city.............	5 770	1 727	9.7	1 826	0.0	13.4	2.2	20 608	62.4	4.3	49.9	17.0	33.1

Table B-5. Cities — Education, Labor Force, and Income

City	Full-year full-time employed (percent)								Children under 18 years in families (percent, except where noted)						Total employed by class of worker (percent)			
						American Indian and Alaska Native	Asian, Hawaiian, and Pacific Islander	Hispanic or Latino[1]				With one parent who is in labor force	+/− U.S. percent of children with no stay-at-home parent	+/− U.S. percent two-income couples				Unpaid family worker
	Total	Men	Women	Non-Hispanic White	Black or African American				Number	Both in labor force	Father only in labor force				Private	Government	Self-employed	
	24	25	26	27	28	29	30	31	32	33	34	35	36	37	38	39	40	41
UNITED STATES....	40.5	50.0	31.6	42.3	36.3	33.6	38.9	34.8	67 882 626	43.2	21.9	21.4	0.0	0.0	75.3	14.6	9.8	0.3
ALABAMA	39.6	49.9	30.4	42.0	32.8	37.7	37.6	39.4	1 049 873	40.4	21.4	22.9	-1.3	-3.4	75.0	15.5	9.2	0.3
Auburn city	23.2	28.9	17.4	22.2	26.8	28.8	31.2	27.4	6 381	42.4	27.7	23.2	1.0	2.8	62.7	28.0	8.6	0.7
Bessemer city..............	30.7	36.5	26.2	32.6	29.8	62.1	12.7	19.2	7 398	20.4	10.4	35.9	-8.3	-12.5	78.5	16.0	5.5	0.0
Birmingham city...........	35.9	41.2	31.6	40.0	34.3	40.4	27.4	39.4	53 831	26.4	9.3	39.4	1.2	-5.4	78.1	16.3	5.3	0.2
Decatur city	41.2	53.3	30.5	42.3	37.4	51.8	43.8	35.0	12 973	39.0	23.7	24.5	-1.1	-2.8	77.3	13.4	9.2	0.1
Dothan city	42.4	53.4	33.1	44.9	35.9	52.3	44.9	34.2	13 716	37.8	18.6	27.0	0.2	0.6	77.0	13.2	9.5	0.3
Florence city	31.3	41.9	22.7	31.6	30.2	16.9	18.0	44.4	7 654	32.6	25.1	26.8	-5.2	-12.7	73.5	16.6	9.6	0.3
Gadsden city	29.9	39.1	22.5	29.8	29.8	39.0	43.8	31.5	7 910	26.4	18.2	32.9	-5.3	-12.6	78.8	13.0	8.0	0.2
Homewood city	43.8	52.6	36.4	44.1	43.9	43.1	32.8	42.7	4 962	50.8	19.9	22.2	8.4	9.4	76.9	14.4	8.4	0.2
Hoover city	50.8	65.4	37.4	51.1	55.6	44.7	50.5	39.9	15 083	49.8	34.8	11.1	-3.7	5.0	77.9	11.5	10.3	0.2
Huntsville city	42.1	51.9	33.3	43.9	38.0	46.3	36.2	45.3	34 315	40.9	19.5	19.5	3.6	-2.1	72.1	19.5	8.3	0.2
Madison city	55.4	69.2	42.0	56.2	55.2	40.1	45.7	48.6	8 378	52.9	25.1	17.1	5.4	13.4	72.1	20.6	7.0	0.3
Mobile city	36.6	45.8	29.0	40.1	32.6	29.7	31.9	35.2	48 355	32.3	16.6	32.0	-0.3	-4.5	75.2	16.1	8.5	0.2
Montgomery city	43.1	51.8	35.7	48.6	36.9	38.4	49.7	53.4	48 489	35.2	15.2	30.5	1.1	2.0	67.3	24.5	7.9	0.2
Phenix City city	39.4	49.5	31.2	42.5	35.4	46.2	50.0	38.3	6 956	35.5	11.9	29.1	0.0	2.9	77.3	16.8	5.4	0.5
Prichard city	27.1	31.1	24.1	29.8	26.8	0.0	0.0	23.3	7 950	18.2	7.4	41.6	-4.8	-15.7	80.0	14.4	5.5	0.1
Tuscaloosa city	31.6	39.2	25.0	32.0	31.8	55.9	17.8	25.1	14 484	33.8	15.0	33.8	3.0	-2.8	69.6	24.2	5.6	0.6
ALASKA	38.1	43.9	31.9	41.9	47.3	20.1	32.0	37.5	180 009	45.4	21.4	20.7	1.5	5.0	62.4	26.8	10.6	0.3
Anchorage municipality .	44.6	51.9	37.1	47.5	46.0	29.0	33.5	39.6	71 592	46.4	21.2	21.1	2.9	9.3	67.9	22.0	9.9	0.2
Fairbanks city	41.3	51.0	30.8	43.3	53.0	19.7	27.1	49.2	8 374	43.5	25.2	20.8	-0.3	3.1	64.9	24.7	10.0	0.5
Juneau city and borough	45.0	50.3	39.8	46.5	44.8	35.8	44.1	42.3	7 951	53.4	16.3	22.8	11.6	13.8	49.2	39.8	10.7	0.3
ARIZONA	38.4	47.1	29.9	40.0	40.5	26.8	39.4	35.3	1 270 112	37.6	24.8	22.1	-4.9	-6.3	74.6	15.2	9.9	0.3
Apache Junction city	33.9	40.9	27.5	32.6	54.1	42.4	71.5	51.3	5 958	37.0	24.6	26.1	-1.5	-16.7	79.7	11.9	8.1	0.3
Avondale city...............	45.9	56.4	35.5	53.4	54.6	40.7	43.7	36.6	11 068	37.5	26.6	20.2	-6.9	4.8	77.2	16.7	6.0	0.0
Bullhead City city	33.8	37.7	30.0	33.6	24.7	40.7	31.3	34.4	6 913	36.3	12.6	33.0	4.7	-11.9	84.0	9.0	0.5	0.4
Casa Grande city	36.4	46.2	27.3	37.3	40.7	31.7	19.4	35.5	7 402	33.3	20.6	31.7	0.4	-8.9	70.2	21.5	7.8	0.6
Chandler city	51.9	63.1	41.1	54.8	53.5	52.1	48.4	41.5	50 231	44.2	28.2	18.8	-1.6	8.1	81.0	11.9	7.0	0.1
Flagstaff city	37.9	46.8	29.4	38.4	36.0	36.2	49.3	36.9	11 960	45.7	16.2	24.4	5.5	10.1	62.6	27.6	9.5	0.3
Gilbert town	54.3	68.9	40.5	54.6	58.6	60.0	48.0	53.8	36 535	50.6	31.9	12.2	-1.8	11.2	77.5	13.0	9.2	0.3
Glendale city	45.6	55.8	35.8	47.8	44.7	41.8	43.2	39.1	61 471	41.5	22.4	21.9	-1.2	3.9	77.9	14.1	7.7	0.2
Lake Havasu City city ..	30.9	37.0	25.2	30.2	28.7	36.9	42.4	38.7	7 536	46.0	16.8	25.4	6.8	-16.8	72.9	12.5	14.2	0.4
Mesa city	42.0	52.6	31.8	42.2	49.6	40.0	40.2	40.5	102 480	40.9	28.4	20.6	-3.1	-3.4	80.8	10.9	8.1	0.2
Oro Valley town............	35.0	45.2	25.5	34.1	47.4	68.4	47.4	39.5	6 161	47.8	38.8	8.9	-7.9	-13.1	70.9	16.0	12.8	0.3
Peoria city	45.3	56.6	35.3	44.3	51.0	47.5	49.2	49.9	29 637	49.9	22.8	19.1	4.4	1.9	76.6	15.1	8.1	0.2
Phoenix city	43.1	51.3	34.6	47.6	39.1	39.9	43.2	34.7	350 141	33.9	23.8	23.7	-7.0	-1.2	79.0	11.7	9.1	0.2
Prescott city	24.9	30.8	19.4	24.2	6.1	29.8	23.3	34.3	5 126	41.8	20.2	28.6	5.8	-18.6	64.0	17.0	18.3	0.6
Scottsdale city	42.9	53.7	33.1	43.0	41.0	31.3	43.9	42.5	37 668	38.9	33.3	19.1	-6.6	-7.3	75.8	7.8	16.2	0.3
Sierra Vista city	41.1	53.0	29.2	40.3	53.7	51.5	33.1	38.9	8 952	42.8	24.3	23.9	2.1	-3.6	60.6	32.2	7.0	0.2
Surprise city	29.3	37.5	21.6	27.6	45.6	37.8	34.0	33.1	5 746	41.0	28.0	19.2	-4.4	-20.9	78.9	13.2	7.8	0.2
Tempe city	42.5	49.6	34.7	43.8	46.4	43.0	31.4	39.5	29 302	41.6	23.5	23.5	0.5	3.3	76.9	15.8	7.2	0.2
Tucson city	35.8	43.8	28.4	36.8	35.9	35.3	29.0	34.4	110 926	34.0	20.0	28.5	-2.1	-4.3	72.6	18.9	8.3	0.2
Yuma city	35.4	45.6	25.5	37.1	43.2	32.8	41.0	32.3	21 549	38.9	23.1	22.2	-3.5	-6.8	65.4	25.9	8.4	0.4
ARKANSAS..............	38.8	47.8	30.5	40.2	31.3	38.0	38.2	37.6	633 653	43.1	20.2	22.3	0.8	-2.4	73.6	14.9	11.1	0.4
Conway city	39.1	51.0	28.5	39.1	40.6	66.2	19.7	39.8	9 527	47.6	20.6	22.6	5.6	9.6	73.3	18.0	8.3	0.4
Fayetteville city	35.1	42.1	27.8	35.5	32.6	39.4	27.5	34.0	10 731	37.0	27.6	22.8	-4.8	2.0	73.9	17.8	8.2	0.2
Fort Smith city	40.0	50.1	30.7	40.5	36.0	43.3	46.3	36.5	19 362	40.7	19.2	23.7	-0.2	-0.6	82.1	8.9	8.7	0.3
Hot Springs city	32.4	40.4	25.7	32.4	33.0	35.2	21.2	36.2	6 581	36.0	16.8	31.9	3.3	-7.6	75.4	12.5	11.4	0.7
Jacksonville city	46.2	57.4	35.4	48.4	43.4	56.7	26.6	41.5	8 018	41.2	20.1	24.0	0.6	2.8	73.6	19.9	6.4	0.1
Jonesboro city	38.8	49.1	29.7	40.2	32.3	39.0	22.8	19.5	12 145	46.5	20.0	21.8	3.7	4.1	73.9	15.5	10.3	0.2
Little Rock city	43.1	51.0	36.3	46.2	38.8	37.5	41.9	35.2	41 527	35.6	17.7	31.0	2.0	2.1	70.7	20.5	8.6	0.2
North Little Rock city	43.2	52.1	35.8	46.3	36.6	49.1	16.3	44.8	14 215	35.5	12.6	34.1	5.0	2.6	71.0	19.5	9.2	0.3
Pine Bluff city	31.6	36.9	27.1	36.7	28.2	51.4	41.4	34.6	13 452	30.4	10.8	33.4	-0.8	-3.7	69.6	22.4	7.5	0.5
Rogers city	45.9	57.5	35.4	46.4	77.2	49.0	73.0	41.3	10 904	46.3	23.6	19.1	0.8	3.6	83.1	7.8	8.8	0.3
Springdale city.............	44.0	55.3	33.2	45.2	48.2	40.5	43.6	39.4	12 715	47.0	21.6	19.1	1.5	1.9	82.6	8.6	8.7	0.2
Texarkana city	36.3	45.5	28.3	39.9	27.6	55.2	49.2	31.3	6 440	34.3	15.4	33.5	3.2	-0.9	75.3	15.5	9.0	0.2
West Memphis city........	38.4	45.4	32.8	45.3	31.7	57.1	47.4	46.2	7 979	26.3	12.2	36.2	-2.1	-2.9	79.4	13.8	6.6	0.2
CALIFORNIA..............	36.5	45.1	28.1	39.5	34.3	32.3	36.9	31.4	8 565 858	37.1	24.3	20.1	-7.4	-4.5	73.7	14.7	11.2	0.4
Alameda city	43.8	52.4	35.9	47.0	44.9	43.7	37.4	42.5	14 513	42.6	22.3	19.8	-2.2	4.7	72.9	15.7	11.0	0.4
Alhambra city	32.8	38.9	27.6	29.3	28.2	37.1	32.1	35.8	18 300	36.8	22.6	21.0	-6.8	-7.6	74.5	16.7	8.4	0.5
Anaheim city	39.7	49.3	30.3	43.1	43.8	35.0	39.9	35.8	91 034	35.2	24.8	19.7	-9.7	-4.9	81.9	9.7	8.1	0.3
Antioch city	42.2	52.7	32.7	43.3	47.8	57.8	41.2	38.2	28 105	42.2	24.5	21.1	-1.3	2.7	78.3	14.3	7.3	0.2
Apple Valley town	31.6	42.7	21.6	32.0	28.3	38.4	35.3	31.5	15 744	35.5	26.8	22.6	-6.5	-11.0	65.7	20.0	13.9	0.4
Arcadia city.................	34.6	44.0	26.5	31.5	24.6	43.1	36.7	39.9	11 896	46.9	26.1	15.6	-2.1	-4.0	69.5	11.9	18.0	0.5
Atascadero city............	36.3	44.3	27.8	37.1	10.2	39.9	56.0	32.8	6 651	42.1	24.3	25.0	2.5	3.0	57.9	26.0	16.0	0.2

[1] Hispanic or Latino persons may be of any race.

Table B-5. Cities — Education, Labor Force, and Income

City	Percent who worked at home	Percent of the population 5 years and over with a disability	Veterans as a percent of the population 18 years and over	Occupation for employed population 16 years and over (percent)						Industry for employed population 16 years and over (percent)					
				Management, professional, and related occupations	Service occupations	Sales and office occupations	Farming, fishing, and forestry occupations	Construction, extraction, and maintenance occupations	Production, transportation and material moving occupations	Agriculture, forestry, fishing, and mining	Construction and manufacturing	Wholesale and retail trade	Transportation and warehousing, and utilities	Service industries	Public administration
	42	43	44	45	46	47	48	49	50	51	52	53	54	55	56
UNITED STATES....	3.3	19.3	12.6	33.6	14.9	26.7	0.7	9.4	14.6	1.9	20.9	15.3	5.2	51.9	4.8
ALABAMA	2.1	23.2	13.5	29.5	13.5	25.9	0.8	11.3	19.0	1.9	26.0	15.8	5.3	45.8	5.2
Auburn city	2.4	12.8	6.2	45.5	17.6	25.3	0.8	3.7	7.1	1.3	10.5	13.6	1.6	69.7	3.4
Bessemer city..............	0.4	29.5	13.0	22.0	20.3	27.4	0.1	10.5	19.7	1.1	19.4	15.5	5.3	53.5	5.2
Birmingham city............	1.2	27.6	12.1	28.0	19.3	29.8	0.1	7.4	15.4	0.4	14.5	15.4	5.4	59.7	4.6
Decatur city	1.6	21.2	13.2	30.5	13.1	24.9	0.4	9.8	21.3	1.0	32.9	14.9	3.5	43.0	4.5
Dothan city	1.4	21.7	15.3	33.4	15.2	27.5	0.3	9.2	14.4	0.5	19.5	18.6	7.6	50.2	3.6
Florence city	1.9	23.0	13.0	31.8	15.7	28.7	0.2	7.2	16.4	0.4	21.7	18.1	4.7	51.1	3.9
Gadsden city	1.6	28.3	14.3	25.4	16.3	24.8	0.5	8.4	24.6	0.7	26.7	15.8	4.0	48.4	4.4
Homewood city	2.5	14.0	8.8	52.8	10.5	27.9	0.3	3.7	4.9	0.5	9.0	14.5	3.1	70.2	2.6
Hoover city	3.9	11.6	11.6	52.8	7.6	29.9	0.1	5.5	4.1	0.5	12.9	17.0	4.1	62.8	2.7
Huntsville city	2.4	18.9	16.0	44.3	13.7	23.9	0.2	6.0	11.9	0.3	21.7	12.6	2.6	53.6	9.3
Madison city	2.2	10.7	17.8	56.8	7.5	23.6	0.0	3.4	8.7	0.0	26.2	13.1	3.2	45.5	12.0
Mobile city	1.8	23.7	13.5	34.0	16.4	27.4	0.2	8.7	13.3	0.6	17.5	16.6	4.7	56.4	4.1
Montgomery city...........	1.7	21.8	14.4	37.0	15.7	29.3	0.1	6.6	11.4	0.5	12.9	15.0	4.0	55.5	12.1
Phenix City city	0.7	25.0	14.1	28.1	14.4	26.8	0.3	9.6	20.8	0.5	26.8	14.3	3.4	48.6	6.3
Prichard city	1.4	29.2	9.3	16.2	25.1	22.2	0.1	12.8	23.8	0.3	23.2	12.6	6.4	53.4	4.1
Tuscaloosa city	2.2	20.0	11.1	36.3	15.9	28.0	0.2	5.7	13.8	1.1	15.4	16.3	2.7	61.0	3.5
ALASKA	4.1	14.9	16.4	34.4	15.6	26.1	1.5	11.6	10.8	4.9	10.6	14.2	8.9	50.8	10.7
Anchorage municipality .	3.7	14.9	16.7	36.8	15.1	28.5	0.3	9.7	9.6	3.1	8.4	15.7	9.4	53.8	9.7
Fairbanks city	4.8	16.3	17.0	30.4	18.6	28.6	0.3	12.4	9.7	2.0	9.6	16.2	8.8	54.9	8.4
Juneau city and borough	4.3	13.7	12.4	42.3	13.4	26.8	1.8	8.6	7.0	5.2	7.5	11.3	6.5	47.0	22.6
ARIZONA	3.7	19.3	14.9	32.7	16.2	28.5	0.6	11.0	10.9	1.5	18.9	15.6	5.0	53.7	5.4
Apache Junction city	2.2	26.8	23.1	18.9	21.4	26.8	0.2	17.1	15.7	0.7	26.0	16.8	4.9	46.3	5.2
Avondale city	2.1	16.3	12.4	28.7	15.4	26.5	2.1	11.5	15.8	2.5	22.5	14.9	8.1	43.8	8.2
Bullhead City city	1.9	29.2	20.8	16.6	38.4	26.8	0.6	10.0	7.6	0.8	8.4	13.4	2.8	72.4	2.2
Casa Grande city	2.2	20.9	15.0	28.1	20.3	23.8	1.4	10.2	16.2	4.0	20.8	14.5	3.0	48.1	9.5
Chandler city	3.1	13.3	11.8	40.8	11.6	28.7	0.5	8.0	10.4	0.7	25.7	16.0	5.4	48.6	3.8
Flagstaff city	3.5	14.9	9.7	37.9	19.4	27.0	0.4	7.1	8.2	1.1	10.7	16.0	3.3	62.8	6.1
Gilbert town	4.1	10.8	11.9	43.6	10.5	30.7	0.2	6.9	8.2	0.6	22.6	17.4	5.9	49.1	4.4
Glendale city	2.6	18.3	13.8	31.4	14.2	30.2	0.4	11.9	11.9	0.6	20.1	16.5	5.5	51.2	6.1
Lake Havasu City city ...	3.5	21.3	21.9	22.9	18.7	31.1	0.1	13.9	13.4	0.3	19.8	18.4	5.8	51.0	4.6
Mesa city	3.1	17.9	14.5	30.9	14.5	30.1	0.2	12.1	12.3	0.4	23.5	16.5	4.9	51.5	3.3
Oro Valley town............	5.4	14.4	21.9	52.1	11.5	26.3	0.1	4.3	5.7	1.2	20.9	13.9	4.2	54.1	5.7
Peoria city	2.8	18.4	17.3	33.9	13.2	31.6	0.1	10.8	10.4	0.3	17.6	17.1	6.9	51.5	6.4
Phoenix city	3.3	19.1	11.6	30.9	15.9	29.1	0.3	12.0	12.0	0.4	20.2	15.2	4.8	54.8	4.6
Prescott city	6.5	20.0	21.3	37.4	18.4	24.9	0.3	9.7	9.3	1.0	15.8	14.6	3.3	60.0	5.3
Scottsdale city	7.1	14.7	14.2	46.9	11.6	33.1	0.0	3.8	4.5	0.3	13.5	17.5	3.4	62.9	2.4
Sierra Vista city	1.7	19.6	25.9	34.0	21.7	29.4	0.2	7.9	6.9	0.7	7.4	15.1	3.2	55.4	18.3
Surprise city	3.3	19.9	23.0	27.9	20.1	30.1	1.5	9.9	10.4	1.9	16.6	15.6	5.5	53.1	7.3
Tempe city	3.2	15.0	10.1	39.7	14.6	29.4	0.1	6.8	9.4	0.1	16.6	14.8	5.1	59.8	3.7
Tucson city	2.9	21.3	14.0	32.0	19.1	28.2	0.2	10.9	9.6	0.6	16.6	14.8	4.0	58.6	5.4
Yuma city	1.5	20.4	15.7	30.2	18.8	28.7	2.5	9.8	10.0	3.9	11.3	18.3	4.6	49.6	12.5
ARKANSAS................	2.6	23.6	14.1	27.7	14.1	25.1	1.5	10.6	21.0	3.7	26.4	16.3	5.9	43.4	4.3
Conway city..................	2.2	16.8	9.8	36.4	14.2	28.9	0.3	7.5	12.6	0.8	20.0	14.9	3.3	57.6	3.5
Fayetteville city............	3.1	16.8	9.8	40.4	15.7	27.1	0.3	5.4	11.0	0.9	16.0	17.1	4.4	59.6	2.0
Fort Smith city	1.8	23.3	13.9	28.7	13.3	24.3	0.5	7.8	25.4	1.1	31.2	15.5	4.5	45.1	2.5
Hot Springs city............	2.6	29.5	15.8	27.9	23.7	23.6	0.5	9.7	14.5	1.2	18.3	15.8	3.3	58.0	3.3
Jacksonville city	1.3	21.6	20.0	25.4	16.5	31.6	0.1	9.4	17.0	0.2	17.8	17.9	7.9	48.1	8.1
Jonesboro city	2.4	22.5	11.9	31.8	14.6	27.2	0.6	7.9	17.9	1.5	20.8	18.8	4.2	51.8	2.9
Little Rock city	2.2	20.2	13.1	41.6	13.8	29.0	0.1	5.7	9.8	0.4	11.6	14.7	4.7	61.5	7.0
North Little Rock city.....	2.1	24.2	15.8	31.5	15.3	30.5	0.1	8.7	13.9	0.3	13.9	15.9	7.6	55.6	6.8
Pine Bluff city	1.8	25.9	13.4	26.0	18.2	24.3	0.5	7.6	23.4	1.0	26.3	15.1	5.2	43.3	9.2
Rogers city	1.8	18.9	12.4	29.9	12.2	26.4	0.2	8.7	22.5	0.6	29.4	25.1	4.6	38.4	1.9
Springdale city.............	2.2	17.7	12.1	25.5	13.5	27.4	1.0	10.3	22.4	1.3	31.0	18.7	6.8	40.1	2.1
Texarkana city	1.3	24.6	14.0	28.6	17.7	24.8	0.4	10.0	18.4	0.9	23.0	17.6	5.8	46.7	5.9
West Memphis city........	1.1	24.7	11.4	23.7	16.1	27.8	0.8	11.2	20.4	1.4	22.2	17.5	8.8	46.2	4.0
CALIFORNIA..............	3.8	19.2	10.4	36.0	14.8	26.8	1.3	8.4	12.7	1.9	19.3	15.2	4.7	54.3	4.5
Alameda city................	4.0	18.1	12.0	48.2	11.7	26.2	0.2	5.7	8.1	0.1	12.8	13.3	7.3	61.8	4.8
Alhambra city	2.2	19.8	5.0	36.8	14.0	30.2	0.0	5.9	13.1	0.1	18.3	16.0	4.9	56.3	4.4
Anaheim city................	2.4	19.2	7.9	27.5	15.6	28.3	0.3	9.5	18.8	0.3	27.0	16.8	3.7	49.5	2.7
Antioch city	2.8	16.3	12.8	29.1	15.1	31.2	0.2	13.2	11.3	0.4	19.1	17.8	6.7	51.6	4.3
Apple Valley town	4.5	20.9	18.2	31.1	15.5	26.7	0.2	12.5	14.0	1.3	14.5	15.9	9.2	53.3	5.9
Arcadia city..................	3.7	14.4	8.0	50.5	8.8	31.8	0.0	3.7	5.2	0.2	13.1	18.3	3.6	62.0	2.8
Atascadero city............	4.1	18.6	16.1	32.7	19.8	24.9	0.6	12.0	10.1	1.1	16.0	15.5	5.3	53.7	8.4

Table B-5. Cities — **Education, Labor Force, and Income**

City	Median household income	Median family income: All families	Median family income: Families with children: Married-couple	Median family income: Families with children: Male householder	Median family income: Families with children: Female householder	Median nonfamily household income	Median income for full-year, full-time workers: Men	Median income for full-year, full-time workers: Women	Per capita income	Households by source of income (percent): With earnings	Households by source of income (percent): With interest, dividend, or rental income	Households by source of income (percent): With Social Security income	Households by source of income (percent): With public assistance income	Households by source of income (percent): With retirement income	Households with income over $100,000 (percent)	+/− U.S. percent for income over $100,000	Households with income below poverty (percent)	Families with children with income below poverty (percent)
	57	58	59	60	61	62	63	64	65	66	67	68	69	70	71	72	73	74
UNITED STATES	41 994	50 046	59 461	29 907	20 284	25 705	38 349	28 135	21 587	80.5	35.9	25.7	3.4	16.7	12.3	0.0	11.8	13.6
ALABAMA	34 135	41 657	51 129	26 284	15 403	17 866	33 992	23 585	18 189	77.0	27.1	28.0	2.2	17.9	7.6	-4.7	16.7	18.2
Auburn city	17 206	55 619	73 716	28 125	17 386	9 677	42 074	27 080	16 431	85.0	32.5	12.5	0.8	8.9	7.9	-4.4	41.5	14.0
Bessemer city	23 066	28 230	41 678	25 568	12 573	12 655	29 868	22 357	12 232	67.5	14.2	35.3	4.9	18.0	2.8	-9.5	27.4	33.7
Birmingham city	26 735	31 851	45 189	22 111	15 602	18 594	28 835	24 376	15 663	74.9	17.1	28.9	3.4	15.0	4.5	-7.8	23.3	29.6
Decatur city	37 192	47 574	57 263	32 297	15 106	21 310	38 384	23 635	20 431	79.0	34.5	25.8	2.1	18.9	9.4	-2.9	14.5	19.4
Dothan city	35 000	45 025	56 852	28 942	13 758	19 443	36 284	23 671	20 539	76.8	31.0	27.8	2.0	16.4	10.0	-2.3	15.9	20.7
Florence city	28 330	40 577	51 631	21 591	13 153	15 234	35 952	22 010	19 464	71.6	31.5	30.8	2.7	21.1	7.9	-4.4	21.3	22.2
Gadsden city	24 823	31 740	42 236	21 741	13 011	14 642	30 246	20 474	15 610	64.6	24.5	39.2	3.1	21.8	5.0	-7.3	21.8	29.1
Homewood city	45 431	60 256	78 202	37 857	33 911	30 000	41 801	35 747	25 491	85.7	44.7	19.3	0.4	12.6	14.8	2.5	7.7	5.1
Hoover city	61 982	79 912	90 026	68 977	36 269	35 724	58 119	35 950	33 361	87.9	48.5	18.7	0.4	13.9	27.0	14.7	4.0	2.6
Huntsville city	41 074	52 202	65 094	25 287	17 538	25 501	41 538	27 078	24 015	81.0	38.4	23.6	2.5	21.4	13.0	0.7	12.7	16.2
Madison city	63 849	74 532	79 423	47 639	26 142	36 722	59 861	33 433	27 821	92.3	47.8	10.9	1.0	15.3	22.7	10.4	6.5	0.0
Mobile city	31 445	39 752	52 213	23 413	12 181	19 533	32 450	22 702	18 072	76.2	26.8	28.3	2.9	17.8	7.7	-4.6	20.2	26.9
Montgomery city	35 627	44 297	56 621	25 192	16 856	23 277	32 950	25 933	19 385	79.9	30.2	25.3	2.5	18.6	9.6	-2.7	16.0	20.8
Phenix City city	26 720	33 740	47 272	29 038	12 451	15 798	29 887	21 784	14 619	72.6	18.0	28.8	4.6	15.2	3.4	-8.9	21.6	24.8
Prichard city	19 544	23 519	37 437	16 696	10 757	10 010	26 806	17 535	10 626	68.6	9.5	31.7	5.8	14.8	2.8	-9.5	35.0	42.8
Tuscaloosa city	27 731	41 753	56 887	30 575	16 025	15 047	32 490	25 528	19 129	78.0	27.8	24.4	2.2	16.3	8.2	-4.1	25.3	21.3
ALASKA	51 571	59 036	65 353	35 386	25 203	33 796	43 856	32 624	22 660	89.5	72.4	13.7	8.7	14.7	16.1	3.8	8.3	9.3
Anchorage municipality	55 546	63 682	69 621	38 140	26 325	37 503	43 971	33 606	25 287	90.8	69.6	12.4	7.0	14.4	18.8	6.5	6.4	7.4
Fairbanks city	40 577	46 785	49 295	33 636	20 330	27 391	31 745	28 227	19 814	87.2	61.8	14.6	9.7	13.7	9.9	-2.4	10.3	10.2
Juneau city and borough	62 034	70 284	77 664	38 750	29 634	37 363	50 000	35 533	26 719	89.9	78.1	13.1	5.7	17.0	19.7	7.4	5.1	5.5
ARIZONA	40 558	46 723	53 815	28 171	21 517	26 828	36 110	27 570	20 275	78.7	34.6	27.1	2.9	18.5	10.8	-1.5	11.8	15.2
Apache Junction city	33 170	37 726	44 160	34 239	22 039	21 154	31 946	24 211	16 806	65.9	33.0	43.6	2.2	26.2	2.7	-9.6	10.3	13.7
Avondale city	49 153	51 004	55 443	31 063	23 707	31 000	35 781	28 265	16 919	88.8	23.8	16.1	4.1	11.9	11.1	-1.2	11.1	13.3
Bullhead City city	30 221	33 914	38 007	23 980	15 643	20 666	25 081	20 683	16 250	71.9	26.2	38.6	4.1	23.7	4.0	-8.3	12.6	19.9
Casa Grande city	36 212	40 827	50 836	20 847	18 983	24 054	35 307	25 233	15 917	77.1	27.4	30.3	4.0	20.5	7.0	-5.3	14.8	18.2
Chandler city	58 416	62 720	66 042	40 042	31 101	40 730	45 618	32 424	23 904	91.2	34.9	13.8	1.6	11.4	16.6	4.3	5.7	6.2
Flagstaff city	37 146	48 427	57 592	24 621	18 277	24 867	32 457	25 243	18 637	89.5	33.4	13.1	2.6	10.8	9.9	-2.4	16.3	15.6
Gilbert town	68 032	70 994	75 484	46 935	32 336	47 052	50 883	33 499	24 795	95.0	38.7	10.3	0.8	9.8	21.5	9.2	3.0	3.0
Glendale city	45 015	51 162	59 559	30 183	23 267	27 994	36 655	28 888	19 124	86.4	29.3	18.5	2.8	14.2	11.3	-1.0	10.3	12.2
Lake Havasu City city	36 499	41 393	51 514	28 598	20 848	22 813	33 007	22 196	20 403	64.2	40.6	45.8	2.0	31.3	7.3	-5.0	8.2	11.1
Mesa city	42 817	49 232	57 408	31 575	25 395	27 813	36 575	27 897	19 601	79.8	34.9	26.3	2.1	17.5	9.6	-2.7	7.9	9.0
Oro Valley town	61 037	67 563	78 773	51 250	24 063	40 223	58 798	32 057	31 134	69.7	61.6	36.8	0.6	32.2	20.6	8.3	3.4	2.4
Peoria city	52 199	58 388	65 832	41 268	32 146	31 244	41 496	30 056	22 726	78.0	39.7	28.6	1.1	21.9	12.1	-0.2	4.7	4.4
Phoenix city	41 207	46 467	51 522	27 857	22 631	29 787	34 204	28 532	19 833	86.1	28.6	19.1	2.9	12.0	11.5	-0.8	12.4	16.7
Prescott city	35 446	46 481	54 800	30 208	17 500	21 492	33 090	23 950	22 565	62.8	49.3	43.4	1.8	31.1	9.7	-2.6	12.8	13.8
Scottsdale city	57 484	73 846	91 616	41 577	31 351	37 929	52 808	35 921	39 158	80.2	49.2	27.2	1.0	17.2	26.0	13.7	5.8	5.1
Sierra Vista city	38 427	44 077	46 525	27 938	20 503	26 887	31 881	25 025	18 436	79.2	35.4	25.0	2.6	28.5	6.6	-5.7	9.4	13.5
Surprise city	44 156	47 899	49 828	27 292	21 250	30 398	34 661	27 003	21 451	62.1	48.6	47.3	2.1	37.7	7.5	-4.8	6.1	11.9
Tempe city	42 361	55 237	64 931	29 398	26 035	30 565	36 952	29 558	22 406	88.7	34.3	14.8	1.7	11.3	12.6	0.3	13.9	12.2
Tucson city	30 981	37 344	43 462	25 011	17 534	21 565	29 668	23 970	16 322	79.6	31.2	24.5	3.8	16.4	5.0	-7.3	16.9	20.1
Yuma city	35 374	39 693	43 418	24 651	19 116	22 567	30 930	25 002	16 730	75.8	31.5	30.0	3.5	20.7	7.6	-4.7	13.4	18.4
ARKANSAS	32 182	38 663	46 222	23 707	15 497	17 999	30 623	21 837	16 904	76.8	28.3	30.4	2.9	16.3	6.0	-6.3	15.8	18.1
Conway city	37 063	47 912	60 935	30 897	18 542	18 494	35 477	25 886	18 509	84.6	31.4	18.6	2.1	11.2	9.5	-2.8	16.8	13.2
Fayetteville city	31 345	45 074	54 105	32 697	16 425	20 324	30 968	23 297	18 311	86.6	32.0	15.6	1.9	10.1	7.9	-4.4	20.3	17.8
Fort Smith city	32 157	41 012	49 167	20 137	15 779	20 496	30 836	23 141	18 994	77.5	31.8	28.2	3.3	14.9	8.1	-4.2	15.0	19.9
Hot Springs city	26 040	32 819	38 433	24 958	12 681	16 784	27 336	21 099	17 961	66.5	30.9	41.7	4.0	21.5	5.8	-6.5	18.4	25.7
Jacksonville city	35 460	40 381	43 352	26 429	15 100	21 341	28 850	22 162	16 369	85.7	26.1	20.6	4.3	20.6	4.2	-8.1	13.2	17.6
Jonesboro city	32 196	42 082	52 013	25 776	12 367	18 402	32 543	22 326	17 884	81.9	28.9	24.0	2.9	13.3	7.3	-5.0	17.7	20.1
Little Rock city	37 572	47 446	63 478	27 270	18 828	26 119	36 815	27 702	23 209	82.8	33.1	21.9	2.7	14.2	11.6	-0.7	13.1	17.2
North Little Rock city	35 578	43 595	55 480	25 250	16 022	22 152	31 977	25 783	19 662	78.3	31.0	29.1	3.2	16.8	7.8	-4.5	14.9	21.5
Pine Bluff city	27 247	34 362	46 546	19 219	15 000	16 624	31 362	21 933	14 637	75.5	21.4	30.9	5.0	14.7	5.0	-7.3	23.3	30.8
Rogers city	40 474	45 876	52 728	23 611	16 547	23 507	31 761	22 375	19 761	82.4	31.4	24.0	2.2	13.8	10.9	-1.4	11.2	13.3
Springdale city	36 729	42 170	47 588	20 455	20 346	22 172	29 379	21 492	16 855	82.7	30.2	24.5	1.6	13.0	6.8	-5.5	10.8	13.4
Texarkana city	31 343	37 157	51 178	24 395	11 660	18 771	35 966	22 132	17 130	75.3	26.1	28.3	3.1	17.4	6.1	-6.2	19.1	26.5
West Memphis city	27 399	32 465	45 466	18 393	12 287	18 490	31 300	21 564	13 679	78.4	17.0	25.4	5.1	13.2	5.3	-7.0	25.8	34.1
CALIFORNIA	47 493	53 025	60 318	31 161	22 200	32 024	41 526	32 432	22 711	82.5	35.0	22.3	4.9	15.4	17.3	5.0	11.8	15.3
Alameda city	56 285	68 625	80 764	37 083	31 620	40 483	50 749	41 183	30 982	83.7	47.0	21.2	3.0	17.6	22.6	10.3	7.1	9.5
Alhambra city	39 213	43 245	45 184	30 625	22 717	26 797	35 053	29 490	17 350	82.2	33.4	20.3	6.0	10.6	9.4	-2.9	13.3	16.4
Anaheim city	47 122	49 969	51 250	28 975	25 847	32 335	34 960	29 762	18 266	87.9	28.5	18.7	3.6	12.9	14.5	2.2	10.5	14.4
Antioch city	60 359	64 723	74 163	40 590	24 868	34 340	50 761	35 217	22 152	87.6	30.3	17.9	4.2	15.7	19.1	6.8	7.7	8.9
Apple Valley town	40 421	45 070	55 833	23 413	15 635	24 288	42 744	31 034	17 830	73.5	31.1	32.4	7.4	24.4	9.7	-2.6	14.0	20.1
Arcadia city	56 100	66 657	76 828	41 100	33 357	32 791	52 397	36 731	28 400	80.2	51.7	25.1	2.1	14.9	23.9	11.6	8.3	8.1
Atascadero city	48 725	55 009	63 093	42 179	22 781	28 095	42 394	30 959	20 029	81.2	40.3	25.2	2.5	19.3	11.0	-1.3	8.3	10.3

STATE Place code	City	High school graduates			College graduates		College graduates (percent)				
		Total population 25 years and over	Percent with a high school diploma or less	Percent with a high school diploma or more	Percent with a bachelor's degree or more	+/− U.S. percent with bachelor's degree or more	Non-Hispanic White	Black or African American	American Indian and Alaska Native	Asian, Hawaiian, and Pacific Islander	Hispanic or Latino[1]
		1	2	3	4	5	6	7	8	9	10
	CALIFORNIA—Cont'd										
06 03386	Azusa city	23 725	59.2	60.7	14.2	-10.2	24.2	18.9	5.1	45.8	5.3
06 03526	Bakersfield city	142 060	47.5	75.9	19.3	-5.1	25.1	9.6	10.9	36.1	6.8
06 03666	Baldwin Park city	40 417	73.6	47.5	9.0	-15.4	9.0	20.2	7.3	33.1	3.8
06 04870	Bell city	19 045	82.7	35.1	4.0	-20.4	9.4	18.5	11.3	27.1	2.6
06 04982	Bellflower city	42 270	55.8	70.8	12.9	-11.5	12.2	12.7	9.1	37.0	5.6
06 04996	Bell Gardens city	20 942	84.1	31.3	4.0	-20.4	8.9	0.0	6.9	46.8	3.2
06 05108	Belmont city	18 793	19.7	94.2	51.7	27.3	50.5	32.9	0.0	68.5	34.7
06 05290	Benicia city	17 930	25.9	91.7	37.3	12.9	38.7	27.5	10.0	48.1	22.1
06 06000	Berkeley city	66 133	16.4	92.2	64.3	39.9	78.4	20.0	25.1	63.8	39.8
06 06308	Beverly Hills city	25 078	22.2	90.8	54.5	30.1	55.6	52.7	21.8	62.5	33.5
06 08100	Brea city	23 098	30.2	88.4	33.5	9.1	34.0	11.1	29.5	62.7	16.7
06 08786	Buena Park city	48 066	48.7	75.8	19.7	-4.7	16.1	20.7	10.1	43.2	5.5
06 08954	Burbank city	70 523	38.2	83.1	29.0	4.6	30.8	36.3	20.1	51.6	13.0
06 09066	Burlingame city	21 111	22.1	92.9	47.9	23.5	48.9	22.3	0.0	62.1	23.5
06 09710	Calexico city	14 961	69.0	47.4	9.1	-15.3	20.0	32.6	0.0	19.5	8.6
06 10046	Camarillo city	38 973	30.1	90.6	32.9	8.5	33.6	45.5	18.8	50.0	16.7
06 10345	Campbell city	27 211	27.1	89.7	39.7	15.3	40.6	23.3	11.5	52.7	16.3
06 11194	Carlsbad city	54 655	21.1	93.1	45.7	21.3	48.2	48.7	27.5	54.8	19.8
06 11530	Carson city	55 241	50.8	70.6	18.1	-6.3	10.6	22.4	8.2	32.9	5.2
06 12048	Cathedral City city	25 700	54.8	69.0	14.7	-9.7	20.9	8.1	37.7	28.5	4.5
06 12524	Ceres city	19 149	63.3	67.0	8.3	-16.1	10.1	12.2	0.0	12.6	3.8
06 12552	Cerritos city	34 351	25.5	90.7	43.7	19.3	30.8	32.5	13.3	55.4	17.1
06 13014	Chico city	31 072	29.7	87.3	33.6	9.2	35.9	24.3	20.2	34.9	19.6
06 13210	Chino city	40 039	55.3	70.7	13.0	-11.4	16.0	11.3	12.5	40.2	6.9
06 13214	Chino Hills city	40 032	26.4	89.9	37.6	13.2	34.7	45.1	20.6	60.8	18.4
06 13392	Chula Vista city	107 496	43.8	78.5	22.2	-2.2	25.9	23.9	16.5	39.2	14.1
06 13588	Citrus Heights city	55 087	39.9	88.5	18.2	-6.2	18.4	23.7	5.0	33.3	12.4
06 13756	Claremont city	20 829	22.0	92.4	52.4	28.0	56.8	37.1	34.4	63.7	27.9
06 14218	Clovis city	41 135	38.2	85.0	23.1	-1.3	24.8	26.1	15.3	33.2	14.1
06 14890	Colton city	25 738	56.2	68.8	12.2	-12.2	18.4	13.3	8.8	43.7	5.1
06 15044	Compton city	46 604	73.1	48.0	5.9	-18.5	10.7	9.2	9.8	19.6	2.1
06 16000	Concord city	80 130	38.4	84.7	25.9	1.5	27.9	22.0	13.3	41.3	10.5
06 16350	Corona city	72 375	40.8	80.6	22.0	-2.4	25.5	24.8	12.5	42.8	9.1
06 16532	Costa Mesa city	71 622	38.0	79.1	29.1	4.7	35.1	35.2	12.5	42.9	8.1
06 16742	Covina city	29 422	44.7	81.9	18.8	-5.6	18.8	17.4	9.1	43.9	11.0
06 17568	Culver City city	28 340	28.1	87.2	41.2	16.8	45.6	51.8	0.0	53.2	16.8
06 17610	Cupertino city	34 521	13.6	95.5	65.4	41.0	59.3	40.9	22.7	75.8	41.0
06 17750	Cypress city	30 168	32.1	89.7	31.2	6.8	28.9	24.9	20.3	49.9	15.6
06 17918	Daly City city	69 660	38.7	82.0	29.1	4.7	27.2	18.9	16.5	37.6	11.9
06 17946	Dana Point city	25 264	24.5	90.7	41.0	16.6	44.4	43.1	15.0	43.2	17.1
06 17988	Danville town	28 443	14.6	96.6	59.4	35.0	59.9	55.9	52.5	69.0	36.5
06 18100	Davis city	30 375	11.5	96.4	68.6	44.2	71.3	50.4	46.4	75.0	42.1
06 18394	Delano city	21 789	78.0	48.7	5.5	-18.9	10.3	2.4	3.9	14.5	2.0
06 19192	Diamond Bar city	36 322	26.2	90.7	42.3	17.9	36.6	39.6	25.6	57.3	18.9
06 19766	Downey city	65 773	52.6	72.3	17.3	-7.1	20.1	18.4	17.9	43.4	10.4
06 20018	Dublin city	20 995	34.3	86.3	32.9	8.5	36.5	9.5	12.2	57.5	16.5
06 20956	East Palo Alto city	15 170	69.8	48.2	10.6	-13.8	44.7	9.5	31.1	16.1	3.3
06 21712	El Cajon city	57 867	50.1	79.2	14.5	-9.9	16.4	9.9	7.3	23.9	6.7
06 21782	El Centro city	21 582	56.1	62.9	14.0	-10.4	28.4	8.9	10.4	40.5	7.5
06 22230	El Monte city	62 422	75.7	44.2	7.1	-17.3	9.4	3.3	2.1	17.2	3.3
06 22678	Encinitas city	40 674	21.1	91.1	50.0	25.6	54.2	34.2	31.4	61.9	18.0
06 22804	Escondido city	79 691	48.6	72.6	20.1	-4.3	25.3	20.2	10.0	34.4	6.1
06 23042	Eureka city	17 033	45.1	81.7	16.9	-7.5	18.4	0.0	10.5	9.8	6.3
06 23182	Fairfield city	56 512	39.5	85.0	20.4	-4.0	24.2	15.5	1.1	67.0	8.6
06 24638	Folsom city	36 010	30.2	88.9	37.6	13.2	39.9	10.2	11.2	67.0	19.2
06 24680	Fontana city	66 706	59.6	65.4	10.3	-14.1	12.2	14.1	7.6	36.7	4.8
06 25338	Foster City city	21 232	14.9	95.6	59.8	35.4	57.0	54.4	45.5	69.1	35.5
06 25380	Fountain Valley city	37 554	29.7	88.6	34.4	10.0	34.1	34.5	13.3	42.1	15.7
06 26000	Fremont city	136 242	28.5	88.4	43.2	18.8	34.5	31.0	23.0	63.2	16.3
06 27000	Fresno city	236 704	51.1	69.1	19.0	-5.4	28.2	11.4	6.6	22.8	7.0
06 28000	Fullerton city	80 010	37.0	81.8	31.3	6.9	34.2	26.5	13.9	52.9	9.7
06 28168	Gardena city	38 196	51.8	74.0	16.6	-7.8	18.2	15.1	8.5	26.4	5.1
06 29000	Garden Grove city	103 456	54.8	67.8	15.0	-9.4	18.8	22.4	6.7	17.8	5.1
06 29504	Gilroy city	24 105	50.0	70.1	19.1	-5.3	29.5	34.1	17.3	31.4	6.8
06 30000	Glendale city	135 054	40.2	79.0	32.1	7.7	32.4	28.2	12.6	53.7	13.9
06 30014	Glendora city	32 253	34.6	87.1	25.7	1.3	26.3	31.6	0.9	52.4	13.5
06 31960	Hanford city	24 658	51.9	74.5	14.4	-10.0	19.4	7.4	7.7	28.5	5.1
06 32548	Hawthorne city	48 336	56.9	66.8	12.7	-11.7	20.9	12.2	4.2	26.1	5.9
06 33000	Hayward city	87 792	50.7	75.1	19.9	-4.5	20.4	22.6	6.3	36.3	6.5
06 33182	Hemet city	41 594	57.4	73.5	10.8	-13.6	11.8	13.3	11.2	25.4	4.0
06 33434	Hesperia city	36 550	58.1	72.6	8.0	-16.4	8.7	17.2	7.4	22.1	3.3

[1] Hispanic or Latino persons may be of any race.

Table B-5. Cities — Education, Labor Force, and Income

City	School enrollment			Population 16 to 19 years				Employment status, 2000			Work status in 1999 of the population 16 years and over — Worked in 1999		
	Grades kindergarten through 12	College or graduate school	Percent private	Number	Percent in armed forces	Percent high school graduates	Percent not enrolled, not grads, not in armed forces, not employed	Total population 16 years and over	Percent in labor force	Unemployment rate	Full-time	Part-time	Did not work in 1999
	11	12	13	14	15	16	17	18	19	20	21	22	23
CALIFORNIA—Cont'd													
Azusa city	10 077	5 024	23.9	3 788	0.0	6.9	5.7	32 098	61.2	9.1	52.0	16.0	32.0
Bakersfield city	60 709	16 233	7.8	15 981	0.0	10.2	5.2	175 535	63.6	8.5	53.0	14.4	32.6
Baldwin Park city	20 685	4 110	6.7	5 170	0.0	8.9	8.0	51 899	56.0	9.9	52.5	11.3	36.1
Bell city	9 720	2 006	6.1	2 668	0.0	8.8	10.4	25 083	55.5	10.8	50.7	10.9	38.5
Bellflower city	17 019	5 594	13.2	4 055	0.0	9.0	5.5	51 688	61.7	8.0	55.7	12.9	31.4
Bell Gardens city	13 482	1 961	3.1	3 165	0.0	10.3	7.7	28 180	53.0	12.6	51.6	9.5	38.9
Belmont city	3 383	2 016	29.8	871	0.0	0.6	0.7	20 756	70.7	3.0	60.3	14.9	24.8
Benicia city	6 229	1 912	12.0	1 466	0.0	7.5	1.8	20 516	71.7	3.7	57.0	18.5	24.4
Berkeley city	11 009	27 016	14.5	7 127	0.0	3.9	1.4	89 901	65.8	5.5	47.7	27.0	25.2
Beverly Hills city	5 589	2 436	25.0	1 616	0.0	3.0	0.0	28 065	59.9	5.4	49.8	14.3	35.9
Brea city	7 047	3 103	13.6	2 038	0.0	8.3	0.3	27 319	69.3	3.7	57.8	15.8	26.4
Buena Park city	17 160	6 026	11.4	4 260	0.0	9.1	4.7	57 518	64.0	6.0	55.8	13.6	30.6
Burbank city	17 589	7 201	17.5	4 330	0.0	10.9	3.0	80 339	65.7	6.0	57.1	13.0	29.9
Burlingame city	3 990	2 070	19.8	1 028	0.0	7.3	3.8	23 206	67.8	2.2	58.3	15.3	26.4
Calexico city	7 788	2 220	4.4	2 168	0.0	9.5	3.8	18 755	52.9	14.3	43.0	14.2	42.7
Camarillo city	10 565	4 030	13.7	2 756	0.3	6.9	3.6	44 217	63.1	3.5	52.7	15.0	32.3
Campbell city	5 970	2 962	14.6	1 459	0.0	9.5	4.3	30 858	73.0	3.4	64.1	13.5	22.3
Carlsbad city	13 444	5 100	12.4	3 265	0.5	5.6	2.8	61 582	66.4	3.8	55.3	15.8	28.9
Carson city	20 139	6 999	13.4	5 417	0.0	5.0	3.7	66 988	60.6	7.9	53.0	12.5	34.5
Cathedral City city	9 869	1 499	4.5	2 499	0.0	13.2	5.5	30 890	60.3	7.1	50.6	14.4	35.0
Ceres city	9 088	1 371	5.7	2 458	0.0	14.5	8.2	23 854	64.0	13.8	54.1	13.7	32.2
Cerritos city	10 655	5 772	13.9	3 171	0.0	2.8	0.6	40 728	62.5	4.2	54.7	14.1	31.2
Chico city	8 986	16 895	3.7	5 084	0.1	6.3	1.8	48 500	62.8	9.5	43.2	29.0	27.8
Chino city	15 209	4 815	10.9	4 112	0.2	10.5	6.5	50 386	57.9	7.4	56.2	15.4	28.4
Chino Hills city	16 320	5 464	14.7	4 056	0.0	6.1	1.6	47 127	71.5	3.9	63.4	13.0	23.5
Chula Vista city	38 206	14 327	10.2	9 324	1.1	9.3	4.8	128 458	61.8	6.1	52.3	14.0	33.7
Citrus Heights city	16 021	6 003	12.2	4 654	0.0	14.8	2.0	66 092	66.5	4.5	55.3	15.3	29.3
Claremont city	5 661	7 407	49.1	3 518	0.4	3.5	1.0	28 086	62.6	8.6	46.1	23.6	30.3
Clovis city	15 980	5 325	7.0	4 241	0.0	8.7	1.8	49 672	67.6	6.2	54.7	17.5	27.8
Colton city	12 318	3 330	9.7	3 228	0.2	12.8	6.9	32 971	63.0	8.8	53.4	13.1	33.4
Compton city	26 942	4 398	7.3	6 338	0.0	10.3	12.3	60 618	51.8	13.7	46.9	9.4	43.7
Concord city	22 672	8 053	12.1	6 597	0.2	10.0	6.7	94 576	66.8	5.2	57.3	15.0	27.7
Corona city	29 056	8 427	10.6	7 349	0.0	12.1	4.9	86 985	69.8	5.4	61.3	12.8	25.8
Costa Mesa city	18 307	10 678	16.3	5 018	0.0	6.5	6.9	85 940	69.0	4.7	59.6	15.8	24.6
Covina city	10 042	3 948	12.1	2 655	0.2	13.0	2.6	35 293	64.5	5.7	55.3	13.9	30.9
Culver City city	6 269	2 865	17.5	1 434	0.0	10.5	2.9	31 572	67.9	5.4	57.4	15.6	27.0
Cupertino city	10 472	3 732	12.0	2 215	0.0	1.9	0.4	38 467	63.7	2.3	56.3	12.0	31.7
Cypress city	10 280	3 983	12.2	2 707	0.6	6.2	2.0	35 443	67.5	5.1	55.8	15.0	29.0
Daly City city	17 593	10 804	20.6	5 328	0.0	7.3	4.3	83 045	63.7	3.8	58.0	13.9	28.1
Dana Point city	5 312	2 414	16.9	1 680	0.0	7.6	2.1	28 714	68.4	3.8	56.0	16.7	27.3
Danville town	9 022	1 810	12.8	1 949	0.0	6.3	0.5	31 318	69.0	3.2	57.9	16.1	26.0
Davis city	8 439	21 196	4.9	6 004	0.0	2.8	0.4	50 301	65.8	4.4	46.6	31.9	21.4
Delano city	9 529	1 479	6.4	2 589	0.0	11.6	9.5	27 583	48.5	30.2	55.2	8.5	36.3
Diamond Bar city	12 364	6 191	12.9	3 438	0.0	4.2	1.3	43 044	66.0	5.7	57.3	14.3	28.4
Downey city	24 209	8 554	12.0	6 704	0.0	8.5	4.4	79 395	59.5	6.5	52.8	12.6	34.5
Dublin city	4 722	1 731	14.1	1 270	0.0	12.5	5.5	24 352	61.7	3.1	63.8	10.4	22.8
East Palo Alto city	7 910	1 292	10.0	2 042	0.0	9.0	13.1	20 037	61.4	7.8	56.7	13.1	30.2
El Cajon city	19 163	6 996	8.2	5 152	1.6	16.2	5.4	70 893	64.2	7.5	52.7	15.0	32.3
El Centro city	10 101	2 650	3.6	2 623	0.5	8.1	6.6	26 614	55.8	11.7	49.3	13.1	37.6
El Monte city	29 573	6 884	6.3	7 523	0.0	9.1	10.9	80 444	56.0	9.9	49.5	12.3	38.1
Encinitas city	10 007	4 208	13.5	2 641	0.0	6.9	3.9	46 306	70.9	3.9	59.1	16.8	24.1
Escondido city	28 636	7 268	9.9	7 710	0.3	11.5	7.7	97 670	63.6	6.1	54.7	14.2	31.0
Eureka city	4 351	2 101	3.5	1 326	0.0	20.1	4.8	20 671	57.3	9.7	43.8	18.6	37.7
Fairfield city	21 097	6 352	10.0	6 004	6.5	18.1	6.6	70 553	65.9	6.0	57.2	13.9	28.9
Folsom city	9 406	3 490	12.3	2 174	0.0	5.7	2.0	40 582	62.4	7.2	58.2	13.6	28.2
Fontana city	36 572	6 550	7.1	8 239	0.3	12.4	6.6	83 873	62.1	8.7	56.1	12.2	31.7
Foster City city	4 557	1 925	14.2	1 063	0.0	6.7	0.0	23 353	70.3	2.2	62.8	12.5	24.7
Fountain Valley city	9 904	5 017	14.1	2 934	0.0	7.1	1.6	43 466	66.3	4.1	54.8	16.3	28.9
Fremont city	37 374	15 467	15.5	9 196	0.1	9.1	2.2	156 083	68.2	3.9	61.6	11.5	26.9
Fresno city	100 385	33 456	5.9	28 779	0.0	8.9	7.5	301 154	59.8	11.2	48.5	15.6	35.9
Fullerton city	23 213	14 049	12.8	7 253	0.1	9.9	5.0	97 722	64.4	5.7	50.2	16.4	30.5
Gardena city	11 222	4 431	13.4	2 863	0.0	11.2	4.6	44 285	58.3	7.4	52.7	11.2	36.1
Garden Grove city	35 958	13 066	9.5	9 016	0.0	9.0	4.1	122 976	60.6	6.8	53.1	13.0	33.9
Gilroy city	9 957	2 058	9.9	2 429	0.0	11.4	6.4	29 324	69.6	5.6	60.5	14.5	25.0
Glendale city	34 109	19 274	17.8	9 726	0.0	8.9	3.2	156 251	58.7	7.2	48.4	14.7	36.9
Glendora city	10 612	4 181	15.1	2 827	0.0	5.4	1.3	37 768	65.6	4.2	52.6	17.0	30.4
Hanford city	10 112	2 292	8.2	2 706	0.0	10.5	9.7	30 033	61.2	11.3	52.0	14.9	33.1
Hawthorne city	19 070	6 132	10.2	4 515	0.0	13.2	7.7	59 676	61.5	10.4	55.7	13.0	31.3
Hayward city	27 165	10 491	12.7	7 425	0.0	10.9	5.7	105 947	63.8	6.3	57.4	12.3	30.3
Hemet city	9 446	2 310	7.9	2 197	0.0	14.0	9.6	46 740	40.4	10.1	33.3	11.0	55.7
Hesperia city	15 795	3 400	6.8	4 202	0.0	14.8	4.5	44 357	56.9	10.5	46.5	12.8	40.7

City	Full-year full-time employed (percent)								Children under 18 years in families (percent, except where noted)						Total employed by class of worker (percent)			
										With two parents		With one parent who is in labor force	+/- U.S. percent of children with no stay-at-home parent	+/- U.S. percent two-income couples				
	Total	Men	Women	Non-Hispanic White	Black or African American	American Indian and Alaska Native	Asian, Hawaiian, and Pacific Islander	Hispanic or Latino[1]	Number	Both in labor force	Father only in labor force				Private	Government	Self-employed	Unpaid family worker
	24	25	26	27	28	29	30	31	32	33	34	35	36	37	38	39	40	41
CALIFORNIA—Cont'd																		
Azusa city	32.8	42.2	24.0	33.6	44.6	40.8	34.9	31.4	12 502	31.4	22.8	21.6	-11.6	-8.1	81.0	12.3	6.6	0.2
Bakersfield city	35.3	45.7	25.8	39.3	27.3	35.8	33.9	30.2	75 451	38.3	22.1	22.9	-3.4	-1.5	69.5	20.6	9.6	0.3
Baldwin Park city	30.7	38.0	23.6	28.9	30.0	35.3	33.6	30.4	23 763	26.0	23.2	19.7	-18.9	-15.8	82.1	10.6	6.9	0.4
Bell city	27.7	38.5	16.9	25.0	12.1	33.8	30.6	28.2	11 907	23.6	27.8	20.3	-20.7	-22.3	78.5	12.0	8.8	0.8
Bellflower city	37.8	47.2	29.2	38.1	46.2	34.8	34.0	36.6	21 478	31.6	20.9	24.9	-8.1	-5.5	79.4	13.1	7.3	0.1
Bell Gardens city	27.3	38.4	16.0	23.6	7.9	37.0	34.3	27.5	16 008	19.3	25.0	19.9	-25.4	-26.7	85.4	7.8	6.7	0.2
Belmont city	46.7	57.2	36.8	46.6	44.7	100.0	47.6	42.6	4 747	54.6	26.0	13.2	3.2	5.7	78.2	10.7	11.0	0.1
Benicia city	44.6	54.9	35.1	44.9	46.5	8.0	45.0	40.6	7 173	50.9	19.5	21.6	7.9	8.5	68.7	19.3	11.8	0.2
Berkeley city	29.1	34.4	24.2	34.4	24.4	27.4	18.2	25.4	13 472	44.4	15.4	25.7	5.5	6.8	59.5	26.3	14.0	0.3
Beverly Hills city	36.5	47.3	27.8	35.5	50.6	37.3	39.6	45.2	6 508	34.0	36.8	15.0	-15.6	-16.3	61.7	7.2	30.6	0.6
Brea city	44.5	56.2	33.6	45.5	62.8	48.9	45.0	38.9	8 564	44.8	26.3	18.2	-1.6	4.0	75.1	15.2	9.4	0.4
Buena Park city	39.5	49.5	30.0	41.7	46.0	38.7	37.8	36.9	21 213	35.6	23.0	21.5	-7.5	-3.9	80.8	10.5	8.3	0.4
Burbank city	40.3	47.1	34.2	39.3	53.1	37.3	44.7	40.1	21 368	42.9	19.5	22.0	0.3	-0.7	75.2	11.8	12.7	0.3
Burlingame city	44.0	54.8	34.6	43.5	40.6	69.2	44.5	46.7	5 134	51.6	24.0	13.9	0.9	2.5	75.9	9.9	13.9	0.3
Calexico city	20.3	26.6	15.0	35.9	14.3	17.0	37.7	19.4	13 673	29.7	27.3	22.0	-12.9	-20.9	67.3	22.5	9.5	0.7
Camarillo city	40.8	54.3	28.8	39.6	42.4	65.7	45.7	41.8	13 673	44.6	29.1	16.0	-4.0	-1.0	69.9	17.6	12.1	0.4
Campbell city	48.3	58.8	38.0	48.9	55.3	34.7	46.2	44.8	7 760	42.9	24.4	24.0	2.3	3.0	79.7	9.9	10.0	0.4
Carlsbad city	41.9	55.0	29.8	41.7	55.7	40.4	48.8	40.5	17 623	42.2	31.9	16.7	-5.7	-0.8	69.8	13.2	16.7	0.3
Carson city	35.0	40.3	30.2	33.5	37.9	42.9	36.8	32.1	22 388	40.7	17.7	22.1	-1.8	-4.4	75.2	18.1	6.4	0.3
Cathedral City city	34.1	42.2	25.9	36.1	36.2	20.8	36.3	31.6	12 461	34.9	24.3	19.2	-10.5	-9.2	76.5	9.1	14.2	0.2
Ceres city	35.3	46.4	25.0	38.0	39.0	53.1	27.6	31.4	11 072	40.8	21.2	21.7	-2.1	-7.2	76.9	14.1	8.7	0.3
Cerritos city	40.4	48.2	33.4	41.9	45.3	47.7	38.5	43.6	11 887	49.9	25.1	11.1	-3.6	0.2	68.9	16.2	14.4	0.5
Chico city	26.6	32.7	20.7	27.7	29.1	27.0	19.3	21.5	11 794	39.8	18.9	23.3	-1.5	1.7	69.9	20.2	9.6	0.4
Chino city	39.7	47.3	29.7	43.3	39.6	45.1	39.1	36.4	17 913	43.6	21.3	18.0	-3.0	1.7	76.3	15.3	8.2	0.2
Chino Hills city	49.5	62.6	37.0	51.2	57.8	40.5	47.2	47.6	21 066	51.3	29.3	11.0	-2.3	7.8	71.5	17.2	11.0	0.3
Chula Vista city	37.5	48.0	28.0	38.7	47.0	42.7	40.1	35.1	47 522	37.3	24.9	22.1	-5.2	-5.0	69.6	21.3	8.8	0.3
Citrus Heights city	41.2	49.7	33.3	41.0	38.5	30.5	38.9	42.9	20 030	42.2	21.4	24.6	2.2	2.6	75.4	16.0	8.4	0.2
Claremont city	30.0	40.1	21.3	30.0	31.7	45.3	23.1	35.4	6 535	47.5	24.4	16.2	-0.9	-0.1	67.1	20.2	12.4	0.3
Clovis city	40.8	52.0	30.9	42.2	39.5	29.5	32.7	40.1	19 994	44.2	22.4	21.5	1.1	3.2	68.5	22.0	9.1	0.4
Colton city	35.6	45.8	26.4	42.8	41.8	35.0	38.9	31.1	15 301	31.1	24.7	23.6	-9.9	-7.4	76.7	16.1	6.9	0.3
Compton city	27.1	33.3	21.4	28.8	27.4	22.1	22.9	26.9	30 652	19.1	22.2	23.9	-21.6	-21.4	79.6	15.1	4.8	0.4
Concord city	41.6	51.0	32.8	43.8	43.5	33.6	41.1	35.5	28 788	42.1	24.7	20.2	-2.3	-1.3	79.8	11.1	8.9	0.2
Corona city	45.8	57.4	34.9	49.5	51.5	41.7	41.1	40.3	39 609	45.5	25.7	16.7	-2.4	4.5	75.4	15.2	9.1	0.3
Costa Mesa city	42.9	51.4	33.9	45.8	53.1	30.5	39.5	37.0	23 036	34.3	26.7	20.9	-9.4	-0.8	77.6	9.0	13.0	0.3
Covina city	40.0	48.8	32.5	38.8	34.2	46.7	38.6	42.5	12 365	42.2	15.8	27.3	4.9	0.9	76.3	16.1	7.4	0.2
Culver City city	40.3	46.4	35.3	43.2	42.9	25.8	37.9	34.7	7 639	42.9	22.4	22.6	0.9	2.8	70.0	15.2	14.5	0.3
Cupertino city	44.5	59.6	29.7	43.6	49.0	20.1	45.3	45.6	13 316	42.7	40.3	9.7	-12.2	-3.2	81.0	8.2	10.3	0.4
Cypress city	41.6	52.5	31.9	41.7	49.9	29.6	38.9	42.4	12 078	48.8	23.3	20.7	4.9	3.4	75.0	14.5	10.1	0.3
Daly City city	39.2	44.0	34.6	35.3	40.6	39.7	41.8	36.7	21 418	45.0	16.1	18.7	-0.9	1.6	78.3	14.9	6.5	0.3
Dana Point city	42.2	52.7	32.0	42.6	74.5	23.3	42.9	40.5	6 668	42.5	29.1	20.6	-1.5	-2.0	69.5	10.9	19.0	0.6
Danville town	47.2	64.4	31.7	46.7	55.6	50.0	50.3	49.5	11 938	46.7	41.0	8.4	-9.5	0.9	73.9	9.5	16.4	0.1
Davis city	30.0	38.0	23.1	34.9	29.3	30.6	17.1	27.5	10 898	50.8	24.1	17.8	4.0	9.7	51.5	41.4	6.8	0.3
Delano city	18.1	22.5	11.9	22.3	33.4	16.0	20.8	14.9	11 778	38.5	18.1	18.1	-8.0	-22.0	76.0	17.1	6.6	0.3
Diamond Bar city	42.9	53.1	33.4	44.4	54.1	54.9	40.7	44.0	14 532	46.6	29.0	13.3	-4.7	1.2	69.1	16.3	14.0	0.5
Downey city	36.1	45.0	28.2	33.5	39.0	35.7	40.3	37.0	28 865	36.7	19.5	21.7	-6.2	-4.7	73.7	14.6	11.1	0.7
Dublin city	47.3	54.9	38.6	52.3	35.8	26.2	49.7	34.2	5 901	50.7	25.8	17.5	3.6	10.8	79.2	12.3	8.4	0.1
East Palo Alto city	35.6	41.9	28.9	44.0	33.0	0.0	41.2	34.6	8 644	28.5	16.7	23.9	-12.2	-11.8	81.4	8.8	9.4	0.4
El Cajon city	37.1	46.3	28.5	37.9	43.4	46.6	34.2	33.5	24 661	33.1	22.1	29.0	-2.5	-4.6	77.7	13.3	8.8	0.3
El Centro city	28.8	36.9	21.3	36.8	24.4	25.5	45.0	25.4	12 006	33.8	20.9	22.9	-7.9	-10.9	60.5	30.3	8.9	0.3
El Monte city	29.3	38.8	19.8	28.3	17.4	28.6	30.2	29.4	35 250	25.7	23.7	20.2	-18.7	-15.9	82.9	10.4	6.4	0.3
Encinitas city	44.2	56.6	32.4	45.0	39.7	44.4	52.7	37.4	12 806	41.4	34.2	17.2	-6.0	2.4	68.1	12.6	19.1	0.2
Escondido city	38.3	49.0	28.1	40.5	46.5	37.7	36.9	34.1	37 170	36.4	24.5	21.3	-6.9	-4.3	77.1	11.1	11.4	0.4
Eureka city	28.7	33.1	24.5	29.2	34.9	24.0	29.0	30.0	5 378	30.5	14.2	31.2	-2.9	-7.3	68.2	18.4	12.7	0.7
Fairfield city	41.8	51.5	32.2	43.4	42.2	37.8	39.9	37.1	26 398	40.7	24.7	21.3	-2.6	-1.5	73.0	20.3	6.5	0.1
Folsom city	42.4	46.8	36.7	45.8	16.9	31.1	54.3	30.7	12 300	48.3	31.8	14.6	-1.7	5.4	70.0	19.8	10.2	0.0
Fontana city	37.3	48.4	26.8	41.8	39.6	38.0	40.5	34.1	45 213	35.6	24.1	16.6	-12.4	-5.7	80.2	13.9	5.7	0.1
Foster City city	49.9	61.8	38.8	49.8	57.8	54.5	49.7	50.5	5 964	49.1	32.3	12.5	-3.0	2.1	80.7	8.8	10.2	0.2
Fountain Valley city	41.9	53.2	31.4	44.1	55.3	44.8	38.1	39.7	12 306	49.1	26.1	14.6	-0.9	1.7	72.6	14.3	12.6	0.5
Fremont city	46.9	58.3	35.6	48.0	56.9	45.7	46.5	43.7	50 450	50.0	29.7	14.1	-5.5	1.6	83.2	9.4	7.1	0.3
Fresno city	30.4	37.0	24.3	36.7	24.7	25.6	20.0	27.2	130 157	29.3	21.1	23.2	-12.1	-7.1	70.8	20.0	8.9	0.3
Fullerton city	38.3	48.7	28.2	39.5	46.7	33.6	34.2	38.0	29 872	38.0	20.3	17.5	-9.1	-5.9	76.2	12.5	10.9	0.4
Gardena city	35.9	42.7	29.7	36.5	40.5	45.5	36.1	31.8	13 674	31.7	17.2	24.8	-8.1	-10.0	77.0	13.8	8.6	0.6
Garden Grove city	36.3	45.5	27.3	40.3	33.8	36.2	33.1	34.9	43 540	39.0	24.5	16.3	-9.3	-6.5	81.1	9.9	8.7	0.3
Gilroy city	41.7	52.6	31.0	47.5	53.2	36.4	50.0	35.8	12 213	39.0	23.1	22.5	-3.1	3.9	79.5	12.4	7.8	0.3
Glendale city	33.1	40.9	26.1	30.6	41.8	45.1	39.5	35.9	42 207	39.9	25.9	13.6	-11.1	-7.6	73.4	11.8	14.2	0.6
Glendora city	39.9	51.2	29.8	39.7	55.8	47.8	43.7	38.4	12 880	44.2	28.1	18.4	-2.0	1.9	71.9	16.7	11.0	0.5
Hanford city	33.4	41.2	26.2	39.5	30.7	20.5	27.5	25.2	12 257	39.5	22.3	23.2	-1.9	-3.1	63.2	28.0	8.1	0.6
Hawthorne city	35.3	42.6	28.9	37.3	38.8	39.1	36.1	31.3	24 282	26.5	17.4	29.9	-8.2	-10.3	79.3	14.5	5.8	0.4
Hayward city	40.0	47.4	32.8	39.4	49.2	47.0	42.1	36.1	34 759	38.0	19.7	22.0	-4.6	-2.7	82.0	12.1	5.7	0.2
Hemet city	21.7	29.7	15.5	18.9	28.9	35.4	25.5	31.7	12 269	29.7	25.2	22.1	-8.5	-25.6	75.7	14.2	9.7	0.4
Hesperia city	32.8	45.4	21.1	34.4	25.1	36.9	41.4	29.8	19 063	31.4	31.4	20.4	-12.8	-11.6	73.2	17.4	8.7	0.6

[1] Hispanic or Latino persons may be of any race.

City	Percent who worked at home	Percent of the population 5 years and over with a disability	Veterans as a percent of the population 18 years and over	Occupation for employed population 16 years and over (percent)						Industry for employed population 16 years and over (percent)					
				Management, professional, and related occupations	Service occupations	Sales and office occupations	Farming, fishing, and forestry occupations	Construction, extraction, and maintenance occupations	Production, transportation and material moving occupations	Agriculture, forestry, fishing, and mining	Construction and manufacturing	Wholesale and retail trade	Transportation and warehousing, and utilities	Service industries	Public administration
	42	43	44	45	46	47	48	49	50	51	52	53	54	55	56
CALIFORNIA—Cont'd															
Azusa city	2.0	22.5	6.7	23.6	17.7	28.0	0.5	9.9	20.3	0.5	25.8	16.8	3.7	49.8	3.3
Bakersfield city	2.6	19.9	11.2	32.0	17.6	26.2	3.0	9.7	11.6	7.8	12.0	16.3	5.1	52.0	6.8
Baldwin Park city	1.9	24.0	4.5	15.0	18.1	26.4	0.3	10.7	29.5	0.3	29.6	16.6	6.0	45.3	2.3
Bell city	2.8	22.0	3.1	12.5	15.5	24.5	0.6	11.3	35.7	0.4	34.6	19.5	5.3	38.0	2.2
Bellflower city	2.0	20.3	9.5	24.4	15.7	31.3	0.1	10.3	18.2	0.2	22.8	17.8	7.3	48.4	3.5
Bell Gardens city	1.6	26.5	2.3	8.9	16.7	24.9	1.2	9.8	38.5	0.3	35.7	19.7	6.0	36.8	1.5
Belmont city	3.3	13.9	10.8	54.4	7.0	26.6	0.0	6.1	5.9	0.3	18.4	15.0	5.8	56.9	3.8
Benicia city	4.2	15.8	14.4	45.7	12.6	26.0	0.3	7.1	8.3	0.4	17.7	13.4	5.5	57.0	6.0
Berkeley city	6.8	14.9	6.4	61.4	9.6	20.3	0.1	3.6	5.0	0.1	7.8	8.9	2.7	76.7	3.8
Beverly Hills city	8.0	17.6	7.4	60.0	7.6	27.9	0.1	1.6	2.8	0.1	7.9	16.4	1.7	72.1	1.7
Brea city	2.9	14.7	10.7	44.2	10.7	31.0	0.0	4.9	9.1	0.2	20.8	16.7	3.5	54.4	4.4
Buena Park city	2.0	18.0	9.0	29.0	13.6	30.8	0.2	9.4	17.0	0.2	25.1	17.5	5.2	49.2	2.9
Burbank city	4.0	18.2	8.8	41.1	11.7	30.7	0.1	8.0	9.0	0.2	14.3	13.5	3.8	64.7	3.4
Burlingame city	4.7	14.1	8.6	52.4	10.7	26.6	0.0	5.5	4.8	0.1	13.6	15.2	6.8	61.6	2.7
Calexico city	3.1	19.2	3.1	19.0	18.8	32.5	11.7	6.9	11.2	12.4	8.6	24.1	5.1	42.2	7.7
Camarillo city	4.6	16.0	16.1	42.7	12.6	27.6	0.6	8.1	8.4	1.5	20.6	14.7	2.5	52.2	8.5
Campbell city	3.0	15.2	9.4	50.3	10.3	24.9	0.0	6.4	8.0	0.2	29.3	13.6	3.3	51.4	2.3
Carlsbad city	8.3	13.8	14.0	49.2	11.7	27.9	0.3	5.6	5.3	0.3	17.7	15.0	3.2	60.2	3.5
Carson city	1.8	22.5	9.8	26.8	14.4	31.0	0.2	7.7	20.0	0.4	22.7	15.7	9.5	47.7	4.1
Cathedral City city	3.2	23.8	11.3	22.0	30.5	25.4	0.3	13.1	8.7	0.5	14.6	14.5	4.1	63.5	2.8
Ceres city	2.3	23.2	11.2	19.1	17.7	26.1	2.2	12.3	22.7	2.5	26.5	17.8	5.9	42.7	4.6
Cerritos city	2.5	13.9	8.3	48.1	8.3	31.3	0.0	4.5	7.7	0.1	18.7	18.7	6.5	51.3	4.6
Chico city	3.8	16.0	9.1	35.3	19.5	28.5	1.3	6.3	9.0	2.3	10.2	18.2	2.5	63.3	3.4
Chino city	2.8	16.3	9.2	28.5	13.5	29.4	0.9	9.4	18.4	1.4	24.3	17.5	7.1	45.1	4.6
Chino Hills city	3.3	11.6	8.4	45.0	10.1	29.5	0.1	6.4	8.8	0.3	19.2	18.1	5.8	50.0	6.6
Chula Vista city	3.0	19.3	13.9	33.0	16.9	29.8	0.2	9.7	10.4	0.2	17.1	15.7	4.3	53.9	8.8
Citrus Heights city	3.1	20.1	16.2	29.0	14.6	33.5	0.1	12.8	10.2	0.2	15.7	19.7	4.5	51.9	7.8
Claremont city	4.9	15.2	11.2	57.4	10.4	22.1	0.1	4.8	5.2	0.3	11.8	8.5	2.8	72.8	3.8
Clovis city	2.3	18.9	12.5	35.2	14.6	29.6	1.2	9.4	10.0	2.0	14.5	17.7	5.2	52.5	8.1
Colton city	2.3	19.2	9.6	22.2	17.1	26.9	0.4	11.4	22.0	0.6	19.9	18.0	7.5	49.2	4.9
Compton city	2.0	23.6	6.4	15.0	17.9	25.1	0.3	9.2	32.4	0.2	28.7	15.6	8.0	43.9	3.6
Concord city	3.2	18.9	11.2	34.0	17.8	27.9	0.1	10.9	9.3	0.3	15.5	15.9	4.9	59.6	3.8
Corona city	3.4	15.6	9.6	32.8	12.7	29.6	0.3	9.3	15.4	0.5	25.7	16.8	5.3	46.0	5.6
Costa Mesa city	3.7	16.1	8.6	35.9	16.9	29.8	0.3	7.7	9.3	0.3	19.6	16.5	2.8	60.4	1.5
Covina city	2.3	19.0	10.3	30.5	14.3	31.8	0.0	9.4	13.9	0.1	19.8	16.9	6.0	52.4	4.8
Culver City city	4.4	18.7	9.7	49.8	11.5	27.3	0.0	5.4	6.0	0.1	10.8	12.3	4.9	69.2	2.7
Cupertino city	4.1	10.0	8.2	71.0	4.2	17.8	0.2	2.4	4.3	0.3	35.9	11.2	1.6	49.5	1.5
Cypress city	2.7	14.7	12.6	42.2	11.0	29.0	0.1	8.1	9.7	0.3	22.3	15.8	5.1	53.0	3.7
Daly City city	1.5	21.2	7.1	29.4	16.9	34.8	0.3	7.0	11.6	0.4	12.6	17.1	9.9	55.8	4.2
Dana Point city	6.1	15.1	12.3	42.5	14.5	28.9	0.1	7.8	6.2	0.3	18.4	17.2	3.4	58.1	2.6
Danville town	6.6	11.1	11.4	58.1	5.7	28.5	0.1	4.0	3.6	0.5	16.8	16.5	3.0	60.7	2.6
Davis city	3.9	9.0	6.3	60.5	11.2	20.5	0.4	2.7	4.7	0.7	6.0	9.7	2.5	73.7	7.4
Delano city	1.6	24.2	5.8	15.7	15.2	19.9	25.8	4.9	18.6	30.3	9.3	17.5	5.0	31.8	6.2
Diamond Bar city	3.0	13.2	7.4	47.4	7.7	32.1	0.1	5.1	7.5	0.3	17.7	20.2	5.0	52.3	4.6
Downey city	2.6	20.5	7.9	28.7	12.4	33.3	0.0	8.8	16.7	0.1	24.1	18.3	5.8	47.3	4.4
Dublin city	3.2	12.7	9.9	46.7	10.5	28.7	0.1	7.2	6.8	0.3	17.3	10.6	4.5	55.8	3.5
East Palo Alto city	2.0	22.1	5.0	18.2	31.9	23.2	0.3	11.9	14.5	0.3	20.4	13.7	3.7	60.1	1.9
El Cajon city	2.7	21.9	14.5	25.4	17.9	32.4	0.1	12.7	11.5	0.2	18.2	17.5	4.3	54.5	5.3
El Centro city	3.5	20.9	9.1	28.5	21.0	25.3	6.7	8.2	10.4	8.1	9.3	17.1	6.1	47.0	12.4
El Monte city	1.7	22.1	4.5	15.4	16.2	22.6	0.6	11.3	33.8	0.7	36.1	16.3	4.6	40.1	2.3
Encinitas city	7.8	13.9	10.0	50.7	13.5	24.5	0.3	6.3	4.7	0.8	15.4	15.0	2.8	63.3	2.7
Escondido city	3.4	19.9	12.6	27.9	18.7	25.9	1.5	11.6	14.3	1.9	23.9	16.5	3.4	51.1	3.2
Eureka city	5.5	27.5	15.9	24.3	24.1	28.0	1.7	9.2	12.7	3.7	12.1	17.5	3.9	57.0	5.7
Fairfield city	2.7	19.7	17.5	29.3	17.0	28.5	0.4	10.9	13.9	0.7	18.5	15.9	6.3	50.3	8.3
Folsom city	5.6	15.3	13.4	51.9	10.9	26.3	0.7	4.9	5.3	1.2	19.1	14.4	3.5	50.9	10.9
Fontana city	2.1	19.0	7.8	20.8	14.5	28.4	0.3	11.8	24.2	0.4	25.5	19.5	8.5	41.9	4.2
Foster City city	3.6	11.6	9.3	61.9	6.1	24.7	0.0	3.6	3.6	0.1	16.6	16.5	5.7	58.6	2.5
Fountain Valley city	3.9	15.0	10.4	43.6	10.2	30.8	0.0	6.4	8.9	0.1	22.0	17.3	3.5	53.2	4.0
Fremont city	2.7	14.2	8.2	49.8	7.8	24.7	0.1	6.3	11.3	0.2	30.9	15.7	4.1	46.6	2.5
Fresno city	2.9	22.1	9.9	30.4	17.4	28.4	2.8	8.0	12.9	3.6	13.4	16.3	4.3	55.4	7.0
Fullerton city	2.4	16.6	9.8	37.0	12.7	29.5	0.2	6.8	13.7	0.2	23.0	17.1	4.2	52.8	2.6
Gardena city	1.9	20.1	9.7	27.9	15.9	29.8	0.2	7.3	18.8	0.3	22.1	17.1	9.0	47.0	4.4
Garden Grove city	1.9	21.9	7.8	25.0	15.7	26.5	0.3	10.4	22.1	0.4	30.0	15.6	4.0	47.4	2.7
Gilroy city	2.6	17.2	9.2	28.6	14.2	28.1	3.2	10.9	15.0	3.5	26.3	20.2	3.6	42.4	4.0
Glendale city	3.0	23.3	6.0	40.5	12.3	30.4	0.1	6.4	10.3	0.2	15.0	15.6	3.8	62.1	3.4
Glendora city	3.1	16.9	11.4	39.9	12.3	28.7	0.2	8.9	9.9	0.2	20.7	15.6	4.5	54.5	4.4
Hanford city	1.9	20.1	13.8	30.0	22.1	23.1	3.9	7.9	13.0	6.9	13.9	14.2	3.4	47.5	14.1
Hawthorne city	1.6	21.7	7.3	23.3	19.4	33.0	0.2	7.5	16.7	0.2	16.6	14.0	10.8	53.9	4.5
Hayward city	1.9	22.8	9.7	26.7	13.5	30.0	0.2	10.9	18.7	0.2	23.9	19.0	7.9	45.9	3.1
Hemet city	3.1	29.5	19.7	22.7	21.2	26.6	1.4	12.0	16.2	1.9	18.3	19.2	4.8	52.0	3.7
Hesperia city	4.1	20.7	14.7	20.9	15.2	26.2	0.2	16.8	20.7	0.7	22.4	17.9	9.2	44.5	5.4

City	Median household income	Median family income: All families	Median family income: Families with children: Married-couple	Median family income: Families with children: Male householder	Median family income: Families with children: Female householder	Median nonfamily household income	Median income for full-year, full-time workers: Men	Median income for full-year, full-time workers: Women	Per capita income	Households by source of income (percent): With earnings	Households by source of income (percent): With interest, dividend, or rental income	Households by source of income (percent): With Social Security income	Households by source of income (percent): With public assistance income	Households by source of income (percent): With retirement income	Households with income over $100,000 (percent)	+/– U.S. percent for income over $100,000	Households with income below poverty (percent)	Families with children with income below poverty (percent)
	57	58	59	60	61	62	63	64	65	66	67	68	69	70	71	72	73	74
CALIFORNIA—Cont'd																		
Azusa city	39 191	40 918	47 368	25 234	20 925	28 015	31 248	27 344	13 412	84.8	22.0	18.1	6.3	13.0	8.0	-4.3	15.3	19.4
Bakersfield city	39 982	45 556	53 008	25 549	15 864	24 939	40 175	28 202	17 678	81.7	27.8	21.5	6.7	13.6	10.0	-2.3	15.5	20.1
Baldwin Park city	41 629	41 256	42 953	24 926	17 460	19 030	27 338	22 463	11 562	89.2	16.7	19.4	9.4	10.6	7.9	-4.4	16.3	18.7
Bell city	29 946	30 504	32 524	25 677	14 789	16 138	22 883	17 214	9 905	87.2	10.7	14.0	8.4	8.6	3.8	-8.5	21.2	26.4
Bellflower city	39 362	42 822	46 952	33 036	22 561	25 532	33 877	28 782	15 982	84.2	21.9	19.9	6.6	11.9	8.1	-4.2	13.4	16.4
Bell Gardens city	30 597	30 419	31 745	24 688	15 812	14 902	21 225	17 169	8 415	89.4	9.5	10.1	14.0	7.2	3.8	-8.5	25.2	29.0
Belmont city	80 905	95 722	113 855	64 333	42 098	48 078	65 092	48 185	42 812	85.3	59.1	21.4	0.7	17.9	38.7	26.4	3.9	2.4
Benicia city	67 617	77 974	95 138	51 063	35 197	41 460	60 524	40 951	31 226	86.5	45.8	20.7	1.4	18.5	28.1	15.8	4.2	4.6
Berkeley city	44 485	70 434	93 198	41 912	30 259	29 115	51 914	42 224	30 477	82.9	50.5	18.1	2.3	13.7	20.8	8.5	18.3	11.6
Beverly Hills city	70 945	102 611	120 987	83 945	35 294	49 394	81 790	48 267	65 507	80.0	49.9	26.2	1.8	9.2	37.9	25.6	8.6	9.9
Brea city	59 759	68 423	80 939	41 591	40 038	36 465	51 322	36 423	26 307	85.0	43.1	22.1	1.6	17.1	21.9	9.6	5.1	5.2
Buena Park city	50 336	52 327	60 074	31 893	28 581	31 503	38 351	30 809	18 031	87.7	27.9	20.9	3.6	14.1	13.1	0.8	9.2	10.8
Burbank city	47 467	56 767	62 708	37 614	29 128	35 347	42 480	36 192	25 713	82.4	35.6	20.8	3.8	13.2	15.1	2.8	9.6	12.0
Burlingame city	68 526	91 309	111 576	78 492	40 250	46 421	60 769	49 825	43 565	83.2	52.7	23.3	1.2	15.0	32.1	19.8	5.1	4.8
Calexico city	28 929	30 277	34 820	20 083	16 282	9 979	29 192	19 789	9 981	83.2	13.5	32.2	14.8	10.0	6.3	-6.0	23.5	26.8
Camarillo city	62 457	72 676	78 709	37 349	36 109	34 611	53 722	37 911	28 635	76.9	50.9	31.7	1.5	24.1	24.5	12.2	4.7	5.4
Campbell city	67 214	78 663	93 530	38 629	40 058	51 201	55 108	45 043	34 441	88.0	42.6	17.7	1.6	11.8	28.0	15.7	4.8	4.3
Carlsbad city	65 145	77 151	93 336	45 143	32 418	41 875	58 825	40 569	34 863	82.1	47.9	24.2	1.3	17.4	28.4	16.1	5.3	6.0
Carson city	52 284	54 886	60 351	36 333	36 043	27 078	34 715	31 524	17 107	85.2	22.9	24.8	5.5	19.8	13.7	1.4	8.4	9.3
Cathedral City city	38 887	42 461	46 365	28 879	29 335	26 505	30 067	26 162	16 215	78.9	25.4	28.5	3.7	14.8	9.3	-3.0	11.5	13.1
Ceres city	40 736	43 587	51 512	34 000	17 886	22 078	35 886	25 153	14 420	83.0	23.8	22.7	7.1	14.7	6.8	-5.5	12.5	12.8
Cerritos city	73 030	76 944	81 093	58 241	45 403	40 236	50 984	38 530	25 249	90.7	47.1	18.4	2.6	15.2	29.9	17.6	4.8	4.6
Chico city	29 359	43 077	53 014	23 125	17 949	19 280	36 646	26 926	16 970	80.4	30.5	19.2	5.2	13.0	6.7	-5.6	25.6	17.7
Chino city	55 401	59 638	66 902	39 318	28 571	28 385	36 175	30 730	17 574	89.0	26.4	17.8	3.7	12.1	16.4	4.1	7.3	7.9
Chino Hills city	78 374	81 794	85 756	48 350	37 391	54 186	56 399	39 197	26 182	94.8	38.7	9.5	1.0	9.5	32.7	20.4	4.4	4.7
Chula Vista city	44 861	50 136	58 186	31 371	24 921	26 571	38 603	29 281	18 556	82.3	30.9	24.1	3.8	20.2	11.8	-0.5	9.8	11.6
Citrus Heights city	43 859	51 207	58 109	35 378	25 881	30 460	39 436	30 145	20 744	80.5	32.8	26.0	4.0	21.6	8.4	-3.9	7.1	8.4
Claremont city	65 910	78 389	83 108	68 214	31 791	37 610	60 191	38 691	28 843	80.1	53.4	28.2	2.3	22.7	27.5	15.2	7.2	9.6
Clovis city	42 283	50 859	62 289	35 615	21 430	23 207	40 697	29 437	18 690	83.9	31.9	21.5	4.2	14.9	10.3	-2.0	9.7	10.5
Colton city	35 777	37 911	45 181	22 569	17 486	24 958	32 424	25 504	13 460	85.6	15.5	17.1	7.1	12.2	6.2	-6.1	17.9	21.6
Compton city	31 819	33 021	36 280	25 977	16 995	17 038	23 590	25 318	10 389	78.7	11.2	23.3	14.9	16.6	5.7	-6.6	26.0	30.2
Concord city	55 597	62 093	71 528	38 810	31 787	36 393	46 600	35 751	24 727	84.8	39.8	21.5	3.2	16.8	18.1	5.8	6.8	7.4
Corona city	59 615	63 505	70 944	35 031	28 424	39 505	45 606	32 280	21 001	91.5	27.5	14.7	2.4	10.9	17.6	5.3	7.2	7.5
Costa Mesa city	50 732	55 456	58 121	33 125	27 420	39 786	39 629	33 586	23 342	88.2	34.5	17.2	2.3	10.6	16.0	3.7	9.3	12.4
Covina city	48 474	55 111	65 788	34 107	20 960	27 620	41 481	33 144	20 231	83.7	31.1	23.0	4.0	15.1	13.6	1.3	10.6	12.9
Culver City city	51 792	61 451	74 057	39 000	36 391	41 112	48 601	42 456	29 025	84.9	45.7	22.5	2.3	15.2	18.7	6.4	6.8	8.3
Cupertino city	100 411	109 455	122 216	78 267	60 492	62 413	93 749	60 435	44 749	85.8	63.7	18.5	1.0	14.0	50.3	38.0	4.7	4.0
Cypress city	64 377	70 060	78 153	38 542	36 373	38 004	52 247	37 467	25 798	85.8	44.7	22.2	2.7	17.6	24.5	12.2	5.6	6.2
Daly City city	62 310	68 365	74 889	34 653	36 621	33 801	38 997	32 993	21 900	86.6	38.9	25.0	2.8	16.8	22.3	10.0	6.7	5.7
Dana Point city	63 043	73 373	78 639	52 121	37 974	50 195	53 609	39 783	37 938	83.9	43.8	21.7	1.0	15.5	28.5	16.2	6.0	5.3
Danville town	114 064	125 867	142 508	44 479	56 900	61 597	100 001	56 078	50 773	88.3	63.9	19.1	0.5	16.0	59.3	47.0	1.8	1.5
Davis city	42 454	74 051	83 743	50 417	33 208	21 819	52 667	36 861	22 937	88.0	50.1	12.3	1.1	11.8	18.9	6.6	22.6	6.9
Delano city	28 143	29 026	32 715	15 969	12 319	11 695	40 015	21 745	11 068	83.9	11.7	22.4	10.1	11.4	5.1	-7.2	27.5	31.0
Diamond Bar city	68 871	71 911	78 985	49 828	36 138	42 402	51 960	38 243	25 472	90.7	43.5	14.1	2.0	10.5	28.0	15.7	6.3	5.2
Downey city	45 667	50 017	55 747	33 468	22 275	28 045	36 765	29 677	18 197	83.0	28.4	23.8	4.1	14.7	12.5	0.2	9.3	12.4
Dublin city	77 283	83 123	94 958	60 481	43 102	61 854	56 829	42 349	29 451	94.1	43.7	12.4	1.7	11.2	32.5	20.2	2.3	2.8
East Palo Alto city	45 006	44 342	50 663	29 219	32 795	28 867	27 003	27 331	13 774	89.7	19.8	19.7	5.0	11.5	12.9	0.6	13.9	15.3
El Cajon city	35 566	40 045	47 049	25 457	19 538	25 256	33 641	25 985	16 698	80.3	25.6	22.6	6.9	15.6	7.3	-5.0	14.1	19.6
El Centro city	33 161	36 910	42 727	30 000	13 539	21 066	37 395	25 015	13 874	81.1	19.0	25.5	11.2	13.8	7.5	-4.8	20.5	25.5
El Monte city	32 439	32 402	33 843	23 194	16 394	16 692	22 137	20 241	10 316	85.9	17.0	16.9	12.1	9.0	6.3	-6.0	23.1	28.1
Encinitas city	63 954	78 104	92 514	40 536	34 375	43 325	52 368	39 728	34 336	86.9	49.6	18.1	1.1	13.5	28.7	16.4	5.8	5.4
Escondido city	42 567	48 456	52 569	27 384	23 688	26 073	33 915	28 656	18 241	80.9	31.4	25.5	3.9	17.6	11.9	-0.4	10.3	14.1
Eureka city	25 849	33 438	40 860	20 493	12 413	17 367	30 187	22 844	16 174	71.8	32.1	29.0	9.6	17.4	4.4	-7.9	21.1	26.4
Fairfield city	51 151	55 503	62 166	27 649	24 607	32 510	40 402	31 415	20 617	85.5	32.0	19.6	4.3	21.1	14.7	2.4	8.3	10.3
Folsom city	73 175	82 448	93 336	42 019	39 167	43 584	61 503	43 483	30 210	86.5	48.3	17.8	1.9	15.4	30.4	18.1	3.9	3.4
Fontana city	45 782	46 957	51 214	28 286	18 238	24 966	36 461	26 672	14 208	89.2	15.8	14.1	6.8	9.9	8.8	-3.5	12.5	15.0
Foster City city	95 279	106 099	118 983	100 495	54 821	66 042	81 207	52 116	45 754	89.5	56.3	16.5	0.9	13.3	47.2	34.9	2.7	1.4
Fountain Valley city	69 734	74 502	83 672	52 321	35 362	41 421	51 290	37 022	26 521	87.6	49.2	22.9	2.6	17.8	28.6	16.3	3.5	3.8
Fremont city	76 579	82 199	93 037	52 147	42 184	52 792	60 628	41 415	31 411	89.8	45.9	15.8	2.5	12.1	33.5	21.2	4.5	4.6
Fresno city	32 236	35 892	42 100	21 383	15 516	22 226	33 295	27 301	15 010	79.5	24.5	21.5	10.7	13.4	7.6	-4.7	20.7	28.2
Fullerton city	50 269	57 345	62 023	34 159	25 933	33 052	41 495	32 339	23 370	85.0	38.4	21.5	2.8	15.3	17.4	5.1	9.8	12.1
Gardena city	38 988	44 906	51 968	24 934	19 736	24 626	34 467	30 151	17 263	80.2	25.7	22.5	6.6	14.0	8.8	-3.5	14.8	18.0
Garden Grove city	47 754	49 697	51 403	31 982	24 589	30 739	34 501	27 185	16 209	85.7	28.0	20.1	5.9	14.2	12.5	0.2	11.5	14.2
Gilroy city	62 135	65 330	75 031	41 157	27 013	40 254	46 185	35 643	22 071	88.8	31.2	17.5	4.2	13.7	23.0	10.7	7.5	10.0
Glendale city	41 805	47 633	50 762	37 059	27 345	30 433	40 555	34 869	22 227	80.4	30.9	20.0	8.5	11.1	14.8	2.5	13.8	18.6
Glendora city	60 013	66 674	73 835	46 611	35 154	31 820	50 638	35 769	25 993	85.2	40.2	24.3	2.2	17.2	21.0	8.7	5.4	5.9
Hanford city	37 582	41 395	50 324	31 250	16 532	23 440	38 974	27 000	17 504	80.2	26.0	24.7	8.0	17.2	8.7	-3.6	14.0	20.5
Hawthorne city	31 887	35 149	41 782	23 140	20 329	25 110	30 020	28 094	15 022	86.2	16.3	13.3	8.2	9.6	6.2	-6.1	18.4	22.8
Hayward city	51 177	54 712	62 230	35 905	29 263	35 668	38 697	31 881	19 695	84.4	30.6	22.0	4.3	17.2	14.3	2.0	8.5	9.7
Hemet city	26 839	33 579	43 108	22 371	14 243	17 855	31 655	24 644	16 226	52.2	34.9	51.3	4.8	28.3	3.3	-9.0	13.6	23.6
Hesperia city	40 201	43 004	50 656	27 630	18 763	20 940	40 504	26 325	15 487	77.7	24.0	29.3	7.9	20.1	6.6	-5.7	12.3	15.8

Table B-5. Cities — Education, Labor Force, and Income

STATE Place code	City	High school graduates			College graduates		College graduates (percent)				
		Total population 25 years and over	Percent with a high school diploma or less	Percent with a high school diploma or more	Percent with a bachelor's degree or more	+/- U.S. percent with bachelor's degree or more	Non-Hispanic White	Black or African American	American Indian and Alaska Native	Asian, Hawaiian, and Pacific Islander	Hispanic or Latino[1]
		1	2	3	4	5	6	7	8	9	10
	CALIFORNIA—Cont'd										
06 33588	Highland city	24 657	51.6	72.0	16.1	-8.3	20.2	11.3	17.1	34.6	6.9
06 34120	Hollister city	19 303	51.6	72.3	15.0	-9.4	24.5	10.7	13.8	27.2	5.6
06 36000	Huntington Beach city	131 982	26.7	89.6	36.0	11.6	37.1	32.3	22.9	48.7	17.9
06 36056	Huntington Park city	31 390	82.7	32.2	4.7	-19.7	15.0	23.6	5.5	28.4	3.8
06 36294	Imperial Beach city	15 320	50.1	77.0	11.7	-12.7	12.9	12.6	10.2	21.4	6.2
06 36448	Indio city	26 303	67.5	55.7	8.6	-15.8	17.7	3.8	5.2	25.7	4.2
06 36546	Inglewood city	64 589	56.4	63.7	13.3	-11.1	17.7	19.5	15.0	27.0	3.7
06 36770	Irvine city	88 960	15.1	95.3	58.4	34.0	57.9	35.7	25.5	66.8	38.6
06 39220	Laguna Hills city	21 025	25.0	91.0	39.3	14.9	40.9	51.9	0.0	55.2	18.7
06 39248	Laguna Niguel city	41 898	17.4	95.2	47.8	23.4	49.2	36.0	16.8	57.9	26.9
06 39290	La Habra city	36 104	49.9	73.4	18.2	-6.2	22.7	28.5	11.5	52.1	6.7
06 39486	Lake Elsinore city	16 007	50.2	71.3	8.6	-15.8	10.6	10.3	7.3	21.8	4.1
06 39496	Lake Forest city	38 060	28.4	88.7	33.9	9.5	36.7	33.4	6.5	44.5	12.5
06 39892	Lakewood city	51 138	39.3	85.1	20.7	-3.7	18.7	21.3	16.1	40.4	11.8
06 40004	La Mesa city	38 412	31.4	89.6	27.6	3.2	29.0	18.1	17.6	37.2	18.0
06 40032	La Mirada city	29 489	40.1	84.5	25.2	0.8	22.9	34.4	25.9	55.3	12.5
06 40130	Lancaster city	69 282	47.7	78.3	15.8	-8.6	18.4	12.3	6.4	35.4	6.1
06 40340	La Puente city	22 423	72.8	49.7	7.8	-16.6	10.6	17.5	2.9	34.1	4.0
06 40830	La Verne city	20 448	30.8	88.7	31.6	7.2	33.0	40.7	0.0	61.8	14.6
06 40886	Lawndale city	18 353	62.7	63.4	12.5	-11.9	14.6	20.4	17.7	27.1	6.0
06 41992	Livermore city	47 453	30.4	89.6	31.6	7.2	33.7	27.5	13.4	42.6	14.0
06 42202	Lodi city	35 047	52.6	72.9	15.6	-8.8	18.5	0.0	3.8	21.4	5.1
06 42524	Lompoc city	24 975	50.7	74.4	13.8	-10.6	18.3	8.9	8.5	23.7	4.4
06 43000	Long Beach city	277 410	46.2	72.7	23.9	-0.5	36.4	13.8	14.9	26.9	8.1
06 43280	Los Altos city	20 128	10.3	97.2	71.3	46.9	70.5	48.3	52.5	77.6	64.4
06 44000	Los Angeles city	2 308 887	50.0	66.6	25.5	1.1	42.6	17.1	11.9	42.0	6.1
06 44028	Los Banos city	14 681	58.3	69.8	9.9	-14.5	15.1	5.9	4.8	13.2	3.5
06 44112	Los Gatos town	21 403	13.8	96.0	58.9	34.5	59.6	37.0	17.6	68.8	36.9
06 44574	Lynwood city	34 020	80.6	79.5	4.5	-19.9	13.1	11.5	2.8	15.7	2.1
06 45022	Madera city	22 755	70.2	52.8	9.3	-15.1	17.5	11.0	2.7	31.0	0.4
06 45400	Manhattan Beach city	25 067	11.3	96.8	67.6	43.2	68.6	32.4	29.9	68.4	53.0
06 45484	Manteca city	29 506	53.9	78.3	11.0	-13.4	12.0	11.8	6.7	26.4	4.6
06 45778	Marina city	16 307	53.8	71.8	14.3	-10.1	21.0	6.0	13.2	16.1	5.4
06 46114	Martinez city	25 201	29.2	91.1	32.1	7.7	32.3	20.8	29.7	52.1	17.4
06 46492	Maywood city	13 756	86.8	29.6	2.3	-22.1	2.2	0.0	8.0	41.4	2.1
06 46870	Menlo Park city	22 454	20.8	89.0	61.7	37.3	72.1	9.3	83.8	66.6	21.8
06 46898	Merced city	34 422	54.0	68.5	13.6	-10.8	22.4	10.9	13.7	8.8	3.2
06 47766	Milpitas city	41 089	34.1	83.2	36.5	12.1	28.7	19.0	13.9	48.2	10.3
06 48256	Mission Viejo city	61 480	22.1	93.8	41.2	16.8	42.3	46.5	15.2	55.3	20.3
06 48354	Modesto city	114 658	49.8	75.0	16.5	-7.9	19.8	14.3	5.5	19.2	0.0
06 48648	Monrovia city	23 634	41.6	78.0	25.1	0.7	32.1	10.7	5.1	46.6	10.1
06 48788	Montclair city	18 765	62.7	60.4	9.6	-14.8	13.6	13.9	0.0	21.7	4.2
06 48816	Montebello city	37 862	61.8	62.1	14.3	-10.1	17.6	24.2	3.3	44.0	7.6
06 48872	Monterey city	20 809	24.2	91.6	46.2	21.8	49.0	43.6	20.6	48.8	22.3
06 48914	Monterey Park city	42 271	48.8	71.6	25.1	0.7	29.3	16.3	11.1	31.0	8.4
06 49138	Moorpark city	17 947	31.7	84.7	34.2	9.8	39.7	45.5	32.5	63.4	9.8
06 49270	Moreno Valley city	74 976	50.2	74.5	14.0	-10.4	16.5	15.4	8.6	36.2	5.8
06 49278	Morgan Hill city	20 658	30.8	86.8	33.5	9.1	39.2	28.1	4.9	49.1	11.0
06 49670	Mountain View city	52 353	22.8	89.0	55.3	30.9	60.5	44.0	23.6	67.4	17.9
06 50076	Murrieta city	26 664	34.2	90.0	23.0	-1.4	23.6	27.7	17.1	42.7	13.2
06 50258	Napa city	48 000	41.9	79.2	23.3	-1.1	27.3	16.8	11.4	41.1	6.7
06 50398	National City city	30 325	66.6	57.2	9.0	-15.4	10.3	16.1	0.0	18.6	3.7
06 50916	Newark city	26 582	44.0	79.2	24.2	-0.2	22.9	27.7	6.7	42.6	7.4
06 51182	Newport Beach city	54 755	12.9	96.7	58.5	34.1	59.1	49.3	20.6	64.3	43.7
06 52526	Norwalk city	59 257	63.5	63.0	10.6	-13.8	9.4	14.9	5.2	37.9	3.9
06 52582	Novato city	33 603	27.4	90.5	37.0	12.6	39.1	27.2	31.4	44.0	17.3
06 53000	Oakland city	261 402	43.7	73.9	30.9	6.5	61.9	16.4	16.3	24.9	10.4
06 53070	Oakley city	14 827	45.6	84.8	13.7	-10.7	13.9	24.5	0.0	32.7	7.8
06 53322	Oceanside city	100 688	41.4	80.8	22.2	-2.2	28.3	13.9	23.0	23.0	7.4
06 53896	Ontario city	85 671	61.1	62.5	10.5	-13.9	14.5	16.4	8.6	32.6	4.5
06 53980	Orange city	82 138	39.2	80.4	28.0	3.6	33.0	25.5	5.4	47.7	7.9
06 54652	Oxnard city	96 399	60.0	59.5	13.7	-10.7	26.1	19.2	13.4	29.8	4.5
06 54806	Pacifica city	26 438	29.9	91.5	33.8	9.4	34.3	42.6	12.6	43.7	18.5
06 55156	Palmdale city	63 006	50.9	74.0	13.3	-11.1	16.4	12.2	12.6	39.1	4.7
06 55184	Palm Desert city	31 802	30.7	88.9	31.4	7.0	34.5	36.3	14.8	41.4	8.1
06 55254	Palm Springs city	32 777	40.1	81.7	26.6	2.2	30.9	10.2	9.2	31.7	6.7
06 55282	Palo Alto city	43 566	9.4	96.2	74.4	50.0	76.1	49.4	30.0	79.0	41.0
06 55520	Paradise town	19 368	41.1	85.7	19.4	-5.0	19.9	57.9	5.8	31.0	8.2
06 55618	Paramount city	28 128	70.7	50.0	7.0	-17.4	10.4	13.9	11.3	23.3	3.4
06 56000	Pasadena city	90 934	33.9	79.5	41.3	16.9	58.7	21.2	10.0	62.6	12.7
06 56700	Perris city	18 332	65.1	61.0	6.6	-17.8	7.6	11.0	1.7	19.3	3.6

[1] Hispanic or Latino persons may be of any race.

City	School enrollment			Population 16 to 19 years				Employment status, 2000			Work status in 1999 of the population 16 years and over		
											Worked in 1999		
	Grades kindergarten through 12	College or graduate school	Percent private	Number	Percent in armed forces	Percent high school graduates	Percent not enrolled, not grads, not in armed forces, not employed	Total population 16 years and over	Percent in labor force	Unemployment rate	Full-time	Part-time	Did not work in 1999
	11	12	13	14	15	16	17	18	19	20	21	22	23
CALIFORNIA—Cont'd													
Highland city	12 317	2 898	9.1	2 936	0.0	8.1	6.7	30 267	63.0	10.4	52.4	13.2	34.4
Hollister city	8 718	1 778	8.4	1 866	0.0	16.0	3.9	23 561	69.3	7.4	62.7	13.8	23.5
Huntington Beach city	31 435	17 604	14.3	8 459	0.0	7.7	2.5	152 059	70.5	3.9	59.2	15.8	25.0
Huntington Park city	16 874	2 737	4.6	4 269	0.0	9.2	10.4	41 519	55.4	11.8	52.5	11.1	36.4
Imperial Beach city	5 877	1 979	8.1	1 887	1.9	21.4	10.6	19 947	66.2	10.9	54.9	14.6	30.5
Indio city	12 778	1 798	4.1	3 297	0.0	14.0	10.9	33 252	58.3	8.2	53.6	11.4	35.0
Inglewood city	27 450	7 796	13.6	6 490	0.1	8.7	8.1	79 516	59.4	10.2	52.9	12.2	35.0
Irvine city	25 786	25 750	9.5	11 487	0.0	3.4	0.7	113 539	68.5	5.1	54.2	20.0	25.8
Laguna Hills city	6 498	2 342	13.2	1 707	0.0	6.6	1.0	24 071	65.6	4.5	55.0	15.3	29.8
Laguna Niguel city	11 893	4 356	16.4	2 381	0.0	4.3	1.0	46 796	70.6	3.7	60.2	15.6	24.2
La Habra city	12 918	4 167	11.2	3 065	0.0	10.7	7.2	43 379	64.3	6.5	55.9	13.1	31.0
Lake Elsinore city	7 898	1 245	6.2	1 853	0.4	16.2	6.4	19 701	62.3	7.1	53.1	12.8	34.1
Lake Forest city	11 791	4 221	12.2	3 220	0.0	9.4	1.6	44 638	72.6	3.3	61.3	16.2	22.5
Lakewood city	16 419	6 853	15.0	4 286	0.1	10.1	3.3	59 782	65.9	5.0	56.1	13.8	30.1
La Mesa city	7 756	6 318	12.6	2 167	0.9	11.6	1.9	44 882	65.5	4.8	52.7	16.1	31.2
La Mirada city	9 708	5 144	26.0	3 166	0.0	6.7	0.9	35 869	62.5	5.5	49.9	17.3	32.8
Lancaster city	29 771	7 562	12.8	7 719	0.0	12.6	9.4	84 383	58.2	11.1	48.8	13.3	37.9
La Puente city	10 756	2 280	6.7	2 820	0.0	10.4	8.7	28 637	57.9	9.2	52.4	11.2	36.4
La Verne city	6 730	2 948	23.2	2 194	0.0	7.5	1.0	24 649	66.7	5.1	53.0	16.8	30.2
Lawndale city	7 715	2 201	10.3	1 780	0.0	11.6	8.3	22 480	63.6	7.7	56.5	13.6	29.9
Livermore city	15 192	4 408	10.1	3 582	0.0	9.3	3.9	54 756	72.9	3.4	61.4	16.0	22.6
Lodi city	11 752	2 782	11.6	3 336	0.0	11.1	6.7	42 693	61.2	7.4	51.6	13.3	35.1
Lompoc city	9 549	2 220	4.8	2 351	0.0	10.4	7.5	30 088	57.2	9.1	47.7	13.3	39.0
Long Beach city	99 704	40 948	9.3	26 989	0.0	9.9	8.4	339 395	61.7	9.4	52.0	13.8	34.2
Los Altos city	4 952	1 334	23.2	937	0.0	2.6	1.8	21 693	59.7	1.8	51.5	14.5	34.0
Los Angeles city	750 743	287 532	16.3	202 241	0.1	7.1	8.8	2 809 852	60.2	9.3	51.9	14.1	34.0
Los Banos city	6 692	994	4.4	1 580	0.0	6.6	10.2	17 687	60.8	13.5	54.0	13.4	32.5
Los Gatos town	4 424	1 827	21.0	987	0.0	6.3	3.3	23 277	67.0	2.9	56.7	14.5	28.8
Lynwood city	20 703	3 123	5.8	5 004	0.0	11.9	10.4	45 775	52.7	12.9	52.8	9.7	37.5
Madera city	11 012	1 985	4.8	2 966	0.0	9.9	11.0	29 507	59.2	18.7	50.2	13.9	35.9
Manhattan Beach city	5 359	1 713	16.0	977	0.0	4.3	1.1	27 051	73.1	2.7	63.6	13.4	22.9
Manteca city	11 842	2 426	7.6	3 281	0.0	13.3	3.4	35 554	63.0	8.1	53.2	14.6	32.2
Marina city	4 271	2 495	10.8	1 428	0.0	5.3	7.2	20 197	51.9	8.1	57.0	14.1	28.9
Martinez city	6 294	2 147	16.5	2 043	0.0	11.4	3.1	29 099	68.6	3.8	59.1	15.2	25.7
Maywood city	7 614	1 245	3.7	1 955	0.0	10.0	7.9	18 538	56.9	11.4	54.5	10.3	35.2
Menlo Park city	4 629	1 879	26.6	1 004	0.0	3.0	4.5	24 761	64.0	2.6	56.4	12.6	31.0
Merced city	16 927	4 076	6.6	4 550	0.0	10.8	6.4	44 173	58.0	13.1	47.7	14.9	37.5
Milpitas city	11 435	5 330	16.3	3 254	0.0	12.2	4.5	48 753	64.6	3.7	64.3	10.7	25.0
Mission Viejo city	19 169	6 817	13.8	4 736	0.1	7.4	0.5	70 280	69.2	3.5	57.5	17.0	25.5
Modesto city	43 222	11 539	8.0	12 016	0.1	12.6	6.2	138 652	61.5	10.1	51.1	14.7	34.2
Monrovia city	7 562	2 467	16.5	1 711	0.0	8.9	6.2	27 504	65.8	6.9	55.7	14.9	29.4
Montclair city	8 222	1 906	7.8	2 367	0.0	12.6	8.9	23 453	58.7	9.0	50.8	13.5	35.6
Montebello city	13 864	4 905	12.9	3 514	0.0	7.5	6.0	45 994	54.5	8.7	47.7	13.0	39.3
Monterey city	3 577	3 275	24.2	1 866	45.9	52.5	1.2	25 340	69.7	3.1	57.5	16.8	25.7
Monterey Park city	10 156	5 778	15.0	2 798	0.5	4.7	5.1	48 754	52.9	5.8	44.3	13.5	42.2
Moorpark city	8 193	1 998	8.8	2 063	0.0	5.1	2.7	21 779	72.5	4.4	60.2	16.1	23.7
Moreno Valley city	40 913	9 471	8.1	10 898	0.1	12.1	4.6	95 754	64.6	8.5	54.1	14.1	31.8
Morgan Hill city	7 452	1 920	14.1	2 135	0.0	8.3	6.7	24 444	70.3	5.2	60.7	15.7	23.6
Mountain View city	8 439	6 068	24.2	2 047	0.0	11.5	4.7	58 994	71.8	2.8	65.5	11.5	23.0
Murrieta city	11 599	2 632	11.5	2 779	0.0	9.5	1.6	31 123	64.3	4.6	52.1	16.3	31.6
Napa city	14 322	4 293	11.8	3 735	0.0	9.6	4.1	55 931	64.4	4.5	53.7	15.4	30.9
National City city	13 054	3 082	5.3	4 002	11.5	19.4	7.3	39 841	57.2	9.3	49.6	13.0	37.4
Newark city	8 933	3 102	13.7	2 620	0.0	9.5	4.5	32 171	66.9	5.0	61.4	12.1	26.5
Newport Beach city	8 421	5 570	25.1	2 091	0.0	6.2	0.2	60 044	65.8	3.0	56.5	14.3	29.1
Norwalk city	25 286	6 941	9.7	6 612	0.0	10.9	8.4	73 541	58.3	8.3	52.9	11.8	35.3
Novato city	8 588	2 976	13.2	2 309	0.3	6.1	3.0	37 862	68.7	3.6	54.8	19.2	26.0
Oakland city	76 159	31 244	16.4	19 832	0.0	9.1	9.9	309 498	61.6	8.3	52.2	14.4	33.4
Oakley city	6 581	1 387	8.4	1 618	0.0	10.3	1.9	17 727	70.7	3.3	60.4	15.4	24.3
Oceanside city	32 386	10 227	8.8	8 417	1.1	14.2	6.3	120 983	63.2	5.4	54.4	13.6	32.0
Ontario city	39 938	8 314	7.1	10 602	0.4	12.6	8.4	108 520	63.2	8.9	55.9	12.3	31.8
Orange city	25 157	10 043	17.5	6 628	0.0	7.2	4.9	97 515	66.5	4.9	57.2	15.5	27.3
Oxnard city	40 175	9 822	7.1	10 962	0.2	9.7	8.5	122 231	63.1	7.4	57.0	11.9	31.2
Pacifica city	7 048	3 047	22.0	1 805	0.0	7.6	1.7	30 527	72.3	3.5	61.4	16.4	22.2
Palmdale city	34 002	6 297	7.8	7 661	0.0	10.6	5.1	76 832	62.8	9.8	52.9	12.9	34.1
Palm Desert city	5 222	2 492	13.9	1 452	1.3	17.5	5.0	34 992	52.0	4.3	43.2	14.9	41.9
Palm Springs city	5 403	1 906	10.8	1 478	0.0	13.7	9.5	36 283	52.4	6.2	44.5	13.5	42.1
Palo Alto city	9 504	4 318	22.7	2 221	0.0	5.0	1.7	47 814	66.9	1.9	57.5	15.2	27.3
Paradise town	4 498	1 282	14.5	1 169	0.0	9.6	2.0	21 561	48.6	6.8	36.6	16.3	47.1
Paramount city	14 938	3 169	7.2	3 391	0.0	10.3	10.3	36 631	58.2	11.5	53.7	11.4	34.9
Pasadena city	22 529	13 562	28.1	5 773	0.0	7.4	3.7	105 992	63.8	6.7	54.3	13.9	31.8
Perris city	10 619	1 538	6.6	2 141	0.0	12.5	9.2	23 013	59.0	11.6	52.3	11.7	36.0

Table B-5. Cities — Education, Labor Force, and Income

City	Full-year full-time employed (percent)								Children under 18 years in families (percent, except where noted)						Total employed by class of worker (percent)			
										With two parents									
	Total	Men	Women	Non-Hispanic White	Black or African American	American Indian and Alaska Native	Asian, Hawaiian, and Pacific Islander	Hispanic or Latino[1]	Number	Both in labor force	Father only in labor force	With one parent who is in labor force	+/- U.S. percent of children with no stay-at-home parent	+/- U.S. percent two-income couples	Private	Government	Self-employed	Unpaid family worker
	24	25	26	27	28	29	30	31	32	33	34	35	36	37	38	39	40	41
CALIFORNIA—Cont'd																		
Highland city	35.9	45.7	27.0	41.2	29.9	37.8	32.9	31.0	14 727	33.9	23.0	22.4	-8.3	-2.8	68.3	22.5	8.8	0.4
Hollister city	41.4	53.4	29.7	48.5	39.5	43.8	45.2	35.0	11 291	42.1	23.4	19.5	-3.0	1.8	77.3	15.0	7.3	0.4
Huntington Beach city	44.9	55.8	34.2	46.5	44.6	51.9	42.1	38.1	40 189	43.4	28.0	18.1	-3.1	2.7	74.8	12.5	12.4	0.4
Huntington Park city	26.6	35.1	18.2	27.7	27.9	30.2	22.7	26.6	19 788	23.9	26.0	18.3	-22.4	-20.7	85.4	8.3	6.0	0.3
Imperial Beach city	37.2	46.9	27.7	42.2	46.0	29.6	27.6	31.8	7 373	28.1	22.5	34.8	-1.7	-8.5	71.7	20.3	7.7	0.3
Indio city	29.8	36.9	22.8	29.9	21.6	22.5	44.0	29.8	16 079	33.2	21.1	24.2	-7.2	-7.9	78.3	13.7	7.7	0.4
Inglewood city	32.7	37.7	28.4	27.0	36.2	21.9	35.5	29.1	33 205	23.5	19.1	29.0	-12.1	-12.7	73.2	18.8	7.9	0.2
Irvine city	41.0	52.5	30.4	45.3	43.7	35.8	34.3	39.5	32 665	42.5	34.8	13.7	-8.4	2.8	71.7	15.1	12.9	0.3
Laguna Hills city	42.9	56.5	30.8	42.2	70.5	21.8	49.7	40.6	7 866	45.0	36.0	11.2	-8.4	-1.0	71.8	9.8	17.4	0.9
Laguna Niguel city	47.2	62.0	33.7	47.2	51.9	47.7	47.9	47.9	16 181	43.9	35.9	14.4	-6.3	2.3	73.6	9.9	16.0	0.4
La Habra city	39.3	49.7	29.3	40.9	44.0	35.4	35.3	37.8	16 101	37.5	22.6	20.7	-6.4	-4.2	79.0	12.5	8.4	0.2
Lake Elsinore city	37.0	49.3	25.0	41.2	34.5	40.1	52.6	29.2	9 928	33.0	30.0	18.4	-13.2	-6.9	81.2	10.4	8.1	0.2
Lake Forest city	47.9	60.2	36.5	49.8	49.7	31.4	43.0	43.8	15 174	48.7	26.0	17.2	1.3	8.7	79.8	9.1	10.6	0.5
Lakewood city	41.6	50.3	33.8	41.5	44.4	50.2	41.4	42.4	20 539	46.5	20.5	18.9	0.8	1.8	76.1	15.8	7.7	0.3
La Mesa city	40.6	51.4	31.2	40.4	47.6	59.1	34.0	42.0	10 400	42.2	22.0	27.3	4.9	-0.1	72.1	18.3	9.4	0.3
La Mirada city	38.2	50.0	27.9	35.8	48.7	32.5	40.6	40.8	11 510	49.2	24.2	13.2	-2.2	-2.0	73.9	17.1	8.7	0.3
Lancaster city	34.3	43.2	25.3	37.0	27.9	23.0	33.1	32.1	35 326	32.3	24.3	25.1	-7.2	-8.2	69.4	22.8	7.5	0.3
La Puente city	31.0	39.3	22.7	30.7	36.1	11.8	35.6	30.4	11 855	29.5	27.5	21.3	-13.8	-12.7	82.2	10.0	7.6	0.2
La Verne city	40.3	50.0	31.7	39.4	41.3	20.0	41.8	42.4	7 722	54.7	21.9	15.7	5.8	2.8	70.8	17.8	11.0	0.4
Lawndale city	35.8	41.6	30.1	36.5	42.3	36.3	34.0	34.0	9 356	30.2	21.3	23.7	-10.7	-8.2	84.9	7.8	7.0	0.3
Livermore city	49.1	61.7	36.5	50.1	43.3	59.0	42.9	44.5	19 943	49.0	27.7	15.2	-0.4	6.0	73.7	18.0	8.0	0.3
Lodi city	35.1	45.5	25.4	37.6	23.8	23.3	27.3	30.8	15 359	35.7	25.9	22.8	-6.1	-5.1	77.0	13.9	9.0	0.2
Lompoc city	33.1	37.2	28.3	36.1	33.0	37.1	31.6	28.9	11 395	41.8	19.4	21.5	-1.3	-1.2	71.9	19.6	8.3	0.2
Long Beach city	34.5	42.4	27.2	40.2	33.2	33.8	28.7	30.3	124 391	26.7	19.8	25.0	-12.9	-6.8	75.2	15.9	8.6	0.3
Los Altos city	41.0	55.6	27.9	38.5	67.7	77.4	52.4	38.4	6 409	47.4	40.3	6.6	-10.6	-5.6	75.5	8.1	16.2	0.2
Los Angeles city	31.9	38.6	37.4	28.9	27.0	32.1	28.2	896 816	28.2	23.3	22.0	-14.4	-10.8	75.5	10.6	13.5	0.4
Los Banos city	33.1	43.2	23.3	37.3	34.5	23.0	33.0	28.5	8 640	37.9	27.6	16.3	-10.4	-11.6	74.8	16.0	0.0	0.2
Los Gatos town	43.4	58.7	30.1	44.3	35.2	77.2	47.8	44.5	5 968	42.0	38.1	13.7	-8.9	-0.3	74.7	9.3	15.5	0.4
Lynwood city	27.9	36.4	19.0	18.2	31.1	21.7	24.1	27.7	23 761	24.4	20.8	18.0	-22.2	-19.1	81.7	11.1	6.9	0.3
Madera city	24.6	31.2	17.9	32.5	24.5	10.9	21.4	20.9	13 964	33.6	24.5	22.3	-8.7	-15.2	74.2	17.6	7.8	0.5
Manhattan Beach city	50.2	61.9	38.4	50.5	46.8	87.3	51.5	44.5	7 448	47.8	35.1	11.8	-5.0	3.5	70.9	11.2	17.8	0.2
Manteca city	37.4	48.8	26.8	38.8	34.2	37.9	43.2	32.1	14 518	39.0	27.1	18.8	-6.8	-4.1	77.7	15.9	6.2	0.2
Marina city	34.8	38.0	30.2	38.5	37.9	25.8	32.4	29.0	4 722	38.4	17.0	26.5	0.3	-3.7	70.0	21.3	8.5	0.2
Martinez city	45.5	54.0	37.4	46.9	39.0	42.5	48.0	35.4	7 662	50.5	22.9	19.6	5.5	9.2	71.8	17.9	10.1	0.3
Maywood city	27.5	36.9	17.6	23.4	18.5	26.5	20.7	27.6	9 605	22.8	26.7	19.5	-22.3	-20.2	87.1	7.0	5.8	0.1
Menlo Park city	42.4	53.6	32.7	43.1	38.1	79.7	44.3	38.4	6 199	36.4	33.8	10.8	9.4	-2.0	77.3	8.6	13.9	0.2
Merced city	28.0	35.6	21.0	34.1	20.7	37.0	15.9	25.5	20 859	31.2	19.4	24.2	-9.2	-8.1	71.9	20.2	7.5	0.4
Milpitas city	46.4	53.9	38.0	50.7	39.4	35.4	48.2	35.7	14 375	47.3	21.0	16.5	-0.8	5.4	86.3	7.8	5.7	0.2
Mission Viejo city	45.1	59.7	31.7	44.6	45.1	00.0	40.0	45.0	24 520	47.2	33.5	12.6	-4.8	2.3	75.4	11.9	12.2	0.4
Modesto city	34.3	44.4	25.3	36.7	31.8	40.3	29.5	28.7	52 813	36.9	22.4	21.3	-6.4	-5.3	74.0	15.4	9.5	0.4
Monrovia city	38.1	45.7	31.5	41.9	23.3	24.9	36.5	35.9	9 436	35.4	16.8	27.6	-1.6	-1.1	74.0	14.3	11.6	0.2
Montclair city	34.2	41.6	26.9	35.4	32.6	32.9	33.9	34.1	9 924	31.3	24.2	19.4	-13.9	-10.7	79.9	12.8	6.7	0.5
Montebello city	31.5	40.9	23.2	25.7	29.4	34.6	31.9	16 512	27.1	20.9	24.3	-13.2	-14.4	74.4	17.1	8.0	0.5
Monterey city	40.1	50.0	30.7	41.0	39.2	44.9	32.0	36.5	4 779	39.1	30.6	22.2	-3.3	-1.8	66.2	19.4	14.1	0.3
Monterey Park city	29.0	36.2	22.5	25.2	51.5	22.9	28.4	31.7	11 940	36.4	19.9	20.1	-8.1	-14.6	73.6	14.3	11.4	0.7
Moorpark city	46.0	60.9	31.5	49.9	55.7	57.5	46.9	35.2	10 172	48.4	30.1	12.0	-4.2	6.0	74.8	13.7	11.2	0.3
Moreno Valley city	37.0	46.8	28.1	42.1	36.1	30.3	36.5	33.0	48 292	34.9	25.8	22.2	-7.5	-3.5	72.8	19.6	7.3	0.3
Morgan Hill city	46.7	59.3	34.4	48.7	46.4	40.4	49.1	40.8	9 648	48.1	28.3	16.5	0.0	5.8	76.7	11.9	11.1	0.3
Mountain View city	48.3	57.6	38.3	50.6	52.1	56.2	48.5	40.0	11 851	43.9	26.8	15.9	-4.8	2.5	85.5	6.5	7.9	0.1
Murrieta city	40.8	55.5	27.2	40.7	57.9	32.9	38.5	37.8	14 376	48.0	33.1	11.7	-4.9	-2.9	69.2	17.3	13.4	0.1
Napa city	38.0	46.8	29.7	39.7	25.4	38.1	42.2	32.8	17 694	42.4	25.3	18.6	-3.6	-1.5	72.9	15.1	11.6	0.4
National City city	30.1	39.3	20.6	36.0	38.4	28.8	27.2	28.5	14 947	24.9	20.3	24.8	-14.9	-17.8	78.8	14.0	6.8	0.4
Newark city	45.5	56.1	35.1	49.5	42.9	46.1	47.6	38.6	10 992	43.1	23.3	15.3	-6.2	-0.2	83.4	11.1	5.3	0.2
Newport Beach city	43.5	57.0	30.5	43.1	45.5	51.0	42.1	52.7	10 912	32.8	45.8	15.4	-16.4	-12.1	68.1	9.0	22.2	0.7
Norwalk city	34.4	42.9	26.3	34.9	40.0	28.8	34.5	33.8	29 971	35.0	22.4	19.6	-10.0	-9.9	80.6	12.6	6.6	0.2
Novato city	41.6	53.0	31.5	41.9	47.8	46.7	40.9	38.5	10 820	48.0	22.0	19.9	3.3	5.1	72.9	12.3	14.5	0.3
Oakland city	33.7	38.5	29.4	42.3	31.8	30.5	29.6	28.1	89 842	27.1	17.0	28.4	-9.1	-5.5	72.4	17.1	10.1	0.3
Oakley city	47.0	61.4	32.7	49.2	47.0	47.9	41.8	41.7	8 096	49.6	28.2	13.1	-1.9	4.7	76.4	15.4	8.2	0.0
Oceanside city	39.0	49.6	29.0	39.9	49.8	38.9	35.3	35.5	40 586	40.1	24.9	21.1	-3.4	-4.2	74.5	14.7	10.4	0.4
Ontario city	36.6	45.4	27.9	40.9	41.1	32.1	38.5	00.5	49 239	31.4	25.4	21.0	-12.2	-8.6	80.7	12.2	6.8	0.3
Orange city	42.5	51.7	33.4	44.9	45.4	43.0	42.9	37.5	30 936	42.0	25.8	19.1	-3.5	0.6	76.8	11.5	11.5	0.2
Oxnard city	34.9	42.3	27.2	40.6	44.2	27.3	36.2	31.7	48 821	37.5	20.7	19.4	-7.7	-4.4	78.4	14.0	7.2	0.4
Pacifica city	46.2	55.8	37.1	46.3	45.2	31.0	47.0	47.0	8 440	57.2	16.6	18.0	10.6	9.5	75.0	16.0	8.9	0.1
Palmdale city	37.0	49.5	25.8	41.6	35.6	31.8	38.4	31.3	40 665	34.5	26.1	20.0	-10.1	-5.9	73.7	18.2	7.7	0.5
Palm Desert city	29.9	37.2	23.6	29.3	32.9	16.8	42.7	30.8	6 604	28.9	29.4	24.4	-7.4	-18.9	69.5	10.9	19.0	0.5
Palm Springs city	29.2	35.5	22.5	27.5	32.6	35.5	36.4	33.5	6 763	28.2	26.9	23.1	-13.3	-17.4	71.5	9.6	18.6	0.4
Palo Alto city	43.6	56.1	31.8	43.1	44.3	49.1	45.7	46.7	11 965	50.3	31.9	12.2	-2.1	2.0	76.8	9.6	13.5	0.2
Paradise town	26.1	34.7	19.1	26.1	57.9	30.8	30.1	18.7	5 171	41.6	22.1	21.4	-1.6	-12.6	64.5	16.9	17.2	1.3
Paramount city	31.7	40.6	23.4	31.8	41.2	28.1	39.3	29.4	18 923	23.9	24.2	23.4	-17.3	-16.5	81.9	10.8	7.1	0.2
Pasadena city	37.7	44.9	31.0	40.3	35.4	30.4	39.1	34.4	28 416	35.4	23.1	21.4	-7.8	-2.5	73.3	13.9	12.5	0.4
Perris city	31.7	42.3	22.0	38.8	35.4	33.6	32.1	27.1	13 002	28.8	26.8	21.3	-14.5	-12.4	80.5	13.0	6.2	0.3

[1] Hispanic or Latino persons may be of any race.

City	Percent who worked at home	Percent of the population 5 years and over with a disability	Veterans as a percent of the population 18 years and over	Occupation for employed population 16 years and over (percent)						Industry for employed population 16 years and over (percent)					
				Management, professional, and related occupations	Service occupations	Sales and office occupations	Farming, fishing, and forestry occupations	Construction, extraction, and maintenance occupations	Production, transportation and material moving occupations	Agriculture, forestry, fishing, and mining	Construction and manufacturing	Wholesale and retail trade	Transportation and warehousing, and utilities	Service industries	Public administration
	42	43	44	45	46	47	48	49	50	51	52	53	54	55	56
CALIFORNIA—Cont'd															
Highland city............	3.0	19.6	12.4	28.9	19.4	25.2	0.5	11.3	14.7	0.8	16.8	16.4	6.5	53.4	6.1
Hollister city.................	2.3	17.1	8.9	29.3	15.7	24.9	3.7	12.2	14.2	4.5	24.4	18.5	4.4	42.5	5.8
Huntington Beach city ...	4.3	14.1	11.3	44.0	11.1	30.0	0.1	7.0	7.8	0.2	21.4	16.7	4.2	53.8	3.7
Huntington Park city......	1.4	21.8	2.2	11.8	15.6	24.4	0.5	9.2	38.3	0.2	36.0	21.6	5.1	35.9	1.2
Imperial Beach city.......	3.0	22.0	17.5	22.8	22.1	28.8	0.9	13.0	12.6	0.5	17.6	16.0	4.1	52.4	9.4
Indio city......................	2.6	21.1	7.6	17.2	29.4	22.7	4.7	15.5	10.5	5.6	15.9	14.4	3.6	57.2	3.3
Inglewood city..............	1.9	22.0	7.7	24.6	20.5	30.7	0.2	7.6	16.3	0.3	14.7	12.4	11.1	56.4	5.2
Irvine city.....................	5.4	11.1	7.0	57.7	7.6	28.1	0.1	2.4	4.3	0.2	16.8	15.2	2.5	62.6	2.8
Laguna Hills city...........	6.4	14.6	11.2	45.3	13.5	30.7	0.0	5.0	5.5	0.2	17.8	15.4	3.2	61.0	2.4
Laguna Niguel city	7.2	10.7	9.9	50.3	9.1	31.9	0.0	3.5	5.1	0.1	17.3	17.0	3.6	58.7	3.4
La Habra city................	1.9	20.2	9.8	28.6	16.3	29.6	0.4	9.3	15.8	0.3	23.2	18.9	5.2	48.8	3.6
Lake Elsinore city.........	3.8	17.5	12.6	21.9	15.9	29.1	0.6	15.0	17.6	0.9	29.2	18.9	5.6	42.5	2.9
Lake Forest city...........	4.1	13.4	10.7	41.3	11.9	33.1	0.1	5.9	7.7	0.1	20.6	19.1	3.7	53.9	2.6
Lakewood city...............	3.0	17.7	12.3	34.0	12.9	30.0	0.0	10.1	13.0	0.2	21.9	17.2	7.2	49.4	4.1
La Mesa city................	3.7	18.1	15.1	37.0	15.2	30.9	0.1	8.6	8.2	0.1	13.9	15.8	3.9	60.3	5.9
La Mirada city..............	2.3	17.1	11.5	36.1	12.0	32.4	0.0	7.2	12.3	0.2	21.2	18.7	5.9	48.7	5.3
Lancaster city	2.6	20.6	15.4	32.3	17.4	26.2	0.1	11.5	12.5	0.6	18.8	14.5	5.7	52.1	8.3
La Puente city..............	1.6	20.9	5.6	15.4	16.5	24.0	0.1	11.2	32.8	0.1	31.0	18.0	5.7	43.2	2.0
La Verne city................	2.4	18.5	11.6	43.3	12.6	27.8	0.0	7.0	9.3	0.4	17.9	15.2	4.4	56.7	5.3
Lawndale city...............	1.2	20.4	6.9	20.6	21.0	30.5	0.0	10.8	17.2	0.1	21.3	16.8	7.9	52.0	1.8
Livermore city...............	3.1	13.5	11.8	41.8	12.4	26.0	0.1	10.3	9.4	0.5	21.1	16.8	3.8	54.8	3.0
Lodi city......................	2.6	22.7	12.5	27.6	14.8	25.8	4.2	10.5	17.0	5.1	21.8	17.1	5.3	46.0	4.7
Lompoc city..................	2.1	21.1	16.6	26.1	20.4	26.1	4.4	10.4	12.6	7.4	17.3	15.0	3.0	49.3	7.9
Long Beach city	2.9	20.9	9.5	34.3	15.8	27.2	0.1	7.7	14.8	0.4	19.5	14.8	6.6	54.9	3.7
Los Altos city...............	7.1	11.6	13.5	74.7	4.0	16.0	0.1	2.3	2.9	0.2	28.5	9.3	0.8	60.2	1.1
Los Angeles city...........	4.1	21.7	6.4	34.2	16.0	26.7	0.2	7.7	15.2	0.2	18.5	14.3	4.0	60.8	2.3
Los Banos city..............	1.9	20.6	11.0	27.0	17.2	21.6	5.4	12.9	15.8	8.6	23.0	17.0	7.7	40.5	3.2
Los Gatos town	5.7	12.0	11.2	64.4	5.1	23.4	0.2	3.4	3.4	0.2	27.8	11.7	1.7	56.7	1.8
Lynwood city.................	1.3	20.1	3.8	12.5	15.3	26.0	0.4	10.6	35.1	0.4	31.9	17.9	7.2	39.9	2.8
Madera city..................	2.5	22.9	7.8	19.9	18.1	21.2	13.9	8.7	18.3	17.8	18.8	13.3	4.1	39.6	6.4
Manhattan Beach city ...	6.0	11.4	10.2	64.3	6.3	24.4	0.0	2.9	2.1	0.1	17.0	11.3	4.0	64.8	2.8
Manteca city................	2.7	20.7	13.5	24.8	14.2	28.7	1.5	13.1	17.8	2.0	21.6	18.0	7.0	46.4	5.0
Marina city...................	2.5	19.1	14.2	26.3	23.3	28.8	3.7	8.6	9.3	3.6	12.0	14.9	3.0	58.7	7.7
Martinez city.................	3.9	16.2	13.2	41.3	10.1	31.0	0.1	10.6	7.0	0.3	17.2	15.7	5.2	55.2	6.5
Maywood city................	2.1	22.4	2.4	10.2	14.4	20.9	0.5	11.3	42.8	0.3	41.0	17.5	6.1	33.4	1.8
Menlo Park city	6.6	14.2	11.3	62.8	9.2	19.0	0.1	3.6	5.3	0.2	16.3	11.3	2.2	68.1	1.8
Merced city..................	2.6	22.2	11.8	27.4	18.1	24.9	4.4	9.6	15.5	5.3	16.4	14.2	4.1	54.0	5.9
Milpitas city.................	1.5	17.0	6.9	45.5	8.3	23.2	0.4	6.1	16.4	0.6	44.7	11.5	3.3	37.9	2.0
Mission Viejo city	5.1	12.6	11.6	46.7	10.3	31.3	0.0	5.1	6.5	0.1	18.9	17.8	3.3	56.6	3.3
Modesto city.................	2.9	22.1	11.3	28.4	15.9	27.7	1.3	10.6	16.1	1.8	20.9	18.0	5.2	50.0	4.1
Monrovia city................	2.8	19.8	9.6	37.3	15.5	29.3	0.3	7.0	10.7	0.3	17.6	16.2	3.4	58.1	4.4
Montclair city...............	1.9	22.2	8.6	19.3	16.6	27.9	0.8	11.7	23.6	0.8	26.6	15.7	7.1	45.7	4.0
Montebello city.............	2.1	22.0	6.8	25.8	14.4	32.6	0.1	7.6	19.6	0.3	21.5	16.8	6.5	50.5	4.4
Monterey city................	3.9	17.9	12.9	46.3	15.2	24.7	1.3	7.2	5.3	1.3	9.5	15.0	2.5	66.7	4.9
Monterey Park city	2.7	21.0	6.3	34.3	15.1	31.6	0.0	4.9	14.0	0.1	18.7	17.9	4.8	54.6	3.9
Moorpark city...............	4.1	13.2	9.0	40.7	14.7	27.7	1.1	6.0	9.8	1.3	22.6	14.4	2.3	54.1	5.3
Moreno Valley city........	3.0	17.9	11.7	25.2	14.9	30.7	0.4	11.3	17.6	0.6	20.9	18.1	7.1	47.4	5.9
Morgan Hill city	3.2	13.8	10.7	44.5	11.0	25.3	1.4	9.8	7.9	1.8	29.3	15.4	3.5	45.8	4.2
Mountain View city	3.4	14.5	7.9	62.5	9.4	17.9	0.3	4.1	5.8	0.4	27.4	10.2	1.8	58.5	1.6
Murrieta city.................	5.6	12.9	16.2	34.6	14.3	30.2	0.2	10.1	10.6	0.9	21.1	18.8	5.0	47.8	6.4
Napa city.....................	3.5	19.2	12.4	32.7	18.6	24.0	2.9	9.6	12.2	3.4	21.6	15.1	3.0	52.1	4.8
National City city	6.1	24.5	10.1	15.4	26.2	25.4	0.9	12.7	19.4	1.0	21.0	14.9	4.1	54.2	4.9
Newark city..................	1.7	16.9	9.4	32.2	11.8	28.9	0.1	9.4	17.6	0.1	30.6	16.9	6.6	42.6	3.2
Newport Beach city.......	7.3	12.6	13.1	57.6	7.3	29.1	0.1	2.7	3.2	0.1	15.1	15.0	2.5	65.6	1.8
Norwalk city.................	1.9	22.5	7.5	21.1	15.0	30.0	0.1	10.7	23.2	0.3	27.3	17.2	7.4	44.8	2.9
Novato city...................	5.6	16.8	11.5	43.4	14.3	28.1	0.1	7.7	6.4	0.2	11.5	16.3	3.4	64.0	4.7
Oakland city	4.1	22.9	8.1	39.2	15.8	25.1	0.2	7.4	12.3	0.2	14.9	12.7	6.2	61.4	4.5
Oakley city...................	3.2	15.4	12.3	25.2	15.9	29.9	0.4	15.7	12.9	0.5	22.6	17.9	6.5	47.9	4.6
Oceanside city..............	3.7	20.0	17.4	31.5	17.1	27.5	1.0	9.1	13.7	1.2	20.2	16.2	4.5	52.7	5.2
Ontario city..................	2.2	20.0	7.5	20.7	15.1	27.0	1.5	11.6	24.0	2.1	27.1	17.5	6.7	42.8	3.9
Orange city...................	3.5	17.3	9.5	37.0	13.7	29.7	0.2	8.1	11.3	0.3	22.5	15.2	3.1	55.2	3.7
Oxnard city..................	1.9	20.8	10.0	21.6	15.1	24.9	9.8	9.0	19.6	10.7	21.2	16.5	3.5	42.5	5.6
Pacifica city.................	2.7	15.1	11.6	39.1	12.8	28.8	0.1	9.9	9.3	0.3	15.0	14.9	9.6	55.3	5.0
Palmdale city................	2.6	17.6	11.1	28.2	16.1	27.6	0.1	12.1	15.9	0.3	22.6	15.6	6.2	50.5	4.8
Palm Desert city...........	6.1	19.9	17.4	37.3	21.1	29.4	0.2	7.3	4.8	0.5	11.0	14.7	3.0	67.2	3.5
Palm Springs city	5.9	26.8	17.4	31.5	25.0	29.2	0.2	8.0	6.1	0.3	10.2	15.0	4.1	68.0	2.4
Palo Alto city	6.6	12.5	9.0	76.0	4.8	14.8	0.0	2.0	2.4	0.1	20.7	7.9	0.9	68.0	2.3
Paradise town	4.8	25.6	18.3	30.4	20.4	25.7	0.2	11.1	12.3	0.8	14.5	16.0	4.6	59.8	4.2
Paramount city..............	1.6	21.2	5.1	18.0	15.7	26.2	0.2	10.5	29.3	0.3	31.5	16.6	7.3	42.2	2.0
Pasadena city...............	3.8	20.4	7.8	48.0	15.7	23.3	0.1	5.1	7.8	0.2	11.6	11.1	3.4	69.9	3.7
Perris city	2.0	22.2	8.8	17.7	17.4	24.9	0.4	14.5	25.1	0.8	30.0	17.1	5.3	42.4	4.4

City	Median household income	Median family income: All families	Median family income: Families with children: Married-couple	Families with children: Male householder	Families with children: Female householder	Median nonfamily household income	Median income for full-year, full-time workers: Men	Median income for full-year, full-time workers: Women	Per capita income	Households by source of income (percent): With earnings	With interest, dividend, or rental income	With Social Security income	With public assistance income	With retirement income	Households with income over $100,000 (percent)	+/− U.S. percent for income over $100,000	Households with income below poverty (percent)	Families with children with income below poverty (percent)
	57	58	59	60	61	62	63	64	65	66	67	68	69	70	71	72	73	74
CALIFORNIA—Cont'd																		
Highland city	41 230	43 649	49 607	22 344	15 908	26 220	40 346	28 108	16 039	84.5	23.7	19.8	9.9	16.1	10.9	-1.4	17.7	24.1
Hollister city	56 104	57 494	63 459	41 743	28 000	34 773	42 226	29 705	18 857	90.1	25.2	17.2	4.7	12.3	17.6	5.3	7.9	8.4
Huntington Beach city	64 824	74 378	86 299	40 745	34 986	45 629	53 424	39 391	31 964	86.9	43.6	19.5	2.0	15.3	26.4	14.1	5.6	6.6
Huntington Park city	28 941	29 844	31 618	16 883	18 813	14 513	21 335	17 165	9 340	86.8	11.0	16.0	9.9	6.7	4.0	-8.3	23.9	27.9
Imperial Beach city	35 882	37 352	40 484	24 257	19 963	27 624	30 950	24 641	16 003	85.5	19.9	17.8	6.5	15.2	5.9	-6.4	13.9	20.1
Indio city	34 624	35 564	38 968	23 852	17 767	20 500	26 269	21 545	13 525	81.3	19.1	23.7	6.4	13.7	6.7	-5.6	17.7	22.3
Inglewood city	34 269	36 541	38 789	25 296	21 557	25 497	29 246	30 533	14 776	82.4	13.8	17.4	8.5	12.4	6.8	-5.5	19.5	24.8
Irvine city	72 057	85 624	96 303	56 364	40 366	46 150	66 866	43 492	32 196	89.1	49.3	13.4	1.0	10.1	32.3	20.0	8.7	5.8
Laguna Hills city	70 234	81 334	94 020	52 500	41 765	39 836	61 456	40 559	36 133	83.4	49.7	22.8	1.5	15.4	32.3	20.0	5.0	4.9
Laguna Niguel city	80 733	93 613	106 136	60 694	39 500	51 615	71 002	41 339	39 167	89.7	49.8	16.4	1.3	13.1	38.9	26.6	3.8	3.2
La Habra city	47 652	51 971	59 130	30 962	26 912	28 188	37 719	31 105	18 923	83.9	31.1	24.0	3.1	14.5	13.1	0.8	10.0	13.6
Lake Elsinore city	41 884	47 563	56 270	19 489	14 597	22 297	42 270	27 406	15 413	83.5	18.2	21.0	6.1	11.8	10.2	-2.1	16.1	18.6
Lake Forest city	67 967	75 121	82 209	46 541	38 952	44 336	53 595	37 925	28 583	90.6	42.1	15.8	1.1	11.3	27.2	14.9	4.2	4.1
Lakewood city	58 214	63 342	72 051	50 641	33 075	32 408	46 304	35 852	22 095	83.2	37.9	25.3	3.2	18.4	16.6	4.3	6.9	7.8
La Mesa city	41 693	50 398	58 823	40 762	25 576	29 442	38 780	31 028	22 372	77.6	38.3	26.3	2.1	18.7	8.4	-3.9	9.1	8.8
La Mirada city	61 632	66 598	73 560	56 848	39 688	30 874	48 673	32 353	22 404	80.6	42.1	31.3	2.6	20.9	19.6	7.3	4.6	4.9
Lancaster city	41 127	44 681	55 109	28 814	17 676	27 358	41 513	29 001	16 935	80.6	24.8	21.3	9.3	17.4	9.7	-2.6	14.1	18.9
La Puente city	41 222	41 079	44 931	27 171	18 696	21 647	26 933	22 555	11 336	87.3	16.6	22.0	7.2	12.3	7.8	-4.5	16.4	20.8
La Verne city	61 326	70 344	83 187	44 375	37 072	28 218	51 740	35 697	26 689	82.1	45.4	25.1	1.3	18.1	22.8	10.5	4.9	3.1
Lawndale city	39 012	37 909	41 105	27 083	24 101	30 260	29 589	30 138	13 702	88.9	18.5	15.1	8.3	9.1	6.1	-6.2	14.0	19.5
Livermore city	75 322	82 421	91 066	52 005	35 870	46 680	60 822	39 800	31 062	88.4	45.5	15.7	2.1	16.6	30.4	18.1	4.4	5.7
Lodi city	39 570	47 020	53 793	26 230	20 143	23 655	39 129	28 237	18 719	77.5	31.7	28.5	4.7	18.0	10.2	-2.1	13.1	19.0
Lompoc city	37 587	42 199	49 130	23 229	18 990	25 531	35 988	27 269	15 509	79.6	29.7	24.1	6.5	19.2	6.3	-6.0	13.4	17.3
Long Beach city	37 270	40 002	44 792	24 005	15 733	31 387	37 494	32 850	19 040	81.5	27.3	17.7	8.8	12.3	12.0	-0.3	18.2	27.2
Los Altos city	126 740	148 201	192 180	127 355	69 423	61 092	100 001	70 850	66 776	79.5	79.1	30.1	0.7	22.1	61.0	48.7	1.8	1.9
Los Angeles city	36 687	39 942	42 144	22 950	17 263	29 011	32 742	30 782	20 671	82.4	27.3	18.4	6.9	10.4	13.6	1.3	18.6	25.3
Los Banos city	43 690	45 304	53 053	32 938	17 250	22 900	38 523	28 256	15 582	84.2	22.0	23.3	5.3	13.0	7.9	-4.4	11.4	11.9
Los Gatos town	94 319	119 194	151 611	82 545	51 303	60 176	93 882	59 303	56 094	83.2	61.0	22.9	0.7	16.8	47.8	35.5	3.5	4.5
Lynwood city	35 888	35 808	37 390	24 688	16 016	16 020	23 074	20 100	0 512	88.6	11.6	12.3	12.4	9.7	4.9	-7.4	21.8	24.4
Madera city	31 033	31 927	37 198	22 321	14 629	17 988	30 679	23 565	11 674	81.0	18.4	24.1	12.5	13.4	5.8	-6.5	25.1	33.9
Manhattan Beach city	100 750	122 686	156 624	75 291	59 375	66 888	89 357	57 033	61 136	87.1	61.6	17.1	0.6	13.5	50.5	38.2	3.7	2.4
Mantoca city	46 677	51 587	58 692	31 380	26 279	27 465	43 754	29 535	18 241	83.1	25.8	22.4	4.8	17.7	10.1	-2.2	8.7	9.2
Marina city	43 000	46 139	53 086	27 386	20 239	28 872	47 047	27 858	18 860	85.1	30.1	21.0	6.4	19.7	10.1	-2.2	11.0	15.8
Martinez city	63 010	77 411	00 574	57 002	36 807	39 488	53 253	41 481	29 701	83.7	45.7	20.2	2.1	18.1	24.0	11.7	5.5	4.3
Maywood city	30 480	30 361	31 807	28 036	16 118	17 917	20 871	17 229	8 926	89.9	9.9	12.5	8.5	7.1	3.2	-8.1	20.4	27.1
Menlo Park city	84 609	105 550	134 833	50 905	47 939	61 462	85 635	54 750	53 341	81.2	62.7	23.9	1.8	17.0	43.2	30.9	5.0	6.4
Merced city	30 429	32 470	40 281	22 757	13 813	21 277	32 743	25 467	13 115	78.1	24.8	23.4	13.1	16.7	5.3	-7.0	21.9	30.1
Milpitas city	84 429	84 827	92 796	51 890	38 681	65 294	51 744	37 002	27 823	92.7	43.9	14.4	2.5	10.2	38.8	26.5	3.8	4.2
Mission Viejo city	78 248	86 902	94 278	68 542	39 158	46 811	64 792	40 063	33 302	87.5	49.8	20.7	1.1	16.2	34.9	22.6	3.2	3.3
Modesto city	40 394	45 681	52 223	28 364	18 631	25 203	09 554	27 708	17 797	79.9	29.3	24.8	6.2	16.8	9.6	-2.7	12.9	18.0
Monrovia city	45 375	49 703	57 310	35 743	24 814	31 435	41 502	33 022	21 686	83.7	33.1	21.9	5.6	13.2	14.7	2.4	10.3	13.4
Montclair city	40 797	42 815	47 940	23 080	26 507	25 645	31 359	27 439	13 556	85.5	21.2	23.0	6.4	10.7	8.1	-4.2	14.5	17.9
Montebello city	38 805	41 257	47 625	25 697	19 904	23 041	30 895	26 943	15 125	79.3	25.2	28.1	7.8	14.3	9.2	-3.1	15.4	20.0
Monterey city	49 109	58 757	62 269	36 151	30 842	35 694	41 587	32 473	27 133	81.2	47.7	25.1	1.1	18.6	15.2	2.9	7.0	6.8
Monterey Park city	40 724	43 507	46 071	27 578	21 364	22 985	35 240	29 745	17 661	77.7	38.8	28.1	7.8	16.2	12.3	0.0	14.0	18.9
Moorpark city	76 642	78 909	83 312	53 750	36 289	47 250	57 000	36 733	25 383	94.4	42.0	13.8	2.0	9.5	30.4	18.1	4.8	5.9
Moreno Valley city	47 387	48 965	55 155	28 295	21 479	30 313	40 191	27 461	14 983	89.4	19.7	16.4	6.7	14.6	9.9	-2.4	12.0	14.9
Morgan Hill city	81 958	90 134	97 772	51 528	40 089	43 029	65 129	43 650	33 047	89.2	45.2	16.1	2.3	14.2	39.3	27.0	4.2	4.6
Mountain View city	69 362	80 379	93 171	44 250	36 975	57 104	66 177	45 411	39 693	88.2	49.3	15.2	1.4	11.1	31.5	19.2	5.6	5.7
Murrieta city	60 911	65 904	75 073	44 750	31 023	31 018	50 210	34 823	23 290	82.4	38.8	24.3	1.2	19.3	19.9	7.6	4.4	3.7
Napa city	49 154	58 788	65 349	37 614	26 966	31 562	42 098	32 209	23 642	78.8	41.3	27.3	2.8	22.9	15.7	3.4	7.3	9.5
National City city	29 826	31 497	34 209	25 541	13 899	16 890	22 380	20 645	11 582	80.9	17.3	23.7	9.2	15.9	3.7	-8.6	20.1	26.5
Newark city	69 350	71 351	80 168	41 583	41 019	49 635	47 229	36 003	23 641	90.0	38.7	18.1	2.5	15.4	26.3	14.0	5.3	5.1
Newport Beach city	83 455	111 166	148 093	55 476	43 681	59 683	81 587	46 853	63 015	81.9	57.4	25.0	0.9	14.0	42.5	30.2	4.8	2.9
Norwalk city	46 047	47 524	51 826	31 667	24 941	26 600	31 902	26 622	14 022	85.9	23.6	22.4	6.2	15.5	8.8	-3.5	10.1	12.3
Novato city	63 453	74 434	87 539	46 818	34 138	42 090	57 507	41 990	32 402	84.8	50.9	23.5	2.1	18.5	27.0	14.7	4.5	5.6
Oakland city	40 055	44 384	53 258	31 508	20 339	32 044	39 002	35 794	21 936	80.3	31.5	19.6	7.9	13.3	14.5	2.2	16.1	22.8
Oakley city	65 589	68 888	72 288	51 544	35 919	41 302	50 418	35 433	21 895	89.8	28.5	16.5	1.9	15.1	17.8	5.5	4.5	3.2
Oceanside city	46 301	52 232	57 666	30 332	24 487	30 226	36 422	29 492	20 329	78.6	36.8	28.0	2.9	21.7	12.1	-0.2	9.2	12.6
Ontario city	42 452	44 031	47 154	29 000	21 356	30 025	32 110	26 566	14 244	88.5	19.4	17.3	6.1	12.1	8.4	-3.9	12.8	15.3
Orange city	58 994	64 573	67 876	40 313	31 215	37 474	43 629	35 267	24 294	87.6	37.4	20.0	2.6	14.3	21.9	9.6	7.4	10.0
Oxnard city	48 603	49 150	51 323	36 101	22 410	32 072	31 440	26 174	15 288	87.1	27.3	22.8	5.2	17.8	12.7	0.4	11.6	14.7
Pacifica city	71 737	78 361	91 340	51 384	40 994	45 776	51 427	40 651	30 183	88.2	44.8	20.2	1.2	16.8	28.4	16.1	2.7	1.2
Palmdale city	46 941	49 293	57 331	33 357	18 692	29 934	43 590	30 330	16 384	85.5	23.0	16.4	8.2	13.8	11.2	-1.1	13.8	16.2
Palm Desert city	48 316	58 183	61 351	31 218	29 788	31 773	45 702	33 778	33 463	67.0	50.0	41.0	1.2	22.1	19.2	6.9	8.3	11.4
Palm Springs city	35 973	45 318	47 005	20 036	17 792	28 943	35 851	28 595	25 957	68.3	40.7	41.9	2.1	22.3	12.7	0.4	12.1	22.2
Palo Alto city	90 377	117 574	150 457	85 807	59 167	56 197	95 869	63 008	56 257	82.7	65.2	23.1	1.0	15.1	45.6	33.3	4.5	4.1
Paradise town	31 863	41 228	51 083	26 083	15 758	19 853	36 756	25 911	19 267	60.7	40.5	46.1	4.8	29.3	5.7	-6.6	11.7	15.7
Paramount city	36 749	37 276	41 113	26 305	17 979	25 073	28 217	23 277	11 487	87.6	13.2	16.1	9.3	10.3	5.2	-7.1	18.6	23.0
Pasadena city	46 012	53 639	58 693	27 865	19 715	35 890	42 086	37 275	28 186	82.2	38.5	20.1	5.2	12.3	19.6	7.3	12.9	17.3
Perris city	35 522	36 063	40 231	20 417	15 701	23 774	32 308	25 399	11 425	85.5	13.3	18.6	9.3	11.5	5.1	-7.2	18.9	21.0

Table B-5. Cities — Education, Labor Force, and Income

STATE Place code	City	High school graduates			College graduates		College graduates (percent)				
		Total population 25 years and over	Percent with a high school diploma or less	Percent with a high school diploma or more	Percent with a bachelor's degree or more	+/– U.S. percent with bachelor's degree or more	Non-Hispanic White	Black or African American	American Indian and Alaska Native	Asian, Hawaiian, and Pacific Islander	Hispanic or Latino[1]
		1	2	3	4	5	6	7	8	9	10
	CALIFORNIA—Cont'd										
06 56784	Petaluma city	36 376	33.4	85.9	30.1	5.7	32.1	16.1	5.9	47.7	11.2
06 56924	Pico Rivera city	37 044	70.9	55.1	7.1	-17.3	8.1	13.9	5.2	40.6	5.5
06 57456	Pittsburg city	33 388	50.2	75.7	14.7	-9.7	15.8	12.1	3.7	31.0	5.5
06 57526	Placentia city	29 970	36.3	81.5	31.3	6.9	34.9	34.2	26.2	52.1	12.0
06 57764	Pleasant Hill city	23 555	24.4	93.1	42.5	18.1	42.2	26.1	24.1	56.8	29.5
06 57792	Pleasanton city	42 370	20.5	94.2	47.3	22.9	45.7	50.4	40.9	70.9	24.6
06 58072	Pomona city	78 809	63.7	54.9	12.8	-11.6	23.6	15.8	8.6	37.4	4.3
06 58240	Porterville city	21 791	61.4	61.7	11.0	-13.4	14.9	5.0	3.8	17.7	5.2
06 58520	Poway city	29 788	25.1	93.1	39.3	14.9	41.2	23.1	7.5	49.4	18.8
06 59451	Rancho Cucamonga city	77 297	35.6	86.0	23.3	-1.1	24.8	24.0	13.4	48.1	12.6
06 59514	Rancho Palos Verdes city	30 023	16.1	95.8	58.0	33.6	55.3	55.2	23.5	70.8	36.6
06 59587	Rancho Santa Margarita city	28 949	18.0	95.1	43.8	19.4	44.8	41.9	45.7	62.3	22.6
06 59920	Redding city	52 101	40.2	85.2	19.4	-5.0	20.1	15.4	7.4	17.1	13.1
06 59962	Redlands city	40 274	31.6	86.6	35.2	10.8	40.3	18.3	22.4	52.9	15.0
06 60018	Redondo Beach city	47 851	21.4	92.5	48.0	23.6	49.5	47.1	22.2	61.0	28.8
06 60102	Redwood City city	51 677	34.6	82.9	35.7	11.3	41.3	21.0	24.3	64.3	10.2
06 60466	Rialto city	47 766	61.2	66.5	8.7	-15.7	10.6	11.7	9.5	28.9	4.1
06 60620	Richmond city	62 662	46.5	75.4	22.4	-2.0	36.2	13.9	13.2	38.2	7.5
06 62000	Riverside city	146 189	48.1	74.9	19.1	-5.3	24.1	17.5	11.3	40.9	7.2
06 62364	Rocklin city	23 029	22.3	94.4	36.1	11.7	35.6	37.8	21.8	56.8	29.4
06 62546	Rohnert Park city	25 518	35.5	88.0	24.7	0.3	24.3	29.3	16.5	42.9	16.0
06 62896	Rosemead city	32 879	65.7	53.2	12.9	-11.5	22.6	17.2	20.5	16.7	4.3
06 62938	Roseville city	53 006	30.0	90.9	31.4	7.0	32.3	47.6	26.7	45.9	15.0
06 64000	Sacramento city	254 921	44.2	77.3	23.9	-0.5	31.9	13.6	14.2	24.8	10.3
06 64224	Salinas city	84 514	63.2	56.0	12.3	-12.1	23.3	8.4	6.6	27.8	4.0
06 65000	San Bernardino city	99 325	60.6	64.9	11.6	-12.8	16.8	10.8	9.3	29.5	4.5
06 65028	San Bruno city	27 680	37.6	84.5	26.2	1.8	25.2	12.5	8.6	44.1	12.8
06 65042	San Buenaventura (Ventura) city	67 718	33.9	85.7	29.2	4.8	33.0	25.4	19.5	45.7	12.1
06 65070	San Carlos city	20 393	20.8	94.6	49.8	25.4	49.8	27.3	0.0	68.4	30.0
06 65084	San Clemente city	34 599	26.4	90.7	36.1	11.7	39.2	24.4	4.7	56.6	14.8
06 66000	San Diego city	779 242	34.2	82.8	35.0	10.6	45.1	15.7	15.8	37.7	11.9
06 66070	San Dimas city	23 056	30.6	87.3	28.4	4.0	27.9	29.7	25.4	57.4	16.6
06 67000	San Francisco city	595 805	32.7	81.2	45.0	20.6	63.2	18.1	28.0	31.6	20.3
06 67042	San Gabriel city	26 962	49.1	69.2	24.6	0.2	31.8	14.4	13.1	29.0	10.9
06 68000	San Jose city	570 755	39.8	78.3	31.6	7.2	39.2	28.0	14.4	40.4	8.9
06 68028	San Juan Capistrano city	21 758	37.5	81.6	30.7	6.3	37.7	7.4	7.2	65.4	9.3
06 68084	San Leandro city	55 846	45.3	80.9	23.3	-1.1	22.2	24.5	9.7	33.6	12.8
06 68154	San Luis Obispo city	23 220	24.1	91.1	40.9	16.5	43.6	16.2	28.8	41.3	20.0
06 68196	San Marcos city	34 030	46.6	75.1	20.0	-4.4	24.6	25.2	12.2	33.9	6.3
06 68252	San Mateo city	67 134	32.2	85.9	38.6	14.2	43.2	25.5	27.9	50.3	11.2
06 68294	San Pablo city	17 347	63.7	62.4	10.4	-14.0	9.8	10.4	5.3	23.0	4.5
06 68364	San Rafael city	40 684	29.5	84.7	43.6	19.2	51.4	28.9	20.1	49.7	11.7
06 68378	San Ramon city	30 297	15.3	96.5	52.7	28.3	51.3	47.5	47.1	69.0	33.1
06 69000	Santa Ana city	178 745	72.8	43.2	9.2	-15.2	25.9	14.4	4.7	18.1	2.9
06 69070	Santa Barbara city	61 096	33.8	81.3	39.6	15.2	52.5	16.9	19.7	49.0	10.1
06 69084	Santa Clara city	70 097	30.2	86.9	42.4	18.0	40.7	34.5	21.5	59.0	14.8
06 69088	Santa Clarita city	93 648	32.6	87.6	29.1	4.7	30.8	29.6	12.3	56.3	12.7
06 69112	Santa Cruz city	33 896	25.4	89.1	44.4	20.0	48.4	35.0	19.5	52.5	18.6
06 69196	Santa Maria city	43 768	61.7	61.0	11.0	-13.4	18.2	17.5	6.7	20.7	3.0
06 70000	Santa Monica city	67 176	21.0	91.0	54.8	30.4	59.9	25.8	20.7	62.8	23.4
06 70042	Santa Paula city	16 544	64.9	57.8	8.6	-15.8	18.0	6.9	0.0	29.5	3.2
06 70098	Santa Rosa city	97 503	36.4	84.2	27.6	3.2	31.7	18.2	8.2	26.0	8.9
06 70224	Santee city	33 609	38.9	88.4	17.0	-7.4	17.6	14.9	0.0	29.2	9.1
06 70280	Saratoga city	20 952	11.2	96.5	68.2	43.8	65.7	44.0	100.0	78.9	41.0
06 70742	Seaside city	18 831	53.3	70.1	17.5	-6.9	29.3	13.7	2.2	13.3	4.9
06 72016	Simi Valley city	71 130	36.7	86.9	24.9	0.5	25.2	31.3	15.7	46.5	12.1
06 73080	South Gate city	50 032	80.6	39.9	4.9	-19.5	11.1	5.8	6.9	37.6	3.8
06 73262	South San Francisco city	40 422	44.2	79.8	25.2	0.8	18.8	28.4	9.2	46.9	9.0
06 73962	Stanton city	22 001	60.9	62.7	11.9	-12.5	16.9	23.9	10.1	20.2	2.5
06 75000	Stockton city	138 343	54.1	68.2	15.4	-9.0	22.1	9.5	7.1	18.0	6.2
06 75630	Suisun City city	15 187	40.0	85.6	17.3	-7.1	16.3	16.2	8.3	24.8	10.2
06 77000	Sunnyvale city	95 278	24.0	89.4	50.8	26.4	49.8	24.8	22.2	67.2	15.6
06 78120	Temecula city	32 843	31.8	90.1	25.0	0.6	27.0	16.6	19.0	38.9	13.2
06 78148	Temple City city	22 330	37.0	83.5	28.5	4.1	21.8	29.8	0.0	42.3	13.9
06 78582	Thousand Oaks city	78 458	24.1	91.4	42.2	17.8	43.6	50.3	20.4	72.2	15.0
06 80000	Torrance city	97 014	29.6	90.6	36.4	12.0	33.4	34.6	21.5	50.5	16.6
06 80238	Tracy city	33 055	43.8	81.5	18.0	-6.4	20.2	18.5	3.8	35.2	6.0
06 80644	Tulare city	24 546	64.9	65.0	8.2	-16.2	12.0	5.0	7.9	17.4	3.2
06 80812	Turlock city	32 628	54.1	70.4	19.1	-5.3	22.7	18.8	21.1	28.1	7.4
06 80854	Tustin city	42 967	35.7	79.9	33.4	9.0	41.4	22.6	23.4	50.4	8.6
06 81204	Union City city	42 039	40.6	80.5	29.5	5.1	22.6	24.2	18.8	43.1	8.7

[1] Hispanic or Latino persons may be of any race.

City	School enrollment			Population 16 to 19 years				Employment status, 2000			Work status in 1999 of the population 16 years and over		
											Worked in 1999		
	Grades kindergarten through 12	College or graduate school	Percent private	Number	Percent in armed forces	Percent high school graduates	Percent not enrolled, not grads, not in armed forces, not employed	Total population 16 years and over	Percent in labor force	Unemployment rate	Full-time	Part-time	Did not work in 1999
	11	12	13	14	15	16	17	18	19	20	21	22	23
CALIFORNIA—Cont'd													
Petaluma city	10 833	3 223	10.3	2 615	0.0	9.5	2.7	41 818	70.4	4.3	56.5	18.7	24.9
Pico Rivera city	15 118	3 590	8.5	4 155	0.2	8.4	6.1	45 882	55.2	7.2	49.6	10.5	39.9
Pittsburg city	13 346	3 815	12.1	3 211	0.0	13.8	5.4	41 024	65.0	7.3	57.5	12.8	29.8
Placentia city	9 540	3 986	13.5	2 670	0.1	6.9	7.6	35 704	68.9	4.3	58.5	15.2	26.3
Pleasant Hill city	5 049	2 979	15.5	1 451	0.0	10.1	3.0	26 542	69.7	3.7	56.7	16.2	27.1
Pleasanton city	13 598	3 331	9.4	2 867	0.0	6.6	0.8	47 468	72.8	2.6	62.5	15.4	22.1
Pomona city	38 928	11 574	7.8	10 489	0.1	9.5	8.3	102 875	57.8	9.9	51.1	13.4	35.5
Porterville city	10 447	2 266	4.3	2 713	0.0	9.7	8.5	27 563	58.6	12.3	49.2	12.7	38.1
Poway city	12 072	3 627	10.2	3 400	0.0	6.9	1.4	35 411	68.2	3.3	55.9	17.3	26.8
Rancho Cucamonga city	30 060	10 693	10.5	8 307	0.0	9.0	4.4	94 364	69.4	5.4	58.5	15.5	26.0
Rancho Palos Verdes city	7 684	2 375	13.5	1 679	0.0	1.1	0.4	32 925	57.4	2.6	47.7	15.1	37.2
Rancho Santa Margarita city	11 162	3 296	14.9	2 016	0.2	4.6	2.3	32 807	78.2	3.0	67.6	14.8	17.6
Redding city	16 165	5 372	11.8	4 837	0.0	10.7	5.0	62 334	58.7	7.7	45.4	16.9	37.6
Redlands city	12 774	6 584	22.8	4 262	0.0	7.9	2.7	49 099	65.2	6.4	51.0	18.1	30.9
Redondo Beach city	8 151	5 136	18.3	2 036	0.0	7.4	0.4	52 642	75.8	4.1	66.6	12.8	20.6
Redwood City city	12 128	4 923	20.1	3 048	0.0	9.0	7.2	59 567	69.6	3.3	62.5	13.3	24.1
Rialto city	26 594	4 954	7.0	6 593	0.1	13.2	7.6	60 745	59.8	10.5	51.4	11.6	37.1
Richmond city	20 656	7 193	12.4	5 213	0.0	11.3	7.8	75 004	61.9	7.7	53.2	13.9	32.9
Riverside city	59 107	24 206	10.6	18 616	0.0	10.2	5.1	186 224	62.4	7.9	51.9	15.5	32.6
Rocklin city	8 220	2 705	9.0	2 160	0.0	7.1	1.7	26 874	71.1	2.7	60.1	16.5	23.4
Rohnert Park city	7 997	5 402	9.0	3 028	0.0	9.3	2.0	32 871	72.1	3.9	57.0	21.1	21.9
Rosemead city	11 757	4 406	8.3	3 403	0.0	6.1	5.8	40 335	54.2	7.5	45.3	14.9	39.8
Roseville city	16 019	4 839	7.5	3 945	0.0	11.5	2.3	60 650	64.2	4.0	54.2	15.3	30.5
Sacramento city	84 577	34 052	9.7	22 824	0.8	11.6	6.9	307 682	60.1	7.9	50.7	14.5	34.8
Salinas city	36 292	7 752	6.7	10 386	0.3	7.9	10.4	107 452	58.1	12.0	54.7	11.9	33.4
San Bernardino city	48 404	11 359	7.5	12 039	0.0	11.9	12.0	126 114	55.8	11.3	47.2	13.5	39.3
San Bruno city	7 331	3 304	18.7	1 997	0.0	10.3	2.3	32 063	68.5	2.7	58.0	14.9	26.2
San Buenaventura (Ventura) city	19 216	7 494	13.7	5 214	0.0	11.2	4.7	78 495	67.0	5.0	55.6	15.7	28.7
San Carlos city	4 387	1 458	21.8	906	0.0	6.6	1.9	21 982	70.3	2.0	60.1	14.9	25.0
San Clemente city	8 682	3 358	15.3	2 004	0.0	12.6	2.0	39 027	66.7	3.8	55.4	16.3	28.3
San Diego city	217 691	133 927	12.7	69 115	5.7	12.7	4.3	959 432	65.7	5.8	55.1	16.0	28.9
San Dimas city	7 128	3 057	21.6	2 265	0.0	5.7	1.5	27 283	66.0	5.4	54.7	16.0	29.3
San Francisco city	88 461	85 159	24.9	26 234	0.2	8.5	4.2	676 376	66.3	4.6	57.5	14.2	28.3
San Gabriel city	7 244	3 770	15.3	1 726	0.0	5.7	3.3	31 081	58.1	6.6	60.4	13.1	36.4
San Jose city	173 848	73 669	12.2	48 471	0.0	8.3	5.3	682 152	66.9	4.3	60.4	12.7	26.9
San Juan Capistrano city	7 307	1 854	16.3	1 842	0.7	10.9	2.8	25 435	60.9	4.1	50.9	15.7	33.4
San Leandro city	13 190	5 711	16.6	3 490	0.0	10.2	3.0	63 549	62.9	5.2	55.6	12.9	31.5
San Luis Obispo city	4 681	15 596	3.8	3 894	0.0	4.3	0.5	38 618	61.8	7.4	43.0	30.9	26.1
San Marcos city	11 752	3 920	7.3	2 833	0.5	8.3	6.0	40 602	64.9	5.5	54.5	14.5	31.0
San Mateo city	14 129	5 794	17.1	3 863	0.0	9.4	5.2	75 583	65.7	2.8	57.6	14.4	28.0
San Pablo city	7 230	2 027	8.4	1 627	0.0	11.2	5.3	21 313	56.1	9.4	51.9	12.1	36.0
San Rafael city	7 934	3 470	19.8	2 331	0.0	10.0	6.7	46 392	65.1	3.7	54.3	17.2	28.6
San Ramon city	8 536	2 824	12.6	2 101	0.0	4.0	1.2	34 073	77.0	1.8	66.8	14.8	18.4
Santa Ana city	85 228	17 973	5.4	22 797	0.2	9.8	11.2	233 350	59.4	8.0	56.2	11.3	32.5
Santa Barbara city	13 917	12 243	19.8	5 729	0.0	5.6	2.9	75 768	67.0	5.8	51.1	20.3	28.6
Santa Clara city	14 303	11 581	30.6	5 249	0.0	7.1	1.5	83 827	68.6	3.4	60.3	13.9	25.8
Santa Clarita city	33 918	10 805	12.0	8 434	0.0	9.7	2.4	110 020	72.0	4.8	60.4	16.1	23.6
Santa Cruz city	6 918	11 428	8.1	4 502	0.0	6.8	1.9	45 984	68.7	6.1	49.7	27.1	23.2
Santa Maria city	17 287	4 006	6.0	5 084	0.0	10.5	8.2	55 559	60.6	8.6	50.6	13.1	36.3
Santa Monica city	9 051	7 686	22.5	2 100	0.0	6.3	2.7	73 115	69.5	7.4	57.6	15.5	26.9
Santa Paula city	6 676	1 211	7.9	1 827	0.0	12.7	11.2	20 631	59.2	8.0	52.9	12.5	34.7
Santa Rosa city	27 144	10 693	10.6	8 408	0.0	12.4	5.4	115 926	65.5	4.4	53.1	17.8	29.1
Santee city	11 791	3 548	8.8	3 412	0.0	11.0	2.4	40 001	70.6	4.4	58.8	15.2	26.0
Saratoga city	6 225	1 512	22.1	1 325	0.0	3.8	0.2	22 959	59.2	1.8	51.0	14.3	34.7
Seaside city	6 820	2 193	11.0	1 658	1.6	9.4	6.9	23 043	65.0	4.7	55.3	15.8	28.8
Simi Valley city	24 067	6 991	12.7	6 240	0.1	7.9	2.3	83 334	71.5	4.2	60.5	14.9	24.6
South Gate city	26 337	5 857	6.2	6 697	0.0	9.7	10.0	65 419	54.7	10.0	53.4	10.7	35.9
South San Francisco city	11 000	5 038	21.7	3 208	0.0	9.5	4.1	47 516	65.2	3.8	58.3	13.7	28.0
Stanton city	8 346	2 205	8.1	2 009	0.0	11.3	9.0	26 592	60.1	7.9	53.2	12.1	34.7
Stockton city	59 451	17 207	12.1	16 792	0.1	10.0	6.7	172 996	58.9	12.4	49.5	13.6	37.0
Suisun City city	6 598	1 893	11.1	1 664	0.0	12.3	1.6	18 478	70.6	6.1	59.3	16.0	24.6
Sunnyvale city	17 962	9 901	18.8	4 440	0.0	10.3	4.3	107 360	70.1	3.3	63.4	11.4	25.3
Temecula city	14 722	3 591	11.2	3 531	0.3	13.2	3.5	39 474	68.6	4.7	57.7	16.2	26.1
Temple City city	6 283	2 934	15.3	1 701	0.0	6.9	0.4	26 220	60.6	5.0	51.3	14.4	34.2
Thousand Oaks city	22 742	8 372	16.2	6 140	0.0	7.3	1.7	89 817	68.5	3.8	55.9	17.7	26.5
Torrance city	24 522	11 314	14.5	6 320	0.0	5.6	2.2	109 862	64.1	3.9	54.5	14.1	31.4
Tracy city	14 810	2 830	9.1	3 344	0.0	11.0	6.0	39 135	69.3	5.8	60.8	13.5	25.7
Tulare city	11 359	1 915	5.6	2 912	0.0	13.9	5.4	30 322	58.7	10.7	50.2	13.0	36.8
Turlock city	12 663	4 237	8.6	3 423	0.0	11.0	5.2	40 644	60.4	9.2	49.6	16.0	34.4
Tustin city	12 965	5 299	10.4	3 094	0.0	8.0	3.6	51 088	71.8	4.7	64.0	13.5	22.5
Union City city	14 068	5 420	12.9	3 620	0.0	6.6	3.9	50 222	65.6	5.1	60.1	11.7	28.3

City	Full-year full-time employed (percent)								Children under 18 years in families (percent, except where noted)						Total employed by class of worker (percent)			
										With two parents		With one parent who is in labor force	+/− U.S. percent of children with no stay-at-home parent	+/− U.S. percent two-income couples				Unpaid family worker
	Total	Men	Women	Non-Hispanic White	Black or African American	American Indian and Alaska Native	Asian, Hawaiian, and Pacific Islander	Hispanic or Latino[1]	Number	Both in labor force	Father only in labor force				Private	Government	Self-employed	
	24	25	26	27	28	29	30	31	32	33	34	35	36	37	38	39	40	41
CALIFORNIA—Cont'd																		
Petaluma city	43.5	55.3	32.5	44.0	35.6	39.9	46.2	38.7	13 577	50.5	25.1	16.0	1.9	5.6	73.2	14.1	12.3	0.4
Pico Rivera city	35.7	46.0	26.0	28.9	19.5	34.6	39.1	36.3	17 765	32.4	22.8	20.3	-11.9	-14.5	79.5	13.7	6.4	0.4
Pittsburg city	40.6	47.3	34.1	43.2	41.2	31.6	41.5	36.9	16 019	38.9	20.8	21.3	-4.4	-0.5	78.3	14.9	6.7	0.1
Placentia city	42.9	53.6	32.7	46.5	41.7	28.7	45.8	34.4	11 981	44.5	27.9	16.2	-3.9	3.9	76.8	13.8	9.1	0.3
Pleasant Hill city	44.5	55.5	34.7	45.6	35.8	56.2	40.4	41.1	6 803	48.6	26.6	17.0	1.0	4.2	75.0	13.0	11.7	0.3
Pleasanton city	50.2	66.2	35.0	49.7	55.5	58.6	51.1	49.5	17 441	46.8	36.1	12.0	-5.8	5.0	77.8	12.2	9.6	0.4
Pomona city	29.8	37.7	21.8	33.6	29.2	22.5	27.8	29.1	46 165	28.2	23.2	19.6	-16.8	-11.3	79.6	12.9	7.2	0.3
Porterville city	26.5	32.0	21.4	30.5	10.3	22.5	21.8	23.3	12 825	36.0	18.1	26.5	-2.1	-2.9	65.8	25.2	8.6	0.4
Poway city	44.7	58.8	31.3	46.0	39.9	41.3	42.0	37.1	14 258	47.1	31.8	14.6	-2.9	3.8	73.5	14.2	12.1	0.2
Rancho Cucamonga city	44.3	55.3	33.6	46.0	46.1	31.7	42.1	41.3	36 498	46.8	22.9	20.4	2.6	7.7	72.7	17.1	9.9	0.4
Rancho Palos Verdes city	37.7	52.4	24.4	36.1	48.3	33.3	39.0	43.5	9 309	46.0	39.5	9.2	-9.4	-9.5	64.4	14.0	21.1	0.5
Rancho Santa Margarita city	56.0	73.0	40.1	57.2	62.4	44.8	48.9	52.7	15 811	49.8	34.0	11.8	-3.0	10.6	78.0	12.1	9.6	0.2
Redding city	32.3	41.6	24.0	33.1	32.1	25.4	22.2	27.7	19 713	37.8	19.8	25.6	-1.2	-6.6	69.9	18.0	11.8	0.3
Redlands city	36.6	47.0	27.8	37.1	35.5	45.3	35.7	35.7	15 639	39.7	21.0	26.5	1.6	0.0	66.4	23.5	9.7	0.4
Redondo Beach city	52.3	61.0	43.5	53.5	58.2	45.1	53.4	43.4	11 264	47.2	22.7	21.1	3.7	9.5	75.9	10.8	13.2	0.2
Redwood City city	46.1	55.2	37.1	48.7	43.1	40.7	50.4	38.7	16 426	45.0	21.0	19.4	-0.2	5.3	79.6	8.6	11.5	0.3
Rialto city	33.4	42.5	25.5	35.4	35.2	28.4	30.7	31.8	31 137	30.6	23.0	23.3	-10.7	-7.7	74.7	19.2	5.7	0.5
Richmond city	35.7	41.0	30.9	42.4	33.2	37.4	34.9	32.4	24 519	30.3	15.3	28.8	-5.5	-4.4	73.5	18.0	8.3	0.2
Riverside city	35.1	44.4	26.4	38.9	33.8	22.8	25.6	32.0	70 633	35.1	23.5	22.4	-7.1	-3.5	71.6	19.6	8.5	0.3
Rocklin city	46.2	57.6	35.6	46.3	54.9	38.7	38.8	48.1	10 567	50.0	27.3	16.6	2.0	6.2	72.3	18.3	9.0	0.4
Rohnert Park city	43.0	53.8	33.3	44.1	34.9	43.6	40.8	41.4	10 049	47.8	23.2	21.7	4.9	6.6	78.6	13.6	7.6	0.3
Rosemead city	29.1	35.8	22.9	27.7	20.0	24.1	28.6	29.5	13 461	30.6	24.0	17.9	-16.1	-13.6	79.5	12.1	8.1	0.4
Roseville city	42.8	54.2	32.6	42.8	50.4	48.9	42.7	42.4	20 893	46.2	26.8	18.7	0.3	-2.5	74.0	17.2	8.5	0.2
Sacramento city	34.7	40.0	29.8	38.8	32.4	32.7	29.5	32.0	101 333	28.7	19.2	25.5	-10.4	-6.7	65.1	27.0	7.6	0.3
Salinas city	26.4	29.6	22.8	37.3	23.4	26.2	33.0	20.6	42 918	37.0	20.3	17.8	-9.8	-8.6	77.2	15.4	7.2	0.2
San Bernardino city	29.3	36.4	22.7	33.0	27.2	24.8	24.5	27.4	59 422	24.3	21.6	25.9	-14.4	-12.2	70.9	21.3	7.4	0.3
San Bruno city	43.2	51.3	35.6	44.2	58.0	39.4	45.1	37.8	8 705	52.0	18.0	16.5	3.9	4.8	77.9	13.2	8.6	0.3
San Buenaventura (Ventura) city	39.9	49.0	31.5	41.1	39.0	39.2	41.2	36.1	23 978	42.6	22.3	22.6	0.6	2.1	67.9	19.4	12.3	0.4
San Carlos city	48.5	60.9	37.6	47.3	63.8	0.0	57.6	47.3	6 087	54.4	29.6	11.8	1.6	9.5	76.6	9.6	13.7	0.1
San Clemente city	42.3	55.2	29.3	42.1	66.1	27.7	50.2	41.8	11 530	42.6	32.9	16.5	-5.5	-2.8	69.6	11.9	18.2	0.3
San Diego city	38.9	47.6	30.1	42.6	38.7	35.3	36.5	31.6	273 089	36.3	24.9	21.0	-7.3	-2.9	72.8	16.5	10.3	0.3
San Dimas city	41.5	51.7	32.5	42.0	39.6	56.3	43.1	40.1	8 400	43.5	29.3	18.6	-2.5	2.7	71.4	15.2	12.8	0.6
San Francisco city	39.1	44.6	33.5	45.8	27.2	34.7	34.4	33.1	101 572	42.0	18.6	19.3	-3.3	-0.9	76.8	11.7	11.2	0.2
San Gabriel city	34.3	41.2	28.2	35.6	44.3	67.0	33.9	34.2	8 591	37.3	24.0	18.1	-9.2	-3.0	75.4	14.4	9.8	0.4
San Jose city	43.5	52.6	34.1	47.6	47.8	35.2	43.6	37.2	217 299	41.4	23.7	18.5	-4.7	1.3	82.7	9.8	7.2	0.3
San Juan Capistrano city	36.7	49.2	25.0	38.7	30.5	47.8	32.0	32.5	8 805	33.6	35.9	16.7	-14.3	-10.9	72.4	10.2	17.0	0.3
San Leandro city	40.3	48.3	33.0	37.2	48.6	42.3	43.2	40.2	16 417	41.8	15.1	25.3	2.5	-1.3	77.7	14.9	7.2	0.2
San Luis Obispo city	24.5	30.0	18.6	25.1	25.1	30.6	19.1	25.0	5 944	46.6	23.3	20.7	2.7	0.4	66.1	22.2	11.6	0.2
San Marcos city	38.8	49.6	28.5	39.8	51.5	34.7	42.1	35.0	14 648	41.6	28.4	16.2	-6.8	-1.8	79.0	10.5	10.2	0.2
San Mateo city	43.4	52.7	34.7	44.2	39.4	42.2	47.1	38.4	17 753	44.1	25.0	17.0	-3.5	0.9	77.6	10.2	11.9	0.3
San Pablo city	31.5	38.9	24.6	27.7	39.5	11.9	32.5	28.4	8 689	25.0	21.5	23.1	-16.5	-10.6	77.8	14.7	6.9	0.6
San Rafael city	36.8	46.0	28.2	38.9	44.3	39.6	39.0	28.1	10 183	40.9	22.7	20.3	-3.4	-0.7	70.0	9.9	19.7	0.4
San Ramon city	55.3	69.0	42.2	56.0	53.7	47.2	52.1	54.5	11 400	53.7	28.8	13.6	2.7	13.0	79.3	10.4	10.0	0.3
Santa Ana city	33.0	40.5	24.8	39.0	36.4	21.2	35.4	31.3	99 434	29.4	25.9	16.1	-19.1	-13.4	85.5	7.7	6.5	0.3
Santa Barbara city	35.9	45.2	26.9	35.6	28.5	24.4	33.7	37.0	16 576	37.3	26.3	20.7	-6.6	-2.1	70.2	14.0	15.4	0.3
Santa Clara city	44.0	54.4	33.4	45.2	45.4	26.1	43.8	41.8	18 907	42.8	26.8	18.4	-3.4	-0.6	85.9	7.9	6.0	0.2
Santa Clarita city	45.5	58.1	33.6	46.4	50.0	43.9	43.7	41.5	44 205	45.9	31.0	15.2	-3.5	4.9	74.0	15.0	10.7	0.3
Santa Cruz city	31.8	40.7	23.2	32.6	31.8	35.4	25.0	30.7	8 811	36.8	24.1	26.3	-1.5	3.3	64.4	20.8	14.6	0.3
Santa Maria city	29.3	36.9	21.6	31.0	36.5	26.1	32.9	27.2	21 973	40.4	20.6	20.1	-4.1	-8.7	80.5	11.0	8.1	0.4
Santa Monica city	38.3	45.6	31.7	40.1	30.5	44.4	35.3	34.3	11 562	41.7	25.5	20.3	-2.6	0.9	69.2	10.3	20.0	0.5
Santa Paula city	30.4	36.8	23.7	32.4	41.9	29.8	39.9	29.3	8 384	35.2	25.0	19.6	-9.8	-10.2	76.3	15.2	7.8	0.7
Santa Rosa city	38.5	48.0	29.8	38.6	39.1	39.9	38.1	37.4	33 285	45.0	20.5	22.0	2.4	2.4	75.0	12.8	11.9	0.3
Santee city	46.9	58.7	36.4	48.4	35.2	40.3	46.2	38.1	14 239	51.0	20.3	22.6	9.0	10.4	74.0	17.1	8.9	0.1
Saratoga city	41.6	58.7	25.9	38.5	45.9	100.0	51.2	32.8	7 641	47.4	42.7	3.9	-13.3	-5.9	72.5	8.6	18.2	0.6
Seaside city	36.7	46.0	27.3	42.9	32.5	25.4	34.3	31.4	8 611	33.9	27.1	20.9	-9.8	-1.9	76.9	12.8	10.1	0.3
Simi Valley city	47.8	58.7	37.2	49.4	50.8	49.0	48.3	39.6	30 135	46.8	27.4	16.8	-1.0	5.3	76.9	11.3	11.5	0.2
South Gate city	29.0	39.1	19.5	28.6	31.5	32.9	40.9	28.9	31 523	25.0	27.6	17.2	-22.4	-19.6	83.2	10.0	6.5	0.3
South San Francisco city	42.7	49.9	35.9	39.5	45.2	33.2	46.5	42.3	13 429	51.0	16.5	17.8	4.2	3.7	79.5	12.8	7.5	0.2
Stanton city	35.9	45.6	26.5	35.4	52.7	43.6	33.4	36.0	10 172	35.2	23.1	19.0	-10.4	-10.1	86.6	7.8	5.5	0.2
Stockton city	30.7	37.0	24.9	36.9	30.4	27.1	23.9	27.3	72 115	30.5	20.0	23.5	-10.6	-8.4	74.5	18.1	7.1	0.3
Suisun City city	45.1	54.9	35.5	49.8	47.5	55.6	38.6	38.4	7 727	47.4	20.7	19.8	2.6	6.1	70.1	23.6	6.1	0.2
Sunnyvale city	48.0	59.1	36.1	50.1	52.6	49.7	47.2	41.8	25 541	41.3	31.5	16.3	-7.0	-3.6	86.6	6.5	6.8	0.1
Temecula city	43.2	58.6	28.7	44.8	52.7	41.5	39.2	36.7	19 131	45.8	32.9	12.4	-6.4	0.9	73.0	15.8	11.0	0.2
Temple City city	37.0	45.6	29.7	37.2	17.0	59.0	35.8	39.6	7 595	44.6	20.6	18.1	-1.9	-1.3	71.2	15.2	13.3	0.2
Thousand Oaks city	43.0	57.3	29.7	42.9	52.3	45.9	50.5	39.3	29 068	44.9	34.7	12.5	-7.2	0.2	72.6	12.1	15.0	0.3
Torrance city	41.5	51.7	32.1	41.9	44.4	43.9	41.5	39.7	30 255	46.3	26.3	16.3	-2.0	-1.2	74.2	12.7	12.5	0.6
Tracy city	46.1	59.7	33.1	48.9	56.5	49.3	44.5	37.6	18 704	45.0	29.1	13.8	-5.8	2.9	80.4	12.6	6.7	0.3
Tulare city	32.6	41.9	24.2	36.1	28.7	29.4	27.6	28.6	13 904	33.4	22.2	21.1	-10.1	-8.1	74.0	16.2	9.6	0.3
Turlock city	32.5	43.4	22.9	34.0	24.2	47.4	30.7	28.3	15 407	40.8	23.2	16.9	-6.9	-5.3	72.2	17.6	10.0	0.3
Tustin city	47.8	57.3	39.2	53.4	54.2	45.0	44.5	39.1	17 077	41.0	22.7	20.0	-3.6	6.0	81.2	9.7	8.8	0.4
Union City city	44.2	53.4	35.3	47.0	48.6	57.6	44.1	40.8	17 384	46.3	19.7	17.3	-1.0	3.3	83.5	10.5	5.8	0.2

[1] Hispanic or Latino persons may be of any race.

Table B-5. Cities — Education, Labor Force, and Income

City	Percent who worked at home	Percent of the population 5 years and over with a disability	Veterans as a percent of the population 18 years and over	Occupation for employed population 16 years and over (percent)						Industry for employed population 16 years and over (percent)					
				Management, professional, and related occupations	Service occupations	Sales and office occupations	Farming, fishing, and forestry occupations	Construction, extraction, and maintenance occupations	Production, transportation and material moving occupations	Agriculture, forestry, fishing, and mining	Construction and manufacturing	Wholesale and retail trade	Transportation and warehousing, and utilities	Service industries	Public administration
	42	43	44	45	46	47	48	49	50	51	52	53	54	55	56
CALIFORNIA—Cont'd															
Petaluma city................	4.7	15.6	11.6	36.5	14.6	28.0	0.6	9.8	10.4	1.0	17.6	15.5	4.7	56.7	4.5
Pico Rivera city............	1.4	22.6	8.0	19.4	14.7	28.8	0.3	9.2	27.5	0.2	26.1	19.3	8.1	42.5	3.8
Pittsburg city...............	2.2	21.1	11.6	24.0	19.1	29.8	0.1	13.2	13.7	0.6	17.5	15.5	7.3	54.9	4.2
Placentia city...............	3.4	12.8	10.5	39.3	12.6	28.5	0.4	7.2	12.0	0.6	24.4	16.0	3.9	51.8	3.4
Pleasant Hill city..........	5.0	14.7	12.1	48.9	10.7	26.9	0.1	8.2	5.2	0.4	14.3	15.9	4.2	61.1	4.1
Pleasanton city.............	4.6	10.9	10.8	52.2	8.7	28.6	0.0	4.7	5.8	0.1	21.3	17.3	4.0	54.2	3.1
Pomona city.................	2.1	21.9	6.3	22.2	17.2	24.6	0.4	11.4	24.3	0.5	27.8	16.4	4.8	47.2	3.3
Porterville city.............	2.6	21.3	9.9	26.5	17.6	23.6	10.6	8.1	13.6	11.2	12.2	17.7	3.6	49.0	6.4
Poway city...................	4.8	12.1	17.0	44.4	14.1	26.6	0.1	7.5	7.3	0.3	19.8	14.8	4.0	56.6	4.5
Rancho Cucamonga city....	3.0	14.8	10.6	35.6	13.2	30.5	0.2	8.5	12.0	0.4	19.2	17.8	6.7	50.5	5.5
Rancho Palos Verdes city..	6.7	12.9	13.9	62.9	5.0	24.0	0.2	3.2	4.8	0.3	17.3	14.7	5.9	50.9	4.9
Rancho Santa Margarita city..	4.4	8.3	8.9	50.3	9.8	30.9	0.2	4.7	4.2	0.3	20.6	16.3	4.0	54.5	4.3
Redding city.................	3.9	21.9	16.0	31.9	20.4	29.0	0.3	7.9	10.5	1.1	11.6	18.2	4.7	58.3	6.0
Redlands city................	2.8	17.5	12.9	45.8	14.3	23.9	0.1	7.0	8.8	0.8	12.0	12.6	4.9	63.4	6.3
Redondo Beach city......	4.3	13.9	9.7	53.1	10.0	26.5	0.0	5.4	4.9	0.1	20.5	13.5	5.8	56.5	3.6
Redwood City city.........	2.9	15.9	8.6	42.3	15.0	24.0	0.3	9.3	9.1	0.5	19.8	14.3	4.1	58.8	2.6
Rialto city...................	2.5	19.8	10.5	20.2	16.1	28.5	0.2	11.2	23.6	0.4	23.1	19.4	8.3	43.3	5.5
Richmond city...............	2.9	21.6	9.2	32.9	18.1	26.4	0.2	9.0	13.3	0.3	15.7	13.6	7.5	57.8	5.0
Riverside city...............	3.0	18.4	10.5	30.9	15.5	26.6	0.4	11.5	15.2	0.6	21.6	15.5	4.6	52.7	5.1
Rocklin city.................	6.0	13.5	15.0	43.8	10.8	31.1	0.0	7.2	7.1	0.2	16.5	18.5	4.1	52.0	8.6
Rohnert Park city..........	2.8	16.9	10.8	30.7	15.4	32.5	0.1	10.1	11.3	0.3	21.0	17.9	4.6	52.4	3.7
Rosemead city..............	1.6	23.9	3.9	22.3	18.2	27.6	0.1	7.1	24.8	0.2	25.9	17.2	4.4	49.5	2.8
Roseville city...............	4.2	16.0	16.5	41.8	12.1	29.2	0.2	8.4	8.3	0.2	18.5	17.0	5.0	50.9	8.3
Sacramento city............	2.9	22.7	11.7	36.2	16.2	28.6	0.4	7.6	11.0	0.6	12.4	13.2	4.7	54.4	14.8
Salinas city.................	1.9	22.6	8.1	21.4	16.2	24.0	14.9	9.1	14.4	15.2	13.3	19.8	3.7	42.1	5.9
San Bernardino city.......	2.8	22.4	11.0	23.3	19.9	26.7	0.4	11.4	18.2	0.7	18.1	17.0	6.5	51.8	6.0
San Bruno city..............	2.4	15.7	9.9	32.2	15.8	32.3	0.1	9.4	10.2	0.1	13.9	18.1	10.6	52.6	4.7
San Buenaventura (Ventura) city..	4.1	18.1	13.4	39.2	13.7	27.6	0.8	8.7	10.0	2.2	17.0	14.8	4.0	54.1	7.9
San Carlos city.............	4.7	12.3	10.3	56.1	8.1	25.9	0.0	5.5	4.5	0.2	19.3	13.8	5.3	58.7	2.8
San Clemente city.........	5.2	13.9	14.2	40.9	13.5	29.2	0.2	8.5	7.8	0.3	18.5	16.8	4.9	55.7	3.8
San Diego city..............	4.0	17.7	12.8	41.8	15.9	26.4	0.2	6.7	9.0	0.3	15.4	13.0	3.7	62.3	5.3
San Dimas city.............	3.3	18.5	12.5	42.2	12.3	29.8	0.2	6.7	8.9	0.3	17.9	16.1	4.0	56.4	5.2
San Francisco city........	4.6	20.3	7.0	48.3	14.3	25.6	0.1	4.2	7.5	0.2	10.1	12.8	4.5	69.1	3.3
San Gabriel city............	2.6	20.4	5.5	34.0	16.2	29.8	0.0	5.6	14.4	0.2	18.6	16.5	4.4	56.9	3.4
San Jose city...............	2.5	18.5	7.7	40.8	12.3	24.4	0.3	7.9	14.3	0.4	33.9	13.7	3.3	46.0	2.7
San Juan Capistrano city..	4.4	16.5	11.8	35.2	16.6	29.8	0.7	8.6	9.2	0.4	18.6	17.3	3.5	57.3	3.0
San Leandro city...........	2.4	22.1	11.3	32.8	11.7	31.7	0.2	8.6	15.1	0.3	20.1	16.3	8.8	49.7	4.7
San Luis Obispo city.....	4.7	14.3	9.0	39.0	19.7	28.6	0.9	5.5	6.3	1.0	10.5	14.7	3.5	66.1	4.3
San Marcos city............	4.2	16.7	12.8	29.0	15.8	27.0	1.6	11.1	15.5	1.4	26.9	17.5	3.4	48.1	2.6
San Mateo city.............	3.5	18.2	9.1	43.2	13.6	27.9	0.1	7.4	7.9	0.2	16.4	15.5	6.6	58.5	2.7
San Pablo city..............	1.6	25.5	6.2	20.2	23.4	25.8	0.7	13.8	16.2	0.8	19.8	12.9	9.0	53.3	4.2
San Rafael city.............	6.5	20.1	9.7	45.1	16.7	25.2	0.1	7.1	5.9	0.3	12.7	14.6	2.6	66.8	2.9
San Ramon city.............	4.8	10.0	10.2	54.8	6.0	30.6	0.0	4.5	4.0	0.3	15.9	17.8	4.6	58.0	3.5
Santa Ana city.............	1.6	21.9	4.2	16.5	21.4	22.4	1.7	11.3	26.7	1.5	32.8	14.5	2.7	46.5	2.0
Santa Barbara city	5.5	17.9	9.1	40.9	18.7	25.3	0.6	6.6	8.0	0.9	14.2	12.9	2.9	65.9	3.2
Santa Clara city............	2.3	15.7	8.5	51.3	9.3	23.2	0.2	5.5	10.6	0.1	34.4	12.4	2.8	47.7	2.7
Santa Clarita city..........	3.2	13.1	9.9	40.9	14.1	28.0	0.0	8.2	8.9	0.4	18.9	14.3	4.3	57.1	5.0
Santa Cruz city.............	5.7	15.2	8.2	45.1	16.1	23.6	0.8	7.6	6.7	1.0	16.3	13.3	1.8	64.4	3.2
Santa Maria city...........	1.3	23.6	11.1	17.8	16.4	23.4	18.7	9.0	14.8	21.4	14.7	17.0	3.0	39.9	3.9
Santa Monica city.........	8.0	16.6	7.3	60.3	9.4	23.3	0.0	3.3	3.7	0.0	8.5	11.2	2.2	75.9	2.1
Santa Paula city...........	1.8	22.2	8.2	18.2	14.5	27.6	11.5	11.2	17.0	13.0	21.5	16.8	4.5	38.6	5.6
Santa Rosa city............	4.4	19.1	13.3	34.1	15.9	27.7	0.9	8.9	12.4	1.1	21.4	15.6	4.0	54.1	3.8
Santee city..................	3.3	15.0	17.2	31.4	14.5	32.3	0.1	12.1	9.6	0.0	20.1	16.3	4.2	52.1	7.3
Saratoga city...............	7.1	9.4	12.0	72.5	3.7	18.7	0.0	2.2	2.9	0.1	35.0	10.6	1.0	50.8	2.5
Seaside city.................	1.9	19.0	12.2	20.4	34.5	23.7	2.4	9.0	10.0	2.6	11.3	13.8	3.0	65.1	4.3
Simi Valley city............	3.7	16.0	11.5	38.2	12.4	30.7	0.2	8.4	10.1	0.5	21.9	15.7	3.4	54.9	3.6
South Gate city	1.4	20.9	3.2	15.0	14.2	27.7	0.4	9.6	33.1	0.3	33.1	18.8	6.0	40.4	1.4
South San Francisco city..	1.8	17.8	8.6	30.1	14.5	32.0	0.4	9.7	13.3	0.5	15.4	17.1	10.8	52.1	4.1
Stanton city.................	1.9	22.4	7.5	19.6	16.4	27.3	0.1	11.6	24.8	0.1	34.3	14.8	4.3	43.7	2.8
Stockton city................	2.4	22.5	10.3	26.5	16.2	27.7	4.1	8.5	17.0	4.2	16.8	16.2	6.3	50.3	6.2
Suisun City city............	2.4	19.0	17.9	26.0	16.8	30.2	0.2	12.3	14.5	0.5	16.7	17.1	8.7	47.3	9.8
Sunnyvale city..............	2.6	14.2	8.7	59.5	9.0	19.4	0.1	4.3	7.6	0.1	34.5	11.5	1.6	50.5	1.8
Temecula city...............	4.1	13.0	14.8	35.5	14.8	28.8	0.2	8.7	12.0	0.5	22.8	17.7	4.9	48.7	5.4
Temple City city	3.5	17.6	8.7	37.9	12.3	32.0	0.1	7.9	9.9	0.2	17.3	17.2	5.7	55.3	4.3
Thousand Oaks city	5.9	15.2	11.8	48.6	11.5	28.0	0.1	5.4	6.4	0.5	19.4	13.9	2.6	59.9	3.7
Torrance city................	3.5	16.2	10.8	45.7	10.1	30.0	0.0	6.2	7.9	0.2	21.5	16.4	6.7	51.6	3.6
Tracy city...................	3.2	16.8	12.0	30.7	12.1	29.7	0.8	10.9	15.7	1.2	25.3	18.6	5.9	44.6	4.5
Tulare city..................	2.8	21.2	8.9	20.7	17.3	27.4	5.9	10.5	18.2	8.0	21.4	15.6	5.6	43.3	6.2
Turlock city.................	2.7	20.4	9.6	30.2	15.0	25.3	3.5	8.3	17.6	5.5	21.2	15.6	4.2	49.4	4.1
Tustin city...................	3.1	15.7	8.8	40.5	13.1	29.6	0.1	5.6	11.1	0.1	22.5	15.7	3.1	56.0	2.7
Union City city.............	1.9	19.3	7.4	35.7	11.3	26.6	0.2	7.4	18.8	0.3	28.0	16.5	7.6	45.2	2.5

City	Median household income	Median family income: All families	Median family income: Families with children: Married-couple	Median family income: Families with children: Male householder	Median family income: Families with children: Female householder	Median nonfamily household income	Median income for full-year, full-time workers: Men	Median income for full-year, full-time workers: Women	Per capita income	Households by source of income (percent): With earnings	Households by source of income (percent): With interest, dividend, or rental income	Households by source of income (percent): With Social Security income	Households by source of income (percent): With public assistance income	Households by source of income (percent): With retirement income	Households with income over $100,000 (percent)	+/− U.S. percent for income over $100,000	Households with income below poverty (percent)	Families with children with income below poverty (percent)
	57	58	59	60	61	62	63	64	65	66	67	68	69	70	71	72	73	74
CALIFORNIA—Cont'd																		
Petaluma city	61 679	71 158	80 992	44 028	31 513	36 538	51 202	37 871	27 087	84.4	45.3	23.1	1.1	18.3	23.1	10.8	5.1	4.6
Pico Rivera city	41 564	45 422	49 615	26 970	20 364	15 460	29 904	25 140	13 011	79.6	16.5	30.8	5.7	15.8	8.2	-4.1	12.6	13.3
Pittsburg city	50 557	54 472	59 952	43 056	26 319	32 086	40 197	31 900	18 241	86.2	24.3	20.6	5.0	16.2	12.5	0.2	10.2	12.1
Placentia city	62 803	68 976	74 304	41 615	31 528	41 688	49 091	35 275	23 843	88.2	42.4	20.3	2.2	15.7	22.9	10.6	6.1	8.8
Pleasant Hill city	67 489	79 001	88 554	60 057	46 450	46 584	60 449	45 428	33 076	83.6	50.6	22.2	1.3	18.4	27.1	14.8	5.1	3.9
Pleasanton city	90 859	102 796	116 020	76 359	44 034	53 053	79 241	46 085	41 623	90.5	52.9	14.9	1.1	13.5	44.3	32.0	2.4	2.4
Pomona city	40 021	40 852	43 858	25 315	20 218	25 687	30 593	26 850	13 336	86.1	22.0	18.2	8.1	11.6	10.1	-2.2	17.7	21.7
Porterville city	32 046	35 136	42 002	22 417	15 310	18 440	31 849	24 649	12 745	78.0	21.0	24.7	11.0	16.6	4.9	-7.4	20.5	27.3
Poway city	71 708	77 875	88 314	38 036	31 023	37 331	56 624	35 948	29 788	88.0	50.9	19.1	2.0	19.2	32.0	19.7	3.8	4.4
Rancho Cucamonga city	60 931	66 446	73 901	44 432	31 163	36 118	48 700	32 815	23 702	90.1	31.2	14.9	2.4	12.5	20.9	8.6	6.0	6.0
Rancho Palos Verdes city	95 503	105 586	123 338	93 488	63 859	56 524	86 096	49 792	46 250	81.1	65.1	30.5	0.9	24.0	47.5	35.2	2.7	2.6
Rancho Santa Margarita city	78 475	88 216	98 114	48 214	37 448	47 307	62 008	41 302	31 531	95.1	39.4	6.9	1.2	6.7	34.9	22.6	2.4	2.1
Redding city	34 194	41 164	51 036	25 149	17 177	20 339	36 800	25 784	18 207	73.5	32.7	30.6	7.2	20.2	7.5	-4.8	13.8	18.0
Redlands city	48 155	56 254	65 437	27 109	26 250	32 710	43 659	34 368	24 237	81.7	36.2	24.1	4.6	19.2	17.0	4.7	9.2	11.4
Redondo Beach city	69 173	80 543	91 527	55 278	34 281	54 665	58 319	46 069	38 305	88.9	45.7	15.0	1.8	11.0	29.6	17.3	5.1	6.0
Redwood City city	66 748	73 798	82 098	40 643	41 089	47 867	51 367	41 904	34 042	85.9	46.8	19.4	1.9	13.4	29.9	17.6	5.1	5.0
Rialto city	41 254	42 638	50 127	32 171	22 698	24 497	35 229	27 262	13 375	84.7	17.2	20.5	8.7	15.2	8.4	-3.9	14.2	17.1
Richmond city	44 210	46 659	54 392	29 698	22 276	35 603	38 392	35 079	19 788	82.1	28.8	21.6	6.3	16.3	12.0	-0.3	13.8	18.8
Riverside city	41 646	47 254	54 568	29 294	19 994	25 909	37 719	29 300	17 882	83.0	26.8	21.3	5.6	15.3	11.7	-0.6	14.1	15.9
Rocklin city	64 737	72 245	86 364	29 412	33 293	34 714	56 598	36 545	26 910	85.8	42.9	19.7	2.0	15.9	24.4	12.1	4.7	4.1
Rohnert Park city	51 942	61 420	69 885	42 692	32 596	32 244	42 413	31 920	23 035	86.5	36.3	19.4	2.3	14.0	14.2	1.9	8.0	4.1
Rosemead city	36 181	36 552	35 743	21 696	18 114	22 329	27 320	23 048	12 146	84.0	26.5	20.9	10.9	12.2	7.3	-5.0	19.1	26.3
Roseville city	57 367	65 929	80 029	42 560	32 308	36 594	51 000	36 053	27 021	79.0	45.7	27.1	2.2	21.7	18.3	6.0	5.1	5.3
Sacramento city	37 049	42 051	47 931	26 786	20 851	28 512	36 644	31 907	18 721	78.3	29.4	22.6	8.5	16.8	9.4	-2.9	15.9	22.5
Salinas city	43 720	44 667	47 438	30 709	21 135	29 644	36 448	27 818	14 495	85.9	25.5	21.4	5.7	15.1	9.8	-2.5	12.8	16.6
San Bernardino city	31 140	33 357	41 328	24 432	14 248	21 506	31 446	26 500	12 925	78.3	18.7	21.8	11.9	14.6	5.4	-6.9	23.5	30.2
San Bruno city	62 081	70 251	81 884	52 059	35 259	40 788	48 266	37 155	26 360	86.3	43.4	21.7	1.5	16.6	22.2	9.9	5.0	3.7
San Buenaventura (Ventura) city	52 298	60 466	68 988	44 293	25 408	33 443	45 568	32 500	25 065	82.3	40.6	25.4	2.7	18.5	17.2	4.9	7.5	10.0
San Carlos city	88 460	103 971	125 992	103 297	46 607	48 592	75 053	54 426	46 628	82.9	61.0	24.4	1.1	17.3	42.8	30.5	2.8	1.6
San Clemente city	63 507	76 261	87 654	41 328	34 831	40 582	53 813	37 716	34 169	83.2	44.9	23.9	1.2	16.5	28.7	16.4	5.4	7.5
San Diego city	45 733	53 060	59 588	29 486	21 481	33 882	38 653	31 812	23 609	83.4	38.1	20.1	3.9	16.1	15.6	3.3	12.1	15.9
San Dimas city	62 885	72 124	84 760	50 438	38 854	35 996	54 474	36 924	28 321	85.0	42.3	22.7	2.7	16.1	24.9	12.6	5.2	5.3
San Francisco city	55 221	63 545	72 158	34 770	27 433	46 457	48 203	40 938	34 556	81.3	46.3	21.0	3.9	13.0	24.7	12.4	10.2	11.8
San Gabriel city	41 791	45 287	49 896	30 507	25 145	27 073	32 342	30 114	16 807	83.5	33.8	19.4	6.5	11.8	11.7	-0.6	14.0	16.3
San Jose city	70 243	74 813	83 876	43 866	32 013	48 486	50 414	37 741	26 697	88.9	39.2	16.7	3.7	13.1	30.8	18.5	7.1	8.1
San Juan Capistrano city	62 392	69 481	70 682	48 929	40 341	36 446	49 085	36 563	29 926	80.4	47.9	26.1	1.4	17.8	25.8	13.5	7.1	10.3
San Leandro city	51 081	60 266	69 755	42 382	34 306	33 886	41 970	34 637	23 895	79.4	41.6	27.8	2.8	20.1	14.9	2.6	6.5	6.3
San Luis Obispo city	31 926	56 319	75 523	36 875	22 868	20 328	45 053	28 110	20 386	81.2	43.5	21.0	1.3	14.5	10.5	-1.8	24.3	7.7
San Marcos city	45 908	51 292	57 644	30 306	25 523	25 788	37 482	27 813	18 657	80.1	35.3	27.4	2.0	19.9	12.5	0.2	9.1	11.1
San Mateo city	64 757	76 223	85 845	52 383	39 107	45 449	52 069	42 468	36 176	81.1	51.4	25.8	1.1	16.5	28.5	16.2	5.2	5.5
San Pablo city	37 184	42 042	44 519	23 100	19 902	20 121	31 787	28 481	14 303	80.1	18.9	20.3	8.2	13.9	7.1	-5.2	17.2	20.7
San Rafael city	60 994	74 398	82 935	48 047	29 911	44 299	52 421	41 580	35 762	81.6	48.5	23.4	2.5	15.3	27.9	15.6	7.8	9.5
San Ramon city	95 856	106 321	119 020	79 492	57 115	67 080	76 727	50 974	42 336	93.1	57.0	12.2	0.7	12.3	47.6	35.3	2.0	1.3
Santa Ana city	43 412	41 050	40 452	29 748	22 451	32 003	23 921	21 949	12 152	90.5	20.2	16.0	5.7	10.6	10.1	-2.2	15.4	19.6
Santa Barbara city	47 498	57 880	61 411	33 203	29 654	35 563	38 300	33 274	26 466	80.5	44.1	25.1	2.0	14.7	17.7	5.4	10.8	13.0
Santa Clara city	69 466	77 189	87 519	50 429	39 179	53 207	60 302	44 938	31 755	86.3	43.8	18.2	2.2	13.5	29.3	17.0	6.6	6.1
Santa Clarita city	66 717	73 588	81 310	52 794	36 582	41 368	55 669	37 646	26 841	89.3	38.8	16.8	2.1	12.8	25.8	13.5	5.7	5.9
Santa Cruz city	50 605	62 231	72 529	41 364	25 750	33 694	46 754	35 737	25 758	84.8	46.1	18.4	2.7	12.3	19.4	7.1	13.1	10.6
Santa Maria city	36 541	39 277	41 516	25 714	16 369	22 525	29 421	23 274	13 780	78.9	28.0	29.3	6.3	19.1	6.8	-5.5	14.9	21.6
Santa Monica city	50 714	75 989	100 604	40 699	36 713	40 820	58 884	44 820	42 874	82.1	44.5	18.1	2.3	9.8	23.6	11.3	9.9	8.4
Santa Paula city	41 651	45 419	49 511	37 500	19 776	21 507	33 086	26 175	15 736	78.1	28.7	29.3	4.8	20.0	10.8	-1.5	12.7	16.7
Santa Rosa city	50 931	59 659	67 415	40 645	29 922	32 972	41 128	31 458	24 495	79.4	43.2	27.1	2.8	18.7	15.8	3.5	7.1	8.0
Santee city	53 624	57 874	66 140	41 991	27 643	30 046	42 582	31 290	21 311	86.7	34.6	21.0	2.9	18.4	12.7	0.4	5.6	5.8
Saratoga city	139 895	155 246	174 973	116 767	57 143	57 781	100 001	67 466	65 400	83.2	76.0	26.6	0.7	18.8	67.1	54.8	2.6	2.6
Seaside city	41 393	43 259	44 037	26 509	20 612	26 524	30 400	27 004	15 183	86.3	30.5	21.1	4.7	16.6	7.8	-4.5	10.5	12.9
Simi Valley city	70 370	75 140	81 688	47 153	38 284	42 295	51 750	36 059	26 586	89.7	38.7	17.9	2.2	14.4	26.4	14.1	4.7	5.1
South Gate city	35 695	35 789	39 795	26 958	18 485	20 852	25 679	20 604	10 602	88.8	15.6	17.0	8.0	8.5	5.3	-7.0	17.5	20.7
South San Francisco city	61 764	66 598	78 073	41 290	35 292	34 899	41 987	36 214	23 562	83.4	42.1	27.1	2.0	20.5	21.3	9.0	4.9	5.1
Stanton city	39 127	40 162	42 468	31 071	26 422	26 879	28 214	26 613	14 197	83.0	23.1	20.7	5.8	13.1	6.6	-5.7	13.3	17.6
Stockton city	35 453	40 434	46 473	26 957	16 013	21 792	36 035	27 263	15 405	78.2	24.9	23.2	10.5	16.4	8.2	-4.1	19.5	26.0
Suisun City city	60 848	63 616	70 550	42 344	29 375	35 794	42 409	31 789	20 386	91.5	28.4	15.5	3.8	19.1	14.4	2.1	5.9	5.6
Sunnyvale city	74 409	81 634	96 048	56 413	41 188	60 167	66 432	45 256	36 524	87.8	49.7	18.1	1.8	13.0	33.7	21.4	4.7	5.2
Temecula city	59 516	62 270	69 407	46 944	27 104	36 983	50 342	32 341	21 557	89.6	32.3	15.9	1.7	16.0	17.0	4.7	6.2	6.8
Temple City city	48 722	54 455	59 147	31 731	25 990	31 230	40 848	32 831	20 267	84.4	42.0	22.2	3.4	15.3	13.2	0.9	8.8	9.7
Thousand Oaks city	76 815	86 041	97 231	49 000	39 004	45 088	65 810	41 694	34 314	86.5	49.3	21.5	1.5	16.5	35.1	22.8	4.4	4.5
Torrance city	56 489	67 098	79 222	43 125	31 623	36 362	52 241	38 483	28 144	82.1	45.4	24.4	2.0	16.7	21.0	8.7	6.5	6.3
Tracy city	62 794	67 464	75 568	39 563	31 667	33 922	50 667	35 692	21 397	88.4	29.4	15.6	2.9	13.9	18.5	6.2	6.2	5.9
Tulare city	33 637	36 935	41 349	28 300	14 353	19 496	31 797	24 365	13 655	79.8	20.3	24.1	9.6	12.8	6.0	-6.3	17.6	23.2
Turlock city	39 050	45 501	53 872	31 058	16 939	21 095	36 567	27 828	16 844	79.1	29.7	25.2	6.4	15.9	8.2	-4.1	14.9	16.4
Tustin city	55 985	60 092	61 236	36 917	32 750	44 802	43 975	34 604	25 932	91.3	36.9	14.1	2.4	9.9	21.3	9.0	6.1	8.8
Union City city	71 926	74 910	80 696	38 661	37 076	37 449	46 200	35 544	22 890	90.4	35.1	17.1	4.7	14.3	28.4	16.1	5.7	5.9

Table B-5. Cities — Education, Labor Force, and Income

STATE Place code	City	High school graduates			College graduates		College graduates (percent)				
		Total population 25 years and over	Percent with a high school diploma or less	Percent with a high school diploma or more	Percent with a bachelor's degree or more	+/− U.S. percent with bachelor's degree or more	Non-Hispanic White	Black or African American	American Indian and Alaska Native	Asian, Hawaiian, and Pacific Islander	Hispanic or Latino[1]
		1	2	3	4	5	6	7	8	9	10
	CALIFORNIA—Cont'd										
06 81344	Upland city	43 311	38.0	83.8	26.7	2.3	29.0	24.7	4.9	48.6	13.8
06 81554	Vacaville city	57 088	41.8	83.9	19.4	−5.0	22.4	9.5	11.2	30.5	8.9
06 81666	Vallejo city	74 155	42.7	81.7	21.1	−3.3	19.8	15.5	9.0	33.3	10.2
06 82590	Victorville city	36 777	52.9	76.7	10.6	−13.8	12.0	12.6	9.7	23.4	5.1
06 82994	Visalia city	53 916	46.2	76.4	18.9	−5.5	23.4	11.5	3.5	23.1	8.4
06 82996	Vista city	53 004	46.3	75.9	19.6	−4.8	26.0	13.1	11.1	37.6	5.4
06 83332	Walnut city	18 699	25.5	88.8	41.9	17.5	33.5	35.1	0.0	54.8	13.3
06 83346	Walnut Creek city	49 986	17.6	95.0	54.0	29.6	53.8	42.6	46.7	69.1	30.5
06 83668	Watsonville city	24 045	71.0	49.1	8.7	−15.7	20.5	3.6	14.4	15.0	3.1
06 04200	West Covina city	65 008	44.4	78.2	21.9	−2.5	20.4	20.7	11.8	42.7	10.1
06 84410	West Hollywood city	31 725	25.4	91.1	46.8	22.4	48.2	30.3	19.8	67.5	29.6
06 84550	Westminster city	57 313	50.2	71.5	18.1	−6.3	22.3	16.3	9.9	19.0	6.2
06 84816	West Sacramento city	19 201	60.2	69.9	9.8	−14.6	11.8	3.7	6.4	14.5	3.8
06 85292	Whittier city	51 648	44.6	78.8	21.9	−2.5	30.2	17.4	15.9	50.6	11.6
06 86328	Woodland city	29 924	51.9	73.0	18.0	−6.4	24.8	5.9	12.3	20.2	5.8
06 86832	Yorba Linda city	37 459	21.5	93.4	41.5	17.1	40.0	56.9	21.3	63.6	27.3
06 86972	Yuba City city	22 202	52.5	72.6	14.4	−10.0	15.5	15.8	12.6	22.8	6.0
06 87042	Yucaipa city	26 261	46.6	80.9	14.3	−10.1	15.3	2.5	8.1	33.1	6.3
08 00000	COLORADO	2 776 632	36.3	86.9	32.7	8.3	37.0	20.5	14.1	41.9	10.4
08 03455	Arvada city	67 370	35.0	90.9	29.0	4.6	30.0	27.4	16.3	36.8	17.3
08 04000	Aurora city	172 456	39.8	85.0	24.6	0.2	28.6	19.8	18.5	26.8	9.4
08 07850	Boulder city	56 232	14.1	94.7	66.9	42.5	69.5	48.8	38.5	78.0	29.3
08 09280	Broomfield city	24 316	27.9	93.1	37.9	13.5	38.9	66.7	29.0	47.5	21.5
08 16000	Colorado Springs city	228 576	31.2	90.9	33.6	9.2	37.0	19.2	11.7	37.1	14.1
08 20000	Denver city	374 478	41.1	78.0	34.5	10.1	47.8	17.8	13.7	40.3	7.8
08 24785	Englewood city	22 215	45.7	84.2	23.0	−1.4	24.1	24.9	2.1	56.4	10.3
08 27425	Fort Collins city	67 081	22.1	94.0	48.4	24.0	50.3	40.0	18.3	68.1	22.0
08 31660	Grand Junction city	28 158	41.8	84.9	26.2	1.8	28.2	24.7	6.0	29.2	0.1
08 32155	Greeley city	42 310	43.4	79.3	26.4	2.0	31.9	30.6	3.2	59.8	8.3
08 43000	Lakewood city	98 169	35.3	89.3	32.8	8.4	35.4	30.2	19.6	45.9	13.0
08 45255	Littleton city	27 669	29.0	91.3	40.1	15.7	42.1	33.8	24.2	35.1	17.2
08 45970	Longmont city	45 215	37.4	86.5	31.3	6.9	34.7	40.8	22.6	46.1	8.5
08 46465	Loveland city	33 206	37.5	90.4	27.5	3.1	28.3	0.0	17.3	45.5	15.4
08 54330	Northglenn city	20 132	45.9	84.7	19.4	−5.0	21.2	41.6	9.8	16.1	11.8
08 62000	Pueblo city	66 175	52.5	78.6	16.8	7.6	21.9	14.6	8.0	44.4	8.8
08 77290	Thornton city	49 787	45.5	85.1	19.9	−4.5	21.9	25.6	1.4	35.6	9.4
08 83835	Westminster city	84 683	36.1	89.1	31.3	6.9	33.9	38.0	10.5	35.5	16.0
08 84440	Wheat Ridge city	23 603	44.5	85.6	25.1	0.7	26.6	16.1	28.3	33.0	11.6
09 00000	CONNECTICUT	2 295 617	44.5	84.0	31.4	7.0	34.2	13.7	15.7	57.2	11.3
09 08000	Bridgeport city	84 458	66.3	65.0	12.2	−12.2	18.0	8.9	10.6	30.5	5.1
09 08420	Bristol city	41 867	57.1	80.8	16.2	−8.2	16.3	10.1	16.0	43.5	8.1
09 18430	Danbury city	51 223	51.7	77.0	27.1	2.7	30.2	17.2	17.4	48.0	10.2
09 37000	Hartford city	69 868	69.6	60.8	12.4	−12.0	27.8	7.7	14.1	37.8	5.1
09 46450	Meriden city	38 504	57.4	77.6	16.4	−8.0	18.4	8.9	13.3	55.0	6.4
09 47290	Middletown city	30 480	46.2	83.6	30.4	6.0	31.9	15.4	25.0	55.7	25.0
09 47500	Milford city	37 480	42.4	88.6	29.3	4.9	28.6	24.1	52.3	61.4	25.4
09 49880	Naugatuck borough	20 451	52.6	83.0	19.0	−5.4	17.5	23.3	0.0	75.8	13.0
09 50370	New Britain city	44 987	63.9	69.0	16.6	−7.8	18.5	15.0	4.6	35.2	6.8
09 52000	New Haven city	72 171	54.6	73.6	27.1	2.7	41.4	12.5	15.1	77.3	10.5
09 52280	New London city	15 348	54.8	78.4	19.6	−4.8	25.2	12.4	14.6	24.9	7.1
09 55990	Norwalk city	58 885	42.3	82.8	34.2	9.8	40.9	16.2	19.5	66.5	10.4
09 56200	Norwich city	24 125	55.0	79.4	18.9	−5.5	19.8	8.9	5.3	44.7	9.3
09 68100	Shelton city	27 013	41.9	87.3	29.9	5.5	29.6	25.8	31.3	55.0	22.2
09 73000	Stamford city	82 886	42.3	82.2	39.6	15.2	47.9	17.0	26.4	68.5	11.8
09 76500	Torrington city	24 916	59.0	78.4	15.7	−8.7	15.8	13.2	0.0	20.6	10.8
09 80000	Waterbury city	69 791	62.6	71.7	13.9	−10.5	16.8	7.0	5.0	41.6	4.7
09 82800	West Haven city	35 341	55.7	81.0	19.1	−5.3	18.8	14.9	0.0	64.0	10.0
10 00000	DELAWARE	514 658	48.8	82.6	25.0	0.6	26.9	14.4	13.2	61.0	13.5
10 21200	Dover city	19 823	40.6	83.3	28.8	4.4	33.5	21.3	19.5	39.4	11.1
10 50670	Newark city	12 610	24.7	93.4	51.3	26.9	51.6	23.3	70.4	81.2	52.1
10 77580	Wilmington city	46 855	55.7	74.4	21.4	−3.0	40.0	9.1	12.6	43.2	6.3
11 00000	DISTRICT OF COLUMBIA	384 535	42.8	77.8	39.1	14.7	80.6	17.5	28.1	58.1	24.8
11 50000	Washington city	384 535	42.8	77.8	39.1	14.7	80.6	17.5	28.1	58.1	24.8

[1] Hispanic or Latino persons may be of any race.

City	School enrollment			Population 16 to 19 years				Employment status, 2000			Work status in 1999 of the population 16 years and over		
											Worked in 1999		
	Grades kindergarten through 12	College or graduate school	Percent private	Number	Percent in armed forces	Percent high school graduates	Percent not enrolled, not grads, not in armed forces, not employed	Total population 16 years and over	Percent in labor force	Unemployment rate	Full-time	Part-time	Did not work in 1999
	11	12	13	14	15	16	17	18	19	20	21	22	23
CALIFORNIA—Cont'd													
Upland city	14 456	5 560	16.0	3 711	0.0	11.4	2.7	51 618	65.9	5.7	54.0	15.4	30.6
Vacaville city	18 355	5 101	9.2	4 619	0.0	12.4	2.7	67 294	60.7	4.3	55.2	13.5	31.3
Vallejo city	24 723	7 690	14.2	6 766	0.2	10.5	3.8	87 934	63.4	7.6	54.8	14.1	31.1
Victorville city	16 715	3 664	5.3	3 925	0.0	12.3	9.4	44 294	56.3	9.9	45.9	13.6	40.4
Visalia city	21 415	5 944	8.8	5 741	0.0	9.2	5.1	65 741	63.8	8.3	52.8	14.8	32.4
Vista city	19 242	5 443	8.6	5 234	1.0	13.9	5.6	65 902	64.3	6.9	54.7	14.4	30.8
Walnut city	7 038	3 525	12.4	2 251	0.0	4.7	0.2	22 979	63.4	3.7	54.1	14.5	31.3
Walnut Creek city	8 637	4 097	16.8	2 317	0.0	4.5	1.5	54 476	57.9	3.6	48.5	14.3	37.3
Watsonville city	11 378	1 841	6.4	2 952	0.0	11.0	9.9	30 909	63.9	12.4	55.6	13.8	30.6
West Covina city	22 761	9 466	15.3	6 173	0.4	8.3	3.8	78 496	61.6	7.0	53.9	13.2	32.9
West Hollywood city	1 701	2 922	24.0	468	0.0	11.8	6.0	33 981	69.7	6.7	58.6	15.0	26.4
Westminster city	17 316	7 831	9.6	4 662	0.0	8.4	4.3	67 455	59.8	5.5	51.5	14.7	33.8
West Sacramento city ...	7 255	1 829	5.5	1 804	0.0	12.4	9.9	22 994	57.2	9.5	48.1	14.0	37.9
Whittier city	17 904	6 897	19.3	5 138	0.0	9.1	5.8	62 628	62.0	6.0	53.3	14.2	32.4
Woodland city	10 811	2 705	8.5	2 957	0.0	13.5	5.4	36 149	64.7	7.2	56.4	14.6	29.0
Yorba Linda city	13 790	4 614	16.4	3 399	0.0	5.4	1.2	43 471	71.6	3.1	57.7	17.6	24.7
Yuba City city	7 995	1 741	6.4	2 092	0.0	14.8	7.4	27 004	61.7	13.0	53.5	13.6	32.9
Yucaipa city	9 458	2 378	10.3	2 485	0.0	10.1	2.7	30 828	60.0	6.4	47.7	15.7	36.6
COLORADO	804 108	282 832	11.7	243 396	0.9	12.4	5.9	3 325 197	70.1	4.3	60.7	16.1	23.2
Arvada city	20 441	5 278	14.1	5 570	0.0	12.0	4.6	78 579	72.2	3.6	61.5	16.7	21.9
Aurora city	53 950	15 259	10.9	15 007	0.4	15.0	7.1	207 931	72.8	4.1	66.3	13.1	20.7
Boulder city	10 174	24 703	8.7	8 801	0.0	4.7	1.9	82 257	71.6	6.7	53.8	27.6	18.6
Broomfield city	8 317	2 242	12.0	2 052	0.0	12.4	2.0	28 260	75.9	3.8	65.5	17.3	17.2
Colorado Springs city	68 243	23 769	15.8	20 586	0.9	14.4	5.5	275 792	70.8	4.4	61.2	15.7	23.1
Denver city	83 908	38 309	18.3	26 299	0.0	13.3	12.6	445 977	67.7	5.7	60.7	13.4	25.9
Englewood city	4 570	1 896	16.1	1 393	0.0	16.3	6.2	26 021	69.5	4.0	60.3	13.9	25.9
Fort Collins city	18 056	24 882	5.8	9 825	0.1	7.7	2.3	95 935	72.4	5.2	56.4	25.8	17.9
Grand Junction city	6 536	3 266	10.6	2 760	0.0	13.0	7.5	34 257	61.7	5.9	49.7	18.4	31.9
Greeley city	13 883	11 226	6.4	6 765	0.1	7.9	6.0	59 039	66.5	7.2	55.5	20.2	24.3
Lakewood city	23 292	9 209	15.8	7 024	0.0	13.3	5.1	115 720	70.8	3.4	61.4	15.3	23.3
Littleton city	7 207	2 205	13.3	2 171	0.7	16.2	3.4	32 267	69.6	2.8	59.2	15.4	25.5
Longmont city	14 252	3 199	11.2	3 814	0.0	13.1	6.2	53 402	72.5	3.5	62.1	15.5	22.4
Loveland city	10 009	2 486	12.4	2 714	0.1	13.9	4.6	38 584	70.1	3.2	58.5	16.9	24.5
Northglenn city	5 960	1 553	8.7	1 814	0.0	20.0	7.1	24 135	72.3	4.7	63.3	14.4	22.2
Pueblo city	18 987	6 022	6.1	6 304	0.0	10.3	9.7	79 762	55.7	7.2	46.5	15.5	38.0
Thornton city	17 052	4 261	9.9	4 688	0.0	18.6	6.3	60 253	76.3	3.7	68.5	14.0	17.5
Westminster city	19 892	6 102	12.3	5 281	0.1	14.3	4.5	76 853	77.7	3.3	67.9	15.1	17.0
Wheat Ridge city	4 969	1 597	14.0	1 413	0.0	9.2	6.0	26 829	64.4	4.5	55.3	14.3	30.5
CONNECTICUT	639 968	204 212	17.2	169 277	0.6	8.9	4.4	2 652 316	66.6	5.2	55.4	16.2	28.4
Bridgeport city	30 096	8 312	20.5	7 952	0.0	10.2	10.0	104 020	61.2	10.5	52.2	14.6	33.2
Bristol city	10 480	2 550	14.6	2 637	0.0	11.6	3.3	47 736	68.6	4.6	57.6	15.0	27.4
Danbury city	11 782	4 753	15.8	3 811	0.0	11.7	4.1	60 459	69.0	3.9	59.6	14.5	25.9
Hartford city	28 107	7 672	11.1	8 274	0.0	8.4	16.0	88 699	56.9	15.9	46.9	14.7	38.5
Meriden city	11 458	2 534	13.1	2 583	0.0	11.5	5.8	44 704	66.1	4.8	56.0	15.4	28.5
Middletown city	6 743	2 882	24.1	1 498	0.0	8.7	5.0	34 603	68.3	4.4	59.4	14.7	25.9
Milford city	8 899	2 465	18.4	2 121	0.0	8.7	4.0	41 761	70.4	4.1	58.8	15.2	26.0
Naugatuck borough	6 371	1 606	13.9	1 701	0.0	11.6	2.9	23 606	69.8	5.3	58.4	15.0	26.6
New Britain city	13 560	5 882	12.8	4 370	0.0	11.1	6.9	56 041	62.3	8.9	51.5	15.9	32.6
New Haven city	24 278	17 115	35.5	9 366	0.0	7.2	7.0	95 568	60.0	13.8	49.5	17.8	32.7
New London city	4 317	3 413	30.8	2 093	11.6	21.3	1.7	20 410	65.8	6.8	54.1	18.2	27.7
Norwalk city	13 149	4 457	18.7	2 989	0.0	8.6	4.1	66 368	70.8	4.8	60.4	14.2	25.4
Norwich city	6 802	1 611	13.7	1 815	0.0	8.9	7.5	28 462	66.5	5.6	54.5	15.8	29.7
Shelton city	6 783	1 874	20.6	1 578	0.0	6.8	0.4	30 135	69.9	3.2	58.1	15.3	26.5
Stamford city	19 126	5 660	19.0	4 269	0.0	10.3	3.5	93 723	67.9	4.3	59.8	12.6	27.5
Torrington city	6 192	1 274	9.6	1 588	0.0	15.9	3.8	28 025	65.7	4.7	53.2	16.4	30.4
Waterbury city	21 232	4 665	18.2	5 178	0.2	12.9	9.2	81 430	61.2	8.6	52.0	13.7	34.3
West Haven city	9 165	3 867	21.5	2 455	0.0	9.6	4.4	41 578	67.9	5.3	56.6	15.1	28.3
DELAWARE	143 780	51 407	19.5	44 154	0.3	11.5	5.6	610 289	65.7	5.1	57.3	14.6	28.1
Dover city	5 412	4 253	16.1	2 418	3.9	7.2	2.5	25 596	63.8	7.0	56.9	14.9	28.2
Newark city	2 548	12 468	15.7	5 128	0.0	2.0	0.3	25 587	64.3	12.6	49.7	32.2	18.1
Wilmington city	14 426	3 291	16.1	4 096	0.0	13.3	15.7	56 086	60.1	9.6	54.3	12.4	33.3
DISTRICT OF COLUMBIA	88 568	59 498	32.7	32 400	1.0	8.2	6.7	469 041	63.6	10.7	55.8	13.1	31.1
Washington city	88 568	59 498	32.7	32 400	1.0	8.2	6.7	469 041	63.6	10.7	55.8	13.1	31.1

Table B-5. Cities — Education, Labor Force, and Income

City	Full-year full-time employed (percent)								Children under 18 years in families (percent, except where noted)						Total employed by class of worker (percent)			
				Non-Hispanic White	Black or African American	American Indian and Alaska Native	Asian, Hawaiian, and Pacific Islander	Hispanic or Latino[1]		With two parents		With one parent who is in labor force	+/- U.S. percent of children with no stay-at-home parent	+/- U.S. percent two-income couples				Unpaid family worker
	Total	Men	Women						Number	Both in labor force	Father only in labor force				Private	Government	Self-employed	
	24	25	26	27	28	29	30	31	32	33	34	35	36	37	38	39	40	41
CALIFORNIA—Cont'd																		
Upland city	38.5	48.6	29.5	39.0	42.8	22.0	35.0	37.5	17 758	38.5	25.8	22.0	-4.1	-1.6	72.3	15.4	12.0	0.4
Vacaville city	41.0	46.8	33.8	43.4	32.3	32.1	44.5	35.2	22 712	45.6	23.5	21.8	2.8	5.7	71.0	22.2	6.7	0.1
Vallejo city	37.9	43.1	33.2	37.8	38.7	31.9	39.0	35.5	29 350	39.7	17.6	25.3	0.4	-0.3	73.7	19.8	6.2	0.3
Victorville city	32.3	45.2	21.1	34.1	26.9	28.2	27.4	31.8	20 301	30.4	25.6	26.5	-7.7	-14.3	71.6	19.7	8.3	0.4
Visalia city	36.0	46.0	27.2	38.6	24.4	27.2	22.8	33.6	27 024	39.4	20.0	22.4	-2.8	-1.7	68.4	21.2	10.1	0.4
Vista city	37.9	48.2	27.8	40.6	46.7	31.5	41.1	32.7	24 661	35.2	24.7	23.5	-5.9	-5.0	77.1	12.1	10.5	0.3
Walnut city	40.3	49.6	31.6	40.6	40.2	45.5	39.3	43.9	7 920	55.4	25.5	8.5	-0.7	2.2	71.0	16.1	12.5	0.5
Walnut Creek city	36.4	48.2	26.8	35.2	54.5	34.0	39.7	42.3	11 119	45.8	31.9	14.7	-4.1	-7.0	75.1	11.2	13.5	0.2
Watsonville city	26.4	31.9	21.0	33.2	30.4	27.7	27.2	24.0	13 447	43.3	13.8	19.8	-1.5	-6.7	82.1	10.9	6.7	0.3
West Covina city	37.3	45.7	29.7	35.8	37.2	41.4	37.0	38.7	27 467	42.6	21.4	19.2	-2.8	-2.6	75.5	16.1	8.2	0.3
West Hollywood city	38.7	45.4	30.5	38.2	33.2	40.4	45.0	45.8	1 879	45.4	17.7	21.3	2.1	-10.9	75.2	7.1	17.5	0.2
Westminster city	37.4	45.8	29.2	40.2	53.1	33.2	33.1	39.7	21 293	38.3	24.5	16.6	-9.7	-7.6	78.2	11.3	10.1	0.5
West Sacramento city	31.5	37.5	25.9	33.2	19.5	32.6	23.1	30.6	8 809	29.8	20.4	25.0	-9.8	-11.1	66.3	23.6	9.7	0.4
Whittier city	38.0	47.8	29.0	36.0	31.1	40.2	39.9	39.7	21 833	39.2	21.9	20.9	-4.5	-2.4	74.2	16.7	8.8	0.4
Woodland city	39.1	48.6	30.2	43.0	24.3	33.2	36.1	33.4	13 670	43.0	22.1	20.2	-1.4	0.1	72.6	19.1	8.2	0.1
Yorba Linda city	46.5	60.4	33.5	47.0	54.9	54.4	44.9	47.0	16 669	48.9	34.3	11.1	-4.6	3.8	71.0	13.1	15.5	0.5
Yuba City city	31.7	39.7	24.3	36.4	35.4	27.0	25.8	21.5	9 763	38.8	19.3	22.5	-3.3	-7.0	72.9	17.5	9.1	0.5
Yucaipa city	35.1	45.5	25.6	35.2	34.1	24.5	31.3	35.2	11 205	41.2	24.8	22.1	-1.3	-5.4	69.8	19.3	10.6	0.2
COLORADO	44.9	54.6	35.2	46.3	44.6	39.4	42.5	38.6	1 043 072	47.2	22.9	19.6	2.2	5.8	73.7	13.9	12.0	0.3
Arvada city	49.1	60.4	38.4	49.1	51.0	50.2	47.0	50.2	25 854	52.4	22.2	18.8	6.6	8.3	75.7	13.8	10.4	0.2
Aurora city	50.1	57.5	42.8	53.9	51.2	41.1	42.0	38.2	71 499	43.1	18.0	25.0	3.5	8.0	80.2	11.9	7.6	0.2
Boulder city	34.2	41.8	26.1	34.6	30.2	20.5	30.1	33.7	13 054	45.6	25.0	19.8	0.8	5.7	68.5	18.6	12.6	0.3
Broomfield city	52.2	64.0	40.4	52.8	53.3	37.6	42.9	53.0	10 961	52.8	24.2	16.4	4.6	10.8	79.2	12.7	8.0	0.1
Colorado Springs city	46.2	58.1	35.0	46.5	49.0	45.0	41.7	44.9	91 237	45.7	25.0	21.3	2.4	5.4	76.2	13.5	10.0	0.3
Denver city	42.8	49.5	36.1	47.1	38.5	35.2	37.4	36.1	110 483	32.7	19.3	26.7	-5.2	-0.4	76.8	13.4	9.5	0.2
Englewood city	45.3	54.4	36.3	45.8	44.9	40.2	40.4	45.7	5 940	44.3	17.8	28.2	7.9	3.9	81.0	8.9	10.0	0.2
Fort Collins city	38.0	48.4	27.6	38.5	38.2	33.4	32.3	35.9	24 499	49.3	27.7	16.4	1.1	8.5	70.9	18.6	10.1	0.4
Grand Junction city	33.3	42.1	25.2	33.5	34.6	38.8	36.5	31.8	8 431	44.5	21.7	22.0	1.9	-2.4	71.6	14.5	13.2	0.7
Greeley city	36.7	46.5	27.6	37.8	33.6	41.5	24.5	34.7	18 709	45.9	20.8	19.2	0.5	4.2	72.9	17.9	8.9	0.3
Lakewood city	47.3	56.3	38.7	48.0	47.7	41.8	42.4	43.7	30 298	44.9	20.2	26.0	6.3	5.0	74.9	14.6	10.4	0.1
Littleton city	45.9	56.4	36.4	45.8	47.7	63.4	53.0	42.4	8 983	48.3	24.3	21.6	5.3	5.5	76.7	10.5	12.6	0.2
Longmont city	47.1	59.2	35.5	49.2	57.3	24.7	51.0	37.2	18 814	46.1	23.2	20.8	2.3	7.5	78.7	10.9	10.1	0.3
Loveland city	45.0	57.5	33.5	45.4	59.8	44.4	33.2	42.8	13 127	54.6	21.6	17.2	7.2	6.9	75.8	12.6	11.3	0.2
Northglenn city	49.3	58.3	40.5	50.7	42.5	52.8	46.7	45.6	7 986	49.7	16.6	24.9	10.0	5.3	81.9	11.1	6.6	0.3
Pueblo city	32.7	00.5	27.6	33.7	26.6	34.5	38.1	31.6	23 685	36.5	13.2	31.4	3.3	-7.4	74.6	17.6	7.4	0.4
Thornton city	54.0	65.5	42.6	55.1	56.7	63.1	53.2	49.9	23 346	49.0	20.4	21.8	0.2	12.7	81.3	11.0	7.4	0.3
Westminster city	54.3	65.6	43.2	55.7	55.2	53.3	49.6	49.5	25 942	52.1	20.8	19.4	6.9	12.5	80.4	11.1	8.3	0.2
Wheat Ridge city	41.6	50.7	33.6	41.3	44.7	24.7	43.5	44.1	6 017	44.0	17.4	26.9	7.2	0.8	74.0	14.2	11.6	0.2
CONNECTICUT	43.4	54.0	33.7	44.4	39.4	38.8	44.6	37.4	802 658	48.0	21.2	20.7	4.1	4.6	76.7	13.3	9.8	0.2
Bridgeport city	37.4	43.0	32.5	35.9	39.6	26.5	38.6	36.6	35 913	29.3	11.4	35.9	0.6	-4.2	81.6	11.7	6.6	0.1
Bristol city	46.9	57.1	37.7	46.9	47.5	29.8	54.0	46.3	13 393	51.1	14.0	27.0	13.5	6.7	82.8	10.4	6.7	0.2
Danbury city	45.5	66.6	34.9	46.3	34.2	36.5	53.2	42.7	15 246	50.4	19.4	19.2	5.0	7.5	81.3	9.3	9.3	0.1
Hartford city	31.1	34.5	28.1	32.1	32.7	19.3	30.1	28.4	32 718	17.8	5.9	45.0	-1.8	-10.8	80.9	14.9	4.1	0.1
Meriden city	44.8	53.9	36.7	45.6	48.7	42.6	43.5	40.4	13 971	41.4	14.6	27.0	3.8	4.3	81.0	12.2	6.6	0.2
Middletown city	46.5	54.8	39.0	47.5	42.3	10.7	42.3	46.6	8 729	47.5	16.4	25.9	8.8	6.8	78.7	15.6	5.7	0.0
Milford city	48.1	59.1	38.4	47.9	53.6	59.6	52.8	48.3	11 337	56.8	19.0	17.0	9.2	7.8	78.9	11.9	9.0	0.2
Naugatuck borough	47.9	57.8	37.6	48.0	50.3	0.0	49.4	47.4	8 108	46.6	21.9	22.6	4.6	5.7	81.6	12.6	5.7	0.2
New Britain city	36.6	42.9	31.0	35.9	45.0	20.1	43.3	34.2	16 034	34.1	10.6	35.0	4.5	-3.6	82.2	12.6	5.1	0.1
New Haven city	31.4	35.5	27.8	32.4	31.7	37.7	26.1	29.7	27 867	22.8	10.6	40.4	-1.4	-5.9	77.8	16.5	5.5	0.1
New London city	38.8	46.3	31.9	38.2	42.4	42.1	39.1	40.3	5 339	26.1	14.6	45.3	6.8	-3.5	81.1	14.4	4.3	0.2
Norwalk city	46.7	55.9	38.3	48.3	44.1	55.9	53.8	39.6	17 084	46.0	21.0	21.8	3.2	5.7	80.2	8.6	10.9	0.3
Norwich city	42.7	53.3	33.4	43.1	40.6	17.8	56.9	46.5	8 165	41.3	10.9	33.2	11.8	4.9	78.8	14.8	6.2	0.2
Shelton city	47.5	59.9	36.3	47.6	49.8	100.0	34.9	51.8	8 702	61.3	20.9	13.2	9.9	8.5	77.9	11.1	10.8	0.2
Stamford city	46.4	56.4	37.2	47.7	44.7	45.5	52.1	41.5	24 438	42.7	23.1	22.7	0.8	2.0	78.9	8.8	11.9	0.3
Torrington city	42.7	53.9	32.6	42.6	39.9	47.4	45.5	48.0	7 817	49.8	20.6	20.3	5.5	5.3	81.2	9.9	8.5	0.5
Waterbury city	38.9	46.9	32.1	40.0	38.6	43.6	33.6	36.0	26 580	32.9	12.3	35.8	4.1	-3.4	80.4	13.9	5.6	0.2
West Haven city	44.6	53.9	36.4	44.1	46.8	47.4	47.8	44.0	11 570	45.3	14.1	29.5	10.2	4.6	80.5	13.5	5.8	0.2
DELAWARE	43.9	52.9	35.7	44.5	41.7	43.2	44.2	41.6	181 743	45.8	18.5	25.1	6.3	3.2	77.7	13.8	8.3	0.2
Dover city	41.2	50.8	33.1	44.7	34.9	49.8	40.0	45.0	7 089	37.9	12.8	34.4	7.7	2.8	64.5	28.4	7.1	0.0
Newark city	26.8	35.5	19.8	26.8	33.9	39.6	20.0	22.7	3 358	53.2	25.8	14.2	2.8	5.8	78.1	16.9	4.9	0.2
Wilmington city	38.0	40.9	35.4	42.5	35.9	55.7	35.4	32.3	16 215	23.4	8.5	46.6	5.4	1.4	80.0	14.6	5.3	0.1
DISTRICT OF COLUMBIA	38.5	42.9	34.8	49.2	32.8	39.4	35.3	39.1	99 374	23.1	9.1	41.0	-0.5	-0.6	66.7	25.9	7.3	0.1
Washington city	38.5	42.9	34.8	49.2	32.8	39.4	35.3	39.1	99 374	23.1	9.1	41.0	-0.5	-0.6	66.7	25.9	7.3	0.1

[1] Hispanic or Latino persons may be of any race.

| City | Percent who worked at home | Percent of the population 5 years and over with a disability | Veterans as a percent of the population 18 years and over | Occupation for employed population 16 years and over (percent) | | | | | | Industry for employed population 16 years and over (percent) | | | | | |
| | | | | Management, professional, and related occupations | Service occupations | Sales and office occupations | Farming, fishing, and forestry occupations | Construction, extraction, and maintenance occupations | Production, transportation and material moving occupations | Agriculture, forestry, fishing, and mining | Construction and manufacturing | Wholesale and retail trade | Transportation and warehousing, and utilities | Service industries | Public administration |
	42	43	44	45	46	47	48	49	50	51	52	53	54	55	56
CALIFORNIA—Cont'd															
Upland city	3.1	18.0	11.4	36.0	13.5	29.7	0.2	8.4	12.2	0.6	20.1	15.7	5.5	53.3	4.8
Vacaville city	2.4	16.4	17.8	31.1	15.6	27.9	0.4	11.9	13.1	0.3	19.2	16.9	6.8	46.4	10.3
Vallejo city	2.9	21.3	14.0	29.3	17.9	28.8	0.2	10.3	13.5	0.5	16.3	13.3	8.5	55.8	5.8
Victorville city	3.0	20.8	14.9	25.6	18.9	27.2	0.3	11.9	16.2	0.8	16.5	17.0	9.1	49.5	7.1
Visalia city	3.3	18.6	11.7	34.1	17.2	26.2	3.1	7.5	11.9	4.2	14.6	16.0	3.9	53.3	8.1
Vista city	3.2	19.9	13.8	27.9	17.1	27.6	1.5	11.1	14.8	1.4	24.5	18.0	3.6	48.5	4.1
Walnut city	2.8	12.9	8.0	48.0	8.2	30.7	0.0	4.8	8.4	0.0	17.1	19.2	6.3	52.3	5.1
Walnut Creek city	5.7	17.4	13.7	55.5	9.0	27.6	0.1	4.1	3.6	0.2	11.4	13.4	3.6	68.5	2.9
Watsonville city	1.6	20.8	5.5	16.8	17.9	19.9	17.0	9.9	18.6	17.6	20.6	17.6	3.1	38.7	2.5
West Covina city	1.8	19.0	9.5	31.7	12.1	33.2	0.0	8.4	14.6	0.1	19.9	17.6	6.5	51.2	4.6
West Hollywood city	6.9	24.5	6.2	54.1	13.0	26.0	0.0	2.6	4.3	0.2	6.8	12.0	3.1	76.1	1.9
Westminster city	2.4	22.4	8.6	29.7	14.0	27.7	0.2	8.6	19.8	0.4	28.2	16.7	3.9	48.4	2.6
West Sacramento city	2.4	26.1	12.4	20.8	19.7	29.5	1.2	12.6	16.2	2.2	17.0	16.6	7.7	43.8	12.6
Whittier city	2.1	18.9	9.7	33.7	12.1	31.5	0.0	7.9	14.7	0.2	20.7	17.6	6.5	50.0	5.1
Woodland city	2.9	21.0	10.7	27.2	15.7	28.0	3.1	9.7	16.2	4.3	16.0	20.0	5.3	48.0	6.4
Yorba Linda city	5.4	9.9	10.9	49.9	8.0	30.6	0.1	5.4	6.0	0.2	22.4	18.0	4.1	51.2	4.1
Yuba City city	2.1	22.0	14.4	26.7	16.7	26.2	3.9	11.1	15.3	6.1	17.7	17.1	4.7	47.9	6.4
Yucaipa city	3.1	21.8	15.2	29.5	17.5	25.7	0.5	13.3	13.5	1.2	19.2	14.9	5.8	53.6	5.4
COLORADO	4.9	16.3	13.9	37.4	13.9	27.2	0.6	10.5	10.5	2.0	18.2	15.2	4.9	55.1	4.6
Arvada city	4.4	15.0	15.3	35.8	11.9	31.3	0.1	10.2	10.8	0.6	19.6	16.9	5.7	51.8	5.4
Aurora city	3.0	17.6	14.9	30.7	13.7	32.5	0.1	11.0	12.0	0.5	15.4	17.0	7.4	55.2	4.5
Boulder city	6.5	10.8	6.6	53.6	14.4	22.6	0.1	4.2	5.2	0.3	12.9	13.4	1.6	69.3	2.6
Broomfield city	3.6	11.7	13.8	44.2	10.4	27.2	0.0	7.4	10.9	0.5	22.9	15.5	5.3	51.7	4.1
Colorado Springs city	3.8	16.0	19.4	38.2	14.7	27.9	0.1	8.9	10.3	0.3	18.6	14.9	3.5	58.1	4.5
Denver city	3.7	20.7	11.2	37.9	15.2	26.3	0.2	10.0	10.4	0.6	15.1	13.3	4.8	61.7	4.6
Englewood city	2.9	23.3	14.2	30.1	15.1	28.9	0.1	13.9	11.8	0.5	19.6	17.4	4.0	55.9	2.6
Fort Collins city	4.3	11.5	9.4	42.9	15.6	24.3	0.5	7.0	9.7	0.9	20.7	15.0	2.7	57.6	3.2
Grand Junction city	4.4	23.3	16.4	32.4	17.9	27.6	0.6	10.0	11.5	2.2	16.0	16.6	4.7	55.8	4.7
Greeley city	2.7	18.7	10.7	30.7	15.7	27.1	0.9	11.0	14.8	1.9	21.3	15.6	3.4	53.3	4.5
Lakewood city	4.0	16.7	13.8	38.9	12.3	29.2	0.1	10.4	9.2	0.9	16.2	15.4	4.7	56.3	6.6
Littleton city	5.2	15.3	13.0	41.3	11.2	30.8	0.1	8.8	7.8	0.8	16.6	16.5	3.1	58.9	4.2
Longmont city	4.4	15.6	12.9	37.5	13.0	26.8	0.3	9.7	12.7	0.9	27.8	15.1	4.0	49.0	3.1
Loveland city	4.0	15.5	15.1	33.0	12.8	27.6	0.4	11.6	14.6	1.1	27.6	18.1	3.2	46.4	3.6
Northglenn city	2.8	15.9	15.3	28.8	13.5	29.7	0.2	12.6	15.3	0.5	19.5	18.7	7.2	50.8	3.3
Pueblo city	2.6	25.2	16.3	26.6	19.3	29.0	0.3	11.7	13.0	0.7	16.9	16.4	4.6	55.2	6.3
Thornton city	2.9	16.0	13.3	28.6	11.6	31.5	0.1	13.0	15.2	0.8	22.6	17.3	9.1	46.4	3.8
Westminster city	4.0	13.9	12.4	37.5	11.6	29.3	0.1	10.1	11.4	0.7	21.4	16.9	5.9	51.1	4.1
Wheat Ridge city	4.1	21.6	13.7	31.6	15.1	29.9	0.1	11.4	11.9	0.9	18.2	16.4	5.1	54.5	5.0
CONNECTICUT	3.1	17.5	12.1	39.1	14.3	26.5	0.2	8.0	12.0	0.4	20.8	14.4	3.9	56.5	4.0
Bridgeport city	1.4	25.6	8.1	21.8	21.5	27.9	0.1	9.4	19.2	0.1	23.4	15.5	4.6	52.9	3.4
Bristol city	1.3	21.4	13.3	28.6	14.6	28.0	0.1	9.9	18.8	0.2	29.5	13.9	3.0	49.9	3.5
Danbury city	2.8	17.9	8.7	32.5	17.0	25.4	0.1	10.9	14.2	0.2	27.8	15.5	3.0	51.5	2.0
Hartford city	1.7	27.2	6.3	21.6	26.5	27.8	0.4	6.8	16.9	0.5	15.9	12.5	5.0	60.7	5.4
Meriden city	1.9	20.8	13.2	28.9	16.8	27.8	0.1	9.4	16.9	0.2	25.3	15.7	4.2	50.1	4.5
Middletown city	1.6	18.2	11.2	43.3	14.4	24.3	0.0	7.3	10.7	0.3	19.7	13.2	3.5	58.0	5.2
Milford city	2.3	16.8	13.4	39.5	12.0	27.8	0.1	8.7	11.9	0.1	23.7	15.2	4.7	52.9	3.5
Naugatuck borough	1.1	18.9	12.7	30.3	15.6	25.1	0.1	10.1	19.0	0.1	29.8	15.3	3.7	46.1	5.0
New Britain city	1.2	24.7	9.6	25.5	19.7	25.2	0.2	7.6	21.8	0.4	24.8	15.3	3.1	52.0	4.5
New Haven city	2.6	22.5	7.5	37.3	18.8	23.5	0.3	5.9	14.2	0.4	14.9	11.7	4.0	65.2	3.8
New London city	3.7	24.2	13.3	27.5	27.9	25.9	0.1	7.0	11.5	0.1	16.4	14.6	3.7	59.7	5.6
Norwalk city	3.7	17.3	9.6	40.8	14.2	26.9	0.1	9.0	9.1	0.1	20.0	15.7	3.2	58.8	2.2
Norwich city	1.5	24.2	16.2	27.6	28.0	24.2	0.3	9.0	10.8	0.6	16.3	13.5	3.0	60.3	6.3
Shelton city	2.7	14.4	12.6	41.0	11.9	27.2	0.0	9.0	10.9	0.2	24.7	16.4	3.0	52.3	3.4
Stamford city	3.8	20.1	8.0	42.0	15.3	26.5	0.1	7.6	8.4	0.3	16.3	13.3	3.7	64.1	2.4
Torrington city	1.8	21.4	13.5	25.4	17.3	26.4	0.2	10.9	19.8	0.4	30.5	16.7	2.9	45.8	3.7
Waterbury city	1.4	24.1	11.1	25.1	20.1	24.6	0.1	8.8	21.4	0.3	26.5	15.5	3.7	49.0	5.0
West Haven city	1.2	20.3	12.0	27.5	16.6	31.1	0.1	9.3	15.5	0.1	19.9	18.3	5.8	51.6	4.2
DELAWARE	3.0	18.4	14.3	35.3	14.6	27.6	0.5	9.5	12.5	1.1	20.6	14.3	4.8	54.0	5.2
Dover city	2.7	18.5	17.7	35.4	18.2	28.8	0.3	7.0	10.3	0.6	14.0	16.3	3.7	51.8	13.6
Newark city	2.4	11.6	6.9	44.7	17.7	25.9	0.2	4.7	6.9	0.2	12.7	13.6	2.8	68.3	2.5
Wilmington city	2.6	23.6	11.1	33.0	21.6	27.2	0.1	5.9	12.1	0.2	13.8	11.5	3.8	64.1	6.4
DISTRICT OF COLUMBIA	3.8	21.9	9.7	51.1	16.1	22.8	0.1	4.8	5.2	0.1	5.5	6.9	3.6	69.0	15.0
Washington city	3.8	21.9	9.7	51.1	16.1	22.8	0.1	4.8	5.2	0.1	5.5	6.9	3.6	69.0	15.0

Table B-5. Cities — Education, Labor Force, and Income

City	Median house-hold income	Median family income — All families	Married-couple	Male house-holder	Female house-holder	Median nonfamily house-hold income	Median income full-year full-time Men	Women	Per capita income	With earnings	With interest, dividend, or rental income	With Social Security income	With public assis-tance income	With retire-ment income	House-holds with income over $100,000 (percent)	+/- U.S. percent for income over $100,000 (percent)	House-holds with income below poverty (percent)	Families with children with income below poverty (percent)
	57	58	59	60	61	62	63	64	65	66	67	68	69	70	71	72	73	74
CALIFORNIA—Cont'd																		
Upland city	48 734	57 471	64 301	24 031	23 359	29 155	45 269	30 686	23 343	83.5	33.6	21.9	3.4	16.8	17.3	5.0	10.6	13.4
Vacaville city	57 667	63 950	72 081	42 066	29 397	34 808	46 129	32 377	21 557	85.9	33.0	19.6	3.1	20.7	17.3	5.0	5.2	6.1
Vallejo city	50 030	56 805	66 488	35 686	26 468	30 041	41 144	33 034	20 415	81.4	27.4	22.9	5.0	22.9	14.2	1.9	9.3	10.3
Victorville city	36 187	39 988	51 280	30 125	18 069	20 067	40 930	26 630	14 454	75.8	21.8	27.7	7.7	18.9	5.3	-7.0	16.0	19.9
Visalia city	41 349	45 830	51 777	26 661	16 907	26 667	37 680	27 466	18 422	81.8	29.8	23.1	7.4	15.0	11.5	-0.8	13.5	19.7
Vista city	42 594	45 649	52 182	27 475	22 491	32 119	34 612	26 640	18 027	84.2	31.9	21.8	3.1	16.1	10.3	-2.0	10.5	14.3
Walnut city	81 015	82 977	88 170	64 028	48 646	38 077	53 671	36 549	25 196	92.2	46.0	12.6	2.9	10.3	34.7	22.4	6.6	6.1
Walnut Creek city	63 238	83 794	104 530	61 028	43 958	41 600	70 329	46 967	39 875	69.8	62.4	36.9	0.7	26.2	27.0	14.7	3.5	3.4
Watsonville city	37 617	40 293	46 102	26 354	19 010	23 898	27 230	22 599	13 205	82.2	24.1	27.2	5.7	15.2	7.9	-4.4	15.9	19.7
West Covina city	53 002	57 614	63 263	32 679	29 564	30 767	39 420	31 675	19 342	85.7	31.9	23.1	4.4	15.6	15.2	2.9	8.3	8.9
West Hollywood city	38 914	41 463	53 606	31 691	27 109	37 557	46 707	36 486	38 302	79.3	32.8	16.1	2.6	6.8	13.6	1.3	10.7	9.8
Westminster city	49 450	52 677	53 786	36 250	27 466	29 989	37 965	29 178	18 218	84.5	31.5	22.1	7.0	14.9	15.4	3.1	11.0	15.0
West Sacramento city	31 718	30 071	00 000	20 508	17 231	22 148	30 558	15 245	74.8	21.9	26.5	10.9	17.6	5.4	-6.9	18.8	24.0
Whittier city	49 256	55 726	63 548	38 164	24 772	30 136	40 985	34 747	21 409	81.4	31.9	25.9	3.7	15.1	16.2	3.9	9.2	11.4
Woodland city	44 449	48 689	51 610	30 750	22 637	27 763	35 776	27 887	18 042	83.1	32.8	24.1	5.0	16.6	9.2	-3.1	10.2	13.0
Yorba Linda city	89 593	96 132	103 779	55 900	46 927	51 737	70 003	43 586	36 173	90.6	50.7	16.4	1.4	13.9	43.4	31.1	2.9	2.8
Yuba City city	32 858	39 381	46 952	28 708	16 436	22 579	36 379	24 057	15 928	80.5	26.0	24.4	6.7	19.0	6.3	-6.0	15.3	20.3
Yucaipa city	39 144	48 683	57 724	35 038	21 554	20 897	41 179	26 686	18 949	74.3	32.7	32.1	4.9	20.1	11.2	-1.1	10.7	11.4
COLORADO	47 203	55 883	63 532	33 223	24 551	30 728	40 105	30 268	24 049	85.8	40.6	19.9	2.5	14.6	14.2	1.9	8.8	9.2
Arvada city	55 541	63 273	71 762	37 083	29 554	33 300	43 847	31 672	24 679	86.2	45.5	21.5	1.5	16.9	16.1	3.8	5.0	5.2
Aurora city	46 507	52 551	57 958	35 896	28 359	33 385	36 794	30 683	21 095	89.0	32.9	16.3	2.3	14.1	9.7	-2.6	7.6	10.2
Boulder city	44 748	70 257	86 887	41 563	24 652	32 013	44 169	33 415	27 262	87.2	53.3	14.1	1.6	11.1	17.9	5.6	15.8	9.2
Broomfield city	63 903	70 551	74 770	41 855	35 243	37 778	50 667	32 430	26 488	90.2	45.5	14.9	1.5	13.8	20.7	8.4	4.5	3.0
Colorado Springs city	45 081	53 478	60 883	30 483	22 437	28 198	38 980	27 047	22 496	85.8	40.3	19.7	2.7	18.1	11.6	-0.7	8.4	9.4
Denver city	39 500	48 195	53 613	31 064	21 171	31 233	35 316	31 432	24 101	82.9	35.2	21.0	3.4	12.9	11.5	-0.8	12.1	16.6
Englewood city	38 943	47 290	54 150	28 977	25 417	29 854	33 303	29 336	20 904	81.1	36.1	23.7	2.0	13.2	6.3	-6.0	8.1	7.0
Fort Collins city	44 459	59 332	68 460	39 128	25 000	26 965	41 733	29 555	22 133	88.4	47.8	15.6	1.7	11.0	12.4	0.1	13.6	7.6
Grand Junction city	33 152	43 851	51 803	24 500	18 556	20 043	33 278	23 674	19 692	74.9	40.2	32.2	3.4	18.0	7.8	-4.5	12.3	11.9
Greeley city	36 414	45 904	51 706	26 645	18 850	21 623	33 900	25 478	17 775	83.6	36.4	21.9	3.1	12.4	7.9	-4.4	16.0	15.1
Lakewood city	48 109	57 171	66 559	35 061	26 068	35 044	40 620	31 962	25 575	85.4	43.8	20.8	1.9	16.2	12.5	0.2	6.3	8.1
Littleton city	50 583	64 671	74 421	45 893	33 491	30 979	45 456	35 171	28 681	81.9	45.0	24.3	2.2	17.0	18.6	6.3	6.0	6.5
Longmont city	51 174	58 037	66 157	33 750	25 691	31 988	41 592	30 560	23 409	85.9	42.7	18.5	2.5	14.1	14.5	2.2	7.3	8.6
Loveland city	47 119	54 337	61 332	27 165	20 000	26 218	40 057	27 226	21 889	82.2	43.3	25.4	2.4	17.0	10.6	-1.7	5.9	5.6
Northglenn city	48 276	52 888	59 493	39 048	30 239	32 154	36 754	28 851	20 253	87.0	33.5	21.9	1.7	16.1	7.9	-4.4	5.2	5.7
Pueblo city	29 650	35 620	44 956	26 536	15 119	18 425	30 507	22 873	16 026	70.9	30.3	33.3	5.9	22.6	4.8	-7.5	17.2	21.8
Thornton city	54 445	58 742	64 159	38 696	26 976	36 235	40 739	30 528	21 471	91.9	32.0	13.7	2.0	10.9	11.7	-0.6	4.3	5.8
Westminster city	56 323	63 776	71 123	45 239	31 250	40 073	42 222	32 249	25 482	91.5	39.0	14.1	1.4	11.7	15.7	3.4	4.5	4.6
Wheat Ridge city	38 983	47 512	59 010	00 006	24 318	27 660	37 432	29 491	22 636	76.6	40.6	30.3	2.5	19.9	8.5	-3.8	8.2	10.1
CONNECTICUT	53 935	65 521	78 589	36 199	24 626	30 873	47 156	34 929	28 766	81.2	44.4	27.0	3.7	17.6	20.2	7.9	8.0	8.6
Bridgeport city	34 658	39 571	51 036	28 214	19 128	22 366	33 605	27 670	16 306	77.1	23.4	26.5	8.1	14.0	7.3	-5.0	18.3	22.1
Bristol city	47 422	58 259	69 904	35 020	23 170	28 042	41 006	31 304	23 362	80.2	39.8	28.1	3.1	19.8	10.8	-1.5	6.8	7.7
Danbury city	53 664	61 899	67 295	30 481	24 691	34 810	40 095	32 034	24 500	84.5	37.1	23.6	2.8	14.1	17.7	5.4	7.7	7.9
Hartford city	24 820	27 051	42 149	20 441	15 915	17 932	29 126	26 700	13 428	72.8	15.9	23.3	15.7	11.5	4.0	-8.3	29.1	35.8
Meriden city	43 237	52 788	64 246	31 363	20 091	27 469	40 873	30 766	20 597	79.1	35.6	27.7	6.0	15.9	9.8	-2.5	10.6	14.1
Middletown city	47 162	60 845	72 578	35 000	25 185	33 518	46 714	35 682	25 720	82.9	40.9	24.9	3.1	16.4	15.6	3.3	7.6	7.0
Milford city	61 183	71 226	81 125	44 239	36 835	39 080	49 730	37 839	28 882	82.6	48.8	28.3	2.1	19.6	19.5	7.2	4.3	3.4
Naugatuck borough	51 247	59 216	66 285	33 250	22 865	28 890	43 519	30 533	22 757	83.2	37.5	25.0	3.3	16.8	11.4	-0.9	6.5	8.0
New Britain city	34 185	41 056	56 561	26 915	17 470	24 320	35 711	27 374	18 404	74.8	31.5	29.8	8.0	19.3	6.2	-6.1	15.1	20.3
New Haven city	29 604	35 950	50 953	23 750	17 618	19 687	35 133	29 421	16 393	75.7	23.6	22.8	11.2	10.9	6.9	-5.4	23.5	28.6
New London city	33 809	38 942	48 934	29 792	20 929	26 824	31 950	26 218	18 437	77.5	29.6	26.1	7.9	14.6	5.8	-6.5	14.6	19.8
Norwalk city	59 839	68 219	79 125	40 035	27 138	41 356	48 930	39 392	31 781	86.5	44.7	23.9	2.5	13.4	24.7	12.4	6.7	8.0
Norwich city	39 181	49 155	60 262	29 868	21 685	22 917	36 534	28 155	20 742	78.2	35.2	28.8	5.2	19.0	8.3	-4.0	12.0	13.7
Shelton city	67 292	75 523	83 675	43 158	33 141	35 453	51 328	37 657	29 893	83.4	50.3	27.9	1.9	19.5	26.2	13.9	3.8	3.3
Stamford city	60 556	69 337	82 279	38 553	31 875	40 144	50 508	38 436	34 987	83.8	37.8	25.0	2.6	12.5	27.8	15.5	7.8	7.0
Torrington city	41 841	54 375	60 539	32 841	21 310	24 125	38 844	29 509	21 406	75.9	41.6	33.2	3.5	19.5	8.7	-3.6	7.8	7.0
Waterbury city	34 285	42 300	55 021	28 250	18 950	20 622	36 175	28 299	17 701	74.9	27.7	30.3	7.7	17.0	7.1	-5.2	15.6	19.1
West Haven city	42 393	51 631	63 015	34 958	24 938	28 741	38 880	31 388	21 121	80.4	28.0	28.0	4.9	16.1	9.9	-2.4	8.7	10.5
DELAWARE	47 381	55 257	67 131	31 963	23 690	29 891	40 442	30 394	23 305	81.3	39.0	26.9	2.7	21.0	14.0	1.7	8.8	9.9
Dover city	38 669	48 338	60 020	36 429	18 942	25 909	36 687	26 968	19 445	79.8	34.9	25.5	3.7	22.3	8.9	-3.4	13.0	17.7
Newark city	48 758	75 188	77 809	20 208	25 500	26 243	47 737	34 643	20 376	85.1	47.8	21.1	1.3	17.6	18.5	6.2	17.8	6.6
Wilmington city	35 116	40 241	54 813	25 817	20 951	26 846	35 580	30 520	20 236	76.7	26.1	27.3	6.6	17.4	9.7	-2.6	18.9	24.1
DISTRICT OF COLUMBIA	40 127	46 283	73 909	27 385	19 656	34 130	41 567	37 236	28 659	78.6	31.4	19.5	5.5	17.9	16.4	4.1	17.1	24.5
Washington city	40 127	46 283	73 909	27 385	19 656	34 130	41 567	37 236	28 659	78.6	31.4	19.5	5.5	17.9	16.4	4.1	17.1	24.5

Table B-5. Cities — Education, Labor Force, and Income

STATE Place code	City	High school graduates			College graduates		College graduates (percent)				
		Total population 25 years and over	Percent with a high school diploma or less	Percent with a high school diploma or more	Percent with a bachelor's degree or more	+/− U.S. percent with bachelor's degree or more	Non-Hispanic White	Black or African American	American Indian and Alaska Native	Asian, Hawaiian, and Pacific Islander	Hispanic or Latino[1]
		1	2	3	4	5	6	7	8	9	10
12 00000	FLORIDA..................	11 024 645	48.9	79.9	22.3	-2.1	24.7	12.4	14.9	40.3	17.5
12 00950	Altamonte Springs city ..	28 740	31.5	89.8	31.2	6.8	32.0	26.8	27.9	56.4	23.6
12 01700	Apopka city.................	16 579	43.5	81.7	22.0	-2.4	24.2	17.0	0.0	39.1	14.8
12 02681	Aventura city	21 694	34.2	89.4	38.7	14.3	36.7	62.8	0.0	50.6	44.2
12 07300	Boca Raton city............	55 137	27.1	92.0	44.2	19.8	45.8	20.5	36.8	58.0	31.0
12 07525	Bonita Springs city	26 498	47.1	83.2	25.5	1.1	28.1	0.0	25.9	30.8	4.7
12 07875	Boynton Beach city	44 564	49.2	80.5	20.7	-3.7	23.6	9.4	0.0	40.4	16.3
12 07950	Bradenton city	35 393	51.6	79.8	20.5	-3.9	23.4	10.1	0.0	19.5	6.7
12 10275	Cape Coral city	73 451	50.1	85.5	17.5	-6.9	17.7	24.6	4.9	37.9	11.9
12 12875	Clearwater city	79 049	44.4	84.4	23.9	-0.5	25.8	6.9	17.8	38.6	15.5
12 13275	Coconut Creek city........	33 215	41.3	87.6	27.1	2.7	25.9	31.7	0.0	41.1	32.4
12 14125	Cooper City city............	17 227	30.5	92.1	38.2	13.8	38.0	52.4	100.0	52.2	31.8
12 14250	Coral Gables city..........	28 731	19.3	91.7	58.3	33.9	66.7	19.4	52.9	59.6	52.1
12 14400	Coral Springs city.........	72 334	33.9	89.6	33.9	9.5	36.1	25.1	22.2	39.0	27.1
12 16475	Davie town	49 801	44.9	84.5	25.8	1.4	25.6	28.6	11.0	48.2	22.8
12 16525	Daytona Beach city	41 995	49.5	79.6	18.8	-5.6	20.0	14.8	10.1	39.6	15.6
12 16725	Deerfield Beach city	50 580	50.5	79.3	21.2	-3.2	23.0	8.0	25.7	48.8	20.6
12 17100	Delray Beach city	45 474	42.6	81.0	29.3	4.9	35.9	9.4	12.2	42.4	20.2
12 17200	Deltona city	45 776	52.8	82.5	13.4	-11.0	13.4	17.0	0.0	29.8	11.2
12 18575	Dunedin city	28 547	42.2	86.6	22.4	-2.0	22.4	11.9	0.0	65.6	16.5
12 24000	Fort Lauderdale city	111 300	45.3	79.0	27.9	3.5	36.4	5.2	15.2	30.1	22.7
12 24125	Fort Myers city	29 875	58.3	70.7	18.3	-6.1	25.7	6.1	6.5	38.6	6.4
12 24300	Fort Pierce city	23 612	65.1	59.7	12.7	-11.7	19.0	5.2	59.6	30.7	5.5
12 25175	Gainesville city	50 574	29.6	87.8	42.8	18.4	49.6	13.9	28.4	80.2	46.9
12 27322	Greenacres city	19 574	54.1	79.8	17.4	-7.0	18.8	9.8	0.0	35.8	10.8
12 28450	Hallandale city..............	28 304	57.7	73.2	19.8	-4.6	20.8	7.5	0.0	40.1	22.8
12 30000	Hialeah city..................	155 607	73.0	49.8	10.4	-14.0	13.7	9.7	1.9	41.1	10.0
12 32000	Hollywood city	100 018	49.8	79.6	21.9	-2.5	24.7	13.0	5.7	32.9	15.9
12 32275	Homestead city	17 570	70.7	50.5	9.8	-14.6	20.7	3.9	17.6	33.3	4.3
12 35000	Jacksonville city	468 364	47.3	82.3	21.1	-3.3	23.6	13.2	17.5	34.3	21.9
12 35875	Jupiter town	29 190	32.9	91.4	34.7	10.3	35.6	39.4	20.7	55.7	13.9
12 36550	Key West city	19 384	40.2	84.7	27.3	2.9	31.6	10.5	16.7	62.2	13.5
12 36950	Kissimmee city	28 995	52.9	78.0	16.3	-8.1	18.2	10.6	12.0	36.6	12.1
12 38250	Lakeland city	53 542	51.0	79.2	20.9	-3.5	23.5	8.7	6.1	50.9	15.7
12 39075	Lake Worth city	23 393	57.6	66.5	16.4	-8.0	20.0	11.4	0.0	31.1	9.8
12 39425	Largo city....................	54 645	52.1	83.4	16.4	-8.0	15.7	17.6	21.3	47.0	20.2
12 39525	Lauderdale Lakes city ...	19 962	66.2	67.9	12.5	-11.9	14.5	11.7	0.0	10.4	14.6
12 39550	Lauderhill city	37 193	53.9	75.9	16.2	-8.2	19.2	12.8	0.0	41.2	18.5
12 43125	Margate city	39 455	53.5	80.2	17.0	-7.4	17.4	19.1	11.8	23.6	13.4
12 43975	Melbourne city..............	49 935	44.1	85.3	21.3	-3.1	22.1	9.8	12.8	37.0	20.0
12 45000	Miami city	252 504	67.1	52.7	16.2	-8.2	46.0	6.5	9.8	43.3	13.4
12 45025	Miami Beach city..........	69 290	41.7	78.8	33.5	9.1	45.6	17.6	14.3	46.3	24.9
12 45975	Miramar city.................	44 035	45.6	82.3	20.7	-3.7	20.4	20.9	30.9	31.8	19.5
12 49425	North Lauderdale city....	19 043	55.8	77.6	13.5	-10.9	15.5	13.7	0.0	17.6	9.2
12 49450	North Miami city	36 360	58.8	67.0	15.8	-8.6	30.7	9.0	28.0	37.6	13.4
12 49475	North Miami Beach city .	25 875	59.1	68.3	14.2	-10.2	20.7	7.4	13.7	24.5	13.6
12 50575	Oakland Park city	21 820	49.8	77.8	21.2	-3.2	23.8	13.7	37.8	37.9	17.3
12 50750	Ocala city	30 629	50.2	79.1	19.4	-5.0	21.5	9.5	24.8	35.8	16.7
12 53000	Orlando city	125 473	42.3	82.2	28.2	3.8	36.3	12.4	14.0	41.4	18.7
12 53150	Ormond Beach city	27 741	37.4	88.0	29.1	4.7	29.2	23.3	7.8	50.9	24.8
12 53575	Oviedo city	16 350	26.2	93.3	41.3	16.9	44.3	25.1	15.3	57.2	29.0
12 54000	Palm Bay city	52 306	48.0	83.7	16.7	-7.7	16.3	14.2	5.7	37.1	18.2
12 54075	Palm Beach Gardens city	26 047	26.4	94.0	43.8	19.4	44.5	16.8	82.4	48.3	33.2
12 54200	Palm Coast city	25 752	47.0	85.6	19.5	-4.9	19.1	21.7	38.7	36.6	15.5
12 54700	Panama City city	24 651	50.5	79.2	18.9	-5.5	21.5	7.0	17.1	28.7	18.1
12 55775	Pembroke Pines city	93 607	38.5	88.0	28.7	4.3	25.8	36.3	7.3	51.7	28.7
12 55925	Pensacola city	38 280	37.6	84.6	32.4	8.0	40.8	11.2	5.4	26.4	34.9
12 56975	Pinellas Park city..........	32 830	58.3	80.2	11.9	-12.5	11.4	14.8	9.4	22.1	11.0
12 57425	Plantation city	58 498	33.0	91.0	36.7	12.3	37.9	30.3	60.9	47.8	34.2
12 57550	Plant City city	18 596	56.4	71.3	16.6	-7.8	19.2	10.6	0.0	48.6	6.4
12 58050	Pompano Beach city	58 729	51.4	77.2	21.6	-2.8	26.1	6.1	7.6	23.6	22.2
12 58575	Port Orange city	33 725	49.9	84.7	17.0	-7.4	16.3	49.8	25.8	37.7	16.0
12 58715	Port St. Lucie city.........	62 007	51.1	83.7	15.0	-9.4	14.9	13.5	0.0	23.1	16.9
12 60975	Riviera Beach city	18 987	56.6	72.6	17.7	-6.7	32.9	8.5	0.0	38.8	13.0
12 63000	St. Petersburg city........	175 242	46.1	81.9	22.8	-1.6	26.1	10.1	22.0	24.4	20.2
12 63650	Sanford city	23 681	55.3	76.3	14.0	-10.4	16.0	5.9	37.5	45.7	17.8
12 64175	Sarasota city	38 323	47.4	80.1	25.7	1.3	30.7	5.0	18.5	46.1	9.2
12 69700	Sunrise city.................	58 187	49.1	83.7	20.0	-4.4	20.0	16.6	15.3	27.6	21.3
12 70600	Tallahassee city	79 856	26.8	89.9	45.0	20.6	52.4	27.9	22.5	66.5	37.7
12 70675	Tamarac city................	45 571	53.8	83.5	17.3	-7.1	17.4	14.9	0.0	29.1	15.7
12 71000	Tampa city...................	198 697	48.4	77.1	25.4	1.0	34.1	9.9	22.0	38.5	14.7
12 71900	Titusville city................	28 405	46.0	84.4	19.2	-5.2	20.1	11.9	6.3	32.3	13.0

[1]Hispanic or Latino persons may be of any race.

Table B-5. Cities — Education, Labor Force, and Income

City	School enrollment			Population 16 to 19 years				Employment status, 2000			Work status in 1999 of the population 16 years and over		
	Grades kindergarten through 12	College or graduate school	Percent private	Number	Percent in armed forces	Percent high school graduates	Percent not enrolled, not grads, not in armed forces, not employed	Total population 16 years and over	Percent in labor force	Unemployment rate	Full-time	Part-time	Did not work in 1999
	11	12	13	14	15	16	17	18	19	20	21	22	23
FLORIDA.................	2 775 141	886 825	14.5	794 066	0.7	10.2	6.3	12 744 825	58.6	5.5	51.5	12.5	36.0
Altamonte Springs city ..	5 951	3 054	19.5	1 711	0.0	14.3	7.7	33 776	74.9	3.8	66.3	13.4	20.3
Apopka city................	5 091	1 193	15.3	1 254	0.0	12.0	9.0	19 359	71.3	4.5	64.2	11.6	24.2
Aventura city	1 756	1 212	39.8	424	0.0	19.3	1.9	22 960	48.0	5.4	43.6	10.1	46.3
Boca Raton city...........	10 951	6 254	34.6	3 815	0.0	5.8	2.1	62 987	59.1	5.8	47.6	15.8	36.7
Bonita Springs city	3 215	570	9.7	1 059	0.0	7.6	8.3	28 851	48.0	2.3	42.2	11.6	46.3
Boynton Beach city	8 419	2 718	12.3	2 114	0.4	6.0	9.1	49 418	56.6	4.6	49.5	12.0	38.5
Bradenton city	7 947	1 707	8.9	2 036	0.0	9.3	7.0	40 212	54.7	4.8	48.0	11.5	40.5
Cape Coral city	17 042	3 442	12.2	4 467	0.3	15.3	4.4	81 736	60.6	3.7	52.6	12.4	34.9
Clearwater city	15 132	5 573	16.5	4 453	0.0	12.4	7.5	89 618	60.2	4.1	51.7	12.9	35.4
Coconut Creek city.......	5 114	2 149	16.3	916	0.0	12.1	5.2	35 916	58.5	3.1	51.4	11.1	37.5
Cooper City city...........	7 253	1 901	14.1	1 733	0.0	6.9	1.4	20 013	74.9	2.7	62.8	16.1	21.1
Coral Gables city	5 475	6 829	65.0	3 234	0.0	4.8	1.7	35 546	62.2	5.9	52.3	17.8	29.8
Coral Springs city.........	28 385	6 207	14.9	7 695	0.0	6.5	3.4	86 052	72.6	4.8	62.1	14.4	23.5
Davie town	14 752	5 772	20.7	3 752	0.0	10.8	4.3	57 971	69.3	4.3	61.3	12.8	25.9
Daytona Beach city.......	8 251	9 058	38.7	4 644	0.2	8.5	5.4	54 221	56.6	10.2	45.9	16.1	38.0
Deerfield Beach city	7 413	3 203	18.6	1 925	0.0	10.6	10.9	55 612	53.4	5.1	47.1	10.7	42.2
Delray Beach city	8 926	2 570	17.5	2 318	0.0	6.6	7.5	50 525	54.0	5.8	46.4	12.6	41.1
Deltona city	14 658	2 862	8.7	4 120	0.0	11.0	4.0	53 301	61.9	4.7	52.9	12.8	34.3
Dunedin city	4 296	1 530	18.1	1 132	0.0	6.2	5.4	30 969	53.6	3.5	45.3	12.8	41.9
Fort Lauderdale city	23 122	7 348	21.7	6 551	0.0	9.5	11.4	126 162	61.3	6.3	54.6	12.1	33.3
Fort Myers city	9 159	1 829	11.8	2 681	0.0	16.6	12.5	36 746	59.4	6.2	55.4	10.5	34.1
Fort Pierce city	7 546	1 470	7.2	2 091	0.0	8.8	11.9	28 485	55.1	8.8	45.5	12.5	42.0
Gainesville city	12 693	30 412	4.8	11 130	0.0	4.3	1.5	80 637	60.9	9.7	45.6	26.5	27.9
Greenacres city	3 899	1 132	9.5	1 079	0.0	7.9	13.6	22 222	55.0	3.7	48.9	10.3	40.8
Hallandale city	3 584	1 537	18.0	737	0.0	10.3	6.5	30 391	47.2	7.2	40.0	9.9	50.1
Hialeah city................	41 878	11 965	11.3	11 079	0.0	7.8	8.5	180 274	50.8	10.1	51.3	8.9	39.8
Hollywood city	22 308	7 638	19.8	5 778	0.0	9.9	5.3	112 796	61.4	5.6	54.1	12.3	33.5
Homestead city	7 064	1 100	6.4	2 014	0.0	8.8	18.9	22 002	62.6	10.3	56.9	9.5	33.7
Jacksonville city	144 621	40 855	15.8	40 232	2.1	12.2	6.8	559 805	67.2	4.9	61.0	11.0	27.2
Jupiter town	6 054	1 523	17.9	1 506	0.0	8.4	2.1	32 116	61.7	3.3	53.5	13.1	33.4
Key West city	3 062	1 207	11.8	748	5.6	26.5	2.4	21 785	70.1	2.8	64.7	10.6	24.6
Kissimmee city	9 308	2 508	10.4	2 624	0.0	9.9	6.3	36 277	68.2	5.2	63.1	12.2	24.7
Lakeland city	12 072	5 097	24.3	3 830	0.0	8.3	5.9	63 218	56.6	7.5	47.9	12.6	39.5
Lake Worth city	6 052	1 595	11.8	2 007	0.0	5.4	12.2	28 046	62.6	7.1	54.4	11.7	33.9
Largo city	7 867	2 450	13.5	2 163	0.3	14.6	5.0	59 868	53.3	3.9	46.4	11.1	42.5
Lauderdale Lakes city ...	6 969	1 721	11.9	1 737	0.0	6.6	6.9	23 840	56.5	9.2	49.3	10.7	39.9
Lauderhill city	11 525	3 155	11.7	3 080	0.0	11.3	4.5	43 750	61.1	6.9	53.6	10.9	35.5
Margate city	8 203	2 323	11.4	2 240	0.0	14.5	3.9	44 016	58.7	4.5	52.4	10.3	37.3
Melbourne city.............	11 122	5 221	25.3	4 042	0.0	9.1	4.7	58 551	59.2	5.4	49.4	13.9	36.7
Miami city	65 023	20 704	12.3	17 940	0.0	8.2	10.7	292 022	50.3	11.7	47.2	10.6	42.3
Miami Beach city..........	9 722	7 157	26.9	2 942	1.3	15.0	5.0	77 643	66.8	7.4	50.7	11.9	37.3
Miramar city	16 534	5 726	15.1	4 119	0.0	7.1	2.8	52 293	69.5	6.8	64.5	10.3	25.2
North Lauderdale city....	7 442	1 983	12.2	2 109	0.0	12.6	7.1	23 618	69.7	5.7	64.0	10.6	25.4
North Miami city	14 467	6 076	15.2	3 903	0.0	7.3	5.8	44 887	59.4	11.6	52.4	13.2	34.4
North Miami Beach city .	8 950	2 840	10.2	2 584	0.0	7.5	6.3	31 048	57.6	10.2	51.7	11.3	37.0
Oakland Park city.........	4 775	1 849	15.4	1 230	1.0	15.9	8.7	25 260	71.0	6.0	61.9	11.8	26.3
Ocala city	7 845	2 386	14.1	2 359	0.3	14.1	9.0	36 252	56.2	7.4	49.0	11.9	39.0
Orlando city	29 573	11 463	14.4	7 880	0.0	15.8	6.6	148 702	68.5	5.0	62.7	11.5	25.8
Ormond Beach city	5 421	1 381	16.1	1 382	0.0	2.7	2.4	30 335	53.5	3.3	43.7	14.1	42.2
Oviedo city	6 479	2 094	9.3	1 495	0.0	4.2	3.5	19 203	75.5	2.8	63.2	16.6	20.2
Palm Bay city	16 173	4 350	11.9	4 225	0.1	7.9	4.9	60 776	62.4	5.0	53.1	13.2	33.7
Palm Beach Gardens city	5 120	1 523	25.1	1 603	0.0	7.9	1.6	28 880	60.5	3.3	50.7	14.6	34.6
Palm Coast city	4 780	1 285	9.1	1 131	0.0	9.8	2.7	27 883	46.4	3.7	38.5	13.0	48.5
Panama City city	6 543	1 844	9.4	1 766	0.6	8.9	8.8	28 986	56.4	5.6	50.5	12.0	37.6
Pembroke Pines city	26 038	8 646	16.5	6 170	0.0	9.4	1.2	105 519	64.7	3.7	57.4	11.6	31.0
Pensacola city	9 820	3 671	14.8	3 008	0.0	6.5	8.9	44 966	59.7	6.4	49.5	14.7	35.9
Pinellas Park city..........	6 842	1 686	16.5	1 757	0.0	10.2	6.2	36 704	60.4	3.9	54.3	10.5	35.1
Plantation city	14 666	5 510	26.1	3 717	0.0	9.7	3.1	66 208	68.9	3.9	61.2	12.0	26.8
Plant City city	6 406	939	8.1	1 875	0.0	11.1	8.1	22 225	61.2	5.6	56.2	11.0	32.7
Pompano Beach city	10 752	3 079	17.5	2 967	0.0	7.4	15.9	65 938	53.8	6.6	49.1	10.9	39.9
Port Orange city	6 918	2 302	14.6	1 939	0.4	11.2	4.1	37 443	57.4	2.9	47.8	14.0	38.2
Port St. Lucie city.........	16 249	3 529	10.4	4 139	0.0	10.6	5.4	69 727	59.2	4.1	50.4	13.0	36.5
Riviera Beach city	7 171	1 014	9.5	1 587	0.0	11.8	9.2	22 222	57.1	8.0	50.9	10.9	30.2
St. Petersburg city........	40 332	13 396	18.1	10 914	0.5	10.4	6.8	199 857	62.4	5.1	54.6	12.4	33.0
Sanford city	7 342	1 996	10.8	1 845	0.0	12.1	7.8	28 481	63.2	5.8	59.3	10.8	29.9
Sarasota city	7 254	2 706	13.3	2 080	0.0	8.8	9.0	43 834	56.5	5.9	49.5	13.0	37.5
Sunrise city................	16 355	4 818	15.5	4 204	0.0	9.5	5.0	66 628	63.9	5.7	56.0	11.3	32.6
Tallahassee city	18 983	45 144	6.6	16 233	0.1	4.9	1.5	127 242	67.0	11.1	50.9	23.6	25.6
Tamarac city...............	5 306	2 423	12.1	1 243	0.0	13.9	3.3	49 069	49.1	6.2	42.6	9.2	48.1
Tampa city	55 779	20 461	17.0	16 189	0.5	9.0	8.2	236 481	64.0	8.5	56.9	12.8	30.3
Titusville city	7 105	1 696	9.8	1 919	0.0	14.0	6.2	32 272	56.6	6.3	46.7	13.1	40.3

Table B-5. Cities — **Education, Labor Force, and Income**

City	Full-year full-time employed (percent): Total	Men	Women	Non-Hispanic White	Black or African American	American Indian and Alaska Native	Asian, Hawaiian, and Pacific Islander	Hispanic or Latino[1]	Children under 18 years in families (percent, except where noted): Number	With two parents: Both in labor force	With two parents: Father only in labor force	With one parent who is in labor force	+/– U.S. percent of children with no stay-at-home parent	+/– U.S. percent two-income couples	Total employed by class of worker (percent): Private	Govern-ment	Self-employed	Unpaid family worker
	24	25	26	27	28	29	30	31	32	33	34	35	36	37	38	39	40	41
FLORIDA	38.2	46.3	30.8	38.4	37.0	38.8	41.3	38.0	3 383 513	40.4	20.0	24.8	0.6	-7.0	74.8	13.7	11.1	0.3
Altamonte Springs city	50.7	61.4	41.2	52.2	55.0	33.3	53.2	40.1	8 008	45.3	18.0	25.8	6.5	9.2	81.9	9.0	8.9	0.2
Apopka city	48.4	57.5	40.4	50.1	45.4	53.8	51.7	44.8	6 910	39.2	19.8	25.5	0.1	7.4	80.9	11.4	7.6	0.2
Aventura city	31.3	41.5	23.3	28.4	44.5	0.0	38.4	40.3	2 449	29.6	32.7	19.4	-15.6	-20.7	70.5	9.3	19.8	0.4
Boca Raton city	35.9	46.9	25.8	36.0	30.3	48.7	32.6	37.8	13 685	40.8	33.8	15.8	-8.0	-10.9	70.8	8.5	20.2	0.4
Bonita Springs city	30.7	38.0	22.9	27.9	64.5	9.3	33.1	47.7	4 286	40.2	24.9	24.4	0.0	-21.5	79.1	5.7	15.1	0.1
Boynton Beach city	37.9	46.8	30.5	34.8	46.7	24.7	43.5	46.9	10 572	43.8	16.6	25.5	4.7	-9.2	77.2	11.5	11.0	0.3
Bradenton city	35.4	43.2	28.7	33.8	37.5	33.3	42.8	42.9	9 914	36.9	17.6	31.5	3.8	-9.2	78.5	11.8	9.5	0.2
Cape Coral city	40.9	48.0	34.3	41.0	31.9	37.1	47.8	40.7	21 860	54.1	16.2	21.1	10.6	-3.0	74.4	12.8	12.5	0.3
Clearwater city	39.0	46.6	32.4	39.1	38.1	40.0	38.5	38.7	19 069	37.4	18.6	29.1	1.9	-6.3	79.1	9.6	11.0	0.2
Coconut Creek city	41.2	52.2	32.0	38.9	56.6	44.4	50.7	47.7	7 499	51.7	21.8	15.4	2.5	-4.5	77.6	11.4	10.6	0.4
Cooper City city	51.5	64.0	40.1	52.3	48.8	100.0	47.3	50.0	8 560	57.7	21.9	14.3	7.4	14.7	67.0	19.0	13.7	0.2
Coral Gables city	39.0	50.2	29.5	36.3	17.3	15.7	29.6	43.7	7 155	41.7	33.3	13.8	-9.1	-3.5	68.9	10.5	20.2	0.4
Coral Springs city	49.7	62.0	38.6	51.2	48.7	30.2	46.5	44.9	34 593	45.9	24.4	19.4	0.7	7.4	77.1	9.6	13.0	0.3
Davie town	48.6	58.6	39.4	49.3	53.0	54.6	45.2	46.0	18 912	47.9	19.9	21.7	5.0	5.3	75.7	13.8	10.4	0.1
Daytona Beach city	30.4	33.7	27.2	30.7	29.3	33.7	27.8	31.2	9 915	26.3	13.6	40.0	1.7	-11.3	78.9	12.5	8.4	0.2
Deerfield Beach city	35.8	44.1	28.9	34.2	38.5	38.1	54.8	40.7	9 513	37.6	17.5	29.7	2.7	-11.7	78.4	9.5	11.9	0.2
Delray Beach city	34.3	42.6	27.0	31.6	37.3	17.9	39.1	45.7	9 688	33.9	17.7	32.5	1.8	-14.1	76.1	9.8	13.7	0.4
Deltona city	41.3	50.9	32.5	42.9	38.0	34.1	35.0	35.3	17 692	44.4	22.5	20.9	0.7	-5.0	78.7	12.2	8.9	0.2
Dunedin city	35.4	43.9	28.5	35.6	36.5	41.0	26.9	34.3	5 337	43.6	22.6	26.9	5.9	-9.4	74.8	11.2	13.7	0.3
Fort Lauderdale city	40.2	46.9	32.7	42.0	35.6	53.6	40.9	40.2	26 109	29.1	18.9	33.1	-2.4	-6.7	76.1	9.5	14.0	0.4
Fort Myers city	39.0	45.9	32.4	40.3	36.4	40.8	45.1	38.8	10 976	27.5	13.5	40.6	3.5	-5.5	80.3	11.4	8.1	0.1
Fort Pierce city	30.3	37.5	23.4	31.3	26.9	36.2	32.4	37.9	8 648	24.2	12.9	34.1	-6.3	-11.9	79.4	11.4	8.8	0.3
Gainesville city	29.1	33.8	24.7	30.9	28.3	53.4	19.7	19.7	15 350	38.1	14.6	29.7	3.2	4.7	57.8	34.5	7.3	0.5
Greenacres city	38.1	46.4	31.1	35.4	54.7	50.0	46.0	42.9	5 268	37.7	20.4	30.8	3.9	-14.6	76.7	13.0	10.0	0.3
Hallandale city	29.0	36.6	22.7	23.9	40.9	65.0	38.6	38.9	4 319	29.0	17.6	38.2	2.6	-23.4	77.0	10.0	12.7	0.3
Hialeah city	34.8	43.6	27.0	32.3	29.4	12.5	21.5	35.0	48 498	32.4	17.3	20.7	-11.5	-18.8	82.6	7.5	9.7	0.2
Hollywood city	39.5	48.0	31.9	39.3	39.9	53.8	38.0	40.4	27 776	38.0	19.5	26.1	-0.5	-4.5	76.8	11.2	11.7	0.3
Homestead city	34.7	41.0	28.1	43.4	30.6	6.1	23.9	31.7	9 589	26.1	15.1	31.9	-6.6	-7.1	81.3	13.4	5.3	0.0
Jacksonville city	46.6	55.6	38.5	48.7	41.6	45.1	48.1	45.2	182 867	38.9	18.5	27.9	2.2	2.5	79.1	12.9	7.9	0.2
Jupiter town	42.1	52.1	32.7	41.9	31.2	41.4	52.6	43.5	7 789	46.0	26.7	17.8	-0.8	-6.1	75.1	9.7	15.0	0.2
Key West city	45.5	51.3	38.2	46.4	46.0	49.1	67.1	38.1	3 844	46.6	15.3	21.8	3.8	4.7	63.4	19.0	17.0	0.7
Kissimmee city	45.3	52.3	38.8	50.1	40.0	54.3	41.6	41.7	11 707	35.4	16.9	28.7	-0.5	1.9	86.7	7.9	5.3	0.2
Lakeland city	35.0	43.4	27.9	34.3	36.7	24.3	37.7	36.2	15 133	35.5	14.4	36.7	7.6	-9.3	76.2	15.1	8.4	0.3
Lake Worth city	36.5	43.7	28.6	35.3	35.7	33.2	49.3	37.0	7 178	30.6	22.2	29.5	-4.5	-10.8	75.7	12.1	11.9	0.3
Largo city	35.8	43.3	29.5	34.7	51.3	54.5	56.9	42.0	10 144	46.3	15.3	27.5	9.2	-11.2	78.9	10.4	10.4	0.3
Lauderdale Lakes city	33.2	39.5	28.4	14.3	42.1	0.0	44.6	28.1	7 781	31.0	9.8	40.5	6.9	-9.7	82.2	12.3	5.3	0.2
Lauderhill city	38.7	44.7	34.1	29.2	44.2	73.1	37.9	43.6	13 933	34.1	10.3	36.9	6.4	-3.0	80.0	12.2	7.5	0.3
Margate city	41.0	50.3	32.9	38.4	51.4	10.3	42.5	45.0	10 569	42.7	21.9	23.6	1.7	-4.6	79.7	11.3	8.7	0.3
Melbourne city	37.4	46.2	29.3	37.8	34.5	33.4	32.2	41.5	13 367	40.5	21.0	25.2	1.1	-6.8	80.7	10.9	8.3	0.2
Miami city	29.5	36.0	23.1	39.5	26.0	26.5	39.3	28.5	70 620	24.0	13.7	30.2	-10.4	-18.1	77.5	10.6	11.6	0.3
Miami Beach city	33.6	40.6	26.3	36.2	35.0	12.5	35.0	31.6	11 066	31.3	24.3	24.5	-8.8	-15.7	76.0	7.8	16.0	0.2
Miramar city	49.5	57.5	42.6	48.8	50.2	42.1	43.7	49.5	21 176	44.5	15.6	23.3	3.2	6.2	76.4	14.8	8.7	0.2
North Lauderdale city	49.3	56.5	43.0	49.5	50.7	40.7	47.5	47.8	9 126	34.9	15.6	34.2	4.5	6.4	82.9	8.5	8.6	0.1
North Miami city	36.1	41.6	31.2	34.4	37.2	46.5	34.1	35.2	15 580	32.8	12.1	28.7	-3.1	-9.3	78.1	12.6	9.1	0.3
North Miami Beach city	36.4	43.4	30.3	32.5	39.1	37.2	31.7	36.9	9 997	31.9	16.5	27.4	-5.3	-9.4	80.7	8.3	10.6	0.3
Oakland Park city	44.3	50.2	37.8	46.2	45.3	24.3	27.6	39.9	6 054	32.8	16.4	38.8	7.0	1.0	78.3	10.6	11.0	0.0
Ocala city	34.5	43.1	27.2	36.9	26.4	31.3	27.1	34.0	9 409	32.8	17.2	35.6	3.8	-4.3	72.6	16.5	10.4	0.5
Orlando city	45.5	54.0	37.7	50.2	38.2	44.0	40.5	41.6	37 597	29.4	15.3	35.6	0.4	0.5	82.8	9.9	7.2	0.1
Ormond Beach city	34.0	43.6	25.8	33.5	42.2	50.0	34.8	46.4	6 737	45.5	23.9	19.8	0.7	-10.8	70.1	13.6	16.0	0.3
Oviedo city	51.2	65.7	37.6	53.4	42.2	39.4	48.2	44.9	8 380	54.3	27.6	13.8	3.5	10.8	75.9	15.1	8.9	0.1
Palm Bay city	40.8	48.7	33.5	42.0	36.2	45.5	29.2	37.6	19 930	43.1	21.1	23.9	2.4	-4.7	79.1	12.1	8.6	0.2
Palm Beach Gardens city	39.9	50.6	30.6	40.1	42.1	17.6	46.0	33.9	6 317	44.9	29.3	19.8	0.1	-7.3	71.5	10.9	17.0	0.6
Palm Coast city	27.9	34.4	22.2	28.4	22.7	54.3	33.7	28.8	5 936	50.5	17.2	19.0	4.9	-19.9	73.0	14.6	12.1	0.2
Panama City city	36.7	43.2	30.7	38.6	28.7	16.1	45.3	30.5	7 602	41.5	17.0	27.6	4.5	-2.3	71.8	18.6	9.4	0.2
Pembroke Pines city	44.8	56.1	35.6	41.9	50.9	41.9	47.9	47.4	33 650	50.9	22.7	16.9	3.2	3.3	73.9	16.4	9.5	0.2
Pensacola city	37.4	47.1	29.1	40.0	30.2	40.1	41.6	39.4	11 807	30.3	20.3	33.0	-1.3	-7.0	70.0	18.4	11.3	0.2
Pinellas Park city	43.2	51.1	36.2	42.5	50.7	67.9	52.2	47.2	9 047	44.9	15.9	28.2	8.5	-2.3	80.7	10.8	8.2	0.3
Plantation city	48.4	57.7	40.4	48.3	50.0	66.4	47.8	48.5	18 414	49.1	20.3	22.5	7.0	3.6	73.8	13.7	12.3	0.2
Plant City city	40.5	49.5	32.2	43.3	34.9	35.4	28.2	32.8	8 272	31.2	21.8	27.0	-6.4	-5.0	79.9	13.3	6.8	0.0
Pompano Beach city	35.5	43.4	27.8	35.2	34.2	39.2	47.2	38.4	12 171	30.6	16.2	31.0	-3.0	-14.6	78.7	8.7	12.4	0.3
Port Orange city	37.4	44.6	31.0	37.1	51.6	40.5	30.8	41.0	8 599	43.8	20.1	24.9	4.1	-6.4	73.7	13.8	12.3	0.2
Port St. Lucie city	39.7	47.1	32.9	39.8	34.8	44.4	46.1	40.5	20 316	46.4	20.1	22.1	3.9	-6.9	77.5	12.6	9.7	0.3
Riviera Beach city	36.5	39.2	34.1	30.5	39.5	61.9	36.9	42.1	8 052	19.7	8.2	45.1	0.2	-12.4	74.7	15.7	9.4	0.2
St. Petersburg city	41.3	48.3	35.2	41.8	38.3	51.0	46.0	43.8	48 915	37.6	14.7	32.2	5.2	-0.5	77.6	12.1	10.1	0.3
Sanford city	42.2	48.5	35.9	46.2	32.7	36.5	54.6	42.6	8 987	35.2	14.2	32.2	2.8	1.8	78.2	15.0	6.6	0.2
Sarasota city	36.5	44.0	29.5	36.0	33.4	59.2	50.3	42.0	8 570	27.0	16.5	35.9	-1.7	-9.6	76.0	9.5	13.9	0.6
Sunrise city	42.9	52.9	34.7	40.3	48.2	39.4	44.5	46.2	20 203	46.0	16.7	25.5	6.9	0.7	79.2	12.0	8.8	0.0
Tallahassee city	34.8	40.5	29.8	38.3	29.1	41.6	35.9	25.3	24 525	38.3	16.2	32.2	5.9	7.9	56.6	36.2	7.0	0.2
Tamarac city	33.5	40.2	28.3	28.5	53.2	0.0	47.8	45.0	7 228	42.7	14.2	30.7	8.8	-15.5	80.4	10.8	8.7	0.1
Tampa city	40.5	48.6	33.1	45.7	33.0	49.5	38.8	34.8	67 390	31.7	16.6	31.3	-1.6	-2.5	77.9	12.9	8.9	0.3
Titusville city	36.2	46.7	26.8	36.6	31.4	44.3	43.3	39.7	8 736	38.2	19.4	33.2	6.8	-11.7	71.4	20.8	7.4	0.4

[1]Hispanic or Latino persons may be of any race.

Table B-5. Cities — Education, Labor Force, and Income

| City | Percent who worked at home | Percent of the population 5 years and over with a disability | Veterans as a percent of the population 18 years and over | Occupation for employed population 16 years and over (percent) | | | | | | Industry for employed population 16 years and over (percent) | | | | | |
| | | | | Management, professional, and related occupations | Service occupations | Sales and office occupations | Farming, fishing, and forestry occupations | Construction, extraction, and maintenance occupations | Production, transportation and material moving occupations | Agriculture, forestry, fishing, and mining | Construction and manufacturing | Wholesale and retail trade | Transportation and warehousing, and utilities | Service industries | Public administration |
	42	43	44	45	46	47	48	49	50	51	52	53	54	55	56
FLORIDA	3.0	22.2	15.2	31.5	16.9	29.5	0.9	10.3	10.8	1.3	15.3	17.5	5.3	55.4	5.2
Altamonte Springs city	2.7	18.6	12.4	38.9	13.4	32.5	0.0	7.6	7.6	0.1	14.1	17.9	4.1	60.9	2.9
Apopka city	2.6	20.1	13.5	33.8	12.8	31.6	1.8	8.8	11.3	1.5	14.8	19.6	5.8	54.5	3.8
Aventura city	5.7	24.4	12.5	48.6	9.5	36.2	0.1	2.7	2.9	0.1	7.2	22.4	4.6	61.2	4.6
Boca Raton city	6.1	16.9	13.7	45.6	13.4	30.9	0.1	5.2	4.8	0.2	11.6	17.2	2.9	65.6	2.6
Bonita Springs city	5.8	21.8	20.7	24.6	21.7	27.2	1.8	18.0	6.8	1.8	22.8	19.8	2.5	51.4	1.8
Boynton Beach city	2.6	23.2	14.7	29.6	21.1	29.7	0.5	10.6	8.3	0.9	14.4	18.1	3.4	59.3	4.0
Bradenton city	2.3	25.0	17.5	28.0	19.5	26.3	1.8	10.6	13.7	1.7	19.0	17.3	3.3	54.3	4.4
Cape Coral city	2.8	20.3	17.9	28.6	16.5	32.3	0.3	12.8	9.5	0.4	17.6	19.4	3.9	53.9	4.8
Clearwater city	4.1	23.1	16.5	34.1	16.3	31.0	0.3	7.8	10.5	0.3	14.7	18.2	3.8	59.6	3.4
Coconut Creek city	2.8	17.9	14.6	37.6	12.9	33.8	0.3	8.7	6.7	0.3	13.8	19.9	4.6	56.3	5.1
Cooper City city	3.3	9.8	10.1	45.3	12.8	29.3	0.1	6.8	5.7	0.2	9.9	15.8	6.7	60.7	6.8
Coral Gables city	5.5	13.4	6.6	59.9	9.4	25.3	0.0	2.5	2.9	0.1	7.6	13.4	4.3	71.1	3.5
Coral Springs city	3.9	15.1	0.0	39.5	12.8	32.9	0.1	7.6	7.0	0.2	13.6	21.0	4.0	57.5	3.6
Davie town	2.6	16.9	11.4	34.1	15.3	30.0	0.3	11.6	8.8	0.4	16.4	18.3	5.9	55.0	5.0
Daytona Beach city	2.1	24.8	16.1	26.1	23.3	29.4	0.2	8.4	12.6	0.3	13.6	15.2	4.0	62.8	3.9
Deerfield Beach city	2.4	26.1	13.7	30.7	18.8	30.3	0.5	10.3	9.4	0.7	16.8	18.4	4.4	56.1	3.5
Delray Beach city	4.3	24.9	14.0	33.6	22.1	26.9	0.5	7.9	9.0	0.4	12.8	18.7	4.0	60.9	3.2
Deltona city	2.5	22.2	17.9	26.6	16.0	31.1	0.1	13.8	12.4	0.2	18.7	18.1	5.2	53.2	4.5
Dunedin city	3.8	26.1	18.4	35.2	16.5	33.0	0.3	7.8	7.3	0.1	13.7	17.3	4.3	60.8	3.9
Fort Lauderdale city	3.8	23.2	12.5	33.4	20.1	27.4	0.3	9.1	9.8	0.4	12.9	16.3	5.4	61.8	3.3
Fort Myers city	1.8	25.2	12.3	25.6	23.4	27.5	1.1	12.7	9.8	1.0	15.8	18.5	2.6	58.2	4.0
Fort Pierce city	2.0	30.5	12.9	19.9	19.3	20.5	9.0	15.8	15.5	7.8	20.6	17.3	3.7	46.7	4.0
Gainesville city	3.1	15.7	9.4	45.9	17.6	26.3	0.3	4.4	5.5	0.5	6.9	11.9	2.4	73.1	5.2
Greenacres city	1.9	25.1	15.4	24.9	21.4	28.4	0.3	13.7	11.2	0.7	16.8	17.0	5.6	54.8	5.0
Hallandale city	3.2	27.5	11.9	27.7	20.5	32.4	0.1	8.3	11.0	0.2	13.2	21.2	6.1	55.7	3.7
Hialeah city	1.1	25.8	2.1	16.5	14.2	30.7	0.3	14.3	24.0	0.3	26.6	20.8	8.8	41.1	2.3
Hollywood city	2.8	22.7	11.9	31.3	16.9	29.7	0.4	11.6	10.0	0.4	13.8	17.7	6.0	58.2	4.0
Homestead city	1.0	24.8	7.6	17.2	19.7	21.4	14.3	17.5	9.8	13.0	17.7	19.0	4.4	40.3	5.6
Jacksonville city	1.9	21.5	17.2	31.2	14.0	32.6	0.2	9.5	12.4	0.3	14.4	16.4	7.9	56.1	4.8
Jupiter town	4.0	17.2	15.5	40.5	16.0	28.8	0.3	7.8	6.7	0.2	14.5	16.6	5.2	59.9	3.6
Key West city	5.7	20.0	15.2	29.8	26.7	26.2	2.2	9.1	0.0	0.3	9.8	13.5	5.0	59.3	10.0
Kissimmee city	1.2	24.2	10.8	20.7	27.9	29.7	0.2	11.2	10.3	0.2	12.3	15.8	5.3	64.0	2.4
Lakeland city	2.2	25.3	16.9	30.8	16.9	28.6	0.4	7.6	15.7	1.3	14.2	20.3	6.1	53.1	5.1
Lake Worth city	2.6	22.1	10.7	21.8	25.3	22.8	2.4	17.3	10.4	2.4	20.2	13.0	4.8	56.0	3.7
Largo city	2.2	28.1	19.1	29.2	16.6	32.7	0.1	9.0	12.4	0.0	18.0	19.1	3.5	54.7	4.7
Lauderdale Lakes city	0.8	27.3	7.9	20.0	26.8	27.3	0.3	11.7	13.8	0.2	15.9	17.3	5.5	58.2	3.0
Lauderhill city	1.5	25.6	9.0	26.2	20.0	32.3	0.3	10.4	10.8	0.3	13.3	18.5	4.2	58.8	5.0
Margate city	1.8	23.7	14.0	27.5	15.4	34.5	0.1	12.5	9.9	0.2	17.2	21.0	4.0	53.0	4.5
Melbourne city	1.9	24.0	19.9	31.4	18.2	28.9	0.3	10.2	11.0	0.3	21.3	18.3	3.4	51.8	4.9
Miami city	2.1	29.4	4.2	23.8	22.1	26.2	0.5	13.6	13.0	0.5	17.7	16.4	6.2	55.8	3.3
Miami Beach city	5.4	25.7	5.6	40.3	21.1	26.9	0.2	4.8	6.8	0.3	8.0	15.2	4.0	69.2	3.2
Miramar city	1.9	16.6	7.6	31.3	16.3	33.1	0.4	9.2	9.9	0.5	12.0	17.9	9.0	54.9	5.7
North Lauderdale city	1.9	23.4	8.0	23.6	19.1	31.7	0.2	13.8	11.7	0.5	18.7	19.3	5.0	53.1	3.5
North Miami city	2.0	25.3	5.3	24.3	25.0	28.5	0.0	8.4	13.8	0.1	11.0	16.4	7.0	62.2	3.4
North Miami Beach city	1.6	22.2	6.0	22.0	22.6	32.1	0.1	10.2	13.0	0.2	13.3	19.7	5.8	58.0	3.0
Oakland Park city	2.0	23.7	9.8	26.4	21.3	27.0	0.2	11.8	13.2	0.3	17.4	16.7	6.1	55.4	4.1
Ocala city	2.6	24.3	16.0	31.8	18.9	27.1	0.8	9.4	12.0	1.2	18.2	16.1	3.6	55.6	5.4
Orlando city	2.2	22.2	12.1	33.3	19.2	30.0	0.2	7.5	9.8	0.4	12.2	14.4	5.8	63.8	3.4
Ormond Beach city	3.4	19.6	19.1	40.3	14.9	30.2	0.1	7.7	6.8	0.3	14.4	16.0	3.6	60.2	5.4
Oviedo city	4.1	11.4	13.9	43.8	12.7	30.1	0.1	6.7	6.5	0.5	14.4	16.4	5.1	58.4	5.2
Palm Bay city	2.1	22.2	18.9	29.4	18.8	27.5	0.2	12.1	12.1	0.4	24.9	16.5	3.3	50.4	4.5
Palm Beach Gardens city	5.4	16.0	15.8	46.9	12.3	30.3	0.2	4.6	5.7	0.2	11.5	16.4	4.0	64.0	4.0
Palm Coast city	2.9	20.5	22.9	28.0	20.6	29.9	0.1	10.6	10.8	0.8	18.9	18.9	4.2	52.6	4.5
Panama City city	2.2	26.0	18.2	32.2	20.8	27.7	0.4	8.6	10.4	0.5	13.7	15.9	4.7	57.7	7.5
Pembroke Pines city	3.0	15.3	10.9	40.7	12.5	32.2	0.2	7.3	7.2	0.2	11.3	18.5	8.3	55.2	6.6
Pensacola city	3.0	22.6	18.7	38.3	17.9	26.8	0.6	7.7	8.7	0.7	10.6	15.1	4.9	61.9	6.8
Pinellas Park city	2.2	27.6	18.9	23.2	15.1	32.5	0.3	10.8	18.1	0.3	23.9	20.4	4.3	46.5	4.6
Plantation city	3.4	15.6	10.9	43.0	12.0	32.2	0.1	6.5	6.2	0.2	11.9	17.5	5.0	59.9	5.6
Plant City city	2.0	22.7	13.1	25.5	15.3	28.1	2.5	10.1	18.5	3.5	20.2	21.5	5.4	46.0	3.4
Pompano Beach city	2.6	20.6	14.0	28.6	18.5	30.0	0.5	11.4	11.0	0.5	16.9	18.3	5.5	56.0	2.8
Port Orange city	2.2	22.4	20.5	30.1	17.6	31.4	0.3	11.1	9.5	0.1	15.4	19.1	4.5	55.3	5.6
Port St. Lucie city	2.2	22.6	17.0	26.6	17.6	32.0	0.1	12.5	10.7	0.6	16.1	21.6	5.3	50.7	5.7
Riviera Beach city	2.3	25.0	14.3	24.5	25.1	26.1	0.2	9.3	14.7	0.3	13.2	14.3	6.7	59.9	5.6
St. Petersburg city	3.1	25.0	16.4	34.0	16.7	28.3	0.1	8.2	12.7	0.1	16.1	15.2	4.4	60.2	4.0
Sanford city	2.2	25.0	14.4	27.0	18.3	29.3	0.3	12.1	15.0	0.5	19.9	17.7	5.8	51.3	4.7
Sarasota city	3.5	25.0	14.6	29.0	23.1	26.6	0.4	11.1	9.8	0.6	16.2	16.0	3.1	60.7	3.4
Sunrise city	1.8	21.0	11.1	31.7	15.7	34.1	0.1	8.9	9.5	0.1	12.6	20.3	6.3	56.0	4.7
Tallahassee city	2.4	13.1	9.2	46.0	15.4	28.7	0.1	4.6	5.2	0.2	5.7	13.4	2.0	60.8	17.9
Tamarac city	1.9	27.7	16.8	28.4	15.7	36.0	0.1	10.6	9.0	0.1	13.7	19.7	4.9	56.6	4.9
Tampa city	2.6	24.1	12.8	34.0	16.3	30.1	0.2	8.6	10.9	0.3	13.5	16.6	4.6	60.9	4.2
Titusville city	2.0	22.0	21.2	33.6	16.7	25.9	0.1	10.8	13.0	0.3	19.4	14.2	4.9	49.7	11.4

City	Median household income	Median family income: All families	Median family income: Families with children: Married-couple	Median family income: Families with children: Male householder	Median family income: Families with children: Female householder	Median nonfamily household income	Median income for full-year, full-time workers: Men	Median income for full-year, full-time workers: Women	Per capita income	Households by source of income (percent): With earnings	Households by source of income (percent): With interest, dividend, or rental income	Households by source of income (percent): With Social Security income	Households by source of income (percent): With public assistance income	Households by source of income (percent): With retirement income	Households with income over $100,000 (percent)	+/− U.S. percent for income over $100,000	Households with income below poverty (percent)	Families with children with income below poverty (percent)
	57	58	59	60	61	62	63	64	65	66	67	68	69	70	71	72	73	74
FLORIDA	38 819	45 625	55 511	27 357	20 553	24 799	33 980	26 236	21 557	74.7	35.3	32.7	2.8	19.9	10.4	-1.9	11.7	14.2
Altamonte Springs city	41 578	49 082	56 378	27 273	26 315	33 183	35 621	29 741	23 216	87.4	29.8	18.4	1.3	11.6	8.2	-4.1	7.4	9.6
Apopka city	43 651	49 380	52 909	27 177	21 799	29 272	33 537	27 355	19 189	87.7	29.9	21.9	3.0	12.8	10.2	-2.1	8.8	10.8
Aventura city	44 526	59 507	69 539	10 000	40 509	33 131	53 803	40 455	41 092	63.0	50.5	43.5	0.9	14.3	19.7	7.4	9.3	10.2
Boca Raton city	60 248	77 861	101 236	40 500	28 456	37 851	59 063	35 456	45 628	74.3	55.2	32.4	1.2	17.0	30.7	18.4	6.9	6.0
Bonita Springs city	46 603	53 436	51 920	24 375	23 281	30 036	32 231	25 703	37 958	61.1	53.4	48.0	1.6	32.2	17.9	5.6	5.2	8.1
Boynton Beach city	39 845	47 546	53 672	37 500	23 750	26 808	34 074	26 917	22 573	68.0	42.3	39.9	1.6	21.1	8.2	-4.1	8.8	12.8
Bradenton city	34 902	42 366	50 849	22 955	20 833	23 789	29 028	24 560	20 133	66.9	38.4	40.2	2.7	24.4	6.0	-6.3	11.9	17.7
Cape Coral city	43 410	47 503	55 390	31 996	24 375	27 607	34 618	25 746	21 021	74.4	38.4	36.1	1.2	25.5	8.2	-4.1	6.7	7.7
Clearwater city	36 494	46 228	57 968	28 309	19 344	24 429	31 747	25 957	22 786	72.4	39.1	34.8	2.9	20.5	9.4	-2.9	10.9	14.5
Coconut Creek city	43 980	55 131	69 026	33 021	25 638	31 098	41 409	31 971	25 590	68.1	44.3	39.5	0.9	18.8	10.5	-1.8	6.9	8.5
Cooper City city	75 166	78 172	84 444	54 042	37 063	44 479	54 113	35 033	27 474	91.7	46.2	16.1	1.4	10.7	28.1	15.8	3.1	3.5
Coral Gables city	66 839	98 553	140 117	50 083	44 087	40 477	72 500	40 914	46 163	82.6	48.5	26.2	1.0	12.4	35.5	23.2	7.6	5.8
Coral Springs city	58 459	64 193	76 801	36 905	28 395	34 772	46 436	31 478	25 282	91.0	32.6	13.4	1.3	7.9	22.7	10.4	7.4	8.3
Davie town	47 014	56 290	72 962	32 800	25 426	28 511	40 193	30 685	23 271	86.3	29.3	20.8	2.3	11.7	15.8	3.5	10.1	9.6
Daytona Beach city	25 439	33 514	41 016	21 346	13 806	18 287	26 472	20 952	17 530	70.8	28.9	32.9	3.5	19.3	5.3	-7.0	22.4	29.6
Deerfield Beach city	34 041	44 853	52 568	30 078	20 610	23 964	35 815	28 893	23 296	62.5	39.4	42.7	1.5	18.0	8.7	-3.6	11.5	15.9
Delray Beach city	43 371	51 195	56 914	26 364	22 804	32 123	35 580	29 473	29 350	65.9	46.1	41.6	1.7	19.9	15.1	2.8	9.9	13.9
Deltona city	39 736	42 122	50 119	32 866	22 929	25 182	31 852	24 456	16 648	77.6	31.4	33.5	2.3	20.9	5.1	-7.2	7.3	8.8
Dunedin city	34 813	47 620	61 647	28 900	24 205	22 162	33 258	27 977	23 460	65.8	43.6	44.6	1.7	24.8	8.1	-4.2	8.6	8.1
Fort Lauderdale city	37 887	46 175	54 260	20 928	17 781	30 858	35 709	28 081	27 798	77.5	34.1	26.7	2.5	12.4	14.3	2.0	14.7	23.5
Fort Myers city	28 514	32 477	44 858	23 485	15 473	21 594	26 709	20 983	17 312	75.3	23.2	27.6	4.9	14.1	6.6	-5.7	19.5	26.3
Fort Pierce city	25 121	29 458	35 365	22 813	11 698	18 600	21 631	20 679	14 345	68.3	24.2	36.8	6.0	18.8	4.6	-7.7	25.4	37.5
Gainesville city	28 164	44 263	55 530	22 734	16 643	18 700	32 208	26 506	16 779	81.8	35.4	18.8	2.8	13.7	7.7	-4.6	26.1	21.7
Greenacres city	36 941	41 250	48 861	33 056	24 568	27 191	30 783	25 528	19 298	67.0	34.9	42.2	2.3	22.7	5.3	-7.0	6.3	7.5
Hallandale city	28 266	37 171	41 582	22 469	17 309	21 421	31 986	25 528	22 464	56.5	39.9	47.6	2.7	17.3	6.6	-5.7	15.7	22.1
Hialeah city	29 492	31 621	36 841	22 838	17 357	12 891	23 823	18 564	12 402	80.2	14.2	29.7	9.6	11.9	4.1	-8.2	20.3	20.1
Hollywood city	36 714	44 849	51 435	26 285	21 503	25 973	34 704	28 177	22 097	76.4	31.3	29.9	2.9	12.9	10.1	-2.2	12.7	15.2
Homestead city	26 775	26 409	30 693	21 522	13 185	21 769	23 720	20 800	11 357	80.9	14.6	18.5	9.4	10.3	4.0	-8.3	28.2	37.6
Jacksonville city	40 316	47 243	56 742	29 311	20 902	26 074	34 787	26 566	20 337	83.5	28.4	22.1	2.6	16.0	9.3	-3.0	11.9	13.8
Jupiter town	54 945	64 873	74 977	41 648	32 375	38 283	46 473	34 877	35 088	77.0	50.8	32.0	0.6	19.4	22.9	10.6	4.6	4.6
Key West city	43 021	50 895	55 968	28 375	26 220	34 520	31 678	26 201	26 316	83.8	33.9	21.2	1.5	14.7	12.2	-0.1	10.1	8.6
Kissimmee city	33 949	36 361	42 486	22 209	20 425	25 264	26 557	21 396	15 071	88.2	17.9	17.8	3.8	10.8	3.7	-8.6	14.0	17.0
Lakeland city	33 119	40 468	51 709	31 307	17 761	22 845	33 305	24 760	19 760	69.8	34.9	37.7	3.4	23.2	6.8	-5.5	13.7	17.8
Lake Worth city	30 034	35 374	39 536	26 944	17 272	22 401	25 297	23 634	15 517	77.4	25.7	27.1	2.9	13.0	4.5	-7.8	18.0	22.4
Largo city	32 217	41 523	51 671	24 924	23 571	22 333	30 902	25 293	20 848	63.7	38.0	43.4	1.9	25.7	4.4	-7.9	8.7	10.4
Lauderdale Lakes city	26 932	32 641	41 822	19 947	17 107	16 380	26 637	21 178	14 039	69.0	19.6	33.4	3.6	14.5	3.0	-9.3	21.7	27.7
Lauderhill city	32 515	36 723	48 278	30 764	19 845	23 880	30 246	25 515	17 243	75.1	24.7	29.1	2.7	12.7	6.0	-6.3	15.7	21.3
Margate city	38 722	48 254	54 852	36 771	27 301	22 433	36 414	27 470	20 308	69.6	34.8	37.5	1.4	19.4	7.1	-5.2	9.2	8.7
Melbourne city	34 571	42 760	55 272	26 706	20 117	22 561	34 026	23 505	19 175	73.1	36.5	34.2	2.5	24.6	6.3	-6.0	11.0	14.0
Miami city	23 483	27 225	33 193	17 982	12 570	13 417	24 899	20 637	15 128	72.1	17.3	28.2	9.9	11.2	6.8	-5.5	29.4	32.8
Miami Beach city	27 322	33 440	44 232	23 594	17 215	23 204	35 497	27 959	27 853	72.2	26.6	25.6	4.8	9.6	11.7	-0.6	22.2	24.8
Miramar city	50 289	52 952	60 800	29 138	28 661	30 109	35 145	29 058	18 462	89.7	21.4	16.3	2.1	9.4	11.7	-0.6	8.1	8.3
North Lauderdale city	40 050	41 990	50 132	30 625	23 097	30 000	29 483	25 240	15 557	88.6	18.5	16.6	2.5	6.9	5.1	-7.2	11.7	14.2
North Miami city	29 778	31 760	37 735	20 061	17 850	22 126	25 888	21 293	14 581	83.9	18.1	18.2	5.8	7.6	6.5	-5.8	21.8	26.6
North Miami Beach city	31 377	35 047	40 570	21 250	16 698	21 669	27 250	22 872	14 699	80.6	22.9	22.9	3.5	9.2	5.6	-6.7	18.8	24.8
Oakland Park city	35 493	38 571	45 833	23 512	20 888	30 314	31 041	26 029	18 873	84.8	24.1	19.7	3.4	9.2	5.7	-6.6	13.0	18.5
Ocala city	30 888	38 190	51 875	25 160	16 923	20 523	31 050	25 069	18 021	70.6	30.5	35.9	3.5	21.2	6.6	-5.7	15.7	21.8
Orlando city	35 732	40 648	49 730	27 889	17 804	29 715	31 456	25 958	21 216	84.3	27.7	20.5	2.9	12.4	7.7	-4.6	12.9	21.2
Ormond Beach city	43 364	52 496	72 828	31 333	25 337	26 400	40 777	27 843	26 364	67.5	50.8	43.2	1.3	29.4	13.5	1.2	5.9	6.8
Oviedo city	64 119	66 288	70 594	37 875	29 744	42 407	48 671	31 865	23 831	93.9	41.3	13.5	1.5	14.4	19.2	6.9	4.0	4.3
Palm Bay city	36 508	41 636	49 831	31 675	21 326	22 651	31 854	23 019	16 992	77.4	30.2	31.9	2.2	22.0	4.5	-7.8	9.1	10.3
Palm Beach Gardens city	59 776	74 548	86 142	36 685	38 913	37 262	51 316	35 314	42 975	76.5	55.7	33.0	1.3	19.5	26.1	13.8	5.5	6.2
Palm Coast city	41 570	45 818	50 241	28 350	20 278	26 117	35 272	26 062	21 490	60.2	47.6	52.0	1.2	42.1	8.0	-4.3	6.3	11.9
Panama City city	31 572	40 890	49 407	21 500	15 726	18 993	31 667	22 147	17 830	73.9	32.4	31.0	4.6	19.8	5.8	-6.5	17.1	22.0
Pembroke Pines city	52 629	61 480	72 319	47 688	35 356	30 317	46 101	34 013	23 843	79.0	37.7	29.2	1.2	14.6	15.7	3.4	6.1	4.6
Pensacola city	34 779	42 868	58 073	26 396	14 960	24 186	35 004	24 841	21 438	75.0	35.7	30.3	3.8	23.7	9.0	-3.3	14.8	21.7
Pinellas Park city	35 048	41 072	49 281	32 154	23 653	23 074	28 924	25 290	18 701	72.2	34.3	35.3	2.7	21.1	4.1	-8.2	9.1	10.0
Plantation city	53 746	65 029	78 163	29 847	34 041	35 098	47 001	34 454	28 250	84.2	36.3	22.3	1.1	13.4	20.5	8.2	6.4	6.0
Plant City city	37 584	43 328	55 821	31 042	19 528	24 510	34 454	24 852	18 815	81.3	25.7	28.7	2.8	15.0	8.9	-3.4	12.4	15.4
Pompano Beach city	36 073	44 195	50 915	22 571	15 617	28 706	31 932	27 993	23 938	68.8	37.5	36.2	2.3	16.0	10.9	-1.4	14.2	23.8
Port Orange city	38 783	44 684	57 500	25 750	21 145	23 703	34 496	23 782	20 628	70.1	41.9	40.4	1.6	28.0	6.0	-6.3	7.7	8.7
Port St. Lucie city	40 509	44 162	51 851	28 625	22 422	27 375	32 407	24 695	18 059	74.7	34.9	36.5	2.0	24.3	5.6	-6.7	7.0	9.1
Riviera Beach city	32 111	36 133	41 203	25 850	16 823	21 482	27 622	22 189	19 847	73.2	24.3	33.2	5.7	17.7	9.9	-2.4	19.9	28.3
St. Petersburg city	34 597	43 198	55 269	28 187	20 388	24 618	31 649	26 644	21 107	75.9	33.4	31.2	3.3	17.4	7.6	-4.7	12.1	14.9
Sanford city	31 163	36 687	43 360	26 146	18 278	21 304	29 477	22 337	15 219	79.8	20.9	26.4	4.8	13.9	4.8	-7.5	16.2	19.4
Sarasota city	34 077	40 398	41 940	28 173	15 952	26 233	27 323	24 689	23 197	70.8	38.5	36.9	2.9	18.0	9.1	-3.2	14.0	23.5
Sunrise city	40 998	47 908	58 382	36 325	28 976	24 149	36 197	29 137	18 713	75.5	29.6	31.8	1.6	14.4	7.3	-5.0	9.1	9.4
Tallahassee city	30 571	49 359	63 193	25 129	18 763	19 862	34 312	28 837	18 981	85.0	31.6	15.2	2.1	11.5	8.0	-4.3	24.6	17.6
Tamarac city	34 290	41 927	52 884	30 259	26 865	22 713	33 724	29 339	22 243	57.3	36.0	51.6	1.3	20.4	6.0	-6.3	8.6	10.1
Tampa city	34 415	40 517	54 605	25 339	18 654	25 576	32 477	26 881	21 953	80.0	28.9	25.9	4.4	14.2	10.5	-1.8	16.3	21.1
Titusville city	35 607	42 453	51 379	28 676	17 252	21 769	36 727	24 821	18 901	70.2	36.8	37.1	3.6	27.7	7.2	-5.1	11.9	14.7

Table B-5. Cities — Education, Labor Force, and Income

STATE Place code	City	High school graduates			College graduates		College graduates (percent)				
		Total population 25 years and over	Percent with a high school diploma or less	Percent with a high school diploma or more	Percent with a bachelor's degree or more	+/− U.S. percent with bachelor's degree or more	Non-Hispanic White	Black or African American	American Indian and Alaska Native	Asian, Hawaiian, and Pacific Islander	Hispanic or Latino[1]
		1	2	3	4	5	6	7	8	9	10
	FLORIDA—Cont'd										
12 75812	Wellington village	23 979	28.6	92.2	38.0	13.6	39.3	34.0	31.8	53.4	27.1
12 76582	Weston city..................	30 798	18.9	95.5	50.9	26.5	52.8	49.8	55.9	61.5	46.2
12 76600	West Palm Beach city ...	56 549	46.9	75.5	26.9	2.5	37.9	12.1	32.5	44.1	12.5
12 78275	Winter Haven city	18 878	56.5	75.8	16.7	-7.7	18.7	8.0	X	35.9	9.4
12 78325	Winter Springs city	20 623	30.9	92.1	36.3	11.9	37.9	23.4	0.0	34.7	29.5
13 00000	GEORGIA..................	5 185 965	50.1	78.6	24.3	-0.1	27.7	15.5	18.1	43.8	13.6
13 01052	Albany city..................	45 809	54.7	72.5	18.2	-6.2	26.0	12.6	9.1	21.7	17.0
13 01696	Alpharetta city	22 591	17.1	95.2	57.1	32.7	57.7	45.1	23.6	79.4	46.7
13 03436	Athens-Clarke County ...	51 845	40.6	81.0	39.8	15.4	52.9	11.3	14.8	76.4	21.3
13 04000	Atlanta city..................	268 246	45.4	76.9	34.6	10.2	67.9	12.7	23.6	52.8	20.8
13 04200	Augusta-Richmond County	122 592	51.7	78.0	18.7	-5.7	24.2	12.5	8.9	27.8	16.6
13 19000	Columbus city..............	114 045	49.3	78.9	20.3	-4.1	26.4	12.0	21.4	30.7	15.8
13 21380	Dalton city	17 173	63.0	59.0	18.3	-6.1	26.7	6.3	10.1	38.6	2.7
13 25720	East Point city	23 230	56.6	75.9	17.6	-6.8	15.7	19.0	26.2	32.7	3.7
13 31908	Gainesville city	15 131	56.7	66.2	24.2	-0.2	37.7	7.3	0.0	8.5	2.5
13 38964	Hinesville city	15 892	41.9	90.0	17.3	-7.1	24.3	11.2	11.3	16.8	13.4
13 44340	LaGrange city	15 726	59.4	70.5	21.0	-3.4	32.0	7.5	15.6	23.6	18.2
13 49000	Macon city	60 148	60.3	72.3	17.2	-7.2	29.2	7.8	0.0	45.9	19.4
13 49756	Marietta city	37 005	39.1	82.2	34.1	9.7	43.0	23.6	10.4	55.1	13.8
13 59724	Peachtree City city	20 222	21.7	96.2	46.2	21.8	48.2	32.2	15.4	45.6	24.5
13 66668	Rome city	22 397	60.7	68.1	18.9	-5.5	26.1	4.6	19.7	26.6	2.9
13 67284	Roswell city	53 703	20.5	92.8	52.6	28.2	57.4	38.0	26.7	60.2	16.9
13 69000	Savannah city	80 319	52.2	76.1	20.2	-4.2	30.3	11.1	3.2	34.5	22.5
13 71492	Smyrna city	28 695	34.2	85.8	40.3	15.9	43.1	39.2	58.4	66.1	15.2
13 78800	Valdosta city	24 244	50.3	75.7	24.9	0.5	37.5	10.0	20.3	23.4	17.6
13 80508	Warner Robins city........	30 909	49.0	83.5	16.7	-7.7	17.9	12.6	4.4	31.1	16.5
15 00000	HAWAII..................	802 477	43.9	84.6	26.2	1.8	37.3	21.0	21.5	24.5	13.3
15 14650	Hilo CDP	26 554	45.5	85.9	24.3	-0.1	32.7	12.8	18.9	26.8	13.7
15 17000	Honolulu CDP	267 587	42.6	83.4	31.1	6.7	45.1	23.6	23.7	28.4	18.9
15 23150	Kailua CDP..................	25 094	31.9	92.8	39.4	15.0	50.3	24.6	38.4	33.7	24.9
15 28250	Kaneohe CDP	23 670	41.0	89.7	29.5	5.1	44.1	21.0	0.0	28.1	14.5
15 51050	Mililani Town CDP........	18 247	29.5	94.3	31.8	7.4	40.7	21.6	0.0	34.7	11.6
15 62600	Pearl City CDP.............	20 792	46.7	86.7	20.1	-4.3	17.3	17.7	47.4	22.3	8.4
15 77750	Waimalu CDP..............	20 284	34.5	90.6	32.4	8.0	39.0	35.5	4.7	33.9	16.5
15 79700	Waipahu CDP	21 085	64.6	68.6	11.1	-13.3	9.2	9.6	X	12.1	8.3
16 00000	IDAHO	787 505	43.8	84.7	21.7	-2.7	22.6	22.4	9.5	00.0	6.6
16 08830	Boise City city	117 575	30.1	91.1	33.6	9.2	34.1	30.8	16.5	43.7	18.2
16 12250	Caldwell city	14 408	61.2	68.8	11.7	-12.7	13.3	47.1	4.7	37.6	4.8
16 16750	Coeur d'Alene city........	22 031	43.3	85.6	19.5	-4.9	19.7	0.0	7.5	31.5	14.6
16 39700	Idaho Falls city	30 503	38.0	87.7	28.2	3.8	29.5	34.9	7.8	38.4	10.7
16 46540	Lewiston city................	20 463	46.5	86.2	19.6	-4.8	19.7	19.4	11.4	37.3	4.5
16 52120	Meridian city	20 588	34.4	92.2	27.1	2.7	27.4	0.0	7.5	31.3	16.7
16 56260	Nampa city	29 571	52.0	77.0	16.0	-8.4	18.0	17.3	3.3	12.1	5.0
16 64090	Pocatello city	29 262	34.9	88.7	27.9	3.5	28.5	24.2	9.7	48.0	14.0
16 82810	Twin Falls city	21 056	48.5	81.5	16.5	-7.9	17.3	0.0	17.0	13.4	6.3
17 00000	ILLINOIS..................	7 973 671	46.3	81.4	26.1	1.7	28.8	14.7	13.3	57.4	9.1
17 00243	Addison village	22 344	55.8	73.5	19.5	-4.9	19.8	16.4	0.0	50.9	6.6
17 01114	Alton city....................	19 957	52.0	81.2	16.1	-8.3	18.2	7.5	7.2	42.9	14.9
17 02154	Arlington Heights village ...	54 025	26.6	92.7	46.5	22.1	45.9	34.9	28.9	73.6	14.6
17 03012	Aurora city	83 551	46.3	75.6	29.9	5.5	39.5	22.1	9.5	64.4	6.1
17 04013	Bartlett village..............	23 114	29.9	92.3	38.3	13.9	37.0	40.3	X	59.2	22.0
17 04845	Belleville city...............	28 591	46.5	83.8	17.6	-6.8	18.0	12.4	0.0	45.5	27.6
17 05573	Berwyn city	34 638	54.5	74.6	17.2	-7.2	20.0	5.8	11.6	43.1	8.8
17 06613	Bloomington city...........	40 943	35.1	89.8	39.7	15.3	39.7	32.3	0.0	72.9	24.1
17 07133	Bolingbrook village	33 668	36.1	87.2	29.2	4.8	30.1	29.9	0.0	52.3	8.8
17 09447	Buffalo Grove village.....	28 025	18.7	95.3	55.9	31.5	55.7	48.8	70.3	66.5	32.1
17 09642	Burbank city	18 152	64.8	73.6	9.3	-15.1	8.8	0.0	0.0	41.1	9.0
17 10487	Calumet City city	24 513	50.9	80.7	13.9	-10.5	10.9	17.6	0.0	28.7	6.3
17 11332	Carol Stream village......	24 266	35.1	89.9	32.0	7.6	31.6	14.5	0.0	54.4	15.7
17 11358	Carpentersville village ...	16 991	61.5	66.7	12.2	-12.2	15.7	18.7	0.0	36.2	3.9
17 12385	Champaign city	34 354	28.3	91.6	44.3	19.9	47.9	15.9	18.9	74.7	35.6
17 14000	Chicago city.................	1 815 896	51.2	71.8	25.5	1.1	42.3	13.5	14.7	48.0	8.5
17 14026	Chicago Heights city	19 441	58.7	71.7	12.3	-12.1	17.9	8.5	0.0	41.0	4.2
17 14351	Cicero town	44 871	77.4	48.2	6.1	-18.3	9.5	3.5	5.7	43.1	3.9
17 17887	Crystal Lake city...........	23 276	31.2	91.5	36.2	11.8	37.3	47.1	20.0	65.1	10.0

[1] Hispanic or Latino persons may be of any race.

Table B-5. Cities — Education, Labor Force, and Income

City	School enrollment			Population 16 to 19 years				Employment status, 2000			Work status in 1999 of the population 16 years and over		
											Worked in 1999		
	Grades kindergarten through 12	College or graduate school	Percent private	Number	Percent in armed forces	Percent high school graduates	Percent not enrolled, not grads, not in armed forces, not employed	Total population 16 years and over	Percent in labor force	Unemployment rate	Full-time	Part-time	Did not work in 1999
	11	12	13	14	15	16	17	18	19	20	21	22	23
FLORIDA—Cont'd													
Wellington village	9 479	1 726	14.4	2 393	0.0	3.6	2.3	27 693	69.1	2.8	59.1	15.1	25.7
Weston city..............	11 478	2 854	23.1	2 306	0.0	7.7	1.1	34 640	68.3	3.6	60.2	13.4	26.5
West Palm Beach city ...	13 310	4 778	19.1	3 814	0.0	9.6	9.6	66 212	60.5	5.4	54.5	11.4	34.1
Winter Haven city.........	3 802	826	13.4	1 077	0.0	5.1	5.7	21 424	49.9	6.1	43.9	10.1	46.0
Winter Springs city	6 507	1 799	11.9	1 784	0.0	6.5	3.5	23 926	70.4	3.9	59.6	15.1	25.3
GEORGIA..............	1 598 291	436 555	12.1	471 799	1.7	11.2	7.3	6 250 687	66.1	5.4	59.0	12.5	28.5
Albany city..................	16 168	5 478	10.0	5 645	12.1	12.7	7.3	58 170	58.3	11.2	49.3	12.3	38.4
Alpharetta city	6 302	1 506	18.2	1 339	0.0	8.3	1.6	25 755	76.5	3.2	68.1	12.4	19.5
Athens-Clarke County ...	13 088	29 695	7.2	10 245	1.1	5.6	4.7	85 219	64.8	10.1	49.2	27.6	23.2
Atlanta city..................	69 309	35 436	21.6	25 146	0.3	8.4	9.4	333 209	64.0	14.0	56.0	12.6	31.4
Augusta-Richmond County	41 134	11 630	10.4	13 139	12.5	20.5	5.7	152 037	62.3	8.4	53.8	13.2	32.9
Columbus city...............	36 797	10 058	9.1	12 458	14.4	23.2	6.9	142 185	63.7	6.3	54.6	13.3	32.2
Dalton city	5 094	717	5.5	1 619	0.0	9.3	25.9	21 383	60.4	4.3	57.9	8.8	33.3
East Point city	8 295	2 070	14.3	2 147	0.0	9.3	13.8	28 767	66.0	8.7	59.9	11.9	28.2
Gainesville city	4 119	1 130	14.5	1 767	0.0	9.5	19.6	19 840	58.7	5.1	54.3	10.6	35.1
Hinesville city	6 935	1 529	5.7	2 023	7.2	20.3	8.4	21 185	72.1	6.2	63.9	12.9	23.2
LaGrange city	5 732	1 153	14.8	1 698	0.0	9.2	6.5	19 593	61.3	5.4	53.2	12.4	34.4
Macon city	19 279	6 105	16.7	6 110	0.1	10.0	11.6	73 919	56.2	10.0	48.4	13.5	38.0
Marietta city.................	8 517	4 892	18.5	2 865	0.0	14.5	9.1	46 704	73.4	5.7	65.6	11.9	22.5
Peachtree City city	8 159	1 077	11.0	1 969	0.6	5.3	1.5	23 155	69.7	2.3	57.8	16.3	26.0
Rome city	6 368	1 949	16.5	2 264	0.0	14.5	12.1	27 686	56.7	7.8	49.8	12.6	37.5
Roswell city	14 610	3 867	17.3	4 177	0.0	5.1	4.2	62 527	73.9	3.4	65.4	13.8	20.8
Savannah city...............	25 695	10 611	17.5	8 126	4.5	14.8	6.0	101 525	60.5	7.8	50.8	15.1	34.0
Smyrna city	5 324	2 780	16.5	1 390	0.0	10.6	13.2	33 608	74.3	5.5	68.9	10.3	20.9
Valdosta city	8 384	6 082	6.8	3 188	0.0	6.0	5.4	33 495	63.9	6.8	51.9	18.4	29.7
Warner Robins city........	9 996	2 649	7.2	2 509	0.2	13.3	8.0	36 761	66.1	5.6	58.9	12.0	29.0
HAWAII.....................	223 185	79 748	18.2	64 343	4.1	17.1	3.6	950 055	64.5	5.9	53.4	15.2	31.4
Hilo CDP	8 235	3 377	6.3	2 781	0.0	9.0	3.4	32 054	58.8	10.2	44.4	16.5	39.1
Honolulu CDP	54 506	32 365	24.2	16 552	1.2	12.6	3.2	308 618	60.7	5.7	50.1	15.2	34.7
Kailua CDP...................	7 058	2 517	32.6	1 935	0.7	10.1	2.8	28 818	68.3	4.6	55.1	16.4	28.4
Kaneohe CDP	6 832	2 371	22.9	1 970	0.0	14.4	3.0	27 510	65.0	5.3	53.6	15.0	31.3
Mililani Town CDP.........	6 025	2 302	17.9	1 657	0.0	7.0	1.2	21 761	75.1	4.1	64.8	14.5	20.7
Pearl City CDP..............	4 363	2 201	16.2	1 605	18.3	26.5	1.3	25 912	64.2	4.5	54.6	13.6	31.9
Waimalu CDP................	4 856	2 333	21.3	1 559	1.2	7.8	0.8	23 972	73.3	4.6	62.2	14.3	23.5
Waipahu CDP	6 907	1 699	12.0	1 954	0.7	15.9	5.0	25 349	57.6	9.1	46.5	14.3	39.1
IDAHO......................	270 423	77 392	10.1	87 734	0.3	14.0	4.0	969 872	66.1	5.7	55.2	17.9	26.8
Boise City city	34 180	13 232	9.1	10 886	0.1	18.2	2.7	144 192	72.5	4.2	60.6	17.5	21.9
Caldwell city	5 311	1 130	14.6	1 811	0.0	12.3	13.0	18 688	65.3	6.1	56.2	14.1	29.7
Coeur d'Alene city........	6 215	2 181	8.7	2 257	0.4	19.8	5.1	27 099	64.9	7.9	52.8	18.4	28.8
Idaho Falls city	11 001	2 309	4.5	3 383	0.0	16.4	4.2	37 435	66.6	5.6	55.0	18.2	26.9
Lewiston city	5 379	2 162	7.7	1 798	0.0	16.0	2.7	24 723	63.9	4.5	50.3	17.9	31.8
Meridian city	7 611	1 488	9.0	1 563	0.0	17.3	1.5	23 919	76.0	2.8	64.2	16.2	19.7
Nampa city	10 507	2 697	14.6	3 072	0.0	17.4	8.8	37 482	67.3	6.9	57.8	14.4	27.8
Pocatello city	9 273	7 547	4.9	3 797	0.2	17.5	3.6	39 445	68.8	6.7	51.5	23.8	24.7
Twin Falls city	6 295	2 201	6.9	2 235	0.0	17.0	3.6	26 196	64.4	6.2	52.4	18.0	29.6
ILLINOIS...................	2 387 464	810 038	17.5	704 632	0.8	10.6	5.7	9 530 946	65.4	6.0	56.0	15.2	28.9
Addison village	6 592	1 888	15.5	2 159	0.0	11.9	8.9	27 353	67.1	4.2	60.6	12.9	26.5
Alton city.....................	5 704	1 795	16.2	1 535	0.0	19.5	6.0	23 383	60.3	7.4	50.1	14.9	35.0
Arlington Heights village	12 769	3 780	22.1	3 144	0.0	3.1	1.6	60 502	67.5	2.4	56.3	16.8	26.9
Aurora city...................	29 774	7 333	16.4	7 813	0.2	11.8	10.0	101 962	71.4	5.8	66.0	12.3	21.7
Bartlett village..............	7 743	1 859	12.8	1 666	0.0	7.5	1.8	25 997	76.9	2.3	67.0	14.9	18.1
Belleville city	7 448	2 660	18.0	2 268	0.0	13.9	5.7	33 321	63.9	5.1	53.7	15.1	31.2
Berwyn city	9 664	3 230	18.0	2 697	0.0	13.9	7.6	41 316	63.8	5.9	57.2	12.2	30.5
Bloomington city...........	11 357	6 150	20.3	3 718	0.0	11.3	4.4	50 528	73.9	3.9	62.2	17.3	20.5
Bolingbrook village	12 542	3 212	12.3	3 338	0.0	11.9	3.8	40 038	77.0	4.9	67.0	14.9	18.1
Buffalo Grove village.....	9 250	2 241	11.1	2 152	0.3	10.6	1.2	31 805	73.8	2.1	63.2	16.4	20.4
Burbank city	5 300	1 571	19.4	1 664	0.0	12.6	2.8	21 775	64.7	5.5	53.4	15.9	30.6
Calumet City city	8 177	2 441	14.7	1 957	0.0	10.5	5.5	28 836	64.1	8.0	54.9	13.6	31.4
Carol Stream village......	8 957	2 431	12.3	2 307	0.0	11.9	3.4	28 982	76.9	3.4	67.5	15.9	16.6
Carpentersville village ...	6 756	1 251	7.0	1 897	0.0	13.3	11.3	21 191	67.9	5.9	63.3	13.0	23.7
Champaign city	8 805	22 395	5.4	8 022	0.1	5.3	1.2	57 103	66.2	7.1	50.8	30.2	19.0
Chicago city	555 241	209 810	24.3	158 717	0.1	11.0	10.2	2 215 574	61.3	10.1	53.8	12.4	33.8
Chicago Heights city	7 613	1 628	15.2	1 839	0.0	15.3	7.0	23 456	59.6	11.1	50.8	13.6	35.7
Cicero town	20 449	3 385	12.2	5 762	0.4	15.3	12.1	58 719	57.6	9.6	56.7	10.7	32.6
Crystal Lake city...........	8 960	2 035	11.5	2 045	0.0	6.9	3.0	26 844	72.5	3.6	59.5	18.0	22.4

Table B-5. Cities — Education, Labor Force, and Income

City	Full-year full-time employed (percent)								Children under 18 years in families (percent, except where noted)						Total employed by class of worker (percent)			
										With two parents		With one parent who is in labor force	+/- U.S. percent of children with no stay-at-home parent	+/- U.S. percent two-income couples				
	Total	Men	Women	Non-Hispanic White	Black or African American	American Indian and Alaska Native	Asian, Hawaiian, and Pacific Islander	Hispanic or Latino¹	Number	Both in labor force	Father only in labor force				Private	Government	Self-employed	Unpaid family worker
	24	25	26	27	28	29	30	31	32	33	34	35	36	37	38	39	40	41
FLORIDA—Cont'd																		
Wellington village	46.4	58.8	35.0	47.6	41.2	63.6	36.9	43.0	11 472	49.0	27.2	15.3	-0.3	5.3	69.0	13.9	16.9	0.2
Weston city	47.5	62.6	33.8	50.8	51.6	83.1	41.2	40.5	15 764	43.4	40.0	10.2	-11.0	-1.0	74.7	11.3	13.8	0.2
West Palm Beach city	40.5	49.3	32.1	41.6	39.5	40.1	46.6	38.5	15 265	31.4	14.1	35.0	1.8	-6.4	75.0	13.2	11.6	0.2
Winter Haven city	32.2	39.8	25.9	31.4	33.2	0.0	28.5	36.9	4 683	32.7	15.3	31.1	-0.8	-15.7	77.2	13.1	9.4	0.3
Winter Springs city	47.0	57.1	37.8	47.4	41.7	72.7	50.1	44.5	8 390	46.0	28.0	17.5	-1.1	3.1	75.5	13.4	10.9	0.2
GEORGIA	44.3	54.0	35.1	46.7	39.4	41.2	41.5	39.9	2 015 574	41.2	21.3	24.1	0.7	2.3	75.3	14.9	9.5	0.3
Albany city	34.5	40.8	29.3	41.3	30.2	10.9	31.8	56.0	18 817	28.9	10.1	38.1	2.4	-0.8	69.2	22.7	7.7	0.5
Alpharetta city	54.8	69.0	41.5	55.0	61.0	54.5	50.9	50.0	9 415	45.1	40.5	10.6	-8.9	2.9	84.2	6.4	9.3	0.1
Athens-Clarke County	29.7	36.0	23.8	27.6	35.8	30.2	21.1	34.9	16 844	35.7	16.1	32.6	3.7	2.0	64.5	28.7	6.6	0.2
Atlanta city	37.3	43.4	31.5	50.0	29.7	35.1	30.4	38.4	81 609	19.2	12.7	41.6	-3.8	-4.4	76.8	13.2	9.9	0.2
Augusta-Richmond County	38.3	45.2	32.0	40.2	36.8	30.2	00.2	04.0	18 711	29.9	16.9	33.8	-0.9	-4.3	68.6	24.5	6.8	0.2
Columbus city	39.5	47.8	31.9	42.4	36.3	36.3	38.4	36.8	45 997	35.6	17.0	31.7	2.7	-0.6	72.8	19.1	7.9	0.3
Dalton city	39.4	50.4	28.5	41.4	43.7	29.5	29.4	36.0	6 845	41.1	24.6	17.0	-6.5	-6.9	81.6	9.7	8.6	0.1
East Point city	41.1	46.7	36.2	28.9	44.1	36.5	32.8	38.4	10 231	24.3	9.7	45.3	5.0	-1.5	78.3	16.1	5.6	0.0
Gainesville city	37.8	48.6	27.2	39.7	31.1	17.6	31.1	38.0	5 516	32.0	24.7	23.5	-9.1	-6.3	78.7	12.0	9.2	0.2
Hinesville city	48.1	64.5	32.7	52.2	45.7	73.2	42.3	42.4	9 900	36.6	24.3	24.7	-3.3	2.4	60.5	32.2	7.1	0.2
LaGrange city	38.2	47.9	30.6	39.6	36.6	83.3	23.3	41.5	6 791	29.2	12.7	40.1	4.7	-1.1	78.3	13.8	7.5	0.4
Macon city	33.7	42.0	27.5	35.8	32.0	12.9	35.8	41.7	24 013	24.9	9.1	42.7	3.0	-6.1	74.9	17.9	7.0	0.2
Marietta city	47.5	54.5	40.6	48.4	49.4	61.3	43.2	42.8	11 750	31.0	21.9	34.0	0.4	4.0	85.3	7.3	7.3	0.1
Peachtree City city	46.5	64.2	30.3	46.1	51.4	81.6	51.5	43.0	9 885	45.3	38.9	12.0	-7.3	2.4	78.3	13.8	7.7	0.2
Rome city	33.0	41.0	25.9	33.5	31.9	34.9	36.2	31.5	7 573	34.4	15.7	31.0	0.8	-5.8	77.3	14.7	7.9	0.2
Roswell city	51.1	63.6	38.7	52.2	57.1	32.0	45.7	42.8	18 993	46.0	35.1	12.9	-5.7	6.1	82.0	6.9	10.8	0.2
Savannah city	36.2	42.6	30.6	39.7	33.3	18.3	33.2	37.9	30 041	29.4	10.8	39.6	4.4	-2.5	74.4	17.0	8.5	0.2
Smyrna city	52.9	59.6	46.8	54.0	56.0	50.0	47.7	42.7	7 137	38.1	18.9	27.2	0.7	0.7	83.2	9.9	6.7	0.2
Valdosta city	36.4	46.7	27.9	40.4	32.5	28.4	22.1	32.0	10 471	31.1	12.8	35.4	1.9	2.4	69.8	22.2	7.8	0.2
Warner Robins city	44.9	56.3	34.7	45.9	43.6	23.5	36.6	43.0	12 685	34.5	18.8	35.3	5.2	-2.6	63.3	30.7	5.8	0.2
HAWAII	39.6	46.1	33.2	43.2	54.4	41.8	38.0	37.3	271 881	46.8	17.5	21.3	3.5	0.2	67.8	21.0	10.8	0.4
Hilo CDP	32.3	36.4	28.5	29.7	52.3	18.1	34.3	27.1	9 261	41.4	12.7	26.6	3.4	-4.9	59.3	29.2	10.8	0.7
Honolulu CDP	37.0	42.9	31.3	41.7	46.5	44.1	35.1	39.8	65 695	45.2	18.7	20.9	1.5	-4.6	68.8	19.4	11.4	0.4
Kailua CDP	43.1	50.7	35.8	43.5	50.5	37.5	43.9	39.3	8 539	53.7	18.3	21.3	10.4	5.7	63.7	20.4	15.2	0.7
Kaneohe CDP	43.0	49.9	36.6	48.9	60.7	50.0	42.0	40.9	8 095	56.9	10.4	22.5	14.8	4.3	64.0	29.2	6.3	0.5
Mililani Town CDP	52.3	59.4	45.2	58.5	64.5	89.5	52.2	42.2	7 404	62.1	14.8	16.7	14.2	15.4	61.5	32.4	5.9	0.2
Pearl City CDP	41.4	48.8	33.0	55.0	50.9	28.6	36.3	42.7	5 184	46.8	17.0	25.3	7.5	-6.7	64.9	27.2	7.6	0.2
Waimalu CDP	49.1	56.0	42.0	56.9	75.9	59.8	46.6	41.6	5 809	54.1	14.4	19.5	9.0	10.2	65.0	27.0	7.8	0.2
Waipahu CDP	31.0	33.5	28.7	30.3	31.3	0.0	31.2	32.6	7 231	36.1	13.6	28.0	-0.5	-13.0	80.2	15.0	4.6	0.2
IDAHO	38.0	48.3	27.8	38.5	40.9	33.1	36.3	32.7	352 685	48.7	26.9	16.7	0.8	1.6	70.0	16.4	13.2	0.5
Boise City city	45.2	55.0	35.7	45.5	40.5	35.5	43.5	45.5	45 296	48.5	24.5	20.9	4.8	8.2	74.6	14.9	10.3	0.2
Caldwell city	37.2	45.3	29.7	38.1	38.2	19.9	24.1	35.4	7 384	41.5	21.5	26.3	3.2	-0.7	78.1	13.1	8.8	0.1
Coeur d'Alene city	35.5	44.5	27.5	35.6	21.9	38.0	31.0	35.2	8 034	43.7	21.3	26.9	6.0	-0.8	75.3	13.3	11.1	0.2
Idaho Falls city	38.9	51.2	27.3	39.5	38.6	38.6	39.6	32.3	14 349	44.8	28.1	19.8	0.0	2.5	72.1	17.6	10.0	0.3
Lewiston city	37.0	46.1	28.5	37.5	27.7	28.5	22.2	30.1	6 812	53.2	15.8	22.8	11.4	2.2	75.0	15.9	8.8	0.2
Meridian city	52.1	66.5	38.6	52.0	56.4	32.0	59.9	56.3	11 473	49.2	31.0	15.6	0.2	13.4	77.1	12.3	10.4	0.2
Nampa city	41.1	51.6	31.5	41.6	46.8	47.4	56.2	36.7	15 567	46.8	24.8	20.1	2.3	3.3	78.2	12.4	9.0	0.4
Pocatello city	35.3	44.7	26.7	35.6	38.6	34.1	29.7	31.1	13 149	48.4	24.7	20.1	3.9	4.9	68.8	22.0	8.9	0.2
Twin Falls city	35.5	45.4	26.5	36.1	10.0	13.2	36.8	29.7	8 485	47.4	19.5	24.3	7.1	3.3	73.2	13.9	12.6	0.3
ILLINOIS	41.6	51.1	32.7	43.8	32.9	37.9	41.8	38.1	3 046 677	44.1	22.1	20.8	0.3	1.8	78.6	12.7	8.4	0.3
Addison village	44.8	54.0	35.6	46.5	52.7	55.6	45.2	39.4	8 999	49.6	18.0	13.5	-1.5	0.4	84.0	7.2	8.6	0.3
Alton city	36.5	43.6	30.6	38.5	30.6	8.2	10.9	35.7	7 174	37.2	12.5	34.3	6.9	-2.4	83.4	11.6	4.6	0.4
Arlington Heights village	45.5	60.4	32.3	45.1	64.5	57.9	48.9	43.7	17 367	53.9	32.7	8.1	-2.6	3.4	80.9	9.5	9.5	0.1
Aurora city	47.6	58.0	37.3	52.0	44.4	38.5	52.4	40.0	43 010	41.9	25.0	18.7	-4.0	5.2	86.0	8.7	5.2	0.1
Bartlett village	57.5	73.3	42.8	57.7	63.8	X	54.2	58.0	11 680	56.8	31.2	8.3	0.5	13.7	84.7	7.7	7.4	0.2
Belleville city	41.3	49.6	34.1	42.0	36.8	47.1	50.2	37.3	9 329	47.5	14.7	26.3	9.2	4.3	80.8	12.7	6.4	0.1
Berwyn city	42.1	49.9	35.0	40.4	48.0	52.2	43.9	44.3	13 348	41.6	26.4	16.9	-6.1	-3.1	84.7	8.9	6.3	0.1
Bloomington city	48.2	57.6	39.6	48.4	49.0	18.9	42.0	47.3	15 338	51.6	19.3	23.7	10.7	12.5	81.5	11.7	6.7	0.1
Bolingbrook village	53.4	64.1	43.0	55.3	56.3	51.2	44.1	45.9	17 351	50.9	20.5	18.8	5.1	14.4	83.7	9.8	6.2	0.3
Buffalo Grove village	51.4	66.7	37.5	52.3	43.2	31.3	47.2	39.9	11 937	57.7	29.3	7.9	1.0	12.1	78.9	9.1	11.7	0.3
Burbank city	42.5	53.8	31.7	42.2	48.8	63.0	37.7	48.0	6 676	46.7	23.2	17.3	-0.6	-4.2	86.2	8.2	5.3	0.3
Calumet City city	41.0	47.8	35.7	35.6	45.3	100.0	51.6	41.2	10 405	34.6	12.6	37.2	7.2	-2.2	80.3	15.3	4.1	0.3
Carol Stream village	54.5	67.4	42.2	55.6	55.2	58.9	52.6	47.9	11 719	57.2	23.7	12.4	5.0	16.4	85.7	8.6	5.6	0.1
Carpentersville village	43.0	51.1	34.6	49.9	36.9	21.1	50.7	33.5	9 313	39.0	21.7	17.1	-8.5	1.0	89.8	5.8	4.2	0.2
Champaign city	30.3	35.5	25.0	32.2	29.8	36.3	17.2	22.7	11 371	51.4	16.3	23.9	10.7	6.4	63.8	30.1	5.9	0.2
Chicago city	36.6	42.4	31.3	45.2	28.8	33.1	36.9	34.7	675 233	26.9	17.1	30.4	-7.3	-6.9	78.9	14.3	6.7	0.2
Chicago Heights city	34.9	40.3	29.9	36.4	30.7	14.0	33.5	39.1	9 660	29.2	17.7	33.6	-1.8	-10.6	80.4	14.5	5.1	0.0
Cicero town	35.1	44.8	24.9	33.7	31.0	18.6	35.6	35.5	27 287	27.8	26.7	15.9	-20.9	-17.2	89.4	6.6	3.7	0.3
Crystal Lake city	48.0	65.4	31.9	47.9	72.7	65.7	43.3	49.5	11 817	52.4	31.2	11.0	-1.2	6.8	83.6	8.5	7.5	0.4

¹Hispanic or Latino persons may be of any race.

Table B-5. Cities — Education, Labor Force, and Income

| City | Percent who worked at home | Percent of the population 5 years and over with a disability | Veterans as a percent of the population 18 years and over | Occupation for employed population 16 years and over (percent) | | | | | | Industry for employed population 16 years and over (percent) | | | | | |
				Management, professional, and related occupations	Service occupations	Sales and office occupations	Farming, fishing, and forestry occupations	Construction, extraction, and maintenance occupations	Production, transportation and material moving occupations	Agriculture, forestry, fishing, and mining	Construction and manufacturing	Wholesale and retail trade	Transportation and warehousing, and utilities	Service industries	Public administration
	42	43	44	45	46	47	48	49	50	51	52	53	54	55	56
FLORIDA—Cont'd															
Wellington village	6.6	12.5	12.0	44.3	13.5	30.7	0.6	5.0	5.8	2.3	11.2	16.2	4.1	60.9	5.3
Weston city...................	5.7	9.9	9.0	51.7	10.1	30.5	0.0	3.2	4.6	0.2	10.8	21.7	5.9	56.1	5.3
West Palm Beach city...	2.3	25.6	10.4	32.1	22.4	25.7	0.8	9.0	10.0	1.1	13.6	14.0	4.2	61.6	5.6
Winter Haven city..........	1.1	29.5	18.1	26.2	19.1	29.2	1.2	10.2	14.1	1.9	12.7	20.6	4.9	55.8	4.1
Winter Springs city........	4.5	15.6	15.3	43.4	11.7	30.4	0.1	7.6	6.9	0.1	15.9	18.0	4.7	56.9	4.3
GEORGIA.................	2.8	19.7	12.8	32.7	13.4	26.8	0.6	10.8	15.7	1.4	22.7	15.8	6.0	49.0	5.0
Albany city...................	1.4	24.8	13.0	30.5	18.3	25.4	0.4	9.0	16.4	0.9	19.6	15.2	3.7	52.4	8.2
Alpharetta city..............	5.7	11.0	9.7	54.6	9.1	27.6	0.1	4.4	4.0	0.1	14.9	17.2	3.4	63.0	1.4
Athens-Clarke County ...	2.3	16.1	7.8	36.9	17.8	24.7	0.7	5.3	14.5	1.1	16.2	15.0	2.4	61.7	3.7
Atlanta city...................	3.8	22.2	9.2	40.6	16.4	25.6	0.2	6.0	11.2	0.4	12.9	12.7	5.9	63.2	4.9
Augusta-Richmond County	1.4	24.4	16.9	30.5	18.4	25.3	0.2	9.7	16.0	0.4	18.4	15.4	5.5	54.6	5.8
Columbus city...............	1.8	23.2	18.3	30.7	16.8	26.7	0.2	9.1	16.5	0.4	20.9	13.6	3.6	55.4	6.0
Dalton city	1.4	23.6	9.8	23.3	9.4	21.2	1.3	6.2	38.6	1.6	52.6	12.2	2.1	29.5	2.0
East Point city	1.6	25.8	12.0	23.2	17.5	30.8	0.1	10.4	18.1	0.1	16.0	15.3	11.5	51.0	6.1
Gainesville city.............	1.7	22.6	9.0	27.9	12.6	20.2	1.4	10.4	27.5	1.9	36.9	15.2	2.8	40.2	2.9
Hinesville city...............	2.0	15.1	23.4	25.8	21.3	27.9	0.4	9.9	14.6	0.7	13.3	15.8	4.9	52.1	13.1
LaGrange city...............	0.9	24.7	11.3	27.6	14.7	23.0	0.0	8.4	26.3	0.3	34.7	15.3	2.7	44.2	2.8
Macon city	1.6	25.5	12.4	27.9	20.2	27.3	0.3	8.8	15.5	0.7	15.9	15.2	4.5	56.9	6.8
Marietta city	2.6	18.0	9.6	33.5	13.9	29.4	0.6	13.5	9.3	0.3	21.1	17.8	3.6	54.9	2.3
Peachtree City city	4.8	10.4	18.0	46.4	10.2	25.9	0.0	5.2	12.3	0.4	15.9	13.5	19.6	45.8	4.8
Rome city	1.7	26.6	11.0	27.4	16.7	22.9	0.6	7.3	25.1	0.6	30.1	14.1	2.8	49.3	3.0
Roswell city	5.7	12.5	10.7	48.5	10.1	30.2	0.1	5.9	5.2	0.3	14.7	17.6	3.4	62.3	1.7
Savannah city...............	2.4	24.9	14.5	28.6	20.7	27.1	0.1	9.5	14.0	0.2	15.0	16.1	5.4	58.2	5.1
Smyrna city	2.9	18.4	11.7	42.7	11.5	28.9	0.1	7.7	9.1	0.2	16.2	15.5	7.3	57.0	3.8
Valdosta city	1.8	20.1	13.0	29.2	18.6	28.8	0.6	7.2	15.6	1.2	16.5	18.3	4.2	54.3	5.6
Warner Robins city........	1.3	20.0	22.1	28.5	16.4	28.0	0.1	14.3	12.8	0.2	16.3	15.5	4.3	44.9	18.9
HAWAII.....................	3.6	18.4	13.1	32.2	20.9	28.1	1.3	8.6	8.9	2.3	9.5	15.4	6.2	58.5	8.1
Hilo CDP	4.4	18.0	14.0	33.6	18.6	28.2	2.2	8.4	8.9	4.0	8.8	16.0	6.7	55.4	9.1
Honolulu CDP	3.1	20.0	12.3	35.7	20.2	29.8	0.5	6.1	7.8	0.7	7.6	15.7	5.7	62.9	7.5
Kailua CDP	4.9	13.2	14.9	43.5	15.7	26.4	0.3	7.6	6.5	0.4	9.5	13.8	6.1	61.1	9.2
Kaneohe CDP	3.0	15.8	16.3	37.6	16.3	28.8	0.6	9.0	7.6	0.9	8.9	13.0	6.5	57.8	13.0
Mililani Town CDP........	1.5	11.1	18.5	37.7	14.1	31.0	0.3	9.5	7.4	0.4	11.4	15.8	8.8	49.5	14.1
Pearl City CDP	3.1	18.8	16.5	27.0	18.5	34.3	0.3	10.6	9.2	0.7	11.0	16.9	7.8	52.1	11.5
Waimalu CDP	1.7	13.2	17.4	36.6	15.5	32.6	0.2	7.9	7.2	0.4	8.7	18.5	8.2	52.1	12.3
Waipahu CDP	2.1	26.8	9.8	14.7	32.9	26.4	1.7	9.8	14.5	1.9	12.8	17.6	5.8	56.2	5.7
IDAHO	4.7	17.1	14.8	31.4	15.6	25.3	2.7	10.8	14.2	5.8	21.2	16.2	4.7	47.1	5.1
Boise City city	4.0	15.5	13.9	38.8	14.9	28.0	0.3	8.0	9.9	0.7	20.7	16.7	4.1	51.4	6.5
Caldwell city	2.5	19.6	11.0	23.8	18.6	22.1	2.7	10.8	22.0	3.8	28.8	16.3	4.6	41.6	4.9
Coeur d'Alene city........	3.1	19.9	14.9	27.8	19.4	28.2	0.5	11.9	12.2	2.1	18.8	20.3	2.9	52.2	3.7
Idaho Falls city	3.5	16.5	14.4	37.9	14.8	27.9	1.4	8.1	9.9	1.9	13.1	19.5	3.6	56.8	5.1
Lewiston city................	2.1	19.9	17.1	26.9	18.0	26.6	1.0	10.1	17.4	1.8	21.8	14.9	4.0	52.1	5.5
Meridian city	3.8	13.5	13.9	37.2	13.4	29.9	0.3	9.8	9.5	0.4	26.2	17.7	4.2	46.4	5.1
Nampa city	3.8	18.2	12.7	26.2	15.7	25.0	1.2	13.3	18.7	1.8	29.8	15.7	5.1	43.6	4.1
Pocatello city	2.6	16.2	13.3	33.8	16.3	28.3	0.4	9.0	12.2	0.9	17.0	15.5	4.9	57.1	4.6
Twin Falls city	3.7	22.3	13.9	26.7	18.3	27.5	2.3	9.4	15.8	2.8	18.6	18.9	5.2	50.4	4.0
ILLINOIS...................	3.1	17.6	10.9	34.2	13.9	27.6	0.3	8.2	15.7	1.1	21.7	14.9	6.0	52.3	4.0
Addison village	1.7	16.4	7.8	26.9	11.5	29.6	0.1	10.2	21.7	0.2	30.4	17.5	6.8	43.3	1.9
Alton city....................	1.5	23.9	16.2	25.5	22.3	26.2	0.2	7.5	18.4	0.4	19.4	14.6	5.3	57.3	3.0
Arlington Heights village	3.7	14.0	11.3	50.5	7.5	29.8	0.0	4.8	7.3	0.2	18.8	16.3	5.0	57.3	2.4
Aurora city..................	2.7	17.2	7.9	33.3	12.4	25.9	0.3	7.6	20.5	0.4	27.3	15.8	5.2	48.9	2.4
Bartlett village..............	3.4	10.8	8.9	43.2	7.9	31.9	0.0	7.2	9.8	0.2	24.0	19.1	5.6	49.1	2.0
Belleville city...............	2.2	20.8	15.7	28.7	19.3	29.7	0.0	8.3	14.0	0.2	15.3	14.8	7.1	57.6	5.1
Berwyn city..................	1.6	20.3	9.0	26.2	14.1	30.0	0.0	9.6	20.1	0.1	23.9	15.9	6.1	51.2	2.8
Bloomington city..........	2.7	13.6	10.9	40.7	13.9	28.1	0.2	6.7	10.4	0.2	13.6	11.7	3.5	68.3	2.7
Bolingbrook village	3.0	12.4	10.3	36.8	11.5	28.8	0.1	9.2	13.7	0.2	20.9	16.2	7.7	52.0	3.0
Buffalo Grove village.....	4.1	9.5	7.8	54.9	6.2	29.3	0.0	4.0	5.6	0.0	19.9	20.1	2.3	55.7	2.0
Burbank city	0.9	17.5	11.2	16.8	15.1	30.5	0.0	12.2	25.4	0.0	26.3	18.7	10.5	41.7	2.7
Calumet City city	0.8	19.8	11.9	24.6	14.0	32.7	0.1	8.9	19.7	0.2	18.3	13.8	10.4	51.8	5.6
Carol Stream village......	2.9	10.8	6.9	37.7	9.0	33.4	0.0	6.8	13.1	0.1	23.3	20.3	6.3	47.2	2.8
Carpentersville village ...	1.4	19.1	8.1	19.7	14.6	29.4	0.4	11.1	24.7	0.8	32.1	16.4	5.8	43.6	1.4
Champaign city	3.4	12.4	8.1	45.1	16.3	25.7	0.3	4.0	8.7	0.5	9.7	13.6	2.9	69.9	3.2
Chicago city.................	2.4	22.8	7.3	33.5	16.6	27.0	0.1	6.6	16.2	0.1	17.5	12.0	6.8	58.8	4.8
Chicago Heights city	1.4	19.3	11.5	24.0	20.0	26.4	0.1	7.6	21.9	0.2	22.8	15.1	6.1	51.2	4.6
Cicero town	1.1	22.6	5.6	11.2	16.6	24.2	0.5	12.0	35.5	0.1	38.1	14.9	5.0	39.9	2.0
Crystal Lake city...........	3.3	11.1	10.6	40.7	10.4	29.7	0.1	7.2	11.9	0.4	25.9	16.5	4.6	51.0	1.5

Table B-5. Cities — Education, Labor Force, and Income

City	Median household income	Median family income				Median nonfamily household income	Median income for full-year, full-time workers		Per capita income	Households by source of income (percent)					Households with income over $100,000 (percent)	+/− U.S. percent for income over $100,000	Households with income below poverty (percent)	Families with children with income below poverty (percent)
		All families	Married-couple	Male householder	Female householder		Men	Women		With earnings	With interest, dividend, or rental income	With Social Security income	With public assistance income	With retirement income				
	57	58	59	60	61	62	63	64	65	66	67	68	69	70	71	72	73	74
FLORIDA—Cont'd																		
Wellington village	70 271	77 078	83 173	48 929	33 023	42 098	56 155	34 925	30 726	89.6	45.0	20.0	1.4	13.2	29.9	17.6	4.4	3.8
Weston city	80 920	88 145	99 988	60 962	36 827	40 952	66 765	39 467	35 490	90.5	45.1	14.7	1.0	8.9	37.6	25.3	4.7	5.4
West Palm Beach city	36 774	42 074	49 469	22 768	15 908	30 144	30 823	27 155	23 188	77.9	30.6	27.3	3.3	12.8	11.5	-0.8	15.6	23.7
Winter Haven city	31 884	39 657	46 674	26 098	20 445	20 485	31 499	22 628	20 383	62.2	35.4	44.7	3.5	24.8	5.4	-6.9	14.5	19.7
Winter Springs city	53 247	62 682	80 532	35 464	28 864	30 484	46 978	30 811	26 166	86.7	42.5	23.7	1.3	18.7	21.0	8.7	3.9	3.6
GEORGIA	42 433	49 280	59 178	29 371	20 011	26 509	36 710	27 336	21 154	83.8	28.8	21.9	2.9	14.4	12.3	0.0	12.6	13.9
Albany city	28 639	33 843	50 639	21 533	13 884	18 178	31 063	23 223	15 485	74.4	21.8	26.8	7.2	15.8	6.7	-5.6	24.3	30.8
Alpharetta city	71 207	92 718	111 057	40 648	38 657	45 470	64 960	40 127	39 432	92.3	45.4	12.5	0.1	9.1	33.6	21.3	4.7	4.2
Athens-Clarke County	28 403	41 607	54 500	26 994	15 161	17 310	31 301	23 680	17 123	85.1	31.4	17.1	2.7	10.7	8.2	-4.1	27.5	21.8
Atlanta city	34 770	37 231	69 022	23 984	14 547	30 814	37 157	30 808	25 772	80.1	26.8	20.6	5.5	11.6	15.1	2.8	20.7	31.9
Augusta-Richmond County	33 086	38 509	47 995	22 947	15 839	21 903	31 110	23 765	17 088	80.0	23.2	25.0	5.2	19.4	6.4	-5.9	17.9	23.1
Columbus city	34 798	41 244	51 089	28 343	17 832	21 860	31 635	25 267	18 202	80.1	24.9	26.1	4.3	20.6	8.0	-1.3	15.1	18.6
Dalton city	34 312	41 111	42 088	30 099	22 306	21 888	29 519	25 037	20 575	81.3	30.2	25.2	3.0	9.5	11.7	-0.6	14.1	15.5
East Point city	31 874	36 099	45 949	28 382	19 980	25 278	27 639	26 165	15 175	82.9	16.9	19.7	5.5	14.6	5.3	-7.0	17.9	23.8
Gainesville city	36 605	43 734	45 000	27 208	15 560	24 550	25 143	25 877	19 128	78.3	29.4	25.9	3.1	11.9	12.0	-0.3	18.1	22.7
Hinesville city	35 013	36 221	41 050	27 944	12 337	26 698	29 203	21 481	14 300	90.1	17.6	8.8	5.1	16.2	4.3	-8.0	14.1	18.6
LaGrange city	29 719	36 438	53 633	26 078	16 054	19 424	30 128	22 704	16 640	77.5	23.6	28.7	5.2	13.2	8.4	-3.9	20.5	25.7
Macon city	27 405	33 699	50 358	25 284	13 842	17 465	30 733	23 880	16 082	73.0	21.1	29.9	6.3	18.0	5.7	-6.6	24.0	31.8
Marietta city	40 645	47 340	56 717	26 367	21 738	32 173	31 828	30 695	23 409	87.6	26.4	15.7	2.5	9.7	11.6	-0.7	12.6	17.4
Peachtree City city	76 458	84 398	93 411	56 044	30 082	42 098	67 184	35 708	31 667	89.5	54.5	16.6	0.7	17.6	34.0	21.7	2.3	2.5
Rome city	30 930	37 775	47 000	23 622	15 679	17 666	30 960	23 601	17 327	72.7	26.7	33.8	4.3	18.2	7.9	-4.4	19.6	23.4
Roswell city	71 726	85 946	101 785	41 300	36 209	46 289	56 865	37 236	36 012	91.9	46.4	13.7	0.8	11.2	34.0	21.7	4.1	4.1
Savannah city	29 038	36 410	49 712	27 236	14 975	19 119	30 018	23 215	16 921	76.3	21.7	29.0	4.6	13.7	5.8	-6.5	20.8	26.5
Smyrna city	47 572	53 821	65 202	27 917	28 728	40 175	40 075	35 937	27 637	89.1	31.9	15.1	1.2	11.8	14.2	1.9	7.8	9.1
Valdosta city	29 046	38 174	51 349	20 905	13 371	18 746	28 950	21 543	16 472	79.9	24.5	22.6	4.8	13.8	7.9	-4.4	23.3	26.9
Warner Robins city	38 401	44 217	50 683	31 778	18 128	27 171	35 371	25 667	18 121	82.0	27.5	20.5	2.0	24.7	4.8	-7.5	11.6	16.8
HAWAII	49 820	56 961	61 332	30 830	21 954	30 272	36 808	29 831	21 525	82.9	45.5	27.8	7.2	21.2	16.6	4.3	10.5	11.3
Hilo CDP	39 139	48 150	61 154	24 420	17 807	20 152	38 369	29 324	18 220	74.6	46.5	35.9	9.9	24.1	9.9	-2.4	15.7	18.9
Honolulu CDP	45 112	56 311	59 997	28 947	22 967	29 671	38 235	30 893	24 191	78.8	48.4	30.9	6.1	21.7	17.0	4.7	12.1	12.2
Kailua CDP	72 784	79 118	94 132	47 000	32 064	42 188	49 831	37 052	29 299	86.2	60.7	29.5	4.3	26.0	31.8	19.5	4.9	5.7
Kaneohe CDP	66 006	71 316	76 954	45 893	27 321	35 746	41 729	32 420	23 476	83.8	56.4	33.1	6.1	28.9	24.2	11.9	5.6	6.8
Mililani Town CDP	73 067	76 338	76 416	39 868	28 750	43 354	49 499	32 932	24 427	93.9	54.8	16.0	3.8	21.4	26.1	13.8	3.3	4.0
Pearl City CDP	62 036	67 246	65 682	43 750	25 375	24 649	31 591	30 022	21 683	82.1	55.0	40.7	5.4	37.9	21.5	9.2	5.5	8.4
Waimalu CDP	61 210	70 740	77 319	39 583	23 992	40 119	42 315	33 222	25 913	91.4	51.5	18.9	3.6	21.2	22.4	10.1	5.1	6.2
Waipahu CDP	49 444	51 855	55 604	37 778	17 564	20 694	29 129	24 506	14 484	82.5	34.5	38.2	16.1	27.4	17.5	5.2	13.5	13.8
IDAHO	37 572	43 490	49 381	27 714	18 494	21 861	34 323	23 991	17 041	82.2	36.4	25.2	3.4	16.6	7.3	-5.0	11.2	12.2
Boise City city	42 432	52 014	61 680	30 328	22 182	27 700	38 536	26 932	22 696	85.4	40.5	19.5	3.0	14.3	10.9	-1.4	8.3	8.6
Caldwell city	30 848	35 158	39 583	22 386	17 798	18 409	27 725	22 103	13 657	80.6	25.9	26.2	5.8	13.8	3.8	-8.5	14.9	18.2
Coeur d'Alene city	33 001	39 491	49 301	27 939	16 408	21 136	33 422	22 505	17 454	78.0	36.4	27.8	4.8	15.4	4.3	-8.0	12.9	13.8
Idaho Falls city	40 512	47 431	53 630	27 143	20 206	22 194	40 469	24 009	18 857	81.5	39.9	25.4	3.8	17.7	8.4	-3.9	10.8	12.1
Lewiston city	36 606	45 410	56 835	26 172	14 539	20 058	35 870	23 780	19 091	75.0	39.1	32.4	5.7	19.8	6.0	-6.3	12.7	14.5
Meridian city	53 276	57 077	61 515	36 985	22 681	29 580	41 124	27 797	20 150	89.9	35.7	14.3	1.7	11.0	11.0	-1.3	5.4	6.2
Nampa city	34 758	39 434	43 800	27 109	18 830	20 750	29 372	22 446	14 491	81.5	27.5	25.6	3.7	13.6	3.3	-9.0	11.6	12.5
Pocatello city	34 326	41 884	46 898	27 500	15 281	20 025	35 542	24 273	17 425	82.3	37.6	23.4	4.6	13.4	7.0	-5.3	15.5	16.1
Twin Falls city	32 641	38 632	44 041	24 375	17 570	20 155	31 679	21 882	16 439	78.7	33.9	28.6	3.9	15.9	4.7	-7.6	12.9	15.6
ILLINOIS	46 590	55 545	65 628	32 231	22 200	28 368	41 870	30 081	23 104	81.7	39.7	24.7	3.3	15.4	14.4	2.1	10.1	11.6
Addison village	54 090	59 007	61 158	35 813	23 802	33 575	40 804	28 647	21 201	87.0	39.0	19.2	1.9	11.9	17.3	5.0	7.8	11.4
Alton city	31 213	37 910	47 446	28 125	14 192	18 898	33 906	23 428	16 817	72.9	31.5	31.0	5.6	19.4	4.4	-7.9	18.1	23.0
Arlington Heights village	67 807	84 488	97 504	57 708	37 438	39 608	60 802	40 590	33 544	82.3	59.9	26.7	1.1	16.7	28.6	16.3	2.7	2.0
Aurora city	54 861	61 113	68 006	32 044	27 973	35 504	41 932	30 735	22 131	90.6	33.2	14.0	2.4	9.7	17.5	5.2	7.1	8.2
Bartlett village	79 718	86 503	90 663	51 823	43 125	41 591	60 793	37 058	29 652	92.7	43.8	13.5	1.1	8.2	33.0	20.7	1.8	1.6
Belleville city	35 979	46 426	56 719	26 172	17 321	22 196	34 639	25 012	18 990	76.5	38.1	30.8	3.7	19.1	5.5	-6.8	11.7	14.4
Berwyn city	43 833	51 767	55 030	32 426	26 231	28 300	36 149	27 392	19 113	80.3	37.8	29.1	3.1	16.2	9.1	-3.2	8.3	8.9
Bloomington city	46 496	61 093	73 093	31 458	25 103	28 509	43 727	30 107	24 751	85.9	42.6	19.3	2.4	13.8	15.1	2.8	8.6	6.7
Bolingbrook village	67 852	71 527	76 166	48 472	37 639	40 816	47 795	34 702	23 468	94.3	36.0	12.1	1.9	9.4	22.0	10.5	3.7	3.0
Buffalo Grove village	80 525	92 583	100 937	58 750	40 677	46 134	65 898	42 520	36 696	90.3	57.8	17.2	0.5	9.1	37.2	24.9	2.1	1.9
Burbank city	49 388	56 279	63 736	32 667	38 875	24 868	40 111	27 254	18 923	80.8	42.2	33.3	2.5	20.2	10.7	-1.6	5.1	6.3
Calumet City city	38 902	45 998	59 221	39 022	27 235	25 228	37 842	30 979	18 123	78.8	27.7	27.5	3.1	17.8	5.8	-6.5	11.2	15.0
Carol Stream village	64 893	74 984	81 724	36 466	29 153	34 672	50 840	32 347	25 152	91.9	40.8	12.7	1.6	8.9	22.2	9.9	3.9	2.9
Carpentersville village	54 526	55 921	56 899	36 369	28 869	36 658	38 388	27 438	17 424	91.0	26.8	17.3	2.8	12.0	11.7	-0.6	7.1	9.8
Champaign city	32 795	52 628	62 142	30 859	18 084	20 027	37 593	28 251	18 664	86.4	40.4	16.8	2.8	12.8	8.2	-4.1	21.4	11.5
Chicago city	38 625	42 724	51 504	27 222	19 070	30 646	36 696	31 170	20 175	80.0	29.2	21.6	6.9	12.2	11.6	-0.7	17.4	23.1
Chicago Heights city	36 958	42 681	53 524	24 438	16 689	18 856	35 631	26 846	14 963	77.9	25.6	29.2	6.9	18.9	7.3	-5.0	16.3	20.9
Cicero town	38 044	40 883	43 458	30 554	20 680	23 298	28 081	21 626	12 489	83.7	26.5	21.1	4.1	10.8	5.2	-7.1	13.7	16.4
Crystal Lake city	66 872	75 396	80 897	45 625	30 270	36 404	53 715	33 482	26 146	85.9	49.3	21.0	0.6	14.1	22.7	10.4	3.3	3.7

STATE Place code	City	High school graduates			College graduates		College graduates (percent)				
		Total population 25 years and over	Percent with a high school diploma or less	Percent with a high school diploma or more	Percent with a bachelor's degree or more	+/− U.S. percent with bachelor's degree or more	Non-Hispanic White	Black or African American	American Indian and Alaska Native	Asian, Hawaiian, and Pacific Islander	Hispanic or Latino[1]
		1	2	3	4	5	6	7	8	9	10
	ILLINOIS—Cont'd										
17 18563	Danville city	22 066	58.7	75.2	15.7	-8.7	17.9	5.9	23.1	66.4	6.3
17 18823	Decatur city	53 061	55.4	80.8	17.0	-7.4	19.1	5.0	17.1	53.1	9.9
17 19161	DeKalb city	17 096	33.6	87.6	38.0	13.6	38.6	36.5	43.8	60.6	19.4
17 19642	Des Plaines city	41 547	46.5	81.9	24.7	0.3	24.5	26.5	9.1	51.9	7.7
17 20292	Dolton village	15 292	43.8	82.6	15.4	-9.0	12.1	15.8	23.1	60.9	1.2
17 20591	Downers Grove village..	33 442	27.3	93.0	46.4	22.0	45.9	33.4	28.9	71.5	18.9
17 22255	East St. Louis city	18 098	62.5	66.3	9.1	-15.3	20.4	8.8	60.0	0.0	5.9
17 23074	Elgin city	57 348	51.2	73.8	20.5	-3.9	26.4	16.5	2.7	38.9	4.8
17 23256	Elk Grove Village village	23 742	37.3	90.3	31.6	7.2	29.1	38.2	100.0	59.7	18.5
17 23620	Elmhurst city	28 890	28.9	91.4	45.1	20.7	45.0	18.4	14.3	67.9	31.0
17 23724	Elmwood Park village....	17 657	52.1	80.0	19.5	-4.9	19.5	18.3	30.0	67.3	8.0
17 24582	Evanston city	47 326	19.0	91.4	62.4	38.0	75.5	23.5	36.6	85.6	32.7
17 27884	Freeport city	17 689	52.9	82.2	17.1	-7.3	18.3	6.6	16.3	79.5	7.9
17 28326	Galesburg city	22 624	55.0	79.2	14.9	-9.5	16.2	4.2	0.0	47.5	5.4
17 29730	Glendale Heights village	19 496	43.4	81.5	26.7	2.3	24.2	29.7	0.0	43.6	12.5
17 29756	Glen Ellyn village	17 689	18.2	94.5	58.8	34.4	60.9	31.5	29.2	64.5	23.1
17 29938	Glenview village	28 855	20.0	94.3	55.9	31.5	55.9	34.1	0.0	70.5	26.6
17 30926	Granite City city	21 065	61.5	77.8	9.8	-14.6	10.0	14.2	7.1	3.8	2.2
17 32018	Gurnee village	18 359	24.4	94.1	47.8	23.4	46.7	46.9	26.9	71.3	31.0
17 32746	Hanover Park village.....	22 295	49.9	78.7	20.2	-4.2	19.0	24.6	0.0	48.0	7.3
17 33383	Harvey city	16 234	58.8	69.6	8.2	-16.2	8.3	8.4	0.0	66.7	4.7
17 34722	Highland Park city	21 499	18.5	91.7	61.6	37.2	65.3	45.9	20.9	66.2	14.9
17 35411	Hoffman Estates village	31 543	33.9	89.6	35.9	11.5	34.3	28.0	19.7	55.7	16.6
17 38570	Joliet city	64 520	51.5	78.8	18.6	-5.8	22.9	9.3	8.6	45.6	5.3
17 38934	Kankakee city	16 665	61.7	68.3	13.2	-11.2	17.5	7.9	7.1	36.0	1.9
17 42028	Lansing village	19 017	49.8	86.6	18.2	-6.2	17.9	17.3	15.8	57.7	10.4
17 44407	Lombard village	29 144	34.2	90.4	36.0	11.6	33.4	41.5	10.3	71.6	22.4
17 47774	Maywood village	15 520	57.6	74.5	10.3	-14.1	25.6	9.1	0.0	33.3	5.4
17 49867	Moline city	29 201	47.5	84.1	20.8	-3.6	21.7	18.4	12.9	76.2	6.1
17 51089	Mount Prospect village..	39 184	38.1	85.7	35.4	11.0	35.6	31.0	7.0	55.3	8.2
17 51349	Mundelein village	18 591	38.3	83.5	39.9	15.5	45.4	42.7	0.0	72.6	6.2
17 51622	Naperville city	78 846	15.3	96.3	60.6	36.2	60.2	43.7	16.5	77.9	35.6
17 53000	Niles village	22 805	47.8	81.4	24.8	0.4	22.0	16.0	0.0	54.9	13.2
17 53234	Normal town	20 113	28.6	93.9	42.4	18.0	42.5	26.4	18.5	73.1	31.2
17 53481	Northbrook village	23 573	16.4	95.6	62.2	37.8	62.2	24.3	0.0	72.7	28.9
17 53559	North Chicago city........	14 943	51.2	76.3	14.8	-9.6	22.6	8.6	0.0	49.2	6.1
17 54638	Oak Forest city	18 126	44.1	89.3	22.5	-1.9	22.6	17.7	X	45.4	10.1
17 54820	Oak Lawn village	39 138	50.8	83.5	20.9	-3.5	21.0	19.3	20.0	38.8	14.4
17 54885	Oak Park village	36 438	16.0	94.4	62.1	37.7	69.0	39.9	0.0	81.1	42.2
17 56640	Orland Park village........	34 865	38.9	89.9	31.7	7.3	30.3	42.1	20.9	70.6	27.2
17 57225	Palatine village	43 592	30.2	89.1	41.4	17.0	43.5	23.0	25.0	65.9	10.1
17 57875	Park Ridge city	26 520	26.2	92.4	46.2	21.8	45.8	54.7	54.5	67.5	29.9
17 58447	Pekin city	22 834	56.5	81.6	13.4	-11.0	13.9	0.0	0.0	48.5	14.1
17 59000	Peoria city	70 288	42.9	82.8	28.0	3.6	31.4	10.0	7.4	69.4	19.3
17 62367	Quincy city	26 691	52.6	82.7	19.3	-5.1	19.6	7.0	0.0	53.9	40.8
17 65000	Rockford city	96 187	53.4	77.8	19.8	-4.6	22.9	8.2	4.3	33.9	6.5
17 65078	Rock Island city	25 161	49.8	82.9	18.7	-5.7	20.7	6.1	5.4	27.1	15.6
17 66040	Round Lake Beach village	14 217	54.3	75.0	16.1	-8.3	19.1	28.8	25.5	33.4	4.3
17 66703	St. Charles city	18 134	30.3	91.6	42.9	18.5	44.2	23.8	0.0	70.4	12.7
17 68003	Schaumburg village.......	52 141	31.3	91.8	38.9	14.5	35.0	38.6	40.3	66.3	22.2
17 70122	Skokie village	44 300	33.4	87.4	42.6	18.2	41.1	26.1	21.5	56.4	25.7
17 72000	Springfield city	75 366	41.6	87.4	30.6	6.2	32.3	15.4	32.3	62.9	30.9
17 73157	Streamwood village.......	23 535	43.4	85.3	26.5	2.1	24.2	34.5	24.5	58.4	10.1
17 75484	Tinley Park village........	31 729	41.4	89.5	24.8	0.4	24.2	29.3	0.0	56.5	13.5
17 77005	Urbana city	17 760	24.7	90.8	53.5	29.1	53.9	18.2	0.0	87.5	65.3
17 79293	Waukegan city	50 596	60.8	66.5	16.3	-8.1	26.4	13.2	0.0	44.1	3.9
17 81048	Wheaton city	35 326	19.5	94.4	57.3	32.9	58.8	32.0	39.5	67.0	24.5
17 81087	Wheeling village	22 907	41.8	82.6	32.1	7.7	34.5	21.6	15.2	61.1	5.7
17 82075	Wilmette village	18 389	11.0	96.8	72.6	48.2	73.6	11.1	0.0	74.9	40.0
17 83245	Woodridge village	19 894	29.9	90.0	39.0	14.6	37.9	30.6	0.0	65.0	16.5
18 00000	INDIANA	3 893 278	55.1	82.1	19.4	-5.0	19.9	12.1	10.3	57.0	11.3
18 01468	Anderson city	38 997	61.5	77.4	13.1	-11.3	13.8	9.4	8.6	25.9	13.7
18 05860	Bloomington city	31 329	25.1	91.2	54.8	30.4	53.4	41.4	43.7	83.6	69.3
18 10342	Carmel city	24 599	17.0	97.0	58.4	34.0	58.2	48.7	11.3	67.6	74.6
18 14734	Columbus city	25 879	46.7	84.8	27.6	3.2	26.7	16.9	13.6	76.6	15.2
18 19486	East Chicago city	18 777	73.4	60.6	7.1	-17.3	9.6	8.4	6.6	25.0	5.1
18 20728	Elkhart city	31 608	63.7	71.5	13.4	-11.0	16.5	4.2	0.0	36.7	3.6
18 22000	Evansville city	80 088	55.8	80.7	16.7	-7.7	17.5	5.8	4.6	55.5	12.8
18 23278	Fishers town.................	24 393	13.3	98.2	60.1	35.7	60.4	58.3	9.1	70.7	49.1

[1] Hispanic or Latino persons may be of any race.

City	School enrollment			Population 16 to 19 years				Employment status, 2000			Work status in 1999 of the population 16 years and over		
											Worked in 1999		
	Grades kindergarten through 12	College or graduate school	Percent private	Number	Percent in armed forces	Percent high school graduates	Percent not enrolled, not grads, not in armed forces, not employed	Total population 16 years and over	Percent in labor force	Unemployment rate	Full-time	Part-time	Did not work in 1999
	11	12	13	14	15	16	17	18	19	20	21	22	23
ILLINOIS—Cont'd													
Danville city	6 097	1 314	11.1	1 912	0.3	16.0	9.4	26 407	53.7	9.2	48.6	13.4	38.0
Decatur city	14 049	5 140	23.1	4 825	0.0	11.8	9.8	64 420	61.2	9.0	50.7	15.4	33.9
DeKalb city	4 402	15 623	4.5	5 352	0.0	4.4	1.6	32 798	66.0	10.0	47.4	34.0	18.6
Des Plaines city	9 731	3 097	15.6	2 565	0.0	11.7	3.6	47 069	63.3	3.9	55.8	13.6	30.6
Dolton village	6 524	1 523	13.8	1 544	0.0	10.8	2.7	18 451	67.7	7.2	59.7	12.7	27.6
Downers Grove village..	8 955	2 960	23.3	2 340	0.0	4.2	1.7	38 115	68.3	2.8	57.1	16.9	26.0
East St. Louis city	7 997	1 152	5.4	2 108	0.0	13.7	11.0	22 297	50.3	17.0	40.6	13.9	45.5
Elgin city	18 436	5 259	15.1	5 251	0.0	12.0	6.9	69 536	70.6	5.8	64.1	13.2	22.8
Elk Grove Village village	6 487	1 785	14.6	1 625	0.0	7.0	1.0	27 085	74.1	3.1	61.3	17.9	20.8
Elmhurst city	7 987	2 801	28.5	2 122	0.0	6.3	1.4	33 012	67.7	2.8	55.3	18.1	26.6
Elmwood Park village....	4 356	1 439	29.9	1 349	0.0	6.4	1.9	20 438	64.8	3.9	53.7	15.9	30.4
Evanston city	10 789	14 761	54.9	6 056	0.0	4.1	1.1	60 908	67.5	7.0	56.7	20.6	22.7
Freeport city	4 675	1 438	15.8	1 544	0.0	13.8	7.8	20 770	62.9	8.0	52.9	15.0	31.4
Galesburg city	5 211	2 394	23.8	1 976	0.0	7.2	9.7	27 453	57.9	7.7	49.2	17.1	33.8
Glendale Heights village	5 912	2 153	15.3	1 729	0.0	11.7	1.6	24 012	75.3	4.4	68.9	14.1	17.1
Glen Ellyn village	5 284	1 645	20.2	1 313	0.0	5.3	2.4	20 167	68.6	2.1	58.2	16.9	24.9
Glenview village	8 165	2 324	21.3	2 006	0.0	4.7	0.7	32 216	66.0	2.3	54.7	17.2	28.2
Granite City city	6 023	1 454	8.8	1 762	0.0	10.3	7.0	24 704	61.9	7.6	52.7	13.4	34.0
Gurnee village	5 912	1 734	16.1	1 113	0.0	5.2	0.8	20 573	75.4	2.3	67.7	14.0	18.3
Hanover Park village.....	8 504	1 813	11.0	2 493	0.0	13.4	6.5	27 719	74.3	4.5	67.0	13.5	19.5
Harvey city	8 062	1 464	6.6	2 029	0.2	9.9	8.6	20 504	58.5	14.9	47.7	15.6	36.6
Highland Park city	6 214	1 152	13.6	1 257	0.0	3.8	0.9	23 696	68.7	2.8	55.3	18.9	25.8
Hoffman Estates village	10 854	3 353	14.1	3 154	0.3	7.5	2.8	37 710	73.3	3.2	63.7	15.5	20.9
Joliet city	20 792	5 022	17.2	5 981	0.1	12.5	15.0	77 970	64.4	6.5	56.6	13.4	30.0
Kankakee city	5 909	1 199	14.5	1 541	0.0	13.8	10.5	20 222	59.5	10.0	50.5	13.5	36.0
Lansing village	5 098	1 305	25.6	1 457	0.5	13.7	2.2	22 151	64.9	4.6	52.5	10.5	31.0
Lombard village	6 919	3 285	29.5	1 858	0.0	11.2	2.3	33 426	69.9	4.5	58.8	16.2	25.0
Maywood village............	6 468	1 470	13.7	1 784	0.2	15.4	7.7	19 382	63.9	11.7	54.7	11.7	33.6
Moline city	7 759	2 183	10.3	2 551	0.0	7.4	5.5	34 578	66.1	5.8	54.5	16.3	29.3
Mount Prospect village..	9 169	3 242	18.0	2 534	0.0	6.6	7.3	45 174	67.9	3.5	58.1	14.7	27.2
Mundelein village	6 647	1 681	14.5	1 618	0.0	7.2	4.1	22 034	72.7	3.0	68.1	12.7	19.2
Naperville city.............	30 266	7 634	15.8	6 960	0.0	4.2	1.5	91 188	73.0	2.8	62.1	16.9	21.0
Niles village	4 061	1 924	22.8	1 425	0.0	6.4	3.8	25 780	55.3	3.7	47.6	12.5	39.8
Normal town	5 670	17 075	6.0	5 877	0.0	3.0	0.7	38 339	70.3	11.4	49.0	34.9	16.1
Northbrook village	6 580	1 420	16.4	1 410	0.0	3.7	1.7	25 957	62.6	2.0	51.0	18.5	30.4
North Chicago city........	6 030	2 070	14.5	6 488	73.4	75.4	2.7	28 116	76.1	3.8	65.1	14.1	20.9
Oak Forest city	5 490	1 423	24.8	1 512	0.0	10.3	2.2	21 570	70.8	3.8	57.2	18.6	24.2
Oak Lawn village...........	9 237	2 626	31.3	2 578	0.4	11.2	2.5	44 583	58.5	4.0	48.5	14.7	36.8
Oak Park village	9 244	4 365	24.2	2 124	0.0	6.9	0.8	41 210	75.2	3.2	54.1	15.9	30.0
Orland Park village.......	9 660	3 085	20.6	2 807	0.2	6.4	1.5	40 289	63.4	2.8	51.7	17.5	30.7
Palatine village	11 153	3 639	16.1	2 942	0.0	8.4	3.5	50 826	75.0	3.2	66.0	13.9	20.1
Park Ridge city	6 859	2 057	26.5	1 778	0.0	3.4	0.4	29 696	63.1	1.9	51.0	17.7	31.3
Pekin city	5 779	1 436	9.4	1 712	0.0	16.6	2.4	26 834	60.9	4.7	54.7	14.5	30.7
Peoria city	20 634	9 402	30.5	6 667	0.1	9.2	5.6	86 749	62.2	7.4	51.0	17.5	31.4
Quincy city	7 188	2 354	29.1	2 517	0.0	10.7	4.2	31 953	63.7	6.2	49.4	18.5	32.1
Rockford city	28 465	6 418	20.9	7 934	0.1	11.0	8.7	113 996	64.3	7.3	54.0	15.4	30.6
Rock Island city	6 813	3 721	30.0	2 918	0.0	9.4	5.0	31 657	63.1	8.6	50.6	18.3	31.1
Round Lake Beach village	5 858	1 068	11.6	1 405	0.0	14.3	6.3	17 421	74.5	3.9	68.2	11.6	20.1
St. Charles city	5 921	1 379	12.3	1 969	0.0	8.5	11.9	21 439	71.8	2.3	58.7	17.8	23.5
Schaumburg village.......	12 033	5 022	16.3	3 708	0.0	8.8	1.9	60 525	75.0	3.1	64.7	15.1	20.2
Skokie village	11 493	4 856	23.2	3 241	0.0	6.5	0.6	50 711	61.8	4.0	51.6	15.9	32.6
Springfield city	19 711	5 985	20.6	5 635	0.3	13.1	6.3	88 375	67.7	4.9	58.8	14.0	27.2
Streamwood village.......	7 323	1 932	14.2	1 856	0.0	10.5	3.1	27 534	74.9	4.0	67.5	13.2	19.3
Tinley Park village........	9 668	2 476	14.1	2 529	0.0	10.4	2.5	37 027	69.6	2.8	57.6	16.8	25.6
Urbana city	3 661	15 147	2.6	4 962	0.1	3.3	0.8	31 391	61.5	6.5	44.4	33.1	22.5
Waukegan city.............	18 784	4 181	12.1	5 418	0.8	16.2	10.0	63 637	67.6	9.6	63.1	10.0	26.9
Wheaton city	10 969	5 572	31.7	3 584	0.0	3.4	3.0	42 658	68.2	3.5	54.8	20.2	24.9
Wheeling village	5 801	2 094	14.8	1 725	0.0	10.0	4.5	27 137	73.3	2.7	65.4	13.6	21.0
Wilmette village	6 301	1 094	21.2	1 266	0.0	2.1	0.0	20 184	63.8	2.6	51.9	18.2	29.9
Woodridge village..........	6 018	2 046	17.0	1 679	0.0	9.1	3.6	23 588	74.6	3.3	66.4	14.6	19.0
INDIANA..................	1 142 156	352 687	14.2	360 606	0.0	10.6	5.1	4 683 717	66.6	4.9	57.0	15.8	27.2
Anderson city	9 917	3 181	21.2	3 552	0.0	13.8	6.2	47 183	60.6	8.2	51.4	15.5	33.1
Bloomington city............	5 844	31 805	3.9	10 429	0.0	4.0	0.8	61 672	58.9	4.8	45.5	35.7	18.8
Carmel city	8 383	1 557	17.0	1 815	0.4	6.6	0.8	27 528	70.8	2.3	59.2	17.4	23.4
Columbus city	6 837	1 628	12.2	1 735	0.0	10.5	7.6	30 030	65.6	3.7	57.6	14.2	28.3
East Chicago city	7 353	1 343	10.5	2 090	0.0	9.8	6.6	23 594	52.3	15.4	44.5	12.1	43.4
Elkhart city	9 464	1 564	8.2	2 664	0.0	16.9	13.6	38 291	69.2	6.0	62.2	13.2	24.6
Evansville city..............	19 779	7 883	19.8	6 804	0.0	11.3	9.5	97 118	64.2	6.6	54.1	15.7	30.3
Fishers town.................	7 277	1 720	13.3	1 084	0.0	8.1	0.7	27 112	82.6	1.7	73.6	13.8	12.7

Table B-5. Cities — Education, Labor Force, and Income

City	Full-year full-time employed (percent)								Children under 18 years in families (percent, except where noted)						Total employed by class of worker (percent)			
										With two parents		With one parent who is in labor force	+/− U.S. percent of children with no stay-at-home parent	+/− U.S. percent two-income couples				
	Total	Men	Women	Non-Hispanic White	Black or African American	American Indian and Alaska Native	Asian, Hawaiian, and Pacific Islander	Hispanic or Latino[1]	Number	Both in labor force	Father only in labor force				Private	Govern-ment	Self-employed	Unpaid family worker
	24	25	26	27	28	29	30	31	32	33	34	35	36	37	38	39	40	41
ILLINOIS—Cont'd																		
Danville city	33.4	40.0	26.8	36.1	25.5	33.3	39.1	28.7	7 713	31.5	18.5	30.7	-2.4	-4.2	76.8	15.7	7.3	0.3
Decatur city	37.6	47.0	29.6	38.7	32.6	26.8	38.9	39.5	18 354	35.4	16.6	33.3	4.1	-3.8	82.5	10.9	6.4	0.2
DeKalb city	27.4	33.1	22.0	29.2	17.4	58.8	9.5	32.5	6 381	48.2	21.8	20.4	4.0	8.6	68.9	26.1	4.7	0.3
Des Plaines city	43.5	54.0	34.1	42.9	54.2	56.3	45.4	46.2	12 473	51.0	23.8	13.7	0.1	0.9	83.0	8.5	8.3	0.1
Dolton village	43.7	47.4	40.8	32.0	46.2	23.5	42.6	46.4	7 393	38.0	8.0	38.5	11.9	4.6	74.1	21.5	4.3	0.0
Downers Grove village	45.5	59.8	32.6	45.1	48.0	18.0	46.4	54.3	11 703	54.7	28.3	10.1	0.2	6.6	79.0	11.2	9.5	0.3
East St. Louis city	23.8	24.7	23.1	25.7	23.7	0.0	68.0	24.8	9 168	10.4	5.1	50.9	-3.3	-15.6	75.2	20.1	4.6	0.2
Elgin city	46.6	55.3	38.2	48.9	45.8	43.4	52.8	41.2	25 432	47.7	19.2	17.3	0.4	6.3	84.9	10.1	4.9	0.1
Elk Grove Village village	50.4	62.9	39.0	50.3	67.4	100.0	49.4	50.2	8 447	57.9	26.5	11.4	4.7	9.3	84.1	8.3	7.4	0.2
Elmhurst city	45.0	58.5	33.0	44.8	36.7	34.7	48.8	48.1	10 968	56.3	30.8	9.8	1.5	6.8	79.8	10.7	9.2	0.3
Elmwood Park village	41.7	53.5	31.5	41.4	23.7	18.6	43.3	45.2	5 482	51.8	22.6	19.6	6.8	2.1	85.0	7.3	7.6	0.2
Evanston city	38.2	45.5	31.8	39.5	38.9	42.6	24.4	35.4	13 916	47.7	17.5	23.2	6.3	10.8	77.2	11.1	11.5	0.2
Freeport city	40.1	46.8	34.4	40.3	35.9	67.9	54.9	38.2	6 138	44.5	13.7	32.4	12.3	0.4	82.0	10.4	7.4	0.2
Galesburg city	33.8	40.4	27.4	35.4	19.7	17.6	16.1	40.1	6 761	44.6	15.6	27.9	7.9	-1.2	80.2	13.0	6.8	0.0
Glendale Heights village	51.8	61.2	42.0	55.5	56.0	51.0	47.5	43.5	8 178	51.2	18.3	13.7	0.3	9.9	86.8	8.0	5.0	0.2
Glen Ellyn village	45.8	61.2	31.7	45.8	46.2	0.0	40.5	52.8	7 439	41.8	45.6	7.9	-14.9	1.3	77.7	11.2	11.1	0.1
Glenview village	43.8	57.4	31.7	43.6	44.5	0.0	45.5	44.6	10 555	50.3	33.8	10.1	-4.2	0.9	72.1	9.1	18.4	0.4
Granite City city	39.2	49.0	30.4	39.2	50.6	33.8	41.1	41.6	7 414	38.8	18.6	28.4	2.6	-5.4	83.1	11.7	5.0	0.2
Gurnee village	56.0	70.4	43.1	56.9	57.3	50.0	53.8	47.9	8 636	53.6	31.8	9.8	-1.2	10.7	81.6	10.1	8.0	0.3
Hanover Park village	52.5	61.9	42.8	55.8	51.8	72.7	49.5	47.0	11 342	49.1	22.5	16.1	0.6	10.6	88.0	7.0	4.9	0.1
Harvey city	30.1	33.1	27.6	24.5	30.6	17.0	37.0	30.5	9 173	22.2	10.3	39.2	-3.2	-16.6	79.5	16.4	3.9	0.1
Highland Park city	42.8	59.6	26.9	42.3	50.2	0.0	43.2	46.5	8 341	51.8	36.1	8.5	-4.3	2.0	69.5	8.7	21.2	0.6
Hoffman Estates village	51.0	63.2	39.3	53.2	54.9	27.8	44.1	45.6	13 871	49.6	26.5	14.2	-0.8	9.9	84.7	8.0	7.1	0.2
Joliet city	41.1	50.5	32.1	44.5	34.0	34.3	46.3	34.8	29 126	43.8	22.9	21.4	0.6	1.6	82.6	12.2	4.9	0.2
Kankakee city	35.9	41.5	31.0	35.1	33.8	17.5	44.7	48.2	7 415	31.4	13.7	36.3	3.1	-0.4	77.3	16.5	6.1	0.1
Lansing village	41.7	54.2	30.8	41.0	44.2	42.4	55.4	45.6	6 664	43.3	28.2	20.3	-1.0	-3.7	81.2	12.4	6.0	0.4
Lombard village	47.7	59.1	37.0	47.9	55.2	55.1	47.5	42.1	9 247	54.6	26.2	14.0	4.0	6.3	83.7	9.9	6.4	0.1
Maywood village	38.1	39.7	36.8	34.0	37.7	0.0	88.1	41.3	7 367	27.6	11.5	40.8	3.8	-2.0	78.4	17.7	3.9	0.0
Moline city	41.3	49.1	34.4	41.4	44.4	38.2	34.3	41.2	10 000	45.0	19.9	26.0	6.4	-1.0	81.0	12.1	6.7	0.2
Mount Prospect village	45.3	57.9	33.2	45.2	49.2	38.4	43.3	47.8	12 492	53.5	24.6	12.4	1.3	2.1	83.0	9.0	7.7	0.3
Mundelein village	52.3	63.3	41.0	54.7	50.3	35.1	48.7	47.1	9 199	50.5	27.8	11.8	-2.3	8.9	82.8	9.8	7.3	0.1
Naperville city	50.8	68.4	34.5	51.1	51.6	55.5	49.2	45.9	40 527	47.5	41.4	6.9	-10.2	5.8	81.1	9.3	9.4	0.2
Niles village	36.8	46.9	28.3	35.8	27.6	14.8	44.8	37.9	5 025	51.1	24.1	12.7	-0.8	-5.8	80.9	9.3	9.5	0.3
Normal town	29.6	36.2	23.9	30.3	26.8	69.0	17.6	23.6	7 494	53.2	19.3	22.0	10.6	9.6	76.4	18.3	5.1	0.3
Northbrook village	41.4	58.9	26.0	40.5	26.8	100.0	50.3	53.5	8 293	49.5	39.7	6.2	-8.9	-0.1	67.7	9.5	22.5	0.3
North Chicago city	37.1	38.8	34.3	38.7	36.9	31.5	34.1	36.0	7 944	37.2	18.9	26.6	-0.8	2.2	72.5	23.6	3.6	0.3
Oak Forest city	46.1	59.7	33.0	47.3	32.3	X	48.8	34.3	7 196	60.6	24.0	11.3	7.3	9.0	83.5	10.1	6.4	0.1
Oak Lawn village	38.2	50.9	27.3	38.1	47.2	75.4	31.3	40.9	11 849	49.9	29.5	12.5	-2.2	-6.3	82.2	9.8	7.8	0.2
Oak Park village	50.9	60.7	42.9	51.2	50.3	85.7	50.3	50.3	12 292	49.5	22.2	20.6	5.5	15.0	74.5	15.6	9.8	0.1
Orland Park village	41.2	55.8	28.3	41.1	54.3	78.9	42.3	44.0	12 285	51.0	31.7	10.0	-3.6	-1.1	77.5	10.8	11.5	0.2
Palatine village	51.9	62.8	41.2	52.8	55.3	50.9	48.4	47.7	15 420	51.2	28.7	12.8	-0.6	8.5	82.9	9.0	7.9	0.1
Park Ridge city	40.9	54.9	28.8	40.7	45.5	40.9	49.3	38.4	8 972	55.4	29.7	10.7	1.5	-0.3	73.3	10.8	15.7	0.2
Pekin city	40.1	48.2	32.3	40.4	23.5	38.1	57.6	56.4	7 493	56.6	13.8	23.6	15.6	1.4	82.7	10.2	7.0	0.1
Peoria city	36.5	45.0	29.3	38.1	30.8	21.9	44.2	29.9	26 584	39.0	19.0	33.2	1.6	-3.0	81.7	11.3	6.8	0.1
Quincy city	37.8	48.0	29.1	38.5	29.5	29.2	38.3	24.2	9 006	58.6	11.0	22.8	16.8	6.3	79.4	13.2	7.3	0.1
Rockford city	39.9	49.1	31.8	41.1	34.3	42.6	40.7	39.3	36 997	39.4	14.5	32.4	7.7	0.4	82.9	9.9	7.0	0.2
Rock Island city	36.8	43.7	30.8	37.9	30.5	32.8	32.5	39.0	8 489	41.7	14.2	32.7	9.8	-0.5	79.7	13.5	6.3	0.5
Round Lake Beach village	51.5	61.5	41.3	55.1	59.6	51.0	38.8	43.4	8 510	47.7	22.4	16.5	-0.4	10.6	87.5	7.0	5.3	0.2
St. Charles city	46.4	60.2	32.9	46.9	23.8	44.6	49.3	43.4	7 226	54.4	29.6	12.4	2.2	9.0	80.3	10.1	9.5	0.1
Schaumburg village	52.6	64.9	41.2	52.8	61.5	58.2	47.2	56.1	15 787	52.3	25.3	15.2	2.9	8.0	84.8	7.9	7.1	0.2
Skokie village	39.4	48.2	31.7	36.3	39.6	23.9	48.9	47.2	13 851	56.9	21.9	12.4	4.7	2.0	75.7	11.1	12.6	0.6
Springfield city	46.6	55.4	39.2	48.6	35.1	38.1	39.3	47.8	25 471	44.9	15.4	30.1	10.4	7.8	61.9	31.4	6.5	0.2
Streamwood village	53.2	63.8	42.9	56.1	53.8	62.4	45.0	42.9	9 825	48.2	22.0	18.3	1.9	8.9	87.1	7.3	5.5	0.2
Tinley Park village	46.7	61.2	33.7	47.2	27.6	100.0	54.7	35.6	12 448	56.3	27.8	11.2	2.9	8.7	82.7	10.1	7.0	0.1
Urbana city	24.5	27.0	21.7	27.9	23.6	41.3	11.6	16.5	4 835	39.8	18.1	30.7	5.9	0.5	55.3	40.5	3.8	0.3
Waukegan city	43.5	50.6	36.2	46.6	42.6	47.7	47.7	40.5	24 694	39.2	18.3	24.3	-1.1	0.0	82.5	12.6	4.7	0.2
Wheaton city	43.1	57.6	29.8	43.0	43.3	60.7	44.5	41.8	14 273	47.7	39.8	8.6	-8.3	4.5	79.0	11.5	9.4	0.1
Wheeling village	50.8	62.3	39.8	53.4	57.9	53.1	49.1	41.2	7 687	56.1	19.5	13.5	5.0	10.1	86.7	7.0	6.1	0.3
Wilmette village	42.1	59.3	27.4	42.2	16.9	25.0	41.8	42.3	8 286	44.7	43.4	7.4	-12.5	-1.3	69.3	7.4	22.6	0.7
Woodridge village	51.5	64.2	39.1	52.9	49.7	48.3	46.3	47.7	8 020	48.4	24.0	16.9	0.7	9.3	82.4	10.3	7.2	0.1
INDIANA	43.4	54.1	33.3	44.2	37.0	39.5	37.1	38.6	1 493 290	47.6	21.7	21.3	4.3	3.6	80.6	10.9	8.2	0.3
Anderson city	37.8	46.5	30.4	38.8	32.8	17.4	27.0	44.2	13 098	35.1	18.2	32.6	3.1	-6.1	82.8	10.4	6.6	0.2
Bloomington city	23.1	27.0	19.4	24.1	19.9	29.6	10.7	21.1	8 085	42.4	17.3	26.9	4.7	4.6	66.9	26.9	6.1	0.2
Carmel city	48.9	66.1	32.9	48.9	68.6	52.2	46.6	36.8	11 287	51.5	36.3	8.9	-4.2	5.5	79.4	8.3	12.3	0.1
Columbus city	45.0	59.5	32.0	44.8	53.3	50.8	45.1	47.4	9 540	41.4	28.6	20.3	-2.9	-0.1	84.0	9.3	6.6	0.1
East Chicago city	28.6	36.0	22.2	26.9	26.0	11.2	17.1	30.9	8 958	20.6	17.8	35.7	-8.3	-22.1	81.2	16.2	2.5	0.1
Elkhart city	44.0	54.3	34.4	45.4	42.3	15.9	30.1	39.9	13 648	39.8	15.7	30.1	5.3	3.4	88.3	6.0	5.6	0.1
Evansville city	41.0	49.5	33.8	41.7	33.6	59.3	45.5	41.8	26 036	43.0	14.4	29.9	8.3	2.5	84.8	8.7	6.2	0.2
Fishers town	61.0	76.7	46.4	61.4	64.9	73.3	52.7	52.1	12 432	56.7	30.5	9.6	1.7	17.2	83.6	7.5	8.9	0.0

[1] Hispanic or Latino persons may be of any race.

Table B-5. Cities — **Education, Labor Force, and Income**

| City | Percent who worked at home | Percent of the population 5 years and over with a disability | Veterans as a percent of the population 18 years and over | Occupation for employed population 16 years and over (percent) | | | | | | Industry for employed population 16 years and over (percent) | | | | | |
| | | | | Management, professional, and related occupations | Service occupations | Sales and office occupations | Farming, fishing, and forestry occupations | Construction, extraction, and maintenance occupations | Production, transportation and material moving occupations | Agriculture, forestry, fishing, and mining | Construction and manufacturing | Wholesale and retail trade | Transportation and warehousing, and utilities | Service industries | Public administration |
	42	43	44	45	46	47	48	49	50	51	52	53	54	55	56
ILLINOIS—Cont'd															
Danville city	2.4	23.7	14.0	27.1	18.3	24.8	0.4	7.5	21.8	1.0	23.1	17.8	5.1	48.5	4.5
Decatur city	2.0	21.5	14.7	27.4	16.9	26.5	0.3	8.9	20.1	1.2	24.8	15.2	7.3	47.8	3.8
DeKalb city	2.4	13.0	7.3	37.0	18.1	27.5	0.2	5.5	11.7	1.1	15.6	14.2	3.2	63.2	2.7
Des Plaines city	2.5	17.9	10.7	32.2	12.3	31.5	0.1	9.1	14.7	0.1	24.1	17.3	6.9	49.2	2.3
Dolton village	2.6	17.5	11.7	27.3	14.4	33.5	0.0	6.2	18.6	0.0	14.1	10.6	14.3	55.1	6.0
Downers Grove village	4.3	12.3	10.9	49.0	8.1	30.2	0.0	5.0	7.7	0.1	16.5	15.7	5.5	60.0	2.2
East St. Louis city	2.6	32.1	11.5	21.9	30.8	23.6	0.1	5.2	18.4	0.2	12.9	9.3	8.3	64.0	5.4
Elgin city	2.1	17.7	9.0	28.0	15.0	25.5	0.3	8.6	22.6	0.2	30.8	14.3	4.7	47.3	2.7
Elk Grove Village village	2.4	13.5	11.1	36.7	9.2	34.9	0.0	7.4	11.8	0.1	24.1	19.8	8.4	45.3	2.4
Elmhurst city	3.2	11.6	11.2	47.4	7.8	31.6	0.0	5.7	7.5	0.1	17.4	16.0	5.4	58.7	2.5
Elmwood Park village	1.5	17.0	8.3	27.2	12.9	33.3	0.1	10.0	16.4	0.1	26.2	16.8	6.5	47.4	3.1
Evanston city	6.1	13.2	7.1	60.7	9.1	22.3	0.0	2.8	5.1	0.2	10.1	8.8	2.6	75.9	2.6
Freeport city	1.8	21.3	13.9	28.1	14.7	26.1	0.1	7.8	23.2	0.3	33.6	12.0	3.7	47.8	2.6
Galesburg city	1.8	20.4	13.6	26.7	19.8	23.0	0.5	8.0	22.0	1.1	19.5	16.3	7.3	50.8	5.0
Glendale Heights village	1.5	16.3	7.4	30.7	10.1	31.8	0.1	8.0	19.3	0.1	27.7	19.6	7.6	42.6	2.4
Glen Ellyn village	5.7	11.0	10.2	53.3	8.0	29.2	0.0	3.3	6.2	0.2	15.9	16.2	4.1	61.0	2.6
Glenview village	5.0	12.1	11.5	53.6	8.0	28.1	0.1	4.0	6.1	0.1	16.3	15.7	3.1	62.2	2.5
Granite City city	1.2	22.9	16.8	21.8	17.2	27.5	0.2	9.3	24.0	0.7	24.4	16.7	6.1	48.1	4.0
Gurnee village	3.0	11.4	9.5	50.4	7.6	28.6	0.1	5.6	7.6	0.4	30.2	16.7	3.1	46.5	3.2
Hanover Park village	1.5	15.1	7.4	26.4	13.4	31.5	0.1	8.8	19.9	0.0	26.4	18.8	7.9	45.3	1.6
Harvey city	2.2	24.5	11.3	20.0	21.9	28.5	0.3	7.3	22.0	0.3	17.7	13.1	10.3	55.2	3.5
Highland Park city	6.3	11.9	10.2	55.6	10.4	27.3	0.0	3.2	3.5	0.0	11.4	16.2	0.9	69.6	1.9
Hoffman Estates village	2.7	12.7	8.4	41.2	9.6	31.2	0.1	6.1	11.9	0.1	22.7	18.2	6.6	50.7	1.7
Joliet city	1.8	17.4	10.7	27.6	16.2	27.4	0.2	10.4	18.3	0.2	23.0	15.8	7.3	48.7	5.0
Kankakee city	2.0	24.1	11.3	22.5	21.5	22.1	0.8	7.8	25.4	1.2	19.0	17.5	6.3	49.2	6.0
Lansing village	2.1	15.5	14.1	29.8	13.3	29.2	0.1	12.6	15.0	0.2	22.6	15.5	8.2	48.7	4.9
Lombard village	2.7	14.0	10.8	39.9	8.0	35.4	0.0	7.4	9.2	0.2	18.1	18.6	6.4	53.7	3.1
Maywood village	1.7	21.7	9.7	20.7	17.9	33.2	0.3	4.7	20.0	0.1	10.3	12.4	11.6	49.5	4.1
Moline city	2.1	16.9	14.4	29.3	17.5	27.3	0.1	7.4	18.4	0.3	25.1	14.6	5.2	50.1	4.8
Mount Prospect village	2.2	15.5	11.1	39.4	10.4	31.3	0.1	5.9	12.9	0.1	22.3	17.5	6.5	51.4	2.2
Mundelein village	3.3	13.2	7.9	41.3	12.8	25.0	0.3	7.9	12.8	0.4	25.5	15.3	2.9	53.3	2.8
Naperville city	5.6	7.9	7.9	56.0	7.5	28.2	0.0	3.6	4.7	0.2	18.2	15.8	4.0	59.6	2.1
Niles village	2.0	18.0	10.3	31.3	13.2	32.4	0.1	8.2	14.9	0.2	22.9	19.1	5.3	49.5	2.9
Normal town	2.5	10.0	8.0	35.5	19.5	32.4	0.1	4.8	7.6	0.3	9.0	15.3	2.5	70.1	2.8
Northbrook village	6.6	11.2	12.3	57.7	4.7	31.6	0.0	2.6	3.3	0.1	13.1	16.7	2.2	66.0	1.7
North Chicago city	6.6	19.0	13.1	25.2	22.3	26.8	0.4	5.3	20.1	0.4	22.5	14.5	4.8	49.8	8.0
Oak Forest city	2.4	13.6	12.7	32.2	11.4	31.6	0.1	12.0	12.8	0.1	19.4	18.0	6.0	53.8	2.9
Oak Lawn village	2.1	18.4	13.8	31.9	10.7	31.2	0.1	12.0	14.1	0.1	20.2	16.0	7.7	52.3	2.9
Oak Park village	5.1	11.0	7.9	60.5	7.9	23.8	0.0	2.8	5.1	0.0	10.2	10.0	4.4	71.9	3.5
Orland Park village	2.1	12.8	13.1	40.5	9.4	32.1	0.0	8.1	9.9	0.1	19.6	17.3	5.6	54.5	2.9
Palatine village	2.5	14.4	9.1	43.8	10.5	30.0	0.1	5.7	10.0	0.1	22.8	17.2	5.4	52.7	1.8
Park Ridge city	4.0	12.9	12.4	50.3	8.3	29.5	0.0	5.2	6.7	0.0	17.6	14.6	4.4	60.4	2.9
Pekin city	1.6	20.5	14.7	24.7	17.4	29.7	0.1	8.1	20.0	0.5	23.4	18.0	4.6	49.4	4.1
Peoria city	2.0	18.7	12.2	38.3	17.7	26.4	0.1	5.7	11.8	0.2	19.6	14.1	3.3	59.0	3.8
Quincy city	2.3	19.2	15.8	27.2	18.4	28.4	0.1	7.5	18.4	0.9	21.3	17.7	3.7	52.6	3.8
Rockford city	2.3	21.0	12.1	29.1	14.8	26.0	0.2	7.3	22.6	0.3	29.8	14.3	5.0	47.7	2.8
Rock Island city	1.7	19.1	14.2	27.3	18.5	28.5	0.4	7.6	17.8	0.4	19.6	15.5	5.2	54.3	4.9
Round Lake Beach village	2.4	14.4	9.3	23.3	15.3	30.4	0.3	11.4	19.3	0.3	32.5	19.7	3.7	41.6	2.1
St. Charles city	3.8	12.0	10.5	42.8	9.8	31.8	0.1	6.5	8.9	0.2	21.7	19.5	3.8	51.8	3.1
Schaumburg village	2.7	12.4	9.8	44.3	8.6	32.2	0.0	5.3	9.6	0.0	20.3	18.3	6.2	52.9	2.2
Skokie village	3.5	18.3	9.0	46.3	10.5	29.1	0.0	4.3	9.7	0.0	16.5	17.5	3.2	59.9	2.8
Springfield city	2.1	18.7	13.8	40.3	15.6	29.9	0.1	6.4	7.7	0.4	8.0	11.8	4.0	54.9	20.9
Streamwood village	2.3	13.6	9.8	33.1	11.3	32.1	0.1	9.3	14.1	0.1	23.8	19.3	7.5	47.4	1.9
Tinley Park village	1.7	12.9	11.3	36.2	11.0	30.2	0.1	11.4	11.3	0.1	21.1	17.0	6.2	52.3	3.4
Urbana city	3.2	11.2	5.7	52.9	14.8	21.7	0.3	3.6	6.7	0.4	7.6	10.0	2.6	76.5	2.9
Waukegan city	1.6	19.0	10.0	22.6	17.9	24.6	0.1	9.7	25.0	0.5	33.1	13.5	3.6	45.0	4.3
Wheaton city	4.5	9.2	9.3	53.8	8.8	28.0	0.0	4.2	5.2	0.1	14.1	13.8	2.7	66.4	2.8
Wheeling village	1.9	16.5	7.2	35.2	12.4	31.3	0.1	6.2	14.8	0.2	24.9	18.0	4.0	50.6	1.5
Wilmette village	7.1	10.2	11.4	66.8	4.5	24.6	0.0	1.8	2.1	0.1	10.9	11.6	1.6	74.0	1.8
Woodridge village	2.7	12.5	8.6	43.2	10.3	29.6	0.0	6.9	10.0	0.2	18.9	17.2	5.7	55.2	2.8
INDIANA	2.9	19.0	13.1	28.7	14.2	25.3	0.4	10.0	21.4	1.4	29.5	15.2	5.2	45.4	3.3
Anderson city	2.4	25.0	14.5	22.8	19.0	26.9	0.1	9.5	21.6	0.2	25.5	17.8	3.3	48.6	4.6
Bloomington city	3.3	10.7	6.1	43.9	20.0	25.4	0.1	4.1	6.4	0.3	8.8	12.3	1.7	74.1	2.7
Carmel city	5.1	9.5	10.8	56.2	8.1	28.2	0.1	3.1	4.3	0.2	18.8	17.0	2.8	59.2	2.0
Columbus city	2.1	19.7	13.1	35.1	12.2	23.3	0.1	6.4	22.9	0.2	39.4	13.5	3.5	40.7	2.8
East Chicago city	1.5	25.6	10.0	17.3	21.7	23.8	0.1	9.1	28.0	0.2	28.9	12.9	4.2	47.8	6.0
Elkhart city	2.1	23.7	11.6	20.0	11.4	21.4	0.3	7.6	39.3	0.3	51.7	12.3	2.9	31.1	1.7
Evansville city	1.8	23.4	13.9	25.0	17.3	28.6	0.1	9.0	19.9	0.3	22.3	17.7	5.9	51.1	2.7
Fishers town	4.9	6.0	8.0	55.5	7.2	30.6	0.1	2.9	3.8	0.3	17.9	17.2	2.3	60.2	2.2

City	Median household income	Median family income: All families	Median family income: Families with children: Married-couple	Median family income: Families with children: Male householder	Median family income: Families with children: Female householder	Median nonfamily household income	Median income for full-year, full-time workers: Men	Median income for full-year, full-time workers: Women	Per capita income	Households by source of income (percent): With earnings	Households by source of income (percent): With interest, dividend, or rental income	Households by source of income (percent): With Social Security income	Households by source of income (percent): With public assistance income	Households by source of income (percent): With retirement income	Households with income over $100,000 (percent)	+/– U.S. percent for income over $100,000	Households with income below poverty (percent)	Families with children with income below poverty (percent)
	57	58	59	60	61	62	63	64	65	66	67	68	69	70	71	72	73	74
ILLINOIS—Cont'd																		
Danville city	30 431	39 308	51 607	22 750	14 236	18 047	33 207	23 828	16 476	71.0	32.3	35.1	5.7	20.3	5.3	-7.0	16.7	21.3
Decatur city	33 111	42 379	56 217	27 254	15 119	20 996	37 707	23 351	19 009	74.3	34.7	31.0	4.6	19.5	6.7	-5.6	14.9	20.9
DeKalb city	35 153	53 017	60 551	24 725	15 658	20 701	37 519	26 922	16 261	86.3	38.7	17.2	2.3	12.2	7.4	-4.9	22.2	12.9
Des Plaines city	53 638	65 806	70 990	48 519	31 959	30 479	43 558	31 589	24 146	78.4	49.9	32.5	1.4	19.5	14.3	2.0	4.7	4.1
Dolton village	48 020	52 725	66 189	48 226	34 853	26 618	39 727	32 419	18 102	85.9	21.1	23.0	3.7	16.4	8.6	-3.7	8.2	8.7
Downers Grove village	65 539	80 604	91 321	41 172	36 852	34 053	58 683	38 178	31 580	81.5	57.7	27.1	0.9	18.1	26.6	14.3	2.9	1.7
East St. Louis city	21 324	24 567	41 926	22 457	12 395	11 598	28 519	22 449	11 169	67.9	9.2	32.6	14.3	17.8	3.2	-9.1	34.5	42.0
Elgin city	52 605	58 404	62 870	33 472	24 366	35 233	40 287	29 140	21 112	86.9	35.1	18.9	2.1	11.3	13.6	1.3	6.5	9.5
Elk Grove Village village	62 132	71 834	78 796	54 732	39 821	36 830	50 829	35 209	28 515	87.9	48.4	23.2	1.1	15.1	20.5	8.2	2.7	1.3
Elmhurst city	69 794	81 496	90 600	54 318	43 750	36 825	59 361	38 680	32 015	82.2	61.8	28.4	0.5	18.2	29.1	16.8	3.1	2.7
Elmwood Park village	47 315	58 358	66 520	47 639	27 500	30 168	41 280	30 115	22 526	80.3	43.2	32.5	1.6	17.1	11.3	-1.0	6.1	5.5
Evanston city	56 335	78 886	98 158	46 591	28 694	37 588	55 388	40 845	33 645	86.4	52.4	19.5	2.1	12.5	26.0	13.7	10.2	7.2
Freeport city	35 399	43 787	56 846	25 938	19 250	22 051	36 411	25 756	18 680	75.1	41.1	31.7	2.9	19.3	4.8	-7.5	12.2	16.2
Galesburg city	31 987	41 796	50 796	20 250	15 372	20 075	32 635	21 863	17 214	71.7	41.7	36.8	4.2	21.6	4.9	-7.4	13.0	19.6
Glendale Heights village	56 285	64 115	68 057	40 677	28 380	41 173	41 516	30 745	21 911	94.0	33.2	11.6	2.0	7.8	13.4	1.1	5.4	6.7
Glen Ellyn village	74 846	95 332	108 257	61 406	40 337	36 135	72 302	39 134	39 783	85.8	59.0	22.1	1.0	13.7	36.7	24.4	3.2	2.3
Glenview village	80 730	96 552	110 292	51 842	40 500	41 530	70 149	41 840	43 384	84.9	64.6	27.6	1.0	15.1	40.4	28.1	2.3	1.8
Granite City city	35 615	42 130	50 448	30 938	16 538	20 799	35 395	24 331	17 691	74.3	34.6	32.4	3.7	23.1	4.5	-7.8	11.5	13.5
Gurnee village	75 742	88 932	97 175	39 219	33 618	40 517	61 003	39 957	31 517	90.5	51.1	14.4	1.3	10.8	31.5	19.2	3.4	2.2
Hanover Park village	61 358	63 990	67 454	45 000	31 492	38 741	40 545	30 000	19 960	93.9	34.1	11.5	1.8	7.4	15.6	3.3	5.0	6.0
Harvey city	31 958	35 378	41 944	22 344	19 375	17 944	31 071	25 676	12 336	79.6	12.1	24.7	12.3	16.0	4.6	-7.7	22.2	26.3
Highland Park city	100 967	117 235	137 795	61 429	44 063	42 230	92 626	42 673	55 331	85.6	69.7	28.2	0.9	12.9	50.6	38.3	3.3	2.9
Hoffman Estates village	65 937	73 685	79 221	63 929	34 318	43 088	51 170	35 339	26 669	92.9	44.6	14.3	1.3	9.8	24.8	12.5	3.9	4.7
Joliet city	47 761	55 870	62 790	34 137	22 671	26 797	42 413	30 027	19 390	81.5	32.0	23.7	3.4	14.2	10.8	-1.5	9.5	10.4
Kankakee city	30 469	36 428	49 210	27 000	16 696	19 065	31 479	24 118	15 479	75.3	26.6	29.5	6.7	16.3	5.0	-7.3	19.0	25.3
Lansing village	47 554	56 901	63 611	43 542	33 036	27 244	46 214	30 115	22 547	79.5	41.3	31.0	1.7	19.6	9.4	-2.9	5.3	6.0
Lombard village	60 015	69 686	75 999	42 250	37 667	39 924	50 591	36 540	27 667	85.1	50.3	24.3	0.8	16.8	18.9	6.6	4.1	2.4
Maywood village	41 942	46 776	61 641	35 313	26 648	19 779	32 083	27 918	14 915	82.0	18.4	28.7	9.4	18.9	8.9	-3.4	13.6	14.3
Moline city	39 363	48 207	55 625	31 719	19 195	24 485	39 900	25 831	21 557	78.1	39.9	28.0	2.9	21.5	8.4	-3.9	9.1	12.3
Mount Prospect village	57 165	67 262	74 462	38 750	28 026	35 690	46 200	33 125	26 464	82.9	51.4	27.6	1.6	15.7	19.3	7.0	4.3	5.0
Mundelein village	69 651	75 083	78 170	19 444	35 539	44 759	50 804	35 325	26 280	92.5	44.6	14.4	1.2	10.4	25.9	13.6	3.6	4.4
Naperville city	88 771	101 590	107 807	52 464	46 198	46 401	78 284	40 999	35 551	92.4	58.8	12.6	0.6	9.5	42.8	30.5	2.2	1.9
Niles village	48 627	58 215	66 679	40 729	39 464	29 276	40 857	31 024	23 543	71.6	52.7	40.8	1.4	20.3	12.7	0.4	5.1	4.7
Normal town	40 379	60 644	70 381	34 000	20 827	23 917	41 911	28 958	17 775	86.5	43.5	17.3	1.1	13.2	10.4	-1.9	18.3	8.3
Northbrook village	95 665	110 778	126 510	52 188	55 524	37 786	90 705	48 833	50 765	82.2	71.0	30.9	0.7	16.4	48.2	35.9	2.6	1.3
North Chicago city	38 180	40 485	41 944	23 458	22 442	27 708	34 205	23 887	14 564	87.6	23.2	16.0	4.8	11.8	6.6	-5.7	14.2	15.5
Oak Forest city	60 073	68 862	75 677	42 857	32 604	30 592	50 214	30 884	23 487	87.7	42.8	20.3	1.3	15.3	16.0	3.7	4.3	3.2
Oak Lawn village	47 585	60 057	70 297	43 125	31 000	28 995	46 721	31 295	23 877	73.2	51.6	38.4	1.1	24.0	13.2	0.9	5.4	5.7
Oak Park village	59 183	81 703	104 381	49 219	36 914	39 251	53 637	41 644	36 340	87.3	46.6	17.2	1.3	11.3	25.7	13.4	6.3	5.5
Orland Park village	67 574	77 507	90 212	59 671	37 331	35 715	60 435	35 896	30 467	80.3	56.6	31.1	0.8	22.1	27.1	14.8	3.3	3.3
Palatine village	63 321	76 270	83 479	36 394	37 250	41 898	51 058	36 030	30 661	89.7	48.2	17.1	1.3	11.1	24.0	11.7	4.0	4.5
Park Ridge city	73 154	87 795	101 620	61 500	52 361	39 539	65 602	41 685	36 046	79.7	67.5	33.5	0.5	20.5	31.4	19.1	3.0	2.7
Pekin city	37 972	46 346	56 376	29 079	16 157	21 104	37 128	22 282	19 616	76.3	36.8	31.1	3.1	21.3	6.8	-5.5	9.8	10.7
Peoria city	36 397	46 882	61 371	24 318	15 211	23 819	41 690	26 316	20 512	77.9	36.9	26.4	6.0	17.7	9.8	-2.5	15.9	23.0
Quincy city	30 956	40 718	51 244	23 832	15 238	19 492	31 453	21 680	17 479	74.5	40.6	33.9	3.8	17.8	4.4	-7.9	12.7	14.8
Rockford city	37 667	45 465	57 146	31 313	18 482	24 511	38 197	26 195	19 781	78.3	34.0	27.1	4.5	15.2	8.7	-3.6	13.0	16.3
Rock Island city	34 729	45 127	54 341	34 583	15 410	22 422	34 469	24 779	19 202	73.9	39.4	30.8	4.1	24.0	6.4	-5.9	13.5	19.1
Round Lake Beach village	59 359	61 637	65 136	39 630	26 947	31 133	39 713	28 546	18 113	91.8	24.1	11.8	2.3	7.8	12.4	0.1	5.0	3.8
St. Charles city	69 424	82 828	92 890	52 232	38 281	39 043	57 842	36 152	33 969	86.7	53.1	19.6	0.8	13.0	29.8	17.5	3.5	3.0
Schaumburg village	60 941	72 631	79 235	48 600	37 841	43 014	52 122	36 837	30 587	88.8	47.4	16.5	0.8	11.2	20.0	7.7	3.2	2.8
Skokie village	57 375	68 253	75 269	50 104	36 418	32 602	47 128	34 872	27 136	78.8	53.0	33.3	3.0	15.5	21.1	8.8	5.7	5.6
Springfield city	39 388	51 298	65 481	26 875	19 520	26 315	38 114	29 881	23 324	80.0	38.9	26.7	3.4	19.0	10.0	-2.3	10.3	13.9
Streamwood village	65 076	68 771	71 557	32 250	38 929	50 026	45 136	33 875	23 961	93.9	39.0	13.2	1.7	10.5	18.0	5.7	2.3	2.6
Tinley Park village	61 648	71 858	78 433	44 107	37 849	35 006	51 096	35 634	25 207	83.4	46.3	24.7	0.9	17.5	18.0	5.7	2.7	1.8
Urbana city	27 819	42 655	54 612	32 813	18 750	18 298	35 000	27 219	15 969	83.6	41.0	16.1	2.5	11.7	6.7	-5.6	25.4	19.3
Waukegan city	42 335	47 341	51 608	30 162	22 618	27 799	30 980	26 066	17 368	84.7	26.4	18.7	3.1	14.6	9.7	-2.6	12.0	14.6
Wheaton city	73 385	90 475	101 659	63 594	35 500	43 543	66 536	40 174	34 147	87.6	61.2	19.9	1.0	14.6	33.6	21.3	3.2	3.5
Wheeling village	55 491	63 088	67 638	39 196	36 570	40 365	42 238	33 611	24 989	87.8	41.5	17.6	1.6	10.3	14.6	2.3	4.9	4.5
Wilmette village	106 773	122 515	146 988	106 047	58 611	51 220	100 001	51 769	55 611	83.3	71.7	29.5	0.5	15.4	54.0	41.7	2.6	1.7
Woodridge village	61 944	71 546	77 416	46 033	33 516	38 351	50 919	34 392	27 851	92.4	41.9	13.3	1.6	10.3	22.3	10.0	3.9	4.0
INDIANA	41 567	50 261	59 025	30 623	20 793	23 689	38 138	26 046	20 397	81.8	35.6	26.0	2.6	17.0	9.2	-3.1	9.5	10.2
Anderson city	32 577	39 552	49 804	24 884	17 969	21 972	32 093	23 645	19 142	73.8	30.7	33.4	3.8	25.7	5.5	-6.8	11.9	18.4
Bloomington city	25 377	50 054	65 000	29 423	20 283	16 722	34 180	26 802	16 481	85.0	40.5	16.2	2.6	11.2	8.2	-4.1	27.7	14.1
Carmel city	81 583	94 210	103 631	64 306	40 540	37 135	73 530	40 012	38 906	89.1	60.9	17.9	0.3	14.3	38.5	26.2	2.5	2.3
Columbus city	41 723	52 296	61 039	32 557	19 640	25 024	41 373	25 840	22 055	80.9	41.0	26.7	2.5	17.5	10.2	-2.1	8.9	9.7
East Chicago city	26 538	31 778	45 864	26 736	12 136	16 543	32 977	22 084	13 517	70.0	20.1	31.0	8.8	20.9	4.6	-7.7	25.2	30.8
Elkhart city	34 863	40 514	47 494	26 816	18 374	24 417	31 057	24 033	17 890	83.0	26.2	24.9	5.1	12.8	5.8	-6.5	12.2	16.4
Evansville city	31 963	41 091	50 870	25 538	17 724	20 737	31 552	22 478	18 388	76.5	33.9	30.5	4.4	17.3	4.9	-7.4	13.1	16.7
Fishers town	75 638	81 971	86 275	59 028	43 341	47 853	60 438	39 335	31 891	95.6	50.7	7.6	0.3	6.5	27.5	15.2	1.8	1.2

STATE Place code	City	Total population 25 years and over	Percent with a high school diploma or less	Percent with a high school diploma or more	Percent with a bachelor's degree or more	+/− U.S. percent with bachelor's degree or more	Non-Hispanic White	Black or African American	American Indian and Alaska Native	Asian, Hawaiian, and Pacific Islander	Hispanic or Latino[1]
		1	2	3	4	5	6	7	8	9	10
	INDIANA—Cont'd										
18 25000	Fort Wayne city	128 039	49.6	83.2	19.4	−5.0	22.0	8.4	6.9	32.2	5.9
18 27000	Gary city	61 790	62.4	72.7	10.1	−14.3	15.4	9.5	0.0	39.7	5.9
18 28386	Goshen city	17 984	62.5	71.9	18.5	−5.9	20.4	2.3	0.0	49.4	5.7
18 29898	Greenwood city	23 322	46.0	87.6	23.7	−0.7	23.4	33.1	0.0	54.1	16.8
18 31000	Hammond city	52 272	63.6	75.6	11.3	−13.1	12.5	9.8	0.0	34.4	6.5
18 34114	Hobart city	17 130	56.1	84.3	14.2	−10.2	14.2	26.3	0.0	50.0	5.5
18 36000	Indianapolis city	509 247	48.0	81.3	25.5	1.1	29.3	13.3	11.0	56.8	13.9
18 38358	Jeffersonville city	18 532	56.2	80.3	14.9	−9.5	15.3	10.6	12.5	47.8	6.6
18 40392	Kokomo city	30 257	58.5	79.4	15.8	−8.6	15.9	12.4	45.3	56.4	9.2
18 40788	Lafayette city	35 312	51.2	83.1	23.7	−0.7	24.8	16.9	14.6	56.5	7.8
18 42426	Lawrence city	24 454	43.2	85.6	26.8	2.4	27.3	24.5	38.4	45.2	12.3
18 46908	Marion city	19 871	65.9	73.3	13.4	−11.0	14.3	6.5	24.8	56.6	7.9
18 48528	Merrillville town	20 587	50.0	86.6	20.2	−4.2	18.8	26.1	0.0	47.8	14.3
18 48798	Michigan City city	21 616	63.5	76.3	12.1	−12.3	14.0	6.5	15.1	0.0	6.2
18 49932	Mishawaka city	30 056	55.6	80.8	18.1	−6.3	17.3	27.7	0.0	59.1	14.8
18 51876	Muncie city	37 584	58.7	75.8	19.0	−5.4	19.6	8.9	0.0	72.6	27.3
18 52326	New Albany city	24 888	57.0	76.1	15.9	−8.5	15.8	13.7	0.0	51.4	7.0
18 54180	Noblesville city	18 403	32.7	90.8	40.9	16.5	41.1	19.6	0.0	86.9	36.6
18 61092	Portage city	21 503	63.8	82.1	10.1	−14.3	10.4	15.9	0.0	0.0	6.6
18 64260	Richmond city	25 657	62.1	74.6	13.8	−10.6	14.1	8.3	0.0	34.0	15.3
18 71000	South Bend city	66 715	53.6	77.7	20.3	−4.1	24.5	7.6	13.9	52.3	8.3
18 75428	Terre Haute city	35 843	55.8	77.7	19.7	−4.7	20.1	10.6	7.0	77.6	14.0
18 78326	Valparaiso city	16 857	38.2	90.6	34.5	10.1	34.1	47.5	85.3	61.3	23.1
18 82862	West Lafayette city	10 159	14.0	96.2	69.7	45.3	66.4	68.1	0.0	90.9	78.5
19 00000	**IOWA**	1 895 856	50.0	86.1	21.2	−3.2	21.3	14.7	9.9	42.4	11.0
19 01855	Ames city	22 932	17.0	95.3	58.6	34.2	56.6	69.5	10.8	80.4	46.4
19 02305	Ankeny city	16 495	27.3	95.5	39.1	14.7	39.5	53.6	X	31.7	12.7
19 06355	Bettendorf city	20 963	30.3	92.6	38.8	14.4	38.9	35.0	15.0	61.7	27.4
19 09550	Burlington city	10 010	60.1	90.0	18.1	−6.0	16.7	6.5	14.0	36.1	4.9
19 11755	Cedar Falls city	18 779	32.5	92.6	39.2	14.8	38.6	38.0	37.9	74.7	40.0
19 12000	Cedar Rapids city	78 178	39.2	90.1	28.4	4.0	28.5	12.2	20.7	53.4	23.2
19 14430	Clinton city	18 374	56.2	84.2	14.9	−9.5	14.9	6.4	8.6	64.6	11.3
19 16860	Council Bluffs city	37 129	57.6	81.3	13.9	−10.5	14.0	5.0	18.4	28.3	11.6
19 19000	Davenport city	62 343	48.2	83.4	21.5	−2.9	22.8	10.6	7.2	29.6	11.4
19 21000	Des Moines city	128 664	50.5	83.0	21.8	−2.6	23.4	14.2	16.3	17.4	8.9
19 22395	Dubuque city	37 210	53.4	84.9	23.3	−1.1	23.4	22.2	14.1	53.6	12.5
19 28515	Fort Dodge city	16 296	50.6	83.8	19.4	−5.0	19.7	11.3	50.0	38.3	4.8
19 38595	Iowa City city	31 933	20.6	94.8	55.9	31.5	55.7	33.9	31.4	77.7	43.7
19 49485	Marion city	17 270	35.8	92.0	29.1	4.7	29.0	23.5	10.4	59.3	18.1
19 49755	Marshalltown city	17 302	56.6	79.0	18.0	−6.4	19.6	8.5	0.0	19.1	1.8
19 50160	Mason City city	19 326	47.0	86.5	20.0	−4.4	20.8	0.0	0.0	11.2	6.5
19 73335	Sioux City city	52 836	54.2	79.7	19.0	−5.4	21.0	11.1	2.3	11.7	2.8
19 79950	Urbandale city	19 336	25.2	96.2	43.7	19.3	44.4	32.7	14.9	35.9	29.8
19 82425	Waterloo city	44 516	52.8	83.8	19.4	−5.0	20.7	9.1	11.9	50.8	11.9
19 83910	West Des Moines city ...	30 455	21.9	96.3	48.5	24.1	49.1	31.7	0.0	69.9	18.9
20 00000	**KANSAS**	1 701 207	43.8	86.0	25.8	1.4	27.2	14.9	14.9	40.0	9.7
20 18250	Dodge City city	14 075	53.4	68.4	17.3	−7.1	25.4	9.5	0.0	0.0	4.1
20 21275	Emporia city	14 469	49.7	79.7	23.8	−0.6	28.1	9.7	17.3	15.0	5.2
20 25325	Garden City city	15 627	57.4	66.9	14.5	−9.9	21.9	0.0	21.7	14.9	3.0
20 33625	Hutchinson city	26 943	47.9	82.3	17.2	−7.2	18.3	8.2	6.0	25.5	6.2
20 36000	Kansas City city	89 540	61.0	73.4	11.7	−12.7	13.3	10.7	3.8	20.4	5.6
20 38900	Lawrence city	40 744	25.6	92.8	47.7	23.3	48.5	33.9	25.8	71.4	34.7
20 39000	Leavenworth city	22 555	44.6	84.5	27.0	2.6	29.6	18.3	7.7	20.7	13.1
20 39075	Leawood city	18 251	9.6	98.1	68.0	43.6	68.4	57.5	0.0	67.1	70.7
20 39350	Lenexa city	26 038	19.3	96.7	49.8	25.4	49.9	42.3	30.5	69.7	27.8
20 44250	Manhattan city	20 284	23.3	94.9	48.2	23.8	48.4	25.4	53.0	75.5	32.9
20 52575	Olathe city	55 828	27.9	92.7	39.9	15.5	41.3	29.5	34.8	45.0	17.8
20 53775	Overland Park city	100 477	19.0	95.8	52.1	27.7	52.6	50.2	23.3	67.0	29.5
20 62700	Salina city	29 352	48.3	86.1	20.3	−4.1	21.4	17.1	16.0	11.9	7.1
20 64500	Shawnee city	31 587	28.2	93.5	39.5	15.1	40.2	42.7	5.3	43.8	21.2
20 71000	Topeka city	80 126	47.3	85.9	25.3	0.9	28.0	11.6	13.8	43.7	12.2
20 79000	Wichita city	216 488	44.8	83.8	25.3	0.9	28.6	12.6	13.5	24.5	9.4
21 00000	**KENTUCKY**	2 646 397	59.4	74.1	17.1	−7.3	17.4	10.7	13.9	52.0	13.0
21 08902	Bowling Green city	27 526	48.9	77.9	26.9	2.5	29.5	10.1	13.3	45.1	7.6
21 17848	Covington city	27 804	63.5	71.3	13.3	−11.1	13.9	7.0	7.8	43.1	9.5
21 28900	Frankfort city	18 458	50.7	79.2	24.9	0.5	25.1	23.2	10.3	70.6	10.6
21 35866	Henderson city	18 423	60.8	76.6	14.0	−10.4	14.2	6.3	0.0	64.9	40.4

[1]Hispanic or Latino persons may be of any race.

Table B-5. Cities — **Education, Labor Force, and Income**

City	School enrollment			Population 16 to 19 years				Employment status, 2000			Work status in 1999 of the population 16 years and over		
											Worked in 1999		
	Grades kindergarten through 12	College or graduate school	Percent private	Number	Percent in armed forces	Percent high school graduates	Percent not enrolled, not grads, not in armed forces, not employed	Total population 16 years and over	Percent in labor force	Unemploy-ment rate	Full-time	Part-time	Did not work in 1999
	11	12	13	14	15	16	17	18	19	20	21	22	23
INDIANA—Cont'd													
Fort Wayne city	39 640	12 569	21.7	12 157	0.0	11.9	5.0	156 045	68.8	6.2	57.3	16.6	26.0
Gary city	22 967	4 897	9.8	6 672	0.0	11.4	7.7	75 511	55.9	14.9	45.7	14.0	40.3
Goshen city	5 193	1 260	19.3	1 791	0.0	10.4	7.9	22 556	67.6	4.0	59.9	14.9	25.2
Greenwood city	6 064	1 630	17.0	1 739	0.0	12.1	2.5	27 802	71.9	2.9	61.8	14.9	23.3
Hammond city	15 916	3 929	14.5	4 733	0.0	14.2	8.9	62 796	60.6	8.9	51.0	14.6	34.3
Hobart city	4 502	1 202	10.2	1 365	0.5	16.1	3.2	20 074	64.5	5.1	51.9	17.3	30.8
Indianapolis city	143 486	42 822	20.0	42 009	0.0	12.4	8.4	610 196	68.9	5.5	60.5	14.1	25.4
Jeffersonville city	4 642	1 185	11.7	1 380	0.0	15.3	6.7	21 619	68.2	5.9	59.5	13.2	27.3
Kokomo city	7 507	1 629	10.3	2 180	1.1	16.2	6.7	35 661	62.9	6.0	54.2	13.5	32.3
Lafayette city	8 877	5 144	8.7	2 783	0.0	16.7	5.4	44 615	70.0	4.5	58.7	17.8	23.5
Lawrence city	8 143	1 606	14.0	2 131	0.0	12.8	4.2	28 757	75.6	4.7	66.8	14.0	19.2
Marion city	5 024	2 278	28.6	1 880	0.0	11.7	6.9	24 597	57.2	8.8	49.7	15.0	35.3
Merrillville town	5 691	1 942	10.5	1 692	0.5	11.2	2.1	24 127	66.3	4.4	55.5	15.5	29.0
Michigan City city	5 819	1 658	13.6	1 585	0.0	12.9	9.4	25 508	59.2	5.6	53.5	15.3	31.3
Mishawaka city	7 766	3 179	22.2	2 623	0.0	12.4	3.4	36 841	68.6	4.1	57.1	17.0	25.9
Muncie city	9 376	13 983	3.4	6 041	0.0	5.8	2.4	55 391	61.2	9.7	45.4	25.1	29.4
New Albany city	6 536	1 747	14.7	1 809	0.0	9.1	9.0	29 263	65.0	4.8	55.6	14.9	29.5
Noblesville city	5 635	1 186	9.3	1 421	0.0	7.2	4.3	21 280	72.0	2.7	62.5	17.1	20.4
Portage city	6 353	1 447	8.9	1 890	0.0	13.2	3.7	25 790	65.7	4.8	55.5	16.0	28.5
Richmond city	6 384	2 391	16.1	2 372	0.0	13.4	11.2	31 046	62.8	9.1	52.3	16.0	31.7
South Bend city	19 947	6 466	21.7	5 651	0.0	11.8	10.3	80 679	63.7	8.2	53.7	15.8	30.5
Terre Haute city	9 314	9 022	12.4	4 617	0.0	5.9	3.5	48 066	58.0	8.2	48.1	19.4	32.4
Valparaiso city	4 231	3 751	39.6	2 174	0.0	8.4	2.9	22 401	64.8	4.3	53.3	20.8	25.9
West Lafayette city	2 161	17 210	3.9	3 438	0.0	1.4	0.4	26 386	58.2	10.5	47.1	35.4	17.6
IOWA	552 637	187 306	13.8	178 931	0.1	9.2	2.8	2 281 274	68.2	4.2	56.1	18.2	25.7
Ames city	5 190	21 428	2.6	6 558	0.0	3.8	0.4	44 175	69.3	5.4	47.5	37.3	15.2
Ankeny city	5 230	2 080	11.0	1 638	0.0	9.2	1.5	20 361	80.8	3.8	65.1	19.6	15.4
Bettendorf city	6 395	1 626	13.4	1 824	0.0	7.9	1.8	24 097	69.4	3.6	57.3	17.8	24.8
Burlington city	4 682	1 084	12.6	1 496	0.0	11.3	4.3	21 080	65.1	6.3	51.4	17.6	31.0
Cedar Falls city	4 931	10 845	4.5	3 855	0.0	3.6	0.7	30 691	68.9	4.0	46.1	33.3	20.6
Cedar Rapids city	21 405	7 673	17.9	7 057	0.0	11.6	2.9	94 226	71.5	4.0	59.9	17.3	22.8
Clinton city	5 184	1 302	13.7	1 484	0.0	7.1	6.4	21 671	62.1	6.0	51.7	15.6	32.7
Council Bluffs city	10 980	2 444	9.3	3 456	0.0	12.6	6.6	44 907	67.6	4.5	58.7	14.6	26.7
Davenport city	18 132	7 928	22.6	5 420	0.0	13.8	5.1	75 506	67.4	6.1	54.9	18.5	26.7
Des Moines city	34 110	11 605	20.6	10 460	0.0	14.7	6.0	154 365	70.2	6.7	60.5	15.1	24.4
Dubuque city	9 999	4 549	40.8	3 433	0.1	7.9	1.1	45 399	67.4	5.4	52.4	19.9	27.7
Fort Dodge city	4 474	1 367	14.6	1 639	0.0	11.5	4.9	19 720	63.3	4.8	51.5	17.7	30.8
Iowa City city	7 573	21 759	4.4	6 765	0.2	4.1	0.7	53 494	71.4	4.2	49.2	35.7	15.2
Marion city	5 064	1 189	11.2	1 411	0.0	8.5	0.0	20 310	76.3	2.8	62.3	18.0	19.7
Marshalltown city	4 932	984	8.9	1 541	0.0	10.3	7.7	20 448	62.7	5.3	53.2	14.5	32.2
Mason City city	5 073	1 552	14.2	1 638	0.0	9.2	2.3	22 963	66.6	5.4	53.5	18.1	28.5
Sioux City city	16 654	4 254	19.0	5 200	0.0	10.9	5.2	64 557	68.3	4.4	57.1	16.9	26.0
Urbandale city	5 791	1 392	17.5	1 437	0.6	13.0	0.4	22 284	76.6	2.3	64.6	16.9	18.5
Waterloo city	12 444	4 185	14.6	3 562	0.2	12.3	3.6	53 386	64.0	6.0	52.3	16.8	30.9
West Des Moines city	7 833	2 964	21.6	1 861	0.0	10.2	1.9	35 876	77.5	1.7	67.1	15.0	17.9
KANSAS	529 202	176 453	11.5	166 014	0.7	10.0	4.0	2 059 160	67.5	4.2	57.5	16.2	26.2
Dodge City city	5 371	1 042	7.3	1 659	0.0	11.7	8.6	18 035	68.8	5.6	60.3	12.6	27.1
Emporia city	4 975	3 746	2.7	2 360	0.0	11.1	4.8	20 708	68.6	6.9	53.4	21.0	25.6
Garden City city	6 388	1 316	5.8	1 982	0.0	6.0	10.4	19 825	69.6	5.3	62.5	13.6	23.8
Hutchinson city	7 093	1 838	9.3	2 287	0.0	11.9	4.4	32 265	60.1	5.8	55.0	13.8	31.2
Kansas City city	30 248	6 504	11.8	8 689	0.0	13.8	11.2	109 206	63.1	8.5	57.1	12.1	30.7
Lawrence city	10 785	24 192	5.6	8 068	0.1	5.1	1.0	66 862	70.7	5.1	51.1	30.8	18.1
Leavenworth city	6 797	2 375	16.2	1 709	2.2	14.5	2.7	26 582	59.7	4.0	58.0	13.3	28.7
Leawood city	6 665	1 008	27.1	1 511	0.0	1.9	0.7	20 404	66.3	1.6	53.3	20.3	26.4
Lenexa city	7 645	2 636	17.1	2 095	0.0	6.1	0.3	31 001	76.9	2.5	64.4	17.6	18.0
Manhattan city	5 100	17 769	3.4	5 481	1.0	6.3	0.9	38 661	69.4	7.1	50.6	32.2	17.1
Olathe city	20 099	5 962	14.6	5 551	0.0	8.7	2.4	67 396	78.9	2.6	67.0	17.4	15.6
Overland Park city	27 620	7 552	16.9	6 940	0.0	8.0	2.1	114 576	72.3	2.3	61.5	16.2	22.3
Salina city	8 886	2 070	14.2	2 749	0.0	8.5	4.2	35 204	69.0	3.6	58.8	16.1	25.1
Shawnee city	9 206	2 676	18.0	2 467	0.0	11.4	1.3	36 592	75.9	1.9	65.8	15.6	18.7
Topeka city	20 728	6 687	15.8	6 789	0.0	16.0	7.7	95 771	65.0	4.7	56.5	14.1	29.4
Wichita city	66 438	22 026	15.6	18 510	0.1	11.9	6.7	260 390	67.8	5.3	59.6	13.9	26.5
KENTUCKY	738 747	206 367	13.3	228 979	0.8	11.9	7.1	3 161 542	60.9	5.7	52.4	13.6	34.0
Bowling Green city	7 155	8 989	4.8	4 472	0.0	7.5	5.0	40 313	65.1	7.8	50.2	22.0	27.8
Covington city	7 946	1 591	16.4	2 138	0.0	16.7	12.4	33 213	63.3	6.2	57.4	12.2	30.3
Frankfort city	4 215	1 991	9.1	1 514	0.0	10.8	5.7	22 230	64.3	8.3	57.3	12.7	30.0
Henderson city	4 667	792	10.4	1 449	0.0	15.9	6.3	21 664	61.6	6.1	53.9	12.4	33.7

Table B-5. Cities — Education, Labor Force, and Income

City	Full-year full-time employed (percent)								Children under 18 years in families (percent, except where noted)						Total employed by class of worker (percent)			
				Non-Hispanic White	Black or African American	American Indian and Alaska Native	Asian, Hawaiian, and Pacific Islander	Hispanic or Latino[1]		With two parents		With one parent who is in labor force	+/- U.S. percent of children with no stay-at-home parent	+/- U.S. percent two-income couples				Unpaid family worker
	Total	Men	Women						Number	Both in labor force	Father only in labor force				Private	Government	Self-employed	
	24	25	26	27	28	29	30	31	32	33	34	35	36	37	38	39	40	41
INDIANA—Cont'd																		
Fort Wayne city	43.3	53.3	34.2	44.8	37.5	44.1	35.5	41.4	52 610	41.0	17.8	29.1	5.5	4.8	84.7	8.9	6.2	0.2
Gary city	30.1	34.3	26.9	30.7	29.9	45.8	24.7	32.3	26 724	18.8	9.8	43.9	-1.9	-12.0	76.6	18.1	5.2	0.2
Goshen city	43.1	54.2	31.8	43.8	20.8	18.0	27.2	43.8	6 973	45.1	21.6	20.4	0.9	3.2	88.4	5.4	6.1	0.1
Greenwood city	48.7	61.9	37.1	49.0	48.3	0.0	34.9	56.0	8 736	51.0	21.1	21.4	7.8	9.1	85.3	9.0	5.6	0.1
Hammond city	35.9	45.2	27.4	36.9	36.4	26.7	27.7	32.5	21 245	34.0	19.1	29.2	-1.4	-10.0	85.2	10.4	4.2	0.2
Hobart city	40.9	52.8	29.9	40.7	54.5	30.2	59.4	37.9	5 715	46.9	27.4	19.7	2.0	-3.0	84.8	9.7	5.3	0.1
Indianapolis city	46.1	54.2	38.7	48.2	40.6	36.6	46.9	40.1	189 050	39.9	16.5	30.2	5.5	5.3	81.7	10.6	7.5	0.1
Jeffersonville city	47.3	56.3	39.3	48.0	43.8	67.8	47.8	40.8	6 186	41.9	14.2	30.9	8.2	6.5	79.9	13.7	6.3	0.1
Kokomo city	40.7	52.4	30.6	41.2	38.0	49.0	35.0	36.2	10 683	37.9	21.0	29.0	2.3	-5.1	84.6	9.6	5.6	0.2
Lafayette city	43.5	52.6	34.8	44.9	43.5	40.8	31.8	31.3	12 158	44.1	19.4	23.2	2.7	4.3	78.1	15.6	5.9	0.3
Lawrence city	53.7	62.4	45.6	54.8	53.5	35.5	54.7	40.7	10 907	51.6	15.4	26.9	13.9	13.1	80.4	11.3	8.2	0.1
Marion city	34.3	42.6	27.4	33.4	39.5	19.5	42.9	40.7	6 659	38.9	12.8	34.3	8.6	-4.7	82.9	10.8	6.1	0.3
Merrillville town	43.1	56.0	31.9	40.4	49.9	52.7	47.7	48.0	7 137	48.3	23.6	19.6	3.3	1.9	81.8	12.6	5.4	0.1
Michigan City city	38.8	44.0	33.6	40.6	34.7	59.8	25.6	31.7	7 532	34.7	12.7	39.0	9.1	-2.5	82.9	11.7	5.0	0.4
Mishawaka city	44.0	56.0	33.5	44.2	46.7	36.1	42.4	44.4	10 533	44.0	17.4	28.3	7.7	3.3	86.6	7.8	5.5	0.1
Muncie city	28.9	36.4	22.6	29.3	29.4	32.0	15.0	18.1	12 309	35.5	16.6	31.8	2.7	-5.4	77.2	17.3	5.1	0.4
New Albany city	42.8	52.1	34.8	42.7	42.2	47.6	52.2	60.5	8 610	41.3	14.5	29.8	6.5	2.5	81.0	11.5	7.4	0.2
Noblesville city	49.5	66.2	33.7	49.8	43.4	71.4	63.1	35.7	8 307	56.1	23.7	14.2	5.7	13.0	79.5	11.5	8.9	0.1
Portage city	43.3	56.6	30.8	43.7	49.6	51.1	11.1	40.0	8 258	38.4	28.9	21.9	-4.3	-2.6	85.4	9.5	5.0	0.1
Richmond city	36.5	46.5	27.9	36.7	36.1	38.3	31.7	34.7	8 532	44.3	15.0	27.7	7.4	0.8	83.9	9.6	6.0	0.5
South Bend city	38.4	47.9	30.2	39.9	34.7	50.0	34.2	36.3	26 646	35.8	17.6	32.4	3.6	1.5	83.3	10.0	6.5	0.2
Terre Haute city	32.2	39.3	25.4	33.0	27.5	30.5	19.3	23.3	11 845	33.1	19.4	30.4	-1.1	-2.2	78.4	15.3	5.8	0.4
Valparaiso city	38.2	50.6	27.2	38.1	34.3	0.0	32.9	47.0	5 662	45.1	26.8	21.9	2.4	2.5	80.7	12.1	7.1	0.1
West Lafayette city	17.8	21.1	13.2	18.2	17.7	67.6	13.5	20.4	2 888	48.8	33.9	12.8	-3.0	-1.7	63.1	32.0	4.2	0.7
IOWA	43.3	52.9	34.3	43.8	33.0	30.3	38.5	38.1	703 382	59.1	15.3	17.9	12.4	9.1	74.8	13.6	11.1	0.4
Ames city	28.5	32.7	23.9	29.8	19.9	10.0	16.6	26.9	7 173	61.0	17.4	14.3	10.7	12.8	56.3	37.9	5.5	0.3
Ankeny city	53.6	65.0	43.3	53.7	52.0	0.0	48.7	64.7	7 178	63.4	18.2	15.9	14.7	22.0	80.0	13.7	6.2	0.2
Bettendorf city	43.2	58.7	31.0	43.6	39.1	70.0	30.7	43.1	6 042	53.3	26.2	15.7	4.4	5.1	76.6	12.8	10.3	0.0
Burlington city	39.1	50.2	29.2	39.9	27.1	26.0	36.9	21.5	6 225	49.2	14.8	24.1	8.7	2.6	81.7	10.7	7.4	0.0
Cedar Falls city	31.1	40.4	23.0	31.4	30.1	8.1	21.4	36.2	6 243	56.7	16.6	18.9	11.0	7.5	70.7	22.0	7.2	0.1
Cedar Rapids city	47.8	57.5	38.9	48.5	35.3	46.5	46.9	41.3	28 086	54.3	16.2	21.4	11.1	10.1	84.0	9.7	6.2	0.1
Clinton city	38.2	48.5	29.0	38.5	30.3	13.6	43.4	37.4	6 540	50.2	15.6	24.5	10.1	-4.3	82.7	10.0	7.0	0.3
Council Bluffs city	45.8	53.5	38.8	46.2	30.2	38.9	43.1	44.8	14 091	46.1	12.1	28.4	9.9	6.6	82.4	10.8	6.8	0.1
Davenport city	41.6	49.7	34.2	42.8	30.8	35.8	44.8	37.4	23 952	47.4	14.2	26.4	9.2	4.5	82.0	11.0	7.0	0.1
Des Moines city	46.5	53.3	40.2	48.0	38.2	36.9	42.0	38.9	45 834	46.6	15.4	25.4	7.4	7.0	81.1	12.4	6.4	0.1
Dubuque city	40.0	49.8	31.5	40.4	33.3	22.9	34.4	31.0	10 002	57.0	14.6	18.8	11.2	7.1	85.4	8.8	5.6	0.3
Fort Dodge city	39.0	48.1	31.2	39.6	35.6	29.6	38.5	22.9	5 903	52.9	12.6	24.1	12.4	7.2	80.2	12.0	7.6	0.2
Iowa City city	33.1	39.5	26.9	33.6	28.5	29.0	28.0	34.9	9 835	56.8	19.3	15.9	8.1	10.8	59.5	34.8	5.5	0.2
Marion city	51.2	62.2	40.9	51.0	54.3	51.4	80.2	49.2	6 821	65.7	12.9	15.3	16.4	17.5	82.7	10.1	7.2	0.0
Marshalltown city	39.6	48.8	30.8	40.4	37.5	10.0	33.7	33.8	5 988	45.0	19.0	25.8	6.2	3.4	77.4	14.8	7.7	0.1
Mason City city	40.9	50.5	32.8	41.4	26.0	15.9	64.0	27.2	6 547	58.3	11.3	23.4	17.1	6.5	81.5	9.2	9.0	0.3
Sioux City city	43.0	51.9	34.9	43.6	36.2	24.7	54.0	38.8	21 697	50.0	15.3	22.6	8.0	8.6	82.4	9.9	7.5	0.3
Urbandale city	55.2	65.6	45.9	55.5	40.9	35.9	67.3	43.9	7 484	64.0	20.3	12.2	11.6	16.1	77.7	13.2	8.9	0.3
Waterloo city	38.7	46.0	32.1	40.2	28.0	21.8	47.9	33.0	16 108	43.3	16.0	26.2	4.9	1.1	80.5	11.7	7.6	0.2
West Des Moines city	56.3	67.9	46.2	57.1	51.3	41.0	48.3	48.3	11 217	56.4	21.4	15.4	7.2	12.8	80.8	10.7	8.3	0.2
KANSAS	43.9	54.5	33.8	44.7	38.4	40.4	40.0	40.1	680 064	51.6	20.8	18.9	5.9	6.3	73.3	15.5	10.8	0.4
Dodge City city	43.6	53.6	32.9	47.0	33.8	10.7	28.1	39.1	7 306	47.9	19.8	19.0	2.3	7.0	78.0	14.4	7.4	0.2
Emporia city	38.7	50.2	28.0	38.0	40.9	56.1	43.8	40.9	6 462	45.1	19.4	24.1	4.6	3.6	74.4	19.0	6.2	0.3
Garden City city	44.5	54.2	34.7	47.7	28.6	33.7	52.9	40.0	8 671	45.6	18.9	16.7	-2.3	6.8	75.8	15.0	8.7	0.5
Hutchinson city	39.3	47.3	31.2	40.0	32.7	33.2	38.1	37.0	9 104	46.2	16.8	28.1	9.7	0.2	79.6	12.5	7.8	0.1
Kansas City city	40.6	47.6	34.2	42.9	36.6	38.7	44.9	39.9	38 545	31.9	15.2	33.2	0.5	-3.2	79.0	15.1	5.6	0.2
Lawrence city	34.4	41.0	27.9	35.6	36.0	28.9	22.3	26.2	14 478	50.8	19.9	22.0	8.2	12.3	68.1	24.5	7.2	0.1
Leavenworth city	39.6	45.7	32.6	42.3	30.8	15.0	38.1	32.2	9 242	42.0	17.2	29.6	21.7	1.6	65.4	28.4	5.8	0.3
Leawood city	44.2	62.8	26.9	44.0	51.4	76.7	44.4	49.3	8 407	48.0	42.6	5.9	-10.7	-1.6	73.9	6.5	19.3	0.3
Lenexa city	51.9	63.6	41.0	52.1	43.4	59.2	45.8	55.8	10 252	55.9	26.0	13.4	4.7	14.6	81.7	9.3	8.8	0.1
Manhattan city	29.7	35.4	23.7	29.6	38.5	28.0	25.4	25.8	6 829	51.5	20.5	20.1	7.0	8.5	57.9	35.6	6.2	0.3
Olathe city	54.8	68.1	42.1	55.5	52.7	43.8	49.4	49.3	27 914	57.0	22.6	15.8	8.2	17.8	80.2	11.7	8.0	0.1
Overland Park city	50.0	64.0	37.4	50.4	53.1	42.7	45.1	46.7	37 521	51.9	30.5	12.2	-0.5	7.1	79.6	10.0	10.3	0.1
Salina city	45.6	55.4	36.4	46.0	44.2	62.2	53.2	38.0	11 237	53.0	14.5	21.5	9.9	9.3	79.7	11.4	8.7	0.2
Shawnee city	53.9	65.3	43.2	54.4	49.7	85.0	51.1	49.7	12 507	50.9	22.3	13.0	8.3	14.5	79.7	11.7	8.5	0.2
Topeka city	43.2	50.0	37.2	44.1	39.9	37.0	35.3	41.1	27 601	43.8	15.1	29.6	8.8	5.5	72.7	20.6	6.6	0.1
Wichita city	45.7	56.3	35.8	47.5	39.1	43.7	39.9	41.4	87 757	43.9	21.4	23.1	2.4	3.2	81.0	11.3	7.4	0.2
KENTUCKY	38.7	48.1	30.0	39.0	35.9	34.5	39.7	37.3	939 639	43.1	21.8	19.7	-1.8	-2.9	75.5	14.4	9.6	0.4
Bowling Green city	34.2	43.1	26.2	34.3	32.9	24.8	35.6	36.3	9 246	36.4	19.8	28.6	0.4	2.1	76.1	16.7	6.9	0.3
Covington city	42.7	51.2	34.9	43.9	33.9	34.5	40.9	42.2	10 281	33.0	15.7	31.3	-0.3	1.1	83.6	11.3	4.9	0.2
Frankfort city	42.7	49.9	36.5	45.2	31.6	53.6	17.4	31.8	5 667	46.5	12.1	29.2	11.1	5.2	53.1	40.1	6.8	0.1
Henderson city	40.9	50.3	32.7	41.2	39.7	0.0	37.9	38.2	6 048	40.9	17.8	25.2	1.5	1.5	82.1	9.8	7.6	0.5

[1]Hispanic or Latino persons may be of any race.

Table B-5. Cities — Education, Labor Force, and Income

City	Percent who worked at home	Percent of the population 5 years and over with a disability	Veterans as a percent of the population 18 years and over	Occupation for employed population 16 years and over (percent)						Industry for employed population 16 years and over (percent)					
				Management, professional, and related occupations	Service occupations	Sales and office occupations	Farming, fishing, and forestry occupations	Construction, extraction, and maintenance occupations	Production, transportation and material moving occupations	Agriculture, forestry, fishing, and mining	Construction and manufacturing	Wholesale and retail trade	Transportation and warehousing, and utilities	Service industries	Public administration
	42	43	44	45	46	47	48	49	50	51	52	53	54	55	56
INDIANA—Cont'd															
Fort Wayne city	2.0	19.3	12.2	28.7	14.8	27.9	0.1	8.1	20.4	0.2	26.7	17.0	4.6	49.0	2.4
Gary city	1.7	26.9	13.4	20.6	24.0	26.8	0.0	7.3	21.3	0.1	22.3	11.8	6.3	53.8	5.7
Goshen city	1.8	18.5	9.7	24.8	12.1	20.0	0.3	7.7	35.1	0.4	46.7	11.9	2.1	37.6	1.3
Greenwood city	1.9	16.3	12.6	35.6	12.0	30.0	0.1	10.0	12.3	0.1	21.5	18.9	6.9	49.9	2.6
Hammond city	1.5	22.1	13.8	20.5	17.6	28.7	0.0	10.9	22.4	0.1	25.5	15.8	7.0	48.1	3.6
Hobart city	2.1	17.9	15.1	25.3	14.2	26.9	0.1	15.1	18.5	0.4	29.2	16.6	6.5	43.2	4.2
Indianapolis city	2.5	20.3	12.5	32.9	14.9	28.3	0.1	8.6	15.2	0.2	19.8	16.4	6.3	53.1	4.3
Jeffersonville city	1.3	20.1	15.2	26.9	14.9	29.8	0.0	8.9	19.6	0.1	23.8	13.8	7.7	47.6	7.0
Kokomo city	1.8	23.7	15.0	23.7	17.3	21.1	0.1	9.7	28.0	0.2	37.5	14.1	3.0	41.2	4.0
Lafayette city	2.2	19.1	12.5	29.8	16.7	24.1	0.3	8.0	21.2	0.5	28.0	14.1	3.0	52.2	2.2
Lawrence city	2.5	17.3	13.7	36.0	11.4	31.0	0.1	8.7	12.8	0.2	21.8	18.1	4.7	49.7	5.4
Marion city	2.7	25.8	14.4	23.0	18.7	21.5	0.1	7.2	29.5	0.5	33.1	13.3	2.9	47.7	2.5
Merrillville town	1.5	17.8	14.2	28.3	14.3	28.0	0.1	9.6	19.7	0.2	24.9	14.2	7.0	49.7	3.9
Michigan City city	1.4	23.1	15.3	21.3	21.3	25.7	0.2	9.3	22.2	0.4	28.2	15.2	4.3	46.2	5.7
Mishawaka city	1.3	20.0	13.1	27.1	15.5	29.0	0.1	8.2	20.1	0.1	26.4	18.9	4.1	47.8	2.6
Muncie city	2.5	20.8	11.1	27.7	20.4	28.0	0.2	6.6	17.1	0.2	18.9	16.1	3.3	58.7	2.7
New Albany city	2.0	21.9	15.2	25.5	15.7	28.1	0.1	9.9	20.8	0.1	26.9	14.3	5.8	48.1	4.8
Noblesville city	3.9	13.4	11.9	43.9	10.3	28.1	0.1	7.2	10.3	0.6	22.9	16.9	2.1	54.0	3.5
Portage city	1.2	18.4	15.0	20.7	16.8	23.5	0.0	15.7	23.2	0.1	33.6	12.5	8.2	43.2	2.4
Richmond city	1.7	24.2	14.1	23.8	17.0	25.2	0.3	8.0	25.7	0.4	30.0	16.9	3.2	47.0	2.5
South Bend city	2.4	21.8	12.7	28.2	16.9	25.6	0.1	7.2	22.0	0.2	24.8	16.0	4.1	52.4	2.5
Terre Haute city	1.8	22.7	12.1	28.5	20.5	28.6	0.2	6.9	15.2	0.4	17.4	19.6	2.9	56.4	3.3
Valparaiso city	2.9	14.4	11.9	38.3	14.4	26.5	0.0	9.2	11.7	0.1	21.6	14.7	3.4	57.3	2.7
West Lafayette city	2.7	9.5	4.9	52.7	16.9	20.6	1.1	2.6	6.0	1.3	10.4	12.5	0.8	73.3	1.7
IOWA	4.7	16.6	13.3	31.3	14.8	25.9	1.1	8.9	18.1	4.4	23.2	15.6	4.9	48.4	3.4
Ames city	3.2	8.3	7.0	47.3	15.6	24.5	1.2	4.7	6.7	1.4	10.1	12.4	2.2	69.3	4.6
Ankeny city	3.2	11.0	10.8	40.9	11.9	32.4	0.2	5.2	9.3	0.8	12.5	18.4	4.5	59.2	4.6
Bettendorf city	3.0	12.9	14.5	42.2	12.2	27.9	0.1	6.1	11.5	0.2	22.1	17.3	5.6	50.5	4.3
Burlington city	2.5	19.2	15.7	24.3	15.0	25.7	0.2	10.1	24.7	0.5	30.0	18.9	5.9	41.4	3.3
Cedar Falls city	2.7	13.2	10.5	37.3	17.9	28.8	0.4	5.5	10.2	0.8	15.1	16.8	2.8	61.9	2.7
Cedar Rapids city	2.3	16.1	14.8	34.6	12.4	30.2	0.2	7.3	15.3	0.4	23.1	16.3	4.5	53.0	2.7
Clinton city	2.3	22.9	16.4	22.2	16.9	25.0	0.2	8.9	26.9	0.8	30.0	14.9	5.6	46.3	2.4
Council Bluffs city	2.0	21.6	15.4	23.5	17.0	31.0	0.2	10.2	18.1	0.6	19.1	17.4	7.5	52.3	3.1
Davenport city	2.5	18.4	13.9	28.7	17.4	28.4	0.1	7.7	17.7	0.2	21.8	17.5	5.1	51.1	4.2
Des Moines city	2.3	20.2	12.5	29.1	16.2	31.1	0.2	9.4	14.0	0.3	16.4	16.1	5.4	56.9	4.9
Dubuque city	2.3	17.3	13.7	29.6	17.0	27.1	0.4	6.4	19.5	0.6	22.3	17.6	3.8	53.7	2.0
Fort Dodge city	1.4	18.8	14.4	28.3	17.7	26.7	0.6	7.4	19.3	1.8	21.5	18.9	5.4	48.1	4.2
Iowa City city	2.5	11.9	6.6	43.6	17.2	27.0	0.2	4.2	7.8	0.3	8.7	13.5	2.2	73.3	2.0
Marion city	3.1	14.0	13.8	35.2	13.8	31.4	0.0	7.2	12.4	0.3	24.1	17.9	4.1	51.1	2.5
Marshalltown city	1.9	18.8	15.0	26.9	17.1	23.2	0.5	8.3	24.1	1.1	33.3	13.5	3.4	45.7	3.0
Mason City city	2.5	18.1	13.6	27.8	16.6	27.9	0.2	7.7	19.7	0.4	23.9	18.2	4.0	50.6	2.8
Sioux City city	2.2	18.7	13.8	27.1	16.6	27.2	0.3	8.3	20.5	0.7	28.9	15.9	4.5	46.9	3.1
Urbandale city	4.2	10.4	12.3	45.8	10.3	31.8	0.1	4.7	7.3	0.7	11.6	16.7	3.7	62.2	5.1
Waterloo city	2.0	22.0	14.7	27.6	15.6	26.6	0.2	8.5	21.5	0.4	26.4	16.1	4.1	50.1	2.9
West Des Moines city	3.7	11.7	11.2	50.0	9.7	30.4	0.1	4.3	5.5	0.2	10.0	15.6	4.0	66.1	4.1
KANSAS	4.0	17.6	13.5	33.9	14.4	25.8	1.0	9.9	15.0	3.8	21.5	14.8	5.2	50.1	4.4
Dodge City city	1.4	18.3	9.0	22.8	14.5	23.1	2.0	10.1	27.5	3.5	33.5	14.5	4.7	40.5	3.3
Emporia city	1.9	17.1	10.3	24.1	18.1	24.1	0.9	8.2	24.6	0.8	27.6	15.3	3.5	48.4	4.3
Garden City city	2.6	15.6	8.6	24.0	14.6	22.8	1.9	9.8	26.9	4.2	31.2	15.5	5.2	39.2	4.5
Hutchinson city	2.2	22.8	14.9	27.3	18.6	26.5	0.4	8.4	18.7	1.2	22.6	17.7	4.4	50.1	4.1
Kansas City city	2.0	24.7	13.1	21.5	17.4	27.8	0.3	11.5	21.4	0.4	21.8	15.5	8.5	48.8	5.0
Lawrence city	3.2	13.0	7.8	41.9	17.3	25.3	0.1	6.1	9.1	0.4	13.0	14.0	2.7	66.1	3.8
Leavenworth city	2.7	22.6	22.9	30.4	22.4	27.8	0.2	8.7	10.5	0.3	12.4	13.6	4.2	56.5	13.0
Leawood city	6.7	8.5	14.5	62.0	6.2	27.6	0.0	2.0	2.3	0.2	11.1	15.8	2.7	68.4	1.8
Lenexa city	4.6	9.8	11.0	48.2	9.4	31.0	0.0	4.9	6.5	0.3	13.9	18.5	4.5	59.7	3.1
Manhattan city	2.9	10.0	9.2	39.9	19.1	27.1	0.8	7.0	6.3	1.3	8.5	14.8	1.7	69.0	4.8
Olathe city	4.0	12.5	10.9	43.0	11.5	29.3	0.1	7.3	8.8	0.2	17.1	17.6	5.0	56.7	3.3
Overland Park city	5.1	11.9	12.2	50.9	9.5	30.2	0.0	4.1	5.3	0.2	12.9	16.7	3.7	63.6	2.9
Salina city	3.3	18.5	14.8	27.3	16.5	26.5	0.3	10.4	19.0	1.1	24.6	16.2	3.8	51.0	3.2
Shawnee city	3.9	11.7	12.2	43.4	9.6	29.7	0.2	7.5	9.6	0.3	17.7	17.2	6.1	55.5	3.2
Topeka city	2.2	22.8	15.8	33.0	15.5	29.5	0.3	8.5	13.2	0.6	15.0	14.6	5.8	54.1	9.9
Wichita city	2.3	19.0	13.6	31.6	14.3	27.2	0.2	10.7	16.0	0.5	29.4	15.0	3.8	48.0	3.3
KENTUCKY	2.7	23.7	12.5	28.7	14.3	25.4	0.9	11.0	19.7	3.3	24.8	15.5	6.0	46.1	4.3
Bowling Green city	1.7	20.6	10.5	29.1	16.9	29.9	0.6	5.9	17.6	0.9	21.8	18.7	3.9	51.5	3.2
Covington city	1.4	25.7	13.4	23.6	18.6	29.8	0.1	9.3	18.7	0.4	20.5	16.3	7.1	50.5	5.3
Frankfort city	2.1	23.6	13.2	35.6	14.2	28.2	0.1	8.2	13.7	0.6	18.3	11.3	2.0	39.8	28.0
Henderson city	1.9	25.1	12.4	24.3	14.8	26.1	0.3	9.7	24.8	1.7	31.0	15.8	4.2	44.1	3.1

Table B-5. Cities — Education, Labor Force, and Income

City	Median house-hold income	All families	Married-couple	Male house-holder	Female house-holder	Median nonfamily house-hold income	Men	Women	Per capita income	With earnings	With interest, dividend, or rental income	With Social Security income	With public assis-tance income	With retire-ment income	House-holds with income over $100,000 (percent)	+/- U.S. percent for income over $100,000	House-holds with income below poverty (percent)	Families with children with income below poverty (percent)
			Families with children															
	57	58	59	60	61	62	63	64	65	66	67	68	69	70	71	72	73	74
INDIANA—Cont'd																		
Fort Wayne city	36 518	45 040	54 461	27 186	19 594	24 187	35 436	25 639	18 517	82.0	32.9	24.8	3.1	15.7	6.1	-6.2	11.3	14.5
Gary city	27 195	32 205	51 534	25 795	14 323	16 493	35 861	25 334	14 383	72.8	16.1	31.9	11.0	21.3	5.3	-7.0	24.4	31.5
Goshen city	39 383	46 877	52 400	27 083	22 235	23 232	32 912	24 456	18 899	81.9	39.1	28.0	2.0	13.5	6.3	-6.0	7.1	9.7
Greenwood city	46 176	57 298	64 523	43 929	27 520	28 428	40 872	29 929	23 003	83.7	36.0	22.4	1.3	14.4	10.6	-1.7	7.0	7.4
Hammond city	35 528	42 221	50 742	29 099	18 897	22 164	36 540	26 153	16 254	76.7	30.2	29.3	5.0	19.1	4.4	-7.9	13.6	18.1
Hobart city	47 759	55 078	58 721	42 639	25 893	27 416	45 746	27 320	21 508	79.5	39.5	32.3	1.6	22.0	8.5	-3.8	4.7	5.3
Indianapolis city	40 154	48 979	61 696	30 229	20 872	27 756	37 126	28 717	21 789	83.7	29.8	22.5	3.1	15.4	9.8	-2.5	10.9	13.7
Jeffersonville city	37 234	45 264	54 292	26 723	21 596	22 153	33 994	25 427	19 656	81.1	30.8	24.4	3.1	17.2	6.8	-5.5	10.8	11.8
Kokomo city	36 258	45 353	56 221	36 875	16 756	22 857	39 957	25 767	20 083	75.8	29.7	29.6	4.4	22.6	6.2	-6.1	12.4	15.9
Lafayette city	35 859	45 480	52 335	22 699	20 307	23 743	34 288	24 200	19 217	83.8	36.6	23.1	2.7	15.1	5.8	-6.5	11.5	13.1
Lawrence city	47 838	56 609	68 260	26 875	30 539	31 239	40 287	31 171	22 543	90.1	30.0	17.3	2.3	14.1	12.5	0.2	5.8	7.2
Marion city	30 440	37 717	44 017	26 719	15 461	17 653	31 004	24 583	16 378	71.0	30.0	35.8	4.3	21.8	5.8	-6.5	16.1	20.2
Merrillville town	49 545	56 355	64 468	39 609	33 873	31 315	43 350	29 557	22 293	80.7	30.2	20.0	1.4	21.1	8.6	-3.7	4.9	4.2
Michigan City city	33 732	39 520	50 887	29 286	18 909	23 515	33 556	24 121	16 995	80.2	29.3	28.9	4.7	16.4	4.2	-8.1	11.8	15.5
Mishawaka city	33 986	41 947	53 076	31 194	20 496	23 622	34 367	24 309	18 434	80.9	32.1	25.5	2.7	14.5	4.2	-8.1	10.1	11.6
Muncie city	26 613	36 398	44 461	25 541	15 686	18 001	30 933	22 433	15 814	75.5	28.9	29.7	4.3	18.5	3.8	-8.5	22.5	21.3
New Albany city	34 923	41 993	54 223	23 704	14 102	22 619	32 311	25 423	18 365	78.7	33.2	28.6	4.2	18.3	4.8	-7.5	13.1	19.8
Noblesville city	61 455	70 914	80 761	33 182	17 221	29 300	50 144	33 479	28 813	87.6	43.3	17.8	1.6	12.8	21.4	9.1	5.4	6.1
Portage city	47 500	54 316	61 211	35 111	21 767	25 812	46 616	26 344	20 146	82.4	33.2	24.9	2.8	18.9	7.4	-4.9	6.9	9.0
Richmond city	30 210	38 346	46 159	21 492	14 489	19 342	31 640	21 754	17 096	74.1	31.4	32.7	4.7	17.6	4.5	-7.8	15.4	20.3
South Bend city	32 439	39 046	49 460	28 333	15 954	22 961	32 494	24 931	17 121	78.4	33.8	29.0	5.1	17.1	5.1	-7.2	14.1	21.2
Terre Haute city	28 018	37 618	46 644	22 712	14 389	18 008	30 350	22 158	15 728	74.2	31.1	31.4	4.7	18.7	4.6	-7.7	19.5	21.8
Valparaiso city	45 799	60 637	67 551	31 027	30 462	24 774	47 808	28 615	22 509	81.5	42.6	25.0	1.7	16.1	10.5	-1.8	10.1	8.2
West Lafayette city	24 869	71 510	79 573	30 000	31 750	16 143	50 396	31 625	18 337	86.6	50.5	14.6	0.7	10.4	11.9	-0.4	37.1	10.0
IOWA	39 469	48 005	55 946	28 788	20 453	22 454	34 320	24 987	19 674	80.4	43.5	28.6	2.9	14.6	7.3	-5.0	9.3	9.3
Ames city	36 042	56 439	64 888	33 375	18 773	22 777	38 840	29 229	18 881	88.1	49.3	15.1	1.5	11.2	9.6	-2.7	19.7	9.2
Ankeny city	55 162	66 433	72 598	35 750	26 852	31 508	42 629	30 030	25 143	90.2	47.9	16.2	1.0	10.3	14.1	1.8	4.4	4.0
Bettendorf city	54 217	66 620	74 799	45 208	28 989	30 108	50 046	29 945	28 053	83.2	54.9	22.3	1.7	17.8	17.1	4.8	4.8	4.2
Burlington city	33 770	40 912	51 579	28 646	14 136	20 901	34 193	23 731	16 450	75.0	30.7	30.8	4.7	17.8	4.9	-7.4	11.3	17.7
Cedar Falls city	40 226	56 158	64 735	27 917	22 236	21 843	38 762	27 270	19 140	81.9	49.9	23.8	1.9	15.0	9.8	-2.5	16.1	8.2
Cedar Rapids city	43 704	54 286	64 945	35 148	23 168	26 979	38 048	27 065	22 589	82.4	44.5	25.1	2.7	16.5	8.9	-3.4	7.7	8.0
Clinton city	34 159	43 157	53 044	28 188	18 065	19 288	35 692	21 826	17 320	73.4	39.7	34.4	4.5	20.1	3.7	-8.6	11.8	16.7
Council Bluffs city	36 221	42 715	52 275	27 826	19 962	22 191	31 249	24 284	18 143	80.2	32.0	28.9	4.1	15.6	5.3	-7.0	10.2	13.1
Davenport city	37 242	45 944	55 766	24 500	16 429	23 200	35 556	25 631	18 828	80.8	37.2	24.3	4.7	18.0	6.4	-5.9	13.0	17.3
Des Moines city	38 408	46 590	53 131	28 378	20 792	25 070	32 342	26 558	19 467	82.3	33.8	24.7	3.9	14.3	6.3	-6.0	10.4	12.5
Dubuque city	36 785	46 564	54 651	30 125	19 516	21 821	32 223	23 637	19 616	78.0	47.1	30.0	3.0	19.2	6.5	-5.8	9.2	8.8
Fort Dodge city	33 361	42 555	51 870	22 250	22 066	20 035	32 080	24 289	18 018	76.5	38.8	32.6	5.0	15.6	4.9	-7.4	11.5	12.2
Iowa City city	34 977	57 568	72 658	34 196	19 740	21 348	36 547	30 095	20 269	88.7	46.5	14.7	2.2	10.5	10.4	-1.9	21.6	10.2
Marion city	48 591	59 110	68 044	28 958	20 208	27 976	41 608	27 156	23 158	84.0	40.0	22.4	2.8	17.1	11.3	-1.0	5.2	6.5
Marshalltown city	35 688	45 315	52 034	29 554	17 977	20 768	33 991	25 102	19 113	76.8	39.1	30.6	4.1	16.2	5.5	-6.8	11.8	14.6
Mason City city	33 852	45 160	55 100	19 524	18 621	20 300	33 725	22 354	18 899	76.2	42.9	32.6	3.1	15.4	5.9	-6.4	11.1	11.9
Sioux City city	37 429	45 751	54 617	24 782	17 781	22 153	32 041	23 626	18 666	80.6	35.1	28.1	3.2	14.5	7.0	-5.3	10.4	12.0
Urbandale city	59 744	70 548	77 490	36 667	37 500	34 155	47 465	34 307	29 021	88.3	52.7	20.0	1.0	14.0	17.9	5.6	3.3	4.5
Waterloo city	34 092	42 731	51 136	23 606	18 120	20 744	32 231	23 559	18 558	75.9	39.3	30.2	4.8	19.8	5.8	-6.5	13.1	16.4
West Des Moines city	54 139	70 600	82 421	37 297	32 437	36 312	46 628	32 078	31 405	88.3	47.4	17.2	1.4	12.7	18.7	6.4	4.3	4.6
KANSAS	40 624	49 624	56 918	29 587	21 194	23 002	36 188	25 978	20 506	81.8	39.1	26.2	2.4	14.8	9.3	-3.0	10.1	10.0
Dodge City city	37 156	41 672	45 382	21 111	20 297	22 116	27 192	22 668	15 538	84.1	29.8	21.8	3.5	10.2	6.1	-6.2	12.0	15.8
Emporia city	30 809	41 571	46 733	31 545	15 896	17 373	28 725	21 214	15 157	80.9	32.8	23.6	3.6	12.4	3.8	-8.5	18.7	17.7
Garden City city	37 752	43 471	46 126	25 372	20 482	20 878	29 900	21 543	15 200	87.9	27.9	19.8	2.2	9.0	4.7	-7.6	12.3	13.6
Hutchinson city	32 645	40 094	51 314	21 678	20 041	20 600	31 598	22 024	17 964	75.9	36.4	30.5	3.3	16.1	4.8	-7.5	13.2	15.3
Kansas City city	33 011	39 491	48 285	28 204	19 608	20 722	31 555	25 398	15 737	79.1	22.9	26.8	4.6	15.9	4.7	-7.6	16.3	19.0
Lawrence city	34 669	51 545	59 347	29 048	21 757	21 120	35 259	28 391	19 378	87.9	38.0	14.9	2.0	9.5	8.5	-3.8	19.9	10.3
Leavenworth city	40 681	48 836	56 317	21 484	21 310	24 684	39 932	24 939	18 785	82.0	38.9	24.5	3.6	23.1	5.9	-6.4	9.0	9.5
Leawood city	102 496	113 058	124 721	36 250	49 886	45 392	95 359	46 197	49 139	86.5	70.2	23.7	0.3	15.0	51.7	39.4	1.8	0.4
Lenexa city	61 990	76 321	84 608	43 261	36 326	36 015	51 542	33 375	30 212	90.3	50.2	14.8	0.7	11.8	23.2	10.9	3.5	2.7
Manhattan city	30 463	48 289	60 040	30 234	20 528	18 497	32 633	25 853	16 566	87.3	43.4	16.5	1.0	12.9	7.9	-4.4	24.1	10.9
Olathe city	61 111	68 498	73 119	40 990	30 965	31 856	46 350	30 836	24 498	92.3	40.5	11.7	1.4	9.6	17.2	4.9	4.0	3.4
Overland Park city	62 116	77 176	90 968	47 500	36 530	38 624	54 545	35 405	32 069	86.9	52.0	20.5	0.6	14.2	24.6	12.3	3.3	2.7
Salina city	36 066	45 433	52 165	26 250	21 850	22 141	32 104	23 027	18 593	81.1	37.2	27.0	2.2	13.9	5.6	-6.7	9.7	10.0
Shawnee city	59 626	70 288	77 024	31 484	30 857	35 153	47 067	32 007	28 142	89.5	47.9	18.3	1.2	13.6	19.7	7.4	3.8	3.0
Topeka city	35 928	45 803	54 951	26 602	20 971	23 075	33 644	26 426	19 555	77.8	36.7	29.0	3.4	18.3	6.5	-5.8	11.9	13.6
Wichita city	39 939	49 247	57 197	29 966	20 855	25 591	37 229	26 618	20 647	82.0	34.2	23.5	3.1	14.7	8.3	-4.0	10.7	12.7
KENTUCKY	33 672	40 939	49 851	24 350	15 713	18 972	33 836	24 194	18 093	76.5	29.0	28.5	3.8	17.5	7.2	-5.1	16.2	18.1
Bowling Green city	29 047	40 320	51 984	25 104	11 437	19 716	30 911	23 578	17 621	79.2	29.2	24.7	3.7	13.7	7.2	-5.1	21.5	24.3
Covington city	30 735	38 307	50 958	25 814	15 128	21 232	31 634	25 160	16 841	77.5	23.6	26.6	6.3	13.4	4.2	-8.1	17.2	22.5
Frankfort city	34 980	47 855	54 341	25 764	15 869	23 239	32 729	25 938	20 512	75.6	35.1	27.9	2.5	23.4	6.4	-5.9	15.2	17.3
Henderson city	30 427	39 887	49 779	15 857	14 861	18 061	33 545	22 931	17 925	74.1	29.0	29.3	4.3	17.6	5.2	-7.1	16.1	21.9

Table B-5. Cities — Education, Labor Force, and Income

STATE Place code	City	High school graduates — Total population 25 years and over	Percent with a high school diploma or less	Percent with a high school diploma or more	College graduates — Percent with a bachelor's degree or more	+/− U.S. percent with bachelor's degree or more	College graduates (percent) — Non-Hispanic White	Black or African American	American Indian and Alaska Native	Asian, Hawaiian, and Pacific Islander	Hispanic or Latino[1]
		1	2	3	4	5	6	7	8	9	10
	KENTUCKY—Cont'd										
21 37918	Hopkinsville city	19 295	56.1	76.1	16.0	−8.4	19.4	5.6	9.1	64.5	8.5
21 40222	Jeffersontown city	17 856	33.6	90.7	32.6	8.2	32.5	29.7	25.0	57.3	33.5
21 46027	Lexington-Fayette	167 235	36.6	85.8	35.6	11.2	38.7	14.5	17.7	67.3	14.6
21 48000	Louisville city	169 442	52.8	76.1	21.3	−3.1	26.6	8.2	20.8	43.1	15.5
21 58620	Owensboro city	35 988	56.1	78.5	17.8	−6.6	18.2	7.3	11.8	64.2	14.5
21 58836	Paducah city	18 092	54.5	76.6	18.6	−5.8	21.8	6.4	0.0	19.1	8.6
21 65226	Richmond city	13 729	48.4	76.9	25.7	1.3	26.6	10.0	34.6	75.3	2.5
22 00000	**LOUISIANA**	2 775 468	57.6	74.8	18.7	−5.7	21.7	10.9	9.2	35.2	19.5
22 00975	Alexandria city	29 132	57.1	72.4	19.5	−4.9	29.9	8.6	30.7	54.2	21.1
22 05000	Baton Rouge city	132 639	43.3	80.1	31.7	7.3	45.3	15.6	25.3	47.4	34.5
22 08920	Bossier City city	34 277	49.0	82.5	18.2	−6.2	20.9	8.6	9.7	22.3	11.3
22 36255	Houma city	19 948	64.6	69.5	14.3	−10.1	17.3	4.4	1.8	45.3	9.4
22 39475	Kenner city	44 673	50.6	78.5	21.3	−3.1	24.6	11.3	7.5	44.1	15.5
22 40735	Lafayette city	68 136	42.2	81.7	31.3	6.9	37.6	12.1	24.3	50.5	21.5
22 41155	Lake Charles city	44 779	54.1	75.4	20.2	−4.2	28.2	8.7	14.4	38.3	26.3
22 51410	Monroe city	29 438	48.8	74.1	26.9	2.5	44.8	11.9	25.7	48.5	8.0
22 54035	New Iberia city	19 759	70.6	64.9	12.3	−12.1	15.4	6.1	37.5	10.4	14.2
22 55000	New Orleans city	300 568	48.8	74.7	25.8	1.4	47.6	13.4	17.1	31.5	27.1
22 70000	Shreveport city	124 960	51.8	79.0	22.2	−2.2	32.2	10.1	13.1	43.5	19.8
22 70805	Slidell city	16 873	46.6	82.8	22.0	−2.4	23.2	14.4	18.4	21.8	17.4
23 00000	**MAINE**	869 893	50.8	85.4	22.9	−1.5	22.9	22.5	12.1	31.7	21.6
23 02795	Bangor city	20 847	44.3	87.0	26.5	2.1	26.7	13.6	25.5	39.8	38.4
23 38740	Lewiston city	23 794	65.6	72.3	12.6	−11.8	12.4	13.6	18.1	24.5	12.7
23 60545	Portland city	45 297	37.6	88.3	36.4	12.0	37.5	25.4	15.9	19.3	23.1
24 00000	**MARYLAND**	3 495 595	42.9	83.8	31.4	7.0	34.9	20.3	21.2	54.7	21.4
24 01600	Annapolis city	24 630	37.9	82.4	38.7	14.3	52.9	6.3	21.7	48.4	18.7
24 04000	Baltimore city	419 581	59.8	68.4	19.1	−5.3	32.9	10.0	16.7	51.8	24.6
24 08775	Bowie city	33 738	25.6	94.7	43.0	18.6	41.2	45.7	58.9	56.2	41.4
24 30325	Frederick city	34 710	42.8	84.2	29.9	5.5	32.6	9.9	15.2	55.8	23.1
24 31175	Gaithersburg city	34 989	29.5	85.6	46.5	22.1	57.7	27.2	64.3	61.0	13.4
24 36075	Hagerstown city	24 029	66.1	73.0	11.8	−12.6	11.9	8.2	0.0	26.4	4.6
24 67675	Rockville city	33 216	27.1	89.1	52.9	28.5	57.7	24.0	19.0	67.4	23.3
25 00000	**MASSACHUSETTS**	4 273 275	42.5	84.8	33.2	8.8	34.6	19.7	19.2	49.6	14.1
25 00765	Agawam city	20 158	49.0	87.5	21.4	−3.0	20.9	30.9	29.3	45.2	30.6
25 02690	Attleboro city	28 635	50.0	81.9	23.5	−0.9	23.5	28.3	0.0	33.9	17.3
25 03600	Barnstable Town city	34 695	35.7	90.4	32.2	7.8	33.6	10.1	21.4	38.8	12.6
25 05595	Beverly city	27 633	37.0	90.8	36.5	12.1	36.4	22.7	0.0	63.1	31.5
25 07000	Boston city	377 574	45.1	78.9	35.6	11.2	48.8	15.6	14.4	37.0	15.3
25 09000	Brockton city	59 428	59.9	75.9	14.0	−10.4	15.0	14.8	10.2	21.6	10.1
25 11000	Cambridge city	66 315	22.7	89.5	65.1	40.7	70.6	28.2	42.4	80.8	47.7
25 13205	Chelsea city	21 597	70.6	59.5	10.0	−14.4	15.1	14.2	0.0	7.2	3.8
25 13660	Chicopee city	37 695	63.2	74.9	12.3	−12.1	12.5	14.0	26.7	22.0	5.5
25 21990	Everett city	26 399	64.1	76.2	14.7	−9.7	15.5	15.3	58.1	16.8	5.4
25 23000	Fall River city	61 177	69.5	56.6	10.7	−13.7	10.6	10.7	5.4	18.1	6.7
25 23875	Fitchburg city	24 863	59.8	75.4	15.4	−9.0	16.9	12.0	27.9	10.6	6.7
25 25100	Franklin city	18 736	30.6	92.9	42.7	18.3	42.5	40.4	23.8	57.5	30.8
25 26150	Gloucester city	21 598	45.8	85.7	27.5	3.1	27.6	42.9	X	49.2	15.6
25 29405	Haverhill city	39 354	47.5	83.6	23.4	−1.0	23.9	25.2	34.7	51.1	8.7
25 30840	Holyoke city	24 509	59.6	70.0	16.9	−7.5	22.4	16.2	18.4	29.1	3.5
25 34550	Lawrence city	40 940	71.4	58.2	10.0	−14.4	14.5	7.6	2.1	14.5	5.7
25 35075	Leominster city	27 797	50.8	81.4	21.9	−2.5	22.7	20.8	0.0	38.5	9.8
25 37000	Lowell city	64 421	60.9	71.2	18.1	−6.3	18.5	19.6	21.8	24.1	6.6
25 37490	Lynn city	57 093	59.7	74.2	16.4	−8.0	18.2	14.7	25.0	14.7	8.5
25 37875	Malden city	40 572	49.6	83.4	26.2	1.8	23.5	25.8	56.2	42.6	23.1
25 38715	Marlborough city	25 512	37.9	87.3	35.6	11.2	34.6	43.9	0.0	71.1	17.4
25 39835	Medford city	39 762	45.9	85.6	31.7	7.3	31.0	26.8	24.4	60.0	24.3
25 40115	Melrose city	19 697	32.8	91.6	40.1	15.7	39.9	32.1	42.3	46.7	42.9
25 40710	Methuen city	29 962	51.4	81.8	23.0	−1.4	23.6	13.2	14.9	32.9	12.9
25 45000	New Bedford city	61 709	70.1	57.6	10.7	−13.7	11.2	8.6	14.3	30.7	4.9
25 45560	Newton city	57 687	17.6	94.5	68.0	43.6	68.8	56.5	35.9	68.6	46.8
25 46330	Northampton city	19 714	32.0	88.7	46.1	21.7	45.9	56.4	56.3	69.7	29.2
25 52490	Peabody city	34 274	49.6	85.1	23.1	−1.3	23.4	10.2	27.6	53.0	9.9
25 53960	Pittsfield city	32 063	51.8	84.4	20.5	−3.9	20.8	9.9	0.0	48.5	3.6
25 55745	Quincy city	65 520	43.5	85.2	31.8	7.4	31.7	32.8	8.8	31.1	38.8
25 56585	Revere city	33 723	63.7	76.7	13.5	−10.9	13.5	20.3	6.7	25.6	7.6
25 59105	Salem city	28 169	43.2	85.2	31.1	6.7	32.2	25.1	0.0	42.8	17.6

[1] Hispanic or Latino persons may be of any race.

City	School enrollment			Population 16 to 19 years				Employment status, 2000			Work status in 1999 of the population 16 years and over		
							Percent not enrolled, not grads, not in armed forces, not employed				Worked in 1999		
	Grades kindergarten through 12	College or graduate school	Percent private	Number	Percent in armed forces	Percent high school graduates		Total population 16 years and over	Percent in labor force	Unemploy-ment rate	Full-time	Part-time	Did not work in 1999
	11	12	13	14	15	16	17	18	19	20	21	22	23
KENTUCKY—Cont'd													
Hopkinsville city............	5 969	1 188	12.2	1 747	1.0	12.7	11.6	23 105	58.5	5.3	53.0	11.3	35.7
Jeffersontown city........	4 882	1 398	24.9	1 296	0.0	12.1	0.5	20 509	71.5	2.6	63.3	14.2	22.6
Lexington-Fayette.........	40 156	31 508	12.7	15 177	0.2	8.0	4.9	210 783	69.8	5.4	58.2	18.2	23.6
Louisville city...............	45 721	17 181	18.5	13 628	0.0	10.3	9.3	201 949	60.8	7.4	50.8	15.1	34.1
Owensboro city	9 377	2 465	18.8	3 108	0.0	12.4	4.1	42 718	61.7	6.9	51.7	15.0	33.3
Paducah city..............	4 482	950	11.2	1 238	0.0	8.3	8.1	20 927	53.4	7.7	46.1	12.0	41.9
Richmond city.............	3 076	7 465	3.6	2 635	0.0	6.3	4.0	22 746	62.9	5.9	49.3	26.0	24.7
LOUISIANA	923 702	258 000	17.2	289 111	0.4	10.4	8.0	3 394 546	59.4	7.3	51.2	13.0	35.8
Alexandria city............	9 905	1 581	11.3	3 133	0.2	10.2	14.3	35 380	53.2	8.9	45.4	11.7	43.0
Baton Rouge city.........	41 232	31 556	14.9	18 306	0.0	7.5	6.1	178 626	61.8	8.3	49.2	19.0	31.8
Bossier City city	11 525	3 199	6.8	3 389	6.8	15.8	6.0	42 188	66.5	5.1	58.4	11.9	29.7
Houma city	6 747	1 140	21.7	2 024	0.0	5.8	5.5	24 238	56.2	7.1	50.6	12.2	37.2
Kenner city	14 733	3 617	33.7	3 965	0.3	7.2	5.5	53 432	66.9	5.9	56.9	14.9	28.2
Lafayette city	21 099	10 512	18.7	7 377	0.0	9.1	6.6	85 898	65.0	8.1	52.3	16.7	30.9
Lake Charles city	13 668	4 850	14.7	4 670	0.0	12.0	5.4	55 394	60.1	9.1	49.6	14.4	36.0
Monroe city.................	11 754	5 220	9.1	4 431	0.1	7.4	10.4	39 294	59.4	12.8	46.5	16.0	37.5
New Iberia city	7 362	904	10.8	1 949	0.0	11.9	11.2	23 946	54.3	11.6	45.2	12.3	42.5
New Orleans city..........	99 998	39 625	26.1	30 841	0.3	9.6	8.0	370 138	57.8	9.4	48.4	14.4	37.3
Shreveport city	40 529	11 067	9.9	12 703	0.5	11.3	10.0	152 931	60.8	10.1	52.5	12.0	35.5
Slidell city	5 230	1 145	15.6	1 426	0.0	10.6	4.3	19 602	61.5	4.4	51.6	14.0	34.4
MAINE	236 267	67 216	12.4	69 770	0.3	10.0	3.4	1 010 318	65.3	4.7	53.7	17.4	28.9
Bangor city	5 065	2 675	17.3	2 038	0.0	12.3	5.3	25 732	64.2	5.5	51.0	17.8	31.1
Lewiston city...............	5 529	3 195	31.5	2 199	0.0	10.6	4.4	29 116	61.1	6.8	50.4	16.7	32.9
Portland city...............	9 286	4 795	14.7	2 776	0.2	12.2	3.0	53 543	69.1	4.8	56.6	17.5	25.9
MARYLAND	1 024 955	354 477	18.1	277 834	0.7	11.6	4.8	4 085 942	67.8	4.7	50.6	13.8	26.6
Annapolis city.............	5 507	2 495	27.5	1 705	0.0	9.8	11.3	28 815	70.2	3.4	60.3	14.9	24.8
Baltimore city..............	125 546	48 736	22.6	38 950	0.0	12.0	11.6	507 504	60.0	10.7	49.8	12.4	37.8
Bowie city	9 578	3 695	25.4	2 354	0.0	7.3	2.3	38 053	74.5	2.2	66.3	14.0	19.7
Frederick city	9 221	3 353	16.7	2 302	0.7	13.9	5.1	40 617	73.1	4.5	64.1	13.0	22.8
Gaithersburg city	8 837	3 399	14.9	2 315	0.0	8.7	6.2	40 802	73.7	4.4	66.1	12.9	21.0
Hagerstown city	6 454	1 001	6.6	1 511	0.0	18.0	9.7	28 136	64.4	4.5	55.9	12.1	32.0
Rockville city	8 296	2 891	18.8	2 065	0.0	7.1	4.9	37 388	67.0	3.2	59.5	14.0	26.5
MASSACHUSETTS ...	1 129 778	473 403	23.9	330 827	0.1	8.2	3.7	5 010 241	66.2	4.6	54.4	17.4	28.1
Agawam city................	4 620	1 510	15.2	1 401	0.0	9.1	2.2	22 817	68.0	4.1	54.8	17.9	27.2
Attleboro city...............	7 736	1 895	17.1	2 020	0.0	8.5	3.7	32 449	70.6	3.7	59.1	15.5	25.4
Barnstable Town city.....	8 119	1 702	12.0	2 155	0.0	8.2	2.1	38 017	61.9	4.7	47.6	20.1	32.4
Beverly city	6 381	3 034	30.6	2 010	0.4	4.1	1.0	32 119	69.2	6.8	54.9	17.9	27.2
Boston city..................	92 704	85 847	45.2	36 529	0.0	6.5	4.7	484 995	63.6	7.2	54.9	15.3	29.8
Brockton city	20 648	5 049	11.3	5 319	0.0	13.0	8.0	70 803	64.5	6.7	53.0	15.3	31.8
Cambridge city	9 929	26 613	68.5	6 733	0.0	5.2	1.2	89 303	67.1	6.1	57.5	20.5	22.0
Chelsea city................	7 403	1 737	16.9	1 865	0.0	12.4	9.9	26 394	53.8	7.3	48.2	11.5	40.3
Chicopee city..............	9 658	2 759	17.5	2 853	0.6	6.8	10.0	43 773	62.4	4.8	50.8	16.5	32.7
Everett city	6 202	2 216	22.4	1 779	0.0	13.5	5.6	30 721	62.5	5.0	53.6	14.7	31.7
Fall River city	16 772	3 725	13.0	4 743	0.0	12.0	8.7	72 237	59.1	7.0	48.7	14.3	37.0
Fitchburg city	7 829	2 769	11.9	2 374	0.0	6.9	7.0	30 162	63.5	8.4	51.2	16.9	31.9
Franklin city	6 053	1 599	17.5	1 530	0.0	4.0	2.2	21 257	73.8	4.2	58.9	20.0	21.2
Gloucester city	5 004	1 289	17.2	1 317	0.8	11.6	2.1	24 397	66.1	4.9	54.0	16.8	29.2
Haverhill city	10 909	3 437	16.5	2 695	0.0	15.8	4.2	45 386	68.0	3.7	57.6	15.3	27.1
Holyoke city	8 873	2 006	15.3	2 349	0.0	10.7	10.6	29 299	54.5	6.7	45.1	14.9	40.0
Lawrence city	17 802	3 457	15.0	4 713	0.0	9.5	10.7	51 287	54.9	8.4	50.7	12.2	37.1
Leominster city	7 995	1 951	17.7	2 051	0.0	17.3	4.5	31 832	66.4	4.0	55.0	16.5	28.5
Lowell city	20 952	7 854	14.3	6 404	0.0	12.0	9.0	79 637	64.2	6.5	53.9	14.8	31.3
Lynn city....................	18 037	4 606	13.4	4 900	0.0	11.3	5.9	67 779	61.7	6.2	50.7	16.2	33.1
Malden city	8 146	4 106	28.1	2 256	0.0	13.8	3.8	46 255	67.3	4.0	58.4	13.8	27.8
Marlborough city	6 047	1 776	22.1	1 387	0.0	15.1	0.6	28 690	73.4	3.4	62.9	14.9	22.2
Medford city................	7 614	5 703	45.8	3 124	0.0	9.7	2.6	46 929	64.2	3.6	53.5	16.3	30.1
Melrose city................	4 186	1 403	21.9	1 085	0.0	5.7	0.0	21 747	69.0	2.0	56.1	17.5	26.4
Methuen city...............	8 365	2 490	17.7	1 875	0.0	6.4	2.7	33 991	64.0	4.3	54.0	15.4	30.6
New Bedford city..........	17 678	3 596	10.1	5 131	0.6	12.2	9.7	73 287	57.7	8.7	47.0	14.6	38.4
Newton city	13 234	9 367	43.1	5 442	0.0	1.8	0.3	68 063	68.1	2.9	57.3	17.8	24.8
Northampton city...........	3 915	4 561	41.0	2 057	0.0	4.1	0.5	24 658	68.9	4.1	50.6	24.2	25.2
Peabody city	8 122	2 504	19.2	2 002	0.0	3.8	1.4	38 465	65.8	3.8	52.1	17.9	30.0
Pittsfield city	7 855	2 032	10.6	2 218	0.0	16.2	4.1	36 463	62.1	6.0	47.8	19.0	33.3
Quincy city..................	11 530	6 354	31.2	3 306	0.0	9.3	3.2	74 258	66.8	3.4	57.3	14.0	28.7
Revere city	7 677	2 406	20.6	1 933	0.0	14.8	4.3	38 473	58.5	5.9	48.2	14.5	37.3
Salem city..................	6 168	3 515	15.9	1 975	0.0	8.1	3.1	33 128	69.2	5.4	56.4	17.4	26.3

Table B-5. Cities — Education, Labor Force, and Income

City	Full-year full-time employed (percent)								Children under 18 years in families (percent, except where noted)						Total employed by class of worker (percent)			
										With two parents		With one parent who is in labor force	+/− U.S. percent of children with no stay-at-home parent	+/− U.S. percent two-income couples				Unpaid family worker
	Total	Men	Women	Non-Hispanic White	Black or African American	American Indian and Alaska Native	Asian, Hawaiian, and Pacific Islander	Hispanic or Latino[1]	Number	Both in labor force	Father only in labor force				Private	Government	Self-employed	
	24	25	26	27	28	29	30	31	32	33	34	35	36	37	38	39	40	41
KENTUCKY—Cont'd																		
Hopkinsville city............	38.7	47.4	31.5	41.1	32.2	52.4	33.5	41.4	7 453	32.7	15.2	35.3	3.4	-1.2	73.5	17.4	8.9	0.2
Jeffersontown city	50.7	61.7	40.9	50.8	50.4	53.1	58.7	42.7	6 504	54.5	19.5	20.0	9.9	8.4	82.2	11.0	6.7	0.1
Lexington-Fayette.........	43.4	51.4	35.8	44.9	39.0	39.0	35.4	30.9	52 507	45.9	19.9	24.4	5.7	7.2	74.4	17.3	8.0	0.3
Louisville city	36.9	43.3	31.4	39.7	31.0	34.9	34.6	32.3	55 859	28.8	11.0	37.3	1.5	-2.0	78.7	13.5	7.5	0.3
Owensboro city	39.0	49.4	30.2	39.3	36.9	28.0	37.4	32.8	12 076	44.8	19.5	23.7	3.9	-1.8	80.6	11.4	7.6	0.4
Paducah city................	33.1	43.6	24.7	33.9	30.3	10.4	54.2	35.4	5 590	33.2	13.8	34.5	3.1	-7.2	75.8	14.0	10.0	0.2
Richmond city	30.1	38.4	22.8	30.0	27.9	31.7	37.5	46.6	4 450	34.1	21.1	30.6	0.1	-0.4	73.7	19.7	5.9	0.6
LOUISIANA	36.4	45.0	28.6	39.7	29.5	32.1	34.3	35.5	1 126 561	36.3	19.8	26.7	-1.6	-4.3	72.8	17.4	9.4	0.3
Alexandria city	31.3	37.3	26.5	34.3	28.6	31.5	33.0	25.0	11 662	28.9	12.0	35.3	-0.4	-6.5	67.5	22.8	9.4	0.4
Baton Rouge city..........	33.8	40.3	28.2	36.9	30.9	39.0	28.4	32.2	51 005	29.5	16.6	35.2	0.1	-2.7	67.8	23.5	8.5	0.2
Bossier City city	44.4	56.4	33.6	45.9	40.4	24.9	35.9	42.3	14 990	41.1	18.8	30.0	6.5	0.5	73.5	18.6	7.7	0.2
Houma city...................	34.7	44.2	25.8	37.0	30.0	18.7	38.8	25.6	8 052	31.6	20.8	25.2	-7.8	-9.6	73.8	9.4	0.5	
Kenner city	43.0	53.9	33.2	45.7	36.9	54.8	47.0	39.1	17 984	40.1	19.7	27.4	2.9	1.5	78.1	11.7	9.9	0.3
Lafayette city	37.0	46.0	28.8	39.9	30.1	41.2	32.0	26.1	26 117	38.0	22.2	26.8	0.2	-1.7	73.9	14.2	11.7	0.3
Lake Charles city	35.2	43.7	27.8	36.9	32.8	28.2	32.4	38.4	16 788	35.7	16.1	32.1	3.2	-5.6	76.2	16.0	7.6	0.2
Monroe city	31.6	38.2	26.4	37.5	26.9	31.3	39.7	28.2	13 831	26.4	11.5	41.9	3.7	0.4	70.8	20.6	8.5	0.1
New Iberia city	30.5	39.2	23.4	34.2	25.4	51.8	23.4	8.7	8 844	28.3	17.5	28.4	-7.9	-10.8	77.4	13.1	9.0	0.5
New Orleans city	33.1	38.5	28.5	39.4	30.0	35.9	29.4	33.7	114 871	24.7	10.4	39.9	0.0	-2.6	70.5	20.4	8.8	0.3
Shreveport city	38.0	45.7	31.6	42.1	33.7	31.7	39.3	35.8	48 750	31.3	12.0	39.2	5.9	-1.8	73.9	17.8	8.0	0.3
Slidell city	39.2	53.4	27.3	40.6	33.3	38.2	12.2	32.8	6 339	43.4	21.7	23.9	2.7	-4.1	73.4	17.7	8.6	0.3
MAINE	40.6	50.4	31.6	40.8	38.3	34.1	36.8	35.4	287 045	51.4	18.0	20.3	7.1	4.2	72.8	14.5	12.4	0.3
Bangor city	38.7	47.4	31.2	39.0	28.5	38.3	34.7	39.7	6 018	45.8	17.9	22.4	3.6	8.1	76.3	15.0	8.4	0.2
Lewiston city	37.6	45.4	30.6	38.1	27.2	48.7	24.5	5.4	6 939	44.2	10.3	30.3	9.9	1.8	81.4	11.1	7.2	0.3
Portland city	42.7	49.7	36.4	43.3	39.2	42.7	28.3	40.9	11 542	44.8	13.1	26.2	6.4	9.3	79.3	10.6	9.9	0.1
MARYLAND	46.5	55.3	38.6	47.4	45.2	47.3	44.5	42.5	1 267 484	46.3	18.7	24.2	5.9	6.5	68.9	22.3	8.5	0.2
Annapolis city	46.0	55.5	37.9	48.8	37.8	66.7	48.8	55.3	7 094	33.1	12.0	36.8	5.3	8.6	69.4	20.2	10.1	0.2
Baltimore city...............	34.7	38.5	31.4	38.7	32.6	27.8	29.6	33.5	137 315	22.3	9.7	42.6	0.3	-6.3	71.6	22.3	5.9	0.2
Bowie city....................	55.3	64.6	47.2	52.1	61.3	66.7	56.2	56.8	12 625	58.0	18.6	17.0	10.4	13.3	61.8	30.7	7.4	0.1
Frederick city	51.5	63.4	40.8	51.7	50.3	65.0	43.0	53.3	12 631	46.8	18.1	26.5	8.7	9.7	74.4	19.0	6.3	0.2
Gaithersburg city	49.7	60.0	40.2	51.8	52.0	56.3	51.2	39.7	12 591	44.5	22.5	21.7	1.6	8.1	74.5	17.3	8.1	0.1
Hagerstown city	43.8	55.0	34.4	43.7	45.3	62.5	42.0	42.1	8 760	34.5	15.3	34.4	4.3	-0.4	79.9	14.5	5.4	0.1
Rockville city	45.9	55.0	37.6	48.1	41.3	31.8	43.3	42.8	10 532	49.0	25.1	16.9	1.3	7.2	64.8	25.1	10.0	0.1
MASSACHUSETTS ...	42.3	53.2	32.5	43.3	38.7	33.9	39.3	34.0	1 434 842	48.2	20.1	19.1	2.7	4.9	77.3	13.5	9.0	0.2
Agawam city	44.2	58.5	31.7	44.0	37.2	51.1	53.7	54.9	5 941	55.5	20.3	16.6	7.5	7.6	77.7	13.4	8.5	0.3
Attleboro city	48.5	59.5	38.5	48.4	50.7	64.7	51.5	47.2	10 018	55.5	17.6	19.1	10.0	9.5	83.1	9.4	7.4	0.1
Barnstable Town city.....	35.0	43.9	27.0	34.6	38.1	25.0	48.0	35.0	10 051	44.9	19.8	20.0	4.8	-3.0	69.7	12.7	17.2	0.4
Beverly city..................	43.1	54.9	33.1	42.8	58.1	80.6	60.4	39.2	8 353	53.7	20.0	17.7	6.8	8.6	78.3	11.4	10.1	0.2
Boston city	38.4	43.6	33.8	41.7	36.9	28.3	28.1	33.4	106 516	29.0	12.2	31.3	-4.3	-1.3	80.3	13.3	6.3	0.1
Brockton city	41.9	50.0	34.8	41.8	45.5	20.9	46.4	37.9	24 601	37.9	12.2	29.7	3.0	2.6	83.0	12.2	4.7	0.1
Cambridge city	36.4	41.2	32.0	40.1	32.5	25.1	25.4	29.7	12 785	35.5	19.3	25.9	-3.2	1.6	81.1	10.7	8.0	0.1
Chelsea city.................	33.8	40.2	27.3	31.5	36.8	15.9	33.0	36.0	8 681	28.3	10.7	28.2	-8.1	-12.0	82.1	12.7	5.0	0.2
Chicopee city	41.3	51.6	32.3	42.3	39.8	28.6	29.0	28.5	11 560	40.0	16.1	25.9	1.3	0.2	80.0	15.2	4.7	0.0
Everett city	39.8	49.9	30.8	39.3	43.7	35.1	34.0	37.5	7 741	36.5	17.1	22.7	-5.4	-4.8	80.7	13.5	5.5	0.3
Fall River city	37.6	46.5	30.2	38.4	28.6	29.8	24.7	26.5	21 085	37.0	11.4	28.4	0.8	-3.8	83.5	11.9	4.5	0.2
Fitchburg city	38.3	48.6	29.2	38.6	40.9	11.3	47.1	33.0	9 596	37.3	16.0	27.2	-0.1	-2.4	80.0	14.7	5.3	0.1
Franklin city.................	48.5	64.3	33.6	49.0	42.1	39.3	39.0	27.3	8 854	55.4	32.2	7.7	-1.5	11.3	80.1	11.0	8.7	0.3
Gloucester city	43.4	55.2	32.8	43.4	53.0	0.0	38.6	45.8	6 411	46.9	21.6	21.1	3.4	5.2	73.4	12.2	14.1	0.3
Haverhill city	46.8	59.7	35.8	47.4	46.4	30.9	45.1	40.9	14 439	46.5	19.5	23.2	5.1	6.9	78.4	13.7	7.7	0.2
Holyoke city	33.5	42.3	26.3	38.6	38.1	0.0	35.5	22.5	10 917	23.9	12.3	27.4	-13.3	-2.5	73.4	21.2	5.3	0.1
Lawrence city	34.5	40.7	29.2	37.0	33.6	30.3	41.5	32.2	21 176	23.9	9.2	34.8	-5.9	-7.8	83.1	11.2	5.5	0.2
Leominster city	44.1	57.5	32.4	44.4	49.9	46.2	45.1	40.4	10 273	41.2	20.9	23.7	0.3	3.8	77.8	13.1	8.9	0.2
Lowell city	41.3	50.2	32.9	42.5	45.9	25.3	38.7	35.4	26 554	36.1	12.7	26.6	-1.9	1.9	81.5	13.8	4.5	0.1
Lynn city	39.3	49.4	30.2	40.2	43.9	12.5	33.2	35.9	22 035	34.4	13.5	27.5	-2.7	-0.3	78.9	15.3	5.7	0.1
Malden city	46.8	55.1	39.2	46.4	49.3	44.4	44.7	50.1	10 756	43.0	21.0	19.6	-2.0	1.7	81.5	12.0	6.4	0.1
Marlborough city...........	49.5	61.7	38.0	50.0	37.9	12.0	51.2	44.0	8 172	53.4	21.0	15.9	4.7	10.4	82.2	9.0	8.7	0.1
Medford city.................	41.2	51.4	32.4	41.1	43.1	15.4	41.2	40.7	9 771	50.6	22.3	16.3	2.3	0.4	80.2	12.6	7.0	0.1
Melrose city	45.5	59.4	33.6	45.3	40.3	0.0	46.7	66.5	5 909	62.3	20.6	11.5	9.2	10.6	76.3	15.0	8.6	0.1
Methuen city	43.6	55.7	33.0	43.7	17.1	15.9	54.3	42.8	10 385	51.3	17.5	16.2	2.9	5.1	78.7	13.8	7.2	0.3
New Bedford city..........	34.5	42.5	27.7	35.9	32.1	23.1	34.7	22.0	21 681	34.5	11.5	32.1	2.0	-7.1	81.4	13.1	5.4	0.1
Newton city..................	44.0	55.6	34.4	44.2	34.4	40.0	49.4	35.3	17 427	63.0	22.5	8.4	6.8	8.8	74.1	10.5	15.3	0.1
Northampton city	36.8	48.0	28.6	37.7	20.1	48.1	36.1	24.6	4 659	54.8	14.4	23.7	13.9	11.7	70.3	19.2	10.5	0.0
Peabody city	42.5	54.7	31.8	42.8	53.4	0.0	42.3	36.5	10 457	58.2	17.4	16.2	9.8	4.9	78.8	13.7	7.2	0.3
Pittsfield city................	37.0	47.4	28.1	37.2	36.5	17.2	44.3	37.6	9 954	44.2	14.6	30.1	9.7	-1.3	77.7	13.8	8.2	0.3
Quincy city	45.2	53.8	37.6	45.4	44.4	20.4	45.0	47.8	14 997	49.5	16.4	19.5	4.4	2.2	79.8	13.8	6.2	0.2
Revere city	36.7	45.7	28.5	36.9	38.5	37.3	28.6	36.5	9 386	37.0	19.4	21.3	-6.3	-8.1	77.4	14.9	7.5	0.2
Salem city....................	44.9	54.5	36.8	45.7	43.3	24.6	38.2	40.5	7 763	43.3	15.9	24.4	3.1	5.6	78.2	13.6	8.0	0.1

[1] Hispanic or Latino persons may be of any race.

City	Percent who worked at home	Percent of the population 5 years and over with a disability	Veterans as a percent of the population 18 years and over	Occupation for employed population 16 years and over (percent)						Industry for employed population 16 years and over (percent)					
				Management, professional, and related occupations	Service occupations	Sales and office occupations	Farming, fishing, and forestry occupations	Construction, extraction, and maintenance occupations	Production, transportation and material moving occupations	Agriculture, forestry, fishing, and mining	Construction and manufacturing	Wholesale and retail trade	Transportation and warehousing, and utilities	Service industries	Public administration
	42	43	44	45	46	47	48	49	50	51	52	53	54	55	56
KENTUCKY—Cont'd															
Hopkinsville city	1.7	26.3	16.2	26.6	17.9	24.9	0.5	7.9	22.1	1.4	26.3	16.2	3.6	47.5	4.9
Jeffersontown city	2.6	13.5	12.5	40.1	10.8	30.1	0.3	7.1	11.7	0.4	17.5	17.7	6.0	54.7	3.6
Lexington-Fayette	2.5	17.7	11.4	40.4	14.6	26.1	1.0	6.7	11.2	2.1	17.4	15.3	3.5	58.1	3.6
Louisville city	1.8	24.8	12.5	30.7	18.2	26.8	0.2	7.5	16.5	0.4	17.5	13.1	6.1	58.6	4.3
Owensboro city	1.5	24.8	15.6	29.4	16.5	24.1	0.3	10.3	19.3	1.2	25.9	15.6	5.2	49.1	2.9
Paducah city	2.5	27.3	13.9	31.1	18.8	27.9	0.4	7.3	14.4	1.0	17.5	18.9	6.0	52.9	3.8
Richmond city	2.0	21.4	7.7	27.5	20.1	30.2	0.6	8.0	13.7	1.2	20.2	18.1	3.6	53.2	3.7
LOUISIANA	2.1	21.8	12.1	29.9	16.7	26.8	0.8	11.7	14.1	4.2	18.0	15.4	5.3	51.3	5.8
Alexandria city	1.9	27.4	14.3	32.8	23.0	27.8	0.2	5.8	10.3	1.2	9.7	17.5	3.4	61.6	6.6
Baton Rouge city	2.4	21.0	10.6	36.7	17.2	28.4	0.1	7.2	10.3	0.6	13.4	14.5	3.6	60.4	7.5
Bossier City city	1.7	19.4	18.4	28.5	19.9	28.3	0.1	10.8	12.5	1.2	13.6	16.3	5.5	57.1	6.3
Houma city	2.2	26.0	12.0	26.0	15.3	28.9	0.6	13.9	15.3	9.5	14.7	16.3	6.0	48.9	4.6
Kenner city	2.2	20.0	9.8	31.4	16.5	29.0	0.4	11.8	10.8	1.4	16.6	17.7	5.8	54.2	4.2
Lafayette city	2.9	18.5	11.5	39.6	15.6	27.5	0.1	8.2	9.0	8.3	9.1	16.6	4.4	57.8	3.7
Lake Charles city	1.9	22.9	14.3	28.8	22.4	26.7	0.1	10.1	11.9	1.2	17.5	15.0	4.0	57.6	4.7
Monroe city	1.4	22.3	10.1	32.6	22.3	28.8	0.1	6.6	9.7	0.6	12.6	15.3	3.1	62.8	5.6
New Iberia city	2.1	23.9	11.1	24.5	18.4	25.1	0.9	14.2	16.9	11.6	15.4	17.5	4.0	47.6	4.0
New Orleans city	2.7	23.2	10.8	34.7	22.1	25.8	0.2	6.8	10.4	1.0	10.1	12.4	5.9	64.1	6.4
Shreveport city	1.9	22.3	13.5	30.2	20.7	26.7	0.2	8.1	14.0	1.2	15.8	15.1	4.4	59.2	4.4
Slidell city	2.6	20.9	16.6	34.3	15.1	29.2	0.2	11.2	10.1	2.0	17.6	16.9	5.1	51.0	7.4
MAINE	4.4	20.0	15.9	31.5	15.3	25.9	1.7	10.3	15.3	2.6	21.1	17.0	4.3	50.6	4.5
Bangor city	4.4	22.6	14.2	34.8	18.6	29.7	0.5	7.5	9.0	1.0	10.6	19.2	5.4	60.0	3.8
Lewiston city	2.3	26.6	16.1	25.0	15.8	31.3	0.2	9.3	18.4	0.4	22.6	20.1	3.8	49.5	3.6
Portland city	3.6	20.4	11.8	39.7	16.3	28.5	0.4	5.2	9.9	0.5	11.6	17.2	3.8	63.9	3.0
MARYLAND	3.3	17.6	13.3	41.3	13.9	26.4	0.3	8.6	9.5	0.6	14.2	13.3	4.9	56.5	10.5
Annapolis city	4.2	17.2	12.7	42.9	18.8	24.9	0.2	6.4	6.9	0.2	10.4	13.4	3.6	63.3	9.2
Baltimore city	2.3	27.2	11.2	32.4	20.0	27.1	0.1	7.0	13.4	0.1	12.9	11.6	5.6	60.5	9.3
Bowie city	3.8	13.5	15.3	52.7	11.3	24.9	0.0	5.9	5.2	0.2	8.6	11.8	4.5	57.3	17.6
Frederick city	3.0	17.1	13.7	39.2	15.1	25.9	0.2	9.9	9.8	0.4	16.9	15.5	3.2	57.0	7.0
Gaithersburg city	2.9	14.4	7.8	48.6	14.9	23.8	0.1	6.6	6.1	0.2	12.5	11.3	3.0	64.7	8.3
Hagerstown city	2.5	23.4	14.0	21.2	19.0	29.1	0.1	11.5	19.2	0.6	23.9	16.7	5.0	47.2	6.7
Rockville city	4.9	13.8	10.6	55.6	12.3	22.0	0.0	5.2	4.8	0.1	8.7	10.6	2.3	66.9	11.4
MASSACHUSETTS	3.1	18.5	11.5	41.1	14.1	25.9	0.2	7.5	11.3	0.4	18.3	14.4	4.2	58.4	4.3
Agawam city	2.2	16.9	14.7	33.2	14.1	30.5	0.1	8.0	14.1	0.5	19.3	17.4	7.5	51.0	4.4
Attleboro city	1.0	18.5	13.8	33.6	12.2	26.6	0.1	8.1	19.4	0.3	31.3	16.4	3.7	45.0	3.3
Barnstable Town city	4.8	19.7	16.3	35.3	20.0	26.1	0.4	10.5	7.7	0.4	14.0	16.8	4.6	59.2	4.9
Beverly city	3.3	17.1	12.9	42.4	13.2	28.9	0.1	6.5	9.0	0.2	18.2	15.8	3.4	59.3	3.1
Boston city	2.4	21.9	6.4	43.3	17.8	25.6	0.1	4.9	8.3	0.1	9.8	10.5	4.1	70.4	5.1
Brockton city	1.1	26.7	11.6	23.9	18.0	30.0	0.1	7.7	20.4	0.2	19.2	19.8	5.6	51.6	3.6
Cambridge city	5.3	14.2	4.9	66.8	8.9	17.8	0.1	2.1	4.3	0.0	6.8	7.2	1.9	81.1	2.9
Chelsea city	2.1	30.4	8.9	17.9	25.2	25.3	0.8	7.3	23.4	0.5	19.9	14.4	6.5	54.5	4.2
Chicopee city	1.4	24.1	16.3	22.8	16.7	27.4	0.2	9.5	23.4	0.2	26.5	17.3	6.6	45.2	4.2
Everett city	0.7	24.2	10.3	24.9	19.1	31.1	0.2	10.9	13.8	0.2	18.3	13.5	7.5	55.5	5.0
Fall River city	1.0	27.3	10.4	22.4	18.6	24.8	0.3	9.7	24.3	0.3	30.6	16.2	3.4	45.5	4.1
Fitchburg city	2.1	23.5	12.8	27.2	17.0	25.7	0.1	8.6	21.4	0.1	27.6	16.5	3.0	47.9	4.8
Franklin city	4.4	12.3	10.4	46.7	10.6	26.1	0.2	8.3	8.1	0.4	21.3	17.3	3.3	54.1	3.6
Gloucester city	4.3	16.9	13.0	36.1	15.1	25.4	2.0	8.0	13.4	2.5	23.8	14.4	4.3	51.5	3.5
Haverhill city	2.7	20.9	12.9	34.3	14.0	26.6	0.0	8.1	17.0	0.1	27.2	14.1	4.7	49.6	4.2
Holyoke city	2.0	28.1	12.6	30.4	18.6	25.5	0.1	7.1	18.3	0.2	20.6	15.7	4.3	52.9	6.2
Lawrence city	2.0	29.4	6.4	20.7	19.4	24.2	0.4	7.5	27.9	0.3	30.1	15.1	4.3	46.5	3.8
Leominster city	2.2	18.9	13.0	32.8	14.5	26.8	0.2	8.0	17.7	0.5	30.6	14.8	3.1	46.1	5.0
Lowell city	1.3	23.2	9.1	28.4	16.0	24.4	0.1	8.6	22.6	0.2	29.5	13.2	4.0	49.0	4.1
Lynn city	1.4	25.4	11.2	25.8	19.9	28.2	0.3	8.7	17.2	0.3	20.5	16.2	6.1	51.9	5.0
Malden city	1.7	21.8	9.8	35.6	17.0	29.1	0.0	7.4	10.9	0.1	14.6	13.1	6.2	61.8	4.3
Marlborough city	2.6	17.1	11.1	42.0	15.1	24.7	0.2	6.7	10.5	0.1	22.6	17.3	3.5	53.4	3.1
Medford city	1.9	19.9	11.0	42.1	13.9	28.5	0.0	7.0	8.5	0.1	13.1	14.1	4.4	63.4	4.9
Melrose city	2.8	15.2	12.1	48.6	10.7	27.0	0.0	6.6	7.1	0.0	13.5	11.8	5.1	63.6	5.9
Methuen city	1.8	19.4	12.2	36.0	12.8	27.1	0.1	8.5	15.4	0.2	26.7	15.1	4.3	47.9	5.9
New Bedford city	1.2	26.1	10.2	20.8	19.8	23.6	1.0	9.8	25.1	1.1	27.9	16.6	3.7	45.8	5.0
Newton city	6.5	12.6	8.5	65.3	7.8	21.0	0.1	2.5	3.3	0.1	8.9	10.7	1.7	75.6	3.1
Northampton city	4.4	16.5	11.0	50.2	14.8	21.6	0.2	5.2	8.1	0.2	11.3	11.6	2.3	70.5	4.1
Peabody city	1.8	18.8	13.4	36.4	13.7	30.2	0.1	8.1	11.4	0.4	19.6	18.0	6.2	51.5	4.3
Pittsfield city	1.7	21.4	14.5	32.4	20.6	27.7	0.5	7.9	11.0	0.7	18.7	16.4	2.9	56.8	4.4
Quincy city	1.4	18.6	11.2	40.1	15.0	29.7	0.1	7.2	7.9	0.1	12.8	13.1	4.6	64.1	5.3
Revere city	1.0	27.4	10.5	25.5	18.8	32.9	0.2	9.2	13.3	0.4	15.1	15.2	9.9	53.4	6.0
Salem city	2.8	19.8	11.2	37.4	15.1	29.5	0.2	6.0	11.9	0.3	16.1	14.8	3.9	61.1	3.7

Table B-5. Cities — **Education, Labor Force, and Income**

City	Median household income	Median family income: All families	Median family income: Families with children: Married-couple	Median family income: Families with children: Male householder	Median family income: Families with children: Female householder	Median nonfamily household income	Median income for full-year, full-time workers: Men	Median income for full-year, full-time workers: Women	Per capita income	Households by source of income (percent): With earnings	Households by source of income (percent): With interest, dividend, or rental income	Households by source of income (percent): With Social Security income	Households by source of income (percent): With public assistance income	Households by source of income (percent): With retirement income	Households with income over $100,000 (percent)	+/− U.S. percent for income over $100,000	Households with income below poverty (percent)	Families with children with income below poverty (percent)
	57	58	59	60	61	62	63	64	65	66	67	68	69	70	71	72	73	74
KENTUCKY—Cont'd																		
Hopkinsville city	30 419	37 598	50 804	24 464	15 888	16 757	31 759	21 995	15 796	75.4	27.0	29.9	4.1	18.8	4.6	-7.7	17.1	19.9
Jeffersontown city	51 999	60 951	69 479	41 719	23 269	33 269	43 222	30 640	23 977	87.5	40.6	20.3	1.2	17.8	12.7	0.4	5.0	6.1
Lexington-Fayette	39 813	53 264	65 931	25 614	19 535	24 770	37 114	27 830	23 109	85.4	35.4	19.6	2.1	14.7	11.5	-0.8	12.9	12.6
Louisville city	28 843	36 696	51 826	24 092	14 309	20 687	31 231	25 237	18 193	73.9	27.1	28.9	4.9	17.1	6.0	-6.3	20.1	28.0
Owensboro city	31 867	41 333	51 579	23 828	14 640	18 228	34 532	22 500	17 968	74.8	32.2	31.4	4.0	19.4	5.0	-7.3	15.7	19.4
Paducah city	26 137	34 092	51 961	24 464	11 505	16 107	33 686	22 842	18 417	66.0	30.0	36.7	5.5	18.8	6.5	-5.8	21.8	29.1
Richmond city	25 533	36 222	45 612	12 375	15 257	15 879	31 064	22 577	15 815	79.7	21.5	21.8	4.5	11.6	4.1	-8.2	26.6	25.9
LOUISIANA	32 566	39 774	51 507	25 613	14 101	18 393	35 108	22 778	16 912	78.1	25.9	25.2	3.3	14.8	7.4	-4.9	19.1	22.1
Alexandria city	26 097	31 978	53 117	19 107	13 498	15 823	31 385	21 130	16 242	71.8	24.3	29.6	5.3	17.5	7.5	-4.8	25.7	32.7
Baton Rouge city	30 368	40 266	57 515	26 444	14 565	19 680	35 896	24 063	18 512	80.2	29.3	22.4	3.2	15.1	9.3	-3.0	22.8	26.6
Bossier City city	36 561	42 642	51 635	33 073	17 656	21 478	32 060	22 905	17 032	82.1	28.2	23.8	3.0	19.7	6.4	-5.9	14.4	16.9
Houma city	34 471	40 679	56 974	20 735	14 978	18 713	36 373	23 061	17 720	74.4	28.2	30.2	3.1	13.4	8.2	-4.1	19.0	22.9
Kenner city	39 946	45 866	59 421	27 219	17 068	27 202	35 740	24 798	19 615	86.4	29.5	20.1	2.8	12.6	10.4	-1.9	12.2	15.9
Lafayette city	35 996	47 783	61 502	32 183	16 665	21 058	40 360	24 887	21 031	81.9	33.2	22.0	1.8	12.0	10.8	-1.5	16.7	16.3
Lake Charles city	30 774	37 774	53 917	24 907	13 192	18 663	35 008	21 619	17 922	75.8	26.8	28.9	3.3	16.4	7.8	-4.5	19.7	24.7
Monroe city	25 864	33 263	54 167	26 250	11 129	15 840	33 057	22 879	15 933	74.0	22.8	26.4	4.5	12.9	7.8	-4.5	29.2	36.0
New Iberia city	26 079	30 828	42 670	23 578	8 960	15 265	30 895	17 610	13 084	73.3	23.3	29.8	5.2	14.2	4.2	-8.1	26.9	35.1
New Orleans city	27 133	32 338	51 346	19 879	13 166	19 453	31 675	24 777	17 258	75.8	23.7	24.7	5.4	13.4	7.8	-4.5	25.6	33.5
Shreveport city	30 526	37 126	52 350	23 416	14 317	20 415	32 193	22 298	17 759	77.1	25.1	26.5	3.8	16.3	7.4	-4.9	20.5	27.6
Slidell city	42 856	48 298	58 065	33 207	18 200	22 904	41 598	27 009	19 947	78.8	35.8	29.2	2.5	20.3	10.7	-1.6	12.2	14.0
MAINE	37 240	45 179	53 839	27 407	17 632	21 715	34 180	25 151	19 533	78.5	37.8	28.9	4.8	17.4	7.1	-5.2	11.5	11.9
Bangor city	29 740	42 047	57 656	27 969	13 155	20 824	33 480	24 855	19 295	75.7	33.9	26.4	6.8	16.6	7.4	-4.9	17.0	17.6
Lewiston city	29 191	40 061	49 774	22 500	16 582	16 848	30 956	22 331	17 905	71.5	32.5	34.0	7.8	15.0	4.2	-8.1	16.8	19.2
Portland city	35 650	48 763	61 688	29 250	18 159	27 035	32 872	28 753	22 698	78.9	38.2	24.4	5.4	13.6	7.0	-5.3	13.1	16.7
MARYLAND	52 868	61 876	74 531	36 405	27 166	32 654	42 857	33 301	25 614	83.8	39.2	22.5	2.4	18.7	18.1	5.8	8.3	8.7
Annapolis city	49 243	56 984	72 917	34 554	20 517	36 667	41 111	31 384	27 180	82.7	39.0	21.6	2.6	18.5	16.4	4.1	11.5	16.6
Baltimore city	30 078	35 438	54 653	25 800	18 281	20 884	32 401	27 478	16 978	74.0	22.2	27.7	7.3	16.9	6.3	-6.0	21.8	26.2
Bowie city	76 778	82 403	86 276	63 281	47 601	55 332	54 956	41 320	30 703	90.4	49.0	17.3	0.6	22.4	28.7	16.4	1.7	1.0
Frederick city	47 700	56 778	65 496	35 720	23 497	33 595	39 271	28 799	23 053	85.8	33.7	19.7	2.4	15.5	11.5	-0.8	6.8	7.3
Gaithersburg city	59 879	66 669	75 691	42 669	32 464	46 350	45 724	37 045	27 323	90.0	42.3	13.3	2.1	12.0	21.8	9.5	5.6	6.3
Hagerstown city	30 796	38 149	48 139	28 202	12 567	20 725	31 797	23 326	17 153	75.8	24.8	26.1	4.3	14.8	3.8	-8.5	17.0	23.0
Rockville city	68 074	79 051	85 871	39 306	27 545	42 827	56 371	39 929	30 518	85.4	55.6	20.9	1.2	18.8	29.8	17.5	6.6	8.0
MASSACHUSETTS	50 502	61 664	74 589	34 532	22 138	29 774	45 130	33 281	25 952	80.1	42.1	26.2	2.9	16.5	17.7	5.4	9.8	10.1
Agawam city	49 390	59 088	66 701	34 250	35 614	30 072	41 647	31 232	22 562	81.6	40.4	28.9	1.5	18.0	10.4	-1.9	6.4	5.7
Attleboro city	50 807	59 112	65 841	32 177	30 993	28 014	41 247	29 663	22 660	83.8	37.8	24.3	2.3	13.9	11.5	-0.8	7.1	5.0
Barnstable Town city	46 811	54 026	70 426	33 173	20 528	28 793	42 657	31 427	25 554	74.5	44.4	35.0	1.7	23.4	13.6	1.3	8.2	11.1
Beverly city	53 984	66 486	78 142	38 269	26 474	33 172	45 982	36 247	28 626	80.4	44.7	27.2	2.7	18.5	18.4	6.1	6.3	6.1
Boston city	39 629	44 151	56 425	30 098	20 093	32 761	38 764	33 690	23 353	79.1	31.4	18.7	4.1	10.9	12.8	0.5	18.7	22.2
Brockton city	39 507	46 235	55 954	29 565	19 327	22 420	35 479	27 603	17 163	77.8	26.9	25.7	5.6	14.8	7.9	-4.4	15.0	17.3
Cambridge city	47 979	59 423	74 634	32 386	25 510	41 548	46 733	40 521	31 156	83.1	49.8	16.9	2.2	10.6	19.6	7.3	12.6	12.6
Chelsea city	30 161	32 130	42 105	19 559	19 478	18 588	28 310	26 608	14 628	71.5	20.3	24.2	7.3	12.4	6.6	-5.7	23.8	24.9
Chicopee city	35 672	44 136	53 785	33 519	18 741	23 259	36 285	26 972	18 646	73.1	34.9	33.9	4.2	22.0	4.9	-7.4	11.4	16.0
Everett city	40 661	49 876	57 279	35 200	22 851	26 565	36 639	31 141	19 845	76.5	31.4	28.2	3.6	17.0	7.9	-4.4	11.6	14.3
Fall River city	29 014	37 671	50 606	25 066	14 310	16 271	31 913	23 762	16 118	69.8	28.1	30.1	6.5	17.0	4.2	-8.1	18.1	21.7
Fitchburg city	37 004	43 291	56 334	24 196	17 538	22 922	36 404	27 211	17 256	74.6	31.5	30.7	5.9	17.8	6.6	-5.7	14.6	18.5
Franklin city	71 174	81 826	89 707	61 071	36 364	35 406	60 526	36 862	27 849	87.7	45.9	19.7	1.3	13.8	28.2	15.9	3.8	3.0
Gloucester city	47 722	58 459	66 221	31 927	17 774	31 652	42 470	31 433	25 595	79.3	40.6	27.5	2.5	15.6	12.9	0.6	9.7	10.8
Haverhill city	49 833	59 772	71 365	30 767	23 691	28 828	41 928	32 617	23 280	80.3	34.6	24.4	3.0	15.0	13.4	1.1	9.9	11.3
Holyoke city	30 441	36 130	55 385	20 032	13 128	19 750	35 968	27 979	15 913	69.0	29.1	32.6	11.2	17.7	5.9	-6.4	23.9	33.9
Lawrence city	27 983	31 809	45 210	25 957	16 758	15 502	28 899	24 023	13 360	74.8	19.1	24.5	9.0	11.1	5.0	-7.3	24.3	26.7
Leominster city	44 893	54 660	67 068	29 038	21 214	27 009	41 338	31 098	21 769	79.2	36.2	25.1	3.4	16.3	11.1	-1.2	10.1	10.4
Lowell city	39 192	45 901	56 563	30 398	18 826	25 606	34 454	28 099	17 557	78.5	26.5	23.2	5.8	12.8	8.1	-4.2	15.7	19.2
Lynn city	37 364	45 295	58 263	29 286	18 779	21 600	35 526	28 736	17 492	75.8	29.3	26.6	6.3	15.6	8.1	-4.2	17.1	19.1
Malden city	45 654	55 557	59 847	32 188	23 111	30 446	38 889	31 843	22 004	80.4	34.7	25.2	2.4	14.7	10.9	-1.4	9.9	10.7
Marlborough city	56 879	70 385	78 128	42 500	26 875	36 105	50 021	33 867	28 723	85.9	41.7	21.3	2.0	13.4	20.4	8.1	7.5	6.8
Medford city	52 476	62 409	72 945	42 361	32 375	34 676	44 233	36 327	24 707	78.3	45.8	31.4	1.7	19.1	16.7	4.4	7.3	5.4
Melrose city	62 811	78 144	87 619	46 635	32 857	31 762	51 850	40 594	30 347	80.2	48.3	30.2	1.6	20.3	23.3	11.0	5.1	2.5
Methuen city	49 627	59 831	71 432	32 917	21 432	25 942	42 207	32 387	22 305	77.0	39.0	31.1	2.8	19.9	13.4	1.1	7.9	9.3
New Bedford city	27 569	35 708	49 738	27 650	13 453	15 660	32 413	23 001	15 602	69.2	27.7	31.7	7.1	17.4	4.2	-8.1	21.0	25.3
Newton city	86 052	105 289	131 101	70 313	53 864	49 872	70 471	49 894	45 708	83.5	65.1	25.9	1.4	14.7	42.8	30.5	4.3	3.9
Northampton city	41 808	56 844	66 603	41 346	30 795	29 818	38 367	31 485	24 022	81.6	46.4	23.8	2.1	15.9	11.8	-0.5	11.3	7.4
Peabody city	54 829	65 483	74 448	37 891	27 500	27 406	45 721	33 234	24 827	78.9	43.3	32.2	1.5	20.8	17.5	5.2	6.6	4.8
Pittsfield city	35 655	46 228	56 903	31 094	17 756	21 643	36 703	27 466	20 549	72.8	43.6	33.6	3.6	22.0	7.7	-4.6	11.7	16.2
Quincy city	47 121	59 735	66 817	41 728	27 255	35 513	41 605	35 419	26 001	78.3	41.5	28.7	2.1	19.3	13.7	1.4	7.5	9.1
Revere city	37 067	45 865	54 405	24 464	17 392	22 333	37 496	31 730	19 698	72.1	31.3	30.8	3.1	17.4	9.0	-3.3	15.0	17.8
Salem city	44 033	55 635	67 793	28 333	24 873	28 707	40 175	32 194	23 857	79.4	37.3	27.0	2.9	16.9	12.1	-0.2	10.4	12.1

Table B-5. Cities — Education, Labor Force, and Income

STATE Place code	City	Total population 25 years and over	Percent with a high school diploma or less	Percent with a high school diploma or more	Percent with a bachelor's degree or more	+/- U.S. percent with bachelor's degree or more	College graduates (percent) Non-Hispanic White	Black or African American	American Indian and Alaska Native	Asian, Hawaiian, and Pacific Islander	Hispanic or Latino[1]
		1	2	3	4	5	6	7	8	9	10
	MASSACHUSETTS— Cont'd										
25 62535	Somerville city	53 693	43.2	80.6	40.6	16.2	42.7	27.7	31.5	59.2	22.3
25 67000	Springfield city	90 800	59.5	73.4	15.4	-9.0	19.4	13.3	8.0	15.4	6.0
25 69170	Taunton city	37 856	60.4	74.8	15.1	-9.3	15.2	12.3	38.3	42.5	8.4
25 72600	Waltham city	39 912	40.0	85.4	38.4	14.0	37.8	32.8	30.9	67.5	20.5
25 73440	Watertown city	25 300	32.7	87.4	47.2	22.8	47.1	46.0	0.0	64.2	32.2
25 76030	Westfield city	25 439	47.4	84.9	24.2	-0.2	24.7	39.6	5.0	44.4	10.7
25 81035	Woburn city	26 829	44.3	88.1	29.5	5.1	27.3	30.1	6.3	73.3	19.7
25 82000	Worcester city	108 769	52.7	76.7	23.3	-1.1	25.9	17.5	11.1	25.3	8.8
26 00000	MICHIGAN	6 415 941	47.9	83.4	21.8	-2.6	22.7	12.8	10.3	60.5	12.9
26 01380	Allen Park city	20 994	47.5	87.3	19.7	-4.7	19.2	6.9	29.8	73.8	16.8
26 03000	Ann Arbor city	64 672	13.3	95.7	69.3	44.9	70.9	30.7	20.00	87.2	60.4
26 05920	Battle Creek city	34 274	50.4	82.4	17.2	-7.2	19.0	8.7	1.7	41.9	8.7
26 06020	Bay City city	23 993	56.8	80.8	12.8	-11.6	13.2	5.6	9.5	41.1	4.6
26 12060	Burton city	19 429	56.6	81.9	11.2	-13.2	10.4	24.7	0.0	43.8	13.6
26 21000	Dearborn city	62 726	46.6	78.0	26.4	2.0	27.1	21.7	10.2	63.9	22.6
26 21020	Dearborn Heights city	40 793	55.8	79.0	16.7	-7.7	16.1	14.6	17.3	47.3	16.5
26 22000	Detroit city	563 979	60.4	69.6	11.0	-13.4	15.2	10.1	12.3	43.8	5.8
26 24120	East Lansing city	15 292	10.4	96.9	70.4	46.0	69.2	62.7	29.1	87.9	51.5
26 24290	Eastpointe city	23 307	59.7	79.3	11.3	-13.1	10.9	15.2	11.0	28.1	19.6
26 27400	Farmington Hills city	57 572	26.0	91.7	47.9	23.5	45.2	48.1	0.0	81.4	47.6
26 29000	Flint city	73 722	57.6	74.5	11.3	-13.1	14.2	8.3	9.7	43.9	10.4
26 31420	Garden City city	20 310	58.0	81.1	9.0	-15.4	8.9	9.9	15.3	14.1	18.9
26 34000	Grand Rapids city	118 579	48.1	78.0	23.8	-0.6	29.8	10.2	6.6	26.5	6.5
26 38640	Holland city	20 094	49.3	78.5	26.9	2.5	32.1	8.8	35.5	27.6	7.1
26 40680	Inkster city	18 374	58.7	74.3	12.1	-12.3	7.4	8.8	11.0	64.7	6.3
26 41420	Jackson city	21 942	53.6	77.3	13.1	-11.3	14.9	5.6	0.0	41.5	9.3
26 42160	Kalamazoo city	39 884	39.4	84.2	32.7	8.3	38.2	11.4	22.8	71.9	12.0
26 42820	Kentwood city	28 518	37.4	89.2	31.5	7.1	32.0	22.0	10.0	70.9	21.5
26 46000	Lansing city	73 763	44.4	82.4	21.2	-3.2	23.1	16.6	15.5	34.5	9.8
26 47800	Lincoln Park city	26 982	66.1	74.7	6.9	-17.5	6.7	12.0	8.6	45.0	4.3
26 49000	Livonia city	70 332	38.6	88.8	29.7	5.3	29.3	18.4	15.6	59.0	25.3
26 50560	Madison Heights city	21 791	54.8	78.8	18.5	-5.9	15.3	34.4	0.0	60.7	30.0
26 53780	Midland city	26 782	29.1	92.2	41.9	17.5	40.8	56.8	6.8	77.7	44.9
26 56020	Mount Pleasant city	8 894	32.8	88.2	40.3	15.9	40.4	25.0	7.3	76.9	21.6
26 50020	Muskegon city	26 104	59.4	77.7	8.7	-15.7	11.0	4.8	4.0	24.5	2.8
26 59440	Novi city	31 216	22.8	94.0	49.1	24.7	47.1	46.9	0.0	74.1	38.0
26 59920	Oak Park city	18 942	40.5	82.2	27.2	2.8	29.1	24.4	39.4	36.6	31.8
26 65440	Pontiac city	39 297	63.6	68.9	10.3	-14.1	12.4	9.5	8.0	19.9	3.0
26 65560	Portage city	29 391	31.2	92.6	36.8	12.4	36.0	34.8	41.7	71.0	29.2
26 65820	Port Huron city	20 476	58.9	76.8	11.3	-13.1	11.9	7.0	4.7	41.0	2.7
26 69035	Rochester Hills city	46 378	25.6	92.7	47.3	22.9	45.1	52.5	0.0	78.0	43.2
26 69800	Roseville city	33 081	62.6	76.2	7.2	-17.2	6.7	12.4	8.0	26.1	8.4
26 70040	Royal Oak city	44 980	31.4	91.5	39.9	15.5	40.1	28.1	28.3	61.3	33.4
26 70520	Saginaw city	36 227	61.7	73.1	10.4	-14.0	14.1	6.7	0.0	47.5	4.3
26 70760	St. Clair Shores city	46 530	49.4	84.4	18.1	-6.3	17.6	30.1	11.2	54.7	29.5
26 74900	Southfield city	55 416	32.0	87.3	36.7	12.3	34.6	36.6	23.2	69.5	37.6
26 74960	Southgate city	21 122	58.4	80.5	12.7	-11.7	11.9	20.2	7.2	57.2	8.8
26 76460	Sterling Heights city	83 774	45.2	84.0	23.0	-1.4	21.4	33.9	12.6	52.5	22.1
26 79000	Taylor city	41 876	65.2	75.2	7.0	-17.4	6.3	8.8	13.4	38.1	7.9
26 80700	Troy city	54 239	25.2	92.2	50.0	25.6	46.0	57.1	8.7	77.1	53.3
26 84000	Warren city	95 949	58.9	76.9	13.0	-11.4	12.3	12.3	9.6	39.9	11.1
26 86000	Westland city	58 687	53.4	81.1	16.1	-8.3	13.8	20.5	12.1	74.2	15.6
26 88900	Wyandotte city	19 278	56.9	79.7	12.7	-11.7	12.4	16.1	5.1	47.3	14.8
26 88940	Wyoming city	42 462	51.6	81.9	17.0	-7.4	18.2	8.4	12.2	14.4	9.7
27 00000	MINNESOTA	3 164 345	40.9	87.9	27.4	3.0	28.0	18.7	8.8	36.1	14.0
27 01486	Andover city	15 484	30.9	94.5	28.0	3.6	27.9	55.3	16.8	12.2	48.6
27 01900	Apple Valley city	28 645	24.1	95.4	41.0	16.6	41.8	26.3	22.7	35.8	12.0
27 06382	Blaine city	27 958	42.1	91.2	19.7	-4.7	19.7	30.1	4.6	30.1	10.1
27 06616	Bloomington city	61 059	31.3	92.2	35.4	11.0	36.3	24.9	15.6	30.1	17.7
27 07948	Brooklyn Center city	19 082	47.9	86.9	16.7	-7.7	16.7	17.9	32.4	14.2	19.8
27 07966	Brooklyn Park city	41 307	34.6	90.5	27.3	2.9	28.2	25.9	11.3	25.9	22.3
27 08794	Burnsville city	38 127	27.1	93.9	36.8	12.4	38.2	25.3	12.4	29.4	18.2
27 13114	Coon Rapids city	38 182	39.8	91.9	21.4	-3.0	21.3	26.9	9.0	31.9	22.6
27 13456	Cottage Grove city	18 410	35.8	94.5	23.9	-0.5	23.7	21.9	6.9	47.1	30.5
27 17000	Duluth city	54 358	41.1	87.7	28.2	3.8	28.8	20.8	8.5	29.2	9.8
27 17288	Eagan city	40 244	20.2	96.0	47.7	23.3	48.9	39.1	9.9	49.2	19.4
27 18116	Eden Prairie city	34 829	14.7	97.2	57.1	32.7	57.8	33.4	17.1	57.9	52.1
27 18188	Edina city	34 453	16.3	96.9	58.5	34.1	58.8	34.2	26.4	65.9	43.5
27 22814	Fridley city	18 611	43.6	89.4	24.4	0.0	24.8	18.4	22.4	29.6	7.4

[1] Hispanic or Latino persons may be of any race.

City	School enrollment			Population 16 to 19 years				Employment status, 2000			Work status in 1999 of the population 16 years and over		
											Worked in 1999		
	Grades kindergarten through 12	College or graduate school	Percent private	Number	Percent in armed forces	Percent high school graduates	Percent not enrolled, not grads, not in armed forces, not employed	Total population 16 years and over	Percent in labor force	Unemployment rate	Full-time	Part-time	Did not work in 1999
	11	12	13	14	15	16	17	18	19	20	21	22	23
MASSACHUSETTS— Cont'd													
Somerville city	8 315	11 452	51.7	3 545	0.0	9.1	3.8	67 455	70.6	3.5	60.8	15.8	23.4
Springfield city	32 506	10 897	21.1	9 601	0.0	9.1	9.4	112 767	58.8	8.5	47.8	17.1	35.1
Taunton city	10 038	2 485	14.9	2 547	0.0	11.8	6.4	43 556	68.2	4.3	56.6	15.6	27.8
Waltham city	6 637	9 070	50.6	4 257	0.0	5.0	1.6	51 037	69.0	5.4	57.0	18.8	24.1
Watertown city	3 281	3 096	44.2	1 181	0.0	10.8	0.8	28 728	68.9	2.4	59.8	15.2	25.0
Westfield city	7 119	4 185	10.7	2 913	0.0	6.0	3.5	31 600	66.2	4.9	52.7	19.2	28.1
Woburn city	5 846	1 788	22.1	1 504	0.0	13.8	1.3	30 312	69.2	3.0	56.9	16.5	26.6
Worcester city	30 588	18 338	30.8	11 442	0.0	9.1	4.2	136 269	60.8	6.3	50.1	17.4	32.4
MICHIGAN	1 971 459	635 836	12.3	566 976	0.0	9.1	4.9	7 630 645	64.6	5.8	53.9	16.5	29.6
Allen Park city	4 924	1 690	15.5	1 222	0.0	7.4	3.7	23 616	59.3	3.5	50.3	14.3	35.4
Ann Arbor city	13 174	36 892	7.6	11 366	0.1	2.4	0.6	97 052	65.9	4.2	52.8	27.6	19.6
Battle Creek city	10 570	2 397	9.8	2 902	0.0	10.8	13.7	40 478	61.1	6.6	52.3	15.2	32.6
Bay City city	7 060	1 763	13.1	1 922	0.0	10.7	7.1	28 445	62.2	6.8	48.9	17.4	33.7
Burton city	6 089	1 286	11.8	1 577	0.0	7.4	8.6	22 811	63.6	5.5	54.6	14.6	30.8
Dearborn city	19 869	6 741	14.6	5 105	0.0	7.1	6.9	73 385	55.8	5.3	45.9	13.4	40.7
Dearborn Heights city ...	9 481	3 436	20.6	2 699	0.0	9.9	3.7	46 632	58.5	4.8	49.7	13.7	36.6
Detroit city	228 639	48 926	12.2	53 909	0.1	12.6	10.5	683 613	56.3	13.8	48.7	11.9	39.4
East Lansing city	3 099	29 329	4.3	9 887	0.0	1.0	0.2	43 032	63.6	10.4	39.0	45.1	15.9
Eastpointe city	6 262	1 613	17.0	1 552	0.0	12.8	3.5	26 658	64.8	4.1	54.9	14.0	31.1
Farmington Hills city	14 387	5 228	17.1	3 805	0.0	9.5	1.3	65 386	66.5	2.9	57.5	14.9	27.7
Flint city	28 066	6 236	8.9	7 337	0.0	11.4	11.7	90 146	58.5	12.9	48.9	15.6	35.5
Garden City city	5 749	1 471	10.7	1 621	0.0	11.9	3.4	23 405	65.6	4.7	56.0	15.2	28.8
Grand Rapids city	38 645	15 383	28.4	13 265	0.0	8.2	9.3	149 929	65.8	6.3	54.6	17.4	28.0
Holland city	6 731	4 152	38.1	2 786	0.0	7.6	3.1	26 999	67.1	5.0	53.6	21.9	24.4
Inkster city	6 726	1 574	10.7	1 705	0.0	12.0	7.4	21 968	60.3	10.3	51.0	12.4	36.6
Jackson city	7 397	1 723	13.3	1 903	0.0	7.0	18.6	26 546	64.0	8.1	54.3	15.0	30.8
Kalamazoo city	11 055	19 725	11.5	8 607	0.0	5.8	3.4	62 928	67.5	12.4	50.1	26.3	23.6
Kentwood city	8 873	2 756	16.6	2 101	0.0	10.1	3.0	34 209	74.3	3.9	62.9	16.3	20.7
Lansing city	23 258	10 192	10.7	6 111	0.0	10.1	8.3	90 077	68.6	6.3	56.7	17.4	25.9
Lincoln Park city	7 019	1 676	12.7	1 807	0.0	15.1	5.5	31 255	63.3	6.2	54.2	14.0	31.8
Livonia city	18 585	6 548	15.8	4 985	0.0	5.2	1.0	79 433	64.8	3.1	52.2	17.2	30.6
Madison Heights city	5 145	1 903	11.2	1 325	0.0	9.0	3.3	25 021	65.2	3.9	56.4	14.5	29.1
Midland city	8 097	3 425	17.2	2 592	0.0	6.7	2.2	32 222	64.1	4.2	50.0	19.8	30.3
Mount Pleasant city	2 143	14 287	3.5	5 585	0.0	1.4	0.7	23 368	61.9	9.2	42.6	40.6	16.8
Muskegon city	7 811	1 873	11.1	2 102	0.0	13.0	6.6	30 779	53.0	7.1	47.4	15.3	37.4
Novi city	9 617	2 848	10.1	2 224	0.0	5.9	1.2	35 863	74.0	2.2	63.0	16.1	20.9
Oak Park city	6 720	2 217	22.2	1 723	0.0	5.3	3.1	22 323	64.0	5.4	55.9	15.2	28.9
Pontiac city	15 100	3 117	7.2	3 460	0.2	10.5	9.3	47 821	62.1	10.3	54.2	13.7	32.2
Portage city	8 892	2 923	10.1	2 287	0.4	10.2	2.0	34 418	71.1	3.7	58.1	17.3	24.6
Port Huron city	6 192	1 292	6.6	1 788	0.0	10.8	11.7	24 633	64.0	7.7	52.9	16.3	30.8
Rochester Hills city	13 836	4 707	17.3	3 420	0.0	4.2	0.4	52 951	69.7	2.4	58.4	16.8	24.8
Roseville city	8 195	2 136	11.2	2 168	0.0	15.2	6.0	38 070	64.7	5.7	54.5	14.2	31.3
Royal Oak city	7 761	5 118	16.9	2 374	0.0	9.1	2.1	50 644	71.8	2.4	61.6	14.2	24.2
Saginaw city	15 070	2 790	7.1	3 601	0.0	9.1	13.1	44 017	58.8	13.1	45.7	17.3	37.0
St. Clair Shores city	9 795	3 106	15.4	2 886	0.0	8.4	2.9	52 026	60.1	4.4	50.8	14.6	34.5
Southfield city	12 893	7 080	20.4	3 690	0.0	9.1	2.9	63 446	65.7	4.6	57.7	13.4	28.9
Southgate city	5 023	1 752	12.6	1 536	0.0	10.0	4.9	24 419	62.8	4.9	53.0	14.8	32.2
Sterling Heights city	22 944	8 173	12.7	6 473	0.1	8.4	2.3	97 973	68.1	3.5	56.6	16.2	27.1
Taylor city	13 243	2 691	12.2	3 496	0.0	15.6	6.5	49 822	63.4	6.5	55.6	13.4	30.9
Troy city	16 490	5 471	13.4	4 062	0.0	3.8	0.9	62 358	69.7	3.3	58.9	16.2	24.9
Warren city	23 690	6 747	11.2	6 427	0.1	9.8	4.1	109 960	61.3	4.7	52.1	14.3	33.6
Westland city	14 400	4 737	11.4	3 821	0.0	14.6	5.6	68 423	67.1	4.5	57.1	14.7	28.2
Wyandotte city	4 792	1 469	16.3	1 472	0.0	16.3	4.0	22 456	64.8	5.8	53.9	14.8	31.3
Wyoming city	14 363	3 539	14.1	4 059	0.0	12.6	3.9	52 051	73.7	4.6	61.9	17.0	21.2
MINNESOTA	975 733	296 258	14.3	293 223	0.1	8.5	2.8	3 781 756	71.2	4.1	57.9	19.2	22.9
Andover city	7 140	1 030	14.3	1 537	0.0	6.8	2.5	18 076	82.1	2.1	66.9	19.6	13.5
Apple Valley city	10 396	2 335	8.4	2 974	0.0	6.2	1.0	33 808	80.7	2.5	66.4	19.3	14.3
Blaine city	9 695	2 114	9.9	2 700	0.0	8.7	3.7	33 338	80.4	3.1	67.9	18.2	13.9
Bloomington city	13 190	4 518	17.0	3 577	0.0	8.7	2.2	69 656	70.7	2.7	58.9	17.9	23.2
Brooklyn Center city	5 385	1 471	9.6	1 524	0.0	18.2	4.5	22 494	70.1	5.0	57.4	16.5	26.1
Brooklyn Park city	14 200	4 150	12.0	4 068	0.0	9.4	4.2	50 058	78.8	3.4	67.7	17.0	15.3
Burnsville city	11 815	3 371	12.8	3 284	0.5	11.4	1.3	46 122	79.8	2.7	65.7	19.1	15.1
Coon Rapids city	13 011	2 956	11.5	3 626	0.0	12.6	3.9	45 963	78.4	3.8	65.3	18.4	16.4
Cottage Grove city	7 292	1 317	10.9	1 912	0.0	9.2	0.4	21 707	80.1	2.7	66.4	18.6	15.0
Duluth city	14 025	11 678	12.6	6 561	0.2	8.2	2.2	70 664	64.3	7.5	47.6	23.8	28.6
Eagan city	13 550	3 589	15.0	2 994	0.0	8.4	1.4	46 552	82.1	2.0	69.6	17.6	12.8
Eden Prairie city	12 234	2 530	14.2	2 687	0.0	5.9	1.1	39 864	79.2	2.1	66.8	17.9	15.3
Edina city....................	8 274	1 619	17.2	1 991	0.0	2.8	0.7	37 985	61.4	1.7	49.4	17.9	32.7
Fridley city	4 575	1 337	11.1	1 034	0.0	10.6	2.4	21 801	73.5	3.0	62.0	16.9	21.1

Table B-5. Cities — Education, Labor Force, and Income

City	Full-year full-time employed (percent)								Children under 18 years in families (percent, except where noted)						Total employed by class of worker (percent)			
										With two parents		With one parent who is in labor force	+/− U.S. percent of children with no stay-at-home parent	+/− U.S. percent two-income couples				
	Total	Men	Women	Non-Hispanic White	Black or African American	American Indian and Alaska Native	Asian, Hawaiian, and Pacific Islander	Hispanic or Latino[1]	Number	Both in labor force	Father only in labor force				Private	Government	Self-employed	Unpaid family worker
	24	25	26	27	28	29	30	31	32	33	34	35	36	37	38	39	40	41
MASSACHUSETTS—Cont'd																		
Somerville city	44.0	50.8	37.6	44.4	46.9	44.1	37.7	47.0	10 508	41.3	18.2	23.3	0.0	2.3	82.5	10.7	6.6	0.3
Springfield city	34.8	42.6	28.2	37.5	36.0	33.6	35.2	26.0	40 101	27.9	9.8	33.8	-2.9	-2.0	76.3	18.2	5.3	0.2
Taunton city	46.8	57.6	37.1	47.3	50.3	55.6	34.1	42.5	13 209	49.9	12.3	22.9	8.2	8.8	79.5	14.8	5.6	0.1
Waltham city	43.4	51.4	35.8	43.8	45.0	54.5	39.0	43.8	8 820	53.4	21.4	16.4	5.2	4.2	83.2	9.6	7.0	0.2
Watertown city	47.7	55.6	41.0	47.5	56.7	100.0	47.2	58.5	4 552	48.5	21.5	16.3	0.2	5.2	80.2	9.9	9.9	0.1
Westfield city	40.7	53.9	28.5	41.0	30.2	48.3	62.5	33.4	9 187	46.8	23.2	17.2	-0.6	6.8	74.1	17.9	7.8	0.2
Woburn city	46.0	57.8	35.0	45.9	44.3	17.2	47.4	51.9	7 558	54.5	21.1	17.2	7.1	5.3	81.9	10.9	7.0	0.1
Worcester city	36.6	45.5	28.5	37.6	37.2	36.9	36.1	30.3	38 129	36.8	13.7	27.9	0.1	0.2	79.3	14.9	5.5	0.3
MICHIGAN	40.1	50.5	30.5	41.6	32.8	37.1	39.3	36.6	2 456 837	44.2	21.9	22.8	2.4	0.1	79.9	11.4	8.4	-0.3
Allen Park city	39.7	52.0	29.0	39.5	49.1	29.0	29.5	45.8	6 338	55.1	25.8	13.6	4.1	-4.7	84.6	9.9	5.3	0.2
Ann Arbor city	33.2	40.2	26.4	34.8	33.2	35.9	24.6	28.4	18 284	47.8	25.8	18.3	1.5	5.3	68.0	24.1	7.7	0.2
Battle Creek city	38.3	45.0	32.3	39.7	33.2	14.2	35.8	40.7	13 404	38.6	15.7	33.1	7.1	-0.7	78.8	13.6	7.3	0.3
Bay City city	36.7	46.5	27.9	37.5	24.2	46.5	30.3	30.2	9 006	43.3	14.6	26.1	4.8	0.4	81.5	11.4	7.0	0.2
Burton city	39.8	50.2	30.2	40.1	38.6	29.9	56.0	33.5	8 001	41.7	23.2	26.0	3.1	-2.6	84.8	7.0	8.1	0.1
Dearborn city	34.0	45.9	22.5	34.4	35.5	30.0	39.5	40.8	26 117	29.5	40.7	12.6	-22.5	-14.1	81.3	10.2	8.1	0.4
Dearborn Heights city ...	38.9	51.1	27.8	38.8	48.0	33.3	32.8	36.3	12 597	44.6	27.9	17.3	-2.7	-9.1	85.1	7.7	6.9	0.2
Detroit city	30.4	33.1	28.2	30.4	30.7	29.0	29.4	25.8	261 080	18.7	8.9	45.0	-0.9	-11.4	77.9	17.2	4.6	0.3
East Lansing city	16.7	19.5	14.1	17.1	14.5	28.1	12.4	21.9	4 099	45.4	24.7	21.9	3.3	6.9	69.0	25.7	4.3	0.1
Eastpointe city	43.3	55.8	31.9	43.1	48.0	37.0	42.9	51.6	8 010	45.0	26.9	19.4	-0.2	0.4	85.3	9.3	5.4	0.1
Farmington Hills city.....	44.7	58.9	31.7	43.5	55.8	63.9	48.5	41.5	18 375	49.0	32.7	12.4	-3.2	0.0	80.7	7.6	11.3	0.4
Flint city	31.5	36.4	27.5	36.4	27.2	35.1	34.9	31.0	34 464	22.6	11.1	44.6	2.6	-9.0	81.1	12.5	6.1	0.3
Garden City city	44.5	57.5	32.2	44.6	48.8	42.4	27.1	57.3	7 229	44.4	25.7	23.0	2.8	-4.6	86.1	7.1	6.7	0.1
Grand Rapids city	39.6	48.4	31.5	41.4	34.6	27.2	43.0	37.2	49 442	38.0	17.5	27.3	0.7	3.0	85.4	8.2	6.1	0.3
Holland city	36.9	49.6	25.9	35.5	35.3	31.0	55.4	39.8	8 456	51.3	17.6	19.7	6.4	6.9	86.2	7.1	6.3	0.4
Inkster city	34.6	41.6	28.7	37.7	33.1	28.4	42.0	40.3	7 968	24.6	12.2	42.7	2.7	-11.4	83.5	11.0	4.8	0.1
Jackson city	39.4	48.3	31.7	41.5	32.9	19.2	18.9	34.7	9 960	31.1	16.9	36.3	2.8	2.2	82.4	10.7	6.7	0.2
Kalamazoo city	30.6	36.3	25.3	30.8	31.5	33.2	15.2	31.6	14 405	33.8	13.0	39.2	8.4	5.7	79.8	13.7	6.2	0.3
Kentwood city	50.5	64.0	38.5	50.4	59.0	35.1	44.6	45.3	11 704	48.5	23.6	20.8	4.7	8.1	88.1	6.0	5.7	0.3
Lansing city	42.0	48.4	36.5	44.5	38.1	36.0	31.5	36.6	29 698	34.6	13.7	35.1	5.1	2.2	75.0	18.8	6.1	0.1
Lincoln Park city	41.6	53.3	30.5	41.8	34.7	20.9	47.3	40.6	9 162	40.8	21.7	24.3	0.5	-8.1	87.8	7.4	4.5	0.3
Livonia city	42.3	56.8	29.1	42.1	49.6	69.5	46.0	37.3	23 507	54.8	27.7	12.3	2.5	2.0	83.1	9.4	7.2	0.3
Madison Heights city.....	43.4	54.5	33.0	42.5	57.6	74.2	44.1	64.8	6 427	42.8	24.6	20.2	-1.6	-2.8	87.4	7.1	5.4	0.1
Midland city	39.4	52.3	28.0	39.3	35.8	40.0	46.3	35.7	10 361	46.1	31.2	18.6	0.1	-1.5	82.0	10.8	7.1	0.2
Mount Pleasant city......	17.3	21.6	14.0	17.4	9.3	19.6	20.7	22.9	2 871	46.0	16.2	30.1	11.5	6.7	72.9	22.2	4.6	0.3
Muskegon city	32.0	35.0	27.0	35.4	26.6	27.3	30.0	29.4	9 392	31.1	10.2	39.2	5.7	-2.4	83.2	11.1	5.5	0.2
Novi city	50.6	67.6	34.9	51.2	60.2	65.8	45.8	40.6	12 797	47.9	38.9	8.2	-8.5	5.4	85.8	6.9	7.1	0.2
Oak Park city	41.9	49.0	36.0	36.5	47.8	64.1	39.2	48.8	8 001	42.8	18.2	25.9	4.1	1.8	81.6	10.8	7.2	0.5
Pontiac city	36.3	42.7	30.5	37.9	35.1	40.0	40.9	35.3	18 164	22.7	13.5	40.9	-1.0	-7.5	85.0	9.0	4.2	0.2
Portage city	46.7	59.5	35.2	46.6	46.5	60.4	47.9	46.9	11 609	52.6	23.7	18.9	6.9	6.2	79.0	11.7	9.1	0.2
Port Huron city	37.1	47.1	28.3	37.5	33.6	21.2	37.3	34.7	8 083	36.8	14.7	36.3	8.5	-0.8	84.2	8.5	6.9	0.3
Rochester Hills city	47.4	64.1	32.1	46.9	60.3	21.1	52.9	41.7	17 525	48.1	36.3	10.7	-5.8	2.1	82.9	8.2	8.7	0.3
Roseville city	42.6	55.0	31.4	42.6	45.4	48.2	40.9	40.0	10 724	40.7	25.6	24.6	0.7	-4.5	87.3	6.7	5.8	0.2
Royal Oak city	40.3	50.8	39.5	49.3	43.1	50.4	47.3	60.8	10 299	50.9	29.3	14.2	0.5	5.1	83.7	7.6	8.6	0.1
Saginaw city	31.3	37.5	26.2	36.8	24.2	21.2	24.4	32.8	17 984	24.2	9.4	44.0	3.6	-7.0	79.6	15.0	5.3	0.1
St. Clair Shores city	40.6	52.8	29.9	40.4	50.2	52.5	48.6	51.8	12 282	46.2	27.6	17.7	-0.7	-5.9	83.5	8.2	8.1	0.2
Southfield city	43.4	50.8	37.4	35.2	50.4	32.8	43.4	39.3	15 683	43.1	16.0	27.8	6.3	0.3	78.6	12.6	8.4	0.4
Southgate city	41.5	55.1	29.1	41.2	43.0	34.4	49.4	45.0	6 150	50.6	22.4	18.3	4.3	-3.8	86.1	8.0	5.9	0.1
Sterling Heights city	45.3	58.7	32.8	45.4	51.1	47.2	44.0	47.4	29 305	51.6	29.4	11.7	-1.3	1.6	85.5	7.8	6.5	0.3
Taylor city	41.8	52.7	32.0	42.3	39.2	34.5	33.9	39.8	16 746	32.3	23.4	28.4	-3.9	-8.3	87.9	6.9	5.0	0.2
Troy city	47.0	62.4	32.4	46.3	52.7	51.9	50.1	49.6	20 906	52.1	33.7	8.5	-4.0	3.4	81.6	7.8	10.4	0.2
Warren city	39.9	51.9	28.9	39.7	52.9	31.4	39.2	39.5	30 405	42.6	25.3	21.1	-0.9	-7.9	86.3	7.8	5.8	0.1
Westland city	44.7	56.7	33.9	44.8	44.5	49.0	46.8	46.6	19 268	42.0	26.4	23.4	0.8	-0.8	87.3	7.9	4.7	0.1
Wyandotte city	41.6	53.7	30.4	42.0	21.4	52.3	24.5	34.5	6 031	46.9	23.6	20.8	3.1	-3.2	85.6	8.8	5.5	0.2
Wyoming city	48.4	60.1	37.2	48.8	48.1	47.0	52.8	43.4	18 555	50.1	20.2	20.9	6.4	7.8	89.2	5.3	5.3	0.2
MINNESOTA.............	44.7	54.6	35.2	45.5	37.1	34.1	38.5	37.8	1 239 179	57.3	16.9	17.7	10.4	11.0	77.1	12.4	10.2	0.3
Andover city	57.1	72.1	41.6	57.0	84.2	46.3	47.9	40.7	9 334	67.2	19.4	7.8	10.4	22.2	77.6	12.7	9.5	0.2
Apple Valley city..........	55.2	67.8	43.6	55.5	52.0	20.0	59.8	49.6	13 193	63.3	19.0	14.3	13.0	20.2	81.1	11.9	7.0	0.1
Blaine city	56.6	67.7	45.8	56.9	58.6	49.5	59.1	47.9	12 630	59.9	14.6	18.5	13.8	19.6	84.1	9.5	6.3	0.1
Bloomington city	47.2	56.7	38.5	47.5	43.0	40.4	48.9	40.4	16 987	54.3	18.4	20.4	10.1	7.7	82.2	8.6	9.0	0.1
Brooklyn Center city.....	45.0	53.1	37.7	45.1	53.0	48.9	34.6	40.1	6 868	52.1	8.9	28.3	15.8	6.2	84.1	9.7	6.2	0.1
Brooklyn Park city	54.8	64.0	46.0	57.2	49.7	53.2	45.5	52.9	18 589	54.3	14.5	21.7	11.4	18.4	83.5	10.3	6.1	0.1
Burnsville city	52.1	62.2	42.5	53.2	43.3	38.3	48.8	34.6	15 339	56.6	17.3	18.9	10.9	16.4	83.7	9.2	6.8	0.3
Coon Rapids city	54.4	66.3	43.5	54.6	53.3	53.4	61.0	45.4	17 013	56.6	15.4	21.1	13.1	17.3	82.3	11.2	6.5	0.1
Cottage Grove city	56.7	67.1	46.4	57.2	43.7	55.4	46.4	46.7	9 717	66.8	15.1	14.4	16.6	19.7	79.7	14.2	6.0	0.1
Duluth city	33.3	41.9	25.7	33.7	21.4	29.5	28.1	35.3	17 399	48.0	16.6	25.8	9.2	5.5	75.1	17.3	7.3	0.3
Eagan city	58.5	70.5	47.1	59.8	54.3	38.2	45.6	52.0	18 525	62.3	20.2	13.2	10.9	20.4	82.4	10.8	6.7	0.1
Eden Prairie city	55.1	68.5	42.5	55.6	49.5	41.0	50.7	43.6	16 505	54.5	30.8	10.4	0.3	12.4	82.8	7.6	9.4	0.2
Edina city	39.6	55.3	26.8	39.3	46.6	44.4	42.1	55.6	10 762	52.2	32.2	10.0	-2.4	-2.6	75.6	9.6	14.7	0.1
Fridley city	49.1	57.4	41.0	49.2	51.8	40.5	47.8	43.8	5 961	52.4	13.4	23.6	11.4	10.3	82.5	11.1	6.3	0.1

[1] Hispanic or Latino persons may be of any race.

Table B-5. Cities — Education, Labor Force, and Income

City	Percent who worked at home	Percent of the population 5 years and over with a disability	Veterans as a percent of the population 18 years and over	Occupation for employed population 16 years and over (percent) Management, professional, and related occupations	Service occupations	Sales and office occupations	Farming, fishing, and forestry occupations	Construction, extraction, and maintenance occupations	Production, transportation and material moving occupations	Industry for employed population 16 years and over (percent) Agriculture, forestry, fishing, and mining	Construction and manufacturing	Wholesale and retail trade	Transportation and warehousing, and utilities	Service industries	Public administration
	42	43	44	45	46	47	48	49	50	51	52	53	54	55	56
MASSACHUSETTS— Cont'd															
Somerville city	2.4	19.4	5.8	47.9	16.3	22.2	0.0	5.0	8.5	0.1	11.4	10.5	3.1	71.5	3.5
Springfield city	2.0	27.6	11.3	27.1	21.6	26.2	0.3	7.1	17.8	0.3	17.8	15.2	5.6	55.4	5.8
Taunton city	1.1	20.1	11.8	26.3	16.5	27.5	0.2	9.8	19.8	0.2	24.4	20.7	5.4	44.9	4.5
Waltham city	2.4	17.9	9.0	45.3	12.9	27.2	0.1	5.8	8.8	0.2	16.5	13.1	2.6	64.2	3.5
Watertown city	4.2	19.1	8.2	55.4	9.6	23.5	0.1	4.6	6.7	0.2	11.9	12.3	3.1	69.6	3.0
Westfield city	2.1	16.0	13.2	32.5	15.1	28.0	0.2	8.9	15.4	0.6	21.8	17.8	6.4	49.8	3.7
Woburn city	1.8	17.0	13.2	38.4	12.9	29.3	0.1	8.4	10.9	0.1	18.5	17.2	5.1	55.9	3.2
Worcester city	1.7	24.0	10.5	33.2	17.9	26.3	0.1	6.4	16.3	0.2	19.1	15.3	4.4	56.8	4.3
MICHIGAN	2.8	18.7	12.4	31.5	14.8	25.6	0.5	9.2	18.5	1.1	28.5	15.1	4.1	47.5	3.6
Allen Park city	1.2	16.6	15.4	33.6	12.3	28.4	0.0	9.6	16.0	0.0	28.7	13.7	6.5	47.6	3.5
Ann Arbor city	4.4	11.2	5.9	61.0	12.4	19.7	0.2	2.7	4.0	0.2	11.2	9.9	1.9	74.8	2.0
Battle Creek city	2.2	22.8	15.0	26.7	18.4	25.5	0.1	6.6	22.8	0.1	28.4	13.6	4.7	47.1	6.1
Bay City city	2.9	21.3	13.9	24.9	18.8	27.5	0.4	9.7	18.7	0.5	22.4	19.8	4.8	49.6	2.9
Burton city	1.8	20.1	14.1	22.6	16.4	23.9	0.1	14.0	23.1	0.3	31.8	18.2	4.2	43.0	2.5
Dearborn city	1.6	19.5	10.5	37.8	13.3	26.9	0.1	7.3	14.7	0.0	26.1	17.5	4.6	49.0	2.7
Dearborn Heights city	1.8	21.1	13.9	28.1	13.8	29.9	0.0	11.0	17.2	0.0	28.3	17.4	6.3	45.3	2.7
Detroit city	1.8	28.3	10.2	21.6	21.6	26.8	0.2	7.2	22.5	0.2	22.5	11.9	6.7	52.7	6.1
East Lansing city	2.6	8.8	3.6	44.6	20.8	27.3	0.4	2.6	4.3	1.0	4.4	10.8	1.1	77.9	4.8
Eastpointe city	1.5	19.8	14.0	23.0	16.3	28.3	0.0	11.1	21.2	0.1	30.2	15.7	4.4	46.6	3.0
Farmington Hills city	2.9	13.1	9.9	53.3	8.2	26.6	0.0	4.5	7.4	0.1	23.6	16.9	2.4	55.0	2.0
Flint city	1.9	25.9	11.5	21.0	23.7	22.4	0.1	8.2	24.6	0.2	28.0	13.8	3.2	51.2	3.5
Garden City city	0.9	18.6	15.3	22.6	13.7	29.1	0.0	12.9	21.6	0.1	31.6	18.0	6.5	41.3	2.5
Grand Rapids city	2.7	20.1	9.8	29.2	16.7	24.9	0.7	6.7	21.7	0.6	27.0	17.1	2.8	50.5	2.1
Holland city	2.4	15.6	8.1	29.0	14.7	23.9	0.7	5.2	26.5	0.8	37.1	13.9	2.3	43.9	2.1
Inkster city	0.8	23.8	12.1	21.6	20.0	25.2	0.1	8.7	24.4	0.1	26.7	13.0	8.7	48.1	3.4
Jackson city	2.0	23.0	12.4	23.0	22.3	22.3	0.0	7.4	25.0	0.2	28.2	15.0	4.0	47.9	4.7
Kalamazoo city	3.2	18.6	8.0	32.2	20.9	25.4	0.8	5.9	14.7	0.7	19.6	14.2	2.8	60.7	2.0
Kentwood city	2.7	14.9	11.3	35.0	11.0	28.9	0.1	5.5	19.4	0.1	28.9	19.1	3.6	46.5	1.9
Lansing city	2.5	21.0	11.3	27.9	18.9	28.8	0.2	8.3	15.9	0.3	17.5	14.8	3.9	54.0	9.5
Lincoln Park city	1.2	23.1	14.5	17.5	15.6	28.9	0.1	13.1	25.0	0.0	29.6	17.5	9.1	41.2	2.6
Livonia city	2.1	14.2	12.5	41.1	11.1	27.6	0.0	8.2	12.0	0.1	27.6	15.3	4.3	50.1	2.6
Madison Heights city	2.0	20.8	11.2	29.5	13.8	28.6	0.1	10.9	17.1	0.1	29.5	17.1	3.6	47.5	2.1
Midland city	3.1	13.6	11.8	46.2	14.7	23.7	0.1	5.8	9.5	0.2	32.3	11.7	2.1	51.3	2.4
Mount Pleasant city	2.7	10.3	5.1	29.2	28.5	32.2	0.3	3.6	6.1	0.4	6.9	16.5	1.2	72.9	2.0
Muskegon city	2.5	28.1	12.9	19.1	21.9	23.4	0.2	6.6	28.7	0.3	33.5	13.8	2.3	45.4	4.8
Novi city	2.5	9.3	8.5	53.0	8.4	25.8	0.0	4.3	8.5	0.1	29.3	16.3	2.6	49.9	1.8
Oak Park city	2.4	20.0	10.1	34.8	13.7	30.7	0.0	4.9	15.9	0.0	21.8	17.1	4.5	53.4	3.2
Pontiac city	1.1	25.4	10.0	18.5	21.4	25.0	0.4	9.5	25.2	0.4	30.7	12.8	3.6	48.6	3.9
Portage city	3.2	15.1	13.1	39.0	11.9	28.4	0.3	7.1	13.3	0.5	26.8	16.6	3.8	49.1	3.2
Port Huron city	3.4	23.3	13.4	20.6	18.6	25.1	0.1	8.1	27.5	0.1	32.2	15.6	4.9	43.7	3.5
Rochester Hills city	3.2	12.8	10.3	53.3	8.1	25.6	0.1	5.1	7.8	0.1	30.6	15.8	1.6	50.0	1.9
Roseville city	1.2	21.0	13.4	19.5	16.1	29.0	0.1	13.6	21.6	0.2	32.9	18.5	3.9	42.3	2.3
Royal Oak city	2.8	14.8	11.4	48.0	10.7	26.2	0.1	6.4	8.6	0.0	22.9	14.8	2.4	57.6	2.3
Saginaw city	2.5	24.1	11.0	21.3	26.0	26.0	0.5	7.2	19.1	0.4	20.8	17.1	3.5	53.4	4.6
St. Clair Shores city	2.3	19.8	14.5	31.4	12.8	30.3	0.0	9.9	15.6	0.2	27.7	16.9	3.4	48.8	3.2
Southfield city	2.4	20.8	10.8	43.9	10.1	28.4	0.1	4.9	12.6	0.0	21.8	13.7	4.4	56.7	3.4
Southgate city	1.0	19.7	13.8	27.3	14.0	28.2	0.0	11.9	18.6	0.2	27.5	15.6	8.9	45.4	2.4
Sterling Heights city	1.6	16.0	10.7	35.5	12.3	29.9	0.1	7.7	14.6	0.1	30.9	18.0	2.5	45.3	3.3
Taylor city	1.2	21.2	12.9	17.5	16.6	26.8	0.1	13.3	25.7	0.1	31.0	15.2	8.0	43.6	2.2
Troy city	2.9	12.0	9.2	54.8	8.4	25.3	0.0	4.3	7.2	0.1	26.4	15.8	2.6	53.0	2.1
Warren city	1.3	19.9	13.4	25.4	14.9	27.8	0.1	10.2	21.7	0.1	32.7	16.2	3.8	44.4	2.9
Westland city	1.3	18.9	12.9	27.0	14.5	27.6	0.1	10.0	20.8	0.1	30.6	16.1	6.5	44.4	2.3
Wyandotte city	1.1	19.4	15.2	22.9	15.7	28.6	0.1	12.7	20.1	0.2	29.7	13.5	6.7	47.4	2.5
Wyoming city	2.0	17.4	10.4	23.4	12.3	27.8	0.5	9.0	26.9	0.4	34.8	21.4	3.3	38.7	1.4
MINNESOTA	4.6	15.0	12.8	35.8	13.7	26.5	0.7	8.4	14.9	2.6	22.2	15.5	5.1	51.2	3.4
Andover city	3.6	9.6	10.9	36.9	10.5	28.6	0.1	10.0	13.8	0.3	27.9	17.8	5.7	44.6	3.7
Apple Valley city	3.8	10.9	13.2	40.6	11.2	32.0	0.1	6.8	9.3	0.3	16.1	16.4	9.9	54.3	2.9
Blaine city	2.8	13.9	13.4	30.9	11.8	28.9	0.1	9.3	19.0	0.3	30.0	16.5	5.6	44.8	2.8
Bloomington city	3.4	14.9	14.8	41.0	10.1	32.0	0.1	6.4	10.4	0.1	18.2	17.2	6.2	55.9	2.3
Brooklyn Center city	2.8	18.2	15.7	28.0	13.7	30.8	0.3	8.9	18.4	0.3	23.7	16.7	6.0	51.0	2.4
Brooklyn Park city	3.1	13.6	11.1	34.3	12.4	30.0	0.0	7.1	16.2	0.1	23.7	16.9	4.9	51.4	3.1
Burnsville city	3.7	14.3	11.7	39.4	13.0	31.5	0.0	6.7	9.4	0.2	17.4	17.5	7.7	54.4	2.8
Coon Rapids city	2.7	13.3	13.5	32.9	12.0	29.1	0.1	9.8	16.2	0.1	27.1	17.3	5.2	47.0	3.3
Cottage Grove city	2.9	10.9	13.5	32.3	12.4	31.3	0.2	9.3	14.5	0.7	23.2	16.3	7.9	47.1	4.9
Duluth city	3.1	19.0	13.2	34.3	19.8	28.1	0.2	7.3	10.4	0.8	9.9	17.3	6.3	61.3	4.5
Eagan city	4.0	9.7	10.6	49.0	9.6	27.7	0.1	5.3	8.4	0.1	16.5	15.0	9.8	55.3	3.3
Eden Prairie city	4.9	8.7	9.3	53.0	8.1	29.0	0.0	3.5	6.4	0.4	19.2	18.0	3.7	57.2	1.4
Edina city	6.8	12.1	13.9	55.2	7.7	30.7	0.0	2.2	4.1	0.1	13.0	16.3	3.3	64.9	2.4
Fridley city	2.4	16.2	14.7	31.5	11.8	29.5	0.2	9.2	17.7	0.4	26.8	17.8	4.8	46.9	3.3

Table B-5. Cities — Education, Labor Force, and Income

City	Median house-hold income	All families	Married-couple	Male house-holder	Female house-holder	Median nonfamily house-hold income	Men	Women	Per capita income	With earnings	With interest, dividend, or rental income	With Social Security income	With public assis-tance income	With retire-ment income	House-holds with income over $100,000 (percent)	+/- U.S. percent for income over $100,000	House-holds with income below poverty (percent)	Families with children with income below poverty (percent)
	57	58	59	60	61	62	63	64	65	66	67	68	69	70	71	72	73	74
MASSACHUSETTS—Cont'd																		
Somerville city	46 315	51 243	56 122	29 318	22 248	40 605	37 263	32 138	23 628	84.1	42.2	19.4	2.2	10.7	13.3	1.0	12.3	13.0
Springfield city	30 417	36 285	51 578	28 568	15 364	20 189	33 663	27 263	15 232	72.6	25.8	28.3	8.6	15.6	5.0	-7.3	21.4	29.4
Taunton city	42 932	52 433	63 142	29 479	19 051	26 186	37 887	28 647	19 899	79.3	34.2	25.7	3.7	16.4	8.0	-4.3	10.7	12.1
Waltham city	54 010	64 595	71 700	47 969	35 332	38 054	44 381	34 998	26 364	82.6	45.0	24.6	1.9	14.7	18.9	6.6	7.6	4.1
Watertown city	59 764	67 441	69 364	23 889	31 489	48 875	48 128	40 996	33 262	82.1	50.5	25.8	1.7	13.8	22.4	10.1	6.6	7.8
Westfield city	45 240	55 327	62 446	29 464	23 102	23 925	39 817	28 823	20 600	78.2	39.5	27.6	3.7	17.5	9.8	-2.5	11.5	12.1
Woburn city	54 897	66 364	73 312	35 417	24 531	35 964	45 947	34 905	26 207	80.9	43.9	28.6	1.7	17.9	16.8	4.5	6.7	7.8
Worcester city	35 623	42 988	56 382	29 722	16 473	23 945	36 893	29 774	18 614	75.4	30.3	27.3	6.0	15.0	8.2	-4.1	16.8	20.9
MICHIGAN	44 667	53 457	65 021	32 208	21 208	26 194	42 962	29 256	22 168	80.2	38.0	26.2	3.6	19.2	12.7	0.4	10.1	11.3
Allen Park city	51 992	63 350	72 683	53 958	34 663	29 619	50 705	31 869	24 980	72.0	52.0	36.8	1.0	29.3	12.9	0.6	3.6	2.7
Ann Arbor city	46 299	71 293	80 912	50 074	31 111	30 719	50 441	37 641	26 419	87.5	51.8	14.9	1.3	11.4	18.4	6.1	15.0	6.0
Battle Creek city	35 491	43 564	56 157	29 962	19 367	22 985	37 683	27 449	18 424	75.9	32.3	29.0	6.0	20.1	7.1	-5.2	14.0	15.8
Bay City city	30 425	38 252	45 967	22 344	17 004	18 784	32 901	22 412	16 550	72.0	31.6	30.9	6.2	20.1	5.3	-7.0	14.3	16.3
Burton city	44 050	50 332	56 660	37 647	22 559	24 764	41 910	28 974	20 548	78.7	32.1	26.8	4.3	24.3	8.6	-3.7	9.4	7.9
Dearborn city	44 560	53 060	55 300	35 978	26 875	29 344	46 405	35 303	21 488	72.4	45.6	33.0	5.1	22.6	13.8	1.5	12.2	19.1
Dearborn Heights city	48 222	54 392	64 832	46 050	26 359	31 426	45 878	30 369	22 829	74.6	45.3	36.0	1.7	27.2	10.9	-1.4	5.3	7.1
Detroit city	29 526	33 853	51 357	26 414	18 774	19 228	34 621	27 365	14 717	74.8	14.9	26.7	11.4	18.1	6.3	-6.0	24.3	28.6
East Lansing city	28 217	61 985	72 148	36 719	20 952	19 945	44 873	32 000	16 333	85.9	47.1	14.5	1.0	12.0	12.1	-0.2	31.2	14.2
Eastpointe city	46 261	54 895	63 023	40 324	26 275	24 546	42 016	28 658	20 665	76.1	37.4	33.6	2.1	21.7	8.0	-4.3	6.8	6.4
Farmington Hills city	67 493	88 138	101 389	57 589	40 034	40 475	64 150	40 765	36 134	83.3	54.5	23.7	1.1	17.0	30.8	18.5	4.2	3.0
Flint city	28 015	31 424	45 883	23 897	14 363	20 379	34 901	25 261	15 733	75.1	19.6	26.7	11.1	20.2	5.5	-6.8	23.7	32.4
Garden City city	51 841	58 530	65 049	53 229	27 650	29 963	45 897	29 170	21 651	81.0	37.7	29.4	1.4	21.6	10.2	-2.1	5.4	4.5
Grand Rapids city	37 224	44 224	54 359	29 638	19 747	25 835	34 029	26 909	17 661	80.8	32.8	23.7	4.9	13.9	6.6	-5.7	13.9	17.3
Holland city	42 291	50 316	58 015	30 000	22 342	28 967	37 130	27 603	18 823	80.8	40.2	26.6	2.3	17.4	8.6	-3.7	10.0	9.9
Inkster city	35 950	41 176	54 487	35 781	21 740	21 500	39 002	27 252	16 711	76.2	18.0	26.9	8.7	21.5	6.2	-6.1	18.1	22.0
Jackson city	31 294	39 072	46 560	24 500	15 606	18 490	32 696	24 708	15 230	76.6	25.2	27.0	8.4	15.9	4.0	-8.3	18.5	23.0
Kalamazoo city	31 189	42 438	54 541	24 519	17 179	21 386	33 178	26 156	16 897	81.4	32.6	21.4	5.3	13.1	6.8	-5.5	21.9	21.2
Kentwood city	46 812	55 615	63 707	43 108	21 439	20 900	41 160	28 343	22 463	85.9	37.2	20.2	2.3	12.3	10.2	-2.1	6.1	7.6
Lansing city	34 833	41 283	50 525	27 076	17 906	25 606	33 916	27 892	17 924	82.1	29.0	22.2	5.9	16.5	4.7	-7.0	15.5	20.1
Lincoln Park city	42 515	49 747	60 813	34 318	21 611	27 145	40 762	27 337	20 140	77.5	32.6	30.7	2.9	22.0	6.5	-5.8	7.8	10.0
Livonia city	63 018	72 720	81 396	68 631	38 804	33 732	56 316	36 108	27 923	78.9	57.4	31.6	1.2	24.7	21.8	9.5	3.2	2.6
Madison Heights city	42 326	51 364	62 308	34 000	27 284	30 359	41 974	29 976	21 429	80.4	33.3	25.8	3.2	17.7	7.8	-4.5	8.4	8.3
Midland city	48 444	64 949	80 994	34 194	24 038	23 046	55 056	31 947	26 818	78.4	55.5	26.2	2.4	20.9	19.6	7.3	9.3	7.8
Mount Pleasant city	24 572	43 927	58 090	22 426	17 868	17 696	32 472	24 723	13 177	85.0	33.9	16.8	1.9	11.3	5.7	-6.6	34.6	15.7
Muskegon city	27 929	32 640	44 444	25 379	16 133	18 294	29 769	23 079	14 283	74.1	22.3	29.9	7.6	18.1	3.2	-9.1	19.3	24.1
Novi city	71 918	91 369	106 527	45 600	30 069	44 623	67 078	39 335	35 992	90.2	53.3	15.4	0.8	12.3	32.1	19.8	2.1	2.3
Oak Park city	48 697	57 656	64 504	44 286	34 853	32 474	41 451	36 883	21 677	83.3	32.7	25.0	5.2	15.3	12.3	0.0	9.7	10.0
Pontiac city	31 207	36 391	48 606	24 244	17 373	21 272	32 593	25 622	15 842	79.2	16.2	23.4	7.6	17.7	5.8	-6.5	20.9	23.9
Portage city	49 410	61 285	72 970	38 438	26 167	27 102	43 809	30 368	25 414	83.5	44.1	23.7	1.4	16.9	15.0	2.7	4.7	5.0
Port Huron city	31 327	39 869	49 856	26 649	16 884	18 451	32 386	23 264	17 100	76.2	29.1	29.1	7.3	17.9	5.5	-6.8	17.2	19.4
Rochester Hills city	74 912	89 653	99 022	72 768	30 994	41 163	71 064	41 302	35 070	85.9	55.0	20.7	0.8	16.8	33.8	21.5	3.5	3.4
Roseville city	41 220	49 244	57 513	33 347	24 688	26 143	40 361	27 035	19 823	77.8	34.5	30.2	2.4	21.2	6.0	-6.3	8.3	9.4
Royal Oak city	52 252	68 109	77 514	45 139	36 327	39 019	51 339	37 266	30 990	82.3	49.3	24.0	1.3	16.6	15.8	3.5	4.6	3.0
Saginaw city	26 485	29 945	47 079	21 786	13 252	14 778	32 088	23 658	13 816	74.3	21.6	26.9	11.9	18.3	4.2	-8.1	25.8	33.9
St. Clair Shores city	49 047	59 245	67 517	36 917	32 478	30 516	47 374	31 813	25 009	72.7	46.1	36.8	1.1	26.0	11.3	-1.0	4.3	3.9
Southfield city	51 802	64 543	78 603	46 023	35 591	36 893	50 016	39 090	28 096	81.3	34.8	26.4	2.4	18.4	17.1	4.8	7.6	7.1
Southgate city	46 927	56 710	65 130	47 292	31 798	28 762	47 021	29 429	23 219	75.5	39.6	31.4	2.0	23.3	9.9	-2.4	6.2	3.5
Sterling Heights city	60 494	70 140	76 113	49 531	28 970	33 290	52 090	32 218	24 958	84.0	47.3	24.4	2.1	19.0	19.1	6.8	5.4	6.0
Taylor city	42 944	48 304	58 625	37 051	18 106	26 873	41 653	26 760	19 638	80.9	28.5	25.9	4.1	20.9	9.3	-3.0	10.3	13.9
Troy city	77 538	92 058	97 868	56 979	49 028	45 502	69 065	42 182	35 936	87.3	57.7	21.0	1.0	16.4	36.2	23.9	3.2	2.1
Warren city	44 626	52 444	60 908	36 328	24 333	27 809	42 033	29 505	21 407	76.7	39.7	32.4	2.8	24.5	9.6	-2.7	7.2	8.4
Westland city	46 308	55 323	65 242	35 851	26 050	31 175	46 020	30 932	22 615	79.8	35.5	26.2	2.1	19.6	9.4	-2.9	6.9	7.1
Wyandotte city	43 740	54 106	63 196	47 993	23 234	26 823	44 290	28 579	22 185	76.8	38.6	33.2	1.8	23.5	8.2	-4.1	6.1	7.6
Wyoming city	43 164	50 002	56 421	33 942	25 872	27 700	36 257	26 154	19 287	87.2	32.9	20.5	2.2	13.3	7.0	-5.3	6.8	7.5
MINNESOTA	47 111	56 874	66 428	32 454	24 335	27 913	40 408	29 670	23 198	83.4	44.0	23.9	3.4	13.7	12.6	0.3	7.9	7.6
Andover city	76 241	78 785	79 636	60 078	31 304	47 604	51 020	35 156	26 317	95.9	47.4	8.7	0.6	8.6	25.6	13.3	1.9	1.6
Apple Valley city	69 752	79 335	85 533	43 875	36 820	38 895	51 435	35 013	29 477	92.4	48.6	12.7	1.2	10.5	25.6	13.3	2.3	1.7
Blaine city	59 219	63 831	68 224	36 563	33 878	38 866	40 908	31 125	22 777	93.2	36.7	13.9	2.3	11.0	12.9	0.6	2.9	2.9
Bloomington city	54 628	67 135	77 061	45 917	29 021	35 664	45 203	33 885	29 782	83.2	52.7	27.1	2.1	18.7	17.7	5.4	4.0	3.8
Brooklyn Center city	44 570	52 006	62 184	33 571	26 778	27 385	36 587	28 599	19 665	81.1	39.1	29.2	4.8	20.1	6.8	-5.5	6.0	7.5
Brooklyn Park city	56 572	64 297	70 996	31 284	29 645	35 228	41 951	31 643	23 199	91.7	38.2	12.6	3.6	9.6	15.2	2.9	5.1	5.6
Burnsville city	57 965	67 979	77 423	32 468	28 750	38 404	46 194	33 042	27 093	90.6	42.8	15.0	2.3	11.7	17.9	5.6	4.8	5.4
Coon Rapids city	55 550	62 260	69 321	44 922	28 400	35 418	41 790	30 840	22 915	89.9	36.7	16.6	2.9	12.8	12.4	0.1	4.3	5.2
Cottage Grove city	65 825	68 953	74 188	41 908	32 644	38 103	46 506	32 255	23 348	93.1	42.2	14.4	1.6	12.3	17.3	5.0	1.9	2.5
Duluth city	33 766	46 394	59 575	28 165	19 264	20 091	36 043	25 797	18 969	75.4	41.4	28.6	6.3	17.6	6.7	-5.6	15.1	13.7
Eagan city	67 388	80 062	90 373	39 792	32 445	44 778	52 481	36 483	30 167	94.3	47.9	10.3	1.8	8.7	25.3	13.0	2.7	2.7
Eden Prairie city	78 328	93 258	105 307	42 500	41 083	50 787	64 439	40 682	38 854	93.8	53.8	10.0	1.6	7.5	36.2	23.9	3.1	3.5
Edina city	66 019	93 496	118 100	79 472	39 583	36 472	71 346	44 064	44 195	74.4	65.6	36.1	1.6	20.8	32.4	20.1	3.3	3.0
Fridley city	48 372	55 381	63 650	33 958	21 689	32 390	38 915	30 461	23 022	85.8	40.8	22.9	4.5	17.0	9.5	-2.8	6.8	10.2

STATE Place code	City	High school graduates			College graduates		College graduates (percent)				
		Total population 25 years and over	Percent with a high school diploma or less	Percent with a high school diploma or more	Percent with a bachelor's degree or more	+/− U.S. percent with bachelor's degree or more	Non-Hispanic White	Black or African American	American Indian and Alaska Native	Asian, Hawaiian, and Pacific Islander	Hispanic or Latino[1]
		1	2	3	4	5	6	7	8	9	10
	MINNESOTA—Cont'd										
27 31076	Inver Grove Heights city	18 822	36.5	92.0	29.6	5.2	29.4	26.9	0.0	77.4	8.7
27 35180	Lakeville city	25 192	26.0	95.6	35.7	11.3	36.3	33.5	12.7	35.8	8.9
27 39878	Mankato city	16 441	35.5	88.1	32.2	7.8	32.3	26.4	18.6	46.2	21.7
27 40166	Maple Grove city	31 658	23.6	96.7	41.7	17.3	41.3	40.8	15.7	59.7	49.0
27 40382	Maplewood city	23 676	41.9	90.1	25.6	1.2	24.6	36.9	26.6	50.2	20.5
27 43000	Minneapolis city	243 409	35.8	85.0	37.4	13.0	45.3	14.0	7.7	31.8	13.3
27 43252	Minnetonka city	36 351	19.9	95.9	51.6	27.2	51.5	45.2	14.6	63.7	58.8
27 43864	Moorhead city	17 370	37.0	87.7	29.5	5.1	31.0	27.0	1.9	20.4	4.7
27 47680	Oakdale city	16 941	37.9	92.9	24.3	−0.1	24.3	14.7	0.0	33.8	27.5
27 51730	Plymouth city	43 490	19.1	96.2	51.0	26.6	51.3	35.7	3.3	67.9	37.7
27 54214	Richfield city	24 308	38.3	89.7	27.3	2.9	28.5	20.1	0.0	33.5	10.4
27 54880	Rochester city	55 537	30.4	91.0	38.1	13.7	38.5	16.7	20.4	55.7	13.0
27 55852	Roseville city	23 740	30.3	91.4	42.3	17.9	41.7	28.3	23.9	63.0	35.5
27 56896	St. Cloud city	32 535	37.5	89.1	29.6	5.2	30.1	14.1	5.8	24.6	25.0
27 57220	St. Louis Park city	32 093	26.7	92.8	43.2	18.8	44.3	22.8	33.1	50.1	26.7
27 58000	St. Paul city	174 204	41.9	83.8	32.0	7.6	37.6	16.3	14.1	17.2	12.9
27 59998	Shoreview city	17 306	23.1	96.0	46.9	22.5	46.7	54.0	41.0	60.4	21.5
27 71032	Winona city	14 666	44.0	82.9	26.3	1.9	26.4	3.7	8.3	47.9	8.1
27 71428	Woodbury city	29 482	19.3	96.4	49.3	24.9	48.9	60.1	23.4	62.1	33.2
28 00000	MISSISSIPPI	1 757 517	56.5	72.9	16.9	−7.5	20.1	10.1	9.1	35.2	12.1
28 06220	Biloxi city	31 052	44.6	81.9	19.2	−5.2	20.6	14.0	14.4	16.3	12.8
28 15380	Columbus city	16 069	54.6	72.1	22.9	−1.5	35.7	9.4	0.0	35.8	19.3
28 29180	Greenville city	24 332	59.8	68.8	17.5	−6.9	26.7	11.9	12.5	40.0	12.7
28 29700	Gulfport city	44 790	48.9	79.2	19.1	−5.3	23.1	10.0	15.5	26.3	18.9
28 31020	Hattiesburg city	24 066	42.9	79.1	28.9	4.5	43.1	10.6	0.0	52.9	21.5
28 36000	Jackson city	108 734	42.4	79.1	27.1	2.7	41.8	18.9	18.2	55.4	23.8
28 46640	Meridian city	25 252	54.0	72.3	17.6	−6.8	24.9	8.9	10.8	56.3	15.5
28 55360	Pascagoula city	16 077	52.9	78.5	15.6	−8.8	18.2	8.6	18.0	23.3	5.9
28 69280	Southaven city	18 550	52.6	82.6	14.3	−10.1	14.6	9.8	10.0	28.6	6.8
28 74840	Tupelo city	22 187	41.5	81.2	26.7	2.3	31.8	10.5	25.6	59.8	5.6
28 76720	Vicksburg city	16 360	52.6	73.6	19.1	−5.3	29.9	9.3	24.3	66.3	8.1
29 00000	MISSOURI	3 634 906	51.4	81.3	21.6	−2.8	22.3	13.2	12.9	50.1	16.1
29 03160	Ballwin city	20 772	23.9	94.9	46.7	22.3	47.2	19.9	20.6	56.6	21.0
29 06652	Blue Springs city	29 611	37.4	92.4	27.4	3.0	27.8	21.3	13.3	43.6	14.0
29 11242	Cape Girardeau city	21 571	46.5	81.6	29.3	4.9	30.3	16.9	15.3	64.1	12.1
29 13600	Chesterfield city	32 689	16.9	95.9	60.6	36.2	59.8	56.1	45.7	76.6	53.1
29 15670	Columbia city	45 650	26.7	91.1	50.5	26.1	52.7	23.3	42.8	72.9	44.3
29 24778	Florissant city	33 681	47.4	85.9	17.4	−7.0	17.2	18.4	0.0	36.3	24.9
29 27190	Gladstone city	18 541	41.4	90.3	25.1	0.7	25.2	33.0	14.5	44.1	17.4
29 31276	Hazelwood city	17 206	45.9	87.4	22.5	−1.9	23.0	20.9	0.0	19.0	23.8
29 35000	Independence city	76 559	55.5	82.9	15.2	−9.2	15.3	12.5	12.9	32.2	12.1
29 37000	Jefferson City city	27 183	42.4	85.1	30.8	6.4	32.2	17.8	9.7	65.4	24.8
29 37592	Joplin city	28 922	49.6	81.5	20.7	−3.7	21.1	12.6	12.0	38.6	11.5
29 38000	Kansas City city	287 046	45.4	82.5	25.7	1.3	32.7	11.9	17.3	35.8	10.8
29 39044	Kirkwood city	19 370	21.1	94.2	51.5	27.1	54.0	16.3	0.0	62.5	74.8
29 41348	Lee's Summit city	45 693	28.3	93.1	37.3	12.9	37.0	51.8	18.9	45.0	33.7
29 42032	Liberty city	16 232	37.3	90.4	32.0	7.6	33.0	23.4	9.4	36.3	16.0
29 46586	Maryland Heights city	17 842	34.8	88.2	38.7	14.3	36.3	42.7	20.0	70.3	14.9
29 54074	O'Fallon city	27 578	37.8	90.4	27.2	2.8	26.9	27.9	0.0	54.0	35.0
29 60788	Raytown city	21 143	46.2	87.3	19.5	−4.9	18.9	24.4	32.8	30.1	13.5
29 64082	St. Charles city	38 753	43.8	86.4	26.6	2.2	26.7	19.1	28.5	64.0	20.3
29 64550	St. Joseph city	47 401	56.1	80.9	17.1	−7.3	17.5	9.6	27.9	30.7	8.8
29 65000	St. Louis city	221 951	56.2	71.3	19.1	−5.3	28.2	8.8	11.3	33.0	16.6
29 65126	St. Peters city	32 046	36.2	91.4	27.2	2.8	27.0	22.7	10.9	48.2	25.5
29 70000	Springfield city	95 232	47.7	82.8	23.0	−1.4	23.5	12.4	9.8	39.7	16.5
29 75220	University City city	25 195	29.7	87.4	45.0	20.6	67.8	15.6	0.0	75.6	52.6
29 79820	Wildwood city	20 715	16.1	96.6	57.4	33.0	56.9	67.7	100.0	85.6	42.3
30 00000	MONTANA	586 621	44.1	87.2	24.4	0.0	25.2	33.2	10.5	38.9	15.4
30 06550	Billings city	58 834	40.7	88.7	28.5	4.1	29.4	44.0	13.0	42.5	11.7
30 08950	Bozeman city	14 318	21.0	94.3	49.5	25.1	49.8	50.0	37.8	74.4	19.8
30 11390	Butte-Silver Bow	23 097	49.2	85.1	21.7	−2.7	22.2	18.2	8.4	45.6	9.8
30 32800	Great Falls city	37 527	45.6	87.2	22.4	−2.0	23.2	22.9	7.5	24.9	16.5
30 35600	Helena city	16 995	31.4	92.7	39.8	15.4	40.8	27.1	6.8	52.0	22.4
30 50200	Missoula city	33 964	30.4	91.5	38.0	13.6	38.4	65.4	23.9	47.6	34.6

[1] Hispanic or Latino persons may be of any race.

Table B-5. Cities — Education, Labor Force, and Income

City	School enrollment			Population 16 to 19 years				Employment status, 2000			Work status in 1999 of the population 16 years and over		
											Worked in 1999		
	Grades kindergarten through 12	College or graduate school	Percent private	Number	Percent in armed forces	Percent high school graduates	Percent not enrolled, not grads, not in armed forces, not employed	Total population 16 years and over	Percent in labor force	Unemployment rate	Full-time	Part-time	Did not work in 1999
	11	12	13	14	15	16	17	18	19	20	21	22	23
MINNESOTA—Cont'd													
Inver Grove Heights city	5 998	1 437	13.3	1 651	0.0	10.0	2.4	22 526	78.3	2.5	65.1	17.8	17.1
Lakeville city	11 095	1 630	8.4	2 369	0.8	9.2	0.8	29 056	82.2	2.1	68.4	18.9	12.7
Mankato city	3 991	9 235	10.2	3 775	0.0	4.6	0.3	27 543	72.0	5.8	48.5	33.3	18.3
Maple Grove city	11 821	2 331	9.6	3 051	0.0	5.7	0.6	36 747	83.3	1.9	68.4	19.8	11.8
Maplewood city	6 292	1 662	18.9	1 845	0.3	15.9	2.5	27 298	69.4	3.0	56.6	17.8	25.6
Minneapolis city	61 171	43 383	16.5	22 082	0.0	8.9	5.8	306 378	72.1	5.8	58.5	19.3	22.1
Minnetonka city	9 315	2 258	17.9	2 316	0.0	3.7	0.8	40 895	73.6	2.3	59.7	18.9	21.3
Moorhead city	5 635	6 505	24.9	3 553	0.0	4.5	1.8	25 724	68.4	5.5	51.9	26.2	21.9
Oakdale city	5 683	1 382	17.6	1 402	0.0	9.5	2.6	19 724	76.4	2.4	64.7	17.0	18.3
Plymouth city	13 170	3 298	17.6	3 202	0.0	7.5	2.5	50 054	76.4	2.4	64.7	17.9	17.4
Richfield city	4 864	1 570	17.3	1 582	0.0	15.0	2.5	28 221	71.1	3.0	58.8	17.7	23.5
Rochester city	16 049	4 996	15.0	4 203	0.0	7.3	2.5	65 670	72.2	4.2	58.3	19.4	22.3
Roseville city	4 577	2 840	31.5	1 730	0.0	5.1	2.0	28 319	65.5	2.4	52.0	19.1	28.0
St. Cloud city	9 332	11 381	12.4	5 320	0.3	9.3	1.7	48 299	71.5	4.4	53.2	27.6	19.2
St. Louis Park city	5 860	2 628	19.3	1 383	0.5	10.4	4.8	36 614	75.2	3.0	62.9	16.3	20.8
St. Paul city	58 145	25 718	25.8	17 605	0.2	9.0	5.7	217 409	69.1	5.7	56.4	18.6	25.0
Shoreview city	5 458	1 397	17.4	1 333	0.0	3.2	0.4	19 999	76.1	1.7	61.9	20.4	17.7
Winona city	3 763	6 707	20.3	3 063	0.0	3.9	0.7	22 743	66.5	6.8	48.9	28.5	22.5
Woodbury city	9 743	2 335	15.7	2 042	0.0	3.1	2.1	33 444	78.5	2.2	66.1	18.0	15.9
MISSISSIPPI	582 848	152 997	11.1	184 029	1.2	9.9	7.8	2 158 941	59.4	7.3	52.4	11.9	35.7
Biloxi city	8 582	2 848	10.8	3 702	30.2	38.9	5.7	39 638	66.8	5.4	59.4	12.9	27.7
Columbus city	5 059	1 917	11.8	1 566	0.0	5.9	7.8	19 968	57.9	10.1	48.8	13.4	37.7
Greenville city	9 921	1 377	12.6	2 687	0.0	5.4	10.0	30 083	57.1	13.5	47.5	11.8	40.7
Gulfport city	13 501	3 409	12.1	4 157	6.3	16.9	10.0	54 680	63.6	6.7	57.0	12.2	30.8
Hattiesburg city	6 808	9 445	11.5	3 800	0.0	9.0	4.9	36 135	60.8	9.5	45.7	21.9	32.4
Jackson city	39 237	14 522	16.4	12 065	0.0	7.5	7.5	137 200	62.2	9.9	53.6	14.4	32.2
Meridian city	7 929	2 259	6.9	2 372	0.4	8.7	9.9	30 282	54.6	9.3	45.1	12.7	42.2
Pascagoula city	4 924	1 056	7.5	1 447	5.5	20.2	7.0	19 834	61.0	8.6	56.7	10.4	32.9
Southaven city	5 621	1 345	12.9	1 377	0.0	8.9	8.1	21 955	71.4	3.8	63.5	12.2	24.3
Tupelo city	7 015	1 361	7.9	1 756	0.0	8.9	5.5	25 853	66.6	4.6	60.4	11.8	27.8
Vicksburg city	5 320	979	10.3	1 507	0.0	10.0	10.1	19 720	59.9	8.7	52.6	12.1	35.3
MISSOURI	1 057 556	319 515	16.7	323 992	0.7	11.2	5.6	4 331 369	65.2	5.3	55.7	15.0	29.3
Ballwin city	6 120	1 918	29.1	1 533	0.0	7.5	2.9	23 689	70.3	2.0	57.9	18.2	23.9
Blue Springs city	10 266	2 620	9.3	3 023	0.0	11.4	3.3	35 542	76.6	3.2	65.6	15.3	19.1
Cape Girardeau city	5 400	5 264	11.7	2 968	0.0	6.9	6.1	28 973	65.3	6.3	49.9	21.6	28.5
Chesterfield city	9 252	2 427	32.1	2 368	0.0	3.2	0.5	36 869	65.7	2.5	54.5	17.4	28.1
Columbia city	11 709	22 162	8.4	8 355	0.0	5.9	2.0	69 857	70.2	6.8	51.5	28.5	20.0
Florissant city	9 176	2 654	26.4	2 492	0.5	9.4	4.5	39 039	66.8	4.3	55.5	15.8	28.8
Gladstone city	4 037	1 272	16.9	1 279	0.5	12.7	3.0	21 421	68.2	2.8	60.1	14.0	26.0
Hazelwood city	4 655	1 730	19.4	1 443	0.0	9.9	4.4	20 549	73.0	4.3	62.9	14.9	22.2
Independence city	19 370	4 036	12.4	5 723	0.0	13.4	8.5	89 279	65.4	5.0	57.0	13.7	29.3
Jefferson City city	5 924	3 042	24.0	1 968	0.0	10.4	3.3	32 261	62.1	4.9	56.3	14.0	29.7
Joplin city	7 210	3 333	19.3	2 699	0.0	12.7	6.7	35 996	64.4	7.8	52.2	17.6	30.2
Kansas City city	81 207	26 433	18.5	22 399	0.0	12.5	7.6	340 707	66.5	6.3	59.4	13.3	27.3
Kirkwood city	4 667	1 643	31.7	1 394	0.0	3.7	2.8	21 863	66.8	2.6	63.6	17.9	28.6
Lee's Summit city	14 900	3 527	11.3	3 683	0.0	8.9	3.7	52 324	73.3	2.6	62.9	15.1	22.1
Liberty city	5 322	1 806	20.8	1 734	0.0	8.0	2.4	19 749	71.1	3.5	60.4	17.0	22.5
Maryland Heights city	4 034	1 655	21.0	1 146	0.0	9.8	4.3	20 943	74.3	2.8	64.1	15.0	20.9
O'Fallon city	10 392	2 037	15.2	2 212	0.0	5.4	3.1	31 957	76.9	3.2	65.4	16.2	18.4
Raytown city	5 064	1 414	12.7	1 491	0.0	14.2	4.6	24 389	63.2	3.5	55.6	13.0	31.3
St. Charles city	10 209	4 907	31.2	3 503	0.2	11.1	4.4	47 661	71.9	6.8	59.5	17.6	22.9
St. Joseph city	13 001	4 469	10.2	4 480	0.0	12.0	8.5	58 006	60.8	6.4	53.8	14.5	31.7
St. Louis city	67 241	24 410	27.0	19 036	0.0	10.4	10.3	268 036	60.5	11.3	51.0	13.8	35.2
St. Peters city	11 765	2 897	19.8	3 032	0.0	7.0	1.7	37 675	76.9	2.1	64.1	17.2	18.7
Springfield city	21 015	20 908	17.6	10 239	0.2	11.0	5.4	125 002	64.5	6.6	51.5	19.7	28.8
University City city	6 121	4 246	41.3	1 657	0.0	11.9	2.7	30 031	67.0	4.3	57.7	16.2	26.1
Wildwood city	8 162	1 488	21.0	1 947	0.0	2.6	3.1	23 442	72.6	2.3	59.5	19.7	20.8
MONTANA	176 805	51 255	8.3	55 369	0.6	11.0	4.4	701 168	65.4	6.3	53.1	18.6	28.2
Billings city	15 980	5 375	10.0	4 877	0.0	12.1	3.2	70 301	67.7	4.2	54.5	19.3	26.3
Bozeman city	3 105	8 681	4.0	2 853	0.0	7.8	1.7	23 835	73.2	9.5	57.0	27.5	15.5
Butte-Silver Bow	6 390	2 458	11.7	1 981	0.0	9.7	4.0	27 369	62.0	6.8	49.1	18.4	32.5
Great Falls city	10 819	2 280	11.6	2 936	3.2	18.8	3.9	43 951	63.7	6.6	51.6	16.9	31.5
Helena city	4 296	1 736	18.9	1 743	0.6	11.1	0.6	20 733	68.3	5.8	54.4	19.0	26.6
Missoula city	8 438	10 256	6.2	4 207	0.2	11.0	2.1	46 882	70.1	7.5	52.5	25.4	22.0

City	Full-year full-time employed (percent)								Children under 18 years in families (percent, except where noted)						Total employed by class of worker (percent)			
				Non-Hispanic White	Black or African American	American Indian and Alaska Native	Asian, Hawaiian, and Pacific Islander	Hispanic or Latino[1]		With two parents		With one parent who is in labor force	+/- U.S. percent of children with no stay-at-home parent	+/- U.S. percent two-income couples				Unpaid family worker
	Total	Men	Women						Number	Both in labor force	Father only in labor force				Private	Government	Self-employed	
	24	25	26	27	28	29	30	31	32	33	34	35	36	37	38	39	40	41
MINNESOTA—Cont'd																		
Inver Grove Heights city	53.8	64.2	43.9	54.4	52.1	45.7	54.7	43.5	7 945	60.3	14.5	19.8	15.5	18.1	82.9	12.1	5.0	0.1
Lakeville city	57.6	72.6	42.4	58.3	47.0	51.1	36.3	38.4	15 206	60.6	22.8	11.7	7.7	20.6	81.3	10.8	7.7	0.2
Mankato city	32.3	38.1	26.8	33.0	18.2	35.4	10.2	55.0	5 259	51.5	13.1	24.6	11.5	9.2	78.8	15.3	5.5	0.4
Maple Grove city	58.5	71.4	46.0	58.7	51.0	46.4	56.4	60.0	15 253	65.4	20.7	10.2	11.0	22.4	81.7	10.2	7.9	0.1
Maplewood city	46.1	56.7	36.8	46.2	46.7	44.0	48.0	43.8	8 369	59.3	16.0	17.8	12.5	8.7	78.8	13.9	7.2	0.1
Minneapolis city	41.6	47.1	36.1	45.6	33.7	29.2	30.2	33.9	76 991	35.1	14.3	29.7	0.2	9.6	78.4	13.9	7.5	0.2
Minnetonka city	47.9	60.7	36.5	48.1	47.0	12.9	48.9	43.1	11 542	56.5	26.3	13.7	5.6	10.7	77.1	9.6	13.0	0.3
Moorhead city	34.5	43.0	27.4	35.2	19.9	24.6	23.3	27.8	6 995	58.0	11.5	24.5	17.9	12.6	74.3	17.7	7.7	0.2
Oakdale city	53.2	63.9	43.9	53.8	34.1	40.0	62.1	51.7	7 582	60.1	15.4	18.6	14.1	17.3	78.7	16.3	5.0	0.1
Plymouth city	52.7	65.8	40.2	53.0	42.4	47.4	56.9	47.1	17 441	55.5	28.1	12.6	3.5	11.9	82.1	7.2	10.5	0.2
Richfield city	46.2	53.9	39.0	46.7	45.4	46.4	48.5	41.6	6 714	50.9	13.8	27.0	13.3	8.7	84.0	9.4	6.6	0.0
Rochester city	45.8	56.6	35.9	47.2	25.9	48.9	40.6	31.9	21 429	54.0	21.4	16.7	6.1	10.5	84.3	9.0	6.6	0.1
Roseville city	41.7	53.2	32.0	41.3	41.3	62.3	48.0	38.3	6 040	60.0	17.1	17.0	12.4	4.9	73.6	18.8	7.4	0.1
St. Cloud city	38.1	44.3	31.9	38.9	21.6	26.9	26.0	36.3	11 698	55.9	15.1	21.1	12.4	13.0	79.7	13.5	6.7	0.1
St. Louis Park city	50.3	58.3	43.3	51.0	44.6	54.4	45.2	37.1	8 087	56.4	15.5	23.1	14.9	13.0	84.1	7.7	7.9	0.2
St. Paul city	40.9	48.2	34.5	43.9	34.9	35.6	29.3	36.1	73 081	39.4	15.0	24.9	-0.3	6.7	77.6	15.2	6.9	0.2
Shoreview city	51.3	63.1	40.9	51.4	41.6	52.2	56.4	39.6	6 700	62.4	19.1	15.6	13.4	15.9	77.2	13.8	8.9	0.2
Winona city	33.9	42.6	26.4	34.7	24.7	3.6	23.6	10.4	4 600	55.5	18.7	17.9	8.8	9.4	79.6	13.3	6.5	0.6
Woodbury city	55.1	69.5	41.9	55.1	58.6	56.9	54.4	51.4	13 997	58.2	26.7	10.4	4.0	15.8	80.9	12.5	6.6	0.0
MISSISSIPPI	36.9	45.4	29.3	40.8	29.8	36.7	36.7	35.6	711 441	37.3	17.2	27.7	0.4	-2.5	72.7	17.6	9.3	0.4
Biloxi city	41.4	48.9	33.8	42.5	38.5	43.6	33.0	44.7	11 643	40.9	18.3	27.2	3.5	-0.7	71.1	20.2	8.4	0.3
Columbus city	32.9	43.3	24.9	37.0	27.7	100.0	37.8	81.6	5 999	28.5	13.1	37.3	1.2	-3.9	72.3	18.7	8.9	0.1
Greenville city	31.7	39.9	25.3	40.8	26.7	21.6	56.6	41.5	11 355	27.3	7.5	42.3	5.0	-3.4	74.4	18.4	7.1	0.1
Gulfport city	40.3	47.1	33.8	42.8	35.1	42.3	43.0	42.7	16 723	37.5	12.3	32.9	5.8	-0.7	73.0	18.6	8.3	0.2
Hattiesburg city	30.2	36.8	24.7	31.3	29.5	48.1	4.3	25.8	8 357	26.5	11.2	44.0	5.9	-3.4	72.4	19.5	7.6	0.5
Jackson city	36.2	41.3	32.0	39.1	34.9	34.0	32.7	31.5	47 394	28.9	10.1	39.4	3.7	1.0	68.4	23.6	7.8	0.2
Meridian city	31.9	41.0	24.8	36.5	27.2	50.0	52.3	28.7	9 957	27.1	10.9	37.2	-0.3	-5.2	72.1	20.3	7.2	0.3
Pascagoula city	39.2	49.5	28.9	40.5	36.3	12.9	47.2	43.0	6 639	36.1	17.3	31.9	3.4	-2.8	75.4	16.2	8.2	0.2
Southaven city	50.4	64.0	38.1	50.8	47.7	30.9	56.9	43.8	7 477	46.6	22.5	21.6	3.6	5.6	83.3	9.5	7.2	0.1
Tupelo city	45.9	58.0	36.0	47.3	41.4	50.0	31.5	61.3	8 796	41.9	19.2	26.8	4.1	4.7	80.2	10.7	8.9	0.2
Vicksburg city	37.8	47.5	30.2	41.1	35.4	26.9	32.2	29.9	6 678	28.9	10.5	44.6	8.9	-0.4	70.6	20.9	8.2	0.3
MISSOURI	42.1	51.3	33.7	43.0	36.0	38.4	40.0	40.1	1 350 334	47.2	19.4	22.5	5.1	2.7	77.2	12.8	9.7	0.4
Ballwin city	47.3	60.2	35.5	47.3	50.9	32.5	53.7	36.6	8 316	57.8	27.3	11.1	4.3	6.6	83.5	7.8	8.3	0.4
Blue Springs city	53.5	64.5	43.3	53.9	54.6	48.1	40.9	45.7	13 540	56.9	18.4	18.8	11.1	15.3	78.0	13.1	8.7	0.2
Cape Girardeau city	36.4	45.3	28.5	37.3	30.4	39.4	21.2	23.5	6 837	45.5	17.0	25.1	6.0	3.3	75.8	15.8	8.3	0.1
Chesterfield city	44.8	62.3	29.5	44.4	46.6	65.7	50.8	46.0	11 436	51.4	35.8	8.0	-5.2	2.1	80.8	6.9	12.0	0.3
Columbia city	36.3	42.8	30.5	37.3	32.0	33.2	29.2	31.3	15 709	50.7	16.0	24.2	10.3	10.5	64.1	28.7	7.0	0.2
Florissant city	44.7	54.0	36.8	43.4	56.4	38.5	53.2	45.3	11 910	50.5	15.3	25.8	11.7	2.4	84.7	10.7	4.5	0.1
Gladstone city	48.2	57.2	40.1	48.3	52.7	39.5	43.1	45.3	5 313	51.1	21.6	22.0	8.5	3.4	80.6	9.9	9.2	0.3
Hazelwood city	50.2	58.7	42.7	51.2	49.8	100.0	37.7	37.0	6 180	42.0	22.6	20.6	28.6	6.2	6.6	85.6	8.7	5.7	0.0
Independence city	43.5	53.1	35.0	43.6	45.3	36.9	36.2	46.7	25 499	44.1	18.3	26.3	5.8	-0.5	81.8	11.0	7.0	0.2
Jefferson City city	43.6	45.3	41.8	47.9	22.2	26.4	40.1	33.2	7 614	55.9	10.5	22.7	14.0	11.5	58.5	34.4	6.8	0.3
Joplin city	39.3	50.8	29.3	39.4	40.4	36.7	42.5	45.4	9 979	40.8	22.3	24.6	0.8	-2.7	82.2	9.1	8.6	0.2
Kansas City city	44.3	51.1	38.1	48.4	36.9	41.5	42.3	38.6	103 352	35.5	15.0	32.4	3.3	3.0	79.3	13.2	7.3	0.2
Kirkwood city	42.5	56.6	31.4	43.2	33.2	87.8	45.4	46.9	6 117	64.5	32.2	16.4	-2.4	2.7	78.5	9.2	12.2	0.2
Lee's Summit city	52.1	66.3	39.7	51.8	59.3	48.4	60.4	52.8	20 357	57.9	21.4	15.9	9.2	12.1	79.3	11.8	8.8	0.1
Liberty city	47.5	59.2	37.3	47.9	45.7	50.0	50.0	37.5	6 990	50.7	23.8	21.8	7.9	12.3	80.2	10.8	8.7	0.2
Maryland Heights city	51.3	59.7	43.2	51.6	58.9	47.6	43.6	49.8	5 361	47.9	20.0	23.6	6.9	7.5	86.2	7.0	6.5	0.2
O'Fallon city	55.0	70.5	40.4	55.4	39.2	20.5	54.7	53.0	14 880	60.3	23.7	11.5	7.2	13.8	86.4	8.3	5.2	0.1
Raytown city	45.2	54.4	37.6	44.1	51.5	46.3	47.3	61.7	6 390	46.0	18.4	23.9	5.3	0.0	81.0	12.3	6.4	0.2
St. Charles city	46.7	56.9	37.1	46.6	45.5	33.7	60.9	44.9	13 566	55.4	16.8	21.7	12.5	8.2	85.3	8.2	6.3	0.2
St. Joseph city	39.3	47.3	31.9	39.6	31.3	49.1	55.8	46.4	16 571	43.1	19.3	27.5	6.0	-0.1	78.8	13.8	7.2	0.1
St. Louis city	35.7	40.8	31.3	42.0	29.3	32.9	36.4	35.0	80 760	25.5	9.2	42.1	3.0	-2.1	79.7	14.5	5.5	0.2
St. Peters city	52.8	64.6	42.1	53.1	52.8	54.3	47.0	52.0	14 979	59.1	21.8	15.3	9.8	15.1	85.8	8.3	5.7	0.2
Springfield city	36.9	45.5	29.1	37.4	27.6	27.2	34.1	30.2	28 308	40.0	20.0	29.7	5.1	-1.6	81.2	10.2	8.3	0.2
University City city	41.6	48.7	35.8	45.4	37.8	44.0	32.3	42.5	7 647	38.9	15.7	30.4	4.7	5.4	79.4	12.1	8.3	0.2
Wildwood city	47.8	69.5	27.6	47.8	48.5	41.0	59.3	33.7	11 054	54.4	35.9	5.8	-4.4	6.5	82.7	6.7	10.4	0.1
MONTANA	36.4	45.0	28.1	37.2	34.6	25.7	28.5	33.1	218 232	51.2	18.9	20.4	7.0	3.1	64.3	18.3	16.7	0.7
Billings city	39.8	50.1	30.8	40.6	32.1	26.4	33.3	32.9	20 515	50.7	16.6	24.2	10.3	7.9	76.7	12.0	11.1	0.2
Bozeman city	31.3	36.9	25.0	31.5	20.8	25.7	22.1	47.3	4 467	50.3	21.1	18.6	4.3	11.3	66.9	21.4	11.3	0.4
Butte-Silver Bow	35.8	42.9	29.0	36.4	44.4	11.5	5.0	31.0	7 799	51.2	15.1	24.8	11.4	3.9	72.7	16.4	10.3	0.6
Great Falls city	37.8	47.0	29.3	38.3	45.8	20.3	39.0	42.5	13 651	49.0	16.5	26.9	11.3	2.5	71.9	16.5	11.1	0.5
Helena city	40.3	47.7	33.6	40.9	26.7	23.1	21.1	17.6	5 268	52.4	14.6	25.1	12.9	10.8	58.5	31.1	10.2	0.2
Missoula city	33.2	39.7	26.9	33.9	15.5	18.7	24.8	31.4	10 739	45.7	18.8	25.4	6.5	7.6	70.0	18.1	11.6	0.2

[1]Hispanic or Latino persons may be of any race.

Table B-5. Cities — Education, Labor Force, and Income

City	Percent who worked at home	Percent of the population 5 years and over with a disability	Veterans as a percent of the population 18 years and over	Occupation for employed population 16 years and over (percent)						Industry for employed population 16 years and over (percent)					
				Management, professional, and related occupations	Service occupations	Sales and office occupations	Farming, fishing, and forestry occupations	Construction, extraction, and maintenance occupations	Production, transportation and material moving occupations	Agriculture, forestry, fishing, and mining	Construction and manufacturing	Wholesale and retail trade	Transportation and warehousing, and utilities	Service industries	Public administration
	42	43	44	45	46	47	48	49	50	51	52	53	54	55	56
MINNESOTA—Cont'd															
Inver Grove Heights city	2.3	12.9	13.0	38.0	11.5	29.4	0.1	9.1	11.9	0.3	20.0	15.7	8.0	51.2	4.8
Lakeville city	3.9	10.7	13.1	37.9	9.2	32.1	0.2	9.1	11.4	0.2	21.1	18.3	9.3	48.4	2.6
Mankato city	2.4	13.7	9.4	30.1	19.1	28.0	0.5	5.7	16.6	1.1	20.8	17.1	2.7	56.2	2.1
Maple Grove city	3.5	8.0	10.4	46.6	9.4	30.1	0.1	6.3	7.6	0.2	22.2	18.5	3.5	53.0	2.6
Maplewood city	2.6	16.6	14.5	34.5	14.2	29.9	0.1	8.0	13.4	0.2	22.2	15.2	6.2	50.1	6.1
Minneapolis city	3.4	17.2	9.1	41.1	16.2	25.7	0.1	4.8	12.0	0.2	14.1	13.2	4.7	64.8	3.0
Minnetonka city	5.5	12.2	12.7	50.6	8.3	30.0	0.1	4.5	6.5	0.2	18.0	17.3	3.6	58.7	2.2
Moorhead city	2.6	15.7	10.9	32.6	18.9	28.9	0.2	7.8	11.5	1.1	12.9	17.4	3.2	62.4	3.0
Oakdale city	2.2	12.5	12.0	35.3	13.7	32.3	0.1	7.3	11.3	0.1	21.5	15.3	6.6	49.4	7.2
Plymouth city	4.6	9.7	10.2	51.4	8.2	28.7	0.2	4.4	7.0	0.3	19.9	18.2	2.9	57.3	1.4
Richfield city	2.7	18.3	14.0	32.5	15.5	33.1	0.1	6.9	12.0	0.2	16.4	18.8	6.0	55.8	2.7
Rochester city	3.1	14.5	11.7	46.8	14.4	23.1	0.1	6.1	9.5	0.2	20.6	12.5	2.2	62.0	2.5
Roseville city	3.3	14.2	14.0	40.5	10.3	27.2	0.1	4.8	9.2	0.4	15.6	13.9	4.5	60.4	5.2
St. Cloud city	3.0	13.8	12.0	30.9	16.4	30.5	0.2	6.7	15.3	0.6	18.3	20.1	3.1	52.6	2.4
St. Louis Park city	4.0	14.7	11.3	45.8	10.0	30.9	0.1	4.3	8.9	0.2	16.4	17.1	3.1	61.2	2.0
St. Paul city	3.0	17.8	10.3	37.8	15.7	26.3	0.2	6.0	14.0	0.3	16.8	12.5	5.1	60.8	4.4
Shoreview city	3.2	9.8	12.7	52.0	8.7	25.9	0.1	4.9	8.5	0.2	21.3	13.6	4.1	56.5	4.2
Winona city	2.5	15.9	10.9	28.3	19.7	27.2	0.4	4.9	19.5	0.9	27.3	15.1	2.8	51.9	2.0
Woodbury city	4.0	9.5	10.6	52.1	9.3	26.5	0.1	4.9	7.2	0.1	20.9	14.0	5.1	55.2	4.5
MISSISSIPPI	1.9	23.6	12.0	27.4	14.9	24.9	1.2	11.2	20.4	3.4	25.9	15.2	5.4	45.0	5.1
Biloxi city	0.9	25.5	19.9	28.2	24.7	26.8	0.8	9.8	9.6	1.3	12.3	15.4	3.3	60.5	7.2
Columbus city	1.7	21.6	13.0	30.4	14.7	25.6	0.3	10.0	19.0	0.8	27.0	14.7	4.2	49.1	4.1
Greenville city	1.0	23.0	9.6	28.0	15.4	26.3	1.3	7.4	21.7	3.0	23.5	15.7	5.0	46.8	6.0
Gulfport city	1.7	25.9	18.0	26.8	23.5	27.4	0.2	10.6	11.5	0.6	14.7	15.0	4.5	58.6	6.7
Hattiesburg city	1.9	19.8	10.2	31.9	19.9	28.2	0.4	6.2	13.3	1.0	13.9	17.8	2.1	61.9	3.3
Jackson city	1.6	23.0	10.9	31.4	18.1	28.8	0.2	7.5	13.7	0.5	13.2	15.2	5.2	58.6	7.2
Meridian city	1.5	23.5	13.0	30.8	19.3	26.6	1.0	6.7	15.6	1.5	18.7	15.5	4.3	54.6	5.4
Pascagoula city	3.3	23.2	10.7	28.0	16.2	25.8	0.4	14.8	16.1	1.6	32.6	14.1	2.7	43.4	5.5
Southaven city	2.0	17.1	13.6	27.2	13.8	31.7	0.1	12.5	14.7	0.3	10.9	17.1	14.7	45.3	3.9
Tupelo city	1.9	19.3	11.6	34.6	10.9	29.3	0.4	4.7	20.1	0.5	28.0	18.2	2.9	47.5	2.9
Vicksburg city	1.5	24.4	12.3	29.1	20.7	22.5	1.1	8.1	18.6	1.9	21.6	13.3	4.9	50.6	7.8
MISSOURI	3.5	19.0	14.2	31.5	15.0	26.9	0.6	9.8	16.3	2.2	21.7	15.5	5.7	50.3	4.6
Ballwin city	4.1	10.8	13.3	46.8	11.6	29.9	0.1	5.0	6.6	0.1	18.3	18.8	4.1	56.1	2.6
Blue Springs city	3.9	13.9	12.8	36.5	12.1	30.1	0.1	10.1	11.1	0.3	17.3	17.3	6.3	53.2	5.6
Cape Girardeau city	1.8	17.7	13.0	33.1	18.2	28.2	0.1	6.8	13.6	0.4	15.7	19.1	3.4	57.5	3.9
Chesterfield city	5.6	9.0	13.0	57.6	6.8	30.2	0.0	1.8	3.6	0.3	16.6	16.2	3.0	62.2	1.7
Columbia city	2.9	14.1	8.7	46.5	15.9	26.9	0.5	4.0	7.2	0.7	8.5	13.4	2.0	70.8	4.6
Florissant city	2.0	17.8	15.6	29.9	13.5	32.0	0.0	10.6	14.0	0.2	21.9	17.8	6.2	50.0	3.9
Gladstone city	3.2	16.6	17.9	31.1	13.1	34.2	0.1	9.0	12.5	0.6	16.4	18.7	8.5	52.3	3.6
Hazelwood city	1.8	18.4	13.9	33.2	12.3	31.7	0.1	8.6	14.1	0.1	22.6	17.1	6.6	50.9	2.7
Independence city	2.1	20.8	15.9	25.9	14.0	31.7	0.1	10.8	17.4	0.3	20.4	17.4	6.1	51.4	4.4
Jefferson City city	2.3	18.1	15.1	39.6	13.3	30.6	0.3	6.2	10.1	0.5	12.0	12.2	3.2	47.1	25.0
Joplin city	2.4	21.2	13.7	28.7	16.0	28.4	0.2	7.8	18.8	0.5	21.5	16.9	6.7	52.2	2.2
Kansas City city	2.6	21.0	13.1	34.1	16.2	28.6	0.1	7.9	13.0	0.4	15.4	14.6	6.3	57.6	5.7
Kirkwood city	4.5	13.5	14.1	54.6	10.2	26.5	0.0	5.0	5.6	0.2	15.4	15.2	2.8	63.7	2.7
Lee's Summit city	3.6	11.8	13.0	44.6	10.7	28.3	0.1	7.7	8.6	0.2	17.6	15.4	4.1	58.0	4.6
Liberty city	3.5	13.5	13.6	37.9	13.7	29.5	0.2	7.7	11.0	0.5	17.6	16.0	6.3	55.6	4.0
Maryland Heights city	2.9	15.0	10.7	43.8	11.2	28.7	0.3	6.4	9.6	0.3	18.9	16.6	5.1	56.7	2.4
O'Fallon city	3.3	10.4	13.2	35.9	12.6	28.6	0.0	10.3	12.6	0.1	25.0	17.3	5.2	49.3	3.2
Raytown city	2.1	20.0	16.9	30.4	13.6	32.0	0.0	10.1	14.0	0.1	18.7	17.3	5.3	52.8	5.8
St. Charles city	2.6	14.5	14.4	34.4	14.2	28.6	0.1	9.8	12.8	0.4	23.0	15.9	6.1	51.6	3.0
St. Joseph city	2.0	21.6	14.7	27.1	18.1	27.5	0.2	9.4	17.7	0.4	22.9	15.9	5.5	50.1	5.3
St. Louis city	1.7	24.8	11.6	29.7	22.1	26.5	0.1	6.2	15.4	0.3	15.9	12.5	5.8	59.3	6.1
St. Peters city	2.6	12.4	13.2	35.8	11.9	30.8	0.0	9.5	11.8	0.2	21.9	17.4	7.4	50.1	3.0
Springfield city	2.6	20.8	13.5	27.7	18.6	30.3	0.2	7.8	15.5	0.3	16.1	19.0	5.0	57.0	2.5
University City city	3.1	18.8	10.9	51.2	12.9	24.4	0.2	3.2	8.2	0.1	10.4	10.3	4.6	70.8	3.8
Wildwood city	6.5	8.1	10.6	55.4	7.6	28.2	0.2	4.2	4.3	0.4	20.8	17.3	4.0	55.5	2.0
MONTANA	6.4	17.5	16.1	33.1	17.2	25.5	2.2	10.7	11.2	7.9	13.4	15.8	5.4	51.5	6.9
Billings city	3.4	18.1	15.4	31.8	17.2	31.9	0.2	8.0	10.8	1.8	10.6	21.3	5.9	56.4	3.9
Bozeman city	4.8	12.0	8.3	37.6	17.6	25.3	1.0	9.3	9.2	1.8	15.4	15.6	2.0	62.0	3.2
Butte-Silver Bow	2.7	18.8	16.7	32.4	19.4	27.0	0.7	9.4	11.1	4.1	9.4	17.8	9.3	54.3	5.1
Great Falls city	3.2	20.9	19.8	31.2	18.7	30.5	0.5	8.8	10.3	1.4	10.7	18.1	5.0	58.0	6.8
Helena city	4.1	19.0	16.4	44.9	14.8	26.6	0.6	5.9	7.1	1.2	7.8	11.6	2.5	57.0	19.8
Missoula city	4.0	16.5	12.2	35.2	19.0	28.7	0.6	8.1	8.4	2.1	11.3	16.9	3.5	63.2	3.0

Table B-5. Cities — Education, Labor Force, and Income

City	Median house-hold income	Median family income — All families	Median family income — Married-couple	Median family income (Families with children) — Male house-holder	Median family income (Families with children) — Female house-holder	Median nonfamily house-hold income	Median income for full-year, full-time workers — Men	Median income for full-year, full-time workers — Women	Per capita income	With earnings	With interest, dividend, or rental income	With Social Security income	With public assis-tance income	With retire-ment income	House-holds with income over $100,000 (percent)	+/- U.S. percent for income over $100,000	House-holds with income below poverty (percent)	Families with children with income below poverty (percent)
	57	58	59	60	61	62	63	64	65	66	67	68	69	70	71	72	73	74
MINNESOTA—Cont'd																		
Inver Grove Heights city	59 090	68 629	79 886	40 750	27 461	39 944	46 257	32 988	25 493	90.8	43.0	16.2	1.7	13.2	18.8	6.5	4.0	4.2
Lakeville city	72 404	76 542	79 892	50 417	36 223	45 515	52 091	34 594	26 492	95.1	44.0	8.8	1.6	6.5	26.0	13.7	2.1	1.8
Mankato city	33 956	47 297	56 358	32 083	19 158	23 242	31 500	23 088	17 652	83.8	38.7	22.2	3.8	11.5	5.8	-6.5	17.3	12.8
Maple Grove city	76 111	81 873	86 536	46 818	41 324	49 338	53 864	37 930	30 544	94.9	52.8	10.7	0.9	9.2	29.4	17.1	1.3	1.1
Maplewood city	51 596	63 049	72 786	47 955	27 307	31 472	44 965	31 472	24 387	80.6	47.6	27.5	2.5	19.2	13.7	1.4	4.7	4.3
Minneapolis city	37 974	48 602	60 522	29 394	21 954	30 297	35 924	31 357	22 685	85.0	36.9	17.2	6.8	9.8	10.4	-1.9	14.0	18.8
Minnetonka city	69 979	85 437	101 897	61 000	41 250	41 875	60 756	40 093	40 410	85.3	58.3	23.8	1.4	15.1	30.2	17.9	2.9	1.8
Moorhead city	34 781	49 118	59 975	26 917	18 537	18 390	34 048	25 103	17 150	80.5	40.1	26.2	5.6	15.0	6.4	-5.9	16.1	13.1
Oakdale city	56 299	66 680	76 208	44 375	30 417	33 950	44 481	33 422	24 107	86.6	45.6	18.8	2.6	14.2	14.7	2.4	3.8	3.7
Plymouth city	77 008	90 134	105 871	60 096	40 926	45 454	61 036	39 701	36 309	91.3	55.2	15.6	1.4	11.2	33.8	21.5	2.5	2.2
Richfield city	45 519	56 434	65 433	32 083	26 940	30 027	39 925	30 437	24 709	80.9	44.4	27.7	2.7	17.9	9.5	-2.8	5.9	6.9
Rochester city	49 090	60 754	71 545	35 179	25 445	29 554	41 416	30 852	24 811	84.5	48.6	20.9	3.3	15.0	14.2	1.9	7.1	7.5
Roseville city	51 056	65 861	79 686	46 852	29 405	32 317	43 808	33 343	27 755	77.2	59.0	31.4	1.7	21.4	15.8	3.5	4.3	5.6
St. Cloud city	37 346	50 460	61 945	30 552	21 822	23 577	34 947	24 422	19 769	84.8	39.3	20.9	3.5	13.5	8.9	-3.4	13.0	7.0
St. Louis Park city	49 260	63 182	71 930	31 250	29 366	36 478	41 399	33 969	28 970	85.3	47.1	21.5	2.9	12.3	13.0	0.7	5.1	5.6
St. Paul city	38 774	48 925	58 969	29 672	20 476	28 571	35 843	30 216	20 216	82.2	37.7	21.2	8.1	12.2	9.3	-3.0	13.0	17.9
Shoreview city	69 719	82 500	93 445	46 442	41 192	39 741	56 808	38 454	32 399	88.2	59.8	20.4	1.3	15.4	27.7	15.4	2.2	1.6
Winona city	32 845	48 413	56 389	23 854	17 552	20 320	32 132	24 400	16 783	79.9	43.4	28.6	3.9	15.5	5.0	-7.3	16.7	9.8
Woodbury city	76 109	84 997	91 203	56 406	39 840	44 554	60 984	38 440	32 606	92.6	55.2	12.4	0.7	10.7	30.2	17.9	1.3	1.1
MISSISSIPPI	31 330	37 406	47 589	23 153	14 655	16 616	31 246	22 109	15 853	77.2	22.6	27.9	3.5	15.6	6.0	-6.3	19.7	22.2
Biloxi city	34 106	40 685	45 477	25 781	16 570	23 102	29 566	22 141	17 809	79.9	29.0	26.5	2.4	21.4	5.9	-6.4	14.3	16.9
Columbus city	27 393	32 596	48 480	25 880	10 238	18 778	31 630	21 099	16 848	74.1	26.3	29.1	4.4	16.8	7.4	-4.9	23.5	34.0
Greenville city	25 928	30 788	45 436	19 911	11 868	13 295	30 671	21 323	13 992	74.7	17.6	27.8	5.2	13.5	5.6	-6.7	28.4	33.2
Gulfport city	32 779	39 314	48 707	24 526	16 888	21 527	30 146	22 322	17 554	79.4	23.9	26.4	3.1	19.0	5.7	-6.6	16.7	20.7
Hattiesburg city	24 409	32 380	41 905	16 875	14 726	15 967	27 400	20 349	15 102	78.3	21.7	24.0	4.3	12.5	5.7	-6.6	27.0	30.8
Jackson city	30 414	36 003	50 313	22 702	15 332	20 835	30 033	24 258	17 116	80.4	21.2	24.4	4.8	14.5	7.3	-5.0	21.3	27.0
Meridian city	25 085	31 062	50 849	19 643	12 056	15 785	31 024	20 647	15 255	68.8	23.1	33.2	4.1	16.7	5.2	-7.1	27.6	34.7
Pascagoula city	32 042	39 044	48 000	22 500	10 794	19 372	30 985	23 287	16 891	75.4	26.9	27.1	4.5	15.7	6.3	-6.0	19.7	28.1
Southaven city	46 691	52 333	57 626	37 619	25 602	28 080	37 096	27 031	20 759	86.8	24.4	19.9	1.7	14.6	7.6	-4.7	7.0	7.2
Tupelo city	38 401	48 465	63 881	30 469	15 813	23 264	36 309	25 082	22 024	83.4	29.6	22.4	1.9	13.2	9.7	-2.6	13.5	15.9
Vicksburg city	28 466	34 380	50 527	24 926	14 659	18 608	30 775	21 272	16 174	76.3	22.9	29.0	5.1	16.0	5.9	-6.4	20.3	28.5
MISSOURI	37 934	46 044	55 854	26 864	19 614	22 293	35 604	25 552	19 936	79.5	36.2	27.6	3.4	17.0	8.8	-3.5	11.8	12.8
Ballwin city	66 458	77 021	85 852	55 385	36 773	32 244	57 232	33 695	29 520	84.3	55.4	23.7	1.0	18.6	25.8	13.5	4.1	2.7
Blue Springs city	55 402	61 008	67 000	32 955	28 750	31 952	42 476	30 274	23 444	90.1	39.3	17.1	1.2	14.6	14.2	1.9	4.6	5.3
Cape Girardeau city	32 452	43 917	52 860	22 050	17 727	19 491	32 144	21 886	18 918	78.3	36.5	27.9	3.5	15.1	6.8	-5.5	16.3	13.9
Chesterfield city	83 802	102 987	112 954	61 250	43 036	42 277	79 431	41 279	43 288	84.5	65.4	23.4	0.4	17.9	42.1	29.8	3.1	2.5
Columbia city	33 729	52 288	66 842	26 719	20 589	20 835	36 008	27 217	19 507	85.4	41.9	17.0	2.8	12.5	9.4	-2.9	19.5	13.4
Florissant city	44 462	52 195	60 766	32 365	30 514	27 052	38 533	28 392	20 622	78.2	42.4	32.6	1.2	24.7	6.4	-5.9	3.8	4.1
Gladstone city	46 333	55 128	68 318	34 896	25 568	29 863	40 999	29 338	25 105	82.6	44.7	26.7	0.9	19.6	9.9	-2.4	4.4	4.8
Hazelwood city	45 110	52 656	65 114	33 793	27 260	30 804	40 658	28 905	22 311	85.0	38.3	23.2	1.6	19.1	8.7	-3.6	5.7	7.2
Independence city	38 012	45 876	55 118	28 404	21 788	24 268	35 440	26 568	19 384	78.0	34.2	29.7	3.0	19.8	6.0	-6.3	8.6	10.9
Jefferson City city	39 628	52 627	61 827	25 313	20 399	24 835	36 152	26 674	21 268	81.3	44.1	26.5	3.1	18.1	8.0	-4.3	10.7	11.7
Joplin city	30 555	38 888	47 320	21 910	15 226	19 503	29 540	21 415	17 738	78.4	33.3	29.8	4.1	15.6	5.5	-6.8	14.9	16.8
Kansas City city	37 198	46 012	58 493	26 946	20 401	26 283	35 908	28 535	20 753	81.1	30.4	23.2	4.0	14.8	8.3	-4.0	13.4	16.9
Kirkwood city	55 122	72 830	87 203	50 341	28 285	33 355	55 101	37 309	32 012	77.8	59.3	30.6	1.5	19.3	21.3	9.0	4.7	4.8
Lee's Summit city	60 905	70 702	78 051	45 089	32 620	30 431	50 396	34 587	26 891	85.9	46.7	20.7	1.2	16.1	20.1	7.8	3.8	3.7
Liberty city	52 745	61 273	73 563	38 281	27 020	27 549	43 046	29 709	23 415	86.2	43.1	22.0	1.6	16.5	13.3	1.0	5.9	4.9
Maryland Heights city	48 689	58 487	68 601	35 625	34 965	37 834	41 184	30 929	24 918	88.7	42.0	17.9	1.7	12.6	10.1	-2.2	5.6	4.8
O'Fallon city	60 179	64 677	69 582	33 846	26 146	35 735	46 045	29 930	21 774	92.2	38.2	15.8	1.3	14.2	13.2	0.9	3.2	3.4
Raytown city	41 949	50 952	60 988	32 946	26 230	27 107	34 860	27 640	21 634	77.1	40.7	32.4	1.8	21.5	6.9	-5.4	5.3	5.9
St. Charles city	47 782	60 175	68 867	31 849	22 820	30 174	41 582	28 430	23 607	82.7	41.9	23.9	2.0	18.6	13.0	0.7	6.3	7.5
St. Joseph city	32 663	40 995	51 088	27 798	17 004	19 311	31 963	22 192	17 445	75.5	34.1	31.4	4.2	18.1	4.9	-7.4	13.5	14.2
St. Louis city	27 156	32 585	48 632	24 251	15 108	20 560	30 657	25 665	16 108	73.6	23.9	27.7	8.1	15.7	4.6	-7.7	22.1	29.8
St. Peters city	57 898	66 513	71 350	40 658	33 980	33 792	46 623	31 107	22 792	88.8	40.8	18.0	0.8	15.6	13.2	0.9	2.6	2.2
Springfield city	29 563	38 114	44 526	21 533	17 843	19 608	28 870	21 678	17 711	78.2	33.7	27.3	4.1	15.2	5.4	-6.9	15.6	16.4
University City city	40 902	52 539	78 507	31 181	19 710	28 428	43 468	31 313	26 901	82.8	38.2	23.5	3.2	15.6	15.3	3.0	14.1	14.8
Wildwood city	94 006	100 460	103 929	93 509	36 691	41 090	78 736	42 369	38 485	91.8	61.6	13.8	0.3	11.3	45.8	33.5	2.2	2.0
MONTANA	33 024	40 487	46 202	25 095	16 203	19 484	31 591	21 679	17 151	79.6	40.0	27.7	3.3	16.3	5.6	-6.7	14.1	16.4
Billings city	35 147	45 032	54 137	24 286	15 836	21 128	34 236	22 558	19 207	79.4	40.8	27.8	3.4	16.7	6.6	-5.7	11.8	15.6
Bozeman city	32 156	41 723	45 076	22 337	16 685	23 566	29 863	21 368	16 104	88.8	43.0	14.4	1.4	11.1	4.8	-7.5	18.9	14.4
Butte-Silver Bow	30 402	40 018	49 842	23 510	14 525	18 237	32 341	22 449	17 009	74.8	38.2	31.9	4.3	20.9	4.9	-7.4	14.3	17.9
Great Falls city	32 436	40 107	47 164	22 768	15 977	19 991	31 127	21 661	18 059	75.5	40.9	30.2	3.9	20.5	5.5	-6.8	14.2	18.8
Helena city	34 416	50 018	57 803	21 181	15 781	22 377	35 585	26 600	20 020	77.7	48.0	26.0	3.6	19.5	6.0	-6.3	14.8	15.9
Missoula city	30 366	42 103	51 258	26 125	15 343	19 452	31 547	22 804	17 166	82.9	41.6	20.9	3.4	12.4	5.8	-6.5	19.6	19.7

Table B-5. Cities — Education, Labor Force, and Income

STATE Place code	City	High school graduates			College graduates		College graduates (percent)				
		Total population 25 years and over	Percent with a high school diploma or less	Percent with a high school diploma or more	Percent with a bachelor's degree or more	+/− U.S. percent with bachelor's degree or more	Non-Hispanic White	Black or African American	American Indian and Alaska Native	Asian, Hawaiian, and Pacific Islander	Hispanic or Latino[1]
		1	2	3	4	5	6	7	8	9	10
31 00000	NEBRASKA..............	1 087 241	44.7	86.6	23.7	-0.7	24.6	14.1	8.8	41.6	8.5
31 03950	Bellevue city	27 732	36.6	91.5	25.2	0.8	25.7	26.8	15.5	36.5	8.8
31 17670	Fremont city	16 353	56.1	83.6	15.8	-8.6	16.2	34.2	0.0	8.8	5.1
31 19595	Grand Island city	27 330	53.5	81.2	15.8	-8.6	17.5	4.8	10.6	24.5	2.7
31 25055	Kearney city	14 617	33.1	89.8	34.9	10.5	35.5	60.0	12.0	62.5	16.0
31 28000	Lincoln city	136 440	34.3	90.2	33.3	8.9	34.2	17.7	18.0	36.1	19.5
31 37000	Omaha city	247 260	41.1	86.0	28.7	4.3	31.9	11.4	7.0	56.4	9.9
32 00000	NEVADA..........	1 310 176	48.7	80.7	18.2	-6.2	20.7	12.0	8.6	27.1	6.4
32 09700	Carson City	35 953	45.4	82.5	18.5	-5.9	20.1	3.6	13.4	40.3	4.8
32 31900	Henderson city	118 629	39.5	88.5	23.7	-0.7	24.4	21.8	15.4	34.1	12.8
32 40000	Las Vegas city	313 205	50.4	78.5	18.2	-6.2	21.6	12.5	11.4	28.7	6.1
32 51800	North Las Vegas city.....	65 528	61.3	66.5	10.2	-14.2	14.5	8.6	1.4	20.9	3.1
32 60600	Reno city	117 487	41.3	82.4	25.0	0.6	28.6	15.2	10.9	32.7	6.6
32 68400	Sparks city................	42 403	45.7	82.2	17.8	-6.6	19.5	15.9	8.5	26.3	7.0
33 00000	NEW HAMPSHIRE.....	823 987	42.7	87.4	28.7	4.3	28.5	27.8	17.0	54.2	22.7
33 14200	Concord city	27 940	39.5	88.6	30.7	6.3	30.4	12.5	0.0	63.2	32.3
33 18820	Dover city	18 267	37.0	88.1	32.4	8.0	32.7	27.3	22.2	30.3	19.7
33 45140	Manchester city	71 556	49.8	80.7	22.3	-2.1	22.4	19.3	27.2	40.2	9.3
33 50260	Nashua city	58 267	39.9	86.6	31.5	7.1	30.6	30.0	16.4	69.6	18.2
33 65140	Rochester city	19 122	55.1	82.8	15.2	-9.2	15.1	11.3	0.0	37.3	17.8
34 00000	NEW JERSEY..........	5 657 799	47.3	82.1	29.8	5.4	32.3	16.2	16.4	61.9	12.5
34 02080	Atlantic City city............	26 521	68.9	61.8	10.4	-14.0	13.0	8.0	0.0	20.7	4.5
34 03580	Bayonne city	43 359	58.6	78.8	20.9	-3.5	21.2	15.4	38.2	42.8	12.3
34 05170	Bergenfield borough......	17 831	41.8	86.6	32.3	7.9	27.1	35.1	0.0	59.5	17.8
34 10000	Camden city	42 746	77.6	51.0	5.4	10.0	10.4	5.3	0.0	11.0	3.1
34 13690	Clifton city................	55 730	54.5	78.6	23.6	-0.8	24.2	24.1	0.0	47.4	12.3
34 19390	East Orange city	43 509	58.7	72.4	15.0	-9.4	22.7	14.8	15.6	48.9	8.0
34 21000	Elizabeth city	75 912	70.3	61.7	10.1	-12.3	15.0	8.9	8.5	42.1	10.0
34 21480	Englewood city	18 010	42.4	82.7	36.7	12.3	61.8	20.1	0.0	60.5	17.0
34 22470	Fair Lawn borough	22 452	33.8	89.9	44.8	20.4	44.3	38.9	18.5	64.6	36.7
34 24420	Fort Lee borough	27 490	31.1	89.5	48.2	23.8	44.6	47.8	0.0	61.7	28.8
34 25770	Garfield city	20 271	65.9	70.3	14.0	-10.4	14.1	7.9	0.0	44.2	9.3
34 28680	Hackensack city	31 518	47.5	79.7	29.1	4.7	35.8	17.3	30.9	67.5	12.9
34 32250	Hoboken city	28 637	28.8	83.3	59.4	35.0	69.3	17.6	47.8	78.5	18.9
34 36000	Jersey City city............	155 400	53.0	72.6	27.5	3.1	34.2	15.5	23.9	55.4	11.4
34 36510	Kearny town	27 690	63.9	70.9	17.4	-7.0	14.0	5.7	30.3	64.2	14.4
34 40350	Linden city	27 238	62.8	78.2	14.1	-10.3	13.8	11.6	0.0	47.6	11.5
34 41310	Long Branch city	20 774	55.0	76.3	20.2	-4.2	25.4	8.5	28.6	30.7	7.7
34 46680	Millville city	16 998	64.6	74.1	12.2	-12.2	12.9	8.7	0.0	76.0	5.7
34 51000	Newark city................	164 298	72.5	57.9	9.0	-15.4	11.6	8.9	4.8	40.2	5.7
34 51210	New Brunswick city	22 088	64.4	62.6	19.2	-5.2	38.6	10.8	23.3	64.8	4.2
34 55950	Paramus borough..........	18 264	39.8	86.2	38.7	14.3	34.1	12.2	0.0	65.5	32.0
34 56550	Passaic city	38 437	71.0	55.5	13.7	-10.7	27.7	8.2	5.3	42.7	5.8
34 57000	Paterson city	88 077	73.9	58.5	8.2	-16.2	14.1	7.3	8.4	29.6	5.7
34 58200	Perth Amboy city	28 309	73.3	55.7	9.7	-14.7	13.9	16.6	3.7	52.0	6.1
34 59190	Plainfield city	29 821	57.8	70.6	18.5	-5.9	36.6	17.7	0.0	36.6	7.0
34 61530	Rahway city	18 140	55.3	81.5	18.6	-5.8	19.1	16.2	5.9	53.3	9.1
34 65790	Sayreville borough	27 872	51.2	85.6	24.9	0.5	19.1	27.6	0.0	73.4	14.4
34 74000	Trenton city	53 021	69.6	62.2	9.2	-15.2	15.9	6.7	0.0	30.2	3.2
34 74630	Union City city	42 677	71.0	54.4	12.5	-11.9	23.5	15.7	9.5	46.9	9.2
34 76070	Vineland city	37 333	64.3	67.8	14.3	-10.1	18.0	6.7	15.7	40.0	6.6
34 79040	Westfield town..............	20 052	19.8	95.4	62.5	38.1	63.8	26.5	31.6	78.4	57.8
34 79610	West New York town	30 669	67.8	54.4	16.4	-8.0	33.7	31.5	0.0	57.8	10.3
35 00000	NEW MEXICO..........	1 134 801	47.7	78.9	23.5	-0.9	34.3	18.8	7.7	43.0	10.8
35 01780	Alamogordo city	21 962	46.9	81.4	14.6	-9.8	18.4	9.4	18.2	20.9	5.7
35 02000	Albuquerque city	291 485	38.2	85.9	31.8	7.4	42.4	23.7	17.0	38.9	15.2
35 12150	Carlsbad city	16 727	58.3	77.4	14.5	0.0	18.2	10.8	17.4	64.5	5.4
35 16420	Clovis city	19 797	50.4	77.5	15.7	-8.7	20.4	11.2	6.0	31.3	4.3
35 25800	Farmington city	22 911	44.4	83.6	19.7	-4.7	24.0	35.9	8.0	30.6	9.5
35 32520	Hobbs city	16 764	60.2	66.1	12.9	-11.5	17.7	6.3	5.3	37.1	5.1
35 39380	Las Cruces city	43 950	41.9	80.3	28.4	4.0	41.2	24.6	13.5	66.0	14.0
35 63460	Rio Rancho city	32 935	37.2	91.2	24.8	0.4	26.9	22.0	18.3	32.4	17.7
35 64930	Roswell city	28 013	52.4	73.8	16.9	-7.5	23.7	5.8	10.8	57.9	5.5
35 70500	Santa Fe city	43 997	32.6	84.6	40.0	15.6	59.7	36.4	24.2	56.0	15.4

[1] Hispanic or Latino persons may be of any race.

City	School enrollment			Population 16 to 19 years				Employment status, 2000			Work status in 1999 of the population 16 years and over		
											Worked in 1999		
	Grades kindergarten through 12	College or graduate school	Percent private	Number	Percent in armed forces	Percent high school graduates	Percent not enrolled, not grads, not in armed forces, not employed	Total population 16 years and over	Percent in labor force	Unemployment rate	Full-time	Part-time	Did not work in 1999
	11	12	13	14	15	16	17	18	19	20	21	22	23
NEBRASKA	338 004	112 315	15.4	107 180	0.3	9.0	3.4	1 315 715	69.7	3.5	58.2	17.7	24.2
Bellevue city	8 966	3 366	16.8	2 600	1.0	15.0	1.3	33 728	74.2	3.4	62.9	17.2	19.9
Fremont city	4 484	1 440	22.6	1 651	0.0	9.1	3.5	19 813	67.1	3.5	54.8	18.0	27.2
Grand Island city	8 104	1 379	9.3	2 440	0.0	14.1	7.3	32 640	68.5	4.9	58.0	16.3	25.6
Kearney city	4 039	5 314	6.7	2 612	0.0	7.0	2.0	21 845	74.4	3.0	56.1	26.4	17.6
Lincoln city	37 022	28 901	15.0	15 523	0.1	9.1	1.9	179 490	73.4	3.8	60.2	20.9	18.9
Omaha city	72 572	30 118	22.7	22 169	0.1	9.8	6.0	301 033	69.4	4.3	58.6	16.6	24.8
NEVADA	366 909	98 631	7.0	98 513	0.3	12.7	8.3	1 538 516	65.2	6.2	59.9	12.0	28.1
Carson City	9 106	2 995	5.9	2 290	0.0	10.5	7.0	41 517	59.8	4.6	56.1	13.0	30.9
Henderson city	32 036	9 894	8.3	8 238	0.1	12.5	3.1	136 389	68.9	4.6	62.1	12.9	25.0
Las Vegas city	86 860	20 102	8.4	22 568	0.1	13.7	11.9	366 552	63.1	7.0	58.8	10.9	30.3
North Las Vegas city	27 029	4 188	3.8	6 227	0.2	10.1	13.5	79 592	63.6	7.7	62.2	9.6	28.2
Reno city	30 731	15 018	6.8	9 742	0.1	11.0	6.9	142 898	67.1	5.6	60.2	14.8	25.0
Sparks city	13 151	3 580	6.8	3 382	0.0	11.1	8.4	50 561	70.3	4.1	62.0	14.1	23.9
NEW HAMPSHIRE	237 188	74 832	17.9	67 668	0.0	8.9	3.1	960 498	70.5	3.8	58.6	17.7	23.7
Concord city	7 299	2 510	17.0	1 865	0.0	9.5	3.1	32 362	65.3	3.7	56.7	15.8	27.5
Dover city	4 094	2 290	16.6	1 187	0.0	17.2	6.1	21 908	72.0	3.1	60.6	16.3	23.1
Manchester city	18 489	5 948	20.4	5 087	0.1	9.8	5.6	84 151	69.1	3.8	58.9	15.5	25.6
Nashua city	16 201	5 009	22.1	4 206	0.0	10.2	2.6	67 342	71.0	4.2	60.4	15.3	24.3
Rochester city	5 324	1 080	15.1	1 481	0.0	16.4	4.2	22 045	69.2	3.7	58.4	16.0	25.6
NEW JERSEY	1 566 107	470 302	18.5	408 187	0.2	8.9	4.3	6 546 155	64.2	5.8	55.7	13.7	30.5
Atlantic City city	7 786	1 574	12.6	1 903	0.0	9.9	12.9	31 117	56.8	12.9	51.6	10.8	37.7
Bayonne city	10 284	3 377	22.7	2 922	0.0	10.3	4.5	49 645	59.5	6.5	52.6	11.0	36.3
Bergenfield borough	4 777	1 739	22.7	1 354	0.0	8.4	0.4	20 501	67.0	3.6	57.6	14.9	27.6
Camden city	21 164	3 032	8.2	5 750	0.0	8.9	17.1	55 173	49.5	15.9	45.3	11.9	42.8
Clifton city	12 612	4 928	22.2	3 376	0.0	8.4	2.1	63 569	61.7	4.9	55.0	12.0	33.0
East Orange city	14 952	3 991	20.0	3 557	0.4	11.3	8.5	52 169	60.7	13.3	51.8	11.4	36.7
Elizabeth city	24 299	6 455	17.9	6 395	0.0	11.6	8.4	91 834	57.1	9.0	54.2	10.5	35.3
Englewood city	4 534	1 570	33.1	1 033	0.0	9.6	7.8	20 469	65.0	6.0	59.4	11.5	29.1
Fair Lawn borough	5 485	1 652	22.4	1 543	0.0	6.5	0.0	25 274	63.9	2.7	54.3	14.5	31.2
Fort Lee borough	4 514	2 142	27.1	967	0.0	13.1	2.5	29 679	60.0	3.4	52.5	11.6	35.9
Garfield city	5 126	1 717	20.0	1 309	0.0	7.8	4.5	23 824	65.5	7.6	57.9	10.8	31.3
Hackensack city	5 625	2 823	21.1	1 511	0.0	7.8	2.4	35 713	66.0	6.7	61.9	10.3	27.8
Hoboken city	2 997	3 851	48.5	1 092	0.0	6.1	2.9	35 076	76.5	4.4	70.6	9.1	20.3
Jersey City city	46 174	17 838	27.6	12 199	0.1	10.3	8.6	186 834	61.5	10.0	55.8	10.7	33.5
Kearny town	6 831	2 808	20.7	2 008	0.0	11.0	5.4	32 875	57.9	6.8	54.1	12.4	33.5
Linden city	6 818	2 118	16.5	1 881	0.0	8.5	4.1	31 495	63.2	5.6	56.5	11.3	32.2
Long Branch city	5 789	1 894	17.9	1 541	0.0	15.1	10.6	24 530	62.9	7.4	54.4	14.4	31.3
Millville city	5 740	866	7.9	1 403	0.0	7.1	5.7	20 155	64.6	9.3	56.0	11.9	32.1
Newark city	59 032	15 312	17.0	16 968	0.0	13.2	11.4	205 511	52.7	16.1	47.0	10.7	42.4
New Brunswick city	6 799	13 244	5.3	5 052	0.0	7.9	4.4	39 748	67.1	10.6	53.1	23.4	23.5
Paramus borough	4 680	1 466	19.1	1 292	0.0	5.7	2.6	20 553	58.7	2.3	48.7	14.3	37.1
Passaic city	15 034	3 013	23.8	4 384	0.3	12.4	12.4	48 814	58.6	10.3	55.3	9.8	34.9
Paterson city	33 812	6 609	17.2	9 101	0.0	13.0	12.6	109 151	55.4	13.1	54.0	10.7	35.4
Perth Amboy city	10 394	1 970	12.4	2 932	0.0	7.5	11.1	35 254	59.5	10.8	57.0	10.3	32.7
Plainfield city	9 957	2 327	17.4	2 494	0.0	10.9	7.0	36 015	69.3	7.9	61.7	11.1	27.2
Rahway city	4 864	1 283	24.8	1 184	0.0	15.2	2.7	20 773	65.0	6.6	58.9	11.7	29.4
Sayreville borough	6 920	2 111	20.1	1 732	0.0	10.2	1.3	31 806	65.5	4.4	57.0	13.0	30.1
Trenton city	17 930	3 361	18.7	4 233	0.0	11.6	12.9	63 856	56.8	10.5	52.3	10.4	37.3
Union City city	13 547	3 297	16.2	3 798	0.0	11.1	9.4	51 949	56.9	12.4	56.0	9.9	34.1
Vineland city	11 464	2 191	15.1	2 993	0.0	13.7	3.7	43 494	63.5	10.7	54.3	13.4	32.4
Westfield town	5 932	1 236	17.3	1 086	0.0	5.7	1.0	21 950	67.9	2.2	57.2	15.4	27.4
West New York town	7 570	2 306	14.6	2 288	0.0	12.9	11.4	36 714	55.7	10.0	56.0	8.2	35.8
NEW MEXICO	384 924	120 265	9.5	113 028	0.4	11.2	7.5	1 369 176	61.0	7.2	52.2	14.7	33.0
Alamogordo city	7 517	2 386	6.4	1 987	0.5	13.6	8.0	26 299	59.5	6.1	51.4	12.9	35.7
Albuquerque city	79 118	38 858	12.1	25 219	0.0	12.0	6.9	351 189	66.2	5.7	55.7	16.5	27.8
Carlsbad city	5 379	1 083	9.6	1 474	0.0	11.7	7.1	19 673	55.1	6.9	47.2	13.4	39.4
Clovis city	7 289	2 242	3.3	1 943	0.0	12.6	7.1	23 736	60.1	6.6	50.4	14.2	35.4
Farmington city	8 362	2 285	5.7	2 645	0.0	11.3	7.5	28 017	65.0	7.0	54.8	14.9	30.3
Hobbs city	6 712	1 309	5.1	2 008	0.0	9.9	9.3	20 688	54.0	10.4	48.0	12.5	39.5
Las Cruces city	13 770	10 495	5.5	4 609	0.0	11.1	6.4	57 610	60.6	8.4	48.6	20.0	31.5
Rio Rancho city	11 289	3 050	10.9	3 051	0.0	13.0	4.3	38 249	67.9	4.7	58.3	15.1	26.6
Roswell city	9 911	2 653	8.5	3 302	0.4	11.1	8.7	34 134	53.9	9.7	46.0	13.4	40.6
Santa Fe city	9 251	4 681	23.0	3 020	0.0	10.1	8.3	50 924	66.8	4.5	54.8	17.7	27.5

Table B-5. Cities — Education, Labor Force, and Income

City	Full-year full-time employed (percent)								Children under 18 years in families (percent, except where noted)						Total employed by class of worker (percent)			
										With two parents								
	Total	Men	Women	Non-Hispanic White	Black or African American	American Indian and Alaska Native	Asian, Hawaiian, and Pacific Islander	Hispanic or Latino[1]	Number	Both in labor force	Father only in labor force	With one parent who is in labor force	+/− U.S. percent of children with no stay-at-home parent	+/− U.S. percent two-income couples	Private	Government	Self-employed	Unpaid family worker
	24	25	26	27	28	29	30	31	32	33	34	35	36	37	38	39	40	41
NEBRASKA.............	45.2	55.8	35.2	46.0	38.2	32.6	40.4	40.2	430 210	56.7	16.7	18.3	10.4	10.5	73.7	13.7	12.1	0.5
Bellevue city.............	50.4	59.8	41.3	51.4	52.3	29.7	32.2	46.4	11 575	52.3	18.9	22.2	9.9	8.9	76.8	16.4	6.6	0.2
Fremont city	43.1	53.9	33.8	43.1	59.4	29.5	62.5	42.7	5 904	54.0	14.4	23.6	13.0	7.5	82.8	9.5	7.4	0.4
Grand Island city.........	43.3	52.4	34.5	44.3	18.5	39.0	56.3	36.2	10 997	51.8	14.1	22.0	9.2	8.0	78.8	11.6	9.4	0.3
Kearney city	41.4	52.5	31.4	41.6	29.2	46.4	37.4	46.2	5 624	59.3	11.5	22.7	17.4	18.8	76.5	14.9	8.3	0.3
Lincoln city	46.2	54.1	38.4	47.2	38.7	32.7	38.5	36.5	49 748	53.6	16.9	21.6	10.6	13.4	72.3	20.1	7.5	0.2
Omaha city	45.7	55.0	37.1	47.8	36.5	29.5	39.2	41.5	93 652	46.0	15.6	25.8	7.2	8.1	82.0	10.4	7.4	0.2
NEVADA.............	42.4	49.7	34.9	43.7	40.3	40.2	43.4	37.7	475 371	39.6	21.8	23.9	-1.1	-3.1	79.6	12.5	7.7	0.3
Carson City	41.3	48.5	33.6	41.4	33.4	44.3	41.3	41.3	11 629	42.7	16.3	28.9	7.0	0.3	66.1	23.1	10.5	0.2
Henderson city	46.4	55.6	37.4	46.6	44.8	49.0	45.0	46.0	42 078	43.4	25.5	22.0	0.8	-0.7	78.7	12.8	8.3	0.2
Las Vegas city..........	40.6	46.8	34.4	43.0	37.3	41.5	43.0	34.1	113 929	34.9	22.4	25.5	-4.2	-6.9	81.9	10.8	7.1	0.2
North Las Vegas city.....	41.5	47.6	35.1	49.0	40.7	42.9	39.7	32.2	35 843	34.2	21.1	21.8	-8.6	-2.9	83.5	11.7	4.6	0.2
Reno city	42.0	48.8	35.0	43.2	40.2	37.8	41.1	37.5	38 873	39.7	19.7	25.9	1.0	0.3	79.0	12.6	8.1	0.3
Sparks city...............	46.0	54.6	37.8	47.6	45.5	47.5	43.0	39.0	16 638	46.4	18.0	23.4	5.2	5.6	80.3	13.4	6.2	0.1
NEW HAMPSHIRE....	46.5	58.0	35.7	46.7	44.3	37.9	44.3	43.7	297 516	53.7	20.7	18.4	7.5	9.3	76.5	12.8	10.5	0.2
Concord city	44.8	50.7	39.2	45.6	19.2	38.9	28.7	28.7	8 969	53.4	13.2	24.7	13.5	12.5	71.6	19.7	8.5	0.3
Dover city	47.0	56.2	38.7	46.9	44.6	39.0	49.7	60.4	5 242	52.8	16.1	24.5	12.7	10.2	77.7	13.5	8.6	0.2
Manchester city	46.4	56.4	36.9	46.8	44.7	36.1	47.8	40.6	24 223	47.1	15.9	23.3	5.8	8.2	81.6	11.4	6.9	0.1
Nashua city	49.2	61.9	37.1	49.6	51.8	35.7	45.5	45.6	20 379	49.3	19.7	21.9	6.6	6.0	83.7	9.2	7.0	0.1
Rochester city	48.0	59.3	37.9	48.3	47.6	0.0	46.9	21.2	6 883	50.6	16.1	23.8	9.8	8.1	80.3	12.8	6.6	0.3
NEW JERSEY..........	42.4	53.0	32.6	43.0	39.5	36.6	46.1	39.7	1 981 051	44.4	24.6	18.6	-1.6	0.3	77.1	13.9	8.8	0.2
Atlantic City city..........	33.8	38.5	29.5	29.6	31.8	22.6	42.2	37.4	9 337	20.1	8.6	46.0	1.5	-8.2	85.0	9.9	4.9	0.2
Bayonne city.............	39.6	48.8	31.5	39.5	44.8	41.0	36.5	39.5	13 224	39.4	23.2	21.2	-4.0	-5.3	75.7	18.3	5.8	0.2
Bergenfield borough.....	45.1	55.7	35.6	42.6	42.7	0.0	50.1	49.1	6 262	54.8	21.9	12.7	2.9	7.7	79.9	12.4	7.4	0.3
Camden city..............	27.4	29.7	25.4	25.4	27.9	12.4	34.3	26.6	24 098	11.0	8.2	45.7	-7.9	-21.2	80.2	16.0	3.6	0.2
Clifton city................	42.2	52.2	33.3	39.4	50.7	41.9	49.4	47.8	16 359	47.9	20.6	17.2	0.5	-2.6	80.3	11.5	8.0	0.2
East Orange city	37.5	40.5	35.3	24.6	38.1	27.4	33.3	31.8	17 025	20.8	7.7	46.7	2.9	6.4	75.1	20.6	4.1	0.1
Elizabeth city	36.4	42.9	30.2	36.1	33.1	15.5	34.2	37.5	29 245	28.1	17.0	27.7	-8.8	-10.5	84.0	10.5	5.5	0.1
Englewood city	44.3	54.8	35.5	44.9	44.1	82.5	52.2	42.4	5 704	43.6	22.9	18.2	-2.8	0.9	77.3	10.8	11.6	0.3
Fair Lawn borough	43.0	54.5	33.0	42.8	75.2	15.6	43.1	45.9	7 090	57.4	25.7	9.7	2.5	2.6	74.1	13.4	12.2	0.3
Fort Lee borough	40.8	53.2	30.1	39.1	40.3	42.2	41.9	46.7	6 126	35.2	40.2	11.7	-17.7	-11.1	73.8	9.9	16.1	0.3
Garfield city	43.5	53.3	34.3	41.8	50.2	39.1	42.9	49.0	6 403	43.8	23.0	19.3	-1.5	-3.7	85.2	8.5	6.1	0.2
Hackensack city	46.1	52.1	40.2	45.5	46.2	26.1	49.4	46.2	7 254	31.3	19.7	31.0	-2.3	-6.1	82.1	10.4	7.5	0.0
Hoboken city	53.3	58.7	47.7	60.8	30.8	45.9	44.9	29.5	3 670	33.3	15.1	29.5	-1.8	8.8	85.6	8.3	6.0	0.1
Jersey City city..........	39.3	47.0	32.2	40.6	36.2	35.3	43.6	38.0	53 816	27.4	14.7	31.7	-5.5	-7.3	80.3	14.2	5.3	0.2
Kearny town	39.5	47.2	31.5	40.4	14.0	28.6	36.3	42.8	8 301	39.4	24.7	19.6	-5.6	-9.1	81.2	11.6	7.0	0.2
Linden city	44.3	53.0	36.8	42.1	45.7	71.4	47.0	48.8	8 235	48.2	16.0	21.0	4.6	-2.6	80.6	13.5	5.6	0.3
Long Branch city	38.7	47.1	31.2	39.2	36.0	45.2	45.2	40.7	7 001	30.0	24.2	27.5	-7.1	-7.3	74.9	14.8	10.1	0.2
Millville city	41.3	52.0	32.1	41.3	41.9	58.7	52.9	38.5	7 106	38.7	15.0	31.2	5.3	1.1	70.4	22.6	6.9	0.2
Newark city	29.8	33.9	26.1	29.1	29.0	27.8	30.8	31.0	66 391	19.7	9.4	38.3	-6.6	-15.7	79.1	16.0	4.7	0.2
New Brunswick city	31.0	37.4	24.9	20.4	37.5	18.8	21.3	42.0	8 425	24.8	12.1	37.9	-1.9	-8.9	81.7	15.4	2.8	0.1
Paramus borough	39.7	51.3	29.1	37.7	32.5	100.0	50.5	36.8	5 869	56.3	31.2	6.2	-2.1	-0.8	72.3	12.9	14.5	0.3
Passaic city	37.4	46.7	28.2	31.2	37.7	35.9	42.4	39.0	18 960	26.7	21.0	25.5	-12.4	-12.6	87.1	8.3	4.6	0.1
Paterson city	36.3	41.6	31.6	31.5	37.3	16.4	31.3	37.3	40 182	24.5	12.4	32.9	-7.2	-12.0	83.9	12.4	3.6	0.1
Perth Amboy city.........	37.9	44.6	31.5	33.1	40.5	25.2	47.6	39.1	12 345	29.2	14.3	28.4	-7.0	-9.1	84.7	11.2	4.1	0.0
Plainfield city	43.3	46.8	40.0	38.3	46.0	39.6	30.9	40.1	11 514	29.7	10.8	43.8	8.9	4.7	81.7	13.8	4.5	0.1
Rahway city	44.4	54.4	36.0	42.6	47.1	64.7	42.3	45.8	5 914	44.8	18.0	23.0	3.2	-2.2	79.9	14.3	5.7	0.1
Sayreville borough	44.9	56.6	34.2	43.4	57.8	90.6	44.5	51.7	9 304	47.3	27.4	15.6	-1.7	-2.4	80.0	14.2	5.6	0.1
Trenton city	36.5	39.2	34.0	37.1	36.4	35.0	43.2	36.0	20 519	24.1	7.8	41.7	1.2	-5.5	72.1	23.7	4.0	0.2
Union City city	33.1	40.8	25.5	31.1	40.8	36.3	32.6	33.1	15 851	24.6	16.4	28.5	-11.5	-18.1	85.7	8.4	5.9	0.1
Vineland city	39.9	47.4	33.5	39.3	43.4	47.6	47.2	39.0	13 123	42.4	13.6	27.4	5.2	-0.1	72.7	19.6	7.6	0.1
Westfield town	44.0	61.6	28.8	43.7	40.2	42.1	51.2	56.1	8 359	52.0	36.9	7.8	-4.8	4.5	73.7	13.3	12.6	0.4
West New York town	35.0	44.3	26.2	40.7	39.3	11.0	35.5	33.5	9 245	21.9	19.8	29.2	-13.5	-21.1	82.6	9.8	7.3	0.3
NEW MEXICO..........	36.4	45.1	28.2	39.1	38.2	28.0	39.7	34.5	475 039	36.6	21.7	24.4	-3.6	-5.8	65.1	22.7	11.8	0.4
Alamogordo city	36.2	49.4	24.0	37.9	44.6	28.7	33.3	31.6	9 722	38.9	24.7	21.7	-4.0	-7.5	59.2	30.0	10.4	0.4
Albuquerque city	40.9	49.9	32.6	42.1	42.3	36.2	40.1	39.4	102 824	39.1	19.6	27.5	2.0	-0.6	71.3	18.8	9.6	0.3
Carlsbad city	32.8	43.8	23.2	32.2	23.1	29.1	63.6	34.1	6 683	35.2	22.1	28.3	-1.1	-12.9	74.2	16.6	8.9	0.3
Clovis city	36.9	49.6	25.5	38.3	36.3	29.7	38.8	33.8	9 240	34.1	22.2	27.2	-3.3	-5.7	65.9	21.4	12.5	0.2
Farmington city...........	38.6	49.8	28.1	40.2	49.1	32.0	34.0	37.9	10 202	40.1	22.8	24.1	-0.4	-2.6	71.6	17.8	10.2	0.4
Hobbs city	30.4	41.5	20.3	35.0	23.6	19.2	43.5	24.6	8 310	30.2	25.5	20.8	-13.6	-12.0	73.7	16.3	9.3	0.7
Las Cruces city	31.1	38.2	24.6	31.7	34.1	33.1	35.4	30.8	17 563	32.8	17.4	30.4	-1.4	-6.4	61.8	28.3	9.7	0.3
Rio Rancho city	45.7	57.5	35.1	45.3	41.6	46.8	44.3	47.7	14 715	49.9	23.8	18.8	4.1	2.6	76.2	15.3	8.4	0.2
Roswell city	31.1	40.8	22.5	31.2	25.3	24.2	44.8	30.9	11 967	30.9	23.6	25.3	-8.4	-13.2	69.7	18.6	11.2	0.5
Santa Fe city	37.5	45.5	30.4	39.1	52.9	32.7	44.6	35.4	11 721	36.9	17.3	30.5	2.8	1.0	60.7	21.9	16.9	0.5

[1] Hispanic or Latino persons may be of any race.

City	Percent who worked at home	Percent of the population 5 years and over with a disability	Veterans as a percent of the population 18 years and over	Occupation for employed population 16 years and over (percent)						Industry for employed population 16 years and over (percent)					
				Management, professional, and related occupations	Service occupations	Sales and office occupations	Farming, fishing, and forestry occupations	Construction, extraction, and maintenance occupations	Production, transportation and material moving occupations	Agriculture, forestry, fishing, and mining	Construction and manufacturing	Wholesale and retail trade	Transportation and warehousing, and utilities	Service industries	Public administration
	42	43	44	45	46	47	48	49	50	51	52	53	54	55	56
NEBRASKA	4.6	16.0	13.7	33.0	14.6	26.4	1.6	9.3	15.1	5.6	18.7	15.7	6.1	50.0	3.9
Bellevue city	2.4	15.1	23.0	32.4	15.2	30.7	0.3	9.8	11.6	0.1	14.2	16.0	6.7	56.7	6.2
Fremont city	2.0	18.6	14.8	22.8	16.8	29.3	0.4	9.0	21.7	1.4	26.1	19.6	5.2	44.4	3.2
Grand Island city	2.0	19.5	14.2	23.9	16.0	27.8	0.9	10.1	21.2	2.0	25.4	19.4	4.9	45.6	2.7
Kearney city	2.1	14.6	9.4	29.7	18.2	30.4	0.9	8.2	12.7	1.5	18.2	19.9	2.2	54.6	3.6
Lincoln city	2.9	14.7	11.3	36.0	15.3	27.1	0.3	8.0	13.3	0.6	18.0	14.0	4.0	56.6	6.8
Omaha city	2.6	16.9	13.4	34.8	14.2	30.1	0.2	8.0	12.6	0.4	16.1	16.5	5.6	59.0	2.5
NEVADA	2.6	20.6	16.0	25.7	24.6	27.6	0.3	11.4	10.4	1.6	14.2	14.0	5.2	60.6	4.5
Carson City	3.4	20.8	18.0	30.2	18.2	28.2	0.3	9.3	13.8	0.6	21.7	13.9	2.7	47.8	13.3
Henderson city	2.6	16.1	16.3	30.9	21.1	30.1	0.0	9.4	8.5	0.3	14.2	14.7	5.9	60.7	4.2
Las Vegas city	2.4	22.2	15.3	25.5	26.3	27.5	0.1	11.5	9.0	0.3	13.4	13.5	4.5	64.6	3.7
North Las Vegas city	1.3	21.0	12.8	17.9	28.1	25.3	0.1	16.3	12.3	0.2	17.9	12.6	4.9	59.7	4.8
Reno city	2.4	19.6	15.4	29.2	22.0	29.1	0.2	8.5	11.0	0.5	13.8	16.0	5.3	60.9	3.5
Sparks city	2.2	20.5	14.9	24.2	20.4	30.1	0.1	10.0	15.2	0.5	15.6	16.7	7.5	54.8	4.8
NEW HAMPSHIRE	4.0	16.9	15.0	35.8	13.0	26.6	0.4	9.4	14.8	0.9	24.9	17.3	4.1	49.0	3.8
Concord city	3.1	18.9	14.4	39.4	14.0	28.0	0.0	8.1	10.4	0.4	15.7	17.1	2.4	56.0	8.3
Dover city	2.8	15.6	14.9	39.3	12.9	29.3	0.4	5.8	12.2	0.5	19.9	18.1	3.5	54.3	3.7
Manchester city	2.2	21.8	14.1	29.8	14.5	28.6	0.1	9.0	18.0	0.1	24.6	18.1	5.0	48.7	3.5
Nashua city	2.7	17.6	14.5	39.6	11.9	26.2	0.1	6.8	15.4	0.3	28.2	16.6	3.9	48.5	2.5
Rochester city	2.3	20.6	17.6	25.0	15.6	27.4	0.4	9.7	21.9	0.8	29.3	18.9	4.3	42.4	4.3
NEW JERSEY	2.7	18.0	10.6	38.0	13.6	28.5	0.2	7.8	12.0	0.3	17.6	15.7	5.9	55.9	4.5
Atlantic City city	1.2	30.3	10.2	13.7	48.5	22.3	0.2	4.9	10.4	0.2	7.3	8.3	2.5	77.3	4.5
Bayonne city	1.5	23.5	11.1	32.0	14.1	32.1	0.1	7.8	14.0	0.1	14.5	13.4	12.2	54.4	5.4
Bergenfield borough	1.8	17.4	9.8	38.1	14.3	29.3	0.0	7.0	11.3	0.1	14.1	17.9	6.5	58.3	3.1
Camden city	0.9	28.3	8.1	16.8	25.5	25.1	0.3	6.7	25.7	0.2	19.8	16.2	4.7	54.0	5.2
Clifton city	2.0	19.2	10.2	32.3	11.7	30.9	0.0	8.4	16.6	0.2	23.4	17.7	6.1	49.9	2.8
East Orange city	1.9	25.1	8.2	24.6	22.2	32.2	0.0	5.9	15.1	0.1	11.3	12.1	10.7	60.3	5.6
Elizabeth city	1.1	24.4	5.1	18.2	17.8	25.9	0.1	9.5	28.4	0.1	24.7	18.0	10.7	43.3	3.2
Englewood city	3.6	18.2	8.9	38.6	16.0	27.2	0.1	5.6	12.4	0.2	14.8	15.4	5.8	60.6	3.2
Fair Lawn borough	3.7	16.5	10.6	48.1	9.1	29.3	0.0	5.8	7.8	0.1	15.8	16.6	5.1	59.1	3.2
Fort Lee borough	4.2	16.6	8.8	51.6	8.3	30.9	0.0	3.3	5.9	0.1	12.7	20.4	4.1	60.6	2.1
Garfield city	1.4	26.6	7.4	20.5	15.5	28.2	0.5	14.6	20.7	0.3	30.7	19.2	5.9	41.7	2.1
Hackensack city	1.6	21.7	8.2	35.6	14.9	29.8	0.0	6.1	13.6	0.0	16.7	17.3	4.9	58.3	2.8
Hoboken city	2.8	15.7	4.4	61.0	6.6	25.9	0.0	1.9	4.6	0.0	9.7	9.9	2.9	74.9	2.6
Jersey City city	1.8	24.3	5.9	33.0	15.9	30.5	0.1	5.1	15.5	0.1	12.4	15.6	10.0	57.7	4.2
Kearny town	1.0	20.9	7.5	26.8	15.0	29.7	0.1	11.5	17.0	0.0	21.7	15.8	9.1	50.5	2.9
Linden city	0.9	20.4	10.6	23.0	14.9	32.3	0.1	9.2	20.5	0.1	24.9	17.0	9.7	43.6	4.6
Long Branch city	1.9	21.0	9.9	28.6	20.5	28.2	0.2	10.5	12.1	0.2	18.0	15.9	4.6	55.9	5.3
Millville city	2.1	20.4	12.3	24.8	19.9	24.5	0.2	10.8	19.8	0.5	26.4	15.1	4.9	43.5	9.7
Newark city	1.2	29.0	5.9	18.9	21.8	27.5	0.1	10.4	21.2	0.1	20.4	13.4	10.2	51.1	4.7
New Brunswick city	1.3	18.5	3.7	24.9	22.4	26.5	0.5	4.6	21.2	0.3	18.6	16.0	4.3	58.1	2.7
Paramus borough	3.5	13.9	12.2	44.1	9.1	33.3	0.0	6.2	7.2	0.0	16.0	20.9	4.9	54.8	3.4
Passaic city	1.4	25.0	3.8	18.0	17.4	23.6	0.3	7.2	33.5	0.2	29.2	18.6	6.0	43.5	2.4
Paterson city	1.0	29.8	5.0	16.7	20.2	27.7	0.2	7.8	27.4	0.1	25.4	17.6	6.5	47.0	3.5
Perth Amboy city	1.0	24.5	6.4	17.5	17.4	25.0	0.1	8.7	31.3	0.1	26.9	18.9	7.1	43.6	3.4
Plainfield city	1.3	20.0	8.9	24.0	17.7	27.3	0.1	8.4	22.5	0.0	22.6	14.9	7.6	51.5	3.4
Rahway city	1.9	18.6	13.0	30.6	13.4	31.1	0.0	9.6	15.3	0.0	20.4	14.4	9.6	50.2	5.4
Sayreville borough	1.4	16.2	11.7	35.5	11.8	31.3	0.1	9.3	12.0	0.2	17.6	16.8	9.1	52.2	4.0
Trenton city	1.6	26.8	9.3	21.5	25.8	27.6	0.3	8.4	16.3	0.3	15.2	12.0	5.5	53.6	13.4
Union City city	1.4	27.9	3.0	17.1	19.2	24.4	0.1	7.9	31.2	0.1	23.4	19.3	9.4	46.4	1.5
Vineland city	1.9	25.4	9.8	26.3	18.0	24.5	2.0	9.7	19.6	2.4	23.2	14.9	4.2	49.9	5.5
Westfield town	4.9	11.2	10.7	60.5	7.6	24.1	0.1	3.3	4.5	0.1	13.8	11.1	3.8	68.6	2.8
West New York town	1.9	28.9	3.0	19.8	20.1	26.3	0.2	7.2	26.5	0.1	21.7	18.2	8.1	49.6	2.2
NEW MEXICO	4.2	20.4	14.5	34.0	17.0	25.9	1.0	11.4	10.7	4.0	14.5	14.9	4.7	53.9	8.0
Alamogordo city	2.5	20.2	22.4	28.6	18.6	24.0	0.5	15.9	12.4	1.2	14.4	15.8	5.5	49.6	13.5
Albuquerque city	3.6	19.6	15.4	38.5	15.8	29.1	0.1	7.8	8.7	0.4	13.6	15.7	3.9	60.7	5.8
Carlsbad city	2.6	22.0	15.4	25.2	19.9	26.0	0.7	15.5	12.5	8.6	11.7	17.3	4.2	52.6	5.5
Clovis city	2.8	22.1	16.8	27.9	19.0	27.9	1.5	10.5	13.2	3.7	10.9	19.2	7.6	51.3	7.4
Farmington city	3.2	17.6	14.5	30.2	14.9	27.3	0.3	15.1	12.1	10.9	9.9	18.9	7.1	49.1	4.1
Hobbs city	2.5	23.2	10.9	25.5	17.6	23.8	1.5	17.8	13.8	18.0	9.3	16.7	5.2	45.9	5.0
Las Cruces city	3.3	19.0	14.6	36.9	18.2	28.4	0.2	8.5	7.7	1.3	10.9	14.7	3.1	60.9	9.1
Rio Rancho city	3.1	17.3	18.0	34.5	15.1	30.9	0.1	9.5	9.9	0.3	20.6	17.9	5.1	49.8	6.3
Roswell city	2.8	23.3	15.2	27.3	17.4	26.3	2.6	10.7	15.7	6.3	16.6	16.8	5.0	50.4	4.8
Santa Fe city	7.3	18.7	12.7	43.0	16.7	26.2	0.2	8.3	5.5	0.7	10.8	14.2	1.8	60.5	12.1

City	Median house-hold income	Median family income — All families	Families with children — Married-couple	Families with children — Male house-holder	Families with children — Female house-holder	Median nonfamily house-hold income	Median income for full-year, full-time workers — Men	Median income for full-year, full-time workers — Women	Per capita income	Households by source of income (percent) — With earnings	With interest, dividend, or rental income	With Social Security income	With public assis-tance income	With retire-ment income	House-holds with income over $100,000 (percent)	+/– U.S. percent for income over $100,000	House-holds with income below poverty (percent)	Families with children with income below poverty (percent)
	57	58	59	60	61	62	63	64	65	66	67	68	69	70	71	72	73	74
NEBRASKA	39 250	48 032	55 343	27 526	20 480	22 985	33 399	24 635	19 613	82.5	41.6	26.4	2.8	12.8	8.1	-4.2	9.7	10.2
Bellevue city	47 201	54 422	58 081	37 857	23 623	28 003	36 394	26 676	20 903	88.2	40.3	19.8	2.2	22.4	8.9	-3.4	5.3	7.1
Fremont city	36 700	45 259	53 100	24 766	22 125	19 736	32 462	21 737	18 006	77.7	40.4	31.6	2.5	15.5	5.3	-7.0	8.9	8.3
Grand Island city	36 044	43 197	48 665	21 695	17 423	20 465	30 245	21 215	17 071	82.1	39.6	26.3	4.3	12.7	5.7	-6.6	12.1	15.6
Kearney city	34 829	46 650	54 830	24 457	16 929	21 556	30 836	23 592	17 713	85.4	38.0	21.2	2.5	9.9	5.7	-6.6	13.9	11.2
Lincoln city	40 605	52 558	61 000	27 399	20 533	25 451	35 188	26 108	20 984	86.1	42.9	20.1	3.1	13.0	8.9	-3.4	10.2	9.3
Omaha city	40 006	50 821	62 370	30 180	21 215	26 152	35 468	27 395	21 756	82.7	37.0	23.6	3.5	13.7	10.0	-2.3	10.4	12.3
NEVADA	44 581	50 849	57 707	32 114	24 148	30 088	36 812	28 019	21 989	83.5	29.6	23.6	2.3	17.4	11.3	-1.0	9.4	11.4
Carson City	41 809	49 570	58 101	26 607	24 026	27 162	36 035	28 617	20 943	78.2	37.2	29.3	2.7	21.3	9.3	-3.0	9.2	11.7
Henderson city	55 949	61 176	69 883	40 790	30 556	38 233	44 478	31 281	26 815	86.8	35.5	21.8	1.7	18.8	17.4	5.1	5.1	5.7
Las Vegas city	44 069	50 465	58 922	31 049	24 806	29 650	36 500	28 751	22 060	82.2	28.8	24.7	2.5	18.0	12.1	-0.2	10.4	13.1
North Las Vegas city	46 057	46 540	51 039	35 444	23 527	32 180	34 021	26 334	16 023	89.1	20.8	17.2	3.4	14.0	8.3	-4.0	12.4	15.1
Reno city	40 530	49 582	56 619	29 710	21 929	28 733	34 659	27 799	22 520	83.5	31.8	22.4	2.7	14.3	10.4	-1.9	11.2	13.5
Sparks city	45 745	52 029	61 432	36 054	26 974	30 754	36 200	29 884	21 122	86.1	30.8	21.6	1.7	15.4	9.7	-2.6	7.4	9.1
NEW HAMPSHIRE	49 467	57 575	67 028	35 036	24 774	28 945	40 819	28 669	23 844	83.8	41.9	24.7	3.0	16.4	13.8	1.5	6.9	6.5
Concord city	42 447	52 418	65 288	25 000	24 107	28 380	36 422	28 558	21 976	80.6	42.8	26.3	3.5	16.9	8.6	-3.7	8.6	9.9
Dover city	43 873	57 050	69 227	39 712	26 694	31 246	40 003	28 456	23 459	84.2	41.9	21.9	3.2	16.3	10.3	-2.0	7.9	8.4
Manchester city	40 774	50 039	60 433	35 582	19 786	27 379	35 502	27 268	21 244	80.7	36.7	26.1	5.4	15.5	7.6	-4.7	10.4	12.3
Nashua city	51 969	61 102	71 413	38 955	23 407	33 766	45 610	30 044	25 209	84.0	41.7	23.2	3.6	15.6	15.9	3.6	6.7	7.5
Rochester city	40 596	47 324	57 369	31 563	17 388	24 244	35 228	24 161	18 859	80.1	32.2	27.7	5.5	19.6	6.2	-6.1	8.7	10.1
NEW JERSEY	55 146	65 370	77 760	35 172	25 473	31 298	48 027	34 636	27 006	81.4	42.4	26.9	2.8	17.1	21.3	9.0	8.3	9.2
Atlantic City city	26 969	31 997	42 646	26 326	18 833	18 282	26 208	24 380	15 402	71.2	16.7	30.3	7.6	14.3	5.3	-7.0	22.5	26.1
Bayonne city	41 566	52 413	61 940	30 727	23 144	24 441	40 762	35 014	21 553	74.1	38.4	32.9	3.3	19.1	11.6	-0.7	11.7	12.0
Bergenfield borough	62 172	71 187	80 733	103 257	35 815	32 889	42 753	35 755	24 706	84.5	43.8	28.9	1.2	18.4	23.2	10.9	3.2	3.4
Camden city	23 421	24 612	36 745	22 192	14 527	14 001	25 857	21 980	9 815	72.8	10.0	23.6	16.3	12.3	2.2	-10.1	34.3	39.3
Clifton city	50 619	60 688	66 786	41 250	30 434	27 652	41 164	33 290	23 638	76.5	47.1	33.9	2.0	17.2	16.0	3.7	6.5	6.5
East Orange city	40 016	42 667	55 875	25 592	22 257	19 506	32 476	30 734	16 488	75.9	15.2	25.7	9.3	14.1	7.6	-4.7	19.1	21.2
Elizabeth city	35 175	38 370	45 911	27 777	18 710	21 785	31 143	24 455	13 114	79.0	20.1	22.0	6.3	11.9	7.2	-5.1	17.9	20.6
Englewood city	58 379	67 194	81 815	39 323	30 850	37 969	43 991	35 564	35 275	83.6	40.0	26.7	3.1	15.2	27.4	15.1	8.4	9.2
Fair Lawn borough	72 127	81 220	92 161	57 679	46 029	36 354	59 264	42 468	32 273	79.2	56.6	32.3	0.7	20.7	29.9	17.6	4.6	2.8
Fort Lee borough	58 161	72 140	76 167	62 969	26 635	40 801	59 149	44 714	37 899	76.4	46.1	29.3	1.1	12.9	25.6	13.3	8.0	8.6
Garfield city	42 748	51 654	56 096	21 205	25 720	23 771	36 731	27 574	19 530	79.5	34.6	29.1	2.3	14.8	9.4	-2.9	7.9	9.2
Hackensack city	49 316	56 953	65 000	33 864	29 868	39 153	40 800	33 913	26 856	85.1	32.6	22.2	2.3	11.0	14.4	2.1	9.5	8.4
Hoboken city	62 550	67 500	85 774	27 871	19 811	60 980	56 369	47 915	43 195	85.5	40.4	16.0	2.4	7.1	28.3	16.0	10.3	17.2
Jersey City city	37 862	41 639	50 506	26 924	18 863	28 368	35 736	31 098	19 410	80.7	24.2	20.3	6.7	10.5	11.5	-0.8	18.0	22.8
Kearny town	47 757	54 596	60 914	35 577	29 375	27 312	40 026	31 125	20 886	82.9	34.9	24.8	2.9	15.5	13.3	1.0	8.7	7.7
Linden city	46 345	54 903	65 129	45 402	30 707	26 476	40 506	30 859	21 314	77.1	39.0	32.6	2.6	18.3	11.2	-1.1	7.0	6.8
Long Branch city	38 651	42 825	51 723	22 404	18 901	31 220	39 481	27 480	20 532	79.6	30.0	24.8	4.4	14.1	10.7	-1.6	15.3	21.0
Millville city	40 378	46 093	58 520	26 741	16 875	23 636	37 473	27 269	18 632	77.9	25.6	28.0	5.5	18.2	8.1	-4.2	13.7	17.8
Newark city	26 913	30 781	44 477	23 419	14 697	14 697	30 203	26 210	13 009	72.2	14.0	24.0	12.6	10.6	5.3	-7.0	28.8	32.6
New Brunswick city	36 080	38 222	42 580	31 544	21 275	27 205	25 795	24 245	14 308	85.4	24.3	18.4	5.7	10.8	8.7	-3.6	23.8	22.4
Paramus borough	76 918	84 406	96 440	27 000	50 292	27 755	60 942	40 709	29 295	81.8	59.5	34.8	0.3	21.7	34.5	22.2	2.5	2.4
Passaic city	33 594	34 935	41 263	23 125	18 109	20 602	24 936	21 680	12 874	81.3	18.7	21.9	6.3	8.8	6.7	-5.6	20.0	23.6
Paterson city	32 778	35 420	43 625	28 285	18 363	18 299	28 640	23 191	13 257	79.7	16.1	22.6	8.7	10.5	7.0	-5.3	21.3	24.5
Perth Amboy city	37 608	40 740	49 992	24 063	17 012	22 760	30 155	22 465	14 989	82.2	22.4	25.4	5.2	14.7	9.0	-3.3	15.9	20.0
Plainfield city	46 683	50 774	67 446	27 167	23 928	27 428	34 617	31 052	19 052	84.2	21.7	23.6	5.9	17.1	15.7	3.4	13.7	17.2
Rahway city	50 729	61 931	67 374	40 521	35 446	29 515	41 610	32 617	22 481	80.2	38.1	30.1	3.4	19.9	13.3	1.0	7.3	6.5
Sayreville borough	58 919	66 256	72 912	38 250	33 051	34 144	48 935	35 989	24 736	83.5	43.2	26.1	1.5	18.6	18.0	5.7	5.2	5.2
Trenton city	31 074	36 681	49 201	27 327	20 168	19 126	30 091	27 451	14 621	75.4	18.4	26.7	7.7	15.1	5.9	-6.4	20.9	23.4
Union City city	30 642	32 246	38 125	20 713	15 748	20 089	26 010	20 373	13 997	81.4	17.1	21.4	6.5	10.2	5.6	-6.7	20.8	24.7
Vineland city	40 076	47 909	58 196	26 071	20 710	22 235	35 821	26 180	18 797	79.6	29.9	29.2	5.2	17.7	9.8	-2.5	12.4	14.8
Westfield town	98 390	112 145	132 390	65 833	38 313	41 395	86 518	47 073	47 187	84.3	69.1	24.7	0.9	18.1	49.4	37.1	2.7	2.8
West New York town	31 980	34 083	37 907	24 375	17 676	19 811	27 004	23 383	16 719	78.4	18.5	24.7	4.5	10.0	8.5	-3.8	20.0	21.7
NEW MEXICO	34 133	39 425	46 011	23 054	16 453	21 791	32 232	24 532	17 261	79.5	30.2	25.5	4.7	17.4	7.6	-4.7	16.8	20.8
Alamogordo city	30 928	35 673	40 012	23 906	11 448	20 189	29 678	19 478	14 662	77.0	29.3	26.5	4.1	23.7	3.1	-9.2	15.4	19.9
Albuquerque city	38 272	46 979	57 271	26 214	19 316	25 882	35 820	27 113	20 884	82.3	36.5	22.8	3.8	17.7	9.7	-2.6	12.7	15.2
Carlsbad city	30 658	35 640	41 623	22 281	16 795	17 690	31 659	19 969	16 496	73.2	28.2	32.2	5.4	18.0	5.0	-7.3	16.0	19.8
Clovis city	28 878	33 622	39 193	24 167	15 613	17 202	28 691	21 071	15 561	76.4	24.5	27.9	6.7	17.0	5.1	-7.2	19.7	25.4
Farmington city	37 663	42 605	50 919	22 813	12 953	22 837	38 651	23 101	18 167	82.9	32.0	23.4	3.4	14.7	7.8	-4.5	14.1	20.2
Hobbs city	28 100	33 017	38 175	17 016	10 509	16 121	32 125	22 378	14 209	74.6	22.3	29.2	7.5	13.7	5.3	-7.0	22.9	28.7
Las Cruces city	30 375	37 670	47 259	23 676	13 019	18 296	31 668	22 484	15 704	78.5	31.7	24.5	5.5	19.7	4.7	-7.6	21.3	26.8
Rio Rancho city	47 169	52 233	58 525	35 033	28 419	30 812	40 407	28 295	20 322	83.7	36.3	24.1	1.9	20.3	7.4	-4.9	4.9	4.6
Roswell city	27 252	31 724	36 627	22 240	14 586	17 059	27 449	22 143	14 589	71.8	29.0	34.8	6.6	18.3	4.4	-7.9	20.1	28.2
Santa Fe city	40 392	49 705	55 949	25 570	22 009	31 399	35 073	29 189	25 454	80.7	42.7	25.3	2.7	18.3	11.7	0.6	11.4	14.9

STATE Place code	City	High school graduates			College graduates		College graduates (percent)				
		Total population 25 years and over	Percent with a high school diploma or less	Percent with a high school diploma or more	Percent with a bachelor's degree or more	+/− U.S. percent with bachelor's degree or more	Non-Hispanic White	Black or African American	American Indian and Alaska Native	Asian, Hawaiian, and Pacific Islander	Hispanic or Latino[1]
		1	2	3	4	5	6	7	8	9	10
36 00000	NEW YORK.............	12 542 536	48.7	79.1	27.4	3.0	31.8	15.8	14.4	41.2	11.5
36 01000	Albany city....................	58 339	43.2	81.2	32.5	8.1	38.9	12.4	23.7	63.2	26.2
36 03078	Auburn city...................	19 390	58.8	74.3	13.6	−10.8	14.5	4.3	11.5	7.5	7.9
36 06607	Binghamton city............	30 827	51.8	78.1	21.3	−3.1	21.7	12.1	0.0	32.5	26.4
36 11000	Buffalo city..................	182 848	54.5	74.6	18.3	−6.1	23.0	10.2	9.6	40.1	13.0
36 24229	Elmira city....................	19 147	61.4	74.2	14.6	−9.8	15.8	9.2	2.8	10.0	4.9
36 27485	Freeport village	28 176	53.6	73.1	20.5	−3.9	26.5	24.7	0.0	43.9	7.7
36 29113	Glen Cove city.............	18 786	48.5	77.6	27.9	3.5	32.7	7.8	7.6	51.5	10.7
36 33139	Hempstead village........	32 349	61.5	66.6	16.0	−8.4	29.1	17.1	9.1	49.5	6.5
36 38077	Ithaca city...................	10 744	27.0	89.5	57.9	33.5	58.9	26.8	46.2	74.7	61.7
36 38264	Jamestown city............	20 795	55.1	79.4	14.8	−9.6	15.5	7.2	5.6	19.4	4.1
36 42554	Lindenhurst village	18 435	56.2	83.5	16.4	−8.0	16.4	9.8	20.9	45.3	12.6
36 43335	Long Beach city............	26 824	36.7	88.7	37.0	12.6	41.0	14.7	30.3	54.9	14.4
36 47042	Middletown city.............	15 805	55.0	74.3	17.0	−7.4	20.0	9.2	11.9	50.6	7.8
36 49121	Mount Vernon city........	45 705	52.1	74.4	24.2	−0.2	31.2	21.0	17.7	52.8	17.6
36 50034	Newburgh city	15 292	69.5	62.1	11.2	−13.2	18.3	8.6	3.7	50.6	4.3
36 50617	New Rochelle city	48 872	43.2	80.0	38.3	13.9	46.4	27.5	25.9	64.0	14.4
36 51000	New York city...............	5 276 946	52.2	72.3	27.4	3.0	41.9	15.8	13.6	36.1	10.5
36 51055	Niagara Falls city	37 186	61.2	76.6	12.5	−11.9	13.4	6.6	17.7	24.5	15.8
36 53682	North Tonawanda city ...	22 539	51.3	85.5	19.5	−4.9	19.3	22.0	22.7	50.4	28.7
36 59223	Port Chester village	18 755	60.4	68.9	20.6	−3.8	29.2	14.5	0.0	65.4	8.2
36 59641	Poughkeepsie city	18 390	55.1	72.3	19.5	−4.9	25.9	8.0	0.0	39.2	15.2
36 63000	Rochester city	132 707	55.6	73.0	20.1	−4.3	29.4	8.2	10.6	33.1	8.2
36 63418	Rome city.....................	24 305	58.6	74.0	15.7	−8.7	17.0	6.8	0.0	36.1	2.9
36 65255	Saratoga Springs city....	17 127	34.4	89.0	38.9	14.5	39.9	16.4	10.5	26.2	37.2
36 65508	Schenectady city	39 762	54.7	77.8	19.0	−5.4	19.9	11.7	22.2	45.9	9.6
36 70420	Spring Valley village......	14 417	54.9	70.1	19.9	−4.5	29.1	15.0	0.0	44.2	4.8
36 73000	Syracuse city................	86 084	52.9	76.2	23.2	−1.2	26.7	8.9	8.6	53.3	14.7
36 75484	Troy city.......................	29 727	54.5	77.7	19.4	−5.0	18.8	10.3	26.2	75.5	12.5
36 76540	Utica city.....................	40 075	57.6	72.6	15.2	−9.2	17.1	6.3	0.0	5.9	6.4
36 76705	Valley Stream village	24 845	48.3	86.2	24.9	0.5	22.9	37.2	23.7	46.8	20.2
36 78608	Watertown city..............	17 032	51.9	82.5	17.3	−7.1	17.4	8.5	12.0	22.2	23.4
36 81677	White Plains city...........	37 983	37.8	82.0	41.1	16.7	53.2	23.2	29.5	72.6	11.8
36 84000	Yonkers city..................	131 749	52.6	76.7	24.8	0.4	28.3	18.4	16.8	53.0	12.9
37 00000	NORTH CAROLINA ...	5 282 994	50.3	78.1	22.5	−1.9	25.2	13.1	10.4	43.0	10.5
37 02140	Asheville city	48 306	41.4	82.3	30.4	6.0	34.9	9.4	12.4	46.6	12.6
37 09060	Burlington city...............	30 454	54.5	74.2	21.7	−2.7	27.3	9.1	32.0	40.6	2.9
37 10740	Cary town	61 114	15.6	95.1	60.7	36.3	61.7	47.7	30.5	73.7	33.4
37 11800	Chapel Hill town	23 625	11.8	94.3	73.7	49.3	80.3	35.8	31.4	83.2	40.0
37 12000	Charlotte city................	352 546	35.0	84.9	36.4	12.0	47.2	18.9	19.7	39.1	13.0
37 14100	Concord city	36 506	47.4	79.2	22.8	−1.6	25.4	13.6	18.1	38.4	4.3
37 19000	Durham city..................	118 100	35.0	82.6	41.8	17.4	55.6	26.3	41.0	77.8	14.4
37 22920	Fayetteville city............	74 800	40.5	84.8	24.2	−0.2	31.5	15.6	11.9	27.9	14.2
37 25580	Gastonia city................	43 911	53.5	72.2	20.2	−4.2	23.5	10.6	13.6	32.0	11.4
37 26880	Goldsboro city	24 606	52.6	76.3	17.2	−7.2	23.3	11.2	0.0	37.4	15.7
37 28000	Greensboro city............	142 293	38.1	84.3	33.9	9.5	42.8	20.6	11.0	31.6	13.5
37 28080	Greenville city..............	31 900	33.3	86.0	38.4	14.0	51.2	15.7	41.5	59.9	20.3
37 31060	Hickory city	24 355	45.7	79.1	28.0	3.6	33.8	6.6	10.3	19.3	2.7
37 31400	High Point city..............	55 703	48.6	77.2	25.5	1.1	33.1	10.8	9.5	23.0	9.2
37 34200	Jacksonville city	26 230	42.6	88.7	17.8	−6.6	21.9	9.7	7.4	12.9	15.1
37 35200	Kannapolis city	24 374	62.8	69.4	12.0	−12.4	12.6	10.9	0.0	9.5	1.2
37 43920	Monroe city..................	16 034	59.5	67.6	15.6	−8.8	21.3	8.0	20.0	59.4	3.5
37 55000	Raleigh city..................	174 393	27.7	88.5	44.9	20.5	54.9	24.2	26.8	59.8	13.6
37 57500	Rocky Mount city	35 407	56.4	74.1	20.1	−4.3	32.2	8.8	25.0	47.1	17.9
37 58860	Salisbury city	17 612	51.2	75.7	24.1	−0.3	30.3	12.9	18.3	21.4	8.1
37 74440	Wilmington city	48 834	40.1	83.0	31.0	6.6	38.0	10.9	17.9	51.0	13.2
37 74540	Wilson city	28 196	57.8	69.3	19.2	−5.2	31.9	6.1	54.0	40.3	3.7
37 75000	Winston-Salem city	120 966	45.0	80.2	30.3	5.9	39.9	16.1	20.7	61.7	7.4
38 00000	NORTH DAKOTA.......	408 585	44.0	83.9	22.0	−2.4	22.4	20.5	9.7	47.4	16.3
38 07200	Bismarck city................	36 133	35.7	87.5	29.4	5.0	30.0	6.2	5.7	39.5	23.3
38 25700	Fargo city	54 319	30.5	91.0	34.4	10.0	34.8	23.2	8.5	61.3	19.4
38 32060	Grand Forks city............	27 429	34.5	89.3	30.3	5.9	30.6	22.1	18.0	54.9	16.7
38 53380	Minot city	23 390	41.6	86.3	24.1	−0.3	24.4	23.9	10.0	27.1	21.3
39 00000	OHIO	7 411 740	53.1	83.0	21.1	−3.3	21.8	11.9	12.4	58.0	15.2
39 01000	Akron city	139 480	55.5	80.0	18.0	−6.4	20.9	8.3	11.1	49.1	17.5
39 03828	Barberton city...............	18 633	66.9	79.2	10.6	−13.8	10.9	4.1	0.0	13.6	19.7
39 04720	Beavercreek city...........	26 181	30.0	92.4	42.9	18.5	41.8	67.5	35.0	62.4	59.0
39 07972	Bowling Green city	11 799	31.5	91.2	44.2	19.8	44.2	62.0	0.0	70.0	15.5

[1] Hispanic or Latino persons may be of any race.

City	School enrollment			Population 16 to 19 years				Employment status, 2000			Work status in 1999 of the population 16 years and over		
											Worked in 1999		
	Grades kindergarten through 12	College or graduate school	Percent private	Number	Percent in armed forces	Percent high school graduates	Percent not enrolled, not grads, not in armed forces, not employed	Total population 16 years and over	Percent in labor force	Unemployment rate	Full-time	Part-time	Did not work in 1999
	11	12	13	14	15	16	17	18	19	20	21	22	23
NEW YORK	3 584 279	1 301 375	21.8	1 017 375	0.3	8.1	5.6	14 805 912	61.1	7.1	51.7	14.1	34.2
Albany city	13 976	16 882	22.6	7 803	0.0	5.4	3.5	78 755	63.6	12.7	50.7	18.7	30.6
Auburn city	4 757	1 424	10.3	1 570	0.0	11.5	8.8	22 894	56.3	6.0	47.4	16.8	35.8
Binghamton city	7 493	5 165	10.4	2 243	0.0	15.2	5.9	38 293	56.0	6.7	44.7	18.0	37.3
Buffalo city	57 805	23 473	19.3	16 610	0.0	10.1	8.9	223 437	58.4	12.5	45.4	17.2	37.5
Elmira city	5 642	2 033	23.8	2 070	0.0	11.8	11.3	24 142	55.0	12.7	47.0	17.0	36.0
Freeport village	9 179	2 208	17.5	2 443	0.0	8.1	4.3	33 452	64.8	5.1	56.8	13.6	29.6
Glen Cove city	4 199	1 647	24.3	1 249	0.0	9.1	3.4	21 644	59.0	5.2	50.5	14.4	35.1
Hempstead village	11 132	6 312	32.0	4 475	0.0	6.4	5.6	42 952	61.6	7.0	53.4	15.4	31.3
Ithaca city	1 907	16 915	74.9	5 411	0.4	1.8	0.1	26 774	56.1	9.4	45.1	35.1	19.8
Jamestown city	5 896	1 297	6.6	1 764	0.0	10.3	8.4	24 530	62.1	8.3	48.4	17.2	34.4
Lindenhurst village	5 628	1 368	12.6	1 208	0.0	8.7	2.3	21 190	65.9	3.7	53.5	15.6	30.8
Long Beach city	4 977	2 274	26.8	1 324	0.0	8.9	1.3	29 711	64.2	5.7	55.7	11.5	32.9
Middletown city	5 283	973	13.8	1 574	0.0	5.7	11.1	19 015	61.1	6.4	52.6	14.0	33.4
Mount Vernon city	13 242	4 245	25.1	3 341	0.0	10.7	4.3	52 875	63.2	7.3	54.7	12.1	33.2
Newburgh city	6 856	1 623	10.1	1 968	0.0	10.4	9.5	19 585	61.0	11.3	52.5	13.5	33.9
New Rochelle city	12 782	5 030	32.3	3 415	0.0	5.6	4.7	56 645	62.3	4.3	53.9	14.0	32.1
New York city	1 494 102	593 664	26.4	414 101	0.0	8.2	7.8	6 279 431	57.8	9.6	50.0	11.4	38.5
Niagara Falls city	10 410	2 630	14.9	2 690	0.0	9.7	5.0	43 186	57.4	10.1	44.4	15.7	39.9
North Tonawanda city	6 002	1 884	15.2	1 911	0.0	10.2	7.3	26 375	66.4	5.1	53.1	17.1	29.8
Port Chester village	4 550	1 437	23.5	1 250	0.0	8.9	6.5	22 215	63.7	5.0	54.4	13.9	31.7
Poughkeepsie city	5 800	2 219	21.5	1 570	0.0	10.4	11.0	22 865	59.5	8.2	49.8	14.7	35.5
Rochester city	46 616	16 714	23.4	12 332	0.1	9.3	9.3	163 495	62.6	10.2	52.2	14.6	33.3
Rome city	5 882	1 213	13.5	1 747	0.0	11.6	5.3	28 186	54.0	7.1	48.2	14.0	37.8
Saratoga Springs city	3 666	3 237	40.6	1 805	3.0	8.9	1.7	21 631	67.5	4.3	55.9	19.2	24.9
Schenectady city	10 811	4 800	25.1	3 327	0.0	9.3	7.6	40 244	60.8	7.5	50.4	15.9	33.7
Spring Valley village	6 151	1 674	35.4	1 597	0.0	3.6	6.3	18 025	66.7	7.1	56.1	14.2	29.7
Syracuse city	27 043	20 840	38.4	11 100	0.1	6.8	7.1	114 165	58.8	9.3	48.3	18.5	33.3
Troy city	7 768	7 239	39.9	3 999	0.0	5.6	7.0	39 454	63.0	11.7	51.4	17.8	30.8
Utica city	10 804	3 842	19.4	3 210	0.2	7.4	4.7	47 540	56.0	8.4	43.9	15.8	40.3
Valley Stream village	6 662	2 576	16.2	2 058	0.0	3.8	6.2	28 831	62.9	3.1	52.0	15.4	32.6
Watertown city	4 939	1 433	11.8	1 488	1.7	13.0	5.8	20 610	58.9	8.0	48.7	15.2	36.0
White Plains city	8 582	3 145	24.6	2 036	0.0	7.7	4.7	40 081	66.1	5.6	56.2	13.7	30.2
Yonkers city	35 665	12 701	30.7	9 626	0.0	8.1	8.6	153 381	58.8	6.7	50.8	12.8	36.4
NORTH CAROLINA	1 445 635	462 275	11.3	428 384	1.8	11.8	6.4	6 290 618	65.7	5.2	58.1	13.0	28.9
Asheville city	10 073	4 655	9.7	3 208	0.2	13.6	6.7	56 962	61.3	6.1	50.9	15.8	33.2
Burlington city	7 966	1 927	11.1	2 244	0.0	10.4	10.7	35 673	64.0	5.5	56.7	12.0	31.4
Cary town	19 886	5 317	11.3	4 194	0.0	4.6	3.5	69 653	76.3	2.6	66.5	14.6	18.8
Chapel Hill town	5 693	19 433	5.0	7 303	0.0	1.3	0.4	42 504	60.3	4.5	45.7	32.9	21.4
Charlotte city	97 127	34 192	16.3	27 346	0.1	8.7	6.5	421 175	71.8	5.5	64.0	13.2	22.0
Concord city	10 319	2 529	11.0	2 498	0.0	8.1	9.1	42 550	70.1	5.4	62.5	12.2	25.3
Durham city	29 809	21 368	28.3	10 691	0.2	6.0	7.1	148 244	67.8	5.6	61.4	14.1	24.5
Fayetteville city	22 548	9 890	14.6	7 368	2.4	12.2	5.2	93 533	66.3	9.8	57.1	13.7	29.2
Gastonia city	12 247	2 631	11.4	3 215	0.0	11.7	10.1	51 367	62.6	6.2	57.8	11.3	30.9
Goldsboro city	7 445	1 955	11.9	2 025	5.3	17.2	7.5	30 109	55.7	8.2	50.8	12.6	36.6
Greensboro city	37 053	23 468	12.6	14 282	0.0	7.5	2.8	178 542	68.7	6.5	58.6	16.7	24.7
Greenville city	8 227	16 392	4.9	6 257	0.2	4.2	1.5	50 387	66.3	8.6	50.3	24.7	24.9
Hickory city	6 368	2 120	16.3	2 037	0.0	9.5	6.6	29 490	67.7	3.6	58.6	13.9	27.5
High Point city	16 286	4 916	17.2	4 553	0.0	8.7	5.8	65 895	68.3	6.1	60.3	13.6	26.1
Jacksonville city	9 896	4 436	7.8	6 580	57.8	68.9	2.0	51 680	80.4	4.0	68.6	13.7	17.8
Kannapolis city	6 489	1 186	8.2	1 851	0.4	11.9	5.3	28 742	64.4	4.8	58.2	10.7	31.1
Monroe city	4 553	876	11.7	1 334	0.0	16.8	10.9	19 852	66.8	6.9	60.1	10.7	29.1
Raleigh city	40 798	35 294	15.0	16 537	0.0	8.1	4.3	224 128	72.7	5.3	63.1	16.3	20.6
Rocky Mount city	11 878	2 634	10.3	3 339	0.0	10.5	9.3	42 394	60.6	9.3	54.2	12.4	33.5
Salisbury city	4 420	2 142	24.4	1 386	0.0	7.4	3.5	21 356	59.1	15.5	50.6	11.3	38.2
Wilmington city	9 883	10 505	8.3	4 885	0.0	7.4	4.9	63 213	63.7	8.5	49.8	19.1	31.1
Wilson city	8 473	2 303	15.0	2 571	0.0	7.5	12.7	33 956	62.2	8.6	54.4	12.7	32.9
Winston-Salem city	31 396	14 066	21.6	10 063	0.0	9.8	7.9	146 408	63.0	5.7	56.1	13.3	30.6
NORTH DAKOTA	123 939	47 003	7.9	43 073	1.0	8.6	2.6	502 306	67.5	4.5	55.7	18.7	25.5
Bismarck city	9 801	3 638	18.0	3 435	0.0	8.5	1.5	44 032	70.6	3.2	58.7	18.1	23.2
Fargo city	13 436	13 086	6.9	5 887	0.1	7.5	2.4	73 615	75.1	4.3	59.6	22.1	18.2
Grand Forks city	7 901	9 858	3.5	4 459	0.0	6.7	1.5	40 066	71.0	4.2	55.2	26.6	18.2
Minot city	6 134	2 999	6.7	2 235	0.9	13.2	3.9	29 125	66.8	4.3	55.1	17.9	27.0
OHIO	2 157 981	652 393	16.0	639 825	0.1	10.5	4.6	8 788 494	64.8	5.0	54.5	15.9	29.6
Akron city	40 268	15 075	11.9	11 980	0.1	12.7	5.6	167 304	64.1	7.4	52.5	15.9	31.5
Barberton city	4 847	882	10.0	1 313	0.0	13.9	4.1	21 753	61.5	6.6	51.2	13.9	34.9
Beavercreek city	7 652	2 379	21.8	2 069	0.0	6.3	0.2	29 807	68.2	2.6	56.4	17.2	26.4
Bowling Green city	2 953	13 658	3.2	5 289	0.2	2.6	1.3	26 278	69.1	14.0	47.4	37.3	15.3

City	Full-year full-time employed (percent)								Children under 18 years in families (percent, except where noted)						Total employed by class of worker (percent)			
										With two parents		With one parent who is in labor force	+/- U.S. percent of children with no stay-at-home parent	+/- U.S. percent two-income couples				
	Total	Men	Women	Non-Hispanic White	Black or African American	American Indian and Alaska Native	Asian, Hawaiian, and Pacific Islander	Hispanic or Latino[1]	Number	Both in labor force	Father only in labor force				Private	Government	Self-employed	Unpaid family worker
	24	25	26	27	28	29	30	31	32	33	34	35	36	37	38	39	40	41
NEW YORK	38.2	47.1	30.1	40.3	34.5	33.0	36.9	32.6	4 383 249	38.9	22.1	21.7	-4.0	-2.8	73.4	17.0	9.4	0.2
Albany city	35.4	40.9	30.7	36.4	35.3	13.6	25.7	31.6	17 298	29.0	9.9	39.6	4.0	0.7	65.9	28.5	5.5	0.1
Auburn city	33.5	41.1	26.1	35.8	17.3	5.6	22.9	17.6	6 125	44.2	11.4	31.6	11.2	3.8	73.1	20.2	6.3	0.3
Binghamton city	31.2	38.2	25.1	32.7	28.1	24.3	18.1	17.5	9 600	38.3	14.6	30.2	3.9	-4.4	71.7	21.9	6.3	0.1
Buffalo city	31.8	37.6	26.9	35.0	28.2	30.0	26.0	24.5	71 285	25.8	10.6	38.9	0.1	-7.6	75.4	19.4	5.0	0.2
Elmira city	31.3	36.0	26.6	33.9	20.2	19.2	30.9	12.0	7 213	30.6	11.8	39.5	5.5	-2.0	75.3	17.8	6.5	0.4
Freeport village	42.4	50.2	35.7	40.3	48.1	80.7	37.6	39.0	10 441	39.3	15.9	25.9	0.6	1.4	74.1	17.3	8.4	0.2
Glen Cove city	38.8	49.4	29.3	38.8	32.2	47.0	34.3	42.6	5 305	36.6	30.0	19.5	-8.5	-5.6	73.9	11.9	13.8	0.5
Hempstead village	36.9	41.7	32.8	20.4	41.4	41.3	37.6	38.5	12 815	29.4	11.8	32.2	-3.0	-1.9	78.9	16.4	4.6	0.1
Ithaca city	17.3	19.4	15.2	19.0	21.7	19.3	9.0	11.1	2 427	34.6	11.2	37.3	7.3	6.0	81.1	11.5	7.2	0.2
Jamestown city	35.2	44.9	26.8	35.6	30.0	36.6	11.1	24.5	7 418	39.5	14.4	29.8	4.7	-1.9	82.2	11.4	6.1	0.3
Lindenhurst village	44.9	59.0	31.7	44.8	36.2	12.5	52.9	45.9	7 223	50.7	27.5	13.1	-0.8	-1.9	77.1	17.0	5.8	0.1
Long Beach city	44.4	53.6	36.1	46.0	38.4	12.8	51.8	35.9	6 035	39.9	23.1	22.7	-2.0	-0.2	70.8	19.4	9.7	0.2
Middletown city	39.4	47.3	32.1	39.7	40.8	44.2	49.5	36.5	6 625	31.8	15.6	28.0	-4.8	0.0	73.8	20.2	5.7	0.2
Mount Vernon city	40.3	45.5	36.3	38.2	40.6	36.4	46.9	42.3	15 739	33.4	13.3	36.2	5.0	-1.4	75.9	17.0	7.0	0.2
Newburgh city	38.0	46.6	30.8	34.7	34.3	15.6	45.8	44.3	8 085	25.8	13.0	37.9	-0.9	-7.4	81.1	14.0	4.6	0.4
New Rochelle city	40.0	50.5	31.1	41.6	37.9	35.1	46.0	36.9	16 402	41.3	26.6	18.0	-5.3	-3.1	75.5	13.1	11.1	0.2
New York city	35.1	42.2	29.1	38.6	33.8	29.7	36.0	30.6	1 767 267	47.0	20.6	25.5	-12.1	-10.3	74.8	16.1	8.9	0.2
Niagara Falls city	32.9	40.0	26.9	33.8	28.6	33.5	23.1	33.5	13 176	33.3	11.3	34.3	3.0	-8.6	81.2	13.4	5.2	0.2
North Tonawanda city	41.6	52.9	31.5	41.8	0.0	56.8	30.7	23.7	7 728	56.2	17.4	16.8	8.4	3.4	80.3	14.1	5.6	0.0
Port Chester village	37.1	43.7	30.5	40.8	36.5	30.9	41.4	33.4	5 880	38.8	24.7	15.6	-10.2	-2.9	81.1	8.0	10.7	0.1
Poughkeepsie city	34.3	38.2	30.7	33.4	35.9	29.2	33.2	34.1	6 832	29.6	8.8	41.9	6.9	-2.6	77.3	15.4	7.1	0.2
Rochester city	37.5	42.6	33.1	41.5	34.0	29.1	33.7	30.4	56 070	22.8	8.4	43.4	1.6	0.1	82.6	11.7	5.6	0.1
Rome city	34.9	41.1	28.3	36.7	21.5	31.0	33.7	20.8	7 275	38.2	18.0	30.0	3.6	-4.6	71.0	23.2	5.6	0.2
Saratoga Springs city	41.0	53.6	29.9	41.5	31.0	36.8	31.9	40.9	4 885	54.4	17.4	23.8	13.6	11.6	68.5	19.9	11.1	0.5
Schenectady city	36.1	41.8	31.1	36.8	33.6	22.1	37.2	28.8	14 030	36.6	10.6	35.2	7.2	-0.4	76.2	17.6	6.0	0.2
Spring Valley village	40.6	46.2	35.2	33.1	45.7	57.6	38.3	39.8	7 470	34.5	23.5	23.0	-7.1	-0.7	77.0	15.7	7.1	0.2
Syracuse city	31.3	36.7	26.8	32.1	31.0	33.5	28.4	23.9	34 063	27.0	10.8	41.2	3.6	-2.5	77.4	16.7	5.8	0.1
Troy city	36.1	40.7	31.8	38.1	33.5	54.4	10.6	25.7	10 366	30.7	14.0	37.4	3.5	-1.2	75.1	20.4	4.3	0.2
Utica city	32.1	40.0	25.3	33.3	24.7	30.4	31.4	29.5	13 680	31.6	13.9	31.3	-1.7	-5.8	76.3	17.0	6.5	0.2
Valley Stream village	41.3	51.9	32.0	39.8	53.2	57.9	40.4	45.3	8 401	50.2	26.9	13.0	-1.4	3.9	72.8	18.3	8.6	0.4
Watertown city	36.7	47.8	27.3	36.5	41.8	44.5	43.1	35.6	6 556	41.9	21.1	25.3	2.6	-2.6	72.0	20.6	7.1	0.3
White Plains city	41.3	51.4	32.8	42.2	39.2	38.4	44.3	40.0	10 160	44.0	24.2	15.0	-5.6	0.5	74.7	13.1	11.9	0.3
Yonkers city	37.6	46.1	30.4	37.9	37.5	30.5	40.7	36.3	44 592	30.3	22.0	24.5	-9.8	-8.2	75.3	16.4	8.2	0.2
NORTH CAROLINA	43.8	53.6	34.7	45.4	39.0	38.3	42.7	40.8	1 837 327	44.2	20.5	23.1	2.7	2.2	75.6	14.5	9.6	0.3
Asheville city	35.3	43.4	28.5	35.8	32.6	25.2	37.4	41.2	12 341	39.8	17.2	30.4	5.6	-2.1	73.8	14.4	11.7	0.2
Burlington city	42.5	50.7	35.5	42.2	45.4	30.1	35.1	38.3	10 319	44.2	15.6	30.5	8.8	1.8	81.2	12.1	6.6	0.1
Cary town	54.4	69.6	39.7	54.9	57.0	53.8	53.4	47.9	27 103	49.5	34.8	11.1	-4.0	8.1	78.5	12.8	8.5	0.2
Chapel Hill town	26.7	33.8	21.1	26.3	27.1	34.7	27.8	28.3	6 903	45.9	21.5	20.8	2.1	3.4	56.2	36.7	6.9	0.2
Charlotte city	48.8	58.2	39.9	51.2	46.8	41.9	47.1	39.0	125 040	38.8	23.2	26.6	0.8	4.2	82.0	9.5	8.2	0.2
Concord city	49.6	61.4	38.8	50.7	48.0	50.6	60.9	39.6	13 900	46.3	22.3	23.5	5.2	8.7	81.8	11.2	6.9	0.1
Durham city	43.7	49.2	38.7	46.2	43.3	51.9	36.7	33.9	39 287	40.5	14.7	30.6	6.5	7.1	76.5	16.7	6.6	0.3
Fayetteville city	41.9	53.8	31.3	45.8	36.6	43.0	36.5	46.4	28 206	36.0	18.7	31.4	2.8	0.1	64.9	25.7	9.3	0.1
Gastonia city	43.6	54.2	34.4	45.2	40.1	52.8	61.0	33.3	15 106	39.8	16.0	28.4	3.6	2.8	80.2	12.1	7.6	0.1
Goldsboro city	36.8	46.1	28.0	41.1	32.2	28.5	43.8	48.3	8 735	28.7	19.6	33.8	-2.1	-5.3	64.9	27.6	7.2	0.3
Greensboro city	42.7	51.4	35.1	43.7	41.4	53.2	40.6	40.6	46 628	38.5	18.3	31.1	5.0	3.6	78.3	13.5	8.1	0.1
Greenville city	33.5	41.7	26.6	34.7	31.0	43.0	34.8	37.7	10 396	34.8	17.7	32.9	3.1	2.0	71.5	22.0	6.2	0.3
Hickory city	45.4	58.2	34.0	45.6	41.0	23.4	50.7	46.6	8 394	44.2	21.0	24.0	5.6	4.3	80.5	10.1	8.9	0.5
High Point city	44.4	54.0	36.0	45.3	43.8	45.3	40.6	40.1	20 884	42.7	16.7	28.2	6.3	7.1	81.6	10.3	8.0	0.1
Jacksonville city	49.9	62.1	28.3	52.6	44.2	54.5	40.6	47.0	15 730	41.0	32.9	17.4	-6.2	-1.8	61.7	29.2	8.8	0.4
Kannapolis city	44.4	53.7	36.3	44.1	43.9	32.0	48.8	52.0	8 209	43.6	18.7	25.9	4.9	2.3	83.1	10.2	6.6	0.2
Monroe city	43.8	52.0	35.5	46.8	43.5	41.8	38.0	36.6	6 253	28.6	20.3	27.9	-8.1	2.1	83.6	10.2	6.1	0.1
Raleigh city	46.7	54.3	39.3	48.2	46.3	37.1	39.8	39.0	54 177	39.5	22.9	27.0	1.9	6.8	75.2	16.6	7.9	0.2
Rocky Mount city	38.3	47.5	31.0	42.8	34.5	68.5	40.3	36.4	14 249	34.4	14.5	29.5	-0.7	-2.3	76.4	16.1	7.2	0.3
Salisbury city	34.9	40.9	29.6	35.6	32.3	64.0	44.0	40.1	5 264	34.5	12.4	36.9	6.8	-2.7	77.2	17.4	5.2	0.3
Wilmington city	34.2	43.1	26.7	35.3	30.4	43.5	26.0	39.7	12 645	31.3	18.1	35.4	2.1	-5.3	73.3	14.9	11.6	0.3
Wilson city	39.0	49.1	30.7	42.8	35.2	34.5	38.9	38.8	10 531	33.5	14.8	34.5	3.4	2.3	77.2	15.4	7.2	0.1
Winston-Salem city	40.7	48.1	34.5	41.3	40.1	50.5	43.3	37.7	39 483	35.9	16.7	31.7	3.0	0.4	81.6	11.2	7.1	0.2
NORTH DAKOTA	40.4	49.6	31.4	40.9	40.9	30.8	30.9	39.1	155 201	60.2	14.9	17.0	12.6	8.8	69.1	16.5	13.9	0.6
Bismarck city	46.0	54.2	38.6	46.9	9.0	28.4	19.8	22.2	12 571	63.9	13.4	17.1	16.4	13.5	71.7	19.3	8.7	0.3
Fargo city	43.6	50.9	36.3	44.2	36.0	30.9	30.5	42.0	18 629	56.3	16.8	20.2	11.9	13.2	79.2	13.4	7.3	0.1
Grand Forks city	38.5	46.1	30.7	38.9	38.7	33.6	17.1	34.8	10 251	56.6	12.5	21.5	13.5	13.9	72.1	21.0	6.7	0.1
Minot city	40.7	50.1	32.1	40.9	47.8	21.0	57.0	53.8	8 150	57.2	11.8	21.3	13.9	7.6	73.2	18.5	8.1	0.3
OHIO	42.0	52.4	32.5	42.9	35.5	36.4	40.8	38.6	2 744 090	45.8	21.2	22.3	3.5	1.8	79.5	12.2	8.0	0.3
Akron city	39.0	47.6	31.5	40.9	34.7	43.9	32.0	33.7	50 938	35.4	14.9	34.1	4.9	-1.1	81.0	12.8	6.0	0.2
Barberton city	38.5	49.6	29.1	39.3	26.3	0.0	51.7	27.2	6 610	35.9	20.0	29.4	0.7	-4.4	85.1	8.6	6.2	0.2
Beavercreek city	47.0	60.9	33.5	46.8	61.5	55.0	47.2	42.9	9 465	58.4	27.0	9.6	3.4	4.2	68.2	22.8	8.9	0.1
Bowling Green city	27.2	32.9	22.2	27.4	14.6	44.8	19.9	32.7	3 696	49.3	14.7	26.2	10.9	10.2	67.9	28.1	3.8	0.3

[1] Hispanic or Latino persons may be of any race.

City	Percent who worked at home	Percent of the population 5 years and over with a disability	Veterans as a percent of the population 18 years and over	Occupation for employed population 16 years and over (percent)						Industry for employed population 16 years and over (percent)					
				Management, professional, and related occupations	Service occupations	Sales and office occupations	Farming, fishing, and forestry occupations	Construction, extraction, and maintenance occupations	Production, transportation and material moving occupations	Agriculture, forestry, fishing, and mining	Construction and manufacturing	Wholesale and retail trade	Transportation and warehousing, and utilities	Service industries	Public administration
	42	43	44	45	46	47	48	49	50	51	52	53	54	55	56
NEW YORK	3.0	20.6	9.5	36.7	16.6	27.1	0.3	7.6	11.7	0.6	15.2	13.8	5.5	59.7	5.2
Albany city	2.4	21.4	9.6	40.9	18.3	28.7	0.0	4.6	7.4	0.1	7.0	12.1	3.3	62.2	15.3
Auburn city	1.8	24.0	14.0	26.1	23.3	24.5	0.4	6.9	18.7	0.5	21.6	17.2	3.7	47.4	9.6
Binghamton city	2.0	24.8	12.8	31.2	21.1	27.0	0.1	5.5	15.1	0.2	17.0	16.5	4.1	57.3	5.0
Buffalo city	1.7	26.2	11.5	29.2	21.1	27.0	0.1	5.5	17.2	0.2	16.3	14.4	5.5	58.4	5.3
Elmira city	2.3	25.8	12.7	27.3	24.3	26.2	0.2	5.8	16.2	0.3	19.5	16.2	3.9	53.4	6.6
Freeport village	2.2	20.9	8.2	27.4	20.6	28.0	0.1	8.2	15.7	0.1	14.6	16.1	7.1	56.6	5.4
Glen Cove city	2.8	16.5	8.6	34.4	20.9	26.8	0.0	9.1	8.9	0.1	16.0	12.6	4.3	63.4	3.5
Hempstead village	1.5	21.2	6.2	21.9	28.3	27.9	0.3	6.7	14.9	0.2	12.4	13.1	6.5	63.4	4.5
Ithaca city	4.9	11.0	3.5	53.8	15.5	24.2	0.5	2.1	3.9	0.9	4.6	6.9	1.0	84.4	2.2
Jamestown city	1.3	24.6	15.4	26.7	20.0	23.4	0.1	6.5	23.3	0.4	26.5	16.9	3.2	49.6	3.3
Lindenhurst village	1.3	16.4	11.0	27.2	16.0	31.3	0.0	11.1	14.3	0.0	20.2	17.5	8.7	47.1	6.5
Long Beach city	2.7	21.8	10.1	42.3	14.5	30.4	0.0	6.0	6.8	0.0	9.8	14.0	6.1	64.1	6.2
Middletown city	1.7	23.7	10.1	26.6	21.2	28.5	1.1	8.2	14.0	1.1	15.0	17.6	4.9	54.1	7.3
Mount Vernon city	2.0	24.1	7.6	34.2	20.3	28.4	0.0	8.2	8.8	0.0	12.1	13.2	6.0	64.6	4.0
Newburgh city	1.5	27.4	8.4	18.0	22.7	23.8	0.3	8.0	27.2	0.6	24.6	17.7	4.3	49.0	3.7
New Rochelle city	2.9	18.0	8.6	42.3	17.0	25.2	0.1	8.4	7.0	0.1	13.0	12.8	4.1	66.6	3.3
New York city	2.9	24.5	5.7	36.8	18.6	27.4	0.0	6.4	10.9	0.1	10.9	12.1	6.5	66.0	4.5
Niagara Falls city	1.7	25.2	14.4	24.3	20.0	29.2	0.1	7.7	18.7	0.2	22.7	16.7	5.6	51.1	3.7
North Tonawanda city	1.5	17.9	15.3	29.8	14.2	28.6	0.2	7.3	19.8	0.2	26.3	17.9	4.9	47.2	3.5
Port Chester village	1.8	24.6	6.1	25.6	27.4	23.9	0.1	11.6	11.4	0.2	18.6	13.4	3.4	62.6	1.8
Poughkeepsie city	3.1	25.1	10.1	30.3	26.9	23.7	0.4	7.2	11.6	0.2	15.2	12.9	3.9	62.8	5.1
Rochester city	2.3	24.9	9.1	31.0	21.1	23.8	0.1	6.3	17.7	0.2	22.0	13.3	3.7	58.0	2.8
Rome city	1.5	23.9	15.5	30.6	21.5	26.2	0.3	6.3	15.2	0.6	16.7	15.5	3.4	55.1	8.7
Saratoga Springs city	4.1	15.7	11.6	43.2	17.5	26.7	0.3	5.0	7.3	0.4	11.8	13.8	2.7	63.8	7.5
Schenectady city	2.6	25.1	12.5	29.7	21.8	28.9	0.1	6.9	12.5	0.4	12.0	16.1	4.2	58.4	9.0
Spring Valley village	1.0	22.2	4.5	25.2	30.3	22.6	0.3	8.0	13.7	0.3	15.9	15.7	3.9	60.5	3.8
Syracuse city	2.0	23.0	10.1	32.6	21.6	25.8	0.2	5.3	14.5	0.2	14.4	13.4	3.9	64.4	3.6
Troy city	2.0	22.6	11.2	32.4	19.1	27.2	0.0	7.5	13.8	0.1	12.1	14.1	5.1	58.9	9.8
Utica city	2.0	25.8	12.0	27.1	21.1	27.9	0.3	5.9	17.7	0.3	17.1	14.5	3.5	58.9	5.8
Valley Stream village	2.0	16.8	11.7	33.5	13.9	35.6	0.0	8.8	8.1	0.1	12.3	15.2	9.0	57.2	6.2
Watertown city	1.7	23.6	16.2	29.7	21.2	28.4	0.3	7.5	12.9	0.4	12.4	18.6	3.5	56.1	0.0
White Plains city	3.5	20.0	8.0	45.9	17.2	25.2	0.1	5.3	6.4	0.3	11.4	13.0	3.7	67.9	3.8
Yonkers city	2.1	23.2	8.8	34.1	17.1	29.9	0.1	8.7	10.1	0.2	13.7	14.1	6.1	61.1	4.9
NORTH CAROLINA	2.7	21.1	13.0	31.2	13.5	24.8	0.8	11.0	18.7	1.6	27.9	14.9	4.6	46.9	4.1
Asheville city	3.4	21.6	14.3	34.5	17.7	25.8	0.4	8.4	13.2	0.5	19.4	16.3	2.9	57.9	3.0
Burlington city	1.6	22.6	12.5	29.2	12.3	25.8	0.3	8.9	23.5	0.3	34.0	14.9	2.3	45.9	2.7
Cary town	4.9	9.0	10.0	59.9	7.4	24.0	0.1	3.9	4.7	0.1	20.5	12.7	3.7	58.7	4.2
Chapel Hill town	4.5	9.2	5.9	56.9	13.2	23.5	0.2	3.0	3.3	0.3	7.6	8.8	1.1	79.5	2.6
Charlotte city	3.2	17.1	10.8	38.1	12.7	29.2	0.1	8.1	11.8	0.2	18.0	15.4	5.8	58.5	2.0
Concord city	2.0	17.5	12.4	32.6	10.8	27.8	1.0	12.0	15.9	0.8	25.8	18.0	5.4	47.6	2.4
Durham city	2.7	18.1	9.5	46.5	13.9	22.8	0.1	7.7	8.9	0.2	16.8	9.7	3.2	66.1	4.0
Fayetteville city	1.6	23.4	21.1	33.3	16.8	26.9	0.1	8.4	14.5	0.3	16.9	16.3	4.5	55.0	6.9
Gastonia city	1.7	24.6	13.4	28.5	12.4	26.3	0.0	8.7	24.1	0.2	32.6	15.6	5.8	42.5	3.4
Goldsboro city	1.2	26.7	17.0	31.0	19.9	24.7	0.3	6.3	17.7	0.8	18.5	16.9	4.0	51.1	8.8
Greensboro city	2.7	18.8	11.3	35.9	13.9	29.1	0.1	7.1	13.9	0.1	21.7	15.5	5.1	55.0	2.6
Greenville city	1.9	17.0	9.0	38.5	17.4	28.3	0.2	5.2	10.3	0.4	15.7	17.2	2.7	60.4	3.5
Hickory city	1.7	20.3	12.2	31.9	12.5	26.1	0.6	5.8	23.1	0.4	35.3	17.5	3.3	41.4	2.1
High Point city	2.3	22.5	12.2	30.3	12.8	28.3	0.2	6.9	21.5	0.4	29.8	16.7	5.4	45.0	2.7
Jacksonville city	3.0	17.2	12.3	30.6	22.8	29.6	0.3	7.6	9.1	0.6	9.1	16.2	3.5	60.6	10.0
Kannapolis city	1.9	27.2	13.1	21.1	15.8	25.0	0.4	13.0	24.6	0.6	33.7	15.8	4.8	41.9	3.1
Monroe city	1.6	23.4	10.4	25.8	13.6	23.8	0.5	14.2	22.1	0.5	35.6	17.7	2.7	40.9	2.7
Raleigh city	3.3	14.6	9.8	45.1	13.1	26.8	0.2	7.1	7.7	0.4	16.9	14.1	3.7	59.2	5.8
Rocky Mount city	2.0	23.2	12.1	30.3	15.2	25.6	0.5	7.8	20.6	0.6	26.6	15.5	4.2	48.6	4.6
Salisbury city	2.1	27.2	14.4	31.4	15.5	21.4	0.0	7.1	24.7	0.1	30.1	13.7	2.9	49.3	3.8
Wilmington city	2.7	22.2	13.4	32.9	19.7	26.3	0.2	9.4	11.5	0.3	16.5	16.5	3.8	59.0	3.9
Wilson city	1.3	26.4	11.1	28.4	15.9	22.4	1.4	9.5	22.4	1.8	31.2	14.3	3.4	45.5	3.8
Winston-Salem city	2.4	19.6	11.7	35.4	15.9	24.7	0.2	7.4	16.4	0.2	21.1	13.1	4.2	58.8	2.6
NORTH DAKOTA	6.0	16.7	12.7	33.3	16.7	26.1	1.7	9.8	12.4	8.2	13.3	16.4	5.7	51.6	4.8
Bismarck city	3.3	17.1	13.2	36.2	16.5	29.6	0.3	7.8	9.6	1.4	10.3	16.7	6.4	55.5	9.6
Fargo city	2.9	15.1	10.4	34.1	15.2	31.2	0.4	7.5	11.5	0.9	14.2	20.3	4.2	57.7	2.7
Grand Forks city	2.8	14.7	11.8	32.0	20.6	26.0	0.4	10.2	10.9	0.8	13.3	17.2	4.7	59.9	4.2
Minot city	2.7	18.6	14.4	33.0	17.8	31.2	0.4	7.9	9.7	1.7	7.6	19.0	5.6	61.3	4.8
OHIO	2.8	18.3	13.5	31.0	14.6	26.4	0.3	8.7	19.0	1.1	26.0	15.5	4.9	48.4	4.1
Akron city	2.0	22.0	13.0	26.0	18.3	28.3	0.1	7.7	19.6	0.1	23.9	15.5	5.6	50.7	4.2
Barberton city	1.3	23.5	16.1	20.1	17.5	27.4	0.2	10.7	24.1	0.2	33.3	15.3	3.8	44.8	2.6
Beavercreek city	3.2	10.4	19.6	51.2	8.9	25.4	0.2	5.4	9.0	0.4	18.3	14.3	3.0	52.4	11.7
Bowling Green city	1.7	11.6	6.3	36.0	21.2	24.6	0.2	3.7	14.2	0.4	15.7	12.4	3.5	64.6	3.4

Table B-5. Cities — **Education, Labor Force, and Income**

City	Median house-hold income	Median family income — All families	Married-couple	Male house-holder	Female house-holder	Median nonfamily house-hold income	Median income for full-year, full-time workers — Men	Women	Per capita income	With earnings	With interest, dividend, or rental income	With Social Security income	With public assis-tance income	With retire-ment income	House-holds with income over $100,000 (percent)	+/− U.S. percent for income over $100,000 (percent)	House-holds with income below poverty (percent)	Families with children with income below poverty (percent)
	57	58	59	60	61	62	63	64	65	66	67	68	69	70	71	72	73	74
NEW YORK	43 393	51 691	63 281	30 373	18 992	27 073	41 188	31 800	23 389	78.1	36.5	26.0	4.9	16.9	15.3	3.0	13.9	16.9
Albany city	30 041	39 932	55 683	23 909	15 934	22 981	32 250	27 944	18 281	75.8	34.0	24.4	6.5	16.3	6.8	−5.5	20.4	26.0
Auburn city	30 281	41 169	55 196	28 250	14 713	17 572	34 876	24 467	17 083	70.1	33.5	34.1	3.9	20.8	4.6	−7.7	15.9	20.7
Binghamton city	25 665	36 137	47 123	19 196	15 193	16 318	29 787	24 157	17 067	69.6	34.8	32.5	6.4	20.4	4.9	−7.4	22.5	25.7
Buffalo city	24 536	30 614	46 935	23 636	12 825	17 107	31 667	24 873	14 991	70.6	25.4	27.7	10.3	17.2	4.1	−8.2	25.4	33.9
Elmira city	27 292	33 592	45 386	21 206	14 549	17 436	32 443	23 514	14 495	71.6	28.6	30.8	6.8	20.6	3.8	−8.5	22.1	27.7
Freeport village	55 948	61 673	67 157	33 917	31 016	35 133	39 209	32 305	21 288	85.1	29.5	24.1	3.0	17.2	19.5	7.2	9.3	11.3
Glen Cove city	55 503	63 021	67 160	29 722	26 716	35 181	45 021	31 192	26 627	78.5	40.6	32.3	1.8	18.0	21.9	9.6	8.8	10.2
Hempstead village	45 234	46 675	52 975	25 000	24 094	24 810	30 248	28 171	15 735	82.3	18.4	21.0	5.5	14.2	13.8	1.5	18.2	17.5
Ithaca city	21 441	42 304	62 500	33 750	24 727	15 918	30 982	29 548	13 408	83.6	44.0	13.7	2.6	7.9	5.8	−6.5	36.7	19.6
Jamestown city	25 837	33 675	44 591	16 711	12 040	16 191	30 903	20 665	15 316	73.5	33.4	30.9	6.9	18.7	3.7	−8.6	17.8	26.1
Lindenhurst village	61 667	67 315	70 156	50 893	31 667	29 311	46 357	32 454	22 150	83.8	37.7	27.6	1.3	21.2	20.2	7.9	7.7	5.4
Long Beach city	56 289	68 222	77 518	39 306	28 256	46 120	51 780	42 050	31 069	81.1	38.7	26.3	2.5	14.5	22.4	10.1	7.9	10.4
Middletown city	39 570	47 760	55 170	25 966	16 050	25 151	36 446	29 286	18 947	77.0	32.1	27.0	7.1	20.7	9.8	−2.5	15.5	21.4
Mount Vernon city	41 128	49 573	63 952	34 044	22 438	28 494	37 198	34 658	20 827	80.0	24.5	25.1	6.1	15.5	13.8	1.5	14.2	15.7
Newburgh city	30 332	32 519	41 092	32 368	15 326	19 793	27 134	22 224	13 360	76.5	18.9	25.3	11.8	16.9	5.0	−7.3	23.5	30.8
New Rochelle city	55 513	72 723	88 774	34 464	25 645	29 780	51 277	40 188	31 956	81.1	40.1	29.1	2.4	16.0	26.4	14.1	11.4	11.6
New York city	38 293	41 887	52 035	28 953	16 760	30 214	38 806	34 213	22 402	76.3	28.8	22.3	7.5	12.4	13.7	1.4	19.7	25.8
Niagara Falls city	26 800	34 377	51 292	24 359	13 975	16 827	32 439	22 876	15 721	68.0	32.3	36.6	7.0	22.3	4.0	−8.3	19.1	25.2
North Tonawanda city	39 154	50 219	59 721	23 661	18 559	20 434	37 051	25 597	19 264	75.9	42.4	31.2	3.1	22.7	6.6	−5.7	8.0	9.1
Port Chester village	45 381	51 025	53 182	31 339	20 819	27 247	34 371	35 115	21 131	81.3	34.6	25.7	2.6	13.4	15.8	3.5	12.4	14.1
Poughkeepsie city	29 389	35 779	57 656	16 618	16 602	19 899	33 998	26 442	16 759	73.2	30.2	27.6	7.3	18.6	7.8	−4.5	21.1	26.5
Rochester city	27 123	31 257	48 924	22 482	14 824	20 736	31 040	25 841	15 588	75.5	22.3	22.0	13.6	13.9	4.7	−7.6	23.5	32.4
Rome city	33 643	42 928	51 757	31 842	13 313	21 377	34 041	25 029	18 604	70.2	39.6	32.8	5.0	27.3	5.8	−6.5	14.2	21.1
Saratoga Springs city	45 130	59 281	66 717	23 398	22 909	26 656	41 246	30 833	26 250	80.6	47.3	26.2	1.5	17.2	13.0	0.7	9.6	10.4
Schenectady city	29 378	36 458	49 605	24 597	14 818	21 873	31 556	26 069	17 076	73.1	32.2	28.3	5.1	19.5	4.2	−8.1	18.2	25.9
Spring Valley village	41 311	42 097	46 455	27 219	25 429	30 117	31 999	26 664	14 861	86.4	19.2	15.4	3.7	11.2	9.2	−3.1	15.8	18.6
Syracuse city	25 000	33 026	48 580	22 221	14 232	17 282	30 925	24 851	15 168	73.3	27.0	26.4	7.4	16.2	5.0	−7.3	25.9	31.1
Troy city	29 844	38 631	54 946	26 384	16 968	19 815	31 275	26 445	16 796	75.6	32.1	26.8	5.0	18.7	4.8	−7.5	19.0	22.2
Utica city	24 916	33 818	41 376	16 985	12 261	15 971	27 882	22 230	15 248	67.3	32.1	35.6	8.6	20.5	3.9	−8.4	23.4	33.5
Valley Stream village	63 243	72 585	79 264	45 250	35 142	26 901	50 948	36 797	25 636	79.5	45.5	34.1	1.4	22.8	23.0	10.7	4.2	3.5
Watertown city	28 429	36 115	42 995	19 490	14 112	16 755	31 637	21 815	16 354	72.7	33.1	29.5	6.9	18.8	4.4	−7.9	19.3	22.6
White Plains city	58 545	71 891	81 929	36 983	23 364	37 329	50 218	38 096	33 825	81.5	44.4	26.5	3.0	16.0	26.5	14.2	8.9	10.6
Yonkers city	44 663	53 233	65 346	30 927	18 625	27 006	42 751	35 697	22 793	75.8	34.3	29.3	5.7	18.2	15.6	3.3	14.4	20.4
NORTH CAROLINA	39 184	46 335	55 255	27 115	19 250	23 240	33 398	25 631	20 307	81.5	30.5	25.3	2.8	16.4	9.4	−2.9	12.4	13.3
Asheville city	32 772	44 029	56 155	25 022	15 317	21 643	31 245	24 529	20 024	73.7	36.2	32.3	3.6	20.1	6.9	−5.4	15.2	17.2
Burlington city	35 301	45 441	57 369	23 373	19 395	21 506	32 335	23 839	19 640	78.4	29.6	29.8	1.6	18.0	7.8	−4.5	13.1	14.2
Cary town	75 122	88 074	98 008	56 033	36 836	45 216	64 317	40 090	32 974	93.8	52.7	10.4	0.5	11.1	32.8	20.5	3.0	2.4
Chapel Hill town	39 140	73 483	93 488	40 357	23 381	21 903	51 816	35 782	24 133	85.6	51.3	16.8	1.2	12.6	20.2	7.9	22.4	8.4
Charlotte city	46 975	56 517	70 897	30 535	24 515	33 185	40 062	30 103	26 823	88.0	33.9	17.6	2.6	11.7	15.9	3.6	9.3	11.0
Concord city	46 094	53 571	66 035	26 774	24 813	25 130	37 647	26 917	21 523	85.9	31.3	21.8	1.3	13.9	12.9	0.6	7.7	8.6
Durham city	41 160	51 162	64 016	26 862	20 757	29 505	35 942	30 973	22 526	84.6	32.1	18.5	2.9	13.6	11.7	−0.6	14.1	16.8
Fayetteville city	36 287	41 210	48 977	26 997	16 544	25 682	32 292	24 553	19 141	81.6	26.9	22.4	4.1	21.2	7.6	−4.7	14.0	17.5
Gastonia city	36 924	44 873	56 644	29 107	17 611	21 467	35 089	25 071	19 592	79.9	25.5	27.6	3.4	15.1	9.8	−2.5	14.7	18.5
Goldsboro city	29 456	34 844	44 813	22 222	15 430	17 835	27 000	22 573	16 614	74.2	24.8	29.4	4.1	20.2	5.1	−7.2	18.6	22.6
Greensboro city	39 661	50 192	63 974	30 518	21 532	27 390	35 643	27 430	22 986	84.4	31.7	21.7	2.5	14.3	11.2	−1.1	11.4	13.4
Greenville city	28 648	44 491	63 461	21 000	16 930	19 885	32 615	26 722	18 476	82.7	26.4	18.2	3.1	12.4	8.1	−4.2	26.0	21.6
Hickory city	37 236	47 522	59 754	24 348	20 540	25 437	32 176	24 484	23 263	81.1	31.8	25.3	2.5	13.4	11.5	−0.8	10.5	13.3
High Point city	40 137	48 057	60 979	27 172	17 587	25 101	34 788	25 979	21 303	83.3	30.9	24.7	3.3	13.2	10.6	−1.7	13.1	16.1
Jacksonville city	32 544	33 763	35 507	25 531	15 190	22 644	17 406	20 456	14 237	88.4	23.8	14.2	3.7	15.2	4.4	−7.9	13.3	16.5
Kannapolis city	35 532	42 445	53 796	26 620	19 358	19 575	31 380	24 002	17 539	79.0	23.8	30.0	3.1	18.1	5.5	−6.8	10.6	12.3
Monroe city	40 457	44 953	48 220	38 929	21 329	24 007	30 851	23 851	17 970	82.9	25.1	23.7	2.9	14.7	8.3	−4.0	13.5	18.8
Raleigh city	46 612	60 003	71 546	35 128	23 550	34 082	40 493	31 296	25 113	88.6	37.9	16.1	1.9	12.2	14.6	2.3	9.9	11.4
Rocky Mount city	32 661	39 929	58 510	19 507	15 905	19 628	32 155	25 298	17 804	77.6	25.3	28.3	6.4	17.1	8.0	−4.3	18.9	23.9
Salisbury city	32 923	41 108	54 325	25 242	16 517	20 794	31 671	25 843	18 864	74.6	28.9	31.7	3.8	17.9	7.2	−5.1	15.7	19.5
Wilmington city	31 099	41 891	55 985	26 833	13 834	22 137	31 440	24 484	21 503	76.4	32.1	27.5	3.5	17.1	8.5	−3.8	19.4	23.0
Wilson city	31 169	41 041	56 587	22 600	14 825	16 505	31 410	23 131	17 813	76.7	24.8	27.7	5.5	18.5	7.9	−4.4	21.3	25.0
Winston-Salem city	37 006	46 595	60 522	29 492	18 244	24 759	33 739	26 976	22 468	78.4	33.5	26.9	3.2	17.3	10.7	−1.6	14.0	17.9
NORTH DAKOTA	34 604	43 654	51 447	26 194	16 538	20 296	31 410	21 552	17 769	80.7	42.4	27.5	2.9	10.8	5.7	−6.6	12.5	12.0
Bismarck city	39 422	51 477	60 540	26 579	17 240	22 455	35 214	23 499	20 789	82.2	44.8	25.1	2.7	14.1	7.3	−5.0	9.7	10.0
Fargo city	35 501	50 486	60 008	29 750	18 413	23 100	32 810	23 107	21 101	86.4	39.6	18.7	2.5	10.2	8.1	−4.2	12.2	9.9
Grand Forks city	34 194	47 491	58 597	28 088	15 974	22 181	31 589	22 269	18 395	85.1	39.4	19.9	2.7	11.3	5.9	−6.4	14.9	14.3
Minot city	32 218	42 804	53 444	27 067	13 750	20 105	31 402	21 026	18 011	78.5	39.3	27.9	2.9	14.4	5.4	−6.9	13.2	14.6
OHIO	40 956	50 037	60 491	30 270	19 627	24 005	38 977	27 152	21 003	79.6	36.6	26.4	3.2	18.9	9.8	−2.5	10.7	12.2
Akron city	31 835	39 381	51 642	28 538	15 447	21 928	32 400	25 120	17 596	76.6	25.4	26.3	6.4	17.8	5.1	−7.2	16.3	21.8
Barberton city	32 178	39 387	50 028	25 331	14 045	20 086	33 600	22 389	17 764	74.3	26.5	32.6	5.4	21.7	4.4	−7.7	13.0	19.8
Beavercreek city	68 801	75 965	80 907	70 417	35 870	38 742	59 547	34 886	30 298	85.3	58.5	20.5	0.7	27.8	24.6	12.3	2.6	2.0
Bowling Green city	30 599	51 804	64 423	32 321	20 634	20 381	35 363	26 075	15 032	87.9	38.3	14.7	1.3	10.7	6.4	−5.9	24.2	12.8

STATE Place code	City	High school graduates			College graduates		College graduates (percent)				
		Total population 25 years and over	Percent with a high school diploma or less	Percent with a high school diploma or more	Percent with a bachelor's degree or more	+/− U.S. percent with bachelor's degree or more	Non-Hispanic White	Black or African American	American Indian and Alaska Native	Asian, Hawaiian, and Pacific Islander	Hispanic or Latino[1]
		1	2	3	4	5	6	7	8	9	10
	OHIO—Cont'd										
39 09680	Brunswick city	21 397	51.6	87.4	19.4	−5.0	19.1	10.3	0.0	58.7	22.5
39 12000	Canton city	51 613	65.6	75.1	11.8	−12.6	13.2	6.0	18.2	20.3	8.9
39 15000	Cincinnati city	207 254	49.1	76.7	26.6	2.2	36.4	10.0	10.5	67.9	39.0
39 16000	Cleveland city..............	296 898	64.2	69.0	11.4	−13.0	15.9	6.5	12.8	41.3	7.8
39 16014	Cleveland Heights city ..	33 522	24.0	91.6	50.0	25.6	67.4	21.9	8.2	82.0	42.9
39 18000	Columbus city	440 987	43.5	83.8	29.0	4.6	32.6	14.3	14.8	59.1	19.3
39 19778	Cuyahoga Falls city.......	34 286	42.3	90.8	25.6	1.2	25.2	29.0	0.0	51.1	25.8
39 21000	Dayton city	100 718	56.8	75.1	14.4	−10.0	16.3	10.9	18.3	52.7	16.9
39 21434	Delaware city................	15 327	45.9	87.7	26.8	2.4	26.7	18.0	21.9	67.2	13.6
39 22694	Dublin city..................	19 718	13.7	97.3	64.7	40.3	64.7	61.0	100.0	66.4	70.6
39 23380	East Cleveland city	16 712	64.1	68.9	8.5	−15.9	28.6	6.8	0.0	25.4	12.6
39 25256	Elyria city	36 097	56.0	81.8	13.1	−11.3	14.3	6.9	6.9	23.8	8.1
39 25704	Euclid city..................	37 394	51.0	82.1	19.6	−4.8	22.0	13.9	0.0	28.2	23.9
39 25914	Fairborn city	19 439	47.8	83.7	21.8	−2.6	20.4	30.2	22.2	48.1	36.3
39 25970	Fairfield city	27 987	42.1	88.9	27.3	2.9	26.4	27.9	42.9	55.2	33.6
39 27048	Findlay city	25 122	49.3	87.6	24.3	−0.1	24.3	18.4	14.3	62.0	10.2
39 29106	Gahanna city	20 933	30.7	93.5	40.4	16.0	40.1	36.5	21.6	66.7	45.8
39 29428	Garfield Heights city......	20 927	61.9	80.2	12.0	−12.4	11.7	9.3	36.9	50.9	9.4
39 32592	Grove City city	17 211	49.1	88.7	22.0	−2.4	22.1	20.1	25.3	44.4	20.9
39 33012	Hamilton city...............	39 011	65.6	73.3	12.2	−12.2	12.5	7.4	0.0	37.6	2.5
39 36610	Huber Heights city........	24 650	44.7	88.2	18.9	−5.5	17.9	23.9	18.3	30.5	26.6
39 39872	Kent city	12 304	36.9	91.7	37.0	12.6	36.7	20.5	18.8	84.2	17.6
39 40040	Kettering city	40 174	35.8	91.0	31.0	6.6	31.1	22.8	5.7	36.9	25.9
39 41664	Lakewood city	39 516	36.3	88.7	35.9	11.5	36.0	25.5	0.0	66.9	31.9
39 41720	Lancaster city	23 364	60.5	83.2	13.3	−11.1	13.3	13.5	0.0	26.9	7.3
39 43554	Lima city	24 551	65.7	75.7	9.5	−14.9	10.9	5.5	9.2	29.0	6.2
39 44856	Lorain city	43 036	63.7	74.3	9.9	−14.5	11.5	6.6	3.8	36.5	4.7
39 47138	Mansfield city..............	33 255	62.2	77.7	13.4	−11.0	15.1	5.6	0.0	38.1	2.1
39 47306	Maple Heights city........	17 705	58.1	82.2	12.9	−11.5	12.7	12.0	10.5	40.4	17.7
39 47754	Marion city	23 068	68.8	75.8	8.8	−15.0	9.8	8.1	10.2	34.7	2.2
39 48244	Massillon city	21 039	64.5	81.0	12.4	−12.0	12.9	6.3	15.2	8.3	20.7
39 48790	Medina city	15 649	39.9	90.7	32.5	8.1	32.9	15.9	0.0	49.5	16.4
39 49056	Mentor city	34 041	40.8	89.2	27.4	3.0	27.2	4.8	0.0	52.8	31.8
39 49840	Middletown city............	34 115	61.3	76.9	13.1	−11.3	13.7	5.8	12.2	49.5	23.8
39 54040	Newark city	30 178	59.8	80.7	14.7	−9.7	14.9	6.9	0.0	25.9	9.4
39 50002	North Olmsted city........	23 540	40.9	90.4	27.1	2.7	26.3	24.8	0.0	62.6	28.0
39 57008	North Royalton city.......	19 469	42.6	90.1	29.4	5.0	28.6	17.1	0.0	60.5	38.3
39 61000	Parma city	60 623	53.7	83.4	17.8	−6.6	16.9	19.8	0.0	61.7	16.8
39 66390	Reynoldsburg city.........	21 100	42.0	90.4	27.1	2.7	26.2	32.2	0.0	41.7	31.7
39 70380	Sandusky city	18 189	63.9	79.6	11.2	−13.2	12.5	7.2	0.0	17.5	1.3
39 71682	Shaker Heights city	20 328	16.4	94.6	61.7	37.3	75.9	35.1	0.0	80.6	56.0
39 74118	Springfield city	40 996	61.6	76.6	12.7	−11.7	13.3	9.0	10.7	69.5	4.1
39 74944	Stow city	21 431	35.7	93.0	36.2	11.8	36.1	30.1	21.1	67.1	16.8
39 75098	Strongsville city	29 733	33.3	93.0	37.0	12.6	36.0	36.7	0.0	70.8	25.1
39 77000	Toledo city	197 020	54.0	79.7	16.8	−7.6	18.7	9.6	14.0	55.3	8.7
39 77504	Trotwood city...............	18 335	54.6	77.9	15.0	−9.4	11.7	17.9	9.4	0.0	30.6
39 79002	Upper Arlington city.......	23 812	12.5	97.9	67.5	43.1	67.7	6.6	0.0	76.2	65.9
39 80892	Warren city	30 612	66.4	77.3	10.9	−13.5	12.2	5.8	0.0	34.5	5.6
39 83342	Westerville city	22 607	26.9	94.6	44.6	20.2	45.0	34.1	0.0	51.4	39.1
39 83622	Westlake city...............	22 925	29.6	92.1	45.3	20.9	43.9	53.7	0.0	76.6	50.9
39 88000	Youngstown city............	52 631	68.4	73.2	9.7	−14.7	12.8	5.7	8.6	30.3	5.2
39 88084	Zanesville city..............	16 399	66.4	73.6	11.4	−13.0	11.3	11.1	18.4	35.4	34.6
40 00000	OKLAHOMA	2 203 173	50.9	80.6	20.3	−4.1	21.7	13.7	13.2	36.7	9.6
40 04450	Bartlesville city	23 262	41.3	86.3	30.7	6.3	33.4	12.8	10.4	22.5	19.8
40 09050	Broken Arrow city.........	45 896	32.5	91.7	30.9	6.5	31.2	36.0	21.5	38.5	25.1
40 23200	Edmond city	42 085	22.6	94.2	47.8	23.4	48.6	32.2	44.1	66.1	26.4
40 23950	Enid city....................	30 884	52.9	81.7	20.0	−4.4	20.8	5.7	10.4	26.6	12.9
40 41850	Lawton city.................	53 060	45.1	85.4	19.3	−5.1	22.7	11.2	13.0	21.2	11.6
40 48350	Midwest City city	34 078	45.7	85.6	17.0	−7.4	17.5	14.2	14.2	20.3	15.0
40 49200	Moore city..................	25 018	45.0	87.1	16.8	−7.6	16.7	25.0	14.5	20.7	12.3
40 50050	Muskogee city	24 820	54.6	75.3	17.5	−6.9	19.2	13.2	12.8	46.8	9.7
40 52500	Norman city	55 108	29.7	90.3	39.8	15.4	39.8	33.9	31.0	64.8	26.3
40 55000	Oklahoma City city	323 219	44.9	81.3	24.0	−0.4	27.5	14.6	13.3	31.7	7.2
40 59850	Ponca City city	16 908	49.0	83.2	21.5	−2.9	22.7	4.0	10.5	42.3	13.3
40 66800	Shawnee city...............	17 292	54.2	77.8	18.5	−5.9	19.9	10.1	9.9	25.7	8.5
40 70300	Stillwater city	18 334	25.0	91.6	48.0	23.6	47.7	29.1	37.4	80.6	41.6
40 75000	Tulsa city...................	253 054	40.9	84.4	28.3	3.9	32.5	14.2	20.7	39.8	9.6

[1] Hispanic or Latino persons may be of any race.

Table B-5. Cities — Education, Labor Force, and Income

City	School enrollment			Population 16 to 19 years				Employment status, 2000			Work status in 1999 of the population 16 years and over		
											Worked in 1999		
	Grades kindergarten through 12	College or graduate school	Percent private	Number	Percent in armed forces	Percent high school graduates	Percent not enrolled, not grads, not in armed forces, not employed	Total population 16 years and over	Percent in labor force	Unemployment rate	Full-time	Part-time	Did not work in 1999
	11	12	13	14	15	16	17	18	19	20	21	22	23
OHIO—Cont'd													
Brunswick city	7 094	1 377	16.0	1 688	0.0	10.2	1.2	25 066	72.1	3.0	60.2	17.0	22.8
Canton city	15 557	3 749	16.4	4 469	0.1	13.4	7.4	61 798	60.5	7.8	50.4	15.4	34.2
Cincinnati city	57 811	29 312	21.4	19 166	0.0	10.0	10.7	257 766	63.1	7.3	53.5	16.6	29.9
Cleveland city	100 543	23 468	19.7	25 926	0.1	10.9	11.7	354 854	57.4	11.2	49.5	12.6	37.9
Cleveland Heights city ..	9 136	5 036	36.5	2 414	0.0	10.2	3.4	39 427	70.1	3.7	58.8	16.8	24.4
Columbus city	119 554	76 580	13.7	39 849	0.1	11.3	5.5	555 471	71.0	4.9	60.9	16.3	22.8
Cuyahoga Falls city.......	7 855	2 636	15.0	2 114	0.0	14.0	2.6	39 396	67.0	3.3	55.5	16.1	28.3
Dayton city	30 165	16 973	31.2	11 207	0.4	11.4	9.7	128 872	59.5	9.2	51.2	15.7	33.1
Delaware city................	4 045	2 559	32.0	1 638	0.0	11.4	2.0	19 516	73.1	10.6	61.9	15.6	22.5
Dublin city...................	7 354	1 387	15.2	1 521	0.0	3.8	1.1	22 211	73.4	2.1	62.9	15.7	21.4
East Cleveland city	6 357	1 244	10.4	1 514	0.0	15.7	6.1	19 974	55.3	15.0	46.3	12.3	41.4
Elyria city....................	10 039	2 526	14.8	2 754	0.0	12.2	8.9	42 597	66.9	5.1	57.1	15.4	27.5
Euclid city	8 825	3 007	24.8	2 403	0.0	7.2	3.7	42 208	62.3	5.1	54.0	12.6	33.4
Fairborn city.................	4 898	4 667	8.3	2 060	0.2	10.7	5.3	26 111	65.9	5.8	53.3	19.9	26.7
Fairfield city	7 774	2 025	17.0	2 118	0.0	12.2	2.2	33 003	72.0	3.0	62.5	14.6	22.9
Findlay city	6 527	3 145	26.3	2 271	0.6	9.6	2.7	30 697	68.0	3.2	57.5	16.8	25.7
Gahanna city	6 904	1 705	20.1	1 832	0.0	5.7	2.5	24 215	74.1	2.8	63.0	15.8	21.2
Garfield Heights city......	5 720	1 215	20.5	1 542	0.6	11.5	2.9	24 025	63.5	5.9	52.9	14.2	32.9
Grove City city..............	5 685	1 207	17.7	1 300	0.0	10.2	2.8	19 998	72.9	3.4	63.5	14.6	21.9
Hamilton city................	11 204	1 821	14.5	3 413	0.0	16.3	7.9	46 872	61.0	5.5	53.1	13.6	33.3
Huber Heights city........	7 528	2 154	15.3	2 095	0.0	13.1	4.1	29 022	70.0	4.5	59.5	14.7	25.8
Kent city	3 117	11 041	3.2	4 179	0.0	3.1	0.3	23 956	69.1	5.7	46.4	35.9	17.7
Kettering city	9 576	3 652	20.3	2 581	0.2	7.8	3.9	45 981	66.4	3.3	54.1	17.0	28.9
Lakewood city	8 546	3 696	20.5	2 594	0.0	10.8	3.6	46 109	72.2	3.6	60.9	15.3	23.8
Lancaster city	5 926	1 269	12.7	1 649	0.0	14.6	6.0	27 518	63.8	4.2	53.9	15.4	30.7
Lima city	7 903	1 969	12.5	2 712	0.0	13.1	8.6	30 391	57.7	9.4	47.9	15.6	36.5
Lorain city	14 473	2 428	13.8	3 583	0.0	14.3	6.9	50 979	61.0	6.5	52.2	14.1	33.7
Mansfield city	8 395	1 947	11.4	2 218	0.0	13.9	6.4	38 679	57.6	6.4	50.0	14.8	35.2
Maple Heights city........	5 250	1 317	18.5	1 260	0.0	12.0	2.1	20 114	64.6	5.2	58.2	11.7	30.1
Marion city	6 692	1 211	7.9	1 672	0.0	12.9	9.9	27 304	59.4	5.7	52.7	12.8	34.5
Massillon city	5 870	993	14.9	1 690	0.0	11.1	9.9	24 412	62.8	4.6	52.6	13.8	33.6
Medina city	5 113	1 004	12.7	1 171	0.0	12.2	3.7	18 193	70.7	2.9	59.2	16.9	23.9
Mentor city..................	10 223	2 157	16.6	2 755	0.0	12.4	0.9	38 879	72.5	2.7	58.9	17.4	23.7
Middletown city.............	8 897	1 647	10.8	2 607	0.0	20.0	5.1	40 248	62.4	5.4	54.1	13.8	32.1
Newark city..................	8 203	1 787	14.4	2 485	0.0	15.0	7.8	35 723	64.0	5.3	54.6	15.3	30.1
North Olmsted city	6 329	1 608	22.8	1 840	0.0	11.7	2.6	27 072	68.5	3.1	55.2	17.7	27.1
North Royalton city........	5 526	1 685	24.9	1 360	0.0	9.3	0.4	22 516	72.8	3.6	59.4	17.1	23.5
Parma city	14 198	4 103	24.7	3 829	0.2	12.7	3.1	68 768	62.8	3.9	52.2	15.2	32.7
Reynoldsburg city.........	6 359	1 653	17.0	1 699	0.0	5.7	2.2	24 542	73.3	3.5	62.0	16.2	21.8
Sandusky city	5 453	799	15.1	1 395	0.0	17.2	4.3	21 561	64.7	6.7	55.2	14.3	30.4
Shaker Heights city	5 895	1 753	24.8	1 238	0.0	7.6	1.0	22 466	68.4	3.5	58.0	15.2	26.8
Springfield city.............	11 587	4 155	21.6	4 002	0.0	9.7	11.3	50 253	60.8	8.6	51.6	15.1	33.3
Stow city	6 356	1 846	16.2	1 576	0.0	10.6	0.4	24 589	70.9	2.9	59.2	17.3	23.4
Strongsville city	8 720	2 137	22.1	2 170	0.0	10.8	1.6	33 642	71.6	3.0	57.3	19.3	23.4
Toledo city...................	59 656	23 969	18.2	17 399	0.0	10.7	7.9	239 663	63.5	7.7	51.5	17.0	31.5
Trotwood city...............	5 695	1 372	12.8	1 466	0.0	3.1	4.4	21 249	58.0	6.3	50.2	13.6	36.2
Upper Arlington city.......	6 536	1 880	15.1	1 634	0.0	3.6	1.1	26 306	64.5	1.5	51.7	19.4	28.9
Warren city	8 661	1 673	11.2	2 433	0.0	11.5	10.4	35 910	55.8	9.0	47.4	13.3	39.3
Westerville city.............	7 466	3 073	26.2	2 485	0.0	6.5	1.0	27 041	71.1	2.3	58.2	20.1	21.8
Westlake city	5 789	1 482	31.8	1 531	0.0	4.8	1.8	25 476	63.5	2.8	52.7	15.8	31.5
Youngstown city............	15 976	4 513	15.9	4 587	0.0	15.0	9.0	63 130	51.2	11.3	41.6	14.7	43.7
Zanesville city..............	4 866	785	7.9	1 240	0.0	15.0	7.9	19 389	59.3	7.9	50.4	14.0	35.6
OKLAHOMA..............	667 503	203 262	9.2	213 273	1.1	11.3	5.6	2 666 724	62.1	5.2	54.2	13.8	32.0
Bartlesville city	6 712	1 439	12.1	1 854	0.0	11.9	5.6	27 097	58.1	5.4	49.4	13.5	37.1
Broken Arrow city.........	17 312	4 301	14.7	4 753	0.0	8.4	2.4	54 521	73.3	2.9	63.0	15.8	21.3
Edmond city	14 154	7 057	10.9	4 840	0.1	9.8	0.8	51 877	70.2	3.0	58.2	17.6	24.2
Enid city	8 699	1 785	9.7	2 560	0.0	9.2	7.5	36 837	62.5	5.2	53.9	14.1	32.0
Lawton city...................	18 391	6 081	5.7	6 715	26.7	37.4	5.0	70 019	65.4	5.7	55.9	14.4	29.7
Midwest City city	10 750	3 196	9.5	3 051	1.1	16.3	2.8	41 320	64.8	5.0	58.1	12.3	29.6
Moore city....................	8 964	2 469	8.8	2 644	0.3	6.2	5.4	30 370	71.1	3.6	62.6	14.7	22.6
Muskogee city	7 056	1 477	4.4	2 133	0.0	10.6	8.3	29 591	54.7	8.2	48.7	11.2	40.1
Norman city	14 716	20 405	5.3	7 902	0.1	5.6	2.0	78 013	67.7	5.0	53.3	23.1	23.6
Oklahoma City city	92 741	31 046	13.9	28 644	0.9	11.9	7.9	391 394	64.4	5.2	57.8	13.0	29.2
Ponca City city	4 942	804	8.8	1 379	0.0	13.1	7.8	19 888	59.9	8.4	51.4	12.7	35.9
Shawnee city................	4 819	3 074	21.9	2 030	0.0	13.5	6.3	22 451	59.1	6.8	48.4	16.7	34.8
Stillwater city ...	4 229	15 908	1.8	4 244	0.7	3.9	0.8	33 776	65.9	5.4	47.0	31.8	21.2
Tulsa city	69 313	25 888	21.7	21 436	0.0	11.1	7.5	306 527	66.0	5.4	57.6	13.9	28.6

Table B-5. Cities — **Education, Labor Force, and Income**

City	Full-year full-time employed (percent)								Children under 18 years in families (percent, except where noted)						Total employed by class of worker (percent)			
												With two parents							
	Total	Men	Women	Non-Hispanic White	Black or African American	American Indian and Alaska Native	Asian, Hawaiian, and Pacific Islander	Hispanic or Latino[1]	Number	Both in labor force	Father only in labor force	With one parent who is in labor force	+/− U.S. percent of children with no stay-at-home parent	+/− U.S. percent two-income couples	Private	Government	Self-employed	Unpaid family worker
	24	25	26	27	28	29	30	31	32	33	34	35	36	37	38	39	40	41
OHIO—Cont'd																		
Brunswick city	49.4	63.1	36.5	49.4	45.0	37.9	50.5	68.3	8 968	57.5	22.0	13.0	5.9	8.6	85.0	9.1	5.8	0.1
Canton city	36.5	45.2	29.2	37.4	33.0	27.8	32.3	31.7	19 590	30.8	17.3	34.4	0.6	-3.8	84.3	10.3	5.2	0.1
Cincinnati city	38.4	44.5	33.1	42.0	33.1	30.2	36.6	41.6	74 443	26.4	12.2	39.2	1.0	1.8	79.9	13.0	6.9	0.2
Cleveland city	34.6	40.3	29.7	40.1	30.0	33.4	32.5	32.4	122 939	21.4	11.6	40.9	-2.3	-9.7	80.2	14.9	4.7	0.2
Cleveland Heights city ..	44.2	51.7	37.9	44.9	44.3	49.2	36.1	49.7	11 036	42.4	17.6	26.4	4.2	7.2	75.3	15.6	8.9	0.2
Columbus city	46.5	53.6	39.9	48.8	41.5	37.0	37.9	44.4	160 779	38.5	15.7	31.5	5.4	7.8	78.6	15.5	5.7	0.2
Cuyahoga Falls city	43.9	55.1	34.3	44.1	42.5	40.2	53.6	29.6	10 776	48.9	23.4	20.6	4.9	3.6	82.0	11.4	6.5	0.1
Dayton city	35.1	40.2	30.6	37.2	32.6	27.6	29.9	34.2	37 464	26.2	12.3	40.8	2.4	-4.5	78.7	16.4	4.7	0.2
Delaware city	46.3	56.4	37.5	46.4	44.1	34.1	50.9	61.1	6 037	44.6	21.7	25.0	5.0	10.7	80.4	12.9	6.6	0.2
Dublin city	52.8	71.4	35.1	52.8	68.7	45.5	51.7	39.2	10 240	48.3	42.7	5.7	-10.6	3.2	77.7	11.6	10.6	0.2
East Cleveland city	31.0	31.8	30.4	17.9	31.6	0.0	54.9	22.4	7 117	14.9	6.2	51.3	1.6	-14.0	78.6	15.3	5.9	0.3
Elyria city	43.8	54.2	34.5	44.7	41.2	30.4	34.7	34.3	13 765	40.4	16.3	29.9	5.7	1.6	84.4	10.1	5.4	0.1
Euclid city	41.6	48.2	36.3	40.1	45.1	64.7	44.9	34.0	11 365	42.1	15.5	31.6	0.1	0.1	80.5	13.7	5.7	0.1
Fairborn city	39.2	48.0	31.2	40.7	30.2	55.6	19.5	35.6	6 433	38.3	20.0	27.8	1.5	-5.8	75.4	19.6	4.9	0.1
Fairfield city	50.2	61.0	40.3	50.0	56.1	55.0	49.4	42.9	9 768	52.2	22.8	18.4	6.0	8.0	83.3	9.5	7.0	0.2
Findlay city	44.4	55.6	34.5	44.4	55.7	40.0	31.2	49.3	8 970	47.9	21.1	23.3	6.6	3.8	85.0	8.7	6.1	0.2
Gahanna city	52.5	65.3	40.9	52.4	48.1	53.5	67.1	65.2	9 075	57.1	24.7	13.2	5.7	12.6	76.1	15.3	8.5	0.2
Garfield Heights city	42.5	51.3	35.3	42.0	45.5	47.7	42.2	34.9	6 932	44.9	19.7	25.5	5.8	2.1	83.6	10.7	5.6	0.1
Grove City city	52.3	62.7	42.9	52.4	52.8	36.1	34.6	56.7	7 446	57.2	16.9	19.3	11.9	11.0	75.7	18.0	6.2	0.1
Hamilton city	39.9	48.6	32.1	41.0	30.2	27.5	36.9	33.2	14 643	38.8	17.8	27.6	1.8	-2.6	82.3	11.9	5.6	0.2
Huber Heights city	48.4	59.2	38.4	48.3	50.2	36.0	45.8	52.8	9 997	49.0	22.6	20.1	4.5	3.5	81.7	13.8	4.5	0.1
Kent city	28.5	38.0	20.7	29.1	27.0	20.0	9.2	32.8	4 402	37.7	16.1	32.6	5.7	4.9	76.4	19.8	3.6	0.3
Kettering city	43.4	54.3	33.8	43.5	43.5	45.5	37.2	35.6	12 692	52.1	19.8	21.9	9.4	1.8	80.0	11.5	8.3	0.2
Lakewood city	48.2	58.6	39.0	48.5	47.1	27.4	47.1	48.2	11 712	42.5	24.7	24.1	2.0	5.5	81.4	10.5	7.9	0.1
Lancaster city	41.4	52.6	31.9	41.5	37.8	19.1	31.3	33.5	8 238	47.1	16.5	25.6	8.1	0.1	81.2	11.3	7.2	0.3
Lima city	34.5	40.3	28.8	36.5	29.0	36.3	27.4	33.0	10 045	26.8	11.6	42.6	4.8	-5.3	83.7	11.6	4.5	0.3
Lorain city	38.4	48.1	30.2	39.2	34.6	36.8	54.3	38.7	18 235	30.6	15.5	35.6	1.0	6.3	84.2	10.9	4.6	0.3
Mansfield city	36.1	43.3	29.3	37.2	32.1	35.2	36.0	33.5	10 923	36.8	17.3	30.6	2.8	-0.8	79.7	12.7	7.4	0.2
Maple Heights city	45.7	53.5	39.2	40.0	50.0	1.6	48.2	32.6	6 357	45.3	13.0	32.1	12.8	2.4	81.6	13.6	4.3	0.4
Marion city	40.0	45.6	34.4	41.5	25.4	13.3	48.3	29.8	8 298	40.9	14.5	30.5	1.0	1.8	81.7	11.9	6.2	0.2
Massillon city	40.7	50.5	32.2	41.7	32.1	20.8	45.3	45.9	7 219	41.3	20.8	28.9	5.6	-2.4	85.0	8.8	6.1	0.1
Medina city	47.5	63.8	33.2	48.0	31.1	32.3	48.2	43.7	7 473	50.5	28.5	14.1	0.0	7.8	81.2	10.4	8.0	0.5
Mentor city	49.2	61.4	37.8	49.1	43.9	50.0	45.0	63.5	12 706	57.8	22.2	14.4	7.6	9.3	83.3	10.0	6.6	0.2
Middletown city	40.4	50.7	31.4	40.6	38.4	40.7	60.4	46.9	12 196	37.8	16.4	31.8	5.0	-2.1	85.7	8.3	6.0	0.0
Newark city	41.8	50.8	34.1	42.0	37.2	38.9	31.7	49.1	11 030	41.8	19.3	26.3	3.5	2.4	83.5	10.7	5.7	0.1
North Olmsted city	46.7	56.3	36.1	45.6	72.9	34.3	47.9	40.2	7 917	56.4	22.0	16.2	8.0	4.3	80.1	11.8	8.0	0.1
North Royalton city	49.0	62.3	36.5	49.5	43.5	100.0	24.8	64.9	6 812	59.5	25.4	10.2	5.1	8.5	80.2	11.2	8.4	0.2
Parma city	42.8	55.6	31.4	42.6	42.9	27.3	43.2	55.2	18 268	51.8	23.5	17.5	4.7	-1.9	84.3	10.1	5.4	0.2
Reynoldsburg city	51.4	60.9	43.1	51.6	52.4	82.6	32.3	53.8	8 250	49.8	16.3	27.1	12.3	8.5	77.2	16.3	6.3	0.2
Sandusky city	42.2	50.2	35.3	43.2	38.0	0.0	44.8	46.1	6 637	39.9	12.1	34.8	10.1	3.0	82.0	11.5	6.2	0.3
Shaker Heights city	45.3	59.1	34.4	46.9	43.2	0.0	43.6	46.7	7 429	51.2	20.6	23.0	9.6	6.7	69.4	17.3	13.3	0.1
Springfield city	37.9	46.6	30.5	38.4	36.5	32.6	50.0	28.4	15 478	37.4	15.0	32.9	5.7	-2.1	82.0	12.7	5.0	0.3
Stow city	47.5	60.6	35.4	47.5	51.8	24.2	54.6	43.9	8 215	56.0	27.0	10.5	1.9	8.6	80.3	11.4	8.1	0.1
Strongsville city	47.1	62.8	32.6	47.2	47.5	0.0	48.6	46.6	11 386	52.5	32.1	10.3	-1.8	6.3	80.1	11.1	8.7	0.0
Toledo city	38.1	46.3	30.9	40.7	30.7	38.6	27.2	35.0	76 666	36.1	14.4	33.3	4.8	-1.2	82.2	12.0	5.7	0.2
Trotwood city	37.1	43.0	32.5	32.3	40.7	49.1	19.0	36.9	6 520	33.0	11.3	36.8	5.2	-8.2	78.0	16.5	4.6	0.2
Upper Arlington city	42.1	57.4	29.0	42.5	68.6	25.4	30.2	44.6	8 217	50.3	34.4	11.4	-2.9	1.8	64.4	19.3	16.2	0.1
Warren city	34.5	43.7	27.0	34.8	33.4	27.4	44.0	29.6	11 573	30.9	13.1	39.0	5.3	-7.8	82.8	11.3	5.9	0.1
Westerville city	47.2	61.0	35.2	47.3	55.3	0.0	47.4	36.9	9 429	53.2	30.5	11.7	0.3	9.5	77.5	14.4	8.1	0.1
Westlake city	43.9	58.9	31.2	43.9	56.9	6.7	44.5	46.1	7 119	53.0	34.2	10.1	-1.5	1.1	76.5	11.0	12.4	0.1
Youngstown city	28.6	33.2	24.6	31.1	25.5	32.9	42.0	26.9	18 521	24.4	10.5	41.8	1.6	-12.8	80.9	13.4	5.5	0.2
Zanesville city	36.6	44.9	29.9	37.2	32.6	67.3	52.8	35.5	6 535	34.9	12.9	33.5	3.8	-3.3	82.0	11.0	6.6	0.4
OKLAHOMA	39.6	49.2	30.5	40.5	34.6	36.7	36.9	38.1	832 936	42.9	23.1	21.9	0.2	-1.7	71.3	16.8	11.4	0.5
Bartlesville city	37.0	46.8	28.5	36.7	33.5	44.5	25.9	44.8	8 206	46.0	25.9	19.5	0.9	-9.3	80.0	9.7	10.0	0.3
Broken Arrow city	50.8	66.7	36.2	51.3	52.1	46.5	47.2	45.6	22 519	51.5	26.9	14.7	1.6	8.6	81.3	9.3	9.3	0.1
Edmond city	45.3	57.6	34.4	47.2	36.4	45.0	20.9	38.9	18 271	49.8	29.2	16.1	1.3	8.7	69.5	17.8	12.4	0.3
Enid city	40.1	51.6	29.7	40.2	40.6	39.2	41.2	37.8	10 824	43.0	25.5	21.9	0.3	-1.8	72.1	14.8	12.5	0.6
Lawton city	39.0	49.7	27.0	39.7	39.6	35.9	32.8	36.1	23 736	37.7	25.3	24.1	-2.8	-3.7	65.3	26.2	8.3	0.2
Midwest City city	43.6	54.8	34.0	42.9	45.1	39.2	51.3	47.2	13 527	35.8	17.6	34.6	5.8	-2.6	66.0	26.6	7.0	0.4
Moore city	48.8	59.8	38.6	49.2	50.7	50.6	49.0	48.6	11 445	46.6	22.4	20.9	2.9	0.0	70.9	21.5	7.4	0.2
Muskogee city	33.6	41.6	26.7	33.6	28.9	36.3	36.6	42.1	8 787	32.8	21.4	27.9	-3.9	-11.2	73.7	17.0	9.1	0.2
Norman city	38.6	46.2	31.0	40.0	29.0	36.8	27.7	32.5	19 324	47.8	24.1	18.8	2.0	6.2	63.1	26.6	9.9	0.4
Oklahoma City city	42.6	51.6	34.3	44.7	36.5	40.4	42.9	37.4	119 882	37.9	19.9	26.8	0.1	0.7	74.8	14.8	10.1	0.3
Ponca City city	37.6	48.2	28.6	37.6	40.6	35.2	61.3	36.2	6 420	43.3	23.2	25.2	3.9	-5.7	78.7	11.5	9.4	0.5
Shawnee city	33.5	41.3	26.5	34.2	29.6	30.7	26.9	36.6	6 425	36.0	18.4	29.2	0.6	-3.8	71.9	19.2	8.6	0.2
Stillwater city	28.1	33.6	22.5	29.3	28.4	27.6	15.7	23.0	5 647	47.0	21.2	23.1	5.5	7.1	56.4	36.6	6.5	0.5
Tulsa city	42.2	52.4	33.1	43.8	36.3	41.1	37.1	41.6	90 496	37.0	23.1	27.2	-0.4	-1.1	80.5	9.1	10.1	0.3

[1] Hispanic or Latino persons may be of any race.

City	Percent who worked at home	Percent of the population 5 years and over with a disability	Veterans as a percent of the population 18 years and over	Occupation for employed population 16 years and over (percent)						Industry for employed population 16 years and over (percent)					
				Management, professional, and related occupations	Service occupations	Sales and office occupations	Farming, fishing, and forestry occupations	Construction, extraction, and maintenance occupations	Production, transportation and material moving occupations	Agriculture, forestry, fishing, and mining	Construction and manufacturing	Wholesale and retail trade	Transportation and warehousing, and utilities	Service industries	Public administration
	42	43	44	45	46	47	48	49	50	51	52	53	54	55	56
OHIO—Cont'd															
Brunswick city	2.4	14.0	12.8	31.0	12.6	28.1	0.1	11.1	17.0	0.1	27.5	17.5	5.5	46.5	2.9
Canton city	1.4	22.1	13.4	21.5	20.0	26.3	0.1	7.9	24.1	0.3	26.8	16.6	4.1	48.4	3.9
Cincinnati city	2.6	22.0	10.5	35.8	17.9	26.3	0.1	6.4	13.5	0.1	17.0	13.2	4.7	60.8	4.1
Cleveland city	1.6	26.2	11.6	22.5	20.9	26.7	0.1	7.5	22.3	0.2	22.7	13.1	6.0	52.6	5.4
Cleveland Heights city	3.8	15.6	9.8	53.5	12.0	22.6	0.0	3.3	8.6	0.1	12.3	11.1	4.0	68.7	3.8
Columbus city	2.3	18.2	10.9	35.5	15.2	30.1	0.1	6.5	12.7	0.2	13.9	17.1	5.3	57.8	5.8
Cuyahoga Falls city	2.2	17.0	14.3	34.5	13.5	30.6	0.0	7.5	13.9	0.1	22.9	18.2	4.5	50.5	3.8
Dayton city	1.6	24.7	13.1	25.7	21.1	25.3	0.1	7.8	20.0	0.2	21.5	13.2	5.1	53.0	7.0
Delaware city	3.3	16.2	13.1	37.3	13.1	28.0	0.3	6.5	14.7	0.5	21.7	14.9	3.9	53.5	5.5
Dublin city	5.4	6.8	9.9	59.8	6.5	28.3	0.1	2.0	3.3	0.2	16.4	17.0	3.1	59.9	3.4
East Cleveland city	1.9	25.8	11.5	20.4	27.4	27.2	0.0	6.0	19.0	0.1	17.1	11.3	5.3	62.1	4.0
Elyria city	1.6	21.6	15.3	24.0	17.2	24.9	0.3	9.4	24.3	0.5	31.3	14.6	4.4	44.8	4.4
Euclid city	1.5	21.5	14.1	30.6	15.2	30.8	0.0	6.8	16.5	0.0	24.1	14.5	4.5	52.3	4.5
Fairborn city	1.1	18.9	17.6	30.8	18.9	27.4	0.1	9.0	13.8	0.2	17.5	15.8	4.2	53.7	8.7
Fairfield city	2.3	14.6	13.7	39.4	10.4	30.6	0.1	7.1	12.4	0.2	23.7	18.7	5.0	49.5	2.9
Findlay city	2.6	15.7	13.2	30.1	15.0	22.7	0.2	8.0	24.0	1.3	31.3	16.3	5.1	44.1	1.9
Gahanna city	3.7	11.7	13.5	46.5	10.1	29.7	0.0	5.7	8.1	0.0	15.2	18.4	5.1	54.4	6.9
Garfield Heights city	1.6	21.6	13.2	23.9	15.1	34.6	0.0	8.0	18.3	0.0	24.2	19.3	5.1	47.7	3.6
Grove City city	2.0	15.2	14.6	34.0	13.1	32.6	0.0	8.6	11.6	0.1	16.5	17.9	7.4	49.1	8.9
Hamilton city	1.5	22.3	14.5	22.6	16.7	28.0	0.1	10.8	21.8	0.2	27.9	15.7	5.8	46.0	4.3
Huber Heights city	1.7	17.2	19.3	30.1	13.9	27.5	0.1	8.5	19.9	0.2	24.4	17.4	6.9	44.1	7.0
Kent city	2.3	13.6	7.1	32.1	20.9	29.0	0.1	4.8	13.1	0.2	15.2	17.2	3.1	62.1	2.2
Kettering city	2.9	16.1	15.3	39.5	12.0	28.8	0.2	6.5	13.0	0.1	21.4	15.9	2.8	55.4	4.3
Lakewood city	2.6	15.1	10.4	41.0	13.8	28.0	0.0	6.7	10.4	0.1	18.0	14.5	3.4	60.5	3.4
Lancaster city	2.1	21.5	16.3	23.8	17.1	29.2	0.1	11.4	18.5	0.1	24.7	20.4	4.1	46.3	4.4
Lima city	1.6	24.0	14.5	18.4	20.8	22.0	0.5	8.5	29.9	0.8	30.5	16.5	4.5	42.6	5.1
Lorain city	1.3	21.7	15.3	20.4	16.7	25.7	0.6	9.6	27.0	0.6	32.4	14.5	4.5	43.6	4.4
Mansfield city	1.6	22.5	14.5	23.2	19.1	23.7	0.0	8.2	25.8	0.1	29.2	15.3	3.4	46.1	5.9
Maple Heights city	1.0	18.2	14.5	25.2	14.8	30.6	0.2	7.2	21.9	0.1	24.3	16.5	5.7	48.7	4.6
Marion city	1.2	25.3	14.3	19.2	17.6	25.9	0.4	8.0	28.9	0.9	32.8	13.6	3.6	42.9	6.2
Massillon city	1.3	20.9	15.1	22.2	16.5	26.1	0.2	7.9	27.1	0.3	32.6	16.1	4.5	43.6	2.8
Medina city	2.9	15.1	12.9	36.2	12.1	29.8	0.1	7.4	14.3	0.4	25.4	18.4	4.0	49.0	2.9
Mentor city	2.2	13.3	14.0	36.1	11.1	28.7	0.2	7.0	16.9	0.3	30.0	17.1	3.6	45.8	3.2
Middletown city	1.7	23.1	14.0	24.3	16.3	25.5	0.1	9.6	24.2	0.1	34.0	14.5	3.5	44.9	3.0
Newark city	1.9	21.7	15.2	23.7	18.0	28.3	0.1	9.0	20.9	0.4	25.7	15.7	3.9	49.8	4.5
North Olmsted city	2.9	14.4	13.9	37.7	12.4	30.6	0.2	7.3	11.8	0.3	20.6	16.7	4.5	53.3	4.6
North Royalton city	3.9	13.6	11.8	37.1	11.6	30.1	0.2	8.4	12.7	0.1	23.3	15.9	5.3	52.5	2.9
Parma city	1.6	17.4	14.0	30.0	14.2	31.9	0.0	8.6	15.3	0.0	22.5	17.9	5.1	50.7	3.7
Reynoldsburg city	2.2	15.3	16.4	36.0	13.8	31.7	0.0	6.6	11.8	0.2	16.6	18.9	5.2	51.3	7.8
Sandusky city	1.4	21.5	14.5	19.0	21.1	24.9	0.2	7.8	27.1	0.6	29.2	15.6	3.2	47.1	4.3
Shaker Heights city	4.1	16.5	11.8	63.3	7.7	21.7	0.0	1.7	5.5	0.0	11.3	9.9	3.4	71.7	3.8
Springfield city	1.6	24.6	15.1	24.4	17.9	25.2	0.3	8.1	24.1	0.4	26.3	14.6	4.2	49.6	4.9
Stow city	2.9	12.9	12.5	42.3	11.9	27.2	0.0	6.1	12.5	0.2	24.2	16.3	4.7	52.5	2.1
Strongsville city	3.4	11.4	12.9	42.2	10.1	30.8	0.1	6.3	10.4	0.1	21.4	17.7	5.9	51.0	3.9
Toledo city	1.5	22.7	12.6	25.7	17.9	26.7	0.1	8.3	21.3	0.2	23.7	16.4	5.5	50.6	3.5
Trotwood city	1.5	25.7	15.1	24.6	15.8	27.2	0.0	7.3	25.1	0.1	25.3	13.3	7.8	46.6	6.9
Upper Arlington city	5.8	10.6	13.2	64.1	6.2	24.7	0.0	2.0	2.9	0.3	8.1	14.2	2.6	69.4	5.3
Warren city	1.7	23.9	15.9	21.1	19.0	23.3	0.2	8.3	28.1	0.0	32.9	12.5	4.3	45.7	4.5
Westerville city	3.9	10.6	12.3	47.6	10.8	29.8	0.1	4.7	7.0	0.1	13.1	16.5	3.7	61.5	5.2
Westlake city	3.9	13.0	12.0	52.9	8.8	27.8	0.0	4.7	5.8	0.1	17.6	14.9	3.2	60.1	4.2
Youngstown city	1.7	26.3	14.4	18.7	24.1	25.5	0.2	7.2	24.2	0.4	21.7	15.8	4.4	52.0	5.6
Zanesville city	2.0	25.6	13.2	22.8	18.2	25.4	0.4	7.5	25.7	0.4	28.4	16.0	3.7	48.3	3.2
OKLAHOMA	3.1	21.6	14.7	30.3	15.5	26.6	0.9	11.3	15.4	4.1	19.5	15.4	5.6	49.5	5.9
Bartlesville city	2.3	22.9	15.8	37.6	15.3	25.5	0.2	8.7	12.8	4.0	22.5	18.2	2.6	49.6	3.1
Broken Arrow city	3.4	13.8	13.8	38.0	11.4	31.5	0.1	9.1	9.9	1.0	16.9	18.5	8.1	53.1	2.4
Edmond city	4.0	13.4	12.4	45.7	11.6	30.6	0.2	5.9	6.1	2.6	11.4	16.3	3.3	59.9	6.5
Enid city	2.2	22.4	15.3	26.5	20.3	25.7	0.6	12.4	14.6	4.2	18.1	17.1	5.5	49.5	5.7
Lawton city	2.0	19.4	19.6	28.6	21.3	26.5	0.4	9.5	13.6	1.0	15.0	15.7	3.7	55.8	8.7
Midwest City city	2.3	22.9	20.1	28.0	15.8	29.9	0.1	12.0	14.2	1.0	15.7	13.9	4.4	49.0	15.9
Moore city	1.6	18.5	17.3	28.2	13.9	30.5	0.1	12.6	14.7	0.8	18.2	16.8	6.1	46.5	11.6
Muskogee city	1.8	28.2	16.3	27.0	18.4	25.2	0.9	10.2	18.3	0.7	23.0	16.6	5.5	48.7	5.5
Norman city	2.7	14.4	11.8	41.4	16.2	26.9	0.2	7.8	7.6	1.4	12.1	14.5	3.6	62.0	6.3
Oklahoma City city	2.7	21.5	13.9	31.3	15.3	29.6	0.2	10.0	13.6	1.4	17.7	16.0	4.2	53.4	7.3
Ponca City city	2.6	23.2	15.7	32.0	17.7	24.3	0.2	9.9	15.9	2.0	27.6	18.2	3.3	45.9	3.0
Shawnee city	1.8	23.8	14.4	28.5	18.2	27.0	0.2	10.5	15.5	1.1	19.6	15.5	3.3	53.0	7.4
Stillwater city	3.1	13.0	7.7	41.3	17.2	26.8	0.6	4.7	9.5	1.3	10.4	13.7	1.8	69.4	3.5
Tulsa city	3.1	20.5	13.4	34.5	14.4	29.7	0.1	9.3	12.0	1.4	16.8	15.7	6.3	57.0	2.8

City	Median household income	Median family income: All families	Median family income: Families with children: Married-couple	Median family income: Families with children: Male householder	Median family income: Families with children: Female householder	Median nonfamily household income	Median income for full-year, full-time workers: Men	Median income for full-year, full-time workers: Women	Per capita income	Households by source of income (percent): With earnings	Households by source of income (percent): With interest, dividend, or rental income	Households by source of income (percent): With Social Security income	Households by source of income (percent): With public assistance income	Households by source of income (percent): With retirement income	Households with income over $100,000 (percent)	+/− U.S. percent for income over $100,000	Households with income below poverty (percent)	Families with children with income below poverty (percent)
	57	58	59	60	61	62	63	64	65	66	67	68	69	70	71	72	73	74
OHIO—Cont'd																		
Brunswick city	56 288	62 080	67 530	40 982	27 500	31 724	43 639	28 640	21 937	87.9	41.3	19.2	1.9	15.4	10.9	-1.4	4.3	5.0
Canton city	28 730	35 680	45 414	22 581	13 674	17 983	31 158	22 073	15 544	73.6	23.7	28.4	7.0	17.0	4.1	-8.2	18.9	24.1
Cincinnati city	29 493	37 543	57 545	24 394	15 336	22 104	34 273	27 617	19 962	76.7	28.0	22.9	5.2	13.5	7.4	-4.9	20.5	27.4
Cleveland city	25 928	30 286	43 765	22 064	14 294	18 684	31 037	24 971	14 291	72.8	19.0	26.1	11.2	14.9	3.4	-8.9	24.6	32.3
Cleveland Heights city	46 731	58 028	72 461	39 375	29 805	31 723	42 710	34 036	25 804	84.2	40.7	19.9	4.5	13.7	15.3	3.0	11.5	9.1
Columbus city	37 897	47 391	60 059	28 159	20 833	28 378	35 730	29 556	20 450	85.0	28.3	17.2	3.7	12.7	7.4	-4.9	13.8	15.7
Cuyahoga Falls city	42 263	52 372	61 237	42 561	22 500	26 250	40 940	29 195	22 550	78.0	38.0	28.9	2.2	20.9	7.1	-5.2	7.2	8.0
Dayton city	27 423	34 978	50 157	25 105	15 261	18 443	31 326	25 537	15 547	74.2	20.0	26.4	6.2	19.3	4.0	-8.3	21.8	27.4
Delaware city	46 030	54 463	64 167	35 278	27 008	27 986	39 037	29 852	20 633	84.0	35.3	23.9	2.9	16.0	8.9	-3.4	7.5	7.1
Dublin city	91 162	104 829	111 722	52 279	50 089	46 596	78 727	45 693	41 122	92.6	59.0	10.9	0.6	10.7	45.1	32.8	2.8	2.3
East Cleveland city	20 542	26 053	41 424	16 522	14 878	13 998	26 444	22 366	12 602	69.0	11.6	23.5	12.8	16.4	2.6	-9.7	30.6	36.7
Elyria city	38 156	45 846	55 130	25 074	17 065	24 738	35 666	24 921	19 344	80.8	30.4	26.2	4.1	19.4	6.7	-5.6	10.7	15.9
Euclid city	35 151	45 278	56 551	31 505	24 237	20 500	37 006	29 445	19 664	72.4	34.4	31.4	4.0	20.2	4.5	-7.8	10.7	10.2
Fairborn city	36 889	44 608	53 765	28 438	18 625	25 805	36 185	26 187	18 662	81.5	32.0	22.3	3.3	23.1	5.0	-0.7	13.8	13.2
Fairfield city	50 316	61 233	69 036	42 552	30 386	35 267	43 268	30 665	24 556	87.8	42.3	20.1	1.0	15.5	12.0	-0.3	4.0	3.8
Findlay city	40 883	49 986	57 296	25 426	19 931	25 493	36 977	24 762	21 328	81.9	38.5	25.0	2.4	17.6	9.4	-2.9	8.9	10.3
Gahanna city	66 031	74 260	82 825	39 200	46 061	36 155	52 414	37 130	29 040	88.1	49.4	17.6	1.0	16.7	25.1	12.8	4.0	3.2
Garfield Heights city	39 278	47 557	56 153	47 750	23 232	22 254	36 138	26 964	18 988	74.8	38.7	33.3	3.3	21.8	4.4	-7.9	8.4	10.2
Grove City city	52 064	62 059	69 188	44 063	25 308	29 552	41 465	31 236	22 305	85.3	37.6	20.9	1.0	20.4	13.0	0.7	4.4	5.1
Hamilton city	35 365	41 936	50 955	28 474	18 399	21 204	33 576	24 582	17 493	76.0	27.8	29.9	4.7	19.7	4.8	-7.5	13.5	15.9
Huber Heights city	49 073	53 579	60 724	36 351	28 591	31 567	41 224	29 764	20 951	85.2	33.9	21.2	1.9	24.0	9.0	-3.3	6.1	6.7
Kent city	29 582	44 440	60 000	25 417	12 467	19 773	32 694	25 645	15 015	84.0	30.4	16.7	3.5	13.9	7.0	-5.3	25.5	24.2
Kettering city	45 051	55 849	65 223	32 478	26 388	30 462	42 311	30 325	27 009	77.5	46.5	29.2	1.1	24.8	11.1	-1.2	5.2	5.0
Lakewood city	40 527	53 433	61 624	31 797	25 039	30 674	39 559	30 968	23 945	82.4	39.0	21.1	2.9	12.7	9.2	-3.1	8.8	10.0
Lancaster city	33 321	39 773	49 608	26 364	17 942	20 882	31 123	23 828	17 648	75.6	31.7	31.2	4.6	21.1	4.6	-7.7	11.2	13.9
Lima city	27 067	32 405	44 219	26 250	14 973	17 569	30 056	23 372	13 882	72.8	21.1	29.5	6.1	18.1	3.1	-9.2	21.9	29.0
Lorain city	33 917	39 454	51 133	29 800	14 858	19 705	35 174	23 973	16 340	76.1	27.5	30.4	5.2	21.7	5.5	-6.8	16.1	22.3
Mansfield city	30 176	37 541	46 094	20 337	15 945	19 333	31 475	22 536	17 726	73.8	28.6	31.0	4.7	18.5	5.2	-7.1	15.1	22.1
Maple Heights city	40 414	48 580	60 395	38 125	30 579	25 197	35 660	28 605	18 676	77.6	32.2	29.7	2.2	18.9	4.5	-7.8	6.2	7.5
Marion city	33 124	40 000	49 417	26 500	10 000	20 117	31 661	23 190	16 247	76.6	25.5	30.4	4.0	19.4	3.9	-8.4	13.0	16.6
Massillon city	32 734	41 058	51 584	21 616	19 839	19 238	32 568	23 381	17 633	75.9	29.9	31.1	3.2	21.4	5.1	7.0	10.7	14.6
Medina city	50 226	57 435	65 586	37 813	19 696	26 605	43 881	27 547	21 709	84.5	40.3	20.7	2.3	14.4	12.5	0.2	6.0	7.3
Mentor city	57 230	65 322	75 841	40 875	36 078	32 066	45 835	31 853	24 592	84.9	46.7	24.3	0.8	19.7	16.0	3.7	3.1	2.4
Middletown city	36 215	43 867	56 060	31 993	19 705	21 269	36 224	25 451	19 773	76.2	27.1	30.3	3.8	21.9	6.5	-5.8	12.6	14.6
Newark city	34 791	42 138	50 902	26 641	17 755	21 499	34 058	25 670	17 819	77.4	30.9	29.4	3.8	20.2	5.5	-6.8	12.6	15.7
North Olmsted city	52 542	62 422	70 422	40 688	32 708	30 731	47 037	31 276	24 329	82.4	50.5	27.0	1.3	20.8	13.7	1.4	4.0	3.9
North Royalton city	57 398	69 983	80 859	34 850	34 650	31 996	48 777	32 058	26 610	85.4	52.0	22.2	0.9	16.5	18.1	5.8	3.3	1.4
Parma city	43 920	52 436	60 274	36 500	26 981	25 680	40 586	28 733	21 290	75.2	46.7	34.7	1.3	23.8	7.3	-5.0	5.0	5.8
Reynoldsburg city	51 108	60 183	69 926	40 962	26 918	31 316	41 432	31 054	23 388	85.0	36.0	20.9	1.7	18.6	11.2	-1.1	5.5	7.0
Sandusky city	31 133	37 749	50 864	28 125	17 592	21 103	31 781	22 354	18 111	76.8	29.1	28.0	3.9	17.6	4.0	-8.3	14.2	18.9
Shaker Heights city	63 983	85 893	114 909	62 386	33 139	34 859	65 813	40 035	41 354	81.6	50.6	26.5	1.8	16.2	30.3	18.0	6.9	7.1
Springfield city	32 193	39 890	50 919	22 044	16 075	20 870	32 913	23 970	16 660	74.6	26.5	30.4	5.9	20.9	5.4	-6.9	15.5	20.7
Stow city	57 525	67 822	75 871	46 645	30 292	33 884	49 305	31 479	25 509	85.3	46.0	21.5	1.0	17.3	16.2	3.9	4.9	4.1
Strongsville city	68 660	76 964	87 090	55 962	42 935	34 871	57 511	34 493	29 722	86.0	55.0	22.9	0.9	18.1	26.0	13.7	2.7	1.7
Toledo city	32 546	41 175	54 265	26 542	15 220	21 562	36 023	25 709	17 388	76.6	28.7	26.7	5.5	17.9	5.2	-7.1	17.1	22.2
Trotwood city	34 931	40 426	52 334	27 458	21 743	23 865	34 639	27 127	18 329	75.7	22.4	30.5	3.7	27.6	6.6	-5.7	13.9	18.1
Upper Arlington city	72 116	90 208	105 660	60 313	45 089	43 220	71 468	43 330	42 025	80.4	67.3	28.7	0.2	22.1	32.8	20.5	2.9	1.9
Warren city	30 147	36 158	46 417	22 500	14 776	19 423	32 879	24 784	16 808	70.6	27.5	32.7	6.4	23.5	4.3	-8.0	18.1	25.3
Westerville city	69 135	82 163	93 489	29 712	29 915	30 563	56 938	37 398	29 401	87.2	52.5	20.6	1.1	16.3	29.6	17.3	4.3	4.1
Westlake city	64 963	81 223	93 187	53 750	50 288	40 771	61 977	38 490	37 142	81.2	58.2	27.1	0.5	18.5	26.6	14.3	2.8	1.6
Youngstown city	24 201	30 701	41 676	22 327	13 423	14 017	30 309	21 735	13 293	67.4	21.8	35.0	8.9	22.3	2.7	-9.6	23.6	32.1
Zanesville city	26 642	31 932	43 132	19 271	12 717	18 379	28 827	20 938	15 192	72.8	22.3	32.2	8.8	18.4	3.0	-9.3	20.1	27.9
OKLAHOMA	33 400	40 709	47 652	24 745	16 657	19 331	31 973	23 450	17 646	78.6	30.5	27.2	5.1	16.4	6.6	-5.7	14.6	16.5
Bartlesville city	35 827	44 617	52 104	25 179	17 660	19 247	36 491	24 221	21 195	71.6	40.8	34.6	3.8	21.5	10.9	-1.4	12.9	15.4
Broken Arrow city	53 507	58 891	64 491	38 929	26 318	29 566	43 506	28 401	21 555	89.6	36.8	16.6	1.9	11.7	13.0	0.7	5.0	4.6
Edmond city	54 556	65 230	72 708	40 101	29 219	25 423	50 168	29 469	26 517	86.4	45.4	17.2	2.4	14.8	19.0	6.7	8.7	5.8
Enid city	32 227	39 113	45 744	23 949	15 441	19 229	31 197	21 269	17 471	78.4	35.7	29.2	5.1	16.6	5.3	-7.0	13.8	17.6
Lawton city	32 521	37 831	42 555	26 151	13 173	20 360	29 400	22 370	15 397	81.3	25.0	21.4	6.2	20.7	4.7	-7.6	16.3	19.7
Midwest City city	35 027	40 604	44 419	27 257	17 469	24 305	32 469	23 593	17 220	79.7	30.3	25.1	4.9	23.3	4.2	-8.1	12.0	18.4
Moore city	43 409	47 773	50 585	35 048	22 026	27 043	35 190	25 864	17 689	87.8	29.3	17.5	3.6	17.4	5.5	-6.8	6.6	9.5
Muskogee city	26 418	33 358	41 433	20 682	14 930	16 140	29 475	21 247	15 351	70.5	25.8	35.3	7.5	19.7	4.6	-7.7	18.5	22.3
Norman city	36 713	51 189	59 686	31 644	20 792	19 598	36 854	27 056	20 630	84.9	37.6	17.8	2.8	13.5	9.9	-2.4	16.7	10.8
Oklahoma City city	34 947	42 689	51 296	25 236	16 324	23 212	32 337	25 294	19 098	81.3	30.9	22.3	5.2	15.6	7.8	-4.5	14.7	19.1
Ponca City city	31 406	39 846	47 931	20 156	15 846	19 579	33 328	20 759	17 732	71.8	36.8	33.4	5.4	17.1	6.6	-5.7	14.4	18.7
Shawnee city	27 659	35 690	42 049	25 357	13 838	16 477	30 738	21 818	15 676	73.2	29.3	32.2	7.1	19.1	5.1	-7.2	17.5	21.8
Stillwater city	25 432	41 938	51 960	27 321	16 995	14 271	32 489	23 739	15 789	85.3	34.3	15.3	2.4	10.7	6.6	-5.7	29.4	15.7
Tulsa city	35 316	44 518	55 001	25 616	17 179	23 790	34 295	26 288	21 534	80.8	32.8	24.0	4.4	13.8	9.7	-2.6	13.0	17.4

STATE Place code	City	High school graduates			College graduates		College graduates (percent)				
		Total population 25 years and over	Percent with a high school diploma or less	Percent with a high school diploma or more	Percent with a bachelor's degree or more	+/- U.S. percent with bachelor's degree or more	Non-Hispanic White	Black or African American	American Indian and Alaska Native	Asian, Hawaiian, and Pacific Islander	Hispanic or Latino[1]
		1	2	3	4	5	6	7	8	9	10
41 00000	OREGON	2 250 998	41.1	85.1	25.1	0.7	26.0	17.8	12.2	37.2	9.6
41 01000	Albany city....................	26 281	43.5	84.7	18.4	-6.0	19.3	11.0	5.4	16.1	6.2
41 05350	Beaverton city	48 907	27.9	90.0	39.1	14.7	41.1	26.3	19.8	50.7	12.8
41 05800	Bend city	33 914	33.7	90.2	29.4	5.0	30.3	0.0	8.7	40.0	8.2
41 15800	Corvallis city	26 539	19.1	93.0	53.1	28.7	53.8	56.3	31.7	68.0	29.5
41 23850	Eugene city	86 004	27.8	91.5	37.3	12.9	38.0	34.3	21.3	53.9	19.1
41 31250	Gresham city.................	55 587	45.2	83.1	18.4	-6.0	19.1	14.8	6.8	28.5	7.7
41 34100	Hillsboro city.................	42 529	37.5	84.2	29.5	5.1	31.0	25.3	15.7	58.7	7.1
41 38500	Keizer city....................	20 740	42.3	84.7	20.4	-4.0	21.7	13.7	18.2	20.4	4.9
41 40550	Lake Oswego city........	24 631	10.4	97.7	62.0	37.6	62.1	57.8	25.7	70.6	46.9
41 45000	McMinnville city	15 782	49.1	81.8	20.8	-3.6	22.9	25.5	11.9	20.7	5.9
41 47000	Medford city.................	41 804	46.4	83.3	21.1	-3.3	22.2	13.4	13.7	27.7	6.9
41 55200	Oregon City city	16 088	41.5	86.2	18.4	-6.0	18.3	22.8	24.4	31.0	13.7
41 59000	Portland city	363 851	36.6	85.7	32.6	8.2	35.9	15.3	14.4	26.3	14.5
41 64900	Salem city....................	86 209	42.4	81.5	24.1	-0.3	26.6	9.5	11.5	25.4	6.9
41 69600	Springfield city..............	32 374	50.3	81.5	13.8	-10.6	14.1	17.8	11.9	25.2	10.1
41 73650	Tigard city....................	27 142	27.4	90.8	36.5	12.1	37.6	34.8	42.6	42.7	13.3
42 00000	PENNSYLVANIA........	8 266 284	56.2	81.9	22.4	-2.0	23.2	12.0	13.2	48.8	12.0
42 02000	Allentown city	68 718	63.8	72.7	15.4	-9.0	18.0	7.5	4.9	29.5	4.7
42 02184	Altoona city..................	32 755	67.9	82.0	12.1	-12.3	12.1	9.8	6.0	37.2	13.6
42 06064	Bethel Park borough	23 980	36.4	92.9	37.8	13.4	37.6	19.6	53.5	69.1	35.7
42 06088	Bethlehem city..............	46 071	54.8	78.4	23.8	-0.6	26.0	17.2	10.3	65.2	7.1
42 13208	Chester city	21 174	71.2	68.7	8.5	-15.9	10.3	7.4	0.0	66.4	6.7
42 21648	Easton city...................	15 813	64.8	71.7	14.9	-9.5	17.1	8.6	0.0	12.2	3.1
42 24000	Erie city	65 260	61.7	79.9	17.4	-7.0	19.1	6.3	6.8	26.8	7.7
42 32800	Harrisburg city..............	30 712	63.4	72.4	14.3	-10.1	24.7	7.8	15.9	14.8	3.8
42 41216	Lancaster city...............	33 183	69.5	66.6	14.0	-10.4	19.0	7.2	6.2	21.2	3.6
42 52330	Municipality of Monroeville borough...	21 605	38.8	89.2	35.6	11.2	34.5	28.5	0.0	75.5	35.0
42 53368	New Castle city	17 909	67.9	77.5	12.0	-12.4	12.4	2.7	0.0	55.4	32.1
42 54656	Norristown borough	20 092	64.6	71.5	13.3	-11.1	15.6	10.0	17.1	26.1	4.7
42 60000	Philadelphia city............	966 197	62.1	71.2	17.9	-6.5	24.1	10.3	9.9	32.6	9.2
42 61000	Pittsburgh city...............	218 813	51.5	81.3	26.2	1.8	28.9	12.2	12.8	75.8	40.3
42 61536	Plum borough................	18 555	45.0	90.5	28.0	3.6	27.3	31.2	X	69.3	63.8
42 63624	Reading city	47 530	75.0	62.3	8.6	-15.8	11.5	5.8	2.5	15.3	2.8
42 69000	Scranton city	51 268	63.5	78.2	15.6	-8.8	15.8	8.6	6.8	26.3	8.7
42 73808	State College borough ..	10 919	14.1	95.9	69.2	44.8	65.8	61.5	31.3	88.8	85.0
42 85152	Wilkes-Barre city	29 129	64.5	76.8	12.8	-11.6	12.9	8.4	0.0	23.4	12.9
42 85312	Williamsport city............	18 387	59.9	77.2	16.3	-8.1	17.3	8.7	7.5	28.3	16.8
42 87048	York city	24 579	71.7	69.0	10.6	-13.8	13.0	6.0	5.1	23.4	3.9
44 00000	RHODE ISLAND	694 573	49.8	78.0	25.6	1.2	27.3	16.7	14.1	35.9	8.6
44 19180	Cranston city	55 886	49.9	78.8	24.6	0.2	25.1	16.0	11.7	29.1	18.0
44 22960	East Providence city	34 489	58.3	71.1	18.0	-6.4	18.6	15.6	16.3	53.3	4.3
44 49960	Newport city.................	17 428	34.3	87.0	41.5	17.1	44.5	14.3	8.2	54.8	16.3
44 54640	Pawtucket city...............	48 132	63.8	66.2	14.3	-10.1	15.9	16.1	15.9	21.6	7.0
44 59000	Providence city.............	96 154	57.3	65.8	24.4	0.0	35.2	15.0	10.4	28.4	6.6
44 74300	Warwick city	61 276	47.2	85.0	24.5	0.1	24.0	29.4	4.1	48.9	33.0
44 80780	Woonsocket city	28 109	68.0	64.0	10.1	-14.3	10.4	9.3	28.2	14.9	2.8
45 00000	SOUTH CAROLINA ...	2 596 010	53.6	76.3	20.4	-4.0	24.3	9.9	11.2	39.8	14.1
45 00550	Aiken city....................	17 161	37.0	84.6	38.1	13.7	48.0	10.7	17.0	60.6	33.5
45 01360	Anderson city	17 134	57.3	70.3	20.0	-4.4	26.4	5.0	0.0	47.1	15.9
45 13330	Charleston city	60 358	36.0	83.7	37.5	13.1	49.0	14.7	29.7	56.0	26.3
45 16000	Columbia city................	65 798	37.9	82.3	35.7	11.3	53.2	13.9	24.3	62.9	25.2
45 25810	Florence city	20 068	48.4	76.2	26.4	2.0	38.2	9.0	0.0	59.9	13.2
45 29815	Goose Creek city	15 260	39.8	89.8	20.6	-3.8	21.3	16.0	5.0	31.3	22.6
45 30850	Greenville city..............	37 171	41.4	79.0	34.2	9.8	47.9	7.7	0.0	43.5	18.1
45 34045	Hilton Head Island town	25 639	25.7	92.5	45.9	21.5	51.6	14.6	10.8	32.3	12.8
45 48535	Mount Pleasant town	32 430	20.1	94.0	52.6	28.2	55.1	18.3	10.9	72.8	37.2
45 50875	North Charleston city	46 879	55.9	72.8	13.8	-10.6	18.0	8.8	25.5	23.1	9.7
45 61405	Rock Hill city	30 252	49.1	75.2	24.3	-0.1	32.7	9.3	0.0	23.7	23.0
45 68290	Spartanburg city............	25 012	51.4	72.4	26.0	1.6	40.2	8.6	20.3	41.7	30.2
45 70270	Summerville town..........	17 885	41.1	86.1	26.7	2.3	29.9	11.6	40.9	55.1	9.9
45 70405	Sumter city	24 012	47.6	78.0	22.5	-1.9	30.2	12.6	0.0	35.0	17.0
46 00000	SOUTH DAKOTA.......	474 359	48.3	84.6	21.5	-2.9	22.3	19.3	8.5	39.2	11.7
46 52980	Rapid City city	37 484	40.1	87.3	26.7	2.3	28.7	7.4	9.0	36.8	8.1
46 59020	Sioux Falls city.............	78 107	40.5	88.5	27.8	3.4	28.8	20.4	7.1	30.7	7.1

[1]Hispanic or Latino persons may be of any race.

City	School enrollment			Population 16 to 19 years				Employment status, 2000			Work status in 1999 of the population 16 years and over		
											Worked in 1999		
	Grades kindergarten through 12	College or graduate school	Percent private	Number	Percent in armed forces	Percent high school graduates	Percent not enrolled, not grads, not in armed forces, not employed	Total population 16 years and over	Percent in labor force	Unemployment rate	Full-time	Part-time	Did not work in 1999
	11	12	13	14	15	16	17	18	19	20	21	22	23
OREGON	621 408	204 811	11.7	191 546	0.1	12.3	5.4	2 673 782	65.2	6.5	53.7	17.2	29.1
Albany city	7 517	2 299	8.9	2 343	0.0	11.1	7.7	31 345	67.1	8.1	54.4	17.2	28.3
Beaverton city	13 804	4 172	12.4	4 057	0.0	14.7	5.3	58 878	72.9	4.5	62.6	15.7	21.8
Bend city	9 154	2 943	10.0	2 564	0.0	16.4	1.8	40 410	68.8	4.3	56.6	18.2	25.3
Corvallis city	6 484	15 006	3.6	4 997	0.0	5.9	0.6	41 406	61.1	5.3	49.3	27.2	23.5
Eugene city	21 034	22 174	7.1	9 422	0.0	10.2	2.9	112 884	65.3	6.2	49.6	23.8	26.6
Gresham city	17 048	4 650	11.4	5 151	0.2	14.4	8.4	67 974	69.3	6.4	57.7	15.8	26.4
Hillsboro city	13 018	3 893	11.6	3 760	0.0	14.1	8.8	52 057	73.7	4.9	63.8	14.2	22.1
Keizer city	6 479	1 441	6.7	1 715	0.0	14.9	7.3	24 277	68.7	7.2	57.7	16.0	26.3
Lake Oswego city	6 999	2 082	13.7	1 731	0.0	4.9	2.1	27 655	68.4	3.2	57.0	17.2	25.8
McMinnville city	4 900	2 142	28.3	1 883	0.0	11.6	7.2	20 314	61.4	8.3	50.6	17.6	31.8
Medford city	11 360	2 500	10.2	3 157	0.3	17.2	6.0	49 032	61.9	7.4	50.4	16.1	33.5
Oregon City city	4 547	1 508	12.0	1 391	0.0	13.4	6.3	19 440	70.2	5.9	59.8	16.8	23.4
Portland city	79 423	41 429	18.4	25 478	0.0	12.4	5.3	429 528	68.8	6.5	57.1	17.0	25.9
Salem city	24 208	8 385	16.4	8 325	0.0	15.0	8.8	105 863	62.5	8.3	53.8	16.2	29.0
Springfield city	9 587	3 010	5.5	2 987	0.0	21.4	6.2	40 006	68.1	8.7	54.4	18.3	27.3
Tigard city	7 238	2 420	13.9	2 021	0.0	13.7	4.7	31 809	72.2	4.7	60.4	16.7	22.8
PENNSYLVANIA	2 228 837	703 163	21.4	672 849	0.1	9.3	4.0	9 693 040	61.9	5.7	51.9	15.2	32.9
Allentown city	19 687	6 180	23.1	5 936	0.0	11.0	10.9	82 784	60.0	7.2	52.4	14.3	33.4
Altoona city	8 447	3 038	11.6	3 521	0.1	11.0	4.0	39 468	59.3	9.1	46.5	16.8	36.7
Bethel Park borough	6 222	1 392	17.8	1 484	0.0	3.8	0.5	26 590	63.6	3.5	52.0	16.0	32.0
Bethlehem city	11 167	8 348	42.7	5 327	0.0	6.6	4.0	58 319	58.9	7.9	49.2	17.0	33.8
Chester city	8 102	2 458	19.3	2 394	0.0	13.6	3.0	26 936	59.0	16.7	49.7	14.3	36.0
Easton city	4 637	3 026	34.4	2 062	0.0	6.5	4.6	20 745	60.3	7.2	56.0	14.8	29.2
Erie city	19 129	6 986	37.2	6 262	0.0	9.8	5.2	80 069	60.8	8.1	49.1	17.2	33.7
Harrisburg city	9 980	1 700	14.0	2 572	0.0	13.5	10.5	36 625	63.6	9.8	57.5	12.0	30.5
Lancaster city	11 303	3 427	20.4	3 795	0.0	10.5	14.1	42 236	63.3	7.8	55.4	14.9	29.7
Municipality of Monroeville borough	4 651	1 284	18.0	1 200	0.0	12.4	1.2	24 004	61.8	3.8	51.0	15.3	33.7
New Castle city	4 506	863	7.2	1 018	0.0	11.6	11.1	20 631	53.2	9.5	43.1	14.2	40.7
Norristown borough	5 641	1 238	17.7	1 638	0.0	15.3	11.7	24 312	66.0	7.0	55.6	12.8	31.6
Philadelphia city	298 504	115 671	32.4	88 916	0.0	10.1	7.4	1 174 798	55.9	10.9	46.7	13.3	40.0
Pittsburgh city	50 034	44 020	31.8	21 955	0.0	8.7	4.4	275 396	58.5	10.1	48.2	16.8	35.0
Plum borough	4 990	1 356	15.5	1 275	0.0	8.0	0.4	20 932	66.7	4.5	54.3	16.0	29.7
Reading city	17 691	3 515	15.0	4 898	0.0	11.0	12.3	59 101	58.4	9.2	52.2	13.0	34.9
Scranton city	12 424	6 470	39.5	4 945	0.0	7.4	3.2	62 472	56.7	7.3	45.9	16.6	37.5
State College borough	1 401	27 314	3.3	6 767	0.2	0.9	0.3	36 520	60.3	9.7	41.9	39.9	18.2
Wilkes-Barre city	6 623	3 866	33.6	2 738	0.0	8.1	4.5	35 568	55.0	8.9	45.4	15.8	38.8
Williamsport city	4 970	3 813	25.5	2 608	0.5	0.8	5.0	24 536	61.3	12.6	50.0	18.5	31.4
York city	8 444	1 745	17.1	2 285	0.0	17.5	11.6	30 390	64.6	9.6	54.6	14.7	30.7
RHODE ISLAND	190 389	84 009	22.7	61 409	0.3	8.7	4.6	827 797	64.6	5.6	52.6	17.4	30.0
Cranston city	13 516	4 771	19.4	4 233	0.0	13.2	7.8	64 096	60.9	4.8	50.2	15.9	33.9
East Providence city	8 134	2 456	19.1	2 068	0.0	10.2	2.7	39 290	62.4	5.5	51.6	15.6	32.8
Newport city	3 809	3 001	37.5	1 740	8.1	13.3	5.7	21 770	70.1	6.8	57.2	18.2	24.7
Pawtucket city	13 994	3 892	18.9	3 684	0.0	16.7	7.9	56 657	63.2	7.1	53.5	13.9	32.6
Providence city	34 614	26 310	37.6	15 673	0.0	6.0	7.3	133 072	57.7	9.3	48.6	18.0	33.4
Warwick city	14 241	4 635	18.1	3 843	0.0	11.3	3.4	69 281	66.5	4.1	53.4	17.0	29.5
Woonsocket city	8 128	1 792	12.8	2 179	0.0	13.9	8.3	33 181	62.2	6.4	50.9	14.8	34.3
SOUTH CAROLINA	767 586	216 839	12.0	235 984	3.0	13.2	6.4	3 114 016	63.4	5.7	55.8	12.8	31.5
Aiken city	4 288	1 748	13.0	1 501	0.4	10.1	6.7	20 262	58.8	6.6	48.8	13.5	37.7
Anderson city	3 961	1 528	19.5	1 301	0.0	10.7	9.7	20 267	54.2	7.9	46.0	12.9	41.1
Charleston city	14 400	14 276	19.3	7 394	0.3	5.5	2.7	78 897	62.2	6.5	52.7	17.0	30.3
Columbia city	17 527	19 625	14.1	11 866	22.3	25.2	6.1	95 695	64.5	8.9	51.7	19.3	29.0
Florence city	5 903	1 290	14.5	1 647	0.0	7.5	7.7	23 587	60.8	7.0	51.0	13.1	35.9
Goose Creek city	6 012	1 739	13.4	3 209	54.7	61.7	1.3	21 327	76.4	3.1	66.1	14.5	19.4
Greenville city	8 613	5 217	33.4	3 355	0.0	9.0	3.4	46 253	65.7	6.5	55.6	15.0	29.4
Hilton Head Island town	4 289	950	24.1	1 070	0.7	19.0	1.8	28 604	55.5	1.8	48.2	14.0	37.8
Mount Pleasant town	8 451	2 323	22.8	1 899	0.7	7.7	3.1	36 578	69.9	2.2	61.3	14.0	24.7
North Charleston city	16 040	4 732	14.7	5 009	2.7	14.8	9.3	59 589	63.8	8.7	56.7	12.7	30.5
Rock Hill city	9 275	5 084	7.8	3 374	0.1	10.9	4.7	38 810	68.0	9.9	57.4	15.6	27.0
Spartanburg city	7 523	2 754	20.3	2 554	0.0	8.3	11.6	30 660	58.9	9.2	49.7	14.7	35.7
Summerville town	6 154	1 443	13.2	1 508	0.0	11.9	3.2	21 103	66.7	4.1	58.4	12.1	29.6
Sumter city	8 189	2 813	16.8	2 475	5.9	16.0	6.1	30 063	61.8	8.1	53.2	13.4	33.3
SOUTH DAKOTA	152 642	42 894	9.7	49 305	0.3	10.2	4.7	577 129	68.4	4.4	57.0	17.4	25.5
Rapid City city	10 831	4 216	10.0	3 844	0.4	13.8	4.0	46 430	68.8	4.7	57.6	17.9	24.5
Sioux Falls city	22 248	7 433	19.9	7 227	0.1	13.4	3.8	96 178	74.8	3.2	63.2	17.1	19.7

Table B-5. Cities — Education, Labor Force, and Income

City	Full-year full-time employed (percent)								Children under 18 years in families (percent, except where noted)						Total employed by class of worker (percent)			
										With two parents		With one parent who is in labor force	+/- U.S. percent of children with no stay-at-home parent	+/- U.S. percent two-income couples				
	Total	Men	Women	Non-Hispanic White	Black or African American	American Indian and Alaska Native	Asian, Hawaiian, and Pacific Islander	Hispanic or Latino[1]	Number	Both in labor force	Father only in labor force				Private	Government	Self-employed	Unpaid family worker
	24	25	26	27	28	29	30	31	32	33	34	35	36	37	38	39	40	41
OREGON	37.3	46.7	28.2	37.6	34.0	34.5	38.5	34.5	796 563	45.7	23.8	20.7	1.8	-0.1	72.5	14.4	12.7	0.4
Albany city	39.3	50.4	29.1	39.8	41.9	25.5	40.1	32.3	10 269	49.3	19.5	21.6	6.3	3.7	75.7	14.9	9.1	0.2
Beaverton city	46.1	57.1	35.6	46.6	50.9	37.0	46.4	42.9	18 371	41.9	29.8	21.3	-1.4	4.7	81.5	9.3	9.1	0.2
Bend city	37.8	47.6	28.5	38.0	21.5	24.2	43.8	35.9	12 259	46.7	23.1	22.3	4.4	4.0	72.6	11.6	15.3	0.5
Corvallis city	27.4	35.8	19.2	28.4	28.2	11.6	20.4	25.0	8 431	48.0	24.1	17.0	0.4	1.9	63.4	29.0	7.4	0.2
Eugene city	32.8	41.0	25.1	33.3	30.7	38.4	22.5	32.3	27 062	44.3	21.7	24.1	3.8	2.4	68.6	18.7	12.4	0.4
Gresham city	41.1	51.3	31.6	42.0	36.8	41.3	45.1	35.1	23 221	43.4	22.9	23.6	2.4	3.9	79.9	11.4	8.5	0.2
Hillsboro city	45.9	56.6	34.5	47.1	55.8	44.4	45.9	39.3	18 831	43.1	31.8	17.2	-4.3	4.5	83.4	9.4	7.0	0.1
Keizer city	40.7	49.5	32.7	42.6	15.5	46.7	40.8	25.1	8 908	49.7	17.9	23.1	8.2	3.4	68.0	22.6	9.2	0.1
Lake Oswego city	44.5	59.4	31.3	44.3	50.8	37.2	46.5	40.9	8 415	46.2	36.8	12.2	-6.2	0.2	68.7	12.6	18.4	0.3
McMinnville city	34.2	44.4	24.7	33.8	56.8	44.7	30.5	36.7	6 473	44.9	24.2	21.8	2.1	-3.3	74.7	16.0	9.0	0.3
Medford city	34.5	44.4	25.7	35.0	47.3	35.5	33.8	28.8	15 267	44.1	20.5	24.9	4.4	-2.1	74.0	12.2	13.6	0.3
Oregon City city	43.7	55.6	32.3	44.0	36.9	40.8	45.2	41.1	6 356	42.0	23.7	25.5	2.9	9.5	75.2	15.3	9.4	0.1
Portland city	39.6	47.0	32.6	40.5	33.0	34.2	38.4	38.6	103 278	42.5	21.2	24.1	2.0	3.4	77.1	11.9	10.7	0.3
Salem city	35.9	42.3	29.5	37.0	26.6	41.0	32.5	28.9	32 129	42.3	20.5	25.1	2.8	0.5	67.7	22.2	9.8	0.3
Springfield city	37.4	47.5	28.0	37.7	42.9	39.8	35.9	33.3	13 288	42.4	16.8	27.8	5.6	2.8	79.0	11.9	8.7	0.4
Tigard city	45.7	57.8	34.5	46.2	38.2	48.0	44.5	42.9	10 161	45.0	25.7	20.9	1.3	5.7	80.6	8.9	10.1	0.4
PENNSYLVANIA	40.0	50.4	30.6	41.0	33.4	34.9	36.7	33.2	2 774 571	45.4	22.7	20.7	1.5	-0.3	80.0	11.3	8.4	0.3
Allentown city	38.4	47.4	30.5	38.8	42.9	32.8	36.0	35.9	24 437	31.8	14.9	33.7	0.9	-5.4	85.7	8.6	5.5	0.2
Altoona city	34.7	44.8	26.1	34.8	30.9	19.0	20.7	36.2	10 796	40.6	18.0	27.8	3.8	-4.0	80.7	12.7	6.3	0.2
Bethel Park borough	42.8	56.5	30.8	43.2	29.5	14.3	29.9	51.8	7 761	54.0	30.8	10.8	0.2	-0.1	81.4	10.6	7.9	0.0
Bethlehem city	35.7	43.1	29.1	36.4	38.7	51.3	20.3	33.2	14 030	42.4	16.3	25.8	3.6	-2.0	85.1	9.3	5.4	0.2
Chester city	32.5	33.2	32.0	25.7	35.7	32.1	24.2	20.8	9 559	21.4	6.4	48.7	5.5	-4.3	82.3	15.3	2.4	0.5
Easton city	38.4	45.5	31.5	39.5	36.9	23.8	28.3	36.1	5 671	32.1	22.4	30.8	-1.7	-0.8	82.3	11.6	5.8	0.3
Erie city	35.8	43.9	28.9	36.6	34.7	22.8	29.1	24.4	24 834	35.0	15.7	34.4	4.8	-1.9	85.7	9.5	4.6	0.2
Harrisburg city	41.0	45.1	37.6	44.4	40.5	24.1	48.1	28.7	12 406	17.9	7.6	49.8	3.1	-4.9	72.8	23.1	4.8	0.2
Lancaster city	40.0	46.5	34.1	41.7	37.8	30.1	38.8	36.7	13 985	29.0	12.9	38.3	2.7	0.2	87.9	7.4	4.6	0.1
Municipality of Monroeville borough	40.9	53.2	30.4	40.2	49.2	42.3	44.6	41.2	5 797	49.5	26.3	18.0	2.9	-1.7	82.5	8.8	8.6	0.1
New Castle city	31.1	39.7	24.2	31.2	29.9	30.4	45.7	43.4	5 940	33.0	16.7	29.2	-2.4	-11.1	80.0	13.1	6.7	0.2
Norristown borough	42.6	50.1	35.7	43.5	41.4	33.3	35.7	45.4	6 819	30.9	12.0	40.5	6.8	2.3	84.9	10.3	4.6	0.2
Philadelphia city	33.2	38.7	28.6	36.5	31.1	25.7	27.3	26.0	343 503	25.3	12.1	37.0	-2.3	-8.4	77.8	16.5	5.5	0.2
Pittsburgh city	33.5	39.6	28.2	35.6	29.5	28.1	22.8	30.6	61 490	30.8	15.0	35.6	1.8	-5.7	80.7	12.5	6.6	0.2
Plum borough	44.3	56.7	32.7	44.1	46.1	X	57.5	31.4	6 617	49.2	30.8	13.9	-1.5	-0.3	84.6	8.4	6.9	0.1
Reading city	35.5	42.1	29.6	38.2	37.8	37.2	33.3	29.7	22 228	24.1	13.5	32.9	-7.6	-10.9	84.8	9.8	5.1	0.2
Scranton city	33.8	43.2	26.0	33.9	33.0	57.4	43.2	28.8	14 951	42.6	18.6	22.3	0.3	-3.6	81.0	12.4	6.1	0.5
State College borough	12.9	15.7	9.9	13.5	13.1	43.2	9.9	7.7	2 015	44.1	21.9	19.7	4.2	0.1	68.6	27.1	3.9	0.4
Wilkes-Barre city	32.6	40.8	25.2	32.9	27.7	0.0	38.2	31.9	8 142	39.7	17.8	28.9	4.0	-2.7	79.9	14.9	5.1	0.2
Williamsport city	34.1	37.9	30.4	34.1	34.4	30.2	31.6	33.8	6 351	33.2	16.9	37.1	5.7	-3.1	83.8	10.4	5.4	0.4
York city	39.0	46.7	32.3	41.1	37.9	42.2	41.7	31.7	10 402	24.7	13.1	43.5	3.6	-2.1	86.2	8.7	5.0	0.1
RHODE ISLAND	40.0	50.2	31.0	41.0	33.8	34.7	34.0	33.0	237 201	46.6	17.0	21.0	3.0	3.3	77.3	13.8	8.7	0.2
Cranston city	39.5	48.5	31.3	40.3	20.4	24.9	37.6	37.8	16 152	52.1	18.0	18.9	6.4	1.4	76.3	14.5	9.0	0.2
East Providence city	40.0	50.5	31.5	40.2	42.6	46.6	44.2	25.6	10 200	48.5	14.1	24.6	8.5	-0.6	81.2	10.8	7.6	0.4
Newport city	41.7	53.6	31.1	42.4	35.5	36.8	49.8	31.6	4 947	36.7	16.1	33.9	6.0	6.0	72.6	14.4	12.7	0.2
Pawtucket city	40.9	49.5	33.5	40.9	39.8	61.7	45.8	40.2	17 380	38.5	12.1	26.9	0.8	-0.3	84.5	10.1	5.2	0.2
Providence city	30.7	37.4	24.8	31.4	31.1	27.4	26.1	29.9	42 020	25.0	12.3	28.4	-11.2	-6.0	82.1	11.6	5.9	0.4
Warwick city	43.6	54.8	33.8	43.5	46.7	49.4	36.1	44.7	18 079	54.7	17.7	19.0	9.1	4.1	78.7	13.3	7.9	0.1
Woonsocket city	39.2	49.5	30.3	39.8	39.3	29.6	44.0	26.4	10 622	32.6	15.2	24.4	-7.6	0.3	86.1	8.6	5.1	0.2
SOUTH CAROLINA	41.7	51.0	33.2	44.2	35.8	42.5	40.3	39.8	937 333	41.4	18.6	25.8	2.6	0.1	75.0	15.9	8.8	0.3
Aiken city	36.4	47.7	27.1	38.3	30.8	75.0	32.9	46.7	5 297	43.3	20.1	26.7	5.4	-4.2	71.1	21.1	7.8	0.0
Anderson city	33.3	41.9	26.4	33.1	33.5	0.0	40.8	34.1	4 959	25.5	19.4	36.9	-2.2	-7.5	76.4	13.9	9.4	0.3
Charleston city	36.5	44.3	29.9	39.6	29.5	50.7	34.2	43.6	17 802	36.0	16.9	30.9	2.3	1.9	68.5	21.8	9.4	0.3
Columbia city	34.0	39.3	29.0	37.6	30.0	38.9	24.7	34.3	20 429	29.6	17.8	37.5	2.5	-2.7	64.4	28.0	7.3	0.2
Florence city	37.9	48.2	29.9	43.8	29.4	18.2	50.0	44.0	7 015	33.0	13.8	35.8	4.2	-0.7	73.0	18.2	8.6	0.1
Goose Creek city	48.4	58.5	36.4	49.5	48.9	35.7	39.8	39.9	8 279	49.1	26.7	15.6	0.1	6.2	71.2	20.4	8.2	0.1
Greenville city	39.2	48.0	31.5	41.7	33.2	45.9	43.2	44.0	10 216	31.9	17.1	33.8	1.1	-0.4	82.2	9.0	8.5	0.3
Hilton Head Island town	36.0	45.9	25.9	34.5	42.3	32.3	40.1	42.9	5 465	42.9	26.6	18.4	-3.3	-14.8	72.2	7.5	20.0	0.3
Mount Pleasant town	49.4	63.2	37.2	50.0	38.1	86.8	51.3	53.0	11 692	45.4	34.2	13.9	-5.3	4.8	65.6	19.7	14.3	0.3
North Charleston city	40.3	47.5	33.3	42.9	37.4	38.2	42.7	39.9	20 167	28.2	13.8	36.5	0.1	-4.8	74.6	18.7	6.3	0.3
Rock Hill city	42.1	52.9	33.5	42.9	40.5	61.5	37.9	41.0	11 599	41.0	14.4	32.3	8.7	4.2	81.0	12.4	6.5	0.2
Spartanburg city	33.8	44.3	26.2	34.2	32.8	47.1	44.1	32.3	8 891	25.7	14.0	39.6	0.7	-3.9	78.4	13.9	7.5	0.3
Summerville town	44.9	57.9	33.6	47.4	35.9	56.8	44.4	29.4	7 664	42.3	21.9	21.0	-1.3	3.4	73.5	19.6	6.8	0.2
Sumter city	38.2	50.3	28.1	42.0	33.3	22.0	43.2	48.4	10 328	39.2	18.1	28.4	3.0	-2.4	69.4	21.1	9.0	0.4
SOUTH DAKOTA	42.8	51.7	34.2	44.3	33.4	24.6	39.4	38.4	191 501	57.8	13.4	19.5	12.7	10.7	69.2	15.3	14.7	0.8
Rapid City city	41.8	50.4	33.7	43.7	32.4	20.9	31.9	45.3	14 090	47.8	14.2	27.1	10.3	8.9	75.8	15.0	9.1	0.1
Sioux Falls city	49.6	57.1	42.6	50.8	35.2	22.3	48.9	40.2	29 764	60.2	13.3	20.0	15.6	16.8	83.8	8.4	7.5	0.3

[1] Hispanic or Latino persons may be of any race.

City	Percent who worked at home	Percent of the population 5 years and over with a disability	Veterans as a percent of the population 18 years and over	Occupation for employed population 16 years and over (percent)						Industry for employed population 16 years and over (percent)					
				Management, professional, and related occupations	Service occupations	Sales and office occupations	Farming, fishing, and forestry occupations	Construction, extraction, and maintenance occupations	Production, transportation and material moving occupations	Agriculture, forestry, fishing, and mining	Construction and manufacturing	Wholesale and retail trade	Transportation and warehousing, and utilities	Service industries	Public administration
	42	43	44	45	46	47	48	49	50	51	52	53	54	55	56
OREGON	5.0	18.8	15.1	33.1	15.3	26.1	1.7	9.1	14.7	3.2	21.3	16.5	4.7	49.9	4.4
Albany city..................	3.5	19.8	15.9	28.5	16.9	24.8	1.3	9.8	18.7	2.8	26.2	15.4	4.5	47.0	4.2
Beaverton city	4.5	14.8	11.0	43.3	12.7	27.8	0.3	5.5	10.3	0.3	21.8	16.6	3.8	55.1	2.3
Bend city	5.7	15.5	14.2	33.9	14.7	27.3	0.6	12.2	11.4	1.3	20.8	17.7	2.6	54.7	2.8
Corvallis city	3.4	12.8	9.5	48.5	16.4	20.7	1.1	5.0	8.3	2.0	17.3	11.1	1.3	65.2	3.2
Eugene city	4.7	16.4	12.4	39.3	14.7	27.0	0.5	6.6	11.9	0.8	16.8	17.2	3.2	59.0	3.1
Gresham city	3.3	18.2	13.8	26.1	16.5	30.2	1.1	10.1	15.9	1.3	21.0	18.7	6.4	49.1	3.6
Hillsboro city	3.0	15.2	11.4	37.6	12.9	24.9	2.0	8.7	13.9	1.4	34.6	15.3	3.3	42.9	2.6
Keizer city...................	3.8	17.0	17.0	32.2	16.2	28.0	2.2	8.7	12.7	2.8	18.5	14.8	4.1	47.9	11.9
Lake Oswego city.........	7.3	10.6	12.7	57.3	6.8	28.6	0.2	2.7	4.3	0.3	14.7	18.0	3.6	59.6	3.8
McMinnville city	2.8	19.1	14.9	25.3	17.6	26.1	3.1	8.9	19.0	3.3	22.7	17.7	4.9	45.6	5.8
Medford city................	3.5	20.7	18.0	29.2	17.5	29.3	1.4	8.9	13.8	2.0	16.4	21.7	3.9	52.4	3.6
Oregon City city	3.8	18.2	14.5	28.3	16.2	29.2	0.2	11.7	14.4	0.8	22.5	18.2	5.5	46.8	6.2
Portland city................	4.3	19.1	11.9	37.2	15.0	26.5	0.2	7.0	14.0	0.4	17.9	16.1	5.5	56.6	3.4
Salem city...................	3.8	20.1	14.2	32.6	16.7	27.0	2.5	7.9	13.2	2.9	17.0	14.9	3.2	50.5	11.5
Springfield city.............	3.5	22.4	14.4	21.5	18.5	27.8	1.0	10.5	20.7	1.4	23.7	19.1	4.2	47.9	3.5
Tigard city...................	4.5	14.2	12.4	38.3	12.7	31.2	0.2	6.4	11.1	0.7	21.0	18.3	4.0	53.4	2.7
PENNSYLVANIA........	3.0	18.6	13.7	32.6	14.8	27.0	0.5	8.9	16.3	1.3	22.0	15.7	5.4	51.5	4.2
Allentown city...............	1.9	22.3	11.6	24.8	18.0	27.6	0.2	8.1	21.3	0.3	24.8	15.9	4.6	51.5	2.9
Altoona city..................	1.1	23.2	16.1	24.3	19.7	28.8	0.2	10.3	16.8	0.2	17.6	20.3	6.0	51.4	4.6
Bethel Park borough	2.8	13.2	14.9	45.5	9.8	30.5	0.1	7.0	7.1	0.6	14.4	16.7	5.5	59.5	3.3
Bethlehem city..............	2.0	19.5	12.3	33.0	17.2	27.3	0.1	6.7	15.7	0.2	20.5	13.9	3.7	59.0	2.7
Chester city	1.3	23.5	11.1	21.9	30.9	24.7	0.0	5.8	16.7	0.0	15.5	12.2	6.0	61.3	5.0
Easton city..................	1.4	18.1	10.6	24.5	18.3	24.4	0.1	9.4	23.3	0.6	27.2	14.3	4.8	49.6	3.5
Erie city	1.3	21.4	13.3	25.1	20.2	27.2	0.4	6.7	20.5	0.6	24.9	15.2	3.0	52.8	3.4
Harrisburg city..............	1.9	25.5	12.8	25.0	20.1	80.8	0.4	5.5	18.1	0.4	11.3	13.5	6.9	52.5	15.3
Lancaster city...............	2.0	23.7	9.3	21.4	19.3	24.6	0.5	7.0	27.2	0.5	28.4	16.8	3.4	48.9	2.1
Municipality of Monroeville borough...	2.6	16.4	14.7	42.7	13.7	29.1	0.0	6.5	8.0	0.0	13.0	10.9	0.0	60.1	3.3
New Castle city.............	2.3	24.4	14.6	24.6	18.7	29.8	0.2	8.7	18.2	0.4	22.0	17.6	6.5	47.6	5.9
Norristown borough.......	1.1	20.4	12.8	23.8	22.6	27.9	0.3	9.8	15.5	0.6	19.1	16.3	4.2	56.2	3.5
Philadelphia city...........	1.9	25.3	10.9	31.5	19.7	29.6	0.1	6.5	12.5	0.1	12.7	13.4	5.9	60.4	7.4
Pittsburgh city..............	2.4	21.2	12.5	36.9	19.9	27.5	0.1	6.2	9.3	0.2	10.4	12.5	4.6	67.9	4.5
Plum borough...............	2.4	14.0	14.3	36.9	13.2	29.8	0.1	9.3	10.7	0.4	18.6	19.1	4.7	54.5	2.7
Reading city	1.4	25.3	10.8	17.7	18.4	25.8	2.2	6.4	29.7	2.6	30.1	15.6	4.5	44.5	2.6
Scranton city................	1.5	24.7	13.6	25.0	18.2	00.0	0.1	7.6	18.2	0.3	20.1	17.2	5.3	52.6	4.6
State College borough ..	2.9	6.4	3.7	48.1	23.5	22.3	0.4	1.7	4.1	0.6	4.3	9.5	0.7	82.6	2.3
Wilkes-Barre city	1.5	26.1	16.3	24.1	18.3	30.8	0.1	8.4	18.2	0.5	17.5	17.2	4.4	53.4	7.0
Williamsport city	1.3	23.9	12.7	23.7	21.1	26.9	0.2	6.9	21.2	0.2	24.2	17.1	2.1	52.6	4.0
York city	1.4	25.7	11.3	19.0	19.3	25.0	0.6	7.0	29.1	0.6	30.9	16.4	3.2	44.9	3.8
RHODE ISLAND	2.2	20.2	12.8	33.9	15.7	27.1	0.3	7.7	15.2	0.5	21.9	15.5	3.9	53.8	4.5
Cranston city	1.8	21.1	13.0	35.0	15.4	29.4	0.1	6.8	13.4	0.1	19.4	16.9	4.0	53.7	5.9
East Providence city	1.9	22.0	12.9	28.4	15.9	29.4	0.3	8.2	17.7	0.2	24.6	15.2	4.5	52.4	3.1
Newport city	4.3	17.5	12.7	39.0	20.4	25.6	0.6	6.1	8.2	0.7	12.7	13.4	3.7	64.5	5.0
Pawtucket city	1.3	25.9	11.6	23.2	14.9	27.6	0.2	8.1	26.0	0.2	30.3	16.7	4.0	45.2	3.7
Providence city.............	2.5	23.1	7.1	32.9	17.8	23.7	0.2	5.2	20.2	0.2	21.4	11.9	2.5	60.3	3.5
Warwick city	1.8	19.5	15.5	33.6	15.4	30.0	0.3	7.6	13.1	0.4	20.0	16.7	5.3	53.2	4.4
Woonsocket city	1.2	26.3	14.4	20.4	17.1	28.3	0.1	9.5	24.7	0.3	30.3	20.6	4.0	42.1	2.8
SOUTH CAROLINA ...	2.1	22.2	14.0	29.1	14.7	25.2	0.6	11.5	19.0	1.1	27.7	15.2	5.0	46.2	4.7
Aiken city....................	1.9	19.7	16.0	45.9	13.4	21.1	0.5	5.4	13.8	0.7	18.7	12.1	12.4	50.9	5.1
Anderson city...............	2.2	27.7	13.5	29.1	17.4	24.9	0.1	8.8	19.7	0.2	26.4	17.2	3.4	49.2	3.5
Charleston city	2.7	19.5	13.1	40.5	19.1	25.9	0.4	6.8	7.3	0.4	11.4	14.9	3.8	64.5	4.9
Columbia city...............	2.7	20.5	11.3	41.0	17.7	26.3	0.3	5.9	8.8	0.4	10.1	12.4	3.1	64.5	9.5
Florence city................	1.4	23.6	12.9	37.4	15.9	25.1	0.1	8.0	13.4	0.2	19.7	13.9	3.8	57.4	4.9
Goose Creek city	0.9	18.7	18.2	31.7	13.4	29.4	0.0	12.4	13.2	0.3	20.8	14.8	7.2	48.8	8.1
Greenville city..............	2.4	20.2	10.4	37.8	17.7	24.7	0.3	6.8	12.6	0.4	19.9	14.8	2.8	59.8	2.1
Hilton Head Island town	5.9	14.6	18.1	34.3	18.5	27.5	0.4	14.2	5.1	0.3	20.0	15.1	2.0	60.0	2.6
Mount Pleasant town	4.3	14.6	14.5	50.9	11.8	25.9	0.3	5.6	5.5	0.3	13.7	14.7	4.7	62.1	4.5
North Charleston city	1.0	24.8	16.9	21.1	21.7	28.4	0.3	12.5	16.0	0.4	18.3	17.4	6.5	50.6	6.9
Rock Hill city	1.9	21.3	11.8	30.1	15.5	27.3	0.2	8.3	18.7	0.3	25.2	17.3	4.3	50.2	2.6
Spartanburg city...........	2.4	25.5	11.7	32.3	17.5	24.2	0.2	6.6	19.2	0.3	26.0	15.0	2.7	53.5	2.6
Summerville town..........	2.0	19.8	20.9	36.3	12.6	26.6	0.5	10.1	13.9	1.1	22.0	15.2	6.1	48.9	6.8
Sumter city	1.5	24.4	15.3	31.5	15.7	26.3	0.4	6.9	19.2	0.9	26.5	15.0	2.8	48.7	6.0
SOUTH DAKOTA.......	6.5	16.7	14.4	32.6	15.6	26.5	1.9	9.1	14.2	8.1	17.3	15.3	4.7	49.8	4.8
Rapid City city	2.4	17.9	17.0	32.8	17.1	29.5	0.4	8.6	11.5	1.1	15.6	17.6	3.7	56.7	5.2
Sioux Falls city	2.7	16.2	12.8	31.1	13.2	33.2	0.3	7.8	14.4	0.8	17.5	17.4	4.4	57.0	2.9

City	Median house-hold income	Median family income — All families	Median family income — Families with children — Married-couple	Median family income — Families with children — Male house-holder	Median family income — Families with children — Female house-holder	Median nonfamily house-hold income	Median income for full-year, full-time workers — Men	Median income for full-year, full-time workers — Women	Per capita income	Households by source of income (percent) — With earnings	With interest, dividend, or rental income	With Social Security income	With public assis-tance income	With retire-ment income	House-holds with income over $100,000 (percent)	+/- U.S. percent for income over $100,000	House-holds with income below poverty (percent)	Families with children with income below poverty (percent)
	57	58	59	60	61	62	63	64	65	66	67	68	69	70	71	72	73	74
OREGON	40 916	48 680	56 294	29 546	19 921	25 761	37 680	27 915	20 940	80.2	39.6	25.8	3.6	17.2	10.0	-2.3	10.8	12.4
Albany city	39 409	46 094	53 872	28 341	18 596	23 113	37 336	25 242	18 570	79.3	37.0	25.6	3.6	16.2	6.6	-5.7	10.9	14.3
Beaverton city	47 863	60 289	68 110	30 000	27 649	32 553	42 465	31 871	25 419	88.7	43.0	15.6	2.7	11.4	15.2	2.9	6.7	7.8
Bend city	40 857	49 387	57 358	24 937	19 006	26 642	34 405	25 919	21 624	81.3	40.5	22.5	3.2	16.1	9.5	-2.8	9.1	11.0
Corvallis city	35 236	53 208	61 602	28 068	17 346	21 318	41 902	30 084	19 317	83.5	48.7	18.4	2.0	13.3	9.8	-2.5	20.0	13.8
Eugene city	35 850	48 527	59 697	28 844	18 360	22 100	36 526	27 811	21 315	80.8	43.0	22.1	2.9	14.9	9.6	-2.7	17.3	13.7
Gresham city	43 442	51 126	60 077	30 316	20 827	27 308	38 921	28 978	19 588	84.3	34.0	20.5	4.4	15.7	8.8	-3.5	10.0	13.7
Hillsboro city	51 737	57 379	62 054	27 346	24 032	36 207	41 733	31 026	21 680	90.0	37.9	14.8	2.5	11.0	12.9	0.6	7.6	9.2
Keizer city	45 052	49 977	58 424	28 792	23 292	27 226	38 378	28 052	20 119	82.8	36.5	24.3	3.2	18.7	9.1	-3.2	8.3	9.1
Lake Oswego city	71 597	94 587	110 655	51 094	40 943	39 680	70 672	42 264	42 166	84.7	58.9	20.0	0.8	16.2	35.2	22.9	4.0	2.4
McMinnville city	38 953	44 013	50 581	32 917	19 615	22 184	35 336	25 406	17 085	75.7	35.2	29.6	3.1	18.8	6.4	-5.9	12.3	12.7
Medford city	36 481	43 972	51 276	21 559	15 855	22 631	35 756	24 341	20 170	73.8	38.8	32.1	5.0	19.1	8.2	-4.1	12.4	17.1
Oregon City city	45 531	51 597	57 214	32 308	20 724	28 438	39 462	30 098	19 870	86.3	34.0	19.9	4.8	14.0	7.8	-4.5	8.4	10.1
Portland city	40 146	50 271	58 697	30 476	21 642	28 877	36 068	30 255	22 643	82.1	39.7	21.8	4.3	13.9	10.2	-2.1	11.9	13.2
Salem city	38 881	46 409	53 619	30 128	19 625	25 856	35 630	27 521	19 141	79.0	37.1	26.1	4.5	18.3	8.0	-4.3	12.3	16.3
Springfield city	33 031	38 399	45 593	28 138	13 460	20 932	31 441	23 805	15 616	81.9	29.9	22.9	6.3	13.5	4.0	-8.3	16.5	22.2
Tigard city	51 581	61 656	69 558	35 408	22 355	32 123	45 548	31 874	25 110	85.6	45.0	20.0	2.3	14.3	15.8	3.5	5.6	7.6
PENNSYLVANIA	40 106	49 184	60 167	29 595	19 585	22 205	38 176	27 365	20 880	76.7	40.4	30.4	3.1	19.7	10.3	-2.0	11.0	12.1
Allentown city	32 016	37 356	45 535	25 617	15 966	22 489	30 985	24 604	16 282	74.9	32.3	30.3	5.2	18.1	4.9	-7.4	15.6	23.7
Altoona city	28 248	36 758	43 431	22 052	12 368	15 457	29 890	21 621	15 213	71.3	32.8	34.9	4.6	16.6	3.4	-8.9	17.0	20.8
Bethel Park borough	53 791	64 390	75 762	39 773	31 250	28 377	50 430	33 912	25 867	77.9	57.0	33.8	0.8	22.9	15.8	3.5	3.9	3.7
Bethlehem city	35 815	45 354	57 760	27 614	17 305	22 260	36 416	26 652	18 987	72.0	41.5	35.1	3.4	23.3	7.4	-4.9	13.0	17.6
Chester city	25 703	30 336	43 697	27 147	16 851	15 474	30 198	24 509	13 052	72.9	13.9	28.8	9.6	14.8	4.2	-8.1	26.1	30.7
Easton city	33 162	38 704	45 816	26 615	16 324	22 972	33 153	24 622	15 949	79.0	25.1	26.2	3.4	13.4	4.3	-8.0	16.0	18.2
Erie city	28 387	36 446	45 801	24 240	14 646	17 369	31 335	22 302	14 972	74.5	34.1	30.1	6.4	18.1	3.1	-9.2	17.6	22.2
Harrisburg city	26 920	29 556	45 734	22 356	16 169	22 174	28 506	25 190	15 787	78.8	19.6	22.3	7.6	16.7	4.3	-8.0	22.3	32.1
Lancaster city	29 770	34 623	43 663	24 048	16 076	21 819	28 628	22 442	13 955	80.8	26.1	24.1	6.7	12.3	3.2	-9.1	18.8	24.9
Municipality of Monroeville borough	44 653	53 474	67 572	35 104	24 826	26 499	42 243	30 894	24 031	77.8	47.2	33.0	1.3	22.2	12.4	0.1	6.5	8.6
New Castle city	25 598	32 539	40 565	23 438	10 375	14 505	30 661	21 600	13 730	67.6	29.3	40.1	8.0	19.6	3.1	-9.2	19.6	29.4
Norristown borough	35 714	42 357	58 238	22 056	21 176	25 716	32 787	27 633	17 977	80.2	22.6	26.0	7.5	14.3	6.0	-6.3	15.3	20.3
Philadelphia city	30 746	37 036	56 212	24 017	17 875	20 323	35 342	29 239	16 509	71.8	24.3	28.5	8.7	17.4	6.3	-6.0	21.8	26.0
Pittsburgh city	28 588	38 795	53 856	25 420	15 353	19 101	33 328	26 122	18 816	72.4	32.6	30.0	5.5	17.3	7.0	-5.3	20.3	24.2
Plum borough	48 386	52 807	62 524	30 089	25 637	30 458	41 672	28 514	20 863	82.2	44.5	26.9	2.0	17.9	9.9	-2.4	5.3	5.4
Reading city	26 698	31 067	40 893	22 683	15 305	17 107	28 784	22 596	13 086	74.6	23.2	28.8	7.9	15.0	3.4	-8.9	23.6	31.4
Scranton city	28 805	39 233	49 179	25 270	14 483	16 633	31 735	22 323	16 174	68.6	35.9	40.0	4.0	19.8	4.1	-8.2	15.0	16.9
State College borough	21 186	54 949	70 185	25 972	26 397	16 416	35 609	28 886	12 155	85.5	42.2	12.1	1.0	10.2	6.7	-5.6	40.2	11.2
Wilkes-Barre city	26 711	36 630	47 188	23 359	13 989	15 680	29 738	23 257	15 050	67.2	33.7	37.1	4.3	20.5	3.3	-9.0	18.0	19.9
Williamsport city	25 946	33 844	40 452	19 920	15 530	15 755	27 060	21 105	14 707	75.1	30.0	30.5	5.3	14.7	4.5	-7.8	21.3	22.2
York city	26 475	30 762	41 065	23 203	14 280	19 533	26 956	20 976	13 439	78.1	23.2	26.8	6.2	12.8	2.0	-10.3	21.7	29.3
RHODE ISLAND	42 090	52 781	63 706	29 776	17 252	23 561	39 202	28 472	21 688	77.4	37.0	27.9	4.6	17.4	11.5	-0.8	12.4	14.2
Cranston city	44 108	55 241	66 379	38 125	24 538	24 752	40 838	29 444	21 978	75.5	40.9	32.8	3.3	19.7	11.2	-1.1	8.4	8.4
East Providence city	39 108	48 463	56 955	35 688	19 504	22 016	35 124	27 315	19 527	74.2	35.4	33.8	3.8	20.3	6.3	-6.0	10.2	10.2
Newport city	40 669	54 116	64 702	23 333	13 301	30 073	40 745	28 375	25 441	79.1	39.8	23.0	6.2	18.0	12.5	0.2	13.6	22.4
Pawtucket city	31 775	39 038	50 677	24 409	13 475	19 906	31 697	24 168	17 008	73.6	27.3	28.1	6.7	14.1	5.1	-7.2	17.4	22.7
Providence city	26 867	32 058	44 002	19 719	12 933	18 130	30 041	24 363	15 525	74.2	25.6	22.3	10.2	10.6	7.0	-5.3	27.9	34.3
Warwick city	46 483	56 225	64 870	39 273	25 452	27 221	40 274	30 144	23 410	77.2	38.6	31.3	2.6	19.7	10.3	-2.0	6.7	6.1
Woonsocket city	30 819	38 353	49 369	23 281	11 156	19 256	31 904	25 373	16 223	72.1	25.1	27.4	9.1	14.1	4.4	-7.9	19.0	26.8
SOUTH CAROLINA	37 082	44 227	53 649	27 291	17 982	21 508	33 279	24 187	18 795	79.9	27.2	26.5	2.5	17.9	8.1	-4.2	14.1	15.7
Aiken city	44 172	56 033	70 785	25 982	15 373	24 745	51 847	26 852	23 172	73.4	41.9	31.8	2.7	24.2	14.3	2.0	13.5	18.2
Anderson city	27 716	39 176	53 410	18 214	14 325	16 364	30 646	22 455	18 577	68.6	27.7	36.2	3.1	20.2	6.4	-5.9	20.9	24.0
Charleston city	35 295	48 705	65 166	33 500	15 586	24 253	35 053	27 810	22 414	78.1	33.9	24.3	2.1	18.7	11.3	-1.0	18.7	20.6
Columbia city	31 141	39 589	59 560	23 241	14 975	23 230	31 456	25 400	18 853	80.4	29.2	22.6	3.2	14.9	9.5	-2.8	20.6	24.7
Florence city	35 388	42 250	62 386	23 814	14 233	22 320	36 352	24 418	20 336	77.3	29.9	27.9	3.7	16.7	9.9	-2.4	17.9	22.0
Goose Creek city	45 919	47 937	51 163	37 931	20 577	30 926	33 701	24 147	16 905	91.4	30.4	14.1	1.5	17.0	7.5	-4.8	6.6	7.8
Greenville city	33 144	44 125	66 418	29 196	16 088	24 343	36 181	26 096	23 242	78.0	30.0	26.3	2.2	13.2	11.6	-0.7	15.9	19.4
Hilton Head Island town	60 438	71 211	71 595	41 000	24 375	40 234	40 448	31 216	36 621	71.9	56.2	38.5	1.2	28.6	25.3	13.0	5.5	9.8
Mount Pleasant town	61 054	71 165	82 093	53 365	31 295	39 408	51 496	32 323	30 823	86.0	46.9	18.2	0.8	17.1	21.8	9.5	5.0	4.2
North Charleston city	29 307	32 868	43 427	25 941	13 036	22 529	27 377	21 284	14 361	81.7	18.6	21.8	3.6	18.1	3.3	-9.0	20.5	28.0
Rock Hill city	37 336	45 697	59 688	27 835	21 774	24 191	32 872	25 065	18 929	82.3	27.1	23.3	2.9	14.3	8.2	-4.1	13.8	13.3
Spartanburg city	28 735	36 108	54 904	26 375	13 395	18 947	31 401	23 864	18 136	73.7	23.6	32.7	4.2	16.7	7.0	-5.3	21.9	30.8
Summerville town	43 635	51 469	57 533	26 184	20 607	24 673	39 934	26 257	20 103	82.7	30.5	22.4	1.9	20.9	9.9	-2.4	9.2	8.5
Sumter city	31 590	38 668	47 248	25 239	18 826	17 282	28 398	23 161	16 949	76.3	28.7	30.1	3.9	18.8	7.5	-4.8	16.6	18.7
SOUTH DAKOTA	35 282	43 237	50 872	24 255	17 977	20 672	30 723	22 172	17 562	81.4	41.0	28.0	3.0	12.7	5.9	-6.4	12.5	13.9
Rapid City city	35 978	44 818	56 060	23 393	16 733	22 807	32 344	22 601	19 445	81.2	39.7	26.7	3.6	16.3	7.1	-5.2	11.8	16.3
Sioux Falls city	41 221	51 516	60 097	27 176	21 600	25 306	33 594	25 483	21 374	86.0	39.4	22.1	2.3	12.3	9.1	-3.2	8.1	8.9

Table B-5. Cities — Education, Labor Force, and Income

STATE Place code	City	High school graduates			College graduates		College graduates (percent)				
		Total population 25 years and over	Percent with a high school diploma or less	Percent with a high school diploma or more	Percent with a bachelor's degree or more	+/− U.S. percent with bachelor's degree or more	Non-Hispanic White	Black or African American	American Indian and Alaska Native	Asian, Hawaiian, and Pacific Islander	Hispanic or Latino[1]
		1	2	3	4	5	6	7	8	9	10
47 00000	TENNESSEE............	3 744 928	55.7	75.9	19.6	−4.8	20.5	12.9	14.8	46.7	14.1
47 03440	Bartlett city	25 915	34.4	93.2	28.2	3.8	27.9	28.7	20.0	45.7	34.2
47 14000	Chattanooga city	104 198	49.5	77.6	21.5	−2.9	27.0	9.3	25.1	51.0	16.3
47 15160	Clarksville city	59 579	43.4	85.3	19.8	−4.6	23.1	10.6	3.0	17.8	15.6
47 15400	Cleveland city	23 295	49.1	76.0	22.3	−2.1	22.6	11.1	0.0	42.4	30.5
47 16420	Collierville town	19 498	25.7	93.2	41.2	16.8	43.1	20.4	21.2	41.4	26.7
47 16540	Columbia city	21 381	58.4	75.9	15.1	−9.3	17.4	6.9	0.0	66.7	5.8
47 27740	Franklin city	27 052	29.5	89.3	42.3	17.9	46.7	14.6	22.9	56.0	10.4
47 28960	Germantown city	24 765	13.0	98.0	60.0	35.6	60.1	57.6	45.0	66.4	43.3
47 33280	Hendersonville city	26 891	38.5	89.2	26.4	2.0	26.2	29.0	24.4	46.1	16.1
47 37640	Jackson city	36 686	51.0	77.7	22.7	−1.7	29.8	11.5	22.5	57.8	10.7
47 38320	Johnson City city	36 756	44.4	78.8	29.4	5.0	29.6	16.9	73.9	75.4	20.6
47 39560	Kingsport city	31 971	50.6	76.5	23.6	−0.8	24.1	12.7	0.0	64.6	22.1
47 40000	Knoxville city	110 317	49.9	78.4	24.6	0.2	26.0	10.5	21.4	62.6	26.4
47 48000	Memphis city	398 824	51.6	76.4	20.9	−3.5	33.2	11.3	13.2	47.5	12.6
47 51560	Murfreesboro city	39 243	41.7	83.4	30.8	6.4	33.0	19.2	13.8	38.6	11.9
47 52004	Nashville-Davidson........	377 734	43.1	81.5	30.5	6.1	34.1	20.2	15.9	50.0	14.4
47 55120	Oak Ridge city	19 456	34.4	89.3	37.9	13.5	39.1	18.7	24.5	71.3	31.0
47 69420	Smyrna town	15 690	52.8	79.9	19.8	−4.6	20.2	12.5	24.1	57.8	6.4
48 00000	TEXAS................	12 790 893	49.2	75.7	23.2	−1.2	30.0	15.3	15.7	47.2	8.9
48 01000	Abilene city	68 635	48.3	79.1	22.0	−2.4	26.6	11.9	15.8	27.7	5.7
48 01924	Allen city....................	26 169	19.0	95.6	47.5	23.1	47.9	50.9	34.7	60.0	32.3
48 03000	Amarillo city	107 811	46.3	79.3	20.5	−3.9	24.6	7.8	17.0	23.7	5.4
48 04000	Arlington city...............	203 373	36.0	84.9	30.4	6.0	34.5	27.0	15.3	36.3	12.5
48 05000	Austin city,..................	401 137	33.6	83.4	40.4	16.0	52.4	19.0	26.9	66.3	15.5
48 06128	Baytown city	39 284	50.2	72.0	13.6	−10.8	19.0	6.8	21.3	34.7	3.6
48 07000	Beaumont city	71 188	49.2	80.6	21.5	−2.9	31.3	9.0	4.5	53.0	11.7
48 07132	Bedford city	32 109	27.0	93.4	36.2	10.8	35.9	31.8	16.8	48.3	21.3
48 08236	Big Spring city	16 857	62.6	67.8	11.1	−13.3	17.6	12.8	0.0	44.1	2.7
48 10768	Brownsville city	76 081	65.5	51.7	13.4	−11.0	33.0	35.1	2.9	55.4	10.8
48 10912	Bryan city	36 005	50.4	72.8	26.0	1.6	37.3	7.9	9.2	72.7	7.9
48 13024	Carrollton city	70 088	31.0	86.4	37.0	12.6	42.4	39.2	19.4	34.7	14.0
48 13492	Cedar Hill city	19 362	33.9	89.8	28.3	3.9	26.8	33.7	23.8	43.2	16.4
48 13552	Cedar Park city	15 668	25.3	93.7	36.6	12.2	34.9	60.4	33.3	64.4	35.3
48 15364	Cleburne city	16 338	59.2	72.5	14.0	−10.4	16.3	9.0	6.3	32.5	2.7
48 15976	College Station city	23 301	18.4	93.8	58.1	33.7	59.2	20.0	43.8	82.3	43.9
48 16432	Conroe city..................	21 294	58.2	66.8	18.3	−6.1	25.3	10.1	0.0	13.7	4.5
48 16612	Coppell city	21 984	13.0	96.6	62.6	38.2	63.9	63.3	40.0	63.3	47.7
48 16624	Copperas Cove city.......	15 944	38.4	91.6	17.1	−7.3	19.1	13.0	12.5	23.2	9.2
48 17000	Corpus Christi city........	170 242	48.9	75.8	19.6	−4.8	29.9	14.0	10.2	43.6	10.0
48 19000	Dallas city...................	734 162	49.3	70.4	27.7	3.3	47.5	13.5	17.0	50.0	6.5
48 19624	Deer Park city	17 442	44.2	88.5	16.5	−7.9	17.8	18.6	6.8	18.7	8.3
48 19792	Del Rio city..................	20 307	67.5	57.3	13.6	−10.8	27.6	26.0	14.5	54.8	9.4
48 19972	Denton city	43 912	36.9	83.2	35.5	11.1	40.0	19.6	37.9	69.6	10.9
48 20092	DeSoto city	24 327	33.7	88.4	30.2	5.8	31.1	30.4	0.0	45.8	18.1
48 21628	Duncanville city	22 880	39.1	85.9	27.5	3.1	29.9	27.5	48.0	44.4	9.6
48 22660	Edinburg city	26 395	59.4	61.2	19.4	−5.0	38.7	13.9	0.0	78.0	15.8
48 24000	El Paso city	334 043	53.9	68.6	18.3	−6.1	36.1	21.7	14.2	40.9	12.0
48 24768	Euless city	30 238	35.5	88.5	29.5	5.1	31.7	25.1	19.7	37.8	14.8
48 25452	Farmers Branch city......	18 148	45.8	76.2	27.2	2.8	35.0	38.1	30.9	39.3	6.0
48 26232	Flower Mound town.......	31 330	14.5	97.4	53.1	28.7	53.2	57.5	20.4	68.8	46.7
48 27000	Fort Worth city.............	324 605	51.3	72.8	22.3	−2.1	32.4	11.4	16.0	35.7	6.7
48 27648	Friendswood city	18 407	25.7	92.4	38.6	14.2	40.0	28.5	30.4	46.7	26.7
48 27684	Frisco city	21 616	18.8	94.5	49.8	25.4	51.8	47.0	58.7	73.9	25.5
48 28068	Galveston city...............	37 385	50.3	74.4	23.7	−0.7	33.7	8.1	10.3	70.0	8.8
48 29000	Garland city	131 291	47.5	78.3	21.8	−2.6	25.9	21.0	19.1	30.0	6.9
48 29336	Georgetown city	18 484	34.8	87.0	36.6	12.2	41.7	21.9	0.0	30.0	9.1
48 30464	Grand Prairie city	75 540	51.1	74.9	19.3	−5.1	22.9	26.2	16.7	30.1	6.3
48 30644	Grapevine city	26 784	24.5	91.8	43.2	18.8	45.1	40.3	82.9	65.6	20.5
48 31928	Haltom City city	24 804	58.9	73.3	12.4	−12.0	12.9	25.5	11.3	15.1	5.2
48 32372	Harlingen city	34 325	57.6	66.2	16.8	−7.6	29.9	30.0	5.3	72.2	9.3
48 35000	Houston city	1 201 154	50.0	70.4	27.0	2.6	46.0	15.9	16.0	47.2	7.9
48 35528	Huntsville city	19 628	55.6	72.2	22.4	−2.0	34.1	7.7	8.6	56.3	3.6
48 35576	Hurst city	23 931	38.4	87.7	24.5	0.1	25.8	18.0	9.6	38.4	11.0
48 37000	Irving city	120 993	42.7	78.0	30.0	5.6	34.5	29.7	11.3	58.0	8.8
48 38632	Keller city	16 789	20.1	95.6	44.6	20.2	44.9	36.7	41.9	62.1	29.3
48 39148	Killeen city	46 926	38.8	89.3	15.7	−8.7	20.2	11.0	13.8	17.4	12.1
48 39352	Kingsville city...............	14 210	54.6	67.6	20.5	−3.9	33.0	9.2	18.3	54.9	14.3
48 40588	Lake Jackson city..........	16 237	28.2	91.9	35.3	10.9	37.8	24.4	0.0	69.9	15.7
48 41212	Lancaster city...............	15 741	46.5	80.6	18.9	−5.5	18.7	20.5	57.4	7.2	8.0

[1] Hispanic or Latino persons may be of any race.

City	School enrollment			Population 16 to 19 years				Employment status, 2000			Work status in 1999 of the population 16 years and over		
											Worked in 1999		
	Grades kindergarten through 12	College or graduate school	Percent private	Number	Percent in armed forces	Percent high school graduates	Percent not enrolled, not grads, not in armed forces, not employed	Total population 16 years and over	Percent in labor force	Unemployment rate	Full-time	Part-time	Did not work in 1999
	11	12	13	14	15	16	17	18	19	20	21	22	23
TENNESSEE............	1 037 539	287 550	13.0	312 760	0.2	12.4	5.2	4 445 909	63.5	5.4	55.9	13.0	31.1
Bartlett city	9 011	2 147	17.3	2 515	0.0	7.8	4.5	30 048	73.1	2.2	62.6	14.9	22.5
Chattanooga city	25 766	10 080	15.6	8 117	0.0	11.4	6.5	124 509	61.4	7.6	52.8	13.8	33.4
Clarksville city	20 914	7 339	7.1	6 007	8.3	20.5	2.8	76 581	71.4	5.8	61.9	13.9	24.2
Cleveland city	5 865	3 948	29.9	2 609	0.0	9.1	3.8	29 848	61.6	5.8	51.4	16.3	32.3
Collierville town	8 181	1 386	11.8	1 741	0.0	5.0	3.4	22 304	73.1	2.7	61.4	16.4	22.2
Columbia city	5 971	1 216	14.0	2 041	0.0	19.1	4.8	25 548	64.9	5.4	55.9	12.6	31.5
Franklin city	8 120	1 478	14.0	1 886	0.0	12.1	2.9	31 081	74.2	3.2	64.9	14.2	20.9
Germantown city	8 605	1 799	27.5	2 261	0.0	2.7	0.3	28 249	68.6	1.9	57.0	16.7	26.3
Hendersonville city	7 906	1 647	11.5	2 258	0.0	12.6	2.0	31 277	71.6	3.6	62.0	14.5	23.5
Jackson city.................	11 419	4 079	27.6	3 795	0.0	12.6	5.6	45 699	64.2	8.8	54.7	14.6	30.7
Johnson City city..........	8 053	6 678	6.5	3 426	0.0	7.6	3.8	45 666	61.6	5.6	49.3	18.7	32.1
Kingsport city	7 507	1 227	5.8	1 805	0.2	9.7	7.6	35 770	52.5	5.8	45.6	12.5	41.8
Knoxville city	24 359	23 601	8.7	11 688	0.0	10.1	5.0	142 967	60.3	6.5	50.5	18.1	31.4
Memphis city	134 638	37 729	12.8	38 209	0.0	10.5	8.5	487 758	63.0	8.6	55.6	12.6	31.9
Murfreesboro city	11 129	11 532	5.9	5 281	0.0	8.7	2.1	55 140	70.7	7.6	56.1	20.8	23.0
Nashville-Davidson........	90 547	41 321	27.6	32 378	0.0	10.0	6.6	456 655	67.4	5.2	60.6	13.9	25.5
Oak Ridge city.............	4 899	1 144	4.6	1 240	0.0	13.0	1.6	21 902	58.2	5.4	48.3	15.0	36.7
Smyrna town	4 828	1 084	11.7	1 430	0.0	16.5	5.2	19 142	74.5	2.8	66.9	12.7	20.5
TEXAS....................	4 355 276	1 202 890	9.2	1 289 185	0.9	11.0	7.1	15 617 373	63.6	6.0	57.3	12.5	30.3
Abilene city	22 749	10 380	26.4	8 910	3.1	13.2	8.9	89 857	63.1	8.2	55.2	16.0	28.8
Allen city	10 385	2 332	8.0	2 401	0.0	7.2	1.1	29 796	78.3	2.5	70.3	13.4	16.3
Amarillo city	34 554	9 992	7.3	10 509	0.1	13.5	8.0	130 592	65.8	5.5	57.0	13.9	29.2
Arlington city	66 207	23 963	11.9	19 187	0.1	10.6	6.2	248 147	74.0	4.2	66.1	13.2	20.7
Austin city	100 419	80 623	8.6	40 339	0.1	9.9	6.9	523 758	71.9	4.4	62.9	15.9	21.2
Baytown city	14 698	3 476	4.6	4 168	0.0	9.8	7.8	48 861	60.9	7.6	56.4	10.5	33.1
Beaumont city	24 013	5 976	10.6	7 286	0.0	9.0	7.7	86 764	60.0	8.1	51.9	13.8	34.4
Bedford city	7 824	2 608	12.2	2 602	0.3	11.2	1.1	38 002	76.2	2.3	67.4	13.3	19.3
Big Spring city	4 795	1 400	6.3	1 450	0.0	15.2	13.5	19 988	45.2	7.7	51.5	9.3	39.1
Brownsville city............	36 747	8 394	5.8	9 839	0.0	5.2	8.2	96 647	52.4	13.0	45.1	11.9	43.0
Bryan city	12 772	9 121	4.4	4 848	0.0	9.1	4.4	50 344	64.6	5.3	56.1	18.0	25.9
Carrollton city	21 719	5 742	12.7	5 599	0.0	9.4	3.8	81 759	77.6	3.0	70.6	12.0	17.3
Cedar Hill city..............	7 711	2 035	16.5	2 126	0.0	10.5	2.5	22 933	76.9	3.6	70.5	11.7	17.8
Cedar Park city	5 620	1 007	5.7	1 254	0.0	11.2	2.0	17 937	78.3	1.9	73.1	11.5	15.5
Cleburne city	5 378	842	6.9	1 613	0.8	15.3	8.5	19 688	61.7	5.4	54.2	11.5	34.3
College Station city	6 807	36 328	2.8	11 581	0.1	2.5	0.5	59 083	61.9	12.8	42.6	37.1	20.3
Conroe city	6 996	1 457	8.0	2 523	0.0	8.6	16.3	27 750	64.7	7.0	59.1	11.4	29.4
Coppell city	9 044	1 402	10.4	1 612	0.0	4.3	1.1	24 455	78.6	1.9	70.5	12.8	16.6
Copperas Cove city.......	6 260	1 739	4.6	1 774	3.7	18.4	3.7	21 184	74.2	5.7	67.2	12.6	20.2
Corpus Christi city........	58 806	16 658	7.0	17 730	0.6	10.8	7.5	208 475	62.6	7.2	53.9	13.8	32.3
Dallas city...................	218 554	56 366	13.8	65 182	0.0	10.9	12.6	904 860	65.1	6.7	61.5	10.2	28.3
Deer Park city	6 682	1 730	4.2	2 187	0.0	8.1	3.1	21 389	71.1	5.6	63.4	11.7	24.9
Del Rio city	8 089	1 121	6.2	2 067	0.2	7.9	9.7	24 502	55.8	10.9	49.4	10.9	39.7
Denton city	11 609	18 770	6.0	6 730	0.1	8.8	3.3	65 848	70.6	7.3	53.7	24.4	21.9
DeSoto city.................	8 033	2 404	16.4	2 115	0.0	10.3	2.2	28 307	72.7	4.3	66.7	11.0	22.3
Duncanville city	7 710	1 730	14.3	2 109	0.0	15.2	1.0	27 004	69.0	3.2	63.7	11.7	24.6
Edinburg city	11 539	4 037	4.1	3 787	0.0	5.1	16.4	34 424	56.7	9.7	50.0	12.3	37.8
El Paso city	134 162	41 132	7.9	36 351	0.2	8.9	6.1	408 552	57.1	9.0	50.4	12.8	36.8
Euless city	7 898	2 616	10.7	2 121	0.0	14.9	5.0	35 641	76.6	2.8	70.9	11.1	18.0
Farmers Branch city......	5 453	1 055	17.6	1 471	0.0	12.0	8.6	21 553	69.2	3.4	65.5	10.6	23.8
Flower Mound town.......	11 868	2 292	8.6	2 455	0.0	6.8	2.2	35 090	77.5	2.5	68.0	14.4	17.6
Fort Worth city..............	106 568	28 331	15.9	31 531	0.2	12.5	9.3	399 651	64.3	6.0	59.1	12.1	28.9
Friendswood city	6 731	1 570	9.1	1 686	0.0	5.5	1.2	21 176	70.6	3.7	62.4	12.7	24.9
Frisco city	5 729	1 374	10.5	1 005	0.0	14.1	0.8	23 736	78.9	2.3	73.6	10.5	16.0
Galveston city	9 963	4 874	7.3	3 403	0.6	10.9	6.1	45 372	59.7	10.1	53.0	13.1	33.9
Garland city	47 207	10 096	9.3	13 314	0.0	9.8	8.2	158 599	70.4	4.6	65.4	11.1	23.4
Georgetown city	4 825	2 093	22.1	1 911	0.0	10.7	1.9	22 529	58.9	2.9	52.2	14.9	32.8
Grand Prairie city	28 032	6 359	9.3	7 843	0.3	14.1	7.2	92 274	70.4	5.4	65.7	11.3	23.0
Grapevine city	9 159	1 892	8.0	2 446	0.0	8.5	1.5	31 260	77.8	2.5	69.9	13.4	16.6
Haltom City city	7 301	1 511	9.2	2 013	0.0	16.9	8.1	29 745	68.8	5.0	62.7	11.6	25.6
Harlingen city	13 235	2 807	6.8	3 694	0.2	8.7	6.2	41 906	51.9	8.9	46.2	11.4	42.5
Houston city	387 528	115 225	10.6	109 467	0.0	9.7	10.7	1 472 506	63.2	7.6	58.1	11.2	30.6
Huntsville city	4 921	7 857	6.5	3 558	0.3	9.5	8.5	30 374	46.9	11.9	46.3	20.2	33.6
Hurst city	6 640	1 594	10.1	1 922	0.0	12.0	5.2	28 047	70.0	3.9	62.2	12.4	25.4
Irving city	32 902	11 826	12.7	9 355	0.1	12.4	8.8	147 795	74.0	4.3	69.5	10.0	20.5
Keller city	6 761	1 147	10.8	1 322	0.0	7.3	1.9	18 829	75.3	2.0	64.8	15.8	19.4
Killeen city	16 782	5 609	6.9	5 032	5.7	21.1	7.8	63 200	73.6	6.3	66.3	11.9	21.8
Kingsville city	4 940	4 175	6.4	1 954	0.0	6.1	4.7	19 465	59.9	11.7	46.2	17.4	36.4
Lake Jackson city..........	6 247	1 323	9.0	1 506	0.0	5.3	5.3	19 289	66.2	4.1	59.7	11.6	28.7
Lancaster city..............	5 910	1 345	14.1	1 308	0.0	12.2	4.1	18 802	68.7	7.7	65.8	9.3	24.9

Table B-5. Cities — **Education, Labor Force, and Income**

City	Full-year full-time employed (percent) Total	Men	Women	Non-Hispanic White	Black or African American	American Indian and Alaska Native	Asian, Hawaiian, and Pacific Islander	Hispanic or Latino[1]	Children under 18 years in families Number	Both in labor force	Father only in labor force	With one parent who is in labor force	+/- U.S. percent of children with no stay-at-home parent	+/- U.S. percent two-income couples	Private	Government	Self-employed	Unpaid family worker
	24	25	26	27	28	29	30	31	32	33	34	35	36	37	38	39	40	41
TENNESSEE	41.8	51.6	32.7	42.6	38.1	42.2	40.5	40.0	1 308 599	42.6	21.4	22.9	0.9	-0.4	76.2	13.9	9.6	0.3
Bartlett city	52.4	65.0	40.8	52.5	53.5	55.0	50.0	48.7	11 217	60.6	22.1	12.9	8.9	12.5	75.6	16.8	7.3	0.2
Chattanooga city	38.7	46.6	31.9	40.3	35.5	35.1	42.1	40.2	31 503	33.1	14.3	36.0	4.5	-1.3	77.5	14.5	7.8	0.2
Clarksville city	46.8	61.5	32.3	48.1	46.1	45.6	28.3	44.2	28 523	42.3	25.8	20.7	-1.6	2.8	70.5	21.6	7.7	0.2
Cleveland city	37.1	48.1	28.0	37.0	39.1	0.0	37.1	37.6	7 801	39.0	27.2	22.1	-3.5	-0.9	79.2	11.6	8.7	0.5
Collierville town	51.9	72.2	32.7	52.5	45.7	12.1	54.5	61.3	10 440	47.5	36.6	11.6	-5.5	7.6	80.4	10.6	8.9	0.1
Columbia city	41.9	53.1	32.5	42.1	39.9	52.0	69.0	45.3	7 621	36.8	21.3	29.8	2.0	0.3	80.2	11.4	8.1	0.3
Franklin city	51.0	65.2	38.2	52.7	41.7	32.7	45.7	45.7	11 507	46.6	31.1	16.4	-1.6	9.2	81.7	8.5	9.4	0.4
Germantown city	47.6	66.5	30.2	47.7	50.2	92.5	43.3	47.7	10 287	44.3	43.1	9.0	-11.3	0.4	75.4	10.1	14.2	0.3
Hendersonville city	48.6	61.7	36.7	48.9	50.8	68.9	46.5	37.9	10 212	50.6	24.8	18.1	4.1	7.1	77.9	11.1	10.6	0.4
Jackson city	39.2	47.5	32.5	41.0	36.8	31.7	33.6	33.7	14 335	38.3	12.6	32.6	6.3	1.3	79.8	13.9	6.0	0.2
Johnson City city	35.8	45.4	27.2	35.7	35.0	64.5	37.4	35.2	10 364	39.5	24.5	23.6	-1.5	-4.5	74.7	16.1	8.7	0.5
Kingsport city	34.0	44.8	25.4	34.0	35.8	18.8	41.1	41.0	9 237	34.7	23.7	23.9	-6.0	-10.7	79.4	9.5	10.6	0.4
Knoxville city	35.6	43.8	28.5	36.5	31.4	38.3	28.6	29.0	31 544	33.8	18.6	26.7	-4.1	-3.1	74.5	17.1	8.1	0.3
Memphis city	39.7	46.1	34.3	43.6	37.2	44.4	41.2	37.3	163 180	26.6	11.4	40.9	2.9	-0.1	77.3	15.8	6.7	0.1
Murfreesboro city	41.7	50.4	33.2	42.5	36.9	52.8	44.8	44.8	14 494	45.0	23.7	23.0	3.4	4.2	77.6	14.9	7.3	0.2
Nashville-Davidson	45.0	53.0	37.8	47.1	40.4	46.5	39.4	41.7	117 003	38.3	18.1	30.0	3.7	3.8	78.2	12.2	9.4	0.2
Oak Ridge city	36.9	49.4	26.5	36.3	38.9	61.9	34.7	53.7	5 889	44.3	21.2	24.9	4.6	-5.4	71.9	19.9	8.1	0.1
Smyrna town	52.7	64.2	41.8	53.7	49.3	66.7	56.0	43.8	6 584	47.8	18.2	23.9	7.1	11.6	82.2	9.1	8.4	0.2
TEXAS	41.0	50.4	31.9	44.6	38.1	39.4	41.6	35.0	5 503 509	39.0	25.2	20.6	-5.0	-2.5	75.3	14.6	9.8	0.3
Abilene city	36.8	43.9	29.7	38.2	29.2	37.3	44.0	35.0	27 393	45.8	20.5	22.4	3.6	1.1	73.0	17.4	9.2	0.4
Allen city	59.0	75.4	43.2	60.3	55.4	49.6	52.6	48.9	14 874	49.4	35.8	10.7	-4.5	11.4	83.3	8.6	7.7	0.5
Amarillo city	42.1	52.4	33.0	43.4	34.9	37.4	41.6	39.2	45 407	41.6	22.4	24.7	1.7	0.8	74.8	14.8	10.0	0.3
Arlington city	50.0	60.3	40.0	52.2	54.4	56.6	38.9	42.6	89 095	44.4	23.6	20.5	0.3	7.5	79.6	12.2	8.0	0.2
Austin city	44.8	52.4	36.8	47.2	41.7	40.7	35.8	42.6	137 082	38.2	22.9	25.0	-1.4	5.3	72.6	18.6	8.6	0.2
Baytown city	38.4	50.0	27.7	41.6	36.8	38.8	39.7	32.7	18 770	30.1	29.6	22.1	-12.4	-11.8	82.6	11.7	5.6	0.1
Beaumont city	36.1	44.1	29.2	39.8	32.1	41.8	36.5	36.1	28 440	32.5	17.2	31.6	-0.5	-3.9	73.1	18.7	8.0	0.2
Bedford city	55.0	65.1	45.7	55.7	53.4	45.5	53.1	48.8	10 005	53.2	22.4	20.1	8.7	12.9	81.2	10.5	8.0	0.3
Big Spring city	30.4	33.0	26.9	34.8	27.6	43.0	18.1	25.2	5 430	37.2	19.7	31.0	3.6	-6.0	66.2	25.3	8.2	0.3
Brownsville city	26.9	35.4	19.9	31.6	33.2	29.5	41.3	26.2	45 021	27.9	25.5	19.2	-17.5	-17.8	70.8	19.5	9.3	0.4
Bryan city	36.9	43.1	30.9	40.1	30.1	24.0	21.7	35.2	16 138	37.7	19.2	25.6	-1.3	1.8	65.4	26.7	7.6	0.3
Carrollton city	55.5	66.2	45.1	58.9	62.0	55.7	45.0	47.1	29 277	48.6	24.2	17.9	1.9	13.8	82.7	8.0	9.1	0.2
Cedar Hill city	57.0	66.3	48.8	56.5	61.5	54.6	41.7	48.9	9 954	55.4	15.7	20.6	11.4	17.9	75.9	16.6	7.5	0.1
Cedar Park city	60.0	74.4	45.9	61.1	63.5	25.3	49.1	53.8	8 281	53.2	26.5	15.2	3.8	14.9	78.1	15.2	6.6	0.1
Cleburne city	39.4	51.1	28.8	39.7	30.9	44.2	24.8	40.6	6 734	45.5	25.1	18.8	-0.3	1.4	80.2	11.2	8.3	0.3
College Station city	21.9	26.9	16.7	22.0	27.6	24.0	20.0	19.7	9 415	48.2	26.2	14.4	-2.0	4.6	57.3	37.2	4.9	0.6
Conroe city	39.3	49.5	29.0	43.0	31.9	27.5	45.3	34.0	9 215	36.1	23.1	24.7	-3.8	-1.4	76.7	14.2	8.8	0.3
Coppell city	60.1	76.8	44.2	60.6	60.2	77.1	50.0	57.3	12 314	50.1	37.3	10.2	-4.3	11.4	81.8	7.0	11.0	0.2
Copperas Cove city	50.8	64.7	37.2	51.9	55.3	61.6	41.6	43.9	9 256	46.6	21.3	22.6	4.6	4.7	60.7	31.5	7.3	0.5
Corpus Christi city	38.1	48.1	29.0	41.1	32.9	41.3	43.9	36.0	72 262	36.0	22.0	25.1	-3.5	-3.9	71.3	18.4	9.9	0.4
Dallas city	42.5	50.0	34.9	49.0	39.1	39.0	45.2	36.7	284 869	28.2	22.9	26.2	-10.2	-7.0	82.1	8.6	9.0	0.2
Deer Park city	49.0	58.7	39.6	49.0	50.0	47.7	34.4	44.6	7 813	54.8	22.6	16.8	7.0	3.9	81.9	13.0	4.9	0.3
Del Rio city	31.4	41.7	22.2	45.5	61.9	36.8	28.1	27.7	10 161	36.3	24.5	17.6	-10.7	-12.9	63.6	26.1	9.3	1.1
Denton city	36.6	45.0	28.7	39.0	30.6	37.6	15.7	33.2	15 290	39.2	25.0	24.4	-1.0	3.2	71.7	20.9	7.1	0.3
DeSoto city	53.2	61.1	46.4	49.6	58.1	44.6	47.9	49.8	10 006	54.3	13.9	21.9	11.6	13.5	72.6	19.1	8.2	0.2
Duncanville city	49.5	59.7	41.0	47.7	56.5	57.9	44.5	47.9	9 576	43.7	20.6	23.4	2.5	6.9	75.0	15.3	9.4	0.3
Edinburg city	29.1	34.3	24.3	33.9	39.4	34.7	48.4	28.1	15 135	34.1	23.6	20.4	-10.1	-8.0	63.0	27.3	9.5	0.2
El Paso city	33.8	44.4	24.8	39.4	41.0	30.8	36.4	31.9	163 639	30.8	25.3	22.5	-11.3	-12.8	70.7	20.9	8.1	0.3
Euless city	56.1	64.1	48.2	58.6	51.8	59.9	48.4	47.8	11 069	42.1	25.4	24.3	1.8	8.5	85.1	7.1	6.7	0.1
Farmers Branch city	47.6	57.1	37.8	49.2	46.8	45.1	40.0	45.8	7 071	48.7	20.1	17.5	1.6	1.3	84.6	6.6	8.4	0.3
Flower Mound town	57.6	75.8	40.0	57.6	65.3	58.6	49.9	59.4	17 452	48.7	39.4	8.5	-7.4	9.4	83.6	8.2	7.9	0.2
Fort Worth city	42.2	51.7	33.3	45.7	38.2	38.9	41.0	38.4	139 371	33.3	23.1	24.4	-6.9	-3.5	81.2	11.2	7.4	0.2
Friendswood city	47.5	61.9	34.3	47.8	51.7	54.4	39.8	48.3	8 384	46.5	35.0	13.7	-4.4	6.6	69.9	18.1	11.8	0.3
Frisco city	61.1	77.3	45.9	61.7	71.5	69.4	67.4	51.4	10 058	52.4	33.3	9.8	-2.4	11.3	82.9	8.9	7.9	0.2
Galveston city	35.7	39.7	32.1	38.8	28.2	18.6	43.9	36.3	12 211	30.3	15.6	34.6	0.3	-7.0	60.5	31.5	7.7	0.3
Garland city	49.0	57.9	40.6	51.7	51.7	43.8	44.5	42.9	60 581	42.0	22.3	21.3	-1.3	5.3	81.8	9.4	8.4	0.3
Georgetown city	36.9	45.0	29.3	36.0	32.9	68.4	32.8	42.6	6 255	51.8	21.6	19.2	6.4	-2.5	72.8	16.4	10.5	0.3
Grand Prairie city	48.9	58.8	39.5	52.2	53.2	55.7	42.3	42.2	36 470	40.8	19.3	23.6	-0.2	4.3	81.7	11.4	6.7	0.2
Grapevine city	55.3	66.9	43.7	57.6	50.9	45.4	45.5	42.0	11 909	51.1	27.9	15.3	1.8	11.9	83.7	8.8	7.4	0.1
Haltom City city	46.3	57.2	35.6	46.4	55.2	42.5	45.8	44.5	9 827	37.6	25.3	23.6	-3.4	-2.4	84.2	8.2	7.3	0.3
Harlingen city	31.7	40.7	24.1	28.3	37.2	34.4	46.8	32.8	16 249	34.1	24.4	17.8	-12.7	-14.1	67.9	21.8	10.0	0.2
Houston city	39.4	47.3	31.8	46.6	36.5	37.4	38.6	34.3	493 088	29.0	24.3	24.8	-10.8	-8.5	79.7	11.1	8.9	0.2
Huntsville city	23.5	22.6	24.9	27.2	17.6	65.0	11.3	19.2	4 874	40.8	19.4	27.7	3.9	0.4	57.4	35.0	7.2	0.4
Hurst city	49.1	59.5	39.6	49.0	57.8	30.3	50.5	47.6	8 775	45.2	21.2	25.6	6.2	3.9	82.1	9.8	7.9	0.2
Irving city	51.1	59.2	42.9	55.2	55.7	50.2	47.0	43.1	45 190	37.8	22.9	24.4	-2.4	2.3	85.5	7.7	6.6	0.2
Keller city	55.0	73.5	37.3	55.0	64.9	54.2	56.2	55.1	9 218	52.6	37.6	5.7	-6.3	8.1	79.9	10.3	9.7	0.1
Killeen city	48.5	62.7	34.4	51.2	51.2	44.1	35.4	42.8	24 547	39.7	22.4	26.8	1.9	2.8	65.7	28.6	5.6	0.1
Kingsville city	29.3	37.9	21.3	34.2	23.8	34.5	17.1	27.8	6 357	35.3	21.7	19.4	-9.9	-8.4	64.6	27.4	7.4	0.5
Lake Jackson city	46.1	61.3	31.8	46.1	54.6	27.7	43.8	45.1	7 902	48.5	29.8	13.6	-2.5	0.6	77.8	13.7	8.4	0.1
Lancaster city	47.8	53.6	43.1	42.9	52.9	63.1	61.8	41.0	7 281	38.2	15.4	30.7	4.3	4.9	69.8	22.2	7.6	0.3

[1] Hispanic or Latino persons may be of any race.

City	Percent who worked at home	Percent of the population 5 years and over with a disability	Veterans as a percent of the population 18 years and over	Occupation for employed population 16 years and over (percent)						Industry for employed population 16 years and over (percent)					
				Management, professional, and related occupations	Service occupations	Sales and office occupations	Farming, fishing, and forestry occupations	Construction, extraction, and maintenance occupations	Production, transportation and material moving occupations	Agriculture, forestry, fishing, and mining	Construction and manufacturing	Wholesale and retail trade	Transportation and warehousing, and utilities	Service industries	Public administration
	42	43	44	45	46	47	48	49	50	51	52	53	54	55	56
TENNESSEE............	2.6	22.0	13.1	29.5	13.7	26.1	0.6	10.3	19.9	1.4	26.2	15.6	6.3	46.5	4.0
Bartlett city	3.1	14.9	15.1	39.4	11.7	32.2	0.0	8.2	8.5	0.1	13.9	16.2	10.9	51.8	7.1
Chattanooga city	2.1	24.1	13.7	31.4	16.6	27.1	0.1	6.7	18.1	0.2	21.7	14.6	6.1	54.0	3.4
Clarksville city	1.7	19.8	20.7	27.3	17.8	26.1	0.2	9.3	19.3	0.5	22.4	15.8	5.1	49.4	6.7
Cleveland city	1.9	20.7	12.3	30.5	13.3	25.4	0.2	8.0	22.6	0.5	29.7	15.0	3.3	48.5	3.0
Collierville town	3.7	9.2	13.1	43.8	9.7	31.1	0.0	5.3	10.2	0.4	19.2	18.7	15.7	42.7	3.3
Columbia city	1.9	20.4	13.0	23.7	15.7	25.1	0.5	10.3	24.8	0.6	31.7	15.2	3.8	45.0	3.6
Franklin city	4.8	12.8	8.6	44.8	10.7	29.3	0.3	6.1	8.9	0.2	18.2	15.9	2.2	61.0	2.6
Germantown city	5.3	9.1	14.6	52.8	7.2	30.5	0.0	3.4	6.0	0.2	14.2	16.6	11.3	55.2	2.6
Hendersonville city	3.2	16.1	13.8	36.6	11.6	33.7	0.1	8.3	9.7	0.3	17.6	20.6	4.9	52.9	3.8
Jackson city	2.0	22.6	11.6	31.7	15.1	25.8	0.3	6.5	20.7	0.2	26.0	15.7	4.0	50.5	3.6
Johnson City city	2.1	23.9	14.9	35.1	15.5	29.3	0.2	6.8	13.1	0.6	20.2	17.6	3.0	56.1	2.5
Kingsport city	2.3	25.9	15.3	34.0	15.2	27.5	0.2	9.1	13.9	0.4	28.4	17.3	2.9	48.2	2.7
Knoxville city	2.3	23.3	12.1	32.6	17.9	29.1	0.2	7.8	12.4	0.2	14.9	18.3	4.5	58.6	3.5
Memphis city	1.7	23.6	11.3	29.5	16.1	29.7	0.1	7.9	16.6	0.2	15.7	15.7	11.4	52.1	4.9
Murfreesboro city	2.4	16.5	11.4	34.1	15.0	27.5	0.2	7.7	15.4	0.6	21.8	17.0	5.2	52.2	3.3
Nashville-Davidson.......	3.1	20.1	11.5	37.2	13.8	28.5	0.1	8.4	11.9	0.2	15.9	14.9	4.6	59.6	4.7
Oak Ridge city	2.6	19.5	17.9	46.6	13.6	25.5	0.1	5.5	8.8	0.3	13.5	12.3	3.3	66.8	3.9
Smyrna town	2.1	16.7	12.9	29.4	10.9	28.3	0.1	11.0	20.2	0.6	28.2	20.2	5.6	42.2	3.2
TEXAS...............	2.8	19.2	11.7	33.3	14.6	27.2	0.7	10.9	13.2	2.7	19.9	15.9	5.8	51.2	4.5
Abilene city.................	1.8	20.2	13.8	32.5	20.1	26.8	0.3	9.7	10.6	1.5	11.9	14.6	5.2	60.8	6.0
Allen city...................	4.3	9.1	10.1	54.4	8.0	27.3	0.1	5.3	4.8	0.7	20.2	17.1	2.6	56.7	2.7
Amarillo city...............	2.3	19.8	12.9	29.0	17.8	28.4	0.3	10.4	14.1	1.0	17.6	18.8	5.6	51.9	5.1
Arlington city..............	2.7	15.8	11.6	36.1	12.5	30.7	0.1	8.4	12.3	0.3	20.0	17.5	7.8	50.9	3.5
Austin city..................	3.4	15.5	9.2	43.1	13.2	26.0	0.1	9.0	8.6	0.4	20.3	13.1	2.6	56.2	7.4
Baytown city...............	1.3	19.7	10.6	26.8	13.4	25.1	0.0	17.4	17.2	1.1	31.9	14.0	5.7	44.5	2.8
Beaumont city	2.0	23.2	13.0	32.4	18.8	26.5	0.3	9.5	12.6	1.0	18.5	15.8	5.1	52.3	7.3
Bedford city	3.1	12.6	13.6	42.2	10.2	32.9	0.0	6.2	8.5	0.4	14.7	16.2	12.0	53.5	3.3
Big Spring city	1.3	23.6	12.4	31.8	23.9	19.2	1.1	10.9	13.2	5.5	15.7	11.7	3.9	54.8	8.4
Brownsville city	2.2	23.5	6.2	27.6	18.5	26.7	1.0	9.4	16.9	1.5	18.9	17.1	5.4	52.1	4.9
Bryan city	1.8	17.1	9.6	32.4	17.5	25.1	0.4	11.6	13.0	2.2	18.0	13.7	3.3	58.4	4.4
Carrollton city	3.6	12.3	9.9	42.3	9.8	31.5	0.2	6.2	10.0	0.5	17.8	19.0	5.7	55.2	1.9
Cedar Hill city	2.1	14.1	11.6	39.4	9.1	33.0	0.0	6.7	11.8	0.3	17.2	16.7	7.8	52.6	5.4
Cedar Park city	2.4	10.6	14.9	47.6	8.2	28.6	0.1	6.9	8.7	0.7	25.1	16.8	3.6	47.2	6.7
Cleburne city	1.6	25.6	12.2	24.9	14.1	25.5	0.3	13.2	22.0	0.8	29.8	18.3	6.5	40.7	3.9
College Station city	2.7	7.7	4.6	46.1	17.0	25.9	0.6	4.7	5.7	1.5	6.7	12.7	2.0	73.9	3.1
Conroe city	1.5	23.3	11.1	24.7	22.0	25.6	0.2	13.8	13.8	1.5	19.7	17.1	4.1	52.7	4.9
Coppell city	4.9	7.7	8.3	59.2	5.8	27.8	0.0	2.8	4.4	0.6	15.3	17.5	5.4	59.4	1.7
Copperas Cove city.......	1.9	17.9	27.5	29.3	21.1	28.1	0.2	11.2	10.2	0.4	12.3	13.8	5.1	54.1	14.3
Corpus Christi city........	2.2	20.9	14.6	30.7	17.3	28.2	0.2	12.2	11.4	1.7	15.4	15.6	4.6	56.2	6.6
Dallas city..................	2.8	21.8	8.2	33.0	14.8	27.7	0.1	11.2	13.1	0.5	19.9	15.3	5.3	56.9	2.1
Deer Park city	0.9	15.5	13.1	31.5	10.9	29.0	0.0	10.9	17.7	1.0	31.7	13.5	7.4	43.2	3.2
Del Rio city	1.6	21.1	11.8	26.5	22.1	24.3	1.1	12.0	14.0	2.2	17.1	16.3	5.4	47.2	11.8
Denton city	2.2	15.4	8.8	35.2	16.9	29.5	0.2	8.4	9.8	0.7	15.1	16.5	3.2	60.9	3.6
DeSoto city	2.5	14.6	14.0	41.2	12.0	29.7	0.0	6.2	10.8	0.7	14.0	13.2	8.8	58.0	5.3
Duncanville city	2.8	16.4	12.7	37.6	10.3	32.1	0.0	7.8	12.1	0.4	16.2	17.8	6.5	55.0	4.1
Edinburg city	2.1	20.2	7.3	36.6	16.8	26.3	1.2	8.2	10.8	2.7	10.5	16.2	5.0	58.7	6.9
El Paso city	2.2	20.3	12.4	31.3	16.9	29.1	0.2	7.6	14.9	0.3	17.8	15.9	6.7	53.0	6.4
Euless city	2.4	14.1	11.7	38.0	10.7	33.3	0.0	7.2	10.8	0.2	15.0	17.1	14.5	51.4	1.8
Farmers Branch city......	3.6	15.2	11.6	32.3	13.3	29.7	0.2	9.4	15.2	0.6	22.3	17.4	4.6	52.9	2.2
Flower Mound town.......	6.4	6.5	12.0	54.5	7.9	28.0	0.0	4.3	5.3	0.7	13.7	17.5	8.7	57.4	2.0
Fort Worth city..............	2.1	21.0	11.1	30.2	14.8	27.2	0.1	11.5	16.1	0.5	23.3	16.5	6.8	49.7	3.3
Friendswood city	4.3	11.9	14.0	48.2	9.8	25.8	0.2	8.1	7.9	1.4	19.9	14.2	6.9	51.1	6.6
Frisco city	4.3	8.6	9.1	54.5	7.3	27.9	0.2	5.2	5.0	1.0	17.6	17.3	3.8	58.4	1.9
Galveston city	2.2	21.4	11.9	35.2	24.2	24.0	0.3	8.3	8.0	0.8	9.5	11.6	3.5	69.6	4.9
Garland city	2.4	18.2	10.7	31.9	11.7	30.2	0.1	11.6	14.4	0.4	25.3	17.2	4.1	50.5	2.5
Georgetown city	4.1	17.0	16.0	39.6	13.0	28.1	0.2	9.6	9.5	1.1	23.2	14.0	3.2	51.5	7.1
Grand Prairie city	2.0	18.7	10.9	30.1	11.4	31.0	0.1	10.7	16.8	0.2	23.6	17.9	9.1	46.0	3.2
Grapevine city	4.1	10.6	11.9	45.3	11.3	29.0	0.0	5.8	8.6	0.5	14.6	16.9	11.3	54.2	2.5
Haltom City city	2.0	20.8	13.1	22.3	13.9	30.8	0.1	14.3	18.6	0.4	29.2	19.6	8.3	39.9	2.4
Harlingen city	2.7	20.2	11.8	33.8	20.3	25.2	0.5	9.3	10.9	0.8	13.7	15.3	3.8	58.5	7.9
Houston city	2.3	20.5	8.2	33.9	15.7	26.4	0.1	11.0	12.9	1.9	18.7	15.3	6.2	55.0	2.8
Huntsville city	1.5	15.9	9.3	32.9	25.6	26.3	1.1	5.9	8.1	2.5	9.1	14.0	1.9	55.2	17.3
Hurst city	2.5	17.9	15.2	35.9	12.8	31.4	0.1	8.5	11.3	0.6	17.7	16.0	10.3	52.9	2.7
Irving city	2.2	17.4	8.7	35.6	12.1	29.5	0.2	10.5	12.1	0.3	19.4	16.4	7.0	55.1	1.8
Keller city	6.2	8.6	12.8	48.2	10.1	27.9	0.0	6.2	7.6	0.7	18.4	14.5	14.6	48.8	3.0
Killeen city	1.1	18.0	25.0	25.7	21.2	30.8	0.2	9.0	13.1	0.2	10.0	17.5	5.8	55.2	11.3
Kingsville city..............	1.3	19.5	11.1	31.7	20.3	24.0	1.1	11.5	11.5	5.5	13.9	12.5	5.9	55.3	6.8
Lake Jackson city........	2.4	15.2	13.1	44.9	11.1	22.4	0.2	10.0	11.4	0.8	38.2	12.2	5.1	40.5	3.2
Lancaster city.............	2.2	18.1	13.6	31.6	10.3	32.8	0.3	10.5	14.5	0.7	18.5	13.1	9.1	51.8	6.9

Table B-5. Cities — **Education, Labor Force, and Income**

City	Median house-hold income	Median family income: All families	Median family income: Families with children: Married-couple	Median family income: Families with children: Male house-holder	Median family income: Families with children: Female house-holder	Median nonfamily house-hold income	Median income for full-year, full-time workers: Men	Median income for full-year, full-time workers: Women	Per capita income	Households by source of income (percent): With earnings	Households by source of income (percent): With interest, dividend, or rental income	Households by source of income (percent): With Social Security income	Households by source of income (percent): With public assis-tance income	Households by source of income (percent): With retire-ment income	House-holds with income over $100,000 (percent)	+/− U.S. percent for income over $100,000	House-holds with income below poverty (percent)	Families with children with income below poverty (percent)
	57	58	59	60	61	62	63	64	65	66	67	68	69	70	71	72	73	74
TENNESSEE	36 360	43 517	52 047	26 932	17 912	21 032	33 643	24 832	19 393	79.7	29.4	26.5	3.5	16.2	8.3	-4.0	14.0	15.0
Bartlett city	66 369	69 962	74 256	52 292	44 327	38 077	46 834	33 843	24 616	89.4	45.0	20.1	0.7	19.2	17.3	5.0	2.7	2.7
Chattanooga city	32 006	41 318	52 847	25 189	16 203	20 861	32 062	24 289	19 689	75.9	27.9	29.2	4.8	17.8	7.6	-4.7	17.1	22.2
Clarksville city	37 548	41 421	45 779	25 957	19 039	25 021	30 955	23 279	16 686	86.8	25.4	17.0	3.5	18.2	5.7	-6.6	10.8	11.8
Cleveland city	30 098	40 150	46 373	21 296	15 425	16 142	31 465	22 195	18 316	77.8	28.5	28.0	3.3	15.7	6.7	-5.6	17.7	18.3
Collierville town	80 575	84 830	92 580	49 886	29 063	34 615	66 041	34 139	30 252	92.3	45.7	13.3	1.0	11.8	35.5	23.2	3.0	2.4
Columbia city	35 879	42 822	52 744	27 679	15 650	22 549	35 981	22 793	18 004	79.3	28.2	26.9	2.8	16.4	7.4	-4.9	13.2	15.7
Franklin city	56 431	69 431	80 460	50 458	29 426	34 933	50 926	32 154	27 276	89.7	41.5	14.6	1.6	9.3	20.7	8.4	6.7	6.7
Germantown city	94 609	103 726	111 259	88 493	46 544	47 676	82 750	41 042	44 021	89.6	63.0	18.7	0.3	15.2	46.8	34.5	2.3	2.3
Hendersonville city	50 108	57 625	67 982	37 647	25 747	28 297	41 485	29 091	24 165	86.3	37.2	21.7	1.6	15.7	14.7	2.4	6.3	7.4
Jackson city	33 194	40 922	54 339	25 833	16 532	21 978	34 778	24 348	18 495	79.6	27.4	26.9	4.4	15.0	7.8	-4.5	17.0	20.2
Johnson City city	30 835	40 977	53 648	21 250	14 974	18 498	32 093	23 064	20 364	76.6	33.6	29.3	3.8	17.2	8.3	-4.0	17.1	17.7
Kingsport city	30 524	40 183	51 005	24 135	11 524	10 020	35 241	21 098	20 549	68.2	36.2	35.9	5.3	20.1	8.9	-3.4	18.0	23.8
Knoxville city	27 492	37 708	47 175	25 343	14 079	18 387	29 902	23 583	18 171	76.5	28.1	26.8	4.5	15.4	5.7	-0.0	21.2	22.9
Memphis city	32 285	37 767	52 666	26 811	18 029	23 471	31 840	25 836	17 838	80.2	21.4	23.0	5.7	13.8	7.3	-5.0	18.6	24.4
Murfreesboro city	39 705	52 654	65 206	27 326	20 925	22 343	36 821	27 146	20 219	85.9	31.0	18.7	2.2	12.5	9.7	-2.6	15.3	11.0
Nashville-Davidson	39 797	49 317	59 548	29 829	20 075	28 553	35 187	28 679	23 069	84.0	31.5	21.5	3.6	14.1	10.6	-1.7	11.9	15.7
Oak Ridge city	41 950	57 087	72 402	30 956	18 773	25 593	46 590	28 922	24 793	70.9	50.7	35.6	3.5	29.4	13.3	1.0	10.4	15.2
Smyrna town	44 405	51 550	59 835	25 573	19 784	29 156	37 438	27 780	19 704	90.2	23.8	15.4	2.7	10.8	7.6	-4.7	8.7	9.5
TEXAS	39 927	45 861	52 372	27 667	19 769	25 623	35 893	26 827	19 617	83.9	29.2	21.6	3.2	13.2	11.5	-0.8	14.0	16.6
Abilene city	33 007	40 028	44 447	21 656	16 925	20 003	30 056	21 657	16 577	81.8	31.1	25.3	3.2	16.3	5.9	-6.4	14.8	16.1
Allen city	78 924	82 747	88 271	46 645	40 909	47 348	61 760	36 828	28 575	96.6	45.4	7.4	0.5	6.3	31.6	19.3	2.5	2.6
Amarillo city	34 940	42 536	49 366	22 996	17 736	20 512	32 091	23 752	18 621	81.5	29.8	25.1	3.1	13.9	7.3	-5.0	14.0	16.8
Arlington city	47 622	56 080	61 592	35 775	24 313	31 511	39 776	30 131	22 445	91.3	30.3	12.9	2.0	10.3	13.0	0.7	8.8	10.4
Austin city	42 689	54 091	63 311	29 851	23 796	31 485	36 550	30 708	24 163	89.7	35.2	12.8	1.8	10.1	13.6	1.3	12.8	13.0
Baytown city	40 559	45 346	48 776	31 186	16 151	25 724	38 022	25 491	17 641	82.4	24.8	21.7	2.8	13.0	9.8	-2.5	13.6	18.6
Beaumont city	32 559	40 825	54 831	24 622	14 926	20 807	36 800	25 258	18 632	76.7	27.8	27.0	4.7	15.1	8.9	-3.4	18.5	24.3
Bedford city	54 436	71 017	80 056	41 750	31 420	31 560	44 667	34 352	29 400	90.7	38.7	15.2	0.7	13.1	19.4	7.1	3.5	3.8
Big Spring city	28 257	35 448	43 302	23 125	15 822	15 703	28 632	22 494	14 119	71.5	23.6	34.8	4.6	17.4	4.9	7.1	21.7	24.6
Brownsville city	24 468	26 186	29 875	20 660	10 343	11 940	22 234	17 597	9 762	78.8	16.0	25.7	12.0	9.5	4.1	-8.2	33.6	39.0
Bryan city	31 672	41 433	48 294	30 431	14 023	19 201	30 589	23 714	15 770	85.0	30.0	19.3	4.0	13.2	6.2	-6.1	21.0	21.9
Carrollton city	62 406	68 672	75 097	44 338	35 019	42 374	46 441	34 350	26 746	94.6	37.1	10.8	0.8	8.2	23.2	10.9	4.5	5.8
Cedar Hill city	60 136	63 416	70 000	40 227	29 129	38 958	42 196	32 999	23 389	93.8	27.9	10.9	1.2	10.3	16.3	4.0	4.7	6.0
Cedar Park city	67 527	70 587	74 046	55 500	32 287	42 102	50 467	33 050	24 767	94.8	38.5	9.4	0.8	9.3	18.9	6.6	3.3	4.6
Cleburne city	35 481	41 975	47 795	31 917	21 000	17 652	32 947	22 530	16 762	76.8	24.6	28.4	2.6	13.8	6.5	-5.8	14.0	14.5
College Station city	21 180	53 147	61 945	28 958	14 107	11 992	40 118	27 191	15 170	89.0	35.7	7.7	0.7	6.0	9.1	-3.2	39.2	16.1
Conroe city	34 123	37 201	42 455	26 250	16 818	24 811	30 182	23 465	16 841	82.0	24.2	23.0	4.4	11.6	7.2	-5.1	16.1	22.4
Coppell city	96 935	106 630	114 261	64 688	45 789	51 040	78 818	45 768	40 219	96.4	51.2	6.4	0.6	5.6	48.2	35.9	1.9	1.8
Copperas Cove city	37 869	40 517	41 542	28 795	18 730	25 394	27 687	22 900	15 995	92.4	23.1	12.7	2.3	21.7	4.9	-7.4	8.6	11.1
Corpus Christi city	36 414	41 672	50 328	23 290	17 051	22 917	32 787	23 624	17 419	81.9	26.4	23.8	4.7	15.2	8.0	-4.3	16.3	19.5
Dallas city	37 628	40 921	45 191	25 634	20 309	31 759	31 650	29 067	22 183	86.0	25.8	17.3	2.9	9.2	12.4	0.1	14.4	21.0
Deer Park city	61 334	66 516	72 669	51 733	30 354	34 609	51 571	31 497	24 440	89.1	34.2	16.1	1.0	12.7	21.2	8.9	4.8	5.0
Del Rio city	27 387	30 788	32 326	14 853	13 529	12 554	29 415	18 255	12 199	79.4	19.5	26.8	6.1	13.5	5.2	-7.1	25.1	30.4
Denton city	35 422	51 419	59 957	27 219	22 063	21 250	35 012	26 841	19 365	87.6	28.3	15.7	1.8	10.1	9.6	-2.7	18.0	11.9
DeSoto city	57 699	66 986	76 476	39 643	30 682	29 115	42 882	34 128	25 650	88.0	30.9	17.9	1.3	14.7	19.0	6.7	6.0	6.4
Duncanville city	51 654	57 064	63 763	36 406	30 486	30 054	40 361	30 730	22 924	87.4	34.4	20.2	1.4	16.4	15.0	2.7	5.0	6.3
Edinburg city	28 938	30 634	36 386	27 250	12 164	16 586	28 547	21 336	11 854	83.5	15.8	20.1	9.8	8.9	5.4	-6.9	27.3	31.6
El Paso city	32 124	35 432	39 436	23 895	15 742	19 831	30 334	22 177	14 388	81.8	22.9	24.8	6.2	15.7	6.9	-5.4	20.4	25.2
Euless city	49 582	54 697	60 239	37 336	33 594	38 789	40 094	33 287	23 764	93.4	29.9	10.2	0.8	7.9	10.7	-1.6	6.0	8.5
Farmers Branch city	54 734	57 531	55 833	42 557	32 176	42 612	35 729	28 663	24 921	86.6	39.5	22.5	0.6	13.2	19.7	7.4	4.9	6.5
Flower Mound town	95 416	98 055	101 445	50 000	43 750	59 119	71 059	42 048	34 699	96.8	50.1	7.0	0.5	6.2	46.2	33.9	2.2	2.7
Fort Worth city	37 074	42 939	50 099	28 019	19 428	25 978	32 225	26 520	18 800	83.7	25.1	20.4	3.1	12.2	8.9	-3.4	14.2	17.6
Friendswood city	69 384	77 293	86 168	52 279	38 860	36 104	61 568	36 272	28 615	88.5	47.2	17.3	1.0	15.5	26.8	14.5	3.3	3.2
Frisco city	79 149	84 150	86 085	45 625	38 934	46 931	60 492	38 323	34 089	95.1	42.5	8.8	0.9	7.6	30.8	18.5	2.9	2.5
Galveston city	28 895	35 049	43 804	21 335	16 353	19 998	30 806	26 841	18 275	77.0	26.3	25.8	4.3	15.1	7.6	-4.7	21.2	27.5
Garland city	49 156	53 545	58 188	37 123	29 825	31 891	36 446	30 088	20 000	89.9	28.1	16.2	2.1	11.3	12.3	0.0	7.6	9.3
Georgetown city	54 098	63 338	73 194	40 625	23 102	25 551	42 434	28 750	24 287	76.4	45.3	31.7	1.7	25.0	17.7	5.4	7.0	8.0
Grand Prairie city	46 816	51 449	59 359	30 775	22 333	31 066	35 938	29 080	18 978	90.2	24.3	15.5	2.4	10.7	10.4	-1.9	9.9	12.2
Grapevine city	71 680	84 940	96 078	30 769	38 750	41 390	57 007	40 140	31 549	93.8	43.7	10.8	1.1	8.5	30.8	18.5	4.7	3.6
Haltom City city	38 818	42 706	49 163	29 531	23 168	27 407	33 699	26 623	17 740	86.0	22.9	21.0	2.0	12.9	6.4	-5.9	9.8	10.2
Harlingen city	30 296	34 015	37 537	21 761	14 138	18 232	28 004	22 421	13 886	73.2	26.1	32.0	7.3	16.3	6.3	-6.0	21.7	27.7
Houston city	36 616	40 443	43 995	24 647	19 309	29 789	32 782	28 093	20 101	85.3	25.7	17.4	3.0	9.7	11.8	-0.5	16.3	21.8
Huntsville city	27 075	46 750	47 778	19 551	20 190	16 137	28 336	23 643	13 576	81.4	25.4	19.3	2.5	13.7	7.4	-4.9	25.6	20.0
Hurst city	50 369	57 955	64 854	30 081	27 474	31 079	41 515	30 355	23 247	84.2	37.1	23.3	1.6	18.0	13.8	1.5	5.7	8.0
Irving city	44 956	50 172	51 664	27 908	26 549	36 902	36 364	30 940	23 419	92.0	27.8	11.8	1.2	7.9	11.9	-0.4	8.6	11.8
Keller city	86 232	90 129	92 282	73 333	36 944	54 018	68 813	35 496	31 986	94.8	50.2	10.7	0.3	11.2	38.1	25.8	1.3	1.3
Killeen city	34 461	36 674	40 719	26 467	16 828	26 376	27 691	22 348	15 323	90.5	20.0	11.7	3.1	17.7	3.4	-8.9	11.7	15.8
Kingsville city	27 624	31 882	40 893	16 172	10 025	13 193	31 890	20 134	13 003	77.0	21.0	25.0	8.1	13.8	4.9	-7.4	27.5	32.0
Lake Jackson city	60 901	69 053	82 409	32 171	24 097	32 557	61 063	31 264	25 877	84.8	47.0	20.6	1.4	17.9	22.2	9.9	7.2	7.3
Lancaster city	43 773	48 498	58 823	39 000	30 661	30 670	34 172	31 245	18 731	87.5	21.4	17.8	2.4	11.4	8.4	-3.9	7.8	8.3

Table B-5. Cities — **Education, Labor Force, and Income**

STATE Place code	City	High school graduates			College graduates		College graduates (percent)				
		Total population 25 years and over	Percent with a high school diploma or less	Percent with a high school diploma or more	Percent with a bachelor's degree or more	+/− U.S. percent with bachelor's degree or more	Non-Hispanic White	Black or African American	American Indian and Alaska Native	Asian, Hawaiian, and Pacific Islander	Hispanic or Latino[1]
		1	2	3	4	5	6	7	8	9	10
	TEXAS—Cont'd										
48 41440	La Porte city	19 508	49.7	83.6	13.2	−11.2	14.1	13.8	8.6	13.4	8.5
48 41464	Laredo city	93 821	63.5	54.8	14.7	−9.7	37.0	24.5	6.7	44.1	13.0
48 41980	League City city	29 095	29.1	90.9	35.5	11.1	37.5	41.9	5.2	36.5	19.2
48 42508	Lewisville city	47 915	34.4	87.0	32.4	8.0	34.8	36.3	16.0	48.4	14.0
48 43888	Longview city	45 509	47.7	80.3	20.6	−3.8	24.7	10.1	17.0	44.3	6.6
48 45000	Lubbock city	114 674	44.3	79.5	26.6	2.2	34.4	10.4	14.4	65.1	7.9
48 45072	Lufkin city	20 439	51.6	72.6	20.6	−3.8	28.3	6.6	22.4	24.1	7.7
48 45384	McAllen city	62 678	53.7	65.3	23.6	−0.8	41.0	27.9	10.8	68.6	17.4
48 45744	McKinney city	32 570	32.6	83.2	39.1	14.7	45.3	19.0	40.1	65.8	12.6
48 46452	Mansfield city	17 529	35.3	86.9	32.8	8.4	34.8	37.4	25.0	63.3	11.0
48 47892	Mesquite city	75 479	46.5	83.0	18.5	−5.9	17.7	25.3	18.5	42.9	9.2
48 48072	Midland city	58 501	41.3	80.6	27.2	2.8	35.9	10.2	29.1	50.1	6.1
48 48768	Mission city	26 655	62.8	59.0	17.9	−6.5	28.2	52.7	0.0	74.0	13.8
48 48804	Missouri City city	32 954	23.2	92.2	44.5	20.1	50.4	37.7	42.9	62.6	20.8
48 50256	Nacogdoches city	14 760	44.9	75.6	30.4	6.0	40.8	9.6	20.6	62.0	6.4
48 50820	New Braunfels city	24 263	52.0	78.0	24.6	0.2	31.8	23.2	8.8	42.4	6.5
48 52356	North Richland Hills city	35 392	33.9	90.0	26.1	1.7	26.5	38.0	30.2	28.1	18.8
48 53388	Odessa city	54 240	55.2	70.7	14.7	−9.7	20.1	7.9	7.1	59.0	5.2
48 55080	Paris city	16 725	57.9	74.0	15.2	−9.2	18.2	5.1	9.1	30.7	9.6
48 56000	Pasadena city	80 614	60.8	67.1	12.7	−11.7	17.3	19.5	15.8	39.6	4.3
48 56348	Pearland city	24 354	34.8	87.9	29.1	4.7	29.9	44.0	17.2	40.7	17.9
48 57200	Pharr city	25 135	73.2	47.3	11.2	−13.2	22.8	0.0	13.1	65.2	8.9
48 58016	Plano city	144 046	18.3	93.9	53.3	28.9	54.4	46.1	26.5	72.4	24.7
48 58820	Port Arthur city	35 576	64.9	69.7	9.3	−15.1	12.1	7.5	7.0	13.8	5.5
48 61796	Richardson city	60 882	22.8	91.5	47.7	23.3	50.8	31.5	26.2	56.1	19.1
48 63500	Round Rock city	36 269	32.1	89.6	32.9	8.5	37.6	27.3	18.5	50.0	15.9
48 63572	Rowlett city	27 162	30.8	92.4	32.5	8.1	32.2	41.1	21.1	50.5	17.3
48 64472	San Angelo city	53 460	51.7	76.1	20.1	−4.3	26.1	12.6	16.1	30.7	6.2
48 65000	San Antonio city	696 022	49.1	75.1	21.6	−2.8	37.0	17.0	12.3	40.3	10.5
48 65516	San Juan city	13 222	75.0	45.4	8.3	−16.1	19.2	15.3	0.0	X	7.4
48 65600	San Marcos city	14 717	44.4	79.5	29.0	4.6	43.5	12.7	28.9	66.7	11.8
48 67496	Sherman city	21 798	48.1	78.5	20.1	−4.3	22.0	10.9	22.0	49.5	8.1
48 68636	Socorro city	14 470	77.7	44.5	4.3	−20.1	19.1	0.0	4.2	59.3	3.4
48 70808	Sugar Land city	39 752	20.0	93.4	53.7	29.3	54.0	51.2	26.8	60.5	33.0
48 72176	Temple city	35 193	46.5	79.8	22.9	−1.5	28.6	7.7	29.1	45.3	7.5
48 72368	Texarkana city	22 337	49.9	79.0	20.4	−4.0	26.7	6.4	21.7	66.0	10.1
48 72392	Texas City city	26 416	56.0	76.6	11.5	−12.9	13.8	7.3	30.4	38.9	6.8
48 72530	The Colony city	15 828	33.9	90.6	24.0	−0.4	25.0	22.5	12.4	44.0	14.4
48 74144	Tyler city	52 125	41.8	78.8	27.5	3.1	37.0	11.5	13.5	60.2	2.9
48 75428	Victoria city	37 322	51.0	75.6	18.5	−5.9	27.0	9.4	10.4	54.6	6.8
48 76000	Waco city	62 302	54.5	71.6	18.6	−5.8	26.6	8.2	5.7	53.0	4.9
48 77272	Weslaco city	15 790	66.3	55.9	13.5	−10.9	29.0	0.0	24.5	65.6	8.2
48 79000	Wichita Falls city	62 652	48.2	79.7	21.5	−2.9	25.3	10.3	16.3	20.7	8.4
49 00000	UTAH	1 197 892	36.9	87.7	26.1	1.7	27.7	19.8	9.1	31.1	9.8
49 07690	Bountiful city	24 100	25.4	93.8	35.6	11.2	36.0	36.8	26.9	41.8	14.3
49 13850	Clearfield city	12 489	45.0	86.6	14.8	−9.6	15.4	18.7	5.5	11.1	8.4
49 20120	Draper city	14 514	26.7	91.1	33.5	9.1	35.9	15.6	0.0	43.5	9.9
49 43660	Layton city	31 054	32.8	91.6	27.1	2.7	28.3	17.1	11.9	32.0	10.3
49 45860	Logan city	18 147	29.3	88.9	34.5	10.1	36.3	32.8	5.9	53.6	8.5
49 49710	Midvale city	15 628	45.8	82.6	20.7	−3.7	22.7	35.7	22.0	44.1	6.4
49 53230	Murray city	20 292	34.4	90.5	25.5	1.1	25.7	23.9	11.8	32.0	21.5
49 55980	Ogden city	43 859	51.6	76.0	16.9	−7.5	20.1	7.0	8.7	29.5	4.6
49 57300	Orem city	39 978	23.9	91.5	35.3	10.9	36.6	46.3	13.8	39.3	18.9
49 62470	Provo city	39 837	25.3	89.4	35.7	11.3	38.5	25.4	21.5	47.4	15.5
49 64340	Riverton city	12 329	35.3	93.2	23.3	−1.1	23.2	72.5	40.0	23.6	21.6
49 65110	Roy city	18 196	40.5	89.7	16.3	−8.1	16.5	15.2	25.4	32.8	8.2
49 65330	St. George city	28 855	38.5	87.8	22.0	−2.4	23.0	19.0	13.1	17.4	4.3
49 67000	Salt Lake City city	110 848	36.3	83.4	34.9	10.5	40.3	16.2	9.7	36.9	9.4
49 67440	Sandy city	47 893	26.8	93.6	34.7	10.3	35.1	43.3	35.8	44.1	18.9
49 70850	South Jordan city	14 714	26.6	95.8	30.9	6.5	31.2	29.8	55.8	40.4	15.2
49 75360	Taylorsville city	31 548	40.8	87.5	17.8	−6.6	18.3	33.4	16.7	22.3	10.7
49 82950	West Jordan city	34 076	38.6	89.3	20.2	−4.2	21.3	40.4	2.8	19.8	8.0
49 83470	West Valley City city	58 128	53.0	78.4	11.4	−13.0	12.6	12.5	8.2	9.6	5.6
50 00000	VERMONT	404 223	45.9	86.4	29.4	5.0	29.4	34.8	18.1	46.1	36.8
50 10675	Burlington city	22 629	35.1	87.7	42.0	17.6	42.5	33.6	27.6	34.5	43.8

[1] Hispanic or Latino persons may be of any race.

Table B-5. Cities — Education, Labor Force, and Income

City	School enrollment			Population 16 to 19 years				Employment status, 2000			Work status in 1999 of the population 16 years and over		
											Worked in 1999		
	Grades kindergarten through 12	College or graduate school	Percent private	Number	Percent in armed forces	Percent high school graduates	Percent not enrolled, not grads, not in armed forces, not employed	Total population 16 years and over	Percent in labor force	Unemployment rate	Full-time	Part-time	Did not work in 1999
	11	12	13	14	15	16	17	18	19	20	21	22	23
TEXAS—Cont'd													
La Porte city	7 160	1 819	6.2	2 046	0.0	9.6	2.8	23 589	70.4	5.1	63.3	10.9	25.8
Laredo city	46 118	10 513	6.0	12 541	0.0	8.2	10.4	120 272	53.5	9.0	49.5	11.6	38.9
League City city	9 515	2 791	11.1	2 303	0.0	5.6	4.0	33 370	73.5	4.0	66.7	11.6	21.7
Lewisville city	13 052	5 051	9.5	3 554	0.0	15.9	4.2	58 818	80.4	3.5	73.2	12.1	14.7
Longview city	14 561	3 314	12.1	4 804	0.0	11.4	10.8	55 843	61.1	7.3	53.7	13.3	33.0
Lubbock city	36 219	29 065	7.6	15 312	0.0	10.2	3.9	155 614	65.1	6.0	54.1	19.0	26.9
Lufkin city	6 262	1 691	6.6	2 006	0.0	9.5	8.2	24 875	59.5	6.9	51.8	13.3	34.8
McAllen city	25 294	6 968	6.1	7 151	0.0	7.9	5.0	77 366	57.6	8.7	50.0	12.4	37.6
McKinney city	10 867	2 526	7.5	2 923	0.0	14.4	15.6	39 123	70.1	3.5	64.3	12.5	23.2
Mansfield city	6 698	1 195	9.7	1 659	0.0	9.7	6.6	20 608	73.1	3.9	66.3	13.8	20.0
Mesquite city	28 445	5 519	9.3	7 428	0.1	11.1	4.6	90 938	73.8	3.7	67.8	11.4	20.8
Midland city	21 781	4 807	11.7	6 189	0.0	9.2	5.0	70 017	64.3	5.4	55.2	14.0	30.8
Mission city	10 944	2 379	4.1	2 006	0.2	5.2	8.0	32 818	50.7	10.6	45.8	10.0	44.1
Missouri City city	12 438	3 360	11.5	3 407	0.0	6.7	2.3	38 309	73.5	4.5	67.0	11.4	21.6
Nacogdoches city	4 697	8 276	4.4	3 583	0.0	4.6	2.6	24 745	63.1	15.5	45.9	24.5	29.6
New Braunfels city	7 011	1 250	9.3	1 955	0.0	17.4	5.9	28 298	62.6	3.7	55.4	12.4	32.2
North Richland Hills city	11 116	2 832	10.6	3 100	0.0	11.5	5.2	42 110	74.5	3.8	65.5	13.9	20.6
Odessa city	20 488	4 630	4.3	6 220	0.1	10.0	4.7	67 017	60.7	7.3	53.4	12.9	33.7
Paris city	4 685	1 084	6.2	1 456	0.0	12.4	6.7	19 935	55.3	6.4	48.8	12.1	39.2
Pasadena city	31 878	6 411	6.4	8 933	0.0	11.1	10.7	101 455	62.2	7.1	57.4	11.1	31.5
Pearland city	7 872	2 137	10.5	1 975	0.0	10.7	1.7	27 986	72.5	3.9	64.7	12.5	22.8
Pharr city	11 857	1 972	3.2	3 216	0.0	9.8	8.8	32 041	50.7	10.5	45.0	11.3	43.1
Plano city	44 709	11 759	11.4	10 977	0.1	9.2	2.0	164 895	75.3	3.1	68.3	12.1	19.6
Port Arthur city	12 356	2 028	5.3	3 850	0.0	13.5	8.3	43 268	52.8	13.3	44.2	11.7	44.1
Richardson city............	16 805	7 135	13.3	4 949	0.0	6.9	3.1	71 347	71.8	3.2	62.7	14.7	22.6
Round Rock city	13 205	2 760	9.0	3 110	0.0	11.6	3.1	42 963	77.4	3.4	71.8	11.3	16.9
Rowlett city.................	10 803	2 072	10.2	2 359	0.0	8.0	2.8	30 953	76.7	2.8	68.4	13.2	18.3
San Angelo city	17 199	6 665	4.6	6 692	7.6	18.5	4.3	68 643	63.8	6.6	53.4	15.4	31.3
San Antonio city	240 693	74 407	12.2	69 641	1.0	11.2	7.6	852 647	62.7	6.1	56.0	13.2	30.8
San Juan city	7 345	1 217	1.0	1 066	0.0	8.5	10.7	17 340	51.6	10.2	45.6	12.9	41.5
San Marcos city	3 321	13 367	3.0	3 726	0.0	5.0	2.8	29 625	68.9	8.7	46.4	33.7	19.9
Sherman city	5 983	2 441	18.9	2 190	0.0	12.1	8.6	27 392	60.0	5.3	53.5	13.8	32.6
Socorro city	8 080	1 465	2.7	2 332	0.0	7.8	8.8	18 837	52.1	13.2	47.0	10.9	42.1
Sugar Land city	16 340	3 580	14.3	4 329	0.0	5.2	1.4	46 259	69.5	4.1	60.5	13.7	25.8
Temple city	10 155	2 832	9.7	2 888	0.0	15.7	4.5	41 650	61.7	5.2	54.9	12.4	32.7
Texarkana city	7 018	1 459	5.0	2 014	0.0	12.7	6.6	26 648	56.2	9.5	49.1	12.0	38.9
Texas City city	8 663	2 180	4.6	2 523	0.0	9.6	6.0	31 592	59.2	7.7	53.9	10.5	35.6
The Colony city	6 607	1 330	6.4	1 580	0.0	11.7	0.9	10 744	70.1	2.9	72.4	12.3	15.3
Tyler city	15 438	5 328	10.4	5 435	0.0	12.1	6.3	64 674	61.2	5.8	52.7	14.0	33.3
Victoria city.................	13 050	2 974	10.0	3 527	0.0	13.3	5.3	44 890	65.0	4.9	57.6	12.6	29.9
Waco city....................	20 426	17 821	32.9	10 610	0.0	7.6	6.3	88 061	58.7	11.5	48.6	17.3	34.2
Weslaco city	6 135	1 072	3.5	1 656	0.0	8.8	9.8	19 267	52.5	14.3	46.1	10.0	43.9
Wichita Falls city	18 767	7 787	8.3	8 624	28.8	40.6	6.3	81 304	63.7	5.5	56.0	14.8	29.3
UTAH	508 724	186 743	10.6	173 747	0.1	13.8	3.9	1 600 279	69.0	4.9	54.5	20.9	24.5
Bountiful city	9 005	2 906	6.5	2 772	0.0	9.7	1.5	30 528	66.3	3.3	49.2	22.5	28.3
Clearfield city...............	6 207	1 401	6.3	2 259	0.4	19.9	10.5	17 565	72.8	7.7	60.2	17.0	22.7
Draper city	5 655	1 795	11.3	1 371	0.0	12.3	3.4	18 146	61.1	1.6	58.2	20.7	21.2
Layton city	14 459	3 649	6.0	4 458	0.9	18.8	1.9	40 481	75.2	4.3	61.4	18.6	19.9
Logan city	5 867	13 414	2.2	4 207	0.0	11.5	3.0	33 757	70.2	6.4	47.8	32.5	19.7
Midvale city	4 261	1 644	10.9	1 806	0.0	17.2	8.5	20 925	73.0	5.1	60.9	15.0	24.1
Murray city	6 467	2 469	7.4	2 264	0.0	16.9	1.9	26 036	71.4	4.6	58.0	19.0	23.1
Ogden city	15 021	4 825	5.4	5 180	0.2	16.4	9.3	57 363	65.7	8.6	54.2	16.9	29.0
Orem city	20 604	9 580	15.3	7 333	0.0	14.7	2.7	58 268	68.8	4.6	50.7	24.7	24.7
Provo city	14 048	37 799	59.2	14 167	0.1	14.5	1.5	84 575	65.9	6.3	43.1	36.9	20.0
Riverton city	7 569	1 077	4.6	1 702	0.0	9.6	2.4	15 516	75.3	2.4	61.0	18.9	20.0
Roy city	7 662	1 589	4.6	2 062	0.4	17.2	3.8	22 925	74.5	4.5	62.8	16.5	20.8
St. George city	9 645	3 479	4.7	4 093	0.0	15.3	2.3	37 257	57.5	6.1	42.6	19.3	38.1
Salt Lake City city	28 767	20 493	11.0	10 469	0.0	13.2	6.6	143 161	68.4	5.8	55.7	18.9	25.5
Sandy city	23 765	5 927	10.1	7 282	0.1	11.7	1.8	61 874	74.6	2.9	57.8	21.5	20.7
South Jordan city	9 261	1 608	4.8	2 710	0.0	9.5	0.3	19 474	72.5	2.7	56.1	22.6	21.3
Taylorsville city............	12 911	3 551	6.0	4 419	0.0	16.6	4.1	42 352	75.6	4.4	63.6	18.0	18.4
West Jordan city	17 900	3 228	6.2	5 523	0.1	16.0	4.0	45 470	78.8	4.2	64.3	19.5	16.2
West Valley City city	24 780	5 196	5.1	7 814	0.0	15.1	6.3	76 161	72.5	5.8	62.4	16.2	21.4
VERMONT	114 318	40 318	16.5	36 432	0.1	10.2	2.5	479 140	69.3	4.2	56.8	18.8	24.4
Burlington city...............	4 738	9 237	16.2	3 323	0.0	5.0	1.7	33 294	68.0	5.4	55.7	23.4	21.0

City	Full-year full-time employed (percent)								Children under 18 years in families (percent, except where noted)						Total employed by class of worker (percent)			
				Non-Hispanic White	Black or African American	American Indian and Alaska Native	Asian, Hawaiian, and Pacific Islander	Hispanic or Latino[1]		With two parents		With one parent who is in labor force	+/− U.S. percent of children with no stay-at-home parent	+/− U.S. percent two-income couples				Unpaid family worker
	Total	Men	Women						Number	Both in labor force	Father only in labor force				Private	Government	Self-employed	
	24	25	26	27	28	29	30	31	32	33	34	35	36	37	38	39	40	41
TEXAS—Cont'd																		
La Porte city	48.5	59.8	37.7	51.3	39.6	49.1	33.3	41.0	8 777	47.9	26.5	16.5	-0.2	3.9	83.1	11.9	4.9	0.2
Laredo city	31.5	42.7	21.7	36.6	26.2	24.2	34.2	31.2	58 398	29.2	27.9	16.1	-19.3	-15.6	67.8	20.2	11.6	0.5
League City city	52.4	65.9	39.1	53.9	56.8	55.8	40.8	44.2	12 863	50.3	29.1	13.9	-0.4	6.8	74.1	17.8	8.0	0.1
Lewisville city	57.2	66.4	48.0	59.5	57.8	48.3	49.3	48.4	19 641	47.6	26.5	18.3	1.3	13.6	85.7	8.6	5.5	0.1
Longview city	38.1	47.7	29.4	40.4	32.4	23.8	42.9	35.1	18 139	37.0	21.7	27.1	-0.5	-2.5	78.6	11.1	10.0	0.3
Lubbock city	38.5	46.2	31.4	38.4	34.1	40.1	30.3	40.8	45 733	42.9	17.5	24.8	3.1	2.9	69.6	20.8	9.3	0.3
Lufkin city	36.9	48.3	27.5	37.3	33.2	35.0	35.2	42.6	8 120	37.3	18.6	27.1	-0.2	-1.9	73.9	16.2	9.8	0.1
McAllen city	32.9	42.5	24.6	38.7	50.2	30.8	36.2	31.3	30 682	36.7	25.1	17.6	-10.3	-10.3	66.9	19.4	13.2	0.5
McKinney city	49.0	63.2	34.7	51.2	37.1	47.1	50.1	44.6	15 818	42.6	35.4	14.9	-7.1	4.1	82.6	9.2	8.1	0.2
Mansfield city	52.7	65.2	39.8	53.8	42.0	30.9	40.9	50.8	8 808	55.1	28.1	11.5	2.0	9.0	78.1	11.6	10.4	0.0
Mesquite city	52.7	62.4	44.1	53.3	55.7	47.6	51.1	48.5	36 065	48.0	20.0	22.1	5.5	10.7	80.4	12.2	7.2	0.2
Midland city	40.8	52.7	30.4	43.4	35.1	47.3	35.8	35.7	26 747	41.8	27.8	19.2	-3.6	-1.7	72.9	14.1	12.5	0.4
Mission city	26.8	33.4	21.2	22.6	39.2	36.1	47.2	27.9	14 044	34.3	25.8	17.7	-12.6	-16.7	67.1	20.4	12.0	0.5
Missouri City city	52.8	62.2	44.3	52.7	56.3	65.9	47.6	44.2	15 501	52.7	23.3	15.1	3.2	11.8	74.6	16.0	9.1	0.3
Nacogdoches city	27.4	34.6	21.5	27.9	24.6	43.3	27.7	29.1	5 797	34.6	13.5	30.4	0.4	2.0	67.0	24.9	7.6	0.6
New Braunfels city	40.3	52.1	29.8	39.6	50.2	35.0	30.3	41.5	9 128	49.0	18.9	22.5	6.9	0.1	73.3	15.0	11.4	0.3
North Richland Hills city	52.0	63.8	40.9	52.0	44.6	57.5	51.6	53.1	14 537	50.1	24.4	19.3	4.8	9.5	81.6	9.9	8.3	0.2
Odessa city	36.8	47.3	27.4	41.2	27.2	41.0	40.5	31.6	25 396	35.4	26.2	25.0	-4.2	-5.7	75.2	14.9	9.6	0.3
Paris city	33.9	44.0	25.6	34.5	31.9	50.3	18.5	35.9	6 159	32.8	17.9	36.5	4.7	-6.0	76.9	12.9	10.0	0.2
Pasadena city	39.3	50.5	28.3	43.0	36.1	37.4	44.5	34.8	42 190	30.7	30.4	19.7	-14.2	-10.0	82.4	10.4	6.9	0.2
Pearland city	51.4	62.2	41.3	52.0	53.8	61.7	46.7	47.8	10 467	53.8	24.2	14.5	3.7	7.7	76.6	15.2	8.0	0.2
Pharr city	24.3	31.9	17.7	11.8	67.4	25.4	13.5	26.0	14 856	28.6	30.8	15.7	-20.3	-22.7	71.2	17.4	11.2	0.2
Plano city	54.3	68.3	40.6	56.2	59.7	56.9	49.6	41.2	61 747	45.5	37.1	11.9	-7.2	6.3	82.4	7.4	10.0	0.2
Port Arthur city	28.4	34.9	22.8	30.1	27.9	36.1	26.4	25.5	15 198	25.7	20.5	29.0	-9.9	-16.9	75.4	17.0	7.4	0.2
Richardson city	48.7	59.4	38.4	49.8	54.7	33.9	41.6	46.5	21 968	48.2	29.1	16.0	-0.4	4.3	79.3	9.8	10.5	0.4
Round Rock city	57.1	68.6	45.8	57.6	65.8	69.7	44.5	54.3	18 545	50.0	26.0	16.2	1.6	12.8	78.5	14.8	6.7	0.1
Rowlett city	56.1	68.5	44.3	56.2	62.9	65.4	52.4	50.6	14 359	58.3	22.2	13.8	7.5	15.7	76.9	12.8	10.1	0.2
San Angelo city	38.8	47.7	30.9	39.4	35.6	48.8	33.3	38.3	21 478	43.0	17.6	25.5	3.9	-2.6	72.6	17.5	9.7	0.3
San Antonio city	40.1	49.3	31.9	44.3	39.9	38.3	40.8	37.3	305 519	34.5	21.6	25.1	-5.0	-4.5	75.9	15.8	8.1	0.2
San Juan city	25.6	33.9	18.2	21.1	0.0	0.0	X	25.9	8 898	26.9	34.7	12.8	-24.9	-22.7	70.6	16.0	13.1	0.3
San Marcos city	27.3	34.2	20.7	24.5	19.9	12.7	11.7	34.1	4 470	40.0	16.9	29.8	5.2	-0.3	71.8	22.4	5.5	0.3
Sherman city	37.5	47.5	28.4	38.5	34.9	48.1	27.6	33.2	7 858	39.6	23.3	22.9	-2.1	-3.6	80.2	11.1	8.5	0.2
Socorro city	25.7	35.2	17.1	40.7	32.9	26.5	48.1	25.1	9 380	21.8	33.7	15.9	-26.9	-25.3	76.5	13.5	9.5	0.5
Sugar Land city	48.3	63.2	34.8	49.7	52.8	26.6	45.5	49.6	19 447	50.0	33.3	11.8	-2.8	6.5	74.1	10.8	14.7	0.5
Temple city	40.0	51.5	29.9	38.9	40.3	55.2	44.9	42.8	13 509	41.1	20.7	26.5	3.0	-1.2	77.4	14.8	7.4	0.4
Texarkana city	34.3	42.1	27.8	37.5	27.6	64.5	44.5	30.5	8 510	27.5	15.8	34.6	-2.5	-5.4	72.7	16.5	10.7	0.2
Texas City city	38.2	45.7	31.9	42.4	31.7	51.3	34.9	35.5	10 255	36.9	18.2	28.8	1.1	-7.0	72.8	20.5	6.5	0.2
The Colony city	59.7	71.3	48.4	61.8	60.5	48.8	42.4	51.1	8 685	57.7	21.9	14.0	7.1	17.6	85.5	7.6	6.9	0.1
Tyler city	37.7	48.8	28.5	37.6	35.7	47.4	58.4	40.8	20 339	37.3	23.5	24.9	-2.4	-4.4	76.7	12.5	10.5	0.3
Victoria city	41.8	53.3	31.6	42.9	39.1	27.6	41.6	41.4	16 334	44.4	17.7	26.2	6.0	1.2	77.6	13.5	8.7	0.2
Waco city	31.7	38.4	25.9	32.1	29.8	31.1	17.4	34.4	25 961	32.7	17.4	31.1	-0.8	-5.6	79.3	13.5	6.9	0.3
Weslaco city	25.3	32.4	19.4	23.4	0.0	31.6	45.8	25.4	7 976	33.7	22.8	23.1	-7.8	-16.6	70.5	19.8	9.4	0.3
Wichita Falls city	39.3	47.6	30.6	41.0	33.8	31.3	35.8	38.0	23 765	44.2	20.6	23.7	3.3	-1.0	69.7	19.9	10.1	0.4
UTAH	39.3	51.4	27.4	39.6	40.8	28.5	39.0	37.8	689 581	46.5	32.9	13.2	-4.9	2.2	74.3	15.7	9.7	0.3
Bountiful city	38.6	54.1	24.5	38.6	63.2	46.2	39.9	33.2	12 025	45.5	39.9	9.9	-9.2	-2.6	73.2	13.9	12.7	0.2
Clearfield city	43.3	55.5	30.8	44.5	42.1	28.9	31.1	41.2	8 833	45.3	25.3	18.9	-0.4	5.7	72.8	21.5	5.5	0.2
Draper city	41.2	49.6	29.5	43.3	15.3	25.1	43.0	24.7	7 795	44.0	44.6	7.9	-12.7	8.3	76.5	11.5	12.1	0.0
Layton city	47.5	61.6	33.5	48.0	55.4	39.4	47.9	39.6	19 966	47.9	33.2	13.5	-3.2	7.2	70.6	21.8	7.4	0.2
Logan city	28.7	38.2	20.0	28.9	30.6	26.1	20.8	31.5	9 640	45.9	33.4	14.4	-4.3	5.8	71.5	21.7	6.6	0.2
Midvale city	42.6	50.4	34.5	45.0	56.3	30.6	45.9	33.0	6 375	37.7	23.9	29.1	2.2	2.1	83.2	10.8	5.9	0.1
Murray city	44.1	55.6	33.2	44.0	45.9	44.7	51.6	41.2	8 770	49.8	27.4	15.1	0.3	3.1	77.0	13.9	8.9	0.3
Ogden city	36.3	45.2	27.3	37.2	31.6	22.5	36.4	33.7	20 566	41.4	20.9	23.6	0.4	-1.6	74.9	18.3	6.5	0.2
Orem city	35.4	48.1	23.2	35.6	32.3	37.8	31.9	33.4	28 428	38.3	42.9	11.2	-15.1	-2.6	77.2	12.5	10.0	0.4
Provo city	22.3	30.3	15.2	21.8	32.2	22.2	15.6	29.5	22 018	37.7	41.8	9.9	-17.0	-2.8	83.2	9.8	6.8	0.2
Riverton city	51.3	69.9	32.9	51.0	72.7	100.0	56.4	59.9	10 567	51.2	35.8	8.9	-4.5	9.3	74.2	15.2	10.5	0.1
Roy city	49.0	61.1	37.3	49.1	58.1	44.3	57.9	47.3	10 583	56.5	22.7	16.0	7.9	12.7	70.7	22.7	6.5	0.1
St. George city	29.3	40.8	18.9	28.6	11.7	31.0	26.0	37.9	13 521	43.3	35.2	14.9	-6.4	-11.5	74.1	12.3	12.7	0.9
Salt Lake City city	37.7	45.2	30.1	39.0	31.4	34.9	35.1	33.7	39 858	39.5	24.2	20.8	-4.3	1.3	74.7	16.9	8.2	0.2
Sandy city	45.3	59.6	31.4	45.4	60.7	43.9	51.5	41.6	29 636	48.3	35.2	11.8	-4.5	7.8	75.6	12.4	11.7	0.3
South Jordan city	44.4	60.8	27.9	44.1	46.4	54.8	51.1	51.1	11 334	50.0	41.6	5.5	-9.1	6.2	73.8	13.7	12.3	0.2
Taylorsville city	48.0	59.0	37.3	48.1	53.8	42.7	46.2	50.0	17 181	48.1	24.6	19.2	2.7	8.8	81.2	12.3	6.3	0.2
West Jordan city	49.9	62.9	36.9	50.3	74.2	41.8	51.8	46.9	24 747	53.9	28.5	11.6	0.9	14.4	79.2	13.0	7.5	0.2
West Valley City city	46.3	55.5	37.0	47.2	55.2	43.5	45.4	43.8	34 119	46.0	24.2	19.2	0.6	6.1	83.0	11.5	5.4	0.1
VERMONT	42.7	52.6	33.3	42.9	34.4	41.6	35.1	32.7	141 993	55.5	16.1	19.9	10.8	10.2	71.5	14.2	14.1	0.3
Burlington city	35.6	43.5	28.5	35.8	32.4	27.0	31.6	24.8	5 979	45.1	14.5	26.7	7.2	9.0	79.4	12.7	7.8	0.1

[1] Hispanic or Latino persons may be of any race.

City	Percent who worked at home	Percent of the population 5 years and over with a disability	Veterans as a percent of the population 18 years and over	Occupation for employed population 16 years and over (percent)						Industry for employed population 16 years and over (percent)					
				Management, professional, and related occupations	Service occupations	Sales and office occupations	Farming, fishing, and forestry occupations	Construction, extraction, and maintenance occupations	Production, transportation and material moving occupations	Agriculture, forestry, fishing, and mining	Construction and manufacturing	Wholesale and retail trade	Transportation and warehousing, and utilities	Service industries	Public administration
	42	43	44	45	46	47	48	49	50	51	52	53	54	55	56
TEXAS—Cont'd															
La Porte city	1.2	17.0	13.9	27.3	12.9	27.4	0.0	13.9	18.5	1.3	34.6	12.7	7.6	40.2	3.6
Laredo city	2.9	20.2	5.7	27.5	17.6	29.5	0.4	10.7	14.3	2.0	11.6	18.3	14.2	47.1	6.8
League City city	3.0	12.6	12.6	47.9	10.0	24.0	0.3	8.2	9.6	1.8	23.7	13.5	5.6	48.7	6.7
Lewisville city	2.4	12.5	10.2	38.5	11.3	31.9	0.1	8.6	9.7	0.3	18.0	20.7	6.4	52.5	2.1
Longview city	2.4	21.5	12.9	30.3	15.7	27.0	0.3	9.9	16.7	3.0	21.0	17.7	3.9	51.0	3.4
Lubbock city	2.4	19.2	10.4	34.2	17.0	29.7	0.4	8.6	10.1	1.3	11.0	17.9	3.7	61.7	4.4
Lufkin city	2.4	21.9	11.3	32.0	18.5	21.8	0.6	7.8	19.3	1.9	25.9	15.7	2.2	50.4	3.9
McAllen city	2.6	18.9	8.2	37.4	15.8	29.9	0.6	7.1	9.2	1.9	12.1	20.4	4.1	56.3	5.3
McKinney city	3.9	12.6	10.2	43.7	12.3	26.9	0.2	7.5	9.3	0.7	23.2	15.9	2.9	54.2	3.1
Mansfield city	2.7	10.7	12.2	41.2	8.9	28.2	0.2	9.7	11.8	0.8	27.7	18.1	6.2	43.2	4.0
Mesquite city	2.3	16.4	11.4	30.9	12.2	32.6	0.0	11.7	12.6	0.3	18.5	17.7	6.5	53.0	3.9
Midland city	2.3	16.2	11.6	36.9	15.6	28.0	0.1	10.2	9.3	13.9	10.4	15.5	4.1	52.3	3.8
Mission city	1.7	19.9	9.8	30.5	16.8	27.8	1.3	11.0	12.5	2.1	16.9	19.7	4.4	51.4	5.2
Missouri City city	2.3	12.6	10.9	49.2	9.0	28.7	0.0	4.9	8.2	2.9	14.7	13.8	7.0	57.5	4.2
Nacogdoches city	2.3	17.7	8.1	30.9	20.1	28.8	1.4	6.5	12.3	2.4	15.4	17.8	2.6	58.0	3.8
New Braunfels city	2.9	19.4	14.0	32.8	14.9	27.6	0.2	8.6	15.9	1.3	21.6	17.1	4.3	51.2	4.5
North Richland Hills city	2.7	16.7	13.8	36.9	11.5	32.9	0.0	8.6	10.1	0.3	18.2	18.4	10.2	49.5	3.5
Odessa city	2.3	18.0	11.3	25.9	16.2	30.1	0.2	12.8	14.8	7.2	17.1	18.7	3.6	50.3	3.0
Paris city	1.6	29.4	14.4	26.4	20.1	25.1	0.5	9.8	18.2	0.9	23.0	15.9	4.4	52.1	3.7
Pasadena city	1.4	20.0	9.8	23.5	13.3	27.6	0.1	18.6	16.9	1.0	30.9	15.6	6.0	44.0	2.6
Pearland city	2.0	14.9	12.4	40.9	9.3	29.7	0.1	9.6	10.5	2.0	21.9	15.0	6.1	49.3	5.7
Pharr city	1.9	21.6	6.3	23.2	20.3	26.2	2.6	12.4	15.2	3.6	17.3	19.1	4.5	51.9	3.6
Plano city	4.7	10.9	10.1	55.5	8.0	27.3	0.0	4.6	4.5	0.8	17.8	17.3	2.7	59.6	1.8
Port Arthur city	1.5	23.9	12.8	20.8	23.2	23.8	1.1	12.2	18.8	2.9	22.6	15.0	5.4	47.1	7.0
Richardson city	4.3	14.3	11.6	51.9	9.6	27.2	0.1	5.0	6.2	0.6	18.3	16.6	2.9	59.5	2.0
Round Rock city	2.7	12.1	12.7	41.9	10.0	29.2	0.3	8.6	10.2	0.6	28.4	15.0	3.1	45.9	6.9
Rowlett city	2.7	10.7	11.9	45.2	7.9	30.9	0.1	8.1	7.9	0.3	20.5	16.4	5.5	53.1	4.1
San Angelo city	2.1	20.7	14.3	27.8	19.4	29.2	0.6	9.8	13.1	2.5	14.6	16.4	3.0	57.6	6.0
San Antonio city	2.2	21.6	14.5	32.1	16.7	30.0	0.1	10.4	10.7	0.4	14.4	16.0	4.7	59.3	5.3
San Juan city	1.7	20.2	4.9	18.7	18.3	27.3	3.3	13.2	17.1	4.0	18.7	18.3	5.0	49.1	3.1
San Marcos city	1.8	14.7	7.6	30.4	21.5	32.4	0.4	6.7	8.6	0.6	11.4	17.2	2.4	64.7	3.6
Sherman city	2.2	23.4	14.1	30.3	15.9	26.9	0.2	8.8	17.9	0.7	25.6	15.5	3.4	50.9	3.9
Socorro city	2.1	20.4	4.5	13.9	15.7	24.1	0.5	16.9	28.9	0.9	36.0	14.5	6.7	38.8	3.0
Sugar Land city	4.1	10.5	8.5	56.8	7.4	27.1	0.2	3.5	5.0	4.5	15.8	16.6	4.2	56.5	2.4
Temple city	2.0	21.5	17.1	33.7	16.7	25.7	0.1	7.4	16.4	0.6	18.8	17.2	3.9	55.6	3.9
Texarkana city	2.5	24.4	13.8	31.5	17.1	29.1	0.2	6.6	15.5	0.8	15.7	18.8	4.1	54.4	6.2
Texas City city	1.6	22.6	14.6	20.5	16.8	27.9	0.2	13.4	15.2	1.0	22.5	15.0	5.2	50.9	5.4
The Colony city	3.1	14.0	12.3	37.2	9.3	34.4	0.1	9.7	9.4	0.2	18.0	22.0	5.1	51.8	2.7
Tyler city	2.1	22.9	11.8	32.4	16.5	26.9	0.4	8.3	15.5	2.3	18.2	17.7	2.8	55.8	3.2
Victoria city	2.0	19.4	12.7	30.1	16.0	27.1	0.2	12.1	14.4	3.6	21.8	18.0	3.5	49.3	3.8
Waco city	2.3	22.6	11.7	28.6	19.0	27.1	0.3	9.4	15.7	0.5	19.8	16.1	3.0	57.0	3.6
Weslaco city	1.4	22.0	8.7	29.4	18.5	28.1	2.4	8.6	12.9	3.4	12.3	19.1	4.7	56.2	4.3
Wichita Falls city	1.9	20.4	15.0	30.1	19.5	26.2	0.3	9.4	14.5	1.6	17.3	16.3	3.5	53.5	7.8
UTAH	4.2	14.9	10.6	32.5	14.0	28.9	0.5	10.6	13.5	1.9	20.3	16.3	4.9	51.1	5.5
Bountiful city	5.0	14.7	12.0	39.0	10.7	33.5	0.1	7.3	9.3	0.4	15.3	18.8	5.5	55.2	4.8
Clearfield city	2.2	15.4	14.7	21.1	16.4	29.7	0.1	13.7	19.0	0.4	24.7	17.7	3.7	40.5	13.1
Draper city	6.4	9.3	8.5	43.6	10.2	31.0	0.3	8.6	6.2	1.0	19.0	17.5	4.3	54.5	3.7
Layton city	3.4	13.2	15.1	33.8	11.7	31.2	0.4	10.7	12.2	0.7	18.4	19.8	5.5	43.7	11.9
Logan city	3.2	10.9	6.0	32.7	16.3	25.4	1.1	6.7	18.0	1.4	25.0	13.4	2.0	56.3	1.8
Midvale city	2.3	21.5	9.8	27.5	17.7	30.5	0.2	12.0	12.0	0.7	19.7	17.4	4.2	54.8	3.2
Murray city	4.7	15.9	12.1	32.7	12.3	36.5	0.1	8.9	9.6	0.5	16.9	18.5	5.7	53.0	5.4
Ogden city	2.8	21.5	13.0	25.0	16.4	25.6	0.7	12.3	19.9	1.3	26.6	15.8	3.2	43.4	9.7
Orem city	5.2	13.1	7.7	37.9	13.5	28.3	0.1	9.2	11.0	0.5	17.7	18.0	2.3	58.6	2.9
Provo city	4.1	10.3	4.4	38.3	16.1	28.8	0.2	7.1	9.4	0.4	13.7	14.6	1.2	67.9	2.2
Riverton city	5.5	9.6	8.6	30.8	13.0	31.5	0.1	13.9	10.8	1.4	24.1	17.0	6.7	45.0	5.8
Roy city	2.9	14.7	15.3	28.5	12.5	29.3	0.0	12.5	17.2	0.2	27.0	14.9	4.0	39.1	14.8
St. George city	5.0	16.9	15.1	27.3	19.1	29.2	0.3	12.1	12.0	0.7	18.2	20.4	3.9	53.3	3.4
Salt Lake City city	3.2	20.0	9.5	38.3	15.4	26.4	0.1	7.6	12.0	0.5	15.6	12.9	4.9	61.9	4.2
Sandy city	5.4	11.9	9.9	37.7	11.8	34.4	0.1	7.4	8.7	0.7	16.0	19.7	5.2	54.5	3.8
South Jordan city	6.0	9.8	9.1	37.5	10.6	32.7	0.1	9.0	10.2	1.1	20.2	17.6	7.4	49.1	4.5
Taylorsville city	3.2	16.1	10.0	27.3	12.3	34.9	0.0	10.5	15.0	0.5	20.3	17.4	7.6	49.5	4.8
West Jordan city	3.6	13.3	8.9	28.9	11.9	32.8	0.1	12.4	14.0	1.0	21.2	18.2	7.2	47.7	4.8
West Valley City city	2.3	18.9	10.3	20.1	12.7	32.3	0.2	12.6	22.2	0.8	26.2	17.8	8.3	43.1	3.8
VERMONT	5.7	17.1	13.6	36.3	14.6	24.5	1.3	9.3	14.0	3.0	21.7	15.1	3.7	51.8	4.6
Burlington city	3.1	17.0	8.1	39.2	16.4	28.6	0.2	5.2	10.4	0.3	14.5	16.5	2.9	62.7	3.2

City	Median house-hold income	All families	Married-couple	Male house-holder	Female house-holder	Median nonfamily house-hold income	Men	Women	Per capita income	With earnings	With interest, dividend, or rental income	With Social Security income	With public assis-tance income	With retire-ment income	House-holds with income over $100,000 (percent)	+/− U.S. percent for income over $100,000 (percent)	House-holds with income below poverty (percent)	Families with children with income below poverty (percent)
	57	58	59	60	61	62	63	64	65	66	67	68	69	70	71	72	73	74
TEXAS—Cont'd																		
La Porte city	55 810	60 034	64 739	36 971	24 917	35 895	46 890	30 080	21 178	89.4	27.7	14.5	2.1	11.5	12.0	-0.3	7.4	8.5
Laredo city	29 108	30 449	33 606	19 130	12 421	14 852	24 708	19 721	11 084	85.4	14.8	21.9	7.7	9.1	6.4	-5.9	26.7	31.3
League City city	67 838	72 760	76 653	45 179	32 563	43 193	54 250	35 115	27 170	93.0	43.4	12.5	0.7	11.5	22.2	9.9	4.1	4.6
Lewisville city	54 771	63 719	70 072	47 455	31 834	38 251	41 503	32 183	24 703	94.5	27.9	9.4	1.2	7.4	15.1	2.8	5.3	6.1
Longview city	33 858	42 378	52 005	25 972	15 998	21 725	34 895	22 045	18 768	77.7	30.9	28.3	3.7	16.2	7.8	-4.5	15.2	19.5
Lubbock city	31 844	41 418	49 609	21 729	16 981	17 855	31 083	22 347	17 511	83.3	28.8	22.1	3.0	12.5	7.0	-5.3	18.8	18.1
Lufkin city	32 989	40 591	47 226	26 487	12 438	18 009	31 799	20 634	17 613	77.3	30.6	29.2	4.2	15.0	8.4	-3.9	17.7	22.7
McAllen city	33 641	36 050	41 990	17 314	15 747	22 211	30 831	23 406	14 939	82.4	22.6	24.5	6.5	9.8	9.4	-2.9	21.7	26.8
McKinney city	63 366	72 133	81 601	31 667	25 657	32 639	51 180	32 599	28 185	90.6	38.9	15.0	1.5	11.0	25.4	13.1	6.4	6.6
Mansfield city	66 764	71 700	79 118	35 313	24 758	37 346	50 579	31 280	26 446	92.8	38.9	14.2	1.2	11.9	24.9	12.6	3.7	3.3
Mesquite city	50 424	56 357	63 663	35 321	28 684	31 338	38 452	30 565	20 890	91.1	25.7	16.4	1.9	11.3	11.1	-1.2	6.5	6.8
Midland city	39 320	48 290	55 285	25 682	19 163	22 096	39 396	25 789	20 884	83.6	35.2	24.8	2.8	12.6	12.4	0.1	12.0	14.7
Mission city	30 647	33 465	38 479	14 917	14 071	14 710	26 880	20 868	12 796	73.0	24.8	31.2	7.3	14.7	7.2	-5.1	24.1	30.7
Missouri City city	72 434	77 762	81 262	41 047	41 268	41 817	52 324	37 305	27 210	94.9	39.6	13.2	0.9	10.8	28.7	16.4	2.9	3.0
Nacogdoches city	22 700	37 020	52 522	30 469	10 134	11 898	29 957	23 291	14 546	79.4	26.9	20.5	3.8	11.3	7.0	-5.3	31.9	31.4
New Braunfels city	40 078	46 726	52 028	24 063	15 694	24 809	32 104	23 979	18 548	77.8	35.8	29.9	2.5	19.6	7.6	-4.7	10.2	13.8
North Richland Hills city	56 150	64 718	72 575	40 588	31 891	31 741	45 821	30 946	25 516	89.7	36.7	18.1	1.1	14.0	16.4	4.1	4.7	4.6
Odessa city	31 209	36 869	42 065	23 399	15 107	19 001	31 853	22 474	16 096	80.1	25.1	24.7	4.3	11.7	6.2	-6.1	18.0	21.9
Paris city	27 438	34 916	46 020	29 196	13 621	14 774	30 215	20 605	17 137	70.5	24.4	33.9	5.4	17.4	5.4	-6.9	20.2	23.8
Pasadena city	38 522	42 541	45 523	30 096	18 374	25 162	35 132	26 465	16 301	85.1	23.1	18.5	3.0	11.9	8.7	-3.6	14.1	17.8
Pearland city	64 156	70 748	79 386	35 924	36 413	35 365	50 936	35 414	26 306	90.8	43.1	17.2	1.1	13.0	22.6	10.3	4.4	4.7
Pharr city	24 333	25 916	25 564	15 625	10 745	11 291	19 509	17 356	9 462	74.2	16.3	31.0	12.1	12.5	3.3	-9.0	32.1	39.9
Plano city	78 722	91 162	99 809	50 500	37 234	46 741	66 188	40 473	36 514	94.3	46.8	9.5	0.8	8.2	36.8	24.5	3.6	4.0
Port Arthur city	26 455	32 143	41 250	26 765	11 732	14 864	31 413	21 458	14 183	69.1	20.8	33.7	5.9	16.4	4.7	-7.6	24.0	31.1
Richardson city	62 392	72 876	79 645	46 250	35 754	40 180	53 922	36 484	29 551	89.4	46.0	17.3	1.1	12.4	24.0	11.7	5.3	4.9
Round Rock city	60 354	65 471	71 639	35 250	30 877	36 999	43 859	31 432	24 911	94.0	34.1	10.0	1.2	9.4	17.4	5.1	4.0	3.5
Rowlett city	70 947	73 417	78 364	49 315	41 190	42 941	50 362	35 953	26 144	93.1	38.5	11.2	0.6	11.0	22.7	10.4	2.7	2.5
San Angelo city	32 232	38 665	44 571	21 638	15 890	18 759	28 915	21 314	17 289	78.0	30.7	27.9	4.3	18.8	5.6	-6.7	15.6	17.4
San Antonio city	36 214	41 331	47 356	25 115	18 021	25 001	30 917	25 322	17 487	83.1	27.5	22.6	3.9	17.1	8.6	-3.7	15.6	19.7
San Juan city	22 706	23 314	25 884	7 778	11 027	12 246	19 091	17 643	7 945	82.8	9.7	23.2	9.6	9.1	3.3	-9.0	33.2	38.6
San Marcos city	25 809	37 113	42 314	29 453	22 600	17 262	25 951	23 361	13 468	87.7	23.5	16.1	1.7	9.0	3.6	-8.7	29.1	18.1
Sherman city	34 211	42 528	48 543	26 765	21 272	20 549	32 925	24 276	18 717	76.8	32.2	28.8	3.2	16.5	6.1	-6.2	14.1	14.8
Socorro city	24 087	24 336	26 524	19 125	14 750	12 227	19 676	15 524	7 287	85.8	9.2	21.2	9.9	8.7	1.5	-10.8	31.9	34.9
Sugar Land city	81 767	88 639	96 940	65 221	39 516	40 640	66 447	39 672	33 506	91.7	55.2	12.5	0.9	8.4	38.6	26.3	3.9	3.2
Temple city	35 135	42 795	50 509	30 347	17 836	21 241	31 759	22 891	19 360	77.8	30.9	27.1	2.9	17.7	7.8	-4.5	13.7	16.7
Texarkana city	29 727	38 505	59 129	18 993	11 757	17 577	35 938	22 017	17 815	73.6	28.0	27.7	4.4	18.3	8.0	-4.3	22.3	30.5
Texas City city	35 963	42 393	54 457	36 500	16 484	20 896	37 715	25 316	17 057	78.1	25.2	28.5	4.4	19.8	6.4	-5.9	14.3	17.5
The Colony city	64 080	66 203	69 648	41 250	40 417	38 727	45 190	31 019	22 903	96.2	31.7	7.9	1.6	7.6	19.9	7.6	2.8	2.2
Tyler city	34 163	43 618	52 070	25 362	16 796	21 174	32 691	23 816	20 184	78.4	32.6	27.6	2.5	15.7	10.4	-1.9	15.8	19.5
Victoria city	36 829	42 866	53 279	21 012	16 583	22 793	35 463	21 686	19 009	81.7	29.8	25.3	3.5	13.6	9.2	-3.1	14.1	17.7
Waco city	26 264	33 919	40 536	21 855	13 286	16 035	27 978	21 907	14 584	78.4	25.4	26.0	4.1	13.8	5.4	-6.9	25.5	26.9
Weslaco city	26 573	29 315	29 635	15 913	13 540	24 965	20 878	22 676	11 225	72.7	21.4	33.1	9.5	12.6	4.6	-7.7	28.3	32.7
Wichita Falls city	32 554	39 911	44 467	24 679	16 950	20 872	29 167	22 676	16 761	80.6	31.7	25.9	3.4	16.9	5.7	-6.6	14.1	15.6
UTAH	45 726	51 022	56 556	32 364	22 090	26 405	38 046	25 579	18 185	86.1	37.5	20.6	3.1	15.7	11.2	-1.1	8.9	8.7
Bountiful city	55 993	62 905	69 821	36 023	30 109	26 754	47 406	28 605	23 967	82.6	51.3	28.5	2.3	22.2	18.9	6.6	4.8	4.5
Clearfield city	38 946	39 902	41 743	32 232	18 276	27 103	31 015	22 242	13 945	89.6	29.5	13.6	5.2	15.8	4.3	-8.0	10.0	11.2
Draper city	72 341	76 868	79 389	50 268	32 500	34 514	51 548	31 994	22 747	96.2	42.0	10.0	0.6	8.5	27.0	14.7	2.7	2.6
Layton city	52 128	57 193	62 227	35 139	21 266	31 802	41 781	27 238	19 604	91.7	36.4	13.7	3.6	17.6	13.2	0.9	5.9	6.5
Logan city	30 778	33 784	42 338	35 167	18 494	24 148	27 897	20 358	13 765	88.4	38.2	15.1	3.2	9.6	5.5	-6.8	20.3	16.4
Midvale city	40 130	43 322	46 378	38 822	15 933	30 950	31 821	26 194	17 609	85.3	31.9	20.6	3.9	14.4	5.8	-6.5	10.8	14.4
Murray city	45 569	51 482	62 155	36 250	22 424	31 187	36 728	26 913	21 094	85.4	40.3	23.4	2.1	16.4	10.4	-1.9	6.7	8.3
Ogden city	34 047	38 950	43 835	25 146	16 004	21 451	29 975	22 612	16 632	80.4	29.2	24.5	5.6	18.2	6.0	-6.3	15.5	18.7
Orem city	47 529	51 214	56 701	31 813	26 855	29 968	40 583	23 701	16 590	89.0	39.5	19.3	2.8	14.8	13.3	1.0	8.1	7.6
Provo city	34 313	36 393	44 037	30 586	18 359	26 930	33 054	21 380	13 207	90.0	42.3	15.2	2.4	10.3	7.3	-5.0	21.6	14.0
Riverton city	63 980	65 330	66 604	40 192	34 940	35 491	43 914	27 104	17 643	93.3	35.2	12.1	1.2	11.6	15.3	3.0	2.7	2.6
Roy city	49 611	53 763	56 922	32 283	21 633	30 200	38 192	24 973	17 794	89.1	36.1	18.2	2.2	19.7	8.0	-4.3	5.2	6.1
St. George city	36 505	41 788	47 941	19 104	17 404	19 996	32 066	21 838	17 022	70.5	39.5	37.3	3.2	25.0	7.5	-4.8	10.0	13.2
Salt Lake City city	36 944	45 140	51 734	30 589	20 948	25 751	32 177	27 001	20 752	81.8	37.9	21.3	4.2	13.4	10.2	-2.1	13.6	15.5
Sandy city	66 458	70 801	75 186	48 571	32 887	36 809	48 953	30 467	22 928	92.1	43.4	14.1	2.1	11.9	23.2	10.9	3.9	3.4
South Jordan city	75 433	76 809	79 239	63 047	36 207	28 000	54 274	30 847	20 938	91.8	51.9	14.4	0.8	12.8	25.4	13.1	1.5	1.4
Taylorsville city	47 236	51 553	55 994	38 006	25 423	31 963	35 643	25 629	17 812	91.6	33.3	16.6	2.5	12.7	9.3	-3.0	5.7	6.2
West Jordan city	55 794	57 818	61 205	36 619	26 558	33 938	38 708	26 854	17 221	95.5	30.2	11.4	2.0	10.0	11.0	-1.3	4.5	4.8
West Valley City city	45 773	48 593	51 784	30 640	21 393	27 940	32 551	23 376	15 031	90.7	26.8	16.8	3.6	13.0	5.9	-6.4	7.5	9.4
VERMONT	40 856	48 625	56 642	28 817	19 973	24 557	34 148	26 223	20 625	82.2	45.0	26.5	4.8	15.5	8.7	-3.6	9.7	9.7
Burlington city	33 070	46 012	54 552	29 412	16 083	24 642	30 763	25 899	19 011	83.5	40.0	20.6	6.6	11.7	6.8	-5.5	18.6	17.2

Table B-5. Cities — Education, Labor Force, and Income

STATE Place code	City	High school graduates			College graduates		College graduates (percent)				
		Total population 25 years and over	Percent with a high school diploma or less	Percent with a high school diploma or more	Percent with a bachelor's degree or more	+/− U.S. percent with bachelor's degree or more	Non-Hispanic White	Black or African American	American Indian and Alaska Native	Asian, Hawaiian, and Pacific Islander	Hispanic or Latino[1]
		1	2	3	4	5	6	7	8	9	10
51 00000	VIRGINIA..............	4 666 574	44.5	81.5	29.5	5.1	32.4	15.1	19.6	48.5	20.7
51 01000	Alexandria city..............	95 730	25.8	86.8	54.3	29.9	70.0	28.3	55.6	55.4	21.3
51 07784	Blacksburg town..........	12 863	17.8	92.9	64.2	39.8	63.3	45.0	16.7	87.1	48.3
51 14968	Charlottesville city........	22 868	40.6	80.8	40.8	16.4	49.1	8.6	41.9	75.2	47.8
51 16000	Chesapeake city............	125 498	42.6	85.1	24.7	0.3	25.5	20.3	12.3	49.8	32.2
51 21344	Danville city.................	33 196	62.2	68.5	13.9	−10.5	18.0	6.7	14.6	45.4	27.8
51 35000	Hampton city................	92 477	42.5	85.5	21.8	−2.6	24.1	18.7	18.3	24.4	17.4
51 35624	Harrisonburg city	17 448	46.7	76.8	31.2	6.8	34.6	18.5	0.0	29.4	7.2
51 44984	Leesburg town..............	18 261	29.5	89.8	41.3	16.9	45.4	16.3	17.9	41.7	19.9
51 47672	Lynchburg city..............	40 806	49.7	78.0	25.2	0.8	31.3	8.3	10.1	58.0	26.2
51 48952	Manassas city...............	21 188	42.7	81.3	28.1	3.7	33.7	17.2	0.0	31.2	9.9
51 56000	Newport News city	110 083	45.6	84.5	19.9	−4.5	25.0	11.7	18.4	25.2	13.7
51 57000	Norfolk city.................	135 258	51.2	78.4	19.6	−4.8	26.3	9.7	9.3	34.3	16.5
51 61832	Petersburg city..............	22 289	61.7	68.6	14.8	−9.6	21.1	12.4	23.9	34.9	17.0
51 64000	Portsmouth city.............	63 685	54.2	75.2	13.8	−10.6	17.0	10.0	18.2	23.1	18.6
51 67000	Richmond city...............	128 555	48.4	75.2	29.5	5.1	51.4	11.2	22.4	49.0	20.3
51 68000	Roanoke city.................	65 593	54.4	76.0	18.7	−5.7	22.2	7.8	20.9	37.4	19.4
51 76432	Suffolk city..................	41 662	52.8	76.8	17.3	−7.1	21.5	10.8	17.0	40.6	17.0
51 82000	Virginia Beach city	266 627	35.5	90.4	28.1	3.7	30.6	18.1	12.7	33.3	19.1
53 00000	WASHINGTON..........	3 827 507	37.8	87.1	27.7	3.3	28.9	19.4	12.4	35.5	11.1
53 03180	Auburn city	25 569	49.1	82.8	15.6	−8.8	15.9	19.7	11.8	26.6	5.1
53 05210	Bellevue city................	78 035	18.4	94.3	54.1	29.7	54.6	39.1	14.3	62.2	28.7
53 05280	Bollingham city.............	39 202	34.5	88.5	33.0	8.6	33.8	36.6	9.8	34.2	21.0
53 07380	Bothell city..................	19 831	27.0	93.7	38.6	14.2	37.3	17.2	6.2	63.2	28.5
53 07695	Bremerton city..............	22 074	44.0	86.5	14.8	−9.6	15.5	9.3	7.9	18.3	8.9
53 08850	Burien city	22 364	42.4	84.8	21.2	−3.2	23.9	7.8	8.5	21.6	6.2
53 17635	Des Moines city............	19 991	38.3	87.5	22.9	−1.5	24.7	8.0	33.3	24.5	8.7
53 20750	Edmonds city................	28 337	20.0	93.6	36.4	12.0	36.5	23.5	10.1	48.6	27.9
53 22640	Everett city	57 162	42.9	84.4	18.5	−5.9	18.8	16.0	12.8	24.3	10.2
53 23515	Federal Way city...........	51 783	35.9	89.3	26.2	1.8	27.0	18.9	26.1	31.6	10.9
53 35275	Kennewick city..............	32 984	41.6	83.3	22.1	−2.3	24.1	16.8	3.6	35.3	5.8
53 35415	Kent city.....................	49 306	39.8	86.6	24.0	−0.4	25.5	14.1	12.5	29.2	9.8
53 35940	Kirkland city.................	32 761	20.5	95.4	47.4	23.0	47.7	43.1	35.2	54.0	26.6
53 36745	Lacey city....................	20 144	33.8	88.1	26.9	2.5	27.7	28.4	12.9	20.5	24.8
53 38038	Lakewood city...............	37 587	43.1	85.4	21.8	−2.6	25.6	14.3	14.5	15.6	10.8
53 40245	Longview city................	22 676	49.8	81.2	14.6	−9.8	15.2	16.2	4.5	9.9	8.8
53 40840	Lynnwood city...............	22 108	38.6	86.9	22.4	−2.0	21.5	27.2	13.6	32.8	12.1
53 43955	Marysville city..............	15 688	41.7	07.1	19.0	−5.4	18.2	30.3	2.3	40.2	18.7
53 47560	Mount Vernon city	15 567	45.9	78.8	18.6	−5.8	22.8	23.2	3.3	18.2	2.5
53 51300	Olympia city.................	28 217	29.2	91.6	40.3	15.9	41.9	37.1	10.7	35.0	18.9
53 53545	Pasco city....................	16 649	65.7	55.9	10.6	−13.8	16.9	14.5	3.0	21.0	2.2
53 56695	Puyallup city................	20 384	42.3	86.7	22.8	−1.6	23.1	37.8	13.6	24.3	12.5
53 57535	Redmond city................	31 363	17.0	94.5	52.9	28.5	52.5	48.8	53.5	65.9	24.9
53 57745	Renton city	34 002	38.5	86.6	27.8	3.4	27.5	20.3	3.7	39.6	14.4
53 58235	Richland city.................	25 339	27.1	92.6	38.9	14.5	38.5	30.7	22.3	61.8	20.7
53 61115	Sammamish city............	21 303	11.4	98.3	61.5	37.1	60.4	43.1	36.2	77.3	47.5
53 62288	SeaTac city..................	16 574	49.5	81.4	15.3	−9.1	16.7	15.4	7.4	17.9	4.0
53 63000	Seattle city..................	409 582	25.8	89.5	47.2	22.8	53.8	20.1	19.7	36.5	26.1
53 63960	Shoreline city...............	36 975	29.7	90.2	37.3	12.9	37.2	26.6	3.8	45.7	29.6
53 67000	Spokane city.................	126 106	38.2	88.1	25.4	1.0	26.3	12.9	11.6	20.4	16.8
53 70000	Tacoma city..................	123 992	45.5	83.6	20.0	−4.4	22.2	13.5	15.0	16.9	10.2
53 73465	University Place city......	19 466	28.2	92.9	33.9	9.5	36.4	21.0	13.5	31.4	11.8
53 74060	Vancouver city..............	91 013	40.5	86.0	21.7	−2.7	22.0	24.3	11.5	31.1	10.3
53 75775	Walla Walla city............	18 503	46.1	79.4	21.6	−2.8	24.8	14.1	12.4	11.4	3.2
53 77105	Wenatchee city.............	17 500	45.6	78.2	23.4	−1.0	27.2	34.0	4.5	19.3	3.0
53 80010	Yakima city..................	43 820	57.2	69.4	16.0	−8.4	19.9	16.1	8.7	29.3	4.6
54 00000	WEST VIRGINIA........	1 233 581	64.2	75.2	14.8	−9.6	14.6	11.5	12.8	62.1	19.7
54 14600	Charleston city..............	37 821	43.6	83.8	32.6	8.2	34.6	12.8	25.8	75.0	20.4
54 39460	Huntington city.............	33 394	52.3	79.6	22.4	−2.0	23.1	8.9	24.6	58.4	19.8
54 55756	Morgantown city............	12 019	30.9	89.2	47.8	23.4	47.4	25.3	17.1	83.8	39.0
54 62140	Parkersburg city............	23 080	61.1	75.6	12.9	−11.5	12.6	19.5	0.0	39.6	27.3
54 86452	Wheeling city................	21 967	54.1	81.9	23.2	−1.2	23.4	10.2	0.0	72.9	26.5
55 00000	WISCONSIN..............	3 475 878	49.5	85.1	22.4	−2.0	23.1	10.5	10.4	42.5	11.4
55 02375	Appleton city................	44 238	42.2	88.8	29.7	5.3	30.4	19.8	23.5	22.1	12.3
55 06500	Beloit city...................	21 835	62.5	75.6	13.5	−10.9	15.2	5.6	12.0	49.1	1.1
55 10025	Brookfield city..............	26 645	25.0	94.0	49.0	24.6	48.3	35.7	28.0	79.6	43.2
55 22300	Eau Claire city..............	34 491	40.1	90.3	28.9	4.5	29.3	20.5	4.6	24.6	24.0
55 26275	Fond du Lac city	27 479	53.1	83.9	19.0	−5.4	19.4	8.1	9.3	44.8	8.9

[1]Hispanic or Latino persons may be of any race.

City	School enrollment			Population 16 to 19 years				Employment status, 2000			Work status in 1999 of the population 16 years and over		
											Worked in 1999		
	Grades kindergarten through 12	College or graduate school	Percent private	Number	Percent in armed forces	Percent high school graduates	Percent not enrolled, not grads, not in armed forces, not employed	Total population 16 years and over	Percent in labor force	Unemployment rate	Full-time	Part-time	Did not work in 1999
	11	12	13	14	15	16	17	18	19	20	21	22	23
VIRGINIA..................	1 291 600	450 800	13.2	382 918	2.0	12.2	4.0	5 529 980	66.8	4.1	59.6	13.6	26.8
Alexandria city.............	14 135	10 296	24.8	3 819	0.2	11.8	5.3	108 764	74.4	3.1	70.1	10.3	19.6
Blacksburg town..........	2 583	23 895	2.0	7 670	0.1	2.1	0.4	35 972	50.9	8.2	47.0	34.5	18.5
Charlottesville city........	4 959	15 501	5.2	5 798	0.2	3.8	1.5	38 906	56.3	4.3	52.8	24.3	22.9
Chesapeake city............	43 542	10 785	11.6	11 484	1.8	12.3	4.0	148 512	69.0	3.8	60.7	14.1	25.2
Danville city.................	8 649	1 709	10.3	2 475	0.0	11.6	9.5	38 388	57.0	10.0	48.7	12.0	39.3
Hampton city...............	27 044	12 830	21.1	9 310	1.3	13.3	3.0	115 091	62.4	6.0	61.1	14.1	24.8
Harrisonburg city..........	4 247	14 822	8.2	6 261	0.0	2.8	2.5	35 052	59.4	9.3	49.8	29.2	21.0
Leesburg town..............	5 352	1 154	11.7	1 057	0.0	8.4	3.1	20 654	77.1	2.1	69.3	12.9	17.8
Lynchburg city.............	10 830	7 622	37.3	4 792	0.3	6.9	4.2	52 279	59.8	6.7	50.1	17.2	32.7
Manassas city..............	7 433	1 916	15.4	1 923	0.0	8.6	5.6	25 719	74.3	3.7	66.5	14.1	19.4
Newport News city........	35 994	10 611	10.6	10 506	7.7	19.2	4.0	135 532	68.3	5.0	59.9	14.2	25.9
Norfolk city.................	40 850	19 085	13.0	16 165	19.0	27.0	5.6	183 922	67.1	7.0	56.9	15.2	27.9
Petersburg city............	6 381	1 388	8.7	1 704	0.3	13.3	11.2	26 200	56.5	8.7	52.6	11.0	36.3
Portsmouth city............	19 171	5 211	12.2	5 791	9.8	19.7	7.4	77 524	62.1	7.0	53.0	13.5	33.5
Richmond city..............	31 524	19 116	18.1	11 559	0.1	9.9	6.2	158 612	62.4	8.0	55.1	14.8	30.1
Roanoke city................	15 292	3 590	9.3	4 030	0.0	18.1	12.8	75 372	62.7	5.8	55.1	12.8	32.1
Suffolk city.................	13 372	3 129	13.3	3 204	0.0	8.7	6.6	47 731	63.6	4.7	55.6	13.0	31.5
Virginia Beach city........	86 963	26 275	12.1	23 384	5.4	15.8	3.7	321 282	72.9	3.5	63.8	14.3	21.9
WASHINGTON..........	1 127 448	358 414	11.1	335 082	0.9	11.3	4.6	4 553 591	66.5	6.1	55.5	16.5	27.9
Auburn city..................	7 552	1 618	9.2	2 164	0.0	17.4	7.3	30 668	67.1	6.1	57.0	12.8	30.2
Bellevue city................	16 825	6 730	14.6	4 676	0.2	7.4	2.2	88 716	67.5	4.1	57.6	15.4	27.0
Bellingham city.............	7 936	14 583	6.5	5 514	0.0	7.3	1.8	56 689	66.4	10.3	46.5	28.2	25.3
Bothell city.................	5 548	1 594	9.9	1 732	0.0	12.6	2.7	23 267	73.4	3.9	60.8	16.8	22.4
Bremerton city.............	6 066	2 264	7.2	2 204	18.2	32.1	8.5	28 701	64.8	7.7	52.6	15.6	31.8
Burien city..................	5 287	1 426	16.3	1 456	0.0	8.8	5.3	25 461	64.8	3.6	57.1	13.8	29.1
Des Moines city............	5 138	1 566	10.3	1 488	0.0	16.1	5.6	23 124	64.9	5.5	55.4	13.9	30.7
Edmonds city...............	6 209	2 422	18.6	1 962	0.0	9.7	2.5	32 458	64.4	3.6	54.3	16.4	29.3
Everett city.................	15 639	4 450	7.8	5 129	6.8	22.6	5.9	70 887	68.8	7.7	59.9	14.1	26.1
Federal Way city..........	16 587	4 496	11.9	4 428	0.0	12.6	5.5	62 131	72.0	5.2	61.6	15.1	23.3
Kennewick city.............	12 038	2 049	6.3	3 359	0.0	9.5	9.8	40 505	68.2	6.6	57.2	16.2	26.6
Kent city....................	15 032	3 835	8.9	4 215	0.0	16.0	7.1	59 670	71.8	5.7	63.1	13.7	23.2
Kirkland city................	5 800	3 037	18.5	1 851	0.0	12.8	1.1	37 697	75.2	3.0	65.5	14.6	19.9
Lacey city...................	5 442	2 007	12.6	1 566	0.4	11.7	2.3	23 923	65.5	6.3	54.9	14.4	30.7
Lakewood city..............	10 122	2 901	10.9	3 322	2.4	17.0	11.2	45 604	59.3	7.6	51.8	13.8	34.4
Longview city...............	6 485	1 419	6.6	1 879	0.0	11.9	7.6	26 824	59.5	8.2	47.6	16.8	35.6
Lynnwood city..............	5 887	2 340	12.6	1 736	0.5	13.4	4.3	26 329	68.5	5.0	57.4	15.9	26.8
Marysville city..............	5 522	979	6.8	1 358	0.9	14.5	6.6	18 312	69.2	4.8	58.3	15.2	26.5
Mount Vernon city.........	5 462	1 606	8.6	1 862	0.0	10.4	8.4	19 560	65.2	7.6	53.7	16.0	30.4
Olympia city................	7 026	3 799	11.4	2 306	0.0	15.1	3.2	34 301	67.5	4.9	53.8	18.5	27.7
Pasco city...................	8 028	1 153	3.3	2 324	0.0	7.4	17.8	21 769	63.3	12.3	56.1	13.2	30.7
Puyallup city................	6 596	1 663	11.3	1 944	0.0	10.6	3.4	24 743	68.8	5.6	57.9	15.2	26.9
Redmond city...............	7 067	2 828	10.8	1 953	0.0	9.9	1.3	36 719	74.0	3.9	64.1	13.8	22.2
Renton city..................	7 540	3 080	13.1	2 067	0.0	13.6	4.1	39 975	72.1	4.3	63.8	13.5	22.7
Richland city................	8 144	2 141	9.4	2 215	0.0	10.3	2.3	29 382	65.3	4.3	53.9	16.4	29.7
Sammamish city............	8 555	1 393	10.1	1 870	0.0	4.6	1.3	24 035	74.0	1.9	62.3	17.7	20.0
SeaTac city.................	4 744	1 153	11.0	1 457	0.0	18.1	3.7	20 018	67.5	6.0	59.2	12.9	27.9
Seattle city.................	63 726	65 399	21.2	25 099	0.3	9.7	2.8	485 170	70.1	5.1	58.5	17.9	23.6
Shoreline city...............	9 305	3 507	13.4	2 673	0.0	11.1	3.8	42 504	66.2	4.5	54.5	17.1	28.3
Spokane city................	34 960	15 220	15.3	11 627	0.1	12.9	4.3	153 402	64.2	8.9	50.1	18.7	31.2
Tacoma city.................	37 010	12 342	15.4	10 943	0.8	12.5	6.5	148 628	64.2	7.7	53.3	15.8	30.9
University Place city......	6 086	1 755	15.4	1 797	1.6	10.6	3.5	23 312	69.4	4.3	59.0	14.5	26.5
Vancouver city.............	26 325	7 276	9.0	7 191	0.1	12.9	8.0	108 396	67.2	6.6	57.4	14.3	28.3
Walla Walla city...........	5 522	3 048	25.7	2 321	0.0	4.2	3.3	23 814	54.0	10.7	50.8	17.2	32.1
Wenatchee city............	5 908	1 311	10.5	1 656	0.0	9.5	10.0	21 047	61.8	11.4	52.8	15.4	31.8
Yakima city.................	15 329	2 557	8.7	4 246	0.0	14.2	8.7	53 108	58.1	12.4	51.9	13.5	34.6
WEST VIRGINIA......	304 216	92 329	7.7	99 445	0.1	11.8	6.4	1 455 101	54.5	7.3	46.8	12.3	40.9
Charleston city.............	7 986	2 825	16.7	2 368	0.2	13.3	9.7	43 619	59.5	5.8	51.5	12.5	35.9
Huntington city.............	6 676	7 324	6.6	3 759	0.1	9.2	4.3	43 411	54.6	10.7	42.5	18.2	39.3
Morgantown city...........	2 139	12 619	3.7	4 629	0.0	4.0	1.5	24 556	56.7	11.3	42.7	32.5	24.9
Parkersburg city...........	5 185	1 330	9.2	1 699	0.0	14.3	9.5	26 942	55.1	7.6	45.1	14.5	40.4
Wheeling city...............	5 116	2 234	27.3	1 639	0.0	4.8	5.6	25 682	56.0	9.4	43.0	16.0	41.0
WISCONSIN.............	1 049 456	328 537	15.7	319 738	0.0	10.6	3.4	4 157 030	69.1	4.7	57.1	18.1	24.8
Appleton city................	14 537	4 039	18.8	4 333	0.1	10.8	2.0	53 221	72.0	3.4	59.0	19.4	21.7
Beloit city...................	7 169	1 953	19.6	2 344	0.0	10.4	9.4	26 876	64.9	9.2	54.3	16.8	28.9
Brookfield city..............	8 353	1 436	29.1	2 082	0.0	5.7	0.3	29 810	64.9	2.8	48.6	20.4	31.0
Eau Claire city.............	10 092	10 908	7.0	5 604	0.0	5.9	1.8	49 972	70.4	5.0	52.0	27.0	21.0
Fond du Lac city..........	7 837	2 268	21.2	2 520	0.3	16.4	4.7	33 298	67.5	4.6	56.4	18.0	25.5

Table B-5. Cities — Education, Labor Force, and Income

City	Full-year full-time employed (percent)								Children under 18 years in families (percent, except where noted)						Total employed by class of worker (percent)			
										With two parents								
	Total	Men	Women	Non-Hispanic White	Black or African American	American Indian and Alaska Native	Asian, Hawaiian, and Pacific Islander	Hispanic or Latino[1]	Number	Both in labor force	Father only in labor force	With one parent who is in labor force	+/- U.S. percent of children with no stay-at-home parent	+/- U.S. percent two-income couples	Private	Government	Self-employed	Unpaid family worker
	24	25	26	27	28	29	30	31	32	33	34	35	36	37	38	39	40	41
VIRGINIA	45.6	55.6	36.2	46.9	41.4	45.8	44.3	43.5	1 639 504	46.4	21.4	21.5	3.3	4.3	71.6	19.6	8.6	0.2
Alexandria city	53.5	59.9	47.6	59.0	47.9	59.6	43.1	42.7	19 982	36.6	20.7	26.6	-1.4	7.9	70.3	21.8	7.7	0.2
Blacksburg town	16.5	19.3	13.0	17.2	20.6	19.5	7.6	17.4	3 749	36.9	29.4	19.0	-8.7	-1.2	52.6	42.8	4.5	0.1
Charlottesville city	29.0	33.7	25.1	28.2	36.9	41.9	15.5	29.6	6 313	36.2	11.2	37.4	9.0	3.8	58.9	33.2	7.7	0.1
Chesapeake city	47.7	59.3	37.1	50.5	41.0	48.8	48.0	49.2	53 826	48.5	20.7	21.5	5.4	7.3	67.0	25.3	7.5	0.3
Danville city	35.1	43.9	28.2	35.3	34.6	37.8	49.5	32.7	10 339	31.6	10.3	41.5	8.5	-4.2	80.0	13.2	6.6	0.2
Hampton city	46.6	57.2	36.4	50.8	41.6	54.4	38.2	46.4	32 785	38.5	17.0	32.5	6.4	3.2	71.3	22.8	5.8	0.1
Harrisonburg city	25.7	33.1	19.1	26.0	27.3	0.0	19.3	25.5	5 870	46.7	20.4	22.8	4.9	5.3	74.0	19.9	6.0	0.2
Leesburg town	56.7	71.3	43.3	57.5	54.3	20.9	59.4	51.2	7 880	51.2	28.5	16.8	3.4	13.0	74.3	17.5	8.0	0.2
Lynchburg city	35.8	45.2	28.3	34.9	38.6	28.7	33.3	33.8	13 485	35.3	17.1	32.9	3.6	-1.2	80.5	12.1	7.2	0.1
Manassas city	53.1	63.5	42.6	54.6	55.3	51.1	50.6	46.5	9 744	49.4	24.0	17.0	1.8	13.4	75.5	17.9	6.5	0.1
Newport News city	44.3	54.7	34.9	47.0	40.9	37.3	37.5	45.2	46 235	39.2	16.5	31.9	6.5	4.6	72.6	21.0	6.2	0.2
Norfolk city	41.3	51.3	30.8	46.5	33.9	37.4	38.5	45.9	51 472	30.5	15.8	34.6	0.5	-1.8	73.0	20.6	6.2	0.2
Petersburg city	37.4	42.3	33.4	31.3	38.9	0.0	38.4	44.6	7 368	26.4	6.5	46.9	8.7	-4.9	67.9	27.3	4.6	0.3
Portsmouth city	38.9	48.0	30.6	43.1	33.8	39.8	48.4	49.1	22 726	30.7	14.2	40.0	6.1	-1.7	67.3	26.4	6.3	0.1
Richmond city	38.2	44.0	33.3	41.9	35.7	33.4	23.3	35.1	38 128	25.0	9.6	43.0	3.4	0.2	74.0	19.1	6.9	0.1
Roanoke city	42.1	50.1	35.3	43.4	38.2	41.6	40.6	41.7	19 747	34.2	15.3	35.6	5.2	0.1	81.7	11.8	6.4	0.1
Suffolk city	44.0	55.5	34.0	49.1	37.3	54.7	49.2	39.4	16 510	44.0	15.9	26.6	6.0	4.9	70.1	22.0	7.5	0.4
Virginia Beach city	49.5	61.6	38.0	50.3	49.0	48.5	42.1	48.1	111 408	48.3	21.6	21.4	5.1	7.3	71.2	19.4	9.2	0.2
WASHINGTON	39.4	49.3	29.8	40.2	40.8	33.3	37.4	32.6	1 433 592	45.0	24.2	20.1	0.5	0.6	72.8	16.5	10.4	0.3
Auburn city	42.4	52.8	32.6	42.9	44.0	40.4	45.7	35.4	10 168	38.6	18.8	28.8	2.8	0.0	83.2	10.3	6.4	0.1
Bellevue city	42.7	54.2	31.7	42.8	49.1	29.1	42.1	46.2	22 441	45.6	32.2	13.9	-5.1	-2.8	79.2	9.2	11.4	0.2
Bellingham city	28.4	35.3	21.9	28.4	30.3	27.3	24.9	32.9	10 877	44.5	21.8	23.2	3.1	1.4	71.6	16.8	11.3	0.3
Bothell city	47.0	59.4	35.8	47.5	52.3	42.9	48.7	37.0	7 261	51.7	26.6	15.9	3.0	7.2	76.6	13.4	9.4	0.6
Bremerton city	37.0	47.3	26.3	36.7	42.8	29.6	32.4	46.4	8 406	34.7	24.3	27.7	-2.2	-5.3	69.1	24.7	6.2	0.0
Durien city	42.3	48.5	36.5	42.2	49.0	30.0	45.4	38.6	6 520	40.5	16.5	26.5	6.9	1.9	78.7	11.9	9.0	0.4
Des Moines city	42.1	51.1	34.2	42.0	45.5	63.9	39.8	38.5	6 612	43.6	16.7	26.9	5.9	2.9	80.3	11.7	7.9	0.1
Edmonds city	40.4	50.1	31.9	40.2	45.5	32.5	38.8	50.1	7 910	46.0	28.2	19.5	0.9	-0.0	70.7	15.5	13.6	0.2
Everett city	41.9	50.9	32.4	42.6	40.6	40.7	34.7	42.9	21 293	38.8	22.4	20.1	0.0	0.6	80.7	11.8	7.4	0.1
Federal Way city	46.0	56.9	35.8	48.0	50.9	34.7	39.7	37.1	22 225	43.8	20.2	24.6	3.8	4.8	80.1	12.5	7.3	0.1
Kennewick city	41.7	53.2	30.9	43.1	36.8	45.0	43.0	34.2	15 474	41.2	22.0	25.4	2.0	5.0	74.5	17.2	8.0	0.3
Kent city	46.4	57.6	35.6	48.3	46.3	38.1	40.5	39.2	20 584	40.0	20.6	24.1	0.4	4.8	82.3	11.2	6.4	0.1
Kirkland city	51.0	61.0	41.9	51.3	51.7	45.6	46.4	52.1	7 917	48.9	22.3	19.7	4.0	7.4	80.1	8.9	10.7	0.2
Lacey city	40.1	50.5	31.2	40.2	54.2	45.0	33.2	39.7	7 561	47.0	21.0	23.6	6.0	1.2	61.8	31.7	6.0	0.5
Lakewood city	35.5	44.6	27.0	36.1	40.4	36.4	27.1	27.1	13 314	31.3	19.2	31.8	-1.5	-7.9	69.6	21.8	8.3	0.3
Longview city	32.2	43.4	22.2	32.2	47.6	17.2	27.9	36.3	8 508	33.9	24.5	28.9	-1.8	-7.5	78.5	12.8	8.5	0.2
Lynnwood city	40.5	49.9	31.9	41.5	47.9	20.4	35.6	39.5	7 845	43.6	25.4	20.6	-0.4	3.0	79.8	11.9	7.7	0.5
Marysville city	43.9	59.9	29.5	43.8	37.6	37.4	45.6	40.8	7 260	44.1	26.7	17.9	2.4	6.0	77.5	13.2	9.3	0.0
Mount Vernon city	34.5	44.3	25.5	37.9	43.5	20.6	25.7	24.6	7 042	44.5	21.9	20.0	-0.1	1.4	77.0	13.9	9.0	0.1
Olympia city	38.0	45.4	31.4	38.2	44.5	30.5	35.5	40.1	8 802	51.7	15.5	23.6	10.7	6.0	57.1	34.4	8.3	0.2
Pasco city	30.4	37.1	23.5	36.0	22.7	21.1	32.3	25.8	10 570	33.6	21.6	22.3	-8.7	-7.5	80.2	13.1	6.4	0.2
Puyallup city	42.1	55.5	30.3	42.3	55.3	56.3	40.5	32.1	8 653	46.1	25.9	22.4	3.9	4.2	78.7	14.1	6.8	0.3
Redmond city	48.4	60.0	37.0	49.5	32.5	60.4	47.6	39.8	9 455	42.3	33.9	17.5	-4.8	4.8	83.5	7.5	8.9	0.1
Renton city	46.8	55.4	38.7	48.0	44.2	51.9	47.0	38.9	10 298	43.1	20.8	25.4	3.9	6.1	82.7	11.3	5.9	0.1
Richland city	41.8	55.1	29.5	41.4	37.8	56.6	39.8	47.1	10 142	45.7	30.2	18.7	-0.2	-1.2	72.8	19.5	7.4	0.4
Sammamish city	50.6	68.7	33.1	51.1	59.1	45.7	49.7	43.8	11 185	44.7	42.9	7.7	-12.2	5.2	77.4	9.6	12.8	0.2
SeaTac city	43.4	49.4	36.7	45.5	38.6	44.5	37.6	42.0	5 807	42.5	18.1	25.5	3.4	-0.5	83.5	10.6	5.7	0.2
Seattle city	40.4	46.8	34.2	42.9	34.2	28.0	33.8	37.1	81 322	44.3	20.4	23.3	3.0	5.1	74.2	15.6	10.0	0.2
Shoreline city	40.4	49.6	32.0	39.6	45.9	46.5	40.3	47.4	11 421	51.8	20.1	19.0	6.2	3.2	71.8	16.4	11.7	0.1
Spokane city	35.5	43.7	28.2	36.1	30.6	30.1	27.8	35.2	45 397	41.8	20.2	26.0	3.2	-0.4	76.0	14.9	8.9	0.2
Tacoma city	37.3	46.2	29.1	38.0	39.5	33.4	30.2	36.4	46 368	40.2	16.9	27.8	3.4	1.0	75.4	16.6	7.7	0.2
University Place city	45.6	55.2	37.3	46.3	49.7	35.8	36.1	42.1	7 634	45.3	20.6	26.4	7.1	6.4	68.6	21.5	9.7	0.3
Vancouver city	40.4	49.9	31.6	40.8	49.3	36.7	39.6	37.1	36 689	39.5	24.4	24.7	-0.4	-1.0	80.3	11.5	7.9	0.2
Walla Walla city	26.8	31.2	22.1	28.1	11.9	33.9	21.7	22.5	6 453	43.0	18.2	26.0	4.4	-7.7	67.6	22.5	9.4	0.5
Wenatchee city	30.8	38.9	23.4	33.6	20.8	27.1	23.2	18.0	7 385	48.1	19.3	17.1	0.6	-5.2	70.9	17.0	11.8	0.3
Yakima city	29.9	38.2	22.3	33.1	32.5	28.0	38.7	21.8	19 965	32.4	19.1	26.3	-5.9	-8.5	75.9	15.0	9.0	0.2
WEST VIRGINIA	33.2	42.0	25.1	33.4	28.6	26.9	31.6	34.3	380 926	39.5	25.1	18.6	-6.5	-10.5	73.5	17.9	8.2	0.4
Charleston city	38.5	47.2	31.2	39.5	31.5	35.4	45.8	43.4	10 201	35.4	21.3	29.5	0.3	-3.5	68.3	20.5	10.8	0.4
Huntington city	27.8	34.3	22.2	28.2	23.7	19.7	17.2	35.8	8 541	32.5	18.1	27.8	-4.3	-10.0	72.7	19.3	7.5	0.5
Morgantown city	20.8	23.1	18.4	21.1	23.0	25.4	9.6	23.9	2 796	51.5	23.3	16.3	3.2	-1.5	57.2	35.3	6.9	0.6
Parkersburg city	32.8	41.7	25.3	32.9	33.5	65.2	39.7	19.2	6 503	34.7	16.1	30.3	0.4	-9.6	79.2	13.3	7.2	0.2
Wheeling city	32.3	42.4	24.3	32.2	33.0	37.0	23.8	47.7	6 098	39.5	22.1	26.8	1.7	-4.5	79.0	11.9	8.8	0.3
WISCONSIN	43.8	53.6	34.6	44.9	32.8	38.5	35.1	37.0	1 308 767	55.0	16.5	19.4	9.8	8.6	78.2	12.5	9.0	0.3
Appleton city	46.2	57.7	35.5	47.2	41.5	43.7	26.0	34.3	18 633	56.3	20.5	15.2	6.9	11.3	85.9	7.9	6.0	0.2
Beloit city	38.5	48.1	30.2	39.9	33.6	41.9	26.9	37.5	9 135	42.7	11.9	30.7	8.8	-3.5	85.4	9.5	4.9	0.2
Brookfield city	40.6	58.2	24.6	40.1	48.1	58.5	48.2	59.3	10 246	59.2	28.8	7.8	2.4	2.0	79.1	8.4	12.3	0.3
Eau Claire city	37.1	46.3	28.9	37.4	17.4	26.7	34.7	38.5	12 666	56.7	15.7	18.9	11.0	11.1	78.1	15.5	6.3	0.2
Fond du Lac city	44.1	56.9	33.1	45.0	20.1	44.0	28.2	35.2	9 794	53.2	15.3	24.3	12.9	9.9	82.9	11.7	5.3	0.1

[1] Hispanic or Latino persons may be of any race.

Table B-5. Cities — Education, Labor Force, and Income

| City | Percent who worked at home | Percent of the population 5 years and over with a disability | Veterans as a percent of the population 18 years and over | Occupation for employed population 16 years and over (percent) | | | | | | Industry for employed population 16 years and over (percent) | | | | | |
| | | | | Management, professional, and related occupations | Service occupations | Sales and office occupations | Farming, fishing, and forestry occupations | Construction, extraction, and maintenance occupations | Production, transportation and material moving occupations | Agriculture, forestry, fishing, and mining | Construction and manufacturing | Wholesale and retail trade | Transportation and warehousing, and utilities | Service industries | Public administration |
	42	43	44	45	46	47	48	49	50	51	52	53	54	55	56
VIRGINIA	3.2	18.1	14.7	38.2	13.7	25.5	0.5	9.6	12.5	1.3	18.7	14.2	4.6	53.0	8.3
Alexandria city	3.5	15.0	11.1	56.2	11.9	21.2	0.1	5.4	5.2	0.2	7.9	8.7	4.1	64.9	14.2
Blacksburg town	3.6	8.8	4.4	52.2	19.4	20.6	0.6	2.5	4.8	0.8	6.7	10.4	1.4	78.9	1.6
Charlottesville city	5.4	13.7	7.4	44.0	19.5	23.3	0.2	5.7	7.4	0.4	8.7	11.4	2.5	73.6	3.2
Chesapeake city	2.4	18.4	18.1	35.6	13.7	27.5	0.3	11.5	11.5	0.5	18.7	14.7	5.9	51.4	8.9
Danville city	1.4	25.8	14.9	23.9	17.0	25.0	0.2	7.9	26.0	0.1	31.6	16.5	3.0	45.7	3.1
Hampton city	1.5	19.5	25.5	32.1	15.1	27.8	0.3	11.0	13.7	0.3	21.9	15.0	4.1	49.6	8.9
Harrisonburg city	3.7	13.5	6.3	31.2	19.9	26.2	0.7	5.6	16.4	1.3	17.8	15.7	2.0	60.4	2.7
Leesburg town	4.6	11.7	13.2	48.4	12.6	25.6	0.1	6.6	6.6	0.4	11.8	13.2	7.1	59.3	8.3
Lynchburg city	2.4	22.8	12.5	33.3	17.1	26.3	0.2	6.9	16.1	0.4	23.9	15.3	3.8	54.2	2.4
Manassas city	2.4	14.2	14.1	38.5	13.9	27.1	0.1	12.1	8.3	0.2	17.9	14.4	5.4	53.5	8.6
Newport News city	1.6	19.1	18.4	30.5	17.6	27.6	0.3	10.4	13.6	0.3	22.3	15.1	3.8	50.6	7.9
Norfolk city	3.8	23.2	16.9	29.1	19.1	27.7	0.2	10.7	13.2	0.2	14.4	15.9	5.7	56.2	7.6
Petersburg city	1.1	28.2	17.6	24.9	22.0	21.8	0.2	6.8	24.4	0.6	21.6	13.9	5.3	50.0	8.6
Portsmouth city	2.7	25.3	17.3	27.7	16.7	27.8	0.2	12.8	14.7	0.4	22.1	14.9	5.1	49.9	7.6
Richmond city	2.3	24.3	11.6	35.5	18.7	26.9	0.1	6.4	12.5	0.2	13.7	13.2	4.6	61.6	6.7
Roanoke city	1.9	25.5	15.0	26.7	16.9	30.3	0.1	8.7	17.2	0.3	19.3	19.9	5.9	51.8	2.9
Suffolk city	1.7	23.1	16.4	30.9	13.8	25.3	0.4	11.3	18.5	0.9	25.9	15.0	6.3	43.8	8.2
Virginia Beach city	2.8	15.8	19.5	35.9	14.9	30.1	0.1	10.0	9.0	0.2	13.9	16.7	4.4	57.6	7.1
WASHINGTON	4.3	18.2	15.3	35.6	14.9	25.9	1.6	9.4	12.7	2.5	19.5	16.2	5.4	51.4	5.0
Auburn city	2.9	21.1	14.9	26.0	16.8	27.9	0.1	11.8	17.4	0.2	28.1	20.1	5.9	42.7	3.1
Bellevue city	5.1	15.1	12.1	53.1	10.1	26.4	0.1	4.1	6.2	0.2	15.5	16.5	3.5	61.4	2.8
Bellingham city	4.3	16.0	11.3	33.3	18.2	28.4	0.8	7.6	11.7	1.0	16.0	19.0	3.6	57.6	2.9
Bothell city	4.7	15.7	12.3	43.2	11.5	28.3	0.3	7.7	8.9	0.4	20.5	16.3	3.2	55.5	4.1
Bremerton city	2.6	25.5	20.2	25.5	24.6	26.0	0.5	11.5	12.1	0.5	16.8	16.5	3.7	55.0	7.5
Burien city	3.3	21.0	15.3	29.9	16.1	27.9	0.4	9.2	16.4	0.4	21.1	17.1	9.1	49.5	2.8
Des Moines city	3.2	16.2	14.6	32.2	14.6	29.8	0.1	8.9	14.4	0.2	21.4	16.1	10.7	48.1	3.4
Edmonds city	4.8	16.6	15.7	41.3	11.2	30.2	0.3	8.1	8.8	0.7	17.3	17.3	4.6	57.0	3.2
Everett city	4.6	21.3	15.1	27.2	16.2	25.8	0.4	13.4	17.0	0.5	29.2	15.9	5.6	45.3	3.5
Federal Way city	2.9	16.2	14.3	31.4	14.4	31.8	0.1	9.0	13.2	0.2	21.5	17.8	9.2	47.3	4.0
Kennewick city	3.5	18.4	14.4	32.4	16.3	26.4	1.5	10.5	12.9	2.5	14.9	17.1	6.2	54.6	4.7
Kent city	3.2	17.4	13.3	30.5	14.5	29.7	0.2	9.9	15.2	0.3	24.4	18.5	7.7	46.2	2.9
Kirkland city	5.3	13.0	11.3	49.2	9.9	28.0	0.0	6.8	6.2	0.3	16.6	17.4	2.9	60.7	2.2
Lacey city	3.6	19.8	19.3	33.5	18.2	28.9	1.1	8.6	9.7	1.3	11.4	13.9	2.9	50.1	20.4
Lakewood city	2.4	23.3	23.9	31.4	19.1	27.0	0.4	8.1	13.9	0.5	14.3	17.3	5.4	54.5	7.9
Longview city	2.4	23.5	15.7	23.9	19.1	23.3	1.5	11.7	20.5	2.8	28.0	14.4	4.4	46.8	3.6
Lynnwood city	4.0	20.7	12.6	31.3	15.5	29.2	0.2	11.0	12.8	0.3	21.9	19.1	4.0	51.8	2.9
Marysville city	3.0	18.3	16.5	29.0	17.1	26.4	0.5	11.4	15.5	0.7	27.8	15.1	4.4	46.4	5.7
Mount Vernon city	3.4	18.0	13.8	25.4	16.1	26.1	6.5	8.6	17.3	7.2	20.4	19.1	5.0	44.2	4.1
Olympia city	3.4	19.1	14.9	42.4	15.5	27.3	0.5	6.5	7.9	1.2	10.8	12.2	2.6	53.3	19.9
Pasco city	2.7	23.3	9.7	20.1	17.8	21.4	12.3	9.0	19.5	13.3	19.2	17.5	6.9	40.3	2.8
Puyallup city	2.6	17.6	15.3	32.6	14.4	26.3	0.1	11.5	15.1	1.0	22.4	17.7	6.7	48.2	4.0
Redmond city	4.3	13.8	10.1	56.7	8.5	23.8	0.0	4.1	6.9	0.2	17.9	17.4	2.8	60.2	1.6
Renton city	2.6	20.6	12.5	34.3	14.3	30.0	0.2	9.4	11.8	0.2	22.8	18.4	4.9	50.4	3.3
Richland city	3.1	16.1	16.2	50.8	12.5	21.5	0.6	6.2	8.4	0.7	10.4	12.0	5.7	66.6	4.6
Sammamish city	7.6	7.6	10.2	58.9	6.6	24.9	0.3	4.1	5.2	0.4	15.9	16.2	4.2	61.4	1.8
SeaTac city	2.2	21.8	14.5	21.3	17.3	28.7	0.4	12.5	19.8	0.3	23.7	17.0	11.1	44.7	3.1
Seattle city	4.6	17.2	10.2	48.4	13.9	24.4	0.3	4.9	8.2	0.3	12.3	14.3	4.2	65.3	3.5
Shoreline city	4.1	18.4	13.1	40.2	14.5	26.7	0.2	8.1	10.2	0.5	15.6	15.2	5.6	59.5	3.6
Spokane city	3.6	21.3	16.1	32.4	18.7	28.5	0.4	7.9	12.2	0.4	14.1	17.1	4.3	59.3	4.7
Tacoma city	3.7	22.9	17.4	29.2	18.7	25.8	0.6	10.1	15.6	0.9	18.8	15.9	6.4	52.2	5.7
University Place city	2.8	16.0	19.3	40.9	15.6	26.2	0.2	7.3	9.8	0.3	14.0	15.4	4.7	59.3	6.3
Vancouver city	3.6	19.3	15.0	29.1	14.8	28.1	0.4	9.9	17.7	0.7	24.0	17.0	7.6	47.1	3.5
Walla Walla city	3.5	22.4	12.6	35.4	20.9	23.9	2.9	7.3	9.7	3.7	12.4	12.4	3.0	60.8	7.6
Wenatchee city	3.9	20.8	13.4	31.6	17.3	24.6	6.3	8.4	11.8	5.2	13.9	18.8	6.0	52.4	3.6
Yakima city	2.7	24.9	12.4	28.0	18.2	23.1	5.7	8.4	16.5	5.1	18.0	19.7	4.0	48.7	4.5
WEST VIRGINIA	2.4	24.4	14.3	27.9	16.6	26.1	0.7	12.3	16.4	4.1	18.9	15.9	6.0	49.3	5.8
Charleston city	2.8	22.2	13.2	43.6	13.9	28.8	0.1	5.6	8.0	1.0	9.5	13.6	3.8	62.3	9.8
Huntington city	2.1	25.5	13.9	31.1	20.1	32.0	0.2	6.7	9.9	0.3	11.4	16.4	3.7	63.3	4.8
Morgantown city	3.7	14.9	7.1	42.6	20.2	26.4	0.3	4.9	5.6	1.2	7.0	10.7	1.6	76.0	3.4
Parkersburg city	1.5	25.6	16.5	25.2	18.6	30.6	0.2	9.0	16.5	0.3	19.1	19.3	4.5	51.0	5.7
Wheeling city	3.1	21.3	15.9	34.7	20.0	27.7	0.1	6.2	11.4	1.1	11.8	15.3	4.6	63.5	3.7
WISCONSIN	3.9	16.0	12.9	31.3	14.0	25.2	0.9	8.7	19.8	2.8	28.1	14.8	4.5	46.3	3.5
Appleton city	2.1	13.5	12.6	34.3	12.7	26.7	0.2	7.5	18.6	0.2	29.5	15.2	3.3	49.8	1.9
Beloit city	1.1	21.4	13.7	21.7	16.6	22.6	0.2	7.5	31.4	0.5	39.8	13.1	3.4	40.9	2.4
Brookfield city	3.8	10.6	13.8	51.3	7.5	28.1	0.0	4.0	9.0	0.1	21.3	17.5	3.2	55.7	2.2
Eau Claire city	2.4	15.3	11.5	30.2	18.2	29.9	0.3	6.6	14.7	0.5	15.9	21.8	3.2	55.5	3.1
Fond du Lac city	1.3	16.3	14.0	25.6	16.9	24.6	0.6	7.4	24.9	1.1	31.9	14.7	4.9	42.6	4.8

Table B-5. Cities — **Education, Labor Force, and Income**

City	Median household income	Median family income: All families	Median family income: Families with children: Married-couple	Median family income: Families with children: Male householder	Median family income: Families with children: Female householder	Median nonfamily household income	Median income for full-year, full-time workers: Men	Median income for full-year, full-time workers: Women	Per capita income	Households by source of income (percent): With earnings	Households by source of income (percent): With interest, dividend, or rental income	Households by source of income (percent): With Social Security income	Households by source of income (percent): With public assistance income	Households by source of income (percent): With retirement income	Households with income over $100,000 (percent)	+/– U.S. percent for income over $100,000	Households with income below poverty (percent)	Families with children with income below poverty (percent)
	57	58	59	60	61	62	63	64	65	66	67	68	69	70	71	72	73	74
VIRGINIA	46 677	54 169	63 157	31 274	21 602	29 642	39 613	29 164	23 975	83.4	38.2	23.4	2.5	18.8	15.1	2.8	9.6	10.2
Alexandria city	56 054	67 023	70 000	34 455	25 261	49 338	49 365	42 159	37 645	88.9	43.7	13.0	1.4	13.5	22.0	9.7	6.8	11.2
Blacksburg town	22 513	51 810	60 299	32 063	15 966	17 083	38 053	25 608	13 946	88.0	44.1	11.2	1.7	9.1	7.7	-4.6	38.7	21.5
Charlottesville city	31 007	45 110	58 750	28 026	16 606	21 431	32 118	27 432	16 973	83.7	40.1	20.9	2.4	14.2	7.6	-4.7	22.7	19.2
Chesapeake city	50 743	56 302	64 604	35 775	22 530	30 378	40 944	27 273	20 949	86.9	35.5	20.8	2.2	20.9	11.9	-0.4	7.4	8.7
Danville city	26 900	36 024	51 017	21 696	15 063	16 957	30 788	22 083	17 151	71.0	27.1	37.1	5.3	20.9	5.2	-7.1	18.6	27.1
Hampton city	39 532	46 110	52 498	32 527	19 345	25 882	33 092	25 455	19 774	83.8	30.0	23.1	2.9	23.6	6.9	-5.4	10.8	13.4
Harrisonburg city	29 949	45 159	52 413	26 563	20 152	19 204	30 337	23 933	14 898	84.9	35.3	20.3	3.2	10.4	7.0	-5.3	26.5	17.7
Leesburg town	68 861	78 111	87 836	39 000	35 257	42 372	52 322	36 783	30 116	93.1	40.7	12.1	1.3	13.1	27.2	14.9	3.9	3.0
Lynchburg city	32 234	40 844	55 751	22 250	17 452	20 013	32 089	23 689	18 263	75.2	32.8	31.7	3.9	19.0	7.3	-5.0	15.6	19.5
Manassas city	60 409	70 141	77 545	38 250	33 191	38 919	44 695	31 403	24 453	91.7	37.2	12.3	1.3	13.8	19.5	7.2	4.8	5.0
Newport News city	36 597	42 520	50 126	25 576	16 378	25 293	32 375	23 289	17 843	83.0	28.3	21.1	3.8	19.9	5.9	-6.4	13.0	17.0
Norfolk city	31 815	36 891	45 417	27 517	15 247	23 548	26 695	22 506	17 372	80.1	25.8	23.6	4.6	19.5	6.3	-6.0	18.1	23.2
Petersburg city	20 051	33 055	40 300	18 651	17 904	20 896	29 192	22 784	15 989	74.9	19.7	31.9	4.9	24.6	4.4	-7.9	19.1	24.4
Portsmouth city	33 742	39 577	50 989	28 814	17 238	22 239	30 792	24 423	16 507	77.2	25.2	28.2	4.6	23.7	4.8	-7.5	14.9	20.0
Richmond city	31 121	38 348	58 193	24 494	16 735	24 224	31 589	26 580	20 337	77.9	28.3	25.9	4.7	16.4	8.3	-4.0	19.3	26.9
Roanoke city	30 719	37 826	48 056	25 455	16 665	20 472	29 680	22 302	18 468	76.4	27.8	30.3	4.3	16.6	5.0	-7.3	15.3	21.7
Suffolk city	41 115	47 342	55 714	33 060	16 514	22 011	37 408	24 767	18 836	80.9	31.0	26.2	3.5	20.7	9.0	-3.3	13.4	15.6
Virginia Beach city	48 705	53 242	56 781	32 008	24 722	33 184	35 860	26 963	22 365	88.6	37.9	17.7	1.6	20.5	12.1	-0.2	6.3	7.4
WASHINGTON	45 776	53 760	61 575	32 356	21 832	29 394	41 774	30 787	22 973	81.9	40.0	22.9	3.8	17.1	12.6	0.3	9.8	11.2
Auburn city	39 208	45 426	52 335	35 931	21 730	26 907	37 367	28 510	19 630	79.9	28.2	22.3	5.8	15.4	7.0	-5.3	12.1	13.8
Bellevue city	62 338	76 868	88 729	49 821	32 705	41 262	59 907	38 688	36 905	84.1	54.6	21.9	1.9	16.8	26.4	14.1	5.3	5.3
Bellingham city	32 530	47 196	55 887	28 362	18 263	21 373	36 392	26 872	19 483	79.8	42.5	23.8	3.2	14.8	8.0	-4.3	19.5	14.9
Bothell city	59 264	68 580	79 392	37 083	35 568	36 021	50 033	35 476	26 483	87.5	44.6	18.8	1.3	15.1	17.4	5.1	5.2	4.3
Bremerton city	30 950	36 358	40 518	24 318	14 274	22 704	29 654	24 123	16 724	72.9	30.9	23.5	8.2	21.2	4.3	-8.0	17.5	22.6
Burien city	41 577	53 814	64 922	40 265	22 182	27 864	40 232	30 849	23 737	78.8	40.5	26.2	4.4	19.2	11.2	-1.1	9.3	11.3
Des Moines city	48 971	57 003	63 873	36 719	29 390	32 698	41 354	31 292	24 127	83.6	40.4	22.9	3.6	19.1	11.5	-0.8	6.8	9.2
Edmonds city	53 522	66 126	83 768	50 326	32 733	35 170	49 221	35 443	30 076	79.7	53.6	29.0	1.4	20.4	18.5	6.2	4.8	4.1
Everett city	40 100	46 713	55 156	34 557	19 979	30 020	36 680	29 984	20 577	82.5	32.2	20.5	5.1	14.4	7.7	-4.6	10.8	14.3
Federal Way city	49 278	55 833	61 916	31 465	25 026	35 279	42 158	31 318	22 451	87.3	34.5	15.8	4.1	13.9	12.8	0.5	8.2	10.0
Kennewick city	41 213	50 011	57 657	30 617	18 877	26 219	42 780	26 892	20 152	82.6	37.0	22.3	6.1	15.7	9.2	-3.1	10.8	14.7
Kent city	46 046	52 274	60 571	31 500	21 127	34 720	40 924	31 120	21 390	86.7	31.7	15.4	5.3	11.4	10.5	-1.8	9.8	12.7
Kirkland city	60 332	73 395	78 306	42 076	39 146	46 972	51 656	40 971	38 903	88.3	47.2	15.9	1.1	12.1	22.2	9.9	5.2	5.7
Lacey city	43 848	50 923	58 523	32 365	20 325	27 423	40 185	30 579	20 224	77.6	39.4	25.5	3.5	24.3	7.5	-4.8	9.7	11.9
Lakewood city	36 422	42 551	48 522	26 311	17 196	24 893	34 189	27 133	20 569	77.4	30.0	25.4	7.4	23.1	8.4	-3.9	14.2	20.2
Longview city	35 171	43 869	50 274	25 054	15 366	20 383	40 033	27 750	18 559	73.6	37.5	30.7	6.4	18.7	7.4	-4.9	14.5	20.5
Lynnwood city	42 814	51 825	62 027	28 068	25 086	29 566	38 925	30 388	19 971	82.5	34.1	23.1	3.1	16.6	8.9	-3.4	8.5	8.0
Marysville city	47 088	55 796	66 290	36 293	27 184	24 829	44 114	30 831	20 414	81.8	33.9	24.1	2.3	18.6	10.5	-1.8	6.1	4.5
Mount Vernon city	37 999	44 772	48 062	36 000	21 250	23 087	35 378	28 426	17 041	79.7	35.2	27.4	4.6	17.6	6.9	-5.4	13.2	15.7
Olympia city	40 846	54 136	65 958	33 611	21 875	25 962	42 188	32 244	22 590	80.0	44.3	23.2	2.9	17.3	9.6	-2.7	12.5	10.5
Pasco city	34 540	37 342	41 307	21 620	12 934	20 087	30 307	22 741	13 404	82.5	25.3	21.6	8.3	12.8	6.5	-5.8	20.9	27.1
Puyallup city	47 269	57 322	63 325	40 833	26 617	29 131	45 380	28 510	22 401	83.1	34.0	20.7	4.3	15.9	11.6	-0.7	7.0	6.8
Redmond city	66 735	78 430	87 423	45 870	32 392	50 594	60 521	39 973	36 233	89.2	49.3	13.5	1.2	10.4	26.6	14.3	4.6	5.8
Renton city	45 820	55 747	62 199	31 875	26 284	33 465	41 347	32 012	24 346	85.1	38.6	18.5	3.2	13.6	11.5	-0.8	9.0	10.7
Richland city	53 092	61 482	71 454	26 875	23 432	29 833	54 053	31 152	25 494	81.0	49.8	25.2	2.8	22.9	16.3	4.0	7.8	9.1
Sammamish city	101 592	104 356	111 308	59 250	52 500	57 286	81 356	48 542	42 971	95.1	60.2	8.7	0.4	10.3	51.3	39.0	1.9	1.8
SeaTac city	41 202	47 630	52 100	37 500	24 881	31 443	35 394	29 824	19 717	84.3	30.5	20.4	3.8	14.4	7.8	-4.5	10.0	14.1
Seattle city	45 736	62 195	75 786	36 034	26 252	34 537	42 002	35 867	30 306	82.6	46.8	19.6	3.0	13.2	15.9	3.6	10.7	11.1
Shoreline city	51 658	61 450	68 969	41 575	30 588	33 785	41 869	34 787	24 959	81.7	49.2	24.7	2.5	17.6	14.0	1.7	6.5	5.6
Spokane city	32 273	41 316	51 079	24 985	16 599	20 838	32 372	25 709	18 451	76.1	33.5	27.1	6.4	15.7	6.5	-5.8	15.3	17.3
Tacoma city	37 879	45 567	54 014	31 162	19 456	25 853	36 707	28 813	19 130	78.9	30.3	23.3	6.6	17.4	7.5	-4.8	14.1	17.3
University Place city	50 287	60 401	73 352	32 750	22 136	32 268	46 238	30 709	25 544	83.8	41.5	20.9	3.6	19.6	15.4	3.1	6.8	9.4
Vancouver city	41 618	47 696	53 508	33 880	20 362	29 775	38 423	27 856	20 192	82.2	34.0	21.8	5.8	15.0	8.4	-3.9	10.6	14.2
Walla Walla city	31 855	40 856	51 014	22 431	15 705	19 887	33 075	25 344	15 792	71.9	38.9	34.8	5.2	19.5	5.8	-6.5	16.3	20.7
Wenatchee city	34 897	45 982	53 533	28 214	16 903	20 941	36 357	26 457	19 498	75.2	36.4	30.2	5.6	18.6	8.5	-3.8	13.2	16.4
Yakima city	29 475	34 798	40 287	21 619	14 691	18 394	30 562	24 900	15 920	74.3	29.9	29.4	6.5	14.6	6.0	-6.3	19.1	26.4
WEST VIRGINIA	29 696	36 484	42 228	21 310	12 861	16 007	32 044	21 767	16 477	70.6	28.7	33.9	4.0	22.0	5.0	-7.3	18.0	21.4
Charleston city	34 009	47 975	65 783	17 798	13 413	22 185	40 147	27 851	26 017	72.6	36.0	31.8	3.9	19.2	13.1	0.8	16.9	22.7
Huntington city	23 234	34 756	40 000	14 186	11 444	14 005	30 937	21 898	16 717	68.7	28.8	35.4	4.5	19.8	4.6	-7.7	25.4	27.9
Morgantown city	20 649	44 622	55 708	7 054	12 935	11 759	34 316	26 858	14 459	80.9	34.5	19.8	2.3	15.8	6.0	-6.3	37.4	23.1
Parkersburg city	26 990	33 081	37 698	21 550	11 426	18 147	31 353	20 938	16 106	68.2	30.6	37.9	5.3	22.1	3.5	-8.8	17.9	28.1
Wheeling city	27 388	38 708	49 552	22 961	11 394	14 779	31 744	23 179	17 923	65.7	38.7	38.4	3.7	22.6	5.4	-6.9	18.8	21.5
WISCONSIN	43 791	52 911	61 834	31 599	22 057	25 837	38 180	26 644	21 271	81.8	47.2	26.4	1.7	15.7	9.4	-2.9	8.4	8.8
Appleton city	47 285	57 097	66 198	39 099	21 330	27 576	41 402	26 600	22 478	84.1	53.5	22.6	1.4	13.8	10.3	-2.0	5.6	5.7
Beloit city	36 414	42 083	50 070	27 545	20 924	20 577	33 579	24 873	16 912	78.3	34.1	28.6	3.2	15.7	5.6	-6.7	12.2	14.3
Brookfield city	76 225	83 691	95 405	67 292	44 231	41 327	66 462	40 345	37 292	80.9	71.8	30.0	0.4	19.2	33.5	21.2	2.0	2.3
Eau Claire city	36 399	49 320	60 653	26 845	23 395	23 258	33 988	24 400	18 230	82.0	48.3	24.5	1.7	14.9	5.8	-6.5	12.2	8.5
Fond du Lac city	41 113	50 341	57 166	32 054	19 390	23 647	36 393	23 314	18 996	80.8	47.3	27.5	1.6	14.7	5.6	-6.7	7.5	7.4

STATE Place code	City	High school graduates			College graduates		College graduates (percent)				
		Total population 25 years and over	Percent with a high school diploma or less	Percent with a high school diploma or more	Percent with a bachelor's degree or more	+/− U.S. percent with bachelor's degree or more	Non-Hispanic White	Black or African American	American Indian and Alaska Native	Asian, Hawaiian, and Pacific Islander	Hispanic or Latino[1]
		1	2	3	4	5	6	7	8	9	10
	WISCONSIN—Cont'd										
55 27300	Franklin city	20 202	38.0	90.0	29.1	4.7	29.9	5.0	22.5	50.5	26.1
55 31000	Green Bay city	64 507	52.7	82.6	19.3	-5.1	20.5	11.4	10.4	15.2	6.9
55 31175	Greenfield city	25 877	48.5	85.0	20.2	-4.2	20.0	6.2	0.0	51.7	13.1
55 37825	Janesville city	38 971	51.7	87.0	18.9	-5.5	19.1	9.3	22.3	31.3	12.8
55 39225	Kenosha city	56 840	50.9	81.8	18.2	-6.2	19.3	11.0	13.7	49.6	7.3
55 40775	La Crosse city	29 391	43.9	87.8	24.1	-0.3	24.5	9.6	11.5	25.3	15.2
55 48000	Madison city	126 804	25.7	92.4	48.2	23.8	49.4	20.0	26.5	66.4	34.1
55 48500	Manitowoc city	22 940	57.0	83.6	17.1	-7.3	17.4	11.5	0.0	22.3	6.4
55 51000	Menomonee Falls village	22 834	41.2	90.4	30.4	6.0	30.0	55.1	16.7	75.6	22.2
55 53000	Milwaukee city	353 305	55.3	74.8	18.3	-6.1	24.8	9.1	11.2	32.4	8.0
55 56375	New Berlin city	26 328	34.7	92.4	36.8	12.4	35.9	61.2	0.0	70.8	36.3
55 58800	Oak Creek city	18 810	43.7	88.6	24.4	0.0	23.9	39.0	16.7	39.4	20.1
55 60500	Oshkosh city	38 496	51.8	84.0	23.1	-1.3	23.3	7.0	14.3	35.3	26.2
55 66000	Racine city	50 038	55.3	77.2	15.6	-8.8	18.9	6.9	2.2	17.2	5.9
55 72975	Sheboygan city	33 309	58.7	81.2	15.9	-8.5	16.3	17.7	0.0	14.5	7.5
55 78650	Superior city	17 653	48.7	85.9	19.2	-5.2	19.7	21.5	0.0	42.9	13.6
55 84250	Waukesha city	41 765	40.3	89.4	30.6	6.2	31.3	15.1	8.6	66.4	12.1
55 84475	Wausau city	25 128	51.6	80.8	21.5	-2.9	22.3	27.7	8.7	9.9	16.8
55 84675	Wauwatosa city	33 616	26.1	93.4	47.6	23.2	47.4	40.9	27.4	71.6	46.8
55 85300	West Allis city	43 017	53.4	82.7	16.4	-8.0	16.2	5.2	7.5	43.7	9.6
55 85350	West Bend city	18 320	47.6	86.5	22.0	-2.4	22.2	28.1	23.1	10.6	9.5
56 00000	WYOMING	315 663	43.1	87.9	21.9	-2.5	23.0	18.6	8.1	34.3	7.8
56 13150	Casper city	31 884	40.1	89.1	22.1	-2.3	23.0	23.4	2.3	35.8	6.7
56 13900	Cheyenne city	35 199	37.5	89.0	24.5	0.1	27.1	12.3	17.1	24.0	8.4
56 45050	Laramie city	13 812	26.5	94.0	46.7	22.3	49.5	37.8	23.5	65.7	9.6

[1] Hispanic or Latino persons may be of any race.

City	School enrollment			Population 16 to 19 years				Employment status, 2000			Work status in 1999 of the population 16 years and over		
											Worked in 1999		
	Grades kindergarten through 12	College or graduate school	Percent private	Number	Percent in armed forces	Percent high school graduates	Percent not enrolled, not grads, not in armed forces, not employed	Total population 16 years and over	Percent in labor force	Unemploy- ment rate	Full-time	Part-time	Did not work in 1999
	11	12	13	14	15	16	17	18	19	20	21	22	23
WISCONSIN—Cont'd													
Franklin city	5 281	1 706	18.3	1 579	0.0	10.8	6.6	23 463	69.2	2.7	58.8	17.4	23.8
Green Bay city	18 923	6 068	16.2	6 078	0.0	10.3	6.5	79 125	70.3	5.0	59.0	17.3	23.7
Greenfield city	5 284	2 033	23.0	1 640	0.0	9.8	0.9	29 683	66.5	3.2	54.4	16.0	29.6
Janesville city	11 320	2 294	10.7	3 026	0.0	10.5	3.2	45 632	70.0	4.7	57.7	17.3	25.1
Kenosha city..................	18 126	5 981	16.5	5 084	0.3	12.4	5.0	68 467	67.2	6.2	56.4	16.6	27.1
La Crosse city	7 357	10 293	15.2	4 788	0.0	8.7	1.4	43 058	65.2	4.6	50.6	25.0	24.4
Madison city	26 635	43 299	8.1	15 980	0.1	6.5	2.2	175 269	73.1	4.8	56.8	25.3	17.9
Manitowoc city	6 255	1 479	21.4	1 688	0.0	11.6	3.9	26 607	65.7	4.4	53.9	17.4	28.6
Menomonee Falls village	5 946	1 315	21.0	1 439	0.0	13.0	1.1	25 347	70.4	2.7	57.8	17.7	24.5
Milwaukee city.............	131 199	45 872	23.1	37 149	0.0	9.9	8.5	442 845	63.9	9.4	54.2	15.9	29.9
New Berlin city.............	7 361	1 844	28.4	1 843	0.0	9.2	1.1	30 008	72.2	2.8	58.8	18.6	22.6
Oak Creek city	5 158	1 779	10.0	1 426	0.0	12.3	2.3	22 177	76.0	2.1	64.4	16.7	18.9
Oshkosh city.................	9 861	8 651	9.1	4 905	0.1	9.1	1.6	51 387	65.9	5.0	53.8	21.2	24.9
Racine city...................	17 680	3 615	15.9	4 949	0.2	13.5	7.7	60 612	63.9	7.0	55.1	15.5	29.3
Sheboygan city.............	9 688	2 069	18.7	2 831	0.0	11.6	4.3	39 391	68.2	3.8	56.4	16.9	26.7
Superior city	4 713	2 173	10.4	1 642	0.5	9.9	4.1	21 957	65.1	7.7	49.4	20.9	29.7
Waukesha city.............	11 006	4 790	23.4	3 739	0.0	12.0	1.4	50 623	73.2	3.4	60.7	18.3	21.0
Wausau city..................	7 283	1 677	11.3	2 213	0.0	13.1	3.0	29 947	64.7	4.4	53.0	17.4	29.6
Wauwatosa city.............	8 338	3 063	31.1	1 957	0.0	7.4	3.2	37 607	66.9	2.2	55.0	17.4	27.6
West Allis city..............	9 894	3 324	20.7	2 885	0.0	13.1	2.5	49 708	67.1	4.4	56.0	16.1	27.8
West Bend city	5 378	1 113	19.5	1 584	0.0	20.9	1.5	21 637	70.9	4.0	58.6	18.1	23.3
WYOMING	98 562	29 697	5.4	32 130	0.6	11.4	3.8	381 912	67.5	5.2	58.0	16.9	25.1
Casper city	9 502	3 177	3.3	3 118	0.0	12.0	3.9	38 535	68.4	4.9	55.9	17.2	26.9
Cheyenne city	9 807	2 555	7.2	2 774	0.6	11.5	4.1	41 432	66.7	4.9	58.4	14.0	27.6
Laramie city..................	3 306	9 656	7.8	3 068	0.0	5.8	0.9	23 063	67.2	5.6	54.9	28.9	16.2

City	Full-year full-time employed (percent)								Children under 18 years in families (percent, except where noted)						Total employed by class of worker (percent)			
										With two parents		With one parent who is in labor force	+/− U.S. percent of children with no stay-at-home parent	+/− U.S. percent two-income couples				
	Total	Men	Women	Non-Hispanic White	Black or African American	American Indian and Alaska Native	Asian, Hawaiian, and Pacific Islander	Hispanic or Latino[1]	Number	Both in labor force	Father only in labor force				Private	Government	Self-employed	Unpaid family worker
	24	25	26	27	28	29	30	31	32	33	34	35	36	37	38	39	40	41
WISCONSIN—Cont'd																		
Franklin city	48.1	54.8	40.8	50.5	9.3	53.6	57.2	47.5	6 772	64.0	20.9	12.4	11.8	14.9	82.7	9.8	7.2	0.3
Green Bay city	45.3	54.6	36.5	46.2	40.1	43.6	33.7	38.0	24 852	50.2	14.4	24.3	9.9	7.6	84.2	9.9	5.8	0.1
Greenfield city	44.1	54.6	35.3	43.7	46.8	56.6	42.7	52.9	6 546	58.5	15.5	18.4	12.3	6.2	84.5	8.5	6.8	0.2
Janesville city	44.0	54.6	34.2	44.3	30.6	48.7	40.3	40.4	14 693	54.0	15.8	24.7	14.1	6.5	83.2	10.8	5.9	0.1
Kenosha city	42.3	50.6	34.5	43.3	35.8	37.5	44.1	36.2	23 330	46.2	15.6	27.0	8.6	4.5	84.0	11.2	4.8	0.1
La Crosse city	34.2	42.7	26.9	34.6	21.3	26.8	28.3	31.4	9 189	51.4	16.4	23.7	10.5	3.2	79.7	14.5	5.6	0.2
Madison city	40.8	47.2	34.8	42.3	37.3	29.5	26.9	35.0	34 850	54.7	13.8	22.1	12.2	12.8	65.5	28.5	6.0	0.1
Manitowoc city	42.7	54.3	32.4	43.0	56.4	28.1	38.4	38.0	7 948	55.2	15.5	21.3	11.9	5.4	83.6	10.1	6.2	0.1
Menomonee Falls village	47.5	59.9	36.1	47.1	62.7	45.8	61.8	68.9	8 067	63.3	20.9	12.0	10.7	10.1	84.3	8.1	7.5	0.1
Milwaukee city	37.9	44.0	32.6	41.9	33.0	37.9	34.6	33.5	153 691	28.0	10.7	37.3	0.7	-0.8	80.4	15.0	4.5	0.1
New Berlin city	50.2	63.5	37.7	50.1	57.7	75.8	47.7	56.8	9 311	62.7	23.0	9.2	7.3	8.8	83.4	8.5	8.0	0.1
Oak Creek city	53.5	64.8	42.6	53.8	50.2	33.3	46.7	60.0	6 866	61.9	20.4	11.7	9.0	14.1	84.1	11.1	4.8	0.0
Oshkosh city	38.5	45.4	31.8	39.5	10.2	30.2	30.9	34.4	12 373	57.3	12.1	22.2	14.9	8.9	78.8	16.5	4.6	0.2
Racine city	39.8	47.1	33.1	43.5	30.0	50.6	29.1	34.2	21 906	37.4	13.3	32.4	5.2	1.3	84.0	11.4	4.5	0.2
Sheboygan city	44.3	55.6	33.7	45.4	40.5	28.0	30.5	41.0	12 508	53.5	16.0	20.5	9.4	8.1	86.8	8.7	4.4	0.2
Superior city	36.1	44.1	29.0	36.6	41.9	27.2	15.7	13.8	5 849	45.4	14.8	28.2	9.0	1.2	78.9	14.5	6.2	0.3
Waukesha city	48.1	58.7	38.0	48.5	25.8	52.7	43.1	46.4	15 066	55.3	20.1	17.8	8.5	11.8	85.5	9.2	5.1	0.2
Wausau city	40.8	49.9	32.6	41.6	41.0	31.4	31.1	43.1	9 318	47.4	16.6	19.5	2.3	4.3	81.1	11.3	7.4	0.3
Wauwatosa city	44.1	55.4	34.6	44.2	34.2	37.8	47.2	50.3	10 703	59.6	20.0	14.7	9.7	9.7	81.3	10.3	8.3	0.1
West Allis city	44.9	54.6	36.0	45.0	35.2	55.9	40.0	43.0	12 607	51.8	13.6	23.3	10.5	5.8	85.3	9.7	4.9	0.1
West Bend city	46.4	58.7	35.3	46.3	69.0	31.3	38.1	56.7	7 187	57.2	18.5	19.3	11.9	10.1	85.2	9.9	4.7	0.2
WYOMING	40.6	51.1	30.2	41.1	39.2	28.2	34.3	37.8	121 984	51.3	21.3	20.1	6.8	4.8	66.1	20.4	13.0	0.5
Casper city	40.1	51.2	30.0	40.5	19.3	22.9	46.9	37.7	12 175	47.5	19.4	25.0	7.9	4.1	73.0	15.9	10.9	0.2
Cheyenne city	43.5	52.2	35.4	44.4	42.6	24.2	32.1	39.4	12 146	50.9	16.7	24.6	10.9	6.2	63.2	27.4	9.2	0.2
Laramie city	31.7	37.5	25.3	31.1	30.3	39.8	21.3	42.8	4 501	47.3	22.5	20.0	2.7	6.7	59.6	31.6	8.6	0.3

[1] Hispanic or Latino persons may be of any race.

City	Percent who worked at home	Percent of the population 5 years and over with a disability	Veterans as a percent of the population 18 years and over	Occupation for employed population 16 years and over (percent)						Industry for employed population 16 years and over (percent)					
				Management, professional, and related occupations	Service occupations	Sales and office occupations	Farming, fishing, and forestry occupations	Construction, extraction, and maintenance occupations	Production, transportation and material moving occupations	Agriculture, forestry, fishing, and mining	Construction and manufacturing	Wholesale and retail trade	Transportation and warehousing, and utilities	Service industries	Public administration
	42	43	44	45	46	47	48	49	50	51	52	53	54	55	56
WISCONSIN—Cont'd															
Franklin city	3.5	13.2	12.1	40.0	9.4	27.7	0.0	8.1	14.8	0.2	26.5	13.8	7.7	49.1	2.7
Green Bay city	1.8	18.0	12.6	26.6	15.0	28.0	0.3	9.1	20.9	0.5	27.5	17.2	5.5	46.0	3.3
Greenfield city	1.8	18.4	13.6	32.0	11.9	32.2	0.0	7.6	16.3	0.2	24.2	17.1	5.5	50.7	2.4
Janesville city	2.0	17.1	14.2	26.6	13.6	24.9	0.2	8.9	25.8	0.5	34.1	17.6	4.5	40.3	2.9
Kenosha city	1.8	18.8	13.0	28.4	15.9	26.7	0.1	7.5	21.3	0.2	30.9	15.3	4.3	45.7	3.7
La Crosse city	2.3	16.3	12.2	27.9	20.4	29.1	0.2	6.6	15.9	0.3	18.9	19.0	3.3	55.4	3.1
Madison city	3.1	13.5	8.7	46.9	14.1	25.7	0.2	4.4	8.7	0.5	11.4	12.9	2.9	65.6	6.6
Manitowoc city	1.8	16.0	14.7	24.0	15.8	23.1	0.6	8.7	27.8	0.8	39.1	13.5	3.7	39.8	3.1
Menomonee Falls village	3.1	12.0	14.3	39.6	9.0	29.6	0.1	8.0	13.7	0.3	28.7	17.2	4.1	48.2	1.5
Milwaukee city	1.7	22.2	10.7	28.0	18.6	26.2	0.2	6.0	21.1	0.4	22.2	12.8	5.1	54.9	4.5
New Berlin city	2.8	11.8	12.0	43.4	7.9	29.4	0.1	7.9	11.4	0.2	24.3	16.6	4.4	52.7	1.8
Oak Creek city	1.8	13.1	12.2	33.3	11.7	28.1	0.4	9.5	17.0	0.3	26.4	14.7	10.3	44.0	4.2
Oshkosh city	1.7	15.7	12.0	28.3	18.1	26.8	0.2	6.0	20.6	0.3	26.0	17.3	3.8	48.6	4.1
Racine city	1.7	20.0	12.3	25.2	16.0	25.5	0.1	7.2	25.9	0.2	33.8	15.1	3.9	42.9	4.2
Sheboygan city	1.5	18.0	13.2	22.6	15.3	21.6	0.4	6.0	34.0	0.4	43.4	13.1	2.1	38.8	2.1
Superior city	1.6	19.7	14.9	25.8	20.1	30.4	0.4	8.2	15.1	0.8	13.2	17.6	8.0	56.2	4.1
Waukesha city	1.9	14.9	11.0	36.0	12.8	28.4	0.1	7.4	15.3	0.3	26.7	16.4	4.1	49.8	2.7
Wausau city	2.3	18.0	14.0	30.6	14.5	28.7	0.5	6.4	19.3	0.8	25.5	18.5	3.7	49.3	2.1
Wauwatosa city	3.6	12.9	12.2	50.5	8.5	28.5	0.1	4.3	8.0	0.1	17.6	14.3	3.6	62.1	2.3
West Allis city	1.5	18.1	14.1	26.9	15.0	29.9	0.1	9.4	18.8	0.2	25.0	17.0	4.6	49.6	3.6
West Bend city	2.4	15.1	11.9	29.4	12.9	26.0	0.1	8.1	23.5	0.3	36.2	13.1	3.3	44.9	2.1
WYOMING	4.3	17.1	15.8	30.0	16.7	24.2	1.5	14.8	12.8	10.7	13.5	14.1	6.6	48.9	6.3
Casper city	2.7	18.3	14.0	29.7	16.1	30.6	0.2	12.8	10.7	5.9	12.8	18.8	4.8	52.5	5.2
Cheyenne city	3.1	18.4	19.0	33.0	15.2	28.5	0.2	10.6	12.4	1.1	12.1	15.4	6.9	50.4	14.1
Laramie city	3.3	12.4	9.8	40.5	19.3	23.7	1.0	7.1	8.4	2.0	9.2	11.9	3.0	69.9	3.9

City	Median house-hold income	Median family income — All families	Median family income — Married-couple	Families with children — Male house-holder	Families with children — Female house-holder	Median nonfamily house-hold income	Men	Women	Per capita income	With earnings	With interest, dividend, or rental income	With Social Security income	With public assis-tance income	With retire-ment income	House-holds with income over $100,000 (percent)	+/– U.S. percent for income over $100,000	House-holds with income below poverty (percent)	Families with children with income below poverty (percent)
	57	58	59	60	61	62	63	64	65	66	67	68	69	70	71	72	73	74
WISCONSIN—Cont'd																		
Franklin city	64 315	75 532	81 757	50 865	42 969	36 569	49 165	35 297	27 474	87.2	59.5	21.8	0.3	16.4	20.8	8.5	2.7	2.2
Green Bay city	38 820	48 678	57 698	28 333	21 016	24 618	34 445	24 864	19 269	81.8	41.0	23.5	2.5	12.3	6.5	-5.8	10.1	11.2
Greenfield city	44 230	56 272	67 000	39 688	36 667	29 851	40 778	31 126	23 755	76.6	52.6	32.6	0.5	23.8	9.2	-3.1	4.2	6.0
Janesville city	45 961	55 133	64 395	34 226	24 853	28 427	41 732	27 296	22 224	81.6	44.4	25.4	1.5	18.8	9.8	-2.5	6.3	6.8
Kenosha city	41 902	51 016	62 517	27 143	22 244	25 390	39 652	27 433	19 578	80.7	38.7	26.3	2.2	18.3	8.0	-4.3	8.8	10.5
La Crosse city	31 103	43 047	51 326	26 614	18 347	21 269	31 561	22 567	17 650	78.2	42.6	30.3	1.4	17.0	5.2	-7.1	15.6	13.1
Madison city	41 941	59 840	67 535	32 948	24 636	30 075	37 680	31 514	23 498	86.7	51.9	17.7	1.6	12.7	10.7	-1.6	13.7	9.3
Manitowoc city	38 203	47 635	57 070	33 250	19 988	22 548	35 857	24 361	19 954	75.8	51.3	32.8	1.0	17.3	5.2	-7.1	7.1	8.2
Menomonee Falls village	57 952	68 952	78 923	51 500	38 125	30 692	48 059	33 037	27 454	81.2	58.7	29.7	0.7	19.9	17.0	4.7	2.5	1.9
Milwaukee city	32 216	37 879	52 283	26 820	17 138	24 306	33 151	26 648	16 181	79.3	31.2	24.0	4.6	14.5	4.7	-7.6	18.2	25.7
New Berlin city	67 576	75 565	86 923	55 900	30 139	39 876	51 757	35 488	29 789	85.6	64.3	25.7	0.6	19.7	24.8	12.5	2.1	2.0
Oak Creek city	53 779	63 381	71 835	42 875	32 743	35 272	44 831	31 683	23 586	87.1	46.0	18.9	0.7	14.2	11.3	-1.0	4.0	2.1
Oshkosh city	37 636	48 843	56 066	32 019	21 462	24 222	34 932	25 258	18 964	80.3	45.4	26.3	1.4	16.9	5.5	-6.8	10.0	8.5
Racine city	37 164	45 150	55 145	29 457	18 491	23 740	35 668	25 325	17 705	78.8	35.7	27.7	2.7	18.3	5.2	-7.1	12.3	16.7
Sheboygan city	40 066	47 718	54 861	30 918	23 002	25 661	36 339	25 313	19 270	78.2	45.4	28.4	1.6	15.8	4.4	-7.9	7.8	9.4
Superior city	31 921	41 093	50 799	22 039	18 324	20 060	34 915	22 852	17 253	75.6	39.8	30.0	2.8	16.0	3.9	-8.4	13.4	15.8
Waukesha city	50 084	60 841	66 638	40 160	25 087	31 326	41 571	30 239	23 242	85.8	47.0	22.1	1.3	14.5	10.6	-1.7	5.4	4.5
Wausau city	36 831	47 065	54 576	28 664	21 131	23 021	34 153	24 961	20 227	76.2	49.6	31.4	2.3	18.7	7.9	-4.4	9.5	12.8
Wauwatosa city	54 519	68 030	77 917	43 500	35 525	34 024	48 971	36 268	28 834	77.1	61.9	30.6	1.1	20.2	15.3	3.0	4.2	3.6
West Allis city	39 394	50 732	59 430	33 889	22 879	26 607	38 162	26 980	20 914	77.0	47.3	29.8	1.4	20.1	5.0	-7.3	6.6	8.1
West Bend city	48 315	56 299	61 172	28 125	26 250	29 337	40 372	25 031	22 116	81.0	50.2	28.1	1.6	15.9	9.0	-3.3	4.8	5.8
WYOMING	37 892	45 685	51 815	29 194	17 122	21 689	35 831	22 397	19 134	82.5	38.2	24.5	2.6	14.6	6.7	-5.6	11.2	12.4
Casper city	36 567	46 267	52 138	26 861	17 899	22 347	36 024	22 278	19 409	80.7	40.4	26.8	2.8	15.1	6.4	-5.9	11.1	13.9
Cheyenne city	38 856	46 771	52 213	27 406	20 498	24 480	34 694	25 462	19 809	79.5	40.8	27.1	2.3	20.6	5.8	-6.5	9.1	10.0
Laramie city	27 319	43 395	50 202	21 648	10 764	16 162	32 296	22 531	16 036	88.2	41.2	14.7	1.8	9.3	4.7	-7.6	24.1	16.9

Migration, Housing, and Transportation

(For explanation of symbols, see page xi.)

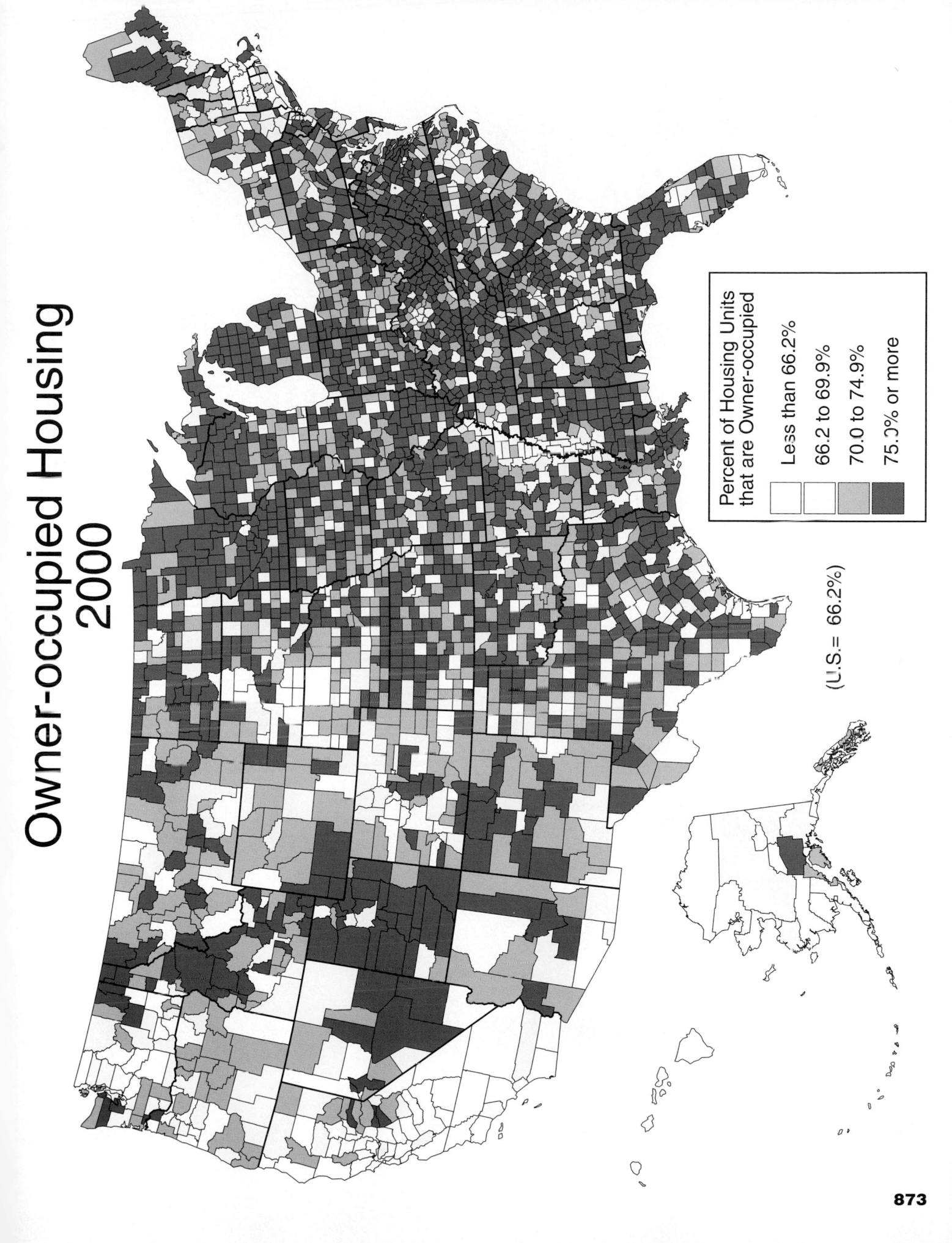

Owner-occupied Housing 2000

Percent of Housing Units
that are Owner-occupied

Less than 66.2%

66.2 to 69.9%

70.0 to 74.9%

75.0% or more

(U.S. = 66.2%)

873

Population Who Lived in a Different House 5 Years Ago
2000

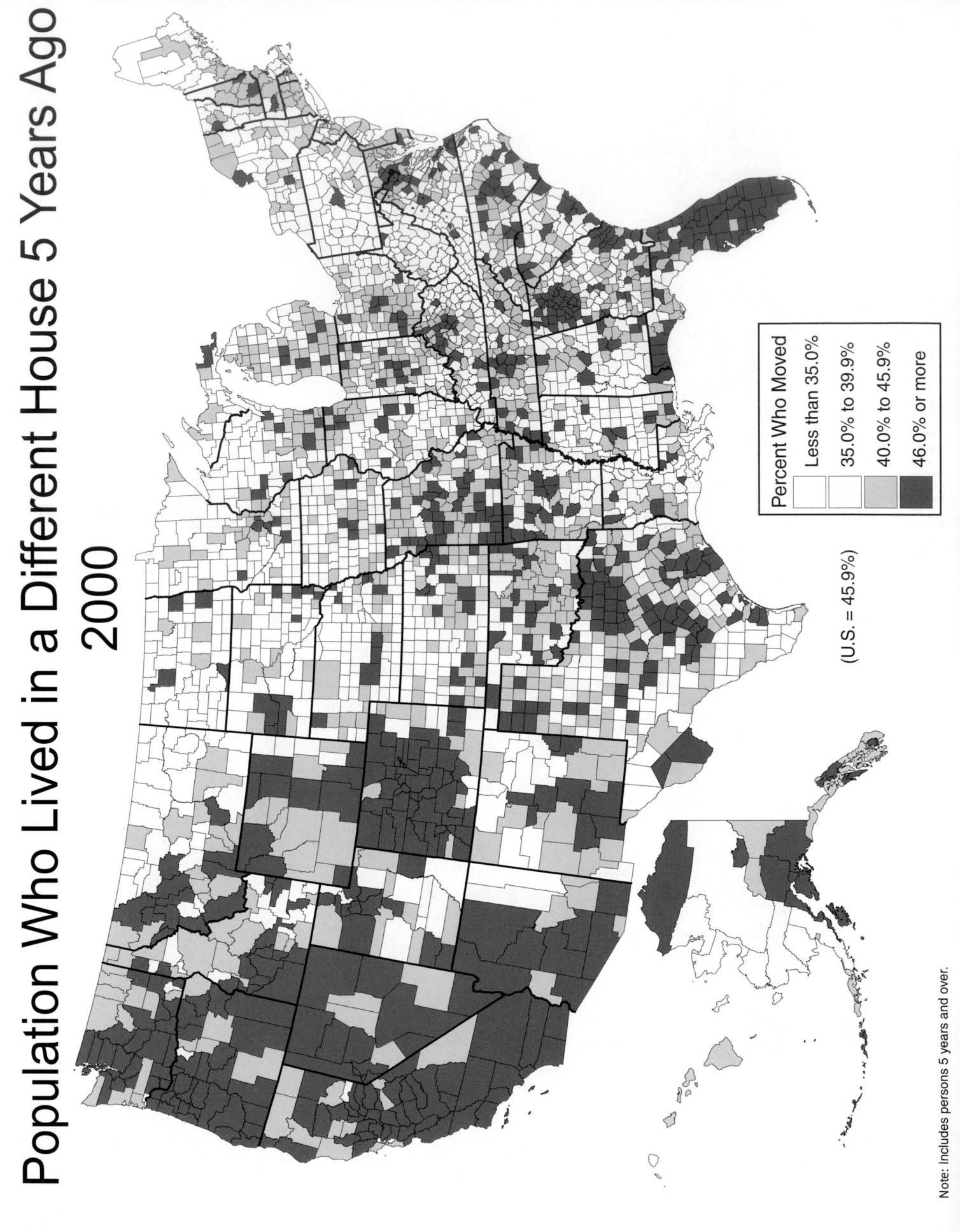

Percent Who Moved

Less than 35.0%

35.0% to 39.9%

40.0% to 45.9%

46.0% or more

(U.S. = 45.9%)

Note: Includes persons 5 years and over.

Median Home Value

2000

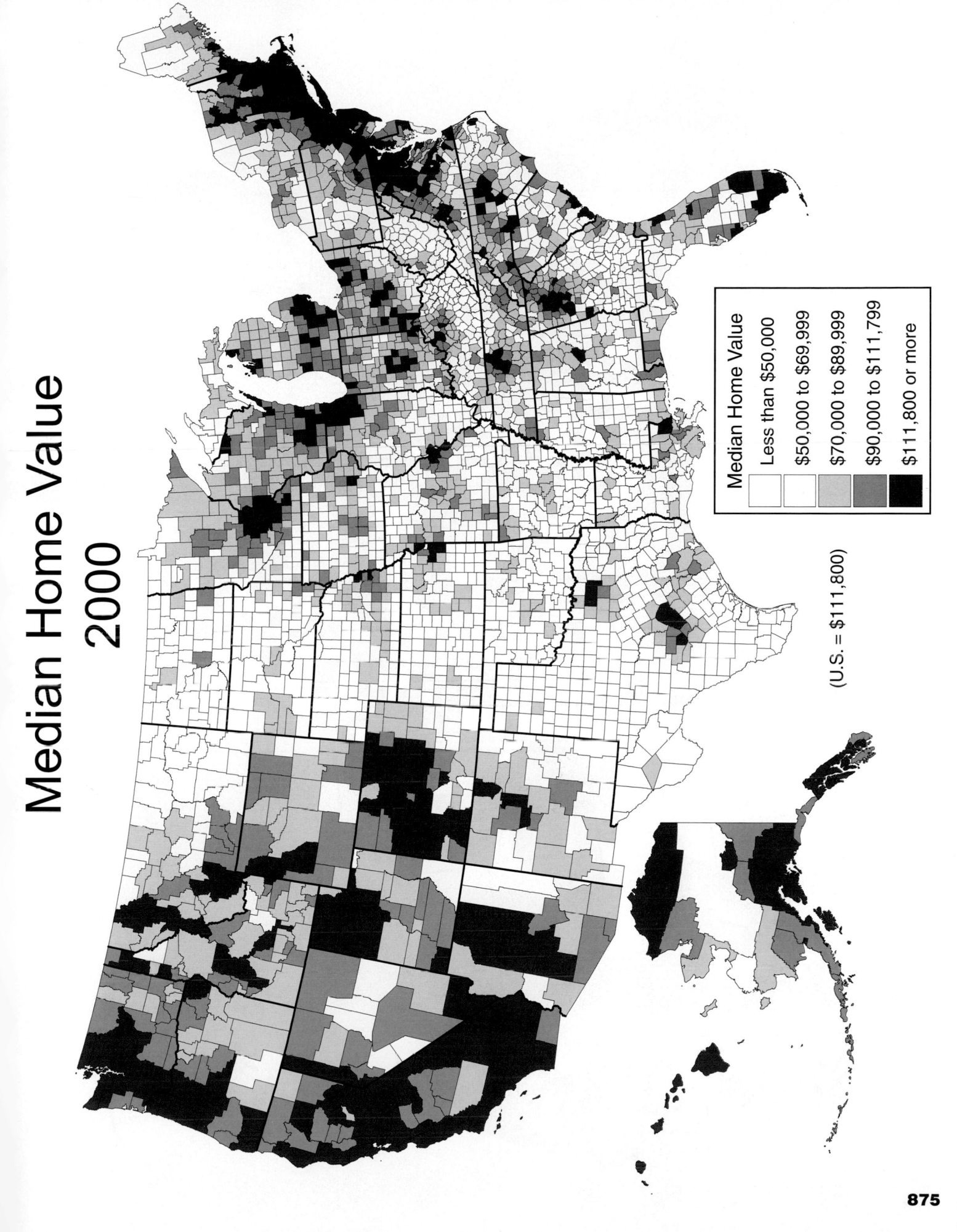

Median Home Value

- Less than $50,000
- $50,000 to $69,999
- $70,000 to $89,999
- $90,000 to $111,799
- $111,800 or more

(U.S. = $111,800)

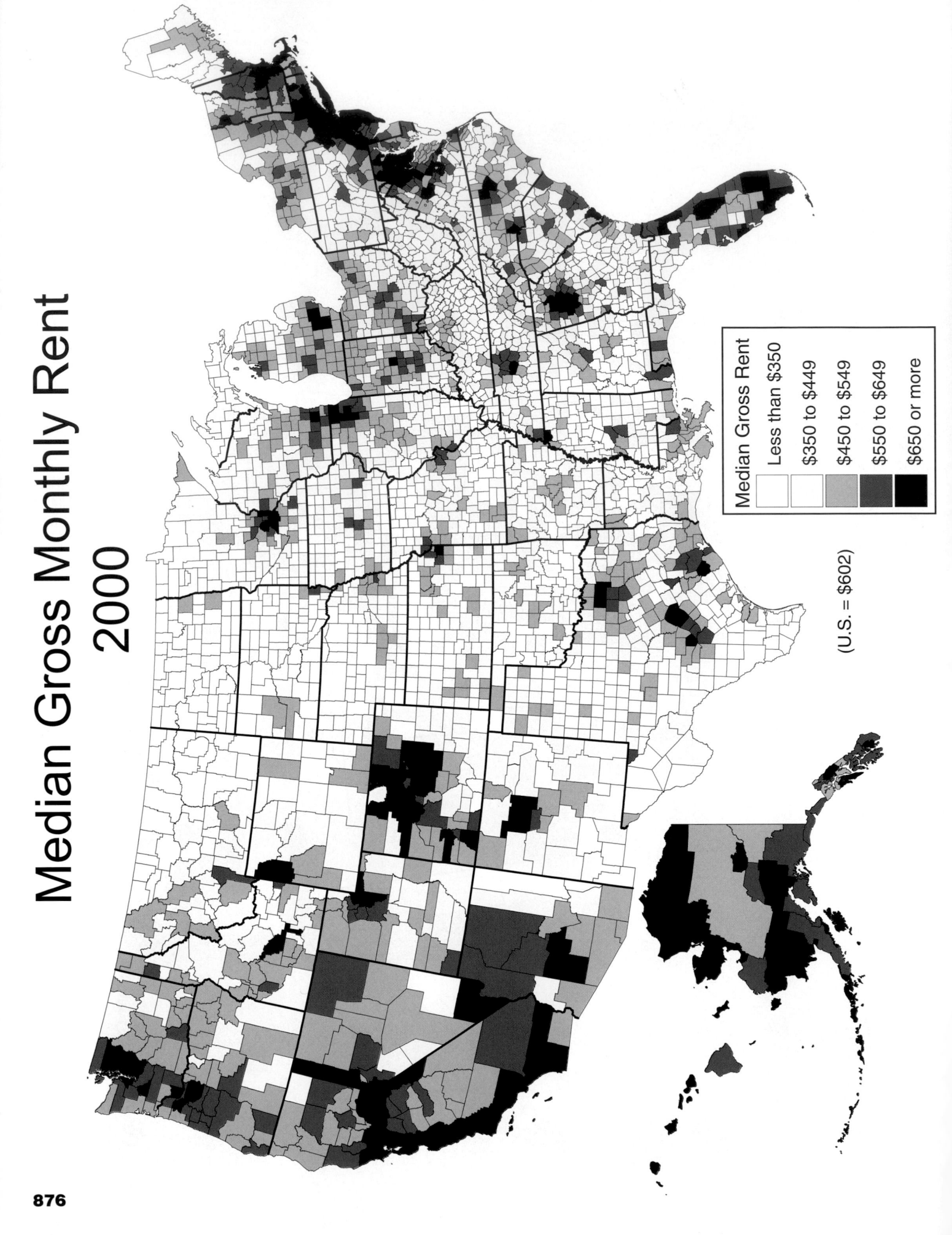

Median Gross Monthly Rent
2000

Median Gross Rent

Less than $350
$350 to $449
$450 to $549
$550 to $649
$650 or more

(U.S. = $602)

Migration, Housing, and Transportation

The census is officially named the U.S. Census of Population and Housing because it is conducted from an address list of housing units. (No comparably comprehensive national list of individuals exists; such a list is necessary for a census, so census takers will know when they are done.) Before the census, the U.S. Postal Service sends the Census Bureau its address list. The bureau then scours the country to update the list for recent construction or demolition, and asks local governments to review it for accuracy. As a result, the census is the nation's primary source for information about where Americans live, what their housing is like, and how they get from home to work.

Table C-1.1. Migration, United States, 2000

(Number, percent.)

Residence in 2000, race, and Hispanic origin	Total population 5 years and over	Residence in 1995 (percent)								
		Same house	Same county, different house	Same state, different county	Another state					From outside the United States
					Total from another state	From Northeast states	From Midwest states	From Southern states	From Western states	
Total Population										
United States	262 375 152	54.1	24.9	9.7	8.4	1.7	1.8	2.9	2.1	2.9
Northeast	50 224 209	60.9	22.0	7.8	6.1	3.1	0.6	1.7	0.8	3.1
Midwest	60 054 144	56.3	24.8	10.3	6.9	0.6	2.8	2.0	1.4	1.8
South	93 431 879	52.5	24.1	10.5	10.2	2.0	1.8	4.8	1.6	2.8
West	58 664 920	48.8	29.0	9.2	9.2	1.0	1.6	2.0	4.7	3.8
Non-Hispanic White										
United States	183 342 983	56.9	22.9	10.2	8.9	1.7	2.1	3.0	2.1	1.1
Northeast	37 141 066	64.2	20.6	7.7	6.2	3.1	0.7	1.7	0.8	1.3
Midwest	49 238 785	58.5	23.2	10.9	6.6	0.6	2.9	1.9	1.2	0.8
South	62 135 688	54.9	21.9	11.2	10.8	2.0	2.1	5.1	1.5	1.1
West	34 827 444	50.6	26.4	9.9	11.5	1.2	2.2	2.4	5.7	1.6
Black or African American										
United States	31 616 957	51.3	30.6	8.4	7.4	1.6	1.3	3.5	0.9	2.3
Northeast	5 567 226	56.6	27.1	8.1	4.6	2.2	0.4	1.8	0.3	3.6
Midwest	5 892 068	50.4	35.3	6.7	6.0	0.5	2.4	2.3	0.8	1.7
South	17 377 637	51.2	29.5	8.9	8.4	1.8	1.2	4.5	0.9	2.0
West	2 780 026	43.6	34.8	9.9	9.0	1.0	1.6	3.5	2.8	2.7
American Indian and Alaska Native										
United States	2 243 344	50.5	26.5	12.4	8.7	0.7	1.6	2.7	3.8	1.8
Northeast	147 359	49.3	27.1	10.7	8.2	3.1	0.8	2.6	1.7	4.7
Midwest	371 782	45.4	26.0	16.8	10.3	0.3	4.1	2.8	3.1	1.5
South	668 959	49.3	24.4	14.3	10.1	1.0	1.5	5.0	2.6	1.8
West	1 055 244	53.1	27.9	10.0	7.4	0.2	0.8	1.2	5.2	1.5
Asian, Hawaiian, or Pacific Islander										
United States	9 867 605	45.9	22.6	8.7	8.8	2.3	1.5	2.2	2.9	14.0
Northeast	1 988 776	46.3	18.8	8.6	9.3	4.6	1.1	1.8	1.8	16.9
Midwest	1 107 227	38.7	20.8	9.5	12.3	2.2	3.8	2.6	3.7	18.7
South	1 808 034	38.9	18.7	10.8	14.5	3.4	2.2	5.1	3.9	17.1
West	4 963 568	49.9	26.0	7.7	5.7	0.9	0.8	1.2	2.7	10.7
Hispanic or Latino										
United States	31 569 576	44.5	31.8	7.8	6.4	1.3	0.7	1.8	2.5	9.6
Northeast	4 765 821	48.5	28.4	7.9	5.3	3.1	0.3	1.2	0.7	9.9
Midwest	2 733 912	41.0	30.1	7.1	10.3	0.8	2.3	3.2	4.0	11.6
South	10 410 350	43.3	28.7	8.3	8.0	1.9	0.9	2.7	2.4	11.7
West	13 659 493	44.7	35.6	7.5	4.7	0.3	0.4	1.1	3.0	7.5

Source: Census 2000 Summary File 3—United States, U.S. Census Bureau, 2002. Tables P24 and PCT64A-I.
[1]Hispanic or Latino persons may be of any race.

Internal Migration

Perhaps the most sought-after information from the census is how many people had moved recently, and from where to where. Each individual is asked where they lived

Table C-1.2.
Westerners moved most; Easterners moved least.
Population Who Lived in the Same House in 1995 and 2000, Selected States

(Percentage of population in the same house.)

State	Percent	State	Percent
Nevada	37.4	Pennsylvania	63.5
Colorado	44.1	West Virginia	63.3
Arizona	44.3	New York	61.8
Alaska	46.2	New Jersey	59.8
Oregon	46.8	Maine	59.6

Source: Census 2000 Summary File 3—United States, U.S. Census Bureau, 2002. Table P24.

five years earlier, and the response is measured against their current address. In essence, the results provide a report card for localities—attractive places simply ''attract'' people from less attractive places.

In 2000, fully 46 percent of Americans (aged 5 and older) said they were living in a different house from the one they lived in 1995. (See Table C-1.1.) Over half of them were still living in the same county. An additional 10 percent were living in the same state. Thus, the 8.4 percent of Americans who changed states are of particular interest, since they contributed to transforming both the states they left, and the states they chose.

Regionally, the South delivered over a third of these interstate migrants, and the West nearly a quarter. The overall pattern of regional concentration is reflected in the racial and ethnic composition of interstate migrants. African Americans were most likely to move to the South, while American Indians were most likely to move from the West.

Table C-1.3. Housing Tenure and Household Type by Age of Householder, United States, 2000

(Number, percent.)

Household type	Total households	Age of householder				
		15 to 24 years	25 to 44 years	45 to 64 years	65 to 74 years	75 years and over
TOTAL OCCUPIED UNITS	105 480 101	5 348 242	41 888 441	35 608 728	11 727 702	10 906 988
Owner-Occupied Units	69 816 513	921 685	23 995 835	27 345 166	9 482 167	8 071 660
Owner-Occupied (percent)	66.2	17.2	57.3	76.8	80.9	74.0
Family households	50.4	12.1	48.1	60.9	55.7	38.6
Married-couple families	42.3	8.0	40.1	52.2	47.6	30.2
Other families	8.1	4.1	8.0	8.7	8.1	8.4
Male householder, no wife present	2.2	1.9	2.5	2.3	1.6	1.7
Female householder, no husband present	5.9	2.2	5.5	6.4	6.4	6.7
Nonfamily households	15.8	5.2	9.2	15.9	25.2	35.4
Not living alone	2.3	2.4	2.5	2.5	1.7	1.2
Male	1.3	1.5	1.6	1.3	0.9	0.5
Female	1.0	0.9	0.9	1.2	0.8	0.7
Living alone	13.5	2.7	6.7	13.4	23.5	34.2
Male	5.1	1.8	4.2	5.6	6.4	7.6
Female	8.3	0.9	2.5	7.8	17.2	26.6
Renter-Occupied Units	35 663 588	4 426 557	17 892 606	8 263 562	2 245 535	2 835 328
Renter-Occupied (percent)	33.8	82.8	42.7	23.2	19.1	26.0
Family households	17.9	36.8	26.6	12.0	6.9	6.1
Married-couple families	9.9	15.9	14.7	7.0	4.5	4.0
Other families	8.0	20.9	11.9	5.1	2.4	2.0
Male householder, no wife present	1.8	5.7	2.7	1.2	0.5	0.4
Female householder, no husband present	6.1	15.2	9.2	3.9	1.9	1.7
Nonfamily households	15.9	46.0	16.1	11.2	12.2	19.9
Not living alone	3.6	24.7	4.4	1.4	0.6	0.4
Male	2.1	12.8	2.8	0.8	0.3	0.2
Female	1.5	11.9	1.6	0.6	0.2	0.2
Living alone	12.4	21.3	11.7	9.8	11.7	19.5
Male	5.7	10.7	7.0	4.8	3.8	3.7
Female	6.6	10.6	4.7	5.0	7.9	15.8

Source: Census 2000 Summary File 3—United States, U.S. Census Bureau, 2002. Table H19.

By and large, migrants tend to stay within their region. People tend to move for either work or retirement, but they don't like to move far from their families and friends. However, states like Colorado that are attractive to young adults drew movers from several sources: people from within the state, people from other states in the West, and people moving from other regions, notably the South. Arizona is another state with above-average in-migration. High proportions of the state's movers were simply changing residences within their county, while a high proportion came from the West, the Midwest (presumably retirees), and outside the United States (such as from Mexico).

Interstate migrants are most likely to be young adults, moving around the country for work and personal experience before they settle down. The top states for new residents from outside the state are particularly popular with young people, as they tend to appreciate states with attractive outdoor recreation opportunities. These states are particularly alluring when the economy is offering plentiful jobs, as it was during the 1990s. In contrast, states with relatively few in-migrants are becoming "older" states because they are not attracting or keeping young people. (See Tables C-1.2. and C-2.)

Several states attracted large numbers of people from outside the United States: these include the "usual suspects" (California, Florida, and New York) as well as Hawaii and Nevada. Nevada's plentiful jobs also attracted large numbers of Americans from out of state, mostly from other Western states (and mostly non-Hispanic whites).

Owning or Renting

Year after year, polls show that owning one's home is an essential component of the American dream. Census 2000 found that home ownership was at a record high for

Table C-1.4.
Where home ownership flourishes.
Home Ownership, Selected States, 2000

(Percent of units.)

State	High home-ownership rates	State	Low home-ownership rates
West Virginia	75.2	New York	53.0
Minnesota	74.5	Hawaii	56.5
Michigan	73.8	California	56.9
Alabama	72.5	Rhode Island	60.0
Mississippi	72.4	Nevada	60.9

Source: Census 2000 Summary File 3—United States, U.S. Census Bureau, 2002. Table H7.

Table C-1.5. Home ownership Rate by Race and Hispanic Origin, United States, 2000

(Number, percent.)

Race and Hispanic origin	Total households	Owners (percent)
Total Households	105 480 101	66.2
One race only	103 509 636	66.6
White	83 715 168	71.3
Black or African American	11 977 309	46.3
American Indian and Alaska Native	765 474	55.7
Asian	3 117 356	53.2
Native Hawaiian or Other Pacific Islander	98 739	45.5
Some other race	3 835 590	40.4
Two or more races	1 970 465	46.6
Hispanic or Latino[1]	9 179 764	45.7
White alone, not Hispanic or Latino	79 086 566	72.4

Source: Census 2000 Summary File 3—United States, U.S. Census Bureau, 2002. Tables H11, H12, and H13.
[1] Hispanic or Latino persons may be of any race.

Americans: owners occupied fully two-thirds of American housing units. (See Table C-1.3.) Times were good, and the big bulge of baby boomers swelled the numbers of Americans in the prime home ownership years.

An owned home is the most valuable investment for all but the wealthiest Americans, and it takes time to acquire one. Thus, renters outnumber owners under age 45, and owners outnumber renters at age 45 and older. This pattern holds across households, including single-person households. However, married-couple households have the highest rates of home ownership; they also become homeowners earlier than people in other household types. Indeed, the increasingly large proportion of homeowners among single-person households at older ages no doubt includes formerly married people living in the family home after death or divorce.

Households that own their home tend to be slightly larger than those that rent. There are relatively few differences among the states: only homeowners in Utah and Hawaii have an average household that exceeds three people. However, as the map on page 873 shows, there is a great deal of difference in home ownership rates.

States with high average rates of home ownership tend to be states where the population is relatively stable. (See Table C-1.4.) In contrast, home ownership lags in states where the population is growing and/or population density is high. Homes tend to cost more in these conditions; there can also be a shortage of adequate units. However, since home ownership becomes easier as incomes rise with age, state-by-state differences tend to be erased for older Americans. On average, young adults are far less likely to

Table C-1.6. Mean and Median Household Income By Age and Tenure, United States, 2000

(Dollars.)

Household type	All house-holds	Age of householder		
		15 to 34 years	35 to 64 years	65 years and over
Mean Household Income				
Total occupied housing units	56 474	44 942	66 660	41 676
Owner occupied	66 699	59 570	76 538	46 229
Renter occupied	36 457	35 605	40 486	25 944
Median Household Income				
Total occupied housing units	41 851	. . .	. . .	. . .
Owner occupied	51 323	. . .	. . .	. . .
Renter occupied	27 362	. . .	. . .	. . .

Source: Census 2000 Summary File 3—United States, U.S. Census Bureau, 2002. Tables H14, HCT12, and HCT14.
. . . = Data not available.

Table C-1.7.
Owner-estimated housing value is a guide to local housing costs.

Median Owner-Estimated Housing Value, Selected States, 2000

(Dollars.)

State	High median value	State	Low median value
Hawaii	249 300	West Virginia	66 000
California	198 900	Arkansas	67 400
Massachusetts	182 800	Mississippi	64 700
New Jersey	167 900	Oklahoma	67 700
Connecticut	160 600	North Dakota	68 300

Source: Census 2000 Summary File 3—United States, U.S. Census Bureau, 2002. Table H85.

own their homes in expensive states like New York, Hawaii, and California. The gap narrows by middle age, and almost vanishes among older people in most states.

The stark differences in the demographics of home ownership are by race and ethnic origin. (See Table C-1.5.) Close to three in four non-Hispanic white households live in a home they own, while American Indians (many of whom live on reservations) are the only other group where the majority of householders are owners. Renters slightly outnumber owners for blacks, Asians, and Hispanics. Put another way, non-Hispanic whites constitute over 80 percent of all homeowners.

The younger age profile of minorities compared with non-Hispanic whites plays a part in these differences; but differences in income, along with differences in location, are particularly important. (See Table C-1.6.) The average income of homeowners is nearly double that of renters, no matter what the age group, so a higher proportion of younger people tends to lower the ownership rate for any demographic group. Living in a big city makes a difference too: all racial and ethnic origin groups are less likely to be homeowners if they live in metropolitan areas. In general, housing is much less expensive in small towns and rural areas. The difference in location is particularly stark for African Americans.

States where income levels tend to be high show higher than average household income for renters as well as owners. This pattern has its parallel in states with lower than average household income. Since housing is a strictly local product, builders build in accordance with local income levels. No wonder lower housing costs are a common selling point for recruiting employers to poorer states. (See Table C-1.7.)

On average, renters devote a relatively high share of their monthly income to rent: fully 25 percent. (See Table C-1.8.) Even owners with a mortgage spend relatively less on their housing—22 percent of monthly household income. (Those with no mortgage spend little more than 10 percent.) In part, this difference reflects the age profile of renters. Nearly two-thirds of renters are under age 45, before income tends to peak—whether from climbing a career ladder or joining two incomes into one family household, or both. (Remember, two-earner married couples aged 45 to 64 have the nation's top incomes.) For renters, housing costs tend to peak as a percentage of income under age 45. For owners, they peak for people aged 45 to 64.

All in all, Census 2000 bears out Americans' continued preference for investing in their homes to the maximum extent. Given longer life expectancy, and potentially longer work and earning lives, these data provide an insight into a major housing trend of the 1990s. Instead of moving to smaller, less expensive houses when their children left home, as housing experts predicted on the basis of past practice, higher-earning baby boomers traded up, not down. More highly educated than their predecessors, and much more likely to have two earners in a household, their incomes were still rising after their children had grown. This is just one example of how policymakers need to understand the new demographics of home ownership, rather than assume the demographics of the past.

Table C-1.8. Owner and Renter Costs as a Percent of Income, United States, 2000

(Number, percent.)

Characteristic	All units	Age of householder						
		15 to 64 years				65 years and over		
		Total 15 to 64 years	15 to 24 years	25 to 44 years	45 to 64 years	Total 65 years and over	65 to 74 years	75 years and over
Median Monthly Owner Costs as a Percent of Income								
Total owner-occupied housing units	18.7	. . .	. . .	. . .	. . .	. . .	. . .	. . .
Units with a mortgage	21.7	. . .	. . .	. . .	. . .	. . .	. . .	. . .
Units without a mortgage	10.5	. . .	. . .	. . .	. . .	. . .	. . .	. . .
Monthly Owner Costs as a Percent of Income								
Total specified owner-occupied units	55 212 108	41 707 722	563 472	19 214 697	21 929 553	13 504 386	7 367 350	6 137 036
Owner costs are less than 20 percent of income	54.0	51.5	34.7	44.7	57.8	62.0	62.7	61.1
Owner costs are 20.0 to 24.9 percent of income	13.9	15.5	16.2	18.2	13.0	9.2	9.2	9.2
Owner costs are 25.0 to 29.9 percent of income	9.4	10.4	12.5	12.5	8.5	6.4	6.4	6.4
Owner costs are 30.0 to 34.9 percent	6.0	6.5	8.7	7.7	5.4	4.6	4.6	4.6
Owner costs are 35.0 percent or more of income	15.8	15.5	26.0	16.3	14.5	16.7	16.3	17.3
Not computed	0.8	0.7	1.8	0.6	0.8	1.2	0.9	1.5
Median Gross Rent as a Percent of Income								
Median gross rent as a percent of income	25.5	. . .	. . .	. . .	. . .	. . .	. . .	. . .
Total specified renter-occupied units	35 199 502	30 192 038	4 398 440	17 666 980	8 126 618	5 007 464	2 211 342	2 796 122
Gross rent is less than 20 percent of income	32.4	34.5	23.5	36.6	35.9	19.8	23.1	17.2
Gross rent is 20.0 to 24.9 percent of income	12.8	13.3	11.6	14.2	12.1	9.7	10.3	9.3
Gross rent is 25.0 to 29.9 percent of income	10.4	10.2	9.7	10.4	9.9	11.8	12.4	11.4
Gross rent is 30.0 to 34.9 percent of income	7.3	7.2	7.7	7.2	6.9	8.3	8.5	8.2
Gross rent is 35.0 percent or more of income	29.5	27.9	39.8	25.3	27.2	39.0	35.4	41.8
Not computed	7.5	6.9	7.7	6.3	7.9	11.3	10.3	12.2

Source: Census 2000 Summary File 3—United States, U.S. Census Bureau, 2002. Tables H70, H71, H95, and H96.
. . . = Data not available.

Table C-1.9.
Population density influences vehicle ownership.
Households With No Car or With Three or More Cars, Selected States, 2000

(Percentage of households.)

State	Percent with no car	State	Percent with three or more cars
New York	29.7	Wyoming	27.5
Pennsylvania	12.8	Utah	26.1
Massachusetts	12.7	Idaho	25.7
Louisiana	11.9	South Dakota	25.3
Illinois	11.8	Montana	25.2

Source: Census 2000 Summary File 3—United States, U.S. Census Bureau, 2002. Table H44.

Means of Transportation

The automobile is widely considered a hallmark of American life, and Census 2000 corroborated that view. It found that over 95 percent of owner-occupied housing units had at least one vehicle. (See Table C-1.11.) Nearly half had two vehicles, and the share of housing units with four or more vehicles exceeded the share without any at all. The census also found that nearly 80 percent of renter-occupied units had one or more cars. The primary difference was that renters tended to have just one car, while owners tended to have two or more.

Vehicle ownership falls off as householders age. Still, among householders aged 75 and older, fully 85 percent of owners and half of renters have at least one vehicle.

Three out of four Americans drive their cars to work—alone, and another eighth car pool. (See Table C-1.10.) Less than 5 percent take public transportation, and almost as many walk, bicycle, or use "other means." Americans' average commute (excluding those who work at home) is 25 minutes.

Commuting patterns are influenced by local conditions, so broad national averages are not very revealing. Walking or biking are generally more popular in a climate with good weather, and the presence or absence of public transport obviously determines how many people use it. For instance, 15 percent of New Yorkers take the subway to work (as do 18 percent of people who live in the District of Columbia)—not many other Americans have this option.

Table C-1.10. Means of Transportation to Work, United States, 2000

(Number, percent, minutes.)

State	Number	Percent
Total Workers 16 Years and Over	12 827 922	100.0
Car, truck, or van	11 273 610	87.9
Drove alone	97 102 050	75.7
Carpooled	15 634 051	12.2
Public transportation	6 067 703	4.7
Bus or trolley bus	3 206 682	2.5
Streetcar or trolley car	72 713	0.1
Subway or elevated	1 885 961	1.5
Railroad	658 097	0.5
Ferryboat	44 106	0.0
Taxicab	200 144	0.2
Motorcycle	142 424	0.1
Bicycle	488 497	0.4
Walked	3 758 982	2.9
Other means	901 298	0.7
Worked at home	4 184 223	3.3
For Total Persons Who Did Not Work at Home		
Mean travel time to work (minutes)	25.5	
Total Persons Who Did Not Work at Home	12 409 500	100.0
Less than 30 minutes	81 292 940	65.5
Public transportation	1 397 634	1.1
Other means	79 895 306	64.4
30 to 44 minutes	23 703 903	19.1
Public transportation	1 579 223	1.3
Other means	22 124 680	17.8
45 to 59 minutes	9 200 414	7.4
Public transportation	1 050 742	0.8
Other means	8 149 672	6.6
60 or more minutes	9 897 748	8.0
Public transportation	2 040 104	1.6
Other means	7 857 644	6.3

Source: Census 2000 Summary File 3—United States, U.S. Census Bureau, 2002. Tables P30, P32, and P33

Table C-1.11. Vehicles Available, United States, 2000

(Number, percent.)

Occupancy status and age	All occupied housing units	Number of vehicles available						
		No vehicles	One or more vehicles	One vehicle	Two vehicles	Three vehicles	Four vehicles	Five or more vehicles
NUMBER								
Owner-Occupied Units	69 816 513	3 165 468	66 651 045	19 383 222	31 569 310	11 395 458	3 157 985	1 145 070
Householder 15 to 64 years	52 262 686	1 429 845	50 832 841	. . .	. . .	. . .	. . .	. . .
Householder 15 to 24 years	921 685	44 025	877 660	. . .	. . .	. . .	. . .	. . .
Householder 25 to 44 years	23 995 835	594 482	23 401 353	. . .	. . .	. . .	. . .	. . .
Householder 45 to 64 years	27 345 166	791 338	26 553 828	. . .	. . .	. . .	. . .	. . .
Householder 65 years and over ...	17 553 827	1 735 623	15 818 204	. . .	. . .	. . .	. . .	. . .
Householder 65 to 74 years	9 482 167	525 319	8 956 848	. . .	. . .	. . .	. . .	. . .
Householder 75 years and over	8 071 660	1 210 304	6 861 356	. . .	. . .	. . .	. . .	. . .
Renter-Occupied Units	35 663 588	7 695 599	27 967 989	16 740 391	8 892 610	1 744 511	392 801	197 676
Householder 15 to 64 years	30 582 725	5 471 461	25 111 264	. . .	. . .	. . .	. . .	. . .
Householder 15 to 24 years	4 426 557	720 423	3 706 134	. . .	. . .	. . .	. . .	. . .
Householder 25 to 44 years	17 892 606	2 859 247	15 033 359	. . .	. . .	. . .	. . .	. . .
Householder 45 to 64 years	8 263 562	1 891 791	6 371 771	. . .	. . .	. . .	. . .	. . .
Householder 65 years and over ...	5 080 863	2 224 138	2 856 725	. . .	. . .	. . .	. . .	. . .
Householder 65 to 74 years	2 245 535	808 123	1 437 412	. . .	. . .	. . .	. . .	. . .
Householder 75 years and over	2 835 328	1 416 015	1 419 313	. . .	. . .	. . .	. . .	. . .
PERCENT								
Owner-Occupied Units	100.0	4.5	95.5	27.8	45.2	16.3	4.5	1.6
Householder 15 to 64 years	100.0	2.7	97.3	. . .	. . .	. . .	. . .	. . .
Householder 15 to 24 years	100.0	4.8	95.2	. . .	. . .	. . .	. . .	. . .
Householder 25 to 44 years	100.0	2.5	97.5	. . .	. . .	. . .	. . .	. . .
Householder 45 to 64 years	100.0	2.9	97.1	. . .	. . .	. . .	. . .	. . .
Householder 65 years and over	100.0	9.9	90.1	. . .	. . .	. . .	. . .	. . .
Householder 65 to 74 years	100.0	5.5	94.5	. . .	. . .	. . .	. . .	. . .
Householder 75 years and over	100.0	15.0	85.0	. . .	. . .	. . .	. . .	. . .
Renter-Occupied Units	100.0	21.6	78.4	46.9	24.9	4.9	1.1	0.6
Householder 15 to 64 years	100.0	17.9	82.1	. . .	. . .	. . .	. . .	. . .
Householder 15 to 24 years	100.0	16.3	83.7	. . .	. . .	. . .	. . .	. . .
Householder 25 to 44 years	100.0	16.0	84.0	. . .	. . .	. . .	. . .	. . .
Householder 45 to 64 years	100.0	22.9	77.1	. . .	. . .	. . .	. . .	. . .
Householder 65 years and over	100.0	43.8	56.2	. . .	. . .	. . .	. . .	. . .
Householder 65 to 74 years	100.0	36.0	64.0	. . .	. . .	. . .	. . .	. . .
Householder 75 years and over	100.0	49.9	50.1	. . .	. . .	. . .	. . .	. . .

Source: Census 2000 Summary File 3—United States, U.S. Census Bureau, 2002. Tables H44 and H45.
. . . = Data not available.

Table C-2. States — **Migration, Housing, and Transportation**

FIPS CODE	STATE	Total population 5 years and over	Residence in 1995 (percent)			Different state				Outside the United States
			Same house	Same county, different house	Same state, different county	Northeast states	Midwest states	Southern states	Western states	
		1	2	3	4	5	6	7	8	9
00	UNITED STATES....	262 375 152	54.1	24.9	9.7	1.7	1.8	2.9	2.1	2.9
01	ALABAMA	4 152 278	57.4	24.7	8.8	0.6	1.3	5.1	0.9	1.2
02	ALASKA	579 740	46.2	27.7	7.5	1.2	2.2	4.7	8.3	2.2
04	ARIZONA	4 752 724	44.3	30.6	4.5	1.8	4.0	3.0	8.0	3.9
05	ARKANSAS	2 492 205	53.3	24.8	10.5	0.4	2.6	5.0	2.1	1.4
06	CALIFORNIA	31 416 629	50.2	30.9	9.8	0.8	0.9	1.3	1.6	4.5
08	COLORADO	4 006 285	44.1	23.0	13.5	1.5	3.8	4.4	6.4	3.4
09	CONNECTICUT	3 184 514	58.2	25.1	5.3	4.7	0.7	1.9	0.9	3.3
10	DELAWARE	732 378	56.0	25.5	2.3	7.3	0.9	4.8	0.8	2.4
11	DISTRICT OF COLUMBIA	539 658	49.9	23.5	X	4.7	1.9	12.4	2.0	5.6
12	FLORIDA	15 043 603	48.9	25.7	8.7	4.5	2.6	3.8	1.3	4.3
13	GEORGIA	7 594 476	49.2	21.1	13.8	2.0	1.9	7.2	1.6	3.2
15	HAWAII	1 134 351	56.8	26.0	2.1	1.2	1.3	3.5	5.1	4.1
16	IDAHO	1 196 793	49.6	23.9	9.4	0.4	1.4	1.7	11.8	1.8
17	ILLINOIS	11 547 505	56.8	26.1	8.3	0.7	2.3	1.7	1.1	3.1
18	INDIANA	5 657 818	55.0	25.5	10.2	0.6	3.5	2.7	1.1	1.3
19	IOWA	2 738 499	56.9	23.3	10.6	0.3	4.3	1.5	1.7	1.4
20	KANSAS	2 500 360	52.4	24.3	10.2	0.5	4.2	3.6	2.8	2.1
21	KENTUCKY	3 776 230	55.9	24.7	9.7	0.6	3.4	3.5	0.9	1.2
22	LOUISIANA	4 153 367	59.0	24.5	9.3	0.5	0.7	3.9	1.1	1.0
23	MAINE	1 204 164	59.6	22.9	7.7	4.8	0.8	2.2	1.2	0.9
24	MARYLAND	4 945 043	55.7	21.9	9.4	2.9	0.9	5.1	1.2	3.0
25	MASSACHUSETTS ...	5 954 249	58.5	22.8	7.8	4.0	0.8	1.7	1.1	3.5
26	MICHIGAN	9 268 782	57.3	25.1	10.9	0.6	1.8	1.7	0.9	1.7
27	MINNESOTA	4 591 491	57.0	20.3	13.1	0.5	4.0	1.4	1.8	1.8
28	MISSISSIPPI	2 641 453	58.5	22.5	9.4	0.4	1.4	5.9	1.0	1.0
29	MISSOURI	5 226 022	53.6	23.5	12.5	0.5	3.7	3.0	1.8	1.3
30	MONTANA	847 362	53.6	22.5	9.9	0.7	2.5	1.8	8.1	0.8
31	NEBRASKA	1 594 700	54.7	23.4	10.5	0.4	3.9	2.0	3.3	1.8
32	NEVADA	1 853 720	37.4	30.6	2.8	2.0	3.3	3.3	16.6	4.1
33	NEW HAMPSHIRE	1 160 340	55.4	22.3	6.9	9.6	0.9	2.2	1.3	1.4
34	NEW JERSEY	7 856 268	59.8	20.7	8.7	4.2	0.5	1.5	0.6	4.0
35	NEW MEXICO	1 689 911	54.4	23.7	7.5	0.9	1.7	4.3	5.2	2.3
36	NEW YORK	17 749 110	61.8	21.8	8.2	1.6	0.5	1.3	0.7	4.1
37	NORTH CAROLINA	7 513 165	53.0	22.3	9.8	3.0	1.6	6.2	1.4	2.6
38	NORTH DAKOTA	603 106	56.8	21.8	10.2	0.4	5.3	1.3	3.0	1.2
39	OHIO	10 599 968	57.5	26.3	9.5	1.0	1.4	2.4	0.8	1.1
40	OKLAHOMA	3 215 719	51.3	25.1	11.8	0.4	2.3	4.5	2.8	1.7
41	OREGON	3 199 323	46.8	27.0	11.1	0.6	1.2	1.4	9.3	2.6
42	PENNSYLVANIA	11 555 538	63.5	21.7	7.6	2.3	0.8	2.1	0.6	1.4
44	RHODE ISLAND	985 184	58.1	24.4	5.1	6.4	0.6	1.8	1.1	2.6
45	SOUTH CAROLINA	3 748 669	55.9	22.3	8.3	2.6	1.6	6.6	1.1	1.6
46	SOUTH DAKOTA	703 820	55.7	21.2	11.8	0.3	5.3	1.4	3.2	1.0
47	TENNESSEE	5 315 920	53.9	25.2	8.7	0.9	2.4	6.2	1.3	1.5
48	TEXAS	19 241 518	49.6	27.0	12.5	0.6	1.5	2.8	2.2	3.8
49	UTAH	2 023 875	49.3	26.6	8.9	0.7	1.3	2.1	8.0	3.2
50	VERMONT	574 842	59.1	21.2	6.3	7.6	0.9	2.1	1.5	1.3
51	VIRGINIA	6 619 266	52.2	18.1	14.2	3.1	1.5	6.0	1.9	3.1
53	WASHINGTON	5 501 398	48.6	27.5	9.5	0.8	1.4	2.1	7.0	3.2
54	WEST VIRGINIA	1 706 931	63.3	21.0	7.0	1.4	1.8	4.4	0.5	0.5
55	WISCONSIN	5 022 073	56.5	24.6	11.0	0.4	3.9	1.2	1.2	1.3
56	WYOMING	462 809	51.3	24.1	7.8	0.8	3.5	2.6	8.9	1.1

Table C-2. States — Migration, Housing, and Transportation

STATE	Non-Hispanic White population 5 years and over	Residence in 1995, non-Hispanic White population (percent)								Black or African American population 5 years and over	Residence in 1995, Black or African American population (percent)							
		Same house	Same county, different house	Same state, different county	Different state Northeast states	Midwest states	Southern states	Western states	Outside the United States		Same house	Same county, different house	Same state, different county	Different state Northeast states	Midwest states	Southern states	Western states	Outside the United States
	10	11	12	13	14	15	16	17	18	19	20	21	22	23	24	25	26	27
UNITED STATES....	183 342 983	56.9	22.9	10.2	1.7	2.1	3.0	2.1	1.1	31 616 957	51.3	30.6	8.4	1.6	1.3	3.5	0.9	2.3
ALABAMA	2 940 696	58.5	23.2	9.6	0.5	1.2	5.7	0.8	0.6	1 062 097	57.0	29.8	6.3	0.8	1.5	3.1	0.6	1.0
ALASKA	396 986	46.3	27.2	6.9	1.4	2.7	5.0	9.0	1.5	20 025	29.6	29.8	4.8	2.7	2.5	18.2	6.6	5.8
ARIZONA	3 096 865	44.9	29.4	4.6	2.4	5.4	3.4	8.5	1.4	142 035	37.2	35.6	3.7	2.1	5.1	5.8	6.8	3.8
ARKANSAS	1 973 388	54.7	23.9	10.9	0.4	2.7	5.1	1.8	0.6	381 001	52.7	31.5	8.1	0.2	2.3	3.2	1.0	1.0
CALIFORNIA	14 992 633	53.4	27.0	11.1	1.2	1.3	1.8	2.4	1.8	2 056 702	46.7	35.6	10.8	0.7	0.9	2.2	0.9	2.2
COLORADO	3 017 474	46.4	22.0	13.5	1.7	4.4	4.6	6.1	1.4	146 774	36.6	26.4	16.1	1.7	3.2	7.3	4.6	4.0
CONNECTICUT	2 488 020	62.7	22.4	5.5	4.4	0.8	1.8	0.9	1.5	280 388	47.8	36.8	4.3	4.0	0.4	2.3	0.5	3.8
DELAWARE	536 532	59.9	23.5	2.3	6.8	0.9	4.9	0.8	1.0	137 021	47.9	32.7	2.4	8.4	0.6	4.8	0.6	2.6
DISTRICT OF COLUMBIA	153 802	38.4	15.8	0.0	11.1	4.8	18.8	4.5	6.6	320 956	58.0	27.5	0.0	1.4	0.6	9.4	0.6	2.5
FLORIDA	9 946 524	51.6	23.3	9.3	4.8	3.5	4.4	1.4	1.7	2 120 383	47.5	32.7	7.8	3.0	0.9	3.4	0.7	4.0
GEORGIA	4 807 358	53.1	19.0	14.5	1.7	1.9	7.3	1.3	1.2	2 148 084	47.0	27.1	12.2	2.4	1.9	6.3	1.2	2.0
HAWAII	264 082	41.7	23.3	2.3	3.4	3.9	8.9	12.7	3.8	19 009	17.1	17.7	1.0	6.0	4.9	32.9	11.8	8.6
IDAHO	1 059 756	50.9	23.7	9.3	0.5	1.4	1.6	11.8	0.9	4 626	33.2	17.7	8.3	0.5	3.6	8.8	15.0	12.9
ILLINOIS	7 933 797	60.0	23.0	9.0	0.7	2.7	1.7	1.1	1.3	1 709 053	54.4	34.9	5.0	0.3	1.6	1.8	0.6	1.5
INDIANA	4 885 617	57.0	24.5	10.7	0.6	3.3	2.5	0.9	0.5	460 134	45.8	37.7	5.7	0.6	4.6	3.2	1.0	1.4
IOWA	2 551 044	58.5	23.1	10.6	0.3	4.1	1.3	1.4	0.7	53 984	38.3	31.8	10.1	0.5	8.6	4.0	2.2	4.6
KANSAS	2 096 378	54.9	23.5	10.6	0.5	4.2	3.2	2.3	0.8	137 795	43.6	32.1	7.5	0.4	5.0	6.0	2.9	2.5
KENTUCKY	3 385 210	57.6	24.2	9.8	0.5	3.3	3.1	0.8	0.6	270 040	45.5	33.9	7.6	0.9	3.9	5.3	0.9	2.0
LOUISIANA	2 622 919	60.3	22.5	10.1	0.5	0.7	4.3	0.9	0.6	1 320 400	58.3	29.0	7.6	0.3	0.6	2.6	0.9	0.7
MAINE	1 164 263	60.2	23.0	7.6	4.6	0.8	2.1	1.2	0.7	5 461	32.6	17.0	12.1	12.8	1.6	7.1	3.7	13.1
MARYLAND	3 096 149	60.4	19.1	9.7	3.1	1.0	4.2	1.2	1.4	1 358 340	49.6	28.4	9.1	2.2	0.6	6.9	0.6	2.7
MASSACHUSETTS ...	4 904 185	61.9	21.6	7.7	3.9	0.8	1.5	1.0	1.7	310 180	49.9	28.2	9.0	3.4	0.6	2.4	0.5	6.0
MICHIGAN	7 332 649	59.1	23.5	11.6	0.5	1.9	1.5	0.9	1.0	1 287 672	54.6	33.5	6.8	0.4	1.2	1.8	0.5	1.2
MINNESOTA	4 079 867	59.8	19.7	13.1	0.5	3.8	1.1	1.4	0.7	150 905	31.3	31.4	10.7	1.2	9.8	3.7	2.0	9.9
MISSISSIPPI	1 623 827	58.2	20.8	10.5	0.4	1.1	7.3	1.0	0.6	943 105	60.4	26.3	7.2	0.2	1.8	2.8	0.6	0.7
MISSOURI	4 400 166	55.2	22.8	12.5	0.5	3.7	2.9	1.7	0.7	571 781	48.3	30.6	12.2	0.4	3.3	2.7	1.1	1.5
MONTANA	762 533	54.2	22.4	9.5	0.7	2.5	1.9	8.1	0.6	2 144	27.8	17.4	12.7	4.6	6.8	9.9	13.9	6.9
NEBRASKA	1 404 202	57.0	22.9	10.8	0.4	3.9	1.7	2.7	0.6	61 234	45.1	33.2	5.1	0.9	5.0	5.0	2.4	3.2
NEVADA	1 229 733	41.0	29.6	3.4	2.4	3.9	3.5	15.0	1.3	121 587	31.2	38.6	1.5	2.1	4.8	4.6	14.3	2.9
NEW HAMPSHIRE	1 105 554	56.3	22.4	6.8	9.4	0.8	2.1	1.2	0.9	8 240	34.0	20.3	8.9	20.3	1.5	5.4	0.9	8.8
NEW JERSEY	5 230 861	65.4	17.6	9.0	4.0	0.5	1.5	0.6	1.4	1 040 456	54.0	28.5	8.3	3.7	0.3	1.9	0.3	3.1
NEW MEXICO	775 397	51.5	22.1	7.6	1.6	3.0	5.9	6.8	1.5	30 633	38.6	27.9	9.5	2.1	2.5	9.6	5.7	4.2
NEW YORK	11 108 223	65.2	20.6	7.9	1.8	0.6	1.4	0.7	1.8	2 759 747	59.8	24.3	8.9	1.0	0.3	1.4	0.3	4.0
NORTH CAROLINA ...	5 320 140	55.8	20.6	10.2	2.9	1.9	6.4	1.3	0.9	1 602 536	51.3	29.4	8.7	2.9	0.7	4.7	0.6	1.6
NORTH DAKOTA	556 518	57.9	21.8	9.9	0.3	5.2	1.1	2.9	0.9	3 299	21.3	15.9	10.1	3.9	11.1	17.1	8.2	12.5
OHIO	8 952 532	59.5	24.7	9.9	0.9	1.4	2.3	0.7	0.6	1 181 757	49.2	38.4	6.0	0.9	1.2	2.4	0.6	1.3
OKLAHOMA	2 409 739	53.6	24.0	11.9	0.4	2.4	4.4	2.6	0.7	236 242	42.6	33.5	10.0	0.7	2.5	5.9	2.7	2.1
OREGON	2 697 503	49.1	26.3	11.5	0.6	1.3	1.3	8.8	1.0	48 543	37.6	34.9	7.5	1.0	1.8	3.5	9.3	4.4
PENNSYLVANIA	9 772 445	65.8	20.6	7.6	2.0	0.8	2.0	0.6	0.7	1 118 387	55.9	29.9	6.6	2.5	0.5	2.2	0.4	2.0
RHODE ISLAND	814 134	61.8	22.5	5.5	6.1	0.6	1.6	0.9	0.9	41 673	42.5	34.3	3.5	7.3	0.8	3.4	1.2	7.0
SOUTH CAROLINA ...	2 499 123	56.3	21.0	8.7	2.6	2.0	7.5	1.1	0.8	1 093 109	58.6	26.1	7.3	2.3	0.5	3.9	0.4	0.9
SOUTH DAKOTA	624 762	57.0	21.0	11.5	0.3	5.3	1.3	2.9	0.7	4 014	22.1	17.8	10.0	1.5	14.8	9.5	7.2	17.0
TENNESSEE	4 240 551	55.7	23.5	9.5	0.9	2.4	6.3	1.1	0.6	852 486	50.6	35.4	4.8	0.5	2.3	4.5	0.7	1.1
TEXAS	10 288 660	61.2	23.6	15.3	0.8	1.9	3.5	2.4	1.3	2 195 706	47.0	33.3	10.4	0.6	1.2	3.9	1.5	2.2
UTAH	1 737 915	51.8	26.2	9.4	0.7	1.3	2.0	7.3	1.3	14 445	29.4	28.7	7.7	2.1	4.2	8.3	10.6	8.9
VERMONT	553 381	59.8	21.3	6.1	7.5	0.8	2.0	1.4	1.0	2 694	29.9	21.8	8.5	21.5	2.5	5.9	2.6	7.4
VIRGINIA	4 675 191	55.3	16.9	13.9	2.9	1.6	6.0	1.9	1.5	1 283 823	49.0	22.5	15.2	3.3	0.9	5.6	1.1	2.3
WASHINGTON	4 383 290	51.2	26.6	9.8	0.8	1.4	1.9	6.6	1.7	170 549	36.0	34.2	7.7	1.4	2.3	6.5	7.2	4.6
WEST VIRGINIA	1 615 870	64.1	21.0	6.9	1.3	1.8	4.2	0.5	0.3	52 308	50.4	26.0	8.1	2.8	2.9	8.0	0.6	1.2
WISCONSIN	4 421 253	58.8	23.1	11.3	0.4	3.8	1.1	1.0	0.5	270 440	40.8	43.4	5.9	0.3	5.2	2.1	0.6	1.7
WYOMING	413 277	52.1	23.7	7.7	0.7	3.7	2.5	8.7	0.8	2 954	31.9	21.9	6.7	3.2	3.4	13.2	13.3	6.4

Table C-2. States — **Migration, Housing, and Transportation**

STATE	American Indian and Alaska Native population 5 years and over	Residence in 1995, American Indian and Alaska Native population (percent) Same house	Same county, different house	Same state, different county	Different state North-east states	Mid-west states	Southern states	Western states	Outside the United States	Asian, Hawaiian, and Pacific Islander population 5 years and over	Residence in 1995, Asian, Hawaiian, and Pacific Islander population (percent) Same house	Same county, different house	Same state, different county	Different state North-east states	Mid-west states	Southern states	Western states	Outside the United States
	28	29	30	31	32	33	34	35	36	37	38	39	40	41	42	43	44	45
UNITED STATES....	2 243 344	50.5	26.5	12.4	0.7	1.6	2.7	3.8	1.8	9 867 605	45.9	22.6	8.7	2.3	1.5	2.2	2.9	14.0
ALABAMA	21 519	53.4	21.6	14.4	0.5	1.1	7.0	0.9	1.1	28 820	39.6	14.9	8.9	2.1	3.3	7.6	3.3	20.4
ALASKA	88 163	57.1	27.7	11.3	0.1	0.3	0.8	2.2	0.4	26 566	36.9	27.0	4.1	0.7	1.7	2.3	16.1	11.3
ARIZONA................	229 059	60.8	23.8	8.0	0.2	0.7	0.8	4.7	1.1	90 715	36.2	24.2	2.9	1.8	3.6	3.6	10.5	17.2
ARKANSAS.............	17 064	42.2	23.2	14.0	0.4	2.9	12.2	4.0	1.1	19 048	39.1	14.5	9.7	2.5	2.7	5.3	6.1	20.1
CALIFORNIA...........	288 559	46.4	35.3	11.3	0.2	0.5	1.2	2.4	2.7	3 572 797	49.7	26.8	9.1	0.9	0.7	1.0	1.1	10.8
COLORADO.............	39 662	40.0	25.7	14.2	0.6	3.5	3.2	10.8	2.0	90 584	36.3	18.6	11.2	2.1	2.9	3.9	9.0	16.1
CONNECTICUT	8 752	44.7	30.2	7.4	5.6	0.8	3.7	2.5	5.1	77 023	39.7	18.4	4.4	10.0	1.7	3.0	2.5	20.2
DELAWARE	2 897	53.8	27.7	4.3	3.0	1.4	5.2	0.3	4.3	15 183	36.4	17.8	1.7	12.3	3.3	3.7	2.3	22.6
DISTRICT OF COLUMBIA.............	1 862	41.7	28.0	0.0	2.0	2.5	16.2	2.8	6.8	14 414	28.7	13.5	0.0	10.4	2.8	14.1	5.3	25.1
FLORIDA.................	51 260	40.9	24.5	13.6	3.9	2.9	6.4	2.6	5.2	254 710	41.6	20.3	9.7	4.6	2.1	3.9	3.5	14.3
GEORGIA................	22 267	36.1	15.6	21.8	3.2	2.5	10.3	4.8	5.7	163 185	31.5	15.3	16.2	4.2	2.5	7.6	4.1	18.5
HAWAII...................	3 062	40.0	30.1	4.0	0.9	1.6	9.9	8.9	4.5	586 986	66.4	24.1	1.7	0.2	0.3	0.5	1.8	4.9
IDAHO....................	15 956	46.4	22.2	12.2	0.2	1.1	1.2	15.2	1.4	11 790	40.4	18.0	6.9	1.0	2.2	2.2	11.6	17.6
ILLINOIS.................	28 215	43.8	32.2	10.6	0.5	2.6	2.5	3.1	4.7	398 497	43.3	22.7	8.5	1.8	2.8	2.1	2.2	16.7
INDIANA.................	15 927	39.3	26.2	16.9	0.7	6.0	5.1	3.7	2.2	54 675	32.7	14.2	8.9	3.5	7.0	4.3	4.5	25.0
IOWA.....................	8 442	35.2	23.3	19.0	0.4	10.5	4.2	5.4	2.0	33 142	36.4	19.6	9.3	1.5	5.5	2.3	4.9	20.4
KANSAS..................	22 685	41.7	25.5	13.4	0.3	3.9	8.6	4.8	1.8	42 477	36.2	20.6	7.4	1.9	5.0	3.7	4.8	20.4
KENTUCKY..............	8 615	39.6	12.8	20.6	1.1	7.3	10.5	5.4	2.8	27 859	31.2	14.6	7.8	3.4	5.1	7.0	3.9	27.1
LOUISIANA.............	23 864	55.6	23.6	11.9	0.5	0.6	4.6	2.2	1.0	52 693	45.8	19.0	9.4	2.3	1.4	5.4	3.9	12.8
MAINE....................	6 884	49.4	25.5	12.8	3.9	0.8	3.5	1.7	2.5	7 824	44.2	15.2	7.1	9.0	2.3	2.6	3.2	16.4
MARYLAND..............	14 878	47.6	24.6	10.6	3.2	0.9	7.0	2.8	3.3	197 957	45.1	18.1	8.4	4.0	1.5	4.6	2.2	16.1
MASSACHUSETTS ...	14 374	47.3	28.7	9.2	5.0	0.9	2.6	2.1	4.3	222 848	38.9	19.7	9.1	5.9	2.0	2.6	3.8	18.1
MICHIGAN	56 021	47.7	27.6	17.3	0.3	1.6	2.5	1.7	1.2	163 181	34.7	19.7	11.2	2.9	3.3	2.3	3.2	22.6
MINNESOTA............	49 433	43.9	25.2	20.9	0.3	4.4	0.9	2.8	1.6	127 373	38.6	22.9	11.3	1.3	4.2	1.9	6.5	13.2
MISSISSIPPI	10 801	54.9	17.4	13.6	0.4	1.6	9.0	2.0	1.2	17 171	39.5	12.8	13.1	2.6	2.9	9.5	5.8	13.8
MISSOURI...............	24 579	40.5	20.8	19.0	0.3	6.2	7.9	4.2	1.1	58 762	36.8	16.5	10.2	2.5	6.0	4.0	5.0	18.9
MONTANA...............	49 660	54.2	24.8	13.7	0.1	1.5	0.6	4.3	0.8	4 513	42.4	15.7	8.3	1.3	2.0	2.3	11.5	16.6
NEBRASKA..............	13 847	42.4	26.1	14.4	0.1	7.7	2.3	5.5	1.6	20 140	34.2	18.8	6.4	1.3	4.8	3.6	5.9	24.9
NEVADA..................	24 420	45.7	27.4	4.6	0.5	2.1	2.2	15.9	1.7	91 555	31.7	25.3	1.5	1.6	2.0	2.5	23.4	12.1
NEW HAMPSHIRE.....	2 563	46.7	15.8	15.5	11.9	1.3	4.3	4.0	0.6	14 421	35.3	12.5	6.4	11.5	3.7	3.1	4.7	22.8
NEW JERSEY...........	16 693	49.9	24.9	9.2	4.3	0.5	2.8	1.7	6.7	447 849	44.7	17.3	9.0	7.3	1.2	1.7	1.3	17.5
NEW MEXICO...........	156 481	65.7	20.1	7.1	0.3	0.5	1.0	4.8	0.5	17 969	40.9	19.4	5.5	2.6	2.5	5.6	9.4	14.1
NEW YORK..............	72 748	51.5	27.8	10.6	1.2	0.7	1.9	1.1	5.2	987 517	50.4	19.9	8.7	2.0	0.7	1.2	1.2	15.9
NORTH CAROLINA ...	92 953	60.4	20.8	10.6	0.9	1.0	3.6	1.3	1.4	105 881	31.6	17.0	9.0	5.9	2.9	8.3	7.3	17.9
NORTH DAKOTA.......	27 955	48.6	25.2	16.2	0.2	5.1	0.7	3.2	0.8	3 332	34.7	11.3	8.2	3.0	5.3	5.3	3.8	28.3
OHIO	25 123	44.8	27.0	15.9	0.7	1.5	5.4	3.4	1.4	124 764	35.7	18.5	9.7	3.8	3.2	3.6	2.7	22.9
OKLAHOMA.............	242 229	51.3	28.0	14.5	0.1	1.1	2.5	2.1	0.4	44 344	38.1	20.5	7.8	1.5	1.8	4.0	5.2	21.1
OREGON.................	40 253	38.8	32.4	13.7	0.2	1.1	1.4	11.0	1.5	99 161	38.5	23.3	8.3	1.4	1.4	1.7	9.8	15.6
PENNSYLVANIA.......	18 246	47.2	23.1	14.5	3.9	1.2	4.9	2.3	2.9	204 244	41.9	16.2	9.3	6.2	1.8	3.5	2.9	18.2
RHODE ISLAND	4 613	40.9	39.3	4.2	7.5	0.5	1.6	2.2	3.8	22 576	46.4	21.2	4.2	8.5	1.6	2.8	4.1	11.2
SOUTH CAROLINA ...	13 780	45.5	19.9	15.7	2.0	2.3	9.3	2.9	2.4	35 366	36.9	13.9	9.6	4.6	2.7	8.6	6.0	17.7
SOUTH DAKOTA......	54 417	50.6	24.3	15.6	0.1	4.9	0.8	3.1	0.5	4 459	32.4	15.0	9.5	1.4	8.6	4.1	8.1	20.8
TENNESSEE............	14 679	42.1	17.6	16.1	1.7	3.8	11.3	4.0	3.5	52 048	36.6	17.7	6.7	3.0	3.4	7.4	4.8	20.4
TEXAS...................	105 578	43.6	27.4	15.7	0.4	1.2	5.0	3.9	2.7	527 132	38.6	22.2	11.6	1.9	2.1	3.1	3.9	16.7
UTAH.....................	25 932	50.7	23.3	10.3	0.3	1.3	1.3	10.9	1.9	46 697	39.2	25.9	4.6	1.1	1.3	1.9	10.1	15.8
VERMONT	2 486	42.9	24.6	17.7	7.7	2.3	2.0	2.3	0.6	4 474	38.0	16.6	7.7	7.6	1.7	2.9	3.6	21.9
VIRGINIA................	21 114	45.7	15.0	17.3	4.3	1.7	8.5	4.6	2.8	243 028	40.7	15.8	12.9	3.2	1.4	5.5	3.0	17.5
WASHINGTON..........	83 734	44.9	32.5	10.6	0.4	0.8	1.4	8.0	1.4	321 223	42.3	25.6	6.4	1.2	1.2	1.9	7.6	13.7
WEST VIRGINIA	3 599	50.1	16.2	17.8	1.7	3.2	8.3	1.0	1.6	9 195	41.9	8.7	8.4	7.3	3.2	7.3	2.0	21.2
WISCONSIN............	45 138	46.9	26.2	18.7	0.1	4.0	1.0	1.8	1.3	76 425	37.8	22.9	10.2	1.7	5.1	2.0	5.5	14.8
WYOMING	10 303	52.0	24.6	9.2	0.3	1.7	1.8	9.7	0.6	3 012	46.5	14.4	4.9	3.2	3.1	3.4	10.5	14.0

Table C-2. States — **Migration, Housing, and Transportation**

| STATE | Hispanic or Latino[1] population 5 years and over | Residence in 1995, Hispanic or Latino[1] population (percent) | | | | | | | | Total occupied housing units | | | |
| | | Same house | Same county, different house | Same state, different county | Northeast states | Midwest states | Southern states | Western states | Outside the United States | Total occupied housing units | Owner-occupied | Renter-occupied | Percent owner-occupied |
	46	47	48	49	50	51	52	53	54	55	56	57	58
UNITED STATES....	31 569 576	44.5	31.8	7.8	1.3	0.7	1.8	2.5	9.6	105 480 101	69 816 513	35 663 588	66.2
ALABAMA	64 417	30.5	17.9	10.7	1.3	2.0	12.0	6.5	19.1	1 737 080	1 258 686	478 394	72.5
ALASKA	22 474	32.1	29.2	6.0	2.8	1.4	8.0	13.6	6.9	221 600	138 503	83 097	62.5
ARIZONA	1 144 449	41.2	35.3	3.6	0.4	0.8	1.6	7.1	9.9	1 901 327	1 293 637	607 690	68.0
ARKANSAS	74 627	26.4	19.3	9.9	0.6	2.7	9.0	13.0	19.0	1 042 696	723 458	319 238	69.4
CALIFORNIA	9 792 887	46.5	37.4	7.8	0.2	0.2	0.6	0.7	6.7	11 502 870	6 546 237	4 956 633	56.9
COLORADO	655 931	37.7	26.9	12.9	0.5	1.3	3.0	7.5	10.1	1 658 238	1 116 305	541 933	67.3
CONNECTICUT	286 424	36.0	38.4	4.0	6.1	0.4	1.5	0.9	12.6	1 301 670	869 742	431 928	66.8
DELAWARE	32 960	36.7	30.6	1.4	9.7	0.8	4.4	1.7	14.6	298 736	216 046	82 690	72.3
DISTRICT OF COLUMBIA	41 068	40.0	25.6	0.0	3.5	0.9	10.1	2.3	17.6	248 338	101 216	147 122	40.8
FLORIDA	2 489 063	40.5	29.9	6.7	4.8	0.9	1.8	1.3	14.0	6 337 929	4 441 711	1 896 218	70.1
GEORGIA	381 522	23.1	17.8	10.7	3.0	2.0	9.2	6.3	27.8	3 006 369	2 029 293	977 076	67.5
HAWAII	76 906	43.6	35.2	3.5	1.3	0.9	5.3	7.0	3.2	403 240	227 783	175 457	56.5
IDAHO	88 458	38.3	28.9	10.7	0.2	0.7	2.0	10.5	8.8	469 645	339 913	129 732	72.4
ILLINOIS	1 054 257	40.0	34.0	4.9	0.4	0.0	1.2	2.0	10.0	4 591 779	3 009 124	1 582 655	67.0
INDIANA	184 818	35.4	25.4	7.7	1.1	5.6	5.0	5.7	14.2	2 336 306	1 669 083	667 223	71.4
IOWA	70 137	30.4	24.0	9.3	0.9	5.5	5.4	10.1	14.4	1 149 276	831 427	317 849	72.3
KANSAS	161 981	36.3	26.4	7.7	0.5	2.9	4.9	7.9	13.3	1 037 891	718 873	319 018	69.3
KENTUCKY	49 770	25.8	16.2	10.8	2.2	4.8	11.0	6.7	22.6	1 590 647	1 125 298	465 349	70.7
LOUISIANA	98 892	45.2	22.4	10.4	1.6	1.2	8.2	3.2	7.8	1 656 053	1 124 995	531 058	67.9
MAINE	8 238	37.8	17.9	11.1	13.8	2.0	8.2	4.9	4.3	518 200	370 920	147 280	71.6
MARYLAND	204 098	38.1	25.3	7.6	3.4	0.5	7.4	2.8	14.8	1 980 859	1 341 594	639 265	67.7
MASSACHUSETTS ...	384 024	37.3	35.2	6.3	5.0	0.4	1.9	1.3	12.7	2 443 580	1 508 248	935 332	61.7
MICHIGAN	283 872	41.4	27.6	9.5	1.0	2.6	4.8	3.3	9.7	3 785 661	2 793 346	992 315	73.8
MINNESOTA	123 105	29.9	21.5	11.6	1.8	3.7	7.2	8.5	15.8	1 895 127	1 412 724	482 403	74.5
MISSISSIPPI	34 263	34.0	11.5	13.8	0.9	2.3	13.7	5.9	17.8	1 046 434	757 151	289 283	72.4
MISSOURI	102 691	34.1	19.6	11.3	1.2	4.9	8.7	8.0	12.2	2 194 594	1 542 310	652 284	70.3
MONTANA	16 286	38.5	24.2	13.7	1.0	2.0	2.6	15.4	2.7	358 667	247 700	110 967	69.1
NEBRASKA	81 218	32.2	24.3	8.5	0.6	3.6	4.4	12.6	13.9	666 184	449 306	216 878	67.4
NEVADA	345 928	28.2	32.6	1.4	0.7	1.1	2.5	21.1	12.4	751 165	457 245	293 920	60.9
NEW HAMPSHIRE.....	17 645	29.9	25.6	7.0	16.1	0.9	3.9	4.8	11.8	474 606	330 783	143 823	69.7
NEW JERSEY	1 019 444	44.5	30.4	7.3	4.4	0.2	1.1	0.6	11.4	3 064 645	2 011 298	1 053 347	65.6
NEW MEXICO	695 697	56.4	26.3	7.3	0.2	0.5	2.9	3.3	3.0	677 971	474 435	203 536	70.0
NEW YORK	2 615 563	54.8	25.2	9.0	1.0	0.2	0.9	0.5	8.5	7 056 860	3 739 247	3 317 613	53.0
NORTH CAROLINA ...	328 240	21.8	17.7	8.6	4.0	1.5	9.9	6.2	30.2	3 132 013	2 172 270	959 743	69.4
NORTH DAKOTA	6 686	36.2	16.7	12.5	1.2	7.7	9.6	10.2	5.8	257 152	171 310	85 842	66.6
OHIO	189 238	40.1	29.0	9.0	2.7	2.0	4.7	3.3	9.1	4 445 773	3 072 514	1 373 259	69.1
OKLAHOMA	154 994	34.6	25.8	8.7	0.7	1.8	8.6	6.4	13.4	1 342 293	918 141	424 152	68.4
OREGON	237 123	29.3	32.7	8.5	0.3	0.6	1.2	13.1	14.5	1 333 723	856 890	476 833	64.2
PENNSYLVANIA	349 250	40.1	29.3	7.9	8.0	0.7	2.5	1.5	10.0	4 777 003	3 406 167	1 370 836	71.3
RHODE ISLAND	90 340	33.0	36.9	2.4	9.0	0.4	1.7	1.4	14.0	408 424	245 150	163 274	60.0
SOUTH CAROLINA ...	83 028	25.7	15.0	8.1	5.5	2.0	12.6	5.4	25.8	1 533 854	1 107 619	426 235	72.2
SOUTH DAKOTA	9 046	34.1	17.4	10.9	1.4	6.6	6.2	17.5	5.8	290 245	197 907	92 338	68.2
TENNESSEE	105 775	23.1	18.1	8.3	1.9	3.4	12.0	7.6	25.5	2 232 905	1 561 461	671 444	69.9
TEXAS	5 963 049	49.2	31.2	8.3	0.3	0.7	1.0	1.8	7.5	7 393 354	4 717 294	2 676 060	63.8
UTAH	173 658	30.3	31.0	5.4	0.5	0.6	2.0	13.0	17.1	701 281	501 659	199 622	71.5
VERMONT	4 885	41.6	14.4	9.4	14.5	1.9	5.6	6.8	5.7	240 634	169 777	70 857	70.6
VIRGINIA	293 823	31.1	18.7	15.1	4.5	1.0	7.5	4.7	17.5	2 699 173	1 837 958	861 215	68.1
WASHINGTON	381 873	34.3	32.8	8.6	0.6	0.7	2.2	10.3	10.6	2 271 398	1 466 985	804 413	64.6
WEST VIRGINIA	10 761	46.5	12.4	13.7	4.6	4.3	9.2	3.8	5.4	736 481	553 626	182 855	75.2
WISCONSIN	166 863	33.4	31.7	8.5	0.7	4.5	3.4	3.8	14.0	2 084 544	1 426 660	657 884	68.4
WYOMING	27 823	44.4	29.4	8.1	0.6	1.8	2.7	9.1	3.9	193 608	135 488	58 120	70.0

[1] Hispanic or Latino persons may be of any race.

Items 46—58

Table C-2. States — **Migration, Housing, and Transportation**

STATE	Homeownership by age of householder											
	15 to 24 years		25 to 44 years		45 to 64 years		65 to 74 years		75 to 84 years		85 years and over	
	Number of householders	Percent owners	Number of householders	Percent owners	Number of householders	Percent owners	Number of householders	Percent owners	Number of householders	Percent owners	Number of householders	Percent owners
	59	60	61	62	63	64	65	66	67	68	69	70
UNITED STATES....	5 348 242	17.2	41 888 441	57.3	35 608 728	76.8	11 727 702	80.9	8 424 936	76.6	2 482 052	65.3
ALABAMA	99 161	28.1	653 185	65.4	590 117	81.6	213 315	84.4	140 257	80.2	41 045	72.2
ALASKA	13 440	15.4	102 986	55.0	82 017	75.6	14 665	79.3	6 950	74.3	1 542	63.5
ARIZONA	116 491	18.0	742 305	58.5	612 253	78.2	227 235	86.7	160 094	83.2	42 949	68.6
ARKANSAS	62 233	23.6	383 869	59.9	348 011	79.7	129 883	84.4	90 924	79.6	27 776	70.1
CALIFORNIA	523 056	11.0	4 878 855	44.5	3 880 866	68.7	1 142 384	75.9	832 793	75.1	244 916	65.9
COLORADO	104 583	16.7	719 459	60.7	561 705	79.9	146 029	82.7	97 542	76.7	28 920	61.1
CONNECTICUT	43 075	11.6	509 035	58.0	452 995	77.2	145 360	78.5	114 889	72.8	36 316	60.9
DELAWARE	13 885	19.3	117 000	64.3	100 496	82.0	37 250	85.9	23 912	81.7	6 193	67.5
DISTRICT OF COLUMBIA	16 702	6.3	102 502	28.7	78 799	52.4	25 653	56.6	18 795	60.8	5 887	58.3
FLORIDA	270 287	18.4	2 232 244	58.0	2 045 804	77.9	898 337	86.2	690 103	84.2	201 154	73.5
GEORGIA	168 562	19.9	1 316 016	59.7	1 008 693	79.2	285 874	82.8	177 892	78.6	49 332	69.2
HAWAII	15 257	8.3	146 561	39.6	148 301	66.5	48 497	75.2	35 079	75.4	9 545	72.2
IDAHO	32 610	21.8	183 492	65.8	158 516	83.3	48 108	87.8	35 607	82.9	11 312	72.1
ILLINOIS	216 302	16.9	1 858 854	59.4	1 535 559	77.6	498 108	79.9	369 498	76.6	113 458	67.0
INDIANA	136 583	21.5	921 950	65.7	779 722	81.9	256 778	83.6	185 789	77.7	55 484	66.0
IOWA	72 017	19.7	420 985	66.6	375 152	83.2	133 696	85.2	110 304	78.4	37 122	66.0
KANSAS	70 571	17.6	401 837	62.2	334 858	81.0	111 980	85.3	88 621	78.9	30 024	65.5
KENTUCKY	90 795	25.4	619 894	63.6	540 655	80.0	181 620	83.6	122 699	80.1	34 984	73.2
LOUISIANA	97 864	23.0	645 839	59.9	565 132	77.2	187 895	82.4	124 619	79.9	34 704	72.1
MAINE	22 194	19.1	192 422	65.3	184 156	81.7	61 712	81.0	43 744	72.8	13 972	62.2
MARYLAND	76 128	15.9	811 751	59.3	709 950	78.4	204 983	79.8	141 064	74.2	36 983	62.0
MASSACHUSETTS	93 549	9.0	972 382	52.7	822 100	74.0	272 485	73.3	214 320	66.4	68 744	53.4
MICHIGAN	186 213	23.1	1 497 095	67.8	1 298 792	83.5	413 758	85.3	301 765	79.4	88 038	66.6
MINNESOTA	105 211	21.1	784 498	71.7	622 155	86.1	186 455	84.9	145 243	73.5	51 565	53.5
MISSISSIPPI	58 020	29.7	402 125	64.2	356 593	81.0	123 878	85.5	80 678	83.7	25 140	77.2
MISSOURI	125 402	21.0	846 870	63.3	726 426	81.0	254 913	83.7	183 664	77.2	57 319	64.3
MONTANA	22 016	17.7	128 416	60.8	128 873	80.0	40 607	83.0	29 682	78.0	9 073	63.3
NEBRASKA	44 844	13.5	258 372	60.1	211 153	79.7	73 055	83.5	58 153	77.5	20 607	65.7
NEVADA	39 835	17.2	308 179	52.3	262 127	70.3	83 988	76.4	47 315	74.0	9 721	60.8
NEW HAMPSHIRE	17 708	12.2	193 708	63.6	168 863	80.0	49 882	80.0	34 437	70.5	10 008	60.0
NEW JERSEY	80 404	14.0	1 205 682	56.2	1 076 702	74.4	357 612	77.1	267 286	73.6	76 959	63.2
NEW MEXICO	39 892	23.4	258 068	61.5	238 318	79.3	78 399	85.2	49 495	82.2	13 799	71.0
NEW YORK	257 977	9.9	2 765 248	43.4	2 455 672	62.4	815 359	65.2	580 391	61.8	182 213	50.1
NORTH CAROLINA	182 233	20.9	1 267 069	61.3	1 046 865	80.3	349 737	84.2	227 187	79.6	58 922	71.4
NORTH DAKOTA	20 254	12.8	94 097	61.4	80 758	80.9	29 059	80.6	24 299	71.1	8 685	55.7
OHIO	234 637	16.3	1 719 123	61.7	1 500 286	79.8	513 819	82.3	375 833	76.9	102 075	64.3
OKLAHOMA	92 870	20.5	499 923	59.1	446 652	79.1	158 909	85.2	109 512	82.0	34 427	73.1
OREGON	80 754	11.2	502 240	53.3	467 881	77.0	138 545	82.3	109 248	77.7	35 055	61.0
PENNSYLVANIA	186 036	16.9	1 731 782	63.8	1 621 131	81.0	621 578	81.6	484 917	75.3	131 559	64.8
RHODE ISLAND	19 010	8.6	156 272	52.4	134 839	72.3	47 229	71.2	39 208	62.7	11 866	50.1
SOUTH CAROLINA	81 705	25.6	594 786	64.1	537 288	81.3	178 634	86.0	113 016	82.9	28 425	73.6
SOUTH DAKOTA	20 091	17.8	107 698	64.4	92 673	79.7	33 680	80.6	26 949	70.7	9 154	53.7
TENNESSEE	124 347	22.4	874 563	61.7	766 895	80.0	253 495	84.1	166 318	80.6	47 287	70.9
TEXAS	469 921	15.7	3 185 434	54.4	2 402 421	76.2	727 323	83.3	472 607	80.4	135 648	70.1
UTAH	61 764	21.1	304 067	66.4	214 110	84.9	62 701	88.4	45 365	86.2	13 274	78.0
VERMONT	11 046	14.2	90 987	63.0	88 206	82.0	26 245	81.3	18 287	73.5	5 863	66.2
VIRGINIA	133 807	15.3	1 109 878	58.8	943 899	80.0	278 295	83.0	184 159	78.4	49 135	69.7
WASHINGTON	128 366	11.6	929 524	55.3	783 114	77.3	215 158	81.8	163 654	76.9	51 582	59.7
WEST VIRGINIA	36 580	27.2	246 892	67.5	262 827	82.7	99 183	85.4	69 916	83.6	21 083	78.9
WISCONSIN	118 211	12.5	820 453	62.6	687 904	80.9	224 460	81.6	176 638	71.5	56 878	57.6
WYOMING	13 743	21.9	71 969	62.3	69 448	81.3	19 899	85.7	14 219	79.4	4 330	66.1

Table C-2. States — **Migration, Housing, and Transportation**

STATE	Homeownership by race and Hispanic origin of householder									
	Non-Hispanic White		Black or African American		American Indian and Alaska Native		Asian, Hawaiian, and Pacific Islander		Hispanic or Latino[1]	
	Number of householders	Percent owners	Number of householders	Percent owners	Number of householders	Percent owners	Number of householders	Percent owners	Number of householders	Percent owners
	71	72	73	74	75	76	77	78	79	80
UNITED STATES....	79 086 566	72.4	11 977 309	46.3	765 474	55.7	3 216 095	53.0	9 179 764	45.7
ALABAMA	1 274 202	78.0	413 096	57.6	8 306	67.5	9 609	49.0	19 211	44.3
ALASKA	166 839	66.0	7 361	34.3	26 556	59.8	7 090	47.0	6 413	43.3
ARIZONA	1 400 209	72.8	53 969	44.1	67 501	61.2	30 850	56.4	331 004	55.0
ARKANSAS	853 217	73.8	145 427	49.9	6 656	58.5	6 051	52.9	20 747	39.4
CALIFORNIA	6 684 001	64.9	777 973	38.9	96 339	45.9	1 139 172	55.0	2 564 765	43.7
COLORADO	1 330 288	71.2	59 214	45.8	14 027	49.9	30 789	55.1	205 570	52.9
CONNECTICUT	1 061 707	73.9	105 069	36.7	3 271	48.3	25 885	49.0	90 025	27.7
DELAWARE	228 480	79.2	51 897	50.6	1 161	65.8	5 254	52.3	9 546	41.8
DISTRICT OF COLUMBIA	83 515	48.7	139 407	38.8	756	29.9	6 541	24.7	14 089	23.5
FLORIDA	4 574 292	76.4	750 541	50.2	19 400	59.8	84 003	60.5	844 253	55.8
GEORGIA	2 021 482	76.1	802 456	50.8	8 036	58.7	50 819	55.1	99 026	37.3
HAWAII	121 168	49.3	7 352	17.1	1 125	30.4	202 617	65.8	20 983	36.1
IDAHO	429 163	74.0	1 468	50.7	5 436	58.6	3 819	63.3	24 238	51.9
ILLINOIS	3 412 380	71.7	623 009	42.2	9 903	51.3	135 371	54.5	368 822	48.6
INDIANA	2 053 032	74.9	184 385	45.2	6 299	54.5	19 630	46.5	54 753	48.6
IOWA	1 089 933	73.9	20 573	37.7	2 630	47.5	10 377	44.4	19 957	46.6
KANSAS	900 492	72.4	54 402	43.9	8 229	55.7	14 426	50.1	48 217	50.8
KENTUCKY	1 440 592	73.7	110 412	41.5	3 451	53.3	9 397	42.3	14 988	34.5
LOUISIANA	1 106 415	75.7	477 599	51.8	8 657	68.1	16 627	52.9	33 561	51.7
MAINE	504 979	72.2	1 952	36.7	2 735	51.4	2 279	45.5	2 267	45.5
MARYLAND	1 305 629	75.8	524 833	51.2	5 667	58.7	63 815	60.9	57 766	48.1
MASSACHUSETTS	2 089 971	66.9	113 697	31.3	5 432	41.4	73 122	41.0	120 414	21.4
MICHIGAN	3 090 407	78.7	491 341	50.7	20 265	60.4	55 085	49.8	82 323	54.6
MINNESOTA	1 736 866	77.5	54 818	32.0	16 318	49.1	35 753	52.3	33 868	42.9
MISSISSIPPI	685 273	78.8	338 957	60.6	3 615	67.7	4 827	51.3	9 490	45.8
MISSOURI	1 883 009	73.9	225 730	47.2	9 819	60.3	20 710	46.8	31 893	49.1
MONTANA	331 164	70.6	853	34.2	15 879	50.4	1 425	47.9	5 156	48.9
NEBRASKA	603 677	70.1	24 513	39.0	4 184	37.1	6 322	42.2	23 320	46.3
NEVADA	550 502	66.0	48 561	40.0	9 084	55.1	30 397	57.5	98 756	45.9
NEW HAMPSHIRE	456 520	70.8	3 146	37.7	948	54.3	4 495	42.5	5 457	36.4
NEW JERSEY	2 186 195	75.7	382 563	40.0	5 599	50.9	145 195	54.8	310 971	33.1
NEW MEXICO	362 928	71.9	12 290	45.5	47 160	68.9	6 163	54.4	244 157	69.3
NEW YORK	4 774 916	65.0	1 030 805	29.1	25 108	36.6	320 412	39.6	829 673	19.5
NORTH CAROLINA	2 327 753	75.7	625 913	52.6	34 821	69.6	32 850	50.9	89 055	31.5
NORTH DAKOTA	242 291	68.1	1 098	18.7	8 957	45.2	1 085	37.0	2 136	33.3
OHIO	3 799 281	73.4	487 408	42.7	10 272	49.9	45 712	47.3	61 058	47.2
OKLAHOMA	1 056 720	72.3	92 114	44.0	85 759	64.2	14 566	47.2	46 176	45.7
OREGON	1 178 598	66.9	18 630	37.0	14 378	48.9	33 879	53.9	62 704	36.6
PENNSYLVANIA	4 133 241	74.8	431 578	49.6	7 040	54.2	67 670	48.5	107 686	43.5
RHODE ISLAND	351 661	66.1	16 790	29.0	1 619	28.2	6 884	40.7	24 853	21.1
SOUTH CAROLINA	1 078 242	77.5	407 979	61.0	5 336	62.3	11 377	53.5	22 723	38.7
SOUTH DAKOTA	267 612	70.6	1 346	33.5	15 406	39.2	1 319	34.0	2 596	42.6
TENNESSEE	1 830 552	74.4	330 932	50.6	5 981	56.7	17 369	49.1	30 083	34.8
TEXAS	4 487 574	70.8	838 663	46.5	39 186	55.0	178 734	52.6	1 787 141	56.1
UTAH	622 048	74.1	4 780	39.2	7 765	54.2	13 683	58.3	46 172	50.4
VERMONT	233 486	71.2	866	30.0	1 067	50.6	1 230	42.3	1 549	55.4
VIRGINIA	2 006 000	74.0	492 371	51.3	8 242	57.1	78 760	56.7	81 939	44.1
WASHINGTON	1 911 072	67.9	67 454	37.2	29 299	50.5	107 103	56.2	106 982	41.0
WEST VIRGINIA	701 286	76.3	21 581	49.9	1 498	62.1	3 201	49.0	3 738	58.5
WISCONSIN	1 888 800	71.7	97 933	32.4	15 909	47.2	21 484	41.6	48 326	37.7
WYOMING	176 894	71.2	1 204	39.6	3 387	55.3	862	63.5	9 168	59.0

[1] Hispanic or Latino persons may be of any race.

Table C-2. States — Migration, Housing, and Transportation

	Homeownership by household type																	
	Family households										Nonfamily households							
			Married-couple family households				Other family households						Two or more adults		Male living alone		Female living alone	
			Total		With children		Total		With children									
STATE	Number of house-holders	Per-cent owners	Number of house-holders	Per-cent owners	Number of house-holders	Per-cent owners	Number of house-holders	Per-cent owners	Number of house-holders	Per-cent owners	Number of house-holders	Per-cent owners	Number of house-holders	Per-cent owners	Number of house-holders	Per-cent owners	Number of house-holders	Per-cent owners
	81	82	83	84	85	86	87	88	89	90	91	92	93	94	95	96	97	98
UNITED STATES....	72 080 574	73.8	55 142 741	81.0	25 253 608	76.7	16 937 833	50.4	9 565 652	39.9	33 399 527	49.8	6 171 545	39.3	11 430 624	47.2	15 797 358	55.7
ALABAMA	1 221 557	78.7	915 980	85.8	396 363	81.8	305 577	57.2	168 247	45.7	515 523	57.7	61 596	41.3	184 099	55.7	269 828	62.9
ALASKA	152 987	69.2	117 618	74.7	64 231	70.9	35 369	50.8	24 600	44.5	68 613	47.5	16 540	45.1	29 602	47.3	22 471	49.7
ARIZONA	1 293 167	74.7	1 000 121	81.0	437 578	74.3	293 046	53.2	174 282	44.4	608 160	53.9	136 227	44.4	208 160	49.9	263 773	62.0
ARKANSAS	735 026	75.2	571 826	82.1	240 026	75.5	163 200	51.0	95 508	39.4	307 670	55.5	41 070	41.8	109 215	52.2	157 385	61.4
CALIFORNIA	7 959 705	63.0	5 959 811	70.1	3 050 023	63.2	1 999 894	41.9	1 109 233	30.5	3 543 165	43.2	836 037	34.6	1 179 080	39.8	1 528 048	50.6
COLORADO	1 088 487	76.3	869 023	82.0	413 065	78.4	219 464	53.7	134 692	46.5	569 751	50.2	133 995	40.5	198 538	48.0	237 218	57.6
CONNECTICUT	883 566	75.4	682 607	83.4	311 500	81.7	200 959	48.4	110 280	35.0	418 104	48.7	73 844	42.2	137 091	44.6	207 169	53.7
DELAWARE	205 242	78.9	155 215	86.2	66 876	82.9	50 027	56.2	28 813	45.0	93 494	57.9	18 806	47.1	30 064	57.1	44 624	62.9
DISTRICT OF COLUMBIA	115 243	49.8	56 893	64.1	20 992	58.1	58 350	35.8	28 787	21.7	133 095	32.9	24 350	30.9	46 475	29.7	62 270	36.1
FLORIDA	4 226 853	75.9	3 225 058	82.6	1 236 739	76.1	1 001 795	54.6	554 706	44.3	2 111 076	58.4	423 716	47.9	691 529	53.5	995 831	66.2
GEORGIA	2 121 564	74.2	1 570 716	82.3	746 855	78.4	550 848	51.1	311 695	41.4	884 805	51.4	174 228	37.3	294 149	49.2	416 428	58.8
HAWAII	288 220	62.2	218 901	66.1	98 502	56.9	69 319	49.8	31 584	30.2	115 020	42.2	26 849	34.2	42 808	40.3	45 363	48.7
IDAHO	336 969	78.4	278 730	83.2	133 738	78.8	58 239	55.6	37 932	47.9	132 676	57.0	27 442	43.4	46 754	55.5	58 480	64.5
ILLINOIS	3 119 231	75.4	2 383 013	83.0	1 131 245	80.1	736 218	50.9	393 251	40.1	1 472 548	50.1	242 767	38.7	512 148	47.1	717 633	56.0
INDIANA	1 607 583	79.5	1 265 751	86.1	566 258	83.1	341 832	54.9	206 353	44.8	728 723	53.7	123 345	43.7	251 856	51.9	353 522	58.4
IOWA	771 813	81.6	639 463	86.6	278 783	83.7	132 350	57.5	83 259	48.7	377 463	53.4	64 360	39.9	126 389	51.5	186 714	59.4
KANSAS	704 264	77.9	574 292	83.5	264 823	79.3	129 972	52.9	81 903	45.1	333 627	51.1	53 319	35.2	118 040	48.6	162 268	58.2
KENTUCKY	1 108 424	77.5	867 580	83.9	381 108	79.5	240 844	54.4	139 182	43.0	482 223	55.3	68 258	42.2	170 964	51.9	243 001	61.4
LOUISIANA	1 160 674	74.4	817 561	83.8	379 304	80.0	343 113	52.0	196 206	41.0	495 379	52.8	76 210	39.7	179 682	49.2	239 487	59.7
MAINE	341 645	81.1	275 462	86.7	115 080	84.7	66 183	57.8	42 738	49.5	176 555	53.1	36 607	50.6	56 302	53.1	83 646	54.2
MARYLAND	1 365 313	75.1	1 008 719	83.1	469 665	80.9	356 594	52.5	196 908	41.7	615 546	51.3	120 076	43.9	196 660	49.6	298 810	55.4
MASSACHUSETTS ...	1 583 423	72.8	1 213 494	80.6	557 093	79.7	369 929	47.3	196 247	43.5	860 157	41.3	175 679	32.8	269 425	39.2	415 053	46.4
MICHIGAN	2 584 296	81.7	1 967 990	88.8	887 286	86.5	616 306	59.2	356 480	48.9	1 201 365	56.7	207 740	47.2	427 364	56.4	566 261	60.3
MINNESOTA	1 259 605	85.0	1 030 296	90.3	485 054	90.1	229 309	61.4	144 139	54.2	635 522	53.8	126 103	47.4	220 302	55.1	289 117	55.5
MISSISSIPPI	750 344	77.0	526 652	85.3	238 153	81.1	223 692	57.6	127 648	46.4	296 090	60.5	38 254	40.4	107 969	57.7	149 867	67.6
MISSOURI	1 481 739	78.7	1 151 097	85.6	503 321	82.2	330 642	54.6	199 819	44.7	712 855	52.8	112 938	42.7	249 305	50.4	350 612	57.8
MONTANA	238 005	77.8	193 220	83.1	82 921	78.4	44 785	54.7	29 214	47.1	120 662	51.9	22 235	40.2	44 889	51.0	53 538	57.5
NEBRASKA	444 936	77.1	363 157	83.2	167 189	79.6	81 779	50.2	51 518	41.0	221 248	48.0	37 738	34.0	77 656	44.1	105 854	55.8
NEVADA	500 500	68.0	377 297	74.5	168 569	68.7	123 203	48.1	72 310	40.0	250 665	46.6	63 882	42.9	96 214	42.4	90 569	53.8
NEW HAMPSHIRE.....	324 872	79.1	265 094	84.7	122 286	83.6	59 778	54.6	36 862	45.3	149 734	49.2	33 709	45.1	51 229	47.0	64 796	53.1
NEW JERSEY	2 162 967	72.8	1 658 754	80.1	789 189	78.0	504 213	48.8	243 816	35.9	901 678	48.4	150 325	40.3	293 922	45.0	457 431	53.3
NEW MEXICO	468 179	76.4	345 133	82.7	160 457	77.6	123 046	58.8	76 123	50.4	209 792	55.7	37 618	47.0	78 414	52.8	93 760	61.6
NEW YORK	4 661 308	61.3	3 336 850	71.1	1 553 732	68.2	1 324 458	36.5	695 632	26.5	2 395 552	36.9	413 015	31.2	794 902	34.5	1 187 635	40.4
NORTH CAROLINA ...	2 169 023	76.0	1 664 266	83.0	717 748	78.4	504 757	52.8	284 240	42.9	962 990	54.4	167 927	38.6	328 630	52.6	466 433	61.3
NORTH DAKOTA	166 731	78.5	138 578	84.3	62 814	82.1	28 153	49.7	17 845	41.7	90 421	44.7	15 029	29.1	33 431	47.3	41 961	48.3
OHIO	3 002 638	77.8	2 309 170	85.6	1 011 543	82.5	693 468	51.7	405 750	39.3	1 443 135	51.1	227 609	40.3	503 452	48.9	712 074	56.1
OKLAHOMA	925 194	74.9	725 136	81.5	316 182	75.3	200 058	51.0	120 403	40.7	417 099	54.0	58 458	37.0	150 259	49.9	208 382	61.7
OREGON	881 211	72.8	702 700	79.6	303 263	73.3	178 511	46.3	110 262	36.7	452 512	47.5	104 794	38.6	147 856	45.2	199 862	54.0
PENNSYLVANIA	3 219 482	80.4	2 493 003	86.8	1 058 249	85.0	726 479	58.5	379 330	44.5	1 557 521	52.6	236 451	42.8	523 479	51.4	797 591	56.2
RHODE ISLAND	266 165	70.4	199 078	79.4	87 385	76.9	67 087	43.7	38 380	29.2	142 259	40.6	25 614	34.7	46 535	38.6	70 110	44.0
SOUTH CAROLINA ...	1 077 068	78.3	793 569	85.5	340 801	81.6	283 499	58.3	158 190	48.2	456 786	57.8	73 668	41.0	161 168	55.7	221 950	64.9
SOUTH DAKOTA	194 996	78.2	158 945	84.4	72 050	82.0	36 051	51.2	23 518	43.7	95 249	47.6	15 229	38.5	34 633	48.3	45 387	50.1
TENNESSEE	1 554 144	77.0	1 187 690	83.9	507 102	79.7	366 454	54.4	204 616	42.6	678 761	53.8	102 432	40.3	238 141	50.1	338 188	60.6
TEXAS	5 270 998	71.1	4 045 537	77.7	2 036 604	72.6	1 225 461	49.2	705 882	39.6	2 122 356	45.8	370 714	33.9	774 157	41.4	977 485	53.8
UTAH	537 929	77.3	448 152	81.4	249 620	80.5	89 777	57.0	52 566	48.3	163 352	52.5	38 687	31.8	53 997	51.4	70 668	64.7
VERMONT	158 314	80.4	128 206	85.8	56 649	83.7	30 108	57.4	19 972	49.5	82 320	51.6	19 095	44.4	26 419	50.8	36 806	55.9
VIRGINIA	1 856 191	75.3	1 441 731	82.0	655 288	78.1	414 460	51.8	232 118	40.9	842 982	52.3	166 434	38.8	281 065	51.0	395 483	58.9
WASHINGTON	1 504 473	73.5	1 193 941	80.2	550 619	75.6	310 532	47.7	196 710	39.2	766 925	47.1	172 785	39.3	265 837	44.7	328 303	53.2
WEST VIRGINIA	505 768	81.6	400 642	86.6	159 738	81.9	105 126	62.6	54 583	49.3	230 713	61.0	31 116	47.7	78 544	58.1	121 053	66.4
WISCONSIN	1 391 503	79.1	1 121 763	86.0	502 171	84.1	269 740	50.4	165 450	40.5	693 041	47.0	135 031	37.3	237 617	47.7	320 393	50.6
WYOMING	131 039	77.7	107 260	82.7	47 778	78.2	23 779	55.2	15 870	47.6	62 569	53.8	11 594	43.5	24 208	51.2	26 767	60.7

Table C-2. States — **Migration, Housing, and Transportation**

STATE	Homeownership by household size				Average household size		Median household income		
	One-person households		Two or more person households						
	Number of householders	Percent owners	Number of householders	Percent owners	Owner-occupied households	Renter-occupied households	All households	Owner-occupied households	Renter-occupied households
	99	100	101	102	103	104	105	106	107
UNITED STATES....	27 227 982	52.1	78 252 119	71.1	2.71	2.36	41 851	51 323	27 362
ALABAMA	453 927	60.0	1 283 153	76.9	2.59	2.25	33 903	40 619	19 870
ALASKA	52 073	48.3	169 527	66.9	2.90	2.48	51 441	63 384	35 406
ARIZONA	471 933	56.7	1 429 394	71.8	2.71	2.48	40 388	48 411	27 332
ARKANSAS	266 600	57.6	776 096	73.4	2.54	2.38	32 097	38 238	21 167
CALIFORNIA	2 707 128	45.9	8 795 742	60.3	2.95	2.78	47 288	62 155	31 912
COLORADO	435 756	53.2	1 222 482	72.4	2.67	2.26	47 009	57 099	30 335
CONNECTICUT	344 260	50.1	957 410	72.8	2.69	2.22	53 736	67 350	31 318
DELAWARE	74 688	60.6	224 048	76.2	2.63	2.30	47 012	54 951	30 429
DISTRICT OF COLUMBIA	108 745	33.4	139 593	46.5	2.34	2.03	39 827	65 288	28 754
FLORIDA	1 687 360	61.0	4 650 569	73.4	2.51	2.35	38 665	45 122	26 707
GEORGIA	710 577	54.9	2 295 792	71.4	2.73	2.47	42 288	51 421	27 657
HAWAII	88 171	44.6	315 069	59.8	3.11	2.66	49 536	64 653	33 755
IDAHO	105 234	60.5	364 411	75.8	2.76	2.51	37 570	44 143	23 940
ILLINOIS	1 220 781	52.3	3 361 998	72.8	2.80	2.29	46 304	56 715	29 065
INDIANA	605 378	55.7	1 730 928	76.9	2.66	2.19	41 425	49 688	25 550
IOWA	313 103	56.2	836 173	78.4	2.59	2.10	39 358	46 120	24 581
KANSAS	280 308	54.2	757 583	74.9	2.65	2.20	40 509	48 572	25 898
KENTUCKY	413 965	57.5	1 176 682	75.4	2.57	2.23	33 549	40 460	21 295
LOUISIANA	419 169	55.2	1 236 884	72.2	2.72	2.41	32 427	40 554	20 138
MAINE	139 948	53.8	378 252	78.2	2.55	2.00	37 072	43 973	22 516
MARYLAND	495 470	53.1	1 485 389	72.6	2.75	2.30	52 640	64 860	32 351
MASSACHUSETTS ...	684 478	43.5	1 759 102	68.8	2.74	2.13	50 284	64 506	30 082
MICHIGAN	993 625	58.6	2 792 036	79.2	2.68	2.21	44 533	52 353	26 153
MINNESOTA	509 419	55.3	1 385 708	81.6	2.71	1.99	47 033	55 338	26 551
MISSISSIPPI	257 836	63.5	788 598	75.3	2.67	2.52	31 232	36 822	19 603
MISSOURI	599 917	54.7	1 594 677	76.1	2.60	2.17	37 828	45 667	23 698
MONTANA	98 427	54.5	260 240	74.6	2.56	2.20	33 014	40 004	20 836
NEBRASKA	183 510	50.8	482 674	73.8	2.65	2.17	39 179	47 466	25 857
NEVADA	186 783	47.9	564 382	65.2	2.74	2.43	44 316	54 626	31 269
NEW HAMPSHIRE	116 025	50.4	358 581	75.9	2.72	2.08	49 224	58 048	31 478
NEW JERSEY	751 353	50.1	2 313 292	70.7	2.85	2.37	54 820	66 770	34 100
NEW MEXICO	172 174	57.6	505 797	74.2	2.74	2.37	33 974	40 432	22 267
NEW YORK	1 982 537	38.0	5 074 323	58.8	2.83	2.36	43 070	58 956	28 851
NORTH CAROLINA ...	795 063	57.7	2 336 950	73.3	2.56	2.34	39 061	46 287	26 140
NORTH DAKOTA	75 392	47.9	181 760	74.4	2.61	2.00	34 483	42 209	22 062
OHIO	1 215 526	53.1	3 230 247	75.1	2.63	2.16	40 846	50 093	25 116
OKLAHOMA	358 641	56.8	983 652	72.6	2.56	2.32	33 243	40 387	21 807
OREGON	347 718	50.3	986 005	69.2	2.61	2.32	40 818	50 713	27 197
PENNSYLVANIA	1 321 070	54.3	3 455 933	77.8	2.64	2.09	39 987	47 611	24 601
RHODE ISLAND	116 645	41.8	291 779	67.3	2.70	2.12	41 827	56 559	24 361
SOUTH CAROLINA	383 118	61.0	1 150 736	75.9	2.61	2.32	36 951	43 179	23 855
SOUTH DAKOTA	80 020	49.3	210 225	75.4	2.64	2.20	35 271	42 834	21 935
TENNESSEE	576 329	56.2	1 656 576	74.7	2.58	2.24	36 239	43 217	23 266
TEXAS	1 751 642	48.3	5 641 712	68.6	2.89	2.50	39 745	49 279	27 506
UTAH	124 665	58.9	576 616	74.3	3.30	2.68	45 661	53 701	28 733
VERMONT	63 225	53.8	177 409	76.5	2.60	2.08	40 750	48 440	25 163
VIRGINIA	676 548	55.6	2 022 625	72.3	2.63	2.33	46 600	55 845	30 750
WASHINGTON	594 140	49.4	1 677 258	70.0	2.67	2.29	45 610	56 307	29 853
WEST VIRGINIA	199 504	63.1	536 884	79.7	2.47	2.18	29 663	34 632	16 794
WISCONSIN	558 010	49.3	1 526 534	75.4	2.67	2.12	43 624	52 546	27 500
WYOMING	50 975	56.2	142 633	74.9	2.59	2.21	37 671	45 157	24 183

Table C-2. States — **Migration, Housing, and Transportation**

STATE	Total occupied housing units	Owner-occupied units Total	15 to 34 years	35 to 64 years	65 years and over	Renter-occupied units Total	15 to 34 years	35 to 64 years	65 years and over	Median housing value (owner estimated)	With a mortgage	Without a mortgage	Median gross rent	Median gross rent as a percent of income
	108	109	110	111	112	113	114	115	116	117	118	119	120	121
UNITED STATES....	56 474	66 699	59 570	76 538	46 229	36 457	35 605	40 486	25 944	111 800	21.7	10.5	602	25.5
ALABAMA	45 786	52 735	44 678	60 631	39 162	27 502	25 346	31 894	20 602	76 700	19.8	9.9	447	24.8
ALASKA	62 426	73 877	60 239	79 204	58 785	43 340	38 735	48 790	31 577	137 400	22.3	9.9	720	24.8
ARIZONA	53 751	62 590	57 062	72 040	45 599	34 935	32 878	38 886	28 018	109 400	22.1	9.9	619	26.6
ARKANSAS..............	42 686	49 268	44 449	56 232	37 213	27 769	27 007	30 614	21 419	67 400	19.4	9.9	453	24.4
CALIFORNIA............	65 383	82 115	75 605	93 202	56 950	43 285	42 673	46 901	29 488	198 900	25.3	9.9	747	27.7
COLORADO.............	61 204	72 549	63 971	81 631	48 352	37 834	37 096	41 499	26 740	160 100	22.6	9.9	671	26.4
CONNECTICUT	73 964	90 057	79 721	105 029	56 577	41 558	42 051	46 344	27 984	160 600	22.4	13.1	681	25.4
DELAWARE	59 885	68 167	62 300	78 067	47 871	38 246	37 292	41 976	29 331	122 000	20.8	9.9	639	24.3
DISTRICT OF COLUMBIA	63 727	97 634	77 836	113 986	72 712	40 400	40 553	43 692	29 350	153 500	22.2	9.9	618	24.8
FLORIDA..................	53 324	61 197	55 506	70 440	47 893	34 881	33 410	38 483	27 357	93 200	22.8	10.5	641	27.5
GEORGIA.................	56 456	66 554	59 597	75 433	44 186	35 484	35 056	38 792	23 315	100 600	20.8	9.9	613	24.9
HAWAII....................	62 794	77 980	66 343	85 151	66 500	43 079	37 722	48 668	33 586	249 300	26.3	9.9	779	27.2
IDAHO....................	48 092	54 984	48 584	62 526	39 462	30 034	27 847	34 599	22 548	102 100	21.5	9.9	515	25.3
ILLINOIS..................	61 249	72 758	67 257	83 806	47 929	37 589	37 925	41 151	26 052	127 800	21.7	11.1	605	24.4
INDIANA..................	52 068	60 140	54 460	69 328	40 074	31 875	30 722	36 597	22 374	92 500	19.3	9.9	521	23.9
IOWA......................	48 984	56 109	52 087	64 796	39 234	30 348	29 794	34 297	22 998	82 100	19.1	9.9	470	23.2
KANSAS..................	51 963	60 695	53 056	70 044	42 872	32 285	30 693	37 105	23 829	81 000	19.3	9.9	498	23.4
KENTUCKY..............	45 124	52 138	47 000	59 456	37 356	28 162	27 547	30 687	21 771	79 600	19.6	9.9	445	24.0
LOUISIANA	44 706	52 792	46 025	60 341	38 231	27 576	25 792	30 897	21 081	77 500	19.6	9.9	466	25.8
MAINE	47 219	54 404	50 178	61 280	38 584	29 123	30 343	32 161	20 066	94 300	21.4	12.1	497	25.3
MARYLAND	67 314	79 901	68 773	89 697	56 586	40 898	40 281	44 896	29 273	143 300	22.2	9.9	689	24.7
MASSACHUSETTS ...	66 116	81 877	78 845	94 722	50 450	40 701	45 355	43 883	24 195	182 800	21.9	12.4	684	25.5
MICHIGAN	57 293	65 484	58 756	75 293	43 608	34 235	32 814	39 117	24 752	110 300	19.6	9.9	546	24.4
MINNESOTA............	59 241	67 905	62 105	77 302	43 447	33 869	34 632	38 010	24 017	118 100	20.0	9.9	566	24.7
MISSISSIPPI............	42 247	48 073	42 213	54 835	35 823	26 998	25 126	30 584	20 145	64 700	20.4	9.9	439	25.0
MISSOURI...............	49 917	58 182	52 077	66 505	41 669	30 376	29 369	33 985	23 436	86 900	19.5	9.9	484	24.0
MONTANA...............	42 434	49 430	43 470	55 519	36 828	26 817	24 799	30 113	22 573	95 800	22.2	10.4	447	25.3
NEBRASKA..............	49 550	58 094	53 752	66 851	40 489	31 851	30 201	35 946	25 787	86 900	19.7	10.5	491	23.0
NEVADA..................	57 222	69 041	62 799	77 093	51 283	38 836	37 914	42 089	28 413	132 500	23.8	9.9	699	26.5
NEW HAMPSHIRE.....	60 777	70 483	66 413	78 729	46 743	38 453	38 871	43 029	25 040	127 500	22.3	13.6	646	24.2
NEW JERSEY...........	72 985	88 128	83 404	102 484	54 930	44 071	47 110	47 790	27 423	167 900	23.7	15.3	751	25.5
NEW MEXICO...........	45 487	52 354	42 599	58 736	41 718	29 479	26 712	33 250	24 192	94 600	22.2	9.9	503	26.6
NEW YORK...............	61 550	78 909	73 402	90 020	54 273	41 985	43 912	45 598	28 419	147 600	23.2	13.6	672	26.8
NORTH CAROLINA ...	51 142	59 184	53 428	67 576	41 417	32 941	32 604	36 038	23 274	95 800	21.3	9.9	548	24.3
NORTH DAKOTA.......	43 532	51 115	47 846	58 155	36 642	28 401	26 268	33 409	24 030	68 300	19.4	10.2	412	22.3
OHIO	52 734	62 091	56 610	71 418	42 390	31 800	30 808	35 093	25 352	100 500	20.6	10.6	515	24.2
OKLAHOMA	44 369	51 777	45 144	59 198	38 911	28 334	25 852	32 400	22 757	67 700	19.2	9.9	456	24.3
OREGON	52 762	63 402	60 057	72 137	43 631	33 642	32 500	36 847	26 640	145 800	23.2	10.5	620	26.9
PENNSYLVANIA........	52 548	60 712	56 391	71 192	40 011	32 263	32 802	35 686	24 122	94 800	21.6	12.2	531	25.0
RHODE ISLAND	54 461	69 268	65 599	79 272	46 835	32 229	31 917	36 906	22 870	130 500	22.7	13.4	553	25.7
SOUTH CAROLINA ...	48 236	54 942	48 433	62 086	40 918	30 811	29 700	34 194	21 921	83 100	20.5	9.9	510	24.4
SOUTH DAKOTA.......	44 748	52 367	47 540	59 515	38 281	28 418	27 110	33 213	21 799	74 300	19.7	10.5	426	22.9
TENNESSEE............	48 574	56 442	49 444	64 494	40 558	30 278	29 201	33 434	22 934	88 300	21.1	9.9	505	24.8
TEXAS.....................	54 225	64 827	56 194	73 917	45 242	35 536	33 227	40 083	25 399	77 800	20.1	10.9	574	24.4
UTAH......................	56 938	65 681	54 886	75 826	46 227	34 968	33 291	39 647	26 671	142 600	22.9	9.9	597	24.9
VERMONT	51 212	59 620	52 457	66 616	42 852	31 066	31 676	34 241	21 151	111 200	22.4	13.9	553	26.2
VIRGINIA.................	61 607	71 831	63 037	81 027	50 278	39 788	38 636	43 490	29 764	118 800	21.4	9.9	650	24.5
WASHINGTON..........	58 504	70 101	66 972	78 351	48 227	37 354	36 380	40 963	27 604	158 800	23.8	10.4	663	26.5
WEST VIRGINIA	39 998	45 063	39 186	51 382	34 955	24 661	22 305	28 070	20 909	66 000	19.5	9.9	401	25.8
WISCONSIN.............	53 756	62 917	58 903	71 743	41 902	33 889	33 730	37 927	25 097	109 900	20.9	11.2	540	23.4
WYOMING	47 601	54 859	45 034	61 820	41 011	30 679	27 631	35 878	22 879	91 500	19.7	9.9	437	22.5

Table C-2. States — **Migration, Housing, and Transportation**

STATE	Households who pay 35 percent or more of income for housing expenses, by tenure, age of householder, and household income (percent)													
	Owner-occupied households							Renter-occupied households						
	Total	15 to 24 years	25 to 44 years	45 to 64 years	65 years and over	Households with income under $50,000	Households with income over $100,000	Total	15 to 24 years	25 to 44 years	45 to 64 years	65 years and over	Households with income under $50,000	Households with income over $100,000
	122	123	124	125	126	127	128	129	130	131	132	133	134	135
UNITED STATES....	15.8	26.0	16.3	14.5	16.7	29.8	1.8	29.5	39.8	25.3	27.2	39.0	37.6	0.3
ALABAMA	13.9	24.3	13.0	13.0	15.9	23.6	0.7	27.4	42.0	23.3	25.2	28.9	31.6	0.0
ALASKA	16.2	31.8	17.5	14.3	17.3	40.3	0.7	25.4	33.3	23.1	22.5	39.5	36.6	0.0
ARIZONA	16.2	27.6	16.8	15.6	15.7	31.4	1.1	30.9	41.2	26.0	27.3	44.9	38.5	0.1
ARKANSAS	12.7	19.8	12.0	11.9	14.2	20.2	0.3	26.7	37.0	23.6	24.6	29.4	30.4	0.0
CALIFORNIA	23.2	38.7	26.1	22.1	20.5	46.2	4.3	34.1	44.9	30.2	32.4	47.3	47.3	0.4
COLORADO	16.6	33.9	18.1	15.1	15.4	35.8	1.3	30.4	42.2	25.5	27.7	41.2	39.8	0.1
CONNECTICUT	17.1	31.1	17.3	14.1	21.3	41.7	2.2	29.0	37.9	25.3	27.3	37.1	39.6	0.7
DELAWARE	13.8	29.8	14.3	12.1	15.0	30.8	0.5	26.7	35.9	21.9	25.0	37.8	34.8	1.2
DISTRICT OF COLUMBIA	18.6	37.9	19.5	17.6	18.9	40.9	2.2	28.2	45.1	23.6	26.1	35.2	37.4	0.8
FLORIDA	18.5	29.1	19.2	18.0	18.1	33.4	1.7	33.0	41.7	28.6	30.9	43.6	41.0	0.3
GEORGIA	15.2	27.2	14.6	14.2	17.7	30.9	1.2	28.1	39.0	24.3	26.8	36.1	36.0	0.1
HAWAII	22.1	37.5	30.4	22.7	15.2	40.0	4.2	29.1	37.8	27.3	27.9	33.8	41.1	0.6
IDAHO	14.5	24.9	15.3	13.5	14.2	25.3	0.7	28.1	35.2	24.9	24.1	36.1	32.7	0.4
ILLINOIS	14.9	24.3	15.8	13.3	15.7	30.4	1.7	28.3	39.3	23.4	26.0	39.1	36.9	0.2
INDIANA	11.2	18.9	10.8	10.0	13.1	21.5	0.7	26.4	38.3	21.3	21.9	35.7	31.8	0.2
IOWA	9.6	15.4	9.7	8.5	10.9	17.0	0.3	24.8	36.5	19.6	20.9	29.0	29.0	0.0
KANSAS	10.5	19.1	10.3	9.6	11.6	19.5	0.7	25.0	37.4	19.2	21.2	33.4	30.2	0.1
KENTUCKY	12.3	18.7	11.6	12.1	13.3	21.0	0.6	25.6	34.8	22.2	24.0	30.6	29.7	0.0
LOUISIANA	14.2	22.3	13.9	13.7	15.0	23.9	0.6	29.8	41.9	26.4	26.9	35.2	34.5	0.3
MAINE	14.7	23.4	14.5	13.3	16.8	25.6	0.7	27.4	33.6	24.7	26.0	31.5	32.0	0.0
MARYLAND	16.1	30.5	16.9	14.6	16.9	38.0	1.5	27.0	36.8	22.5	25.0	39.5	37.3	0.4
MASSACHUSETTS	16.2	25.8	16.5	13.9	19.7	38.4	1.5	28.6	40.8	24.3	27.1	35.8	39.4	0.3
MICHIGAN	12.7	21.9	13.0	11.4	14.1	25.7	0.9	28.4	39.4	24.0	24.5	37.6	35.6	0.0
MINNESOTA	11.1	21.4	11.5	9.7	12.2	24.0	0.8	27.1	34.4	21.3	23.3	38.3	33.5	0.3
MISSISSIPPI	16.0	25.7	14.7	15.0	18.6	25.2	0.5	27.6	38.1	24.6	25.8	30.8	30.8	0.1
MISSOURI	11.6	19.6	11.4	10.9	12.5	21.2	0.8	26.3	36.3	22.0	23.0	33.7	31.0	0.1
MONTANA	15.3	33.1	16.8	14.8	13.7	24.4	0.4	28.2	41.4	24.3	23.9	32.0	31.6	0.0
NEBRASKA	10.6	17.9	10.4	9.4	12.1	19.2	0.6	23.5	34.0	18.4	19.0	32.7	28.0	0.2
NEVADA	19.8	32.4	20.5	18.0	21.2	43.2	1.2	30.5	37.5	27.0	27.7	44.6	40.7	0.1
NEW HAMPSHIRE	15.3	26.2	14.8	13.4	20.0	35.7	0.6	25.6	35.1	20.9	23.5	36.0	34.2	0.0
NEW JERSEY	20.5	34.1	21.1	17.0	25.2	47.9	2.3	29.9	37.1	25.7	28.1	42.8	40.2	0.0
NEW MEXICO	16.0	29.3	17.0	15.5	14.8	26.4	0.7	30.5	42.0	27.1	27.7	35.7	35.7	0.2
NEW YORK	19.6	36.1	21.3	17.0	21.5	39.2	2.3	33.4	45.5	30.5	30.2	41.3	45.0	0.8
NORTH CAROLINA	15.0	25.4	14.4	13.9	17.0	27.8	1.0	26.7	37.4	22.3	25.1	34.6	32.7	0.1
NORTH DAKOTA	9.7	17.7	8.9	8.7	11.8	16.5	0.3	22.6	34.6	15.1	17.4	30.4	25.6	0.0
OHIO	13.2	23.0	13.1	12.0	14.8	25.2	0.8	27.4	37.1	22.9	24.4	36.7	33.0	0.1
OKLAHOMA	12.1	22.4	11.8	11.3	12.8	19.6	0.5	26.7	37.5	22.7	23.0	33.4	30.7	0.1
OREGON	17.5	31.8	19.6	15.9	16.9	33.7	1.2	32.2	43.7	26.9	27.8	45.9	39.7	0.0
PENNSYLVANIA	15.1	26.0	15.1	13.4	17.0	26.9	1.0	28.6	40.4	23.1	26.1	37.3	34.8	0.3
RHODE ISLAND	17.1	37.9	17.0	14.4	20.8	37.6	0.9	28.9	41.9	24.7	25.3	35.3	35.3	0.0
SOUTH CAROLINA	14.3	19.5	13.5	13.6	16.1	25.3	1.1	26.8	36.6	22.5	25.7	35.2	32.0	0.1
SOUTH DAKOTA	10.4	18.1	9.8	9.5	11.9	17.3	1.0	22.7	31.5	17.3	18.2	29.8	25.6	0.0
TENNESSEE	14.4	24.6	14.2	13.4	15.6	24.7	1.0	27.2	37.9	23.6	24.8	33.4	32.1	0.1
TEXAS	13.6	24.2	13.3	12.3	15.6	25.8	1.1	27.1	40.0	22.6	24.0	39.6	34.3	0.2
UTAH	16.2	32.5	20.1	12.8	12.8	32.4	1.6	27.7	31.4	25.2	25.2	36.9	34.4	0.3
VERMONT	16.2	22.3	15.3	14.4	20.7	30.6	0.5	29.5	41.9	25.5	28.2	32.1	34.8	0.6
VIRGINIA	14.1	24.0	14.7	12.9	15.0	29.4	1.2	26.3	37.8	21.8	24.5	36.8	35.2	0.3
WASHINGTON	18.1	35.2	20.3	16.8	16.6	37.2	1.9	30.8	41.6	26.1	27.4	44.0	40.0	0.1
WEST VIRGINIA	11.9	23.9	12.4	11.4	11.7	17.8	0.5	28.3	44.3	25.6	24.7	26.4	31.5	0.0
WISCONSIN	12.0	20.0	11.9	10.5	14.6	24.4	0.7	25.4	35.8	19.3	21.9	35.8	31.4	0.1
WYOMING	11.3	19.9	12.0	10.7	11.0	20.0	1.1	23.3	37.8	18.2	20.5	24.8	27.4	0.0

Table C-2. States — **Migration, Housing, and Transportation**

STATE	Total number of workers 16 years and over	Drove alone	Carpooled	Public trans-portation	Motor-cycle or bicycle	Walked	Other means	Worked at home	Time for all workers who did not work at home	Time on public trans-portation	Time by all other means	Total households	No vehicles	One vehicle	Two vehicles	Three or more vehicles	Average vehicles available
	136	137	138	139	140	141	142	143	144	145	146	147	148	149	150	151	152
UNITED STATES....	128 279 228	75.7	12.2	4.7	0.5	2.9	0.7	3.3	25.5	47.7	24.3	105 480 101	10.3	34.2	38.4	17.1	1.7
ALABAMA	1 900 089	83.0	12.3	0.5	0.1	1.3	0.7	2.1	24.8	44.7	24.7	1 737 080	8.3	32.3	38.2	21.3	1.8
ALASKA	290 597	66.5	15.5	1.8	0.6	7.3	4.2	4.1	19.6	28.0	19.4	221 600	10.9	33.9	38.2	17.1	1.7
ARIZONA	2 210 395	74.1	15.4	1.9	1.4	2.6	0.9	3.7	24.9	44.9	24.5	1 901 327	7.4	38.6	39.0	14.9	1.7
ARKANSAS..............	1 160 101	79.9	14.1	0.4	0.2	1.9	0.8	2.6	21.9	35.9	21.8	1 042 696	8.1	34.9	40.7	16.4	1.7
CALIFORNIA	14 525 322	71.8	14.5	5.1	1.1	2.9	0.8	3.8	27.7	47.8	26.6	11 502 870	9.5	34.1	37.7	18.6	1.7
COLORADO..............	2 191 626	75.1	12.2	3.2	0.9	3.0	0.6	4.9	24.3	41.6	23.7	1 658 238	6.4	31.6	40.5	21.5	1.9
CONNECTICUT	1 640 823	80.0	9.4	4.0	0.2	2.7	0.5	3.1	24.4	55.1	23.1	1 301 670	9.6	33.1	40.7	16.6	1.7
DELAWARE	373 070	79.2	11.5	2.8	0.3	2.6	0.6	3.0	24.0	41.3	23.5	298 736	8.0	34.1	41.4	16.5	1.7
DISTRICT OF COLUMBIA............	260 884	38.4	11.0	33.2	1.2	11.8	0.6	3.8	29.7	38.3	25.2	248 338	36.9	43.5	15.5	4.1	0.9
FLORIDA	6 910 168	78.8	12.9	1.9	0.8	1.7	0.9	3.0	26.2	46.5	25.8	6 337 929	8.1	41.4	38.2	12.3	1.6
GEORGIA	3 832 803	77.5	14.5	2.3	0.2	1.7	0.9	2.8	27.7	47.4	27.2	3 006 369	8.3	32.3	39.8	19.6	1.8
HAWAII	563 154	63.9	19.0	6.3	1.4	4.8	0.9	3.6	26.1	44.9	24.8	403 240	11.0	37.0	35.7	16.3	1.7
IDAHO	594 654	77.0	12.3	1.1	0.8	3.5	0.6	4.7	20.0	57.9	19.6	469 645	4.7	27.7	41.9	25.7	2.0
ILLINOIS..................	5 745 731	73.2	10.9	8.7	0.4	3.1	0.7	3.1	28.0	48.8	26.0	4 591 779	11.8	35.4	37.6	15.1	1.6
INDIANA...................	2 910 612	81.8	11.0	1.0	0.3	2.4	0.6	2.9	22.6	43.9	22.4	2 336 306	7.2	32.4	40.3	20.1	1.8
IOWA.......................	1 469 763	78.6	10.8	1.0	0.4	4.0	0.5	4.7	18.5	28.0	18.4	1 149 276	6.4	30.5	40.4	22.6	1.9
KANSAS..................	1 311 343	81.5	10.6	0.5	0.3	2.5	0.6	4.0	19.0	34.3	19.0	1 037 891	5.7	31.6	40.9	21.8	1.9
KENTUCKY..............	1 781 733	80.2	12.6	1.2	0.2	2.4	0.7	2.7	23.5	35.9	23.4	1 590 647	9.3	33.3	39.4	18.0	1.7
LOUISIANA..............	1 831 057	78.1	13.6	2.4	0.5	2.2	1.1	2.1	25.7	43.1	25.2	1 656 053	11.9	37.0	38.0	13.1	1.6
MAINE	615 144	78.6	11.3	0.8	0.3	4.0	0.7	4.4	22.7	34.1	22.6	518 200	7.6	34.4	41.9	16.0	1.7
MARYLAND..............	2 591 670	73.7	12.4	7.2	0.2	2.5	0.6	3.3	31.2	51.4	29.5	1 980 859	11.2	33.4	37.7	17.7	1.7
MASSACHUSETTS ...	3 102 837	73.8	9.0	8.7	0.4	4.3	0.5	3.1	27.0	43.6	25.3	2 443 580	12.7	37.0	37.7	12.6	1.5
MICHIGAN	4 540 372	83.2	9.7	1.3	0.3	2.2	0.5	2.8	24.1	42.7	23.9	3 785 661	7.7	33.7	40.7	17.9	1.8
MINNESOTA	2 541 611	77.6	10.4	3.2	0.5	3.3	0.5	4.6	21.9	35.0	21.4	1 895 127	7.7	31.2	42.2	19.0	1.8
MISSISSIPPI	1 164 118	79.4	15.2	0.6	0.2	1.9	0.9	1.9	24.6	46.3	24.5	1 046 434	9.2	34.2	37.8	18.8	1.7
MISSOURI................	2 629 296	80.5	11.6	1.5	0.2	2.1	0.6	3.5	23.8	40.6	23.5	2 194 594	8.3	34.1	39.8	17.9	1.7
MONTANA................	422 159	73.9	11.9	0.7	1.0	5.5	0.6	6.4	17.7	43.3	17.5	358 667	6.1	29.9	38.9	25.2	2.0
NEBRASKA..............	873 197	80.0	10.5	0.7	0.4	3.2	0.5	4.6	18.0	34.8	17.8	666 184	6.3	31.0	40.4	22.3	1.9
NEVADA...................	923 155	74.5	14.7	3.9	0.8	2.7	0.8	2.6	23.3	50.5	22.1	751 165	8.7	37.9	37.8	15.5	1.7
NEW HAMPSHIRE.....	638 565	81.8	9.8	0.7	0.3	2.9	0.6	4.0	25.3	47.3	25.1	474 606	5.8	31.1	44.5	18.7	1.8
NEW JERSEY...........	3 876 433	73.0	10.6	9.6	0.3	3.1	0.7	2.7	30.0	56.6	27.1	3 064 645	12.7	34.8	37.9	14.7	1.6
NEW MEXICO	759 177	75.8	14.8	0.8	0.8	2.8	0.8	4.2	21.9	37.8	21.8	677 971	6.7	35.0	38.2	20.0	1.8
NEW YORK...............	8 211 916	56.3	9.2	24.4	0.3	6.2	0.5	3.0	31.7	50.5	25.4	7 056 860	29.7	33.0	27.3	10.0	1.2
NORTH CAROLINA ...	3 837 773	79.4	14.0	0.9	0.3	1.9	0.8	2.7	24.0	37.3	23.8	3 132 013	7.5	32.3	39.9	20.3	1.8
NORTH DAKOTA.......	319 481	77.7	10.0	0.4	0.4	5.0	0.5	6.0	15.8	26.1	15.8	257 152	6.6	30.1	39.1	24.2	1.9
OHIO	5 307 502	82.8	9.3	2.1	0.2	2.4	0.5	2.8	22.9	39.5	22.5	4 445 773	8.6	33.5	39.4	18.6	1.8
OKLAHOMA	1 539 792	80.0	13.2	0.5	0.3	2.1	0.8	3.1	21.7	33.8	21.7	1 342 293	7.0	34.9	39.9	18.1	1.8
OREGON	1 601 378	73.2	12.2	4.2	1.2	3.6	0.7	5.0	22.2	39.3	21.5	1 333 723	7.5	32.8	39.9	19.9	1.8
PENNSYLVANIA........	5 556 311	76.5	10.4	5.2	0.3	4.1	0.5	3.0	25.2	45.2	24.0	4 777 003	12.8	34.9	37.5	14.8	1.6
RHODE ISLAND	490 905	80.1	10.4	2.5	0.3	3.8	0.6	2.2	22.5	44.5	21.9	408 424	10.9	36.4	38.3	14.3	1.6
SOUTH CAROLINA ...	1 822 969	79.4	14.0	0.8	0.3	2.3	1.0	2.1	24.3	41.4	24.2	1 533 854	9.0	33.6	39.1	18.3	1.7
SOUTH DAKOTA......	372 648	77.3	10.4	0.5	0.3	4.5	0.5	6.5	16.6	29.4	16.5	290 245	6.1	29.9	38.7	25.3	2.0
TENNESSEE	2 618 404	81.7	12.5	0.8	0.2	1.5	0.7	2.6	24.5	41.7	24.3	2 232 905	7.7	32.3	39.9	20.1	1.8
TEXAS.....................	9 157 875	77.7	14.5	1.9	0.4	1.9	0.9	2.8	25.4	46.7	25.0	7 393 354	7.4	36.0	40.9	15.7	1.7
UTAH.......................	1 032 858	75.5	14.1	2.2	0.6	2.8	0.6	4.2	21.3	42.2	20.8	701 281	5.1	26.9	41.9	26.1	2.0
VERMONT	311 839	75.2	11.9	0.7	0.4	5.6	0.6	5.7	21.6	31.3	21.6	240 634	6.8	33.6	43.1	16.4	1.8
VIRGINIA..................	3 481 820	77.1	12.7	3.6	0.3	2.3	0.8	3.2	27.0	44.3	26.3	2 699 173	7.7	31.6	39.6	21.2	1.8
WASHINGTON...........	2 785 479	73.3	12.8	4.9	0.7	3.2	0.7	4.3	25.5	44.3	24.5	2 271 398	7.4	31.7	39.4	21.5	1.8
WEST VIRGINIA........	718 106	80.3	12.7	0.8	0.1	2.9	0.7	2.4	26.2	41.2	26.1	736 481	10.8	35.4	38.4	15.3	1.6
WISCONSIN.............	2 690 704	79.5	9.9	2.0	0.5	3.7	0.4	3.9	20.8	37.4	20.5	2 084 544	7.9	32.5	41.5	18.1	1.8
WYOMING	239 809	75.4	13.2	1.4	0.6	4.4	0.7	4.3	17.8	49.1	17.3	193 608	4.6	29.2	38.7	27.5	2.0

Table C-3. States and Counties — Migration, Housing, and Transportation

STATE/County code	MSA/PMSA/NECMA code[1]	STATE County	Residence in 1995 (percent)						Occupied housing units		Householders 65 years and over	
			Total population 5 years and over	Same house	Same county, different house	Same state, different county	Different state	Outside the United States	Number	Percent owner-occupied	Number	Percent owner-occupied
			1	2	3	4	5	6	7	8	9	10
00 000	...	UNITED STATES....	262 375 152	54.1	24.9	9.7	8.4	2.9	105 480 101	66.2	22 634 690	77.6
01 000	...	ALABAMA	4 152 278	57.4	24.7	8.8	7.9	1.2	1 737 080	72.5	394 617	81.7
01 001	5240	Autauga County	40 526	55.1	19.6	13.3	11.1	0.9	16 003	80.8	3 054	87.2
01 003	5160	Baldwin County	131 862	53.2	21.9	9.5	14.2	1.3	55 336	79.6	14 503	87.1
01 005	...	Barbour County	27 238	60.5	21.0	9.3	7.5	1.6	10 409	73.2	2 670	77.6
01 007	...	Bibb County	19 429	64.3	15.1	15.2	4.2	1.3	7 421	80.2	1 735	82.3
01 009	1000	Blount County	47 360	59.4	19.5	15.3	4.7	1.1	19 265	83.5	4 545	82.8
01 011	...	Bullock County	11 003	59.4	17.4	16.4	4.3	2.6	3 986	74.4	1 099	85.0
01 013	...	Butler County	20 009	62.2	27.3	5.9	4.4	0.2	8 398	76.2	2 309	78.6
01 015	0450	Calhoun County	105 320	57.1	27.2	6.9	7.8	1.0	45 307	72.5	10 943	83.9
01 017	...	Chambers County	34 148	63.6	24.3	5.1	6.6	0.4	14 522	75.7	3 838	83.8
01 019	...	Cherokee County	22 558	63.4	16.9	7.5	11.4	0.8	9 719	81.7	2 403	83.1
01 021	...	Chilton County	36 939	61.8	20.7	12.1	4.7	0.8	15 287	82.2	3 681	82.6
01 023	...	Choctaw County	14 849	69.7	20.5	4.8	4.4	0.0	6 063	86.3	1 573	85.5
01 025	...	Clarke County	25 791	69.8	20.1	6.1	3.5	0.4	10 578	81.1	2 606	86.7
01 027	...	Clay County	13 393	68.1	17.7	10.4	3.3	0.5	5 765	77.2	1 543	76.8
01 029	...	Cleburne County	13 280	66.9	17.7	5.3	9.6	0.7	5 590	80.4	1 365	86.0
01 031	...	Coffee County	40 914	55.3	19.9	10.1	12.1	2.6	17 421	71.4	4 231	81.8
01 033	2650	Colbert County	51 637	62.2	23.4	9.1	4.8	0.6	22 461	75.7	5 675	80.6
01 035	...	Conecuh County	13 256	71.1	17.3	6.7	4.5	0.4	5 792	81.1	1 596	78.7
01 037	...	Coosa County	11 467	66.2	12.9	17.6	2.9	0.4	4 682	84.8	1 202	85.9
01 039	...	Covington County	35 423	63.1	23.1	6.6	6.7	0.4	15 640	77.7	4 724	82.4
01 041	...	Crenshaw County	12 859	65.4	19.3	10.7	4.2	0.3	5 577	76.6	1 649	76.8
01 043	...	Cullman County	72 614	59.2	24.7	9.5	5.6	1.0	30 706	78.1	7 225	80.4
01 045	2180	Dale County	45 333	51.8	18.5	9.8	16.3	3.6	18 878	64.2	4 032	82.1
01 047	...	Dallas County	42 959	65.0	25.8	3.9	4.3	0.9	17 841	65.7	4 504	74.4
01 049	...	DeKalb County	60 078	60.2	23.0	8.7	6.6	1.4	25 113	78.7	5 939	81.0
01 051	5240	Elmore County	61 694	53.3	17.1	20.5	8.3	0.8	22 737	81.4	4 729	84.5
01 053	...	Escambia County	36 076	61.3	22.3	7.9	7.9	0.5	14 297	77.1	3 514	86.5
01 055	2880	Etowah County	96 773	61.6	24.9	7.5	5.1	0.8	41 615	74.4	11 871	81.2
01 057	...	Fayette County	17 424	66.6	19.9	8.7	4.4	0.0	7 102	77.2	2 049	74.3
01 059	...	Franklin County	29 285	61.8	22.3	6.6	7.5	1.8	12 259	74.3	3 151	80.4
01 061	...	Geneva County	24 316	64.2	20.0	8.2	7.1	0.6	10 477	80.6	2 912	84.4
01 063	...	Greene County	9 226	71.1	17.5	6.8	4.2	0.4	3 931	75.6	1 031	82.9
01 065	...	Hale County	15 785	68.1	17.2	9.8	4.2	0.6	6 415	80.2	1 578	81.7
01 067	...	Henry County	15 238	66.0	15.6	12.1	5.5	0.8	6 525	80.9	1 826	85.2
01 069	2180	Houston County	82 828	54.0	27.9	7.6	9.6	0.9	35 834	69.5	7 775	78.9
01 071	...	Jackson County	50 517	61.6	23.6	7.2	7.2	0.4	21 615	77.9	4 940	80.5
01 073	1000	Jefferson County	618 995	56.7	29.4	6.1	6.4	1.4	263 265	66.5	61 747	80.8
01 075	...	Lamar County	15 001	65.3	22.9	5.9	5.2	0.6	6 468	76.9	1 798	75.6
01 077	2650	Lauderdale County	82 805	60.0	24.9	7.7	0.0	0.7	36 088	73.2	8 727	82.7
01 079	2030	Lawrence County	32 625	65.4	21.0	9.3	4.1	0.3	13 538	83.1	2 972	85.3
01 081	0580	Lee County	107 968	44.1	20.8	19.6	14.1	1.4	45 702	62.1	6 270	79.3
01 083	3440	Limestone County	61 239	59.3	22.2	10.4	7.5	0.6	24 688	77.3	5 198	81.3
01 085	...	Lowndes County	12 465	75.7	11.8	9.0	3.2	0.3	4 909	83.4	1 193	88.3
01 087	...	Macon County	22 558	59.2	20.7	8.7	9.7	1.8	8 950	67.3	2 401	76.2
01 089	3440	Madison County	257 992	50.4	28.3	6.3	13.0	2.0	109 955	69.9	19 184	83.2
01 091	...	Marengo County	20 967	68.4	19.1	8.2	3.3	0.9	8 767	79.2	2 168	85.7
01 093	...	Marion County	29 360	61.9	22.6	9.5	5.3	0.7	12 697	77.9	3 489	79.1
01 095	...	Marshall County	76 750	56.2	25.6	10.0	6.2	1.9	32 547	74.7	7 760	80.2
01 097	5160	Mobile County	370 583	58.1	29.9	3.4	7.3	1.3	150 179	68.9	32 917	81.4
01 099	...	Monroe County	22 519	69.0	20.6	6.2	3.9	0.2	9 383	80.4	2 259	84.7
01 101	5240	Montgomery County	208 155	51.9	28.1	8.8	9.7	1.4	86 068	64.0	18 366	77.6
01 103	2030	Morgan County	103 716	56.8	26.5	8.5	7.1	1.1	43 602	73.1	9 423	79.6
01 105	...	Perry County	10 983	65.0	20.7	9.3	4.7	0.4	4 333	73.8	1 286	81.1
01 107	...	Pickens County	19 521	67.3	21.2	5.7	5.3	0.4	8 086	79.2	2 238	80.5
01 109	...	Pike County	27 629	57.0	24.1	11.1	6.2	1.6	11 933	67.2	2 789	80.4
01 111	...	Randolph County	20 929	66.3	20.2	5.4	7.8	0.3	8 642	79.1	2 478	84.3
01 113	1800	Russell County	46 183	56.9	21.0	5.7	14.6	1.7	19 741	62.4	4 649	76.9
01 115	1000	St. Clair County	60 566	59.2	18.1	16.8	5.4	0.4	24 143	83.7	4 867	88.0
01 117	1000	Shelby County	132 542	48.9	17.7	20.9	11.3	1.2	54 631	80.9	7 950	87.7
01 119	...	Sumter County	13 744	67.1	18.7	7.1	6.5	0.5	5 708	72.3	1 452	83.5
01 121	...	Talladega County	75 278	60.4	21.9	11.5	5.6	0.6	30 674	76.4	7 581	81.7
01 123	...	Tallapoosa County	38 899	63.1	23.2	9.4	3.9	0.4	16 656	76.3	4 466	80.5
01 125	8600	Tuscaloosa County	154 505	51.0	27.8	12.1	7.5	1.6	64 517	63.5	12 654	79.5
01 127	...	Walker County	66 242	63.9	24.3	7.4	4.0	0.5	28 364	80.0	7 149	84.9

[1]MSA = Metropolitan Statistical Area. PMSA = Primary MSA. NECMA = New England County Metropolitan Area. See the Appendix A for explanation of these concepts. See Appendix B for list of metropolitan areas identified by type, with component counties.

Table C-3. States and Counties — **Migration, Housing, and Transportation**

STATE County	Owner-occupied by household type (percent)								Median household income			Median housing value (owner estimated)	Median monthly owner costs as a percent of income	
	Family-households					Nonfamily households								
		Married-couple family		Other family										
	Total family households	Total	With own children under 18 years	Total	With own children under 18 years	Total nonfamily households	Two or more adults	Living alone	All households	Owner-occupied households	Renter-occupied households		With a mortgage	Without a mortgage
	11	12	13	14	15	16	17	18	19	20	21	22	23	24
UNITED STATES....	73.8	81.0	76.7	50.4	39.9	49.8	39.3	52.1	41 851	51 323	27 362	111 800	21.7	10.5
ALABAMA	78.7	85.8	81.8	57.2	45.7	57.7	41.3	60.0	33 903	40 619	19 870	76 700	19.8	9.9
Autauga County	83.3	86.8	81.0	70.3	64.6	72.0	60.4	73.4	41 953	46 209	26 996	82 500	19.4	9.9
Baldwin County	84.4	88.5	83.8	65.4	56.7	66.5	55.7	68.1	40 174	43 965	26 480	105 300	20.8	9.9
Barbour County	78.0	87.0	82.4	58.4	50.9	61.1	58.6	61.3	25 080	30 613	12 335	57 200	20.4	10.2
Bibb County................	84.7	88.9	87.5	69.4	55.3	66.2	56.1	67.3	31 402	35 217	17 583	57 400	19.2	9.9
Blount County................	87.2	89.5	87.1	72.5	60.2	70.9	64.5	71.5	35 054	38 324	19 736	76 900	19.6	10.3
Bullock County	76.3	88.9	88.6	62.0	48.7	70.5	65.0	70.9	20 720	24 717	11 804	54 000	29.6	11.6
Butler County	80.4	89.0	85.8	61.5	50.9	66.4	61.5	66.8	24 745	29 896	12 881	48 600	20.5	12.3
Calhoun County	78.4	85.4	77.9	56.2	42.6	59.2	40.2	61.9	31 422	37 538	18 027	65 700	19.0	9.9
Chambers County	79.7	87.8	82.3	61.4	51.3	66.2	53.7	67.2	29 795	33 953	17 247	56 700	18.3	10.7
Cherokee County	83.6	87.7	82.0	62.1	52.7	76.3	82.2	75.9	31 247	34 347	19 448	63 500	19.9	10.2
Chilton County.............	85.8	89.7	86.6	68.5	57.7	71.9	54.0	73.9	32 032	35 610	17 633	70 500	20.6	9.9
Choctaw County	88.8	91.7	92.1	80.4	73.8	80.1	92.0	79.4	25 218	27 434	12 269	46 800	18.4	10.5
Clarke County	84.0	87.7	84.7	73.4	65.1	73.6	53.4	74.8	27 743	30 967	17 971	53 000	18.0	10.1
Clay County..................	83.6	88.0	84.9	66.1	61.6	61.7	60.6	61.9	27 539	32 085	14 485	58 000	19.9	9.9
Cleburne County	84.7	87.8	83.6	66.6	63.2	68.2	58.6	69.5	30 727	33 485	18 839	62 100	20.9	9.9
Coffee County	75.8	81.8	75.9	53.8	45.2	59.9	44.2	61.7	33 142	38 306	20 428	70 200	18.8	9.9
Colbert County	81.0	87.8	85.7	56.2	42.1	62.4	46.4	63.9	31 806	37 450	18 076	68 200	20.0	10.4
Conecuh County	85.4	92.3	93.9	68.8	59.1	71.9	82.1	71.3	21 974	26 917	10 604	48 700	20.5	12.3
Coosa County	88.0	90.9	89.7	77.8	65.7	75.9	64.4	77.0	29 162	31 719	16 640	53 300	21.0	9.9
Covington County.........	82.0	87.8	82.4	59.1	46.0	68.3	60.9	68.9	26 215	29 405	15 612	52 900	19.5	11.0
Crenshaw County	81.2	87.4	83.3	64.1	52.9	66.0	65.0	66.1	25 783	29 057	13 305	48 200	19.1	10.6
Cullman County............	83.3	86.8	83.6	64.8	56.0	63.8	47.9	65.6	32 069	36 441	20 631	78 800	21.6	9.9
Dale County	66.6	73.2	60.2	45.0	33.3	57.9	42.3	59.9	31 493	38 504	21 846	62 800	18.7	9.9
Dallas County	69.5	83.6	77.2	49.6	39.1	56.6	56.7	56.6	23 559	32 311	11 485	57 100	19.9	10.3
DeKalb County	82.5	86.2	81.6	66.5	58.0	68.0	74.9	67.3	29 792	32 933	19 019	61 700	20.0	10.8
Elmore County	85.0	88.4	83.1	70.4	61.1	69.1	49.5	71.5	40 933	45 112	25 829	88 300	19.5	9.9
Escambia County	80.4	87.1	81.8	61.0	46.4	69.2	53.0	71.0	27 979	32 606	16 504	56 700	19.1	9.9
Etowah County	79.2	85.5	78.4	59.4	43.8	62.6	45.3	64.3	31 073	36 466	18 090	66 500	19.7	9.9
Fayette County	83.6	87.9	86.1	62.2	54.6	60.9	60.5	60.9	28 678	32 976	13 716	56 100	20.0	9.9
Franklin County	79.1	84.4	79.0	56.7	48.4	61.0	31.5	63.4	27 181	32 592	15 578	60 700	20.6	10.0
Geneva County	83.4	88.4	83.8	64.6	52.4	73.6	48.1	75.5	26 176	30 327	15 129	52 400	20.2	9.9
Greene County	77.0	84.1	82.2	68.5	56.0	72.8	42.1	74.2	20 151	23 547	11 597	42 600	24.6	13.2
Hale County	84.7	90.7	87.0	73.9	67.9	68.6	94.3	67.2	25 919	29 698	11 899	50 500	19.7	9.9
Henry County	84.3	89.6	89.1	69.1	56.0	71.9	58.2	73.0	29 792	33 817	14 429	57 900	19.8	11.2
Houston County	76.2	83.9	80.0	52.2	39.6	53.3	46.7	54.1	34 372	42 199	19 854	74 500	17.9	9.9
Jackson County.............	82.4	87.2	83.2	63.6	53.3	65.6	67.6	65.4	32 090	36 660	18 777	62 400	19.3	9.9
Jefferson County	73.7	83.4	79.6	52.4	38.6	51.6	36.0	53.8	36 534	45 976	22 919	88 100	20.2	9.9
Lamar County	80.9	85.8	82.5	62.0	50.5	65.8	80.8	64.9	27 962	31 649	14 481	49 400	21.3	9.9
Lauderdale County........	81.0	86.9	82.0	56.6	42.2	55.1	35.5	57.7	33 348	40 932	16 877	80 900	19.8	9.9
Lawrence County	86.4	90.2	89.4	69.4	59.1	72.9	58.1	74.1	31 430	35 513	18 400	64 700	20.5	11.0
Lee County..................	78.1	85.4	82.6	56.9	49.2	38.0	21.8	45.0	30 707	45 615	13 502	85 500	19.8	9.9
Limestone County	82.0	87.5	84.1	58.3	50.1	63.8	52.4	64.9	37 482	43 246	20 863	80 700	18.9	9.9
Lowndes County	85.5	90.3	88.1	78.7	71.7	78.0	80.7	77.7	23 039	26 202	9 282	46 700	22.6	12.7
Macon County	74.3	86.6	83.0	60.3	47.4	55.8	31.3	59.4	21 210	29 545	11 438	61 100	22.3	11.7
Madison County	78.2	85.7	82.5	51.5	41.1	51.4	36.9	53.6	44 688	55 689	25 146	98 300	18.6	9.9
Marengo County	82.8	89.9	88.5	67.0	57.3	69.8	64.3	70.1	28 059	32 896	12 206	53 800	18.7	9.9
Marion County	82.5	87.3	80.7	61.0	53.9	66.3	71.9	65.9	27 284	31 514	16 000	55 900	20.3	9.9
Marshall County	79.3	84.7	79.3	56.7	43.3	62.4	48.8	63.7	32 018	38 354	18 360	76 200	20.7	9.9
Mobile County	74.5	84.2	80.0	51.6	38.4	54.9	39.3	57.3	33 431	41 423	19 103	76 600	20.1	9.9
Monroe County..............	84.4	90.2	87.4	67.7	60.4	70.0	63.9	70.4	28 992	31 980	14 111	51 900	18.6	9.9
Montgomery County......	70.5	80.7	75.8	49.5	38.8	51.4	39.8	53.1	35 888	46 026	22 141	84 900	20.0	9.9
Morgan County..............	79.6	85.5	82.5	55.0	39.8	55.8	43.1	57.1	37 548	45 667	21 395	82 800	19.2	9.9
Perry County	75.1	85.0	80.2	61.8	49.7	70.7	69.8	70.7	20 239	25 770	11 102	39 200	22.4	11.7
Pickens County	83.3	90.4	85.7	66.6	59.9	68.6	68.3	68.6	25 637	29 720	12 965	57 400	20.2	10.4
Pike County..................	76.8	86.5	84.2	55.4	48.1	49.8	27.1	54.2	25 789	33 798	13 012	58 200	20.6	9.9
Randolph County	83.0	88.7	84.7	63.7	49.2	69.3	56.3	70.7	28 434	32 131	17 370	59 900	20.8	9.9
Russell County	66.7	77.3	67.4	45.6	34.1	53.3	48.1	54.0	27 249	32 847	19 391	66 100	21.0	11.1
St. Clair County............	86.8	89.8	85.4	71.5	62.1	73.6	62.3	75.1	37 432	40 549	25 801	81 200	20.5	9.9
Shelby County	88.0	90.6	89.7	72.2	66.6	60.1	44.0	62.8	55 248	61 789	32 429	136 200	19.7	9.9
Sumter County	78.8	87.9	84.6	67.6	53.6	60.8	37.6	64.3	19 133	23 510	9 636	40 700	22.5	10.9
Talladega County	80.7	87.6	84.9	60.4	48.8	65.4	56.1	66.2	31 044	35 821	15 622	62 000	20.3	9.9
Tallapoosa County	80.9	87.4	83.7	62.1	45.0	65.1	68.1	64.8	30 638	36 203	17 689	65 000	20.7	9.9
Tuscaloosa County	74.6	84.1	82.6	49.2	38.5	42.8	22.7	47.4	33 632	45 783	17 302	95 400	20.4	9.9
Walker County...............	84.0	88.1	84.6	69.6	57.5	69.4	68.2	69.5	28 856	32 037	16 534	55 600	20.0	10.0

STATE County	Median gross rent	Percent who pay 35 percent or more of income for housing expenses		Means of transportation to work (percent except where noted)							Vehicles available (percent of households)		
		Owners	Renters	Number of workers 16 years and over	Car, truck, or van		Public transportation	Other means	Walked		No vehicles	One vehicle	Two or more vehicles
					Drove alone	Carpooled							
	25	26	27	28	29	30	31	32	33		34	35	36
UNITED STATES....	602	15.8	29.5	128 279 228	75.7	12.2	4.7	1.2	2.9		10.3	34.2	55.5
ALABAMA	447	13.9	27.4	1 900 089	83.0	12.3	0.5	0.8	1.3		8.3	32.3	59.5
Autauga County	537	11.1	22.2	19 808	83.2	13.3	0.2	0.8	0.7		5.2	27.7	67.1
Baldwin County	566	14.1	26.2	62 219	82.8	11.1	0.3	1.0	1.2		4.2	31.6	64.2
Barbour County	333	16.2	28.0	10 023	78.7	16.4	0.2	0.7	1.8		12.5	33.6	53.9
Bibb County.................	348	15.0	21.9	7 875	79.5	16.2	0.5	1.0	1.3		9.7	28.2	62.1
Blount County	385	13.0	16.5	22 255	78.8	17.0	0.2	0.6	1.0		5.4	24.5	70.1
Bullock County	324	21.0	37.6	3 382	71.3	18.8	0.0	1.7	5.1		17.6	37.1	45.3
Butler County	328	17.6	27.7	7 881	78.9	15.7	0.1	1.7	0.6		12.1	34.8	53.2
Calhoun County	413	11.7	27.8	47 181	85.1	10.6	0.5	0.9	1.2		7.9	32.0	60.1
Chambers County	374	12.3	28.2	15 480	82.1	14.5	0.3	0.5	1.4		10.2	35.0	54.9
Cherokee County	362	14.6	21.5	10 014	81.5	14.8	0.2	0.4	0.9		6.0	27.2	66.8
Chilton County	385	15.4	20.5	17 151	78.9	16.7	0.2	0.8	1.0		7.0	26.5	66.4
Choctaw County	284	13.7	17.9	5 382	75.3	19.9	0.0	0.6	1.0		11.0	31.1	57.9
Clarke County	343	14.2	20.0	10 226	80.4	15.3	0.3	1.1	1.6		11.3	32.4	56.4
Clay County	272	13.8	18.3	5 828	83.9	12.0	0.3	0.3	1.7		8.4	27.3	64.2
Cleburne County	378	12.5	20.1	6 060	80.2	16.0	0.3	1.0	1.3		6.1	26.4	67.5
Coffee County	415	9.8	22.4	18 974	83.2	11.8	0.2	1.7	1.1		7.5	30.5	62.0
Colbert County	414	15.1	27.9	22 593	87.1	10.2	0.2	0.5	0.9		6.4	29.7	63.9
Conecuh County	289	19.4	25.9	4 771	77.9	16.7	0.1	0.8	1.2		11.6	35.7	52.7
Coosa County	295	11.4	22.7	4 750	83.1	13.7	0.4	0.7	0.7		8.1	26.4	65.5
Covington County	340	13.2	23.3	15 116	80.3	13.4	0.1	1.5	1.7		8.8	31.9	59.3
Crenshaw County.........	279	13.0	20.7	5 400	72.5	20.4	0.1	1.5	2.4		11.5	31.8	56.7
Cullman County............	398	15.0	21.2	34 619	81.8	12.7	0.2	0.5	1.4		6.3	27.2	66.5
Dale County	398	13.0	19.5	21 313	82.7	10.9	0.5	1.4	2.6		6.3	34.0	59.6
Dallas County	350	17.3	30.7	15 003	81.8	14.2	0.9	0.9	1.1		16.2	37.4	46.4
DeKalb County	370	14.9	17.6	28 637	81.1	13.5	0.2	0.8	1.3		6.1	29.1	64.8
Elmore County	486	12.4	22.8	28 143	84.4	12.1	0.2	0.4	0.7		4.1	25.2	70.7
Escambia County	351	14.2	21.7	14 316	81.1	14.4	0.7	1.1	1.6		9.2	31.7	59.1
Etowah County	395	13.3	25.0	42 636	84.5	11.9	0.1	0.7	0.9		7.6	32.3	60.1
Fayette County.............	283	11.9	18.0	7 294	84.0	12.0	0.1	0.9	1.4		8.1	29.3	62.5
Franklin County	335	16.1	21.8	12 839	79.0	16.4	0.5	0.7	1.0		8.3	29.4	62.3
Geneva County	319	15.8	23.3	10 614	82.7	11.4	0.0	1.3	1.4		7.9	31.7	60.4
Greene County	235	19.8	20.3	3 064	75.9	17.2	0.8	0.7	2.0		16.3	38.7	45.0
Hale County	295	16.8	20.6	5 725	77.2	17.3	0.3	1.0	1.6		15.6	31.5	52.9
Henry County	336	14.2	22.5	6 612	82.4	13.6	0.2	0.6	0.6		9.1	31.6	59.2
Houston County	413	12.0	25.1	39 962	85.7	10.3	0.6	1.0	0.9		8.3	34.2	57.6
Jackson County............	370	11.8	19.8	24 394	83.4	12.6	0.2	0.8	1.3		7.2	26.2	66.6
Jefferson County	500	15.4	28.4	292 449	83.3	11.7	1.1	0.7	1.3		9.9	36.1	54.0
Lamar County	282	15.1	22.5	6 420	85.3	10.7	0.3	0.9	1.7		8.2	28.2	63.7
Lauderdale County	420	12.4	29.7	35 478	85.3	10.4	0.2	0.6	1.6		6.0	28.9	65.1
Lawrence County	361	14.7	22.3	14 479	84.4	12.3	0.0	0.6	0.8		7.7	25.7	66.6
Lee County	449	12.5	44.1	52 119	84.1	10.8	0.5	0.9	1.9		6.8	34.3	58.9
Limestone County	392	10.6	20.0	29 283	83.9	12.3	0.3	0.6	1.0		6.6	26.2	67.2
Lowndes County	298	20.6	28.6	4 405	76.1	18.9	0.5	1.3	0.9		15.1	33.4	51.5
Macon County	352	20.2	32.8	7 982	74.2	18.5	0.3	0.9	4.1		18.8	36.1	45.1
Madison County	503	10.8	26.1	134 044	83.9	11.3	0.4	0.7	1.3		5.6	31.2	63.3
Marengo County...........	305	15.6	23.2	7 955	78.9	15.1	1.0	1.0	2.6		14.4	33.7	51.9
Marion County	328	14.0	19.6	12 593	84.6	11.5	0.3	0.7	1.2		8.9	29.6	61.5
Marshall County	406	13.2	20.0	36 048	82.3	13.1	0.1	0.7	1.0		6.9	29.2	63.9
Mobile County	476	15.4	31.4	162 389	82.7	12.5	0.8	0.9	1.3		8.9	35.3	55.8
Monroe County	351	12.9	26.6	9 053	82.1	11.3	0.2	3.0	1.2		10.5	32.6	56.8
Montgomery County......	526	14.9	30.2	96 943	82.7	12.4	0.7	0.8	1.6		9.8	37.5	52.7
Morgan County.............	429	11.2	23.5	49 769	85.5	10.7	0.2	0.7	1.0		6.3	29.9	63.9
Perry County	341	18.8	33.1	3 424	73.8	20.1	0.3	0.6	3.8		16.6	39.0	44.4
Pickens County	245	16.1	18.2	7 524	82.3	13.7	0.2	0.9	0.9		11.8	32.3	55.8
Pike County	334	13.5	30.2	12 527	79.1	14.7	0.3	1.0	2.9		11.4	35.9	52.6
Randolph County	312	14.0	17.5	8 978	76.7	18.7	0.0	0.8	1.7		7.9	29.4	62.8
Russell County	428	16.8	26.5	19 859	81.9	13.9	0.8	1.1	1.3		12.6	35.8	51.6
St. Clair County	482	13.0	18.5	27 773	81.7	14.3	0.1	0.7	1.1		4.8	25.6	69.6
Shelby County..............	635	11.8	21.6	73 773	86.2	9.0	0.1	0.4	1.0		3.4	26.0	70.6
Sumter County	298	18.3	27.8	4 568	77.3	13.9	2.1	1.9	3.2		19.4	37.9	42.7
Talladega County	351	14.8	23.2	31 443	83.9	12.2	0.7	0.8	1.2		10.2	30.0	59.7
Tallapoosa County	358	14.2	24.9	17 009	82.2	14.0	0.2	0.9	0.8		9.4	30.3	60.3
Tuscaloosa County	487	13.6	36.2	73 292	84.0	10.6	0.5	0.7	2.2		8.4	34.5	57.1
Walker County..............	368	15.5	23.2	27 448	83.7	12.9	0.2	1.0	0.8		7.5	30.4	62.1

Table C-3. States and Counties — **Migration, Housing, and Transportation**

STATE/County code	MSA/PMSA/NECMA code[1]	STATE County	Residence in 1995 (percent)						Occupied housing units		Householders 65 years and over	
			Total population 5 years and over	Same house	Same county, different house	Same state, different county	Different state	Outside the United States	Number	Percent owner-occupied	Number	Percent owner-occupied
			1	2	3	4	5	6	7	8	9	10
		ALABAMA—Cont'd										
01 129	...	Washington County	16 759	74.5	14.5	7.0	3.7	0.3	6 705	88.2	1 490	91.8
01 131	...	Wilcox County	12 100	69.1	20.5	6.3	3.6	0.5	4 776	83.3	1 299	83.2
01 133	...	Winston County	23 293	62.9	20.7	10.9	4.8	0.6	10 107	80.0	2 377	79.3
02 000	...	ALASKA	579 740	46.2	27.7	7.5	16.5	2.2	221 600	62.5	23 157	76.7
02 013	...	Aleutians East Borough	2 586	56.5	7.2	4.2	27.9	4.2	526	58.4	42	90.5
02 016	...	Aleutians West Census Area	5 220	38.3	16.9	6.8	31.2	6.8	1 270	27.8	61	67.2
02 020	0380	Anchorage Municipality	240 627	41.6	32.2	5.4	17.9	2.8	94 822	60.0	8 779	73.6
02 050	...	Bethel Census Area	14 405	63.3	24.4	6.3	5.4	0.6	4 226	60.9	566	80.2
02 060	...	Bristol Bay Borough	1 169	56.1	16.9	14.6	12.0	0.3	490	51.0	47	76.6
02 068	...	Denali Borough	1 795	54.5	11.9	11.9	20.2	1.5	785	64.7	38	94.7
02 070	...	Dillingham Census Area	4 435	65.3	17.4	9.1	7.4	0.8	1 529	60.6	222	77.5
02 090	...	Fairbanks North Star Borough	76 200	39.4	26.1	6.7	24.8	3.0	29 777	54.0	2 593	70.8
02 100	...	Haines Borough	2 266	52.2	20.0	13.3	12.8	1.7	991	69.7	166	74.1
02 110	...	Juneau City and Borough	28 711	45.1	31.2	8.2	13.9	1.4	11 543	63.8	1 252	75.2
02 122	...	Kenai Peninsula Borough	46 359	53.8	24.6	8.8	12.1	0.7	18 438	73.7	2 260	81.1
02 130	...	Ketchikan Gateway Borough	13 135	48.7	28.6	8.4	13.2	1.1	5 399	60.7	716	77.1
02 150	...	Kodiak Island Borough	12 567	39.1	27.7	7.8	20.9	4.5	4 424	54.8	457	77.2
02 164	...	Lake and Peninsula Borough	1 675	73.4	10.8	8.9	6.2	0.7	588	67.5	72	80.6
02 170	...	Matanuska-Susitna Borough	55 170	49.4	21.8	14.1	13.5	1.2	20 556	78.8	2 387	84.6
02 180	...	Nome Census Area	8 395	62.3	24.3	6.7	6.1	0.6	2 693	58.2	396	83.3
02 185	...	North Slope Borough	6 679	51.6	29.3	8.9	8.4	1.8	2 109	48.8	201	90.5
02 188	...	Northwest Arctic Borough	6 444	60.2	25.8	7.7	5.9	0.4	1 780	56.3	243	86.8
02 201	...	Prince of Wales-Outer Ketchikan Cens	5 706	54.9	26.6	8.1	9.8	0.5	2 262	70.1	254	79.5
02 220	...	Sitka City and Borough	8 317	43.0	26.0	9.0	20.7	1.3	3 278	58.1	438	72.1
02 232	...	Skagway-Hoonah-Angoon Census Area	3 251	59.7	17.0	10.8	12.1	0.5	1 369	63.6	172	77.3
02 240	...	Southeast Fairbanks Census Area	5 739	55.9	15.2	8.7	17.0	3.2	2 098	69.1	284	82.7
02 261	...	Valdez-Cordova Census Area	9 533	52.1	21.0	11.1	14.0	1.8	3 884	67.8	419	80.9
02 270	...	Wade Hampton Census Area	6 288	75.0	17.6	4.4	2.8	0.2	1 602	66.4	260	76.5
02 280	...	Wrangell-Petersburg Census Area	6 234	55.9	27.0	6.5	9.8	0.7	2 587	70.4	453	77.3
02 282	...	Yakutat City and Borough	760	54.2	19.2	11.8	14.5	0.3	265	59.6	22	72.7
02 290	...	Yukon-Koyukuk Census Area	6 074	62.3	19.4	11.6	6.3	0.4	2 309	67.2	357	84.9
04 000	...	ARIZONA	4 752 724	44.3	30.6	4.5	16.8	3.9	1 901 327	68.0	430 278	83.6
04 001	...	Apache County	63 202	70.6	14.4	6.9	7.4	0.7	19 971	74.3	3 952	87.1
04 003	...	Cochise County	110 047	46.4	22.9	7.4	19.0	4.3	43 893	67.3	11 425	83.9
04 005	2620	Coconino County	107 775	46.2	23.0	13.8	15.4	1.6	40 448	61.4	5 735	85.8
04 007	...	Gila County	48 370	54.5	18.8	16.3	9.7	0.7	20 140	78.7	6 532	89.7
04 009	...	Graham County	30 909	57.5	18.8	13.6	7.6	2.4	10 116	73.2	2 538	84.9
04 011	...	Greenlee County	7 855	57.1	20.9	10.9	10.2	0.9	3 117	51.0	580	87.2
04 012	...	La Paz County	18 774	54.2	17.3	4.6	22.2	1.7	8 362	78.1	3 370	90.5
04 013	6200	Maricopa County	2 832 694	41.6	34.1	2.4	17.4	4.6	1 132 886	67.5	230 086	82.6
04 015	4120	Mohave County	145 803	46.2	21.3	4.2	26.9	1.4	62 809	73.6	20 725	87.1
04 017	...	Navajo County	89 175	60.6	20.0	11.9	6.4	1.2	30 043	75.5	6 418	88.1
04 019	8520	Pima County	788 868	46.2	31.2	4.5	15.1	3.1	332 350	64.3	77 969	80.9
04 021	6200	Pinal County	167 639	47.2	19.3	15.9	15.3	2.3	61 364	77.4	18 642	90.0
04 023	...	Santa Cruz County	35 184	55.2	28.6	5.9	5.7	4.6	11 809	68.0	2 560	80.5
04 025	...	Yavapai County	158 931	44.1	21.7	12.9	19.6	1.7	70 171	73.4	23 356	85.7
04 027	9360	Yuma County	147 498	46.1	27.4	2.8	18.6	5.1	53 848	72.2	16 390	88.7
05 000	...	ARKANSAS	2 492 205	53.3	24.8	10.5	10.1	1.4	1 042 696	69.4	248 583	81.0
05 001	...	Arkansas County	19 372	60.8	25.7	8.5	4.5	0.4	8 457	67.8	2 096	80.5
05 003	...	Ashley County	22 588	61.6	26.4	4.9	6.5	0.6	9 384	76.2	2 313	78.8
05 005	...	Baxter County	36 699	55.0	19.5	7.5	17.9	0.2	17 052	79.7	6 628	87.7
05 007	2580	Benton County	141 889	45.2	24.0	8.0	20.5	2.3	58 212	72.2	14 103	86.6
05 009	...	Boone County	31 824	53.5	22.8	9.3	13.7	0.7	13 851	73.3	3 663	84.5
05 011	...	Bradley County	11 855	62.8	19.1	8.1	8.8	1.2	4 834	72.5	1 378	83.6
05 013	...	Calhoun County	5 431	65.0	16.3	14.1	3.5	1.1	2 317	82.2	654	87.6
05 015	...	Carroll County	23 779	53.5	20.4	7.2	15.7	3.1	10 189	73.0	2 475	84.4
05 017	...	Chicot County	13 145	61.8	22.3	6.6	8.2	1.1	5 205	69.6	1 623	78.3
05 019	...	Clark County	22 142	50.5	22.5	16.1	8.6	2.4	8 912	65.6	2 265	81.4
05 021	...	Clay County	16 553	59.6	26.3	5.7	8.1	0.3	7 417	74.9	2 466	82.6
05 023	...	Cleburne County	22 822	56.7	16.9	14.8	11.0	0.6	10 190	80.6	3 289	86.6
05 025	...	Cleveland County	8 001	64.4	17.3	12.6	4.6	1.0	3 273	82.2	809	89.1
05 027	...	Columbia County	24 019	58.5	25.7	7.4	7.4	1.0	9 981	71.3	2 950	78.9

[1]MSA = Metropolitan Statistical Area. PMSA = Primary MSA. NECMA = New England County Metropolitan Area. See the Appendix A for explanation of these concepts. See Appendix B for list of metropolitan areas identified by type, with component counties.

STATE County	Owner-occupied by household type (percent)								Median household income			Median housing value (owner estimated)	Median monthly owner costs as a percent of income	
	Family-households					Nonfamily households								
		Married-couple family		Other family										
	Total family households	Total	With own children under 18 years	Total	With own children under 18 years	Total nonfamily households	Two or more adults	Living alone	All households	Owner-occupied households	Renter-occupied households		With a mortgage	Without a mortgage
	11	12	13	14	15	16	17	18	19	20	21	22	23	24

ALABAMA—Cont'd														
Washington County.......	89.7	92.8	94.4	77.3	71.0	83.3	68.9	84.0	31 223	33 342	16 369	51 800	18.1	9.9
Wilcox County	85.5	89.2	84.5	80.7	76.9	77.8	74.1	78.1	16 620	19 196	8 496	39 500	24.6	11.9
Winston County	84.6	88.3	82.6	67.5	64.2	67.7	63.6	67.9	28 320	31 121	15 453	53 200	19.9	9.9
ALASKA	69.2	74.7	70.9	50.8	44.5	47.5	45.1	48.3	51 441	63 384	35 406	137 400	22.3	9.9
Aleutians East Borough	67.9	68.1	67.5	67.6	66.3	39.5	29.4	42.0	46 250	47 708	45 469	98 800	15.8	11.1
Aleutians West Census Area.................	36.6	33.5	35.2	46.3	31.7	15.4	12.9	16.2	60 071	60 313	60 040	95 700	21.8	14.8
Anchorage Municipality.	67.3	74.2	70.4	44.8	39.3	44.8	42.6	45.6	55 441	71 772	35 414	152 300	22.6	9.9
Bethel Census Area......	67.1	68.7	70.0	64.2	53.5	41.7	44.6	41.0	35 990	34 505	38 849	77 400	22.3	15.5
Bristol Bay Borough	63.2	66.9	69.2	45.3	45.0	31.2	55.6	25.3	52 647	57 778	49 688	136 200	21.8	11.7
Denali Borough	80.1	82.4	79.4	71.6	63.5	43.7	46.3	43.2	54 896	62 386	41 442	108 300	20.1	9.9
Dillingham Census Area	68.3	72.8	73.9	58.0	39.8	41.0	34.3	42.3	42 703	42 837	42 500	108 200	19.8	16.8
Fairbanks North Star Borough...............	59.7	63.6	56.6	44.2	36.5	41.2	37.4	42.3	48 591	65 153	33 479	128 800	22.1	9.9
Haines Borough	78.0	81.7	78.6	61.7	55.2	53.2	49.3	54.2	40 919	50 117	25 682	122 900	20.8	9.9
Juneau City and Borough..................	73.4	79.4	76.9	51.9	43.5	44.1	40.0	45.4	62 496	76 873	37 402	179 200	23.0	9.9
Kenai Peninsula Borough..................	80.0	85.5	83.0	57.2	54.1	59.4	60.7	59.1	46 655	54 450	29 153	115 300	21.2	9.9
Ketchikan Gateway Borough..................	69.0	76.4	75.2	44.8	34.3	43.8	32.4	46.8	51 603	65 551	35 662	160 300	24.2	9.9
Kodiak Island Borough..	58.0	61.2	57.8	45.0	42.9	45.9	34.7	49.3	53 613	70 127	41 882	152 800	21.2	10.8
Lake and Peninsula Borough..................	74.8	74.5	78.2	75.4	76.8	50.0	63.0	47.6	37 500	40 511	32 917	91 600	20.3	15.7
Matanuska-Susitna Borough..................	83.3	88.5	86.6	62.0	56.3	66.4	68.4	65.8	50 698	55 848	29 041	122 500	22.0	9.9
Nome Census Area.......	66.0	64.9	64.5	67.5	58.0	39.3	31.4	41.3	41 306	39 211	45 203	79 000	20.2	18.1
North Slope Borough	56.2	55.3	58.8	57.5	50.8	29.3	22.0	31.3	63 750	67 313	61 083	113 900	17.8	10.6
Northwest Arctic Borough..................	60.7	63.7	65.0	56.I	48.0	39.8	38.2	40.2	45 449	42 300	48 684	94 900	24.9	16.5
Prince of Wales-Outer Ketchikan Cens.....	74.3	77.3	75.3	64.3	55.7	60.9	61.9	60.7	40 439	43 411	35 742	91 500	21.0	12.6
Sitka City and Borough.	67.9	73.8	68.5	45.4	37.6	37.0	34.6	37.7	51 490	64 462	35 313	174 700	24.4	9.9
Skagway-Hoonah-Angoon Census Area.	70.9	71.7	65.0	68.0	56.3	51.I	60.9	48.9	41 647	44 792	38 300	120 000	23.7	11.9
Southeast Fairbanks Census Area	70.4	73.8	65.8	56.2	49.2	65.9	54.4	68.3	38 186	45 952	27 197	90 900	18.1	9.9
Valdez-Cordova Census Area	73.5	78.4	75.7	54.2	48.7	56.8	59.8	56.0	49 031	60 201	35 205	117 400	19.6	11.8
Wade Hampton Census Area..................	70.0	69.9	72.3	70.0	66.6	51.0	45.5	52.0	30 265	28 774	34 444	40 000	22.6	15.9
Wrangell-Petersburg Census Area	74.9	80.3	77.0	52.6	53.5	60.4	76.2	57.4	46 195	51 004	33 523	140 100	24.2	14.1
Yakutat City and Borough..................	70.6	73.3	70.8	65.5	63.9	42.9	72.7	34.9	47 188	54 167	33 958	97 600	21.1	9.9
Yukon-Koyukuk Census Area..................	72.3	73.9	69.0	70.0	64.0	58.1	63.2	57.2	28 990	29 125	28 826	62 000	21.6	15.3
ARIZONA	74.7	81.0	74.3	53.2	44.4	53.9	44.4	56.7	40 388	48 411	27 332	109 400	22.1	9.9
Apache County..............	75.6	78.4	73.9	70.6	62.7	70.1	63.1	70.8	22 994	22 083	25 402	39 200	19.9	9.9
Cochise County............	71.2	76.6	64.6	51.0	38.0	58.0	47.6	59.7	32 102	38 207	23 837	80 200	21.1	9.9
Coconino County..........	70.2	76.8	73.1	50.4	43.0	43.3	27.8	50.9	38 296	47 796	27 275	124 700	22.1	9.9
Gila County	81.3	86.2	74.2	62.7	49.8	72.7	70.8	72.9	30 374	33 675	21 580	90 100	23.3	10.7
Graham County	75.5	80.9	73.9	58.8	49.6	66.0	52.1	68.3	29 344	34 957	19 098	72 800	20.8	10.2
Greenlee County	53.0	53.8	41.4	49.8	37.0	45.8	33.7	47.2	38 878	34 315	41 577	59 800	19.4	9.9
La Paz County	80.2	85.1	69.2	58.9	52.9	73.7	70.5	74.5	25 691	26 505	22 070	54 000	21.9	9.9
Maricopa County	74.6	81.2	75.6	51.9	43.7	52.7	43.4	55.6	45 167	54 648	30 063	122 000	22.0	9.9
Mohave County	76.7	82.5	69.6	52.7	41.8	66.5	57.4	69.1	31 366	34 084	24 842	79 500	23.3	10.4
Navajo County	77.7	82.7	75.5	64.8	57.4	68.0	60.6	69.1	28 659	31 942	21 210	69 200	20.4	9.9
Pima County	73.3	80.3	74.3	51.6	42.4	48.2	40.4	50.3	36 532	46 347	23 673	102 600	22.3	9.9
Pinal County................	79.9	85.2	73.9	60.9	52.0	70.4	67.2	71.2	35 658	39 140	24 416	76 300	22.2	9.9
Santa Cruz County.......	70.3	74.1	67.8	54.9	54.9	58.0	53.9	58.6	29 452	34 688	20 509	92 800	26.1	10.3
Yavapai County	79.0	83.2	71.9	57.6	45.5	62.2	51.4	64.9	34 710	38 632	24 678	114 700	24.3	9.9
Yuma County	73.8	78.3	67.5	54.2	43.1	66.8	60.2	68.2	31 880	35 809	23 435	72 100	22.5	9.9
ARKANSAS..............	75.2	82.1	75.5	51.0	39.4	55.5	41.8	57.6	32 097	38 238	21 167	67 400	19.4	9.9
Arkansas County...........	71.7	79.9	68.6	49.9	33.4	58.3	62.6	57.8	30 282	36 991	18 979	52 600	18.8	10.3
Ashley County..............	80.3	87.0	80.5	56.9	41.4	64.6	40.7	66.8	32 144	36 664	19 697	49 200	18.1	10.4
Baxter County..............	85.1	89.7	82.3	56.5	38.6	67.8	51.5	69.8	29 261	32 100	19 066	79 900	21.2	9.9
Benton County.............	77.0	81.5	73.0	52.5	43.8	57.8	44.4	60.4	40 268	45 266	28 624	92 900	19.7	9.9
Boone County..............	79.7	83.7	78.3	60.0	44.7	57.1	54.5	57.4	30 115	34 177	18 134	73 900	20.8	9.9
Bradley County............	76.4	83.1	76.0	56.4	40.6	63.1	60.7	63.2	25 519	29 937	13 926	44 600	19.1	11.9
Calhoun County...........	82.9	86.1	79.2	71.3	63.8	80.4	63.0	81.7	28 147	29 847	22 969	35 200	17.0	10.6
Carroll County	76.9	80.9	69.9	60.3	55.5	64.0	44.6	67.7	27 764	30 809	21 243	80 200	23.1	11.8
Chicot County..............	72.2	80.6	72.3	57.8	42.9	63.5	53.8	64.5	21 493	25 742	15 046	40 800	23.5	14.8
Clark County................	74.2	81.9	75.3	48.3	35.4	49.2	21.1	54.5	28 610	35 530	15 326	62 000	19.2	9.9
Clay County................	78.6	82.5	74.3	56.2	43.1	67.0	53.2	68.6	25 047	27 882	17 892	40 100	18.8	11.5
Cleburne County..........	85.1	89.3	82.0	61.0	50.5	68.6	63.0	69.2	31 340	34 055	19 197	77 600	21.9	10.4
Cleveland County.........	85.8	88.9	85.8	70.2	60.4	70.4	56.6	71.5	32 250	35 825	19 583	47 800	17.7	9.9
Columbia County..........	76.4	84.6	79.7	54.4	42.5	60.5	43.3	62.3	27 283	33 081	16 740	49 000	21.0	11.5

STATE County	Median gross rent	Percent who pay 35 percent or more of income for housing expenses		Means of transportation to work (percent except where noted)						Vehicles available (percent of households)		
		Owners	Renters	Number of workers 16 years and over	Car, truck, or van		Public transportation	Other means	Walked	No vehicles	One vehicle	Two or more vehicles
					Drove alone	Carpooled						
	25	26	27	28	29	30	31	32	33	34	35	36

STATE County	25	26	27	28	29	30	31	32	33	34	35	36
ALABAMA—Cont'd												
Washington County.......	269	12.7	17.0	6 719	74.7	19.3	1.0	1.0	2.1	8.2	28.7	63.1
Wilcox County	250	23.4	18.4	3 377	76.2	19.1	0.6	1.2	1.2	20.1	34.8	45.1
Winston County.............	329	14.9	18.5	10 428	80.9	13.6	0.2	0.9	1.4	7.7	30.1	62.1
ALASKA	720	16.2	25.4	290 597	66.5	15.5	1.8	4.8	7.3	10.9	33.9	55.2
Aleutians East Borough	710	19.6	18.4	1 047	26.7	7.6	1.1	6.0	57.7	27.9	37.8	34.2
Aleutians West Census Area...........................	892	18.1	8.9	3 217	38.4	8.7	3.2	13.8	34.7	20.7	42.1	37.2
Anchorage Municipality .	736	15.8	28.3	131 228	74.4	14.6	2.0	2.6	2.7	6.4	35.1	58.5
Bethel Census Area......	814	17.2	20.5	5 310	18.7	14.0	6.1	27.3	31.1	58.4	25.2	16.4
Bristol Bay Borough	778	16.3	11.2	568	63.6	10.4	0.0	4.9	16.5	10.8	38.8	50.4
Denali Borough	568	6.9	11.2	913	56.7	12.5	6.9	2.6	12.0	5.7	35.2	59.1
Dillingham Census Area	761	23.8	17.3	1 718	33.4	21.6	1.9	17.3	22.1	38.8	36.8	24.4
Fairbanks North Star Borough......................	679	14.2	22.1	40 504	72.8	16.8	0.7	1.7	4.2	6.5	33.7	59.8
Haines Borough	588	11.5	25.7	947	56.8	15.8	2.3	2.4	11.0	8.1	37.5	54.4
Juneau City and Borough......................	863	14.8	27.3	16 216	62.9	18.5	4.3	1.9	8.0	7.4	37.1	55.5
Kenai Peninsula Borough......................	609	17.1	25.7	19 760	69.6	12.5	0.4	7.2	4.8	6.0	32.8	61.2
Ketchikan Gateway Borough......................	775	17.7	26.2	6 973	60.7	20.7	2.6	3.0	8.6	12.9	39.5	47.6
Kodiak Island Borough..	791	15.2	21.9	6 632	62.8	18.8	1.2	4.6	9.9	9.5	36.1	54.4
Lake and Peninsula Borough......................	591	24.1	16.8	562	15.7	9.4	0.0	36.1	29.7	42.9	37.9	19.2
Matanuska-Susitna Borough......................	700	16.9	32.9	24 649	68.9	16.3	0.6	5.2	2.6	3.7	27.3	69.1
Nome Census Area.......	755	21.0	18.4	3 055	24.4	11.9	1.4	20.7	38.4	55.6	29.1	15.3
North Slope Borough	902	13.6	14.3	2 838	23.9	27.2	10.6	9.3	26.6	48.5	39.9	11.6
Northwest Arctic Borough......................	842	23.9	16.0	2 344	9.8	11.9	0.5	22.7	50.7	71.6	21.0	7.4
Prince of Wales-Outer Ketchikan Cens..........	580	14.7	17.7	2 516	46.5	24.3	1.1	7.6	16.5	16.3	41.1	42.6
Sitka City and Borough .	768	15.7	28.2	4 420	56.6	20.0	0.5	6.6	12.1	11.8	36.0	52.1
Skagway-Hoonah-Angoon Census Area.	515	16.9	10.3	1 420	43.7	13.8	2.5	8.2	27.0	26.2	37.3	36.6
Southeast Fairbanks Census Area	516	12.9	20.2	2 050	65.3	13.4	0.3	2.7	15.0	8.9	32.5	58.6
Valdez-Cordova Census Area	634	14.8	18.8	4 395	60.6	14.7	1.0	3.5	14.6	8.6	37.6	53.8
Wade Hampton Census Area...........................	552	19.1	12.0	1 787	2.2	4.8	0.3	42.5	47.2	75.9	16.9	7.2
Wrangell-Petersburg Census Area	648	20.5	25.0	2 882	54.4	18.8	0.7	8.0	13.6	14.6	38.6	46.8
Yakutat City and Borough......................	622	12.6	13.1	435	40.5	24.6	3.7	9.2	16.6	15.5	41.5	43.0
Yukon-Koyukuk Census Area...........................	464	21.8	15.3	2 211	18.5	10.0	0.5	20.6	46.0	53.8	26.8	19.4
ARIZONA	619	16.2	30.9	2 210 395	74.1	15.4	1.9	2.3	2.6	7.4	38.6	54.0
Apache County.............	342	14.6	12.5	15 854	65.6	20.2	0.6	1.6	8.6	16.4	38.9	44.7
Cochise County.............	470	14.3	22.9	46 866	73.4	14.9	0.3	1.7	5.8	7.1	36.8	56.1
Coconino County..........	629	15.0	31.0	54 283	68.1	16.5	0.7	3.3	7.6	6.9	34.2	58.9
Gila County	501	17.2	26.4	17 729	75.5	14.7	0.3	1.6	3.7	7.5	37.1	55.4
Graham County.............	449	15.9	27.0	10 517	71.1	19.1	0.3	2.2	3.7	8.5	33.4	58.2
Greenlee County...........	291	11.8	8.7	3 341	74.6	20.0	0.2	0.5	1.9	4.9	29.5	65.5
La Paz County	442	14.5	22.5	6 455	70.3	15.8	0.0	3.1	6.9	5.6	40.3	54.1
Maricopa County	666	16.2	31.1	1 406 442	74.7	15.2	2.1	2.3	2.1	7.0	38.7	54.3
Mohave County	559	18.2	28.0	59 219	74.0	18.1	0.6	2.0	2.4	5.7	37.3	57.1
Navajo County..............	396	14.4	20.0	28 965	69.5	19.1	0.7	1.4	5.8	12.9	35.4	51.7
Pima County.................	544	16.1	33.9	369 261	73.8	14.7	2.5	2.7	2.6	9.0	40.1	50.9
Pinal County	509	15.3	25.6	59 992	73.8	17.9	0.2	2.0	2.8	6.6	41.0	52.4
Santa Cruz County........	475	21.2	30.8	12 687	74.2	15.8	0.8	1.5	3.7	8.4	32.3	59.3
Yavapai County	600	18.0	35.6	67 109	75.1	13.7	0.3	1.6	3.4	4.8	35.6	59.6
Yuma County	508	17.0	26.8	51 675	73.7	16.0	1.1	3.0	4.3	7.2	40.3	52.5
ARKANSAS...............	453	12.7	26.7	1 160 101	79.9	14.1	0.4	1.0	1.9	8.1	34.9	57.1
Arkansas County..........	392	13.4	25.4	9 220	82.1	12.1	0.1	1.1	1.7	8.7	36.3	55.0
Ashley County	414	14.1	25.2	9 469	83.7	11.8	0.1	1.2	1.5	10.3	33.1	56.6
Baxter County	435	13.2	26.2	14 835	80.8	14.0	0.1	0.7	1.8	5.7	36.9	57.4
Benton County	528	11.5	22.4	70 922	80.7	12.9	0.2	0.9	2.0	4.3	31.0	64.7
Boone County	414	14.1	29.1	14 900	79.9	13.2	0.1	0.9	2.0	6.7	30.9	62.5
Bradley County.............	326	13.3	26.0	4 576	72.2	19.5	0.0	1.7	4.0	10.1	36.5	53.4
Calhoun County............	368	12.0	16.4	2 302	80.2	14.6	0.3	2.5	1.4	10.0	32.1	57.9
Carroll County	433	17.3	24.3	11 469	72.6	15.2	0.1	1.1	3.7	6.1	32.4	61.5
Chicot County	336	20.2	19.2	4 817	71.4	20.0	0.7	1.7	4.2	20.4	34.0	45.6
Clark County	396	11.6	32.4	10 543	76.3	13.9	0.3	0.7	6.6	11.5	34.1	54.4
Clay County	320	14.3	17.7	7 415	81.6	13.2	0.1	0.9	1.7	8.9	34.8	56.3
Cleburne County	419	16.3	19.9	9 624	78.0	16.5	0.1	0.4	2.0	6.4	32.0	61.6
Cleveland County..........	370	9.2	21.5	3 587	77.3	16.8	0.1	0.9	1.8	7.3	29.3	63.5
Columbia County..........	381	15.3	26.9	10 419	80.5	11.4	0.6	1.7	4.2	11.5	34.0	54.4

Table C-3. States and Counties — Migration, Housing, and Transportation

STATE/ County code	MSA/PMSA/ NECMA code¹	STATE County	Total population 5 years and over	Residence in 1995 (percent) Same house	Same county, different house	Same state, different county	Different state	Outside the United States	Occupied housing units Number	Percent owner-occupied	Householders 65 years and over Number	Percent owner-occupied
			1	2	3	4	5	6	7	8	9	10
		ARKANSAS—Cont'd										
05 029	...	Conway County	19 055	61.7	19.0	12.7	5.9	0.8	7 967	78.0	2 171	87.2
05 031	3700	Craighead County	76 589	47.2	29.6	13.5	8.7	1.0	32 301	63.9	6 362	79.4
05 033	2720	Crawford County	49 255	52.6	24.7	13.1	9.2	0.4	19 702	75.9	4 118	83.9
05 035	4920	Crittenden County	46 571	53.2	27.9	7.5	10.2	1.1	18 471	60.3	3 405	76.6
05 037	...	Cross County	18 189	58.9	24.9	9.7	6.2	0.3	7 391	70.7	1 822	79.0
05 039	...	Dallas County	8 746	61.1	20.6	12.1	5.8	0.3	3 519	73.9	1 098	81.1
05 041	...	Desha County	14 202	61.3	26.5	7.6	3.9	0.7	5 922	63.5	1 490	74.6
05 043	...	Drew County	17 467	55.8	22.5	14.1	7.2	0.5	7 337	68.9	1 683	80.5
05 045	4400	Faulkner County	80 153	45.6	23.9	19.8	9.7	1.0	31 882	68.6	5 413	80.2
05 047	...	Franklin County	16 623	60.4	20.4	11.7	7.4	0.2	6 882	78.0	1 809	80.1
05 049	...	Fulton County	10 990	59.8	15.4	11.0	13.7	0.1	4 810	81.1	1 521	88.8
05 051	...	Garland County	83 249	52.6	23.8	9.9	12.8	1.0	37 813	71.2	12 900	83.3
05 053	...	Grant County	15 390	60.2	16.6	16.1	6.6	0.5	6 241	80.2	1 245	84.7
05 055	...	Greene County	34 826	52.8	28.4	9.8	8.6	0.4	14 750	71.3	3 557	77.8
05 057	...	Hempstead County	21 801	57.4	22.7	10.4	6.5	3.0	8 959	69.3	2 213	80.0
05 059	...	Hot Spring County	28 372	57.3	21.5	13.9	6.7	0.6	12 004	78.0	3 197	87.0
05 061	...	Howard County	13 319	57.9	23.3	10.5	6.3	2.0	5 471	72.0	1 414	80.8
05 063	...	Independence County	32 016	57.5	24.4	9.9	6.9	1.3	13 467	74.4	3 392	79.5
05 065	...	Izard County	12 572	55.3	18.9	13.1	11.4	1.4	5 440	80.1	1 869	87.3
05 067	...	Jackson County	17 369	65.6	22.1	8.3	3.6	0.3	6 971	69.6	2 002	76.1
05 069	6240	Jefferson County	78 470	56.5	29.0	7.5	5.6	1.4	30 555	66.1	7 334	79.8
05 071	...	Johnson County	21 291	53.5	21.9	12.0	9.9	2.7	8 738	73.0	2 232	82.6
05 073	...	Lafayette County	8 047	68.6	18.1	6.7	6.1	0.5	3 434	78.4	999	85.5
05 075	...	Lawrence County	16 657	56.2	25.6	11.7	5.9	0.6	7 108	71.2	2 000	76.1
05 077	...	Lee County	11 749	55.3	21.2	16.8	6.1	0.6	4 182	63.6	1 128	77.7
05 079	...	Lincoln County	13 684	54.4	14.3	22.7	8.5	0.1	4 265	76.2	1 121	81.6
05 081	...	Little River County	12 668	59.4	22.6	7.2	10.4	0.3	5 465	76.5	1 361	77.1
05 083	...	Logan County	21 021	56.6	24.6	11.0	7.2	0.5	8 693	77.2	2 297	83.2
05 085	4400	Lonoke County	40 131	51.3	19.5	17.6	10.8	0.9	15 262	75.9	3 575	80.1
05 087	...	Madison County	13 323	63.7	13.2	14.6	7.7	0.8	5 463	79.0	1 354	85.8
05 089	...	Marion County	15 324	55.6	15.9	9.1	18.9	0.5	6 776	80.0	2 120	87.0
05 091	8360	Miller County	37 423	54.9	23.5	6.8	14.0	0.8	15 007	67.9	3 486	81.6
05 093	...	Mississippi County	47 798	54.1	33.3	3.7	8.4	0.5	19 349	58.9	4 451	70.3
05 095	...	Monroe County	9 541	61.2	23.8	9.6	4.9	0.5	4 105	64.9	1 173	71.6
05 097	...	Montgomery County	8 690	63.9	15.0	12.0	8.4	0.7	3 785	82.8	1 137	85.8
05 099	...	Nevada County	9 311	63.0	18.7	12.1	5.4	0.8	3 893	74.8	1 170	76.5
05 101	...	Newton County	8 108	62.2	13.4	14.0	9.9	0.6	3 500	81.5	919	85.0
05 103	...	Ouachita County	27 026	62.3	25.1	6.9	5.1	0.6	11 613	71.4	3 312	82.2
05 105	...	Perry County	9 573	60.4	15.9	16.3	6.8	0.6	3 989	82.1	958	86.8
05 107	...	Phillips County	24 190	60.5	28.2	5.1	5.8	0.4	9 711	56.3	2 654	72.0
05 109	...	Pike County	10 595	64.4	15.2	11.9	7.7	0.7	4 504	78.6	1 231	84.6
05 111	...	Poinsett County	23 862	59.1	26.4	9.7	4.4	0.4	10 026	66.8	2 478	72.5
05 113	...	Polk County	18 902	56.4	25.4	6.2	11.2	0.9	8 047	78.4	2 237	85.3
05 115	...	Pope County	51 044	50.8	27.1	11.8	9.8	0.6	20 701	71.2	4 241	81.4
05 117	...	Prairie County	8 974	64.3	18.8	12.7	4.0	0.3	3 894	72.8	1 152	78.6
05 119	4400	Pulaski County	335 566	50.4	29.9	7.9	9.9	1.9	147 942	60.9	28 618	76.9
05 121	...	Randolph County	17 105	56.9	25.9	8.4	7.8	1.1	7 265	74.5	1 981	80.0
05 123	...	St. Francis County	27 089	54.1	28.0	11.2	5.0	2.9	10 043	63.2	2 382	73.8
05 125	4400	Saline County	78 144	54.7	19.3	16.8	8.6	0.6	31 778	80.7	6 353	86.4
05 127	...	Scott County	10 183	58.2	21.8	9.9	8.6	1.5	4 323	74.2	1 055	83.8
05 129	...	Searcy County	7 814	63.9	17.8	9.3	8.8	0.2	3 523	77.7	1 078	77.2
05 131	2720	Sebastian County	106 590	49.9	27.3	8.8	12.1	2.0	45 300	63.5	9 665	76.8
05 133	...	Sevier County	14 504	55.3	25.4	6.3	9.8	3.2	5 708	74.2	1 421	79.8
05 135	...	Sharp County	16 147	56.6	15.2	15.9	12.2	0.1	7 211	80.1	2 536	87.4
05 137	...	Stone County	10 857	62.5	19.0	8.4	9.8	0.2	4 768	77.9	1 399	81.9
05 139	...	Union County	42 828	60.6	26.3	5.7	6.3	1.1	17 989	72.9	4 874	84.2
05 141	...	Van Buren County	15 338	59.7	16.1	14.2	9.4	0.6	6 825	81.1	2 468	85.8
05 143	2580	Washington County	145 934	42.9	27.5	12.3	13.8	3.5	60 151	59.4	10 180	80.5
05 145	...	White County	62 937	50.2	24.1	13.4	11.1	1.2	25 148	73.0	6 097	80.8
05 147	...	Woodruff County	8 125	63.0	22.6	9.4	4.6	0.4	3 531	65.6	1 001	73.1
05 149	...	Yell County	19 769	51.6	22.8	12.4	9.8	3.4	7 922	72.9	1 962	81.5
06 000	...	CALIFORNIA	31 416 629	50.2	30.9	9.8	4.6	4.5	11 502 870	56.9	2 220 093	74.5
06 001	5775	Alameda County	1 346 666	50.8	25.2	13.0	5.1	5.9	523 366	54.7	90 904	70.8
06 003	...	Alpine County	1 147	57.9	10.5	17.6	12.9	1.1	483	67.9	72	91.7
06 005	...	Amador County	33 690	53.4	17.0	25.5	3.4	0.6	12 759	75.4	4 121	88.2

¹MSA = Metropolitan Statistical Area. PMSA = Primary MSA. NECMA = New England County Metropolitan Area. See the Appendix A for explanation of these concepts. See Appendix B for list of metropolitan areas identified by type, with component counties.

Table C-3. States and Counties — **Migration, Housing, and Transportation**

STATE County	Owner-occupied by household type (percent)								Median household income			Median housing value (owner estimated)	Median monthly owner costs as a percent of income	
	Family-households					Nonfamily households								
		Married-couple family		Other family										
	Total family households	Total	With own children under 18 years	Total	With own children under 18 years	Total nonfamily households	Two or more adults	Living alone	All households	Owner-occupied households	Renter-occupied households		With a mortgage	Without a mortgage
	11	12	13	14	15	16	17	18	19	20	21	22	23	24
ARKANSAS—Cont'd														
Conway County	81.6	86.7	82.4	61.8	46.7	68.8	58.4	69.9	30 727	35 548	18 954	58 100	18.8	12.2
Craighead County	71.7	79.7	73.6	44.6	32.3	46.8	25.7	51.9	32 409	42 228	20 208	74 800	19.4	9.9
Crawford County	79.2	83.8	79.0	58.7	48.5	64.7	59.0	65.6	32 913	36 798	21 292	68 000	19.7	9.9
Crittenden County	65.5	76.9	70.4	44.8	32.6	46.5	38.2	47.8	30 030	39 455	19 267	65 900	20.8	9.9
Cross County	74.3	79.8	70.3	57.5	44.9	60.1	47.2	61.3	29 120	33 590	19 688	52 400	20.6	11.8
Dallas County	79.2	82.9	75.8	68.3	61.1	61.3	22.9	63.2	25 799	29 647	17 092	36 300	18.3	10.2
Desha County	67.1	80.2	74.9	42.7	29.9	54.6	46.7	55.2	23 804	31 753	13 027	42 400	18.7	10.4
Drew County	76.1	82.3	74.7	57.2	45.1	52.6	37.4	55.4	28 245	35 297	17 129	52 100	18.0	11.1
Faulkner County	77.6	83.9	81.3	52.2	44.2	46.7	29.1	51.8	38 155	47 076	22 235	85 000	19.1	9.9
Franklin County	83.6	87.1	82.7	66.5	59.0	63.5	53.9	64.6	30 580	33 698	17 393	58 300	20.3	9.9
Fulton County	84.3	87.6	77.5	64.5	53.6	72.8	73.9	72.6	25 728	28 268	17 038	59 200	22.3	11.7
Garland County	76.8	83.2	74.9	51.9	37.3	59.7	48.6	61.3	31 434	36 779	20 107	77 200	20.5	9.9
Grant County	84.7	86.6	80.0	71.7	63.3	65.5	42.0	68.5	36 856	40 556	24 605	60 800	17.6	9.9
Greene County	76.6	81.5	75.7	53.5	41.2	57.3	47.7	58.6	31 024	37 010	20 349	63 200	19.2	9.9
Hempstead County	73.6	82.0	75.3	51.3	37.8	58.7	40.7	61.2	28 846	33 523	19 055	49 100	18.7	10.4
Hot Spring County	81.4	85.9	78.2	60.6	44.3	68.2	54.1	69.7	31 472	34 238	21 463	56 800	18.7	9.9
Howard County	77.5	83.6	77.9	55.6	37.1	58.0	40.1	59.8	28 384	32 892	19 591	54 700	19.5	10.6
Independence County	79.2	83.8	76.3	57.2	44.3	62.0	66.4	61.6	31 558	36 146	19 457	57 700	19.1	10.2
Izard County	85.2	89.0	84.3	63.4	46.3	68.6	64.4	69.1	26 071	30 072	14 969	58 100	21.5	10.8
Jackson County	74.4	81.1	75.8	51.8	38.8	58.6	51.9	59.2	25 255	31 243	16 250	42 100	18.5	12.2
Jefferson County	70.5	81.1	71.0	47.0	33.2	55.7	49.2	56.4	31 413	39 531	19 670	53 800	18.1	11.1
Johnson County	77.7	82.4	76.4	56.8	42.3	61.2	41.6	64.2	27 853	31 705	19 280	56 500	19.7	9.9
Lafayette County	81.3	86.6	83.1	66.7	57.1	71.8	68.3	72.0	24 926	28 013	14 978	33 900	19.7	12.0
Lawrence County	77.0	80.3	70.6	62.3	54.2	57.3	41.4	59.0	27 050	30 947	16 725	45 100	19.5	10.8
Lee County	65.7	81.6	77.3	41.8	25.9	58.5	25.0	60.6	20 142	26 349	13 790	38 900	21.5	12.1
Lincoln County	79.3	84.5	83.0	64.0	54.0	67.4	53.5	69.4	29 608	33 306	17 342	45 000	19.2	11.7
Little River County	80.3	85.4	79.0	63.2	59.0	66.9	96.3	64.7	29 326	34 089	17 184	50 400	18.1	9.9
Logan County	80.5	85.6	80.1	57.9	44.5	68.3	54.7	69.8	28 567	31 471	18 906	54 000	19.1	9.9
Lonoke County	80.0	84.4	80.4	59.5	47.6	61.6	49.1	63.6	39 983	46 282	22 462	76 900	18.6	9.9
Madison County	82.3	84.5	78.3	69.7	59.8	69.1	68.7	69.1	28 501	31 852	19 792	71 500	19.8	9.9
Marion County	84.1	87.4	77.9	60.2	47.6	69.7	70.4	69.6	26 766	29 464	19 841	69 600	21.4	11.5
Miller County	71.9	81.3	75.9	46.4	36.6	58.2	56.9	58.4	30 951	36 795	19 503	60 200	17.8	10.0
Mississippi County	62.8	72.2	62.1	41.5	26.6	48.5	41.1	49.4	27 604	35 625	18 036	51 900	19.0	11.1
Monroe County	69.6	79.7	74.9	47.0	30.5	55.4	49.2	56.1	22 410	28 593	13 333	39 100	21.8	11.5
Montgomery County	85.6	87.8	84.4	74.1	66.2	75.2	80.0	74.6	27 716	30 551	16 034	53 700	19.5	10.1
Nevada County	78.9	86.0	78.4	58.8	42.8	64.8	55.7	65.3	27 014	30 375	12 417	39 100	17.9	11.2
Newton County	83.9	88.3	83.6	62.0	53.1	75.5	79.5	75.1	24 532	27 207	15 196	56 500	21.8	9.9
Ouachita County	75.2	84.7	75.5	48.4	34.0	62.8	59.0	63.1	29 307	34 705	17 962	47 200	18.5	10.9
Perry County	84.5	87.8	85.5	66.0	56.3	75.6	58.9	77.9	30 811	32 652	21 629	55 700	19.9	10.1
Phillips County	58.8	76.3	66.5	33.7	20.9	50.2	44.9	50.6	22 009	31 234	14 150	43 600	19.9	12.8
Pike County	82.2	86.7	80.1	57.9	51.3	69.0	61.8	69.7	27 807	30 489	19 125	48 000	20.7	10.9
Poinsett County	70.6	76.5	68.6	50.0	34.3	57.2	49.1	58.1	26 299	31 877	16 680	46 800	19.8	10.8
Polk County	83.6	86.2	78.7	70.6	62.4	65.0	55.9	66.0	25 186	28 368	17 010	57 500	21.5	10.7
Pope County	77.9	82.9	78.4	56.4	45.7	53.5	38.0	56.5	32 268	38 881	21 059	66 600	18.5	9.9
Prairie County	77.1	81.4	74.0	61.7	50.9	61.8	57.5	62.3	29 500	33 265	19 375	50 300	20.7	10.5
Pulaski County	68.8	78.8	72.6	43.2	32.3	46.3	37.3	47.7	37 914	49 457	25 044	82 200	19.4	9.9
Randolph County	78.9	83.1	77.8	60.0	52.1	62.6	66.5	62.3	27 878	32 294	15 850	51 600	19.0	9.9
St. Francis County	67.3	80.7	73.2	44.0	27.3	52.7	57.7	52.1	26 250	32 319	14 118	50 700	20.4	11.7
Saline County	84.1	87.9	82.8	63.9	55.0	69.4	65.6	70.0	42 470	46 453	27 179	82 300	18.9	9.9
Scott County	78.9	83.9	79.1	54.2	43.1	61.9	42.0	64.1	26 422	29 574	18 550	46 400	18.3	10.7
Searcy County	83.7	88.2	85.2	62.0	52.3	63.6	64.3	63.5	21 567	24 609	12 593	47 300	21.7	11.3
Sebastian County	70.8	78.6	72.8	45.0	34.6	48.0	34.7	50.2	33 776	42 605	23 087	71 300	18.4	9.9
Sevier County	76.5	82.6	74.6	51.7	43.6	67.4	43.8	70.5	29 603	32 603	21 968	50 400	18.1	9.9
Sharp County	83.0	87.1	82.1	61.5	50.2	72.8	67.8	73.4	25 195	27 078	18 598	52 100	22.0	11.7
Stone County	82.9	84.7	77.0	70.3	63.0	64.2	56.6	64.8	22 430	25 821	15 953	60 100	23.7	11.8
Union County	76.7	85.3	78.7	54.4	43.3	63.5	56.3	64.1	29 663	34 966	18 644	49 300	19.2	11.5
Van Buren County	85.5	88.8	80.5	68.5	57.2	70.6	62.3	71.6	27 281	29 631	19 247	57 900	22.6	9.9
Washington County	69.5	75.7	70.5	44.5	38.5	39.8	24.6	44.5	34 458	45 235	22 854	88 300	19.4	9.9
White County	78.6	83.1	77.6	57.7	47.8	57.3	47.4	58.5	32 079	37 645	20 775	64 700	19.4	10.5
Woodruff County	69.5	78.7	69.7	48.7	33.2	56.9	47.2	57.8	21 989	28 638	13 810	33 700	17.8	13.0
Yell County	75.9	81.1	72.1	57.7	45.9	64.4	44.1	67.0	28 556	32 722	20 973	56 700	19.9	11.6
CALIFORNIA	63.0	70.1	63.2	41.9	30.5	43.2	34.6	45.9	47 288	62 155	31 912	198 900	25.3	9.9
Alameda County	63.0	70.4	66.2	42.9	30.3	39.2	34.0	41.0	55 600	75 328	37 431	291 900	25.0	9.9
Alpine County	77.0	84.9	87.3	58.1	41.3	54.2	54.2	54.1	40 781	50 625	30 750	181 000	24.2	9.9
Amador County	79.6	85.4	76.2	53.5	40.6	64.9	56.0	66.6	41 884	47 695	28 967	153 700	24.8	10.9

STATE County	Median gross rent	Percent who pay 35 percent or more of income for housing expenses		Means of transportation to work (percent except where noted)						Vehicles available (percent of households)		
		Owners	Renters	Number of workers 16 years and over	Car, truck, or van		Public transportation	Other means	Walked	No vehicles	One vehicle	Two or more vehicles
					Drove alone	Carpooled						
	25	26	27	28	29	30	31	32	33	34	35	36
ARKANSAS—Cont'd												
Conway County	414	12.3	26.3	8 420	79.0	14.7	0.1	1.1	1.7	6.4	33.7	59.9
Craighead County	454	13.1	31.9	39 290	83.1	11.7	0.1	0.7	1.9	6.1	36.6	57.3
Crawford County	405	10.9	22.0	22 969	82.0	13.9	0.3	0.9	1.0	5.9	31.8	62.3
Crittenden County	486	15.8	32.7	20 154	79.6	15.6	0.5	1.3	1.9	14.1	39.0	46.9
Cross County	420	16.3	24.5	7 899	81.1	14.0	0.2	1.0	1.7	9.9	36.1	54.0
Dallas County	380	9.2	22.4	3 509	75.2	16.8	0.4	1.7	4.5	11.1	41.0	47.9
Desha County	354	13.1	25.2	5 340	75.6	18.5	0.0	1.4	1.9	18.2	35.7	46.0
Drew County	374	12.1	27.2	7 892	78.6	14.9	0.2	1.8	2.9	8.5	33.7	57.9
Faulkner County	499	10.6	31.0	41 855	78.7	15.3	0.2	1.0	2.0	5.8	31.9	62.3
Franklin County	376	13.0	26.8	7 498	77.4	16.1	0.2	1.8	2.1	7.2	31.7	61.1
Fulton County	337	13.1	28.7	4 474	78.2	14.9	0.1	0.8	1.6	5.1	31.3	63.6
Garland County	478	12.5	29.0	36 185	78.9	13.9	1.0	1.1	2.4	8.5	38.7	52.8
Grant County	435	7.2	20.2	7 449	82.3	14.2	0.2	0.8	1.2	4.6	29.5	66.0
Greene County	431	12.9	23.8	16 811	83.0	12.8	0.1	0.8	1.0	7.1	31.9	61.0
Hempstead County	397	13.0	24.4	10 075	76.6	17.5	0.2	1.6	1.1	10.3	34.4	55.3
Hot Spring County	409	10.8	19.4	13 282	81.1	14.2	0.2	1.0	1.1	7.0	31.4	61.6
Howard County	369	16.5	19.9	6 293	76.5	15.9	0.1	1.6	3.3	9.2	32.5	58.3
Independence County	423	11.9	21.7	15 100	80.4	13.9	0.1	0.7	2.2	7.4	31.5	61.2
Izard County	336	14.7	24.7	4 815	78.6	14.9	0.3	0.6	1.4	6.3	36.3	57.4
Jackson County	339	13.5	24.6	6 875	82.9	12.6	0.2	1.2	1.4	9.5	38.3	52.3
Jefferson County	463	14.1	30.0	32 715	80.6	15.1	0.5	0.8	1.2	11.2	38.0	50.8
Johnson County	411	12.3	24.0	9 491	76.0	16.1	0.1	1.1	3.6	7.5	33.7	58.8
Lafayette County	319	13.4	24.4	3 111	72.5	20.2	0.5	0.7	2.0	13.0	36.5	50.5
Lawrence County	367	14.5	26.1	7 139	79.5	12.7	0.3	1.4	3.2	8.5	33.3	58.2
Lee County	314	18.5	27.4	3 519	74.7	19.1	0.1	2.6	1.9	17.8	36.2	46.0
Lincoln County	385	12.0	21.1	4 535	76.5	18.6	0.3	1.1	2.1	11.1	34.0	54.8
Little River County	372	13.2	24.8	5 746	83.0	11.9	0.4	1.5	1.8	8.7	34.1	57.3
Logan County	380	12.2	22.9	9 056	77.0	15.6	0.1	1.1	2.3	7.4	30.2	62.4
Lonoke County	490	10.5	25.6	25 006	82.0	13.7	0.2	1.0	1.1	6.0	27.5	66.6
Madison County	358	15.3	19.7	6 404	60.3	19.1	0.0	0.7	2.6	7.1	25.6	67.3
Marion County	388	14.5	19.9	6 021	74.2	18.5	0.3	1.2	2.0	5.4	32.5	62.1
Miller County	439	11.3	27.8	16 626	84.8	11.8	0.2	0.9	0.9	8.8	36.7	54.5
Mississippi County	422	15.2	29.2	20 112	80.2	15.6	0.2	1.1	1.9	12.5	39.4	48.1
Monroe County	280	18.2	23.0	3 731	77.3	14.1	0.2	2.0	3.6	16.3	37.6	46.1
Montgomery County	321	11.3	15.7	3 728	73.0	17.8	0.1	1.3	3.4	6.4	29.1	64.5
Nevada County	339	14.2	22.5	4 179	79.5	15.4	0.4	2.0	1.0	10.3	35.7	54.0
Newton County	335	12.1	22.7	3 435	69.8	21.2	0.3	1.0	2.5	9.0	31.3	59.7
Ouachita County	355	13.0	25.1	11 210	81.0	13.7	0.6	1.2	1.7	11.0	36.5	52.6
Perry County	408	13.8	17.2	4 380	76.7	16.8	0.8	0.8	1.4	5.3	28.7	66.0
Phillips County	357	16.4	33.1	8 800	76.3	18.0	0.7	2.0	1.7	20.9	38.4	40.7
Pike County	366	14.4	15.2	4 832	76.2	14.9	0.6	1.8	2.8	7.1	31.2	61.7
Poinsett County	346	12.7	22.7	10 460	80.2	15.0	0.1	1.1	1.9	10.0	36.2	53.8
Polk County	361	14.7	22.1	8 316	78.1	13.4	0.3	1.2	3.3	6.4	34.0	59.6
Pope County	427	11.4	24.0	24 280	81.7	13.3	0.1	1.0	1.6	5.3	31.7	63.0
Prairie County	336	16.5	14.9	4 055	80.7	12.7	0.1	0.5	2.7	9.3	32.0	58.7
Pulaski County	539	12.7	28.0	174 066	81.6	12.9	1.3	0.9	1.2	8.4	39.7	51.9
Randolph County	362	11.8	25.6	7 439	79.8	13.8	0.1	1.6	1.3	6.5	32.4	61.0
St. Francis County	403	16.7	35.3	9 707	76.8	17.2	0.5	2.4	1.2	16.1	38.1	45.8
Saline County	525	9.0	23.8	39 456	84.3	11.7	0.2	0.6	0.9	4.1	28.5	67.4
Scott County	343	10.3	19.2	4 636	70.3	20.4	0.0	0.9	2.4	7.4	33.6	59.0
Searcy County	293	14.4	22.8	3 072	72.5	19.0	0.5	1.3	2.5	7.9	30.5	61.5
Sebastian County	428	11.2	24.5	52 350	81.1	14.0	0.7	1.0	1.2	8.3	36.3	55.4
Sevier County	398	14.5	23.2	6 691	73.1	21.1	0.1	1.6	1.4	6.4	32.8	60.8
Sharp County	379	16.0	22.8	5 858	76.6	15.9	0.1	0.9	2.3	5.7	36.2	58.1
Stone County	349	12.3	16.0	4 293	71.3	17.7	0.7	1.4	2.5	8.1	31.5	60.4
Union County	408	14.7	28.5	18 271	83.3	12.1	0.1	1.0	1.9	10.6	36.2	53.2
Van Buren County	372	12.5	23.9	5 969	74.8	18.1	0.1	1.7	1.9	6.6	34.8	58.6
Washington County	490	11.9	30.3	76 093	79.0	13.3	0.5	1.1	2.6	5.7	35.3	59.0
White County	416	12.6	25.2	28 654	78.6	14.5	0.3	1.1	2.7	6.7	31.9	61.4
Woodruff County	291	16.2	22.2	3 451	78.7	16.1	0.1	0.8	2.7	14.8	38.0	47.2
Yell County	372	13.3	16.6	8 925	72.4	19.4	0.2	1.5	3.8	7.0	33.0	59.9
CALIFORNIA	747	23.2	34.1	14 525 322	71.8	14.5	5.1	1.9	2.9	9.5	34.1	56.4
Alameda County	852	22.4	32.5	678 910	66.4	13.8	10.6	2.5	3.2	10.9	34.9	54.2
Alpine County	659	16.4	29.1	613	51.9	15.7	0.5	2.6	24.8	6.2	30.6	63.1
Amador County	685	19.6	31.5	13 378	76.8	12.9	0.3	1.3	3.5	5.8	28.5	65.8

Table C-3. States and Counties — Migration, Housing, and Transportation

			Residence in 1995 (percent)						Occupied housing units		Householders 65 years and over	
STATE/ County code	MSA/PMSA/ NECMA code[1]	STATE County	Total population 5 years and over	Same house	Same county, different house	Same state, different county	Different state	Outside the United States	Number	Percent owner-occupied	Number	Percent owner-occupied
			1	2	3	4	5	6	7	8	9	10
		CALIFORNIA—Cont'd										
06 007	1620	Butte County	191 504	47.9	27.9	17.9	4.2	1.9	79 566	60.7	21 039	82.6
06 009	...	Calaveras County	38 831	55.0	15.8	25.2	3.5	0.6	16 469	78.7	4 759	89.4
06 011	...	Colusa County	17 275	57.6	22.5	13.0	1.6	5.2	6 097	63.3	1 306	80.9
06 013	5775	Contra Costa County	883 762	53.2	24.1	14.5	4.6	3.7	344 129	69.3	67 152	81.1
06 015	...	Del Norte County	26 026	45.5	21.3	22.5	9.2	1.6	9 170	63.8	2 308	75.8
06 017	6920	El Dorado County	147 368	52.7	21.0	19.4	5.6	1.3	58 939	74.7	12 727	85.3
06 019	2840	Fresno County	732 422	51.0	35.7	8.0	2.2	3.1	252 940	56.5	49 530	74.4
06 021	...	Glenn County	24 459	57.3	25.7	12.3	2.5	2.2	9 172	64.0	2 261	79.0
06 023	...	Humboldt County	119 423	51.3	28.9	13.3	5.4	1.2	51 238	57.6	10 834	80.5
06 025	...	Imperial County	131 530	52.1	27.3	12.2	3.3	5.1	39 384	58.3	9 095	69.3
06 027	...	Inyo County	16 962	54.3	24.1	15.1	5.3	1.3	7 703	65.9	2 240	84.2
06 029	0680	Kern County	606 633	47.2	34.9	10.5	3.8	3.6	208 652	62.1	40 739	78.7
06 031	...	Kings County	119 256	42.3	24.2	22.6	4.8	6.1	34 418	55.9	6 291	74.2
06 033	...	Lake County	55 255	51.9	22.4	20.0	4.3	1.3	23 974	70.5	7 547	86.2
06 035	...	Lassen County	32 185	45.5	15.1	31.9	4.2	3.3	9 625	68.1	2 165	81.0
06 037	4480	Los Angeles County	8 791 096	52.0	35.7	3.8	3.3	5.3	3 133 774	47.9	556 224	67.2
06 039	2840	Madera County	113 722	52.8	24.8	16.3	2.4	3.6	36 155	66.2	8 476	83.2
06 041	7360	Marin County	234 008	54.8	21.9	13.4	5.8	4.1	100 650	63.6	21 923	79.2
06 043	...	Mariposa County	16 311	53.0	18.8	22.6	5.3	0.4	6 613	69.9	1 915	83.3
06 045	...	Mendocino County	81 075	56.1	26.1	12.2	3.5	2.1	33 266	61.3	7 912	78.3
06 047	4940	Merced County	192 259	50.5	29.8	14.3	2.2	3.3	63 815	58.7	12 474	77.0
06 049	...	Modoc County	8 940	59.8	18.0	14.0	6.2	2.0	3 784	70.7	1 026	79.3
06 051	...	Mono County	12 097	38.0	27.9	23.2	8.2	2.8	5 137	60.1	608	89.8
06 053	7120	Monterey County	370 950	48.8	28.5	11.1	5.4	6.2	121 236	54.7	25 342	76.6
06 055	8720	Napa County	116 795	53.0	25.0	13.6	4.4	4.0	45 402	65.1	11 600	79.0
06 057	...	Nevada County	87 813	52.3	21.6	19.8	5.3	1.0	36 894	75.8	10 139	86.7
06 059	5945	Orange County	2 632 408	48.0	33.3	9.7	4.1	4.9	935 287	61.4	169 273	78.8
06 061	6920	Placer County	232 679	47.4	19.4	25.2	6.4	1.7	93 382	73.2	20 422	82.8
06 063	...	Plumas County	19 853	56.2	16.8	19.3	6.9	0.9	9 000	70.1	2 535	85.2
06 065	6780	Riverside County	1 425 927	46.7	28.8	17.0	4.7	2.8	506 218	68.8	122 795	82.0
06 067	6920	Sacramento County	1 136 050	47.5	32.1	12.4	4.4	3.6	453 602	58.2	86 079	76.0
06 069	...	San Benito County	48 623	49.3	21.8	22.4	2.9	3.6	15 885	68.1	2 558	79.9
06 071	6780	San Bernardino County.	1 568 725	48.2	29.9	14.6	4.6	2.7	528 594	64.5	90 480	79.9
06 073	7320	San Diego County	2 617 718	45.1	34.5	7.1	9.2	4.2	994 677	55.4	196 534	75.3
06 075	7360	San Francisco County...	745 650	54.2	19.7	10.2	9.3	6.7	329 700	35.0	68 613	51.7
06 077	8120	San Jòaquin County......	519 445	51.2	29.1	13.8	2.8	3.0	181 629	60.4	36 484	73.9
06 079	7460	San Luis Obispo County	234 524	46.7	26.2	20.9	4.6	1.6	92 739	61.5	23 326	81.9
06 081	7360	San Mateo County	662 509	56.6	20.7	12.6	4.3	5.9	254 103	61.5	53 583	78.2
06 083	7480	Santa Barbara County ..	373 862	48.3	29.2	12.8	5.5	4.1	136 622	56.1	32 370	77.4
06 085	7400	Santa Clara County.......	1 564 066	51.2	28.0	7.6	5.3	8.0	565 863	59.8	91 763	76.6
06 087	7485	Santa Cruz County.......	240 233	50.6	27.7	13.8	4.5	3.5	91 139	60.0	16 355	78.8
06 089	6690	Shasta County	153 584	50.0	30.2	13.3	5.5	0.9	63 426	66.1	15 850	80.7
06 091	...	Sierra County	3 409	61.1	13.9	17.8	6.8	0.4	1 520	70.9	426	82.6
06 093	...	Siskiyou County	42 028	55.1	23.6	13.4	6.8	1.0	18 556	67.2	5 560	82.7
06 095	8720	Solano County	366 302	49.9	24.7	16.4	5.6	3.5	130 403	65.2	22 343	77.8
06 097	7500	Sonoma County	431 580	52.0	28.9	12.1	4.0	3.0	172 403	64.1	37 981	78.4
06 099	5170	Stanislaus County	411 833	50.8	31.1	12.7	2.7	2.7	145 146	61.9	28 439	75.2
06 101	9340	Sutter County	73 266	51.6	25.5	15.7	3.6	3.6	27 033	61.5	5 675	79.9
06 103	...	Tehama County	52 486	52.5	23.8	18.7	3.9	1.2	21 013	67.7	5 986	80.8
06 105	...	Trinity County	12 494	59.0	18.7	18.3	3.6	0.4	5 587	71.3	1 509	86.8
06 107	8780	Tulare County	335 395	53.1	33.6	8.1	2.2	3.0	110 385	61.5	22 683	78.5
06 109	...	Tuolumne County	51 965	49.4	21.1	23.7	5.3	0.6	21 004	71.2	6 589	85.7
06 111	8735	Ventura County	697 367	51.7	28.8	11.5	4.9	3.1	243 234	67.6	46 466	80.0
06 113	9270	Yolo County	157 792	41.8	23.4	24.2	5.1	5.5	59 375	53.1	10 376	75.3
06 115	9340	Yuba County	55 394	47.2	23.5	17.5	8.6	3.2	20 535	54.0	4 311	75.7
08 000	...	COLORADO..............	4 006 285	44.1	23.0	13.5	16.1	3.4	1 658 238	67.3	272 491	78.3
08 001	2080	Adams County...............	333 734	43.8	21.7	18.6	11.7	4.2	128 156	70.6	18 220	81.7
08 003	...	Alamosa County...........	13 975	51.8	20.5	16.8	9.5	1.3	5 467	64.0	981	73.1
08 005	2080	Arapahoe County	454 817	44.3	19.8	16.1	15.9	3.9	190 909	68.0	26 355	78.3
08 007	...	Archuleta County	9 359	42.0	20.2	9.8	27.3	0.6	3 980	76.8	853	88.6
08 009	...	Baca County.................	4 268	63.1	18.7	4.8	12.6	0.8	1 905	76.5	635	86.0
08 011	...	Bent County.................	5 652	49.7	12.5	19.2	18.0	0.6	2 003	67.7	571	81.6
08 013	1125	Boulder County	273 719	40.8	24.4	10.0	21.1	3.9	114 680	64.7	14 819	77.2
08 015	...	Chaffee County	15 544	48.2	21.3	15.1	14.5	1.0	6 584	73.3	1 816	84.5
08 017	...	Cheyenne County	2 090	62.3	17.2	11.8	7.4	1.2	880	75.0	275	86.9

[1]MSA = Metropolitan Statistical Area. PMSA = Primary MSA. NECMA = New England County Metropolitan Area. See the Appendix A for explanation of these concepts. See Appendix B for list of metropolitan areas identified by type, with component counties.

Table C-3. States and Counties — **Migration, Housing, and Transportation**

STATE County	Owner-occupied by household type (percent)								Median household income			Median housing value (owner estimated)	Median monthly owner costs as a percent of income	
	Family-households					Nonfamily households								
	Total family households	Married-couple family		Other family		Total nonfamily households	Two or more adults	Living alone	All households	Owner-occupied households	Renter-occupied households		With a mortgage	Without a mortgage
		Total	With own children under 18 years	Total	With own children under 18 years									
	11	12	13	14	15	16	17	18	19	20	21	22	23	24
CALIFORNIA—Cont'd														
Butte County	70.6	78.4	68.6	45.2	34.3	44.5	23.6	52.6	31 769	41 725	20 489	116 200	24.1	10.3
Calaveras County	81.9	87.1	80.0	54.9	40.3	70.8	63.3	72.6	41 235	45 445	27 252	156 300	26.1	12.3
Colusa County	65.2	70.5	62.5	44.2	34.9	57.5	48.5	58.8	34 971	41 903	25 304	111 000	24.5	11.3
Contra Costa County	74.8	81.4	77.3	50.9	40.3	55.9	47.5	58.2	63 400	76 591	40 174	253 800	24.7	9.9
Del Norte County	68.0	77.3	63.1	44.6	35.6	54.6	67.7	51.5	29 286	37 968	18 145	101 500	22.3	10.9
El Dorado County	79.9	85.8	80.3	51.1	41.6	60.4	51.2	63.5	51 380	61 154	31 278	191 500	25.5	11.3
Fresno County	60.1	68.7	59.5	37.9	26.9	46.1	33.7	49.2	34 500	47 718	22 114	102 600	24.2	10.8
Glenn County	65.7	72.3	62.0	41.0	29.1	59.3	42.2	62.8	32 144	38 085	22 372	97 800	22.7	9.9
Humboldt County	67.1	76.0	67.1	43.4	33.0	43.4	30.0	43.5	31 070	41 836	19 717	128 500	23.8	9.9
Imperial County	60.0	66.3	59.3	43.4	30.8	51.4	47.1	52.1	31 368	43 469	20 188	93 800	24.5	10.9
Inyo County	71.2	77.6	66.2	47.9	36.0	56.2	42.6	58.1	35 269	40 625	26 944	128 500	22.1	10.2
Kern County	65.3	73.4	65.8	42.7	33.3	52.3	42.0	54.5	35 265	46 204	22 590	89 400	23.5	10.5
Kings County	58.0	65.2	56.1	36.6	27.0	48.4	40.2	50.6	35 345	46 772	24 948	96 500	23.2	9.9
Lake County	71.2	80.6	66.1	43.8	33.9	69.3	59.9	71.5	29 980	34 331	21 812	105 600	26.7	13.8
Lassen County	73.6	80.2	70.0	45.0	35.0	55.0	40.9	50.7	35 745	41 905	24 004	105 100	22.9	10.0
Los Angeles County	53.9	61.4	54.5	35.9	24.2	34.8	29.8	36.2	42 030	62 180	29 395	201 400	26.6	9.9
Madera County	68.0	74.5	63.9	44.2	32.1	59.3	49.6	61.6	36 112	43 083	24 476	118 300	25.0	10.9
Marin County	72.9	78.3	75.1	51.2	44.1	49.3	43.6	51.1	71 047	91 363	47 738	493 300	25.2	9.9
Mariposa County	74.4	79.4	69.0	53.3	35.4	60.3	70.2	58.3	34 449	39 845	23 629	138 700	24.1	9.9
Mendocino County	64.4	72.6	60.5	38.9	29.8	55.2	47.8	57.2	35 791	44 360	25 645	165 000	24.3	11.0
Merced County	61.2	69.1	61.3	38.1	26.6	49.7	36.2	52.7	35 619	46 430	23 943	110 900	24.7	10.8
Modoc County	73.3	78.8	62.6	50.2	43.0	65.3	64.7	65.4	27 239	33 117	18 298	72 900	20.0	10.3
Mono County	68.0	73.9	64.1	41.0	35.6	47.5	39.2	51.4	44 427	52 109	31 295	189 500	28.1	9.9
Monterey County	58.1	63.4	54.0	39.7	27.7	45.4	40.3	46.8	48 165	60 686	36 271	254 800	26.4	9.9
Napa County	69.7	76.0	66.1	48.3	35.9	55.3	50.7	56.4	51 660	62 952	37 619	242 200	25.4	9.9
Nevada County	81.1	86.7	79.8	57.1	48.7	62.8	57.9	64.2	45 572	51 561	29 333	199 300	26.6	11.4
Orange County	66.0	71.3	64.4	46.2	34.0	49.7	36.3	54.1	58 500	73 745	40 451	253 000	25.1	9.9
Placer County	79.6	85.3	81.7	53.3	44.1	55.9	50.2	57.5	57 285	66 991	35 015	208 800	24.6	9.9
Plumas County	76.1	81.0	66.5	48.3	35.0	57.3	54.0	57.0	36 207	44 010	22 074	128 800	23.8	10.7
Riverside County	72.6	79.4	73.1	49.1	38.6	58.1	52.2	59.7	42 811	52 288	26 858	135 000	25.4	10.5
Sacramento County	65.0	73.9	67.2	42.6	31.6	45.0	38.4	46.9	43 612	57 468	29 245	141 100	23.7	9.9
San Benito County	70.6	74.0	60.6	51.2	41.0	57.3	46.0	60.0	57 600	69 002	30 002	200 000	27.0	0.0
San Bernardino County	67.6	75.5	69.7	45.7	34.9	54.2	44.2	56.7	41 839	52 375	27 005	124 900	24.8	10.3
San Diego County	62.0	68.8	60.9	40.2	28.2	42.0	30.8	46.1	46 887	62 537	32 133	212 000	25.6	9.9
San Francisco County	50.5	54.4	54.2	40.0	27.0	22.5	18.6	24.3	54 886	77 917	45 275	422 700	25.2	9.9
San Joaquin County	64.3	73.1	65.6	38.7	27.8	49.1	40.9	51.1	41 216	54 613	25 780	139 800	24.5	9.9
San Luis Obispo County	70.9	77.3	70.2	45.1	34.9	45.0	27.7	52.1	42 200	54 479	27 740	218 600	26.5	9.9
San Mateo County	68.6	73.0	68.3	51.5	40.0	46.7	37.7	49.6	70 483	85 619	51 771	449 900	25.7	9.9
Santa Barbara County	63.5	68.7	58.3	43.9	31.2	41.6	28.3	47.1	46 493	61 060	32 252	264 100	26.5	9.9
Santa Clara County	66.4	71.0	66.7	48.8	35.5	44.3	34.6	48.1	74 003	91 407	54 010	422 600	24.2	9.9
Santa Cruz County	67.3	73.9	66.8	46.2	35.6	47.6	36.7	52.6	53 820	66 340	36 276	350 000	26.7	9.9
Shasta County	71.1	79.6	69.2	43.5	30.9	54.8	46.0	56.9	34 308	41 217	22 074	112 900	25.2	11.6
Sierra County	78.1	84.4	73.7	45.4	35.8	57.0	62.7	55.9	36 706	43 051	24 044	128 200	22.8	11.0
Siskiyou County	71.9	79.0	64.9	43.5	32.5	58.1	51.3	59.3	29 481	36 738	19 220	98 800	22.7	11.2
Solano County	69.3	76.5	71.4	46.6	35.9	52.8	48.0	54.1	54 027	66 114	36 235	174 900	24.8	9.9
Sonoma County	70.6	76.8	69.7	48.9	39.9	51.6	43.3	54.5	52 798	64 189	37 503	265 200	26.0	9.9
Stanislaus County	65.4	72.9	66.1	42.6	31.9	51.0	42.9	53.0	40 202	50 838	26 356	123 900	24.3	9.9
Sutter County	66.2	73.8	65.3	39.1	25.6	47.8	42.4	48.8	38 253	50 384	24 656	119 900	23.4	9.9
Tehama County	70.5	76.7	63.2	49.4	38.9	60.9	53.3	62.5	30 979	37 337	21 361	97 000	23.5	10.7
Trinity County	75.7	82.2	65.7	51.5	40.9	62.8	57.1	63.9	27 406	31 984	18 853	103 300	26.4	9.9
Tulare County	63.6	70.9	61.8	42.4	31.7	53.5	35.4	57.2	33 669	42 762	22 582	96 500	24.4	9.9
Tuolumne County	76.2	83.6	72.5	45.5	33.3	60.5	52.9	62.3	39 105	45 152	25 371	143 600	25.1	10.1
Ventura County	71.3	76.3	70.4	51.9	40.7	56.1	48.6	58.3	59 292	71 551	39 315	238 800	25.2	9.9
Yolo County	63.7	70.7	64.9	41.1	32.4	34.7	17.0	44.8	40 527	60 527	24 785	164 400	23.9	9.9
Yuba County	55.9	62.3	49.3	37.7	23.1	49.0	44.1	50.3	30 612	39 457	23 137	89 500	24.6	10.2
COLORADO	76.3	82.0	78.4	53.7	46.5	50.2	40.5	53.2	47 009	57 099	30 335	160 100	22.6	9.9
Adams County	75.8	81.8	77.2	56.8	49.7	57.0	48.9	59.5	47 215	54 691	32 067	141 700	23.6	9.9
Alamosa County	72.1	77.4	71.1	53.5	47.7	47.1	36.1	49.2	29 331	40 045	17 175	84 600	20.7	10.1
Arapahoe County	76.4	82.5	80.8	53.9	47.6	51.8	45.2	53.5	53 371	65 274	34 075	166 000	21.8	9.9
Archuleta County	80.7	86.5	82.0	55.1	49.0	66.7	61.0	68.1	37 287	41 300	25 469	156 200	24.5	9.9
Baca County	79.6	84.2	75.2	54.8	46.1	70.1	56.6	71.4	27 839	30 857	20 563	49 300	20.4	11.3
Bent County	73.2	80.2	71.0	46.0	40.0	55.2	23.9	59.1	28 398	32 636	21 029	57 900	21.4	10.4
Boulder County	77.4	82.5	81.3	54.1	51.2	45.5	32.7	52.1	55 678	71 595	33 189	231 000	22.3	9.9
Chaffee County	79.2	84.1	76.9	50.1	38.7	61.8	54.4	63.3	33 814	38 420	23 445	146 500	24.7	9.9
Cheyenne County	82.5	85.4	78.4	64.3	58.8	58.1	23.5	60.5	37 037	41 458	24 375	63 700	18.4	9.9

STATE County	Median gross rent	Percent who pay 35 percent or more of income for housing expenses		Means of transportation to work (percent except where noted)						Vehicles available (percent of households)		
		Owners	Renters	Number of workers 16 years and over	Car, truck, or van		Public transportation	Other means	Walked	No vehicles	One vehicle	Two or more vehicles
					Drove alone	Carpooled						
	25	26	27	28	29	30	31	32	33	34	35	36
CALIFORNIA—Cont'd												
Butte County	563	19.3	41.8	80 809	74.3	13.3	1.1	3.6	3.4	7.7	35.3	57.1
Calaveras County	599	24.7	29.4	15 863	73.9	15.2	0.3	1.1	2.7	5.8	26.1	68.1
Colusa County	494	19.5	26.2	7 052	67.9	19.2	0.4	3.3	5.6	7.5	31.3	61.2
Contra Costa County	898	21.4	31.9	442 008	70.2	13.5	9.0	1.5	1.5	6.5	30.5	63.0
Del Norte County	519	18.0	38.3	8 844	73.9	15.5	1.3	1.7	4.0	10.3	36.5	53.2
El Dorado County	702	22.8	32.7	72 119	75.8	13.3	1.8	1.1	2.2	4.6	26.5	68.9
Fresno County	534	20.7	36.3	294 942	74.2	16.7	1.7	1.9	2.4	11.2	35.7	53.1
Glenn County	458	17.6	22.9	10 342	71.3	15.9	0.3	1.7	4.6	8.1	30.3	61.6
Humboldt County	537	17.7	42.2	54 034	71.6	13.1	1.0	2.2	6.5	8.7	36.5	54.8
Imperial County	504	21.4	35.4	43 204	72.7	17.0	1.7	1.9	3.7	11.1	34.0	54.9
Inyo County	516	13.2	26.0	7 884	70.4	14.7	0.7	3.3	7.2	8.4	34.6	57.0
Kern County	518	20.2	34.9	229 733	73.8	18.4	1.4	1.8	1.9	10.4	33.9	55.7
Kings County	533	18.3	28.9	41 944	73.5	17.0	1.6	2.0	3.3	9.3	34.9	55.8
Lake County	567	24.3	34.5	19 886	72.2	15.4	0.4	1.3	3.3	8.5	35.2	56.3
Lassen County	561	13.6	29.3	9 911	76.7	13.0	0.5	1.2	3.6	7.8	27.9	64.3
Los Angeles County	704	26.8	35.8	3 858 750	70.4	15.1	6.6	1.6	2.9	12.6	37.0	50.5
Madera County	562	22.4	32.9	40 958	73.1	18.1	0.7	1.4	2.4	8.1	30.2	61.7
Marin County	1 162	24.8	34.7	126 646	65.5	10.7	10.1	1.9	3.0	5.1	34.9	60.0
Mariposa County	502	18.9	25.6	6 646	63.5	16.6	1.4	2.8	10.2	5.7	28.9	65.4
Mendocino County	600	19.4	31.0	37 663	71.6	14.1	0.6	1.8	5.1	7.9	34.9	57.2
Merced County	518	21.6	32.1	73 346	72.9	18.5	0.7	1.8	3.0	10.4	31.9	57.7
Modoc County	429	15.6	24.8	3 534	72.8	10.7	0.1	2.1	6.3	7.6	31.2	61.2
Mono County	682	27.5	29.8	7 105	62.4	15.9	3.0	1.8	9.5	5.1	34.0	60.9
Monterey County	776	24.9	30.5	164 517	68.7	19.5	2.2	2.2	3.8	7.1	33.4	59.5
Napa County	818	20.4	30.0	57 393	72.7	14.8	1.4	1.9	4.1	6.2	32.4	61.5
Nevada County	746	24.5	33.4	40 673	75.4	12.7	0.7	0.9	2.7	4.7	27.7	67.5
Orange County	923	23.1	33.3	1 313 987	76.5	13.3	2.8	1.7	2.0	5.8	31.1	63.1
Placer County	780	20.3	30.5	116 409	80.1	10.1	1.0	1.2	1.7	4.9	27.0	68.0
Plumas County	525	17.1	29.7	8 287	74.3	13.0	0.3	1.4	5.5	6.4	29.9	63.7
Riverside County	660	23.3	36.0	590 516	73.4	17.6	1.4	1.8	1.9	7.1	34.7	58.3
Sacramento County	659	19.1	32.9	536 310	75.4	14.4	3.1	1.7	2.1	8.7	37.1	54.2
San Benito County	765	26.6	29.3	23 105	73.1	18.4	1.3	1.6	2.6	4.9	23.5	71.6
San Bernardino County	648	22.5	35.1	658 708	73.6	17.5	1.9	1.4	2.4	8.0	32.4	59.7
San Diego County	761	23.2	34.1	1 299 503	73.9	13.0	3.4	1.9	3.4	8.0	34.8	57.1
San Francisco County	928	22.9	28.2	418 553	40.5	10.8	31.1	3.6	9.4	28.6	42.0	29.4
San Joaquin County	617	21.1	35.7	213 629	74.6	17.0	1.4	1.8	2.3	9.5	32.2	58.3
San Luis Obispo County	719	23.0	40.4	107 807	73.9	13.5	1.0	2.4	3.7	5.3	33.2	61.6
San Mateo County	1 144	23.4	31.1	354 096	72.3	12.8	7.4	1.7	2.1	6.1	31.8	62.1
Santa Barbara County	830	24.5	38.2	179 445	69.4	15.8	2.4	3.8	4.0	6.9	34.0	59.2
Santa Clara County	1 185	21.1	29.6	828 927	77.3	12.2	3.5	2.0	1.8	5.7	29.0	65.3
Santa Cruz County	924	25.9	37.2	126 106	69.5	14.2	3.3	3.2	4.4	6.3	31.4	62.3
Shasta County	563	22.1	36.9	64 487	79.7	12.0	0.9	1.2	2.2	7.0	34.2	58.7
Sierra County	513	18.5	26.8	1 502	68.6	18.2	0.0	1.2	7.7	8.1	27.8	64.1
Siskiyou County	471	17.9	34.1	16 706	70.2	13.7	0.6	1.3	5.8	8.1	32.9	59.0
Solano County	797	21.3	30.2	174 571	73.3	17.7	2.7	1.6	1.6	6.6	29.1	64.4
Sonoma County	864	23.0	32.6	224 947	74.7	12.6	2.4	1.7	3.1	5.8	31.6	62.7
Stanislaus County	611	20.9	35.1	170 169	76.9	15.0	1.0	1.5	2.4	8.6	32.1	59.3
Sutter County	506	19.4	30.4	30 383	78.2	14.8	0.6	1.5	1.9	7.9	31.6	60.5
Tehama County	486	19.1	30.0	20 640	75.4	13.7	0.6	1.7	2.7	7.7	31.7	60.5
Trinity County	487	20.6	32.5	4 401	69.9	14.3	0.3	1.4	5.7	5.8	32.5	61.7
Tulare County	516	20.6	32.7	130 744	72.2	18.7	0.9	2.2	2.5	9.7	33.3	57.0
Tuolumne County	611	19.4	37.5	19 878	77.4	12.0	0.6	1.3	2.9	5.5	29.7	64.8
Ventura County	892	23.5	31.3	345 658	75.9	15.1	1.1	1.7	2.1	5.0	28.0	66.9
Yolo County	687	18.9	43.4	75 151	67.2	13.2	3.7	8.3	3.8	8.4	34.8	56.7
Yuba County	488	20.6	28.9	21 990	73.2	17.8	0.7	1.8	2.4	9.5	33.8	56.7
COLORADO	671	16.6	30.4	2 191 626	75.1	12.2	3.2	1.5	3.0	6.4	31.6	62.0
Adams County	705	18.1	29.3	178 572	76.0	14.4	4.3	0.9	1.4	5.9	30.0	64.2
Alamosa County	408	15.6	30.4	6 766	69.2	15.2	0.0	2.0	9.0	8.4	32.7	58.8
Arapahoe County	735	15.2	29.3	260 271	78.8	10.9	3.2	0.9	1.6	5.6	33.6	60.8
Archuleta County	627	20.2	30.4	4 465	70.6	15.4	0.1	1.6	3.8	5.1	24.8	70.1
Baca County	295	14.0	11.7	1 990	69.6	13.3	0.0	1.5	5.5	3.8	28.4	67.8
Bent County	415	14.5	25.3	2 159	75.7	11.9	0.3	0.7	5.3	6.2	32.8	61.1
Boulder County	825	16.4	36.6	159 786	70.8	10.4	4.9	3.5	4.1	5.4	31.9	62.7
Chaffee County	517	17.4	30.6	6 665	72.3	13.1	0.5	1.8	4.0	5.3	28.2	66.5
Cheyenne County	362	8.0	18.0	1 041	69.3	11.3	0.0	0.8	6.2	5.0	25.3	69.7

Table C-3. States and Counties — Migration, Housing, and Transportation

STATE/ County code	MSA/PMSA/ NECMA code[1]	STATE County	Total population 5 years and over	Residence in 1995 (percent)					Occupied housing units		Householders 65 years and over	
				Same house	Same county, different house	Same state, different county	Different state	Outside the United States	Number	Percent owner-occupied	Number	Percent owner-occupied
			1	2	3	4	5	6	7	8	9	10
		COLORADO—Cont'd										
08 019	...	Clear Creek County	8 770	52.7	12.8	19.0	14.4	1.2	4 019	75.9	501	90.2
08 021	...	Conejos County............	7 749	68.8	16.4	8.5	5.8	0.5	2 980	78.6	910	85.9
08 023	...	Costilla County	3 464	65.4	11.2	10.0	12.0	1.4	1 503	78.5	509	87.2
08 025	...	Crowley County	5 276	42.2	10.6	37.4	9.6	0.2	1 358	72.9	384	80.7
08 027	...	Custer County	3 317	45.4	14.1	18.4	21.5	0.6	1 480	78.9	348	87.4
08 029	...	Delta County	26 174	52.0	20.2	13.6	12.5	1.7	11 058	77.5	3 681	85.2
08 031	2080	Denver County	517 349	42.7	24.3	12.5	13.9	6.6	239 235	52.5	43 704	68.0
08 033	...	Dolores County	1 750	55.7	14.2	15.0	14.3	0.7	785	76.1	192	85.9
08 035	2080	Douglas County............	158 773	34.3	11.7	27.0	24.6	2.4	60 924	87.9	4 023	89.1
08 037	...	Eagle County	38 770	35.0	24.0	10.8	21.6	8.6	15 148	63.7	783	80.7
08 039	...	Elbert County	18 606	44.1	9.3	31.9	13.7	0.9	6 770	89.4	717	92.5
08 041	1720	El Paso County	477 912	40.4	27.2	4.5	24.0	4.0	192 409	64.7	29 228	78.8
08 043	...	Fremont County	43 946	41.1	19.8	29.1	9.6	0.5	15 232	76.0	4 372	80.6
08 045	...	Garfield County	40 474	39.9	27.3	14.1	15.3	3.4	16 229	65.1	2 462	73.2
08 047	...	Gilpin County	4 485	43.4	5.9	33.9	15.7	1.1	2 043	78.5	234	92.3
08 049	...	Grand County	11 731	42.2	20.4	18.3	17.2	2.0	5 075	68.3	626	81.6
08 051	...	Gunnison County	13 306	36.8	25.3	14.8	21.6	1.5	5 649	58.4	595	82.0
08 053	...	Hinsdale County	742	50.0	17.0	9.0	23.0	0.9	359	64.9	69	87.0
08 055	...	Huerfano County	7 512	51.1	18.1	16.7	13.5	0.6	3 082	70.6	992	82.5
08 057	...	Jackson County	1 490	57.7	18.2	11.5	12.3	0.3	661	67.9	148	85.1
08 059	2080	Jefferson County	494 065	50.9	21.0	14.0	12.3	1.8	206 067	72.5	32 278	78.5
08 061	...	Kiowa County	1 527	64.4	18.5	9.3	7.6	0.3	665	71.3	191	85.9
08 063	...	Kit Carson County........	7 521	57.4	17.5	8.1	14.8	2.3	2 990	72.1	763	79.4
08 065	...	Lake County	7 199	44.6	20.4	15.1	12.6	7.3	2 977	68.1	404	87.1
08 067	...	La Plata County............	41 643	45.4	22.4	9.1	22.1	1.0	17 342	68.4	2 697	83.6
08 069	2670	Larimer County............	236 326	41.5	26.2	12.3	18.2	1.9	97 164	67.7	15 058	81.1
08 071	...	Las Animas County......	14 388	58.3	19.5	8.3	12.4	1.5	6 173	70.4	1 972	83.7
08 073	...	Lincoln County	5 765	43.9	15.4	27.7	11.7	1.4	2 058	68.9	591	76.3
08 075	...	Logan County	19 270	53.1	21.3	16.6	7.3	1.7	7 551	69.8	2 090	81.1
08 077	2995	Mesa County............	109 124	45.1	29.1	10.4	14.5	0.9	45 823	72.7	11 173	82.5
08 079	...	Mineral County	794	50.6	13.1	8.3	26.7	1.3	377	73.2	106	80.2
08 081	...	Moffat County	12 318	49.5	21.1	13.5	14.7	1.3	4 983	72.0	793	74.7
08 083	...	Montezuma County	22 095	52.5	24.9	6.5	15.4	0.8	9 201	74.8	2 080	84.6
08 085	...	Montrose County	31 229	48.6	21.7	14.9	13.6	1.2	13 043	74.9	3 453	80.5
08 087	...	Morgan County............	24 856	50.0	26.8	9.7	10.0	3.4	9 539	68.5	2 331	77.7
08 089	...	Otero County	19 042	56.2	26.5	9.2	6.8	1.3	7 920	69.2	2 187	79.4
08 091	...	Ouray County	3 559	46.1	14.0	15.6	23.4	0.9	1 576	73.0	310	89.4
08 093	...	Park County	13 654	41.5	9.5	28.6	19.3	1.1	5 894	87.8	638	91.5
08 095	...	Phillips County	4 170	54.7	20.5	12.0	10.4	2.5	1 781	76.3	527	83.5
08 097	...	Pitkin County	14 260	44.0	23.6	0.7	18.0	4.8	6 807	50.1	707	82.0
08 099	...	Prowers County	13 323	51.7	25.3	9.0	9.9	4.0	5 307	66.2	1 356	79.9
08 101	6560	Pueblo County..............	132 161	51.5	30.2	8.5	8.8	0.9	54 579	70.4	14 607	81.5
08 103	...	Rio Blanco County	5 639	51.3	21.5	13.8	12.0	1.4	2 306	70.4	426	80.5
08 105	...	Rio Grande County	11 583	56.6	20.0	12.6	8.9	1.9	4 701	70.8	1 236	81.8
08 107	...	Routt County	18 605	41.1	24.5	11.0	21.8	1.6	7 953	69.3	751	82.2
08 109	...	Saguache County..........	5 515	50.8	18.0	16.8	11.7	2.7	2 300	69.4	435	83.4
08 111	...	San Juan County	532	50.0	18.0	9.8	21.8	0.4	269	67.3	37	89.2
08 113	...	San Miguel County	6 305	35.3	22.6	11.0	27.4	3.7	3 015	51.6	177	84.2
08 115	...	Sedgwick County	2 594	64.1	13.2	13.1	8.6	0.9	1 165	73.4	407	84.0
08 117	...	Summit County	22 307	29.1	21.9	11.9	30.1	7.1	9 120	59.0	443	88.3
08 119	...	Teller County................	19 399	41.4	14.8	20.3	22.3	1.3	7 993	80.9	905	91.0
08 121	...	Washington County	4 615	64.2	15.1	13.8	5.9	0.9	1 989	73.7	609	83.4
08 123	3060	Weld County................	166 956	42.5	26.4	17.7	10.6	2.8	63 247	68.7	10 710	77.6
08 125	...	Yuma County	9 192	57.3	19.3	12.5	7.3	3.6	3 800	71.1	1 040	81.6
09 000	...	CONNECTICUT	3 184 514	58.2	25.1	5.3	8.2	3.3	1 301 670	66.8	296 565	74.1
09 001	5483	Fairfield County	819 251	57.3	25.0	2.1	10.6	5.0	324 232	69.2	73 060	78.2
09 003	3283	Hartford County............	802 702	58.0	27.7	4.5	6.4	3.4	335 098	64.2	78 847	73.2
09 005	...	Litchfield County	171 567	63.7	19.7	9.1	6.4	1.1	71 551	75.2	16 516	76.3
09 007	3283	Middlesex County..........	145 545	59.0	18.9	12.3	8.3	1.5	61 341	72.1	13 216	74.0
09 009	5483	New Haven County	771 758	58.5	26.9	4.8	6.8	3.0	319 040	63.1	75 743	70.6
09 011	5523	New London County	242 931	55.2	25.0	5.8	12.2	1.7	99 835	66.7	21 782	75.1
09 013	3283	Tolland County	128 308	59.3	14.5	17.0	7.5	1.7	49 431	73.5	9 059	78.6
09 015	...	Windham County..........	102 452	58.9	23.4	8.5	7.5	1.7	41 142	67.4	8 342	67.5

[1]MSA = Metropolitan Statistical Area. PMSA = Primary MSA. NECMA = New England County Metropolitan Area. See the Appendix A for explanation of these concepts. See Appendix B for list of metropolitan areas identified by type, with component counties.

Table C-3. States and Counties — Migration, Housing, and Transportation

STATE County	Owner-occupied by household type (percent)								Median household income			Median housing value (owner estimated)	Median monthly owner costs as a percent of income	
	Family-households					Nonfamily households								
		Married-couple family		Other family										
	Total family households	Total	With own children under 18 years	Total	With own children under 18 years	Total nonfamily households	Two or more adults	Living alone	All households	Owner-occupied households	Renter-occupied households		With a mortgage	Without a mortgage
	11	12	13	14	15	16	17	18	19	20	21	22	23	24
COLORADO—Cont'd														
Clear Creek County	84.1	87.0	83.1	67.9	65.1	60.7	51.8	63.2	50 389	56 090	30 735	193 500	23.4	9.9
Conejos County	81.7	87.3	83.0	64.8	53.1	69.8	60.3	70.7	24 729	28 376	15 474	54 400	20.8	12.6
Costilla County	82.5	85.9	79.5	71.5	66.4	69.6	62.0	70.5	19 724	21 418	13 802	56 500	28.3	14.3
Crowley County	77.5	82.3	77.5	60.2	47.5	61.6	28.3	66.0	27 727	30 395	21 750	65 000	21.6	11.8
Custer County	82.8	84.3	71.9	69.4	64.9	68.3	36.7	72.8	35 000	40 141	25 700	157 600	23.1	9.9
Delta County	81.2	85.0	77.0	62.0	50.2	67.7	52.6	69.7	32 726	36 216	21 852	116 000	24.4	9.9
Denver County	64.2	72.7	67.0	44.4	34.3	40.8	36.5	42.0	39 317	52 589	28 022	160 100	23.2	9.9
Dolores County	79.1	84.2	74.3	56.6	50.9	69.3	63.2	70.4	32 406	34 856	25 000	74 800	20.1	9.9
Douglas County	92.1	93.4	93.4	78.1	76.3	68.9	64.8	70.4	82 578	86 955	48 767	237 600	22.5	9.9
Eagle County	75.2	78.4	76.3	57.8	60.7	46.7	38.0	54.6	62 353	73 138	47 743	300 900	25.8	9.9
Elbert County	91.7	92.8	91.1	82.3	78.3	77.3	72.8	78.6	62 694	67 092	35 139	235 400	24.9	9.9
El Paso County	72.1	77.7	72.4	49.4	41.6	47.4	37.7	50.0	46 658	56 759	30 759	143 600	22.5	9.9
Fremont County	80.2	84.6	78.9	60.8	50.6	66.7	54.1	68.6	34 480	39 607	22 469	99 400	22.8	9.9
Garfield County	71.4	76.1	69.7	49.9	43.0	50.6	51.5	50.3	46 402	55 410	32 819	185 300	23.9	9.9
Gilpin County	85.5	88.1	88.2	65.5	68.5	67.1	60.4	69.8	52 071	56 138	35 917	187 600	25.9	9.9
Grand County	78.0	82.4	75.9	47.0	39.4	51.5	39.0	57.5	48 648	55 540	36 366	196 900	22.6	9.9
Gunnison County	77.6	80.8	76.0	59.2	53.7	37.2	20.9	49.4	36 580	49 480	23 493	179 700	25.2	9.9
Hinsdale County	73.2	77.9	61.4	37.9	31.6	46.9	39.1	48.9	37 153	44 205	26 042	218 100	24.0	9.9
Huerfano County	76.6	81.8	73.8	56.9	35.7	60.6	61.4	60.4	26 162	28 916	19 005	79 700	24.5	12.7
Jackson County	69.6	70.6	57.8	63.6	52.6	64.5	60.7	65.1	31 780	34 926	27 900	84 700	21.7	9.9
Jefferson County	80.3	85.4	83.4	57.6	50.1	55.6	47.0	58.1	57 075	67 258	35 810	184 200	21.9	9.9
Kiowa County	76.1	83.2	73.8	38.9	45.5	61.0	28.6	63.3	30 516	33 854	20 804	52 100	18.8	11.3
Kit Carson County	77.6	81.3	75.4	55.3	46.9	59.4	55.8	59.7	33 229	40 199	23 500	78 200	19.4	9.9
Lake County	75.2	78.8	71.9	60.5	58.3	55.4	43.5	59.6	37 674	42 247	28 250	102 600	22.9	9.9
La Plata County	79.6	84.8	82.5	59.7	55.1	49.2	37.9	54.6	40 213	49 875	25 323	174 500	23.3	9.9
Larimer County	78.8	83.6	81.1	54.7	48.8	46.7	30.7	54.4	48 484	59 785	29 257	168 200	22.5	9.9
Las Animas County	75.8	81.0	72.5	60.6	43.3	59.6	55.6	60.1	28 111	32 766	17 318	86 300	23.2	10.9
Lincoln County	73.2	76.9	71.2	56.5	55.8	59.6	53.5	60.4	32 019	36 516	27 298	78 700	21.5	11.4
Logan County	77.2	81.1	70.4	56.5	49.1	54.6	48.8	55.5	32 571	39 216	21 578	86 200	20.6	11.6
Mesa County	78.7	84.5	79.0	54.2	44.3	59.3	47.0	62.2	35 680	41 872	22 459	113 800	23.0	9.9
Mineral County	83.7	84.6	72.0	76.7	81.8	52.4	31.6	56.1	33 967	36 042	27 361	129 000	18.9	9.9
Moffat County	80.0	85.7	80.9	55.1	46.2	51.0	52.7	50.7	41 592	49 505	26 472	96 300	19.2	9.9
Montezuma County	80.7	85.9	78.6	61.8	54.5	60.4	54.1	61.5	32 228	37 545	20 911	106 400	21.8	9.9
Montrose County	78.8	83.1	76.5	58.7	49.7	65.1	67.9	64.6	34 856	39 897	23 382	112 800	23.7	9.9
Morgan County	73.8	77.8	69.8	55.0	51.2	53.9	40.3	56.2	34 606	40 294	24 328	94 300	21.9	10.3
Otero County	74.8	82.1	72.1	50.7	41.5	56.8	48.5	57.8	29 602	35 370	17 439	67 700	20.1	9.9
Ouray County	79.5	81.5	74.2	66.0	56.3	55.9	42.7	58.7	42 388	48 986	29 667	238 600	29.1	9.9
Park County	90.6	92.1	89.1	79.9	75.7	80.5	72.7	83.1	51 866	54 554	38 214	174 600	24.5	9.9
Phillips County	80.1	82.4	78.1	64.8	55.6	67.8	52.8	69.4	32 382	35 566	25 729	82 400	21.1	9.9
Pitkin County	76.0	80.6	79.8	55.3	53.9	44.2	37.5	47.4	60 058	72 357	45 102	497 000	26.5	9.9
Prowers County	72.1	78.6	70.8	42.4	29.6	52.2	33.2	55.6	29 458	34 319	20 833	65 500	21.0	9.9
Pueblo County	76.3	84.6	77.9	53.4	40.1	57.5	47.8	59.3	32 617	39 806	19 468	93 100	22.3	9.9
Rio Blanco County	78.0	82.9	73.5	54.0	45.8	51.7	36.2	54.3	36 042	42 072	25 080	95 200	17.7	9.9
Rio Grande County	76.4	81.0	71.2	54.7	44.9	55.7	42.8	57.4	30 611	35 103	20 322	80 500	23.5	9.9
Routt County	81.7	85.3	82.1	62.6	62.6	50.1	42.8	54.6	53 387	60 271	39 983	246 200	24.0	9.9
Saguache County	73.8	84.7	67.7	57.4	46.9	60.3	57.7	60.9	25 327	28 538	17 765	67 700	21.8	9.9
San Juan County	70.8	74.8	47.1	60.5	57.6	62.6	60.0	63.0	30 208	33 125	14 375	131 900	25.3	11.7
San Miguel County	64.2	70.0	63.4	39.4	44.5	40.2	33.2	44.3	48 551	64 628	36 653	297 900	21.9	9.9
Sedgwick County	77.8	82.2	73.2	47.1	40.7	63.5	76.5	62.8	28 838	31 571	21 574	59 900	21.1	9.9
Summit County	73.7	77.5	75.9	52.4	58.7	42.4	34.2	52.1	56 487	66 467	42 807	268 800	23.3	9.9
Teller County	84.8	86.4	82.1	73.0	70.4	69.4	64.1	71.0	50 733	54 089	40 818	160 600	23.7	9.9
Washington County	79.1	81.3	72.8	66.0	56.0	60.5	55.8	61.0	32 234	35 321	24 398	76 800	19.6	9.9
Weld County	76.4	81.1	77.1	54.6	48.2	48.9	32.9	54.4	42 152	51 443	24 646	136 600	23.9	9.9
Yuma County	74.8	77.7	70.6	55.0	48.3	62.5	50.0	63.9	33 196	37 650	22 923	80 400	20.2	9.9
CONNECTICUT	75.4	83.4	81.7	48.4	35.0	48.7	42.2	50.1	53 736	67 350	31 318	160 600	22.4	13.1
Fairfield County	76.3	83.1	81.6	50.6	37.4	52.2	42.1	54.4	65 014	80 790	37 255	265 100	23.1	13.8
Hartford County	73.3	83.1	81.1	45.1	31.2	46.2	38.2	47.8	50 678	65 561	29 511	142 500	21.9	12.9
Litchfield County	82.6	87.2	86.4	60.2	48.3	58.5	57.5	58.8	56 136	65 028	32 089	155 900	22.7	13.2
Middlesex County	82.2	87.2	87.6	58.7	47.0	52.4	49.4	53.1	59 049	68 421	36 849	163 400	22.1	12.5
New Haven County	72.1	81.5	79.6	44.6	30.7	45.5	41.0	46.4	48 544	63 116	28 430	145 500	22.9	13.8
New London County	75.0	81.8	77.2	50.6	37.5	49.3	42.8	50.8	50 599	61 549	32 177	139 700	21.8	11.8
Tolland County	85.2	89.2	90.2	62.5	52.5	47.2	38.7	49.8	58 826	70 035	32 494	150 500	21.1	11.5
Windham County	75.8	83.8	82.1	48.8	38.7	48.9	49.7	48.7	45 082	55 050	26 179	117 500	21.6	11.4

STATE County	Percent who pay 35 percent or more of income for housing expenses		Means of transportation to work (percent except where noted)						Vehicles available (percent of households)		
			Car, truck, or van								
	Median gross rent	Owners	Renters	Number of workers 16 years and over	Drove alone	Carpooled	Public transportation	Other means	Walked	No vehicles	One vehicle	Two or more vehicles
	25	26	27	28	29	30	31	32	33	34	35	36
COLORADO—Cont'd												
Clear Creek County	648	18.8	32.6	5 556	72.8	13.2	2.1	0.6	3.7	2.9	25.7	71.3
Conejos County	332	17.3	26.0	3 052	72.3	16.2	0.4	0.6	3.6	8.6	28.1	63.3
Costilla County	316	21.6	25.4	1 115	71.5	18.1	0.2	2.0	3.7	11.3	35.5	53.2
Crowley County	367	14.0	14.1	1 355	72.1	13.7	0.6	1.1	6.4	7.7	28.4	63.9
Custer County	476	19.0	27.8	1 468	64.4	20.9	0.0	0.0	3.9	4.9	19.3	75.9
Delta County	504	16.9	27.6	11 211	69.8	14.3	0.1	0.8	5.4	4.9	26.7	68.5
Denver County	631	19.2	30.6	278 715	68.3	13.5	8.4	1.8	4.3	13.9	43.1	43.0
Dolores County	510	15.2	25.1	794	68.8	16.1	0.0	1.3	7.1	4.6	30.7	64.7
Douglas County	1 053	16.2	26.8	96 167	81.0	8.0	1.5	0.9	0.8	1.4	17.0	81.6
Eagle County	1 007	24.6	27.4	25 020	65.6	16.1	8.5	1.0	3.6	3.0	27.7	69.3
Elbert County	655	23.3	24.8	10 580	76.2	12.8	1.1	0.9	2.1	1.8	13.2	85.0
El Paso County	657	16.3	29.3	263 805	78.0	12.0	1.0	1.2	3.7	5.4	31.6	63.1
Fremont County	496	16.4	31.7	16 077	75.5	15.1	0.5	1.3	2.3	6.4	30.4	63.3
Garfield County	657	19.4	28.2	22 540	64.8	20.8	3.0	1.2	5.0	4.7	28.6	66.6
Gilpin County	642	24.0	34.1	2 008	73.0	15.5	1.2	1.0	4.1	2.6	25.1	72.3
Grand County	655	15.8	21.5	7 329	67.4	16.2	1.3	1.8	5.7	3.5	26.6	69.9
Gunnison County	593	21.2	38.5	7 916	56.6	15.7	2.9	6.3	11.9	4.0	32.1	63.9
Hinsdale County	510	14.1	24.8	433	50.8	16.4	0.5	3.0	10.9	4.7	26.7	68.5
Huerfano County	419	18.3	28.9	2 838	67.2	17.3	0.4	1.6	5.0	11.4	31.7	56.9
Jackson County	388	12.5	22.5	785	52.0	10.1	0.4	0.6	17.3	4.2	24.2	71.6
Jefferson County	760	14.6	28.2	286 304	79.6	9.9	3.3	0.9	1.3	4.0	28.8	67.2
Kiowa County	366	15.0	14.3	737	70.6	11.1	0.5	0.7	7.9	5.6	26.8	67.7
Kit Carson County	420	13.0	18.5	3 626	72.0	12.4	0.4	0.9	6.3	6.8	26.0	67.2
Lake County	558	16.1	29.7	3 961	59.6	28.5	3.4	1.1	4.1	6.3	27.3	66.4
La Plata County	655	18.1	35.4	22 481	69.5	13.6	1.0	2.4	5.2	5.1	27.3	67.6
Larimer County	678	15.0	33.9	134 615	77.4	11.0	0.9	3.0	2.7	4.0	28.3	67.7
Las Animas County	397	16.2	26.3	5 946	72.7	16.6	0.5	0.5	4.6	10.2	33.5	56.3
Lincoln County	447	12.5	17.7	2 453	69.4	12.2	0.0	1.6	6.6	4.4	29.3	66.3
Logan County	451	15.1	26.4	9 209	76.0	13.5	0.0	1.0	3.9	5.7	31.7	62.7
Mesa County	527	15.7	33.8	54 101	77.1	12.1	0.5	2.3	2.8	5.1	31.4	63.5
Mineral County	500	7.0	7.1	402	50.7	28.1	0.2	2.0	10.9	4.0	31.6	64.5
Moffat County	460	10.1	17.0	6 767	70.1	22.0	1.4	0.9	2.3	6.1	24.9	69.0
Montezuma County	459	16.2	28.1	10 371	73.0	16.8	0.3	1.7	3.5	6.1	29.0	64.9
Montrose County	521	19.2	29.2	14 855	71.3	15.9	0.3	1.5	3.8	5.7	29.6	64.7
Morgan County	482	12.9	23.9	11 693	76.6	14.9	0.1	1.4	3.3	6.0	29.9	64.1
Otero County	372	13.5	26.5	8 205	74.5	14.2	0.6	0.6	5.4	8.6	32.1	59.3
Ouray County	696	24.2	35.6	1 778	58.7	13.9	0.3	1.9	11.4	3.3	26.4	70.3
Park County	806	22.0	30.1	7 737	66.0	20.7	2.3	0.8	2.0	2.2	19.8	78.0
Phillips County	388	12.4	17.2	1 954	70.7	12.4	0.0	0.6	5.5	5.2	30.2	64.6
Pitkin County	947	27.0	28.4	9 443	51.0	11.4	10.6	4.0	12.9	4.2	37.7	58.0
Prowers County	400	11.9	22.0	6 573	75.2	15.7	0.3	1.6	3.7	8.0	31.9	60.1
Pueblo County	409	16.4	35.3	58 749	79.4	13.6	0.7	1.1	1.9	9.4	32.5	58.2
Rio Blanco County	399	8.8	19.1	2 896	70.6	16.7	0.2	1.2	6.7	4.4	25.5	70.1
Rio Grande County	382	17.4	25.5	5 282	70.0	16.6	0.0	1.6	3.7	7.6	28.6	63.8
Routt County	740	21.7	28.2	12 009	68.7	15.1	2.1	2.3	5.7	3.5	27.8	68.7
Saguache County	404	17.5	27.3	2 440	61.8	19.3	0.0	2.9	6.6	8.9	33.2	57.9
San Juan County	561	19.0	54.5	292	49.7	14.4	0.0	1.7	21.6	8.2	35.7	56.1
San Miguel County	811	24.9	31.9	4 370	45.1	12.9	3.4	10.5	19.8	6.4	36.4	57.2
Sedgwick County	301	8.8	14.4	1 307	68.0	12.9	0.2	1.4	7.1	4.5	27.8	67.7
Summit County	874	21.2	24.3	15 959	65.7	12.5	5.0	2.2	8.7	3.3	29.0	67.8
Teller County	767	19.7	21.7	10 806	74.5	15.3	0.4	0.8	3.1	2.4	21.9	75.7
Washington County	341	12.1	15.0	2 321	63.1	11.2	0.1	0.9	9.3	3.0	25.6	71.4
Weld County	564	18.4	32.2	86 210	78.5	12.7	0.4	1.3	2.9	5.6	26.8	67.6
Yuma County	375	10.3	19.5	4 715	74.8	10.9	0.0	0.5	2.6	4.6	29.4	66.1
CONNECTICUT	681	17.1	29.0	1 640 823	80.0	9.4	4.0	0.7	2.7	9.6	33.1	57.3
Fairfield County	838	20.7	30.5	419 237	74.7	9.6	8.1	0.8	2.3	8.6	31.3	60.1
Hartford County	645	14.9	29.2	403 863	82.2	9.0	3.5	0.7	2.1	11.2	34.7	54.1
Litchfield County	660	17.1	24.0	93 934	83.5	8.6	1.0	0.6	2.4	5.4	29.8	64.9
Middlesex County	701	15.3	23.1	80 715	84.6	7.5	1.2	0.6	2.8	6.0	31.0	63.0
New Haven County	666	18.0	31.5	388 050	80.7	9.7	3.2	0.8	3.2	12.3	35.6	52.1
New London County	646	14.5	22.9	129 553	81.1	9.9	1.6	0.9	3.8	7.1	32.9	60.0
Tolland County	662	12.5	26.7	71 434	82.5	8.5	1.3	0.5	4.4	4.4	27.9	67.7
Windham County	548	13.9	24.7	54 037	80.8	12.9	0.6	0.7	2.5	8.1	30.9	61.1

Table C-3. States and Counties — Migration, Housing, and Transportation

STATE/ County code	MSA/PMSA/ NECMA code[1]	STATE County	Total population 5 years and over	Residence in 1995 (percent)					Occupied housing units		Householders 65 years and over	
				Same house	Same county, different house	Same state, different county	Different state	Outside the United States	Number	Percent owner-occupied	Number	Percent owner-occupied
			1	2	3	4	5	6	7	8	9	10
10 000	...	DELAWARE	732 378	56.0	25.5	2.3	13.9	2.4	298 736	72.3	67 355	82.7
10 001	2190	Kent County	117 562	55.6	24.3	5.2	12.8	2.0	47 224	70.0	9 856	82.1
10 003	9160	New Castle County	467 203	55.3	27.3	1.2	13.7	2.6	188 935	70.1	38 315	79.4
10 005	...	Sussex County	147 613	58.3	21.0	3.5	15.3	2.0	62 577	80.7	19 184	89.6
11 000	...	DISTRICT OF COLUMBIA..	539 658	49.9	23.5	X	20.9	5.6	248 338	40.8	50 335	58.4
11 001	8840	District of Columbia......	539 658	49.9	23.5	X	20.9	5.6	248 338	40.8	50 335	58.4
12 000	...	FLORIDA..................	15 043 603	48.9	25.7	8.7	12.4	4.3	6 337 929	70.1	1 789 594	84.0
12 001	2900	Alachua County	206 860	39.9	23.4	22.4	10.9	3.4	87 509	54.9	13 848	83.9
12 003	...	Baker County	20 670	59.0	16.4	18.2	5.9	0.6	7 043	81.3	1 212	92.1
12 005	6015	Bay County	139 213	49.4	26.5	6.2	15.9	2.0	59 597	68.6	13 017	85.1
12 007	...	Bradford County	24 690	58.1	14.8	20.6	5.8	0.7	8 497	79.0	2 276	87.7
12 009	4900	Brevard County	451 553	51.6	25.6	6.4	14.5	1.9	198 195	74.6	61 049	86.8
12 011	2680	Broward County	1 520 842	47.1	27.2	9.0	10.6	6.1	654 445	69.5	173 341	83.9
12 013	...	Calhoun County	12 264	67.1	16.6	12.3	3.4	0.6	4 468	80.2	1 136	89.3
12 015	6580	Charlotte County	136 659	52.5	17.0	8.6	20.7	1.2	63 864	83.7	30 891	90.2
12 017	...	Citrus County	113 648	53.5	17.4	10.8	17.6	0.8	52 634	85.6	23 705	92.9
12 019	3600	Clay County	131 720	49.8	15.8	16.2	15.9	2.2	50 243	77.9	8 103	84.3
12 021	5345	Collier County	238 077	44.2	22.7	7.1	19.7	6.2	102 973	75.6	38 231	88.9
12 023	...	Columbia County	52 904	53.0	20.1	16.6	9.4	0.9	20 925	77.1	5 237	85.3
12 027	...	DeSoto County	30 331	48.3	20.7	11.9	11.1	8.0	10 746	74.7	3 829	90.2
12 029	...	Dixie County..............	13 080	60.2	13.3	20.9	4.7	0.9	5 205	86.5	1 513	92.8
12 031	3600	Duval County	723 198	48.9	29.7	6.6	12.2	2.6	303 747	63.1	54 361	77.0
12 033	6080	Escambia County	276 629	47.7	25.7	7.5	16.8	2.3	111 049	67.3	26 251	83.4
12 035	2020	Flagler County	47 707	48.1	15.8	11.6	23.3	1.2	21 294	84.1	8 976	91.5
12 037	...	Franklin County	10 551	59.5	16.3	13.6	8.5	2.1	4 096	79.2	1 158	88.7
12 039	8240	Gadsden County	42 047	64.7	18.5	10.2	5.5	1.2	15 867	78.0	3 597	87.5
12 041	...	Gilchrist County...........	13 615	59.4	10.2	23.7	6.1	0.6	5 021	86.2	1 191	92.8
12 043	...	Glades County	9 966	53.0	11.3	22.9	10.5	2.2	3 852	81.6	1 231	91.8
12 045	...	Gulf County	12 723	57.9	16.8	15.5	8.7	1.0	4 931	81.0	1 511	89.3
12 047	...	Hamilton County	12 564	54.0	14.8	15.8	6.1	9.3	4 161	77.3	1 062	89.6
12 049	...	Hardee County	24 870	55.3	23.0	11.0	5.8	5.1	8 166	73.4	2 439	89.3
12 051	...	Hendry County	33 340	51.2	22.6	11.5	6.6	8.1	10 850	72.4	2 339	88.7
12 053	8280	Hernando County	124 914	54.9	17.1	11.1	15.9	0.9	55 425	86.5	25 351	93.7
12 055	...	Highlands County	82 787	52.9	20.6	10.7	12.9	2.9	37 471	79.7	18 231	89.3
12 057	8280	Hillsborough County......	931 276	46.0	30.0	7.5	12.5	4.0	391 357	64.1	77 597	79.8
12 059	...	Holmes County	17 531	57.2	18.1	16.4	7.7	0.6	6 921	81.6	2 062	88.8
12 061	...	Indian River County	107 745	52.1	20.5	10.6	14.8	1.9	49 137	77.6	20 912	86.3
12 063	...	Jackson County...........	44 253	61.8	17.6	12.4	7.3	0.9	16 620	77.9	4 675	85.8
12 065	...	Jefferson County	12 244	60.4	16.1	17.8	4.8	0.9	4 695	80.9	1 216	88.7
12 067	...	Lafayette County	6 620	53.7	14.0	22.1	6.0	4.1	2 142	80.4	514	95.1
12 069	5960	Lake County	199 560	49.5	18.3	15.9	14.7	1.5	88 413	81.5	34 905	89.9
12 071	2700	Lee County................	417 783	47.7	24.4	6.1	18.7	3.1	188 599	76.5	70 186	88.5
12 073	8240	Leon County	225 718	41.0	25.9	19.5	11.2	2.4	96 521	57.0	12 882	81.2
12 075	...	Levy County	32 501	54.6	15.7	20.1	8.8	0.9	13 867	83.6	4 262	91.7
12 077	...	Liberty County	6 641	58.6	12.4	20.2	3.6	5.2	2 222	81.7	463	88.8
12 079	...	Madison County	17 646	65.5	17.6	11.9	4.1	0.9	6 629	78.4	1 696	88.4
12 081	7510	Manatee County	249 004	47.3	24.1	9.9	16.1	2.6	112 460	73.7	42 853	86.3
12 083	5790	Marion County	245 837	50.3	22.7	11.1	14.6	1.2	106 755	79.8	40 959	90.9
12 085	2710	Martin County	121 277	50.0	18.9	14.5	14.5	2.2	55 288	79.8	22 941	91.6
12 086	5000	Miami-Dade County	2 108 512	50.2	32.9	2.2	4.9	9.8	776 774	57.8	174 102	65.4
12 087	...	Monroe County............	76 301	48.2	21.5	9.3	17.0	4.0	35 086	62.4	7 779	82.2
12 089	3600	Nassau County............	54 148	55.0	18.8	13.2	12.2	0.8	21 980	80.7	4 561	85.9
12 091	2750	Okaloosa County	159 735	46.4	22.1	6.3	21.0	4.1	66 269	66.4	13 422	84.0
12 093	...	Okeechobee County	33 568	51.5	24.8	13.0	7.3	3.5	12 593	74.9	3 646	89.9
12 095	5960	Orange County	835 287	42.3	26.2	11.7	13.8	6.0	336 286	60.7	56 670	79.6
12 097	5960	Osceola County	161 025	40.0	21.5	11.8	17.6	9.0	60 977	67.8	12 289	82.5
12 099	8960	Palm Beach County	1 069 257	49.5	26.0	7.3	12.9	4.4	474 175	74.7	170 020	87.2
12 101	8280	Pasco County	326 884	52.2	18.8	13.2	14.1	1.6	147 566	82.4	58 541	89.9
12 103	8280	Pinellas County	876 588	50.4	27.5	5.9	13.5	2.7	414 968	70.8	136 990	82.9
12 105	3980	Polk County	453 180	51.1	27.6	7.9	11.2	2.2	187 233	73.4	56 473	86.0
12 107	...	Putnam County	66 043	60.6	19.0	11.7	7.5	1.2	27 839	80.0	8 766	88.1
12 109	3600	St. Johns County	116 709	45.9	18.5	14.9	19.3	1.4	49 614	76.4	12 577	86.2
12 111	2710	St. Lucie County...........	182 029	51.9	22.3	11.3	12.3	2.2	76 933	78.0	27 209	91.7
12 113	6080	Santa Rosa County......	109 975	48.6	18.0	13.9	16.9	2.6	43 793	80.4	8 337	90.4

[1]MSA = Metropolitan Statistical Area. PMSA = Primary MSA. NECMA = New England County Metropolitan Area. See the Appendix A for explanation of these concepts. See Appendix B for list of metropolitan areas identified by type, with component counties.

Table C-3. States and Counties — **Migration, Housing, and Transportation**

STATE County	Owner-occupied by household type (percent)								Median household income			Median housing value (owner estimated)	Median monthly owner costs as a percent of income	
	Family-households					Nonfamily households								
		Married-couple family		Other family										
	Total family households	Total	With own children under 18 years	Total	With own children under 18 years	Total nonfamily households	Two or more adults	Living alone	All households	Owner-occupied households	Renter-occupied households		With a mortgage	Without a mortgage
	11	12	13	14	15	16	17	18	19	20	21	22	23	24
DELAWARE	78.9	86.2	82.9	56.2	45.0	57.9	47.1	60.6	47 012	54 951	30 429	122 000	20.8	9.9
Kent County	75.0	82.4	76.8	53.1	43.2	57.4	50.3	59.2	40 618	47 482	26 666	103 300	21.7	9.9
New Castle County	78.4	86.2	84.3	55.8	44.4	52.9	41.2	56.0	51 966	62 416	32 125	132 900	20.4	9.9
Sussex County	83.3	89.2	83.3	60.2	49.0	74.5	66.9	76.2	39 371	42 438	25 860	99 700	21.7	9.9
DISTRICT OF COLUMBIA	49.8	64.1	58.1	35.8	21.7	32.9	30.9	33.4	39 827	65 288	28 754	153 500	22.2	9.9
District of Columbia	49.8	64.1	58.1	35.8	21.7	32.9	30.9	33.4	39 827	65 288	28 754	153 500	22.2	9.9
FLORIDA	75.9	82.6	76.1	54.6	44.3	58.4	47.9	61.0	38 665	45 122	26 707	93 200	22.8	10.5
Alachua County	71.5	80.6	79.8	48.1	39.4	34.9	18.9	43.8	31 372	47 699	18 194	88 400	20.9	9.9
Baker County	85.2	91.9	89.2	61.0	54.4	65.6	57.5	67.0	39 977	43 083	22 958	65 500	18.4	9.9
Bay County	75.1	81.6	74.0	53.0	41.5	54.8	41.0	57.9	35 894	41 899	24 915	83 700	21.1	9.9
Bradford County	82.9	88.1	84.4	65.4	51.7	68.5	64.4	69.2	32 840	36 821	20 057	64 000	20.6	9.9
Brevard County	80.0	86.1	79.1	60.5	49.1	61.9	53.6	63.8	39 882	45 369	26 750	87 600	21.6	9.9
Broward County	74.6	81.7	77.6	54.7	45.0	60.6	51.3	63.0	41 510	48 576	30 433	102 800	24.5	13.1
Calhoun County	84.1	86.3	82.2	76.9	72.4	70.9	39.0	74.2	26 262	28 991	17 892	50 200	21.8	10.6
Charlotte County	87.4	90.7	78.9	66.9	54.3	75.5	66.3	77.3	36 365	38 216	27 131	87 700	24.1	11.6
Citrus County	89.2	93.0	84.0	67.5	56.6	77.6	68.0	79.4	31 059	32 656	21 341	71 100	21.8	9.9
Clay County	82.0	85.7	82.0	65.0	56.7	62.7	51.9	65.5	48 619	53 393	33 824	97 400	20.8	9.9
Collier County	79.1	84.7	72.9	50.4	42.2	67.6	53.5	71.1	48 219	53 544	35 077	149 000	23.9	9.9
Columbia County	81.4	86.3	82.0	66.2	55.1	66.4	62.3	67.3	30 829	34 009	22 210	63 300	20.8	10.3
DeSoto County	78.8	85.1	71.5	53.2	51.3	64.4	36.2	74.5	30 660	33 199	22 766	55 700	22.5	9.9
Dixie County	88.3	91.8	83.5	75.8	69.3	82.0	76.2	83.4	25 771	27 156	18 750	45 100	23.4	10.8
Duval County	70.4	78.8	74.1	50.2	39.7	48.5	41.7	50.3	40 539	49 645	28 123	86 100	20.7	9.9
Escambia County	72.5	80.8	71.9	52.1	38.5	56.6	43.3	59.6	35 294	42 267	23 672	81 700	21.0	9.9
Flagler County	86.6	89.4	80.7	68.3	54.0	76.8	67.7	78.8	40 311	42 426	27 833	109 400	23.8	9.9
Franklin County	83.0	91.3	84.6	55.3	46.3	71.8	63.4	73.2	26 690	30 144	18 494	74 600	24.1	11.1
Gadsden County	80.2	87.7	83.6	66.4	52.7	72.2	69.9	72.5	31 692	36 542	17 300	61 200	21.1	10.1
Gilchrist County	90.3	92.0	90.9	83.0	74.4	74.4	67.6	75.9	30 203	32 058	19 495	63 600	21.9	11.1
Glades County	84.4	88.8	80.3	63.9	57.9	74.6	61.4	77.8	30 845	31 704	27 567	60 200	19.7	10.4
Gulf County	84.3	89.9	82.5	65.5	48.8	72.4	53.3	74.0	30 208	33 585	19 000	67 900	22.3	10.0
Hamilton County	79.6	86.3	83.4	65.7	50.0	71.3	50.4	73.9	25 425	30 299	15 101	45 900	17.9	10.9
Hardee County	74.6	78.9	70.2	60.0	54.7	69.4	43.0	75.9	29 907	32 496	23 380	53 400	20.3	10.4
Hendry County	75.2	81.0	76.3	58.4	52.9	63.0	49.4	68.2	33 486	38 434	21 010	56 600	19.8	9.9
Hernando County	88.8	92.0	82.3	72.5	60.8	80.5	70.9	82.3	32 460	34 163	24 398	79 700	23.4	10.5
Highlands County	82.6	87.5	72.8	58.1	45.3	73.2	61.5	75.2	30 053	32 204	21 171	62 000	21.7	9.9
Hillsborough County	72.8	80.7	76.2	50.7	40.6	47.8	41.1	49.8	40 587	50 193	27 964	91 800	21.7	10.7
Holmes County	84.2	87.6	83.0	71.0	59.5	75.1	72.9	75.4	27 441	30 754	15 711	53 200	21.4	9.9
Indian River County	82.2	86.9	79.4	59.6	49.1	68.3	56.3	70.4	39 685	44 172	20 500	91 000	21.0	10.2
Jackson County	81.6	86.3	81.9	67.1	59.1	69.2	46.0	71.5	29 457	33 128	19 924	59 300	19.0	9.9
Jefferson County	81.4	89.2	85.8	70.5	61.1	72.5	49.7	76.1	33 553	37 826	17 974	69 900	21.3	9.9
Lafayette County	80.1	84.8	71.3	62.3	51.0	81.5	60.3	84.7	30 514	33 246	20 489	60 800	17.6	11.7
Lake County	85.5	89.8	82.2	63.0	51.4	71.8	65.9	72.9	36 884	40 216	24 358	83 700	21.9	9.9
Lee County	81.3	86.6	76.2	56.8	46.6	66.4	56.5	68.8	40 307	44 223	29 027	96 700	23.0	10.6
Leon County	73.3	82.3	81.1	51.8	46.6	35.8	18.7	43.7	37 280	54 691	20 619	100 600	21.1	9.9
Levy County	85.3	89.4	84.3	71.1	60.8	79.7	70.8	81.6	26 917	28 579	18 343	55 100	22.1	11.1
Liberty County	84.2	89.3	86.1	69.3	63.9	76.2	61.0	70.9	29 367	31 620	20 395	49 900	18.9	9.9
Madison County	81.8	90.1	88.7	64.9	56.3	69.9	49.5	72.4	26 571	29 603	16 169	51 900	23.5	12.6
Manatee County	77.9	84.4	74.6	51.4	38.6	65.7	52.3	68.5	38 343	42 668	27 927	96 000	22.9	10.5
Marion County	83.3	88.4	81.3	63.0	50.8	71.6	64.8	72.9	31 841	34 289	23 432	70 100	21.6	9.9
Martin County	84.6	88.9	78.5	60.5	48.6	70.6	58.6	72.8	43 225	48 952	26 986	114 400	22.2	9.9
Miami-Dade County	62.9	69.9	66.3	48.1	38.1	45.4	43.3	45.9	35 768	48 173	22 773	113 200	26.6	13.5
Monroe County	69.1	74.6	64.9	45.0	35.2	53.0	45.8	56.1	41 995	48 995	34 287	195 700	28.0	13.4
Nassau County	85.6	89.5	86.8	66.1	53.1	65.5	59.0	66.9	45 787	50 922	28 116	98 000	21.4	9.9
Okaloosa County	71.7	76.8	66.6	50.4	39.5	53.7	40.7	57.0	41 358	49 096	30 438	96 800	21.2	9.9
Okeechobee County	78.2	82.8	70.6	61.6	53.4	66.2	51.7	70.2	30 345	33 641	23 258	64 100	20.8	11.1
Orange County	69.7	77.3	73.5	50.0	41.6	43.3	33.6	47.1	41 142	50 936	29 924	100 300	22.9	10.5
Osceola County	71.9	78.2	71.6	51.8	43.9	55.7	43.6	59.9	38 143	43 400	29 868	92 500	23.8	11.5
Palm Beach County	79.4	85.7	79.2	54.9	45.0	66.0	56.2	68.2	44 878	51 281	30 657	115 000	23.2	11.1
Pasco County	85.9	90.0	84.0	67.6	55.6	75.2	69.8	76.3	32 896	35 684	22 669	67 800	22.2	10.5
Pinellas County	78.1	84.5	79.4	57.2	45.1	60.3	53.2	61.8	37 003	42 199	27 027	85 600	22.4	11.5
Polk County	78.2	84.6	76.2	55.7	44.0	61.6	53.8	63.2	35 972	40 762	25 395	69 800	20.8	9.9
Putnam County	82.9	89.4	83.0	61.4	49.6	73.1	70.0	73.7	28 249	32 016	16 151	54 100	18.9	9.9
St. Johns County	83.8	87.3	84.9	66.1	56.1	60.0	48.0	63.4	50 055	56 455	30 869	140 700	21.9	9.9
St. Lucie County	79.7	85.8	76.5	55.8	44.7	74.0	65.5	76.1	36 453	39 899	25 810	81 500	23.0	11.1
Santa Rosa County	84.0	88.5	84.2	63.2	55.3	68.6	55.3	71.6	41 673	45 848	25 946	96 300	21.5	9.9

STATE County	Median gross rent	Percent who pay 35 percent or more of income for housing expenses — Owners	Renters	Means of transportation to work (percent except where noted) — Number of workers 16 years and over	Car, truck, or van — Drove alone	Carpooled	Public transportation	Other means	Walked	Vehicles available (percent of households) — No vehicles	One vehicle	Two or more vehicles
	25	26	27	28	29	30	31	32	33	34	35	36
DELAWARE	639	13.8	26.7	373 070	79.2	11.5	2.8	1.0	2.6	8.0	34.1	57.9
Kent County	573	14.9	26.4	59 813	79.7	12.9	0.8	1.2	2.3	7.8	32.6	59.6
New Castle County	670	13.3	27.8	245 134	79.0	10.9	3.9	0.9	2.8	8.8	34.6	56.6
Sussex County	507	14.8	22.1	68 123	79.5	12.4	0.7	1.1	2.2	5.8	33.8	60.4
DISTRICT OF COLUMBIA................	618	18.6	28.2	260 884	38.4	11.0	33.2	1.9	11.8	36.9	43.5	19.5
District of Columbia.......	618	18.6	28.2	260 884	38.4	11.0	33.2	1.9	11.8	36.9	43.5	19.5
FLORIDA..................	641	18.5	33.0	6 910 168	78.8	12.9	1.9	1.7	1.7	8.1	41.4	50.4
Alachua County............	553	15.1	43.9	102 713	74.7	12.7	2.4	3.6	3.2	7.3	40.1	52.7
Baker County	399	9.7	17.8	9 147	79.8	16.3	0.2	1.0	0.7	6.6	28.9	64.5
Bay County	536	13.6	27.5	67 548	81.0	13.1	0.3	1.7	1.6	6.6	37.4	55.9
Bradford County	430	14.6	20.9	9 314	78.5	12.8	0.4	2.7	2.7	8.7	32.4	59.0
Brevard County	604	15.1	30.4	205 079	83.4	10.7	0.3	1.7	1.3	5.3	40.9	53.8
Broward County	757	23.4	35.5	743 543	80.0	12.0	2.3	1.4	1.3	9.4	43.7	46.9
Calhoun County	353	13.6	22.2	4 444	77.4	16.7	0.5	1.4	2.0	10.6	34.4	55.0
Charlotte County	626	18.8	29.4	49 631	81.7	12.4	0.2	1.7	0.7	5.5	46.1	48.4
Citrus County	478	13.2	29.9	37 912	81.0	13.0	0.3	1.3	1.4	5.2	44.2	50.6
Clay County................	668	12.8	21.7	67 753	84.1	11.0	0.2	1.5	1.0	3.3	27.7	68.9
Collier County	753	20.4	28.1	103 068	74.4	14.9	1.9	2.2	1.8	4.9	42.6	52.6
Columbia County	448	15.6	25.4	22 707	80.5	13.6	0.1	2.2	1.3	7.4	36.6	56.0
DeSoto County.............	442	13.9	23.1	12 567	52.3	33.1	8.3	2.2	1.6	8.2	45.9	45.9
Dixie County...............	322	17.7	23.8	4 506	76.9	14.5	0.3	2.6	0.6	7.0	35.9	57.2
Duval County	604	15.3	26.9	374 292	79.5	13.1	2.0	1.7	1.8	9.1	38.4	52.5
Escambia County	533	15.1	31.7	128 323	76.9	11.5	1.4	1.8	6.0	8.4	38.4	53.3
Flagler County..............	698	17.8	29.9	18 449	81.4	11.7	0.7	1.7	1.2	3.3	40.7	56.0
Franklin County	419	17.5	26.6	3 869	73.6	19.1	0.4	1.6	2.5	8.4	39.8	51.8
Gadsden County	386	15.9	27.2	17 743	74.2	20.9	0.6	0.6	1.8	11.9	35.5	52.6
Gilchrist County	420	15.9	18.2	5 685	75.7	15.6	0.7	2.1	1.5	4.0	35.2	60.8
Glades County	474	15.5	21.3	3 583	67.9	22.6	2.6	2.7	1.3	6.6	41.5	51.9
Gulf County	413	14.9	21.0	4 621	77.3	16.0	0.1	1.3	1.5	7.4	36.7	55.9
Hamilton County	352	16.0	27.3	4 076	76.8	15.4	0.8	3.1	2.2	11.8	35.4	52.8
Hardee County	446	15.7	23.4	9 790	64.5	26.9	1.3	2.3	2.3	8.3	39.0	52.7
Hendry County	479	15.6	27.8	14 307	63.7	22.6	8.0	2.0	1.8	7.8	38.4	53.8
Hernando County	550	16.9	32.2	43 189	81.5	13.4	0.2	1.2	0.8	5.0	46.6	48.3
Highlands County..........	479	13.9	29.5	29 342	74.1	19.3	1.2	1.2	1.7	7.3	50.3	42.3
Hillsborough County......	623	16.8	30.2	470 753	79.5	13.1	1.4	1.6	1.6	8.1	39.9	52.0
Holmes County............	387	13.3	25.4	6 741	80.0	12.4	0.0	0.6	2.2	7.7	36.2	56.0
Indian River County	615	16.3	32.2	44 876	80.4	12.2	0.4	1.9	1.3	6.0	43.7	50.3
Jackson County	368	11.3	21.6	16 965	81.6	12.2	0.2	1.2	1.6	10.5	34.3	55.2
Jefferson County..........	385	20.6	24.6	5 445	75.3	19.5	0.8	1.1	1.0	9.6	32.4	58.0
Lafayette County..........	420	13.5	26.4	2 475	73.2	18.3	0.0	2.0	3.8	6.2	34.9	58.9
Lake County................	534	14.7	30.8	81 463	80.6	12.8	0.4	1.6	1.4	5.4	44.4	50.3
Lee County..................	646	17.6	30.5	182 581	78.7	13.7	0.8	1.9	1.5	5.8	46.1	48.2
Leon County	606	14.6	42.7	120 019	79.4	13.5	1.6	1.1	1.9	7.1	38.8	54.1
Levy County	413	17.8	27.2	12 699	74.7	17.6	0.2	1.6	2.0	5.6	39.3	55.1
Liberty County	350	16.4	19.9	2 356	70.7	24.0	0.0	1.7	1.6	7.5	34.7	57.8
Madison County	347	21.2	24.6	6 736	76.5	15.5	0.1	2.4	2.7	12.2	33.6	54.2
Manatee County...........	637	16.9	31.2	111 002	79.7	13.2	0.5	1.7	1.5	6.5	46.3	47.2
Marion County	513	14.3	29.1	96 304	80.6	13.2	0.2	1.3	1.4	5.8	45.2	49.0
Martin County..............	633	17.1	30.5	50 241	79.2	12.1	0.4	2.0	1.4	5.4	44.9	49.7
Miami-Dade County	647	28.1	39.0	899 323	73.8	14.6	5.2	1.5	2.2	14.3	38.8	46.9
Monroe County	820	28.0	33.5	41 617	67.2	11.1	1.0	10.2	5.3	8.9	42.1	49.0
Nassau County............	553	14.5	23.5	26 795	80.1	13.5	0.2	1.6	1.1	5.6	28.4	66.0
Okaloosa County..........	601	13.5	23.2	82 148	82.8	11.7	0.3	1.6	1.5	4.1	33.6	62.3
Okeechobee County	486	14.3	25.5	13 701	67.8	22.9	3.4	2.0	1.6	7.8	41.0	51.2
Orange County.............	699	18.7	32.7	439 323	79.9	12.2	2.5	1.5	1.4	7.3	37.7	55.0
Osceola County............	714	20.5	35.1	77 863	78.2	15.8	1.1	1.7	1.4	5.7	37.9	56.3
Palm Beach County	739	19.7	33.8	475 572	79.6	11.9	1.4	1.6	1.4	7.9	44.2	47.9
Pasco County	518	15.1	31.4	131 390	80.0	13.9	0.3	1.5	1.3	6.1	47.0	46.9
Pinellas County	616	17.7	31.0	418 625	79.7	11.0	1.9	1.8	2.0	9.2	47.0	43.8
Polk County.................	501	14.2	26.8	202 341	79.9	14.3	0.7	1.6	1.4	7.2	41.5	51.3
Putnam County	384	15.1	26.8	25 758	78.0	16.9	0.7	1.5	1.0	9.5	37.4	53.1
St. Johns County..........	724	15.0	32.1	58 878	81.2	10.8	0.6	1.8	2.0	4.2	35.4	60.4
St. Lucie County...........	621	19.3	34.0	76 261	80.0	13.9	1.0	1.5	1.0	5.6	44.2	50.2
Santa Rosa County.......	540	15.6	28.3	51 801	83.0	11.4	0.3	1.4	0.9	3.5	29.5	66.9

Table C-3. States and Counties — Migration, Housing, and Transportation

			Residence in 1995 (percent)						Occupied housing units		Householders 65 years and over	
STATE/ County code	MSA/PMSA/ NECMA code[1]	STATE County	Total population 5 years and over	Same house	Same county, different house	Same state, different county	Different state	Outside the United States	Number	Percent owner-occupied	Number	Percent owner-occupied
			1	2	3	4	5	6	7	8	9	10
		FLORIDA—Cont'd										
12 115	7510	Sarasota County	313 327	51.4	22.3	6.8	17.0	2.5	149 937	79.1	64 360	89.1
12 117	5960	Seminole County	341 949	46.9	20.0	16.1	13.8	3.2	139 572	69.5	24 333	80.1
12 119	...	Sumter County	51 222	43.9	11.7	18.9	24.0	1.5	20 779	86.4	9 379	94.2
12 121	...	Suwannee County	32 789	56.8	16.9	18.3	6.4	1.6	13 460	81.0	3 641	82.6
12 123	...	Taylor County	18 111	61.0	19.8	13.1	5.4	0.8	7 176	79.8	1 838	86.5
12 125	...	Union County	12 707	55.3	12.9	23.0	7.3	1.6	3 367	74.5	628	84.7
12 127	2020	Volusia County	421 553	51.7	23.6	8.9	13.9	1.9	184 723	75.3	63 025	86.3
12 129	...	Wakulla County	21 496	55.8	14.1	22.6	7.1	0.3	8 450	84.2	1 473	91.1
12 131	...	Walton County	38 441	52.5	17.1	14.3	14.3	1.8	16 548	79.0	4 243	92.4
12 133	...	Washington County	19 709	56.4	15.1	19.2	7.2	2.0	7 931	81.9	2 083	87.4
13 000	...	GEORGIA................	7 594 476	49.2	21.1	13.8	12.7	3.2	3 006 369	67.5	513 098	80.0
13 001	...	Appling County	16 110	64.8	20.4	7.7	5.1	2.0	6 606	79.0	1 507	82.1
13 003	...	Atkinson County	6 885	60.2	21.5	9.2	5.4	3.7	2 717	74.2	517	82.8
13 005	...	Bacon County	9 325	61.0	21.7	10.0	6.2	1.2	3 600	74.0	020	84.0
13 007	...	Baker County	3 783	68.3	14.9	11.6	3.9	1.3	1 514	77.6	416	88.0
13 009	...	Baldwin County	42 429	55.0	20.3	17.0	7.2	0.5	14 758	66.4	2 749	82.8
13 011	...	Banks County	13 319	60.9	12.6	21.7	3.6	1.2	5 364	81.0	1 092	86.1
13 013	0520	Barrow County	42 429	47.5	18.6	23.6	9.3	1.1	16 354	75.5	2 809	77.6
13 015	0520	Bartow County	70 158	51.3	22.6	16.1	8.9	1.1	27 176	75.2	4 608	83.0
13 017	...	Ben Hill County	16 192	58.6	25.6	8.7	4.6	2.5	6 673	66.7	1 568	73.6
13 019	...	Berrien County	14 995	59.9	19.5	11.9	7.8	0.9	6 261	75.6	1 442	83.6
13 021	4680	Bibb County	142 519	53.0	29.6	9.3	7.1	1.0	59 667	58.8	13 536	74.1
13 023	...	Bleckley County	10 959	66.4	16.8	11.8	4.5	0.6	4 372	76.1	1 155	82.3
13 025	...	Brantley County	13 572	65.8	14.3	14.4	5.2	0.3	5 436	86.9	1 001	91.3
13 027	...	Brooks County	15 400	60.4	17.5	13.1	8.2	0.8	6 155	76.9	1 418	83.8
13 029	7520	Bryan County	21 631	47.5	13.4	19.7	17.6	1.9	8 089	78.0	1 033	83.9
13 031	...	Bulloch County	52 761	44.7	20.2	25.0	8.1	2.0	20 743	58.1	3 468	79.8
13 033	...	Burke County	20 452	63.4	21.0	9.9	4.5	1.3	7 934	76.0	1 646	77.2
13 035	...	Butts County	18 301	49.4	15.9	29.5	4.7	0.4	6 455	76.6	1 173	83.6
13 037	...	Calhoun County	5 967	59.9	15.5	18.7	3.9	2.0	1 962	71.6	561	78.6
13 039	...	Camden County	00 000	00.0	10.4	6.6	31.1	1.0	11 705	62.2	1 764	77.0
13 043	...	Candler County	8 845	57.7	22.9	10.1	6.4	2.9	3 375	73.2	773	78.5
13 045	0520	Carroll County	81 071	50.0	25.1	16.0	7.6	1.4	31 568	70.5	5 943	79.8
13 047	1560	Catoosa County	49 654	54.3	18.1	10.4	16.9	0.3	20 425	77.0	4 124	85.5
13 049	...	Charlton County	9 637	62.1	13.5	7.9	16.3	0.2	3 342	80.7	701	84.5
13 051	7520	Chatham County	216 600	50.5	27.1	6.0	13.8	2.6	89 865	60.4	20 603	76.4
13 053	1800	Chattahoochee County .	13 630	15.4	4.3	7.9	63.3	9.1	2 932	27.9	160	90.0
13 055	...	Chattooga County	23 841	60.5	23.2	10.5	4.7	1.1	9 577	75.4	2 460	84.5
13 057	0520	Cherokee County	129 888	48.1	14.3	20.7	14.6	2.4	49 495	83.9	5 774	89.5
13 059	0500	Clarke County	96 051	33.9	21.1	27.7	12.6	4.6	39 706	42.1	5 539	77.1
13 061	...	Clay County	3 129	60.9	21.4	9.4	8.0	0.4	1 347	74.2	302	77.3
13 063	0520	Clayton County	216 690	41.5	20.0	20.5	13.8	4.2	82 243	60.6	8 567	85.0
13 065	...	Clinch County	6 389	57.9	23.3	10.3	4.3	4.2	2 512	72.4	521	76.4
13 067	0520	Cobb County	564 574	43.8	20.6	11.6	19.3	4.7	227 487	68.2	25 021	84.2
13 069	...	Coffee County	34 522	54.6	25.6	10.0	7.8	2.0	13 354	74.4	2 554	82.0
13 071	...	Colquitt County	38 890	54.5	25.9	9.7	7.3	2.7	15 495	66.7	3 742	77.9
13 073	0600	Columbia County..........	83 135	53.3	15.1	14.4	14.9	2.2	31 120	82.1	4 521	86.2
13 075	...	Cook County	14 522	55.4	24.9	10.9	7.5	1.3	5 882	74.9	1 409	85.2
13 077	0520	Coweta County	82 117	47.7	20.0	19.0	11.2	2.1	31 442	78.0	4 552	80.1
13 079	...	Crawford County	11 749	65.4	8.7	21.6	4.2	0.1	4 461	84.8	666	86.0
13 081	...	Crisp County	20 244	58.0	26.8	9.0	4.9	1.4	8 337	60.5	2 004	74.9
13 083	1560	Dade County	14 264	59.8	14.4	6.8	17.8	1.3	5 633	80.2	1 193	83.7
13 085	...	Dawson County	14 860	50.1	11.1	28.7	9.4	0.7	6 069	81.4	989	86.0
13 087	...	Decatur County	26 042	57.7	24.4	7.3	9.3	1.4	10 380	72.5	2 515	82.7
13 089	0520	DeKalb County	619 018	43.8	21.5	12.1	15.9	6.7	249 339	58.5	34 061	77.5
13 091	...	Dodge County	17 996	59.3	23.6	12.8	3.5	0.8	7 062	73.8	1 760	84.7
13 093	...	Dooly County	10 764	57.7	19.7	18.6	2.4	1.6	3 909	71.4	896	83.5
13 095	0120	Dougherty County	88 735	52.1	29.6	9.7	6.9	1.7	35 552	53.5	7 500	73.7
13 097	0520	Douglas County............	85 459	51.0	19.0	18.3	10.3	1.4	32 822	74.8	4 185	83.6
13 099	...	Early County	11 471	59.9	25.4	8.4	5.6	0.6	4 695	72.4	1 345	77.9
13 101	...	Echols County	3 502	57.9	6.5	19.8	8.0	7.8	1 264	75.7	259	86.5
13 103	7520	Effingham County.........	34 701	53.5	16.5	18.2	10.9	0.8	13 151	82.7	2 060	85.4
13 105	...	Elbert County	19 247	63.1	22.0	8.5	5.5	0.9	8 004	75.9	2 040	82.0
13 107	...	Emanuel County	20 410	65.1	20.6	9.1	2.6	2.6	8 045	71.2	2 135	75.2
13 109	...	Evans County.............	9 804	50.9	21.0	19.9	5.6	2.5	3 778	71.4	866	88.3

[1]MSA = Metropolitan Statistical Area. PMSA = Primary MSA. NECMA = New England County Metropolitan Area. See the Appendix A for explanation of these concepts. See Appendix B for list of metropolitan areas identified by type, with component counties.

STATE County	Owner-occupied by household type (percent)								Median household income			Median monthly owner costs as a percent of income	
	Family-households					Nonfamily households						Median housing value (owner estimated)	With a mortgage	Without a mortgage
		Married-couple family		Other family										
	Total family households	Total	With own children under 18 years	Total	With own children under 18 years	Total nonfamily households	Two or more adults	Living alone	All households	Owner-occupied households	Renter-occupied households			
	11	12	13	14	15	16	17	18	19	20	21	22	23	24
FLORIDA—Cont'd														
Sarasota County	84.2	88.3	79.8	62.9	50.4	70.2	60.7	72.2	41 794	45 771	30 705	112 000	23.5	10.7
Seminole County	77.3	82.7	80.3	56.8	46.6	51.4	43.5	53.8	49 139	58 243	33 855	115 100	21.4	9.9
Sumter County	87.5	91.4	75.9	66.1	49.4	83.6	81.2	84.0	32 202	34 110	21 336	74 600	22.1	9.9
Suwannee County	84.6	87.9	83.0	72.6	68.7	71.6	71.0	71.7	29 904	32 382	17 935	57 900	20.0	10.6
Taylor County	82.2	89.2	82.6	61.2	49.9	73.6	65.1	75.0	29 815	32 984	18 584	53 900	20.7	10.0
Union County	77.2	82.4	75.0	60.6	48.5	64.8	29.0	71.1	33 762	36 958	24 239	56 000	20.3	9.9
Volusia County	81.3	86.7	80.0	61.7	48.9	63.9	55.0	66.1	35 188	39 449	24 543	83 000	22.9	10.6
Wakulla County	87.1	90.0	88.0	78.5	73.1	76.0	75.3	76.1	37 394	41 120	22 633	79 900	22.4	9.9
Walton County	82.0	87.4	80.4	61.0	46.7	72.6	57.1	75.3	31 980	35 079	22 591	77 500	22.4	9.9
Washington County	83.8	88.6	84.2	66.5	55.8	76.9	74.4	77.2	27 864	31 196	17 894	64 400	21.2	9.9
GEORGIA	74.2	82.3	78.4	51.1	41.4	51.4	37.3	54.9	42 288	51 421	27 657	100 600	20.8	9.9
Appling County	82.7	88.0	85.6	64.0	59.2	68.4	65.5	68.6	30 472	34 659	16 208	51 300	19.1	10.5
Atkinson County	77.1	82.2	79.0	62.2	58.7	66.2	44.4	69.2	26 498	30 942	18 045	32 500	20.5	11.1
Bacon County	79.6	85.3	84.0	61.6	40.9	61.0	39.7	62.7	26 260	32 080	13 681	46 400	20.6	11.1
Baker County	79.5	85.4	84.7	66.7	56.8	72.7	57.9	74.1	29 135	31 392	21 250	50 200	22.4	9.9
Baldwin County	75.1	82.9	81.7	59.5	49.7	48.8	21.1	56.9	35 421	43 740	23 177	70 400	19.9	9.9
Banks County	83.7	87.3	82.0	62.9	58.2	71.6	58.0	73.6	38 140	41 515	25 324	81 800	20.2	9.9
Barrow County	79.0	83.9	80.7	59.7	51.7	63.9	53.8	66.4	43 886	49 713	28 561	98 700	22.5	10.7
Bartow County	79.0	83.6	78.9	58.8	46.5	62.3	51.8	64.3	43 795	50 160	28 971	92 700	20.2	9.9
Ben Hill County	70.2	78.4	75.4	52.5	42.1	58.5	41.2	60.5	26 765	31 923	15 736	51 700	20.5	11.8
Berrien County	78.8	84.9	80.2	57.9	52.1	67.1	60.4	68.1	29 824	34 827	18 050	53 900	19.3	9.9
Bibb County	66.1	81.4	77.6	38.6	26.3	43.9	32.0	46.0	34 329	48 339	20 113	82 700	20.1	9.9
Bleckley County	81.4	88.7	84.6	62.3	58.4	62.9	52.2	64.2	33 218	37 692	19 187	60 600	18.3	9.9
Brantley County	89.5	91.0	89.2	82.9	81.3	78.4	86.4	77.2	30 157	31 459	21 622	39 400	18.2	9.9
Brooks County	79.7	86.6	83.6	64.6	52.3	69.6	53.2	71.6	26 880	30 779	16 413	55 400	22.1	11.4
Bryan County	81.5	86.4	83.1	62.6	57.2	63.0	56.4	64.0	48 101	55 818	30 023	94 900	20.0	11.5
Bulloch County	73.4	81.9	78.1	47.3	41.0	35.2	12.1	49.8	28 812	41 516	15 294	80 300	19.1	9.9
Burke County	80.2	89.0	86.7	65.3	51.0	64.6	66.1	64.4	28 293	32 575	13 870	51 800	20.8	9.9
Butts County	80.0	85.3	79.7	64.3	54.6	66.2	68.3	65.8	39 483	45 296	25 374	86 100	20.9	11.0
Calhoun County	77.1	86.0	79.6	62.9	51.9	59.2	37.8	61.0	24 850	29 550	14 357	44 400	20.0	11.6
Camden County	65.8	70.6	68.2	46.2	39.4	54.3	47.0	56.2	40 890	47 432	30 926	79 200	21.0	10.4
Candler County	75.9	84.8	82.9	53.7	41.9	66.1	47.7	68.5	25 779	31 875	14 484	47 600	19.1	12.2
Carroll County	76.6	83.4	79.8	53.6	43.4	53.7	36.6	58.2	38 691	45 569	22 355	87 800	21.0	9.9
Catoosa County	82.7	87.1	83.6	62.4	49.7	59.8	46.2	61.9	40 048	45 672	22 389	86 100	19.1	9.9
Charlton County	84.3	87.8	82.3	73.2	65.2	69.8	71.4	69.5	28 732	31 817	15 163	51 400	21.5	14.1
Chatham County	67.9	78.0	71.8	45.2	32.4	45.6	33.1	48.5	37 644	49 133	24 041	91 500	21.6	11.1
Chattahoochee County .	24.7	22.1	13.3	38.8	29.8	55.8	48.2	57.5	36 898	36 250	37 253	56 000	19.4	12.6
Chattooga County	78.0	84.3	77.3	58.6	47.2	68.9	58.6	70.3	30 469	33 302	22 305	58 000	19.6	9.9
Cherokee County	86.8	90.3	88.4	66.8	59.8	72.4	60.6	75.9	60 677	65 764	37 173	138 300	21.1	9.9
Clarke County	59.1	71.3	64.5	34.6	22.6	25.3	11.8	34.5	28 365	49 078	18 244	102 600	20.2	9.9
Clay County	78.4	91.5	92.8	59.3	54.5	64.7	62.8	64.9	22 285	29 682	10 331	41 600	22.7	11.1
Clayton County	65.2	75.1	70.1	47.2	38.9	48.7	38.4	51.5	42 638	50 575	32 416	90 900	21.2	9.9
Clinch County	77.6	87.6	86.2	53.9	42.7	59.0	58.2	59.1	26 720	31 250	15 270	43 700	17.8	9.9
Cobb County	77.0	83.5	81.7	51.1	44.9	48.4	34.4	53.1	58 283	70 643	39 517	145 300	20.1	9.9
Coffee County	77.9	83.4	79.3	61.5	55.0	64.5	53.9	66.3	30 677	35 224	21 154	49 800	20.1	9.9
Colquitt County	71.5	82.3	75.5	44.4	38.3	54.3	40.3	56.1	28 167	35 398	16 696	55 500	19.3	11.1
Columbia County	84.7	88.6	85.2	65.7	53.3	70.3	61.9	71.8	55 372	60 862	33 243	110 200	20.1	9.9
Cook County	79.1	84.6	81.4	64.8	59.8	63.5	53.8	64.7	28 009	31 262	20 426	53 200	22.2	12.1
Coweta County	82.7	89.4	88.5	57.3	49.5	60.6	51.8	62.4	52 428	59 750	28 169	121 400	20.4	9.9
Crawford County	87.4	93.2	91.4	64.9	62.1	75.3	63.3	77.0	38 162	40 796	21 029	69 600	20.4	9.9
Crisp County	63.9	78.5	76.0	37.1	27.5	52.0	39.9	53.4	26 203	37 164	13 982	64 400	19.4	11.1
Dade County	84.2	86.5	82.7	72.5	59.7	67.4	73.7	66.7	35 826	37 920	24 962	74 400	20.0	9.9
Dawson County	84.8	87.4	81.8	70.2	66.7	70.0	63.6	71.5	47 157	51 422	35 227	133 600	22.2	10.2
Decatur County	76.9	85.1	78.6	59.8	46.9	60.5	21.9	64.5	29 450	33 665	19 311	61 800	20.7	11.1
DeKalb County	66.0	75.3	69.6	48.7	40.3	45.6	35.5	49.3	48 726	61 483	35 183	133 500	21.5	9.9
Dodge County	79.0	88.0	84.1	57.2	45.4	61.8	43.0	63.2	27 397	33 616	16 177	45 300	20.1	9.9
Dooly County	74.5	84.6	76.7	55.1	40.9	63.6	41.4	65.7	27 596	34 726	14 357	51 500	18.9	11.7
Dougherty County	58.6	73.5	62.3	36.6	24.2	42.3	27.2	44.9	30 456	41 986	19 535	69 500	20.5	10.9
Douglas County	80.9	86.1	82.4	62.2	55.6	55.5	43.7	59.0	49 621	55 312	34 158	99 600	20.4	9.9
Early County	76.6	87.1	84.9	56.8	45.4	62.5	47.7	64.0	26 081	32 220	13 354	46 600	17.8	11.5
Echols County	80.4	83.7	75.8	70.5	59.7	61.9	20.7	77.1	25 199	26 845	16 023	56 700	21.4	18.5
Effingham County.........	84.8	89.0	87.2	66.1	55.2	74.2	64.9	75.9	45 947	50 300	25 771	87 400	20.0	9.9
Elbert County	79.7	87.3	81.4	58.8	51.6	66.0	35.9	68.3	28 861	32 797	16 677	59 600	21.1	9.9
Emanuel County	76.6	86.5	81.3	52.4	43.7	57.5	51.1	58.4	24 497	30 564	12 200	46 800	20.1	11.6
Evans County...............	74.3	83.3	75.7	51.6	42.2	64.2	39.2	67.4	26 662	31 890	16 310	52 900	22.5	9.9

STATE County	Median gross rent	Percent who pay 35 percent or more of income for housing expenses		Means of transportation to work (percent except where noted)						Vehicles available (percent of households)		
		Owners	Renters	Number of workers 16 years and over	Car, truck, or van		Public transportation	Other means	Walked	No vehicles	One vehicle	Two or more vehicles
					Drove alone	Carpooled						
	25	26	27	28	29	30	31	32	33	34	35	36
FLORIDA—Cont'd												
Sarasota County	711	18.3	32.7	132 765	80.8	10.1	0.8	2.0	1.6	6.0	46.2	47.8
Seminole County	731	15.7	29.1	187 594	83.1	10.1	0.7	1.3	1.0	4.5	33.7	61.8
Sumter County	410	12.5	23.7	14 698	81.2	12.8	0.2	1.6	1.1	5.3	51.6	43.1
Suwannee County	394	15.8	23.6	13 496	74.4	17.7	0.2	2.2	2.1	7.5	36.3	56.2
Taylor County	389	15.3	22.6	7 218	76.8	15.9	0.2	2.2	2.9	11.0	34.1	54.9
Union County	345	14.0	14.8	3 955	81.9	12.1	0.5	2.2	1.0	6.9	30.7	62.5
Volusia County	597	17.8	33.9	185 915	78.7	13.5	1.0	1.9	1.9	7.1	42.4	50.5
Wakulla County	506	14.7	35.1	10 475	78.7	15.4	0.6	0.4	1.5	5.6	31.8	62.6
Walton County	486	17.3	26.1	16 968	77.1	15.3	0.3	1.8	1.8	5.2	36.9	58.0
Washington County	383	14.1	27.5	7 831	78.2	16.0	0.3	1.1	1.9	8.0	33.9	58.1
GEORGIA	613	15.2	28.1	3 832 803	77.5	14.5	2.3	1.1	1.7	8.3	32.3	59.4
Appling County	351	13.1	26.9	7 583	76.3	19.1	0.3	1.4	1.4	7.2	31.2	61.6
Atkinson County	288	15.1	21.6	3 146	70.3	21.0	0.8	2.7	1.7	7.3	36.4	56.3
Bacon County	316	16.3	29.0	4 195	79.0	15.3	0.3	1.5	1.3	10.1	35.3	54.6
Baker County	311	17.4	13.6	1 543	78.3	17.1	0.5	0.8	1.4	8.5	35.0	56.5
Baldwin County	478	13.9	26.5	17 115	81.2	14.3	0.5	0.9	1.2	9.4	33.8	56.9
Banks County	424	14.3	21.8	6 928	78.7	15.0	0.4	1.1	1.2	6.6	22.3	71.1
Barrow County	583	14.5	24.9	22 616	77.8	18.4	0.4	0.7	0.3	6.3	24.6	69.1
Bartow County	575	12.1	23.3	35 953	80.4	14.9	0.5	1.0	0.9	5.2	26.2	68.6
Ben Hill County	371	16.7	29.8	7 203	79.0	16.3	0.7	1.7	1.2	12.7	39.2	48.1
Berrien County	369	13.1	24.1	7 286	79.8	14.2	0.6	1.7	0.8	7.4	34.2	58.4
Bibb County	474	14.3	30.5	63 229	79.9	14.2	1.6	0.9	1.4	12.4	36.1	51.4
Bleckley County	373	11.4	23.7	4 699	80.7	12.9	0.2	1.1	2.0	9.1	30.6	60.2
Brantley County	382	11.9	12.7	6 080	76.1	18.7	0.5	1.2	0.9	5.2	28.6	66.2
Brooks County	353	20.4	26.3	6 767	75.6	19.4	0.4	1.1	0.9	8.8	34.6	56.7
Bryan County	541	13.3	25.4	10 996	82.7	12.5	0.3	1.2	0.7	4.5	26.1	69.4
Bulloch County	436	12.3	41.0	24 248	78.3	14.4	0.4	1.8	2.9	7.0	33.1	59.9
Burke County	315	20.9	22.4	8 104	70.0	15.5	0.7	2.0	1.6	16.1	28.6	55.3
Butts County	480	13.6	25.8	7 924	80.4	16.0	0.1	0.7	0.5	5.9	27.8	66.3
Calhoun County	201	19.5	24.5	2 070	73.4	22.0	0.7	1.1	2.3	16.1	35.1	48.8
Camden County	551	13.6	14.2	21 066	76.9	14.3	0.4	2.3	4.7	5.8	28.7	65.5
Candler County	353	17.5	31.3	3 595	69.0	24.3	0.3	1.8	1.8	7.3	40.8	51.9
Carroll County	488	14.1	30.2	39 730	79.0	15.5	0.3	1.1	1.9	6.9	29.0	64.1
Catoosa County	482	11.6	28.3	26 710	85.6	11.4	0.2	0.7	0.7	3.9	28.3	67.8
Charlton County	394	19.8	30.1	3 484	77.7	17.4	0.1	1.3	1.2	11.5	32.6	55.9
Chatham County	589	17.0	33.4	104 853	76.4	13.4	3.2	1.6	2.9	11.9	37.1	51.1
Chattahoochee County	581	17.2	4.8	8 538	51.6	14.6	0.6	2.9	24.9	4.5	27.7	67.8
Chattooga County	380	13.0	17.0	10 497	77.5	16.5	0.2	1.1	2.5	7.9	32.9	59.2
Cherokee County	740	15.4	25.9	74 075	81.2	11.8	0.4	1.1	0.6	2.9	21.8	75.2
Clarke County	540	13.3	43.5	48 241	75.1	14.4	2.4	1.6	4.3	8.4	37.3	54.3
Clay County	265	20.2	22.6	1 204	69.7	22.5	0.0	1.2	3.2	17.2	36.6	46.2
Clayton County	699	15.8	27.5	112 580	76.3	18.2	1.5	1.0	1.4	5.5	37.8	56.7
Clinch County	256	11.0	16.1	2 545	75.0	18.6	0.5	2.8	2.9	15.4	30.1	54.5
Cobb County	806	13.3	26.8	325 412	80.8	12.0	1.3	0.9	1.0	3.8	31.1	65.1
Coffee County	380	15.0	21.5	15 350	79.1	16.1	0.6	1.7	1.0	9.0	37.1	53.9
Colquitt County	370	14.9	28.8	17 806	71.8	22.4	0.8	1.2	2.0	11.3	37.4	51.3
Columbia County	620	12.7	24.3	43 507	86.2	10.3	0.1	0.7	0.6	3.2	22.3	74.5
Cook County	404	19.4	25.2	6 616	80.1	13.2	0.5	1.9	1.9	8.9	34.0	57.1
Coweta County	628	13.5	28.3	43 506	81.1	14.0	0.4	1.0	0.5	5.6	24.7	69.6
Crawford County	420	14.1	26.5	5 309	83.5	13.2	0.4	1.0	0.6	6.2	26.6	67.2
Crisp County	368	15.1	35.4	8 638	78.0	16.3	1.1	0.9	1.1	16.5	33.6	50.0
Dade County	406	12.9	18.9	6 983	76.6	14.5	0.8	1.0	3.3	6.4	25.9	67.8
Dawson County	685	17.7	26.1	8 082	78.9	15.0	0.0	0.3	1.6	3.1	23.5	73.4
Decatur County	384	16.6	24.1	11 087	75.9	17.5	0.7	1.7	1.4	10.1	33.2	56.7
DeKalb County	767	16.8	29.9	341 110	70.5	15.4	8.2	1.1	1.8	9.1	39.0	51.9
Dodge County	321	13.4	25.1	7 457	78.6	16.6	0.2	2.0	0.9	11.1	32.4	56.5
Dooly County	313	12.5	31.1	4 160	79.2	17.0	0.2	1.6	1.0	14.4	33.3	52.3
Dougherty County	469	17.8	32.2	38 026	78.1	15.9	1.1	0.8	2.5	12.9	38.9	48.1
Douglas County	731	12.8	29.0	46 176	81.6	14.3	0.5	0.7	0.5	4.6	26.8	68.5
Early County	292	11.1	28.0	4 818	72.1	20.4	0.6	2.2	2.1	14.9	36.1	49.0
Echols County	390	16.2	24.6	1 661	70.3	21.6	1.3	1.4	5.0	4.3	31.1	64.6
Effingham County	500	11.6	20.6	17 211	83.5	14.1	0.2	0.6	0.4	4.0	25.6	70.4
Elbert County	327	14.6	23.7	8 576	77.5	15.0	0.2	3.1	1.7	10.6	26.1	63.3
Emanuel County	296	18.2	29.5	8 739	72.2	19.2	0.4	2.9	2.9	13.3	35.7	51.0
Evans County	371	17.6	29.4	4 161	70.6	16.3	0.4	5.4	5.9	10.2	39.2	50.5

STATE/ County code	MSA/PMSA/ NECMA code[1]	STATE County	Residence in 1995 (percent)						Occupied housing units		Householders 65 years and over	
			Total population 5 years and over	Same house	Same county, different house	Same state, different county	Different state	Outside the United States	Number	Percent owner-occupied	Number	Percent owner-occupied
			1	2	3	4	5	6	7	8	9	10
		GEORGIA—Cont'd										
13 111	...	Fannin County	18 746	60.8	16.3	11.3	11.4	0.1	8 369	82.6	2 609	85.6
13 113	0520	Fayette County	86 007	51.3	13.1	16.3	17.1	2.2	31 524	86.6	5 053	87.9
13 115	...	Floyd County	84 524	53.8	27.9	8.8	7.8	1.7	34 028	66.8	8 297	76.7
13 117	0520	Forsyth County	88 989	40.6	11.7	26.4	18.8	2.5	34 565	88.1	4 091	88.4
13 119	...	Franklin County	18 999	59.9	16.0	17.1	6.6	0.3	7 888	79.3	2 017	82.7
13 121	0520	Fulton County	759 179	42.8	23.5	11.9	17.0	4.8	321 242	52.0	47 240	66.4
13 123	...	Gilmer County	21 733	51.8	16.5	18.0	10.5	3.2	9 071	78.1	2 134	87.8
13 125	...	Glascock County	2 391	60.0	15.1	19.7	4.1	1.1	1 004	80.2	291	84.2
13 127	...	Glynn County	63 224	52.4	24.9	9.6	11.1	2.0	27 208	65.5	6 836	77.3
13 129	...	Gordon County	40 940	52.9	24.5	11.5	8.5	2.6	16 173	71.7	3 001	81.3
13 131	...	Grady County	22 021	56.5	25.1	8.2	8.0	2.2	8 797	73.3	2 087	81.9
13 133	...	Greene County	13 432	56.4	20.9	14.8	6.9	1.0	5 477	76.2	1 308	89.2
13 135	0520	Gwinnett County	541 751	41.7	19.9	15.2	17.6	5.6	202 317	72.4	18 086	85.2
13 137	...	Habersham County	33 709	55.4	19.9	15.4	6.2	3.1	13 259	76.2	3 229	84.4
13 139	...	Hall County	128 040	47.8	24.7	12.2	8.8	6.5	47 381	71.1	8 530	82.6
13 141	...	Hancock County	9 505	70.9	11.1	14.9	2.7	0.3	3 237	76.5	890	81.1
13 143	...	Haralson County	23 915	58.5	20.6	16.2	4.3	0.4	9 826	75.2	2 201	79.1
13 145	1800	Harris County	22 279	56.0	12.1	20.2	10.2	1.5	8 822	86.1	1 997	90.7
13 147	...	Hart County	21 610	61.4	17.4	14.4	6.1	0.7	9 106	80.8	2 431	86.8
13 149	...	Heard County	10 132	62.5	13.8	17.5	5.6	0.6	4 043	77.3	880	77.2
13 151	0520	Henry County	109 726	45.2	15.1	28.3	10.2	1.2	41 373	85.3	5 377	90.6
13 153	4680	Houston County	103 033	47.3	23.4	9.6	16.6	3.1	40 911	68.5	6 463	86.8
13 155	...	Irwin County	9 257	65.7	17.3	13.0	3.1	0.9	3 644	76.8	831	81.0
13 157	...	Jackson County	38 605	50.6	18.1	23.7	6.6	1.0	15 057	74.9	2 916	78.0
13 159	...	Jasper County	10 645	56.4	16.1	23.9	3.5	0.3	4 175	79.1	876	85.7
13 161	...	Jeff Davis County	11 714	60.6	22.8	10.5	5.0	1.1	4 828	77.4	1 060	87.1
13 163	...	Jefferson County	16 080	65.6	22.4	7.6	3.2	1.1	6 339	72.2	1 552	77.9
13 165	...	Jenkins County	7 979	61.5	20.7	11.2	4.3	2.2	3 214	73.4	772	83.4
13 167	...	Johnson County	7 976	70.1	16.6	8.2	4.4	0.8	3 130	79.8	863	85.3
13 169	4680	Jones County	22 130	63.5	12.3	19.2	4.5	0.5	8 659	85.8	1 524	90.4
13 171	...	Lamar County	14 932	57.3	16.5	19.5	5.5	1.1	5 712	72.4	1 390	83.5
13 173	...	Lanier County	6 715	52.3	15.5	18.0	11.9	2.3	2 593	76.3	485	82.1
13 175	...	Laurens County	41 716	58.9	26.1	8.6	5.4	1.0	17 083	71.3	3 822	79.2
13 177	0120	Lee County	22 942	52.9	16.0	21.2	8.2	1.7	8 229	78.3	958	84.6
13 179	...	Liberty County	55 210	32.7	13.8	8.5	36.6	8.5	19 383	50.7	1 451	83.3
13 181	...	Lincoln County	7 929	67.4	16.3	10.6	5.3	0.4	3 251	81.8	886	84.7
13 183	...	Long County	9 187	47.0	10.4	15.3	22.6	4.7	3 574	66.2	372	88.4
13 185	...	Lowndes County	85 728	45.7	25.1	10.6	16.0	2.7	32 654	60.8	5 915	76.8
13 187	...	Lumpkin County	19 708	47.1	15.4	25.2	10.0	2.2	7 537	72.3	1 308	82.3
13 189	0600	McDuffie County	19 690	60.0	23.8	11.2	4.4	0.7	7 970	71.4	1 691	80.4
13 191	...	McIntosh County	10 150	59.9	16.0	14.8	8.2	1.1	4 202	83.5	929	89.0
13 193	...	Macon County	13 041	68.2	18.4	8.5	3.3	1.6	4 834	73.2	1 239	85.0
13 195	0500	Madison County	23 957	65.1	15.3	14.0	4.9	0.6	9 800	80.2	1 866	85.2
13 197	...	Marion County	6 678	56.5	14.5	17.5	8.3	3.2	2 668	78.1	509	80.9
13 199	...	Meriwether County	21 017	63.5	17.1	14.0	4.5	0.9	8 248	74.1	2 057	84.7
13 201	...	Miller County	6 005	67.6	16.2	10.2	5.7	0.2	2 487	76.9	652	83.4
13 205	...	Mitchell County	22 238	61.2	20.9	12.5	4.3	1.1	8 063	72.0	1 828	80.6
13 207	...	Monroe County	20 405	65.0	12.5	17.3	4.4	0.8	7 719	79.4	1 325	83.3
13 209	...	Montgomery County	7 720	57.2	14.7	20.2	5.9	1.9	2 919	78.2	638	86.1
13 211	...	Morgan County	14 441	59.3	18.6	17.2	4.1	0.8	5 558	77.6	1 168	87.2
13 213	...	Murray County	33 542	56.9	21.0	15.1	5.8	1.2	13 286	73.7	2 031	82.2
13 215	1800	Muscogee County	172 678	47.8	26.9	6.3	15.9	3.1	69 819	56.4	14 864	76.2
13 217	0520	Newton County	57 211	50.2	19.5	22.0	7.3	1.1	21 997	77.7	3 957	81.7
13 219	0500	Oconee County	24 392	51.3	12.4	22.6	12.1	1.5	9 051	80.2	1 234	87.4
13 221	...	Oglethorpe County	11 789	66.3	11.1	17.8	4.0	0.8	4 849	82.5	938	85.2
13 223	0520	Paulding County	73 976	46.8	14.2	27.4	10.9	0.8	28 089	86.8	3 039	85.6
13 225	4680	Peach County	22 133	56.0	17.8	16.8	7.5	1.8	8 436	68.4	1 891	84.1
13 227	0520	Pickens County	21 523	56.7	17.9	19.0	5.9	0.4	8 960	82.1	1 827	85.3
13 229	...	Pierce County	14 612	62.5	18.2	13.0	5.3	1.1	5 958	80.7	1 381	87.5
13 231	...	Pike County	12 745	57.4	13.6	24.6	3.8	0.5	4 755	81.5	984	82.4
13 233	...	Polk County	35 477	57.6	24.9	10.6	4.9	1.9	14 012	71.3	3 280	80.2
13 235	...	Pulaski County	8 961	59.0	13.8	18.8	6.9	1.5	3 407	73.7	914	86.0
13 237	...	Putnam County	17 632	58.2	15.6	19.9	4.7	1.6	7 402	79.5	1 778	87.6
13 239	...	Quitman County	2 457	62.8	13.1	8.5	15.4	0.2	1 047	80.4	350	92.0
13 241	...	Rabun County	14 202	59.8	19.2	7.7	11.1	2.3	6 279	79.4	1 815	85.7
13 243	...	Randolph County	7 249	64.1	19.2	9.1	5.7	2.0	2 909	68.8	809	76.9

[1]MSA = Metropolitan Statistical Area. PMSA = Primary MSA. NECMA = New England County Metropolitan Area. See the Appendix A for explanation of these concepts. See Appendix B for list of metropolitan areas identified by type, with component counties.

STATE County	Owner-occupied by household type (percent)								Median household income			Median monthly owner costs as a percent of income	
	Family-households					Nonfamily households							
		Married-couple family		Other family									
	Total family households	Total	With own children under 18 years	Total	With own children under 18 years	Total nonfamily households	Two or more adults	Living alone	All households	Owner-occupied households	Renter-occupied households	Median housing value (owner estimated)	With a mortgage	Without a mortgage
	11	12	13	14	15	16	17	18	19	20	21	22	23	24
GEORGIA—Cont'd														
Fannin County	85.7	89.8	84.9	64.4	51.2	74.7	68.1	75.3	30 300	32 842	18 983	81 000	23.0	9.9
Fayette County	90.6	92.4	91.1	77.4	71.8	67.2	56.2	69.0	71 329	76 590	41 616	170 200	21.4	9.9
Floyd County	72.2	80.1	71.6	46.5	32.4	53.0	34.3	55.9	35 550	43 170	23 975	81 700	20.2	9.9
Forsyth County	90.2	92.3	91.3	74.5	75.9	78.1	70.5	79.8	68 352	72 613	35 188	177 900	20.7	9.9
Franklin County	82.6	86.4	83.1	68.1	64.1	70.4	72.2	70.2	32 453	36 455	20 128	72 900	21.8	9.9
Fulton County	63.0	76.8	76.1	37.2	25.7	36.8	29.8	38.9	46 995	72 357	30 194	175 800	21.8	10.7
Gilmer County	80.5	84.5	75.8	61.2	52.1	71.1	53.4	74.3	35 080	37 448	25 065	86 200	23.0	9.9
Glascock County	83.2	86.2	78.5	70.4	53.6	72.3	65.2	73.0	29 000	32 531	20 391	50 100	17.1	11.9
Glynn County	71.8	80.7	73.8	46.9	36.1	51.9	34.4	54.9	37 609	48 284	23 958	97 200	21.5	10.7
Gordon County	75.6	79.4	72.7	59.1	51.0	59.1	42.8	61.8	38 213	43 536	26 670	80 800	19.2	9.9
Grady County	76.2	84.1	80.8	57.5	47.4	65.1	56.2	66.5	27 701	33 546	16 529	64 100	22.2	13.1
Greene County	78.2	87.5	80.5	58.1	48.7	70.8	67.0	71.3	33 067	39 614	19 736	69 600	21.1	10.6
Gwinnett County	79.2	83.9	82.6	57.3	52.4	51.6	42.6	54.5	60 244	70 163	39 905	140 600	20.7	9.9
Habersham County	79.6	83.9	76.8	58.5	51.1	66.4	43.2	69.7	36 142	40 964	25 194	90 100	22.3	9.9
Hall County	75.0	80.3	73.6	53.3	46.3	58.5	36.4	63.8	44 559	51 646	30 630	111 500	21.3	9.9
Hancock County	78.6	87.1	85.0	69.0	58.1	70.6	86.7	70.0	22 010	25 945	10 321	46 600	26.7	13.7
Haralson County	80.3	84.6	77.4	65.0	56.8	60.6	57.7	61.0	31 575	37 453	19 060	70 800	20.6	10.2
Harris County	88.3	91.3	88.9	74.7	64.8	77.8	65.4	79.7	47 713	52 578	25 720	113 700	20.9	9.9
Hart County	85.4	90.2	87.1	68.4	62.3	68.1	60.4	68.8	32 392	36 123	18 853	78 500	21.4	9.9
Heard County	80.7	88.9	87.2	55.0	41.0	66.5	40.0	70.2	31 803	36 277	20 996	66 000	22.1	9.9
Henry County	88.4	91.4	89.9	73.2	66.1	71.8	64.8	73.4	57 178	60 726	37 880	120 000	21.5	9.9
Houston County	72.9	80.7	74.5	48.3	38.5	55.8	44.5	57.6	43 603	51 721	28 673	84 500	19.2	9.9
Irwin County	80.2	87.0	86.0	61.9	44.5	66.5	38.4	68.9	30 195	33 136	18 750	48 100	21.2	12.3
Jackson County	78.6	83.9	79.7	57.4	49.7	62.8	56.4	64.0	39 873	45 443	25 482	89 900	21.7	10.2
Jasper County	81.3	87.0	81.7	62.3	46.1	72.5	80.2	71.3	40 044	42 903	25 000	82 600	21.6	9.9
Jeff Davis County	81.5	89.1	85.3	60.0	47.0	64.8	36.7	67.6	27 193	29 462	19 922	47 400	21.2	10.8
Jefferson County	75.5	85.9	84.4	59.1	47.5	63.2	42.1	64.8	26 255	31 376	15 053	45 600	22.0	10.7
Jenkins County	76.2	85.4	79.1	61.5	56.8	66.6	51.7	68.8	24 847	29 485	15 121	43 500	24.1	10.2
Johnson County	83.5	91.3	86.7	65.9	54.0	70.4	80.0	69.8	23 988	26 883	11 143	37 900	21.0	10.8
Jones County	88.3	91.6	89.7	76.1	67.4	77.4	52.5	80.7	42 788	45 516	27 292	79 000	20.0	9.9
Lamar County	77.3	86.1	81.4	53.4	32.7	57.7	42.7	60.0	36 517	43 226	22 656	80 100	20.9	9.9
Lanier County	79.6	84.0	79.6	65.8	56.4	66.9	62.6	67.6	28 867	31 763	19 943	50 300	22.5	12.9
Laurens County	76.3	86.0	81.0	52.4	43.1	58.5	38.2	60.7	31 988	39 233	17 644	61 700	19.2	9.9
Lee County	81.3	85.7	83.5	61.8	00.0	00.0	66.0	61.2	49 066	54 602	32 609	92 600	19.4	9.9
Liberty County	51.9	55.5	47.2	40.3	31.5	46.1	32.2	50.1	33 772	41 756	28 010	73 800	22.6	11.0
Lincoln County	83.2	89.7	84.6	63.9	50.2	77.8	82.6	77.2	30 913	34 569	25 040	67 200	21.8	13.1
Long County	69.5	71.4	66.8	63.6	61.7	56.4	51.8	57.7	30 113	32 500	25 046	53 700	26.7	11.3
Lowndes County	68.6	78.0	71.7	45.6	34.9	43.9	23.1	50.3	32 095	44 424	21 205	79 800	20.5	9.9
Lumpkin County	80.4	84.4	79.0	61.2	53.9	52.6	27.3	60.6	38 182	45 282	25 711	101 000	22.1	9.9
McDuffie County	75.5	85.3	83.9	53.3	36.7	59.6	48.4	61.0	31 944	38 777	18 696	65 900	20.7	9.9
McIntosh County	86.7	90.4	87.8	76.6	70.9	75.5	76.1	75.4	29 817	32 164	19 500	53 500	24.2	11.6
Macon County	76.6	85.3	79.8	62.5	50.9	64.2	64.9	64.1	24 674	29 774	16 304	48 100	20.2	12.2
Madison County	84.2	87.8	83.7	68.7	60.1	68.5	58.2	70.4	36 310	40 065	22 942	79 100	20.0	9.9
Marion County	83.3	88.7	85.9	69.5	62.8	64.8	54.9	66.2	29 014	32 373	11 615	58 100	20.9	13.4
Meriwether County	77.4	85.8	79.4	61.1	44.2	64.9	49.0	66.9	32 092	38 638	17 404	66 800	19.4	10.4
Miller County	80.9	87.2	84.3	63.5	56.4	66.9	30.9	70.0	27 833	30 297	15 750	49 000	22.4	11.6
Mitchell County	73.2	83.6	79.7	55.0	42.4	68.4	80.1	67.2	26 645	32 575	15 362	55 500	20.0	12.2
Monroe County	83.2	90.1	88.1	60.0	42.5	66.2	68.0	65.9	43 839	50 319	24 762	87 100	19.5	9.9
Montgomery County	82.6	86.0	83.0	72.3	66.4	67.3	57.0	68.7	28 966	33 466	18 227	50 000	21.0	9.9
Morgan County	79.7	84.5	83.1	65.1	54.6	70.6	63.0	71.7	39 384	44 077	25 181	97 600	22.4	9.9
Murray County	77.3	81.3	77.2	61.8	57.4	61.4	45.0	64.5	36 498	40 877	26 326	68 700	19.8	9.9
Muscogee County	61.4	72.3	64.5	39.8	27.4	45.6	33.0	47.8	34 787	46 136	24 311	83 100	21.1	9.9
Newton County	81.2	87.8	83.8	60.4	51.3	65.4	51.9	68.2	44 599	50 554	26 311	99 900	21.7	10.1
Oconee County	82.8	87.4	85.4	56.3	50.8	69.0	45.3	73.4	55 501	61 338	33 027	145 900	20.5	9.9
Oglethorpe County	86.8	90.1	85.2	75.6	71.2	71.0	58.7	73.1	35 755	39 147	21 208	79 300	22.5	11.0
Paulding County	88.9	91.8	89.9	71.9	66.1	77.5	75.4	78.1	52 063	55 185	31 988	103 600	21.1	9.9
Peach County	73.2	87.8	84.7	43.8	32.0	56.3	26.8	63.9	34 891	44 869	18 254	72 500	20.6	10.7
Pickens County	86.2	89.9	86.2	66.2	53.4	68.4	70.1	68.2	41 261	44 550	25 153	101 000	21.3	9.9
Pierce County	84.0	87.5	82.8	69.1	61.6	71.0	55.7	72.4	30 100	32 561	16 483	52 000	22.0	10.9
Pike County	84.5	88.1	86.0	66.8	54.3	69.8	75.4	69.0	43 506	48 149	28 171	99 900	20.8	9.9
Polk County	75.8	83.4	75.0	53.1	40.6	58.6	39.3	61.3	31 897	37 470	21 181	72 600	20.4	9.9
Pulaski County	78.2	86.2	76.8	57.2	50.1	63.7	78.6	61.8	31 189	36 152	17 674	71 400	21.3	12.1
Putnam County	81.9	88.9	84.4	56.9	49.6	72.4	65.2	73.5	36 794	41 954	19 784	83 600	20.0	9.9
Quitman County	82.5	89.0	81.4	66.7	46.2	75.0	65.6	76.2	25 469	27 647	20 670	44 300	16.8	11.3
Rabun County	83.7	87.4	79.5	65.4	51.6	69.8	67.9	70.0	33 851	37 692	24 518	97 100	23.4	9.9
Randolph County	73.0	82.8	75.1	55.5	43.4	59.7	44.2	60.6	22 029	25 913	12 759	40 800	23.5	12.6

Table C-3. States and Counties — Migration, Housing, and Transportation

STATE County	Median gross rent	Percent who pay 35 percent or more of income for housing expenses — Owners	Renters	Means of transportation to work (percent except where noted) — Number of workers 16 years and over	Car, truck, or van — Drove alone	Carpooled	Public transportation	Other means	Walked	Vehicles available (percent of households) — No vehicles	One vehicle	Two or more vehicles
	25	26	27	28	29	30	31	32	33	34	35	36
GEORGIA—Cont'd												
Fannin County	391	15.3	20.3	8 105	76.5	17.8	0.3	0.8	1.3	7.0	30.8	62.2
Fayette County	890	14.0	29.0	45 231	84.5	9.4	0.8	1.2	0.4	2.1	20.3	77.6
Floyd County	476	13.9	25.6	39 622	79.8	15.6	0.4	0.8	1.4	8.4	31.3	60.2
Forsyth County	683	14.8	23.5	51 224	81.6	11.2	0.5	0.8	0.6	2.4	18.8	78.8
Franklin County	377	15.2	22.2	8 844	80.4	13.5	0.1	1.2	1.6	6.4	27.6	66.0
Fulton County	709	19.1	30.2	385 442	71.4	11.6	9.3	1.1	2.2	15.2	38.2	46.6
Gilmer County	482	16.6	18.3	10 213	73.3	19.6	1.0	1.3	1.5	5.1	29.4	65.5
Glascock County	313	14.0	14.3	1 065	73.2	20.8	0.6	0.7	2.3	7.7	25.8	66.5
Glynn County	533	16.0	28.8	31 425	80.0	13.4	0.5	1.8	1.8	8.2	35.3	56.5
Gordon County	486	11.6	18.8	22 017	78.4	17.5	0.7	0.9	0.8	6.0	28.4	65.6
Grady County	368	21.7	31.2	9 919	73.8	18.5	0.3	1.8	1.6	9.3	34.5	56.1
Greene County	386	20.2	22.3	5 609	71.9	18.5	0.6	2.0	2.5	12.5	29.1	58.5
Gwinnett County	824	14.4	26.0	309 797	79.7	14.1	0.8	0.8	0.8	3.1	27.1	69.8
Habersham County	467	14.6	20.4	16 482	79.2	15.0	0.2	0.6	2.6	6.5	27.2	66.2
Hall County	619	15.0	25.6	65 402	76.4	17.9	1.1	1.1	1.3	6.1	27.7	66.2
Hancock County	277	20.9	24.5	2 881	62.4	29.8	1.8	3.5	1.5	20.4	32.5	47.1
Haralson County	395	15.0	25.8	11 040	75.8	19.0	0.5	0.9	0.8	7.5	28.0	64.5
Harris County	411	14.4	22.8	11 811	84.9	11.8	0.3	0.5	0.6	4.5	23.6	71.9
Hart County	381	15.0	24.7	10 275	78.9	15.0	0.8	0.4	1.4	7.8	30.0	62.2
Heard County	428	17.6	20.7	4 488	72.7	22.5	0.2	0.7	0.9	8.0	26.5	65.5
Henry County	740	14.0	20.9	60 381	83.0	13.2	0.4	0.6	0.5	2.4	21.5	76.0
Houston County	558	12.3	23.7	53 089	83.3	12.3	0.6	1.1	1.2	5.8	31.7	62.6
Irwin County	343	15.6	20.6	4 021	81.8	12.9	0.1	0.8	1.7	9.9	32.8	57.3
Jackson County	501	15.4	22.3	19 132	79.3	15.5	0.1	0.8	0.9	6.0	26.7	67.3
Jasper County	442	20.3	21.4	5 123	74.5	18.4	0.2	2.4	1.9	7.9	27.3	64.8
Jeff Davis County	368	16.9	23.0	5 132	78.5	17.0	0.0	2.0	0.4	7.5	35.8	56.7
Jefferson County	300	14.1	22.2	5 841	73.5	19.6	0.3	0.7	1.8	17.6	31.0	51.4
Jenkins County	327	20.9	23.6	3 268	74.4	19.3	0.2	3.2	1.8	13.7	32.6	53.6
Johnson County	259	18.6	30.8	2 969	79.7	14.9	0.5	1.3	1.7	11.9	33.8	54.4
Jones County	447	12.8	19.2	10 543	85.7	11.3	0.0	0.4	0.4	4.7	25.5	69.7
Lamar County	441	18.4	24.0	7 026	78.5	16.9	0.6	1.7	0.9	9.4	28.4	62.2
Lanier County	394	20.1	24.9	2 985	77.8	16.2	0.0	1.8	2.4	9.8	34.4	55.8
Laurens County	392	12.6	26.8	18 986	79.6	16.4	0.4	1.0	1.0	9.4	34.7	55.9
Lee County	587	12.6	17.6	11 902	85.3	12.1	0.3	0.5	0.6	3.7	24.3	72.0
Liberty County	529	19.3	19.7	28 743	72.1	17.9	0.3	1.8	6.4	6.6	37.2	56.2
Lincoln County	377	17.4	8.4	3 377	77.2	17.5	0.0	1.5	1.2	7.7	33.4	59.0
Long County	456	20.8	17.5	4 409	74.3	19.6	0.8	1.7	1.4	6.6	32.3	61.0
Lowndes County	495	14.9	32.0	41 303	79.9	14.4	0.3	1.2	2.5	8.1	34.0	57.9
Lumpkin County	534	16.8	29.4	10 118	75.3	18.2	0.3	1.1	3.1	4.2	27.7	68.0
McDuffie County	389	16.5	23.1	8 846	79.1	16.8	0.4	0.8	1.4	13.5	30.1	56.4
McIntosh County	369	19.8	21.4	4 347	78.7	15.0	0.3	1.4	2.2	8.5	35.5	56.0
Macon County	331	15.2	23.1	4 724	69.4	21.6	1.9	0.9	3.9	17.2	34.8	48.0
Madison County	452	12.9	19.9	12 257	79.8	14.2	0.2	0.8	1.8	6.2	25.9	67.9
Marion County	317	17.7	30.4	2 972	68.8	24.9	0.1	2.5	1.4	13.0	27.6	59.4
Meriwether County	427	16.5	27.4	8 893	76.5	17.8	0.5	1.3	1.2	10.9	32.2	56.9
Miller County	317	17.1	19.6	2 800	75.5	17.1	0.4	2.1	2.0	8.1	31.8	60.0
Mitchell County	337	16.9	27.9	8 722	74.2	19.6	0.5	1.6	2.3	13.4	34.8	51.7
Monroe County	461	14.5	23.6	10 316	83.0	13.3	0.1	1.0	1.3	8.5	23.4	68.1
Montgomery County	323	13.9	22.2	3 483	71.3	21.1	0.0	1.2	4.7	8.1	33.3	58.7
Morgan County	470	19.5	19.7	7 278	77.5	16.0	0.0	0.8	1.8	6.0	27.9	66.1
Murray County	446	13.1	20.1	17 441	80.2	17.2	0.2	0.6	0.4	6.2	31.5	62.3
Muscogee County	500	15.6	26.8	82 977	75.5	14.6	1.5	2.0	4.7	11.7	38.5	49.8
Newton County..............	597	15.4	30.8	28 560	81.4	14.3	0.4	1.0	0.7	5.9	26.6	67.5
Oconee County	589	12.1	22.5	12 903	82.5	12.7	0.3	0.9	0.7	3.3	21.8	74.9
Oglethorpe County	457	17.2	22.0	5 928	82.1	13.5	0.4	0.5	1.2	6.4	25.9	67.7
Paulding County	628	13.9	25.7	40 830	83.5	12.3	0.3	0.9	0.4	3.3	21.3	75.3
Peach County	412	17.1	30.0	9 731	76.6	17.0	0.8	1.2	2.9	12.1	32.4	55.5
Pickens County	470	15.1	27.7	11 116	78.7	17.4	0.4	0.8	0.7	4.5	27.3	68.2
Pierce County	328	13.7	22.9	6 847	79.6	15.6	0.1	1.7	0.9	8.3	29.2	62.5
Pike County	470	16.1	15.8	6 149	79.9	15.1	0.4	1.1	1.1	4.6	23.3	72.0
Polk County	425	13.9	25.2	15 552	75.2	20.7	0.3	0.9	0.9	10.5	29.0	60.5
Pulaski County	369	19.4	21.3	3 894	79.7	14.8	0.2	2.0	1.9	9.4	31.4	59.1
Putnam County	355	15.0	24.8	8 055	73.5	20.8	0.5	1.4	1.9	7.9	26.0	66.1
Quitman County	323	10.3	17.4	902	71.5	22.7	0.0	2.4	1.2	11.2	33.0	55.8
Rabun County	439	15.9	19.0	6 429	74.7	19.1	0.6	0.4	1.6	5.8	29.0	65.2
Randolph County	251	17.2	21.0	2 671	72.3	18.0	0.9	1.7	5.9	19.4	36.7	43.8

STATE/ County code	MSA/PMSA/ NECMA code[1]	STATE County	Total population 5 years and over	Same house	Same county, different house	Same state, different county	Different state	Outside the United States	Number	Percent owner-occupied	Number	Percent owner-occupied
					Residence in 1995 (percent)				Occupied housing units		Householders 65 years and over	
			1	2	3	4	5	6	7	8	9	10
		GEORGIA—Cont'd										
13 245	0600	Richmond County........	185 414	50.7	25.9	7.7	13.5	2.3	73 920	57.9	14 511	77.0
13 247	0520	Rockdale County........	65 480	52.0	15.8	17.4	11.2	3.6	24 052	74.5	3 973	85.8
13 249	...	Schley County............	3 456	58.3	18.5	16.1	5.2	1.9	1 435	76.3	299	75.3
13 251	...	Screven County..........	14 356	65.1	21.2	9.2	3.9	0.7	5 797	77.7	1 532	83.2
13 253	...	Seminole County........	8 692	60.7	20.7	11.8	6.7	0.2	3 573	80.8	982	89.2
13 255	0520	Spalding County.........	54 144	53.4	26.6	13.3	5.4	1.2	21 519	62.8	4 370	77.8
13 257	...	Stephens County........	23 818	58.6	23.6	9.4	7.4	1.1	9 951	72.7	2 388	83.4
13 259	...	Stewart County..........	4 917	65.6	18.1	10.4	4.9	1.0	2 007	72.5	505	80.6
13 261	...	Sumter County	30 563	57.8	24.5	10.9	5.8	1.0	12 025	63.9	2 445	76.5
13 263	...	Talbot County............	6 101	71.8	14.6	9.8	3.3	0.5	2 538	82.7	737	86.8
13 265	...	Taliaferro County........	1 945	72.8	11.4	13.2	2.5	0.1	870	77.1	312	83.0
13 267	...	Tattnall County...........	20 981	49.4	17.4	24.5	6.6	2.0	7 057	70.5	1 659	78.6
13 269	...	Taylor County............	8 188	67.0	19.1	10.2	3.3	0.5	3 281	76.8	875	83.4
13 271	...	Telfair County............	11 092	73.3	15.4	8.6	1.9	0.8	4 140	78.3	1 114	83.8
13 273	...	Terrell County............	10 119	62.2	21.5	10.6	4.8	0.9	4 002	66.3	1 043	75.8
13 275	...	Thomas County............	39 872	56.3	28.8	6.7	7.7	0.6	16 309	70.0	4 059	79.9
13 277	...	Tift County..................	35 439	54.0	26.4	10.0	6.5	3.1	13 919	67.2	2 865	78.5
13 279	...	Toombs County............	23 987	58.6	21.9	10.3	7.2	2.0	9 877	65.5	2 105	77.3
13 281	...	Towns County............	8 897	56.1	12.7	16.1	14.3	0.9	3 998	85.2	1 498	91.9
13 283	...	Treutlen County..........	6 363	65.5	18.6	10.9	3.9	1.1	2 531	74.9	657	74.1
13 285	...	Troup County............	54 556	53.1	28.4	8.9	8.3	1.4	21 920	64.5	5 015	78.2
13 287	...	Turner County............	8 744	63.6	20.1	11.3	2.7	2.3	3 435	71.4	886	76.2
13 289	4680	Twiggs County	9 847	71.2	10.5	14.4	3.7	0.3	3 832	82.7	924	89.7
13 291	...	Union County	16 460	57.2	15.3	11.8	15.6	0.2	7 159	82.3	2 477	86.4
13 293	...	Upson County	25 841	62.9	23.6	9.1	3.6	0.9	10 722	69.9	2 542	78.1
13 295	1560	Walker County	57 134	61.6	19.9	8.1	9.8	0.6	23 605	77.0	5 782	85.8
13 297	0520	Walton County	55 798	50.4	19.3	23.5	5.8	1.0	21 307	76.5	3 617	80.9
13 299	...	Ware County	33 238	53.0	24.2	14.8	7.0	1.1	13 475	70.3	3 426	82.0
13 301	...	Warren County	5 891	66.7	18.7	11.6	2.2	0.8	2 435	76.8	651	77.4
13 303	...	Washington County.......	19 828	63.6	21.1	10.5	4.1	0.7	7 435	74.1	1 659	83.1
13 305	...	Wayne County............	24 811	53.1	22.7	14.7	8.4	1.2	9 324	70.5	1 961	86.4
13 307	...	Webster County	2 236	69.5	10.6	14.4	3.5	1.7	911	81.1	274	90.4
13 309	...	Wheeler County	5 815	57.7	11.3	21.4	8.4	1.1	2 011	77.4	575	83.5
13 311	...	White County	18 703	51.4	15.9	21.3	10.8	0.6	7 731	79.3	2 007	85.0
13 313	...	Whitfield County	76 966	52.4	25.3	6.7	9.5	6.1	29 385	67.6	5 702	82.4
13 315	...	Wilcox County	8 048	61.6	12.8	18.7	6.8	0.1	2 785	79.9	752	86.3
13 317	...	Wilkes County	10 066	61.0	19.7	8.1	4.4	0.8	4 314	75.5	1 245	80.0
13 319	...	Wilkinson County	9 475	68.2	15.5	13.2	2.2	1.0	3 827	82.3	895	90.3
13 321	...	Worth County	20 416	64.9	17.1	13.1	4.6	0.4	8 106	76.2	1 937	77.2
15 000	...	HAWAII....................	1 134 351	56.8	26.0	2.1	11.0	4.1	403 240	56.5	93 121	75.0
15 001	...	Hawaii County	139 793	57.7	26.5	4.8	8.5	2.5	52 985	64.5	12 363	80.6
15 003	3320	Honolulu County..........	819 914	56.3	26.1	1.2	11.7	4.7	286 450	54.5	66 986	73.6
15 005	...	Kalawao County	147	90.5	0.0	9.5	0.0	0.0	115	0.0	64	0.0
15 007	...	Kauai County	54 822	62.8	23.0	4.1	8.3	1.9	20 183	61.3	4 758	77.7
15 009	...	Maui County	119 675	55.8	26.2	4.2	10.9	3.0	43 507	57.5	8 950	76.3
16 000	...	IDAHO.....................	1 196 793	49.6	23.9	9.4	15.3	1.8	469 645	72.4	95 027	84.1
16 001	1080	Ada County	277 902	43.7	29.7	7.5	17.1	2.0	113 408	70.7	18 103	80.9
16 003	...	Adams County............	3 331	60.3	13.8	13.0	12.2	0.7	1 421	79.0	390	87.2
16 005	6340	Bannock County..........	69 452	49.4	26.9	10.4	12.2	1.1	27 192	70.6	5 078	86.8
16 007	...	Bear Lake County	5 985	64.1	17.6	4.2	14.0	0.1	2 259	83.2	683	87.6
16 009	...	Benewah County..........	8 572	61.2	17.8	6.2	13.6	1.1	3 580	78.4	973	82.8
16 011	...	Bingham County..........	38 065	61.9	21.3	9.5	6.1	1.3	13 317	79.4	2 795	89.1
16 013	...	Blaine County............	17 837	47.6	22.3	6.9	19.3	3.9	7 780	68.7	947	81.9
16 015	...	Boise County..............	6 236	51.0	10.6	22.0	14.9	1.5	2 616	83.3	510	91.8
16 017	...	Bonner County	34 741	56.2	17.4	5.2	20.5	0.6	14 693	77.8	3 103	87.0
16 019	...	Bonneville County	75 742	53.0	25.8	7.8	12.6	0.8	28 753	74.7	5 581	84.0
16 021	...	Boundary County	9 160	57.5	19.7	5.7	16.2	0.9	3 707	78.4	844	87.3
16 023	...	Butte County	2 709	63.4	17.1	10.8	8.6	0.1	1 089	77.1	310	84.8
16 025	...	Camas County	946	52.7	14.0	25.1	7.5	0.7	396	77.8	94	87.2
16 027	1080	Canyon County	119 519	45.3	26.6	12.2	13.9	2.0	45 018	73.3	9 212	82.1
16 029	...	Caribou County	6 756	64.9	18.6	6.5	9.4	0.5	2 560	79.5	614	90.1
16 031	...	Cassia County	19 663	58.1	19.7	12.1	8.7	1.3	7 060	72.6	1 746	85.2
16 033	...	Clark County	937	54.6	12.7	13.0	11.2	8.4	340	68.2	74	94.6
16 035	...	Clearwater County	8 498	60.1	17.3	10.6	11.3	0.7	3 456	77.9	930	83.0

[1]MSA = Metropolitan Statistical Area. PMSA = Primary MSA. NECMA = New England County Metropolitan Area. See the Appendix A for explanation of these concepts. See Appendix B for list of metropolitan areas identified by type, with component counties.

Table C-3. States and Counties — **Migration, Housing, and Transportation**

	Owner-occupied by household type (percent)								Median household income				Median monthly owner costs as a percent of income	
STATE County	Family-households					Nonfamily households								
		Married-couple family		Other family										
	Total family households	Total	With own children under 18 years	Total	With own children under 18 years	Total nonfamily households	Two or more adults	Living alone	All households	Owner-occupied households	Renter-occupied households	Median housing value (owner estimated)	With a mortgage	Without a mortgage
	11	12	13	14	15	16	17	18	19	20	21	22	23	24
GEORGIA—Cont'd														
Richmond County	62.7	74.6	66.9	42.8	31.5	48.0	35.7	50.2	32 606	42 304	21 972	73 600	21.5	9.9
Rockdale County	79.4	85.6	82.0	55.1	47.2	56.3	38.9	60.4	53 518	61 230	36 348	117 800	19.9	9.9
Schley County	78.0	86.6	84.2	57.3	55.5	71.8	75.0	71.5	31 658	35 932	17 241	48 700	21.8	12.0
Screven County	81.4	87.3	84.9	67.8	60.7	68.7	67.9	68.8	28 496	31 869	14 478	51 800	21.3	11.8
Seminole County	80.7	86.9	79.6	65.5	49.9	81.0	56.8	83.4	27 351	30 066	18 730	52 200	19.7	11.4
Spalding County	67.4	80.1	73.5	40.0	29.8	50.2	36.6	52.8	36 288	45 943	24 000	84 700	21.1	10.1
Stephens County	77.3	81.7	76.3	57.9	45.9	61.7	56.2	62.4	29 832	34 529	21 295	74 000	21.6	11.5
Stewart County	76.2	84.5	79.9	64.7	50.4	65.1	60.3	65.6	24 921	28 486	15 679	37 400	18.0	10.3
Sumter County	69.5	81.9	79.3	46.9	33.9	50.1	41.1	51.5	30 701	38 361	17 979	60 700	19.9	9.9
Talbot County	83.2	93.2	96.4	64.6	56.9	81.4	86.2	80.9	26 078	29 449	13 462	46 300	18.9	11.4
Taliaferro County	80.1	87.2	87.3	69.5	58.2	71.8	65.2	72.3	23 523	28 125	11 250	43 100	18.6	9.9
Tattnall County	75.0	82.3	78.4	55.3	47.1	60.2	32.0	64.3	27 582	33 502	18 963	52 100	19.7	12.0
Taylor County	82.3	90.2	85.4	66.4	57.6	64.0	63.6	64.1	25 280	29 291	10 824	48 900	19.3	11.9
Telfair County	81.8	88.3	82.3	64.8	53.6	70.4	70.0	70.4	26 151	29 448	13 657	39 900	19.5	11.6
Terrell County	71.5	85.6	76.6	49.8	42.6	51.9	42.9	52.8	26 711	34 054	15 443	57 900	22.1	11.7
Thomas County	74.1	81.9	75.5	55.3	45.3	60.3	52.3	61.5	31 082	37 550	20 387	68 100	20.7	11.2
Tift County	72.8	80.8	75.3	52.5	39.8	52.2	27.9	56.0	32 650	39 574	20 666	67 100	19.1	9.9
Toombs County	71.1	79.4	70.7	50.6	40.8	52.9	29.5	55.9	26 636	32 963	18 847	55 200	20.5	9.9
Towns County	89.1	91.3	84.1	70.3	52.5	75.8	73.5	76.0	32 359	34 058	23 650	113 600	22.8	9.9
Treutlen County	80.4	86.8	83.7	65.5	58.4	60.8	78.5	59.0	24 639	30 595	11 115	44 600	22.8	9.9
Troup County	69.3	80.2	74.1	45.8	35.4	52.3	35.3	54.8	35 268	43 433	22 398	81 200	19.5	11.1
Turner County	75.5	81.8	77.2	62.7	50.5	59.4	67.1	58.6	25 765	31 898	14 432	47 900	19.9	13.6
Twiggs County	84.8	89.6	84.6	74.6	70.3	76.4	51.0	79.4	31 095	33 654	20 946	50 200	18.0	12.0
Union County	87.1	90.3	82.9	68.4	49.5	69.6	67.9	69.8	31 498	35 702	17 600	106 100	22.8	9.9
Upson County	74.8	84.0	78.6	52.9	37.6	57.1	51.9	57.6	31 481	38 026	19 317	63 100	20.3	10.7
Walker County	80.6	85.1	78.6	64.3	50.0	66.7	50.2	68.7	32 337	36 951	21 552	68 900	21.0	9.9
Walton County	80.5	87.1	84.2	54.2	43.1	61.2	50.7	63.7	46 578	54 653	26 214	111 000	21.2	9.9
Ware County	75.6	82.6	77.9	56.2	44.6	58.3	44.0	59.8	28 100	33 121	18 513	52 500	19.5	10.9
Warren County	79.2	89.6	83.9	60.7	52.8	71.4	58.3	72.8	26 357	29 985	11 063	46 400	19.2	13.7
Washington County	77.6	87.2	84.8	59.7	47.6	64.7	42.8	67.1	30 334	37 115	15 606	55 900	21.2	10.8
Wayne County	81.0	87.0	83.2	57.9	48.9	62.7	54.6	63.5	32 659	37 951	19 035	56 200	18.0	9.9
Webster County	81.9	87.6	83.5	68.5	58.2	80.2	63.6	81.9	28 831	31 857	20 163	42 500	17.2	9.9
Wheeler County	82.7	85.6	79.8	75.5	66.5	65.0	63.8	65.1	23 750	26 650	13 083	45 900	18.4	12.6
White County	82.9	86.0	77.7	65.9	50.3	68.6	56.7	70.3	35 691	39 955	22 205	104 200	24.0	9.9
Whitfield County	71.0	76.2	68.3	50.3	43.1	57.1	47.0	58.8	39 259	46 771	27 711	86 000	18.7	9.9
Wilcox County	82.5	86.7	80.5	70.5	68.0	73.4	66.1	74.0	27 839	31 551	17 594	43 300	19.5	10.4
Wilkes County	80.9	89.7	87.4	60.4	50.2	63.5	65.9	63.3	28 235	33 932	15 243	58 000	22.5	12.7
Wilkinson County	84.9	90.9	88.8	71.5	62.6	75.0	94.4	72.8	32 921	36 089	17 344	51 900	21.3	9.9
Worth County	79.5	86.4	82.6	58.3	45.4	65.8	59.0	66.7	32 544	38 081	16 678	58 400	21.0	9.9
HAWAII	62.2	66.1	56.9	49.8	30.2	42.2	34.2	44.6	49 536	64 653	33 755	249 300	26.3	9.9
Hawaii County	69.7	76.0	68.2	52.4	38.6	52.3	45.2	54.4	39 336	47 634	26 640	155 400	24.7	9.9
Honolulu County	60.1	63.4	53.2	49.5	27.2	40.1	31.7	42.6	51 745	70 041	34 973	274 600	26.4	9.9
Kalawao County	0.0	0.0	X	X	X	0.0	X	0.0	9 375	0	9 375	0	0.0	0.0
Kauai County	67.3	72.8	66.2	50.4	36.1	45.5	40.3	47.0	44 968	55 216	31 179	214 600	26.0	9.9
Maui County	64.9	70.6	65.1	47.6	30.4	41.1	32.9	44.5	48 837	60 738	35 888	241 900	27.9	9.9
IDAHO	78.4	83.2	78.8	55.6	47.9	57.0	43.4	60.5	37 570	44 143	23 940	102 100	21.5	9.9
Ada County	78.6	84.1	82.6	54.5	47.9	53.2	43.7	56.2	46 104	55 578	27 387	122 400	21.1	9.9
Adams County	81.9	85.1	74.3	58.6	50.6	70.8	72.2	70.6	28 829	31 996	20 395	99 500	23.9	9.9
Bannock County	78.6	83.3	80.9	58.1	47.8	51.2	34.6	55.8	36 678	45 761	20 024	87 000	20.0	9.9
Bear Lake County	86.8	90.0	86.7	61.7	51.6	71.8	35.0	74.7	31 890	34 359	22 143	71 400	20.3	10.0
Benewah County	83.2	87.7	81.8	61.6	55.9	66.6	72.1	65.5	30 380	34 077	21 061	81 200	21.5	9.9
Bingham County	83.0	88.2	84.9	58.0	50.0	64.1	50.2	65.7	36 268	41 452	20 756	81 700	19.5	9.9
Blaine County	76.3	79.3	77.2	59.0	58.1	56.0	49.2	58.6	51 048	59 815	32 782	266 500	25.5	9.9
Boise County	86.6	89.1	83.8	71.7	67.9	74.2	74.1	74.2	38 651	41 707	25 938	112 100	23.9	9.9
Bonner County	83.4	88.0	83.4	60.2	52.9	64.9	64.2	65.1	32 835	36 875	20 548	115 500	24.2	11.2
Bonneville County	81.3	85.8	84.1	58.6	50.7	55.3	41.0	57.8	41 831	49 844	21 968	91 000	19.5	9.9
Boundary County	84.2	87.7	84.2	67.5	63.8	62.7	72.6	61.0	30 559	34 986	22 295	101 200	23.7	9.9
Butte County	83.5	88.3	84.0	57.3	41.4	59.4	79.3	57.1	30 257	37 212	15 188	69 100	18.2	10.1
Camas County	82.1	86.3	83.3	42.9	42.1	65.7	15.0	77.6	35 769	39 167	25 000	91 100	24.5	10.6
Canyon County	76.8	81.3	75.8	57.1	50.8	62.4	55.5	63.9	36 034	41 508	23 801	93 800	22.3	9.9
Caribou County	84.6	86.9	81.8	64.4	51.4	62.1	60.0	62.4	38 393	41 250	24 762	77 300	18.5	9.9
Cassia County	75.8	80.2	72.8	51.3	45.5	61.1	40.4	63.8	33 666	39 344	21 215	79 800	20.5	9.9
Clark County	67.7	72.2	61.5	49.0	45.5	69.8	38.5	75.3	31 364	32 222	25 000	54 300	18.9	10.1
Clearwater County	82.4	86.8	79.6	59.0	49.8	66.3	63.6	66.8	31 803	35 675	21 094	77 500	20.4	9.9

Table C-3. States and Counties — **Migration, Housing, and Transportation**

STATE County	Percent who pay 35 percent or more of income for housing expenses — Median gross rent	Owners	Renters	Means of transportation to work (percent except where noted) — Number of workers 16 years and over	Car, truck, or van — Drove alone	Carpooled	Public transportation	Other means	Walked	Vehicles available (percent of households) — No vehicles	One vehicle	Two or more vehicles
	25	26	27	28	29	30	31	32	33	34	35	36
GEORGIA—Cont'd												
Richmond County	505	17.5	29.6	84 849	76.5	14.6	1.3	1.2	5.0	12.1	39.5	48.4
Rockdale County	757	14.0	27.2	32 931	79.7	15.6	0.6	0.8	0.4	4.2	27.3	68.5
Schley County	358	22.3	17.9	1 577	76.0	19.8	0.3	0.8	1.4	11.4	34.0	54.6
Screven County	341	15.8	30.6	5 865	76.8	17.1	0.5	0.4	2.1	10.2	35.3	54.4
Seminole County	362	17.5	25.9	3 656	78.5	15.4	1.2	2.1	1.4	11.7	31.4	56.9
Spalding County	537	15.2	31.8	24 931	76.1	19.2	1.1	0.9	1.4	11.1	31.8	57.1
Stephens County	422	16.5	24.7	11 795	82.3	12.8	0.2	0.7	2.3	7.5	30.3	62.2
Stewart County	245	10.6	22.2	1 892	65.1	27.1	2.3	1.7	2.6	19.7	36.5	43.7
Sumter County	399	15.2	27.6	13 963	76.5	18.6	0.2	0.8	2.4	12.9	35.6	51.5
Talbot County	307	15.7	25.9	2 475	73.9	22.5	0.7	0.5	1.0	17.7	34.1	48.2
Taliaferro County	285	11.0	28.0	744	72.0	23.0	0.1	0.4	2.3	15.9	37.0	47.1
Tattnall County	338	13.4	22.7	7 880	71.7	18.6	0.4	4.4	2.2	10.6	35.7	53.8
Taylor County	302	12.6	25.4	3 028	76.2	18.4	0.3	0.9	1.9	13.9	34.5	51.6
Telfair County	311	14.3	23.0	4 091	79.6	16.1	0.2	1.8	0.8	11.5	38.4	50.1
Terrell County	314	15.5	24.9	4 070	70.0	21.2	0.7	0.4	2.6	16.8	32.9	50.3
Thomas County	446	17.4	24.4	17 833	79.6	16.0	0.5	0.8	1.2	11.0	36.1	52.9
Tift County	431	12.4	26.9	16 912	77.3	16.2	0.3	1.6	2.9	9.6	36.5	53.9
Toombs County	393	16.7	25.3	10 823	78.1	17.0	0.7	0.9	2.1	10.3	37.5	52.2
Towns County	435	15.9	25.8	3 680	73.8	16.4	0.2	0.6	4.5	6.8	30.2	63.0
Treutlen County	309	12.0	23.3	2 222	75.7	19.4	0.2	0.8	2.7	12.5	34.9	52.6
Troup County	482	14.4	27.6	26 339	78.7	16.2	1.7	1.1	1.0	11.6	34.0	54.3
Turner County	347	17.7	27.7	3 842	73.6	20.6	0.0	1.0	1.7	12.5	35.4	52.1
Twiggs County	390	15.4	23.6	4 086	77.9	17.5	0.2	0.8	0.7	13.9	27.5	58.7
Union County	389	15.6	25.5	7 090	77.6	17.1	0.0	0.3	1.4	4.2	30.5	65.4
Upson County	414	13.2	26.3	11 252	77.0	15.8	1.0	2.1	2.1	9.7	34.3	56.0
Walker County	441	13.7	23.7	27 223	83.1	13.0	0.3	0.8	1.2	6.7	32.4	60.9
Walton County	558	14.8	28.3	29 031	79.1	14.9	0.2	1.3	1.1	6.1	23.7	70.2
Ware County	401	14.0	30.3	13 562	79.1	14.7	1.5	1.0	1.5	10.5	36.7	52.8
Warren County	317	17.9	28.0	2 290	69.7	23.5	0.2	2.4	1.3	15.0	30.9	54.1
Washington County	342	14.4	31.3	7 643	79.4	16.0	1.0	0.8	1.5	13.3	34.0	52.7
Wayne County	371	9.6	22.8	10 125	80.5	14.1	0.5	1.0	1.6	7.8	32.5	59.7
Webster County	202	14.4	11.0	070	76.0	19.1	0.0	2.2	1.5	10.6	34.2	55.1
Wheeler County	249	15.7	20.4	2 049	69.9	23.1	0.0	1.9	2.2	11.2	36.7	52.1
White County	525	16.0	25.7	9 463	79.8	13.5	0.2	0.8	2.0	4.5	25.6	69.8
Whitfield County	484	10.1	19.1	38 909	77.0	18.2	0.6	0.9	1.6	6.6	31.4	62.0
Wilcox County	298	14.1	23.2	2 911	78.0	15.4	0.4	1.5	1.6	11.5	31.5	56.9
Wilkes County	359	18.8	25.8	4 457	74.0	18.7	0.4	1.3	2.2	13.9	32.2	53.9
Wilkinson County	366	14.9	29.2	4 060	77.6	17.0	0.4	0.9	2.7	8.0	30.7	61.2
Worth County	367	16.0	26.7	9 213	80.2	15.9	0.4	1.2	0.3	10.5	29.0	60.5
HAWAII	779	22.1	29.1	563 154	63.9	19.0	6.3	2.4	4.8	11.0	37.0	52.0
Hawaii County	645	20.0	30.7	63 401	68.6	19.7	0.7	1.9	3.0	6.9	36.8	56.3
Honolulu County	802	22.0	28.9	412 250	61.4	19.4	8.3	2.4	5.6	12.8	37.5	49.7
Kalawao County	525	X	11.3	58	75.9	0.0	0.0	24.1	0.0	11.3	54.8	33.9
Kauai County	739	22.5	30.0	26 183	74.9	15.8	0.7	1.4	1.9	6.0	33.5	60.4
Maui County	788	26.1	29.1	61 262	71.1	17.2	0.8	3.2	2.8	6.4	36.0	57.7
IDAHO	515	14.5	28.1	594 654	77.0	12.3	1.1	1.4	3.5	4.7	27.7	67.6
Ada County	617	13.4	31.7	155 666	80.9	10.2	0.8	1.9	1.9	4.6	29.4	66.0
Adams County	395	15.0	28.2	1 374	63.4	13.7	0.7	2.5	6.8	3.2	26.2	70.7
Bannock County	443	11.7	31.7	35 122	78.6	12.8	1.7	1.1	2.9	5.5	29.4	65.1
Bear Lake County	345	10.1	18.2	2 443	69.5	19.6	0.9	0.9	4.0	5.8	23.2	71.0
Benewah County	380	16.1	17.8	3 427	78.0	10.7	0.2	1.4	5.5	5.1	25.0	69.9
Bingham County	411	11.2	22.9	17 685	73.9	14.1	3.1	0.3	3.0	3.9	22.1	74.0
Blaine County	740	22.0	26.2	10 592	69.1	13.2	1.3	2.6	5.2	3.0	29.7	67.3
Boise County	495	19.3	20.8	3 050	66.2	22.8	0.3	0.8	5.0	3.1	23.8	73.1
Bonner County	518	20.0	33.1	15 570	73.4	14.2	0.4	1.8	3.5	5.0	26.5	68.5
Bonneville County	485	10.4	30.4	37 765	77.6	10.0	5.6	0.5	1.9	4.9	27.5	67.6
Boundary County	452	15.6	23.0	3 830	71.1	17.2	0.0	1.3	5.1	3.2	25.2	71.5
Butte County	335	12.7	31.7	1 203	60.6	20.9	4.9	1.2	5.2	4.9	25.3	69.8
Camas County	477	15.2	20.0	495	65.1	18.6	0.0	0.6	7.1	3.3	25.0	71.7
Canyon County	509	16.1	26.2	58 983	77.0	14.4	0.3	1.5	3.0	4.9	28.3	66.7
Caribou County	398	10.0	17.1	2 944	75.4	13.7	0.0	0.4	4.5	4.4	21.5	74.1
Cassia County	403	11.8	20.5	8 841	76.0	13.5	0.2	1.1	4.2	5.2	26.7	68.1
Clark County	347	10.6	9.9	443	65.0	19.6	0.0	0.7	7.0	2.6	36.2	61.2
Clearwater County	396	10.5	23.8	3 207	74.2	12.1	0.1	1.3	7.4	4.2	25.1	70.7

STATE/ County code	MSA/PMSA/ NECMA code[1]	STATE County	Residence in 1995 (percent)						Occupied housing units		Householders 65 years and over	
			Total population 5 years and over	Same house	Same county, different house	Same state, different county	Different state	Outside the United States	Number	Percent owner-occupied	Number	Percent owner-occupied
			1	2	3	4	5	6	7	8	9	10
		IDAHO—Cont'd										
16 037	...	Custer County	4 111	59.1	17.2	11.1	12.4	0.1	1 770	74.7	452	85.0
16 039	...	Elmore County	26 736	31.3	19.4	7.5	32.3	9.4	9 092	57.4	1 266	83.7
16 041	...	Franklin County	10 227	59.1	19.6	3.9	15.9	1.5	3 476	80.8	812	93.0
16 043	...	Fremont County	10 922	64.9	13.9	12.7	7.0	1.5	3 885	84.3	965	89.3
16 045	...	Gem County	14 112	55.7	19.4	12.7	11.1	1.2	5 539	79.9	1 502	91.7
16 047	...	Gooding County	13 084	50.1	24.0	15.3	7.8	2.7	5 046	72.4	1 383	84.9
16 049	...	Idaho County	14 700	58.7	17.1	10.2	13.7	0.3	6 084	77.0	1 692	85.2
16 051	...	Jefferson County	17 487	61.2	15.6	12.6	9.2	1.5	5 901	84.7	1 181	91.0
16 053	...	Jerome County..............	16 863	54.2	19.1	14.2	11.0	1.6	6 298	70.0	1 571	87.0
16 055	...	Kootenai County............	101 260	46.8	25.7	5.8	21.1	0.7	41 308	74.5	8 581	83.1
16 057	...	Latah County	33 038	41.0	19.4	16.8	19.9	2.9	13 059	58.7	1 854	87.9
16 059	...	Lemhi County	7 407	59.9	18.7	6.4	13.6	1.3	3 275	76.1	983	83.2
16 061	...	Lewis County................	3 564	66.8	10.0	13.9	9.1	0.3	1 554	74.5	475	76.6
16 063	...	Lincoln County	3 737	55.8	14.9	16.6	10.9	1.8	1 447	74.4	364	88.7
16 065	...	Madison County	25 504	39.5	13.4	16.7	28.5	1.9	7 129	59.2	966	82.5
16 067	...	Minidoka County	18 569	63.0	18.3	10.1	6.2	2.3	6 973	76.9	1 813	91.3
16 069	...	Nez Perce County........	35 173	54.5	23.2	8.1	13.6	0.7	15 286	68.7	4 010	82.2
16 071	...	Oneida County	3 821	66.5	16.1	4.6	12.0	0.8	1 430	82.3	387	86.3
16 073	...	Owyhee County	9 828	51.4	14.6	18.4	12.3	3.4	3 710	69.7	901	81.7
16 075	...	Payette County	19 047	51.4	20.8	8.2	18.4	1.2	7 371	74.2	1 722	85.4
16 077	...	Power County	6 920	61.1	18.0	12.4	6.8	1.7	2 560	74.5	447	89.0
16 079	...	Shoshone County.........	12 996	55.3	22.6	7.5	13.9	0.7	5 906	72.6	1 654	81.3
16 081	...	Teton County	5 481	52.1	19.1	5.8	19.6	3.4	2 078	73.7	321	90.0
16 083	...	Twin Falls County	59 528	51.5	25.8	10.0	10.6	2.1	23 853	68.3	5 695	81.8
16 085	...	Valley County	7 334	57.3	14.3	14.7	13.4	0.4	3 208	79.1	729	84.1
16 087	...	Washington County.......	9 293	53.3	20.8	10.6	13.4	1.9	3 762	73.8	1 314	85.6
17 000	...	ILLINOIS..................	11 547 505	56.8	26.1	8.3	5.8	3.1	4 591 779	67.3	981 064	77.2
17 001	...	Adams County..............	64 046	59.0	28.2	5.1	7.3	0.4	26 860	73.8	7 363	80.2
17 003	...	Alexander County..........	8 988	63.5	17.6	10.4	8.4	0.1	3 808	72.0	1 093	83.6
17 005	...	Bond County	16 645	55.7	17.1	19.2	7.7	0.4	6 155	79.6	1 714	85.2
17 007	6880	Boone County	38 686	53.7	18.8	20.4	5.0	2.1	14 597	78.6	2 677	78.9
17 009	...	Brown County	6 674	54.5	13.1	24.9	7.4	0.1	2 108	74.1	618	81.7
17 011	...	Bureau County	33 416	66.0	19.1	10.5	4.1	0.3	14 182	76.0	4 288	81.8
17 013	...	Calhoun County	4 813	69.7	16.7	8.8	4.7	0.1	2 046	80.8	683	83.7
17 015	...	Carroll County	15 741	63.7	20.3	11.4	4.2	0.5	6 794	76.7	2 106	84.9
17 017	...	Cass County	12 782	59.0	21.3	10.3	5.2	4.3	5 347	75.2	1 543	85.4
17 019	1400	Champaign County	169 301	42.5	24.0	20.9	8.5	4.1	70 597	55.7	11 745	79.6
17 021	...	Christian County...........	33 238	63.2	23.3	9.6	3.6	0.3	13 921	76.2	4 238	78.5
17 023	...	Clark County	15 997	65.0	18.1	8.5	8.1	0.3	6 971	77.5	2 068	84.2
17 025	...	Clay County.................	13 706	66.7	20.4	9.6	3.2	0.1	5 839	79.8	1 791	85.7
17 027	7040	Clinton County	33 415	67.3	17.1	11.2	3.7	0.7	12 754	80.3	3 478	85.4
17 029	...	Coles County...............	50 382	48.4	22.9	23.6	4.5	0.7	21 043	61.9	4 867	77.8
17 031	1600	Cook County	4 991 310	57.0	30.9	2.5	4.9	4.6	1 974 181	57.9	417 884	71.6
17 033	...	Crawford County	19 333	62.8	24.2	6.0	6.8	0.3	7 842	80.2	2 317	85.6
17 035	...	Cumberland County	10 538	65.0	18.1	15.0	1.7	0.2	4 368	82.0	1 242	87.0
17 037	1600	DeKalb County	83 370	45.7	18.7	27.6	5.7	2.4	31 674	59.6	5 543	76.3
17 039	...	De Witt County	15 766	60.9	21.8	12.9	4.0	0.4	6 770	74.9	1 721	77.9
17 041	...	Douglas County............	18 551	66.6	17.9	10.6	4.3	0.6	7 574	76.9	1 942	85.9
17 043	1600	DuPage County	838 650	57.3	19.3	12.9	6.7	3.7	325 601	76.4	52 877	81.7
17 045	...	Edgar County	18 570	63.6	24.2	6.3	5.7	0.2	7 874	74.6	2 297	81.5
17 047	...	Edwards County...........	6 581	69.2	15.8	12.2	2.8	0.0	2 905	81.2	904	83.1
17 049	...	Effingham County.........	31 793	61.1	24.1	10.6	3.8	0.4	13 001	76.0	3 035	83.5
17 051	...	Fayette County	20 488	60.2	19.6	16.7	3.0	0.5	8 146	79.7	2 213	87.3
17 053	...	Ford County	13 296	64.2	15.5	16.8	3.1	0.3	5 639	76.0	1 729	81.1
17 055	...	Franklin County	36 788	63.1	22.6	9.8	4.3	0.1	16 408	77.7	5 217	86.7
17 057	...	Fulton County	36 113	61.4	22.8	13.1	2.4	0.3	14 877	76.3	4 616	81.3
17 059	...	Gallatin County.............	6 105	65.7	19.6	8.2	5.8	0.7	2 726	81.1	880	84.4
17 061	...	Greene County	13 834	63.0	21.5	11.4	3.6	0.5	5 757	76.4	1 737	85.3
17 063	1600	Grundy County	35 023	57.0	20.9	16.6	4.9	0.6	14 293	72.3	3 022	76.7
17 065	...	Hamilton County	8 133	64.1	18.6	13.4	3.4	0.5	3 462	81.5	1 097	85.6
17 067	...	Hancock County	18 999	67.4	19.8	5.2	7.3	0.2	8 069	80.3	2 355	88.1
17 069	...	Hardin County	4 525	65.2	19.3	11.6	3.0	0.8	1 987	80.5	654	83.3
17 071	...	Henderson County	7 740	68.5	14.3	7.2	9.9	0.1	3 365	78.9	835	84.7
17 073	1960	Henry County	47 974	63.8	20.3	10.2	5.2	0.5	20 056	78.8	5 647	84.2
17 075	...	Iroquois County	29 388	65.2	19.3	11.2	3.7	0.7	12 220	76.4	3 626	84.9

[1]MSA = Metropolitan Statistical Area. PMSA = Primary MSA. NECMA = New England County Metropolitan Area. See the Appendix A for explanation of these concepts. See Appendix B for list of metropolitan areas identified by type, with component counties.

Table C-3. States and Counties — **Migration, Housing, and Transportation**

STATE County	Owner-occupied by household type (percent)								Median household income			Median monthly owner costs as a percent of income	
	Family-households					Nonfamily households							
		Married-couple family		Other family									
	Total family households	Total	With own children under 18 years	Total	With own children under 18 years	Total nonfamily households	Two or more adults	Living alone	All households	Owner-occupied households	Renter-occupied households	Median housing value (owner estimated)	With a mortgage	Without a mortgage
	11	12	13	14	15	16	17	18	19	20	21	22	23	24

IDAHO—Cont'd

Custer County	79.2	81.9	67.6	60.5	56.4	65.1	51.3	67.2	31 357	36 940	21 300	89 700	19.6	9.9
Elmore County	59.4	61.7	49.1	47.7	39.1	51.3	38.3	53.8	35 417	40 875	27 367	88 900	21.8	9.9
Franklin County	82.3	84.4	80.1	63.8	47.3	73.2	46.9	74.7	36 262	39 613	28 462	96 300	21.5	9.9
Fremont County	88.7	90.2	86.6	75.9	73.5	68.2	57.9	69.5	33 567	36 230	22 813	78 300	22.2	9.9
Gem County	81.4	86.3	79.5	53.5	31.4	75.2	52.3	79.1	34 305	38 306	21 210	99 500	22.8	10.0
Gooding County	74.8	79.2	68.2	50.0	48.3	65.6	47.8	68.9	31 920	34 380	25 465	83 200	21.4	9.9
Idaho County	81.2	86.4	80.0	53.1	43.2	67.1	56.2	68.9	29 284	31 644	19 025	89 900	21.6	9.9
Jefferson County	86.6	89.5	87.0	65.7	54.4	75.3	45.0	79.0	37 729	40 539	23 780	89 400	21.9	9.9
Jerome County	72.6	78.3	68.0	39.7	26.0	61.4	42.6	65.3	34 869	39 992	24 309	90 700	22.0	10.5
Kootenai County	80.3	85.6	81.8	57.0	48.3	59.6	52.2	61.6	37 616	42 911	24 190	116 400	23.8	9.9
Latah County	72.8	76.7	72.1	48.4	46.2	37.5	19.9	46.6	32 680	48 961	18 316	118 200	21.4	9.9
Lemhi County	80.4	85.7	77.6	45.9	37.3	67.2	72.6	66.2	29 720	32 182	18 476	91 300	23.8	9.9
Lewis County	81.5	84.4	77.5	64.0	57.7	59.8	57.1	60.2	31 780	35 125	19 509	78 200	19.6	10.7
Lincoln County	76.3	79.8	74.1	57.5	44.4	69.5	66.7	70.0	32 979	35 806	24 479	78 100	20.5	9.9
Madison County	70.0	77.5	80.0	50.7	51.0	27.0	0.0	61.0	32 500	44 005	20 042	99 000	21.0	0.0
Minidoka County	79.0	81.9	73.2	63.8	57.4	69.5	41.2	73.5	31 900	34 940	22 230	74 500	21.5	9.9
Nez Perce County	76.6	83.8	77.7	48.5	37.8	53.2	44.6	55.4	36 409	44 339	21 169	102 900	19.9	9.9
Oneida County	85.3	89.1	89.0	54.2	53.3	72.0	100.0	71.7	33 350	36 710	17 938	88 300	23.1	9.9
Owyhee County	72.6	75.7	69.0	56.3	53.5	61.1	57.1	61.8	28 133	31 490	22 454	83 100	23.1	9.9
Payette County	77.9	82.4	72.3	58.5	46.4	62.7	37.9	67.2	33 011	37 551	22 597	88 200	23.3	9.9
Power County	78.4	80.5	79.3	66.4	55.0	61.4	39.7	64.1	32 247	37 409	22 628	82 100	22.1	14.1
Shoshone County	77.5	83.6	74.0	52.7	42.9	63.2	61.7	63.4	28 419	32 587	19 321	65 800	20.6	10.8
Teton County	78.0	81.2	78.7	60.7	58.0	63.2	45.1	69.8	41 524	44 488	35 944	131 800	23.9	9.9
Twin Falls County	72.9	79.1	70.5	47.7	39.7	56.8	40.9	60.3	34 666	40 683	23 183	92 800	21.0	9.9
Valley County	85.0	88.8	82.9	57.4	51.1	64.7	63.4	64.9	36 260	39 287	27 582	134 200	24.9	9.9
Washington County	78.2	81.4	68.7	61.0	41.1	61.9	48.8	63.8	30 591	32 679	24 132	91 800	22.6	11.8

ILLINOIS .... | 75.4 | 83.0 | 80.1 | 50.9 | 40.1 | 50.1 | 38.7 | 52.3 | 46 304 | 56 715 | 29 065 | 127 800 | 21.7 | 11.1 |

Adams County	81.4	87.5	84.7	53.5	42.2	58.0	45.5	59.8	34 856	40 991	21 200	73 100	18.6	10.2
Alexander County	76.4	86.3	77.8	55.1	46.5	63.6	71.8	63.2	25 768	31 675	12 092	32 600	19.7	11.6
Bond County	84.0	87.8	82.6	62.4	52.8	69.1	56.9	70.9	37 681	42 156	20 494	68 200	18.3	9.9
Boone County	82.1	88.0	86.3	57.6	52.6	61.7	60.0	61.8	52 117	60 170	30 000	100 000	22.2	10.5
Brown County	84.4	88.1	84.9	58.2	46.8	54.3	34.8	56.3	35 408	40 942	20 042	50 800	15.3	9.9
Bureau County	81.0	85.0	79.9	60.6	53.1	64.4	59.8	64.9	40 030	44 914	27 020	78 900	19.1	10.8
Calhoun County	84.0	87.7	84.8	60.0	59.8	73.2	55.4	75.3	34 459	37 412	25 952	69 300	19.2	11.7
Carroll County	81.6	84.5	75.8	66.4	58.0	65.6	60.3	66.3	37 000	40 596	25 967	71 100	19.3	9.9
Cass County	77.7	83.3	74.3	53.2	46.4	69.6	53.6	72.4	34 787	39 331	25 000	54 400	17.7	10.3
Champaign County	73.9	80.7	79.4	48.3	41.3	32.6	17.8	38.6	37 613	54 057	21 362	91 200	19.2	9.9
Christian County	82.9	87.4	82.2	62.8	53.2	61.7	56.0	62.3	36 372	40 850	21 455	61 700	18.5	11.3
Clark County	82.8	88.8	85.2	55.8	51.0	65.5	56.4	66.2	35 678	38 983	23 462	64 000	18.2	10.4
Clay County	85.1	88.3	83.7	70.7	59.2	68.1	67.2	68.2	30 877	33 757	20 193	50 200	19.0	9.9
Clinton County	85.6	90.8	80.5	60.8	46.0	66.4	47.5	60.2	43 364	47 856	26 250	80 500	19.0	10.3
Coles County	78.8	85.3	81.7	52.6	49.0	38.7	16.8	46.4	32 492	43 815	17 421	70 800	19.4	9.9
Cook County	66.0	75.3	71.7	45.3	32.0	42.9	31.4	45.3	45 433	59 682	30 634	154 300	23.1	11.9
Crawford County	84.5	90.2	85.4	57.1	45.6	70.3	57.2	71.8	32 688	36 952	21 676	53 900	18.6	10.4
Cumberland County	85.1	89.3	86.5	65.5	52.8	74.3	70.6	74.8	36 146	39 220	22 533	68 200	20.4	9.9
DeKalb County	74.1	80.5	78.2	45.8	35.7	34.4	15.3	42.6	45 928	60 802	25 940	133 900	22.7	11.7
De Witt County	80.9	85.0	81.5	60.2	50.8	61.5	47.9	63.5	41 942	48 876	24 496	75 400	17.8	9.9
Douglas County	81.3	85.8	80.6	58.4	47.0	65.5	68.5	65.1	39 314	44 686	25 507	70 800	18.6	9.9
DuPage County	84.1	87.7	87.6	63.7	56.6	56.2	45.3	58.5	67 234	77 234	42 583	187 600	22.3	11.4
Edgar County	79.8	83.3	77.9	63.7	55.0	63.7	48.1	65.7	35 000	39 083	21 669	56 400	18.1	10.7
Edwards County	86.7	89.2	86.9	70.6	65.8	68.2	58.6	69.1	32 134	35 842	18 958	45 800	18.8	10.9
Effingham County	83.5	88.4	84.5	60.1	50.5	58.1	35.0	61.1	39 555	44 217	25 331	83 700	19.2	10.8
Fayette County	84.7	88.5	85.3	68.3	60.6	68.5	56.0	70.0	32 134	35 000	21 289	59 300	19.2	10.2
Ford County	81.2	83.7	79.8	67.9	62.2	64.1	63.0	64.1	38 032	41 875	26 275	71 200	18.7	9.9
Franklin County	82.6	88.3	83.3	59.1	46.3	67.7	55.5	69.1	28 053	31 742	16 639	45 900	19.9	12.6
Fulton County	81.6	86.1	81.6	60.1	50.4	64.3	62.5	64.6	33 656	38 225	20 696	58 400	18.6	11.0
Gallatin County	84.6	88.6	82.2	65.4	63.7	73.8	58.0	75.4	25 675	28 630	12 409	42 700	19.7	11.5
Greene County	80.1	84.9	79.2	60.7	50.7	67.2	57.9	68.3	31 581	33 986	22 694	49 200	19.3	10.2
Grundy County	79.4	84.2	81.0	55.7	45.8	54.1	44.7	55.8	51 519	60 503	33 125	125 300	20.8	10.3
Hamilton County	84.6	89.2	84.2	56.8	45.0	74.1	93.8	72.7	30 773	34 965	16 855	48 100	18.2	10.1
Hancock County	85.4	87.4	82.5	74.0	64.9	68.5	48.6	71.1	36 524	40 181	24 660	58 900	17.5	9.9
Hardin County	84.9	90.7	79.3	58.9	61.3	70.5	86.0	69.3	26 928	30 188	16 111	42 300	16.9	10.0
Henderson County	82.9	86.6	79.0	62.9	52.5	69.1	61.5	70.4	37 057	40 620	25 548	53 500	17.3	9.9
Henry County	83.8	88.1	85.2	61.3	49.6	66.1	60.0	66.9	39 840	44 600	25 904	78 600	18.9	10.7
Iroquois County	80.5	84.8	81.2	57.1	46.3	66.4	51.9	68.4	37 953	41 817	27 659	79 400	18.9	11.5

Table C-3. States and Counties — Migration, Housing, and Transportation

STATE County	Median gross rent	Percent who pay 35 percent or more of income for housing expenses		Means of transportation to work (percent except where noted)						Vehicles available (percent of households)		
		Owners	Renters	Number of workers 16 years and over	Car, truck, or van		Public transportation	Other means	Walked	No vehicles	One vehicle	Two or more vehicles
					Drove alone	Carpooled						
	25	26	27	28	29	30	31	32	33	34	35	36

STATE County	25	26	27	28	29	30	31	32	33	34	35	36
IDAHO—Cont'd												
Custer County	378	11.2	14.7	1 905	61.7	18.5	2.2	1.4	6.3	3.6	26.6	69.9
Elmore County	473	14.7	13.4	12 449	76.1	14.9	0.4	2.3	3.8	4.0	28.6	67.4
Franklin County	481	16.1	19.5	4 838	72.7	14.0	0.2	0.6	5.2	2.8	18.9	78.3
Fremont County	420	14.4	19.7	5 044	76.6	14.2	0.6	0.7	3.0	3.9	22.5	73.6
Gem County	502	18.5	32.4	6 227	76.6	13.5	0.1	0.9	2.7	3.8	26.1	70.1
Gooding County	480	16.6	20.6	6 155	69.0	17.5	0.2	1.7	4.9	3.6	25.6	70.8
Idaho County	410	13.4	25.3	5 788	70.0	12.2	0.3	1.5	7.0	5.4	25.8	68.8
Jefferson County	433	15.4	18.2	8 227	72.8	12.6	3.7	0.9	2.9	3.1	20.0	76.8
Jerome County	480	15.2	21.2	7 931	76.5	11.6	0.0	2.1	3.5	3.6	28.3	68.1
Kootenai County	571	20.1	32.4	49 351	80.8	11.1	0.2	1.3	2.2	4.3	26.8	68.9
Latah County	469	12.0	42.2	16 837	66.1	13.5	0.8	2.5	13.6	5.5	31.5	63.0
Lemhi County	390	14.9	19.7	3 097	69.0	14.7	0.3	0.2	5.0	4.7	23.1	72.2
Lewis County	342	11.5	18.6	1 483	70.8	10.3	0.1	0.9	10.5	7.1	27.5	65.4
Lincoln County	464	11.6	16.2	1 769	63.3	19.8	2.4	1.1	6.2	3.3	27.7	69.0
Madison County	298	12.2	18.8	11 451	65.0	11.6	0.7	0.8	16.3	6.1	23.5	70.4
Minidoka County	394	14.1	18.9	8 657	78.2	12.5	0.1	1.7	2.1	3.4	28.5	68.1
Nez Perce County	462	13.2	29.7	17 551	83.5	9.5	0.5	0.8	3.3	6.4	28.0	65.6
Oneida County	484	14.1	21.8	1 739	64.9	22.8	0.2	0.2	3.9	3.3	23.4	73.3
Owyhee County	383	16.9	17.9	4 314	69.3	15.8	0.2	1.3	6.0	4.5	27.3	68.2
Payette County	460	16.8	23.8	8 670	77.3	13.6	0.0	1.0	3.0	4.3	30.0	65.8
Power County	388	16.9	13.9	3 252	72.8	17.3	0.1	0.6	3.7	4.6	26.1	69.3
Shoshone County	389	14.3	25.4	5 280	74.0	15.2	0.2	1.3	6.4	7.4	31.4	61.2
Teton County	603	17.7	16.1	2 938	61.4	18.0	0.8	1.8	8.5	2.1	23.1	74.8
Twin Falls County	489	13.8	25.7	29 405	80.1	11.4	0.7	0.9	2.3	5.1	28.6	66.4
Valley County	505	22.2	23.0	3 469	75.1	14.1	0.2	1.6	4.4	2.7	25.8	71.5
Washington County	457	15.8	17.4	4 187	68.5	15.9	0.1	1.3	4.9	4.8	29.6	65.6
ILLINOIS	605	14.9	28.3	5 745 731	73.2	10.9	8.7	1.0	3.1	11.8	35.4	52.8
Adams County	402	9.1	23.4	32 936	83.8	8.8	0.6	0.9	2.8	8.0	33.0	59.0
Alexander County	265	18.1	24.8	3 198	76.7	15.8	1.1	0.8	3.9	16.7	37.6	45.7
Bond County	385	9.5	22.9	7 659	75.9	11.6	0.7	0.7	6.0	5.0	32.5	62.4
Boone County	531	14.9	20.8	19 755	80.9	13.1	0.4	0.8	1.4	5.5	26.4	68.0
Brown County	316	5.4	18.6	2 503	80.5	11.0	0.1	1.2	2.8	6.7	31.8	61.5
Bureau County	432	10.5	17.0	17 184	82.1	9.5	0.1	1.3	2.5	5.9	30.9	63.2
Calhoun County	350	10.7	18.5	2 292	73.0	17.5	0.3	0.3	2.6	6.2	27.1	66.8
Carroll County	385	10.8	13.2	7 621	76.1	12.9	0.3	1.0	4.2	5.4	33.0	61.6
Cass County	419	9.3	19.6	6 411	72.3	20.1	0.2	0.3	2.7	5.8	31.5	62.7
Champaign County	540	10.2	39.7	91 368	69.4	11.0	4.9	2.5	8.5	9.5	39.2	51.3
Christian County	407	11.0	24.4	15 728	78.3	14.6	0.6	1.0	2.0	7.8	32.7	59.6
Clark County	422	10.9	20.0	7 802	82.6	10.6	0.2	0.8	2.2	5.2	32.3	62.4
Clay County	348	9.8	16.3	6 393	81.6	10.7	1.0	0.6	2.2	6.9	33.9	59.2
Clinton County	430	8.7	20.3	17 084	80.2	11.2	0.7	0.9	2.5	5.9	29.1	65.0
Coles County	438	12.0	38.5	25 694	77.1	11.2	0.4	1.5	7.0	7.4	37.4	55.2
Cook County	648	18.4	30.0	2 371 161	62.9	12.3	17.3	1.1	4.0	19.1	40.4	40.5
Crawford County	372	12.1	25.0	8 497	84.0	9.2	0.4	0.6	1.8	4.9	33.5	61.6
Cumberland County	372	10.8	19.1	5 366	83.1	10.7	0.1	0.5	1.6	4.8	27.5	67.7
DeKalb County	577	13.8	35.1	44 810	77.6	9.4	1.3	1.6	6.8	5.8	32.4	61.8
De Witt County	409	10.7	17.9	8 301	80.4	12.5	0.2	0.3	3.0	5.3	30.8	63.8
Douglas County	431	6.9	16.5	9 423	75.9	11.5	0.1	3.0	3.7	9.7	30.0	60.4
DuPage County	837	15.5	24.5	469 373	79.6	7.5	6.7	0.8	1.8	4.4	30.0	65.6
Edgar County	391	8.8	20.1	8 806	80.9	13.4	0.1	0.7	1.9	5.8	33.2	61.0
Edwards County	319	8.0	15.0	3 296	77.6	12.7	0.4	0.1	3.9	6.4	30.0	63.6
Effingham County	436	11.3	19.1	17 077	84.1	8.8	0.3	1.2	1.5	6.3	31.6	62.1
Fayette County	384	11.2	20.8	9 188	81.3	11.2	0.1	0.8	2.1	5.5	30.8	63.7
Ford County	412	9.0	15.4	6 774	78.2	10.6	0.2	1.1	3.9	6.0	31.5	62.5
Franklin County	380	12.4	25.8	15 675	82.8	11.2	0.1	0.7	2.0	8.5	36.9	54.6
Fulton County	390	10.5	21.2	15 884	78.9	13.8	0.2	1.0	2.3	8.2	31.2	60.7
Gallatin County	272	11.8	26.2	2 569	79.3	13.9	0.3	1.1	1.3	7.8	33.3	58.9
Greene County	369	11.8	17.0	6 202	76.1	13.8	0.0	1.2	2.9	6.3	31.4	62.3
Grundy County	602	11.3	20.5	18 246	85.3	8.9	0.6	0.5	1.5	4.6	29.1	66.3
Hamilton County	308	8.5	25.1	3 643	82.4	10.9	0.7	0.6	1.5	8.3	28.3	63.4
Hancock County	363	7.9	17.1	9 864	81.4	9.4	0.3	0.7	2.8	4.1	29.2	66.7
Hardin County	246	10.2	19.8	1 765	78.4	14.3	0.6	1.3	2.0	10.1	31.0	59.0
Henderson County	374	8.5	17.0	3 944	77.8	14.0	0.0	0.5	2.3	4.1	28.8	67.1
Henry County	419	8.4	17.9	24 617	82.4	9.5	0.1	1.0	2.6	6.2	29.2	64.7
Iroquois County	446	10.7	19.5	14 728	80.0	9.7	0.3	0.8	3.2	4.2	31.1	64.7

Table C-3. States and Counties — **Migration, Housing, and Transportation**

STATE/ County code	MSA/PMSA/ NECMA code[1]	STATE County	Residence in 1995 (percent)						Occupied housing units		Householders 65 years and over	
			Total population 5 years and over	Same house	Same county, different house	Same state, different county	Different state	Outside the United States	Number	Percent owner-occupied	Number	Percent owner-occupied
			1	2	3	4	5	6	7	8	9	10
		ILLINOIS—Cont'd										
17 077	...	Jackson County	56 632	44.3	19.7	24.4	8.3	3.3	24 215	53.3	4 256	80.8
17 079	...	Jasper County	9 535	71.6	15.9	9.2	3.3	0.0	3 930	83.2	1 114	86.3
17 081	...	Jefferson County	37 707	59.7	22.8	11.0	5.9	0.6	15 374	74.4	4 106	78.9
17 083	7040	Jersey County	20 389	60.8	19.0	14.1	5.6	0.6	8 096	77.7	2 085	77.0
17 085	...	Jo Daviess County	21 047	63.1	18.4	9.4	8.4	0.7	9 218	77.3	2 641	81.0
17 087	...	Johnson County	12 293	59.5	11.7	21.3	6.9	0.7	4 183	84.9	1 242	85.4
17 089	1600	Kane County	368 883	54.0	21.2	14.6	5.9	4.3	133 901	76.0	21 042	81.0
17 091	3740	Kankakee County	96 675	57.3	26.3	10.3	5.1	0.9	38 182	69.4	8 669	77.9
17 093	1600	Kendall County	50 195	54.3	14.6	24.7	5.6	0.8	18 798	84.1	3 047	83.5
17 095	...	Knox County	52 615	57.8	23.2	11.3	6.2	1.5	22 056	71.6	6 300	77.4
17 097	1600	Lake County	591 519	52.2	22.1	11.9	10.0	3.8	216 297	77.8	33 353	82.3
17 099	...	La Salle County	104 571	63.6	21.5	9.6	4.6	0.7	43 417	75.1	12 059	82.6
17 101	...	Lawrence County	14 590	62.7	23.0	7.0	6.7	0.6	6 309	77.0	1 943	82.1
17 103	...	Lee County	34 101	60.1	19.8	15.3	4.1	0.7	13 253	73.9	3 384	79.2
17 105	...	Livingston County	37 361	60.1	19.9	15.5	4.3	0.2	14 374	74.2	3 884	80.6
17 107	...	Logan County	29 493	56.1	23.1	14.0	5.0	0.4	11 113	71.0	2 979	00.0
17 109	...	McDonough County	31 527	48.7	18.8	23.7	6.6	2.2	12 360	63.1	2 972	80.9
17 111	1600	McHenry County	239 110	55.9	19.1	17.0	6.2	1.8	89 403	83.1	13 274	85.2
17 113	1040	McLean County	140 745	46.4	24.7	19.0	8.2	1.7	56 746	66.4	9 565	80.1
17 115	2040	Macon County	107 397	55.8	29.7	8.3	5.5	0.6	46 561	71.7	11 751	81.9
17 117	...	Macoupin County	46 195	62.7	22.1	11.0	3.8	0.4	19 253	79.0	5 628	84.0
17 119	7040	Madison County	242 611	58.6	26.7	7.4	6.8	0.6	101 953	73.8	24 935	80.1
17 121	...	Marion County	39 029	61.0	24.9	10.0	4.0	0.1	16 619	76.6	4 723	81.2
17 123	...	Marshall County	12 462	66.4	17.8	13.0	2.8	0.1	5 225	80.2	1 466	84.4
17 125	...	Mason County	15 107	66.9	20.0	10.5	2.5	0.1	6 389	76.7	1 877	87.3
17 127	...	Massac County	14 220	62.7	21.9	7.0	7.9	0.4	6 261	78.6	1 840	83.8
17 129	7880	Menard County	11 765	58.4	18.7	17.9	4.4	0.5	4 873	78.9	1 145	83.1
17 131	...	Mercer County	16 000	64.8	16.9	11.4	6.7	0.3	6 624	79.7	1 839	81.8
17 133	7040	Monroe County	25 806	61.5	16.6	12.1	9.5	0.4	10 275	80.2	2 172	83.5
17 135	...	Montgomery County	28 895	63.8	20.2	11.1	4.5	0.4	11 507	78.4	3 352	83.0
17 137	...	Morgan County	34 689	58.6	23.6	12.8	4.3	0.7	14 039	70.3	3 660	75.1
17 139	...	Moultrie County	13 363	61.3	19.5	15.0	3.9	0.4	5 405	78.4	1 416	79.1
17 141	6880	Ogle County	47 040	50.0	20.7	14.0	4.4	1.5	10 270	74.5	4 000	80.5
17 143	6120	Peoria County	170 926	54.9	28.4	9.4	5.9	1.2	72 733	67.8	17 201	78.8
17 145	...	Perry County	21 869	63.1	19.9	13.8	3.0	0.3	8 504	78.6	2 706	85.5
17 147	...	Piatt County	15 357	65.6	15.8	14.8	3.7	0.1	6 475	80.3	1 717	85.8
17 149	...	Pike County	16 383	64.3	22.7	7.6	5.1	0.3	6 876	77.2	2 272	82.7
17 151	...	Pope County	4 191	58.9	14.4	18.4	7.9	0.4	1 769	82.1	590	85.1
17 153	...	Pulaski County	6 881	65.1	19.9	10.6	3.8	0.6	2 893	75.7	895	83.6
17 155	...	Putnam County	5 726	67.0	13.4	16.5	3.0	0.2	2 415	82.3	659	85.9
17 157	...	Randolph County	32 021	65.6	18.9	10.6	4.6	0.2	12 084	79.4	3 496	85.1
17 159	...	Richland County	15 173	61.9	23.4	8.0	6.4	0.3	6 660	76.4	1 973	84.8
17 161	1960	Rock Island County	139 859	58.5	26.1	5.5	8.3	1.5	60 712	69.7	15 487	76.1
17 163	7040	St. Clair County	238 509	56.7	27.4	4.7	10.0	1.3	96 810	67.0	22 740	80.7
17 165	...	Saline County	25 190	60.9	24.6	9.7	4.8	0.1	10 992	76.5	3 443	81.7
17 167	7880	Sangamon County	176 953	55.0	31.0	8.4	4.9	0.7	78 722	70.0	16 954	78.5
17 169	...	Schuyler County	6 772	66.9	18.8	11.1	2.7	0.4	2 975	79.0	895	86.4
17 171	...	Scott County	5 197	67.1	16.8	11.9	4.1	0.2	2 222	77.6	607	81.1
17 173	...	Shelby County	21 540	66.7	16.9	13.8	2.4	0.1	9 056	81.0	2 726	88.2
17 175	...	Stark County	5 919	67.3	15.8	14.2	2.5	0.2	2 525	77.4	827	85.7
17 177	...	Stephenson County	46 002	59.7	24.6	9.8	5.2	0.7	19 785	74.8	5 241	80.9
17 179	6120	Tazewell County	120 430	60.5	23.6	11.0	4.2	0.7	50 327	76.1	12 688	80.6
17 181	...	Union County	17 339	60.3	23.5	10.9	4.7	0.6	7 290	75.4	2 083	78.0
17 183	...	Vermilion County	78 361	59.7	28.9	5.1	5.7	0.6	33 406	71.8	9 203	80.4
17 185	...	Wabash County	12 191	62.9	22.3	6.7	7.8	0.3	5 192	75.2	1 432	81.1
17 187	...	Warren County	17 682	63.5	17.2	14.3	4.3	0.7	7 166	74.4	1 907	85.7
17 189	...	Washington County	14 279	66.3	17.3	11.5	4.7	0.2	5 848	81.0	1 745	85.0
17 191	...	Wayne County	16 129	64.6	22.8	8.1	4.3	0.1	7 143	79.6	2 153	84.8
17 193	...	White County	14 611	64.4	21.1	7.9	6.5	0.2	6 534	78.0	2 019	82.4
17 195	...	Whiteside County	56 861	60.3	27.6	5.9	5.6	0.5	23 684	74.5	6 365	82.3
17 197	1600	Will County	460 465	54.2	17.3	21.2	5.8	1.5	167 542	83.2	25 682	83.3
17 199	...	Williamson County	57 647	59.0	22.9	11.6	5.9	0.4	25 358	73.6	6 957	81.8
17 201	6880	Winnebago County	258 830	56.0	29.7	6.2	6.2	1.9	107 980	70.1	23 046	78.4
17 203	6120	Woodford County	33 155	63.2	16.3	15.9	4.3	0.3	12 797	82.7	3 276	84.4

[1]MSA = Metropolitan Statistical Area. PMSA = Primary MSA. NECMA = New England County Metropolitan Area. See the Appendix A for explanation of these concepts. See Appendix B for list of metropolitan areas identified by type, with component counties.

Table C-3. States and Counties — **Migration, Housing, and Transportation**

STATE County	Owner-occupied by household type (percent)								Median household income				Median monthly owner costs as a percent of income	
	Family-households					Nonfamily households								
		Married-couple family		Other family										
	Total family households	Total	With own children under 18 years	Total	With own children under 18 years	Total nonfamily households	Two or more adults	Living alone	All households	Owner-occupied households	Renter-occupied households	Median housing value (owner estimated)	With a mortgage	Without a mortgage
	11	12	13	14	15	16	17	18	19	20	21	22	23	24
ILLINOIS—Cont'd														
Jackson County	72.7	81.9	78.3	44.0	36.1	31.9	16.6	37.5	24 813	41 010	13 137	63 400	19.0	10.1
Jasper County	90.4	93.5	91.0	65.4	60.2	64.2	49.5	65.6	35 891	40 708	20 194	65 700	17.6	9.9
Jefferson County	82.1	87.7	84.7	57.1	52.0	57.5	43.8	59.3	33 006	39 204	18 937	60 000	19.8	11.7
Jersey County	83.5	87.8	83.5	59.2	47.6	62.6	65.3	62.2	42 011	46 923	24 783	82 600	18.6	11.0
Jo Daviess County	85.5	88.7	84.9	66.2	53.9	59.5	59.9	59.5	40 330	44 724	24 138	93 500	20.7	9.9
Johnson County	89.4	92.3	88.4	72.7	61.1	72.6	82.2	71.3	33 771	36 265	17 396	63 400	19.2	9.9
Kane County	81.8	88.0	86.1	55.3	47.2	57.3	53.4	58.2	58 888	68 175	33 946	157 800	23.1	11.9
Kankakee County	76.3	83.9	80.7	51.2	38.7	53.2	45.2	54.7	41 612	50 084	26 266	95 800	21.6	11.3
Kendall County	87.7	90.4	89.3	69.1	56.4	69.9	66.4	70.7	63 682	68 424	39 777	156 100	23.8	12.3
Knox County	79.7	86.4	81.0	53.5	40.1	56.0	53.6	56.4	35 033	41 532	21 316	63 400	18.2	10.4
Lake County	83.2	88.0	86.4	59.1	50.3	60.5	54.0	61.8	66 953	78 209	35 493	191 600	23.1	12.2
La Salle County	81.5	86.6	82.4	59.4	46.8	60.9	57.7	61.3	40 338	46 439	25 734	86 500	19.9	11.4
Lawrence County	82.4	87.0	79.6	62.6	52.6	65.5	52.1	66.9	30 109	32 622	21 172	45 000	18.8	11.2
Lee County	80.6	85.4	81.2	57.5	48.3	59.0	58.0	59.2	41 342	46 585	26 813	83 400	19.9	9.9
Livingston County	80.2	84.6	80.5	59.7	53.6	60.4	51.2	61.6	41 067	45 602	26 776	78 300	19.7	10.1
Logan County	77.4	82.7	77.4	52.0	42.5	58.2	52.7	59.0	39 436	45 660	26 227	74 900	19.2	11.0
McDonough County	79.6	85.7	80.4	49.0	33.1	40.9	19.0	48.3	32 484	42 713	16 053	60 800	17.7	9.9
McHenry County	88.1	91.1	90.1	68.2	60.3	65.8	64.2	66.2	64 638	70 827	36 898	167 400	23.4	12.1
McLean County	80.2	85.7	85.4	56.2	50.1	43.4	24.3	50.2	46 634	59 749	26 838	109 300	19.5	9.9
Macon County	79.2	88.4	82.6	49.9	38.4	56.7	50.0	57.7	37 834	46 085	21 150	68 500	18.1	10.0
Macoupin County	83.6	88.3	84.5	59.8	48.4	67.8	71.5	67.4	36 143	40 320	22 930	67 200	19.2	11.0
Madison County	80.8	87.7	84.1	57.0	44.6	58.2	45.1	60.6	41 356	49 222	23 663	76 500	19.0	10.6
Marion County	83.1	89.1	84.7	60.9	50.8	62.0	53.9	63.0	35 006	39 638	17 759	53 500	18.5	9.9
Marshall County	86.2	88.6	85.9	71.5	64.8	64.7	55.9	65.7	41 793	46 014	25 685	77 400	19.0	9.9
Mason County	80.6	85.7	79.7	55.7	41.7	66.6	60.9	67.3	35 731	40 300	24 038	59 600	18.9	10.4
Massac County	83.8	89.2	84.0	61.1	49.6	67.0	63.4	67.5	31 509	35 968	17 841	60 800	19.2	11.1
Menard County	83.3	88.7	83.2	56.8	50.1	67.1	63.3	67.6	46 522	51 514	24 105	92 700	19.5	9.9
Mercer County	82.6	85.3	81.6	65.5	58.6	71.2	74.3	70.9	40 964	45 187	30 202	70 900	19.1	9.9
Monroe County	86.1	90.1	86.3	60.0	57.7	61.9	59.4	62.2	55 409	60 987	35 742	125 900	19.8	9.9
Montgomery County	83.4	88.8	83.1	60.2	51.9	67.1	58.8	68.1	33 312	37 834	20 930	55 300	19.3	10.7
Morgan County	79.7	85.0	83.8	56.7	48.7	51.8	51.6	51.8	36 766	44 730	21 653	73 300	19.1	9.9
Moultrie County	84.6	87.5	83.6	65.7	57.9	61.0	51.7	62.0	40 314	44 366	27 800	73 400	18.6	10.5
Ogle County	80.7	84.2	80.5	61.6	54.8	57.5	59.2	57.2	45 323	52 585	29 225	104 100	20.7	10.0
Peoria County	77.3	86.6	84.0	48.1	36.5	50.2	39.6	52.1	39 985	50 630	22 393	85 300	19.2	9.9
Perry County	84.6	90.1	86.2	59.6	50.3	65.4	54.5	66.7	32 742	37 082	19 987	54 400	17.9	10.6
Piatt County	86.3	89.5	86.1	66.7	62.5	64.3	62.5	64.6	45 521	49 203	31 438	82 100	19.0	10.1
Pike County	82.7	86.1	82.4	65.4	53.2	64.4	54.5	65.2	30 833	34 282	21 250	54 800	18.6	10.2
Pope County	87.2	90.7	86.8	73.0	58.7	70.5	78.7	69.7	29 365	32 196	14 844	60 200	19.5	11.1
Pulaski County	78.9	87.6	83.7	55.7	48.6	68.9	51.4	70.4	25 326	30 177	13 936	34 800	17.6	10.3
Putnam County	85.5	88.4	87.2	69.1	59.1	73.7	76.6	73.4	45 037	48 505	29 083	88 200	19.3	9.9
Randolph County	84.4	88.9	85.0	61.9	51.8	68.1	62.7	68.9	36 758	40 585	24 092	64 100	18.7	9.9
Richland County	83.1	88.9	84.8	59.0	48.9	62.3	37.1	66.4	30 958	36 027	18 030	62 100	20.0	10.1
Rock Island County	78.1	85.5	80.8	53.6	42.7	54.1	50.3	54.8	38 600	47 150	22 414	77 800	18.9	10.6
St. Clair County	72.3	81.9	76.4	50.5	38.4	54.7	53.2	54.9	39 017	48 010	25 253	74 200	20.0	11.2
Saline County	82.1	86.4	81.8	63.3	58.9	65.4	57.4	66.0	28 568	32 608	16 126	46 600	19.1	11.9
Sangamon County	79.2	87.5	86.2	52.8	45.6	53.9	44.6	55.6	42 736	52 190	26 460	87 600	19.9	9.9
Schuyler County	85.4	87.4	82.8	69.1	47.7	64.4	46.8	66.5	34 783	36 907	25 966	53 300	18.3	11.1
Scott County	80.7	83.9	82.0	63.2	48.2	70.1	67.2	70.4	36 595	40 802	24 205	56 900	17.7	11.0
Shelby County	85.1	88.5	82.0	65.7	59.8	70.3	58.7	71.4	37 317	41 084	24 730	67 400	18.7	9.9
Stark County	81.7	84.8	77.1	63.6	44.9	67.3	71.0	67.0	35 757	38 668	26 098	63 600	18.4	11.1
Stephenson County	82.1	88.3	84.0	52.9	42.7	58.9	57.4	59.1	40 419	46 380	23 852	80 400	19.7	10.7
Tazewell County	83.5	88.3	84.8	58.3	47.9	57.6	58.9	57.4	45 401	52 682	25 710	89 300	18.7	9.9
Union County	81.2	86.4	82.3	61.1	54.1	62.9	62.1	63.0	30 980	36 186	16 025	60 400	18.6	11.5
Vermilion County	78.2	85.9	80.3	53.0	42.5	58.6	51.0	59.6	34 200	40 074	21 425	54 600	17.6	10.6
Wabash County	82.7	86.7	80.3	59.0	43.6	58.3	43.5	60.3	34 293	40 056	17 237	49 900	19.4	9.9
Warren County	79.9	84.0	78.6	62.9	53.6	61.7	60.7	61.8	36 087	40 325	25 566	60 000	17.8	9.9
Washington County	84.9	87.0	81.4	72.7	58.9	70.3	63.0	71.0	40 882	44 470	27 829	74 000	19.7	10.8
Wayne County	84.3	88.0	84.8	66.1	53.9	68.6	58.0	69.7	30 409	34 119	19 024	47 100	17.9	9.9
White County	82.7	86.7	84.3	58.6	49.2	68.4	57.1	69.6	29 878	32 796	18 219	43 000	18.2	10.6
Whiteside County	80.7	86.6	81.8	56.1	47.5	59.1	56.3	59.5	40 177	46 194	24 691	75 700	18.8	9.9
Will County	88.5	92.9	91.9	66.4	57.9	63.9	61.8	64.4	62 033	68 521	32 160	152 200	22.7	11.3
Williamson County	80.0	85.9	80.8	55.7	44.6	60.5	52.7	61.6	31 890	38 290	18 779	61 200	19.5	11.0
Winnebago County	78.5	86.4	83.5	51.3	41.1	51.8	49.8	52.2	43 832	53 142	26 206	90 900	20.6	11.7
Woodford County	87.3	90.0	88.2	65.7	56.3	67.9	70.7	67.5	51 040	55 901	31 756	103 200	19.2	9.9

STATE County	Median gross rent	Percent who pay 35 percent or more of income for housing expenses		Means of transportation to work (percent except where noted)						Vehicles available (percent of households)		
		Owners	Renters	Number of workers 16 years and over	Car, truck, or van		Public transportation	Other means	Walked	No vehicles	One vehicle	Two or more vehicles
					Drove alone	Carpooled						
	25	26	27	28	29	30	31	32	33	34	35	36

STATE County	25	26	27	28	29	30	31	32	33	34	35	36
ILLINOIS—Cont'd												
Jackson County	409	11.4	42.3	27 609	73.3	13.0	1.2	2.1	7.8	11.2	39.9	48.9
Jasper County	363	9.1	23.1	4 911	78.0	10.7	0.0	1.0	4.6	5.8	25.2	69.0
Jefferson County	392	12.7	22.9	17 335	83.7	9.1	0.8	1.1	2.2	8.9	32.7	58.4
Jersey County	424	9.1	22.7	10 223	81.9	8.8	0.6	1.1	3.9	4.8	27.0	68.2
Jo Daviess County	393	12.2	24.0	11 386	75.8	10.4	0.3	0.4	5.2	6.5	28.5	65.0
Johnson County	351	12.2	27.4	4 311	83.0	11.1	0.8	0.7	1.4	5.9	29.5	64.6
Kane County	686	16.9	26.4	192 862	79.8	11.5	2.7	1.0	1.6	5.5	28.5	66.0
Kankakee County	539	14.8	29.9	47 255	81.1	11.6	1.1	1.1	2.6	7.3	35.8	56.9
Kendall County	720	14.9	20.5	28 364	82.8	8.8	2.1	0.3	1.1	2.9	22.2	74.8
Knox County	411	9.4	23.0	25 130	80.6	10.2	0.9	1.2	4.1	8.4	34.7	56.9
Lake County	742	18.5	26.8	317 442	76.4	10.2	4.6	1.7	2.9	4.6	28.0	67.4
La Salle County	474	12.1	21.5	50 158	82.3	10.5	0.4	1.0	2.6	6.4	35.1	58.6
Lawrence County	360	12.1	14.6	6 944	82.9	10.0	0.7	0.6	2.3	6.1	33.2	60.7
Lee County	468	9.6	16.9	16 114	81.8	9.9	0.7	0.9	2.7	6.5	30.9	62.6
Livingston County	404	10.0	10.0	17 000	00.0	10.4	0.0	0.5	0.5	5.5	00.0	50.4
Logan County	455	11.1	19.7	13 763	81.0	11.1	0.6	1.2	2.1	5.4	34.1	60.5
McDonough County	393	7.8	35.5	15 531	72.5	10.5	1.3	1.7	9.8	7.3	36.1	56.6
McHenry County	761	16.7	26.6	133 257	82.4	8.6	3.1	0.8	1.3	3.5	24.4	72.1
McLean County	533	10.3	27.5	79 370	79.7	9.9	1.1	0.8	5.2	6.0	33.5	60.5
Macon County	448	10.3	27.2	51 709	84.4	9.4	0.9	0.7	2.1	8.2	35.3	56.5
Macoupin County	422	10.7	22.6	22 456	81.1	11.3	0.2	0.8	2.6	5.6	30.3	64.1
Madison County	490	11.0	27.7	121 852	83.9	9.7	1.5	0.7	1.9	7.0	33.9	59.1
Marion County	371	10.3	24.5	18 518	83.8	9.6	0.3	0.8	2.4	7.3	35.6	57.1
Marshall County	410	9.8	14.6	6 492	79.9	10.3	0.6	1.0	3.3	4.4	29.6	66.0
Mason County	390	10.1	20.4	6 991	78.6	13.6	0.2	0.7	2.3	5.7	30.8	63.6
Massac County	373	15.1	26.1	6 589	82.5	10.4	0.3	1.6	1.9	9.2	33.5	57.4
Menard County	455	9.7	20.6	6 448	80.8	12.7	0.2	0.3	1.5	4.4	28.9	66.7
Mercer County	392	10.9	12.7	7 881	82.9	9.7	0.0	1.3	1.8	4.5	26.1	69.5
Monroe County	562	11.5	17.1	14 092	86.2	7.9	0.0	0.7	0.0	3.3	22.9	73.0
Montgomery County	388	12.9	22.5	12 776	79.2	12.3	0.2	1.1	2.1	6.3	34.9	58.8
Morgan County	420	10.2	23.0	17 176	78.6	11.7	0.4	1.6	3.9	8.5	32.3	59.3
Moultrie County	436	10.0	21.0	6 700	70.0	0.0	0.0	2.0	3.6	6.0	00.1	60.0
Ogle County	489	12.2	19.3	24 544	82.0	9.4	0.4	0.9	3.2	4.6	28.6	66.8
Peoria County	490	10.8	28.5	84 003	82.9	9.6	2.0	0.6	2.7	9.1	36.7	54.2
Perry County	370	10.6	21.2	9 039	80.8	11.8	0.3	0.8	2.9	8.5	33.1	58.3
Piatt County	460	9.4	17.7	8 375	83.4	7.5	0.2	0.9	3.2	4.6	27.8	67.6
Pike County	341	12.3	15.9	7 611	80.4	11.1	0.4	0.8	2.5	6.6	30.8	62.6
Pope County	257	13.6	18.3	1 840	76.1	10.5	0.3	2.3	6.0	8.3	29.7	62.0
Pulaski County	305	13.1	26.6	2 801	78.5	13.1	0.8	1.1	2.4	12.2	35.9	51.9
Putnam County	445	5.3	20.1	2 777	82.0	10.4	0.3	0.7	2.1	4.1	30.1	65.8
Randolph County	393	9.3	20.0	13 768	80.1	12.2	0.3	0.9	2.5	5.4	31.3	63.3
Richland County	385	11.0	28.4	7 124	84.1	0.3	0.2	0.6	1.7	7.3	33.2	50.5
Rock Island County	450	10.3	24.3	70 250	82.8	10.1	1.4	0.9	2.6	8.6	36.6	54.8
St. Clair County	503	13.2	28.1	113 479	81.6	10.5	2.9	0.6	1.8	10.4	35.2	54.3
Saline County	347	12.3	24.5	10 456	82.8	10.5	0.7	0.9	2.1	10.0	35.3	54.7
Sangamon County	503	10.4	24.9	96 474	81.9	11.0	1.7	0.7	2.1	8.2	37.4	54.3
Schuyler County	341	9.7	14.2	3 560	78.4	13.4	0.0	1.6	2.0	4.8	29.4	65.8
Scott County	326	10.9	9.5	2 698	79.7	12.6	0.1	0.4	2.5	4.2	29.5	66.2
Shelby County	418	9.4	16.4	10 500	78.7	13.3	0.6	0.8	1.7	3.8	29.9	66.3
Stark County	397	9.4	13.7	2 652	77.3	12.1	0.1	0.9	3.4	5.1	32.1	62.8
Stephenson County	433	10.2	22.2	23 210	81.7	10.0	0.6	0.4	2.5	7.7	32.6	59.7
Tazewell County	471	9.4	21.4	62 028	85.3	9.6	0.5	0.7	1.4	5.5	31.1	63.4
Union County	341	9.2	26.9	7 421	80.9	11.4	0.8	0.7	1.9	10.0	33.4	56.6
Vermilion County	420	10.4	25.6	34 948	81.6	12.1	0.6	0.7	2.0	9.9	35.3	54.8
Wabash County	337	8.1	21.7	6 152	76.6	14.7	0.1	0.9	3.7	7.6	32.1	60.3
Warren County	376	7.6	21.7	9 027	78.8	11.0	0.1	0.8	4.5	7.2	32.6	60.2
Washington County	424	8.7	10.4	7 557	80.2	8.6	0.6	1.1	2.4	4.2	28.2	67.6
Wayne County	308	11.0	17.0	7 499	80.1	12.6	0.7	0.8	2.0	6.6	30.2	63.2
White County	313	10.3	19.1	6 678	81.0	11.7	0.4	1.0	2.2	6.9	33.7	59.5
Whiteside County	463	10.0	22.1	27 986	80.9	11.7	0.7	1.2	2.5	7.1	31.2	61.7
Will County	630	15.1	25.2	241 887	82.9	8.3	4.1	0.7	1.1	4.0	25.8	70.3
Williamson County	400	12.1	26.5	26 721	85.7	9.5	0.1	0.7	1.8	7.8	36.3	55.9
Winnebago County	514	12.8	25.2	132 631	83.6	10.6	1.1	0.8	1.4	7.8	33.8	58.3
Woodford County	484	8.9	16.1	17 461	82.9	8.9	0.0	0.8	2.7	3.8	24.3	71.9

STATE/ County code	MSA/PMSA/ NECMA code[1]	STATE County	Total population 5 years and over	Same house	Same county, different house	Same state, different county	Different state	Outside the United States	Number	Percent owner-occupied	Number	Percent owner-occupied
					Residence in 1995 (percent)					Occupied housing units		Householders 65 years and over	
			1	2	3	4	5	6	7	8	9	10
18 000	...	INDIANA..................	5 657 818	55.0	25.5	10.2	8.0	1.3	2 336 306	71.4	498 051	79.4
18 001	2760	Adams County............	30 947	66.0	23.3	6.3	4.0	0.3	11 818	77.0	2 920	72.9
18 003	2760	Allen County..............	306 500	52.7	31.4	5.9	8.3	1.6	128 745	71.0	24 642	77.6
18 005	...	Bartholomew County.....	66 182	54.4	26.5	9.6	7.5	2.1	27 936	74.2	5 766	82.1
18 007	...	Benton County............	8 830	61.9	17.3	15.2	5.0	0.5	3 558	75.8	922	84.2
18 009	...	Blackford County..........	13 147	60.4	24.3	12.0	3.1	0.1	5 690	78.6	1 499	84.7
18 011	3480	Boone County.............	42 722	57.1	18.9	15.9	7.5	0.6	17 081	78.7	3 322	78.9
18 013	...	Brown County.............	14 163	63.7	10.7	18.8	6.1	0.8	5 897	85.0	1 275	90.4
18 015	...	Carroll County.............	18 796	63.0	15.4	15.7	5.2	0.6	7 718	79.7	1 890	86.6
18 017	...	Cass County..............	38 063	59.7	23.8	9.8	5.4	1.4	15 715	73.6	4 121	80.6
18 019	4520	Clark County..............	89 910	54.8	24.6	8.7	11.0	0.8	38 751	70.0	7 999	77.4
18 021	8320	Clay County...............	24 826	61.6	23.0	10.7	4.3	0.5	10 216	79.1	2 801	81.0
18 023	3920	Clinton County............	31 414	57.9	25.2	9.3	4.3	3.1	12 545	72.9	3 095	78.2
18 025	...	Crawford County..........	10 058	62.7	17.7	11.7	7.9	0.1	4 181	82.9	964	82.5
18 027	...	Daviess County...........	27 556	67.1	21.3	6.6	4.0	1.0	10 894	78.6	2 830	80.9
18 029	1640	Dearborn County.........	42 986	60.7	18.3	5.1	15.6	0.3	16 832	78.6	3 534	79.1
18 031	...	Decatur County...........	22 712	60.6	25.1	9.3	4.1	0.9	9 389	73.2	2 070	80.2
18 033	2760	DeKalb County............	37 225	56.7	26.4	10.6	5.9	0.3	15 134	81.5	2 936	83.8
18 035	5280	Delaware County...........	111 756	52.0	26.8	13.8	6.1	1.2	47 131	67.2	10 283	83.9
18 037	...	Dubois County............	36 842	66.0	22.4	6.4	4.2	1.0	14 813	78.0	3 308	77.9
18 039	2330	Elkhart County............	168 052	51.3	30.8	6.1	8.8	3.0	66 154	72.2	13 292	78.4
18 041	...	Fayette County............	23 925	58.0	28.8	9.1	3.7	0.4	10 199	71.6	2 760	78.5
18 043	4520	Floyd County..............	66 298	57.1	21.5	10.1	11.0	0.3	27 511	72.5	5 413	77.5
18 045	...	Fountain County...........	16 771	61.2	20.6	11.0	6.8	0.4	7 041	77.9	1 951	82.8
18 047	...	Franklin County...........	20 617	62.5	16.6	9.9	10.7	0.2	7 868	81.4	1 623	84.1
18 049	...	Fulton County.............	19 166	60.8	21.5	12.2	4.9	0.7	8 082	78.3	2 132	84.3
18 051	...	Gibson County............	30 402	64.5	20.2	8.8	5.9	0.6	12 847	77.9	3 422	82.4
18 053	...	Grant County..............	68 963	55.5	28.4	6.8	8.4	0.9	28 319	73.2	7 353	78.1
18 055	...	Greene County............	31 105	62.6	22.0	11.1	4.1	0.2	13 372	80.0	3 449	81.6
18 057	3480	Hamilton County..........	165 990	46.1	18.4	20.1	14.1	1.3	65 933	80.9	8 480	81.4
18 059	3480	Hancock County..........	51 664	56.9	18.3	20.1	4.5	0.2	20 718	81.4	3 992	81.9
18 061	4520	Harrison County...........	32 121	62.6	15.4	11.9	9.5	0.5	12 917	84.1	2 603	87.2
18 063	3480	Hendricks County.........	96 527	53.8	16.2	21.3	7.9	0.8	37 275	82.9	5 995	84.4
18 065	...	Henry County..............	45 532	62.5	24.1	9.4	3.9	0.2	19 486	77.1	4 980	82.5
18 067	3850	Howard County...........	78 943	55.9	28.5	8.9	6.0	0.7	34 800	71.7	7 677	80.4
18 069	2760	Huntington County........	35 508	58.5	26.0	10.0	5.2	0.3	14 242	77.0	2 983	86.0
18 071	...	Jackson County............	38 381	58.3	25.1	9.2	5.9	1.5	16 052	74.2	3 643	83.7
18 073	...	Jasper County.............	27 959	60.3	17.3	15.7	6.2	0.5	10 686	77.5	2 416	80.9
18 075	...	Jay County	20 188	63.7	23.8	8.0	4.0	0.5	8 405	77.8	2 339	82.6
18 077	...	Jefferson County..........	29 761	55.5	22.6	11.9	9.5	0.5	12 148	74.6	2 757	80.2
18 079	...	Jennings County...........	25 501	55.8	22.8	16.2	5.0	0.3	10 134	79.1	1 953	84.4
18 081	3480	Johnson County...........	106 625	51.8	19.1	20.2	8.1	0.8	42 434	76.5	7 099	77.6
18 083	...	Knox County..............	36 970	56.1	24.6	12.0	6.2	1.0	15 552	68.9	4 058	79.0
18 085	...	Kosciusko County........	68 606	56.6	25.3	10.6	6.4	1.1	27 283	78.9	5 546	83.2
18 087	...	LaGrange County.........	31 509	62.9	20.3	10.1	5.6	1.0	11 225	81.4	2 205	83.3
18 089	2960	Lake County..............	450 115	61.5	25.8	2.3	9.2	1.1	181 633	69.0	43 098	79.4
18 091	...	LaPorte County	103 061	58.3	25.1	9.1	6.7	0.8	41 050	75.2	9 964	82.2
18 093	...	Lawrence County	42 948	59.2	28.3	7.3	4.8	0.5	18 535	78.9	4 447	79.5
18 095	3480	Madison County...........	124 968	59.7	27.2	7.8	4.6	0.8	53 052	74.2	13 922	83.1
18 097	3480	Marion County............	796 858	47.2	34.3	8.3	7.9	2.3	352 164	59.3	65 472	72.0
18 099	...	Marshall County..........	41 833	59.8	22.6	10.8	5.4	1.4	16 519	76.8	3 805	81.6
18 101	...	Martin County.............	9 703	66.3	20.0	10.2	3.4	0.1	4 183	81.3	1 141	83.1
18 103	...	Miami County.............	33 755	58.0	20.9	14.9	5.7	0.5	13 716	76.0	3 387	84.4
18 105	1020	Monroe County...........	114 507	39.0	22.0	20.7	14.6	3.6	46 898	53.9	7 097	77.4
18 107	...	Montgomery County......	35 167	56.7	26.7	10.3	5.3	1.0	14 595	73.3	3 430	79.0
18 109	3480	Morgan County............	61 860	58.5	20.0	16.5	4.8	0.2	24 437	79.7	4 566	79.4
18 111	...	Newton County............	13 670	63.5	13.8	15.1	7.1	0.6	5 340	80.0	1 207	85.7
18 113	...	Noble County	42 637	56.8	23.2	12.0	5.9	2.0	16 696	78.0	3 169	80.1
18 115	1640	Ohio County..............	5 293	62.6	14.1	12.5	10.7	0.2	2 201	77.6	514	79.0
18 117	...	Orange County	18 036	63.4	21.3	9.9	5.0	0.3	7 621	79.2	1 839	82.6
18 119	...	Owen County	20 362	59.0	15.4	21.2	4.0	0.4	8 282	81.6	1 692	85.4
18 121	...	Parke County	16 297	61.3	15.4	17.8	5.0	0.5	6 415	80.3	1 699	82.5
18 123	...	Perry County	17 886	62.0	20.8	9.9	6.7	0.5	7 270	79.2	2 008	78.2
18 125	...	Pike County................	12 018	61.7	20.1	14.1	3.8	0.3	5 119	82.7	1 480	87.4
18 127	2960	Porter County.............	137 274	57.4	20.6	11.3	9.8	0.9	54 649	76.6	10 324	81.7
18 129	2440	Posey County.............	25 327	64.9	19.3	10.7	4.7	0.3	10 205	81.9	2 457	82.9
18 131	...	Pulaski County	12 888	62.5	18.6	15.4	3.3	0.3	5 170	80.7	1 419	87.7

[1]MSA = Metropolitan Statistical Area. PMSA = Primary MSA. NECMA = New England County Metropolitan Area. See the Appendix A for explanation of these concepts. See Appendix B for list of metropolitan areas identified by type, with component counties.

STATE County	Owner-occupied by household type (percent)								Median household income				Median monthly owner costs as a percent of income	
	Family-households				Nonfamily households									
		Married-couple family		Other family										
	Total family households	Total	With own children under 18 years	Total	With own children under 18 years	Total nonfamily households	Two or more adults	Living alone	All households	Owner-occupied households	Renter-occupied households	Median housing value (owner estimated)	With a mortgage	Without a mortgage
	11	12	13	14	15	16	17	18	19	20	21	22	23	24
INDIANA	79.5	86.1	83.1	54.9	44.8	53.7	43.7	55.7	41 425	49 688	25 550	92 500	19.3	9.9
Adams County	85.1	88.3	87.5	67.4	61.3	54.5	51.8	54.7	40 790	45 372	25 397	86 800	18.1	9.9
Allen County	79.9	87.7	86.1	53.6	45.1	52.8	47.0	54.0	42 519	51 331	26 403	87 100	18.4	9.9
Bartholomew County	80.1	84.8	80.5	58.7	48.2	59.2	51.1	60.6	43 696	50 844	28 255	99 300	19.8	9.9
Benton County	79.5	82.4	79.4	63.5	52.6	66.2	51.6	68.2	39 513	43 158	29 330	76 100	19.7	11.7
Blackford County	83.4	87.5	78.7	64.9	51.3	66.7	73.1	65.9	35 000	39 883	22 727	60 100	18.4	9.9
Boone County	85.3	88.5	86.5	65.8	56.2	59.3	48.1	61.8	49 686	56 095	31 492	130 600	20.3	10.4
Brown County	88.5	89.9	84.6	79.0	68.8	74.6	72.9	75.0	43 693	46 359	30 611	118 300	22.2	9.9
Carroll County	83.5	86.5	79.8	64.3	53.1	69.1	48.9	72.3	42 192	46 443	31 115	86 600	18.4	9.9
Cass County	79.4	85.2	78.5	55.3	42.2	60.1	52.1	61.3	38 897	44 771	27 010	71 400	17.1	9.9
Clark County	77.5	83.6	79.0	57.6	44.5	53.5	49.3	54.2	39 814	46 814	25 350	87 700	19.4	9.9
Clay County	83.8	88.3	85.4	62.5	48.3	66.5	61.5	67.1	36 175	39 763	23 578	71 900	19.0	10.6
Clinton County	77.1	83.5	77.7	50.3	45.3	62.1	54.3	63.5	40 388	46 323	27 055	85 500	18.5	11.5
Crawford County	86.5	90.3	86.4	71.2	67.3	73.2	71.2	73.6	32 341	35 288	18 942	63 500	20.0	10.7
Daviess County	84.8	89.1	85.2	63.8	53.2	62.4	40.0	66.0	36 660	39 186	20 200	72 800	18.1	9.9
Dearborn County	84.2	89.1	86.9	61.4	49.0	60.5	57.2	61.1	47 749	54 557	25 207	123 100	19.9	9.9
Decatur County	77.6	82.5	77.5	54.9	45.8	61.0	51.8	62.6	40 311	45 307	28 697	88 100	19.3	9.9
DeKalb County	87.6	91.0	88.2	70.4	64.2	65.6	56.0	67.2	44 963	49 475	27 891	87 300	19.2	9.9
Delaware County	77.8	85.1	79.2	50.9	43.9	49.0	24.8	56.3	34 420	44 273	19 659	74 400	18.5	9.9
Dubois County	86.5	90.0	90.2	66.6	55.0	55.2	45.1	56.7	43 861	50 130	26 703	92 000	18.3	9.9
Elkhart County	79.1	85.7	82.4	52.8	44.9	54.1	50.1	55.0	44 479	51 325	29 412	95 600	18.7	9.9
Fayette County	78.2	82.8	77.0	59.8	44.7	56.1	51.3	56.9	38 555	45 395	25 584	78 800	17.9	9.9
Floyd County	79.6	87.8	85.8	50.4	36.7	54.5	46.9	56.1	43 838	53 477	24 918	104 400	19.7	9.9
Fountain County	82.8	87.1	82.7	62.2	55.1	65.8	56.5	67.2	37 949	40 836	25 640	66 700	18.2	9.9
Franklin County	85.9	88.7	85.9	70.1	56.3	65.5	63.0	65.9	43 877	49 028	26 062	98 700	20.0	9.9
Fulton County	83.2	88.4	84.5	58.9	48.6	66.3	63.1	66.8	38 961	42 467	26 179	76 800	18.3	10.0
Gibson County	83.6	88.3	84.6	60.5	50.3	64.0	61.0	64.4	37 168	42 292	21 740	71 200	18.6	10.0
Grant County	80.1	87.0	81.4	54.1	43.6	57.8	51.3	58.8	36 119	42 723	21 918	68 000	18.2	9.9
Greene County	84.9	89.1	84.8	61.3	52.2	68.3	75.9	67.4	33 845	38 533	17 338	66 300	18.2	10.1
Hamilton County	87.3	90.7	91.3	61.4	56.0	59.0	53.7	60.2	70 613	79 502	37 596	163 600	19.8	9.9
Hancock County	86.6	89.8	88.4	64.9	59.3	62.6	55.1	63.8	55 847	61 309	31 603	130 700	19.7	9.9
Harrison County	87.6	90.8	88.4	71.6	61.6	73.4	63.0	75.3	43 583	46 920	27 902	94 300	19.2	9.9
Hendricks County	87.9	90.4	88.2	70.8	64.3	65.2	61.4	65.9	55 450	60 384	35 000	132 100	19.7	9.9
Henry County	82.6	87.3	81.9	59.7	47.6	63.0	58.3	63.6	38 233	43 536	22 375	84 700	18.0	9.9
Howard County	78.5	86.4	82.3	51.0	41.9	57.3	50.0	58.3	43 117	52 436	24 186	87 000	17.5	9.9
Huntington County	81.9	86.3	83.2	60.7	55.7	64.4	48.2	67.2	41 633	46 936	26 943	82 800	18.5	9.9
Jackson County	79.1	83.9	79.6	57.6	46.8	61.8	40.8	65.8	39 055	44 066	26 767	83 900	18.6	9.9
Jasper County	83.7	87.7	84.2	59.4	44.8	56.8	55.9	56.9	43 433	48 971	29 467	106 200	19.1	9.9
Jay County	82.6	86.8	82.9	61.6	52.9	65.7	50.0	68.1	35 381	39 180	23 738	66 100	18.1	10.1
Jefferson County	82.1	88.3	84.0	57.9	50.8	57.2	49.5	58.5	37 595	43 693	23 341	84 700	19.0	9.9
Jennings County	83.6	86.3	80.4	70.9	60.1	65.5	59.9	66.8	38 768	41 400	26 670	77 000	19.4	9.9
Johnson County	83.6	87.9	87.0	61.2	54.2	55.7	52.8	56.2	52 832	60 198	31 086	120 100	19.9	9.9
Knox County	77.1	83.9	78.5	49.3	36.9	53.5	31.1	57.1	31 299	39 604	16 920	63 400	18.2	9.9
Kosciusko County	84.0	87.7	83.0	64.6	54.8	64.8	57.1	66.3	44 084	48 413	29 754	91 500	18.9	9.9
LaGrange County	85.3	88.7	86.2	64.2	57.4	66.8	64.8	67.1	42 699	46 064	28 231	107 100	20.1	9.9
Lake County	75.4	85.4	81.0	51.1	35.5	54.0	47.8	55.0	41 557	50 760	25 069	96 300	19.9	10.9
LaPorte County	81.3	87.9	85.1	54.6	46.7	61.1	56.6	61.9	41 273	47 781	24 614	92 300	19.8	9.9
Lawrence County	84.7	88.3	83.7	67.8	57.4	65.2	57.1	66.4	36 496	41 517	20 764	74 200	18.8	9.9
Madison County	80.3	86.9	80.4	57.2	44.7	60.7	56.0	61.4	38 523	44 906	22 700	80 500	18.9	9.9
Marion County	69.3	80.5	77.8	44.7	35.6	43.9	38.2	45.3	40 248	52 214	27 044	97 200	20.2	9.9
Marshall County	82.4	86.2	82.4	64.0	53.7	60.8	54.7	61.9	42 329	46 561	28 821	88 900	19.1	9.9
Martin County	85.9	88.4	84.7	72.2	61.8	71.1	73.7	70.8	35 532	40 708	20 539	60 700	18.9	9.9
Miami County	80.6	84.8	76.7	60.7	50.6	64.2	59.9	64.7	39 046	43 456	26 169	69 400	17.3	9.9
Monroe County	74.8	80.2	79.6	54.4	47.5	30.8	15.7	37.8	33 137	52 100	18 820	107 500	19.5	9.9
Montgomery County	80.0	85.3	79.2	53.9	49.9	57.3	49.2	58.5	41 309	47 546	26 740	88 900	18.9	9.9
Morgan County	84.5	88.6	86.3	64.2	52.3	62.9	59.3	63.7	48 102	53 666	27 089	114 400	19.7	10.2
Newton County	84.0	86.7	80.2	67.4	48.0	67.7	60.7	69.0	40 800	44 648	26 096	88 600	20.7	11.9
Noble County	83.8	88.2	84.5	61.6	56.0	61.9	57.9	62.7	42 824	48 710	26 427	89 700	19.0	9.9
Ohio County	83.9	85.8	82.3	72.2	56.8	60.4	77.4	57.5	41 794	48 342	21 875	106 500	19.4	10.1
Orange County	85.6	88.9	87.9	70.3	57.6	63.7	64.5	63.6	31 375	35 686	17 674	63 500	19.8	9.9
Owen County	85.1	89.7	85.9	63.6	56.2	71.0	65.0	72.0	36 438	39 781	25 522	82 300	20.7	9.9
Parke County	85.0	88.7	83.0	67.7	56.3	67.8	58.9	69.0	35 469	39 269	22 162	66 300	17.5	9.9
Perry County	87.0	91.7	91.5	64.8	50.3	61.5	70.1	60.3	35 852	41 074	16 624	72 500	17.6	9.9
Pike County	87.8	89.8	87.2	76.0	71.5	69.2	46.3	71.7	34 382	37 764	21 973	57 200	18.1	9.9
Porter County	83.7	88.5	86.1	61.2	53.0	57.7	48.9	59.7	52 873	60 672	31 781	123 000	19.6	9.9
Posey County	86.6	90.5	86.3	61.4	50.9	67.9	77.5	66.6	44 278	52 109	21 782	87 600	18.3	9.9
Pulaski County	84.8	87.9	85.2	71.4	66.0	69.0	62.3	69.8	35 600	38 516	26 754	73 200	19.0	9.9

Table C-3. States and Counties — **Migration, Housing, and Transportation**

STATE County	Median gross rent	Percent who pay 35 percent or more of income for housing expenses — Owners	Renters	Means of transportation to work (percent except where noted) — Number of workers 16 years and over	Car, truck, or van — Drove alone	Carpooled	Public transportation	Other means	Walked	Vehicles available (percent of households) — No vehicles	One vehicle	Two or more vehicles
	25	26	27	28	29	30	31	32	33	34	35	36
INDIANA	521	11.2	26.4	2 910 612	81.8	11.0	1.0	0.9	2.4	7.2	32.4	60.4
Adams County	393	9.2	19.1	15 735	78.3	13.9	0.3	1.8	2.0	11.0	27.3	61.6
Allen County	506	9.6	25.7	164 549	84.1	10.4	0.6	0.6	1.5	7.1	34.1	58.8
Bartholomew County	570	10.5	25.2	35 116	84.4	10.3	0.5	0.9	1.1	5.5	28.6	65.9
Benton County	488	10.7	15.4	4 617	78.5	13.5	0.6	0.6	2.1	3.7	29.5	66.9
Blackford County	396	9.4	23.5	6 569	82.6	10.8	0.3	0.7	1.6	5.4	29.5	65.2
Boone County	545	15.2	23.4	22 679	83.9	8.8	0.1	0.8	1.4	3.4	26.0	70.5
Brown County	569	14.8	24.0	7 354	81.4	11.7	0.7	0.7	1.2	2.4	22.7	74.8
Carroll County	453	9.2	16.8	9 865	80.2	11.8	0.4	1.1	1.9	4.7	25.7	69.6
Cass County	440	8.0	19.7	19 118	81.2	11.9	1.1	1.0	1.7	6.3	33.1	60.6
Clark County	511	11.6	23.6	48 343	84.2	10.9	0.7	0.7	1.4	6.7	34.2	59.1
Clay County	419	10.4	23.2	11 927	82.0	12.5	0.4	0.9	1.3	6.0	28.8	65.2
Clinton County	495	12.4	21.4	15 010	79.4	14.2	0.6	1.8	1.5	6.8	29.9	63.3
Crawford County	390	12.2	20.6	4 563	74.9	17.8	0.7	2.0	0.6	6.6	23.7	69.7
Daviess County	363	10.4	19.8	13 069	72.4	18.2	0.1	1.7	2.7	12.7	29.1	58.3
Dearborn County	504	11.0	25.4	22 711	83.0	11.7	0.5	0.9	1.5	5.6	23.1	71.3
Decatur County	490	10.8	18.1	12 329	80.6	13.4	0.1	0.5	2.3	5.7	28.1	66.2
DeKalb County	480	8.2	17.4	20 289	83.6	10.8	0.3	0.9	1.9	3.2	28.0	68.8
Delaware County	465	11.1	34.5	54 400	81.2	9.4	1.1	0.9	4.8	7.3	34.6	58.1
Dubois County	440	7.7	18.1	20 692	85.2	9.4	0.0	0.6	1.9	5.8	26.2	68.0
Elkhart County	541	10.0	21.0	91 778	79.4	13.4	0.5	1.5	2.0	7.6	31.6	60.9
Fayette County	442	11.4	21.8	11 559	79.3	16.1	0.0	0.7	1.6	7.2	31.9	60.9
Floyd County	517	11.1	24.6	35 297	85.5	9.4	0.7	0.7	1.2	6.7	29.5	63.8
Fountain County	439	9.6	16.9	8 026	78.6	14.3	0.0	0.6	2.5	5.5	29.1	65.3
Franklin County	407	10.8	16.6	10 515	80.8	13.3	0.1	0.4	2.2	4.9	20.4	74.7
Fulton County	456	10.2	20.5	9 912	82.0	11.2	0.4	0.4	1.2	5.4	30.8	63.9
Gibson County	427	9.7	24.4	15 592	83.8	10.2	0.2	0.8	2.7	6.1	29.5	64.5
Grant County	428	10.7	21.7	32 377	79.9	11.1	0.4	1.1	4.5	7.7	33.2	59.1
Greene County	375	9.5	25.9	14 928	78.6	14.6	0.1	0.9	2.5	6.0	29.7	64.3
Hamilton County	709	10.9	23.3	94 561	87.2	6.4	0.2	0.6	0.9	2.4	23.3	74.3
Hancock County	571	11.8	17.0	28 214	86.1	8.4	0.1	0.8	1.2	3.4	23.4	73.2
Harrison County	475	8.3	14.9	17 364	81.5	12.7	0.1	0.6	1.2	3.2	23.5	73.2
Hendricks County	644	11.8	18.9	53 022	89.1	6.0	0.2	0.8	0.6	2.4	23.4	74.2
Henry County	464	10.3	25.8	21 677	84.0	10.4	0.2	0.4	2.0	5.4	28.4	66.2
Howard County	509	9.8	25.9	38 709	84.7	10.3	0.4	1.0	1.4	7.3	34.6	58.1
Huntington County	488	9.7	18.4	19 317	81.4	10.2	0.2	1.1	3.3	5.1	29.2	65.8
Jackson County	495	9.9	23.4	19 963	81.6	12.5	0.4	1.1	1.5	6.3	29.2	64.5
Jasper County	486	11.2	19.8	13 614	81.7	10.0	0.3	1.2	3.2	4.8	24.9	70.4
Jay County	387	9.5	16.2	10 131	80.8	12.5	0.2	1.1	2.0	7.2	27.7	65.1
Jefferson County	419	8.9	20.1	15 032	81.2	10.6	0.6	1.0	4.1	6.6	29.9	63.6
Jennings County	490	12.5	19.4	12 962	79.4	16.1	0.3	0.6	1.4	4.6	24.8	70.7
Johnson County	599	10.2	23.3	58 816	86.2	8.8	0.1	0.9	1.5	4.0	26.2	69.8
Knox County	403	10.2	30.1	17 829	82.6	9.8	0.2	0.9	4.2	7.8	34.6	57.6
Kosciusko County	502	9.8	17.8	36 711	78.8	13.8	0.6	1.4	1.8	5.4	28.5	66.1
LaGrange County	477	10.3	14.8	15 700	60.3	24.6	0.5	5.2	2.7	22.8	21.0	56.1
Lake County	544	14.4	28.8	208 957	80.7	11.3	3.2	0.8	2.0	10.6	36.3	53.0
LaPorte County	495	11.4	25.8	50 121	83.6	9.8	1.0	1.0	2.0	7.3	33.4	59.3
Lawrence County	447	10.5	23.9	21 301	80.1	14.6	0.5	1.2	1.2	6.7	28.5	64.7
Madison County	490	10.5	26.6	58 916	81.8	12.0	0.5	0.8	2.3	7.2	34.5	58.3
Marion County	567	13.3	28.3	424 598	80.4	12.2	2.3	0.8	1.9	9.7	40.0	50.4
Marshall County	500	9.8	21.2	21 792	78.7	12.8	0.4	1.7	3.1	6.6	26.9	66.5
Martin County	356	8.8	16.3	4 698	77.9	16.4	0.1	0.2	1.6	6.6	29.2	64.3
Miami County	452	7.8	19.5	16 258	81.4	11.2	0.5	1.0	2.3	5.8	29.5	64.7
Monroe County	560	11.3	44.7	60 423	73.6	10.3	1.8	2.2	8.6	8.0	37.1	54.9
Montgomery County	477	9.7	18.6	18 129	81.8	11.1	0.2	0.6	3.4	6.9	30.6	62.4
Morgan County	531	11.7	20.9	33 152	82.8	11.2	0.3	1.2	1.8	3.6	23.5	72.9
Newton County	472	13.6	20.1	6 857	80.7	12.5	0.5	0.9	2.5	4.0	28.7	67.3
Noble County	470	8.8	18.7	22 670	80.5	13.8	0.3	0.8	2.0	5.6	28.3	66.1
Ohio County	463	8.4	18.9	2 794	83.4	10.7	0.0	0.8	1.9	7.4	24.1	68.5
Orange County	385	13.1	18.7	8 599	81.3	13.2	0.1	0.4	1.7	7.1	29.9	63.0
Owen County	455	10.1	20.4	10 100	76.6	17.1	0.1	0.8	1.8	4.8	25.9	69.3
Parke County	381	9.4	21.8	7 318	79.1	12.4	0.2	1.2	2.6	5.6	27.3	67.1
Perry County	370	7.7	22.1	8 602	76.4	17.3	0.2	1.0	1.3	7.9	27.5	64.6
Pike County	339	10.8	11.7	5 785	78.5	14.4	0.1	0.9	1.7	4.2	27.1	68.8
Porter County	625	11.1	26.0	72 441	85.5	7.8	1.3	0.7	2.1	4.1	28.6	67.3
Posey County	419	8.7	23.3	12 866	86.2	7.7	0.0	0.7	2.1	5.1	24.3	70.6
Pulaski County	397	11.1	15.3	6 175	81.0	10.4	0.3	1.1	1.6	3.6	29.1	67.3

Table C-3. States and Counties — **Migration, Housing, and Transportation**

STATE/ County code	MSA/PMSA/ NECMA code[1]	STATE County	Total population 5 years and over	Residence in 1995 (percent)					Occupied housing units		Householders 65 years and over	
				Same house	Same county, different house	Same state, different county	Different state	Outside the United States	Number	Percent owner-occupied	Number	Percent owner-occupied
			1	2	3	4	5	6	7	8	9	10
		INDIANA—Cont'd										
18 133	...	Putnam County	33 858	53.7	19.9	19.4	6.5	0.5	12 374	78.6	2 943	83.5
18 135	...	Randolph County	25 569	62.5	21.7	9.2	6.2	0.4	10 937	75.9	2 864	84.5
18 137	...	Ripley County	24 521	61.6	20.4	10.0	7.3	0.6	9 842	76.9	2 331	76.9
18 139	...	Rush County	16 993	59.7	24.7	12.6	2.9	0.1	6 923	74.1	1 800	84.3
18 141	7800	St. Joseph County	246 865	55.2	26.1	5.3	11.7	1.7	100 743	71.7	24 213	81.4
18 143	4520	Scott County	21 246	59.1	24.6	10.5	5.4	0.4	8 832	75.8	1 729	82.8
18 145	3480	Shelby County	40 519	58.6	23.6	12.9	4.0	1.0	16 561	73.4	3 334	82.8
18 147	...	Spencer County	19 135	65.9	16.9	10.4	6.3	0.5	7 569	83.4	1 738	77.9
18 149	...	Starke County	22 024	61.5	18.3	12.3	7.1	0.7	8 740	80.8	2 215	86.2
18 151	...	Steuben County	31 021	53.6	24.5	10.5	10.4	1.1	12 738	78.3	2 599	84.3
18 153	...	Sullivan County	20 514	60.6	20.9	13.0	4.9	0.6	7 819	79.8	2 157	82.0
18 155	...	Switzerland County	8 501	59.8	18.7	11.8	9.7	0.0	3 435	77.8	680	79.3
18 157	3920	Tippecanoe County	140 093	38.3	24.6	19.0	13.2	4.8	55 226	55.9	8 752	78.1
18 159	3850	Tipton County	15 576	64.2	16.3	15.8	3.3	0.4	6 469	79.9	1 616	78.9
18 161	...	Union County	6 848	65.4	16.4	10.4	7.7	0.1	2 793	75.0	625	79.4
18 163	2440	Vanderburgh County	161 284	54.3	29.2	8.2	7.4	0.8	70 623	66.8	17 404	70.1
18 165	8320	Vermillion County	15 698	64.1	20.2	8.6	6.8	0.3	6 762	79.2	1 767	80.9
18 167	8320	Vigo County	99 390	52.6	27.5	9.5	9.1	1.3	40 998	67.4	10 168	77.0
18 169	...	Wabash County	32 919	60.6	24.5	10.2	4.5	0.2	13 215	75.9	3 478	82.2
18 171	...	Warren County	7 915	66.0	9.6	19.7	4.8	0.0	3 219	80.9	756	85.8
18 173	2440	Warrick County	48 933	58.2	19.5	14.4	7.3	0.6	19 438	83.3	3 501	82.1
18 175	...	Washington County	25 391	60.9	21.3	10.4	7.1	0.2	10 264	81.1	2 124	83.9
18 177	...	Wayne County	66 735	56.9	29.2	5.0	8.2	0.7	28 469	68.7	7 279	76.4
18 179	2760	Wells County	25 756	62.1	21.6	12.0	3.9	0.4	10 402	80.8	2 384	86.3
18 181	...	White County	23 686	59.3	20.5	12.9	6.0	1.3	9 727	76.6	2 624	83.9
18 183	2760	Whitley County	28 646	61.0	20.0	15.1	3.6	0.4	11 711	83.3	2 505	86.7
19 000	...	**IOWA**	2 738 499	56.9	23.3	10.6	7.8	1.4	1 149 276	72.3	281 122	80.0
19 001	...	Adair County	7 790	66.0	16.8	10.6	6.4	0.2	3 398	75.3	1 169	81.6
19 003	...	Adams County	4 223	65.4	16.1	13.8	4.5	0.2	1 867	74.8	689	80.6
19 005	...	Allamakee County	13 812	64.1	18.7	8.1	4.9	4.1	5 722	76.5	1 709	82.0
19 007	...	Appanoose County	12 950	60.2	25.3	9.0	5.1	0.3	5 779	74.1	1 740	79.0
19 009	...	Audubon County	6 444	70.4	15.4	9.3	4.4	0.5	2 773	79.0	887	87.4
19 011	...	Benton County	23 674	60.8	16.6	17.2	5.0	0.3	9 746	79.4	2 579	85.2
19 013	8920	Black Hawk County	120 253	54.5	24.6	12.2	6.0	2.7	49 683	68.9	11 812	77.6
19 015	...	Boone County	24 631	60.6	20.2	14.3	4.6	0.3	10 374	75.6	2 689	83.2
19 017	...	Bremer County	22 029	62.0	15.9	16.3	5.6	0.2	8 860	78.1	2 444	82.1
19 019	...	Buchanan County	19 649	62.9	21.0	11.8	4.2	0.1	7 933	78.1	2 179	84.2
19 021	...	Buena Vista County	19 226	55.9	18.8	10.4	10.4	4.6	7 499	70.5	2 114	80.5
19 023	...	Butler County	14 444	69.0	15.9	11.8	3.2	0.2	6 175	80.4	1 928	86.2
19 025	...	Calhoun County	10 556	62.9	17.0	14.9	5.0	0.1	4 513	77.4	1 661	79.1
19 027	...	Carroll County	20 126	68.0	20.1	7.8	3.9	0.3	8 486	74.3	2 623	78.5
19 029	...	Cass County	13 895	65.3	20.5	8.9	4.9	0.4	6 120	74.6	1 935	81.1
19 031	...	Cedar County	17 088	60.9	18.5	15.7	4.7	0.3	7 147	76.9	1 865	80.2
19 033	...	Cerro Gordo County	43 618	58.7	25.0	9.8	5.9	0.6	19 374	71.5	5 202	78.1
19 035	...	Cherokee County	12 338	66.8	18.8	9.3	5.0	0.1	5 378	73.5	1 704	83.3
19 037	...	Chickasaw County	12 347	67.8	19.3	9.7	2.8	0.3	5 192	80.4	1 568	85.4
19 039	...	Clarke County	8 569	56.9	17.8	16.9	7.6	0.8	3 584	72.3	1 098	77.4
19 041	...	Clay County	16 288	60.3	21.3	10.8	6.9	0.6	7 259	69.2	2 083	76.1
19 043	...	Clayton County	17 612	67.3	18.5	8.1	5.5	0.6	7 375	76.6	2 192	83.5
19 045	...	Clinton County	46 949	59.5	25.8	6.7	7.4	0.6	20 105	72.9	5 076	79.4
19 047	...	Crawford County	15 845	62.5	17.7	8.7	7.6	3.5	6 441	73.1	1 883	81.8
19 049	2120	Dallas County	37 444	52.2	15.3	22.5	8.7	1.2	15 584	76.4	2 894	79.8
19 051	...	Davis County	7 936	64.7	20.7	8.4	5.8	0.4	3 207	79.8	930	82.9
19 053	...	Decatur County	8 208	53.8	17.6	10.7	16.6	1.3	3 337	71.1	1 012	77.6
19 055	...	Delaware County	17 231	66.8	20.4	9.4	3.3	0.1	6 834	78.0	1 686	82.0
19 057	...	Des Moines County	39 769	59.0	26.6	6.8	6.8	0.8	17 270	74.2	4 744	80.7
19 059	...	Dickinson County	15 558	59.1	19.1	13.1	8.5	0.2	7 103	78.0	2 188	84.5
19 061	2200	Dubuque County	83 184	60.0	25.4	5.5	7.9	1.3	33 690	73.5	7 908	79.6
19 063	...	Emmet County	10 438	61.3	22.5	7.8	7.6	0.7	4 450	75.2	1 344	84.4
19 065	...	Fayette County	20 718	62.1	21.0	10.8	5.4	0.6	8 778	75.6	2 660	83.6
19 067	...	Floyd County	15 869	61.4	23.5	10.2	4.4	0.4	6 828	74.1	2 058	79.7
19 069	...	Franklin County	10 094	66.7	15.8	11.4	4.2	2.0	4 356	74.8	1 346	83.1
19 071	...	Fremont County	7 576	61.5	15.8	10.8	11.3	0.6	3 199	74.5	1 033	80.2
19 073	...	Greene County	9 758	64.8	18.8	10.5	5.2	0.7	4 205	75.6	1 408	78.9
19 075	...	Grundy County	11 696	68.4	13.5	14.7	3.2	0.2	4 984	79.7	1 474	83.7

[1]MSA = Metropolitan Statistical Area. PMSA = Primary MSA. NECMA = New England County Metropolitan Area. See the Appendix A for explanation of these concepts. See Appendix B for list of metropolitan areas identified by type, with component counties.

STATE County	Owner-occupied by household type (percent)								Median household income			Median housing value (owner estimated)	Median monthly owner costs as a percent of income	
	Family-households				Nonfamily households									
		Married-couple family		Other family										
	Total family households	Total	With own children under 18 years	Total	With own children under 18 years	Total nonfamily households	Two or more adults	Living alone	All households	Owner-occupied households	Renter-occupied households		With a mortgage	Without a mortgage
	11	12	13	14	15	16	17	18	19	20	21	22	23	24
INDIANA—Cont'd														
Putnam County	84.0	87.6	85.6	62.8	49.7	63.0	58.2	63.7	38 800	43 580	25 128	94 900	20.8	10.1
Randolph County	80.3	85.1	77.9	57.6	41.0	65.0	52.7	66.8	34 446	39 386	21 162	67 000	17.9	10.4
Ripley County	83.6	87.0	84.9	67.5	56.9	57.5	59.7	57.3	41 300	46 006	24 466	97 900	19.2	9.9
Rush County	78.3	83.1	77.2	57.3	49.7	62.5	49.4	64.5	38 839	42 415	27 475	86 100	18.3	10.8
St. Joseph County........	80.0	87.5	84.5	55.7	44.2	55.2	49.3	56.4	40 131	47 964	24 443	85 800	19.2	9.9
Scott County.................	79.4	84.2	78.5	61.0	47.0	65.4	60.8	66.1	34 898	39 268	22 054	74 700	19.3	9.9
Shelby County..............	80.3	84.8	83.3	60.4	48.9	54.6	42.7	56.9	43 698	50 330	30 976	99 000	18.5	9.9
Spencer County	88.4	91.6	90.3	69.5	59.7	67.0	74.7	66.0	42 364	46 949	23 359	85 400	18.6	9.9
Starke County	84.2	87.7	80.8	68.4	57.7	71.2	73.6	70.9	37 192	41 202	22 135	80 500	20.5	9.9
Steuben County	84.3	88.9	83.0	65.1	56.1	64.2	55.0	66.4	44 128	48 667	29 896	98 600	19.1	9.9
Sullivan County	83.5	87.7	83.4	64.1	49.1	70.7	80.6	69.3	33 372	37 045	19 429	57 900	18.6	11.1
Switzerland County	82.4	86.0	84.2	67.7	56.7	65.2	56.5	67.0	36 875	40 811	23 993	85 200	20.8	11.4
Tippecanoe County	71.9	77.5	75.3	49.4	45.0	32.9	16.2	40.7	38 483	55 036	22 339	110 100	19.7	9.9
Tipton County	84.4	86.2	83.3	73.3	65.7	67.1	57.1	68.3	48 811	52 898	32 149	87 000	16.6	9.9
Union County	77.8	82.9	79.5	45.6	37.2	67.2	64.1	67.6	36 953	40 682	26 339	84 700	19.8	10.8
Vanderburgh County	77.3	85.1	83.4	51.8	40.3	48.8	36.4	51.1	36 665	46 330	21 651	81 100	18.8	9.9
Vermillion County	84.1	88.3	87.3	65.5	56.7	68.1	81.6	66.3	34 163	39 022	18 150	59 700	18.1	9.9
Vigo County.................	77.8	85.0	80.6	54.4	45.8	49.0	34.2	52.1	33 021	42 879	19 368	71 800	18.5	9.9
Wabash County............	82.5	87.5	85.7	60.5	50.9	59.4	53.5	60.3	40 172	45 358	26 221	78 700	17.3	9.9
Warren County	83.9	87.3	83.0	60.6	52.6	71.8	63.9	73.1	40 972	44 347	27 891	77 100	20.2	9.9
Warrick County	88.4	91.6	91.2	68.8	59.9	64.8	65.8	64.7	49 068	54 163	28 004	100 900	19.4	9.9
Washington County	85.3	88.1	84.9	71.1	62.1	69.1	63.2	70.0	36 521	39 881	23 452	77 400	19.5	9.9
Wayne County	76.1	83.7	77.8	46.7	33.9	53.1	54.8	52.8	34 574	42 670	20 977	80 700	19.1	9.9
Wells County	86.0	89.8	88.9	67.3	60.3	66.4	61.7	67.0	43 711	47 870	28 028	88 100	18.6	9.9
White County................	80.9	84.7	76.5	63.6	51.9	64.9	57.0	66.4	40 432	44 511	29 591	85 800	19.5	10.8
Whitley County	89.3	92.7	90.1	73.1	66.0	65.8	57.3	67.1	46 163	50 885	30 123	96 600	19.0	9.9
IOWA........................	81.6	86.6	83.7	57.5	48.7	53.4	39.9	56.2	39 358	46 120	24 581	82 100	19.1	9.9
Adair County	81.4	83.8	74.8	63.8	50.0	61.9	56.5	62.4	35 111	39 803	24 487	63 000	17.6	9.9
Adams County	80.2	84.4	79.6	46.4	42.2	63.5	62.8	63.6	30 161	33 425	22 177	56 500	17.1	11.1
Allamakee County	83.6	86.7	79.5	64.1	50.9	61.1	45.7	63.3	33 803	37 168	22 175	69 900	19.0	10.2
Appanoose County	83.4	87.8	82.8	63.9	53.3	55.5	51.8	56.0	28 407	32 113	17 264	49 300	17.9	10.4
Audubon County	82.1	86.3	81.0	51.7	46.0	72.0	49.1	73.6	32 347	34 805	26 440	58 400	17.1	9.9
Benton County	84.7	88.4	84.6	61.8	51.5	64.8	44.0	67.6	42 307	46 382	27 879	85 800	19.6	9.9
Black Hawk County.......	80.1	86.3	83.2	56.3	45.7	48.6	29.1	54.7	37 069	46 087	21 501	76 200	18.4	9.9
Boone County	83.2	88.2	85.3	56.3	45.2	58.7	48.5	60.4	40 754	45 629	27 618	77 100	18.8	11.0
Bremer County	86.9	89.9	87.3	65.5	59.8	56.2	27.2	60.5	40 690	47 242	25 137	90 800	18.6	9.9
Buchanan County	82.7	86.9	83.0	56.0	51.4	66.2	59.8	67.0	37 542	42 207	23 198	76 200	19.0	10.3
Buena Vista County	79.7	83.8	78.4	55.0	49.4	51.0	30.2	54.8	35 586	40 334	23 871	65 900	18.3	10.2
Butler County	84.2	87.3	81.9	62.4	48.7	70.6	60.1	71.6	36 066	38 892	25 549	66 500	18.0	10.8
Calhoun County	84.1	88.3	86.1	57.4	51.2	63.9	55.2	64.5	32 553	36 706	21 023	56 700	18.9	9.9
Carroll County	83.9	88.7	86.2	52.7	44.9	54.7	45.0	55.8	37 624	43 531	24 836	77 500	18.6	9.9
Cass County	82.4	87.9	84.3	54.8	47.0	58.8	51.5	59.6	32 523	37 516	22 716	63 900	17.6	9.9
Cedar County	83.2	85.4	83.4	69.2	65.8	60.6	47.8	62.9	42 516	46 408	30 601	86 400	19.4	10.6
Cerro Gordo County......	82.8	89.4	88.9	52.6	45.3	51.3	42.4	52.8	35 852	43 612	20 616	76 100	19.1	10.7
Cherokee County	78.9	83.0	75.1	51.9	48.5	62.5	47.9	64.3	35 230	38 114	28 340	60 400	18.2	10.6
Chickasaw County	86.7	89.5	87.5	65.7	55.8	65.3	63.7	65.5	37 702	41 790	24 342	73 000	18.5	9.9
Clarke County	77.0	81.2	75.7	55.9	43.2	61.1	60.4	61.2	33 761	38 938	24 500	71 900	19.1	12.1
Clay County	78.4	85.5	81.4	43.3	30.9	50.4	40.2	51.6	35 589	41 282	22 923	75 700	18.5	9.9
Clayton County.............	82.2	85.0	78.6	67.0	60.1	63.4	57.2	64.3	33 897	36 962	25 055	71 300	18.7	9.9
Clinton County	81.6	87.4	85.0	56.4	44.2	54.3	45.6	55.8	37 390	44 620	22 233	72 600	18.5	9.9
Crawford County	80.5	86.2	82.2	50.1	37.8	55.3	47.8	56.2	33 954	38 174	23 346	60 000	18.6	9.9
Dallas County	84.2	88.5	86.7	59.4	49.8	56.4	46.7	58.3	48 287	57 091	26 450	105 800	20.7	9.9
Davis County	85.6	89.0	87.5	60.6	61.0	65.2	43.3	68.5	33 047	38 261	20 964	60 900	17.9	12.6
Decatur County	80.0	85.3	77.5	47.4	40.8	54.6	48.1	55.6	27 068	31 555	16 411	51 900	19.2	11.9
Delaware County...........	85.4	88.1	85.1	68.0	58.0	57.2	56.7	57.2	37 435	42 828	23 228	83 900	19.5	10.8
Des Moines County.......	82.5	89.3	85.6	55.0	45.2	57.6	51.2	58.6	36 463	42 430	21 208	69 000	18.4	9.9
Dickinson County	85.4	89.7	86.7	56.9	50.6	63.2	50.0	65.1	39 247	44 541	24 290	94 700	20.3	9.9
Dubuque County	83.0	88.1	85.2	57.0	47.8	52.3	43.0	53.9	39 611	46 927	23 338	91 900	19.4	9.9
Emmet County	84.1	88.7	84.1	59.3	46.0	58.0	45.9	59.5	33 716	38 263	23 894	55 700	17.2	10.0
Fayette County.............	81.8	87.2	83.9	57.6	46.4	62.5	50.7	64.2	32 341	36 298	21 216	62 500	18.1	9.9
Floyd County................	82.5	88.2	85.1	51.0	44.6	55.7	35.6	58.0	35 370	39 890	21 147	68 900	18.6	10.0
Franklin County	80.1	85.1	80.3	51.3	45.7	63.0	63.0	62.9	36 004	41 573	25 526	58 900	16.8	9.9
Fremont County	79.9	84.5	77.9	56.4	48.0	61.7	56.4	62.4	37 294	42 794	23 844	68 000	17.7	9.9
Greene County.............	81.2	83.7	83.7	70.1	60.4	63.3	72.4	62.5	33 785	38 164	21 462	54 600	18.0	10.7
Grundy County	83.8	85.9	82.0	66.2	58.6	68.8	60.4	69.4	39 329	43 304	29 798	74 200	18.4	9.9

STATE County	Median gross rent	Percent who pay 35 percent or more of income for housing expenses		Means of transportation to work (percent except where noted)	Car, truck, or van					Vehicles available (percent of households)		
		Owners	Renters	Number of workers 16 years and over	Drove alone	Carpooled	Public transportation	Other means	Walked	No vehicles	One vehicle	Two or more vehicles
	25	26	27	28	29	30	31	32	33	34	35	36
INDIANA—Cont'd												
Putnam County	462	13.6	20.2	15 658	79.4	10.9	0.1	1.1	5.3	3.8	28.6	67.5
Randolph County	392	9.3	23.6	12 362	80.7	11.6	0.2	0.6	3.1	6.1	28.4	65.5
Ripley County	478	10.6	19.9	12 651	79.4	12.8	0.3	0.6	2.8	6.0	25.9	68.1
Rush County	446	11.3	17.9	8 653	78.1	12.9	0.8	0.3	2.2	6.3	29.4	64.2
St. Joseph County........	535	10.9	28.1	125 416	81.2	10.3	1.2	0.7	3.9	8.3	35.9	55.8
Scott County................	463	11.1	22.8	10 362	82.4	12.6	0.4	1.0	1.4	5.6	28.2	66.2
Shelby County..............	528	10.0	20.9	21 797	84.0	9.6	0.3	1.4	2.2	4.2	30.3	65.5
Spencer County	423	9.0	16.6	9 945	83.7	10.4	0.1	0.6	1.4	4.3	22.9	72.7
Starke County	431	13.2	18.9	9 787	80.4	13.9	0.2	0.9	1.8	5.5	31.4	63.1
Steuben County	520	10.4	16.7	17 182	82.3	11.3	0.5	0.7	2.3	4.8	31.4	63.8
Sullivan County	375	10.6	20.4	8 381	84.4	11.3	0.0	0.4	1.4	6.2	27.9	65.9
Switzerland County	444	16.7	21.0	4 066	78.5	13.2	0.0	1.1	2.7	6.6	26.5	67.0
Tippecanoe County.......	565	10.6	37.4	73 345	77.3	10.0	1.5	1.6	6.8	6.9	36.2	56.8
Tipton County	480	9.8	17.8	8 132	86.2	8.9	0.0	0.6	1.7	2.7	28.1	69.2
Union County	450	10.0	19.8	3 428	82.6	8.8	0.0	0.4	3.4	5.3	27.1	67.7
Vanderburgh County	458	10.6	28.2	83 576	83.9	9.5	1.2	0.7	2.6	10.5	35.9	53.6
Vermillion County	378	10.8	15.8	7 509	84.8	10.3	0.2	0.6	1.8	6.6	29.5	63.9
Vigo County.................	445	10.0	29.2	47 249	81.5	11.0	0.3	1.0	4.1	8.8	36.4	54.7
Wabash County............	425	6.2	15.0	16 810	80.7	11.2	0.2	0.8	3.8	4.6	31.7	63.7
Warren County	419	13.1	10.9	4 112	82.7	11.8	0.0	0.8	1.4	2.3	24.7	73.0
Warrick County	478	9.5	17.9	26 470	89.3	6.7	0.2	0.2	0.7	3.0	21.7	75.3
Washington County	418	11.1	19.5	13 001	79.3	14.0	0.4	1.2	1.3	6.7	24.6	68.6
Wayne County..............	446	10.9	25.6	33 111	81.4	11.1	0.6	1.2	2.9	8.7	33.0	58.3
Wells County	458	7.1	16.3	13 980	84.8	7.6	0.4	0.6	2.0	4.0	28.0	68.0
White County	526	11.7	15.1	12 441	78.2	13.2	0.2	1.1	2.8	4.2	31.8	64.0
Whitley County	453	9.9	16.2	16 095	85.2	9.2	0.2	0.8	1.3	4.2	28.3	67.6
IOWA........................	470	9.6	24.8	1 469 763	78.6	10.8	1.0	0.9	4.0	6.4	30.5	63.1
Adair County	373	7.8	16.7	4 105	74.9	12.5	0.4	1.2	3.8	5.9	28.5	65.6
Adams County	333	5.5	15.0	2 205	76.5	8.2	0.7	1.1	4.8	5.2	27.3	67.5
Allamakee County	348	9.3	17.8	7 172	67.1	14.2	0.1	1.1	7.5	5.9	28.0	66.1
Appanoose County........	346	11.5	25.4	5 842	79.7	11.5	0.2	1.3	2.7	7.6	31.3	61.0
Audubon County	351	8.2	13.1	3 178	76.1	8.6	0.1	0.3	3.5	5.5	26.9	67.5
Benton County	385	9.6	17.4	12 641	76.9	13.7	0.3	0.4	2.4	5.0	23.4	71.6
Black Hawk County.......	472	8.4	33.2	62 897	82.8	8.4	0.8	0.9	4.2	7.7	31.8	60.5
Boone County	443	9.1	17.1	13 435	79.0	12.4	0.2	0.7	2.6	5.6	28.3	66.0
Bremer County	400	7.7	15.6	11 829	78.5	7.5	0.2	0.5	6.6	4.8	24.8	70.4
Buchanan County..........	376	10.0	17.5	9 794	77.9	8.7	0.3	1.2	5.0	7.3	27.1	65.6
Buena Vista County	417	9.5	19.9	9 643	72.2	12.0	0.2	1.2	7.8	6.1	31.9	62.1
Butler County	351	7.8	17.8	7 279	76.9	9.1	0.2	0.9	4.0	4.3	25.1	70.6
Calhoun County	315	9.5	19.0	4 926	78.4	10.5	0.2	0.6	4.4	4.5	31.1	64.4
Carroll County.............	403	8.4	18.3	10 873	78.7	8.8	0.7	0.6	3.8	6.5	31.2	62.3
Cass County................	357	7.5	17.7	7 267	77.1	10.6	0.4	0.6	4.1	7.2	32.0	60.8
Cedar County	441	9.1	14.8	9 618	77.4	13.3	0.3	0.6	3.6	5.0	24.4	70.6
Cerro Gordo County......	404	9.8	23.6	23 267	83.3	7.6	1.2	0.8	3.3	8.6	32.6	58.7
Cherokee County	353	9.2	14.2	6 445	77.8	9.7	0.1	1.4	4.5	5.4	29.0	65.6
Chickasaw County........	325	7.0	17.5	6 109	74.3	8.9	0.4	1.0	4.9	5.4	25.4	70.1
Clarke County..............	449	8.3	17.1	4 477	71.7	18.3	0.7	0.2	2.3	6.2	28.0	65.8
Clay County.................	379	7.6	18.2	9 015	80.4	9.9	0.6	1.3	3.2	7.3	31.8	61.0
Clayton County............	353	9.6	13.0	9 321	69.1	12.1	0.2	0.9	6.4	5.2	28.9	65.9
Clinton County.............	399	9.0	25.6	23 883	80.5	10.4	0.8	0.8	3.0	7.4	30.5	62.1
Crawford County..........	362	9.2	17.8	8 170	75.8	13.6	0.1	0.4	3.1	6.6	24.9	68.5
Dallas County..............	529	12.0	20.2	21 746	81.5	11.8	0.3	0.6	1.8	3.6	26.7	69.7
Davis County................	352	9.0	16.3	3 915	69.5	11.9	0.7	2.1	3.9	10.0	24.6	65.4
Decatur County	340	9.1	25.3	4 034	67.1	13.5	0.7	1.5	9.4	7.7	30.0	62.3
Delaware County..........	370	9.1	24.5	9 191	73.7	9.5	0.2	0.7	3.9	4.9	25.0	70.0
Des Moines County.......	439	9.7	22.0	20 688	81.7	11.1	0.6	1.1	2.3	7.5	32.6	59.9
Dickinson County	416	11.0	14.4	8 309	80.0	10.3	0.1	1.1	3.5	4.3	30.8	64.8
Dubuque County	434	8.0	23.8	45 167	81.9	8.2	0.6	0.5	4.8	7.2	31.8	61.0
Emmet County	322	7.7	12.8	5 420	76.8	13.9	0.8	0.7	2.5	6.7	29.1	64.2
Fayette County	360	8.6	21.7	10 319	73.9	9.6	0.1	1.1	5.9	6.2	31.4	62.4
Floyd County	357	8.3	15.7	7 724	81.4	7.6	0.3	1.0	2.5	6.1	30.1	63.8
Franklin County............	374	9.1	17.1	5 204	72.8	11.5	0.3	1.2	4.0	5.8	28.3	65.9
Fremont County	391	8.7	19.1	3 860	80.3	11.0	0.2	0.6	2.6	5.3	27.1	67.6
Greene County	342	13.0	15.5	4 565	77.4	11.7	0.3	0.9	3.7	7.3	29.5	63.1
Grundy County	376	8.6	15.5	6 078	78.7	7.5	0.1	1.1	5.1	4.3	27.0	68.6

Table C-3. States and Counties — **Migration, Housing, and Transportation**

STATE/ County code	MSA/PMSA/ NECMA code[1]	STATE County	Total population 5 years and over	Residence in 1995 (percent) Same house	Same county, different house	Same state, different county	Different state	Outside the United States	Occupied housing units Number	Percent owner-occupied	Householders 65 years and over Number	Percent owner-occupied
			1	2	3	4	5	6	7	8	9	10
		IOWA—Cont'd										
19 077	...	Guthrie County..............	10 738	62.1	15.1	17.6	4.9	0.3	4 641	79.6	1 539	82.5
19 079	...	Hamilton County...........	15 380	62.6	19.6	11.1	6.1	0.7	6 692	72.8	2 020	79.6
19 081	...	Hancock County............	11 371	66.1	16.6	11.2	5.3	0.7	4 795	78.2	1 365	84.4
19 083	...	Hardin County................	17 726	60.8	19.8	13.6	5.3	0.4	7 628	74.6	2 451	80.4
19 085	...	Harrison County	14 733	60.6	22.9	7.1	9.2	0.2	6 115	76.6	1 803	76.8
19 087	...	Henry County.................	19 128	58.2	22.5	12.9	6.0	0.4	7 626	73.1	1 866	77.0
19 089	...	Howard County	9 362	65.0	18.5	9.2	7.0	0.2	3 974	79.2	1 274	84.3
19 091	...	Humboldt County	9 824	66.4	16.7	11.6	4.6	0.8	4 295	75.9	1 497	82.3
19 093	...	Ida County....................	7 402	69.5	17.6	8.8	4.0	0.1	3 213	73.2	1 085	82.6
19 095	...	Iowa County..................	14 714	65.9	17.3	12.9	3.8	0.1	6 163	77.9	1 711	81.9
19 097	...	Jackson County............	19 098	65.4	19.3	9.6	5.6	0.2	8 078	75.8	2 249	80.4
19 099	...	Jasper County..............	34 874	59.6	21.1	13.9	4.9	0.5	14 689	75.7	3 872	79.2
19 101	...	Jefferson County...........	15 305	56.4	25.1	8.9	7.4	2.2	6 649	67.4	1 456	76.3
19 103	3500	Johnson County............	104 761	40.4	22.3	19.6	14.3	3.4	44 080	56.7	5 454	79.3
19 105	...	Jones County................	19 087	59.9	20.2	14.0	5.5	0.4	7 560	75.8	2 047	77.3
19 107	...	Keokuk County.............	10 728	68.1	16.9	11.3	3.6	0.1	4 586	78.8	1 556	84.3
19 109	...	Kossuth County............	16 189	68.6	17.8	8.1	5.3	0.2	6 974	77.6	2 262	83.1
19 111	...	Lee County...................	35 779	61.9	24.1	4.8	8.5	0.6	15 161	75.5	4 262	79.4
19 113	1360	Linn County.................	178 464	52.3	28.5	9.3	8.7	1.2	76 753	72.7	15 597	81.0
19 115	...	Louisa County..............	11 316	63.9	17.0	11.4	6.2	1.5	4 519	77.3	1 095	86.3
19 117	...	Lucas County...............	8 849	61.6	20.3	13.1	5.0	0.0	3 811	78.4	1 219	82.9
19 119	...	Lyon County.................	10 973	68.7	18.5	5.3	7.2	0.3	4 428	81.7	1 344	86.9
19 121	...	Madison County	13 050	59.9	17.6	17.2	5.0	0.2	5 326	78.0	1 367	78.5
19 123	...	Mahaska County	20 840	57.8	21.8	12.4	7.1	0.9	8 880	71.1	2 327	77.9
19 125	...	Marion County..............	30 084	56.2	21.2	14.9	7.1	0.7	12 017	75.5	3 001	75.7
19 127	...	Marshall County...........	36 808	57.7	23.9	8.9	7.4	2.1	15 338	73.8	3 922	77.2
19 129	...	Mills County.................	13 616	57.2	19.8	10.2	12.4	0.5	5 324	79.5	1 280	84.8
19 131	...	Mitchell County.............	10 203	69.4	15.3	9.2	5.8	0.4	4 294	81.5	1 507	83.3
19 133	...	Monona County............	9 484	65.4	18.6	9.0	6.9	0.1	4 211	76.2	1 607	86.2
19 135	...	Monroe County.............	7 496	63.7	18.8	13.1	4.3	0.2	3 228	78.5	1 064	78.5
19 137	...	Montgomery County	11 055	59.1	20.6	10.8	8.9	0.6	4 886	73.2	1 510	81.0
19 139	...	Muscatine County	38 801	58.4	27.1	7.3	5.9	1.3	15 847	75.4	3 398	79.0
19 141	...	O'Brien County	14 204	66.4	17.6	10.0	5.4	0.6	6 001	76.8	1 893	87.5
19 143	...	Osceola County............	6 578	70.0	15.0	7.8	6.9	0.3	2 778	77.8	812	85.7
19 145	...	Page County	16 047	58.0	20.6	12.8	8.2	0.3	6 708	71.7	2 107	77.5
19 147	...	Palo Alto County	9 563	61.1	18.8	13.3	6.0	0.8	4 119	74.0	1 383	83.7
19 149	...	Plymouth County...........	23 199	62.2	21.4	10.4	5.6	0.5	9 372	77.4	2 617	82.9
19 151	...	Pocahontas County.......	8 236	70.1	13.4	11.4	4.9	0.2	3 617	79.2	1 211	84.6
19 153	2120	Polk County.................	346 421	49.8	29.7	9.1	8.8	2.6	149 112	68.8	27 787	76.1
19 155	5920	Pottawattamie County ...	81 997	56.5	27.0	5.2	10.7	0.6	33 844	71.1	7 820	79.5
19 157	...	Poweshiek County	17 754	55.6	21.1	11.9	10.4	1.0	7 398	71.9	1 974	76.7
19 159	...	Ringgold County............	5 143	63.6	14.8	13.6	7.5	0.4	2 245	75.5	866	78.5
19 161	...	Sac County..................	10 872	68.8	17.1	9.9	3.8	0.5	4 746	76.8	1 613	81.6
19 163	1960	Scott County.................	147 593	54.0	27.8	5.3	11.6	1.2	62 334	70.5	12 210	80.6
19 165	...	Shelby County..............	12 405	67.8	18.1	7.2	6.5	0.3	5 173	77.1	1 592	84.8
19 167	...	Sioux County................	29 541	63.1	19.5	6.7	8.9	1.9	10 693	80.4	3 040	84.8
19 169	...	Story County	75 811	39.3	19.5	24.2	12.6	4.4	29 383	58.3	4 754	78.4
19 171	...	Tama County................	16 855	61.9	19.2	13.2	5.1	0.5	7 018	77.6	2 070	83.0
19 173	...	Taylor County...............	6 576	63.4	18.8	8.0	9.0	0.8	2 824	76.6	979	83.8
19 175	...	Union County................	11 554	61.4	20.0	10.0	7.6	1.1	5 242	72.0	1 434	76.2
19 177	...	Van Buren County..........	7 380	65.1	16.4	12.3	6.0	0.1	3 181	79.3	1 038	83.0
19 179	...	Wapello County.............	33 953	60.2	22.8	9.6	6.7	0.6	14 784	75.6	4 055	82.1
19 181	2120	Warren County..............	37 915	60.7	17.2	16.6	4.8	0.8	14 708	79.9	3 145	77.0
19 183	...	Washington County.......	19 283	61.3	18.8	13.6	5.7	0.5	8 056	75.3	2 265	78.3
19 185	...	Wayne County..............	6 393	60.3	20.0	13.3	6.2	0.3	2 821	79.5	1 018	81.1
19 187	...	Webster County............	37 665	58.4	25.5	10.1	5.4	0.6	15 878	71.2	4 169	78.6
19 189	...	Winnebago County.........	11 088	60.8	18.7	12.1	7.1	1.4	4 749	76.1	1 483	83.5
19 191	...	Winneshiek County	20 249	60.4	18.6	8.6	10.8	1.4	7 734	73.6	2 307	76.0
19 193	7720	Woodbury County	96 157	55.1	27.8	4.6	10.1	2.3	39 151	68.6	8 872	77.4
19 195	...	Worth County...............	7 464	64.9	16.6	12.9	5.3	0.4	3 278	79.0	1 004	84.0
19 197	...	Wright County	13 530	64.8	19.5	10.3	4.5	0.9	5 940	74.1	1 973	75.8
20 000	...	KANSAS...................	2 500 360	52.4	24.3	10.2	11.1	2.1	1 037 891	69.3	230 625	80.3
20 001	...	Allen County.................	13 486	59.9	23.2	11.3	5.1	0.4	5 775	74.9	1 602	82.8
20 003	...	Anderson County...........	7 611	58.3	20.3	13.4	7.8	0.2	3 221	80.0	1 065	80.9
20 005	...	Atchison County............	15 715	59.2	21.0	8.5	10.9	0.4	6 275	73.5	1 756	85.6

[1]MSA = Metropolitan Statistical Area. PMSA = Primary MSA. NECMA = New England County Metropolitan Area. See the Appendix A for explanation of these concepts. See Appendix B for list of metropolitan areas identified by type, with component counties.

Table C-3. States and Counties — **Migration, Housing, and Transportation**

STATE County	Owner-occupied by household type (percent)								Median household income			Median monthly owner costs as a percent of income	
	Family-households					Nonfamily households							
		Married-couple family		Other family									
	Total family households	Total	With own children under 18 years	Total	With own children under 18 years	Total nonfamily households	Two or more adults	Living alone	All households	Owner-occupied households	Renter-occupied households	Median housing value (owner estimated)	With a mortgage	Without a mortgage
	11	12	13	14	15	16	17	18	19	20	21	22	23	24
IOWA—Cont'd														
Guthrie County	85.1	88.6	86.5	64.6	57.7	66.8	61.8	67.5	35 970	38 936	25 653	67 200	19.5	11.7
Hamilton County	79.5	83.2	78.0	57.9	55.8	57.7	42.9	59.5	37 719	42 386	26 599	71 900	18.5	10.8
Hancock County	83.2	85.8	81.0	64.4	54.2	66.1	46.0	68.3	38 218	40 896	28 828	61 500	18.2	9.9
Hardin County	81.6	85.1	79.4	59.0	54.2	60.3	45.9	62.1	35 502	38 882	25 011	58 400	18.1	10.2
Harrison County	83.6	86.7	81.3	64.4	54.9	59.9	58.7	60.1	38 099	41 941	23 036	78 700	19.6	10.5
Henry County	81.7	87.5	87.4	53.9	44.0	53.8	52.9	53.9	39 372	45 170	23 780	75 500	17.7	9.9
Howard County	86.8	90.0	87.0	66.7	63.9	64.2	47.7	66.3	34 297	38 613	23 234	64 500	19.8	10.3
Humboldt County	82.5	86.8	79.4	57.4	51.6	62.3	52.5	63.2	37 728	42 936	23 278	72 300	17.9	9.9
Ida County	80.7	84.5	78.7	53.0	38.8	57.4	49.4	58.1	34 685	40 048	25 087	59 400	17.1	9.9
Iowa County	86.9	90.0	89.8	64.3	58.0	57.1	43.6	59.3	40 984	45 331	25 733	88 400	19.0	9.9
Jackson County	82.6	87.0	83.0	59.7	45.1	60.6	47.2	62.4	34 672	39 627	22 788	80 300	19.4	10.9
Jasper County	84.2	88.2	84.4	62.0	53.9	56.0	54.5	56.3	41 857	46 983	27 574	83 400	19.3	10.4
Jefferson County	75.9	79.7	73.7	58.2	57.2	51.8	41.8	53.5	33 160	40 296	24 216	72 700	19.3	10.5
Johnson County	77.1	82.4	82.6	52.5	48.1	33.0	20.3	39.7	39 825	60 772	21 997	123 700	20.3	9.9
Jones County	82.2	87.0	83.8	54.6	43.6	61.2	58.7	61.7	37 646	43 061	26 720	81 500	20.0	9.9
Keokuk County	84.0	88.3	84.0	57.9	47.8	67.3	53.9	68.7	33 739	37 227	23 297	55 200	17.7	10.4
Kossuth County	82.1	85.5	80.6	54.7	41.1	67.6	61.2	68.2	34 762	37 568	26 278	57 200	17.6	9.9
Lee County	84.0	89.2	83.9	62.1	52.2	57.7	62.6	57.0	36 216	41 504	20 786	61 100	18.2	10.5
Linn County	83.1	88.6	87.8	58.0	49.5	52.9	42.5	55.5	45 939	53 790	27 363	97 200	19.3	9.9
Louisa County	81.1	85.6	81.1	55.7	49.2	66.5	50.6	69.1	38 829	43 006	25 531	66 400	17.6	9.9
Lucas County	86.5	90.6	87.7	64.5	54.0	61.1	62.9	60.9	30 845	34 779	15 257	59 200	18.8	12.0
Lyon County	86.5	88.4	85.7	66.6	55.2	68.1	59.2	68.7	37 103	39 954	26 046	68 600	18.0	9.9
Madison County	83.9	88.3	83.1	59.2	48.8	61.0	41.8	63.7	41 827	46 536	26 185	93 300	21.2	11.8
Mahaska County	78.5	83.7	78.9	51.7	44.1	54.1	48.7	54.9	37 488	43 262	24 066	69 100	16.6	9.9
Marion County	84.5	87.9	85.9	62.8	56.7	53.3	59.5	52.5	42 252	47 418	26 297	87 100	18.8	9.9
Marshall County	81.3	86.9	82.8	58.4	50.9	57.5	46.5	59.5	38 215	45 357	24 290	70 900	19.0	10.8
Mills County	85.7	89.1	85.6	65.0	54.6	61.6	68.0	60.6	42 844	47 923	25 747	95 200	20.5	11.5
Mitchell County	88.0	90.4	86.1	72.4	66.7	66.6	62.4	67.0	35 085	37 873	22 571	70 600	18.2	9.9
Monona County	80.9	83.5	77.3	68.2	57.9	67.4	45.6	69.9	33 225	34 981	26 418	55 100	19.5	9.9
Monroe County	85.4	89.8	86.7	63.0	53.7	63.6	56.8	64.5	34 718	37 843	20 250	58 000	17.3	11.7
Montgomery County	81.4	86.4	79.4	62.5	50.0	56.7	46.3	58.0	32 725	38 189	20 182	58 800	19.5	10.1
Muscatine County	81.8	87.0	81.0	59.0	50.3	59.4	60.5	59.1	41 932	49 116	22 785	82 200	19.1	9.9
O'Brien County	83.7	86.1	81.5	58.0	52.7	61.7	31.9	65.0	36 056	39 545	26 353	59 300	17.4	9.9
Osceola County	83.6	86.1	85.1	63.6	57.7	64.4	54.8	65.3	34 442	37 097	27 411	55 100	17.7	9.9
Page County	81.4	87.4	82.4	51.4	38.4	52.0	53.0	51.8	35 491	41 311	20 554	61 700	17.4	9.9
Palo Alto County	82.2	85.4	76.9	61.0	61.5	58.9	26.8	63.4	31 920	35 537	24 155	55 900	17.7	10.7
Plymouth County	84.3	87.4	84.7	61.4	50.9	59.0	52.7	59.9	41 508	46 880	25 493	90 100	19.2	10.7
Pocahontas County	83.9	88.1	84.8	54.9	42.8	69.1	60.0	69.8	33 137	35 038	25 313	44 200	17.0	9.9
Polk County	79.6	85.5	84.3	56.7	46.7	48.9	41.8	50.7	45 830	56 160	28 413	100 100	20.2	10.8
Pottawattamie County	77.9	84.8	81.2	53.8	42.4	55.3	49.6	56.5	40 106	46 688	26 366	84 800	19.6	10.8
Poweshiek County	81.3	86.4	83.1	53.2	47.9	53.6	44.9	55.0	37 950	44 716	24 608	81 800	18.9	9.9
Ringgold County	79.2	84.5	78.4	45.5	34.7	67.7	70.3	67.4	29 297	32 990	19 156	50 400	18.2	10.7
Sac County	82.4	86.4	79.8	58.9	46.0	64.8	53.1	65.8	32 804	36 221	22 588	54 500	17.9	9.9
Scott County	79.7	86.2	83.5	54.9	46.5	51.5	42.6	53.4	42 650	51 866	23 738	90 400	19.2	9.9
Shelby County	82.9	85.8	80.8	59.4	44.7	62.2	42.9	64.6	37 450	42 122	25 684	77 000	19.0	9.9
Sioux County	87.1	89.1	87.3	64.3	58.5	59.6	43.1	61.1	40 460	43 556	24 175	85 400	19.1	9.9
Story County	76.8	81.2	81.2	51.8	47.9	32.5	14.4	42.8	40 542	56 680	22 809	110 600	19.6	9.9
Tama County	82.6	86.2	79.6	62.0	51.8	65.2	49.0	67.5	37 242	40 873	25 806	67 900	18.3	11.1
Taylor County	80.0	83.8	75.3	53.4	44.3	69.3	51.7	72.1	31 316	33 904	22 431	43 500	17.2	10.4
Union County	82.8	86.9	79.8	58.4	53.1	52.5	48.9	53.0	32 100	38 633	20 242	59 000	17.0	11.1
Van Buren County	84.2	87.2	82.7	66.2	58.7	68.8	64.4	69.4	31 062	32 665	23 060	49 100	18.2	11.5
Wapello County	82.9	87.7	82.9	63.8	59.0	61.4	51.5	63.4	32 230	36 194	20 399	51 600	18.4	10.5
Warren County	87.5	91.2	90.7	67.2	59.1	55.3	52.3	55.8	50 074	55 187	25 827	102 600	19.7	9.9
Washington County	83.5	86.3	82.4	67.0	57.1	56.0	43.7	57.6	39 193	43 988	25 789	84 200	19.4	9.9
Wayne County	84.7	86.7	83.8	72.1	70.5	68.3	56.9	69.1	29 298	31 784	20 600	42 900	18.3	11.6
Webster County	80.8	86.5	83.0	56.4	47.5	53.5	42.9	55.2	35 548	42 181	22 496	65 900	17.3	10.4
Winnebago County	84.0	87.4	84.8	61.5	51.9	60.1	39.0	62.7	38 198	42 598	25 788	64 200	16.4	9.9
Winneshiek County	84.6	87.4	85.1	60.6	52.9	51.2	33.4	54.5	38 249	42 700	23 634	90 300	19.1	9.9
Woodbury County	77.6	84.0	81.4	55.3	45.8	49.5	40.3	51.3	38 096	45 884	24 533	75 400	19.3	10.6
Worth County	84.1	86.8	79.8	69.0	59.2	67.8	73.1	67.0	36 458	39 697	24 042	60 300	17.6	9.9
Wright County	81.6	84.0	78.2	64.5	60.2	59.5	46.3	60.9	36 223	41 503	22 139	54 800	17.3	9.9
KANSAS	77.9	83.5	79.3	52.9	45.1	51.1	35.2	54.2	40 509	48 572	25 898	81 000	19.3	9.9
Allen County	81.7	88.9	83.4	52.4	44.3	60.9	45.5	63.1	31 371	37 634	19 173	43 400	17.4	9.9
Anderson County	86.2	89.9	88.8	64.1	57.9	65.0	48.8	66.6	32 922	36 526	23 024	61 300	19.6	9.9
Atchison County	81.1	86.5	75.7	60.0	51.8	57.0	48.5	58.3	34 883	39 980	23 011	57 300	18.6	10.8

STATE County	Median gross rent	Percent who pay 35 percent or more of income for housing expenses		Means of transportation to work (percent except where noted)						Vehicles available (percent of households)		
		Owners	Renters	Number of workers 16 years and over	Car, truck, or van		Public transportation	Other means	Walked	No vehicles	One vehicle	Two or more vehicles
					Drove alone	Carpooled						
	25	26	27	28	29	30	31	32	33	34	35	36

IOWA—Cont'd												
Guthrie County	389	12.7	16.3	5 592	73.6	15.0	0.1	0.5	3.8	4.4	26.3	69.3
Hamilton County	422	10.3	17.0	8 393	77.3	13.0	0.2	1.1	3.3	4.9	31.2	63.9
Hancock County	353	9.1	13.8	5 986	73.1	14.2	0.2	0.6	3.6	3.5	26.8	69.7
Hardin County	403	8.5	17.0	8 781	78.1	10.2	0.1	1.0	4.1	5.2	30.6	64.2
Harrison County	418	10.4	21.0	7 367	75.7	14.8	0.1	0.8	2.9	6.3	24.6	69.1
Henry County	428	9.6	20.1	9 780	79.9	11.5	0.4	0.8	4.0	6.1	27.8	66.0
Howard County	333	7.4	15.6	4 706	71.3	12.2	0.3	0.6	5.1	5.9	27.8	66.3
Humboldt County	362	5.9	17.1	4 846	81.2	9.0	0.3	0.8	3.2	4.7	30.1	65.2
Ida County	338	7.8	15.9	3 699	77.1	9.4	0.3	0.9	4.5	5.2	29.4	65.4
Iowa County	412	8.6	13.4	8 211	71.3	16.9	0.1	0.6	3.8	4.8	27.3	68.0
Jackson County	386	10.1	17.4	10 211	74.3	12.4	0.3	1.1	4.7	6.0	28.1	65.9
Jasper County	448	10.2	17.6	18 376	78.7	11.8	0.5	0.7	3.2	6.1	28.0	65.9
Jefferson County	426	12.0	25.3	8 213	74.2	10.2	0.2	1.4	5.9	6.6	34.1	59.4
Johnson County	564	10.4	41.7	63 087	68.2	11.3	5.3	2.2	10.0	7.8	35.8	56.4
Jones County	416	9.3	17.1	9 614	77.0	11.0	0.0	0.5	4.0	5.5	25.8	68.7
Keokuk County	372	9.2	18.3	5 246	74.4	14.4	0.1	0.8	4.6	5.4	25.2	69.5
Kossuth County	347	8.5	14.9	8 110	74.6	11.7	0.4	0.8	3.3	4.5	28.3	67.1
Lee County	398	8.8	23.3	17 099	80.9	10.6	0.3	0.9	3.5	7.6	29.6	62.9
Linn County	510	8.8	23.6	102 234	82.3	10.3	1.1	0.7	2.6	6.2	31.4	62.5
Louisa County	419	7.1	17.1	5 752	78.3	14.4	0.5	0.5	1.7	3.9	25.8	70.3
Lucas County	326	9.4	21.6	4 318	77.9	11.4	0.3	1.2	3.0	8.1	25.0	66.9
Lyon County	350	8.5	12.4	5 845	73.0	10.9	0.3	0.6	4.8	3.6	24.6	71.7
Madison County	445	14.6	21.1	6 998	78.2	13.5	0.2	0.5	1.7	3.9	23.8	72.3
Mahaska County	420	7.8	23.4	10 660	77.4	12.8	0.2	1.1	2.6	6.9	28.5	64.7
Marion County	472	8.8	27.2	16 046	75.1	12.9	0.7	0.9	6.1	6.1	25.4	68.4
Marshall County	458	11.4	28.5	18 853	79.6	12.8	0.5	1.0	2.6	6.8	30.4	62.8
Mills County	465	12.5	20.6	7 315	79.1	12.8	0.1	0.7	1.8	4.7	24.0	71.3
Mitchell County	334	7.1	16.7	5 061	71.1	10.8	0.2	0.8	5.5	6.7	26.9	66.4
Monona County	384	9.1	15.7	4 615	73.9	12.9	0.2	1.2	5.4	7.9	28.8	63.3
Monroe County	399	6.8	17.4	3 582	82.5	10.7	0.2	0.5	3.0	6.2	29.3	64.5
Montgomery County	361	9.9	26.9	5 450	79.5	11.0	0.3	0.6	3.4	7.3	32.9	59.8
Muscatine County	460	9.9	23.5	20 538	79.8	11.5	0.9	1.4	2.7	6.4	30.0	63.6
O'Brien County	373	7.5	15.5	7 265	74.2	11.7	0.9	1.5	5.6	6.9	27.9	65.2
Osceola County	374	8.9	15.3	3 327	72.2	10.8	0.1	1.1	6.7	5.4	28.7	65.9
Page County	407	9.7	26.1	7 537	80.5	9.6	0.3	0.3	3.9	6.3	33.5	60.2
Palo Alto County	337	9.5	21.2	4 863	74.9	11.0	0.6	0.3	5.0	4.3	31.9	63.8
Plymouth County	416	8.7	19.8	12 483	80.0	8.9	0.1	0.5	3.2	5.0	26.0	69.0
Pocahontas County	315	8.5	14.2	3 870	72.7	11.9	0.0	0.7	4.3	5.5	29.6	64.9
Polk County	574	11.7	25.3	198 183	82.0	10.4	1.9	0.6	2.0	6.8	33.7	59.5
Pottawattamie County	537	10.6	26.5	44 047	81.6	12.1	0.5	0.7	2.0	6.7	31.4	61.9
Poweshiek County	432	9.2	16.3	9 556	68.6	12.3	0.1	2.2	11.3	5.2	31.7	63.1
Ringgold County	368	11.8	20.0	2 376	73.4	13.1	0.2	0.6	4.5	5.2	28.9	65.9
Sac County	329	8.4	17.4	5 466	75.7	9.8	0.2	0.3	5.7	6.2	29.2	64.7
Scott County	496	10.8	28.9	78 460	84.8	8.7	0.7	0.8	1.9	7.4	32.7	59.9
Shelby County	399	7.6	19.3	6 534	75.0	10.5	0.1	0.6	5.3	4.1	26.4	69.5
Sioux County	385	7.6	16.4	16 646	73.3	7.7	0.2	1.1	10.4	4.4	25.1	70.6
Story County	575	9.2	36.7	43 861	71.3	9.4	4.1	2.1	9.6	4.6	32.4	63.0
Tama County	418	9.2	15.4	8 390	76.9	11.4	0.0	0.9	3.9	5.5	26.5	68.1
Taylor County	352	7.3	16.7	3 205	73.9	14.3	0.1	0.5	3.1	4.5	25.7	69.8
Union County	344	6.9	20.9	6 080	80.3	9.7	1.6	1.1	2.6	7.2	30.4	62.4
Van Buren County	334	9.5	13.5	3 700	70.3	15.1	0.3	1.0	4.0	5.4	28.4	66.1
Wapello County	419	9.8	27.0	16 223	81.1	12.3	1.0	1.1	1.6	7.7	32.7	59.6
Warren County	494	9.7	22.2	21 745	79.6	11.9	0.4	0.8	2.8	3.5	24.9	71.7
Washington County	424	10.7	19.0	10 618	72.4	13.7	0.4	0.8	3.7	5.9	28.7	65.4
Wayne County	303	10.8	14.3	3 045	70.2	14.8	0.0	1.3	3.5	4.8	28.9	66.4
Webster County	408	8.1	22.6	18 363	83.7	10.1	0.4	0.6	2.2	6.0	34.1	59.9
Winnebago County	341	6.8	14.8	5 960	71.7	14.3	0.1	0.6	6.9	5.4	30.2	64.4
Winneshiek County	389	6.4	18.1	11 665	68.5	8.2	0.2	0.8	14.6	5.1	28.6	66.4
Woodbury County	494	9.9	24.7	51 233	78.7	13.6	1.0	0.8	2.9	9.1	31.4	59.5
Worth County	357	10.1	15.7	4 006	77.7	11.1	0.3	0.9	3.7	5.9	24.3	69.8
Wright County	350	7.1	17.9	6 861	75.9	12.9	0.4	1.3	4.6	4.7	33.3	62.0
KANSAS	498	10.5	25.0	1 311 343	81.5	10.6	0.5	0.9	2.5	5.7	31.6	62.7
Allen County	365	8.7	22.5	6 731	79.2	12.7	0.1	1.0	2.3	5.6	30.5	63.9
Anderson County	365	9.0	16.6	3 743	76.8	14.6	0.4	1.1	2.3	5.2	29.0	65.8
Atchison County	378	11.8	20.2	7 665	78.7	12.4	0.5	0.7	4.1	8.0	29.4	62.6

Table C-3. States and Counties — **Migration, Housing, and Transportation**

STATE/ County code	MSA/PMSA/ NECMA code[1]	STATE County	Residence in 1995 (percent)						Occupied housing units		Householders 65 years and over	
			Total population 5 years and over	Same house	Same county, different house	Same state, different county	Different state	Outside the United States	Number	Percent owner-occupied	Number	Percent owner-occupied
			1	2	3	4	5	6	7	8	9	10
		KANSAS—Cont'd										
20 007	...	Barber County	5 039	65.7	18.5	9.5	6.1	0.3	2 235	75.3	751	81.9
20 009	...	Barton County	26 397	60.1	24.1	9.2	5.0	1.5	11 393	72.0	3 313	83.2
20 011	...	Bourbon County	14 465	56.9	24.1	9.2	9.3	0.5	6 161	74.1	1 917	77.5
20 013	...	Brown County	10 044	61.6	20.1	8.7	9.2	0.5	4 318	71.3	1 453	78.9
20 015	9040	Butler County	55 373	53.5	21.7	15.6	8.4	0.7	21 527	77.7	4 798	83.4
20 017	...	Chase County	2 855	57.9	19.1	14.2	8.2	0.7	1 246	73.5	369	80.5
20 019	...	Chautauqua County	4 154	63.0	14.9	11.3	10.7	0.1	1 796	81.8	705	89.9
20 021	...	Cherokee County	21 058	58.4	23.6	5.7	11.9	0.4	8 875	76.2	2 480	81.8
20 023	...	Cheyenne County	3 016	62.2	20.0	6.1	11.2	0.6	1 360	77.4	547	89.8
20 025	...	Clark County	2 252	57.5	15.9	15.9	9.2	1.5	979	76.5	332	84.0
20 027	...	Clay County	8 338	65.4	17.4	9.8	6.6	0.8	3 617	77.0	1 135	83.5
20 029	...	Cloud County	9 778	62.2	18.8	13.0	4.9	1.0	4 163	74.4	1 343	84.1
20 031	...	Coffey County	8 352	61.8	19.3	13.0	5.6	0.3	3 489	78.3	900	86.7
20 033	...	Comanche County	1 859	60.4	18.3	11.0	10.3	0.1	872	73.5	314	79.6
20 035	...	Cowley County	33 962	55.3	24.9	9.5	8.7	1.6	14 039	70.9	3 831	79.1
20 037	...	Crawford County	35 871	50.7	24.0	13.0	10.4	2.0	15 504	64.3	3 962	80.7
20 039	...	Decatur County	3 309	64.1	17.6	7.7	8.9	1.6	1 494	76.0	535	83.2
20 041	...	Dickinson County	18 244	60.8	19.8	11.9	6.9	0.6	7 903	74.8	2 265	78.3
20 043	...	Doniphan County	7 726	63.3	16.8	7.7	11.8	0.5	3 173	74.6	919	80.7
20 045	4150	Douglas County	94 411	37.0	23.1	20.9	15.9	3.0	38 486	51.9	5 195	75.1
20 047	...	Edwards County	3 254	66.1	16.0	10.8	5.3	1.8	1 455	77.5	479	84.6
20 049	...	Elk County	3 132	67.0	12.6	13.4	6.6	0.4	1 412	80.8	536	83.2
20 051	...	Ellis County	25 932	56.3	20.5	16.9	5.3	1.1	11 193	63.3	2 629	77.9
20 053	...	Ellsworth County	6 251	62.7	13.9	17.3	5.7	0.4	2 481	79.6	850	86.6
20 055	...	Finney County	36 275	45.3	28.4	8.2	12.3	5.8	12 948	64.8	1 797	81.1
20 057	...	Ford County	29 441	49.6	26.8	7.7	8.4	7.4	10 852	64.8	2 123	72.3
20 059	...	Franklin County	23 092	53.9	23.6	14.3	7.8	0.5	9 452	73.5	2 193	76.9
20 061	...	Geary County	25 367	40.3	18.2	5.8	28.4	7.3	10 458	50.4	1 671	80.8
20 063	...	Gove County	2 895	72.2	11.2	11.4	5.1	0.1	1 245	79.7	474	85.9
20 065	...	Graham County	2 819	67.2	15.2	10.0	7.4	0.2	1 263	79.3	473	90.1
20 067	...	Grant County	7 241	55.0	23.5	9.5	10.5	1.6	2 742	74.7	427	84.8
20 069	...	Gray County	5 432	58.9	15.4	16.3	5.4	4.1	2 045	72.7	411	85.6
20 071	...	Greeley County	1 436	60.7	14.1	12.5	8.5	1.1	602	75.1	174	88.5
20 073	...	Greenwood County	7 220	57.3	20.5	14.8	6.9	0.5	3 234	75.3	1 147	79.9
20 075	...	Hamilton County	2 477	52.0	19.8	10.0	13.0	5.2	1 054	69.7	336	83.9
20 077	...	Harper County	6 168	62.1	20.5	10.5	6.7	0.2	2 773	74.6	973	84.3
20 079	9040	Harvey County	30 692	54.3	21.6	14.1	8.5	1.5	12 581	71.9	3 385	78.5
20 081	...	Haskell County	3 922	59.5	16.0	12.6	8.0	3.9	1 481	72.2	299	85.3
20 083	...	Hodgeman County	1 984	65.7	13.1	15.7	4.6	1.0	796	78.4	257	81.7
20 085	...	Jackson County	11 782	62.7	16.9	14.9	4.9	0.6	4 727	80.6	1 222	86.2
20 087	...	Jefferson County	17 245	60.1	16.0	10.0	4.5	0.6	6 000	85.1	1 555	86.6
20 089	...	Jewell County	3 620	67.0	15.6	7.8	9.1	0.6	1 695	79.9	685	86.6
20 091	3760	Johnson County	417 449	50.0	23.3	6.6	18.0	2.2	174 570	72.3	28 459	78.1
20 093	...	Kearny County	4 123	60.5	19.6	10.6	6.6	2.7	1 542	73.5	333	87.7
20 095	...	Kingman County	8 160	63.6	16.6	14.5	4.9	0.4	3 371	78.1	1 111	84.7
20 097	...	Kiowa County	3 094	57.5	17.5	15.4	8.6	1.1	1 365	71.8	467	83.3
20 099	...	Labette County	21 464	57.3	24.3	9.1	8.9	0.5	9 194	73.3	2 609	81.4
20 101	...	Lane County	2 036	66.4	19.7	8.4	5.0	0.5	910	77.0	275	85.1
20 103	3760	Leavenworth County	63 875	46.7	19.5	11.7	19.0	3.1	23 071	67.0	4 357	80.4
20 105	...	Lincoln County	3 395	64.0	14.8	14.4	6.6	0.2	1 529	78.7	580	83.6
20 107	...	Linn County	8 976	57.7	16.2	18.8	7.1	0.2	3 807	82.5	1 187	90.0
20 109	...	Logan County	2 846	67.2	12.2	12.3	7.6	0.7	1 243	76.3	428	89.3
20 111	...	Lyon County	33 464	46.5	26.8	15.6	7.9	3.2	13 691	60.9	2 556	75.4
20 113	...	McPherson County	27 838	56.5	22.6	13.8	5.9	1.2	11 205	73.9	3 004	79.2
20 115	...	Marion County	12 619	58.6	17.8	17.4	6.0	0.2	5 114	79.9	1 728	83.9
20 117	...	Marshall County	10 427	66.1	18.9	7.3	7.1	0.6	4 458	79.7	1 537	84.6
20 119	...	Meade County	4 260	58.0	15.2	13.8	10.4	2.7	1 728	73.9	531	89.1
20 121	3760	Miami County	26 442	55.7	16.8	18.3	8.8	0.3	10 365	78.5	2 189	82.2
20 123	...	Mitchell County	6 580	63.3	19.1	11.5	5.3	0.8	2 850	74.7	970	84.2
20 125	...	Montgomery County	34 025	55.3	25.5	8.1	10.7	0.5	14 903	71.7	4 444	79.5
20 127	...	Morris County	5 760	61.8	20.3	11.8	5.9	0.3	2 539	78.2	826	87.0
20 129	...	Morton County	3 215	58.8	19.5	6.9	11.1	3.7	1 306	71.6	309	88.0
20 131	...	Nemaha County	9 956	68.8	17.7	7.7	5.6	0.1	3 959	80.5	1 298	82.9
20 133	...	Neosho County	15 964	60.1	21.7	12.1	5.8	0.3	6 739	74.5	1 914	83.3
20 135	...	Ness County	3 274	66.8	15.1	12.7	5.2	0.3	1 516	76.1	557	81.3
20 137	...	Norton County	5 675	60.2	14.2	15.3	10.1	0.2	2 266	77.9	813	81.7

[1]MSA = Metropolitan Statistical Area. PMSA = Primary MSA. NECMA = New England County Metropolitan Area. See the Appendix A for explanation of these concepts. See Appendix B for list of metropolitan areas identified by type, with component counties.

Table C-3. States and Counties — **Migration, Housing, and Transportation**

STATE County	Owner-occupied by household type (percent)								Median household income			Median monthly owner costs as a percent of income	
	Family-households					Nonfamily households							
		Married-couple family		Other family									
	Total family households	Total	With own children under 18 years	Total	With own children under 18 years	Total nonfamily households	Two or more adults	Living alone	All households	Owner-occupied households	Renter-occupied households	Median housing value (owner estimated)	With a mortgage	Without a mortgage
	11	12	13	14	15	16	17	18	19	20	21	22	23	24
KANSAS—Cont'd														
Barber County	78.9	82.9	73.9	50.3	45.9	67.7	26.8	70.2	33 474	35 565	26 902	33 500	17.1	9.9
Barton County	78.5	85.0	76.8	47.4	40.4	59.2	38.4	61.6	31 946	37 708	20 334	53 900	19.0	11.0
Bourbon County	81.6	86.4	78.9	59.3	48.1	58.3	47.9	59.5	31 520	36 716	19 254	49 400	19.0	11.4
Brown County	77.4	84.2	77.5	48.5	45.9	58.1	54.5	58.4	31 629	36 820	20 938	54 600	18.3	10.9
Butler County	83.8	87.4	84.5	63.2	53.9	59.5	47.7	61.1	44 940	51 506	25 938	83 200	19.2	10.8
Chase County	78.9	82.5	75.6	59.5	57.5	63.0	55.3	63.8	32 898	36 357	24 643	52 000	18.5	9.9
Chautauqua County	82.4	86.2	79.9	61.4	48.9	80.3	89.5	80.0	28 404	29 483	21 726	34 100	16.2	12.1
Cherokee County	79.5	85.0	79.8	57.8	42.9	68.3	60.2	69.3	30 656	34 276	20 200	48 400	18.1	10.5
Cheyenne County	78.5	80.9	70.4	62.9	56.0	75.0	62.5	75.5	30 747	31 984	26 667	52 800	17.4	11.0
Clark County	77.3	80.8	69.9	49.4	34.8	74.7	60.0	75.3	33 586	37 974	25 000	44 800	18.7	9.9
Clay County	83.9	87.4	84.5	59.1	50.8	61.5	49.1	62.9	34 290	38 538	21 875	55 400	18.5	9.9
Cloud County	82.9	88.2	83.4	52.2	37.2	59.1	38.8	62.0	31 814	35 438	18 704	45 100	17.3	9.9
Coffey County	82.3	87.3	82.0	49.4	44.1	68.0	48.8	69.7	38 226	42 224	26 604	63 500	15.7	9.9
Comanche County	79.6	80.3	74.9	74.6	69.2	62.5	71.4	62.3	29 313	33 750	20 486	31 800	18.0	9.9
Cowley County	76.9	82.8	75.1	50.4	44.1	57.6	38.9	59.8	33 650	40 465	21 338	55 200	18.8	11.6
Crawford County	75.0	81.6	75.4	49.6	40.8	47.6	16.5	55.9	29 534	38 185	18 886	55 000	19.2	11.3
Decatur County	80.4	82.5	73.2	65.0	58.5	67.9	45.5	69.4	30 035	32 923	22 656	45 200	19.4	12.0
Dickinson County	81.7	86.0	80.9	56.2	48.9	59.8	52.6	60.6	35 991	40 796	22 829	65 400	19.1	9.9
Doniphan County	80.5	84.7	78.8	61.1	50.8	61.7	38.7	64.7	31 924	35 990	20 889	53 200	16.7	10.9
Douglas County	71.4	78.4	77.9	43.2	40.5	27.7	14.5	35.2	37 584	56 603	22 837	115 600	20.5	9.9
Edwards County	79.9	82.8	72.5	61.4	58.6	73.0	61.3	73.7	30 871	33 547	22 583	38 400	18.2	11.0
Elk County	85.9	87.5	81.9	75.2	61.6	71.2	87.5	70.6	27 045	29 470	18 105	31 000	19.4	11.3
Ellis County	78.8	84.6	83.3	53.4	50.2	39.1	18.6	45.1	32 109	42 990	19 012	84 100	20.6	10.2
Ellsworth County	85.0	88.6	84.1	58.8	55.7	69.1	54.4	70.2	35 216	38 639	24 297	45 200	16.9	11.2
Finney County	70.7	75.2	68.1	52.8	49.2	46.4	28.4	50.8	37 819	46 011	24 646	76 200	20.6	9.9
Ford County	71.6	79.4	75.2	42.3	38.5	46.5	18.9	52.0	37 826	45 338	25 755	64 600	19.3	10.9
Franklin County	79.9	85.1	82.7	57.2	47.8	57.0	58.1	56.8	39 220	45 625	25 551	76 600	19.1	11.7
Geary County	51.2	55.0	42.1	37.6	26.4	48.0	36.2	50.5	31 703	41 456	25 499	65 700	20.9	12.1
Gove County	84.9	85.3	77.6	81.5	66.7	68.0	84.6	67.4	34 044	36 276	27 625	51 200	18.4	9.9
Graham County	85.8	89.4	80.3	58.8	50.0	66.1	45.2	67.8	31 018	32 683	22 411	42 900	20.1	10.6
Grant County	79.5	84.1	83.0	47.0	53.7	58.5	56.0	58.7	40 325	46 019	26 604	68 500	19.4	9.9
Gray County	75.8	80.2	76.5	43.1	39.1	62.7	51.0	64.1	40 304	44 698	30 871	69 900	18.3	9.9
Greeley County	75.8	77.2	66.9	62.5	56.7	73.3	33.3	76.2	36 310	41 250	29 688	57 000	20.1	10.3
Greenwood County	79.6	84.2	74.0	47.6	39.2	66.5	78.7	65.3	30 361	33 792	18 963	37 900	19.3	11.1
Hamilton County	76.9	82.0	75.5	50.0	38.0	54.2	37.5	56.0	32 586	40 542	22 188	57 000	18.6	11.0
Harper County	81.7	85.4	79.1	60.2	54.5	61.0	59.4	61.2	29 592	33 795	21 071	46 400	17.6	12.1
Harvey County	79.6	84.3	80.5	53.8	40.4	53.3	44.5	54.4	40 964	47 645	25 031	76 000	18.4	9.9
Haskell County	74.8	77.7	69.8	47.8	35.9	62.5	36.4	64.4	38 079	43 346	25 833	64 500	18.6	9.9
Hodgeman County	82.3	82.8	80.3	78.9	72.0	67.8	57.9	68.7	35 897	37 847	28 214	50 300	17.7	9.9
Jackson County	85.1	89.3	83.6	62.5	55.8	67.3	55.7	68.5	40 589	43 256	28 393	79 100	19.1	10.4
Jefferson County	88.6	90.9	86.7	73.2	68.7	73.6	62.3	75.3	45 516	48 191	30 533	86 900	19.9	9.9
Jewell County	86.7	87.9	80.2	73.4	58.5	67.6	51.0	69.2	30 527	32 050	21 923	29 000	17.2	9.9
Johnson County	82.9	87.2	87.7	56.7	51.9	47.9	36.9	50.4	61 249	72 470	37 341	149 300	19.7	9.9
Kearny County	77.3	80.4	74.7	59.7	54.6	60.2	53.1	60.9	40 118	42 083	28 667	65 200	19.3	9.9
Kingman County	81.1	83.6	79.6	66.9	62.3	70.5	49.2	72.0	36 817	39 360	26 915	61 200	18.2	9.9
Kiowa County	77.8	81.9	73.5	44.0	33.3	59.1	47.6	59.7	31 813	37 000	22 569	43 600	16.7	10.0
Labette County	79.8	86.2	79.1	56.3	48.6	59.9	49.7	60.9	31 171	34 811	21 497	44 300	18.5	11.3
Lane County	80.4	83.6	78.8	53.1	54.2	70.0	47.1	71.4	35 139	38 715	25 625	48 400	17.3	11.1
Leavenworth County	71.2	76.3	64.1	47.9	35.7	54.3	52.6	54.5	47 660	55 451	33 480	101 600	19.7	9.9
Lincoln County	83.3	83.8	78.0	79.4	71.6	68.8	68.6	68.8	30 520	32 039	21 020	41 300	19.7	9.9
Linn County	85.4	88.2	80.2	66.7	53.2	74.6	63.7	76.0	35 491	39 518	20 719	67 300	18.9	10.9
Logan County	80.1	82.3	74.8	65.8	68.8	68.2	50.0	69.9	32 212	34 601	26 300	53 300	18.9	9.9
Lyon County	73.6	79.8	76.5	46.6	41.5	39.0	18.0	45.1	32 815	42 987	20 776	67 300	19.1	10.6
McPherson County	82.7	86.3	84.3	53.2	43.4	52.1	35.3	54.3	41 095	46 436	23 548	83 300	18.6	9.9
Marion County	86.2	88.8	85.6	66.2	58.9	63.5	51.8	64.7	33 801	36 921	21 034	59 000	18.8	10.4
Marshall County	84.8	88.4	87.3	57.6	35.1	69.1	46.8	71.2	31 947	35 167	23 375	51 300	17.1	9.9
Meade County	75.8	77.9	70.7	57.8	41.8	68.9	50.0	70.0	36 250	39 119	30 031	55 500	18.3	9.9
Miami County	84.5	89.0	87.5	57.9	44.8	60.4	51.5	62.1	46 779	52 875	28 134	116 400	20.6	12.1
Mitchell County	83.3	87.2	85.0	57.1	40.7	58.2	24.5	61.8	32 500	36 948	22 269	56 300	19.3	11.0
Montgomery County	78.8	85.2	79.6	51.8	42.2	56.8	35.2	58.9	30 703	36 242	18 309	47 500	18.6	11.3
Morris County	83.9	86.9	82.1	63.8	58.9	64.8	66.0	64.7	31 924	36 495	21 451	52 200	17.7	9.9
Morton County	77.3	80.9	76.9	53.6	45.7	55.7	38.5	57.1	37 404	43 601	26 080	63 100	16.6	9.9
Nemaha County	88.3	91.0	89.5	67.3	64.1	62.8	52.0	63.8	34 036	38 554	20 288	61 700	18.8	9.9
Neosho County	81.4	86.8	79.3	54.8	45.4	58.3	47.3	59.4	31 785	36 578	20 376	47 200	17.9	10.4
Ness County	82.2	85.9	80.4	52.8	39.4	64.9	54.8	65.5	32 625	36 304	24 375	41 600	18.4	9.9
Norton County	83.8	86.3	75.3	67.4	64.2	66.8	44.4	68.7	31 102	34 071	22 006	49 400	19.8	10.9

Table C-3. States and Counties — **Migration, Housing, and Transportation**

STATE County	Median gross rent	Percent who pay 35 percent or more of income for housing expenses		Means of transportation to work (percent except where noted)							Vehicles available (percent of households)		
		Owners	Renters	Number of workers 16 years and over	Car, truck, or van		Public transportation	Other means	Walked		No vehicles	One vehicle	Two or more vehicles
					Drove alone	Carpooled							
	25	26	27	28	29	30	31	32	33		34	35	36

KANSAS—Cont'd													
Barber County	354	8.3	7.1	2 517	78.0	9.3	0.8	1.9	4.7		4.3	32.6	63.1
Barton County	390	10.7	23.3	13 387	84.4	9.0	0.2	1.1	2.0		5.9	32.8	61.3
Bourbon County	356	10.7	25.9	7 309	75.4	18.1	0.1	0.6	1.7		6.6	32.1	61.3
Brown County	342	11.5	19.4	4 883	80.6	9.8	0.0	0.8	2.7		6.7	32.0	61.3
Butler County	485	11.4	24.4	27 789	84.2	9.9	0.1	0.6	1.8		3.4	25.4	71.2
Chase County	349	10.9	13.2	1 519	78.0	11.1	0.3	0.9	2.6		5.1	28.4	66.5
Chautauqua County	365	7.9	23.8	1 701	73.7	13.6	0.1	1.5	5.1		5.6	27.2	67.2
Cherokee County	381	10.2	23.5	10 119	81.8	11.5	0.1	0.8	2.2		5.7	31.3	63.0
Cheyenne County	314	7.0	12.3	1 493	71.0	10.6	0.0	1.5	5.0		4.4	31.7	63.9
Clark County	386	8.8	13.4	1 110	76.9	10.4	0.4	0.8	5.7		3.9	32.7	63.4
Clay County	333	9.7	10.5	4 293	74.3	13.5	0.2	0.6	4.0		5.1	28.5	66.4
Cloud County	312	6.7	17.6	4 888	79.4	10.1	0.2	0.4	4.0		5.4	30.4	64.2
Coffey County	394	7.7	14.9	4 370	80.0	10.9	0.0	0.6	1.9		5.0	25.0	70.0
Comanche County	294	10.6	14.0	963	77.5	8.3	0.7	0.8	6.1		5.4	28.8	65.8
Cowley County	417	10.0	24.9	16 205	82.0	10.7	0.1	0.8	2.7		6.0	32.4	61.5
Crawford County	451	11.9	33.5	18 030	82.4	9.8	0.3	1.0	3.0		7.4	32.5	60.1
Decatur County	354	10.2	10.8	1 586	74.6	10.5	0.1	1.3	3.9		2.9	28.0	69.0
Dickinson County	377	9.2	18.5	9 639	79.9	11.5	0.3	0.7	2.8		4.5	29.1	66.4
Doniphan County	379	10.2	22.2	3 826	79.7	9.9	0.1	0.9	4.3		6.3	27.4	66.3
Douglas County	560	11.3	38.6	54 496	76.9	10.3	1.0	1.4	6.7		5.6	34.7	59.7
Edwards County	350	9.9	15.1	1 574	77.1	12.8	0.3	0.4	4.4		6.2	30.7	63.2
Elk County	301	10.1	12.2	1 303	72.6	14.7	0.0	0.7	3.4		7.5	29.0	63.5
Ellis County	431	11.3	29.4	14 764	84.0	8.6	0.0	0.9	4.0		5.3	34.4	60.3
Ellsworth County	336	8.5	12.7	2 944	75.7	13.6	0.0	0.5	4.0		4.9	27.8	67.3
Finney County	491	12.6	24.4	18 287	74.0	18.9	0.4	1.3	2.3		6.1	32.9	60.9
Ford County	451	11.9	22.0	14 966	75.7	18.0	0.5	1.8	1.7		6.1	32.5	61.4
Franklin County	465	11.2	24.1	12 161	76.1	16.3	0.4	1.1	2.3		6.1	27.7	66.2
Geary County	461	13.5	19.5	13 414	76.1	15.0	0.7	2.3	3.7		8.1	37.0	54.9
Gove County	330	11.0	10.4	1 467	69.3	8.0	0.0	0.7	8.5		4.1	25.9	70.0
Graham County	320	14.5	11.5	1 387	73.5	12.5	0.2	0.9	5.2		4.4	28.1	67.5
Grant County	436	12.1	14.5	3 448	77.6	14.6	0.0	0.8	1.4		4.2	33.0	62.7
Gray County	418	8.4	11.6	2 776	77.0	10.7	0.0	0.3	4.3		2.3	29.0	68.7
Greeley County	000	14.7	10.0	601	83.5	10.2	0.7	0.4	7.3		2.7	28.1	69.3
Greenwood County	322	9.6	19.1	3 361	68.2	20.1	0.2	0.9	5.1		6.5	27.4	66.1
Hamilton County	373	10.9	18.1	1 174	72.7	14.7	0.0	2.6	5.1		4.7	30.9	64.3
Harper County	356	11.4	21.2	2 944	76.2	12.1	0.2	0.5	4.8		5.9	31.5	62.6
Harvey County	448	8.2	19.5	16 020	81.7	8.6	0.5	1.1	3.7		5.5	30.1	64.5
Haskell County	446	7.3	14.1	1 892	74.7	11.0	0.1	1.2	5.1		4.1	29.2	66.8
Hodgeman County	360	6.9	17.8	986	73.2	9.9	0.0	0.2	4.6		4.3	24.9	70.9
Jackson County	453	10.7	21.3	6 062	75.5	16.1	0.4	1.2	2.0		3.9	22.8	73.4
Jefferson County	447	11.9	17.6	8 876	77.7	14.6	0.1	0.9	2.3		3.3	19.8	76.9
Jewell County	266	6.6	13.9	1 785	75.0	8.3	0.2	0.6	4.8		5.1	24.6	70.3
Johnson County	702	10.8	22.3	243 908	86.7	6.9	0.3	0.5	0.8		3.2	29.1	67.7
Kearny County	465	11.6	14.9	1 914	76.9	13.4	0.0	1.5	2.6		3.6	26.0	70.4
Kingman County	397	7.4	13.8	3 965	76.6	14.1	0.1	0.7	2.6		3.1	27.3	69.6
Kiowa County	336	8.2	21.5	1 563	75.5	8.8	0.3	0.7	8.0		6.6	28.3	65.1
Labette County	375	10.0	19.5	10 676	81.5	9.9	0.2	1.0	3.4		8.5	29.4	62.1
Lane County	365	9.9	11.1	1 059	75.1	9.3	0.0	1.2	5.9		5.1	23.6	71.3
Leavenworth County	551	9.9	16.7	31 223	80.9	11.0	0.5	1.1	3.0		5.9	26.1	68.0
Lincoln County	296	8.9	13.0	1 813	72.8	12.0	0.6	0.9	4.2		4.8	24.9	70.3
Linn County	412	11.8	22.5	4 317	72.0	19.8	0.3	1.2	2.5		4.9	23.9	71.3
Logan County	360	9.7	18.3	1 483	79.3	6.9	0.0	0.9	5.8		3.4	30.3	66.3
Lyon County	420	10.0	30.3	17 807	76.4	14.4	0.4	1.3	4.4		7.4	34.2	58.4
McPherson County	416	7.4	19.6	14 925	80.1	8.1	0.4	1.2	4.7		5.1	28.5	66.4
Marion County	374	8.4	19.4	6 236	75.3	9.4	0.7	1.0	6.7		5.0	27.8	67.2
Marshall County	324	8.7	13.3	5 228	76.6	10.4	0.1	0.6	5.4		5.7	29.5	64.9
Meade County	395	8.5	13.9	2 010	77.6	11.5	0.0	0.5	3.2		3.7	29.8	66.5
Miami County	499	10.2	22.4	14 310	81.3	12.2	0.5	0.4	1.6		5.2	22.7	72.1
Mitchell County	346	8.9	15.0	3 346	77.6	8.7	0.1	0.4	6.7		6.5	30.4	63.1
Montgomery County	401	11.8	25.2	16 244	80.7	11.6	0.2	1.5	3.2		7.9	33.6	58.5
Morris County	368	8.2	18.3	2 963	79.5	7.2	0.0	0.7	2.7		4.6	29.2	66.2
Morton County	413	6.8	19.6	1 594	77.9	13.7	0.3	0.9	3.8		2.0	30.1	67.9
Nemaha County	321	9.0	19.8	4 929	79.0	8.5	0.2	0.5	2.8		5.2	26.9	67.9
Neosho County	375	10.1	22.3	7 911	82.0	10.6	0.1	1.1	1.9		5.0	30.7	64.4
Ness County	340	9.4	13.7	1 666	71.9	12.1	0.4	0.7	7.2		2.9	29.2	67.9
Norton County	329	12.8	15.8	2 468	81.7	7.7	0.6	0.4	4.4		6.4	29.9	63.7

STATE/ County code	MSA/PMSA/ NECMA code[1]	STATE County	Residence in 1995 (percent)						Occupied housing units		Householders 65 years and over	
			Total population 5 years and over	Same house	Same county, different house	Same state, different county	Different state	Outside the United States	Number	Percent owner-occupied	Number	Percent owner-occupied
			1	2	3	4	5	6	7	8	9	10
		KANSAS—Cont'd										
20 139	...	Osage County	15 575	60.2	18.3	17.1	4.2	0.2	6 490	79.8	1 686	81.4
20 141	...	Osborne County	4 250	68.9	13.4	12.3	5.1	0.2	1 940	78.6	738	86.3
20 143	...	Ottawa County	5 816	59.1	17.0	18.8	4.3	0.7	2 430	82.2	646	85.4
20 145	...	Pawnee County	6 838	64.3	14.1	14.6	6.7	0.3	2 739	74.4	836	79.9
20 147	...	Phillips County	5 664	63.6	21.4	8.2	6.9	0.0	2 496	77.9	785	85.1
20 149	...	Pottawatomie County	16 872	56.9	17.9	17.1	7.3	0.9	6 771	78.5	1 513	84.6
20 151	...	Pratt County	9 036	59.7	18.5	13.7	7.7	0.4	3 963	73.4	1 249	79.0
20 153	...	Rawlins County	2 838	69.2	16.4	6.2	8.2	0.0	1 269	76.8	486	87.2
20 155	...	Reno County	60 643	54.9	26.9	10.9	6.5	0.8	25 498	70.7	6 713	79.7
20 157	...	Republic County	5 574	65.0	18.5	9.7	6.4	0.3	2 557	78.9	1 001	81.5
20 159	...	Rice County	10 116	57.1	18.0	17.0	7.4	0.6	4 050	76.6	1 249	83.2
20 161	...	Riley County	59 348	30.9	15.7	27.5	21.0	5.0	22 137	47.3	3 118	79.7
20 163	...	Rooks County	5 366	64.8	17.6	12.6	5.0	0.1	2 362	77.1	837	84.5
20 165	...	Rush County	3 379	65.0	14.6	15.4	4.9	0.1	1 548	82.4	530	90.6
20 167	...	Russell County	7 009	67.6	17.5	9.4	5.3	0.2	3 207	75.2	1 202	83.9
20 169	...	Saline County	49 949	51.6	27.4	11.5	8.5	1.0	21 436	69.0	4 849	79.5
20 171	...	Scott County	4 777	55.1	28.0	11.0	5.8	0.2	2 045	74.4	621	82.4
20 173	9040	Sedgwick County	417 591	49.3	32.3	6.0	9.9	2.4	176 444	66.2	34 103	79.4
20 175	...	Seward County	20 371	45.2	24.0	7.3	15.1	8.3	7 419	64.1	1 201	79.2
20 177	8440	Shawnee County	158 281	53.6	30.4	7.9	7.1	1.1	68 920	67.5	15 372	75.8
20 179	...	Sheridan County	2 672	72.6	12.9	9.8	4.3	0.3	1 124	82.3	356	86.2
20 181	...	Sherman County	6 346	57.7	17.8	12.7	11.2	0.6	2 758	68.9	770	81.0
20 183	...	Smith County	4 345	70.4	16.2	8.1	5.2	0.1	1 953	79.7	785	82.5
20 185	...	Stafford County	4 521	62.7	16.2	13.8	5.8	1.5	2 010	77.7	708	87.7
20 187	...	Stanton County	2 216	54.2	20.8	11.6	9.6	3.8	858	67.8	207	88.4
20 189	...	Stevens County	4 985	63.0	19.7	8.0	7.3	2.0	1 988	75.4	491	88.4
20 191	...	Sumner County	24 200	60.2	18.5	14.4	6.6	0.4	9 888	76.7	2 610	82.8
20 193	...	Thomas County	7 624	59.6	17.4	16.0	6.3	0.7	3 226	69.0	824	84.8
20 195	...	Trego County	3 152	68.8	14.0	12.2	4.5	0.5	1 412	81.4	491	88.0
20 197	...	Wabaunsee County	6 465	64.6	12.8	17.2	5.2	0.2	2 633	82.9	703	82.6
20 199	...	Wallace County	1 657	68.4	12.9	10.0	7.9	0.9	674	76.6	204	88.7
20 201	...	Washington County	6 113	70.6	14.6	9.5	5.0	0.4	2 673	79.5	1 048	86.1
20 203	...	Wichita County	2 325	60.7	20.6	10.1	7.0	1.6	967	74.3	274	84.3
20 205	...	Wilson County	9 721	58.5	22.7	12.8	5.7	0.3	4 203	78.1	1 292	83.7
20 207	...	Woodson County	3 596	63.4	15.2	17.6	3.7	0.1	1 642	81.4	651	88.3
20 209	3760	Wyandotte County	145 220	53.9	25.7	6.2	10.3	3.9	59 700	62.9	12 411	78.4
21 000	...	KENTUCKY	3 776 230	55.9	24.7	9.7	8.4	1.2	1 590 647	70.7	339 303	81.2
21 001	...	Adair County	16 159	58.5	23.9	9.4	7.2	1.0	6 747	80.1	1 829	85.9
21 003	...	Allen County	16 604	57.1	24.7	10.3	7.5	0.4	6 910	79.0	1 721	85.2
21 005	...	Anderson County	17 677	57.3	21.1	15.0	6.0	0.7	7 320	79.8	1 306	89.7
21 007	...	Ballard County	7 772	61.4	22.6	7.1	8.5	0.4	3 395	81.9	873	80.3
21 009	...	Barren County	35 627	56.0	28.1	9.1	6.3	0.5	15 346	72.3	3 768	79.1
21 011	...	Bath County	10 351	61.7	20.4	12.3	5.4	0.3	4 445	79.8	1 053	85.7
21 013	...	Bell County	28 257	63.1	24.1	5.3	6.9	0.5	12 004	67.5	2 757	76.8
21 015	1640	Boone County	79 175	48.1	18.4	16.3	15.5	1.6	31 258	74.2	4 646	77.2
21 017	4280	Bourbon County	18 101	55.5	26.9	12.9	3.8	1.0	7 681	65.5	1 713	80.6
21 019	3400	Boyd County	47 033	58.9	23.5	7.0	9.8	0.8	20 010	72.9	5 024	81.7
21 021	...	Boyle County	26 163	51.7	22.6	16.5	8.0	1.2	10 574	69.3	2 737	83.2
21 023	...	Bracken County	7 738	62.9	21.3	9.2	6.4	0.2	3 228	76.9	757	80.2
21 025	...	Breathitt County	15 175	68.5	19.9	7.7	3.4	0.5	6 170	76.5	1 363	80.9
21 027	...	Breckinridge County	17 515	62.6	19.9	10.8	6.2	0.5	7 324	81.9	1 827	83.0
21 029	4520	Bullitt County	56 802	58.6	17.6	18.6	4.8	0.4	22 171	83.9	3 155	89.6
21 031	...	Butler County	12 177	64.4	20.1	10.9	3.5	1.1	5 059	79.5	1 142	82.6
21 033	...	Caldwell County	12 362	62.7	22.3	9.9	4.8	0.2	5 431	77.4	1 626	83.9
21 035	...	Calloway County	32 511	51.5	20.4	13.1	12.5	2.4	13 862	68.3	3 451	87.0
21 037	1640	Campbell County	82 536	58.9	23.2	8.4	8.8	0.7	34 742	69.0	7 323	77.8
21 039	...	Carlisle County	5 032	63.8	17.6	10.7	7.9	0.0	2 208	84.0	618	91.3
21 041	...	Carroll County	9 455	51.3	27.7	11.8	8.4	0.8	3 940	66.8	891	75.2
21 043	3400	Carter County	25 154	66.2	21.2	6.2	6.3	0.1	10 342	81.0	2 487	87.7
21 045	...	Casey County	14 505	63.7	21.0	9.2	4.9	1.1	6 260	81.1	1 819	84.1
21 047	1660	Christian County	65 108	41.1	20.8	6.2	28.1	3.8	24 857	55.3	4 381	79.0
21 049	4280	Clark County	30 963	52.0	27.8	13.2	6.4	0.7	13 015	68.6	2 923	79.6
21 051	...	Clay County	23 170	66.1	20.3	7.8	5.2	0.6	8 556	74.8	1 732	80.6
21 053	...	Clinton County	9 026	67.3	22.5	4.2	4.6	1.3	4 086	77.2	1 147	80.3
21 055	...	Crittenden County	8 890	64.9	18.5	9.6	6.7	0.4	3 829	80.3	1 106	87.2

[1]MSA = Metropolitan Statistical Area. PMSA = Primary MSA. NECMA = New England County Metropolitan Area. See the Appendix A for explanation of these concepts. See Appendix B for list of metropolitan areas identified by type, with component counties.

Table C-3. States and Counties — **Migration, Housing, and Transportation**

STATE County	Owner-occupied by household type (percent)								Median household income			Median monthly owner costs as a percent of income	
	Family-households				Nonfamily households								
		Married-couple family		Other family									
	Total family households	Total	With own children under 18 years	Total	With own children under 18 years	Total nonfamily households	Two or more adults	Living alone	All households	Owner-occupied households	Renter-occupied households	Median housing value (owner estimated)	With a mortgage	Without a mortgage
	11	12	13	14	15	16	17	18	19	20	21	22	23	24
KANSAS—Cont'd														
Osage County	85.5	89.2	84.3	65.6	58.3	63.9	74.1	62.5	37 869	42 833	21 994	71 500	19.3	9.9
Osborne County	83.2	86.8	84.2	58.7	39.3	70.8	57.4	71.7	29 069	30 808	20 662	36 200	17.5	9.9
Ottawa County	86.9	91.4	90.0	59.9	57.6	70.7	75.9	70.1	37 787	42 241	22 898	61 600	19.0	9.9
Pawnee County	81.6	88.2	80.3	45.4	39.4	60.5	74.0	59.7	34 983	41 909	21 893	50 000	18.4	9.9
Phillips County	85.6	87.5	83.5	67.9	57.9	60.9	53.2	61.6	35 269	38 622	23 158	51 600	17.4	9.9
Pottawatomie County	83.9	86.5	82.7	67.0	60.9	63.8	51.8	65.7	40 266	44 243	27 551	80 400	19.2	9.9
Pratt County	79.9	85.4	80.8	49.8	44.9	60.4	50.4	61.4	35 347	41 284	20 221	57 400	18.9	9.9
Rawlins County	80.4	82.1	75.3	69.9	49.2	69.8	55.6	70.8	31 906	33 590	23 250	41 600	20.8	11.2
Reno County	78.1	84.6	79.9	47.8	39.3	54.8	40.0	56.9	35 627	41 792	22 253	66 000	19.0	9.9
Republic County	86.9	89.1	80.2	61.5	62.1	63.7	55.4	64.3	30 404	33 951	17 004	40 200	19.0	10.2
Rice County	81.0	84.9	78.2	58.6	52.9	66.3	58.0	66.9	35 050	38 740	23 568	44 600	18.5	9.9
Riley County	63.2	67.2	60.9	43.9	38.0	27.2	11.9	36.6	31 781	50 911	20 132	89 100	18.7	9.9
Rooks County	82.2	85.0	74.2	66.7	54.9	67.5	55.4	68.4	30 113	32 000	24 545	40 500	18.9	11.6
Rush County	87.1	90.0	85.9	69.4	64.7	73.2	67.4	73.8	31 632	33 313	22 375	33 100	17.9	11.4
Russell County	82.9	86.2	80.7	65.9	56.1	61.8	53.7	62.7	29 695	35 000	17 606	43 900	19.0	10.0
Saline County	78.1	84.3	80.0	51.6	44.1	51.1	37.5	53.6	37 145	44 616	24 247	83 700	19.6	9.9
Scott County	79.7	84.3	83.4	55.3	55.9	62.2	31.7	65.5	37 986	45 234	24 028	69 300	17.9	10.9
Sedgwick County	75.0	81.5	77.7	51.8	43.4	48.2	41.6	49.3	42 298	52 162	26 824	80 400	19.3	9.9
Seward County	70.2	75.6	70.6	48.3	40.3	46.1	29.5	50.1	37 147	44 832	24 269	63 100	19.4	9.9
Shawnee County	77.2	85.1	81.4	50.1	41.8	49.4	41.1	50.8	40 774	50 634	24 571	79 600	19.0	9.9
Sheridan County	86.4	90.1	84.9	56.2	47.9	72.0	20.0	73.7	33 500	34 901	23 750	57 300	20.2	10.9
Sherman County	76.9	82.4	74.1	45.9	33.9	54.6	23.3	61.6	32 359	36 125	22 647	62 400	19.9	12.0
Smith County	82.7	85.9	79.0	56.5	48.4	73.4	30.4	75.0	28 276	30 206	22 000	39 800	17.6	10.9
Stafford County	82.0	84.2	75.6	67.1	62.9	69.9	43.4	72.0	30 841	33 075	23 313	37 900	18.6	10.8
Stanton County	71.2	74.9	62.5	51.0	47.5	58.2	42.3	60.3	39 565	46 500	28 393	64 600	18.2	9.9
Stevens County	79.2	82.8	72.6	60.1	63.0	64.4	48.3	65.4	40 047	46 190	25 878	69 600	18.8	9.9
Sumner County	83.1	86.8	81.4	63.3	53.8	60.1	51.2	61.0	39 514	44 667	22 875	63 800	18.5	11.1
Thomas County	78.7	84.6	75.7	40.7	32.0	49.0	37.5	50.7	37 290	44 912	21 172	76 300	18.0	9.9
Trego County	84.8	84.4	78.6	80.9	80.9	74.8	54.8	76.2	30 426	32 021	23 333	49 500	18.5	11.0
Wabaunsee County	86.2	86.6	84.1	83.7	76.6	73.5	60.6	75.0	41 377	43 883	28 636	69 500	18.1	9.9
Wallace County	90.9	93.9	78.1	53.2	46.9	66.3	60.2	66.1	32 593	38 750	21 875	43 500	19.5	10.3
Washington County	84.0	86.1	79.6	66.5	44.9	70.5	54.7	71.7	29 570	31 546	23 967	37 500	17.2	0.0
Wichita County	75.9	78.3	72.0	63.5	52.9	69.2	28.6	70.4	34 345	39 063	28 523	52 900	17.9	10.6
Wilson County	83.7	87.7	83.0	61.8	49.5	66.3	48.5	68.2	29 833	33 340	18 242	40 800	18.5	11.6
Woodson County	86.4	89.4	81.6	71.3	63.6	72.3	62.5	73.0	25 283	27 160	15 431	42 700	20.9	12.2
Wyandotte County	68.5	78.1	69.5	50.1	39.9	51.9	47.6	52.7	33 666	41 496	23 366	53 400	19.5	11.1
KENTUCKY	77.5	83.9	79.5	54.4	43.0	55.3	42.2	57.5	33 549	40 460	21 295	79 600	19.6	9.9
Adair County	84.8	88.4	84.2	68.9	58.3	68.8	63.8	69.3	23 708	27 175	13 142	56 200	20.6	9.9
Allen County	81.6	86.4	84.6	60.8	51.4	71.3	72.2	71.2	30 660	34 011	17 078	65 100	20.0	9.9
Anderson County	83.2	87.3	83.6	63.9	52.4	69.1	53.1	71.9	44 625	47 901	30 608	91 200	18.9	9.9
Ballard County	87.4	91.0	88.3	67.1	58.1	67.8	77.9	66.8	32 350	37 078	17 857	56 800	17.6	9.9
Barren County	77.3	82.9	79.4	51.2	40.5	59.3	47.1	60.4	31 234	36 144	20 803	73 600	19.1	9.9
Bath County	83.3	86.8	77.4	67.2	58.6	70.7	67.8	71.1	26 206	29 174	15 476	53 600	20.0	9.9
Bell County	72.0	78.3	72.9	54.6	38.2	56.1	37.4	57.4	18 896	23 335	11 852	41 700	21.8	9.9
Boone County	81.3	86.4	86.1	56.7	48.3	53.0	48.8	53.9	53 274	61 015	31 889	124 600	19.9	9.9
Bourbon County	69.7	76.3	68.9	47.8	34.5	55.3	59.9	54.6	35 250	43 647	21 457	87 600	19.8	9.9
Boyd County	77.8	83.9	77.4	53.7	41.5	61.2	56.8	61.6	32 685	39 538	18 735	65 600	18.7	9.9
Boyle County	75.2	82.4	75.5	48.9	35.6	55.8	42.4	57.6	34 811	42 819	21 083	84 600	18.7	9.9
Bracken County	79.0	83.6	78.0	60.0	54.2	71.3	47.2	74.6	33 967	38 703	20 923	68 300	18.5	9.9
Breathitt County	79.4	82.9	80.6	69.2	58.3	68.5	59.1	69.4	18 855	21 601	12 271	32 000	21.5	9.9
Breckinridge County	86.4	90.4	86.7	67.1	60.8	69.7	80.5	68.6	30 183	33 622	16 693	61 100	20.5	9.9
Bullitt County	86.2	90.3	87.7	67.4	58.8	74.7	66.1	76.5	45 093	48 119	27 037	99 400	19.8	9.9
Butler County	82.6	87.7	83.8	57.8	42.7	70.9	58.7	72.4	29 633	32 534	18 568	54 400	19.3	9.9
Caldwell County	81.1	85.6	80.3	58.6	48.6	68.2	58.2	68.8	28 710	33 498	17 399	54 400	19.9	9.9
Calloway County	80.8	84.6	80.8	62.2	54.3	47.6	18.6	55.4	29 785	37 559	17 434	77 400	20.8	9.9
Campbell County	77.1	84.8	83.6	52.4	39.2	52.8	40.7	54.7	41 746	50 759	24 413	97 400	19.8	9.9
Carlisle County	86.0	89.4	88.5	71.0	61.2	79.1	60.8	80.7	30 093	32 401	21 490	48 600	21.0	9.9
Carroll County	72.9	82.6	73.3	44.8	34.3	52.8	44.7	54.4	35 417	43 011	20 391	75 600	18.6	9.9
Carter County	84.4	87.9	83.6	68.2	58.8	70.7	65.6	71.3	26 438	30 231	14 170	47 100	18.6	10.9
Casey County	85.1	88.3	82.0	70.8	61.8	71.5	70.2	71.6	21 456	23 544	12 058	45 900	22.1	11.1
Christian County	57.4	62.9	48.8	38.3	27.8	49.1	32.4	51.8	31 113	39 219	24 720	71 300	20.0	9.9
Clark County	72.3	78.4	71.0	49.2	32.9	58.6	49.0	60.3	39 247	48 096	24 729	91 800	19.3	9.9
Clay County	77.6	81.4	76.8	64.2	56.4	66.1	71.9	65.5	16 386	18 726	11 276	34 500	21.0	12.1
Clinton County	83.0	85.9	85.4	69.4	67.6	64.3	53.3	65.5	19 599	22 327	12 540	42 200	19.3	13.4
Crittenden County	83.6	88.7	84.1	59.0	46.9	72.5	58.3	73.6	28 366	32 101	15 078	48 100	19.0	9.9

Table C-3. States and Counties — **Migration, Housing, and Transportation**

STATE County	Median gross rent	Percent who pay 35 percent or more of income for housing expenses — Owners	Renters	Number of workers 16 years and over	Car, truck, or van — Drove alone	Carpooled	Public transportation	Other means	Walked	No vehicles	One vehicle	Two or more vehicles
	25	26	27	28	29	30	31	32	33	34	35	36
KANSAS—Cont'd												
Osage County	398	9.3	21.0	8 089	78.5	14.0	0.2	1.0	2.1	4.5	24.7	70.8
Osborne County	314	7.2	9.9	2 068	74.9	8.9	0.6	0.6	5.3	5.8	30.8	63.4
Ottawa County	372	11.1	20.7	3 058	79.8	11.6	0.2	0.3	2.7	4.0	21.1	74.9
Pawnee County	332	7.3	13.1	3 227	81.2	11.2	0.0	0.1	4.1	3.7	35.4	61.0
Phillips County	296	7.8	16.6	2 836	76.8	9.5	0.1	1.3	4.2	5.3	26.8	67.9
Pottawatomie County	464	10.8	21.8	9 016	80.4	10.9	0.1	0.9	2.5	3.6	24.1	72.3
Pratt County	389	8.9	27.3	4 721	79.2	11.0	0.2	0.6	2.6	5.2	33.5	61.3
Rawlins County	328	9.6	16.1	1 347	68.3	12.2	1.2	0.6	7.1	6.4	27.0	66.7
Reno County	442	10.0	27.2	29 998	82.6	10.4	0.3	1.0	1.8	6.6	31.2	62.2
Republic County	288	8.3	16.4	2 767	78.4	7.1	0.5	1.7	1.6	4.3	30.0	65.7
Rice County	340	8.9	16.8	4 920	77.7	10.8	0.5	0.8	5.8	5.8	27.1	67.1
Riley County	475	7.9	34.4	34 591	71.2	10.0	0.4	2.6	12.3	4.6	34.3	61.0
Rooks County	325	7.1	13.3	2 578	78.9	10.4	0.2	0.4	5.3	5.2	29.0	65.7
Rush County	328	8.3	15.8	1 627	75.4	11.5	0.1	1.3	5.0	4.7	26.7	68.6
Russell County	325	8.3	17.6	3 354	79.7	8.4	0.5	0.9	2.6	5.0	30.9	64.1
Saline County	457	9.9	25.1	27 461	84.2	8.7	0.5	1.1	1.5	5.0	31.4	63.6
Scott County	402	7.7	22.0	2 748	79.9	11.0	0.0	0.5	2.8	4.4	28.4	67.1
Sedgwick County	511	10.4	25.3	218 599	84.8	9.8	0.7	0.8	1.4	6.4	34.6	59.0
Seward County	467	8.1	24.2	9 478	72.9	21.4	0.2	1.9	1.5	7.0	37.5	55.5
Shawnee County	494	9.9	29.0	83 741	83.4	11.3	0.9	0.6	1.2	7.3	35.2	57.4
Sheridan County	286	10.6	16.9	1 360	72.5	7.0	0.0	1.3	6.7	4.4	25.4	70.1
Sherman County	414	14.2	23.8	3 333	80.1	7.9	0.2	1.6	2.8	3.7	30.0	66.3
Smith County	283	8.7	9.2	2 048	74.2	9.9	0.3	0.9	5.6	5.3	24.1	70.6
Stafford County	353	7.7	14.4	2 169	75.7	12.0	0.1	1.2	5.5	5.5	32.7	61.8
Stanton County	406	11.5	11.3	1 141	71.4	17.6	0.0	1.6	6.1	4.1	30.9	65.0
Stevens County	450	4.9	18.0	2 380	80.3	10.5	0.0	1.1	2.8	3.2	32.4	64.4
Sumner County	416	10.1	21.4	11 535	80.5	11.3	0.2	0.3	2.5	4.1	27.7	68.3
Thomas County	373	9.6	17.9	4 000	82.8	6.6	0.1	0.6	3.1	4.8	29.5	65.7
Trego County	326	12.6	14.5	1 537	78.3	9.6	0.0	1.3	3.1	4.6	29.1	66.3
Wabaunsee County	378	6.1	14.3	3 444	77.3	13.7	0.3	0.8	3.3	2.7	20.1	77.2
Wallace County	361	12.4	14.7	857	70.7	7.9	0.6	1.1	7.9	2.8	22.1	75.1
Washington County	286	7.4	10.5	3 160	72.0	12.0	0.1	0.9	5.7	5.1	28.1	66.8
Wichita County	451	10.5	17.0	1 136	76.2	10.3	0.9	1.1	3.3	3.1	28.4	68.5
Wilson County	382	13.0	25.4	4 634	79.6	11.4	0.0	1.4	2.5	6.3	30.2	63.5
Woodson County	321	15.2	18.5	1 579	74.3	15.3	0.5	1.3	1.9	5.9	29.7	64.4
Wyandotte County	492	13.8	27.2	66 696	78.1	16.3	1.4	1.0	1.3	11.3	38.6	50.1
KENTUCKY	445	12.3	25.6	1 781 733	80.2	12.6	1.2	0.9	2.4	9.3	33.3	57.4
Adair County	315	17.9	22.8	7 222	77.6	12.3	1.3	1.0	2.6	10.9	31.6	57.5
Allen County	357	16.1	23.1	7 573	77.1	16.1	0.2	1.2	2.1	8.8	29.7	61.5
Anderson County	523	11.8	21.2	9 335	84.4	11.1	0.2	1.4	0.7	4.9	22.7	72.5
Ballard County	349	10.2	18.3	3 760	87.0	8.6	0.0	0.6	1.3	5.9	32.3	61.8
Barren County	383	12.4	21.0	17 215	81.9	13.0	0.2	0.5	0.9	8.4	28.7	62.9
Bath County	317	10.0	22.5	4 337	77.0	16.8	0.3	1.0	2.2	9.2	30.3	60.5
Bell County	309	13.3	25.0	8 816	79.1	15.7	0.3	0.8	2.6	16.9	37.5	45.5
Boone County	596	10.5	24.0	44 507	84.6	10.1	1.1	0.6	0.9	5.0	27.6	67.4
Bourbon County	416	11.2	25.9	9 103	78.2	14.2	0.1	0.9	3.1	10.7	31.1	58.2
Boyd County................	407	12.2	23.6	19 106	84.9	10.5	0.3	0.8	1.6	10.6	34.6	54.8
Boyle County	419	13.1	21.2	12 184	78.0	12.2	0.5	0.8	4.9	8.0	35.1	56.9
Bracken County............	337	13.6	18.7	3 818	71.6	21.1	0.1	1.0	2.6	6.8	27.1	66.0
Breathitt County	297	12.1	27.3	4 764	71.3	21.0	1.4	0.9	2.8	18.5	36.1	45.4
Breckinridge County......	360	12.4	25.2	7 798	74.4	17.6	0.7	1.5	2.2	8.3	29.0	62.7
Bullitt County	499	12.4	21.0	30 648	84.9	11.2	0.4	0.7	1.0	4.1	24.0	71.9
Butler County	338	14.4	22.8	5 796	78.4	17.1	0.1	0.2	1.5	7.9	28.3	63.8
Caldwell County	348	10.4	17.6	5 639	80.5	12.2	0.0	1.2	1.5	7.6	29.2	63.2
Calloway County	427	13.0	31.7	15 532	79.7	10.7	0.9	0.6	5.2	5.3	37.4	57.3
Campbell County	512	10.4	26.9	42 820	79.1	11.4	3.6	0.7	2.9	10.4	35.7	53.8
Carlisle County	273	15.9	15.7	2 202	81.2	13.2	0.1	0.8	2.0	4.3	33.1	62.6
Carroll County..............	389	9.3	25.1	4 466	80.8	13.7	0.1	1.1	1.6	10.5	31.7	57.8
Carter County...............	365	13.1	27.0	10 258	71.3	20.0	0.3	0.7	3.6	11.1	27.9	61.0
Casey County...............	295	16.2	21.7	6 089	71.2	19.6	0.6	1.2	2.7	11.5	31.1	57.4
Christian County	458	13.4	20.3	33 000	74.0	13.9	0.6	1.8	7.2	9.7	35.8	54.5
Clark County	476	11.3	23.2	15 487	84.0	12.1	0.3	0.4	1.1	8.2	30.2	61.7
Clay County.................	292	15.4	26.0	6 374	75.6	19.1	0.5	1.1	1.8	14.1	38.9	47.0
Clinton County.............	294	14.5	24.1	3 935	80.5	15.6	0.4	0.8	0.4	10.5	32.4	57.2
Crittenden County	331	9.6	29.2	3 832	78.0	14.8	0.3	1.1	2.1	9.8	30.3	59.9

STATE/ County code	MSA/PMSA/ NECMA code[1]	STATE County	Residence in 1995 (percent)						Occupied housing units		Householders 65 years and over	
			Total population 5 years and over	Same house	Same county, different house	Same state, different county	Different state	Outside the United States	Number	Percent owner-occupied	Number	Percent owner-occupied
			1	2	3	4	5	6	7	8	9	10
		KENTUCKY—Cont'd										
21 057	...	Cumberland County	6 746	66.5	20.0	8.0	5.4	0.2	2 976	77.6	863	84.4
21 059	5990	Daviess County	85 314	55.1	31.9	6.4	6.1	0.5	36 033	70.3	8 258	77.7
21 061	...	Edmonson County........	10 958	64.1	16.6	11.8	7.3	0.2	4 648	85.6	1 113	91.1
21 063	...	Elliott County	6 311	69.1	13.9	12.9	3.9	0.1	2 638	82.3	628	86.0
21 065	...	Estill County	14 370	58.3	27.5	11.1	3.1	0.0	6 108	73.9	1 452	77.9
21 067	4280	Fayette County	244 455	42.5	29.2	13.5	11.4	3.4	108 288	55.3	17 060	73.5
21 069	...	Fleming County	12 882	61.3	23.8	8.7	5.9	0.4	5 367	78.8	1 227	83.0
21 071	...	Floyd County	39 873	68.3	19.7	6.4	5.2	0.5	16 881	76.2	3 786	86.3
21 073	...	Franklin County	44 777	51.1	28.2	12.3	6.9	1.5	19 907	64.8	4 502	77.2
21 075	...	Fulton County	7 282	56.2	21.9	8.1	13.0	0.8	3 237	64.2	1 008	76.3
21 077	1640	Gallatin County	7 265	54.8	16.5	19.3	9.4	0.1	2 902	77.0	458	71.4
21 079	...	Garrard County	13 904	52.0	19.7	22.6	5.0	0.6	5 741	76.4	1 192	82.2
21 081	1640	Grant County	20 596	51.4	19.2	20.8	8.0	0.6	8 175	74.1	1 365	79.8
21 083	...	Graves County	34 584	60.2	24.9	7.1	7.0	0.8	14 841	77.9	3 926	83.5
21 085	...	Grayson County	22 525	58.0	27.5	9.7	4.4	0.4	9 596	77.3	2 317	86.7
21 087	...	Green County	10 921	60.4	15.2	11.4	4.5	0.4	4 706	78.4	1 248	82.9
21 089	3400	Greenup County	34 736	64.2	18.8	8.6	8.1	0.3	14 536	81.8	3 693	88.5
21 091	...	Hancock County	7 799	57.4	22.7	11.5	8.0	0.3	3 215	82.5	659	82.5
21 093	...	Hardin County	87 416	48.5	23.5	7.7	16.9	3.3	34 497	66.9	5 743	82.3
21 095	...	Harlan County	31 168	70.3	23.9	3.0	2.4	0.3	13 291	73.5	3 289	82.5
21 097	...	Harrison County	16 819	55.2	25.4	13.0	6.1	0.3	7 012	70.5	1 658	77.0
21 099	...	Hart County	16 303	60.9	22.2	11.3	5.0	0.6	6 769	77.3	1 622	85.2
21 101	2440	Henderson County	42 006	55.5	29.6	6.3	8.1	0.5	18 095	67.3	4 180	76.8
21 103	...	Henry County	14 015	57.6	18.8	17.4	5.3	0.9	5 844	77.4	1 220	87.1
21 105	...	Hickman County	4 985	67.1	18.7	9.1	5.0	0.0	2 188	81.4	618	87.2
21 107	...	Hopkins County	43 705	61.9	25.7	6.3	5.6	0.4	18 820	74.7	4 566	83.9
21 109	...	Jackson County............	12 614	66.3	20.0	9.2	4.2	0.3	5 307	80.2	1 141	88.3
21 111	4520	Jefferson County	647 008	53.6	32.0	4.1	8.4	1.8	287 012	64.9	62 690	79.5
21 113	4280	Jessamine County........	36 159	47.4	20.8	18.5	12.4	0.9	13 867	67.1	2 192	80.4
21 115	...	Johnson County	22 018	65.3	23.5	6.9	3.8	0.5	9 103	76.4	2 001	87.9
21 117	1640	Kenton County	140 369	55.3	23.7	9.4	10.8	0.8	59 444	66.4	11 073	72.9
21 119	...	Knott County	10 007	71.9	17.6	6.7	3.1	0.6	6 717	79.6	1 407	87.5
21 121	...	Knox County	29 564	62.6	22.3	8.9	5.6	0.6	12 416	71.4	2 870	80.2
21 123	...	Larue County	12 575	60.1	20.5	15.0	4.2	0.2	5 275	80.3	1 405	82.9
21 125	...	Laurel County	48 965	59.3	21.8	11.7	6.8	0.4	20 353	77.0	4 158	84.9
21 127	...	Lawrence County	14 661	63.2	20.5	8.6	7.6	0.0	5 954	78.0	1 381	86.5
21 129	...	Lee County	7 513	82.9	19.1	12.0	5.8	0.2	2 985	76.8	795	80.6
21 131	...	Leslie County	11 640	75.1	17.3	5.7	1.8	0.1	4 885	82.1	1 013	86.0
21 133	...	Letcher County	23 868	72.6	19.0	4.0	4.1	0.2	10 085	80.8	2 363	86.9
21 135	...	Lewis County	13 218	68.6	19.8	5.6	5.8	0.2	5 422	81.2	1 201	87.1
21 137	...	Lincoln County	21 753	56.3	22.3	14.0	6.9	0.4	9 206	78.9	2 117	86.0
21 139	...	Livingston County	9 282	68.0	14.7	12.9	4.2	0.1	3 996	85.2	975	89.6
21 141	...	Logan County	24 745	56.0	27.3	7.9	7.4	0.5	10 506	75.2	2 594	84.7
21 143	...	Lyon County	7 777	67.2	9.4	16.3	6.5	0.6	2 898	82.2	876	88.9
21 145	...	McCracken County........	61 594	56.8	24.1	7.7	10.9	0.5	27 736	68.7	7 075	75.3
21 147	...	McCreary County	15 960	61.0	27.0	3.6	8.2	0.2	6 520	75.6	1 342	86.1
21 149	...	McLean County	9 279	63.2	20.5	11.5	4.1	0.7	3 984	80.3	1 032	84.2
21 151	4280	Madison County	66 370	44.0	27.0	18.1	9.8	1.0	27 152	59.7	4 482	77.8
21 153	...	Magoffin County	12 391	71.8	20.4	5.6	2.0	0.2	5 024	81.9	872	86.0
21 155	...	Marion County	17 011	63.0	21.0	11.7	3.1	1.2	6 613	78.2	1 450	85.2
21 157	...	Marshall County	28 535	64.1	17.9	9.3	8.2	0.5	12 412	82.6	3 444	87.5
21 159	...	Martin County...............	11 683	69.2	20.1	6.1	4.6	0.0	4 776	79.3	915	85.0
21 161	...	Mason County	15 731	59.0	24.3	9.2	6.6	0.8	6 847	67.4	1 707	75.6
21 163	...	Meade County	24 040	52.1	15.6	16.5	13.5	2.2	9 470	73.9	1 358	87.0
21 165	...	Menifee County	6 172	64.0	15.2	14.6	5.9	0.3	2 537	81.2	523	85.1
21 167	...	Mercer County	19 457	54.8	26.1	12.5	5.7	0.8	8 423	74.5	2 110	85.8
21 169	...	Metcalfe County	9 399	61.8	20.0	10.9	6.9	0.4	4 016	79.3	965	85.9
21 171	...	Monroe County	11 022	60.6	26.4	5.5	6.2	1.2	4 741	75.1	1 259	80.9
21 173	...	Montgomery County	21 026	54.9	25.6	13.2	5.8	0.5	8 902	71.5	2 083	75.7
21 175	...	Morgan County	13 190	64.4	16.3	13.4	5.5	0.4	4 752	79.9	1 223	85.4
21 177	...	Muhlenberg County	29 965	67.0	23.5	5.7	3.6	0.2	12 357	82.9	3 220	88.0
21 179	...	Nelson County	34 741	57.1	24.6	12.5	5.1	0.6	13 953	78.0	2 470	89.6
21 181	...	Nicholas County	6 385	58.5	22.5	13.9	5.0	0.1	2 710	74.8	624	73.4
21 183	...	Ohio County	21 500	62.8	23.1	9.7	4.0	0.5	8 899	80.2	2 285	86.4
21 185	4520	Oldham County	43 130	53.5	12.1	20.3	13.5	0.7	14 856	86.8	1 832	89.1
21 187	...	Owen County	9 917	57.3	19.3	17.4	5.6	0.4	4 086	78.2	1 033	82.5

[1]MSA = Metropolitan Statistical Area. PMSA = Primary MSA. NECMA = New England County Metropolitan Area. See the Appendix A for explanation of these concepts. See Appendix B for list of metropolitan areas identified by type, with component counties.

Table C-3. States and Counties — Migration, Housing, and Transportation

STATE County	Owner-occupied by household type (percent)								Median household income			Median housing value (owner estimated)	Median monthly owner costs as a percent of income	
		Family-households				Nonfamily households								
		Married-couple family		Other family										
	Total family households	Total	With own children under 18 years	Total	With own children under 18 years	Total nonfamily households	Two or more adults	Living alone	All households	Owner-occupied households	Renter-occupied households		With a mortgage	Without a mortgage
	11	12	13	14	15	16	17	18	19	20	21	22	23	24

KENTUCKY—Cont'd

STATE County	11	12	13	14	15	16	17	18	19	20	21	22	23	24
Cumberland County	82.8	86.9	76.1	67.5	56.4	65.8	60.5	66.1	21 590	25 014	14 426	50 800	20.9	10.8
Daviess County	76.9	82.8	79.7	53.7	43.8	55.4	45.4	56.7	36 803	45 350	20 836	80 600	18.4	9.9
Edmonson County	88.3	92.1	88.7	67.5	55.2	77.6	79.8	77.3	25 102	27 556	15 273	54 800	21.9	12.2
Elliott County	86.9	92.0	88.0	63.3	54.1	69.6	57.1	70.7	20 742	24 315	8 848	43 700	22.0	10.8
Estill County	77.9	83.7	79.2	57.7	50.2	63.1	74.3	62.1	23 859	29 346	13 750	44 900	21.4	9.9
Fayette County	68.7	77.5	75.9	41.6	32.9	36.4	24.0	40.2	39 568	57 236	24 463	109 700	19.2	9.9
Fleming County	81.6	86.1	82.5	61.8	50.9	71.1	71.1	71.1	28 154	31 539	17 381	58 400	18.9	9.9
Floyd County	79.5	83.3	77.6	64.7	51.3	67.1	68.4	67.1	21 074	25 065	11 212	43 300	21.0	9.9
Franklin County	73.1	81.0	74.1	46.1	33.4	49.7	37.9	51.6	39 664	50 575	24 603	89 200	18.5	9.9
Fulton County	70.8	80.2	73.5	48.3	37.3	51.8	48.1	52.1	24 002	30 785	12 416	42 600	18.4	10.1
Gallatin County	81.3	85.8	83.3	62.7	56.4	64.9	72.2	63.4	36 429	41 476	21 397	82 100	20.3	10.2
Garrard County	80.2	84.9	79.5	57.1	51.8	64.5	77.1	62.6	33 787	40 893	18 929	80 500	20.1	9.9
Grant County	77.8	81.6	76.3	63.6	55.2	62.3	61.5	62.4	39 232	44 060	27 039	84 200	20.6	9.9
Graves County	82.4	88.0	83.3	58.9	48.1	66.8	56.8	67.7	30 763	35 786	14 911	62 400	19.9	9.9
Grayson County	81.4	85.7	77.3	60.1	48.9	66.5	56.1	67.9	27 740	30 272	18 396	63 000	21.3	9.9
Green County	83.2	87.5	85.0	63.0	42.2	65.7	56.4	66.6	25 325	30 013	13 722	55 000	19.4	10.6
Greenup County	84.4	87.0	82.1	70.9	57.1	73.2	51.7	74.8	32 072	36 136	19 423	60 600	18.8	9.9
Hancock County	86.8	90.6	87.8	66.8	57.6	68.9	67.3	69.1	36 373	39 337	21 364	62 500	18.2	9.9
Hardin County	72.2	77.2	69.6	51.7	43.1	51.8	44.1	52.9	37 459	44 524	26 555	84 700	19.6	9.9
Harlan County	77.6	81.8	77.7	63.3	54.4	63.5	57.2	64.0	18 456	22 040	11 351	37 600	22.7	11.3
Harrison County	75.5	82.2	75.5	45.8	37.0	57.5	54.9	57.9	36 026	42 114	23 553	82 400	18.0	9.9
Hart County	80.3	86.1	84.0	57.0	48.7	69.8	54.8	71.8	25 835	29 539	16 680	58 100	20.3	10.3
Henderson County	75.7	83.7	77.2	43.5	30.8	47.9	40.1	49.0	35 551	45 837	19 838	72 900	18.2	9.9
Henry County	81.0	86.1	77.0	61.2	50.0	67.0	48.6	70.2	37 294	43 570	23 003	80 200	19.9	9.9
Hickman County	84.7	88.8	86.1	69.5	63.7	73.1	66.7	73.4	32 074	35 713	17 550	48 500	18.2	9.9
Hopkins County	79.9	85.9	82.2	57.3	43.3	61.8	56.4	62.3	30 708	34 870	19 865	52 400	18.3	9.9
Jackson County	84.1	87.9	86.5	68.9	63.8	68.7	69.1	68.6	20 384	22 102	11 630	44 000	25.9	11.3
Jefferson County	73.7	83.8	80.2	48.8	34.9	49.4	40.5	51.1	39 298	50 148	24 093	100 800	19.7	9.9
Jessamine County	71.5	75.8	71.3	52.7	42.5	52.4	41.5	54.9	40 024	50 248	26 049	98 700	20.4	9.9
Johnson County	79.3	83.9	79.3	58.9	41.6	67.4	62.1	67.8	24 786	27 937	15 280	51 200	19.7	11.0
Kenton County	76.5	84.3	83.5	52.1	40.1	46.3	38.2	48.0	43 855	54 507	26 378	102 900	19.6	9.9
Knott County	82.9	84.1	79.6	78.4	69.3	70.2	63.9	70.7	20 170	22 185	12 227	36 200	21.6	9.9
Knox County	76.2	82.5	74.5	55.3	40.3	59.3	57.6	59.5	18 648	22 307	11 773	43 500	23.6	10.9
Larue County	86.4	90.5	88.8	66.7	55.2	63.3	59.1	63.9	32 256	36 954	16 042	73 900	20.6	9.9
Laurel County	80.3	85.1	81.6	60.4	51.3	66.9	53.5	68.7	26 591	30 269	17 107	64 100	21.8	9.9
Lawrence County	80.3	83.7	81.2	64.6	43.7	71.0	70.5	71.1	21 797	25 126	13 228	43 300	20.4	9.9
Lee County	80.8	87.1	83.6	55.2	45.7	66.6	83.3	65.5	18 478	22 640	9 583	39 100	23.4	12.1
Leslie County	85.5	89.6	89.6	71.4	65.9	71.7	49.0	73.7	18 904	20 925	9 552	29 900	22.1	10.7
Letcher County	82.7	86.7	82.7	67.9	56.3	75.3	81.2	74.8	21 098	23 575	12 481	35 700	20.9	9.9
Lewis County	83.5	87.5	81.3	66.8	60.6	74.4	77.6	74.0	21 943	24 427	11 229	39 000	21.9	10.2
Lincoln County	82.0	86.0	81.1	63.9	52.3	70.5	43.8	73.9	27 100	30 614	17 440	60 800	20.2	11.0
Livingston County	90.2	91.8	89.4	81.5	80.2	72.1	65.2	73.1	31 605	33 440	24 538	56 400	19.1	9.9
Logan County	79.6	84.9	80.7	59.6	52.2	63.6	52.1	64.9	32 314	37 491	21 071	65 700	19.6	10.6
Lyon County	86.6	90.5	81.0	63.8	49.4	71.5	36.4	74.5	31 080	33 450	20 859	72 800	17.7	9.9
McCracken County	77.1	85.3	81.1	48.9	39.2	52.0	47.0	52.6	34 211	41 981	19 343	79 800	18.9	9.9
McCreary County	77.6	84.3	80.2	56.0	45.0	70.3	64.7	70.9	19 381	21 800	13 573	36 600	23.0	9.9
McLean County	84.6	89.1	84.3	65.6	55.9	68.8	71.7	68.5	29 176	32 409	15 141	52 000	18.1	10.7
Madison County	70.3	77.8	72.5	40.6	30.7	37.9	18.7	43.6	33 034	43 724	21 464	87 500	19.1	9.9
Magoffin County	84.7	88.0	87.1	73.0	61.4	72.5	52.8	73.8	19 469	21 918	10 717	36 700	22.0	14.3
Marion County	82.0	89.6	87.9	58.6	47.0	68.4	54.3	70.4	30 281	34 267	16 442	70 200	19.9	9.9
Marshall County	88.0	91.9	87.7	63.3	51.7	68.1	61.9	68.7	34 888	39 054	18 321	78 100	19.2	9.9
Martin County	83.1	87.0	84.9	68.5	56.3	67.0	58.5	67.8	18 460	20 628	9 614	44 500	23.5	12.0
Mason County	73.5	80.9	75.6	47.0	34.7	53.7	41.9	55.1	30 028	36 954	18 834	71 200	20.5	9.9
Meade County	76.0	78.6	71.1	63.3	52.2	66.0	53.2	68.3	37 403	41 113	28 367	75 500	19.5	9.9
Menifee County	84.1	88.3	81.1	62.3	43.6	72.2	86.5	70.3	21 912	25 125	10 208	47 100	26.4	10.1
Mercer County	78.0	83.7	75.3	53.1	34.8	65.4	57.6	66.3	35 286	40 998	21 684	85 000	19.2	9.9
Metcalfe County	83.4	87.1	84.9	66.7	53.9	68.6	75.3	68.1	23 675	27 716	13 848	52 200	19.9	11.8
Monroe County	79.4	85.7	80.2	57.6	47.0	64.2	49.4	65.2	22 411	26 952	11 892	56 000	22.5	11.3
Montgomery County	77.7	83.1	77.2	55.4	51.9	55.0	42.5	56.9	31 455	35 731	20 843	75 900	20.2	9.9
Morgan County	84.0	87.4	84.0	65.9	62.5	67.5	63.6	67.9	21 720	24 413	13 561	46 300	23.2	10.0
Muhlenberg County	87.9	92.0	88.5	68.2	54.7	69.1	64.3	69.5	28 523	31 241	13 601	51 600	18.9	9.9
Nelson County	82.6	89.3	86.3	60.2	52.4	65.2	61.0	65.9	38 589	43 627	20 433	86 500	19.1	9.9
Nicholas County	79.7	85.0	81.0	62.3	60.7	62.2	62.6	62.2	29 557	34 283	17 017	59 100	18.4	9.9
Ohio County	83.0	87.4	83.6	62.8	51.9	72.2	66.7	72.8	28 774	32 336	17 438	52 100	18.2	10.2
Oldham County	90.4	93.5	92.1	69.7	60.0	69.7	71.8	69.3	63 321	69 889	25 932	158 700	19.6	9.9
Owen County	82.2	84.9	80.7	69.0	52.2	66.9	73.8	65.9	33 114	38 474	19 855	72 000	21.5	9.9

STATE County	Percent who pay 35 percent or more of income for housing expenses			Means of transportation to work (percent except where noted)						Vehicles available (percent of households)		
				Number of workers 16 years and over	Car, truck, or van							
	Median gross rent	Owners	Renters		Drove alone	Carpooled	Public transportation	Other means	Walked	No vehicles	One vehicle	Two or more vehicles
	25	26	27	28	29	30	31	32	33	34	35	36
KENTUCKY—Cont'd												
Cumberland County	242	14.9	14.3	2 756	76.9	18.3	0.0	0.4	1.7	12.6	30.7	56.7
Daviess County	415	9.6	24.7	42 298	85.1	10.3	0.3	0.8	1.5	8.0	32.7	59.3
Edmonson County........	310	17.6	17.0	4 606	76.9	14.6	0.4	0.9	1.8	7.6	28.4	64.1
Elliott County	232	15.8	30.8	2 109	66.1	26.4	0.5	1.0	1.8	13.0	32.1	54.9
Estill County	332	12.1	26.7	5 351	77.1	19.0	0.3	1.0	1.3	13.5	29.5	57.0
Fayette County............	528	11.0	30.6	136 793	79.9	11.2	1.3	1.1	4.0	7.9	39.0	53.1
Fleming County	318	10.4	17.4	5 895	77.4	14.5	0.4	0.7	2.6	9.9	29.3	60.9
Floyd County	332	12.2	27.0	12 284	80.6	14.1	0.2	0.8	2.1	13.9	35.7	50.4
Franklin County	482	8.9	26.3	23 288	79.7	14.6	0.5	0.6	2.1	8.1	36.1	55.7
Fulton County...............	343	17.1	28.3	2 787	77.6	18.4	0.0	1.0	0.4	14.6	38.9	46.6
Gallatin County	422	13.6	21.6	3 589	76.0	15.2	0.2	1.8	3.4	7.6	28.8	63.6
Garrard County	390	13.3	26.5	6 786	75.9	18.0	0.3	0.5	1.1	6.1	27.4	66.5
Grant County	505	12.7	20.6	10 262	78.7	15.6	0.6	0.7	1.3	5.1	28.0	66.9
Graves County	354	12.3	28.7	15 614	81.0	12.3	0.3	1.6	1.5	9.0	32.3	58.7
Grayson County	353	12.9	20.0	9 919	75.9	18.0	0.2	0.7	1.7	8.8	29.3	61.9
Green County...............	326	14.5	28.8	4 733	79.3	13.4	0.3	0.8	1.6	8.7	30.5	60.8
Greenup County...........	412	12.2	21.5	13 798	85.5	10.2	0.2	0.6	1.5	6.1	31.6	62.3
Hancock County	438	11.7	20.5	3 705	87.5	8.4	0.2	0.7	0.6	4.9	23.6	71.5
Hardin County	443	11.5	19.0	44 815	79.3	11.6	0.7	1.9	3.1	6.5	31.1	62.4
Harlan County	306	15.5	24.6	8 742	80.6	13.0	1.1	1.4	2.5	16.4	37.8	45.8
Harrison County	403	9.9	19.2	8 293	78.6	14.8	0.3	0.4	1.5	6.8	31.5	61.7
Hart County	312	13.5	21.9	6 945	73.2	15.2	0.6	0.4	2.0	11.1	29.9	59.0
Henderson County	408	9.4	23.3	20 810	82.8	12.2	0.6	1.0	1.3	8.8	34.2	57.0
Henry County	444	12.2	19.4	6 993	76.6	16.8	0.3	0.7	1.9	7.1	28.5	64.4
Hickman County	282	17.2	16.0	2 164	80.0	13.7	0.7	1.0	2.0	7.9	30.0	62.2
Hopkins County	363	11.8	21.5	19 065	83.3	12.7	0.2	0.9	1.2	9.7	31.5	58.9
Jackson County............	301	18.3	26.8	4 514	74.0	19.3	0.6	0.4	2.1	12.6	30.2	57.2
Jefferson County..........	494	12.7	27.2	329 091	80.8	11.0	3.1	0.8	2.0	11.3	37.5	51.2
Jessamine County........	535	12.4	27.0	18 885	78.5	13.4	0.2	0.8	3.4	6.5	28.2	65.3
Johnson County	338	16.3	24.1	7 943	81.1	14.1	0.5	0.8	1.7	10.8	34.2	55.1
Kenton County..............	517	10.2	25.3	76 169	80.8	11.0	3.4	0.7	2.1	10.0	33.6	56.4
Knott County	293	15.8	22.4	4 987	76.1	15.1	0.8	1.4	4.1	12.6	37.1	50.3
Knox County.................	327	19.5	30.9	9 880	80.1	14.3	0.4	1.0	2.4	14.7	36.6	48.7
Larue County	342	12.6	24.2	5 827	80.8	11.4	0.1	1.0	1.8	7.2	26.1	66.7
Laurel County	377	14.6	26.0	21 180	81.1	13.3	0.3	0.9	1.8	9.1	32.2	58.8
Lawrence County	362	11.9	27.7	4 800	77.5	16.3	0.4	1.0	2.1	11.8	32.9	55.3
Lee County..................	268	20.8	24.4	2 188	77.3	17.4	0.4	1.9	2.1	12.6	30.0	60.7
Leslie County	278	14.7	22.7	3 360	79.2	14.4	2.0	1.0	2.4	13.9	34.8	51.3
Letcher County............	309	13.5	21.9	7 582	81.8	13.0	0.8	1.0	1.7	12.7	36.1	51.1
Lewis County	269	15.0	17.6	4 851	73.9	19.3	0.3	0.9	2.1	10.9	31.9	57.2
Lincoln County	378	15.3	18.1	9 683	78.1	14.6	0.2	0.9	2.1	8.3	30.3	61.4
Livingston County.........	362	10.2	21.3	4 431	86.8	7.6	0.3	0.7	1.9	5.4	26.9	67.7
Logan County	415	13.6	23.1	12 167	81.4	12.1	0.3	1.0	1.6	8.3	29.6	62.1
Lyon County.................	398	11.2	27.4	2 739	86.7	9.7	0.0	0.8	0.9	5.7	29.0	65.3
McCracken County.......	419	12.6	26.8	28 888	84.9	9.6	0.7	1.0	1.1	8.7	36.2	55.0
McCreary County	320	15.5	25.5	5 345	77.0	17.2	0.5	1.3	1.3	12.0	38.5	49.5
McLean County	318	9.0	22.4	4 206	83.5	12.1	0.2	0.0	1.8	7.0	30.9	62.1
Madison County	428	11.9	28.7	34 494	77.1	12.6	0.6	0.8	6.2	7.7	32.8	59.6
Magoffin County	294	21.7	31.4	3 795	72.2	20.5	1.4	0.9	2.5	15.5	31.8	52.7
Marion County	353	11.6	24.2	7 543	76.3	16.5	0.8	0.6	1.7	10.4	27.4	62.2
Marshall County	407	11.1	22.1	13 162	83.1	11.1	0.2	1.0	1.7	4.7	29.8	65.5
Martin County	286	18.2	25.5	3 038	78.4	16.2	0.8	1.6	1.2	14.4	34.7	50.8
Mason County..............	369	12.7	24.7	7 560	76.8	14.6	1.2	0.7	2.5	9.3	33.5	57.2
Meade County..............	431	12.8	13.1	11 466	83.0	13.0	0.0	0.8	0.6	5.1	27.5	67.4
Menifee County	233	22.8	23.5	2 261	68.8	22.6	0.2	1.9	3.2	8.7	30.7	60.7
Mercer County..............	411	9.3	21.0	9 610	81.8	13.2	0.0	0.2	1.4	7.2	29.4	63.5
Metcalfe County	310	14.5	24.7	4 094	79.3	11.7	1.3	0.5	1.2	7.6	30.0	62.4
Monroe County.............	304	16.2	26.7	4 707	79.6	12.0	0.3	0.9	2.5	12.0	30.7	57.2
Montgomery County	420	14.3	22.5	9 872	81.4	14.5	0.2	0.7	1.4	10.0	29.8	60.1
Morgan County.............	310	18.7	23.5	4 241	73.8	18.5	0.6	0.7	3.7	11.2	32.9	55.9
Muhlenberg County.......	330	12.2	23.3	11 797	80.9	13.3	0.4	1.4	1.6	8.0	30.7	61.3
Nelson County..............	426	10.1	24.1	17 594	81.8	12.6	0.3	0.6	1.4	6.0	28.2	65.8
Nicholas County	296	8.2	18.3	2 037	72.4	22.0	0.1	1.0	1.1	11.6	28.6	59.8
Ohio County	350	14.0	22.9	9 290	77.7	16.0	0.3	1.3	1.6	8.4	27.9	63.7
Oldham County	499	11.0	20.3	21 716	85.5	8.8	0.4	0.5	0.9	2.8	20.4	76.8
Owen County	357	16.6	19.2	4 543	71.4	20.8	0.4	0.8	1.8	6.9	29.0	64.1

Items 25—36

Table C-3. States and Counties — Migration, Housing, and Transportation

STATE/ County code	MSA/PMSA/ NECMA code[1]	STATE County	Total population 5 years and over	Same house	Same county, different house	Same state, different county	Different state	Outside the United States	Occupied housing units Number	Percent owner-occupied	Householders 65 years and over Number	Percent owner-occupied
			1	2	3	4	5	6	7	8	9	10
		KENTUCKY—Cont'd										
21 189	...	Owsley County	4 574	70.9	17.2	8.3	3.6	0.0	1 894	78.4	441	77.3
21 191	1640	Pendleton County..........	13 400	57.2	20.1	17.4	4.9	0.5	5 170	77.9	954	82.1
21 193	...	Perry County	27 672	72.2	18.6	5.6	3.3	0.2	11 460	77.4	2 479	84.0
21 195	...	Pike County	64 554	67.5	23.5	3.8	4.8	0.3	27 612	78.7	6 043	84.6
21 197	...	Powell County	12 323	56.6	26.3	13.4	3.7	0.1	5 044	74.0	975	83.2
21 199	...	Pulaski County	52 874	58.2	25.5	7.7	8.0	0.7	22 719	76.0	5 612	85.5
21 201	...	Robertson County	2 135	60.4	18.6	16.1	4.9	0.1	866	77.9	221	82.8
21 203	...	Rockcastle County	15 583	64.1	22.1	9.3	4.5	0.1	6 544	79.6	1 519	86.6
21 205	...	Rowan County..............	20 919	50.3	20.9	19.3	8.0	1.6	7 927	69.7	1 609	81.0
21 207	...	Russell County	15 415	64.4	22.3	7.5	5.5	0.3	6 941	79.4	1 763	85.4
21 209	4280	Scott County	30 583	44.9	23.3	21.5	8.7	1.5	12 110	69.8	1 920	76.9
21 211	...	Shelby County	30 945	49.0	22.7	18.2	7.3	2.8	12 104	72.7	2 251	84.5
21 213	...	Simpson County	15 204	53.5	28.1	8.7	8.7	1.0	6 415	71.8	1 500	80.1
21 215	...	Spencer County	10 907	49.9	15.2	27.3	6.8	0.7	4 251	82.6	574	84.3
21 217	...	Taylor County..............	21 598	58.5	26.0	10.2	4.9	0.4	9 233	72.3	2 442	79.9
21 219	...	Todd County	11 087	60.7	19.2	8.4	11.0	0.7	4 569	76.5	1 166	87.8
21 221	...	Trigg County	11 843	60.7	17.2	8.7	12.2	1.1	5 215	81.3	1 423	88.8
21 223	...	Trimble County	7 580	54.6	18.8	14.8	11.4	0.4	3 137	80.6	693	83.4
21 225	...	Union County	14 677	60.7	20.4	7.7	9.8	1.3	5 710	77.9	1 385	87.4
21 227	...	Warren County	86 711	45.7	26.8	12.9	12.3	2.4	35 365	64.0	6 427	79.0
21 229	...	Washington County	10 258	62.6	18.7	13.3	5.0	0.4	4 121	79.9	1 083	86.9
21 231	...	Wayne County..............	18 581	63.3	24.4	5.6	5.8	0.8	7 913	76.4	1 923	81.9
21 233	...	Webster County	13 241	60.2	19.9	11.9	6.4	1.5	5 560	78.0	1 439	84.2
21 235	...	Whitley County	33 566	61.6	21.3	9.5	7.0	0.6	13 780	72.7	3 004	80.9
21 237	...	Wolfe County	6 605	64.7	21.0	8.7	5.0	0.5	2 816	73.8	516	78.3
21 239	4280	Woodford County	21 808	55.0	17.2	17.9	8.4	1.5	8 893	72.4	1 550	80.5
22 000	...	LOUISIANA	4 153 367	59.0	24.5	9.3	6.1	1.0	1 656 053	67.9	347 218	80.5
22 001	3880	Acadia Parish	54 250	64.3	22.7	8.0	4.5	0.5	21 142	72.2	4 732	85.5
22 003	...	Allen Parish	23 782	57.0	17.8	9.5	15.4	0.3	8 102	76.0	1 994	86.6
22 005	0760	Ascension Parish	70 403	59.6	20.6	14.0	4.9	0.9	26 691	82.2	3 924	85.9
22 007	...	Assumption Parish	21 758	72.0	15.9	10.4	1.3	0.4	8 239	84.1	1 834	88.4
22 009	...	Avoyelles Parish...........	38 630	67.2	21.9	7.0	3.6	0.3	14 736	74.4	3 695	81.2
22 011	...	Beauregard Parish	30 731	57.9	22.1	12.4	6.7	0.8	12 104	79.8	2 550	88.4
22 013	...	Bienville Parish.............	14 747	66.4	19.1	9.9	4.4	0.2	6 108	77.8	1 816	84.7
22 015	7680	Bossier Parish	90 997	50.5	21.4	12.7	13.6	1.8	36 628	69.5	6 899	84.4
22 017	7680	Caddo Parish	234 713	55.1	30.5	6.1	7.4	0.9	97 974	63.8	22 314	80.1
22 019	3960	Calcasieu Parish	170 236	55.5	31.2	5.7	6.9	0.7	68 613	71.5	14 563	83.4
22 021	...	Caldwell Parish	9 905	60.5	21.5	13.3	4.5	0.2	3 941	79.2	968	83.0
22 023	...	Cameron Parish	9 349	68.7	14.0	13.5	3.1	0.7	3 592	85.2	704	92.8
22 025	...	Catahoula Parish	10 219	67.4	18.8	10.9	2.6	0.3	4 082	83.0	1 062	85.6
22 027	...	Claiborne Parish	15 856	59.9	24.5	9.3	6.1	0.2	6 270	75.8	1 907	87.9
22 029	...	Concordia Parish	18 773	65.2	20.3	6.3	7.7	0.5	7 521	76.1	1 967	87.2
22 031	...	De Soto Parish	23 700	65.5	18.5	11.6	3.8	0.6	9 691	76.6	2 612	82.4
22 033	0760	East Baton Rouge Parish	383 818	51.8	29.6	10.1	6.7	1.8	156 365	61.6	27 265	81.6
22 035	...	East Carroll Parish	8 706	64.8	21.0	6.7	5.6	1.8	2 969	62.1	795	77.7
22 037	...	East Feliciana Parish	19 975	63.1	13.3	20.9	2.2	0.6	6 699	82.4	1 468	85.1
22 039	...	Evangeline Parish	32 603	64.3	22.7	9.3	3.1	0.6	12 736	69.4	3 124	74.0
22 041	...	Franklin Parish	19 738	65.0	23.0	8.4	3.3	0.4	7 754	76.2	2 111	84.7
22 043	...	Grant Parish	17 295	61.8	19.8	13.5	4.7	0.2	7 073	81.7	1 637	90.3
22 045	...	Iberia Parish	67 467	64.8	24.9	6.6	3.0	0.6	25 381	73.4	5 439	83.5
22 047	...	Iberville Parish.............	31 127	66.3	17.2	14.2	2.0	0.3	10 674	77.3	2 321	84.3
22 049	...	Jackson Parish.............	14 425	64.3	21.5	11.0	3.2	0.1	6 086	77.3	1 739	86.9
22 051	5560	Jefferson Parish	425 529	61.4	23.7	8.4	5.0	1.4	176 234	63.9	36 284	78.3
22 053	...	Jefferson Davis Parish ..	29 034	65.3	22.1	8.3	3.9	0.3	11 480	74.9	2 800	82.6
22 055	3880	Lafayette Parish	176 774	53.3	27.4	11.6	6.3	1.4	72 372	66.1	12 176	79.3
22 057	3350	Lafourche Parish	83 754	66.9	22.2	7.6	2.7	0.6	32 057	77.9	6 809	87.3
22 059	...	La Salle Parish	13 419	60.7	22.9	11.2	4.9	0.3	5 291	83.5	1 391	89.9
22 061	...	Lincoln Parish	39 947	49.8	20.9	17.9	9.6	1.8	15 235	59.9	3 174	80.8
22 063	0760	Livingston Parish	84 981	58.1	19.5	16.4	5.6	0.4	32 630	83.8	5 496	88.4
22 065	...	Madison Parish	12 614	60.8	23.4	9.2	5.6	1.0	4 469	61.9	1 032	83.0
22 067	...	Morehouse Parish	28 876	63.7	26.2	5.4	4.5	0.2	11 382	71.6	3 055	79.8
22 069	...	Natchitoches Parish	36 319	56.2	22.3	14.1	6.5	0.9	14 263	64.5	3 544	80.6
22 071	5560	Orleans Parish	451 739	56.8	28.6	6.0	7.1	1.4	188 251	46.5	38 961	63.4
22 073	5200	Ouachita Parish............	136 644	56.3	28.8	8.5	6.0	0.4	55 216	64.1	11 919	77.2
22 075	5560	Plaquemines Parish	24 841	65.5	16.4	12.1	5.3	0.6	9 021	78.9	1 779	90.8

[1] MSA = Metropolitan Statistical Area. PMSA = Primary MSA. NECMA = New England County Metropolitan Area. See the Appendix A for explanation of these concepts. See Appendix B for list of metropolitan areas identified by type, with component counties.

STATE County	Owner-occupied by household type (percent)								Median household income				Median monthly owner costs as a percent of income	
	Family-households					Nonfamily households								
	Married-couple family			Other family										
	Total family households	Total	With own children under 18 years	Total	With own children under 18 years	Total nonfamily households	Two or more adults	Living alone	All households	Owner-occupied households	Renter-occupied households	Median housing value (owner estimated)	With a mortgage	Without a mortgage
	11	12	13	14	15	16	17	18	19	20	21	22	23	24
KENTUCKY—Cont'd														
Owsley County	82.1	87.6	89.2	66.7	63.2	68.1	69.2	68.0	16 059	19 171	7 623	34 500	26.4	18.3
Pendleton County	81.4	86.3	80.6	55.8	50.2	65.8	68.9	65.4	37 959	43 367	22 177	78 800	20.5	9.9
Perry County	81.0	85.7	82.3	65.1	55.3	66.7	71.2	66.3	22 254	25 772	11 220	41 300	21.0	9.9
Pike County	82.1	86.4	82.6	65.6	52.8	69.2	67.3	69.3	23 700	26 946	14 068	49 100	21.6	9.9
Powell County	76.7	80.6	73.5	62.3	54.9	66.1	64.2	66.5	25 663	29 323	17 957	53 800	22.0	10.3
Pulaski County	80.6	85.0	78.5	61.3	48.8	63.8	55.2	64.7	27 197	30 873	15 461	64 800	19.1	9.9
Robertson County	79.2	84.4	72.6	58.1	46.6	74.7	66.7	75.8	30 291	35 107	14 531	60 900	16.9	9.9
Rockcastle County	83.9	87.0	81.5	71.4	60.3	67.8	71.8	67.4	23 810	28 098	10 923	45 200	21.6	10.1
Rowan County	78.0	84.3	80.0	53.2	46.9	53.8	22.3	62.4	27 800	33 651	15 055	65 700	19.2	9.9
Russell County	83.6	87.9	81.1	64.0	51.2	69.9	72.6	69.6	22 347	25 216	14 010	54 100	23.3	10.5
Scott County	75.1	80.9	76.3	51.8	40.3	54.2	47.7	55.5	46 443	57 853	26 595	105 500	17.9	9.9
Shelby County	77.4	83.6	79.3	51.2	43.2	58.4	43.6	61.8	45 299	53 698	26 216	122 600	19.8	9.9
Simpson County	74.0	70.0	73.1	54.4	45.8	64.0	53.1	65.5	36 218	40 506	27 250	81 100	20.7	9.9
Spencer County	86.3	89.6	86.6	64.7	51.8	67.8	71.4	67.2	47 351	50 050	21 929	114 200	20.1	9.9
Taylor County	77.0	85.0	79.5	46.7	38.5	60.4	61.8	60.3	28 562	33 693	15 636	70 000	20.5	9.9
Todd County	78.8	83.3	75.1	62.8	52.5	70.1	52.0	72.2	29 476	32 892	20 471	57 800	18.6	10.8
Trigg County	82.9	86.7	81.5	62.7	52.8	77.3	66.4	78.5	32 774	35 662	26 745	71 300	19.6	9.9
Trimble County	83.1	86.7	81.3	67.4	57.9	73.5	70.7	74.1	36 070	40 206	23 201	74 400	20.2	9.9
Union County	82.7	88.9	83.8	61.1	50.3	66.1	67.7	65.9	34 227	39 398	19 778	56 200	18.7	9.9
Warren County	74.0	81.4	77.3	46.0	38.0	43.6	23.3	49.0	36 250	46 406	22 158	95 300	19.4	9.9
Washington County	83.7	89.5	83.1	57.6	48.3	69.4	42.1	72.5	32 412	36 521	18 233	73 700	20.1	9.9
Wayne County	80.8	85.4	80.9	61.7	54.5	63.9	67.8	63.6	20 830	24 267	12 154	44 000	20.2	10.5
Webster County	82.6	85.6	78.8	70.2	63.0	65.5	46.1	67.3	31 336	35 159	19 560	44 200	17.5	9.9
Whitley County	78.3	83.7	78.8	59.9	49.5	58.1	39.5	60.0	21 898	26 490	11 653	49 500	20.5	10.4
Wolfe County	79.2	83.6	77.3	64.7	60.9	60.4	39.5	61.6	20 046	22 985	11 426	37 900	25.2	9.9
Woodford County	78.2	83.8	81.8	52.6	40.5	54.7	40.9	57.2	48 380	58 759	27 573	119 700	19.0	9.9
LOUISIANA	74.4	83.8	80.0	52.0	41.0	52.8	39.7	55.2	32 427	40 554	20 138	77 500	19.6	9.9
Acadia Parish	74.8	83.9	80.0	48.5	34.8	64.6	57.4	65.6	26 541	32 157	15 286	54 800	18.3	10.4
Allen Parish	77.7	82.7	78.2	61.1	49.1	71.2	60.0	72.1	27 902	31 928	17 865	51 800	20.8	9.9
Ascension Parish	85.6	91.2	89.7	67.2	59.8	70.1	65.8	70.9	40 570	50 001	22 141	89 900	18.5	9.9
Assumption Parish	86.5	91.0	89.3	72.8	67.2	76.3	70.6	77.3	31 635	34 712	16 793	58 400	17.7	9.9
Avoyelles Parish	77.5	85.8	80.6	55.8	45.1	66.5	66.5	66.5	23 873	28 179	12 342	52 000	20.8	9.9
Beauregard Parish	83.4	87.8	83.4	64.6	57.7	69.3	45.6	72.4	33 012	35 790	23 889	55 600	18.1	9.9
Bienville Parish	79.9	88.2	83.7	61.9	51.0	73.1	68.1	73.4	23 619	27 741	12 716	40 600	19.7	11.4
Bossier Parish	74.2	81.7	76.4	51.9	40.5	56.4	42.7	58.6	38 961	46 119	25 277	79 000	19.1	9.9
Caddo Parish	70.0	81.2	74.9	49.6	35.9	51.6	41.4	53.2	31 453	41 077	20 253	70 600	19.1	9.9
Calcasieu Parish	77.4	85.3	80.8	54.4	42.5	56.7	44.1	59.1	35 346	42 162	20 825	70 300	17.8	9.9
Caldwell Parish	82.5	88.9	84.2	60.5	47.0	70.8	67.8	71.2	27 247	32 238	12 327	46 400	19.3	11.0
Cameron Parish	86.5	92.6	88.7	70.7	60.7	75.1	67.7	76.3	34 482	36 548	23 021	51 000	17.7	9.9
Catahoula Parish	87.0	92.8	89.0	70.0	61.3	71.6	75.4	71.3	22 012	25 506	12 467	38 000	19.2	11.2
Claiborne Parish	77.9	86.5	81.2	60.7	45.6	70.9	73.1	70.7	25 435	31 121	14 060	48 300	21.1	11.2
Concordia Parish	78.6	87.7	83.2	59.9	49.4	69.5	55.5	70.7	22 386	26 584	12 540	47 200	21.5	11.7
De Soto Parish	80.0	87.9	83.1	62.0	49.1	68.1	57.3	69.3	28 357	32 311	14 519	53 600	18.9	11.2
East Baton Rouge Parish	71.1	82.2	79.1	47.0	36.6	43.2	22.9	48.7	37 090	51 003	21 759	96 600	19.2	9.9
East Carroll Parish	64.6	78.3	66.9	47.7	35.3	55.4	36.8	56.8	19 755	25 896	11 413	36 200	25.8	13.3
East Feliciana Parish	84.9	90.4	87.0	71.9	68.0	74.6	56.5	76.1	32 277	35 744	16 898	67 000	20.2	9.9
Evangeline Parish	74.1	84.1	79.3	47.0	39.8	57.1	53.7	57.3	20 339	28 158	9 309	48 300	20.4	10.2
Franklin Parish	78.6	86.8	83.8	58.3	40.0	69.5	64.8	70.0	23 079	26 486	12 220	42 400	20.9	12.0
Grant Parish	82.6	89.2	84.0	61.1	49.1	79.1	64.9	81.1	29 289	31 507	16 506	50 900	19.8	10.0
Iberia Parish	76.8	85.9	82.2	54.1	42.4	62.9	58.1	63.7	31 258	37 115	16 258	64 700	18.6	9.9
Iberville Parish	80.8	88.4	84.8	65.9	58.8	66.6	61.9	67.2	29 339	33 672	16 892	64 000	18.4	9.9
Jackson Parish	79.6	85.3	79.4	63.3	49.0	71.7	57.8	72.7	28 075	32 609	14 831	49 900	18.5	10.1
Jefferson Parish	72.2	81.1	77.5	50.2	35.9	45.9	36.6	47.6	38 239	47 517	26 110	102 800	20.5	9.9
Jefferson Davis Parish	78.8	85.4	81.9	58.1	44.6	63.4	55.6	64.3	27 329	32 041	16 042	56 400	19.5	10.6
Lafayette Parish	76.1	85.1	83.6	51.9	43.9	45.1	34.6	48.0	36 384	46 096	22 104	91 400	18.6	9.9
Lafourche Parish	82.3	89.1	86.3	58.7	49.1	64.2	50.2	67.4	34 592	38 676	20 891	71 100	18.4	9.9
La Salle Parish	85.3	89.2	84.0	66.8	58.9	78.8	52.5	81.5	28 136	31 017	17 250	43 300	19.1	12.7
Lincoln Parish	70.7	82.0	79.4	43.8	31.6	41.0	13.2	50.6	27 039	41 023	12 472	72 300	19.7	9.9
Livingston Parish	86.7	90.1	87.1	71.6	65.9	73.3	70.4	73.9	38 927	42 018	26 819	79 600	19.4	9.9
Madison Parish	62.3	78.5	68.5	37.4	24.5	61.0	60.9	61.0	20 582	27 026	13 401	43 900	21.7	11.7
Morehouse Parish	75.4	85.3	76.7	55.1	39.5	61.0	53.3	61.7	25 082	31 799	12 608	46 600	19.7	10.4
Natchitoches Parish	70.7	81.9	77.4	45.6	35.9	51.6	30.9	55.9	25 414	33 092	12 666	61 500	20.2	9.9
Orleans Parish	54.3	71.1	66.5	36.1	24.5	34.6	29.4	35.6	27 129	42 157	17 827	88 100	22.9	11.4
Ouachita Parish	70.8	82.7	78.1	45.0	34.9	48.7	33.2	51.4	31 649	42 149	18 289	74 000	18.9	9.9
Plaquemines Parish	81.0	84.5	81.1	68.9	53.9	71.5	59.4	74.0	37 803	40 009	31 415	68 900	19.8	9.9

STATE County	Percent who pay 35 percent or more of income for housing expenses			Means of transportation to work (percent except where noted)						Vehicles available (percent of households)		
					Car, truck, or van							
	Median gross rent	Owners	Renters	Number of workers 16 years and over	Drove alone	Carpooled	Public transportation	Other means	Walked	No vehicles	One vehicle	Two or more vehicles
	25	26	27	28	29	30	31	32	33	34	35	36
KENTUCKY—Cont'd												
Owsley County	276	23.7	29.8	1 339	71.8	20.8	0.0	1.3	2.2	14.8	37.4	47.8
Pendleton County..........	428	11.5	23.4	6 467	76.2	16.8	0.8	0.9	2.2	6.6	26.4	67.0
Perry County	302	12.1	24.0	8 811	79.5	15.3	1.1	0.8	1.5	15.1	34.3	50.6
Pike County	352	14.4	27.9	21 600	82.7	11.2	0.4	0.9	3.0	12.0	33.8	54.2
Powell County	406	16.4	26.9	5 223	75.9	18.8	0.3	1.0	1.7	9.3	33.9	56.8
Pulaski County	360	11.9	27.9	22 884	82.5	11.6	0.3	0.7	1.5	8.6	33.0	58.5
Robertson County	250	14.0	16.1	922	72.1	20.3	0.4	1.2	1.1	7.3	31.8	61.0
Rockcastle County	282	15.5	21.9	6 418	74.2	18.6	0.5	1.1	1.8	11.6	30.4	58.1
Rowan County	421	10.2	26.2	9 560	74.4	13.9	0.3	0.6	8.5	9.0	33.0	58.0
Russell County	313	17.0	26.1	6 463	82.8	11.0	0.0	0.6	1.5	9.8	32.9	57.3
Scott County	513	8.6	22.4	16 536	80.3	12.9	0.3	0.8	2.5	5.8	29.3	64.8
Shelby County	495	12.8	20.4	16 726	79.1	12.9	0.9	0.6	2.2	6.5	25.1	68.4
Simpson County............	469	13.0	17.2	7 726	79.1	15.6	0.3	0.7	1.6	8.4	30.4	61.2
Spencer County	426	7.0	18.8	5 896	83.8	12.4	0.2	0.5	0.5	4.7	20.5	74.8
Taylor County	349	13.5	24.2	9 769	79.9	12.2	0.1	0.8	3.6	9.5	32.7	57.8
Todd County	388	11.9	22.9	5 411	73.9	15.3	0.3	1.9	2.0	11.5	30.3	58.2
Trigg County	399	14.3	17.6	5 448	82.1	11.9	0.1	1.2	1.4	7.0	28.3	64.7
Trimble County..............	392	13.0	19.7	3 680	76.8	17.8	0.1	1.2	1.1	5.8	28.6	65.6
Union County	337	12.2	20.9	6 742	76.4	15.8	0.5	1.2	3.8	6.6	29.9	63.5
Warren County	490	12.8	27.8	46 106	79.7	13.1	0.5	0.9	3.4	7.4	32.8	59.8
Washington County	352	12.2	18.7	4 787	77.5	12.8	0.3	1.1	3.6	7.5	31.0	61.5
Wayne County	313	15.3	28.7	7 281	82.4	12.2	0.3	0.7	1.7	11.1	31.6	57.3
Webster County	331	11.0	21.5	6 063	77.2	17.0	0.3	0.8	2.2	8.1	27.0	64.9
Whitley County	352	13.5	28.9	12 746	76.6	16.1	0.9	1.0	3.0	11.8	35.8	52.5
Wolfe County	250	16.3	21.4	2 202	68.9	23.9	1.3	1.0	1.8	12.3	32.9	54.8
Woodford County	488	8.9	22.3	12 377	83.1	11.1	0.0	0.4	1.9	5.9	26.0	68.1
LOUISIANA	466	14.2	29.8	1 831 057	78.1	13.6	2.4	1.6	2.2	11.9	37.0	51.1
Acadia Parish	332	13.1	24.5	21 064	79.3	14.9	0.2	1.6	2.4	11.1	36.3	52.6
Allen Parish	350	15.5	21.7	7 819	78.5	15.8	0.5	2.3	0.9	8.8	39.2	52.0
Ascension Parish	450	10.2	20.6	34 633	85.0	10.2	0.1	1.1	1.7	6.9	30.5	62.7
Assumption Parish	368	10.0	19.1	8 597	76.9	16.6	0.3	1.4	3.0	12.6	32.1	55.2
Avoyelles Parish...........	320	16.3	28.6	13 892	76.8	17.0	0.5	2.0	2.0	12.9	36.4	50.6
Beauregard Parish	383	12.1	18.0	12 616	79.6	14.1	0.6	1.8	1.5	7.6	34.1	58.3
Bienville Parish.............	335	15.6	25.2	5 243	75.4	18.7	0.4	1.6	2.0	15.5	35.4	49.1
Bossier Parish..............	488	11.0	22.4	45 520	83.4	11.6	0.7	1.4	1.3	7.7	34.0	58.3
Caddo Parish	463	13.7	29.7	104 075	79.9	13.4	2.3	1.1	1.6	12.8	38.5	48.7
Calcasieu Parish	465	10.7	27.8	77 899	83.6	11.3	0.4	1.4	1.6	8.0	37.2	54.8
Caldwell Parish	334	15.5	28.7	3 851	77.5	18.0	0.3	0.9	2.1	10.7	34.6	54.7
Cameron Parish	412	9.2	17.6	4 071	79.9	14.2	0.1	1.4	1.4	6.6	35.4	58.1
Catahoula Parish...........	267	15.3	20.2	3 591	76.9	15.5	0.7	2.9	2.4	11.7	32.5	55.8
Claiborne Parish...........	318	13.0	25.3	5 586	77.8	15.5	0.7	1.3	2.7	13.8	35.6	50.7
Concordia Parish	305	17.2	34.0	6 725	79.9	14.0	0.1	2.3	1.4	13.4	39.3	47.3
De Soto Parish.............	313	14.1	21.6	9 421	78.3	16.9	0.5	1.5	1.5	13.2	32.3	54.4
East Baton Rouge Parish	510	13.6	32.9	188 996	81.2	11.6	1.4	1.1	2.3	8.7	37.8	53.5
East Carroll Parish	277	21.6	26.8	2 646	74.5	19.7	0.8	1.4	2.8	21.9	40.5	37.7
East Feliciana Parish	344	15.5	19.0	7 433	81.1	13.3	0.3	1.5	1.8	10.1	34.8	55.1
Evangeline Parish	289	19.0	35.9	10 777	80.5	13.8	0.1	1.9	1.8	13.5	36.9	49.7
Franklin Parish	313	15.1	27.1	7 151	78.8	14.3	0.1	2.4	2.5	12.7	35.0	52.4
Grant Parish	374	10.6	24.8	7 076	78.0	16.2	0.7	1.4	1.3	7.9	32.1	59.9
Iberia Parish	388	12.7	28.4	27 043	80.4	13.8	0.6	1.5	1.5	10.8	36.4	52.8
Iberville Parish..............	341	14.8	24.9	11 144	81.1	12.4	0.2	2.6	2.8	13.0	35.7	51.3
Jackson Parish	325	12.6	21.4	6 039	82.2	13.4	0.5	1.1	1.3	11.8	33.4	54.8
Jefferson Parish	544	14.9	29.3	209 611	78.5	13.7	2.6	1.4	1.7	9.3	40.3	50.4
Jefferson Davis Parish ..	353	13.3	25.0	11 353	80.0	14.0	0.1	1.9	1.6	8.5	38.2	53.4
Lafayette Parish	475	12.4	27.5	87 053	83.6	9.6	1.2	1.6	1.4	8.3	37.1	54.6
Lafourche Parish	402	10.9	24.7	36 348	78.5	14.7	0.7	1.8	2.3	9.4	34.5	56.1
La Salle Parish..............	329	13.6	22.6	5 291	79.7	15.1	0.3	1.6	0.7	9.3	33.3	57.4
Lincoln Parish...............	436	13.4	41.6	17 094	78.8	13.5	0.2	1.3	4.4	10.6	35.8	53.6
Livingston Parish...........	481	11.9	21.4	40 267	83.1	13.1	0.3	0.9	0.8	5.0	30.3	64.7
Madison Parish	334	14.2	26.5	4 168	71.3	21.1	1.2	1.0	4.0	19.2	40.8	40.0
Morehouse Parish	362	14.6	29.6	10 792	76.6	18.1	1.0	1.1	1.5	15.4	34.3	50.3
Natchitoches Parish	370	16.7	36.9	14 603	74.7	17.2	0.5	1.5	3.5	13.6	36.9	49.5
Orleans Parish	488	20.9	36.1	188 703	60.3	16.1	13.7	2.0	5.2	27.3	42.3	30.4
Ouachita Parish............	444	12.8	31.8	63 027	82.1	12.4	1.2	1.1	1.4	11.8	36.2	52.0
Plaquemines Parish	521	14.9	17.2	10 074	76.8	15.2	0.8	2.6	2.2	9.6	35.9	54.5

Table C-3. States and Counties — Migration, Housing, and Transportation

STATE/ County code	MSA/PMSA/ NECMA code[1]	STATE County	Total population 5 years and over	Residence in 1995 (percent)					Occupied housing units		Householders 65 years and over	
				Same house	Same county, different house	Same state, different county	Different state	Outside the United States	Number	Percent owner-occupied	Number	Percent owner-occupied
			1	2	3	4	5	6	7	8	9	10
		LOUISIANA—Cont'd										
22 077	...	Pointe Coupee Parish ...	21 207	72.3	17.2	8.2	1.9	0.3	8 397	77.7	2 159	85.1
22 079	0220	Rapides Parish.............	117 515	59.9	26.7	7.4	5.2	0.8	47 120	68.0	10 823	80.9
22 081	...	Red River Parish..........	8 879	66.4	21.6	7.9	3.8	0.2	3 414	76.2	976	84.9
22 083	...	Richland Parish	19 389	64.4	21.6	10.4	3.4	0.2	7 490	72.3	2 146	80.9
22 085	...	Sabine Parish	21 920	63.9	21.8	8.1	5.6	0.6	9 221	81.0	2 603	87.1
22 087	5560	St. Bernard Parish.......	63 073	65.1	23.6	8.0	2.8	0.4	25 123	74.7	6 374	82.2
22 089	5560	St. Charles Parish	44 565	66.5	15.5	12.9	4.2	0.9	16 422	81.4	2 803	90.9
22 091	...	St. Helena Parish	9 762	74.1	12.1	11.1	2.5	0.3	3 873	85.0	969	90.4
22 093	5560	St. James Parish	19 735	78.8	15.0	4.9	1.2	0.1	6 992	85.6	1 472	94.1
22 095	5560	St. John the Baptist Parish	39 577	65.2	16.9	13.4	3.6	0.9	14 283	81.0	2 372	83.6
22 097	3880	St. Landry Parish	80 870	65.5	23.3	8.0	2.8	0.5	32 328	70.7	8 111	78.3
22 099	3880	St. Martin Parish	44 915	68.3	17.8	11.2	2.4	0.3	17 164	81.7	3 334	86.1
22 101	...	St. Mary Parish	49 547	64.2	25.4	5.3	4.4	0.7	19 317	73.9	4 152	89.8
22 103	5560	St. Tammany Parish	177 000	54.7	20.2	13.9	10.3	0.9	69 253	80.5	12 199	84.9
22 105	...	Tangipahoa Parish	93 315	61.5	21.0	11.8	4.6	1.0	36 558	73.3	7 133	83.3
22 107	...	Tensas Parish	6 180	66.0	18.3	11.1	4.0	0.6	2 416	69.4	697	85.8
22 109	3350	Terrebonne Parish	96 728	62.4	25.6	6.6	4.9	0.6	35 997	75.5	6 618	83.8
22 111	...	Union Parish.................	21 183	60.6	19.3	12.2	7.3	0.6	8 857	81.2	2 264	89.4
22 113	...	Vermilion Parish	49 948	64.4	22.9	8.6	3.1	1.0	19 832	77.0	4 917	86.3
22 115	...	Vernon Parish	47 546	44.6	16.1	7.2	27.8	4.4	18 260	56.7	3 076	85.9
22 117	...	Washington Parish.........	40 837	64.3	22.1	8.6	4.6	0.3	16 467	76.5	4 576	83.8
22 119	7680	Webster Parish.............	39 235	63.3	23.0	7.5	5.8	0.4	16 501	74.5	4 399	86.1
22 121	0760	West Baton Rouge Parish	20 086	66.7	15.5	15.0	2.5	0.3	7 663	78.8	1 504	86.9
22 123	...	West Carroll Parish	11 580	65.5	18.0	10.2	6.0	0.2	4 458	79.0	1 345	82.8
22 125	...	West Feliciana Parish ...	14 441	47.9	10.2	36.0	5.4	0.5	3 645	74.5	670	85.1
22 127	...	Winn Parish	15 834	60.5	20.7	13.4	5.2	0.3	5 930	74.7	1 666	83.0
23 000	...	MAINE	1 204 164	59.6	22.9	7.7	9.0	0.9	518 200	71.6	119 428	75.8
23 001	4243	Androscoggin County....	97 643	56.7	27.8	7.2	7.6	0.7	42 028	63.4	9 358	65.1
23 003	...	Aroostook County.........	70 183	67.8	22.1	3.4	5.6	1.1	30 356	73.1	8 292	72.2
23 005	6403	Cumberland County	250 237	54.2	25.8	7.4	11.2	1.3	107 989	66.7	22 691	73.0
23 007	...	Franklin County	27 970	62.1	18.8	12.4	6.1	0.6	11 806	76.0	2 796	80.4
23 009	...	Hancock County	49 291	61.7	19.6	7.3	10.3	1.1	21 864	75.6	5 649	81.4
23 011	...	Kennebec County..........	110 706	60.8	23.3	8.8	6.5	0.5	47 683	71.2	10 784	75.9
23 013	...	Knox County	37 552	59.5	23.3	7.3	9.2	0.7	16 608	74.0	4 464	81.0
23 015	...	Lincoln County	31 979	64.9	16.4	8.7	9.5	0.5	14 158	83.1	3 910	87.3
23 017	...	Oxford County	51 888	65.1	19.5	8.0	6.8	0.5	22 314	77.0	5 618	78.6
23 019	0733	Penobscot County........	137 190	58.4	25.0	9.1	6.5	1.0	58 096	69.8	12 583	74.8
23 021	...	Piscataquis County	16 408	67.1	17.6	8.1	6.1	1.0	7 278	79.4	2 107	78.7
23 023	...	Sagadahoc County.......	36 000	57.6	16.1	13.9	11.4	1.1	14 117	72.0	2 876	78.4
23 025	...	Somerset County	47 991	65.7	19.7	9.0	5.1	0.5	20 496	77.9	4 562	80.3
23 027	...	Waldo County	34 234	63.4	17.1	9.7	9.5	0.3	14 726	79.8	3 314	83.2
23 029	...	Washington County.......	32 232	66.7	19.2	5.1	7.9	1.0	14 118	77.6	3 921	79.4
23 031	...	York County	175 651	58.0	22.5	6.0	12.8	0.7	74 563	72.6	16 503	76.3
24 000	...	MARYLAND	4 945 043	55.7	21.9	9.4	10.0	3.0	1 980 859	67.7	383 030	76.0
24 001	1900	Allegany County	71 215	64.4	20.7	4.7	9.8	0.4	29 322	70.1	8 894	78.1
24 003	0720	Anne Arundel County....	456 969	55.7	20.7	10.1	11.2	2.3	178 670	75.5	30 949	85.8
24 005	0720	Baltimore County..........	709 509	58.1	18.4	15.5	6.0	2.0	299 877	67.6	70 860	74.4
24 009	8840	Calvert County	69 584	58.6	15.7	15.6	9.1	1.0	25 447	85.2	4 175	83.9
24 011	...	Caroline County	27 934	59.8	20.0	13.1	5.9	1.2	11 097	74.0	2 569	83.3
24 013	0720	Carroll County	140 776	61.7	17.3	14.6	5.5	0.8	52 503	82.0	9 565	79.4
24 015	9160	Cecil County	80 035	55.9	23.9	6.6	12.9	0.7	31 223	74.9	5 571	80.8
24 017	8840	Charles County	111 916	55.6	19.7	12.6	10.3	1.9	41 668	78.2	5 677	79.6
24 019	...	Dorchester County	29 004	64.6	22.0	8.2	4.5	0.5	12 706	70.1	3 733	78.2
24 021	8840	Frederick County...........	181 218	55.3	20.8	11.9	10.6	1.4	70 060	75.8	11 404	78.7
24 023	...	Garrett County.............	28 033	67.0	18.7	6.6	7.5	0.2	11 476	77.9	2 663	83.1
24 025	0720	Harford County	202 967	58.4	20.0	11.1	8.9	1.5	79 667	78.0	14 028	82.2
24 027	0720	Howard County	229 797	51.9	16.7	16.0	12.1	3.3	90 043	73.8	10 713	74.6
24 029	...	Kent County	18 318	58.5	19.5	10.0	10.7	1.3	7 666	70.3	2 407	80.6
24 031	8840	Montgomery County	813 460	52.7	23.2	4.4	12.8	6.9	324 565	68.7	58 785	78.3
24 033	8840	Prince George's County..	743 851	52.7	24.3	5.3	13.6	4.1	286 610	61.8	38 594	78.0
24 035	0720	Queen Anne's County ...	37 981	56.5	16.4	19.4	6.8	0.9	15 315	83.2	3 403	87.7
24 037	...	St. Mary's County	79 992	51.0	20.0	9.9	17.3	1.8	30 642	71.8	4 463	84.0
24 039	...	Somerset County	23 590	61.9	17.7	12.6	6.7	1.1	8 361	69.7	2 232	79.6
24 041	...	Talbot County	32 065	56.6	21.5	11.7	9.2	1.0	14 307	71.6	4 441	79.7

[1]MSA = Metropolitan Statistical Area. PMSA = Primary MSA. NECMA = New England County Metropolitan Area. See the Appendix A for explanation of these concepts. See Appendix B for list of metropolitan areas identified by type, with component counties.

	Owner-occupied by household type (percent)								Median household income				Median monthly owner costs as a percent of income	
STATE County	Family-households					Nonfamily households								
		Married-couple family		Other family										
	Total family households	Total	With own children under 18 years	Total	With own children under 18 years	Total nonfamily households	Two or more adults	Living alone	All households	Owner-occupied households	Renter-occupied households	Median housing value (owner estimated)	With a mortgage	Without a mortgage
	11	12	13	14	15	16	17	18	19	20	21	22	23	24
LOUISIANA—Cont'd														
Pointe Coupee Parish ...	80.1	86.5	82.6	62.3	52.3	70.9	74.7	70.4	30 311	35 035	17 717	68 400	21.2	9.9
Rapides Parish............	72.9	83.3	78.3	48.3	35.5	56.3	45.8	57.7	29 710	37 024	18 710	68 300	19.9	9.9
Red River Parish..........	78.7	87.0	82.6	59.8	46.9	69.1	71.3	68.9	23 242	27 281	14 551	45 100	23.9	10.7
Richland Parish...........	74.6	82.0	71.8	55.8	43.7	65.8	63.2	66.1	23 860	29 730	12 136	50 800	20.7	10.3
Sabine Parish...............	84.3	89.4	84.4	64.8	48.7	72.6	67.8	73.0	26 481	30 107	12 088	48 200	19.7	10.2
St. Bernard Parish.......	79.4	85.3	81.0	63.0	50.6	61.9	47.4	64.3	35 523	40 744	23 332	82 900	19.4	9.9
St. Charles Parish........	84.9	91.1	90.4	66.1	55.7	67.1	65.8	67.3	45 040	51 112	24 938	96 300	19.5	9.9
St. Helena Parish.........	87.4	89.5	87.3	82.7	80.9	78.8	74.5	79.3	24 826	26 231	18 958	55 100	20.6	12.1
St. James Parish..........	88.0	92.2	91.1	77.6	68.1	76.3	66.7	77.4	35 497	39 179	16 813	69 300	17.9	9.9
St. John the Baptist Parish	84.4	90.7	89.1	69.2	63.0	68.0	65.0	68.5	39 208	43 525	21 788	79 000	19.7	9.9
St. Landry Parish	74.2	84.2	80.2	51.7	38.8	61.6	57.6	62.0	22 961	28 856	11 812	53 800	19.6	11.3
St. Martin Parish..........	84.7	91.1	88.8	67.5	59.6	72.3	67.9	73.1	30 527	34 418	16 076	59 400	19.5	9.9
St. Mary Parish............	76.9	84.5	78.3	58.7	48.4	65.6	60.5	66.4	27 992	31 538	20 719	63 100	18.5	11.1
St. Tammany Parish	85.3	89.6	88.8	66.9	59.2	64.8	56.4	66.4	47 453	53 266	27 842	116 000	19.9	9.9
Tangipahoa Parish........	80.2	87.1	83.9	62.2	54.8	56.8	35.6	61.4	29 123	34 621	16 718	73 000	21.0	9.9
Tensas Parish	70.3	78.0	69.4	55.3	40.3	67.4	69.5	67.2	19 976	25 529	12 199	42 500	24.8	13.0
Terrebonne Parish	80.0	85.8	82.9	61.8	52.5	61.3	51.1	63.7	34 936	39 527	23 871	72 200	18.9	9.9
Union Parish.................	84.0	88.3	82.9	69.4	56.3	73.9	62.2	75.1	28 635	31 744	18 596	53 000	19.6	10.8
Vermilion Parish...........	80.8	86.6	82.7	62.4	50.8	66.7	59.9	67.8	29 157	33 931	16 178	58 900	19.0	9.9
Vernon Parish...............	57.3	58.8	45.5	51.1	42.4	54.9	38.3	56.8	30 968	35 343	26 652	56 400	19.2	9.9
Washington Parish........	79.2	86.9	81.2	62.1	51.6	69.7	59.7	70.6	24 222	27 673	15 247	52 800	22.5	11.3
Webster Parish.............	78.5	86.4	80.7	57.1	43.0	65.0	50.1	66.4	28 566	33 301	16 195	51 900	19.0	9.9
West Baton Rouge Parish	81.8	89.8	88.5	64.7	57.4	69.7	58.6	71.5	36 803	42 690	19 809	74 400	18.7	9.9
West Carroll Parish	81.8	86.4	82.2	63.6	54.7	71.4	47.7	73.8	24 043	26 768	16 683	42 300	18.0	12.6
West Feliciana Parish ...	78.6	85.7	79.9	57.6	48.7	61.8	34.9	63.9	38 240	45 033	23 953	87 100	21.5	9.9
Winn Parish..................	76.7	84.2	79.6	56.4	44.8	69.4	49.1	70.9	25 246	28 757	14 366	37 800	20.2	11.6
MAINE	81.1	86.7	84.7	57.8	49.5	53.1	50.6	53.8	37 072	43 973	22 516	94 300	21.4	12.1
Androscoggin County....	74.5	82.8	80.9	46.7	40.1	42.9	46.1	42.1	35 655	45 781	21 151	86 800	21.4	12.5
Aroostook County.........	83.6	88.4	85.5	59.5	48.2	51.0	55.6	50.2	28 830	34 534	15 590	58 400	19.2	12.1
Cumberland County	79.0	84.7	84.6	55.3	48.2	45.9	39.2	47.9	43 780	54 140	27 856	129 800	21.9	12.6
Franklin County	84.2	89.6	86.7	63.0	54.0	60.0	54.3	61.8	31 461	36 836	18 218	76 300	21.3	11.6
Hancock County............	83.8	87.9	84.8	64.1	58.1	60.1	60.8	60.0	35 634	40 913	22 456	104 000	22.4	11.6
Kennebec County..........	80.8	87.3	85.2	56.9	49.4	52.8	54.9	52.4	36 322	43 486	20 963	84 200	20.8	12.0
Knox County.................	82.1	86.8	83.7	61.1	53.2	59.1	57.0	59.6	36 824	41 862	24 010	110 200	22.7	12.0
Lincoln County	87.9	90.8	87.1	73.5	67.2	73.1	66.4	74.6	38 724	41 725	24 316	114 500	22.7	11.8
Oxford County	84.0	89.3	87.1	61.6	52.3	61.9	65.1	61.1	33 497	38 108	20 313	80 300	21.3	11.7
Penobscot County.........	80.8	86.9	84.8	56.3	47.7	48.9	43.6	50.5	33 891	41 826	19 741	77 400	20.5	12.1
Piscataquis County	86.1	89.7	85.1	71.0	64.8	65.9	76.8	63.8	27 950	31 537	16 250	62 900	20.2	12.8
Sagadahoc County........	80.1	87.1	81.7	52.0	39.1	54.4	48.0	55.9	41 805	49 721	26 684	108 600	21.9	11.1
Somerset County	84.6	89.7	86.2	64.2	56.6	63.0	64.8	62.5	30 487	34 789	18 248	67 000	20.2	11.6
Waldo County	85.6	89.1	85.5	70.3	64.5	67.2	67.0	67.2	33 914	37 532	22 516	85 600	21.7	11.8
Washington County.......	84.3	87.8	85.1	69.9	60.9	64.7	62.2	65.2	26 021	29 431	16 095	66 200	20.7	13.2
York County	80.6	86.0	84.6	55.6	45.0	55.6	54.3	56.0	43 277	50 694	25 775	119 500	22.0	12.2
MARYLAND	75.1	83.1	80.9	52.5	41.7	51.3	43.9	53.1	52 640	64 860	32 351	143 300	22.2	9.9
Allegany County	79.4	85.2	80.1	56.5	43.0	53.3	34.3	56.7	30 910	37 663	16 834	70 100	19.8	10.9
Anne Arundel County....	80.9	86.2	82.8	60.5	48.8	61.3	54.0	63.3	61 648	69 691	39 524	156 500	22.4	9.9
Baltimore County..........	76.5	83.6	81.8	54.7	43.2	49.8	40.2	51.9	50 497	60 737	32 740	125 700	21.3	9.9
Calvert County	88.7	92.7	92.3	70.6	63.5	71.3	75.4	70.3	65 724	70 980	37 064	170 800	22.4	9.9
Caroline County	78.0	86.4	81.3	54.7	40.7	63.0	52.5	65.5	38 609	44 888	25 559	101 600	23.4	10.5
Carroll County	86.9	90.3	89.8	66.5	57.5	64.0	63.4	64.1	60 103	66 159	32 110	163 300	22.8	9.9
Cecil County	80.6	86.3	82.7	57.9	49.2	58.2	54.3	59.3	50 284	56 401	31 447	130 200	22.2	9.9
Charles County	82.3	88.5	85.7	62.4	52.4	63.7	56.8	65.6	62 309	70 671	38 232	153 500	22.6	9.9
Dorchester County	75.3	85.2	79.9	48.7	35.0	59.4	58.2	59.6	33 723	40 982	20 946	88 000	22.5	11.3
Frederick County..........	82.0	86.6	87.0	58.3	47.8	57.8	49.6	60.1	60 305	68 689	35 735	161 000	22.4	9.9
Garrett County..............	83.4	87.4	82.1	63.4	54.2	63.2	55.4	64.4	32 254	36 811	19 427	84 500	21.6	9.9
Harford County.............	83.6	88.6	87.2	61.0	50.1	60.2	57.8	60.7	57 046	64 466	33 075	145 500	21.8	9.9
Howard County	81.7	86.1	87.3	60.0	51.8	52.0	44.7	54.1	74 006	86 933	44 315	198 600	21.9	9.9
Kent County	77.2	83.6	74.1	53.8	48.8	56.3	39.5	59.3	39 500	46 745	26 587	121 000	22.2	11.3
Montgomery County	75.6	80.9	79.6	53.8	45.3	53.1	42.2	55.9	71 594	87 650	44 987	210 600	21.5	9.9
Prince George's County .	67.6	77.7	72.5	49.6	38.8	48.6	39.0	51.1	54 879	69 585	36 405	143 700	23.9	9.9
Queen Anne's County...	87.5	91.4	88.7	67.7	61.5	70.0	63.8	71.6	56 173	61 690	31 676	160 000	23.2	11.0
St. Mary's County.........	77.6	82.9	78.0	56.2	48.8	56.0	51.0	57.3	54 721	63 540	34 522	148 000	22.0	9.9
Somerset County	75.5	84.9	79.0	53.9	42.0	58.6	44.9	60.9	29 921	37 450	16 232	76 500	21.5	11.7
Talbot County...............	79.6	86.2	81.7	51.8	37.5	55.0	41.9	57.3	43 699	52 524	25 796	151 500	22.5	9.9

STATE County	Median gross rent	Percent who pay 35 percent or more of income for housing expenses		Means of transportation to work (percent except where noted)						Vehicles available (percent of households)		
		Owners	Renters	Number of workers 16 years and over	Car, truck, or van		Public transportation	Other means	Walked	No vehicles	One vehicle	Two or more vehicles
					Drove alone	Carpooled						
	25	26	27	28	29	30	31	32	33	34	35	36
LOUISIANA—Cont'd												
Pointe Coupee Parish ...	343	15.8	21.6	8 779	79.4	15.9	0.6	1.4	1.2	10.5	33.7	55.8
Rapides Parish	434	14.2	31.1	49 957	78.7	13.9	1.3	1.5	2.2	11.1	38.0	50.9
Red River Parish	325	19.2	20.6	3 105	77.5	17.9	0.1	1.6	0.9	14.5	35.1	50.3
Richland Parish	329	16.3	28.6	7 488	77.1	16.8	0.3	1.4	2.9	13.8	36.0	50.1
Sabine Parish	309	12.0	21.8	8 288	74.8	16.8	0.6	2.4	2.3	10.2	35.2	54.5
St. Bernard Parish	489	12.2	26.1	28 739	78.7	16.1	0.8	1.6	1.4	10.3	36.8	52.9
St. Charles Parish	507	12.4	23.7	21 134	84.1	11.5	0.6	1.1	1.4	6.4	29.1	64.5
St. Helena Parish	326	19.1	20.0	3 624	78.9	15.5	0.6	0.5	1.7	12.1	36.6	51.4
St. James Parish	317	11.6	13.4	7 566	80.5	14.9	0.4	0.9	2.1	10.2	33.1	56.6
St. John the Baptist Parish	489	14.8	24.6	17 466	79.7	15.4	0.3	1.6	1.5	9.5	32.3	58.2
St. Landry Parish	320	15.9	30.5	28 583	80.0	13.2	0.7	1.8	2.4	15.4	36.8	47.8
St. Martin Parish	353	14.9	24.0	18 676	78.9	14.8	0.4	1.8	1.8	10.9	33.9	55.2
St. Mary Parish	397	12.5	23.3	19 826	78.2	12.4	0.6	3.5	3.3	13.2	38.3	48.5
St. Tammany Parish	593	14.4	29.4	87 130	80.2	13.7	0.3	1.3	0.8	4.4	29.9	65.7
Tangipahoa Parish	427	16.3	31.5	40 017	78.7	14.0	0.5	1.6	2.6	10.3	36.6	53.2
Tensas Parish	265	22.4	27.2	2 142	69.2	21.5	0.7	1.7	3.5	21.8	32.0	46.2
Terrebonne Parish	460	12.9	23.8	40 514	79.6	12.4	0.9	3.5	1.6	9.2	37.0	53.8
Union Parish	351	14.5	19.7	9 062	78.5	16.9	0.2	1.4	0.8	10.8	31.7	57.6
Vermilion Parish	342	13.3	23.2	20 675	81.7	11.7	0.6	2.1	2.0	9.4	36.5	54.1
Vernon Parish	411	11.6	14.0	22 910	73.2	17.4	0.5	2.0	5.6	7.7	38.1	54.2
Washington Parish	330	15.7	27.3	14 663	75.7	17.9	0.5	1.9	2.1	11.4	39.5	49.0
Webster Parish	360	12.4	29.3	16 362	79.7	15.3	0.9	1.0	1.3	10.8	34.7	54.5
West Baton Rouge Parish	439	12.5	26.3	9 284	81.6	12.5	0.5	1.6	2.0	9.2	36.0	54.8
West Carroll Parish	326	15.9	18.7	4 060	77.1	16.8	0.4	1.8	1.9	8.9	35.6	55.5
West Feliciana Parish ...	411	11.1	15.5	4 303	83.1	11.6	0.8	1.2	0.5	8.7	30.4	60.9
Winn Parish	341	15.0	26.1	5 412	80.3	14.6	0.1	1.3	2.0	13.8	36.5	49.7
MAINE	497	14.7	27.4	615 144	78.6	11.3	0.8	0.9	4.0	7.6	34.4	58.0
Androscoggin County....	433	13.8	24.3	50 869	70.0	13.4	0.9	1.0	4.0	11.1	35.5	53.4
Aroostook County	364	12.3	23.0	31 957	79.7	11.4	0.5	0.9	4.0	8.5	35.7	55.8
Cumberland County	615	15.9	28.4	137 256	78.9	9.5	1.6	1.0	4.4	8.6	35.1	56.3
Franklin County	432	15.2	30.6	13 379	76.9	12.4	0.3	0.8	4.7	6.4	32.1	61.5
Hancock County	514	16.2	26.5	24 782	74.5	11.2	0.5	1.2	6.3	6.1	33.8	60.1
Kennebec County	439	13.1	28.5	56 351	79.2	11.4	0.8	0.9	3.6	8.0	35.0	56.6
Knox County	517	16.5	28.7	18 829	74.6	11.1	0.4	1.3	5.5	6.6	36.1	57.3
Lincoln County	541	16.3	26.7	15 869	76.5	12.3	0.2	1.0	3.8	5.8	31.4	62.8
Oxford County	418	14.3	22.8	25 090	76.6	14.0	0.5	0.0	3.4	6.8	33.1	60.1
Penobscot County	468	13.3	31.2	68 652	79.2	10.7	0.9	0.9	4.6	7.7	35.3	56.9
Piscataquis County	373	12.5	22.4	7 115	77.0	11.8	0.1	1.0	6.2	6.7	33.9	59.5
Sagadahoc County	551	13.5	24.6	17 864	78.1	11.6	0.5	1.0	4.4	5.1	32.9	62.1
Somerset County	421	13.2	29.1	22 767	77.3	13.1	0.2	1.0	3.8	7.0	34.3	58.7
Waldo County	494	16.2	27.7	16 861	76.9	13.2	0.2	1.1	2.7	6.3	32.0	61.7
Washington County	408	15.6	22.9	13 743	76.0	12.1	0.5	1.2	5.3	8.5	35.5	56.1
York County	568	15.2	27.8	93 760	81.3	10.9	0.8	0.7	2.4	5.9	32.7	61.4
MARYLAND	689	16.1	27.0	2 591 670	73.7	12.4	7.2	0.8	2.5	11.2	33.4	55.3
Allegany County	381	11.5	29.1	29 571	80.6	12.8	0.6	0.4	4.1	10.9	34.5	54.7
Anne Arundel County....	798	15.3	22.3	255 858	80.3	10.7	2.5	0.8	2.3	5.3	28.7	66.0
Baltimore County	670	14.5	26.6	373 496	79.7	10.8	4.0	0.6	2.0	8.9	36.7	54.5
Calvert County	837	16.3	27.0	37 556	77.6	16.1	1.3	0.6	0.8	3.7	21.2	75.1
Caroline County	482	17.0	21.4	14 093	77.0	14.7	0.3	1.1	1.8	6.5	31.4	62.1
Carroll County	638	14.3	27.7	77 592	83.1	9.8	1.3	0.5	1.5	4.3	21.4	74.3
Cecil County	617	14.9	23.3	42 055	83.2	10.7	0.6	0.9	1.6	6.0	27.7	66.3
Charles County	858	15.3	26.3	61 698	77.5	15.9	2.4	0.7	0.9	4.7	24.7	70.6
Dorchester County	456	17.6	28.0	13 984	76.9	15.0	1.0	1.3	2.0	12.0	33.0	55.1
Frederick County	719	14.7	25.0	102 318	79.3	12.4	1.4	0.6	2.4	5.0	25.2	69.9
Garrett County	382	14.6	23.0	12 943	77.3	13.7	0.4	0.5	2.9	7.8	31.4	60.8
Harford County	648	13.3	22.4	111 704	83.4	10.4	1.0	0.8	1.4	5.6	27.0	67.4
Howard County	879	14.2	24.5	134 992	81.9	9.4	2.5	0.5	1.1	4.3	26.4	69.3
Kent County	526	18.3	23.8	9 062	73.5	11.4	0.5	2.0	7.9	8.5	32.4	59.1
Montgomery County	914	15.0	26.7	455 331	68.9	10.9	12.6	0.7	1.9	7.5	34.3	58.2
Prince George's County	737	20.0	24.9	397 403	66.8	16.2	11.9	0.9	2.2	10.5	38.6	50.9
Queen Anne's County ...	622	19.2	25.5	20 852	79.2	11.7	0.6	1.0	2.0	4.0	24.3	71.7
St. Mary's County	719	14.1	22.2	43 264	79.8	12.5	1.4	1.4	1.8	5.4	26.6	68.0
Somerset County	429	19.1	33.7	9 100	75.8	14.2	1.2	2.0	4.0	13.3	31.8	54.9
Talbot County	552	16.8	25.8	16 030	79.0	10.1	1.0	1.2	3.4	7.5	31.9	60.6

Table C-3. States and Counties — **Migration, Housing, and Transportation**

STATE/County code	MSA/PMSA/NECMA code[1]	STATE County	Residence in 1995 (percent)						Occupied housing units		Householders 65 years and over	
			Total population 5 years and over	Same house	Same county, different house	Same state, different county	Different state	Outside the United States	Number	Percent owner-occupied	Number	Percent owner-occupied
			1	2	3	4	5	6	7	8	9	10
		MARYLAND—Cont'd										
24 043	3180	Washington County	123 780	57.4	23.2	11.4	7.4	0.7	49 726	65.6	12 320	74.5
24 045	...	Wicomico County	79 444	54.0	24.8	9.7	10.1	1.4	32 218	66.5	6 969	78.8
24 047	...	Worcester County	44 260	55.3	19.2	13.8	10.8	0.9	19 694	75.0	6 271	84.3
24 510	0720	Baltimore city	609 345	57.1	28.2	6.5	6.1	2.1	257 996	50.3	62 344	62.4
25 000	...	MASSACHUSETTS ...	5 954 249	58.5	22.8	7.8	7.5	3.5	2 443 580	61.7	555 549	68.2
25 001	0743	Barnstable County	211 653	57.6	21.6	10.5	8.8	1.4	94 822	77.8	32 986	85.5
25 003	6323	Berkshire County	127 950	61.5	25.4	2.7	9.2	1.1	56 006	66.9	15 820	72.3
25 005	1123	Bristol County	500 806	62.4	24.9	6.3	4.9	1.5	205 411	61.6	48 253	63.7
25 007	...	Dukes County	14 146	61.2	20.2	6.8	9.2	2.5	6 421	71.3	1 472	83.4
25 009	1123	Essex County	675 622	58.7	25.4	6.9	6.0	2.9	275 419	63.5	64 621	66.8
25 011	...	Franklin County	67 878	61.4	22.0	9.1	6.2	1.2	29 466	67.0	6 719	77.3
25 013	8003	Hampden County	426 558	58.7	29.0	4.1	5.3	2.9	175 288	61.9	43 192	70.3
25 015	8003	Hampshire County	145 599	53.9	16.7	14.4	12.3	2.7	55 991	65.0	12 213	72.9
25 017	1123	Middlesex County	1 373 758	57.9	21.9	6.6	9.0	4.7	561 220	61.8	119 351	69.1
25 019	...	Nantucket County	8 981	54.3	18.2	12.5	10.7	4.4	3 699	63.1	590	77.6
25 021	1123	Norfolk County	608 488	62.2	16.6	11.6	6.6	2.9	248 827	69.7	61 232	71.5
25 023	1123	Plymouth County	439 945	63.5	20.0	11.0	4.1	1.4	168 361	75.6	35 196	76.8
25 025	1123	Suffolk County	651 708	49.3	22.3	9.1	11.8	7.5	278 722	33.9	50 919	46.3
25 027	1123	Worcester County	701 157	59.0	25.5	6.3	6.5	2.8	283 927	64.1	62 985	67.0
26 000	...	MICHIGAN	9 268 782	57.3	25.1	10.9	5.0	1.7	3 785 661	73.8	803 561	81.0
26 001	...	Alcona County	11 202	64.7	9.9	21.2	3.6	0.6	5 132	89.5	1 864	92.5
26 003	...	Alger County	9 431	66.5	16.8	11.0	5.0	0.6	3 785	82.4	1 111	82.9
26 005	3000	Allegan County	98 039	57.9	20.2	16.5	4.6	0.9	38 165	82.9	7 405	88.0
26 007	...	Alpena County	29 600	63.6	22.7	9.8	3.6	0.3	12 818	79.3	3 610	85.0
26 009	...	Antrim County	21 810	57.7	17.3	18.7	5.9	0.4	9 222	85.0	2 596	91.7
26 011	...	Arenac County	16 361	64.7	15.1	17.1	2.7	0.5	6 710	84.3	1 836	89.2
26 013	...	Baraga County	8 273	66.5	18.4	10.5	4.1	0.5	3 353	77.7	902	81.4
26 015	...	Barry County	52 919	61.4	15.0	19.2	4.1	0.3	21 035	85.9	4 191	88.1
26 017	6960	Bay County	103 467	65.1	24.1	7.7	2.8	0.3	43 930	79.3	10 760	85.3
26 019	...	Benzie County	15 061	57.7	14.7	22.3	4.8	0.5	6 500	85.8	1 735	90.3
26 021	0870	Berrien County	151 825	57.7	26.4	4.0	9.9	2.0	63 569	72.2	15 645	83.5
26 023	...	Branch County	42 921	58.3	22.7	11.2	6.4	1.3	16 349	78.9	3 924	83.7
26 025	3720	Calhoun County	129 025	57.1	27.4	8.9	5.7	1.0	54 100	73.0	12 444	81.7
26 027	...	Cass County	47 996	61.2	17.4	9.2	11.8	0.4	19 676	81.9	4 665	90.5
26 029	...	Charlevoix County	24 369	59.2	19.0	15.8	5.4	0.6	10 400	81.2	2 562	86.6
26 031	...	Cheboygan County	24 896	61.3	16.2	15.7	6.2	0.5	10 835	82.8	3 137	89.4
26 033	...	Chippewa County	36 493	53.5	23.0	17.1	5.1	1.3	13 474	74.0	3 255	84.1
26 035	...	Clare County	29 444	58.9	17.1	19.6	3.9	0.5	12 686	82.2	3 497	88.2
26 037	4040	Clinton County	60 284	63.2	15.0	18.5	2.9	0.4	23 653	85.2	4 425	90.2
26 039	...	Crawford County	13 477	57.8	14.7	22.8	4.0	0.6	5 625	82.8	1 601	88.6
26 041	...	Delta County	36 481	66.5	19.3	8.0	5.8	0.4	15 836	79.6	4 171	80.7
26 043	...	Dickinson County	25 939	65.0	20.4	5.6	8.8	0.3	11 386	80.1	3 310	83.1
26 045	4040	Eaton County	97 148	56.9	18.6	19.4	4.4	0.7	40 167	74.1	7 381	80.3
26 047	...	Emmet County	29 490	56.7	20.7	16.0	5.8	0.7	12 577	75.5	2 998	78.1
26 049	2640	Genesee County	404 586	56.8	31.2	7.5	3.9	0.7	169 825	73.2	33 274	82.8
26 051	...	Gladwin County	24 587	60.8	17.3	19.1	2.5	0.2	10 561	85.6	3 160	89.2
26 053	...	Gogebic County	16 563	66.6	18.3	5.2	8.9	1.0	7 425	78.7	2 681	82.2
26 055	...	Grand Traverse County	72 878	54.4	22.1	16.4	6.0	1.1	30 396	77.3	6 214	85.6
26 057	...	Gratiot County	39 779	58.9	20.3	16.6	3.4	0.8	14 501	77.5	3 535	83.9
26 059	...	Hillsdale County	43 505	58.0	22.1	13.0	6.4	0.4	17 335	79.9	3 941	87.1
26 061	...	Houghton County	34 058	56.8	17.2	16.7	8.0	1.4	13 793	71.5	3 813	80.9
26 063	...	Huron County	34 093	69.0	18.9	9.1	2.6	0.5	14 597	83.5	4 626	88.3
26 065	4040	Ingham County	261 790	46.5	25.4	18.7	6.3	3.1	108 593	60.7	17 952	75.4
26 067	...	Ionia County	57 310	59.7	19.9	16.3	3.2	1.0	20 606	80.1	4 032	82.1
26 069	...	Iosco County	26 040	57.4	18.4	18.3	5.5	0.4	11 727	82.0	3 823	88.8
26 071	...	Iron County	12 568	67.2	18.4	6.2	7.9	0.2	5 748	82.5	2 299	85.2
26 073	...	Isabella County	59 998	43.3	18.3	32.0	4.7	1.7	22 425	63.3	3 751	84.2
26 075	3520	Jackson County	147 975	59.0	26.4	9.4	4.6	0.7	58 168	76.5	13 413	82.5
26 077	3720	Kalamazoo County	223 228	49.8	27.2	14.7	6.8	1.5	93 479	65.8	17 464	76.0
26 079	...	Kalkaska County	15 490	57.5	13.4	24.4	4.0	0.7	6 428	85.4	1 497	90.3
26 081	3000	Kent County	530 219	52.4	30.2	8.7	6.0	2.7	212 890	70.3	37 199	78.6
26 083	...	Keweenaw County	2 195	66.8	6.7	20.0	6.1	0.3	998	89.3	344	90.4
26 085	...	Lake County	10 739	55.9	11.9	27.0	4.9	0.3	4 704	82.9	1 544	88.2
26 087	2160	Lapeer County	82 051	60.5	18.2	17.8	2.9	0.7	30 729	85.0	5 143	82.5

[1]MSA = Metropolitan Statistical Area. PMSA = Primary MSA. NECMA = New England County Metropolitan Area. See the Appendix A for explanation of these concepts. See Appendix B for list of metropolitan areas identified by type, with component counties.

Table C-3. States and Counties — Migration, Housing, and Transportation

STATE County	Owner-occupied by household type (percent)								Median household income			Median housing value (owner estimated)	Median monthly owner costs as a percent of income	
	Family-households					Nonfamily households								
		Married-couple family		Other family										
	Total family households	Total	With own children under 18 years	Total	With own children under 18 years	Total nonfamily households	Two or more adults	Living alone	All households	Owner-occupied households	Renter-occupied households		With a mortgage	Without a mortgage
	11	12	13	14	15	16	17	18	19	20	21	22	23	24

MARYLAND—Cont'd														
Washington County	73.2	80.2	76.3	44.9	32.5	48.9	40.8	50.6	40 315	49 080	26 435	113 500	21.4	10.4
Wicomico County	73.1	83.3	79.1	46.1	34.8	52.4	38.1	56.7	38 723	48 010	23 807	91 600	20.5	10.6
Worcester County	80.4	87.3	77.3	54.2	42.2	63.8	53.4	66.1	40 419	45 315	26 231	116 600	22.6	9.9
Baltimore city	58.6	74.2	71.6	44.0	30.9	39.3	37.6	39.6	29 743	41 359	19 809	69 900	22.5	12.5

| MASSACHUSETTS | 72.8 | 80.6 | 79.7 | 47.3 | 33.5 | 41.3 | 32.8 | 43.5 | 50 284 | 64 506 | 30 682 | 182 800 | 21.9 | 12.4 |

Barnstable County	83.9	89.2	84.5	60.5	48.6	66.7	60.3	68.0	45 977	51 480	29 257	178 000	23.1	12.4
Berkshire County	78.9	86.3	83.5	53.9	41.3	46.6	45.1	46.9	39 038	49 420	22 621	115 100	21.2	11.7
Bristol County	71.3	80.3	78.8	42.4	28.0	40.3	40.8	40.2	43 275	57 525	24 614	147 100	21.6	11.9
Dukes County	79.2	83.5	80.9	64.9	59.3	59.7	52.0	61.8	45 310	51 379	35 026	315 500	25.9	13.9
Essex County	73.3	81.3	80.2	47.0	32.2	43.4	41.1	43.9	51 213	67 750	28 548	206 800	22.3	12.6
Franklin County	78.7	85.6	83.3	54.7	44.1	47.3	43.2	48.6	40 730	50 466	23 750	121 400	21.7	12.2
Hampden County	68.9	81.7	77.3	42.3	28.9	46.1	42.9	46.7	39 637	52 411	21 892	113 700	21.6	12.7
Hampshire County	79.9	85.1	83.9	59.2	47.6	42.0	30.2	46.4	45 908	57 700	27 615	142 600	21.4	11.5

Middlesex County	74.2	79.4	80.1	52.9	38.9	39.0	27.3	42.5	60 483	76 552	39 631	244 400	21.7	12.1
Nantucket County	77.2	80.8	79.8	60.5	64.4	44.2	34.2	48.5	55 547	69 893	42 333	583 500	26.3	11.8
Norfolk County	81.4	85.2	86.6	64.1	49.6	46.0	34.1	48.8	62 852	75 606	38 569	226 700	21.7	12.4
Plymouth County	82.6	88.9	88.0	58.8	43.5	56.5	56.7	56.5	55 496	65 518	29 130	174 200	22.5	12.7
Suffolk County	42.7	53.2	50.1	27.5	15.6	25.0	17.1	27.9	39 001	59 836	30 307	201 300	22.9	13.0
Worcester County	74.1	81.9	80.9	46.6	34.2	43.0	39.1	43.9	47 569	61 125	27 645	142 600	21.2	12.3

| MICHIGAN | 81.7 | 88.8 | 86.5 | 59.2 | 48.9 | 56.7 | 47.2 | 58.6 | 44 533 | 52 353 | 26 153 | 110 300 | 19.6 | 9.9 |

Alcona County	91.9	94.3	87.4	77.0	67.0	84.0	82.1	84.3	31 416	32 520	19 063	84 700	21.0	9.9
Alger County	88.1	92.3	90.4	63.4	60.9	70.1	64.8	71.0	35 692	39 087	21 406	76 500	19.9	9.9
Allegan County	87.4	92.2	89.4	64.7	59.5	69.5	70.1	69.4	45 868	50 173	28 560	111 300	20.2	9.9
Alpena County	87.1	92.4	89.8	63.5	50.0	62.7	54.4	64.0	34 039	40 189	17 877	78 900	10.7	9.9
Antrim County	88.8	91.8	86.3	72.1	62.2	75.0	61.0	77.1	38 348	40 897	24 266	103 300	21.8	10.7
Arenac County	87.7	92.7	88.7	64.5	54.3	76.1	76.8	76.0	33 241	36 779	16 806	75 400	19.8	10.8
Baraga County	84.5	90.0	80.4	62.9	50.7	64.2	57.5	65.1	33 428	39 227	18 276	66 400	18.3	9.9
Barry County	88.0	92.7	90.6	71.9	68.1	73.2	67.4	74.5	46 833	50 440	27 452	109 600	20.4	9.9

Bay County	87.2	90.3	90.5	65.3	55.7	62.2	57.8	62.9	38 647	45 244	20 515	83 600	18.8	10.8
Benzie County	90.1	93.1	89.4	73.1	63.9	75.3	68.3	76.9	37 453	40 193	23 333	104 700	22.2	9.9
Berrien County	78.3	86.8	81.4	51.8	40.1	59.3	53.6	60.2	38 291	45 572	22 558	93 300	19.4	9.9
Branch County	84.0	89.4	85.1	63.1	52.7	66.4	68.6	66.0	38 537	42 645	26 120	83 300	19.3	9.9
Calhoun County	80.6	87.1	82.5	61.3	52.6	57.3	51.6	58.3	38 937	45 915	24 920	81 300	19.0	10.1
Cass County	85.4	90.0	84.5	66.0	57.9	72.5	61.5	74.7	41 338	44 621	27 882	90 800	19.5	9.9
Charlevoix County	85.8	90.9	88.6	61.9	53.0	70.4	67.6	70.9	39 935	43 704	25 494	110 400	20.4	9.9
Cheboygan County	86.7	90.4	84.7	69.0	58.0	73.5	68.2	74.3	33 438	36 071	19 552	89 600	21.5	9.9
Chippewa County	81.6	88.7	83.9	56.4	45.9	58.6	44.9	61.4	34 234	40 146	19 748	75 800	18.9	9.9

Clare County	86.9	92.0	86.1	67.5	58.4	71.7	74.0	71.3	29 091	31 011	17 896	69 900	20.8	9.9
Clinton County	89.5	92.8	90.9	70.2	64.3	71.4	67.9	72.2	52 423	57 139	30 495	121 100	19.2	9.9
Crawford County	86.5	92.3	88.6	62.9	54.3	73.3	73.3	73.3	33 389	36 307	20 254	78 500	19.8	9.9
Delta County	87.7	92.1	89.3	63.7	52.6	62.7	58.2	63.3	35 250	41 461	18 243	77 000	18.6	9.9
Dickinson County	86.1	90.8	88.3	62.5	51.8	68.1	61.4	68.9	34 724	39 986	19 412	64 800	18.4	11.0
Eaton County	82.9	88.7	88.1	58.8	50.7	53.1	48.1	54.1	49 033	57 278	29 345	112 400	19.2	9.9
Emmet County	85.3	89.0	85.2	67.4	62.0	55.0	46.8	56.6	40 184	45 757	25 084	123 600	22.2	9.9
Genesee County	79.9	89.6	86.2	57.4	46.8	58.7	53.5	59.7	41 999	50 876	22 627	90 800	18.8	9.9
Gladwin County	88.6	92.3	88.3	68.7	58.9	77.6	75.2	78.0	31 673	33 883	19 604	83 000	22.0	10.0

Gogebic County	86.9	91.6	88.3	67.3	50.6	65.2	56.3	66.2	27 002	30 781	16 917	42 600	18.7	11.5
Grand Traverse County	84.9	89.1	88.8	65.6	60.1	60.8	50.6	63.5	43 019	48 622	29 392	123 300	21.0	9.9
Gratiot County	82.2	87.8	84.9	58.5	47.1	65.7	57.3	67.3	36 896	41 727	22 975	75 900	18.1	9.9
Hillsdale County	85.0	89.9	85.6	60.0	51.3	66.4	60.9	67.5	40 400	44 094	25 510	87 600	19.5	9.9
Houghton County	84.2	88.8	85.4	65.4	54.8	53.0	31.2	58.6	29 044	35 592	16 218	57 000	18.5	10.4
Huron County	88.3	92.4	88.7	67.0	57.4	72.2	61.0	73.4	35 375	38 824	20 754	79 700	18.6	9.9
Ingham County	74.9	83.2	81.2	51.5	44.5	40.3	26.3	45.4	40 579	54 759	23 489	97 700	19.5	9.9
Ionia County	85.7	90.6	88.4	66.1	59.0	64.3	67.7	63.6	42 904	48 222	23 128	93 500	18.8	9.9
Iosco County	87.3	92.5	84.8	62.0	51.5	71.3	69.6	71.5	31 245	34 106	18 418	78 500	21.0	10.1

Iron County	88.0	93.0	89.5	66.2	56.3	73.1	73.6	73.1	28 688	31 932	16 622	51 100	18.7	11.1
Isabella County	82.0	88.1	85.4	59.4	55.3	37.6	14.6	54.9	34 363	45 506	19 543	88 400	18.6	9.9
Jackson County	82.5	89.7	86.6	57.7	47.2	62.2	57.8	63.1	42 751	49 691	24 794	96 300	19.0	9.9
Kalamazoo County	79.7	88.0	80.8	52.1	44.3	42.6	27.4	47.8	41 924	54 107	23 642	105 200	19.1	9.9
Kalkaska County	88.9	92.9	88.3	69.3	60.2	76.2	70.6	77.6	35 808	38 150	23 004	81 100	21.4	10.3
Kent County	80.0	87.3	86.6	54.5	47.8	49.9	39.3	52.6	46 076	54 959	28 582	111 600	19.4	9.9
Keweenaw County	94.8	96.0	92.5	88.0	86.9	81.0	33.3	85.7	27 857	29 911	15 341	49 300	18.9	9.9
Lake County	86.0	91.1	81.7	65.4	54.8	77.3	79.4	76.9	26 206	29 290	14 049	59 000	22.5	11.2
Lapeer County	90.1	92.8	91.1	75.4	65.0	67.1	66.5	67.3	51 643	56 118	29 267	139 400	20.3	9.9

Items 11—24

STATE County	Percent who pay 35 percent or more of income for housing expenses		Means of transportation to work (percent except where noted)							Vehicles available (percent of households)		
				Car, truck, or van								
	Median gross rent	Owners	Renters	Number of workers 16 years and over	Drove alone	Carpooled	Public transportation	Other means	Walked	No vehicles	One vehicle	Two or more vehicles
	25	26	27	28	29	30	31	32	33	34	35	36

MARYLAND—Cont'd												
Washington County.......	482	13.8	23.0	60 597	80.6	11.9	1.1	1.0	2.1	9.4	31.7	58.9
Wicomico County	567	13.8	31.8	41 621	78.8	12.4	1.6	1.2	2.5	9.5	33.4	57.2
Worcester County	574	16.0	25.1	21 177	79.5	10.3	1.4	1.3	2.5	7.8	34.6	57.6
Baltimore city.............	498	20.5	33.0	249 373	54.7	15.2	19.5	1.1	7.1	35.9	40.3	23.8
MASSACHUSETTS ...	684	16.2	28.6	3 102 837	73.8	9.0	8.7	1.0	4.3	12.7	37.0	50.3
Barnstable County........	723	18.3	30.5	99 197	81.3	8.1	1.4	1.3	2.6	5.0	38.5	56.6
Berkshire County........	499	14.6	27.6	64 058	79.2	9.7	1.5	0.8	5.3	11.0	39.8	49.2
Bristol County..............	499	14.8	26.3	254 121	81.7	10.7	2.6	0.8	2.2	11.7	35.9	52.4
Dukes County.............	741	26.4	23.4	7 598	72.2	8.3	1.5	2.9	5.2	3.7	36.0	60.3
Essex County	665	17.0	28.7	343 631	78.7	9.4	4.9	0.9	2.8	11.1	36.0	52.9
Franklin County	541	13.8	27.7	37 053	79.3	10.1	1.2	0.9	3.4	7.8	36.6	55.7
Hampden County	535	15.4	30.3	202 127	81.4	10.3	2.5	0.7	3.0	14.7	38.1	47.2
Hampshire County	631	14.9	31.8	81 424	74.1	7.8	2.5	1.3	10.1	7.3	37.0	55.7
Middlesex County.........	835	15.9	27.2	763 636	72.1	8.2	10.3	1.2	4.6	10.5	36.4	53.1
Nantucket County.........	1 016	28.5	35.2	5 346	65.2	15.6	0.2	2.9	9.7	5.2	35.4	59.3
Norfolk County	853	16.3	27.7	331 653	72.9	7.4	12.3	0.7	3.0	8.8	35.6	55.5
Plymouth County..........	679	17.7	28.8	231 671	80.9	9.1	5.4	0.7	1.4	7.0	30.7	62.3
Suffolk County.............	791	20.5	32.1	320 979	43.7	9.8	30.9	1.5	11.8	33.2	44.7	22.1
Worcester County	580	14.7	26.1	360 343	82.6	9.3	1.7	0.7	3.0	9.8	35.5	54.7
MICHIGAN	546	12.7	28.4	4 540 372	83.2	9.7	1.3	0.7	2.2	7.7	33.7	58.6
Alcona County..............	411	14.0	25.9	3 808	79.0	11.4	0.1	0.8	1.8	3.4	34.6	62.0
Alger County................	376	11.0	17.1	3 713	76.0	12.0	1.0	0.9	6.0	6.2	33.2	60.6
Allegan County............	515	11.4	21.2	51 192	82.8	10.4	0.3	0.8	1.6	4.2	27.2	68.5
Alpena County.............	370	10.1	25.8	13 666	83.8	8.0	0.4	1.2	2.4	7.4	32.8	59.9
Antrim County..............	460	15.1	22.7	9 740	78.3	12.4	0.4	0.8	2.7	4.1	32.1	63.9
Arenac County	399	14.6	28.6	6 444	82.5	10.8	0.1	0.6	1.8	6.1	31.4	62.4
Baraga County	339	9.3	21.8	3 440	75.2	15.1	0.4	1.1	4.0	9.5	34.1	56.4
Barry County	493	11.7	21.6	26 921	83.2	10.4	0.1	0.3	1.7	3.9	24.0	72.1
Bay County.................	440	11.0	26.5	50 106	87.3	7.2	0.6	0.6	1.6	6.8	33.4	59.8
Benzie County..............	486	14.2	21.8	7 120	80.2	11.1	0.5	1.0	2.9	4.1	30.0	65.9
Berrien County.............	476	12.4	28.9	75 081	81.6	10.7	0.6	1.0	2.9	7.9	35.2	56.9
Branch County	477	12.2	19.4	20 737	78.3	13.0	0.4	1.4	2.5	6.8	30.4	62.8
Calhoun County	484	12.1	27.2	61 649	82.3	10.5	1.0	0.8	2.7	8.2	35.6	56.2
Cass County................	471	13.2	19.5	24 271	82.7	10.7	0.3	0.6	2.0	4.9	29.2	65.9
Charlevoix County	470	11.9	23.4	11 782	81.0	10.6	0.6	1.1	2.4	4.6	32.6	62.8
Cheboygan County	440	14.6	29.2	10 089	78.8	13.5	0.3	0.6	2.3	4.8	34.3	60.9
Chippewa County.........	426	10.7	28.2	14 918	74.5	14.3	1.7	1.1	4.9	7.4	37.7	54.9
Clare County	397	15.4	25.2	11 390	79.9	12.6	0.5	0.8	2.3	7.9	35.8	56.3
Clinton County.............	511	9.9	18.5	32 405	83.1	10.1	0.3	0.4	1.8	3.1	24.4	72.5
Crawford County	453	14.3	32.7	5 745	83.2	10.6	0.5	0.4	1.7	6.7	32.6	60.7
Delta County	383	10.0	22.6	17 116	83.4	9.9	0.8	0.8	2.4	6.7	33.1	60.2
Dickinson County	417	9.8	28.8	12 038	81.5	12.2	0.1	0.9	3.0	7.0	33.6	59.3
Eaton County	569	10.2	23.2	52 704	82.9	10.5	0.8	0.5	2.0	4.6	30.4	65.0
Emmet County	513	15.0	26.7	14 917	77.5	13.0	0.2	0.5	4.0	5.9	33.5	60.6
Genesee County	507	12.6	32.0	187 588	84.3	10.6	1.2	0.6	1.2	7.8	35.6	56.6
Gladwin County	395	15.1	20.6	9 518	79.3	11.6	0.4	1.2	2.1	6.6	32.6	60.9
Gogebic County	340	11.2	23.9	6 590	77.0	13.3	0.5	0.3	5.5	10.0	40.1	49.9
Grand Traverse County	614	13.6	24.2	39 292	81.9	9.8	0.7	1.2	2.2	4.7	30.6	64.7
Gratiot County	424	9.4	22.2	17 428	79.8	11.0	0.0	1.1	4.0	5.3	33.0	61.7
Hillsdale County	434	11.1	18.0	21 624	81.2	9.9	0.2	0.8	3.6	5.7	29.7	64.6
Houghton County	368	10.6	31.4	14 918	72.5	11.1	0.8	0.9	10.9	9.8	36.1	54.1
Huron County	383	10.3	21.3	15 355	78.2	10.6	0.6	0.8	4.3	5.7	34.2	60.1
Ingham County............	542	11.9	35.1	139 263	78.8	9.8	2.2	1.1	5.2	8.0	38.0	54.0
Ionia County................	468	10.7	22.7	26 669	81.6	11.5	0.2	0.8	2.0	4.3	28.0	67.7
Iosco County...............	416	12.6	29.1	9 957	83.4	9.9	0.3	1.1	1.7	6.3	37.7	56.0
Iron County.................	346	9.5	22.0	4 916	77.8	13.6	0.2	0.5	4.5	7.9	36.8	55.2
Isabella County	462	10.5	37.2	30 755	77.9	9.8	0.5	1.3	7.2	6.1	31.3	62.7
Jackson County............	505	10.0	28.2	70 317	83.5	10.6	0.5	0.7	1.9	7.5	31.8	60.7
Kalamazoo County.......	529	9.9	32.2	118 232	83.0	9.0	1.3	0.7	2.9	6.9	34.8	58.3
Kalkaska County	468	15.0	24.0	7 243	76.8	16.1	0.5	0.9	2.0	4.6	30.9	64.5
Kent County	554	11.0	26.1	284 236	83.4	9.5	1.1	0.9	2.1	7.0	33.7	59.3
Keweenaw County	263	8.4	21.4	894	75.5	10.9	0.0	0.2	6.8	6.4	34.2	59.4
Lake County	387	17.4	32.0	3 795	74.9	16.5	0.7	1.5	2.6	7.8	37.2	55.0
Lapeer County..............	541	12.7	22.9	40 141	83.6	11.3	0.3	0.5	1.4	3.7	23.2	73.1

Table C-3. States and Counties — Migration, Housing, and Transportation

STATE/ County code	MSA/PMSA/ NECMA code[1]	STATE County	Residence in 1995 (percent)						Occupied housing units		Householders 65 years and over	
			Total population 5 years and over	Same house	Same county, different house	Same state, different county	Different state	Outside the United States	Number	Percent owner-occupied	Number	Percent owner-occupied
			1	2	3	4	5	6	7	8	9	10
		MICHIGAN—Cont'd										
26 089	...	Leelanau County	20 044	61.2	12.8	17.9	7.1	0.9	8 436	84.7	2 310	93.9
26 091	0440	Lenawee County	92 699	58.1	24.4	10.6	6.2	0.7	35 930	78.2	8 080	83.4
26 093	0440	Livingston County	145 664	55.0	16.9	21.9	5.5	0.7	55 384	88.1	7 810	87.1
26 095	...	Luce County	6 665	59.0	14.9	20.7	4.3	1.1	2 481	79.6	658	83.7
26 097	...	Mackinac County	11 383	63.9	14.4	16.4	4.7	0.7	5 067	79.1	1 463	87.7
26 099	2160	Macomb County	737 174	58.3	25.4	11.3	3.2	1.9	309 203	78.9	70 833	81.9
26 101	...	Manistee County	23 247	62.5	17.5	14.9	4.7	0.4	9 860	81.0	2 864	89.5
26 103	...	Marquette County	61 409	58.3	23.0	10.7	7.4	0.5	25 767	69.8	5 933	77.6
26 105	...	Mason County	26 721	60.2	20.6	12.3	6.5	0.4	11 406	78.3	3 101	82.2
26 107	...	Mecosta County	38 146	51.6	15.4	26.3	5.2	1.5	14 915	73.6	3 335	89.9
26 109	...	Menominee County	23 811	65.9	20.2	4.6	9.1	0.1	10 529	79.5	2 882	82.9
26 111	6960	Midland County	77 546	59.7	20.5	12.8	5.7	1.3	31 769	78.4	6 524	80.4
26 113	...	Missaukee County	13 548	64.9	14.5	17.2	3.1	0.2	5 450	83.5	1 341	90.2
26 115	2160	Monroe County	136 291	61.0	21.7	8.3	8.2	0.7	53 772	80.9	10 771	80.9
26 117	...	Montcalm County	57 225	56.6	19.2	18.0	3.7	0.6	22 079	81.6	4 810	86.1
26 119	...	Montmorency County	9 856	60.0	14.4	22.2	3.2	0.2	4 455	86.1	1 507	92.2
26 121	3000	Muskegon County	158 669	58.6	28.7	8.1	4.2	0.5	63 330	77.7	14 517	82.0
26 123	...	Newaygo County	44 614	60.5	17.2	17.3	4.4	0.6	17 599	84.5	3 869	87.6
26 125	2160	Oakland County	1 114 228	55.8	24.7	10.8	5.9	2.8	471 115	74.8	87 173	76.0
26 127	...	Oceana County	25 165	62.6	17.4	13.2	5.0	1.8	9 778	82.7	2 481	88.4
26 129	...	Ogemaw County	20 523	61.1	15.7	19.5	3.3	0.3	8 842	85.0	2 672	91.6
26 131	...	Ontonagon County	7 484	71.2	15.9	6.3	6.3	0.3	3 456	84.9	1 161	88.3
26 133	...	Osceola County	21 755	61.1	17.5	17.1	3.8	0.5	8 861	81.3	2 113	88.7
26 135	...	Oscoda County	8 942	62.0	13.7	20.9	3.3	0.1	3 921	85.3	1 292	90.6
26 137	...	Otsego County	21 844	55.6	19.4	19.4	5.1	0.4	8 995	81.9	2 016	82.8
26 139	3000	Ottawa County	220 333	55.0	21.9	15.9	6.1	1.0	81 662	80.8	14 491	84.3
26 141	...	Presque Isle County	13 712	69.9	14.6	12.8	2.5	0.2	6 155	85.5	2 083	88.2
26 143	...	Roscommon County	24 380	58.4	15.4	22.3	3.7	0.3	11 250	85.8	4 013	93.5
26 145	6960	Saginaw County	195 858	61.5	26.0	8.1	3.5	0.8	80 430	73.8	18 984	79.7
26 147	2160	St. Clair County	153 105	58.4	25.5	12.4	3.1	0.6	62 072	79.6	13 391	82.8
26 149	...	St. Joseph County	57 924	57.8	26.5	6.9	7.6	1.2	23 381	76.9	5 388	83.6
26 151	...	Sanilac County	41 000	60.5	18.7	14.8	2.7	0.4	16 871	81.9	4 345	88.3
26 153	...	Schoolcraft County	8 405	62.2	20.0	12.3	5.0	0.5	3 606	81.0	1 001	91.1
26 155	...	Shiawassee County	66 861	63.1	21.4	12.3	2.9	0.4	26 896	80.1	5 516	83.2
26 157	...	Tuscola County	54 665	64.4	19.8	13.4	2.2	0.3	21 454	84.1	4 586	89.5
26 159	3720	Van Buren County	71 045	61.1	19.5	12.6	5.7	1.1	27 982	79.5	6 200	84.2
26 161	0440	Washtenaw County	302 785	43.0	22.8	17.7	11.7	4.7	125 327	59.7	17 055	79.1
26 163	2160	Wayne County	1 909 251	60.0	29.9	4.3	3.6	2.2	768 440	66.6	173 387	77.4
26 165	...	Wexford County	28 536	55.8	21.0	17.1	5.6	0.5	11 824	79.2	2 715	84.5
27 000	...	**MINNESOTA**	4 591 491	57.0	20.3	13.1	7.7	1.8	1 895 127	74.5	383 263	76.4
27 001	...	Aitkin County	14 607	63.2	12.7	20.6	3.2	0.3	6 644	85.3	2 259	82.9
27 003	5120	Anoka County	275 716	59.2	17.0	17.8	5.0	1.1	106 428	83.4	13 683	76.4
27 005	...	Becker County	28 118	61.8	18.5	11.9	7.4	0.4	11 844	80.4	3 226	77.6
27 007	...	Beltrami County	36 846	56.4	21.3	15.0	6.2	1.1	14 337	74.5	3 011	76.1
27 009	6980	Benton County	31 756	55.7	15.1	24.5	3.9	0.8	13 065	67.1	2 331	65.8
27 011	...	Big Stone County	5 551	74.9	13.1	7.3	4.5	0.3	2 377	85.1	850	85.9
27 013	...	Blue Earth County	52 798	51.9	19.4	20.0	7.2	1.5	21 062	66.4	4 380	75.3
27 015	...	Brown County	25 487	64.6	19.6	7.8	7.6	0.5	10 598	80.1	3 239	78.0
27 017	...	Carlton County	29 805	65.9	17.1	12.3	4.2	0.5	12 064	82.0	3 258	78.5
27 019	5120	Carver County	64 052	55.4	14.5	19.8	8.7	1.6	24 356	83.5	3 485	71.8
27 021	...	Cass County	25 770	62.8	13.4	18.8	4.6	0.5	10 893	86.0	3 315	85.6
27 023	...	Chippewa County	12 327	65.5	17.3	11.3	5.6	0.3	5 361	76.5	1 672	71.2
27 025	5120	Chisago County	37 974	57.3	13.1	24.5	4.8	0.3	14 454	87.0	2 530	77.0
27 027	2520	Clay County	48 078	54.3	17.9	11.0	15.6	1.2	18 670	71.6	4 261	74.9
27 029	...	Clearwater County	7 927	67.1	18.4	9.3	5.0	0.2	3 330	81.6	959	76.7
27 031	...	Cook County	4 938	57.8	17.2	17.3	6.9	0.9	2 350	78.2	563	81.0
27 033	...	Cottonwood County	11 461	68.9	17.0	8.3	5.3	0.5	4 917	80.4	1 761	81.1
27 035	...	Crow Wing County	51 804	55.7	22.6	16.2	5.0	0.6	22 250	79.6	6 043	81.9
27 037	5120	Dakota County	328 482	54.3	20.1	15.4	8.6	1.6	131 151	78.2	16 779	76.7
27 039	...	Dodge County	16 390	62.4	17.0	13.4	6.4	0.8	6 420	84.4	1 428	80.3
27 041	...	Douglas County	30 999	60.7	19.3	15.1	4.6	0.3	13 276	77.2	3 729	76.6
27 043	...	Faribault County	15 318	69.5	16.1	8.9	5.1	0.4	6 652	80.6	2 352	82.4
27 045	...	Fillmore County	19 886	66.7	17.3	9.7	6.1	0.2	8 228	80.7	2 495	82.2
27 047	...	Freeborn County	30 787	64.3	22.2	7.2	5.4	0.8	13 356	78.7	3 937	81.7
27 049	...	Goodhue County	41 483	62.5	19.0	11.5	6.4	0.6	16 983	78.9	4 059	76.9

[1]MSA = Metropolitan Statistical Area. PMSA = Primary MSA. NECMA = New England County Metropolitan Area. See the Appendix A for explanation of these concepts. See Appendix B for list of metropolitan areas identified by type, with component counties.

Table C-3. States and Counties — Migration, Housing, and Transportation

STATE County	Owner-occupied by household type (percent)								Median household income				Median monthly owner costs as a percent of income	
	Family-households				Nonfamily households									
		Married-couple family		Other family										
	Total family households	Total	With own children under 18 years	Total	With own children under 18 years	Total nonfamily households	Two or more adults	Living alone	All households	Owner-occupied households	Renter-occupied households	Median housing value (owner estimated)	With a mortgage	Without a mortgage
	11	12	13	14	15	16	17	18	19	20	21	22	23	24
MICHIGAN—Cont'd														
Leelanau County	87.9	91.4	87.3	65.2	53.3	75.7	64.2	77.7	47 110	50 640	32 432	164 900	22.4	9.9
Lenawee County	84.2	89.5	86.1	60.8	49.2	61.9	57.8	62.6	45 748	51 876	27 033	110 300	19.5	9.9
Livingston County	92.7	95.1	94.8	76.7	70.1	70.9	67.6	71.6	67 441	72 486	34 860	185 900	20.2	9.9
Luce County	84.4	90.3	87.0	52.3	42.5	67.6	59.2	68.5	31 698	35 069	18 155	68 200	19.3	9.9
Mackinac County	84.5	89.3	83.8	61.1	48.8	68.1	58.8	69.7	33 503	36 542	22 721	89 800	21.3	10.1
Macomb County	86.6	90.8	89.6	70.1	58.8	62.1	56.8	63.0	51 903	59 310	31 167	134 900	19.6	10.2
Manistee County	86.8	92.7	87.8	61.0	49.5	68.5	56.0	70.5	34 303	38 389	20 578	79 200	18.8	10.3
Marquette County	83.1	88.5	84.8	60.8	50.7	46.1	31.4	49.8	35 067	44 289	19 774	75 700	18.0	9.9
Mason County	84.0	89.8	85.9	58.6	50.9	65.4	61.0	66.1	34 816	39 697	20 233	83 300	18.9	10.3
Mecosta County	83.5	89.4	84.3	58.8	53.2	54.0	30.7	62.7	33 865	40 079	17 388	86 400	19.6	9.9
Menominee County	85.9	92.2	91.8	58.7	46.1	66.8	68.4	66.6	32 652	36 987	19 019	65 600	18.4	9.9
Midland County	87.1	90.9	90.0	65.6	58.0	56.5	45.0	59.0	45 236	52 896	22 430	96 300	18.1	9.9
Missaukee County	86.9	90.7	86.4	65.5	56.7	73.7	63.4	75.6	35 215	36 972	24 894	78 400	20.0	10.0
Monroe County	86.7	91.0	88.2	68.0	57.2	63.9	60.8	64.4	51 596	57 609	26 885	126 600	19.2	9.9
Montcalm County	86.0	90.2	86.7	68.2	61.6	69.2	64.6	70.1	37 242	41 011	23 560	83 300	20.3	10.3
Montmorency County	90.6	93.2	85.9	75.4	64.0	76.3	65.7	77.8	29 876	31 071	20 878	77 400	22.7	9.9
Muskegon County	83.4	91.2	89.4	61.1	50.6	64.4	66.5	64.0	38 039	44 373	20 463	84 400	19.2	9.9
Newaygo County	88.8	92.2	88.8	72.9	67.6	72.5	66.7	73.5	37 347	40 737	21 864	84 800	20.2	10.9
Oakland County	84.3	88.6	88.5	65.4	57.5	55.2	51.5	56.0	61 829	72 320	36 652	173 800	20.0	10.1
Oceana County	85.8	89.9	83.9	69.2	61.3	73.3	66.8	74.5	35 155	38 112	22 014	79 600	20.0	10.1
Ogemaw County	88.4	92.8	86.5	66.8	54.5	76.9	72.0	77.7	30 701	32 515	21 063	77 100	22.2	9.9
Ontonagon County	90.6	93.9	89.2	72.4	55.0	74.6	78.2	74.1	29 609	32 021	16 555	45 300	16.7	9.9
Osceola County	85.6	90.6	86.4	63.9	54.7	70.0	67.1	70.6	34 006	37 245	21 356	72 600	19.2	10.4
Oscoda County	88.2	91.5	85.8	68.7	59.6	78.6	81.4	78.1	28 050	30 208	18 542	70 700	22.8	9.9
Otsego County	88.2	92.2	89.6	67.3	56.3	64.8	57.2	66.3	40 927	44 851	24 290	101 500	20.1	9.9
Ottawa County	87.9	91.3	90.3	66.6	60.5	58.7	38.9	63.7	52 316	58 178	32 220	128 800	19.6	9.9
Presque Isle County	91.8	94.4	92.3	74.4	65.6	71.8	74.4	71.6	31 974	34 295	17 639	78 000	19.9	10.0
Roscommon County	89.8	94.2	88.3	66.0	55.0	77.4	67.9	78.8	30 033	32 107	18 587	76 600	20.7	9.9
Saginaw County	80.9	90.1	87.5	56.1	45.3	57.5	48.6	59.0	38 527	46 260	21 501	84 900	18.3	9.9
St. Clair County	86.1	91.2	88.2	64.8	55.2	62.8	55.5	64.1	46 129	52 483	24 889	122 700	20.5	10.5
St. Joseph County	83.2	88.8	85.4	62.3	56.9	61.4	55.7	62.7	40 409	45 381	25 612	84 400	18.6	9.9
Sanilac County	85.8	89.9	84.9	65.3	53.2	71.8	63.1	73.0	37 142	40 385	25 059	91 000	19.9	10.4
Schoolcraft County	87.5	92.2	89.1	65.5	56.7	68.7	80.5	67.4	30 630	34 512	16 234	66 600	19.4	10.3
Shiawassee County	85.7	90.2	87.8	67.0	56.9	63.9	57.9	65.1	42 843	48 290	24 382	97 100	19.2	9.9
Tuscola County	88.7	92.2	89.2	71.9	64.6	70.7	63.0	71.9	40 431	44 283	25 532	88 300	18.7	9.9
Van Buren County	84.1	89.7	86.1	62.7	54.3	67.4	64.4	68.1	39 317	44 275	23 162	90 100	19.5	9.9
Washtenaw County	76.2	82.9	82.5	50.2	40.1	36.1	23.2	41.1	51 773	72 031	30 123	170 100	20.5	9.9
Wayne County	72.8	84.8	81.3	53.4	40.1	54.1	48.9	55.0	40 570	51 060	24 138	96 200	19.8	11.1
Wexford County	85.6	90.8	88.9	64.3	56.4	63.6	56.4	65.2	35 447	38 674	22 093	78 300	19.9	10.4
MINNESOTA	85.0	90.3	90.1	61.4	54.2	53.8	47.4	55.3	47 033	55 338	26 551	118 100	20.0	9.9
Aitkin County	90.7	94.1	92.0	70.0	63.0	74.1	79.0	73.4	31 250	33 348	18 659	86 200	21.6	9.9
Anoka County	89.7	94.1	93.5	70.0	62.2	64.5	66.6	63.9	57 741	63 058	30 299	129 000	20.4	9.9
Becker County	87.4	92.1	91.3	63.6	53.3	64.8	67.7	64.4	34 753	40 037	17 564	84 100	20.5	10.2
Beltrami County	82.7	90.2	90.1	62.0	55.7	56.7	41.3	61.1	33 392	39 861	18 871	74 300	19.2	9.9
Benton County	82.6	88.3	90.7	57.5	52.4	38.3	26.1	42.6	41 838	51 095	25 835	99 300	19.6	9.9
Big Stone County	91.3	93.7	89.1	76.2	70.5	71.8	76.5	71.5	30 734	33 322	15 703	46 700	18.8	9.9
Blue Earth County	82.9	88.8	89.6	57.6	56.8	41.2	24.3	48.8	38 837	48 884	22 794	95 400	19.8	9.9
Brown County	88.6	91.2	91.2	72.3	64.4	62.1	44.2	64.0	39 638	44 895	22 447	85 200	18.8	9.9
Carlton County	89.9	93.9	92.5	70.5	62.5	63.8	64.0	63.8	39 826	44 705	19 626	86 200	19.6	10.1
Carver County	89.8	92.9	94.0	69.0	64.8	62.2	69.7	60.2	64 883	72 508	31 470	168 700	21.7	9.9
Cass County	90.2	94.3	92.8	68.9	65.2	75.6	72.7	76.0	34 149	36 709	18 823	96 200	22.3	10.6
Chippewa County	86.6	90.7	92.3	61.7	51.4	55.6	55.2	55.7	35 816	41 888	20 500	67 500	18.8	10.1
Chisago County	92.2	95.1	95.1	77.6	73.9	70.0	84.3	66.1	52 119	55 996	25 595	133 200	22.0	9.9
Clay County	84.3	90.8	89.5	55.4	48.8	46.5	34.1	50.0	37 346	48 101	16 574	84 300	20.0	9.9
Clearwater County	87.6	92.1	91.7	66.5	60.2	68.1	60.6	68.9	30 699	34 107	16 380	61 800	17.9	9.9
Cook County	87.7	90.7	88.5	70.6	64.6	63.3	70.7	61.9	36 903	42 375	22 500	107 200	22.0	9.9
Cottonwood County	88.9	91.8	88.9	69.5	56.4	61.7	59.7	61.9	32 054	36 903	17 727	55 500	17.0	9.9
Crow Wing County	87.5	92.6	90.4	62.4	57.1	62.3	59.8	62.8	37 487	42 923	19 629	104 800	20.3	9.9
Dakota County	86.2	90.6	91.5	64.1	57.3	57.6	51.1	59.4	61 807	70 078	35 701	148 500	20.3	9.9
Dodge County	89.4	92.1	90.9	73.0	68.5	68.6	64.6	69.4	47 601	52 127	26 420	99 200	19.7	10.4
Douglas County	87.8	91.7	91.1	61.9	59.4	54.0	46.6	55.4	37 588	43 854	18 894	101 500	20.6	9.9
Faribault County	87.3	89.7	87.5	70.4	64.3	67.0	63.5	67.4	34 370	37 803	22 346	54 200	16.8	9.9
Fillmore County	87.3	90.4	88.3	66.7	57.8	65.7	61.3	66.4	36 731	40 737	22 073	84 600	19.2	9.9
Freeborn County	87.1	92.0	89.0	61.6	54.2	61.2	60.4	61.3	36 882	41 729	20 910	76 000	18.3	9.9
Goodhue County	87.2	92.1	91.4	59.5	53.4	59.3	63.4	58.6	46 908	53 254	25 652	119 300	20.3	9.9

STATE County	Median gross rent	Percent who pay 35 percent or more of income for housing expenses		Number of workers 16 years and over	Means of transportation to work (percent except where noted)					Vehicles available (percent of households)		
					Car, truck, or van							
		Owners	Renters		Drove alone	Carpooled	Public transportation	Other means	Walked	No vehicles	One vehicle	Two or more vehicles
	25	26	27	28	29	30	31	32	33	34	35	36
MICHIGAN—Cont'd												
Leelanau County	565	14.9	18.9	9 715	79.0	10.0	0.6	0.6	2.8	3.0	28.3	68.7
Lenawee County	517	11.6	21.7	45 822	83.3	10.1	0.3	0.7	2.6	4.8	29.7	65.5
Livingston County	681	12.4	26.9	79 729	87.1	7.7	0.2	0.5	1.1	2.9	20.9	76.2
Luce County	430	10.5	26.3	2 341	75.7	13.1	0.2	0.9	3.8	4.9	37.2	57.9
Mackinac County	429	13.7	19.0	4 607	71.2	13.2	1.9	4.3	4.4	8.3	36.2	55.5
Macomb County	603	12.1	24.8	383 664	89.0	7.5	0.5	0.5	0.9	5.7	33.2	61.1
Manistee County	424	10.0	21.9	10 080	78.1	12.5	0.4	0.8	3.0	6.0	34.4	59.6
Marquette County.........	398	8.1	27.6	30 045	80.3	10.9	0.6	0.8	5.0	8.2	31.7	60.1
Mason County	425	11.3	24.5	12 392	81.4	9.7	0.9	0.8	2.6	7.4	33.1	59.4
Mecosta County	470	11.6	38.4	17 071	74.1	12.9	0.9	1.2	6.1	6.1	34.5	59.4
Menominee County	353	8.5	21.6	11 617	81.3	10.7	0.3	1.4	3.0	7.4	32.7	59.9
Midland County	498	8.9	29.3	38 207	86.6	7.7	0.5	0.7	1.3	4.6	29.0	66.3
Missaukee County........	460	11.3	23.4	6 170	76.6	12.5	0.9	0.7	3.6	4.5	30.0	65.5
Monroe County	549	11.0	27.3	68 835	88.1	8.2	0.4	0.4	1.0	5.0	27.5	67.5
Montcalm County	455	12.3	23.4	25 927	77.0	14.5	0.1	0.8	2.6	5.4	30.4	64.2
Montmorency County	431	16.3	20.1	3 271	79.8	12.6	0.1	0.7	1.6	4.4	34.8	60.8
Muskegon County.........	453	11.6	30.1	75 376	84.0	10.4	0.6	0.9	1.4	7.4	33.4	59.2
Newaygo County	447	12.7	25.7	20 096	78.9	14.5	0.3	0.7	1.7	4.9	29.6	65.5
Oakland County	707	14.1	25.6	603 761	88.2	6.8	0.5	0.5	1.1	5.4	32.2	62.5
Oceana County	427	12.5	23.0	11 153	77.0	13.8	0.3	0.8	3.2	4.4	29.8	65.8
Ogemaw County	432	16.0	23.3	8 032	81.8	9.9	0.3	1.0	2.1	5.7	33.2	61.1
Ontonagon County	321	8.1	16.7	3 090	73.4	13.3	1.0	0.9	6.1	7.2	32.6	60.2
Osceola County	409	11.0	23.5	9 809	78.1	13.1	0.4	0.8	2.7	6.5	31.7	61.8
Oscoda County	393	15.3	25.7	3 232	78.0	11.4	0.0	2.1	3.2	7.1	34.9	58.0
Otsego County	540	11.3	25.4	10 652	81.8	10.6	0.7	0.4	1.9	4.4	31.5	64.2
Ottawa County	579	9.9	22.9	121 120	85.9	7.2	0.5	0.6	2.6	3.6	25.7	70.7
Presque Isle County......	345	11.0	17.3	5 298	80.2	11.1	0.2	1.0	2.1	5.6	32.5	61.9
Roscommon County.......	420	14.0	27.9	8 719	80.9	11.8	0.6	1.1	2.0	5.9	39.9	54.1
Saginaw County	497	11.1	33.1	89 177	85.9	8.4	0.6	0.7	1.6	8.0	34.8	57.3
St. Clair County	537	13.7	28.7	76 437	83.7	10.6	0.5	0.8	1.7	6.0	30.7	63.3
St. Joseph County	456	10.3	22.4	29 237	79.8	12.7	0.3	1.2	2.4	7.2	31.1	61.7
Sanilac County	448	13.6	20.5	19 126	77.2	12.6	0.4	0.8	2.8	5.0	32.1	62.9
Schoolcraft County	345	10.5	30.3	3 204	74.4	13.8	0.8	1.0	4.8	7.4	33.5	59.1
Shiawassee County	482	11.8	24.9	33 514	83.0	10.4	0.1	0.7	2.1	4.7	28.3	67.0
Tuscola County	445	9.7	19.7	25 274	83.2	10.6	0.2	0.6	2.0	4.2	28.8	66.9
Van Buren County........	451	13.5	24.8	34 763	82.6	12.0	0.2	0.8	1.9	5.0	29.5	65.5
Washtenaw County	687	12.9	33.2	169 169	76.0	8.5	3.2	1.4	7.4	6.8	36.5	56.7
Wayne County...............	530	15.2	30.7	827 311	80.1	11.7	3.8	0.7	1.9	13.8	39.0	47.2
Wexford County	451	13.5	22.9	13 606	78.8	13.4	0.4	0.9	2.6	7.1	32.2	60.6
MINNESOTA	566	11.1	27.1	2 541 611	77.6	10.4	3.2	0.9	3.3	7.7	31.2	61.2
Aitkin County	409	15.5	25.9	6 098	74.1	11.8	0.4	1.1	4.7	6.1	32.2	61.7
Anoka County	649	10.2	28.9	162 802	82.4	10.1	2.7	0.5	1.1	4.6	24.6	70.8
Becker County..............	364	12.1	25.0	13 630	76.2	12.7	0.4	0.9	2.8	6.8	29.6	63.6
Beltrami County............	414	11.9	30.0	17 713	72.3	14.7	0.9	0.9	6.1	8.1	31.3	60.6
Benton County..............	480	10.3	20.1	18 652	81.3	10.1	1.4	0.9	1.9	8.0	28.8	63.2
Big Stone County	231	9.5	15.9	2 457	72.0	11.1	0.5	0.5	6.4	8.2	29.9	61.9
Blue Earth County........	487	9.7	29.7	30 876	76.9	10.4	1.6	0.8	5.8	7.3	30.8	62.0
Brown County...............	399	8.7	25.2	13 585	75.9	9.1	0.6	0.9	6.2	7.4	31.0	61.6
Carlton County	395	10.6	21.3	14 100	82.1	10.9	0.2	0.6	2.5	6.5	29.8	63.7
Carver County	637	13.2	24.2	37 317	82.6	8.7	0.8	0.4	1.9	3.5	22.8	73.7
Cass County.................	371	15.5	23.8	11 436	74.3	12.6	0.9	1.5	3.8	6.0	28.5	65.4
Chippewa County	401	8.5	25.2	6 256	76.9	10.6	0.4	0.5	3.5	5.3	32.1	62.6
Chisago County............	506	14.4	22.0	20 772	81.0	12.6	0.2	0.9	1.1	4.0	21.8	74.2
Clay County	421	9.5	36.8	25 430	77.4	10.1	0.8	0.8	7.2	7.3	30.7	62.0
Clearwater County	340	12.8	24.1	3 491	73.7	13.0	0.6	1.2	5.2	7.4	27.7	64.9
Cook County	456	14.3	18.4	2 597	67.8	13.5	0.1	1.0	10.1	5.2	38.5	56.3
Cottonwood County.......	308	7.1	21.1	5 799	73.1	10.8	0.5	1.1	5.6	6.1	32.5	61.4
Crow Wing County	458	12.3	28.6	25 420	81.1	10.6	0.5	0.7	2.7	7.0	29.8	63.1
Dakota County	722	10.4	24.1	197 794	83.5	9.0	2.3	0.7	1.0	4.2	28.1	67.7
Dodge County	386	10.3	16.5	9 205	77.8	11.2	0.9	0.4	3.3	4.6	23.8	71.6
Douglas County	411	11.5	27.1	16 283	79.0	9.2	0.4	0.8	3.1	6.9	28.5	64.5
Faribault County...........	347	8.3	17.6	7 621	74.6	10.1	0.6	1.0	5.5	5.9	31.2	62.8
Fillmore County	350	9.3	18.7	10 649	68.3	12.0	1.9	0.8	5.7	6.9	27.5	65.6
Freeborn County	368	8.7	24.9	15 801	80.6	10.1	0.4	0.7	2.9	7.2	31.3	61.4
Goodhue County	477	10.5	27.6	23 092	79.4	9.9	1.1	0.5	3.6	7.2	25.9	67.0

STATE/ County code	MSA/PMSA/ NECMA code[1]	STATE County	Total population 5 years and over	Residence in 1995 (percent)					Occupied housing units		Householders 65 years and over	
				Same house	Same county, different house	Same state, different county	Different state	Outside the United States	Number	Percent owner-occupied	Number	Percent owner-occupied
			1	2	3	4	5	6	7	8	9	10
		MINNESOTA—Cont'd										
27 051	...	Grant County	5 968	64.7	17.3	13.8	4.1	0.1	2 534	82.2	878	80.4
27 053	5120	Hennepin County	1 043 809	51.8	26.0	8.2	10.2	3.7	456 129	66.2	79 349	72.9
27 055	3870	Houston County	18 572	65.4	19.2	5.9	9.2	0.4	7 633	81.1	1 943	79.7
27 057	...	Hubbard County	17 368	59.8	14.1	19.3	6.5	0.3	7 435	83.4	2 167	80.9
27 059	5120	Isanti County	29 271	61.8	12.0	22.3	3.6	0.4	11 236	85.2	2 127	74.4
27 061	...	Itasca County	41 680	63.3	20.3	10.7	5.0	0.7	17 789	82.9	4 792	80.6
27 063	...	Jackson County	10 682	68.3	15.6	9.2	6.6	0.3	4 556	79.1	1 446	84.3
27 065	...	Kanabec County	14 108	61.2	15.7	19.8	3.1	0.3	5 759	84.0	1 372	80.5
27 067	...	Kandiyohi County	38 620	60.4	21.9	10.6	5.9	1.2	15 936	75.5	4 010	76.8
27 069	...	Kittson County	4 963	72.3	15.8	5.6	5.6	0.6	2 167	82.7	733	81.7
27 071	...	Koochiching County	13 607	66.0	21.2	6.2	5.6	1.0	6 040	80.4	1 813	78.7
27 073	...	Lac qui Parle County	7 664	72.4	13.9	9.0	4.4	0.3	3 316	80.7	1 193	78.9
27 075	...	Lake County	10 499	68.2	14.7	11.5	5.2	0.3	4 646	84.0	1 364	83.8
27 077	...	Lake of the Woods County	4 326	67.1	16.6	7.3	8.0	1.0	1 903	85.4	471	75.2
27 079	...	Le Sueur County	23 833	65.3	14.5	15.5	4.2	0.5	9 630	82.9	2 399	83.1
27 081	...	Lincoln County	6 070	67.7	16.2	9.5	6.4	0.2	2 653	80.4	999	78.1
27 083	...	Lyon County	23 744	56.6	21.8	12.0	7.6	2.0	9 715	68.4	2 441	71.2
27 085	...	McLeod County	32 472	61.0	19.9	13.0	5.4	0.7	13 449	78.5	2 983	73.4
27 087	...	Mahnomen County	4 812	70.4	14.0	11.1	3.7	0.7	1 969	77.3	628	78.3
27 089	...	Marshall County	9 564	71.8	14.1	9.1	4.5	0.6	4 101	83.8	1 252	80.4
27 091	...	Martin County	20 659	64.7	20.8	8.7	5.5	0.3	9 067	77.4	2 909	81.6
27 093	...	Meeker County	21 189	64.1	16.4	16.0	3.1	0.3	8 590	81.5	2 369	75.8
27 095	...	Mille Lacs County	20 979	58.4	17.9	19.6	3.7	0.4	8 638	79.8	2 330	77.0
27 097	...	Morrison County	29 559	67.4	18.6	11.3	2.5	0.2	11 816	82.0	3 200	79.1
27 099	...	Mower County	36 203	60.9	21.8	8.6	7.1	1.6	15 582	78.3	4 775	81.3
27 101	...	Murray County	8 670	72.4	15.8	6.8	4.8	0.3	3 722	84.5	1 262	86.3
27 103	...	Nicollet County	28 021	55.0	13.0	22.8	8.0	1.2	10 642	75.6	2 104	78.8
27 105	...	Nobles County	19 410	65.0	18.2	5.3	9.7	1.8	7 939	75.1	2 394	81.5
27 107	...	Norman County	7 008	65.8	16.5	9.9	7.3	0.6	3 010	81.1	1 042	80.8
27 109	6820	Olmsted County	115 459	54.8	21.9	7.5	12.7	3.1	47 807	76.0	8 694	77.5
27 111	...	Otter Tail County	53 980	63.2	18.7	10.4	6.8	0.9	22 671	80.0	6 975	75.9
27 113	...	Pennington County	12 747	60.2	20.3	12.7	6.0	0.7	5 525	74.6	1 423	75.1
27 115	...	Pine County	25 116	60.1	15.1	20.2	4.2	0.3	9 939	83.7	2 546	83.2
27 117	...	Pipestone County	9 314	68.1	16.6	7.1	8.1	0.2	4 069	77.5	1 363	83.6
27 119	2985	Polk County	29 456	62.0	20.2	7.5	9.4	0.8	12 070	74.0	3 437	74.9
27 121	...	Pope County	10 690	65.7	16.3	13.8	4.0	0.2	4 513	80.8	1 419	76.9
27 123	5120	Ramsey County	476 014	53.8	21.7	12.9	8.8	2.8	201 236	63.5	38 824	71.1
27 125	...	Red Lake County	4 063	71.4	15.0	9.5	3.9	0.2	1 727	79.4	516	76.2
27 127	...	Redwood County	15 770	69.3	18.6	8.5	3.5	0.1	6 674	80.0	2 052	80.4
27 129	...	Renville County	16 158	69.5	15.2	10.7	4.2	0.4	6 779	81.0	2 148	83.1
27 131	...	Rice County	53 208	52.3	20.5	14.7	10.4	2.2	18 888	77.9	3 887	78.5
27 133	...	Rock County	9 165	68.0	17.9	4.7	8.6	0.7	3 843	78.0	1 260	79.4
27 135	...	Roseau County	15 129	67.1	20.4	7.0	4.5	0.9	6 190	84.1	1 339	81.8
27 137	2240	St. Louis County	190 105	60.8	22.8	9.6	6.0	0.8	82 619	74.7	21 284	76.7
27 139	5120	Scott County	81 314	52.8	14.5	23.4	8.2	1.1	30 692	86.6	3 418	77.2
27 141	5120	Sherburne County	59 074	54.1	11.6	29.9	4.1	0.3	21 581	84.0	2 467	70.1
27 143	...	Sibley County	14 281	68.6	12.8	13.2	4.3	1.1	5 772	80.9	1 688	82.8
27 145	6980	Stearns County	124 571	57.1	19.7	16.8	5.2	1.1	47 604	73.8	9 538	79.6
27 147	...	Steele County	31 356	57.5	22.4	12.2	6.2	1.8	12 846	80.2	2 957	84.3
27 149	...	Stevens County	9 519	53.1	17.9	20.6	7.6	0.9	3 751	70.2	1 107	72.7
27 151	...	Swift County	11 311	61.4	15.8	9.2	12.3	1.3	4 353	77.1	1 493	71.5
27 153	...	Todd County	22 999	66.0	15.1	14.0	4.0	0.9	9 342	82.9	2 656	81.2
27 155	...	Traverse County	3 903	70.2	14.9	7.2	7.5	0.2	1 717	80.5	722	80.5
27 157	...	Wabasha County	20 378	63.6	16.9	12.5	5.8	1.2	8 277	82.5	1 965	81.6
27 159	...	Wadena County	12 844	62.1	16.8	16.3	4.6	0.1	5 426	77.4	1 699	77.2
27 161	...	Waseca County	18 216	60.4	20.4	12.1	6.8	0.3	7 059	80.0	1 695	82.2
27 163	5120	Washington County	185 760	58.3	14.5	18.1	8.0	1.2	71 462	85.8	9 692	79.3
27 165	...	Watonwan County	11 081	68.3	17.9	6.6	5.5	1.8	4 627	77.0	1 429	78.7
27 167	...	Wilkin County	6 683	64.0	15.9	9.1	10.7	0.3	2 752	80.6	710	76.3
27 169	...	Winona County	47 205	54.8	22.2	11.1	10.8	1.2	18 744	71.0	4 159	78.2
27 171	5120	Wright County	82 485	58.4	16.6	19.9	4.7	0.4	31 465	84.3	4 961	75.2
27 173	...	Yellow Medicine County	10 447	68.5	13.8	11.8	5.4	0.4	4 439	79.3	1 390	81.0

[1]MSA = Metropolitan Statistical Area. PMSA = Primary MSA. NECMA = New England County Metropolitan Area. See the Appendix A for explanation of these concepts. See Appendix B for list of metropolitan areas identified by type, with component counties.

STATE County	Total family households	Married-couple family Total	With own children under 18 years	Other family Total	With own children under 18 years	Total nonfamily households	Two or more adults	Living alone	All households	Owner-occupied households	Renter-occupied households	Median housing value (owner estimated)	With a mortgage	Without a mortgage
	11	12	13	14	15	16	17	18	19	20	21	22	23	24
MINNESOTA—Cont'd														
Grant County	88.6	90.4	88.6	77.0	72.8	67.7	62.0	68.4	33 750	37 273	20 259	59 400	18.5	10.5
Hennepin County	79.8	86.8	87.5	55.5	48.5	46.7	41.1	48.3	51 654	65 819	30 216	141 100	20.1	9.9
Houston County	89.7	93.6	94.4	69.2	63.5	60.0	56.1	60.5	40 916	46 348	21 741	92 600	19.2	9.9
Hubbard County	88.8	92.7	91.3	67.5	61.3	69.2	74.6	68.4	35 153	39 478	18 721	91 400	20.4	9.9
Isanti County	91.1	94.0	94.4	77.3	71.3	67.4	68.4	67.2	50 141	54 330	22 891	116 800	21.2	9.9
Itasca County	89.7	93.1	90.4	71.5	61.4	67.2	60.7	68.2	36 164	40 514	20 180	79 100	19.9	9.9
Jackson County	86.1	88.1	82.4	70.5	65.1	63.7	53.0	64.8	36 594	40 319	24 855	63 400	17.9	9.9
Kanabec County	88.5	92.3	90.8	70.8	65.4	72.2	83.5	70.3	39 070	42 243	23 726	89 800	21.2	9.9
Kandiyohi County	85.3	90.8	89.9	57.6	51.8	53.7	42.9	55.9	39 535	46 703	20 923	91 700	20.3	9.9
Kittson County	87.7	89.8	84.8	75.9	57.3	72.5	85.7	71.4	32 543	34 983	18 542	41 600	17.1	9.9
Koochiching County	88.5	94.5	93.1	60.7	52.6	64.9	66.0	64.8	35 718	40 351	15 933	63 700	17.9	9.9
Lao qui Parle County	88.9	90.3	88.2	76.3	73.3	63.8	66.7	63.0	32 772	36 583	20 325	53 100	17.5	9.9
Lake County	89.8	92.2	89.9	76.7	70.0	71.7	77.4	70.8	40 171	43 884	18 977	75 600	17.5	9.9
Lake of the Woods County	91.5	93.8	93.0	76.5	76.5	73.5	75.0	73.3	32 813	37 077	16 111	62 700	21.0	9.9
Le Sueur County	89.1	92.8	91.1	67.9	57.6	66.9	65.5	67.2	45 571	50 012	26 540	109 600	20.2	9.9
Lincoln County	87.4	89.6	88.8	69.1	56.3	66.1	58.7	66.7	31 427	34 083	21 150	51 300	18.8	10.5
Lyon County	80.8	86.6	85.3	47.8	42.4	45.1	29.3	48.9	38 977	46 870	22 197	82 400	18.6	9.9
McLeod County	88.8	92.1	92.9	69.0	65.2	54.3	52.7	54.6	46 389	52 892	24 904	105 700	20.1	9.9
Mahnomen County	81.0	90.0	85.2	57.0	43.6	69.0	68.0	69.1	29 161	32 500	18 375	61 900	17.9	9.9
Marshall County	91.6	93.3	93.3	78.4	77.0	66.1	65.0	66.2	34 701	38 068	18 188	52 600	17.5	9.9
Martin County	84.9	90.0	85.1	56.9	43.4	61.9	55.1	62.6	34 643	40 230	19 880	64 200	18.1	9.9
Meeker County	88.8	91.7	90.6	70.0	62.8	62.6	62.4	62.7	40 842	46 445	22 250	93 700	19.3	9.9
Mille Lacs County	87.6	92.2	90.0	67.7	61.8	62.1	72.5	60.2	36 847	41 742	19 272	94 000	21.0	11.0
Morrison County	88.4	92.5	91.4	66.4	57.2	65.3	65.7	65.3	36 824	41 102	19 073	86 600	19.2	10.1
Mower County	87.5	92.3	92.3	66.4	57.8	59.7	50.7	61.1	36 567	41 955	19 922	74 400	18.5	9.9
Murray County	89.1	90.5	87.1	74.8	71.2	73.7	61.1	75.1	34 847	37 009	23 421	58 100	18.6	9.9
Nicollet County	86.0	91.4	91.4	54.1	46.3	52.9	36.0	57.9	46 031	53 544	25 625	110 700	19.2	9.9
Nobles County	82.1	86.9	80.1	54.2	47.7	58.7	41.7	60.9	35 418	40 606	23 158	64 500	18.1	9.9
Norman County	87.5	89.6	89.4	73.5	60.0	67.0	74.5	67.7	32 712	36 055	20 865	49 100	17.2	10.7
Olmsted County	86.4	90.6	90.2	64.0	59.5	54.0	49.7	55.1	51 175	59 956	27 000	111 700	18.5	9.9
Otter Tail County	88.0	92.6	92.4	64.8	57.1	59.5	50.0	60.8	35 284	40 423	18 095	84 400	19.1	9.9
Pennington County	85.4	91.1	90.5	59.9	51.1	54.6	46.9	50.1	34 187	40 866	19 198	60 700	17.4	9.9
Pine County	89.8	93.5	91.6	73.5	67.3	69.4	68.5	69.6	37 348	41 509	20 023	87 400	21.0	8.8
Pipestone County	85.7	90.2	85.4	56.0	52.6	60.7	41.6	62.2	31 814	36 009	21 604	53 600	17.7	10.3
Polk County	83.8	89.6	88.3	56.2	47.8	53.8	42.6	55.3	34 988	41 970	18 331	72 700	19.0	9.9
Pope County	89.3	91.7	91.4	71.0	61.1	62.2	63.8	62.0	35 678	39 505	19 855	79 900	19.4	10.1
Ramsey County	75.9	83.5	82.9	53.1	41.8	44.9	41.5	45.7	45 595	59 553	27 349	122 800	19.9	9.9
Red Lake County	86.5	90.4	92.0	65.2	51.3	65.7	62.7	66.1	31 490	36 127	18 542	48 700	17.3	9.9
Redwood County	87.4	90.1	87.8	70.4	67.5	61.4	61.9	64.7	37 169	41 578	22 328	62 700	17.6	9.9
Renville County	87.4	89.8	86.0	69.7	58.8	67.4	65.5	67.6	37 751	41 195	25 777	61 000	17.7	9.9
Rice County	86.3	91.7	91.0	60.6	53.0	57.8	54.4	58.5	48 412	54 618	28 451	124 200	20.9	10.6
Rock County	85.0	88.0	85.8	57.4	55.2	60.8	38.6	62.3	37 851	41 551	21 150	73 500	18.4	10.4
Roseau County	90.2	93.5	95.6	72.3	67.6	68.5	74.9	67.7	39 836	42 887	23 136	69 500	19.1	9.9
St. Louis County	86.2	92.2	91.9	62.2	53.4	55.6	44.2	57.9	36 155	43 568	17 536	74 600	18.9	9.9
Scott County	91.3	95.0	95.3	68.5	61.0	69.5	73.4	68.2	66 359	71 380	29 245	160 900	21.4	9.9
Sherburne County	91.6	95.0	95.5	70.4	67.3	58.0	60.1	57.0	57 081	61 587	27 887	139 400	21.4	9.9
Sibley County	86.3	90.2	88.2	61.4	48.6	67.8	63.9	68.4	41 093	45 026	24 870	88 000	19.4	9.9
Stearns County	87.0	91.7	92.4	61.6	54.2	45.8	30.4	51.4	42 418	50 270	24 247	102 100	19.6	9.9
Steele County	87.9	92.7	90.0	61.9	55.8	61.6	52.3	63.4	46 259	51 759	26 351	103 400	20.2	9.9
Stevens County	86.5	90.2	91.1	55.3	40.9	42.3	23.1	47.4	37 245	44 669	16 069	71 400	17.8	9.9
Swift County	87.1	89.9	85.4	68.2	61.6	57.4	63.6	56.8	35 226	40 885	21 786	63 000	17.9	9.9
Todd County	90.1	93.3	91.7	70.2	63.6	66.1	62.7	66.5	31 984	36 325	16 462	70 400	19.9	10.1
Traverse County	87.1	91.7	91.2	63.8	51.5	67.6	64.7	67.8	30 625	34 521	18 750	41 100	19.5	10.0
Wabasha County	89.1	91.7	90.3	71.8	66.3	66.0	68.4	65.6	42 601	47 265	25 214	96 900	19.9	9.9
Wadena County	84.7	89.6	88.0	62.0	51.7	62.3	52.9	63.4	30 380	35 209	14 398	64 600	17.9	11.3
Waseca County	87.8	92.5	91.7	62.8	54.2	61.1	54.9	62.1	41 805	47 177	25 100	89 600	19.5	10.1
Washington County	91.1	94.2	94.9	72.1	66.2	68.2	66.8	68.5	66 183	71 677	32 626	156 200	20.9	9.9
Watonwan County	83.5	86.9	83.3	66.1	58.7	63.1	65.0	62.9	35 559	39 788	21 228	62 200	17.2	9.9
Wilkin County	89.2	92.1	90.8	72.8	60.7	60.5	67.6	59.4	38 441	43 538	17 222	64 700	18.0	9.9
Winona County	85.5	90.2	88.4	61.4	51.4	46.8	31.0	52.0	38 966	47 546	21 347	96 400	19.7	9.9
Wright County	90.4	93.6	94.3	71.8	66.1	64.7	74.4	62.1	54 174	59 749	27 085	134 500	21.2	9.9
Yellow Medicine County	87.2	90.0	88.5	68.7	61.5	63.2	39.9	66.1	34 609	38 556	19 875	60 900	17.8	9.9

STATE County	Median gross rent	Percent who pay 35 percent or more of income for housing expenses — Owners	Renters	Means of transportation to work (percent except where noted) — Number of workers 16 years and over	Car, truck, or van — Drove alone	Carpooled	Public transportation	Other means	Walked	Vehicles available (percent of households) — No vehicles	One vehicle	Two or more vehicles
	25	26	27	28	29	30	31	32	33	34	35	36
MINNESOTA—Cont'd												
Grant County	359	11.3	20.1	2 959	73.3	9.8	0.1	0.5	5.7	4.7	28.0	67.3
Hennepin County	654	12.4	28.6	607 567	74.9	9.5	7.2	1.3	3.1	10.7	36.5	52.8
Houston County	392	8.3	17.0	10 009	75.6	9.8	0.3	0.9	5.0	5.4	29.3	65.3
Hubbard County	382	12.5	17.8	7 862	77.9	12.0	0.5	0.5	2.9	5.5	28.4	66.1
Isanti County	527	14.2	31.4	16 085	80.0	13.1	0.5	0.7	1.8	4.8	21.9	73.3
Itasca County	406	11.8	23.8	18 909	80.0	11.8	0.6	0.7	2.8	7.0	28.9	64.1
Jackson County	357	7.1	17.1	5 596	76.6	8.9	0.4	0.8	3.5	4.5	29.4	66.2
Kanabec County	446	10.8	19.1	7 038	76.8	14.3	0.3	0.5	2.6	5.1	25.7	69.2
Kandiyohi County	435	10.2	25.2	20 815	78.5	11.3	1.4	0.6	3.1	6.8	30.1	63.2
Kittson County	347	8.1	16.1	2 255	69.9	14.5	0.7	0.0	6.6	5.0	32.7	62.3
Koochiching County	348	9.3	23.0	6 358	78.3	11.0	0.6	1.4	4.3	7.6	35.0	57.5
Lac qui Parle County	348	6.8	19.5	3 800	72.0	9.0	0.5	0.8	6.6	5.3	26.9	67.8
Lake County	435	8.5	24.4	5 114	75.4	12.6	0.0	1.0	5.9	6.4	30.8	62.8
Lake of the Woods County	338	12.9	24.1	2 123	68.2	14.5	0.0	1.2	6.6	6.9	25.9	67.2
Le Sueur County	433	11.1	17.3	13 204	78.2	11.3	0.4	0.9	3.8	5.3	26.0	68.8
Lincoln County	326	11.3	15.7	3 066	72.1	8.7	0.2	0.6	5.7	4.8	30.5	64.7
Lyon County	445	7.4	24.2	13 216	75.8	11.2	1.4	0.7	5.7	7.0	31.9	61.1
McLeod County	465	9.6	19.6	18 233	78.4	11.1	0.5	0.7	3.5	4.5	28.2	67.3
Mahnomen County	302	9.6	24.6	2 200	66.4	14.9	0.5	1.3	6.4	6.7	33.3	60.0
Marshall County	317	8.6	17.3	4 460	73.2	13.6	0.0	0.7	4.6	5.2	27.1	67.7
Martin County	342	9.4	21.0	10 620	79.1	8.9	0.7	1.0	3.9	7.2	34.2	58.7
Meeker County	441	11.0	25.5	10 969	77.4	11.0	0.2	1.1	3.9	5.6	27.3	67.1
Mille Lacs County	409	13.6	23.4	10 531	74.6	14.6	0.1	0.9	4.0	7.1	29.0	63.9
Morrison County	404	11.1	25.1	14 849	73.6	12.6	0.2	0.8	4.1	7.0	27.1	66.0
Mower County	380	9.2	24.4	18 336	79.1	10.4	1.6	0.8	3.6	7.5	34.6	57.9
Murray County	373	10.9	19.8	4 489	69.7	12.0	0.8	1.1	5.5	4.2	27.2	68.6
Nicollet County	488	9.2	22.9	16 542	76.6	8.6	0.3	0.8	8.8	4.7	28.8	66.5
Nobles County	388	9.2	20.6	10 012	70.7	15.6	1.0	0.6	4.6	7.5	30.1	62.4
Norman County	374	8.9	21.4	3 328	70.7	12.2	0.3	1.2	7.0	5.2	29.9	64.9
Olmsted County	556	7.8	28.6	65 891	77.2	11.3	3.1	0.9	3.8	6.6	31.9	61.5
Otter Tail County	391	10.3	26.4	26 150	75.9	11.1	0.5	0.7	4.6	6.5	28.4	65.1
Pennington County	349	8.0	23.0	6 558	77.2	13.4	1.3	0.6	2.7	7.2	33.7	59.0
Pine County	431	12.2	22.2	11 602	75.2	14.0	0.3	1.1	3.1	5.7	28.7	65.6
Pipestone County	365	7.3	20.1	4 889	75.7	8.9	0.0	1.0	6.5	6.0	32.9	61.2
Polk County	396	9.6	30.6	14 186	77.2	10.9	0.4	0.8	5.3	8.0	31.7	60.4
Pope County	363	10.3	25.5	5 285	75.3	8.2	0.2	0.8	4.2	6.5	27.4	66.1
Ramsey County	606	11.8	29.7	260 287	75.0	11.0	6.0	1.0	3.8	11.8	37.9	50.3
Red Lake County	282	8.2	15.0	1 903	72.7	12.4	0.2	0.4	6.0	6.9	27.3	65.7
Redwood County	371	6.9	17.0	8 061	72.2	10.3	1.1	1.3	5.8	5.5	32.6	61.9
Renville County	382	8.2	18.1	8 176	73.4	11.0	0.6	0.7	5.2	5.4	28.8	65.8
Rice County	519	12.1	20.4	28 604	71.1	12.0	0.7	1.5	9.8	6.7	29.1	64.2
Rock County	394	8.4	23.4	4 850	70.0	13.4	0.3	0.8	5.5	7.0	29.0	64.0
Roseau County	442	9.8	20.5	8 358	68.0	21.7	0.3	1.0	3.6	4.7	27.8	67.6
St. Louis County	415	10.4	30.1	92 771	78.3	10.9	2.2	0.7	4.3	10.2	33.8	55.9
Scott County	655	11.3	26.3	48 858	83.5	9.4	0.9	0.4	1.2	3.1	19.2	77.6
Sherburne County	570	11.1	25.8	34 084	81.2	12.4	0.4	0.5	1.3	3.5	18.6	77.9
Sibley County	426	9.4	17.9	7 839	71.8	14.3	0.2	0.8	4.6	4.5	26.6	69.0
Stearns County	473	9.6	24.4	71 453	77.2	9.4	1.2	0.8	5.6	6.0	28.0	66.0
Steele County	471	9.9	20.5	17 848	79.7	11.0	0.2	1.0	2.9	5.6	29.3	65.2
Stevens County	385	10.0	31.2	5 152	68.5	9.0	1.8	1.5	11.3	8.5	30.2	61.3
Swift County	362	8.3	24.1	5 160	75.6	9.0	0.5	1.2	5.4	7.6	30.9	61.5
Todd County	346	12.1	22.8	11 019	71.8	11.7	0.1	1.2	5.0	6.6	29.5	63.9
Traverse County	374	8.8	29.8	1 634	68.7	7.8	0.1	0.4	8.6	5.0	32.8	62.1
Wabasha County	434	10.0	22.5	11 174	73.1	10.1	1.7	1.0	5.5	5.3	25.8	68.9
Wadena County	337	12.1	26.2	5 831	73.9	12.0	1.0	0.8	4.2	8.7	32.2	59.1
Waseca County	402	8.5	18.0	9 652	77.9	12.0	0.9	0.3	3.1	5.6	27.0	67.3
Washington County	699	11.9	27.6	107 454	83.7	9.4	1.3	0.5	1.1	3.3	24.1	72.7
Watonwan County	338	8.3	19.9	5 495	72.4	13.9	0.1	1.1	6.2	8.7	30.9	60.4
Wilkin County	339	8.5	16.2	3 414	77.1	9.3	0.3	1.1	4.0	6.9	28.6	64.5
Winona County	425	9.4	27.4	26 103	75.4	9.3	1.0	1.5	7.3	8.1	32.0	59.9
Wright County	526	11.9	22.4	47 284	80.3	12.6	0.3	0.6	1.4	3.8	22.3	73.9
Yellow Medicine County	357	10.0	22.7	5 165	75.0	9.9	0.1	0.5	5.7	5.5	29.0	65.5

STATE/ County code	MSA/PMSA/ NECMA code[1]	STATE County	Total population 5 years and over	Residence in 1995 (percent)					Occupied housing units		Householders 65 years and over	
				Same house	Same county, different house	Same state, different county	Different state	Outside the United States	Number	Percent owner-occupied	Number	Percent owner-occupied
			1	2	3	4	5	6	7	8	9	10
28 000	...	MISSISSIPPI	2 641 453	58.5	22.5	9.4	8.6	1.0	1 046 434	72.4	229 696	84.0
28 001	...	Adams County	32 148	64.5	24.4	3.3	7.4	0.3	13 677	70.2	3 606	81.9
28 003	...	Alcorn County	32 280	63.7	22.0	5.4	8.2	0.7	14 224	73.5	3 383	81.2
28 005	...	Amite County	12 772	74.4	11.0	7.5	6.9	0.2	5 271	85.9	1 383	87.9
28 007	...	Attala County	18 398	64.2	20.0	8.9	6.3	0.6	7 567	77.7	2 296	87.7
28 009	...	Benton County	7 443	65.5	17.2	10.7	6.1	0.5	2 999	84.3	873	93.5
28 011	...	Bolivar County	37 622	62.9	24.0	7.1	5.2	0.7	13 776	61.1	3 054	76.0
28 013	...	Calhoun County	14 119	67.4	22.6	5.8	3.4	0.8	6 019	76.2	1 695	85.6
28 015	...	Carroll County	10 195	71.4	11.1	13.2	3.8	0.5	4 071	84.8	1 129	89.9
28 017	...	Chickasaw County	17 983	69.0	18.5	9.0	2.9	0.7	7 253	77.8	1 798	86.3
28 019	...	Choctaw County	9 093	69.3	16.3	9.2	4.6	0.7	3 686	81.3	1 049	87.8
28 021	...	Claiborne County	11 047	69.2	13.5	11.6	4.3	1.4	3 685	80.3	858	88.1
28 023	...	Clarke County	16 725	69.6	17.0	8.7	4.2	0.5	6 978	84.2	1 865	90.3
28 025	...	Clay County	20 386	63.6	23.6	7.2	5.1	0.6	8 152	73.4	1 935	86.7
28 027	...	Coahoma County	27 875	60.8	28.2	4.9	5.3	0.8	10 553	57.3	2 601	68.1
28 029	...	Copiah County	26 898	65.8	18.5	9.8	5.2	0.7	10 112	79.8	2 694	85.5
28 031	...	Covington County	17 905	68.1	18.5	9.8	3.4	0.3	7 126	84.9	1 739	90.7
28 033	4920	DeSoto County	98 866	48.5	19.7	6.8	23.9	1.0	38 792	79.2	6 024	88.6
28 035	3285	Forrest County	67 835	48.6	22.8	17.3	9.8	1.6	27 183	60.4	5 496	81.0
28 037	...	Franklin County	7 888	67.1	17.6	8.0	6.9	0.4	3 211	86.1	859	93.0
28 039	...	George County	17 751	62.6	21.2	8.4	7.0	0.9	6 742	86.2	1 385	88.8
28 041	...	Greene County	12 366	60.5	12.7	19.7	5.8	1.3	4 148	86.9	922	89.0
28 043	...	Grenada County	21 663	59.5	23.7	10.1	6.0	0.7	8 820	69.1	2 149	80.8
28 045	0920	Hancock County	40 235	56.6	18.3	8.1	16.3	0.6	16 897	79.6	3 760	88.8
28 047	0920	Harrison County	175 868	49.0	25.8	5.9	17.5	1.8	71 538	62.7	14 576	80.8
28 049	3560	Hinds County	232 375	54.2	30.4	8.5	6.1	0.8	91 030	63.9	18 009	80.6
28 051	...	Holmes County	19 931	68.9	19.5	4.9	6.0	0.7	7 314	73.2	1 968	82.4
28 053	...	Humphreys County	10 369	67.7	23.2	6.3	2.2	0.6	3 765	61.4	954	73.4
28 055	...	Issaquena County	2 139	61.0	11.5	23.4	3.9	0.2	726	67.4	182	74.2
28 057	...	Itawamba County	21 372	66.2	17.8	11.2	4.6	0.2	8 773	82.5	2 127	87.3
28 059	0920	Jackson County	122 189	56.6	23.3	6.4	12.3	1.5	47 676	74.6	9 106	86.1
28 061	...	Jasper County	16 910	72.8	14.2	8.7	4.1	0.2	6 708	86.8	1 834	91.1
28 063	...	Jefferson County	9 029	71.0	15.2	8.2	4.0	1.6	2 709	80.4	854	89.2
28 065	...	Jefferson Davis County .	12 971	69.5	16.8	8.5	5.1	0.1	5 177	84.5	1 321	92.8
28 067	...	Jones County	60 411	63.2	22.7	7.0	5.4	1.7	24 275	76.8	6 175	86.3
28 069	...	Kemper County	9 745	72.1	13.6	9.7	3.7	0.9	3 909	83.9	1 106	92.0
28 071	...	Lafayette County	36 686	43.9	17.6	20.3	15.9	2.3	14 073	60.6	2 460	82.2
28 073	3285	Lamar County	36 206	51.1	17.8	19.5	10.9	0.7	14 396	75.8	2 656	87.8
28 075	...	Lauderdale County	72 554	57.3	26.4	6.5	8.9	0.9	29 990	67.8	7 063	78.9
28 077	...	Lawrence County	12 356	68.2	17.0	8.2	5.9	0.6	5 040	84.3	1 159	94.2
28 079	...	Leake County	19 452	66.9	19.4	9.3	3.8	0.7	7 611	82.0	2 101	90.6
28 081	...	Lee County	70 111	55.2	27.4	9.8	7.0	0.6	29 200	69.2	5 369	81.2
28 083	...	Leflore County	34 986	56.9	29.1	8.0	4.4	1.6	13 066	53.3	3 147	67.0
28 085	...	Lincoln County	30 880	60.6	22.7	10.6	5.6	0.4	12 538	78.1	3 267	84.8
28 087	...	Lowndes County	56 830	55.7	26.1	6.2	11.0	1.0	22 849	66.6	4 402	81.0
28 089	3560	Madison County	68 859	52.3	18.5	18.5	9.7	1.0	27 219	70.8	4 328	77.4
28 091	...	Marion County	23 878	59.6	26.1	8.7	5.2	0.4	9 336	80.4	2 453	89.1
28 093	...	Marshall County	32 518	67.5	15.2	6.3	10.0	1.0	12 163	80.5	2 780	85.3
28 095	...	Monroe County	35 487	65.0	23.2	7.0	4.5	0.4	14 603	79.0	3 615	88.5
28 097	...	Montgomery County	11 437	67.3	19.7	9.9	2.5	0.5	4 690	76.9	1 314	83.0
28 099	...	Neshoba County	26 468	63.4	20.6	10.8	4.7	0.5	10 694	79.5	2 782	82.6
28 101	...	Newton County	20 300	63.2	21.3	10.9	4.2	0.4	8 221	81.8	2 231	89.8
28 103	...	Noxubee County	11 531	71.5	19.5	3.9	4.2	0.8	4 470	79.7	1 218	87.1
28 105	...	Oktibbeha County	40 351	42.2	21.8	21.9	12.0	2.2	15 945	55.6	2 618	83.2
28 107	...	Panola County	31 689	65.8	19.3	8.7	5.9	0.2	12 232	77.9	2 995	86.4
28 109	...	Pearl River County	45 197	56.4	21.6	5.1	16.2	0.7	18 078	79.8	4 048	87.9
28 111	...	Perry County	11 226	65.4	15.4	14.7	4.2	0.2	4 420	84.6	905	86.5
28 113	...	Pike County	36 069	62.8	21.7	8.1	7.1	0.4	14 792	74.3	3 725	87.1
28 115	...	Pontotoc County	24 760	60.9	21.1	11.9	5.3	0.8	10 097	78.1	2 382	82.7
28 117	...	Prentiss County	23 816	64.2	21.0	10.6	4.1	0.1	9 821	78.0	2 295	84.6
28 119	...	Quitman County	9 306	67.0	19.6	8.3	4.9	0.2	3 565	68.8	860	82.1
28 121	3560	Rankin County	107 265	51.0	20.7	18.9	8.2	1.2	42 089	77.2	6 743	87.2
28 123	...	Scott County	26 284	62.7	22.3	7.3	6.0	1.8	10 183	78.4	2 316	89.8
28 125	...	Sharkey County	6 032	69.3	18.5	8.6	3.1	0.5	2 163	65.7	513	73.9
28 127	...	Simpson County	25 698	65.5	19.1	10.8	3.9	0.6	10 076	81.2	2 467	90.2
28 129	...	Smith County	15 060	69.3	17.1	9.7	3.1	0.9	6 046	87.0	1 537	91.8
28 131	...	Stone County	12 689	55.7	20.1	14.1	9.3	0.8	4 747	81.3	977	88.3

[1]MSA = Metropolitan Statistical Area. PMSA = Primary MSA. NECMA = New England County Metropolitan Area. See the Appendix A for explanation of these concepts. See Appendix B for list of metropolitan areas identified by type, with component counties.

STATE County	Owner-occupied by household type (percent)								Median household income			Median housing value (owner estimated)	Median monthly owner costs as a percent of income	
	Family-households					Nonfamily households								
		Married-couple family		Other family										
	Total family households	Total	With own children under 18 years	Total	With own children under 18 years	Total nonfamily households	Two or more adults	Living alone	All households	Owner-occupied households	Renter-occupied households	Median housing value (owner estimated)	With a mortgage	Without a mortgage
	11	12	13	14	15	16	17	18	19	20	21	22	23	24
MISSISSIPPI	77.0	85.3	81.1	57.6	46.4	60.5	40.4	63.5	31 232	36 822	19 603	64 700	20.4	9.9
Adams County	74.1	85.0	80.5	56.1	43.7	61.3	45.5	62.9	25 488	31 630	14 248	57 900	22.3	11.1
Alcorn County	79.7	85.0	82.3	60.6	47.2	59.0	33.2	61.3	29 135	34 383	17 952	58 700	19.6	9.9
Amite County	88.2	92.1	91.6	77.8	68.8	79.4	64.6	80.5	26 049	28 824	13 556	51 200	20.8	10.7
Attala County	79.4	87.2	78.7	60.4	50.5	73.6	54.6	75.0	24 543	27 586	16 135	47 400	21.2	9.9
Benton County	85.4	89.6	86.0	72.6	56.8	81.5	56.1	84.4	25 170	27 595	18 854	50 700	21.6	10.6
Bolivar County	64.7	77.0	68.7	50.6	37.7	52.2	28.1	55.7	23 286	31 949	14 052	51 300	20.3	11.1
Calhoun County	79.9	87.0	83.4	62.5	49.9	67.0	31.1	69.6	27 275	31 791	17 511	46 500	20.4	10.1
Carroll County	85.9	91.2	92.7	70.6	54.5	81.6	81.0	81.6	28 822	30 888	20 691	51 200	19.3	12.3
Chickasaw County	81.0	87.8	82.6	66.5	62.1	69.1	48.0	70.5	25 465	30 350	16 521	46 800	21.0	11.8
Choctaw County	84.6	89.0	81.6	71.4	59.6	72.8	76.5	72.4	26 174	28 807	15 938	54 100	21.4	11.2
Claiborne County	82.3	90.0	87.2	71.7	62.5	75.9	65.1	77.0	22 295	24 854	12 899	42 200	22.0	12.5
Clarke County	85.1	89.5	86.6	73.2	64.8	82.1	69.4	83.2	26 676	29 794	16 474	47 700	18.5	9.9
Clay County	76.6	88.5	82.1	57.0	45.0	65.0	37.4	66.9	26 754	33 367	15 632	58 000	19.8	9.9
Coahoma County	61.6	77.6	70.7	44.2	34.5	47.2	31.0	49.1	22 428	31 549	13 992	48 200	21.3	12.7
Copiah County	82.9	89.5	86.1	70.5	62.1	71.0	54.5	72.6	26 173	29 271	14 533	52 300	21.7	12.5
Covington County	86.6	91.7	91.7	75.2	70.9	79.8	74.0	80.2	26 309	28 253	15 924	49 800	22.0	11.1
DeSoto County	82.7	87.1	83.1	64.8	56.9	67.0	60.3	68.4	48 114	53 364	32 781	101 200	20.3	9.9
Forrest County	71.0	81.6	79.4	50.1	42.0	41.7	21.6	47.0	27 179	36 267	17 358	64 800	21.1	10.9
Franklin County	86.6	92.0	86.1	69.9	62.2	84.7	85.0	84.7	24 618	27 621	11 950	44 300	23.0	9.9
George County	88.7	90.8	89.4	77.9	71.7	77.1	47.4	80.1	35 248	37 740	23 033	60 100	19.2	9.9
Greene County	89.9	92.0	88.4	80.4	70.0	77.3	73.1	77.6	28 733	30 971	15 263	49 700	19.4	11.4
Grenada County	73.4	83.4	77.1	50.0	36.5	58.2	35.8	60.6	27 904	33 605	17 371	64 000	21.5	9.9
Hancock County	84.1	88.9	83.2	67.0	54.6	69.1	60.0	71.0	35 337	39 116	22 682	82 100	21.4	9.9
Harrison County	68.5	76.3	69.0	49.2	37.2	50.3	39.3	52.8	35 502	43 069	25 668	82 000	20.4	9.9
Hinds County	70.2	83.2	79.0	50.1	37.3	49.9	33.1	52.7	33 957	43 530	20 203	72 100	20.8	9.9
Holmes County	75.7	86.1	84.9	65.8	55.6	66.9	64.6	67.1	17 530	21 710	10 291	39 700	26.1	14.1
Humphreys County	62.7	78.2	72.5	46.5	34.6	57.8	43.8	58.9	21 169	26 057	14 495	46 000	20.5	14.1
Issaquena County	69.2	78.1	77.3	52.0	38.5	63.1	55.6	64.1	19 708	24 236	13 417	43 900	21.3	13.6
Itawamba County	85.0	88.9	85.6	67.1	52.8	75.1	74.5	75.2	31 200	33 392	20 924	55 300	19.0	9.9
Jackson County	78.9	85.5	79.3	58.5	46.5	61.2	45.2	64.3	39 143	44 959	24 976	75 400	19.5	9.9
Jasper County	88.2	90.8	89.1	82.5	76.5	82.7	69.1	83.3	24 559	26 168	16 396	47 600	23.7	11.4
Jefferson County	81.7	92.4	88.4	71.0	67.4	77.4	78.5	77.4	18 366	21 174	9 955	41 900	22.8	15.8
Jefferson Davis County	86.0	91.0	86.8	76.8	68.3	80.5	79.8	80.6	21 414	23 501	13 115	45 100	24.8	11.7
Jones County	81.0	88.7	84.3	59.4	48.6	65.7	44.6	68.2	28 648	32 785	18 604	54 000	19.8	9.9
Kemper County	85.4	91.1	90.5	74.5	63.4	80.1	80.9	80.1	24 081	26 701	12 708	46 500	22.2	11.2
Lafayette County	77.1	84.4	80.5	52.3	45.8	37.6	11.9	48.6	27 770	40 366	16 023	83 900	20.8	10.2
Lamar County	82.2	87.3	86.6	59.2	46.0	56.9	19.2	65.6	37 438	42 843	23 244	86 000	20.1	9.9
Lauderdale County	72.3	82.6	77.1	50.6	35.4	58.1	42.7	59.9	30 759	37 246	17 309	62 000	19.9	9.9
Lawrence County	84.8	89.5	83.9	68.9	57.4	82.8	66.7	83.9	28 188	31 367	15 827	51 300	20.4	10.6
Leake County	83.3	88.9	86.3	69.0	55.3	78.4	41.7	81.5	26 955	29 502	18 438	50 400	20.8	9.9
Lee County	74.9	84.1	90.0	47.6	40.1	55.0	41.0	57.0	36 141	43 869	23 023	79 100	19.0	9.9
Leflore County	57.9	76.8	72.9	38.2	25.9	43.1	32.3	44.2	21 153	31 183	13 414	52 700	22.7	10.6
Lincoln County	81.4	87.7	84.1	59.9	46.3	68.9	63.7	69.4	27 390	32 283	15 710	57 400	20.7	10.9
Lowndes County	71.9	82.0	74.7	48.4	35.9	52.9	36.8	55.0	32 257	40 839	17 677	71 400	20.5	9.9
Madison County	79.5	87.3	87.3	59.1	50.2	49.3	40.2	50.6	46 859	59 125	28 475	110 900	18.9	9.9
Marion County	83.2	88.5	84.0	68.6	58.7	72.3	77.9	71.9	23 942	26 941	16 092	52 800	22.2	12.2
Marshall County	82.5	89.5	86.8	69.2	60.0	74.7	68.6	75.4	28 893	32 420	17 335	60 200	23.5	11.1
Monroe County	81.5	88.4	85.9	63.2	47.4	72.2	62.9	73.0	30 303	34 171	17 083	59 400	20.9	9.9
Montgomery County	77.5	85.2	81.3	61.6	51.2	75.6	68.1	76.0	25 382	29 290	14 096	48 600	22.0	11.5
Neshoba County	81.9	88.5	88.2	65.0	56.5	73.2	66.2	73.8	28 091	31 342	18 146	54 000	20.6	11.2
Newton County	83.8	88.4	84.8	71.4	60.2	76.4	60.7	77.6	27 768	31 515	15 142	50 000	20.1	10.3
Noxubee County	81.3	86.2	82.6	74.1	65.4	75.7	80.0	75.5	22 029	25 343	12 985	41 300	22.8	11.1
Oktibbeha County	71.2	78.3	79.2	55.8	47.5	33.9	10.5	45.8	24 352	38 923	13 761	76 300	19.7	9.9
Panola County	79.3	86.8	81.3	64.8	54.5	73.7	54.6	75.9	26 623	30 694	16 776	48 400	21.5	10.4
Pearl River County	81.5	87.1	81.1	61.5	50.8	74.6	64.4	75.9	30 684	34 459	18 728	70 200	21.5	10.4
Perry County	86.2	89.9	86.8	72.1	61.0	79.3	61.7	81.1	27 201	30 048	17 679	46 900	20.9	11.1
Pike County	77.2	87.2	82.0	58.9	48.6	67.1	49.8	68.3	23 930	27 945	14 127	53 400	22.7	12.6
Pontotoc County	82.9	87.1	84.0	66.8	61.0	62.9	57.1	63.3	31 991	36 754	20 967	59 800	19.5	9.9
Prentiss County	82.0	87.7	82.0	63.0	49.6	67.4	52.0	68.9	28 606	32 333	19 240	53 400	19.9	9.9
Quitman County	72.3	82.6	78.5	60.3	49.1	60.6	44.2	62.2	20 604	25 541	13 444	34 700	22.6	12.7
Rankin County	81.7	87.2	84.2	61.5	53.3	64.1	48.4	66.9	44 709	50 568	29 902	88 500	19.0	9.9
Scott County	80.0	86.0	82.4	67.3	56.7	73.8	49.3	77.7	26 726	29 455	18 619	42 600	22.0	10.8
Sharkey County	67.8	77.8	72.8	54.9	42.8	59.8	33.9	62.6	22 399	28 397	14 636	43 400	20.2	9.9
Simpson County	82.4	86.5	84.0	70.5	62.2	77.6	49.7	79.9	27 731	30 035	19 623	51 900	22.6	12.6
Smith County	87.9	90.3	89.7	78.9	67.8	83.9	66.2	84.8	30 623	31 906	22 115	54 000	19.6	11.1
Stone County	82.4	87.6	82.4	60.8	51.6	77.8	58.8	80.0	31 465	35 785	20 921	69 900	20.0	12.9

STATE County	Median gross rent	Percent who pay 35 percent or more of income for housing expenses		Means of transportation to work (percent except where noted)						Vehicles available (percent of households)		
		Owners	Renters	Number of workers 16 years and over	Car, truck, or van		Public transportation	Other means	Walked	No vehicles	One vehicle	Two or more vehicles
					Drove alone	Carpooled						
	25	26	27	28	29	30	31	32	33	34	35	36
MISSISSIPPI	439	16.0	27.6	1 164 118	79.4	15.2	0.6	1.0	1.9	9.2	34.2	56.6
Adams County	375	18.7	32.0	12 633	79.3	14.6	1.2	1.0	1.7	9.9	38.6	51.5
Alcorn County	355	13.4	23.3	14 535	83.9	11.3	0.3	0.7	1.7	8.2	31.2	60.7
Amite County	291	17.6	21.6	4 872	77.6	14.6	0.8	1.5	1.5	10.3	31.7	58.0
Attala County	349	16.8	25.7	7 238	75.6	19.3	0.9	1.1	1.4	13.4	36.7	49.9
Benton County	368	17.6	24.4	2 814	80.0	15.8	1.3	1.1	0.5	7.0	34.0	59.0
Bolivar County	377	18.9	31.1	13 885	75.1	18.2	1.0	1.2	2.9	16.8	39.5	43.7
Calhoun County	321	13.4	18.4	6 182	76.4	19.9	0.3	0.4	1.5	11.2	32.8	56.0
Carroll County	340	18.9	11.0	4 373	77.7	19.1	0.5	0.5	0.8	9.1	31.3	59.6
Chickasaw County	349	15.4	25.6	7 846	77.6	17.8	0.3	0.9	1.8	9.9	33.7	56.4
Choctaw County	332	15.9	24.1	3 470	76.5	18.1	0.6	1.1	0.7	11.2	29.5	59.3
Claiborne County	312	22.9	31.7	3 687	69.9	20.8	1.4	0.5	6.2	15.4	40.1	44.5
Clarke County	355	16.8	20.6	6 541	79.9	16.1	0.6	1.0	1.1	10.4	32.5	57.0
Clay County	364	19.6	28.1	8 604	77.3	17.1	0.5	1.5	2.3	11.3	37.0	51.7
Coahoma County	360	22.3	27.8	9 952	69.4	21.3	3.8	1.5	2.5	19.0	39.1	41.9
Copiah County	363	17.3	25.0	10 718	75.9	19.0	0.6	1.5	2.0	11.1	35.3	53.6
Covington County	343	19.7	23.9	7 266	76.7	17.6	0.3	1.2	1.0	0.5	34.1	57.3
DeSoto County	657	13.1	22.0	52 647	85.5	11.2	0.2	0.6	0.3	3.6	27.7	68.7
Forrest County	438	18.2	32.8	31 559	80.1	12.9	0.3	1.1	3.6	8.2	39.7	52.1
Franklin County	273	14.9	25.9	2 963	79.7	15.1	0.6	1.1	2.3	11.0	30.8	58.3
George County	428	13.6	18.8	7 207	69.4	25.8	0.1	1.1	2.2	4.0	29.4	66.6
Greene County	338	13.9	25.3	4 122	72.0	22.3	0.4	1.8	1.2	7.6	29.8	62.7
Grenada County	371	19.2	25.5	9 174	79.6	16.8	0.9	0.9	1.1	13.3	33.5	53.3
Hancock County	510	16.5	27.7	17 053	78.8	14.4	0.4	2.1	0.9	5.0	35.5	59.5
Harrison County	543	15.1	26.9	87 885	79.1	13.0	0.5	1.2	4.7	6.6	37.7	55.7
Hinds County	503	17.0	32.3	107 388	79.0	15.6	0.9	0.8	2.1	9.8	38.2	52.0
Holmes County	265	26.2	24.4	6 113	67.3	27.6	1.6	1.1	1.6	23.0	36.7	40.3
Humphreys County	313	16.2	24.5	3 573	65.7	26.1	1.5	1.2	4.4	17.3	42.6	40.1
Issaquena County	225	17.5	18.3	685	71.2	18.4	1.3	1.6	4.5	17.2	36.5	46.3
Itawamba County	384	13.3	19.9	9 915	81.0	15.8	0.1	0.3	0.9	6.2	27.7	66.2
Jackson County	522	13.1	26.5	58 112	81.8	13.6	0.4	1.0	0.9	5.9	30.7	63.3
Jasper County	315	21.4	19.1	6 481	76.7	19.1	0.2	0.8	1.3	12.4	31.0	56.6
Jefferson County	276	23.1	32.0	2 004	76.4	20.7	0.5	0.2	0.3	15.8	39.2	45.0
Jefferson Davis County	321	25.2	26.1	4 600	76.4	18.4	0.9	1.7	0.0	11.6	35.4	53.0
Jones County	374	14.6	22.7	26 495	79.9	14.9	0.8	1.1	1.5	8.2	32.2	59.6
Kemper County	233	21.4	17.0	3 816	73.0	21.9	0.7	0.7	1.0	13.7	34.5	51.9
Lafayette County	507	16.8	42.9	17 269	78.3	13.5	0.1	1.0	4.6	6.5	35.3	58.3
Lamar County	523	13.9	27.9	17 967	84.1	10.7	0.6	1.0	1.1	4.8	29.4	66.1
Lauderdale County	404	16.0	27.1	31 587	81.1	12.7	0.4	1.2	3.0	11.9	35.0	53.1
Lawrence County	351	18.2	24.3	4 958	75.0	19.1	0.6	2.0	1.5	7.4	30.7	61.9
Loake County	345	17.6	18.7	7 568	73.6	21.1	1.0	1.3	1.0	10.2	33.7	56.1
Lee County	441	12.3	22.2	35 569	83.9	12.3	0.3	0.7	1.1	8.1	32.7	59.2
Leflore County	325	21.1	29.4	12 184	74.1	18.5	1.8	1.3	2.7	18.7	41.5	39.8
Lincoln County	366	14.8	27.1	12 700	80.1	15.0	0.4	1.2	1.3	9.2	33.6	58.3
Lowndes County	416	15.3	30.1	25 310	79.7	15.0	0.1	0.8	2.7	9.9	32.9	57.2
Madison County	590	13.8	26.0	34 902	82.6	12.6	0.3	0.6	0.8	6.8	32.4	60.8
Marion County	345	18.2	25.3	9 350	79.0	15.3	0.5	2.4	1.1	8.0	36.4	55.7
Marshall County	375	22.0	22.7	13 494	77.3	18.0	0.3	1.2	1.4	9.9	31.9	58.2
Monroe County	362	14.2	25.9	15 303	82.2	14.4	0.1	0.8	0.7	10.0	31.4	58.6
Montgomery County	347	17.2	26.2	4 620	77.6	18.3	0.6	1.4	0.8	13.3	33.0	53.6
Neshoba County	343	16.3	18.5	11 780	80.2	15.3	0.4	1.1	1.2	9.1	33.8	57.1
Newton County	345	15.0	24.3	8 778	80.0	15.2	0.3	0.5	1.4	9.0	32.7	58.3
Noxubee County	270	19.5	22.2	3 991	75.2	17.8	1.0	1.4	2.2	18.0	35.5	46.5
Oktibbeha County	473	16.6	42.0	18 401	79.1	13.4	0.8	0.8	4.1	8.8	35.9	55.3
Panola County	387	16.2	27.4	12 673	78.0	18.1	0.4	1.1	1.3	9.9	36.1	54.1
Pearl River County	421	17.1	25.6	18 875	78.4	15.5	0.3	1.8	1.6	6.4	31.7	61.9
Perry County	310	16.5	17.9	4 565	76.7	17.0	1.0	1.8	1.1	9.7	27.4	62.9
Pike County	380	19.3	32.0	13 953	80.5	15.0	0.2	1.2	1.3	11.1	35.0	53.9
Pontotoc County	391	11.7	23.1	12 191	80.5	16.2	0.0	0.8	1.0	7.3	29.4	63.3
Prentiss County	325	13.5	16.3	10 811	81.7	14.8	0.1	0.5	1.2	8.3	30.8	60.9
Quitman County	303	20.2	25.4	3 416	67.9	23.7	2.1	1.8	2.6	17.0	39.8	43.2
Rankin County	576	11.4	20.8	56 240	84.7	11.1	0.2	0.8	0.6	4.3	29.9	65.8
Scott County	370	17.3	22.8	11 246	72.7	19.2	0.5	1.5	3.9	11.2	34.6	54.3
Sharkey County	283	17.3	24.0	2 155	72.2	19.4	1.1	1.9	3.6	17.7	39.9	42.4
Simpson County	376	19.3	21.6	10 374	74.9	19.0	0.6	0.6	2.4	9.4	31.7	58.8
Smith County	331	14.0	17.0	6 417	74.6	17.5	0.4	1.7	1.0	8.2	30.3	61.5
Stone County	429	15.9	19.7	5 805	78.3	14.0	0.4	1.6	1.8	7.0	27.8	65.2

STATE/ County code	MSA/PMSA/ NECMA code[1]	STATE County	Total population 5 years and over	Same house	Same county, different house	Same state, different county	Different state	Outside the United States	Number	Percent owner-occupied	Number	Percent owner-occupied
						Residence in 1995 (percent)			Occupied housing units		Householders 65 years and over	
			1	2	3	4	5	6	7	8	9	10
		MISSISSIPPI—Cont'd										
28 133	...	Sunflower County.........	31 979	62.5	20.3	12.5	4.0	0.6	9 637	61.9	2 111	72.9
28 135	...	Tallahatchie County	13 893	70.6	17.7	8.0	3.2	0.4	5 263	76.1	1 377	84.6
28 137	...	Tate County.................	23 546	60.8	16.8	12.1	9.9	0.3	8 850	78.3	2 029	85.1
28 139	...	Tippah County..............	19 495	64.6	21.3	7.5	5.1	1.4	8 108	78.1	1 892	88.5
28 141	...	Tishomingo County	18 057	67.5	18.6	5.7	7.5	0.7	7 917	78.7	2 081	87.8
28 143	...	Tunica County	8 451	56.7	23.4	6.2	12.9	0.8	3 258	51.8	662	69.3
28 145	...	Union County	23 513	63.5	19.4	10.5	5.9	0.7	9 786	77.6	2 467	85.4
28 147	...	Walthall County	14 081	68.1	19.2	6.0	6.1	0.6	5 571	83.2	1 275	91.5
28 149	...	Warren County	45 912	58.7	27.4	6.3	7.3	0.4	18 756	68.3	3 938	78.7
28 151	...	Washington County.......	57 754	59.9	29.3	4.4	5.2	1.3	22 158	59.5	4 993	80.9
28 153	...	Wayne County...............	19 608	67.3	22.0	5.2	4.9	0.6	7 857	84.9	1 602	89.3
28 155	...	Webster County	9 624	63.2	19.3	12.4	4.6	0.5	3 905	78.4	1 033	84.2
28 157	...	Wilkinson County	9 723	71.0	13.8	7.8	6.4	1.1	3 578	83.1	938	93.2
28 159	...	Winston County	18 790	66.5	21.1	7.9	4.0	0.5	7 578	79.6	2 014	90.2
28 161	...	Yalobusha County........	12 203	63.9	20.5	11.0	4.5	0.1	5 260	79.0	1 420	84.0
28 163	...	Yazoo County...............	26 041	57.8	24.4	11.1	5.1	1.7	9 178	68.9	2 293	80.8
29 000	...	MISSOURI................	5 226 022	53.6	23.5	12.5	9.1	1.3	2 194 594	70.3	495 896	79.1
29 001	...	Adair County	23 685	43.6	19.1	22.2	13.9	1.2	9 669	60.4	2 014	81.4
29 003	7000	Andrew County	15 474	59.2	15.7	18.0	6.5	0.5	6 273	80.0	1 510	83.2
29 005	...	Atchison County	6 148	63.0	20.4	8.5	7.8	0.3	2 722	69.2	905	77.0
29 007	...	Audrain County	24 186	57.5	21.3	15.0	5.8	0.4	9 844	74.1	2 790	85.8
29 009	...	Barry County	31 736	52.4	21.8	10.6	14.0	1.3	13 398	75.7	3 635	83.4
29 011	...	Barton County	11 578	57.7	21.8	11.3	9.0	0.2	4 895	73.4	1 286	80.9
29 013	...	Bates County	15 634	56.8	20.7	14.9	7.1	0.4	6 511	75.0	1 903	81.5
29 015	...	Benton County	16 375	56.1	14.7	19.2	9.6	0.5	7 420	82.2	2 437	89.2
29 017	...	Bollinger County	11 291	61.0	16.7	15.3	6.8	0.1	4 576	81.6	1 230	81.8
29 019	1740	Boone County	127 143	39.7	27.8	18.9	11.2	2.3	53 094	57.5	7 350	79.0
29 021	7000	Buchanan County	80 639	55.1	27.6	9.4	7.3	0.6	33 557	67.5	8 397	77.3
29 023	...	Butler County	38 277	55.8	26.2	9.7	7.6	0.7	16 718	68.9	4 695	77.5
29 025	...	Caldwell County	8 397	55.4	18.4	21.3	4.7	0.2	3 523	77.4	993	80.2
29 027	...	Callaway County	38 330	52.9	20.7	18.8	6.6	1.0	14 416	76.8	2 710	82.5
29 029	...	Camden County	35 307	49.4	18.9	17.0	13.7	1.0	15 779	82.3	4 709	89.7
29 031	...	Cape Girardeau County ..	64 678	51.7	26.2	11.8	9.2	1.1	26 980	68.4	5 942	78.3
29 033	...	Carroll County	9 640	63.5	23.6	8.7	4.1	0.1	4 169	74.0	1 293	80.3
29 035	...	Carter County	5 587	59.2	18.7	13.2	8.5	0.4	2 378	76.7	649	78.0
29 037	3760	Cass County	76 039	52.5	19.8	16.6	10.4	0.7	30 168	79.6	6 217	79.5
29 039	...	Cedar County	12 984	58.2	19.2	12.9	9.2	0.5	5 685	78.3	1 997	87.3
29 041	...	Chariton County	8 007	70.0	16.3	10.2	3.3	0.2	3 469	80.5	1 222	83.7
29 043	7920	Christian County...........	50 144	42.5	19.2	24.1	13.5	0.7	20 425	75.9	3 563	84.1
29 045	...	Clark County	6 960	66.6	18.4	5.7	9.3	0.0	2 966	78.5	754	78.8
29 047	3760	Clay County	170 777	49.5	23.7	14.1	11.7	1.0	72 558	70.7	12 600	81.4
29 049	3760	Clinton County..............	17 741	53.7	15.6	22.2	8.2	0.2	7 152	79.0	1 709	79.6
29 051	...	Cole County	66 644	52.5	23.7	15.7	7.0	1.1	27 040	67.8	5 375	77.7
29 053	...	Cooper County	15 688	53.8	20.4	17.9	5.9	2.1	5 932	74.2	1 581	79.4
29 055	...	Crawford County	21 332	56.7	21.4	16.4	5.2	0.4	8 858	76.7	2 315	82.3
29 057	...	Dade County	7 467	61.2	16.6	14.4	7.5	0.3	3 202	78.8	1 000	84.6
29 059	...	Dallas County	14 640	58.1	15.2	17.0	9.2	0.4	6 030	79.2	1 563	84.5
29 061	...	Daviess County	7 451	56.8	20.2	15.2	7.5	0.3	3 178	76.8	996	84.3
29 063	...	DeKalb County	10 978	51.7	11.2	29.3	6.3	1.4	3 528	73.4	1 144	72.2
29 065	...	Dent County	13 969	54.0	24.9	12.6	8.3	0.2	5 982	74.1	1 704	78.3
29 067	...	Douglas County	12 313	62.1	16.1	9.4	11.9	0.5	5 201	79.0	1 441	83.5
29 069	...	Dunklin County.............	30 771	56.1	28.5	7.1	7.9	0.5	13 411	65.9	3 662	78.4
29 071	7040	Franklin County	87 359	57.5	24.9	13.2	4.2	0.3	34 945	78.0	7 546	84.3
29 073	...	Gasconade County	14 440	61.8	16.9	16.1	4.5	0.7	6 171	80.3	1 904	84.3
29 075	...	Gentry County	6 428	60.5	21.6	11.4	6.0	0.4	2 747	74.5	954	78.9
29 077	7920	Greene County..............	225 739	45.9	29.2	13.0	11.1	0.8	97 859	63.6	21 088	78.5
29 079	...	Grundy County	9 779	59.1	20.8	12.1	7.8	0.2	4 382	71.8	1 374	76.2
29 081	...	Harrison County	8 268	59.6	22.0	9.9	7.6	0.9	3 658	74.7	1 170	79.8
29 083	...	Henry County	20 665	52.7	24.6	15.7	6.8	0.2	9 133	73.0	2 566	79.0
29 085	...	Hickory County	8 546	58.7	14.5	16.7	9.7	0.4	3 911	84.5	1 453	90.9
29 087	...	Holt County	5 093	66.5	18.5	9.1	5.9	0.1	2 237	74.4	801	76.3
29 089	...	Howard County	9 641	58.9	17.4	17.2	5.9	0.5	3 836	75.2	1 098	81.3
29 091	...	Howell County	34 717	53.3	24.5	9.5	12.3	0.4	14 762	73.5	4 030	78.7
29 093	...	Iron County	10 072	58.8	20.6	15.8	4.4	0.3	4 197	75.9	1 076	82.7
29 095	3760	Jackson County............	609 212	52.0	30.4	5.4	10.3	1.8	266 294	62.9	56 554	73.1

[1]MSA = Metropolitan Statistical Area. PMSA = Primary MSA. NECMA = New England County Metropolitan Area. See the Appendix A for explanation of these concepts. See Appendix B for list of metropolitan areas identified by type, with component counties.

STATE County	Owner-occupied by household type (percent)								Median household income			Median housing value (owner estimated)	Median monthly owner costs as a percent of income	
	Family-households				Nonfamily households									
		Married-couple family		Other family										
	Total family households	Total	With own children under 18 years	Total	With own children under 18 years	Total nonfamily households	Two or more adults	Living alone	All households	Owner-occupied households	Renter-occupied households		With a mortgage	Without a mortgage
	11	12	13	14	15	16	17	18	19	20	21	22	23	24
MISSISSIPPI—Cont'd														
Sunflower County	64.6	77.5	73.9	47.7	37.0	53.3	23.6	57.5	24 714	32 475	17 352	49 100	21.5	11.3
Tallahatchie County	80.1	86.9	84.2	69.4	64.3	65.5	53.9	66.6	22 100	25 184	13 778	37 600	24.0	12.9
Tate County	82.4	87.7	85.4	66.4	55.3	65.2	47.6	67.5	35 404	40 000	21 183	73 800	20.1	9.9
Tippah County	81.2	86.3	82.1	62.3	53.2	69.9	46.3	72.0	29 735	31 993	20 551	53 900	21.5	10.2
Tishomingo County	81.9	86.3	81.2	61.0	51.3	71.2	51.0	72.6	28 594	31 162	19 040	54 900	19.1	9.9
Tunica County	55.3	67.4	65.5	43.2	36.5	44.6	21.2	49.5	23 170	28 482	18 276	50 800	19.4	12.6
Union County	81.1	86.7	82.7	57.0	51.0	67.6	38.9	70.2	32 429	35 816	21 026	61 800	20.0	9.9
Walthall County	85.2	90.2	86.0	72.0	57.4	77.6	63.3	78.6	23 055	26 858	15 401	57 200	23.9	11.7
Warren County	73.5	85.6	79.2	49.2	37.5	55.6	44.2	57.0	34 841	42 457	20 226	70 400	19.9	9.9
Washington County	62.3	76.7	66.8	43.4	28.0	52.3	30.7	55.0	25 429	33 714	17 156	52 200	21.2	11.7
Wayne County	86.5	91.9	88.4	72.3	65.4	80.0	90.7	79.4	26 038	28 026	16 271	42 900	20.1	10.1
Webster County	81.6	88.1	83.4	56.2	40.6	69.4	67.9	69.5	29 636	33 100	16 365	52 600	20.5	11.0
Wilkinson County	84.5	90.2	88.8	76.1	67.2	79.9	83.1	79.6	18 739	21 883	10 519	39 700	24.7	12.8
Winston County	81.2	89.5	85.5	60.4	40.0	75.2	43.0	77.8	28 030	31 265	17 347	57 000	19.7	9.9
Yalobusha County	82.4	87.6	86.8	71.4	58.4	71.4	69.0	71.6	26 815	29 662	16 226	47 700	21.0	10.7
Yazoo County	71.4	85.9	79.5	52.1	41.8	62.3	51.9	63.4	25 021	31 177	13 495	49 400	21.3	9.9
MISSOURI	78.7	85.6	82.2	54.6	44.7	52.8	42.7	54.7	37 828	45 667	23 698	86 900	19.5	9.9
Adair County	75.6	81.0	74.8	47.7	44.9	41.1	14.3	51.7	27 394	37 584	14 427	73 400	18.7	9.9
Andrew County	85.3	91.1	89.9	53.7	49.6	64.4	56.5	65.7	40 825	45 090	25 967	86 400	18.0	9.9
Atchison County	77.5	81.8	75.2	55.6	43.9	53.8	37.8	55.6	30 870	35 134	23 398	51 600	17.4	10.8
Audrain County	79.9	86.0	81.3	53.8	43.8	61.3	48.2	62.8	31 899	37 088	21 528	66 500	18.2	9.9
Barry County	81.5	86.4	80.0	57.6	45.4	60.5	52.1	61.5	28 681	32 573	19 563	69 500	21.3	9.9
Barton County	79.5	84.6	79.2	55.3	38.5	59.1	42.3	61.3	29 394	33 774	19 338	58 600	18.1	10.9
Bates County	79.7	83.9	77.8	56.3	46.6	63.8	47.1	66.2	30 714	34 323	22 446	65 700	19.5	11.2
Benton County	85.8	90.0	80.1	60.8	50.2	73.7	67.4	74.6	26 948	29 736	17 138	66 800	22.2	9.9
Bollinger County	86.5	89.7	86.2	67.1	58.5	66.5	63.8	66.8	30 243	33 248	18 095	61 900	19.3	9.9
Boone County	72.9	80.2	79.0	47.4	43.9	34.9	22.1	40.2	37 383	53 277	22 382	100 800	19.7	9.9
Buchanan County	75.4	83.2	77.2	49.7	40.4	52.6	39.0	55.1	34 621	41 727	21 711	72 500	18.5	9.9
Butler County	74.6	81.3	74.1	50.4	39.1	56.9	50.4	57.8	27 299	32 980	16 768	58 100	18.4	9.9
Caldwell County	80.2	88.2	81.0	53.4	47.0	65.5	55.5	65.5	30 773	34 600	20 038	63 000	19.9	10.2
Callaway County	83.1	88.7	85.1	59.5	51.3	60.7	51.1	63.0	39 390	44 288	24 269	83 300	18.9	9.9
Camden County	86.9	91.1	85.3	60.5	50.8	70.4	64.1	71.8	35 704	38 045	25 571	107 000	21.9	9.9
Cape Girardeau County	79.3	86.1	83.9	49.9	43.0	46.7	28.8	50.8	36 056	44 874	21 241	91 800	18.9	9.9
Carroll County	80.8	85.9	81.7	46.2	30.6	58.8	54.4	59.3	30 579	33 721	21 583	55 600	18.9	11.2
Carter County	82.2	85.5	77.8	67.8	64.2	63.9	67.6	63.5	22 907	26 946	14 519	50 200	21.4	9.9
Cass County	85.1	89.3	85.6	62.8	55.0	61.7	64.1	61.3	49 395	54 344	28 895	104 600	19.6	9.9
Cedar County	83.1	86.8	80.5	59.0	41.9	67.6	67.3	67.7	26 737	30 251	14 840	61 600	21.0	10.5
Chariton County	85.0	88.5	84.8	63.7	51.1	71.1	59.0	72.1	31 715	34 231	20 474	52 700	17.2	9.9
Christian County	80.5	84.6	81.6	57.7	51.5	60.3	48.7	62.4	37 825	43 555	25 027	96 100	20.7	9.9
Clark County	84.1	85.9	84.7	73.6	68.6	65.1	74.3	63.9	29 385	32 120	20 404	52 700	18.7	9.9
Clay County	79.9	86.0	83.8	54.6	47.7	49.7	41.7	51.4	48 084	56 974	31 121	104 400	19.7	9.9
Clinton County	84.3	89.4	87.6	57.3	48.4	63.8	65.7	63.5	41 148	47 062	24 080	91 800	19.7	10.2
Cole County	79.5	87.3	85.6	46.1	37.2	44.7	32.3	46.8	43 033	53 915	25 035	96 800	18.8	9.9
Cooper County	80.0	84.9	79.7	56.1	49.1	60.8	55.0	61.7	35 059	38 995	25 238	77 500	19.6	9.9
Crawford County	80.8	85.1	78.5	57.2	48.0	66.0	47.1	68.8	30 927	34 812	19 676	69 800	21.5	9.9
Dade County	81.8	85.5	75.2	61.7	48.1	71.1	73.9	70.9	29 672	31 795	20 278	63 600	20.4	10.2
Dallas County	83.8	88.4	81.0	59.7	53.7	66.8	64.1	67.2	27 035	30 299	16 587	70 200	22.9	10.2
Daviess County	80.7	85.5	77.0	49.5	36.5	67.0	68.1	66.9	30 759	33 039	21 346	64 900	19.2	10.7
DeKalb County	81.5	86.0	82.4	54.7	45.3	54.8	51.7	55.2	31 297	36 584	18 896	70 400	19.0	9.9
Dent County	78.5	84.3	78.7	50.1	39.5	63.0	62.7	63.0	27 283	32 058	18 012	62 400	20.5	9.9
Douglas County	83.5	87.2	82.3	62.5	52.1	67.9	70.9	67.6	25 646	27 765	18 000	67 700	22.3	11.3
Dunklin County	70.2	78.6	68.2	42.9	28.9	56.5	52.3	57.0	25 012	31 958	14 705	45 500	18.1	10.2
Franklin County	83.9	88.7	86.1	61.2	50.1	61.8	53.5	63.4	42 907	47 709	26 750	93 500	19.1	9.9
Gasconade County	84.8	88.6	83.3	64.1	56.2	70.1	59.3	71.5	34 816	38 078	24 679	76 800	19.6	9.9
Gentry County	81.7	86.0	80.3	56.8	44.8	58.0	47.6	58.5	28 505	31 304	20 825	54 100	18.5	10.7
Greene County	74.7	81.6	78.2	49.2	40.6	44.6	29.0	48.7	33 927	42 529	21 620	88 200	20.2	9.9
Grundy County	79.5	83.7	72.5	58.8	46.2	57.2	66.4	56.2	27 148	32 257	17 434	47 100	17.6	9.9
Harrison County	81.3	85.6	82.0	59.0	49.0	59.8	67.2	59.3	29 086	32 635	19 962	49 600	18.1	10.4
Henry County	80.2	83.7	78.0	65.3	58.3	57.1	61.3	56.6	30 861	34 010	21 463	65 800	19.6	10.7
Hickory County	89.0	91.6	84.1	69.1	57.9	74.2	60.9	76.1	25 281	26 784	15 841	61 400	22.2	9.9
Holt County	82.3	86.0	80.6	65.6	48.0	57.7	47.3	58.5	29 910	32 449	17 195	50 700	17.7	9.9
Howard County	82.2	86.7	82.6	62.7	51.0	59.6	65.5	58.8	31 588	38 025	20 075	67 500	19.1	9.9
Howell County	78.4	83.5	77.5	53.7	42.4	60.7	59.9	60.7	25 411	30 021	14 949	66 300	21.2	9.9
Iron County	80.4	86.0	80.6	54.7	46.4	65.1	64.5	65.2	26 061	30 207	15 978	53 500	19.8	9.9
Jackson County	72.8	82.9	79.5	49.4	39.0	46.3	41.7	47.2	39 100	49 911	25 699	84 900	19.8	10.6

Table C-3. States and Counties — **Migration, Housing, and Transportation**

STATE County	Median gross rent	Percent who pay 35 percent or more of income for housing expenses — Owners	Renters	Means of transportation to work (percent except where noted) — Car, truck, or van — Number of workers 16 years and over	Drove alone	Carpooled	Public transportation	Other means	Walked	Vehicles available (percent of households) — No vehicles	One vehicle	Two or more vehicles
	25	26	27	28	29	30	31	32	33	34	35	36
MISSISSIPPI—Cont'd												
Sunflower County.........	357	20.7	25.9	10 273	74.7	19.1	1.0	1.2	2.3	14.1	38.7	47.2
Tallahatchie County	285	22.5	22.8	4 994	70.7	22.3	2.1	1.3	2.7	15.4	37.2	47.4
Tate County..................	410	16.9	26.3	10 503	77.2	16.5	0.2	1.2	2.3	7.7	30.6	61.7
Tippah County.............	353	16.6	21.9	8 551	81.7	13.3	0.2	1.1	1.6	8.0	30.2	61.8
Tishomingo County	353	13.2	18.4	7 833	83.6	12.6	0.4	1.0	1.4	5.4	30.0	64.6
Tunica County..............	459	16.4	25.7	3 571	73.8	19.5	1.0	2.0	2.9	15.7	44.0	40.2
Union County	401	13.3	22.8	11 233	82.8	14.3	0.1	0.7	0.9	7.6	28.1	64.3
Walthall County	346	22.5	30.8	5 529	75.6	18.3	0.7	2.2	0.6	10.2	34.2	55.6
Warren County	466	14.1	29.9	21 537	80.6	14.9	1.2	0.7	0.8	9.7	36.0	54.3
Washington County.......	423	20.2	33.5	22 314	74.9	19.6	0.9	1.7	1.9	15.9	38.9	45.3
Wayne County..............	334	17.0	24.6	7 577	78.4	16.3	0.6	0.9	1.0	10.7	32.2	57.1
Webster County............	319	11.4	24.0	4 111	81.7	13.9	0.3	1.2	1.2	8.5	30.3	61.3
Wilkinson County	269	17.5	13.0	2 893	76.3	16.8	0.9	1.3	2.4	16.7	38.2	45.1
Winston County............	370	17.8	29.0	7 683	77.8	17.9	0.4	0.9	1.0	9.7	32.6	57.7
Yalobusha County.........	304	17.0	24.7	4 956	78.1	17.3	0.5	1.2	1.4	11.0	36.3	52.7
Yazoo County...............	346	18.7	30.0	9 100	76.2	19.9	0.9	0.9	0.8	15.2	35.2	49.6
MISSOURI.................	484	11.6	26.3	2 629 296	80.5	11.6	1.5	0.8	2.1	8.3	34.1	57.7
Adair County	418	10.8	41.6	11 740	72.4	12.0	0.3	1.6	10.4	8.0	35.5	56.6
Andrew County.............	435	8.1	23.2	8 102	80.9	11.8	0.1	0.9	1.5	4.4	26.8	68.8
Atchison County	317	11.0	13.4	3 009	77.8	12.0	0.2	0.6	4.1	7.3	32.6	60.1
Audrain County............	384	9.9	18.8	11 278	77.2	12.1	0.3	0.9	1.5	9.8	33.4	56.9
Barry County	377	13.3	22.3	14 523	73.6	17.6	0.2	1.7	2.3	6.6	32.6	60.8
Barton County..............	354	11.5	17.7	5 817	75.0	15.1	0.0	0.9	2.0	6.7	30.6	62.6
Bates County...............	413	11.6	24.5	7 292	74.6	14.4	0.5	1.5	2.9	6.3	29.5	64.2
Benton County..............	364	13.3	26.3	6 492	72.8	15.3	0.5	0.8	2.3	6.2	33.0	60.8
Bollinger County...........	337	10.3	15.4	5 273	75.8	15.9	1.2	0.5	2.1	6.0	26.3	67.7
Boone County	523	9.9	34.5	71 967	77.4	12.5	0.7	1.5	4.7	6.5	36.0	57.4
Buchanan County.........	435	9.8	26.8	38 702	82.6	11.6	0.8	0.8	1.8	9.3	36.6	54.2
Butler County	354	10.3	23.3	16 618	81.3	12.3	1.1	1.0	1.9	10.7	37.3	52.0
Caldwell County	336	11.3	16.7	4 007	74.4	16.4	0.1	0.4	1.9	6.7	31.3	62.0
Callaway County	418	9.3	20.4	19 441	78.8	14.8	0.5	0.5	2.5	5.5	29.9	64.7
Camden County	454	15.8	19.1	16 075	76.5	14.7	0.2	0.9	2.3	4.2	31.4	64.4
Cape Girardeau County	440	11.3	27.7	34 235	82.7	10.2	0.4	0.7	3.2	7.4	34.0	58.6
Carroll County	323	10.9	14.4	4 578	74.2	16.4	0.2	1.0	1.8	7.1	30.5	62.4
Carter County...............	303	14.5	18.8	2 195	73.8	16.2	0.1	2.5	3.0	6.5	38.3	55.2
Cass County................	543	10.0	22.4	40 755	82.5	11.6	0.3	0.7	1.1	4.3	26.7	68.9
Cedar County	324	14.8	26.8	5 209	73.0	15.8	0.2	1.2	3.0	8.6	32.2	59.2
Chariton County	317	9.3	17.4	3 803	77.2	12.1	0.0	0.8	2.2	7.7	28.3	64.1
Christian County...........	511	14.3	26.1	27 421	82.9	11.0	0.1	0.6	0.9	3.8	28.1	68.0
Clark County	316	8.3	20.1	3 388	77.8	12.5	0.4	0.8	2.9	7.0	28.9	64.1
Clay County.................	576	9.8	21.0	96 971	84.8	10.2	0.5	0.7	1.0	4.7	32.7	62.7
Clinton County.............	442	12.3	20.6	8 981	80.1	12.6	0.5	0.8	1.5	5.1	27.9	67.0
Cole County	441	7.7	20.6	35 879	79.8	14.4	0.9	0.4	1.6	6.8	33.7	59.5
Cooper County	426	10.7	20.2	7 326	76.9	15.4	0.4	1.1	2.5	5.8	27.6	66.6
Crawford County	387	13.2	24.4	9 509	77.4	16.2	0.3	0.9	1.8	5.8	31.8	62.4
Dade County	297	13.0	12.9	3 392	72.1	16.8	0.2	0.7	3.0	5.1	29.3	65.6
Dallas County..............	353	17.7	24.5	6 425	76.2	14.6	0.1	1.2	1.9	7.5	30.6	61.9
Daviess County	331	11.8	19.7	3 540	67.2	17.5	0.2	2.0	4.8	9.1	27.7	63.2
DeKalb County.............	332	11.4	18.2	3 980	76.0	13.2	0.3	1.2	2.2	7.7	30.1	62.3
Dent County	337	10.3	25.5	5 977	79.6	13.5	0.5	1.2	1.3	8.7	31.5	59.8
Douglas County............	305	15.4	18.5	5 311	72.0	16.3	0.0	1.1	2.5	7.7	32.0	60.2
Dunklin County.............	323	13.2	27.4	12 999	79.1	13.5	0.5	1.3	2.4	12.4	36.9	50.7
Franklin County	471	9.2	21.6	45 363	81.6	12.9	0.3	0.7	1.2	5.9	27.7	66.4
Gasconade County	374	10.5	18.8	6 960	77.2	15.5	0.5	0.6	2.1	6.1	30.1	63.8
Gentry County	294	9.1	13.5	2 951	77.5	14.8	0.1	0.5	2.1	7.0	33.4	59.6
Greene County	462	12.2	30.0	119 180	82.1	10.3	0.8	1.1	2.4	7.1	36.1	56.8
Grundy County.............:	325	8.6	20.5	4 681	75.8	13.5	0.4	1.1	3.0	8.2	37.3	54.5
Harrison County	336	10.9	19.4	4 109	74.8	13.1	0.6	1.2	3.5	7.2	30.5	62.3
Henry County	394	13.0	21.0	9 838	78.6	15.0	0.1	0.4	1.8	6.9	32.9	60.2
Hickory County............	342	14.3	20.9	2 866	73.1	15.8	0.2	1.0	1.7	4.3	31.4	64.2
Holt County	272	8.5	11.9	2 468	79.1	11.2	0.1	0.6	2.8	6.7	30.0	63.3
Howard County	380	10.0	24.3	4 853	73.5	13.9	0.1	0.3	6.2	8.8	28.5	62.7
Howell County	350	14.8	24.3	15 521	80.4	11.8	0.3	1.3	1.7	7.5	32.1	60.4
Iron County..................	347	9.9	26.5	4 075	76.3	16.3	0.1	0.8	2.3	8.7	32.4	58.9
Jackson County............	536	13.4	27.4	310 789	80.5	11.5	2.7	0.8	1.8	10.8	38.3	50.9

STATE/ County code	MSA/PMSA/ NECMA code[1]	STATE County	Residence in 1995 (percent)						Occupied housing units		Householders 65 years and over	
			Total population 5 years and over	Same house	Same county, different house	Same state, different county	Different state	Outside the United States	Number	Percent owner-occupied	Number	Percent owner-occupied
			1	2	3	4	5	6	7	8	9	10
		MISSOURI—Cont'd										
29 097	3710	Jasper County	97 127	48.2	28.6	8.7	13.4	1.2	41 412	67.0	9 772	80.7
29 099	7040	Jefferson County	183 819	57.7	22.8	14.5	4.5	0.5	71 499	83.4	11 303	85.6
29 101	...	Johnson County	44 928	41.1	19.4	20.6	16.2	2.6	17 410	61.5	2 896	79.8
29 103	...	Knox County	4 083	61.5	18.2	14.7	5.6	0.0	1 791	77.1	618	81.2
29 105	...	Laclede County	30 275	54.1	26.9	10.0	8.6	0.4	12 760	72.8	3 161	79.4
29 107	3760	Lafayette County	30 956	56.7	21.8	15.6	5.5	0.5	12 569	75.4	3 153	81.2
29 109	...	Lawrence County	32 695	54.9	21.2	15.3	8.0	0.7	13 568	74.3	3 439	83.3
29 111	...	Lewis County	9 760	56.8	20.3	8.8	13.6	0.5	3 956	76.5	1 038	74.4
29 113	7040	Lincoln County	36 085	54.0	20.2	19.4	6.1	0.2	13 851	80.8	2 562	83.5
29 115	...	Linn County	12 933	58.9	24.8	10.9	5.0	0.4	5 697	77.0	1 944	79.4
29 117	...	Livingston County	13 672	56.1	25.0	13.2	5.0	0.8	5 736	70.8	1 692	77.7
29 119	...	McDonald County	20 003	49.3	20.6	7.2	20.5	2.4	8 113	71.5	1 624	81.2
29 121	...	Macon County	14 775	59.3	21.9	11.3	7.3	0.2	6 501	75.9	2 012	79.4
29 123	...	Madison County	11 097	56.0	24.3	14.4	5.0	0.3	4 711	76.0	1 381	81.6
29 125	...	Maries County	8 326	62.4	14.3	17.3	5.1	0.9	3 519	81.5	881	86.8
29 127	...	Marion County	26 422	54.2	27.5	10.1	7.5	0.6	11 066	70.4	3 096	76.6
29 129	...	Mercer County	3 550	59.9	15.1	12.0	12.8	0.2	1 600	76.8	562	79.2
29 131	...	Miller County	21 952	56.5	21.4	16.3	5.3	0.4	9 284	75.0	2 438	79.2
29 133	...	Mississippi County	12 462	60.1	26.5	7.1	5.8	0.5	5 383	63.5	1 469	79.9
29 135	...	Moniteau County	13 832	56.6	17.8	20.1	4.8	0.7	5 259	77.7	1 329	82.1
29 137	...	Monroe County	8 706	59.3	18.5	17.3	4.7	0.2	3 656	78.5	1 068	79.6
29 139	...	Montgomery County	11 437	60.4	19.3	15.4	4.3	0.6	4 775	78.7	1 361	83.9
29 141	...	Morgan County	18 161	55.9	16.9	16.2	10.4	0.6	7 850	82.9	2 341	85.9
29 143	...	New Madrid County	18 455	58.8	22.3	12.9	5.8	0.2	7 824	66.1	2 009	78.6
29 145	3710	Newton County	48 986	51.7	21.1	14.0	12.5	0.7	20 140	76.6	4 634	84.6
29 147	...	Nodaway County	20 882	50.4	21.1	14.8	12.7	1.0	8 138	63.8	1 899	76.5
29 149	...	Oregon County	9 713	56.6	19.3	8.4	15.5	0.2	4 263	78.3	1 323	82.7
29 151	...	Osage County	12 202	67.9	16.4	11.9	3.3	0.4	4 922	83.0	1 174	85.5
29 153	...	Ozark County	9 047	62.1	15.8	8.5	12.8	0.8	3 950	81.6	1 239	85.6
29 155	...	Pemiscot County	18 397	54.9	31.4	6.0	7.0	0.7	7 855	58.4	2 078	72.6
29 157	...	Perry County	16 893	64.6	23.5	7.4	4.2	0.4	6 904	79.9	1 797	87.0
29 159	...	Pettis County	36 649	52.7	25.7	11.2	8.7	1.7	15 568	72.5	3 823	81.8
29 161	...	Phelps County	37 539	46.7	20.7	17.1	10.6	1.9	15 683	65.6	3 599	75.9
29 163	...	Pike County	17 377	54.7	21.2	15.7	6.8	1.6	6 451	74.1	1 762	83.4
29 165	3760	Platte County	68 717	49.3	15.9	17.7	15.5	1.6	29 278	67.4	4 127	74.7
29 167	...	Polk County	25 192	51.2	19.0	19.2	9.7	1.0	9 917	73.0	2 574	83.1
29 169	...	Pulaski County	38 014	36.6	16.2	5.8	36.4	6.1	13 433	58.0	2 273	84.8
29 171	...	Putnam County	4 883	64.5	18.5	8.1	8.0	0.9	2 228	77.2	657	82.5
29 173	...	Ralls County	9 077	61.3	16.0	17.9	4.7	0.0	3 736	82.3	898	89.1
29 175	...	Randolph County	23 052	53.1	26.3	14.8	5.0	0.8	9 199	72.0	2 379	78.4
29 177	3760	Ray County	21 809	60.9	19.7	13.7	5.5	0.2	8 743	79.5	1 061	80.8
29 179	...	Reynolds County	6 308	59.1	20.6	15.1	5.0	0.2	2 721	77.1	769	78.3
29 181	...	Ripley County	12 697	60.4	22.0	9.7	7.5	0.4	5 416	78.0	1 512	80.6
29 183	7040	St. Charles County	262 259	50.9	22.7	16.9	8.7	0.9	101 663	82.0	15 622	83.8
29 185	...	St. Clair County	9 138	57.7	14.8	19.4	8.0	0.1	4 040	79.5	1 327	82.4
29 186	...	Ste. Genevieve County .	16 780	66.6	16.8	12.2	4.3	0.0	6 586	82.3	1 726	81.7
29 187	...	St. Francois County	52 288	52.9	26.0	15.4	5.1	0.6	20 793	73.2	5 193	81.7
29 189	7040	St. Louis County	952 458	59.2	19.6	11.9	7.8	1.5	404 312	74.1	92 966	82.0
29 195	...	Saline County	22 257	51.4	27.1	11.5	8.5	1.4	9 015	60.1	2 453	77.3
29 197	...	Schuyler County	3 934	62.5	18.0	10.7	8.5	0.3	1 725	75.2	514	73.9
29 199	...	Scotland County	4 630	66.0	20.1	7.1	6.8	0.1	1 902	76.7	579	80.5
29 201	...	Scott County	37 543	56.0	26.7	10.7	6.1	0.5	15 626	69.3	3 615	77.6
29 203	...	Shannon County	7 823	62.4	18.9	12.1	6.4	0.2	3 319	79.7	884	83.3
29 205	...	Shelby County	6 413	59.5	22.1	13.3	4.9	0.2	2 745	75.1	851	77.0
29 207	...	Stoddard County	28 039	56.5	25.5	11.3	6.3	0.4	12 064	72.3	3 420	80.2
29 209	...	Stone County	27 076	53.1	15.0	14.4	17.0	0.5	11 822	81.2	3 606	89.0
29 211	...	Sullivan County	6 710	58.1	17.7	11.0	10.4	2.9	2 925	71.7	856	77.0
29 213	...	Taney County	37 312	45.9	22.0	11.8	19.5	0.8	16 158	68.9	4 172	83.8
29 215	...	Texas County	21 678	58.5	20.1	10.6	10.0	0.8	9 378	76.6	2 798	80.9
29 217	...	Vernon County	19 031	54.7	25.4	11.1	8.3	0.5	7 966	72.3	1 937	81.2
29 219	7040	Warren County	22 937	57.5	15.1	21.2	5.6	0.6	9 185	83.1	2 062	86.2
29 221	...	Washington County	21 788	61.7	19.7	13.3	5.0	0.3	8 406	79.9	1 842	85.0
29 223	...	Wayne County	12 560	62.2	18.0	13.3	6.2	0.2	5 551	78.2	1 751	82.9
29 225	7920	Webster County	28 710	51.9	21.3	17.9	8.6	0.3	11 073	78.0	2 362	81.7
29 227	...	Worth County	2 254	64.2	20.3	10.5	5.1	0.0	1 009	76.8	357	83.2
29 229	...	Wright County	16 721	53.1	23.7	13.3	9.6	0.4	7 081	73.1	2 088	78.7

[1]MSA = Metropolitan Statistical Area. PMSA = Primary MSA. NECMA = New England County Metropolitan Area. See the Appendix A for explanation of these concepts. See Appendix B for list of metropolitan areas identified by type, with component counties.

STATE County	Owner-occupied by household type (percent)								Median household income			Median monthly owner costs as a percent of income	
	Family-households				Nonfamily households								
		Married-couple family		Other family									
	Total family households	Total	With own children under 18 years	Total	With own children under 18 years	Total nonfamily households	Two or more adults	Living alone	All households	Owner-occupied households	Renter-occupied households	Median housing value (owner estimated)	With a mortgage	Without a mortgage
	11	12	13	14	15	16	17	18	19	20	21	22	23	24

MISSOURI—Cont'd

STATE County	11	12	13	14	15	16	17	18	19	20	21	22	23	24
Jasper County	74.0	80.6	73.5	50.4	41.0	52.3	34.9	55.6	31 415	37 351	21 425	67 200	18.5	9.9
Jefferson County	87.3	91.3	88.8	71.5	63.6	70.5	68.4	71.0	46 206	50 818	26 997	93 300	19.1	9.9
Johnson County	71.3	76.1	68.4	47.7	40.4	40.5	22.0	48.1	35 420	46 061	21 986	88 000	19.6	9.9
Knox County	80.9	83.4	80.1	67.2	46.9	69.0	80.4	67.8	26 810	29 958	17 284	50 400	17.7	12.2
Laclede County	78.9	84.0	77.9	53.1	43.1	56.8	51.7	57.6	29 491	35 220	18 999	70 400	19.7	9.9
Lafayette County	80.9	86.0	80.8	56.9	49.3	61.0	48.3	62.9	37 914	44 585	24 501	78 700	18.7	9.9
Lawrence County	79.1	84.6	77.8	54.8	43.5	61.5	48.9	63.0	30 796	35 588	18 537	68 500	20.6	9.9
Lewis County	85.0	89.1	86.7	66.0	61.9	58.2	64.7	57.2	30 656	34 655	17 580	52 700	16.2	9.9
Lincoln County	85.4	90.2	88.4	63.9	56.3	65.9	58.4	67.4	42 816	47 308	26 106	94 900	19.4	9.9
Linn County	82.6	88.9	86.9	57.7	50.4	66.1	66.2	66.1	27 667	31 995	16 073	46 300	18.6	11.5
Livingston County	78.3	84.1	80.3	51.2	45.8	55.8	46.9	56.6	31 996	37 428	19 675	63 500	18.7	9.9
McDonald County	75.0	81.6	76.9	51.0	45.9	62.4	51.9	64.4	27 123	31 333	18 342	58 100	18.7	10.8
Macon County	83.7	87.9	80.8	65.0	55.7	59.7	57.4	59.9	30 135	34 167	17 953	61 300	19.3	9.9
Madison County	80.3	84.9	81.4	58.8	48.7	65.9	54.0	67.6	25 720	28 869	16 506	54 900	20.4	11.4
Maries County	86.0	88.9	83.5	70.3	63.3	70.1	81.3	68.9	32 013	35 686	22 257	71 900	18.9	9.9
Marion County	78.1	85.0	81.2	48.2	37.2	53.6	45.0	54.7	31 652	40 046	17 549	67 400	17.3	9.9
Mercer County	83.0	87.3	86.6	56.7	46.7	63.7	50.0	64.9	29 485	31 850	19 420	40 000	17.1	10.9
Miller County	81.9	86.4	81.5	63.1	52.6	59.2	50.9	60.6	30 912	34 899	19 253	70 000	20.8	9.9
Mississippi County	65.3	75.2	65.2	42.8	31.0	59.7	48.2	60.7	22 791	29 036	15 091	45 200	19.2	11.4
Moniteau County	82.5	87.6	86.8	56.8	46.9	65.9	57.9	67.1	36 812	41 063	22 213	74 500	18.5	9.9
Monroe County	82.8	84.7	82.8	73.1	64.7	68.2	63.1	68.8	31 223	33 691	23 220	63 300	18.3	9.9
Montgomery County	82.7	86.5	78.8	66.9	54.1	69.6	62.6	70.6	33 407	36 561	21 821	69 000	18.5	10.2
Morgan County	87.0	89.9	84.3	69.3	58.4	72.8	80.6	71.6	30 334	33 086	18 636	76 100	20.1	9.9
New Madrid County	70.2	79.0	72.9	44.6	30.1	56.3	36.5	58.5	26 756	32 121	16 943	44 000	17.3	10.2
Newton County	81.4	85.4	79.0	60.1	48.7	63.5	50.1	65.9	35 036	38 551	23 515	73 500	19.1	9.9
Nodaway County	79.8	83.5	80.2	60.2	55.9	40.0	16.4	48.2	31 724	40 794	17 263	73 600	17.7	9.9
Oregon County	82.9	86.0	80.1	68.6	55.9	66.9	60.2	67.7	22 184	24 258	14 343	53 600	24.2	11.3
Osage County	89.4	92.7	90.7	69.6	58.1	65.7	50.9	67.9	39 782	43 692	19 500	84 100	18.8	9.9
Ozark County	83.9	86.8	79.4	66.7	50.9	75.3	70.8	75.8	25 685	27 472	15 357	63 300	22.6	9.9
Pemiscot County	62.4	75.7	64.5	36.1	27.0	49.9	43.6	50.6	22 044	30 654	12 659	41 200	19.3	12.1
Perry County	84.9	89.6	86.9	58.7	45.7	67.5	52.0	70.0	36 716	40 779	22 514	80 400	18.6	9.9
Pettis County	78.5	83.6	78.0	60.0	52.6	59.6	49.2	61.6	31 580	36 721	21 984	67 600	19.1	9.9
Phelps County	76.5	82.3	77.0	50.2	38.9	44.8	28.2	48.1	29 497	38 859	17 029	72 800	18.1	9.9
Pike County	81.0	86.7	79.7	58.0	49.5	58.4	60.0	58.2	32 362	37 145	21 190	68 400	19.3	9.9
Platte County	78.5	84.1	83.3	52.7	45.5	42.3	31.4	44.9	55 662	65 950	37 541	127 800	19.4	9.9
Polk County	79.5	83.6	78.0	56.1	47.3	55.8	34.2	60.0	29 413	33 861	18 863	77 600	21.0	9.9
Pulaski County	61.1	63.7	49.8	48.5	38.3	48.8	41.1	50.1	34 337	37 475	30 508	70 900	20.6	9.9
Putnam County	82.8	86.2	79.8	60.7	54.5	65.2	51.9	66.8	26 261	29 172	16 289	47 900	20.0	12.9
Ralls County	86.2	89.3	83.0	62.1	49.7	70.6	56.1	73.6	36 739	39 678	23 393	69 300	18.2	9.9
Randolph County	77.7	83.7	77.8	55.6	44.6	59.6	53.5	60.4	31 160	36 564	20 690	52 000	18.5	10.7
Ray County	84.5	89.3	85.5	55.7	48.3	64.5	62.5	64.8	41 764	47 915	21 938	85 200	18.4	10.9
Reynolds County	82.7	87.1	78.2	58.8	51.2	63.8	57.8	64.5	25 203	29 136	17 500	52 100	19.5	10.5
Ripley County	83.2	86.5	81.3	66.6	56.9	65.2	63.8	65.3	23 386	26 165	14 618	46 500	21.0	11.5
St. Charles County	88.2	92.1	91.4	67.5	61.5	62.4	58.2	63.5	57 198	62 960	33 194	122 600	19.5	9.9
St. Clair County	84.6	88.0	80.5	68.0	62.4	67.9	66.9	68.0	25 584	28 269	18 974	58 100	20.3	10.7
Ste. Genevieve County	87.4	91.6	89.4	66.7	58.3	67.5	63.9	68.1	38 416	41 733	21 889	84 400	18.5	9.9
St. Francois County	79.7	86.3	80.8	55.3	46.7	57.2	52.9	57.8	31 321	36 930	18 433	67 400	19.0	9.9
St. Louis County	82.9	89.2	88.3	62.2	50.6	56.2	41.2	58.8	50 517	59 871	30 463	114 800	19.3	9.9
Saline County	73.8	81.1	74.1	47.9	40.6	59.6	63.2	59.0	32 735	39 399	21 119	62 800	18.0	9.9
Schuyler County	83.7	86.1	81.5	68.3	60.0	56.0	71.4	54.7	27 364	33 582	17 196	52 200	17.0	10.1
Scotland County	81.1	83.8	77.0	63.2	60.2	66.7	59.1	67.3	27 364	30 739	17 784	49 100	19.0	10.2
Scott County	74.4	82.9	76.1	47.6	34.9	56.2	43.7	57.6	31 356	38 353	18 735	63 000	18.5	9.9
Shannon County	83.5	86.9	81.5	67.4	58.8	70.2	76.5	69.5	21 110	23 342	12 191	46 800	21.3	10.4
Shelby County	80.8	83.7	77.7	62.4	50.5	63.5	70.3	62.6	29 105	32 488	19 318	49 900	17.9	9.9
Stoddard County	76.8	-81.8	73.7	53.3	43.1	61.6	51.5	62.6	27 055	31 125	18 070	56 800	18.9	10.5
Stone County	84.6	88.1	80.7	61.9	51.3	70.9	57.8	73.3	32 480	35 390	21 531	90 900	22.7	9.9
Sullivan County	77.0	83.6	75.1	51.4	35.5	60.6	56.3	61.1	26 229	29 954	19 419	47 000	18.6	12.2
Taney County	75.3	79.5	71.6	54.3	47.0	55.0	44.2	57.4	30 945	35 060	23 421	81 000	21.8	9.9
Texas County	81.6	87.2	79.2	56.3	45.5	64.1	53.9	65.1	24 369	27 620	14 870	62 300	21.6	9.9
Vernon County	79.4	84.2	77.6	59.4	42.4	57.0	65.5	55.9	29 949	35 849	17 421	61 400	18.8	10.8
Warren County	87.0	91.5	88.4	63.2	55.1	71.6	71.5	71.7	41 159	45 128	23 661	101 600	19.4	9.9
Washington County	83.3	87.8	83.1	65.5	58.9	70.0	65.8	70.7	26 925	30 102	16 209	49 900	18.8	10.3
Wayne County	81.8	86.7	79.2	60.5	44.0	69.9	66.7	70.3	24 156	26 786	15 689	41 200	18.9	9.9
Webster County	82.3	86.6	83.1	57.3	50.1	63.8	61.3	64.2	31 590	34 907	22 694	81 900	21.2	9.9
Worth County	82.4	85.6	78.9	62.9	65.1	65.1	76.9	64.1	27 472	30 607	18 235	34 300	18.6	9.9
Wright County	78.4	84.1	78.1	52.9	40.4	60.1	45.8	61.6	24 601	29 000	14 918	65 600	23.4	10.5

STATE County	Median gross rent	Percent who pay 35 percent or more of income for housing expenses		Means of transportation to work (percent except where noted)						Vehicles available (percent of households)		
		Owners	Renters	Number of workers 16 years and over	Car, truck, or van		Public transportation	Other means	Walked	No vehicles	One vehicle	Two or more vehicles
					Drove alone	Carpooled						
	25	26	27	28	29	30	31	32	33	34	35	36

MISSOURI—Cont'd

STATE County	25	26	27	28	29	30	31	32	33	34	35	36
Jasper County	441	10.2	26.2	48 176	82.6	11.3	0.2	0.9	2.2	7.4	35.0	57.6
Jefferson County	502	10.1	23.3	98 030	84.3	12.2	0.2	0.4	0.8	4.3	26.9	68.8
Johnson County	475	10.4	29.1	23 890	76.9	13.8	0.3	0.7	4.6	5.4	30.5	64.1
Knox County	282	10.2	13.6	1 885	72.6	13.5	0.1	0.3	3.6	8.7	27.5	63.8
Laclede County	371	12.7	21.1	14 740	78.1	13.9	0.3	0.8	1.9	7.1	34.3	58.6
Lafayette County	426	9.0	21.1	15 798	78.4	14.6	0.1	0.8	2.2	6.3	29.6	64.1
Lawrence County	404	13.2	22.4	15 679	79.3	12.7	0.2	0.8	1.9	6.8	32.6	60.5
Lewis County	273	10.4	20.4	4 996	74.4	11.2	0.0	0.9	6.6	7.2	30.4	62.5
Lincoln County	460	10.6	22.8	18 386	82.1	12.7	0.1	0.4	1.1	5.4	25.0	69.6
Linn County	322	10.9	19.9	6 172	77.8	13.0	0.3	0.8	2.2	7.5	34.6	57.9
Livingston County	357	11.0	24.9	6 554	74.9	15.2	0.5	1.3	2.9	8.8	33.9	57.3
McDonald County	382	14.9	23.0	9 590	67.5	22.2	0.4	1.1	2.5	7.2	33.9	58.8
Macon County	308	12.2	17.2	7 312	76.9	13.4	0.2	1.1	2.5	7.3	31.7	61.0
Madison County	354	14.5	26.4	4 745	80.0	14.9	0.0	1.2	1.1	8.9	31.6	59.5
Maries County	351	9.9	18.0	4 075	69.9	20.8	0.1	0.9	2.3	5.7	29.8	64.6
Marion County	358	8.6	21.6	12 663	82.3	11.7	0.4	0.7	2.0	8.0	31.3	66.9
Mercer County	286	7.9	19.0	1 731	74.2	12.5	0.1	1.0	2.5	5.3	32.0	62.8
Miller County	367	12.6	17.7	10 727	74.9	17.3	0.2	0.9	2.0	6.4	31.4	62.1
Mississippi County	327	14.5	30.5	5 283	74.8	17.2	0.3	2.0	2.7	16.0	36.8	47.2
Moniteau County	370	9.3	13.5	6 669	73.8	17.6	0.1	1.1	2.4	8.1	28.4	63.6
Monroe County	337	10.8	14.5	4 218	76.6	11.7	0.1	0.9	2.1	7.4	27.8	64.9
Montgomery County	385	11.3	21.1	5 419	77.2	14.4	0.3	0.6	2.5	6.5	28.1	65.3
Morgan County	367	12.7	23.4	8 081	69.9	17.3	0.3	1.0	2.9	7.5	29.9	62.6
New Madrid County	330	11.2	24.2	7 987	83.7	10.2	0.3	1.4	2.2	12.2	37.6	50.2
Newton County	421	11.0	18.8	24 482	79.5	13.7	0.2	1.4	1.6	5.5	30.2	64.3
Nodaway County	392	6.8	31.6	10 886	74.7	12.3	0.2	1.2	7.6	5.3	34.3	60.4
Oregon County	339	17.3	24.8	3 765	76.2	14.3	0.1	0.9	1.8	10.2	31.1	58.8
Osage County	343	7.3	17.8	6 525	67.2	24.1	0.2	0.6	2.1	6.2	21.6	72.2
Ozark County	336	17.9	24.3	3 757	73.2	15.5	0.3	0.6	2.8	5.3	27.1	67.6
Pemiscot County	333	14.8	32.8	7 158	80.0	14.2	0.4	1.4	2.2	14.3	41.4	44.3
Perry County	422	11.6	21.8	8 954	79.8	13.4	0.6	0.7	1.7	5.9	28.3	65.7
Pettis County	426	9.2	24.2	18 286	79.8	13.4	0.5	1.1	1.7	7.7	33.3	59.0
Phelps County	396	9.4	30.9	17 438	75.8	13.0	0.5	1.3	5.4	8.6	35.9	55.5
Pike County	356	11.8	16.9	7 457	76.1	13.5	1.0	1.3	3.8	9.5	29.0	61.5
Platte County	640	10.8	19.6	40 998	85.8	8.9	0.3	0.6	1.0	4.0	30.5	65.5
Polk County	391	12.3	28.4	11 741	76.7	12.7	0.1	0.8	3.9	5.5	30.3	64.2
Pulaski County	439	11.9	10.0	20 635	66.0	12.1	2.2	3.2	13.9	6.2	31.3	62.5
Putnam County	278	13.2	23.3	2 175	74.3	15.1	0.0	1.4	2.3	9.0	28.9	62.1
Ralls County	400	9.1	21.0	4 784	81.8	12.0	0.3	0.5	1.4	4.4	25.7	69.9
Randolph County	384	11.1	20.5	10 513	78.1	15.9	0.5	1.0	1.7	8.8	33.4	57.8
Ray County	455	10.0	24.4	10 829	79.4	14.7	0.4	0.6	1.2	5.5	27.5	67.1
Reynolds County	317	11.9	26.7	2 383	75.1	16.7	0.8	0.7	2.9	9.1	29.5	61.4
Ripley County	306	14.5	24.5	4 842	70.0	10.7	0.2	1.1	2.0	7.1	36.4	56.4
St. Charles County	624	10.0	22.3	149 111	87.1	8.1	0.3	0.6	0.8	3.6	25.0	71.4
St. Clair County	290	12.9	16.5	3 774	72.8	15.1	0.1	0.6	1.2	6.9	32.6	60.5
Ste. Genevieve County	306	9.7	26.0	8 343	80.5	12.8	0.4	0.5	1.9	5.8	27.3	66.9
St. Francois County	402	10.7	26.5	21 908	80.2	14.4	0.6	0.8	1.3	7.0	35.2	57.8
St. Louis County	601	11.6	26.3	498 319	84.9	8.4	1.7	0.6	1.3	6.4	35.5	58.1
Saline County	391	8.9	20.4	11 203	76.2	14.9	0.3	1.0	4.4	7.4	36.7	55.9
Schuyler County	276	10.2	12.9	1 905	74.9	13.8	0.0	0.6	2.9	6.4	29.7	63.9
Scotland County	313	10.2	22.1	2 301	70.4	13.3	0.2	0.6	3.4	5.0	29.3	65.7
Scott County	393	11.8	26.2	17 934	82.9	12.0	0.5	0.8	1.0	9.2	36.4	54.4
Shannon County	283	15.0	22.2	3 093	72.2	18.5	0.8	1.0	1.7	8.6	29.6	61.8
Shelby County	294	10.3	15.7	3 105	76.6	10.1	0.2	0.6	3.7	5.4	34.5	60.1
Stoddard County	352	11.4	21.4	12 784	81.1	11.1	0.1	0.9	3.8	8.0	33.4	58.6
Stone County	468	14.8	28.6	11 640	75.5	15.5	0.1	0.4	2.4	4.8	30.0	65.2
Sullivan County	328	13.8	18.6	3 217	72.1	15.0	0.2	1.7	4.2	9.7	30.6	59.7
Taney County	483	14.6	24.4	18 558	75.4	15.7	0.2	0.9	3.3	5.0	37.4	57.6
Texas County	308	16.1	24.8	9 075	75.3	13.9	0.4	1.4	1.9	7.9	31.7	60.4
Vernon County	364	9.4	25.3	9 102	75.9	14.6	0.4	1.2	2.9	7.7	31.7	60.6
Warren County	466	10.6	19.1	11 978	80.8	13.2	0.1	0.9	1.5	4.4	27.3	68.3
Washington County	364	12.9	25.1	8 526	75.3	19.5	0.2	1.0	1.8	9.3	29.8	60.9
Wayne County	317	11.2	23.7	4 551	75.7	16.0	0.7	1.5	0.9	8.8	34.0	57.2
Webster County	398	14.5	23.4	13 511	77.3	14.7	0.4	1.0	1.9	7.5	24.8	67.8
Worth County	258	9.6	19.0	1 063	75.4	13.4	0.7	1.2	2.9	6.2	30.0	63.7
Wright County	308	15.6	21.7	7 270	72.7	15.1	0.1	0.8	1.7	7.9	31.1	61.0

STATE/ County code	MSA/PMSA/ NECMA code[1]	STATE County	Residence in 1995 (percent)						Occupied housing units		Householders 65 years and over	
			Total population 5 years and over	Same house	Same county, different house	Same state, different county	Different state	Outside the United States	Number	Percent owner-occupied	Number	Percent owner-occupied
			1	2	3	4	5	6	7	8	9	10
		MISSOURI—Cont'd										
29 510	7040	St. Louis city..............	324 769	50.7	29.3	8.9	7.4	3.7	147 076	46.9	34 383	61.2
30 000	...	MONTANA	847 362	53.6	22.5	9.9	13.2	0.8	358 667	69.1	79 362	78.9
30 001	...	Beaverhead County	8 660	53.8	17.9	12.8	15.1	0.4	3 684	63.7	844	76.4
30 003	...	Big Horn County...........	11 481	61.1	22.0	7.8	8.4	0.7	3 924	64.9	744	80.2
30 005	...	Blaine County.............	6 429	65.5	19.6	10.3	4.0	0.6	2 501	61.0	649	73.3
30 007	...	Broadwater County	4 157	54.3	16.3	17.4	11.4	0.6	1 752	79.3	430	84.0
30 009	...	Carbon County.............	9 062	57.3	15.7	13.0	13.4	0.7	4 065	74.2	1 087	84.5
30 011	...	Carter County.............	1 306	73.8	10.8	6.8	8.6	0.0	543	74.6	170	82.4
30 013	3040	Cascade County............	75 002	52.8	24.5	7.5	13.4	1.8	32 547	64.9	7 331	75.1
30 015	...	Chouteau County	5 583	64.4	11.7	16.9	6.5	0.6	2 226	68.6	600	82.2
30 017	...	Custer County	11 005	57.7	22.6	9.9	9.4	0.4	4 768	70.1	1 225	78.8
30 019	...	Daniels County	1 924	69.2	16.5	7.1	5.8	1.4	892	77.9	305	77.7
30 021	...	Dawson County	8 568	62.8	16.9	9.8	10.1	0.5	3 625	74.0	998	80.9
30 023	...	Deer Lodge County......	9 027	65.2	15.4	9.3	9.8	0.3	3 995	73.9	1 224	81.6
30 025	...	Fallon County.............	2 701	67.0	16.7	9.0	7.1	0.1	1 140	77.3	355	85.1
30 027	...	Fergus County.............	11 279	59.3	21.8	11.2	7.5	0.2	4 860	73.7	1 489	78.4
30 029	...	Flathead County...........	70 037	52.4	24.9	6.1	15.8	0.8	29 588	73.3	5 996	78.9
30 031	...	Gallatin County............	63 905	40.8	24.3	13.2	20.3	1.4	26 323	62.4	3 618	83.5
30 033	...	Garfield County............	1 194	66.4	19.7	7.5	5.6	0.8	532	73.3	183	76.5
30 035	...	Glacier County	12 171	62.2	24.3	6.7	5.8	0.9	4 304	62.0	783	81.0
30 037	...	Golden Valley County ...	991	65.7	8.6	18.3	7.5	0.0	365	77.5	112	80.4
30 039	...	Granite County	2 692	61.5	12.0	13.6	12.8	0.1	1 200	74.0	333	83.2
30 041	...	Hill County..................	15 457	55.4	23.5	12.0	8.5	0.7	6 457	64.4	1 498	74.0
30 043	...	Jefferson County	9 516	55.4	12.0	20.7	11.5	0.3	3 747	83.2	682	86.5
30 045	...	Judith Basin County	2 207	68.2	11.7	14.5	5.5	0.0	951	77.2	277	80.1
30 047	...	Lake County	24 749	53.9	20.4	11.3	14.0	0.4	10 192	71.5	2 518	87.2
30 049	...	Lewis and Clark County	52 205	53.2	22.7	10.4	13.0	0.8	22 850	70.0	4 228	78.3
30 051	...	Liberty County.............	2 049	74.2	11.0	11.4	3.2	0.2	833	71.9	243	77.8
30 053	...	Lincoln County	17 892	55.6	23.5	4.8	15.7	0.3	7 764	76.5	1 882	80.6
30 055	...	McCone County	1 864	72.6	11.6	10.2	5.3	0.3	810	77.7	255	84.3
30 057	...	Madison County	6 524	56.6	15.3	13.2	14.5	0.3	2 956	70.4	811	83.1
30 059	...	Meagher County...........	1 829	64.7	15.4	11.5	7.8	0.5	803	73.2	252	82.5
30 061	...	Mineral County	3 695	52.3	18.7	10.3	17.8	0.9	1 584	73.0	324	82.7
30 063	5140	Missoula County	90 465	45.4	25.5	10.8	17.3	1.0	38 439	61.9	6 253	73.6
30 065	...	Musselshell County	4 266	59.8	15.4	14.5	10.2	0.1	1 878	76.9	556	77.2
30 067	...	Park County	14 788	51.9	22.1	9.3	15.4	1.3	6 828	66.4	1 681	76.3
30 069	...	Petroleum County	459	65.8	6.5	19.6	7.6	0.4	211	74.4	72	80.6
30 071	...	Phillips County	4 373	64.8	20.9	9.0	4.5	0.8	1 848	70.5	560	73.4
30 073	...	Pondera County	6 009	66.4	14.2	12.7	6.0	0.6	2 410	70.2	723	77.7
30 075	...	Powder River County	1 747	66.9	12.3	12.0	8.8	0.1	737	72.9	205	84.8
30 077	...	Powell County	6 847	53.4	15.0	19.7	11.1	0.8	2 422	71.3	681	78.4
30 079	...	Prairie County	1 148	67.2	12.9	9.1	10.4	0.3	537	77.7	183	83.1
30 081	...	Ravalli County	34 000	48.1	21.0	9.8	20.4	0.6	14 289	75.7	3 646	81.5
30 083	...	Richland County...........	9 063	64.5	20.4	7.5	7.3	0.3	3 878	72.3	1 047	80.6
30 085	...	Roosevelt County	9 764	68.8	19.4	6.1	4.9	0.8	3 581	65.3	813	79.3
30 087	...	Rosebud County	8 618	58.8	21.7	11.6	7.3	0.5	3 307	67.2	628	71.7
30 089	...	Sanders County	9 743	56.7	16.2	8.7	17.4	1.0	4 273	76.5	1 189	82.6
30 091	...	Sheridan County	3 887	72.6	14.7	7.0	5.4	0.3	1 741	80.1	605	84.1
30 093	...	Silver Bow County	32 672	59.0	22.5	8.8	9.3	0.5	14 432	70.4	3 670	76.6
30 095	...	Stillwater County	7 755	55.0	14.7	14.8	14.7	0.8	3 234	76.0	801	81.6
30 097	...	Sweet Grass County	3 393	55.3	17.0	12.1	14.6	1.0	1 476	74.1	438	82.0
30 099	...	Teton County..............	6 057	61.8	15.8	14.0	7.6	0.7	2 538	75.7	739	81.6
30 101	...	Toole County...............	5 001	60.6	17.0	15.1	6.8	0.4	1 962	71.5	542	75.3
30 103	...	Treasure County	813	63.7	14.0	12.1	9.8	0.4	357	71.4	102	85.3
30 105	...	Valley County	7 283	69.7	13.6	10.2	6.3	0.2	3 150	75.9	963	87.4
30 107	...	Wheatland County........	2 127	69.0	14.0	11.0	6.1	0.0	853	72.2	270	77.0
30 109	...	Wibaux County	1 011	69.8	10.4	8.8	9.4	1.6	421	73.2	134	82.1
30 111	0880	Yellowstone County	120 912	52.3	27.5	8.6	11.0	0.6	52 084	69.2	11 415	77.9
31 000		NEBRASKA..............	1 594 700	54.7	23.4	10.5	9.7	1.8	666 184	67.4	151 815	78.8
31 001	...	Adams County.............	29 093	54.2	22.8	13.4	7.3	2.4	12 141	66.8	3 155	72.1
31 003	...	Antelope County...........	7 003	69.4	17.0	10.0	3.4	0.2	2 953	76.4	994	85.4
31 005	...	Arthur County	429	64.8	8.4	18.2	8.6	0.0	185	63.8	43	86.0
31 007	...	Banner County	782	68.0	3.5	19.9	7.0	1.5	311	64.6	99	83.8

[1]MSA = Metropolitan Statistical Area. PMSA = Primary MSA. NECMA = New England County Metropolitan Area. See the Appendix A for explanation of these concepts. See Appendix B for list of metropolitan areas identified by type, with component counties.

STATE County	Owner-occupied by household type (percent)								Median household income			Median monthly owner costs as a percent of income		
	Family-households					Nonfamily households								
		Married-couple family		Other family								Median housing value (owner estimated)	With a mortgage	Without a mortgage
	Total family households	Total	With own children under 18 years	Total	With own children under 18 years	Total nonfamily households	Two or more adults	Living alone	All households	Owner-occupied households	Renter-occupied households			
	11	12	13	14	15	16	17	18	19	20	21	22	23	24
MISSOURI—Cont'd														
St. Louis city	56.4	72.0	67.6	40.9	27.2	36.3	37.4	36.1	27 033	38 787	19 054	63 500	20.1	11.4
MONTANA	77.8	83.1	78.4	54.7	47.1	51.9	40.2	54.5	33 014	40 004	20 836	95 800	22.2	10.4
Beaverhead County	74.9	79.1	74.6	47.2	41.0	43.6	22.8	48.0	29 034	38 374	18 472	86 300	21.6	10.2
Big Horn County	65.5	69.6	61.9	56.0	50.1	62.4	64.5	62.2	27 584	30 124	22 971	59 300	20.5	11.1
Blaine County	64.0	70.3	60.8	46.9	36.3	53.4	50.0	53.8	25 099	31 767	18 505	55 000	19.7	12.0
Broadwater County	83.3	84.7	83.0	75.1	74.8	68.6	51.0	70.7	32 982	34 808	24 519	84 100	22.4	10.2
Carbon County	79.3	83.5	78.7	54.8	40.2	63.9	56.7	65.0	32 114	36 087	25 000	109 700	22.1	11.0
Carter County	78.0	80.5	75.7	61.2	42.9	66.5	60.0	66.9	25 903	28 125	19 808	51 900	27.5	13.1
Cascade County	73.5	79.5	71.7	50.2	40.9	48.1	45.5	48.6	32 732	40 983	20 828	89 600	22.1	10.1
Chouteau County	70.0	74.4	66.1	47.1	35.6	65.0	60.9	65.5	29 661	34 022	21 741	70 000	24.6	11.5
Custer County	78.7	81.9	78.2	67.9	57.2	53.9	42.5	55.8	30 017	35 894	18 750	62 800	19.3	11.7
Daniels County	84.8	86.9	82.9	67.7	69.6	66.5	55.9	67.7	27 938	30 781	17 625	46 500	20.7	11.7
Dawson County	82.2	87.0	80.9	60.0	49.8	55.8	35.0	57.9	31 236	35 958	17 250	58 700	18.5	11.4
Deer Lodge County	81.8	87.4	86.9	58.3	45.3	60.3	38.6	62.6	26 172	32 346	15 044	70 800	21.6	12.4
Fallon County	80.9	83.3	76.8	65.5	50.0	68.6	73.3	68.1	29 489	32 546	21 250	52 100	17.8	11.4
Fergus County	80.7	83.3	78.0	66.2	59.6	60.1	66.7	59.4	30 396	33 905	19 706	70 800	21.4	9.9
Flathead County	80.6	84.6	81.3	61.9	57.8	57.0	51.4	58.3	34 617	40 455	22 028	118 600	24.8	9.9
Gallatin County	75.6	80.9	77.0	47.6	43.3	40.9	26.3	49.2	38 220	48 626	25 583	140 000	23.2	9.9
Garfield County	80.4	81.5	80.3	71.8	57.7	57.3	64.3	56.7	24 688	28 333	21 176	49 000	21.1	14.0
Glacier County	63.8	70.1	63.7	50.0	39.9	56.1	64.2	55.2	27 292	33 338	18 366	60 100	18.1	13.9
Golden Valley County	81.6	82.9	87.1	62.5	63.6	67.3	71.4	66.7	28 750	33 977	17 188	58 400	19.9	11.2
Granite County	80.1	83.1	75.6	66.4	67.9	62.3	55.8	63.2	27 436	30 167	18 889	83 300	25.4	11.1
Hill County	74.5	81.3	75.8	46.0	40.0	45.2	29.0	48.4	30 957	38 636	17 193	74 600	21.6	11.1
Jefferson County	88.0	89.7	84.1	74.2	74.2	67.6	61.5	68.7	41 472	46 209	21 076	127 700	21.6	9.9
Judith Basin County	79.3	80.5	76.3	68.8	53.3	72.2	66.7	72.7	28 565	30 581	22 303	62 600	19.6	11.6
Lake County	77.0	83.4	73.5	55.7	46.1	57.8	46.9	59.8	28 382	34 075	17 166	120 900	24.3	11.0
Lewis and Clark County	81.1	86.4	83.0	58.6	51.4	49.3	50.6	49.0	36 989	45 015	22 395	105 800	22.0	9.9
Liberty County	79.6	81.1	74.1	65.5	58.3	53.5	38.5	54.3	30 563	35 515	20 526	59 800	25.6	9.9
Lincoln County	83.2	88.0	82.8	58.9	51.7	61.3	53.7	62.5	26 561	30 608	14 257	79 000	22.0	11.4
McCone County	79.9	82.9	76.2	52.5	40.7	71.2	66.7	71.6	29 191	33 750	20 481	45 600	21.4	12.1
Madison County	78.2	80.5	70.2	58.1	42.5	55.7	42.3	58.3	29 798	34 401	22 264	116 300	22.9	11.8
Meagher County	78.0	81.8	71.1	51.5	40.7	64.3	60.0	64.7	29 625	31 304	20 179	68 400	23.2	11.5
Mineral County	80.0	84.8	76.3	51.6	44.2	58.2	57.0	58.4	27 413	31 850	17 727	87 000	25.7	11.5
Missoula County	76.0	82.4	79.8	51.3	46.0	40.3	27.6	45.6	34 559	46 316	20 281	128 700	23.5	10.1
Musselshell County	80.9	84.2	79.4	59.9	50.0	69.3	67.9	69.5	28 615	30 511	17 404	61 300	20.1	12.3
Park County	76.5	79.8	75.1	59.2	52.2	50.1	44.2	51.2	31 334	36 250	21 672	99 200	23.1	11.9
Petroleum County	81.6	84.7	73.2	58.8	53.8	60.0	28.6	63.5	23 750	28 438	17 188	51 000	20.0	16.9
Phillips County	77.7	82.0	74.7	54.2	53.2	55.0	32.1	57.4	28 529	35 398	17 800	56 500	21.0	9.9
Pondera County	74.4	78.2	73.3	55.3	50.7	59.5	49.1	60.5	30 076	34 019	20 570	72 200	21.1	12.7
Powder River County	75.9	78.1	71.2	57.9	45.5	65.2	50.0	67.4	28 898	31 150	22 500	59 700	19.0	12.7
Powell County	75.9	79.4	73.8	60.0	53.5	62.0	46.2	64.3	30 563	32 727	24 150	76 000	19.7	9.9
Prairie County	81.9	83.8	68.9	57.7	38.9	69.4	75.0	68.9	25 404	27 150	20 962	39 400	16.7	10.7
Ravalli County	81.6	85.9	80.9	55.1	44.6	61.1	61.6	61.0	32 289	36 606	21 931	134 700	25.4	9.9
Richland County	79.1	83.5	81.5	55.1	43.6	57.7	43.7	59.3	32 485	37 229	21 776	59 200	19.0	10.4
Roosevelt County	68.9	83.2	78.5	44.9	36.4	55.7	44.4	57.1	24 809	30 699	15 213	47 600	18.3	13.1
Rosebud County	72.8	80.7	75.8	48.6	36.1	51.6	47.9	51.9	36 035	42 839	22 786	55 900	17.4	10.5
Sanders County	81.2	84.9	81.1	61.2	56.6	66.6	63.4	67.1	26 329	28 876	18 750	89 800	24.7	11.4
Sheridan County	85.5	89.6	83.8	54.2	32.7	69.7	71.8	69.6	29 413	32 896	17 500	44 100	19.7	10.9
Silver Bow County	80.1	86.7	84.1	55.5	46.6	54.8	41.4	57.1	30 659	37 797	16 696	73 600	21.2	11.0
Stillwater County	80.3	82.6	76.0	61.4	52.9	64.6	54.1	65.9	38 561	41 613	30 339	103 200	19.8	9.9
Sweet Grass County	79.0	81.0	79.2	63.8	50.0	64.4	54.7	65.8	32 370	36 328	24 706	107 900	21.7	11.3
Teton County	82.5	86.3	80.8	55.5	45.3	60.2	49.4	61.6	30 373	34 841	19 242	77 400	22.9	10.7
Toole County	78.6	80.4	76.0	68.3	62.2	57.0	63.3	56.3	30 266	36 287	20 726	59 400	20.9	10.7
Treasure County	75.3	77.3	63.0	62.5	41.2	63.6	60.0	63.9	29 940	34 635	15 962	45 500	20.5	11.4
Valley County	84.1	88.6	83.7	60.4	41.9	58.3	56.8	58.5	31 058	36 584	19 021	59 200	18.3	10.5
Wheatland County	77.5	80.3	68.5	63.3	61.5	63.3	72.2	62.8	25 396	27 419	19 609	54 800	20.4	11.5
Wibaux County	82.9	85.4	74.8	67.5	50.0	52.6	36.4	54.0	27 574	32 667	16 406	51 500	21.3	9.9
Yellowstone County	78.4	85.0	82.7	53.2	45.2	51.3	42.6	53.1	36 889	45 595	21 343	97 200	21.2	9.9
NEBRASKA	77.1	83.2	79.6	50.2	41.0	48.0	34.0	50.8	39 179	47 466	25 857	86 900	19.7	10.5
Adams County	77.5	83.3	81.1	50.9	39.9	45.9	30.0	48.9	37 305	44 819	23 306	75 600	19.7	9.9
Antelope County	80.0	82.1	75.5	64.2	54.8	68.0	44.7	69.4	29 661	31 829	23 986	49 800	18.3	11.9
Arthur County	66.2	69.8	69.4	51.7	25.0	55.0	100.0	52.6	28 958	31 042	22 361	48 800	11.3	9.9
Banner County	69.2	69.4	59.5	66.7	50.0	50.0	69.2	45.9	31 736	32 708	26 136	67 000	30.3	9.9

STATE County	Median gross rent	Percent who pay 35 percent or more of income for housing expenses		Means of transportation to work (percent except where noted)						Vehicles available (percent of households)		
		Owners	Renters	Number of workers 16 years and over	Car, truck, or van		Public transportation	Other means	Walked	No vehicles	One vehicle	Two or more vehicles
					Drove alone	Carpooled						
	25	26	27	28	29	30	31	32	33	34	35	36
MISSOURI—Cont'd												
St. Louis city	442	15.7	32.4	140 747	68.9	13.6	10.7	1.0	4.0	25.2	45.8	29.1
MONTANA	447	15.3	28.2	422 159	73.9	11.9	0.7	1.7	5.5	6.1	29.9	64.0
Beaverhead County	392	15.4	28.8	4 403	69.5	10.0	0.5	1.3	11.4	5.0	30.9	64.2
Big Horn County	356	14.3	16.9	4 576	64.9	21.0	0.1	1.5	7.6	8.4	33.7	57.9
Blaine County	295	17.4	18.4	2 749	61.2	16.7	0.4	1.7	9.3	9.3	31.9	58.8
Broadwater County	409	14.5	24.0	1 995	67.5	14.8	0.0	1.5	6.5	3.3	24.7	72.0
Carbon County	439	11.9	20.2	4 468	66.0	12.8	0.9	2.2	6.6	4.5	28.3	67.2
Carter County	325	14.8	11.2	742	33.3	9.2	0.4	2.0	11.2	3.5	19.7	76.8
Cascade County	414	14.9	25.2	37 275	80.5	10.6	0.8	0.9	3.3	8.2	32.1	59.7
Chouteau County	287	17.6	11.7	2 548	61.2	10.8	0.5	2.2	10.2	5.7	24.4	69.9
Custer County	373	11.2	25.8	5 480	77.8	9.9	0.2	1.2	5.0	5.7	33.1	61.2
Daniels County	346	12.2	21.9	895	59.8	10.6	0.0	0.6	12.4	7.3	25.4	67.3
Dawson County	346	14.2	17.0	4 291	72.7	12.7	0.0	1.6	5.3	5.2	28.9	66.0
Deer Lodge County	321	13.8	18.3	3 744	75.3	14.3	0.1	1.0	5.6	9.1	31.0	59.8
Fallon County	322	12.2	7.4	1 408	73.2	9.6	0.1	0.4	7.0	5.4	23.1	71.5
Fergus County	413	15.0	23.7	5 472	67.4	11.7	0.3	0.7	8.1	6.5	27.7	65.7
Flathead County	484	19.9	27.4	34 045	77.0	12.2	0.4	1.3	4.0	4.6	27.7	67.7
Gallatin County	555	16.9	32.7	36 773	70.6	12.5	0.3	2.6	6.9	3.1	28.9	68.0
Garfield County	319	14.5	8.6	646	60.2	10.2	0.0	0.0	15.6	3.4	23.1	73.5
Glacier County	351	13.8	21.8	4 692	63.1	22.3	0.1	1.2	8.0	10.6	35.4	54.0
Golden Valley County	348	6.7	28.3	512	39.5	14.3	0.0	1.2	13.9	6.8	23.0	70.1
Granite County	381	16.7	25.8	1 261	65.1	11.4	0.4	2.1	10.4	3.9	27.6	68.5
Hill County	364	14.5	27.3	7 335	78.0	10.5	0.2	1.3	5.8	8.4	30.4	61.3
Jefferson County	419	14.1	25.7	4 842	75.2	14.0	0.2	0.9	3.7	4.5	19.6	75.8
Judith Basin County	340	9.7	13.3	1 056	55.7	11.5	0.2	0.6	10.3	5.4	21.3	73.3
Lake County	403	16.9	26.7	10 815	71.2	14.5	0.4	1.0	4.4	4.2	28.6	67.2
Lewis and Clark County	457	13.9	29.2	28 411	75.9	12.1	0.4	1.1	5.5	6.0	30.0	63.9
Liberty County	340	18.6	7.8	881	52.9	7.8	0.0	2.6	17.7	10.1	22.3	67.6
Lincoln County	374	16.4	31.4	6 721	74.3	10.7	0.1	2.4	5.2	7.9	27.8	64.4
McCone County	406	12.3	12.9	997	60.4	10.9	0.4	0.7	11.2	3.3	22.1	74.6
Madison County	460	18.5	25.4	3 109	62.7	15.1	0.1	1.1	9.1	4.5	25.5	70.0
Meagher County	373	17.8	20.2	891	61.7	14.8	0.0	1.0	8.9	7.6	28.3	64.1
Mineral County	418	22.5	28.5	1 629	68.0	16.6	0.0	1.3	7.4	5.3	30.0	64.7
Missoula County	530	17.8	39.7	49 448	73.3	11.0	1.3	4.3	5.5	6.2	31.4	62.4
Musselshell County	350	14.2	23.9	1 888	68.3	10.7	0.3	1.0	11.1	5.1	27.5	67.4
Park County	443	14.5	25.9	7 712	68.5	11.7	1.4	2.0	7.1	5.8	33.1	61.1
Petroleum County	330	13.8	30.0	228	35.1	14.9	0.0	1.3	24.6	0.9	37.4	61.6
Phillips County	320	10.8	14.1	2 115	62.3	11.8	0.1	0.9	14.5	4.5	27.3	68.2
Pondera County	367	17.2	17.0	2 691	65.0	11.2	0.2	1.8	12.0	5.3	28.6	66.1
Powder River County	346	10.9	8.4	922	58.1	8.6	0.0	0.0	13.3	1.8	23.9	74.4
Powell County	411	9.9	23.0	2 553	66.9	13.1	0.1	0.6	9.3	7.7	26.5	65.7
Prairie County	283	8.6	9.3	569	51.5	7.2	0.4	2.3	30.1	3.9	25.7	70.4
Ravalli County	502	22.5	29.1	15 362	69.7	14.3	0.2	1.3	4.7	3.5	27.5	69.0
Richland County	347	9.6	13.9	4 410	75.3	11.5	0.0	0.8	4.4	5.4	30.2	64.4
Roosevelt County	323	11.4	25.3	3 792	69.4	12.8	0.2	1.1	9.3	8.3	36.9	54.8
Rosebud County	350	11.6	20.1	3 873	69.4	16.0	0.2	1.9	9.2	6.9	27.8	65.3
Sanders County	390	18.9	25.5	3 903	65.0	16.3	0.5	1.5	7.3	4.4	28.2	67.4
Sheridan County	290	8.9	17.0	1 816	65.7	10.5	0.2	0.9	10.5	5.6	28.7	65.7
Silver Bow County	362	12.3	26.7	15 601	81.2	10.5	0.6	0.8	4.2	9.8	31.3	58.9
Stillwater County	439	13.2	15.3	3 847	63.0	15.8	5.3	0.9	6.1	3.6	21.7	74.7
Sweet Grass County	429	14.6	18.8	1 753	57.2	15.9	2.1	1.2	9.0	5.6	30.8	63.6
Teton County	362	14.7	20.8	2 669	64.2	10.6	0.1	1.8	9.0	6.9	21.9	71.2
Toole County	372	11.1	18.2	2 239	67.8	13.2	0.0	0.8	9.6	8.6	30.7	60.7
Treasure County	283	5.8	15.3	429	62.2	9.8	0.5	0.7	13.1	5.0	26.3	68.6
Valley County	351	11.5	23.8	3 470	74.5	9.9	0.5	0.2	7.0	4.3	29.8	65.9
Wheatland County	315	14.6	17.2	1 013	45.9	10.3	0.2	0.8	15.7	4.0	28.3	67.8
Wibaux County	281	8.3	14.6	497	63.8	11.7	0.0	1.4	4.8	5.0	27.1	67.9
Yellowstone County	474	13.4	29.7	64 697	81.4	9.8	1.1	1.1	2.5	6.7	32.1	61.2
NEBRASKA	491	10.6	23.5	873 197	80.0	10.5	0.7	0.9	3.2	6.3	31.0	62.7
Adams County	445	8.7	23.2	15 853	80.9	10.7	0.2	0.6	4.0	7.0	30.6	62.4
Antelope County	327	12.3	12.7	3 628	72.8	8.4	0.1	0.3	5.8	5.0	27.1	67.9
Arthur County	286	3.6	10.2	251	58.2	6.8	0.0	0.8	12.0	3.8	17.3	78.9
Banner County	246	9.1	4.4	394	56.6	16.2	0.8	0.8	8.4	0.6	22.8	76.5

Table C-3. States and Counties — **Migration, Housing, and Transportation**

STATE/ County code	MSA/PMSA/ NECMA code[1]	STATE County	Residence in 1995 (percent)						Occupied housing units		Householders 65 years and over	
			Total population 5 years and over	Same house	Same county, different house	Same state, different county	Different state	Outside the United States	Number	Percent owner-occupied	Number	Percent owner-occupied
			1	2	3	4	5	6	7	8	9	10
		NEBRASKA—Cont'd										
31 009	...	Blaine County	549	74.3	7.1	14.4	4.2	0.0	238	65.1	79	87.3
31 011	...	Boone County	5 889	68.2	19.0	10.3	2.3	0.2	2 454	75.2	841	84.4
31 013	...	Box Butte County	11 370	58.4	24.2	6.7	9.8	0.9	4 780	70.1	1 114	75.7
31 015	...	Boyd County	2 318	75.0	14.3	7.8	2.8	0.1	1 014	80.4	419	89.3
31 017	...	Brown County	3 338	66.7	16.2	11.4	5.5	0.2	1 530	74.4	526	83.8
31 019	...	Buffalo County	39 470	47.8	24.8	18.8	7.6	1.0	15 930	63.6	3 329	78.8
31 021	...	Burt County	7 345	63.5	17.9	11.7	6.5	0.3	3 155	75.9	1 106	77.2
31 023	...	Butler County	8 157	69.0	13.8	12.0	4.7	0.6	3 426	75.5	1 009	82.7
31 025	5920	Cass County	22 641	57.9	17.0	17.3	7.5	0.3	9 161	79.7	1 934	81.5
31 027	...	Cedar County	9 022	72.7	16.3	7.3	3.5	0.2	3 623	80.3	1 227	86.6
31 029	...	Chase County	3 840	61.8	17.8	9.5	10.7	0.2	1 662	77.1	533	87.8
31 031	...	Cherry County	5 772	60.0	18.5	10.2	11.0	0.3	2 508	62.2	683	82.3
31 033	...	Cheyenne County	9 195	59.3	18.4	9.3	12.2	0.8	4 071	72.8	1 206	84.7
31 035	...	Clay County	6 635	65.4	14.6	13.6	5.7	0.8	2 756	77.8	815	84.0
31 037	...	Colfax County	9 709	61.0	17.2	10.1	7.2	4.3	3 682	75.4	1 075	83.3
31 039	...	Cuming County	9 548	67.5	16.1	10.5	4.7	1.2	3 945	71.5	1 296	81.7
31 041	...	Custer County	11 134	63.8	19.7	10.9	5.4	0.2	4 826	73.2	1 584	81.3
31 043	7720	Dakota County	18 557	51.8	20.7	5.4	18.0	4.1	7 095	67.5	1 307	77.0
31 045	...	Dawes County	8 604	47.7	16.5	17.6	17.4	0.8	3 512	62.6	921	77.1
31 047	...	Dawson County	22 320	52.6	23.1	9.2	10.3	4.8	8 824	69.1	2 135	80.6
31 049	...	Deuel County	2 008	56.6	18.1	12.3	12.9	0.1	908	78.0	332	89.2
31 051	...	Dixon County	5 951	67.7	12.5	10.2	8.5	1.1	2 413	76.3	740	85.9
31 053	...	Dodge County	33 861	57.3	23.1	11.9	6.9	0.9	14 433	67.9	4 065	75.4
31 055	5920	Douglas County	429 561	52.6	27.8	5.8	11.3	2.4	182 194	63.2	33 856	76.2
31 057	...	Dundy County	2 168	68.6	12.0	8.0	10.1	1.3	961	72.4	346	84.7
31 059	...	Fillmore County	6 252	64.7	17.8	13.2	3.9	0.3	2 689	74.7	882	84.4
31 061	...	Franklin County	3 377	71.0	13.9	10.1	4.5	0.5	1 485	81.3	548	91.8
31 063	...	Frontier County	2 928	61.3	10.6	19.7	8.1	0.3	1 192	73.0	348	90.8
31 065	...	Furnas County	5 014	65.1	17.2	10.6	6.0	0.2	2 278	76.6	858	80.1
31 067	...	Gage County	21 632	60.2	22.6	10.9	5.8	0.5	9 316	71.4	2 817	77.7
31 069	...	Garden County	2 209	60.4	15.2	10.9	13.1	0.4	1 020	70.8	344	92.2
31 071	...	Garfield County	1 812	68.6	14.6	10.8	5.8	0.2	813	72.0	288	74.7
31 073	...	Gosper County	2 035	64.1	11.9	20.5	3.3	0.1	863	75.6	276	89.5
31 075	...	Grant County	708	64.3	14.8	16.4	4.5	0.0	292	67.8	71	91.5
31 077	...	Greeley County	2 560	73.2	13.2	11.1	2.3	0.2	1 077	78.4	426	90.1
31 079	...	Hall County	49 462	54.4	25.7	10.1	7.1	2.7	20 366	65.9	4 575	76.0
31 081	...	Hamilton County	8 772	65.5	16.5	13.3	4.6	0.1	3 503	75.2	872	82.2
31 083	...	Harlan County	3 592	64.6	13.9	14.1	7.2	0.3	1 597	80.2	626	85.3
31 085	...	Hayes County	1 026	66.2	12.4	13.4	7.1	1.0	430	71.9	141	85.8
31 087	...	Hitchcock County	2 980	64.2	13.6	8.8	12.8	0.6	1 287	78.0	445	80.0
31 089	...	Holt County	10 877	69.9	17.1	8.4	4.3	0.4	4 608	73.5	1 477	83.5
31 091	...	Hooker County	748	69.3	10.7	15.6	4.4	0.0	335	74.0	116	85.3
31 093	...	Howard County	6 179	63.5	14.4	18.0	3.8	0.3	2 546	77.2	775	86.3
31 095	...	Jefferson County	7 908	66.2	21.9	7.5	4.3	0.1	3 527	75.7	1 346	77.5
31 097	...	Johnson County	4 259	66.0	13.2	14.5	5.1	1.1	1 887	75.0	662	81.4
31 099	...	Kearney County	6 455	58.6	14.1	20.5	6.1	0.7	2 643	74.0	694	87.8
31 101	...	Keith County	8 363	55.8	21.2	10.7	11.6	0.6	3 707	73.1	1 006	80.4
31 103	...	Keya Paha County	924	76.2	9.3	7.1	7.1	0.2	409	71.4	136	81.5
31 105	...	Kimball County	3 869	62.8	15.1	8.2	13.6	0.3	1 727	76.5	546	89.2
31 107	...	Knox County	8 847	68.9	18.4	8.0	4.5	0.2	3 811	74.9	1 433	84.6
31 109	4360	Lancaster County	233 685	46.6	30.6	11.2	9.2	2.4	99 187	60.5	17 160	73.9
31 111	...	Lincoln County	32 336	52.9	27.5	8.9	9.9	0.8	14 076	69.2	3 485	79.6
31 113	...	Logan County	734	63.9	11.9	18.0	6.3	0.0	316	71.5	91	93.4
31 115	...	Loup County	665	72.8	8.7	12.8	5.7	0.0	289	77.5	96	92.7
31 117	...	McPherson County	497	70.6	8.7	17.1	3.6	0.0	202	67.3	66	86.4
31 119	...	Madison County	32 785	54.3	25.0	12.7	6.4	1.6	13 436	65.8	3 302	73.6
31 121	...	Merrick County	7 685	63.2	16.4	16.3	3.8	0.4	3 209	74.3	1 008	81.9
31 123	...	Morrill County	5 106	59.5	17.2	13.5	9.2	0.6	2 138	71.4	635	87.4
31 125	...	Nance County	3 792	66.8	12.9	14.8	5.2	0.2	1 577	74.8	523	83.2
31 127	...	Nemaha County	7 229	57.8	17.2	12.7	12.1	0.3	3 047	72.5	984	77.7
31 129	...	Nuckolls County	4 795	69.4	14.6	10.5	5.2	0.3	2 218	80.0	787	88.3
31 131	...	Otoe County	14 402	58.3	20.5	12.1	8.8	0.3	6 060	74.0	1 818	82.0
31 133	...	Pawnee County	2 946	67.9	11.7	13.2	6.1	1.1	1 330	81.0	550	87.8
31 135	...	Perkins County	3 026	63.8	14.3	11.3	10.1	0.5	1 275	75.6	406	81.5
31 137	...	Phelps County	9 135	62.9	20.3	11.0	5.7	0.1	3 844	73.2	1 188	84.0
31 139	...	Pierce County	7 380	65.9	15.6	14.1	4.2	0.2	2 979	77.8	911	88.4

[1]MSA = Metropolitan Statistical Area. PMSA = Primary MSA. NECMA = New England County Metropolitan Area. See the Appendix A for explanation of these concepts. See Appendix B for list of metropolitan areas identified by type, with component counties.

STATE County	Owner-occupied by household type (percent)								Median household income			Median monthly owner costs as a percent of income	
	Family-households					Nonfamily households							
		Married-couple family		Other family									
	Total family households	Total	With own children under 18 years	Total	With own children under 18 years	Total nonfamily households	Two or more adults	Living alone	All households	Owner-occupied households	Renter-occupied households	Median housing value (owner estimated)	With a mortgage	Without a mortgage
	11	12	13	14	15	16	17	18	19	20	21	22	23	24
NEBRASKA—Cont'd														
Blaine County	61.1	61.9	43.3	50.0	0.0	74.6	42.9	78.1	25 147	25 288	24 844	27 500	28.8	11.8
Boone County	79.6	82.8	77.8	54.4	40.7	65.2	80.0	64.4	31 283	33 061	25 189	58 700	18.7	11.8
Box Butte County	76.8	82.3	78.0	48.4	43.3	54.7	56.1	54.5	39 471	45 781	26 440	68 100	17.1	10.4
Boyd County	83.9	84.0	72.4	81.6	81.6	73.6	65.2	74.2	25 926	27 031	21 375	27 600	17.9	12.3
Brown County	80.0	83.0	79.1	60.9	49.4	63.8	61.7	64.0	28 413	31 331	20 938	47 600	19.5	11.1
Buffalo County	76.7	83.0	80.5	47.2	43.9	39.8	15.5	48.5	36 405	45 276	23 930	87 600	20.5	11.0
Burt County	82.6	86.2	81.4	60.0	57.0	59.1	46.6	60.2	33 979	37 262	23 139	63 600	20.1	11.7
Butler County	83.1	84.4	80.8	72.4	57.2	58.8	39.8	60.7	36 242	39 903	27 246	65 400	18.8	9.9
Cass County	84.2	87.8	83.3	64.2	61.0	66.6	68.8	66.1	46 405	51 035	31 381	96 000	20.3	10.9
Cedar County	86.5	89.4	83.4	62.0	51.3	65.5	57.3	66.2	33 035	35 264	24 482	58 700	19.7	11.6
Chase County	80.2	83.0	70.5	59.0	49.4	69.9	52.4	71.5	29 427	36 129	24 662	56 800	17.8	10.6
Cherry County	65.6	67.5	55.6	55.7	42.9	54.7	41:4	56.0	29 427	34 938	24 894	65 500	20.5	11.2
Cheyenne County	79.7	85.1	77.0	53.5	50.3	59.3	38.0	62.0	33 166	38 254	23 258	56 800	19.2	10.5
Clay County	82.1	85.3	83.0	58.0	46.8	66.4	64.0	66.6	33 835	37 116	23 363	52 600	18.6	11.0
Colfax County	79.5	82.6	78.8	59.1	51.2	65.4	50.8	67.4	35 938	37 957	29 950	60 100	17.2	9.9
Cuming County	75.9	79.1	73.1	51.5	37.8	61.5	54.2	62.3	33 133	36 514	24 862	72 500	19.4	9.9
Custer County	78.6	82.0	72.9	51.8	41.4	61.2	55.3	61.6	30 644	34 543	21 617	52 300	18.1	10.1
Dakota County	73.0	81.5	75.9	45.8	34.8	52.9	49.1	53.7	38 694	46 446	24 311	76 400	19.1	10.4
Dawes County	75.6	79.6	74.0	50.4	43.8	43.6	31.8	47.2	28 931	37 892	17 096	57 600	17.9	9.9
Dawson County	74.6	79.3	70.3	50.8	40.8	55.2	33.8	58.9	36 410	41 336	25 903	64 300	19.0	10.9
Deuel County	84.3	85.8	76.1	75.3	65.5	65.6	44.0	67.5	32 500	37 143	21 711	51 100	17.0	11.3
Dixon County	81.0	83.9	77.2	61.5	54.5	64.9	49.4	66.8	34 149	38 082	25 750	62 900	19.3	10.5
Dodge County	76.5	81.3	77.5	53.3	43.4	50.0	40.9	51.6	37 447	43 293	25 045	81 900	18.8	10.3
Douglas County	75.3	83.9	82.8	49.3	38.8	42.4	35.5	43.9	42 913	56 052	27 155	99 600	19.8	10.5
Dundy County	77.2	77.1	62.2	77.8	73.9	62.8	50.0	63.8	27 131	30 968	22 411	36 300	15.7	11.2
Fillmore County	80.7	84.5	79.3	54.6	34.3	62.3	54.7	62.9	35 057	37 867	26 582	55 200	18.7	10.9
Franklin County	82.7	85.2	74.0	66.4	64.4	78.4	66.7	79.1	28 750	29 420	25 694	38 500	19.9	12.0
Frontier County	79.6	81.6	71.9	57.4	47.1	57.1	12.5	62.8	33 770	36 889	26 029	60 300	20.6	11.0
Furnas County	83.0	86.0	83.3	63.5	57.8	64.7	66.7	64.6	30 365	32 350	21 983	39 400	18.8	10.8
Gage County	79.3	83.9	78.4	50.8	46.5	55.6	38.2	58.2	34 814	39 571	25 236	72 900	19.3	10.3
Garden County	70.6	74.1	56.5	50.5	17.3	71.2	64.0	71.7	25 815	27 583	22 750	47 600	20.4	11.5
Garfield County	79.0	80.8	74.9	51.5	60.0	60.6	50.0	61.3	27 831	30 643	20 481	46 200	22.0	13.2
Gosper County	79.6	80.6	70.3	69.4	55.3	62.8	20.0	65.0	36 156	39 018	31 118	71 600	18.2	11.3
Grant County	69.2	71.4	60.0	52.0	57.9	63.2	0.0	64.2	34 808	35 000	34 167	30 800	16.0	9.9
Greeley County	81.8	85.3	76.7	61.5	35.2	71.2	66.7	71.3	28 669	30 722	23 750	40 300	21.3	11.3
Hall County	74.6	82.0	75.4	42.5	32.7	45.8	31.8	48.4	37 264	45 721	22 586	82 500	20.6	10.8
Hamilton County	80.3	83.2	79.4	58.6	48.3	58.2	50.7	58.9	40 266	44 463	28 638	78 300	19.7	9.9
Harlan County	84.7	87.3	77.3	54.2	39.6	71.4	64.4	72.3	30 996	33 192	22 578	48 300	17.4	12.1
Hayes County	70.4	71.3	57.5	60.0	X	75.6	60.0	76.3	26 429	25 885	28 229	48 300	24.6	11.1
Hitchcock County	81.1	83.9	75.0	64.4	51.4	70.7	51.5	72.5	28 750	30 885	21 250	41 300	19.3	9.9
Holt County	79.6	82.2	77.1	60.8	40.6	59.9	64.5	59.5	30 672	32 214	24 979	63 600	19.5	12.8
Hooker County	76.6	77.6	70.8	50.0	50.0	69.0	100.0	65.8	27 847	29 643	22 708	43 700	14.9	10.1
Howard County	80.3	84.7	80.0	49.3	39.3	69.3	85.1	67.5	33 059	37 216	25 438	72 500	21.5	12.3
Jefferson County	83.5	88.2	81.1	57.6	39.9	59.5	59.6	59.4	32 686	36 003	20 820	44 700	17.7	9.9
Johnson County	79.3	82.9	74.7	55.7	48.6	66.2	53.6	67.5	32 239	34 974	24 259	57 200	17.6	11.7
Kearney County	77.8	81.6	73.0	52.0	43.9	63.9	54.2	65.1	39 274	44 634	27 194	77 300	19.1	10.4
Keith County	78.1	81.6	74.9	57.5	54.6	62.3	64.3	62.0	32 945	38 030	22 601	66 700	19.5	11.9
Keya Paha County	73.7	76.4	62.5	50.0	44.4	65.5	62.5	65.7	23 750	25 179	21 023	38 000	25.0	12.9
Kimball County	82.4	86.2	78.7	59.1	32.9	65.0	68.8	64.6	30 898	34 351	21 900	48 500	19.0	11.8
Knox County	78.3	81.1	71.6	56.5	47.7	67.8	51.9	68.9	27 435	29 752	21 047	45 900	19.0	12.5
Lancaster County	75.4	83.4	82.2	43.2	36.4	36.6	22.7	41.2	41 860	55 984	25 243	105 100	20.5	9.9
Lincoln County	77.6	83.5	79.3	45.1	34.2	52.3	46.8	53.2	36 388	43 215	23 248	77 300	19.2	11.8
Logan County	70.6	71.1	62.7	66.7	60.0	73.9	50.0	76.3	33 750	36 667	27 500	61 400	22.5	11.6
Loup County	77.6	76.5	70.1	88.9	66.7	77.4	66.7	78.2	25 804	27 308	21 375	46 400	20.7	11.8
McPherson County	66.0	67.6	56.8	52.9	33.3	72.5	X	72.5	26 000	26 786	23 750	44 700	17.5	9.9
Madison County	76.8	83.1	80.8	45.3	38.0	43.9	27.7	47.0	35 633	45 405	22 292	78 900	20.0	10.4
Merrick County	79.6	83.9	76.2	56.0	50.9	60.5	42.7	62.5	34 694	37 991	26 212	64 900	20.8	10.9
Morrill County	73.9	77.7	68.0	48.7	37.8	65.5	51.6	67.1	29 940	33 750	24 076	50 300	17.8	11.0
Nance County	80.9	84.7	77.4	54.0	39.3	60.3	47.1	61.3	31 198	35 871	21 500	50 600	17.8	10.6
Nemaha County	79.9	82.7	75.2	63.0	53.2	58.6	31.7	62.6	32 266	38 807	22 128	61 900	17.4	9.9
Nuckolls County	85.5	88.6	82.0	56.4	47.8	69.8	32.8	72.9	28 976	31 031	21 154	35 900	19.0	11.3
Otoe County	79.7	84.1	80.8	52.7	46.9	61.1	50.0	62.7	36 961	41 712	25 430	82 000	19.5	11.0
Pawnee County	84.1	87.4	81.7	63.3	55.2	75.5	75.0	75.6	28 608	30 889	20 893	39 000	18.1	11.8
Perkins County	80.7	83.5	79.0	55.7	54.5	63.4	76.0	62.5	33 831	37 647	26 563	56 000	17.8	9.9
Phelps County	80.3	83.1	77.3	55.2	52.1	56.6	47.1	57.7	37 651	42 192	26 096	71 400	17.9	11.3
Pierce County	82.2	84.5	79.7	65.9	47.4	66.7	42.3	69.2	32 061	35 313	25 000	65 200	19.1	12.1

STATE County	Median gross rent	Percent who pay 35 percent or more of income for housing expenses — Owners	Renters	Means of transportation to work (percent except where noted) — Number of workers 16 years and over	Car, truck, or van — Drove alone	Carpooled	Public transportation	Other means	Walked	Vehicles available (percent of households) — No vehicles	One vehicle	Two or more vehicles
	25	26	27	28	29	30	31	32	33	34	35	36
NEBRASKA—Cont'd												
Blaine County	365	19.7	12.2	271	47.2	14.0	0.0	0.7	15.1	5.9	21.0	73.1
Boone County	310	11.9	12.3	2 944	73.3	10.3	0.1	1.1	4.8	4.4	25.0	70.7
Box Butte County	411	9.9	20.6	5 715	79.5	8.6	0.2	1.4	4.8	5.4	29.1	65.5
Boyd County	261	13.4	10.2	1 153	62.9	11.9	0.2	0.9	9.5	5.8	26.2	67.9
Brown County	347	8.8	17.2	1 730	73.5	9.4	0.0	1.2	5.5	4.6	31.5	63.9
Buffalo County	495	11.3	28.0	23 078	84.4	7.9	0.1	0.6	3.2	4.0	28.1	67.9
Burt County	395	12.0	16.1	3 710	75.4	10.8	0.1	0.8	4.2	5.5	26.0	68.5
Butler County	389	9.5	10.3	4 302	75.2	11.2	0.2	1.0	3.8	5.5	22.8	71.7
Cass County................	502	11.9	21.4	12 582	81.4	12.6	0.0	0.5	1.7	4.3	22.3	73.3
Cedar County	350	10.5	18.2	4 562	70.7	10.8	0.0	0.3	5.9	4.4	24.8	70.8
Chase County	335	10.7	14.7	1 939	75.3	10.4	0.0	0.5	6.5	3.7	25.2	71.2
Cherry County	424	11.9	14.8	3 166	62.2	9.4	0.2	1.3	13.3	4.9	31.3	63.8
Cheyenne County	388	10.4	17.2	4 975	78.9	12.2	0.0	0.5	2.7	5.7	34.0	60.3
Clay County.................	363	9.9	12.0	3 323	77.0	8.8	0.3	0.8	5.4	3.2	26.1	70.7
Colfax County	410	9.0	9.6	5 199	67.1	18.5	0.2	1.1	5.4	5.2	27.6	67.2
Cuming County	398	10.9	13.9	5 161	73.2	9.8	0.0	0.3	5.5	3.7	29.8	66.5
Custer County	333	11.0	15.0	5 679	71.4	9.8	0.1	0.8	5.1	5.2	26.1	68.6
Dakota County	516	9.1	26.0	9 842	76.9	17.4	0.3	1.1	1.6	5.7	31.8	62.5
Dawes County	394	10.9	36.3	4 696	72.2	10.3	0.1	0.9	10.8	6.1	27.7	66.3
Dawson County	453	9.5	19.1	11 138	74.6	16.8	0.1	1.8	2.5	4.6	29.0	66.4
Deuel County	338	9.7	10.6	1 049	77.2	8.8	0.0	1.1	7.1	4.5	24.4	71.0
Dixon County	401	8.6	13.1	3 100	72.6	13.1	0.3	0.8	5.3	5.3	24.9	69.7
Dodge County	485	11.2	23.3	18 091	82.7	9.4	0.1	1.0	3.4	6.6	30.8	62.6
Douglas County	541	11.4	25.6	236 799	82.4	10.5	1.6	0.7	2.1	8.8	36.2	55.1
Dundy County	286	9.4	10.3	1 116	72.0	8.5	0.0	1.3	9.8	3.9	26.0	70.1
Fillmore County	367	8.8	13.9	3 175	74.7	9.2	0.0	0.3	6.0	4.9	27.1	68.0
Franklin County	361	11.2	12.6	1 621	77.1	9.8	0.1	0.7	4.3	3.8	25.1	71.0
Frontier County	368	7.1	17.1	1 600	66.3	9.6	0.3	0.7	9.4	4.1	22.8	73.1
Furnas County.............	314	11.7	12.7	2 381	77.1	9.6	0.0	0.8	6.7	5.8	27.9	66.3
Gage County................	421	10.6	18.8	11 540	81.5	9.5	0.2	0.9	2.2	5.2	28.7	66.2
Garden County.............	325	7.9	11.2	1 126	64.8	11.9	0.0	0.9	12.5	4.2	27.9	67.8
Garfield County	010	11.0	26.1	901	69.9	9.3	0.0	2.0	6.3	6.2	29.0	64.8
Gosper County.............	406	11.0	15.7	1 043	76.0	11.6	0.0	0.2	5.4	3.5	20.3	76.2
Grant County................	369	7.7	7.0	408	58.8	4.9	1.0	1.2	10.8	2.7	19.2	78.1
Greeley County	306	12.3	11.9	1 259	62.2	10.8	0.0	0.7	11.0	5.1	25.2	69.7
Hall County..................	456	11.3	25.3	26 622	82.5	11.6	0.3	0.8	1.9	5.9	31.5	62.5
Hamilton County...........	420	9.2	13.2	4 722	80.3	8.2	0.0	0.8	3.2	2.7	23.3	74.1
Harlan County..............	370	8.3	16.5	1 745	75.2	10.8	0.0	0.2	5.3	3.4	27.8	68.8
Hayes County...............	296	16.4	3.1	521	60.5	11.5	0.0	0.8	8.6	2.8	17.7	79.5
Hitchcock County	329	8.5	13.5	1 419	71.4	8.8	0.0	1.0	7.1	2.9	25.7	71.4
Holt County	323	13.4	10.6	5 656	72.5	8.5	0.0	0.8	6.6	4.8	26.5	68.7
Hooker County	204	11.4	14.7	368	68.8	9.2	0.0	1.4	9.8	3.9	21.8	74.3
Howard County	403	14.5	12.3	3 296	75.8	10.2	0.2	1.2	3.8	4.3	21.8	73.9
Jefferson County	349	8.4	20.5	4 008	75.9	13.5	0.0	0.2	2.9	4.9	29.9	65.2
Johnson County	378	9.6	22.1	2 128	75.3	12.8	0.3	0.7	3.6	6.8	24.9	68.3
Kearney County	453	8.9	17.9	3 515	79.4	9.3	0.3	0.6	4.4	2.5	21.2	76.3
Keith County................	404	10.1	15.9	4 383	78.0	11.0	0.0	1.2	4.3	5.4	28.0	66.6
Keya Paha County	277	16.2	18.3	464	51.9	10.8	0.0	1.3	11.0	4.2	20.5	75.3
Kimball County	381	11.8	22.9	1 937	74.3	12.5	0.0	0.2	6.1	3.6	29.7	66.6
Knox County	264	10.6	10.3	4 339	68.1	10.8	0.0	0.9	8.0	6.3	27.1	66.6
Lancaster County	519	9.8	28.7	138 151	80.6	10.2	1.2	1.6	3.2	4.6	34.4	58.8
Lincoln County	427	11.7	23.1	16 666	83.4	9.1	0.1	1.1	2.4	5.0	30.1	64.8
Logan County...............	340	10.7	4.4	383	61.9	9.7	0.0	0.3	8.1	1.6	15.5	82.9
Loup County.................	278	14.8	12.2	320	54.4	8.8	1.3	0.6	11.9	1.7	23.9	74.4
McPherson County........	269	6.0	0.0	256	43.4	5.1	0.0	0.0	9.0	2.0	14.9	83.2
Madison County	434	10.6	25.5	17 594	80.7	10.4	0.4	1.1	2.8	7.8	30.4	61.8
Merrick County	401	11.9	16.7	3 965	77.8	11.8	0.2	0.3	3.8	4.5	24.2	71.3
Morrill County	370	10.8	15.0	2 494	72.9	10.6	0.3	0.7	5.7	4.7	26.4	68.8
Nance County	352	8.0	18.4	1 863	73.0	12.2	0.0	0.8	5.2	3.7	25.7	70.6
Nemaha County	360	13.8	18.9	3 640	76.5	9.8	0.1	0.7	5.1	6.5	30.4	63.1
Nuckolls County	315	10.7	16.4	2 397	73.2	11.3	0.1	0.5	5.8	5.5	29.9	64.6
Otoe County.................	434	11.8	14.9	7 593	76.8	12.9	0.3	0.7	2.6	5.1	27.7	67.2
Pawnee County............	309	9.3	16.0	1 471	70.2	12.8	0.1	1.2	5.9	6.9	26.1	67.0
Perkins County.............	389	8.9	22.7	1 529	74.8	7.0	0.1	0.7	5.6	5.3	20.9	73.7
Phelps County..............	378	10.5	14.6	4 899	78.6	10.4	0.2	0.7	4.6	3.7	23.7	72.6
Pierce County...............	372	9.0	19.7	3 880	76.5	9.1	0.1	0.5	4.6	4.9	23.7	71.4

STATE/ County code	MSA/PMSA/ NECMA code[1]	STATE County	Total population 5 years and over	Residence in 1995 (percent)					Occupied housing units		Householders 65 years and over	
				Same house	Same county, different house	Same state, different county	Different state	Outside the United States	Number	Percent owner-occupied	Number	Percent owner-occupied
			1	2	3	4	5	6	7	8	9	10
		NEBRASKA—Cont'd										
31 141	...	Platte County..............	29 407	60.1	21.2	10.7	6.4	1.5	12 076	73.3	2 861	80.8
31 143	...	Polk County..............	5 324	66.8	13.2	15.2	4.3	0.4	2 259	76.9	736	87.6
31 145	...	Red Willow County.......	10 740	61.2	20.1	9.9	8.4	0.3	4 710	70.6	1 353	78.0
31 147	...	Richardson County.......	9 054	63.1	24.1	5.1	7.7	0.0	3 993	74.7	1 371	79.6
31 149	...	Rock County..............	1 655	69.0	13.4	11.1	6.5	0.0	763	73.1	266	89.8
31 151	...	Saline County..............	13 051	58.7	16.0	15.6	7.7	2.0	5 188	70.8	1 501	76.7
31 153	5920	Sarpy County..............	112 578	46.4	16.2	15.6	19.0	2.8	43 426	69.2	5 331	80.3
31 155	...	Saunders County	18 576	64.2	15.1	15.7	4.5	0.6	7 498	79.6	2 024	84.5
31 157	...	Scotts Bluff County	34 493	57.1	25.5	5.7	10.6	1.1	14 887	66.2	4 156	76.2
31 159	...	Seward County.............	15 562	55.2	16.9	18.4	8.7	0.8	6 013	72.0	1 619	75.4
31 161	...	Sheridan County	5 834	62.0	17.8	8.4	11.6	0.2	2 549	69.9	867	81.1
31 163	...	Sherman County	3 147	70.7	12.7	12.0	4.5	0.0	1 394	80.6	530	87.0
31 165	...	Sioux County..............	1 396	60.5	11.6	17.7	10.2	0.0	605	66.8	177	87.6
31 167	...	Stanton County	5 973	66.2	9.2	19.7	3.9	1.1	2 297	80.1	496	86.5
31 169	...	Thayer County.............	5 727	68.3	17.3	9.4	4.7	0.3	2 541	80.0	910	85.7
31 171	...	Thomas County	687	71.5	7.9	10.2	10.5	0.0	325	73.5	99	89.9
31 173	...	Thurston County...........	6 474	60.9	23.4	6.8	7.8	1.1	2 255	60.8	613	80.3
31 175	...	Valley County	4 390	66.7	16.3	13.3	3.2	0.5	1 965	75.8	724	80.5
31 177	5920	Washington County........	17 585	56.6	17.1	16.5	8.9	0.9	6 940	77.3	1 557	81.3
31 179	...	Wayne County.............	9 328	50.7	15.3	24.3	8.5	1.3	3 437	64.8	844	82.8
31 181	...	Webster County	3 854	66.2	15.8	11.6	6.0	0.4	1 708	78.3	608	81.3
31 183	...	Wheeler County	827	77.3	6.4	13.2	3.1	0.0	352	70.2	100	88.0
31 185	...	York County	13 753	59.2	19.9	10.6	9.2	1.0	5 722	69.6	1 586	72.6
32 000	...	NEVADA....................	1 853 720	37.4	30.6	2.8	25.1	4.1	751 165	60.9	141 024	74.5
32 001	...	Churchill County..........	22 202	45.4	20.8	6.9	24.3	2.5	8 912	65.8	1 833	81.9
32 003	4120	Clark County	1 272 872	34.5	32.5	0.9	27.4	4.7	512 253	59.1	93 609	73.2
32 005	...	Douglas County...........	39 164	48.9	16.9	6.3	26.7	1.2	16 401	74.2	3 802	89.1
32 007	...	Elko County................	41 470	47.6	26.1	6.0	18.4	1.9	15 638	69.8	1 872	74.8
32 009	...	Esmeralda County.........	940	53.1	16.0	11.5	18.3	1.2	455	66.4	129	72.1
32 011	...	Eureka County	1 557	59.4	8.0	13.7	15.7	3.2	666	74.0	151	75.5
32 013	...	Humboldt County	14 808	45.8	22.2	10.6	19.3	2.0	5 733	73.0	787	79.9
32 015	...	Lander County.............	5 364	56.0	20.4	7.5	15.2	0.9	2 093	77.1	258	86.8
32 017	...	Lincoln County	3 897	55.8	12.6	15.3	14.5	1.8	1 540	74.7	504	74.8
32 019	...	Lyon County	32 277	44.1	16.0	17.7	21.1	1.1	13 007	75.9	3 087	84.5
32 021	...	Mineral County	4 807	56.0	21.8	7.2	13.6	1.4	2 197	72.7	682	85.5
32 023	4120	Nye County	30 602	41.1	13.3	19.6	24.8	1.2	13 309	76.4	4 018	87.0
32 027	...	Pershing County...........	6 267	48.4	16.1	16.4	17.1	2.0	1 962	69.4	389	86.9
32 029	...	Storey County	3 251	49.1	4.5	23.4	21.7	1.2	1 462	79.7	261	86.6
32 031	6720	Washoe County.............	316 402	41.2	32.4	3.5	19.4	3.4	132 084	59.3	23 841	71.8
32 033	...	White Pine County.........	8 631	52.5	16.7	11.2	18.8	0.7	3 282	76.5	790	85.1
32 510	...	Carson City	49 209	46.1	22.4	11.3	17.7	2.5	20 171	63.1	5 011	75.4
33 000	...	NEW HAMPSHIRE.....	1 160 340	55.4	22.3	6.9	14.0	1.4	474 606	69.7	94 327	74.4
33 001	...	Belknap County...........	53 328	55.9	21.5	11.6	10.2	0.8	22 459	74.1	5 265	80.2
33 003	...	Carroll County	41 581	58.8	17.7	8.1	14.4	0.9	18 351	77.7	4 984	86.8
33 005	...	Cheshire County	70 018	57.5	22.3	5.6	13.7	0.8	28 299	70.9	6 710	77.2
33 007	...	Coos County	31 434	64.1	22.6	4.3	8.4	0.6	13 961	71.1	4 073	71.9
33 009	...	Grafton County	77 524	54.5	19.7	6.3	18.2	1.4	31 598	68.6	6 906	79.5
33 011	1123	Hillsborough County......	355 128	53.6	25.6	4.9	13.5	2.5	144 455	64.9	25 648	66.7
33 013	...	Merrimack County	128 235	55.6	21.7	11.5	10.2	1.0	51 843	69.5	10 549	72.9
33 015	1123	Rockingham County.......	259 267	57.1	19.7	5.5	16.7	1.0	104 529	75.6	17 876	77.2
33 017	1123	Strafford County...........	105 623	50.3	22.8	10.9	14.9	1.1	42 581	64.4	8 003	75.7
33 019	...	Sullivan County	38 202	59.6	22.2	6.0	11.7	0.6	16 530	72.1	4 313	79.0
34 000	...	NEW JERSEY...........	7 856 268	59.8	20.7	8.7	6.8	4.0	3 064 645	65.6	701 857	74.2
34 001	0560	Atlantic County	236 405	57.6	26.9	6.2	5.9	3.4	95 024	66.3	21 964	73.5
34 003	0875	Bergen County	829 455	62.8	19.3	5.8	7.4	4.8	330 817	67.2	83 136	76.5
34 005	6160	Burlington County..........	396 629	60.0	19.1	9.3	9.8	1.8	154 371	77.4	33 185	85.1
34 007	6160	Camden County	474 661	63.0	22.2	6.3	6.7	1.8	185 744	70.0	42 151	73.7
34 009	0560	Cape May County	97 148	61.1	20.2	7.6	10.2	0.9	42 148	74.3	13 705	81.3
34 011	8760	Cumberland County	137 590	60.9	26.1	6.8	3.5	2.7	49 143	67.9	12 325	75.6
34 013	5640	Essex County	736 536	57.9	25.3	6.7	5.2	4.9	283 736	45.6	61 090	56.7
34 015	6160	Gloucester County	238 232	65.4	17.4	9.8	6.7	0.6	90 717	79.9	18 465	81.8
34 017	3640	Hudson County	571 095	53.8	24.9	4.9	8.1	8.2	230 546	30.6	45 632	42.8
34 019	5015	Hunterdon County	113 866	61.8	12.8	15.6	8.2	1.6	43 678	83.7	7 333	84.3

[1]MSA = Metropolitan Statistical Area. PMSA = Primary MSA. NECMA = New England County Metropolitan Area. See the Appendix A for explanation of these concepts. See Appendix B for list of metropolitan areas identified by type, with component counties.

STATE County	Total family households	Owner-occupied by household type (percent) Family-households Married-couple family Total	With own children under 18 years	Other family Total	With own children under 18 years	Nonfamily households Total nonfamily households	Two or more adults	Living alone	Median household income All households	Owner-occupied households	Renter-occupied households	Median housing value (owner estimated)	Median monthly owner costs as a percent of income With a mortgage	Without a mortgage
	11	12	13	14	15	16	17	18	19	20	21	22	23	24
NEBRASKA—Cont'd														
Platte County	82.5	86.9	83.6	56.1	43.9	51.8	38.6	53.9	39 299	45 860	25 342	80 000	18.4	9.9
Polk County	80.8	82.8	76.4	59.6	54.1	68.0	50.7	69.9	37 564	40 078	27 656	63 300	17.9	9.9
Red Willow County	80.5	86.3	83.5	47.6	38.0	49.9	34.7	51.9	32 154	38 101	22 552	59 000	18.6	12.0
Richardson County	80.7	86.8	83.7	54.3	48.4	63.9	69.7	63.2	29 502	33 474	20 356	42 000	17.6	10.7
Rock County	78.8	81.5	65.8	65.1	47.8	62.5	19.0	66.3	25 614	27 266	21 797	42 200	22.9	11.9
Saline County	78.8	83.5	77.3	55.3	55.9	54.2	35.5	57.6	36 600	41 405	26 604	70 900	18.9	10.6
Sarpy County	76.2	80.5	76.9	54.4	44.1	46.2	38.5	48.2	53 746	62 594	33 508	112 000	20.1	9.9
Saunders County	85.0	88.4	86.2	62.7	51.8	64.8	54.1	66.3	41 600	46 091	26 390	92 800	20.0	10.7
Scotts Bluff County	73.6	80.4	73.4	47.9	40.1	50.0	44.7	50.6	31 892	39 181	21 826	70 900	19.2	11.5
Seward County	80.8	83.4	79.9	57.9	50.5	51.0	33.7	54.2	42 546	48 894	26 693	91 000	19.6	10.4
Sheridan County	74.7	79.2	67.7	50.2	38.3	60.0	46.9	61.1	29 323	32 053	20 429	47 700	19.1	11.9
Sherman County	84.7	86.6	78.5	70.5	59.0	72.1	51.6	73.6	28 125	29 351	22 426	45 000	19.6	12.4
Sioux County	70.1	72.2	57.3	50.0	11.8	57.9	40.0	61.2	29 680	30 000	28 036	57 300	25.0	10.5
Stanton County	80.0	86.4	80.2	66.1	57.3	67.3	64.5	67.7	36 823	40 322	30 250	70 100	21.0	10.6
Thayer County	83.6	87.0	81.8	57.4	49.3	72.7	79.5	72.4	30 816	32 976	25 639	43 200	18.1	11.0
Thomas County	71.8	76.7	69.6	25.0	0.0	76.8	33.3	79.2	27 019	27 361	26 250	37 800	12.8	9.9
Thurston County	61.9	71.8	59.9	41.1	34.6	57.3	46.3	58.5	27 760	32 544	22 394	53 400	16.6	10.6
Valley County	81.4	84.5	78.3	59.3	45.8	64.5	45.7	66.0	28 105	31 806	19 702	47 200	19.1	11.9
Washington County	82.1	86.6	84.2	57.1	43.7	63.2	51.6	65.1	48 600	55 462	30 262	122 300	20.7	11.1
Wayne County	77.8	82.0	76.5	50.8	49.4	41.0	9.9	53.9	32 509	42 098	20 051	79 700	17.8	11.8
Webster County	85.0	87.2	80.8	64.5	52.1	65.7	56.8	66.3	29 972	32 098	21 250	44 800	19.2	11.3
Wheeler County	72.4	76.1	65.9	40.0	23.5	65.1	20.0	67.3	26 000	26 161	25 625	42 700	18.8	10.7
York County	80.3	84.1	80.5	50.6	38.2	45.3	21.5	48.0	37 240	43 193	25 098	76 600	18.9	10.6
NEVADA	68.0	74.5	68.7	48.1	40.0	46.6	42.9	47.9	44 316	54 626	31 269	132 500	23.8	9.9
Churchill County	68.4	72.3	61.7	49.6	43.4	58.4	56.4	58.8	41 177	48 272	30 800	106 300	20.6	9.9
Clark County	66.2	73.0	67.2	46.9	38.6	45.0	42.0	46.1	44 331	55 268	31 457	132 200	23.9	9.9
Douglas County	70.6	83.0	73.6	55.3	47.1	62.3	59.0	63.3	51 567	57 521	35 108	174 200	24.2	9.9
Elko County	75.9	81.3	79.6	52.5	48.9	52.9	50.0	53.6	47 674	53 483	31 960	106 200	20.2	9.9
Esmeralda County	74.4	76.7	56.9	61.5	76.2	55.8	66.7	53.7	33 083	36 667	28 750	47 400	18.8	9.9
Eureka County	70.7	92.3	77.2	65.2	54.1	62.8	60.0	63.3	41 731	46 518	27 375	65 600	20.2	9.9
Humboldt County	79.7	82.9	82.1	66.1	63.7	55.4	49.8	56.6	47 065	54 122	31 496	93 200	19.1	9.9
Lander County	81.0	85.7	87.8	57.4	50.3	66.2	43.7	70.4	45 807	50 447	29 188	66 000	16.5	9.9
Lincoln County	80.9	84.9	76.5	61.2	53.6	62.9	67.3	62.5	29 896	37 857	14 138	74 300	18.9	10.7
Lyon County	78.3	82.3	77.2	62.3	51.0	69.1	69.9	68.9	40 544	43 583	31 307	103 800	23.7	9.9
Mineral County	77.4	83.1	69.9	63.3	48.7	64.6	66.7	64.2	32 809	36 069	24 489	54 900	18.4	9.9
Nye County	82.2	85.9	76.1	63.5	52.1	64.0	55.0	66.2	35 695	37 840	28 046	96 300	23.2	9.9
Pershing County	74.1	79.7	78.6	52.5	38.0	58.2	47.5	60.5	40 027	45 038	29 625	79 500	18.7	11.5
Storey County	85.2	87.5	84.9	70.9	50.0	60.0	60.0	62.6	46 182	50 580	33 750	122 400	23.2	9.9
Washoe County	67.9	74.2	69.4	47.7	40.2	44.2	40.0	45.6	45 632	58 868	30 784	149 500	24.4	9.9
White Pine County	81.9	86.6	81.8	64.1	58.3	66.2	78.7	64.2	37 143	41 662	26 607	65 600	19.6	13.1
Carson City	69.6	75.8	64.4	50.8	40.8	50.4	44.6	51.6	41 777	50 908	30 117	136 300	22.6	9.9
NEW HAMPSHIRE	79.1	84.7	83.6	54.6	45.3	49.2	45.1	50.4	49 224	58 048	31 478	127 500	22.3	13.6
Belknap County	81.3	86.8	83.7	56.3	47.1	57.9	51.3	59.7	43 627	50 067	28 243	104 100	22.6	13.2
Carroll County	83.8	88.7	84.0	60.9	52.0	65.3	63.1	65.8	39 703	43 750	28 063	117 800	23.3	13.4
Cheshire County	81.2	85.9	84.3	61.7	53.8	50.2	42.1	52.6	42 110	50 179	27 714	104 100	23.1	14.5
Coos County	80.4	86.7	81.7	56.8	47.4	53.3	57.7	52.4	33 393	40 036	20 504	69 300	19.6	14.7
Grafton County	78.9	84.0	80.8	55.7	44.8	50.1	40.9	52.9	41 869	49 950	27 312	106 000	21.3	12.7
Hillsborough County	74.9	81.3	81.0	47.4	38.0	43.2	43.0	43.3	53 247	65 934	33 939	135 500	22.1	13.7
Merrimack County	79.0	84.3	83.4	57.2	47.3	48.9	48.4	49.0	48 214	57 158	30 177	115 100	21.9	13.0
Rockingham County	84.0	88.2	88.2	62.2	53.4	54.4	50.1	55.7	57 911	66 039	37 036	158 300	22.8	13.4
Strafford County	76.5	83.3	81.5	50.6	42.5	41.7	32.0	45.7	44 541	53 931	30 561	112 100	22.3	14.2
Sullivan County	79.6	85.4	83.0	53.7	44.0	56.0	54.0	56.5	40 640	47 284	26 255	89 600	22.1	14.1
NEW JERSEY	72.8	80.1	78.0	48.8	35.9	48.4	40.3	50.1	54 820	68 770	34 103	167 900	23.7	15.3
Atlantic County	73.7	82.7	79.2	51.4	39.8	51.6	47.1	52.6	43 788	53 079	27 778	118 300	24.7	15.8
Bergen County	75.0	78.8	77.1	58.0	42.9	47.6	37.4	49.3	64 912	79 926	42 010	240 800	24.5	15.7
Burlington County	83.7	87.8	85.8	66.3	55.3	60.8	56.5	61.7	58 220	65 930	37 194	134 000	23.3	14.5
Camden County	78.0	87.0	86.6	55.0	42.5	51.1	46.7	51.9	47 645	59 365	26 995	110 200	23.3	15.6
Cape May County	80.1	85.7	78.5	58.3	44.1	63.4	55.5	64.6	41 297	48 760	26 657	138 000	24.8	16.1
Cumberland County	72.7	83.6	70.4	49.3	37.1	55.8	50.0	56.9	38 675	48 809	22 136	89 200	22.8	14.0
Essex County	53.6	67.5	65.6	30.3	19.4	28.3	25.0	28.9	44 306	73 805	28 315	188 400	24.2	16.1
Gloucester County	86.2	91.5	91.5	65.3	51.7	61.8	54.7	63.3	53 854	61 436	28 303	118 200	23.1	14.5
Hudson County	35.7	42.5	36.8	23.6	13.9	22.2	15.4	24.0	39 976	60 524	32 992	162 800	26.5	17.9
Hunterdon County	89.9	92.2	92.8	71.7	61.7	64.8	62.2	65.4	80 012	87 676	41 658	246 700	23.7	14.1

STATE County	Median gross rent	Percent who pay 35 percent or more of income for housing expenses — Owners	Renters	Means of transportation to work (percent except where noted) — Number of workers 16 years and over	Car, truck, or van — Drove alone	Carpooled	Public transportation	Other means	Walked	Vehicles available (percent of households) — No vehicles	One vehicle	Two or more vehicles
	25	26	27	28	29	30	31	32	33	34	35	36
NEBRASKA—Cont'd												
Platte County...............	429	7.5	21.8	16 056	80.9	9.5	0.2	0.9	2.3	5.3	28.6	66.1
Polk County................	387	8.4	13.1	2 753	76.2	10.2	0.0	0.7	4.4	3.4	27.2	69.4
Red Willow County.......	393	11.5	21.1	5 710	80.6	10.1	0.4	0.5	3.5	4.3	30.3	65.4
Richardson County.......	298	8.7	10.2	4 303	78.5	12.0	0.1	0.5	3.7	6.8	31.5	61.8
Rock County...............	282	15.3	14.9	894	63.9	9.8	0.0	0.6	8.1	3.8	30.0	66.2
Saline County..............	443	8.1	20.1	6 983	70.7	16.8	0.2	1.0	5.5	4.5	26.1	69.3
Sarpy County..............	607	9.6	16.6	66 535	86.1	9.2	0.2	0.5	1.0	3.0	26.0	71.0
Saunders County	474	11.3	16.4	10 183	80.1	10.3	0.0	0.5	3.2	5.2	21.2	73.6
Scotts Bluff County	433	10.4	27.5	17 042	80.5	11.7	0.1	1.3	2.6	6.4	32.0	61.6
Seward County.............	449	11.5	22.4	8 588	73.6	12.5	0.2	1.2	7.1	4.0	25.5	70.5
Sheridan County	369	10.1	20.7	2 980	65.1	12.4	0.2	0.7	7.6	5.8	29.2	65.0
Sherman County	350	12.2	15.2	1 615	70.3	10.2	0.4	0.6	6.7	7.2	26.3	66.4
Sioux County	413	4.3	10.4	712	53.9	12.6	0.3	1.8	8.0	2.3	21.5	76.2
Stanton County	411	11.2	11.3	3 291	75.0	10.9	0.0	0.7	2.9	2.7	21.0	76.3
Thayer County..............	321	9.2	12.6	2 853	75.5	8.4	0.0	0.8	6.7	4.3	27.6	68.0
Thomas County............	300	7.3	6.9	381	59.6	10.2	0.0	2.9	19.2	3.7	31.4	64.9
Thurston County...........	301	9.4	13.6	2 520	69.6	15.5	1.1	0.8	7.0	9.6	31.8	58.6
Valley County	289	11.8	22.0	2 206	73.3	7.4	0.0	1.3	7.0	6.9	28.4	64.7
Washington County.......	539	10.8	20.1	10 043	83.3	9.1	0.0	0.6	2.5	4.2	24.2	71.5
Wayne County.............	404	9.2	27.6	5 381	73.5	9.5	0.1	0.7	8.9	2.9	26.5	70.6
Webster County	301	12.5	12.3	1 786	73.6	10.6	0.0	0.4	5.9	4.4	27.1	68.4
Wheeler County	270	9.2	3.6	453	65.3	5.3	0.2	1.3	6.0	4.0	25.3	70.7
York County................	439	8.1	18.9	7 205	76.9	10.5	0.0	1.1	5.7	5.3	30.4	64.3
NEVADA..................	699	19.8	30.5	923 155	74.5	14.7	3.9	1.6	2.7	8.7	37.9	53.3
Churchill County	595	9.4	18.1	10 977	74.0	17.1	0.1	1.2	3.8	5.7	28.9	65.4
Clark County	716	20.5	31.6	631 236	74.6	14.7	4.4	1.7	2.3	9.5	40.2	50.3
Douglas County...........	780	20.2	28.8	18 936	79.0	10.9	0.4	1.6	2.1	2.7	26.4	70.9
Elko County................	583	14.0	18.0	21 278	64.2	18.1	8.8	1.1	5.3	4.9	30.6	64.5
Esmeralda County........	381	4.6	11.5	429	63.9	12.6	1.9	1.4	14.2	4.6	38.9	56.5
Eureka County	469	14.4	11.1	712	64.0	13.1	4.4	1.8	9.1	8.0	28.1	64.0
Humboldt County	531	11.9	11.7	6 931	60.5	24.1	9.0	0.9	3.7	5.4	26.8	67.8
Lander County.............	496	6.4	15.3	2 476	66.1	25.0	0.2	0.7	4.5	5.5	27.7	66.7
Lincoln County	328	10.6	14.5	1 453	66.3	14.2	1.0	2.5	12.5	10.7	32.1	57.2
Lyon County	591	19.0	24.1	15 141	75.7	17.3	0.1	0.7	2.6	4.5	25.9	69.6
Mineral County	398	13.5	16.4	2 029	72.4	14.1	0.3	1.2	7.7	5.2	38.1	56.6
Nye County	541	18.4	22.4	12 080	70.4	18.0	1.8	1.4	4.9	4.4	31.5	64.1
Pershing County	498	11.4	18.5	2 242	69.9	18.4	0.6	1.6	6.3	5.4	34.9	59.7
Storey County	513	19.6	22.6	1 745	77.8	11.7	0.7	0.5	6.2	5.9	24.4	69.7
Washoe County............	675	19.6	30.3	168 922	75.3	13.8	3.2	1.6	3.2	8.9	35.1	56.1
White Pine County	452	10.4	18.3	3 286	71.3	15.7	1.6	0.7	5.7	6.1	30.4	63.6
Carson City	650	15.6	31.0	23 282	77.7	13.9	0.6	1.8	2.7	6.5	36.4	57.2
NEW HAMPSHIRE.....	646	15.3	25.6	638 565	81.8	9.8	0.7	0.8	2.9	5.8	31.1	63.2
Belknap County	588	16.3	25.8	28 253	80.8	11.2	0.5	0.8	2.7	5.5	32.5	62.0
Carroll County	552	18.4	25.0	20 785	79.6	9.9	0.3	1.3	3.3	4.3	33.0	62.7
Cheshire County	596	17.4	27.1	37 235	78.8	11.5	0.4	0.5	4.3	5.3	31.5	63.2
Coos County	399	13.3	25.1	15 230	78.8	11.4	0.2	1.4	4.4	8.0	38.0	53.9
Grafton County	560	13.6	24.6	41 333	72.8	12.2	0.7	1.3	7.7	6.5	34.8	58.7
Hillsborough County......	694	14.4	25.3	198 868	83.3	9.5	0.9	0.7	2.1	6.8	31.0	62.1
Merrimack County	613	13.3	25.6	69 676	81.2	10.7	0.6	0.6	2.8	6.1	31.4	62.4
Rockingham County......	717	17.1	25.0	148 703	84.8	7.8	0.8	0.8	1.7	3.7	27.4	68.9
Strafford County	623	14.1	27.6	58 403	80.3	10.4	1.0	1.0	4.2	6.2	32.6	61.2
Sullivan County	537	14.6	25.5	20 079	79.4	12.7	0.4	0.7	2.2	6.8	31.1	62.1
NEW JERSEY..........	751	20.5	29.9	3 876 433	73.0	10.6	9.6	0.9	3.1	12.7	34.8	52.5
Atlantic County	677	22.6	30.7	112 659	73.1	11.5	7.7	1.4	4.4	15.5	36.9	47.6
Bergen County	872	23.3	29.3	427 462	72.8	9.7	11.0	0.6	2.8	8.9	35.5	55.6
Burlington County	758	17.9	26.3	207 471	82.7	9.2	2.9	0.7	1.6	5.1	32.7	62.2
Camden County	635	20.1	31.9	230 408	74.0	11.4	8.8	1.0	2.5	12.6	36.5	50.9
Cape May County	650	22.9	31.7	44 022	80.1	9.4	1.8	1.5	4.3	9.8	41.6	48.6
Cumberland County	616	18.4	34.7	57 387	78.3	13.7	2.2	1.5	2.1	13.4	36.7	49.9
Essex County	675	23.3	31.8	328 214	61.5	12.0	18.6	0.9	4.2	25.4	37.1	37.5
Gloucester County	645	17.7	30.3	122 267	82.0	9.9	2.6	0.9	2.0	6.3	31.0	62.7
Hudson County	703	28.6	29.2	264 544	42.0	13.0	33.6	1.0	8.6	35.1	43.1	21.8
Hunterdon County	867	18.5	28.7	62 359	82.5	7.3	1.7	0.7	1.8	3.4	22.8	73.7

STATE/ County code	MSA/PMSA/ NECMA code[1]	STATE County	Total population 5 years and over	Residence in 1995 (percent)					Occupied housing units		Householders 65 years and over	
				Same house	Same county, different house	Same state, different county	Different state	Outside the United States	Number	Percent owner-occupied	Number	Percent owner-occupied
			1	2	3	4	5	6	7	8	9	10
		NEW JERSEY— Cont'd										
34 021	8480	Mercer County	328 588	57.4	21.9	7.5	9.1	4.1	125 807	67.0	28 119	74.6
34 023	5015	Middlesex County	701 409	57.5	18.9	10.1	7.0	6.4	265 815	66.7	57 056	79.8
34 025	5190	Monmouth County	573 303	61.1	20.0	8.6	7.9	2.3	224 236	74.6	48 551	75.4
34 027	5640	Morris County	437 746	61.1	16.4	11.8	6.9	3.9	169 711	76.0	32 002	80.0
34 029	5190	Ocean County	478 826	60.4	19.7	12.9	5.8	1.2	200 402	83.2	73 096	90.5
34 031	0875	Passaic County	452 743	59.4	24.6	7.3	3.6	5.1	163 856	55.6	36 594	66.9
34 033	6160	Salem County	60 428	67.2	19.5	7.7	4.5	1.0	24 295	73.0	6 030	77.3
34 035	5015	Somerset County	275 485	55.5	15.4	16.5	8.2	4.5	108 984	77.2	19 402	81.9
34 037	5640	Sussex County	134 380	64.0	15.9	13.3	6.0	0.8	50 831	82.7	7 998	81.9
34 039	5640	Union County	486 355	60.0	19.8	9.5	4.9	5.0	186 124	61.6	45 525	73.0
34 041	5640	Warren County	95 388	60.0	16.5	14.9	7.0	1.6	38 660	72.8	8 498	75.5
35 000	...	**NEW MEXICO**	1 689 911	54.4	23.7	7.5	12.1	2.3	677 971	70.0	141 693	82.8
35 001	0200	Bernalillo County	518 381	48.9	29.8	6.1	12.6	2.5	220 936	63.6	42 020	78.4
35 003	...	Catron County	3 394	57.7	9.0	10.1	23.0	0.1	1 584	80.4	453	90.1
35 005	...	Chaves County	56 978	55.6	25.9	6.5	10.3	1.7	22 561	70.9	6 167	78.1
35 006	...	Cibola County	23 585	67.4	16.5	9.3	6.2	0.6	8 327	77.1	1 748	86.5
35 007	...	Colfax County	13 423	56.4	21.1	8.1	13.3	1.2	5 821	72.7	1 668	85.0
35 009	...	Curry County	41 329	44.5	26.3	7.1	17.7	4.4	16 766	59.4	3 441	83.1
35 011	...	De Baca County	2 128	67.3	15.3	11.3	6.1	0.1	922	77.8	340	85.9
35 013	4100	Dona Ana County	161 181	53.1	24.4	7.1	12.6	2.9	59 556	67.5	12 238	83.6
35 015	...	Eddy County	47 952	59.0	25.8	5.6	8.9	0.7	19 379	74.3	4 775	85.0
35 017	...	Grant County	28 911	58.5	23.9	5.3	11.5	0.8	12 146	74.5	3 293	90.1
35 019	...	Guadalupe County	4 424	62.2	15.7	14.5	6.3	1.2	1 655	74.1	417	84.2
35 021	...	Harding County	786	73.0	11.5	9.4	5.6	0.5	371	75.2	173	85.5
35 023	...	Hidalgo County	5 473	64.4	17.9	4.3	11.3	2.1	2 152	67.8	548	78.5
35 025	...	Lea County	51 266	56.5	27.6	4.9	9.5	1.5	19 699	72.6	4 642	81.6
35 027	...	Lincoln County	10 440	50.2	10.2	12.0	16.9	1.7	8 202	77.2	2 406	85.3
35 028	7490	Los Alamos County	17 275	59.6	17.6	6.0	14.6	2.2	7 497	78.6	1 383	91.3
35 029	...	Luna County	23 130	57.3	21.6	5.4	12.4	3.2	9 397	75.0	3 158	84.0
35 031	...	McKinley County	67 873	69.8	18.8	3.1	7.6	0.7	21 476	72.4	3 601	88.3
35 033	...	Mora County	4 857	69.3	9.9	12.4	8.0	0.5	2 017	82.5	627	91.7
35 035	...	Otero County	57 857	48.1	19.3	6.3	18.9	7.4	22 984	66.9	4 906	86.6
35 037	...	Quay County	9 592	62.3	19.8	8.3	8.3	1.3	4 201	70.5	1 398	83.1
35 039	...	Rio Arriba County	38 419	71.3	14.3	7.8	5.1	1.4	15 044	81.7	3 132	91.4
35 041	...	Roosevelt County	16 660	49.6	23.3	12.3	13.3	1.5	6 639	62.7	1 518	84.6
35 043	0200	Sandoval County	83 382	56.6	11.6	16.0	14.7	1.1	31 411	83.6	5 885	85.5
35 045	...	San Juan County	104 783	57.2	25.9	4.5	11.5	0.9	37 711	75.3	6 931	84.4
35 047	...	San Miguel County	28 186	63.2	19.1	9.4	6.9	1.5	11 134	73.2	2 249	81.4
35 049	7490	Santa Fe County	121 557	53.4	21.6	7.0	13.9	4.2	52 482	68.6	9 857	80.8
35 051	...	Sierra County	12 668	50.6	16.5	13.4	18.4	1.2	6 113	74.8	2 614	84.3
35 053	...	Socorro County	16 854	58.5	18.2	12.1	9.4	1.8	6 675	71.0	1 407	84.5
35 055	...	Taos County	28 347	64.4	16.5	4.9	12.8	1.4	12 675	75.5	2 731	85.6
35 057	...	Torrance County	15 725	53.6	11.2	20.2	14.4	0.7	6 024	83.9	1 199	90.6
35 059	...	Union County	3 945	60.4	19.6	5.8	12.6	1.7	1 733	72.9	529	82.2
35 061	0200	Valencia County	61 142	56.3	16.5	17.3	8.4	1.5	22 681	83.9	4 239	90.8
36 000	...	**NEW YORK**	17 749 110	61.8	21.8	8.2	4.1	4.1	7 056 860	53.0	1 577 963	62.2
36 001	0160	Albany County	278 018	56.7	23.9	13.3	4.1	1.9	120 512	57.7	27 742	69.7
36 003	...	Allegany County	47 130	60.4	19.8	12.6	5.9	1.2	18 009	73.9	4 529	82.3
36 005	5600	Bronx County	1 225 092	60.5	22.8	8.2	2.2	6.3	463 212	19.5	89 587	29.7
36 007	0960	Broome County	189 216	59.4	25.3	9.1	4.8	1.4	80 749	65.1	21 357	76.1
36 009	...	Cattaraugus County	78 785	63.8	21.6	9.7	4.5	0.5	32 023	74.4	8 198	80.9
36 011	8160	Cayuga County	77 917	64.6	22.0	9.6	3.4	0.3	30 558	72.0	7 642	75.9
36 013	3610	Chautauqua County	131 677	60.9	26.7	6.9	4.9	0.7	54 515	69.3	14 543	75.2
36 015	2335	Chemung County	85 707	60.0	26.0	7.6	5.8	0.5	35 049	68.9	9 073	79.8
36 017	...	Chenango County	48 341	63.3	22.6	10.1	3.6	0.3	19 926	75.3	4 767	76.9
36 019	...	Clinton County	75 795	57.9	24.3	11.4	4.9	1.5	29 423	68.5	6 116	75.1
36 021	...	Columbia County	59 722	62.9	20.5	11.2	4.4	1.0	24 796	70.5	6 362	77.6
36 023	...	Cortland County	45 718	54.6	25.2	16.1	3.3	0.8	18 210	64.3	4 058	68.0
36 025	...	Delaware County	45 612	65.1	17.2	12.6	4.7	0.4	19 270	75.7	5 798	81.5
36 027	2281	Dutchess County	263 037	59.5	20.7	12.2	5.7	1.9	99 536	68.9	21 276	76.3
36 029	1280	Erie County	892 879	62.9	28.1	4.0	3.4	1.6	380 873	65.3	100 614	74.3
36 031	...	Essex County	36 908	61.9	17.5	12.5	7.2	1.0	15 028	73.8	4 099	81.3
36 033	...	Franklin County	48 620	65.8	21.4	13.6	5.9	3.2	17 931	70.3	4 379	72.3
36 035	...	Fulton County	51 998	62.7	22.8	10.2	3.6	0.8	21 884	72.1	6 299	77.7

[1]MSA = Metropolitan Statistical Area. PMSA = Primary MSA. NECMA = New England County Metropolitan Area. See the Appendix A for explanation of these concepts. See Appendix B for list of metropolitan areas identified by type, with component counties.

STATE County	Owner-occupied by household type (percent)								Median household income			Median housing value (owner estimated)	Median monthly owner costs as a percent of income	
	Family-households				Nonfamily households									
		Married-couple family		Other family										
	Total family households	Total	With own children under 18 years	Total	With own children under 18 years	Total nonfamily households	Two or more adults	Living alone	All households	Owner-occupied households	Renter-occupied households		With a mortgage	Without a mortgage
	11	12	13	14	15	16	17	18	19	20	21	22	23	24
NEW JERSEY— Cont'd														
Mercer County	75.2	82.9	81.6	51.9	38.3	48.9	45.4	49.7	56 525	71 016	33 553	143 600	22.5	14.7
Middlesex County	73.7	78.1	75.7	55.8	41.4	48.6	32.9	52.4	61 145	71 867	42 481	164 400	23.2	14.8
Monmouth County	82.9	88.3	88.2	58.8	45.9	53.6	51.9	53.9	64 070	77 141	32 258	195 800	23.7	15.1
Morris County	84.1	87.2	87.3	65.2	53.9	52.9	45.5	54.5	77 236	89 412	46 970	250 400	22.9	13.6
Ocean County	85.8	89.3	84.5	68.9	56.1	77.4	66.4	79.1	46 395	50 119	32 005	128 000	24.7	16.6
Passaic County	60.5	70.5	65.5	35.6	22.5	42.1	33.7	43.8	48 772	68 154	31 591	185 300	24.8	16.5
Salem County	79.2	87.1	85.0	55.0	39.8	57.2	53.4	57.8	45 078	55 158	25 026	104 600	22.7	14.0
Somerset County	83.2	86.6	87.0	64.5	56.9	61.6	52.0	63.7	76 771	87 936	48 028	222 400	22.5	14.4
Sussex County	88.0	91.5	92.1	67.9	54.0	65.2	60.5	66.3	64 978	71 678	36 680	157 600	24.2	14.6
Union County	68.6	76.1	72.9	46.8	31.2	43.8	33.1	45.8	55 026	71 572	35 485	185 200	23.6	16.0
Warren County	81.0	86.6	85.9	54.5	41.0	52.5	48.8	53.3	55 352	65 240	34 317	156 400	24.2	14.9
NEW MEXICO	76.4	82.7	77.6	58.8	50.4	55.7	47.0	57.6	33 974	40 432	22 267	94 600	22.2	9.9
Bernalillo County	72.8	80.9	76.3	52.0	43.0	47.2	41.3	48.7	38 723	49 883	24 445	123 200	23.0	9.9
Catron County	84.2	86.8	76.3	72.3	66.3	73.0	72.7	73.0	23 698	25 762	16 685	81 200	28.8	10.6
Chaves County	75.5	80.9	75.4	59.1	53.0	58.8	50.4	59.8	28 406	33 117	19 756	56 700	19.8	9.9
Cibola County	80.8	86.5	81.0	68.5	57.3	65.9	55.4	67.5	27 819	30 350	20 959	54 400	19.1	9.9
Colfax County	75.4	81.4	73.4	54.8	42.7	66.7	47.0	68.9	30 859	35 081	23 053	73 900	20.6	10.0
Curry County	63.1	70.4	58.2	40.8	32.0	50.3	33.2	52.7	28 662	35 595	21 229	61 800	20.3	9.9
De Baca County	79.1	82.5	79.6	62.1	43.1	75.2	72.2	75.3	25 417	29 115	17 596	51 300	21.1	11.0
Dona Ana County	74.0	81.1	76.2	53.6	46.4	50.6	34.0	55.5	29 648	36 557	17 579	74 000	21.0	9.9
Eddy County	79.1	85.8	80.6	54.4	45.5	61.7	50.6	63.1	32 122	37 347	19 306	60 900	18.6	9.9
Grant County	79.6	86.9	78.7	57.9	45.3	62.4	47.6	64.7	28 804	33 996	17 267	82 600	22.8	9.9
Guadalupe County	79.8	86.9	78.6	61.2	57.3	60.8	63.6	60.6	25 201	27 820	16 932	51 500	21.6	13.7
Harding County	77.2	82.7	71.2	57.1	10.0	72.0	71.4	72.1	25 662	30 250	16 389	32 300	37.5	10.0
Hidalgo County	71.3	79.8	71.0	48.1	36.7	58.9	66.1	58.1	24 138	28 780	15 870	51 900	19.6	10.3
Lea County	75.9	82.3	76.7	52.9	44.8	62.8	48.4	64.5	29 287	34 669	18 478	47 300	17.8	9.9
Lincoln County	81.6	87.3	79.6	58.2	51.3	67.4	60.1	68.7	33 397	37 525	20 174	90 900	22.4	9.9
Los Alamos County	87.0	88.7	85.6	73.0	66.2	57.4	46.4	58.8	77 432	86 375	45 227	213 000	19.4	9.9
Luna County	78.8	86.0	76.6	57.5	46.6	66.1	57.4	67.2	20 796	24 230	13 139	52 300	20.5	9.9
McKinley County	74.3	79.5	76.7	66.1	57.7	65.8	57.0	67.1	24 880	26 613	21 334	44 300	20.3	9.9
Mora County	86.0	91.5	85.5	73.5	67.6	74.8	75.7	74.6	23 733	26 568	12 750	73 200	18.9	13.2
Otero County	69.4	73.2	63.7	55.5	44.6	60.0	52.0	61.0	30 912	34 198	25 425	68 700	21.5	9.9
Quay County	75.5	81.8	71.7	53.4	36.1	60.1	38.5	62.5	24 405	27 739	16 114	52 700	21.4	12.1
Rio Arriba County	85.0	88.7	84.7	77.1	71.5	73.3	68.4	74.2	29 258	31 521	19 540	88 600	23.5	10.8
Roosevelt County	68.7	73.9	64.6	50.4	37.8	49.4	32.4	53.7	26 799	32 392	18 133	56 700	20.0	9.9
Sandoval County	86.6	88.9	85.9	78.2	71.6	74.5	70.6	75.4	44 686	47 235	31 205	111 600	22.8	9.9
San Juan County	79.2	84.2	79.9	65.1	58.7	62.5	49.8	64.9	33 322	37 782	22 890	77 000	19.6	9.9
San Miguel County	79.0	85.7	83.8	67.2	60.5	61.0	65.4	60.1	26 489	30 817	15 281	82 400	27.1	12.3
Santa Fe County	77.9	83.6	80.0	61.6	53.5	52.7	49.4	53.6	41 901	50 813	27 368	169 100	23.9	9.9
Sierra County	82.2	86.7	76.7	63.3	52.5	64.1	68.8	63.4	24 114	27 076	13 460	62 200	23.4	9.9
Socorro County	77.9	83.6	77.0	64.3	56.6	56.6	55.0	57.0	23 542	29 161	15 575	70 100	21.9	12.3
Taos County	80.7	87.2	85.2	66.4	56.4	67.1	57.0	69.2	26 673	30 587	18 438	124 900	26.5	11.3
Torrance County	86.5	89.8	86.2	76.0	68.7	77.3	78.2	77.2	30 642	33 454	18 240	79 400	24.5	11.7
Union County	77.0	81.0	66.7	59.8	52.4	64.3	71.1	63.8	27 847	31 964	16 875	53 800	20.6	10.5
Valencia County	86.5	91.5	88.6	71.4	67.0	75.5	68.5	77.3	34 095	36 987	20 804	91 700	23.9	9.9
NEW YORK	61.3	71.1	68.2	36.5	26.5	36.9	31.2	38.0	43 070	58 956	28 851	147 600	23.2	13.6
Albany County	71.8	81.5	79.6	44.4	30.2	37.4	27.4	39.8	43 077	59 178	27 277	113 100	20.9	11.1
Allegany County	82.1	87.6	83.6	58.3	47.6	56.4	47.8	58.5	32 031	37 954	17 404	51 300	19.8	12.1
Bronx County	21.0	31.1	25.4	12.2	7.3	16.4	14.1	16.8	27 315	52 240	23 108	183 800	28.5	13.7
Broome County	76.8	84.8	81.5	50.3	36.7	45.6	35.2	47.9	35 211	45 626	20 278	74 000	19.9	11.7
Cattaraugus County	81.0	87.1	83.6	58.4	48.8	60.6	60.2	60.6	33 676	39 030	20 038	59 000	20.0	12.2
Cayuga County	80.4	86.8	84.0	58.3	47.6	53.9	52.2	54.2	37 395	44 792	21 205	72 900	21.4	13.6
Chautauqua County	78.3	86.3	82.4	50.0	38.8	51.3	42.1	53.1	33 271	40 937	18 828	62 700	20.6	13.1
Chemung County	76.6	85.6	83.1	49.9	38.2	53.5	50.5	54.1	36 126	44 452	20 839	66 200	20.7	12.7
Chenango County	82.5	88.7	85.6	60.1	49.9	60.0	66.1	58.6	33 656	39 366	20 444	58 300	20.4	12.1
Clinton County	79.7	86.4	84.3	54.5	45.0	47.2	42.2	48.8	37 190	46 120	20 496	77 400	20.1	11.1
Columbia County	77.3	83.4	78.4	53.6	39.1	56.7	55.2	57.0	41 830	50 491	26 084	111 200	22.5	12.2
Cortland County	77.0	84.0	82.2	52.4	44.0	41.6	31.7	45.0	34 977	44 728	20 222	73 600	21.3	12.8
Delaware County	82.3	87.9	83.8	59.9	46.8	62.8	56.5	64.1	32 404	37 717	20 804	74 800	21.7	12.7
Dutchess County	78.1	84.6	83.3	51.3	37.5	47.8	42.3	49.0	53 086	65 006	31 188	150 800	22.9	12.4
Erie County	75.4	85.4	83.5	47.6	32.2	47.2	37.8	48.9	38 211	50 091	21 087	88 200	21.7	13.6
Essex County	82.6	88.9	85.4	64.0	52.5	57.2	50.9	58.5	34 702	40 384	21 357	76 800	20.7	12.8
Franklin County	80.1	87.5	84.1	58.1	50.1	51.3	54.1	50.7	31 214	38 135	18 771	59 500	19.4	13.1
Fulton County	79.6	86.0	81.4	58.6	50.4	57.0	53.5	57.7	33 410	39 228	20 353	63 200	21.6	13.8

	Percent who pay 35 percent or more of income for housing expenses		Means of transportation to work (percent except where noted)						Vehicles available (percent of households)		
				Car, truck, or van							
STATE County	Median gross rent	Owners	Renters	Number of workers 16 years and over	Drove alone	Carpooled	Public transportation	Other means	Walked	No vehicles	One vehicle	Two or more vehicles
	25	26	27	28	29	30	31	32	33	34	35	36
NEW JERSEY— Cont'd												
Mercer County..............	727	18.5	28.1	163 257	73.3	11.0	6.9	1.1	4.5	11.7	34.2	54.1
Middlesex County.........	845	18.5	26.5	363 176	74.4	11.1	8.7	0.9	2.8	8.6	34.6	56.8
Monmouth County........	759	21.4	32.1	291 938	75.7	9.2	8.9	0.9	2.0	7.8	31.3	61.0
Morris County..............	883	18.5	24.2	239 839	81.2	8.2	4.2	0.9	1.8	4.8	27.3	67.9
Ocean County..............	819	21.1	36.6	209 328	82.7	10.5	1.9	0.8	1.5	8.3	39.5	52.2
Passaic County	747	22.8	33.2	210 378	71.2	13.5	8.1	1.2	3.9	16.2	34.9	49.0
Salem County...............	602	16.2	30.6	28 748	83.8	9.4	1.2	1.2	2.2	9.8	33.5	56.8
Somerset County	898	18.3	25.7	151 284	81.7	8.0	4.1	1.1	1.6	5.0	28.9	66.1
Sussex County	790	21.2	28.8	72 728	83.9	9.4	1.4	0.6	1.3	4.2	24.0	71.8
Union County	752	21.0	29.1	238 606	71.0	11.6	10.6	1.2	3.2	12.7	35.3	52.0
Warren County	689	20.2	29.3	50 358	81.4	10.9	1.2	0.8	2.4	7.4	30.5	62.1
NEW MEXICO.........	503	16.0	30.5	759 177	75.8	14.8	0.8	1.6	2.8	6.7	35.0	58.2
Bernalillo County	560	17.5	33.5	261 708	77.4	13.0	1.5	1.7	2.5	6.8	37.4	55.7
Catron County	392	15.9	23.4	1 240	56.0	17.7	0.0	2.2	9.6	4.5	34.3	61.2
Chaves County	402	14.4	28.1	22 689	77.7	14.2	0.5	1.4	2.7	7.6	35.7	56.8
Cibola County..............	355	10.6	19.4	8 509	73.7	18.2	0.5	1.0	2.8	8.6	31.9	59.5
Colfax County..............	414	13.4	23.0	5 963	70.9	17.9	0.5	0.7	4.5	6.2	30.6	63.2
Curry County...............	427	16.2	21.5	19 133	78.7	13.7	0.2	1.4	2.9	7.9	37.0	55.2
De Baca County...........	371	11.5	19.2	893	75.4	11.8	0.6	1.0	5.8	7.7	31.9	60.4
Dona Ana County.........	445	14.0	34.4	66 761	77.2	14.6	0.5	1.7	2.5	6.3	34.2	59.5
Eddy County................	394	10.6	24.8	20 185	77.1	15.2	1.5	1.1	2.3	6.2	35.0	58.8
Grant County...............	419	14.3	29.9	11 185	73.1	14.9	0.3	1.7	4.6	6.7	33.8	59.5
Guadalupe County	322	13.9	21.6	1 554	74.3	17.2	0.1	1.6	4.3	11.2	32.1	56.7
Harding County	367	13.6	19.1	360	60.6	16.7	0.8	1.1	6.9	10.8	27.2	62.0
Hidalgo County............	267	13.6	22.0	2 090	70.7	17.5	0.5	1.7	7.7	10.5	33.6	55.9
Lea County..................	388	14.0	24.9	19 828	78.8	14.9	0.1	1.7	1.7	6.5	35.5	58.0
Lincoln County	468	15.8	28.7	8 337	73.0	15.5	0.2	0.9	3.6	4.4	34.5	61.1
Los Alamos County.......	666	8.0	18.4	9 476	81.6	9.3	0.2	2.3	2.6	2.4	27.1	70.5
Luna County................	337	14.8	28.2	6 982	73.8	19.2	0.1	1.3	2.8	10.5	36.3	53.2
McKinley County	374	11.7	18.7	21 427	63.1	22.5	0.7	2.2	5.8	12.5	41.8	45.7
Mora County................	357	13.4	25.4	1 675	61.5	23.3	0.8	2.8	7.3	7.0	31.4	61.5
Otero County...............	441	14.2	23.4	24 896	74.3	17.4	0.3	2.1	2.7	6.6	33.9	59.5
Quay County	311	13.2	15.1	3 996	72.5	17.7	0.2	0.6	3.7	8.7	36.9	54.4
Rio Arriba County........	394	15.2	22.3	16 239	69.9	20.1	0.3	1.4	3.6	9.9	29.9	63.3
Roosevelt County	391	15.7	30.3	7 496	77.0	13.4	0.1	1.5	3.8	5.5	34.0	60.5
Sandoval County..........	726	16.2	31.0	38 371	79.9	12.5	0.5	1.4	1.4	4.8	29.6	65.6
San Juan County..........	459	12.9	25.5	43 667	78.7	15.0	0.1	1.3	1.9	6.5	32.3	61.2
San Miguel County.......	430	21.7	38.1	11 113	71.3	19.8	0.3	1.3	3.8	9.8	34.3	55.9
Santa Fe County..........	690	20.1	34.2	60 050	71.4	15.0	0.0	1.4	3.1	5.4	34.6	60.0
Sierra County..............	348	15.0	31.1	4 362	68.0	17.5	0.0	2.3	5.5	9.6	36.9	53.5
Socorro County	362	14.3	32.0	7 002	68.5	14.6	0.6	3.9	8.3	9.0	38.1	52.9
Taos County................	531	21.4	37.1	13 164	71.7	14.8	0.1	1.8	4.6	6.4	37.3	56.4
Torrance County	458	23.5	30.8	6 652	69.9	20.3	0.3	0.9	3.7	5.3	31.9	62.8
Union County	376	15.4	27.9	1 875	73.3	13.1	0.0	1.5	3.5	3.6	36.3	60.1
Valencia County	490	18.8	31.3	26 696	77.3	16.4	0.2	0.9	1.4	4.1	27.4	68.5
NEW YORK..............	672	19.6	33.4	8 211 916	56.3	9.2	24.4	0.8	6.2	29.7	33.0	37.3
Albany County..............	611	13.1	30.6	141 842	76.8	9.8	5.6	0.5	4.7	14.3	38.8	46.9
Allegany County...........	423	13.9	33.4	21 021	71.0	11.7	0.7	0.9	11.6	8.5	35.9	55.6
Bronx County	620	30.1	36.2	415 075	27.0	9.3	53.7	0.8	7.2	61.6	28.8	9.6
Broome County............	462	11.8	33.1	89 552	79.5	10.2	2.8	0.7	4.3	12.4	38.5	49.1
Cattaraugus County	425	13.1	27.8	36 941	76.6	12.6	0.7	1.0	5.6	9.7	37.1	53.2
Cayuga County	482	15.0	31.8	36 784	80.2	10.9	1.0	0.8	3.7	9.6	34.9	55.5
Chautauqua County	438	14.7	31.9	61 734	78.5	11.0	1.2	0.9	5.1	11.2	38.1	50.7
Chemung County	493	13.3	32.6	38 451	81.1	10.6	1.1	0.8	4.1	11.2	38.4	50.4
Chenango County	439	13.4	28.2	22 246	76.6	13.1	0.7	0.6	4.5	7.9	35.2	56.9
Clinton County.............	479	13.1	31.7	34 420	77.2	12.7	1.4	0.6	5.0	9.1	34.6	56.3
Columbia County..........	553	16.2	27.7	28 929	75.7	11.7	2.3	1.1	4.1	7.9	35.4	56.7
Cortland County	471	13.7	33.5	22 163	74.1	12.0	2.2	1.0	6.2	10.6	34.8	54.6
Delaware County	451	15.2	33.1	20 243	73.7	12.5	1.1	0.8	6.2	7.9	37.8	54.3
Dutchess County..........	707	17.2	31.0	128 437	78.5	9.6	4.2	0.7	3.9	7.7	30.8	61.5
Erie County	516	15.2	36.1	421 809	80.9	9.7	4.1	0.6	2.7	15.1	38.6	46.3
Essex County	452	13.9	27.9	16 104	75.2	14.2	0.6	0.7	4.6	7.7	37.1	55.2
Franklin County	409	13.6	29.3	19 681	76.9	11.8	0.9	1.3	4.7	9.9	38.0	52.2
Fulton County...............	458	16.0	29.5	23 763	79.6	12.6	1.4	0.6	3.1	9.1	37.6	53.3

Table C-3. States and Counties — **Migration, Housing, and Transportation**

STATE/ County code	MSA/PMSA/ NECMA code[1]	STATE County	Total population 5 years and over	Residence in 1995 (percent)					Occupied housing units		Householders 65 years and over	
				Same house	Same county, different house	Same state, different county	Different state	Outside the United States	Number	Percent owner-occupied	Number	Percent owner-occupied
			1	2	3	4	5	6	7	8	9	10
		NEW YORK—Cont'd										
36 037	6840	Genesee County	56 738	65.8	20.6	10.5	2.6	0.6	22 770	72.9	5 254	75.6
36 039	...	Greene County	45 678	64.9	16.9	11.4	6.2	0.5	18 256	72.2	4 823	78.9
36 041	...	Hamilton County	5 150	69.7	13.3	12.1	4.6	0.2	2 362	79.3	700	85.6
36 043	8680	Herkimer County	60 861	66.4	20.5	9.5	3.2	0.4	25 734	71.2	7 416	74.1
36 045	...	Jefferson County	103 563	51.6	23.0	5.9	16.3	3.3	40 068	59.8	8 334	73.5
36 047	5600	Kings County	2 285 223	62.9	22.9	4.5	2.8	7.0	880 727	27.1	187 391	36.1
36 049	...	Lewis County	25 301	71.2	16.9	7.3	4.2	0.5	10 040	77.0	2 533	78.6
36 051	6840	Livingston County	60 796	59.0	18.6	18.8	2.6	0.9	22 150	74.5	4 655	77.3
36 053	8160	Madison County	65 323	61.4	18.4	14.0	5.3	0.9	25 368	74.9	5 878	78.7
36 055	6840	Monroe County	688 804	57.4	30.0	5.9	4.5	2.2	286 512	65.1	59 926	71.9
36 057	0160	Montgomery County	46 781	64.4	23.6	9.4	2.2	0.6	20 038	67.1	6 246	71.3
36 059	5380	Nassau County	1 248 676	69.9	16.5	9.6	1.9	2.1	447 387	80.3	119 326	85.8
36 061	5600	New York County	1 462 015	56.9	17.0	8.4	10.6	7.1	738 644	20.1	140 513	22.9
36 063	1280	Niagara County	206 730	65.7	24.7	6.5	2.4	0.8	87 846	69.9	22 413	76.7
36 065	8680	Oneida County	222 067	63.5	24.5	6.7	3.1	2.3	90 496	67.2	24 713	74.5
36 067	8160	Onondaga County	428 522	57.7	28.0	7.0	5.4	1.8	181 153	64.5	41 567	74.1
36 069	6840	Ontario County	94 145	60.2	20.7	13.1	5.2	0.8	38 370	73.6	8 718	76.8
36 071	5660	Orange County	315 429	58.9	21.9	10.9	6.4	1.9	114 788	67.0	21 916	72.1
36 073	6840	Orleans County	41 389	60.1	21.9	14.1	2.4	1.4	15 363	75.6	3 686	81.4
36 075	8160	Oswego County	114 830	60.7	25.1	10.8	2.9	0.4	45 522	72.8	9 382	75.8
36 077	...	Otsego County	58 752	58.5	19.3	16.8	4.7	0.7	23 291	73.0	6 092	81.2
36 079	5600	Putnam County	89 138	64.3	11.7	18.7	3.5	1.8	32 703	82.2	5 424	84.9
36 081	5600	Queens County	2 088 870	61.8	20.7	7.2	2.2	8.1	782 664	42.8	177 102	57.1
36 083	0160	Rensselaer County........	143 234	62.8	20.3	11.1	4.5	1.3	59 894	64.9	13 693	76.2
36 085	5600	Richmond County	414 402	63.2	20.1	11.6	2.4	2.6	156 341	63.8	31 240	69.0
36 087	5600	Rockland County	265 002	64.5	19.3	8.5	4.3	3.4	92 675	71.7	19 289	75.5
36 089	...	St. Lawrence County.....	105 957	59.0	24.3	9.4	6.2	1.1	40 506	70.6	9 464	75.3
36 091	0160	Saratoga County	187 572	58.5	19.8	13.4	7.4	0.8	78 165	72.0	15 136	75.7
36 093	0160	Schenectady County	137 584	61.1	22.7	10.7	3.9	1.5	59 684	65.4	15 855	74.8
36 095	0160	Schoharie County..........	29 826	63.8	19.6	13.0	3.3	0.3	11 991	75.3	3 011	80.3
36 097	...	Schuyler County	18 100	63.7	17.7	13.8	4.8	0.0	7 374	77.2	1 830	81.3
36 099	...	Seneca County	31 524	62.3	21.2	11.1	4.7	0.7	12 630	73.7	3 055	80.2
36 101	...	Steuben County	92 702	62.4	24.6	7.2	5.3	0.4	39 071	73.2	9 612	79.0
36 103	5380	Suffolk County	1 319 377	64.7	22.4	8.2	2.7	2.0	469 299	79.8	97 033	83.4
36 105	...	Sullivan County	69 707	59.7	18.8	14.5	5.5	1.5	27 661	68.1	7 273	78.3
36 107	0960	Tioga County	48 539	65.1	18.0	10.2	6.2	0.5	19 725	77.8	4 295	85.3
36 109	...	Tompkins County	92 300	41.9	18.3	15.6	18.5	5.7	36 420	53.8	6 210	69.5
36 111	...	Ulster County	168 093	61.6	19.9	12.4	4.7	1.3	67 499	68.0	15 329	78.2
36 113	2975	Warren County	59 829	61.5	21.4	11.2	5.2	0.7	25 726	69.9	6 415	79.2
36 115	2975	Washington County.......	57 619	62.9	18.1	12.6	6.0	0.3	22 458	74.3	5 352	81.2
36 117	6840	Wayne County	87 737	63.4	21.7	11.6	2.8	0.5	34 908	77.6	7 129	75.9
36 119	5600	Westchester County	859 662	61.2	21.4	8.9	3.9	4.6	337 142	60.1	80 435	68.9
36 121	...	Wyoming County..........	41 142	67.6	16.5	11.6	2.7	1.5	14 906	76.9	3 355	81.0
36 123	...	Yates County	22 990	60.6	21.1	12.8	5.0	0.4	9 029	77.0	2 505	81.0
37 000	...	NORTH CAROLINA ...	7 513 165	53.0	22.3	9.8	12.2	2.6	3 132 013	69.4	635 846	81.4
37 001	3120	Alamance County..........	122 378	54.5	24.5	8.9	9.4	2.8	51 584	70.1	11 639	83.3
37 003	3290	Alexander County..........	31 319	63.5	18.3	11.2	6.2	0.9	13 137	80.5	2 517	86.6
37 005	...	Alleghany County	10 126	64.9	17.3	8.5	6.5	2.8	4 593	79.0	1 355	86.6
37 007	...	Anson County	23 676	67.7	18.8	8.0	4.8	0.8	9 204	76.0	2 395	84.5
37 009	...	Ashe County.................	23 091	64.6	20.7	8.0	5.9	0.7	10 411	81.0	2 949	86.9
37 011	...	Avery County	16 304	61.2	14.5	13.6	8.9	1.9	6 532	80.5	1 736	91.0
37 013	...	Beaufort County	42 255	62.1	23.7	7.1	6.0	1.2	18 319	75.1	4 678	82.0
37 015	...	Bertie County	18 567	68.0	19.6	7.0	5.0	0.4	7 743	74.9	2 252	79.2
37 017	...	Bladen County..............	30 051	69.9	14.3	9.5	4.8	1.5	12 897	77.8	3 374	80.0
37 019	9200	Brunswick County	69 144	53.9	17.0	13.3	14.5	1.2	30 438	82.2	8 213	90.5
37 021	0480	Buncombe County........	194 791	53.0	24.8	7.7	12.8	1.7	85 776	70.3	20 435	81.4
37 023	3290	Burke County	83 645	59.6	20.4	11.4	7.2	1.4	34 528	74.1	7 700	83.9
37 025	1520	Cabarrus County	121 743	53.4	18.2	13.9	12.5	2.1	49 519	74.7	9 636	83.2
37 027	3290	Caldwell County	72 503	60.9	24.8	8.1	5.2	1.0	30 768	74.9	6 928	84.2
37 029	...	Camden County	6 507	55.0	12.8	16.7	14.7	0.8	2 662	83.5	630	91.7
37 031	...	Carteret County............	56 465	54.5	22.3	11.4	10.8	1.0	25 204	76.6	6 655	88.0
37 033	...	Caswell County	22 133	66.8	11.6	14.4	6.5	0.7	8 670	79.4	2 110	85.3
37 035	3290	Catawba County	132 318	56.2	22.5	9.6	9.1	2.6	55 533	72.6	11 413	83.7
37 037	6640	Chatham County	46 331	59.5	13.9	13.8	9.0	3.8	19 741	77.2	4 844	83.8
37 039	...	Cherokee County	22 990	64.9	15.1	4.4	14.9	0.7	10 336	82.1	3 208	84.3

[1]MSA = Metropolitan Statistical Area. PMSA = Primary MSA. NECMA = New England County Metropolitan Area. See the Appendix A for explanation of these concepts. See Appendix B for list of metropolitan areas identified by type, with component counties.

STATE County	Owner-occupied by household type (percent)								Median household income			Median housing value (owner estimated)	Median monthly owner costs as a percent of income	
	Family-households				Nonfamily households									
	Married-couple family		Other family											
	Total family households	Total	With own children under 18 years	Total	With own children under 18 years	Total nonfamily households	Two or more adults	Living alone	All households	Owner-occupied households	Renter-occupied households		With a mortgage	Without a mortgage
	11	12	13	14	15	16	17	18	19	20	21	22	23	24
NEW YORK—Cont'd														
Genesee County	82.0	87.7	84.8	59.3	47.3	52.2	49.3	52.8	40 629	48 303	24 304	82 700	21.8	12.5
Greene County	79.7	86.9	84.8	53.8	39.7	57.6	57.8	57.6	36 229	43 032	22 328	91 900	22.4	13.4
Hamilton County	86.8	89.3	83.5	72.6	58.7	64.6	66.7	64.3	32 401	35 783	21 172	88 200	21.9	12.0
Herkimer County	80.1	86.8	84.4	57.6	45.3	53.3	44.8	55.1	32 914	39 691	18 750	65 100	19.9	13.0
Jefferson County	65.5	70.3	60.4	46.0	34.1	46.0	46.0	46.0	33 876	42 549	23 355	66 100	20.0	13.1
Kings County	30.9	38.7	35.0	19.6	11.6	19.4	15.4	20.2	31 726	55 387	25 880	229 200	27.2	12.9
Lewis County	83.6	88.2	85.6	61.5	48.1	59.5	61.1	59.2	34 450	39 121	19 652	63 300	19.1	11.6
Livingston County	83.4	89.1	87.6	60.8	54.0	54.5	43.9	58.1	42 092	50 484	22 241	86 300	21.7	12.6
Madison County	83.8	88.7	86.9	64.0	54.5	55.0	53.2	55.5	40 033	46 825	24 565	78 700	21.2	12.7
Monroe County	76.2	86.7	86.1	46.4	35.3	44.7	40.6	45.6	44 805	58 926	24 391	98 200	21.5	12.7
Montgomery County	75.6	83.7	79.1	50.7	35.4	51.3	40.1	53.4	32 329	40 220	21 308	64 300	21.3	14.5
Nassau County	85.3	88.7	87.3	70.1	55.2	62.4	52.2	64.1	71 846	80 428	41 937	240 200	24.9	15.8
New York County	22.6	30.7	30.5	9.3	8.4	18.4	13.9	19.4	46 823	95 950	39 657	361 100	21.3	9.9
Niagara County	79.1	87.6	86.1	51.3	37.2	51.3	48.3	51.8	38 330	40 010	20 388	80 900	21.4	13.6
Oneida County	76.8	84.9	81.5	50.8	37.7	49.1	45.4	49.7	35 995	45 647	20 379	73 200	20.8	12.7
Onondaga County	76.2	85.6	84.4	48.8	36.6	43.9	38.4	45.1	40 812	54 191	21 998	84 900	20.9	13.2
Ontario County	82.0	88.1	86.4	56.6	46.3	54.8	50.0	56.0	44 362	52 108	25 910	91 100	21.6	12.9
Orange County	73.7	80.3	77.3	48.8	36.4	48.0	44.0	48.8	51 895	64 516	31 905	141 500	23.2	13.8
Orleans County	80.8	88.9	84.5	55.2	45.4	63.0	59.0	64.0	37 696	43 780	21 256	71 000	22.4	13.2
Oswego County	81.1	87.8	84.8	57.0	47.5	54.5	49.2	56.1	36 686	44 241	20 174	69 800	20.4	12.7
Otsego County	82.9	88.5	85.5	61.1	52.2	54.7	43.6	57.9	33 562	39 756	20 501	74 400	21.5	13.0
Putnam County	87.5	90.4	89.6	70.8	59.1	64.1	61.1	64.8	72 228	81 242	41 382	205 500	24.4	14.3
Queens County	47.5	52.3	46.0	36.8	24.9	32.2	21.1	34.5	42 069	56 360	34 252	206 200	27.5	12.8
Rensselaer County	74.8	83.9	81.0	46.3	33.3	45.9	41.9	46.9	42 586	54 691	25 953	99 600	21.7	12.1
Richmond County	71.6	78.5	76.7	49.5	32.3	42.4	39.5	42.8	54 011	67 839	32 281	216 600	23.4	11.7
Rockland County	78.2	82.4	78.4	58.3	46.3	50.0	46.0	50.7	67 821	84 504	35 611	234 300	24.3	14.2
St. Lawrence County	79.5	86.1	81.9	56.0	46.1	52.8	51.9	53.0	32 343	39 595	17 094	59 100	19.3	11.3
Saratoga County	81.9	86.1	85.1	61.3	53.6	50.1	43.5	51.8	49 326	57 000	32 237	112 600	21.5	11.8
Schenectady County	75.8	85.1	82.7	47.2	33.1	47.1	40.2	48.3	41 322	54 272	24 149	92 300	21.8	12.7
Schoharie County	82.9	88.1	83.3	61.7	49.1	58.8	57.1	59.2	37 031	42 143	21 821	82 800	22.4	13.1
Schuyler County	83.1	88.6	81.1	62.3	55.2	63.0	63.4	62.9	36 067	40 996	21 038	66 500	21.3	12.0
Seneca County	80.7	86.8	85.3	58.0	47.5	59.0	58.2	59.2	37 351	43 989	21 268	70 400	20.8	13.2
Steuben County	81.4	87.8	84.4	59.2	50.4	56.4	53.9	56.9	35 355	41 806	20 530	63 100	19.9	11.7
Suffolk County	85.1	88.8	88.2	68.8	55.7	61.8	55.4	63.4	65 149	72 320	39 139	183 500	25.3	16.2
Sullivan County	73.5	81.8	76.7	46.7	31.8	57.4	49.6	59.0	36 665	44 610	22 232	90 400	23.8	14.6
Tioga County	83.7	89.7	88.1	56.4	48.2	62.3	58.3	63.2	40 523	46 246	23 357	72 900	20.4	11.4
Tompkins County	74.2	80.1	78.6	51.9	47.3	31.1	22.3	35.1	37 305	54 655	21 433	96 300	21.6	11.5
Ulster County	77.2	84.3	81.4	53.3	40.5	51.2	45.3	52.8	42 340	51 888	25 977	111 500	22.5	13.1
Warren County	78.8	86.0	83.8	53.0	42.7	52.1	42.9	54.2	38 764	46 371	24 662	94 600	22.5	12.3
Washington County	80.3	85.8	80.8	59.1	45.3	60.1	57.3	60.7	37 647	43 817	23 568	78 800	22.2	13.3
Wayne County	85.1	91.1	90.0	62.1	53.4	58.6	64.0	57.2	44 621	51 874	23 001	84 100	21.8	13.1
Westchester County	67.2	74.4	72.2	42.0	29.0	43.5	34.9	45.0	63 307	89 675	37 305	285 800	24.1	15.4
Wyoming County	83.0	88.0	84.1	61.0	51.7	61.0	59.5	61.3	39 811	44 529	23 575	75 300	21.7	12.3
Yates County	83.5	90.0	85.9	58.1	49.5	62.1	63.7	61.7	34 494	39 944	21 896	76 000	22.9	13.5
NORTH CAROLINA ...	76.0	83.0	78.4	52.8	42.9	54.4	38.6	57.7	39 061	46 287	26 140	95 800	21.3	9.9
Alamance County	76.0	82.1	77.5	56.6	47.4	57.2	40.5	60.5	38 827	44 609	27 075	96 200	21.7	9.9
Alexander County	83.5	88.5	84.0	61.1	50.6	71.8	62.8	73.3	38 419	42 468	26 148	84 100	20.5	9.9
Alleghany County	83.9	87.1	77.7	63.8	61.8	68.1	61.0	69.0	29 564	32 910	18 598	86 400	21.6	10.3
Anson County	77.6	86.4	84.3	60.4	46.9	71.7	64.3	72.3	29 948	34 105	19 613	60 400	21.1	10.9
Ashe County	85.5	89.1	81.7	67.1	54.3	70.0	51.9	72.0	28 374	31 326	18 255	86 800	22.4	9.9
Avery County	85.8	88.5	82.1	72.5	55.6	68.3	40.6	71.9	31 295	34 678	20 557	78 900	20.9	9.9
Beaufort County	79.7	87.4	81.7	55.1	46.2	63.7	50.4	65.3	31 061	36 775	17 141	69 500	21.6	11.3
Bertie County	77.7	85.8	82.2	61.6	52.5	68.1	55.6	69.2	25 142	27 496	16 694	53 500	23.3	12.2
Bladen County	83.0	89.7	82.9	68.0	61.8	66.2	63.4	66.5	26 602	30 950	14 460	55 900	21.1	11.6
Brunswick County	85.1	89.2	80.6	68.0	59.4	74.4	68.7	75.6	35 890	39 013	23 104	95 200	23.3	10.9
Buncombe County	78.5	83.5	78.9	54.9	49.2	55.0	40.6	57.9	36 626	42 534	24 513	102 200	22.2	9.9
Burke County	79.1	84.0	78.8	61.9	52.1	62.0	49.1	64.0	35 499	40 051	26 239	77 600	20.4	9.9
Cabarrus County	79.1	85.2	82.7	54.8	44.2	62.0	49.7	64.4	45 757	52 340	30 579	108 900	21.0	10.9
Caldwell County	79.5	85.1	80.3	59.0	47.1	62.3	56.0	63.3	35 723	40 460	23 973	79 800	20.6	9.9
Camden County	84.1	88.6	84.6	61.7	44.4	81.6	59.6	85.3	38 916	40 959	27 111	93 600	21.6	11.2
Carteret County	82.2	87.2	80.0	58.3	49.3	64.2	52.2	66.3	38 236	43 103	24 446	106 400	22.2	9.9
Caswell County	82.6	88.5	85.4	65.0	58.7	69.9	66.3	70.3	34 747	39 393	21 133	74 300	19.6	9.9
Catawba County	78.6	84.7	79.3	55.9	46.2	58.0	45.2	60.4	40 704	46 507	28 549	95 100	20.6	9.9
Chatham County	82.4	87.2	83.1	61.9	50.7	64.9	56.6	66.6	43 363	49 571	29 781	113 300	21.2	9.9
Cherokee County	85.5	89.8	84.1	63.8	56.6	73.6	84.5	72.5	28 063	30 567	17 545	75 500	22.7	9.9

Table C-3. States and Counties — **Migration, Housing, and Transportation**

STATE County	Median gross rent	Percent who pay 35 percent or more of income for housing expenses — Owners	Renters	Means of transportation to work (percent except where noted) — Car, truck, or van — Number of workers 16 years and over	Drove alone	Carpooled	Public transportation	Other means	Walked	Vehicles available (percent of households) — No vehicles	One vehicle	Two or more vehicles
	25	26	27	28	29	30	31	32	33	34	35	36
NEW YORK—Cont'd												
Genesee County	517	14.0	26.5	29 042	82.8	9.8	0.3	1.1	3.4	7.5	33.8	58.7
Greene County.............	508	16.9	32.8	19 964	78.1	11.7	1.4	0.7	3.9	8.5	35.9	55.5
Hamilton County	457	11.9	27.5	2 260	78.4	8.0	0.4	1.1	8.1	4.7	36.0	59.3
Herkimer County	420	15.7	29.3	28 622	77.3	12.5	1.1	0.5	5.2	10.1	38.8	51.1
Jefferson County	486	13.9	23.3	49 526	75.3	10.8	0.9	0.8	8.1	9.6	37.5	52.9
Kings County	672	28.6	36.2	901 027	22.4	8.0	57.4	1.1	8.8	57.0	33.1	10.0
Lewis County...............	444	11.8	29.7	11 660	75.0	10.2	0.4	1.4	6.8	5.7	29.5	64.7
Livingston County..........	541	13.8	33.9	29 772	77.8	11.4	0.4	0.4	6.5	5.7	31.0	63.3
Madison County	509	14.6	24.2	31 945	78.5	9.6	0.6	0.9	6.4	7.2	33.9	58.9
Monroe County	612	14.9	36.4	345 019	82.0	8.4	2.7	0.7	3.4	11.5	36.2	52.3
Montgomery County......	464	16.8	30.3	21 288	76.9	12.1	2.4	1.0	4.2	11.8	39.3	49.0
Nassau County	964	24.5	31.8	619 586	69.4	8.6	15.7	0.7	2.7	7.7	29.8	62.5
New York County	796	24.0	30.4	753 114	7.6	3.4	59.6	1.7	21.9	77.5	20.2	2.3
Niagara County	479	13.9	32.3	98 541	85.2	8.4	1.1	0.5	2.8	11.1	36.8	52.1
Oneida County	470	13.4	32.0	100 800	80.2	11.3	1.5	0.7	3.8	12.3	37.5	50.2
Onondaga County	550	14.3	34.2	211 646	80.1	9.9	2.6	0.7	3.9	12.7	37.4	49.9
Ontario County	564	13.7	31.2	49 951	81.8	9.3	0.8	0.5	4.0	7.3	32.6	60.1
Orange County............	714	18.7	32.4	152 489	76.6	11.1	4.7	0.8	4.2	10.6	29.7	59.7
Orleans County	519	15.1	34.8	18 238	80.2	13.1	0.4	0.8	2.3	6.2	34.7	59.0
Oswego County	507	14.3	34.2	52 833	80.7	11.6	0.8	0.6	3.7	8.9	34.3	56.7
Otsego County	485	15.4	35.8	26 975	73.2	12.5	1.4	0.7	6.8	7.6	36.0	56.4
Putnam County	913	21.9	30.0	48 167	79.1	8.2	7.2	0.6	1.6	4.2	23.3	72.4
Queens County	775	27.9	32.7	931 709	34.3	10.2	47.4	0.7	5.7	37.7	41.1	21.2
Rensselaer County........	547	13.7	28.1	73 830	78.9	11.1	2.8	0.7	3.9	11.5	36.3	52.1
Richmond County	742	20.9	30.4	191 145	54.3	12.1	28.4	0.7	2.9	18.4	38.2	43.4
Rockland County	884	22.1	35.2	132 302	73.7	11.0	8.2	0.7	2.8	8.8	29.6	61.6
St. Lawrence County.....	428	11.6	32.6	44 341	75.9	11.1	0.4	1.0	7.2	9.1	38.2	52.7
Saratoga County	638	14.1	24.6	101 950	83.4	9.2	0.9	0.5	2.4	5.6	32.4	62.0
Schenectady County	572	13.8	33.2	66 425	80.7	9.0	3.0	0.8	3.5	12.4	38.1	49.4
Schoharie County..........	506	15.1	31.3	13 759	77.6	12.0	1.2	0.7	4.1	6.9	32.4	60.7
Schuyler County	466	14.0	27.8	8 362	76.9	12.8	1.1	0.7	3.4	6.1	31.5	62.4
Seneca County	521	13.0	32.8	14 486	81.3	10.2	0.5	0.8	3.1	7.7	33.7	58.6
Steuben County	468	12.1	30.5	43 108	77.4	13.4	0.5	0.8	3.9	9.4	35.8	54.7
Suffolk County	945	24.6	35.6	670 406	78.1	10.0	6.8	0.8	1.7	5.4	26.8	67.7
Sullivan County	545	21.5	34.8	29 544	76.7	12.4	2.5	0.5	4.2	10.7	37.3	52.1
Tioga County	468	11.4	28.0	24 332	80.2	12.8	0.7	0.9	2.2	7.0	30.0	63.0
Tompkins County	611	14.0	42.8	47 394	59.8	12.2	4.8	1.3	16.8	11.4	41.0	47.6
Ulster County	626	17.9	35.2	81 726	78.1	10.4	2.2	0.8	3.8	8.5	34.9	56.7
Warren County	557	16.1	30.2	29 360	80.8	10.7	1.1	0.8	3.4	8.3	36.4	55.3
Washington County	509	15.5	28.9	26 843	78.9	11.6	0.6	0.7	3.5	7.3	34.7	57.9
Wayne County	527	13.9	29.2	44 792	82.5	10.7	0.5	0.6	2.8	6.4	31.1	62.6
Westchester County	839	23.5	31.7	425 052	61.6	9.5	20.4	0.6	4.0	15.2	35.8	49.0
Wyoming County	482	13.5	26.8	18 474	79.7	10.2	0.5	0.6	4.6	5.9	31.5	62.5
Yates County	467	15.0	30.1	10 916	71.2	13.3	0.5	1.4	7.0	9.9	32.3	57.8
NORTH CAROLINA ...	548	15.0	26.7	3 837 773	79.4	14.0	0.9	1.1	1.9	7.5	32.3	60.2
Alamance County.........	557	14.6	25.5	63 698	81.5	14.1	0.1	0.9	1.3	6.2	31.8	62.0
Alexander County........	439	13.2	22.2	17 999	82.0	12.7	0.0	1.2	1.7	5.5	24.5	70.0
Alleghany County	363	14.1	21.7	5 042	73.8	20.2	0.5	0.6	1.9	9.1	27.0	63.9
Anson County..............	404	18.0	29.1	9 805	76.6	18.8	0.2	1.3	1.0	11.4	33.1	55.6
Ashe County................	375	14.0	18.6	11 082	76.2	16.0	0.0	1.6	1.0	8.7	28.8	62.5
Avery County..............	430	14.8	19.6	7 049	72.7	19.5	0.2	0.5	3.3	8.1	28.4	63.5
Beaufort County	405	17.8	29.2	18 497	78.6	14.6	0.5	1.0	2.0	9.9	31.8	58.3
Bertie County	358	19.7	26.9	7 352	74.9	20.3	0.3	0.5	2.5	14.6	32.7	52.7
Bladen County..............	350	17.9	24.6	12 842	80.2	14.7	0.5	1.3	1.2	9.3	35.8	54.9
Brunswick County.........	535	17.4	30.0	31 962	78.5	14.0	0.6	1.9	1.6	7.5	32.5	61.8
Buncombe County.........	551	15.3	29.0	99 133	79.6	13.0	0.8	0.8	2.0	7.7	33.9	58.4
Burke County	450	10.7	20.1	42 214	81.8	13.7	0.2	1.3	1.2	6.8	30.7	62.5
Cabarrus County..........	566	12.6	21.5	65 982	83.3	12.3	0.4	0.7	1.1	6.0	28.1	65.9
Caldwell County	446	12.3	20.0	38 970	79.9	16.5	0.0	1.0	0.8	6.5	27.1	66.4
Camden County	514	17.6	26.5	3 151	79.0	15.7	0.4	1.1	0.9	4.8	23.6	71.6
Carteret County............	511	15.3	27.0	27 214	78.1	15.4	0.3	1.3	1.6	5.9	32.8	61.2
Caswell County	390	15.1	20.1	9 917	76.4	19.1	0.3	1.2	1.2	9.0	26.8	64.1
Catawba County...........	525	13.5	20.5	73 984	81.6	14.4	0.3	1.0	1.0	5.7	29.9	64.5
Chatham County	579	14.2	22.2	24 657	76.9	15.8	0.2	1.1	1.4	5.9	28.7	65.4
Cherokee County	350	14.9	21.8	10 004	77.5	16.6	0.1	0.8	1.8	8.4	30.4	61.2

STATE/ County code	MSA/PMSA/ NECMA code[1]	STATE County	Total population 5 years and over	Residence in 1995 (percent)					Occupied housing units		Householders 65 years and over	
				Same house	Same county, different house	Same state, different county	Different state	Outside the United States	Number	Percent owner-occupied	Number	Percent owner-occupied
			1	2	3	4	5	6	7	8	9	10
		NORTH CAROLINA—Cont'd										
37 041	...	Chowan County............	13 652	65.6	18.7	6.3	8.8	0.6	5 580	72.3	1 811	76.9
37 043	...	Clay County................	8 412	58.3	14.7	7.7	18.8	0.5	3 847	84.6	1 358	90.5
37 045	...	Cleveland County.........	89 835	60.2	24.0	8.2	6.5	1.1	37 046	72.9	8 515	81.9
37 047	...	Columbus County........	51 125	69.6	19.3	5.5	5.1	0.5	21 308	76.4	5 548	80.3
37 049	...	Craven County............	84 793	48.5	19.8	7.9	21.8	2.0	34 582	66.7	7 887	85.2
37 051	2560	Cumberland County	278 459	45.5	22.1	4.7	23.0	4.7	107 358	59.4	15 543	82.8
37 053	5720	Currituck County	17 091	58.4	11.9	7.6	21.5	0.6	6 902	81.5	1 455	89.6
37 055	...	Dare County	28 425	49.8	21.7	6.9	20.1	1.5	12 690	74.5	2 671	87.5
37 057	3120	Davidson County	137 610	60.2	21.4	10.9	5.4	2.0	58 156	74.2	11 993	83.0
37 059	3120	Davie County...............	32 589	59.7	16.4	14.5	8.5	0.9	13 750	83.3	3 206	88.5
37 061	...	Duplin County	45 674	61.3	20.6	8.8	4.7	4.6	18 267	74.9	4 451	83.1
37 063	6640	Durham County	207 994	44.2	24.1	10.2	16.1	5.3	89 015	54.2	13 907	73.6
37 065	6895	Edgecombe County.......	51 964	58.0	25.1	10.7	4.8	1.3	20 392	64.0	4 713	73.1
37 067	3120	Forsyth County	285 762	52.5	24.9	8.7	11.0	2.9	123 851	65.6	26 074	78.8
37 069	6640	Franklin County	43 919	58.1	15.1	16.4	8.3	2.2	17 843	77.8	3 551	82.7
37 071	1520	Gaston County	177 684	58.3	25.4	8.0	6.4	2.0	73 936	68.9	16 131	80.9
37 073	...	Gates County	9 916	66.9	12.6	6.8	13.4	0.3	3 901	82.0	997	90.3
37 075	...	Graham County............	7 528	67.6	18.9	4.7	8.4	0.4	3 354	82.7	949	84.9
37 077	...	Granville County...........	45 543	57.7	15.5	16.0	8.1	2.7	16 654	75.1	3 486	81.1
37 079	...	Greene County	17 698	60.9	15.8	14.8	5.7	2.8	6 696	74.7	1 579	80.6
37 081	3120	Guilford County	393 748	49.4	27.0	9.0	11.4	3.1	168 667	62.7	32 126	77.3
37 083	...	Halifax County	53 830	65.5	22.0	6.1	5.6	0.8	22 122	67.0	5 850	77.5
37 085	...	Harnett County	84 164	51.3	17.1	16.5	12.2	2.9	33 800	70.3	5 974	81.5
37 087	...	Haywood County	51 206	60.5	22.2	6.4	10.3	0.5	23 100	77.3	6 802	86.3
37 089	...	Henderson County	84 283	54.1	20.4	9.0	14.1	2.3	37 414	78.8	11 988	87.4
37 091	...	Hertford County	21 369	67.9	17.9	7.0	6.4	0.8	8 953	70.0	2 379	78.2
37 093	...	Hoke County	30 636	51.2	14.0	19.3	10.8	4.7	11 373	75.0	1 526	82.3
37 095	...	Hyde County	5 562	65.7	15.9	10.2	7.0	0.0	2 186	78.4	632	84.8
37 097	...	Iredell County	114 173	55.1	19.4	9.8	13.9	1.8	47 360	75.3	9 763	86.7
37 099	...	Jackson County	31 471	54.8	16.0	16.2	11.9	1.1	13 191	72.5	3 235	84.5
37 101	6640	Johnston County	112 146	52.1	18.6	16.7	10.2	2.4	46 595	73.4	8 298	74.6
37 103	...	Jones County	9 758	67.2	13.0	13.0	5.8	0.9	4 061	79.6	973	85.7
37 105	...	Lee County	45 672	56.6	21.6	9.2	9.1	3.4	18 466	71.7	3 902	83.8
37 107	...	Lenoir County	55 807	58.8	27.6	7.6	4.4	1.6	23 862	67.0	5 733	73.4
37 109	1520	Lincoln County	59 686	58.8	17.0	14.5	7.1	2.7	24 041	78.5	4 684	84.9
37 111	...	McDowell County	39 596	60.2	22.9	10.1	5.1	1.7	16 604	77.2	4 097	83.4
37 113	...	Macon County	28 318	58.1	15.5	5.8	19.8	0.8	12 828	81.3	4 535	91.7
37 115	0480	Madison County	18 441	59.7	16.1	14.2	9.1	0.9	8 000	76.5	2 016	83.5
37 117	...	Martin County	24 038	67.0	19.5	8.4	4.5	0.7	10 020	71.8	2 579	81.2
37 119	1520	Mecklenburg County	645 187	43.6	26.3	6.4	19.6	4.2	273 416	62.3	37 923	76.8
37 121	...	Mitchell County............	14 912	66.0	18.1	10.7	4.0	0.0	6 551	80.9	1 937	87.2
37 123	...	Montgomery County......	24 998	61.2	18.6	11.1	5.8	3.2	9 848	76.5	2 508	81.4
37 125	...	Moore County	70 591	56.0	19.9	9.1	13.2	1.8	30 713	78.6	9 850	87.5
37 127	6895	Nash County	81 664	56.0	23.5	12.9	6.6	1.1	33 644	67.7	7 580	73.2
37 129	9200	New Hanover County....	151 073	45.4	24.6	13.2	15.2	1.6	68 183	64.7	13 569	78.8
37 131	...	Northampton County......	20 838	68.3	14.9	9.0	6.8	1.0	8 691	76.8	2 571	81.6
37 133	3605	Onslow County	137 170	35.8	18.4	6.2	36.1	3.5	48 122	58.1	6 321	84.2
37 135	6640	Orange County..............	112 444	41.2	15.9	20.5	17.8	4.6	45 863	57.6	6 532	78.7
37 137	...	Pamlico County	12 266	67.6	14.6	9.7	7.5	0.6	5 178	82.1	1 657	89.1
37 139	...	Pasquotank County.......	32 769	53.3	22.3	10.3	12.8	1.3	12 907	65.7	3 237	79.3
37 141	...	Pender County	38 726	55.8	15.2	17.7	9.4	1.9	16 054	82.6	3 570	87.9
37 143	...	Perquimans County	10 800	61.3	13.5	11.0	13.8	0.5	4 645	78.6	1 398	87.6
37 145	...	Person County	33 337	63.0	21.2	9.7	5.8	0.4	14 085	74.6	3 360	81.4
37 147	3150	Pitt County...................	125 238	44.7	27.4	16.5	9.8	1.6	52 539	58.1	8 599	73.2
37 149	...	Polk County	17 328	62.1	12.3	8.1	16.3	1.2	7 908	78.6	2 896	79.1
37 151	3120	Randolph County	121 584	59.5	20.8	10.7	6.4	2.6	50 659	76.6	10 227	84.2
37 153	...	Richmond County	43 386	59.2	23.4	9.3	6.7	1.4	17 873	72.0	4 343	84.5
37 155	...	Robeson County	113 682	61.9	23.5	7.3	5.0	2.4	43 677	72.8	8 709	77.0
37 157	...	Rockingham County......	86 160	62.5	23.6	6.8	5.7	1.4	36 989	73.7	9 551	81.6
37 159	1520	Rowan County	121 745	57.7	22.5	10.4	7.6	1.8	49 940	73.6	11 241	85.3
37 161	...	Rutherford County........	58 945	60.9	25.6	6.7	6.1	0.7	25 191	74.5	6 667	82.6
37 163	...	Sampson County..........	55 708	60.2	21.0	10.9	4.7	3.3	22 273	73.5	5 175	80.0
37 165	...	Scotland County...........	33 380	58.8	22.4	8.3	9.2	1.3	13 399	69.1	2 718	76.7
37 167	...	Stanly County...............	54 491	61.1	20.4	11.6	5.9	1.0	22 223	76.2	5 578	84.1
37 169	3120	Stokes County	41 833	63.1	15.8	15.7	4.7	0.7	17 579	82.0	3 348	86.8
37 171	...	Surry County	66 940	62.5	22.2	6.8	6.5	1.9	28 408	76.3	7 352	81.2

[1]MSA = Metropolitan Statistical Area. PMSA = Primary MSA. NECMA = New England County Metropolitan Area. See the Appendix A for explanation of these concepts. See Appendix B for list of metropolitan areas identified by type, with component counties.

Table C-3. States and Counties — **Migration, Housing, and Transportation**

STATE County	Owner-occupied by household type (percent)								Median household income			Median housing value (owner estimated)	Median monthly owner costs as a percent of income	
	Family-households					Nonfamily households								
		Married-couple family		Other family										
	Total family households	Total	With own children under 18 years	Total	With own children under 18 years	Total nonfamily households	Two or more adults	Living alone	All households	Owner-occupied households	Renter-occupied households	Median housing value (owner estimated)	With a mortgage	Without a mortgage
	11	12	13	14	15	16	17	18	19	20	21	22	23	24
NORTH CAROLINA—Cont'd														
Chowan County	77.0	85.6	79.5	52.3	41.0	60.2	75.5	58.6	30 941	37 120	16 475	76 100	21.6	11.8
Clay County	87.7	89.1	78.4	79.0	72.5	77.1	83.0	76.5	31 369	33 481	19 485	91 100	22.7	9.9
Cleveland County	77.5	85.3	79.3	52.6	41.9	60.3	51.1	61.5	35 165	40 702	22 592	77 600	20.3	10.2
Columbus County	80.5	86.7	83.1	64.9	55.7	66.3	56.9	67.2	26 364	30 785	15 534	64 100	22.9	11.9
Craven County	70.5	75.6	66.2	50.9	37.9	56.7	38.0	60.0	35 746	43 295	25 098	86 100	21.1	10.3
Cumberland County	63.2	69.1	60.6	47.0	37.0	49.2	35.7	52.2	37 226	45 619	27 363	84 900	23.2	10.8
Currituck County	83.7	89.0	83.7	59.7	52.5	74.7	55.0	80.0	40 394	43 651	26 371	95 500	23.4	9.9
Dare County	80.3	84.0	81.1	60.5	51.0	62.7	53.1	65.8	42 628	48 839	30 425	128 600	24.7	9.9
Davidson County	78.7	85.1	82.1	52.3	39.1	61.8	49.3	63.9	38 703	45 170	25 393	91 700	20.4	9.9
Davie County	86.9	90.3	86.6	71.0	65.0	72.6	60.7	74.2	40 507	44 412	25 539	103 300	21.1	9.9
Duplin County	77.4	83.4	77.1	60.3	53.9	68.3	47.7	71.2	30 137	33 511	20 457	63 400	21.7	11.9
Durham County	64.0	74.7	69.9	39.2	29.8	38.8	27.8	42.0	43 219	59 945	28 668	128 300	21.3	9.9
Edgecombe County	67.7	79.1	74.0	48.3	34.3	54.2	41.9	55.9	30 566	37 791	19 320	63 400	21.7	11.9
Forsyth County	73.2	82.3	77.9	46.6	35.0	50.7	40.2	52.5	41 870	53 054	25 980	108 900	20.2	9.9
Franklin County	80.2	86.2	81.8	60.7	50.1	71.3	68.8	71.7	38 443	42 623	24 467	85 600	22.3	11.9
Gaston County	73.9	80.9	74.9	50.6	38.3	55.5	40.1	58.2	39 256	46 223	27 366	86 600	20.8	11.0
Gates County	84.5	91.0	88.6	61.4	53.5	74.7	66.4	75.9	35 775	39 208	23 341	66 200	19.2	12.0
Graham County	86.9	89.7	85.2	72.6	62.8	72.2	89.6	70.6	27 145	29 433	15 462	64 500	19.4	11.2
Granville County	78.9	86.7	82.5	58.6	50.0	64.9	60.4	65.5	39 583	45 906	22 500	88 100	21.1	9.9
Greene County	75.8	83.7	79.7	58.4	45.2	71.0	63.0	71.7	32 013	35 813	18 734	63 700	22.5	10.3
Guilford County	71.4	81.1	76.5	43.5	34.4	46.1	28.8	50.2	42 514	54 129	27 963	112 600	21.1	9.9
Halifax County	71.6	83.7	78.3	49.5	39.2	56.7	47.4	57.7	26 216	33 186	16 465	60 800	21.3	12.9
Harnett County	75.8	82.0	77.1	57.6	48.8	56.4	42.5	59.6	34 928	41 055	22 986	80 600	21.7	11.0
Haywood County	81.8	85.1	77.8	66.6	51.5	67.0	64.2	67.4	33 602	37 436	22 299	89 400	22.0	9.9
Henderson County	82.8	87.0	80.5	61.2	48.8	69.2	59.3	70.5	38 242	42 368	25 696	114 200	21.1	9.9
Hertford County	74.0	85.2	86.2	52.3	41.6	60.6	46.3	62.3	26 290	31 464	18 539	53 800	24.5	11.4
Hoke County	78.3	84.2	81.6	65.3	58.3	63.6	47.9	66.3	33 274	36 100	21 262	70 700	24.2	11.4
Hyde County	82.6	84.4	76.1	77.1	65.3	70.1	52.1	72.0	28 716	30 176	24 444	60 100	23.7	13.4
Iredell County	80.2	85.9	81.5	57.0	45.7	62.0	49.9	64.1	41 828	47 436	27 535	105 000	21.3	9.9
Jackson County	82.1	86.6	80.7	65.5	59.1	54.5	31.7	61.0	32 392	38 493	20 382	93 100	19.6	9.9
Johnston County	77.7	83.4	79.8	55.4	49.2	62.0	55.7	63.2	40 640	48 252	23 323	97 100	21.8	11.1
Jones County	82.1	89.4	85.8	63.1	52.4	72.7	69.9	73.1	30 755	34 159	17 027	65 400	21.9	11.7
Lee County	77.2	84.9	78.9	53.5	39.4	57.2	42.7	59.8	39 203	46 358	24 543	89 500	20.7	10.2
Lenoir County	73.1	84.1	78.8	48.3	39.7	54.1	45.6	55.2	30 984	39 293	17 849	69 000	21.9	11.5
Lincoln County	82.2	86.3	83.0	63.1	47.3	66.9	56.8	68.9	41 487	46 546	27 395	92 500	20.5	9.9
McDowell County	81.8	85.9	80.6	64.8	55.2	65.0	61.8	65.5	32 135	35 590	23 020	64 800	19.4	9.9
Macon County	84.8	88.1	78.8	68.6	58.0	73.5	60.7	75.2	31 901	34 007	22 125	97 400	21.5	9.9
Madison County	81.1	84.7	79.0	65.8	56.2	65.9	45.3	68.9	31 016	35 117	20 174	84 100	20.7	9.9
Martin County	75.5	86.8	79.6	48.5	33.0	62.1	56.0	62.6	28 666	34 475	16 778	61 600	21.4	12.2
Mecklenburg County	71.9	81.2	79.2	43.9	35.4	45.1	34.2	48.2	50 311	64 111	33 113	139 000	21.4	9.9
Mitchell County	84.2	88.3	83.2	61.6	48.2	72.1	62.9	73.0	30 303	32 559	21 084	70 400	21.4	9.9
Montgomery County	79.7	84.3	79.4	64.6	55.5	67.6	65.2	67.8	32 478	36 627	20 945	67 500	20.9	9.9
Moore County	83.6	88.0	80.5	63.8	55.7	66.0	54.2	67.6	41 176	46 338	25 817	111 900	21.9	9.9
Nash County	73.6	82.1	78.9	47.4	37.9	52.9	41.5	54.5	37 195	45 216	22 372	85 600	20.3	10.7
New Hanover County	76.2	84.1	81.0	45.9	36.9	46.5	30.2	52.1	40 025	50 993	23 840	127 900	23.0	10.2
Northampton County	81.2	90.0	83.9	62.2	50.0	67.1	59.0	67.8	26 891	32 194	14 201	52 400	20.6	13.4
Onslow County	60.8	63.5	56.1	49.7	40.6	49.4	30.0	54.4	33 697	40 844	27 033	78 200	22.1	9.9
Orange County	74.5	81.1	81.4	50.1	45.9	34.8	18.4	43.4	42 845	63 611	25 894	161 600	21.4	9.9
Pamlico County	84.6	89.5	86.1	65.5	46.3	75.9	77.2	75.8	33 477	37 639	21 120	75 100	23.2	10.2
Pasquotank County	69.6	80.8	71.4	43.4	31.2	56.5	44.3	58.5	30 597	37 779	19 833	78 000	23.0	13.7
Pender County	85.8	89.2	85.3	72.0	61.0	73.8	67.0	75.0	36 389	39 825	22 042	86 900	23.5	9.9
Perquimans County	82.9	89.4	81.8	61.6	44.5	67.1	54.1	68.9	30 517	34 504	16 525	71 400	23.9	13.2
Person County	79.1	85.8	81.0	59.1	44.6	62.7	57.6	63.4	36 809	42 490	22 716	85 500	20.7	10.1
Pitt County	71.2	81.0	80.5	48.0	41.4	37.0	20.0	43.1	32 579	46 576	19 199	82 000	20.5	11.3
Polk County	84.6	86.5	79.4	72.5	68.1	66.2	61.2	66.8	36 447	39 813	27 400	103 900	22.2	9.9
Randolph County	81.1	85.9	80.5	61.5	52.4	63.7	52.0	65.5	38 442	42 895	26 099	86 100	20.0	9.9
Richmond County	75.4	84.9	78.7	55.7	42.4	64.0	46.2	66.2	28 646	33 446	19 107	54 100	20.0	12.6
Robeson County	77.3	86.8	84.1	60.1	51.9	60.0	55.0	60.8	28 084	32 873	15 819	53 100	21.3	11.6
Rockingham County	78.2	84.8	78.5	56.8	43.5	62.5	44.8	64.6	33 498	38 953	21 545	77 800	21.0	9.9
Rowan County	78.2	84.9	79.9	54.8	46.8	61.9	47.8	64.1	37 670	42 338	26 550	88 000	20.9	10.1
Rutherford County	79.2	85.4	80.9	56.5	45.1	62.6	50.0	64.0	31 065	36 080	20 586	71 300	21.0	10.2
Sampson County	78.0	84.2	79.6	59.8	52.5	61.3	48.1	63.1	31 787	36 352	20 149	66 400	20.5	11.8
Scotland County	72.3	83.0	78.0	49.9	35.1	60.7	53.8	61.5	31 138	40 906	17 490	62 900	19.8	9.9
Stanly County	79.5	85.2	79.8	54.5	45.7	67.5	51.2	69.3	36 583	41 016	25 660	84 100	21.4	10.7
Stokes County	85.4	88.6	84.1	69.9	57.3	71.9	70.5	72.1	38 861	42 111	25 890	84 000	20.6	9.9
Surry County	81.2	85.2	80.2	64.7	58.6	63.5	51.4	64.7	33 172	37 223	21 467	78 800	20.9	9.9

STATE County	Median gross rent	Percent who pay 35 percent or more of income for housing expenses		Means of transportation to work (percent except where noted)						Vehicles available (percent of households)		
		Owners	Renters	Number of workers 16 years and over	Car, truck, or van		Public transportation	Other means	Walked	No vehicles	One vehicle	Two or more vehicles
					Drove alone	Carpooled						
	25	26	27	28	29	30	31	32	33	34	35	36

NORTH CAROLINA—Cont'd

STATE County	25	26	27	28	29	30	31	32	33	34	35	36
Chowan County	429	14.6	26.6	5 974	70.0	17.8	0.5	2.8	5.1	14.7	34.3	51.1
Clay County	408	16.1	24.1	3 696	78.5	17.2	0.2	0.5	1.0	5.5	32.4	62.2
Cleveland County	447	15.6	25.0	43 976	81.7	13.7	0.1	0.8	1.6	8.2	29.6	62.1
Columbus County	379	19.4	27.7	20 551	80.1	14.4	0.2	1.6	1.8	10.0	34.2	55.8
Craven County	501	14.9	23.4	41 848	77.8	15.6	0.6	1.2	2.6	7.9	33.9	58.2
Cumberland County	581	19.4	24.7	143 202	77.2	14.2	0.8	1.4	4.2	7.6	34.5	57.9
Currituck County	590	19.2	32.2	8 603	79.8	15.4	0.4	1.7	0.5	4.4	26.8	68.8
Dare County	638	20.1	23.8	15 419	76.8	14.2	0.1	1.9	2.2	3.3	33.8	62.9
Davidson County	464	12.8	24.1	72 893	81.9	14.4	0.3	0.7	1.1	6.1	27.5	66.4
Davie County	493	12.4	23.8	16 634	83.2	12.6	0.1	0.7	0.9	6.2	25.7	68.1
Duplin County	399	17.2	20.2	21 284	73.4	20.1	0.1	2.4	1.5	8.6	31.7	59.7
Durham County	658	16.2	30.3	112 433	74.8	15.9	3.0	0.9	2.6	9.3	37.6	53.1
Edgecombe County	442	18.8	30.8	22 192	77.4	16.5	1.6	1.1	1.5	14.8	35.0	49.6
Forsyth County	523	12.9	26.0	147 838	80.5	12.8	1.5	0.8	1.9	8.6	34.4	57.0
Franklin County	488	17.3	24.0	22 248	78.4	17.1	0.3	1.2	1.0	6.7	28.8	64.5
Gaston County	535	14.1	25.1	89 341	83.7	12.7	0.3	0.7	1.0	6.8	32.4	60.8
Gates County	448	14.6	28.4	4 266	77.1	17.3	0.0	1.1	2.1	9.0	27.0	64.0
Graham County	319	15.5	24.0	3 244	67.8	28.0	0.2	1.2	1.7	8.4	30.4	61.2
Granville County	481	13.7	26.7	20 494	81.0	14.9	0.1	1.0	1.2	8.4	28.0	63.7
Greene County	405	18.5	26.6	7 600	78.1	18.3	0.4	1.1	0.7	9.9	32.2	58.0
Guilford County	590	14.4	27.7	213 079	81.2	12.0	1.3	1.0	1.7	7.8	34.9	57.3
Halifax County	399	17.8	29.2	20 617	78.0	17.2	0.3	1.0	1.7	16.3	32.1	51.6
Harnett County	486	17.1	25.5	40 599	79.1	16.2	0.4	1.2	1.3	7.9	30.9	61.2
Haywood County	455	14.4	23.7	23 721	81.3	13.7	0.5	0.5	1.3	6.6	32.6	60.8
Henderson County	513	12.6	25.9	38 711	80.8	13.9	0.2	0.7	1.2	5.0	33.6	61.3
Hertford County	410	21.7	24.4	8 453	71.7	22.3	0.8	1.2	2.1	13.1	34.0	52.9
Hoke County	504	20.6	27.6	14 204	75.8	19.2	0.5	1.5	0.9	9.1	31.8	59.2
Hyde County	383	18.9	27.9	2 194	73.2	14.0	0.8	4.6	4.2	9.6	41.9	48.5
Iredell County	540	13.9	23.2	60 191	82.7	12.5	0.2	0.9	0.9	5.8	28.3	66.0
Jackson County	430	12.3	28.8	15 369	76.3	16.5	0.3	0.7	3.6	7.5	32.0	60.5
Johnston County	498	15.1	25.9	58 675	79.9	15.8	0.4	0.8	0.9	7.0	28.7	64.3
Jones County	396	19.8	29.1	4 267	78.0	17.3	0.2	1.5	1.1	9.6	31.7	58.7
Lee County	497	14.2	23.1	22 893	78.3	16.9	0.5	1.2	1.4	7.6	31.5	60.8
Lenoir County	405	16.8	27.5	25 187	80.1	14.7	0.6	1.0	1.6	13.4	32.6	54.0
Lincoln County	482	12.9	19.3	31 803	82.1	14.7	0.0	0.6	0.5	5.4	24.7	69.9
McDowell County	411	10.5	20.8	19 228	77.4	18.8	0.4	0.7	0.7	7.6	30.0	62.4
Macon County	485	13.2	28.6	12 576	80.2	12.9	0.2	0.7	1.4	6.3	33.9	59.8
Madison County	367	13.9	23.9	8 570	79.0	13.5	0.2	1.1	2.6	7.9	28.7	63.5
Martin County	400	20.0	29.2	10 487	78.8	16.0	0.2	1.8	1.2	12.0	00.5	54.2
Mecklenburg County	693	15.9	27.0	362 991	79.2	12.5	2.6	0.9	1.4	6.9	36.2	56.9
Mitchell County	070	12.0	21.0	6 026	76.0	21.1	0.0	0.3	1.1	9.5	29.3	61.2
Montgomery County	407	14.1	22.0	11 550	74.4	20.5	0.3	0.8	1.4	9.0	29.5	61.5
Moore County	528	14.6	25.5	32 018	80.5	12.8	0.1	1.0	1.5	5.5	32.4	62.1
Nash County	494	15.1	26.0	38 844	82.5	13.4	0.4	0.8	1.0	8.7	30.7	60.6
New Hanover County	631	19.1	37.4	80 088	82.4	10.7	0.9	1.4	1.7	7.6	35.8	56.6
Northampton County	386	17.8	24.6	7 789	78.6	16.5	0.3	1.1	2.0	16.1	30.4	53.5
Onslow County	518	16.1	18.7	79 399	66.7	17.2	0.8	2.5	10.4	6.2	33.3	60.5
Orange County	684	14.9	40.5	60 860	70.1	11.7	4.2	2.5	7.0	7.8	33.9	58.3
Pamlico County	466	18.9	25.2	4 939	74.3	16.5	0.7	1.9	3.1	8.6	33.7	57.7
Pasquotank County	493	20.5	29.5	14 552	75.1	17.1	1.5	1.9	2.9	12.9	32.7	54.4
Pender County	491	19.1	29.6	17 732	80.2	13.9	0.1	1.3	1.2	6.4	30.4	63.2
Perquimans County	419	18.9	29.4	4 434	76.2	15.6	0.7	0.9	2.3	9.3	30.8	59.9
Person County	455	15.0	23.2	16 531	79.2	16.5	0.2	0.8	0.9	6.0	28.6	65.4
Pitt County	471	15.4	34.8	63 307	80.5	12.8	0.8	1.3	2.4	8.9	36.9	54.2
Polk County	515	14.5	25.3	7 776	78.1	14.1	0.1	0.9	2.0	6.4	30.3	63.2
Randolph County	463	11.5	20.6	65 803	81.4	13.9	0.1	1.1	1.4	5.1	28.4	66.5
Richmond County	404	14.3	26.5	18 984	76.5	17.3	0.6	1.2	2.8	12.2	34.8	53.0
Robeson County	389	18.1	28.0	47 222	75.3	20.5	0.2	1.2	1.2	11.0	34.9	54.1
Rockingham County	437	15.0	24.3	41 638	80.6	15.3	0.1	0.7	1.2	8.3	29.7	62.0
Rowan County	496	13.8	23.0	60 299	81.2	14.2	0.3	1.0	1.2	7.1	30.6	62.3
Rutherford County	404	13.5	23.4	27 673	82.1	13.0	0.1	0.7	1.6	7.8	31.4	60.8
Sampson County	387	15.0	23.0	26 014	78.4	15.9	0.5	1.6	1.7	9.0	30.5	60.5
Scotland County	433	14.6	27.8	13 996	81.7	12.9	0.1	1.7	1.8	9.9	36.5	53.6
Stanly County	463	13.7	22.0	27 488	82.0	13.2	0.2	0.5	1.6	5.9	27.1	67.0
Stokes County	449	14.2	18.7	21 709	81.6	14.1	0.1	0.4	0.8	5.4	24.3	70.2
Surry County	411	13.2	21.7	33 458	78.4	16.5	0.2	1.1	1.4	7.7	28.9	63.4

Table C-3. States and Counties — Migration, Housing, and Transportation

STATE/ County code	MSA/PMSA/ NECMA code[1]	STATE County	Residence in 1995 (percent)						Occupied housing units		Householders 65 years and over	
			Total population 5 years and over	Same house	Same county, different house	Same state, different county	Different state	Outside the United States	Number	Percent owner-occupied	Number	Percent owner-occupied
			1	2	3	4	5	6	7	8	9	10
		NORTH CAROLINA—Cont'd										
37 173	...	Swain County	12 193	67.0	14.0	9.3	9.0	0.7	5 137	76.9	1 293	80.0
37 175	...	Transylvania County	27 886	57.5	17.6	7.1	16.5	1.3	12 320	79.4	4 137	90.6
37 177	...	Tyrrell County	3 958	63.1	13.3	13.0	8.5	2.1	1 537	74.8	439	88.2
37 179	1520	Union County	113 722	53.2	17.0	14.7	12.6	2.5	43 390	80.6	7 217	86.0
37 181	...	Vance County	39 882	58.5	23.9	9.5	6.2	1.8	16 199	66.2	3 639	72.6
37 183	6640	Wake County	582 978	41.7	25.7	10.1	18.0	4.5	242 040	65.9	29 225	78.5
37 185	...	Warren County	18 847	62.8	14.6	12.6	9.2	0.9	7 708	77.2	2 207	83.1
37 187	...	Washington County	12 823	67.9	19.9	5.6	5.5	1.1	5 367	73.5	1 374	82.8
37 189	...	Watauga County	41 021	46.5	16.1	22.2	13.4	1.6	16 540	62.9	3 196	86.0
37 191	2980	Wayne County	105 621	53.0	25.9	7.3	10.8	3.0	42 612	65.3	8 842	75.5
37 193	...	Wilkes County	61 500	64.7	21.7	6.6	5.2	1.7	26 650	77.9	6 442	87.1
37 195	...	Wilson County	68 861	55.6	28.2	8.4	5.7	2.1	28 613	61.2	6 153	71.5
37 197	3120	Yadkin County	33 964	64.5	17.5	11.4	4.8	1.8	14 505	80.3	3 512	86.4
37 199	...	Yancey County	16 800	66.4	17.5	7.0	6.8	2.3	7 472	80.2	2 169	86.2
38 000	...	NORTH DAKOTA	603 106	56.8	21.8	10.2	10.0	1.2	257 152	66.6	62 043	73.4
38 001	...	Adams County	2 482	66.1	18.4	6.0	8.7	0.8	1 121	70.9	394	71.8
38 003	...	Barnes County	11 152	62.1	20.5	11.9	4.6	0.8	4 884	71.1	1 516	74.7
38 005	...	Benson County	6 332	66.5	20.5	8.9	3.9	0.3	2 328	68.3	665	77.7
38 007	...	Billings County	850	72.9	5.9	12.2	8.5	0.5	366	76.2	96	91.7
38 009	...	Bottineau County	6 864	67.4	15.3	11.2	5.0	1.1	2 962	80.0	963	79.4
38 011	...	Bowman County	3 094	64.0	17.2	9.7	9.0	0.0	1 358	79.5	439	83.6
38 013	...	Burke County	2 162	75.2	13.5	6.6	4.7	0.0	1 013	84.6	400	86.3
38 015	1010	Burleigh County	65 105	54.8	23.7	13.2	7.9	0.4	27 670	68.0	5 615	69.9
38 017	2520	Cass County	115 059	44.8	28.4	10.7	14.3	1.8	51 315	54.4	8 258	60.6
38 019	...	Cavalier County	4 622	76.8	11.0	6.9	4.8	0.5	2 017	81.5	708	84.7
38 021	...	Dickey County	5 436	64.0	13.9	9.0	12.5	0.6	2 283	71.4	779	74.1
38 023	...	Divide County	2 214	73.6	11.8	10.1	3.7	0.9	1 005	81.9	435	82.1
38 025	...	Dunn County	3 399	70.1	11.7	12.9	5.1	0.2	1 378	79.9	404	81.9
38 027	...	Eddy County	2 607	72.0	11.7	13.7	2.7	0.0	1 164	75.3	407	77.6
38 029	...	Emmons County	4 094	71.6	18.1	5.7	4.3	0.3	1 786	84.2	720	83.6
38 031	...	Foster County	3 558	61.0	19.9	12.8	5.3	0.9	1 540	74.3	549	76.7
38 033	...	Golden Valley County	1 818	68.9	9.9	8.2	12.9	0.1	761	77.8	239	83.7
38 035	2985	Grand Forks County	61 929	42.9	27.3	9.3	17.8	2.7	25 435	53.7	4 055	71.0
38 037	...	Grant County	2 714	75.2	11.9	6.9	5.2	0.8	1 195	79.6	458	80.1
38 039	...	Griggs County	2 627	74.6	13.5	7.2	4.1	0.6	1 178	78.4	449	78.4
38 041	...	Hettinger County	2 593	77.3	13.2	3.5	5.9	0.0	1 152	84.3	462	84.6
38 043	...	Kidder County	2 625	75.3	12.3	10.6	1.8	0.1	1 158	81.9	459	83.4
38 045	...	LaMoure County	4 493	72.0	15.4	7.2	5.2	0.2	1 942	81.0	706	81.9
38 047	...	Logan County	2 179	76.4	12.1	8.0	3.1	0.4	963	85.4	385	88.1
38 049	...	McHenry County	5 682	71.6	12.6	10.5	4.8	0.5	2 526	81.5	853	81.6
38 051	...	McIntosh County	3 248	71.7	17.9	5.7	4.5	0.3	1 467	82.8	686	86.2
38 053	...	McKenzie County	5 394	70.1	14.0	8.8	6.6	0.5	2 151	73.9	592	81.8
38 055	...	McLean County	8 868	71.0	14.0	10.5	4.3	0.1	3 815	82.3	1 238	83.1
38 057	...	Mercer County	8 246	73.6	12.8	7.9	5.1	0.6	3 346	84.4	778	82.0
38 059	1010	Morton County	23 682	62.3	16.4	14.6	6.2	0.4	9 889	75.6	2 431	74.6
38 061	...	Mountrail County	6 198	66.2	18.0	10.8	4.4	0.6	2 560	72.6	752	79.3
38 063	...	Nelson County	3 571	70.6	12.7	10.1	6.0	0.6	1 628	80.3	679	81.3
38 065	...	Oliver County	1 963	76.9	9.9	9.5	3.7	0.0	791	85.6	203	82.3
38 067	...	Pembina County	8 148	68.9	17.6	8.2	4.8	0.5	3 535	78.3	1 095	80.0
38 069	...	Pierce County	4 414	65.0	15.9	13.7	4.3	1.1	1 964	73.1	742	77.0
38 071	...	Ramsey County	11 401	55.8	23.3	14.2	5.3	1.4	4 957	64.9	1 458	62.1
38 073	...	Ransom County	5 544	64.6	15.7	11.7	7.5	0.5	2 350	75.5	765	72.0
38 075	...	Renville County	2 493	70.1	10.1	12.4	6.4	1.0	1 085	77.7	349	79.4
38 077	...	Richland County	16 944	60.2	15.3	13.9	9.9	0.7	6 885	69.5	1 751	74.2
38 079	...	Rolette County	12 506	64.4	23.1	7.1	4.4	0.9	4 556	67.4	908	71.7
38 081	...	Sargent County	4 113	66.1	16.5	10.0	7.1	0.3	1 786	79.6	547	77.1
38 083	...	Sheridan County	1 655	80.6	8.3	7.3	3.8	0.0	731	84.8	305	85.2
38 085	...	Sioux County	3 606	53.8	28.3	5.9	11.9	0.2	1 095	46.1	155	59.4
38 087	...	Slope County	729	77.1	5.5	6.3	10.2	1.0	313	87.2	96	96.9
38 089	...	Stark County	21 336	61.8	20.6	8.3	8.9	0.5	8 932	70.3	2 299	71.9
38 091	...	Steele County	2 128	71.7	11.1	11.2	5.6	0.4	923	76.9	305	78.7
38 093	...	Stutsman County	20 768	58.6	21.6	12.1	7.4	0.4	8 954	67.2	2 465	67.2
38 095	...	Towner County	2 747	71.4	16.2	8.8	3.2	0.4	1 218	74.9	429	75.1
38 097	...	Traill County	7 964	60.9	16.6	14.4	7.3	0.8	3 341	72.4	992	70.1
38 099	...	Walsh County	11 686	69.9	17.8	6.8	5.1	0.4	5 029	76.8	1 602	82.0

[1]MSA = Metropolitan Statistical Area. PMSA = Primary MSA. NECMA = New England County Metropolitan Area. See the Appendix A for explanation of these concepts. See Appendix B for list of metropolitan areas identified by type, with component counties.

Table C-3. States and Counties — **Migration, Housing, and Transportation**

STATE County	Owner-occupied by household type (percent)								Median household income			Median monthly owner costs as a percent of income		
	Family-households					Nonfamily households								
		Married-couple family		Other family										
	Total family households	Total	With own children under 18 years	Total	With own children under 18 years	Total nonfamily households	Two or more adults	Living alone	All households	Owner-occupied households	Renter-occupied households	Median housing value (owner estimated)	With a mortgage	Without a mortgage
	11	12	13	14	15	16	17	18	19	20	21	22	23	24

NORTH CAROLINA—Cont'd														
Swain County	80.6	85.4	80.8	66.8	58.6	67.4	67.9	67.4	27 843	31 815	17 763	80 000	20.0	9.9
Transylvania County	83.9	87.7	81.1	63.5	48.1	68.9	53.3	71.1	38 094	42 937	22 696	106 900	20.8	9.9
Tyrrell County	77.3	86.1	77.2	56.4	48.1	68.9	40.0	70.6	25 021	28 000	16 464	49 700	23.4	17.9
Union County	83.6	88.7	86.4	59.6	50.3	68.6	56.1	71.1	50 354	55 443	30 779	123 300	21.7	9.9
Vance County	71.0	82.0	75.8	49.9	40.4	53.9	49.2	54.6	30 856	37 813	18 427	70 800	21.9	11.5
Wake County	76.9	84.0	83.4	47.5	41.1	44.7	31.7	48.9	54 965	69 441	33 677	156 200	21.1	9.9
Warren County	80.8	87.7	82.8	64.0	55.7	68.3	60.2	69.1	28 340	32 000	16 637	64 500	21.5	11.5
Washington County	76.0	88.4	81.1	47.9	37.3	67.2	63.6	67.6	28 742	34 565	14 669	63 700	21.4	11.4
Watauga County	81.4	86.1	82.6	57.0	44.6	38.1	12.7	50.9	32 624	42 945	19 167	128 200	22.2	9.9
Wayne County	70.6	78.3	72.4	48.9	42.9	52.1	38.5	54.5	33 790	41 227	23 417	77 000	20.8	10.3
Wilkes County	82.6	86.3	82.4	65.0	54.4	65.3	52.5	66.7	34 108	37 750	22 518	80 400	20.0	9.9
Wilson County	67.7	80.2	74.4	39.8	30.9	46.4	28.0	49.2	33 453	43 245	21 135	79 300	22.1	11.5
Yadkin County	82.1	86.8	82.7	58.8	46.6	75.1	52.2	77.5	36 325	40 277	26 037	81 100	21.7	9.9
Yancey County	84.3	88.2	81.1	64.1	50.6	69.6	56.8	70.9	29 864	32 963	19 393	81 400	19.9	9.9
NORTH DAKOTA	78.5	84.3	82.1	49.7	41.7	44.7	29.1	47.9	34 483	42 209	22 062	68 300	19.4	10.2
Adams County	79.4	82.6	76.8	55.8	53.0	55.2	59.3	54.9	28 630	30 881	21 413	38 800	17.8	12.1
Barnes County	84.6	87.8	86.7	67.5	54.8	46.9	27.9	49.4	31 187	38 071	18 768	55 600	19.1	9.9
Benson County	69.8	81.5	75.3	46.5	36.2	64.2	74.0	63.3	27 051	32 798	17 448	32 200	15.7	10.2
Billings County	83.7	84.3	83.2	79.4	66.7	58.7	70.0	57.6	31 731	33 194	26 250	50 800	19.3	9.9
Bottineau County	88.0	90.9	86.9	65.0	45.7	64.7	67.9	64.4	30 291	33 533	20 754	44 900	18.7	10.9
Bowman County	86.2	88.7	86.4	63.2	54.4	66.2	63.6	66.4	31 667	33 494	25 074	50 800	17.3	9.9
Burke County	88.2	89.2	83.9	82.5	80.5	77.2	70.6	77.6	25 477	26 528	20 000	28 300	18.4	10.9
Burleigh County	81.1	87.8	88.2	48.0	39.1	43.0	34.3	44.8	41 163	51 276	23 945	92 100	20.0	10.1
Cass County	72.9	81.1	83.3	36.8	35.2	28.3	19.1	31.4	37 966	53 605	24 075	93 900	20.3	9.9
Cavalier County	88.8	90.1	87.9	77.7	70.4	65.7	51.9	66.3	31 949	34 720	22 115	42 100	18.8	9.9
Dickey County	78.6	81.9	77.7	55.4	51.0	57.5	54.0	57.7	29 671	35 607	18 782	50 100	18.7	9.9
Divide County	87.0	88.7	79.2	79.7	79.1	71.5	72.7	71.4	29 563	31 910	19 375	30 900	19.4	10.8
Dunn County	85.6	88.9	85.1	68.6	54.8	66.2	70.4	65.5	29 490	31 854	17 663	43 500	18.8	9.9
Eddy County	85.5	87.0	82.2	70.6	51.6	57.0	63.2	56.7	29 025	31 707	19 567	35 000	16.2	10.7
Emmons County	88.7	91.7	88.7	67.9	59.6	73.9	81.6	73.3	25 756	26 584	18 194	39 800	19.3	12.7
Foster County	85.4	89.2	89.4	62.2	48.9	51.9	61.9	51.0	31 667	37 833	19 605	54 900	18.3	11.2
Golden Valley County	84.1	86.3	77.9	65.5	61.9	64.6	80.0	64.0	30 528	32 209	21 484	42 000	18.1	9.9
Grand Forks County	67.1	73.4	70.1	40.5	32.4	31.8	15.6	37.3	35 633	49 897	24 013	87 100	20.6	11.6
Grant County	85.4	87.1	77.7	70.5	53.7	68.2	82.6	67.4	23 163	24 975	17 250	28 500	20.2	12.4
Griggs County	84.9	86.6	80.7	65.1	38.5	65.3	44.0	66.8	29 722	33 469	19 519	37 900	17.8	10.7
Hettinger County	90.2	91.7	88.0	75.0	60.5	71.3	50.0	72.0	29 183	30 881	17 639	33 100	17.0	9.9
Kidder County	87.4	88.6	82.3	78.5	60.0	69.9	81.8	69.2	25 233	26 613	20 000	40 500	19.4	12.3
LaMoure County	89.4	90.4	87.2	79.0	71.6	63.4	85.2	62.4	29 851	32 424	20 069	38 600	17.6	10.7
Logan County	91.2	91.9	91.0	82.2	75.0	73.2	53.8	74.9	28 341	29 847	20 750	33 100	17.0	12.0
McHenry County	87.5	90.6	89.6	69.8	63.8	68.9	78.6	68.0	27 135	30 483	18 875	37 700	18.3	10.0
McIntosh County	88.8	91.0	87.3	62.2	57.9	70.9	72.2	70.8	26 074	26 991	21 250	29 500	17.9	12.7
McKenzie County	77.4	84.9	78.7	44.2	31.0	65.0	56.9	65.7	29 148	32 196	21 447	46 800	16.5	9.9
McLean County	88.0	91.8	88.3	59.6	50.2	68.3	65.8	68.5	31 999	35 410	17 917	51 400	15.9	9.9
Mercer County	91.0	94.6	92.7	60.7	52.3	66.0	67.3	65.9	42 095	47 155	18 125	61 000	14.9	10.1
Morton County	84.1	89.5	88.5	57.2	46.3	55.3	42.6	57.2	36 723	41 957	19 654	66 800	19.8	9.9
Mountrail County	77.3	85.1	76.5	52.3	42.3	62.3	57.7	62.8	26 299	29 583	19 315	40 500	18.4	12.4
Nelson County	87.1	89.0	80.4	76.8	61.3	69.0	56.5	69.5	29 471	31 647	17 426	36 000	19.3	10.4
Oliver County	91.3	92.8	90.2	74.0	51.9	66.8	85.0	64.6	36 198	39 922	20 000	62 100	16.5	10.1
Pembina County	86.9	90.0	89.5	66.7	53.8	61.2	57.9	61.4	36 688	41 211	24 333	53 200	17.8	9.9
Pierce County	83.7	89.5	89.3	47.2	20.5	53.0	60.0	52.5	26 779	30 673	18 929	53 900	19.3	12.8
Ramsey County	79.2	86.3	87.2	49.6	40.4	39.2	57.5	36.6	35 527	42 911	18 468	59 700	18.1	9.9
Ransom County	88.3	91.4	87.7	62.9	55.3	50.2	35.4	51.5	37 353	41 436	21 006	59 200	17.5	10.0
Renville County	85.3	87.2	85.2	71.4	65.6	60.2	72.7	59.3	30 734	33 586	19 444	47 300	19.2	10.6
Richland County	82.5	86.6	87.4	60.0	48.9	45.7	28.2	49.3	36 177	43 150	21 250	65 200	19.2	11.0
Rolette County	71.5	83.0	74.8	52.5	47.7	56.0	58.2	55.7	25 887	32 346	13 101	46 300	15.8	9.9
Sargent County	86.6	89.1	89.7	66.9	58.1	63.6	54.0	64.6	36 667	39 877	25 500	44 700	16.1	9.9
Sheridan County	88.5	90.5	86.0	72.4	45.5	75.8	75.0	75.9	24 398	26 304	16 250	27 800	21.4	11.1
Sioux County	46.1	59.0	52.0	34.8	33.0	46.1	45.9	46.1	22 825	26 813	20 476	37 500	17.4	11.1
Slope County	92.8	92.9	89.4	92.0	87.5	73.9	100.0	72.7	25 288	27 813	15 000	25 700	12.5	9.9
Stark County	81.9	86.9	86.7	52.1	38.9	47.1	29.4	49.8	32 283	40 079	17 926	69 800	19.3	11.0
Steele County	83.9	84.6	80.8	75.0	69.7	61.1	45.8	62.5	35 799	39 875	25 104	39 800	19.3	9.9
Stutsman County	80.1	85.8	83.6	51.1	43.2	45.1	43.5	45.3	33 780	41 560	19 769	63 900	18.9	10.1
Towner County	84.0	86.5	86.7	65.6	57.6	58.4	41.7	59.4	32 704	36 689	19 537	40 300	16.6	10.3
Traill County	82.8	87.2	85.9	57.8	45.2	51.6	40.4	53.3	36 970	42 817	22 229	60 200	17.6	10.6
Walsh County	84.2	88.3	85.2	62.7	51.1	62.4	40.8	64.2	34 115	37 752	21 753	50 900	19.1	10.5

STATE County	Median gross rent	Owners	Renters	Number of workers 16 years and over	Drove alone	Carpooled	Public transportation	Other means	Walked	No vehicles	One vehicle	Two or more vehicles
	25	26	27	28	29	30	31	32	33	34	35	36
NORTH CAROLINA—Cont'd												
Swain County	384	10.0	24.5	5 230	77.1	15.6	0.0	1.4	2.5	6.9	35.1	57.9
Transylvania County	468	11.3	22.7	12 254	79.7	14.4	0.2	0.9	2.2	5.9	31.6	62.5
Tyrrell County	375	25.8	26.4	1 531	65.1	23.8	1.2	2.0	3.5	12.3	39.0	48.7
Union County	587	14.9	23.1	61 217	81.4	13.0	0.4	0.8	0.9	4.5	24.1	71.4
Vance County	441	17.6	30.5	17 911	76.8	19.2	0.3	1.1	1.4	12.3	33.0	54.7
Wake County...............	727	13.4	28.4	338 602	81.1	11.2	1.2	1.0	1.7	4.9	32.1	63.1
Warren County	395	18.6	27.1	7 149	75.2	18.2	0.4	1.4	1.6	10.7	31.0	58.3
Washington County.......	403	19.7	32.5	5 308	76.0	17.8	0.9	2.1	1.1	13.7	32.7	53.5
Watauga County	548	15.3	43.3	20 985	74.5	13.7	0.8	0.7	6.2	5.6	32.3	62.1
Wayne County..............	455	14.2	21.9	49 590	80.5	14.0	0.4	1.3	2.0	8.9	32.4	58.7
Wilkes County	416	12.4	18.7	31 041	79.7	16.4	0.0	0.5	0.9	8.3	25.9	65.8
Wilson County	469	18.2	31.5	32 890	78.8	15.7	1.0	1.5	1.5	11.4	33.9	54.7
Yadkin County..............	438	15.2	16.3	17 267	80.0	15.7	0.2	0.6	1.2	5.3	25.6	69.1
Yancey County	371	10.9	19.4	7 665	73.2	20.7	0.4	0.8	2.0	9.8	27.6	62.6
NORTH DAKOTA......	412	9.7	22.6	319 481	77.7	10.0	0.4	0.8	5.0	6.6	30.1	63.3
Adams County..............	295	10.1	10.8	1 209	69.1	9.8	0.0	0.0	7.4	5.9	29.4	64.7
Barnes County.............	324	9.9	19.1	5 597	72.1	11.9	0.0	1.7	7.5	7.1	29.0	63.9
Benson County.............	292	10.2	12.5	2 350	63.2	17.8	1.1	1.7	6.4	9.3	30.8	59.9
Billings County	392	18.6	0.0	443	50.6	7.4	0.0	0.0	12.9	1.1	20.2	78.7
Bottineau County..........	365	9.9	21.3	3 130	72.6	10.8	0.3	1.1	7.4	3.8	28.3	67.9
Bowman County............	316	7.1	8.5	1 632	72.3	7.4	0.0	1.0	8.0	3.3	26.5	70.2
Burke County	285	10.6	14.4	998	66.8	6.0	0.4	1.5	11.3	6.3	21.2	72.5
Burleigh County............	446	9.4	25.9	37 217	83.4	9.0	0.4	0.6	2.6	6.9	30.1	63.0
Cass County.................	463	9.8	24.9	69 743	83.5	8.0	0.4	1.0	3.8	7.0	34.0	59.0
Cavalier County............	313	7.5	16.4	2 091	74.5	7.9	0.4	1.0	8.7	3.2	25.9	70.9
Dickey County..............	332	9.6	18.4	2 832	63.5	10.5	0.0	1.4	13.6	5.1	33.5	61.5
Divide County	293	10.6	20.0	962	67.4	10.5	0.5	2.0	11.7	5.0	26.9	68.2
Dunn County	231	10.2	9.4	1 606	65.1	6.0	0.2	1.0	6.7	5.4	24.3	70.2
Eddy County	294	9.4	15.8	1 193	68.7	10.1	0.0	0.3	7.8	6.7	29.2	64.1
Emmons County............	271	16.9	11.7	1 854	57.5	8.6	0.3	0.5	10.6	5.7	26.0	68.3
Foster County..............	342	12.2	18.8	1 749	71.8	9.8	0.0	0.8	8.5	5.2	28.4	66.4
Golden Valley County ...	323	8.6	11.4	835	67.2	9.9	0.0	0.6	10.1	3.9	28.1	67.9
Grand Forks County......	477	11.3	25.6	35 038	80.3	10.0	0.9	1.0	4.5	6.8	34.4	58.8
Grant County................	257	12.4	12.9	1 239	51.4	9.8	0.2	1.1	11.5	6.9	23.1	70.0
Griggs County..............	274	8.0	9.1	1 271	66.9	9.8	0.1	1.7	8.2	7.4	21.1	71.6
Hettinger County	225	7.1	15.9	1 115	65.0	7.4	0.4	0.3	9.6	6.0	24.1	69.9
Kidder County	260	13.0	19.5	1 156	58.4	7.4	0.0	0.8	11.1	7.3	21.2	71.5
LaMoure County............	287	8.2	13.0	2 079	62.9	9.3	0.1	0.7	11.0	4.1	23.7	72.2
Logan County...............	277	11.1	10.1	952	57.6	10.0	0.2	0.4	13.8	4.3	24.8	70.9
McHenry County	267	11.5	19.5	2 579	65.9	11.9	0.1	0.5	7.8	6.1	23.5	70.4
McIntosh County	280	10.6	16.5	1 411	61.7	10.3	0.1	0.5	11.1	5.7	27.6	66.7
McKenzie County	274	11.3	10.4	2 424	67.4	10.6	0.9	0.4	6.6	6.2	25.9	67.9
McLean County.............	291	8.8	11.7	4 012	67.8	14.1	0.1	0.7	7.8	5.0	23.0	72.0
Mercer County..............	325	5.1	17.4	4 067	72.2	14.7	0.1	0.2	6.2	4.1	19.2	76.6
Morton County..............	405	9.4	27.5	12 792	78.7	10.4	0.4	0.8	3.3	6.5	25.8	67.6
Mountrail County	337	11.5	17.8	2 695	69.0	14.1	0.4	0.6	5.5	5.6	30.7	63.7
Nelson County	275	9.4	10.7	1 620	70.6	10.6	0.0	0.2	11.3	5.9	30.2	63.9
Oliver County	280	11.8	13.6	987	62.0	15.1	0.4	0.0	6.0	3.3	13.9	82.8
Pembina County............	361	8.7	16.0	3 961	73.9	14.2	0.1	0.8	6.3	4.8	27.9	67.3
Pierce County...............	374	10.4	24.8	2 040	65.2	8.3	0.0	0.5	8.9	6.2	28.5	65.3
Ramsey County.............	324	7.2	18.5	5 657	76.5	11.9	0.9	0.9	5.5	9.5	30.5	60.0
Ransom County.............	304	6.3	14.7	2 851	73.1	12.0	0.0	0.8	6.1	6.4	26.3	67.3
Renville County	326	12.2	15.6	1 249	67.2	9.2	0.4	0.2	8.5	3.8	24.5	71.7
Richland County	374	8.5	19.9	8 646	74.4	10.9	0.0	0.8	6.6	5.4	29.9	64.7
Rolette County..............	281	10.7	25.2	4 482	71.4	18.5	0.3	0.5	4.5	10.6	33.9	55.5
Sargent County	340	6.4	11.0	2 110	63.6	12.9	0.0	1.1	11.1	4.8	22.5	72.8
Sheridan County	264	14.8	15.4	660	57.6	5.0	0.9	0.6	11.1	5.3	24.9	69.8
Sioux County................	235	15.7	7.3	1 144	65.5	16.7	1.0	1.2	10.0	12.4	39.2	48.4
Slope County................	325	10.9	0.0	396	50.0	6.6	0.0	0.8	10.1	0.0	23.0	77.0
Stark County	342	10.5	28.4	11 064	78.3	10.1	0.1	1.0	4.7	8.1	28.9	63.0
Steele County	271	7.7	3.3	1 056	71.0	6.4	0.0	0.8	9.0	3.0	22.5	74.4
Stutsman County..........	366	7.2	19.2	10 884	77.4	10.3	0.6	0.6	5.3	8.2	30.2	61.6
Towner County	309	12.2	19.7	1 333	64.8	11.3	0.2	1.3	9.8	5.4	27.0	67.6
Traill County	344	7.6	19.5	3 906	76.3	10.3	0.1	1.3	7.2	5.3	28.8	66.0
Walsh County................	361	10.0	14.4	5 740	75.8	12.1	0.1	1.6	5.9	6.3	29.4	64.3

STATE/ County code	MSA/PMSA/ NECMA code[1]	STATE County	Residence in 1995 (percent)						Occupied housing units		Householders 65 years and over	
			Total population 5 years and over	Same house	Same county, different house	Same state, different county	Different state	Outside the United States	Number	Percent owner-occupied	Number	Percent owner-occupied
			1	2	3	4	5	6	7	8	9	10
		NORTH DAKOTA— Cont'd										
38 101	...	Ward County	54 555	50.9	23.2	7.8	15.2	3.0	23 041	62.7	4 987	74.0
38 103	...	Wells County	4 879	70.9	16.6	6.8	5.4	0.3	2 215	76.5	889	73.8
38 105	...	Williams County	18 630	61.0	25.2	5.7	7.8	0.3	8 095	71.6	2 131	77.4
39 000	...	OHIO	10 599 968	57.5	26.3	9.5	5.6	1.1	4 445 773	69.1	991 727	78.4
39 001	...	Adams County	25 599	60.8	25.5	9.8	3.7	0.2	10 501	73.9	2 425	79.5
39 003	4320	Allen County	101 269	58.8	27.2	8.7	4.7	0.6	40 646	72.1	10 027	81.8
39 005	...	Ashland County	49 026	60.7	20.6	14.1	3.9	0.6	19 524	75.6	4 606	83.0
39 007	1680	Ashtabula County	96 005	61.8	25.5	7.5	4.7	0.5	39 397	74.1	9 687	81.0
39 009	...	Athens County	59 224	44.4	19.1	26.2	8.1	2.2	22 501	60.4	3 797	83.0
39 011	4320	Auglaize County	43 498	62.9	22.5	10.8	3.3	0.5	17 376	77.9	4 155	80.1
39 013	9000	Belmont County	66 691	67.4	20.5	6.5	5.2	0.4	28 309	75.0	8 800	80.5
39 015	1640	Brown County...............	39 307	59.1	18.1	18.5	4.1	0.2	15 555	79.5	3 179	84.3
39 017	3200	Butler County	309 892	51.0	26.0	13.4	8.5	1.1	123 082	71.6	22 935	80.9
39 019	1320	Carroll County	27 147	66.0	16.9	13.8	3.0	0.3	11 126	80.0	2 548	82.8
39 021	...	Champaign County	36 332	60.6	20.7	15.3	2.9	0.5	14 952	76.0	3 267	81.1
39 023	2000	Clark County	135 109	57.7	29.2	8.3	4.3	0.4	56 648	71.5	14 001	79.0
39 025	1640	Clermont County	164 386	54.3	22.7	14.6	7.7	0.7	66 013	74.8	10 732	79.8
39 027	...	Clinton County	37 631	53.2	26.0	15.0	4.9	0.4	15 416	68.9	3 227	76.6
39 029	9320	Columbiana County......	105 439	63.8	23.0	7.0	5.8	0.5	42 973	76.0	11 143	82.1
39 031	...	Coshocton County........	34 320	64.4	24.1	8.3	2.7	0.5	14 356	76.0	3 644	75.7
39 033	4800	Crawford County	43 933	64.0	24.2	8.0	3.2	0.6	18 957	72.5	4 805	81.7
39 035	1680	Cuyahoga County	1 303 066	59.6	29.6	4.5	4.5	1.8	571 457	63.2	145 935	73.5
39 037	...	Darke County	49 747	65.6	23.1	6.6	4.5	0.2	20 419	76.6	4 968	83.6
39 039	...	Defiance County	36 791	63.3	22.8	8.4	5.1	0.4	15 138	79.6	3 211	88.4
39 041	1840	Delaware County	101 246	46.6	14.3	28.0	10.4	0.7	39 674	80.4	5 464	85.4
39 043	...	Erie County	74 817	61.7	23.4	11.2	3.3	0.4	31 727	72.0	7 736	80.4
39 045	1040	Fairfield County	114 162	56.7	21.0	15.7	6.2	0.4	45 425	76.2	8 946	82.4
39 047	...	Fayette County	26 576	58.5	26.8	12.2	3.6	0.9	11 054	66.6	2 737	76.8
39 049	1840	Franklin County	992 062	46.4	33.1	9.6	7.9	2.9	438 778	56.9	69 296	74.3
00 051	0100	Fulton County...............	39 048	63.2	19.2	11.8	5.6	0.2	15 480	80.1	3 270	83.9
39 053	...	Gallia County...............	29 123	61.8	25.4	7.9	4.7	0.2	12 060	74.8	2 678	83.1
39 055	1680	Geauga County	84 836	67.6	13.1	14.7	4.3	0.3	31 630	87.3	6 355	89.0
39 057	2000	Greene County.............	139 268	52.9	18.3	16.3	10.7	1.8	55 312	69.6	10 872	85.0
39 059	...	Guernsey County	38 024	59.9	25.5	10.4	4.0	0.2	16 094	73.4	3 980	79.2
39 061	1640	Hamilton County	788 968	55.4	31.4	5.1	6.4	1.6	346 790	59.8	75 569	70.9
39 063	...	Hancock County...........	66 351	56.3	25.9	10.3	6.5	1.0	27 898	73.1	6 022	82.7
39 065	...	Hardin County	29 860	57.5	24.0	14.1	3.9	0.4	11 963	73.0	2 780	81.2
39 067	...	Harrison County	14 927	67.5	16.9	10.9	4.3	0.5	6 398	77.5	1 704	82.5
39 069	...	Henry County	27 257	66.7	19.8	9.7	3.4	0.4	10 935	80.5	2 755	88.5
39 071	...	Highland County	37 935	56.4	24.4	15.1	3.9	0.3	15 587	75.3	3 849	79.0
39 073	...	Hocking County	26 359	60.5	21.1	15.4	2.5	0.5	10 843	75.6	2 440	82.3
39 075	...	Holmes County	34 949	68.3	20.7	8.5	1.8	0.6	11 337	76.9	2 220	80.9
39 077	...	Huron County	55 002	58.4	26.5	10.7	3.6	0.8	22 307	72.2	5 152	80.1
39 079	...	Jackson County	30 545	59.1	26.5	9.0	4.9	0.6	12 619	73.8	2 843	81.6
39 081	8080	Jefferson County	70 040	69.3	20.3	4.7	5.2	0.5	30 417	74.3	9 243	81.9
39 083	...	Knox County.................	51 116	56.0	23.2	13.2	6.6	1.1	19 075	75.7	4 952	83.1
39 085	1680	Lake County	213 646	62.4	23.1	9.4	3.8	1.2	89 700	77.5	20 423	81.8
39 087	3400	Lawrence County	58 476	65.2	22.7	2.7	9.1	0.3	24 732	74.8	6 241	82.1
39 089	1840	Licking County	135 588	55.9	24.3	14.2	5.3	0.3	55 609	74.4	11 406	79.7
39 091	...	Logan County...............	42 848	58.6	25.9	11.7	2.9	1.0	17 956	75.6	4 301	83.4
39 093	1680	Lorain County...............	264 988	59.4	26.0	9.0	4.8	0.9	105 836	74.1	23 182	82.3
39 095	8400	Lucas County	424 043	56.6	31.1	5.3	5.9	1.2	182 847	65.3	40 641	77.2
39 097	1840	Madison County	37 674	56.2	19.3	20.0	3.4	1.0	13 672	72.3	2 886	76.5
39 099	9320	Mahoning County	242 267	64.2	24.3	6.4	4.5	0.7	102 587	72.8	30 007	78.9
39 101	...	Marion County	62 297	59.5	26.9	9.5	3.5	0.5	24 578	72.9	5 942	79.9
39 103	1680	Medina County	140 512	60.1	17.6	16.5	5.3	0.6	54 542	81.2	9 983	80.9
39 105	...	Meigs County	21 772	66.3	20.2	8.6	4.5	0.3	9 234	79.4	2 233	85.8
39 107	...	Mercer County	37 887	66.2	23.5	7.1	3.0	0.3	14 756	80.2	3 917	83.3
39 109	2000	Miami County	92 444	56.4	26.3	11.5	5.4	0.5	38 437	72.3	8 493	81.4
39 111	...	Monroe County..............	14 371	68.9	18.4	7.3	5.2	0.1	6 021	80.7	1 549	85.7
39 113	2000	Montgomery County......	522 180	54.3	30.6	7.2	6.8	1.1	229 229	64.7	51 128	77.1
39 115	...	Morgan County	13 980	62.7	19.7	13.4	4.0	0.2	5 890	78.2	1 587	84.9
39 117	...	Morrow County	29 538	59.3	16.3	20.4	3.8	0.2	11 499	82.2	2 216	84.5
39 119	...	Muskingum County	78 982	60.5	26.3	9.1	3.8	0.3	32 518	73.5	8 011	81.6
39 121	...	Noble County	13 336	60.4	13.5	21.5	4.0	0.7	4 546	79.8	1 329	80.8

[1]MSA = Metropolitan Statistical Area. PMSA = Primary MSA. NECMA = New England County Metropolitan Area. See the Appendix A for explanation of these concepts. See Appendix B for list of metropolitan areas identified by type, with component counties.

STATE County	Owner-occupied by household type (percent)								Median household income			Median monthly owner costs as a percent of income		
	Family-households				Nonfamily households									
		Married-couple family		Other family										
	Total family households	Total	With own children under 18 years	Total	With own children under 18 years	Total nonfamily households	Two or more adults	Living alone	All households	Owner-occupied households	Renter-occupied households	Median housing value (owner estimated)	With a mortgage	Without a mortgage
	11	12	13	14	15	16	17	18	19	20	21	22	23	24
NORTH DAKOTA— Cont'd														
Ward County	72.0	77.0	69.6	46.9	39.5	44.1	31.3	46.9	33 543	42 401	23 381	74 200	19.0	9.9
Wells County	85.3	86.7	84.7	72.6	63.7	59.8	76.3	58.9	31 997	36 455	19 250	40 500	19.2	9.9
Williams County	81.2	87.3	83.4	53.0	46.0	53.4	35.2	55.8	31 611	37 447	18 824	53 500	18.5	10.4
OHIO	77.8	85.6	82.5	51.7	39.3	51.1	40.3	53.1	40 846	50 093	25 116	100 500	20.6	10.6
Adams County..............	77.4	83.5	76.5	54.6	42.5	64.6	59.7	65.3	29 001	33 628	18 147	65 100	20.5	11.4
Allen County................	78.4	87.6	83.5	48.0	39.9	57.3	45.1	59.0	37 170	44 317	21 778	80 600	18.8	9.9
Ashland County............	81.6	86.1	82.5	58.2	50.3	60.0	46.5	62.1	39 080	44 453	25 193	97 800	20.1	10.7
Ashtabula County.........	80.0	85.8	80.9	58.1	44.5	59.7	48.1	61.8	35 984	41 624	22 810	85 100	20.9	11.2
Athens County.............	78.5	83.5	80.6	60.4	53.1	37.0	15.5	48.5	27 174	38 197	13 722	75 800	20.2	9.9
Auglaize County...........	83.7	88.2	86.2	59.8	49.1	61.8	46.4	63.8	43 419	48 294	30 285	91 700	18.7	9.9
Belmont County............	81.1	88.1	82.8	56.0	39.7	61.9	55.4	62.6	29 495	34 344	16 678	63 300	19.0	10.3
Brown County...............	83.3	86.8	83.5	68.9	61.8	67.8	73.6	66.6	38 104	42 328	22 464	87 600	20.6	9.9
Butler County	79.9	86.3	84.0	53.6	40.8	50.5	33.3	54.7	47 702	58 388	28 360	119 200	20.4	10.1
Carroll County	83.4	87.4	82.7	61.5	47.9	70.7	56.1	73.1	35 787	39 944	21 117	88 500	20.4	9.9
Champaign County	81.3	86.1	80.4	58.5	52.1	61.8	57.2	62.6	42 843	48 636	27 193	94 800	20.6	10.6
Clark County	77.2	85.4	78.5	50.5	37.7	58.4	48.4	60.1	39 829	47 364	23 681	88 300	19.7	10.1
Clermont County	81.9	87.1	84.5	57.4	47.0	53.9	49.8	54.8	49 195	57 753	29 187	116 600	21.0	10.2
Clinton County.............	76.4	82.8	76.2	49.4	41.3	49.8	38.0	52.0	40 523	48 937	26 098	95 900	21.0	9.9
Columbiana County......	81.7	87.0	83.1	59.5	46.6	61.5	59.5	61.7	34 045	39 066	20 831	78 300	20.3	10.7
Coshocton County........	81.6	85.5	81.3	61.2	53.7	62.2	59.9	62.5	34 569	39 882	21 746	77 100	19.5	9.9
Crawford County	77.8	84.2	78.5	54.0	40.7	60.4	54.5	61.3	35 833	41 426	23 081	78 700	18.7	9.9
Cuyahoga County	72.9	83.6	81.6	49.3	34.2	47.2	41.0	48.1	38 943	50 607	24 144	110 100	22.1	12.4
Darke County	81.8	86.7	81.2	57.0	44.0	62.2	52.9	63.4	39 324	44 092	26 196	93 800	19.1	9.9
Defiance County...........	85.3	90.3	85.9	63.4	56.7	64.4	56.4	65.8	44 644	48 235	28 920	85 400	19.1	9.9
Delaware County..........	87.2	91.1	90.5	58.4	50.4	57.1	46.9	59.7	67 046	76 966	34 719	188 000	20.9	9.9
Erie County	79.6	87.2	82.6	50.5	37.8	55.0	45.6	56.4	42 362	50 658	25 829	107 400	20.2	10.3
Fairfield County	81.7	86.8	84.0	55.0	44.2	59.2	45.8	61.7	47 824	55 920	28 434	129 300	21.0	9.9
Fayette County	71.8	79.0	70.0	44.0	33.9	54.0	43.9	55.8	36 289	42 923	25 886	87 000	20.5	10.5
Franklin County	68.7	79.0	76.6	42.4	33.1	38.9	27.7	42.2	42 520	57 375	28 409	113 700	21.2	10.9
Fulton County..............	85.4	88.0	84.8	70.1	62.7	63.3	45.2	65.7	44 297	49 441	29 943	104 000	20.9	9.9
Gallia County..............	80.1	86.0	80.5	56.5	47.0	61.9	56.3	62.7	30 060	35 231	15 933	68 200	19.4	11.9
Geauga County	91.5	94.0	92.4	74.1	63.1	71.5	61.1	73.5	60 187	65 096	33 879	179 000	21.5	10.9
Greene County............	77.8	84.1	77.3	49.3	37.5	49.8	30.9	54.8	48 232	59 576	27 694	121 900	20.5	9.9
Guernsey County	79.6	86.8	82.2	55.2	45.7	58.8	50.6	60.1	30 211	35 594	19 055	66 200	19.6	10.4
Hamilton County...........	72.2	83.7	83.0	43.4	30.9	40.1	31.1	41.7	40 882	56 452	24 095	109 000	20.7	11.2
Hancock County	81.4	87.1	83.9	54.9	44.8	54.7	38.2	57.8	43 813	51 064	26 528	97 500	18.6	9.9
Hardin County..............	80.3	85.7	81.5	57.4	42.0	57.0	34.6	61.1	34 770	40 573	20 078	73 500	19.3	10.1
Harrison County............	82.5	87.2	83.0	56.9	43.8	65.2	56.6	66.5	30 895	34 625	18 426	58 500	18.6	9.9
Henry County	84.6	89.0	83.7	59.6	49.1	69.6	64.7	70.3	41 921	46 264	27 727	85 400	19.1	10.5
Highland County...........	80.5	86.3	81.6	56.1	44.2	60.8	59.6	60.9	35 184	39 963	22 178	83 000	20.1	10.2
Hocking County............	80.0	84.6	77.1	57.3	49.9	63.9	70.0	63.0	34 237	40 281	19 428	81 400	19.9	10.1
Holmes County............	80.8	83.6	82.6	61.4	50.3	60.0	49.2	61.7	37 065	41 236	27 754	114 800	22.2	9.9
Huron County	78.9	84.8	79.6	55.3	44.6	54.1	37.5	57.0	40 410	46 482	26 723	93 800	19.7	10.0
Jackson County...........	77.8	84.3	79.2	57.9	43.4	63.1	66.8	62.6	30 253	35 261	17 938	65 500	21.0	11.5
Jefferson County	80.5	87.6	81.9	55.7	39.6	61.1	53.8	61.9	30 639	36 297	18 150	62 600	19.1	9.9
Knox County................	81.5	87.2	81.5	52.8	39.7	60.5	48.9	62.2	38 719	44 433	24 317	94 900	20.7	10.5
Lake County................	84.7	89.3	86.8	65.5	51.4	60.7	52.9	62.1	48 624	54 869	31 263	125 400	21.7	11.1
Lawrence County	78.8	84.2	77.6	60.2	47.0	64.5	58.3	65.2	28 766	33 375	17 162	64 500	20.1	10.4
Licking County.............	81.0	87.0	83.9	55.0	44.3	57.4	53.4	58.2	43 940	51 713	25 725	110 700	20.6	9.9
Logan County..............	79.7	85.6	81.8	54.8	45.4	65.7	61.5	66.4	41 224	46 916	26 563	86 600	19.1	10.9
Lorain County..............	80.4	88.4	84.5	52.9	36.4	57.8	46.6	59.8	44 870	53 087	24 945	113 800	21.1	10.6
Lucas County	74.7	85.2	82.2	48.9	36.8	48.8	39.6	50.7	37 563	48 910	22 052	88 500	19.9	11.6
Madison County...........	78.6	83.7	77.1	55.0	45.7	54.8	44.7	56.6	44 617	50 873	30 500	100 400	21.4	11.3
Mahoning County	80.7	88.9	86.0	57.7	42.8	56.5	48.3	57.5	35 235	42 627	20 036	79 900	20.5	11.6
Marion County	78.8	85.0	78.8	56.3	47.2	58.8	56.2	59.2	38 686	44 406	24 103	77 000	19.4	10.6
Medina County	87.1	90.9	89.9	63.8	50.3	61.0	56.9	61.7	55 234	61 489	29 994	145 500	21.8	10.0
Meigs County	82.6	87.8	82.4	61.6	52.1	71.6	63.2	72.8	27 379	30 574	16 468	55 100	21.6	9.9
Mercer County.............	85.4	89.1	88.6	60.6	48.4	64.6	56.5	65.5	42 336	47 056	24 642	93 500	19.7	9.9
Miami County	78.5	84.7	79.0	51.7	40.0	55.6	44.3	57.5	44 099	51 445	28 332	112 300	20.2	9.9
Monroe County............	86.0	90.1	86.6	63.4	45.8	66.1	60.0	66.9	30 654	34 948	16 290	61 500	18.9	9.9
Montgomery County......	73.3	82.8	78.4	47.5	35.1	49.2	37.2	51.4	40 089	50 918	25 285	94 800	20.9	11.4
Morgan County............	81.1	86.0	80.1	59.4	43.2	71.0	70.1	71.2	29 467	33 880	16 417	66 800	18.8	9.9
Morrow County............	86.2	89.4	84.7	61.4	64.2	68.0	58.6	69.5	41 030	44 641	25 346	97 100	21.6	11.0
Muskingum County	79.4	86.8	82.4	52.2	39.7	59.5	56.9	60.0	35 096	40 972	21 444	81 400	19.2	10.1
Noble County	84.7	89.4	87.0	58.5	45.2	66.5	62.5	66.9	32 403	36 740	19 477	66 300	18.8	10.3

Table C-3. States and Counties — **Migration, Housing, and Transportation**

STATE County	Percent who pay 35 percent or more of income for housing expenses			Means of transportation to work (percent except where noted)						Vehicles available (percent of households)		
	Median gross rent	Owners	Renters	Number of workers 16 years and over	Car, truck, or van		Public transportation	Other means	Walked	No vehicles	One vehicle	Two or more vehicles
					Drove alone	Carpooled						
	25	26	27	28	29	30	31	32	33	34	35	36
NORTH DAKOTA— Cont'd												
Ward County	408	9.9	22.0	29 818	81.7	10.6	0.5	0.4	2.8	6.7	29.8	63.5
Wells County	267	12.2	19.9	2 125	68.7	7.8	0.8	0.8	9.8	5.8	28.6	65.6
Williams County	331	10.4	18.8	9 481	79.5	10.2	0.1	1.3	4.3	6.5	30.6	63.0
OHIO	515	13.2	27.4	5 307 502	82.8	9.3	2.1	0.7	2.4	8.6	33.5	58.0
Adams County.............	381	14.5	23.1	11 133	75.9	14.5	0.8	1.1	3.0	8.7	29.6	61.7
Allen County................	446	11.2	27.4	47 096	84.9	9.3	0.8	0.7	2.2	7.6	32.9	59.5
Ashland County............	471	11.6	22.5	24 737	82.6	8.3	0.5	0.8	4.0	6.8	28.4	64.8
Ashtabula County.........	473	13.5	25.2	45 689	81.0	12.5	1.0	1.0	2.2	7.4	32.3	60.3
Athens County..............	469	12.9	45.8	25 586	70.0	9.5	0.6	1.4	14.5	8.5	34.1	57.4
Auglaize County...........	457	7.8	20.1	23 282	84.5	7.3	0.4	1.3	3.0	4.1	28.7	67.3
Belmont County............	362	10.9	24.4	27 889	84.1	9.5	0.7	0.6	2.3	10.0	33.3	56.7
Brown County,.............	433	12.8	22.1	18 691	79.0	14.9	0.4	0.8	1.6	5.6	23.7	70.7
Butler County	569	11.6	28.1	160 314	84.2	9.1	0.9	0.6	2.6	6.1	29.4	64.5
Carroll County	411	10.9	23.0	12 882	83.7	9.4	0.6	0.5	2.3	4.8	26.1	69.1
Champaign County	469	12.0	19.3	18 905	82.3	12.2	0.1	0.6	2.2	6.1	28.0	65.9
Clark County	487	12.5	27.3	65 887	82.6	11.3	1.1	0.8	2.2	7.7	34.0	58.3
Clermont County	552	12.6	25.0	88 372	84.5	9.9	1.1	0.7	1.0	4.9	25.9	69.2
Clinton County	494	12.9	23.2	19 949	81.9	10.5	0.5	0.5	3.2	6.9	29.2	63.9
Columbiana County.......	421	11.8	23.6	49 461	83.5	9.4	0.6	0.6	2.7	6.9	31.3	61.7
Coshocton County........	385	9.7	18.6	16 585	79.2	12.2	1.1	1.1	2.7	9.3	27.7	63.0
Crawford County	418	10.8	22.9	21 442	83.2	10.3	0.2	1.2	2.7	7.0	31.8	61.2
Cuyahoga County	541	16.7	30.5	622 876	78.8	9.1	6.2	0.8	2.5	13.7	40.0	46.3
Darke County	447	10.6	22.7	25 303	83.6	9.1	0.3	0.8	2.2	4.8	27.7	67.5
Defiance County	472	10.0	19.4	19 540	84.6	9.8	0.3	0.8	2.2	4.1	28.5	67.3
Delaware County...........	639	12.5	22.5	57 840	86.1	7.0	0.3	0.6	1.4	2.9	21.6	75.5
Erie County	498	12.8	24.2	37 016	88.1	7.1	0.5	0.6	1.5	6.2	33.2	60.7
Fairfield County	550	12.5	22.4	60 465	85.4	9.1	0.4	0.4	1.4	4.7	25.6	69.7
Fayette County..............	489	11.2	22.8	13 433	81.3	12.4	0.5	0.8	1.7	6.7	31.8	61.5
Franklin County............	595	14.3	28.0	548 655	80.9	9.9	3.1	0.8	2.7	8.6	38.4	53.0
Fulton County	484	11.6	18.4	20 855	84.7	0.0	0.0	0.7	2.1	4.1	24.7	71.2
Gallia County................	391	12.4	30.9	11 813	84.0	9.8	0.5	0.6	3.0	8.3	30.1	61.6
Geauga County	592	15.9	22.4	44 499	82.3	9.5	1.0	0.6	1.2	6.9	20.9	72.2
Greene County	587	12.1	28.7	72 958	84.4	8.3	0.3	0.6	3.5	5.2	28.8	66.0
Guernsey County	385	12.8	25.1	16 644	81.0	11.1	0.8	1.0	2.8	7.9	31.1	61.1
Hamilton County...........	485	14.0	28.8	398 465	78.9	9.7	5.0	0.7	2.9	13.5	36.9	49.6
Hancock County...........	487	8.8	22.5	35 845	84.3	8.4	0.7	0.8	2.7	4.7	31.3	64.0
Hardin County	405	9.9	28.0	14 390	76.9	10.9	0.5	0.7	6.8	7.3	30.9	61.8
Harrison County	385	10.1	27.7	6 585	80.9	11.8	0.5	0.4	3.3	5.6	28.3	66.1
Henry County	480	8.3	21.6	13 911	84.9	9.2	0.4	0.5	1.9	3.7	28.5	67.8
Highland County...........	434	13.3	20.6	17 662	79.1	13.9	0.3	0.4	1.9	6.8	28.8	64.4
Hocking County............	386	11.5	25.8	11 829	80.6	13.9	0.4	0.7	1.9	7.8	26.6	65.6
Holmes County.............	422	12.1	13.9	16 456	53.7	21.9	1.5	3.6	6.7	31.2	18.4	50.5
Huron County	474	11.2	22.3	27 571	84.9	8.6	0.6	0.9	2.3	5.6	30.4	64.0
Jackson County............	408	16.9	29.5	13 026	83.4	11.2	0.4	0.3	1.8	8.8	28.9	62.3
Jefferson County	378	11.1	25.2	28 793	84.8	8.5	0.3	0.5	3.6	10.6	33.7	55.7
Knox County	446	12.2	21.7	25 064	77.5	11.3	0.7	1.0	4.9	6.0	29.8	64.3
Lake County	623	13.5	26.4	116 830	87.4	7.7	0.9	0.5	1.3	4.8	32.0	63.3
Lawrence County	421	13.8	29.6	23 136	86.7	8.8	0.6	0.7	1.4	8.5	33.6	57.9
Licking County..............	504	12.6	24.7	71 213	83.5	9.9	0.5	0.6	2.2	6.1	28.0	65.9
Logan County...............	489	11.4	21.5	21 962	82.0	10.7	0.2	1.0	2.1	5.6	30.7	63.8
Lorain County...............	518	13.7	27.2	132 895	84.4	9.3	0.8	0.8	2.4	6.6	31.4	62.0
Lucas County	484	13.6	29.8	207 585	84.5	9.2	1.8	0.7	1.9	9.7	38.9	51.5
Madison County	510	11.0	20.1	17 828	83.5	10.0	0.3	1.0	1.8	6.2	27.3	66.4
Mahoning County	446	13.9	28.7	109 102	86.6	8.4	0.9	0.6	1.5	9.6	35.8	54.6
Marion County..............	500	11.1	27.1	29 138	83.6	10.9	0.8	0.9	1.6	9.0	32.1	58.9
Medina County	625	13.8	24.5	76 548	87.0	7.0	0.7	0.7	1.0	4.0	23.8	72.2
Meigs County,..............	351	15.5	22.7	8 752	80.8	11.7	0.7	1.6	1.6	9.2	26.7	64.1
Mercer County..............	433	10.1	21.7	19 742	83.2	9.3	0.1	0.5	2.4	3.3	27.0	69.7
Miami County	522	11.2	23.5	49 799	86.4	8.0	0.5	0.7	1.6	5.0	29.3	65.7
Monroe County.............	352	9.5	24.8	5 768	77.2	13.1	1.6	0.7	3.0	7.6	25.8	66.6
Montgomery County......	525	14.5	27.9	259 419	83.7	8.6	2.7	0.6	2.2	9.8	36.7	53.5
Morgan County.............	347	10.2	24.7	5 858	77.4	12.2	0.2	1.3	2.1	6.8	27.4	65.8
Morrow County.............	455	12.3	22.8	15 083	82.2	11.6	0.3	0.6	1.6	4.3	22.8	72.9
Muskingum County	406	12.3	25.5	37 774	81.4	12.0	0.7	0.6	2.9	7.4	31.1	61.4
Noble County	368	11.5	23.1	5 028	80.5	10.6	0.8	1.2	2.8	7.9	24.8	67.2

Table C-3. States and Counties — Migration, Housing, and Transportation

STATE/ County code	MSA/PMSA/ NECMA code[1]	STATE County	Total population 5 years and over	Residence in 1995 (percent)					Occupied housing units		Householders 65 years and over	
				Same house	Same county, different house	Same state, different county	Different state	Outside the United States	Number	Percent owner-occupied	Number	Percent owner-occupied
			1	2	3	4	5	6	7	8	9	10
		OHIO—Cont'd										
39 123	...	Ottawa County	38 851	64.1	18.5	13.5	3.6	0.3	16 474	80.7	4 525	87.4
39 125	...	Paulding County	18 959	66.9	19.3	8.7	4.6	0.5	7 773	83.9	1 646	88.3
39 127	...	Perry County	31 571	65.0	19.8	13.1	1.9	0.2	12 500	79.4	2 843	82.6
39 129	1840	Pickaway County..........	49 601	57.5	17.8	20.6	3.4	0.8	17 599	74.6	3 915	78.4
39 131	...	Pike County	25 830	57.6	25.0	13.5	3.5	0.4	10 444	70.1	2 383	69.8
39 133	0080	Portage County	142 803	55.6	20.3	18.0	5.1	0.9	56 449	71.3	10 900	81.9
39 135	...	Preble County	39 644	61.0	22.8	11.6	4.5	0.2	16 001	78.9	3 643	83.9
39 137	...	Putnam County	32 195	71.8	19.2	7.0	1.8	0.2	12 200	84.1	3 058	87.3
39 139	4800	Richland County	120 597	59.4	26.7	8.8	4.6	0.5	49 534	71.6	12 033	78.9
39 141	...	Ross County	68 826	58.1	26.5	10.3	4.4	0.7	27 136	73.5	6 072	80.5
39 143	...	Sandusky County	57 716	63.6	23.5	9.2	3.2	0.5	23 717	75.3	5 797	81.5
39 145	...	Scioto County	74 199	62.3	26.6	6.4	4.3	0.4	30 871	70.1	7 941	74.1
39 147	...	Seneca County	55 050	62.6	23.6	10.1	3.3	0.4	22 292	75.1	5 456	83.6
39 149	...	Shelby County	44 330	59.8	25.6	9.7	4.2	0.8	17 636	74.4	3 827	80.2
39 151	1320	Stark County	354 010	61.8	26.9	6.7	4.1	0.5	148 316	72.4	36 602	79.0
39 153	0080	Summit County	506 987	58.4	26.4	9.2	5.0	1.0	217 788	70.2	50 267	79.7
39 155	9320	Trumbull County	211 361	64.1	25.3	5.9	4.2	0.4	89 020	74.3	23 308	81.3
39 157	...	Tuscarawas County	84 907	62.3	25.4	8.9	3.1	0.4	35 653	75.0	8 873	81.3
39 159	...	Union County	37 821	51.8	19.9	21.1	6.7	0.4	14 346	77.5	2 473	80.2
39 161	...	Van Wert County	27 769	64.5	21.8	8.6	4.6	0.4	11 587	81.7	2 914	88.0
39 163	...	Vinton County	11 872	62.7	17.4	17.1	2.7	0.1	4 892	77.8	1 116	82.3
39 165	1640	Warren County	145 961	48.9	18.6	22.1	9.4	1.0	55 966	78.5	9 319	78.7
39 167	6020	Washington County.......	59 540	64.3	21.7	5.5	8.3	0.3	25 137	76.2	6 299	83.2
39 169	...	Wayne County	103 735	60.1	24.3	10.4	4.4	0.9	40 445	73.3	8 666	82.7
39 171	...	Williams County	36 702	59.2	25.6	8.1	6.7	0.4	15 105	76.8	3 415	83.2
39 173	8400	Wood County	114 025	53.4	18.4	20.5	6.6	1.1	45 172	70.6	8 842	80.8
39 175	...	Wyandot County	21 394	64.6	21.7	10.8	2.6	0.3	8 882	74.7	2 161	84.0
40 000	...	OKLAHOMA	3 215 719	51.3	25.1	11.8	10.0	1.7	1 342 293	68.4	302 848	82.7
40 001	...	Adair County	19 439	60.2	24.8	6.7	7.8	0.6	7 471	73.3	1 821	82.3
40 003	...	Alfalfa County	5 837	63.3	12.5	16.4	7.0	0.7	2 199	81.7	795	89.1
40 005	...	Atoka County	13 070	58.2	18.3	14.8	8.4	0.3	4 964	76.4	1 434	80.2
40 007	...	Beaver County	5 521	64.0	12.8	8.3	12.6	2.4	2 245	79.1	671	92.3
40 009	...	Beckham County	18 534	49.6	26.1	11.0	12.4	0.9	7 356	71.1	2 053	83.1
40 011	...	Blaine County	11 275	55.8	19.7	14.5	8.7	1.2	4 159	76.9	1 291	88.8
40 013	...	Bryan County	34 271	52.0	26.1	9.1	11.9	0.8	14 422	69.3	3 761	81.9
40 015	...	Caddo County	28 189	58.0	21.7	12.0	7.2	1.1	10 957	73.5	3 144	85.4
40 017	5880	Canadian County	81 771	53.1	20.4	17.5	8.0	1.0	31 484	78.9	5 206	82.9
40 019	...	Carter County	42 515	55.3	27.7	8.9	7.7	0.5	17 992	71.1	4 825	82.4
40 021	...	Cherokee County	39 641	51.4	22.2	16.9	8.1	1.3	16 175	66.8	3 713	78.5
40 023	...	Choctaw County	14 354	59.7	23.0	8.5	8.4	0.4	6 220	70.9	1 829	79.6
40 025	...	Cimarron County	2 936	63.8	15.4	6.2	10.7	3.9	1 257	72.6	407	84.0
40 027	5880	Cleveland County	194 674	45.9	23.1	18.3	10.6	2.1	79 186	67.0	11 500	81.5
40 029	...	Coal County	5 639	62.6	17.7	11.8	7.6	0.3	2 373	75.3	731	80.4
40 031	4200	Comanche County	106 069	42.6	24.2	6.3	23.0	3.9	39 808	60.3	7 243	83.2
40 033	...	Cotton County	6 179	60.1	16.8	12.2	10.1	0.9	2 614	76.4	757	83.2
40 035	...	Craig County	14 079	56.1	21.6	14.4	7.6	0.3	5 620	74.9	1 614	80.2
40 037	8560	Creek County	62 822	58.3	21.0	14.5	5.9	0.2	25 289	78.0	5 714	84.4
40 039	...	Custer County	24 588	50.0	23.8	18.3	6.8	1.1	10 136	63.7	2 319	81.8
40 041	...	Delaware County	34 813	52.0	17.1	15.3	14.9	0.7	14 838	79.2	4 286	87.4
40 043	...	Dewey County	4 508	66.2	14.5	14.6	4.1	0.6	1 962	79.0	649	87.7
40 045	...	Ellis County	3 871	67.6	13.8	11.1	7.4	0.1	1 769	80.7	567	89.8
40 047	2340	Garfield County	53 944	51.7	27.7	8.1	11.2	1.4	23 175	70.2	5 966	84.1
40 049	...	Garvin County	25 484	56.4	24.0	11.0	7.9	0.7	10 865	73.9	3 280	83.9
40 051	...	Grady County	42 476	56.6	21.5	15.8	5.5	0.5	17 341	75.7	4 142	85.5
40 053	...	Grant County	4 869	62.3	17.6	13.3	6.3	0.5	2 089	78.8	716	88.5
40 055	...	Greer County	5 780	55.5	18.4	17.4	7.7	1.0	2 237	74.8	821	83.3
40 057	...	Harmon County	3 117	62.1	18.7	10.3	8.3	0.6	1 266	77.2	422	91.5
40 059	...	Harper County	3 401	63.4	15.5	10.4	9.4	1.2	1 509	78.7	489	89.2
40 061	...	Haskell County	11 001	56.6	22.9	12.6	7.6	0.3	4 624	77.3	1 318	83.8
40 063	...	Hughes County	13 334	57.4	19.0	15.2	7.8	0.6	5 319	75.8	1 780	84.0
40 065	...	Jackson County	26 053	44.2	23.7	8.7	20.6	2.8	10 590	60.3	2 307	80.3
40 067	...	Jefferson County	6 401	58.5	19.2	10.9	10.4	1.1	2 716	74.1	869	80.2
40 069	...	Johnston County	9 849	56.5	21.7	13.4	8.1	0.3	4 057	73.7	1 119	84.2
40 071	...	Kay County	44 704	55.7	24.7	8.8	9.7	1.1	19 157	71.7	5 291	84.7
40 073	...	Kingfisher County..........	13 066	60.9	21.8	12.2	4.0	1.2	5 247	78.2	1 457	87.3

[1]MSA = Metropolitan Statistical Area. PMSA = Primary MSA. NECMA = New England County Metropolitan Area. See the Appendix A for explanation of these concepts. See Appendix B for list of metropolitan areas identified by type, with component counties.

STATE County	Total family households	Married-couple family Total	Married-couple family With own children under 18 years	Other family Total	Other family With own children under 18 years	Total nonfamily households	Two or more adults	Living alone	All households	Owner-occupied households	Renter-occupied households	Median housing value (owner estimated)	With a mortgage	Without a mortgage
	11	12	13	14	15	16	17	18	19	20	21	22	23	24
OHIO—Cont'd														
Ottawa County	84.9	89.5	86.0	63.1	54.0	70.0	57.0	71.8	44 238	48 324	30 284	109 200	19.9	10.1
Paulding County	87.9	90.9	85.0	73.9	66.0	72.9	63.6	74.4	40 608	43 227	26 920	72 500	18.1	9.9
Perry County	82.9	87.1	81.5	63.7	52.2	68.7	70.6	68.4	34 521	38 418	22 460	71 700	19.2	9.9
Pickaway County	79.4	84.7	79.0	55.7	43.6	59.7	59.4	59.8	42 494	49 757	25 499	105 500	20.7	9.9
Pike County	74.8	81.3	78.9	52.2	44.9	57.3	42.6	59.9	31 905	37 779	20 706	68 700	18.5	9.9
Portage County	81.4	87.7	86.4	55.9	44.1	48.0	32.6	52.7	43 980	52 669	25 285	118 300	20.9	10.0
Preble County	83.1	87.2	83.1	61.5	51.2	65.7	60.4	66.6	42 100	46 797	27 121	96 800	20.4	9.9
Putnam County	89.0	91.5	90.6	73.5	65.6	68.0	61.8	68.6	46 118	50 102	29 683	91 300	18.3	9.9
Richland County	79.1	86.1	80.5	52.4	40.4	54.6	47.7	55.7	37 431	44 458	23 571	87 900	19.9	10.1
Ross County	79.3	84.9	80.7	58.2	45.5	59.5	54.2	60.4	36 859	42 298	22 824	81 600	19.3	9.9
Sandusky County	80.8	86.8	82.7	58.4	45.1	61.4	48.4	63.7	40 661	46 560	27 493	88 900	19.0	9.9
Scioto County	77.0	84.2	79.0	53.6	45.6	54.5	46.5	55.6	27 887	33 665	16 446	59 900	19.7	10.4
Seneca County	81.2	86.6	83.7	60.1	51.6	60.3	42.7	63.6	37 976	42 419	25 174	81 100	18.6	9.9
Shelby County	80.2	80.0	82.0	52.5	00.8	57.7	16.8	59.5	44 486	51 150	29 463	97 900	19.2	9.9
Stark County	80.1	87.1	84.0	54.1	41.1	54.8	49.3	55.8	39 927	47 041	24 611	100 000	20.0	9.9
Summit County	79.0	86.9	84.9	53.4	39.7	52.8	42.9	54.8	42 173	51 807	24 670	108 000	21.0	11.2
Trumbull County	80.7	87.4	82.8	58.1	40.8	59.5	53.2	60.3	38 328	44 758	23 133	84 400	18.9	9.9
Tuscarawas County	80.7	85.8	81.4	57.9	50.1	60.8	56.3	61.5	35 471	40 173	23 405	86 000	20.3	9.9
Union County	83.9	88.7	85.4	54.3	44.9	57.4	58.8	57.0	51 862	58 343	29 459	126 200	20.8	10.9
Van Wert County	86.4	91.0	89.4	64.0	50.8	69.1	50.6	71.1	39 193	43 211	26 998	74 700	18.4	9.9
Vinton County	82.4	87.0	82.8	66.4	58.4	65.4	64.4	65.6	29 112	33 139	14 985	60 300	19.1	9.9
Warren County	84.4	88.6	87.9	58.4	50.3	58.3	48.4	60.2	57 699	65 293	33 303	142 500	20.2	10.1
Washington County	82.1	87.9	83.6	55.3	45.7	62.3	54.8	63.6	34 175	40 679	20 000	76 200	19.0	9.9
Wayne County	80.5	85.3	82.3	55.6	41.8	53.4	47.5	54.5	41 582	48 000	26 364	104 900	20.1	9.9
Williams County	83.5	88.7	84.2	59.4	54.1	60.2	55.5	60.9	40 612	45 582	26 250	84 600	19.3	9.9
Wood County	83.6	88.5	86.9	61.0	51.9	45.1	21.8	52.4	44 431	54 689	24 778	111 200	19.7	10.2
Wyandot County	79.4	84.3	80.6	53.7	42.3	63.1	48.2	64.9	39 013	43 607	28 002	81 900	17.9	9.9
OKLAHOMA	74.9	81.5	75.3	51.0	40.7	54.0	37.0	56.8	33 243	40 387	21 807	67 700	19.2	9.9
Adair County	75.5	79.8	71.3	60.9	51.1	66.8	58.1	67.5	24 981	27 929	18 813	46 900	21.6	11.4
Alfalfa County	84.8	87.1	79.0	70.3	60.2	75.1	65.6	75.5	30 101	31 262	23 417	31 300	18.6	9.9
Atoka County	82.0	88.0	84.2	58.0	48.6	62.8	58.0	63.2	24 500	26 889	14 283	50 100	19.1	12.4
Beaver County	79.8	81.7	72.7	68.6	55.8	76.9	54.5	78.4	36 544	38 975	28 009	50 000	10.0	0.0
Beckham County	75.3	81.8	75.9	46.6	36.6	62.2	38.5	64.9	27 692	32 307	18 353	51 600	17.8	9.9
Blaine County	79.4	82.7	76.6	63.1	47.5	71.0	53.8	71.7	28 784	32 810	19 740	41 800	17.9	10.5
Bryan County	75.6	81.5	72.0	53.3	42.0	55.2	27.8	59.6	27 825	33 112	18 875	54 000	19.0	9.9
Caddo County	75.6	80.6	73.2	59.3	46.9	67.9	53.8	69.2	27 320	30 882	18 741	44 800	18.6	10.0
Canadian County	83.7	87.5	84.8	65.8	57.7	62.5	54.8	63.8	45 293	50 408	26 020	86 000	18.6	9.9
Carter County	76.3	83.1	76.2	51.8	44.0	58.7	44.9	60.0	29 065	34 398	19 797	56 000	19.2	10.4
Cherokee County	74.1	80.0	74.9	54.7	44.5	50.5	27.3	55.7	26 428	32 440	16 602	62 500	19.9	9.9
Choctaw County	74.7	82.3	72.3	51.9	37.3	62.2	50.0	63.3	23 022	27 290	15 072	44 000	18.4	9.9
Cimarron County	76.1	79.7	68.5	52.6	47.5	64.6	68.8	64.4	30 575	34 194	19 770	41 200	15.1	9.9
Cleveland County	77.5	83.2	81.2	53.7	47.5	44.4	25.3	50.2	41 564	51 733	23 620	86 000	19.2	9.9
Coal County	79.2	82.9	74.5	64.1	48.0	66.5	70.7	66.1	23 398	26 238	14 853	40 000	19.7	11.0
Comanche County	64.6	72.3	61.5	40.5	28.6	48.9	33.4	51.5	33 883	42 268	23 674	70 500	19.7	9.9
Cotton County	80.1	85.0	77.1	58.2	45.8	67.4	74.5	66.9	27 259	31 867	15 071	50 300	18.1	11.3
Craig County	79.3	83.9	77.3	57.4	43.6	64.6	50.3	66.0	30 743	33 365	20 701	58 000	19.2	9.9
Creek County	81.5	84.9	79.8	67.9	59.9	67.5	66.4	67.6	33 231	37 075	22 132	63 200	19.2	9.9
Custer County	72.3	78.6	75.8	50.0	41.1	47.5	26.0	53.0	28 613	38 525	17 520	65 200	19.0	9.9
Delaware County	81.6	85.7	76.9	61.2	52.5	72.8	61.8	74.4	27 723	30 339	20 343	67 200	22.7	10.7
Dewey County	82.6	85.4	79.2	59.3	43.5	71.3	52.8	72.5	27 917	29 254	23 194	42 800	18.0	11.0
Ellis County	81.1	84.8	77.6	55.5	43.0	79.8	83.9	79.5	27 944	30 019	21 806	37 700	17.5	10.3
Garfield County	75.4	80.2	72.7	54.1	42.5	59.0	42.9	61.4	32 917	37 437	23 123	59 100	18.9	9.9
Garvin County	77.2	80.5	70.8	63.1	52.4	65.9	55.9	67.0	28 022	32 050	19 410	48 000	18.9	11.0
Grady County	79.6	85.4	80.0	54.2	42.6	64.3	55.2	65.5	32 685	37 890	20 108	61 400	18.9	9.9
Grant County	80.9	83.8	83.0	62.6	55.0	73.9	50.0	75.4	29 047	31 292	22 287	40 000	19.2	9.9
Greer County	80.5	86.5	77.9	56.7	39.4	64.6	48.0	65.7	25 707	28 926	14 307	33 700	17.7	11.2
Harmon County	79.3	84.8	77.3	54.7	33.7	72.3	26.7	74.2	22 617	25 458	14 141	29 700	17.5	11.6
Harper County	83.1	84.8	75.5	71.9	59.7	69.6	40.0	72.3	33 278	36 944	25 433	40 800	14.0	9.9
Haskell County	79.4	83.7	78.4	59.7	51.2	71.4	86.4	70.7	24 402	27 614	17 721	46 900	18.4	10.5
Hughes County	78.6	84.9	78.1	54.6	40.9	69.5	67.2	69.7	22 637	25 904	15 888	38 500	20.8	11.6
Jackson County	63.0	68.6	53.0	39.5	31.0	53.4	30.6	56.6	30 230	37 174	24 176	58 900	19.5	11.5
Jefferson County	79.3	83.6	73.3	53.4	44.6	62.7	57.8	63.1	23 952	26 648	16 114	34 700	19.0	12.2
Johnston County	76.4	81.5	72.0	56.9	41.8	66.8	40.2	70.1	24 362	27 500	17 220	43 800	18.4	11.0
Kay County	77.1	82.9	73.0	54.0	41.4	60.1	40.5	62.7	30 619	36 652	20 356	53 900	18.4	10.4
Kingfisher County	81.6	85.0	77.8	64.2	54.2	68.2	45.1	70.3	36 550	40 750	23 278	64 400	17.7	9.9

STATE County	Percent who pay 35 percent or more of income for housing expenses			Means of transportation to work (percent except where noted)						Vehicles available (percent of households)		
					Car, truck, or van							
	Median gross rent	Owners	Renters	Number of workers 16 years and over	Drove alone	Carpooled	Public transportation	Other means	Walked	No vehicles	One vehicle	Two or more vehicles
	25	26	27	28	29	30	31	32	33	34	35	36
OHIO—Cont'd												
Ottawa County	496	12.2	22.0	19 434	85.3	8.0	0.4	0.7	2.4	4.1	30.4	65.4
Paulding County	393	8.3	17.5	9 640	84.1	9.7	0.6	0.6	2.5	4.7	24.9	70.3
Perry County	415	12.9	17.8	14 385	78.9	14.8	0.8	0.9	2.0	7.4	26.5	66.1
Pickaway County	494	12.1	27.6	21 921	84.2	10.7	0.3	0.5	1.8	4.9	26.2	68.9
Pike County	424	13.4	28.3	10 208	80.7	13.8	0.4	0.9	2.3	8.3	29.0	62.7
Portage County	544	12.6	30.5	78 023	84.0	8.5	0.6	0.6	3.6	5.0	28.6	66.4
Preble County	492	10.1	21.1	20 226	83.5	10.7	0.3	0.6	1.8	4.5	23.9	71.5
Putnam County	446	8.3	16.7	16 905	84.1	10.1	0.4	0.6	2.1	3.9	23.9	72.2
Richland County	451	11.9	24.8	57 131	84.7	9.3	0.7	0.7	1.7	7.5	32.1	60.3
Ross County	430	10.8	23.8	30 409	83.1	11.5	0.6	0.9	2.2	7.1	29.9	63.0
Sandusky County	462	10.1	20.2	29 971	84.8	9.3	0.8	0.8	2.2	5.6	29.6	64.8
Scioto County	378	13.9	27.6	28 356	83.3	10.4	0.7	1.0	2.3	9.9	33.7	56.4
Seneca County	433	8.5	21.0	28 274	82.5	9.3	1.0	1.1	3.6	6.0	31.4	62.7
Shelby County	499	9.1	24.8	23 582	86.3	8.3	0.2	0.6	1.7	4.3	30.6	65.1
Stark County	486	12.1	25.0	177 234	86.2	7.8	1.1	0.7	1.9	7.1	31.9	61.0
Summit County	546	14.1	28.5	258 414	85.9	7.9	1.6	0.6	1.5	8.2	33.9	57.9
Trumbull County	461	10.9	26.0	97 485	87.1	8.4	0.2	0.9	1.3	7.0	34.3	58.7
Tuscarawas County	443	11.1	22.9	42 093	84.5	9.9	0.2	1.2	1.7	7.3	29.7	63.0
Union County	574	10.8	20.4	20 416	83.6	10.7	0.2	0.6	1.6	4.1	23.6	72.4
Van Wert County	412	7.9	14.1	14 375	84.7	9.6	0.2	0.6	2.2	4.3	29.4	66.3
Vinton County	391	11.6	27.3	4 795	79.1	15.3	0.4	0.6	2.2	8.5	28.6	62.9
Warren County	613	10.8	22.5	76 548	86.0	8.6	0.8	0.4	0.9	3.6	24.1	72.3
Washington County	400	9.9	26.5	28 171	84.2	8.6	0.2	0.9	3.3	6.7	30.7	62.6
Wayne County	492	10.9	21.4	54 487	79.5	9.7	0.4	1.0	4.2	8.1	28.0	64.0
Williams County	476	9.4	21.4	19 641	83.4	10.0	0.4	0.8	2.5	5.2	29.8	65.0
Wood County	508	10.7	31.0	61 207	84.6	7.8	0.4	1.0	4.1	4.4	31.7	63.9
Wyandot County...........	408	8.9	11.9	11 317	83.6	10.0	0.2	1.0	2.0	4.9	28.8	66.3
OKLAHOMA	456	12.1	26.7	1 539 792	80.0	13.2	0.5	1.1	2.1	7.0	34.9	58.1
Adair County	342	16.2	20.8	8 215	71.2	21.5	0.8	1.2	1.7	9.8	34.8	55.5
Alfalfa County	282	8.1	11.6	2 330	79.0	11.0	0.2	0.6	3.8	5.3	29.7	65.0
Atoka County................	327	13.2	25.2	4 749	76.5	15.3	0.4	1.4	2.6	7.8	35.7	56.5
Beaver County	389	9.3	5.9	2 684	80.8	10.8	0.3	1.0	2.5	3.3	26.5	70.2
Beckham County	353	10.1	19.3	7 735	79.4	14.4	0.1	1.0	2.2	8.1	34.6	57.4
Blaine County	332	9.0	25.5	4 462	80.7	12.1	0.1	1.0	2.8	5.1	30.3	64.6
Bryan County	375	12.8	26.7	15 382	80.1	15.0	0.1	0.9	1.8	7.2	34.9	57.8
Caddo County	329	11.0	17.4	11 211	77.6	15.1	0.3	1.0	2.2	7.8	33.9	58.3
Canadian County	510	11.5	26.9	43 206	85.6	10.0	0.1	0.6	0.9	3.8	27.1	69.1
Carter County	416	13.4	24.8	18 939	81.4	12.5	0.4	1.3	1.4	8.2	36.5	55.3
Cherokee County	389	14.5	33.4	17 489	73.2	18.5	0.5	1.3	3.1	8.7	33.8	57.5
Choctaw County	302	13.7	25.7	5 591	77.9	15.3	0.2	1.3	1.7	10.0	36.4	53.6
Cimarron County	284	7.3	12.7	1 389	74.3	14.5	0.1	1.4	4.5	5.6	32.1	62.2
Cleveland County	526	11.4	33.1	104 629	84.0	10.0	0.4	1.2	1.8	4.3	31.6	64.1
Coal County	287	11.4	22.2	2 245	71.9	19.2	0.7	1.2	2.1	9.1	35.4	55.5
Comanche County	452	13.7	26.5	51 684	73.3	13.9	1.0	2.2	7.3	8.2	35.4	56.4
Cotton County	328	12.3	19.1	2 668	81.3	13.0	0.1	1.0	1.8	6.0	34.2	59.7
Craig County	396	10.6	21.3	6 277	77.3	14.2	0.2	1.5	2.3	6.5	32.7	60.7
Creek County	428	13.4	21.0	28 817	80.9	13.5	0.1	1.0	1.7	6.1	30.1	63.8
Custer County	371	9.5	31.7	12 192	80.5	13.0	0.2	1.2	2.6	5.6	34.5	59.9
Delaware County	390	16.5	24.5	14 477	75.6	16.0	0.4	1.3	2.5	4.3	33.2	62.5
Dewey County	303	10.3	13.2	2 103	78.3	11.9	0.1	0.6	3.5	5.2	27.5	67.3
Ellis County	339	8.5	16.9	1 915	76.1	11.4	0.0	1.4	4.1	5.2	27.8	67.0
Garfield County	436	11.0	26.0	26 712	81.6	12.2	0.3	1.0	1.9	6.4	35.1	58.5
Garvin County	388	12.1	20.9	11 318	78.7	14.5	0.3	1.1	1.7	6.6	35.2	58.2
Grady County	396	11.7	21.7	20 290	80.8	13.3	0.1	1.1	1.4	6.4	29.0	64.6
Grant County................	391	11.7	15.6	2 308	74.6	12.1	0.0	0.9	3.4	3.7	27.7	68.6
Greer County	290	8.0	15.7	2 038	84.9	9.3	0.2	1.3	1.5	7.4	33.0	59.6
Harmon County	274	12.2	28.1	1 250	78.3	14.6	0.5	0.7	3.0	9.7	34.1	56.2
Harper County	315	4.3	13.3	1 702	78.1	12.1	0.3	0.9	3.8	4.2	26.2	69.6
Haskell County	301	14.1	28.6	4 533	72.4	17.7	0.6	0.7	2.2	10.6	32.5	56.9
Hughes County	309	14.2	23.2	4 862	77.4	15.7	0.3	0.5	3.2	8.4	35.9	55.7
Jackson County............	429	15.6	20.5	12 531	81.8	11.2	0.4	2.1	2.9	6.7	37.4	55.9
Jefferson County	261	15.3	14.9	2 564	74.5	17.5	0.3	1.6	2.1	9.6	31.6	58.9
Johnston County	321	13.9	22.8	4 112	74.8	18.7	0.2	1.1	2.7	8.8	34.5	56.7
Kay County...................	414	12.5	25.7	20 039	81.0	12.8	0.1	0.8	2.1	6.8	36.2	57.0
Kingfisher County..........	384	8.7	17.6	6 567	81.5	12.7	0.1	0.2	1.8	4.3	28.2	67.5

Table C-3. States and Counties — Migration, Housing, and Transportation

STATE/ County code	MSA/PMSA/ NECMA code[1]	STATE County	Total population 5 years and over	Residence in 1995 (percent)					Occupied housing units		Householders 65 years and over	
				Same house	Same county, different house	Same state, different county	Different state	Outside the United States	Number	Percent owner-occupied	Number	Percent owner-occupied
			1	2	3	4	5	6	7	8	9	10
		OKLAHOMA—Cont'd										
40 075	...	Kiowa County	9 633	60.1	18.6	14.0	6.2	1.0	4 208	75.2	1 397	85.7
40 077	...	Latimer County	9 974	57.1	19.4	17.1	5.3	1.0	3 951	74.5	1 096	83.8
40 079	...	Le Flore County	44 821	55.4	25.1	8.2	9.8	1.5	17 861	75.1	4 391	84.0
40 081	...	Lincoln County	29 999	58.0	18.8	17.0	5.8	0.4	12 178	80.1	2 935	85.9
40 083	5880	Logan County	31 872	54.7	15.0	19.9	9.7	0.7	12 389	78.4	2 605	83.8
40 085	...	Love County	8 309	60.9	18.6	9.5	10.5	0.6	3 442	81.8	1 023	89.9
40 087	5880	McClain County	25 946	54.5	17.0	21.0	6.6	0.8	10 331	81.3	2 276	87.4
40 089	...	McCurtain County	31 808	61.6	26.1	4.5	7.1	0.8	13 216	73.3	3 281	84.3
40 091	...	McIntosh County	18 420	58.1	17.4	17.1	6.8	0.6	8 085	78.9	2 727	85.3
40 093	...	Major County	7 117	67.6	14.8	12.2	4.9	0.4	3 046	81.0	917	93.6
40 095	...	Marshall County	12 343	55.6	19.3	12.7	10.2	2.1	5 371	79.2	1 759	87.2
40 097	...	Mayes County	35 754	54.8	21.8	14.9	8.3	0.3	14 823	77.0	3 691	84.7
40 099	...	Murray County	11 824	57.5	19.0	15.6	6.8	1.2	5 003	74.2	1 338	89.1
40 101	...	Muskogee County	64 579	53.9	27.4	11.0	6.9	0.8	26 458	69.6	7 199	79.1
40 103	...	Noble County	10 713	58.1	22.2	15.4	4.2	0.2	4 504	75.2	1 093	85.0
40 105	...	Nowata County	9 897	59.3	18.0	12.0	10.2	0.5	4 147	77.7	1 298	84.3
40 107	...	Okfuskee County	11 077	59.4	17.2	17.5	5.1	0.8	4 270	76.0	1 275	84.9
40 109	5880	Oklahoma County	612 796	47.7	31.1	8.3	10.0	2.8	266 834	60.4	54 173	81.0
40 111	...	Okmulgee County	37 044	55.6	21.6	15.3	6.4	1.0	15 300	72.6	4 310	84.2
40 113	8560	Osage County	41 777	61.1	13.7	18.7	6.0	0.5	16 617	80.5	3 895	85.2
40 115	...	Ottawa County	30 965	53.2	25.2	7.9	12.6	1.0	12 984	73.9	3 914	80.0
40 117	...	Pawnee County	15 587	57.4	17.4	17.8	7.0	0.4	6 383	80.0	1 574	87.9
40 119	...	Payne County	64 636	39.2	22.9	23.7	11.2	3.1	26 680	55.9	4 586	83.2
40 121	...	Pittsburg County	41 512	55.4	22.7	13.1	8.1	0.6	17 157	76.0	5 035	85.8
40 123	...	Pontotoc County	32 983	52.1	26.7	13.5	6.9	0.8	13 978	67.0	3 571	79.9
40 125	5880	Pottawatomie County	61 001	54.4	22.1	15.6	7.2	0.7	24 540	72.2	6 115	81.7
40 127	...	Pushmataha County	10 937	60.7	18.8	12.4	7.6	0.5	4 739	77.8	1 469	82.1
40 129	...	Roger Mills County	3 251	65.9	15.3	13.3	5.4	0.2	1 428	78.8	472	89.8
40 131	8560	Rogers County	65 728	54.6	18.7	17.0	9.1	0.7	25 724	81.1	4 857	84.8
40 133	...	Seminole County	23 267	58.2	22.6	12.4	6.5	0.3	9 575	72.3	2 880	83.4
40 135	2720	Sequoyah County	36 179	55.7	24.7	7.9	11.2	0.5	14 761	75.2	3 633	83.4
40 137	...	Stephens County	40 355	60.0	24.0	8.3	7.2	0.4	17 463	75.6	5 172	86.7
40 139	...	Texas County	18 374	48.1	21.4	6.5	18.0	6.0	7 153	67.1	1 398	89.3
40 141	...	Tillman County	8 739	60.9	19.9	9.7	7.7	1.8	3 594	77.2	1 207	87.2
40 143	8560	Tulsa County	522 152	46.5	31.0	8.1	11.9	2.4	226 892	61.8	44 089	79.0
40 145	8560	Wagoner County	53 408	56.4	13.2	20.9	8.8	0.7	21 010	81.0	3 975	88.0
40 147	...	Washington County	46 125	54.0	22.8	10.2	11.5	1.5	20 179	74.0	5 689	83.7
40 149	...	Washita County	10 802	59.4	15.3	16.3	8.2	0.8	4 506	74.7	1 381	85.7
40 151	...	Woods County	8 676	52.5	20.0	18.1	8.7	0.7	3 684	69.6	1 117	90.4
40 153	...	Woodward County	17 265	55.0	22.7	14.2	7.5	0.6	7 141	72.0	1 728	85.1
41 000	...	OREGON	3 199 323	46.8	27.0	11.1	12.5	2.6	1 333 723	64.2	282 848	77.9
41 001	...	Baker County	15 839	53.9	22.4	12.5	10.8	0.4	6 883	70.0	2 086	83.5
41 003	1890	Benton County	74 282	42.3	19.4	20.8	14.5	3.1	30 145	57.3	4 947	78.4
41 005	6440	Clackamas County	316 516	51.8	20.8	15.5	9.9	2.0	128 201	71.1	24 358	77.2
41 007	...	Clatsop County	33 621	47.9	25.1	9.6	15.5	1.9	14 703	64.2	3 571	78.6
41 009	6440	Columbia County	40 734	53.4	22.4	14.9	8.7	0.5	16 375	76.1	3 292	83.9
41 011	...	Coos County	59 732	53.6	25.3	7.8	12.4	0.9	26 213	68.2	7 947	81.6
41 013	...	Crook County	17 953	46.1	25.3	18.0	9.7	0.8	7 354	74.2	1 676	81.5
41 015	...	Curry County	20 269	52.3	18.5	8.5	20.0	0.7	9 543	72.9	3 769	84.3
41 017	...	Deschutes County	108 293	40.6	26.5	15.6	16.3	1.0	45 595	72.3	10 072	85.3
41 019	...	Douglas County	94 748	52.2	28.3	7.6	11.3	0.6	39 821	71.7	11 489	82.3
41 021	...	Gilliam County	1 828	56.3	15.9	19.5	8.0	0.2	819	69.6	262	89.7
41 023	...	Grant County	7 482	56.1	22.5	12.3	8.4	0.7	3 246	73.3	865	87.1
41 025	...	Harney County	7 164	46.2	25.1	16.7	11.4	0.5	3 036	72.6	632	86.6
41 027	...	Hood River County	18 932	52.0	24.3	8.3	11.8	3.6	7 248	64.9	1 784	72.5
41 029	4890	Jackson County	170 324	46.5	30.4	6.9	15.1	1.1	71 532	66.5	18 668	77.9
41 031	...	Jefferson County	17 610	45.5	22.6	20.0	11.0	1.0	6 727	71.3	1 561	84.8
41 033	...	Josephine County	71 725	51.1	26.2	7.3	15.0	0.5	31 000	70.0	9 959	82.4
41 035	...	Klamath County	59 705	48.5	26.7	9.1	14.9	0.9	25 205	68.0	6 299	80.5
41 037	...	Lake County	7 042	55.1	18.9	12.9	12.4	0.7	3 084	68.8	838	81.4
41 039	2400	Lane County	304 463	46.8	31.1	7.7	12.5	1.8	130 453	62.3	28 211	79.4
41 041	...	Lincoln County	42 327	46.8	24.4	14.6	12.5	1.8	19 296	65.7	5 609	81.3
41 043	...	Linn County	96 024	51.0	26.7	12.4	9.1	0.9	39 541	67.9	9 945	79.1
41 045	...	Malheur County	29 285	51.0	21.9	10.8	12.4	3.9	10 221	63.8	2 753	75.2
41 047	7080	Marion County	262 794	44.9	31.2	11.0	9.3	3.5	101 641	62.9	21 873	77.0

[1]MSA = Metropolitan Statistical Area. PMSA = Primary MSA. NECMA = New England County Metropolitan Area. See the Appendix A for explanation of these concepts. See Appendix B for list of metropolitan areas identified by type, with component counties.

STATE County	Owner-occupied by household type (percent)								Median household income			Median monthly owner costs as a percent of income	
	Family-households					Nonfamily households							
		Married-couple family		Other family									
	Total family households	Total	With own children under 18 years	Total	With own children under 18 years	Total nonfamily households	Two or more adults	Living alone	All households	Owner-occupied households	Renter-occupied households	Median housing value (owner estimated)	With a mortgage	Without a mortgage
	11	12	13	14	15	16	17	18	19	20	21	22	23	24

OKLAHOMA—Cont'd

	11	12	13	14	15	16	17	18	19	20	21	22	23	24
Kiowa County	79.5	86.5	79.3	56.0	43.7	66.5	57.5	67.2	25 924	30 400	15 659	37 200	17.5	11.1
Latimer County	78.1	85.8	78.3	53.1	43.4	65.1	47.8	66.7	23 837	28 091	13 488	47 900	19.8	10.5
Le Flore County	78.6	83.8	77.5	57.5	50.5	65.1	40.1	68.2	26 972	31 153	17 162	51 500	19.0	11.0
Lincoln County	83.8	87.5	81.5	65.9	57.4	68.6	54.7	70.1	31 033	34 045	21 298	55 600	19.2	10.3
Logan County	83.1	87.5	82.4	62.6	55.9	65.7	58.9	66.7	36 857	41 463	22 244	68 600	19.0	10.2
Love County	84.1	88.0	83.2	66.8	57.8	75.1	58.2	77.0	31 780	34 928	20 369	52 100	20.1	9.9
McClain County	82.9	86.8	82.0	62.5	52.4	75.5	65.5	76.8	36 849	41 131	23 535	72 800	18.9	9.9
McCurtain County	76.0	83.1	76.1	56.0	47.0	65.9	46.9	67.4	23 943	28 434	15 061	45 500	19.2	10.5
McIntosh County	81.4	86.6	77.6	58.4	47.8	72.9	70.4	73.2	25 861	28 493	16 353	55 100	20.2	11.5
Major County	82.3	86.0	79.4	53.7	45.7	77.7	59.4	79.3	30 571	33 834	20 888	53 100	16.9	9.9
Marshall County	82.4	87.0	78.8	62.9	52.4	71.4	54.5	73.2	26 630	29 499	17 593	49 300	19.8	11.2
Mayes County	80.9	85.0	78.7	60.6	51.6	66.2	54.2	67.6	31 382	35 396	21 656	63 800	18.2	9.9
Murray County	75.9	80.3	69.5	54.6	43.1	69.8	61.0	70.8	30 097	34 315	22 535	51 500	17.4	10.7
Muskogee County	75.0	82.0	74.7	52.6	41.9	57.1	48.8	58.1	28 170	34 539	18 080	57 100	19.6	10.1
Noble County	79.3	83.9	75.4	57.7	51.6	64.9	55.4	66.1	34 227	37 694	24 321	54 700	18.0	9.9
Nowata County	81.3	85.0	77.1	62.3	59.3	68.2	61.5	68.8	29 798	33 628	20 393	47 700	18.6	9.9
Okfuskee County	80.3	84.5	79.0	65.5	52.0	66.2	59.8	66.7	24 196	27 243	16 637	44 700	19.4	11.3
Oklahoma County	67.8	77.0	70.4	43.0	31.9	47.2	32.8	49.9	34 783	45 302	22 990	74 400	19.8	9.9
Okmulgee County	76.6	82.7	75.8	54.9	42.6	63.0	50.8	64.2	27 450	31 861	16 978	49 900	19.4	10.5
Osage County	84.3	88.4	84.2	66.5	57.0	69.8	66.3	70.2	34 110	38 773	18 948	61 000	18.7	9.9
Ottawa County	79.3	85.0	77.2	57.2	41.4	61.0	64.7	60.6	27 401	31 609	17 479	50 300	18.5	9.9
Pawnee County	83.0	86.4	79.9	65.6	60.0	71.1	67.1	71.6	31 700	33 887	24 915	52 200	19.3	11.9
Payne County	71.7	79.1	75.6	42.5	38.8	34.1	15.9	41.4	28 589	42 043	15 527	73 200	18.7	9.9
Pittsburg County	79.4	84.5	77.8	59.0	47.1	67.9	57.5	68.8	28 582	32 487	16 150	51 400	18.3	10.1
Pontotoc County	75.0	83.1	76.4	45.0	33.6	50.0	29.2	53.0	26 659	34 300	17 259	58 600	20.1	11.1
Pottawatomie County	77.0	82.4	75.2	57.0	46.0	59.5	41.8	62.1	31 637	36 785	20 922	59 500	18.8	10.2
Pushmataha County	82.3	87.1	78.9	62.2	48.8	67.4	52.9	68.8	22 038	25 224	13 676	44 700	19.8	10.5
Roger Mills County	80.8	82.7	76.4	68.7	60.6	74.1	38.5	76.4	30 000	33 628	21 576	51 700	20.6	9.9
Rogers County	85.3	89.0	85.8	64.8	55.7	65.6	60.8	66.1	43 887	49 393	24 129	89 000	18.8	9.9
Seminole County	75.7	80.9	70.3	58.3	43.1	63.7	42.8	66.0	25 212	28 459	16 992	41 600	19.7	11.2
Sequoyah County	78.6	84.4	77.2	54.3	43.1	65.1	58.6	66.0	27 276	31 676	16 071	56 600	19.9	10.7
Stephens County	78.9	84.2	75.4	53.5	43.5	66.6	51.6	67.6	30 563	34 659	19 104	55 900	19.1	9.9
Texas County	71.7	76.4	66.4	46.3	36.7	54.3	14.8	64.3	35 981	41 563	26 339	61 500	18.4	9.9
Tillman County	79.5	83.9	74.7	60.8	50.4	71.8	66.1	72.1	25 152	27 342	17 547	32 100	19.0	11.6
Tulsa County	70.5	78.5	73.9	44.6	35.1	45.3	33.3	47.4	38 138	49 716	25 243	85 000	19.2	9.9
Wagoner County	84.1	88.6	84.4	62.2	52.2	69.0	59.7	70.3	41 308	46 107	23 209	83 000	19.0	9.9
Washington County	80.2	85.3	79.8	56.7	47.4	59.4	53.3	60.0	35 912	41 758	20 873	63 400	17.0	9.9
Washita County	77.0	81.2	72.1	55.6	45.2	68.6	43.4	71.0	29 643	32 428	21 496	43 000	17.9	9.9
Woods County	77.7	83.3	70.2	51.4	40.4	56.8	27.6	61.4	28 945	35 319	16 989	47 800	16.8	9.9
Woodward County	77.8	82.1	75.6	55.5	48.4	57.6	48.9	58.6	33 786	38 697	22 090	58 200	19.0	9.9
OREGON	72.8	79.6	73.3	46.3	36.7	47.5	38.6	50.3	40 818	50 713	27 197	145 800	23.2	10.5
Baker County	75.8	80.7	69.6	50.8	38.0	57.8	57.7	57.8	29 978	33 768	21 522	88 800	24.9	11.6
Benton County	72.9	78.3	75.1	43.7	39.8	32.9	20.6	39.0	41 878	61 480	22 832	166 500	21.4	9.9
Clackamas County	78.6	84.1	80.2	52.5	44.2	52.0	44.3	54.1	51 680	62 195	32 551	193 700	23.2	10.2
Clatsop County	71.2	77.3	67.0	48.0	36.6	51.3	46.4	52.3	35 964	45 160	24 033	138 800	24.0	10.8
Columbia County	80.7	85.9	80.8	54.3	43.8	63.1	69.1	61.7	45 452	51 676	27 433	146 600	22.5	9.9
Coos County	73.7	80.4	67.8	46.3	33.6	57.1	47.9	59.1	31 202	37 069	20 562	94 900	21.8	11.8
Crook County	77.9	82.2	71.0	55.6	47.0	63.9	58.8	65.1	36 300	40 887	26 792	99 600	22.5	11.1
Curry County	77.9	81.5	66.6	55.5	41.5	63.8	56.7	65.1	30 135	32 647	22 989	125 000	25.7	10.2
Deschutes County	79.1	84.4	78.5	50.9	44.3	56.2	44.7	60.2	41 593	48 447	27 875	140 700	23.4	10.6
Douglas County	77.1	82.6	74.0	52.8	38.3	58.7	54.1	59.7	33 084	38 216	23 000	98 900	22.1	10.1
Gilliam County	71.9	74.6	60.2	55.3	38.1	65.1	51.4	67.1	33 510	37 083	27 734	78 500	19.1	13.5
Grant County	78.0	81.7	72.7	59.8	51.1	62.7	57.1	63.5	32 185	35 686	25 667	82 400	21.4	9.9
Harney County	76.7	79.8	70.1	62.3	56.1	63.1	59.9	63.7	31 267	34 457	25 215	75 900	19.7	12.1
Hood River County	69.9	73.7	60.5	52.8	38.9	52.0	34.6	55.9	38 315	46 100	27 355	150 600	24.4	9.9
Jackson County	73.1	79.8	71.0	47.4	35.6	52.5	43.5	55.0	36 283	44 061	24 108	132 100	23.5	10.3
Jefferson County	73.6	79.0	67.8	52.3	42.8	63.4	50.2	66.6	35 527	39 006	26 750	100 700	22.9	11.7
Josephine County	74.7	81.2	67.4	49.0	38.5	59.5	50.2	61.4	31 042	36 220	21 160	119 300	24.3	9.9
Klamath County	74.7	81.8	72.6	47.5	39.2	53.3	41.5	56.0	31 308	38 587	20 684	87 000	19.9	9.9
Lake County	73.2	77.7	67.7	51.2	44.3	58.9	53.4	59.8	29 663	33 628	23 822	65 800	18.4	9.9
Lane County	72.8	80.4	73.5	45.2	35.4	44.2	31.8	48.9	36 684	46 924	23 168	136 000	23.3	9.9
Lincoln County	71.4	79.9	67.5	41.7	32.5	55.5	49.4	56.9	32 690	39 154	24 082	136 900	25.9	12.1
Linn County	73.1	79.9	71.9	44.4	33.3	54.8	49.6	55.9	37 421	45 348	24 421	122 900	23.1	11.4
Malheur County	69.3	75.0	66.4	45.7	34.3	49.5	36.6	51.9	30 412	37 420	21 092	86 300	20.5	9.9
Marion County	69.0	76.6	68.7	42.4	33.8	49.1	39.5	51.7	40 530	50 501	27 248	128 700	23.5	10.1

STATE County	Median gross rent	Percent who pay 35 percent or more of income for housing expenses		Means of transportation to work (percent except where noted)						Vehicles available (percent of households)		
		Owners	Renters	Number of workers 16 years and over	Car, truck, or van		Public transportation	Other means	Walked	No vehicles	One vehicle	Two or more vehicles
					Drove alone	Carpooled						
	25	26	27	28	29	30	31	32	33	34	35	36
OKLAHOMA—Cont'd												
Kiowa County	312	11.0	24.3	4 106	79.0	14.5	0.1	0.4	2.9	6.3	38.4	55.3
Latimer County	327	12.9	22.8	3 899	75.6	14.6	0.0	2.2	3.5	7.9	34.6	57.5
Le Flore County	372	13.6	25.1	18 813	77.3	16.3	0.3	1.2	2.0	8.0	32.4	59.6
Lincoln County	397	11.8	20.4	13 716	77.0	17.0	0.0	0.7	1.5	5.4	29.4	65.2
Logan County	417	13.3	23.2	15 744	78.0	13.8	0.2	1.2	2.4	5.0	28.7	66.3
Love County	388	11.4	14.2	3 840	77.9	16.3	0.2	1.3	2.1	4.8	29.3	66.0
McClain County	446	11.3	18.8	12 862	80.6	13.3	0.0	0.8	0.8	4.1	26.4	69.5
McCurtain County	302	12.7	20.9	13 019	77.6	15.3	0.3	1.4	2.0	9.7	36.3	54.0
McIntosh County	375	15.2	28.6	7 146	74.7	15.5	0.6	1.4	2.1	7.0	34.6	58.4
Major County	345	7.8	15.7	3 571	76.9	12.7	0.1	1.7	2.2	4.0	27.2	68.8
Marshall County	354	13.8	18.7	5 214	76.3	16.4	0.0	1.1	2.8	7.4	33.5	59.2
Mayes County	394	10.2	20.9	16 242	79.7	13.6	0.2	0.8	2.3	6.1	29.2	64.7
Murray County	377	11.9	19.6	5 461	79.1	14.8	0.0	0.7	1.7	6.0	34.1	59.9
Muskogee County	396	13.8	28.6	26 773	78.2	16.2	0.3	1.0	1.6	9.0	37.6	53.4
Noble County	388	11.5	18.6	5 272	83.3	11.1	0.0	1.5	1.5	4.2	28.7	67.1
Nowata County	354	9.5	21.9	4 448	74.1	10.7	0.3	1.1	1.7	0.5	34.0	55.5
Okfuskee County	316	13.4	17.3	4 054	70.7	19.9	0.1	1.0	3.4	8.9	33.7	57.3
Oklahoma County	483	12.5	27.9	305 058	80.8	12.7	0.8	1.1	1.7	7.8	39.7	52.5
Okmulgee County	369	12.2	22.8	15 329	76.8	14.9	0.2	1.4	2.6	10.5	34.1	55.5
Osage County	359	12.1	20.2	18 916	79.9	14.6	0.2	0.8	1.4	6.3	30.2	63.5
Ottawa County	355	9.8	22.1	13 934	78.2	14.3	0.2	1.4	2.6	8.0	32.5	59.5
Pawnee County	419	13.9	21.9	7 151	77.3	16.7	0.2	0.9	1.8	5.3	28.8	66.0
Payne County	459	10.8	42.8	33 094	75.6	11.9	0.2	1.8	7.2	6.4	36.4	57.3
Pittsburg County	386	10.6	27.1	16 352	81.1	14.2	0.1	0.9	0.8	9.1	34.7	56.2
Pontotoc County	377	12.4	27.1	15 389	81.0	14.3	0.1	0.7	1.8	7.1	34.9	58.0
Pottawatomie County	431	9.9	26.0	27 763	80.9	14.1	0.2	1.0	1.7	7.1	32.8	60.1
Pushmataha County	276	14.3	17.9	4 195	74.0	17.7	0.2	1.3	2.6	10.5	31.8	57.7
Roger Mills County	314	11.3	11.7	1 603	74.2	12.8	0.2	1.3	3.1	4.3	26.8	68.9
Rogers County	480	10.7	23.9	32 891	82.8	12.5	0.1	0.4	0.8	4.7	24.8	70.5
Seminole County	375	15.8	26.5	9 386	77.2	15.3	0.1	1.1	2.9	8.7	30.1	55.2
Sequoyah County	354	14.6	24.0	15 596	78.6	15.9	0.2	1.4	1.4	7.5	34.1	58.4
Stephens County	391	12.2	23.3	17 571	82.1	13.0	0.0	1.0	1.6	6.1	32.5	61.3
Texas County	450	9.7	15.5	9 419	74.0	17.7	0.4	0.0	0.0	6.0	30.0	63.6
Tillman County	335	10.4	17.5	3 446	80.8	14.1	0.2	0.5	1.6	8.4	35.3	56.3
Tulsa County	520	12.1	26.9	271 055	80.8	12.4	0.9	0.9	1.9	7.7	38.0	54.3
Wagoner County	469	12.3	22.6	26 958	83.1	12.3	0.1	0.8	0.7	5.0	26.8	68.1
Washington County	406	8.1	24.9	20 989	78.8	15.4	0.2	1.3	1.5	6.9	33.7	59.4
Washita County	373	10.9	18.3	4 986	78.2	13.3	0.0	1.2	2.5	4.4	32.0	63.6
Woods County	359	7.1	27.5	4 190	80.9	9.8	0.0	1.7	4.1	4.4	36.2	59.4
Woodward County	396	10.8	19.9	8 326	80.7	12.2	0.0	0.8	2.4	5.2	31.2	63.6
OREGON	620	17.5	32.2	1 601 378	73.2	12.2	4.2	1.9	3.6	7.5	32.8	59.7
Baker County	453	16.4	31.8	6 643	67.7	13.7	0.5	2.1	5.4	7.3	28.7	64.1
Benton County	597	13.5	41.6	37 747	70.7	10.4	1.6	5.2	7.7	5.7	33.2	61.2
Clackamas County	702	18.0	29.5	166 890	78.2	10.3	3.1	0.9	2.1	4.9	27.7	67.4
Clatsop County	543	18.6	31.8	16 685	74.1	11.2	1.3	2.2	6.1	8.3	35.0	56.7
Columbia County	581	15.7	28.0	19 726	78.7	13.4	0.2	1.0	2.1	4.6	25.5	69.9
Coos County	499	15.4	34.4	25 010	77.1	12.4	0.6	1.6	3.1	7.5	34.1	58.4
Crook County	538	15.1	22.9	7 998	70.9	18.0	0.1	1.3	4.3	5.4	27.5	67.1
Curry County	550	18.9	27.9	7 831	74.4	12.9	0.3	1.1	3.8	6.0	35.7	58.3
Deschutes County	644	17.9	33.6	54 721	75.2	13.1	0.8	2.2	2.3	4.2	26.7	69.1
Douglas County	489	16.1	28.6	40 930	78.2	11.7	0.4	1.8	3.1	6.0	29.9	64.0
Gilliam County	484	17.4	19.5	926	73.3	11.8	0.0	0.5	7.8	3.9	33.5	62.6
Grant County	432	11.7	16.3	3 297	74.0	11.4	0.2	1.3	4.9	5.2	26.8	68.0
Harney County	453	15.5	18.0	3 376	68.3	12.6	0.0	1.3	9.1	4.7	30.3	65.0
Hood River County	538	16.9	24.5	9 245	72.2	12.4	0.4	1.1	6.5	6.9	27.5	65.6
Jackson County	597	18.0	36.0	79 197	77.4	10.9	0.7	1.8	3.6	6.0	32.4	61.6
Jefferson County	501	18.1	22.9	8 036	71.3	19.4	0.0	0.9	2.7	3.7	26.8	69.5
Josephine County	534	17.6	35.5	27 822	77.6	11.2	0.2	1.4	2.9	5.9	31.4	62.7
Klamath County	475	14.2	33.7	25 902	78.2	11.3	0.7	1.7	3.0	7.0	30.2	62.9
Lake County	401	13.5	21.7	2 997	68.9	14.1	0.1	1.2	9.6	6.2	30.6	63.1
Lane County	604	17.3	38.3	152 737	71.6	12.2	3.3	3.7	4.2	7.9	33.9	58.2
Lincoln County	575	22.9	33.1	18 963	72.5	14.9	0.6	1.3	4.6	7.2	39.4	53.4
Linn County	580	16.4	36.9	45 373	79.3	11.8	0.3	1.1	2.9	6.8	28.6	64.6
Malheur County	443	12.7	26.9	11 117	72.8	14.1	0.1	1.0	4.4	6.9	28.8	64.3
Marion County	574	17.8	31.1	124 872	72.8	16.1	2.1	1.6	3.0	7.2	33.6	59.2

Table C-3. States and Counties — Migration, Housing, and Transportation

STATE/ County code	MSA/PMSA/ NECMA code[1]	STATE County	Residence in 1995 (percent)						Occupied housing units		Householders 65 years and over	
			Total population 5 years and over	Same house	Same county, different house	Same state, different county	Different state	Outside the United States	Number	Percent owner-occupied	Number	Percent owner-occupied
			1	2	3	4	5	6	7	8	9	10
		OREGON—Cont'd										
41 049	...	Morrow County..............	10 058	46.5	18.7	18.3	13.3	3.3	3 776	73.1	769	85.4
41 051	6440	Multnomah County........	618 617	44.9	29.9	8.2	12.9	4.2	272 098	56.9	47 790	72.3
41 053	7080	Polk County.................	58 294	47.7	18.7	23.0	8.7	2.0	23 058	68.4	5 521	76.3
41 055	...	Sherman County	1 835	62.6	15.5	12.6	8.0	1.3	797	70.4	231	92.6
41 057	...	Tillamook County	23 033	53.7	21.6	14.2	8.8	1.7	10 200	71.9	3 373	84.5
41 059	...	Umatilla County	65 317	50.9	26.0	7.9	13.1	2.1	25 195	64.9	5 516	77.9
41 061	...	Union County	23 009	50.1	24.5	13.4	10.8	1.3	9 740	66.6	2 371	78.0
41 063	...	Wallowa County	6 874	57.2	22.4	9.8	10.1	0.6	3 029	71.8	902	84.9
41 065	...	Wasco County..............	22 260	50.2	25.0	12.7	10.9	1.3	9 401	68.4	2 583	80.4
41 067	6440	Washington County.......	410 641	41.2	27.1	11.9	15.2	4.5	169 162	60.5	25 085	73.2
41 069	...	Wheeler County	1 480	56.4	12.1	20.4	10.4	0.7	653	72.1	241	86.3
41 071	6440	Yamhill County	79 213	47.6	24.2	15.8	10.1	2.3	28 732	69.6	6 000	80.7
42 000	...	PENNSYLVANIA........	11 555 538	63.5	21.7	7.6	5.8	1.4	4 777 003	71.3	1 238 054	77.4
42 001	...	Adams County..............	85 917	60.4	18.2	9.3	10.8	1.3	33 652	76.8	7 581	81.2
42 003	6280	Allegheny County	1 210 720	64.6	24.7	4.4	4.9	1.4	537 150	67.0	152 093	75.1
42 005	...	Armstrong County	68 513	70.9	17.5	9.1	2.3	0.3	29 005	77.3	8 734	81.8
42 007	6280	Beaver County	171 594	68.5	21.2	6.2	3.7	0.4	72 576	74.9	21 958	80.3
42 009	...	Bedford County.............	46 945	70.6	18.4	6.4	4.4	0.2	19 768	80.2	5 475	82.5
42 011	6680	Berks County................	350 815	61.1	24.4	7.9	4.8	1.8	141 570	74.0	35 887	78.6
42 013	0280	Blair County..................	121 866	66.7	24.0	5.5	3.5	0.3	51 518	72.9	14 060	77.8
42 015	...	Bradford County............	58 944	66.4	21.1	5.1	7.1	0.4	24 453	75.5	6 333	78.7
42 017	6160	Bucks County	559 308	63.2	18.9	9.5	7.0	1.3	218 725	77.3	45 373	78.8
42 019	6280	Butler County	162 972	63.3	19.1	11.1	5.8	0.6	65 862	77.8	14 803	76.5
42 021	3680	Cambria County............	144 857	71.7	18.6	6.0	3.0	0.6	60 531	74.7	20 339	79.8
42 023	...	Cameron County	5 699	70.2	18.5	7.5	3.7	0.2	2 465	75.0	825	79.6
42 025	0240	Carbon County..............	55 750	69.2	17.5	9.5	3.4	0.4	23 701	78.2	6 902	81.6
42 027	8050	Centre County	129 506	46.9	17.4	21.7	10.5	3.6	49 323	60.2	8 979	79.7
42 029	6160	Chester County	404 444	58.6	17.9	12.1	9.4	2.0	157 905	76.3	30 593	80.0
42 031	...	Clarion County..............	39 484	63.0	18.0	15.0	3.5	0.6	16 052	72.2	4 153	80.2
42 033	...	Clearfield County...........	78 881	70.1	18.4	7.6	3.7	0.3	32 785	79.2	9 228	82.4
42 035	...	Clinton County..............	35 849	63.7	19.7	12.5	3.5	0.5	14 773	73.0	4 241	74.8
42 037	7560	Columbia County	61 028	62.6	20.8	11.9	3.9	0.8	24 915	72.2	6 526	79.4
42 039	...	Crawford County	85 025	62.9	21.7	9.3	5.8	0.3	34 678	75.4	8 781	79.2
42 041	3240	Cumberland County	202 010	57.3	20.1	13.7	7.5	1.4	83 015	73.0	19 455	78.3
42 043	3240	Dauphin County............	236 801	59.0	24.5	9.4	5.6	1.5	102 670	65.4	23 215	75.2
42 045	6160	Delaware County...........	516 387	64.4	19.6	8.4	5.8	1.8	206 320	71.9	55 237	79.1
42 047	...	Elk County....................	33 086	74.4	18.4	4.8	2.1	0.3	14 124	79.4	4 066	80.6
42 049	2360	Erie County..................	263 678	60.2	28.3	4.8	5.3	1.2	106 507	69.2	25 937	75.3
42 051	6280	Fayette County..............	140 254	70.9	20.7	5.0	3.2	0.3	59 969	73.1	17 753	79.3
42 053	...	Forest County...............	4 765	68.6	8.8	15.9	6.4	0.3	2 000	82.6	684	82.7
42 055	...	Franklin County.............	121 121	62.8	23.3	5.3	7.6	1.0	50 633	74.0	13 063	79.0
42 057	...	Fulton County...............	13 370	70.5	16.8	7.0	5.4	0.2	5 660	79.0	1 364	83.6
42 059	...	Greene County..............	38 564	67.0	19.8	7.5	5.2	0.4	15 060	74.1	4 159	81.1
42 061	...	Huntingdon County	43 120	68.2	16.6	11.1	3.9	0.2	16 759	77.6	4 379	81.4
42 063	...	Indiana County	85 184	64.3	17.3	14.3	3.5	0.7	34 123	71.8	8 768	80.8
42 065	...	Jefferson County...........	43 396	69.5	18.2	8.8	3.2	0.3	18 375	77.2	5 305	78.4
42 067	...	Juniata County	21 301	67.9	19.8	8.5	3.3	0.5	8 584	77.7	2 235	78.7
42 069	7560	Lackawanna County......	202 210	69.2	21.4	4.5	4.3	0.7	86 218	67.6	27 139	71.3
42 071	4000	Lancaster County	438 090	60.2	27.2	6.4	4.9	1.3	172 560	70.9	38 891	73.8
42 073	...	Lawrence County...........	89 361	67.9	20.7	6.7	4.1	0.5	37 091	77.3	11 682	79.2
42 075	3240	Lebanon County............	112 993	62.6	23.7	8.7	4.0	1.0	46 551	72.7	12 071	76.6
42 077	0240	Lehigh County	293 518	58.9	23.3	8.8	6.7	2.2	121 906	68.8	30 627	71.9
42 079	7560	Luzerne County.............	303 358	69.1	22.3	4.7	3.4	0.5	130 687	70.3	41 342	73.6
42 081	9140	Lycoming County...........	113 461	61.0	26.0	8.5	3.8	0.7	47 003	69.5	12 460	76.9
42 083	...	McKean County.............	43 338	64.1	22.9	5.8	6.7	0.5	18 024	74.8	4 990	78.4
42 085	7610	Mercer County	113 496	65.3	21.4	6.9	6.0	0.4	46 712	76.2	13 993	81.6
42 087	...	Mifflin County................	43 591	68.5	22.9	6.2	2.2	0.2	18 413	74.1	5 315	79.1
42 089	...	Monroe County..............	130 412	57.2	15.6	7.0	19.2	1.1	49 454	78.3	9 845	85.0
42 091	6160	Montgomery County......	702 662	61.2	18.7	11.9	6.2	2.0	286 098	73.5	69 074	76.3
42 093	...	Montour County.............	17 220	65.2	15.0	14.1	5.2	0.5	7 085	72.8	1 715	78.4
42 095	0240	Northampton County	251 979	61.7	18.9	8.5	9.3	1.5	101 541	73.3	26 044	78.1
42 097	...	Northumberland County	89 719	67.9	19.5	8.9	3.4	0.4	38 835	73.6	11 839	75.0
42 099	3240	Perry County.................	40 955	67.3	18.5	12.0	1.9	0.3	16 695	79.6	3 514	80.7
42 101	6160	Philadelphia County	1 419 977	61.9	25.3	3.8	5.7	3.3	590 071	59.3	148 201	73.7
42 103	5660	Pike County..................	43 628	60.4	9.2	6.0	24.0	0.4	17 433	84.8	4 435	91.2

[1]MSA = Metropolitan Statistical Area. PMSA = Primary MSA. NECMA = New England County Metropolitan Area. See the Appendix A for explanation of these concepts. See Appendix B for list of metropolitan areas identified by type, with component counties.

Table C-3. States and Counties — Migration, Housing, and Transportation

	Owner-occupied by household type (percent)								Median household income				Median monthly owner costs as a percent of income	
	Family-households					Nonfamily households								
		Married-couple family		Other family										
STATE County	Total family households	Total	With own children under 18 years	Total	With own children under 18 years	Total nonfamily households	Two or more adults	Living alone	All households	Owner-occupied households	Renter-occupied households	Median housing value (owner estimated)	With a mortgage	Without a mortgage
	11	12	13	14	15	16	17	18	19	20	21	22	23	24
OREGON—Cont'd														
Morrow County	75.3	79.7	73.3	54.7	50.0	65.6	58.8	67.3	37 481	41 050	28 640	82 700	19.8	9.9
Multnomah County	69.0	77.4	73.3	44.9	34.5	41.4	37.6	42.7	41 288	55 234	27 236	156 600	23.8	11.9
Polk County	77.8	82.8	75.6	52.7	42.0	46.3	32.7	50.8	42 350	52 599	25 031	143 200	23.4	9.9
Sherman County	72.1	74.1	67.6	61.4	41.8	66.5	66.7	66.5	35 594	37 813	27 500	73 000	18.9	9.9
Tillamook County	76.6	80.6	69.3	57.2	44.3	62.3	51.5	64.4	34 346	38 903	24 911	135 600	23.3	9.9
Umatilla County	69.7	76.9	70.1	43.5	36.0	53.0	40.1	55.9	35 998	42 874	25 555	94 000	20.7	9.9
Union County	75.4	81.1	73.0	46.4	39.7	48.1	37.7	50.7	33 591	40 751	19 624	94 500	20.5	12.0
Wallowa County	76.5	82.6	74.0	42.1	31.0	61.4	57.1	62.0	31 986	36 755	21 294	118 900	22.7	11.3
Wasco County	73.9	80.4	68.3	49.0	38.6	56.1	47.1	57.5	35 699	42 482	22 087	100 900	21.9	11.4
Washington County	69.8	76.0	73.4	40.7	32.6	41.1	31.4	44.1	52 054	66 645	35 015	180 400	22.7	9.9
Wheeler County	74.2	77.4	58.3	45.7	44.4	67.8	86.7	64.6	28 882	32 688	23 750	82 100	23.6	10.6
Yamhill County	74.8	80.6	74.7	48.1	38.5	54.2	38.8	58.7	44 390	52 153	30 143	146 500	23.6	10.5
PENNSYLVANIA	80.4	86.8	85.0	58.5	44.5	52.6	42.8	54.3	39 987	47 611	24 601	94 800	21.6	12.2
Adams County	82.5	87.1	84.0	60.0	48.4	60.7	56.1	61.8	42 913	48 228	28 360	109 500	23.3	10.9
Allegheny County	78.8	86.6	86.1	54.6	38.8	47.7	35.9	49.6	38 154	48 066	22 791	83 500	20.9	12.9
Armstrong County	82.9	87.2	83.9	63.7	50.7	63.6	57.7	64.3	31 694	35 975	20 006	63 800	20.5	12.4
Beaver County	81.7	88.1	85.4	57.0	43.4	59.3	51.9	60.3	36 963	42 896	22 323	83 200	21.1	13.0
Bedford County	85.4	88.7	85.5	67.5	56.2	65.8	63.0	66.2	32 647	35 737	21 337	77 900	21.9	11.2
Berks County	81.9	87.7	85.7	57.9	46.2	55.8	49.9	57.1	44 456	51 927	26 648	104 400	21.4	12.0
Blair County	81.3	87.4	83.7	60.1	45.8	54.9	49.7	55.7	32 846	39 161	18 449	71 100	20.4	11.5
Bradford County	82.4	87.0	82.8	61.9	53.9	58.6	57.5	58.8	34 986	39 655	21 989	74 000	20.5	11.2
Bucks County	85.6	89.3	89.3	66.5	54.9	54.0	51.2	54.7	59 443	67 604	36 426	161 900	23.0	13.0
Butler County	86.6	90.0	90.0	68.0	55.3	56.2	45.6	58.2	42 248	48 791	23 528	105 300	21.0	10.7
Cambria County	82.8	88.6	87.0	61.4	43.6	58.1	47.1	59.2	30 192	34 925	17 827	61 400	20.2	12.3
Cameron County	84.9	90.3	86.6	64.2	47.2	55.7	56.8	55.6	32 077	35 880	21 458	61 500	20.4	12.1
Carbon County	83.5	88.2	83.5	65.0	52.1	66.2	64.6	66.5	35 176	39 586	21 802	81 000	23.1	12.6
Centre County	80.1	83.4	82.0	61.2	54.5	32.6	12.7	44.2	36 295	49 642	20 365	109 400	22.2	9.9
Chester County	85.0	89.9	89.5	63.0	52.0	53.9	50.9	50.9	65 037	75 403	38 516	178 900	21.8	11.9
Clarion County	81.6	86.8	83.8	57.0	42.3	52.8	29.9	58.5	30 984	36 821	17 169	68 000	18.9	10.1
Clearfield County	85.9	90.5	86.4	65.8	51.8	63.5	58.8	64.1	31 407	35 724	18 573	59 300	21.3	12.0
Clinton County	81.5	86.9	82.7	58.3	47.8	55.1	40.7	58.2	30 880	37 190	17 360	75 400	21.1	13.0
Columbia County	81.2	86.5	82.5	58.0	45.2	54.4	37.8	58.6	33 944	39 944	20 762	85 800	20.8	11.0
Crawford County	82.9	88.4	84.3	58.9	47.5	58.9	51.4	60.3	33 688	39 105	20 303	70 600	19.8	12.0
Cumberland County	82.7	86.9	83.8	61.0	50.2	52.8	42.4	54.9	46 628	54 509	29 532	116 500	21.1	9.9
Dauphin County	75.0	83.9	81.1	49.4	36.7	47.7	43.5	48.5	41 496	51 409	27 280	98 700	20.9	11.5
Delaware County	81.1	87.7	87.2	60.7	44.0	52.3	42.1	53.9	49 742	59 597	30 319	127 000	22.3	13.8
Elk County	87.4	91.8	91.0	67.7	51.4	61.5	59.1	61.8	37 769	43 079	21 488	77 400	19.8	10.1
Erie County	79.2	86.9	84.3	53.7	40.0	48.8	40.7	50.4	36 578	44 782	21 072	82 500	20.4	11.6
Fayette County	78.9	85.6	79.8	57.3	40.5	60.4	52.8	61.2	27 582	33 111	16 242	60 600	20.8	11.1
Forest County	88.2	92.4	80.4	66.5	53.1	71.6	82.8	60.8	27 284	30 357	15 038	50 600	18.8	11.0
Franklin County	80.8	84.9	79.4	58.4	45.6	56.4	52.4	57.1	40 379	46 100	27 139	95 100	20.6	9.9
Fulton County	83.8	87.4	83.4	66.5	56.0	66.6	66.8	66.5	35 060	38 435	22 482	82 200	21.0	10.4
Greene County	78.9	85.6	82.3	52.6	36.8	62.5	48.3	64.6	30 235	36 463	16 203	55 800	19.1	12.2
Huntingdon County	83.7	87.9	84.8	64.2	51.8	62.8	55.9	63.7	33 274	37 626	21 091	71 800	20.5	11.2
Indiana County	82.9	86.8	83.2	64.5	50.7	49.8	22.5	57.2	30 214	36 449	16 627	68 300	21.2	11.2
Jefferson County	84.0	89.2	84.9	61.8	46.7	60.8	61.0	60.8	31 575	36 138	17 275	59 600	19.8	10.8
Juniata County	82.9	86.4	83.2	59.8	51.3	61.8	55.7	62.7	34 820	38 234	25 694	86 900	20.7	9.9
Lackawanna County	77.8	84.2	82.6	56.3	36.9	48.7	37.9	50.0	34 386	42 701	20 846	91 100	21.8	13.5
Lancaster County	78.9	84.0	82.1	52.7	42.4	50.0	42.3	51.6	45 464	53 136	29 748	118 300	22.0	9.9
Lawrence County	84.5	90.3	87.0	62.9	45.3	60.4	53.1	61.2	33 147	39 264	17 118	71 100	20.3	12.4
Lebanon County	80.4	85.8	81.5	54.9	41.5	54.5	48.0	55.6	40 738	48 115	25 709	99 200	21.4	10.7
Lehigh County	78.8	85.5	84.0	53.3	39.5	48.1	45.1	48.7	43 413	53 713	26 041	112 100	21.8	12.4
Luzerne County	79.5	86.1	83.6	58.0	38.9	53.5	44.5	54.6	33 616	40 640	20 630	83 500	21.1	13.2
Lycoming County	78.9	85.7	81.1	52.4	41.0	49.6	36.7	52.1	34 044	40 930	21 348	84 700	20.9	12.1
McKean County	82.5	89.8	87.1	55.8	43.5	58.9	52.0	60.0	33 177	39 132	18 810	54 200	18.9	11.3
Mercer County	83.6	89.0	86.5	62.2	48.9	59.5	57.2	59.8	34 619	39 975	20 571	75 100	20.1	11.7
Mifflin County	80.5	84.7	80.4	61.9	50.8	58.8	54.7	59.3	31 867	36 544	18 453	72 300	21.1	11.6
Monroe County	82.8	87.0	85.5	63.0	54.0	65.7	57.2	68.1	46 341	51 248	29 054	123 900	24.3	13.4
Montgomery County	83.5	87.5	88.7	63.1	51.0	50.8	41.7	52.7	60 617	70 631	37 946	158 900	22.1	12.4
Montour County	83.1	87.6	85.8	59.8	50.5	50.9	39.6	52.6	37 747	42 426	24 524	91 500	21.5	9.9
Northampton County	81.2	87.3	84.9	55.3	41.5	54.8	46.0	56.5	44 993	53 104	26 456	118 800	22.4	12.6
Northumberland County	81.4	86.7	83.7	59.5	47.2	58.5	53.8	59.2	31 243	36 475	18 867	70 000	20.7	11.3
Perry County	84.5	88.2	84.8	66.7	57.7	65.4	64.7	65.5	41 817	46 116	26 631	95 000	21.7	9.9
Philadelphia County	68.2	78.9	76.6	55.8	42.1	45.7	34.6	47.7	30 431	37 773	21 365	61 000	21.5	13.4
Pike County	87.3	90.0	86.0	71.4	61.8	77.4	79.0	77.0	44 047	47 412	30 174	117 500	24.5	13.7

STATE County	Median gross rent	Percent who pay 35 percent or more of income for housing expenses		Means of transportation to work (percent except where noted)							Vehicles available (percent of households)		
		Owners	Renters	Number of workers 16 years and over	Car, truck, or van		Public transportation	Other means	Walked	No vehicles	One vehicle	Two or more vehicles	
					Drove alone	Carpooled							
	25	26	27	28	29	30	31	32	33	34	35	36	
OREGON—Cont'd													
Morrow County	473	11.1	16.9	4 517	72.9	16.5	0.1	1.3	4.1	4.2	24.8	70.9	
Multnomah County	633	19.5	32.9	335 182	65.6	12.0	11.1	2.3	4.6	12.7	38.4	48.9	
Polk County	565	17.9	34.3	28 772	74.5	14.1	0.8	1.4	3.9	5.9	28.8	65.3	
Sherman County	390	10.5	28.7	809	71.6	8.5	0.0	0.6	9.8	5.9	24.7	69.4	
Tillamook County	532	16.1	25.6	10 754	70.8	14.9	0.6	1.8	5.4	5.8	35.1	59.1	
Umatilla County	481	13.2	22.7	30 646	79.3	12.8	0.1	1.2	2.9	5.6	29.7	64.7	
Union County	487	12.8	33.4	10 772	74.0	11.5	0.1	1.7	6.2	7.7	27.9	64.4	
Wallowa County	451	18.3	25.0	2 989	70.6	11.2	0.2	1.3	7.1	5.3	28.4	66.4	
Wasco County	488	15.7	29.4	10 068	75.6	13.5	0.3	1.0	4.8	7.0	29.3	63.7	
Washington County	720	16.4	27.6	229 632	75.1	11.1	5.8	1.2	2.2	5.6	33.5	60.9	
Wheeler County	410	13.8	19.0	608	54.6	16.1	1.0	0.7	8.7	2.6	28.9	68.5	
Yamhill County	623	17.9	29.5	38 588	75.3	13.8	0.4	1.4	4.4	4.8	26.6	68.6	
PENNSYLVANIA	531	15.1	28.6	5 556 311	76.5	10.4	5.2	0.8	4.1	12.8	34.9	52.3	
Adams County	509	15.2	21.0	45 475	80.9	10.5	0.2	0.8	4.3	5.2	27.4	67.4	
Allegheny County	516	15.0	29.9	582 362	72.1	10.0	10.5	0.7	4.1	16.2	39.4	44.3	
Armstrong County	395	13.3	24.0	29 788	82.0	10.2	0.4	0.8	3.5	8.5	34.3	57.2	
Beaver County	438	14.4	24.0	81 203	83.6	9.7	1.2	0.7	2.9	9.4	35.1	55.4	
Bedford County	401	13.7	21.3	22 074	79.1	12.3	0.1	1.0	2.7	6.2	28.4	65.4	
Berks County	545	14.1	26.6	177 831	81.1	10.0	1.7	0.8	3.6	10.6	30.7	58.6	
Blair County	411	12.9	28.3	56 733	82.2	10.4	0.5	0.9	3.7	9.8	35.9	54.3	
Bradford County	414	13.1	22.4	27 404	77.5	11.4	0.3	1.0	4.9	7.0	33.1	60.0	
Bucks County	736	17.3	26.2	303 586	83.0	8.3	2.8	0.6	1.7	5.1	28.9	66.0	
Butler County	487	13.3	28.7	81 104	84.9	8.3	0.4	0.5	2.8	5.7	30.6	63.7	
Cambria County	361	12.5	24.2	60 303	81.7	10.7	1.2	0.7	3.5	12.0	35.9	52.0	
Cameron County	368	12.3	16.4	2 483	77.4	13.3	0.1	0.9	6.2	8.9	39.8	51.2	
Carbon County	458	18.1	26.8	25 868	81.8	11.9	0.7	0.6	3.2	8.1	33.0	58.9	
Centre County	565	12.5	42.1	63 097	66.7	11.6	3.9	1.4	12.4	9.0	35.6	55.5	
Chester County	754	15.5	26.3	218 153	80.7	8.6	2.6	0.6	2.5	5.2	28.3	66.5	
Clarion County	383	10.7	30.0	17 652	79.0	9.6	0.3	0.7	6.8	7.3	34.1	58.7	
Clearfield County	376	13.5	23.9	35 093	81.9	11.8	0.2	0.9	2.5	7.7	33.6	58.6	
Clinton County	411	14.4	29.0	16 443	77.2	12.6	0.1	0.8	6.2	9.9	33.5	56.6	
Columbia County	448	12.3	27.8	29 334	79.4	10.5	0.3	1.0	6.2	7.5	32.9	59.6	
Crawford County	406	12.3	26.2	38 871	77.8	11.3	0.4	0.8	5.4	9.2	35.5	55.3	
Cumberland County	576	11.5	24.1	105 860	82.1	9.2	0.6	0.9	4.2	5.5	33.3	61.2	
Dauphin County	557	13.7	24.6	121 202	78.5	12.2	2.4	0.8	3.4	11.4	36.7	51.9	
Delaware County	662	17.5	32.1	253 922	75.4	9.7	7.8	0.7	3.7	11.3	37.7	51.0	
Elk County	418	9.8	18.8	16 486	84.2	10.1	0.4	0.2	3.0	7.7	34.3	57.9	
Erie County	445	13.0	28.4	126 797	79.9	11.2	1.4	1.0	4.3	10.5	37.7	51.8	
Fayette County	367	14.4	28.6	57 946	83.1	11.6	0.4	0.5	2.5	11.5	35.2	53.3	
Forest County	337	9.0	19.5	1 809	74.0	13.8	0.9	1.6	6.1	6.8	35.4	57.9	
Franklin County	455	10.6	19.5	61 973	81.7	10.5	0.3	0.9	2.6	6.0	29.2	64.8	
Fulton County	389	14.3	21.8	6 619	78.4	14.4	0.2	0.6	2.5	5.7	26.4	67.9	
Greene County	367	13.1	25.3	14 878	81.5	11.0	0.1	0.7	3.4	9.5	33.8	56.7	
Huntingdon County	380	13.1	17.9	18 614	73.6	15.5	0.3	0.9	5.8	7.9	29.2	62.9	
Indiana County	426	13.7	35.4	36 913	77.2	10.1	0.4	0.9	8.3	8.3	34.1	57.6	
Jefferson County	377	11.6	26.2	19 569	81.3	10.4	0.2	0.9	3.9	8.5	33.8	57.7	
Juniata County	395	9.9	13.6	10 432	71.6	19.3	0.5	0.7	3.0	6.4	25.2	68.4	
Lackawanna County	440	15.8	25.2	94 532	80.5	12.2	0.9	0.6	3.7	13.7	36.7	49.7	
Lancaster County	572	12.6	25.4	231 674	78.2	10.2	1.2	1.3	4.4	9.8	30.8	59.5	
Lawrence County	424	12.5	28.8	40 285	84.4	7.9	0.7	0.7	3.3	9.6	34.7	55.7	
Lebanon County	470	12.6	21.2	58 810	81.0	10.3	0.6	0.9	3.2	8.3	31.9	59.8	
Lehigh County	586	13.9	28.9	147 930	81.7	9.8	1.6	0.7	3.5	10.6	33.4	56.1	
Luzerne County	434	15.4	25.5	141 168	81.9	11.1	1.0	0.6	3.2	12.9	36.3	50.8	
Lycoming County	449	14.0	29.4	54 029	80.3	11.3	1.1	1.0	4.0	10.1	34.8	55.1	
McKean County	416	11.9	28.8	19 709	79.0	12.3	0.5	0.8	5.0	9.4	38.2	52.4	
Mercer County	443	11.6	26.2	51 120	83.2	9.2	0.3	0.8	3.2	7.9	37.2	54.9	
Mifflin County	384	12.1	25.1	20 193	77.1	13.1	0.3	0.9	4.0	10.5	31.6	58.0	
Monroe County	658	22.0	32.0	62 270	77.5	13.0	3.4	0.6	2.2	5.0	29.0	66.0	
Montgomery County	757	16.3	25.8	379 832	80.5	8.3	4.4	0.6	2.6	6.3	32.8	60.9	
Montour County	459	13.7	21.5	8 051	82.7	8.4	0.6	0.7	3.4	8.3	33.5	58.2	
Northampton County	576	15.2	27.1	125 671	82.3	9.6	1.1	0.6	4.1	8.5	31.5	60.0	
Northumberland County	389	12.1	23.2	41 141	79.9	12.0	0.3	1.1	4.2	11.2	36.4	52.4	
Perry County	473	13.8	19.8	21 391	77.8	15.2	0.5	0.7	2.2	6.3	26.6	67.1	
Philadelphia County	569	19.4	36.0	569 761	49.2	12.8	25.4	1.6	9.1	35.7	42.0	22.2	
Pike County	701	21.0	32.8	19 302	78.7	12.8	2.9	0.5	1.7	3.9	31.0	65.1	

STATE/ County code	MSA/PMSA/ NECMA code[1]	STATE County	Total population 5 years and over	Residence in 1995 (percent)					Occupied housing units		Householders 65 years and over	
				Same house	Same county, different house	Same state, different county	Different state	Outside the United States	Number	Percent owner-occupied	Number	Percent owner-occupied
			1	2	3	4	5	6	7	8	9	10
		PENNSYLVANIA— Cont'd										
42 105	...	Potter County	16 974	64.9	17.6	9.3	7.5	0.6	7 005	77.4	1 882	80.1
42 107	...	Schuylkill County	143 026	69.5	20.1	6.3	3.7	0.3	60 530	77.9	20 027	80.9
42 109	...	Snyder County	35 421	67.8	16.1	11.0	4.6	0.5	13 654	76.5	3 402	79.0
42 111	3680	Somerset County	75 700	70.6	19.9	5.8	2.6	1.0	31 222	78.0	9 414	81.0
42 113	...	Sullivan County	6 285	70.1	10.8	14.1	4.7	0.4	2 660	80.4	893	84.5
42 115	...	Susquehanna County	39 822	70.0	16.0	7.2	6.4	0.4	16 529	79.5	4 291	82.0
42 117	...	Tioga County	39 139	62.5	20.9	9.4	6.9	0.4	15 925	76.1	4 172	81.7
42 119	...	Union County	39 637	57.3	12.1	17.4	10.4	2.8	13 178	73.4	3 365	73.6
42 121	...	Venango County	54 307	67.2	20.2	8.0	4.0	0.5	22 747	76.4	6 087	80.2
42 123	...	Warren County	41 426	67.7	22.2	5.3	4.6	0.2	17 696	78.2	4 668	81.3
42 125	6280	Washington County	191 658	68.9	18.8	7.9	3.9	0.5	81 130	77.1	24 082	80.4
42 127	...	Wayne County	45 043	67.0	14.9	7.7	9.8	0.6	18 350	80.5	5 312	84.6
42 129	6280	Westmoreland County	350 893	70.0	18.7	7.7	3.2	0.4	149 813	78.0	44 528	82.6
42 131	7560	Wyoming County	26 470	65.5	17.4	11.5	5.1	0.5	10 762	79.0	2 351	84.1
42 133	9280	York County	358 615	60.2	24.7	6.4	7.8	0.9	148 219	76.1	31 919	80.9
44 000	...	RHODE ISLAND	985 184	58.1	24.4	5.1	9.8	2.6	408 424	60.0	98 303	65.3
44 001	6483	Bristol County	47 964	63.5	16.7	7.4	11.3	1.1	19 033	71.2	5 006	77.5
44 003	6483	Kent County	157 191	63.6	19.7	10.1	5.8	0.8	67 320	71.6	16 437	71.0
44 005	...	Newport County	80 396	55.4	20.6	3.7	18.1	2.2	35 228	61.6	8 380	73.7
44 007	6483	Providence County	583 278	56.6	27.7	2.9	9.3	3.5	239 936	53.2	58 517	59.3
44 009	6483	Washington County	116 355	57.5	19.9	9.8	11.6	1.1	46 907	72.9	9 963	77.6
45 000	...	SOUTH CAROLINA	3 748 669	55.9	22.3	8.3	11.8	1.6	1 533 854	72.2	320 075	83.8
45 001	...	Abbeville County	24 403	64.0	18.6	10.2	6.5	0.7	10 131	80.4	2 671	84.8
45 003	0600	Aiken County	133 139	59.7	23.5	4.3	11.3	1.1	55 587	75.7	12 156	86.5
45 005	...	Allendale County	10 451	72.2	16.6	5.1	5.7	0.4	3 915	72.5	1 028	84.0
45 007	3160	Anderson County	154 711	58.8	25.2	8.0	7.3	0.7	65 649	76.3	14 773	82.9
45 009	...	Bamberg County	15 007	65.6	18.3	9.8	5.2	1.2	6 123	74.8	1 646	84.0
45 011	...	Barnwell County	21 850	67.8	21.3	6.1	4.6	0.3	9 021	75.5	1 918	79.7
45 013	...	Beaufort County	112 783	43.9	18.0	4.6	30.0	3.5	45 532	73.3	12 211	91.8
45 015	1440	Berkeley County	132 615	52.9	17.1	12.6	16.0	1.4	49 922	74.2	7 662	90.2
45 017	...	Calhoun County	14 235	70.8	10.7	13.3	4.5	0.6	5 917	84.3	1 425	88.1
45 019	1440	Charleston County	289 926	49.6	25.5	7.1	15.9	2.0	123 326	61.1	24 426	79.8
45 021	3160	Cherokee County	48 722	61.2	24.2	6.5	7.3	0.7	20 495	73.9	4 164	81.0
45 023	...	Chester County	31 813	66.0	19.1	8.5	6.1	0.4	12 860	78.3	2 995	88.5
45 025	...	Chesterfield County	39 878	65.2	19.7	4.6	9.1	1.4	16 557	76.2	3 552	84.1
45 027	...	Clarendon County	30 529	64.4	17.9	9.5	7.4	0.8	11 812	79.1	3 184	86.6
45 029	...	Colleton County	35 628	64.2	18.3	9.5	6.8	1.1	14 470	80.2	3 261	85.6
45 031	...	Darlington County	62 811	64.2	21.8	7.5	5.6	0.9	25 793	77.0	5 254	81.6
45 033	...	Dillon County	28 497	64.6	24.3	5.7	4.7	0.7	11 199	72.0	2 420	74.8
45 035	1440	Dorchester County	89 935	52.4	16.9	14.2	15.1	1.5	34 709	75.0	5 894	81.2
45 037	0600	Edgefield County	23 161	62.6	17.7	10.5	7.3	1.8	8 270	80.4	1 875	80.7
45 039	...	Fairfield County	21 913	70.5	16.3	8.6	4.2	0.5	8 774	77.5	2 214	85.3
45 041	2655	Florence County	117 636	59.6	24.3	7.6	7.5	0.9	47 147	73.0	9 619	81.7
45 043	...	Georgetown County	52 353	62.0	17.4	7.7	12.2	0.8	21 659	81.3	5 305	88.9
45 045	3160	Greenville County	354 190	51.5	25.5	6.9	13.5	2.5	149 556	68.2	29 171	81.0
45 047	...	Greenwood County	61 657	54.6	26.6	10.3	6.9	1.6	25 729	69.3	6 140	82.4
45 049	...	Hampton County	19 957	68.8	16.0	10.2	4.6	0.3	7 444	78.1	1 852	86.6
45 051	5330	Horry County	185 564	49.3	22.3	5.6	21.1	1.7	81 800	73.0	19 754	88.7
45 053	...	Jasper County	19 167	60.5	12.8	13.3	10.1	3.3	7 042	77.8	1 665	87.0
45 055	...	Kershaw County	49 292	60.5	18.1	12.3	8.5	0.6	20 188	82.0	4 314	86.6
45 057	...	Lancaster County	57 411	62.7	22.8	6.2	7.3	1.0	23 178	75.2	5 060	86.3
45 059	...	Laurens County	64 984	61.4	19.9	12.5	5.2	1.0	26 290	77.4	5 848	83.3
45 061	...	Lee County	18 833	67.6	15.0	10.9	4.6	1.9	6 886	79.3	1 746	84.6
45 063	1760	Lexington County	201 383	55.2	21.0	12.7	9.8	1.3	83 240	77.2	13 756	86.4
45 065	...	McCormick County	9 552	59.1	12.3	9.9	18.0	0.8	3 558	81.1	1 056	86.6
45 067	...	Marion County	33 033	63.6	24.1	6.1	4.8	1.3	13 301	73.4	3 219	83.3
45 069	...	Marlboro County	26 855	67.6	20.6	5.5	5.9	0.4	10 478	70.8	2 361	79.2
45 071	...	Newberry County	33 875	63.9	20.1	9.2	5.0	1.9	14 026	76.7	3 727	83.5
45 073	...	Oconee County	62 175	59.4	22.8	6.3	10.7	0.8	27 283	78.4	6 807	86.1
45 075	...	Orangeburg County	85 592	65.0	20.8	7.2	6.2	0.7	34 118	75.6	8 497	84.3
45 077	3160	Pickens County	103 955	52.6	19.6	15.8	10.3	1.6	41 306	73.4	8 063	85.2
45 079	1760	Richland County	300 624	49.0	22.7	11.4	14.3	2.5	120 101	61.4	20 163	79.4
45 081	...	Saluda County	17 939	67.7	14.6	9.7	4.8	3.3	7 127	80.6	1 753	89.1
45 083	3160	Spartanburg County	236 811	56.3	27.1	6.7	8.5	1.4	97 735	72.0	20 991	81.5

[1]MSA = Metropolitan Statistical Area. PMSA = Primary MSA. NECMA = New England County Metropolitan Area. See the Appendix A for explanation of these concepts. See Appendix B for list of metropolitan areas identified by type, with component counties.

STATE County	Total family households	Total	With own children under 18 years	Total	With own children under 18 years	Total nonfamily households	Two or more adults	Living alone	All households	Owner-occupied households	Renter-occupied households	Median housing value (owner estimated)	With a mortgage	Without a mortgage
	11	12	13	14	15	16	17	18	19	20	21	22	23	24
PENNSYLVANIA—Cont'd														
Potter County	82.4	86.6	81.1	61.9	49.4	64.6	56.6	65.8	32 179	36 463	21 444	70 500	20.4	11.9
Schuylkill County	85.1	89.8	87.1	67.9	51.5	63.6	61.9	63.8	32 580	36 940	19 372	63 900	20.4	12.5
Snyder County	83.6	87.8	84.7	59.9	43.8	57.4	49.0	59.1	35 996	40 315	23 007	87 800	21.5	10.7
Somerset County	84.4	88.3	84.8	64.8	47.3	62.6	59.3	63.0	30 715	34 712	18 924	66 900	21.6	10.8
Sullivan County	87.2	90.7	87.9	68.7	49.0	67.2	65.3	67.5	30 000	33 669	20 741	80 800	20.9	12.1
Susquehanna County	84.9	89.1	85.6	66.3	55.7	66.1	65.6	66.2	33 689	37 500	20 765	84 500	22.5	12.5
Tioga County	82.5	87.5	81.9	58.3	49.5	61.0	52.7	62.7	31 928	36 885	19 091	72 200	21.4	11.2
Union County	83.2	87.0	85.6	57.9	46.0	50.1	45.5	50.9	40 248	46 915	21 763	97 200	20.7	9.9
Venango County	83.6	89.4	85.8	61.1	49.9	59.3	61.4	59.0	32 406	37 661	18 193	55 800	19.0	11.0
Warren County	86.0	89.7	86.1	68.5	58.9	61.5	56.3	62.3	35 683	40 122	21 848	62 800	18.8	11.0
Washington County	84.4	89.7	87.2	62.1	44.8	60.5	50.1	61.9	37 437	43 826	20 452	85 400	20.2	11.0
Wayne County	84.9	89.3	84.9	65.6	52.6	69.8	69.2	69.9	34 202	37 840	21 201	103 900	24.1	12.1
Westmoreland County	84.9	89.3	86.7	64.4	48.5	61.8	53.5	62.7	37 095	42 651	21 847	87 600	20.9	11.7
Wyoming County	84.0	87.7	84.3	67.2	56.8	66.1	58.1	67.4	36 610	40 867	23 281	91 600	22.6	12.5
York County	83.7	89.1	87.2	58.9	47.5	57.3	51.0	58.8	45 193	51 484	27 648	108 200	22.0	10.5
RHODE ISLAND	70.4	79.4	76.9	43.7	29.2	40.6	34.7	41.8	41 827	56 559	24 361	130 500	22.7	13.4
Bristol County	81.1	85.8	85.3	59.3	38.9	47.6	39.3	49.1	50 972	63 960	28 015	163 500	22.9	14.7
Kent County	81.4	86.7	87.7	59.6	45.4	51.6	50.4	51.8	47 375	56 416	27 720	116 800	22.9	14.1
Newport County	71.2	77.1	70.4	48.5	31.8	44.9	37.6	46.6	50 146	61 177	32 125	163 200	23.2	13.0
Providence County	63.6	74.7	71.2	37.3	23.7	34.6	28.9	35.8	36 648	53 439	22 114	122 100	22.7	13.5
Washington County	82.4	87.8	86.0	58.5	46.5	52.4	40.3	56.3	52 810	63 908	29 006	157 200	22.5	12.2
SOUTH CAROLINA	78.3	85.5	81.6	58.3	48.2	57.8	41.0	61.0	36 951	43 179	23 855	83 100	20.5	9.9
Abbeville County	84.2	89.7	87.0	68.0	54.9	70.5	50.8	72.4	32 468	36 105	19 120	64 200	19.4	11.0
Aiken County	80.8	87.7	83.5	60.3	50.4	63.0	47.6	65.3	37 556	43 693	21 839	76 800	19.5	9.9
Allendale County	76.6	87.1	86.2	63.3	48.3	64.2	54.5	65.2	21 332	25 761	11 193	44 300	24.6	14.5
Anderson County	82.0	88.5	85.2	60.3	50.0	61.3	48.2	63.1	36 686	41 667	21 329	81 400	19.8	9.9
Bamberg County	79.8	87.0	83.2	68.2	57.7	63.3	50.7	64.4	23 614	29 116	13 893	50 300	20.0	10.9
Barnwell County	79.4	89.2	86.5	59.6	51.5	65.7	56.3	66.7	29 149	33 917	16 294	51 500	18.4	10.5
Beaufort County	76.1	80.3	66.0	58.0	51.7	65.6	44.9	70.6	46 886	53 982	33 002	168 100	23.4	9.9
Berkeley County	77.5	81.8	75.5	63.5	56.2	63.9	52.1	66.8	39 616	44 102	28 729	79 900	20.4	9.9
Calhoun County	86.9	91.4	90.1	75.1	67.7	77.5	72.3	78.1	32 190	35 555	18 875	60 600	18.9	10.9
Charleston County	70.4	79.8	76.1	48.6	36.7	45.0	29.2	49.9	37 808	49 604	25 005	117 700	22.1	11.0
Cherokee County	78.8	87.0	86.3	57.5	49.2	61.3	55.3	62.1	33 743	39 443	21 270	66 600	19.5	9.9
Chester County	81.8	89.4	85.2	66.1	53.5	69.2	61.7	70.1	32 336	36 126	20 332	60 200	18.6	9.9
Chesterfield County	80.3	87.4	84.9	64.0	54.6	66.2	58.0	67.2	29 187	33 977	17 060	54 400	19.8	9.9
Clarendon County	81.8	90.5	86.2	63.9	56.5	71.7	74.5	71.4	26 842	31 702	14 517	59 700	19.3	10.8
Colleton County	83.5	89.4	86.7	70.1	62.7	71.5	63.1	72.5	30 213	32 682	18 659	62 200	22.3	10.9
Darlington County	80.9	88.2	85.0	65.9	54.2	67.0	54.9	68.6	30 987	36 158	17 773	59 800	19.2	9.9
Dillon County	76.2	84.9	81.0	61.9	51.7	61.1	52.4	62.0	26 366	32 493	13 426	50 000	19.7	10.9
Dorchester County	80.8	86.1	82.6	63.6	54.0	56.3	42.3	58.8	42 939	49 039	29 276	92 200	20.9	9.9
Edgefield County	84.5	90.0	87.9	68.5	60.0	67.7	64.6	68.0	34 690	40 233	16 708	73 000	20.9	9.9
Fairfield County	79.3	86.1	79.8	65.7	56.4	72.7	74.6	72.5	29 685	34 299	17 088	63 100	21.9	9.9
Florence County	78.5	86.9	84.2	59.3	47.4	58.4	43.1	60.4	34 845	40 973	20 909	71 900	19.6	9.9
Georgetown County	85.2	89.8	85.3	71.9	61.8	70.6	62.5	71.8	35 164	39 179	21 318	83 700	21.4	10.4
Greenville County	75.7	83.4	80.8	49.9	39.3	51.8	35.4	54.7	40 986	50 210	26 676	102 700	20.3	9.9
Greenwood County	74.4	84.5	76.8	49.3	39.1	58.0	34.3	62.5	34 475	40 525	21 835	75 000	19.5	9.9
Hampton County	81.6	88.4	85.3	66.9	59.5	69.3	63.3	70.0	28 369	31 982	18 268	51 400	20.1	11.8
Horry County	78.9	85.3	80.8	57.4	48.2	60.9	43.5	65.9	36 215	40 898	26 481	95 400	21.9	9.9
Jasper County	81.2	84.2	79.8	74.2	64.3	68.6	57.0	70.6	30 191	33 064	20 561	64 900	23.0	10.5
Kershaw County	85.5	90.7	87.7	69.7	59.1	71.9	60.4	73.5	38 526	41 989	22 764	77 000	19.3	9.9
Lancaster County	79.7	88.0	85.9	56.6	45.5	63.1	44.8	65.9	34 691	40 229	23 139	71 100	19.8	9.9
Laurens County	81.6	88.6	83.2	63.9	54.8	66.7	59.8	67.7	33 827	38 226	20 194	67 600	19.8	9.9
Lee County	83.5	91.5	87.6	70.9	66.4	68.8	71.2	68.6	26 590	30 968	13 544	47 600	20.6	11.6
Lexington County	83.0	88.8	86.8	61.1	53.8	62.1	45.5	66.1	44 254	50 797	27 441	92 700	19.6	9.9
McCormick County	83.5	89.4	85.2	69.7	66.3	74.2	97.2	72.3	32 594	36 362	15 400	56 200	22.6	10.2
Marion County	76.7	86.8	83.2	60.8	47.4	64.9	54.6	66.1	26 285	31 172	15 757	55 600	19.4	11.4
Marlboro County	76.5	86.0	80.8	59.9	47.3	57.4	59.7	57.2	26 651	32 439	15 536	49 000	20.7	10.1
Newberry County	80.5	88.3	85.0	62.4	55.1	67.7	50.9	69.7	32 926	38 121	18 121	69 100	20.8	9.9
Oconee County	84.0	88.6	83.8	64.0	53.3	63.7	57.3	64.6	36 595	41 122	21 082	79 700	19.3	9.9
Orangeburg County	80.1	88.3	85.0	64.8	57.4	65.3	45.3	68.2	29 086	33 673	17 534	59 800	20.3	9.9
Pickens County	82.9	87.7	84.7	63.0	53.0	52.2	22.9	61.9	36 189	42 357	20 506	84 800	19.6	9.9
Richland County	71.0	81.0	77.5	47.8	36.7	44.5	28.5	48.3	39 921	51 811	25 676	95 000	20.9	9.9
Saluda County	82.3	88.0	83.2	66.0	59.7	75.7	54.7	78.7	35 541	39 592	20 484	68 600	19.4	9.9
Spartanburg County	77.7	85.4	81.5	54.3	42.2	57.7	46.8	59.4	37 332	44 367	23 765	84 400	20.5	9.9

STATE County	Median gross rent	Percent who pay 35 percent or more of income for housing expenses		Means of transportation to work (percent except where noted)							Vehicles available (percent of households)		
				Number of workers 16 years and over	Car, truck, or van								
		Owners	Renters		Drove alone	Carpooled	Public transportation	Other means	Walked		No vehicles	One vehicle	Two or more vehicles
	25	26	27	28	29	30	31	32	33		34	35	36

PENNSYLVANIA— Cont'd													
Potter County	432	13.9	26.3	7 649	73.4	14.3	0.1	0.9	6.4		6.1	37.7	56.2
Schuylkill County	379	13.6	21.4	62 702	79.7	12.6	0.4	0.6	4.0		12.7	33.9	53.4
Snyder County	439	12.4	22.8	17 573	75.9	10.5	0.6	1.8	6.6		7.5	29.0	63.5
Somerset County	366	13.2	23.3	34 049	79.2	12.4	0.3	0.6	3.1		8.3	33.6	58.1
Sullivan County	346	14.7	22.0	2 691	70.7	13.3	0.4	0.9	10.2		5.8	34.6	59.6
Susquehanna County....	427	15.7	26.5	18 685	78.3	12.5	0.2	0.8	3.8		6.4	31.6	62.0
Tioga County...............	421	13.7	25.5	17 859	75.0	12.7	0.4	0.9	5.7		5.9	34.4	59.7
Union County	473	11.3	27.3	16 002	76.9	10.0	0.1	1.3	8.0		8.0	29.0	63.0
Venango County	382	12.0	25.8	24 055	80.4	11.7	0.7	1.2	3.3		8.6	36.0	55.4
Warren County	401	10.6	18.7	20 062	78.4	12.5	0.6	1.1	4.4		6.6	36.7	56.7
Washington County.......	423	12.5	26.0	89 534	82.5	9.9	1.3	0.6	3.2		9.5	33.4	57.1
Wayne County	481	18.6	28.6	19 909	80.1	10.4	1.0	0.9	3.5		6.4	33.0	60.5
Westmoreland County...	432	13.9	24.5	165 205	84.7	8.7	0.9	0.5	2.9		8.4	34.6	57.0
Wyoming County	470	17.3	23.7	12 464	81.3	10.9	0.4	0.5	3.2		5.4	30.3	64.3
York County	531	13.5	23.7	193 126	84.3	9.5	0.6	0.8	2.2		0.0	20.3	61.1
RHODE ISLAND	553	17.1	28.9	490 905	80.1	10.4	2.5	1.0	3.8		10.9	36.4	52.6
Bristol County..............	578	19.2	24.5	24 323	82.0	8.7	2.3	0.8	3.4		7.0	30.6	62.4
Kent County	613	16.8	26.2	83 793	86.6	8.8	1.2	0.5	1.2		7.2	33.3	59.5
Newport County	689	18.4	25.2	43 684	80.1	8.3	1.4	1.2	5.2		7.9	36.7	55.4
Providence County........	527	17.2	30.0	276 324	77.4	11.8	3.3	1.1	4.5		14.1	39.0	46.9
Washington County.......	645	15.7	29.2	62 781	82.8	8.4	1.4	0.7	3.5		4.1	29.9	66.0
SOUTH CAROLINA ...	510	14.3	26.8	1 822 969	79.4	14.0	0.8	1.3	2.3		9.0	33.6	57.4
Abbeville County	367	14.3	27.9	11 334	79.9	14.6	0.6	0.7	2.5		8.4	30.1	61.4
Aiken County	475	12.6	26.9	62 802	81.6	13.9	0.3	1.0	1.5		7.3	32.9	59.8
Allendale County	305	23.1	25.8	3 414	72.1	19.5	1.6	1.4	3.5		21.8	37.4	40.7
Anderson County	454	12.1	26.3	76 098	83.3	12.6	0.3	0.8	1.4		7.7	30.8	61.5
Bamberg County	299	19.5	24.8	5 822	71.7	20.8	0.4	2.1	3.0		15.2	39.0	45.8
Barnwell County	384	16.0	27.6	9 272	77.8	16.7	0.6	1.4	1.8		13.9	32.7	53.4
Beaufort County	690	19.1	24.4	55 790	71.2	14.4	1.2	3.1	5.5		5.5	35.1	58.4
Berkeley County	562	15.2	20.5	65 990	78.6	13.6	0.4	1.0	4.0		6.7	32.1	61.2
Calhoun County	370	14.6	22.5	6 417	78.1	17.2	0.6	1.4	0.9		8.9	29.5	61.6
Charleston County	605	17.9	33.6	143 921	76.6	12.8	2.5	1.9	3.5		11.9	37.6	50.5
Cherokee County	401	14.2	21.0	22 999	79.0	16.7	0.5	1.9	0.8		10.2	33.4	56.5
Chester County	409	14.5	24.6	14 456	79.0	17.5	0.4	1.1	1.1		10.8	32.9	56.3
Chesterfield County.......	391	13.1	26.3	17 306	80.0	15.3	0.2	1.4	1.4		11.2	33.4	55.4
Clarendon County	320	16.9	26.6	11 675	77.2	17.8	0.5	0.7	2.0		13.3	37.0	49.7
Colleton County	405	20.1	25.0	14 627	72.0	21.6	1.3	1.7	1.4		12.5	34.1	53.3
Darlington County	374	14.0	27.1	28 234	80.0	13.4	0.9	1.6	2.4		11.7	35.3	53.1
Dillon County...............	335	16.3	27.5	12 170	76.0	18.0	0.5	2.2	1.7		15.0	35.6	49.4
Dorchester County	568	13.6	22.7	44 282	82.0	12.7	0.5	1.3	1.3		6.5	31.9	61.6
Edgefield County	361	15.4	23.5	9 434	80.6	15.2	0.7	0.7	0.9		8.8	28.8	62.4
Fairfield County	395	19.4	26.4	9 870	77.2	18.7	0.4	1.6	1.1		13.2	29.9	56.9
Florence County	452	14.8	27.2	54 482	80.6	13.9	1.0	1.4	1.4		10.4	33.7	55.9
Georgetown County	489	16.7	26.9	23 162	76.3	16.9	1.4	1.4	1.9		10.0	33.9	56.1
Greenville County.........	544	13.2	25.5	185 461	81.6	12.4	0.4	1.0	2.2		7.6	34.3	58.2
Greenwood County	440	11.6	24.5	29 747	81.5	14.5	0.1	0.8	2.1		10.6	33.5	55.9
Hampton County	370	16.8	24.6	7 619	73.2	19.1	1.6	2.2	2.3		15.2	34.5	50.4
Horry County	594	15.4	28.0	95 732	79.0	14.4	0.5	1.7	1.7		6.5	38.5	55.0
Jasper County	493	17.0	26.1	8 431	68.4	25.8	1.2	1.0	1.6		12.1	34.1	53.7
Kershaw County	455	14.3	20.4	24 599	79.6	16.1	0.4	1.1	1.3		8.1	28.7	63.2
Lancaster County	427	13.5	22.6	27 442	78.9	17.8	0.4	0.7	1.1		9.0	29.5	61.5
Laurens County............	448	13.7	29.6	30 661	79.9	15.6	0.2	0.9	1.9		9.5	31.9	58.6
Lee County..................	330	16.5	26.6	7 310	71.3	21.3	2.3	1.3	2.4		16.8	35.2	48.0
Lexington County	548	11.6	24.6	109 259	83.1	11.6	0.3	0.9	1.2		5.3	30.6	64.0
McCormick County	304	17.1	22.1	3 267	73.3	20.6	0.5	1.2	2.6		11.0	33.4	55.5
Marion County	386	16.5	27.9	13 854	74.2	18.1	1.3	3.3	1.3		15.8	38.1	46.1
Marlboro County...........	342	15.6	28.2	10 828	76.4	17.3	1.3	2.0	1.7		18.0	34.4	47.5
Newberry County	385	13.0	21.7	15 581	80.3	15.1	0.7	1.2	1.4		10.9	31.1	58.0
Oconee County	424	9.6	21.7	29 544	80.7	14.7	0.3	1.0	1.2		6.2	29.6	64.2
Orangeburg County.......	389	15.8	26.3	35 970	77.6	17.0	0.6	1.2	1.8		12.8	35.1	52.1
Pickens County	479	11.3	34.4	52 130	80.7	12.8	0.3	0.9	3.1		5.9	30.3	63.7
Richland County	570	15.5	29.1	155 968	76.7	12.2	2.0	1.5	5.4		9.0	37.4	53.6
Saluda County..............	394	12.3	21.2	8 584	76.4	19.4	0.2	0.8	1.0		9.1	29.3	61.6
Spartanburg County.......	485	13.2	25.3	117 096	82.2	13.3	0.5	0.6	1.4		8.4	31.8	59.9

STATE/ County code	MSA/PMSA/ NECMA code[1]	STATE County	Total population 5 years and over	Residence in 1995 (percent)					Occupied housing units		Householders 65 years and over	
				Same house	Same county, different house	Same state, different county	Different state	Outside the United States	Number	Percent owner-occupied	Number	Percent owner-occupied
			1	2	3	4	5	6	7	8	9	10
		SOUTH CAROLINA—Cont'd										
45 085	8140	Sumter County	96 890	55.0	23.5	5.8	12.9	2.8	37 728	69.5	7 527	80.4
45 087	...	Union County	28 054	68.3	22.8	5.1	3.6	0.3	12 087	76.7	3 015	83.9
45 089	...	Williamsburg County	34 689	74.9	14.4	6.5	3.7	0.6	13 714	80.7	3 393	86.4
45 091	1520	York County	153 591	52.3	24.8	5.1	16.6	1.2	61 051	73.1	10 543	84.4
46 000	...	SOUTH DAKOTA	703 820	55.7	21.2	11.8	10.3	1.0	290 245	68.2	69 783	73.2
46 003	...	Aurora County	2 889	66.9	12.8	9.3	10.2	0.8	1 165	76.1	367	79.8
46 005	...	Beadle County	16 090	61.0	24.2	8.1	6.0	0.7	7 210	67.7	2 171	70.2
46 007	...	Bennett County	3 260	61.1	18.3	12.1	8.5	0.0	1 123	59.5	250	74.4
46 009	...	Bon Homme County	6 897	61.7	14.1	16.8	7.1	0.3	2 635	76.1	927	79.3
46 011	...	Brookings County	26 601	45.5	20.4	19.4	13.3	1.3	10 665	58.2	1 966	69.9
46 013	...	Brown County	33 208	55.3	25.4	9.9	8.9	0.5	14 638	66.3	3 671	68.9
46 015	...	Brule County	5 047	63.0	15.2	12.6	9.1	0.1	1 998	71.2	597	73.4
46 017	...	Buffalo County	1 822	68.6	15.2	14.5	1.6	0.1	526	43.2	90	70.0
46 019	...	Butte County	8 539	54.9	21.4	9.1	14.1	0.4	3 516	73.4	867	75.9
46 021	...	Campbell County	1 688	80.0	11.7	2.5	5.5	0.2	725	82.1	266	84.6
46 023	...	Charles Mix County	8 546	67.0	19.2	7.1	6.2	0.4	3 343	68.3	1 078	74.9
46 025	...	Clark County	3 912	68.9	14.7	12.0	3.1	1.4	1 598	80.7	583	80.1
46 027	...	Clay County	12 806	39.4	15.2	25.8	17.1	2.5	4 878	54.4	882	75.4
46 029	...	Codington County	24 107	56.4	24.5	12.5	6.0	0.6	10 357	70.1	2 234	71.2
46 031	...	Corson County	3 796	65.7	17.8	7.6	8.4	0.4	1 271	59.2	324	66.7
46 033	...	Custer County	6 931	55.7	12.2	14.1	17.9	0.1	2 970	77.0	827	79.2
46 035	...	Davison County	17 527	52.5	22.5	17.3	7.0	0.7	7 585	61.8	2 005	58.7
46 037	...	Day County	5 922	69.3	15.9	8.2	6.1	0.4	2 586	76.1	954	73.6
46 039	...	Deuel County	4 239	68.5	15.4	9.8	6.0	0.2	1 843	80.0	585	80.2
46 041	...	Dewey County	5 432	54.8	25.4	12.5	6.8	0.4	1 863	55.3	402	68.9
46 043	...	Douglas County	3 253	73.1	13.9	7.9	4.9	0.2	1 321	81.0	497	82.7
46 045	...	Edmunds County	4 120	68.8	14.0	11.6	5.4	0.2	1 681	82.0	584	81.7
46 047	...	Fall River County	7 081	60.3	15.9	7.9	15.6	0.3	3 127	69.5	1 051	77.6
46 049	...	Faulk County	2 504	73.9	12.5	10.6	2.6	0.4	1 014	81.5	376	87.2
46 051	...	Grant County	7 389	67.0	16.2	8.4	8.0	0.5	3 116	77.4	957	70.1
46 053	...	Gregory County	4 572	71.2	17.1	5.6	5.9	0.2	2 022	74.7	808	76.6
46 055	...	Haakon County	2 075	67.0	17.1	11.1	4.9	0.0	870	76.9	280	86.4
46 057	...	Hamlin County	5 180	65.5	17.8	11.7	4.8	0.3	2 048	81.8	620	83.2
46 059	...	Hand County	3 543	73.1	15.8	8.1	2.8	0.2	1 543	74.1	615	72.7
46 061	...	Hanson County	2 900	72.8	8.3	13.0	5.0	0.9	1 115	79.2	307	79.8
46 063	...	Harding County	1 298	69.5	15.3	6.9	7.9	0.5	525	73.7	152	84.2
46 065	...	Hughes County	15 403	57.6	19.1	14.6	7.7	1.0	6 512	66.2	1 231	62.1
46 067	...	Hutchinson County	7 606	69.9	14.8	10.5	4.7	0.1	3 190	78.8	1 290	78.1
46 069	...	Hyde County	1 529	69.7	12.2	13.9	4.3	0.0	679	71.6	238	81.5
46 071	...	Jackson County	2 673	68.1	15.1	11.8	4.7	0.3	945	63.6	252	72.2
46 073	...	Jerauld County	2 213	75.0	14.2	7.2	3.5	0.0	987	72.1	395	75.2
46 075	...	Jones County	1 136	67.4	17.2	13.4	2.0	0.0	509	72.5	159	78.0
46 077	...	Kingsbury County	5 507	65.9	16.5	12.5	4.9	0.3	2 406	76.1	911	73.0
46 079	...	Lake County	10 667	58.1	18.1	15.4	8.1	0.3	4 372	70.5	1 191	78.1
46 081	...	Lawrence County	20 762	48.6	20.4	16.4	14.2	0.5	8 881	64.8	2 184	69.7
46 083	7760	Lincoln County	22 198	53.1	11.5	25.0	9.9	0.5	8 782	79.7	1 736	74.4
46 085	...	Lyman County	3 562	65.3	15.2	11.7	7.1	0.7	1 400	68.8	380	84.2
46 087	...	McCook County	5 445	62.2	15.4	15.6	6.5	0.3	2 204	78.9	663	73.3
46 089	...	McPherson County	2 740	73.2	14.1	7.7	4.5	0.5	1 227	83.2	534	79.4
46 091	...	Marshall County	4 308	73.3	16.1	5.1	5.5	0.0	1 844	77.9	635	79.7
46 093	...	Meade County	22 418	50.2	13.6	17.0	16.7	2.6	8 805	68.2	1 577	77.5
46 095	...	Mellette County	1 893	67.2	11.4	14.0	7.2	0.3	694	65.0	167	80.8
46 097	...	Miner County	2 738	71.1	14.9	9.2	4.6	0.2	1 212	76.4	449	77.7
46 099	7760	Minnehaha County	137 416	49.0	27.8	9.5	11.7	2.0	57 996	64.7	10 405	68.9
46 101	...	Moody County	6 176	63.0	16.4	10.8	8.7	1.1	2 526	72.5	659	76.9
46 103	6660	Pennington County	82 286	47.7	27.2	9.7	14.1	1.3	34 641	66.2	6 831	73.7
46 105	...	Perkins County	3 169	74.3	14.9	4.7	4.9	1.3	1 429	76.6	515	77.7
46 107	...	Potter County	2 571	67.9	19.4	8.0	4.6	0.2	1 145	79.1	424	79.5
46 109	...	Roberts County	9 334	65.4	17.7	8.5	8.1	0.3	3 683	68.9	1 021	76.6
46 111	...	Sanborn County	2 528	69.1	16.3	9.5	4.9	0.1	1 043	77.7	338	78.7
46 113	...	Shannon County	11 078	67.7	19.4	5.6	6.4	0.9	2 785	49.6	435	62.5
46 115	...	Spink County	7 001	67.5	18.5	9.1	4.4	0.4	2 847	73.8	947	68.7
46 117	...	Stanley County	2 620	59.7	11.8	20.5	7.6	0.3	1 111	76.6	210	87.6
46 119	...	Sully County	1 466	65.3	15.6	11.9	7.1	0.1	630	75.9	174	81.0
46 121	...	Todd County	7 932	59.3	24.9	8.7	6.8	0.2	2 462	45.0	375	73.6

[1]MSA = Metropolitan Statistical Area. PMSA = Primary MSA. NECMA = New England County Metropolitan Area. See the Appendix A for explanation of these concepts. See Appendix B for list of metropolitan areas identified by type, with component counties.

STATE County	Total family households	Total	With own children under 18 years	Total	With own children under 18 years	Total nonfamily households	Two or more adults	Living alone	All households	Owner-occupied households	Renter-occupied households	Median housing value (owner estimated)	With a mortgage	Without a mortgage
	11	12	13	14	15	16	17	18	19	20	21	22	23	24
SOUTH CAROLINA—Cont'd														
Sumter County	73.9	80.2	74.3	59.5	51.6	57.2	41.9	59.4	33 632	40 014	22 632	67 000	19.5	9.9
Union County	82.8	90.3	86.2	64.4	55.1	61.9	51.7	62.9	31 600	36 631	16 892	56 600	19.7	10.6
Williamsburg County	84.8	90.5	87.4	73.9	64.3	69.1	67.0	69.3	24 523	28 103	11 716	49 100	20.9	10.9
York County	79.0	85.8	83.3	54.9	43.5	56.8	42.3	60.3	44 542	52 241	28 227	104 900	20.7	9.9
SOUTH DAKOTA.......	78.2	84.4	82.0	51.2	43.7	47.6	38.5	49.3	35 271	42 834	21 935	74 300	19.7	10.5
Aurora County	81.8	84.8	78.8	58.1	43.2	62.4	31.6	64.2	29 913	32 394	22 891	37 700	16.6	10.9
Beadle County	80.8	86.8	82.5	48.6	40.6	45.1	44.7	45.1	30 979	39 887	18 273	57 500	18.1	12.0
Bennett County	61.9	76.0	68.3	31.8	24.8	53.1	44.7	54.6	24 623	30 167	15 893	39 500	18.2	10.2
Bon Homme County......	82.9	86.4	84.8	53.6	38.3	61.1	57.1	61.4	30 464	32 555	21 929	52 300	17.9	12.3
Brookings County..........	78.2	84.1	85.9	46.5	41.4	29.9	15.5	35.6	35 490	48 949	20 431	84 800	19.2	9.9
Brown County	80.9	86.6	84.8	54.2	46.2	40.5	35.3	41.4	34 792	43 900	19 896	69 500	18.7	10.8
Brule County	81.8	86.4	84.4	54.8	52.1	49.7	43.3	50.4	31 913	36 433	22 344	61 800	19.7	12.1
Buffalo County..............	44.3	58.4	53.5	30.9	26.2	38.1	0.0	43.5	13 021	19 464	9 922	30 900	17.5	25.0
Butte County	79.0	80.5	77.9	72.1	66.8	59.9	28.5	64.9	29 328	32 400	20 430	52 300	21.1	14.4
Campbell County..........	85.5	85.0	79.5	93.3	100.0	73.8	100.0	73.3	28 233	30 284	20 000	31 300	19.1	11.7
Charles Mix County......	73.5	81.5	74.7	47.5	38.9	56.1	51.5	56.4	25 728	29 910	17 052	53 800	20.2	12.8
Clark County	86.7	88.7	84.7	71.0	54.7	66.7	80.0	65.6	30 284	32 577	16 528	42 300	20.8	12.0
Clay County.................	71.5	78.7	79.2	40.4	34.4	33.1	20.9	38.4	27 554	44 331	15 027	73 700	18.6	9.9
Codington County	81.8	87.2	86.5	56.5	50.5	46.6	40.1	47.8	36 309	43 499	18 883	80 400	19.8	10.5
Corson County	60.4	75.5	68.4	33.8	31.0	55.3	41.0	57.3	20 688	23 547	17 538	22 500	18.7	11.2
Custer County	82.7	86.8	79.7	50.4	50.0	63.7	71.9	62.3	35 505	40 660	22 500	81 900	21.2	10.0
Davison County	78.6	86.0	84.4	43.9	31.5	32.3	35.9	31.6	33 518	46 730	19 804	69 600	18.4	11.3
Day County	84.7	90.0	85.8	56.9	45.4	59.8	64.1	59.5	30 250	34 665	20 542	36 600	17.5	10.3
Deuel County	87.8	90.2	86.5	67.4	55.8	62.9	61.5	63.0	32 350	35 932	20 300	53 000	19.4	10.8
Dewey County	56.6	69.5	66.2	41.2	35.1	51.4	48.1	51.8	23 616	28 537	18 523	32 900	18.1	14.9
Douglas County............	87.7	89.8	89.3	65.4	55.3	63.6	33.3	64.6	28 476	30 000	22 946	40 500	18.6	12.6
Edmunds County	86.1	88.1	86.5	66.1	50.0	71.2	62.5	71.8	32 392	34 312	23 942	44 100	17.8	12.7
Fall River County	79.6	84.1	70.8	58.8	46.6	51.7	59.7	50.7	28 509	33 131	19 189	53 000	19.9	13.1
Faulk County	86.6	89.2	85.5	61.2	59.0	69.7	86.7	68.8	30 086	31 850	19 375	34 100	17.1	10.1
Grant County	87.1	88.4	88.0	75.3	65.9	55.3	52.5	55.5	32 500	37 129	16 944	60 500	17.5	9.9
Gregory County............	82.6	87.3	84.1	51.5	36.8	60.9	54.3	61.3	22 770	26 681	16 188	35 500	18.9	11.9
Haakon County	82.5	83.2	79.3	77.1	66.7	62.6	50.0	63.5	29 628	30 054	28 661	46 500	17.8	11.8
Hamlin County..............	87.5	90.2	89.5	64.2	58.4	67.7	57.5	68.4	33 750	37 218	20 500	53 000	19.7	12.5
Hand County	81.8	84.1	77.6	64.2	62.5	57.5	55.6	57.6	31 639	35 272	19 000	46 400	19.0	10.0
Hanson County.............	81.4	83.5	79.3	49.1	55.6	72.3	44.4	74.3	32 882	37 135	22 308	52 000	18.4	11.9
Harding County	75.1	75.2	67.5	75.0	56.3	70.8	75.0	70.4	25 491	25 703	25 208	47 100	23.6	17.8
Hughoo County	80.5	86.3	88.6	49.3	40.9	37.9	43.9	37.1	43 182	53 139	22 480	86 900	18.2	9.9
Hutchinson County.......	85.6	87.0	84.4	72.9	61.2	64.1	51.0	64.8	29 444	32 935	20 513	47 100	18.1	12.1
Hyde County	74.9	77.7	68.9	58.8	51.1	64.5	56.3	65.2	30 607	32 679	25 662	39 200	21.0	12.2
Jackson County............	66.2	77.9	74.0	40.2	33.1	56.6	50.0	57.5	24 246	26 116	21 333	32 100	18.3	12.2
Jerauld County	78.1	78.9	60.7	72.0	66.0	60.3	47.6	61.2	30 363	33 578	18 036	44 600	17.7	10.6
Jones County	79.6	82.9	82.6	65.0	58.5	60.2	30.8	62.4	30 046	36 193	17 222	38 500	17.1	12.3
Kingsbury County..........	84.8	87.7	84.5	63.0	48.0	58.2	59.4	58.2	31 173	37 083	18 140	48 000	17.2	9.9
Lake County	81.9	85.6	81.5	51.3	46.0	49.6	32.0	53.3	34 918	41 977	20 532	73 900	20.2	9.9
Lawrence County	78.8	83.9	81.5	55.8	46.9	41.2	32.1	43.5	31 914	40 339	18 483	82 300	21.4	11.8
Lincoln County	87.7	91.3	92.5	60.6	54.3	54.2	54.8	54.1	47 955	54 006	27 500	103 500	20.3	9.9
Lyman County	73.1	84.1	76.4	45.3	30.8	57.5	36.6	59.9	29 009	33 490	20 035	43 500	17.6	11.8
McCook County	85.4	86.4	82.2	77.3	66.3	63.2	70.9	62.4	35 904	39 688	23 971	64 600	18.5	11.6
McPherson County.......	90.9	91.2	88.1	86.4	81.8	67.6	47.4	68.6	22 630	24 848	14 500	26 500	18.2	13.9
Marshall County	83.2	87.4	82.5	61.7	50.0	66.8	64.3	67.0	30 457	33 636	17 167	44 900	18.3	11.4
Meade County	70.7	73.0	64.9	57.7	51.5	60.5	61.5	60.3	37 002	41 650	28 894	78 400	20.9	11.3
Mellette County	65.9	74.5	68.0	50.3	45.3	62.7	58.3	63.3	23 000	31 181	14 766	28 700	12.2	11.8
Miner County	84.1	87.7	81.5	58.2	43.1	62.1	46.7	63.3	29 628	31 520	20 333	31 800	21.2	10.2
Minnehaha County	78.1	85.3	86.4	48.3	43.3	39.7	32.1	41.6	42 680	53 081	26 608	98 000	20.2	9.9
Moody County	80.5	86.0	81.8	54.2	48.4	54.5	60.2	53.5	35 789	40 266	23 704	61 600	19.3	9.9
Pennington County........	74.7	82.1	78.4	49.1	40.0	48.6	45.2	49.4	37 571	45 988	22 532	83 800	20.9	9.9
Perkins County	86.2	88.4	85.4	72.9	71.1	58.3	52.4	58.6	27 551	30 612	16 607	34 200	19.5	12.6
Potter County	88.2	90.5	90.8	73.0	62.7	60.4	47.4	61.1	30 208	34 097	17 721	43 500	19.9	10.5
Roberts County	72.5	83.5	75.8	40.8	33.0	60.2	61.6	60.1	28 226	32 484	18 275	46 200	18.8	10.1
Sanborn County	84.5	86.8	83.7	69.7	58.7	61.7	60.4	61.9	32 863	36 667	23 224	36 400	16.1	9.9
Shannon County	48.3	52.4	49.3	45.5	41.9	56.5	73.8	53.4	20 782	24 074	18 229	23 100	18.6	10.1
Spink County................	81.6	84.4	83.3	62.7	55.2	57.3	75.0	55.6	32 037	35 684	20 233	36 700	18.5	10.9
Stanley County	83.6	87.6	88.3	56.3	58.2	60.2	71.2	57.9	41 328	46 581	28 542	75 200	18.4	9.9
Sully County	84.6	84.6	78.6	84.2	71.4	55.6	65.4	54.0	32 500	36 607	25 789	54 200	19.2	10.6
Todd County.................	46.1	51.1	38.9	42.3	34.7	41.3	28.7	43.7	20 967	24 861	17 617	29 400	19.9	11.9

STATE County	Median gross rent	Percent who pay 35 percent or more of income for housing expenses		Number of workers 16 years and over	Means of transportation to work (percent except where noted)					Vehicles available (percent of households)		
		Owners	Renters		Car, truck, or van		Public transportation	Other means	Walked	No vehicles	One vehicle	Two or more vehicles
					Drove alone	Carpooled						
	25	26	27	28	29	30	31	32	33	34	35	36
SOUTH CAROLINA—Cont'd												
Sumter County	461	13.1	21.6	44 325	80.4	14.5	0.8	1.4	1.2	11.0	32.2	56.8
Union County	373	12.5	20.8	12 565	79.6	17.2	0.4	0.8	1.4	12.7	32.5	54.8
Williamsburg County	291	16.6	29.0	13 443	71.4	20.0	4.5	1.1	1.5	15.8	34.0	50.2
York County	581	12.6	25.3	79 996	82.1	13.4	0.3	1.0	1.2	6.9	29.1	64.1
SOUTH DAKOTA	426	10.4	22.7	372 648	77.3	10.4	0.5	0.8	4.5	6.1	29.9	64.0
Aurora County	309	10.5	12.0	1 422	67.5	10.4	0.1	1.1	6.0	2.1	26.3	71.6
Beadle County	366	9.1	25.9	8 372	77.5	10.0	0.9	0.4	4.5	7.0	32.9	60.2
Bennett County	358	14.5	30.2	1 232	60.8	13.9	1.3	0.8	16.5	9.9	39.5	50.6
Bon Homme County	300	11.2	16.2	3 065	68.6	10.2	0.1	0.7	6.8	5.8	26.3	67.9
Brookings County	396	5.5	25.0	16 054	76.4	10.7	0.2	1.1	6.7	4.6	30.8	64.5
Brown County	375	10.0	22.8	18 668	82.2	8.9	0.4	0.7	3.6	6.9	32.8	60.3
Brule County	378	10.8	13.6	2 492	71.5	9.3	0.0	0.8	6.7	6.7	27.2	66.1
Buffalo County	319	20.0	17.6	435	67.8	13.6	0.9	2.5	4.4	15.8	38.0	46.2
Butte County	401	14.0	20.6	4 348	70.7	14.3	0.3	0.6	5.3	2.7	25.5	71.9
Campbell County	279	18.0	4.4	829	56.2	9.8	0.2	1.4	11.2	1.9	24.6	73.5
Charles Mix County	307	12.6	18.8	3 606	68.4	11.0	0.4	1.7	5.9	9.0	32.4	58.5
Clark County	334	10.2	19.2	1 866	60.8	10.2	0.4	0.3	8.9	7.2	25.9	66.9
Clay County..................	440	10.2	40.6	6 763	69.9	10.1	0.5	2.2	11.9	4.9	36.7	58.4
Codington County	401	10.4	28.6	13 762	82.7	7.6	0.9	1.1	2.6	6.7	28.8	64.5
Corson County	266	15.1	17.9	1 219	55.9	11.2	1.2	2.7	18.5	9.7	32.3	58.1
Custer County	349	11.6	17.1	3 371	72.1	12.0	0.8	1.2	5.7	4.9	26.7	68.5
Davison County	388	8.6	24.9	9 494	78.0	10.4	0.2	0.7	4.4	8.6	31.3	60.1
Day County	303	8.4	12.6	2 687	69.8	8.9	0.1	0.2	7.6	6.0	30.8	63.2
Deuel County	303	8.9	15.4	2 205	71.6	10.5	0.0	1.2	5.0	5.0	23.3	71.7
Dewey County	308	13.6	25.9	1 929	55.1	22.4	1.3	1.6	11.4	9.8	38.7	51.5
Douglas County	300	8.2	20.4	1 594	60.5	8.5	0.3	0.8	10.5	4.4	25.3	70.3
Edmunds County...........	270	9.5	8.3	1 943	64.9	10.5	0.1	0.7	9.8	6.6	22.3	71.1
Fall River County	369	10.1	26.6	3 140	71.7	14.2	0.1	1.5	5.0	8.4	30.2	61.4
Faulk County	270	7.6	14.5	1 147	57.3	7.2	0.0	3.0	14.1	7.6	27.1	65.3
Grant County	350	11.1	29.9	3 742	74.8	11.5	0.0	0.5	3.7	6.2	29.0	64.9
Gregory County	264	12.5	13.0	2 172	65.5	8.2	0.2	0.9	5.1	6.0	28.1	65.9
Haakon County	364	7.4	8.9	1 135	64.2	10.5	0.0	1.4	9.8	4.4	26.1	69.5
Hamlin County...............	329	12.7	11.5	2 469	71.9	12.2	0.6	0.4	5.5	4.5	23.7	71.8
Hand County	306	10.7	11.3	1 839	64.2	7.1	0.4	1.2	7.8	7.1	27.0	65.9
Hanson County	322	6.6	3.2	1 457	70.2	11.3	0.0	0.1	6.3	7.6	22.5	69.9
Harding County	318	24.7	14.6	678	44.2	12.5	0.0	0.4	11.4	1.5	26.1	72.4
Hughes County	404	7.0	19.3	8 812	77.9	13.9	0.2	0.5	3.6	5.5	33.5	61.1
Hutchinson County........	314	10.0	15.6	3 589	66.0	8.1	0.0	0.7	9.2	4.9	28.6	66.5
Hyde County	310	13.6	11.3	788	60.5	8.6	0.3	0.5	9.6	3.1	28.4	68.5
Jackson County.............	335	13.2	21.9	950	63.1	11.1	0.0	0.7	8.5	7.1	29.6	63.3
Jerauld County	317	7.0	19.3	1 092	68.0	8.2	0.0	0.0	7.3	8.6	26.6	64.7
Jones County	338	9.4	16.7	636	66.0	13.1	0.5	0.0	7.7	3.9	21.4	74.7
Kingsbury County	315	7.4	13.6	2 685	68.0	12.6	0.0	1.0	7.0	5.6	25.4	69.0
Lake County	382	11.0	21.3	5 848	76.1	12.6	0.1	0.5	5.1	3.7	28.4	67.9
Lawrence County	416	15.5	26.6	10 325	77.7	11.5	0.2	0.5	6.2	5.0	30.9	64.1
Lincoln County	559	10.9	25.6	13 176	83.8	8.5	0.1	0.7	2.0	2.8	20.0	77.2
Lyman County	288	12.0	16.0	1 690	66.7	9.8	0.0	1.1	8.1	7.9	27.4	64.7
McCook County.............	375	9.5	14.0	2 761	69.5	12.8	0.0	1.4	5.3	5.0	23.9	71.1
McPherson County........	253	13.8	16.7	1 181	54.7	10.8	0.0	0.9	11.3	10.4	25.3	64.4
Marshall County	302	10.2	13.1	1 958	69.1	10.0	0.3	1.0	6.6	6.5	26.0	67.5
Meade County	468	14.4	14.7	12 440	79.2	11.6	0.0	0.5	2.8	4.2	25.2	70.7
Mellette County	279	15.5	32.2	764	54.1	13.9	1.0	0.9	9.3	11.0	27.4	61.7
Miner County	333	13.1	16.4	1 385	67.7	10.1	0.0	0.7	6.3	3.0	28.3	68.7
Minnehaha County	516	9.2	23.0	81 957	83.7	9.4	0.8	0.6	2.3	6.1	31.8	62.1
Moody County	381	11.3	11.2	3 336	73.1	10.9	0.1	1.1	4.6	5.6	25.7	68.7
Pennington County	497	10.8	27.0	44 988	82.9	10.4	0.6	0.7	2.3	6.1	30.5	63.5
Perkins County	293	10.0	18.1	1 595	56.7	9.9	0.0	0.8	10.9	5.7	26.5	67.8
Potter County	318	11.5	22.4	1 273	70.1	7.0	0.0	1.6	11.2	3.4	28.3	68.3
Roberts County	305	10.3	16.4	4 170	69.4	12.6	0.1	0.7	7.9	7.4	29.3	63.3
Sanborn County	301	12.1	10.5	1 339	71.5	11.9	0.0	0.7	4.1	3.1	23.3	73.6
Shannon County	304	8.9	12.3	2 564	61.7	21.8	1.0	1.1	11.8	14.9	44.0	41.0
Spink County	325	9.1	17.0	3 151	69.3	10.6	0.2	1.1	5.1	6.9	28.6	64.5
Stanley County.............	440	8.4	23.0	1 699	80.3	8.7	0.0	0.2	1.9	3.5	26.1	70.4
Sully County	343	9.5	8.8	783	68.1	9.5	0.0	0.6	6.3	2.7	24.0	73.3
Todd County	272	16.2	19.0	2 575	61.5	20.9	2.3	2.2	8.9	16.2	37.3	46.5

STATE/ County code	MSA/PMSA/ NECMA code[1]	STATE County	Total population 5 years and over	Residence in 1995 (percent)					Occupied housing units		Householders 65 years and over	
				Same house	Same county, different house	Same state, different county	Different state	Outside the United States	Number	Percent owner-occupied	Number	Percent owner-occupied
			1	2	3	4	5	6	7	8	9	10
		SOUTH DAKOTA— Cont'd										
46 123	...	Tripp County	6 032	69.7	20.8	6.0	3.4	0.1	2 550	75.0	868	75.9
46 125	...	Turner County	8 359	65.5	14.7	13.2	6.3	0.4	3 510	77.4	1 195	78.7
46 127	...	Union County	11 727	54.4	14.4	7.4	22.9	1.0	4 927	74.5	1 145	78.6
46 129	...	Walworth County	5 614	57.9	18.4	13.9	9.5	0.3	2 506	71.2	876	80.1
46 135	...	Yankton County	20 292	54.9	20.0	11.5	12.9	0.7	8 187	69.1	1 936	72.5
46 137	...	Ziebach County	2 247	64.8	13.0	14.2	7.1	0.9	741	59.6	144	80.6
47 000	...	TENNESSEE	5 315 920	53.9	25.2	8.7	10.7	1.5	2 232 905	69.9	467 100	81.5
47 001	3840	Anderson County	67 274	61.5	20.3	9.7	7.9	0.7	29 780	72.5	7 901	82.3
47 003	...	Bedford County	34 861	51.4	26.9	11.4	6.5	3.7	13 905	73.5	3 140	83.8
47 005	...	Benton County	15 695	61.9	20.8	8.7	8.3	0.2	6 863	80.6	2 031	89.6
47 007	...	Bledsoe County	11 654	56.9	14.9	20.2	7.7	0.4	4 430	81.7	933	85.1
47 009	3840	Blount County	99 662	55.6	23.4	9.6	10.8	0.9	42 667	75.9	9 682	87.1
47 011	...	Bradley County	82 248	53.0	25.5	7.3	12.4	1.2	34 281	68.6	6 815	78.5
47 013	...	Campbell County	37 513	61.6	24.1	5.4	8.1	0.8	16 125	73.4	4 180	00.0
47 015	...	Cannon County	11 946	63.5	16.2	14.6	5.0	0.7	4 998	78.5	1 302	81.3
47 017	...	Carroll County	27 755	59.5	21.2	11.1	7.8	0.5	11 779	79.0	3 236	92.0
47 019	3660	Carter County	53 614	59.5	23.0	9.0	8.0	0.5	23 486	74.9	5 874	85.1
47 021	5360	Cheatham County	33 310	57.4	13.9	20.3	8.0	0.3	12 878	83.6	1 958	90.8
47 023	3580	Chester County	14 502	57.4	16.9	15.0	10.1	0.7	5 660	77.3	1 268	78.7
47 025	...	Claiborne County	28 180	62.6	22.0	4.4	10.4	0.6	11 799	78.5	2 784	86.9
47 027	...	Clay County	7 575	64.6	19.7	7.6	7.7	0.4	3 379	80.0	904	85.4
47 029	...	Cocke County	31 556	62.8	22.5	6.4	8.0	0.4	13 762	75.5	3 066	83.4
47 031	...	Coffee County	44 806	56.1	23.2	11.2	8.6	0.9	18 885	71.5	4 390	83.8
47 033	...	Crockett County	13 607	66.8	15.3	11.0	5.5	1.5	5 632	74.9	1 420	84.3
47 035	...	Cumberland County	44 266	55.9	21.5	7.3	14.8	0.5	19 508	80.6	6 262	89.1
47 037	5360	Davidson County	532 311	45.5	29.0	7.9	14.2	3.3	237 405	55.3	42 441	74.5
47 039	...	Decatur County	11 072	65.0	17.7	10.4	6.6	0.4	4 908	80.1	1 332	88.2
47 041	...	DeKalb County	16 378	58.8	21.8	11.0	7.4	1.1	6 984	75.0	1 759	85.0
47 043	5360	Dickson County	40 181	56.1	23.9	12.5	7.0	0.5	16 473	76.1	3 448	84.1
47 045	...	Dyer County	34 019	61.0	21.6	7.8	8.0	0.8	14 751	65.6	3 398	76.6
47 047	4920	Fayette County	26 867	61.9	12.9	19.8	5.0	0.3	10 467	80.3	2 400	81.6
47 049	...	Fentress County	15 621	59.1	27.0	7.6	6.2	0.2	6 693	79.1	1 587	86.3
47 051	...	Franklin County	36 923	57.8	21.4	10.2	9.7	1.0	15 003	78.5	4 137	86.1
47 053	...	Gibson County	45 206	58.9	26.1	9.0	5.4	0.6	19 518	72.1	5 401	83.8
47 055	...	Giles County	27 646	62.6	22.7	6.6	7.6	0.5	11 713	75.4	2 990	83.1
47 057	...	Grainger County	19 408	65.8	15.6	12.7	5.4	0.7	8 270	83.6	1 781	87.7
47 059	...	Greene County	59 210	59.1	24.3	7.2	8.5	0.8	25 756	76.7	6 296	86.7
47 061	...	Grundy County	13 362	67.6	18.9	8.3	5.0	0.3	5 562	82.1	1 207	90.8
47 063	...	Hamblen County	54 365	55.5	23.9	9.3	8.1	3.2	23 211	72.5	5 148	82.4
47 065	1560	Hamilton County	289 008	54.0	28.2	4.1	11.4	1.5	124 444	65.9	28 981	77.0
47 067	...	Hancock County	6 433	71.0	16.5	6.7	5.1	0.6	2 769	78.7	000	80.8
47 069	...	Hardeman County	26 439	58.0	19.4	8.1	13.4	1.1	9 412	74.1	2 477	79.9
47 071	...	Hardin County	24 064	58.4	23.2	10.3	7.8	0.3	10 426	77.3	2 612	86.9
47 073	3660	Hawkins County	50 242	61.3	19.7	10.5	8.0	0.5	21 936	78.7	4 695	82.8
47 075	...	Haywood County	18 384	60.6	25.6	7.8	5.2	0.8	7 558	65.9	1 856	80.9
47 077	...	Henderson County	23 870	58.8	23.3	11.1	6.2	0.6	10 306	79.2	2 474	84.1
47 079	...	Henry County	29 421	55.5	24.0	8.0	12.3	0.2	13 019	77.4	3 699	84.9
47 081	...	Hickman County	20 828	55.8	17.5	16.9	9.6	0.3	8 081	80.2	1 689	83.2
47 083	...	Houston County	7 552	64.6	19.5	8.1	7.4	0.5	3 216	77.0	899	81.3
47 085	...	Humphreys County	16 884	61.4	21.2	10.4	6.6	0.3	7 238	77.9	1 721	87.2
47 087	...	Jackson County	10 331	64.2	15.3	12.2	7.9	0.3	4 466	80.8	1 132	88.0
47 089	...	Jefferson County	41 601	55.9	16.1	16.4	10.4	1.1	17 155	77.9	3 641	86.6
47 091	...	Johnson County	16 634	63.3	20.2	6.7	9.4	0.5	6 827	79.7	1 771	84.8
47 093	3840	Knox County	358 859	52.0	27.2	8.9	10.5	1.3	157 872	66.9	32 234	81.3
47 095	...	Lake County	7 577	58.2	18.1	18.6	4.4	0.7	2 410	60.0	758	71.8
47 097	...	Lauderdale County	25 264	56.6	26.2	11.2	5.4	0.5	9 567	65.0	2 190	72.7
47 099	...	Lawrence County	37 272	60.9	27.4	5.2	6.1	0.3	15 480	77.1	3 789	88.4
47 101	...	Lewis County	10 645	59.2	22.2	11.2	7.2	0.2	4 381	79.5	1 067	83.4
47 103	...	Lincoln County	29 464	57.7	25.4	6.0	10.4	0.6	12 503	76.2	3 465	82.7
47 105	3840	Loudon County	36 824	57.9	17.8	13.5	10.0	0.8	15 944	79.1	4 289	86.7
47 107	...	McMinn County	45 890	58.7	23.0	10.5	7.3	0.6	19 721	75.7	4 765	83.1
47 109	...	McNairy County	23 127	61.5	20.3	8.7	9.2	0.3	9 980	80.0	2 706	86.1
47 111	...	Macon County	18 919	57.6	20.5	12.5	8.4	1.0	7 916	78.6	1 704	83.5
47 113	3580	Madison County	85 527	50.8	27.8	10.5	9.7	1.2	35 552	67.0	7 538	78.6
47 115	1560	Marion County	26 129	64.7	21.3	6.9	6.8	0.4	11 037	80.5	2 560	87.8

[1]MSA = Metropolitan Statistical Area. PMSA = Primary MSA. NECMA = New England County Metropolitan Area. See the Appendix A for explanation of these concepts. See Appendix B for list of metropolitan areas identified by type, with component counties.

Table C-3. States and Counties — Migration, Housing, and Transportation

STATE County	Owner-occupied by household type (percent)								Median household income			Median housing value (owner estimated)	Median monthly owner costs as a percent of income	
	Family-households					Nonfamily households								
		Married-couple family		Other family										
	Total family households	Total	With own children under 18 years	Total	With own children under 18 years	Total nonfamily households	Two or more adults	Living alone	All households	Owner-occupied households	Renter-occupied households		With a mortgage	Without a mortgage
	11	12	13	14	15	16	17	18	19	20	21	22	23	24
SOUTH DAKOTA— Cont'd														
Tripp County	81.8	86.8	85.1	51.6	35.5	60.6	40.5	62.6	28 136	33 438	14 619	45 500	20.0	11.6
Turner County	84.5	86.2	80.0	70.6	67.7	60.3	54.3	61.0	35 307	38 782	25 399	61 200	20.4	11.5
Union County	81.2	85.2	82.3	54.2	46.4	57.2	50.5	58.3	44 147	48 424	31 921	85 200	19.9	11.1
Walworth County	76.8	86.2	79.2	44.9	34.5	60.4	84.3	58.3	28 113	34 739	17 399	40 500	20.8	11.5
Yankton County	80.2	85.6	83.0	52.2	46.3	47.5	39.8	48.7	35 350	42 126	21 491	73 800	19.5	9.9
Ziebach County	60.8	75.8	68.0	40.5	34.9	54.8	53.3	55.0	18 869	24 113	11 146	41 200	24.1	12.6
TENNESSEE	77.0	83.9	79.7	54.4	42.6	53.8	40.3	56.2	36 239	43 217	23 266	88 300	21.1	9.9
Anderson County	78.5	85.4	80.4	53.0	40.4	59.2	48.5	60.4	35 345	41 309	20 580	83 400	19.9	9.9
Bedford County	77.6	84.6	79.4	52.1	43.6	61.4	50.7	63.4	36 855	41 695	23 757	78 900	20.8	9.9
Benton County	83.5	87.2	80.1	66.1	48.5	73.3	66.3	74.1	28 129	29 806	20 313	62 800	20.6	9.9
Bledsoe County	85.6	87.9	82.3	75.2	66.6	69.7	47.2	72.2	29 324	32 091	19 510	63 700	25.2	9.9
Blount County	81.0	85.5	80.9	60.7	46.3	62.7	53.2	64.2	37 647	43 371	23 176	96 600	20.9	9.9
Bradley County	75.6	81.2	75.0	52.2	40.8	50.1	32.2	53.4	35 011	42 379	21 697	88 300	20.9	9.9
Campbell County	78.1	82.8	78.2	60.4	46.3	61.5	56.2	62.1	25 357	29 286	14 831	57 700	23.3	10.1
Cannon County	84.2	85.8	81.9	77.3	64.9	62.6	49.0	63.7	31 906	35 878	18 919	80 500	20.9	9.9
Carroll County	81.7	86.3	78.1	64.6	54.2	72.3	56.0	74.2	30 242	33 288	19 836	58 300	19.9	9.9
Carter County	80.0	84.2	78.7	64.8	53.3	63.0	47.9	64.9	27 300	31 270	18 390	68 300	20.7	9.9
Cheatham County	85.2	89.5	85.5	65.2	56.3	77.3	73.3	78.2	45 556	49 109	29 016	105 100	21.5	9.9
Chester County	81.2	86.5	81.4	61.2	50.9	65.5	57.2	66.4	34 298	40 167	16 962	71 700	19.4	9.9
Claiborne County	82.1	85.6	81.7	68.3	56.4	68.2	49.5	70.3	25 753	28 955	16 484	63 200	20.4	9.9
Clay County	83.0	86.6	81.2	69.0	49.0	73.2	66.1	74.0	23 699	26 930	14 797	51 700	20.0	13.6
Cocke County	80.7	86.5	79.5	64.6	54.0	62.5	48.1	64.2	25 699	29 433	14 826	63 300	22.1	9.9
Coffee County	76.9	83.2	77.7	50.9	38.9	57.4	47.1	58.8	35 185	41 486	20 860	79 600	19.9	9.9
Crockett County	77.3	82.4	74.1	56.4	52.0	68.6	71.1	68.4	30 252	33 998	21 267	64 000	20.5	9.9
Cumberland County	84.0	89.0	81.9	60.0	48.6	70.7	57.2	72.5	30 664	33 434	18 841	83 500	22.7	9.9
Davidson County	65.5	75.2	70.7	43.6	31.6	41.1	31.3	43.5	39 612	51 964	27 808	114 200	21.9	9.9
Decatur County	84.1	88.9	85.9	62.3	56.1	70.5	41.7	72.7	28 968	31 957	18 807	56 200	18.8	9.9
DeKalb County	78.0	84.7	78.5	51.4	37.9	67.3	61.9	67.9	30 041	33 881	19 028	83 200	20.7	9.9
Dickson County	81.0	87.2	82.3	57.8	46.7	62.0	57.2	62.7	38 651	44 726	21 952	93 900	20.8	9.9
Dyer County	71.1	79.7	73.0	43.6	27.3	51.8	36.0	53.7	32 623	40 361	21 390	72 300	19.5	10.0
Fayette County	85.7	90.6	86.6	69.1	53.7	62.7	68.7	61.9	40 155	45 411	17 922	96 800	22.9	9.9
Fentress County	81.9	86.1	82.2	65.5	54.2	71.8	76.3	71.4	23 237	25 936	14 277	51 300	22.3	10.5
Franklin County	82.5	86.7	78.9	64.5	52.8	66.5	56.6	67.6	35 862	40 139	21 310	80 200	19.8	9.9
Gibson County	76.1	83.8	76.7	49.6	38.1	62.9	46.6	64.6	30 689	36 001	21 351	65 500	19.8	9.9
Giles County	80.7	87.2	83.4	56.8	40.5	62.3	51.5	63.5	34 659	40 249	21 798	74 700	19.4	9.9
Grainger County	85.9	88.9	84.1	70.2	62.2	76.9	66.9	78.2	27 970	30 064	18 255	65 200	21.3	9.9
Greene County	81.0	85.0	80.6	63.8	52.1	66.1	53.8	67.7	30 184	34 039	19 892	74 500	20.0	9.9
Grundy County	85.0	88.7	84.4	71.2	61.6	74.0	86.0	72.8	23 289	26 362	11 445	48 500	22.7	11.6
Hamblen County	77.6	84.0	78.9	53.7	42.5	59.8	42.1	62.7	32 168	38 008	21 873	82 100	20.3	9.9
Hamilton County	73.9	82.1	78.2	49.0	36.3	49.4	40.3	50.9	38 509	48 854	24 128	93 000	19.9	9.9
Hancock County	83.6	86.5	81.4	73.9	56.7	67.3	76.5	66.5	18 938	22 883	9 798	49 300	21.1	9.9
Hardeman County	77.8	85.0	79.7	61.5	53.0	64.7	49.6	66.2	28 871	32 218	18 018	57 400	20.9	10.6
Hardin County	81.7	85.1	80.0	66.1	50.7	66.2	62.7	66.6	28 443	32 324	18 621	63 100	20.9	10.5
Hawkins County	83.6	88.0	83.9	63.4	49.3	65.4	62.1	65.8	31 308	34 886	20 086	75 000	20.3	9.9
Haywood County	69.1	78.5	68.4	51.7	36.7	57.6	54.8	57.9	27 831	34 887	17 228	66 400	21.6	10.8
Henderson County	84.9	89.0	87.3	69.8	62.6	64.4	41.3	67.1	31 929	35 754	17 806	65 800	21.3	9.9
Henry County	80.9	85.7	78.7	61.9	53.1	69.3	50.4	71.9	30 044	32 313	21 257	68 600	21.6	9.9
Hickman County	83.0	85.9	81.1	69.6	60.3	72.1	68.3	72.6	31 325	33 991	19 269	75 900	22.4	9.9
Houston County	80.9	86.2	84.0	59.6	45.8	66.9	69.4	66.6	29 508	33 065	16 338	61 900	19.6	9.9
Humphreys County	81.7	88.0	78.1	52.7	44.6	68.3	66.2	68.5	35 721	40 380	21 413	75 700	18.6	9.9
Jackson County	83.5	87.4	81.4	69.3	57.3	74.1	64.1	75.6	26 543	29 537	15 833	65 500	21.6	11.3
Jefferson County	83.0	87.9	84.6	61.5	50.0	63.6	45.9	66.5	32 429	36 948	19 735	81 000	21.3	9.9
Johnson County	82.9	85.3	77.9	73.4	58.2	72.1	81.0	70.9	23 591	26 467	14 181	61 300	23.9	10.4
Knox County	78.0	84.8	82.4	53.2	40.6	47.2	32.9	50.4	37 380	48 551	20 770	95 700	20.7	9.9
Lake County	65.1	76.5	71.2	35.5	15.4	49.7	26.2	51.6	22 057	30 451	13 521	50 900	20.4	11.4
Lauderdale County	70.6	77.9	69.9	51.8	37.1	50.6	50.4	50.6	29 784	36 778	20 974	58 100	19.7	10.9
Lawrence County	81.1	85.7	78.2	61.1	48.3	65.8	46.8	67.7	30 205	33 543	20 440	72 800	20.5	10.5
Lewis County	85.1	88.5	85.5	71.0	52.5	64.4	71.6	63.3	30 881	35 016	17 783	61 500	19.2	9.9
Lincoln County	81.6	86.9	79.9	61.4	48.6	61.7	33.4	64.4	33 091	39 217	19 550	74 300	19.8	10.2
Loudon County	83.0	87.1	77.8	64.0	47.0	68.0	50.6	70.3	39 861	43 867	25 574	92 900	20.1	9.9
McMinn County	80.8	85.0	80.8	62.5	47.7	62.4	48.6	64.0	31 482	35 999	20 463	76 200	20.3	9.9
McNairy County	83.3	88.1	82.4	62.4	49.8	71.7	67.9	72.2	29 912	32 005	19 605	56 900	20.1	9.9
Macon County	82.6	87.2	84.5	62.3	51.5	67.7	55.0	69.1	30 494	35 359	18 040	65 900	20.0	9.9
Madison County	73.9	83.7	79.3	48.2	33.8	51.0	38.5	53.1	36 776	46 235	21 660	82 700	19.9	9.9
Marion County	83.9	88.2	83.2	67.3	53.6	70.9	52.5	72.7	31 269	34 172	21 847	66 700	20.8	9.9

STATE County	Median gross rent	Percent who pay 35 percent or more of income for housing expenses		Means of transportation to work (percent except where noted)						Vehicles available (percent of households)		
		Owners	Renters	Number of workers 16 years and over	Car, truck, or van		Public transportation	Other means	Walked	No vehicles	One vehicle	Two or more vehicles
					Drove alone	Carpooled						
	25	26	27	28	29	30	31	32	33	34	35	36
SOUTH DAKOTA— Cont'd												
Tripp County................	302	13.7	18.3	2 996	68.0	12.3	0.2	0.6	6.1	6.0	28.4	65.6
Turner County..............	363	9.6	15.5	4 414	70.9	10.8	0.1	0.8	5.7	4.3	21.9	73.7
Union County	505	11.9	15.4	6 715	79.4	10.4	0.2	0.5	2.9	4.6	25.8	69.6
Walworth County..........	381	14.1	25.8	2 594	76.1	6.6	0.8	1.1	8.0	8.3	35.0	56.7
Yankton County............	396	10.8	20.9	10 614	80.4	8.7	0.3	1.0	4.2	6.0	31.8	62.2
Ziebach County............	331	20.1	38.5	670	45.2	24.8	1.0	1.2	8.7	14.2	37.1	48.7
TENNESSEE..............	505	14.4	27.2	2 618 404	81.7	12.5	0.8	0.8	1.5	7.7	32.3	60.0
Anderson County	450	11.7	28.6	30 688	86.4	9.5	0.2	0.5	1.3	7.5	30.6	61.9
Bedford County	488	14.5	23.8	18 252	78.2	15.3	0.6	0.7	1.8	6.4	27.7	65.9
Benton County	367	12.5	17.2	6 499	80.2	14.3	0.2	1.2	1.1	6.5	32.1	61.4
Bledsoe County............	343	14.1	19.5	4 830	76.2	19.3	0.0	0.8	1.3	6.8	28.2	65.0
Blount County	450	11.8	24.0	49 250	84.9	10.4	0.3	0.7	1.3	5.3	29.3	65.3
Bradley County............	455	14.7	26.5	41 355	85.0	12.4	0.1	0.4	1.3	5.3	29.5	65.3
Campbell County..........	356	17.5	27.2	14 256	80.9	15.0	0.0	1.6	0.6	11.2	33.8	54.0
Cannon County	382	11.7	25.5	5 818	76.3	17.3	0.1	1.6	1.2	7.0	26.5	66.5
Carroll County	384	12.3	25.0	12 471	82.0	13.0	0.2	1.2	1.8	6.0	33.0	61.1
Carter County..............	393	11.6	21.7	25 043	82.4	13.3	0.4	0.4	1.9	7.6	29.0	63.4
Cheatham County	588	14.0	24.7	17 985	79.1	16.7	0.3	1.0	0.7	4.4	21.5	74.1
Chester County............	401	12.2	31.3	6 905	79.8	13.5	0.0	0.6	3.9	6.7	29.7	63.6
Claiborne County	353	15.1	23.5	11 497	80.4	14.5	0.3	1.0	0.9	7.5	29.7	62.8
Clay County.................	252	15.2	19.2	3 383	79.0	15.0	0.9	0.4	1.9	8.3	30.6	61.0
Cocke County..............	334	12.4	22.4	13 837	78.5	16.6	0.2	0.9	1.4	9.0	30.0	61.0
Coffee County..............	445	12.1	24.7	21 648	82.4	13.3	0.3	0.9	0.8	5.7	30.6	63.7
Crockett County	393	15.9	26.9	6 209	82.0	12.3	0.1	0.5	2.1	7.7	34.1	58.2
Cumberland County	418	13.8	27.7	18 614	82.5	12.6	0.3	0.8	1.6	5.8	29.4	64.8
Davidson County	615	15.3	27.8	285 980	78.6	13.3	1.8	0.9	2.3	8.7	40.5	50.8
Decatur County	346	13.5	22.3	5 062	79.8	15.6	0.1	1.3	0.9	7.7	29.3	63.0
DeKalb County.............	389	12.2	30.0	7 798	76.3	14.5	0.2	1.8	3.6	7.4	31.4	61.3
Dickson County............	506	12.8	28.8	20 274	79.3	15.9	0.3	0.7	0.9	6.2	29.7	64.1
Dyer County	424	14.1	24.7	16 204	84.0	12.4	0.5	0.7	0.7	7.5	35.0	57.5
Fayette County.............	383	19.4	26.1	12 558	80.3	14.3	0.6	1.0	0.8	8.3	27.5	64.3
Fentress County...........	322	18.4	26.3	6 166	78.9	15.8	0.2	0.7	1.4	8.9	33.0	58.2
Franklin County............	439	12.5	21.0	17 258	80.0	12.6	0.1	1.0	3.2	6.4	27.4	66.2
Gibson County	398	13.3	20.5	20 998	84.6	11.7	0.2	1.1	0.9	7.8	34.1	58.1
Giles County................	427	10.7	22.6	13 605	82.5	11.4	0.4	0.8	2.0	9.3	26.9	63.9
Grainger County...........	348	13.4	20.8	8 781	81.5	13.6	0.3	0.3	1.3	6.8	24.7	68.5
Greene County	377	12.6	20.2	28 365	83.9	11.0	0.3	0.5	1.2	6.1	30.2	63.7
Grundy County.............	339	16.9	25.7	5 298	73.0	19.0	0.0	1.3	1.6	7.7	32.9	59.4
Hamblen County...........	418	13.2	23.3	27 039	84.6	12.9	0.2	0.4	0.9	6.1	31.4	62.5
Hamilton County...........	510	12.9	27.4	146 824	82.4	11.9	1.0	0.7	1.7	8.4	33.4	58.2
Hancock County	206	14.6	17.6	2 407	71.4	20.8	0.1	0.6	0.6	13.9	32.2	53.0
Hardeman County	387	17.9	26.5	9 968	78.9	16.6	0.2	1.4	0.8	10.6	31.6	57.8
Hardin County	371	17.0	22.1	10 632	80.7	14.3	0.2	0.9	1.9	8.0	31.4	60.6
Hawkins County	395	12.3	21.1	22 167	85.9	10.5	0.4	0.7	0.4	8.2	26.7	65.1
Haywood County	400	21.0	25.7	8 305	78.5	17.6	0.2	1.8	1.0	13.4	35.5	51.1
Henderson County	412	13.7	25.8	11 553	84.7	11.0	0.2	1.0	0.8	7.3	30.7	62.0
Henry County	403	15.3	21.5	13 487	82.5	12.8	0.2	0.8	1.3	7.5	31.6	60.9
Hickman County	430	17.8	23.9	8 913	76.5	18.5	0.1	0.6	0.7	6.7	30.8	62.5
Houston County	394	17.0	21.7	3 258	81.1	14.7	0.5	0.1	1.2	6.1	32.2	61.7
Humphreys County	398	9.9	17.6	7 985	80.3	15.1	0.2	0.6	1.6	7.0	26.7	66.3
Jackson County............	314	16.2	14.6	4 514	79.0	16.0	0.3	0.8	1.2	6.5	25.9	67.6
Jefferson County	420	13.7	23.9	20 211	82.4	10.8	0.2	1.0	2.6	5.9	25.8	68.3
Johnson County	344	16.9	19.8	6 169	76.2	19.1	0.1	0.8	0.8	8.0	30.7	61.2
Knox County................	493	13.9	30.0	184 824	84.5	9.2	0.7	0.6	2.2	7.4	33.9	58.6
Lake County................	287	14.2	22.6	2 317	81.0	13.3	0.4	1.3	2.4	11.1	43.4	45.5
Lauderdale County........	407	17.6	25.3	10 067	83.3	13.0	0.3	0.6	1.2	10.7	35.5	53.8
Lawrence County	395	13.5	22.1	16 820	80.8	13.6	0.0	0.8	1.4	7.7	30.2	62.1
Lewis County...............	357	12.6	16.4	4 764	77.1	17.2	0.1	1.0	2.4	7.8	28.0	64.2
Lincoln County	388	12.3	22.4	14 430	80.6	14.9	0.4	0.7	0.7	7.3	27.0	65.8
Loudon County	462	13.3	22.1	17 671	83.7	10.6	0.2	1.3	0.9	6.0	26.0	68.0
McMinn County	409	13.2	22.4	21 427	83.0	12.4	0.2	0.5	1.6	7.2	28.9	63.9
McNairy County............	356	14.1	22.2	10 646	81.7	12.4	0.3	1.3	1.2	7.9	29.6	62.5
Macon County..............	364	11.6	25.1	9 255	73.7	21.0	0.4	0.6	1.3	6.9	27.4	65.7
Madison County	510	12.1	29.0	42 881	84.1	10.7	0.8	0.9	1.6	9.9	32.0	58.1
Marion County..............	420	14.7	23.2	11 766	81.9	14.6	0.0	0.6	0.7	8.1	27.6	64.4

STATE/County code	MSA/PMSA/NECMA code[1]	STATE County	Residence in 1995 (percent)						Occupied housing units		Householders 65 years and over	
			Total population 5 years and over	Same house	Same county, different house	Same state, different county	Different state	Outside the United States	Number	Percent owner-occupied	Number	Percent owner-occupied
			1	2	3	4	5	6	7	8	9	10
		TENNESSEE— Cont'd										
47 117	...	Marshall County	25 015	54.5	23.1	12.8	8.7	1.0	10 307	73.0	2 143	82.2
47 119	...	Maury County	64 643	54.8	24.6	9.8	9.8	1.0	26 444	72.8	5 516	83.0
47 121	...	Meigs County	10 319	58.3	15.1	19.0	7.5	0.1	4 304	81.9	870	89.7
47 123	...	Monroe County	36 528	58.0	21.4	10.5	9.4	0.7	15 329	78.3	3 615	85.2
47 125	1660	Montgomery County	123 542	42.1	22.8	4.4	25.7	5.1	48 330	63.5	6 714	81.4
47 127	...	Moore County................	5 434	66.8	11.4	16.7	4.9	0.3	2 211	83.7	587	85.5
47 129	...	Morgan County	18 617	67.4	17.7	10.0	4.4	0.5	6 990	82.8	1 576	90.8
47 131	...	Obion County	30 396	59.6	24.4	6.8	8.3	0.9	13 182	71.5	3 373	81.0
47 133	...	Overton County	18 882	65.9	16.0	12.0	5.6	0.6	8 110	80.8	2 097	85.5
47 135	...	Perry County	7 166	66.4	14.1	11.1	8.2	0.2	3 023	85.8	768	83.3
47 137	...	Pickett County	4 670	66.5	17.2	6.7	9.5	0.1	2 091	84.3	654	89.0
47 139	...	Polk County	15 011	65.9	15.3	10.1	8.5	0.2	6 448	80.8	1 531	86.5
47 141	...	Putnam County	58 541	48.3	24.9	14.5	10.7	1.6	24 865	65.6	5 290	82.3
47 143	...	Rhea County	26 681	58.4	23.7	9.2	7.9	0.7	11 184	75.4	2 672	83.9
47 145	...	Roane County	48 880	62.3	19.5	10.2	7.5	0.5	21 200	77.5	5 458	83.3
47 147	5360	Robertson County	50 734	56.6	19.4	15.3	6.8	1.9	19 906	76.5	4 023	77.8
47 149	5360	Rutherford County	168 311	44.4	24.7	17.3	12.2	1.5	66 443	69.8	8 746	81.3
47 151	...	Scott County	19 660	65.3	23.8	3.1	7.5	0.4	8 203	76.5	1 617	83.1
47 153	...	Sequatchie County	10 554	57.9	22.4	13.2	6.0	0.5	4 463	76.2	970	83.9
47 155	3840	Sevier County................	67 000	54.3	21.5	8.7	14.8	0.8	28 467	73.3	5 701	86.3
47 157	4920	Shelby County	829 246	51.2	33.7	2.1	11.1	1.9	338 366	63.1	60 204	77.3
47 159	...	Smith County.................	16 551	57.3	21.8	14.5	5.8	0.6	6 878	78.8	1 596	82.3
47 161	...	Stewart County	11 661	56.7	16.3	12.3	13.8	0.9	4 930	79.3	1 240	86.9
47 163	3660	Sullivan County	144 563	60.2	24.6	5.3	9.2	0.6	63 556	75.8	16 403	85.5
47 165	5360	Sumner County	121 789	51.8	22.1	14.0	11.0	1.2	48 941	75.5	8 405	79.8
47 167	4920	Tipton County	47 682	52.9	20.2	15.3	10.5	1.2	18 106	76.2	3 280	81.2
47 169	...	Trousdale County	6 800	62.7	12.5	15.2	8.1	1.6	2 780	76.3	677	85.8
47 171	3660	Unicoi County	16 697	64.9	18.0	7.3	9.5	0.2	7 516	76.6	1 960	80.8
47 173	3840	Union County	16 608	62.2	17.8	14.4	5.5	0.1	6 742	80.9	1 338	90.3
47 175	...	Van Buren County..........	5 186	69.8	11.2	13.2	5.7	0.1	2 180	85.6	555	88.3
47 177	...	Warren County	35 764	54.6	29.2	8.5	5.5	2.3	15 181	72.9	3 688	80.5
47 179	3660	Washington County	100 816	54.4	21.7	12.2	10.6	1.1	44 195	68.2	9 272	78.9
47 181	...	Wayne County	15 979	58.9	18.1	15.8	6.7	0.4	5 936	82.9	1 533	89.2
47 183	...	Weakley County	32 868	53.5	23.2	13.8	7.8	1.6	13 599	68.8	3 196	80.2
47 185	...	White County.................	21 719	62.6	22.5	8.4	6.0	0.6	9 229	79.7	2 342	87.4
47 187	5360	Williamson County	117 355	48.2	14.9	16.7	18.6	1.5	44 725	81.5	6 038	84.9
47 189	5360	Wilson County	82 813	53.8	19.2	17.3	9.1	0.6	32 798	81.4	5 433	87.5
48 000	...	**TEXAS**....................	19 241 518	49.6	27.0	12.5	7.1	3.8	7 393 354	63.8	1 335 578	80.9
48 001	...	Anderson County	51 995	61.3	17.8	9.9	9.5	1.5	15 678	73.9	4 113	84.8
48 003	...	Andrews County	12 075	63.3	20.6	12.2	3.3	0.6	4 601	79.7	1 133	85.3
48 005	...	Angelina County	74 243	57.0	26.4	11.6	3.7	1.3	28 685	72.4	6 813	82.8
48 007	...	Aransas County	21 309	48.9	20.2	20.3	9.2	1.3	9 132	75.1	3 015	86.9
48 009	9080	Archer County	8 299	60.5	12.9	22.2	3.7	0.6	3 345	81.2	846	87.7
48 011	...	Armstrong County	2 033	60.0	11.4	23.9	4.6	0.2	802	79.1	249	89.2
48 013	...	Atascosa County	35 459	60.9	17.2	17.3	3.6	1.0	12 816	78.5	2 831	84.1
48 015	...	Austin County...............	22 056	58.1	18.3	18.6	3.4	1.6	8 747	77.2	2 362	86.7
48 017	...	Bailey County	6 069	57.1	25.6	11.2	5.1	1.1	2 348	71.3	588	85.4
48 019	...	Bandera County	16 690	49.5	11.7	31.3	6.3	1.2	7 010	82.9	1 770	91.8
48 021	0640	Bastrop County	53 475	52.0	15.4	24.7	5.8	2.1	20 097	80.3	3 885	85.8
48 023	...	Baylor County	3 871	57.2	22.5	16.1	4.1	0.2	1 791	72.6	693	71.4
48 025	...	Bee County	30 465	43.8	19.9	32.5	3.3	0.5	9 061	65.5	2 202	78.9
48 027	3810	Bell County	216 793	39.5	24.0	11.9	19.4	5.3	85 507	55.7	13 557	80.2
48 029	7240	Bexar County	1 283 614	51.2	30.9	7.0	8.1	2.9	488 942	61.2	93 571	78.6
48 031	...	Blanco County	7 888	54.3	14.1	23.4	6.7	1.5	3 303	78.6	931	85.8
48 033	...	Borden County	704	69.3	4.1	22.4	3.4	0.7	292	73.3	81	87.7
48 035	...	Bosque County	16 216	55.3	18.3	21.7	3.5	1.1	6 726	77.5	2 133	83.7
48 037	8360	Bowie County	83 487	52.8	26.1	9.6	10.9	0.6	33 058	70.9	8 161	84.9
48 039	1145	Brazoria County	223 313	53.1	23.6	16.5	4.7	2.0	81 954	74.0	13 727	85.7
48 041	1260	Brazos County	142 773	32.1	23.1	32.6	7.3	4.9	55 202	45.6	6 738	79.1
48 043	...	Brewster County	8 407	48.9	15.4	23.4	8.1	4.3	3 669	59.4	893	75.6
48 045	...	Briscoe County	1 680	65.8	13.1	18.9	2.2	0.0	724	77.1	239	90.8
48 047	...	Brooks County	7 326	71.9	19.6	7.1	1.3	0.1	2 711	73.1	808	91.0
48 049	...	Brown County	35 355	50.1	26.7	17.9	4.7	0.6	14 306	72.2	4 044	84.9
48 051	...	Burleson County	15 321	63.3	15.2	17.9	3.1	0.5	6 363	79.6	1 759	87.9
48 053	...	Burnet County	31 900	51.3	16.8	24.7	5.7	1.5	13 133	78.4	3 965	88.2

[1]MSA = Metropolitan Statistical Area. PMSA = Primary MSA. NECMA = New England County Metropolitan Area. See the Appendix A for explanation of these concepts. See Appendix B for list of metropolitan areas identified by type, with component counties.

STATE County	Owner-occupied by household type (percent)								Median household income			Median housing value (owner estimated)	Median monthly owner costs as a percent of income	
	Family-households					Nonfamily households								
		Married-couple family		Other family										
	Total family households	Total	With own children under 18 years	Total	With own children under 18 years	Total nonfamily households	Two or more adults	Living alone	All households	Owner-occupied households	Renter-occupied households		With a mortgage	Without a mortgage
	11	12	13	14	15	16	17	18	19	20	21	22	23	24
TENNESSEE— Cont'd														
Marshall County	78.6	84.1	79.7	56.3	42.5	57.8	45.6	59.4	38 627	45 424	23 610	85 000	19.5	9.9
Maury County	78.0	85.0	82.2	55.3	44.7	58.2	35.3	61.5	41 167	48 190	25 743	95 400	19.7	9.9
Meigs County	85.8	88.5	81.3	72.5	65.8	69.6	79.1	68.2	28 994	32 361	16 864	71 600	21.4	9.9
Monroe County	83.7	87.0	81.5	69.5	61.8	63.7	62.4	63.8	29 990	32 889	20 361	71 900	20.9	9.9
Montgomery County	68.3	72.6	68.4	51.3	41.5	49.4	40.0	51.7	38 876	46 127	28 391	84 500	21.8	9.9
Moore County	85.6	89.3	79.4	66.2	51.9	77.3	81.6	76.9	36 039	39 365	23 224	89 700	21.3	10.2
Morgan County	87.1	90.9	86.9	71.4	64.1	69.9	57.9	71.3	27 911	30 402	18 470	56 000	22.8	9.9
Obion County	76.7	83.2	74.8	49.8	36.3	58.7	41.7	60.5	32 495	37 863	21 486	64 700	18.9	10.7
Overton County	84.9	87.8	81.0	74.4	58.1	69.7	70.1	69.7	26 652	29 661	18 450	67 800	21.4	10.6
Perry County	90.5	92.5	90.1	80.2	73.9	73.7	74.2	73.6	28 627	30 966	18 859	54 200	21.2	9.9
Pickett County	88.1	90.0	82.5	75.6	71.6	74.8	63.6	75.4	24 625	26 304	14 775	69 900	22.1	10.9
Polk County	86.1	86.8	85.0	82.1	69.0	65.8	50.8	67.6	30 014	33 508	19 146	63 900	19.3	9.9
Putnam County	76.4	82.1	75.7	53.1	46.1	44.8	19.5	51.2	30 936	39 438	19 190	89 400	21.6	9.9
Rhea County	77.8	82.4	76.9	58.3	48.1	68.9	71.2	68.5	30 635	34 698	19 439	70 100	19.9	9.9
Roane County	82.9	87.7	82.1	61.7	50.7	63.7	45.5	65.8	33 212	39 386	18 181	79 400	20.0	9.9
Robertson County	80.8	86.0	82.8	57.7	47.5	61.3	48.7	63.6	42 706	49 024	25 799	105 300	21.5	9.9
Rutherford County	79.0	85.2	84.1	54.8	46.1	46.7	30.2	52.6	46 149	55 219	26 173	111 600	20.9	9.9
Scott County	81.1	86.5	83.1	60.1	48.1	63.8	54.2	64.7	24 106	26 912	15 109	51 100	23.1	12.5
Sequatchie County	78.4	84.3	80.1	56.9	45.9	69.6	77.2	68.9	30 856	34 514	22 106	74 800	23.8	9.9
Sevier County	78.5	82.9	76.9	59.3	47.9	59.0	50.0	60.9	34 745	38 997	24 774	101 200	21.6	9.9
Shelby County	70.7	82.3	79.1	50.4	39.1	47.0	35.9	49.1	39 501	51 413	24 977	90 800	21.7	10.4
Smith County	83.7	87.0	82.1	67.0	53.7	64.6	54.0	65.7	36 143	39 656	21 736	86 800	21.6	9.9
Stewart County	81.7	85.4	75.5	58.6	45.2	72.0	88.3	70.7	32 774	37 262	21 080	74 000	21.2	9.9
Sullivan County	81.4	85.7	80.0	62.0	48.9	62.2	53.6	63.1	33 571	38 622	20 173	82 600	20.3	9.9
Sumner County	81.0	86.6	82.7	56.1	46.0	58.3	51.0	59.7	46 194	52 702	26 770	121 000	21.5	9.9
Tipton County	80.0	86.7	83.0	57.4	47.9	62.3	53.9	63.5	41 638	47 482	22 395	87 400	21.0	9.9
Trousdale County	79.8	85.0	80.3	59.3	51.4	60.7	50.4	60.6	31 530	35 989	21 731	78 300	19.7	10.5
Unicoi County	82.1	86.0	76.1	64.2	57.1	63.7	47.7	65.2	30 284	34 091	18 310	76 800	19.6	9.9
Union County	82.8	86.7	84.7	65.1	53.0	73.8	68.9	74.3	27 363	30 420	18 419	65 600	23.1	9.9
Van Buren County	87.8	90.7	88.3	77.3	74.0	70.1	77.4	79.9	27 660	29 339	17 717	52 000	21.3	9.9
Warren County	78.0	83.9	78.6	54.0	45.5	60.0	39.5	63.0	31 221	36 797	17 215	73 000	20.7	9.9
Washington County	77.6	83.8	79.4	52.9	40.0	49.1	35.6	51.8	32 974	40 973	20 082	90 900	20.9	9.9
Wayne County	86.3	89.9	86.1	70.5	54.7	73.8	63.4	75.0	26 717	29 106	16 645	51 300	21.7	9.9
Weakley County	78.6	84.5	81.7	53.1	42.6	48.4	24.1	53.5	29 825	37 115	17 121	66 500	19.7	9.9
White County	82.5	86.6	80.6	65.7	56.7	71.7	65.4	72.4	29 099	31 441	20 368	72 800	22.0	9.9
Williamson County	87.0	90.1	90.8	66.4	58.4	59.0	51.1	60.5	69 138	78 344	37 484	204 700	21.3	9.9
Wilson County	85.1	89.2	86.7	64.8	55.8	68.0	65.5	68.4	50 054	55 952	27 086	133 000	21.0	9.9
TEXAS	71.1	77.7	72.6	49.2	39.6	45.8	33.9	48.3	39 745	49 279	27 506	77 800	20.1	10.9
Anderson County	76.6	83.6	77.5	54.0	43.7	66.8	58.7	67.6	32 123	35 656	22 126	56 500	20.0	12.7
Andrews County	83.1	86.0	78.9	67.3	66.1	68.1	42.9	69.3	34 131	35 895	24 490	38 900	19.0	9.9
Angelina County	77.1	83.4	78.3	54.0	44.9	59.1	40.1	61.6	33 191	38 799	21 139	57 000	19.0	10.2
Aransas County	76.9	82.7	72.6	64.0	50.5	66.2	69.3	65.7	30 334	32 384	23 644	65 400	20.8	12.4
Archer County	84.2	86.6	83.4	67.4	62.1	72.0	70.7	72.2	38 484	42 182	24 743	62 100	19.4	11.4
Armstrong County	81.3	81.0	71.1	64.2	88.6	71.3	77.8	71.0	37 045	39 063	29 167	65 700	15.0	11.9
Atascosa County	81.9	86.5	84.7	65.3	54.2	66.2	67.0	66.0	32 570	36 997	10 605	48 800	19.5	10.9
Austin County	81.4	85.9	81.7	59.4	54.9	65.0	45.6	67.5	38 948	43 062	28 629	84 400	18.8	10.2
Bailey County	73.2	75.5	62.8	57.0	52.4	65.6	58.3	66.3	29 023	31 670	20 841	38 300	19.3	11.5
Bandera County	86.4	88.6	82.2	73.8	61.1	73.8	50.5	78.2	38 942	42 619	26 750	85 900	20.2	9.9
Bastrop County	83.1	86.5	83.0	68.6	58.5	72.6	75.6	71.9	43 674	48 087	27 873	86 700	19.9	10.1
Baylor County	80.5	85.9	78.1	49.7	30.7	57.4	100.0	56.5	25 104	30 813	12 196	37 300	22.5	12.5
Bee County	70.3	77.3	68.4	51.8	39.5	52.7	49.7	53.1	28 169	34 299	18 588	48 300	19.2	10.2
Bell County	61.3	66.1	57.7	43.0	34.3	40.7	32.2	42.6	36 865	46 956	27 614	75 700	20.6	9.9
Bexar County	68.6	75.5	69.7	50.6	37.7	43.1	34.9	44.9	38 200	48 276	26 473	71 800	20.5	9.9
Blanco County	80.8	83.6	76.2	64.9	57.7	72.9	65.1	74.2	39 731	43 266	27 159	98 300	20.5	9.9
Borden County	71.9	75.3	60.5	54.3	47.8	77.3	40.0	80.0	29 444	30 577	22 500	50 000	43.0	9.9
Bosque County	79.7	81.4	70.3	68.6	58.0	71.8	71.5	71.9	34 142	37 424	24 701	60 500	19.5	12.2
Bowie County	75.5	85.1	80.1	48.8	33.9	59.7	41.5	61.8	33 053	40 313	19 664	61 600	18.9	10.4
Brazoria County	78.8	84.4	80.8	54.7	45.4	57.7	47.0	59.8	48 191	56 591	29 882	81 000	18.5	9.9
Brazos County	63.2	72.0	68.3	34.5	28.2	23.6	9.6	34.2	28 802	53 100	16 736	88 200	19.7	10.6
Brewster County	69.1	71.6	65.1	60.2	63.5	44.0	36.5	45.4	27 456	33 036	18 707	63 600	19.1	12.4
Briscoe County	80.2	83.1	78.4	64.6	60.0	69.5	60.0	70.0	28 167	31 618	18 438	33 900	17.0	10.1
Brooks County	73.1	79.5	65.9	60.5	48.5	73.1	45.2	75.1	18 836	21 826	10 692	33 000	19.1	15.4
Brown County	77.3	83.7	74.6	51.6	37.7	60.4	51.3	61.6	31 007	36 430	18 630	48 100	19.0	11.8
Burleson County	82.2	86.1	81.4	65.9	57.7	72.8	66.1	73.6	32 811	35 783	24 534	53 100	19.2	11.5
Burnet County	81.9	86.4	77.4	58.0	46.3	68.5	64.3	69.3	37 535	42 098	22 985	85 900	21.2	11.3

Table C-3. States and Counties — Migration, Housing, and Transportation

STATE County	Median gross rent	Percent who pay 35 percent or more of income for housing expenses — Owners	Renters	Number of workers 16 years and over	Car, truck, or van — Drove alone	Carpooled	Public transportation	Other means	Walked	Vehicles available (percent of households) — No vehicles	One vehicle	Two or more vehicles
	25	26	27	28	29	30	31	32	33	34	35	36
TENNESSEE— Cont'd												
Marshall County	444	11.6	23.7	12 754	80.8	14.0	0.4	0.6	1.2	6.0	29.0	65.0
Maury County	514	13.3	25.3	33 602	82.9	13.2	0.3	0.7	1.0	6.0	29.8	64.2
Meigs County	365	13.4	18.1	4 353	79.3	16.1	0.8	0.9	1.0	5.7	28.6	65.6
Monroe County.............	396	11.8	24.0	15 885	82.3	13.3	0.2	0.7	1.0	6.6	30.2	63.2
Montgomery County......	549	15.8	22.4	65 700	81.6	12.3	0.9	1.2	2.1	6.0	30.1	64.0
Moore County..............	402	11.4	18.7	2 707	88.8	6.4	0.0	0.2	1.1	3.8	25.3	70.9
Morgan County	397	15.9	18.7	7 275	79.6	16.1	0.2	0.7	1.3	7.5	26.0	66.5
Obion County	393	11.1	21.0	14 515	83.5	12.4	0.4	0.7	0.9	6.3	32.1	61.5
Overton County	345	14.0	22.2	8 602	82.9	12.0	0.2	1.3	1.8	7.2	28.7	64.1
Perry County	365	14.1	21.1	3 167	74.5	19.2	0.2	0.7	0.8	6.4	27.6	66.1
Pickett County	241	11.5	12.1	2 110	80.1	14.2	0.3	0.0	0.5	6.4	29.2	64.4
Polk County	345	12.9	16.6	6 786	75.5	18.5	0.4	0.5	2.0	6.4	28.0	65.6
Putnam County	441	14.0	31.3	28 985	80.6	12.9	0.2	1.2	2.4	5.8	32.0	62.2
Rhea County	384	12.8	23.9	12 260	77.7	17.4	0.2	0.5	1.6	6.9	30.6	62.4
Roane County	398	12.5	22.8	22 333	86.1	10.3	0.2	0.9	0.7	6.9	28.6	64.5
Robertson County	502	14.6	23.5	27 248	79.9	15.1	0.3	0.9	0.9	6.4	24.8	68.7
Rutherford County	601	12.5	32.0	94 489	83.1	12.6	0.2	0.7	1.0	4.0	28.2	67.8
Scott County................	347	17.7	22.8	7 728	82.6	14.1	0.3	0.7	1.3	7.2	32.5	60.2
Sequatchie County	382	17.3	23.3	4 805	83.4	13.9	0.3	0.3	1.3	6.0	27.7	66.3
Sevier County..............	513	13.9	24.9	34 389	80.6	13.2	0.5	0.8	1.6	4.7	29.6	65.8
Shelby County..............	566	17.4	30.8	402 560	80.2	13.1	2.1	0.9	1.5	11.2	38.6	50.1
Smith County...............	401	14.0	23.0	8 034	82.3	12.2	0.4	0.9	0.9	7.5	25.7	66.8
Stewart County	420	11.3	18.5	5 080	78.3	16.7	0.5	2.5	0.3	8.3	22.8	68.9
Sullivan County	419	12.3	26.7	67 101	86.1	9.5	0.2	0.6	1.2	7.3	28.7	64.0
Sumner County	594	14.3	28.1	64 756	82.9	12.1	0.3	0.8	0.8	5.2	26.7	68.1
Tipton County	470	15.9	25.4	23 192	82.9	13.1	0.3	1.1	0.5	6.7	27.8	65.4
Trousdale County.........	452	15.0	22.9	3 248	76.1	18.3	0.3	1.6	0.7	7.6	28.0	64.4
Unicoi County	380	10.0	24.2	7 472	85.6	11.2	0.0	0.9	0.5	7.3	27.5	65.1
Union County	388	15.9	30.6	7 302	81.0	15.1	0.0	0.5	1.5	6.6	27.2	66.2
Van Buren County.........	346	13.4	14.3	2 471	72.2	21.0	0.3	1.7	1.4	7.7	30.0	62.4
Warren County	416	12.2	26.9	17 505	78.5	15.0	0.2	0.6	2.4	7.8	28.6	63.5
Washington County	446	14.0	29.4	50 659	85.0	10.4	0.4	0.6	1.5	7.4	31.5	61.0
Wayne County..............	322	13.3	19.9	5 915	79.3	14.7	0.8	1.6	2.0	7.8	27.4	64.7
Weakley County	391	11.5	27.0	15 572	82.2	10.4	0.2	0.8	3.5	6.5	31.8	61.7
White County................	392	13.5	20.2	10 088	81.8	12.4	0.1	1.5	1.2	8.3	28.1	63.6
Williamson County	744	14.6	23.8	64 650	83.6	9.3	0.2	0.9	0.7	2.6	21.3	76.1
Wilson County	567	13.0	25.3	45 839	83.3	11.6	0.3	0.9	0.6	4.2	22.9	72.9
TEXAS.....................	574	13.6	27.1	9 157 875	77.7	14.5	1.9	1.3	1.9	7.4	36.0	56.6
Anderson County	456	16.7	24.7	16 702	79.3	16.0	0.3	0.7	1.4	8.0	34.9	57.0
Andrews County	397	11.5	19.0	4 915	83.8	11.3	0.1	1.5	1.0	6.8	37.3	55.9
Angelina County	461	12.4	29.6	33 278	80.0	15.2	0.1	1.2	1.1	8.0	33.7	58.3
Aransas County	475	16.1	22.3	8 473	75.1	16.3	0.2	2.3	2.8	5.8	40.8	53.4
Archer County	424	10.2	13.7	4 278	80.3	12.1	0.2	1.1	1.9	3.5	26.9	69.6
Armstrong County	436	12.6	21.0	965	79.6	11.7	0.2	1.2	1.2	2.6	21.6	75.8
Atascosa County	398	12.8	27.4	15 166	73.7	20.2	0.0	1.6	2.1	7.7	32.2	60.1
Austin County...............	475	10.9	18.1	10 573	79.8	13.3	0.1	1.2	1.6	7.3	28.4	64.4
Bailey County	383	12.5	14.4	2 671	79.3	14.5	0.0	0.7	3.1	4.9	35.9	59.2
Bandera County	477	15.9	23.7	7 715	75.1	16.1	0.1	0.9	2.6	3.3	31.4	65.2
Bastrop County	549	13.0	22.9	26 114	74.6	20.4	0.2	0.9	1.3	6.0	28.5	65.5
Baylor County	271	13.9	15.6	1 524	84.4	9.4	0.0	0.4	1.6	6.2	38.7	55.1
Bee County	416	11.8	22.9	9 748	74.9	17.3	0.6	1.9	1.9	8.8	39.2	52.1
Bell County	543	13.1	22.3	112 585	78.9	14.2	0.3	1.4	3.6	6.9	36.4	56.8
Bexar County	556	13.8	27.6	607 860	75.7	14.7	3.3	1.2	2.5	9.6	37.2	53.2
Blanco County	479	12.5	19.6	3 900	75.1	14.4	0.3	0.5	2.6	4.1	29.0	67.0
Borden County	225	22.8	5.8	340	85.6	5.0	0.0	0.9	5.6	1.4	24.0	74.7
Bosque County.............	432	13.2	16.9	7 004	74.0	19.7	0.2	0.4	1.8	4.6	31.6	63.8
Bowie County	459	12.0	28.6	35 493	82.4	12.4	0.2	1.0	1.7	9.8	34.0	56.2
Brazoria County	542	10.2	23.2	104 832	82.8	12.6	0.3	1.0	1.1	4.7	29.7	65.6
Brazos County.............	584	12.9	49.3	70 562	76.5	13.2	1.0	3.5	3.3	6.6	36.2	57.3
Brewster County	370	14.5	31.8	4 015	68.3	15.8	0.0	3.7	7.4	6.4	43.9	49.7
Briscoe County	301	8.7	19.1	768	78.0	14.5	0.0	1.0	2.3	5.7	34.3	60.1
Brooks County..............	250	18.3	33.8	2 409	71.2	22.0	0.0	1.7	2.4	18.5	35.6	46.0
Brown County...............	441	12.0	28.7	15 301	82.6	11.7	0.3	1.3	1.8	5.7	36.5	57.8
Burleson County...........	443	8.6	21.8	6 868	76.5	17.5	0.0	1.6	1.1	8.0	32.4	59.6
Burnet County	509	13.9	26.9	14 651	76.2	16.2	0.1	1.8	1.8	4.7	33.2	62.1

STATE/ County code	MSA/PMSA/ NECMA code[1]	STATE County	Residence in 1995 (percent)						Occupied housing units		Householders 65 years and over	
			Total population 5 years and over	Same house	Same county, different house	Same state, different county	Different state	Outside the United States	Number	Percent owner-occupied	Number	Percent owner-occupied
			1	2	3	4	5	6	7	8	9	10
		TEXAS—Cont'd										
48 055	0640	Caldwell County	29 786	55.2	17.1	24.4	2.4	0.9	10 816	69.6	2 435	79.1
48 057	...	Calhoun County	19 083	59.6	24.1	10.9	2.9	2.4	7 442	72.8	1 896	88.0
48 059	...	Callahan County	12 205	57.2	16.3	19.5	6.4	0.6	5 061	80.8	1 510	90.9
48 061	1240	Cameron County	303 696	58.5	28.2	5.0	4.3	4.0	97 267	67.7	23 298	81.3
48 063	...	Camp County	10 810	54.1	23.1	17.9	2.5	2.5	4 336	74.8	1 112	88.0
48 065	...	Carson County	6 141	64.6	12.5	16.9	5.8	0.3	2 470	83.6	673	94.2
48 067	...	Cass County	28 613	62.2	21.5	10.3	5.6	0.4	12 190	78.6	3 551	86.6
48 069	...	Castro County	7 574	63.7	21.1	12.4	1.9	0.9	2 761	71.0	642	81.6
48 071	3360	Chambers County	24 205	57.7	16.3	21.1	3.6	1.2	9 139	83.6	1 596	90.3
48 073	...	Cherokee County	43 370	56.5	23.2	14.7	2.7	2.8	16 651	73.8	4 530	86.2
48 075	...	Childress County	7 315	63.7	19.9	9.6	4.5	2.2	2 474	70.7	769	83.7
48 077	...	Clay County	10 360	61.0	13.1	20.5	5.1	0.3	4 323	83.0	1 184	90.3
48 079	...	Cochran County	3 460	63.6	19.2	12.0	2.8	2.5	1 309	74.1	377	89.1
48 081	...	Coke County	3 710	57.1	11.8	25.5	3.6	1.9	1 544	78.8	582	84.9
48 083	...	Coleman County	8 719	59.6	18.7	18.1	0.1	0.6	3 889	74.6	1 436	82.9
48 085	1920	Collin County	449 510	38.1	19.9	22.0	15.5	4.5	181 970	68.7	15 298	77.2
48 087	...	Collingsworth County	2 995	63.4	21.4	8.4	6.0	0.8	1 294	78.9	499	87.2
48 089	...	Colorado County	19 150	65.9	16.2	13.3	2.6	2.0	7 641	76.7	2 475	83.4
48 091	7240	Comal County	73 182	51.5	17.1	23.1	6.7	1.6	29 066	77.2	7 070	87.0
48 093	...	Comanche County	13 128	59.3	19.5	16.2	3.5	1.4	5 522	76.2	1 879	83.2
48 095	...	Concho County	3 831	48.8	8.1	23.3	19.7	0.1	1 058	75.0	354	83.3
48 097	...	Cooke County	33 835	53.2	21.7	17.1	6.3	1.8	13 643	72.1	3 676	85.6
48 099	3810	Coryell County	69 046	39.4	10.1	16.2	28.4	5.8	19 950	54.8	2 638	85.6
48 101	...	Cottle County	1 808	63.3	18.6	15.5	2.0	0.6	820	71.6	342	78.9
48 103	...	Crane County	3 723	67.5	15.7	10.7	3.5	2.6	1 360	85.3	309	95.5
48 105	...	Crockett County	3 835	68.2	17.5	11.2	3.2	0.0	1 524	71.5	381	78.5
48 107	...	Crosby County	6 526	58.0	23.8	16.3	1.5	0.5	2 512	69.3	809	79.7
48 109	...	Culberson County	2 754	68.0	15.0	10.0	5.7	1.3	1 052	70.4	208	80.8
48 111	...	Dallam County	5 688	53.7	19.9	14.4	11.0	0.0	2 317	63.0	526	79.3
48 113	1920	Dallas County...............	2 038 325	45.3	32.6	8.4	6.9	6.7	807 621	52.6	114 435	76.4
48 115	...	Dawson County	14 126	58.1	17.2	14.3	9.7	0.7	4 726	73.4	1 519	84.7
48 117	...	Deaf Smith County.......	16 953	57.4	27.3	0.0	0.6	1.7	6 180	67.4	1 420	78.0
48 119	...	Delta County	5 048	56.6	17.8	21.1	3.7	0.8	2 094	77.1	568	87.5
48 121	1920	Denton County	397 853	37.7	22.2	23.5	13.5	3.1	158 903	64.5	13 445	77.8
48 123	...	DeWitt County	18 898	61.7	20.0	16.1	1.2	0.9	7 207	76.6	2 421	83.0
48 125	...	Dickens County	2 634	61.2	13.9	18.7	5.7	0.5	980	77.7	343	84.0
48 127	...	Dimmit County	9 419	68.5	21.0	6.3	3.5	0.7	3 308	73.9	912	85.4
48 129	...	Donley County	3 648	57.9	18.8	16.3	6.6	0.4	1 578	74.4	606	83.5
48 131	...	Duval County	12 153	70.7	15.1	11.8	2.1	0.4	4 350	80.8	1 226	86.9
48 133	...	Eastland County	17 206	57.7	19.3	17.7	4.0	1.5	7 321	76.7	2 661	84.8
48 135	5800	Ector County	111 545	57.1	29.4	8.8	3.6	1.1	43 846	68.6	8 547	81.3
48 137	...	Edwards County	2 033	71.1	11.6	14.7	2.1	0.6	801	79.7	270	89.6
48 139	1920	Ellis County	102 901	50.9	20.9	20.9	5.3	2.0	37 020	76.2	6 710	83.2
48 141	2320	El Paso County	621 288	55.2	30.4	2.4	6.9	5.1	210 022	63.6	40 868	76.0
48 143	...	Erath County	30 891	47.5	24.6	20.5	4.9	2.6	12 568	63.1	2 838	83.4
48 145	...	Falls County	17 495	62.3	16.8	16.1	3.2	1.7	6 496	71.7	1 950	81.0
48 147	...	Fannin County	29 410	50.9	18.2	23.8	5.9	1.3	11 105	74.7	3 190	82.4
48 149	...	Fayette County	20 692	62.5	18.3	14.6	2.7	1.9	8 722	78.2	3 050	85.0
48 151	...	Fisher County	4 096	63.6	15.2	18.6	2.0	0.6	1 785	76.8	713	84.0
48 153	...	Floyd County	7 180	60.7	23.9	12.8	1.7	0.9	2 730	74.0	757	85.9
48 155	...	Foard County	1 528	63.4	17.0	16.4	3.1	0.1	664	75.0	247	82.2
48 157	3360	Fort Bend County.........	327 666	52.0	16.0	20.7	7.4	3.9	110 915	80.8	10 405	84.5
48 159	...	Franklin County	8 897	56.6	13.5	23.2	4.3	2.4	3 754	79.0	1 187	84.5
48 161	...	Freestone County.........	16 995	63.6	16.0	16.6	2.5	1.2	6 588	78.6	1 935	88.1
48 163	...	Frio County..................	15 018	64.7	24.9	8.3	1.5	0.6	4 743	69.0	1 153	78.1
48 165	...	Gaines County	13 290	59.6	26.0	9.6	2.9	1.9	4 681	78.6	915	89.6
48 167	2920	Galveston County..........	232 804	52.4	25.1	14.4	5.7	2.3	94 782	66.2	18 344	78.6
48 169	...	Garza County	4 549	58.1	15.8	19.8	4.0	2.3	1 663	70.9	411	84.9
48 171	...	Gillespie County	19 783	60.1	15.2	18.7	5.0	1.0	8 521	77.5	3 308	85.6
48 173	...	Glasscock County	1 297	71.8	8.0	15.0	1.3	3.9	483	67.3	88	93.2
48 175	...	Goliad County	6 496	60.9	14.8	21.4	2.6	0.3	2 644	80.3	774	87.3
48 177	...	Gonzales County...........	17 359	61.3	21.6	11.6	2.4	3.1	6 782	69.2	2 305	77.9
48 179	...	Gray County	21 422	59.0	23.7	11.8	4.6	0.9	8 793	77.4	2 769	84.8
48 181	7640	Grayson County	103 405	51.3	26.1	13.4	7.9	1.2	42 849	70.5	11 033	82.1
48 183	4420	Gregg County	103 667	52.0	26.8	13.9	5.7	1.5	42 687	64.1	10 331	78.0
48 185	...	Grimes County	22 160	58.2	14.8	21.5	4.6	1.0	7 753	77.8	1 983	84.3

[1]MSA = Metropolitan Statistical Area. PMSA = Primary MSA. NECMA = New England County Metropolitan Area. See the Appendix A for explanation of these concepts. See Appendix B for list of metropolitan areas identified by type, with component counties.

Table C-3. States and Counties — Migration, Housing, and Transportation

STATE County	Total family households	Family-households Married-couple family Total	With own children under 18 years	Other family Total	With own children under 18 years	Total nonfamily households	Two or more adults	Living alone	Median household income All households	Owner-occupied households	Renter-occupied households	Median housing value (owner estimated)	With a mortgage	Without a mortgage
	11	12	13	14	15	16	17	18	19	20	21	22	23	24
TEXAS—Cont'd														
Caldwell County	73.2	78.3	71.4	56.2	46.4	58.9	64.4	58.0	36 602	42 313	26 235	68 100	20.4	10.6
Calhoun County	76.0	82.4	74.7	53.6	43.7	62.9	50.4	64.7	35 349	39 598	23 495	51 400	17.2	9.9
Callahan County	82.3	85.8	75.6	64.0	48.4	76.6	41.3	79.8	32 330	34 448	22 279	49 600	20.3	10.6
Cameron County	69.9	74.6	66.9	55.8	42.3	57.4	50.0	58.4	26 031	31 387	16 441	48 000	22.2	12.1
Camp County	77.4	84.5	77.2	51.8	31.4	67.3	22.2	70.3	31 243	34 707	22 236	57 700	18.8	12.4
Carson County	85.5	87.1	82.6	76.1	63.8	77.5	61.8	78.4	39 669	41 677	30 333	52 900	16.3	9.9
Cass County	81.5	87.7	82.1	58.7	44.9	71.6	56.9	72.9	28 273	31 466	16 520	49 600	19.1	10.9
Castro County	72.1	77.1	69.8	50.5	31.3	67.4	53.8	68.3	30 082	35 451	20 605	50 300	18.1	11.3
Chambers County	85.3	87.7	85.6	72.3	61.9	76.9	58.5	80.2	47 609	51 430	30 361	71 100	18.0	9.9
Cherokee County	76.9	83.4	75.6	55.7	46.6	65.3	50.8	66.7	29 233	33 034	20 852	51 600	20.7	11.9
Childress County	75.9	84.3	80.7	39.5	11.9	60.2	37.7	62.0	28 694	35 991	17 846	44 600	18.0	11.3
Clay County	84.9	87.2	81.7	69.3	51.7	77.8	75.8	78.0	35 570	37 455	27 803	52 100	18.6	12.2
Cochran County	76.1	78.3	64.7	66.5	53.4	67.0	47.1	68.2	27 482	27 727	26 250	28 400	18.8	10.3
Coke County	82.2	85.2	74.6	64.5	49.5	71.0	77.4	70.6	29 267	32 568	17 400	47 000	18.7	9.9
Coleman County	77.4	79.3	66.1	67.8	55.7	69.0	65.1	69.3	25 600	28 414	16 398	37 300	19.3	12.4
Collin County	79.9	84.2	85.3	53.0	49.3	38.4	34.8	39.2	70 292	86 099	43 072	151 600	20.5	10.8
Collingsworth County	84.3	90.3	85.8	53.6	28.7	65.8	64.3	65.8	25 242	30 361	16 118	37 600	17.6	13.2
Colorado County	81.4	87.0	82.9	57.3	51.9	65.2	49.4	67.1	32 118	37 126	20 269	60 200	19.3	10.3
Comal County	81.9	86.5	81.3	58.9	48.4	62.6	53.1	64.3	46 093	51 418	30 497	102 100	20.3	9.9
Comanche County	79.0	83.8	73.2	54.1	43.6	69.2	75.2	68.7	28 439	31 774	19 133	48 000	17.8	12.1
Concho County	79.3	79.0	69.3	81.0	67.7	64.1	53.8	64.6	31 381	33 672	22 857	47 600	19.1	10.3
Cooke County	75.9	80.5	70.6	54.3	41.1	61.4	48.5	63.2	37 582	42 805	25 525	73 200	19.2	10.8
Coryell County	56.2	59.2	45.7	42.5	31.7	49.6	43.4	51.0	36 244	44 058	29 673	69 400	19.8	10.8
Cottle County	75.2	79.5	60.6	57.4	43.9	64.2	57.1	64.4	25 000	30 039	18 021	30 200	15.8	11.4
Crane County	86.8	90.4	87.8	69.2	47.2	79.6	47.6	82.2	32 404	35 136	21 500	37 300	17.2	12.0
Crockett County	76.6	81.1	80.2	57.3	50.4	57.2	46.4	58.0	27 682	31 844	19 609	48 900	16.8	11.6
Crosby County	70.6	74.3	61.3	55.4	46.6	65.7	50.0	67.2	25 078	29 688	17 863	36 000	18.9	10.7
Culberson County	72.5	73.9	69.4	67.3	56.8	64.0	64.3	64.0	25 850	27 281	19 554	32 300	20.4	13.5
Dallam County	64.1	68.5	62.6	47.9	42.1	59.9	20.0	62.3	27 472	31 760	24 535	44 200	18.3	9.9
Dallas County	60.5	68.9	63.0	39.5	30.8	36.9	29.9	38.6	43 119	57 950	32 057	90 800	20.5	11.3
Dawson County	77.0	82.7	73.6	53.1	38.6	62.6	94.6	61.6	27 588	31 929	17 087	41 000	18.9	12.0
Deaf Smith County	70.7	76.8	67.9	50.5	39.4	55.0	59.0	54.7	29 549	34 613	22 169	47 300	19.0	10.4
Delta County	78.5	82.9	78.4	58.1	49.0	73.8	54.8	75.1	30 077	34 214	19 191	40 500	21.4	13.8
Denton County	76.5	82.1	82.0	48.8	43.2	36.1	28.8	38.6	57 808	74 199	35 038	127 000	20.6	10.8
DeWitt County	80.9	86.7	82.3	60.1	52.8	66.1	47.4	67.8	28 722	31 786	17 342	49 600	17.8	10.4
Dickens County	81.3	84.7	77.9	59.0	59.0	71.0	64.0	71.5	25 069	27 765	17 083	27 100	18.3	13.8
Dimmit County	74.6	80.0	74.6	60.5	36.5	71.2	50.8	73.3	21 250	24 258	13 056	29 300	20.8	12.5
Donley County	81.8	86.1	75.5	56.0	43.0	59.3	56.0	59.5	29 286	34 550	19 167	45 800	18.4	10.9
Duval County	83.2	85.8	81.0	75.9	60.6	73.5	58.2	74.7	22 405	23 508	18 209	28 900	19.4	11.4
Eastland County	81.0	85.3	75.5	61.5	44.0	67.0	60.7	67.6	26 862	30 618	14 744	37 100	18.8	12.1
Ector County	75.7	83.0	79.4	52.9	46.1	49.9	40.4	51.2	31 012	37 034	20 191	42 800	19.0	10.1
Edwards County	81.7	83.9	72.2	76.2	71.2	73.8	82.4	73.1	25 286	25 774	21 375	44 000	25.0	12.7
Ellis County	79.6	84.4	79.7	58.1	49.9	62.2	54.7	63.5	50 175	56 315	31 720	88 000	19.6	11.0
El Paso County	67.8	73.5	67.6	52.5	40.2	47.4	41.7	48.2	30 858	38 738	20 054	67 100	21.7	10.1
Erath County	73.2	77.5	68.9	49.7	37.2	44.2	19.6	50.6	30 830	37 855	20 713	68 200	19.8	11.7
Falls County	74.7	81.6	75.5	57.7	47.2	65.2	56.4	66.1	27 217	31 667	16 392	41 900	19.7	10.2
Fannin County	79.9	85.4	77.5	56.6	43.7	61.2	54.8	61.8	34 690	39 938	21 867	58 200	18.7	11.5
Fayette County	83.8	87.5	85.0	63.7	57.4	64.9	58.3	65.3	34 152	38 305	21 825	75 900	18.6	9.9
Fisher County	80.4	86.6	82.7	47.4	30.6	68.3	59.3	68.8	27 759	32 679	16 316	33 200	16.7	12.3
Floyd County	74.0	77.8	65.0	55.4	45.2	73.6	73.9	73.6	27 148	31 911	17 946	38 600	18.8	11.0
Foard County	80.3	82.7	71.7	69.2	57.4	64.4	53.8	65.1	26 190	30 938	17 500	27 300	18.0	12.7
Fort Bend County	84.4	88.3	87.4	66.5	62.5	61.8	55.9	62.8	63 963	72 026	35 327	110 800	20.3	10.3
Franklin County	82.9	86.9	76.8	56.6	45.9	68.5	49.4	70.3	31 258	34 420	20 991	64 300	19.7	13.1
Freestone County	80.7	85.2	78.4	61.5	49.2	73.5	66.2	74.1	31 406	35 230	22 388	55 100	18.7	11.3
Frio County	71.9	79.0	70.1	53.7	38.0	59.1	41.8	60.9	24 144	27 316	16 250	34 200	21.1	12.8
Gaines County	80.2	82.1	76.7	69.4	58.9	72.1	60.3	72.9	30 784	34 023	21 918	42 300	18.7	9.9
Galveston County	73.2	80.5	76.2	50.7	39.2	50.0	44.0	51.1	42 230	54 251	25 637	81 900	20.4	11.8
Garza County	74.7	83.2	75.6	48.7	31.8	60.2	56.1	60.6	26 678	30 893	20 682	41 500	22.9	10.9
Gillespie County	82.4	85.3	76.0	62.4	47.4	65.2	39.6	67.7	37 072	40 491	27 327	105 200	22.7	9.9
Glasscock County	73.6	73.9	69.4	68.4	60.0	48.8	28.6	51.4	35 313	40 568	30 000	65 000	19.6	9.9
Goliad County	84.7	87.5	82.6	68.8	59.0	67.0	61.9	67.5	34 375	38 667	18 152	61 800	18.8	9.9
Gonzales County	72.3	78.1	68.0	53.0	46.4	60.9	47.5	62.2	27 962	33 464	19 266	50 700	19.1	10.2
Gray County	82.2	86.3	81.7	58.9	49.8	66.7	64.2	66.8	31 272	35 348	20 252	36 900	17.3	9.9
Grayson County	77.0	82.7	74.8	54.7	44.2	55.1	45.3	56.6	37 351	43 898	25 582	67 800	19.3	11.8
Gregg County	71.0	79.0	72.8	46.8	35.7	48.2	32.8	50.5	34 532	43 257	23 845	72 500	19.1	10.0
Grimes County	80.1	84.6	80.3	66.3	54.0	71.7	71.8	71.6	31 460	34 805	20 588	57 100	19.3	12.2

STATE County	Median gross rent	Percent who pay 35 percent or more of income for housing expenses		Means of transportation to work (percent except where noted)						Vehicles available (percent of households)		
		Owners	Renters	Number of workers 16 years and over	Car, truck, or van					No vehicles	One vehicle	Two or more vehicles
					Drove alone	Carpooled	Public transportation	Other means	Walked			
	25	26	27	28	29	30	31	32	33	34	35	36
TEXAS—Cont'd												
Caldwell County	472	12.7	22.3	13 250	74.7	20.0	0.2	0.9	1.8	6.5	33.1	60.4
Calhoun County	440	7.9	24.0	8 121	78.5	15.4	0.2	1.8	2.2	7.2	34.0	58.8
Callahan County	394	11.9	20.0	5 589	77.6	15.5	0.0	1.4	1.8	4.3	32.1	63.6
Cameron County	413	15.2	30.4	106 769	73.2	19.4	0.8	1.8	2.3	11.6	39.8	48.6
Camp County	402	13.9	18.6	4 518	77.6	14.2	0.2	3.1	2.0	7.4	34.2	58.4
Carson County	398	8.2	11.1	2 958	84.1	10.5	0.0	1.1	1.8	3.2	27.2	69.6
Cass County................	356	13.3	20.3	11 665	80.8	13.2	0.4	1.9	1.6	8.7	33.9	57.4
Castro County	363	13.2	15.9	3 316	75.9	15.7	0.1	2.5	2.4	6.3	33.0	60.8
Chambers County	487	10.7	14.8	11 459	84.4	11.3	0.0	1.0	1.5	5.0	28.0	67.0
Cherokee County	412	14.9	24.1	18 371	75.6	18.0	0.3	1.6	1.7	8.3	34.6	57.1
Childress County..........	347	7.7	19.6	2 529	79.5	14.9	0.0	0.8	0.6	7.8	36.4	55.8
Clay County.................	394	13.5	12.8	5 249	79.5	13.0	0.2	1.1	2.1	3.6	27.9	68.5
Cochran County	381	10.4	14.9	1 316	76.3	14.0	0.5	1.7	3.9	4.4	37.1	58.5
Coke County	280	10.4	18.3	1 421	82.4	11.3	0.2	0.5	2.2	5.1	34.1	60.8
Coleman County	310	14.9	19.6	3 550	79.9	14.2	0.1	1.0	2.2	6.6	35.4	58.1
Collin County...............	798	13.0	21.5	263 601	83.5	9.5	0.8	0.7	1.0	2.6	28.8	68.6
Collingsworth County	293	11.9	20.2	1 243	83.3	9.3	0.0	0.7	3.7	6.6	32.0	61.4
Colorado County..........	375	13.2	17.9	8 579	75.0	15.7	0.5	1.4	3.8	10.0	31.4	58.6
Comal County	626	12.2	26.3	35 943	80.6	13.1	0.1	1.2	1.2	4.1	29.8	66.1
Comanche County	353	11.2	22.7	5 807	74.2	14.5	0.0	0.6	2.8	6.9	33.3	59.8
Concho County	373	13.2	19.8	1 175	73.4	14.9	0.3	0.9	3.4	5.6	32.7	61.7
Cooke County	458	11.4	22.5	16 183	77.5	16.0	0.8	0.8	1.2	5.2	31.1	63.7
Coryell County..............	548	13.8	17.7	33 927	68.1	19.7	0.2	1.7	8.4	4.2	34.8	61.0
Cottle County	218	9.6	12.6	806	72.7	20.0	0.2	1.5	2.1	9.9	36.3	53.8
Crane County	403	8.3	24.5	1 414	71.7	21.3	0.0	3.8	0.9	6.1	34.1	59.8
Crockett County	315	8.6	18.3	1 754	79.5	11.3	0.3	2.0	2.3	11.7	30.7	57.6
Crosby County	334	13.4	16.9	2 587	79.1	15.3	0.2	1.2	1.0	6.3	35.8	57.9
Culberson County	323	14.9	18.9	1 262	74.7	15.7	1.1	1.7	3.2	6.7	36.6	56.7
Dallam County..............	426	12.5	21.5	2 711	74.8	16.2	0.5	1.8	2.9	5.6	39.3	55.1
Dallas County...............	647	15.1	25.9	1 038 779	74.8	16.1	3.6	1.1	1.7	8.1	40.3	51.6
Dawson County............	341	13.7	21.0	4 888	79.0	14.2	0.1	2.3	1.7	7.9	39.3	52.7
Deaf Smith County.......	371	14.4	22.9	7 010	70.1	13.7	0.5	2.0	1.8	8.9	34.5	56.6
Delta County................	392	12.9	23.1	2 215	78.1	14.9	0.3	1.1	1.3	10.2	34.8	55.0
Denton County.............	725	12.3	27.5	235 672	82.0	10.9	0.7	1.1	1.6	3.4	29.8	66.9
DeWitt County..............	344	10.3	22.2	7 779	77.2	14.4	0.1	1.5	2.0	6.3	37.5	53.3
Dickens County	312	13.9	24.3	975	80.6	11.8	0.7	0.8	2.5	6.1	32.6	61.3
Dimmit County	337	12.9	35.3	3 218	76.5	16.7	0.3	2.5	1.7	11.5	38.4	50.1
Donley County.............	321	15.3	23.6	1 627	82.5	11.2	0.0	1.2	1.8	5.3	36.7	58.0
Duval County...............	292	12.7	16.2	4 226	71.0	20.4	0.0	2.1	3.3	12.9	42.0	45.1
Eastland County...........	360	12.1	23.6	7 479	76.7	16.0	0.1	1.4	3.4	7.0	36.1	56.9
Ector County...............	400	11.7	25.6	49 099	81.7	13.1	0.2	1.2	1.4	7.5	38.9	53.6
Edwards County	400	18.4	15.4	000	67.3	20.1	0.3	0.4	5.6	6.7	31.7	61.5
Ellis County	584	12.9	22.5	52 380	80.8	14.2	0.8	1.1	0.9	4.7	26.1	69.2
El Paso County	468	15.5	31.2	244 464	75.9	16.2	2.2	1.3	2.2	10.4	34.7	54.9
Erath County	450	14.4	30.2	14 763	78.9	12.4	0.1	1.3	3.0	6.1	33.7	60.2
Falls County	343	14.8	22.9	6 265	78.6	14.4	0.2	0.8	2.6	12.2	35.9	51.9
Fannin County	432	12.6	23.6	12 146	78.2	15.2	0.3	0.7	1.5	7.9	29.2	62.9
Fayette County	400	12.6	21.7	9 898	79.4	11.9	0.1	1.2	2.3	7.5	27.8	64.7
Fisher County	274	10.5	15.7	1 823	77.3	14.7	0.2	1.0	3.2	5.4	34.8	59.8
Floyd County	366	10.7	25.0	2 912	81.9	13.1	0.4	0.6	2.1	7.5	32.2	60.3
Foard County	268	13.8	22.0	671	68.6	24.9	0.0	2.1	1.3	7.5	31.3	61.1
Fort Bend County	730	14.6	24.7	163 614	81.6	12.6	1.7	0.8	0.5	2.8	24.2	73.0
Franklin County	404	14.1	18.9	3 797	78.7	12.0	0.3	1.6	2.6	5.2	32.2	62.6
Freestone County.........	378	15.5	20.3	6 830	78.1	14.0	0.0	1.2	3.0	6.2	32.1	61.6
Frio County	335	15.0	23.0	5 205	69.2	22.4	0.1	3.1	3.3	12.1	39.6	48.3
Gaines County	343	13.6	15.9	5 315	76.6	17.9	0.0	1.4	1.8	4.4	35.0	60.5
Galveston County..........	571	13.9	30.3	112 616	78.2	13.6	1.4	2.0	2.3	8.5	35.4	56.2
Garza County	315	21.0	25.4	1 834	79.0	14.9	0.0	1.9	1.1	8.1	41.6	50.3
Gillespie County	529	12.6	19.1	9 157	73.6	15.6	0.1	1.1	2.1	4.4	31.1	64.5
Glasscock County	331	16.3	2.7	594	69.9	13.0	0.0	0.3	6.9	2.7	27.7	69.6
Goliad County	357	8.5	11.4	2 882	74.9	14.3	0.5	0.9	3.3	5.7	29.7	64.6
Gonzales County..........	313	12.6	16.0	7 807	71.1	19.4	0.3	1.2	4.3	11.2	34.6	54.2
Gray County................	403	10.7	22.8	8 604	82.7	13.0	0.2	1.2	1.1	6.0	33.2	60.8
Grayson County...........	518	12.6	24.2	50 013	80.8	13.4	0.2	1.0	1.8	6.2	33.1	60.8
Gregg County..............	474	12.1	26.9	48 310	83.2	11.9	0.2	1.2	1.3	7.2	38.1	54.8
Grimes County	428	13.3	20.7	8 722	75.7	15.9	0.2	1.5	1.9	9.4	33.3	57.3

Table C-3. States and Counties — Migration, Housing, and Transportation

STATE/ County code	MSA/PMSA/ NECMA code[1]	STATE County	Total population 5 years and over	Residence in 1995 (percent)					Occupied housing units		Householders 65 years and over	
				Same house	Same county, different house	Same state, different county	Different state	Outside the United States	Number	Percent owner-occupied	Number	Percent owner-occupied
			1	2	3	4	5	6	7	8	9	10
		TEXAS—Cont'd										
48 187	7240	Guadalupe County	82 868	51.1	18.3	20.8	8.3	1.4	30 900	77.0	6 265	84.3
48 189	...	Hale County	33 605	51.0	28.3	15.9	3.5	1.4	11 975	64.8	3 087	81.0
48 191	...	Hall County	3 505	57.7	19.0	19.3	3.1	0.8	1 548	74.3	580	81.6
48 193	...	Hamilton County	7 773	56.8	18.2	20.4	3.5	1.1	3 374	77.8	1 202	84.7
48 195	...	Hansford County	5 007	58.4	19.1	11.2	6.7	4.7	2 005	74.4	533	88.0
48 197	...	Hardeman County	4 417	59.9	23.1	11.4	5.3	0.3	1 943	73.2	666	84.7
48 199	0840	Hardin County	44 778	62.1	19.9	14.0	3.7	0.3	17 805	82.5	3 947	90.6
48 201	3360	Harris County	3 121 999	47.8	34.5	6.1	5.8	5.8	1 205 516	55.3	161 177	76.6
48 203	4420	Harrison County	58 047	57.8	20.4	15.3	5.3	1.3	23 087	77.2	5 371	86.7
48 205	...	Hartley County	5 209	52.9	8.5	24.9	10.2	3.4	1 604	76.4	472	82.2
48 207	...	Haskell County	5 801	63.2	18.3	16.5	1.6	0.4	2 569	78.9	1 018	92.8
48 209	0640	Hays County	91 596	41.4	15.4	35.5	6.1	1.6	33 410	64.9	4 428	81.6
48 211	...	Hemphill County	3 156	60.4	18.3	13.8	6.5	1.0	1 280	77.3	320	92.2
48 213	1920	Henderson County	68 679	55.4	17.2	21.3	5.2	1.0	28 804	80.0	8 656	89.0
48 215	4880	Hidalgo County	511 643	61.1	25.8	4.3	4.3	4.5	156 824	73.1	34 311	84.2
48 217	...	Hill County....................	30 127	55.0	20.0	18.7	4.0	2.3	12 204	75.0	3 576	82.7
48 219	...	Hockley County	21 063	58.2	22.6	15.3	3.4	0.6	7 994	74.4	1 969	87.4
48 221	2800	Hood County	38 723	48.6	19.3	23.6	7.7	0.8	16 176	81.2	4 641	89.2
48 223	...	Hopkins County	29 908	52.3	26.9	14.5	4.7	1.5	12 286	71.4	3 308	82.1
48 225	...	Houston County	21 919	54.1	19.4	21.2	3.9	1.4	8 259	76.1	2 682	83.6
48 227	...	Howard County	31 645	53.2	19.5	18.5	6.4	2.3	11 389	69.5	3 173	78.5
48 229	...	Hudspeth County	3 056	66.6	12.9	12.2	5.5	2.8	1 092	81.0	213	96.7
48 231	1920	Hunt County	71 535	51.2	20.8	20.5	5.7	1.8	28 742	71.4	6 449	82.5
48 233	...	Hutchinson County.......	22 221	59.1	23.9	10.8	5.4	0.8	9 283	78.9	2 566	88.7
48 235	...	Irion County	1 677	60.9	10.1	28.0	0.8	0.1	694	77.7	185	86.5
48 237	...	Jack County	8 266	50.3	16.4	23.9	5.9	3.5	3 047	76.8	919	89.4
48 239	...	Jackson County	13 356	61.6	21.4	13.0	2.8	1.3	5 336	73.7	1 407	86.6
48 241	...	Jasper County	33 176	62.0	18.3	15.3	3.6	0.7	13 450	80.6	3 859	88.7
48 243	...	Jeff Davis County	2 124	52.8	9.9	25.7	8.1	3.4	896	70.2	254	90.2
48 245	0840	Jefferson County	235 207	57.3	26.4	10.3	4.4	1.6	92 880	65.9	23 751	81.3
48 247	...	Jim Hogg County	4 859	60.2	29.2	9.5	0.6	0.5	1 815	77.6	489	86.3
48 249	...	Jim Wells County	36 159	66.1	19.4	11.9	1.8	0.8	12 961	76.5	3 205	84.4
48 251	2800	Johnson County	117 495	50.3	20.2	22.8	5.4	1.3	43 636	78.9	8 003	85.0
48 253	...	Jones County	19 747	47.9	13.0	35.7	2.9	0.5	6 140	79.2	1 761	84.0
48 255	...	Karnes County	14 608	59.5	17.9	19.3	1.9	1.4	4 454	74.0	1 369	83.6
48 257	1920	Kaufman County	66 188	53.4	18.2	23.0	4.0	1.4	24 367	79.2	4 656	83.5
48 259	...	Kendall County	22 263	50.3	13.7	27.1	7.7	1.2	8 613	79.6	2 014	86.5
48 261	...	Kenedy County	378	72.8	5.3	17.7	3.4	0.8	138	40.6	34	52.9
48 263	...	Kent County	832	62.7	12.5	22.1	2.6	0.0	353	78.5	128	83.6
48 265	...	Kerr County	41 383	51.6	20.4	17.6	9.1	1.3	17 813	73.3	6 959	84.2
48 267	...	Kimble County	4 193	59.8	17.5	16.6	3.9	2.2	1 866	73.6	577	84.6
48 269	...	King County	331	67.4	4.5	26.3	1.2	0.6	108	38.9	26	76.9
48 271	...	Kinney County	3 173	58.5	13.7	18.0	8.4	1.4	1 314	77.9	572	86.5
48 273	...	Kleberg County	29 149	53.2	23.6	14.8	6.4	2.0	10 896	58.6	2 173	79.4
48 275	...	Knox County.................	3 984	63.9	18.4	12.7	2.6	2.5	1 690	75.4	614	84.2
48 277	...	Lamar County	45 106	49.6	31.6	10.4	7.1	1.3	19 077	67.2	5 164	77.2
48 279	...	Lamb County.................	13 593	63.9	20.8	10.2	3.8	1.4	5 360	75.6	1 623	85.2
48 281	...	Lampasas County	16 550	52.3	19.6	17.5	8.2	2.4	6 554	74.0	1 586	86.3
48 283	...	La Salle County	5 437	70.1	15.6	12.0	2.0	0.3	1 819	74.7	517	78.9
48 285	...	Lavaca County	18 080	68.1	16.0	13.8	1.5	0.5	7 669	78.4	2 696	83.8
48 287	...	Lee County	14 555	59.0	16.0	19.9	3.3	1.8	5 663	79.4	1 473	89.2
48 289	...	Leon County	14 502	57.2	18.0	20.3	3.5	1.0	6 189	82.8	1 997	91.3
48 291	3360	Liberty County	65 425	55.0	17.6	22.3	3.7	1.5	23 242	79.0	4 954	86.4
48 293	...	Limestone County	20 632	58.3	21.3	15.7	2.3	2.5	7 906	74.9	2 302	86.5
48 295	...	Lipscomb County	2 875	58.6	14.9	13.7	10.5	2.4	1 205	77.9	369	90.5
48 297	...	Live Oak County	11 719	62.7	15.1	16.8	2.6	2.7	4 230	81.4	1 252	91.5
48 299	...	Llano County	16 425	53.8	14.9	23.9	6.7	0.7	7 879	80.9	3 355	86.5
48 301	...	Loving County	67	65.7	3.0	26.9	4.5	0.0	31	80.6	6	100.0
48 303	4600	Lubbock County	225 526	47.4	29.8	16.2	5.5	1.1	92 516	59.2	17 515	81.0
48 305	...	Lynn County	6 077	63.2	19.9	13.5	2.9	0.4	2 354	74.6	645	88.2
48 307	...	McCulloch County	7 683	58.5	23.4	14.5	2.7	0.9	3 277	72.7	1 095	86.3
48 309	8800	McLennan County	198 274	48.2	29.4	14.7	5.8	1.9	78 859	60.2	17 895	79.9
48 311	...	McMullen County	821	71.6	12.4	14.4	1.0	0.6	355	80.8	126	92.1
48 313	...	Madison County	12 237	51.2	13.7	28.1	5.7	1.3	3 914	77.0	1 206	87.3
48 315	...	Marion County	10 335	60.0	11.4	19.8	8.2	0.6	4 610	82.1	1 512	88.3
48 317	...	Martin County...............	4 342	66.2	15.6	14.7	1.5	2.1	1 624	74.3	430	82.1

[1]MSA = Metropolitan Statistical Area. PMSA = Primary MSA. NECMA = New England County Metropolitan Area. See the Appendix A for explanation of these concepts. See Appendix B for list of metropolitan areas identified by type, with component counties.

STATE County	Owner-occupied by household type (percent)								Median household income			Median housing value (owner estimated)	Median monthly owner costs as a percent of income	
	Family-households					Nonfamily households								
	Married-couple family			Other family										
	Total family households	Total	With own children under 18 years	Total	With own children under 18 years	Total nonfamily households	Two or more adults	Living alone	All households	Owner-occupied households	Renter-occupied households	Median housing value (owner estimated)	With a mortgage	Without a mortgage
	11	12	13	14	15	16	17	18	19	20	21	22	23	24
TEXAS—Cont'd														
Guadalupe County	80.9	85.6	80.3	61.3	53.7	63.5	52.2	65.6	43 666	49 546	28 342	82 400	19.8	9.9
Hale County	67.1	73.6	67.2	41.6	29.2	57.5	32.7	59.9	30 877	38 123	23 525	53 300	19.2	9.9
Hall County	77.8	81.9	74.6	57.7	56.7	67.6	41.2	69.4	22 917	25 034	16 196	24 300	19.3	13.3
Hamilton County	81.7	84.8	76.0	63.2	56.4	68.7	54.1	69.6	31 045	35 523	21 556	57 300	19.0	12.8
Hansford County	75.3	77.3	68.9	59.0	54.3	71.7	41.5	74.3	35 696	40 696	24 741	46 500	17.2	11.3
Hardeman County	76.9	81.8	74.8	53.1	31.5	65.5	53.5	66.4	28 470	33 115	18 676	31 000	17.1	12.1
Hardin County	85.3	89.4	85.2	67.3	59.9	73.2	66.4	74.0	37 510	40 465	25 827	62 100	18.1	10.4
Harris County	63.1	70.7	66.3	41.7	32.7	37.6	30.7	39.1	42 425	58 443	30 015	84 200	19.7	10.6
Harrison County	80.3	86.3	79.7	59.7	50.7	68.4	49.8	70.5	33 468	38 156	20 658	61 700	19.1	10.7
Hartley County	82.7	83.8	76.7	68.2	54.5	56.4	25.0	60.1	45 200	50 870	27 037	87 500	18.2	9.9
Haskell County	79.4	83.5	75.9	56.1	41.7	77.9	62.9	78.6	23 586	25 934	18 040	34 000	21.4	12.9
Hays County	79.7	84.5	81.3	59.1	58.0	35.5	19.1	45.3	45 158	58 621	23 661	116 700	21.0	10.5
Hemphill County	80.0	81.9	72.5	65.1	57.1	69.9	44.4	71.3	35 779	39 808	24 531	55 800	18.3	12.2
Henderson County	80.2	87.3	70.3	61.9	56.0	71.4	63.4	72.5	32 488	35 715	22 278	61 700	19.7	11.1
Hidalgo County	75.7	79.8	75.9	61.4	49.8	58.2	44.1	60.4	24 707	28 322	15 638	46 000	23.0	12.1
Hill County	77.9	82.9	73.9	57.1	46.3	67.5	51.9	69.8	31 513	35 412	20 188	55 200	20.7	12.7
Hockley County	77.3	82.0	73.7	57.8	45.4	65.2	39.0	68.1	30 725	34 796	20 915	47 100	19.1	10.3
Hood County	85.5	88.1	78.5	70.0	64.6	68.1	68.5	68.1	43 712	48 353	29 060	88 800	19.9	10.6
Hopkins County	75.3	80.7	72.2	50.7	41.9	61.0	38.4	64.2	32 190	36 404	23 935	61 600	19.3	12.8
Houston County	79.6	86.0	79.4	60.2	45.9	68.1	57.8	69.1	27 789	30 785	17 971	48 400	22.8	13.1
Howard County	74.6	81.6	71.9	52.2	39.7	57.4	49.0	58.2	30 169	36 019	19 375	38 500	17.8	10.4
Hudspeth County	82.5	84.1	79.9	76.5	72.8	75.4	62.5	76.3	20 991	20 357	24 167	26 300	20.5	13.5
Hunt County	77.9	83.2	77.5	57.0	49.7	54.8	46.3	56.3	36 708	42 848	24 264	61 300	19.4	11.2
Hutchinson County	82.9	87.8	81.4	59.5	45.2	67.4	63.0	67.9	35 979	40 507	19 710	43 100	16.3	9.9
Irion County	81.0	81.5	76.0	77.0	67.6	68.0	61.9	68.8	36 607	40 139	27 750	59 500	19.3	9.9
Jack County	78.5	82.8	75.8	57.5	48.6	72.1	35.2	74.8	32 426	36 039	22 303	47 200	19.3	13.0
Jackson County	75.9	81.5	71.4	51.3	41.2	67.4	54.4	68.3	35 432	41 059	23 542	52 200	17.7	11.1
Jasper County	82.8	87.2	81.8	65.7	57.1	74.2	65.3	75.2	30 756	33 170	20 584	52 900	20.0	9.9
Jeff Davis County	73.5	75.3	57.8	62.5	65.1	62.3	40.0	64.4	31 250	32 917	29 514	76 000	22.8	10.9
Jefferson County	71.7	81.7	75.3	47.9	33.0	53.0	40.6	54.6	34 386	43 192	21 539	58 300	18.5	10.8
Jim Hogg County	70.6	77.7	75.1	66.8	48.4	71.3	100.0	70.3	26 003	28 279	13 875	33 000	20.5	9.9
Jim Wells County	79.9	83.8	77.9	67.0	55.5	64.1	56.7	64.8	28 412	31 199	20 220	40 400	19.5	11.6
Johnson County	82.5	86.0	80.6	64.8	59.1	64.9	58.1	66.2	44 299	49 377	28 065	76 000	18.9	11.3
Jones County	82.1	86.7	82.6	60.7	50.8	70.8	82.1	69.8	29 801	33 880	17 433	37 000	19.8	11.7
Karnes County	75.8	81.8	75.9	59.2	45.5	69.0	53.9	70.6	26 442	29 938	19 559	39 700	19.4	10.2
Kaufman County	82.6	87.5	84.4	61.2	56.4	66.3	67.9	66.1	44 654	50 152	26 176	81 100	20.5	10.8
Kendall County	83.6	86.3	82.4	65.1	54.3	66.1	67.0	65.9	49 735	56 430	27 926	132 900	21.7	9.9
Kenedy County	38.7	39.0	28.9	37.9	28.6	48.1	0.0	52.0	25 000	34 583	21 667	53 300	16.3	9.9
Kent County	79.8	80.9	71.8	72.7	52.6	75.2	40.0	77.0	29 063	31 369	22 813	30 600	18.4	9.9
Kerr County	77.2	81.1	68.2	58.6	48.7	64.6	60.5	65.1	34 421	38 216	25 282	85 700	21.5	10.7
Kimble County	76.6	78.9	62.6	65.4	64.9	66.7	83.9	65.7	28 147	33 232	18 675	60 500	23.2	12.6
King County	44.4	44.4	31.7	X	X	11.1	X	11.1	36 667	37 500	35 833	26 700	0.0	10.8
Kinney County	79.6	84.5	83.4	49.2	33.8	73.5	69.2	73.8	29 083	31 890	22 031	43 100	19.4	11.4
Kleberg County	64.7	72.6	62.9	43.4	29.8	43.4	23.1	49.3	29 410	37 977	17 146	50 500	19.6	11.9
Knox County	78.1	82.7	73.5	55.6	47.0	69.5	71.4	69.5	24 792	27 620	16 927	28 900	18.8	12.7
Lamar County	71.8	80.0	71.9	44.5	33.5	56.0	46.3	56.9	31 302	38 245	20 098	57 900	18.9	12.2
Lamb County	78.0	82.7	75.1	58.8	44.3	60.6	72.9	68.3	28 060	31 766	19 709	35 100	18.7	10.3
Lampasas County	77.1	82.0	74.0	51.4	36.9	64.6	61.8	65.0	36 325	41 806	24 214	73 500	19.9	9.9
La Salle County	79.6	84.2	84.0	68.3	55.6	60.1	14.9	65.2	22 717	25 189	16 932	26 000	19.9	12.2
Lavaca County	82.4	87.1	80.2	60.9	51.0	68.9	53.5	69.9	29 084	32 790	18 376	61 500	18.8	10.0
Lee County	82.1	86.2	80.7	61.8	54.2	71.7	65.6	72.3	35 737	39 651	26 081	70 900	18.9	12.1
Leon County	84.1	88.8	81.7	59.2	53.3	79.2	73.7	79.6	31 344	33 732	20 270	60 800	19.5	12.1
Liberty County	81.8	86.9	83.1	62.1	51.6	69.6	58.3	71.1	37 877	42 077	22 944	55 100	18.7	10.4
Limestone County	77.2	85.0	79.0	52.1	36.0	69.3	62.5	70.1	29 733	33 927	19 688	46 600	19.3	10.9
Lipscomb County	77.8	79.6	70.4	63.3	45.3	78.1	70.0	78.6	32 303	34 393	26 731	40 100	17.0	9.9
Live Oak County	84.4	87.4	82.7	67.9	54.3	73.4	55.4	75.5	32 126	35 339	24 038	53 000	18.5	9.9
Llano County	85.3	87.2	71.6	69.5	68.2	71.3	69.4	71.5	34 741	37 478	26 128	89 200	23.3	10.9
Loving County	68.4	68.4	50.0	X	X	100.0	X	100.0	45 417	45 417	42 500	12 500	0.0	0.0
Lubbock County	69.4	76.7	71.7	47.8	37.5	40.0	23.0	44.8	32 076	43 079	20 680	65 700	19.6	10.1
Lynn County	74.4	77.6	68.0	58.7	54.0	75.1	70.7	75.5	26 476	30 479	19 786	38 500	17.5	10.8
McCulloch County	74.6	77.3	66.2	62.1	54.9	68.6	51.0	70.5	25 242	28 507	15 722	39 400	18.6	13.1
McLennan County	69.1	77.2	70.5	44.8	32.2	41.9	20.1	47.6	33 263	43 466	21 201	66 400	19.6	11.1
McMullen County	78.4	79.1	75.7	74.3	61.1	86.0	100.0	85.7	31 761	31 313	39 375	47 400	38.0	11.1
Madison County	79.4	86.3	79.6	56.6	35.9	70.9	47.6	73.9	29 747	33 077	22 250	55 300	18.6	10.2
Marion County	83.3	87.4	80.2	69.9	63.6	79.4	86.0	78.7	25 131	27 739	13 989	41 000	20.4	12.8
Martin County	77.4	81.4	75.0	55.8	54.5	63.4	43.8	64.3	31 452	35 461	20 227	50 700	21.7	11.0

STATE County	Median gross rent	Percent who pay 35 percent or more of income for housing expenses		Means of transportation to work (percent except where noted)						Vehicles available (percent of households)		
		Owners	Renters	Number of workers 16 years and over	Car, truck, or van		Public transportation	Other means	Walked	No vehicles	One vehicle	Two or more vehicles
					Drove alone	Carpooled						
	25	26	27	28	29	30	31	32	33	34	35	36

TEXAS—Cont'd

STATE County	25	26	27	28	29	30	31	32	33	34	35	36
Guadalupe County	508	10.8	24.3	41 163	79.7	14.7	0.2	1.2	1.7	5.6	27.8	66.6
Hale County	408	11.3	20.5	14 326	79.6	14.5	0.2	1.0	2.6	7.0	35.3	57.7
Hall County	310	10.7	18.1	1 396	79.1	15.5	0.3	0.6	2.1	8.3	43.1	48.6
Hamilton County	388	13.1	17.9	3 376	73.1	15.6	0.1	1.6	3.6	5.2	32.7	62.1
Hansford County	375	11.9	11.9	2 374	76.7	15.8	0.0	1.2	2.9	2.9	31.9	65.2
Hardeman County	327	10.1	25.7	2 093	80.4	14.1	0.0	1.4	2.8	8.1	32.5	59.4
Hardin County	480	11.8	20.0	20 314	84.6	10.8	0.0	1.8	1.0	5.2	33.1	61.7
Harris County	590	14.1	26.2	1 515 593	75.7	14.6	4.1	1.4	1.8	8.7	38.9	52.4
Harrison County	442	12.6	26.5	25 817	81.7	12.9	0.2	0.9	1.8	8.7	30.0	61.3
Hartley County	478	7.1	25.8	1 982	86.6	8.2	0.0	0.1	1.7	4.9	26.9	68.2
Haskell County	329	14.8	17.9	2 360	85.5	7.8	0.1	1.5	2.1	6.2	35.5	58.3
Hays County	628	13.1	41.0	49 578	76.5	14.2	0.6	1.2	3.8	4.4	29.0	66.5
Hemphill County	453	13.1	17.3	1 545	75.4	15.2	0.0	1.2	2.9	2.7	31.5	65.9
Henderson County	464	13.2	24.3	28 958	77.8	16.5	0.1	1.3	1.3	5.8	33.8	60.3
Hidalgo County	401	15.7	28.9	176 308	73.7	19.1	0.3	2.8	1.9	9.6	40.5	49.9
Hill County	436	13.8	26.2	13 144	77.3	16.1	0.1	1.1	2.2	5.9	34.4	59.7
Hockley County	410	11.5	22.0	9 328	77.8	16.1	0.3	1.4	2.1	6.1	35.0	58.9
Hood County	541	12.2	22.1	17 868	79.9	14.3	0.0	0.7	1.2	2.6	30.1	67.2
Hopkins County	430	14.8	23.2	14 223	77.0	14.8	0.1	1.5	2.9	6.2	34.3	59.5
Houston County	376	15.4	22.6	7 843	76.8	15.8	0.4	1.2	2.4	10.1	37.8	52.1
Howard County	414	11.8	28.1	11 853	80.6	14.9	0.2	1.2	1.2	9.4	38.1	52.6
Hudspeth County	317	10.0	12.0	1 105	72.8	15.7	0.1	1.8	8.2	7.2	32.9	59.9
Hunt County	476	12.9	27.4	34 010	77.0	17.0	0.1	0.9	2.1	6.4	32.1	61.5
Hutchinson County	379	8.3	24.6	9 649	83.0	13.1	0.2	0.8	0.7	5.1	32.0	62.9
Irion County	491	11.7	5.1	835	81.9	11.0	0.2	0.6	3.1	3.5	30.3	66.3
Jack County	360	15.6	18.1	3 290	73.6	17.8	0.1	1.3	2.0	7.7	30.6	61.7
Jackson County	406	13.1	21.7	5 967	77.1	15.5	0.0	1.9	2.7	7.1	33.3	59.7
Jasper County	392	14.7	22.2	13 073	79.5	15.8	0.2	1.2	1.2	8.4	34.6	57.0
Jeff Davis County	354	13.0	8.3	1 014	67.8	17.0	0.0	2.8	6.2	4.0	35.4	60.6
Jefferson County	477	12.3	28.8	97 437	82.3	12.4	0.9	1.2	1.5	10.8	38.9	50.3
Jim Hogg County	366	12.1	17.8	1 838	81.2	14.9	0.0	1.3	1.1	12.3	41.0	46.7
Jim Wells County	420	13.3	21.2	13 994	76.8	17.2	0.3	1.2	2.0	9.4	38.6	52.0
Johnson County	540	11.9	21.8	58 393	80.4	14.4	0.1	1.0	1.5	4.5	26.2	69.4
Jones County	376	14.1	17.8	6 808	80.7	14.2	0.1	0.6	1.6	5.9	33.6	60.5
Karnes County	326	11.7	18.6	4 598	72.2	20.4	0.0	1.3	2.0	10.2	36.4	53.4
Kaufman County	533	13.1	25.1	32 704	77.9	16.9	0.2	1.0	1.4	5.5	27.3	67.2
Kendall County	659	16.6	31.5	10 767	78.3	14.0	0.1	1.0	1.8	2.7	27.7	69.6
Kenedy County	425	9.1	0.0	187	47.6	21.9	0.0	3.7	17.1	16.7	37.7	45.7
Kent County	247	8.9	6.0	375	87.5	6.1	0.0	0.5	2.4	1.7	28.6	69.7
Kerr County	536	14.5	29.2	17 034	77.3	14.1	0.3	1.4	2.4	5.5	39.9	54.6
Kimble County	365	12.8	20.0	1 893	75.6	14.3	0.0	1.1	2.6	4.9	37.0	58.0
King County	217	20.0	0.0	148	58.1	27.7	0.0	0.0	14.2	1.9	26.9	71.3
Kinney County	369	9.7	22.7	984	76.7	14.9	0.4	0.9	2.0	7.7	40.3	52.0
Kleberg County	447	13.7	32.0	12 647	75.5	15.8	0.2	2.2	4.9	12.2	39.0	48.8
Knox County	250	11.4	14.7	1 561	81.7	11.1	0.1	1.5	1.1	9.2	36.3	54.5
Lamar County	430	14.7	28.1	20 124	81.3	13.2	0.3	1.1	1.7	9.0	34.1	56.9
Lamb County	342	10.7	19.5	5 641	77.7	14.9	0.1	2.4	1.8	6.7	36.0	57.3
Lampasas County	439	13.2	19.1	7 957	78.7	16.4	0.0	0.9	1.0	5.8	29.7	64.5
La Salle County	276	11.8	23.8	1 803	64.9	25.6	2.3	1.7	2.2	18.6	38.0	43.4
Lavaca County	366	9.6	21.6	8 481	74.4	16.6	0.2	1.1	2.8	7.5	34.9	57.6
Lee County	436	11.5	16.5	7 227	73.4	19.2	0.0	0.5	1.8	5.2	32.8	62.0
Leon County	410	14.8	23.0	5 908	78.1	12.6	0.1	0.9	1.6	7.4	33.9	58.7
Liberty County	450	11.6	23.4	25 983	78.5	16.4	0.2	1.6	1.1	7.6	34.0	58.4
Limestone County	426	14.2	23.7	8 403	79.2	14.6	0.1	2.2	1.4	7.8	36.6	55.6
Lipscomb County	366	12.0	16.3	1 255	72.5	18.2	0.6	1.7	3.1	4.8	32.1	63.1
Live Oak County	366	11.3	12.6	4 175	74.1	18.0	0.0	1.9	3.0	6.7	35.3	58.1
Llano County	547	14.2	24.0	6 450	76.9	14.5	0.0	1.0	2.4	3.6	35.5	61.0
Loving County	575	X	0.0	38	68.4	10.5	0.0	0.0	21.1	0.0	29.0	71.0
Lubbock County	507	12.8	36.2	112 693	80.7	13.1	0.9	1.1	1.8	6.7	38.5	54.7
Lynn County	289	12.5	13.6	2 505	78.1	14.1	0.0	1.3	2.4	5.3	36.6	58.1
McCulloch County	386	12.5	22.1	3 144	83.4	11.7	0.3	1.2	1.1	9.8	37.1	53.1
McLennan County	499	11.8	32.8	92 441	79.1	14.2	0.8	1.1	2.3	8.3	37.2	54.6
McMullen County	420	21.9	12.8	340	73.5	16.5	1.5	0.0	2.1	10.1	31.5	58.3
Madison County	436	12.7	20.7	4 090	74.1	18.1	0.1	0.9	2.2	7.8	35.1	57.2
Marion County	399	16.6	24.0	3 934	76.4	15.1	0.2	2.6	3.4	8.6	38.2	53.2
Martin County	311	11.4	16.3	1 754	80.6	12.5	0.0	0.8	2.9	7.6	32.7	59.7

STATE/County code	MSA/PMSA/NECMA code[1]	STATE County	Total population 5 years and over	Residence in 1995 (percent)					Occupied housing units		Householders 65 years and over	
				Same house	Same county, different house	Same state, different county	Different state	Outside the United States	Number	Percent owner-occupied	Number	Percent owner-occupied
			1	2	3	4	5	6	7	8	9	10
		TEXAS—Cont'd										
48 319	...	Mason County	3 549	65.1	14.0	17.7	3.0	0.2	1 607	80.5	643	84.1
48 321	...	Matagorda County	35 289	58.8	25.6	10.3	2.8	2.5	13 901	66.8	3 173	85.2
48 323	...	Maverick County	42 566	64.7	22.7	5.9	2.7	4.0	13 089	69.5	2 965	69.4
48 325	...	Medina County	36 605	57.4	16.7	18.5	4.2	3.2	12 880	79.7	2 977	88.0
48 327	...	Menard County	2 251	57.0	20.2	18.5	3.5	0.9	990	75.4	321	86.9
48 329	5800	Midland County	107 417	54.0	25.6	13.7	5.3	1.4	42 745	69.5	8 857	79.8
48 331	...	Milam County	22 672	59.2	20.5	15.9	3.4	1.0	9 199	73.0	2 779	83.7
48 333	...	Mills County	4 866	63.0	14.6	19.2	2.6	0.6	2 001	80.9	742	86.8
48 335	...	Mitchell County	9 244	45.6	16.2	22.3	3.4	12.5	2 837	76.0	959	86.5
48 337	...	Montague County	17 980	58.0	19.8	15.9	5.5	0.8	7 770	78.7	2 463	86.6
48 339	3360	Montgomery County	271 298	46.7	19.4	21.2	9.6	3.0	103 296	78.2	16 790	81.2
48 341	...	Moore County	18 263	49.0	28.0	11.2	7.8	4.0	6 774	70.5	1 166	86.7
48 343	...	Morris County	12 302	61.6	18.9	15.5	3.5	0.6	5 215	77.8	1 607	88.7
48 345	...	Motley County	1 332	61.8	15.0	17.3	4.9	1.0	606	77.4	222	85.1
48 347	...	Nacogdoches County	55 391	49.6	21.7	22.2	4.3	2.1	22 006	61.5	4 602	82.3
48 349	...	Navarro County	41 849	55.4	23.7	14.5	3.2	3.2	16 491	70.7	4 337	80.0
48 351	...	Newton County	14 089	67.2	13.4	15.6	2.7	1.0	5 583	84.5	1 462	89.0
48 353	...	Nolan County	14 815	58.6	21.1	17.0	2.6	0.7	6 170	67.4	1 726	83.4
48 355	1880	Nueces County	289 673	53.2	29.6	9.3	6.3	1.6	110 365	61.3	22 568	77.7
48 357	...	Ochiltree County	8 265	58.2	21.6	10.2	6.7	3.3	3 261	72.5	636	90.9
48 359	...	Oldham County	2 040	47.5	12.3	27.7	11.4	1.1	735	66.3	150	94.0
48 361	0840	Orange County	79 262	59.3	25.5	9.5	5.0	0.6	31 642	77.2	7 401	87.0
48 363	...	Palo Pinto County	25 262	52.7	23.2	17.9	4.7	1.5	10 594	71.9	3 014	83.8
48 365	...	Panola County	21 476	62.9	20.2	10.4	5.8	0.6	8 821	80.8	2 491	88.6
48 367	2800	Parker County	82 844	50.8	16.6	26.3	5.4	0.9	31 131	80.6	5 924	86.4
48 369	...	Parmer County	9 223	59.9	19.7	9.2	8.2	3.0	3 322	72.3	796	83.9
48 371	...	Pecos County	15 742	56.8	17.2	17.6	5.6	2.8	5 153	74.2	1 195	89.0
48 373	...	Polk County	38 861	53.7	17.9	22.5	5.1	0.9	15 119	81.6	4 909	88.7
48 375	0320	Potter County	104 175	46.7	24.6	10.2	7.5	2.1	40 760	60.1	9 019	78.5
48 377	...	Presidio County	6 745	56.6	14.9	14.5	5.4	8.7	2 530	70.1	774	77.0
48 379	...	Rains County	8 632	47.5	15.6	30.5	5.4	0.9	3 617	82.7	1 024	87.3
48 381	0320	Randall County	97 128	49.6	22.0	21.2	6.3	0.9	41 240	70.3	8 526	83.7
48 383	...	Reagan County	3 050	67.2	19.3	11.3	1.9	0.3	1 107	78.4	223	82.5
48 385	...	Real County	2 908	58.8	12.8	24.9	3.0	0.5	1 245	77.0	412	89.1
48 387	...	Red River County	13 492	62.1	19.8	14.0	3.7	0.5	5 827	75.0	1 882	84.2
48 389	...	Reeves County	12 205	65.2	18.0	11.0	3.5	1.4	4 091	77.6	1 162	84.2
48 391	...	Refugio County	7 343	63.6	21.3	12.0	2.5	0.6	2 985	74.7	853	83.2
48 393	...	Roberts County	843	53.1	12.2	27.0	7.4	0.2	362	79.6	101	92.1
48 395	...	Robertson County	14 845	59.5	18.0	18.0	3.2	1.2	6 179	71.6	2 018	80.7
48 397	1920	Rockwall County	39 930	46.6	14.9	28.0	8.8	1.8	14 530	82.7	1 935	88.4
48 399	...	Runnels County	10 817	57.7	19.9	17.3	4.0	1.1	4 428	77.4	1 479	85.8
48 401	...	Rusk County	44 429	62.9	16.7	11.7	4.3	1.4	17 364	79.9	5 038	87.2
48 403	...	Sabine County	9 921	62.3	14.7	16.3	6.3	0.5	4 485	86.2	1 753	91.6
48 405	...	San Augustine County	8 435	66.9	15.4	14.8	2.3	0.5	3 575	81.6	1 224	84.7
48 407	...	San Jacinto County	20 888	59.5	10.6	25.9	3.1	0.9	8 651	87.9	2 397	92.0
48 409	1880	San Patricio County	61 822	54.6	20.0	12.9	10.9	1.7	22 093	68.2	4 769	83.5
48 411	...	San Saba County	5 869	56.0	21.2	19.8	2.3	0.7	2 289	75.6	814	83.7
48 413	...	Schleicher County	2 750	65.0	17.8	13.7	2.4	1.2	1 115	75.7	298	84.6
48 415	...	Scurry County	15 338	56.2	22.6	16.8	2.2	2.3	5 756	73.9	1 608	82.0
48 417	...	Shackelford County	3 132	59.6	16.3	20.2	2.8	1.0	1 300	78.7	391	91.8
48 419	...	Shelby County	23 525	63.8	20.5	9.8	3.4	2.4	9 595	78.2	2 734	85.2
48 421	...	Sherman County	2 963	56.4	13.5	14.7	13.1	2.4	1 124	74.2	261	94.6
48 423	8640	Smith County	162 278	51.0	27.7	13.9	5.5	1.9	65 692	69.7	16 010	82.5
48 425	...	Somervell County	6 364	51.7	16.8	25.9	4.7	0.9	2 438	74.7	531	82.9
48 427	...	Starr County	48 044	72.4	18.4	3.5	1.3	4.4	14 410	79.4	2 993	86.0
48 429	...	Stephens County	9 148	57.7	19.9	15.5	4.9	2.0	3 661	72.4	1 089	85.5
48 431	...	Sterling County	1 324	68.1	15.6	13.3	1.4	1.5	513	76.2	131	80.2
48 433	...	Stonewall County	1 612	67.7	17.2	11.6	3.3	0.1	713	78.5	238	87.8
48 435	...	Sutton County	3 778	63.9	21.2	11.6	1.5	1.8	1 515	72.0	369	83.2
48 437	...	Swisher County	7 745	57.0	20.1	16.3	4.1	2.5	2 925	70.4	961	86.3
48 439	2800	Tarrant County	1 332 055	44.9	30.6	11.1	9.4	4.0	533 864	60.8	76 952	80.4
48 441	0040	Taylor County	117 587	46.5	25.2	15.6	10.2	2.5	47 274	61.5	10 173	80.8
48 443	...	Terrell County	1 024	67.0	11.2	13.2	5.1	3.5	443	77.7	131	87.8
48 445	...	Terry County	11 849	59.4	22.2	12.5	2.9	3.1	4 278	71.1	1 116	87.0
48 447	...	Throckmorton County	1 743	65.1	13.9	16.6	3.9	0.5	765	77.3	254	90.6
48 449	...	Titus County	25 659	51.6	26.6	13.0	5.1	3.7	9 552	72.4	2 391	84.9

[1]MSA = Metropolitan Statistical Area. PMSA = Primary MSA. NECMA = New England County Metropolitan Area. See the Appendix A for explanation of these concepts. See Appendix B for list of metropolitan areas identified by type, with component counties.

Table C-3. States and Counties — Migration, Housing, and Transportation

STATE County	Owner-occupied by household type (percent)								Median household income			Median housing value (owner estimated)	Median monthly owner costs as a percent of income	
	Family-households					Nonfamily households								
		Married-couple family		Other family										
	Total family households	Total	With own children under 18 years	Total	With own children under 18 years	Total nonfamily households	Two or more adults	Living alone	All households	Owner-occupied households	Renter-occupied households		With a mortgage	Without a mortgage
	11	12	13	14	15	16	17	18	19	20	21	22	23	24

TEXAS—Cont'd

STATE County	11	12	13	14	15	16	17	18	19	20	21	22	23	24
Mason County	83.2	86.5	81.2	60.3	38.4	74.5	100.0	73.1	29 911	35 161	16 509	69 000	20.4	10.5
Matagorda County	72.0	78.7	72.5	49.1	38.2	53.6	43.0	55.0	32 531	40 490	21 737	56 700	17.8	10.7
Maverick County	73.6	77.7	74.1	59.0	46.4	43.9	27.1	44.8	20 806	25 177	14 019	45 300	21.0	12.0
Medina County	82.3	85.6	81.7	67.4	54.2	69.3	71.3	69.1	36 027	39 192	23 315	65 900	20.6	10.6
Menard County	78.0	81.2	75.4	66.9	59.4	69.9	56.5	71.0	24 716	27 132	20 750	34 400	19.0	14.1
Midland County	77.7	83.5	79.9	53.9	44.9	47.7	33.7	49.4	38 837	48 633	24 293	68 500	19.3	11.1
Milam County	77.3	82.2	73.1	56.0	37.4	62.1	42.0	63.7	33 048	37 708	22 243	53 600	17.9	10.7
Mills County	83.9	86.1	74.1	70.1	63.8	73.9	73.3	73.9	30 408	33 109	15 288	62 400	16.7	11.7
Mitchell County	79.0	83.8	77.6	63.5	38.6	68.8	77.6	68.2	25 907	28 441	20 165	32 300	20.3	14.1
Montague County	82.5	86.0	79.1	64.2	55.6	69.5	57.1	70.5	30 836	35 363	20 769	56 300	19.1	12.0
Montgomery County	83.3	87.6	85.6	60.6	53.8	60.2	54.6	61.4	50 821	59 178	31 191	95 600	19.5	9.9
Moore County	74.4	79.3	71.2	52.8	48.0	55.8	25.8	60.6	35 150	40 720	24 200	53 000	18.3	9.9
Morris County	81.3	87.5	78.4	62.0	48.8	69.0	29.1	72.4	28 580	31 785	18 317	44 100	19.4	11.5
Motley County	79.8	81.6	71.0	68.9	40.7	71.6	56.3	73.1	28 871	30 298	22 375	31 700	15.7	10.8
Nacogdoches County	73.3	81.6	77.0	47.2	36.5	40.5	12.0	49.2	28 637	39 043	15 301	65 500	19.1	9.9
Navarro County	74.5	82.1	74.2	48.8	36.9	60.7	43.9	62.8	31 240	36 931	20 614	55 500	18.9	12.7
Newton County	87.4	90.5	88.2	75.3	60.0	76.4	78.1	76.2	28 613	30 786	16 721	43 100	18.5	9.9
Nolan County	71.0	78.1	66.7	49.2	39.8	58.9	46.1	60.4	26 487	31 772	17 372	35 800	17.1	11.2
Nueces County	67.7	75.6	69.0	47.3	32.2	44.5	33.8	46.9	35 779	45 390	24 073	68 100	21.7	12.0
Ochiltree County	72.9	76.6	71.6	47.3	35.5	71.2	59.6	72.8	37 432	45 850	25 901	46 500	18.5	9.9
Oldham County	65.4	66.4	59.7	55.8	23.1	69.1	81.8	68.2	34 542	35 057	33 750	48 300	19.3	13.3
Orange County	80.9	87.8	81.5	54.4	42.8	65.8	58.0	66.8	37 380	43 049	22 006	57 100	18.0	9.9
Palo Pinto County	74.6	80.7	71.4	51.6	38.5	65.6	50.9	67.6	31 259	35 395	22 705	46 900	19.1	12.5
Panola County	84.2	87.7	83.3	68.2	54.5	71.4	69.7	71.5	31 333	34 726	17 611	51 500	19.4	9.9
Parker County	84.3	88.2	84.2	63.2	58.5	66.9	58.7	68.3	45 554	50 859	27 711	88 200	19.4	11.5
Parmer County	73.5	76.1	70.0	53.5	44.2	67.7	50.8	69.4	30 404	34 761	22 723	49 100	17.6	10.9
Pecos County	77.4	82.0	79.9	57.2	42.8	62.7	55.1	63.8	28 125	30 270	24 464	37 800	18.5	10.3
Polk County	85.2	89.5	82.1	67.4	61.0	72.0	52.6	74.2	30 261	32 846	19 858	50 600	20.4	10.7
Potter County	66.3	74.4	65.7	46.2	35.5	47.0	34.6	49.0	29 446	36 343	21 513	52 000	20.2	10.2
Presidio County	74.4	78.9	74.1	58.5	45.6	57.8	75.0	56.5	19 872	21 353	14 601	31 200	19.6	13.3
Rains County	83.8	87.0	80.8	67.5	56.9	79.4	72.3	80.5	33 068	35 482	23 792	58 400	19.5	12.6
Randall County	80.4	85.1	81.5	56.8	48.2	47.3	35.2	49.7	42 726	52 282	25 579	89 400	18.9	9.9
Reagan County	82.2	86.4	84.0	55.0	53.5	63.3	100.0	62.1	32 730	35 870	23 618	44 100	19.6	11.7
Real County	78.1	81.1	67.3	60.0	46.8	74.5	45.0	76.2	25 603	27 276	21 579	61 200	22.6	11.0
Red River County	78.0	83.9	73.4	58.1	47.5	68.0	53.1	69.3	27 373	31 223	17 463	38 100	17.9	11.0
Reeves County	80.2	86.3	85.2	61.8	45.5	68.8	70.7	68.7	23 194	24 257	18 080	23 400	20.3	13.1
Refugio County	77.6	82.7	73.5	60.3	44.4	67.0	53.4	68.3	29 777	33 518	22 051	39 900	18.2	9.9
Roberts County	80.7	81.4	70.4	70.6	28.6	75.9	X	75.9	42 250	40 500	50 962	53 100	17.3	9.9
Robertson County	73.4	83.4	74.2	46.4	33.9	67.2	75.0	66.5	28 843	34 729	15 767	53 000	20.3	13.5
Rockwall County	86.7	89.8	88.1	66.1	61.8	63.3	61.5	63.7	65 312	72 775	36 890	141 900	20.9	11.2
Runnels County	80.3	83.6	73.0	64.2	50.6	69.9	54.5	70.8	28 546	31 099	21 618	40 600	18.1	12.1
Rusk County	81.3	85.4	78.6	64.8	53.4	76.1	70.0	76.6	32 889	36 441	21 845	57 500	18.8	10.1
Sabine County	88.7	91.3	85.3	73.8	64.7	80.3	66.7	81.7	27 400	28 769	18 576	47 000	19.3	11.5
San Augustine County	85.7	91.9	85.8	62.4	52.0	71.4	80.0	70.8	27 164	29 404	17 351	45 100	21.2	10.9
San Jacinto County	88.9	91.2	86.2	78.2	70.1	84.7	75.0	86.1	32 017	34 248	16 705	54 200	19.5	11.4
San Patricio County	71.5	75.9	69.7	55.9	38.1	56.3	47.9	57.7	34 669	41 579	24 524	61 300	20.3	11.8
San Saba County	79.0	81.8	69.3	63.3	50.7	67.3	47.2	68.4	30 069	32 736	22 028	53 300	18.0	12.0
Schleicher County	75.2	77.2	79.6	63.1	58.5	76.9	62.5	78.2	29 683	32 946	26 042	45 900	19.9	10.9
Scurry County	79.1	84.6	78.0	54.0	42.2	60.4	59.5	60.5	31 467	37 241	18 924	45 000	18.8	12.3
Shackelford County	81.6	83.2	72.4	73.2	57.7	70.9	52.9	71.9	30 707	33 702	24 514	42 100	18.6	13.3
Shelby County	80.6	86.6	81.5	61.4	53.7	71.9	63.6	72.6	28 580	31 757	18 379	50 000	18.0	9.9
Sherman County	74.8	77.1	68.9	58.7	50.6	72.3	15.4	75.3	32 568	36 207	27 500	50 300	15.7	11.1
Smith County	76.1	82.9	76.8	51.5	41.9	53.4	34.1	56.1	36 739	44 184	24 252	76 500	19.8	10.4
Somervell County	79.4	83.9	78.6	53.0	47.3	60.6	40.2	64.2	41 132	45 902	28 482	88 100	18.9	11.6
Starr County	80.0	81.6	79.9	75.0	65.7	75.1	69.7	75.4	16 287	17 561	11 178	35 900	22.9	13.0
Stephens County	76.3	84.8	77.4	45.3	38.1	62.6	58.6	63.0	28 866	32 289	22 214	44 200	19.0	12.4
Sterling County	78.7	80.5	82.6	67.3	74.3	68.1	50.0	68.7	34 479	37 574	22 500	51 200	18.4	11.3
Stonewall County	82.2	86.6	81.6	55.7	38.9	70.2	28.6	73.0	28 350	31 806	19 554	32 500	17.8	10.8
Sutton County	75.0	76.6	64.6	65.9	54.2	61.8	0.0	62.6	34 019	37 473	25 833	45 400	17.6	12.0
Swisher County	70.5	74.6	65.1	52.6	36.5	70.1	58.7	71.1	28 884	31 167	25 256	40 500	19.1	10.4
Tarrant County	69.7	76.7	72.9	46.6	37.5	40.7	32.4	42.5	45 947	59 410	31 507	88 600	20.3	11.2
Taylor County	68.2	74.2	66.5	46.0	36.2	46.6	28.1	50.4	33 701	42 142	23 610	60 000	19.4	10.4
Terrell County	78.5	80.4	77.3	70.7	60.6	75.9	100.0	75.4	23 466	24 412	20 250	26 900	16.2	13.9
Terry County	72.6	77.8	67.0	52.8	41.9	66.3	38.2	68.3	27 472	33 254	18 886	44 000	17.9	13.0
Throckmorton County	76.7	80.0	71.3	59.8	39.5	78.4	53.8	79.9	28 783	30 417	24 167	36 800	17.2	12.0
Titus County	75.6	82.1	74.2	52.0	41.8	62.2	36.9	64.6	32 097	36 086	22 142	60 700	20.5	12.4

Table C-3. States and Counties — **Migration, Housing, and Transportation**

STATE County	Median gross rent	Percent who pay 35 percent or more of income for housing expenses		Means of transportation to work (percent except where noted)						Vehicles available (percent of households)		
		Owners	Renters	Number of workers 16 years and over	Car, truck, or van		Public transportation	Other means	Walked	No vehicles	One vehicle	Two or more vehicles
					Drove alone	Carpooled						
	25	26	27	28	29	30	31	32	33	34	35	36

TEXAS—Cont'd												
Mason County	306	11.1	25.1	1 641	70.1	14.4	0.1	1.5	2.2	5.1	32.8	62.1
Matagorda County	411	11.0	22.7	14 762	74.9	19.3	0.4	1.5	2.0	9.9	34.5	55.5
Maverick County	323	13.4	30.9	12 732	70.2	22.1	0.5	2.6	2.6	12.4	40.1	47.5
Medina County	453	12.9	23.0	15 855	75.1	17.6	0.3	1.4	2.6	6.5	29.9	63.6
Menard County	339	16.2	16.9	984	72.9	18.1	0.2	1.8	1.6	7.1	38.4	54.5
Midland County	464	12.9	25.6	50 805	83.3	12.2	0.2	0.8	1.0	6.0	35.5	58.4
Milam County	390	11.9	21.9	10 128	78.5	14.6	0.0	1.4	2.3	8.1	33.9	58.0
Mills County	369	12.4	20.1	2 114	74.0	15.9	0.0	0.7	2.9	4.1	33.3	62.6
Mitchell County	389	15.9	19.6	2 849	81.5	14.6	0.2	0.6	1.2	9.0	35.2	55.8
Montague County	419	13.0	21.3	7 970	76.8	15.9	0.6	0.8	1.9	5.2	31.5	63.3
Montgomery County	617	12.4	25.3	134 118	80.0	13.2	1.2	1.4	1.0	4.7	29.0	66.4
Moore County	406	9.5	19.6	8 320	74.8	20.4	0.3	1.0	1.7	4.8	29.6	65.7
Morris County	364	14.2	26.0	5 049	85.0	9.8	0.1	1.5	1.5	7.5	35.8	56.6
Motley County	354	7.4	13.5	621	74.1	16.9	0.3	0.5	2.9	8.1	29.4	62.5
Nacogdoches County	465	12.9	39.4	25 105	79.0	13.0	0.3	1.6	3.2	7.9	37.4	54.6
Navarro County	454	14.7	25.8	18 119	77.9	16.6	0.5	1.6	1.4	9.0	35.6	55.5
Newton County	363	11.3	18.5	5 104	74.7	18.3	1.2	2.0	1.1	9.8	35.2	55.0
Nolan County	340	11.1	25.1	6 329	80.5	14.2	0.0	1.3	1.7	8.2	38.6	53.2
Nueces County	548	16.1	30.0	132 006	76.4	15.9	1.9	1.5	1.9	9.5	38.2	52.4
Ochiltree County	431	13.0	18.5	4 043	75.8	19.2	0.2	1.3	1.0	3.1	32.7	64.3
Oldham County	422	16.0	6.7	965	70.6	11.6	0.4	0.6	10.5	5.3	29.4	65.3
Orange County	472	10.1	26.6	34 839	84.3	11.6	0.1	1.2	1.0	7.5	32.6	59.9
Palo Pinto County	455	13.6	24.4	11 741	78.7	15.2	0.1	1.0	2.3	7.5	34.7	57.8
Panola County	368	13.4	25.4	8 851	81.4	12.8	0.1	0.9	2.2	7.1	35.9	56.9
Parker County	548	12.2	24.0	41 031	79.9	14.8	0.1	0.7	1.3	3.8	26.6	69.6
Parmer County	395	9.0	22.5	3 800	75.3	16.1	0.4	1.9	3.3	4.4	33.0	62.6
Pecos County	367	11.2	14.1	6 017	75.8	18.2	0.1	2.2	2.1	6.6	35.0	58.4
Polk County	421	13.6	24.4	13 594	75.7	16.7	0.4	2.0	2.1	8.0	36.8	55.3
Potter County	451	12.7	30.5	45 745	79.0	15.5	0.6	1.3	1.6	8.8	39.6	51.7
Presidio County	276	13.3	19.8	2 352	68.8	20.3	1.0	1.6	5.9	13.1	37.8	49.3
Rains County	454	13.5	22.3	3 812	73.9	17.0	0.3	1.2	2.6	5.0	29.3	65.8
Randall County	504	5.4	20.2	50 012	84.6	10.8	0.2	0.6	1.0	3.4	33.1	63.6
Reagan County	369	10.2	18.1	1 397	74.9	18.8	0.0	1.5	2.1	2.3	36.1	60.6
Real County	433	17.2	24.1	1 153	65.8	16.7	0.8	2.0	8.0	6.0	36.9	57.0
Red River County	328	10.2	20.7	5 859	75.4	16.0	0.3	2.0	2.5	8.2	32.6	59.2
Reeves County	307	12.6	17.4	4 098	77.1	17.5	0.1	2.6	1.4	9.7	40.9	49.3
Refugio County	366	9.8	16.2	3 210	76.9	15.5	0.0	1.8	0.1	0.6	27.0	53.4
Roberts County	380	8.5	7.7	454	80.4	10.4	0.0	1.5	4.2	1.9	25.7	72.4
Robertson County	344	14.9	26.5	6 182	74.0	18.5	0.1	2.0	1.8	14.5	31.5	54.0
Rockwall County	699	14.0	18.9	21 217	83.1	10.8	0.8	0.4	0.7	2.0	23.0	75.0
Runnels County	356	11.3	23.6	4 512	77.5	13.1	0.2	1.2	2.9	7.0	30.8	62.1
Rusk County	419	11.1	21.2	10 560	82.5	12.4	0.2	1.2	1.5	7.1	32.7	60.2
Sabine County	319	15.4	19.8	3 169	75.9	17.2	0.6	2.0	2.3	8.5	34.7	56.8
San Augustine County	317	13.0	27.7	3 150	77.3	15.2	0.3	2.9	2.2	10.8	36.8	52.4
San Jacinto County	380	14.0	22.3	8 200	75.2	17.9	0.1	1.9	1.1	5.8	36.9	57.3
San Patricio County	518	13.2	24.5	26 367	76.1	16.1	0.2	1.7	3.1	7.5	36.3	56.2
San Saba County	402	11.7	17.6	2 392	79.7	14.1	0.1	1.2	2.1	6.5	31.1	62.3
Schleicher County	321	15.0	13.9	1 263	74.7	16.9	0.0	1.0	3.1	5.4	38.0	56.6
Scurry County	392	10.6	18.2	6 344	80.5	13.6	0.0	1.5	2.0	6.4	38.0	55.6
Shackelford County	380	11.4	16.9	1 437	78.3	14.8	0.0	0.9	2.3	4.9	35.1	60.0
Shelby County	327	14.0	22.0	9 606	74.2	15.5	0.6	2.7	3.1	10.8	35.9	53.3
Sherman County	418	8.4	9.8	1 350	82.4	12.6	0.0	0.9	2.3	1.5	34.4	64.1
Smith County	517	13.0	29.9	76 267	81.8	12.8	0.3	1.3	1.1	6.8	34.6	58.6
Somervell County	402	12.3	19.0	3 096	82.6	11.5	0.2	2.0	1.4	4.2	30.2	65.5
Starr County	281	14.1	28.9	13 147	69.2	19.9	0.5	3.2	4.8	14.7	37.8	47.5
Stephens County	400	11.8	16.3	3 867	77.9	17.5	0.0	1.2	1.2	7.3	35.1	57.6
Sterling County	392	9.8	10.9	618	75.9	10.8	0.0	2.3	2.4	4.1	35.3	60.6
Stonewall County	290	12.4	10.9	708	75.6	18.8	0.0	1.1	2.1	5.5	36.9	57.6
Sutton County	362	12.3	16.3	1 817	79.3	12.9	0.6	2.4	1.9	6.7	35.2	58.2
Swisher County	387	10.8	17.9	3 296	82.3	12.7	0.4	1.0	1.7	7.3	35.4	57.3
Tarrant County	612	13.1	25.4	703 035	81.3	13.0	0.6	1.0	1.4	5.6	35.5	58.8
Taylor County	472	11.1	26.9	58 718	81.1	12.6	0.5	1.4	2.5	6.2	37.5	56.2
Terrell County	446	13.6	9.6	461	70.9	8.9	0.0	2.6	13.4	12.6	31.6	55.8
Terry County	388	14.1	29.2	4 674	78.8	14.3	0.1	2.1	2.5	5.3	37.3	57.4
Throckmorton County	327	10.9	12.4	839	77.6	13.8	0.6	1.3	1.4	4.6	32.5	62.9
Titus County	462	16.9	25.1	11 086	79.2	16.2	0.4	0.7	1.3	6.8	35.0	58.2

STATE/ County code	MSA/PMSA/ NECMA code[1]	STATE County	Residence in 1995 (percent)						Occupied housing units		Householders 65 years and over	
			Total population 5 years and over	Same house	Same county, different house	Same state, different county	Different state	Outside the United States	Number	Percent owner-occupied	Number	Percent owner-occupied
			1	2	3	4	5	6	7	8	9	10
		TEXAS—Cont'd										
48 451	7200	Tom Green County	97 019	48.4	26.9	14.5	8.1	2.0	39 503	64.1	9 298	77.9
48 453	0640	Travis County	753 786	37.6	29.3	17.0	10.2	5.9	320 766	51.5	35 222	78.1
48 455	...	Trinity County	12 965	56.3	17.1	21.1	4.1	1.4	5 723	80.8	2 049	88.5
48 457	...	Tyler County	19 645	58.3	17.6	20.0	3.2	0.8	7 775	84.0	2 355	89.6
48 459	4420	Upshur County	33 003	57.8	16.8	19.8	5.0	0.6	13 290	81.7	3 404	87.1
48 461	...	Upton County	3 215	64.7	19.1	13.7	1.9	0.5	1 256	75.6	350	87.7
48 463	...	Uvalde County	23 799	59.2	22.3	13.8	3.3	1.5	8 559	72.0	2 239	84.2
48 465	...	Val Verde County	40 982	55.1	23.7	9.0	7.9	4.3	14 151	66.0	3 137	77.4
48 467	...	Van Zandt County	45 108	57.3	17.1	21.1	3.3	1.3	18 195	80.9	5 135	86.8
48 469	8750	Victoria County	77 789	52.0	31.1	12.1	3.5	1.4	30 071	67.4	6 417	80.9
48 471	...	Walker County	58 854	41.7	14.8	35.2	3.7	4.5	18 303	59.9	3 811	81.5
48 473	3360	Waller County	30 397	48.4	13.8	31.9	3.8	2.0	10 557	72.5	2 029	85.0
48 475	...	Ward County	10 213	59.9	21.2	15.1	3.2	0.7	3 964	78.2	1 011	85.3
48 477	...	Washington County	28 554	57.1	19.9	19.0	2.0	2.1	11 322	73.5	3 230	84.6
48 479	4080	Webb County	172 808	58.8	28.7	4.7	2.4	5.5	50 740	65.7	8 563	74.9
48 481	...	Wharton County	38 401	62.1	24.1	9.8	2.2	1.8	14 799	68.8	3 958	81.1
48 483	...	Wheeler County	4 994	58.7	17.2	16.1	7.0	1.0	2 152	78.0	768	90.4
48 485	9080	Wichita County	122 607	45.9	26.6	11.5	13.4	2.6	48 441	62.3	11 115	80.2
48 487	...	Wilbarger County	13 673	54.1	26.8	13.5	5.0	0.5	5 537	66.3	1 669	76.2
48 489	...	Willacy County	18 409	70.2	17.3	8.0	2.9	1.7	5 584	77.3	1 669	90.8
48 491	0640	Williamson County	228 851	39.6	19.0	26.3	13.1	2.0	86 766	74.2	10 718	81.4
48 493	7240	Wilson County	30 161	57.7	14.4	23.3	3.8	0.8	11 038	85.0	2 347	89.0
48 495	...	Winkler County	6 670	64.1	17.5	9.7	6.7	2.1	2 584	83.2	714	89.9
48 497	...	Wise County	45 490	49.7	17.3	24.9	5.7	2.4	17 178	81.3	3 409	86.7
48 499	...	Wood County	34 846	54.4	18.0	22.1	4.6	0.9	14 583	81.4	5 016	86.9
48 501	...	Yoakum County............	6 781	64.3	21.9	8.8	3.6	1.5	2 469	78.2	523	91.2
48 503	...	Young County	16 885	57.2	21.7	15.1	5.2	0.9	7 167	73.8	2 173	84.4
48 505	...	Zapata County	11 085	65.1	22.1	6.2	4.0	2.6	3 921	81.9	1 198	90.0
48 507	...	Zavala County	10 615	66.8	20.4	5.3	3.7	3.8	3 428	73.0	1 060	90.6
49 000	...	UTAH.......................	2 023 875	49.3	26.6	8.9	12.0	3.2	701 281	71.5	121 340	86.4
49 001	...	Beaver County	5 437	58.4	17.7	12.7	10.0	1.3	1 982	78.9	528	90.9
49 003	...	Box Elder County	38 794	58.9	20.7	12.9	6.4	1.0	13 144	80.0	2 737	88.8
49 005	...	Cache County	82 421	44.1	24.5	13.4	14.5	3.5	27 543	64.6	4 034	89.6
49 007	...	Carbon County	18 936	59.2	20.1	12.3	7.5	0.9	7 413	77.4	1 896	90.2
49 009	...	Daggett County	859	54.7	4.7	27.1	12.8	0.7	340	70.6	79	88.6
49 011	7160	Davis County	215 480	51.9	22.2	12.0	11.9	2.0	71 201	77.6	10 965	91.1
49 013	...	Duchesne County..........	13 081	63.0	17.7	14.2	4.8	0.3	4 559	80.8	958	93.1
49 015	...	Emery County	9 978	65.9	17.0	11.5	4.9	0.7	3 468	82.0	681	89.9
49 017	...	Garfield County	4 326	61.7	15.5	12.3	9.7	0.9	1 576	79.0	414	92.5
49 019	...	Grand County	7 905	51.2	22.9	9.2	15.4	1.3	3 434	70.9	772	85.6
49 021	...	Iron County	30 600	42.1	21.0	17.9	17.4	1.5	10 627	66.3	1 876	89.3
49 023	...	Juab County	7 339	58.8	13.7	22.8	4.2	0.6	2 456	79.6	496	81.7
49 025	2620	Kane County	5 636	57.4	11.5	11.8	18.2	1.0	2 237	78.1	693	87.7
49 027	...	Millard County	11 404	62.7	17.2	12.0	6.2	1.9	3 840	79.6	986	86.3
49 029	...	Morgan County	6 550	60.8	10.0	21.7	6.0	1.5	2 046	88.3	386	93.8
49 031	...	Piute County	1 316	66.9	12.3	11.9	7.4	1.5	509	87.2	164	90.9
49 033	...	Rich County..................	1 816	64.7	13.1	12.4	8.2	1.6	645	83.7	165	85.5
49 035	7160	Salt Lake County..........	818 213	50.0	30.9	4.7	10.3	4.2	295 141	69.0	47 176	82.3
49 037	...	San Juan County	13 010	68.5	15.9	7.2	8.2	0.4	4 089	79.3	780	92.6
49 039	...	Sanpete County	20 889	51.1	18.3	21.4	6.5	2.6	6 547	78.8	1 678	89.9
49 041	...	Sevier County	17 183	58.8	19.4	14.5	6.3	1.0	6 081	82.0	1 636	89.8
49 043	...	Summit County	27 690	43.0	19.1	13.8	20.6	3.6	10 332	75.5	920	92.7
49 045	...	Tooele County	36 245	41.7	19.6	23.8	13.7	1.3	12 677	78.3	2 005	86.1
49 047	...	Uintah County	23 108	59.8	21.6	9.7	8.2	0.6	8 187	77.0	1 794	87.8
49 049	6520	Utah County	328 190	43.2	28.1	7.9	16.9	4.0	99 937	66.8	13 970	88.5
49 051	...	Wasatch County............	13 824	49.5	18.6	17.6	11.7	2.6	4 743	80.6	835	90.5
49 053	...	Washington County	82 121	42.5	23.5	15.7	16.8	1.6	29 939	74.0	9 492	90.2
49 055	...	Wayne County	2 297	62.7	12.0	16.4	8.4	0.4	890	77.6	254	91.7
49 057	7160	Weber County	179 238	51.7	26.1	9.8	9.9	2.5	65 698	74.9	12 970	86.8
50 000	...	VERMONT	574 842	59.1	21.2	6.3	12.1	1.3	240 634	70.6	50 395	76.7
50 001	...	Addison County............	33 909	60.3	18.3	7.6	12.7	1.1	13 068	75.0	2 649	80.8
50 003	...	Bennington County........	35 005	61.6	21.7	2.9	13.1	0.8	14 846	71.4	3 789	78.8
50 005	...	Caledonia County..........	28 062	61.9	20.2	7.7	9.6	0.6	11 663	72.9	2 911	75.2

[1]MSA = Metropolitan Statistical Area. PMSA = Primary MSA. NECMA = New England County Metropolitan Area. See the Appendix A for explanation of these concepts. See Appendix B for list of metropolitan areas identified by type, with component counties.

Table C-3. States and Counties — **Migration, Housing, and Transportation**

STATE County	Owner-occupied by household type (percent)								Median household income			Median housing value (owner estimated)	Median monthly owner costs as a percent of income	
	Family-households				Nonfamily households									
		Married-couple family		Other family										
	Total family households	Total	With own children under 18 years	Total	With own children under 18 years	Total nonfamily households	Two or more adults	Living alone	All households	Owner-occupied households	Renter-occupied households		With a mortgage	Without a mortgage
	11	12	13	14	15	16	17	18	19	20	21	22	23	24

TEXAS—Cont'd

STATE County	11	12	13	14	15	16	17	18	19	20	21	22	23	24
Tom Green County	72.2	78.4	71.8	51.3	40.0	46.7	32.6	49.1	33 025	40 600	22 489	62 700	19.7	10.4
Travis County	65.8	73.4	71.9	43.2	38.6	31.9	25.5	34.5	46 526	65 638	31 569	127 600	21.2	9.9
Trinity County	83.3	87.7	79.6	67.2	61.9	74.7	62.3	76.0	27 231	29 292	19 375	48 300	21.0	13.0
Tyler County	87.1	89.1	83.7	75.6	64.7	75.4	80.9	74.9	29 910	32 183	19 428	46 400	19.6	10.7
Upshur County	84.1	87.0	83.4	71.2	61.9	74.5	78.5	74.0	33 237	36 220	21 709	56 100	19.9	10.5
Upton County	78.9	80.7	71.4	68.9	61.1	65.7	38.5	68.2	28 750	32 639	23 839	30 100	16.3	9.9
Uvalde County	74.0	78.5	73.8	56.5	42.4	64.9	48.3	66.3	27 084	30 919	18 934	43 800	18.8	10.8
Val Verde County	69.6	73.0	65.2	55.9	44.7	51.3	23.7	54.7	28 473	32 546	20 476	53 200	19.7	12.3
Van Zandt County	84.0	87.4	79.7	65.6	54.1	71.3	64.5	72.1	34 582	37 833	21 761	66 700	20.3	11.7
Victoria County	73.2	80.0	73.4	48.8	37.5	50.5	37.7	52.5	38 992	46 406	26 065	68 600	18.5	10.5
Walker County	71.7	78.1	71.2	50.5	45.4	40.2	17.7	48.8	31 180	41 442	19 731	67 700	19.8	10.9
Waller County	76.6	82.8	75.7	57.1	44.9	60.6	41.5	65.2	37 425	46 021	22 390	77 500	20.1	11.5
Ward County	81.2	87.2	82.7	54.2	46.2	69.1	53.1	70.2	29 461	32 991	17 260	31 800	17.1	10.0
Washington County	79.1	85.2	81.7	56.3	46.8	60.5	38.9	63.7	36 326	41 825	23 134	85 600	19.6	9.9
Webb County	68.5	73.3	70.3	54.0	42.8	48.0	43.3	48.5	27 979	34 310	18 012	67 000	24.0	12.5
Wharton County	72.9	78.8	71.0	52.0	40.0	57.6	45.0	59.1	32 250	38 713	21 627	56 700	18.5	10.9
Wheeler County	79.0	81.3	66.3	64.8	56.2	75.9	80.0	75.7	31 188	33 503	24 432	38 900	19.4	10.8
Wichita County	69.1	75.1	66.5	47.5	37.0	47.7	33.4	50.1	33 770	41 820	24 453	59 700	19.6	10.9
Wilbarger County	72.5	78.9	70.3	50.2	42.8	52.5	27.1	54.6	29 008	35 724	20 000	46 300	19.4	13.0
Willacy County	77.6	80.9	73.2	67.4	49.5	76.1	48.1	78.5	21 998	23 876	14 530	33 500	21.8	14.3
Williamson County	80.3	84.5	82.9	58.0	53.9	53.3	47.4	54.9	60 627	68 046	38 964	123 900	20.8	9.9
Wilson County	86.8	89.7	87.9	72.6	64.0	77.6	83.6	76.7	40 113	43 535	24 528	74 200	18.5	10.1
Winkler County	85.2	89.7	88.6	63.2	53.1	76.3	60.5	77.5	30 394	32 314	22 132	27 600	17.0	11.5
Wise County	84.3	86.3	81.8	72.2	67.1	70.8	76.1	69.8	41 890	46 376	26 357	82 300	20.0	11.0
Wood County	84.3	87.5	77.3	67.1	60.8	73.5	72.2	73.6	32 742	35 638	20 489	67 300	20.3	11.7
Yoakum County	79.0	85.3	81.5	48.1	45.6	74.6	20.8	77.6	31 250	34 966	26 000	36 100	17.8	10.7
Young County	76.9	80.8	67.6	56.6	46.9	66.0	43.5	68.0	30 549	35 169	20 660	46 600	18.5	11.7
Zapata County	84.2	87.9	85.7	70.2	62.8	72.4	40.8	74.7	24 095	26 041	11 570	37 100	23.2	9.9
Zavala County	73.3	79.1	69.8	61.2	37.8	71.5	46.4	74.5	16 663	19 236	11 288	24 100	21.3	12.6
UTAH	77.3	81.4	80.5	57.0	48.3	52.5	31.8	58.9	45 661	53 701	28 733	142 600	22.9	9.9
Beaver County	83.0	88.1	85.7	54.1	45.0	64.7	21.2	68.2	34 219	37 744	24 500	89 300	20.9	10.0
Box Elder County	82.2	85.3	82.9	62.1	51.5	69.3	59.0	70.3	44 457	49 891	28 060	117 700	21.7	9.9
Cache County	72.1	74.2	77.7	57.6	49.9	40.3	11.4	58.0	39 585	49 768	25 142	129 700	22.3	9.9
Carbon County	81.8	87.0	81.0	55.4	40.0	66.7	46.6	69.7	33 021	39 105	19 571	85 200	18.6	10.9
Daggett County	74.3	77.6	67.1	51.6	35.0	61.1	33.3	62.9	30 333	34 167	25 000	69 700	17.5	9.9
Davis County	81.2	85.1	83.6	58.9	46.8	59.2	43.4	62.4	53 865	61 224	32 318	153 100	22.1	9.9
Duchesne County	83.4	87.7	84.1	60.1	49.1	69.8	55.8	71.7	31 086	34 007	20 905	80 000	22.8	9.9
Emery County	85.4	89.0	85.8	58.2	44.2	68.2	43.1	70.2	40 000	43 372	21 679	79 200	18.8	9.9
Garfield County	82.5	85.3	77.7	63.3	51.6	68.0	61.1	69.1	35 474	37 882	25 707	90 400	20.9	9.9
Grand County	76.0	84.0	77.3	55.6	38.7	62.1	48.7	65.2	32 134	36 497	20 452	104 100	22.5	9.9
Iron County	72.9	76.7	76.1	50.2	41.5	45.1	13.7	60.5	32 662	40 871	22 198	108 300	24.3	9.9
Juab County	82.5	86.7	88.0	57.8	49.5	67.8	47.1	70.2	38 362	41 158	26 667	113 600	22.6	10.9
Kane County	81.9	84.1	80.5	65.1	55.8	67.5	67.1	67.6	33 983	35 967	26 875	95 900	22.1	9.9
Millard County	82.8	85.9	84.5	60.4	44.8	66.3	59.0	66.7	36 071	40 625	21 685	82 600	19.5	9.9
Morgan County	89.7	90.4	87.9	82.7	72.6	78.9	81.0	78.7	50 500	55 259	32 083	175 400	22.3	9.9
Piute County	89.3	91.9	87.3	71.4	53.8	80.2	100.0	79.3	31 083	34 091	15 417	81 300	20.6	9.9
Rich County	87.1	88.4	85.1	72.7	58.3	70.1	44.4	74.3	40 298	44 205	24 250	83 800	19.5	9.9
Salt Lake County	76.4	81.3	80.5	56.4	48.9	49.0	36.4	52.9	48 192	57 688	30 489	153 500	23.0	9.9
San Juan County	81.2	84.1	83.1	72.3	62.4	72.2	54.3	74.4	27 363	27 753	26 442	57 300	23.2	9.9
Sanpete County	82.7	85.8	82.5	60.2	48.0	65.0	25.8	74.2	33 143	36 588	22 160	104 600	24.5	10.2
Sevier County	83.7	87.7	85.2	56.8	46.1	74.4	64.2	75.2	35 714	38 539	22 482	94 800	21.9	9.9
Summit County	81.1	84.6	84.2	55.4	54.1	60.4	41.6	69.2	65 697	76 970	40 795	281 600	24.3	9.9
Tooele County	81.0	84.6	83.0	61.1	53.2	67.2	60.8	68.2	45 950	50 467	30 141	124 300	23.4	9.9
Uintah County	80.7	84.8	81.4	61.5	48.6	62.1	50.2	64.1	34 412	39 683	21 998	82 800	20.4	9.9
Utah County	72.2	74.9	77.2	54.2	48.3	43.7	15.3	63.3	45 770	55 956	28 166	153 600	23.5	9.9
Wasatch County	82.4	86.1	83.0	59.7	42.8	72.5	46.6	79.3	49 271	52 307	34 744	186 800	24.9	9.9
Washington County	77.4	81.5	74.8	49.7	39.4	61.1	32.2	67.2	37 510	42 261	26 698	131 300	25.8	9.9
Wayne County	80.8	82.4	75.3	66.2	62.3	68.2	28.6	73.8	32 063	34 293	26 016	99 800	21.1	9.9
Weber County	80.0	85.1	82.2	58.8	48.4	58.6	42.7	61.9	44 111	51 232	25 277	122 600	22.5	9.9
VERMONT	80.4	85.8	83.7	57.4	49.5	51.6	44.4	53.8	40 750	48 440	25 163	111 200	22.4	13.9
Addison County	82.2	85.6	81.9	66.1	55.8	58.1	51.2	60.1	43 160	48 562	28 811	116 200	23.3	14.0
Bennington County	79.9	86.6	82.4	53.0	45.2	54.1	52.1	54.6	39 383	46 257	22 160	113 300	22.9	14.1
Caledonia County	81.3	87.2	82.9	58.1	48.8	55.3	58.0	54.6	34 547	41 320	19 484	85 900	21.9	14.4

STATE County	Percent who pay 35 percent or more of income for housing expenses			Means of transportation to work (percent except where noted)						Vehicles available (percent of households)		
					Car, truck, or van							
	Median gross rent	Owners	Renters	Number of workers 16 years and over	Drove alone	Carpooled	Public transportation	Other means	Walked	No vehicles	One vehicle	Two or more vehicles
	25	26	27	28	29	30	31	32	33	34	35	36
TEXAS—Cont'd												
Tom Green County	457	12.1	28.4	47 286	79.4	12.7	0.4	1.2	4.1	7.0	37.9	55.1
Travis County	727	14.5	32.9	433 064	74.9	13.6	3.7	1.9	2.2	6.8	39.3	53.9
Trinity County	403	17.4	20.7	4 925	72.6	19.0	0.5	1.8	3.1	8.0	38.2	53.8
Tyler County	432	11.2	20.0	6 700	75.7	17.7	0.1	1.7	1.5	5.7	36.6	57.7
Upshur County	415	11.1	22.2	14 359	79.2	15.4	0.1	0.8	1.3	5.9	30.8	63.3
Upton County	309	9.5	10.7	1 291	77.8	13.9	0.0	1.5	3.8	6.4	35.5	58.0
Uvalde County.............	414	10.5	23.5	9 740	71.4	18.9	0.3	2.5	3.6	9.8	37.1	53.0
Val Verde County.........	408	14.2	21.7	16 007	75.1	17.7	0.1	2.9	2.2	8.3	35.7	56.0
Van Zandt County	461	14.7	19.8	19 594	76.3	16.1	0.3	0.9	2.2	5.8	30.5	63.8
Victoria County	507	10.5	24.1	37 867	77.8	17.6	0.1	1.1	1.3	7.0	34.7	58.3
Walker County	509	11.8	37.4	21 956	78.9	15.4	0.2	1.3	2.6	8.0	36.5	55.4
Waller County	473	16.9	24.9	13 392	74.0	16.9	0.5	1.5	3.7	7.1	34.7	58.2
Ward County	349	8.2	26.4	3 844	78.3	16.0	0.0	2.3	1.9	8.1	36.1	55.8
Washington County.......	479	13.5	27.2	13 289	78.8	13.8	0.0	0.7	2.1	7.8	32.6	59.6
Webb County	449	19.1	30.7	61 256	71.5	19.3	2.5	1.7	2.1	12.3	36.7	50.9
Wharton County	415	11.6	22.5	17 356	78.0	15.1	0.1	2.1	1.8	9.5	36.5	53.9
Wheeler County	348	12.4	18.4	2 361	76.4	17.9	0.0	0.5	3.5	5.5	33.6	60.9
Wichita County	486	11.8	25.6	61 170	77.9	11.2	0.4	1.2	7.4	6.7	36.4	56.8
Wilbarger County	377	12.1	17.4	6 394	83.8	11.9	0.0	0.8	2.2	8.3	35.2	56.5
Willacy County	301	17.8	20.2	5 883	74.3	17.3	0.5	2.4	3.3	12.9	40.9	46.2
Williamson County	787	11.9	25.4	127 639	82.2	11.8	0.3	0.9	1.0	3.3	26.6	70.2
Wilson County	421	11.5	21.1	13 719	76.4	18.5	0.1	1.2	1.2	4.6	26.6	68.8
Winkler County	370	9.3	22.2	2 502	73.5	22.7	0.4	1.8	1.1	5.9	39.1	55.0
Wise County................	484	14.5	21.5	22 121	77.5	16.0	0.3	1.1	1.8	4.3	25.4	70.4
Wood County	436	13.2	21.3	14 172	77.1	14.5	0.2	0.6	2.5	5.0	33.3	61.7
Yoakum County............	394	15.8	15.1	2 824	77.1	17.0	0.0	2.3	1.7	6.4	28.6	65.1
Young County	389	12.0	18.4	7 758	77.2	16.2	0.1	1.0	2.4	5.7	35.9	58.4
Zapata County	267	13.0	28.7	3 299	75.2	18.5	0.0	1.2	2.5	10.7	39.7	49.6
Zavala County	217	15.4	24.1	2 972	67.6	21.8	0.7	4.6	2.7	16.4	42.0	41.6
UTAH......................	597	16.2	27.7	1 032 858	75.5	14.1	2.2	1.2	2.8	5.1	26.9	68.0
Beaver County	490	15.6	25.2	2 460	73.4	18.7	0.5	1.4	2.5	5.9	23.7	70.4
Box Elder County	514	13.8	21.1	18 030	72.0	19.0	0.8	1.1	2.3	3.9	20.5	75.6
Cache County	509	13.9	26.9	43 731	73.2	14.5	1.5	1.5	4.7	4.2	24.8	71.0
Carbon County	433	10.8	25.7	8 460	77.9	14.6	0.2	0.9	3.3	5.6	25.8	68.6
Daggett County	500	10.9	10.5	377	69.8	8.5	0.0	0.5	8.8	2.9	29.7	67.4
Davis County	637	13.5	23.9	112 717	78.9	12.6	2.2	0.8	1.4	3.2	22.5	74.3
Duchesne County.........	452	14.5	27.9	5 370	74.1	14.8	0.3	1.0	3.6	4.2	25.6	70.2
Emery County	397	9.8	22.0	4 293	73.6	18.0	0.1	1.2	2.9	3.8	20.5	75.7
Garfield County	435	12.5	10.3	1 983	65.8	19.3	0.1	1.7	7.9	2.9	25.9	71.2
Grand County	498	16.7	34.0	3 958	67.7	13.7	0.0	4.8	7.5	5.9	38.4	55.7
Iron County..................	468	18.0	30.1	15 249	74.2	16.0	0.2	1.4	5.3	4.2	26.6	69.2
Juab County	501	16.3	15.6	3 369	67.6	21.4	0.2	2.3	6.3	3.9	20.9	75.2
Kane County	406	14.9	14.4	2 621	71.5	11.3	0.6	1.3	4.9	4.6	30.2	65.2
Millard County	388	10.3	18.1	4 820	68.5	19.4	0.4	1.5	5.0	5.9	24.7	69.4
Morgan County............	580	16.4	23.6	3 168	74.8	15.5	0.6	0.9	3.3	3.3	13.8	82.9
Piute County................	395	16.4	15.5	523	68.8	14.7	0.4	3.4	6.3	3.7	23.0	73.3
Rich County.................	354	13.1	4.5	791	65.7	19.0	0.4	0.6	5.7	3.3	21.7	75.0
Salt Lake County..........	638	16.8	28.5	438 627	76.4	13.1	3.5	1.2	2.0	6.3	29.4	64.3
San Juan County	383	15.3	13.6	4 117	67.0	18.1	0.6	0.7	8.6	10.4	35.6	54.0
Sanpete County	432	17.6	23.4	8 412	67.6	18.7	0.5	1.2	6.8	5.3	22.5	72.2
Sevier County..............	477	14.4	25.0	7 444	76.1	13.3	1.0	1.2	3.5	4.2	23.4	72.5
Summit County.............	909	24.4	25.7	16 295	74.4	12.4	1.2	1.6	3.0	2.7	22.0	75.3
Tooele County	532	16.5	23.3	17 966	67.1	23.1	2.3	0.8	2.9	4.1	26.6	69.3
Uintah County	422	13.1	24.5	10 145	73.2	18.8	0.5	2.0	1.9	5.0	24.3	70.7
Utah County	580	17.3	29.4	163 577	72.5	14.9	1.4	1.3	4.9	3.4	23.7	72.9
Wasatch County...........	731	19.3	24.4	6 860	74.7	16.3	0.3	0.7	2.7	3.0	21.8	75.2
Washington County.......	594	19.6	29.8	35 064	75.8	15.3	0.2	1.4	2.4	3.9	32.2	63.9
Wayne County..............	463	13.8	11.1	1 087	70.6	13.3	0.0	1.6	9.5	4.4	23.0	72.6
Weber County	544	15.5	28.1	91 344	78.7	14.2	1.4	1.1	1.6	6.2	28.0	65.9
VERMONT	553	16.2	29.5	311 839	75.2	11.9	0.7	0.9	5.6	6.8	33.6	59.5
Addison County............	565	18.2	25.8	18 503	71.3	10.8	0.2	1.1	8.6	4.3	30.6	65.1
Bennington County.......	538	18.2	31.0	18 320	76.0	11.7	0.7	1.1	5.1	7.9	34.3	57.8
Caledonia County.........	428	16.9	26.9	14 262	75.7	12.2	0.2	0.4	5.0	8.3	34.0	57.7

STATE/ County code	MSA/PMSA/ NECMA code[1]	STATE County	Total population 5 years and over	Residence in 1995 (percent)					Occupied housing units		Householders 65 years and over	
				Same house	Same county, different house	Same state, different county	Different state	Outside the United States	Number	Percent owner-occupied	Number	Percent owner-occupied
			1	2	3	4	5	6	7	8	9	10
		VERMONT—Cont'd										
50 007	1303	Chittenden County	138 073	51.5	24.0	6.5	15.5	2.5	56 452	66.1	8 693	70.6
50 009	...	Essex County	6 117	68.0	10.1	7.5	13.3	1.1	2 602	79.7	650	83.4
50 011	1303	Franklin County	42 208	62.1	22.5	8.5	6.1	0.7	16 765	75.0	3 141	78.5
50 013	1303	Grand Isle County	6 515	61.1	12.3	16.9	8.2	1.4	2 761	81.3	581	85.0
50 015	...	Lamoille County	21 923	56.8	20.3	9.5	12.3	1.1	9 221	70.8	1 687	78.1
50 017	...	Orange County	26 627	67.2	13.6	9.2	9.4	0.6	10 936	78.1	2 292	85.5
50 019	...	Orleans County	24 813	64.1	20.5	6.4	8.1	1.0	10 446	74.1	2 504	78.5
50 021	...	Rutland County	60 188	62.0	24.2	4.0	9.3	0.5	25 678	69.8	6 408	75.8
50 023	...	Washington County	54 914	59.5	21.7	6.6	10.9	1.3	23 659	68.5	4 927	73.9
50 025	...	Windham County	41 885	59.9	21.1	3.8	14.1	1.2	18 375	67.9	4 052	77.3
50 027	...	Windsor County	54 603	61.2	18.3	4.6	15.0	0.9	24 162	71.5	6 111	78.8
51 000	...	VIRGINIA	6 619 266	52.2	18.1	14.2	12.4	3.1	2 699 173	68.1	511 589	80.1
51 001	...	Accomack County	36 005	60.3	22.0	4.5	10.6	2.6	15 299	75.0	4 645	86.9
51 003	1540	Albemarle County	74 250	49.8	17.4	13.4	15.8	3.5	31 876	65.8	5 861	78.6
51 005	...	Alleghany County	12 202	71.3	13.5	11.5	3.5	0.2	5 149	84.8	1 408	91.0
51 007	...	Amelia County	10 694	63.2	15.0	18.3	3.4	0.0	4 240	82.0	915	90.3
51 009	4640	Amherst County	30 113	63.7	18.2	11.7	5.7	0.7	11 941	78.1	2 972	85.4
51 011	...	Appomattox County	12 871	63.9	18.6	12.2	4.8	0.6	5 322	81.0	1 315	88.4
51 013	8840	Arlington County	179 064	39.3	17.2	11.1	21.7	10.6	86 352	43.3	11 920	63.9
51 015	...	Augusta County	61 958	62.0	19.5	11.3	6.3	0.8	24 818	83.2	5 380	89.4
51 017	...	Bath County	4 823	65.6	14.8	12.9	4.5	2.3	2 053	79.8	517	85.1
51 019	4640	Bedford County	56 881	60.4	11.5	19.1	8.5	0.6	23 838	86.6	5 063	92.3
51 021	...	Bland County	6 563	69.4	10.3	8.4	10.3	1.6	2 568	86.1	709	88.9
51 023	6800	Botetourt County	28 758	63.1	13.4	15.7	7.5	0.3	11 700	87.7	2 535	88.5
51 025	...	Brunswick County	17 549	58.6	14.2	21.3	5.3	0.6	6 277	77.7	1 981	83.6
51 027	...	Buchanan County	25 665	76.4	14.2	6.7	2.6	0.2	10 464	82.9	2 177	88.7
51 029	...	Buckingham County	14 870	56.9	15.4	21.0	6.4	0.3	5 324	77.9	1 354	88.6
51 031	4640	Campbell County	48 064	62.9	17.7	13.5	5.4	0.5	20 639	77.3	4 755	85.7
51 033	...	Caroline County	20 774	67.3	12.6	14.4	5.1	0.5	8 021	82.0	1 789	89.9
51 035	...	Carroll County	27 911	69.5	15.0	7.9	7.1	0.5	12 186	81.7	3 555	87.1
51 036	6760	Charles City County	6 542	74.3	9.9	13.2	2.2	0.3	2 670	84.9	638	82.0
51 037	...	Charlotte County	11 814	66.5	14.4	11.4	7.1	0.6	4 951	77.4	1 565	85.9
51 041	6760	Chesterfield County	242 866	54.8	19.3	13.7	10.6	1.6	93 772	80.9	13 022	87.8
51 043	8840	Clarke County	12 008	59.8	11.2	19.8	8.7	0.5	4 942	75.5	1 228	81.4
51 045	...	Craig County	4 828	65.8	18.9	12.7	2.5	0.1	2 060	81.4	552	87.7
51 047	8840	Culpeper County	32 091	51.7	20.2	18.3	7.8	2.0	12 141	70.5	2 595	80.8
51 049	...	Cumberland County	8 468	64.3	12.6	16.9	5.3	0.9	3 528	77.2	912	80.7
51 051	...	Dickenson County	15 506	72.5	17.0	6.9	3.5	0.1	6 732	82.1	1 740	87.6
51 053	6760	Dinwiddie County	23 233	64.1	14.9	16.2	4.5	0.3	9 107	79.2	1 981	88.9
51 057	...	Essex County	9 519	62.7	18.0	14.5	4.0	0.8	3 995	77.2	1 227	89.3
51 059	8840	Fairfax County	902 189	49.2	18.7	9.5	14.8	7.8	350 714	71.0	46 273	81.0
51 061	8840	Fauquier County	51 566	57.1	15.2	17.1	9.0	1.5	19 842	76.2	3 612	82.6
51 063	...	Floyd County	13 080	64.8	14.8	11.7	7.7	0.9	5 791	81.8	1 450	88.9
51 065	1540	Fluvanna County	18 814	56.6	11.9	18.0	12.0	1.5	7 387	85.3	1 814	92.3
51 067	...	Franklin County	44 747	61.7	17.7	12.7	7.4	0.5	18 963	81.2	4 473	88.1
51 069	...	Frederick County	55 370	56.5	19.7	11.8	11.1	1.0	22 097	80.3	4 079	83.4
51 071	...	Giles County	15 728	68.0	10.4	6.5	6.9	0.2	6 994	79.0	1 911	84.9
51 073	5720	Gloucester County	32 770	59.7	15.1	16.1	8.1	1.1	13 127	81.4	2 637	90.2
51 075	6760	Goochland County	15 999	61.8	9.6	23.2	5.1	0.4	6 158	86.7	1 310	87.2
51 077	...	Grayson County	17 074	68.5	11.2	12.9	6.8	0.5	7 259	81.3	2 041	85.8
51 079	1540	Greene County	14 129	56.9	15.9	19.7	6.9	0.5	5 574	81.5	902	90.5
51 081	...	Greensville County	11 161	63.4	12.9	20.2	3.2	0.2	3 375	78.3	951	84.4
51 083	...	Halifax County	35 201	67.2	21.4	5.9	5.0	0.4	15 018	76.0	4 358	83.3
51 085	6760	Hanover County	80 643	57.0	14.2	20.0	8.3	0.6	31 121	84.3	5 731	89.1
51 087	6760	Henrico County	244 359	50.1	20.7	16.1	10.7	2.5	108 121	65.7	20 161	77.1
51 089	...	Henry County	54 861	66.2	21.8	5.2	5.3	1.5	23 910	76.9	5 870	85.3
51 091	...	Highland County	2 443	76.0	13.1	6.7	4.0	0.2	1 131	83.7	416	84.4
51 093	5720	Isle of Wight County	27 949	63.4	12.4	16.9	6.9	0.4	11 319	80.9	2 415	83.8
51 095	5720	James City County	45 539	49.7	13.6	18.0	17.1	1.4	19 003	77.0	4 727	79.5
51 097	...	King and Queen County	6 270	69.2	8.9	18.4	3.1	0.4	2 673	82.3	741	94.3
51 099	8840	King George County	15 607	57.1	13.4	14.0	13.7	1.8	6 091	71.8	933	90.4
51 101	...	King William County	12 237	64.1	12.0	20.8	2.6	0.5	4 846	85.1	930	86.7
51 103	...	Lancaster County	11 134	63.8	16.5	10.7	8.5	0.5	5 004	83.0	2 117	88.2
51 105	...	Lee County	22 220	64.8	24.0	4.0	7.0	0.2	9 706	74.4	2 534	83.1
51 107	8840	Loudoun County	153 293	40.4	16.0	20.1	19.3	4.2	59 900	79.4	5 735	77.1

[1]MSA = Metropolitan Statistical Area. PMSA = Primary MSA. NECMA = New England County Metropolitan Area. See the Appendix A for explanation of these concepts. See Appendix B for list of metropolitan areas identified by type, with component counties.

Table C-3. States and Counties — Migration, Housing, and Transportation

STATE County	Owner-occupied by household type (percent)								Median household income			Median monthly owner costs as a percent of income	
	Family-households					Nonfamily households						Median housing value (owner estimated)	With a mortgage	Without a mortgage
		Married-couple family		Other family										
	Total family households	Total	With own children under 18 years	Total	With own children under 18 years	Total nonfamily households	Two or more adults	Living alone	All households	Owner-occupied households	Renter-occupied households			
	11	12	13	14	15	16	17	18	19	20	21	22	23	24
VERMONT—Cont'd														
Chittenden County	80.2	85.8	86.3	55.5	49.8	42.4	32.6	46.6	47 724	61 028	28 261	136 500	22.1	12.3
Essex County	83.6	88.6	80.8	63.7	50.9	70.8	71.9	70.6	30 164	32 516	22 067	70 700	20.2	15.1
Franklin County	80.9	86.9	84.5	55.1	46.8	58.8	53.5	60.4	41 711	47 419	26 693	99 900	22.3	14.3
Grand Isle County	86.8	89.6	88.5	70.6	64.4	68.1	63.8	69.5	42 975	46 471	29 740	126 000	23.5	15.2
Lamoille County	81.3	86.1	84.1	62.0	59.8	51.4	44.1	54.3	39 081	45 647	26 351	114 400	23.4	13.7
Orange County	83.5	86.9	83.3	68.1	60.2	65.7	63.5	66.3	39 677	44 544	27 056	98 600	22.6	13.8
Orleans County	81.8	87.8	84.5	58.2	52.1	56.9	53.9	57.6	31 083	35 903	18 772	82 400	21.6	15.2
Rutland County	78.7	84.4	80.7	57.8	44.9	52.9	43.3	55.2	36 509	44 307	21 825	97 200	22.9	14.2
Washington County	79.7	86.1	86.1	52.6	47.2	48.6	46.8	49.1	40 637	50 490	23 994	105 200	22.0	14.4
Windham County	77.3	83.4	79.5	52.7	45.4	52.4	50.1	53.0	38 374	46 097	25 100	112 400	22.7	14.3
Windsor County	80.5	85.0	81.6	59.3	49.9	54.6	46.6	56.4	40 470	47 909	25 000	112 100	22.9	14.4
VIRGINIA	75.3	82.0	78.1	51.8	40.9	52.3	38.8	55.6	46 600	55 845	30 750	118 800	21.4	9.9
Accomack County	78.6	83.9	73.4	63.6	54.3	67.4	45.7	70.7	30 130	32 191	21 864	69 200	22.1	12.0
Albemarle County	76.6	80.4	80.0	59.2	48.6	44.8	27.2	49.3	50 795	63 301	33 905	160 500	20.4	9.9
Alleghany County	87.3	90.8	86.7	64.0	46.4	77.1	69.3	77.8	38 716	42 059	22 756	73 900	18.4	9.9
Amelia County	84.3	88.7	88.0	68.5	47.4	75.0	70.8	75.9	40 161	44 067	27 462	92 200	20.9	9.9
Amherst County	82.3	88.0	83.7	62.0	52.4	66.5	61.7	67.1	37 019	41 244	23 601	87 600	19.6	9.9
Appomattox County	83.1	89.1	86.3	62.2	50.8	74.4	73.3	74.6	36 847	40 185	23 652	80 400	19.4	9.9
Arlington County	55.4	62.0	60.1	31.7	25.5	33.0	22.5	36.4	62 830	88 791	49 200	233 700	19.7	9.9
Augusta County	86.7	89.3	86.4	72.5	63.3	71.7	69.4	72.2	43 097	46 652	26 786	107 000	20.4	9.9
Bath County	84.8	89.3	85.3	57.1	48.4	67.8	71.7	67.4	34 756	37 545	27 813	83 900	18.8	9.9
Bedford County	90.8	93.2	91.1	74.0	68.5	73.0	65.8	74.2	43 528	46 680	29 061	116 100	20.2	9.9
Bland County	91.2	92.6	93.1	82.2	78.8	70.7	51.1	72.2	29 962	31 464	20 543	65 700	18.4	9.9
Botetourt County	90.7	92.8	90.0	75.0	68.3	76.7	78.0	76.5	48 419	51 636	24 653	127 000	19.8	9.9
Brunswick County	79.1	87.7	83.7	59.1	45.0	74.5	56.6	76.8	31 138	35 421	20 703	66 300	20.8	10.4
Buchanan County	86.0	88.8	87.2	73.2	57.1	73.4	49.2	75.4	22 026	25 135	11 902	42 800	22.8	9.9
Buckingham County	82.5	88.0	81.9	67.8	59.3	67.2	61.6	68.3	29 507	33 872	19 000	71 200	21.6	9.9
Campbell County	82.2	87.4	82.9	63.6	51.2	64.9	62.3	65.3	37 020	41 876	24 763	87 600	19.0	9.9
Caroline County	83.6	87.2	80.2	72.5	59.9	77.2	72.8	78.0	39 889	43 533	28 115	89 200	22.1	9.9
Carroll County	85.7	89.5	83.8	66.3	54.5	71.3	50.4	73.2	30 112	33 453	17 221	64 100	19.7	9.9
Charles City County	87.0	90.4	87.3	77.6	72.4	78.6	67.6	80.0	42 744	43 750	31 667	84 000	20.4	10.2
Charlotte County	82.2	87.5	84.1	65.0	53.0	66.7	68.5	66.4	28 709	32 311	18 706	69 600	21.6	10.3
Chesterfield County	85.0	89.5	88.2	64.4	56.8	67.3	58.4	69.4	58 264	64 460	35 655	119 300	20.1	9.9
Clarke County	80.5	83.8	80.4	67.5	63.2	63.4	75.8	60.8	51 723	59 756	32 247	156 500	22.0	9.9
Craig County	84.5	89.4	86.6	61.9	27.6	72.6	59.6	73.9	37 722	41 139	20 676	89 600	22.0	9.9
Culpeper County	75.5	81.2	76.9	53.8	36.1	56.1	41.4	59.7	45 725	55 293	30 151	131 400	21.9	10.1
Cumberland County	83.2	88.9	82.9	67.6	55.9	62.9	75.0	60.5	31 557	38 534	18 520	76 600	22.2	9.9
Dickenson County	85.6	89.5	83.3	71.1	58.2	72.6	58.0	73.8	23 066	25 237	13 203	45 100	23.1	9.9
Dinwiddie County	82.0	86.7	80.8	68.3	59.3	71.2	66.5	72.0	41 312	46 069	27 582	86 800	21.4	9.9
Essex County	80.3	84.1	78.4	67.7	48.5	70.5	58.3	72.7	36 828	40 683	26 348	91 100	21.0	9.9
Fairfax County	76.6	80.3	77.8	57.8	50.3	56.7	41.9	61.4	80 978	95 175	52 816	222 400	20.5	9.9
Fauquier County	81.1	83.5	81.2	68.1	58.1	60.2	54.0	61.9	61 643	70 665	37 179	175 100	21.4	10.1
Floyd County	85.1	88.8	84.8	63.3	57.6	73.2	58.0	74.9	31 877	34 707	22 392	78 300	20.9	9.9
Fluvanna County	86.7	90.1	86.3	71.9	56.4	80.5	69.5	82.6	46 260	48 864	31 783	113 200	21.9	9.9
Franklin County	86.0	89.9	85.3	68.0	53.8	67.7	59.0	69.2	37 860	41 568	22 495	95 300	21.0	9.9
Frederick County	83.8	86.4	84.0	69.8	60.9	69.7	66.5	70.5	47 218	51 709	32 428	114 300	21.1	9.9
Giles County	83.6	86.6	81.3	71.3	49.3	68.2	57.1	69.5	34 781	38 992	21 250	67 500	18.7	9.9
Gloucester County	85.2	90.2	87.4	62.3	51.8	69.7	57.9	72.2	45 234	50 412	26 854	106 300	21.7	9.9
Goochland County	90.9	92.4	89.4	82.9	75.8	73.0	64.4	74.5	56 204	60 667	28 083	150 800	21.0	9.9
Grayson County	86.8	89.7	84.6	72.2	63.3	68.2	56.7	69.5	28 856	31 119	19 256	62 200	18.5	9.9
Greene County	83.8	86.9	84.6	69.4	53.3	73.7	65.8	75.9	45 753	49 684	30 360	108 200	20.6	9.9
Greensville County	79.4	85.2	85.5	64.6	55.8	75.3	48.0	78.5	32 544	36 732	23 214	63 500	19.4	9.9
Halifax County	80.0	86.1	80.1	63.9	51.8	66.6	59.7	67.1	29 809	34 251	20 263	69 300	20.4	10.3
Hanover County	88.3	91.5	89.9	70.9	62.5	69.0	62.3	70.3	59 180	64 416	32 275	146 800	20.8	9.9
Henrico County	74.4	82.6	80.0	49.5	40.8	49.9	37.2	52.7	48 974	59 368	33 562	119 900	21.0	9.9
Henry County	81.4	87.5	82.7	60.2	51.1	65.9	55.7	67.1	31 790	36 287	21 390	69 500	19.2	9.9
Highland County	90.2	90.7	88.6	87.4	88.6	70.3	64.7	70.9	29 767	32 536	24 250	88 000	25.0	9.9
Isle of Wight County	84.8	91.1	89.9	60.1	48.3	67.4	74.5	66.4	45 443	50 782	21 314	115 500	21.9	9.9
James City County	84.3	88.4	87.8	63.5	55.0	56.8	47.2	59.0	55 720	65 593	32 403	157 200	21.6	9.9
King and Queen County	85.8	89.9	89.5	72.5	60.4	73.3	67.0	74.3	35 987	38 013	31 833	82 000	20.6	10.5
King George County	75.9	79.3	73.4	62.0	46.7	59.6	58.6	59.9	49 981	56 390	35 948	122 800	20.9	9.9
King William County	87.9	91.6	92.8	71.8	62.2	75.0	82.9	73.3	50 096	52 573	30 903	104 500	20.6	9.9
Lancaster County	86.1	90.7	83.0	64.3	48.9	76.0	73.0	76.3	33 405	37 522	22 943	118 800	22.7	10.4
Lee County	78.3	82.2	77.3	63.5	50.2	64.8	52.2	65.9	23 227	27 484	12 494	53 400	18.9	9.9
Loudoun County	85.0	88.4	88.7	63.5	61.3	62.4	54.9	64.8	80 903	88 967	50 677	202 300	22.0	9.9

STATE County	Percent who pay 35 percent or more of income for housing expenses			Means of transportation to work (percent except where noted)						Vehicles available (percent of households)		
					Car, truck, or van							
	Median gross rent	Owners	Renters	Number of workers 16 years and over	Drove alone	Carpooled	Public transportation	Other means	Walked	No vehicles	One vehicle	Two or more vehicles
	25	26	27	28	29	30	31	32	33	34	35	36
VERMONT—Cont'd												
Chittenden County	662	13.8	33.1	79 670	76.1	10.8	1.5	1.0	6.5	7.1	33.0	59.9
Essex County	420	14.6	22.3	2 909	75.8	12.7	0.3	1.3	5.4	5.3	34.7	60.1
Franklin County	539	14.7	24.8	22 578	73.3	16.5	0.2	0.4	4.0	6.3	29.8	63.9
Grand Isle County	619	22.2	24.0	3 466	73.8	16.5	0.2	1.3	2.3	4.5	27.7	67.8
Lamoille County	543	19.8	26.9	12 141	74.8	11.0	0.4	1.4	5.5	5.2	32.9	61.9
Orange County	511	16.9	24.0	14 424	74.5	13.2	0.3	0.9	3.9	4.9	30.0	65.2
Orleans County	420	16.0	29.1	11 845	72.7	12.0	0.5	1.0	6.3	6.6	35.0	58.4
Rutland County	517	17.2	30.9	31 048	77.9	11.2	0.6	0.8	4.8	7.9	36.0	56.1
Washington County......	519	15.2	28.7	30 881	74.1	12.5	0.4	0.8	6.2	8.1	34.8	57.1
Windham County..........	552	18.0	27.4	22 895	74.0	11.4	0.7	1.0	6.1	7.8	35.8	56.4
Windsor County............	539	17.8	28.4	28 897	76.4	12.0	0.5	0.8	4.2	5.7	35.2	59.1
VIRGINIA.................	650	14.1	26.3	3 481 820	77.1	12.7	3.6	1.2	2.3	7.7	31.6	60.7
Accomack County	446	17.5	23.8	16 304	76.7	14.3	1.6	2.0	2.6	9.5	36.4	54.1
Albemarle County	712	12.4	30.7	39 137	78.8	12.0	1.7	0.8	1.5	4.4	32.7	62.9
Alleghany County	360	8.7	17.1	5 489	85.3	10.6	0.1	0.6	1.1	5.9	21.2	72.9
Amelia County	480	13.0	18.6	5 483	78.2	16.6	0.5	1.1	0.8	6.0	24.6	69.5
Amherst County	427	13.0	20.9	14 450	79.5	12.0	0.8	1.2	4.1	6.3	29.0	64.7
Appomattox County......	437	8.6	19.3	6 294	81.9	14.0	0.1	1.1	1.0	7.8	27.0	65.2
Arlington County	897	11.7	23.0	116 046	54.9	11.5	23.3	1.4	5.6	12.4	48.4	39.2
Augusta County............	506	11.7	16.9	32 461	84.1	9.7	0.2	0.7	1.7	3.5	22.1	74.5
Bath County	367	11.3	16.3	2 464	78.4	10.4	0.0	0.9	7.7	5.5	21.4	73.2
Bedford County	444	12.0	15.4	29 931	85.2	10.5	0.3	0.5	0.6	3.9	21.6	74.5
Bland County	349	9.2	11.8	2 630	85.4	9.7	0.5	1.1	0.8	7.0	24.9	68.1
Botetourt County	475	10.7	20.6	15 519	86.8	8.8	0.5	0.4	0.5	3.7	19.4	76.9
Brunswick County	349	18.4	15.5	6 363	75.6	16.1	0.8	2.0	2.2	11.6	30.9	57.5
Buchanan County.........	336	13.6	20.6	7 854	82.2	13.9	0.6	0.5	1.4	9.6	29.1	61.3
Buckingham County	370	13.7	20.9	5 668	73.5	16.6	0.8	3.0	2.6	9.2	29.8	61.0
Campbell County...........	427	9.8	21.0	24 806	85.0	9.7	0.2	1.0	1.3	6.6	28.1	65.3
Caroline County	587	16.1	21.6	10 352	77.5	16.1	1.3	1.0	1.5	6.8	25.4	67.8
Carroll County	366	11.5	25.6	13 447	78.8	17.1	0.3	0.8	1.1	8.3	28.6	63.1
Charles City County	420	14.7	17.9	3 357	79.9	14.4	0.7	1.3	0.7	8.6	22.1	69.4
Charlotte County	339	14.2	17.3	5 061	75.3	18.5	0.5	1.1	1.3	10.4	31.2	58.4
Chesterfield County.......	717	11.0	25.4	134 313	85.8	9.5	0.3	0.6	0.8	3.3	24.5	72.2
Clarke County	625	14.2	21.0	6 512	77.3	10.8	0.5	0.9	4.7	5.9	24.9	69.2
Craig County	404	12.0	11.1	2 340	78.9	16.2	0.0	0.9	1.6	6.7	24.2	69.1
Culpeper County	603	13.2	24.4	16 042	74.8	17.7	0.8	0.9	2.3	6.4	26.4	67.2
Cumberland County	456	13.1	28.0	3 956	77.1	17.0	0.3	2.6	1.4	7.9	29.9	62.2
Dickenson County	347	12.4	28.7	5 014	80.7	15.1	0.7	0.7	1.7	10.7	32.9	56.4
Dinwiddie County	566	14.3	24.5	11 314	85.1	10.6	0.3	1.2	0.9	5.1	27.5	67.4
Essex County	539	14.7	21.2	4 771	77.0	15.1	1.1	2.5	2.3	6.6	29.1	64.4
Fairfax County..............	998	13.3	22.8	527 464	73.4	13.1	7.3	0.8	1.3	4.1	29.6	66.4
Fauquier County	705	13.6	25.5	28 224	77.6	12.6	1.0	0.7	3.0	4.0	21.0	75.0
Floyd County	407	11.2	18.1	6 570	73.4	18.6	0.1	0.3	1.4	6.6	24.8	68.6
Fluvanna County	669	14.7	24.2	9 758	77.5	15.4	1.0	0.7	1.2	3.4	26.2	70.4
Franklin County	395	13.4	18.6	22 470	80.3	12.6	0.1	1.1	2.6	6.1	22.9	71.0
Frederick County..........	620	12.5	23.5	30 374	83.4	11.8	0.3	0.3	1.3	3.9	23.8	72.3
Giles County................	375	10.1	23.3	7 295	79.1	16.8	0.2	0.7	0.8	8.5	28.0	63.4
Gloucester County	527	14.5	25.7	16 952	79.3	14.0	0.9	1.2	1.1	3.7	25.1	71.2
Goochland County	589	15.5	27.0	8 299	83.1	10.7	0.2	1.2	1.0	4.6	20.4	75.0
Grayson County	318	8.8	13.6	7 705	73.8	19.5	0.4	0.5	1.4	8.6	26.8	64.5
Greene County.............	622	10.6	21.4	7 925	78.8	15.5	0.5	0.7	1.2	3.7	22.2	74.1
Greensville County........	395	13.6	17.6	3 758	81.1	14.3	0.9	0.6	0.3	8.5	29.5	62.0
Halifax County.............	360	13.5	19.2	14 679	81.1	14.3	0.4	0.9	1.0	10.3	29.7	60.0
Hanover County	686	11.3	21.6	44 460	86.2	8.1	0.2	0.9	1.3	3.6	20.4	76.1
Henrico County	676	12.8	25.1	136 872	84.8	9.8	1.1	0.8	0.9	5.6	36.0	58.3
Henry County	389	12.2	23.2	26 222	79.8	16.0	0.5	1.2	1.1	8.7	29.1	62.2
Highland County...........	339	13.7	18.5	1 106	70.3	19.9	0.0	0.0	1.9	7.6	26.1	66.3
Isle of Wight County......	502	13.5	25.9	13 986	84.3	10.8	0.1	0.5	1.1	5.8	23.0	71.2
James City County........	703	15.2	33.4	21 922	82.0	10.0	0.8	1.0	1.4	5.0	27.2	67.8
King and Queen County	473	14.4	14.5	2 913	77.0	16.6	0.8	1.1	1.2	5.8	24.7	69.5
King George County	622	11.8	13.8	8 187	79.6	13.2	0.9	1.3	2.2	4.6	25.4	70.0
King William County.......	550	10.3	12.3	6 594	82.6	12.9	0.0	0.5	1.3	5.3	23.1	71.6
Lancaster County..........	508	16.9	17.6	4 271	79.1	11.6	1.7	1.8	1.9	7.4	32.3	60.4
Lee County..................	341	11.9	29.8	8 179	80.9	13.7	0.3	0.9	1.3	12.2	33.5	54.3
Loudoun County............	954	13.3	23.4	92 315	81.6	9.8	1.5	0.8	1.2	2.5	23.3	74.2

Table C-3. States and Counties — Migration, Housing, and Transportation

STATE/ County code	MSA/PMSA/ NECMA code[1]	STATE County	Residence in 1995 (percent)						Occupied housing units		Householders 65 years and over	
			Total population 5 years and over	Same house	Same county, different house	Same state, different county	Different state	Outside the United States	Number	Percent owner-occupied	Number	Percent owner-occupied
			1	2	3	4	5	6	7	8	9	10
		VIRGINIA—Cont'd										
51 109	...	Louisa County	24 100	61.2	14.0	17.9	6.5	0.4	9 945	81.4	2 188	86.4
51 111	...	Lunenburg County	12 489	68.6	13.5	9.6	7.3	1.0	4 998	77.8	1 499	87.4
51 113	...	Madison County	11 839	64.1	15.6	12.1	6.6	1.5	4 739	76.9	1 212	84.7
51 115	5720	Mathews County	8 766	62.7	12.1	19.9	4.8	0.6	3 932	84.7	1 384	94.3
51 117	...	Mecklenburg County	30 629	64.9	18.3	8.9	7.4	0.5	12 951	74.3	3 882	81.0
51 119	...	Middlesex County	9 555	58.7	17.6	17.1	6.1	0.5	4 253	83.0	1 392	91.6
51 121	...	Montgomery County	79 589	38.7	18.3	24.8	14.7	3.6	30 997	55.1	4 734	80.9
51 125	...	Nelson County	13 683	66.9	13.2	13.3	6.2	0.4	5 887	80.8	1 660	87.7
51 127	6760	New Kent County	12 667	61.6	10.8	22.9	4.3	0.4	4 925	88.8	901	96.1
51 131	...	Northampton County	12 373	64.7	18.0	8.8	7.0	1.6	5 321	68.7	2 031	79.1
51 133	...	Northumberland County	11 740	64.6	12.4	14.3	7.7	1.0	5 470	87.4	2 318	95.1
51 135	...	Nottoway County	14 855	61.4	14.2	18.1	5.2	1.2	5 664	70.9	1 594	83.2
51 137	...	Orange County	24 368	58.2	16.5	18.4	6.3	0.6	10 150	77.1	2 826	89.5
51 139	...	Page County	21 900	64.2	22.5	8.2	4.7	0.4	9 305	73.9	2 397	85.7
51 141	...	Patrick County	18 277	66.9	16.3	6.9	9.5	0.4	8 141	80.2	2 209	85.9
51 143	1950	Pittsylvania County	58 236	66.2	19.9	8.0	5.3	0.7	24 684	80.1	6 152	85.3
51 145	6760	Powhatan County	21 069	59.2	10.1	24.8	5.9	0.1	7 258	88.9	1 071	89.1
51 147	...	Prince Edward County ..	18 807	54.6	13.7	22.3	8.3	1.1	6 561	68.5	1 830	79.2
51 149	6760	Prince George County ..	31 074	49.8	8.9	17.7	19.4	4.2	10 159	73.1	1 684	89.7
51 153	8840	Prince William County...	257 038	45.6	18.4	15.7	16.2	4.0	94 570	71.7	7 467	75.2
51 155	...	Pulaski County	33 112	62.5	23.2	9.6	4.5	0.2	14 643	73.6	3 545	83.1
51 157	...	Rappahannock County..	6 628	66.1	13.9	14.0	5.5	0.5	2 788	75.4	579	89.6
51 159	...	Richmond County	8 436	59.2	11.3	17.1	8.9	3.6	2 937	77.2	926	85.0
51 161	6800	Roanoke County	81 272	58.0	11.2	20.6	9.2	1.0	34 686	77.1	8 338	80.9
51 163	...	Rockbridge County	19 712	64.7	18.6	8.0	7.8	0.9	8 486	77.6	2 336	86.0
51 165	...	Rockingham County	63 473	62.6	21.0	9.1	6.2	1.1	25 355	78.0	5 886	85.4
51 167	...	Russell County	28 724	67.5	19.2	7.5	4.8	1.0	11 789	81.1	2 711	85.9
51 169	3660	Scott County	22 219	69.5	17.5	5.7	7.1	0.2	9 795	78.3	2 880	80.6
51 171	...	Shenandoah County	33 059	59.0	22.1	10.3	7.7	0.8	14 296	73.1	4 010	85.3
51 173	...	Smyth County	31 314	63.9	22.4	8.2	5.2	0.3	13 493	74.1	3 601	80.1
51 175	...	Southampton County	16 568	63.0	14.6	18.2	3.9	0.3	6 279	74.3	1 674	81.5
51 177	8840	Spotsylvania County	83 753	53.4	15.2	19.1	11.2	1.2	31 308	82.2	4 544	82.6
51 179	8840	Stafford County	85 426	50.2	13.5	18.0	16.2	2.2	30 187	80.6	3 166	90.7
51 181	...	Surry County	6 454	67.3	13.7	15.8	2.9	0.2	2 619	77.0	656	81.7
51 183	...	Sussex County	11 923	62.3	14.6	17.1	5.0	1.0	4 126	69.5	1 183	81.2
51 185	...	Tazewell County	42 209	66.7	20.7	5.1	7.1	0.4	18 277	77.3	4 610	84.8
51 187	8840	Warren County	29 480	56.7	19.3	14.1	9.4	0.5	12 087	74.1	2 451	80.8
51 191	3660	Washington County	48 518	61.6	19.2	9.2	9.7	0.3	21 056	77.3	5 203	87.5
51 193	...	Westmoreland County..	15 852	68.0	14.3	9.6	7.6	0.5	6 846	79.2	2 198	89.8
51 195	...	Wise County	37 847	64.9	21.0	8.7	5.1	0.3	16 013	75.2	3 639	85.7
51 197	...	Wythe County	26 083	65.1	19.5	8.7	6.3	0.4	11 511	77.4	2 859	86.6
51 199	5720	York County	52 569	47.8	10.4	18.1	18.9	4.8	20 000	75.8	3 386	92.0
		Independent Cities										
51 510	8840	Alexandria city	120 272	36.7	15.6	16.6	21.7	9.5	61 889	40.0	7 582	60.3
51 515	4640	Bedford city	5 944	57.5	13.7	21.3	7.2	0.3	2 519	60.3	768	77.6
51 520	3660	Bristol city	16 479	58.3	11.0	15.6	14.6	0.5	7 678	65.0	2 562	76.9
51 530	...	Buena Vista city	5 980	59.7	3.6	28.9	7.7	0.1	2 547	70.6	714	78.7
51 540	1540	Charlottesville city	43 051	35.1	8.7	33.6	18.2	4.4	16 851	40.9	2 865	76.3
51 550	5720	Chesapeake city	185 025	51.9	17.7	16.2	12.6	1.6	69 900	74.9	10 977	81.6
51 560	...	Clifton Forge city	4 056	60.1	13.9	18.0	6.7	1.3	1 841	62.7	656	64.9
51 570	6760	Colonial Heights city	16 072	58.7	14.4	18.9	6.3	1.7	7 027	69.4	1 969	84.4
51 580	...	Covington city	5 901	62.5	4.4	26.7	5.1	1.3	2 835	69.8	948	78.4
51 590	1950	Danville city	45 553	60.0	12.9	19.5	6.8	0.8	20 607	58.0	6 610	72.8
51 595	...	Emporia city	5 346	54.8	5.9	29.2	9.3	0.8	2 226	52.1	659	63.4
51 600	8840	Fairfax city	20 236	47.7	9.3	22.7	10.9	9.4	8 035	69.1	1 461	89.0
51 610	8840	Falls Church city	9 751	47.2	6.3	21.5	17.5	7.5	4 471	60.5	917	68.6
51 620	...	Franklin city	7 946	57.5	13.9	23.6	4.7	0.3	3 384	53.6	875	65.8
51 630	8840	Fredericksburg city	18 186	39.5	13.2	30.5	14.5	2.4	8 102	35.5	1 686	50.2
51 640	...	Galax city	6 463	53.5	13.3	24.2	6.7	2.3	2 950	66.1	858	80.9
51 650	5720	Hampton city	137 303	47.7	19.3	12.0	18.0	3.0	53 887	58.6	9 910	81.8
51 660	...	Harrisonburg city	38 524	33.2	4.5	41.3	16.0	5.1	13 133	39.1	2 115	63.6
51 670	6760	Hopewell city	20 654	54.0	19.9	17.3	7.4	1.4	9 055	55.9	2 031	76.4
51 678	...	Lexington city	6 656	42.0	1.1	24.9	29.9	2.1	2 232	55.2	724	68.4
51 680	4640	Lynchburg city	61 433	51.6	20.5	13.7	12.3	2.0	25 477	58.5	6 817	70.9

[1]MSA = Metropolitan Statistical Area. PMSA = Primary MSA. NECMA = New England County Metropolitan Area. See the Appendix A for explanation of these concepts. See Appendix B for list of metropolitan areas identified by type, with component counties.

STATE County	Owner-occupied by household type (percent)								Median household income			Median monthly owner costs as a percent of income	
	Family-households					Nonfamily households							
		Married-couple family		Other family									
	Total family households	Total	With own children under 18 years	Total	With own children under 18 years	Total nonfamily households	Two or more adults	Living alone	All households	Owner-occupied households	Renter-occupied households	Median housing value (owner estimated)	With a mortgage	Without a mortgage
	11	12	13	14	15	16	17	18	19	20	21	22	23	24

VIRGINIA—Cont'd														
Louisa County	84.3	88.7	85.1	69.2	63.6	73.5	66.3	75.0	39 205	43 075	24 401	96 100	22.3	9.9
Lunenburg County.........	81.3	88.7	80.3	61.7	49.6	70.1	66.9	70.4	27 846	30 090	19 792	62 500	22.1	11.0
Madison County	79.5	81.0	75.6	72.4	55.2	69.6	59.3	71.4	40 518	43 717	28 513	111 800	21.0	9.9
Mathews County	87.4	90.0	81.6	72.3	55.3	77.8	69.7	78.9	42 538	44 667	25 625	111 400	21.0	10.1
Mecklenburg County	78.5	86.4	81.2	55.9	44.4	65.0	48.6	67.2	31 474	35 347	21 494	73 800	21.7	9.9
Middlesex County	85.6	89.6	82.7	69.2	57.1	77.4	63.0	80.0	37 281	41 250	26 307	110 400	22.1	9.9
Montgomery County......	73.9	79.2	76.4	50.0	40.7	31.2	11.4	45.4	32 472	47 098	19 830	101 200	19.9	9.9
Nelson County...............	84.0	87.2	80.5	72.2	66.0	73.1	69.5	73.7	36 701	39 918	26 580	94 000	20.5	9.9
New Kent County	90.3	92.1	92.7	81.4	73.9	82.9	62.9	88.2	53 553	57 851	31 705	131 000	21.2	9.9
Northampton County	71.4	78.8	69.2	54.5	34.1	63.2	54.0	64.3	28 013	32 445	18 690	75 100	23.4	10.6
Northumberland County	88.9	92.0	81.6	70.5	49.8	84.2	83.1	84.3	38 567	41 143	26 367	117 300	22.9	9.9
Nottoway County............	76.0	83.8	73.0	55.7	39.8	59.4	47.6	60.8	30 251	36 343	22 279	72 300	21.7	10.5
Orange County	78.8	83.6	76.2	61.6	47.0	72.4	68.6	73.1	43 305	46 877	29 622	112 800	22.6	9.9
Page County	77.0	83.2	73.1	55.0	40.5	66.0	54.7	67.9	33 435	38 033	23 121	85 900	23.1	9.9
Patrick County	83.3	86.9	76.3	65.7	58.9	72.2	58.9	73.4	28 939	31 753	21 230	70 500	19.2	0.0
Pittsylvania County........	83.8	88.7	84.3	64.3	50.9	69.7	61.5	70.5	35 282	39 384	21 502	74 300	19.6	9.9
Powhatan County	90.8	92.6	91.0	79.3	74.6	80.4	85.1	79.2	54 844	59 356	30 229	140 000	20.5	9.9
Prince Edward County ..	75.6	83.7	78.2	52.1	47.2	55.4	35.0	59.7	30 857	35 477	21 014	87 700	22.5	9.9
Prince George County ...	75.0	79.2	68.6	57.8	44.3	65.0	55.0	66.2	49 714	55 678	31 476	114 100	20.3	9.9
Prince William County...	75.9	81.2	78.0	54.8	47.6	57.2	51.6	59.1	65 754	76 511	41 597	147 900	22.1	9.9
Pulaski County	79.4	86.2	77.6	52.8	39.5	60.6	57.0	61.1	34 067	40 760	20 893	75 200	18.5	9.9
Rappahannock County..	77.5	78.7	68.5	71.1	49.7	70.1	69.8	70.1	45 833	50 928	33 320	166 100	22.1	10.9
Richmond County..........	80.7	86.5	82.1	62.4	53.0	69.5	76.7	68.8	32 489	37 311	21 563	85 500	20.8	9.9
Roanoke County...........	85.1	89.4	88.8	64.2	53.4	57.4	39.8	60.0	47 450	54 172	30 744	117 400	20.1	9.9
Rockbridge County.......	81.6	84.8	79.5	67.4	63.4	67.4	58.5	68.9	36 268	40 259	22 926	94 500	20.9	9.9
Rockingham County......	82.2	85.6	80.8	64.4	50.5	65.7	59.4	66.9	40 968	44 587	29 260	103 200	21.3	9.9
Russell County	84.2	87.6	82.5	68.4	58.7	71.7	62.4	72.3	26 927	29 435	18 099	55 200	20.7	9.9
Scott County.................	81.8	84.9	81.1	66.3	52.4	69.3	55.8	70.2	27 239	30 577	16 969	62 500	19.4	9.9
Shenandoah County	77.5	83.3	73.4	52.4	34.6	62.7	44.0	65.9	39 140	43 585	28 457	101 100	20.9	9.9
Smyth County................	78.5	83.6	77.4	59.0	43.8	63.3	47.9	64.9	29 771	33 580	21 286	62 600	18.8	9.9
Southampton County.....	79.1	86.5	84.3	59.5	53.7	61.7	52.9	62.8	34 227	41 134	20 119	79 500	21.2	9.9
Spotsylvania County	85.5	88.8	86.6	68.4	61.1	69.7	61.8	71.9	57 216	61 496	37 339	125 700	22.0	9.9
Stafford County	84.0	87.6	85.1	63.5	55.3	66.1	57.2	69.2	67 229	72 794	42 422	155 100	22.0	9.9
Surry County	81.2	86.2	79.9	64.0	57.6	65.6	53.6	67.3	38 149	42 063	24 688	82 800	22.3	9.9
Sussex County	70.1	80.3	66.3	49.5	34.2	68.1	68.3	68.1	30 807	36 050	21 853	67 900	21.0	10.5
Tazewell County............	80.8	83.5	78.7	69.6	55.7	68.1	52.9	69.5	27 151	30 204	21 284	55 700	20.5	9.9
Warren County	78.9	84.0	78.8	59.3	50.1	62.8	55.5	64.5	42 487	50 158	28 336	109 700	21.0	9.9
Washington County.......	83.6	86.5	80.6	69.0	51.9	61.6	38.6	64.4	32 767	37 104	22 388	82 300	19.9	9.9
Westmoreland County...	81.5	86.3	75.7	65.7	51.5	74.4	63.6	76.4	37 074	40 224	27 791	91 800	21.8	10.1
Wise County.................	80.3	85.6	80.1	59.7	42.6	62.0	58.3	62.3	26 373	31 514	15 323	53 700	20.7	9.9
Wythe County...............	82.2	87.3	81.7	62.4	51.8	65.6	48.3	67.5	31 939	35 939	20 502	67 400	19.4	9.9
York County	77.5	80.3	71.2	60.8	49.8	69.0	57.6	71.5	57 911	60 401	30 294	149 100	21.7	0.0

Independent Cities														
Alexandria city..............	47.2	55.4	49.2	25.2	17.8	34.0	26.8	35.9	56 161	85 357	44 063	202 400	20.7	9.9
Bedford city	68.8	81.0	74.9	40.7	27.4	45.5	47.1	45.4	29 170	36 518	18 112	89 800	20.9	9.9
Bristol city....................	71.9	79.5	69.7	49.0	26.7	53.6	39.2	55.0	27 012	32 631	16 491	69 400	19.7	10.4
Buena Vista city	73.9	79.9	73.4	53.5	47.7	63.3	17.6	69.3	31 406	35 897	23 793	71 400	21.1	9.9
Charlottesville city	58.4	71.9	67.5	31.4	21.6	26.2	11.5	34.5	31 054	51 822	21 145	117 800	21.6	9.9
Chesapeake city............	78.8	86.1	83.9	53.9	41.8	61.0	52.2	63.2	50 692	59 338	30 069	119 700	23.5	10.6
Clifton Forge city	70.4	82.4	76.5	46.3	19.9	50.4	69.4	48.2	26 042	35 096	15 714	52 400	20.4	11.2
Colonial Heights city	76.6	85.4	76.4	49.6	39.3	54.4	33.5	58.3	42 585	50 065	29 184	94 700	20.3	9.9
Covington city...............	75.1	80.4	70.9	60.0	56.9	61.1	35.6	63.8	29 944	35 786	19 940	50 700	19.3	10.4
Danville city	63.7	78.7	69.4	39.8	24.0	48.5	37.6	49.5	26 753	36 106	17 390	69 800	19.5	9.9
Emporia city	59.0	72.7	59.5	34.6	18.8	40.5	40.3	40.5	29 650	40 865	17 750	67 300	19.7	10.9
Fairfax city....................	74.8	77.8	72.7	61.1	51.8	57.1	42.3	62.8	67 719	79 876	49 286	188 300	20.1	9.9
Falls Church city	71.1	74.3	79.2	59.9	49.9	45.3	41.4	46.2	74 496	94 191	51 811	262 400	20.8	10.7
Franklin city..................	61.9	77.8	76.9	35.2	20.4	36.0	13.4	38.6	31 152	47 287	18 351	93 800	24.5	9.9
Fredericksburg city........	47.6	59.1	56.3	24.9	14.6	24.2	14.6	27.3	34 158	57 351	26 857	134 500	21.7	9.9
Galax city	74.2	80.0	73.4	55.1	42.1	52.4	26.4	54.8	27 744	34 840	16 286	62 900	18.5	9.9
Hampton city	64.6	75.1	66.8	40.5	27.1	46.3	30.6	50.0	39 358	49 978	26 814	90 000	22.8	10.7
Harrisonburg city	57.0	67.4	61.2	26.9	24.0	21.3	7.2	32.1	30 406	51 500	22 668	119 300	19.5	9.9
Hopewell city	60.0	76.6	60.4	32.8	24.9	47.8	43.3	48.8	32 573	43 611	22 939	77 000	21.7	10.5
Lexington city	75.5	76.7	82.4	71.1	61.2	35.9	20.3	39.9	28 737	49 773	13 633	129 800	23.8	9.9
Lynchburg city..............	68.1	81.8	76.4	41.4	28.1	42.9	25.7	45.7	32 243	41 972	20 868	84 900	20.8	9.9

STATE County	Median gross rent	Percent who pay 35 percent or more of income for housing expenses — Owners	Renters	Car, truck, or van — Number of workers 16 years and over	Drove alone	Carpooled	Public transportation	Other means	Walked	Vehicles available (percent of households) — No vehicles	One vehicle	Two or more vehicles
	25	26	27	28	29	30	31	32	33	34	35	36
VIRGINIA—Cont'd												
Louisa County	504	16.9	21.1	12 039	75.8	17.2	0.5	1.0	1.2	6.4	24.3	69.4
Lunenburg County........	394	18.0	23.7	5 016	75.4	17.7	0.6	1.4	2.5	9.4	34.5	56.2
Madison County	494	12.7	18.1	6 057	76.9	12.4	0.2	0.9	3.7	4.6	23.3	72.1
Mathews County	506	11.2	14.2	4 020	75.6	13.7	2.6	1.6	2.1	4.5	25.9	69.7
Mecklenburg County	375	14.5	20.6	13 209	77.9	15.9	0.3	1.2	1.8	9.7	31.4	58.9
Middlesex County	544	12.8	22.4	4 233	79.0	13.9	0.9	0.9	3.4	6.1	27.6	66.3
Montgomery County......	535	11.2	41.2	38 330	77.4	9.8	3.1	1.6	5.2	5.7	31.7	62.6
Nelson County..............	440	14.0	18.1	6 637	70.8	20.5	0.3	1.7	1.5	8.0	23.7	68.3
New Kent County	636	15.2	20.8	6 828	85.0	11.7	0.2	0.3	0.8	3.7	18.0	78.3
Northampton County	382	17.5	25.0	5 069	71.1	16.1	2.2	2.0	3.9	12.6	37.4	50.0
Northumberland County	478	18.5	17.5	4 815	81.2	9.8	1.3	1.6	1.4	6.3	29.8	63.9
Nottoway County...........	438	16.0	25.6	5 896	75.9	17.6	0.7	0.5	1.7	11.2	33.7	55.1
Orange County..............	583	14.2	25.9	11 935	78.6	14.6	0.6	0.5	2.5	5.4	30.1	64.5
Page County.................	441	15.3	24.1	10 847	74.3	18.9	0.2	0.7	1.5	6.8	28.4	64.8
Patrick County	333	9.7	15.0	8 779	76.8	15.6	0.7	0.9	3.0	9.0	24.9	66.1
Pittsylvania County	398	11.3	21.1	28 931	82.1	14.1	0.3	0.7	0.5	7.3	26.7	66.0
Powhatan County..........	623	12.4	23.0	10 423	85.3	9.7	0.4	1.1	0.6	2.7	16.4	81.0
Prince Edward County ..	459	19.3	28.0	7 466	69.5	16.4	1.3	1.0	8.7	10.3	34.4	55.3
Prince George County ..	609	12.5	14.0	15 943	76.3	8.9	2.0	1.3	9.4	3.6	25.6	70.9
Prince William County...	862	14.4	23.3	150 526	72.7	18.8	3.1	1.0	1.4	3.5	26.1	70.4
Pulaski County	382	9.0	21.2	16 183	85.0	10.9	0.2	1.0	1.4	9.1	30.8	60.1
Rappahannock County..	599	16.3	19.1	3 552	74.8	12.9	0.7	0.5	2.1	5.2	20.8	74.0
Richmond County	457	13.2	17.6	3 202	78.6	14.1	0.4	1.2	2.7	11.5	27.2	61.3
Roanoke County	575	11.5	20.2	43 419	87.7	7.7	0.2	0.5	1.1	4.3	28.0	67.7
Rockbridge County	442	12.3	24.9	9 964	79.0	14.0	0.5	0.8	1.1	4.7	25.7	69.6
Rockingham County......	485	12.0	18.6	34 113	79.5	11.6	0.3	1.2	2.2	5.6	24.2	70.3
Russell County	355	11.2	24.2	10 574	82.1	13.4	0.1	0.6	1.2	9.1	27.6	63.3
Scott County.................	335	9.5	18.0	9 054	80.9	13.0	0.5	0.9	1.6	12.5	28.8	58.7
Shenandoah County	468	10.9	21.0	17 463	79.4	13.4	0.2	0.6	2.1	6.3	27.6	66.1
Smyth County................	353	9.8	16.7	14 681	81.2	14.4	0.3	1.0	1.4	9.0	31.2	59.8
Southampton County	409	15.4	27.2	6 945	81.6	12.9	0.6	1.2	1.3	9.1	30.5	60.5
Spotsylvania County	805	14.6	24.4	45 409	79.1	14.2	2.3	0.6	0.7	3.3	22.5	74.2
Stafford County	842	13.4	23.1	48 381	74.1	17.3	2.5	0.8	2.5	2.3	19.4	78.3
Surry County	402	13.9	19.3	3 147	75.1	19.2	0.6	1.0	0.9	7.2	28.5	64.3
Sussex County	434	15.2	24.8	4 181	80.6	14.5	0.7	0.4	1.9	13.6	32.4	54.0
Tazewell County...........	376	11.9	21.8	17 141	84.1	11.4	0.4	0.7	1.5	9.5	31.5	59.0
Warren County	531	14.2	26.7	15 372	72.4	21.2	0.7	0.7	2.5	6.0	28.3	65.7
Washington County.......	412	11.2	20.3	23 495	84.9	9.7	0.1	0.8	1.4	6.7	28.6	64.8
Westmoreland County...	537	17.7	26.0	7 034	77.4	18.0	0.1	0.6	1.9	9.4	29.2	61.4
Wise County.................	353	12.7	26.7	14 636	82.6	12.7	0.3	0.8	2.0	10.5	31.9	57.6
Wythe County................	401	11.6	22.1	13 038	78.7	15.1	0.1	1.2	1.0	9.2	31.0	59.7
York County	708	12.5	16.8	28 636	85.5	9.0	0.5	0.9	1.5	2.6	23.3	74.1
Independent Cities												
Alexandria city..............	861	13.3	23.0	77 190	62.8	13.2	16.4	1.2	3.0	11.2	52.4	36.4
Bedford city	436	11.4	24.2	2 421	73.9	18.2	0.3	0.6	4.3	15.4	31.4	53.2
Bristol city....................	409	11.9	27.1	6 962	84.7	9.6	0.8	0.6	2.5	15.2	38.7	46.1
Buena Vista city	403	12.9	19.5	2 997	77.2	15.2	0.2	1.6	4.0	14.2	33.6	52.2
Charlottesville city	596	14.2	40.5	20 323	60.4	9.7	5.1	2.8	16.5	14.2	41.4	44.4
Chesapeake city...........	642	17.4	28.5	96 977	83.9	10.5	0.9	1.1	1.1	5.7	28.3	66.0
Clifton Forge city	341	10.0	26.8	1 657	74.4	16.4	0.0	0.4	6.2	17.9	37.9	44.2
Colonial Heights city	619	10.3	30.1	8 080	88.5	8.4	0.1	0.4	1.2	5.9	32.9	61.2
Covington city	404	13.4	28.0	2 640	76.2	14.6	0.3	1.7	3.2	15.9	36.0	48.0
Danville city	404	13.2	30.5	19 262	79.9	13.7	2.1	1.0	2.0	17.3	38.6	44.1
Emporia city	437	12.2	26.9	2 173	76.7	16.7	0.6	1.4	3.6	15.1	40.7	44.1
Fairfax city...................	945	10.6	23.9	11 845	73.5	11.6	7.6	0.9	3.4	4.0	32.8	63.2
Falls Church city	965	12.2	25.5	5 853	63.0	11.5	15.9	1.6	3.0	7.5	44.7	47.8
Franklin city	493	17.4	34.7	3 337	76.3	16.6	1.3	0.7	2.2	14.6	38.7	46.7
Fredericksburg city........	651	16.9	33.0	9 659	70.6	12.6	4.3	1.6	7.5	13.2	44.2	42.6
Galax city	346	13.6	25.0	3 013	76.5	19.2	0.3	0.4	2.1	15.1	39.9	45.1
Hampton city	603	17.0	29.8	66 101	79.7	12.9	2.8	1.1	1.9	8.7	36.6	54.7
Harrisonburg city	480	10.9	33.8	18 270	70.7	10.0	3.3	2.8	9.6	9.6	34.2	56.3
Hopewell city	512	15.8	26.4	9 222	82.7	12.8	0.5	0.8	1.0	10.3	40.4	49.3
Lexington city	434	15.4	41.6	2 069	55.7	10.1	0.0	2.7	26.5	14.2	43.0	42.9
Lynchburg city..............	469	13.1	28.7	28 619	76.8	12.3	3.1	0.8	4.7	14.9	37.0	48.1

STATE/ County code	MSA/PMSA/ NECMA code[1]	STATE County	Total population 5 years and over	Residence in 1995 (percent)					Occupied housing units		Householders 65 years and over	
				Same house	Same county, different house	Same state, different county	Different state	Outside the United States	Number	Percent owner-occupied	Number	Percent owner-occupied
			1	2	3	4	5	6	7	8	9	10
		VIRGINIA—Cont'd										
51 683	8840	Manassas city	32 021	48.4	5.6	28.9	12.7	4.4	11 757	69.8	1 200	80.8
51 685	8840	Manassas Park city.......	9 265	39.8	3.0	38.4	13.8	4.9	3 254	78.7	262	79.8
51 690	...	Martinsville city	14 528	58.0	7.0	27.2	6.0	1.7	6 498	60.2	1 959	73.7
51 700	5720	Newport News city	165 897	45.5	22.9	12.5	16.1	3.1	69 686	52.4	12 096	73.9
51 710	5720	Norfolk city	217 818	42.7	23.3	11.8	19.7	2.5	86 210	45.6	17 601	70.1
51 720	...	Norton city	3 690	49.5	23.5	19.3	6.5	1.2	1 730	56.0	415	68.4
51 730	6760	Petersburg city	31 517	55.6	23.6	11.6	7.6	1.6	13 799	51.5	3 609	71.8
51 735	5720	Poquoson city................	10 971	59.4	12.9	17.5	8.9	1.3	4 166	84.1	835	92.3
51 740	5720	Portsmouth city	93 508	51.4	23.4	14.2	10.0	1.0	38 170	58.5	9 434	75.8
51 750	...	Radford city	15 267	31.6	8.2	43.8	14.4	2.1	5 809	44.5	1 065	73.2
51 760	6760	Richmond city................	185 379	48.0	25.3	15.7	8.7	2.3	84 549	46.1	18 247	64.3
51 770	6800	Roanoke city	88 721	53.4	24.4	12.7	8.0	1.4	42 003	56.3	10 404	71.4
51 775	6800	Salem city.....................	23 542	56.3	10.4	23.3	9.1	1.0	9 954	67.6	2 471	79.3
51 790	...	Staunton city	22 570	55.1	6.9	30.5	7.0	0.5	9 676	61.4	2 777	73.5
51 800	5720	Suffolk city	59 081	53.4	17.5	18.5	9.7	1.0	23 283	72.2	4 870	81.7
51 810	5720	Virginia Beach city	394 892	45.8	24.3	8.6	18.3	2.9	154 455	65.6	22 067	78.9
51 820	...	Waynesboro city............	18 289	52.0	8.3	30.0	8.5	1.1	8 332	61.2	2 129	83.5
51 830	5720	Williamsburg city	11 675	28.0	6.3	37.9	24.7	3.1	3 619	44.3	939	78.7
51 840	...	Winchester city.............	22 146	44.1	8.7	29.0	14.8	3.4	10 001	45.7	2 260	67.9
53 000	...	WASHINGTON..........	5 501 398	48.6	27.5	9.5	11.2	3.2	2 271 398	64.6	430 394	77.2
53 001	...	Adams County..............	14 873	56.4	22.0	10.9	5.2	5.5	5 229	68.4	1 154	86.0
53 003	...	Asotin County...............	19 148	51.7	21.2	6.8	20.1	0.2	8 364	67.1	2 246	79.9
53 005	6740	Benton County...............	131 802	51.2	25.5	10.9	10.3	2.2	52 866	68.8	10 280	79.4
53 007	...	Chelan County..............	61 879	51.9	25.8	12.9	6.3	3.0	25 021	64.6	6 459	74.3
53 009	...	Clallam County.............	61 211	54.3	23.7	9.3	11.4	1.2	27 164	72.8	9 158	83.7
53 011	6440	Clark County.................	318 152	44.2	28.5	5.4	18.8	3.1	127 208	67.3	21 134	79.2
53 013	...	Columbia County...........	3 836	58.1	18.6	13.9	8.9	0.5	1 687	69.6	453	81.0
53 015	...	Cowlitz County..............	86 502	52.6	29.6	7.2	9.7	1.0	35 850	67.6	8 098	78.4
53 017	...	Douglas County.............	30 179	54.4	17.5	20.5	5.2	2.4	11 726	71.0	2 675	86.6
53 019	...	Ferry County.................	6 869	54.9	19.2	17.5	8.1	0.3	2 823	73.0	673	84.8
53 021	6740	Franklin County.............	44 504	49.0	23.6	13.0	7.8	6.5	14 840	65.7	2 667	80.1
53 023	...	Garfield County.............	2 288	62.9	16.8	12.6	7.0	0.7	987	73.8	326	86.2
53 025	...	Grant County.................	68 214	50.0	26.9	11.0	7.4	4.7	25 204	66.7	5 612	78.7
53 027	...	Grays Harbor County	62 955	56.7	25.8	10.7	5.7	1.2	26 808	69.1	7 055	83.8
53 029	7600	Island County...............	66 796	46.5	16.0	13.6	21.1	2.7	27 784	70.1	6 525	87.9
53 031	...	Jefferson County..........	24 902	52.9	17.3	15.4	12.9	1.6	11 645	76.1	3 661	88.3
53 033	7600	King County..................	1 632 553	47.6	30.0	6.0	11.7	4.7	710 916	59.8	117 256	73.0
53 035	1150	Kitsap County...............	216 823	48.7	23.4	9.1	16.6	2.2	86 416	67.4	15 495	78.7
53 037	...	Kittitas County..............	31 673	44.0	18.7	27.7	7.4	2.1	13 382	58.3	2 796	79.7
53 039	...	Klickitat County.............	17 977	53.3	21.8	10.5	12.9	1.5	7 473	68.8	1 864	79.7
53 041	...	Lewis County.................	64 103	55.0	20.0	12.1	7.4	1.4	26 306	71.4	7 166	80.3
53 043	...	Lincoln County..............	9 607	59.0	15.4	17.8	6.8	1.0	4 151	76.6	1 194	86.6
53 045	...	Mason County...............	46 757	53.8	17.2	20.1	7.8	1.1	18 912	79.0	5 074	89.1
53 047	...	Okanogan County	37 051	54.4	24.6	13.2	5.5	2.3	15 027	68.6	3 696	81.9
53 049	...	Pacific County...............	20 055	57.0	20.7	12.1	8.9	1.3	9 096	74.7	3 155	84.1
53 051	...	Pend Oreille County......	11 093	59.0	15.9	15.7	8.8	0.6	4 639	77.4	1 195	85.3
53 053	8200	Pierce County...............	651 081	46.9	28.3	10.4	11.3	3.1	260 800	63.5	46 221	77.3
53 055	...	San Juan County	13 539	50.1	19.6	14.0	15.0	1.3	6 466	73.6	1 669	84.7
53 057	...	Skagit County...............	96 277	50.2	25.8	12.6	8.7	2.7	38 852	69.7	9 873	80.4
53 059	...	Skamania County..........	9 222	53.0	17.7	14.9	13.8	0.7	3 755	73.9	712	87.6
53 061	7600	Snohomish County.......	562 924	47.0	27.0	13.6	9.6	2.8	224 852	67.7	35 095	76.0
53 063	7840	Spokane County...........	390 366	50.8	29.5	7.4	10.2	2.0	163 611	65.5	33 749	76.0
53 065	...	Stevens County............	37 615	56.5	17.6	15.8	9.4	0.7	15 017	78.1	3 420	82.3
53 067	5910	Thurston County...........	194 657	48.1	25.7	12.3	11.7	2.1	81 625	66.6	15 512	78.8
53 069	...	Wahkiakum County	3 615	62.2	12.3	16.3	9.2	0.0	1 553	79.7	433	87.8
53 071	...	Walla Walla County.......	51 741	51.1	23.5	10.5	11.5	3.4	19 647	65.2	5 445	75.3
53 073	0860	Whatcom County..........	156 441	45.4	28.0	14.0	9.8	2.8	64 446	63.4	12 565	76.6
53 075	...	Whitman County...........	38 789	38.0	14.4	31.6	11.7	4.3	15 257	47.8	2 519	79.1
53 077	9260	Yakima County..............	203 449	53.8	32.7	5.2	5.5	2.7	73 993	64.4	16 114	76.6
54 000	...	WEST VIRGINIA........	1 706 931	63.3	21.0	7.0	8.1	0.5	736 481	75.2	190 182	84.0
54 001	...	Barbour County............	14 733	67.0	17.0	9.3	6.3	0.3	6 123	78.5	1 734	86.6
54 003	8840	Berkeley County............	70 990	54.7	22.6	5.7	16.5	0.5	29 569	74.1	5 634	80.7
54 005	...	Boone County...............	23 909	66.4	21.0	8.1	4.3	0.2	10 291	78.9	2 482	87.0

[1]MSA = Metropolitan Statistical Area. PMSA = Primary MSA. NECMA = New England County Metropolitan Area. See the Appendix A for explanation of these concepts. See Appendix B for list of metropolitan areas identified by type, with component counties.

Table C-3. States and Counties — Migration, Housing, and Transportation

STATE County	Owner-occupied by household type (percent)								Median household income			Median housing value (owner estimated)	Median monthly owner costs as a percent of income	
	Family-households					Nonfamily households								
		Married-couple family		Other family										
	Total family households	Total	With own children under 18 years	Total	With own children under 18 years	Total nonfamily households	Two or more adults	Living alone	All households	Owner-occupied households	Renter-occupied households		With a mortgage	Without a mortgage
	11	12	13	14	15	16	17	18	19	20	21	22	23	24
VIRGINIA—Cont'd														
Manassas city	76.6	81.4	80.9	58.5	54.8	52.1	52.3	52.1	60 609	72 208	41 095	148 600	21.2	9.9
Manassas Park city	79.0	83.3	82.9	67.0	64.5	77.6	62.6	84.4	60 897	62 772	52 171	115 700	24.3	12.9
Martinsville city	65.9	77.5	71.4	44.7	30.9	50.9	40.5	52.0	27 604	35 567	18 713	69 400	20.3	9.9
Newport News city	58.8	70.8	62.5	34.1	22.3	39.4	31.5	41.2	36 503	50 080	25 508	94 200	22.9	10.5
Norfolk city	51.9	65.7	56.1	29.9	18.3	35.8	26.7	38.7	31 566	45 868	22 961	88 300	24.0	12.2
Norton city	66.0	78.3	64.5	38.9	23.9	39.6	54.5	38.2	23 893	35 078	13 265	53 800	19.6	9.9
Petersburg city	57.3	72.7	55.9	41.6	23.4	42.2	32.6	44.0	28 696	40 017	21 500	68 100	23.1	11.5
Poquoson city	84.9	88.3	82.5	63.3	50.2	80.5	62.8	83.7	60 668	62 533	40 786	149 800	22.1	10.9
Portsmouth city	63.2	78.5	72.2	38.2	24.1	49.1	42.5	50.3	33 712	43 505	22 591	81 000	23.5	12.6
Radford city	71.2	80.6	83.5	38.4	16.7	22.5	6.0	34.1	24 346	46 350	13 550	93 100	17.8	9.9
Richmond city	55.5	74.3	68.2	34.5	20.6	36.0	29.9	37.6	30 934	47 481	21 534	87 400	22.3	12.4
Roanoke city	64.8	77.2	70.5	41.7	26.2	44.5	36.1	45.9	30 681	40 232	21 229	80 100	21.2	9.9
Salem city	75.2	80.7	76.1	54.8	39.6	52.7	48.1	53.5	39 464	46 830	26 954	99 200	20.0	9.9
Staunton city	72.9	82.5	74.9	43.2	36.2	44.1	37.6	45.1	32 949	44 152	21 693	88 000	20.4	9.9
Suffolk city	74.9	86.8	83.7	44.8	31.8	63.8	62.7	64.0	40 533	49 461	21 423	104 500	24.0	11.0
Virginia Beach city	71.5	77.0	72.2	52.0	44.3	49.9	38.4	54.1	48 700	58 460	34 231	121 500	23.9	10.1
Waynesboro city	66.5	77.9	62.4	35.3	25.6	50.8	22.9	54.4	33 333	41 976	23 017	88 500	21.1	9.9
Williamsburg city	60.6	67.8	64.6	37.1	17.3	27.7	9.9	34.3	37 859	57 755	28 142	182 000	20.4	9.9
Winchester city	56.8	66.5	58.4	31.5	22.5	31.2	18.9	34.3	34 427	49 322	26 543	109 800	21.3	9.9
WASHINGTON	73.5	80.2	75.6	47.7	39.2	47.1	39.3	49.4	45 610	56 307	29 853	158 800	23.8	10.4
Adams County	70.5	75.9	69.5	49.1	37.3	60.4	59.0	60.6	33 423	39 316	24 646	79 500	23.0	10.6
Asotin County	71.0	80.4	70.4	40.7	30.1	58.8	44.5	61.5	33 519	41 629	21 711	96 600	20.8	9.9
Benton County	75.6	82.0	77.3	50.1	42.5	51.1	40.5	53.2	46 624	57 353	29 217	111 200	19.8	9.9
Chelan County	71.5	77.7	68.8	41.2	30.0	48.9	43.2	50.1	37 120	48 121	24 060	143 400	24.1	10.8
Clallam County	79.4	85.0	75.4	54.1	42.1	59.5	51.5	61.0	36 429	41 907	23 172	125 200	23.7	9.9
Clark County	73.0	80.4	75.3	44.7	35.0	52.7	45.1	55.0	48 150	57 569	31 743	153 100	24.4	9.9
Columbia County	74.1	79.6	66.1	44.4	33.9	59.9	62.7	59.6	35 337	43 333	22 240	85 500	21.1	10.4
Cowlitz County	73.9	81.9	74.1	44.2	36.4	53.0	47.1	54.4	39 343	48 297	23 941	125 100	22.1	9.9
Douglas County	73.9	80.0	71.3	44.6	36.6	61.8	57.6	62.7	38 950	45 853	25 924	127 100	23.3	9.9
Ferry County	75.3	81.0	68.1	55.1	42.6	67.3	76.5	65.6	30 353	34 180	20 313	87 200	20.8	9.9
Franklin County	69.2	75.9	68.3	46.0	39.3	53.2	53.5	53.1	39 049	49 175	21 361	95 200	20.8	9.9
Garfield County	78.9	81.7	67.5	66.1	54.2	63.0	55.6	64.0	32 452	36 442	23 472	70 800	20.5	10.8
Grant County	71.0	76.6	67.7	48.2	43.0	53.8	48.9	54.8	35 277	40 939	23 619	93 300	21.7	9.9
Grays Harbor County	74.5	83.1	74.5	47.6	35.8	57.9	47.2	60.4	34 102	40 532	21 896	93 500	22.2	11.1
Island County	74.3	77.4	66.2	54.5	45.2	58.8	53.4	60.3	45 366	52 950	30 280	168 400	25.1	9.9
Jefferson County	81.9	88.5	78.9	53.0	44.8	65.2	62.9	65.7	38 171	43 384	22 013	157 400	25.3	11.9
King County	72.7	79.4	78.1	47.1	38.4	41.2	35.5	43.0	52 896	69 052	34 700	226 400	23.9	10.9
Kitsap County	73.9	79.5	73.0	49.4	41.0	51.4	45.4	53.1	46 897	56 791	30 244	145 200	23.8	10.5
Kittitas County	74.1	79.5	70.9	49.1	42.0	36.1	17.9	44.6	32 237	47 043	15 053	134 100	22.2	10.9
Klickitat County	74.9	80.5	68.2	48.2	33.4	52.9	45.8	54.2	34 457	40 185	22 764	111 300	24.1	10.4
Lewis County	76.2	82.4	74.7	50.1	40.3	60.0	53.9	61.3	35 178	41 027	22 920	114 200	23.3	11.1
Lincoln County	79.1	82.2	70.5	57.1	50.2	70.7	64.5	71.7	35 206	38 518	24 464	84 400	22.5	9.9
Mason County	82.6	88.2	79.4	58.0	48.6	70.5	62.3	72.5	39 686	42 964	26 095	120 400	23.3	9.9
Okanogan County	73.3	79.1	67.8	53.7	44.0	57.3	61.1	56.6	29 907	35 221	19 181	90 300	22.0	9.9
Pacific County	79.0	83.5	69.3	53.7	45.2	66.9	56.9	68.8	31 307	34 786	20 915	96 200	24.8	10.8
Pend Oreille County	81.6	88.0	82.9	51.2	45.5	67.2	57.4	68.9	31 360	35 950	17 625	104 100	23.3	9.9
Pierce County	70.3	77.8	72.3	45.5	37.1	48.1	44.3	49.1	44 853	56 286	28 819	144 400	24.4	11.1
San Juan County	80.7	84.9	77.7	57.2	53.7	61.9	57.0	63.0	43 344	48 489	30 453	286 400	28.8	11.9
Skagit County	75.6	81.9	74.1	49.0	39.6	55.7	51.2	56.9	42 442	49 881	28 670	152 900	24.9	11.2
Skamania County	76.4	81.2	76.7	55.5	45.1	67.2	71.7	66.0	39 248	44 855	26 182	144 400	23.2	10.8
Snohomish County	74.8	81.3	79.4	48.9	41.1	50.8	44.6	52.7	52 915	62 915	35 072	188 600	24.6	10.5
Spokane County	75.4	82.9	79.1	49.5	41.5	47.0	35.9	49.6	37 191	47 420	22 696	111 200	23.0	10.0
Stevens County	81.9	86.9	81.8	51.2	50.7	67.6	67.3	67.7	34 524	39 265	20 068	107 800	23.7	10.1
Thurston County	75.2	81.7	76.8	50.6	41.8	48.8	40.4	51.3	46 929	56 353	30 161	138 800	23.2	9.9
Wahkiakum County	85.8	90.1	82.0	62.4	51.3	64.3	54.7	65.9	38 987	41 951	29 028	133 700	20.9	10.4
Walla Walla County	74.1	80.6	71.8	48.0	39.8	46.7	31.5	49.7	35 198	45 869	20 027	109 100	22.2	10.1
Whatcom County	75.4	81.6	77.2	48.6	42.5	42.1	24.3	49.4	40 207	50 466	24 835	149 500	24.3	10.9
Whitman County	68.6	72.6	66.1	45.9	43.2	24.4	8.0	34.3	28 796	49 649	16 367	110 100	20.5	9.9
Yakima County	69.2	76.7	68.0	44.5	35.1	51.0	43.6	52.5	34 879	44 261	22 760	107 200	23.1	9.9
WEST VIRGINIA	81.6	86.6	81.9	62.6	49.3	61.0	47.7	63.1	29 663	34 632	16 794	66 000	19.5	9.9
Barbour County	82.2	85.5	78.7	68.9	52.2	69.7	52.0	72.6	24 389	27 882	12 899	53 000	19.9	9.9
Berkeley County	80.1	85.7	81.6	60.8	54.2	60.1	59.7	60.2	38 492	44 100	24 668	91 000	20.7	9.9
Boone County	82.4	87.2	81.0	64.4	51.1	69.5	76.1	68.9	25 416	29 060	16 296	52 100	19.8	9.9

STATE County	Median gross rent	Percent who pay 35 percent or more of income for housing expenses		Number of workers 16 years and over	Means of transportation to work (percent except where noted)					Vehicles available (percent of households)		
		Owners	Renters		Car, truck, or van		Public transportation	Other means	Walked	No vehicles	One vehicle	Two or more vehicles
					Drove alone	Carpooled						
	25	26	27	28	29	30	31	32	33	34	35	36
VIRGINIA—Cont'd												
Manassas city	801	14.5	22.0	18 145	75.1	16.5	3.0	1.3	1.7	4.7	28.5	66.9
Manassas Park city.......	930	18.9	24.4	5 503	72.8	18.4	2.3	2.7	0.9	4.0	23.4	72.6
Martinsville city	401	15.6	28.9	6 025	78.2	17.4	0.5	0.4	1.5	14.7	40.8	44.5
Newport News city	559	16.8	27.3	86 282	78.7	13.0	2.8	1.2	2.7	11.4	37.3	51.3
Norfolk city	538	21.0	32.1	112 083	66.8	14.2	4.6	3.8	6.8	17.0	41.4	41.6
Norton city	347	12.5	20.3	1 455	77.6	14.3	0.4	1.4	4.0	15.0	40.1	44.9
Petersburg city	495	21.1	30.2	13 176	73.4	18.7	3.3	1.3	2.1	20.9	39.8	39.3
Poquoson city	697	11.9	28.3	5 658	87.8	7.2	0.1	0.9	0.8	2.8	18.8	78.4
Portsmouth city	540	19.8	33.1	43 922	72.8	15.6	3.0	2.5	3.3	14.5	38.5	47.0
Radford city	437	7.2	41.1	6 968	75.0	8.9	0.4	0.7	12.6	8.8	35.0	56.2
Richmond city	540	19.4	33.5	88 924	70.6	12.6	8.3	1.9	4.4	21.6	42.2	36.1
Roanoke city	448	15.2	27.0	43 694	79.7	12.4	3.1	1.2	1.8	12.7	41.2	46.1
Salem city	550	10.9	24.6	12 188	84.2	9.0	0.3	0.7	4.2	6.0	34.2	59.9
Staunton city	466	12.5	24.0	10 913	80.1	12.4	0.2	1.0	3.7	10.1	37.1	52.8
Suffolk city	506	19.0	31.9	28 372	80.4	13.7	1.2	1.7	1.3	10.3	29.6	60.1
Virginia Beach city	734	18.5	27.7	222 648	82.0	10.8	0.7	1.7	2.0	4.7	31.0	64.3
Waynesboro city...........	469	12.8	26.9	8 541	81.9	12.3	0.6	1.6	1.9	9.9	36.5	53.6
Williamsburg city	616	15.0	31.9	4 239	66.6	9.5	1.5	3.2	15.1	10.2	44.6	45.2
Winchester city	547	10.6	26.8	11 917	72.2	17.0	1.9	0.9	4.8	12.3	39.1	48.5
WASHINGTON...........	663	18.1	30.8	2 785 479	73.3	12.8	4.9	1.4	3.2	7.4	31.7	60.8
Adams County..............	430	16.2	21.1	6 373	69.0	18.7	0.1	1.9	4.9	7.5	26.3	66.1
Asotin County...............	494	13.4	31.2	9 067	82.3	9.3	0.1	1.0	2.3	6.1	31.0	62.9
Benton County..............	566	11.6	26.5	65 348	80.2	12.6	1.0	1.1	1.6	5.4	28.4	66.2
Chelan County..............	535	18.4	30.5	27 978	73.5	14.0	1.1	1.5	4.5	7.8	30.0	62.1
Clallam County.............	532	15.9	35.0	24 125	74.0	14.0	1.4	1.6	3.5	6.9	32.9	60.2
Clark County................	684	18.9	31.2	161 471	79.3	11.2	2.6	1.1	1.4	5.7	29.5	64.8
Columbia County...........	467	14.1	20.9	1 699	76.0	11.2	0.5	0.5	6.9	7.7	25.7	66.6
Cowlitz County.............	518	14.6	32.7	39 330	81.6	11.6	0.4	1.3	2.3	7.5	29.3	63.2
Douglas County............	545	17.1	25.4	13 981	75.4	14.2	0.7	1.7	3.5	4.5	27.9	67.6
Ferry County................	380	14.0	23.4	2 572	68.9	13.3	0.4	1.0	8.5	6.3	29.5	64.3
Franklin County	464	13.3	29.4	19 115	60.6	21.1	1.3	1.6	2.1	7.4	28.0	63.8
Garfield County.............	390	11.9	23.4	962	78.5	7.5	0.0	1.0	7.6	4.6	33.1	62.3
Grant County................	476	14.8	25.0	28 809	73.0	17.3	0.6	1.3	3.1	5.8	29.1	65.1
Grays Harbor County	500	16.2	32.8	27 036	75.8	13.6	1.4	1.1	3.9	9.6	31.5	58.9
Island County...............	684	19.6	25.1	32 538	73.6	13.3	2.2	1.7	3.8	3.6	28.2	68.1
Jefferson County	595	19.3	32.3	10 626	68.8	11.5	1.2	3.4	5.4	5.3	31.8	62.9
King County.................	758	19.1	29.8	911 677	68.7	12.0	9.6	1.6	3.6	9.3	35.4	55.3
Kitsap County...............	667	18.3	29.2	106 877	66.3	14.6	8.7	2.3	3.8	4.6	28.6	64.6
Kittitas County..............	407	14.6	46.6	15 200	68.4	14.2	0.5	2.0	8.2	6.7	30.6	62.8
Klickitat County............	498	18.8	29.7	7 664	71.8	15.4	0.7	1.4	4.5	7.8	25.3	66.9
Lewis County................	551	16.2	36.8	26 390	78.8	12.3	0.3	1.0	2.8	6.2	27.3	66.5
Lincoln County	438	13.9	21.7	4 125	71.1	9.8	0.2	1.0	7.9	5.5	23.9	70.6
Mason County...............	579	16.7	29.4	19 037	74.2	16.9	1.2	1.6	1.8	4.4	26.9	68.7
Okanogan County	423	16.7	27.0	15 031	70.3	14.1	0.5	1.4	5.6	6.4	30.7	62.9
Pacific County..............	483	20.0	28.6	7 887	73.7	13.9	0.6	1.8	4.3	7.4	34.4	58.2
Pend Oreille County......	422	15.9	29.8	3 965	72.1	13.9	0.1	1.2	5.9	5.8	26.9	67.3
Pierce County...............	624	19.8	30.8	324 285	76.4	13.3	2.7	1.2	2.9	7.0	31.3	61.7
San Juan County	607	24.4	27.2	6 350	61.9	10.9	2.1	2.5	8.9	4.5	31.5	63.9
Skagit County	668	18.6	32.2	45 453	77.1	13.1	1.0	1.1	3.0	5.8	27.7	66.5
Skamania County..........	579	16.7	32.3	4 261	76.0	14.8	0.5	0.8	2.3	3.5	23.7	72.8
Snohomish County........	766	19.4	28.8	299 861	75.2	14.1	3.9	0.9	1.9	4.9	28.9	66.2
Spokane County...........	532	16.8	33.2	191 195	76.7	12.3	2.8	1.2	2.8	8.8	32.7	58.6
Stevens County............	453	17.6	31.1	15 273	74.6	13.5	0.2	1.0	4.1	5.3	24.6	70.1
Thurston County...........	655	15.9	31.0	100 986	77.2	12.7	2.2	1.4	2.8	6.3	29.8	63.9
Wahkiakum County	519	11.3	26.8	1 532	67.9	22.9	0.3	0.5	4.8	4.4	23.2	72.3
Walla Walla County.......	487	14.6	35.7	23 240	73.0	12.6	0.7	2.3	7.9	8.1	32.9	59.0
Whatcom County...........	622	18.2	38.1	79 263	75.9	10.6	2.0	2.4	4.1	6.7	31.0	62.3
Whitman County............	482	12.2	47.1	18 305	58.1	14.0	5.0	2.1	15.8	7.0	37.5	55.6
Yakima County.............	534	16.2	31.9	86 583	77.5	14.4	0.5	1.4	2.6	7.7	29.7	62.6
WEST VIRGINIA	401	11.9	28.3	718 106	80.3	12.7	0.8	0.9	2.9	10.8	35.4	53.7
Barbour County	330	12.2	28.7	5 984	77.6	13.2	0.2	1.1	4.6	10.5	32.7	56.9
Berkeley County...........	506	12.7	23.7	35 659	80.8	13.8	0.8	1.1	1.7	7.0	32.2	60.8
Boone County	353	15.4	24.3	8 511	83.5	12.6	0.2	0.4	2.2	12.4	35.1	52.5

STATE/ County code	MSA/PMSA/ NECMA code[1]	STATE County	Residence in 1995 (percent)						Occupied housing units		Householders 65 years and over	
			Total population 5 years and over	Same house	Same county, different house	Same state, different county	Different state	Outside the United States	Number	Percent owner-occupied	Number	Percent owner-occupied
			1	2	3	4	5	6	7	8	9	10
		WEST VIRGINIA— Cont'd										
54 007	...	Braxton County	13 961	66.5	19.8	7.7	6.0	0.1	5 771	78.1	1 575	81.4
54 009	8080	Brooke County	24 211	68.8	16.4	5.9	8.6	0.4	10 396	76.6	3 126	81.1
54 011	3400	Cabell County	91 451	56.2	24.7	9.8	8.7	0.7	41 180	64.6	10 709	79.2
54 013	...	Calhoun County	7 199	70.1	14.2	6.7	8.9	0.0	3 071	79.0	854	86.8
54 015	...	Clay County	9 705	66.0	18.7	8.8	6.4	0.1	4 020	79.1	1 038	85.9
54 017	...	Doddridge County	6 958	68.8	9.5	15.9	5.6	0.2	2 845	81.3	761	89.0
54 019	...	Fayette County	44 866	63.7	20.6	8.6	6.5	0.6	18 945	77.2	5 457	88.1
54 021	...	Gilmer County	6 798	57.0	18.6	16.0	7.7	0.7	2 768	72.3	738	87.3
54 023	...	Grant County	10 578	69.5	16.8	7.0	6.2	0.6	4 591	80.8	1 188	83.7
54 025	...	Greenbrier County	32 584	64.3	21.3	6.6	7.6	0.2	14 571	76.5	4 166	84.9
54 027	...	Hampshire County	18 931	66.7	15.1	5.5	12.4	0.3	7 955	81.1	1 943	82.4
54 029	8080	Hancock County	30 950	67.8	19.4	4.5	8.0	0.2	13 678	77.0	3 852	85.6
54 031	...	Hardy County	11 917	64.6	18.6	6.8	9.8	0.2	5 204	80.5	1 220	79.8
54 033	...	Harrison County	64 791	65.1	22.9	5.4	6.0	0.6	27 867	74.8	8 022	84.7
54 035	...	Jackson County	26 323	63.0	21.6	8.8	6.3	0.3	11 061	79.5	2 897	84.9
54 037	8840	Jefferson County	39 552	56.3	18.3	4.6	19.9	0.9	16 165	75.9	3 223	83.0
54 039	1480	Kanawha County	188 674	62.7	25.3	5.8	5.6	0.5	86 226	70.3	22 775	81.2
54 041	...	Lewis County	16 027	62.6	22.5	9.0	5.5	0.3	6 946	73.0	1 919	81.0
54 043	...	Lincoln County	20 779	69.8	18.4	7.4	4.1	0.3	8 664	79.0	2 002	83.3
54 045	...	Logan County	35 564	69.0	21.5	5.6	3.6	0.3	14 880	76.8	4 029	88.7
54 047	...	McDowell County	25 908	75.7	17.8	2.6	3.8	0.2	11 169	79.8	3 115	85.5
54 049	...	Marion County	53 756	65.4	21.3	7.3	5.5	0.5	23 652	74.7	6 838	86.1
54 051	9000	Marshall County	33 618	69.4	19.2	5.6	5.7	0.1	14 207	77.5	3 873	82.3
54 053	...	Mason County	24 482	66.6	21.5	4.9	6.9	0.1	10 587	80.9	2 584	87.2
54 055	...	Mercer County	59 323	63.5	23.1	5.2	8.0	0.2	26 509	76.9	7 976	85.2
54 057	1900	Mineral County	25 587	66.9	19.1	4.0	9.6	0.4	10 784	77.8	2 739	81.2
54 059	...	Mingo County	26 622	72.1	19.5	3.3	5.0	0.1	11 303	77.8	2 624	82.5
54 061	...	Monongalia County	77 809	49.8	18.7	13.2	16.4	2.0	33 446	61.0	5 916	83.6
54 063	...	Monroe County	13 851	63.3	13.3	7.5	15.6	0.3	5 447	84.4	1 629	93.2
54 065	...	Morgan County	14 059	62.1	15.3	4.6	17.4	0.5	6 145	83.3	1 579	91.1
54 067	...	Nicholas County	25 134	68.3	19.4	7.4	4.8	0.2	10 722	82.9	2 840	88.7
54 069	9000	Ohio County	44 988	62.1	20.6	6.4	10.2	0.6	19 733	68.6	5 989	75.7
54 071	...	Pendleton County	7 782	69.7	13.2	5.0	10.3	1.6	3 350	79.2	918	86.2
54 073	...	Pleasants County	7 068	64.3	19.3	10.0	6.0	0.4	2 887	80.5	746	85.7
54 075	...	Pocahontas County.......	8 686	64.3	19.8	6.2	9.3	0.4	3 835	80.3	1 028	87.2
54 077	...	Preston County	27 731	69.9	18.7	5.1	6.0	0.2	11 544	83.1	2 936	87.5
54 079	1480	Putnam County	48 234	59.5	18.4	14.1	7.7	0.4	20 028	84.0	3 862	89.6
54 081	...	Raleigh County	74 888	62.4	22.1	6.4	8.6	0.6	31 793	76.5	8 308	86.5
54 083	...	Randolph County	26 794	63.6	20.5	7.7	7.6	0.6	11 072	75.8	2 989	82.2
54 085	...	Ritchie County	9 772	68.8	18.3	7.3	5.6	0.1	4 184	81.7	1 171	88.6
54 087	...	Roane County	14 551	62.4	20.4	9.9	7.1	0.3	6 161	79.6	1 567	85.6
54 089	...	Summers County	12 395	67.2	17.1	7.1	6.2	0.2	5 530	79.1	1 737	81.8
54 091	...	Taylor County	15 239	67.4	15.2	11.7	5.5	0.2	6 320	79.6	1 692	87.2
54 093	...	Tucker County	6 982	73.6	16.3	6.3	3.7	0.2	3 052	82.5	937	86.0
54 095	...	Tyler County	9 092	66.6	16.0	10.9	6.2	0.3	3 836	83.7	1 119	88.5
54 097	...	Upshur County	22 149	62.3	21.7	7.3	8.3	0.4	8 972	76.7	2 291	86.7
54 099	3400	Wayne County	40 413	66.9	18.7	7.6	6.3	0.5	17 239	78.1	4 477	84.8
54 101	...	Webster County	9 200	69.5	18.8	3.9	7.7	0.2	4 010	79.1	1 076	86.4
54 103	...	Wetzel County	16 712	67.5	20.5	6.7	5.2	0.1	7 164	78.5	1 989	85.1
54 105	...	Wirt County	5 552	61.9	18.8	14.0	5.3	0.0	2 284	83.1	508	83.3
54 107	6020	Wood County	82 863	59.7	27.6	4.3	8.0	0.4	36 275	73.4	9 323	81.5
54 109	...	Wyoming County..........	24 240	75.2	16.5	5.1	3.1	0.1	10 454	83.3	2 462	90.8
55 000	...	WISCONSIN..............	5 022 073	56.5	24.6	11.0	6.7	1.3	2 084 544	68.4	457 976	74.7
55 001	...	Adams County.............	17 740	59.4	11.3	21.4	7.6	0.2	7 900	85.4	2 605	90.2
55 003	...	Ashland County	15 809	62.3	19.6	8.9	8.9	0.3	6 718	70.6	1 830	69.9
55 005	...	Barron County	42 437	58.1	24.0	10.6	6.8	0.5	17 851	75.9	4 787	76.5
55 007	...	Bayfield County	14 209	66.5	14.4	11.1	7.4	0.6	6 207	82.6	1 680	85.7
55 009	3080	Brown County	211 086	53.3	29.0	9.7	6.4	1.6	87 295	65.4	16 223	72.2
55 011	...	Buffalo County	12 993	66.4	15.0	10.4	7.9	0.3	5 511	76.5	1 475	76.9
55 013	...	Burnett County	14 893	62.6	14.4	8.5	14.0	0.6	6 613	84.5	2 053	86.9
55 015	0460	Calumet County	37 779	61.3	14.8	18.8	4.5	0.6	14 910	80.4	2 682	81.4
55 017	2290	Chippewa County..........	51 801	62.7	20.6	11.7	4.6	0.4	21 356	75.6	5 107	78.1
55 019	...	Clark County	31 013	66.3	16.9	11.3	5.0	0.5	12 047	81.3	3 453	81.0
55 021	...	Columbia County	49 239	59.1	18.4	17.2	4.8	0.5	20 439	74.9	4 858	76.0
55 023	...	Crawford County	16 226	62.0	18.0	11.0	8.8	0.1	6 677	76.9	1 845	80.1

[1]MSA = Metropolitan Statistical Area. PMSA = Primary MSA. NECMA = New England County Metropolitan Area. See the Appendix A for explanation of these concepts. See Appendix B for list of metropolitan areas identified by type, with component counties.

STATE County	Owner-occupied by household type (percent)								Median household income			Median monthly owner costs as a percent of income		
	Family-households					Nonfamily households								
		Married-couple family		Other family										
	Total family households	Total	With own children under 18 years	Total	With own children under 18 years	Total nonfamily households	Two or more adults	Living alone	All households	Owner-occupied households	Renter-occupied households	Median housing value (owner estimated)	With a mortgage	Without a mortgage
	11	12	13	14	15	16	17	18	19	20	21	22	23	24
WEST VIRGINIA— Cont'd														
Braxton County	81.3	82.4	75.1	76.3	68.5	70.4	76.9	69.4	24 136	26 677	15 250	52 300	19.5	9.9
Brooke County	84.1	88.8	83.8	65.0	41.5	60.0	76.8	58.2	32 882	37 417	18 896	64 700	19.2	9.9
Cabell County	76.0	83.2	78.2	52.1	40.5	45.8	24.4	50.2	28 778	37 470	15 580	72 800	19.4	9.9
Calhoun County	83.1	83.4	80.9	81.5	68.6	68.1	69.3	67.9	21 770	24 256	13 729	44 800	20.8	9.9
Clay County	83.9	87.9	84.1	69.1	58.4	65.1	74.5	64.6	22 255	26 421	11 673	47 300	21.2	9.9
Doddridge County	84.0	88.6	82.8	66.0	54.3	73.5	83.3	71.8	26 968	29 896	16 178	55 700	18.4	9.9
Fayette County	80.9	86.0	79.7	65.3	49.4	68.7	53.1	70.8	25 032	28 326	14 020	48 100	19.4	10.4
Gilmer County	79.4	85.1	80.4	57.1	50.2	57.8	22.0	68.8	22 945	26 563	13 958	59 600	20.2	10.0
Grant County	86.5	90.2	85.4	68.4	54.2	66.6	56.8	68.3	28 679	31 811	18 714	72 200	21.7	9.9
Greenbrier County........	81.9	86.4	83.5	65.3	53.7	65.1	53.7	66.3	26 778	30 959	14 404	67 300	20.6	9.9
Hampshire County	84.3	88.6	85.8	67.0	56.3	73.0	73.4	73.0	31 450	34 598	20 725	71 200	19.5	9.9
Hancock County	82.3	86.7	82.5	66.4	46.7	64.5	58.3	65.3	33 818	38 223	22 380	67 500	18.9	9.9
Hardy County	86.1	89.4	87.1	70.6	62.0	68.3	69.2	68.2	32 357	35 672	19 590	70 900	19.5	9.9
Harrison County	80.3	85.4	79.9	61.8	48.4	62.5	49.5	64.1	30 304	34 855	17 526	64 700	19.9	10.2
Jackson County............	82.9	87.1	83.7	63.6	47.2	69.7	78.0	68.7	32 337	36 880	16 151	72 000	18.5	9.9
Jefferson County	81.8	87.2	82.6	60.4	49.5	61.8	56.5	63.3	44 325	51 816	24 282	110 500	20.4	9.9
Kanawha County..........	78.1	84.8	79.7	57.1	41.4	55.9	44.9	57.4	33 635	40 502	20 954	75 000	18.3	9.9
Lewis County...............	78.8	83.2	75.8	60.9	47.8	59.8	60.5	59.7	26 926	31 132	14 475	60 700	20.9	9.9
Lincoln County	82.9	86.6	81.3	68.0	57.0	67.0	71.9	66.6	22 738	26 730	11 516	53 600	19.7	9.9
Logan County	79.3	83.5	77.5	64.8	44.5	69.7	62.5	70.3	24 545	28 067	13 910	55 200	21.4	10.2
McDowell County	83.2	87.7	83.0	70.6	59.8	71.7	79.2	71.1	16 922	19 110	10 166	20 800	22.9	11.7
Marion County	82.2	87.4	82.0	61.6	46.7	60.3	37.2	64.5	28 552	33 922	16 077	60 400	19.0	9.9
Marshall County	84.1	88.7	83.4	65.4	49.6	61.1	56.7	61.6	31 318	37 102	15 306	60 500	17.6	9.9
Mason County	84.1	88.6	84.3	64.2	57.7	72.7	75.3	72.5	26 896	31 308	11 455	58 200	19.1	9.9
Mercer County	82.2	86.7	80.8	66.0	52.5	65.7	47.5	67.9	26 690	30 946	16 013	56 200	19.1	9.9
Mineral County	82.9	87.7	82.2	62.4	49.0	65.2	52.0	67.1	31 039	35 038	18 532	69 700	19.8	9.9
Mingo County	82.3	85.7	79.4	69.8	55.2	65.6	74.8	65.0	21 550	25 182	10 976	50 500	21.5	11.1
Monongalia County	80.6	85.1	85.0	63.0	54.9	36.5	18.1	44.3	28 668	41 987	13 404	83 800	19.6	9.9
Monroe County	87.7	91.2	88.5	71.1	47.2	76.3	58.5	78.4	28 001	30 758	19 167	62 000	20.4	9.9
Morgan County	87.0	90.6	84.2	60.1	56.6	74.3	76.0	73.9	34 536	36 741	24 779	85 300	21.5	9.9
Nicholas County	86.7	90.1	86.6	70.7	58.9	72.7	58.8	74.1	27 164	30 056	14 525	52 800	20.5	9.9
Ohio County	78.7	85.8	82.9	54.6	37.3	52.4	47.0	53.1	30 649	38 900	15 364	69 800	18.9	9.9
Pendleton County	81.5	84.3	80.6	70.4	61.5	73.8	64.0	75.4	30 343	32 383	25 531	71 600	19.3	9.9
Pleasants County	83.2	88.4	84.2	59.2	45.5	73.0	54.5	75.5	32 876	36 508	18 333	67 100	18.4	9.9
Pocahontas County.......	84.0	86.3	80.6	72.2	69.4	73.1	62.3	74.7	26 189	28 125	19 329	61 500	21.8	10.2
Preston County	87.4	90.7	88.8	71.5	61.0	71.9	75.7	71.3	28 082	30 905	15 394	56 700	19.4	9.9
Putnam County	87.6	90.5	87.7	72.2	63.3	72.0	57.9	74.0	41 842	45 891	23 630	92 600	18.8	9.9
Raleigh County	80.9	86.8	81.4	58.7	40.3	66.4	54.9	67.8	28 319	32 563	16 644	62 700	20.3	9.9
Randolph County	82.1	86.4	81.7	64.9	56.0	61.8	52.6	63.3	27 179	31 472	16 449	66 600	20.8	9.9
Ritchie County	85.6	88.1	83.5	73.3	59.6	72.0	61.6	73.3	27 408	31 354	18 571	50 800	18.0	9.9
Roane County	81.9	86.6	80.4	60.4	46.2	73.4	75.4	73.1	24 552	27 473	13 986	56 400	19.1	9.9
Summers County	81.3	85.4	76.8	66.0	58.1	74.3	89.8	73.1	21 013	23 966	12 741	53 800	22.7	11.5
Taylor County	83.6	87.7	79.5	66.9	53.9	70.0	58.7	71.7	27 356	30 698	13 459	57 500	20.9	11.3
Tucker County	86.8	89.9	85.1	73.9	65.7	72.9	71.3	73.1	25 365	27 185	18 423	57 200	23.0	9.9
Tyler County................	86.7	89.8	84.5	71.0	57.0	75.2	74.0	75.4	29 038	32 945	16 142	59 800	19.2	9.9
Upshur County	80.9	87.1	81.0	54.9	40.8	66.3	59.8	67.1	26 863	31 343	13 898	66 300	20.9	9.9
Wayne County	83.1	87.0	83.0	65.7	52.5	64.0	62.7	64.1	27 491	31 707	15 048	63 600	19.7	9.9
Webster County	81.9	85.9	77.2	64.8	55.6	72.3	61.9	73.5	21 021	23 902	10 874	39 900	24.1	10.8
Wetzel County	83.0	87.8	80.9	61.4	49.0	67.5	75.2	66.4	30 719	35 820	15 784	59 900	19.0	9.9
Wirt County	85.7	89.5	85.5	66.4	60.1	75.6	65.8	77.2	30 599	33 391	13 899	56 100	15.7	9.9
Wood County	80.6	87.0	81.6	55.6	41.7	57.4	44.9	59.2	33 339	39 725	18 432	74 600	19.1	9.9
Wyoming County	85.5	88.6	84.1	70.4	61.0	77.0	75.4	77.1	23 907	26 448	13 699	38 600	21.0	9.9
WISCONSIN..............	79.1	86.0	84.1	73.7	40.5	47.0	37.3	49.3	43 624	52 546	27 500	109 900	20.9	11.2
Adams County	88.3	91.1	82.9	73.7	64.0	78.8	81.0	78.4	33 197	35 210	23 017	77 800	22.3	12.2
Ashland County	82.3	89.3	87.5	57.6	50.1	50.0	43.6	51.1	31 797	38 427	18 107	61 900	20.2	11.3
Barron County	84.4	88.6	84.7	64.0	55.5	56.5	56.8	56.4	37 029	41 814	21 139	80 000	19.4	10.5
Bayfield County	87.4	91.9	89.3	67.8	58.8	72.1	73.0	71.9	33 289	36 905	18 977	87 500	20.4	12.9
Brown County...............	77.4	85.2	83.9	43.8	35.5	42.0	35.0	43.9	46 293	56 928	28 582	116 100	20.6	11.1
Buffalo County	85.7	88.6	84.6	67.5	52.4	56.4	52.1	57.1	37 370	42 100	24 533	84 800	19.9	10.2
Burnett County	88.3	92.7	87.7	64.4	53.8	76.4	73.3	77.0	34 181	36 261	22 616	84 800	21.5	11.2
Calumet County	88.0	90.8	91.7	68.5	62.5	57.1	52.4	58.1	52 659	57 867	31 927	108 200	19.9	10.5
Chippewa County.........	84.0	89.8	88.2	57.7	46.3	55.7	51.4	56.6	39 536	45 196	24 388	88 400	19.4	9.9
Clark County	87.5	90.5	88.3	69.4	60.6	64.9	57.8	66.0	34 607	38 125	22 022	70 700	19.4	11.9
Columbia County..........	83.8	87.7	85.6	62.1	53.2	54.6	49.7	55.6	45 046	51 333	29 335	118 700	22.7	10.9
Crawford County	84.4	88.7	85.3	63.7	53.7	59.7	56.9	60.1	34 022	38 636	22 171	77 100	19.8	10.0

STATE County	Median gross rent	Percent who pay 35 percent or more of income for housing expenses — Owners	Renters	Number of workers 16 years and over	Car, truck, or van — Drove alone	Carpooled	Public transportation	Other means	Walked	No vehicles	One vehicle	Two or more vehicles
	25	26	27	28	29	30	31	32	33	34	35	36
WEST VIRGINIA—Cont'd												
Braxton County	332	9.7	23.7	5 077	76.3	16.8	0.4	0.4	2.3	12.5	34.0	53.5
Brooke County	379	10.0	28.0	10 645	85.7	8.0	0.2	0.7	3.9	8.6	36.5	54.8
Cabell County	420	11.7	36.2	40 400	80.9	10.4	1.1	1.0	4.5	14.0	38.7	47.3
Calhoun County	302	17.8	18.6	2 471	67.1	23.4	0.0	1.8	1.3	13.6	33.6	52.8
Clay County	278	9.7	23.6	3 128	77.2	19.4	0.2	0.4	1.2	12.3	32.9	54.8
Doddridge County	350	9.6	21.5	2 566	74.6	17.2	0.5	1.4	3.2	8.4	34.8	56.8
Fayette County	357	13.7	26.7	15 787	81.9	12.7	0.4	0.9	2.2	13.4	36.6	50.0
Gilmer County	373	16.8	29.5	2 394	73.1	14.9	0.1	2.0	6.1	9.2	36.1	54.6
Grant County	361	12.4	19.9	4 895	75.3	18.5	0.1	0.7	2.0	8.3	29.3	62.5
Greenbrier County	372	13.7	31.8	13 210	80.6	12.9	0.2	0.6	2.7	10.2	34.1	55.7
Hampshire County	389	11.9	20.0	8 390	69.4	22.9	0.5	0.9	3.3	7.6	28.7	63.7
Hancock County	451	11.2	26.2	14 179	86.1	8.7	1.0	0.3	2.1	7.2	37.5	55.2
Hardy County	375	11.4	24.2	6 012	73.5	17.3	0.2	1.1	3.3	10.2	28.8	61.0
Harrison County	398	12.8	28.0	27 646	82.8	10.7	0.7	0.9	2.5	11.0	36.5	52.5
Jackson County	390	8.9	23.0	11 159	80.7	12.8	0.1	1.1	2.3	8.4	32.0	59.7
Jefferson County	496	14.3	28.2	21 066	72.1	17.7	2.6	0.7	3.4	6.8	28.3	64.9
Kanawha County	444	9.7	25.4	87 563	79.6	12.3	2.3	0.9	2.7	13.0	38.1	48.9
Lewis County	340	13.2	23.7	6 606	79.2	14.4	0.0	0.5	1.3	11.9	31.8	56.3
Lincoln County	322	10.9	29.1	6 986	79.5	16.2	0.3	0.7	1.4	13.6	36.4	50.0
Logan County	368	14.2	28.7	11 826	80.2	14.2	0.2	0.8	2.6	13.4	37.7	48.8
McDowell County	260	15.2	25.9	5 920	83.4	11.2	0.3	1.2	3.2	18.2	41.1	40.7
Marion County	401	10.7	31.6	23 353	82.9	9.7	0.5	1.1	3.5	10.4	36.8	52.8
Marshall County	347	9.4	24.1	14 012	82.3	11.0	0.3	0.6	3.3	9.6	33.2	57.1
Mason County	316	12.7	26.9	9 232	83.5	10.3	0.0	0.8	3.0	10.1	33.2	56.7
Mercer County	372	11.6	30.7	22 905	83.7	11.7	0.4	0.7	1.6	11.4	37.6	51.0
Mineral County	378	13.0	23.7	11 595	79.1	15.2	0.3	0.6	3.0	9.1	30.1	60.8
Mingo County	329	14.1	27.7	7 712	83.2	11.7	0.8	0.9	2.6	14.9	40.9	44.2
Monongalia County	453	12.3	44.9	36 939	75.9	11.6	0.9	1.9	6.7	9.0	38.7	52.3
Monroe County	388	12.6	19.2	5 189	79.4	13.4	0.0	0.7	2.9	7.0	31.3	61.7
Morgan County	447	14.3	22.7	6 512	76.4	18.2	0.4	1.0	2.0	6.6	30.0	63.4
Nicholas County	360	12.7	28.2	9 689	79.3	15.3	0.3	1.2	1.3	10.9	32.2	56.9
Ohio County	374	11.1	25.3	20 306	78.2	10.9	1.6	0.9	5.5	15.0	39.0	46.0
Pendleton County	376	10.7	9.8	3 577	70.7	19.7	0.2	0.2	3.5	7.3	26.6	66.1
Pleasants County	335	9.3	19.2	2 928	85.3	10.6	0.2	0.4	2.4	10.3	31.1	58.6
Pocahontas County	355	13.7	17.7	3 543	72.1	17.2	0.3	1.6	4.0	9.9	31.5	58.6
Preston County	336	10.4	22.4	11 869	76.7	16.4	0.3	1.2	2.2	8.7	30.3	61.0
Putnam County	496	10.4	22.6	23 553	85.2	10.0	0.1	0.6	1.2	5.7	29.7	64.6
Raleigh County	385	14.2	24.7	28 731	83.1	11.9	0.3	0.9	1.9	11.7	35.8	52.5
Randolph County	370	11.5	25.9	11 332	76.8	16.0	0.1	0.7	4.1	10.5	36.9	52.5
Ritchie County	323	10.4	21.5	3 945	80.0	14.4	0.1	0.9	1.5	10.1	32.9	57.0
Roane County	338	11.4	26.4	5 378	74.6	19.3	0.0	0.6	1.9	10.9	34.5	54.6
Summers County	284	15.0	24.0	4 115	79.3	13.7	0.3	1.3	1.8	11.9	36.5	51.6
Taylor County	330	14.7	25.7	6 154	82.9	12.3	0.3	0.9	2.3	10.7	32.8	56.5
Tucker County	370	16.2	19.3	2 918	79.6	14.1	0.2	1.2	2.8	9.2	33.9	56.9
Tyler County	343	12.7	20.8	3 418	78.7	14.3	0.0	0.8	3.3	8.9	34.2	56.9
Upshur County	362	11.9	24.5	9 114	76.2	12.3	0.3	0.9	7.2	10.1	31.8	58.1
Wayne County	382	13.3	27.7	15 851	85.2	9.7	0.5	0.6	2.0	11.0	36.9	52.1
Webster County	285	21.0	24.4	2 809	69.0	22.6	1.0	1.2	2.7	12.6	34.9	52.5
Wetzel County	335	10.2	25.8	6 108	81.8	11.3	0.2	0.6	3.6	11.2	32.9	56.0
Wirt County	313	9.4	30.4	2 230	76.9	18.8	0.0	0.5	1.7	7.6	31.6	60.9
Wood County	429	10.1	29.1	37 650	84.3	10.3	0.7	0.6	2.1	9.1	35.6	55.2
Wyoming County	318	12.4	23.3	7 359	79.4	15.0	0.8	0.8	2.0	11.1	39.2	49.6
WISCONSIN	540	12.0	25.4	2 690 704	79.5	9.9	2.0	0.9	3.7	7.9	32.5	59.6
Adams County	443	15.7	22.5	7 700	78.1	12.4	0.4	1.4	2.6	4.2	30.5	65.3
Ashland County	372	13.6	24.7	7 674	73.1	12.2	0.5	1.7	8.4	9.9	35.2	54.9
Barron County	417	10.9	25.5	22 214	78.5	9.6	0.2	0.6	4.2	6.1	30.3	63.6
Bayfield County	369	13.8	23.2	6 542	73.8	10.2	1.0	0.9	7.5	4.5	29.6	65.9
Brown County	520	10.5	23.1	118 872	84.7	8.4	0.9	0.7	2.8	6.0	32.6	61.5
Buffalo County	399	9.2	19.2	7 129	72.9	10.5	0.2	0.5	5.7	5.0	26.4	68.6
Burnett County	398	12.9	19.7	6 734	75.4	12.9	0.2	0.8	4.5	3.8	30.0	66.2
Calumet County	491	8.5	13.0	21 913	82.7	8.7	0.2	0.6	3.5	3.5	26.5	70.1
Chippewa County	446	10.9	20.4	27 294	81.2	8.9	0.3	0.8	3.1	5.8	28.1	66.1
Clark County	366	11.1	16.2	15 683	68.7	10.1	0.1	1.5	5.8	8.1	26.8	65.2
Columbia County	507	13.6	18.3	26 991	79.7	10.9	0.3	0.6	3.1	5.1	28.9	65.9
Crawford County	394	10.4	16.7	8 127	73.0	11.5	0.5	1.1	5.0	7.0	31.1	62.0

Table C-3. States and Counties — **Migration, Housing, and Transportation**

STATE/ County code	MSA/PMSA/ NECMA code[1]	STATE County	Total population 5 years and over	Residence in 1995 (percent)					Occupied housing units		Householders 65 years and over	
				Same house	Same county, different house	Same state, different county	Different state	Outside the United States	Number	Percent owner-occupied	Number	Percent owner-occupied
			1	2	3	4	5	6	7	8	9	10
		WISCONSIN—Cont'd										
55 025	4720	Dane County	401 058	46.1	29.7	10.8	10.5	2.9	173 484	57.6	25 930	70.8
55 027	...	Dodge County	80 793	58.2	20.1	16.6	3.6	1.5	31 417	73.5	7 357	76.1
55 029	...	Door County	26 657	64.1	19.5	9.5	6.7	0.2	11 828	79.3	3 501	84.7
55 031	2240	Douglas County............	40 721	61.0	22.9	4.1	11.2	0.8	17 808	71.5	4 306	74.8
55 033	...	Dunn County	37 563	53.2	17.9	18.5	9.6	0.9	14 337	69.0	2 834	78.4
55 035	2290	Eau Claire County........	87 682	50.8	23.8	15.8	8.8	0.7	35 822	65.0	7 451	74.2
55 037	...	Florence County	4 854	69.2	12.9	8.2	9.3	0.3	2 133	85.6	600	82.3
55 039	...	Fond du Lac County	91 596	59.5	24.0	10.7	4.6	1.2	36 931	73.0	8 486	76.9
55 041	...	Forest County	9 456	62.1	18.4	14.7	4.5	0.3	4 043	78.9	1 277	83.4
55 043	...	Grant County	47 004	59.4	20.7	12.7	6.7	0.6	18 465	72.4	4 781	77.9
55 045	...	Green County	31 509	58.5	23.1	12.2	5.9	0.3	13 212	73.7	3 300	77.7
55 047	...	Green Lake County.......	18 015	64.1	15.7	15.1	4.5	0.6	7 703	77.2	2 415	79.6
55 049	...	Iowa County	21 329	63.3	17.9	14.3	4.3	0.2	8 764	75.8	1 999	79.3
55 051	...	Iron County	6 597	62.9	15.6	10.8	10.3	0.4	3 083	80.7	1 069	81.9
55 053	...	Jackson County	18 037	60.4	17.5	15.7	5.2	1.1	7 070	75.0	1 949	76.3
55 055	...	Jefferson County	69 342	57.5	20.5	16.0	5.1	0.9	28 205	71.7	6 108	76.5
55 057	...	Juneau County	22 879	61.1	20.4	12.2	6.0	0.3	9 696	76.9	2 717	82.2
55 059	3800	Kenosha County...........	139 358	55.7	24.1	5.2	13.7	1.3	56 057	69.1	11 699	76.9
55 061	...	Kewaunee County	18 993	65.4	18.1	12.1	4.2	0.3	7 623	81.9	1 900	81.8
55 063	3870	La Crosse County	100 683	51.0	26.4	13.9	8.1	0.6	41 599	65.1	8 773	74.2
55 065	...	Lafayette County	15 180	66.7	17.3	10.6	5.0	0.3	6 211	77.4	1 803	81.8
55 067	...	Langlade County	19 575	65.5	19.3	11.8	3.3	0.1	8 452	78.7	2 567	80.8
55 069	...	Lincoln County	27 975	63.5	21.8	9.9	4.2	0.7	11 721	78.3	3 155	76.1
55 071	...	Manitowoc County	78 124	64.6	23.2	7.5	4.0	0.6	32 721	76.0	8 520	76.9
55 073	8940	Marathon County	117 712	61.7	23.7	9.3	4.6	0.7	47 702	75.7	10 228	78.1
55 075	...	Marinette County	41 164	64.2	17.9	9.5	7.9	0.5	17 585	79.5	4 959	78.2
55 077	...	Marquette County	15 088	57.9	14.5	18.3	8.9	0.4	5 986	82.3	1 882	87.1
55 078	...	Menominee County	4 112	69.2	14.2	11.6	4.3	0.6	1 345	74.5	294	84.0
55 079	5080	Milwaukee County........	873 148	52.3	33.7	5.7	5.9	2.4	377 729	52.6	82 136	65.5
55 081	...	Monroe County	38 115	58.4	23.8	9.7	7.2	0.8	15 399	73.7	3 603	75.5
55 083	...	Oconto County	33 579	63.0	15.9	18.4	2.5	0.2	13 979	82.9	3 561	82.7
55 085	...	Oneida County	35 079	61.1	17.1	13.7	7.0	1.0	15 333	79.7	4 561	83.7
55 087	0460	Outagamie County	149 809	57.4	22.5	13.2	5.6	1.3	60 530	72.4	11 305	75.6
55 089	5080	Ozaukee County	77 223	58.9	18.6	14.9	6.8	0.9	30 857	76.3	6 771	80.6
55 091	...	Pepin County................	6 791	65.8	13.6	15.0	5.3	0.3	2 759	79.6	798	75.6
55 093	5120	Pierce County...............	34 716	56.1	16.3	12.3	14.7	0.6	13 015	73.1	2 149	80.3
55 095	...	Polk County..................	38 868	61.4	19.6	7.4	11.1	0.5	16 254	80.1	4 062	76.2
55 097	...	Portage County	63 250	56.1	21.6	16.2	5.3	0.7	25 040	70.9	4 800	77.2
55 099	...	Price County	15 075	65.9	18.0	11.2	4.4	0.5	6 564	80.8	2 037	80.1
55 101	6600	Racine County..............	175 707	57.3	25.9	9.5	5.8	1.5	70 819	70.6	15 647	77.3
55 103	...	Richland County	16 908	62.0	18.6	13.5	5.6	0.3	7 118	74.5	2 092	77.5
55 105	3620	Rock County.................	141 950	55.3	29.4	6.8	7.5	1.1	58 617	71.2	12 378	77.4
55 107	...	Rusk County	14 506	64.4	17.2	11.4	6.4	0.5	6 095	78.6	1 833	81.3
55 109	5120	St. Croix County...........	58 728	56.9	19.3	8.6	14.8	0.4	23 410	76.4	4 004	69.6
55 111	...	Sauk County.................	51 659	59.1	22.4	12.4	5.5	0.6	21 644	73.3	5 210	79.0
55 113	...	Sawyer County	15 330	62.2	17.8	10.7	8.7	0.6	6 640	76.9	1 952	80.4
55 115	...	Shawano County	38 147	62.3	17.6	15.9	3.5	0.7	15 815	78.2	4 408	80.1
55 117	7620	Sheboygan County........	105 384	59.3	26.4	7.9	5.3	1.1	43 545	71.4	10 111	75.6
55 119	...	Taylor County	18 558	67.5	19.2	9.7	3.2	0.4	7 529	80.4	1 972	78.3
55 121	...	Trempealeau County.....	25 376	63.9	20.1	11.1	4.5	0.3	10 747	74.3	2 898	70.7
55 123	...	Vernon County	26 213	64.1	17.7	12.6	5.4	0.3	10 825	79.1	3 024	80.0
55 125	...	Vilas County	20 159	64.7	12.2	14.1	8.3	0.6	9 066	82.0	3 018	87.5
55 127	...	Walworth County...........	88 296	51.6	20.4	15.5	11.2	1.3	34 522	69.1	7 842	77.7
55 129	...	Washburn County	15 212	61.9	17.3	10.8	9.6	0.3	6 604	80.9	1 910	81.1
55 131	5080	Washington County........	109 493	59.9	20.1	15.9	3.4	0.6	43 842	76.0	8 352	75.9
55 133	5080	Waukesha County.........	337 664	58.6	19.6	15.3	5.6	0.9	135 229	76.5	26 960	73.9
55 135	...	Waupaca County...........	48 632	61.4	21.6	12.9	3.8	0.3	19 863	76.9	4 932	75.4
55 137	...	Waushara County	21 969	62.9	14.4	17.7	4.4	0.5	9 336	83.4	2 756	85.3
55 139	0460	Winnebago County........	147 360	53.7	24.1	15.7	5.4	0.9	61 157	68.0	12 907	75.3
55 141	...	Wood County	70 880	63.7	23.4	8.2	4.2	0.6	30 135	74.3	7 529	73.6
56 000		**WYOMING**	462 809	51.3	24.1	7.8	15.7	1.1	193 608	70.0	38 448	81.2
56 001	...	Albany County	30 374	35.6	20.6	19.1	22.5	2.2	13 269	51.3	1 694	88.4
56 003	...	Big Horn County...........	10 650	58.1	18.9	8.9	13.2	0.9	4 312	74.4	1 252	83.2
56 005	...	Campbell County...........	31 201	52.4	25.2	7.1	14.7	0.6	12 207	73.6	1 060	68.0
56 007	...	Carbon County	14 737	53.6	20.6	10.1	15.5	0.2	6 129	70.9	1 322	80.3

[1]MSA = Metropolitan Statistical Area. PMSA = Primary MSA. NECMA = New England County Metropolitan Area. See the Appendix A for explanation of these concepts. See Appendix B for list of metropolitan areas identified by type, with component counties.

Table C-3. States and Counties — Migration, Housing, and Transportation

STATE County	Owner-occupied by household type (percent)								Median household income			Median housing value (owner estimated)	Median monthly owner costs as a percent of income	
	Family-households					Nonfamily households								
		Married-couple family		Other family										
	Total family households	Total	With own children under 18 years	Total	With own children under 18 years	Total nonfamily households	Two or more adults	Living alone	All households	Owner-occupied households	Renter-occupied households		With a mortgage	Without a mortgage
	11	12	13	14	15	16	17	18	19	20	21	22	23	24
WISCONSIN—Cont'd														
Dane County	74.8	81.8	82.0	43.2	37.6	33.5	24.5	37.2	49 067	65 493	30 409	146 600	22.2	10.5
Dodge County	81.7	86.6	84.4	56.3	46.2	53.0	43.1	54.9	45 334	51 180	30 942	108 100	21.5	12.0
Door County	86.7	90.4	86.4	62.9	51.9	63.8	53.2	65.4	38 970	44 589	24 163	122 900	22.2	10.9
Douglas County	83.2	91.1	91.5	53.2	45.6	51.0	40.4	53.2	35 397	42 205	19 251	70 800	19.3	10.4
Dunn County	81.6	86.7	84.3	56.2	48.5	45.5	28.7	52.8	38 727	46 456	23 971	91 900	20.4	11.0
Eau Claire County	80.6	86.6	85.9	50.7	43.2	39.2	21.4	46.2	39 172	49 898	24 644	96 000	19.8	11.0
Florence County	91.2	93.0	93.7	77.3	72.1	74.1	70.8	74.7	34 777	36 512	23 250	81 300	19.9	12.3
Fond du Lac County	83.1	88.0	86.0	56.4	45.9	50.0	41.7	51.7	45 480	52 017	27 156	101 100	19.9	10.8
Forest County	84.3	90.4	85.0	60.7	53.1	66.7	69.0	66.5	32 025	35 927	19 890	76 300	18.9	10.7
Grant County	83.6	88.1	85.1	59.8	50.3	49.0	30.6	53.5	36 273	41 811	21 886	80 000	19.2	9.9
Green County	81.5	86.7	82.7	56.1	45.0	55.6	56.7	55.3	43 119	48 647	28 345	102 700	22.3	11.5
Green Lake County	84.1	87.4	84.6	63.2	55.7	61.4	56.1	62.1	39 152	43 550	26 214	92 100	21.4	11.7
Iowa County	82.0	85.8	83.0	62.8	52.9	60.8	59.0	61.2	42 548	47 907	29 598	99 700	21.4	12.2
Iron County	89.5	93.2	88.9	69.5	61.0	65.5	67.1	65.2	29 595	32 866	17 237	64 300	20.9	13.6
Jackson County	82.9	85.9	81.7	68.7	59.7	57.4	51.4	58.6	36 931	41 131	24 219	78 400	19.5	10.9
Jefferson County	80.1	85.4	82.8	54.7	45.5	51.6	42.7	53.8	46 897	54 101	30 992	123 600	22.3	12.1
Juneau County	82.6	87.8	84.3	60.5	48.0	64.2	62.6	64.5	35 383	39 942	22 788	71 200	20.2	10.8
Kenosha County	77.7	85.1	83.2	51.6	41.2	50.2	40.4	52.4	46 594	57 204	28 384	118 200	21.4	12.5
Kewaunee County	87.7	91.0	89.6	67.8	57.2	66.4	67.3	66.2	44 140	48 193	25 893	94 200	19.9	10.9
La Crosse County	80.2	86.6	85.6	51.9	43.6	40.5	23.7	46.3	39 361	49 808	24 249	94 400	20.6	11.0
Lafayette County	83.3	86.9	83.7	65.0	55.0	63.3	53.1	64.9	37 135	40 885	26 450	79 900	19.7	11.8
Langlade County	85.4	90.1	87.1	61.2	51.0	64.1	63.8	64.1	33 468	38 902	20 275	71 200	20.0	12.0
Lincoln County	87.2	91.8	89.3	61.7	51.0	56.7	45.3	58.5	39 395	44 777	21 421	86 600	19.7	11.2
Manitowoc County	85.4	90.0	89.3	61.1	51.4	55.6	49.8	56.5	43 070	49 431	26 144	91 200	19.0	10.2
Marathon County	84.9	88.9	87.7	62.5	53.6	52.8	47.1	54.0	45 160	51 490	27 726	96 200	19.6	9.9
Marinette County	87.7	91.2	89.2	68.5	59.0	62.5	55.2	63.6	35 376	39 176	21 339	70 100	19.7	10.2
Marquette County	86.8	89.9	85.0	70.4	59.2	71.8	66.4	72.9	35 513	37 207	25 833	87 900	21.7	12.4
Menominee County	74.6	86.4	78.3	59.7	45.6	74.2	72.6	74.7	29 005	36 597	15 402	58 000	19.8	10.3
Milwaukee County	63.3	76.6	73.1	37.2	25.6	36.8	28.8	38.5	37 879	52 042	26 310	100 500	21.1	12.6
Monroe County	80.7	85.0	81.6	61.1	54.9	57.1	53.4	57.9	37 080	42 348	24 185	79 300	20.3	10.1
Oconto County	88.6	91.7	90.0	71.3	64.1	68.3	70.8	67.9	41 239	44 824	24 871	90 000	20.2	10.8
Oneida County	87.5	91.4	88.0	66.4	59.9	62.7	63.4	62.6	37 065	40 688	23 070	103 400	20.7	12.2
Outagamie County	83.5	88.4	88.3	54.2	46.7	46.7	39.3	48.4	49 504	56 944	30 928	105 900	20.3	10.5
Ozaukee County	84.6	88.2	87.7	57.4	48.3	51.5	42.4	53.1	62 106	72 073	37 194	176 600	21.4	11.3
Pepin County	87.5	90.9	90.8	66.4	56.9	60.9	54.2	61.9	37 515	42 194	20 915	83 800	20.6	11.8
Pierce County	84.0	87.7	87.1	62.7	56.2	47.7	30.2	55.0	49 846	57 116	31 016	125 500	21.4	10.7
Polk County	87.2	90.9	88.2	68.5	65.1	63.6	64.8	63.4	41 097	45 789	23 479	100 200	20.8	10.9
Portage County	83.9	89.0	87.9	56.7	50.4	45.3	27.0	52.3	43 075	51 836	24 364	98 200	19.5	9.9
Price County	88.8	91.8	91.9	73.9	68.3	64.7	56.1	66.1	34 744	38 035	20 522	72 500	20.3	12.5
Racine County	78.2	86.5	83.3	47.9	35.3	52.3	50.1	52.7	47 528	56 894	26 617	110 200	20.7	11.5
Richland County	82.2	86.6	81.9	62.0	50.7	58.1	51.3	59.3	33 822	38 700	22 372	81 000	21.1	11.8
Rock County	78.9	86.2	81.6	51.1	42.2	53.9	46.7	55.6	45 318	53 824	28 060	98 300	19.9	10.9
Rusk County	86.9	90.2	86.2	70.4	60.2	60.7	56.2	61.5	31 023	35 199	19 806	65 900	18.7	11.1
St. Croix County	86.0	89.5	90.0	63.7	55.4	50.6	50.5	50.6	54 621	63 505	31 088	141 800	20.6	10.4
Sauk County	81.9	86.7	83.7	57.3	51.7	54.6	50.6	55.6	41 841	47 784	28 644	106 700	21.8	11.3
Sawyer County	82.3	89.0	83.3	56.0	44.2	64.8	69.3	64.0	32 051	37 205	20 122	93 100	20.0	12.1
Shawano County	84.9	89.3	87.6	62.5	53.1	62.0	64.0	61.6	37 905	41 959	23 733	86 000	19.8	10.5
Sheboygan County	81.2	86.7	83.2	49.8	37.8	49.8	42.9	51.1	46 114	52 968	30 074	105 800	20.6	11.4
Taylor County	88.2	91.3	91.6	71.4	62.0	61.0	56.5	61.8	38 194	43 142	24 326	78 800	19.2	11.5
Trempealeau County	83.8	88.0	88.7	64.1	53.6	54.3	53.2	54.5	37 606	43 581	22 257	81 200	18.9	11.5
Vernon County	85.7	89.2	85.9	66.6	56.3	64.1	55.6	65.4	33 072	37 377	20 901	79 300	20.7	12.1
Vilas County	86.8	90.2	84.9	68.4	55.0	70.8	68.1	71.2	33 872	36 699	23 316	118 200	21.8	12.9
Walworth County	79.1	84.8	80.4	52.7	39.2	47.8	32.3	52.5	46 143	55 193	30 275	128 800	22.8	11.8
Washburn County	87.8	91.2	87.7	68.1	60.6	66.0	64.5	66.3	33 780	37 440	21 280	84 600	21.8	12.1
Washington County	83.6	88.5	87.1	53.4	42.1	53.1	45.8	54.9	56 559	62 724	35 741	153 100	21.9	10.2
Waukesha County	85.8	89.2	89.2	62.0	50.6	49.4	43.1	50.9	62 604	71 426	37 997	169 000	21.4	11.3
Waupaca County	84.5	89.0	89.0	60.9	52.2	59.0	58.0	59.2	40 774	46 789	24 354	91 700	19.9	11.5
Waushara County	88.2	91.3	86.7	70.8	64.6	71.8	74.9	71.2	36 894	39 821	22 395	87 100	21.9	10.9
Winnebago County	79.8	86.3	83.9	49.4	40.6	46.2	32.0	50.1	44 269	53 158	27 674	97 000	20.4	10.7
Wood County	83.8	88.0	86.5	60.5	53.0	53.4	56.2	53.0	41 590	48 889	23 822	82 100	18.1	9.9
WYOMING	77.7	82.7	78.2	55.2	47.6	53.8	43.5	56.2	37 671	45 157	24 183	91 500	19.7	9.9
Albany County	68.5	75.3	71.7	41.0	33.5	31.8	15.5	39.7	29 082	47 720	16 704	111 500	19.9	9.9
Big Horn County	79.7	83.1	77.0	60.9	49.0	61.1	57.6	61.6	32 668	36 534	21 684	70 600	18.7	9.9
Campbell County	81.9	86.0	83.0	62.2	60.7	49.5	51.0	49.1	49 060	55 346	30 679	91 700	18.1	9.9
Carbon County	78.6	83.8	76.0	53.7	47.0	54.9	52.3	55.3	35 448	41 600	24 931	69 000	17.0	9.9

STATE County	Median gross rent	Percent who pay 35 percent or more of income for housing expenses		Means of transportation to work (percent except where noted)							Vehicles available (percent of households)		
		Owners	Renters	Number of workers 16 years and over	Car, truck, or van		Public transportation	Other means	Walked	No vehicles	One vehicle	Two or more vehicles
					Drove alone	Carpooled						
	25	26	27	28	29	30	31	32	33	34	35	36
WISCONSIN—Cont'd												
Dane County	641	12.9	30.7	242 542	74.1	9.5	4.2	2.2	6.2	8.0	35.6	56.4
Dodge County	528	12.6	16.9	42 598	80.1	10.8	0.5	0.7	3.4	4.4	30.8	64.7
Door County	481	15.3	23.6	13 614	76.0	10.5	0.8	1.0	4.0	4.4	31.5	64.2
Douglas County	411	10.6	28.1	20 323	80.3	10.6	1.5	0.9	4.3	8.7	33.0	58.3
Dunn County	461	10.7	26.1	20 248	74.9	9.6	0.3	1.0	7.4	4.5	27.2	68.3
Eau Claire County	486	10.0	27.6	48 603	80.3	8.2	1.4	1.1	5.5	6.7	31.2	62.1
Florence County	385	15.1	17.6	2 296	85.6	4.8	0.0	0.3	2.4	5.7	26.9	67.4
Fond du Lac County	500	10.5	22.6	50 732	80.8	10.5	0.5	1.0	3.7	6.1	31.1	62.8
Forest County	325	12.7	14.0	3 961	73.6	13.1	0.5	1.1	6.0	5.9	34.5	59.5
Grant County	395	10.3	21.8	24 705	72.4	11.5	0.3	1.2	6.8	6.2	29.0	64.8
Green County	464	12.3	17.5	17 997	76.3	10.9	0.2	0.8	4.6	5.7	29.5	64.8
Green Lake County	437	12.7	20.0	9 465	74.5	12.5	0.3	0.4	5.7	6.3	30.1	63.6
Iowa County	502	14.1	15.8	12 467	74.6	12.6	0.2	0.5	3.8	4.5	26.7	68.8
Iron County	308	13.6	15.6	2 806	76.1	13.1	0.5	0.5	4.1	9.1	34.3	56.6
Jackson County	397	10.8	22.2	8 760	74.3	12.4	0.7	1.5	3.7	6.9	28.4	64.7
Jefferson County	564	12.5	18.2	39 264	80.7	10.5	0.8	0.8	3.6	5.2	29.5	65.4
Juneau County	433	12.0	22.2	11 220	77.8	11.7	0.2	1.0	4.3	5.8	30.7	63.5
Kenosha County	589	14.0	27.0	72 053	82.8	10.7	1.2	0.8	2.1	6.8	34.3	58.9
Kewaunee County	428	11.2	15.6	10 580	76.6	11.0	0.3	0.5	4.2	4.7	27.8	67.5
La Crosse County	470	11.1	25.9	55 971	81.0	8.8	1.3	1.0	4.9	7.6	33.2	59.2
Lafayette County	404	12.6	16.4	8 421	70.2	12.0	0.5	0.7	5.5	6.6	25.2	68.2
Langlade County	405	11.4	24.1	9 517	78.2	11.7	0.2	1.0	4.2	5.8	31.8	62.4
Lincoln County	433	11.6	20.5	14 319	78.4	12.6	0.5	0.7	3.3	5.7	29.3	64.9
Manitowoc County	433	9.6	17.9	42 406	80.9	10.2	0.5	1.0	3.5	6.9	32.1	61.0
Marathon County	484	10.3	19.5	65 680	81.1	9.5	1.0	0.8	2.6	5.6	29.1	65.3
Marinette County	400	11.4	19.3	19 991	78.2	11.4	0.3	1.3	4.3	6.7	30.6	62.7
Marquette County	456	15.7	18.3	6 513	75.5	13.8	0.1	0.7	3.4	4.3	29.6	66.1
Menominee County	245	14.0	22.7	1 365	70.0	20.4	2.1	1.8	3.4	8.5	38.9	52.6
Milwaukee County	555	13.9	29.9	427 620	75.0	11.5	6.9	0.8	3.7	16.3	41.5	42.2
Monroe County	455	10.9	18.7	19 927	75.6	11.8	0.3	1.0	4.2	8.3	27.9	63.8
Oconto County	429	11.4	10.5	17 444	77.9	12.5	0.2	0.6	2.7	4.4	27.3	68.3
Oneida County	400	10.7	20.0	16 701	81.4	9.5	0.5	0.8	4.1	5.3	32.5	62.2
Outagamie County	534	9.7	19.6	84 571	84.6	7.4	0.8	0.8	3.2	5.3	29.2	65.5
Ozaukee County	642	13.8	18.4	43 544	84.7	7.8	0.5	0.6	2.7	3.4	26.3	70.3
Pepin County	368	11.3	15.7	3 531	73.9	11.5	0.3	0.5	5.1	7.4	26.1	66.5
Pierce County	542	12.3	21.5	20 810	75.1	11.6	0.4	0.7	6.5	3.3	23.9	72.8
Polk County	440	13.4	21.5	20 288	76.9	12.8	0.3	0.6	3.2	5.1	27.3	67.6
Portage County	477	9.1	25.4	35 088	78.5	9.2	0.4	2.0	5.6	5.8	29.7	64.6
Price County	404	12.9	19.9	7 322	75.1	13.0	0.3	0.8	5.4	6.7	30.6	62.6
Racine County	548	11.8	27.5	89 494	83.6	9.9	1.6	0.7	2.0	8.1	32.3	59.5
Richland County	427	12.4	24.4	8 794	72.0	13.1	0.3	0.9	4.5	7.3	29.2	63.5
Rock County	543	10.9	23.0	76 033	83.1	10.1	0.7	0.6	2.7	6.1	31.7	62.2
Rusk County	371	12.4	23.6	6 888	71.6	12.7	0.4	1.1	4.6	5.9	32.3	61.8
St. Croix County	587	11.9	24.0	34 428	80.7	11.7	0.3	0.5	2.2	4.2	23.2	72.6
Sauk County	508	12.8	20.1	28 694	77.4	11.1	0.5	0.8	3.9	5.8	31.5	62.7
Sawyer County	386	16.3	21.1	6 979	73.7	12.1	0.5	1.4	6.2	4.5	33.4	62.1
Shawano County	438	11.1	18.1	19 667	76.1	11.3	0.3	0.9	3.8	6.1	29.3	64.6
Sheboygan County	482	9.9	17.5	58 546	81.0	10.2	0.8	1.3	3.8	7.0	33.7	59.4
Taylor County	405	11.8	16.2	9 700	71.9	11.5	0.5	0.7	4.6	5.8	26.8	67.3
Trempealeau County	380	9.5	16.8	13 863	74.7	11.8	0.2	0.9	5.3	6.5	27.6	65.9
Vernon County	367	11.0	20.2	12 930	71.3	10.7	0.5	1.2	5.4	8.9	27.7	63.4
Vilas County	434	15.2	20.4	8 876	80.2	9.4	0.1	1.0	4.9	3.7	35.0	61.3
Walworth County	588	16.1	26.6	48 172	80.3	9.2	0.8	0.8	4.8	4.8	31.2	64.0
Washburn County	413	14.8	23.7	7 015	75.7	12.0	0.1	1.0	3.7	5.6	29.7	64.6
Washington County	620	11.3	19.4	63 620	85.5	8.6	0.7	0.5	1.4	3.9	26.9	69.2
Waukesha County	726	12.7	24.3	192 602	87.0	7.1	0.7	0.5	1.5	4.2	25.0	70.8
Waupaca County	450	12.2	18.0	24 979	80.6	9.6	0.5	0.6	3.4	5.7	29.0	65.4
Waushara County	448	13.7	18.0	10 288	78.8	11.4	0.3	0.9	3.0	5.2	28.7	66.1
Winnebago County	500	10.4	21.4	81 109	84.5	7.8	0.8	1.0	3.3	5.8	33.1	61.1
Wood County	442	7.2	22.7	36 803	82.2	8.9	0.4	0.7	3.6	6.0	31.8	62.2
WYOMING	437	11.3	23.3	239 809	75.4	13.2	1.4	1.3	4.4	4.6	29.2	66.2
Albany County	464	9.9	42.6	16 822	70.7	11.4	0.6	3.0	10.5	4.3	34.9	60.8
Big Horn County	380	9.8	17.7	4 732	72.8	11.2	0.2	1.8	6.1	4.5	24.8	70.7
Campbell County	463	9.0	15.6	17 778	77.3	13.9	3.8	0.8	2.0	2.8	23.2	74.0
Carbon County	377	6.8	17.3	7 203	73.6	13.5	0.2	1.3	7.6	5.2	29.4	65.4

STATE/ County code	MSA/PMSA/ NECMA code[1]	STATE County	Total population 5 years and over	Residence in 1995 (percent)					Occupied housing units		Householders 65 years and over	
				Same house	Same county, different house	Same state, different county	Different state	Outside the United States	Number	Percent owner-occupied	Number	Percent owner-occupied
			1	2	3	4	5	6	7	8	9	10
		WYOMING—Cont'd										
56 009	...	Converse County	11 264	56.4	20.7	11.2	11.5	0.2	4 694	74.1	1 039	81.6
56 011	...	Crook County	5 591	64.1	14.2	6.5	14.1	1.0	2 308	80.1	586	89.8
56 013	...	Fremont County	33 400	59.2	21.9	6.4	11.9	0.6	13 545	72.8	3 098	81.5
56 015	...	Goshen County	11 802	57.0	18.9	8.3	15.3	0.5	5 061	70.7	1 498	79.0
56 017	...	Hot Springs County	4 662	54.2	20.8	11.0	13.9	0.1	2 108	68.6	588	71.4
56 019	...	Johnson County	6 726	52.6	15.7	9.0	21.8	0.9	2 959	73.7	879	86.1
56 021	1580	Laramie County	76 328	46.3	27.5	4.2	19.8	2.3	31 927	69.1	6 240	80.3
56 023	...	Lincoln County	13 594	59.1	16.3	7.6	16.5	0.5	5 266	81.4	1 154	89.9
56 025	1350	Natrona County	62 306	51.0	29.6	7.4	11.1	0.8	26 819	69.9	5 552	80.8
56 027	...	Niobrara County	2 293	63.5	13.6	10.2	12.2	0.5	1 011	72.9	341	80.4
56 029	...	Park County	24 352	51.1	23.0	7.6	17.6	0.7	10 312	71.3	2 475	81.2
56 031	...	Platte County	8 348	61.8	16.8	9.2	11.2	1.0	3 625	75.8	888	85.0
56 033	...	Sheridan County	25 137	50.1	24.9	8.2	16.2	0.6	11 167	68.9	2 988	75.6
56 035	...	Sublette County	5 565	55.7	17.0	11.7	15.1	0.5	2 371	73.5	477	87.0
56 037	...	Sweetwater County	34 934	54.9	27.4	5.6	11.2	0.9	14 105	75.1	2 156	81.9
56 039	...	Teton County	17 313	39.5	23.7	4.4	29.1	3.3	7 688	54.8	868	80.5
56 041	...	Uinta County	18 107	51.4	26.7	6.1	15.2	0.6	6 823	75.2	866	84.9
56 043	...	Washakie County	7 821	58.5	20.4	10.9	9.6	0.5	3 278	73.1	803	82.3
56 045	...	Weston County.............	6 304	62.7	18.9	8.9	8.9	0.7	2 624	78.0	624	83.5

[1]MSA = Metropolitan Statistical Area. PMSA = Primary MSA. NECMA = New England County Metropolitan Area. See the Appendix A for explanation of these concepts. See Appendix B for list of metropolitan areas identified by type, with component counties.

Table C-3. States and Counties — **Migration, Housing, and Transportation**

STATE County	Owner-occupied by household type (percent)								Median household income			Median monthly owner costs as a percent of income	
	Family-households					Nonfamily households							
		Married-couple family		Other family									
	Total family households	Total	With own children under 18 years	Total	With own children under 18 years	Total nonfamily households	Two or more adults	Living alone	All households	Owner-occupied households	Renter-occupied households	Median housing value (owner estimated)	With a mortgage	Without a mortgage
	11	12	13	14	15	16	17	18	19	20	21	22	23	24
WYOMING—Cont'd														
Converse County	79.3	85.5	79.4	48.2	40.7	60.3	81.4	56.8	38 826	45 938	19 317	82 100	17.3	9.9
Crook County	85.0	86.8	81.2	73.9	66.5	67.7	51.2	70.1	35 000	38 800	26 196	85 800	16.9	9.9
Fremont County	77.5	83.3	76.1	57.8	48.9	62.0	51.3	63.8	32 847	38 185	21 386	85 800	19.5	9.9
Goshen County	76.6	81.5	75.2	52.7	35.4	58.1	60.9	57.6	31 645	36 191	19 480	77 000	20.4	11.6
Hot Springs County	74.7	79.0	74.5	42.6	9.6	57.4	61.1	57.0	29 571	35 820	19 513	79 500	21.0	11.7
Johnson County	76.7	79.7	72.3	61.3	57.7	67.2	66.7	67.3	34 594	38 987	27 132	109 700	21.6	9.9
Laramie County	75.8	81.1	75.6	55.0	45.5	54.9	52.9	55.2	39 488	47 524	25 172	101 200	21.0	9.9
Lincoln County	84.1	86.8	82.2	61.3	54.0	73.3	71.0	73.7	41 224	44 719	29 787	91 800	21.3	9.9
Natrona County	77.7	84.2	79.1	52.9	46.5	54.5	47.4	56.0	36 359	44 518	22 264	81 400	19.1	9.9
Niobrara County	77.0	80.1	75.2	60.6	49.3	64.4	53.1	65.7	29 006	31 563	20 278	66 900	19.0	11.1
Park County	78.1	81.3	79.5	58.1	52.5	56.6	35.8	60.7	35 519	40 537	24 334	106 600	21.2	9.9
Platte County	81.0	83.6	77.2	50.8	50.8	63.4	74.5	62.3	33 974	39 276	24 727	81 000	17.4	9.9
Sheridan County	75.4	80.4	72.6	51.2	39.9	57.5	46.5	59.4	33 717	40 759	21 486	98 300	21.7	10.0
Sublette County	78.9	82.2	78.2	52.1	42.1	59.0	57.1	60.4	38 845	43 535	29 333	113 800	22.1	9.9
Sweetwater County	81.8	87.0	85.3	59.0	49.4	57.5	53.8	58.2	45 871	52 572	27 287	92 800	19.0	9.9
Teton County	68.9	72.3	69.1	52.3	52.3	38.2	36.8	39.1	54 123	64 669	41 270	344 500	25.1	9.9
Uinta County	80.0	84.5	81.5	60.6	56.1	60.0	38.0	63.5	43 907	49 875	28 497	83 700	19.2	9.9
Washakie County	78.5	84.5	82.1	50.4	38.6	60.3	45.7	62.1	36 130	42 083	20 750	81 200	18.9	9.9
Weston County	83.9	87.7	85.4	59.6	49.1	62.8	69.7	61.9	32 967	37 545	20 481	63 900	17.8	9.9

STATE County	Median gross rent	Percent who pay 35 percent or more of income for housing expenses		Means of transportation to work (percent except where noted)						Vehicles available (percent of households)		
		Owners	Renters	Number of workers 16 years and over	Car, truck, or van		Public transportation	Other means	Walked	No vehicles	One vehicle	Two or more vehicles
					Drove alone	Carpooled						
	25	26	27	28	29	30	31	32	33	34	35	36
WYOMING—Cont'd												
Converse County	349	9.9	14.9	5 858	68.3	18.8	4.8	1.0	3.3	6.1	26.1	67.8
Crook County	393	5.3	13.9	2 782	69.3	14.7	0.4	1.4	6.9	3.0	20.2	76.8
Fremont County	381	10.1	20.8	15 644	73.4	14.4	0.3	2.0	6.2	5.4	30.7	63.8
Goshen County	368	12.3	22.9	5 607	76.9	10.2	0.3	0.8	5.6	4.5	31.2	64.3
Hot Springs County.......	366	13.1	14.9	2 382	69.3	14.7	0.3	0.2	8.8	4.8	28.9	66.3
Johnson County	445	11.8	22.6	3 167	70.4	8.8	0.0	1.5	9.1	4.5	27.4	68.1
Laramie County	473	12.4	23.9	39 423	80.4	12.4	0.4	1.0	2.2	5.6	32.1	62.2
Lincoln County	464	13.8	15.1	6 431	68.7	19.4	1.4	0.7	4.2	3.0	23.1	73.9
Natrona County	409	10.0	22.8	32 619	82.7	11.3	0.4	0.9	1.4	5.4	31.2	63.5
Niobrara County	309	8.8	11.7	1 147	66.3	9.4	0.8	3.4	10.2	4.2	27.6	68.2
Park County	435	13.4	21.8	12 126	74.4	13.0	0.1	1.6	5.2	3.4	29.8	66.9
Platte County	362	11.4	13.8	4 275	74.0	9.8	0.0	1.5	8.1	3.9	26.0	70.1
Sheridan County	439	14.5	23.7	13 059	78.9	11.0	0.2	1.2	3.6	7.2	30.6	62.3
Sublette County............	523	12.2	23.9	2 971	71.9	12.2	0.4	1.0	7.6	2.3	24.8	72.9
Sweetwater County.......	428	9.1	18.5	18 494	71.6	16.2	6.4	0.9	2.3	3.3	25.5	71.3
Teton County...............	707	22.4	21.2	11 302	66.2	13.3	2.1	2.6	9.0	3.2	28.2	68.6
Uinta County	433	10.2	18.0	9 236	71.1	18.8	2.8	1.6	2.2	2.9	26.7	70.4
Washakie County	393	10.5	21.4	3 806	77.9	10.0	0.1	0.5	5.4	3.7	30.2	66.1
Weston County..............	364	9.8	20.0	2 945	69.3	13.9	5.1	0.8	5.8	2.4	27.1	70.5

Table C-4. Metropolitan Areas — **Migration, Housing, and Transportation**

CMSA/MSA/PMSA/NECMA code[1]	Area name	Residence in 1995 (percent)						Occupied housing units		Householders 65 years and over	
		Total population 5 years and over	Same house	Same county, different house	Same state, different county	Different state	Outside the United States	Number	Percent owner-occupied	Number	Percent owner-occupied
		1	2	3	4	5	6	7	8	9	10
0040	Abilene, TX..................	117 587	46.5	25.2	15.6	10.2	2.5	47 274	61.5	10 173	80.8
0120	Albany, GA	111 677	52.3	26.8	12.1	7.2	1.7	43 781	58.1	8 458	74.9
0160	Albany-Schenectady-Troy, NY	823 015	59.6	22.0	12.3	4.8	1.4	350 284	64.6	81 683	73.4
0200	Albuquerque, NM	662 905	50.6	26.3	8.4	12.5	2.2	275 028	67.6	52 144	80.2
0220	Alexandria, LA	117 515	59.9	26.7	7.4	5.2	0.8	47 120	68.0	10 823	80.9
0240	Allentown-Bethlehem-Easton, PA	601 247	61.0	20.9	8.7	7.5	1.8	247 148	71.6	63 573	75.5
0280	Altoona, PA	121 866	66.7	24.0	5.5	3.5	0.3	51 518	72.9	14 060	77.8
0320	Amarillo, TX.................	201 303	48.1	23.4	20.1	6.9	1.5	82 000	65.2	17 545	81.0
0380	Anchorage, AK	240 627	41.6	32.2	5.4	17.9	2.8	94 822	60.0	8 779	73.6
0450	Anniston, AL	105 320	57.1	27.2	6.9	7.8	1.0	45 307	72.5	10 943	83.9
0460	Appleton-Oshkosh-Neenah, WI	334 956	56.2	22.4	15.0	5.4	1.1	136 597	71.3	26 894	76.0
0480	Asheville, NC...............	213 232	53.6	24.1	8.3	12.4	1.6	93 776	70.8	22 451	81.6
0500	Athens, GA..................	144 400	42.0	18.7	24.6	11.3	3.4	58 557	54.4	8 639	80.3
0520	Atlanta, GA	3 805 188	44.6	20.3	15.4	16.4	4.3	1 504 871	66.4	196 150	78.8
0580	Auburn-Opalika, AL......	107 968	44.1	20.8	19.6	14.1	1.4	45 702	62.1	6 270	79.3
0600	Augusta-Aiken, GA-SC .	444 539	54.9	22.7	8.2	12.4	1.8	176 867	69.4	34 754	81.9
0640	Austin-San Marcos, TX .	1 157 494	39.4	25.2	20.8	10.1	4.5	471 855	58.3	56 688	79.6
0680	Bakersfield, CA	606 633	47.2	34.9	10.5	3.8	3.6	208 652	62.1	40 739	78.7
0733	Bangor, ME	137 190	58.4	25.0	9.1	6.5	1.0	58 096	69.8	12 583	74.8
0743	Barnstable-Yarmouth, MA	211 653	57.6	21.6	10.5	8.8	1.4	94 822	77.8	32 986	85.5
0760	Baton Rouge, LA...........	559 288	54.3	26.4	11.7	6.1	1.4	223 349	67.9	38 189	83.2
0840	Beaumont-Port Arthur, TX............................	359 247	58.4	25.4	10.6	4.4	1.2	142 327	70.5	35 099	83.5
0860	Bellingham, WA............	156 441	45.4	28.0	14.0	9.8	2.8	64 446	63.4	12 565	76.6
0870	Benton Harbor, MI........	151 825	57.7	26.4	4.0	9.9	2.0	63 569	72.2	15 045	83.5
0880	Billings, MT.................	120 912	52.3	27.5	8.6	11.0	0.6	52 084	69.2	11 415	77.9
0920	Biloxi-Gulfport-Pascagoula, MS	338 292	52.6	24.0	6.4	15.5	1.6	130 111	69.0	27 442	83.6
0960	Binghamton, NY	237 755	60.6	23.8	9.3	5.1	1.2	100 474	67.6	25 652	77.6
1000	Birmingham, AL............	859 463	55.8	20.2	0.7	7.0	1.2	361 304	70.7	79 109	82.1
1010	Bismarck, ND	88 787	56.8	21.7	13.6	7.5	0.4	37 559	70.0	8 046	71.3
1020	Bloomington, IN	114 507	39.0	22.0	20.7	14.6	3.6	46 898	53.9	7 097	77.4
1040	Bloomington-Normal, IL	140 745	46.4	24.7	19.0	8.2	1.7	56 746	66.4	9 565	80.1
1080	Boise City, ID	397 421	44.2	28.7	8.9	16.1	2.0	158 426	71.4	27 315	81.3
1123	Boston-Worcester-Lawrence-Lowell-Brockton, MA-NH	5 671 502	58.0	22.5	7.7	8.4	3.5	2 313 452	61.6	494 084	66.8
1240	Brownsville-Harlingen-San Benito, TX...........	303 696	58.5	28.2	5.0	4.3	4.0	97 267	67.7	23 298	81.3
1260	Bryan-College Station, TX............................	142 773	32.1	23.1	32.6	7.3	4.9	55 202	45.6	6 738	79.1
1280	Buffalo-Niagara Falls, NY	1 099 609	63.5	27.5	4.4	3.2	1.4	468 719	66.2	123 027	74.8
1303	Burlington, VT..............	180 790	54.2	23.3	7.3	13.1	2.1	75 978	68.6	12 415	73.3
1320	Canton-Massillon, OH ...	381 157	62.1	26.2	7.2	4.0	0.5	159 442	72.9	39 150	79.3
1350	Casper, WY	62 306	51.0	29.6	7.4	11.1	0.8	26 819	69.9	5 552	80.8
1360	Cedar Rapids, IA...........	178 464	52.3	28.5	9.3	8.7	1.2	76 753	72.7	15 597	81.0
1400	Champaign-Urbana, IL..	169 301	42.5	24.0	20.9	8.5	4.1	70 597	55.7	11 745	79.6
1480	Charleston, WV	236 908	62.1	23.9	7.5	6.0	0.5	106 254	72.9	26 637	82.4
1440	Charleston-North Charleston, SC	512 476	50.9	21.8	9.7	15.8	1.8	207 957	66.5	37 982	82.1
1520	Charlotte-Gastonia-Rock Hill, NC-SC	1 393 358	49.9	23.8	8.5	14.8	3.0	575 293	68.4	97 375	81.0
1540	Charlottesville, VA........	150 244	47.1	14.1	20.4	15.2	3.2	61 688	62.8	11 442	81.1
1560	Chattanooga, TN-GA ...	436 849	56.4	25.1	5.6	11.7	1.2	185 144	69.9	42 640	79.8
1580	Cheyenne, WY	76 328	46.3	27.5	4.2	19.8	2.3	31 927	69.1	6 240	80.3
14	Chicago-Gary-Kenosha, IL-IN-WI	8 481 933	56.5	26.8	6.9	6.0	3.8	3 302 211	65.2	649 514	75.0
1600	Chicago, IL..................	7 658 511	56.2	27.0	7.0	5.7	4.1	2 971 690	64.6	575 724	74.5
2960	Gary, IN......................	587 389	60.6	24.6	4.4	9.3	1.0	236 282	70.8	53 422	79.9
3740	Kankakee, Il................	96 675	57.3	26.3	10.3	5.1	0.9	38 182	69.4	8 669	77.9
3800	Kenosha, WI................	139 358	55.7	24.1	5.2	13.7	1.3	56 057	69.1	11 699	76.9
1620	Chico-Paradise, CA.......	191 504	47.9	27.9	17.9	4.2	1.9	79 566	60.7	21 039	82.6
21	Cincinnati-Hamilton, OH-KY-IN	1 840 134	54.1	26.3	10.3	8.2	1.2	768 130	67.1	151 601	74.9
1640	Cincinnati, OH-KY-IN .	1 530 242	54.7	26.3	9.6	8.1	1.2	645 048	66.2	128 666	73.8
3200	Hamilton-Middletown, OH	309 892	51.0	26.0	13.4	8.5	1.1	123 082	71.6	22 935	80.9
1660	Clarksville-Hopkinsville, TN-KY.......................	188 650	41.7	22.1	5.0	26.5	4.6	73 187	60.7	11 095	80.5
28	Cleveland-Akron, OH	2 752 843	59.7	26.4	7.9	4.6	1.3	1 166 799	68.8	276 732	77.2
0080	Akron, OH	649 790	57.8	25.1	11.2	5.0	1.0	274 237	70.5	61 167	80.1
1680	Cleveland-Lorain-Elyria, OH	2 103 053	60.3	26.8	6.9	4.5	1.4	892 562	68.3	215 565	76.4
1720	Colorado Springs, CO ...	477 912	40.4	27.2	4.5	24.0	4.0	192 409	64.7	29 228	78.8
1740	Columbia, MO	127 143	39.7	27.8	18.9	11.2	2.3	53 094	57.5	7 350	79.0

[1]MSA = Metropolitan Statistical Area. CMSA = Consolidated MSA. PMSA = Primary MSA. NECMA = New England County Metropolitan Area. See the Appendix A for explanation of these concepts. See Appendix B for list of metropolitan areas identified by type, with component counties.

Table C-4. Metropolitan Areas — **Migration, Housing, and Transportation**

Area name	Owner-occupied by household type (percent)								Median household income			Median housing value (owner estimated)	Median monthly owner costs as a percent of income	
	Family households					Nonfamily households								
	Married-couple family			Other family										
	Total family households	Total	With own children under 18 years	Total	With own children under 18 years	Total nonfamily households	Two or more adults	Living alone	All households	Owner-occupied households	Renter-occupied households	Median housing value (owner estimated)	With a mortgage	Without a mortgage
	11	12	13	14	15	16	17	18	19	20	21	22	23	24
Abilene, TX....................	68.2	74.2	66.5	46.0	36.2	46.6	28.1	50.4	33 701	42 142	23 610	60 000	19.4	10.4
Albany, GA...................	63.6	76.9	69.6	39.5	28.9	44.5	30.1	47.0	34 270	45 191	20 666	75 400	20.1	10.6
Albany-Schenectady-Troy, NY	76.1	84.1	82.0	49.2	36.7	44.3	36.5	46.1	43 158	55 056	26 751	102 200	21.4	12.1
Albuquerque, NM	75.9	83.0	79.0	56.5	48.2	51.1	45.1	52.6	39 030	47 821	24 608	118 500	23.0	9.9
Alexandria, LA	72.9	83.3	78.3	48.3	35.5	56.3	45.8	57.7	29 710	37 024	18 710	68 300	19.9	9.9
Allentown-Bethlehem-Easton, PA	80.3	86.5	84.4	55.2	41.4	52.4	47.1	53.5	42 967	51 726	25 931	111 600	22.1	12.5
Altoona, PA	81.3	87.4	83.7	60.1	45.8	54.9	49.7	55.7	32 846	39 161	18 449	71 100	20.4	11.5
Amarillo, TX..................	73.5	80.3	74.3	50.2	40.4	47.1	34.9	49.3	35 696	45 029	23 143	73 600	19.4	9.9
Anchorage, AK	67.3	74.2	70.4	44.8	39.3	44.8	42.6	45.6	55 441	71 772	35 414	152 300	22.6	9.9
Anniston, AL	78.4	85.4	77.9	56.2	42.6	59.2	40.2	61.9	31 422	37 538	18 027	65 700	19.0	9.9
Appleton-Oshkosh-Neenah, WI	82.4	87.8	87.0	53.3	45.4	47.3	36.3	50.1	47 332	55 597	29 624	102 000	20.3	10.6
Asheville, NC...............	78.7	83.6	78.9	60.3	49.7	55.8	40.9	58.8	36 146	41 851	24 192	99 800	22.1	9.9
Athens, GA	69.5	79.1	75.0	42.4	32.0	32.8	15.0	43.0	33 403	48 973	19 828	102 400	20.2	9.9
Atlanta, GA..................	74.5	82.8	80.5	49.8	41.6	47.9	37.4	51.1	51 772	63 233	33 790	132 600	21.0	9.9
Auburn-Opalika, AL.......	78.1	85.4	82.6	56.9	49.2	38.0	21.8	45.0	30 707	45 615	13 502	85 500	19.8	9.9
Augusta-Aiken, GA-SC .	74.4	83.4	78.6	52.0	40.6	56.6	43.7	58.7	37 768	46 197	22 550	80 800	20.4	9.9
Austin-San Marcos, TX .	71.2	77.8	76.1	48.1	43.6	36.2	28.2	39.3	48 725	63 677	31 684	121 300	21.0	9.9
Bakersfield, CA	65.3	73.4	65.8	42.7	33.3	52.3	42.0	54.5	35 265	46 204	22 590	89 400	23.5	10.5
Bangor, ME	80.8	86.9	84.8	56.3	47.7	48.9	43.6	50.5	33 891	41 826	19 741	77 400	20.5	12.1
Barnstable-Yarmouth, MA	83.9	89.2	84.5	60.5	48.6	66.7	60.3	68.0	45 977	51 480	29 257	178 000	23.1	12.4
Baton Rouge, LA...........	76.0	85.2	82.6	52.7	43.5	49.3	30.2	54.1	38 220	48 742	22 014	92 200	19.2	9.9
Beaumont-Port Arthur, TX..............................	75.7	84.4	78.4	51.0	37.4	57.5	46.2	59.0	35 437	42 549	21 960	58 500	18.4	10.4
Bellingham, WA............	75.4	81.6	77.2	48.6	42.5	42.1	24.3	49.4	40 207	50 466	24 835	149 500	24.3	10.9
Benton Harbor, MI........	78.3	86.8	81.4	51.8	40.1	59.3	53.6	60.2	38 291	45 572	22 558	93 300	19.4	9.9
Billings, MT..................	78.4	85.0	82.7	53.2	45.2	51.3	42.6	53.1	36 889	45 595	21 343	97 200	21.2	9.9
Biloxi-Gulfport-Pascagoula, MS	74.3	81.4	74.7	54.2	42.1	55.9	43.4	58.7	36 630	42 922	25 308	79 500	20.1	9.9
Binghamton, NY	78.3	86.0	83.1	51.4	39.0	48.2	38.8	50.2	36 291	45 787	20 672	73 800	19.9	11.7
Birmingham, AL............	77.8	85.7	82.7	55.7	43.0	54.5	39.1	56.7	38 963	47 341	23 907	93 500	20.1	9.9
Bismarck, ND	81.9	88.2	88.3	50.5	41.3	45.9	35.8	47.9	39 977	48 494	22 783	85 800	20.0	10.1
Bloomington, IN............	74.8	80.2	79.6	54.4	47.5	30.8	15.7	37.8	33 137	52 100	18 820	107 500	19.5	9.9
Bloomington-Normal, IL	80.2	85.7	85.4	56.2	50.1	43.4	24.3	50.2	46 634	59 749	26 838	109 300	19.5	9.9
Boise City, ID	78.1	83.3	80.5	55.3	48.8	55.4	45.9	58.1	42 592	50 733	26 426	114 600	21.4	9.9
Boston-Worcester-Lawrence-Lowell-Brockton, MA-NH	72.9	80.3	80.1	47.5	33.9	40.2	32.2	42.4	52 071	67 134	32 029	186 000	21.9	12.5
Brownsville-Harlingen-San Benito, TX...........	69.9	74.6	66.9	55.8	42.3	57.4	50.0	58.4	26 031	31 387	16 441	48 000	22.2	12.1
Bryan-College Station, TX..............................	63.2	72.0	68.3	34.5	28.2	23.6	9.6	34.2	28 802	53 100	16 736	88 200	19.7	10.6
Buffalo-Niagara Falls, NY	76.1	85.9	84.1	48.2	33.1	48.0	39.5	49.4	38 234	49 730	20 970	86 900	21.6	13.6
Burlington, VT	80.7	86.2	85.9	55.9	49.5	46.0	36.3	49.9	46 094	56 610	27 979	128 100	22.2	13.0
Canton-Massillon, OH ...	80.4	87.1	83.9	54.5	41.5	55.8	49.7	56.9	39 585	46 436	24 383	99 200	20.0	9.9
Casper, WY..................	77.7	84.2	79.1	52.9	46.5	54.5	47.4	56.0	36 359	44 518	22 264	81 400	19.1	9.9
Cedar Rapids, IA...........	83.1	88.6	87.8	58.0	49.5	52.9	42.5	55.5	45 939	53 790	27 363	97 200	19.3	9.9
Champaign-Urbana, IL..	73.9	80.7	79.4	48.3	41.3	32.6	17.8	38.6	37 613	54 057	21 362	91 200	19.2	9.9
Charleston, WV	80.1	86.2	81.8	59.3	45.0	58.1	46.7	59.7	35 307	41 554	21 214	78 400	18.4	9.9
Charleston-North Charleston, SC..........	74.2	81.6	77.3	54.5	44.7	49.9	34.1	54.3	39 319	47 618	26 259	96 700	21.5	10.3
Charlotte-Gastonia-Rock Hill, NC-SC	75.6	83.3	80.4	49.6	39.8	51.9	38.7	55.1	45 915	55 021	31 048	116 200	21.2	9.9
Charlottesville, VA.........	75.3	81.2	79.6	53.1	41.2	41.6	22.3	48.4	44 266	56 285	27 710	135 600	20.8	9.9
Chattanooga, TN-GA	76.8	83.7	79.5	53.7	40.9	53.7	42.7	55.4	37 176	44 837	23 580	86 500	19.9	9.9
Cheyenne, WY..............	75.8	81.1	75.6	55.0	45.5	54.9	52.9	55.2	39 488	47 524	25 172	101 200	21.0	9.9
Chicago-Gary-Kenosha, IL-IN-WI	73.3	81.5	79.2	49.4	37.6	47.6	37.4	49.7	50 724	63 438	31 319	155 100	22.7	11.7
Chicago, IL...............	72.9	81.0	78.9	49.1	37.4	47.0	36.5	49.1	51 349	65 040	31 716	161 700	22.9	11.8
Gary, IN....................	77.3	86.2	82.4	52.7	38.6	54.8	48.1	55.9	44 275	52 843	26 033	102 400	19.8	10.5
Kankakee, IL............	76.3	83.9	80.7	51.2	38.7	53.2	45.2	54.7	41 612	50 084	24 266	95 800	21.6	11.3
Kenosha, WI..............	77.7	85.1	83.2	51.6	41.2	50.2	40.4	52.4	46 594	57 204	28 384	118 200	21.4	12.5
Chico-Paradise, CA.......	70.6	78.4	68.6	45.2	34.3	44.5	23.6	52.6	31 769	41 725	20 489	116 200	24.1	10.3
Cincinnati-Hamilton, OH-KY-IN	77.2	85.4	84.1	49.5	37.7	46.1	37.1	47.8	44 761	56 549	25 860	112 800	20.4	10.3
Cincinnati, OH-KY-IN .	76.6	85.2	84.1	48.8	37.2	45.4	37.9	46.7	44 106	56 205	25 519	111 600	20.4	10.3
Hamilton-Middletown, OH	79.9	86.3	84.0	53.6	40.8	50.5	33.3	54.7	47 702	58 388	28 360	119 200	20.4	10.1
Clarksville-Hopkinsville, TN-KY	64.6	69.4	61.9	46.6	36.6	49.3	38.0	51.8	36 201	43 915	26 774	81 400	21.4	9.9
Cleveland-Akron, OH	77.8	86.4	84.3	52.7	38.0	51.2	43.2	52.6	42 056	52 124	25 072	115 300	21.6	11.6
Akron, OH	79.5	87.1	85.3	53.9	40.5	51.9	40.3	54.4	42 482	51 985	24 797	110 700	21.0	11.0
Cleveland-Lorain-Elyria, OH	77.3	86.2	83.9	52.4	37.3	51.0	44.3	52.0	41 928	52 168	25 139	116 600	21.8	11.8
Colorado Springs, CO ...	72.1	77.7	72.4	49.4	41.6	47.4	37.7	50.0	46 658	56 759	30 759	143 600	22.5	9.9
Columbia, MO	72.9	80.2	79.0	47.4	43.9	34.9	22.1	40.2	37 383	53 277	22 382	100 800	19.7	9.9

Table C-4. Metropolitan Areas — **Migration, Housing, and Transportation**

Area name	Percent who pay 35 percent or more of income for housing expenses		Means of transportation to work (percent except where noted)						Vehicles available (percent of households)		
			Number of workers 16 years and over	Car, truck, or van							
	Median gross rent	Owners	Renters		Drove alone	Carpooled	Public transportation	Other means	Walked	No vehicles	One vehicle	Two or more vehicles
	25	26	27	28	29	30	31	32	33	34	35	36
Abilene, TX..................	472	11.1	26.9	58 718	81.1	12.6	0.5	1.4	2.5	6.2	37.5	56.2
Albany, GA..................	477	16.6	30.8	49 928	79.8	15.0	0.9	0.7	2.0	11.2	36.2	52.6
Albany-Schenectady-Troy, NY	586	13.8	29.5	419 094	79.4	9.9	3.2	0.6	3.8	11.2	36.6	52.2
Albuquerque, NM	563	17.4	33.2	326 775	77.7	13.3	1.3	1.6	2.3	6.4	35.7	57.9
Alexandria, LA..............	434	14.2	31.1	49 957	78.7	13.9	1.3	1.5	2.2	11.1	38.0	50.9
Allentown-Bethlehem-Easton, PA	572	14.9	28.0	299 469	81.9	9.9	1.3	0.6	3.7	9.5	32.6	58.0
Altoona, PA	411	12.9	28.3	56 733	82.2	10.4	0.5	0.9	3.7	9.8	35.9	54.3
Amarillo, TX..................	475	10.9	29.5	99 657	82.0	12.9	0.4	0.9	1.3	6.0	36.3	57.7
Anchorage, AK	736	15.8	28.3	131 228	74.4	14.6	2.0	2.6	2.7	6.4	35.1	58.5
Anniston, AL.................	413	11.7	27.8	47 181	85.1	10.6	0.5	0.9	1.2	7.9	32.0	60.1
Appleton-Oshkosh-Neenah, WI	513	9.9	20.0	187 593	84.4	7.7	0.7	0.9	3.3	5.3	30.6	64.0
Asheville, NC................	543	15.3	28.7	107 703	79.5	13.0	0.8	0.9	2.0	7.7	33.5	58.8
Athens, GA..................	537	12.9	40.6	73 401	77.2	14.1	1.6	1.3	3.2	7.3	33.0	59.8
Atlanta, GA..................	746	15.4	28.5	2 060 632	77.0	10.6	3.7	1.0	1.3	7.3	31.8	60.9
Auburn-Opalika, AL .	449	12.5	44.1	52 119	84.1	10.8	0.5	0.9	1.9	6.8	34.3	58.9
Augusta-Aiken, GA-SC .	500	14.7	27.9	209 438	80.3	13.6	0.7	1.0	2.7	9.0	33.5	57.6
Austin-San Marcos, TX .	721	13.7	32.2	649 645	76.5	13.7	2.6	1.6	2.1	5.9	35.6	58.4
Bakersfield, CA	518	20.2	34.9	229 733	73.8	18.4	1.4	1.8	1.9	10.4	33.9	55.7
Bangor, ME	468	13.3	31.2	68 652	79.2	10.7	0.9	0.9	4.6	7.7	35.3	56.9
Barnstable-Yarmouth, MA......	723	18.3	30.5	99 197	81.3	8.1	1.4	1.3	2.6	5.0	38.5	56.6
Baton Rouge, LA...........	502	12.9	31.1	273 180	82.0	11.7	1.0	1.1	2.0	8.0	35.8	56.2
Beaumont-Port Arthur, TX......	476	11.8	27.8	152 590	83.1	12.0	0.6	1.3	1.3	9.3	36.8	53.9
Bellingham, WA.............	622	18.2	38.1	79 263	75.9	10.6	2.0	2.4	4.1	6.7	31.0	62.3
Benton Harbor, MI........	476	12.4	28.9	75 081	81.6	10.7	0.6	1.0	2.9	7.9	35.2	56.9
Billings, MT..................	474	13.4	29.7	64 697	81.4	9.8	1.1	1.1	2.5	6.7	32.1	61.2
Biloxi-Gulfport-Pascagoula, MS	535	14.5	26.9	163 050	80.0	13.3	0.4	1.2	2.9	6.2	35.0	58.8
Binghamton, NY	463	11.7	32.4	113 884	79.7	10.8	2.3	0.7	3.9	11.3	36.8	51.8
Birmingham, AL.............	507	14.6	27.0	410 250	80.5	11.7	0.8	0.6	1.2	8.4	33.3	58.4
Bismarck, ND................	438	9.4	26.2	50 009	82.2	9.4	0.4	0.6	2.8	6.8	29.0	64.2
Bloomington, IN............	560	11.3	44.7	60 423	73.6	10.3	1.8	2.2	8.6	8.0	37.1	54.9
Bloomington-Normal, IL	533	10.3	27.5	79 370	79.7	9.9	1.1	0.8	5.2	6.0	33.5	60.5
Boise City, ID	593	14.1	30.3	214 649	79.9	11.4	0.7	1.8	2.2	4.7	29.1	66.2
Boston-Worcester-Lawrence-Lowell-Brockton, MA-NH	707	16.1	28.1	3 012 008	74.2	8.9	8.8	1.0	4.0	12.3	35.9	51.8
Brownsville-Harlingen-San Benito, TX..........	413	15.2	30.4	106 769	73.2	19.4	0.8	1.8	2.3	11.6	39.8	48.6
Bryan-College Station, TX........	584	12.9	49.3	70 562	76.5	13.2	1.0	3.5	3.3	6.6	36.2	57.3
Buffalo-Niagara Falls, NY	510	14.9	35.5	520 350	81.7	9.4	3.5	0.6	2.7	14.3	38.3	47.4
Burlington, VT	636	14.3	31.5	105 714	75.4	12.2	1.2	0.9	5.8	6.8	32.1	61.0
Canton-Massillon, OH ...	483	12.1	24.9	190 116	86.0	8.0	1.0	0.7	1.9	6.9	31.5	61.6
Casper, WY..................	409	10.0	22.8	32 619	82.7	11.3	0.4	0.9	1.4	5.4	31.2	63.5
Cedar Rapids, IA...........	510	8.8	23.6	102 234	82.3	10.3	1.1	0.7	2.6	6.2	31.4	62.5
Champaign-Urbana, IL...	540	10.2	39.7	91 368	69.4	11.0	4.9	2.5	8.5	9.5	39.2	51.3
Charleston, WV	449	9.9	25.1	111 116	80.8	11.8	1.8	0.8	2.3	11.6	36.5	51.8
Charleston-North Charleston, SC...........	592	16.5	29.8	254 193	78.1	13.0	1.6	1.6	3.5	9.7	35.3	54.9
Charlotte-Gastonia-Rock Hill, NC-SC	627	14.7	25.5	751 629	80.9	12.9	1.4	0.8	1.2	6.6	32.4	61.0
Charlottesville, VA........	661	12.9	34.5	77 143	73.8	12.2	2.4	1.3	5.4	6.9	33.3	59.8
Chattanooga, TN-GA	495	12.9	26.8	219 506	82.7	12.2	0.8	0.7	1.5	7.6	32.1	60.2
Cheyenne, WY	473	12.4	23.9	39 423	80.4	12.4	0.4	1.0	2.2	5.6	32.1	62.2
Chicago-Gary-Kenosha, IL-IN-WI	659	17.0	29.1	4 218 108	70.5	11.0	11.5	1.0	3.1	13.6	36.1	50.3
Chicago, IL..................	669	17.4	29.2	3 817 402	69.3	11.0	12.5	1.1	3.2	14.2	36.3	49.5
Gary, IN......................	563	13.6	28.3	281 398	81.9	10.4	2.7	0.8	2.0	9.1	34.6	56.3
Kankakee, IL................	539	14.8	29.9	47 255	81.1	11.6	1.1	1.1	2.6	7.3	34.3	56.9
Kenosha, WI................	589	14.0	27.0	72 053	82.8	10.7	1.2	0.8	2.1	6.8	34.3	58.9
Chico-Paradise, CA.......	563	19.3	41.8	80 809	74.3	13.3	1.1	3.6	3.4	7.7	35.3	57.1
Cincinnati-Hamilton, OH-KY-IN	516	12.4	27.4	951 709	81.4	10.0	2.9	0.6	2.3	9.6	32.3	58.1
Cincinnati, OH-KY-IN .	505	12.6	27.3	791 395	80.8	10.2	3.3	0.6	2.2	10.3	32.9	56.8
Hamilton-Middletown, OH	569	11.6	28.1	160 314	84.2	9.1	0.9	0.6	2.6	6.1	29.4	64.5
Clarksville-Hopkinsville, TN-KY......................	519	15.1	21.6	98 700	79.1	12.8	0.8	1.4	3.8	7.2	32.0	60.8
Cleveland-Akron, OH	545	15.1	29.3	1 375 774	82.3	8.7	3.4	0.7	2.1	10.0	35.4	54.6
Akron, OH	545	13.8	28.9	336 437	85.4	8.0	1.4	0.6	2.0	7.5	32.8	59.7
Cleveland-Lorain-Elyria, OH	545	15.5	29.4	1 039 337	81.3	9.0	4.1	0.7	2.2	10.8	36.2	53.0
Colorado Springs, CO...	657	16.3	29.3	263 805	78.0	12.0	1.0	1.2	3.7	5.4	31.6	63.1
Columbia, MO	523	9.9	34.5	71 967	77.4	12.5	0.7	1.5	4.7	6.5	36.0	57.4

Table C-4. Metropolitan Areas — **Migration, Housing, and Transportation**

CMSA/MSA/ PMSA/NECMA code[1]	Area name	Total population 5 years and over	Residence in 1995 (percent) Same house	Same county, different house	Same state, different county	Different state	Outside the United States	Occupied housing units Number	Percent owner-occupied	Householders 65 years and over Number	Percent owner-occupied
		1	2	3	4	5	6	7	8	9	10
1760	Columbia, SC	502 007	51.5	22.0	11.9	12.5	2.1	203 341	67.9	33 919	82.2
1800	Columbus, GA-AL	254 770	48.5	23.3	7.5	17.7	3.0	101 314	59.3	21 670	77.7
1840	Columbus, OH	1 430 333	48.8	29.1	12.5	7.4	2.2	610 757	62.3	101 913	76.4
1880	Corpus Christi, TX	351 495	53.5	27.9	10.0	7.1	1.6	132 458	62.5	27 337	78.7
1890	Corvallis, OR	74 282	42.3	19.4	20.8	14.5	3.1	30 145	57.3	4 947	78.4
1900	Cumberland, MD-WV	96 802	65.1	20.3	4.5	9.7	0.4	40 106	72.2	11 633	78.8
31	Dallas-Fort Worth, TX	4 806 038	44.6	28.3	13.5	8.8	4.8	1 906 764	60.5	267 104	79.3
1920	Dallas, TX	3 234 921	44.1	28.1	13.6	8.8	5.4	1 281 957	58.9	171 584	78.1
2800	Fort Worth-Arlington, TX	1 571 117	45.7	28.8	13.1	8.8	3.6	624 807	63.6	95 520	81.6
1950	Danville, VA	103 789	63.5	16.8	13.1	5.9	0.7	45 291	70.1	12 762	78.8
1960	Davenport-Moline-Rock Island, IA-IL	335 426	57.3	26.0	6.1	9.3	1.2	143 102	71.3	33 344	79.1
2000	Dayton-Springfield, OH	889 001	54.8	28.0	9.3	6.9	1.0	379 626	67.2	84 494	78.9
2020	Daytona Beach, FL	469 260	51.3	22.8	9.2	14.9	1.8	206 017	76.2	72 001	86.9
2030	Decatur, AL	136 341	58.9	25.2	8.6	6.4	0.9	57 140	75.5	12 395	81.0
2040	Decatur, IL	107 397	55.8	29.7	8.3	5.5	0.6	46 561	71.7	11 751	81.9
34	Denver-Boulder-Greeley, CO	2 399 413	44.0	21.7	15.4	15.0	3.9	1 003 218	66.4	150 109	75.9
1125	Boulder-Longmont, CO	273 719	40.8	24.4	10.0	21.1	3.9	114 680	64.7	14 819	77.2
2080	Denver, CO	1 958 738	44.6	21.0	15.9	14.5	4.0	825 291	66.5	124 580	75.6
3060	Greeley, CO	166 956	42.5	26.4	17.7	10.6	2.8	63 247	68.7	10 710	77.6
2120	Des Moines, IA	421 780	51.0	27.3	11.0	8.4	2.3	179 404	70.4	33 826	76.5
35	Detroit-Ann Arbor-Flint, MI	5 077 834	57.4	26.8	9.0	4.7	2.1	2 081 797	72.2	426 917	78.9
0440	Ann Arbor, MI	541 148	48.8	21.5	17.6	9.1	3.0	216 641	70.0	32 945	82.0
2160	Detroit, MI	4 132 100	58.5	27.0	8.0	4.2	2.2	1 695 331	72.4	360 698	78.3
2640	Flint, MI	404 586	56.8	31.2	7.5	3.9	0.7	169 825	73.2	33 274	82.8
2180	Dothan, AL	128 161	53.2	24.6	8.4	11.9	1.8	54 712	67.7	11 807	80.0
2190	Dover, DE	117 562	55.6	24.3	5.2	12.8	2.0	47 224	70.0	9 856	82.1
2200	Dubuque, IA	83 184	60.0	25.4	5.5	7.9	1.3	33 690	73.5	7 908	79.6
2240	Duluth-Superior, MN-WI	230 826	60.9	22.8	8.6	6.9	0.8	100 427	74.1	25 590	76.4
2290	Eau Claire, WI	139 483	55.2	22.6	14.3	7.3	0.6	57 178	68.9	12 558	75.8
2320	El Paso, TX	621 288	55.2	30.4	2.4	6.9	5.1	210 022	63.6	40 868	76.0
2330	Elkhart-Goshen, IN	168 052	51.3	30.8	6.1	8.8	3.0	66 154	72.2	13 292	78.4
2335	Elmira, NY	85 707	60.0	26.0	7.6	5.8	0.5	35 049	68.9	9 073	79.8
2340	Enid, OK	53 944	51.7	27.7	8.1	11.2	1.4	23 175	70.2	5 966	84.1
2360	Erie, PA	263 678	60.2	28.3	4.8	5.3	1.2	106 507	69.2	25 937	75.3
2400	Eugene-Springfield, OR	304 463	46.8	31.1	7.7	12.5	1.8	130 453	62.3	28 211	79.4
2440	Evansville-Henderson, IN-KY	277 550	56.2	26.7	9.2	7.2	0.7	118 361	70.9	27 572	77.6
2520	Fargo-Moorhead, ND-MN	163 137	47.6	25.3	10.8	14.7	1.6	69 985	59.0	12 519	65.4
2560	Fayetteville, NC	278 459	45.5	22.1	4.7	23.0	4.7	107 358	59.4	15 543	82.8
2580	Fayetteville-Springdale-Rogers, AR	287 823	44.0	25.8	10.2	17.1	2.9	118 363	65.7	24 283	84.1
2620	Flagstaff, AZ-UT	113 411	46.8	22.4	13.7	15.5	1.5	42 685	62.3	6 428	86.0
2650	Florence, AL	134 442	60.8	24.3	8.2	6.0	0.6	58 549	74.2	14 402	81.9
2655	Florence, SC	117 636	59.6	24.3	7.6	7.5	0.9	47 147	73.0	9 619	81.7
2670	Fort Collins-Loveland, CO	236 326	41.5	26.2	12.3	18.2	1.9	97 164	67.7	15 058	81.1
2700	Fort Myers-Cape Coral, FL	417 783	47.7	24.4	6.1	18.7	3.1	188 599	76.5	70 186	88.5
2710	Fort Pierce-Port St. Lucie, FL	303 306	51.1	21.0	12.6	13.1	2.2	132 221	78.8	50 150	91.7
2720	Fort Smith, AR-OK	192 024	51.7	26.1	9.7	11.2	1.3	79 763	68.7	17 416	79.8
2750	Fort Walton Beach, FL	159 735	46.4	22.1	6.3	21.0	4.1	66 269	66.4	13 422	84.0
2760	Fort Wayne, IN	464 582	55.4	28.8	7.6	7.1	1.2	192 052	73.9	38 370	79.5
2840	Fresno, CA	846 144	51.3	34.2	9.1	2.2	3.1	289 095	57.7	58 006	75.7
2880	Gadsden, AL	96 773	61.6	24.9	7.5	5.1	0.8	41 615	74.4	11 871	81.2
2900	Gainesville, FL	206 860	39.9	23.4	22.4	10.9	3.4	87 509	54.9	13 848	83.9
2975	Glens Falls, NY	117 448	62.2	19.8	11.9	5.6	0.6	48 184	72.0	11 767	80.1
2980	Goldsboro, NC	105 621	53.0	25.9	7.3	10.8	3.0	42 612	65.3	8 842	75.5
2985	Grand Forks, ND-MN	91 385	49.0	25.0	8.8	15.1	2.1	37 505	60.2	7 492	72.8
2995	Grand Junction, CO	109 124	45.1	29.1	10.4	14.5	0.9	45 823	72.7	11 173	82.5
3000	Grand Rapids-Muskegon-Holland, MI	1 007 260	54.5	27.2	10.9	5.6	1.8	396 047	74.9	73 612	81.3
3040	Great Falls, MT	75 002	52.8	24.5	7.5	13.4	1.8	32 547	64.9	7 331	75.1
3080	Green Bay, WI	211 086	53.3	29.0	9.7	6.4	1.6	87 295	65.4	16 223	72.2
3120	Greensboro—Winston-Salem—High Point, NC	1 169 468	54.2	24.0	9.8	9.4	2.7	498 751	68.7	102 125	80.7
3150	Greenville, NC	125 238	44.7	27.4	16.5	9.8	1.6	52 539	58.1	8 599	73.2
3160	Greenville-Spartanburg-Anderson, SC	898 389	54.7	25.1	8.1	10.4	1.7	374 741	71.5	77 162	81.9
3240	Harrisburg-Lebanon-Carlisle, PA	592 759	59.7	22.4	10.9	5.7	1.3	248 931	70.3	58 255	76.8

[1]MSA = Metropolitan Statistical Area. CMSA = Consolidated MSA. PMSA = Primary MSA. NECMA = New England County Metropolitan Area. See the Appendix A for explanation of these concepts. See Appendix B for list of metropolitan areas identified by type, with component counties.

Table C-4. Metropolitan Areas — **Migration, Housing, and Transportation**

Area name	Owner-occupied by household type (percent)								Median household income			Median housing value (owner estimated)	Median monthly owner costs as a percent of income	
	Family households					Nonfamily households								
		Married-couple family		Other family										
	Total family households	Total	With own children under 18 years	Total	With own children under 18 years	Total nonfamily households	Two or more adults	Living alone	All households	Owner-occupied households	Renter-occupied households		With a mortgage	Without a mortgage
	11	12	13	14	15	16	17	18	19	20	21	22	23	24
Columbia, SC	76.3	84.7	81.9	52.4	42.9	50.6	34.4	54.5	41 516	51 330	26 220	94 000	20.3	9.9
Columbus, GA-AL	63.7	73.2	63.9	43.0	30.6	49.2	37.6	51.1	34 374	44 161	24 220	81 400	21.1	9.9
Columbus, OH..............	73.2	82.1	79.6	45.3	35.9	42.7	31.2	45.8	44 605	57 440	28 446	118 700	21.1	10.4
Corpus Christi, TX........	68.4	75.7	69.1	48.7	33.1	46.1	35.3	48.4	35 599	44 702	24 137	67 100	21.5	12.0
Corvallis, OR	72.9	78.3	75.1	43.7	39.8	32.9	20.6	39.0	41 878	61 480	22 832	166 500	21.4	9.9
Cumberland, MD-WV	80.4	86.0	80.7	58.1	44.7	56.0	37.7	59.2	30 948	36 869	17 133	69 900	19.8	10.4
Dallas-Fort Worth, TX ...	69.2	76.5	72.6	45.1	37.3	40.4	32.8	42.2	47 200	60 936	32 433	96 200	20.4	11.2
Dallas, TX..............	67.9	75.4	71.7	43.4	35.9	39.0	31.8	40.8	48 068	62 726	33 200	102 100	20.5	11.2
Fort Worth-Arlington, TX..............	72.0	78.5	74.3	48.8	40.1	43.4	34.9	45.3	45 750	57 099	31 280	87 500	20.2	11.2
Danville, VA..............	75.4	85.2	79.5	50.2	34.3	58.1	49.0	59.1	31 156	38 212	18 875	72 500	19.5	9.9
Davenport-Moline-Rock Island, IA-IL..............	79.7	86.2	82.7	55.1	45.2	54.5	47.4	55.7	40 617	48 934	23 388	83 300	19.0	10.1
Dayton-Springfield, OH .	75.2	83.6	78.3	48.5	36.2	51.1	38.1	53.5	41 380	51 473	25 662	98 300	20.6	10.7
Daytona Beach, FL	81.9	87.1	80.0	62.2	49.3	65.0	55.9	67.2	35 716	39 839	24 790	85 300	23.0	10.4
Decatur, AL	81.3	86.7	84.2	58.4	44.0	59.5	45.9	60.8	36 097	42 704	21 011	78 300	19.4	9.9
Decatur, IL....................	79.2	00.4	02.0	40.0	38.1	56.7	50.0	57.7	37 834	46 085	21 150	68 500	18.1	10.0
Denver-Boulder-Greeley, CO	76.2	82.3	79.9	53.4	46.7	48.9	41.0	51.4	50 891	62 647	31 595	172 800	22.5	9.9
Boulder-Longmont, CO	77.4	82.5	81.3	54.1	51.2	45.5	32.7	52.1	55 678	71 595	33 189	231 000	22.3	9.9
Denver, CO	76.1	82.4	80.0	53.2	46.1	49.5	43.5	51.1	50 985	62 698	31 816	170 900	22.5	9.9
Greeley, CO	76.4	81.1	77.1	54.6	48.2	48.9	32.9	54.4	42 152	51 443	24 646	136 600	23.9	9.9
Des Moines, IA............	00.8	86.4	85.1	57.7	47.9	49.8	42.6	51.6	46 355	56 138	28 117	100 800	20.2	10.6
Detroit-Ann Arbor-Flint, MI..............	80.2	88.1	86.2	58.6	46.8	55.5	48.6	56.8	48 953	59 056	27 775	127 900	19.8	10.4
Ann Arbor, MI..............	82.7	88.0	87.2	58.1	48.4	45.1	31.6	49.6	54 866	67 646	30 236	163 800	20.2	9.9
Detroit, MI..............	79.9	87.9	86.0	58.8	46.7	56.5	51.8	57.4	48 937	58 775	28 056	127 800	19.8	10.6
Flint, MI..............	79.9	89.6	86.2	57.4	46.8	58.7	53.5	59.7	41 999	50 876	22 627	90 800	18.8	9.9
Dothan, AL	72.9	80.1	72.6	49.8	37.3	54.8	45.2	56.0	33 156	41 030	20 634	70 200	18.1	9.9
Dover, DE...................	75.0	82.4	70.0	50.1	43.2	67.4	50.3	59.2	40 618	47 482	26 666	103 300	21.7	9.9
Dubuque, IA..............	83.0	88.1	85.2	57.0	47.8	52.3	43.0	53.9	39 611	46 927	23 338	91 900	19.4	9.9
Duluth-Superior, MN-WI	85.0	92.0	91.0	60.6	51.0	54.8	43.5	57.1	36 001	43 301	17 996	73 900	19.0	9.9
Eau Claire, WI..............	02.0	07.0	00.0	63.4	44.6	44.5	27.9	49.9	39 015	47 791	24 577	93 100	19.7	10.5
El Paso, TX..............	67.8	73.5	67.6	52.5	40.2	47.4	41.7	48.2	30 858	38 738	20 054	67 100	21.7	10.1
Elkhart-Goshen, IN........	79.1	85.7	82.4	52.8	44.9	54.1	50.1	55.0	44 479	51 325	29 412	95 600	18.7	9.9
Elmira, NY	76.6	85.6	83.1	49.9	38.2	53.5	50.5	54.1	36 126	44 452	20 839	66 200	20.7	12.7
Enid, OK	75.4	80.2	72.7	54.1	42.5	59.0	42.9	61.4	32 917	37 437	23 123	59 100	18.9	9.9
Erie, PA...................	79.2	86.9	84.3	53.7	40.0	48.8	40.7	50.4	36 578	44 782	21 072	82 500	20.4	11.6
Eugene-Springfield, OR	72.8	80.4	73.5	45.2	35.4	44.2	31.8	48.9	36 684	46 924	23 168	136 000	23.3	9.9
Evansville-Henderson, IN-KY..............	80.0	86.8	84.5	53.4	41.9	51.7	42.3	53.4	39 100	46 040	21 842	84 000	18.8	9.9
Fargo-Moorhead, ND-MN..............	70.2	03.9	85.0	42.2	30.3	32.4	22.2	35.7	37 776	51 975	22 435	90 600	20.2	9.9
Fayetteville, NC..............	63.2	69.1	60.6	47.0	37.0	49.2	35.7	52.2	37 226	45 619	27 363	84 900	23.2	10.8
Fayetteville-Springdale-Rogers, AR..............	73.5	78.8	71.8	48.1	41.0	47.3	31.1	51.6	37 238	45 252	25 243	90 700	19.5	9.9
Flagstaff, AZ-UT	70.8	77.3	73.5	50.8	43.4	44.3	28.5	51.8	38 000	46 787	27 261	122 300	22.1	9.9
Florence, AL	81.0	87.3	83.4	56.4	42.1	57.8	38.8	60.0	32 630	39 564	17 173	75 500	19.9	9.9
Florence, SC	78.5	86.9	84.2	59.3	47.4	58.4	43.1	60.4	34 845	40 973	20 909	71 900	19.6	9.9
Fort Collins-Loveland, CO	78.8	83.6	81.1	54.7	48.8	46.7	30.7	54.4	48 484	59 785	29 257	168 200	22.5	9.9
Fort Myers-Cape Coral, FL	81.3	86.6	76.2	56.8	46.6	66.4	56.5	68.8	40 307	44 223	29 027	96 700	23.0	10.6
Fort Pierce-Port St. Lucie, FL..............	81.7	87.1	77.3	57.3	46.0	72.5	62.8	74.6	38 807	42 993	26 411	88 700	22.8	10.2
Fort Smith, AR-OK	74.6	81.1	75.4	49.8	39.3	54.2	42.9	55.9	32 292	38 472	21 710	67 100	18.9	9.9
Fort Walton Beach, FL..	71.7	76.8	66.6	50.4	39.5	53.7	40.7	57.0	41 358	49 096	30 438	96 800	21.2	9.9
Fort Wayne, IN..............	82.0	88.4	86.5	57.5	49.7	55.8	48.8	57.2	42 781	50 236	26 637	87 400	18.5	9.9
Fresno, CA	61.1	69.6	60.1	38.5	27.5	47.5	35.3	50.5	34 740	47 066	22 263	105 000	24.3	10.8
Gadsden, AL	79.2	85.5	78.4	59.4	43.8	62.6	45.3	64.3	31 073	36 466	18 090	66 500	19.7	9.9
Gainesville, FL	71.5	80.6	79.8	48.1	39.4	34.9	18.9	43.8	31 372	47 699	18 194	88 400	20.9	9.9
Glens Falls, NY	79.5	85.9	82.3	55.9	43.9	55.6	49.0	57.0	38 267	45 108	24 230	86 600	22.4	12.7
Goldsboro, NC	70.6	78.3	72.4	48.9	42.9	52.1	30.5	54.5	33 790	41 227	23 417	77 000	20.8	10.3
Grand Forks, ND-MN	72.7	79.0	75.9	45.4	37.2	38.2	19.9	43.2	35 423	46 752	22 658	82 600	20.0	10.8
Grand Junction, CO	78.7	84.5	79.0	54.2	44.3	59.3	47.0	62.2	35 680	41 872	22 459	113 800	23.0	9.9
Grand Rapids-Muskegon-Holland, MI..............	83.0	89.3	88.2	58.5	51.2	55.4	45.2	57.8	46 156	53 162	27 929	111 000	19.5	9.9
Great Falls, MT	73.5	79.5	71.7	50.2	40.9	48.1	45.5	48.6	32 732	40 983	20 828	89 600	22.1	10.1
Green Bay, WI	77.4	85.2	83.9	43.8	35.5	42.0	35.0	43.9	46 293	56 928	28 582	116 100	20.6	11.1
Greensboro—Winston-Salem—High Point, NC	75.6	83.3	79.0	50.1	39.7	53.5	37.8	56.5	40 802	49 072	26 804	99 600	20.8	9.9
Greenville, NC	71.2	81.0	80.5	48.0	41.4	37.0	20.0	43.1	32 579	46 576	19 199	82 000	20.5	11.3
Greenville-Spartanburg-Anderson, SC	78.4	85.5	82.4	54.7	43.9	55.4	38.1	58.4	38 279	45 391	24 251	88 700	20.1	9.9
Harrisburg-Lebanon-Carlisle, PA	79.3	85.6	82.4	54.5	42.4	51.5	45.0	52.7	42 960	51 257	27 490	104 700	21.1	10.5

Table C-4. Metropolitan Areas — **Migration, Housing, and Transportation**

Area name	Percent who pay 35 percent or more of income for housing expenses			Means of transportation to work (percent except where noted)						Vehicles available (percent of households)		
	Median gross rent	Owners	Renters	Number of workers 16 years and over	Car, truck, or van		Public transportation	Other means	Walked	No vehicles	One vehicle	Two or more vehicles
					Drove alone	Carpooled						
	25	26	27	28	29	30	31	32	33	34	35	36
Columbia, SC	565	13.9	27.8	265 227	79.3	11.9	1.3	1.3	3.7	7.5	34.6	57.9
Columbus, GA-AL	485	15.7	25.5	123 185	75.8	14.2	1.2	1.7	5.2	11.0	36.4	52.6
Columbus, OH	586	13.7	27.3	777 922	82.0	9.6	2.3	0.7	2.4	7.5	34.8	57.6
Corpus Christi, TX	545	15.6	29.2	158 373	76.3	16.0	1.6	1.6	2.1	9.1	37.8	53.0
Corvallis, OR	597	13.5	41.6	37 747	70.7	10.4	1.6	5.2	7.7	5.7	33.2	61.2
Cumberland, MD-WV	381	11.9	28.0	41 166	80.2	13.4	0.5	0.5	3.8	10.4	33.3	56.3
Dallas-Fort Worth, TX	649	13.7	25.4	2 527 648	78.8	14.0	1.8	1.0	1.5	6.1	35.6	58.4
Dallas, TX	667	14.1	25.5	1 707 321	77.6	14.3	2.4	1.0	1.5	6.4	36.2	57.4
Fort Worth-Arlington, TX	607	13.0	25.2	820 327	81.2	13.3	0.5	1.0	1.4	5.4	34.3	60.3
Danville, VA	402	12.2	27.3	48 193	81.2	14.0	1.0	0.8	1.1	11.9	32.1	56.0
Davenport-Moline-Rock Island, IA-IL	468	10.2	25.8	173 327	83.6	9.4	0.9	0.9	2.3	7.7	33.8	58.4
Dayton-Springfield, OH	526	13.5	27.6	448 063	84.0	8.9	1.8	0.7	2.4	8.4	34.4	57.3
Daytona Beach, FL	603	17.8	33.7	204 364	79.0	13.3	1.0	1.9	1.8	6.7	42.2	51.1
Decatur, AL	423	11.9	23.3	64 248	85.2	11.1	0.1	0.7	1.0	6.6	28.9	64.5
Decatur, IL	448	10.3	27.2	51 709	84.4	9.4	0.9	0.7	2.1	8.2	35.3	56.5
Denver-Boulder-Greeley, CO	706	16.6	30.5	1 346 025	75.6	11.5	4.3	1.4	2.4	7.0	32.8	60.2
Boulder-Longmont, CO	825	16.4	36.6	159 786	70.8	10.4	4.9	3.5	4.1	5.4	31.9	62.7
Denver, CO	700	16.5	29.5	1 100 029	76.1	11.6	4.6	1.1	2.1	7.3	33.4	59.3
Greeley, CO	564	18.4	32.2	86 210	78.5	12.7	0.4	1.3	2.9	5.6	26.8	67.6
Des Moines, IA	566	11.6	24.8	241 674	81.8	10.7	1.6	0.6	2.1	6.3	32.3	61.4
Detroit-Ann Arbor-Flint, MI	584	13.8	29.0	2 482 457	84.2	9.3	1.8	0.7	1.8	8.7	34.7	56.5
Ann Arbor, MI	665	12.5	31.2	294 720	80.1	8.5	2.0	1.0	4.9	5.5	31.4	63.1
Detroit, MI	583	14.0	28.4	2 000 149	84.8	9.2	1.9	0.6	1.4	9.2	35.1	55.7
Flint, MI	507	12.6	32.0	187 588	84.3	10.6	1.2	0.6	1.2	7.8	35.6	56.6
Dothan, AL	408	12.3	23.0	61 275	84.7	10.5	0.5	1.1	1.5	7.6	34.1	58.3
Dover, DE	573	14.9	26.4	59 813	79.7	12.9	0.8	1.2	2.3	7.8	32.6	59.6
Dubuque, IA	434	8.0	23.8	45 167	81.9	8.2	0.6	0.5	4.8	7.2	31.8	61.0
Duluth-Superior, MN-WI	414	10.4	29.8	113 094	78.7	10.9	2.1	0.8	4.3	10.0	33.7	56.4
Eau Claire, WI	476	10.3	25.5	75 897	80.6	8.5	1.0	1.0	4.7	6.4	30.0	63.6
El Paso, TX	468	15.5	31.2	244 464	75.9	16.2	2.2	1.3	2.2	10.4	34.7	54.9
Elkhart-Goshen, IN	541	10.0	21.0	91 778	79.4	13.4	0.5	1.5	2.0	7.6	31.6	60.9
Elmira, NY	493	13.3	32.6	38 451	81.1	10.6	1.1	0.8	4.1	11.2	38.4	50.4
Enid, OK	436	11.0	26.0	26 712	81.6	12.2	0.3	1.0	1.9	6.4	35.1	58.5
Erie, PA	445	13.0	28.4	126 797	79.9	11.2	1.4	1.0	4.3	10.5	37.7	51.8
Eugene-Springfield, OR	604	17.3	38.3	152 737	71.6	12.2	3.3	3.7	4.2	7.9	33.9	58.2
Evansville-Henderson, IN-KY	450	10.0	26.1	143 722	85.0	9.2	0.8	0.6	2.0	8.6	32.3	59.1
Fargo-Moorhead, ND-MN	455	9.7	27.1	95 173	81.8	8.6	0.5	0.9	4.7	7.1	33.1	59.8
Fayetteville, NC	581	19.4	24.7	143 202	77.2	14.2	0.8	1.4	4.2	7.6	34.5	57.9
Fayetteville-Springdale-Rogers, AR	505	11.7	27.2	147 015	79.8	13.1	0.3	1.0	2.3	5.0	33.2	61.8
Flagstaff, AZ-UT	624	15.0	30.5	56 904	68.2	16.3	0.7	3.2	7.5	6.8	34.0	59.2
Florence, AL	419	13.5	29.0	61 069	86.0	10.3	0.2	0.6	1.3	6.2	29.2	64.6
Florence, SC	452	14.8	27.2	54 482	80.6	13.9	1.0	1.4	1.4	10.4	33.7	55.9
Fort Collins-Loveland, CO	678	15.0	33.9	134 615	77.4	11.0	0.9	3.0	2.7	4.0	28.3	67.7
Fort Myers-Cape Coral, FL	646	17.6	30.5	182 581	78.7	13.7	0.8	1.9	1.5	5.8	46.1	48.2
Fort Pierce-Port St. Lucie, FL	626	18.4	32.6	126 502	79.7	13.2	0.8	1.7	1.2	5.5	44.5	50.0
Fort Smith, AR-OK	413	11.7	23.9	90 915	80.9	14.3	0.5	1.0	1.2	7.6	34.8	57.7
Fort Walton Beach, FL	601	13.5	23.2	82 148	82.8	11.7	0.3	1.6	1.5	4.1	33.6	62.3
Fort Wayne, IN	492	9.3	23.7	249 965	83.6	10.4	0.6	0.8	1.8	6.5	32.2	61.3
Fresno, CA	536	20.9	36.0	335 900	74.1	16.9	1.6	1.9	2.4	10.8	35.0	54.2
Gadsden, AL	395	13.3	25.0	42 636	84.5	11.9	0.1	0.7	0.9	7.6	32.3	60.1
Gainesville, FL	553	15.1	43.9	102 713	74.7	12.7	2.4	3.6	3.2	7.3	40.1	52.7
Glens Falls, NY	535	15.9	29.7	56 203	79.9	11.2	0.9	0.8	3.5	7.9	35.6	56.5
Goldsboro, NC	455	14.2	21.9	49 590	80.5	14.0	0.4	1.3	2.0	8.9	32.4	58.7
Grand Forks, ND-MN	463	10.6	26.6	49 224	79.4	10.3	0.8	1.0	4.8	7.2	33.5	59.3
Grand Junction, CO	527	15.7	33.8	54 101	77.1	12.1	0.5	2.3	2.8	5.1	31.4	63.5
Grand Rapids-Muskegon-Holland, MI	543	10.9	25.8	531 924	84.0	9.2	0.8	0.8	2.1	6.1	31.4	62.5
Great Falls, MT	414	14.9	25.2	37 275	80.5	10.6	0.8	0.9	3.3	8.2	32.1	59.7
Green Bay, WI	520	10.5	23.1	118 872	84.7	8.4	0.9	0.7	2.8	6.0	32.6	61.5
Greensboro—Winston-Salem—High Point, NC	538	13.5	25.7	618 921	81.2	13.1	0.9	0.9	1.6	7.2	32.0	60.8
Greenville, NC	471	15.4	34.8	63 307	80.5	12.8	0.8	1.3	2.4	8.9	36.9	54.2
Greenville-Spartanburg-Anderson, SC	504	12.9	26.2	453 784	81.8	12.9	0.4	0.9	1.9	7.8	32.5	59.7
Harrisburg-Lebanon-Carlisle, PA	544	12.7	23.7	307 263	80.2	11.0	1.3	0.9	3.6	8.5	34.0	57.5

Table C-4. Metropolitan Areas — **Migration, Housing, and Transportation**

CMSA/MSA/ PMSA/NECMA code[1]	Area name	Total population 5 years and over	Residence in 1995 (percent)					Occupied housing units		Householders 65 years and over	
			Same house	Same county, different house	Same state, different county	Different state	Outside the United States	Number	Percent owner-occupied	Number	Percent owner-occupied
		1	2	3	4	5	6	7	8	9	10
3283	Hartford, CT	1 076 555	58.3	24.9	7.0	6.8	2.9	445 870	66.3	101 122	73.8
3285	Hattiesburg, MS	104 041	49.5	21.0	18.1	10.2	1.3	41 579	65.7	8 152	83.2
3290	Hickory-Morganton-Lenoir, NC	319 785	58.9	22.1	9.9	7.4	1.8	133 966	74.3	28 558	84.1
3320	Honolulu, HI	819 914	56.3	26.1	1.2	11.7	4.7	286 450	54.5	66 986	73.6
3350	Houma, LA	180 482	64.5	24.0	7.1	3.9	0.6	68 054	76.7	13 427	85.5
42	Houston-Galveston-Brazoria, TX	4 297 107	48.7	30.5	9.7	6.0	5.0	1 639 401	60.7	229 022	78.4
1145	Brazoria, TX	223 313	53.1	23.6	16.5	4.7	2.0	81 954	74.0	13 727	85.7
2920	Galveston-Texas City, TX	232 804	52.4	25.1	14.4	5.7	2.3	94 782	66.2	18 344	78.6
3360	Houston, TX	3 840 990	48.3	31.3	9.0	6.1	5.3	1 462 665	59.6	196 951	77.9
3400	Huntington-Ashland, WV-KY-OH	297 263	61.6	22.3	7.2	8.4	0.5	128 039	73.0	32 631	82.6
3440	Huntsville, AL	319 231	52.1	27.1	7.1	11.9	1.8	134 643	71.2	24 382	82.8
3480	Indianapolis, IN	1 487 733	50.3	27.8	12.4	8.0	1.6	629 655	67.8	116 182	76.1
3500	Iowa City, IA	104 761	40.1	22.3	19.6	14.3	3.4	44 080	56.7	5 454	79.3
3520	Jackson, MI	147 975	59.0	26.4	9.4	4.6	0.7	58 168	76.5	13 413	82.5
3560	Jackson, MS	408 499	53.0	25.9	12.9	7.3	1.0	160 338	68.5	29 080	81.6
3580	Jackson, TN	100 029	51.7	26.2	11.1	9.8	1.1	41 212	68.4	8 806	78.6
3600	Jacksonville, FL	1 025 775	49.0	26.1	9.1	13.5	2.3	425 584	67.3	79 602	79.7
3605	Jacksonville, NC	137 170	35.8	18.4	6.2	36.1	3.5	48 122	58.1	6 321	84.2
3610	Jamestown, NY	131 677	60.9	26.7	6.9	4.9	0.7	54 515	69.3	14 543	75.2
3620	Janesville-Beloit, WI	141 950	55.3	29.4	6.8	7.5	1.1	58 617	71.2	12 378	77.4
3660	Johnson City-Kingsport-Bristol, TN-VA	453 148	59.6	21.6	8.8	9.4	0.6	199 218	74.2	48 849	83.2
3680	Johnstown, PA	220 557	71.4	19.1	5.9	2.9	0.7	91 753	75.9	29 753	80.2
3700	Jonesboro, AR	76 589	47.2	29.6	13.5	8.7	1.0	32 301	63.9	6 362	79.4
3710	Joplin, MO	146 113	49.3	26.1	10.5	13.1	1.1	61 552	70.1	14 406	81.9
3720	Kalamazoo-Battle Creek, MI	423 298	53.0	26.0	12.6	6.3	1.3	175 561	70.2	36 108	79.4
3760	Kansas City, MO-KS	1 648 237	51.4	25.3	8.6	12.8	1.9	694 468	67.9	133 737	76.6
3810	Killeen-Temple, TX	285 839	30.5	20.6	12.9	21.6	5.4	105 457	55.5	16 195	81.1
3840	Knoxville, TN	646 227	54.4	24.5	9.5	10.5	1.1	281 472	70.5	61 145	83.4
3850	Kokomo, IN	94 519	57.2	26.5	10.0	5.6	0.7	41 269	73.0	9 293	80.1
3870	La Crosse, WI-MN	119 255	53.2	25.3	12.6	8.2	0.6	49 232	67.6	10 716	75.2
3920	Lafayette, IN	171 507	41.9	24.7	17.2	11.6	4.5	67 771	59.1	11 847	78.1
3880	Lafayette, LA	356 809	59.0	24.6	10.2	4.7	0.9	143 006	69.9	28 353	80.8
3960	Lake Charles, LA	170 236	55.5	31.2	5.7	6.9	0.7	68 613	71.5	14 563	83.4
3980	Lakeland-Winter Haven, FL	453 180	51.1	27.6	7.9	11.2	2.2	187 233	73.4	56 473	86.0
4000	Lancaster, PA	438 090	60.2	27.2	6.4	4.9	1.3	172 560	70.9	38 891	73.8
4040	Lansing-East Lansing, MI	410 222	51.3	22.3	18.8	5.4	2.2	172 413	67.2	29 758	78.8
4080	Laredo, TX	172 808	58.8	28.7	4.7	2.4	5.5	50 740	65.7	8 563	74.9
4100	Las Cruces, NM	161 181	53.1	24.4	7.1	12.6	2.9	59 556	67.5	12 238	83.6
4120	Las Vegas, NV-AZ	1 449 277	35.8	30.9	1.6	27.3	4.3	588 371	61.1	118 352	76.1
4150	Lawrence, KS	94 411	37.0	23.1	20.9	15.9	3.0	38 486	51.9	5 195	75.1
4200	Lawton, OK	106 069	42.6	24.2	6.3	23.0	3.9	39 808	60.3	7 243	83.2
4243	Lewiston-Auburn, ME	97 643	56.7	27.8	7.2	7.6	0.7	42 028	63.4	9 358	65.1
4280	Lexington, KY	448 439	45.1	27.0	15.3	10.2	2.3	191 006	59.8	31 840	76.1
4320	Lima, OH	144 767	60.0	25.8	9.4	4.2	0.6	58 022	73.8	14 182	81.3
4360	Lincoln, NE	233 685	46.6	30.6	11.2	9.2	2.4	99 187	60.5	17 160	73.9
4400	Little Rock-North Little Rock, AR	542 994	50.4	26.5	11.8	9.7	1.5	230 864	65.9	43 959	79.0
4420	Longview-Marshall, TX..	194 717	54.7	23.2	15.3	5.5	1.3	79 064	70.9	19 106	82.1
49	Los Angeles-Riverside-Orange County, CA....	15 115 523	50.4	33.7	7.5	3.8	4.6	5 347 107	54.8	985 238	72.8
4480	Los Angeles-Long Beach, CA	8 791 096	52.0	35.7	3.8	3.3	5.3	3 133 774	47.9	556 224	67.2
5945	Orange County, CA....	2 632 408	48.0	33.3	9.7	4.1	4.9	935 287	61.4	169 273	78.8
6780	Riverside-San Bernardino, CA..........	2 994 652	47.5	29.3	15.8	4.6	2.8	1 034 812	66.6	213 275	81.1
8735	Ventura, CA..............	697 367	51.7	28.8	11.5	4.9	3.1	243 234	67.6	46 466	80.0
4520	Louisville, KY-IN.............	956 515	54.7	28.1	7.0	8.8	1.4	412 050	68.6	85 421	80.1
4600	Lubbock, TX	225 526	47.4	29.8	16.2	5.5	1.1	92 516	59.2	17 515	81.0
4640	Lynchburg, VA	202 435	58.7	16.8	15.1	8.4	1.0	84 414	73.9	20 375	82.0
4680	Macon, GA	299 662	52.6	24.7	10.8	10.1	1.7	121 505	65.4	24 338	79.9
4720	Madison, WI	401 058	46.1	29.7	10.8	10.5	2.9	173 484	57.6	25 930	70.8
4800	Mansfield, OH	164 530	60.6	26.1	8.6	4.2	0.5	68 491	71.8	16 838	79.7
4880	McAllen-Edinburg-Mission, TX	511 643	61.1	25.8	4.3	4.3	4.5	156 824	73.1	34 311	84.2
4890	Medford-Ashland, OR ...	170 324	46.5	30.4	6.9	15.1	1.1	71 532	66.5	18 668	77.9
4900	Melbourne-Titusville-Palm Bay, FL............	451 553	51.6	25.6	6.4	14.5	1.9	198 195	74.6	61 049	86.8
4920	Memphis, TN-AR-MS	1 049 232	51.4	31.0	3.9	12.0	1.7	424 202	65.4	75 349	78.5

[1]MSA = Metropolitan Statistical Area. CMSA = Consolidated MSA. PMSA = Primary MSA. NECMA = New England County Metropolitan Area. See the Appendix A for explanation of these concepts. See Appendix B for list of metropolitan areas identified by type, with component counties.

Table C-4. Metropolitan Areas — **Migration, Housing, and Transportation**

Area name	Owner-occupied by household type (percent)								Median household income			Median housing value (owner estimated)	Median monthly owner costs as a percent of income	
	Family households					Nonfamily households								
		Married-couple family		Other family										
	Total family households	Total	With own children under 18 years	Total	With own children under 18 years	Total nonfamily households	Two or more adults	Living alone	All households	Owner-occupied households	Renter-occupied households		With a mortgage	Without a mortgage
	11	12	13	14	15	16	17	18	19	20	21	22	23	24
Hartford, CT	75.9	84.5	83.3	47.8	34.3	47.1	40.0	48.7	52 491	66 460	30 608	146 300	21.8	12.7
Hattiesburg, MS	75.3	84.1	82.8	52.4	43.1	45.8	21.0	52.1	30 747	38 935	18 811	73 200	20.7	9.9
Hickory-Morganton-Lenoir, NC	79.4	85.0	79.9	58.7	48.3	61.2	49.8	63.2	37 817	42 722	26 664	85 600	20.5	9.9
Honolulu, HI	60.1	63.4	53.2	49.5	27.2	40.1	31.7	42.5	51 745	70 041	34 973	274 600	26.4	9.9
Houma, LA	81.1	87.4	84.5	60.4	51.0	62.7	50.7	65.5	34 767	39 089	22 540	71 700	18.6	9.9
Houston-Galveston-Brazoria, TX	68.1	75.3	71.4	45.6	36.9	41.8	34.3	43.4	44 545	58 822	29 969	85 600	19.7	10.5
Brazoria, TX	78.8	84.4	80.8	54.7	45.4	57.7	47.0	59.8	48 191	56 591	29 882	81 000	18.5	9.9
Galveston-Texas City, TX	73.2	80.5	76.2	50.7	39.2	50.0	44.0	51.1	42 230	54 251	25 637	81 900	20.4	11.8
Houston, TX	67.2	74.4	70.5	44.9	36.3	40.6	33.2	42.1	44 458	59 347	30 142	86 200	19.7	10.5
Huntington-Ashland, WV-KY-OH	79.6	85.0	79.7	58.9	46.4	57.6	39.9	60.1	29 452	35 451	16 408	65 100	19.3	9.9
Huntsville, AL	79.0	86.1	82.8	52.7	42.6	53.4	38.6	55.4	43 111	52 891	24 471	95 000	18.7	9.9
Indianapolis, IN	76.9	85.1	83.2	50.4	41.5	49.2	42.9	50.6	45 356	56 161	28 021	109 200	19.9	9.9
Iowa City, IA	77.1	82.4	82.6	52.5	48.1	33.0	20.3	39.7	39 825	60 772	21 997	123 700	20.3	9.9
Jackson, MI	82.5	89.7	86.6	57.7	47.2	62.2	57.8	63.1	42 751	49 691	24 794	96 300	19.0	9.9
Jackson, MS	75.0	85.2	82.2	53.5	42.2	53.1	37.9	55.6	38 781	47 814	22 937	82 400	19.8	9.9
Jackson, TN	75.0	84.2	79.6	49.7	35.4	52.7	40.0	54.7	36 454	44 966	21 149	81 200	19.8	9.9
Jacksonville, FL	74.4	81.6	77.3	53.4	43.1	51.7	44.0	53.7	42 294	51 043	28 881	92 500	20.9	9.9
Jacksonville, NC	60.8	63.5	56.1	49.7	40.6	49.4	30.0	54.4	33 697	40 844	27 033	78 200	22.1	9.9
Jamestown, NY	78.3	86.3	82.4	50.0	38.8	51.3	42.1	53.1	33 271	40 937	18 828	62 700	20.6	13.1
Janesville-Beloit, WI	78.9	86.2	81.6	51.1	42.2	53.9	46.7	55.6	45 318	53 824	28 060	98 300	19.9	10.9
Johnson City-Kingsport-Bristol, TN-VA	80.6	85.3	79.9	60.8	47.0	59.3	45.2	61.1	31 590	36 681	19 727	79 800	20.4	9.9
Johnstown, PA	83.3	88.5	86.2	62.4	44.7	59.5	51.4	60.3	30 380	34 847	18 133	63 400	20.7	11.9
Jonesboro, AR	71.7	79.7	73.6	44.6	32.3	46.8	25.7	51.9	32 409	42 228	20 208	74 800	19.4	9.9
Joplin, MO	76.5	82.3	75.5	53.1	43.0	55.5	39.2	58.6	32 524	37 696	21 826	69 300	18.7	9.9
Kalamazoo-Battle Creek, MI	80.8	88.0	85.4	56.9	48.7	50.1	36.3	53.8	40 636	49 915	23 921	94 600	19.1	9.9
Kansas City, MO-KS	77.3	84.6	82.0	52.0	43.2	48.7	41.8	50.1	46 058	56 242	29 441	104 400	19.7	9.9
Killeen-Temple, TX	60.2	64.7	55.0	42.9	33.8	42.1	33.9	43.9	36 726	46 424	28 057	74 500	20.4	10.0
Knoxville, TN	79.0	85.0	81.2	55.8	42.7	52.8	38.5	55.5	36 753	44 682	21 528	94 000	20.7	9.9
Kokomo, IN	79.5	86.4	82.5	53.6	44.5	58.6	50.9	59.6	44 273	52 487	24 848	87 000	17.3	9.9
La Crosse, WI-MN	81.8	87.8	87.2	54.5	46.7	42.9	25.7	48.3	39 649	49 093	24 000	94 100	20.4	10.5
Lafayette, IN	73.0	78.8	75.8	49.6	45.0	36.8	18.9	44.3	38 842	53 070	22 851	102 900	19.4	9.9
Lafayette, LA	76.5	85.5	83.0	53.3	43.5	53.9	42.0	56.2	30 851	37 752	17 870	71 700	18.8	9.9
Lake Charles, LA	77.4	85.3	80.8	54.4	42.5	56.7	44.1	59.1	35 346	42 162	20 825	70 300	17.8	9.9
Lakeland-Winter Haven, FL	78.2	84.6	76.2	55.7	44.0	61.6	53.8	63.2	35 972	40 762	25 395	69 800	20.8	9.9
Lancaster, PA	78.9	84.0	82.1	52.7	42.4	50.0	42.3	51.6	45 464	53 136	29 748	118 300	22.0	9.9
Lansing-East Lansing, MI	79.4	86.4	84.8	55.0	47.9	45.6	32.0	49.9	44 139	55 866	25 224	106 200	19.4	9.9
Laredo, TX	68.5	73.3	70.3	54.0	42.8	48.0	43.3	48.5	27 979	34 310	18 012	67 000	24.0	12.5
Las Cruces, NM	74.0	81.1	76.2	53.6	46.4	50.6	34.0	55.5	29 648	36 557	17 579	74 000	21.0	9.9
Las Vegas, NV-AZ	67.7	74.4	67.6	47.6	39.1	47.6	43.5	49.0	42 289	51 668	30 961	125 700	23.8	9.9
Lawrence, KS	71.4	78.4	77.9	43.2	40.5	27.7	14.5	35.2	37 584	56 603	22 837	115 600	20.5	9.9
Lawton, OK	64.6	72.3	61.5	40.5	28.6	48.9	33.4	51.5	33 883	42 268	23 674	70 500	19.7	9.9
Lewiston-Auburn, ME	74.5	82.8	80.9	46.7	40.1	42.9	46.1	42.1	35 655	45 781	21 151	86 800	21.4	12.5
Lexington, KY	70.5	78.0	74.7	44.3	34.2	40.5	26.9	44.3	39 117	53 146	24 234	102 500	19.2	9.9
Lima, OH	80.0	87.8	84.4	50.8	42.0	58.5	45.4	60.3	39 422	45 688	23 825	84 500	18.8	9.9
Lincoln, NE	75.4	83.4	82.2	43.2	36.4	36.6	22.7	41.2	41 860	55 984	25 243	105 100	20.5	9.9
Little Rock-North Little Rock, AR	73.5	81.7	76.7	47.5	37.2	49.5	39.1	51.4	38 968	48 173	24 659	82 100	19.2	9.9
Longview-Marshall, TX	76.0	82.7	76.8	54.0	43.5	57.6	43.4	59.6	33 963	40 306	22 652	65 300	19.2	10.3
Los Angeles-Riverside-Orange County, CA	60.2	67.5	60.7	40.1	28.7	41.6	34.6	43.6	45 697	62 118	30 840	193 400	25.9	9.9
Los Angeles-Long Beach, CA	53.9	61.4	54.5	35.9	24.2	34.8	29.8	36.2	42 030	62 180	29 395	201 400	26.6	9.9
Orange County, CA	66.0	71.3	64.4	46.2	34.0	49.7	36.3	54.1	58 500	73 745	40 451	253 000	25.1	9.9
Riverside-San Bernardino, CA	70.0	77.4	71.3	47.2	36.5	56.2	48.4	58.2	42 257	52 334	26 940	129 700	25.1	10.4
Ventura, CA	71.3	76.3	70.4	51.9	40.7	56.1	48.6	58.3	59 292	71 551	39 315	238 800	25.2	9.9
Louisville, KY-IN	76.7	85.3	82.2	51.7	38.5	52.1	44.0	53.6	40 712	50 267	24 464	99 800	19.6	9.9
Lubbock, TX	69.4	76.7	71.7	47.8	37.5	40.0	23.0	44.8	32 076	43 079	20 680	65 700	19.6	10.1
Lynchburg, VA	80.7	88.1	84.3	55.3	43.5	57.8	48.3	59.3	36 982	43 122	23 003	93 400	20.0	9.9
Macon, GA	71.4	82.7	78.1	45.1	33.9	51.0	36.3	53.5	38 339	48 614	22 652	81 400	19.7	9.9
Madison, WI	74.8	81.8	82.0	43.2	37.6	33.5	24.5	37.2	49 067	65 493	30 409	146 400	22.2	10.5
Mansfield, OH	78.7	85.5	79.9	52.9	40.5	56.2	49.6	57.2	36 980	43 416	23 429	85 200	19.5	9.9
McAllen-Edinburg-Mission, TX	75.7	79.8	75.9	61.4	49.8	58.2	44.1	60.4	24 707	28 322	15 638	46 000	23.0	12.1
Medford-Ashland, OR	73.1	79.8	71.0	47.4	35.6	52.5	43.5	55.0	36 283	44 061	24 108	132 100	23.5	10.3
Melbourne-Titusville-Palm Bay, FL	80.9	86.1	79.4	60.5	49.1	61.9	53.6	63.8	39 882	45 369	26 750	87 600	21.6	9.9
Memphis, TN-AR-MS	72.5	83.2	79.7	51.5	40.4	49.0	38.7	51.0	40 108	50 811	25 008	90 900	21.5	9.9

Table C-4. Metropolitan Areas — **Migration, Housing, and Transportation**

Area name	Median gross rent	Percent who pay 35 percent or more of income for housing expenses — Owners	Renters	Means of transportation to work (percent except where noted) — Number of workers 16 years and over	Car, truck, or van — Drove alone	Carpooled	Public transportation	Other means	Walked	Vehicles available (percent of households) — No vehicles	One vehicle	Two or more vehicles
	25	26	27	28	29	30	31	32	33	34	35	36
Hartford, CT	653	14.7	28.3	556 012	82.6	8.7	2.9	0.7	2.5	9.7	33.5	56.8
Hattiesburg, MS	451	16.6	31.6	49 526	81.5	12.1	0.4	1.1	2.7	6.9	36.1	56.9
Hickory-Morganton-Lenoir, NC	478	12.5	20.4	173 167	81.3	14.5	0.2	1.1	1.1	6.1	28.9	65.0
Honolulu, HI	802	22.0	28.9	412 250	61.4	19.4	8.3	2.4	5.6	12.8	37.5	49.7
Houma, LA	431	12.0	24.2	76 862	79.1	13.5	0.8	2.7	1.9	9.3	35.9	54.9
Houston-Galveston-Brazoria, TX	589	13.8	26.2	2 081 607	77.0	14.2	3.3	1.3	1.6	7.8	36.5	55.7
Brazoria, TX	542	10.2	23.2	104 832	82.8	12.6	0.3	1.0	1.1	4.7	29.7	65.6
Galveston-Texas City, TX.............	571	13.9	30.3	112 616	78.2	13.6	1.4	2.0	2.3	8.5	35.4	56.2
Houston, TX	592	14.0	26.0	1 864 159	76.6	14.4	3.6	1.3	1.6	7.9	36.9	55.2
Huntington-Ashland, WV-KY-OH	410	12.5	30.5	122 549	82.9	10.8	0.6	0.8	2.7	10.9	35.2	54.0
Huntsville, AL	486	10.8	25.2	163 327	83.9	11.5	0.3	0.7	1.3	5.8	30.3	64.0
Indianapolis, IN	570	12.2	26.7	795 755	82.8	10.5	1.3	0.8	1.7	7.1	34.0	58.8
Iowa City, IA	564	10.4	41.7	63 087	68.2	11.3	5.3	2.2	10.0	7.8	35.8	56.4
Jackson, MI	505	10.0	28.2	70 317	83.5	10.6	0.5	0.7	1.9	7.5	31.8	60.7
Jackson, MS	528	15.0	29.1	198 530	81.2	13.8	0.6	0.8	1.4	7.9	35.0	57.1
Jackson, TN	502	12.1	29.3	49 786	83.5	11.1	0.7	0.8	1.9	9.4	31.7	58.9
Jacksonville, FL............	616	14.9	26.9	527 718	80.3	12.6	1.5	1.7	1.7	7.7	36.3	56.1
Jacksonville, NC	518	16.1	18.7	79 399	66.7	17.2	0.8	2.5	10.4	6.2	33.3	60.5
Jamestown, NY	438	14.7	31.9	61 734	78.5	11.0	1.2	0.9	5.1	11.2	38.1	50.7
Janesville-Beloit, WI	543	10.9	23.9	75 033	83.1	10.1	0.7	0.6	2.7	6.1	31.7	62.2
Johnson City-Kingsport-Bristol, TN-VA	416	12.2	25.4	211 953	85.0	10.5	0.3	0.6	1.3	8.0	29.5	62.6
Johnstown, PA	363	12.7	23.9	94 352	80.8	11.3	0.9	0.7	3.4	10.8	35.1	54.1
Jonesboro, AR	454	13.1	31.9	39 290	83.1	11.7	0.1	0.7	1.9	6.1	36.6	57.3
Joplin, MO	435	10.5	24.4	72 658	81.5	12.2	0.2	1.1	2.0	6.8	33.5	59.8
Kalamazoo-Battle Creek, MI	508	11.2	30.0	214 644	82.7	9.9	1.0	0.7	2.7	7.0	34.2	58.8
Kansas City, MO-KS	575	11.8	24.7	881 258	82.8	10.4	1.3	0.7	1.4	7.3	33.5	59.2
Killeen-Temple, TX........	544	13.2	21.5	146 512	76.4	15.5	0.3	1.4	4.7	6.4	36.1	57.6
Knoxville, TN	483	13.3	28.3	324 124	84.2	10.0	0.5	0.7	1.9	6.7	31.8	61.4
Kokomo, IN	506	9.8	25.0	46 841	84.9	10.1	0.3	0.9	1.5	6.6	33.5	59.8
La Crosse, WI-MN	463	10.6	25.2	65 980	80.2	9.0	1.1	1.0	4.9	7.3	32.6	60.1
Lafayette, IN	555	11.0	35.5	88 355	77.7	10.7	1.4	1.6	5.9	6.9	35.0	58.0
Lafayette, LA	420	13.6	27.5	155 376	81.0	11.6	0.9	1.6	1.8	10.6	36.5	52.8
Lake Charles, LA	465	10.7	27.8	77 899	83.6	11.3	0.4	1.4	1.6	8.0	37.2	54.8
Lakeland-Winter Haven, Fl	501	14.2	26.8	202 341	79.9	14.3	0.7	1.6	1.4	7.2	41.5	51.3
Lancaster, PA...............	572	12.6	25.4	231 674	78.2	10.2	1.2	1.0	4.4	0.8	30.8	59.5
Lansing-East Lansing, MI	545	11.2	32.0	224 372	80.4	10.0	1.6	0.9	4.0	6.5	34.3	59.1
Laredo, TX	449	19.1	30.7	61 256	71.5	19.3	2.5	1.7	2.1	12.3	36.7	50.9
Las Cruces, NM	445	14.0	34.4	66 761	77.2	14.6	0.5	1.7	2.5	6.3	34.2	59.5
Las Vegas, NV-AZ	703	20.3	31.2	702 535	74.5	15.0	4.1	1.7	2.4	9.0	39.7	51.3
Lawrence, KS	560	11.3	38.6	54 496	76.9	10.3	1.0	1.4	6.7	5.6	34.7	59.7
Lawton, OK	452	13.7	26.5	51 684	73.3	13.9	1.0	2.2	7.3	8.2	35.4	56.4
Lewiston-Auburn, ME....	433	13.8	24.3	50 869	78.0	13.4	0.9	1.0	4.0	11.1	35.5	53.4
Lexington, KY	502	11.0	29.0	243 675	79.8	11.9	0.9	0.9	3.9	7.7	35.2	57.1
Lima, OH	448	10.2	25.6	70 378	84.7	8.6	0.7	0.9	2.5	6.5	31.7	61.8
Lincoln, NE..................	519	9.8	28.7	138 151	80.6	10.2	1.2	1.6	3.2	6.8	34.4	58.8
Little Rock-North Little Rock, AR	530	11.7	27.9	280 383	81.6	13.2	0.9	0.9	1.3	7.3	36.0	56.7
Longview-Marshall, TX..	462	12.1	26.4	88 486	82.1	12.7	0.2	1.1	1.5	7.4	34.5	58.1
Los Angeles-Riverside-Orange County, CA....	733	25.0	35.2	6 767 619	72.4	15.2	4.7	1.6	2.6	10.1	34.9	55.1
Los Angeles-Long Beach, CA	704	26.8	35.8	3 858 750	70.4	15.1	6.6	1.6	2.9	12.6	37.0	50.5
Orange County, CA....	923	23.1	33.3	1 313 987	76.5	13.3	2.8	1.7	2.0	5.8	31.1	63.1
Riverside-San Bernardino, CA..........	653	22.9	35.5	1 249 224	73.5	17.6	1.7	1.6	2.2	7.5	33.5	59.0
Ventura, CA...............	892	23.5	31.3	345 658	75.9	15.1	1.1	1.7	2.1	5.0	28.0	66.9
Louisville, KY-IN...........	496	12.2	26.2	492 821	82.0	10.9	2.2	0.8	1.7	9.5	34.7	55.8
Lubbock, TX	507	12.8	36.2	112 693	80.7	13.1	0.9	1.1	1.8	6.7	38.5	54.7
Lynchburg, VA..............	448	12.0	24.2	100 227	81.6	11.2	1.1	0.8	2.5	8.6	29.2	62.3
Macon, GA	492	13.7	28.0	140 678	81.3	13.6	1.0	1.0	1.3	9.7	33.3	57.0
Madison, WI	641	12.9	30.7	242 542	74.1	9.5	4.2	2.2	6.2	8.0	35.6	56.4
Mansfield, OH	441	11.6	24.3	78 573	84.3	9.6	0.6	0.9	2.0	7.4	32.1	60.6
McAllen-Edinburg-Mission, TX	401	15.7	28.9	176 308	73.7	19.1	0.3	2.8	1.9	9.6	40.5	49.9
Medford-Ashland, OR ...	597	18.0	36.0	79 197	77.4	10.9	0.7	1.8	3.6	6.0	32.4	61.6
Melbourne-Titusville-Palm Bay,FL.............	604	15.1	30.4	205 079	83.4	10.7	0.3	1.7	1.3	5.3	40.9	53.8
Memphis, TN-AR-MS	563	16.9	30.2	511 111	80.9	13.0	1.7	0.9	1.3	10.4	36.9	52.7

Table C-4. Metropolitan Areas — **Migration, Housing, and Transportation**

CMSA/MSA/PMSA/NECMA code[1]	Area name	Residence in 1995 (percent)						Occupied housing units		Householders 65 years and over	
		Total population 5 years and over	Same house	Same county, different house	Same state, different county	Different state	Outside the United States	Number	Percent owner-occupied	Number	Percent owner-occupied
		1	2	3	4	5	6	7	8	9	10
4940	Merced, CA	192 259	50.5	29.8	14.3	2.2	3.3	63 815	58.7	12 474	77.0
56	Miami-Fort Lauderdale, FL	3 629 354	48.9	30.5	5.1	7.3	8.3	1 431 219	63.2	347 443	74.7
2680	Fort Lauderdale, FL ...	1 520 842	47.1	27.2	9.0	10.6	6.1	654 445	69.5	173 341	83.9
5000	Miami, FL	2 108 512	50.2	32.9	2.2	4.9	9.8	776 774	57.8	174 102	65.4
63	Milwaukee-Racine, WI ..	1 573 235	55.1	28.1	9.4	5.7	1.7	658 476	62.1	139 866	69.8
5080	Milwaukee-Waukesha, WI	1 397 528	54.8	28.4	9.3	5.7	1.8	587 657	61.1	124 219	68.8
6600	Racine, WI	175 707	57.3	25.9	9.5	5.8	1.5	70 819	70.6	15 647	77.3
5120	Minneapolis-St. Paul, MN-WI	2 757 395	54.3	21.1	13.5	8.7	2.4	1 136 615	72.4	183 468	73.7
5140	Missoula, MT	90 465	45.4	25.5	10.8	17.3	1.0	38 439	61.9	6 253	73.6
5160	Mobile, AL	502 445	56.8	27.8	5.0	9.1	1.3	205 515	71.7	47 420	83.1
5170	Modesto, CA	411 833	50.8	31.1	12.7	2.7	2.7	145 146	61.9	28 439	75.2
5200	Monroe, LA	136 644	56.3	28.8	8.5	6.0	0.4	55 216	64.1	11 919	77.2
5240	Montgomery, AL	310 375	52.6	24.8	11.7	9.6	1.2	124 808	69.4	26 149	80.0
5280	Muncie, IN	111 756	52.0	26.8	13.8	6.1	1.2	47 131	67.2	10 283	83.9
5330	Myrtle Beach, SC	185 564	49.3	22.3	5.6	21.1	1.7	81 800	73.0	19 754	88.7
5345	Naples, FL	238 077	44.2	22.7	7.1	19.7	6.2	102 973	75.6	38 231	88.9
5360	Nashville, TN	1 146 804	48.1	24.5	12.3	12.9	2.2	479 569	66.0	80 492	78.4
5523	New London-Norwich, CT	242 931	55.2	25.0	5.8	12.2	1.7	99 835	66.7	21 782	75.1
5560	New Orleans, LA	1 246 885	59.6	24.2	8.7	6.3	1.2	505 579	61.8	102 244	74.6
70	New York-Northern New Jersey-Long Island, NY-NJ-CT-PA .	19 775 438	61.1	20.9	7.9	5.1	5.0	7 735 264	53.0	1 704 921	62.5
0875	Bergen-Passaic, NJ ...	1 282 198	61.6	21.2	6.3	6.1	4.9	494 673	63.4	119 730	73.5
2281	Dutchess County, NY.	263 037	59.5	20.7	12.2	5.7	1.9	99 536	68.9	21 276	76.3
3640	Jersey City, NJ	571 095	53.8	24.9	4.9	8.1	8.2	230 546	30.6	45 632	42.8
5015	Middlesex-Somerset-Hunterdon, NJ	1 090 760	57.4	17.4	12.3	7.5	5.4	418 477	71.2	83 791	80.7
5190	Monmouth-Ocean, NJ	1 052 129	60.8	19.9	10.6	7.0	1.8	424 638	78.7	121 647	84.4
5380	Nassau-Suffolk, NY	2 568 053	67.2	19.5	8.9	2.3	2.1	916 686	80.0	216 359	84.7
5483	New Haven-Bridgeport-Stamford-Danbury-Waterbury, CT	1 591 009	57.9	25.9	3.4	8.8	4.0	643 272	66.2	148 803	74.3
5600	New York, NY	8 689 404	61.2	20.8	7.4	4.0	6.6	3 484 108	34.7	730 981	44.3
5640	Newark, NJ	1 890 405	59.9	20.7	9.5	5.7	4.2	729 062	60.8	155 113	68.6
5660	Newburgh, NY-PA......	359 057	59.0	20.4	10.3	8.5	1.8	132 221	69.4	26 351	75.3
8480	Trenton, NJ	328 588	57.4	21.9	7.5	9.1	4.1	125 807	67.0	28 119	74.6
5720	Norfolk-Virginia Beach-Newport News, VA-NC	1 460 854	48.0	20.7	12.9	16.1	2.4	577 659	63.0	104 733	78.6
5790	Ocala, FL	245 837	50.3	22.7	11.1	14.6	1.2	106 755	79.8	40 959	90.9
5800	Odessa-Midland, TX	218 962	55.6	27.5	11.2	4.4	1.3	86 591	69.1	17 404	80.6
5880	Oklahoma City, OK	1 008 060	48.6	27.3	12.1	9.7	2.3	424 764	64.7	81 875	81.5
5920	Omaha, NE-IA	664 362	52.3	25.1	8.1	12.4	2.1	275 565	66.0	50 498	77.5
5960	Orlando, FL	1 537 821	44.0	23.3	13.2	14.3	5.1	625 248	66.3	128 197	82.8
5990	Owensboro, KY	85 314	55.1	31.9	6.4	6.1	0.5	36 033	70.3	8 258	77.7
6015	Panama City, FL	139 213	49.4	26.5	6.2	15.9	2.0	59 597	68.6	13 017	85.1
6020	Parkersburg-Marietta, WV-OH	142 403	61.6	25.1	4.8	8.1	0.3	61 412	74.6	15 622	82.2
6080	Pensacola, FL	386 604	47.9	23.5	9.3	16.8	2.4	154 842	71.0	34 588	85.1
6120	Peoria-Pekin, IL...........	324 511	57.9	25.4	10.7	5.1	0.9	135 857	72.3	33 165	80.0
77	Philadelphia-Wilmington-Atlantic City, PA-NJ-DE-MD....	5 791 109	61.3	21.9	7.3	7.3	2.2	2 320 719	69.9	540 189	77.1
0560	Atlantic-Cape May, NJ	333 553	58.7	24.9	6.6	7.2	2.7	137 172	68.8	35 669	76.5
6160	Philadelphia, PA-NJ ...	4 772 728	62.1	21.1	7.9	6.7	2.2	1 914 246	69.9	448 309	76.9
8760	Vineland-Millville-Bridgeton, NJ	137 590	60.9	26.1	6.8	3.5	2.7	49 143	67.9	12 325	75.6
9160	Wilmington-Newark, DE-MD....................	547 238	55.4	26.8	2.0	13.6	2.3	220 158	70.8	43 886	79.6
6200	Phoenix-Mesa, AZ........	3 000 333	41.9	33.3	3.1	17.3	4.5	1 194 250	68.0	248 728	83.1
6240	Pine Bluff, AR..............	78 470	56.5	29.0	7.5	5.6	1.4	30 555	66.1	7 334	79.8
6280	Pittsburgh, PA	2 228 091	66.4	22.3	5.9	4.4	1.0	966 500	71.3	275 217	77.6
6323	Pittsfield, MA	127 950	61.5	25.4	2.7	9.2	1.1	56 006	66.9	15 820	72.3
6340	Pocatello, ID	69 452	49.4	26.9	10.4	12.2	1.1	27 192	70.6	5 078	86.8
6403	Portland, ME	250 237	54.2	25.8	7.4	11.2	1.3	107 989	66.7	22 691	73.0
79	Portland-Salem, OR-WA............................	2 104 961	45.5	27.3	10.8	13.0	3.5	866 475	63.0	155 053	75.5
6440	Portland-Vancouver, OR-WA......................	1 783 873	45.5	27.0	10.3	13.7	3.5	741 776	62.9	127 659	75.2
7080	Salem, OR................	321 088	45.4	29.0	13.2	9.2	3.3	124 699	63.9	27 394	76.8
6483	Providence-Warwick-Pawtucket, RI	904 788	58.3	24.7	5.2	9.1	2.6	373 196	59.9	89 923	64.5
6520	Provo-Orem, UT............	328 190	43.2	28.1	7.9	16.9	4.0	99 937	66.8	13 970	88.5
6560	Pueblo, CO.................	132 161	51.5	30.2	8.5	8.8	0.9	54 579	70.4	14 607	81.5
6580	Punta Gorda, FL	136 659	52.5	17.0	8.6	20.7	1.2	63 864	83.7	30 891	90.2
6640	Raleigh-Durham-Chapel Hill, NC	1 105 812	44.6	22.8	12.2	16.1	4.3	461 097	64.5	66 357	77.6
6660	Rapid City, SD	82 286	47.7	27.2	9.7	14.1	1.3	34 641	66.2	6 831	73.7

[1]MSA = Metropolitan Statistical Area. CMSA = Consolidated MSA. PMSA = Primary MSA. NECMA = New England County Metropolitan Area. See the Appendix A for explanation of these concepts. See Appendix B for list of metropolitan areas identified by type, with component counties.

Table C-4. Metropolitan Areas — **Migration, Housing, and Transportation**

Area name	Owner-occupied by household type (percent)								Median household income			Median monthly owner costs as a percent of income		
	Family households					Nonfamily households								
		Married-couple family		Other family										
	Total family households	Total	With own children under 18 years	Total	With own children under 18 years	Total nonfamily households	Two or more adults	Living alone	All households	Owner-occupied households	Renter-occupied households	Median housing value (owner estimated)	With a mortgage	Without a mortgage
	11	12	13	14	15	16	17	18	19	20	21	22	23	24
Merced, CA	61.2	69.1	61.3	38.1	26.6	49.7	36.2	52.7	35 619	46 430	23 943	110 900	24.7	10.8
Miami-Fort Lauderdale, FL	68.0	75.2	71.1	50.6	40.9	53.3	47.4	54.7	38 380	48 373	25 680	108 400	25.4	13.3
Fort Lauderdale, FL	74.6	81.7	77.6	54.7	45.0	60.6	51.3	63.0	41 510	48 576	30 433	102 800	24.5	13.1
Miami, FL	62.9	69.9	66.3	48.1	38.1	45.4	43.3	45.9	35 768	48 173	22 773	113 200	26.6	13.5
Milwaukee-Racine, WI	72.9	83.0	81.0	42.4	30.6	41.4	34.1	43.0	45 887	59 643	28 372	128 200	21.2	11.9
Milwaukee-Waukesha, WI	72.3	82.5	80.7	41.8	30.1	40.3	32.6	42.0	45 682	60 048	28 558	130 800	21.3	12.0
Racine, WI	78.2	86.5	83.3	47.9	35.3	52.3	50.1	52.7	47 528	56 894	26 617	110 200	20.7	11.5
Minneapolis-St. Paul, MN-WI	83.6	89.3	89.9	60.1	52.7	51.0	47.3	52.0	54 226	65 042	30 095	139 200	20.4	9.9
Missoula, MT	76.0	82.4	79.8	51.3	46.0	40.3	27.6	45.6	34 559	46 316	20 281	128 700	23.5	10.1
Mobile, AL	77.2	85.5	81.1	54.1	41.7	57.9	43.5	60.1	35 435	42 102	20 642	83 000	20.3	9.9
Modesto, CA	65.4	72.9	66.1	42.6	31.9	51.0	42.9	53.0	40 202	50 838	26 356	123 900	24.3	9.9
Monroe, LA	70.8	82.7	78.1	45.0	34.9	48.7	33.2	51.4	31 649	42 149	18 289	74 000	18.9	9.9
Montgomery, AL	75.3	83.4	78.4	54.6	44.5	55.7	42.7	57.6	37 481	45 844	22 786	85 300	19.8	9.9
Muncie, IN	77.8	85.1	79.2	50.9	43.9	49.0	24.8	56.3	34 420	44 273	19 659	74 400	18.5	9.9
Myrtle Beach, SC	78.9	85.3	80.8	57.4	48.2	60.9	43.5	65.9	30 215	40 090	20 401	95 400	21.0	9.9
Naples, FL	79.1	84.7	72.9	50.4	42.2	67.6	53.5	71.1	48 219	53 544	35 077	149 000	23.9	9.9
Nashville, TN	75.1	82.7	80.4	50.4	39.7	47.0	36.0	49.7	44 044	54 472	27 769	120 800	21.5	9.9
New London-Norwich, CT	75.0	81.8	77.2	50.6	37.5	49.3	42.8	50.8	50 599	61 549	32 177	139 700	21.8	11.8
New Orleans, LA	70.0	81.4	78.8	47.2	35.4	44.7	37.1	46.1	35 183	46 302	21 769	95 800	20.8	9.9
New York-Northern New Jersey-Long Island, NY-NJ-CT-PA	60.7	70.1	67.8	36.2	24.8	36.7	29.8	38.1	50 513	70 843	32 293	199 800	24.2	14.7
Bergen-Passaic, NJ	70.1	76.3	73.5	48.0	32.3	45.9	36.1	47.6	59 072	76 199	37 524	222 700	24.6	15.9
Dutchess County, NY	78.1	84.6	83.3	51.3	37.5	47.8	42.3	49.0	53 086	65 006	31 188	150 800	22.9	12.4
Jersey City, NJ	35.7	42.5	36.8	23.6	13.9	22.2	15.4	24.0	39 976	60 524	32 992	162 800	26.5	17.9
Middlesex-Somerset-Hunterdon, NJ	77.9	82.0	80.8	58.9	46.5	53.6	40.4	56.6	66 519	77 743	43 584	180 600	23.1	14.6
Monmouth Ocean, NJ	84.3	88.8	86.7	63.3	50.3	65.4	58.3	66.5	54 771	62 400	32 175	156 200	24.2	16.1
Nassau-Suffolk, NY	85.2	88.7	87.7	60.4	55.5	62.1	54.1	63.7	68 143	76 153	40 636	212 600	25.1	16.0
New Haven-Bridgeport-Stamford-Danbury-Waterbury, CT	74.3	82.4	80.7	47.5	33.7	48.6	41.5	50.1	55 823	71 059	31 932	189 000	23.0	13.8
New York, NY	40.6	50.2	46.8	23.5	14.8	24.5	18.5	25.7	40 698	66 150	30 880	230 400	25.3	13.5
Newark, NJ	68.9	78.5	77.2	41.6	28.5	40.8	35.4	41.8	56 547	76 556	32 889	196 200	23.6	14.9
Newburgh, NY-PA	75.5	81.7	78.4	50.9	38.9	51.8	48.6	52.4	50 965	61 289	31 776	137 800	23.4	13.8
Trenton, NJ	75.2	82.9	81.6	51.9	38.3	48.9	45.4	49.7	56 525	71 016	33 553	143 600	22.5	14.7
Norfolk-Virginia Beach-Newport News, VA-NC	69.1	78.4	72.8	43.7	32.6	48.4	37.5	51.3	42 358	53 528	27 538	107 100	23.3	10.6
Ocala, FL	83.3	88.4	81.3	63.0	50.8	71.6	64.8	72.9	31 841	34 289	23 432	70 100	21.6	9.9
Odessa-Midland, TX	76.7	83.3	79.6	53.3	45.5	48.8	37.2	50.3	34 538	41 613	22 076	53 500	19.2	10.5
Oklahoma City, OK	72.5	80.3	75.2	47.7	37.6	49.0	33.0	52.2	36 585	46 366	23 137	76 900	19.5	9.9
Omaha, NE-IA	76.3	83.6	81.4	51.1	40.8	45.3	38.3	46.9	44 770	55 739	28 179	100 100	19.8	10.5
Orlando, FL	74.0	80.7	75.9	52.8	43.8	49.7	38.9	53.4	41 719	49 522	30 285	99 500	22.5	9.9
Owensboro, KY	76.9	82.8	79.7	53.7	43.8	55.4	45.4	56.7	36 803	45 350	20 836	80 600	18.4	9.9
Panama City, FL	75.1	81.6	74.0	53.0	41.5	54.8	41.0	57.9	35 894	41 899	24 915	83 700	21.1	9.9
Parkersburg-Marietta, WV-OH	81.2	87.4	82.4	55.5	43.3	59.3	48.9	60.9	33 688	40 137	19 043	75 200	19.1	9.9
Pensacola, FL	76.1	83.4	76.4	54.5	42.5	59.2	46.0	62.2	36 992	43 394	24 128	86 100	21.2	9.9
Peoria-Pekin, IL	80.7	87.7	84.8	52.4	41.0	53.9	47.3	55.0	42 956	51 877	24 051	88 900	19.0	9.9
Philadelphia-Wilmington-Atlantic City, PA-NJ-DE-MD	78.6	86.2	85.4	58.2	45.1	51.4	42.9	53.1	47 181	57 557	28 732	120 300	22.4	13.3
Atlantic-Cape May, NJ	75.7	83.7	79.0	53.0	40.8	55.3	49.2	56.6	42 893	51 789	27 451	123 400	24.7	15.9
Philadelphia, PA-NJ	79.0	86.4	86.1	59.0	45.7	50.8	42.2	52.4	47 204	57 821	28 621	119 400	22.5	13.5
Vineland-Millville-Bridgeton, NJ	72.7	83.6	78.4	49.3	37.1	55.8	50.0	56.9	38 675	48 809	22 136	89 200	22.8	14.0
Wilmington-Newark, DE-MD	78.7	86.2	84.0	56.1	45.1	53.5	42.7	56.3	51 699	61 531	32 035	132 500	20.6	9.9
Phoenix-Mesa, AZ	74.9	81.4	75.5	52.4	44.2	53.4	44.2	56.3	44 526	53 417	29 838	119 600	22.0	9.9
Pine Bluff, AR	70.5	81.1	71.0	47.0	33.2	55.7	49.2	56.4	31 413	39 531	19 670	53 800	18.1	11.1
Pittsburgh, PA	81.1	87.7	86.2	58.1	41.9	52.5	41.1	54.2	37 377	45 434	22 115	84 300	20.9	12.3
Pittsfield, MA	78.9	86.3	83.5	53.9	41.3	46.6	45.1	46.9	39 038	49 420	22 621	115 100	21.2	11.7
Pocatello, ID	78.6	83.3	80.9	58.1	47.8	51.2	34.6	55.8	36 678	45 761	20 024	87 000	20.0	9.9
Portland, ME	79.0	84.7	84.6	55.3	48.2	45.9	39.2	47.9	43 780	54 140	27 856	129 800	21.9	12.6
Portland-Salem, OR-WA	72.0	79.1	74.5	45.3	35.9	45.6	38.6	47.8	46 007	57 633	30 336	162 200	23.5	10.6
Portland-Vancouver, OR-WA	72.3	79.3	75.3	45.6	36.1	45.1	38.7	47.2	46 941	59 141	30 803	167 100	23.5	10.7
Salem, OR	70.6	77.9	70.0	43.9	34.9	48.6	38.1	51.6	40 858	50 882	26 933	131 600	23.5	10.1
Providence-Warwick-Pawtucket, RI	70.4	79.7	77.5	43.3	29.1	40.1	34.4	41.4	41 215	56 159	23 558	127 600	22.7	13.5
Provo-Orem, UT	72.2	74.9	77.2	54.2	48.3	43.7	15.3	63.3	45 770	55 956	28 166	153 600	23.5	9.9
Pueblo, CO	76.3	84.6	77.9	53.4	40.1	57.5	47.8	59.3	32 617	39 806	19 468	93 100	22.3	9.9
Punta Gorda, FL	87.4	90.7	78.9	66.9	54.3	75.5	66.3	77.3	36 365	38 216	27 131	87 700	24.1	11.6
Raleigh-Durham-Chapel Hill, NC	74.8	82.4	80.7	47.6	40.3	45.1	31.1	49.6	48 837	61 661	30 543	138 500	21.3	9.9
Rapid City, SD	74.7	82.1	78.4	49.1	40.0	48.6	45.2	49.4	37 571	45 988	22 532	83 800	20.9	9.9

Table C-4. Metropolitan Areas — **Migration, Housing, and Transportation**

Area name	Median gross rent	Percent who pay 35 percent or more of income for housing expenses		Means of transportation to work (percent except where noted)						Vehicles available (percent of households)		
		Owners	Renters	Number of workers 16 years and over	Car, truck, or van Drove alone	Carpooled	Public transportation	Other means	Walked	No vehicles	One vehicle	Two or more vehicles
	25	26	27	28	29	30	31	32	33	34	35	36
Merced, CA	518	21.6	32.1	73 346	72.9	18.5	0.7	1.8	3.0	10.4	31.9	57.7
Miami-Fort Lauderdale, FL	689	25.9	37.7	1 642 866	76.6	13.4	3.9	1.5	1.8	12.1	41.1	46.9
Fort Lauderdale, FL ...	757	23.4	35.5	743 543	80.0	12.0	2.3	1.4	1.3	9.4	43.7	46.9
Miami, FL	647	28.1	39.0	899 323	73.8	14.6	5.2	1.5	2.2	14.3	38.8	46.9
Milwaukee-Racine, WI ..	577	13.1	28.2	816 880	80.1	9.9	4.0	0.7	2.8	11.5	35.4	53.1
Milwaukee-Waukesha, WI	580	13.3	28.3	727 386	79.7	9.9	4.3	0.7	2.9	11.9	35.8	52.3
Racine, WI	548	11.8	27.5	89 494	83.6	9.9	1.6	0.7	2.0	8.1	32.3	59.5
Minneapolis-St. Paul, MN-WI	641	11.8	28.0	1 595 550	78.3	10.0	4.5	0.9	2.4	8.1	31.6	60.3
Missoula, MT	530	17.8	39.7	49 448	73.3	11.0	1.3	4.3	5.5	6.2	31.4	62.4
Mobile, AL	490	15.1	30.4	224 608	82.8	12.2	0.6	0.9	1.3	7.7	34.3	58.1
Modesto, CA	611	20.9	35.1	170 169	76.9	15.0	1.0	1.5	2.4	8.6	32.1	59.3
Monroe, LA	444	12.8	31.8	63 027	82.1	12.4	1.2	1.1	1.4	11.8	36.2	52.0
Montgomery, AL	522	14.0	28.8	144 894	83.1	12.5	0.6	0.7	1.3	8.2	34.0	57.8
Muncie, IN	465	11.1	34.5	54 400	81.2	9.4	1.1	0.9	4.8	7.3	34.6	58.1
Myrtle Beach, SC	594	15.4	28.0	95 732	79.0	14.4	0.5	1.7	1.7	6.5	38.5	55.0
Naples, FL	753	20.4	28.1	103 068	74.4	14.9	1.9	2.2	1.8	4.9	42.6	52.6
Nashville, TN	610	14.4	27.9	621 221	80.7	12.8	1.0	0.8	1.5	6.5	32.9	60.6
New London-Norwich, CT	646	14.5	22.9	129 553	81.1	9.9	1.6	0.9	3.8	7.1	32.9	60.0
New Orleans, LA	515	16.1	32.4	570 423	73.0	14.6	5.6	1.6	2.7	15.3	38.7	46.0
New York-Northern New Jersey-Long Island, NY-NJ-CT-PA .	740	22.3	32.5	9 319 218	56.3	9.4	24.9	0.9	5.6	28.7	32.4	38.9
Bergen-Passaic, NJ ...	822	23.2	30.9	637 840	72.3	10.9	10.0	0.8	3.1	11.3	35.3	53.4
Dutchess County, NY.	707	17.2	31.0	128 437	78.5	9.6	4.2	0.7	3.9	7.7	30.8	61.5
Jersey City, NJ	703	28.6	29.2	264 544	42.0	13.0	33.6	1.0	8.6	35.1	43.1	21.8
Middlesex-Somerset-Hunterdon, NJ	858	18.5	26.5	576 819	77.2	9.9	6.7	0.9	2.4	7.1	31.9	61.0
Monmouth-Ocean, NJ ..	780	21.2	33.8	501 266	78.7	9.8	6.0	0.8	1.8	8.0	35.2	56.8
Nassau-Suffolk, NY	954	24.5	33.8	1 289 992	73.9	9.3	11.1	0.7	2.2	6.5	28.3	65.2
New Haven-Bridgeport-Stamford-Danbury-Waterbury, CT	726	19.4	31.0	807 287	77.6	9.7	5.8	0.8	2.7	10.4	33.5	56.1
New York, NY	715	25.4	33.6	3 797 591	31.4	8.3	47.0	1.0	9.3	50.0	31.9	18.1
Newark, NJ	729	20.8	29.9	929 745	71.8	10.6	10.6	0.9	3.0	14.9	33.1	52.0
Newburgh, NY-PA	713	19.1	32.4	171 791	76.8	11.3	4.5	0.7	3.9	9.7	29.9	60.4
Trenton, NJ	727	18.5	28.1	163 257	73.3	11.0	6.9	1.1	4.5	11.7	34.2	54.1
Norfolk-Virginia Beach-Newport News, VA-NC	615	17.7	29.3	760 401	78.9	12.1	1.9	1.8	2.7	8.7	33.2	58.2
Ocala, FL	513	14.3	29.1	96 304	80.6	13.2	0.2	1.3	1.4	5.8	45.2	49.0
Odessa-Midland, TX	435	12.3	25.6	99 904	82.5	12.7	0.2	1.0	1.2	6.8	37.3	56.0
Oklahoma City, OK	487	12.1	28.5	509 262	81.8	12.0	0.6	1.1	1.7	6.7	36.2	57.1
Omaha, NE-IA	548	11.0	24.2	370 006	82.9	10.5	1.1	0.7	1.9	7.3	33.2	59.4
Orlando, FL	698	17.6	32.1	786 243	80.6	12.1	1.7	1.5	1.3	6.2	37.8	56.0
Owensboro, KY	415	9.6	24.7	42 298	85.1	10.3	0.3	0.8	1.5	8.0	32.7	59.3
Panama City, FL	536	13.6	27.5	67 548	81.0	13.1	0.3	1.7	1.6	6.6	37.4	55.9
Parkersburg-Marietta, WV-OH	417	10.0	28.1	65 821	84.3	9.6	0.5	0.7	2.6	8.1	33.6	58.2
Pensacola, FL	534	15.2	31.1	180 124	78.6	11.5	1.0	1.7	4.5	7.0	35.9	57.1
Peoria-Pekin, IL	483	10.0	25.5	163 492	83.8	9.5	1.2	0.7	2.2	7.3	33.4	59.3
Philadelphia-Wilmington-Atlantic City, PA-NJ-DE-MD....	651	17.8	31.2	2 815 405	73.3	10.3	8.7	1.0	3.9	15.3	35.6	49.1
Atlantic-Cape May, NJ	671	22.7	30.9	156 681	75.1	10.9	6.0	1.4	4.4	13.8	38.3	47.9
Philadelphia, PA-NJ ...	648	17.9	31.6	2 314 148	72.3	10.1	9.7	0.9	4.1	16.3	35.6	48.1
Vineland-Millville-Bridgeton, NJ	616	18.4	34.7	57 387	78.3	13.7	2.2	1.5	2.1	13.4	36.7	49.9
Wilmington-Newark, DE-MD..................	667	13.5	27.2	287 189	79.6	10.9	3.4	0.9	2.6	8.4	33.6	58.0
Phoenix-Mesa, AZ........	661	16.2	30.9	1 466 434	74.6	15.3	2.0	2.2	2.1	6.9	38.8	54.2
Pine Bluff, AR..............	463	14.1	30.0	32 715	80.6	15.1	0.5	0.8	1.2	11.2	38.0	50.8
Pittsburgh, PA	482	14.4	28.5	1 057 354	77.4	9.7	6.2	0.7	3.6	12.9	37.0	50.1
Pittsfield, MA	499	14.6	27.6	64 058	79.2	9.7	1.5	0.8	5.3	11.0	39.8	49.2
Pocatello, ID.................	443	11.7	31.7	35 122	78.6	12.8	1.7	1.1	2.9	5.5	29.4	65.1
Portland, ME	615	15.9	28.4	137 256	78.9	9.5	1.6	1.0	4.4	8.6	35.1	56.3
Portland-Salem, OR-WA.................	660	18.2	30.9	1 105 133	73.1	12.1	5.7	1.5	3.0	7.9	33.1	59.0
Portland-Vancouver, OR-WA..................	672	18.3	30.7	951 489	73.1	11.5	6.3	1.5	3.0	8.1	33.2	58.8
Salem, OR...................	573	17.8	31.6	153 644	73.1	15.7	1.9	1.6	3.2	7.0	32.7	60.3
Providence-Warwick-Pawtucket, RI	545	17.0	29.2	447 221	80.1	10.6	2.6	0.9	3.7	11.2	36.4	52.4
Provo-Orem, UT	580	17.3	29.4	163 577	72.5	14.9	1.4	1.3	4.9	3.4	23.7	72.9
Pueblo, CO	489	16.4	35.3	58 749	79.4	13.6	0.7	1.1	1.9	9.4	32.5	58.2
Punta Gorda, FL	626	18.8	29.4	49 631	81.7	12.4	0.2	1.7	0.7	5.5	46.1	48.4
Raleigh-Durham-Chapel Hill, NC	686	14.4	29.9	617 475	78.5	12.9	1.7	1.1	2.3	6.3	32.7	60.9
Rapid City, SD	497	10.8	27.0	44 988	82.9	10.4	0.6	0.7	2.3	6.1	30.5	63.5

Table C-4. Metropolitan Areas — **Migration, Housing, and Transportation**

CMSA/MSA/ PMSA/NECMA code[1]	Area name	Total population 5 years and over	Residence in 1995 (percent) Same house	Same county, different house	Same state, different county	Different state	Outside the United States	Occupied housing units Number	Percent owner-occupied	Householders 65 years and over Number	Percent owner-occupied
		1	2	3	4	5	6	7	8	9	10
6680	Reading, PA	350 815	61.1	24.4	7.9	4.8	1.8	141 570	74.0	35 887	78.6
6690	Redding, CA	153 584	50.0	30.2	13.3	5.5	0.9	63 426	66.1	15 850	80.7
6720	Reno, NV	316 402	41.2	32.4	3.5	19.4	3.4	132 084	59.3	23 841	71.8
6740	Richland-Kennewick-Pasco, WA	176 306	50.6	25.0	11.4	9.7	3.3	67 706	68.1	12 947	79.6
6760	Richmond-Petersburg, VA	932 074	53.0	19.5	16.1	9.6	1.9	387 721	67.7	72 356	78.0
6800	Roanoke, VA	222 293	56.6	16.6	17.1	8.5	1.1	98 343	68.5	23 748	77.4
6820	Rochester, MN	115 459	54.8	21.9	7.5	12.7	3.1	47 807	76.0	8 694	77.5
6840	Rochester, NY	1 029 609	58.8	27.0	8.4	4.1	1.7	420 073	68.2	89 368	73.6
6880	Rockford, IL	345 362	56.1	27.2	9.0	5.8	1.9	141 855	71.6	30 421	78.8
6895	Rocky Mount, NC	133 628	56.8	24.1	12.1	5.9	1.2	54 036	66.3	12 293	73.1
82	Sacramento-Yolo, CA	1 673 889	47.4	28.5	15.9	4.8	3.3	665 298	61.3	129 604	77.9
6920	Sacramento, CA	1 516 097	48.0	29.1	15.1	4.8	3.1	605 923	62.1	119 228	78.2
9270	Yolo, CA	157 792	41.8	23.4	24.2	5.1	5.5	59 375	53.1	10 376	75.3
6960	Saginaw-Bay City-Midland, MI	370 871	62.1	24.0	8.0	3.9	0.8	156 129	76.3	36 268	81.5
7120	Salinas, CA	370 950	48.8	28.5	11.1	5.4	6.2	121 236	54.7	25 342	76.6
7160	Salt Lake City-Ogden, UT	1 212 931	50.6	28.6	6.7	10.5	3.5	432 040	71.3	71 111	84.5
7200	San Angelo, TX	97 019	48.4	26.9	14.5	8.1	2.0	39 503	64.1	9 298	77.9
7240	San Antonio, TX	1 469 825	51.3	29.2	8.9	7.9	2.7	559 946	63.4	109 253	79.7
7320	San Diego, CA	2 617 718	45.1	34.5	7.1	9.2	4.2	994 677	55.4	196 534	75.3
84	San Francisco-Oakland-San Jose, CA	6 591 573	52.4	24.8	11.7	5.4	5.7	2 557 158	57.8	482 217	73.2
5775	Oakland, CA	2 230 428	51.7	24.7	13.6	4.9	5.0	867 495	60.5	158 056	75.1
7360	San Francisco, CA	1 642 167	55.2	20.4	11.6	6.8	6.0	684 453	49.0	144 119	65.7
7400	San Jose, CA	1 564 068	51.2	28.0	7.6	5.3	8.0	565 863	59.8	91 763	76.6
7485	Santa Cruz-Watsonville, CA	240 233	50.6	27.7	13.8	4.5	3.5	91 139	60.0	16 355	78.8
7500	Santa Rosa, CA	431 580	52.0	28.9	12.1	4.0	3.0	172 403	64.1	37 981	78.4
8720	Vallejo-Fairfield-Napa, CA	483 097	50.7	24.8	16.7	5.3	3.6	175 805	65.2	33 943	78.2
7460	San Luis Obispo-Atascadero-Paso Robles, CA	234 524	46.7	26.2	20.9	4.6	1.6	92 739	61.5	23 326	81.9
7480	Santa Barbara-Santa Maria-Lompoc, CA	373 862	48.3	29.2	12.8	5.5	4.1	136 622	56.1	32 370	77.4
7490	Santa Fe, NM	138 832	54.2	21.0	6.8	14.0	4.0	59 979	69.8	11 240	82.1
7510	Sarasota-Bradenton, FL	562 331	49.6	23.1	8.1	16.6	2.5	262 397	76.8	107 213	88.0
7520	Savannah, GA	272 932	50.6	24.7	8.6	13.7	2.3	111 105	64.3	23 696	77.5
7560	Scranton—Wilkes-Barre—Hazleton, PA	593 066	68.3	21.6	5.7	3.8	0.6	252 582	69.9	77 358	73.6
91	Seattle-Tacoma-Bremerton, WA	3 324 634	47.5	28.2	8.9	11.8	3.7	1 392 393	62.9	236 104	75.4
1150	Bremerton, WA	216 623	48.7	23.4	9.1	16.6	2.2	86 416	67.4	15 495	78.7
5910	Olympia, WA	194 657	48.1	25.7	12.3	11.7	2.1	81 625	66.6	15 512	78.8
7600	Seattle-Bellevue-Everett, WA	2 262 273	47.4	28.8	8.1	11.5	4.1	963 552	62.0	158 876	74.2
8200	Tacoma, WA	651 081	46.9	28.3	10.4	11.3	3.1	260 800	63.5	46 221	77.3
7610	Sharon, PA	113 496	65.3	21.4	6.9	6.0	0.4	46 712	76.2	13 993	81.6
7620	Sheboygan, WI	105 384	59.3	26.4	7.9	5.3	1.1	43 545	71.4	10 111	75.6
7640	Sherman-Denison, TX	103 405	51.3	26.1	13.4	7.9	1.2	42 849	70.5	11 033	82.1
7680	Shreveport-Bossier City, LA	364 945	54.9	27.4	7.9	8.8	1.1	151 103	66.4	33 612	81.8
7720	Sioux City, IA-NE	114 714	54.6	26.6	4.8	11.4	2.6	46 246	68.4	10 179	77.3
7760	Sioux Falls, SD	159 614	49.6	25.5	11.7	11.5	1.8	66 778	66.7	12 141	69.7
7800	South Bend, IN	246 865	55.2	26.1	5.3	11.7	1.7	100 743	71.7	24 213	81.4
7840	Spokane, WA	390 366	50.8	29.5	7.4	10.2	2.0	163 611	65.5	33 749	76.0
7880	Springfield, IL	188 718	55.2	30.2	9.0	4.9	0.7	83 595	70.5	18 099	78.8
8003	Springfield, MA	572 157	57.5	25.9	6.8	7.1	2.8	231 279	62.6	55 405	70.8
7920	Springfield, MO	304 593	45.9	26.8	15.3	11.3	0.8	129 357	66.8	27 013	79.5
6980	St. Cloud, MN	156 327	56.8	18.7	18.4	5.0	1.1	60 669	72.3	11 869	76.9
7000	St. Joseph, MO	96 113	55.8	25.7	10.7	7.2	0.6	39 830	69.5	9 907	78.2
7040	St. Louis, MO-IL	2 430 416	56.7	23.0	11.3	7.5	1.5	1 012 419	71.4	221 854	78.9
8050	State College, PA	129 506	46.9	17.4	21.7	10.5	3.6	49 323	60.2	8 979	79.7
8080	Steubenville-Weirton, OH-WV	125 201	68.8	19.3	4.9	6.6	0.4	54 491	75.4	16 221	82.6
8120	Stockton-Lodi, CA	519 445	51.2	29.1	13.8	2.8	3.0	181 629	60.4	36 484	73.9
8140	Sumter, SC	96 890	55.0	23.5	5.8	12.9	2.8	37 728	69.5	7 527	80.4
8160	Syracuse, NY	685 852	59.3	26.0	8.6	4.8	1.3	282 601	67.6	64 469	75.0
8240	Tallahassee, FL	267 765	44.7	24.7	18.1	10.3	2.2	112 388	60.0	16 479	82.6
8280	Tampa-St. Petersburg-Clearwater, FL	2 259 662	49.1	26.7	7.9	13.3	3.0	1 009 316	70.8	298 479	84.4
8320	Terre Haute, IN	139 914	55.5	25.9	9.6	8.0	1.0	57 976	70.8	14 736	78.2
8360	Texarkana, TX-Texarkana, AR	120 910	53.4	25.3	8.8	11.9	0.7	48 695	70.0	11 647	83.9
8400	Toledo, OH	577 116	56.4	27.8	8.7	6.0	1.1	243 499	67.3	52 756	78.2
8440	Topeka, KS	158 281	53.6	30.4	7.9	7.1	1.1	68 920	67.5	15 372	75.8

[1]MSA = Metropolitan Statistical Area. CMSA = Consolidated MSA. PMSA = Primary MSA. NECMA = New England County Metropolitan Area. See the Appendix A for explanation of these concepts. See Appendix B for list of metropolitan areas identified by type, with component counties.

Table C-4. Metropolitan Areas — **Migration, Housing, and Transportation**

Area name	Owner-occupied by household type (percent)								Median household income			Median housing value (owner estimated)	Median monthly owner costs as a percent of income	
	Family households					Nonfamily households								
		Married-couple family		Other family										
	Total family households	Total	With own children under 18 years	Total	With own children under 18 years	Total nonfamily households	Two or more adults	Living alone	All households	Owner-occupied households	Renter-occupied households		With a mortgage	Without a mortgage
	11	12	13	14	15	16	17	18	19	20	21	22	23	24
Reading, PA	81.9	87.7	85.7	57.9	46.2	55.8	49.9	57.1	44 456	51 927	26 648	104 400	21.4	12.0
Redding, CA	71.1	79.6	69.2	43.5	30.9	54.8	46.0	56.9	34 308	41 217	22 074	112 900	25.2	11.6
Reno, NV	67.9	74.2	69.4	47.7	40.2	44.2	40.0	45.6	45 632	58 868	30 784	149 500	24.4	9.9
Richland-Kennewick-Pasco, WA	74.1	80.6	75.1	49.0	41.8	51.5	43.0	53.2	44 573	55 334	26 950	107 600	20.0	9.9
Richmond-Petersburg, VA	75.8	85.1	82.3	49.8	39.4	50.7	40.9	53.0	46 597	57 785	27 923	115 000	20.9	9.9
Roanoke, VA	77.2	85.1	82.2	51.5	37.3	51.6	40.8	53.3	39 143	47 918	24 549	101 200	20.4	9.9
Rochester, MN	86.4	90.6	90.2	64.0	59.5	54.0	49.7	55.1	51 175	59 956	27 688	114 700	18.5	9.9
Rochester, NY	78.5	87.5	86.5	50.0	39.5	47.9	44.3	48.8	43 913	55 436	24 206	93 300	21.6	12.8
Rockford, IL	79.4	86.4	83.4	53.0	43.7	53.3	51.7	53.6	44 942	53 919	26 708	95 600	20.8	11.4
Rocky Mount, NC	71.4	81.0	77.3	47.8	36.1	53.4	41.6	55.0	34 695	42 200	21 340	76 200	20.6	11.2
Sacramento-Yolo, CA	68.5	76.8	70.6	44.1	33.7	46.4	37.3	49.1	45 922	59 966	29 510	156 200	24.0	9.9
Sacramento, CA	69.0	77.4	71.2	44.4	33.8	47.7	41.1	49.5	46 426	59 905	30 094	155 600	24.0	9.9
Yolo, CA	63.7	70.7	64.9	41.1	32.4	34.7	17.0	44.8	40 527	60 527	24 785	164 400	23.9	9.9
Saginaw-Bay City-Midland, MI	84.0	91.1	88.9	59.7	49.7	58.7	50.3	60.2	39 766	47 249	21 434	86 700	18.4	9.9
Salinas, CA	58.1	63.4	54.0	39.7	27.7	45.4	40.3	46.8	48 165	60 686	36 271	254 800	26.4	9.9
Salt Lake City-Ogden, UT	77.9	82.6	81.4	57.2	48.5	51.5	37.7	55.4	48 494	57 239	30 202	148 300	22.7	9.9
San Angelo, TX	72.2	78.4	71.8	51.3	40.0	46.7	32.6	49.1	33 025	40 600	22 489	62 700	19.7	10.4
San Antonio, TX	70.4	77.2	71.4	51.7	39.2	45.3	36.7	47.1	39 018	48 458	26 620	74 100	20.4	9.9
San Diego, CA	62.0	68.8	60.9	40.2	28.2	42.0	30.8	46.1	46 887	62 537	32 133	212 000	25.6	9.9
San Francisco-Oakland-San Jose, CA	66.5	72.4	68.3	46.8	35.4	41.7	33.8	44.5	61 813	78 489	43 465	340 800	25.0	9.9
Oakland, CA	67.9	75.2	71.0	45.8	34.1	45.2	38.4	47.3	58 964	75 899	38 248	277 400	24.9	9.9
San Francisco, CA	62.3	67.1	64.8	46.2	35.9	32.5	25.8	35.1	62 855	83 786	47 319	449 400	25.5	9.9
San Jose, CA	66.4	71.0	66.7	48.6	35.5	44.3	34.6	48.1	74 003	91 407	54 010	422 600	24.2	9.9
Santa Cruz-Watsonville, CA	67.3	73.9	66.8	46.2	35.5	47.5	36.7	52.6	53 829	69 349	36 276	353 300	26.7	9.9
Santa Rosa, CA	70.6	76.8	69.7	48.9	39.9	51.6	43.3	54.5	52 798	64 189	37 503	265 200	26.0	9.9
Vallejo-Fairfield-Napa, CA	69.4	76.2	70.2	46.9	35.9	53.6	48.8	54.9	53 347	65 458	36 582	187 200	24.9	9.9
San Luis Obispo-Atascadero-Paso Robles, CA	70.9	77.3	70.2	45.1	34.9	45.0	27.7	52.1	42 200	54 479	27 740	218 600	26.5	9.9
Santa Barbara-Santa Maria-Lompoc, CA	63.5	68.7	58.3	43.9	31.2	41.6	28.3	47.1	46 493	61 060	32 252	264 100	26.5	9.9
Santa Fe, NM	79.2	84.4	80.9	62.3	54.5	53.2	49.3	54.2	45 505	54 677	28 919	174 900	22.9	9.9
Sarasota-Bradenton, FL	81.4	86.6	77.4	57.3	44.4	68.4	57.3	70.7	40 427	44 629	29 341	104 700	23.2	10.6
Savannah, GA	71.4	80.5	76.0	48.1	36.2	48.6	35.9	51.4	39 400	49 808	24 360	91 100	21.2	10.8
Scranton—Wilkes-Barre—Hazleton, PA	79.3	85.6	83.2	57.7	39.7	52.3	41.9	53.8	34 058	41 244	20 799	86 700	21.4	13.1
Seattle-Tacoma-Bremerton, WA	72.9	79.5	76.5	47.5	39.1	44.8	38.9	46.6	50 558	62 875	32 578	186 100	24.1	10.8
Bremerton, WA	73.9	79.5	73.0	49.4	41.0	51.4	45.4	53.1	46 897	56 791	30 244	145 200	23.8	10.5
Olympia, WA	75.2	81.7	76.8	50.6	41.8	48.8	40.4	51.3	46 929	56 353	30 161	138 800	23.2	9.9
Seattle-Bellevue-Everett, WA	73.3	79.8	78.1	47.7	39.4	43.3	37.4	45.2	52 537	66 611	34 640	211 700	24.2	10.8
Tacoma, WA	70.3	77.8	72.3	45.5	37.1	48.1	44.3	49.1	44 853	56 286	28 819	144 400	24.4	11.1
Sharon, PA	83.6	89.0	86.5	62.2	48.9	59.5	57.2	59.8	34 619	39 975	20 571	75 100	20.1	11.7
Sheboygan, WI	81.2	86.7	83.2	49.8	37.8	49.8	42.9	51.1	46 114	52 968	30 074	105 800	20.6	11.4
Sherman-Denison, TX	77.0	82.7	74.8	54.7	44.2	55.1	45.3	56.6	37 351	43 898	25 582	67 800	19.3	11.8
Shreveport-Bossier City, LA	72.0	82.0	76.0	50.8	37.6	54.0	42.3	55.7	32 490	41 229	20 927	70 100	19.1	9.9
Sioux City, IA-NE	76.9	83.6	80.5	53.7	43.8	49.9	41.5	51.7	38 191	45 974	24 488	75 600	19.2	10.6
Sioux Falls, SD	79.5	86.3	87.4	49.8	44.4	41.0	34.0	42.8	43 439	53 187	26 688	98 600	20.2	9.9
South Bend, IN	80.0	87.5	84.5	55.7	44.2	55.2	49.3	56.4	40 131	47 964	24 443	85 800	19.2	9.9
Spokane, WA	75.4	82.9	79.1	49.5	41.5	47.0	35.9	49.6	37 191	47 420	22 696	111 200	23.0	10.0
Springfield, IL	79.5	87.6	85.9	53.0	45.8	54.5	45.3	56.1	42 977	52 128	26 360	87 900	19.8	9.9
Springfield, MA	72.2	82.6	78.9	45.1	31.9	45.0	37.9	46.6	41 005	53 897	23 244	120 900	21.6	12.5
Springfield, MO	76.5	82.7	79.5	51.0	43.1	47.4	32.0	51.2	34 445	41 996	22 011	89 000	20.4	9.9
St. Cloud, MN	86.1	91.0	92.0	60.6	53.7	44.1	29.4	49.4	42 285	50 490	24 811	101 500	19.6	9.9
St. Joseph, MO	77.1	84.7	79.7	50.2	41.6	54.0	40.9	56.5	35 614	42 293	22 166	75 100	18.4	9.9
St. Louis, MO-IL	79.8	87.7	85.7	56.4	45.4	53.8	46.3	55.2	44 316	53 617	25 977	96 200	19.4	9.9
State College, PA	80.1	83.4	82.0	61.2	54.5	32.6	12.7	44.2	36 295	49 642	20 365	109 400	22.2	9.9
Steubenville-Weirton, OH-WV	81.6	87.6	82.4	60.1	41.5	61.7	59.0	62.0	31 880	37 026	19 306	64 400	19.1	9.9
Stockton-Lodi, CA	64.3	73.1	65.6	38.7	27.8	49.1	40.9	51.1	41 216	54 613	25 780	139 800	24.5	9.9
Sumter, SC	73.9	80.2	74.3	59.5	51.6	57.2	41.9	59.4	33 632	40 014	22 632	67 000	19.5	9.9
Syracuse, NY	78.2	86.4	84.6	52.2	40.9	47.3	42.8	48.4	39 715	50 543	21 854	80 600	20.9	13.1
Tallahassee, FL	74.5	83.1	81.4	54.8	47.8	39.1	20.7	47.1	36 354	50 731	20 441	93 600	21.1	9.9
Tampa-St. Petersburg-Clearwater, FL	77.9	84.5	78.7	56.2	44.9	58.5	50.6	60.4	37 303	42 737	26 982	84 800	22.1	10.9
Terre Haute, IN	79.8	86.1	82.5	56.9	47.2	53.5	40.8	55.9	33 855	41 678	19 621	70 200	18.5	9.9
Texarkana, TX-Texarkana, AR	74.3	83.9	78.7	48.0	34.8	59.2	46.7	60.7	32 291	39 173	19 609	61 100	18.6	10.3
Toledo, OH	77.2	86.1	83.4	51.4	39.9	48.8	35.5	51.7	39 616	50 234	22 850	93 600	19.9	11.3
Topeka, KS	77.2	85.1	81.4	50.1	41.8	49.4	41.1	50.8	40 774	50 634	24 571	79 600	19.0	9.9

Table C-4. Metropolitan Areas — **Migration, Housing, and Transportation**

Area name	Median gross rent	Percent who pay 35 percent or more of income for housing expenses		Means of transportation to work (percent except where noted)						Vehicles available (percent of households)		
		Owners	Renters	Number of workers 16 years and over	Car, truck, or van: Drove alone	Car, truck, or van: Carpooled	Public transportation	Other means	Walked	No vehicles	One vehicle	Two or more vehicles
	25	26	27	28	29	30	31	32	33	34	35	36
Reading, PA	545	14.1	26.6	177 831	81.1	10.0	1.7	0.8	3.6	10.6	30.7	58.6
Redding, CA	563	22.1	36.9	64 487	79.7	12.0	0.9	1.2	2.2	7.0	34.2	58.7
Reno, NV	675	19.6	30.3	168 922	75.3	13.8	3.2	1.6	3.2	8.9	35.1	56.1
Richland-Kennewick-Pasco, WA	542	12.0	27.2	84 463	77.8	14.5	1.0	1.2	1.7	5.8	28.5	65.7
Richmond-Petersburg, VA	613	13.5	28.2	491 211	82.0	10.4	2.1	1.0	1.9	8.9	32.1	59.0
Roanoke, VA	497	12.6	24.8	114 820	84.2	9.8	1.4	0.8	1.6	8.0	33.2	58.8
Rochester, MN	556	7.8	28.6	65 891	77.2	11.3	3.1	0.9	3.8	6.6	31.9	61.5
Rochester, NY	594	14.6	35.0	516 814	81.8	9.1	2.0	0.7	3.5	10.0	35.0	55.0
Rockford, IL	512	12.9	24.2	176 930	83.1	10.7	0.9	0.8	1.6	7.1	32.4	60.5
Rocky Mount, NC	471	16.4	27.9	61 036	80.7	14.5	0.8	0.9	1.2	11.0	32.5	56.5
Sacramento-Yolo, CA	673	19.7	33.8	799 989	75.3	13.5	2.7	2.2	2.2	7.8	34.5	57.7
Sacramento, CA	672	19.7	32.6	724 838	76.2	13.6	2.6	1.6	2.0	7.7	34.5	57.8
Yolo, CA	687	18.9	43.4	75 151	67.2	13.2	3.7	8.3	3.8	8.4	34.8	56.7
Saginaw-Bay City-Midland, MI	483	10.7	30.8	177 490	86.4	7.9	0.6	0.6	1.5	7.0	33.2	59.8
Salinas, CA	776	24.9	30.5	164 517	68.7	19.5	2.2	2.2	3.8	7.1	33.4	59.5
Salt Lake City-Ogden, UT	625	16.0	27.9	642 688	77.2	13.1	3.0	1.1	1.8	5.8	28.1	66.2
San Angelo, TX	457	12.1	28.4	47 286	79.4	12.7	0.4	1.2	4.1	7.0	37.9	55.1
San Antonio, TX	556	13.5	27.4	698 685	76.2	14.7	2.9	1.2	2.4	9.0	36.1	54.9
San Diego, CA	761	23.2	34.1	1 299 503	73.9	13.0	3.4	1.9	3.4	8.0	34.8	57.1
San Francisco-Oakland-San Jose, CA	968	22.2	31.0	3 432 157	68.1	12.9	9.5	2.2	3.3	9.9	32.9	57.2
Oakland, CA	868	22.0	32.3	1 120 918	67.9	13.7	10.0	2.1	2.5	9.2	33.1	57.7
San Francisco, CA	1 023	23.6	29.7	899 295	56.5	11.6	18.8	2.6	5.6	16.8	37.2	46.0
San Jose, CA	1 185	21.1	29.6	828 927	77.3	12.2	3.5	2.0	1.8	5.7	29.0	65.3
Santa Cruz-Watsonville, CA	924	25.9	37.2	126 106	69.5	14.2	3.3	3.2	4.4	6.3	31.4	62.3
Santa Rosa, CA	864	23.0	32.6	224 947	74.7	12.6	2.4	1.7	3.1	5.8	31.6	62.7
Vallejo-Fairfield-Napa, CA	802	21.1	30.2	231 964	73.1	17.0	2.4	1.7	2.2	6.5	29.9	63.6
San Luis Obispo-Atascadero-Paso Robles, CA	719	23.0	40.4	107 807	73.9	13.5	1.0	2.4	3.7	5.3	33.2	61.6
Santa Barbara-Santa Maria-Lompoc, CA	830	24.5	38.2	179 445	69.4	15.8	2.4	3.8	4.0	6.9	34.0	59.2
Santa Fe, NM	688	18.1	32.8	73 129	72.7	15.0	0.8	1.5	3.0	5.0	33.7	61.3
Sarasota-Bradenton, FL	673	17.7	32.0	243 767	80.3	11.6	0.7	1.9	1.6	6.2	46.2	47.5
Savannah, GA	582	16.2	32.4	133 060	77.8	13.4	2.5	1.5	2.4	10.4	34.9	54.7
Scranton—Wilkes-Barre—Hazleton, PA	439	15.3	25.6	277 498	81.2	11.4	0.9	0.7	3.7	12.3	35.8	51.9
Seattle-Tacoma-Bremerton, WA	723	19.0	29.8	1 776 224	71.6	12.8	6.8	1.4	3.2	7.7	32.7	59.6
Bremerton, WA	667	18.3	29.2	106 877	66.3	14.3	8.7	2.3	3.8	6.8	28.6	64.6
Olympia, WA	655	15.9	31.0	100 986	77.2	12.7	2.2	1.4	2.8	6.3	29.8	63.9
Seattle-Bellevue-Everett, WA	758	19.2	29.5	1 244 076	70.4	12.6	8.0	1.4	3.2	8.1	33.7	58.2
Tacoma, WA	624	19.8	30.8	324 285	76.4	13.3	2.7	1.2	2.9	7.0	31.3	61.7
Sharon, PA	443	11.6	26.2	51 120	83.2	9.2	0.3	0.8	3.2	7.9	37.2	54.9
Sheboygan, WI	482	9.9	17.5	58 546	81.0	10.2	0.8	1.3	3.8	7.0	33.7	59.4
Sherman-Denison, TX	518	12.6	24.2	50 013	80.8	13.4	0.2	1.0	1.8	6.2	33.1	60.8
Shreveport-Bossier City, LA	460	13.0	28.1	165 957	80.8	13.1	1.7	1.2	1.5	11.3	37.0	51.7
Sioux City, IA-NE	499	9.8	24.9	61 075	78.4	14.2	0.9	0.9	2.7	8.6	31.5	59.9
Sioux Falls, SD	517	9.5	23.2	95 133	83.7	9.3	0.7	0.6	2.3	5.7	30.2	64.1
South Bend, IN	535	10.9	28.1	125 416	81.2	10.3	1.2	0.7	3.9	8.3	35.9	55.8
Spokane, WA	532	16.8	33.2	191 195	76.7	12.3	2.8	1.2	2.8	8.8	32.7	58.6
Springfield, IL	501	10.3	24.7	102 922	81.8	11.1	1.6	0.7	2.1	8.0	36.9	55.1
Springfield, MA	556	15.3	30.6	283 551	79.3	9.6	2.5	0.9	5.0	12.9	37.9	49.3
Springfield, MO	467	12.7	29.2	160 112	81.8	10.8	0.7	1.0	2.1	6.6	33.8	59.5
St. Cloud, MN	475	9.7	23.3	90 105	78.0	9.6	1.2	0.8	4.8	6.4	28.1	65.4
St. Joseph, MO	435	9.6	26.5	46 804	82.3	11.6	0.7	0.9	1.7	8.5	35.0	56.5
St. Louis, MO-IL	525	11.6	27.6	1 238 964	82.6	9.9	2.4	0.6	1.6	9.0	34.4	56.6
State College, PA	565	12.5	42.1	63 097	66.7	11.6	3.9	1.4	12.4	9.0	35.6	55.5
Steubenville-Weirton, OH-WV	395	10.9	26.0	53 617	85.3	8.5	0.4	0.5	3.3	9.4	35.2	55.4
Stockton-Lodi, CA	617	21.1	35.7	213 629	74.6	17.0	1.4	1.8	2.3	9.5	32.2	58.3
Sumter, SC	461	13.1	21.6	44 325	80.4	14.5	0.8	1.4	1.2	11.0	32.2	56.8
Syracuse, NY	535	14.4	33.3	333 208	80.0	10.2	2.0	0.7	4.1	11.2	36.4	52.4
Tallahassee, FL	591	14.8	41.5	137 762	78.7	14.5	1.5	1.0	1.9	7.8	38.3	53.9
Tampa-St. Petersburg-Clearwater, FL	608	16.9	30.7	1 063 957	79.7	12.4	1.4	1.7	1.7	8.1	44.2	47.7
Terre Haute, IN	437	10.2	27.4	66 685	82.0	11.2	0.3	0.9	3.3	8.1	34.3	57.7
Texarkana, TX-Texarkana, AR	453	11.8	28.4	52 119	83.1	12.2	0.2	1.0	1.4	9.5	34.9	55.7
Toledo, OH	488	12.9	29.6	289 647	84.5	8.9	1.4	0.7	2.4	8.3	36.6	55.0
Topeka, KS	494	9.9	29.0	83 741	83.4	11.3	0.9	0.6	1.2	7.3	35.2	57.4

Table C-4. Metropolitan Areas — **Migration, Housing, and Transportation**

CMSA/MSA/PMSA/NECMA code[1]	Area name	Total population 5 years and over	Residence in 1995 (percent)					Occupied housing units		Householders 65 years and over	
			Same house	Same county, different house	Same state, different county	Different state	Outside the United States	Number	Percent owner-occupied	Number	Percent owner-occupied
		1	2	3	4	5	6	7	8	9	10
8520	Tucson, AZ..................	788 868	46.2	31.2	4.5	15.1	3.1	332 350	64.3	77 969	80.9
8560	Tulsa, OK	745 887	49.7	26.9	11.0	10.6	1.8	315 532	66.9	62 530	80.9
8600	Tuscaloosa, AL	154 505	51.0	27.8	12.1	7.5	1.6	64 517	63.5	12 654	79.5
8640	Tyler, TX......................	162 278	51.0	27.7	13.9	5.5	1.9	65 692	69.7	16 010	82.5
8680	Utica-Rome, NY	282 928	64.1	23.7	7.3	3.1	1.9	116 230	68.1	32 129	74.4
8750	Victoria, TX...................	77 789	52.0	31.1	12.1	3.5	1.4	30 071	67.4	6 417	80.9
8780	Visalia-Tulare-Porterville, CA	335 395	53.1	33.6	8.1	2.2	3.0	110 385	61.5	22 683	78.5
8800	Waco, TX	198 274	48.2	29.4	14.7	5.8	1.9	78 859	60.2	17 895	79.9
97	Washington-Baltimore, DC-MD-VA-WV	7 092 599	52.6	20.7	9.9	12.6	4.2	2 871 861	65.0	495 041	74.1
0720	Baltimore, MD	2 387 344	57.0	21.2	11.8	7.9	2.1	974 071	66.9	201 862	73.5
3180	Hagerstown, MD	123 780	57.4	23.2	11.4	7.4	0.7	49 726	65.6	12 320	74.5
8840	Washington, DC-MD-VA-WV..............	4 581 475	50.2	20.4	8.8	15.1	5.5	1 848 064	64.0	280 859	74.5
8920	Waterloo-Cedar Falls, IA...................	120 253	54.5	24.6	12.2	6.0	2.7	49 683	68.9	11 812	77.6
8940	Wausau, WI..................	117 712	61.7	23.7	9.3	4.6	0.7	47 702	75.7	10 228	78.1
8960	West Palm Beach-Boca Raton, FL	1 069 257	49.5	26.0	7.3	12.9	4.4	474 175	74.7	170 020	87.2
9000	Wheeling, WV-OH........	145 297	66.2	20.2	6.3	6.9	0.4	62 249	73.6	18 662	79.3
9080	Wichita Falls, TX...........	130 906	46.8	25.8	12.1	12.8	2.4	51 786	63.5	11 961	80.7
9040	Wichita, KS..................	503 656	50.1	30.5	7.6	9.7	2.2	210 552	67.7	42 286	79.8
9140	Williamsport, PA...........	113 461	61.0	26.0	8.5	3.8	0.7	47 003	69.5	12 460	76.9
9200	Wilmington, NC	220 217	48.1	22.2	13.3	15.0	1.5	98 621	70.1	21 782	83.2
9260	Yakima, WA	203 449	53.8	32.7	5.2	5.5	2.7	73 993	64.4	16 114	76.6
9280	York, PA......................	358 615	60.2	24.7	6.4	7.8	0.9	148 219	76.1	31 919	80.9
9320	Youngstown-Warren, OH............................	559 067	64.1	24.4	6.3	4.6	0.6	234 580	73.9	64 458	80.3
9340	Yuba City, CA	128 660	49.7	24.6	16.5	5.7	3.4	47 568	58.2	9 986	78.0
9360	Yuma, AZ	147 498	46.1	27.4	2.8	18.6	5.1	53 848	72.2	16 390	88.7

[1]MSA = Metropolitan Statistical Area. CMSA = Consolidated MSA. PMSA = Primary MSA. NECMA = New England County Metropolitan Area. See the Appendix A for explanation of these concepts. See Appendix B for list of metropolitan areas identified by type, with component counties.

Table C-4. Metropolitan Areas — **Migration, Housing, and Transportation**

Area name	Owner-occupied by household type (percent)								Median household income			Median monthly owner costs as a percent of income		
	Family households					Nonfamily households								
		Married-couple family		Other family										
	Total family households	Total	With own children under 18 years	Total	With own children under 18 years	Total nonfamily households	Two or more adults	Living alone	All households	Owner-occupied households	Renter-occupied households	Median housing value (owner estimated)	With a mortgage	Without a mortgage
	11	12	13	14	15	16	17	18	19	20	21	22	23	24
Tucson, AZ..................	73.3	80.3	74.3	51.6	42.4	48.2	40.4	50.3	36 532	46 347	23 673	102 600	22.3	9.9
Tulsa, OK..................	74.7	81.6	77.1	50.0	40.4	49.9	38.4	51.8	38 141	47 012	24 752	81 900	19.1	9.9
Tuscaloosa, AL	74.6	84.1	82.6	49.2	38.5	42.8	22.7	47.4	33 632	45 783	17 302	95 400	20.4	9.9
Tyler, TX....................	76.1	82.9	76.8	51.5	41.9	53.4	34.1	56.1	36 739	44 184	24 252	76 500	19.8	10.4
Utica-Rome, NY	77.5	85.3	82.2	52.3	39.4	50.0	45.3	50.8	35 355	44 160	20 121	71 100	20.7	12.8
Victoria, TX.................	73.2	80.0	73.4	48.8	37.5	50.5	37.7	52.5	38 992	46 406	26 065	68 600	18.5	10.5
Visalia-Tulare-Porterville, CA	63.6	70.9	61.8	42.4	31.7	53.5	35.4	57.2	33 669	42 762	22 582	96 500	24.4	9.9
Waco, TX	69.1	77.2	70.5	44.8	32.2	41.9	20.1	47.6	33 263	43 466	21 201	66 400	19.6	11.1
Washington-Baltimore, DC-MD-VA-WV	73.4	81.1	79.2	50.7	40.7	48.1	40.9	50.0	57 123	71 058	35 897	157 400	21.9	9.9
Baltimore, MD	75.3	84.2	82.9	52.3	40.9	49.4	44.2	50.7	49 653	61 563	29 559	132 400	22.0	10.3
Hagerstown, MD	73.2	80.2	76.3	44.9	32.5	48.9	40.8	50.6	40 315	49 080	26 435	113 500	21.4	10.4
Washington, DC-MD-VA-WV......................	72.3	79.6	77.5	49.9	40.8	47.4	39.3	49.6	62 123	77 708	39 706	172 900	21.8	9.9
Waterloo-Cedar Falls, IA.............................	80.1	86.3	83.2	56.3	45.7	48.6	29.1	54.7	37 069	46 087	21 501	76 200	18.4	9.9
Wausau, WI.................	84.9	88.9	87.7	62.5	53.6	52.8	47.1	54.0	45 160	51 490	27 726	96 200	19.6	9.9
West Palm Beach-Boca Raton, FL	79.4	85.7	79.2	54.9	45.0	66.0	56.2	68.2	44 878	51 281	30 657	115 000	23.2	11.1
Wheeling, WV-OH........	81.2	87.6	83.0	57.7	41.1	58.2	52.2	59.0	30 242	36 258	16 016	64 400	18.7	9.9
Wichita Falls, TX	70.2	76.0	67.9	48.4	38.1	48.9	34.7	51.2	34 086	41 853	24 464	59 800	19.6	11.0
Wichita, KS..................	76.3	82.4	78.7	52.9	44.1	49.4	42.2	50.6	42 419	51 836	26 669	80 400	19.2	9.9
Williamsport, PA............	78.9	85.7	81.1	52.4	41.0	49.6	36.7	52.1	34 044	40 930	21 348	84 700	20.9	12.1
Wilmington, NC	79.3	85.9	80.9	55.2	43.7	53.2	36.8	58.2	38 493	46 533	23 693	118 000	23.1	10.5
Yakima, WA	69.2	76.7	68.0	44.5	35.1	51.0	43.6	52.5	34 879	44 261	22 760	107 200	23.1	9.9
York, PA	83.7	89.1	87.2	58.9	47.5	57.3	51.0	58.8	45 193	51 484	27 648	108 200	22.0	10.5
Youngstown-Warren, OH......................	80.9	88.0	84.2	58.1	42.7	58.5	52.2	59.3	36 215	42 633	21 216	81 500	19.8	10.8
Yuba City, CA	61.8	69.1	58.7	38.5	24.4	48.3	43.3	49.5	34 648	45 023	23 951	108 100	23.8	9.9
Yuma, AZ	73.8	78.3	67.5	54.2	43.1	66.8	60.2	68.2	31 880	35 809	23 435	72 100	22.5	9.9

Table C-4. Metropolitan Areas — **Migration, Housing, and Transportation**

Area name	Median gross rent	Percent who pay 35 percent or more of income for housing expenses		Means of transportation to work (percent except where noted)							Vehicles available (percent of households)		
		Owners	Renters	Number of workers 16 years and over	Car, truck, or van		Public transportation	Other means	Walked	No vehicles	One vehicle	Two or more vehicles
					Drove alone	Carpooled						
	25	26	27	28	29	30	31	32	33	34	35	36
Tucson, AZ	544	16.1	33.9	369 261	73.8	14.7	2.5	2.7	2.6	9.0	40.1	50.9
Tulsa, OK	508	12.1	26.1	378 637	81.1	12.6	0.7	0.8	1.6	7.0	35.1	57.8
Tuscaloosa, AL	487	13.6	36.2	73 292	84.0	10.6	0.5	0.7	2.2	8.4	34.5	57.1
Tyler, TX.....................	517	13.0	29.9	76 267	81.8	12.8	0.3	1.3	1.1	6.8	34.6	58.6
Utica-Rome, NY	459	13.9	31.4	129 422	79.6	11.6	1.4	0.7	4.1	11.8	37.8	50.4
Victoria, TX.................	507	10.5	24.1	37 867	77.8	17.6	0.1	1.1	1.3	7.0	34.7	58.3
Visalia-Tulare- Porterville, CA	516	20.6	32.7	130 744	72.2	18.7	0.9	2.2	2.5	9.7	33.3	57.0
Waco, TX	499	11.8	32.8	92 441	79.1	14.2	0.8	1.1	2.3	8.3	37.2	54.6
Washington-Baltimore, DC-MD-VA-WV	744	15.5	26.2	3 839 052	70.4	12.8	9.4	0.9	3.0	12.0	33.9	54.1
Baltimore, MD	626	15.8	28.2	1 223 867	75.5	11.5	6.2	0.8	2.9	14.4	33.4	52.2
Hagerstown, MD	482	13.8	23.0	60 597	80.6	11.9	1.1	1.0	2.1	9.4	31.7	58.9
Washington, DC-MD- VA-WV......................	811	15.3	25.3	2 554 588	67.8	13.4	11.2	1.0	3.0	10.8	34.3	55.0
Waterloo-Cedar Falls, IA	472	8.4	33.2	62 897	82.8	8.4	0.8	0.9	4.2	7.7	31.8	60.5
Wausau, WI.................	484	10.3	19.5	65 680	81.1	9.5	1.0	0.8	2.6	5.6	29.1	65.3
West Palm Beach-Boca Raton, FL	739	19.7	33.8	475 572	79.6	11.9	1.4	1.6	1.4	7.9	44.2	47.9
Wheeling, WV-OH........	364	10.6	24.7	62 207	81.8	10.3	0.9	0.7	3.6	11.5	35.1	53.4
Wichita Falls, TX	484	11.7	25.3	65 448	78.0	11.3	0.4	1.2	7.0	6.5	35.8	57.7
Wichita, KS.................	506	10.4	24.9	262 408	84.6	9.7	0.6	0.8	1.6	6.0	33.4	60.5
Williamsport, PA...........	449	14.0	29.4	54 029	80.3	11.3	1.1	1.0	4.0	10.1	34.8	55.1
Wilmington, NC	615	18.6	36.1	112 050	81.3	11.6	0.8	1.5	1.7	7.1	34.8	58.2
Yakima, WA	534	16.2	31.9	86 583	77.5	14.4	0.5	1.4	2.6	7.7	29.7	62.6
York, PA......................	531	13.5	23.7	193 126	84.3	9.5	0.6	0.8	2.2	6.6	29.3	64.1
Youngstown-Warren, OH	447	12.4	26.9	256 048	86.2	8.6	0.6	0.7	1.7	8.1	34.4	57.5
Yuba City, CA	498	19.9	29.7	52 373	76.1	16.1	0.7	1.6	2.1	8.6	32.6	58.8
Yuma, AZ	508	17.0	26.8	51 675	73.7	16.0	1.1	3.0	4.3	7.2	40.3	52.5

Table C-5. Cities — **Migration, Housing, and Transportation**

STATE Place code	City	Total population 5 years and over	Residence in 1995 (percent)					Occupied housing units		Householders 65 years and over	
			Same house	Same county, different house	Same state, different county	Different state	Outside the United States	Number	Percent owner-occupied	Number	Percent owner-occupied
		1	2	3	4	5	6	7	8	9	10
00 00000	UNITED STATES....	262 375 152	54.1	24.9	9.7	8.4	2.9	105 480 101	66.2	22 634 690	77.6
01 00000	ALABAMA	4 152 278	57.4	24.7	8.8	7.9	1.2	1 737 080	72.5	394 617	81.7
01 03076	Auburn city	41 174	26.7	18.1	31.9	20.5	2.8	18 379	41.2	1 956	72.3
01 05980	Bessemer city	27 472	61.7	30.7	2.7	4.4	0.5	11 636	58.9	3 398	75.5
01 07000	Birmingham city............	226 637	54.7	32.7	5.5	5.5	1.6	98 937	53.5	22 847	75.1
01 20104	Decatur city	50 385	51.6	29.1	8.7	9.0	1.6	21 848	64.0	4 865	73.6
01 21184	Dothan city	53 723	50.4	28.6	9.1	10.8	1.1	23 748	63.1	5 259	76.0
01 26896	Florence city	34 338	51.7	26.8	11.8	8.5	1.2	15 772	58.5	4 080	76.4
01 28696	Gadsden city	36 227	57.5	27.4	7.8	6.0	1.3	16 392	63.4	5 595	75.5
01 35800	Homewood city..............	23 454	43.9	25.7	12.8	14.2	3.4	10 556	55.3	1 949	79.3
01 35896	Hoover city	58 306	44.0	21.2	15.2	16.5	3.1	25 147	66.3	4 303	76.9
01 37000	Huntsville city	148 270	50.8	28.7	6.8	11.4	2.3	66 724	61.7	13 847	80.7
01 45784	Madison city	26 817	37.3	29.2	7.4	22.9	3.2	11 055	70.5	790	83.3
01 50000	Mobile city	184 387	54.9	31.0	4.2	8.1	1.8	78 447	59.4	18 732	77.0
01 51000	Montgomery city	187 508	50.6	28.7	8.8	10.3	1.5	78 438	61.9	16 461	76.7
01 59472	Phenix City city	26 341	51.4	23.0	7.4	16.3	1.9	11 524	52.1	2 753	70.2
01 62496	Prichard city	26 565	66.4	28.4	1.9	2.7	0.6	9 875	58.4	2 449	77.5
01 77256	Tuscaloosa city	74 056	43.0	28.7	16.8	9.5	2.0	31 493	48.1	6 347	76.1
02 00000	ALASKA	579 740	46.2	27.7	7.5	16.5	2.2	221 600	62.5	23 157	76.7
02 03000	Anchorage municipality .	240 627	41.6	32.2	5.4	17.9	2.8	94 822	60.0	8 779	73.6
02 24230	Fairbanks city	27 410	30.1	27.0	6.9	32.3	3.7	11 127	34.7	1 410	58.6
02 36400	Juneau city and borough	28 711	45.1	31.2	8.2	13.9	1.4	11 543	63.8	1 252	75.2
04 00000	ARIZONA	4 752 724	44.3	30.6	4.5	16.8	3.9	1 901 327	68.0	430 278	83.6
04 02830	Apache Junction city	29 132	39.8	12.0	24.4	22.5	1.3	13 701	82.5	5 249	92.3
04 04720	Avondale city	32 425	34.3	41.0	2.7	17.1	4.9	10 635	77.5	988	80.5
04 08220	Bullhead City city	31 735	39.7	23.8	2.9	31.1	2.5	13 912	60.0	4 198	80.5
04 10530	Casa Grande city	23 035	46.4	30.0	7.6	14.3	1.7	8 905	63.5	2 244	78.2
04 12000	Chandler city	160 549	36.5	34.8	2.8	22.2	3.7	62 358	73.5	6 209	77.4
04 23620	Flagstaff city	49 506	34.5	25.9	18.1	19.2	2.2	19 374	48.1	2 018	82.6
04 27400	Gilbert town	98 362	28.2	42.8	2.3	24.8	1.9	35 434	84.9	2 299	86.5
04 27820	Glendale city	200 276	40.9	37.1	2.1	15.6	4.2	75 671	65.0	10 063	74.6
04 39370	Lake Havasu City city ...	39 983	48.3	18.4	4.0	28.1	1.2	17 889	77.7	6 996	87.3
04 46000	Mesa city	364 927	40.2	34.6	3.6	17.7	3.9	146 742	66.5	33 501	83.0
04 51600	Oro Valley town.............	28 293	37.7	24.5	3.6	32.4	1.8	12 337	84.1	4 100	94.1
04 54050	Peoria city	100 276	40.1	38.9	2.0	17.1	1.8	39 245	84.2	9 546	78.6
04 55000	Phoenix city	1 207 309	43.3	34.2	2.0	14.2	6.3	465 864	60.7	68 804	77.3
04 57380	Prescott city	33 211	42.4	21.0	11.7	22.8	2.0	15 387	65.7	5 715	82.4
04 65000	Scottsdale city	192 638	39.8	30.6	1.5	25.1	2.9	90 643	69.6	22 750	80.7
04 66820	Sierra Vista city	34 570	33.6	20.9	4.5	34.0	7.1	14 127	52.3	2 712	81.3
04 71510	Surprise city	28 662	23.4	34.6	2.0	36.1	4.0	12 502	88.1	4 743	92.8
04 73000	Tempe city...................	149 719	38.5	31.7	3.3	21.0	5.5	63 545	51.0	7 814	80.5
04 77000	Tucson city	452 203	42.8	34.3	5.1	13.8	4.0	192 946	53.5	39 499	74.2
04 85540	Yuma city	70 856	43.1	28.3	3.6	20.5	4.4	26 697	63.0	6 810	82.8
05 00000	ARKANSAS.................	2 492 205	53.3	24.8	10.5	10.1	1.4	1 042 696	69.4	248 583	81.0
05 15190	Conway city..................	40 304	35.6	25.0	26.2	11.6	1.6	16 057	55.0	2 513	70.4
05 23290	Fayetteville city.............	53 873	31.5	26.4	21.2	16.8	4.0	23 666	42.1	2 862	77.0
05 24550	Fort Smith city..............	74 225	46.9	28.2	9.2	13.0	2.6	32 351	56.4	7 056	73.1
05 33400	Hot Springs city............	33 508	48.7	26.8	11.5	11.7	1.4	16 061	57.8	5 920	73.8
05 34760	Jacksonville city	27 116	40.1	27.8	6.7	20.5	4.9	10 838	47.3	1 452	77.1
05 35710	Jonesboro city	51 965	43.1	29.9	15.6	10.3	1.2	22 319	58.0	4 212	78.0
05 41000	Little Rock city..............	170 603	48.9	30.7	8.5	9.9	2.0	77 427	57.5	14 814	75.1
05 50450	North Little Rock city.....	56 112	51.5	33.1	6.7	7.7	1.1	25 519	57.5	6 326	74.0
05 55310	Pine Bluff city	50 525	51.6	32.6	8.0	6.1	1.7	19 790	58.9	4 928	76.9
05 60410	Rogers city	35 355	40.4	26.1	8.0	21.7	3.7	14 045	63.1	2 832	79.9
05 66080	Springdale city..............	41 738	39.0	28.7	9.9	16.0	6.3	16 218	60.6	3 251	76.1
05 68810	Texarkana city..............	24 803	50.5	24.1	8.6	15.8	1.1	10 500	61.1	2 301	77.4
05 74540	West Memphis city........	25 335	52.0	29.7	7.7	9.4	1.2	10 057	56.2	1 949	72.1
06 00000	CALIFORNIA..............	31 416 629	50.2	30.9	9.8	4.6	4.5	11 502 870	56.9	2 220 093	74.5
06 00562	Alameda city.................	68 239	50.1	25.6	11.7	7.5	5.1	30 226	47.9	5 903	66.2
06 00884	Alhambra city	80 794	50.4	35.6	2.9	2.0	9.2	29 111	39.2	5 776	56.4
06 02000	Anaheim city.................	297 241	44.5	37.8	8.8	2.8	6.1	96 849	50.1	14 906	69.7
06 02252	Antioch city..................	83 119	49.9	29.2	15.3	3.1	2.5	29 366	70.9	4 045	74.0
06 02364	Apple Valley town	50 447	48.9	34.6	10.5	5.0	1.0	18 575	70.4	4 967	86.3
06 02462	Arcadia city..................	50 627	55.7	28.9	2.7	3.2	9.5	19 134	62.3	4 716	76.0
06 03064	Atascadero city..............	25 100	51.5	32.8	12.1	2.9	0.7	9 530	65.6	1 935	74.9

Table C-5. Cities — **Migration, Housing, and Transportation**

City	Owner-occupied by household type (percent)								Median household income			Median housing value (owner estimated)	Median monthly owner costs as a percent of income	
	Family households					Nonfamily households								
		Married-couple family		Other family										
	Total family households	Total	With own children under 18 years	Total	With own children under 18 years	Total nonfamily households	Two or more adults	Living alone	All households	Owner-occupied households	Renter-occupied households	Median housing value (owner estimated)	With a mortgage	Without a mortgage
	11	12	13	14	15	16	17	18	19	20	21	22	23	24
UNITED STATES....	73.8	81.0	76.7	50.4	39.9	49.8	39.3	52.1	41 851	51 323	27 362	111 800	21.7	10.5
ALABAMA	78.7	85.8	81.8	57.2	45.7	57.7	41.3	60.0	33 903	40 619	19 870	76 700	19.8	9.9
Auburn city	69.7	77.7	76.4	48.7	45.1	22.4	13.4	28.3	17 479	51 624	10 630	116 100	20.2	9.9
Bessemer city	60.1	74.5	64.2	46.2	27.6	56.3	33.7	58.1	22 569	29 623	15 362	56 400	22.7	13.8
Birmingham city............	60.4	74.3	65.4	45.8	30.1	42.9	31.4	44.7	26 479	35 322	18 613	62 200	22.3	11.5
Decatur city	72.5	81.9	78.0	43.2	29.9	45.8	32.2	47.3	36 992	50 672	20 895	88 700	19.3	9.9
Dothan city	71.1	80.7	76.0	45.5	30.3	45.9	35.7	47.1	34 918	46 840	20 158	83 600	17.4	9.9
Florence city	70.2	81.6	74.9	40.0	24.2	40.2	19.3	43.5	28 561	43 598	14 716	82 700	19.7	9.9
Gadsden city	68.6	78.2	64.0	51.6	33.9	54.8	36.1	56.7	25 156	32 277	15 652	49 000	20.5	9.9
Homewood city............	67.7	75.1	72.8	46.9	39.8	39.5	24.8	43.1	44 323	61 521	29 601	156 700	19.6	9.9
Hoover city	77.3	81.9	81.4	46.1	41.8	40.6	20.4	43.9	62 040	83 413	38 690	176 400	19.4	9.9
Huntsville city	71.5	81.8	76.5	43.8	31.9	45.1	29.4	47.4	41 052	55 760	23 603	95 600	18.4	9.9
Madison city	79.2	85.9	84.2	45.5	38.0	47.9	38.2	49.5	63 097	75 533	34 276	137 900	18.5	9.9
Mobile city	66.3	78.5	73.8	44.5	29.6	46.5	28.8	49.3	31 115	41 823	19 223	80 400	20.8	10.0
Montgomery city............	68.5	79.1	73.5	47.7	36.9	49.4	39.0	51.0	35 683	46 564	22 239	84 600	20.0	9.9
Phenix City city	57.4	71.7	62.9	34.4	21.9	41.8	35.5	42.5	26 460	35 839	18 554	72 500	20.7	10.8
Prichard city	59.5	79.2	70.1	41.6	26.8	55.4	69.8	53.9	19 267	28 522	11 531	49 300	20.8	12.7
Tuscaloosa city	62.8	76.3	74.8	36.6	24.6	30.6	12.6	35.6	27 000	46 937	15 349	97 400	20.9	9.9
ALASKA	69.2	74.7	70.9	50.8	44.5	47.5	45.1	48.3	51 441	63 384	35 406	137 400	22.3	9.9
Anchorage municipality .	67.3	74.2	70.4	44.8	39.3	44.8	42.6	45.6	55 441	71 772	35 414	152 300	22.6	9.9
Fairbanks city	39.2	42.8	32.0	28.3	20.9	26.4	23.8	27.0	39 942	63 023	31 203	127 000	23.2	10.9
Juneau city and borough	73.4	79.4	76.9	51.9	43.5	44.1	40.0	45.4	62 496	76 873	37 402	179 200	23.0	9.9
ARIZONA	74.7	81.0	74.3	53.2	44.4	53.9	44.4	56.7	40 388	48 411	27 332	109 400	22.1	9.9
Apache Junction city	84.5	88.1	79.6	70.4	66.0	78.7	74.4	79.9	32 993	34 577	26 623	74 000	25.3	10.5
Avondale city.................	79.9	85.4	81.7	61.4	55.4	66.6	72.3	64.5	49 320	55 390	28 310	122 500	22.5	10.9
Bullhead City city	63.9	71.6	51.5	41.7	24.8	52.3	42.8	55.7	30 087	33 926	23 902	68 400	24.5	10.2
Casa Grande city	68.9	77.0	67.9	47.7	38.1	48.5	40.9	50.0	35 975	43 757	25 409	79 900	21.9	9.9
Chandler city	78.0	82.6	79.4	59.6	54.4	61.4	57.8	62.9	58 204	65 485	38 731	135 100	21.4	9.9
Flagstaff city	59.9	69.8	67.0	31.7	24.0	29.6	16.4	38.4	37 686	57 087	26 139	149 000	21.6	9.9
Gilbert town	87.2	91.0	90.8	65.6	59.4	74.3	72.7	74.9	67 756	72 161	41 002	157 100	22.4	9.9
Glendale city	72.2	79.6	74.8	49.9	40.7	46.4	44.1	47.2	44 997	57 114	27 136	113 300	21.5	10.1
Lake Havasu City city ...	81.8	86.4	74.2	56.4	50.7	67.5	55.2	70.8	36 294	39 569	27 164	96 300	24.1	9.9
Mesa city	72.9	79.8	74.0	47.2	38.2	52.8	40.7	56.5	42 492	50 482	30 665	112 100	22.0	9.9
Oro Valley town............	90.2	91.9	88.1	70.5	63.0	64.6	45.9	68.7	60 989	65 350	40 169	175 500	22.1	9.9
Peoria city	88.5	91.1	89.8	75.5	70.8	71.4	72.5	71.2	52 247	55 772	34 968	121 100	22.4	9.9
Phoenix city	67.9	75.5	70.1	48.4	40.2	46.4	40.5	48.3	41 013	52 343	27 962	107 000	22.0	10.4
Prescott city	76.0	82.6	68.6	47.3	34.7	50.8	30.1	56.1	35 145	43 129	21 627	148 600	23.3	9.9
Scottsdale city	79.7	85.0	83.2	54.5	47.5	54.1	43.2	57.3	57 048	70 452	38 243	205 000	22.4	9.9
Sierra Vista city	56.6	60.8	43.3	40.2	29.6	41.8	19.7	45.7	38 276	51 604	29 725	100 000	20.1	9.9
Surprise city	89.9	92.5	81.0	68.7	52.7	81.5	76.5	82.7	44 040	46 656	24 962	122 400	23.1	9.9
Tempe city...................	66.4	75.0	70.8	41.8	35.4	33.3	22.9	39.9	42 199	60 147	30 388	126 700	19.8	9.9
Tucson city..................	63.1	71.8	65.0	43.8	33.9	39.9	32.1	42.0	30 819	40 961	21 827	91 200	22.7	10.2
Yuma city	65.5	71.6	61.3	45.2	32.9	56.0	47.2	57.9	35 202	42 298	25 929	78 100	21.7	9.9
ARKANSAS...............	75.2	82.1	75.5	51.0	39.4	55.5	41.8	57.6	32 097	38 238	21 167	67 400	19.4	9.9
Conway city.................	68.1	77.5	75.6	36.1	29.3	31.5	17.1	37.1	37 391	53 715	21 264	97 200	19.1	9.9
Fayetteville city............	58.9	67.9	66.2	30.9	29.1	24.2	14.2	28.5	31 186	53 147	20 515	97 700	19.3	9.9
Fort Smith city	64.4	73.5	67.3	38.6	27.6	42.0	28.2	44.4	32 117	44 606	22 733	72 900	18.2	9.9
Hot Springs city	64.0	74.1	63.0	40.3	21.9	49.6	40.4	50.8	25 755	32 589	18 112	69 200	20.8	11.0
Jacksonville city	50.4	57.3	40.8	30.2	17.9	38.5	22.0	41.4	34 347	48 285	26 056	70 100	19.0	9.9
Jonesboro city	67.5	77.5	70.6	37.4	24.6	40.3	19.8	46.0	32 143	45 718	19 702	85 000	19.7	9.9
Little Rock city..............	66.9	78.3	74.9	42.0	33.0	43.0	35.6	44.2	37 598	51 333	25 067	87 300	19.6	9.9
North Little Rock city.....	64.3	77.7	69.3	36.3	25.2	45.9	30.9	48.2	35 518	45 825	22 974	75 100	19.4	9.9
Pine Bluff city	62.6	77.0	64.8	41.2	27.3	51.3	43.9	52.2	27 475	37 397	17 841	50 000	19.5	11.7
Rogers city..................	67.1	74.8	68.5	36.8	32.9	52.3	35.3	55.9	40 600	47 994	29 189	91 100	19.8	9.9
Springdale city..............	64.0	69.6	61.4	42.3	34.0	50.9	37.3	53.6	36 384	45 701	27 334	86 500	18.5	9.9
Texarkana city	65.0	77.5	71.7	37.4	27.3	52.7	57.8	52.0	31 250	39 325	19 381	61 900	17.7	9.9
West Memphis city........	61.8	75.8	68.0	42.6	27.0	42.1	34.4	43.3	27 390	38 833	17 197	62 800	21.1	9.9
CALIFORNIA.............	63.0	70.1	63.2	41.9	30.5	43.2	34.6	45.9	47 288	62 155	31 912	198 900	25.3	9.9
Alameda city	56.5	63.0	57.8	37.8	26.4	35.6	30.1	37.1	55 814	75 598	42 398	331 600	24.9	9.9
Alhambra city	42.8	47.7	39.3	31.0	15.4	30.1	19.2	33.0	39 097	55 629	30 903	204 300	26.7	9.9
Anaheim city	53.1	58.7	49.5	36.2	25.5	40.3	31.6	43.1	46 917	66 608	34 003	204 000	25.9	9.9
Antioch city	74.6	82.9	80.2	46.3	36.7	56.7	55.8	57.0	60 013	71 480	31 673	195 300	25.5	9.9
Apple Valley town	72.3	81.3	71.3	44.3	31.7	64.0	50.2	67.3	40 046	48 338	23 494	109 500	24.4	12.5
Arcadia city	68.0	72.7	66.1	51.2	38.3	45.7	35.8	47.3	56 531	72 388	39 071	372 700	26.7	9.9
Atascadero city.............	72.9	80.4	74.3	47.9	41.4	47.1	45.7	47.5	48 003	58 248	28 857	195 900	26.1	10.1

Table C-5. Cities — **Migration, Housing, and Transportation**

City	Percent who pay 35 percent or more of income for housing expenses		Means of transportation to work (percent except where noted)						Vehicles available (percent of households)		
				Car, truck, or van							
	Median gross rent	Owners	Renters	Number of workers 16 years and over	Drove alone	Carpooled	Public transportation	Other means	Walked	No vehicles	One vehicle	Two or more vehicles
	25	26	27	28	29	30	31	32	33	34	35	36
UNITED STATES....	602	15.8	29.5	128 279 228	75.7	12.2	4.7	1.2	2.9	10.3	34.2	55.5
ALABAMA	447	13.9	27.4	1 900 089	83.0	12.3	0.5	0.8	1.3	8.3	32.3	59.5
Auburn city	446	11.2	54.2	18 610	82.1	9.4	1.2	1.1	3.9	6.2	41.2	52.6
Bessemer city	382	22.3	27.6	9 913	79.7	15.6	1.6	0.9	1.8	17.8	41.4	40.8
Birmingham city............	446	20.1	31.9	96 725	76.9	15.8	2.6	1.0	2.4	16.8	43.2	40.0
Decatur city	429	11.2	26.0	23 929	86.1	10.1	0.2	0.9	1.1	7.8	35.2	57.0
Dothan city	417	10.7	25.1	25 471	85.9	10.3	0.7	0.9	0.9	8.9	37.2	53.9
Florence city	416	13.2	31.8	15 066	86.0	8.8	0.1	0.7	2.5	9.1	36.9	54.1
Gadsden city	361	15.6	26.9	13 869	81.2	14.9	0.3	0.9	1.1	12.2	40.6	47.1
Homewood city............	578	11.0	26.8	13 536	85.7	9.1	0.4	0.4	1.8	4.5	41.0	54.4
Hoover city	712	13.5	22.9	33 422	86.8	8.4	0.1	0.3	0.5	2.6	31.3	66.1
Huntsville city..............	495	11.7	27.8	74 556	83.8	11.2	0.5	0.7	1.5	7.3	36.7	56.0
Madison city	588	8.9	19.5	15 935	87.1	9.9	0.1	0.4	0.4	2.0	28.8	69.2
Mobile city	482	16.7	31.6	80 085	82.2	12.4	1.1	0.9	1.6	10.8	40.6	48.6
Montgomery city............	528	14.7	30.4	87 989	82.6	12.4	0.8	0.8	1.7	10.2	38.6	51.3
Phenix City city	431	16.0	25.9	11 389	82.4	14.1	0.7	0.8	1.3	15.3	39.1	45.6
Prichard city	375	20.7	37.8	8 527	77.1	16.0	2.0	1.4	2.1	19.8	39.4	40.8
Tuscaloosa city	481	14.7	41.6	33 706	81.4	10.8	0.9	0.5	4.1	11.0	41.2	47.7
ALASKA	720	16.2	25.4	290 597	66.5	15.5	1.8	4.8	7.3	10.9	33.9	55.2
Anchorage municipality .	736	15.8	28.3	131 228	74.4	14.6	2.0	2.6	2.7	6.4	35.1	58.5
Fairbanks city	680	15.3	24.4	14 133	67.0	18.4	1.3	2.0	6.4	12.9	41.5	45.6
Juneau city and borough	863	14.8	27.3	16 216	62.9	18.5	4.3	1.9	8.0	7.4	37.1	55.5
ARIZONA	619	16.2	30.9	2 210 395	74.1	15.4	1.9	2.3	2.6	7.4	38.6	54.0
Apache Junction city	541	16.7	29.6	12 392	75.2	18.5	0.2	1.9	1.9	5.6	48.3	46.0
Avondale city	583	16.0	27.3	15 815	72.3	20.7	0.4	2.0	2.0	7.2	29.0	63.8
Bullhead City city	591	18.6	32.3	14 008	68.8	23.1	0.8	2.7	2.9	8.3	44.2	47.4
Casa Grande city	541	16.5	29.9	10 046	77.7	14.9	0.4	2.9	2.0	8.7	41.8	49.5
Chandler city	755	13.0	27.7	91 201	80.0	10.0	0.7	1.0	1.1	3.0	31.4	64.7
Flagstaff city	662	14.6	37.2	28 494	69.4	14.7	0.6	4.5	7.2	6.4	35.1	58.5
Gilbert town	792	14.8	24.6	55 938	82.1	11.3	0.4	1.4	0.7	2.0	22.7	75.3
Glendale city	612	15.5	30.5	103 428	75.4	16.3	1.8	2.0	2.0	7.5	35.7	56.8
Lake Havasu City city ...	609	19.0	28.4	16 217	78.5	13.2	1.2	2.3	1.4	4.2	34.6	61.3
Mesa city	669	14.7	30.6	182 582	75.3	15.7	1.4	2.4	2.1	6.5	40.5	53.0
Oro Valley town............	767	12.9	28.8	12 335	82.5	9.3	0.8	1.2	0.8	1.5	35.9	62.6
Peoria city	941	14.7	39.6	49 507	80.4	14.2	0.4	1.4	0.8	5.2	32.5	62.3
Phoenix city................	622	17.8	30.9	599 592	71.7	17.4	3.3	2.2	2.2	8.9	39.5	51.6
Prescott city..................	571	15.1	43.4	13 321	74.8	10.1	0.6	2.1	5.9	6.6	41.4	52.0
Scottsdale city	844	19.2	31.4	102 824	80.3	7.0	1.1	2.1	1.7	4.0	38.8	56.3
Sierra Vista city	524	10.8	17.1	18 307	72.3	14.4	0.6	1.9	9.1	5.8	40.5	53.8
Surprise city	663	15.1	37.3	10 644	75.8	16.9	0.6	1.7	1.6	3.1	44.7	52.2
Tempe city	715	13.6	34.9	89 233	72.9	12.5	3.0	4.4	4.0	7.3	39.9	52.7
Tucson city	516	17.5	35.4	216 314	71.0	15.7	3.5	3.6	3.4	11.9	44.1	44.0
Yuma city	549	15.8	26.4	30 497	74.0	15.4	0.3	3.3	5.6	8.7	40.4	50.9
ARKANSAS................	453	12.7	26.7	1 160 101	79.9	14.1	0.4	1.0	1.9	8.1	34.9	57.1
Conway city..................	505	8.9	34.1	21 274	78.6	14.5	0.2	1.0	3.5	7.0	35.9	57.2
Fayetteville city..............	480	11.2	36.3	28 844	78.1	12.1	1.0	1.2	4.4	6.8	42.6	50.6
Fort Smith city	424	11.2	25.4	36 144	79.8	14.8	1.0	1.2	1.4	10.1	39.6	50.2
Hot Springs city	455	14.7	31.1	14 355	74.1	15.7	2.2	1.3	4.1	15.5	44.6	40.0
Jacksonville city	489	10.8	22.4	14 568	81.4	14.6	0.4	1.4	0.9	6.4	38.6	55.0
Jonesboro city	461	13.3	34.6	27 102	83.2	11.4	0.2	0.7	2.1	6.7	38.6	54.7
Little Rock city..............	562	13.7	29.7	87 711	81.0	12.7	1.9	0.8	1.5	9.5	42.9	47.7
North Little Rock city.....	512	11.7	29.9	28 196	79.8	14.2	1.4	1.0	1.4	11.4	40.5	48.0
Pine Bluff city	461	15.4	33.9	19 806	77.9	17.3	0.6	0.9	1.4	13.9	42.6	43.6
Rogers city	535	11.5	22.5	18 060	79.8	15.0	0.3	1.4	1.6	5.8	34.5	59.7
Springdale city..............	505	10.2	22.5	21 118	80.2	15.0	0.1	1.1	1.5	6.3	34.9	58.8
Texarkana city..............	447	11.7	28.9	11 025	85.0	11.5	0.2	0.9	1.0	10.4	38.0	51.6
West Memphis city.......	475	16.6	37.1	10 511	80.2	14.7	0.6	1.7	1.8	16.7	39.7	43.6
CALIFORNIA............	747	23.2	34.1	14 525 322	71.8	14.5	5.1	1.9	2.9	9.5	34.1	56.4
Alameda city................	899	20.7	28.8	37 327	63.0	11.9	15.7	2.6	2.6	9.4	42.6	48.0
Alhambra city	721	23.5	33.6	36 538	75.3	14.4	4.6	0.9	2.6	10.4	38.4	51.2
Anaheim city................	818	24.2	36.1	139 343	71.1	17.5	4.6	2.2	2.3	8.1	33.4	58.5
Antioch city	786	22.0	37.7	40 712	74.2	15.5	4.3	1.7	1.5	5.4	26.8	67.8
Apple Valley town	573	21.9	39.4	19 358	76.8	15.5	0.8	1.2	1.2	7.0	32.7	60.3
Arcadia city..................	830	26.2	29.9	22 935	79.9	12.1	2.4	0.7	1.3	5.1	31.9	63.1
Atascadero city............	701	21.7	40.4	12 056	77.6	15.0	0.4	1.4	1.5	4.4	30.4	65.2

Table C-5. Cities — **Migration, Housing, and Transportation**

STATE Place code	City	Total population 5 years and over	Residence in 1995 (percent)					Occupied housing units		Householders 65 years and over	
			Same house	Same county, different house	Same state, different county	Different state	Outside the United States	Number	Percent owner-occupied	Number	Percent owner-occupied
		1	2	3	4	5	6	7	8	9	10
	CALIFORNIA—Cont'd										
06 03386	Azusa city	40 299	47.8	37.3	5.7	2.8	6.4	12 439	50.4	2 017	74.2
06 03526	Bakersfield city	226 174	43.9	40.4	9.4	4.1	2.3	83 428	60.4	14 334	74.6
06 03666	Baldwin Park city	68 385	58.6	33.7	2.5	1.0	4.2	16 962	60.7	2 210	77.5
06 04870	Bell city	32 800	47.8	43.8	2.1	1.2	5.2	8 918	30.9	1 017	49.8
06 04982	Bellflower city	66 112	45.4	43.8	4.3	2.1	4.5	23 336	40.3	3 675	63.1
06 04996	Bell Gardens city	39 021	47.7	41.9	2.7	0.6	7.1	9 466	23.8	744	47.0
06 05108	Belmont city	23 670	56.0	21.0	11.0	6.1	5.8	10 468	60.2	1 994	81.7
06 05290	Benicia city	25 626	56.0	21.5	15.8	5.3	1.4	10 325	70.7	1 646	79.3
06 06000	Berkeley city	98 889	45.4	17.0	22.1	9.5	5.9	44 955	42.7	7 293	72.5
06 06308	Beverly Hills city	32 662	55.2	30.5	2.8	6.0	5.5	15 032	43.5	4 263	62.6
06 08100	Brea city	33 090	53.9	23.4	15.8	3.8	3.2	13 016	64.3	2 533	73.3
06 08786	Buena Park city	72 135	50.8	26.8	14.3	2.1	6.0	23 360	56.9	3 910	81.7
06 08954	Burbank city	94 866	53.6	34.0	3.8	5.3	3.5	41 608	43.6	8 468	61.9
06 09066	Burlingame city	26 546	53.9	20.3	13.1	7.2	5.4	12 497	47.7	2 914	74.0
06 09710	Calexico city	24 952	57.2	28.8	5.5	1.3	7.2	6 801	55.3	1 642	53.2
06 10046	Camarillo city	53 239	51.6	28.5	11.0	6.9	2.0	21 444	73.5	6 299	82.3
06 10345	Campbell city	35 952	50.0	29.9	9.1	4.4	6.6	15 990	48.5	2 531	61.3
06 11194	Carlsbad city	73 024	42.3	33.7	10.6	11.2	2.2	31 486	67.3	6 847	82.4
06 11530	Carson city	83 499	62.0	31.1	2.5	1.5	2.9	24 624	78.0	5 205	85.1
06 12048	Cathedral City city	39 205	43.9	35.4	10.1	6.2	4.3	14 072	64.9	3 515	79.2
06 12524	Ceres city	31 360	50.7	34.9	10.5	1.6	2.3	10 472	66.7	1 726	80.6
06 12552	Cerritos city	49 135	65.3	22.9	5.3	1.9	4.6	15 395	83.5	2 357	90.3
06 13014	Chico city	55 881	30.2	31.2	29.4	5.4	3.9	23 374	39.7	3 688	68.6
06 13210	Chino city	62 853	53.7	18.9	21.0	4.2	2.3	17 376	68.6	2 372	68.0
06 13214	Chino Hills city	61 092	51.9	17.2	26.1	2.6	2.2	20 015	84.9	1 135	90.1
06 13392	Chula Vista city	160 508	47.2	36.3	5.3	6.0	5.2	57 728	57.5	11 881	71.1
06 13588	Citrus Heights city	79 525	46.5	31.9	14.6	4.9	2.1	33 493	57.3	7 128	72.1
06 13756	Claremont city	32 718	49.4	22.7	12.4	11.7	3.8	11 304	67.0	3 047	66.0
06 14218	Clovis city	63 187	49.4	36.8	9.1	3.4	1.3	24 240	60.7	4 154	68.8
06 14890	Colton city	43 346	48.2	32.5	13.0	2.8	3.5	14 586	52.3	1 889	75.5
06 15044	Compton city	83 615	59.0	33.6	2.3	0.9	4.3	22 303	56.9	4 360	81.0
06 16000	Concord city	113 203	51.5	29.0	10.2	4.3	5.0	43 949	62.6	7 734	78.5
06 16350	Corona city	112 884	39.4	25.0	27.5	5.1	3.0	37 824	67.4	4 038	72.5
06 16532	Costa Mesa city	101 202	43.8	36.1	8.6	5.0	6.6	39 188	40.3	5 943	69.7
06 16742	Covina city	43 579	50.7	38.7	5.3	2.2	3.2	16 023	58.7	2 837	77.8
06 17568	Culver City city	36 849	57.2	31.8	3.3	4.6	3.1	16 611	54.4	3 394	72.2
06 17610	Cupertino city	47 532	49.3	20.2	7.4	7.2	15.8	18 217	63.3	3 190	85.7
06 17750	Cypress city	43 836	55.0	23.8	14.4	3.5	3.3	15 646	69.3	2 975	79.8
06 17918	Daly City city	97 300	56.4	15.9	17.9	2.1	7.7	30 727	60.2	6 222	78.2
06 17946	Dana Point city	32 976	46.0	34.1	11.0	6.2	2.7	14 403	61.4	2 979	88.6
06 17988	Danville town	39 243	53.9	19.7	15.2	8.4	2.9	15 027	89.4	2 627	88.5
06 18100	Davis city	57 575	30.5	17.8	39.1	7.8	4.9	22 927	44.5	2 688	76.0
06 18394	Delano city	35 402	47.4	30.5	14.5	1.1	6.5	8 410	59.4	1 497	65.8
06 19192	Diamond Bar city	53 181	56.9	27.5	7.7	2.4	5.6	17 646	82.7	1 974	84.7
06 19766	Downey city	98 790	50.3	41.4	3.2	1.6	3.6	33 989	51.8	6 876	76.6
06 20018	Dublin city	28 256	45.7	29.3	15.7	6.1	3.2	9 330	64.9	795	77.4
06 20956	East Palo Alto city	26 621	54.2	23.2	11.7	1.8	9.1	6 938	43.3	933	72.2
06 21712	El Cajon city	87 249	40.1	42.9	5.1	7.5	4.4	34 222	40.7	6 053	68.9
06 21782	El Centro city	34 635	49.6	32.3	9.6	2.6	5.9	11 448	50.4	2 292	58.3
06 22230	El Monte city	105 077	50.7	38.8	2.2	1.0	7.3	27 036	41.0	3 701	61.5
06 22678	Encinitas city	54 648	49.5	31.6	8.0	8.7	2.2	22 834	64.1	3 832	76.5
06 22804	Escondido city	121 784	40.2	43.7	5.7	5.4	5.0	43 796	53.3	9 593	65.4
06 23042	Eureka city	24 421	43.5	35.8	13.7	6.0	1.1	10 942	46.9	2 583	74.0
06 23182	Fairfield city	88 341	45.0	26.0	15.4	9.7	3.9	30 972	59.6	5 152	79.0
06 24638	Folsom city	48 444	38.9	26.4	23.0	8.4	3.3	17 180	76.3	2 701	80.9
06 24680	Fontana city	115 378	44.8	29.5	20.3	2.3	3.0	33 963	68.2	3 305	75.1
06 25338	Foster City city	27 149	50.0	19.5	11.8	8.8	9.9	11 613	61.6	1 768	84.4
06 25380	Fountain Valley city	51 658	59.6	27.0	6.9	3.8	2.7	18 170	74.7	3 546	86.1
06 26000	Fremont city	188 394	49.4	21.7	14.2	5.0	9.6	68 237	64.5	8 694	78.7
06 27000	Fresno city	388 739	46.2	39.2	8.9	2.6	3.1	139 951	50.7	24 636	69.3
06 28000	Fullerton city	117 165	49.1	30.3	12.0	3.4	5.3	43 581	53.8	8 556	78.8
06 28168	Gardena city	53 399	56.7	36.2	1.9	1.9	3.3	20 336	47.3	4 282	67.9
06 29000	Garden Grove city	152 628	49.8	37.3	5.6	1.8	5.6	45 914	59.5	8 498	74.9
06 29504	Gilroy city	37 774	44.1	39.5	8.0	2.8	5.6	11 894	61.2	1 634	67.4
06 30000	Glendale city	184 012	50.8	35.2	2.5	3.0	8.6	71 804	38.4	15 295	48.4
06 30014	Glendora city	46 638	61.3	29.6	5.7	2.1	1.2	16 857	73.5	3 633	80.8
06 31960	Hanford city	38 270	48.7	32.1	13.5	3.3	2.4	13 913	59.3	2 940	70.5
06 32548	Hawthorne city	75 695	45.6	44.3	2.6	2.6	4.9	28 459	25.8	3 079	57.6
06 33000	Hayward city	128 968	50.0	26.1	13.6	3.0	7.3	44 902	53.3	8 219	75.2
06 33182	Hemet city	54 958	42.3	35.1	14.3	6.9	1.4	25 266	64.2	12 313	80.0
06 33434	Hesperia city	57 612	49.7	34.3	11.6	3.5	0.9	19 920	72.5	4 039	84.8

Table C-5. Cities — Migration, Housing, and Transportation

City	Owner-occupied by household type (percent)								Median household income			Median housing value (owner estimated)	Median monthly owner costs as a percent of income	
	Family households					Nonfamily households								
		Married-couple family		Other family										
	Total family households	Total	With own children under 18 years	Total	With own children under 18 years	Total nonfamily households	Two or more adults	Living alone	All households	Owner-occupied households	Renter-occupied households		With a mortgage	Without a mortgage
	11	12	13	14	15	16	17	18	19	20	21	22	23	24
CALIFORNIA—Cont'd														
Azusa city	50.4	59.3	52.6	32.7	20.9	50.3	33.4	56.0	38 831	51 804	30 355	143 400	26.9	9.9
Bakersfield city	66.2	75.6	71.0	41.2	33.0	44.0	35.5	45.9	39 723	52 931	23 639	103 500	23.8	10.5
Baldwin Park city	61.1	65.8	59.5	50.1	36.0	57.3	51.3	59.3	41 732	50 050	30 806	144 100	26.8	9.9
Bell city	31.1	36.8	33.5	19.2	12.1	29.8	15.1	33.0	29 730	46 491	25 337	164 400	32.1	12.1
Bellflower city	42.4	50.7	44.0	26.3	18.5	34.3	35.1	34.1	39 090	55 842	31 754	172 600	26.0	9.9
Bell Gardens city	23.5	28.6	23.2	13.7	9.7	26.0	17.3	29.2	29 969	43 147	26 788	171 700	33.3	11.8
Belmont city	74.7	77.2	75.6	60.3	60.9	35.0	35.9	34.7	79 109	98 084	54 535	581 800	24.9	9.9
Benicia city	78.6	86.1	84.3	52.4	49.6	52.1	51.8	52.2	65 853	78 931	41 256	263 100	24.5	9.9
Berkeley city	63.7	70.8	69.6	47.5	39.1	27.6	22.4	30.3	44 242	80 324	27 341	374 300	25.0	9.9
Beverly Hills city	60.7	66.1	60.4	35.7	23.2	22.0	20.2	22.3	70 541	125 707	48 179	993 600	29.5	9.9
Brea city	73.2	78.6	74.7	50.9	35.9	42.8	33.1	45.3	58 869	71 504	41 586	248 600	24.3	9.9
Buena Park city	58.7	64.5	55.7	43.4	27.8	50.1	34.8	55.4	50 328	63 066	36 151	197 300	25.0	9.9
Burbank city	52.3	57.9	52.5	36.2	24.7	31.2	28.7	31.7	46 850	66 882	36 258	249 200	26.4	9.9
Burlingame city	64.5	68.1	68.5	48.6	36.3	26.9	21.5	28.3	68 931	96 493	53 144	658 000	25.9	9.9
Calexico city	57.6	64.8	62.4	40.9	27.3	37.7	48.4	36.3	27 887	39 821	17 141	106 300	30.2	10.9
Camarillo city	76.8	80.6	73.4	54.1	43.2	65.4	56.2	67.1	62 289	71 932	43 438	245 000	24.5	9.9
Campbell city	60.4	66.9	61.0	41.1	28.7	32.3	30.5	33.0	66 675	88 685	51 371	422 100	24.6	9.9
Carlsbad city	74.7	80.4	75.9	50.7	43.5	52.4	40.2	56.5	64 978	79 665	44 339	308 800	25.1	9.9
Carson city	79.2	83.1	79.0	68.6	53.2	72.4	60.5	75.3	52 382	58 064	36 168	176 100	25.8	9.9
Cathedral City city	66.2	72.9	65.7	45.5	35.8	62.1	62.7	61.9	37 777	46 201	27 875	113 600	24.9	10.8
Ceres city	67.8	75.9	69.2	43.5	36.6	61.6	46.7	66.5	41 515	50 302	26 244	116 700	24.5	9.9
Cerritos city	83.9	85.5	78.8	75.7	66.6	80.5	63.0	85.4	73 085	79 626	48 720	278 700	24.1	9.9
Chico city	58.7	68.5	63.7	33.4	27.6	21.1	8.3	30.3	29 279	51 240	19 924	138 600	24.1	9.9
Chino city	72.7	77.5	74.0	55.7	45.7	49.9	39.4	52.7	54 300	66 264	33 177	171 100	24.4	12.2
Chino Hills city	87.0	89.8	89.9	69.2	65.1	72.8	73.3	72.7	77 870	83 041	51 361	236 300	25.6	10.1
Chula Vista city	60.9	67.7	61.4	41.5	29.0	46.6	37.1	48.8	44 829	59 663	30 962	187 100	26.6	9.9
Citrus Heights city	65.1	72.2	64.0	45.5	32.6	42.7	35.0	45.0	43 941	53 683	33 738	132 700	23.0	9.9
Claremont city	76.2	81.7	81.7	53.7	44.4	46.3	50.9	45.3	65 616	83 428	34 094	249 300	22.8	9.9
Clovis city	67.2	75.6	72.7	41.4	31.4	42.9	38.1	43.9	42 409	58 503	25 843	122 100	23.6	11.7
Colton city	57.5	67.0	61.4	38.9	28.4	36.4	29.8	38.0	35 146	45 243	25 425	99 800	24.8	9.9
Compton city	57.3	64.3	55.5	47.6	30.3	64.7	41.7	67.8	31 297	41 844	20 235	135 700	30.2	13.2
Concord city	66.2	72.6	64.8	46.5	34.2	54.5	44.7	57.7	55 473	66 988	38 259	220 500	24.3	9.9
Corona city	73.0	79.2	77.5	48.2	36.9	44.0	42.9	44.4	59 794	71 908	37 509	190 900	26.6	9.9
Costa Mesa city	47.7	54.0	45.8	29.6	17.1	29.9	21.6	33.7	50 614	66 807	42 326	263 700	25.8	9.9
Covina city	64.1	73.0	67.2	44.8	29.3	43.1	35.7	45.0	49 288	63 034	32 954	186 200	24.4	9.9
Culver City city	59.7	66.3	60.0	41.7	28.5	47.3	40.4	48.9	52 065	65 849	41 563	271 900	25.9	9.9
Cupertino city	67.6	68.8	62.4	59.8	45.7	50.6	35.2	55.1	100 398	113 266	82 099	634 900	24.0	9.9
Cypress city	72.4	78.4	71.3	51.9	39.6	57.8	44.0	60.6	64 209	74 597	42 083	246 300	24.1	9.9
Daly City city	64.6	69.5	63.6	50.6	34.1	47.0	32.6	52.5	61 837	73 594	46 310	324 200	25.0	9.9
Dana Point city	67.5	72.6	59.1	46.8	36.6	50.6	36.7	55.7	62 955	79 356	47 837	365 400	26.9	9.9
Danville town	91.7	93.4	92.8	78.1	70.3	80.0	83.4	79.2	113 253	118 573	61 536	537 000	25.2	9.9
Davis city	68.2	75.6	76.0	41.2	39.2	21.3	9.0	33.7	42 227	82 630	22 127	233 000	22.4	9.9
Delano city	61.5	68.0	65.9	45.3	36.1	46.3	32.2	49.5	27 644	34 744	18 463	85 600	27.3	11.1
Diamond Bar city	84.8	87.4	86.2	73.6	69.1	71.4	57.1	74.9	69 099	75 306	44 310	237 800	26.0	9.9
Downey city	55.2	63.4	58.5	35.5	20.3	40.8	24.6	44.5	45 363	60 344	34 637	207 400	27.6	9.9
Dublin city	72.4	75.3	77.7	59.8	48.6	47.7	40.6	50.7	77 340	85 121	63 141	327 300	25.9	9.9
East Palo Alto city	48.2	52.6	47.2	40.2	25.9	27.9	20.2	30.3	43 656	60 289	33 685	295 700	28.4	9.9
El Cajon city	44.2	53.7	43.8	23.6	13.0	33.4	22.7	37.0	35 446	51 986	28 218	178 600	26.3	9.9
El Centro city	53.1	59.7	54.2	37.9	27.5	40.7	34.5	41.6	31 951	47 426	20 654	97 700	23.6	11.8
El Monte city	41.5	45.8	37.3	32.8	16.3	38.4	27.0	42.6	32 456	46 625	25 879	153 100	27.1	9.9
Encinitas city	73.8	79.7	78.3	48.8	42.8	48.1	34.3	54.5	63 185	80 751	43 333	343 500	25.2	9.9
Escondido city	58.0	64.9	55.8	35.8	24.8	41.4	31.4	44.2	42 482	57 663	30 431	178 000	25.8	9.9
Eureka city	55.4	67.6	49.7	31.7	21.1	36.8	24.1	40.6	25 923	38 082	18 740	113 600	24.4	10.6
Fairfield city	62.5	69.3	61.3	40.6	27.4	49.6	42.3	51.7	51 107	66 557	34 330	170 600	25.4	9.9
Folsom city	81.7	86.8	86.6	51.6	45.5	61.7	69.6	59.7	73 345	82 592	47 884	223 300	23.7	10.3
Fontana city	70.6	77.8	75.3	48.2	38.3	53.8	53.9	53.8	45 585	55 694	25 423	128 700	26.9	9.9
Foster City city	67.9	69.0	65.5	61.4	57.0	47.9	41.0	50.3	93 519	98 933	85 700	530 200	25.5	9.9
Fountain Valley city	78.9	82.1	77.1	64.4	44.5	59.4	49.9	62.6	69 307	78 291	48 265	285 700	23.9	9.9
Fremont city	69.5	72.9	71.9	53.5	42.2	48.1	39.2	51.6	75 991	88 904	58 184	354 300	24.3	9.9
Fresno city	54.8	65.2	57.2	33.6	24.2	40.8	28.2	44.2	32 083	47 182	21 160	94 900	24.4	11.3
Fullerton city	61.1	67.8	59.1	38.7	25.9	38.0	24.5	42.9	49 833	69 020	35 356	230 500	24.5	9.9
Gardena city	49.9	55.2	44.4	39.4	24.1	41.5	34.3	42.9	38 595	53 396	30 067	173 000	26.1	9.9
Garden Grove city	60.1	64.3	56.9	47.2	31.0	57.3	49.3	59.8	47 414	60 051	33 179	194 500	25.2	9.9
Gilroy city	62.2	70.5	65.6	39.3	26.9	57.0	62.4	55.5	62 613	77 901	41 517	337 200	27.7	10.1
Glendale city	41.7	45.1	39.8	31.0	17.8	30.8	27.3	31.5	41 499	69 934	30 219	290 400	27.7	10.4
Glendora city	78.1	83.5	79.9	58.1	46.1	58.3	54.9	59.0	59 244	68 994	36 649	218 700	25.6	9.9
Hanford city	63.3	72.8	65.3	36.8	28.2	47.8	45.6	48.3	36 640	49 457	22 571	100 800	23.4	10.5
Hawthorne city	30.0	39.9	32.9	16.3	8.4	16.4	11.2	17.7	31 785	58 207	27 064	184 800	27.5	9.9
Hayward city	57.1	63.9	55.8	40.2	26.1	43.8	33.5	47.5	50 841	62 409	40 801	223 800	25.8	9.9
Hemet city	67.1	76.5	58.1	35.9	22.2	59.8	48.4	61.4	26 877	30 907	21 505	69 900	27.0	11.5
Hesperia city	74.1	82.2	76.1	49.2	34.6	66.0	59.3	67.5	40 374	46 726	25 778	94 300	23.5	11.8

Table C-5. Cities — **Migration, Housing, and Transportation**

City	Median gross rent	Percent who pay 35 percent or more of income for housing expenses — Owners	Renters	Means of transportation to work (percent except where noted) — Number of workers 16 years and over	Car, truck, or van — Drove alone	Carpooled	Public transportation	Other means	Walked	Vehicles available (percent of households) — No vehicles	One vehicle	Two or more vehicles
	25	26	27	28	29	30	31	32	33	34	35	36
CALIFORNIA—Cont'd												
Azusa city	743	25.9	34.2	17 520	64.9	19.4	3.9	3.5	6.3	11.8	36.3	51.9
Bakersfield city	564	20.4	38.2	99 769	77.1	15.6	1.7	1.7	1.3	10.1	34.9	55.0
Baldwin Park city	724	26.5	36.6	25 230	65.7	23.8	4.8	1.9	1.8	7.8	27.7	64.5
Bell city	642	38.3	38.0	12 031	57.3	23.9	10.6	2.2	3.2	15.6	39.2	45.3
Bellflower city	704	25.9	32.6	28 542	74.0	17.2	3.4	1.6	1.7	10.9	38.1	51.1
Bell Gardens city	665	39.6	38.4	12 474	55.7	24.4	11.6	2.9	3.8	17.1	35.3	47.6
Belmont city	1 116	21.8	29.2	13 919	81.2	9.6	3.8	0.8	1.4	5.7	31.1	63.2
Benicia city	892	22.1	27.8	13 756	77.6	11.7	4.2	1.3	1.0	3.1	30.9	66.0
Berkeley city	740	21.7	40.6	54 674	43.2	9.6	18.6	6.9	14.9	17.0	45.1	37.9
Beverly Hills city	1 171	32.2	38.5	15 673	75.8	8.0	2.9	1.0	4.3	7.8	43.0	49.2
Brea city	935	19.4	28.7	17 966	83.3	9.0	1.0	0.8	3.0	5.7	28.7	65.6
Buena Park city	841	23.9	32.2	33 562	76.3	14.9	3.0	2.2	1.6	6.7	29.6	63.7
Burbank city	778	23.9	32.3	48 430	77.5	11.8	2.6	1.4	2.7	9.4	40.8	49.7
Burlingame city	1 108	23.7	27.5	15 202	77.2	6.9	7.6	1.2	2.4	7.1	41.3	51.6
Calexico city	517	31.9	44.3	8 220	66.7	20.5	3.3	1.2	5.1	14.9	29.2	55.9
Camarillo city	975	21.7	29.0	26 453	81.6	10.2	0.5	1.3	1.9	4.1	32.3	63.6
Campbell city	1 154	20.2	30.7	21 410	83.1	8.9	1.9	1.5	1.7	5.9	36.5	57.6
Carlsbad city	989	22.5	31.4	38 644	78.1	8.4	2.1	1.7	1.5	4.0	33.2	62.8
Carson city	754	24.3	32.5	36 500	73.9	18.2	2.9	1.3	1.9	6.1	25.8	68.1
Cathedral City city	695	26.1	33.9	16 866	73.9	16.6	2.8	2.1	1.3	7.9	37.9	54.3
Ceres city	607	20.2	36.1	12 839	76.6	16.8	1.1	1.7	1.4	7.3	32.1	60.6
Cerritos city	1 260	22.8	36.4	23 932	81.4	13.3	1.2	0.6	0.9	2.4	16.9	80.7
Chico city	594	19.0	46.1	26 947	70.0	12.6	1.9	6.2	5.5	9.1	37.6	53.3
Chino city	769	20.6	32.6	26 472	74.9	16.8	1.4	1.8	2.2	6.0	25.6	68.4
Chino Hills city	1 035	23.7	26.2	31 769	80.1	13.4	2.0	0.9	0.3	1.8	17.5	80.7
Chula Vista city	707	24.3	32.9	72 813	76.2	13.9	4.2	1.2	1.5	8.9	32.8	58.2
Citrus Heights city	728	17.2	30.6	41 152	79.4	12.7	1.7	1.5	1.6	6.3	35.3	58.4
Claremont city	771	16.4	34.8	15 805	66.9	10.2	2.9	1.5	13.6	6.7	33.6	59.7
Clovis city	580	18.7	36.5	30 959	82.1	12.0	0.6	1.7	1.4	6.9	34.5	58.6
Colton city	618	23.5	34.7	18 354	73.2	19.3	1.8	1.2	2.2	10.8	39.2	50.0
Compton city	597	35.9	44.4	26 282	62.9	22.5	8.4	2.0	2.2	15.3	36.9	47.9
Concord city	880	21.4	32.9	58 700	69.0	14.2	9.6	2.2	1.7	7.6	32.4	60.0
Corona city	812	23.8	30.4	56 209	75.7	16.4	1.2	1.8	1.6	5.4	26.0	68.6
Costa Mesa city	956	25.9	31.6	55 630	73.7	12.5	4.7	2.9	2.4	6.5	36.7	56.8
Covina city	742	22.0	31.0	20 902	77.0	14.0	4.4	0.8	1.5	7.0	33.1	59.9
Culver City city	887	24.7	28.8	19 835	76.9	9.1	4.5	1.6	3.5	6.7	43.4	49.9
Cupertino city	1 693	20.1	25.0	23 772	84.3	8.0	0.9	1.2	1.4	3.3	24.8	71.9
Cypress city	922	18.3	31.0	22 169	82.8	11.0	1.3	0.8	1.4	4.3	27.2	68.5
Daly City city	1 074	22.4	33.2	49 640	57.7	20.3	17.8	1.3	1.3	8.1	33.3	58.6
Dana Point city	1 139	27.0	33.2	18 499	77.1	11.1	2.5	1.2	1.9	3.4	33.3	63.3
Danville town	1 604	24.0	34.1	20 644	79.5	7.1	5.0	1.2	0.6	2.7	18.0	79.3
Davis city	775	15.4	53.1	31 165	60.7	8.9	6.9	15.0	4.6	4.6	36.7	56.8
Delano city	467	27.3	36.3	8 857	65.2	28.5	0.4	1.9	2.4	14.6	32.8	52.6
Diamond Bar city	1 012	27.9	32.5	26 284	81.1	12.6	2.4	0.4	0.4	3.3	21.3	75.4
Downey city	731	26.0	32.1	42 920	75.1	16.5	3.3	1.2	1.3	7.7	34.7	57.6
Dublin city	1 356	22.5	30.0	14 336	79.1	9.6	5.4	1.4	1.3	2.4	27.9	69.7
East Palo Alto city	854	33.2	37.7	11 014	64.0	23.4	6.2	2.8	1.6	10.4	33.7	55.9
El Cajon city	671	22.7	36.5	41 072	74.1	14.8	3.9	1.9	2.7	11.7	39.7	48.6
El Centro city	527	22.5	37.6	12 741	73.4	16.1	1.7	2.1	3.1	11.7	36.4	51.9
El Monte city	672	27.1	39.3	39 211	61.0	22.4	7.3	3.3	4.3	15.4	33.3	51.3
Encinitas city	977	24.9	34.2	31 068	76.9	8.6	2.9	1.8	2.0	3.6	30.7	65.8
Escondido city	746	22.8	37.7	57 073	71.4	18.3	2.8	2.1	2.0	9.5	34.8	55.7
Eureka city	495	18.4	40.1	10 426	68.1	15.0	1.9	1.7	7.7	14.5	43.0	42.6
Fairfield city	778	21.1	27.8	42 519	73.7	18.1	1.9	1.8	1.7	7.0	30.1	62.9
Folsom city	939	17.9	27.4	23 053	79.4	10.2	1.4	1.2	2.2	3.7	30.0	66.3
Fontana city	636	26.1	37.8	46 234	73.2	19.6	2.5	1.4	1.2	7.5	26.9	65.6
Foster City city	1 620	24.8	24.9	15 829	82.0	8.2	3.6	1.3	1.3	2.4	31.9	65.7
Fountain Valley city	1 058	20.1	31.6	27 127	82.7	10.5	0.8	0.8	1.2	4.2	22.3	73.5
Fremont city	1 196	21.6	27.2	100 215	77.4	12.4	5.0	1.4	1.1	4.6	26.1	69.3
Fresno city	538	21.4	39.2	156 569	74.7	16.0	2.5	1.8	2.1	13.6	39.4	47.0
Fullerton city	820	20.5	34.5	58 036	76.0	13.0	3.4	1.9	3.2	7.0	35.3	57.7
Gardena city	710	23.0	31.6	23 363	75.2	15.3	4.1	1.6	1.9	10.3	39.0	50.7
Garden Grove city	827	22.7	37.0	67 705	74.7	17.1	3.5	1.4	1.5	7.3	28.7	64.0
Gilroy city	936	27.4	28.2	18 774	70.1	19.2	3.6	2.8	1.8	6.4	27.7	65.9
Glendale city	758	28.9	40.3	83 340	74.1	14.1	4.4	1.1	3.2	13.1	38.0	48.9
Glendora city	822	22.3	31.8	23 362	80.4	12.4	1.9	0.9	1.4	4.1	28.8	67.2
Hanford city	569	17.6	35.8	16 067	78.4	14.8	1.0	2.2	1.7	10.2	37.4	52.4
Hawthorne city	636	27.1	34.8	31 750	71.5	16.4	6.9	1.2	2.4	14.5	45.8	39.6
Hayward city	921	23.8	32.4	61 696	69.1	18.2	6.7	1.9	2.1	7.9	32.6	59.4
Hemet city	563	20.9	37.8	16 485	73.3	16.6	1.0	3.2	2.8	12.5	52.5	34.9
Hesperia city	625	18.8	35.5	21 960	74.9	17.8	0.7	1.8	0.6	6.2	29.9	63.8

Table C-5. Cities — **Migration, Housing, and Transportation**

STATE Place code	City	Total population 5 years and over	Residence in 1995 (percent)					Occupied housing units		Householders 65 years and over	
			Same house	Same county, different house	Same state, different county	Different state	Outside the United States	Number	Percent owner-occupied	Number	Percent owner-occupied
		1	2	3	4	5	6	7	8	9	10
	CALIFORNIA—Cont'd										
06 33588	Highland city	40 690	45.9	38.5	9.8	3.2	2.5	13 542	66.8	1 999	76.0
06 34120	Hollister city	31 254	45.9	24.7	22.6	3.0	3.7	9 741	66.4	1 342	74.6
06 36000	Huntington Beach city	178 345	50.1	31.1	11.0	5.5	2.3	73 808	60.6	12 812	82.2
06 36056	Huntington Park city	54 969	46.3	43.8	1.6	0.9	7.4	14 864	27.3	1 657	42.5
06 36294	Imperial Beach city	24 771	39.1	39.4	8.9	9.0	3.6	9 272	30.0	1 297	68.2
06 36448	Indio city	44 156	49.6	36.6	5.5	2.6	5.6	13 888	56.1	2 440	78.0
06 36546	Inglewood city	102 331	52.9	39.6	1.9	1.9	3.7	36 817	36.4	4 969	54.5
06 36770	Irvine city	135 071	39.2	28.9	16.5	7.1	8.4	51 190	60.0	6 461	71.0
06 39220	Laguna Hills city	29 403	53.0	28.9	8.2	5.8	4.1	10 930	76.6	2 311	72.4
06 39248	Laguna Niguel city	57 382	49.2	30.7	9.9	7.2	2.9	23 223	75.1	3 242	89.9
06 39290	La Habra city	54 466	48.7	25.9	19.3	1.8	4.3	19 042	56.8	3 837	75.2
06 39486	Lake Elsinore city	26 476	38.0	30.5	24.9	3.9	2.7	8 818	65.0	1 367	81.1
06 39496	Lake Forest city	54 732	50.6	32.0	8.3	4.9	4.2	20 124	71.7	2 709	81.2
06 39892	Lakewood city	73 887	60.8	29.0	5.3	2.3	2.6	26 817	72.0	5 866	85.0
00 40004	La Mesa city	51 668	46.6	35.1	6.2	8.8	3.3	24 154	47.1	6 241	65.7
06 40032	La Mirada city	44 070	60.7	24.7	9.1	2.9	2.6	14 576	82.0	3 935	84.2
06 40130	Lancaster city	109 259	43.2	42.7	7.6	5.0	1.5	38 209	61.2	6 658	74.9
06 40340	La Puente city	37 310	60.0	31.8	2.5	0.7	5.0	9 462	60.8	1 688	76.3
06 40830	La Verne city	30 077	57.8	31.2	6.5	2.4	2.0	11 070	78.1	2 566	86.0
06 40886	Lawndale city	28 851	44.5	45.2	2.9	2.1	5.2	9 561	33.0	1 060	55.5
06 41992	Livermore city	67 831	47.4	28.4	14.3	6.8	3.0	26 065	72.1	3 481	77.6
06 42202	Lodi city	52 586	46.4	34.5	11.1	3.6	4.4	20 694	54.4	5 102	69.1
06 42524	Lompoc city	37 955	50.5	33.9	8.8	4.4	2.5	13 064	51.4	2 594	76.7
06 43000	Long Beach city	423 544	45.2	40.6	6.8	3.2	4.2	163 107	41.1	25 431	65.7
06 43280	Los Altos city	26 023	66.5	18.9	6.5	5.2	2.9	10 468	86.0	3 260	92.7
06 44000	Los Angeles city	3 412 889	49.5	36.9	3.2	3.8	6.5	1 275 358	38.6	220 475	61.0
06 44028	Los Banos city	23 420	46.9	16.5	31.5	2.3	2.7	7 752	68.3	1 418	78.5
06 44112	Los Gatos town	27 122	54.7	24.4	9.8	7.7	3.3	12 013	65.4	2 643	77.3
00 44574	Lynwood city	62 479	54.8	37.3	2.2	1.2	4.5	14 414	47.1	1 154	72.3
06 45022	Madera city	38 095	47.5	35.8	8.6	2.2	5.9	12 019	52.8	2 306	71.5
06 45400	Manhattan Beach city	31 821	55.4	28.1	5.3	9.1	2.0	14 536	64.9	2 418	90.0
00 45404	Manteca city	45 536	49.8	20.0	18.3	3.4	1.8	16 343	63.2	2 652	74.8
06 45778	Marina city	23 704	42.5	29.0	14.5	5.5	8.5	6 749	45.7	1 208	83.9
06 46114	Martinez city	34 112	54.1	29.3	11.1	4.1	1.5	14 359	69.0	2 342	76.1
06 46492	Maywood city	24 880	49.3	41.1	1.7	0.8	7.1	6 469	29.5	526	57.2
06 46870	Menlo Park city	28 834	52.9	16.0	16.6	8.2	6.4	12 426	57.0	3 026	75.9
06 46898	Merced city	58 268	43.5	39.3	11.0	2.8	3.4	20 480	46.2	3 740	66.2
06 47766	Milpitas city	58 215	53.2	27.3	7.4	3.7	8.5	17 137	69.7	1 808	75.9
06 48256	Mission Viejo city	86 509	54.2	29.7	8.5	5.6	2.0	32 329	81.5	5 817	89.3
06 48354	Modesto city	175 424	49.3	32.0	13.1	3.1	2.2	65 103	58.9	12 729	71.2
00 48640	Monrovia city	33 938	49.4	39.7	4.6	3.4	3.0	13 481	48.0	2 394	62.5
06 48788	Montclair city	30 284	53.4	19.7	20.8	1.4	4.8	8 799	60.5	1 474	70.4
06 48816	Montebello city	56 891	58.2	34.8	2.4	0.9	3.6	18 830	47.6	4 378	72.2
06 48872	Monterey city	28 279	38.8	21.5	13.5	18.7	7.4	12 634	38.4	2 981	64.8
06 48914	Monterey Park city	56 693	61.0	27.0	2.2	1.7	8.1	19 531	54.1	5 876	72.2
06 49138	Moorpark city	28 810	57.4	25.7	9.5	4.5	2.8	8 984	82.5	768	88.5
06 49270	Moreno Valley city	130 172	46.3	30.9	17.4	3.3	2.1	39 229	71.3	4 189	83.1
06 49278	Morgan Hill city	30 810	47.1	33.9	8.8	6.9	3.2	10 861	72.8	1 493	78.7
06 49670	Mountain View city	66 229	42.6	22.4	12.0	10.2	12.8	31 159	41.4	4 596	68.3
06 50076	Murrieta city	41 038	42.2	25.9	24.0	6.8	1.1	14 311	80.3	3 025	83.6
06 50258	Napa city	67 831	49.0	30.1	12.2	4.3	4.5	26 965	60.2	6 506	72.2
06 50398	National City city	50 132	48.5	36.3	4.7	5.6	4.9	15 100	35.0	3 318	52.2
06 50916	Newark city	39 536	59.5	19.4	13.7	2.7	4.8	12 992	70.7	1 753	76.8
06 51182	Newport Beach city	67 081	45.1	32.2	12.3	8.1	2.3	33 094	55.5	7 804	76.3
06 52526	Norwalk city	94 380	56.2	35.1	3.7	1.1	3.9	26 894	65.8	4 998	81.3
06 52582	Novato city	44 957	53.7	24.2	13.1	5.6	3.4	18 526	67.5	3 801	80.8
06 53000	Oakland city	371 551	51.5	27.3	10.7	4.8	5.7	150 787	41.4	28 252	57.4
06 53070	Oakley city	23 395	53.4	29.2	13.2	3.1	1.1	7 847	85.0	947	81.2
06 53322	Oceanside city	148 685	44.1	33.9	9.2	8.8	4.0	56 396	62.1	14 128	83.3
06 53896	Ontario city	142 157	48.9	28.2	16.2	2.2	4.5	43 453	57.7	5 400	73.8
06 53980	Orange city	118 941	49.8	36.1	6.8	3.2	4.0	40 803	62.5	7 482	75.8
06 54652	Oxnard city	155 446	51.9	34.1	5.7	2.6	5.7	43 630	57.2	7 542	77.1
06 54806	Pacifica city	36 442	61.7	17.6	14.0	4.4	2.3	14 003	68.6	2 390	75.5
06 55156	Palmdale city	105 886	46.4	42.6	4.8	3.9	2.3	34 344	71.1	4 076	78.1
06 55184	Palm Desert city	39 464	40.4	28.2	16.6	11.3	3.5	19 299	67.2	7 837	78.8
06 55254	Palm Springs city	40 778	47.0	25.5	13.7	9.9	3.9	20 540	60.7	7 673	76.2
06 55282	Palo Alto city	55 823	55.4	16.2	10.8	9.3	8.4	25 327	56.8	6 112	69.7
06 55520	Paradise town	25 270	54.1	26.5	15.1	3.9	0.4	11 571	70.6	4 504	82.9
06 55618	Paramount city	49 287	47.9	42.8	3.8	1.1	4.4	14 006	42.8	1 537	66.8
06 56000	Pasadena city	124 685	49.6	34.0	4.0	5.9	6.5	51 827	45.7	9 915	64.3
06 56700	Perris city	32 298	41.8	33.2	18.9	2.0	4.1	9 636	68.8	1 225	82.2

Table C-5. Cities — **Migration, Housing, and Transportation**

City	Owner-occupied by household type (percent)								Median household income			Median housing value (owner estimated)	Median monthly owner costs as a percent of income	
	Family households					Nonfamily households								
		Married-couple family		Other family										
	Total family households	Total	With own children under 18 years	Total	With own children under 18 years	Total nonfamily households	Two or more adults	Living alone	All households	Owner-occupied households	Renter-occupied households	Median housing value (owner estimated)	With a mortgage	Without a mortgage
	11	12	13	14	15	16	17	18	19	20	21	22	23	24
CALIFORNIA—Cont'd														
Highland city	67.7	78.3	73.3	43.9	29.9	62.8	56.2	64.5	41 355	52 695	21 127	122 200	24.6	9.9
Hollister city	69.4	74.2	70.5	52.0	47.1	51.4	39.3	55.1	55 878	68 760	34 741	262 100	26.9	9.9
Huntington Beach city	68.3	74.9	68.6	44.2	29.7	46.1	29.4	53.1	64 536	79 292	48 858	292 000	24.4	9.9
Huntington Park city	29.2	34.6	28.8	17.7	11.6	16.5	14.2	17.2	28 841	49 019	24 445	162 700	31.4	10.8
Imperial Beach city	31.2	36.0	20.6	22.3	12.5	27.2	15.6	31.5	35 707	50 396	30 803	168 000	25.4	9.9
Indio city	58.3	65.6	57.3	39.5	31.7	47.0	43.2	47.8	34 712	44 649	22 961	92 300	23.8	9.9
Inglewood city	39.2	50.4	42.3	25.2	17.1	29.8	29.3	29.9	33 580	51 878	26 393	170 400	29.3	10.9
Irvine city	67.8	72.7	70.9	47.5	43.3	43.6	25.5	51.3	71 513	89 944	47 955	301 400	24.4	9.9
Laguna Hills city	81.1	85.1	83.2	58.7	51.7	64.1	55.4	66.0	70 473	81 523	41 857	287 000	25.8	9.9
Laguna Niguel city	79.3	83.2	80.6	56.2	44.1	64.1	51.1	68.5	80 233	95 315	51 819	361 700	25.3	9.9
La Habra city	60.1	66.5	56.8	42.3	27.5	47.2	38.0	49.4	47 597	61 191	35 370	190 000	26.3	9.9
Lake Elsinore city	68.8	78.4	73.6	40.8	27.5	50.6	42.1	53.3	42 524	55 664	25 896	138 900	26.8	12.5
Lake Forest city	75.8	81.2	78.8	53.2	43.3	59.9	53.6	62.0	68 542	78 399	46 858	258 500	24.3	9.9
Lakewood city	73.8	78.4	72.5	60.1	46.6	66.3	53.8	69.4	58 137	65 354	40 652	201 800	24.4	9.9
La Mesa city	57.8	66.1	59.7	37.2	20.6	33.5	22.7	36.7	41 505	55 220	32 741	192 800	24.6	9.9
La Mirada city	85.4	87.8	86.4	74.3	64.4	68.8	60.8	70.3	61 303	65 596	31 553	206 400	25.3	9.9
Lancaster city	65.4	77.0	72.6	41.1	33.2	49.9	47.7	50.5	40 535	51 074	25 600	97 800	23.8	9.9
La Puente city	62.6	67.8	60.8	51.5	35.5	49.1	36.4	53.4	40 621	51 350	27 406	145 700	26.1	9.9
La Verne city	81.5	86.1	81.8	61.6	51.0	66.9	50.5	70.9	61 391	69 519	38 772	219 400	24.9	9.9
Lawndale city	34.3	41.7	35.2	22.2	14.9	29.1	21.0	32.1	37 626	51 035	33 049	175 500	29.5	9.9
Livermore city	77.4	83.2	80.3	52.6	44.6	56.3	53.8	57.2	74 421	86 214	44 895	309 100	25.4	9.9
Lodi city	59.1	68.1	57.0	33.1	21.5	43.8	32.4	46.2	39 489	52 665	26 422	139 800	23.5	9.9
Lompoc city	55.5	64.2	52.7	31.5	23.4	41.2	34.1	42.7	37 475	50 734	27 523	143 000	25.3	9.9
Long Beach city	45.7	57.0	48.3	25.5	15.5	33.7	30.9	34.5	37 170	61 197	26 777	198 600	25.9	9.9
Los Altos city	91.7	92.6	92.6	82.2	75.2	67.1	60.9	68.5	126 778	134 616	81 444	973 500	23.5	9.9
Los Angeles city	44.8	52.4	44.5	28.9	18.5	28.0	24.1	29.2	36 541	61 591	26 775	215 600	27.7	10.2
Los Banos city	71.2	78.5	76.1	44.1	33.5	55.3	48.0	56.5	43 497	52 209	27 058	138 200	26.2	9.9
Los Gatos town	78.7	84.0	81.4	51.8	44.3	44.6	35.2	47.5	93 320	118 267	63 345	748 300	24.7	9.9
Lynwood city	48.4	56.0	51.8	32.2	23.0	35.5	22.1	39.2	35 432	48 346	25 596	147 300	30.4	10.1
Madera city	55.0	63.6	55.0	35.2	23.5	44.6	32.1	47.4	30 988	41 036	20 356	92 300	25.9	9.9
Manhattan Beach city	82.4	85.3	85.6	62.6	56.3	40.3	23.3	47.5	100 850	114 978	77 947	669 800	23.6	9.9
Manteca city	68.4	75.6	71.1	44.4	34.6	46.2	39.3	48.0	46 199	56 292	33 232	152 200	25.2	9.9
Marina city	48.3	56.6	44.1	27.2	10.4	39.3	33.8	41.1	43 299	56 488	36 216	233 100	25.5	9.9
Martinez city	76.4	83.4	81.3	50.9	40.9	55.8	47.0	58.4	62 975	77 366	38 387	251 400	23.9	9.9
Maywood city	30.8	35.9	29.9	19.2	11.3	18.6	8.2	22.9	30 701	49 446	25 083	158 800	31.2	10.8
Menlo Park city	69.0	72.2	73.5	55.7	41.6	40.0	31.5	42.6	83 156	107 363	61 334	738 300	25.4	9.9
Merced city	49.5	61.1	53.6	27.5	20.0	37.8	27.2	40.4	30 765	47 824	21 864	103 200	24.2	11.2
Milpitas city	71.9	78.5	72.1	55.4	42.3	59.5	47.3	66.0	84 630	95 928	58 763	363 100	23.5	9.9
Mission Viejo city	84.6	87.7	85.4	66.9	57.1	70.1	63.6	71.9	77 754	85 215	49 536	288 700	24.5	9.9
Modesto city	63.3	72.3	65.9	39.3	29.0	47.3	41.1	48.8	40 588	52 576	26 797	123 800	23.9	9.9
Monrovia city	50.3	58.9	50.4	31.3	20.5	43.1	42.5	43.3	46 076	63 320	34 130	224 200	26.1	9.9
Montclair city	60.9	68.4	62.3	41.0	29.4	58.5	45.2	62.0	41 001	51 682	27 149	132 100	25.5	9.9
Montebello city	49.8	56.9	42.3	35.9	17.8	39.5	19.7	44.4	38 562	54 931	29 400	195 100	26.6	9.9
Monterey city	47.8	52.4	38.1	32.9	20.2	28.1	19.3	30.6	49 051	61 833	41 822	392 200	27.2	9.9
Monterey Park city	55.4	60.7	47.5	41.8	21.4	49.4	38.5	52.3	40 579	55 182	28 155	211 600	26.1	9.9
Moorpark city	83.1	86.0	84.2	66.1	53.8	78.7	69.9	82.3	76 762	83 241	46 484	273 300	26.4	9.9
Moreno Valley city	73.0	81.0	77.7	50.6	42.3	61.0	54.0	63.0	47 741	55 583	28 558	117 800	25.3	11.8
Morgan Hill city	75.8	80.9	73.7	51.7	38.1	61.5	62.3	61.3	82 010	99 680	48 137	405 000	24.5	9.9
Mountain View city	49.4	51.0	49.9	42.9	25.7	33.0	24.0	36.4	69 190	90 371	59 360	464 800	24.0	9.9
Murrieta city	85.9	88.9	87.1	66.3	60.8	53.9	52.2	54.3	60 935	67 005	34 989	190 300	26.3	11.0
Napa city	65.2	71.4	62.0	42.3	31.5	50.4	45.1	51.7	49 313	61 617	36 282	230 500	25.7	9.9
National City city	37.4	43.1	33.6	26.9	13.3	26.6	23.8	27.3	29 663	44 339	23 558	138 800	26.1	9.9
Newark city	72.5	75.4	69.3	61.1	50.2	63.2	50.5	68.2	69 287	76 435	51 729	297 800	25.3	9.9
Newport Beach city	73.5	78.4	79.6	49.3	35.0	36.4	21.7	41.8	83 797	108 531	63 833	675 800	27.0	9.9
Norwalk city	67.0	71.8	66.5	53.5	39.3	59.4	50.6	61.6	46 061	52 164	33 806	160 100	26.5	9.9
Novato city	71.7	77.0	69.9	53.4	44.0	58.9	48.5	61.9	62 495	75 959	44 985	364 800	26.2	9.9
Oakland city	48.8	58.9	52.2	33.5	20.4	31.5	33.7	30.8	39 916	63 950	29 278	227 300	25.4	10.6
Oakley city	87.1	90.3	89.1	67.3	70.2	74.8	74.7	74.8	64 847	69 533	35 933	185 500	26.8	10.6
Oceanside city	66.4	73.2	66.8	41.3	29.5	52.3	37.2	57.2	45 964	56 523	33 362	185 400	26.3	9.9
Ontario city	60.3	67.1	61.8	43.4	32.3	47.3	35.5	50.9	42 090	52 455	30 851	136 300	26.1	9.9
Orange city	66.1	71.3	63.0	47.6	34.5	52.0	43.5	54.7	58 829	73 600	40 716	247 000	24.8	9.9
Oxnard city	58.9	64.2	56.7	43.5	28.9	50.2	41.1	53.4	47 960	60 634	34 292	183 200	25.6	9.9
Pacifica city	76.2	80.4	78.7	60.2	52.2	51.2	42.4	55.2	71 059	80 172	54 881	366 500	25.3	9.9
Palmdale city	73.5	82.3	80.4	50.2	42.5	59.9	56.0	61.2	46 993	55 976	25 224	113 600	25.3	10.1
Palm Desert city	75.1	81.6	67.5	45.0	36.8	55.6	53.9	56.1	48 535	58 554	31 646	176 400	26.4	11.5
Palm Springs city	65.8	73.0	54.2	43.9	27.9	56.1	62.1	54.5	35 609	46 254	24 176	135 700	25.8	13.1
Palo Alto city	72.0	75.2	73.2	53.6	43.7	35.9	30.6	37.4	90 144	119 964	61 245	776 000	21.6	9.9
Paradise town	76.2	82.8	74.4	51.2	35.9	61.3	47.7	63.6	31 812	36 737	20 685	112 300	23.7	12.1
Paramount city	42.3	48.6	43.9	31.3	20.2	45.1	39.0	46.8	36 597	45 957	30 732	136 800	28.0	9.9
Pasadena city	53.5	60.5	53.4	35.5	25.6	35.1	31.3	36.1	46 037	72 907	32 004	268 500	25.9	9.9
Perris city	69.9	79.2	76.3	48.0	39.6	62.9	58.0	64.2	35 042	41 409	21 009	87 100	27.5	11.5

Table C-5. Cities — **Migration, Housing, and Transportation**

City	Median gross rent	Percent who pay 35 percent or more of income for housing expenses		Means of transportation to work (percent except where noted)							Vehicles available (percent of households)		
		Owners	Renters	Number of workers 16 years and over	Car, truck, or van		Public transportation	Other means	Walked		No vehicles	One vehicle	Two or more vehicles
					Drove alone	Carpooled							
	25	26	27	28	29	30	31	32	33		34	35	36
CALIFORNIA—Cont'd													
Highland city	574	19.2	39.7	16 595	74.2	18.5	1.9	1.3	1.1		9.9	30.7	59.4
Hollister city	769	26.8	31.4	14 708	74.4	18.0	1.5	2.1	1.8		6.3	23.8	70.0
Huntington Beach city	985	21.7	28.4	101 300	82.7	9.0	1.1	1.5	1.5		3.9	31.1	65.0
Huntington Park city	590	37.2	37.6	19 695	51.8	21.7	15.4	2.8	6.9		24.4	37.8	37.8
Imperial Beach city	690	21.0	32.3	11 536	68.2	16.6	6.6	2.7	2.9		10.0	40.5	49.5
Indio city	579	21.5	34.1	17 425	65.5	25.5	1.9	2.0	2.5		11.3	36.1	52.6
Inglewood city	673	34.0	38.6	40 881	69.1	18.4	7.5	1.1	2.0		14.9	43.2	41.9
Irvine city	1 272	22.4	36.0	72 870	79.2	8.2	0.7	1.8	4.8		3.9	31.5	64.6
Laguna Hills city	1 184	27.3	41.1	14 704	77.1	13.5	1.4	0.5	1.1		5.7	26.1	68.2
Laguna Niguel city	1 205	24.4	34.1	31 391	81.4	8.9	0.9	0.8	0.8		2.4	26.6	71.0
La Habra city	787	21.9	31.7	25 549	76.8	15.4	2.2	1.4	2.3		6.5	32.9	60.6
Lake Elsinore city	633	25.6	35.6	11 079	72.1	20.0	1.5	1.6	1.0		6.8	30.2	63.0
Lake Forest city	1 085	22.3	33.1	30 777	79.8	12.4	1.4	1.4	0.9		3.4	28.1	68.5
Lakewood city	886	19.6	30.5	36 392	81.7	12.0	1.3	1.1	1.0		5.9	28.2	65.8
La Mesa city	759	18.3	34.4	27 472	80.7	10.2	2.6	1.7	1.2		9.0	41.6	49.4
La Mirada city	870	19.5	38.8	20 753	79.1	12.3	1.4	1.5	3.4		4.5	25.7	69.9
Lancaster city	643	21.2	38.2	42 351	73.4	18.9	2.2	1.3	1.6		9.3	35.6	55.0
La Puente city	678	26.3	34.0	14 640	64.7	25.0	5.4	2.0	1.3		11.5	29.7	58.9
La Verne city	856	23.8	31.0	15 245	78.4	13.3	3.0	0.8	2.0		4.8	26.9	68.4
Lawndale city	783	29.7	32.4	12 839	67.0	20.4	6.9	2.3	2.3		11.2	38.8	50.0
Livermore city	1 035	20.4	31.2	37 874	79.8	10.4	3.3	2.1	1.4		4.2	24.5	71.3
Lodi city	621	18.7	35.4	23 716	76.0	15.8	0.5	2.4	2.7		10.7	37.0	52.3
Lompoc city	639	19.4	34.4	15 379	71.6	20.2	1.2	2.5	2.5		7.5	37.3	55.1
Long Beach city	639	24.1	36.5	184 479	72.6	13.7	6.6	1.7	2.5		15.7	41.9	42.4
Los Altos city	1 727	17.0	30.5	12 559	84.2	4.3	1.5	1.6	1.4		2.9	20.0	77.2
Los Angeles city	672	29.4	37.1	1 494 895	65.7	14.7	10.2	1.6	3.6		16.5	40.3	43.2
Los Banos city	562	23.5	25.3	9 132	65.7	26.9	0.2	1.5	3.8		9.0	28.9	62.1
Los Gatos town	1 331	23.7	27.4	14 890	82.4	8.8	1.0	0.8	1.3		5.1	29.0	65.9
Lynwood city	629	36.9	39.0	20 272	61.1	25.6	8.0	1.4	2.6		13.1	32.8	54.2
Madera city	527	23.8	37.6	13 742	68.2	23.2	1.5	2.7	1.9		14.6	35.2	50.2
Manhattan Beach city	1 358	22.1	20.7	19 030	84.5	6.9	0.4	1.0	1.3		2.7	30.8	66.5
Manteca city	724	21.3	32.8	20 136	76.5	16.3	1.5	1.3	1.7		6.2	32.4	61.4
Marina city	778	23.2	32.9	9 477	75.2	16.0	2.1	1.8	2.4		8.9	37.1	54.0
Martinez city	870	18.3	31.5	18 820	77.4	10.4	5.7	1.1	1.4		5.6	30.6	63.8
Maywood city	602	33.5	38.2	9 071	53.2	23.5	11.6	2.5	7.1		18.0	35.8	46.2
Menlo Park city	1 319	22.0	31.7	15 237	75.5	7.1	4.0	4.5	2.2		5.5	37.9	56.6
Merced city	509	20.7	36.9	21 668	73.8	19.3	0.7	2.0	1.6		15.2	38.3	46.5
Milpitas city	1 279	19.3	29.9	29 850	81.7	12.7	2.3	1.1	0.7		5.0	19.8	75.2
Mission Viejo city	1 145	20.9	35.6	46 324	82.4	9.5	1.0	1.0	0.9		2.6	24.4	73.1
Modesto city	639	20.1	36.6	74 878	78.9	13.7	1.3	1.5	1.7		9.4	34.5	56.1
Monrovia city	746	22.9	31.1	16 477	75.7	13.6	2.9	1.7	3.4		9.7	38.0	52.4
Montclair city	671	22.5	38.9	12 252	71.0	19.7	2.9	2.1	2.4		8.6	32.5	50.9
Montebello city	698	23.7	35.7	22 197	69.8	18.2	6.3	1.1	2.5		12.1	36.7	51.2
Monterey city	888	22.5	30.1	16 699	65.0	9.1	3.1	2.8	16.1		8.0	46.4	45.6
Monterey Park city	722	21.9	35.8	23 826	74.2	15.7	4.4	1.0	1.9		12.0	32.1	55.9
Moorpark city	1 172	26.4	34.4	14 861	78.5	14.2	0.9	0.8	1.5		1.8	18.0	80.3
Moreno Valley city	743	24.4	39.1	55 089	74.2	18.9	1.9	1.3	0.7		6.1	26.4	67.5
Morgan Hill city	1 112	22.6	29.9	15 961	75.5	14.6	4.4	1.3	1.0		4.1	23.1	72.9
Mountain View city	1 222	19.9	26.2	40 321	78.3	8.4	4.8	2.9	2.2		5.7	41.9	52.4
Murrieta city	842	23.8	36.4	18 779	79.3	12.9	0.2	1.2	0.8		3.6	24.4	71.9
Napa city	819	20.5	32.1	33 743	75.0	15.4	1.8	2.2	2.1		7.6	32.9	59.5
National City city	573	25.8	35.6	20 111	61.7	17.8	6.6	3.1	4.8		18.4	35.3	46.3
Newark city	1 093	23.2	27.3	19 994	75.0	16.9	3.4	2.2	0.8		5.0	22.0	73.1
Newport Beach city	1 257	28.3	28.4	37 910	82.6	5.7	0.8	1.7	2.0		3.6	37.9	58.6
Norwalk city	767	24.6	33.2	38 134	73.6	17.5	3.0	1.8	2.3		7.3	29.4	63.3
Novato city	1 146	25.1	37.6	24 588	70.3	12.8	8.4	1.3	1.6		5.6	31.0	63.4
Oakland city	696	25.4	34.6	170 503	55.3	16.6	17.4	2.8	3.7		19.6	41.9	38.4
Oakley city	944	24.4	33.7	11 729	77.6	14.6	2.3	0.9	1.4		4.4	17.9	77.6
Oceanside city	818	24.5	36.4	70 782	73.3	16.3	3.7	1.6	1.3		6.2	37.0	56.8
Ontario city	720	24.4	34.9	60 919	69.8	22.5	2.7	1.4	1.5		8.3	31.7	60.1
Orange city	884	22.0	31.5	60 382	76.5	12.8	2.6	1.6	2.9		6.3	28.8	64.9
Oxnard city	780	24.5	32.7	69 411	67.3	25.2	1.3	2.6	1.6		7.3	29.5	63.2
Pacifica city	1 261	22.6	29.3	20 842	74.9	12.2	8.1	1.2	1.0		3.6	27.6	68.7
Palmdale city	630	24.7	40.0	42 219	69.6	23.2	2.7	1.0	1.0		7.2	28.8	64.0
Palm Desert city	744	23.7	33.9	17 037	77.9	11.2	1.3	1.6	1.9		6.7	46.0	47.3
Palm Springs city	631	26.4	39.5	17 401	73.7	12.2	2.2	2.3	3.7		10.9	50.8	38.3
Palo Alto city	1 349	15.7	30.9	30 950	74.5	6.1	3.4	6.1	3.2		6.6	35.1	58.2
Paradise town	573	18.4	42.8	9 530	77.6	13.9	0.9	1.0	1.8		8.5	39.7	51.8
Paramount city	720	30.2	35.8	18 289	65.2	24.2	3.8	2.4	2.9		12.4	37.7	49.9
Pasadena city	746	25.0	33.5	61 891	70.5	13.3	4.7	2.4	5.3		11.8	41.6	46.6
Perris city	630	29.5	44.2	11 580	67.8	24.5	1.6	1.8	2.3		8.6	34.5	56.9

Table C-5. Cities — **Migration, Housing, and Transportation**

STATE Place code	City	Total population 5 years and over	Residence in 1995 (percent)					Occupied housing units		Householders 65 years and over	
			Same house	Same county, different house	Same state, different county	Different state	Outside the United States	Number	Percent owner-occupied	Number	Percent owner-occupied
		1	2	3	4	5	6	7	8	9	10
	CALIFORNIA—Cont'd										
06 56784	Petaluma city...............	50 951	54.5	22.8	15.5	4.4	2.8	19 965	70.1	3 798	77.0
06 56924	Pico Rivera city............	58 084	64.3	30.2	1.8	0.8	2.9	16 473	70.1	4 065	84.5
06 57456	Pittsburg city...............	52 287	51.6	28.8	11.8	2.9	4.7	17 792	62.8	2 836	74.5
06 57526	Placentia city..............	43 717	50.1	32.9	9.5	2.9	4.7	15 138	68.8	2 697	87.3
06 57764	Pleasant Hill city.........	30 830	52.1	25.0	12.6	6.7	3.6	13 773	63.7	2 803	68.7
06 57792	Pleasanton city............	59 228	48.3	23.3	16.1	8.6	3.7	23 317	73.4	2 945	78.6
06 58072	Pomona city................	135 538	51.1	33.5	9.2	1.7	4.5	37 890	57.2	5 557	70.8
06 58240	Porterville city............	36 175	46.3	39.7	7.7	2.5	3.9	11 970	56.2	2 312	70.3
06 58520	Poway city	45 411	54.9	30.6	5.0	7.4	2.1	15 587	77.6	2 222	80.5
06 59451	Rancho Cucamonga city...................	119 382	50.8	30.3	12.8	3.9	2.2	40 976	70.3	4 525	76.3
06 59514	Rancho Palos Verdes city.......................	39 504	60.8	25.9	3.1	5.9	4.3	15 233	81.9	4 531	94.3
06 59587	Rancho Santa Margarita city............	42 800	37.4	40.5	11.3	8.8	2.0	16 307	77.9	918	62.5
06 59920	Redding city	75 872	42.6	34.8	14.7	6.7	1.2	32 137	56.8	8 136	73.5
06 59962	Redlands city..............	59 695	50.8	30.6	10.9	5.4	2.3	23 669	60.2	4 911	74.4
06 60018	Redondo Beach city.....	59 578	46.6	35.4	6.0	8.6	3.4	28 566	49.5	3 681	65.3
06 60102	Redwood City city........	69 828	49.0	27.5	12.0	4.8	6.7	28 095	53.0	4 657	68.4
06 60466	Rialto city.................	83 135	47.5	32.3	15.5	1.6	3.1	24 479	68.4	3 476	78.4
06 60620	Richmond city..............	92 071	51.5	22.8	17.8	3.2	4.8	34 705	53.4	6 237	77.4
06 62000	Riverside city..............	235 384	47.5	32.2	14.3	2.9	3.1	82 079	56.7	14 036	72.3
06 62364	Rocklin city................	33 726	39.9	19.6	30.8	8.6	1.2	13 284	72.7	1 914	78.3
06 62546	Rohnert Park city	39 639	45.2	29.8	18.4	3.8	2.8	15 553	58.1	2 399	67.9
06 62896	Rosemead city	49 369	57.4	32.9	1.7	1.1	7.0	13 889	48.8	2 655	66.6
06 62938	Roseville city	74 325	40.4	17.4	32.4	7.7	2.2	30 816	69.4	7 067	79.3
06 64000	Sacramento city	378 678	48.6	32.6	11.3	3.7	3.8	154 565	50.1	30 932	70.6
06 64224	Salinas city................	136 924	45.9	33.8	10.1	3.1	7.1	38 227	50.1	6 246	69.8
06 65000	San Bernardino city.......	167 274	45.0	37.5	11.3	3.0	3.3	56 174	52.5	9 468	74.9
06 65028	San Bruno city............	37 796	59.5	22.0	9.8	3.4	5.3	14 650	62.4	2 955	85.8
06 65042	San Buenaventura (Ventura) city............	94 381	47.6	32.3	12.7	5.3	2.2	38 571	58.6	8 249	74.6
06 65070	San Carlos city............	25 762	59.9	21.3	12.0	4.5	2.3	11 360	73.1	2 653	83.3
06 65084	San Clemente city.........	46 741	48.1	32.6	10.2	6.4	2.7	19 391	62.5	4 331	81.6
06 66000	San Diego city.............	1 141 742	43.6	33.8	7.7	9.9	5.0	450 682	49.5	80 334	71.6
06 66070	San Dimas city............	33 019	56.1	32.6	6.5	3.3	1.6	12 233	73.6	2 547	69.6
06 67000	San Francisco city........	745 650	54.2	19.7	10.2	9.3	6.7	329 700	35.0	68 613	51.7
06 67042	San Gabriel city...........	36 835	56.0	31.5	1.7	1.3	9.4	12 535	47.7	2 344	74.1
06 68000	San Jose city..............	825 954	51.8	30.9	6.7	3.7	6.9	276 417	61.8	39 481	74.7
06 68028	San Juan Capistrano city.......................	31 602	49.6	35.6	7.8	4.0	3.1	10 956	79.1	2 788	84.9
06 68064	San Leandro city..........	74 451	54.1	28.7	9.6	3.3	4.4	30 616	60.7	7 767	77.5
06 68154	San Luis Obispo city	42 551	33.5	23.9	35.1	5.4	2.1	18 653	41.8	3 612	76.5
06 68196	San Marcos city	50 457	42.4	39.7	7.0	6.1	4.9	18 176	66.2	4 289	81.4
06 68252	San Mateo city............	86 829	54.5	23.9	10.1	5.0	6.5	37 318	53.9	9 119	70.9
06 68294	San Pablo city.............	27 575	50.6	25.0	15.7	1.7	7.1	9 057	49.8	1 518	63.7
06 68364	San Rafael city............	52 799	50.7	24.5	12.3	4.6	7.9	22 401	53.6	4 923	76.9
06 68378	San Ramon city............	41 255	46.2	17.4	22.3	10.1	4.1	16 805	71.1	1 562	78.0
06 69000	Santa Ana city............	302 982	47.2	39.3	4.0	1.4	8.2	72 882	49.3	9 178	70.4
06 69070	Santa Barbara city	87 085	47.0	28.8	13.4	5.5	5.3	35 706	41.9	8 407	60.1
06 69084	Santa Clara city...........	95 589	45.7	26.0	9.0	6.9	12.3	38 500	46.1	6 741	71.9
06 69088	Santa Clarita city..........	139 374	51.1	35.9	4.8	5.0	3.2	50 685	74.8	6 936	72.4
06 69112	Santa Cruz city............	51 678	40.5	26.0	22.0	7.3	4.1	20 395	46.5	3 132	72.7
06 69196	Santa Maria city...........	70 334	45.7	36.6	8.7	2.9	6.0	22 086	55.9	5 096	79.9
06 70000	Santa Monica city.........	80 707	52.6	28.9	4.1	9.7	4.8	44 497	29.8	8 099	41.5
06 70042	Santa Paula city...........	26 088	53.4	34.4	5.3	2.3	4.6	8 157	57.5	1 865	75.4
06 70098	Santa Rosa city...........	138 333	47.0	34.3	10.8	4.4	3.5	56 063	58.3	13 551	73.5
06 70224	Santee city	49 593	54.4	34.6	3.7	6.2	1.2	18 441	71.0	3 226	86.9
06 70280	Saratoga city	28 280	65.2	22.5	4.3	3.4	4.6	10 464	90.0	2 811	90.7
06 70742	Seaside city	28 797	47.2	26.5	6.1	12.2	8.1	9 841	44.0	1 668	81.8
06 72016	Simi Valley city............	103 365	52.1	28.2	13.8	4.0	1.9	36 478	77.6	4 680	82.1
06 73080	South Gate city	86 773	52.9	40.4	1.3	0.7	4.7	23 217	46.9	2 795	66.3
06 73262	South San Francisco city.......................	56 711	61.1	21.2	11.2	1.7	4.9	19 691	62.6	4 574	76.6
06 73962	Stanton city................	33 535	43.1	37.0	8.7	2.5	8.8	10 708	48.6	2 049	61.2
06 75000	Stockton city...............	222 562	48.5	33.6	11.7	2.6	3.6	78 522	51.9	15 383	67.0
06 75630	Suisun City city	24 054	56.5	22.8	14.0	3.4	3.3	7 989	73.6	793	65.3
06 77000	Sunnyvale city.............	122 733	46.2	23.7	8.2	7.9	14.0	52 534	47.6	8 680	77.9
06 78120	Temecula city..............	52 205	38.0	21.5	28.9	8.8	2.9	18 219	72.9	2 226	85.1
06 78148	Temple City city...........	31 348	58.2	31.5	2.8	1.8	5.8	11 393	63.0	2 314	81.6
06 78582	Thousand Oaks city	109 118	52.3	21.8	16.9	6.6	2.4	41 796	75.5	8 104	82.3
06 80000	Torrance city...............	130 278	54.2	33.2	3.1	3.8	5.6	54 534	56.0	12 100	78.0
06 80238	Tracy city..................	51 702	45.4	17.9	28.6	5.1	3.0	17 581	72.4	2 171	70.5
06 80644	Tulare city.................	39 829	51.7	37.6	7.5	1.5	1.8	13 514	60.7	2 733	73.3
06 80812	Turlock city................	51 126	49.6	31.2	12.9	3.2	3.1	18 343	55.8	3 821	68.1
06 80854	Tustin city..................	62 116	36.1	42.3	9.6	5.3	6.7	23 838	49.7	3 008	74.9
06 81204	Union City city.............	61 853	52.4	25.4	11.6	3.0	7.6	18 628	71.2	2 454	78.8

Table C-5. Cities — **Migration, Housing, and Transportation**

City	Owner-occupied by household type (percent)								Median household income			Median housing value (owner estimated)	Median monthly owner costs as a percent of income	
	Family households					Nonfamily households								
		Married-couple family		Other family										
	Total family households	Total	With own children under 18 years	Total	With own children under 18 years	Total nonfamily households	Two or more adults	Living alone	All households	Owner-occupied households	Renter-occupied households		With a mortgage	Without a mortgage
	11	12	13	14	15	16	17	18	19	20	21	22	23	24

CALIFORNIA—Cont'd

City	11	12	13	14	15	16	17	18	19	20	21	22	23	24
Petaluma city	76.5	81.9	79.4	54.8	45.0	55.2	48.3	57.4	61 503	72 105	42 731	282 800	25.1	9.9
Pico Rivera city	72.3	77.8	70.7	59.4	37.0	57.7	64.6	56.6	41 723	48 537	28 640	165 700	28.4	9.9
Pittsburg city	67.4	74.9	69.9	47.3	34.6	48.8	46.9	49.4	50 183	61 111	33 825	161 700	24.6	11.5
Placentia city	71.1	76.1	68.3	50.5	35.2	60.6	39.6	68.1	62 017	75 203	41 774	258 600	24.7	9.9
Pleasant Hill city	74.7	80.0	77.7	53.9	50.2	45.9	37.4	48.6	66 772	78 777	45 360	287 600	24.5	9.9
Pleasanton city	80.7	84.5	84.3	57.3	48.1	51.5	41.2	54.6	90 359	102 755	59 611	428 200	24.3	9.9
Pomona city	60.3	67.2	62.5	43.8	33.2	45.6	37.4	48.7	39 602	51 341	26 247	134 000	26.7	9.9
Porterville city	59.7	69.6	62.1	37.2	29.8	43.9	23.5	47.7	31 310	43 938	18 770	92 200	24.4	10.3
Poway city	81.1	86.8	84.9	54.1	46.1	60.2	58.0	61.0	71 616	83 987	40 497	272 800	24.2	9.9
Rancho Cucamonga city	75.0	81.7	79.8	53.3	44.0	53.2	45.3	55.5	60 645	70 310	40 484	176 400	25.3	9.9
Rancho Palos Verdes city	84.8	86.3	78.2	73.7	64.2	70.1	70.4	70.0	95 095	101 886	70 326	547 100	24.8	9.9
Rancho Santa Margarita city	83.6	87.6	89.3	62.5	57.0	59.0	48.7	62.3	78 244	89 846	44 968	272 900	26.7	9.9
Redding city	63.8	74.2	65.7	35.2	20.2	40.0	30.2	46.8	31 004	46 002	22 150	116 300	25.0	11.5
Redlands city	67.9	76.1	69.7	44.1	29.7	43.9	36.3	45.7	48 600	63 970	31 851	152 200	22.8	9.9
Redondo Beach city	60.6	66.8	64.0	41.7	30.6	36.9	30.3	39.5	68 500	87 201	53 681	341 600	24.6	9.9
Redwood City city	58.7	65.2	59.8	35.4	25.7	42.8	32.0	46.4	66 935	88 877	49 356	487 600	26.4	9.9
Rialto city	69.7	78.9	74.9	49.5	39.2	61.4	56.0	62.7	40 351	49 828	24 658	113 200	25.8	9.9
Richmond city	56.5	65.8	56.5	40.7	26.2	47.1	41.9	48.5	43 815	56 592	32 467	170 700	26.2	9.9
Riverside city	63.6	73.1	67.4	40.2	28.6	39.6	29.3	43.1	41 506	57 960	26 638	136 000	23.9	9.9
Rocklin city	79.4	84.7	84.5	53.9	46.0	52.2	43.2	55.0	64 206	75 784	37 096	208 600	24.5	11.2
Rohnert Park city	68.6	74.9	73.5	49.5	40.8	39.8	27.6	46.0	52 122	63 690	38 054	222 000	26.7	11.0
Rosemead city	47.1	50.6	43.0	38.9	20.4	57.2	47.9	59.5	36 174	49 157	27 614	179 900	26.7	9.9
Roseville city	77.0	83.5	81.3	48.8	42.1	50.1	48.4	50.5	57 225	67 721	37 953	192 300	24.4	9.9
Sacramento city	57.7	67.3	59.2	38.7	27.7	39.0	33.9	40.3	36 950	51 277	26 299	126 000	24.3	9.9
Salinas city	52.0	58.1	50.7	34.4	24.4	43.4	42.0	43.7	43 280	57 400	32 485	189 500	25.6	9.9
San Bernardino city	55.0	66.4	59.6	35.6	25.2	45.6	35.6	48.3	30 939	43 755	20 248	94 300	24.7	9.9
San Bruno city	66.6	71.7	64.9	48.3	34.1	53.5	37.7	57.6	61 917	69 145	52 162	365 100	26.2	9.9
San Buenaventura (Ventura) city	65.3	72.5	66.8	44.3	33.3	45.7	36.0	48.5	52 166	64 772	37 326	233 400	24.4	9.9
San Carlos city	81.7	85.0	84.7	62.5	51.8	55.5	51.1	56.7	88 077	100 237	57 576	607 100	25.4	9.9
San Clemente city	71.4	76.9	70.0	44.8	38.0	43.7	32.1	48.2	63 099	82 936	43 285	364 800	26.2	9.9
San Diego city	58.4	65.3	57.5	38.1	26.5	36.0	25.3	40.3	45 609	64 206	31 722	220 000	25.2	9.9
San Dimas city	78.4	83.1	81.0	61.0	47.5	59.5	59.3	59.5	62 058	70 497	39 699	218 600	24.5	9.9
San Francisco city	50.5	54.4	54.2	40.0	27.0	22.5	18.6	24.3	54 886	77 917	45 275	422 700	25.2	9.9
San Gabriel city	49.4	54.9	45.5	36.0	17.9	42.5	25.9	47.4	41 709	57 713	31 852	226 700	26.4	9.9
San Jose city	66.4	72.0	67.5	47.4	34.6	48.7	38.7	52.7	69 933	85 756	48 608	375 500	24.4	9.9
San Juan Capistrano city	79.3	83.7	77.3	58.7	47.0	78.6	68.7	80.9	62 483	70 536	45 246	274 100	25.9	9.9
San Leandro city	66.8	74.6	67.9	45.0	30.8	49.3	38.1	51.9	50 735	60 416	40 730	229 700	25.2	9.9
San Luis Obispo city	65.5	70.4	70.2	60.0	53.7	24.0	10.3	36.3	32 055	58 725	29 826	252 900	24.7	9.9
San Marcos city	67.8	72.6	64.9	47.2	28.3	61.6	47.1	65.8	45 931	55 827	35 000	178 400	26.3	9.9
San Mateo city	61.6	65.9	62.4	45.5	33.9	42.5	31.7	45.4	65 109	79 548	52 980	453 600	26.0	9.9
San Pablo city	49.9	58.5	51.8	35.5	25.3	49.5	38.4	51.6	36 859	49 896	27 264	135 500	27.4	10.3
San Rafael city	61.1	68.1	57.7	37.1	26.9	43.6	35.1	46.5	61 080	87 704	41 541	457 000	24.0	9.9
San Ramon city	81.3	84.9	85.6	59.2	57.4	45.7	43.7	46.4	95 209	107 069	70 035	421 000	24.5	9.9
Santa Ana city	50.7	53.8	47.3	41.3	30.0	42.9	36.1	45.7	42 994	55 689	33 530	173 300	26.4	0.0
Santa Barbara city	52.6	58.5	46.8	34.1	24.9	29.6	22.3	32.6	47 108	68 736	36 397	469 300	28.7	9.9
Santa Clara city	52.7	55.7	48.0	42.3	24.0	34.9	21.8	40.3	68 818	80 777	60 891	387 000	23.1	9.9
Santa Clarita city	79.4	83.9	82.8	59.7	53.3	60.6	58.2	61.3	66 554	76 265	41 221	216 900	24.7	9.9
Santa Cruz city	60.3	68.1	63.1	40.5	29.3	31.6	22.4	37.5	50 430	71 586	35 221	397 100	27.6	9.9
Santa Maria city	57.5	68.2	51.0	40.0	23.4	51.0	43.1	52.8	36 623	47 736	25 883	140 000	26.7	9.9
Santa Monica city	47.5	54.5	55.6	27.2	25.4	19.1	19.8	18.9	50 468	90 050	40 695	479 200	26.9	9.9
Santa Paula city	57.5	63.5	50.2	37.6	23.8	57.6	45.1	60.0	40 262	52 438	29 142	166 600	25.4	9.9
Santa Rosa city	65.4	72.6	64.3	42.8	34.7	46.1	35.7	49.6	50 658	62 193	36 817	236 000	25.6	9.9
Santee city	72.7	78.9	73.9	52.9	40.0	65.6	54.9	68.8	52 876	59 391	36 521	172 800	25.0	9.9
Saratoga city	93.3	93.7	92.6	89.2	87.9	74.4	76.3	74.0	138 803	145 005	62 348	1 000 001	23.5	9.9
Seaside city	42.0	42.3	31.4	41.3	26.5	50.0	46.6	51.2	41 537	49 863	36 069	232 200	27.7	9.9
Simi Valley city	81.5	85.8	83.1	63.9	55.5	62.5	59.7	63.6	70 293	77 725	48 157	235 200	25.1	9.9
South Gate city	47.2	53.1	48.1	32.7	22.8	44.7	28.7	48.8	35 247	48 017	26 867	161 400	20.8	0.0
South San Francisco city	66.1	70.3	63.7	52.9	38.8	52.1	36.7	56.2	61 375	71 041	47 429	344 300	26.1	9.9
Stanton city	48.7	51.8	44.9	41.0	31.4	48.2	43.5	49.5	38 424	50 241	29 866	140 200	27.4	9.9
Stockton city	56.2	67.3	58.8	32.0	21.3	41.0	33.3	42.8	35 219	51 274	22 007	117 500	24.0	10.3
Suisun City city	77.1	81.1	80.5	62.2	59.7	58.4	62.0	57.3	60 908	67 471	36 681	161 100	25.1	9.9
Sunnyvale city	54.7	56.9	51.0	45.0	32.4	36.0	26.3	39.8	74 334	86 407	66 556	441 400	23.3	9.9
Temecula city	77.9	82.8	80.9	53.6	48.2	48.5	45.0	49.7	59 703	68 551	36 341	189 500	26.8	9.9
Temple City city	67.5	73.8	67.0	48.7	31.2	49.0	32.5	52.3	48 048	58 478	35 788	233 300	25.7	9.9
Thousand Oaks city	80.9	84.7	81.8	61.1	54.0	59.1	55.3	60.1	76 235	87 049	50 051	312 900	24.7	9.9
Torrance city	64.6	69.8	62.6	44.6	27.1	38.9	33.2	40.1	56 264	71 773	41 518	308 600	25.9	9.9
Tracy city	76.3	82.1	80.7	50.1	43.6	55.4	57.1	54.9	62 752	73 681	38 181	211 700	26.3	9.9
Tulare city	63.9	73.5	65.2	38.8	30.5	47.9	38.2	49.8	33 549	42 905	23 573	92 900	23.9	10.6
Turlock city	61.3	69.4	62.2	35.9	26.7	40.4	30.5	42.8	38 764	52 085	24 764	124 300	23.2	9.9
Tustin city	52.7	58.4	50.5	34.8	25.6	43.5	34.5	46.6	56 019	78 114	42 432	251 000	24.1	9.9
Union City city	73.7	77.2	74.0	60.3	48.5	57.1	45.2	61.4	71 501	80 815	51 490	296 600	25.0	9.9

Table C-5. Cities — **Migration, Housing, and Transportation**

City	Median gross rent	Percent who pay 35 percent or more of income for housing expenses — Owners	Renters	Number of workers 16 years and over	Means of transportation to work (percent except where noted) — Car, truck, or van — Drove alone	Carpooled	Public transportation	Other means	Walked	Vehicles available (percent of households) — No vehicles	One vehicle	Two or more vehicles
	25	26	27	28	29	30	31	32	33	34	35	36
CALIFORNIA—Cont'd												
Petaluma city	946	22.1	30.7	27 600	72.1	13.8	5.0	1.8	2.6	5.7	27.5	66.7
Pico Rivera city	700	27.7	33.9	22 833	72.4	18.2	3.9	1.3	2.8	9.3	30.1	60.6
Pittsburg city	880	22.8	36.1	23 942	67.3	18.9	8.5	1.6	1.5	8.0	29.6	62.4
Placentia city	890	20.6	29.3	23 148	78.5	13.2	1.3	1.8	1.9	4.6	25.7	69.7
Pleasant Hill city	984	19.7	32.8	17 456	72.5	8.2	11.2	1.5	1.6	6.2	33.6	60.3
Pleasanton city	1 219	20.4	25.0	33 269	80.0	8.0	4.9	1.3	1.3	2.9	24.5	72.6
Pomona city	644	29.0	38.5	52 066	66.8	22.0	4.9	2.3	2.0	10.5	32.4	57.1
Porterville city	504	20.1	38.6	13 716	70.5	20.5	1.3	3.0	2.1	12.5	36.5	51.0
Poway city	910	22.1	34.7	22 945	82.4	9.3	1.0	1.2	1.3	3.6	19.9	76.5
Rancho Cucamonga city	872	24.6	29.0	60 635	80.6	12.5	2.0	0.9	1.0	4.3	26.7	69.0
Rancho Palos Verdes city	1 496	22.5	29.7	18 175	83.7	7.4	1.0	0.4	0.7	1.2	21.8	77.1
Rancho Santa Margarita city	1 110	26.1	36.0	24 435	83.3	9.9	0.9	0.6	0.8	2.4	26.8	70.8
Redding city	576	21.3	38.6	33 223	80.3	10.9	1.3	1.2	2.4	8.6	38.2	53.2
Redlands city	689	18.5	32.3	29 334	77.4	12.9	1.4	1.6	3.8	7.1	36.6	56.3
Redondo Beach city	995	22.5	23.5	37 661	83.3	7.4	1.5	2.1	1.4	5.0	37.3	57.7
Redwood City city	1 105	25.0	31.2	39 189	73.9	12.7	4.8	2.8	2.8	7.2	34.2	58.7
Rialto city	631	27.0	40.6	31 542	72.7	20.1	2.4	1.1	1.3	8.7	32.7	58.7
Richmond city	764	23.5	34.2	41 745	59.3	19.6	14.5	1.9	1.9	12.9	39.7	47.4
Riverside city	670	19.8	38.2	104 326	72.1	18.0	2.2	1.8	3.0	9.0	34.1	56.9
Rocklin city	900	19.0	30.6	18 355	81.4	9.4	0.8	1.1	1.4	3.5	26.1	70.4
Rohnert Park city	903	24.7	35.6	22 119	77.9	12.0	3.4	1.7	2.3	6.4	31.5	62.1
Rosemead city	722	25.7	41.1	19 637	69.8	18.6	5.3	2.0	2.6	12.5	30.0	57.6
Roseville city	809	18.2	29.6	36 667	82.3	9.9	1.3	1.3	0.9	5.7	31.2	63.1
Sacramento city	625	20.9	34.6	166 419	71.0	16.3	4.6	2.4	2.8	12.9	42.0	45.1
Salinas city	725	23.4	31.6	52 912	67.8	23.4	2.8	2.0	2.1	8.3	33.4	58.3
San Bernardino city	563	22.8	41.5	60 601	69.3	20.2	3.4	1.8	2.6	15.2	38.1	46.7
San Bruno city	1 162	22.9	34.7	20 958	72.0	14.4	7.9	1.1	2.2	5.0	33.7	61.3
San Buenaventura (Ventura) city	841	20.0	32.2	48 873	79.2	11.2	1.4	1.5	2.6	7.1	34.2	58.8
San Carlos city	1 181	22.1	28.6	14 887	82.6	6.2	3.7	1.3	1.4	5.1	28.3	66.6
San Clemente city	916	25.5	31.0	24 620	79.1	11.2	1.5	1.1	1.9	3.7	30.5	65.8
San Diego city	763	22.8	34.4	580 318	74.0	12.2	4.2	2.0	3.6	9.5	37.7	52.9
San Dimas city	876	22.5	25.5	16 647	79.0	12.7	1.8	1.1	2.1	5.6	27.9	66.4
San Francisco city	928	22.9	28.2	418 553	40.5	10.8	31.1	3.6	9.4	28.6	42.0	29.4
San Gabriel city	759	24.3	34.2	16 355	72.7	15.8	3.9	1.5	3.4	8.1	35.2	56.7
San Jose city	1 123	21.8	32.3	427 984	76.4	14.1	4.1	1.5	1.4	6.1	27.0	66.9
San Juan Capistrano city	1 006	26.6	32.7	14 581	76.2	12.8	2.7	1.7	2.2	5.4	28.5	66.1
San Leandro city	873	20.0	29.0	36 928	70.3	13.1	10.2	2.1	1.9	9.3	35.4	55.3
San Luis Obispo city	724	20.7	53.5	21 684	69.0	10.4	2.9	4.9	8.2	7.5	37.7	54.8
San Marcos city	797	25.5	33.9	24 307	73.1	16.9	1.9	2.0	1.9	6.0	32.1	61.9
San Mateo city	1 168	24.0	30.9	47 247	75.3	11.0	6.2	1.4	2.6	7.1	36.7	56.1
San Pablo city	687	29.4	34.6	10 405	59.3	24.3	11.1	1.8	2.0	17.3	38.0	44.7
San Rafael city	1 040	22.7	37.3	28 460	63.8	11.8	12.4	2.3	3.2	7.4	39.2	53.4
San Ramon city	1 388	21.7	22.0	25 431	79.7	8.8	4.9	0.8	1.0	2.3	24.7	73.0
Santa Ana city	815	25.8	35.1	124 289	60.1	24.7	8.5	2.9	2.2	10.3	32.4	57.2
Santa Barbara city	936	28.9	39.8	46 866	66.0	13.6	4.5	4.1	6.2	9.5	40.9	49.6
Santa Clara city	1 238	18.2	27.5	54 676	78.3	11.4	2.9	1.9	3.2	6.1	36.6	57.3
Santa Clarita city	943	21.6	34.1	73 975	78.0	13.6	3.0	0.9	1.3	4.7	26.8	68.5
Santa Cruz city	941	26.9	41.2	28 971	60.9	12.6	7.3	5.4	8.1	9.2	35.8	54.9
Santa Maria city	675	22.3	37.5	29 874	65.8	28.0	0.7	2.5	1.6	8.6	35.5	55.9
Santa Monica city	792	26.0	30.1	45 933	75.4	6.1	4.1	2.0	4.4	10.7	52.4	36.9
Santa Paula city	689	21.4	35.8	10 973	64.4	28.8	0.8	1.5	2.8	8.8	33.0	58.1
Santa Rosa city	862	21.0	33.6	70 867	77.1	12.3	2.2	1.8	2.2	7.3	35.5	57.2
Santee city	833	19.6	28.9	26 506	82.6	10.2	1.7	1.4	0.8	4.6	29.0	66.3
Saratoga city	1 689	21.4	21.0	13 159	85.4	5.0	0.9	0.7	0.9	3.0	14.2	82.8
Seaside city	810	28.4	25.7	13 944	68.9	17.6	5.6	3.5	2.4	7.3	37.6	55.0
Simi Valley city	1 058	22.7	27.1	56 074	79.6	12.9	1.4	1.3	1.0	3.0	21.6	75.4
South Gate city	620	33.5	34.5	31 333	64.5	21.8	8.0	1.5	2.7	12.8	34.2	53.0
South San Francisco city	1 057	21.9	31.4	29 049	68.2	16.9	9.2	1.3	2.6	8.1	29.9	61.9
Stanton city	793	28.0	41.9	14 356	67.1	19.4	5.2	4.1	2.2	11.0	37.9	51.1
Stockton city	581	21.5	39.6	86 780	73.6	18.0	1.9	1.9	2.2	12.9	35.7	51.5
Suisun City city	870	20.7	30.9	11 905	74.5	18.2	2.6	1.4	1.0	4.7	22.7	72.7
Sunnyvale city	1 270	18.9	23.8	71 736	80.1	10.4	3.8	1.5	1.5	5.4	37.1	57.5
Temecula city	846	25.3	32.3	25 359	78.8	14.2	0.4	1.4	1.1	3.9	25.9	70.2
Temple City city	800	24.6	31.4	14 804	81.0	10.9	2.7	0.7	1.1	4.6	33.3	62.1
Thousand Oaks city	1 131	23.6	32.3	58 284	80.6	9.5	0.7	1.1	2.1	3.6	25.0	71.4
Torrance city	903	23.0	29.6	66 569	82.9	9.8	1.3	1.2	1.3	6.0	35.2	58.8
Tracy city	807	22.8	28.2	24 974	72.5	18.9	2.1	1.7	1.6	5.3	23.3	71.4
Tulare city	541	19.5	31.1	15 407	78.6	14.2	1.1	1.8	1.5	10.5	33.8	55.7
Turlock city	590	19.7	36.5	21 764	79.4	12.5	0.7	1.7	3.0	9.5	34.9	55.7
Tustin city	925	19.2	30.3	34 325	78.2	13.2	2.9	1.1	1.4	4.8	36.7	58.5
Union City city	1 094	21.8	29.1	30 457	73.0	16.1	6.3	1.4	1.3	5.1	21.8	73.1

Table C-5. Cities — **Migration, Housing, and Transportation**

STATE Place code	City	Total population 5 years and over	Residence in 1995 (percent)					Occupied housing units		Householders 65 years and over	
			Same house	Same county, different house	Same state, different county	Different state	Outside the United States	Number	Percent owner-occupied	Number	Percent owner-occupied
		1	2	3	4	5	6	7	8	9	10
	CALIFORNIA—Cont'd										
06 81344	Upland city	63 734	49.0	28.0	15.6	4.0	3.4	24 557	58.9	4 496	79.4
06 81554	Vacaville city	82 548	44.7	27.8	17.5	5.8	4.2	28 111	66.7	4 422	78.3
06 81666	Vallejo city	108 361	54.1	22.5	17.0	3.0	3.4	39 560	63.3	7 633	74.5
06 82590	Victorville city	58 878	47.7	34.7	11.9	4.5	1.1	21 040	64.9	4 759	76.4
06 82954	Visalia city	83 997	47.7	37.8	9.7	3.5	1.3	30 941	62.8	6 251	78.9
06 82996	Vista city	82 347	42.6	39.3	6.5	7.7	3.9	28 993	53.9	5 412	79.7
06 83332	Walnut city	28 606	66.1	22.2	4.3	1.6	5.8	8 260	88.9	766	93.1
06 83346	Walnut Creek city	61 582	52.7	21.9	13.6	7.3	4.5	30 340	68.1	10 954	84.9
06 83668	Watsonville city	40 439	49.8	36.2	5.2	1.3	7.5	11 443	48.0	2 260	71.4
06 84200	West Covina city	96 998	55.8	34.2	4.5	1.8	3.7	31 399	66.6	5 936	77.7
06 84410	West Hollywood city	35 158	44.8	29.3	4.7	13.8	7.4	23 120	21.6	4 410	25.5
06 84550	Westminster city	81 596	53.0	33.0	7.0	2.2	4.8	26 373	60.3	5 459	73.4
06 84816	West Sacramento city	29 185	48.6	23.7	16.7	3.1	7.8	11 396	54.6	2 677	70.4
06 85292	Whittier city	77 328	55.9	34.8	5.3	1.9	2.1	28 333	57.8	6 605	75.4
06 86328	Woodland city	45 201	46.0	33.5	12.5	3.7	4.2	16 727	58.4	3 274	72.7
06 86832	Yorba Linda city	55 208	60.6	23.9	10.1	4.1	1.4	19 226	84.7	2 667	85.2
06 86972	Yuba City city	33 778	41.6	30.4	18.5	5.0	4.5	13 274	47.3	2 537	72.3
06 87042	Yucaipa city	38 597	49.1	33.7	11.5	4.7	1.0	15 193	74.1	4 217	87.3
08 00000	COLORADO	4 006 285	44.1	23.0	13.5	16.1	3.4	1 658 238	67.3	272 491	78.3
08 03455	Arvada city	95 907	53.4	22.8	12.3	10.0	1.6	38 914	75.5	7 255	77.7
08 04000	Aurora city	253 989	40.1	20.1	17.2	16.9	5.8	105 500	63.9	13 269	77.8
08 07850	Boulder city	90 783	33.6	21.5	11.7	26.9	6.2	39 639	49.4	5 113	71.2
08 09280	Broomfield city	35 367	42.9	18.2	21.4	15.6	2.0	13 858	76.6	1 694	82.8
08 16000	Colorado Springs city	333 904	40.1	28.1	4.6	23.1	4.1	141 672	60.8	22 657	75.5
08 20000	Denver city	517 349	42.7	24.3	12.5	13.9	6.6	239 235	52.5	43 704	68.0
08 24785	Englewood city	29 079	44.9	18.0	21.2	13.1	2.9	14 340	52.3	2 682	71.3
08 27425	Fort Collins city	111 340	33.5	26.3	15.3	22.3	2.6	45 828	57.1	5 741	75.5
08 31660	Grand Junction city	39 775	41.6	29.8	11.2	16.2	1.3	17 957	63.0	4 893	72.2
08 32155	Greeley city	71 043	37.2	32.0	14.9	12.8	3.2	27 642	58.5	5 104	71.7
08 43000	Lakewood city	135 404	48.4	21.3	15.8	12.2	2.4	60 577	60.8	11 054	77.4
08 45255	Littleton city	38 212	47.6	20.0	17.4	13.1	1.9	17 389	62.0	3 747	69.2
08 45970	Longmont city	65 757	40.7	29.7	8.5	17.5	3.6	26 725	65.5	4 173	73.7
08 46465	Loveland city	47 109	45.2	29.0	9.6	15.2	1.0	19 728	69.5	4 082	76.9
08 54330	Northglenn city	29 285	48.9	22.2	15.0	11.2	2.7	11 693	67.9	2 089	82.9
08 62000	Pueblo city	95 537	53.9	30.4	7.2	7.5	1.0	40 412	65.6	11 529	78.5
08 77290	Thornton city	75 441	41.2	27.8	17.4	11.8	1.9	28 834	77.9	2 910	79.1
08 83835	Westminster city	94 044	43.1	21.0	18.3	14.7	2.0	38 418	70.1	4 201	74.6
08 84440	Wheat Ridge city	30 026	40.0	23.6	15.2	8.9	2.5	14 591	54.6	4 198	62.9
09 00000	CONNECTICUT	3 184 514	58.2	25.1	5.3	8.2	3.3	1 301 670	66.8	296 565	74.1
09 08000	Bridgeport city	128 328	50.2	34.5	1.9	6.3	7.2	50 307	43.3	10 902	59.2
09 08420	Bristol city	56 303	56.8	30.6	6.2	4.9	1.5	24 886	62.0	5 949	68.0
09 18430	Danbury city	69 942	49.7	26.9	2.6	11.3	9.4	27 183	58.3	4 839	71.1
09 37000	Hartford city	111 380	45.5	37.9	2.3	6.1	8.2	44 986	24.6	8 014	42.4
09 46450	Meriden city	54 273	57.4	29.6	5.4	4.6	3.0	22 951	59.8	5 194	70.4
09 47290	Middletown city	40 363	49.5	23.7	13.0	11.4	2.4	18 554	51.3	3 672	59.4
09 47500	Milford city	49 254	63.9	20.1	8.9	5.5	1.6	20 900	77.3	5 059	81.5
09 49880	Naugatuck borough	28 850	61.1	25.7	6.7	4.0	2.5	11 829	66.5	2 478	69.7
09 50370	New Britain city	67 095	51.0	31.8	4.5	5.6	7.1	28 558	42.7	6 988	66.7
09 52000	New Haven city	115 106	44.1	32.1	3.1	13.9	6.8	47 094	29.6	8 861	42.1
09 52280	New London city	23 964	40.5	30.5	4.6	19.1	5.3	10 181	37.9	2 299	59.4
09 55990	Norwalk city	77 456	56.7	27.2	1.6	9.2	5.3	32 711	62.0	7 060	77.4
09 56200	Norwich city	33 986	51.4	32.0	5.8	8.7	2.1	15 091	52.5	3 768	61.1
09 68100	Shelton city	35 749	65.1	23.3	5.3	4.8	1.5	14 190	81.6	3 014	84.1
09 73000	Stamford city	109 214	53.6	25.2	1.3	11.6	8.3	45 399	56.6	9 800	70.2
09 76500	Torrington city	33 109	61.0	28.8	4.4	4.5	1.3	14 743	64.6	3 910	69.0
09 80000	Waterbury city	99 037	52.5	32.1	5.1	5.6	4.8	42 622	47.6	10 123	59.6
09 82800	West Haven city	49 163	57.3	29.4	3.5	5.9	3.9	21 090	55.1	4 821	71.3
10 00000	DELAWARE	732 378	56.0	25.5	2.3	13.9	2.4	298 736	72.3	67 355	82.7
10 21200	Dover city	30 269	48.6	27.1	4.6	17.0	2.7	12 513	52.7	2 833	65.0
10 50670	Newark city	27 689	39.9	21.3	2.5	31.7	4.6	8 989	54.7	1 627	68.0
10 77580	Wilmington city	67 767	51.4	35.6	1.5	9.4	2.1	28 617	50.1	6 619	63.3
11 00000	DISTRICT OF COLUMBIA	539 658	49.9	23.5	X	20.9	5.6	248 338	40.8	50 335	58.4
11 50000	Washington city	539 658	49.9	23.5	X	20.9	5.6	248 338	40.8	50 335	58.4

Table C-5. Cities — Migration, Housing, and Transportation

City	Owner-occupied by household type (percent)								Median household income			Median housing value (owner estimated)	Median monthly owner costs as a percent of income	
	Family households					Nonfamily households								
		Married-couple family		Other family										
	Total family households	Total	With own children under 18 years	Total	With own children under 18 years	Total nonfamily households	Two or more adults	Living alone	All households	Owner-occupied households	Renter-occupied households		With a mortgage	Without a mortgage
	11	12	13	14	15	16	17	18	19	20	21	22	23	24
CALIFORNIA—Cont'd														
Upland city	65.0	74.8	66.5	35.4	26.4	42.4	31.1	45.5	48 669	67 494	28 586	203 100	24.5	9.9
Vacaville city	71.7	78.7	73.9	47.1	40.0	51.4	41.3	54.5	57 541	67 164	40 380	176 000	24.4	9.9
Vallejo city	67.3	76.0	72.3	46.7	32.9	53.1	51.6	53.5	50 095	61 555	33 500	162 600	24.7	9.9
Victorville city	67.5	75.8	69.2	47.8	39.9	56.5	47.1	58.5	36 204	43 455	22 725	95 600	24.9	13.0
Visalia city	66.8	76.3	68.3	38.2	27.3	51.2	35.8	54.6	41 092	51 096	25 903	112 200	23.6	9.9
Vista city	57.7	65.0	56.8	36.4	26.0	44.0	31.6	48.4	42 757	56 127	32 204	188 700	25.7	9.9
Walnut city	89.9	91.0	90.1	84.1	86.6	75.5	45.1	85.3	81 309	85 133	50 341	280 300	26.9	9.9
Walnut Creek city	76.5	80.7	75.1	53.0	43.2	57.9	40.9	61.2	63 656	72 565	50 439	337 700	23.6	9.9
Watsonville city	46.8	54.9	47.1	26.6	14.5	52.0	45.7	53.5	37 394	52 186	29 150	207 300	28.6	9.9
West Covina city	68.9	74.7	69.5	51.3	38.1	56.9	47.8	59.8	53 140	64 405	35 605	188 400	26.2	9.9
West Hollywood city	21.8	21.9	26.2	21.4	18.4	21.5	24.0	20.8	38 848	64 554	34 345	263 400	32.9	12.1
Westminster city	61.5	65.4	54.4	48.7	33.0	56.0	48.2	58.6	49 299	63 263	32 258	215 900	24.7	9.9
West Sacramento city	56.9	63.4	51.4	42.3	26.7	50.0	46.5	50.8	31 625	42 130	21 055	99 900	24.3	10.4
Whittier city	62.8	71.9	64.9	38.4	24.9	44.3	32.1	46.8	49 033	66 482	34 623	209 800	25.2	9.9
Woodland city	62.2	69.7	61.7	37.1	29.4	47.7	38.0	50.0	44 217	56 490	29 069	149 500	25.1	9.9
Yorba Linda city	86.7	89.5	88.5	66.5	59.1	74.1	63.6	77.1	89 013	96 974	52 194	340 600	24.9	9.9
Yuba City city	52.8	63.1	53.7	26.7	17.0	36.0	26.6	37.8	32 364	46 927	24 025	112 300	24.8	9.9
Yucaipa city	75.9	82.5	74.5	51.8	42.7	70.0	63.9	71.1	38 851	45 966	26 722	116 400	23.5	9.9
COLORADO	76.3	82.0	78.4	53.7	46.5	50.2	40.5	53.2	47 009	57 099	30 335	160 100	22.6	9.9
Arvada city	82.3	87.2	84.2	60.6	52.1	58.6	53.5	59.9	55 184	62 907	32 988	173 200	21.9	9.9
Aurora city	68.9	75.9	71.6	50.4	43.3	54.5	48.1	56.2	46 117	55 312	31 833	139 700	22.6	9.9
Boulder city	69.6	76.0	76.0	46.4	45.8	34.4	21.3	43.5	44 839	71 063	29 859	272 200	22.3	9.9
Broomfield city	82.5	86.0	84.5	63.4	61.3	59.1	51.6	61.6	63 707	70 605	38 992	182 200	22.1	9.9
Colorado Springs city	69.7	76.1	71.9	45.9	38.2	43.5	33.4	46.1	44 833	56 300	29 981	143 300	22.5	9.9
Denver city	64.2	72.7	67.0	44.4	34.3	40.8	36.5	42.0	39 317	52 589	28 022	160 100	23.2	9.9
Englewood city	63.6	70.6	62.7	46.2	35.8	40.2	35.2	41.5	39 315	49 445	31 535	143 300	23.7	9.9
Fort Collins city	73.1	78.4	78.0	50.5	45.4	36.4	21.2	46.6	44 415	61 532	26 977	164 000	22.1	9.9
Grand Junction city	73.7	80.8	77.0	48.1	38.4	47.3	36.2	49.7	32 998	43 254	20 635	114 000	22.5	9.9
Greeley city	70.3	77.7	73.6	43.8	39.9	37.1	17.4	44.5	36 277	50 009	21 899	129 600	23.1	9.9
Lakewood city	69.6	77.7	72.4	43.5	33.6	47.4	36.6	50.5	47 836	59 057	35 302	169 000	22.0	9.9
Littleton city	73.9	80.8	75.0	46.5	41.5	44.4	43.9	44.5	50 254	65 117	31 333	183 800	21.3	9.9
Longmont city	72.4	78.6	74.1	48.4	44.2	49.6	48.1	50.0	50 826	61 254	32 291	173 800	23.2	9.9
Loveland city	76.4	82.0	78.0	49.8	44.1	52.4	49.2	53.1	46 975	55 235	29 548	154 500	22.9	9.9
Northglenn city	77.3	82.1	75.7	61.0	53.6	44.4	42.9	44.8	47 971	55 541	33 581	146 800	23.9	9.9
Pueblo city	71.7	81.8	74.0	49.7	36.0	54.1	42.4	56.0	29 584	36 474	18 155	85 800	22.0	9.9
Thornton city	83.0	88.7	86.6	62.2	55.4	63.0	55.1	65.8	53 837	59 994	36 951	152 100	23.5	10.2
Westminster city	77.6	82.5	82.0	58.4	53.0	54.1	43.4	57.7	56 429	63 870	41 040	165 600	22.4	9.9
Wheat Ridge city	63.0	70.0	62.4	43.5	35.1	43.1	40.5	43.6	38 462	49 593	29 194	165 000	23.8	9.9
CONNECTICUT	75.4	83.4	81.7	48.4	35.0	48.7	42.2	50.1	53 736	67 350	31 318	160 600	22.4	13.1
Bridgeport city	46.5	59.5	52.0	30.8	20.0	37.2	24.3	39.6	34 212	48 106	25 374	107 700	25.0	16.8
Bristol city	72.0	80.0	77.5	47.2	34.1	43.3	41.8	43.6	46 802	59 434	30 781	123 700	22.0	13.0
Danbury city	65.5	71.7	67.4	43.3	26.4	44.0	32.4	47.3	53 523	66 186	38 495	174 600	22.9	13.4
Hartford city	28.6	43.9	35.6	18.2	11.7	18.3	16.3	18.7	24 747	43 025	20 211	95 300	24.6	14.6
Meriden city	67.6	79.5	76.5	38.4	25.5	45.1	43.0	45.5	42 219	55 348	25 744	114 700	22.0	14.1
Middletown city	64.9	73.2	72.8	39.9	25.0	33.7	31.2	34.4	47 067	62 815	35 535	134 400	21.8	12.6
Milford city	85.6	89.0	88.1	70.7	61.1	60.3	51.2	62.4	60 977	67 109	44 063	166 000	22.9	14.4
Naugatuck borough	75.5	82.0	80.9	54.5	40.6	45.2	39.7	46.3	50 807	59 225	32 472	128 200	22.7	11.1
New Britain city	50.4	63.6	55.4	28.7	16.3	31.4	17.6	34.4	34 415	49 027	26 580	97 600	22.7	16.1
New Haven city	36.0	50.6	44.5	20.6	12.0	21.5	20.1	21.8	29 445	54 514	21 811	104 300	24.0	13.9
New London city	45.7	54.5	48.0	26.1	16.6	29.2	28.2	29.4	33 456	48 070	26 089	101 500	24.0	14.2
Norwalk city	68.6	76.6	72.5	45.1	32.1	50.0	45.5	51.2	58 776	74 163	37 495	249 300	24.5	13.2
Norwich city	63.3	74.7	70.2	39.9	28.5	36.0	25.6	38.5	38 636	52 263	25 923	106 200	22.5	13.7
Shelton city	87.7	90.9	90.6	69.6	51.4	64.0	61.8	64.4	68 362	73 937	45 833	209 100	22.2	12.8
Stamford city	65.4	72.7	70.2	43.5	33.4	41.0	28.8	44.1	60 165	77 668	43 412	306 700	25.1	16.2
Torrington city	74.4	81.9	79.6	48.5	37.5	48.8	37.0	51.0	41 728	53 649	27 590	112 100	23.3	15.5
Waterbury city	54.6	68.9	61.7	30.5	18.4	35.7	31.8	36.3	34 089	50 277	23 119	97 800	23.2	13.3
West Haven city	62.8	72.6	68.6	41.8	26.4	42.4	36.7	43.6	41 726	55 690	30 540	117 000	24.2	18.6
DELAWARE	78.9	86.2	82.9	56.2	45.0	57.9	47.1	60.6	47 012	54 951	30 429	122 000	20.8	9.9
Dover city	61.8	76.6	70.3	34.3	24.8	39.3	30.8	41.4	37 866	52 177	24 748	107 700	21.6	9.9
Newark city	79.9	84.7	82.9	56.9	51.8	28.2	14.6	38.8	47 759	76 269	23 006	151 800	18.7	9.9
Wilmington city	56.2	71.5	66.1	41.4	27.1	42.6	35.5	44.0	34 345	48 052	25 179	89 300	20.9	11.4
DISTRICT OF COLUMBIA	49.8	64.1	58.1	35.8	21.7	32.9	30.9	33.4	39 827	65 288	28 754	153 500	22.2	9.9
Washington city	49.8	64.1	58.1	35.8	21.7	32.9	30.9	33.4	39 827	65 288	28 754	153 500	22.2	9.9

Table C-5. Cities — Migration, Housing, and Transportation

City	Median gross rent	Percent who pay 35 percent or more of income for housing expenses		Number of workers 16 years and over	Means of transportation to work (percent except where noted)					Vehicles available (percent of households)		
		Owners	Renters		Car, truck, or van					No vehicles	One vehicle	Two or more vehicles
					Drove alone	Carpooled	Public transportation	Other means	Walked			
	25	26	27	28	29	30	31	32	33	34	35	36
CALIFORNIA—Cont'd												
Upland city	710	20.8	37.9	31 569	77.2	13.6	2.5	1.3	2.2	6.4	35.6	58.0
Vacaville city	842	20.2	29.9	38 374	78.8	14.5	0.7	1.9	1.8	5.3	28.4	66.3
Vallejo city	781	21.8	33.9	50 230	66.6	22.9	5.0	1.3	1.2	9.2	31.3	59.4
Victorville city	584	23.5	38.4	22 025	74.5	18.6	1.1	1.4	1.3	9.4	35.6	55.0
Visalia city	578	18.4	34.6	37 766	79.4	12.4	1.2	2.1	1.5	8.8	34.6	56.6
Vista city	788	23.6	36.3	38 533	73.4	16.7	3.3	1.8	1.7	7.0	35.9	57.1
Walnut city	1 223	28.5	37.2	13 883	76.4	17.6	2.0	0.9	0.4	1.9	11.9	86.2
Walnut Creek city	1 024	19.6	28.8	29 901	69.4	7.7	13.8	1.3	2.0	7.5	42.9	49.6
Watsonville city	742	26.7	34.6	16 604	60.7	25.4	2.9	4.0	5.4	10.3	35.0	54.7
West Covina city	828	24.7	32.8	43 974	75.9	16.0	4.3	1.0	1.1	6.5	26.4	67.1
West Hollywood city	773	39.6	33.8	21 638	74.9	6.1	5.4	1.2	5.5	17.1	57.3	25.6
Westminster city	842	22.5	40.2	37 148	77.4	15.6	2.0	1.3	1.3	7.7	29.6	62.7
West Sacramento city	525	19.9	38.3	11 607	70.9	19.9	2.7	1.9	2.1	14.8	37.4	47.8
Whittier city	723	22.7	30.5	35 596	80.0	12.5	2.5	0.9	2.0	8.3	32.4	59.2
Woodland city	655	20.2	34.0	21 152	74.4	16.3	1.1	2.8	2.4	8.0	33.8	58.2
Yorba Linda city	1 191	22.9	32.6	29 743	83.8	8.8	0.5	0.7	0.8	2.2	17.1	80.7
Yuba City city	496	21.8	32.2	14 042	75.8	17.8	0.7	1.5	2.0	11.2	39.6	49.2
Yucaipa city	610	16.3	37.1	17 036	78.1	15.6	0.7	0.8	1.7	8.4	35.2	56.4
COLORADO	671	16.6	30.4	2 191 626	75.1	12.2	3.2	1.5	3.0	6.4	31.6	62.0
Arvada city	714	15.1	29.0	53 713	82.1	8.5	3.3	0.7	0.9	5.3	26.8	67.9
Aurora city	700	16.3	29.9	142 136	76.7	13.9	4.2	0.8	1.4	7.0	37.5	55.5
Boulder city	818	16.5	44.0	53 828	59.8	8.7	8.3	7.6	9.0	8.7	40.8	50.6
Broomfield city	856	14.4	25.3	20 299	80.5	9.8	3.7	1.1	1.1	3.0	24.3	72.8
Colorado Springs city	652	15.8	30.4	183 806	79.6	11.7	1.2	1.3	2.5	6.3	34.8	58.9
Denver city	631	19.2	30.6	278 715	68.3	13.5	8.4	1.8	4.3	13.9	43.1	43.0
Englewood city	675	18.7	28.7	17 064	75.0	12.6	4.7	1.6	3.2	10.1	40.6	49.3
Fort Collins city	689	14.5	39.0	64 531	76.3	10.2	1.5	5.0	3.6	5.1	32.2	62.7
Grand Junction city	496	14.6	36.6	19 573	75.5	11.9	0.9	3.2	4.1	8.5	36.6	54.9
Greeley city	548	17.2	35.4	35 734	78.5	12.4	0.4	2.1	3.9	8.0	33.0	59.0
Lakewood city	763	14.3	29.3	77 680	77.9	11.7	4.1	0.8	1.5	5.5	36.0	58.4
Littleton city	709	14.0	30.8	21 512	79.4	9.5	3.2	0.8	1.8	7.0	37.8	55.3
Longmont city	769	18.5	31.6	36 789	77.1	13.4	2.1	1.4	1.6	5.4	31.1	63.5
Loveland city	636	14.7	26.8	25 812	82.5	10.8	0.1	1.0	1.6	4.6	30.0	65.5
Northglenn city	692	17.6	24.1	16 382	77.0	12.7	5.0	0.7	1.8	5.2	28.8	66.0
Pueblo city	475	16.1	36.8	40 401	79.1	13.8	0.9	1.3	2.3	11.6	35.9	52.4
Thornton city	802	17.7	29.5	43 499	79.0	12.5	3.9	0.9	0.8	3.4	26.9	69.7
Westminster city	848	14.2	25.7	56 951	79.6	10.7	4.1	0.7	1.0	4.0	29.8	66.2
Wheat Ridge city	651	15.5	31.2	16 183	76.2	11.8	4.7	1.1	2.1	6.6	42.1	51.3
CONNECTICUT	681	17.1	29.0	1 640 823	80.0	9.4	4.0	0.7	2.7	9.6	33.1	57.3
Bridgeport city	671	25.0	35.9	55 272	66.4	18.7	8.4	1.4	3.6	23.8	41.9	34.3
Bristol city	594	15.0	23.1	30 798	85.9	9.8	0.6	0.5	1.8	7.0	36.6	56.4
Danbury city	818	18.1	25.5	39 448	75.9	14.4	3.8	1.1	1.9	7.8	34.0	58.2
Hartford city	560	24.2	37.4	41 009	56.3	16.5	18.6	1.2	5.8	36.1	42.0	21.9
Meriden city	618	16.8	30.7	27 345	83.4	10.4	1.2	0.6	2.5	12.1	37.7	50.3
Middletown city	665	15.7	22.5	22 118	84.2	8.4	1.7	0.5	3.5	10.3	40.2	49.6
Milford city	860	17.2	23.7	27 767	86.0	6.9	3.3	0.4	1.1	5.6	32.8	61.6
Naugatuck borough	631	15.4	22.3	15 263	87.7	9.1	0.5	0.4	1.2	6.4	34.3	59.3
New Britain city	574	17.1	29.9	31 071	77.2	12.2	3.5	1.3	4.6	16.3	43.9	39.8
New Haven city	651	21.7	37.9	47 857	55.7	15.0	11.1	1.9	13.6	29.7	44.2	26.1
New London city	592	19.3	28.8	12 201	66.8	12.2	3.1	2.3	12.0	19.3	45.3	35.5
Norwalk city	875	21.8	30.7	44 061	74.2	10.9	8.5	0.6	2.1	8.7	36.4	54.9
Norwich city	588	17.9	28.5	17 483	78.9	12.4	3.5	0.8	2.9	12.8	39.7	47.5
Shelton city	790	15.4	24.4	20 043	87.1	7.4	1.5	0.3	0.9	3.8	26.9	69.2
Stamford city	1 007	29.6	31.2	59 868	70.1	10.6	10.7	1.0	3.7	10.4	38.1	51.5
Torrington city	591	20.5	28.1	17 220	82.5	11.1	0.7	1.1	2.7	10.3	36.5	53.2
Waterbury city	562	17.9	30.5	44 256	77.5	13.9	3.6	1.0	2.7	19.5	41.7	38.8
West Haven city	689	23.1	33.6	26 166	79.4	11.6	4.8	0.6	2.4	13.1	42.2	44.7
DELAWARE	639	13.8	26.7	373 070	79.2	11.5	2.8	1.0	2.6	8.0	34.1	57.9
Dover city	599	15.7	31.3	14 675	76.8	13.0	1.0	1.5	4.9	11.4	41.1	47.4
Newark city	681	11.3	41.3	14 015	69.5	8.5	4.0	2.7	13.0	7.8	33.3	58.9
Wilmington city	596	18.9	30.7	29 690	62.4	14.5	12.0	1.0	7.6	26.8	44.1	29.1
DISTRICT OF COLUMBIA	618	18.6	28.2	260 884	38.4	11.0	33.2	1.9	11.8	36.9	43.5	19.5
Washington city	618	18.6	28.2	260 884	38.4	11.0	33.2	1.9	11.8	36.9	43.5	19.5

Table C-5. Cities — **Migration, Housing, and Transportation**

STATE Place code	City	Total population 5 years and over	Residence in 1995 (percent)					Occupied housing units		Householders 65 years and over	
			Same house	Same county, different house	Same state, different county	Different state	Outside the United States	Number	Percent owner-occupied	Number	Percent owner-occupied
		1	2	3	4	5	6	7	8	9	10
12 00000	FLORIDA..................	15 043 603	48.9	25.7	8.7	12.4	4.3	6 337 929	70.1	1 789 594	84.0
12 00950	Altamonte Springs city ..	38 933	34.7	18.6	23.9	18.3	4.5	19 006	41.6	3 003	64.2
12 01700	Apopka city.................	23 799	42.8	28.4	14.0	10.0	4.7	9 503	75.0	1 556	89.3
12 02681	Aventura city...............	24 371	47.5	23.4	6.0	11.1	11.9	14 000	71.8	6 134	86.4
12 07300	Boca Raton city............	72 160	49.7	21.3	8.9	14.0	6.1	31 989	75.7	9 484	88.3
12 07525	Bonita Springs city........	31 568	45.1	15.6	9.5	23.9	5.9	14 904	81.7	6 543	93.2
12 07875	Boynton Beach city	56 466	49.1	27.0	7.7	12.6	3.7	26 008	72.8	10 096	86.6
12 07950	Bradenton city	46 843	49.0	27.6	7.3	13.4	2.6	21 492	62.0	8 217	75.3
12 10275	Cape Coral city	96 524	47.4	25.4	5.4	20.1	1.7	40 852	80.0	12 239	90.2
12 12875	Clearwater city.............	102 378	46.4	27.2	5.9	15.3	5.2	48 255	62.0	15 561	76.6
12 13275	Coconut Creek city........	40 601	46.4	26.8	8.2	14.0	4.7	20 076	75.5	7 710	91.4
12 14125	Cooper City city............	26 126	62.1	21.2	8.7	6.0	2.0	9 086	92.2	1 164	96.3
12 14250	Coral Gables city	40 123	49.0	28.0	4.3	10.9	7.8	16 734	66.1	4 411	77.9
12 14400	Coral Springs city.........	109 348	40.3	31.5	6.9	15.1	6.2	39 497	65.0	3 986	69.2
12 16475	Davie town...................	70 543	48.1	30.7	8.1	9.1	4.1	28 600	76.3	4 587	85.8
12 16525	Daytona Beach city	60 920	42.4	27.4	9.0	17.6	3.7	28 634	47.3	8 565	72.5
12 16725	Deerfield Beach city	61 593	49.8	23.1	8.4	11.5	7.2	31 412	70.3	13 162	84.7
12 17100	Delray Beach city	57 120	49.4	25.3	6.8	13.0	5.5	26 757	69.5	10 659	82.8
12 17200	Deltona city	65 422	53.5	17.5	13.0	13.6	2.4	24 906	87.2	6 742	94.9
12 18575	Dunedin city	34 545	51.2	27.0	6.2	13.3	2.3	17 386	71.8	7 073	78.8
12 24000	Fort Lauderdale city	144 317	47.3	30.7	5.5	10.5	6.0	68 448	55.4	16 668	78.5
12 24125	Fort Myers city	44 313	37.8	33.7	8.3	13.7	6.6	19 160	39.6	4 418	54.9
12 24300	Fort Pierce city	34 662	46.5	31.4	8.3	8.0	5.7	14 412	53.0	4 302	80.9
12 25175	Gainesville city	91 253	36.4	23.0	25.7	10.3	4.7	37 278	47.7	6 513	80.1
12 27322	Greenacres city............	25 648	42.0	34.9	4.7	13.6	4.8	12 166	70.4	4 353	87.3
12 28450	Hallandale city..............	33 236	51.7	17.1	12.3	11.4	7.5	18 110	66.0	9 156	80.8
12 30000	Hialeah city..................	213 195	49.7	32.6	1.2	2.6	13.9	70 763	50.8	19 505	56.0
12 32000	Hollywood city	131 121	47.9	25.1	10.9	9.8	6.3	59 628	62.2	16 117	77.6
12 32275	Homestead city	28 675	36.1	43.1	2.8	6.6	11.4	10 065	36.3	1 452	62.6
12 35000	Jacksonville city	682 120	48.9	29.8	6.5	12.1	2.6	284 492	63.2	50 655	77.6
12 35875	Jupiter town	37 231	49.0	24.2	6.4	17.9	2.5	16 943	80.8	4 881	88.0
12 36550	Key West city	24 342	39.3	22.9	8.1	23.7	6.1	11 017	45.6	2 096	69.0
12 36950	Kissimmee city	44 081	31.5	21.0	12.1	20.6	14.9	17 156	44.5	2 296	68.3
12 38250	Lakeland city	73 401	45.9	31.7	8.8	11.6	2.1	33 451	59.9	11 224	80.0
12 39075	Lake Worth city	32 834	44.7	31.2	4.2	8.8	11.0	13 854	52.3	3 378	76.3
12 39425	Largo city....................	66 479	47.2	28.4	5.8	15.8	2.8	34 015	67.8	13 565	83.5
12 39525	Lauderdale Lakes city ...	29 159	47.7	33.2	3.8	6.8	8.5	12 094	61.8	3 869	86.1
12 39550	Lauderhill city	52 898	45.0	32.2	5.5	9.2	8.1	22 723	59.5	6 246	82.0
12 43125	Margate city.................	50 824	52.3	28.4	4.2	10.6	4.5	22 714	80.0	8 103	88.4
12 43975	Melbourne city..............	67 604	46.1	27.8	6.9	16.0	3.2	30 796	62.0	8 681	74.7
12 45000	Miami city	341 205	49.3	34.3	1.4	3.8	11.2	134 359	34.9	38 439	45.0
12 45025	Miami Beach city	84 879	38.0	30.6	3.2	12.2	16.0	46 220	36.6	12 460	49.3
12 45975	Miramar city.................	66 256	42.4	15.2	27.3	8.1	7.0	23 058	80.4	2 550	84.9
12 49425	North Lauderdale city....	29 672	44.6	31.5	4.4	10.5	9.0	10 818	64.1	1 447	86.2
12 49450	North Miami city	55 175	48.9	33.8	3.0	4.8	9.4	20 520	50.2	2 930	76.1
12 49475	North Miami Beach city .	37 945	51.1	31.6	2.2	5.4	9.8	13 989	62.1	2 722	82.3
12 50575	Oakland Park city..........	29 199	40.0	34.3	4.3	10.8	10.5	13 565	50.7	2 010	74.8
12 50750	Ocala city	42 881	43.2	32.2	12.1	10.9	1.7	18 804	56.8	5 795	73.6
12 53000	Orlando city	173 822	36.2	29.7	11.7	15.3	7.1	81 020	40.8	14 175	64.9
12 53150	Ormond Beach city	34 840	55.2	22.9	7.0	14.0	0.9	15 695	81.4	6 047	87.8
12 53575	Oviedo city	24 800	43.5	18.0	17.7	16.5	4.3	8 650	85.7	785	92.0
12 54000	Palm Bay city...............	74 522	52.0	26.3	5.3	14.4	2.0	30 352	75.4	7 519	89.7
12 54075	Palm Beach Gardens city	32 992	48.4	28.7	5.6	14.5	2.8	15 408	78.9	4 664	86.3
12 54200	Palm Coast city	31 950	45.3	15.3	11.4	26.7	1.2	13 850	86.4	6 169	93.2
12 54700	Panama City city	34 296	50.0	26.8	6.7	15.0	1.4	14 797	57.7	3 698	74.0
12 55775	Pembroke Pines city	127 545	42.3	20.3	19.1	11.9	6.3	51 981	80.1	13 540	89.0
12 55925	Pensacola city..............	52 958	54.1	25.5	5.9	13.0	1.5	24 441	63.5	6 817	82.5
12 56975	Pinellas Park city..........	42 700	52.3	30.6	4.4	9.8	3.0	19 464	74.7	5 796	90.6
12 57425	Plantation city..............	78 377	48.6	29.1	6.7	10.6	5.0	33 345	71.5	6 834	83.1
12 57550	Plant City city	27 604	44.6	33.0	9.3	9.8	3.3	10 945	65.9	2 391	82.5
12 58050	Pompano Beach city	74 297	49.4	29.1	5.3	9.8	6.4	35 174	62.5	12 574	77.5
12 58575	Port Orange city	43 306	52.2	26.6	4.7	15.5	1.0	19 430	82.0	6 580	90.5
12 58715	Port St. Lucie city.........	83 567	50.9	19.7	13.3	14.7	1.5	33 902	82.9	10 153	93.2
12 60975	Riviera Beach city	28 174	52.5	32.8	4.2	8.1	2.4	11 516	58.6	3 338	83.9
12 63000	St. Petersburg city........	233 943	49.5	30.0	6.3	11.4	2.8	109 519	63.6	28 582	77.8
12 63650	Sanford city.................	34 707	44.4	26.5	11.6	14.3	3.1	14 096	55.7	2 856	66.2
12 64175	Sarasota city	49 890	44.3	27.1	10.0	13.0	5.6	23 419	58.6	7 567	77.3
12 69700	Sunrise city..................	80 162	49.1	29.3	6.6	9.7	5.4	33 281	74.0	9 527	85.6
12 70600	Tallahassee city	142 852	33.2	24.8	25.3	13.5	3.1	63 174	43.9	7 856	78.6
12 70675	Tamarac city.................	53 597	50.5	29.2	5.5	10.7	4.1	27 420	80.0	13 483	92.4
12 71000	Tampa city...................	283 068	46.4	30.9	7.4	10.8	4.6	124 775	55.1	27 214	71.6
12 71900	Titusville city................	38 320	51.8	29.8	6.0	11.5	0.9	17 220	68.3	5 521	84.8

Table C-5. Cities — **Migration, Housing, and Transportation**

City	Owner-occupied by household type (percent)								Median household income			Median housing value (owner estimated)	Median monthly owner costs as a percent of income	
	Family households					Nonfamily households								
		Married-couple family		Other family										
	Total family households	Total	With own children under 18 years	Total	With own children under 18 years	Total nonfamily households	Two or more adults	Living alone	All households	Owner-occupied households	Renter-occupied households		With a mortgage	Without a mortgage
	11	12	13	14	15	16	17	18	19	20	21	22	23	24
FLORIDA	75.9	82.6	76.1	54.6	44.3	58.4	47.9	61.0	38 665	45 122	26 707	93 200	22.8	10.5
Altamonte Springs city	50.5	58.3	54.2	31.8	21.2	31.5	23.1	33.8	41 014	52 483	35 659	101 500	21.4	9.9
Apopka city	78.2	86.1	82.4	55.7	47.6	65.7	59.3	67.8	43 760	50 628	29 348	98 400	22.7	11.1
Aventura city	76.6	78.3	57.5	68.3	58.3	67.4	63.6	68.0	44 813	43 664	47 083	118 100	26.0	13.1
Boca Raton city	83.6	87.4	88.0	64.1	56.7	61.9	52.0	64.5	59 787	72 261	34 698	195 200	22.8	11.1
Bonita Springs city	85.2	88.6	67.0	59.4	53.2	73.8	59.9	77.6	46 080	49 400	36 907	131 600	23.4	9.9
Boynton Beach city	77.0	82.6	73.7	58.4	48.3	66.4	53.1	69.1	39 583	42 977	31 896	86 200	23.5	11.2
Bradenton city	68.0	77.6	70.5	42.4	32.5	52.8	40.0	55.3	34 606	41 280	25 606	90 300	21.8	9.9
Cape Coral city	82.8	86.7	78.9	65.2	55.2	71.6	62.9	74.2	43 532	46 460	32 629	106 500	23.6	11.7
Clearwater city	69.4	78.1	70.7	45.5	33.5	52.3	42.2	54.5	36 428	44 084	27 063	91 100	22.7	11.7
Coconut Creek city	80.7	83.2	79.9	67.3	60.9	67.8	48.7	71.9	43 494	44 892	40 100	88 600	24.0	12.4
Cooper City city	92.5	94.6	93.1	81.1	73.0	90.5	91.5	90.2	74 298	77 109	41 771	154 100	22.7	12.9
Coral Gables city	78.6	83.6	87.4	58.2	51.7	46.6	41.1	47.9	67 057	99 304	34 905	314 800	23.6	12.1
Coral Springs city	70.6	77.8	76.4	46.8	41.6	43.3	37.6	45.3	58 033	72 452	37 510	166 000	23.7	11.9
Davie town	81.8	88.0	87.8	63.9	57.5	64.1	55.5	67.5	47 146	54 804	29 257	107 100	23.6	11.0
Daytona Beach city	50.7	70.0	65.7	38.7	24.6	35.3	24.0	38.7	25 513	35 107	19 100	74 700	24.0	10.7
Deerfield Beach city	74.0	79.0	65.6	57.6	44.0	66.3	46.8	70.3	34 001	36 552	29 827	76 300	23.8	14.1
Delray Beach city	74.3	81.4	72.4	51.5	41.5	63.4	52.3	65.9	43 040	49 435	31 685	102 700	23.6	11.8
Deltona city	88.0	90.6	86.2	77.1	69.8	84.3	78.6	86.0	39 703	40 850	32 996	82 000	23.2	10.6
Dunedin city	81.4	87.0	85.2	60.2	51.6	59.7	58.8	59.9	34 325	41 366	22 265	86 900	22.8	11.0
Fort Lauderdale city	63.7	75.7	67.4	38.2	27.9	47.6	46.0	48.1	37 261	50 783	26 460	132 600	25.2	13.9
Fort Myers city	47.4	60.8	52.8	29.5	20.0	29.3	24.6	30.7	28 259	38 639	22 609	71 700	22.5	9.9
Fort Pierce city	55.1	68.7	54.4	32.5	19.0	49.7	36.6	52.8	25 273	34 397	17 023	57 000	23.7	12.7
Gainesville city	64.3	74.6	73.9	43.3	34.6	31.5	15.3	40.3	28 310	47 967	17 165	83 700	20.5	9.9
Greenacres city	71.3	77.1	65.0	56.1	47.1	68.8	49.7	73.5	36 650	38 131	33 768	72 400	23.3	10.8
Hallandale city	67.8	76.8	53.5	40.4	21.6	64.4	50.6	66.4	27 646	30 355	23 432	75 100	27.1	13.9
Hialeah city	54.0	58.7	49.7	42.2	31.6	36.9	43.5	35.1	29 234	39 093	20 762	102 300	29.0	14.4
Hollywood city	69.8	77.5	73.2	49.1	37.9	51.8	49.9	52.2	36 633	45 018	27 951	98 300	24.7	13.6
Homestead city	36.2	46.2	35.0	23.4	16.2	36.7	26.1	41.3	27 032	43 521	21 549	80 300	24.1	15.2
Jacksonville city	70.3	78.8	73.0	50.0	30.4	48.7	42.4	50.3	40 138	49 249	27 679	84 100	20.6	9.9
Jupiter town	83.8	86.9	83.8	67.0	64.2	74.4	69.8	75.6	54 730	50 662	40 417	140 700	22.8	10.8
Key West city	53.7	59.3	51.3	37.3	21.0	37.5	35.1	38.9	42 486	54 818	35 435	252 700	29.5	14.7
Kissimmee city	50.2	58.5	52.1	33.6	24.9	31.4	20.9	36.3	34 133	42 286	29 299	90 900	23.6	11.5
Lakeland city	67.9	77.6	66.4	42.7	30.3	47.8	36.4	50.0	32 699	39 254	25 607	71 500	20.9	9.9
Lake Worth city	55.8	64.4	52.1	38.2	30.5	47.9	38.8	50.5	29 502	37 213	23 914	75 300	23.8	13.4
Largo city	76.4	82.8	72.3	54.1	41.8	57.9	43.6	60.7	32 140	34 625	28 423	63 400	22.5	11.6
Lauderdale Lakes city	59.3	73.0	58.8	41.2	28.1	66.2	53.5	68.8	26 905	31 775	21 165	61 600	28.9	17.2
Lauderhill city	60.7	72.4	61.3	42.2	30.6	57.5	44.8	60.2	32 493	38 707	26 246	70 000	25.8	11.7
Margate city	82.6	86.8	83.5	67.5	57.3	75.6	60.5	78.6	38 399	40 129	33 439	82 300	24.2	12.8
Melbourne city	73.8	81.1	76.2	52.4	40.4	44.6	37.3	46.3	34 179	41 528	23 700	80 300	21.9	9.9
Miami city	38.8	45.8	35.7	28.3	15.5	28.4	29.3	28.2	23 084	39 388	17 422	116 400	30.6	15.9
Miami Beach city	44.0	52.9	45.8	24.0	17.6	31.7	27.0	32.7	27 176	46 374	21 588	138 700	28.6	16.5
Miramar city	82.9	87.7	86.8	71.4	66.6	69.2	66.5	70.0	50 279	54 940	31 905	112 600	26.7	12.9
North Lauderdale city	66.1	76.0	72.0	48.9	47.2	58.7	47.1	63.3	39 400	44 316	31 478	87 400	24.9	13.8
North Miami city	53.1	61.7	59.6	40.5	32.2	44.5	40.2	45.5	29 311	38 076	22 586	85 800	31.1	15.1
North Miami Beach city	63.0	71.2	66.8	48.8	42.7	59.9	57.4	60.5	31 325	37 367	23 186	86 900	29.2	13.2
Oakland Park city	54.6	65.8	60.4	36.5	25.4	46.4	45.6	46.7	34 799	43 676	27 190	92 300	25.1	13.6
Ocala city	63.4	73.4	69.2	42.8	30.4	46.8	37.7	48.5	30 890	38 821	22 827	71 700	20.5	11.5
Orlando city	49.4	59.1	51.4	32.9	22.7	31.2	25.3	33.2	35 623	46 924	30 041	97 400	22.4	11.5
Ormond Beach city	86.3	90.2	86.2	66.8	55.9	71.3	68.5	71.9	43 301	47 242	29 773	102 700	22.3	9.9
Oviedo city	88.6	91.4	90.5	73.0	68.3	69.8	58.5	76.0	63 744	67 441	41 988	132 200	21.5	9.9
Palm Bay city	79.3	84.2	77.9	63.2	53.9	65.1	51.7	68.9	36 240	39 637	27 782	76 200	22.2	9.9
Palm Beach Gardens city	83.7	88.4	83.7	60.7	51.4	69.6	62.8	71.1	58 822	67 240	38 528	145 600	22.1	10.1
Palm Coast city	87.0	89.3	81.4	69.1	55.5	84.3	66.0	88.1	41 855	43 069	36 111	110 500	23.9	9.9
Panama City city	66.0	75.2	67.8	43.5	30.1	44.6	26.0	48.5	31 674	41 221	21 741	75 200	20.6	10.5
Pembroke Pines city	83.1	86.2	83.6	70.2	63.4	72.8	57.3	76.1	52 698	57 013	41 543	122 700	23.8	12.0
Pensacola city	71.5	82.2	77.0	50.0	34.7	51.6	40.4	54.1	35 019	43 793	23 102	91 300	21.5	9.9
Pinellas Park city	78.4	83.9	74.4	62.0	55.0	68.4	54.0	71.8	35 007	37 065	29 395	69 300	22.2	13.0
Plantation city	77.9	83.1	79.5	59.6	53.2	58.3	50.0	60.6	53 375	62 080	39 094	138 700	23.3	11.5
Plant City city	70.2	78.3	71.2	49.2	38.8	54.6	34.4	58.8	37 173	45 579	25 573	82 400	21.3	12.4
Pompano Beach city	68.8	77.4	64.7	45.6	31.4	55.6	45.4	58.0	36 143	43 811	27 514	94 700	25.3	12.7
Port Orange city	86.4	89.6	82.4	73.3	64.4	72.8	66.3	74.5	38 568	40 623	28 914	87 100	22.0	10.9
Port St. Lucie city	83.7	87.3	80.7	66.9	58.9	80.4	74.7	82.2	40 629	42 078	33 462	87 700	23.1	11.6
Riviera Beach city	60.1	75.9	55.2	40.3	23.1	55.4	40.4	58.6	31 771	41 337	21 801	87 800	25.1	13.8
St. Petersburg city	73.1	81.3	76.9	55.0	42.4	51.4	51.5	51.4	34 676	42 011	25 324	78 200	22.5	12.1
Sanford city	62.3	70.4	64.0	47.5	35.4	43.7	38.0	45.5	30 954	39 877	23 677	72 800	22.9	10.3
Sarasota city	64.1	72.5	54.9	45.6	29.0	52.8	41.5	55.6	33 888	41 154	25 118	95 600	23.9	12.9
Sunrise city	78.4	83.7	80.8	63.8	58.1	65.2	51.8	68.0	40 825	43 213	34 289	94 100	24.7	14.3
Tallahassee city	62.5	74.2	72.0	40.7	34.6	27.4	13.3	35.0	30 440	53 116	19 352	98 100	21.7	9.9
Tamarac city	80.0	85.4	69.6	60.9	43.3	80.0	61.4	83.2	33 783	33 998	33 149	85 900	25.3	13.8
Tampa city	64.2	73.9	68.8	46.6	34.2	42.9	39.1	43.9	34 233	44 069	25 135	80 700	22.2	11.9
Titusville city	73.8	82.3	69.8	49.8	35.5	58.2	47.0	60.2	35 625	42 087	23 351	72 900	20.2	9.9

Table C-5. Cities — **Migration, Housing, and Transportation**

City	Median gross rent	Percent who pay 35 percent or more of income for housing expenses		Means of transportation to work (percent except where noted)						Vehicles available (percent of households)		
		Owners	Renters	Number of workers 16 years and over	Car, truck, or van — Drove alone	Carpooled	Public transportation	Other means	Walked	No vehicles	One vehicle	Two or more vehicles
	25	26	27	28	29	30	31	32	33	34	35	36
FLORIDA..............	641	18.5	33.0	6 910 168	78.8	12.9	1.9	1.7	1.7	8.1	41.4	50.4
Altamonte Springs city ..	733	16.0	25.8	23 839	82.8	10.8	1.2	0.9	1.7	5.9	49.6	44.5
Apopka city.................	682	17.5	30.3	13 009	81.8	12.8	1.3	1.0	0.6	5.5	35.0	59.5
Aventura city...............	1 256	24.5	34.8	10 190	82.2	7.4	2.0	0.9	1.8	10.8	57.6	31.6
Boca Raton city...........	847	21.2	35.9	34 374	80.9	8.3	0.9	1.9	2.0	4.4	39.7	56.0
Bonita Springs city	721	16.8	23.0	13 283	73.1	16.5	0.5	2.5	1.6	3.4	47.7	48.9
Boynton Beach city	787	18.1	37.7	26 010	81.6	12.1	1.5	1.2	1.1	8.3	48.5	43.2
Bradenton city.............	654	16.4	33.4	20 385	77.8	15.3	1.0	2.2	1.4	11.1	48.5	40.4
Cape Coral city	696	19.2	30.1	46 914	83.5	11.2	0.5	1.4	0.7	3.4	38.7	57.9
Clearwater city............	637	18.8	32.3	50 770	74.6	12.1	3.9	2.2	3.0	10.7	48.1	41.2
Coconut Creek city.......	903	18.5	30.8	19 933	85.6	9.5	0.7	0.9	0.5	6.3	50.8	42.9
Cooper City city...........	988	18.9	31.6	14 369	86.8	8.7	0.1	0.5	0.5	2.4	22.6	75.0
Coral Gables city.........	754	23.4	31.4	20 536	76.8	6.9	2.9	1.3	6.7	6.4	40.7	53.0
Coral Springs city........	899	20.8	34.4	58 510	81.5	11.2	1.0	1.3	1.2	4.5	29.5	66.0
Davie town.................	792	20.6	35.4	37 630	83.2	10.5	0.9	1.6	1.2	4.5	37.4	58.1
Daytona Beach city	530	21.8	36.7	26 998	70.0	15.2	3.8	3.1	5.7	15.7	49.2	35.1
Deerfield Beach city	790	21.0	34.9	27 537	80.7	12.8	1.2	1.6	1.4	14.7	49.6	35.7
Delray Beach city	807	19.5	34.8	25 300	78.1	12.4	1.7	1.6	1.8	8.7	49.4	41.8
Deltona city.................	708	18.4	27.2	30 918	80.5	15.1	0.5	1.1	0.3	3.7	33.7	62.6
Dunedin city................	581	17.3	31.6	15 722	81.5	9.9	1.1	1.6	2.1	8.9	51.1	40.0
Fort Lauderdale city	641	26.7	34.2	70 732	75.2	11.3	4.9	2.4	2.4	12.1	51.0	37.0
Fort Myers city	588	18.4	35.4	20 079	69.1	20.9	2.3	2.5	3.4	18.1	48.5	33.4
Fort Pierce city	517	23.7	38.9	13 900	67.6	22.4	4.0	2.2	1.9	15.0	50.5	34.5
Gainesville city............	540	14.5	45.2	43 060	69.8	12.2	3.2	6.0	5.6	9.3	44.4	46.3
Greenacres city...........	739	17.4	30.6	11 542	79.1	15.9	0.5	2.3	0.3	5.6	53.4	41.0
Hallandale city.............	657	23.5	37.7	12 962	76.6	11.6	4.3	1.7	2.8	19.0	59.2	21.8
Hialeah city.................	614	31.1	41.7	79 947	76.6	16.4	2.9	1.3	1.6	13.5	37.2	49.3
Hollywood city.............	685	24.4	35.9	63 888	77.7	13.1	3.1	1.5	1.8	12.0	46.2	41.8
Homestead city	546	25.2	35.4	12 244	55.1	35.2	2.9	4.2	1.6	19.7	42.6	37.7
Jacksonville city...........	598	15.2	26.8	350 458	79.2	13.4	2.1	1.6	1.8	9.3	38.2	52.5
Jupiter town.................	883	18.8	28.0	18 834	84.3	7.7	0.4	1.9	0.8	2.8	41.0	56.2
Key West city	899	29.9	35.1	14 611	55.8	10.9	1.2	18.4	8.0	15.8	46.3	37.9
Kissimmee city	709	20.2	35.9	22 972	75.7	17.6	2.0	1.6	1.9	7.5	44.1	48.4
Lakeland city...............	528	14.6	28.1	32 387	79.1	12.9	1.8	1.4	2.7	10.8	48.4	40.7
Lake Worth city	556	24.3	32.3	16 091	67.6	23.1	2.4	2.6	1.7	12.6	48.7	38.7
Largo city...................	625	17.3	32.5	29 997	80.8	11.9	1.3	1.8	2.0	8.9	54.9	36.1
Lauderdale Lakes city ...	662	33.9	44.3	11 868	72.6	17.6	7.1	0.6	1.2	16.1	52.3	31.6
Lauderhill city	687	27.9	39.6	24 082	76.7	14.2	5.3	1.3	1.0	13.8	48.8	37.4
Margate city................	805	23.0	33.8	24 196	81.8	12.6	1.3	1.7	0.9	10.3	45.2	44.5
Melbourne city.............	588	14.4	32.3	32 126	82.7	11.6	0.3	1.6	1.9	7.5	46.3	46.2
Miami city...................	535	33.9	40.9	126 539	64.5	16.3	11.4	2.1	3.7	26.7	42.1	31.2
Miami Beach city..........	632	33.4	40.3	39 868	58.2	9.6	11.4	5.1	10.3	32.6	47.5	19.9
Miramar city................	784	28.1	33.2	33 294	80.2	14.5	1.5	1.0	0.9	5.2	30.2	64.6
North Lauderdale city....	794	28.0	35.6	15 222	78.9	15.2	2.6	0.8	0.6	5.3	42.4	52.3
North Miami city...........	613	37.2	40.4	22 914	68.8	14.4	10.6	1.5	2.7	13.7	48.8	37.5
North Miami Beach city.	643	32.5	42.4	15 567	71.1	15.5	9.5	1.0	1.3	13.0	43.7	43.3
Oakland Park city.........	687	24.1	37.6	16 457	75.8	14.1	4.4	1.4	2.3	7.4	52.9	39.6
Ocala city	548	15.5	34.3	18 439	81.4	11.8	0.4	1.7	2.1	11.6	46.9	41.5
Orlando city	700	17.3	31.1	94 809	78.9	11.2	4.1	1.7	1.9	11.1	46.8	42.1
Ormond Beach city	709	16.8	31.8	15 444	84.0	8.7	0.9	1.9	1.1	5.4	40.0	54.6
Oviedo city	901	13.4	28.4	13 928	84.9	8.5	0.1	2.0	0.4	1.4	19.6	79.0
Palm Bay city..............	633	17.2	32.5	35 147	83.5	12.1	0.4	1.5	0.4	4.2	39.0	56.8
Palm Beach Gardens city ..	939	17.5	36.5	16 558	84.6	7.6	0.3	1.0	1.1	3.8	39.7	56.5
Palm Coast city............	814	17.7	30.6	12 177	82.8	11.4	0.7	1.6	0.7	2.7	39.6	57.7
Panama City city..........	526	13.3	29.5	15 173	80.2	13.7	0.7	1.6	1.6	11.3	42.2	46.5
Pembroke Pines city	945	20.9	31.5	64 509	84.0	10.6	0.9	0.9	0.6	7.0	36.6	56.4
Pensacola city.............	536	16.8	32.1	24 587	81.1	10.4	2.1	1.7	1.7	10.8	41.9	47.2
Pinellas Park city..........	614	16.9	26.3	20 876	80.0	12.8	1.1	2.3	1.7	7.4	47.0	45.5
Plantation city..............	938	19.6	37.1	42 890	83.9	10.0	1.2	0.8	0.6	5.1	37.7	57.2
Plant City city..............	561	16.3	30.6	12 566	78.2	16.5	0.4	1.7	1.2	7.4	39.2	53.4
Pompano Beach city	707	26.5	37.3	32 377	76.7	13.0	2.7	2.8	2.2	11.5	51.5	37.0
Port Orange city	682	16.5	32.5	20 589	83.4	11.6	0.5	1.5	0.8	5.5	40.9	53.6
Port St. Lucie city.........	741	18.9	31.0	38 933	84.1	11.7	0.3	1.2	0.5	2.7	38.8	58.5
Riviera Beach city	587	25.9	34.3	11 366	72.5	16.3	4.3	2.4	2.2	15.2	48.9	36.0
St. Petersburg city........	567	18.5	30.7	116 066	78.1	11.8	2.9	1.9	2.2	12.6	45.0	42.3
Sanford city	605	19.1	34.8	16 612	75.6	17.5	1.2	1.8	1.6	11.1	42.8	46.2
Sarasota city...............	648	20.1	34.3	22 820	76.0	12.2	2.5	3.1	2.7	11.5	48.8	39.7
Sunrise city.................	849	23.9	34.8	39 344	83.4	11.4	1.7	0.7	1.1	11.0	41.9	47.2
Tallahassee city	605	16.3	45.0	73 595	78.5	12.8	2.4	1.3	2.6	8.9	43.7	47.4
Tamarac city................	789	20.3	30.9	22 020	83.2	11.0	1.7	1.2	1.0	10.8	54.1	35.1
Tampa city..................	577	18.9	30.3	135 425	76.6	13.7	2.7	2.0	2.3	12.9	44.5	42.6
Titusville city...............	548	13.4	32.8	16 661	83.1	11.5	0.3	1.2	1.8	6.9	43.4	49.7

Table C-5. Cities — **Migration, Housing, and Transportation**

STATE Place code	City	Total population 5 years and over	Residence in 1995 (percent)					Occupied housing units		Householders 65 years and over	
			Same house	Same county, different house	Same state, different county	Different state	Outside the United States	Number	Percent owner-occupied	Number	Percent owner-occupied
		1	2	3	4	5	6	7	8	9	10
	FLORIDA—Cont'd										
12 75812	Wellington village	35 528	42.7	28.8	8.8	16.6	3.1	12 891	82.1	1 925	92.1
12 76582	Weston city	44 798	28.1	26.2	12.3	20.6	12.8	16 544	81.9	1 909	84.5
12 76600	West Palm Beach city ...	76 938	42.8	31.2	6.7	11.8	7.5	34 645	52.1	8 198	64.9
12 78275	Winter Haven city	24 519	48.2	32.3	7.1	10.4	2.1	11 852	58.7	4 757	70.1
12 78325	Winter Springs city	29 414	46.1	22.9	14.9	13.3	2.8	11 742	80.5	2 077	90.0
13 00000	**GEORGIA**	7 594 476	49.2	21.1	13.8	12.7	3.2	3 006 369	67.5	513 098	80.0
13 01052	Albany city	71 080	50.8	30.6	10.2	6.6	1.8	28 687	47.4	6 063	68.8
13 01696	Alpharetta city	31 549	30.4	18.0	14.0	32.1	5.4	13 843	60.2	1 253	75.0
13 03436	Athens-Clarke County ...	96 051	33.9	21.1	27.7	12.6	4.6	39 706	42.1	5 539	77.1
13 04000	Atlanta city	389 992	44.2	26.9	11.6	13.2	4.1	168 242	43.7	30 068	60.2
13 04200	Augusta-Richmond County	185 414	50.7	25.9	7.7	13.5	2.3	73 920	57.9	14 511	77.0
13 19000	Columbus city	172 678	47.8	26.9	6.3	15.9	3.1	69 819	56.4	14 864	76.2
13 21380	Dalton city	25 815	41.5	26.1	7.1	12.8	12.0	9 011	49.7	2 057	70.6
13 25720	East Point city	35 926	48.7	28.5	8.7	10.3	3.7	14 454	45.3	2 065	77.9
13 31908	Gainesville city	23 301	37.5	28.8	10.0	11.2	12.4	8 426	43.7	1 908	63.8
13 38964	Hinesville city	27 359	34.2	15.3	6.9	33.1	10.4	10 583	50.3	575	75.0
13 44340	LaGrange city	24 342	46.2	33.3	8.9	9.3	2.3	10 102	47.5	2 527	66.7
13 49000	Macon city	90 018	53.1	31.0	8.4	6.5	0.9	38 613	49.9	9 660	68.9
13 49756	Marietta city	54 006	28.8	24.0	12.7	23.4	11.1	23 994	37.1	2 998	61.9
13 59724	Peachtree City city	29 922	46.7	13.3	10.3	26.2	3.5	11 004	81.1	1 505	82.0
13 66668	Rome city	32 854	47.4	31.2	9.3	8.8	3.3	13 229	53.5	3 664	65.4
13 67284	Roswell city	74 532	42.1	16.0	13.7	21.6	6.6	30 304	67.1	3 243	80.1
13 69000	Savannah city	122 421	50.8	28.7	5.0	12.9	2.6	51 426	50.3	12 778	69.5
13 71492	Smyrna city	38 266	35.1	20.3	14.1	22.4	8.2	18 455	50.3	2 139	72.9
13 78800	Valdosta city	40 439	45.0	27.1	14.5	11.3	2.1	16 743	47.9	3 314	69.6
13 80508	Warner Robins city	45 312	43.0	26.0	10.1	17.3	3.7	19 658	57.8	3 518	85.7
15 00000	**HAWAII**	1 134 351	56.8	26.0	2.1	11.0	4.1	403 240	56.5	93 121	75.0
15 14650	Hilo CDP	38 509	60.2	27.6	4.5	5.1	2.6	11 681	60.8	4 202	76.3
15 17000	Honolulu CDP	352 992	56.3	27.2	1.5	8.9	6.1	140 328	46.9	39 919	67.4
15 23150	Kailua CDP	34 555	62.1	24.1	1.5	9.9	2.5	12 213	69.8	2 743	90.3
15 28250	Kaneohe CDP	33 140	68.0	22.8	1.1	6.9	1.2	10 978	68.1	3 215	83.1
15 51050	Mililani Town CDP	26 776	66.5	20.6	0.7	9.2	3.0	9 006	76.0	961	91.9
15 62600	Pearl City CDP	29 321	66.2	17.2	0.5	13.0	3.0	8 865	69.7	3 195	86.3
15 77750	Waimalu CDP	27 853	59.4	26.7	0.9	8.9	4.1	10 572	61.5	1 512	88.7
15 79700	Waipahu CDP	30 895	58.6	31.3	1.1	2.3	6.7	7 551	53.5	2 245	67.4
16 00000	**IDAHO**	1 196 793	49.6	23.9	9.4	15.3	1.8	469 645	72.4	95 027	84.1
16 08830	Boise City city	172 899	43.6	29.6	7.5	16.8	2.6	74 501	63.9	12 976	77.7
16 12250	Caldwell city	23 311	40.5	34.0	8.2	14.7	2.6	8 993	65.4	1 905	75.1
16 16750	Coeur d'Alene city	32 365	38.8	31.5	7.4	21.8	0.5	13 940	61.9	3 186	75.5
16 39700	Idaho Falls city	46 457	48.3	28.3	8.4	14.1	1.0	18 835	68.4	3 926	80.5
16 46540	Lewiston city	29 240	52.9	23.7	8.5	14.2	0.7	12 816	67.1	3 423	81.3
16 52120	Meridian city	30 864	34.0	35.2	7.6	22.5	0.7	11 790	83.9	1 311	80.2
16 56260	Nampa city	46 908	36.9	27.9	15.1	18.0	2.2	18 227	69.8	3 075	78.7
16 64090	Pocatello city	47 256	45.8	28.3	10.7	13.9	1.3	19 378	66.2	3 579	87.1
16 82810	Twin Falls city	31 432	47.6	25.8	11.9	12.4	2.4	13 296	62.4	3 037	77.5
17 00000	**ILLINOIS**	11 547 505	56.8	26.1	8.3	5.8	3.1	4 591 779	67.3	981 064	77.2
17 00243	Addison village	32 956	56.6	19.1	12.5	2.9	8.9	11 598	68.3	1 836	89.8
17 01114	Alton city	28 332	55.0	31.0	6.2	7.3	0.6	12 513	65.4	3 356	75.2
17 02154	Arlington Heights village	71 417	60.6	26.6	3.9	4.6	4.3	30 732	76.7	7 852	79.6
17 03012	Aurora city	128 477	44.9	25.2	14.3	9.7	6.0	46 615	70.0	5 297	74.6
17 04013	Bartlett village	32 842	58.5	19.7	15.9	5.1	0.8	12 157	93.5	1 211	93.2
17 04845	Belleville city	39 591	55.3	31.1	5.1	7.5	1.0	17 757	60.6	4 615	73.6
17 05573	Berwyn city	49 734	54.4	37.0	1.7	2.5	4.4	19 702	61.6	5 101	71.3
17 06613	Bloomington city	60 288	44.0	29.2	13.7	10.7	2.4	26 727	63.4	4 377	74.3
17 07133	Bolingbrook village	51 017	54.3	12.6	24.9	5.4	2.8	17 441	85.2	1 338	69.4
17 09447	Buffalo Grove village	39 841	61.1	16.1	12.9	5.7	4.1	15 601	87.1	2 330	93.9
17 09642	Burbank city	26 200	67.6	27.2	0.8	1.4	3.0	9 314	82.8	2 616	84.6
17 10487	Calumet City city	35 885	58.1	36.3	0.9	3.2	1.5	15 128	63.2	3 608	75.5
17 11332	Carol Stream village	36 812	53.8	25.6	10.6	5.5	4.5	13 853	70.0	1 374	49.1
17 11358	Carpentersville village ...	27 140	49.8	18.3	19.3	4.6	7.9	8 738	80.2	1 017	93.4
17 12385	Champaign city	64 592	36.3	21.0	28.7	9.2	4.8	27 142	47.4	3 915	79.0
17 14000	Chicago city	2 678 081	54.4	32.7	1.9	5.6	5.4	1 061 921	43.8	205 209	60.5
17 14026	Chicago Heights city	30 082	63.3	27.8	2.5	3.3	3.0	10 767	63.1	2 499	81.1
17 14351	Cicero town	76 342	52.6	35.3	1.1	2.8	8.2	23 115	55.2	3 920	73.5
17 17887	Crystal Lake city	34 710	55.2	21.1	13.7	8.8	1.2	12 983	79.2	2 303	75.7

Table C-5. Cities — Migration, Housing, and Transportation

City	Total family households	Owner-occupied by household type (percent)							Median household income			Median housing value (owner estimated)	Median monthly owner costs as a percent of income	
		Family households				Nonfamily households								
		Married-couple family		Other family										
		Total	With own children under 18 years	Total	With own children under 18 years	Total nonfamily households	Two or more adults	Living alone	All households	Owner-occupied households	Renter-occupied households		With a mortgage	Without a mortgage
	11	12	13	14	15	16	17	18	19	20	21	22	23	24
FLORIDA—Cont'd														
Wellington village	83.2	87.0	83.4	60.3	50.9	76.8	66.1	80.1	70 522	76 853	47 190	163 000	22.6	10.7
Weston city..................	84.1	86.2	84.5	70.1	66.4	71.4	66.3	72.8	80 485	87 546	45 539	186 800	23.2	11.6
West Palm Beach city ...	61.0	72.9	65.1	38.2	26.8	42.1	38.4	43.1	36 639	48 907	26 284	91 500	23.3	11.9
Winter Haven city.........	68.1	79.0	64.9	40.4	21.5	45.5	54.7	44.2	31 625	40 718	21 206	64 700	22.4	9.9
Winter Springs city	83.7	88.5	84.6	62.1	56.0	70.2	60.3	72.9	53 631	62 423	34 406	124 500	20.7	10.0
GEORGIA................	74.2	82.3	78.4	51.1	41.4	51.4	37.3	54.9	42 288	51 421	27 657	100 600	20.8	9.9
Albany city..................	52.6	69.7	58.0	31.7	19.4	37.3	23.7	39.7	28 140	41 107	18 783	69 200	20.9	10.8
Alpharetta city	74.2	79.7	84.6	42.5	34.9	34.9	27.8	36.9	70 460	97 990	48 834	222 600	20.8	9.9
Athens-Clarke County ...	59.1	71.3	64.5	34.6	22.6	25.3	11.8	34.5	28 365	49 078	18 244	102 600	20.2	9.9
Atlanta city..................	52.1	70.0	64.6	34.4	19.5	35.2	31.5	36.4	34 449	57 058	23 623	144 100	23.2	11.7
Augusta-Richmond County	62.7	74.6	66.9	42.8	31.5	48.0	35.7	50.2	32 606	42 304	21 972	73 600	21.5	9.9
Columbus city..............	61.4	72.3	64.5	39.8	27.4	45.6	33.0	47.8	34 787	46 136	24 311	83 100	21.1	9.9
Dalton city..................	51.6	59.4	48.7	26.2	20.8	42.5	27.0	45.0	34 170	49 811	26 639	99 600	18.9	9.9
East Point city	48.0	65.1	52.6	32.6	20.8	40.4	35.1	42.0	31 924	43 795	25 069	86 600	24.2	10.3
Gainesville city	50.2	59.8	45.7	25.7	12.7	32.0	8.8	37.1	36 650	57 971	27 380	129 500	22.1	10.3
Hinesville city	54.2	60.8	57.5	36.8	30.9	37.0	26.6	40.6	35 561	46 016	27 439	76 300	22.6	10.4
LaGrange city	53.8	69.9	59.3	33.5	23.0	35.8	18.7	38.4	29 170	42 009	20 559	78 800	19.5	12.1
Macon city..................	55.5	74.6	66.4	33.2	20.1	40.3	24.7	42.8	27 332	40 856	17 811	68 000	20.8	10.1
Marietta city................	45.9	58.9	48.0	21.2	15.0	26.6	15.2	30.9	40 706	60 121	32 923	144 400	21.6	9.9
Peachtree City city	86.7	89.4	88.0	64.4	60.0	55.9	34.5	59.0	76 569	84 093	47 995	189 800	20.9	9.9
Rome city...................	60.6	72.5	60.9	36.8	25.4	40.1	27.9	42.1	31 113	44 163	20 736	86 600	19.3	10.1
Roswell city................	75.2	80.8	79.2	45.5	38.6	48.5	35.9	52.5	71 446	93 152	44 722	204 700	20.4	9.9
Savannah city..............	57.1	70.0	59.1	38.4	23.9	39.6	24.7	42.9	28 927	41 129	20 744	78 300	22.8	12.4
Smyrna city.................	55.7	65.3	57.7	32.9	24.3	44.6	41.5	45.4	47 810	58 350	39 136	121 700	21.0	9.9
Valdosta city...............	56.3	70.3	62.0	34.8	21.5	34.7	14.7	41.5	28 617	45 464	19 466	81 600	20.5	9.9
Warner Robins city.......	61.9	73.0	62.4	37.6	28.5	49.2	34.7	51.4	38 315	46 389	28 432	73 900	19.5	9.9
HAWAII..................	62.2	66.1	56.9	49.8	30.2	42.2	34.2	44.6	49 536	64 653	33 755	249 300	26.3	9.9
Hilo CDP	68.5	76.9	67.3	49.0	31.8	42.9	30.7	46.0	39 005	53 931	21 360	152 900	22.6	9.9
Honolulu CDP	54.0	57.4	44.8	44.3	18.8	35.1	26.3	37.4	45 029	65 984	32 259	317 300	25.9	9.9
Kailua CDP	75.8	78.8	72.2	64.7	46.6	50.4	37.4	56.1	72 777	83 207	50 016	355 100	25.9	9.9
Kaneohe CDP	71.8	76.4	67.8	56.6	33.6	53.5	32.5	59.7	65 568	74 738	48 672	286 400	24.8	9.9
Mililani Town CDP........	77.6	81.1	72.9	60.2	42.6	66.5	60.0	68.6	72 178	79 507	52 688	261 200	24.5	9.9
Pearl City CDP.............	74.1	76.0	50.8	68.0	29.0	48.0	41.4	49.0	61 875	71 454	39 245	272 100	22.4	9.9
Waimalu CDP..............	68.6	73.0	64.6	51.6	29.1	43.4	30.5	47.8	61 037	78 283	39 668	242 100	25.3	9.9
Waipahu CDP	56.8	60.6	43.9	46.9	23.2	34.4	32.1	35.1	48 741	68 577	30 828	260 600	25.9	9.9
IDAHO....................	78.4	83.2	78.8	55.6	47.9	57.0	43.4	60.5	37 570	44 143	23 940	102 100	21.5	9.9
Boise City city	73.6	79.9	78.0	50.0	43.1	47.6	37.6	50.8	42 347	53 870	27 108	118 100	20.8	9.9
Caldwell city	68.5	73.8	68.3	53.1	49.9	57.6	53.5	58.8	30 790	35 970	21 665	81 400	22.9	11.0
Coeur d'Alene city........	69.0	77.8	72.8	43.3	33.0	49.4	37.3	53.0	32 799	40 137	22 037	105 300	23.5	10.4
Idaho Falls city	76.5	82.3	79.0	53.4	44.7	49.5	33.3	52.5	40 670	51 012	21 590	88 700	19.2	9.9
Lewiston city...............	75.9	83.7	77.6	46.2	36.6	50.9	43.7	52.6	36 682	46 109	20 718	103 100	19.9	9.9
Meridian city...............	86.4	91.1	91.4	64.2	55.9	73.1	74.1	72.8	52 722	57 243	27 148	119 800	21.8	9.9
Nampa city..................	74.0	79.8	76.3	52.9	44.4	58.9	49.7	61.0	35 148	40 775	24 150	89 900	22.5	9.9
Pocatello city..............	74.9	80.0	77.5	54.6	45.2	48.4	30.7	53.8	34 407	44 454	19 666	83 100	20.0	9.9
Twin Falls city	68.5	77.4	68.4	39.5	31.6	49.9	39.9	52.1	32 720	40 849	21 500	90 800	20.7	9.9
ILLINOIS..................	75.4	83.0	80.1	50.9	40.1	50.1	38.7	52.3	46 304	56 715	29 065	127 800	21.7	11.1
Addison village	73.1	78.1	68.7	51.2	29.6	51.8	42.7	54.7	52 628	63 026	33 654	169 700	24.3	13.6
Alton city....................	71.5	83.1	74.6	49.1	35.1	55.8	42.3	58.0	31 353	38 486	17 633	55 400	18.6	11.6
Arlington Heights village	86.3	88.2	89.3	71.7	59.4	57.4	37.4	60.1	67 629	77 510	43 870	222 900	21.5	11.9
Aurora city..................	76.0	83.1	81.8	51.3	45.5	53.1	47.4	54.6	54 421	65 947	33 405	132 400	22.8	12.3
Bartlett village.............	94.9	96.5	96.1	81.8	78.3	87.0	82.6	88.3	79 215	81 558	44 231	198 600	23.1	14.2
Belleville city...............	71.5	80.8	77.5	48.2	35.7	44.1	39.2	44.8	36 213	46 762	23 986	69 700	20.7	10.7
Berwyn city.................	69.4	74.9	71.9	53.9	40.5	46.5	37.6	48.0	43 101	52 045	31 853	137 400	25.4	13.4
Bloomington city	77.6	83.1	84.1	57.1	53.1	42.7	33.7	44.9	45 628	60 092	28 014	108 200	19.6	9.9
Bolingbrook village	89.4	93.0	91.9	73.9	71.6	65.4	65.1	65.4	67 799	72 627	40 736	141 400	22.9	10.8
Buffalo Grove village.....	91.1	91.9	92.6	84.7	82.6	75.2	56.9	78.3	79 880	84 095	55 819	214 700	22.3	9.9
Burbank city................	86.4	89.7	87.1	75.9	68.1	70.0	68.3	70.2	49 857	53 766	32 453	137 600	22.7	12.4
Calumet City city	69.1	80.3	74.5	52.9	44.3	51.1	62.8	49.9	37 944	45 442	28 166	89 300	23.0	11.2
Carol Stream village......	79.5	86.2	88.3	48.2	48.3	44.2	37.3	45.9	64 554	78 336	36 796	166 200	22.6	13.3
Carpentersville village ...	81.9	87.7	84.9	62.6	57.1	72.2	61.4	75.1	54 120	58 963	33 571	116 300	24.4	12.0
Champaign city	71.9	80.4	80.8	43.6	33.3	26.4	14.1	32.2	32 672	54 477	18 378	89 500	19.3	9.9
Chicago city................	51.3	61.8	56.6	35.7	22.4	32.5	24.1	34.4	37 878	54 068	28 397	144 300	23.8	12.3
Chicago Heights city	67.6	80.8	74.4	45.5	28.9	50.1	42.5	51.3	36 934	48 841	20 542	94 000	23.6	12.2
Cicero town	57.5	63.3	59.4	42.1	34.9	46.4	27.6	50.2	37 108	45 922	28 545	120 200	26.1	14.6
Crystal Lake city...........	86.8	90.3	89.8	63.9	62.2	55.6	40.8	58.5	67 121	74 634	36 694	165 700	23.3	11.1

Table C-5. Cities — **Migration, Housing, and Transportation**

City	Percent who pay 35 percent or more of income for housing expenses			Means of transportation to work (percent except where noted)						Vehicles available (percent of households)		
				Car, truck, or van								
	Median gross rent	Owners	Renters	Number of workers 16 years and over	Drove alone	Carpooled	Public transportation	Other means	Walked	No vehicles	One vehicle	Two or more vehicles
	25	26	27	28	29	30	31	32	33	34	35	36
FLORIDA—Cont'd												
Wellington village	989	18.8	30.4	18 353	81.7	9.1	0.6	1.3	0.6	1.6	25.3	73.1
Weston city..................	1 084	20.7	31.4	22 388	82.9	9.0	0.6	1.1	0.8	2.1	25.9	71.9
West Palm Beach city...	664	23.8	36.6	37 043	76.0	13.8	2.8	2.3	2.8	14.2	46.4	39.4
Winter Haven city.........	495	16.4	34.3	9 855	82.7	12.9	0.8	1.6	1.0	13.3	49.0	37.7
Winter Springs city........	727	14.0	26.2	15 904	84.3	9.4	0.3	1.2	0.3	2.9	30.7	66.5
GEORGIA..............	613	15.2	28.1	3 832 803	77.5	14.5	2.3	1.1	1.7	8.3	32.3	59.4
Albany city...................	466	18.1	33.2	29 415	76.7	16.9	1.3	0.9	2.8	14.9	41.6	43.6
Alpharetta city..............	908	14.9	20.9	18 795	83.6	8.3	1.5	0.4	0.5	2.7	35.6	61.7
Athens-Clarke County ...	540	13.3	43.5	48 241	75.1	14.4	2.4	1.6	4.3	8.4	37.3	54.3
Atlanta city..................	606	22.9	32.5	178 970	64.0	12.4	15.0	1.3	3.5	23.6	42.4	34.1
Augusta-Richmond County	505	17.5	29.6	84 849	76.5	14.6	1.3	1.2	5.0	12.1	39.5	48.4
Columbus city..............	500	15.6	26.8	82 977	75.5	14.6	1.5	2.0	4.7	11.7	38.5	49.8
Dalton city	484	9.8	20.2	12 067	68.9	24.2	1.2	1.2	3.1	10.5	39.2	50.3
East Point city	595	21.2	36.2	16 909	59.2	20.0	17.6	0.2	1.4	20.8	44.1	35.1
Gainesville city.............	606	17.6	27.4	10 811	68.7	21.7	2.6	2.3	3.1	13.1	38.5	48.5
Hinesville city..............	549	19.2	24.6	14 043	80.1	14.6	0.3	1.7	1.3	7.1	38.3	54.6
LaGrange city..............	487	14.3	31.2	11 181	74.2	18.4	3.4	1.5	1.7	16.5	41.5	42.0
Macon city..................	444	15.7	32.3	36 409	75.2	17.3	2.7	1.2	2.1	17.1	40.6	42.3
Marietta city................	767	15.2	30.7	31 705	71.7	18.6	2.9	2.0	2.2	9.8	44.2	46.0
Peachtree City city	990	13.8	27.6	15 533	83.4	8.8	0.8	1.9	0.3	2.1	24.0	74.0
Rome city	443	14.3	27.1	14 135	76.0	17.5	0.8	1.6	2.3	13.6	37.5	48.9
Roswell city	894	14.7	24.9	44 024	79.4	10.4	1.9	1.5	1.1	3.1	29.4	67.5
Savannah city..............	564	20.3	37.1	55 740	70.8	15.3	4.9	2.3	4.3	17.6	42.2	40.2
Smyrna city	776	15.4	26.3	23 085	81.0	12.2	2.2	0.6	1.0	6.2	46.5	47.3
Valdosta city...............	495	17.2	35.3	19 507	76.5	16.5	0.3	1.5	3.3	11.1	39.3	49.6
Warner Robins city........	566	13.2	25.9	22 502	82.7	13.1	0.5	0.9	1.5	7.4	39.9	52.8
HAWAII....................	779	22.1	29.1	563 154	63.9	19.0	6.3	2.4	4.8	11.0	37.0	52.0
Hilo CDP	542	15.0	33.6	16 578	71.6	19.2	0.6	1.4	2.8	10.1	37.3	52.5
Honolulu CDP	760	19.8	30.0	173 069	57.7	18.1	11.6	2.9	6.6	19.4	43.1	37.5
Kailua CDP	1 111	20.6	32.4	18 344	69.6	16.6	4.3	2.3	2.3	5.2	27.9	66.9
Kaneohe CDP	1 075	20.5	32.2	16 699	68.7	20.6	4.7	0.9	2.1	6.2	28.7	65.1
Mililani Town CDP........	1 174	23.7	33.6	15 444	74.6	18.0	3.6	0.6	1.7	2.8	22.6	74.6
Pearl City CDP	798	15.1	22.2	15 568	61.5	20.3	4.5	2.9	7.8	6.6	30.9	62.5
Waimalu CDP..............	962	20.5	31.6	16 481	67.6	22.2	5.4	1.4	1.6	4.9	38.7	56.4
Waipahu CDP	664	22.0	27.8	12 594	57.7	21.1	16.0	1.2	1.9	13.4	32.0	54.6
IDAHO	515	14.5	28.1	594 654	77.0	12.3	1.1	1.4	3.5	4.7	27.7	67.6
Boise City city	613	13.0	32.2	99 005	79.9	10.3	1.2	2.3	2.3	5.6	33.9	60.5
Caldwell city	495	16.9	29.0	11 333	74.8	16.5	0.2	1.8	4.2	7.5	34.2	58.3
Coeur d'Alene city........	555	18.3	36.7	15 915	80.8	10.8	0.3	2.0	3.0	7.3	34.9	57.8
Idaho Falls city	475	8.9	32.1	23 211	78.2	9.9	5.5	0.7	2.1	5.9	31.6	62.5
Lewiston city................	461	13.5	31.1	14 806	84.9	8.6	0.5	0.8	3.1	7.1	29.3	63.6
Meridian city................	629	12.8	31.1	17 458	84.9	10.1	0.0	0.8	0.4	3.0	21.2	75.8
Nampa city	528	16.4	28.9	23 154	76.3	15.1	0.4	1.8	2.5	5.4	33.0	61.6
Pocatello city...............	433	11.6	31.2	24 890	78.2	12.8	1.7	1.3	3.4	6.0	32.7	61.3
Twin Falls city	500	13.3	28.9	15 560	80.6	11.8	1.2	1.0	1.7	6.4	33.6	60.0
ILLINOIS..................	605	14.9	28.3	5 745 731	73.2	10.9	8.7	1.0	3.1	11.8	35.4	52.8
Addison village	688	19.3	24.6	17 335	78.9	13.3	2.6	1.0	2.4	5.2	33.7	61.0
Alton city....................	430	13.7	33.4	12 777	81.3	11.5	2.6	0.9	2.1	12.1	42.2	45.7
Arlington Heights village	933	13.9	26.1	39 292	80.4	5.9	7.8	0.6	1.7	6.2	35.8	58.0
Aurora city	700	16.6	27.8	67 060	74.7	14.2	5.5	1.3	1.6	6.2	32.7	61.1
Bartlett village..............	752	18.1	27.1	19 178	84.5	5.6	5.4	0.8	0.3	2.0	20.8	77.3
Belleville city................	497	11.8	32.8	19 967	81.8	10.6	2.8	0.5	2.1	11.1	40.5	48.5
Berwyn city.................	593	21.4	26.3	24 377	69.0	14.7	10.8	0.7	3.2	14.0	41.6	44.5
Bloomington city...........	525	11.2	22.7	35 310	81.3	10.3	1.4	0.8	3.5	7.7	37.5	54.8
Bolingbrook village........	786	16.2	24.2	28 875	80.7	10.6	4.1	0.6	1.0	3.2	22.9	73.8
Buffalo Grove village.....	1 079	14.7	24.3	22 728	83.3	5.8	5.5	0.5	0.9	2.2	28.7	69.0
Burbank city................	682	17.3	34.7	13 005	79.0	11.4	5.6	1.1	2.0	6.2	32.0	61.8
Calumet City city	630	19.0	27.5	16 569	73.2	11.8	10.9	1.0	2.3	11.7	48.1	40.2
Carol Stream village......	798	15.1	26.8	21 237	84.2	7.7	3.7	0.6	0.9	5.7	27.1	67.2
Carpentersville village ...	675	19.2	28.3	13 323	77.6	17.0	1.1	1.8	1.1	5.7	27.2	67.1
Champaign city	549	11.8	46.4	34 283	64.5	10.8	6.2	2.8	12.3	11.8	42.9	45.3
Chicago city................	616	21.2	30.8	1 192 139	50.1	14.5	26.1	1.3	5.7	28.8	43.5	27.7
Chicago Heights city	566	18.7	36.0	12 131	72.8	15.0	6.5	1.6	2.7	12.6	42.0	45.3
Cicero town	561	24.7	27.9	29 722	57.5	26.4	9.7	1.7	3.7	14.8	41.2	44.0
Crystal Lake city...........	855	14.7	33.6	18 463	83.1	7.2	4.3	0.8	1.3	6.4	25.5	68.1

Items 25—36

Table C-5. Cities — **Migration, Housing, and Transportation**

STATE Place code	City	Total population 5 years and over	Residence in 1995 (percent)					Occupied housing units		Householders 65 years and over	
			Same house	Same county, different house	Same state, different county	Different state	Outside the United States	Number	Percent owner-occupied	Number	Percent owner-occupied
		1	2	3	4	5	6	7	8	9	10
	ILLINOIS—Cont'd										
17 18563	Danville city	31 436	51.8	33.2	6.7	7.4	0.9	13 304	62.0	3 881	71.9
17 18823	Decatur city	76 611	52.3	31.6	9.1	6.1	0.8	34 126	66.5	9 224	79.1
17 19161	DeKalb city	36 729	32.6	18.0	38.7	6.7	4.0	12 986	42.0	1 951	68.1
17 19642	Des Plaines city	55 387	62.6	28.5	2.3	3.1	3.6	22 474	79.7	6 420	81.2
17 20292	Dolton village	23 908	63.4	33.1	0.8	1.8	0.9	8 532	81.3	1 333	82.2
17 20591	Downers Grove village..	45 619	65.7	15.8	11.6	4.9	2.0	19 000	78.5	4 582	76.7
17 22255	East St. Louis city	28 770	65.9	27.2	2.2	3.9	0.9	11 187	53.0	3 074	74.8
17 23074	Elgin city	85 359	51.8	23.7	13.6	4.9	6.0	31 540	70.3	5 076	80.6
17 23256	Elk Grove Village village	32 575	63.1	24.4	5.3	4.8	2.3	13 226	76.6	2 620	75.8
17 23620	Elmhurst city	39 898	65.4	15.9	13.0	4.1	1.6	15 723	82.8	4 318	86.2
17 23724	Elmwood Park village....	23 985	59.3	33.0	1.2	0.9	5.7	9 858	65.6	2 792	71.9
17 24582	Evanston city	70 041	43.9	30.2	3.8	16.8	5.3	29 651	52.6	5 292	67.8
17 27884	Freeport city	24 697	54.3	28.4	9.5	6.7	1.0	11 241	68.2	3 141	76.1
17 28326	Galesburg city	31 835	52.2	24.4	13.4	7.6	2.3	13 234	64.1	3 997	72.1
17 29730	Glendale Heights village	29 141	51.4	23.3	12.7	5.8	6.8	10 739	70.0	860	68.5
17 29756	Glen Ellyn village	24 797	59.0	19.7	9.7	7.6	4.0	10 251	78.0	2 110	83.0
17 29938	Glenview village	38 879	61.8	27.6	2.3	5.8	2.5	15 439	87.3	4 265	90.6
17 30926	Granite City city	29 743	59.9	28.5	3.7	7.5	0.4	12 860	70.4	3 544	74.8
17 32018	Gurnee village	25 897	45.0	27.2	12.0	14.0	1.8	10 539	78.1	1 314	64.7
17 32746	Hanover Park village.....	34 913	55.5	20.6	12.5	4.9	6.5	11 155	82.0	733	91.0
17 33383	Harvey city	27 226	58.4	34.4	1.3	3.4	2.5	8 980	56.7	1 855	73.4
17 34722	Highland Park city	29 071	64.9	14.5	10.4	6.6	3.6	11 507	81.9	3 090	86.5
17 35411	Hoffman Estates village	46 715	55.9	27.7	4.6	5.6	6.3	17 192	76.3	1 734	77.0
17 38570	Joliet city	96 363	48.6	27.2	16.0	5.2	3.0	36 199	70.3	7 163	72.8
17 38934	Kankakee city	25 294	50.9	33.6	8.7	4.9	1.9	10 007	53.1	2 362	61.3
17 42028	Lansing village	26 333	66.0	27.0	1.9	4.5	0.7	11 419	75.4	2 928	83.3
17 44407	Lombard village	39 328	60.2	18.8	12.6	5.5	2.9	16 416	75.0	3 634	81.7
17 47774	Maywood village	24 854	66.4	28.4	1.7	1.8	1.7	7 937	62.9	1 818	77.9
17 49867	Moline city	40 882	56.6	27.8	4.9	8.9	1.8	18 489	67.3	4 773	78.1
17 51089	Mount Prospect village..	53 049	59.3	24.8	3.5	4.4	8.1	21 718	71.3	5 573	86.0
17 51349	Mundelein village	27 769	51.5	21.4	14.0	6.9	6.2	9 833	79.9	1 094	83.7
17 51622	Naperville city	117 630	50.0	16.3	16.2	14.0	3.5	43 715	80.0	4 454	77.2
17 53000	Niles village	28 974	63.2	28.3	1.3	2.1	5.0	12 086	76.2	5 046	79.4
17 53234	Normal town	43 131	34.7	19.1	36.5	7.7	2.0	15 127	54.9	2 225	82.6
17 53481	Northbrook village	31 526	67.1	23.5	3.9	3.6	2.0	12 210	91.6	3 821	87.8
17 53559	North Chicago city........	33 178	24.7	15.5	7.0	46.1	6.7	7 674	36.0	938	64.0
17 54638	Oak Forest city	26 149	68.2	27.0	2.0	1.6	1.2	9 735	81.6	1 624	87.3
17 54820	Oak Lawn village...........	52 446	69.3	25.8	1.3	2.2	1.4	22 276	82.8	8 387	89.0
17 54885	Oak Park village............	48 907	52.8	29.8	3.7	10.4	3.3	23 079	56.3	3 694	61.1
17 56640	Orland Park village........	48 436	63.8	29.4	3.6	2.4	0.7	18 692	91.3	5 223	93.1
17 57225	Palatine village	60 412	49.6	31.0	6.6	6.3	6.6	25 553	69.2	3 853	78.8
17 57875	Park Ridge city	35 555	69.4	25.7	1.5	2.4	1.0	14 185	87.9	4 484	90.1
17 58447	Pekin city	31 614	55.0	29.2	9.9	4.7	1.2	13 337	67.2	3 655	74.7
17 59000	Peoria city	104 558	49.4	31.0	10.6	7.2	1.8	45 132	59.9	10 619	74.2
17 62367	Quincy city	37 827	54.6	30.6	5.6	8.7	0.5	16 502	66.4	4 717	75.2
17 65000	Rockford city	138 274	52.7	31.9	6.7	5.9	2.8	59 201	61.3	13 708	72.9
17 65078	Rock Island city	37 185	57.1	26.6	6.8	8.5	1.0	16 120	65.1	4 510	73.7
17 66040	Round Lake Beach village	22 794	51.1	22.6	13.5	6.3	6.5	7 312	85.7	657	63.6
17 66703	St. Charles city	26 253	52.4	18.5	17.2	9.8	2.1	10 353	73.8	1 720	74.4
17 68003	Schaumburg village.......	70 189	53.1	26.0	7.6	7.1	6.2	31 747	69.4	4 814	77.5
17 70122	Skokie village	60 073	61.4	28.3	1.4	3.1	5.8	23 201	75.1	7 737	81.1
17 72000	Springfield city	105 006	51.0	33.1	9.5	5.5	0.9	48 673	62.8	10 697	72.8
17 73157	Streamwood village.......	33 733	54.4	28.3	8.3	5.7	3.3	12 155	89.5	1 229	96.2
17 75484	Tinley Park village........	45 212	61.0	28.7	6.8	2.8	0.6	17 480	84.8	3 488	83.3
17 77005	Urbana city	34 593	29.3	22.2	28.2	11.6	8.6	14 258	36.8	2 282	66.7
17 79293	Waukegan city	79 554	46.8	31.2	7.5	6.4	8.1	27 777	56.7	4 457	73.2
17 81048	Wheaton city	51 900	56.3	20.4	9.2	10.6	3.5	19 412	74.1	3 488	79.8
17 81087	Wheeling village	32 023	51.4	30.0	4.8	5.6	8.3	13 267	66.5	2 258	70.1
17 82075	Wilmette village	25 712	64.7	25.4	1.4	5.8	2.8	10 043	86.9	2 911	85.9
17 83245	Woodridge village.........	28 836	53.7	19.3	16.0	5.9	5.1	11 369	67.2	995	84.4
18 00000	**INDIANA**	5 657 818	55.0	25.5	10.2	8.0	1.3	2 336 306	71.4	498 051	79.4
18 01468	Anderson city	55 594	51.1	33.2	7.9	6.6	1.3	25 209	63.8	7 239	77.9
18 05860	Bloomington city	66 535	25.9	19.2	29.2	20.2	5.5	26 417	35.5	3 700	73.0
18 10342	Carmel city	34 817	44.5	17.2	16.8	19.1	2.4	13 679	79.0	2 106	74.7
18 14734	Columbus city..............	36 121	47.5	29.4	10.1	10.0	3.1	15 974	64.6	3 535	74.7
18 19486	East Chicago city	29 502	59.7	29.7	1.0	6.7	3.0	11 707	44.6	3 265	63.8
18 20728	Elkhart city	46 709	44.3	32.4	6.1	11.9	5.3	20 167	53.7	4 374	66.6
18 22000	Evansville city..............	114 096	52.7	30.7	7.8	7.9	0.9	52 324	59.9	13 481	73.4
18 23278	Fishers town.................	34 299	30.5	18.1	30.6	19.5	1.3	14 448	77.9	726	70.1

Table C-5. Cities — **Migration, Housing, and Transportation**

City	Owner-occupied by household type (percent)								Median household income			Median housing value (owner estimated)	Median monthly owner costs as a percent of income	
	Family households					Nonfamily households								
		Married-couple family		Other family										
	Total family households	Total	With own children under 18 years	Total	With own children under 18 years	Total nonfamily households	Two or more adults	Living alone	All households	Owner-occupied households	Renter-occupied households		With a mortgage	Without a mortgage
	11	12	13	14	15	16	17	18	19	20	21	22	23	24
ILLINOIS—Cont'd														
Danville city	71.0	82.9	74.0	42.5	35.5	47.2	39.4	48.1	30 732	39 928	18 358	51 800	18.0	11.0
Decatur city	74.2	85.9	77.3	45.9	33.7	53.6	47.3	54.6	33 150	41 515	19 815	60 600	18.3	10.4
DeKalb city	63.6	74.2	72.3	28.8	23.6	19.3	7.2	27.4	35 418	60 786	21 013	126 400	23.5	10.0
Des Plaines city	86.5	89.5	86.9	73.1	63.8	65.5	53.3	67.2	53 327	58 611	37 117	174 800	23.9	11.0
Dolton village	84.1	88.9	89.2	77.3	71.6	71.6	71.8	71.6	48 136	52 606	29 970	92 900	23.9	13.6
Downers Grove village..	87.7	90.9	93.7	67.7	61.5	58.8	52.7	59.7	65 198	75 091	36 260	195 900	21.9	10.8
East St. Louis city	53.6	76.1	58.7	43.4	27.6	51.6	49.9	51.8	20 877	29 986	11 798	41 600	22.9	13.1
Elgin city	75.1	82.6	78.9	49.4	38.6	58.2	52.1	59.5	52 144	60 874	34 015	138 500	24.3	13.4
Elk Grove Village village	82.7	86.2	86.7	62.4	55.3	62.5	57.4	63.4	62 214	69 354	42 331	181 700	22.3	10.1
Elmhurst city	89.7	91.1	92.1	80.1	67.9	65.1	56.6	66.1	68 998	75 009	42 490	204 700	21.6	10.9
Elmwood Park village....	73.2	78.8	79.3	56.4	43.2	50.8	53.2	50.4	47 014	55 913	34 720	171 400	24.4	13.6
Evanston city	66.3	73.4	75.3	44.8	33.4	36.5	19.1	41.0	56 140	81 097	37 060	229 500	22.8	12.3
Freeport city	77.7	87.4	85.0	48.5	39.0	53.4	53.5	53.4	35 433	43 281	21 277	67 700	19.9	11.1
Galesburg city	74.1	83.5	76.8	46.7	32.2	49.2	47.1	49.6	31 421	40 107	19 952	59 700	18.3	10.6
Glendale Heights village	80.9	85.2	87.4	63.3	52.6	44.0	37.8	45.8	56 144	64 857	39 759	139 400	23.5	11.2
Glen Ellyn village	85.5	89.7	88.3	54.9	48.2	59.4	38.2	62.6	74 884	89 864	33 943	253 900	21.4	11.2
Glenview village	89.9	91.7	89.1	76.2	68.3	78.8	78.2	78.9	79 194	87 127	42 370	302 200	22.1	11.2
Granite City city...........	76.1	83.7	77.7	57.5	39.7	59.4	51.8	60.6	35 589	42 058	21 661	56 400	18.8	10.1
Gurnee village	87.9	92.2	93.4	57.7	52.3	53.0	42.3	55.2	75 887	84 891	36 327	194 800	23.0	12.0
Hanover Park village.....	83.8	87.6	85.8	70.3	64.6	73.9	59.8	77.9	61 108	64 585	39 583	139 900	24.1	11.9
Harvey city	58.9	73.5	63.7	42.6	28.0	49.6	43.2	50.6	31 919	40 670	20 420	70 200	24.3	11.2
Highland Park city	86.7	88.5	85.8	69.1	63.4	65.0	49.3	67.1	100 139	113 949	42 130	370 900	22.0	13.4
Hoffman Estates village	83.0	86.6	87.3	66.1	63.8	56.8	47.8	59.3	66 102	74 060	43 944	176 500	22.3	9.9
Joliet city	78.2	86.7	85.1	52.4	41.3	51.9	49.4	52.4	47 380	58 014	26 637	116 600	22.7	10.8
Kankakee city	60.0	75.8	69.3	37.9	26.9	41.2	45.6	40.4	30 037	41 720	19 521	72 300	22.3	12.8
Lansing village	83.4	89.7	88.7	60.4	49.0	58.1	44.6	60.1	48 264	54 308	32 331	115 600	20.4	11.4
Lombard village............	84.2	87.5	88.2	67.7	57.7	58.3	38.3	62.3	59 488	65 330	43 326	163 000	22.9	12.6
Maywood village...........	67.7	81.8	73.4	52.7	35.2	46.1	51.7	45.3	41 320	54 282	25 425	108 300	24.5	12.0
Moline city	76.0	82.9	77.8	51.2	43.1	52.5	46.6	53.4	39 546	48 094	25 321	79 300	19.4	11.2
Mount Prospect village..	78.4	81.2	76.2	62.4	46.6	54.0	36.0	57.2	57 192	66 578	41 391	204 700	22.5	12.4
Mundelein village	82.4	86.6	85.2	59.0	56.7	70.8	59.1	73.8	69 864	78 078	41 265	162 400	23.0	12.0
Naperville city..............	88.1	90.5	92.6	65.3	60.9	52.7	45.5	54.2	88 050	100 555	48 476	248 200	21.3	9.9
Niles village	84.8	87.0	84.7	74.7	61.8	59.4	62.7	59.1	47 731	52 681	32 287	198 000	25.5	13.0
Normal town	76.0	85.6	84.7	41.5	33.5	30.1	10.3	44.4	40 337	61 268	22 840	116 200	19.5	9.9
Northbrook village	94.9	95.6	95.2	88.2	82.6	78.9	73.1	79.3	95 508	101 260	42 661	353 100	21.8	10.3
North Chicago city........	36.5	37.1	26.8	35.0	18.4	34.6	23.1	37.2	37 521	46 058	33 344	101 400	27.5	17.0
Oak Forest city	88.3	93.0	90.9	64.6	50.1	61.2	59.9	61.5	59 613	65 710	32 211	145 900	22.1	11.8
Oak Lawn village...........	88.1	91.3	90.9	75.7	61.9	72.5	49.6	74.7	47 158	51 209	32 469	147 600	22.5	12.6
Oak Park village............	72.7	80.7	85.2	48.8	41.3	35.1	35.1	35.1	58 418	82 959	37 877	206 100	21.2	12.8
Orland Park village........	93.8	95.8	96.2	81.0	74.2	82.7	68.9	84.3	66 912	70 394	39 617	196 700	22.2	11.7
Palatine village	76.6	81.2	81.4	52.9	48.1	55.3	41.5	58.8	62 734	73 500	43 640	183 400	22.2	11.9
Park Ridge city	93.4	94.8	95.3	84.4	75.3	72.8	58.6	74.0	73 733	79 467	38 682	286 000	22.4	12.3
Pekin city	75.7	82.1	76.3	51.0	41.0	51.0	56.1	50.1	37 794	47 359	21 932	76 100	18.3	10.3
Peoria city	70.0	82.4	79.4	41.4	30.0	44.5	33.3	46.6	36 406	50 260	20 920	84 000	19.7	9.9
Quincy city	75.3	84.3	80.8	44.7	33.6	52.1	38.9	53.9	31 077	39 161	20 004	68 900	18.6	10.7
Rockford city	70.2	81.2	77.5	44.5	34.1	45.8	43.2	46.3	37 535	48 428	23 695	79 400	21.0	12.1
Rock Island city	75.2	85.9	83.9	48.1	34.2	50.5	43.7	51.6	34 347	44 525	20 111	69 800	19.1	10.7
Round Lake Beach village	89.2	92.2	91.6	75.2	66.2	69.7	73.6	68.6	59 583	62 263	26 948	122 600	24.3	13.7
St. Charles city.............	83.8	87.8	88.3	61.4	53.0	48.5	47.8	48.7	69 759	83 115	42 800	193 800	22.3	11.5
Schaumburg village.......	78.6	81.9	82.4	64.2	51.5	54.7	37.9	58.2	60 395	65 799	50 608	161 500	22.0	10.2
Skokie village	79.4	83.0	79.1	63.4	46.5	63.2	43.4	65.6	57 665	66 618	38 348	209 700	24.3	11.3
Springfield city.............	74.0	84.8	84.4	47.0	39.0	47.4	37.4	49.1	39 444	51 049	25 145	84 300	19.5	9.9
Streamwood village.......	89.5	92.3	90.6	77.2	69.7	89.3	81.0	91.0	64 519	65 896	51 019	142 800	23.2	11.8
Tinley Park village.........	91.4	94.0	93.6	77.5	63.0	67.1	56.3	68.8	61 083	66 747	35 525	160 900	22.2	11.2
Urbana city	57.6	66.2	66.4	33.4	28.4	20.7	9.3	26.7	28 266	52 648	18 344	89 500	19.6	9.9
Waukegan city..............	62.9	71.7	68.7	41.8	30.7	41.7	36.2	42.9	42 559	55 931	29 928	118 700	24.0	13.1
Wheaton city	82.3	85.8	88.3	56.6	63.4	53.6	40.7	55.6	73 172	86 316	46 424	211 200	21.4	10.1
Wheeling village	77.6	79.0	79.8	70.9	66.4	47.4	35.8	49.6	54 989	61 552	41 814	147 600	24.0	10.9
Wilmette village	92.2	93.3	91.8	82.0	76.5	69.4	81.6	68.2	105 869	115 283	42 396	424 800	21.6	9.9
Woodridge village.........	75.5	82.9	82.7	48.6	39.8	46.3	35.9	48.5	62 106	73 904	42 534	160 200	21.6	10.3
INDIANA	79.5	86.1	83.1	54.9	44.8	53.7	43.7	55.7	41 425	49 688	25 550	92 500	19.3	9.9
Anderson city	70.0	79.4	65.9	48.5	34.1	53.8	47.1	54.9	32 306	39 964	21 837	65 900	19.6	9.9
Bloomington city...........	60.5	68.1	67.5	37.2	32.8	19.2	8.1	25.4	25 087	56 284	16 974	119 300	19.7	9.9
Carmel city	86.9	90.6	90.9	57.2	54.0	50.6	40.5	52.2	81 830	95 076	40 096	201 400	18.7	9.9
Columbus city	72.5	78.9	73.2	48.5	36.7	49.5	42.3	50.7	41 184	52 460	26 442	104 000	20.0	9.9
East Chicago city	49.0	66.6	58.1	29.0	16.5	35.2	32.1	35.5	26 104	39 794	17 981	70 400	18.0	9.9
Elkhart city..................	61.4	70.9	64.5	41.5	33.0	41.2	34.4	42.8	35 117	42 495	27 811	74 200	18.8	9.9
Evansville city	70.2	79.7	76.3	46.8	35.4	45.4	33.1	47.5	31 703	40 622	21 281	69 300	19.2	9.9
Fishers town.................	86.8	89.3	92.6	66.7	66.4	52.7	53.4	52.6	74 683	81 841	45 481	161 300	20.7	9.9

Table C-5. Cities — **Migration, Housing, and Transportation**

City	Median gross rent	Percent who pay 35 percent or more of income for housing expenses		Means of transportation to work (percent except where noted)							Vehicles available (percent of households)		
		Owners	Renters	Number of workers 16 years and over	Car, truck, or van		Public transportation	Other means	Walked		No vehicles	One vehicle	Two or more vehicles
					Drove alone	Carpooled							
	25	26	27	28	29	30	31	32	33		34	35	36
ILLINOIS—Cont'd													
Danville city	410	12.0	28.1	12 584	79.5	13.6	1.2	0.9	2.4		14.3	40.1	45.6
Decatur city	447	11.1	28.8	35 140	82.4	10.7	1.3	0.9	2.7		10.3	40.0	49.6
DeKalb city	565	14.3	42.1	18 871	70.5	9.5	2.5	2.3	12.8		8.6	38.9	52.5
Des Plaines city	764	17.0	28.2	28 223	79.7	9.0	6.7	0.6	1.5		9.3	34.8	55.9
Dolton village	686	21.3	33.2	11 234	67.2	14.5	13.0	1.3	1.4		8.5	39.5	52.0
Downers Grove village	768	13.9	27.3	25 067	77.3	5.5	10.7	0.6	1.6		7.4	31.9	60.7
East St. Louis city	361	21.6	36.1	9 027	67.7	12.0	14.6	0.8	2.4		31.2	41.0	27.8
Elgin city	675	19.3	24.3	45 445	78.3	14.3	2.7	0.8	1.9		7.2	33.5	59.3
Elk Grove Village village	825	12.7	27.1	19 188	85.8	7.2	3.5	0.3	0.9		4.8	32.9	62.3
Elmhurst city	840	13.6	23.6	21 411	79.7	5.6	7.5	0.9	3.1		6.2	30.1	63.7
Elmwood Park village	670	20.4	25.4	12 445	78.1	8.6	8.8	0.8	2.3		12.6	39.5	48.0
Evanston city	856	19.7	34.2	37 655	53.4	8.3	18.4	2.2	11.7		15.2	48.6	36.2
Freeport city	425	10.4	24.2	11 855	81.7	12.2	1.2	0.4	2.7		11.2	40.9	47.9
Galesburg city	412	10.0	25.4	14 493	78.3	11.1	1.6	1.4	5.8		11.5	40.6	47.9
Glendale Heights village	823	18.6	23.9	16 997	81.7	12.2	2.6	0.9	1.1		5.3	30.9	63.8
Glen Ellyn village	736	13.7	26.2	13 388	72.2	6.4	11.7	1.3	2.8		4.9	32.1	62.9
Glenview village	828	17.9	19.4	20 475	77.5	7.1	8.1	0.7	1.5		3.2	28.3	68.6
Granite City city	429	10.1	25.4	13 860	81.1	12.6	2.1	1.1	1.9		10.6	39.2	50.3
Gurnee village	806	15.2	32.5	14 910	85.8	7.6	2.7	0.3	0.6		4.2	28.6	67.2
Hanover Park village	750	17.7	26.2	19 287	77.8	14.2	3.7	0.9	1.8		4.8	25.4	69.9
Harvey city	593	22.4	38.8	9 856	63.3	17.3	13.1	0.5	3.6		21.2	39.9	38.9
Highland Park city	931	19.7	28.0	15 504	69.9	8.3	12.3	0.9	2.2		4.0	27.7	68.3
Hoffman Estates village	888	15.6	25.0	26 331	84.2	7.6	3.3	1.0	1.3		4.2	28.3	67.5
Joliet city	549	15.8	25.9	45 796	81.0	11.8	2.6	1.2	1.6		8.5	34.7	56.8
Kankakee city	491	18.7	35.8	10 630	73.6	17.3	1.4	2.7	3.0		14.6	44.2	41.2
Lansing village	658	13.6	25.6	13 461	81.4	7.7	6.1	0.3	2.3		5.9	39.5	54.6
Lombard village	889	14.1	26.1	21 953	81.3	7.5	6.4	0.6	1.6		6.1	36.2	57.7
Maywood village	638	22.9	39.2	10 686	68.3	15.6	9.4	1.8	3.2		15.4	37.3	47.3
Moline city	474	10.5	21.2	21 172	84.1	9.5	1.9	0.7	1.6		8.0	38.7	53.3
Mount Prospect village	786	14.4	22.5	29 175	78.2	10.4	6.0	1.1	2.1		6.1	36.4	57.5
Mundelein village	774	16.1	25.7	15 314	78.4	12.0	4.1	1.3	0.8		2.5	26.7	70.8
Naperville city	942	13.6	25.0	63 884	78.6	4.9	9.0	0.7	1.4		2.8	23.8	73.4
Niles village	747	17.4	32.2	13 462	78.2	10.7	6.1	1.0	2.0		11.2	38.6	50.1
Normal town	554	9.5	38.9	23 193	75.1	8.7	1.5	1.2	11.0		5.9	35.8	58.3
Northbrook village	1 279	17.1	43.9	15 710	74.8	6.7	9.9	0.6	1.3		2.5	25.6	72.0
North Chicago city	670	28.0	22.2	19 751	41.1	7.4	1.4	16.3	27.2		9.7	40.4	50.0
Oak Forest city	667	14.5	26.9	14 514	78.5	8.7	8.8	0.6	1.0		5.3	28.2	66.6
Oak Lawn village	687	15.2	30.3	24 444	79.1	8.3	8.2	0.4	1.8		8.1	40.1	51.8
Oak Park village	710	15.6	22.3	29 484	60.8	7.6	21.8	0.7	4.0		12.5	47.6	39.9
Orland Park village	760	15.2	26.3	24 459	82.8	6.9	6.5	0.6	1.1		4.2	28.3	67.5
Palatine village	884	15.8	25.2	36 386	80.3	10.0	4.7	1.1	1.4		5.3	35.4	59.3
Park Ridge city	858	15.6	29.9	18 100	77.4	6.2	10.1	0.5	1.8		5.3	31.4	63.3
Pekin city	434	8.9	21.8	15 277	83.0	12.7	0.6	0.7	1.5		8.5	39.0	52.5
Peoria city	496	12.0	31.1	49 161	80.0	10.5	3.2	0.5	3.8		11.8	41.2	47.0
Quincy city	410	8.8	25.1	18 814	83.1	9.2	0.9	1.0	3.6		10.6	40.0	49.4
Rockford city	498	13.3	27.6	66 617	80.7	12.3	1.8	1.0	1.9		11.4	39.6	49.0
Rock Island city	437	11.5	29.2	17 897	79.2	10.0	2.3	1.1	5.7		11.9	40.5	47.7
Round Lake Beach village	827	20.3	21.8	12 201	74.4	18.1	3.0	1.1	0.9		4.7	23.5	71.8
St. Charles city	797	15.1	22.5	14 792	84.6	6.3	3.2	0.5	1.6		4.3	28.7	66.9
Schaumburg village	981	15.0	23.2	43 306	85.4	6.5	4.1	0.4	0.9		5.8	40.2	54.1
Skokie village	800	19.6	27.3	29 632	74.0	11.3	8.1	0.9	2.2		9.4	37.5	53.1
Springfield city	499	10.4	26.8	56 027	80.6	11.2	2.5	0.9	2.6		11.0	42.4	46.6
Streamwood village	1 130	15.7	27.9	19 510	81.4	11.6	3.3	0.6	0.7		1.9	26.3	71.8
Tinley Park village	709	13.8	25.1	24 663	79.1	7.7	10.2	0.5	0.8		4.8	30.5	64.7
Urbana city	537	9.5	44.8	17 441	53.3	10.5	10.9	5.2	17.0		15.7	47.7	36.6
Waukegan city	647	20.5	28.5	37 964	70.0	21.3	3.6	1.5	2.0		10.7	38.8	50.5
Wheaton city	892	13.0	22.7	27 826	75.9	5.8	8.5	1.0	4.2		3.3	33.4	63.3
Wheeling village	885	18.6	25.4	18 933	79.9	12.5	3.3	0.7	1.8		5.2	40.4	54.4
Wilmette village	1 028	15.7	30.4	12 371	66.0	6.2	18.7	0.8	1.3		4.5	30.3	65.2
Woodridge village	756	13.0	22.7	16 835	80.1	8.1	7.0	0.6	1.4		4.3	33.0	62.7
INDIANA	521	11.2	26.4	2 910 612	81.8	11.0	1.0	0.9	2.4		7.2	32.4	60.4
Anderson city	493	12.3	27.5	25 687	77.3	15.2	1.0	0.6	3.6		10.2	42.6	47.2
Bloomington city	557	14.2	48.2	33 338	66.8	9.2	3.0	3.2	14.5		11.0	44.7	44.3
Carmel city	748	8.8	25.4	18 861	87.0	6.4	0.1	0.4	0.9		2.2	23.1	74.7
Columbus city	579	10.4	27.2	18 671	83.6	10.9	0.5	1.3	1.6		7.8	34.1	58.1
East Chicago city	409	12.8	28.0	10 146	72.9	15.1	3.1	1.8	5.6		25.1	43.3	31.5
Elkhart city	537	12.9	22.8	24 324	75.0	18.4	1.3	1.1	2.1		10.3	43.5	46.2
Evansville city	454	11.4	28.4	57 186	81.8	10.7	1.7	0.8	3.2		13.2	40.4	46.4
Fishers town	797	10.9	17.5	21 766	89.9	4.1	0.1	0.6	0.4		1.1	25.6	73.3

Table C-5. Cities — **Migration, Housing, and Transportation**

STATE Place code	City	Total population 5 years and over	Residence in 1995 (percent)					Occupied housing units		Householders 65 years and over	
			Same house	Same county, different house	Same state, different county	Different state	Outside the United States	Number	Percent owner-occupied	Number	Percent owner-occupied
		1	2	3	4	5	6	7	8	9	10
	INDIANA—Cont'd										
18 25000	Fort Wayne city	189 774	50.7	32.4	6.1	8.6	2.2	83 337	61.6	17 031	72.0
18 27000	Gary city	94 183	62.3	28.9	1.6	6.4	0.8	38 244	55.9	9 466	78.0
18 28386	Goshen city	27 084	43.1	33.3	6.9	9.3	7.5	10 668	64.0	2 628	70.9
18 29898	Greenwood city	32 973	46.8	16.0	25.9	9.9	1.4	14 865	62.5	2 609	61.4
18 31000	Hammond city	76 426	60.4	25.2	1.5	11.4	1.4	32 026	63.2	7 864	78.1
18 34114	Hobart city	23 954	61.7	26.3	6.2	5.3	0.5	9 834	80.3	2 436	84.3
18 36000	Indianapolis city	733 924	47.4	34.1	8.3	7.8	2.3	324 373	58.8	60 160	72.1
18 38358	Jeffersonville city	25 667	51.0	26.6	8.5	13.0	0.8	11 705	62.1	2 330	77.3
18 40392	Kokomo city	42 279	51.9	30.8	9.3	7.4	0.7	20 325	60.9	4 758	73.4
18 40788	Lafayette city	52 255	42.1	30.7	12.1	12.1	3.0	24 040	52.6	4 701	76.2
18 42426	Lawrence city	35 819	41.6	36.4	8.3	11.3	2.3	14 913	75.5	2 162	83.7
18 46908	Marion city	29 040	50.3	31.7	8.0	9.3	0.7	12 430	61.6	3 480	67.4
18 48528	Merrillville town	28 823	58.5	28.6	2.8	8.8	1.3	11 763	70.8	3 063	70.6
18 48798	Michigan City city	30 446	53.4	28.6	9.2	8.2	0.6	12 546	60.8	3 122	73.0
18 40000	Mishawaka city	43 121	48.6	30.9	7.3	11.5	1.7	20 310	56.8	4 940	72.3
18 51876	Muncie city	63 508	44.6	28.3	18.4	7.1	1.6	27 320	55.8	6 113	80.4
18 52326	New Albany city	34 938	53.7	25.1	10.8	9.9	0.5	15 918	59.5	3 745	71.2
18 54180	Noblesville city	26 248	45.2	23.9	18.9	11.5	0.4	10 649	75.3	1 624	76.2
18 61092	Portage city	31 089	55.5	22.6	13.6	7.2	1.1	12 706	72.2	2 510	78.4
18 64260	Richmond city	36 453	50.3	33.3	5.2	10.1	1.1	16 343	58.5	4 324	69.9
18 71000	South Bend city	98 014	52.8	29.8	5.0	9.8	2.7	42 801	63.1	10 892	77.5
18 75428	Terre Haute city	55 983	45.8	29.4	12.1	11.0	1.6	22 852	59.3	5 999	72.3
18 78326	Valparaiso city	25 908	44.4	24.6	12.6	16.7	1.7	10 914	54.8	2 350	64.9
18 82862	West Lafayette city	28 222	23.0	14.2	33.6	19.3	9.9	10 493	32.9	1 524	68.4
19 00000	IOWA	2 738 499	56.9	23.3	10.6	7.8	1.4	1 149 276	72.3	281 122	80.0
19 01855	Ames city	48 387	28.6	18.1	31.2	15.4	6.6	18 045	46.1	2 401	77.5
19 02305	Ankeny city	24 717	40.6	28.1	15.7	12.8	2.7	10 270	71.7	1 440	79.4
19 06355	Bettendorf city	29 385	51.8	27.9	5.2	14.0	1.2	12 476	77.1	2 531	76.8
19 09550	Burlington city	25 129	55.2	28.1	7.8	8.0	1.0	11 135	70.1	3 233	77.3
19 11755	Cedar Falls city	34 775	43.7	21.4	26.6	6.6	1.6	12 835	64.4	2 655	79.4
19 12000	Cedar Rapids city	112 239	50.0	29.0	10.0	9.3	1.6	49 010	69.1	10 602	79.8
19 14430	Clinton city	25 991	55.2	29.9	4.5	9.8	0.7	11 431	69.3	2 984	78.6
19 16860	Council Bluffs city	54 185	51.1	30.7	5.6	11.8	0.9	22 900	65.1	6 220	74.3
19 19000	Davenport city	91 010	51.8	28.5	5.6	12.5	1.5	39 119	65.1	7 829	79.6
19 21000	Des Moines city	183 502	50.9	29.9	7.9	8.1	3.3	80 497	64.7	16 759	74.0
19 22395	Dubuque city	53 916	56.5	26.1	6.1	9.7	1.8	22 538	67.7	5 699	75.7
19 28515	Fort Dodge city	23 402	53.3	30.3	10.1	5.6	0.8	10 452	66.3	2 695	76.7
19 38595	Iowa City city	59 628	33.7	21.1	22.5	18.1	4.5	25 195	46.6	3 158	75.9
19 49485	Marion city	24 553	51.8	30.2	9.0	8.3	0.7	10 464	78.1	2 011	81.8
19 49755	Marshalltown city	24 331	53.2	25.4	9.5	8.9	3.0	10 177	70.1	2 708	74.9
19 50160	Mason City city	27 267	54.8	27.3	10.9	6.5	0.6	12 369	67.4	3 385	73.3
19 73335	Sioux City city	78 595	53.3	28.7	4.5	10.7	2.8	32 048	66.3	7 064	75.1
19 79950	Urbandale city	27 194	52.8	27.6	9.5	8.2	1.9	11 471	77.5	1 978	84.6
19 82425	Waterloo city	63 793	55.4	27.4	6.6	6.6	4.0	28 166	67.1	7 029	75.0
19 83910	West Des Moines city ...	42 735	39.8	27.3	16.2	14.3	2.4	19 777	62.2	3 052	73.6
20 00000	KANSAS	2 500 360	52.4	24.3	10.2	11.1	2.1	1 037 891	69.3	230 625	80.3
20 18250	Dodge City city	22 630	47.1	28.0	7.8	8.9	8.3	8 396	60.3	1 530	68.6
20 21275	Emporia city	24 759	39.9	27.9	18.4	9.5	4.4	10 247	53.5	1 814	68.6
20 25325	Garden City city	25 245	43.5	29.5	8.1	13.3	5.6	9 271	60.9	1 421	78.7
20 33625	Hutchinson city	38 031	50.7	28.3	13.0	7.1	1.0	16 324	64.7	4 533	75.5
20 36000	Kansas City city	135 070	54.1	26.0	5.5	10.3	4.1	55 501	62.0	11 476	79.2
20 38900	Lawrence city	75 752	32.1	23.2	23.0	18.0	3.7	31 435	45.8	3 881	72.8
20 39000	Leavenworth city	32 380	37.7	21.8	6.7	29.1	4.7	12 009	50.3	2 298	73.5
20 39075	Leawood city	26 072	59.9	19.6	1.6	17.9	1.0	9 878	92.8	2 009	95.9
20 39350	Lenexa city	37 309	49.7	21.9	7.6	18.0	2.9	15 511	62.9	1 971	62.3
20 44250	Manhattan city	42 940	28.9	17.0	34.4	15.6	4.2	16 981	43.2	2 436	77.0
20 52575	Olathe city	84 490	43.7	26.9	7.6	19.3	2.5	32 307	71.6	2 867	70.5
20 53775	Overland Park city	138 240	47.8	22.8	5.6	20.9	2.8	59 744	68.2	11 067	72.9
20 62700	Salina city	42 430	49.3	28.0	12.1	9.4	1.2	18 531	66.2	4 213	77.3
20 64500	Shawnee city	44 468	51.1	24.9	8.4	13.7	1.9	18 584	74.2	2 620	83.8
20 71000	Topeka city	113 352	50.6	32.3	8.3	7.6	1.3	52 230	60.8	12 205	71.2
20 79000	Wichita city	316 917	47.4	33.5	6.0	10.3	2.9	139 008	61.6	27 665	77.6
21 00000	KENTUCKY	3 776 230	55.9	24.7	9.7	8.4	1.2	1 590 647	70.7	339 303	81.2
21 08902	Bowling Green city	46 157	35.5	27.5	19.2	13.6	4.2	19 185	47.1	3 897	70.8
21 17848	Covington city	40 050	50.6	26.0	10.1	12.5	0.8	18 230	49.3	3 473	53.7
21 28900	Frankfort city	25 767	45.6	29.8	13.6	8.8	2.2	12 283	51.9	3 066	69.9
21 35866	Henderson city	25 556	47.9	34.6	8.0	8.6	0.8	11 715	57.6	2 966	69.9

Table C-5. Cities — Migration, Housing, and Transportation

City	Owner-occupied by household type (percent)								Median household income			Median monthly owner costs as a percent of income	
	Family households					Nonfamily households						Median housing value (owner estimated)		
		Married-couple family		Other family										
	Total family households	Total	With own children under 18 years	Total	With own children under 18 years	Total nonfamily households	Two or more adults	Living alone	All households	Owner-occupied households	Renter-occupied households	Median housing value (owner estimated)	With a mortgage	Without a mortgage
	11	12	13	14	15	16	17	18	19	20	21	22	23	24

INDIANA—Cont'd														
Fort Wayne city	71.2	81.9	78.9	46.9	37.2	46.6	41.1	47.7	36 341	44 720	25 310	73 100	18.6	9.9
Gary city	59.2	77.4	62.5	43.5	24.6	48.9	42.6	49.8	27 195	37 424	17 842	51 900	21.5	13.0
Goshen city	71.4	79.5	73.0	39.0	32.1	48.7	47.4	49.0	39 164	47 859	26 782	86 400	18.8	9.9
Greenwood city	74.9	82.2	83.3	47.1	42.5	40.0	37.3	40.5	46 682	57 949	30 909	112 300	20.6	9.9
Hammond city	70.3	80.8	72.8	48.9	32.5	49.7	47.0	50.1	35 051	42 684	22 838	78 500	19.6	10.9
Hobart city	85.9	89.4	86.9	72.0	61.4	66.7	62.0	67.6	47 681	51 951	30 597	98 300	19.2	10.5
Indianapolis city	68.7	80.1	77.2	44.4	34.8	43.5	38.0	44.8	39 971	52 076	26 901	96 900	20.1	9.9
Jeffersonville city	70.8	80.0	75.4	48.7	32.2	47.6	47.5	47.6	36 892	45 717	24 058	83 600	20.0	9.9
Kokomo city	67.9	79.5	73.8	41.0	29.0	50.5	41.3	51.7	35 709	46 188	23 176	72 800	17.9	9.9
Lafayette city	64.8	71.8	65.2	42.7	33.6	36.4	21.4	40.7	35 532	47 226	25 663	89 300	20.0	9.9
Lawrence city	81.1	89.0	87.7	56.6	52.7	62.9	50.2	66.1	47 716	55 489	30 698	102 900	20.9	9.9
Marion city	70.4	80.7	72.7	45.7	35.3	48.0	40.0	49.2	30 329	37 361	19 882	56 700	18.1	10.4
Merrillville town	80.2	85.8	85.9	61.3	56.6	49.4	48.4	49.5	49 064	55 632	34 226	101 300	20.2	9.9
Michigan City city	66.6	79.9	76.2	43.2	31.6	50.8	45.0	51.8	33 209	41 231	23 763	75 600	20.7	11.3
Mishawaka city	68.8	76.9	73.0	49.4	43.0	40.7	39.3	41.0	33 498	40 374	26 583	74 100	19.3	10.9
Muncie city	67.1	76.4	65.4	45.8	37.4	42.7	20.1	50.7	26 363	35 510	17 608	57 100	19.2	10.4
New Albany city	66.9	79.6	74.5	38.0	22.5	46.9	35.2	49.0	34 755	44 348	23 318	87 000	20.0	11.1
Noblesville city	81.7	89.2	89.0	42.7	36.5	57.0	45.0	59.3	59 536	71 358	27 281	140 600	20.6	9.9
Portage city	77.7	84.4	80.1	56.2	47.0	58.8	49.3	61.0	47 233	53 686	30 531	100 000	19.1	10.4
Richmond city	66.7	77.6	69.4	35.9	23.3	46.1	47.7	45.8	29 795	40 360	19 606	71 200	19.2	10.6
South Bend city	69.8	81.0	76.9	48.3	34.2	52.7	43.3	54.6	32 248	39 684	21 845	66 200	20.0	10.1
Terre Haute city	70.2	80.6	73.5	47.6	37.7	44.8	27.7	48.8	27 906	39 160	16 890	60 100	18.6	9.9
Valparaiso city	70.5	78.0	78.4	42.1	37.2	33.0	22.9	35.5	45 016	61 306	28 265	121 000	20.0	9.9
West Lafayette city	69.9	77.2	83.3	36.2	53.9	13.5	4.0	23.0	24 742	78 457	15 135	144 800	18.2	9.9
IOWA	81.6	86.6	83.7	57.5	48.7	53.4	39.9	56.2	39 358	46 120	24 581	82 100	19.1	9.9
Ames city	69.2	74.8	76.3	40.9	36.5	23.3	9.0	34.2	35 977	62 354	21 567	125 300	19.9	9.9
Ankeny city	81.5	87.6	87.3	48.1	41.8	47.7	32.0	53.1	55 253	67 424	30 462	123 600	19.6	9.9
Bettendorf city	86.1	89.2	87.7	66.7	63.9	56.3	53.1	56.7	53 462	61 525	30 483	114 400	19.5	9.9
Burlington city	79.2	86.9	81.8	52.9	43.5	54.0	49.2	54.7	33 401	40 088	20 234	62 700	18.7	10.0
Cedar Falls city	83.9	88.2	88.0	61.5	59.6	36.7	13.5	51.0	39 743	52 739	21 364	97 400	18.8	9.9
Cedar Rapids city	80.1	87.1	86.3	53.6	44.0	51.1	37.6	54.5	43 231	51 791	26 473	92 900	19.5	9.9
Clinton city	79.1	87.1	82.1	52.5	38.8	51.3	39.8	53.3	34 161	41 845	19 400	61 500	18.5	9.9
Council Bluffs city	72.7	81.7	77.5	49.4	39.7	50.6	46.2	51.6	36 280	43 885	25 163	76 500	19.6	11.4
Davenport city	74.7	83.5	80.0	49.5	40.0	48.4	38.1	50.8	37 328	47 248	21 743	78 900	19.1	9.9
Des Moines city	75.1	82.3	79.0	55.3	43.7	48.7	45.1	49.6	38 036	46 426	25 226	79 900	20.9	11.9
Dubuque city	79.1	86.0	83.4	51.6	42.1	47.8	36.7	49.7	36 809	45 192	22 552	86 400	19.3	9.9
Fort Dodge city	77.8	85.1	80.7	53.3	44.5	48.3	31.7	50.9	33 622	41 475	21 782	64 000	17.0	11.4
Iowa City city	71.7	78.3	79.0	46.5	39.9	26.2	14.1	33.9	34 387	60 650	19 425	121 400	20.5	9.9
Marion city	88.3	92.2	91.2	68.9	64.1	55.9	61.3	54.7	48 037	55 259	26 405	97 800	19.1	10.5
Marshalltown city	78.4	85.6	81.0	54.5	44.9	54.6	40.6	57.2	35 483	43 219	21 425	66 800	19.1	11.8
Mason City city	81.2	89.6	89.7	48.8	41.6	46.4	38.4	47.8	33 615	42 699	19 462	72 500	18.7	10.8
Sioux City city	76.1	83.2	81.4	53.7	44.3	47.1	40.2	48.6	37 037	45 709	24 043	73 100	19.4	10.8
Urbandale city	86.2	89.8	90.0	63.4	53.9	57.5	42.9	61.0	59 192	67 871	32 226	131 100	19.8	9.9
Waterloo city	76.4	84.2	79.8	52.7	40.2	51.2	41.9	53.2	33 780	41 874	20 984	63 800	18.5	10.6
West Des Moines city	77.5	82.9	85.0	47.7	42.3	39.3	22.6	44.4	53 852	71 360	36 101	137 500	20.0	9.9
KANSAS	77.9	83.5	79.3	52.9	45.1	51.1	35.2	54.2	40 509	48 572	25 898	81 000	19.3	9.9
Dodge City city	68.1	77.3	73.0	38.9	35.1	40.7	14.5	46.5	36 962	45 617	25 357	65 800	19.9	10.4
Emporia city	68.0	74.8	71.3	43.7	40.3	32.6	14.1	38.5	30 840	42 998	19 664	65 500	19.4	10.9
Garden City city	68.3	73.4	65.6	49.7	44.3	42.3	23.6	46.8	36 844	45 467	24 427	77 700	20.5	10.0
Hutchinson city	73.2	81.9	79.0	42.8	33.6	50.2	33.8	52.6	32 773	40 225	21 690	63 200	19.0	10.1
Kansas City city	67.4	77.0	67.9	49.9	39.5	51.7	47.1	52.5	32 841	40 812	23 329	51 900	19.6	11.2
Lawrence city	67.1	75.0	75.3	40.5	38.5	23.9	11.9	31.3	34 734	56 094	22 166	112 800	20.4	9.9
Leavenworth city	52.8	57.1	38.6	38.5	26.6	44.9	47.9	44.4	40 210	46 540	32 164	74 400	19.6	10.2
Leawood city	96.1	97.0	97.4	85.2	77.9	76.3	67.2	77.4	103 162	107 883	41 384	274 400	19.6	9.9
Lenexa city	76.6	80.7	83.2	50.3	52.7	33.6	23.0	36.7	61 802	80 923	38 563	156 300	18.7	9.9
Manhattan city	63.9	69.3	69.0	42.7	39.4	23.2	9.6	32.4	30 204	52 868	18 255	93 700	18.5	9.9
Olathe city	80.3	86.6	86.8	46.8	46.2	42.9	42.4	43.0	60 721	71 378	33 051	138 600	20.0	9.9
Overland Park city	80.7	84.6	86.8	55.7	51.1	43.6	28.4	47.0	61 902	76 298	41 214	160 900	19.3	9.9
Salina city	75.9	82.6	78.3	50.7	42.8	48.7	35.6	51.2	35 845	43 541	23 808	81 200	19.7	9.9
Shawnee city	85.4	90.0	89.3	58.8	50.3	46.1	35.5	48.8	58 905	69 196	35 916	141 100	19.8	9.9
Topeka city	71.2	80.8	76.2	46.8	38.4	45.8	36.8	47.3	35 776	44 917	23 662	65 700	19.2	9.9
Wichita city	71.4	78.9	74.6	48.3	39.0	44.8	37.6	46.0	39 639	50 400	26 108	75 000	19.4	9.9
KENTUCKY	77.5	83.9	79.5	54.4	43.0	55.3	42.2	57.5	33 549	40 460	21 295	79 600	19.6	9.9
Bowling Green city	59.1	69.8	61.6	32.8	25.8	31.6	13.9	36.8	29 442	44 607	21 362	97 000	20.2	10.0
Covington city	60.1	74.0	74.4	37.6	26.7	35.8	28.6	37.4	30 973	44 787	20 480	72 300	20.1	10.2
Frankfort city	61.2	72.3	63.1	35.1	21.6	39.9	28.4	41.7	34 481	49 252	23 173	87 600	18.3	9.9
Henderson city	67.5	79.1	70.5	35.8	23.1	40.9	32.6	42.1	30 190	43 337	18 066	70 600	18.3	9.9

Table C-5. Cities — **Migration, Housing, and Transportation**

City	Median gross rent	Percent who pay 35 percent or more of income for housing expenses — Owners	Renters	Means of transportation to work (percent except where noted) — Number of workers 16 years and over	Car, truck, or van — Drove alone	Carpooled	Public transportation	Other means	Walked	Vehicles available (percent of households) — No vehicles	One vehicle	Two or more vehicles
	25	26	27	28	29	30	31	32	33	34	35	36
INDIANA—Cont'd												
Fort Wayne city	490	10.6	26.0	98 784	81.8	12.2	1.2	0.8	2.1	9.2	40.4	50.4
Gary city	469	22.8	32.3	34 633	72.0	18.1	4.7	1.0	2.5	19.4	44.7	35.9
Goshen city	519	8.4	22.0	14 453	76.0	15.9	0.2	2.3	3.9	6.8	38.5	54.7
Greenwood city	610	10.4	25.6	19 095	85.8	10.1	0.1	0.4	1.7	5.3	35.7	59.0
Hammond city	518	12.2	30.6	33 895	77.7	12.7	4.6	0.8	2.6	12.4	43.1	44.5
Hobart city	628	11.7	24.9	12 019	87.9	6.6	1.6	0.8	0.9	5.1	31.2	63.7
Indianapolis city...........	567	13.4	28.6	389 885	80.1	12.3	2.4	0.8	2.0	10.0	40.0	50.1
Jeffersonville city	485	11.8	23.7	13 555	84.0	10.4	1.2	1.0	2.1	8.8	40.7	50.5
Kokomo city..................	498	11.3	25.6	20 646	82.4	12.1	0.5	1.0	2.2	10.4	43.2	46.5
Lafayette city	560	11.0	29.2	29 176	80.3	12.0	1.8	1.3	2.4	8.6	41.7	49.7
Lawrence city	590	13.4	25.4	20 337	83.5	12.3	0.5	0.5	0.7	3.9	34.7	61.4
Marion city	413	12.1	23.0	12 455	76.1	12.6	0.9	1.8	5.9	12.6	41.6	45.8
Morrillville town..............	704	11.3	28.6	15 016	84.2	10.3	2.1	0.7	1.2	7.8	32.7	59.5
Michigan City city	489	14.0	28.1	13 926	80.0	13.2	1.8	1.0	2.6	10.8	44.3	44.8
Mishawaka city	526	11.3	23.4	23 711	82.1	11.8	1.0	0.6	3.2	8.9	45.0	46.1
Muncie city	449	13.1	37.4	29 634	75.4	11.4	1.7	1.2	7.9	10.6	42.5	46.9
New Albany city	503	12.5	25.3	17 703	83.1	11.1	0.9	0.8	2.1	10.1	39.1	50.8
Noblesville city	629	10.6	28.8	14 670	85.5	8.3	0.2	0.7	1.3	4.8	26.7	68.5
Portage city	594	12.1	27.1	15 836	86.6	9.6	1.3	0.9	0.4	4.3	33.6	62.1
Richmond city..............	439	11.8	26.6	17 311	79.1	12.7	1.0	1.4	4.0	12.5	39.8	47.6
South Bend city...........	531	12.7	31.6	46 154	78.4	13.4	2.7	1.0	2.1	12.6	43.4	44.0
Terre Haute city	430	10.9	33.1	25 055	78.5	11.3	0.5	1.3	6.7	12.3	41.5	46.2
Valparaiso city	625	9.6	27.7	13 579	80.9	6.4	0.7	1.3	7.8	8.3	38.6	53.2
West Lafayette city........	614	8.5	59.4	13 250	66.9	7.1	1.9	2.1	19.3	9.4	38.4	52.2
IOWA	470	9.6	24.8	1 469 763	78.6	10.8	1.0	0.9	4.0	6.4	30.5	63.1
Ames city....................	600	8.9	41.4	28 297	65.4	9.1	6.1	3.0	13.2	5.6	36.5	57.9
Ankeny city	596	9.5	23.3	15 629	86.1	7.5	1.8	0.2	1.2	3.8	26.6	69.6
Bettendorf city	572	10.2	23.5	15 956	87.7	7.1	0.4	0.5	1.2	5.5	30.9	63.6
Burlington city..............	437	10.8	22.8	12 685	80.5	12.7	0.6	1.3	2.5	9.5	35.8	54.7
Cedar Falls city	492	7.6	39.4	19 794	80.3	5.7	0.5	1.2	9.6	5.0	31.9	63.1
Cedar Rapids city.........	521	9.3	24.7	63 692	82.3	10.7	1.3	0.9	2.5	7.5	34.9	57.6
Clinton city..................	383	9.3	26.7	12 416	81.5	11.5	1.2	0.9	2.7	9.3	35.2	55.5
Council Bluffs city........	550	11.6	29.1	28 441	81.8	12.5	0.7	0.8	2.1	8.4	36.0	55.5
Davenport city.............	482	11.4	31.7	47 069	83.6	9.7	1.1	0.9	2.2	9.2	36.4	54.4
Des Moines city............	532	13.7	27.1	99 490	78.9	12.5	2.5	0.8	2.9	10.0	38.1	51.9
Dubuque city................	436	8.2	24.5	28 527	81.5	8.8	0.8	0.6	6.1	9.3	36.7	54.0
Fort Dodge city.............	418	7.3	25.0	11 644	85.1	10.1	0.6	0.8	2.1	7.5	39.5	53.0
Iowa City city..............	572	10.9	47.5	35 668	61.0	10.2	7.7	3.0	15.5	10.3	40.5	49.2
Marion city	456	6.9	24.3	14 768	84.9	9.0	1.4	0.8	0.8	5.0	30.1	64.9
Marshalltown city...........	464	12.0	33.1	11 913	78.5	14.8	0.7	1.2	2.9	9.0	35.0	56.0
Mason City city.............	405	9.3	24.2	14 265	84.4	8.0	1.3	0.8	3.0	10.9	36.9	52.2
Sioux City city..............	495	10.3	25.7	41 571	78.6	14.1	1.2	1.0	2.9	10.3	33.1	56.6
Urbandale city	645	8.6	25.5	16 495	85.8	7.7	1.0	0.3	1.0	3.1	29.2	67.8
Waterloo city	467	9.8	32.6	31 497	83.9	10.4	1.2	0.8	1.8	10.2	35.0	54.8
West Des Moines city ...	674	11.3	20.4	27 047	84.2	8.4	2.0	0.6	1.2	3.7	36.4	59.9
KANSAS..................	498	10.5	25.0	1 311 343	81.5	10.6	0.5	0.9	2.5	5.7	31.6	62.7
Dodge City city.............	454	12.3	23.4	11 458	75.8	19.2	0.6	1.9	1.2	7.1	35.2	57.7
Emporia city	421	10.8	31.9	12 960	75.5	14.8	0.4	1.8	5.4	9.0	38.4	52.6
Garden City city............	497	11.9	25.7	12 827	73.3	20.5	0.4	1.4	1.7	7.2	34.5	58.2
Hutchinson city.............	450	10.8	29.3	17 994	84.4	10.6	0.1	0.9	1.7	7.9	36.3	55.8
Kansas City city............	491	14.2	27.4	61 601	77.4	16.8	1.5	1.0	1.3	11.7	39.1	49.2
Lawrence city	555	11.7	39.9	44 131	76.1	10.3	1.1	1.6	7.5	6.0	38.0	56.0
Leavenworth city	540	10.8	16.7	14 995	77.8	12.5	0.8	1.4	4.8	8.8	33.7	57.5
Leawood city	786	13.2	21.4	13 100	88.0	4.1	0.3	0.5	0.4	0.4	17.2	82.4
Lenexa city	763	9.6	24.3	22 971	86.7	6.8	0.3	0.6	0.9	3.2	29.2	67.6
Manhattan city..............	483	8.0	39.4	24 313	75.2	8.6	0.2	2.1	11.0	5.3	36.5	58.2
Olathe city..................	612	10.3	19.1	51 087	85.6	8.7	0.2	0.7	0.9	3.1	24.4	72.4
Overland Park city.........	766	10.6	23.9	79 767	86.8	6.5	0.5	0.5	0.7	3.9	31.0	65.1
Salina city..................	454	9.9	25.8	23 201	84.8	8.8	0.5	1.2	1.4	5.6	34.2	60.3
Shawnee city................	626	10.6	20.8	26 877	88.1	6.9	0.2	0.4	0.5	3.5	28.3	68.2
Topeka city	486	10.7	29.9	58 312	82.2	12.1	1.3	0.7	1.5	9.0	41.6	49.4
Wichita city	505	10.8	26.1	164 725	84.4	10.2	0.8	0.9	1.4	7.4	38.1	54.5
KENTUCKY	445	12.3	25.6	1 781 733	80.2	12.6	1.2	0.9	2.4	9.3	33.3	57.4
Bowling Green city........	485	13.5	29.6	23 777	74.9	15.3	0.7	1.1	6.3	10.7	40.9	48.5
Covington city..............	451	12.6	29.8	19 341	70.1	15.0	7.0	1.2	5.3	21.7	40.2	38.1
Frankfort city	474	9.4	27.5	12 804	78.0	15.8	0.6	0.4	3.1	12.1	43.5	44.4
Henderson city	402	9.4	24.7	12 286	79.4	14.5	0.9	1.4	1.9	11.9	41.1	47.0

Table C-5. Cities — **Migration, Housing, and Transportation**

STATE Place code	City	Total population 5 years and over	Residence in 1995 (percent) Same house	Same county, different house	Same state, different county	Different state	Outside the United States	Occupied housing units Number	Percent owner-occupied	Householders 65 years and over Number	Percent owner-occupied
		1	2	3	4	5	6	7	8	9	10
	KENTUCKY—Cont'd										
21 37918	Hopkinsville city..........	27 953	48.9	30.3	7.8	11.0	1.9	12 215	57.8	2 765	74.3
21 40222	Jeffersontown city	24 540	50.1	31.0	5.0	11.6	2.3	10 614	70.0	1 659	80.7
21 46027	Lexington-Fayette........	244 455	42.5	29.2	13.5	11.4	3.4	108 288	55.3	17 060	73.5
21 48000	Louisville city.............	239 541	51.9	34.3	3.9	7.4	2.4	111 354	52.5	26 167	72.5
21 58620	Owensboro city	50 545	50.8	34.3	7.2	7.3	0.5	22 748	60.4	5 980	71.3
21 58836	Paducah city	24 540	50.6	26.8	9.8	12.1	0.7	11 797	53.2	3 597	61.6
21 65226	Richmond city..............	25 447	32.2	27.2	27.8	11.1	1.7	10 783	35.0	1 617	64.7
22 00000	**LOUISIANA**	4 153 367	59.0	24.5	9.3	6.1	1.0	1 656 053	67.9	347 218	80.5
22 00975	Alexandria city	43 255	57.4	29.9	6.9	5.0	0.8	17 856	57.0	4 534	75.9
22 05000	Baton Rouge city..........	212 357	49.8	29.7	11.5	6.8	2.2	88 886	52.4	17 968	79.1
22 08920	Bossier City city	51 907	45.9	22.1	13.0	16.8	2.2	21 173	60.1	4 032	79.8
22 36255	Houma city.................	29 726	59.1	27.4	6.9	5.3	1.2	11 542	68.0	2 580	77.1
22 39475	Kenner city.................	65 657	58.7	25.4	8.1	5.8	2.0	25 652	60.8	3 931	69.0
22 40735	Lafayette city	103 254	51.6	27.3	12.7	6.7	1.6	43 497	58.3	8 502	76.5
22 41155	Lake Charles city	66 558	53.5	31.0	6.8	7.4	1.3	27 887	57.8	6 673	77.2
22 51410	Monroe city.................	49 001	54.3	29.0	9.5	6.4	0.7	19 432	49.3	4 530	65.3
22 54035	New Iberia city.............	29 956	58.2	30.1	7.4	3.2	1.1	11 820	62.1	2 870	79.7
22 55000	New Orleans city..........	451 739	56.8	28.6	6.0	7.1	1.4	188 251	46.5	38 961	63.4
22 70000	Shreveport city	186 271	54.0	31.3	6.3	7.5	0.9	78 762	59.2	18 049	78.8
22 70805	Slidell city..................	23 947	59.7	19.3	10.2	10.0	0.8	9 515	76.1	2 166	87.1
23 00000	**MAINE**	1 204 164	59.6	22.9	7.7	9.0	0.9	518 200	71.6	119 428	75.8
23 02795	Bangor city.................	29 712	47.1	32.3	10.6	8.1	1.8	13 713	47.4	2 790	60.7
23 38740	Lewiston city...............	33 751	50.0	33.4	5.7	9.9	1.0	15 290	47.3	4 011	55.5
23 60545	Portland city	61 046	44.2	31.2	8.5	13.0	3.1	29 715	42.4	5 955	54.1
24 00000	**MARYLAND**	4 945 043	55.7	21.9	9.4	10.0	3.0	1 980 859	67.7	383 030	76.0
24 01600	Annapolis city	33 490	48.9	27.3	6.8	13.0	4.1	15 306	51.9	2 983	65.4
24 04000	Baltimore city..............	609 345	57.1	28.2	6.5	6.1	2.1	257 996	50.3	62 344	62.4
24 08775	Bowie city..................	46 185	56.3	24.6	6.2	11.1	1.8	18 102	85.2	2 694	87.1
24 30325	Frederick city	48 704	42.0	27.3	12.2	15.1	3.3	20 799	55.9	3 604	60.1
24 31175	Gaithersburg city..........	48 311	42.0	28.3	4.7	15.3	9.7	19 501	53.0	2 487	47.7
24 36075	Hagerstown city...........	33 800	48.4	34.9	5.7	9.9	1.0	15 827	42.1	3 643	56.9
24 67675	Rockville city	44 311	51.1	23.2	3.1	11.4	11.3	17 245	67.9	3 521	73.3
25 00000	**MASSACHUSETTS** ...	5 954 249	58.5	22.8	7.8	7.5	3.5	2 443 580	61.7	555 549	68.2
25 00765	Agawam city...............	26 601	65.2	28.6	2.2	3.5	0.5	11 260	73.6	2 765	75.1
25 02690	Attleboro city..............	39 170	59.8	22.9	7.3	8.4	1.6	16 019	63.8	3 252	65.1
25 03600	Barnstable Town city.....	45 317	56.4	24.8	8.9	7.6	2.2	19 626	76.1	6 168	82.7
25 05595	Beverly city................	37 410	57.2	26.5	7.2	6.9	2.2	15 750	60.0	3 898	63.6
25 07000	Boston city.................	557 376	47.8	22.4	9.3	13.1	7.4	239 528	32.2	41 261	44.5
25 09000	Brockton city...............	87 671	57.4	24.5	11.0	2.9	4.3	33 675	54.5	6 987	64.9
25 11000	Cambridge city............	97 174	38.7	18.1	7.0	25.4	10.8	42 615	32.2	6 745	47.7
25 13205	Chelsea city................	32 314	50.0	24.8	7.4	3.7	14.1	11 888	29.0	2 406	41.6
25 13660	Chicopee city..............	51 838	60.7	29.1	3.8	4.4	2.1	23 117	59.3	6 701	71.5
25 21990	Everett city.................	35 805	57.0	25.3	8.3	3.5	6.0	15 435	41.5	3 754	59.6
25 23000	Fall River city	86 178	58.4	32.2	2.7	4.8	1.9	38 759	34.9	10 012	41.9
25 23875	Fitchburg city..............	36 704	53.8	31.2	6.3	6.1	2.6	14 943	51.5	3 687	59.4
25 25100	Franklin city................	26 708	58.8	20.2	8.9	10.3	1.8	10 152	81.4	1 698	68.1
25 26150	Gloucester city	28 551	63.7	25.6	4.8	4.8	1.1	12 592	59.8	3 073	67.5
25 29405	Haverhill city...............	54 747	52.6	32.3	5.9	7.3	1.9	22 976	60.2	4 681	58.5
25 30840	Holyoke city................	36 726	52.8	29.8	5.6	5.8	5.9	14 967	41.5	3 694	51.7
25 34550	Lawrence city..............	65 730	42.6	37.2	3.4	8.6	8.2	24 463	32.2	4 374	43.1
25 35075	Leominster city............	38 321	57.2	28.7	5.5	4.7	4.0	16 491	57.8	3 867	65.3
25 37000	Lowell city.................	97 516	50.0	31.5	4.5	7.0	6.9	37 887	43.1	6 930	58.1
25 37490	Lynn city...................	82 539	54.3	27.0	8.1	4.6	6.0	33 563	45.6	7 627	53.0
25 37875	Malden city................	53 061	54.5	24.2	8.4	5.2	7.6	23 009	43.3	5 098	47.7
25 38715	Marlborough city...........	33 891	51.8	26.5	6.3	8.3	7.1	14 501	61.0	2 879	68.9
25 39835	Medford city...............	53 060	60.1	22.0	6.2	7.9	3.7	22 067	58.7	6 159	65.5
25 40115	Melrose city................	25 308	66.7	20.4	6.7	5.0	1.1	10 982	67.1	3 034	65.0
25 40710	Methuen city...............	41 077	60.8	25.5	5.9	5.5	2.3	16 532	71.9	4 273	73.4
25 45000	New Bedford city..........	87 592	57.7	32.5	3.5	2.9	3.4	38 178	43.8	10 173	54.4
25 45560	Newton city................	79 230	60.1	13.5	11.2	10.9	4.3	31 201	69.6	8 000	74.5
25 46330	Northampton city..........	27 869	49.5	21.0	10.1	16.0	3.5	11 880	53.5	2 467	67.7
25 52490	Peabody city...............	45 357	67.2	23.7	5.0	2.5	1.5	18 581	71.2	5 272	69.6
25 53960	Pittsfield city	43 057	61.0	29.4	2.4	6.1	1.1	19 704	60.8	5 408	71.5
25 55745	Quincy city.................	83 593	56.0	20.5	12.8	5.6	5.1	38 883	49.1	10 049	56.7
25 56585	Revere city	44 621	62.6	19.6	8.5	3.3	6.0	19 463	49.9	5 220	57.1
25 59105	Salem city..................	38 170	55.0	27.9	7.1	7.2	2.9	17 492	49.1	4 051	62.1

Table C-5. Cities — **Migration, Housing, and Transportation**

City	Owner-occupied by household type (percent)								Median household income			Median monthly owner costs as a percent of income	
	Family households					Nonfamily households						Median housing value (owner estimated)	With a mortgage	Without a mortgage
		Married-couple family		Other family										
	Total family households	Total	With own children under 18 years	Total	With own children under 18 years	Total nonfamily households	Two or more adults	Living alone	All households	Owner-occupied households	Renter-occupied households			
	11	12	13	14	15	16	17	18	19	20	21	22	23	24
KENTUCKY—Cont'd														
Hopkinsville city...........	62.7	75.2	65.1	36.7	27.5	47.7	32.8	49.4	30 223	40 659	20 705	72 300	19.2	9.9
Jeffersontown city	78.3	83.7	82.2	57.0	45.0	51.5	50.8	51.7	51 843	60 017	35 290	122 100	19.1	9.9
Lexington-Fayette..........	68.7	77.5	75.9	41.6	32.9	36.4	24.0	40.2	39 568	57 236	24 463	109 700	19.2	9.9
Louisville city...............	61.4	76.6	69.7	40.6	25.1	41.5	34.7	42.8	28 649	40 199	19 247	81 900	21.1	10.1
Owensboro city	67.4	74.8	68.6	45.7	33.6	48.7	34.8	50.5	31 745	41 703	19 955	76 000	18.6	9.9
Paducah city................	62.3	77.0	69.5	34.5	21.7	41.1	41.9	41.1	26 613	37 649	16 231	61 400	19.2	9.9
Richmond city..............	48.6	60.1	54.2	22.9	12.7	20.6	9.5	25.0	25 642	45 349	19 320	83 300	18.1	9.9
LOUISIANA	74.4	83.8	80.0	52.0	41.0	52.8	39.7	55.2	32 427	40 554	20 138	77 500	19.6	9.9
Alexandria city.............	62.4	80.2	74.3	36.9	24.6	46.6	39.4	47.5	26 002	36 133	15 773	70 700	21.0	9.9
Baton Rouge city..........	62.8	76.3	70.1	41.3	28.9	37.1	17.8	42.5	30 193	46 261	19 215	93 100	19.5	9.9
Bossier City city	65.1	75.0	67.8	39.5	27.6	48.2	29.4	51.6	36 325	45 929	24 467	77 700	19.4	9.9
Houma city	74.5	84.1	79.4	52.8	42.4	52.3	36.2	55.5	33 800	41 667	21 629	79 300	18.7	9.9
Kenner city	68.0	78.2	73.7	42.9	29.4	42.2	37.5	43.2	39 984	51 299	28 143	108 000	20.3	9.0
Lafayette city	70.7	81.5	78.6	44.0	34.3	37.5	24.5	41.1	35 840	50 340	22 306	99 800	18.6	9.9
Lake Charles city	65.6	77.9	69.6	41.6	26.0	43.5	30.2	45.9	30 860	40 844	19 304	70 800	18.0	9.9
Monroe city	56.2	75.4	68.2	34.9	25.1	37.5	24.9	39.8	25 383	40 931	15 221	71 000	19.3	9.9
New Iberia city	65.2	77.0	68.7	43.7	29.8	54.5	48.5	55.5	26 247	33 884	16 527	64 300	19.3	9.9
New Orleans city...........	54.3	71.1	66.5	36.1	24.5	34.6	29.4	35.6	27 129	42 157	17 827	88 100	22.9	11.4
Shreveport city	65.4	77.7	70.5	46.6	32.3	47.8	36.9	49.6	30 509	40 571	20 606	70 700	19.2	9.9
Slidell city	79.9	87.1	81.4	56.0	44.1	64.7	46.1	68.2	43 103	48 422	26 808	90 200	19.0	9.9
MAINE	81.1	86.7	84.7	57.8	49.5	53.1	50.6	53.8	37 072	43 973	22 516	94 300	21.4	12.1
Bangor city	62.5	74.0	72.9	33.3	23.2	30.5	24.8	32.0	29 389	47 246	19 974	83 800	20.4	12.8
Lewiston city	61.9	74.0	68.5	30.2	22.5	28.2	30.4	27.7	28 697	45 326	19 397	85 800	21.9	13.0
Portland city	60.5	70.3	71.2	35.1	26.4	27.2	24.4	28.2	35 390	52 376	26 068	125 200	22.1	13.3
MARYLAND	75.1	83.1	80.9	52.5	41.7	51.3	43.9	53.1	52 640	64 860	32 351	143 300	22.2	9.9
Annapolis city.............	61.7	76.5	74.8	35.1	23.3	38.6	30.8	41.1	49 346	66 423	32 390	161 700	23.1	10.8
Baltimore city...............	58.6	74.2	71.6	44.0	30.9	39.3	37.6	39.6	29 743	41 359	19 809	69 900	22.5	12.5
Bowie city	88.4	90.5	89.2	78.8	72.1	75.8	72.2	76.9	76 511	79 297	57 756	157 800	22.6	9.9
Frederick city	65.2	73.3	74.5	41.3	33.2	41.2	34.3	43.3	47 344	62 002	32 448	134 300	23.4	10.6
Gaithersburg city	59.3	64.9	64.3	41.6	33.6	41.5	34.1	43.5	59 535	77 545	45 094	154 900	22.5	9.9
Hagerstown city	49.4	61.6	55.4	24.5	15.5	31.9	21.9	33.8	30 341	41 902	21 792	89 100	20.8	11.4
Rockville city	73.2	77.2	70.9	56.3	42.0	55.6	48.4	57.5	68 918	81 790	42 036	192 800	21.5	9.9
MASSACHUSETTS ...	72.8	80.6	79.7	47.3	33.5	41.3	32.8	43.5	50 284	64 506	30 682	182 800	21.9	12.4
Agawam city	83.2	88.3	87.8	62.1	45.9	55.0	52.4	55.6	49 254	56 843	32 003	128 700	22.1	12.4
Attleboro city	74.0	80.0	79.8	50.9	41.1	41.4	40.4	41.6	50 417	60 571	33 498	147 200	22.2	10.8
Barnstable Town city.....	82.8	89.3	87.2	58.4	48.8	63.2	53.9	65.2	46 781	53 355	26 846	170 600	23.7	12.9
Beverly city	75.2	80.4	83.0	52.8	37.2	34.2	25.0	36.4	52 648	67 241	35 219	220 100	22.7	12.4
Boston city..................	40.9	51.7	49.3	26.1	15.1	24.1	16.2	27.1	39 329	60 970	30 609	210 100	22.6	12.5
Brockton city...............	62.1	76.1	70.6	37.0	22.6	38.9	41.8	38.2	39 133	53 741	23 818	127 900	23.0	12.9
Cambridge city	43.1	48.0	48.7	30.5	22.5	24.4	15.5	28.0	47 232	78 366	38 048	331 600	20.6	9.9
Chelsea city.................	31.1	39.3	31.1	19.0	9.7	25.3	28.9	24.4	30 280	48 143	24 857	163 200	21.1	14.0
Chicopee city...............	67.4	76.8	67.1	44.5	29.9	46.4	40.4	47.5	35 492	43 124	26 632	102 000	21.9	12.8
Everett city	49.4	56.9	54.0	32.9	20.8	28.6	12.9	32.0	40 003	50 441	32 528	178 800	22.2	13.1
Fall River city	44.1	56.3	51.1	21.4	9.6	20.5	18.4	20.8	28 490	45 690	21 357	133 900	21.5	11.4
Fitchburg city...............	59.9	72.0	65.8	32.5	18.7	37.2	32.9	38.2	37 103	51 145	24 751	107 800	22.3	12.7
Franklin city.................	89.6	93.4	94.7	64.8	57.7	52.4	50.4	52.8	71 262	81 503	33 826	219 800	22.1	11.2
Gloucester city	71.8	79.0	75.6	47.7	29.6	39.4	41.5	39.0	47 697	60 053	32 100	203 400	24.2	13.3
Haverhill city................	70.1	79.6	77.5	42.8	32.1	42.1	44.7	41.5	49 246	63 223	27 952	153 000	22.0	12.3
Holyoke city.................	48.8	67.1	59.5	23.9	14.9	28.7	28.8	28.7	30 192	52 798	18 477	102 400	20.8	12.0
Lawrence city...............	35.2	48.9	45.7	19.7	14.9	25.5	18.0	27.0	27 428	46 019	21 163	116 400	23.3	13.8
Leominster city	68.7	77.6	74.1	42.9	29.3	36.2	32.3	37.0	43 945	59 666	28 802	135 500	23.1	13.3
Lowell city...................	50.9	61.9	56.8	31.3	20.2	29.6	24.3	31.0	38 678	54 505	28 224	130 500	21.7	12.8
Lynn city....................	53.1	64.6	58.7	33.1	19.7	32.9	36.1	32.3	36 452	55 344	23 480	145 300	22.8	12.8
Malden city	55.6	59.9	57.1	43.3	27.3	25.5	20.9	26.7	45 255	58 270	34 968	185 100	23.5	13.0
Marlborough city...........	72.2	75.9	72.8	55.2	35.9	40.5	32.5	42.4	55 007	70 017	39 755	181 500	21.7	12.8
Medford city	70.8	76.6	74.9	54.1	35.2	39.5	27.1	43.8	52 510	62 292	38 912	229 500	23.2	14.2
Melrose city	80.8	84.4	87.8	60.9	43.7	42.0	46.1	41.2	62 985	77 206	39 401	252 500	21.5	12.5
Methuen city................	79.8	85.9	82.0	58.4	39.8	53.4	54.9	53.2	49 237	58 555	30 000	156 100	22.0	14.6
New Bedford city...........	51.0	64.4	57.2	26.9	16.0	31.3	31.7	31.2	27 799	43 137	18 843	113 500	22.4	14.6
Newton city.................	81.7	84.4	86.3	65.7	58.8	46.0	26.1	52.7	85 701	103 066	54 535	416 600	20.5	12.0
Northampton city...........	76.3	80.1	79.5	64.6	59.4	30.7	22.2	33.6	41 680	57 327	29 333	147 100	20.7	11.2
Peabody city................	80.6	85.2	84.4	60.8	43.5	49.3	41.7	50.7	54 245	64 495	30 279	205 800	21.5	11.0
Pittsfield city	72.7	83.8	79.4	44.8	33.1	42.8	40.7	43.1	36 143	48 056	21 771	98 200	21.5	12.3
Quincy city..................	63.5	67.9	69.3	51.1	36.0	32.8	20.7	35.8	46 786	58 424	37 301	181 500	22.9	13.5
Revere city..................	59.2	65.9	62.5	44.9	25.1	35.4	30.3	36.4	36 367	50 506	26 556	172 400	25.8	16.0
Salem city...................	60.9	71.0	67.3	35.9	17.1	34.3	26.6	36.3	43 580	60 532	31 211	188 300	23.0	14.1

Table C-5. Cities — **Migration, Housing, and Transportation**

City	Percent who pay 35 percent or more of income for housing expenses		Means of transportation to work (percent except where noted)						Vehicles available (percent of households)		
				Car, truck, or van								
	Median gross rent	Owners	Renters	Number of workers 16 years and over	Drove alone	Carpooled	Public transportation	Other means	Walked	No vehicles	One vehicle	Two or more vehicles
	25	26	27	28	29	30	31	32	33	34	35	36
KENTUCKY—Cont'd												
Hopkinsville city	424	12.7	29.2	12 506	80.9	13.0	0.6	1.5	2.3	13.1	39.1	47.8
Jeffersontown city	610	11.0	16.4	14 031	85.6	9.5	0.8	0.4	1.1	4.0	32.2	63.8
Lexington-Fayette	528	11.0	30.6	136 793	79.9	11.2	1.3	1.1	4.0	7.9	39.0	53.1
Louisville city	443	15.7	30.8	110 930	73.5	12.6	6.9	1.1	4.1	20.5	43.5	36.1
Owensboro city	406	10.2	25.4	24 097	85.1	10.2	0.5	0.8	1.9	10.8	39.3	49.9
Paducah city	386	13.9	27.6	10 162	81.6	11.7	1.2	1.2	1.7	15.2	44.7	40.1
Richmond city	422	11.6	31.4	13 258	76.3	13.4	0.5	0.7	7.2	11.1	43.9	45.1
LOUISIANA	466	14.2	29.8	1 831 057	78.1	13.6	2.4	1.6	2.2	11.9	37.0	51.1
Alexandria city	430	16.2	37.1	16 889	77.5	13.8	2.8	1.3	2.7	17.5	42.7	39.8
Baton Rouge city	483	14.8	34.7	98 715	77.6	12.4	2.2	1.5	3.8	12.2	42.4	45.4
Bossier City city	484	10.3	23.8	26 072	82.3	11.3	0.8	2.1	1.8	9.3	37.4	53.3
Houma city	417	13.1	24.5	12 411	78.8	12.7	1.6	3.1	1.6	12.8	40.1	47.1
Kenner city	581	16.4	29.9	33 014	77.2	14.5	2.5	1.6	2.1	8.8	37.8	53.5
Lafayette city	485	12.7	29.2	50 350	82.5	9.3	1.8	1.7	1.9	9.9	39.1	51.0
Lake Charles city	462	12.0	29.9	29 665	80.4	13.1	0.7	1.7	2.3	11.6	43.2	45.2
Monroe city	392	14.1	33.1	20 075	76.4	14.9	3.1	1.5	2.8	20.7	40.3	38.9
New Iberia city	400	13.0	31.1	11 243	79.7	14.5	0.8	1.6	1.3	15.4	40.1	44.6
New Orleans city	488	20.9	36.1	188 703	60.3	16.1	13.7	2.0	5.2	27.3	42.3	30.4
Shreveport city	470	14.5	30.2	82 134	78.9	13.8	2.8	0.9	1.7	14.3	40.7	45.1
Slidell city	606	12.4	34.4	11 337	80.3	13.8	0.5	1.6	1.2	5.8	32.2	62.0
MAINE	497	14.7	27.4	615 144	78.6	11.3	0.8	0.9	4.0	7.6	34.4	58.0
Bangor city	475	13.4	34.1	15 334	76.6	10.2	2.3	1.3	5.3	13.5	45.2	41.4
Lewiston city	408	13.4	25.5	16 314	72.4	13.1	1.9	1.6	8.6	18.0	41.7	40.3
Portland city	598	16.6	30.8	34 626	70.7	10.8	4.4	1.6	8.9	18.4	44.3	37.3
MARYLAND	689	16.1	27.0	2 591 670	73.7	12.4	7.2	0.8	2.5	11.2	33.4	55.3
Annapolis city	762	16.9	25.8	19 174	68.8	11.5	7.2	1.3	6.9	15.8	39.0	45.3
Baltimore city	498	20.5	33.0	249 373	54.7	15.2	19.5	1.1	7.1	35.9	40.3	23.8
Bowie city	1 094	14.9	22.4	27 320	76.4	12.2	6.3	0.5	0.9	3.8	25.8	70.4
Frederick city	718	17.1	29.0	27 919	73.9	15.1	1.9	1.2	4.9	10.3	38.7	51.1
Gaithersburg city	904	17.0	27.2	28 145	68.4	13.4	12.2	0.7	2.3	9.7	39.3	51.0
Hagerstown city	441	14.2	26.6	16 993	76.4	13.3	2.2	1.7	3.9	19.7	41.3	39.1
Rockville city	972	15.5	28.6	23 888	67.6	10.7	13.8	0.8	2.2	8.3	34.8	57.0
MASSACHUSETTS	684	16.2	28.6	3 102 837	73.8	9.0	8.7	1.0	4.3	12.7	37.0	50.3
Agawam city	651	13.5	22.0	14 676	89.4	6.8	0.5	0.2	0.9	6.0	35.8	58.3
Attleboro city	610	13.3	22.6	21 540	80.2	10.2	5.3	0.8	1.6	8.1	34.2	57.8
Barnstable Town city	742	19.9	34.0	22 161	80.3	9.1	1.6	1.5	2.7	5.6	37.9	56.5
Beverly city	740	16.7	24.2	20 409	78.1	6.9	7.1	0.9	3.7	9.2	38.7	52.1
Boston city	803	20.0	32.1	278 463	41.5	9.2	32.3	1.6	13.0	34.9	44.4	20.7
Brockton city	625	20.3	30.1	41 523	72.9	15.1	7.5	1.1	2.3	16.7	40.1	43.2
Cambridge city	962	16.5	32.8	54 959	35.0	5.4	25.1	4.9	24.4	27.7	51.5	20.8
Chelsea city	695	12.4	34.3	12 574	47.8	17.6	24.9	1.1	6.6	32.2	47.4	20.3
Chicopee city	530	14.3	26.1	25 440	82.1	11.4	1.4	0.9	2.8	13.6	44.1	42.2
Everett city	729	16.1	31.0	17 818	60.2	13.3	19.9	1.2	4.7	21.7	46.5	31.8
Fall River city	428	14.7	25.8	38 840	78.9	14.8	1.5	0.8	3.1	20.7	44.7	34.7
Fitchburg city	555	16.1	27.5	17 129	76.8	13.3	2.2	1.6	4.0	14.2	41.3	44.5
Franklin city	677	15.7	24.3	14 807	81.9	5.2	6.9	0.4	1.4	5.1	24.8	70.1
Gloucester city	677	21.4	27.0	15 104	78.5	7.7	3.8	0.7	5.0	11.7	38.4	49.9
Haverhill city	658	16.1	29.7	29 241	81.6	10.8	2.3	0.4	2.0	11.4	37.5	51.1
Holyoke city	503	13.2	35.1	14 501	74.7	13.9	3.2	1.4	4.8	26.6	40.5	32.9
Lawrence city	607	20.5	34.8	24 826	64.5	21.8	6.3	2.0	3.3	27.3	43.1	29.6
Leominster city	579	13.8	23.8	19 854	84.3	9.1	1.7	1.0	1.7	9.5	38.9	51.7
Lowell city	627	16.4	28.6	46 764	73.8	15.7	3.4	1.3	4.6	17.1	42.4	40.5
Lynn city	608	17.8	32.2	38 360	70.4	13.2	9.3	1.2	4.6	20.6	42.8	36.5
Malden city	777	20.0	29.0	29 119	59.9	10.2	23.7	0.8	3.6	17.3	46.6	36.1
Marlborough city	811	14.3	27.3	19 839	81.8	10.8	1.3	1.3	2.2	7.6	35.8	56.6
Medford city	819	18.8	27.4	28 416	65.3	9.4	18.1	0.9	4.5	13.3	41.8	44.8
Melrose city	760	14.0	24.7	14 524	70.7	7.9	14.7	0.6	3.3	10.9	37.4	51.8
Methuen city	645	16.2	25.5	20 471	84.9	9.5	1.6	0.8	1.4	8.2	35.5	56.2
New Bedford city	455	17.2	32.0	37 537	74.1	16.1	2.8	1.6	4.2	21.7	44.0	34.3
Newton city	1 083	15.8	25.3	44 217	68.4	6.9	12.3	1.0	4.8	6.7	34.0	59.3
Northampton city	647	15.8	26.9	16 008	70.0	7.1	3.2	1.6	13.7	11.3	43.0	45.7
Peabody city	704	14.4	27.3	23 882	85.9	8.1	2.2	0.7	1.3	8.0	33.2	58.8
Pittsfield city	503	14.5	28.9	20 846	79.8	11.2	2.4	0.9	4.1	14.0	43.1	42.9
Quincy city	808	17.8	25.4	46 991	63.1	10.4	21.3	0.6	3.2	15.5	47.8	36.7
Revere city	726	26.8	32.5	20 529	62.4	12.2	20.8	1.1	2.4	21.1	46.8	32.1
Salem city	705	18.9	27.1	21 318	72.0	9.8	8.7	0.7	5.9	13.2	45.4	41.4

Table C-5. Cities — **Migration, Housing, and Transportation**

STATE Place code	City	Total population 5 years and over	Residence in 1995 (percent)					Occupied housing units		Householders 65 years and over	
			Same house	Same county, different house	Same state, different county	Different state	Outside the United States	Number	Percent owner-occupied	Number	Percent owner-occupied
		1	2	3	4	5	6	7	8	9	10
	MASSACHUSETTS—Cont'd										
25 62535	Somerville city	74 034	44.5	20.4	8.4	16.8	9.9	31 555	30.6	5 426	52.6
25 67000	Springfield city..............	140 488	52.1	34.2	3.1	6.6	3.9	57 130	49.9	13 253	65.1
25 69170	Taunton city.................	52 130	59.6	25.5	10.4	3.3	1.3	22 045	61.2	4 815	67.6
25 72600	Waltham city................	56 476	51.8	22.9	7.3	12.2	5.8	23 207	46.0	5 098	62.3
25 73440	Watertown city..............	31 547	52.2	21.2	10.4	11.5	4.8	14 629	47.1	3 522	68.2
25 76030	Westfield city................	37 521	57.2	26.5	8.5	4.4	3.4	14 797	67.8	3 318	75.4
25 81035	Woburn city..................	35 237	63.0	23.1	4.9	5.7	3.3	14 997	61.2	3 612	76.4
25 82000	Worcester city...............	161 570	50.8	30.0	5.0	7.9	6.3	67 028	43.3	15 934	55.9
26 00000	**MICHIGAN**	9 268 782	57.3	25.1	10.9	5.0	1.7	3 785 661	73.8	803 561	81.0
26 01380	Allen Park city	27 736	70.0	25.1	2.5	1.5	0.9	11 974	87.9	4 173	89.3
26 03000	Ann Arbor city	108 319	36.7	19.7	18.1	17.3	8.1	45 674	45.2	6 375	73.0
26 05920	Battle Creek city............	49 388	52.7	31.0	8.0	6.8	1.4	21 348	65.9	5 040	76.1
26 06020	Bay City city.................	34 262	61.5	27.2	7.5	3.7	0.2	15 208	69.5	3 749	83.4
26 12060	Burton city...................	28 104	57.4	30.8	7.4	3.8	0.5	11 699	80.7	2 287	91.9
26 21000	Dearborn city................	89 714	59.7	26.1	3.4	4.1	6.7	36 770	73.5	10 997	77.9
26 21020	Dearborn Heights city ...	54 519	67.0	24.7	3.1	3.1	2.2	23 276	85.4	7 474	88.1
26 22000	Detroit city	875 384	60.0	32.0	2.8	3.0	2.2	336 428	54.9	71 223	72.8
26 24120	East Lansing city...........	45 551	22.6	13.0	47.3	9.2	7.8	14 426	32.2	1 917	62.4
26 24290	Eastpointe city..............	31 917	63.7	21.4	12.0	2.0	0.9	13 595	87.9	4 139	89.4
26 27440	Farmington Hills city.......	77 330	55.8	20.3	13.0	6.6	4.3	33 559	66.8	7 405	64.8
26 29000	Flint city.....................	113 859	54.6	36.5	4.5	3.7	0.7	48 744	58.9	9 507	78.4
26 31420	Garden City city............	28 227	68.5	25.3	3.3	2.3	0.7	11 479	86.3	2 742	86.6
26 34000	Grand Rapids city	181 859	49.1	30.9	8.5	6.7	4.9	73 291	59.8	14 519	70.7
26 38640	Holland city..................	32 481	47.7	21.0	19.4	9.5	2.3	11 995	67.1	2 961	80.0
26 40680	Inkster city...................	27 701	58.7	31.2	3.5	3.7	2.9	11 169	57.9	2 262	76.3
26 41420	Jackson city..................	33 019	50.8	35.1	7.0	6.1	1.1	14 210	57.6	3 176	75.6
26 42160	Kalamazoo city..............	72 358	40.1	26.5	22.9	7.8	2.7	29 411	47.8	5 083	64.0
26 42820	Kentwood city...............	41 820	46.5	30.8	10.7	8.5	3.6	18 453	61.0	3 070	75.2
26 46000	Lansing city..................	109 428	48.5	30.0	12.7	6.0	2.8	49 569	57.4	8 304	75.5
26 47800	Lincoln Park city...........	37 242	63.0	31.1	2.5	2.6	0.7	16 204	79.1	4 008	90.0
26 49000	Livonia city..................	94 934	68.1	21.5	6.8	2.8	0.8	38 089	88.8	10 536	84.3
26 50560	Madison Heights city.....	29 154	59.5	20.7	10.2	4.4	5.2	13 299	70.1	2 916	69.8
26 53780	Midland city	39 055	54.6	22.5	13.4	7.6	1.9	16 722	69.6	3 881	73.0
26 56020	Mount Pleasant city.......	25 114	22.7	14.5	53.0	6.5	3.4	8 468	34.5	1 273	65.4
26 56320	Muskegon city...............	37 161	50.6	32.5	10.6	5.3	1.1	14 561	57.0	3 477	66.8
26 59440	Novi city......................	44 015	47.9	21.2	15.3	11.1	4.5	18 732	70.9	2 272	76.5
26 59920	Oak Park city................	27 832	62.6	16.7	14.2	3.5	3.0	11 104	74.9	2 638	75.9
26 65440	Pontiac city..................	60 483	49.6	34.9	7.0	6.2	2.4	24 234	52.8	3 978	67.0
26 65560	Portage city..................	41 825	51.7	28.7	9.6	8.6	1.5	18 147	69.0	3 544	75.4
26 65820	Port Huron city..............	29 765	49.1	39.2	6.5	4.3	1.0	12 957	57.1	3 147	68.0
26 69035	Rochester Hills city	64 407	57.8	21.7	9.9	7.1	3.5	26 321	79.2	4 390	74.5
26 69800	Roseville city	45 050	61.1	25.9	8.9	2.7	1.5	19 976	75.2	5 035	78.0
26 70040	Royal Oak city	56 930	59.1	22.7	10.9	5.3	1.9	28 880	70.1	6 415	80.7
26 70520	Saginaw city.................	56 554	56.7	33.5	5.4	3.7	0.6	23 189	63.6	5 089	82.8
26 70760	St. Clair Shores city	59 918	68.5	17.6	10.9	2.2	0.8	27 438	85.8	9 251	85.9
26 74900	Southfield city...............	73 974	51.5	19.3	19.7	5.7	3.7	33 987	54.1	7 754	53.0
26 74960	Southgate city...............	28 498	62.6	29.6	3.4	3.6	0.8	12 836	70.8	3 686	71.6
26 76460	Sterling Heights city	116 666	60.1	20.1	13.3	3.2	3.3	46 319	79.0	9 074	78.1
26 79000	Taylor city....................	60 992	61.1	32.3	2.6	2.9	1.1	24 776	70.8	4 740	81.8
26 80700	Troy city......................	76 000	61.1	20.2	8.1	6.2	4.4	30 018	77.4	5 296	74.1
26 84000	Warren city...................	129 739	63.0	19.3	13.1	2.8	1.9	55 577	80.3	15 408	88.0
26 86000	Westland city................	80 608	52.4	33.8	6.5	5.0	2.4	36 535	62.7	7 997	63.9
26 88900	Wyandotte city..............	26 431	63.7	29.7	2.8	2.9	0.8	11 816	73.1	3 192	79.2
26 88940	Wyoming city................	63 881	51.3	32.4	8.1	5.5	2.8	26 535	67.7	4 263	81.5
27 00000	**MINNESOTA**............	4 591 491	57.0	20.3	13.1	7.7	1.8	1 895 127	74.5	383 263	76.4
27 01486	Andover city	24 220	58.5	20.4	14.1	6.2	0.8	8 107	95.9	479	69.9
27 01900	Apple Valley city...........	42 257	54.2	21.1	12.4	10.7	1.5	16 344	87.9	1 569	77.1
27 06382	Blaine city...................	41 409	59.8	18.2	16.2	4.8	0.9	15 899	90.6	1 425	88.7
27 06616	Bloomington city............	80 711	60.5	21.8	7.7	7.7	2.3	36 396	70.7	8 350	76.5
27 07948	Brooklyn Center city......	27 145	55.7	24.8	8.5	7.3	3.6	11 424	68.9	2 915	77.0
27 07966	Brooklyn Park city.........	61 953	51.4	28.8	8.5	7.6	3.8	24 432	73.2	2 383	82.3
27 08794	Burnsville city..............	55 909	51.3	17.0	19.5	9.9	2.3	23 684	68.3	2 963	76.6
27 13114	Coon Rapids city..........	57 012	59.3	17.9	16.6	5.1	1.0	22 575	80.3	2 702	73.7
27 13456	Cottage Grove city........	27 913	62.5	16.4	14.1	6.0	1.0	9 926	91.7	943	87.2
27 17000	Duluth city...................	82 144	52.9	24.5	13.9	7.6	1.2	35 487	64.2	8 672	67.1
27 17288	Eagan city	58 471	53.4	17.0	16.0	10.8	2.7	23 776	74.8	1 790	80.3
27 18116	Eden Prairie city...........	50 564	49.0	26.1	7.2	13.7	3.9	20 457	78.4	1 724	80.9
27 18188	Edina city....................	44 958	62.2	22.8	4.8	8.7	1.5	20 986	76.4	7 421	71.0
27 22814	Fridley city..................	25 686	56.1	13.6	21.7	6.3	2.2	11 328	67.7	2 229	87.6

Table C-5. Cities — Migration, Housing, and Transportation

City	Owner-occupied by household type (percent)								Median household income			Median housing value (owner estimated)	Median monthly owner costs as a percent of income	
	Family households					Nonfamily households								
		Married-couple family		Other family										
	Total family households	Total	With own children under 18 years	Total	With own children under 18 years	Total nonfamily households	Two or more adults	Living alone	All households	Owner-occupied households	Renter-occupied households	Median housing value (owner estimated)	With a mortgage	Without a mortgage
	11	12	13	14	15	16	17	18	19	20	21	22	23	24
MASSACHUSETTS— Cont'd														
Somerville city	44.6	48.3	43.9	35.5	18.1	18.1	9.1	24.5	46 395	58 041	42 251	262 000	23.3	11.7
Springfield city	54.9	71.9	63.8	33.3	22.2	40.9	38.7	41.3	30 193	44 896	18 881	86 500	22.1	13.8
Taunton city	71.3	81.2	78.6	42.9	27.8	42.0	37.3	43.0	43 051	55 611	29 885	141 300	21.2	10.9
Waltham city	61.1	65.5	65.2	46.0	28.2	28.2	19.3	31.2	53 286	67 432	42 607	246 400	22.8	12.9
Watertown city	58.4	60.6	63.0	51.2	36.0	35.5	16.7	43.9	60 026	66 417	55 271	275 900	22.5	12.7
Westfield city	78.0	84.5	78.8	53.8	36.6	46.1	35.3	48.8	45 879	56 851	25 791	128 900	21.2	12.5
Woburn city	73.9	77.6	76.4	59.3	37.8	38.3	24.5	41.7	55 094	66 008	43 077	217 500	22.6	10.9
Worcester city	52.4	64.5	58.0	29.4	16.8	30.3	22.5	32.2	35 321	52 083	25 503	118 400	21.2	12.4
MICHIGAN	81.7	88.8	86.5	59.2	48.9	56.7	47.2	58.6	44 533	52 353	26 153	110 300	19.6	9.9
Allen Park city	92.6	94.9	95.4	83.1	72.4	77.7	74.9	78.0	51 840	55 066	35 557	118 900	17.9	10.5
Ann Arbor city	65.0	69.4	68.4	47.0	40.3	27.1	14.7	33.1	45 923	76 770	29 828	178 500	20.8	9.9
Battle Creek city	73.5	82.4	77.8	54.8	48.3	53.4	46.8	54.6	35 246	43 966	22 151	70 800	19.4	10.6
Bay City city	78.5	89.0	84.7	54.3	42.8	55.3	49.3	56.2	30 325	37 031	18 119	65 800	19.7	12.3
Burton city	85.6	90.5	87.4	71.7	62.5	69.1	67.1	69.4	43 712	47 990	24 728	81 100	18.9	9.9
Dearborn city	80.1	83.5	81.0	67.5	55.5	61.1	57.3	61.6	43 977	52 420	25 280	129 300	21.2	10.7
Dearborn Heights city ...	89.5	92.2	90.4	80.1	67.1	76.6	70.8	77.4	47 703	50 190	35 046	110 200	19.9	10.4
Detroit city	59.1	75.0	67.2	47.7	34.9	46.9	41.4	47.8	29 274	39 012	20 530	62 800	21.0	11.9
East Lansing city	61.2	67.8	69.9	40.5	37.6	15.9	5.9	23.9	27 456	76 230	17 951	144 100	19.0	9.9
Eastpointe city	92.0	94.9	93.8	83.3	75.3	79.8	81.7	79.5	45 951	49 675	21 870	97 800	19.5	10.9
Farmington Hills city......	80.5	83.3	85.2	63.9	61.5	41.4	30.9	43.3	67 324	87 129	43 779	220 400	20.1	9.9
Flint city	61.2	79.8	69.6	44.1	31.2	54.9	48.8	56.0	27 857	38 309	17 517	49 100	18.7	10.4
Garden City city	91.7	94.5	93.5	81.5	73.0	72.5	67.4	73.3	51 789	54 985	28 785	110 700	19.5	10.6
Grand Rapids city	69.2	81.0	78.6	44.8	37.0	45.0	35.9	47.4	37 081	47 279	24 336	91 100	19.2	9.9
Holland city	75.5	83.4	80.0	46.7	39.6	50.5	30.9	55.4	42 239	50 145	31 244	104 800	19.7	9.9
Inkster city	62.8	74.7	66.8	49.6	35.9	47.9	41.6	49.0	34 956	42 489	24 349	67 300	19.9	10.6
Jackson city	63.6	78.1	72.1	42.1	30.0	48.2	37.1	50.6	30 945	40 773	19 535	64 400	18.8	10.2
Kalamazoo city	64.6	79.5	78.3	40.7	31.1	31.6	19.0	37.5	30 704	46 970	19 642	80 700	19.1	9.9
Kentwood city	73.3	80.6	81.4	47.1	38.6	40.6	22.7	44.3	45 599	54 129	32 995	114 000	19.8	9.9
Lansing city	66.0	77.8	71.6	45.7	37.7	45.9	39.7	47.6	34 477	44 617	23 517	73 000	19.7	10.4
Lincoln Park city	86.2	90.5	88.2	74.9	63.7	65.8	64.4	66.1	42 500	46 746	29 664	83 900	19.1	11.4
Livonia city	94.2	95.7	95.5	85.6	77.4	73.5	75.9	73.2	63 045	67 829	30 425	160 400	18.8	9.9
Madison Heights city	79.0	81.7	78.6	69.9	63.0	56.7	57.4	56.6	42 686	49 472	29 041	108 800	20.3	11.0
Midland city	82.6	87.9	88.0	56.3	49.3	44.8	28.7	48.1	47 265	62 396	21 558	110 400	17.9	9.9
Mount Pleasant city.......	62.2	73.9	67.8	33.7	31.4	17.7	3.8	33.6	24 659	51 306	17 377	95 100	18.2	9.9
Muskegon city	66.4	79.2	72.4	48.7	36.3	43.3	44.2	43.1	27 776	35 407	18 044	60 200	20.1	11.0
Novi city	82.6	84.1	86.9	71.7	64.8	48.1	36.4	50.6	72 023	86 138	50 075	214 600	19.3	9.9
Oak Park city	77.9	83.6	82.1	66.7	55.6	68.2	55.1	70.4	48 072	52 579	31 814	114 300	21.3	12.3
Pontiac city	58.4	72.9	65.2	43.0	32.6	43.1	43.1	43.1	30 800	41 542	21 137	73 400	22.3	12.0
Portage city	82.3	88.2	86.2	55.8	48.3	41.7	34.0	43.3	48 854	61 332	28 273	118 700	18.9	9.9
Port Huron city	65.3	77.6	67.0	41.9	31.6	43.7	35.9	45.2	31 358	42 881	20 430	84 800	20.6	12.1
Rochester Hills city	88.0	90.0	90.0	73.5	67.0	56.0	53.4	56.4	75 758	85 673	42 377	215 100	19.3	9.9
Roseville city	83.0	88.8	86.5	68.7	56.4	61.7	61.0	61.8	41 260	46 866	26 813	97 100	19.9	10.4
Royal Oak city	86.3	89.5	88.6	73.4	62.0	53.7	41.6	56.3	52 252	62 053	36 763	149 400	19.1	11.0
Saginaw city	67.6	84.6	77.0	50.0	38.4	55.9	48.7	57.2	26 389	34 240	15 601	47 000	18.6	11.4
St. Clair Shores city	91.5	94.2	93.5	80.8	71.8	75.9	76.5	75.8	48 878	51 857	30 761	122 500	19.7	10.8
Southfield city	67.2	75.7	78.4	47.9	41.7	35.8	32.8	36.3	51 879	66 669	38 514	151 200	22.2	12.1
Southgate city	84.3	87.3	88.1	72.4	62.3	48.2	46.3	48.5	46 597	53 084	31 229	108 600	18.9	10.9
Sterling Heights city	88.3	91.5	91.5	71.6	58.7	54.7	47.5	55.8	60 240	67 046	33 367	157 800	18.8	9.9
Taylor city	74.0	84.8	79.3	49.5	36.3	62.6	59.2	63.4	42 881	50 207	28 463	91 100	18.6	10.7
Troy city	87.7	89.6	89.0	74.0	69.8	49.3	42.8	50.5	77 232	89 099	47 382	217 800	19.2	9.9
Warren city	86.2	90.6	87.2	73.1	59.2	68.9	61.6	70.2	44 620	48 838	30 397	115 400	19.7	10.9
Westland city	73.7	80.5	79.8	54.0	45.0	45.6	41.1	46.5	45 996	55 206	32 859	115 100	19.4	10.8
Wyandotte city..............	82.9	89.4	87.5	65.0	48.9	56.1	44.6	57.9	44 093	51 521	29 205	102 600	19.9	11.8
Wyoming city	77.4	84.0	82.2	57.7	49.7	48.7	42.7	50.4	42 700	50 409	29 903	91 700	19.7	9.9
MINNESOTA	85.0	90.3	90.1	61.4	54.2	53.8	47.4	55.3	47 033	55 338	26 551	118 100	20.0	9.9
Andover city	97.7	98.9	99.2	83.5	77.4	82.2	93.0	78.1	75 941	77 072	26 855	159 900	20.1	9.9
Apple Valley city............	92.3	95.1	94.4	76.4	73.7	73.8	77.2	73.0	69 429	74 428	34 182	149 900	20.1	9.9
Blaine city	93.6	95.8	95.3	84.2	80.3	80.3	76.1	81.9	59 004	61 758	36 149	117 600	20.0	9.9
Bloomington city	82.3	87.4	87.6	58.5	44.8	50.9	40.4	53.6	55 104	65 518	35 396	144 800	19.2	9.9
Brooklyn Center city	78.1	85.5	82.9	56.9	43.6	52.0	56.9	50.8	44 414	52 296	26 260	104 900	20.6	9.9
Brooklyn Park city	80.6	89.1	87.3	51.1	46.6	55.2	52.9	55.8	56 298	66 896	31 986	129 700	20.0	9.9
Burnsville city	77.9	84.4	83.8	51.0	44.5	49.6	41.5	52.5	57 420	69 792	38 423	149 600	20.0	9.9
Coon Rapids city...........	85.7	91.7	89.9	63.0	53.4	65.4	64.1	65.8	55 654	62 036	31 623	123 300	20.2	9.9
Cottage Grove city	93.7	96.7	97.0	73.5	63.5	78.6	77.9	78.8	65 579	68 067	32 813	137 200	20.9	9.9
Duluth city	79.7	87.7	88.6	55.6	46.1	44.1	30.3	47.8	33 518	44 818	17 781	80 700	19.3	9.9
Eagan city	83.4	87.6	90.2	59.5	51.3	55.7	40.4	61.0	67 151	77 589	44 269	161 000	19.7	9.9
Eden Prairie city	85.7	89.7	92.1	58.9	55.0	59.8	40.5	65.5	78 699	91 375	49 430	193 600	19.5	9.9
Edina city	88.4	90.7	93.8	70.2	64.5	57.1	36.2	59.8	65 887	79 345	36 692	222 600	20.5	9.9
Fridley city	76.8	86.3	82.6	45.7	30.9	51.1	44.5	53.3	48 658	57 166	32 757	117 400	19.4	9.9

Table C-5. Cities — **Migration, Housing, and Transportation**

City	Median gross rent	Percent who pay 35 percent or more of income for housing expenses — Owners	Renters	Means of transportation to work (percent except where noted) — Number of workers 16 years and over	Car, truck, or van — Drove alone	Carpooled	Public transportation	Other means	Walked	Vehicles available (percent of households) — No vehicles	One vehicle	Two or more vehicles
	25	26	27	28	29	30	31	32	33	34	35	36
MASSACHUSETTS—Cont'd												
Somerville city	874	20.6	28.2	44 977	45.3	10.3	29.2	3.4	9.4	22.7	46.2	31.0
Springfield city	517	18.0	33.8	58 967	73.0	14.3	5.8	0.9	4.2	22.5	42.7	34.8
Taunton city	575	13.7	25.3	27 870	82.4	11.8	2.4	1.1	1.3	9.3	38.2	52.4
Waltham city	869	19.4	25.1	32 671	73.0	8.4	8.5	1.0	6.7	10.5	42.6	47.0
Watertown city	1 048	18.2	21.9	18 918	66.3	8.2	15.1	1.3	4.9	10.0	45.2	44.8
Westfield city	590	13.7	28.5	19 553	84.6	7.3	1.4	0.8	3.9	10.0	33.3	56.7
Woburn city	881	16.7	26.3	20 032	84.9	6.6	4.4	0.5	1.7	7.2	38.5	54.3
Worcester city	577	15.2	29.3	75 537	73.6	12.5	4.3	1.0	7.0	18.1	45.0	36.9
MICHIGAN	546	12.7	28.4	4 540 372	83.2	9.7	1.3	0.7	2.2	7.7	33.7	58.6
Allen Park city	595	7.6	18.7	13 272	90.6	6.1	0.5	0.4	1.2	6.8	35.9	57.4
Ann Arbor city	742	13.3	37.9	60 188	62.6	7.9	6.6	2.7	15.8	9.5	44.4	46.0
Battle Creek city	488	13.4	29.6	22 482	81.6	11.5	1.7	0.9	2.1	11.9	41.3	46.9
Bay City city	395	13.8	27.5	16 209	83.6	8.3	1.1	1.0	3.0	11.3	40.0	48.8
Burton city	476	11.1	25.1	13 213	85.5	10.5	0.4	0.5	1.2	5.1	35.3	59.5
Dearborn city	640	16.8	36.5	37 881	86.4	8.2	1.2	0.7	1.9	10.6	41.0	48.4
Dearborn Heights city ...	693	13.0	25.2	25 304	88.1	8.3	0.4	0.4	1.1	6.8	37.7	55.5
Detroit city	486	20.4	33.9	319 449	68.6	17.1	8.7	1.1	2.8	21.9	44.1	34.0
East Lansing city	578	10.4	53.5	23 495	60.5	8.0	4.3	3.2	21.4	9.9	43.7	46.4
Eastpointe city	537	12.3	33.1	16 251	86.8	8.9	1.0	0.6	1.3	7.8	35.3	56.9
Farmington Hills city	840	14.2	25.3	41 626	89.5	5.9	0.3	0.4	1.0	4.9	33.6	61.5
Flint city	476	16.1	40.2	44 114	75.0	15.8	4.0	1.0	2.4	15.9	44.1	39.9
Garden City city	569	10.8	21.4	14 380	89.5	7.3	0.2	0.7	1.4	5.2	31.9	62.9
Grand Rapids city	531	11.5	30.9	90 663	76.5	12.8	2.4	1.6	4.0	11.9	40.6	47.5
Holland city	551	10.7	23.8	16 928	77.1	10.9	1.1	1.0	7.6	7.5	36.9	55.6
Inkster city	557	18.2	25.6	11 402	79.7	14.0	2.2	1.2	2.2	14.9	40.9	44.2
Jackson city	462	12.4	32.1	15 204	78.3	14.1	1.5	1.0	3.0	15.6	42.4	41.9
Kalamazoo city	520	11.7	38.1	36 122	74.4	11.2	3.2	1.1	7.0	12.5	42.7	44.8
Kentwood city	586	11.8	19.9	23 997	87.4	8.1	0.6	0.5	0.7	5.0	40.8	54.2
Lansing city	498	13.2	30.3	56 449	78.7	12.9	2.7	0.8	2.4	11.0	42.7	46.4
Lincoln Park city	522	12.4	23.3	18 096	85.1	10.8	0.8	0.5	1.5	8.5	39.5	52.0
Livonia city	726	9.4	28.6	48 856	90.5	5.6	0.4	0.3	1.1	4.0	28.0	68.1
Madison Heights city	588	14.5	24.8	15 398	88.2	7.6	0.7	0.5	1.1	8.6	41.0	50.5
Midland city	510	8.5	30.1	19 507	87.4	6.3	0.6	0.8	1.8	5.9	34.4	59.7
Mount Pleasant city.......	446	9.2	40.4	12 645	70.0	9.0	0.7	2.1	15.5	10.0	35.7	54.3
Muskegon city	416	14.5	31.4	14 942	76.1	15.3	1.2	2.0	2.9	14.0	43.8	42.3
Novi city	817	9.8	19.6	25 521	91.1	5.2	0.3	0.5	0.5	2.8	31.2	65.9
Oak Park city	748	17.5	36.1	13 164	84.4	9.5	1.1	0.6	2.0	9.6	37.8	52.6
Pontiac city	554	22.0	33.8	25 808	77.1	17.3	1.1	1.2	2.2	15.6	42.6	41.8
Portage city	541	8.8	24.3	23 136	88.4	6.9	0.3	0.4	0.8	4.3	33.5	62.2
Port Huron city	515	15.2	34.0	14 200	74.2	15.0	1.7	1.9	3.8	13.9	41.2	45.0
Rochester Hills city	827	12.2	26.2	35 674	90.4	5.0	0.1	0.5	0.8	4.3	27.1	68.6
Roseville city	569	12.5	27.1	22 618	88.2	7.8	1.0	0.8	1.1	7.1	38.4	54.5
Royal Oak city	639	11.3	21.0	34 934	88.6	5.2	1.0	0.5	1.8	6.6	42.3	51.2
Saginaw city	431	14.9	38.6	21 913	80.9	12.0	1.5	1.1	2.0	14.7	44.3	41.0
St. Clair Shores city	621	11.6	29.3	29 277	88.7	7.1	0.6	0.2	1.0	5.4	39.2	55.4
Southfield city	797	19.7	29.3	38 877	85.6	8.9	1.1	0.5	1.5	9.9	41.9	48.1
Southgate city	604	9.7	22.5	14 203	88.4	7.9	1.0	0.6	1.2	8.1	36.4	55.5
Sterling Heights city	644	11.2	24.2	63 247	90.9	6.2	0.3	0.3	0.7	5.5	28.7	65.8
Taylor city	578	13.1	26.7	28 643	86.5	10.2	0.3	0.9	0.9	7.5	35.2	57.2
Troy city	808	11.5	20.0	41 434	90.0	5.6	0.3	0.5	0.6	3.6	26.5	69.9
Warren city	598	12.4	26.3	62 810	87.1	9.1	0.7	0.6	1.2	6.3	37.2	56.5
Westland city	627	12.2	25.5	42 760	87.2	9.2	0.4	0.6	1.2	7.8	39.7	52.5
Wyandotte city	524	11.2	20.5	13 354	86.7	9.6	0.2	0.6	1.9	8.4	38.3	53.8
Wyoming city	555	9.7	23.2	35 777	84.5	9.7	1.1	0.9	1.8	6.7	36.6	56.7
MINNESOTA	566	11.1	27.1	2 541 611	77.6	10.4	3.2	0.9	3.3	7.7	31.2	61.2
Andover city	772	9.2	59.9	14 314	85.1	8.2	2.2	0.3	0.6	1.9	10.3	87.8
Apple Valley city...........	746	11.1	24.4	26 221	84.2	7.5	3.1	0.8	0.6	3.3	24.8	71.8
Blaine city	702	8.1	24.8	25 636	81.3	11.7	2.5	0.9	0.8	2.6	24.8	72.6
Bloomington city	753	10.8	27.2	47 327	82.5	8.8	2.9	0.8	1.5	5.9	35.2	58.9
Brooklyn Center city......	636	11.5	35.5	14 686	76.9	11.6	5.2	1.4	2.1	8.7	39.3	52.0
Brooklyn Park city	663	12.1	27.7	37 393	79.7	11.3	4.5	0.5	0.8	6.9	30.3	62.9
Burnsville city	779	11.3	23.7	35 224	81.6	10.1	2.9	0.6	1.0	4.4	32.0	63.6
Coon Rapids city...........	736	9.3	31.7	34 144	83.0	9.6	3.5	0.4	0.8	4.4	27.1	68.5
Cottage Grove city	804	10.7	29.4	16 674	83.2	11.1	1.4	0.6	0.8	2.2	18.1	79.7
Duluth city	444	12.5	33.4	41 232	76.6	10.3	4.2	0.8	5.0	14.3	37.4	48.2
Eagan city	806	9.5	21.2	36 969	85.6	6.8	2.2	0.5	1.0	2.4	29.4	68.2
Eden Prairie city	883	10.1	21.9	30 611	83.8	6.9	2.8	0.6	1.0	2.6	28.4	69.0
Edina city	864	14.7	35.3	22 547	81.0	6.5	3.2	0.8	1.6	7.7	35.6	56.7
Fridley city	635	9.6	24.0	15 221	82.6	9.3	3.8	0.6	1.2	7.1	33.8	59.2

Table C-5. Cities — **Migration, Housing, and Transportation**

STATE Place code	City	Total population 5 years and over	Residence in 1995 (percent)					Occupied housing units		Householders 65 years and over	
			Same house	Same county, different house	Same state, different county	Different state	Outside the United States	Number	Percent owner-occupied	Number	Percent owner-occupied
		1	2	3	4	5	6	7	8	9	10
	MINNESOTA—Cont'd										
27 31076	Inver Grove Heights city	27 611	51.7	22.1	17.2	7.2	1.9	11 255	77.4	1 355	86.1
27 35180	Lakeville city	38 690	51.7	23.2	15.0	9.3	0.9	13 609	91.4	786	86.9
27 39878	Mankato city	30 782	40.7	19.5	27.5	10.0	2.3	12 350	52.9	2 357	66.6
27 40166	Maple Grove city	46 544	60.2	23.1	6.5	9.0	1.2	17 525	92.5	1 295	90.6
27 40382	Maplewood city	32 680	61.6	21.2	10.4	5.7	1.0	13 759	75.6	3 237	71.7
27 43000	Minneapolis city	357 867	42.7	28.0	9.8	13.5	6.1	162 363	51.4	23 058	67.9
27 43252	Minnetonka city	48 561	57.4	25.1	6.1	9.7	1.7	21 392	75.7	4 889	73.6
27 43864	Moorhead city	30 328	48.1	18.0	14.0	18.1	1.7	11 651	63.7	2 685	70.7
27 47680	Oakdale city	24 586	56.8	12.5	23.0	6.6	1.0	10 249	80.7	1 513	66.5
27 51730	Plymouth city	61 386	53.6	26.9	7.1	10.0	2.5	24 822	76.6	3 182	83.6
27 54214	Richfield city	32 271	56.7	23.2	8.3	7.8	3.9	15 073	67.5	3 592	81.7
27 54880	Rochester city	78 989	49.3	22.6	7.8	16.0	4.2	33 986	70.9	6 336	73.5
27 55852	Roseville city	32 136	59.5	18.7	12.9	6.8	2.1	14 605	67.4	4 283	75.7
27 56896	St. Cloud city	55 681	44.2	18.4	28.5	7.0	1.9	22 611	56.0	3 931	73.5
27 57220	St. Louis Park city	41 630	51.4	26.2	8.8	10.3	3.4	20 779	63.5	4 169	71.0
27 58000	St. Paul city	265 546	49.1	23.9	12.6	10.8	3.5	112 109	54.8	19 843	65.3
27 59998	Shoreview city	24 468	63.6	17.7	12.1	5.2	1.4	10 125	87.3	1 682	86.6
27 71032	Winona city	25 835	45.3	23.7	14.5	14.6	1.8	10 301	61.0	2 404	73.0
27 71428	Woodbury city	42 016	44.1	13.5	24.1	16.4	1.8	16 676	85.3	1 607	84.4
28 00000	MISSISSIPPI	2 641 453	58.5	22.5	9.4	8.6	1.0	1 046 434	72.4	229 696	84.0
28 06220	Biloxi city	46 973	42.3	24.3	6.6	23.9	2.9	19 619	49.1	4 510	71.6
28 15380	Columbus city	24 159	54.8	27.2	6.7	9.9	1.4	10 083	54.8	2 521	74.9
28 29180	Greenville city	38 097	58.0	30.1	4.1	6.3	1.5	14 769	55.8	3 237	79.3
28 29700	Gulfport city	65 852	48.4	27.1	5.2	17.5	1.8	26 949	58.7	5 607	80.7
28 31020	Hattiesburg city	41 901	40.6	22.9	22.6	11.8	2.1	17 217	44.7	3 410	73.5
28 36000	Jackson city	169 715	52.8	31.9	8.5	6.0	0.8	67 805	57.9	12 996	78.4
28 46640	Meridian city	37 061	55.6	28.4	6.8	8.2	1.0	15 972	56.7	4 447	75.8
28 55360	Pascagoula city	24 142	51.0	31.4	4.4	11.0	2.2	9 855	56.7	2 014	79.2
28 69280	Southaven city	26 856	47.5	21.9	6.3	23.4	1.0	11 039	72.3	1 478	92.9
28 74840	Tupelo city	31 809	49.9	28.7	11.0	9.5	0.9	13 482	62.3	2 539	77.4
28 76720	Vicksburg city	24 082	55.7	30.9	6.4	6.4	0.6	10 365	56.2	2 709	72.3
29 00000	MISSOURI	5 226 022	53.6	23.5	12.5	9.1	1.3	2 194 594	70.3	495 896	79.1
29 03160	Ballwin city	29 022	58.1	22.1	6.6	11.7	1.5	11 809	82.9	2 555	87.7
29 06652	Blue Springs city	44 344	52.3	31.4	6.0	9.9	0.4	17 336	74.1	2 173	77.1
29 11242	Cape Girardeau city	33 426	45.9	26.3	14.9	11.4	1.5	14 369	57.3	3 382	74.0
29 13600	Chesterfield city	44 324	56.3	22.1	5.9	13.3	2.5	18 091	78.1	3 914	80.4
29 15670	Columbia city	79 857	31.7	27.0	23.8	14.1	3.4	33 754	47.2	4 719	75.4
29 24778	Florissant city	47 020	62.3	23.6	8.1	5.3	0.7	20 354	76.8	5 901	82.9
29 27190	Gladstone city	24 842	55.9	23.3	11.2	8.9	0.6	11 485	68.8	2 649	84.0
29 31276	Hazelwood city	24 565	59.3	23.6	9.9	6.1	1.0	10 907	65.0	2 044	76.3
29 35000	Independence city	105 757	54.2	32.2	5.9	7.0	0.8	47 359	67.8	11 847	79.3
29 37000	Jefferson City city	37 119	47.7	23.7	18.6	8.3	1.6	15 815	58.8	3 657	75.9
29 37592	Joplin city	42 370	43.5	27.0	12.0	16.6	0.9	19 156	57.6	4 694	76.9
29 38000	Kansas City city	409 894	49.8	27.1	8.0	12.7	2.4	183 958	57.7	36 679	72.4
29 39044	Kirkwood city	25 631	62.8	21.9	7.6	7.4	0.3	11 781	77.2	3 277	78.2
29 41348	Lee's Summit city	65 321	47.2	32.2	7.1	12.6	0.9	26 499	75.7	4 611	56.4
29 42032	Liberty city	24 359	47.0	25.0	12.5	15.1	0.4	9 448	73.2	1 683	80.9
29 46586	Maryland Heights city	24 447	50.8	21.1	13.3	10.1	4.7	11 269	63.0	1 603	87.9
29 54074	O'Fallon city	41 110	39.8	24.7	22.9	11.5	1.1	15 354	89.6	1 746	90.9
29 60788	Raytown city	28 623	60.0	28.5	4.1	6.8	0.5	12 841	73.9	3 631	81.2
29 64082	St. Charles city	56 210	49.0	23.8	16.5	8.8	1.9	24 084	64.8	4 980	74.7
29 64550	St. Joseph city	69 122	53.2	28.5	10.0	7.7	0.6	28 984	64.8	7 378	75.4
29 65000	St. Louis city	324 769	50.7	29.3	8.9	7.4	3.7	147 076	46.9	34 383	61.2
29 65126	St. Peters city	47 549	56.4	20.5	15.9	6.7	0.6	18 436	85.5	2 427	81.6
29 70000	Springfield city	142 875	41.4	29.6	15.4	12.4	1.2	64 821	53.6	15 128	74.4
29 75220	University City city	35 247	55.6	15.3	13.7	12.3	3.1	16 487	57.8	3 321	68.3
29 79820	Wildwood city	30 618	48.0	23.9	7.0	19.6	1.5	10 922	90.9	1 259	71.5
30 00000	MONTANA	847 362	53.6	22.5	9.9	13.2	0.8	358 667	69.1	79 362	78.9
30 06550	Billings city	83 638	50.1	28.2	9.5	11.5	0.8	37 401	64.0	8 792	75.3
30 08950	Bozeman city	26 598	29.3	24.5	20.1	23.6	2.5	10 926	43.0	1 384	75.5
30 11390	Butte-Silver Bow	32 672	59.0	22.5	8.8	9.3	0.5	14 432	70.4	3 670	76.6
30 32800	Great Falls city	53 004	53.0	26.0	8.3	11.5	1.2	23 785	63.1	5 664	71.8
30 35600	Helena city	24 089	49.1	23.2	11.7	15.3	0.7	11 520	57.0	2 360	72.9
30 50200	Missoula city	53 944	38.4	27.4	13.0	19.8	1.4	24 015	50.2	4 069	64.9

Table C-5. Cities — **Migration, Housing, and Transportation**

City	Owner-occupied by household type (percent)								Median household income			Median monthly owner costs as a percent of income	
	Family households					Nonfamily households							
		Married-couple family		Other family									
	Total family households	Total	With own children under 18 years	Total	With own children under 18 years	Total nonfamily households	Two or more adults	Living alone	All households	Owner-occupied households	Renter-occupied households	Median housing value (owner estimated)	With a mortgage	Without a mortgage
	11	12	13	14	15	16	17	18	19	20	21	22	23	24
MINNESOTA—Cont'd														
Inver Grove Heights city	84.0	89.2	88.9	62.0	52.8	61.4	46.6	66.7	58 925	66 273	37 491	137 800	19.5	9.9
Lakeville city	93.8	96.1	96.6	77.4	73.7	77.8	77.5	77.9	72 481	76 117	35 318	165 400	20.7	9.9
Mankato city	74.3	83.5	86.0	46.4	48.9	31.7	17.5	39.5	33 814	47 463	22 089	91 800	20.0	9.9
Maple Grove city	95.4	96.7	96.7	85.8	83.2	81.3	69.7	84.5	76 124	78 615	51 159	153 800	20.5	9.9
Maplewood city	85.5	89.7	90.1	67.7	52.7	55.7	61.1	54.4	51 411	60 544	27 002	125 900	20.3	9.9
Minneapolis city	66.7	77.2	76.4	47.6	40.2	38.5	35.8	39.4	37 856	53 665	25 769	113 700	20.5	10.7
Minnetonka city	86.9	89.6	91.8	69.7	61.4	53.8	43.8	56.2	69 352	79 885	44 570	182 500	20.0	9.9
Moorhead city	79.7	88.3	86.6	49.3	44.6	39.2	26.5	43.5	33 807	49 550	16 184	84 100	19.8	9.9
Oakdale city	87.7	92.8	94.5	64.3	60.6	64.4	67.1	63.9	56 792	65 518	28 142	134 900	20.7	9.9
Plymouth city	85.0	89.7	91.4	58.0	53.7	56.0	34.5	63.1	76 771	87 892	47 325	191 100	19.2	9.9
Richfield city	79.3	86.9	86.2	56.1	45.0	51.1	46.3	52.3	45 370	56 614	29 086	127 300	19.9	9.9
Rochester city	83.5	88.4	88.0	60.7	56.2	49.2	45.4	50.1	48 765	59 125	26 935	110 900	18.3	9.9
Roseville city	83.1	88.5	88.9	55.8	44.4	45.0	35.7	47.0	50 960	63 627	32 307	139 800	19.2	9.9
St. Cloud city	78.1	86.0	86.4	50.9	44.9	29.7	17.0	36.2	37 225	51 290	23 697	93 400	19.7	9.9
St. Louis Park city	78.4	83.5	84.2	60.5	54.2	47.7	34.9	51.4	49 480	59 738	33 725	131 900	19.9	9.9
St. Paul city	67.8	77.5	76.8	47.4	35.8	39.1	38.7	39.2	38 610	53 658	25 438	105 000	20.3	10.3
Shoreview city	93.1	95.0	93.7	82.3	81.1	73.3	65.0	75.0	69 582	75 610	36 920	153 200	18.6	9.9
Winona city	81.5	88.6	87.7	52.3	36.0	38.7	21.1	45.1	33 378	46 055	18 416	89 800	19.9	9.9
Woodbury city	89.7	91.3	93.3	76.6	73.7	71.4	55.2	75.9	76 385	81 609	51 518	172 700	21.1	9.9
MISSISSIPPI	77.0	85.3	81.1	57.6	46.4	60.5	40.4	63.5	31 232	36 822	19 603	64 700	20.4	9.9
Biloxi city	54.6	61.0	48.0	39.3	27.6	39.5	25.1	42.4	34 372	46 812	26 857	87 700	19.9	9.9
Columbus city	63.1	77.9	68.3	40.1	22.8	40.1	25.9	42.3	27 178	39 624	16 581	67 900	21.1	10.1
Greenville city	58.4	76.1	67.7	37.6	22.6	49.5	29.2	52.2	25 294	35 501	16 657	54 100	21.0	11.5
Gulfport city	64.6	74.4	66.3	46.0	33.1	47.4	34.1	50.5	32 699	41 152	23 616	77 900	21.1	10.4
Hattiesburg city	57.1	70.1	64.8	39.5	31.1	29.6	13.4	34.7	24 334	35 788	17 551	65 400	21.7	10.4
Jackson city	64.3	79.7	74.8	45.6	33.4	45.7	29.3	48.6	30 440	40 956	19 298	64 200	21.6	9.9
Meridian city	61.3	77.8	73.4	39.3	24.0	48.7	31.3	50.7	24 962	33 837	14 952	58 400	20.9	9.9
Pascagoula city	63.1	75.8	64.4	36.3	20.8	42.4	18.7	46.6	32 431	44 390	20 349	68 300	18.1	11.1
Southaven city	76.3	82.0	75.3	55.8	44.1	60.4	52.8	61.9	46 712	53 379	34 685	90 400	19.9	9.9
Tupelo city	69.5	80.7	77.1	40.3	33.0	46.5	37.7	47.8	38 806	51 903	25 039	91 200	19.2	9.9
Vicksburg city	60.4	79.3	66.6	41.9	29.7	45.0	27.2	46.8	28 854	39 158	17 480	62 000	19.5	9.9
MISSOURI	78.7	85.6	82.2	54.6	44.7	52.8	42.7	54.7	37 828	45 667	23 698	86 900	19.5	9.9
Ballwin city	89.2	92.0	92.0	68.4	57.7	63.2	44.4	65.8	66 740	73 778	36 226	155 800	19.3	9.9
Blue Springs city	81.0	86.2	84.4	59.0	56.9	50.8	44.4	52.5	55 150	62 275	34 165	108 200	19.7	9.9
Cape Girardeau city	70.7	80.4	77.8	39.6	29.5	39.0	22.3	43.3	32 013	45 449	20 271	88 800	19.0	9.9
Chesterfield city	88.7	90.8	91.4	69.7	61.8	49.0	30.5	51.8	82 824	100 710	42 888	232 100	18.6	9.9
Columbia city	66.2	75.1	75.2	39.7	36.8	26.8	14.3	32.6	33 604	58 015	20 984	110 700	19.6	9.9
Florissant city	83.7	88.3	85.5	70.0	59.3	62.9	51.4	64.5	44 278	49 028	31 697	75 000	18.4	9.9
Gladstone city	80.0	85.4	82.1	59.1	52.9	48.9	41.6	50.3	46 073	54 526	30 359	100 100	18.9	9.9
Hazelwood city	75.5	82.3	81.0	58.6	49.1	48.1	39.2	49.9	44 686	51 643	34 107	79 400	18.1	9.9
Independence city	76.1	83.9	77.6	52.4	40.3	52.5	43.7	54.0	38 076	44 450	27 255	76 000	19.5	10.1
Jefferson City city	73.3	83.1	79.8	39.6	28.6	38.6	24.7	40.8	39 726	54 785	24 480	97 700	18.7	9.9
Joplin city	66.9	75.6	65.6	41.3	30.2	43.2	21.8	47.6	30 613	38 494	21 250	67 300	18.1	9.9
Kansas City city	68.2	79.6	76.5	46.5	35.9	42.7	38.4	43.6	37 008	48 143	25 980	83 300	20.0	10.9
Kirkwood city	87.7	93.0	92.8	63.7	52.7	60.7	42.5	63.4	55 846	64 072	32 119	157 000	19.0	9.9
Lee's Summit city	85.0	89.7	90.8	59.2	55.4	49.4	50.0	49.3	60 642	71 279	31 146	131 700	19.7	9.9
Liberty city	80.4	87.5	85.8	52.9	44.9	53.8	38.6	56.8	52 511	62 681	28 905	118 800	20.4	9.9
Maryland Heights city	76.6	82.0	82.2	58.1	50.8	44.8	23.9	49.8	49 067	57 308	37 211	107 000	19.7	9.9
O'Fallon city	92.4	95.6	94.7	74.0	68.0	76.6	76.2	76.8	60 360	63 527	31 223	132 800	20.7	9.9
Raytown city	81.1	87.2	82.7	62.6	50.0	60.7	56.7	61.3	41 803	47 391	26 797	79 700	18.9	9.9
St. Charles city	77.3	83.4	82.1	51.9	43.3	43.0	32.4	45.5	47 514	59 219	31 662	113 800	18.5	9.9
St. Joseph city	73.2	81.4	74.7	48.7	39.2	49.9	34.2	52.8	32 674	40 621	21 173	68 800	18.3	9.9
St. Louis city	56.4	72.0	67.6	40.9	27.2	36.3	37.4	36.1	27 033	38 787	19 054	63 500	20.1	11.4
St. Peters city	90.3	93.1	92.6	75.8	73.7	71.0	74.7	70.2	57 771	61 591	34 059	113 000	19.3	9.9
Springfield city	65.3	74.2	68.9	41.6	31.5	39.1	24.4	43.1	29 268	38 498	20 882	78 700	20.3	9.9
University City city	72.3	78.8	78.2	60.0	38.9	39.5	22.1	44.6	41 202	56 867	26 155	103 300	20.7	10.7
Wildwood city	95.3	95.9	97.6	87.2	84.0	63.6	69.1	63.0	94 010	99 593	40 139	241 900	19.9	9.9
MONTANA	77.8	83.1	78.4	54.7	47.1	51.9	40.2	54.5	33 014	40 004	20 836	95 800	22.2	10.4
Billings city	74.4	82.7	79.5	46.9	38.5	47.1	37.0	49.3	35 385	46 052	20 868	96 700	21.2	9.9
Bozeman city	60.5	68.0	61.6	34.8	31.1	27.3	14.7	36.9	32 350	50 084	22 411	134 200	22.5	10.7
Butte-Silver Bow	80.1	86.7	84.1	55.5	46.6	54.8	41.4	57.1	30 659	37 797	16 696	73 600	21.2	11.0
Great Falls city	74.1	82.6	77.3	47.2	37.9	44.8	41.0	45.5	32 207	41 663	18 531	89 700	22.1	9.9
Helena city	72.9	82.4	78.5	42.6	33.4	37.6	31.1	38.8	34 044	48 852	21 277	107 300	21.2	9.9
Missoula city	68.0	76.9	73.3	42.0	35.8	31.2	21.9	35.5	30 636	46 837	18 955	127 900	23.7	10.2

Table C-5. Cities — **Migration, Housing, and Transportation**

City	Median gross rent	Percent who pay 35 percent or more of income for housing expenses		Means of transportation to work (percent except where noted)						Vehicles available (percent of households)		
		Owners	Renters	Number of workers 16 years and over	Car, truck, or van		Public transportation	Other means	Walked	No vehicles	One vehicle	Two or more vehicles
					Drove alone	Carpooled						
	25	26	27	28	29	30	31	32	33	34	35	36
MINNESOTA—Cont'd												
Inver Grove Heights city	767	10.3	24.0	16 780	85.1	9.3	2.2	0.4	0.7	4.1	31.2	64.7
Lakeville city	807	9.3	29.3	22 998	83.2	10.1	1.5	0.7	0.6	1.4	16.1	82.5
Mankato city	496	10.1	32.5	18 251	75.3	10.5	2.7	1.1	8.0	10.2	35.9	53.9
Maple Grove city	891	10.5	16.6	29 715	85.4	7.0	3.0	0.4	0.7	1.1	20.7	78.2
Maplewood city	688	10.5	33.6	18 071	81.7	11.3	3.1	0.4	0.8	6.6	33.6	59.8
Minneapolis city	575	15.0	29.9	203 951	61.6	11.3	14.6	2.5	6.6	19.7	43.4	36.9
Minnetonka city	915	11.5	25.0	29 066	83.3	7.1	2.6	0.6	0.8	3.4	31.7	64.9
Moorhead city	428	8.5	39.1	16 352	76.2	9.5	1.0	1.0	9.8	9.1	35.4	55.5
Oakdale city	654	11.4	31.0	14 560	86.6	7.7	1.7	0.7	1.1	5.0	32.0	63.0
Plymouth city	857	9.8	20.4	36 835	83.9	7.4	2.4	0.8	1.0	2.5	29.1	68.5
Richfield city	638	11.0	30.0	19 187	77.2	9.8	6.4	1.3	2.7	9.7	41.4	48.9
Rochester city	561	7.8	29.8	44 664	76.0	10.9	4.2	1.1	4.7	8.1	37.1	54.8
Roseville city	688	9.0	29.9	17 761	81.0	9.3	2.6	0.8	3.0	6.9	39.4	53.7
St. Cloud city	470	9.8	24.6	32 512	77.5	10.7	2.6	1.1	5.1	9.5	36.1	54.4
St. Louis Park city	716	12.1	27.6	26 441	78.5	8.7	6.1	0.7	2.1	8.2	43.8	48.0
St. Paul city	565	13.8	30.7	139 067	69.2	12.4	8.7	1.3	5.4	16.8	41.3	41.9
Shoreview city	712	8.1	24.2	14 801	85.3	8.4	1.8	0.5	0.8	3.0	30.7	66.3
Winona city	407	9.4	30.0	13 654	75.1	8.1	1.3	2.1	10.9	11.6	39.5	48.8
Woodbury city	991	10.1	26.0	25 334	84.4	9.0	1.5	0.5	0.6	1.9	24.6	73.5
MISSISSIPPI	439	16.0	27.6	1 164 118	79.4	15.2	0.6	1.0	1.9	9.2	34.2	56.6
Biloxi city	531	14.5	23.1	24 641	73.4	12.9	0.7	1.4	10.7	8.1	41.3	50.6
Columbus city	424	17.7	32.3	10 146	75.1	16.7	0.3	0.9	5.3	15.0	38.3	46.6
Greenville city	433	19.8	35.5	14 641	74.6	19.8	1.3	1.6	1.7	17.5	40.1	42.4
Gulfport city	538	16.7	30.2	31 692	79.1	13.6	0.7	1.3	3.5	7.7	42.2	50.2
Hattiesburg city	446	19.0	33.8	19 401	78.7	12.5	0.4	1.3	5.2	11.3	45.7	42.9
Jackson city	497	19.0	33.7	76 046	77.2	17.1	1.2	0.8	2.0	11.2	42.2	46.6
Meridian city	383	18.1	30.7	14 603	79.3	14.3	0.7	1.5	2.7	16.4	41.6	42.0
Pascagoula city	486	12.1	31.3	10 892	78.7	14.4	0.5	1.5	1.6	10.4	39.3	50.3
Southaven city	675	12.3	23.4	14 821	86.6	10.3	0.3	0.5	0.3	2.9	32.0	65.1
Tupelo city	454	11.2	22.6	16 146	84.7	11.2	0.4	0.6	1.3	8.5	36.1	55.3
Vicksburg city	445	14.5	31.8	10 537	78.5	16.7	1.9	0.5	1.0	14.5	41.7	43.8
MISSOURI	484	11.6	26.3	2 629 296	80.5	11.6	1.5	0.8	2.1	8.3	34.1	57.7
Ballwin city	695	9.8	25.2	16 046	88.1	5.9	0.6	0.6	0.7	3.1	26.5	70.4
Blue Springs city	648	11.8	19.6	25 968	85.4	9.2	0.4	0.5	0.6	3.0	26.5	70.5
Cape Girardeau city	436	11.7	30.1	17 337	81.8	9.8	0.7	0.7	5.2	9.9	41.2	48.9
Chesterfield city	838	11.3	27.3	23 378	88.3	4.4	0.3	0.7	0.8	3.1	26.3	70.6
Columbia city	525	9.8	37.6	44 919	75.2	11.7	1.1	2.1	7.0	8.6	40.1	51.3
Florissant city	581	9.0	20.9	24 547	87.4	7.7	1.4	0.6	1.0	5.4	38.7	56.0
Gladstone city	581	9.3	23.0	13 981	85.3	9.9	0.5	0.6	0.5	4.0	38.8	57.3
Hazelwood city	587	10.4	18.1	14 148	86.0	8.7	1.9	0.5	1.1	5.7	39.7	54.5
Independence city	518	11.0	23.5	54 514	83.1	12.3	0.8	0.8	0.9	6.6	39.3	54.1
Jefferson City city	434	8.3	21.5	18 860	80.4	13.0	1.7	0.4	2.2	9.7	39.7	50.6
Joplin city	453	9.7	29.2	21 024	82.7	10.8	0.4	1.2	2.5	8.9	41.7	49.4
Kansas City city	548	14.3	27.4	208 554	78.7	11.8	3.8	0.8	2.3	12.9	40.8	46.3
Kirkwood city	671	9.3	25.5	14 054	85.5	6.9	1.0	0.4	1.8	4.9	38.9	56.2
Lee's Summit city	654	10.6	32.4	36 881	88.3	7.2	0.2	0.2	0.6	5.9	26.4	67.7
Liberty city	551	11.1	21.3	13 350	84.1	9.5	0.3	0.6	2.0	4.7	29.2	66.1
Maryland Heights city	659	9.8	20.3	14 863	88.5	6.4	1.1	0.3	0.8	4.5	38.9	56.6
O'Fallon city	615	11.9	24.4	23 518	85.8	9.0	0.3	0.7	1.0	2.6	20.3	77.0
Raytown city	551	10.1	24.8	14 742	86.4	9.3	0.4	0.6	1.3	4.8	37.7	57.5
St. Charles city	604	9.0	23.1	31 490	86.6	8.2	0.5	0.6	1.4	6.4	34.5	59.1
St. Joseph city	435	9.9	27.8	32 610	82.1	12.1	0.9	0.8	2.0	10.1	39.1	50.9
St. Louis city	442	15.7	32.4	140 747	68.9	13.6	10.7	1.0	4.0	25.2	45.8	29.1
St. Peters city	639	9.0	20.5	27 984	88.4	7.5	0.3	0.7	0.4	2.8	27.5	69.7
Springfield city	452	12.3	31.2	73 930	80.1	11.0	1.3	1.4	3.6	9.3	42.5	48.3
University City city	603	16.7	32.7	18 852	76.5	10.1	4.9	1.3	4.0	11.2	44.0	44.8
Wildwood city	752	12.5	29.7	16 476	87.4	4.7	0.5	0.7	0.3	2.7	14.1	83.2
MONTANA	447	15.3	28.2	422 159	73.9	11.9	0.7	1.7	5.5	6.1	29.9	64.0
Billings city	475	12.8	31.0	45 013	81.9	9.6	1.2	1.2	2.7	8.1	36.1	55.8
Bozeman city	551	16.4	37.8	15 434	67.6	11.9	0.4	4.7	10.7	4.7	37.8	57.4
Butte-Silver Bow	362	12.3	26.7	15 601	81.2	10.5	0.6	0.8	4.2	9.8	31.3	58.9
Great Falls city	407	15.1	28.8	25 840	81.8	10.0	1.0	0.8	3.1	10.0	35.0	55.0
Helena city	442	13.4	28.7	13 139	74.2	10.4	0.7	1.6	9.0	9.6	39.1	51.3
Missoula city	524	18.0	42.9	29 805	69.7	10.0	1.8	6.3	8.1	8.5	37.3	54.2

Table C-5. Cities — **Migration, Housing, and Transportation**

STATE Place code	City	Total population 5 years and over	Residence in 1995 (percent)					Occupied housing units		Householders 65 years and over	
			Same house	Same county, different house	Same state, different county	Different state	Outside the United States	Number	Percent owner-occupied	Number	Percent owner-occupied
		1	2	3	4	5	6	7	8	9	10
31 00000	NEBRASKA.............	1 594 700	54.7	23.4	10.5	9.7	1.8	666 184	67.4	151 815	78.8
31 03950	Bellevue city	41 211	52.0	17.2	11.6	16.2	3.0	16 966	66.0	2 957	81.6
31 17670	Fremont city	23 499	54.1	23.5	13.4	8.1	0.9	10 183	63.4	2 898	71.3
31 19595	Grand Island city...........	39 487	52.3	26.7	10.2	7.8	3.1	16 414	62.6	3 742	73.6
31 25055	Kearney city	25 268	41.6	25.5	23.4	8.3	1.2	10 471	56.1	2 008	73.3
31 28800	Lincoln city	210 329	44.7	31.2	11.8	9.7	2.6	90 488	57.9	15 561	72.3
31 37000	Omaha city	362 048	53.2	27.4	5.7	11.1	2.7	156 858	59.6	30 913	75.3
32 00000	NEVADA..................	1 853 720	37.4	30.6	2.8	25.1	4.1	751 165	60.9	141 024	74.5
32 09700	Carson City	49 209	46.1	22.4	11.3	17.7	2.5	20 171	63.1	5 011	75.4
32 31900	Henderson city	164 110	32.3	31.6	1.1	33.3	1.7	66 541	70.6	10 748	82.0
32 40000	Las Vegas city	442 290	35.5	32.5	0.9	26.0	5.0	176 848	59.1	35 451	71.6
32 51800	North Las Vegas city.....	103 612	35.6	34.1	0.7	22.7	6.9	34 011	70.2	3 501	85.2
32 60600	Reno city	168 592	37.1	32.5	4.1	21.9	4.3	74 023	47.7	14 096	62.8
32 68400	Sparks city	61 730	41.3	35.3	3.1	16.7	3.6	24 650	59.8	4 557	75.3
33 00000	NEW HAMPSHIRE.....	1 160 340	55.4	22.3	6.9	14.0	1.4	474 606	69.7	94 327	74.4
33 14200	Concord city	38 356	47.8	28.9	10.4	11.7	1.3	16 281	51.5	3 481	58.8
33 18820	Dover city	25 347	45.6	23.7	13.4	15.8	1.5	11 573	51.1	2 191	70.2
33 45140	Manchester city	99 771	47.3	30.5	8.0	10.1	4.2	44 247	46.0	9 309	54.5
33 50260	Nashua city	81 071	49.9	27.1	2.8	16.2	3.9	34 614	56.9	6 513	63.6
33 65140	Rochester city	26 567	51.6	30.0	6.0	11.8	0.5	11 434	66.8	2 498	74.0
34 00000	NEW JERSEY..........	7 856 268	59.8	20.7	8.7	6.8	4.0	3 064 645	65.6	701 857	74.2
34 02080	Atlantic City city............	37 546	50.9	31.4	3.0	6.1	8.6	15 848	28.9	4 009	39.4
34 03580	Bayonne city	58 200	62.9	26.9	2.3	4.0	4.1	25 545	40.0	7 495	54.3
34 05170	Bergenfield borough......	24 426	64.6	17.7	3.1	9.1	5.4	8 981	71.1	2 189	80.6
34 10000	Camden city	72 651	55.7	32.1	3.3	5.0	3.9	24 177	46.0	4 433	66.9
34 13690	Clifton city...................	74 029	61.4	20.9	9.7	3.5	4.5	30 244	60.9	9 082	73.6
34 19390	East Orange city	64 257	55.3	32.1	4.0	4.4	4.2	26 031	26.7	5 554	38.0
34 21000	Elizabeth city	111 501	51.6	27.1	7.4	3.9	10.0	40 482	29.8	7 680	50.1
34 21480	Englewood city	24 314	57.5	20.8	3.2	11.8	6.7	9 273	59.3	2 360	68.4
34 22470	Fair Lawn borough	29 933	69.5	14.0	6.4	6.8	4.3	11 906	80.1	3 707	81.0
34 24420	Fort Lee borough	33 369	51.4	18.6	4.1	14.2	11.7	16 544	56.3	4 982	67.9
34 25770	Garfield city	28 056	55.1	22.9	10.6	3.6	7.7	11 250	40.2	2 826	62.8
34 28680	Hackensack city	40 164	48.8	26.2	5.3	10.2	9.5	18 113	32.4	3 171	46.8
34 32250	Hoboken city	37 450	42.3	14.5	14.0	24.1	5.0	19 507	23.0	2 706	17.9
34 36000	Jersey City city	223 948	54.3	25.3	3.5	8.7	8.2	88 632	28.2	15 144	41.6
34 36510	Kearny town	38 211	54.3	22.1	11.1	4.1	8.5	13 539	48.0	2 610	67.4
34 40350	Linden city	37 007	62.5	23.2	6.8	3.1	4.4	15 052	58.7	4 525	73.3
34 41310	Long Branch city	29 326	52.8	31.6	4.9	4.2	6.5	12 594	42.4	2 813	61.7
34 46680	Millville city	24 991	57.7	31.9	5.3	4.1	1.0	10 043	63.8	2 310	69.9
34 51000	Newark city	252 719	54.4	29.6	5.6	3.1	7.3	91 382	23.8	16 001	35.5
34 51210	New Brunswick city	45 251	34.0	24.9	21.3	7.2	12.5	13 057	26.3	2 035	52.5
34 55950	Paramus borough..........	24 404	68.0	20.4	4.0	4.9	2.6	8 082	90.7	2 589	92.5
34 56550	Passaic city	61 096	50.9	30.9	3.8	3.7	10.7	19 458	26.9	3 492	41.1
34 57000	Paterson city	136 673	54.5	32.4	2.9	2.6	7.6	44 710	31.5	7 985	44.8
34 58200	Perth Amboy city...........	43 574	49.1	31.9	3.4	4.8	10.8	14 562	40.6	2 919	59.6
34 59190	Plainfield city	44 203	55.3	23.7	9.5	5.0	6.5	15 137	50.1	2 839	60.7
34 61530	Rahway city..................	24 850	62.5	20.7	9.7	4.5	2.6	10 028	62.9	2 597	74.2
34 65790	Sayreville borough	37 662	60.3	18.3	8.5	6.7	6.2	14 955	67.7	3 262	81.6
34 74000	Trenton city	78 692	55.5	31.3	4.2	4.2	4.7	29 455	45.5	6 934	60.6
34 74630	Union City city	62 243	51.1	28.4	2.9	5.9	11.7	22 872	18.2	3 977	33.3
34 76070	Vineland city	52 977	60.8	27.1	5.0	3.6	3.6	19 930	66.3	5 097	73.4
34 79040	Westfield town	27 251	66.7	14.4	8.1	8.8	2.0	10 622	81.6	2 411	80.8
34 79610	West New York town	42 766	50.6	27.0	3.3	6.4	12.7	16 719	19.9	4 090	22.9
35 00000	NEW MEXICO...........	1 689 911	54.4	23.7	7.5	12.1	2.3	677 971	70.0	141 693	82.8
35 01780	Alamogordo city	32 810	46.2	19.1	6.1	18.7	9.9	13 626	60.5	3 068	84.2
35 02000	Albuquerque city	417 841	46.4	31.2	6.5	13.3	2.7	183 406	60.4	35 155	75.7
35 12150	Carlsbad city	24 065	57.0	27.5	5.3	9.4	0.9	10 064	71.3	2 629	83.0
35 16420	Clovis city....................	29 986	46.1	30.3	6.8	13.4	3.4	12 460	62.2	2 760	81.8
35 25800	Farmington city	34 872	50.9	28.7	4.7	14.9	0.8	13 957	68.7	2 644	81.7
35 32520	Hobbs city	26 170	52.0	31.4	5.4	9.7	1.5	10 099	68.1	2 388	80.5
35 39380	Las Cruces city	69 162	44.6	29.2	10.4	13.6	2.2	29 137	58.5	6 614	80.3
35 63460	Rio Rancho city............	47 895	49.0	11.9	18.8	19.1	1.1	18 965	81.4	3 652	80.2
35 64930	Roswell city	42 097	53.8	26.8	6.9	10.8	1.6	17 110	68.7	5 033	76.5
35 70500	Santa Fe city	58 451	47.7	25.2	5.1	17.2	4.8	27 519	58.2	6 202	76.0

Items 1—10

Table C-5. Cities — **Migration, Housing, and Transportation**

City	Owner-occupied by household type (percent)								Median household income			Median housing value (owner estimated)	Median monthly owner costs as a percent of income	
	Family households					Nonfamily households								
		Married-couple family		Other family										
	Total family households	Total	With own children under 18 years	Total	With own children under 18 years	Total nonfamily households	Two or more adults	Living alone	All households	Owner-occupied households	Renter-occupied households		With a mortgage	Without a mortgage
	11	12	13	14	15	16	17	18	19	20	21	22	23	24
NEBRASKA.............	77.1	83.2	79.6	50.2	41.0	48.0	34.0	50.8	39 179	47 466	25 857	86 900	19.7	10.5
Bellevue city.............	75.3	81.6	77.5	50.9	35.6	43.7	27.5	47.8	46 913	55 556	31 563	96 900	19.7	9.9
Fremont city................	73.4	79.7	76.8	47.8	37.1	44.4	35.3	46.0	36 758	44 879	24 352	85 500	18.6	10.7
Grand Island city..........	72.2	80.7	73.6	39.7	29.8	42.5	30.0	44.9	36 396	45 920	22 011	81 000	20.6	10.9
Kearney city................	72.5	81.5	81.3	41.6	40.5	32.8	11.1	42.2	34 142	46 197	22 639	89 300	20.5	11.2
Lincoln city..................	73.5	82.1	81.2	41.6	34.6	35.1	21.4	39.7	40 629	55 317	25 030	101 600	20.5	9.9
Omaha city..................	71.8	81.4	79.3	47.2	36.2	40.6	33.2	42.3	39 815	52 081	26 740	93 300	19.6	10.4
NEVADA..................	68.0	74.5	68.7	48.1	40.0	46.6	42.9	47.9	44 316	54 626	31 269	132 500	23.8	9.9
Carson City	69.6	75.8	64.4	50.8	40.8	50.4	44.6	51.6	41 777	50 908	30 117	136 300	22.6	9.9
Henderson city	76.9	82.0	78.7	56.7	48.8	55.1	48.0	58.1	55 629	63 513	39 916	151 400	23.3	9.9
Las Vegas city.............	66.4	73.8	67.1	46.4	37.7	44.6	43.8	44.8	43 781	55 647	29 826	133 100	23.8	9.9
North Las Vegas city.....	71.0	77.2	72.7	55.2	47.0	66.9	61.8	69.3	45 935	52 383	29 737	120 900	24.9	9.9
Reno city....................	57.4	65.5	60.1	36.3	28.2	34.9	29.8	36.6	40 447	57 295	29 424	147 900	24.6	9.9
Sparks city.................	64.8	71.1	65.3	46.2	37.1	49.1	49.8	43.0	45 337	56 072	33 246	138 900	24.2	9.9
NEW HAMPSHIRE.....	79.1	84.7	83.6	54.6	45.3	49.2	45.1	50.4	49 224	58 048	31 478	127 500	22.3	13.6
Concord city................	64.0	71.3	73.6	42.1	32.0	33.2	31.3	33.6	42 190	54 524	31 291	105 700	21.7	13.8
Dover city...................	69.0	77.8	74.1	41.0	32.3	28.2	18.4	32.3	43 070	59 780	32 889	130 500	21.3	14.7
Manchester city............	57.1	66.6	64.1	31.1	20.6	29.9	28.6	30.3	40 606	56 477	30 991	114 600	22.9	15.5
Nashua city	66.3	74.4	73.3	37.0	27.2	40.2	38.2	40.7	51 880	66 320	36 332	132 200	21.4	13.7
Rochester city	74.3	82.4	79.6	46.6	41.3	51.3	51.2	51.3	40 279	46 359	27 936	89 300	22.8	14.9
NEW JERSEY	72.8	80.1	78.0	48.8	35.9	48.4	40.3	50.1	54 820	68 770	34 103	167 900	23.7	15.3
Atlantic City city............	34.7	48.1	40.2	23.2	11.1	21.8	22.0	21.8	26 817	45 057	21 524	88 700	23.9	15.4
Bayonne city................	46.5	52.1	43.1	33.7	19.7	28.9	20.4	29.9	41 162	58 312	32 871	169 400	24.1	19.2
Bergenfield borough......	77.5	80.7	78.5	65.1	51.0	51.9	54.4	51.4	62 103	73 297	39 368	184 800	26.0	18.4
Camden city................	47.1	66.6	59.7	36.4	26.4	43.1	35.4	44.8	23 039	32 393	16 145	40 800	24.2	15.2
Clifton city..................	68.6	73.2	68.5	53.1	34.9	44.8	29.5	47.2	50 136	61 130	37 317	183 600	24.9	17.9
East Orange city	34.1	45.7	37.7	25.5	13.6	14.6	20.2	13.7	31 740	56 871	25 461	125 400	27.4	19.3
Elizabeth city	34.1	41.9	33.9	21.9	11.6	19.6	14.5	20.8	35 453	52 969	30 021	154 600	27.0	16.6
Englewood city	63.4	70.6	67.5	46.3	37.2	49.9	50.4	49.8	57 521	81 216	37 339	198 200	24.4	15.8
Fair Lawn borough........	85.9	87.2	89.2	78.3	65.9	62.4	55.7	63.5	72 036	78 704	43 904	216 400	23.3	15.7
Fort Lee borough..........	58.9	60.8	48.4	49.8	32.7	52.7	49.1	53.0	56 664	67 645	42 927	190 100	28.8	17.6
Garfield city................	46.3	49.0	43.3	38.9	20.0	28.0	13.4	31.3	42 456	52 355	38 655	178 400	27.2	21.4
Hackensack city	40.2	45.5	41.7	30.1	19.4	23.7	20.5	24.2	48 997	66 115	41 885	165 100	27.8	17.2
Hoboken city	31.4	39.7	44.4	12.7	11.7	18.4	10.8	22.5	62 604	94 033	53 082	249 300	23.4	20.4
Jersey City city............	32.9	40.4	35.8	22.6	12.9	20.0	17.4	20.7	37 399	58 554	31 504	137 900	26.1	16.9
Kearny town	53.4	58.5	54.5	39.2	20.2	33.2	20.2	36.1	47 189	63 647	37 542	166 600	25.0	18.3
Linden city..................	63.8	68.9	62.0	50.0	31.7	48.4	31.4	51.4	46 011	54 312	37 020	152 100	24.7	17.1
Long Branch city	49.8	60.1	52.7	31.5	16.5	32.1	29.9	32.6	38 357	54 539	29 809	138 800	26.5	18.5
Millville city.................	69.9	82.0	75.4	43.5	32.2	49.7	45.4	50.5	40 179	50 879	21 139	86 300	22.2	13.9
Newark city.................	27.4	38.7	32.7	17.4	9.8	16.2	13.2	16.7	26 644	49 083	21 248	132 800	27.4	14.9
New Brunswick city.......	33.0	38.7	25.9	26.8	13.2	17.8	9.2	24.8	35 558	55 069	30 844	125 700	25.6	16.8
Paramus borough..........	91.7	92.0	90.4	89.2	73.7	84.8	68.9	86.2	77 883	80 618	55 042	286 300	24.7	13.5
Passaic city	29.6	38.8	34.7	16.5	9.6	18.9	12.4	20.6	33 520	55 502	27 846	156 600	29.2	16.8
Paterson city	34.2	44.8	37.2	21.8	13.6	23.1	19.1	23.9	32 214	51 741	26 435	148 500	27.4	16.6
Perth Amboy city..........	42.3	52.1	44.6	25.3	15.0	35.4	22.5	38.2	36 889	53 189	28 832	132 100	25.0	17.8
Plainfield city...............	55.3	67.8	60.3	40.4	26.6	36.4	33.3	37.3	46 281	68 067	31 045	137 500	25.0	17.9
Rahway city.................	71.9	79.7	75.1	51.9	30.2	44.8	41.1	45.5	50 250	59 577	36 811	144 100	24.2	16.8
Sayreville borough	74.5	78.9	74.5	55.9	37.0	49.2	42.4	50.6	58 388	66 283	44 674	152 400	23.6	14.3
Trenton city.................	50.3	65.5	57.9	36.8	22.0	36.8	41.5	35.9	30 654	44 215	22 358	66 200	23.9	16.1
Union City city	19.9	25.1	18.9	12.3	7.3	13.9	8.6	15.4	30 581	47 403	27 747	159 600	35.1	24.2
Vineland city................	71.9	81.6	76.3	51.2	39.7	52.2	47.1	53.2	38 848	51 069	23 482	94 000	22.8	14.1
Westfield town..............	90.7	92.9	94.3	74.3	64.7	50.8	30.9	54.5	99 382	109 999	45 993	338 300	21.5	14.0
West New York town	19.9	24.3	17.8	13.0	12.2	20.0	17.3	20.6	31 750	52 015	28 683	168 900	32.1	12.1
NEW MEXICO...........	76.4	82.7	77.6	58.8	50.4	55.7	47.0	57.6	33 974	40 432	22 267	94 600	22.2	9.9
Alamogordo city	63.4	67.3	56.6	50.0	36.5	53.2	37.9	55.0	30 898	35 808	25 435	68 000	21.3	9.9
Albuquerque city...........	70.6	79.7	75.5	48.1	39.0	44.1	37.4	45.8	38 134	50 415	24 423	123 700	23.0	9.9
Carlsbad city	77.0	84.4	78.0	54.6	44.2	58.0	44.7	59.7	30 946	36 778	18 816	59 300	18.9	9.9
Clovis city...................	66.9	78.4	67.1	38.5	30.2	51.6	32.7	54.4	28 561	35 109	19 955	62 300	20.2	9.9
Farmington city............	75.2	81.5	75.6	55.1	47.2	51.3	37.0	54.2	37 307	45 179	23 792	92 200	19.4	9.9
Hobbs city	71.7	80.0	72.8	45.7	36.7	58.6	41.5	60.7	27 847	34 663	17 249	48 400	17.8	9.9
Las Cruces city	68.3	79.1	72.0	44.7	38.2	41.8	24.2	47.8	30 374	40 945	17 170	83 700	21.2	9.9
Rio Rancho city............	84.6	87.1	83.8	73.4	70.6	72.0	70.3	72.4	46 989	49 870	36 133	111 900	22.8	9.9
Roswell city.................	74.4	80.8	75.4	57.0	49.9	56.0	46.4	57.2	27 056	32 176	18 629	55 800	20.2	9.9
Santa Fe city...............	69.1	75.8	68.6	53.1	39.2	45.1	42.7	45.7	40 184	52 634	28 177	177 200	24.2	9.9

Table C-5. Cities — **Migration, Housing, and Transportation**

City	Median gross rent	Percent who pay 35 percent or more of income for housing expenses		Means of transportation to work (percent except where noted)							Vehicles available (percent of households)		
		Owners	Renters	Number of workers 16 years and over	Car, truck, or van		Public transportation	Other means	Walked	No vehicles	One vehicle	Two or more vehicles
					Drove alone	Carpooled						
	25	26	27	28	29	30	31	32	33	34	35	36
NEBRASKA	491	10.6	23.5	873 197	80.0	10.5	0.7	0.9	3.2	6.3	31.0	62.7
Bellevue city	581	9.7	19.0	23 859	85.1	10.7	0.3	0.5	1.1	4.3	31.7	63.9
Fremont city	497	10.7	24.5	12 625	84.4	9.3	0.1	1.2	3.0	7.8	33.6	58.6
Grand Island city	455	10.7	25.9	21 032	82.6	12.4	0.3	0.8	1.9	6.8	34.2	59.0
Kearney city	509	10.8	31.0	15 553	86.5	7.4	0.2	0.6	3.3	4.9	32.2	62.9
Lincoln city	519	9.7	29.1	124 882	80.7	10.1	1.3	1.7	3.4	7.3	36.2	56.5
Omaha city	537	11.6	25.8	196 801	81.3	11.1	1.9	0.8	2.4	9.8	38.6	51.6
NEVADA	699	19.8	30.5	923 155	74.5	14.7	3.9	1.6	2.7	8.7	37.9	53.3
Carson City	650	15.6	31.0	23 282	77.7	13.9	0.6	1.8	2.7	6.5	36.4	57.2
Henderson city	857	19.3	30.3	88 076	82.1	10.9	1.7	1.3	1.3	3.9	35.4	60.7
Las Vegas city	699	20.4	32.5	210 806	73.8	15.1	4.8	1.8	2.2	10.7	40.3	49.1
North Las Vegas city	644	23.3	31.7	45 714	72.0	19.5	4.4	1.6	1.2	8.7	33.1	58.2
Reno city	650	20.2	30.9	88 851	72.6	14.3	4.4	1.9	4.4	12.3	40.2	47.5
Sparks city	716	17.8	29.4	33 533	76.3	14.2	3.1	1.6	2.5	7.4	36.0	56.6
NEW HAMPSHIRE	646	15.3	25.6	638 565	81.8	9.8	0.7	0.8	2.9	5.8	31.1	63.2
Concord city	647	12.3	25.6	20 045	80.6	10.6	1.2	0.5	4.1	9.5	41.9	48.6
Dover city	639	11.4	24.6	15 022	82.8	10.2	1.0	0.8	2.5	7.3	37.5	55.1
Manchester city	649	15.5	25.9	54 808	81.0	11.9	1.4	0.7	2.9	11.0	40.5	48.6
Nashua city	757	13.3	26.8	44 972	83.5	9.2	1.5	0.7	2.5	8.3	35.3	56.3
Rochester city	601	14.2	29.7	14 407	82.5	12.0	0.6	1.4	1.2	6.7	36.5	56.9
NEW JERSEY	751	20.5	29.9	3 876 433	73.0	10.6	9.6	0.9	3.1	12.7	34.8	52.5
Atlantic City city	561	24.7	31.6	14 639	35.0	11.7	27.9	3.2	21.0	50.3	36.3	13.4
Bayonne city	681	30.0	25.1	26 943	59.2	13.0	17.9	0.3	8.1	25.1	46.0	28.9
Bergenfield borough	855	25.0	32.5	12 972	71.7	11.4	11.6	0.8	2.7	7.8	36.0	56.2
Camden city	522	23.7	38.1	22 161	45.6	22.2	20.8	2.1	8.5	40.6	41.7	17.7
Clifton city	784	23.4	29.3	36 568	77.4	11.2	6.6	0.8	2.1	11.2	38.6	50.2
East Orange city	650	30.2	33.2	26 503	51.0	14.3	27.8	1.4	3.6	37.1	41.5	21.4
Elizabeth city	681	28.0	31.4	46 093	59.0	17.9	14.7	2.2	4.9	25.2	41.8	32.9
Englewood city	825	27.4	28.9	12 067	59.0	14.4	16.6	1.8	4.6	14.5	38.0	47.5
Fair Lawn borough	923	20.0	32.1	15 440	75.0	7.6	11.4	0.2	2.0	5.5	33.2	61.3
Fort Lee borough	1 101	33.4	33.6	16 733	60.8	12.7	17.6	0.6	4.0	13.5	52.2	34.3
Garfield city	777	31.1	28.6	14 100	75.2	14.9	4.6	0.9	3.6	14.2	40.5	45.3
Hackensack city	848	27.1	26.6	21 473	63.3	10.8	15.6	1.7	6.9	15.8	53.5	30.7
Hoboken city	1 002	24.4	22.7	25 306	24.9	4.2	57.2	0.7	10.3	38.3	48.6	13.1
Jersey City city	675	26.9	29.7	100 750	36.4	13.3	39.5	1.0	8.0	40.7	41.6	17.7
Kearny town	769	25.3	27.7	17 296	65.4	12.7	14.0	0.7	6.1	16.0	39.9	44.0
Linden city	795	22.2	28.1	18 381	75.9	11.7	7.1	0.9	3.5	14.7	39.1	46.2
Long Branch city	727	29.9	33.8	13 980	68.8	16.3	6.6	1.9	4.5	15.1	46.4	38.5
Millville city	589	15.6	29.8	11 433	80.5	11.1	2.8	1.3	2.2	14.7	37.1	48.2
Newark city	586	28.5	34.1	87 720	45.3	17.6	26.5	1.4	7.9	44.2	36.2	19.6
New Brunswick city	837	25.4	40.3	23 124	47.7	24.3	11.3	2.6	12.9	23.9	41.0	35.1
Paramus borough	1 483	22.2	37.4	11 576	77.3	10.5	6.6	0.4	1.8	2.6	23.5	74.0
Passaic city	677	33.3	34.1	24 806	45.2	21.1	18.7	3.7	9.8	34.0	39.5	26.5
Paterson city	696	29.0	36.5	50 619	58.0	21.0	12.2	1.9	5.9	29.3	40.3	30.4
Perth Amboy city	732	25.2	36.4	18 173	57.2	25.6	7.0	2.6	6.6	26.9	39.5	33.6
Plainfield city	726	25.7	31.1	22 405	61.7	21.3	8.8	3.1	3.9	17.2	38.1	44.7
Rahway city	732	23.0	25.7	12 203	73.3	10.9	9.4	1.1	3.5	11.7	40.4	47.9
Sayreville borough	795	18.2	20.8	19 516	79.0	9.4	8.6	0.5	1.0	7.3	36.7	56.0
Trenton city	604	23.5	34.3	31 364	59.2	20.0	11.6	1.7	5.9	30.8	40.6	28.6
Union City city	658	41.8	35.2	24 812	33.4	18.2	33.2	1.6	12.2	46.3	39.4	14.4
Vineland city	638	18.7	36.7	23 938	78.2	14.0	2.5	1.6	1.9	14.0	36.8	49.1
Westfield town	1 048	18.1	29.4	14 368	72.7	5.5	14.3	0.6	2.1	3.9	25.4	70.7
West New York town	681	34.3	34.7	17 719	34.6	17.0	30.6	2.0	14.0	43.1	41.4	15.4
NEW MEXICO	503	16.0	30.5	759 177	75.8	14.8	0.8	1.6	2.8	6.7	35.0	58.2
Alamogordo city	456	14.2	26.0	14 413	76.8	16.4	0.3	2.0	2.0	6.8	37.0	56.2
Albuquerque city	560	17.4	34.3	215 222	77.7	12.5	1.7	1.8	2.7	7.2	39.3	53.4
Carlsbad city	411	10.2	27.1	9 872	74.4	16.8	2.4	1.2	2.6	6.3	37.7	56.0
Clovis city	428	16.5	27.3	13 125	81.0	13.3	0.2	1.2	1.4	8.7	38.5	52.8
Farmington city	494	13.7	31.6	16 672	81.8	11.5	0.1	1.2	2.2	6.0	33.0	61.0
Hobbs city	393	10.7	28.6	9 746	78.4	16.2	0.2	1.5	1.2	7.3	38.6	54.1
Las Cruces city	470	15.0	37.9	31 497	77.6	14.1	0.6	1.6	2.8	7.3	39.6	53.1
Rio Rancho city	807	16.5	31.1	24 412	84.4	10.5	0.5	1.0	0.4	3.5	29.4	67.1
Roswell city	411	15.2	30.4	16 370	77.7	14.8	0.7	1.5	2.4	8.4	38.6	53.0
Santa Fe city	707	19.7	35.9	31 893	72.4	13.3	1.5	1.4	4.1	7.3	42.2	50.5

Table C-5. Cities — **Migration, Housing, and Transportation**

STATE Place code	City	Total population 5 years and over	Residence in 1995 (percent)					Occupied housing units		Householders 65 years and over	
			Same house	Same county, different house	Same state, different county	Different state	Outside the United States	Number	Percent owner-occupied	Number	Percent owner-occupied
		1	2	3	4	5	6	7	8	9	10
36 00000	NEW YORK............	17 749 110	61.8	21.8	8.2	4.1	4.1	7 056 860	53.0	1 577 963	62.2
36 01000	Albany city..................	90 185	44.6	28.3	19.1	5.1	3.0	40 709	37.6	8 393	59.6
36 03078	Auburn city	26 808	55.9	29.3	10.6	3.9	0.3	11 411	51.9	3 277	61.6
36 06607	Binghamton city............	44 471	50.3	30.8	10.5	5.2	3.2	21 089	43.0	5 735	59.8
36 11000	Buffalo city..................	271 861	54.1	35.7	4.3	3.6	2.3	122 720	43.5	27 528	62.3
36 24229	Elmira city...................	28 817	49.8	33.0	9.4	7.3	0.5	11 475	48.2	2 773	66.3
36 27485	Freeport village............	40 728	59.6	25.9	8.4	1.4	4.6	13 504	65.2	2 663	74.8
36 29113	Glen Cove city..............	25 133	60.8	25.4	6.8	2.9	4.2	9 461	58.5	2 649	73.3
36 33139	Hempstead village.........	51 968	55.1	23.4	10.3	4.1	7.1	15 176	43.2	2 513	57.3
36 38077	Ithaca city	28 323	19.4	15.4	24.6	31.4	9.1	10 253	25.7	1 365	52.5
36 38264	Jamestown city.............	29 370	53.6	36.0	4.6	4.9	0.9	13 558	51.3	3 445	61.9
36 42554	Lindenhurst village	26 011	71.7	18.2	7.5	1.7	0.9	9 069	80.6	1 834	90.3
36 43335	Long Beach city............	33 862	56.9	27.2	9.7	3.7	2.5	14 923	53.4	3 426	62.5
36 47042	Middletown city............	23 356	49.8	33.0	8.5	4.7	3.9	9 478	45.7	2 092	56.5
36 49121	Mount Vernon city	63 622	59.4	24.3	9.2	2.6	4.4	25 729	36.5	5 703	48.0
36 50034	Newburgh city	25 528	45.0	36.6	8.0	4.1	6.3	9 147	30.6	1 616	45.7
36 50617	New Rochelle city	67 396	60.6	21.9	8.4	3.4	5.6	26 189	50.3	6 951	58.6
36 51000	New York city	7 475 602	61.0	21.0	7.0	4.0	7.0	3 021 588	30.2	625 833	39.8
36 51055	Niagara Falls city	52 046	64.7	28.1	4.0	2.2	0.9	24 101	57.7	7 405	73.9
36 53682	North Tonawanda city ...	31 358	67.3	19.0	10.2	2.4	1.1	13 671	68.7	3 610	73.6
36 59223	Port Chester village.......	25 869	56.8	26.7	3.5	3.5	9.5	9 531	43.2	2 378	56.2
36 59641	Poughkeepsie city	27 676	46.5	33.5	10.9	5.4	3.8	12 014	36.8	2 877	53.1
36 63000	Rochester city	202 726	45.9	39.9	6.2	4.9	3.1	89 003	40.2	14 080	56.6
36 63418	Rome city	32 823	60.9	28.6	5.0	4.5	1.0	13 677	57.0	3 703	71.0
36 65255	Saratoga Springs city	24 768	48.8	23.0	13.2	13.7	1.3	10 784	55.8	2 359	60.0
36 65508	Schenectady city	57 624	49.4	29.4	13.9	4.9	2.4	26 307	44.6	6 353	62.3
36 70420	Spring Valley village......	22 999	56.0	23.1	5.8	2.4	12.7	7 542	31.5	995	38.7
36 73000	Syracuse city................	137 104	44.2	34.8	9.1	8.2	3.7	59 486	40.3	12 707	60.4
36 75484	Troy city.....................	46 084	50.6	24.3	14.9	6.9	3.3	19 996	40.1	4 764	58.0
36 76540	Utica city....................	56 615	55.1	28.0	6.8	2.9	7.2	25 076	48.9	7 418	65.0
36 76705	Valley Stream village	34 305	69.9	12.6	13.8	1.8	1.8	12 492	80.4	3 705	83.3
36 78608	Watertown city..............	24 681	47.0	31.2	6.0	12.7	3.1	11 036	43.0	2 625	60.4
36 81677	White Plains city...........	49 897	59.9	23.4	6.5	4.6	5.6	20 921	52.4	4 972	65.1
36 84000	Yonkers city.................	182 574	61.2	22.0	10.2	2.6	4.0	74 351	43.2	19 887	57.0
37 00000	NORTH CAROLINA ...	7 513 165	53.0	22.3	9.8	12.2	2.6	3 132 013	69.4	635 846	81.4
37 02140	Asheville city...............	65 353	47.6	25.4	9.3	15.2	2.5	30 728	56.3	8 610	71.8
37 09060	Burlington city..............	42 388	51.9	26.3	7.9	9.6	4.4	18 290	59.6	4 654	80.4
37 10740	Cary town	86 906	37.2	22.5	8.0	26.0	6.3	34 887	73.1	2 778	84.8
37 11800	Chapel Hill town	47 226	29.4	12.2	30.9	22.4	5.2	17 932	42.2	2 599	69.8
37 12000	Charlotte city................	503 789	44.0	26.3	6.1	18.7	4.9	215 745	57.5	30 971	75.0
37 14100	Concord city	51 567	46.8	19.0	15.2	16.1	3.0	20 895	67.8	3 899	78.0
37 19000	Durham city	173 810	40.5	25.1	10.6	17.8	6.0	75 021	49.0	11 427	69.8
37 22920	Fayetteville city............	111 753	46.9	24.7	4.8	19.4	4.2	48 432	53.3	8 610	81.3
37 25580	Gastonia city	61 776	51.8	27.7	7.5	9.2	3.8	25 958	57.0	6 188	74.0
37 26880	Goldsboro city	36 002	47.4	25.8	6.9	16.5	3.4	14 645	42.4	3 627	64.2
37 28000	Greensboro city.............	209 434	44.8	28.3	9.9	13.0	4.0	92 221	52.9	17 036	72.7
37 28080	Greenville city..............	57 122	32.4	26.3	25.9	13.7	1.8	25 304	39.2	3 472	66.5
37 31060	Hickory city..................	34 871	44.9	24.1	13.0	14.2	3.8	15 462	55.1	3 438	74.5
37 31400	High Point city..............	79 671	46.5	28.5	9.5	11.4	4.1	33 498	59.4	6 912	71.6
37 34200	Jacksonville city...........	60 331	24.5	14.3	5.1	51.7	4.4	17 216	39.5	2 136	77.7
37 35200	Kannapolis city	34 154	55.1	20.5	12.0	9.4	3.1	14 795	66.7	3 806	81.8
37 43920	Monroe city..................	23 777	47.2	23.5	11.2	10.4	7.7	9 014	56.3	1 774	76.4
37 55000	Raleigh city..................	259 043	37.3	27.3	12.7	16.9	5.7	112 557	51.6	15 010	72.5
37 57500	Rocky Mount city..........	52 265	49.5	26.7	14.9	7.8	1.1	21 552	54.9	4 961	66.1
37 58860	Salisbury city	25 035	48.0	26.6	11.3	11.6	2.5	10 358	53.9	2 900	74.4
37 74440	Wilmington city.............	71 521	41.5	25.9	16.3	14.2	2.1	34 264	48.6	8 036	71.2
37 74540	Wilson city...................	41 085	49.8	31.4	8.9	6.9	3.0	17 250	50.8	3 773	65.3
37 75000	Winston-Salem city	173 229	49.3	26.6	8.3	11.8	4.0	76 277	55.8	17 589	74.3
38 00000	NORTH DAKOTA.......	603 106	56.8	21.8	10.2	10.0	1.2	257 152	66.6	62 043	73.4
38 07200	Bismarck city	52 099	54.8	23.2	13.6	8.0	0.4	23 143	63.3	4 984	67.2
38 25700	Fargo city	84 990	39.7	29.2	12.2	16.7	2.2	39 351	47.1	6 329	56.8
38 32060	Grand Forks city	46 450	41.0	29.3	11.1	16.6	2.0	19 674	50.5	3 061	66.6
38 53380	Minot city....................	34 198	51.9	27.6	9.7	9.1	1.8	15 523	62.4	3 886	70.5
39 00000	OHIO	10 599 968	57.5	26.3	9.5	5.6	1.1	4 445 773	69.1	991 727	78.4
39 01000	Akron city....................	201 588	55.1	31.8	7.3	4.4	1.5	90 092	59.3	20 397	75.8
39 03828	Barberton city	25 832	59.3	30.1	6.4	3.3	0.9	11 540	65.5	3 362	74.5
39 04720	Beavercreek city...........	36 213	60.4	12.0	14.5	11.1	2.1	14 137	84.2	2 598	90.3
39 07972	Bowling Green city	28 513	31.9	19.6	36.7	8.9	2.8	10 206	41.9	1 356	78.4

Table C-5. Cities — **Migration, Housing, and Transportation**

City	Owner-occupied by household type (percent)								Median household income			Median housing value (owner estimated)	Median monthly owner costs as a percent of income	
	Family households					Nonfamily households								
		Married-couple family		Other family										
	Total family households	Total	With own children under 18 years	Total	With own children under 18 years	Total nonfamily households	Two or more adults	Living alone	All households	Owner-occupied households	Renter-occupied households		With a mortgage	Without a mortgage
	11	12	13	14	15	16	17	18	19	20	21	22	23	24
NEW YORK	61.3	71.1	68.2	36.5	26.5	36.9	31.2	38.0	43 070	58 956	28 851	147 600	23.2	13.6
Albany city	52.0	69.1	60.6	30.0	17.9	25.7	17.6	28.1	30 067	51 374	21 580	97 000	22.0	11.6
Auburn city	63.5	75.1	73.6	39.3	24.7	36.1	25.2	38.1	29 794	42 825	18 959	65 200	22.0	14.9
Binghamton city	56.7	68.8	62.4	32.9	19.3	29.5	19.8	31.9	25 711	41 684	16 362	66 100	20.1	12.5
Buffalo city	52.2	69.8	64.6	33.4	20.1	32.8	24.8	34.4	24 175	37 625	16 548	58 800	21.8	13.7
Elmira city	56.5	72.8	67.9	31.4	23.0	36.4	36.7	36.4	26 949	40 491	16 843	52 500	20.5	13.7
Freeport village	67.7	74.0	65.7	55.1	49.2	58.0	57.0	58.3	56 076	70 610	33 391	175 400	27.8	17.3
Glen Cove city	63.4	70.3	60.6	40.8	22.9	46.4	43.1	47.0	55 482	72 557	38 661	262 200	27.2	14.7
Hempstead village	48.6	59.2	52.7	35.8	22.7	26.8	22.8	27.6	44 940	68 976	31 165	165 500	29.3	17.6
Ithaca city	54.0	64.7	65.4	33.9	32.7	14.5	11.2	16.7	21 927	51 179	16 092	96 300	22.7	12.9
Jamestown city	63.5	76.8	70.7	34.5	25.9	34.5	31.9	35.1	25 676	37 896	16 917	50 500	20.2	12.7
Lindenhurst village	84.9	87.9	88.1	72.5	59.6	64.5	62.4	65.0	61 888	68 232	35 841	169 000	26.4	17.8
Long Beach city	63.1	70.0	73.9	43.9	32.1	41.6	33.7	43.4	55 894	69 890	46 112	214 000	24.7	17.6
Middletown city	52.5	67.0	59.8	27.6	15.9	33.8	22.3	36.3	38 659	56 102	25 982	103 200	22.7	13.0
Mount Vernon city	42.2	51.5	44.6	29.2	19.0	25.9	20.3	26.8	40 733	64 404	31 490	224 300	28.4	18.9
Newburgh city	33.3	44.9	36.0	20.1	12.0	25.1	22.5	25.7	29 655	47 098	23 764	93 200	24.9	14.8
New Rochelle city	59.2	66.5	62.6	36.7	22.6	32.2	31.3	32.3	56 147	90 085	35 315	299 900	24.1	16.1
New York city	35.2	43.9	40.0	21.3	13.2	22.2	16.5	23.3	37 786	60 876	30 481	221 200	26.4	12.7
Niagara Falls city	67.1	84.2	78.6	38.3	22.9	43.8	37.5	44.5	26 735	36 834	15 743	59 300	20.8	14.2
North Tonawanda city	80.1	86.9	85.8	51.2	34.9	46.3	34.9	47.8	39 442	49 936	21 989	82 000	21.9	14.1
Port Chester village	46.5	52.0	44.1	32.6	21.5	36.3	8.3	42.3	44 327	60 259	34 695	252 100	28.6	22.3
Poughkeepsie city	43.0	62.8	56.4	18.8	10.6	29.2	21.3	31.3	30 153	52 016	20 623	108 800	22.8	14.1
Rochester city	48.8	69.2	64.2	30.2	20.1	30.3	32.5	29.8	27 004	43 513	18 814	62 100	22.2	14.7
Rome city	66.3	77.9	70.8	38.0	27.9	42.4	39.3	43.0	33 502	46 165	21 014	64 800	20.3	14.2
Saratoga Springs city	74.2	80.4	79.5	49.8	40.6	32.2	24.5	34.1	45 119	61 418	26 844	128 600	21.4	12.9
Schenectady city	52.9	66.5	61.1	32.2	19.8	35.0	27.8	36.4	29 122	42 168	21 581	69 200	22.4	16.4
Spring Valley village	33.8	39.4	33.2	25.1	23.1	25.0	12.5	28.4	41 129	58 750	35 263	132 700	27.2	17.5
Syracuse city	51.9	68.7	65.1	31.1	20.1	28.2	22.5	29.7	25 077	42 984	16 954	67 900	21.4	14.8
Troy city	50.9	67.6	62.0	26.0	15.7	27.3	21.0	28.9	29 688	46 799	21 206	85 100	22.1	13.1
Utica city	58.7	72.8	64.1	34.2	19.6	35.8	30.9	36.5	24 789	37 809	15 636	57 800	22.0	13.2
Valley Stream village	86.2	89.6	89.2	72.2	51.8	60.2	41.7	62.2	63 029	70 417	38 908	202 600	27.0	17.4
Watertown city	53.2	63.6	55.1	27.5	17.9	28.1	23.7	28.9	28 052	43 148	19 023	64 100	21.1	13.5
White Plains city	58.3	63.9	60.3	39.5	27.5	43.2	38.8	44.0	57 447	83 777	38 303	273 000	20.5	14.0
Yonkers city	48.3	58.0	50.0	28.4	14.2	33.0	23.2	34.4	44 046	66 644	30 827	214 100	25.9	15.6
NORTH CAROLINA	76.0	83.0	78.4	52.8	42.9	54.4	38.6	57.7	39 061	46 287	26 140	95 800	21.3	9.9
Asheville city	67.8	76.3	70.4	46.3	36.4	42.7	27.4	46.2	32 452	42 710	21 978	105 200	23.0	11.7
Burlington city	66.0	75.7	67.8	43.2	32.4	47.8	24.9	51.6	34 692	45 004	25 302	94 600	21.4	10.5
Cary town	82.1	85.7	86.2	55.4	52.5	50.0	37.2	54.1	74 938	87 777	44 716	193 000	20.4	9.9
Chapel Hill town	65.3	72.8	74.4	35.7	30.9	22.5	10.9	31.0	39 106	85 998	22 236	217 300	20.4	9.9
Charlotte city	67.0	77.7	75.1	40.1	31.3	42.1	31.2	45.3	46 642	61 670	32 389	131 500	21.5	9.9
Concord city	74.1	82.4	80.0	45.8	37.9	51.4	42.3	53.2	45 500	55 020	30 882	113 700	21.3	11.7
Durham city	58.6	70.3	65.8	35.0	25.7	35.4	24.8	38.6	41 100	59 743	28 130	125 600	21.7	9.9
Fayetteville city	58.9	67.5	59.9	40.0	26.9	42.5	28.5	45.6	36 124	46 555	26 719	87 200	23.6	11.1
Gastonia city	63.1	72.9	65.6	39.3	24.1	43.4	26.8	46.1	36 790	48 213	25 799	92 100	20.7	12.9
Goldsboro city	46.8	57.9	42.8	25.3	16.6	34.3	25.0	35.7	29 103	41 862	22 492	83 400	21.8	10.9
Greensboro city	63.0	74.8	69.0	36.8	27.5	38.5	21.7	42.9	39 604	52 597	28 074	104 700	21.2	9.9
Greenville city	56.0	70.3	70.5	29.4	21.2	23.7	11.1	29.7	28 487	53 389	18 896	92 100	20.4	11.0
Hickory city	63.2	74.1	66.4	34.1	23.2	42.3	28.2	45.2	37 257	50 245	27 961	116 600	21.3	9.9
High Point city	65.5	76.6	70.5	38.9	27.7	47.0	31.9	50.1	39 714	51 984	25 164	101 800	21.9	10.1
Jacksonville city	38.7	40.4	30.4	31.9	25.0	42.4	26.3	46.5	32 392	45 210	27 642	82 800	22.2	10.2
Kannapolis city	69.3	77.1	71.0	49.2	35.9	61.0	41.8	64.4	35 246	40 227	28 106	81 400	21.2	12.3
Monroe city	60.1	73.3	62.8	31.0	22.5	46.8	30.9	50.4	40 099	52 048	28 652	103 600	22.7	10.9
Raleigh city	64.7	75.6	73.5	35.8	29.2	35.5	22.7	40.2	46 562	65 940	31 809	152 400	21.4	9.9
Rocky Mount city	60.9	75.5	71.1	34.8	23.3	41.5	26.9	43.6	32 456	45 877	20 513	85 400	21.7	10.8
Salisbury city	60.1	73.7	63.0	32.9	23.3	44.1	27.7	46.4	33 080	43 856	23 497	91 600	21.8	11.2
Wilmington city	61.9	74.5	68.1	36.8	21.1	34.8	19.1	40.1	30 838	46 073	21 198	121 600	24.6	11.6
Wilson city	58.0	74.0	67.7	31.1	21.9	36.8	19.3	39.6	31 579	47 578	19 762	90 900	22.8	11.3
Winston-Salem city	63.3	75.1	68.1	39.7	27.1	44.2	32.1	46.3	36 806	50 668	24 753	99 000	20.7	9.9
NORTH DAKOTA	78.5	84.3	82.1	49.7	41.7	44.7	29.1	47.9	34 483	42 209	22 062	68 300	19.4	10.2
Bismarck city	77.7	85.5	85.9	43.1	33.6	39.7	31.2	41.5	39 305	50 913	23 829	90 300	19.6	10.5
Fargo city	67.2	76.6	79.7	31.7	29.9	24.4	14.5	27.9	35 430	53 816	23 839	94 100	20.5	9.9
Grand Forks city	67.9	76.9	78.5	37.2	29.5	27.3	12.7	32.8	33 905	51 196	22 025	90 100	20.7	11.9
Minot city	77.6	86.6	85.3	43.0	35.1	39.9	28.5	42.6	32 057	43 093	20 147	74 900	18.8	9.9
OHIO	77.8	85.6	82.5	51.7	39.3	51.1	40.3	53.1	40 846	50 093	25 116	100 500	20.6	10.6
Akron city	68.3	80.8	76.0	46.4	32.5	46.0	36.9	48.0	31 708	41 679	20 524	76 800	21.6	12.1
Barberton city	71.5	80.8	72.3	49.4	32.3	54.5	51.8	55.0	31 805	39 451	20 329	78 500	20.2	10.3
Beavercreek city	89.9	91.9	88.4	72.7	66.1	62.6	50.3	64.9	68 865	73 477	42 417	143 600	19.6	9.9
Bowling Green city	69.0	77.5	75.7	40.1	34.2	20.9	5.7	30.9	30 976	55 138	20 801	122 000	20.2	9.9

Table C-5. Cities — **Migration, Housing, and Transportation**

City	Median gross rent	Percent who pay 35 percent or more of income for housing expenses		Means of transportation to work (percent except where noted)						Vehicles available (percent of households)		
					Car, truck, or van							
		Owners	Renters	Number of workers 16 years and over	Drove alone	Carpooled	Public transportation	Other means	Walked	No vehicles	One vehicle	Two or more vehicles
	25	26	27	28	29	30	31	32	33	34	35	36
NEW YORK..............	672	19.6	33.4	8 211 916	56.3	9.2	24.4	0.8	6.2	29.7	33.0	37.3
Albany city..................	570	15.7	36.8	42 605	61.8	11.2	13.1	0.6	10.8	27.6	43.8	28.6
Auburn city.................	475	15.8	36.1	11 827	78.3	12.2	2.1	0.9	4.6	17.7	43.6	38.7
Binghamton city............	430	12.7	37.5	19 646	70.2	12.9	7.9	1.2	5.8	24.9	43.0	32.2
Buffalo city..................	472	19.1	41.5	110 640	65.4	14.4	12.3	0.9	5.3	31.4	43.1	25.4
Elmira city..................	447	14.5	36.5	11 241	71.9	12.2	2.7	1.4	9.6	22.3	44.0	33.8
Freeport village	860	28.8	35.8	20 045	63.2	13.0	15.2	1.6	4.9	12.6	37.6	49.8
Glen Cove city.............	1 002	25.7	38.6	11 907	74.6	9.6	7.5	1.3	4.2	10.3	36.1	53.6
Hempstead village........	838	34.9	34.1	23 779	48.4	15.0	24.3	1.9	8.8	26.0	35.5	38.5
Ithaca city.................	574	18.0	51.6	13 335	35.7	8.1	7.9	2.2	41.2	24.6	46.4	29.0
Jamestown city.............	407	14.9	35.1	13 624	75.1	13.9	2.7	1.1	5.8	20.0	43.7	36.2
Lindenhurst village	858	25.7	36.3	13 180	76.4	9.9	10.3	0.8	1.2	6.1	27.7	66.2
Long Beach city	1 025	25.7	32.3	17 669	63.7	7.6	20.7	1.3	4.0	14.0	47.1	38.9
Middletown city............	684	17.0	39.2	10 599	73.5	14.5	5.6	0.9	3.7	19.7	38.2	42.1
Mount Vernon city	752	32.7	34.7	30 158	51.3	12.6	27.5	1.1	5.5	29.8	42.0	28.2
Newburgh city	614	22.0	38.0	10 235	58.7	21.8	8.0	2.0	7.9	33.3	36.8	29.9
New Rochelle city	848	24.0	33.4	33 204	60.0	11.9	17.8	0.8	6.6	17.2	38.7	44.0
New York city	705	26.8	37.2	3 192 070	24.9	8.0	52.8	1.0	10.4	55.7	31.6	12.7
Niagara Falls city	436	15.2	38.5	21 679	78.7	10.4	3.1	0.9	5.2	22.5	42.4	35.0
North Tonawanda city ...	502	14.6	31.8	16 205	86.1	9.1	0.5	0.7	2.2	9.9	38.4	51.7
Port Chester village	914	32.7	36.5	13 131	59.4	15.2	14.3	1.0	8.4	21.8	38.1	40.1
Poughkeepsie city	608	18.3	37.6	12 101	66.0	13.3	9.9	0.8	7.0	24.4	42.9	32.7
Rochester city	553	19.7	42.5	89 467	69.6	12.1	8.1	1.4	6.5	25.3	44.2	30.5
Rome city	462	13.5	30.7	13 780	80.1	12.2	1.9	0.8	3.6	14.2	41.5	44.3
Saratoga Springs city	594	15.2	28.6	13 759	74.8	9.8	2.0	0.9	8.4	12.2	37.7	50.1
Schenectady city	548	17.1	35.3	26 426	70.9	11.8	6.5	1.4	6.8	21.5	45.7	32.8
Spring Valley village......	815	29.8	33.0	10 709	60.3	17.7	15.6	1.7	3.7	17.4	43.8	38.7
Syracuse city................	506	17.3	41.2	59 041	65.9	13.7	7.0	1.1	10.1	26.6	44.1	29.4
Troy city......................	519	14.5	32.2	21 346	69.9	10.8	6.6	1.0	9.7	22.5	44.7	32.8
Utica city.....................	430	15.3	39.2	23 634	69.6	16.6	4.3	1.2	6.3	24.7	43.8	31.5
Valley Stream village	955	24.7	30.6	17 368	68.2	9.1	17.1	0.6	3.0	9.2	33.2	57.6
Watertown city..............	457	14.3	29.4	11 013	77.1	13.3	1.8	1.1	5.1	19.2	45.0	35.8
White Plains city............	879	21.1	31.6	26 032	59.7	9.3	19.7	0.7	7.1	17.2	42.8	40.0
Yonkers city..................	735	26.2	33.2	82 251	57.8	12.2	23.1	0.6	4.2	27.1	39.4	33.5
NORTH CAROLINA ...	548	15.0	26.7	3 837 773	79.4	14.0	0.9	1.1	1.9	7.5	32.3	60.2
Asheville city	562	17.2	33.5	32 125	76.4	13.5	2.2	1.2	3.3	12.4	40.5	47.1
Burlington city...............	554	14.3	27.6	21 254	79.7	16.5	0.0	0.9	1.3	8.0	37.4	54.6
Cary town	826	10.9	22.8	51 175	84.2	8.9	0.3	0.8	0.8	2.3	26.0	71.7
Chapel Hill town	690	12.5	47.0	23 543	61.5	9.3	6.5	3.1	15.1	11.3	38.2	50.5
Charlotte city	684	16.6	27.4	280 528	77.8	13.4	3.2	0.9	1.5	8.0	39.0	53.0
Concord city	586	13.1	21.9	27 895	83.3	12.5	0.3	0.9	1.1	7.0	30.5	62.6
Durham city	657	16.5	30.6	93 057	72.7	17.0	3.5	1.0	3.1	10.7	40.3	49.0
Fayetteville city.............	585	20.5	28.2	54 850	81.1	13.3	1.3	1.1	1.7	10.0	39.3	50.8
Gastonia city	559	15.3	29.3	29 541	82.0	13.8	0.6	0.6	1.2	9.8	36.8	53.3
Goldsboro city	451	16.8	22.9	15 022	78.1	14.6	0.6	2.1	3.4	15.5	37.5	47.0
Greensboro city	608	15.2	28.9	112 625	79.3	12.8	1.7	1.2	2.4	8.7	40.5	50.8
Greenville city	482	15.3	38.0	29 795	80.0	11.2	1.6	1.2	4.1	10.1	44.0	46.0
Hickory city	540	14.5	23.7	18 955	80.6	14.5	0.5	0.9	1.8	8.5	37.7	53.7
High Point city	528	16.0	27.8	41 347	79.5	14.1	1.7	1.0	1.4	11.0	35.5	53.5
Jacksonville city	544	15.4	16.8	38 763	55.0	18.0	1.2	3.6	19.2	7.2	37.7	55.2
Kannapolis city	523	15.0	22.7	17 231	80.0	15.0	0.5	1.0	1.5	8.6	35.6	55.8
Monroe city..................	587	19.9	26.5	12 103	75.6	20.1	0.5	1.0	1.3	9.6	36.7	53.7
Raleigh city..................	718	14.2	30.7	151 655	78.7	11.5	2.4	1.3	2.9	7.1	40.5	52.4
Rocky Mount city..........	496	18.0	31.3	22 831	79.7	14.8	1.2	1.1	1.2	14.4	36.5	49.1
Salisbury city	506	15.6	29.3	10 433	77.7	15.8	0.9	0.8	2.7	13.5	41.6	44.9
Wilmington city	602	21.7	38.8	35 912	79.1	11.8	1.9	1.6	3.0	12.2	43.3	44.4
Wilson city	478	19.1	34.7	18 932	77.3	16.8	1.5	1.6	1.5	14.9	37.3	47.8
Winston-Salem city	518	14.1	28.2	85 003	76.4	14.8	2.5	1.0	2.9	11.8	40.3	48.0
NORTH DAKOTA.......	412	9.7	22.6	319 481	77.7	10.0	0.4	0.8	5.0	6.6	30.1	63.3
Bismarck city	447	8.3	26.3	29 789	84.9	8.2	0.5	0.6	2.5	8.0	33.5	58.5
Fargo city	468	10.1	25.9	52 137	83.6	7.7	0.5	1.1	4.4	8.0	37.8	54.2
Grand Forks city...........	477	11.6	29.4	26 721	80.8	9.3	1.1	1.1	5.0	8.0	37.3	54.6
Minot city	405	9.8	29.7	18 458	84.5	8.9	0.7	0.5	2.7	8.5	33.6	58.0
OHIO	515	13.2	27.4	5 307 502	82.8	9.3	2.1	0.7	2.4	8.6	33.5	58.0
Akron city	496	16.8	31.3	97 019	80.8	10.9	3.3	0.8	2.3	13.2	40.9	45.9
Barberton city...............	457	13.3	28.6	12 181	84.8	9.6	1.1	0.4	2.8	9.9	40.0	50.1
Beavercreek city............	821	10.8	23.3	19 533	90.0	5.8	0.1	0.3	0.6	1.7	20.6	77.7
Bowling Green city	495	11.4	39.6	15 097	74.4	9.3	0.6	2.2	11.9	5.7	42.2	52.0

Table C-5. Cities — **Migration, Housing, and Transportation**

STATE Place code	City	Total population 5 years and over	Residence in 1995 (percent)					Occupied housing units		Householders 65 years and over	
			Same house	Same county, different house	Same state, different county	Different state	Outside the United States	Number	Percent owner-occupied	Number	Percent owner-occupied
		1	2	3	4	5	6	7	8	9	10
	OHIO—Cont'd										
39 09680	Brunswick city	31 003	59.2	15.7	20.1	4.2	0.7	11 904	80.9	1 758	82.7
39 12000	Canton city	74 769	56.3	34.4	4.9	3.5	0.8	32 530	59.6	7 937	71.9
39 15000	Cincinnati city	306 954	46.1	38.1	6.0	7.5	2.2	147 991	39.0	28 920	55.9
39 16000	Cleveland city	439 641	55.8	34.8	3.4	3.9	2.0	190 633	48.5	42 204	66.0
39 16014	Cleveland Heights city ..	46 906	57.3	26.1	4.8	8.8	3.0	20 947	62.0	3 921	70.9
39 18000	Columbus city	659 006	41.7	35.1	11.5	8.3	3.4	301 788	49.1	42 612	70.1
39 19778	Cuyahoga Falls city	46 089	57.2	29.1	7.7	5.0	1.0	21 668	65.7	5 233	77.9
39 21000	Dayton city	154 535	51.0	33.6	7.7	6.5	1.3	67 465	52.7	14 610	69.5
39 21434	Delaware city	23 118	41.5	25.9	20.6	11.0	1.0	9 560	59.8	1 749	66.0
39 22694	Dublin city	28 731	44.4	24.5	8.6	18.2	4.4	11 165	77.2	1 090	79.3
39 23380	East Cleveland city	25 203	52.9	42.1	1.4	2.3	1.3	11 210	35.5	2 708	54.1
39 25256	Elyria city	51 401	56.3	33.4	5.4	4.3	0.6	22 419	64.6	5 057	76.8
39 25704	Euclid city	49 408	56.8	32.0	6.4	3.7	1.1	24 353	59.5	7 203	66.9
39 25914	Fairborn city	30 211	44.2	22.0	20.9	10.3	2.6	13 623	51.6	2 528	82.4
39 25970	Fairfield city	39 457	50.3	22.9	17.1	8.4	1.3	16 955	65.3	2 642	85.1
39 27048	Findlay city	36 364	49.6	29.2	11.5	8.3	1.3	15 957	64.9	3 464	81.1
39 29106	Gahanna city	30 162	54.8	29.6	6.9	7.5	1.2	11 925	77.7	1 697	78.2
39 29428	Garfield Heights city	28 752	69.5	25.1	2.9	1.7	0.8	12 377	80.1	3 917	88.8
39 32592	Grove City city	24 942	51.2	34.3	8.4	5.2	0.8	10 247	72.0	1 753	80.9
39 33012	Hamilton city	56 177	53.0	35.2	5.4	5.4	0.9	24 199	60.6	5 870	74.4
39 36610	Huber Heights city	35 473	54.5	28.1	8.0	8.3	1.1	14 403	72.0	2 236	89.2
39 39872	Kent city	26 601	34.9	18.5	35.3	8.4	2.9	9 799	38.2	1 557	63.8
39 40040	Kettering city	54 206	58.2	27.1	7.7	6.2	0.7	25 675	66.5	7 096	77.6
39 41664	Lakewood city	53 244	49.7	32.0	8.3	7.4	2.7	26 693	45.1	5 165	54.0
39 41720	Lancaster city	32 566	48.9	33.0	12.1	5.5	0.4	14 834	59.3	4 010	72.5
39 43554	Lima city	36 919	51.2	34.1	8.7	5.3	0.8	15 441	57.0	3 787	76.7
39 44856	Lorain city	63 288	55.2	34.1	4.9	3.9	1.8	26 407	61.0	6 267	78.6
39 47138	Mansfield city	45 820	53.6	30.8	8.8	5.9	0.8	20 241	57.7	5 624	69.2
39 47306	Maple Heights city	24 555	66.5	27.5	3.5	1.9	0.6	10 489	83.8	2 780	91.3
39 47754	Marion city	32 826	55.1	31.6	8.7	4.2	0.5	13 562	63.3	3 334	73.5
39 48244	Massillon city	29 223	62.3	28.5	5.0	3.8	0.5	12 644	68.6	3 361	74.8
39 48790	Medina city	22 710	46.8	23.8	17.0	11.1	1.3	9 407	66.6	1 697	55.6
39 49056	Mentor city	47 256	67.4	19.7	8.2	3.9	0.9	18 797	87.4	3 746	89.6
39 49840	Middletown city	48 026	51.6	33.1	9.6	5.3	0.4	21 515	60.1	5 395	75.3
39 54040	Newark city	42 727	48.5	36.0	9.6	5.5	0.5	19 332	58.5	4 726	68.7
39 56882	North Olmsted city	32 187	64.7	24.3	5.3	4.6	1.3	13 517	79.7	3 383	88.4
39 57008	North Royalton city	27 164	62.1	27.8	5.8	3.5	0.8	11 250	74.8	2 076	86.7
39 61000	Parma city	80 678	65.9	25.7	3.6	3.4	1.5	35 126	77.5	10 850	86.5
39 66390	Reynoldsburg city	29 832	47.4	27.3	15.4	8.4	1.4	12 876	65.3	2 076	78.2
39 70380	Sandusky city	26 062	54.7	31.7	8.6	4.3	0.6	11 855	56.4	2 972	70.7
39 71682	Shaker Heights city	27 610	58.4	25.6	3.2	9.8	2.9	12 225	65.1	3 263	69.1
39 74118	Springfield city	60 265	50.8	35.6	7.3	5.7	0.0	20 250	56.0	6 006	68.9
39 74944	Stow city	30 026	55.4	26.0	12.7	5.4	0.6	12 317	72.1	2 176	74.4
39 75098	Strongsville city	41 133	60.7	26.9	5.4	6.0	1.1	16 204	82.7	2 948	82.5
39 77000	Toledo city	290 942	55.0	32.4	5.3	6.0	1.3	128 915	59.8	28 963	76.3
39 77504	Trotwood city	25 784	58.2	33.3	3.1	4.3	1.1	11 112	62.5	2 780	72.1
39 79002	Upper Arlington city	31 707	64.6	24.1	4.0	5.6	1.6	13 979	81.1	3 965	82.9
39 80892	Warren city	43 234	55.6	34.0	5.2	4.9	0.4	19 300	58.5	5 537	72.7
39 83342	Westerville city	33 246	58.7	19.7	12.5	8.2	0.8	12 673	79.0	2 228	70.0
39 83622	Westlake city	30 205	56.2	29.3	6.6	6.8	1.2	12 867	75.1	3 320	71.1
39 88000	Youngstown city	76 203	61.0	26.7	5.7	5.5	1.1	32 177	64.0	9 811	79.2
39 88084	Zanesville city	23 635	51.6	35.0	8.6	4.4	0.4	10 654	55.5	2 887	70.4
40 00000	OKLAHOMA	3 215 719	51.3	25.1	11.8	10.0	1.7	1 342 293	68.4	302 848	82.7
40 04450	Bartlesville city	32 589	50.6	24.1	10.1	13.3	1.9	14 563	70.4	4 207	80.8
40 09050	Broken Arrow city	68 954	48.7	25.3	9.6	14.9	1.6	26 202	78.9	3 432	82.3
40 23200	Edmond city	63 655	46.4	27.7	8.4	14.5	2.9	25 271	72.7	3 796	79.0
40 23950	Enid city	43 818	48.8	28.7	8.4	12.5	1.7	18 950	67.1	4 844	82.5
40 41850	Lawton city	85 524	38.6	24.2	6.5	26.2	4.5	31 771	54.7	5 523	81.1
40 48350	Midwest City city	50 302	48.3	32.9	6.0	11.0	1.8	22 150	61.3	4 915	85.2
40 49200	Moore city	37 688	51.9	20.1	16.5	9.9	1.7	14 840	75.6	1 974	81.1
40 50050	Muskogee city	35 509	50.9	31.2	9.8	7.2	0.8	15 559	62.4	4 598	74.3
40 52500	Norman city	90 074	39.6	26.2	18.5	12.6	3.2	38 841	55.3	5 766	80.8
40 55000	Oklahoma City city	469 127	46.6	30.4	10.6	9.5	3.0	204 505	59.5	39 213	80.0
40 59850	Ponca City city	24 000	52.4	24.9	10.7	10.9	1.1	10 653	68.1	2 847	83.8
40 66800	Shawnee city	26 580	47.4	25.0	17.3	9.3	1.1	11 320	60.3	3 205	77.0
40 70300	Stillwater city	37 279	28.1	21.9	31.6	13.5	5.0	15 568	41.6	1 944	75.5
40 75000	Tulsa city	364 847	45.4	31.5	7.9	12.2	3.0	165 842	55.6	33 963	77.2

Table C-5. Cities — **Migration, Housing, and Transportation**

City	Owner-occupied by household type (percent)								Median household income			Median housing value (owner estimated)	Median monthly owner costs as a percent of income	
	Family households					Nonfamily households								
		Married-couple family		Other family										
	Total family households	Total	With own children under 18 years	Total	With own children under 18 years	Total nonfamily households	Two or more adults	Living alone	All households	Owner-occupied households	Renter-occupied households		With a mortgage	Without a mortgage
	11	12	13	14	15	16	17	18	19	20	21	22	23	24
OHIO—Cont'd														
Brunswick city	86.5	91.8	89.3	60.7	44.6	61.6	46.9	65.2	55 796	61 632	31 435	135 300	21.7	9.9
Canton city	67.1	80.0	74.1	45.0	32.0	47.8	46.2	48.1	28 528	37 359	18 196	66 400	20.3	9.9
Cincinnati city	51.3	69.1	66.5	29.7	18.1	27.0	23.1	27.8	29 431	49 208	21 056	93 200	21.3	12.5
Cleveland city	54.6	71.0	64.3	38.8	24.4	39.8	39.5	39.9	25 775	36 142	17 808	71 100	23.4	12.6
Cleveland Heights city ..	76.6	82.5	85.4	62.9	49.8	41.2	33.8	43.2	45 863	61 206	27 752	110 100	21.5	12.5
Columbus city	61.1	73.1	70.4	38.0	29.2	34.6	25.0	37.6	37 693	52 242	27 242	99 100	21.4	11.1
Cuyahoga Falls city	77.2	83.3	80.3	53.2	41.9	47.3	35.9	49.5	42 479	50 852	29 715	106 000	21.1	9.9
Dayton city	59.9	76.4	70.0	39.0	25.0	43.5	33.2	45.5	27 309	38 802	17 728	66 700	21.8	12.1
Delaware city	70.5	79.7	75.2	38.1	31.9	38.6	25.0	42.0	45 839	60 068	30 121	124 400	20.0	10.2
Dublin city	86.6	88.2	89.7	69.8	66.7	44.1	36.6	45.5	92 212	104 659	52 197	241 900	20.8	9.9
East Cleveland city	43.2	62.2	49.5	31.2	13.7	25.2	32.2	24.4	20 597	32 081	15 854	67 200	29.0	15.9
Elyria city	73.0	83.9	78.9	46.1	31.4	48.1	34.4	50.6	38 207	47 547	24 552	92 800	21.0	10.0
Euclid city	69.7	79.7	76.2	50.7	40.2	46.7	47.8	46.5	34 983	43 876	25 332	90 500	21.9	12.4
Fairborn city	62.5	72.8	62.5	35.4	25.2	36.3	18.3	42.6	37 071	48 518	26 027	89 900	20.2	9.9
Fairfield city	75.5	81.1	79.9	50.1	36.0	44.4	23.4	49.3	50 167	60 294	39 978	120 800	19.7	9.9
Findlay city	75.0	82.5	76.8	46.2	34.4	47.4	30.0	51.0	40 782	50 996	25 811	96 100	18.6	9.9
Gahanna city	85.5	89.8	90.0	62.0	55.3	55.0	46.0	57.0	66 512	75 351	40 248	145 600	20.3	10.5
Garfield Heights city	83.9	91.0	89.6	65.2	45.8	72.6	66.4	73.6	38 893	42 297	25 565	88 300	22.1	13.1
Grove City city	79.9	87.5	85.0	46.3	35.9	50.5	42.2	51.9	52 395	63 224	30 716	119 800	21.5	11.0
Hamilton city	67.6	78.0	72.1	43.0	29.8	47.2	36.7	49.0	35 098	43 691	22 880	84 700	20.9	10.8
Huber Heights city	75.8	81.2	76.4	54.4	42.7	60.8	37.1	66.1	49 785	54 781	37 743	92 400	20.1	10.4
Kent city	55.5	72.1	73.1	21.9	16.5	20.9	7.8	28.3	29 230	56 556	19 678	112 700	19.5	11.0
Kettering city	78.4	85.1	81.9	52.4	45.7	47.8	37.5	49.5	44 700	55 316	29 821	110 500	20.2	10.7
Lakewood city	64.3	71.9	72.4	44.3	33.3	28.3	24.0	29.3	40 379	56 926	30 453	117 600	21.4	12.9
Lancaster city	64.4	73.2	67.3	38.1	25.0	49.9	35.8	51.6	33 389	40 799	25 165	92 200	22.0	10.7
Lima city	61.0	78.2	68.9	35.3	28.1	50.2	35.7	52.5	27 039	35 101	18 649	54 700	19.1	10.4
Lorain city	66.1	80.3	72.3	40.3	24.0	50.0	45.6	50.7	34 002	43 823	20 523	85 700	20.8	10.8
Mansfield city	66.3	77.2	68.5	41.3	28.7	44.8	38.5	45.8	29 924	39 852	20 394	71 700	20.5	10.9
Maple Heights city	88.3	93.8	90.4	76.1	66.5	74.7	70.9	75.1	40 479	43 514	27 035	84 800	22.1	13.2
Marion city	69.8	78.4	69.2	48.3	37.3	51.1	47.0	51.8	33 065	40 622	22 416	66 200	19.5	11.5
Massillon city	75.8	84.4	78.7	49.7	41.9	54.3	56.9	53.9	32 688	40 414	20 969	80 900	20.9	11.8
Medina city	75.8	81.8	84.0	45.2	39.3	43.3	39.2	43.8	49 559	60 750	26 377	138 600	22.4	12.8
Mentor city	90.6	93.6	91.8	74.1	60.9	77.6	63.0	80.1	57 177	61 447	36 422	144 100	21.0	10.7
Middletown city	68.1	77.4	69.8	45.7	29.5	45.1	40.5	45.9	35 944	46 177	25 064	89 700	20.5	11.2
Newark city	66.0	76.4	70.6	38.9	26.8	45.4	42.0	46.0	34 445	44 444	22 869	84 900	19.8	9.9
North Olmsted city	87.1	90.0	87.0	73.0	58.1	62.9	39.9	66.4	52 451	57 090	36 646	139 600	21.8	12.8
North Royalton city	84.3	88.0	90.1	63.5	54.9	53.9	33.8	57.5	56 976	65 147	40 603	169 900	23.0	12.0
Parma city	84.7	89.1	87.6	67.2	50.9	63.3	52.3	64.9	43 860	48 446	31 412	113 500	21.7	12.6
Reynoldsburg city	74.4	81.7	78.3	49.4	39.8	44.6	37.0	46.2	50 947	61 460	34 170	120 300	21.3	11.5
Sandusky city	64.6	78.1	71.3	37.4	25.3	44.1	36.5	45.3	30 622	40 026	21 939	74 100	20.2	11.4
Shaker Heights city	77.6	86.0	85.6	51.8	44.0	41.5	29.7	43.1	62 451	85 740	35 688	181 500	19.9	11.7
Springfield city	63.0	75.1	63.9	39.1	26.0	46.9	35.8	48.9	31 716	41 368	21 415	69 300	20.0	10.4
Stow city	82.3	86.2	85.9	56.5	49.7	46.9	38.3	48.7	57 891	66 255	36 968	141 100	20.7	9.9
Strongsville city	89.9	92.3	92.6	72.1	64.1	59.1	53.4	60.1	68 902	75 363	35 556	170 300	21.0	11.0
Toledo city	68.2	80.9	75.2	44.9	32.7	47.0	38.0	48.9	32 236	42 545	20 508	73 700	19.7	11.8
Trotwood city	67.8	80.6	74.7	46.5	32.9	52.0	41.4	53.3	35 006	42 544	23 704	80 700	23.4	12.4
Upper Arlington city	88.6	90.8	90.5	74.1	72.2	65.2	36.3	68.9	72 200	81 211	46 500	211 800	21.1	10.8
Warren city	64.5	77.8	67.1	42.0	26.1	48.3	35.4	49.9	29 970	38 532	18 424	63 500	18.8	10.7
Westerville city	86.1	91.7	91.8	50.5	39.8	56.9	48.0	58.2	69 259	81 886	31 011	159 800	18.9	9.9
Westlake city	88.0	89.8	92.5	73.1	69.5	51.7	38.5	53.4	63 879	72 442	44 143	183 500	21.3	10.3
Youngstown city	68.8	84.2	76.0	49.9	32.9	56.3	45.2	57.7	23 985	30 500	14 094	40 700	20.4	12.2
Zanesville city	60.4	73.4	64.3	36.1	25.9	48.0	49.1	47.8	26 461	33 572	18 774	60 300	20.8	11.7
OKLAHOMA	74.9	81.5	75.3	51.0	40.7	54.0	37.0	56.8	33 243	40 387	21 807	67 700	19.2	9.9
Bartlesville city	77.4	83.2	78.0	51.3	42.6	55.3	46.8	56.0	35 990	43 781	20 636	63 600	16.9	9.9
Broken Arrow city	83.2	87.1	85.4	60.1	55.6	60.0	45.7	62.6	53 258	60 188	32 056	98 500	19.1	9.9
Edmond city	81.8	86.9	86.2	55.8	51.5	46.4	25.1	51.3	54 119	66 606	24 902	118 000	19.5	9.9
Enid city	72.7	78.2	69.3	50.8	39.2	56.0	42.1	58.1	32 174	37 080	22 700	58 800	19.1	9.9
Lawton city	58.6	66.8	55.1	36.3	25.0	45.1	30.9	47.7	32 577	42 235	23 794	69 700	19.8	9.9
Midwest City city	66.0	75.1	62.6	45.1	31.8	52.0	33.2	54.9	34 928	42 166	25 753	61 600	18.9	9.9
Moore city	77.7	82.8	77.1	60.1	52.9	68.2	44.4	72.7	43 454	46 994	31 458	69 500	19.7	9.9
Muskogee city	68.8	77.6	68.4	47.9	35.7	50.7	40.2	52.2	26 111	33 936	18 165	54 300	19.7	9.9
Norman city	70.4	77.6	76.4	44.3	39.2	34.3	17.1	40.7	36 359	52 983	20 121	93 700	18.8	9.9
Oklahoma City city	67.5	77.2	71.9	41.8	30.8	45.6	33.4	47.9	34 621	45 938	22 672	78 100	20.1	9.9
Ponca City city	73.4	80.6	69.5	49.0	35.1	58.0	36.9	60.9	31 226	39 695	20 216	58 300	18.3	10.2
Shawnee city	66.4	73.6	62.1	48.0	36.6	49.0	26.1	52.7	27 578	34 382	19 423	56 100	18.6	10.9
Stillwater city	61.3	70.9	70.8	29.2	26.1	24.1	12.1	30.3	25 204	50 863	14 313	91 700	18.8	9.9
Tulsa city	64.7	74.3	67.5	39.2	28.8	41.8	29.5	44.0	35 261	47 422	24 479	81 900	19.2	9.9

Table C-5. Cities — **Migration, Housing, and Transportation**

City	Percent who pay 35 percent or more of income for housing expenses		Means of transportation to work (percent except where noted)							Vehicles available (percent of households)		
	Median gross rent	Owners	Renters	Number of workers 16 years and over	Car, truck, or van		Public transportation	Other means	Walked	No vehicles	One vehicle	Two or more vehicles
					Drove alone	Carpooled						
	25	26	27	28	29	30	31	32	33	34	35	36
OHIO—Cont'd												
Brunswick city	630	13.2	24.0	17 258	88.5	6.8	1.0	0.8	0.5	3.0	24.9	72.1
Canton city	420	14.6	28.3	33 665	80.1	11.8	2.7	0.9	3.2	15.4	39.6	44.9
Cincinnati city	444	16.6	29.9	147 616	69.5	11.4	10.1	0.9	5.5	23.4	44.0	32.7
Cleveland city	465	21.6	33.8	175 727	67.8	13.5	12.0	1.0	4.0	24.6	43.9	31.5
Cleveland Heights city ..	640	18.3	29.6	26 193	76.9	8.8	5.8	1.1	3.6	10.2	40.5	49.2
Columbus city	586	15.0	29.0	367 387	79.0	10.8	3.9	0.8	3.2	10.3	42.4	47.3
Cuyahoga Falls city......	584	12.4	24.0	25 198	88.2	6.9	1.0	0.3	1.4	6.5	37.5	56.0
Dayton city	448	19.1	33.2	67 339	73.6	11.6	7.0	0.9	5.3	20.0	41.9	38.1
Delaware city...............	581	10.8	26.1	12 490	82.8	8.5	0.4	0.8	4.1	7.4	33.1	59.5
Dublin city...................	929	13.1	26.3	15 802	89.4	4.0	0.4	0.4	0.5	1.5	21.5	77.1
East Cleveland city	472	34.2	37.6	9 203	62.2	13.4	17.9	0.9	3.9	32.8	42.9	24.2
Elyria city...................	514	14.3	28.3	26 422	83.4	10.7	0.9	0.8	2.6	8.4	39.0	52.6
Euclid city	541	14.0	30.9	24 577	81.0	9.6	5.7	0.5	1.7	13.1	46.7	40.2
Fairborn city................	573	10.7	29.3	15 955	84.3	10.2	0.3	0.7	3.4	6.8	39.4	53.8
Fairfield city	667	11.3	17.6	22 736	87.5	8.2	1.1	0.4	0.5	3.6	32.7	63.7
Findlay city	487	8.7	25.3	19 817	82.3	9.2	1.1	1.1	3.7	5.9	37.4	50.0
Gahanna city	682	11.6	17.3	17 339	86.4	8.0	0.9	0.4	0.7	3.3	25.4	71.3
Garfield Heights city......	555	15.8	28.7	14 049	83.4	9.1	3.2	0.7	2.0	8.9	41.0	50.1
Grove City city.............	619	11.4	21.7	13 879	87.0	8.0	1.1	0.9	0.9	5.3	30.3	64.5
Hamilton city	498	12.9	28.1	26 502	79.7	14.6	1.0	0.8	2.5	12.6	36.5	50.9
Huber Heights city........	651	11.3	19.0	19 077	88.3	7.9	0.9	0.5	0.7	3.5	28.6	67.9
Kent city	501	11.5	36.7	15 103	72.8	8.8	2.2	0.8	13.1	8.3	41.6	50.1
Kettering city	570	11.2	25.8	29 079	87.5	6.5	1.1	0.6	1.4	6.0	39.0	55.1
Lakewood city..............	549	13.2	22.1	31 564	76.1	9.0	7.8	0.9	3.6	13.6	46.3	40.1
Lancaster city	510	13.4	25.4	16 436	81.3	12.0	0.5	1.0	3.2	9.5	37.1	53.4
Lima city.....................	426	12.9	31.0	15 545	80.1	14.0	1.7	0.9	1.7	13.9	41.3	44.8
Lorain city...................	485	14.2	29.0	28 211	81.8	13.7	0.7	0.8	1.7	11.0	38.9	50.1
Mansfield city..............	439	13.0	29.6	20 335	83.2	10.9	1.3	0.7	2.4	11.9	40.9	47.1
Maple Heights city........	521	15.9	30.0	12 084	85.2	7.6	4.1	0.6	1.5	7.6	41.3	51.1
Marion city..................	495	12.7	27.7	14 890	82.6	12.1	0.9	1.5	1.8	12.2	38.0	49.8
Massillon city..............	445	14.0	26.2	14 331	84.9	9.4	1.4	0.9	2.0	9.2	35.8	55.1
Medina city..................	628	14.4	30.9	12 310	87.1	6.7	0.7	0.9	1.6	7.0	30.1	63.0
Mentor city..................	700	13.3	24.1	27 067	89.9	5.6	0.9	0.4	1.0	2.9	27.2	69.9
Middletown city............	515	13.7	29.5	23 015	85.7	9.1	1.1	0.7	1.8	9.8	38.5	51.7
Newark city.................	488	11.9	27.4	21 253	83.0	12.0	1.0	0.6	1.5	10.5	37.3	52.2
North Olmsted city........	634	15.3	24.4	17 661	86.1	6.3	2.7	0.5	1.5	4.6	33.3	62.1
North Royalton city........	643	16.4	16.3	15 605	86.6	6.2	1.7	0.6	1.0	2.2	30.8	66.9
Parma city	592	13.0	24.6	40 871	86.5	6.8	3.1	0.6	1.4	7.3	37.7	55.0
Reynoldsburg city.........	653	10.2	21.9	17 078	86.3	7.4	1.3	0.4	1.2	3.6	34.9	61.5
Sandusky city..............	468	13.8	26.1	12 707	84.1	10.5	0.6	1.1	2.3	10.6	43.0	46.4
Shaker Heights city	747	16.7	26.2	14 546	78.5	7.1	8.1	0.7	1.4	7.1	39.5	53.4
Springfield city.............	476	13.2	31.0	27 136	76.3	15.5	1.5	1.1	4.2	12.7	42.9	44.4
Stow city.....................	715	10.8	21.5	16 656	89.9	5.6	0.4	0.6	0.6	4.9	26.6	68.5
Strongsville city	622	12.6	23.1	23 095	86.1	7.1	2.2	0.5	0.7	2.5	24.1	73.4
Toledo city..................	469	14.0	31.1	137 076	82.1	10.7	2.5	0.8	2.3	12.1	42.5	45.4
Trotwood city...............	557	21.0	37.9	11 230	82.8	10.7	3.5	0.7	1.0	10.1	42.4	47.5
Upper Arlington city.......	776	13.7	23.8	16 531	86.0	4.3	1.5	0.9	1.4	3.0	32.6	64.4
Warren city..................	443	12.1	29.7	17 690	84.0	10.7	0.2	1.7	1.8	11.7	44.2	44.2
Westerville city............	623	11.4	22.8	18 467	86.6	6.0	1.0	0.4	2.1	4.7	25.1	70.2
Westlake city	866	14.3	31.6	15 559	87.3	5.3	2.3	0.6	0.6	5.2	33.7	61.1
Youngstown city	401	16.5	33.8	27 934	79.4	12.4	2.7	1.1	2.6	18.0	42.5	39.4
Zanesville city.............	389	15.3	27.5	10 362	77.0	15.8	1.3	1.0	2.9	12.6	43.5	43.9
OKLAHOMA	456	12.1	26.7	1 539 792	80.0	13.2	0.5	1.1	2.1	7.0	34.9	58.1
Bartlesville city	405	7.5	26.2	14 607	79.8	14.6	0.3	1.5	1.5	7.8	36.2	56.0
Broken Arrow city.........	629	9.7	24.4	38 243	85.2	10.0	0.3	0.6	0.6	3.5	24.2	72.3
Edmond city	552	10.6	31.5	34 865	84.7	8.3	0.3	0.8	1.9	3.8	26.6	69.6
Enid city.....................	437	11.2	26.7	21 426	81.5	12.7	0.3	1.0	2.1	7.1	37.4	55.5
Lawton city..................	460	14.0	26.9	41 947	72.2	13.6	1.1	2.5	8.6	9.1	38.1	52.9
Midwest City city	490	11.2	24.9	25 025	82.7	12.6	0.3	0.9	1.2	6.5	40.4	53.2
Moore city...................	619	12.3	22.5	20 459	87.2	9.6	0.1	0.6	0.9	3.7	28.5	67.8
Muskogee city	403	13.8	29.2	14 578	77.0	18.0	0.5	1.2	1.7	11.4	42.9	45.7
Norman city.................	512	11.5	38.7	49 089	81.3	10.3	0.6	1.9	3.0	5.7	37.5	56.9
Oklahoma City city	481	13.2	27.9	234 222	80.4	13.1	1.0	1.1	1.6	8.2	40.1	51.7
Ponca City city	447	13.5	30.3	10 730	82.9	12.5	0.1	0.7	1.2	7.1	40.9	52.1
Shawnee city...............	427	9.0	29.1	12 062	80.6	13.9	0.3	1.4	2.1	10.2	40.6	49.3
Stillwater city...............	468	9.8	47.9	20 536	72.9	10.4	0.3	2.4	10.9	7.1	41.0	51.9
Tulsa city....................	511	13.1	27.5	187 612	79.4	13.1	1.2	1.0	2.2	9.1	42.5	48.4

Table C-5. Cities — **Migration, Housing, and Transportation**

STATE Place code	City	Residence in 1995 (percent)						Occupied housing units		Householders 65 years and over	
		Total population 5 years and over	Same house	Same county, different house	Same state, different county	Different state	Outside the United States	Number	Percent owner-occupied	Number	Percent owner-occupied
		1	2	3	4	5	6	7	8	9	10
41 00000	OREGON	3 199 323	46.8	27.0	11.1	12.5	2.6	1 333 723	64.2	282 848	77.9
41 01000	Albany city..................	37 613	43.3	29.0	15.9	10.8	1.0	16 143	59.4	3 548	68.8
41 05350	Beaverton city..............	70 554	37.2	25.6	13.1	16.8	7.2	30 830	47.9	4 238	62.1
41 05800	Bend city.....................	48 291	35.2	30.0	13.7	19.4	1.6	21 049	63.4	4 181	80.9
41 15800	Corvallis city................	46 963	33.3	19.8	25.2	17.2	4.5	19 641	44.6	3 111	71.3
41 23850	Eugene city..................	130 496	39.0	31.5	10.2	16.4	3.0	57 978	51.7	10 932	71.0
41 31250	Gresham city................	82 970	41.9	34.2	7.8	11.1	5.0	33 298	54.7	5 255	66.0
41 34100	Hillsboro city................	63 457	33.0	34.1	8.6	18.2	6.2	25 030	52.4	2 681	68.6
41 38500	Keizer city...................	29 861	41.8	33.8	11.0	10.9	2.5	12 111	64.7	2 553	79.0
41 40550	Lake Oswego city..........	33 511	50.1	15.5	14.9	16.3	3.2	14 704	71.5	2 560	75.7
41 45000	McMinnville city............	24 619	38.7	33.7	11.8	12.3	3.5	9 374	60.7	2 326	72.5
41 47000	Medford city.................	58 901	42.3	34.9	7.2	14.3	1.4	25 141	57.1	6 718	65.6
41 55200	Oregon City city............	23 460	40.8	32.2	15.8	9.9	1.3	9 511	59.5	1 620	67.0
41 59000	Portland city.................	497 056	45.0	29.2	8.2	13.4	4.2	223 752	55.8	40 319	71.9
41 64900	Salem city...................	126 426	40.0	30.8	14.0	11.7	3.6	50 645	57.0	10 553	72.3
41 69600	Springfield city..............	48 403	41.4	38.4	7.4	11.3	1.4	20 498	53.6	3 399	76.1
41 73650	Tigard city....................	38 029	43.5	23.8	14.5	14.7	3.6	16 511	58.5	2 640	70.6
42 00000	PENNSYLVANIA........	11 555 538	63.5	21.7	7.6	5.8	1.4	4 777 003	71.3	1 238 054	77.4
42 02000	Allentown city...............	99 279	49.8	28.7	8.6	8.6	4.3	42 032	53.0	10 587	63.2
42 02184	Altoona city..................	46 398	63.4	26.3	6.5	3.4	0.3	20 060	65.9	5 501	74.1
42 06064	Bethel Park borough	31 769	72.5	19.4	2.8	4.4	0.9	13 362	80.0	3 901	74.8
42 06088	Bethlehem city..............	67 520	55.1	18.1	12.5	10.6	3.6	28 116	58.1	8 193	70.1
42 13208	Chester city..................	33 824	55.8	30.8	6.6	4.9	2.0	12 814	47.7	2 954	61.7
42 21648	Easton city...................	24 555	48.1	25.8	7.9	15.6	2.6	9 544	48.4	1 893	57.7
42 24000	Erie city......................	96 483	56.2	32.6	3.9	5.1	2.2	40 942	56.2	10 732	68.3
42 32800	Harrisburg city..............	45 204	48.7	32.3	8.9	7.1	3.0	20 593	42.3	3 872	57.1
42 41216	Lancaster city...............	52 019	46.1	35.1	7.6	7.0	4.2	20 940	46.5	3 794	59.9
42 52330	Municipality of Monroeville borough...	27 966	66.8	20.6	5.9	5.2	1.6	12 376	69.7	3 607	75.9
42 53368	New Castle city.............	24 556	62.8	26.7	4.7	5.4	0.4	10 727	64.6	3 521	71.0
42 54656	Norristown borough.......	29 235	54.8	25.3	10.4	5.2	4.3	12 029	48.1	2 584	66.7
42 60000	Philadelphia city...........	1 419 977	61.9	25.3	3.8	5.7	3.3	590 071	59.3	148 201	73.7
42 61000	Pittsburgh city..............	316 760	56.8	27.5	5.9	7.1	2.7	143 739	52.1	38 642	67.9
42 61536	Plum borough...............	25 206	67.5	21.2	6.2	3.9	1.1	10 270	79.8	2 371	80.9
42 63624	Reading city.................	74 390	49.9	31.7	5.4	7.5	5.5	30 108	51.0	7 096	65.1
42 69000	Scranton city	72 558	64.2	24.1	5.0	5.5	1.2	31 303	54.5	10 355	60.3
42 73808	State College borough ..	37 664	18.4	9.9	45.4	18.9	7.5	12 024	22.8	1 425	62.9
42 85152	Wilkes-Barre city...........	41 067	62.8	26.0	5.1	5.5	0.6	17 961	53.5	6 006	62.6
42 85312	Williamsport city	28 847	47.6	30.7	14.8	5.8	1.0	12 219	44.9	2 851	62.3
42 87048	York city......................	37 682	44.9	37.3	6.3	8.3	3.2	16 132	46.9	3 246	65.2
44 00000	RHODE ISLAND........	985 184	58.1	24.4	5.1	9.8	2.6	408 424	60.0	98 303	65.3
44 19180	Cranston city	75 081	62.8	24.5	5.8	5.5	1.4	30 954	66.8	8 807	70.0
44 22960	East Providence city	46 095	64.8	23.4	4.2	6.3	1.3	20 530	59.0	5 998	61.9
44 49960	Newport city	24 880	43.6	26.2	3.6	23.9	2.8	11 566	41.9	2 472	63.6
44 54640	Pawtucket city..............	68 081	56.6	30.4	1.3	6.7	5.0	30 047	44.4	7 177	57.6
44 59000	Providence city.............	161 631	44.6	29.0	3.2	16.6	6.6	62 389	34.6	12 458	50.4
44 74300	Warwick city.................	81 078	65.0	17.9	11.0	5.3	0.8	35 517	72.6	9 585	72.0
44 80780	Woonsocket city............	39 950	51.9	33.9	0.9	10.7	2.6	17 750	35.0	4 021	40.4
45 00000	SOUTH CAROLINA ...	3 748 669	55.9	22.3	8.3	11.8	1.6	1 533 854	72.2	320 075	83.8
45 00550	Aiken city....................	23 723	54.1	24.1	5.2	15.3	1.3	10 276	66.1	2 871	79.6
45 01360	Anderson city	23 587	50.1	31.3	7.1	10.2	1.3	10 605	53.6	3 311	67.8
45 13330	Charleston city	90 702	45.9	26.0	8.6	17.4	2.0	40 454	51.8	9 087	68.4
45 16000	Columbia city...............	109 721	40.9	22.5	14.5	18.9	3.3	42 077	45.5	8 386	68.8
45 25810	Florence city................	28 386	54.0	27.4	8.6	8.9	1.2	11 946	61.7	2 788	79.7
45 29815	Goose Creek city	26 563	35.0	14.6	11.7	36.4	2.3	8 934	63.1	822	83.5
45 30850	Greenville city..............	53 204	46.8	27.8	8.3	14.2	2.8	24 454	47.0	5 763	67.4
45 34045	Hilton Head Island town	32 224	45.7	18.2	2.7	27.5	6.0	14 403	77.7	5 280	93.9
45 48535	Mount Pleasant town	43 737	41.4	26.3	6.5	23.7	2.1	18 906	74.0	2 750	82.5
45 50875	North Charleston city	72 913	42.5	28.9	8.9	16.8	2.9	29 747	46.2	4 529	81.5
45 61405	Rock Hill city................	46 800	43.9	30.5	9.0	14.6	2.0	19 035	53.9	3 369	77.8
45 68290	Spartanburg city...........	36 839	51.5	32.1	6.2	8.6	1.5	15 949	49.9	3 934	65.7
45 70270	Summerville town..........	26 286	47.8	18.6	13.2	18.6	1.8	10 562	65.0	1 987	62.7
45 70405	Sumter city	36 949	45.6	25.5	5.8	19.5	3.7	14 625	53.3	3 509	70.2
46 00000	SOUTH DAKOTA.......	703 820	55.7	21.2	11.8	10.3	1.0	290 245	68.2	69 783	73.2
46 52980	Rapid City city..............	55 386	45.0	28.4	10.7	14.3	1.5	24 012	59.2	5 332	69.9
46 59020	Sioux Falls city..............	114 988	45.6	27.0	11.9	13.2	2.3	49 761	61.0	8 866	66.5

Table C-5. Cities — **Migration, Housing, and Transportation**

City	Owner-occupied by household type (percent)								Median household income			Median housing value (owner estimated)	Median monthly owner costs as a percent of income	
	Family households					Nonfamily households								
		Married-couple family		Other family										
	Total family households	Total	With own children under 18 years	Total	With own children under 18 years	Total nonfamily households	Two or more adults	Living alone	All households	Owner-occupied households	Renter-occupied households		With a mortgage	Without a mortgage
	11	12	13	14	15	16	17	18	19	20	21	22	23	24
OREGON	72.8	79.6	73.3	46.3	36.7	47.5	38.6	50.3	40 818	50 713	27 197	145 800	23.2	10.5
Albany city	66.6	76.6	70.6	32.6	29.0	44.1	39.3	45.2	39 301	51 057	24 312	124 500	22.8	11.2
Beaverton city	59.1	67.3	65.4	30.0	24.1	30.2	17.3	34.1	47 752	69 522	34 421	186 100	22.5	10.4
Bend city	71.7	78.8	74.5	42.2	36.0	48.5	32.9	54.2	40 610	50 580	27 479	138 100	23.2	10.6
Corvallis city	63.4	70.5	68.3	32.6	30.7	24.8	13.5	30.8	35 578	62 259	21 430	154 700	20.9	9.9
Eugene city	68.0	77.4	73.9	38.4	31.7	32.6	21.8	37.4	35 468	52 338	21 883	145 000	23.2	9.9
Gresham city	62.9	71.7	64.6	35.1	27.9	37.0	27.7	39.7	42 981	58 671	29 618	155 800	23.3	10.6
Hillsboro city	61.2	67.5	65.7	33.3	24.6	33.5	25.0	36.4	51 575	64 115	39 538	163 200	23.1	11.1
Keizer city	69.7	78.9	71.5	36.6	31.5	51.5	50.0	51.9	45 150	56 373	29 719	133 600	22.4	9.9
Lake Oswego city	82.6	85.8	86.8	61.4	59.4	50.1	41.6	52.1	71 724	94 297	39 720	286 900	21.3	10.3
McMinnville city	68.4	75.4	68.5	45.0	36.7	43.2	23.0	49.1	38 904	47 714	28 206	130 400	23.2	11.2
Medford city	64.5	73.7	64.5	34.2	24.2	42.9	34.9	44.7	36 135	47 358	24 293	128 500	22.9	10.7
Oregon City city	66.8	77.8	70.4	35.2	23.7	42.0	35.1	44.1	45 024	57 481	30 675	161 900	25.1	10.4
Portland city	68.9	77.6	74.3	45.8	34.8	40.8	37.8	41.8	40 227	53 949	26 724	154 700	23.9	12.1
Salem city	65.5	73.9	68.0	39.6	31.6	41.9	30.5	44.9	38 973	51 619	26 510	126 300	23.6	10.8
Springfield city	60.1	70.6	61.0	33.1	22.6	42.9	30.9	47.1	33 116	44 011	23 131	111 700	23.3	10.5
Tigard city	69.1	76.8	77.0	35.4	30.0	37.9	28.8	40.3	51 641	69 613	32 922	187 100	22.4	10.3
PENNSYLVANIA	80.4	86.8	85.0	58.5	44.5	52.6	42.8	54.3	39 987	47 611	24 601	94 800	21.6	12.2
Allentown city	62.4	73.9	67.7	39.6	26.1	38.9	33.1	40.1	32 235	41 740	22 512	77 000	22.5	13.2
Altoona city	75.1	84.5	79.7	51.7	37.0	50.2	44.9	51.1	28 176	36 745	14 859	57 600	19.9	12.2
Bethel Park borough	90.8	93.6	95.4	73.8	69.3	52.7	61.7	51.9	54 173	61 220	30 794	115 400	20.6	11.6
Bethlehem city	68.7	77.9	72.6	43.7	30.6	41.4	24.2	44.9	35 667	47 546	23 587	97 100	22.0	12.9
Chester city	52.2	71.5	62.4	38.4	23.7	39.7	33.5	40.7	25 608	34 789	17 893	43 300	24.0	15.6
Easton city	58.3	71.0	68.2	36.4	27.0	33.4	22.6	36.2	33 314	43 796	24 603	77 500	23.5	14.5
Erie city	66.6	79.0	72.6	43.3	27.3	40.3	31.4	42.0	28 212	38 744	17 888	64 700	20.9	13.8
Harrisburg city	48.4	65.5	60.3	35.0	24.0	35.2	34.8	35.3	26 824	37 726	20 599	56 900	23.3	15.2
Lancaster city	53.5	66.7	59.9	35.3	26.2	36.8	30.6	38.4	29 509	40 617	21 038	71 900	23.7	11.6
Municipality of Monroeville borough	81.4	85.6	86.7	65.0	49.4	47.5	28.5	49.9	44 172	50 571	31 710	92 500	20.4	12.1
New Castle city	74.1	85.8	79.1	50.4	30.8	48.6	34.8	50.1	25 631	34 120	13 530	43 000	21.1	13.9
Norristown borough	69.1	71.1	67.6	42.5	26.1	32.8	27.1	34.0	35 618	47 373	27 999	85 800	23.5	14.3
Philadelphia city	68.2	78.9	76.6	55.8	42.1	45.7	34.6	47.7	30 431	37 773	21 365	61 000	21.5	13.4
Pittsburgh city	65.7	78.1	76.4	46.0	29.2	37.5	25.3	40.2	28 444	40 080	19 076	60 700	20.8	13.5
Plum borough	87.6	91.1	89.8	68.4	54.2	56.5	38.7	59.6	48 520	51 436	36 004	92 900	21.7	10.9
Reading city	57.9	71.2	62.4	40.3	31.0	40.0	34.2	41.2	26 605	36 043	18 370	45 000	21.2	13.5
Scranton city	66.3	75.4	73.4	44.9	27.2	38.1	25.5	39.8	28 689	39 358	19 294	78 400	22.2	14.2
State College borough	57.4	61.5	60.9	38.9	42.3	9.7	2.5	18.1	21 087	67 692	16 491	147 600	20.3	9.9
Wilkes-Barre city	67.0	77.4	73.7	45.8	27.1	37.0	21.2	39.4	26 268	35 692	17 097	65 500	20.8	13.7
Williamsport city	56.4	68.9	60.8	33.4	23.8	30.4	15.4	34.3	25 988	37 904	18 425	67 900	20.8	13.1
York city	54.3	70.9	60.6	34.8	21.1	36.8	29.2	38.9	26 258	36 425	19 586	56 500	22.1	13.4
RHODE ISLAND	70.4	79.4	76.9	43.7	29.2	40.6	34.7	41.8	41 827	56 559	24 361	130 500	22.7	13.4
Cranston city	77.9	84.3	82.9	57.7	41.5	45.6	40.0	46.5	43 864	54 765	27 774	122 600	23.5	14.0
East Providence city	71.2	79.4	75.9	49.2	33.7	38.5	35.7	38.9	38 788	49 817	25 009	118 800	23.1	12.8
Newport city	51.7	64.8	56.1	26.3	12.5	32.4	26.8	34.0	40 268	60 163	28 989	166 600	23.7	13.7
Pawtucket city	52.0	63.8	56.3	28.2	16.4	32.3	31.7	32.5	31 577	46 510	23 015	101 800	22.2	14.4
Providence city	41.7	56.3	50.8	23.0	15.4	24.8	16.8	27.2	26 587	46 698	18 843	101 700	22.8	12.7
Warwick city	82.4	86.3	87.9	67.2	54.2	54.6	53.4	54.8	46 440	53 163	29 625	111 200	23.1	14.2
Woonsocket city	46.5	58.8	55.2	21.9	14.3	17.3	15.6	17.6	30 898	50 163	22 699	113 800	22.0	13.8
SOUTH CAROLINA	78.3	85.5	81.6	58.3	48.2	57.8	41.0	61.0	36 951	43 179	23 855	83 100	20.5	9.9
Aiken city	74.5	84.7	79.1	44.2	32.9	50.2	26.3	54.0	43 529	54 512	25 352	108 400	20.2	9.9
Anderson city	63.1	77.6	75.5	36.0	18.3	40.0	27.5	41.6	27 758	39 087	18 609	83 800	21.9	11.1
Charleston city	65.5	80.5	78.3	40.7	25.4	35.2	20.4	40.2	35 229	53 121	21 687	137 800	23.0	11.0
Columbia city	55.6	69.9	64.0	32.6	20.3	34.3	22.1	37.6	31 093	48 634	21 031	96 800	21.8	9.9
Florence city	69.1	84.3	79.4	42.9	27.4	47.3	30.7	49.6	35 124	46 371	19 789	89 500	18.9	10.1
Goose Creek city	63.4	64.8	58.7	56.6	49.8	61.6	73.3	58.1	45 954	55 885	31 499	98 500	19.8	9.9
Greenville city	56.2	71.1	68.9	29.5	17.8	36.9	19.3	39.8	32 604	49 118	25 081	112 500	20.3	9.9
Hilton Head Island town	81.6	85.7	69.6	53.7	51.2	68.6	41.9	75.8	60 234	69 331	40 825	280 100	24.2	9.9
Mount Pleasant town	83.1	86.7	88.3	63.6	65.5	54.2	34.5	61.0	61 095	68 253	42 145	180 000	21.3	9.9
North Charleston city	50.6	62.4	52.1	34.6	24.5	38.4	24.6	41.8	29 118	37 526	22 957	64 500	21.8	10.9
Rock Hill city	62.9	74.1	71.3	39.9	28.7	37.3	19.6	42.4	37 009	49 548	27 726	90 100	20.7	10.5
Spartanburg city	56.7	75.2	70.4	32.6	20.8	39.1	26.3	41.0	28 836	43 211	18 206	84 100	21.4	9.9
Summerville town	75.3	81.3	78.5	54.5	47.3	37.5	26.1	39.5	43 238	52 340	30 328	106 600	21.9	10.3
Sumter city	58.7	66.1	55.6	44.1	34.9	41.1	19.6	43.5	31 580	44 809	22 485	76 600	18.8	9.9
SOUTH DAKOTA	78.2	84.4	82.0	51.2	43.7	47.6	38.5	49.3	35 271	42 834	21 935	74 300	19.7	10.5
Rapid City city	68.9	78.0	73.6	41.4	31.1	42.1	35.9	43.5	35 905	47 085	22 219	85 500	20.9	9.9
Sioux Falls city	75.5	83.3	84.6	46.2	40.1	37.2	29.4	39.3	41 341	53 102	26 499	97 300	20.1	9.9

Table C-5. Cities — **Migration, Housing, and Transportation**

City	Median gross rent	Percent who pay 35 percent or more of income for housing expenses		Means of transportation to work (percent except where noted)						Vehicles available (percent of households)		
		Owners	Renters	Number of workers 16 years and over	Car, truck, or van		Public transportation	Other means	Walked	No vehicles	One vehicle	Two or more vehicles
					Drove alone	Carpooled						
	25	26	27	28	29	30	31	32	33	34	35	36
OREGON	620	17.5	32.2	1 601 378	73.2	12.2	4.2	1.9	3.6	7.5	32.8	59.7
Albany city..................	594	15.7	38.5	19 074	82.0	10.1	0.4	1.4	2.6	9.1	32.0	58.9
Beaverton city	706	16.5	26.6	40 341	72.5	10.6	8.3	1.0	3.1	7.5	40.6	51.8
Bend city	649	18.3	34.8	26 106	74.6	12.7	1.4	2.8	2.8	5.8	33.4	60.7
Corvallis city	592	13.4	44.3	23 475	66.2	9.3	2.5	7.5	11.1	7.9	40.0	52.1
Eugene city	621	18.2	42.4	67 823	66.8	11.2	4.9	6.2	6.1	10.6	39.3	50.1
Gresham city	661	17.6	32.9	43 104	72.5	13.3	7.6	1.6	1.8	8.3	34.9	56.8
Hillsboro city	782	16.8	28.0	35 797	73.4	13.8	6.5	1.2	2.2	5.6	33.9	60.5
Keizer city...................	609	15.5	31.8	15 249	78.1	13.7	1.9	1.2	1.4	5.6	32.5	62.0
Lake Oswego city..........	839	15.9	27.6	18 043	78.8	7.7	3.7	0.6	2.0	3.3	32.5	64.2
McMinnville city	611	17.4	32.7	11 244	75.0	14.8	0.4	2.1	4.9	7.8	34.6	57.6
Medford city..................	605	17.6	37.1	27 579	79.3	11.9	0.5	1.8	3.1	8.9	36.0	55.1
Oregon City city	686	21.1	33.2	12 647	77.6	12.4	3.4	0.5	2.3	7.9	29.0	63.1
Portland city	622	19.9	33.0	270 996	63.7	11.9	12.3	2.6	5.2	14.0	39.8	46.2
Salem city	560	17.6	31.7	59 777	71.8	15.4	3.3	2.0	3.7	9.2	37.4	53.4
Springfield city..............	582	16.7	35.5	24 458	73.5	14.3	4.6	2.1	2.0	8.6	38.0	53.4
Tigard city....................	673	13.6	30.6	21 619	77.2	10.4	5.1	1.0	1.7	5.1	37.5	57.4
PENNSYLVANIA........	531	15.1	28.6	5 556 311	76.5	10.4	5.2	0.8	4.1	12.8	34.9	52.3
Allentown city...............	541	16.4	31.5	45 221	71.2	14.6	3.8	1.1	7.4	18.8	42.3	38.9
Altoona city..................	381	13.6	31.5	20 812	79.3	12.8	1.0	1.1	4.6	14.9	40.3	44.8
Bethel Park borough	672	12.3	33.3	16 140	78.4	6.5	10.5	0.8	1.1	6.8	34.0	59.2
Bethlehem city..............	559	15.5	29.3	31 106	76.5	11.3	2.4	0.6	7.2	14.0	41.2	44.8
Chester city	541	23.7	37.9	12 799	56.0	18.8	16.4	1.1	6.4	33.1	42.3	24.7
Easton city	552	19.6	28.3	11 296	66.4	16.9	3.4	1.1	10.9	17.5	40.5	42.0
Erie city	424	15.4	31.7	43 835	73.3	13.9	3.4	1.4	6.6	18.2	44.4	37.4
Harrisburg city	479	22.8	30.7	20 520	58.5	19.1	9.3	1.5	9.7	30.9	43.6	25.5
Lancaster city	488	18.6	31.4	23 890	62.3	15.5	6.5	2.0	11.6	24.2	44.3	31.6
Municipality of Monroeville borough...	684	14.7	32.7	14 085	81.7	8.8	4.9	0.3	1.6	7.8	39.2	52.9
New Castle city	365	14.7	34.4	9 724	79.8	10.6	2.4	0.6	4.3	18.2	41.7	40.1
Norristown borough.......	632	22.6	31.4	14 598	64.2	16.3	8.6	1.8	8.1	21.3	44.2	34.5
Philadelphia city	569	19.4	36.0	569 761	49.2	12.8	25.4	1.6	9.1	35.7	42.0	22.2
Pittsburgh city..............	500	16.9	34.0	141 844	54.8	11.4	20.5	1.2	9.8	29.4	42.7	27.9
Plum borough................	674	14.8	24.9	13 082	84.7	8.7	2.9	0.5	0.8	4.9	29.7	65.4
Reading city	459	17.6	31.7	30 586	60.7	20.1	7.1	2.0	8.8	29.6	39.9	30.5
Scranton city	425	17.5	27.2	32 028	74.2	14.8	1.8	0.7	6.9	20.6	40.8	38.6
State College borough ..	595	11.2	55.4	15 885	37.9	7.2	8.9	2.5	40.6	19.2	46.2	34.7
Wilkes-Barre city	411	16.2	28.6	17 469	73.6	14.2	2.2	1.2	7.4	23.5	40.9	35.5
Williamsport city	424	14.6	33.7	12 899	69.8	14.4	3.7	1.7	9.1	22.6	40.5	36.9
York city......................	439	18.0	31.2	17 345	66.8	17.4	4.5	1.9	8.1	24.1	43.4	32.5
RHODE ISLAND	553	17.1	28.9	490 905	80.1	10.4	2.5	1.0	3.8	10.9	36.4	52.6
Cranston city	615	18.5	25.5	35 991	84.7	9.3	2.4	0.6	1.1	9.2	37.5	53.3
East Providence city	548	15.4	27.2	22 434	82.6	10.1	2.6	1.0	1.8	10.5	41.1	48.4
Newport city.................	646	20.8	27.9	13 976	69.0	9.1	2.5	2.0	13.1	14.5	46.3	39.2
Pawtucket city..............	498	17.0	28.2	32 241	75.8	14.4	3.7	1.3	3.5	16.1	43.3	40.6
Providence city.............	526	19.7	35.2	67 169	60.5	15.4	7.3	2.1	12.2	22.9	43.6	33.5
Warwick city	673	17.3	25.9	43 088	86.5	8.5	1.5	0.5	1.2	6.8	35.4	57.7
Woonsocket city	483	16.2	26.6	18 729	79.3	14.0	1.2	1.0	3.4	17.3	41.2	41.4
SOUTH CAROLINA ...	510	14.3	26.8	1 822 969	79.4	14.0	0.8	1.3	2.3	9.0	33.6	57.4
Aiken city.....................	546	13.1	29.7	10 980	80.4	12.4	0.4	1.4	3.5	8.5	37.8	53.7
Anderson city	454	11.8	30.5	9 962	77.4	14.3	1.2	1.3	3.7	19.2	37.9	43.0
Charleston city	614	20.5	39.6	45 015	73.5	11.6	3.6	2.0	6.6	15.4	40.7	43.9
Columbia city	536	17.8	33.0	54 288	65.4	11.3	4.2	3.1	13.4	15.8	43.1	41.1
Florence city.................	462	14.4	31.2	13 066	80.7	11.9	2.4	1.7	1.8	14.6	37.2	48.2
Goose Creek city	646	13.1	14.3	15 439	69.9	10.7	0.1	1.5	16.8	3.1	29.0	67.9
Greenville city...............	526	16.6	26.6	27 967	73.4	14.0	1.1	1.2	7.8	14.6	45.0	40.5
Hilton Head Island town	847	20.2	24.3	15 354	74.3	14.0	1.5	2.2	2.1	4.5	32.9	62.6
Mount Pleasant town	838	14.5	27.8	24 685	85.6	7.6	0.4	1.3	0.9	3.9	30.4	65.7
North Charleston city	517	16.8	29.2	33 962	70.9	16.9	4.7	2.8	3.8	16.5	43.9	39.6
Rock Hill city	610	13.3	28.7	23 277	78.7	15.7	0.6	1.1	2.0	10.0	37.7	52.3
Spartanburg city	465	15.7	29.9	15 895	75.5	15.0	2.7	1.0	3.5	19.1	40.2	40.6
Summerville town...........	588	15.3	24.5	13 295	83.6	11.9	0.7	0.7	1.1	7.3	33.0	59.7
Sumter city	471	14.0	22.1	16 729	79.7	13.1	1.2	2.1	2.4	15.6	35.4	49.0
SOUTH DAKOTA.......	426	10.4	22.7	372 648	77.3	10.4	0.5	0.8	4.5	6.1	29.9	64.0
Rapid City city..............	496	10.1	27.5	30 053	84.1	9.9	0.8	0.7	2.1	7.8	34.7	57.5
Sioux Falls city	521	8.9	23.9	68 737	84.3	9.2	0.9	0.7	2.3	6.7	34.3	58.9

Table C-5. Cities — **Migration, Housing, and Transportation**

STATE Place code	City	Total population 5 years and over	Residence in 1995 (percent)					Occupied housing units		Householders 65 years and over	
			Same house	Same county, different house	Same state, different county	Different state	Outside the United States	Number	Percent owner-occupied	Number	Percent owner-occupied
		1	2	3	4	5	6	7	8	9	10
47 00000	TENNESSEE.............	5 315 920	53.9	25.2	8.7	10.7	1.5	2 232 905	69.9	467 100	81.5
47 03440	Bartlett city	37 558	55.3	32.9	1.0	9.8	1.0	13 755	92.1	2 066	97.3
47 14000	Chattanooga city	146 369	52.1	30.8	4.4	10.8	2.0	65 568	54.9	16 405	70.4
47 15160	Clarksville city	94 649	37.9	22.7	4.6	28.9	5.9	36 994	57.7	4 655	78.0
47 15400	Cleveland city	34 700	44.8	28.2	8.0	16.8	2.2	15 022	52.3	3 435	68.1
47 16420	Collierville town	29 436	43.1	32.0	3.1	20.6	1.3	10 364	86.4	1 206	87.8
47 16540	Columbia city	30 578	50.3	27.7	9.4	10.8	1.8	13 121	63.3	3 121	79.2
47 27740	Franklin city	38 171	32.5	17.3	18.7	28.8	2.7	16 090	63.5	2 003	72.9
47 28960	Germantown city	35 235	57.4	25.8	1.4	14.4	1.1	13 233	88.8	2 290	92.7
47 33280	Hendersonville city	37 887	46.8	20.1	16.2	16.0	0.8	15 795	71.2	2 498	73.4
47 37640	Jackson city	55 361	44.9	30.6	12.1	10.8	1.6	23 519	56.5	5 103	74.0
47 38320	Johnson City city..........	52 261	47.0	23.5	14.7	13.3	1.5	23 621	56.9	5 349	71.5
47 39560	Kingsport city	42 076	53.6	28.1	8.2	9.2	0.9	19 665	64.5	5 661	78.3
47 40000	Knoxville city	163 524	46.4	29.8	11.6	10.3	1.9	76 597	51.1	16 767	74.4
47 48000	Memphis city	599 671	51.9	34.3	2.0	9.7	2.1	250 810	55.9	48 735	74.8
47 51560	Murfreesboro city	61 160	33.5	28.9	20.3	15.0	2.2	26 669	52.3	4 087	75.7
47 52004	Nashville-Davidson........	532 311	45.5	29.0	7.9	14.2	3.3	237 405	55.3	42 441	74.5
47 55120	Oak Ridge city..............	26 004	58.7	18.0	10.9	11.1	1.3	12 062	68.6	3 805	82.4
47 69420	Smyrna town	23 238	41.7	25.4	17.7	13.4	1.9	9 604	64.8	1 167	77.2
48 00000	TEXAS....................	19 241 518	49.6	27.0	12.5	7.1	3.8	7 393 354	63.8	1 335 578	80.9
48 01000	Abilene city..................	107 647	43.5	23.8	19.6	10.5	2.7	41 547	58.7	8 861	79.9
48 01924	Allen city.....................	38 834	37.1	20.8	20.8	18.7	2.6	14 213	85.7	758	86.3
48 03000	Amarillo city	159 666	49.3	23.7	18.3	6.9	1.7	67 612	63.3	15 007	79.6
48 04000	Arlington city	305 415	40.7	30.6	13.1	10.2	5.4	124 884	54.7	12 553	81.4
48 05000	Austin city...................	609 773	36.0	29.6	17.6	10.1	6.7	265 409	44.9	28 494	75.0
48 06128	Baytown city.................	61 101	50.7	33.6	7.6	4.5	3.6	23 646	59.5	4 131	82.1
48 07000	Beaumont city	105 796	54.0	28.5	10.1	5.4	1.9	44 375	59.9	10 687	77.7
48 07132	Bedford city	44 288	45.7	29.8	11.7	10.5	2.2	20 254	55.1	2 409	66.3
48 08236	Big Spring city	23 792	48.1	19.8	21.7	7.5	2.9	8 174	64.1	2 359	73.0
48 10768	Brownsville city	126 114	57.6	30.7	3.8	2.7	5.2	38 224	61.4	7 947	72.7
48 10912	Bryan city	60 697	40.0	29.6	20.4	5.8	4.1	23 871	51.0	4 030	74.8
48 13024	Carrollton city	100 676	44.4	22.3	18.9	9.1	5.4	39 161	65.5	3 284	79.2
48 13492	Cedar Hill city	29 512	48.6	32.8	10.1	7.4	1.1	10 789	81.1	770	77.5
48 13552	Cedar Park city	23 027	33.1	18.7	30.7	16.1	1.5	8 650	83.7	561	82.4
48 15364	Cleburne city	24 157	48.3	29.6	14.9	5.1	2.2	9 382	66.8	2 231	79.9
48 15976	College Station city	64 784	19.6	16.2	48.6	9.0	6.5	24 657	30.7	1 677	82.1
48 16432	Conroe city	33 523	41.7	28.1	17.4	5.4	7.4	13 168	47.6	2 607	63.0
48 16612	Coppell city..................	32 424	39.3	28.9	12.8	14.2	4.7	12 179	77.2	570	77.0
48 16624	Copperas Cove city.......	26 767	38.9	12.4	15.1	27.6	8.0	10 368	53.8	829	84.6
48 17000	Corpus Christi city	256 350	51.8	30.5	9.4	6.7	1.7	98 808	59.6	19 818	76.5
48 19000	Dallas city...................	1 080 660	43.2	32.6	8.8	6.9	8.4	451 697	43.2	67 213	72.8
48 19624	Deer Park city	26 652	58.4	32.7	5.0	3.1	0.8	9 602	79.2	1 203	91.1
48 19792	Del Rio city..................	31 247	57.5	25.4	8.3	4.8	3.9	10 745	65.2	2 483	75.4
48 19972	Denton city	75 726	32.1	28.8	24.0	9.8	5.3	30 900	41.7	4 042	73.2
48 20092	DeSoto city..................	35 048	52.0	31.8	9.0	6.3	1.0	13 751	72.0	2 305	77.6
48 21628	Duncanville city	33 666	54.3	32.4	7.2	4.2	1.9	12 862	71.9	2 137	82.2
48 22660	Edinburg city	44 044	51.3	33.5	7.6	3.6	4.0	14 279	62.3	2 390	80.3
48 24000	El Paso city	517 224	54.1	31.7	2.4	6.7	5.0	182 177	61.4	37 538	74.9
48 24768	Euless city...................	42 574	40.2	26.5	14.6	13.1	5.6	19 189	43.8	1 562	79.3
48 25452	Farmers Branch city......	26 185	50.8	28.8	9.0	5.2	6.2	9 808	68.3	2 098	90.1
48 26232	Flower Mound town........	45 877	34.8	17.7	19.6	25.9	2.0	16 306	92.7	626	83.9
48 27000	Fort Worth city..............	490 219	44.7	33.0	9.9	7.6	4.8	195 146	55.9	34 182	77.7
48 27648	Friendswood city	26 853	56.0	18.1	17.3	7.6	1.1	10 024	80.4	1 592	71.2
48 27684	Frisco city	29 172	26.1	19.0	31.7	20.6	2.6	12 051	81.7	706	84.7
48 28068	Galveston city	53 530	48.5	29.3	12.7	5.9	3.6	23 806	43.6	5 509	66.7
48 29000	Garland city	198 373	49.3	31.1	7.9	6.5	5.2	73 234	65.6	9 427	80.8
48 29336	Georgetown city	26 542	34.4	20.9	28.0	14.1	2.6	10 430	69.4	2 864	86.6
48 30464	Grand Prairie city	115 998	46.8	28.2	14.1	7.5	3.4	43 618	61.3	5 262	80.1
48 30644	Grapevine city	39 053	41.3	25.2	14.4	14.3	4.8	15 742	65.1	1 218	72.0
48 31928	Haltom City city	36 001	45.7	34.4	7.7	8.7	3.5	15 019	59.1	2 646	81.3
48 32372	Harlingen city	52 358	54.3	29.2	7.8	6.4	2.4	19 029	61.2	5 470	81.2
48 35000	Houston city	1 794 753	46.9	34.2	6.0	5.5	7.3	718 231	45.8	108 378	73.5
48 35528	Huntsville city	33 379	35.2	13.9	44.4	4.5	2.0	10 231	43.4	1 984	76.5
48 35576	Hurst city	33 728	48.3	31.4	8.8	8.3	3.2	14 101	66.0	2 932	83.6
48 37000	Irving city	176 341	35.6	32.0	12.2	10.9	9.3	76 262	37.3	7 229	77.4
48 38632	Keller city	25 006	43.8	23.3	11.3	20.4	1.2	8 800	92.9	698	93.4
48 39148	Killeen city	77 957	33.7	20.5	9.2	27.7	8.9	32 452	46.2	2 576	84.7
48 39352	Kingsville city...............	23 495	50.9	25.0	15.7	6.1	2.2	8 927	54.9	1 765	77.3
48 40588	Lake Jackson city..........	24 565	50.7	31.6	8.9	6.5	2.3	9 599	71.2	1 772	82.1
48 41212	Lancaster city	23 910	52.3	32.9	9.0	4.9	0.9	9 206	65.9	1 321	88.6

Table C-5. Cities — **Migration, Housing, and Transportation**

City	Total family households	Family households Married-couple family Total	With own children under 18 years	Other family Total	With own children under 18 years	Total nonfamily households	Two or more adults	Living alone	Median household income All households	Owner-occupied households	Renter-occupied households	Median housing value (owner estimated)	With a mortgage	Without a mortgage
	11	12	13	14	15	16	17	18	19	20	21	22	23	24
TENNESSEE..............	77.0	83.9	79.7	54.4	42.6	53.8	40.3	56.2	36 239	43 217	23 266	88 300	21.1	9.9
Bartlett city	92.9	94.9	92.4	79.7	74.6	86.7	79.4	87.8	66 598	68 592	44 912	133 000	20.9	9.9
Chattanooga city	63.2	74.6	68.0	41.9	27.8	42.1	35.8	43.2	31 602	43 164	21 738	83 300	21.1	9.9
Clarksville city	62.8	67.5	63.2	45.9	37.6	43.8	36.0	45.9	37 427	45 877	28 124	83 500	21.9	9.9
Cleveland city	63.2	70.9	62.3	40.1	27.5	33.1	18.8	35.6	29 834	44 468	19 563	96 400	22.0	9.9
Collierville town	90.3	92.6	92.3	71.8	64.1	62.3	44.4	65.2	80 261	84 954	40 146	190 600	21.1	10.4
Columbia city	68.7	78.6	74.7	47.0	34.1	52.0	21.8	56.4	35 363	42 802	24 763	86 400	20.2	10.0
Franklin city	72.6	78.5	82.7	47.6	35.7	42.8	37.6	43.8	56 148	71 812	37 043	179 500	21.5	9.9
Germantown city	92.8	94.8	94.0	73.2	68.0	68.4	53.6	69.9	93 863	100 157	53 670	215 200	18.6	9.9
Hendersonville city	79.2	85.2	82.2	52.1	42.4	49.3	45.5	50.0	50 111	59 087	30 422	134 200	21.6	9.9
Jackson city	63.9	76.5	69.5	40.8	26.7	43.2	27.8	45.7	32 850	45 027	21 216	80 500	20.5	9.9
Johnson City city	69.4	77.9	73.1	44.4	31.6	39.1	28.0	41.5	30 775	43 834	18 828	95 300	21.1	9.9
Kingsport city	72.1	81.3	74.3	45.2	29.0	50.9	45.0	51.5	30 581	39 656	17 002	85 400	20.6	9.9
Knoxville city	64.3	75.0	71.2	42.0	26.7	36.5	21.9	39.9	27 421	39 724	17 776	77 800	22.4	10.7
Memphis city	62.8	76.1	70.1	47.2	35.1	43.7	32.5	45.8	32 208	42 018	23 297	72 300	22.4	11.4
Murfreesboro city	66.1	75.2	74.8	37.8	32.6	31.8	14.7	39.1	39 319	57 009	24 135	118 500	21.3	9.9
Nashville-Davidson........	65.5	75.2	70.7	43.6	31.6	41.1	31.3	43.5	39 612	51 964	27 808	114 200	21.9	9.9
Oak Ridge city	76.3	85.2	79.1	44.3	33.2	54.7	40.1	56.1	41 637	55 020	22 368	97 100	19.4	9.9
Smyrna town	72.8	81.0	78.0	46.5	32.5	43.7	35.1	45.9	44 471	57 172	27 824	112 500	20.2	9.9
TEXAS	71.1	77.7	72.6	49.2	39.6	45.8	33.9	48.3	39 745	49 279	27 506	77 800	20.1	10.9
Abilene city	65.6	71.9	63.8	43.5	33.8	44.0	25.9	47.8	32 757	41 823	23 587	60 000	19.4	10.6
Allen city.....................	89.1	91.4	90.6	71.4	71.0	66.3	56.3	68.9	79 311	84 357	43 211	142 200	21.1	10.6
Amarillo city	71.4	78.8	72.5	48.0	38.0	46.1	35.3	47.9	34 903	44 180	23 272	71 600	19.3	9.9
Arlington city	64.8	73.0	65.5	37.7	31.9	32.8	25.5	34.8	47 282	64 015	32 202	94 800	20.0	10.0
Austin city...................	59.3	67.6	65.3	38.1	32.4	28.2	21.5	31.0	42 440	62 517	31 108	120 800	21.2	9.9
Baytown city	64.8	73.4	66.0	40.5	29.7	44.8	28.9	47.6	40 173	49 856	29 642	63 500	18.6	9.9
Beaumont city	66.7	78.1	71.8	44.1	29.4	46.7	35.9	48.3	32 325	44 163	20 864	62 000	18.9	11.5
Bedford city	69.9	75.9	73.5	45.6	40.8	30.8	30.1	30.9	54 904	76 931	35 730	116 400	19.5	9.9
Big Spring city	70.5	79.7	69.5	48.0	34.5	50.7	43.7	51.5	27 577	35 148	17 206	36 300	18.0	10.5
Brownsville city............	63.5	68.3	62.3	51.6	36.2	49.3	47.4	49.5	24 348	31 664	14 844	49 400	22.9	13.6
Bryan city	60.7	70.1	64.7	35.1	25.5	34.6	15.3	42.6	31 528	46 278	21 499	71 600	19.6	10.8
Carrollton city	71.3	77.2	75.2	45.1	38.2	48.8	43.0	50.4	62 241	75 901	41 965	124 000	20.0	9.9
Cedar Hill city	84.0	89.6	89.3	65.4	58.4	68.2	61.4	69.7	59 669	64 567	36 840	96 200	21.9	9.9
Cedar Park city	85.9	88.9	88.1	69.2	65.0	73.5	74.8	73.0	67 566	71 958	41 181	126 600	21.6	11.3
Cleburne city	72.0	77.6	69.8	50.6	39.2	52.5	38.9	54.3	35 324	42 407	24 164	64 900	18.9	13.4
College Station city	55.9	66.1	65.0	22.1	22.8	12.3	5.6	20.2	20 978	69 371	13 575	114 000	19.7	9.9
Conroe city	54.4	63.4	60.4	31.5	26.2	34.1	25.2	36.0	34 339	43 477	27 289	71 800	19.0	9.9
Coppell city..................	84.1	87.0	88.7	63.1	56.3	48.4	48.7	48.4	95 835	109 035	52 484	205 600	20.2	9.9
Copperas Cove city.......	57.3	62.5	55.5	38.4	30.0	41.1	41.3	41.1	38 419	47 934	29 810	71 500	20.7	9.9
Corpus Christi city.........	66.3	74.4	67.8	46.1	31.1	42.7	32.3	45.1	36 235	46 538	24 492	70 500	21.7	12.1
Dallas city...................	51.7	60.8	53.1	33.7	23.4	30.8	25.7	31.9	37 470	52 461	30 611	87 400	20.8	12.0
Deer Park city	83.3	88.4	85.7	58.7	49.9	59.8	46.6	62.9	61 483	69 078	38 224	90 200	18.1	9.9
Del Rio city	69.0	73.2	63.9	54.4	42.8	49.7	23.8	52.4	27 555	33 687	18 946	56 200	19.5	12.9
Denton city	59.4	68.4	66.6	31.6	24.6	21.2	12.0	25.5	35 097	58 053	23 622	98 600	21.9	11.0
DeSoto city	80.0	86.5	83.1	55.4	45.0	45.2	34.4	46.3	57 360	69 131	31 958	108 900	21.6	9.9
Duncanville city	74.6	82.2	74.5	51.6	41.5	61.2	52.4	62.7	51 853	61 118	35 467	88 600	20.3	10.9
Edinburg city	66.2	71.6	67.3	52.4	38.1	45.9	33.7	49.3	28 803	37 105	16 550	57 100	20.8	11.0
El Paso city	65.9	72.2	65.0	50.1	36.4	45.5	40.2	46.3	31 946	41 779	20 023	69 900	21.7	9.9
Euless city	54.4	60.2	56.6	35.8	29.0	27.4	26.9	27.6	49 012	61 919	39 429	94 200	19.3	11.3
Farmers Branch city......	71.2	76.6	66.4	47.6	39.7	61.3	45.0	65.1	53 779	57 885	46 250	97 600	20.6	9.9
Flower Mound town.......	94.2	96.1	96.1	75.1	74.2	79.9	81.7	79.5	95 096	98 249	51 821	181 800	20.4	9.9
Fort Worth city	64.0	71.7	67.0	45.5	34.8	40.5	32.0	42.2	36 871	47 316	27 461	69 700	20.8	11.9
Friendswood city	86.3	89.5	88.5	68.1	60.4	57.4	61.6	56.7	68 493	76 560	40 927	123 900	20.2	9.9
Frisco city	86.9	90.9	90.0	55.9	51.6	60.4	56.8	61.3	78 137	84 908	39 750	156 000	21.1	10.3
Galveston city..............	51.0	61.3	50.6	32.2	17.7	33.4	26.1	34.8	28 950	40 486	21 631	71 900	22.4	13.1
Garland city	69.6	75.9	69.5	49.7	43.0	52.8	41.9	55.1	49 040	58 386	34 375	86 200	20.1	11.1
Georgetown city	76.1	83.0	74.9	44.2	35.8	49.9	29.9	53.4	53 531	63 996	32 819	139 200	21.2	9.9
Grand Prairie city	68.0	74.5	70.6	49.0	37.4	42.3	36.9	43.7	46 484	56 876	32 328	82 000	20.2	10.4
Grapevine city	74.5	79.6	80.9	48.3	47.0	40.4	35.8	41.6	71 576	91 841	41 023	153 700	19.7	11.0
Haltom City city	66.8	73.3	66.1	49.7	40.6	43.7	42.4	44.1	39 111	45 504	31 803	62 400	20.3	11.5
Harlingen city	64.4	69.5	57.7	48.8	34.8	51.0	37.6	52.8	29 840	36 561	21 148	54 600	20.6	10.2
Houston city	52.9	60.7	52.8	36.0	24.7	33.1	25.9	34.6	36 540	51 510	28 484	77 500	20.2	10.8
Huntsville city	59.4	69.1	61.5	35.5	29.9	24.9	9.5	32.6	26 909	43 934	18 404	78 200	20.4	10.6
Hurst city	71.3	78.9	66.8	44.2	30.9	51.4	41.7	53.4	49 856	62 121	32 520	97 800	19.6	10.6
Irving city	46.4	54.3	47.5	25.1	18.0	23.2	17.6	24.6	44 652	61 027	37 379	92 600	19.5	10.1
Keller city....................	93.7	95.1	94.4	72.6	70.8	86.3	86.2	86.3	86 060	90 126	37 450	173 200	20.7	10.9
Killeen city	52.0	56.5	54.9	38.4	31.8	31.7	22.8	34.3	34 691	44 165	28 255	72 500	22.0	9.9
Kingsville city...............	61.2	70.5	59.9	39.0	24.7	40.6	22.1	46.1	27 848	38 118	15 799	48 900	19.7	11.7
Lake Jackson city.........	78.1	84.6	81.2	44.2	40.4	48.3	35.2	50.3	60 613	74 114	33 918	95 400	17.6	9.9
Lancaster city	69.7	78.3	73.1	53.0	44.8	54.3	37.8	56.8	43 784	50 869	36 192	75 700	21.8	12.3

Table C-5. Cities — **Migration, Housing, and Transportation**

City	Median gross rent	Percent who pay 35 percent or more of income for housing expenses		Means of transportation to work (percent except where noted)							Vehicles available (percent of households)		
		Owners	Renters	Number of workers 16 years and over	Car, truck, or van		Public transportation	Other means	Walked	No vehicles	One vehicle	Two or more vehicles
					Drove alone	Carpooled						
	25	26	27	28	29	30	31	32	33	34	35	36
TENNESSEE.............	505	14.4	27.2	2 618 404	81.7	12.5	0.8	0.8	1.5	7.7	32.3	60.0
Bartlett city	821	11.8	14.0	21 226	89.4	7.0	0.0	0.3	0.2	1.6	18.7	79.8
Chattanooga city	495	15.1	29.4	69 127	79.5	13.3	2.0	0.9	2.2	12.8	39.4	47.8
Clarksville city	550	15.9	23.1	50 593	81.3	12.4	1.0	1.3	2.3	6.8	32.4	60.9
Cleveland city	457	16.3	30.7	16 933	83.5	11.7	0.1	0.6	2.1	8.0	37.3	54.7
Collierville town	757	13.8	23.0	15 633	88.4	6.6	0.1	0.9	0.3	1.9	18.7	79.5
Columbia city	516	14.1	26.6	15 451	80.2	15.9	0.2	0.6	1.1	8.2	37.7	54.1
Franklin city	758	15.1	25.2	21 957	82.9	10.2	0.2	1.1	0.9	4.0	32.1	63.9
Germantown city	929	10.7	19.5	18 717	87.9	5.5	0.0	0.8	0.4	1.3	18.6	80.2
Hendersonville city	669	13.3	31.3	21 315	85.2	9.8	0.4	0.9	0.5	3.6	28.8	67.7
Jackson city	514	12.9	30.5	26 268	81.8	12.0	1.3	0.8	2.2	12.5	38.8	48.7
Johnson City city	438	14.1	31.3	26 155	83.3	10.9	0.8	0.8	2.3	10.1	37.6	52.3
Kingsport city	417	12.8	29.6	17 342	85.6	9.6	0.1	0.8	1.5	11.0	36.2	52.8
Knoxville city	467	17.6	32.8	79 042	80.5	10.5	1.5	0.9	4.2	12.0	42.8	45.2
Memphis city	548	19.8	31.8	274 934	76.6	15.7	3.0	1.0	1.9	14.3	44.0	41.7
Murfreesboro city	592	12.3	35.4	35 515	81.7	12.5	0.3	1.1	1.9	6.0	37.0	57.0
Nashville-Davidson........	615	15.3	27.8	285 980	78.6	13.3	1.8	0.9	2.3	8.7	40.5	50.8
Oak Ridge city	487	9.8	31.0	11 887	86.1	8.9	0.4	0.3	1.7	6.9	34.2	58.9
Smyrna town	589	11.5	24.0	13 637	83.3	13.3	0.1	0.6	0.5	4.1	30.4	65.5
TEXAS.....................	574	13.6	27.1	9 157 875	77.7	14.5	1.9	1.3	1.9	7.4	36.0	56.6
Abilene city..................	474	11.5	27.5	51 233	80.9	12.8	0.6	1.4	2.6	6.7	38.8	54.5
Allen city.....................	887	11.9	27.7	22 479	86.1	7.7	1.0	0.4	0.5	1.7	18.3	80.1
Amarillo city.................	475	11.2	29.3	79 604	82.1	13.1	0.4	1.0	1.1	6.7	38.1	55.3
Arlington city................	635	12.4	26.0	172 355	81.9	12.5	0.2	1.1	1.6	4.3	36.9	58.8
Austin city...................	724	14.8	33.5	353 109	73.6	13.9	4.5	2.1	2.5	7.8	42.5	49.7
Baytown city................	529	12.5	23.4	26 910	81.2	14.9	0.1	1.3	1.2	7.1	37.6	55.3
Beaumont city	488	13.8	31.1	46 571	80.2	13.3	1.6	1.2	1.7	12.4	41.4	46.3
Bedford city	696	10.6	23.9	27 876	87.5	8.0	0.0	0.6	0.8	3.2	38.9	58.0
Big Spring city	413	13.1	29.8	8 153	80.2	15.4	0.3	1.6	1.3	11.4	40.9	47.7
Brownsville city............	405	17.5	33.2	43 161	71.7	21.1	1.3	1.6	2.2	13.7	38.7	47.6
Bryan city	566	13.0	40.4	30 078	74.9	17.1	1.0	3.4	1.9	9.1	38.4	52.5
Carrollton city	781	12.5	21.5	60 594	81.2	11.6	1.4	1.0	1.3	2.8	30.0	67.2
Cedar Hill city	743	16.1	25.4	16 728	81.8	14.4	0.7	0.4	0.6	2.4	27.1	70.5
Cedar Park city	849	14.0	31.2	13 472	86.2	9.9	0.2	0.9	0.4	1.7	22.4	76.0
Cleburne city	525	13.6	27.0	11 346	78.8	16.8	0.1	2.1	0.6	8.6	34.0	57.4
College Station city	597	13.1	57.1	30 983	76.8	9.5	1.2	4.3	5.5	5.3	36.6	58.1
Conroe city	559	13.2	27.8	16 393	73.5	20.8	0.4	2.5	1.4	9.5	41.0	49.5
Coppell city	946	13.1	17.4	18 643	87.9	5.7	0.5	0.6	0.4	1.9	22.9	75.2
Copperas Cove city.......	583	14.8	24.2	14 651	76.7	18.2	0.4	1.3	1.6	4.2	35.0	60.9
Corpus Christi city........	555	16.2	30.4	118 869	76.8	15.7	2.1	1.5	1.8	9.5	38.3	52.2
Dallas city...................	623	16.9	26.8	537 006	70.8	17.8	5.5	1.2	1.9	10.9	46.0	43.1
Deer Park city	654	9.5	22.1	14 058	86.8	10.4	0.4	0.9	0.7	2.7	23.5	73.8
Del Rio city..................	402	14.6	25.5	11 916	76.6	17.5	0.2	2.5	1.5	10.3	36.8	52.9
Denton city	625	14.1	39.1	42 412	76.4	13.0	0.8	2.1	5.5	6.6	41.5	51.9
DeSoto city..................	'680	16.4	28.2	19 271	83.4	11.4	1.0	0.9	0.8	3.8	30.9	65.3
Duncanville city	731	16.1	23.8	17 743	81.9	12.2	1.5	1.0	0.6	3.8	31.6	64.5
Edinburg city................	453	14.2	30.7	17 324	75.9	16.8	0.0	2.4	2.8	9.7	40.6	49.7
El Paso city	474	15.7	32.0	208 101	76.5	15.8	2.3	1.2	2.0	11.0	35.1	54.0
Euless city	703	10.6	17.7	26 117	84.0	10.3	0.5	1.1	1.5	3.4	42.4	54.2
Farmers Branch city......	783	13.3	16.6	14 104	75.3	17.0	1.7	0.8	1.6	2.6	33.0	64.4
Flower Mound town.......	1 050	12.0	22.9	26 186	84.1	7.3	0.5	1.3	0.5	0.9	13.0	86.1
Fort Worth city..............	559	14.7	27.7	235 799	77.0	16.7	1.5	1.1	1.7	8.7	40.4	50.9
Friendswood city	855	12.7	29.3	14 168	85.5	8.0	0.7	0.6	0.9	3.1	24.3	72.6
Frisco city	850	12.4	28.2	18 068	85.0	8.9	0.3	0.8	0.6	1.9	21.4	76.7
Galveston city..............	531	17.6	33.5	23 791	65.7	18.0	3.4	4.2	6.6	17.8	47.1	35.1
Garland city	672	13.6	24.4	104 420	78.3	15.2	2.0	1.1	1.0	4.8	33.1	62.1
Georgetown city	669	13.5	27.0	12 691	79.6	11.3	0.1	1.5	3.5	4.1	34.2	61.6
Grand Prairie city	642	13.1	24.8	59 938	81.4	14.2	0.3	1.1	1.1	4.9	33.3	61.8
Grapevine city	764	10.8	19.8	23 339	82.7	11.3	0.2	1.1	0.6	3.5	28.5	68.0
Haltom City city	569	12.3	21.5	19 051	80.1	15.6	0.1	0.9	1.3	4.9	39.1	56.0
Harlingen city	455	12.9	27.5	19 381	76.9	17.4	0.2	1.4	1.4	11.2	42.8	46.0
Houston city	575	15.6	27.0	841 686	71.8	15.9	5.9	1.7	2.3	11.6	44.3	44.1
Huntsville city	515	11.5	40.7	12 184	77.2	15.6	0.3	1.4	4.1	10.1	40.1	49.9
Hurst city	632	9.5	25.9	18 512	83.2	10.7	0.4	1.6	1.6	4.3	32.0	63.6
Irving city	714	12.4	21.5	102 717	77.9	14.7	2.3	1.2	1.7	5.7	45.1	49.2
Keller city....................	792	10.2	29.3	13 531	85.2	6.9	0.1	0.7	1.0	1.7	13.9	84.4
Killeen city	559	16.6	23.7	42 833	80.8	14.4	0.4	1.5	1.9	6.4	42.0	51.6
Kingsville city...............	446	14.3	33.8	10 062	75.1	15.4	0.3	2.4	5.5	13.5	40.4	46.1
Lake Jackson city.........	595	8.0	26.3	12 050	86.2	9.8	0.2	0.8	0.6	4.5	27.9	67.6
Lancaster city	671	16.8	23.6	11 605	80.0	14.8	1.5	0.5	0.9	5.2	37.9	56.9

Table C-5. Cities — **Migration, Housing, and Transportation**

STATE Place code	City	Total population 5 years and over	Residence in 1995 (percent)					Occupied housing units		Householders 65 years and over	
			Same house	Same county, different house	Same state, different county	Different state	Outside the United States	Number	Percent owner-occupied	Number	Percent owner-occupied
		1	2	3	4	5	6	7	8	9	10
	TEXAS—Cont'd										
48 41440	La Porte city	29 565	53.6	34.4	7.3	3.4	1.3	10 905	77.5	1 175	82.3
48 41464	Laredo city	158 427	57.7	29.4	4.8	2.5	5.7	46 907	64.4	8 015	74.1
48 41980	League City city	41 608	47.0	17.5	21.7	11.3	2.5	16 168	77.2	1 499	80.9
48 42508	Lewisville city	70 433	32.2	22.5	26.4	14.7	4.2	30 025	53.8	2 253	68.1
48 43888	Longview city	67 767	50.4	26.8	14.6	6.7	1.5	28 311	58.4	6 806	74.4
48 45000	Lubbock city	185 551	45.7	29.9	17.4	5.8	1.3	77 500	55.8	14 569	80.5
48 45072	Lufkin city	30 160	52.0	28.9	13.5	3.9	1.8	12 241	60.1	3 103	77.7
48 45384	McAllen city	97 025	54.7	28.7	6.1	5.6	5.0	33 101	63.4	7 005	79.0
48 45744	McKinney city	48 902	29.7	25.6	21.4	17.7	5.5	18 178	70.6	2 188	78.7
48 46452	Mansfield city	26 488	42.3	31.3	11.4	12.2	2.7	9 136	87.3	1 001	87.9
48 47892	Mesquite city	115 260	49.3	36.0	7.2	5.2	2.2	44 077	65.5	5 457	78.6
48 48072	Midland city	88 127	52.9	26.2	13.6	5.7	1.5	35 698	66.0	7 761	78.4
48 48768	Mission city	41 689	54.7	28.6	6.5	4.9	5.3	13 863	74.9	3 940	86.5
48 48804	Missouri City city	48 641	54.9	17.8	17.8	6.7	2.9	17 024	91.0	1 418	90.8
48 50256	Nacogdoches city	28 621	40.5	21.1	30.8	4.6	3.0	11 264	44.0	2 018	72.0
48 50820	New Braunfels city	34 241	48.1	21.9	21.5	6.6	1.9	13 647	64.8	3 734	79.8
48 52356	North Richland Hills city	51 647	49.1	30.0	9.4	9.3	2.1	20 724	67.3	3 069	80.7
48 53388	Odessa city	83 665	54.6	30.3	9.7	4.0	1.3	33 680	64.2	6 841	79.9
48 55080	Paris city	23 942	41.8	36.3	11.5	8.9	1.6	10 542	54.0	3 050	71.2
48 56000	Pasadena city	128 775	47.8	38.0	5.3	4.0	4.9	47 063	56.0	7 191	78.8
48 56348	Pearland city	34 684	52.1	17.0	24.7	5.1	1.1	13 150	79.6	1 897	87.0
48 57200	Pharr city	41 723	61.3	26.8	2.9	4.7	4.3	12 810	73.0	3 646	82.9
48 58016	Plano city	204 045	39.7	19.1	19.5	16.3	5.3	80 916	68.9	6 289	67.1
48 58820	Port Arthur city	53 336	59.3	27.8	6.1	4.4	2.3	21 834	62.2	6 585	76.7
48 61796	Richardson city	85 459	47.2	23.2	14.6	8.9	6.2	35 039	64.5	5 228	83.7
48 63500	Round Rock city	54 482	34.2	19.3	28.7	15.0	2.7	20 935	65.3	1 494	68.3
48 63572	Rowlett city	40 462	49.7	29.0	12.2	8.0	1.1	14 248	92.1	1 143	93.9
48 64472	San Angelo city	82 541	46.3	27.4	15.3	8.7	2.3	34 045	60.8	8 205	76.1
48 65000	San Antonio city	1 052 750	51.0	31.8	6.9	7.3	3.0	405 544	58.1	77 925	77.5
48 65516	San Juan city	23 220	64.4	26.4	1.3	3.1	4.9	6 615	77.4	1 251	81.9
48 65600	San Marcos city	32 324	28.6	18.0	45.8	5.9	1.8	12 627	30.1	1 508	63.5
48 67496	Sherman city	32 461	44.7	29.3	14.8	8.6	2.6	13 741	56.2	3 537	73.2
48 68636	Socorro city	25 210	73.8	19.2	0.6	1.9	4.5	6 916	81.9	936	87.6
48 70808	Sugar Land city	59 649	58.7	13.8	14.9	7.5	5.0	20 612	84.5	2 012	87.6
48 72176	Temple city	50 320	44.1	32.6	13.7	7.8	1.8	21 500	55.7	5 420	70.2
48 72368	Texarkana city	32 367	48.9	29.0	7.4	13.9	0.8	13 578	58.8	3 367	79.7
48 72392	Texas City city	38 664	56.5	31.7	7.5	2.6	1.6	15 447	63.4	3 557	80.9
48 72530	The Colony city	24 471	50.8	19.9	17.9	10.1	1.3	8 483	82.2	451	83.4
48 74144	Tyler city	77 655	47.9	28.4	14.6	5.9	3.2	32 705	56.0	8 072	73.7
48 75428	Victoria city	55 843	48.9	32.6	13.0	3.8	1.6	22 104	60.8	4 810	77.7
48 76000	Waco city	105 493	41.7	30.1	18.5	7.0	2.7	42 341	46.3	10 057	73.2
48 77272	Weslaco city	24 339	61.7	27.4	4.3	4.8	1.9	8 197	65.5	2 711	76.2
48 79000	Wichita Falls city	96 586	42.9	26.4	12.5	15.4	2.8	37 878	57.7	8 323	77.5
49 00000	UTAH	2 023 875	49.3	26.6	8.9	12.0	3.2	701 281	71.5	121 340	86.4
49 07690	Bountiful city	37 917	58.9	21.1	10.7	8.1	1.3	13 323	77.9	3 518	90.9
49 13850	Clearfield city	22 702	37.8	24.0	13.5	20.0	4.7	7 918	55.6	942	88.0
49 20120	Draper city	22 829	30.6	40.4	10.3	17.4	1.3	6 319	83.9	410	88.8
49 43660	Layton city	52 695	46.7	22.1	12.3	16.4	2.5	18 250	74.6	2 117	91.4
49 45860	Logan city	38 703	28.1	23.6	21.5	20.8	6.1	13 941	44.2	1 799	86.4
49 49710	Midvale city	24 409	39.2	31.5	6.5	14.5	8.3	10 125	47.9	1 823	85.9
49 53230	Murray city	31 325	51.4	33.2	4.5	7.9	2.9	12 654	67.0	2 678	85.7
49 55980	Ogden city	69 982	44.7	28.5	10.0	12.3	4.5	27 393	61.2	5 808	78.4
49 57300	Orem city	75 356	50.1	27.0	6.1	12.4	4.3	23 386	67.0	3 329	88.9
49 62470	Provo city	96 213	27.6	24.2	9.0	31.6	7.6	29 225	42.7	3 651	84.1
49 64340	Riverton city	22 085	50.4	36.1	5.0	8.0	0.5	6 395	94.8	522	92.9
49 65110	Roy city	29 563	50.6	24.0	14.1	9.2	2.1	10 663	84.1	1 763	94.8
49 65330	St. George city	45 340	39.3	24.5	16.9	16.9	2.4	17 359	67.9	5 887	88.4
49 67000	Salt Lake City city	167 221	43.1	29.4	6.0	13.4	8.1	71 402	51.2	13 938	72.3
49 67440	Sandy city	81 377	59.5	25.0	3.2	10.8	1.4	25 701	84.3	2 749	84.8
49 70850	South Jordan city	26 878	53.9	33.3	3.1	8.7	1.1	7 556	89.5	817	79.1
49 75360	Taylorsville city	52 978	53.0	31.7	4.4	7.5	3.4	18 578	71.1	2 254	93.1
49 82950	West Jordan city	60 548	46.9	37.1	4.1	10.2	1.6	18 863	81.9	1 407	85.0
49 83470	West Valley City city	97 050	49.1	33.3	4.0	8.4	5.1	32 263	72.6	3 543	82.6
50 00000	VERMONT	574 842	59.1	21.2	6.3	12.1	1.3	240 634	70.6	50 395	76.7
50 10675	Burlington city	37 203	37.2	26.7	9.0	22.5	4.6	15 885	41.5	2 578	63.4

Table C-5. Cities — **Migration, Housing, and Transportation**

City	Owner-occupied by household type (percent)								Median household income			Median monthly owner costs as a percent of income		
	Family households					Nonfamily households								
		Married-couple family		Other family										
	Total family households	Total	With own children under 18 years	Total	With own children under 18 years	Total nonfamily households	Two or more adults	Living alone	All households	Owner-occupied households	Renter-occupied households	Median housing value (owner estimated)	With a mortgage	Without a mortgage
	11	12	13	14	15	16	17	18	19	20	21	22	23	24
TEXAS—Cont'd														
La Porte city	81.0	85.0	84.2	62.1	56.8	64.4	57.8	65.8	55 621	61 712	36 444	80 500	18.5	11.9
Laredo city	67.3	72.2	68.8	52.5	40.6	46.8	41.3	47.4	29 043	36 043	18 238	70 400	24.0	12.6
League City city	83.2	86.3	85.7	64.8	62.1	56.4	47.4	58.5	67 799	73 520	46 330	109 200	20.6	11.7
Lewisville city	66.5	72.5	73.9	42.3	36.4	29.6	22.2	32.2	54 607	70 483	40 216	111 900	19.8	11.2
Longview city	66.5	76.6	68.9	40.3	29.4	41.5	26.3	43.7	33 280	44 438	23 086	74 300	19.2	10.2
Lubbock city	67.0	75.0	70.1	44.6	33.5	36.7	20.9	41.5	31 721	44 520	20 483	67 900	19.5	10.2
Lufkin city	67.0	77.0	69.6	41.1	32.0	45.2	17.1	49.3	32 133	41 368	20 519	65 500	19.2	11.1
McAllen city	68.1	72.8	68.0	53.0	40.9	46.0	34.6	48.0	33 435	41 453	21 613	69 800	21.5	11.8
McKinney city	77.9	84.2	84.8	46.4	43.0	45.1	27.3	48.2	62 371	77 550	32 415	145 400	22.1	12.5
Mansfield city	88.7	91.0	89.9	72.7	68.3	78.0	71.8	79.4	66 901	72 050	36 685	119 700	21.3	11.4
Mesquite city	72.4	79.3	75.9	50.3	42.2	45.1	45.5	45.0	50 368	60 459	34 367	85 400	20.1	10.4
Midland city	75.0	81.5	77.7	50.2	40.5	44.1	29.7	45.8	39 041	50 675	24 006	71 400	19.4	11.2
Mission city	76.0	81.7	74.5	56.4	43.5	70.2	66.1	70.6	29 707	34 474	14 757	56 100	23.8	11.7
Missouri City city	92.1	93.4	92.1	86.1	83.7	84.1	82.5	84.3	72 455	76 343	41 885	111 200	20.6	10.0
Nacogdoches city	60.0	73.8	70.4	31.1	24.2	25.2	4.5	33.5	23 278	42 518	13 226	73 500	18.8	9.9
New Braunfels city	71.0	77.3	70.4	49.1	34.0	49.3	28.5	52.3	39 504	45 201	30 035	89 200	20.2	9.9
North Richland Hills city	75.4	81.1	76.5	51.4	43.4	43.9	35.2	46.2	56 245	67 271	37 068	98 900	19.7	10.4
Odessa city	72.1	80.8	76.4	47.3	39.6	44.8	32.5	46.5	30 983	38 558	20 384	46 500	19.2	11.7
Paris city	57.6	68.9	56.7	34.0	22.7	47.5	31.0	49.1	27 259	36 372	19 503	51 800	18.6	13.2
Pasadena city	60.4	67.3	60.7	39.9	30.7	42.7	30.7	45.2	38 178	50 626	27 477	67 600	20.0	10.5
Pearland city	83.9	89.3	88.9	56.6	45.7	60.7	57.0	61.5	62 584	70 966	36 241	114 100	19.3	11.5
Pharr city	75.3	78.2	71.0	65.1	49.3	59.4	58.5	59.5	24 274	29 164	13 667	39 900	23.9	12.1
Plano city	78.7	83.3	84.2	48.9	45.3	39.0	36.2	39.6	77 935	97 020	46 558	161 200	19.9	9.9
Port Arthur city	66.7	78.7	71.0	45.7	30.5	52.6	37.6	54.1	26 236	32 784	16 793	35 700	18.7	11.5
Richardson city	73.2	78.0	75.2	48.5	42.8	43.8	25.5	49.1	62 291	75 849	43 577	130 500	19.8	9.9
Round Rock city	73.0	78.6	78.6	48.1	42.5	41.3	43.7	40.5	60 313	69 260	38 926	119 200	20.4	9.9
Rowlett city	92.9	94.3	93.0	83.3	82.6	86.4	90.8	85.6	71 125	72 129	47 692	116 800	21.1	11.9
San Angelo city	69.4	76.0	69.0	48.8	37.2	43.6	28.0	46.2	32 145	40 395	22 433	61 000	19.7	10.4
San Antonio city	65.8	73.1	67.0	48.7	35.2	40.4	32.0	42.3	36 136	46 342	25 909	67 500	20.5	10.1
San Juan city	78.4	81.9	79.6	66.2	52.8	68.7	34.7	74.3	22 687	26 184	12 361	41 100	25.2	13.7
San Marcos city	51.4	59.0	46.7	35.1	28.9	14.2	5.6	21.4	25 552	42 128	19 721	76 000	22.3	11.0
Sherman city	65.0	71.7	61.0	45.1	33.2	40.5	25.1	43.1	34 381	43 598	25 507	67 500	19.6	11.1
Socorro city	82.8	84.8	82.1	75.9	70.8	71.7	70.1	72.0	23 932	25 731	16 187	48 700	26.3	12.1
Sugar Land city	88.2	91.0	90.5	70.3	66.7	62.6	69.6	61.4	82 273	89 945	42 610	158 300	19.4	10.8
Temple city	65.2	73.7	65.2	38.9	30.1	37.4	36.0	37.6	34 996	46 754	24 842	74 400	19.6	10.2
Texarkana city	64.5	80.1	74.2	37.1	21.3	47.6	32.7	49.6	30 152	41 568	18 397	64 300	19.5	10.1
Texas City city	70.1	78.2	73.0	50.8	34.6	46.6	39.9	47.7	35 647	45 805	22 415	62 800	19.5	12.0
The Colony city	82.3	85.1	84.3	66.7	63.3	81.5	78.5	82.8	64 146	66 078	53 355	95 700	20.5	11.5
Tyler city	64.9	75.0	69.1	38.2	26.9	39.7	19.1	42.9	33 828	48 654	23 392	80 100	19.8	10.7
Victoria city	67.3	75.4	67.4	42.7	31.7	44.0	28.4	46.6	36 046	46 979	25 604	69 400	19.0	11.1
Waco city	56.6	67.3	58.1	35.2	22.1	31.6	13.2	37.5	25 993	37 419	17 639	53 200	20.5	11.6
Weslaco city	69.6	74.4	64.2	56.1	33.0	49.1	45.5	49.5	26 680	33 052	16 394	45 300	22.4	10.9
Wichita Falls city	65.0	71.4	62.7	43.6	32.8	43.5	31.0	45.8	32 634	41 558	24 454	60 900	20.0	10.9
UTAH	77.3	81.4	80.5	57.0	48.3	52.5	31.8	58.9	45 661	53 701	28 733	142 600	22.9	9.9
Bountiful city	81.7	84.6	82.2	62.1	44.7	61.6	30.9	65.9	55 885	64 350	35 790	173 700	21.1	9.9
Clearfield city	56.9	63.1	57.4	37.2	24.7	50.3	33.2	54.4	38 996	46 753	30 246	111 000	23.4	9.9
Draper city	87.9	89.8	90.7	70.6	61.9	57.3	43.4	60.4	72 603	80 151	34 180	241 600	24.4	9.9
Layton city	80.5	85.4	85.3	56.4	46.0	49.7	43.6	51.4	52 109	60 920	31 046	142 900	21.6	9.9
Logan city	52.7	54.3	58.3	44.1	34.3	27.5	7.8	44.9	30 735	45 238	23 944	115 300	21.6	9.9
Midvale city	52.4	58.1	45.6	38.3	23.9	39.1	19.7	45.6	39 483	47 681	32 777	140 400	23.7	9.9
Murray city	72.6	78.3	77.6	50.2	41.1	54.5	31.9	60.5	45 305	52 814	34 487	151 200	22.8	9.9
Ogden city	67.6	74.8	69.5	47.1	36.2	47.6	35.9	50.3	34 370	42 800	21 692	99 200	23.2	9.9
Orem city	70.7	73.4	74.2	56.3	46.5	50.4	26.0	61.3	47 150	57 362	30 456	150 800	21.7	9.9
Provo city	50.9	53.0	58.8	39.7	35.5	24.6	8.7	51.3	34 042	50 861	25 255	144 900	25.1	9.9
Riverton city	95.3	96.7	97.0	82.4	79.9	88.9	72.6	92.5	63 560	64 621	41 250	173 300	24.3	9.9
Roy city	86.0	89.9	88.9	67.9	59.5	76.3	50.8	80.8	49 312	52 289	33 281	121 000	22.6	9.9
St. George city	72.1	77.4	69.0	40.3	31.6	55.1	26.5	62.2	36 946	43 283	26 178	135 100	25.4	9.9
Salt Lake City city	61.4	66.6	64.2	46.6	38.7	38.2	29.6	40.9	36 616	52 525	24 887	152 400	23.2	9.9
Sandy city	87.8	89.8	90.2	74.4	68.9	64.4	57.8	66.5	66 489	72 059	38 641	180 700	21.8	9.9
South Jordan city	93.0	94.3	95.2	78.3	68.5	52.5	75.7	47.9	75 127	77 135	42 375	222 700	23.2	9.9
Taylorsville city	74.7	80.1	78.5	55.3	46.9	58.4	35.0	65.9	47 012	54 174	33 438	134 500	21.7	9.9
West Jordan city	84.8	87.9	88.4	67.4	63.4	64.5	51.2	69.2	55 673	60 189	32 802	152 600	23.8	9.9
West Valley City city	76.7	82.5	80.2	57.6	48.6	55.6	49.0	57.7	45 651	51 136	29 822	125 400	23.3	9.9
VERMONT	80.4	85.8	83.7	57.4	49.5	51.6	44.4	53.8	40 750	48 440	25 163	111 200	22.4	13.9
Burlington city	61.3	70.8	65.8	36.9	27.8	25.6	16.6	30.6	33 020	53 138	22 730	127 600	22.3	12.8

Table C-5. Cities — **Migration, Housing, and Transportation**

City	Percent who pay 35 percent or more of income for housing expenses			Means of transportation to work (percent except where noted)						Vehicles available (percent of households)		
				Car, truck, or van								
	Median gross rent	Owners	Renters	Number of workers 16 years and over	Drove alone	Carpooled	Public transportation	Other means	Walked	No vehicles	One vehicle	Two or more vehicles
	25	26	27	28	29	30	31	32	33	34	35	36
TEXAS—Cont'd												
La Porte city	625	11.2	20.0	15 529	86.1	9.7	0.4	1.4	1.1	3.9	28.2	67.9
Laredo city	454	19.6	31.2	57 382	72.0	18.8	2.5	1.7	2.0	12.3	36.5	51.1
League City city	768	12.3	20.2	23 307	83.7	10.2	1.2	1.2	0.8	2.4	24.9	72.7
Lewisville city	783	11.0	22.7	44 984	82.9	12.6	0.5	0.7	0.9	3.9	33.5	62.6
Longview city	477	12.1	28.3	31 110	82.9	11.8	0.2	1.1	1.5	7.8	41.0	51.2
Lubbock city	514	12.8	37.5	93 289	80.5	12.9	1.1	1.1	2.0	7.1	39.7	53.1
Lufkin city	479	12.5	35.1	13 550	78.6	16.5	0.1	1.4	1.0	10.1	39.3	50.6
McAllen city	487	16.7	28.6	39 868	77.1	16.5	0.4	1.8	1.5	8.5	38.2	53.3
McKinney city	678	15.4	27.4	26 001	80.5	13.2	0.4	0.6	1.4	4.4	28.2	67.4
Mansfield city	647	12.4	14.8	14 215	85.9	10.1	0.2	0.5	0.7	1.9	18.1	80.0
Mesquite city	691	12.1	24.8	63 335	81.0	14.5	0.7	0.7	0.8	4.7	33.4	61.9
Midland city	464	12.2	26.3	41 873	83.3	12.3	0.2	0.9	1.0	6.5	36.8	56.6
Mission city	380	16.9	30.2	14 598	77.3	17.3	0.1	2.3	1.2	9.4	41.0	49.7
Missouri City city	893	14.8	25.8	26 500	83.8	11.4	1.7	0.6	0.3	0.9	21.7	77.4
Nacogdoches city	478	12.9	44.3	12 871	77.0	13.6	0.4	2.0	4.7	10.4	44.1	45.5
New Braunfels city	635	11.1	29.3	16 694	81.1	13.0	0.1	1.2	1.7	6.2	36.6	57.1
North Richland Hills city	702	12.1	22.0	29 686	86.7	8.7	0.1	1.0	0.9	3.4	29.3	67.3
Odessa city	404	12.0	26.2	37 111	82.1	12.7	0.2	1.3	1.4	8.0	40.8	51.2
Paris city	436	15.8	30.7	10 135	80.4	13.9	0.3	1.3	2.4	12.8	42.1	45.1
Pasadena city	534	12.3	27.8	57 462	78.6	16.2	0.6	1.4	1.8	7.4	37.5	55.0
Pearland city	672	11.2	24.2	19 156	87.8	8.3	0.6	0.6	0.8	2.7	24.7	72.6
Pharr city	372	15.7	32.3	14 148	73.0	19.8	0.8	3.1	1.4	11.3	40.6	48.0
Plano city	862	12.4	22.2	118 835	83.1	8.9	1.1	0.9	1.2	2.4	27.0	70.6
Port Arthur city	405	13.6	29.0	19 203	75.4	18.1	0.9	2.2	2.0	15.8	42.2	42.0
Richardson city	827	12.5	25.3	48 908	81.9	9.5	1.7	0.7	1.8	3.4	31.2	65.4
Round Rock city	812	10.1	25.3	31 712	82.9	12.8	0.2	1.0	0.5	3.1	28.9	68.0
Rowlett city	900	11.9	24.2	22 817	84.7	10.3	1.3	0.7	0.4	1.6	17.0	81.4
San Angelo city	458	12.3	29.0	40 184	78.8	12.9	0.4	1.2	4.5	7.6	39.6	52.8
San Antonio city	549	13.9	28.0	491 435	75.6	15.2	3.8	1.1	2.2	10.6	38.9	50.5
San Juan city	364	19.8	33.1	7 733	72.2	20.5	0.8	3.4	1.5	9.1	37.6	53.3
San Marcos city	622	17.4	47.3	18 154	72.9	14.0	1.3	1.9	8.0	7.7	41.4	50.9
Sherman city	538	12.9	28.5	15 255	78.5	15.1	0.2	0.8	3.1	8.2	39.1	52.7
Socorro city	399	16.6	32.0	8 369	75.8	19.0	0.3	2.0	0.7	7.6	31.6	60.9
Sugar Land city	939	15.4	26.9	30 510	84.3	9.3	1.4	0.6	0.2	1.3	20.9	77.9
Temple city	522	12.0	28.1	23 976	79.7	14.6	0.3	0.8	2.6	10.4	39.2	50.4
Texarkana city	470	13.8	30.8	13 357	82.2	11.5	0.4	1.2	2.2	14.0	37.3	48.6
Texas City city	533	13.4	29.8	16 946	79.8	15.1	0.6	1.5	1.4	9.1	37.0	54.0
The Colony city	986	10.2	20.3	14 222	85.8	9.9	0.3	0.7	0.2	2.3	19.3	78.4
Tyler city	514	14.1	32.2	36 809	79.5	14.7	0.6	1.8	1.4	9.4	40.9	49.7
Victoria city	512	10.9	25.3	27 301	76.5	18.8	0.1	1.1	1.5	8.3	38.1	53.6
Waco city	490	13.0	37.4	44 589	74.7	16.4	1.4	1.6	3.5	11.7	44.3	44.0
Weslaco city	398	14.9	27.8	8 505	75.5	17.0	0.3	2.5	3.4	14.9	42.1	43.0
Wichita Falls city	489	12.5	25.9	47 765	76.6	10.7	0.5	1.2	9.1	7.6	38.7	53.7
UTAH	597	16.2	27.7	1 032 858	75.5	14.1	2.2	1.2	2.8	5.1	26.9	68.0
Bountiful city	644	11.0	22.9	19 332	81.1	9.4	2.6	0.7	1.2	3.5	23.3	73.2
Clearfield city	622	15.5	23.7	11 561	78.9	13.8	1.9	0.9	2.3	4.6	32.7	62.8
Draper city	742	21.1	29.4	10 740	81.6	8.9	1.8	0.6	0.7	1.3	17.3	81.5
Layton city	630	12.8	26.9	28 700	77.9	14.6	1.9	1.1	1.2	3.4	25.1	71.5
Logan city	499	12.6	28.8	21 667	70.3	14.6	2.8	2.1	7.0	5.7	32.3	62.0
Midvale city	655	17.4	25.7	14 345	70.7	18.1	5.1	1.1	2.8	8.1	38.5	53.4
Murray city	656	15.6	26.1	17 422	76.3	11.5	4.5	0.6	2.4	5.4	34.6	60.0
Ogden city	504	16.9	31.0	33 789	73.1	17.7	2.3	1.5	2.6	10.7	34.8	54.6
Orem city	639	15.3	27.6	37 687	75.6	15.3	1.4	0.8	1.6	2.9	25.9	71.1
Provo city	521	18.8	32.6	51 013	63.2	15.5	1.8	2.5	12.8	5.3	31.3	63.5
Riverton city	713	17.1	22.7	11 253	80.9	11.0	1.4	0.9	0.3	0.5	12.0	87.5
Roy city	611	16.3	19.1	16 117	83.4	11.7	0.7	0.6	0.8	3.5	24.5	72.0
St. George city	591	18.2	31.8	19 818	75.9	15.4	0.2	1.2	2.4	4.6	36.0	59.5
Salt Lake City city	564	17.8	30.8	90 187	69.3	13.9	6.3	2.3	4.9	12.7	40.2	47.1
Sandy city	768	15.7	24.7	44 232	78.3	11.3	3.2	1.2	0.6	2.4	18.1	79.5
South Jordan city	1 049	13.9	33.6	13 583	81.8	9.3	1.7	0.8	0.4	2.3	12.4	85.3
Taylorsville city	681	14.7	26.3	30 145	80.0	13.1	2.1	0.6	0.9	3.5	27.7	68.9
West Jordan city	730	18.4	25.8	33 934	79.9	12.3	2.3	1.0	0.9	2.5	18.5	78.9
West Valley City city	643	17.7	32.8	50 957	76.6	16.6	2.2	1.0	1.2	5.3	27.7	67.1
VERMONT	553	16.2	29.5	311 839	75.2	11.9	0.7	0.9	5.6	6.8	33.6	59.5
Burlington city	618	14.0	37.6	20 848	62.4	12.0	3.8	1.8	16.8	14.8	42.2	43.0

Table C-5. Cities — **Migration, Housing, and Transportation**

STATE Place code	City	Total population 5 years and over	Residence in 1995 (percent)					Occupied housing units		Householders 65 years and over	
			Same house	Same county, different house	Same state, different county	Different state	Outside the United States	Number	Percent owner-occupied	Number	Percent owner-occupied
		1	2	3	4	5	6	7	8	9	10
51 00000	VIRGINIA..............	6 619 266	52.2	18.1	14.2	12.4	3.1	2 699 173	68.1	511 589	80.1
51 01000	Alexandria city.............	120 272	36.7	15.6	16.6	21.7	9.5	61 889	40.0	7 582	60.3
51 07784	Blacksburg town...........	38 179	20.2	12.0	40.2	21.1	6.5	13 143	30.0	1 100	79.8
51 14968	Charlottesville city........	43 051	35.1	8.7	33.6	18.2	4.4	16 851	40.9	2 865	76.3
51 16000	Chesapeake city.............	185 025	51.9	17.7	16.2	12.6	1.6	69 900	74.9	10 977	81.6
51 21344	Danville city.............	45 553	60.0	12.9	19.5	6.8	0.8	20 607	58.0	6 610	72.8
51 35000	Hampton city.............	137 303	47.7	19.3	12.0	18.0	3.0	53 887	58.6	9 910	81.8
51 35624	Harrisonburg city...........	38 524	33.2	4.5	41.3	16.0	5.1	13 133	39.1	2 115	63.6
51 44984	Leesburg town..............	25 520	39.0	23.0	15.1	19.2	3.7	10 325	67.9	957	69.1
51 47672	Lynchburg city.............	61 433	51.6	20.5	13.7	12.3	2.0	25 477	58.5	6 817	70.9
51 48952	Manassas city.............	32 021	48.4	5.6	28.9	12.7	4.4	11 757	69.8	1 200	80.8
51 56000	Newport News city.......	165 897	45.5	22.9	12.5	16.1	3.1	69 686	52.4	12 096	73.9
51 57000	Norfolk city.............	217 818	42.7	23.3	11.8	19.7	2.5	86 210	45.6	17 601	70.1
51 61832	Petersburg city.............	31 517	55.6	23.6	11.6	7.6	1.6	13 799	51.5	3 609	71.8
51 64000	Portsmouth city.............	93 508	51.4	23.4	14.2	10.0	1.0	38 170	58.5	9 434	75.8
51 67000	Richmond city.............	185 379	48.0	25.3	15.7	8.7	2.3	84 549	46.1	18 247	64.3
51 68000	Roanoke city.............	88 721	53.4	24.4	12.7	8.0	1.4	42 003	56.3	10 404	71.4
51 76432	Suffolk city.............	59 081	53.4	17.5	18.5	9.7	1.0	23 283	72.2	4 870	81.7
51 82000	Virginia Beach city........	394 892	45.8	24.3	8.6	18.3	2.9	154 455	65.6	22 067	78.9
53 00000	WASHINGTON..........	5 501 398	48.6	27.5	9.5	11.2	3.2	2 271 398	64.6	430 394	77.2
53 03180	Auburn city................	37 102	39.0	37.8	9.3	8.6	5.2	16 060	53.9	2 871	72.4
53 05210	Bellevue city.............	103 087	46.9	27.6	4.3	12.8	8.4	45 687	61.3	9 291	74.3
53 05280	Bellingham city............	63 389	34.8	27.6	23.3	11.4	2.9	27 949	47.9	5 539	69.0
53 07380	Bothell city.............	27 913	51.9	20.0	14.9	10.4	2.9	11 951	68.0	1 781	82.4
53 07695	Bremerton city.............	34 022	35.8	29.9	8.7	22.5	3.0	15 085	40.6	3 066	60.0
53 08850	Burien city.............	29 956	52.3	34.2	3.2	6.4	3.9	13 437	56.6	3 043	72.1
53 17635	Des Moines city............	27 491	40.2	33.0	5.7	9.3	2.8	11 375	61.3	2 036	81.6
53 20750	Edmonds city................	37 598	54.3	18.7	15.5	8.7	2.8	16 936	68.3	4 179	79.0
53 22640	Everett city.............	84 120	39.1	33.2	10.2	13.3	4.2	36 355	45.9	5 949	63.8
53 23515	Federal Way city.........	76 700	42.4	30.7	8.9	12.1	5.9	31 468	56.2	4 117	73.4
53 35275	Kennewick city.............	50 556	46.0	26.8	12.4	11.3	2.4	20 869	59.6	3 906	72.3
53 35415	Kent city.............	72 774	36.9	37.2	6.2	13.9	5.8	31 138	48.9	3 748	59.0
53 35940	Kirkland city.............	42 500	41.3	32.3	6.6	15.2	4.6	20 823	56.7	2 989	74.6
53 36745	Lacey city.............	28 625	39.9	27.3	11.8	18.3	2.7	12 371	55.7	3 020	63.2
53 38038	Lakewood city.............	54 044	42.3	30.8	6.7	15.4	4.7	23 763	47.5	4 885	82.2
53 40245	Longview city.............	32 259	49.0	32.4	0.7	10.5	1.5	14 040	67.0	3 660	67.8
53 40840	Lynnwood city.............	31 424	45.2	22.4	15.7	9.7	7.1	13 261	52.8	2 403	62.0
53 43955	Marysville city.............	23 140	39.1	37.3	11.1	11.1	1.5	9 392	63.0	2 106	64.4
53 47560	Mount Vernon city........	24 130	39.9	27.4	14.6	10.8	7.2	9 308	57.2	2 118	68.5
53 51300	Olympia city.............	39 974	41.1	28.4	13.4	14.2	2.9	18 682	50.6	3 696	68.3
53 53545	Pasco city.............	28 475	44.8	25.1	13.4	8.5	8.3	9 614	59.7	1 646	75.5
53 56695	Puyallup city.............	30 290	44.6	34.4	10.1	9.3	1.6	12 775	54.9	2 171	60.7
53 57535	Redmond city.............	42 622	40.2	27.7	5.6	17.4	9.1	19 129	55.3	2 358	59.7
53 57745	Renton city.............	46 480	41.8	33.5	5.7	12.8	6.2	21 689	50.4	3 351	60.7
53 58235	Richland city.............	36 153	51.4	24.3	9.5	11.9	2.9	15 530	66.3	3 558	79.2
53 61115	Sammamish city.............	31 451	48.1	27.8	3.0	17.7	3.3	11 146	89.9	773	94.6
53 62288	SeaTac city.............	23 964	44.2	33.9	5.0	8.9	7.9	9 690	54.0	1 560	86.0
53 63000	Seattle city.............	537 538	44.1	30.2	6.9	14.0	4.8	258 510	48.4	45 947	66.3
53 63960	Shoreline city.............	50 189	55.7	25.5	7.7	6.9	4.2	20 735	68.1	4 445	77.5
53 67000	Spokane city.............	182 420	48.0	32.1	7.3	10.1	2.5	81 674	58.9	18 145	71.5
53 70000	Tacoma city.............	179 684	47.8	30.5	9.2	8.8	3.7	76 110	54.8	14 805	64.2
53 73465	University Place city......	28 247	47.0	31.9	7.5	10.1	3.4	12 176	57.9	2 229	77.3
53 74060	Vancouver city.............	131 474	38.0	29.6	6.2	21.6	4.6	56 640	53.1	10 135	69.6
53 75775	Walla Walla city...........	28 033	49.0	25.4	10.2	10.9	4.5	10 633	59.5	3 140	67.8
53 77105	Wenatchee city.............	25 861	45.9	29.4	14.0	6.9	3.8	10 781	57.5	3 015	68.7
53 80010	Yakima city.............	65 994	46.6	36.8	6.1	7.7	2.9	26 610	53.4	6 834	67.0
54 00000	WEST VIRGINIA........	1 706 931	63.3	21.0	7.0	8.1	0.5	736 481	75.2	190 182	84.0
54 14600	Charleston city.............	50 297	56.0	28.6	6.2	8.4	0.9	24 473	58.0	6 525	72.9
54 39460	Huntington city.............	48 960	51.7	24.5	12.8	10.2	0.9	22 965	54.7	6 494	74.3
54 55756	Morgantown city.............	26 370	33.2	15.6	22.0	25.0	4.2	10 873	40.8	1 984	78.6
54 62140	Parkersburg city.............	31 276	54.2	31.4	4.5	9.3	0.5	14 483	61.9	4 336	74.7
54 86452	Wheeling city.............	29 804	60.9	22.1	6.2	10.0	0.8	13 652	62.6	4 572	70.0
55 00000	WISCONSIN..........	5 022 073	56.5	24.6	11.0	6.7	1.3	2 084 544	68.4	457 976	74.7
55 02375	Appleton city................	65 309	53.6	21.0	15.1	7.9	2.3	26 780	68.8	5 104	75.7
55 06500	Beloit city.............	32 947	50.7	31.3	4.1	11.2	2.7	13 364	62.1	3 151	71.1
55 10025	Brookfield city.............	36 625	63.7	12.5	15.7	6.6	1.5	13 947	90.0	3 907	86.8
55 22300	Eau Claire city.............	58 153	45.5	24.7	19.0	10.0	0.8	23 911	57.4	4 844	72.6
55 26275	Fond du Lac city...........	39 733	50.5	31.0	10.0	6.1	2.4	16 679	62.0	3 772	69.8

Table C-5. Cities — Migration, Housing, and Transportation

City	Owner-occupied by household type (percent)								Median household income			Median housing value (owner estimated)	Median monthly owner costs as a percent of income	
	Family households					Nonfamily households								
		Married-couple family		Other family										
	Total family households	Total	With own children under 18 years	Total	With own children under 18 years	Total nonfamily households	Two or more adults	Living alone	All households	Owner-occupied households	Renter-occupied households	Median housing value (owner estimated)	With a mortgage	Without a mortgage
	11	12	13	14	15	16	17	18	19	20	21	22	23	24
VIRGINIA..................	75.3	82.0	78.1	51.8	40.9	52.3	38.8	55.6	46 600	55 845	30 750	118 800	21.4	9.9
Alexandria city.............	47.2	55.4	49.2	25.2	17.8	34.0	26.8	35.9	56 161	85 357	44 063	202 400	20.7	9.9
Blacksburg town...........	59.1	66.3	63.7	29.0	33.3	13.3	4.6	25.3	22 806	62 280	17 431	136 200	19.1	9.9
Charlottesville city........	58.4	71.9	67.5	31.4	21.6	26.2	11.5	34.5	31 054	51 822	21 145	117 800	21.6	9.9
Chesapeake city...........	78.8	86.1	83.9	53.9	41.8	61.0	52.2	63.2	50 692	59 338	30 069	119 700	23.5	10.6
Danville city................	63.7	78.7	69.4	39.8	24.0	48.5	37.6	49.5	26 753	36 106	17 390	69 800	19.5	9.9
Hampton city...............	64.6	75.1	66.8	40.5	27.1	46.3	30.6	50.0	39 358	49 978	26 814	90 000	22.8	10.7
Harrisonburg city..........	57.0	67.4	61.2	26.9	24.0	21.3	7.2	32.1	30 406	51 500	22 668	119 300	19.5	9.9
Leesburg town.............	77.6	83.8	85.2	50.2	51.9	45.3	37.2	47.7	68 157	82 334	40 586	178 600	22.1	9.9
Lynchburg city.............	68.1	81.8	76.4	41.4	28.1	42.9	25.7	45.7	32 243	41 972	20 868	84 900	20.8	9.9
Manassas city..............	76.6	81.4	80.9	58.5	54.8	52.1	52.3	52.1	60 609	72 208	41 095	148 600	21.2	9.9
Newport News city........	58.8	70.8	62.5	34.1	22.3	39.4	31.5	41.2	36 503	50 080	25 508	94 200	22.9	10.5
Norfolk city.................	51.9	65.7	56.1	29.9	18.3	35.8	26.7	38.7	31 566	45 868	22 961	88 300	24.0	12.2
Petersburg city............	57.3	72.7	55.9	41.6	23.4	42.2	32.6	44.0	28 696	40 017	21 500	68 100	23.1	11.5
Portsmouth city............	63.2	78.5	72.2	38.2	24.1	49.1	42.5	50.3	33 712	43 505	22 591	81 000	23.5	12.6
Richmond city..............	55.5	74.3	68.2	34.5	20.6	36.0	29.9	37.6	30 934	47 481	21 534	87 400	22.3	12.4
Roanoke city	64.8	77.2	70.5	41.7	26.2	44.5	36.1	45.9	30 681	40 232	21 229	80 100	21.2	9.9
Suffolk city.................	74.9	86.8	83.7	44.8	31.8	63.8	62.7	64.0	40 533	49 461	21 423	104 500	24.0	11.0
Virginia Beach city	71.5	77.0	72.2	52.0	44.3	49.9	38.4	54.1	48 700	58 460	34 231	121 500	23.9	10.1
WASHINGTON..........	73.5	80.2	75.6	47.7	39.2	47.1	39.3	49.4	45 610	56 307	29 853	158 800	23.8	10.4
Auburn city.................	59.2	69.4	63.9	34.7	29.5	45.0	42.1	45.8	39 038	50 494	28 171	132 400	25.4	11.3
Bellevue city	72.8	76.4	72.8	53.2	43.9	41.5	33.1	43.8	62 366	79 118	43 468	287 300	23.2	9.9
Bellingham city............	66.2	75.1	71.8	37.6	32.4	29.8	13.6	37.9	33 019	50 319	22 181	148 900	23.9	9.9
Bothell city.................	76.4	80.9	80.9	58.4	51.0	51.4	44.2	53.7	58 442	66 587	41 071	209 600	24.3	9.9
Bremerton city.............	46.6	55.1	41.7	28.1	17.8	33.0	30.3	33.6	31 096	43 854	22 490	101 500	23.9	10.9
Burien city..................	65.3	75.6	68.8	36.8	26.5	43.3	44.7	43.0	41 698	57 003	28 843	172 100	25.3	11.3
Des Moines city............	69.1	76.5	67.3	47.8	40.4	46.9	34.7	50.1	48 806	59 862	33 483	170 000	23.6	9.9
Edmonds city...............	77.0	82.8	82.0	52.6	42.6	52.5	53.3	52.3	53 114	66 447	36 210	229 600	23.5	9.9
Everett city.................	53.3	63.0	56.3	29.9	22.1	34.9	29.7	36.3	39 952	55 261	30 099	161 700	25.4	11.8
Federal Way city	63.6	73.9	68.7	33.9	25.8	40.9	35.2	42.7	49 327	62 606	33 279	165 300	23.3	9.9
Kennewick city	67.5	76.7	72.4	40.5	33.8	42.6	31.3	45.2	40 569	54 861	25 992	106 300	19.6	9.9
Kent city....................	56.5	66.6	62.6	29.5	22.8	36.0	31.5	37.4	46 092	61 808	33 544	168 100	24.2	10.1
Kirkland city................	67.9	73.5	72.1	46.8	42.7	44.2	36.2	46.8	59 314	70 775	48 161	266 400	23.9	12.4
Lacey city	62.6	70.3	67.5	37.5	26.9	42.9	36.1	44.3	43 384	54 375	30 399	127 700	23.7	10.7
Lakewood city	53.6	64.4	51.9	27.6	16.6	37.0	30.5	38.6	36 276	52 195	25 525	139 800	23.8	9.9
Longview city...............	66.9	77.6	65.6	36.9	29.9	41.6	30.8	43.6	34 589	48 325	22 194	118 800	21.7	9.9
Lynnwood city	59.7	67.2	61.3	36.2	24.4	41.1	29.2	44.2	42 864	57 639	31 639	176 500	24.8	10.7
Marysville city	71.7	78.7	76.0	45.3	42.0	42.4	25.2	46.6	46 714	59 109	31 580	169 100	25.1	12.0
Mount Vernon city	64.1	71.4	64.5	39.5	31.6	43.1	35.1	45.3	37 721	50 417	24 874	136 100	24.2	11.9
Olympia city................	65.5	74.5	68.6	38.4	27.6	33.8	25.2	36.5	40 346	57 056	25 471	140 700	22.2	9.9
Pasco city..................	63.6	72.2	64.0	42.5	35.5	47.8	48.4	47.7	34 343	46 187	18 937	86 500	20.8	9.9
Puyallup city...............	66.6	77.3	76.1	30.0	24.8	32.6	29.7	33.4	46 528	62 429	30 860	154 600	23.7	11.1
Redmond city	65.7	69.8	71.2	46.0	38.7	39.7	27.8	43.6	67 273	80 768	52 909	255 200	22.4	9.9
Renton city.................	60.5	69.3	65.8	34.5	21.5	37.4	33.8	38.5	45 823	60 439	33 275	172 800	23.5	10.5
Richland city...............	75.2	81.1	76.6	48.3	37.2	46.9	37.7	48.3	52 561	64 875	33 328	123 000	19.1	9.9
Sammamish city...........	93.0	94.7	94.2	75.4	68.7	69.4	74.9	67.4	101 783	106 994	52 426	362 900	23.4	9.9
SeaTac city	60.0	68.5	56.5	39.3	36.5	44.3	31.8	47.7	41 075	52 062	31 835	147 000	23.6	11.6
Seattle city.................	66.9	74.3	76.0	44.5	34.3	33.7	29.7	35.1	45 572	66 248	31 764	252 100	24.1	11.5
Shoreline city..............	76.2	81.8	79.0	55.8	46.7	52.6	37.7	57.0	51 200	60 306	35 153	200 500	25.8	11.8
Spokane city...............	69.9	79.7	76.3	44.4	36.6	43.4	35.2	45.3	32 230	43 140	20 797	96 100	23.0	10.8
Tacoma city................	64.0	73.2	68.7	42.5	33.8	40.6	39.0	41.0	37 600	50 192	24 940	123 400	24.8	12.9
University Place city......	66.0	76.7	73.7	30.8	22.2	40.9	36.6	42.1	49 708	67 458	30 075	173 600	23.0	10.8
Vancouver city.............	59.9	69.2	61.9	33.2	24.8	41.0	32.4	43.5	41 504	53 441	30 401	140 800	24.5	9.9
Walla Walla city...........	70.6	79.3	71.7	44.0	36.6	41.7	25.9	44.9	31 499	43 129	18 443	97 100	22.2	10.8
Wenatchee city............	66.9	74.9	67.0	36.8	24.6	40.6	30.5	42.5	34 665	49 132	22 695	129 000	23.4	10.5
Yakima city.................	60.3	71.3	62.6	33.3	24.4	41.2	30.5	43.3	29 495	40 967	20 576	100 100	23.2	10.6
WEST VIRGINIA	81.6	86.6	81.9	62.6	49.3	61.0	47.7	63.1	29 663	34 632	16 794	66 000	19.5	9.9
Charleston city	70.9	82.2	77.9	44.9	28.3	41.8	26.9	43.8	34 049	48 666	20 104	100 800	18.3	9.9
Huntington city............	68.5	78.3	71.7	46.2	30.3	38.9	17.3	43.7	23 321	35 228	13 530	65 600	20.0	10.3
Morgantown city...........	70.0	76.2	73.0	50.8	39.9	22.6	6.0	32.9	20 738	45 332	11 197	92 900	20.2	9.9
Parkersburg city	70.0	79.4	70.1	47.5	34.6	49.2	26.4	52.7	27 226	34 914	16 889	63 900	20.2	9.9
Wheeling city...............	74.5	82.8	80.6	51.3	33.2	47.0	45.5	47.2	27 134	37 418	14 203	67 300	19.5	9.9
WISCONSIN.............	79.1	86.0	84.1	50.4	40.5	47.0	37.3	49.3	43 624	52 546	27 500	109 900	20.9	11.2
Appleton city...............	81.1	87.5	86.9	49.4	41.8	44.6	36.8	46.2	47 377	56 979	29 444	97 600	19.7	11.6
Beloit city...................	68.5	80.4	70.9	41.3	35.8	49.6	48.4	49.9	35 897	44 447	22 517	67 500	19.2	11.4
Brookfield city..............	94.0	95.3	96.3	80.9	75.0	73.2	73.2	73.2	75 733	79 376	49 844	188 700	20.9	10.9
Eau Claire city.............	75.5	83.2	82.4	45.0	39.1	33.9	14.1	42.8	36 301	48 656	24 607	91 700	19.7	11.6
Fond du Lac city	74.4	82.5	79.6	43.8	36.9	41.4	31.9	43.4	41 043	50 574	26 078	89 900	19.8	11.6

Table C-5. Cities — **Migration, Housing, and Transportation**

City	Percent who pay 35 percent or more of income for housing expenses		Means of transportation to work (percent except where noted)						Vehicles available (percent of households)		
				Car, truck, or van							
	Median gross rent	Owners	Renters	Number of workers 16 years and over	Drove alone	Carpooled	Public transportation	Other means	Walked	No vehicles	One vehicle	Two or more vehicles
	25	26	27	28	29	30	31	32	33	34	35	36
VIRGINIA	650	14.1	26.3	3 481 820	77.1	12.7	3.6	1.2	2.3	7.7	31.6	60.7
Alexandria city	861	13.3	23.0	77 190	62.8	13.2	16.4	1.2	3.0	11.2	52.4	36.4
Blacksburg town	553	11.2	48.9	16 004	67.4	8.5	7.0	2.2	11.3	6.0	36.1	57.9
Charlottesville city	596	14.2	40.5	20 323	60.4	9.7	5.1	2.8	16.5	14.2	41.4	44.4
Chesapeake city	642	17.4	28.5	96 977	83.9	10.5	0.9	1.1	1.1	5.7	28.3	66.0
Danville city	404	13.2	30.5	19 262	79.9	13.7	2.1	1.0	2.0	17.3	38.6	44.1
Hampton city	603	17.0	29.8	66 101	79.7	12.9	2.8	1.1	1.9	8.7	36.6	54.7
Harrisonburg city	480	10.9	33.8	18 270	70.7	10.0	3.3	2.8	9.6	9.6	34.2	56.3
Leesburg town	847	11.7	25.6	15 340	82.4	10.0	0.7	0.6	1.6	4.0	30.5	65.5
Lynchburg city	469	13.1	28.7	28 619	76.8	12.3	3.1	0.8	4.7	14.9	37.0	48.1
Manassas city	801	14.5	22.0	18 145	75.1	16.5	3.0	1.3	1.7	4.7	28.5	66.9
Newport News city	559	16.8	27.3	86 282	78.7	13.0	2.8	1.2	2.7	11.4	37.3	51.3
Norfolk city	538	21.0	32.1	112 083	66.8	14.2	4.6	3.8	6.8	17.0	41.4	41.6
Petersburg city	495	21.1	30.2	13 176	73.4	18.7	3.3	1.3	2.1	20.9	39.8	39.3
Portsmouth city	540	19.8	33.1	43 922	72.8	15.6	3.0	2.5	3.3	14.5	38.5	47.0
Richmond city	540	10.4	33.5	88 924	70.6	12.6	8.3	1.9	4.4	21.6	42.2	36.1
Roanoke city	448	15.2	27.0	43 694	79.7	12.4	3.1	1.2	1.8	12.7	41.2	46.1
Suffolk city	506	19.0	31.9	28 372	80.4	13.7	1.2	1.7	1.3	10.3	29.6	60.1
Virginia Beach city	734	18.5	27.7	222 648	82.0	10.8	0.7	1.7	2.0	4.7	31.0	64.3
WASHINGTON	663	18.1	30.8	2 785 479	73.3	12.8	4.9	1.4	3.2	7.4	31.7	60.8
Auburn city	639	19.3	31.5	18 922	72.9	15.2	5.0	1.1	3.0	9.3	39.1	51.7
Bellevue city	916	17.8	30.7	56 474	74.0	10.6	6.7	1.0	2.6	5.6	36.1	58.3
Bellingham city	613	15.5	44.0	32 952	69.9	11.7	3.6	3.8	6.8	10.2	38.8	50.9
Bothell city	913	17.5	25.8	16 163	75.4	13.2	4.6	0.7	1.4	3.4	33.4	63.2
Bremerton city	554	16.7	35.0	16 827	55.6	16.4	10.7	3.8	10.8	18.5	39.7	41.8
Burien city	666	20.7	32.2	15 521	68.7	17.1	8.0	1.4	1.5	8.6	39.6	51.8
Des Moines city	705	17.7	29.1	13 831	76.4	12.7	5.5	0.9	1.2	4.6	37.9	57.6
Edmonds city	779	16.7	30.4	19 793	76.4	9.8	6.5	1.0	1.4	4.4	35.3	60.4
Everett city	687	20.9	30.1	43 958	68.7	16.8	4.1	1.4	4.4	9.7	40.0	50.3
Federal Way city	737	18.4	30.3	41 259	73.8	15.4	5.9	0.8	1.3	6.1	34.9	59.1
Kennewick city	541	12.9	28.8	25 480	79.4	13.1	1.3	0.9	1.7	6.7	32.5	60.8
Kent city	724	19.7	28.5	39 629	73.5	14.8	5.7	0.8	1.9	7.5	38.1	54.4
Kirkland city	972	19.2	24.9	27 060	76.0	9.8	5.5	1.3	2.2	4.2	40.6	55.2
Lacey city	677	15.8	29.5	14 416	77.6	13.3	2.1	0.7	2.7	8.1	37.5	54.4
Lakewood city	550	15.7	34.9	24 495	75.3	14.9	3.9	1.2	2.3	10.9	40.4	48.7
Longview city	511	14.4	37.2	14 409	81.6	11.5	0.5	1.6	2.5	10.7	35.9	53.5
Lynnwood city	741	19.0	32.8	16 624	70.3	15.0	7.5	0.7	2.5	9.4	35.9	54.7
Marysville city	724	19.3	28.1	11 801	75.5	16.2	2.1	0.7	2.6	7.1	32.8	60.1
Mount Vernon city	655	17.9	35.0	11 578	74.6	16.5	1.2	1.8	2.6	9.1	33.0	57.9
Olympia city	624	14.7	37.2	21 645	71.1	12.3	5.2	2.4	5.6	11.1	39.7	49.2
Pasco city	466	12.6	33.1	11 768	67.4	24.6	1.8	2.1	1.4	9.8	34.0	56.2
Puyallup city	702	17.7	33.1	15 793	82.5	10.8	1.7	0.8	1.5	7.5	32.0	50.7
Redmond city	1 021	17.1	27.1	25 638	76.1	11.3	4.2	1.2	2.8	5.4	39.3	55.4
Renton city	723	18.0	30.2	26 743	72.8	15.2	6.2	1.0	2.2	8.7	40.5	50.8
Richland city	619	8.4	26.6	18 078	80.5	11.8	1.1	1.5	2.0	6.4	31.1	62.5
Sammamish city	1 121	19.5	24.7	17 146	79.7	8.6	2.1	1.1	0.9	0.9	13.2	85.9
SeaTac city	654	13.9	28.8	12 432	70.4	14.2	8.7	1.0	3.6	8.2	41.2	50.7
Seattle city	721	19.7	30.6	316 493	56.5	11.2	17.6	2.7	7.4	16.3	42.5	41.2
Shoreline city	798	22.2	27.2	26 276	70.0	12.8	10.2	1.0	1.7	6.6	33.8	59.7
Spokane city	509	17.2	35.7	88 299	74.1	12.9	4.2	1.5	3.6	12.7	37.9	49.4
Tacoma city	581	21.4	34.9	86 530	72.4	13.9	5.3	1.3	3.5	12.3	37.4	50.3
University Place city	618	15.6	28.4	15 243	81.2	10.8	2.7	0.5	2.0	4.2	37.1	58.7
Vancouver city	671	19.0	32.8	67 015	76.9	12.6	3.7	1.3	1.8	8.4	37.6	54.0
Walla Walla city	500	17.0	39.6	11 325	70.4	13.6	0.9	3.1	8.4	11.5	37.8	50.7
Wenatchee city	545	16.1	36.6	11 336	74.1	14.8	1.1	1.8	4.3	10.5	35.9	53.6
Yakima city	526	17.4	37.4	26 439	76.5	14.4	1.3	1.9	3.2	12.6	38.1	49.3
WEST VIRGINIA	401	11.9	28.3	718 106	80.3	12.7	0.8	0.9	2.9	10.8	35.4	53.7
Charleston city	439	10.6	26.7	24 015	74.5	11.8	4.8	0.9	5.3	18.9	41.2	39.8
Huntington city	414	13.5	41.5	20 679	75.6	11.4	1.8	1.2	7.9	18.7	43.8	37.5
Morgantown city	431	12.7	53.6	12 084	64.5	9.9	1.6	3.5	16.8	13.1	43.1	43.8
Parkersburg city	418	11.3	32.4	13 395	80.3	12.0	1.7	0.7	3.8	14.4	43.1	42.4
Wheeling city	363	11.4	25.2	12 802	76.1	9.9	2.3	1.1	7.5	19.5	41.2	39.3
WISCONSIN	540	12.0	25.4	2 690 704	79.5	9.9	2.0	0.9	3.7	7.9	32.5	59.6
Appleton city	508	9.8	19.2	36 435	83.5	8.0	1.1	0.9	4.3	6.5	33.7	59.8
Beloit city	509	11.8	28.9	15 547	78.6	13.7	1.1	0.5	5.0	10.3	37.7	52.0
Brookfield city	1 014	12.9	31.3	18 496	89.4	5.4	0.5	0.4	0.4	2.0	20.8	77.2
Eau Claire city	485	10.5	26.8	32 721	79.4	8.5	1.7	1.3	6.7	7.4	35.1	57.5
Fond du Lac city	507	10.3	24.9	21 158	81.1	11.9	1.0	1.4	3.3	8.8	38.5	52.7

Table C-5. Cities — **Migration, Housing, and Transportation**

STATE Place code	City	Total population 5 years and over	Residence in 1995 (percent)					Occupied housing units		Householders 65 years and over	
			Same house	Same county, different house	Same state, different county	Different state	Outside the United States	Number	Percent owner-occupied	Number	Percent owner-occupied
		1	2	3	4	5	6	7	8	9	10
	WISCONSIN—Cont'd										
55 27300	Franklin city	27 820	55.5	27.1	11.8	4.8	0.8	10 612	78.3	1 628	72.9
55 31000	Green Bay city	94 983	49.0	31.1	10.1	7.3	2.5	41 629	56.0	8 412	69.1
55 31175	Greenfield city	33 781	57.8	31.2	5.6	4.2	1.4	15 685	59.6	4 622	64.2
55 37825	Janesville city	55 175	52.0	33.5	6.5	7.4	0.7	23 869	68.1	4 763	76.7
55 39225	Kenosha city	83 881	52.4	27.7	5.2	13.1	1.6	34 546	62.2	7 701	71.5
55 40775	La Crosse city	49 107	43.2	26.3	20.3	9.3	0.9	21 048	50.7	5 170	67.0
55 48000	Madison city	196 989	39.2	28.8	13.8	13.8	4.4	88 845	47.8	12 959	68.6
55 48500	Manitowoc city	31 957	58.7	28.3	6.7	5.4	0.9	14 222	67.6	4 148	72.2
55 51000	Menomonee Falls village	30 445	60.2	14.2	19.6	5.7	0.4	12 855	77.1	3 395	68.8
55 53000	Milwaukee city	549 702	49.0	36.3	5.2	6.4	3.0	232 178	45.3	44 834	64.3
55 56375	New Berlin city	36 112	63.2	10.8	20.4	4.9	0.6	14 505	81.3	3 061	81.1
55 58800	Oak Creek city	26 536	51.9	32.1	8.4	6.2	1.4	11 239	61.5	1 680	58.9
55 60500	Oshkosh city	59 432	45.7	26.8	20.4	6.1	1.0	24 026	57.6	5 158	69.3
55 66000	Racine city	75 192	53.6	31.7	6.9	5.6	2.2	31 498	60.2	7 309	73.6
55 72975	Sheboygan city	47 266	54.8	30.7	5.9	7.3	1.3	20 814	61.0	5 134	72.6
55 78650	Superior city	25 701	56.5	25.4	4.5	12.6	1.0	11 614	61.8	2 970	68.4
55 84250	Waukesha city	59 696	46.2	28.7	14.7	8.2	2.2	25 665	56.4	4 599	58.9
55 84475	Wausau city	35 975	54.7	27.9	9.6	6.2	1.6	15 704	61.7	3 951	68.5
55 84675	Wauwatosa city	44 257	58.6	26.1	7.6	6.9	0.8	20 391	67.8	5 953	64.3
55 85300	West Allis city	57 716	56.2	31.8	7.5	3.5	1.0	27 626	58.0	7 213	64.7
55 85350	West Bend city	26 027	51.8	30.5	14.0	3.6	0.2	11 369	62.0	2 646	65.1
56 00000	WYOMING	462 809	51.3	24.1	7.8	15.7	1.1	193 608	70.0	38 448	81.2
56 13150	Casper city	46 659	50.5	29.6	7.7	11.4	0.9	20 437	67.4	4 433	79.0
56 13900	Cheyenne city	49 540	48.1	27.6	4.7	17.7	1.9	22 282	66.2	4 765	77.9
56 45050	Laramie city	25 771	32.1	20.5	21.0	23.9	2.5	11 375	47.5	1 391	87.2

Table C-5. Cities — **Migration, Housing, and Transportation**

City	Owner-occupied by household type (percent)								Median household income			Median housing value (owner estimated)	Median monthly owner costs as a percent of income	
	Family households					Nonfamily households								
		Married-couple family		Other family										
	Total family households	Total	With own children under 18 years	Total	With own children under 18 years	Total nonfamily households	Two or more adults	Living alone	All households	Owner-occupied households	Renter-occupied households		With a mortgage	Without a mortgage
	11	12	13	14	15	16	17	18	19	20	21	22	23	24
WISCONSIN—Cont'd														
Franklin city	88.3	90.9	91.9	71.3	66.2	52.0	34.2	55.6	65 239	75 009	39 978	153 400	22.0	12.4
Green Bay city	67.9	78.6	74.2	35.9	29.2	38.4	29.1	40.9	38 590	50 562	25 981	96 300	21.1	12.2
Greenfield city	74.3	79.3	80.3	52.9	49.0	39.1	25.2	41.9	43 952	54 415	33 711	121 500	21.8	14.2
Janesville city	77.6	85.1	81.1	50.8	42.0	50.0	37.0	53.2	45 671	55 269	29 033	98 900	19.6	10.6
Kenosha city..................	71.7	81.6	78.6	45.6	35.4	43.9	35.0	45.8	41 536	53 707	26 233	105 800	21.1	12.7
La Crosse city	69.6	78.6	76.0	41.6	29.3	32.5	15.8	38.7	31 025	43 433	21 640	83 200	21.1	12.3
Madison city	68.0	76.3	76.4	38.3	33.0	29.1	19.9	33.4	41 826	62 592	27 783	137 700	22.3	10.8
Manitowoc city..............	79.0	85.4	84.8	53.5	43.7	48.9	41.4	50.0	37 927	45 988	24 582	83 200	18.9	10.0
Menomonee Falls village	87.8	90.7	93.1	67.3	56.9	48.7	50.1	48.5	57 932	66 951	33 203	151 000	21.3	12.5
Milwaukee city	53.2	69.7	62.5	32.1	21.1	34.1	26.2	36.0	32 021	45 139	23 805	79 600	20.9	12.2
New Berlin city	89.8	91.7	92.8	72.0	52.7	54.5	41.6	58.0	67 152	72 760	45 553	161 100	21.1	11.8
Oak Creek city	76.6	79.8	82.2	55.9	40.8	31.0	26.6	32.4	53 445	66 056	38 482	136 700	22.5	12.4
Oshkosh city.................	72.6	81.0	77.4	42.0	33.2	37.7	23.2	42.6	37 522	48 608	25 908	85 500	19.9	10.9
Racine city...................	68.1	81.0	74.8	41.6	30.3	45.0	41.4	45.9	36 702	47 944	22 502	83 400	20.8	12.1
Sheboygan city.............	71.7	80.4	74.4	38.9	27.5	43.7	29.5	46.3	40 066	47 370	29 044	87 500	20.4	12.5
Superior city	76.2	87.9	90.4	43.9	37.5	41.9	29.7	44.7	32 013	40 804	18 925	63 900	19.4	10.8
Waukesha city..............	69.8	76.9	75.7	40.0	28.1	33.6	29.7	34.6	49 806	63 269	34 003	138 000	22.0	11.5
Wausau city.................	74.3	80.2	74.5	50.7	43.0	42.9	35.2	44.4	37 184	47 861	24 922	84 700	19.7	11.5
Wauwatosa city	81.3	85.7	87.0	59.3	53.7	47.1	47.5	47.0	54 519	65 979	33 877	138 500	20.7	12.0
West Allis city	74.3	82.6	80.4	49.4	35.2	37.5	35.4	37.8	39 262	50 213	28 224	99 600	21.4	13.8
West Bend city	72.9	81.0	79.8	36.5	25.7	40.6	32.0	42.6	48 021	57 147	32 903	128 900	22.7	10.2
WYOMING	77.7	82.7	78.2	55.2	47.6	53.8	43.5	56.2	37 671	45 157	24 183	91 500	19.7	9.9
Casper city	76.1	83.4	76.9	50.8	45.0	51.4	42.5	53.2	36 352	45 880	21 779	83 100	18.9	9.9
Cheyenne city	75.0	82.0	79.1	50.5	39.9	50.9	47.2	51.5	38 784	47 542	24 377	100 400	21.2	9.9
Laramie city.................	66.6	74.4	71.1	37.9	31.0	28.4	13.6	36.0	27 720	48 854	16 097	109 200	19.8	9.9

Table C-5. Cities — **Migration, Housing, and Transportation**

City	Median gross rent	Percent who pay 35 percent or more of income for housing expenses		Means of transportation to work (percent except where noted)						Vehicles available (percent of households)		
		Owners	Renters	Number of workers 16 years and over	Car, truck, or van		Public transportation	Other means	Walked	No vehicles	One vehicle	Two or more vehicles
					Drove alone	Carpooled						
	25	26	27	28	29	30	31	32	33	34	35	36
WISCONSIN—Cont'd												
Franklin city	722	14.2	22.5	15 568	87.8	7.0	0.9	0.3	0.4	3.2	26.0	70.8
Green Bay city	495	12.0	25.5	51 993	82.9	10.3	1.3	0.8	2.8	8.4	39.0	52.6
Greenfield city	659	14.0	24.0	18 723	86.2	8.4	1.8	0.3	1.6	7.6	41.5	50.9
Janesville city	567	10.2	23.6	29 853	85.0	9.2	1.0	0.8	2.0	5.9	35.5	58.6
Kenosha city	571	13.3	27.5	42 293	80.9	11.8	1.5	1.0	2.8	8.8	38.9	52.2
La Crosse city	449	11.9	28.3	26 056	75.6	9.0	2.4	1.6	9.1	12.1	41.2	46.7
Madison city	644	13.1	35.6	119 707	65.7	9.6	7.2	3.8	10.7	11.8	42.3	45.9
Manitowoc city	430	9.5	20.1	16 447	81.2	11.1	0.7	1.3	3.8	9.8	39.7	50.5
Menomonee Falls village	702	10.7	29.6	17 076	88.1	7.0	0.7	0.5	0.7	4.8	28.6	66.6
Milwaukee city	527	15.0	32.0	249 889	68.8	13.6	10.3	0.9	4.7	21.4	43.6	35.1
New Berlin city	830	11.2	25.8	20 792	88.8	6.7	0.5	0.4	0.7	2.6	24.2	73.2
Oak Creek city	704	12.2	19.1	16 133	87.6	8.1	1.2	0.4	0.9	4.8	31.2	64.0
Oshkosh city	487	11.1	24.4	31 317	81.5	8.7	1.3	1.1	5.7	7.4	38.8	53.8
Racine city	520	13.5	30.9	35 175	78.3	12.7	3.3	1.0	3.0	13.3	40.0	46.8
Sheboygan city	477	10.6	19.0	25 446	78.8	12.6	1.6	1.7	3.9	10.3	41.9	47.7
Superior city	406	10.4	28.4	12 945	80.0	9.8	2.0	0.8	5.7	11.8	38.1	50.1
Waukesha city	675	12.8	24.0	35 224	83.5	8.5	1.8	0.7	3.6	8.2	34.1	57.6
Wausau city	473	11.2	23.9	18 262	80.5	10.4	2.1	1.2	3.5	10.1	40.2	49.7
Wauwatosa city	702	11.3	28.9	24 299	84.6	6.8	2.2	0.6	2.1	8.1	38.1	53.8
West Allis city	571	12.4	27.8	31 292	81.4	9.4	3.3	0.8	3.5	12.5	42.6	44.9
West Bend city	603	10.2	21.4	14 456	85.0	9.3	1.3	0.7	1.3	7.6	36.3	56.2
WYOMING	437	11.3	23.3	239 809	75.4	13.2	1.4	1.3	4.4	4.6	29.2	66.2
Casper city	408	9.4	23.1	24 607	83.0	11.2	0.5	1.0	1.6	5.8	33.3	60.9
Cheyenne city	470	11.7	25.7	25 941	82.2	11.3	0.5	1.0	1.9	6.6	35.5	57.9
Laramie city	465	8.3	43.9	14 297	69.9	11.6	0.7	3.4	11.2	4.8	38.0	57.3

Appendices

Appendices

APPENDIX A
GEOGRAPHIC CONCEPTS AND CODES

AREAS FOR WHICH DATA ARE PRESENTED

The Who, What, and Where of America: Understanding the Census Results presents data for the Nation (Tables A-1, B-1, and C-1), States (Tables A-2, B-2, and C-2), States and Counties (Tables A-3, B-3, and C-3), Metropolitan Areas (Tables A-4, B-4, and C-4), and Cities with populations of 25,000 or more (Tables A-5, B-5, and C-5),

STATES AND COUNTIES

Data are presented for each of the 50 states, the District of Columbia, and the United States as a whole. The states are arranged alphabetically, and in Tables A-3, B-3, and C-3 counties are arranged alphabetically within each state.

Data are presented for 3,141 counties and county equivalents. Maps of each state, showing their counties and county equivalents and their metropolitan areas are contained in Appendix D.

County equivalents

In Louisiana, the primary divisions of the state are known as parishes rather than counties. In Alaska, the county equivalents are the organized boroughs, together with the census areas that were developed for general statistical purposes by the state of Alaska and the U.S. Bureau of the Census. Four states—Maryland, Missouri, Nevada, and Virginia—have one or more incorporated places that are legally independent of any county and thus constitute primary divisions of their states. Within each state, independent cities are listed alphabetically following the list of counties. A list of independent cities is given at the end of this appendix. The District of Columbia is not divided into counties or county equivalents—data for the entire District are presented as a county equivalent. New York City contains five counties—Bronx, Kings, New York, Queens, and Richmond.

County changes since the 1990 Census

Dade County in Florida officially became Miami-Dade County.

Denali Borough in Alaska was formed primarily from the Yukon-Koyukuk census area and a small part of the Southeast Fairbanks census area.

The Skagway-Yakutat-Angoon census area in Alaska was dissolved and replaced by Yakutat Borough and the Skagway-Hoonah-Angoon census area.

South Boston City in Virginia, formerly an independent city, became a town within Halifax County.

Yellowstone Park in Montana, which had not been part of any county, was dissolved as a county equivalent and became part of Park and Gallatin Counties.

The city of Takoma Park, Maryland, formerly split between Montgomery and Prince George's Counties, moved its boundary, and now lies completely within Montgomery County.

METROPOLITAN AREAS

Tables A-4, B-4, and C-4 present data for 335 metropolitan areas comprising 248 metropolitan statistical areas (MSAs), 17 consolidated metropolitan statistical areas (CMSAs), 58 primary metropolitan statistical areas (PMSAs), and 12 New England county metropolitan areas (NECMAs). The left-hand column of each page provides an alphabetical listing of MSAs, CMSAs, and NECMAs—PMSAs are listed alphabetically under the CMSAs of which they are components.

The metropolitan areas used in this volume are those defined by the U.S. government based on 1990 census data. The U.S. Office of Management and Budget first issued these definitions in December 1992. Additional revisions occurred throughout the decade, with the final revisions dated June 30, 1999.

In general, a metropolitan area is a geographic area consisting of a large population nucleus together with adjacent communities that have a high degree of economic and social integration with that nucleus. The major purpose of defining these areas is to enable all U.S. government agencies to use the same geographic definitions in tabulating and publishing data.

Metropolitan complexes with populations of one million or more may be divided into primary metropolitan statistical areas (PMSAs) with the support of local opinion. When PMSAs are defined, the larger metropolitan area of which they are components is designated a consolidated metropolitan statistical area (CMSA).

For most of the United States, metropolitan areas are defined in terms of counties because counties are the smallest geographical units for which a wide variety of statistical data can be obtained. In New England, however, the metropolitan area definitions are in terms of cities and towns because these subcounty units are of great local significance. An alternative concept for the New England states is the New England county metropolitan area (NECMA). NECMAs, rather than MSAs, CMSAs, and PMSAs, are presented for New England in this volume for consistency with other editions of *County and City Extra*.

In recent years, the Office of Management and Budget has issued new standards that will replace the existing metropolitan statistical areas. These new metropolitan area definitions are based on the 2000 census and follow new rules. The criteria are new, and there are smaller areas called micropolitan areas in addition to metropolitan areas. The new list of 935 metropolitan and micropolitan areas was released in June 2003 as this book was being finalized, and is not used here.

CITIES

Tables A-5, B-5, and C-5 present data for 1,253 cities with 2000 census populations of 25,000 or more. Corresponding data for states are also provided. The states are arranged alphabetically, and the cities are arranged alphabetically within each state.

For Hawaii, data for census designated places (CDPs) are included, since the U.S. Bureau of the Census does not recognize any incorporated places in Hawaii. CDPs are delineated by the U.S. Bureau of the Census, in cooperation with states and localities, as statistical counterparts of incorporated places for purposes of the decennial census. CDPs comprise densely settled concentrations of population that are identifiable by name but are not legally incorporated places.

A consolidated city is an incorporated place that has combined its governmental functions with a county or subcounty entity but contains one or more other semi-independent incorporated places that continue to function as local governments within the consolidated government. Consolidated cities included in this volume are Milford, CT; Athens-Clarke County, GA; Augusta-Richmond County, GA; Columbus, GA; Indianapolis, IN; Butte-Silver Bow, MT; and Nashville-Davidson, TN.

GEOGRAPHIC CODES

Tables A-2 through A-5, B-2 through B-5, and C-2 through C-5 provide, in one or more columns at the beginning of the table, a geographic code or codes for each area.

In Tables A-3, B-3, and C-3 (States and Counties), a five-digit state and county code is given for each state and county. The first two digits indicate the state; the remaining three represent the county. Within each state, the counties are numbered in alphabetical order beginning with 001, with even numbers usually omitted. Independent cities follow the counties and begin with the number 510. In the second column of these tables, a four-digit metropolitan area (MSA, PMSA, or NECMA) code is given for those counties that are within metropolitan areas. In Tables A-2, B-2, and C-2, a two-digit state code is provided. The state code is a sequential numbering, with some gaps, of the states and the District of Columbia in alphabetical order from Alabama (01) to Wyoming (56).

These codes have been established by the U.S. government as Federal Information Processing Standards and are often referred to as *FIPS codes*. They are used by U.S. government agencies and many other organizations for data presentation. The codes are provided in this volume for use in matching the data given here with other data sources in which counties may be identified by FIPS code. The metro area codes will also enable the user to identify the metro area of which a county is a component. Tables A-4, B-4, and C-4 (Metropolitan Areas) provide the same metro area codes for each metropolitan area.

Tables A-5, B-5, and C-5 (Cities) provide, in the first column, a seven-digit state and place code. The first two digits identify the state and are the same as the state FIPS codes described above. The remaining five digits are the place FIPS codes established by the U.S. government. For the seven consolidated cities, the consolidated city code is used instead of the place code.

INDEPENDENT CITIES

Independent cities are not included in any county; data are presented separately in this volume.

MARYLAND:
Baltimore: (Separate from Baltimore County)

MISSOURI:
St. Louis: (Separate from St. Louis County)

NEVADA:
Carson City

VIRGINIA:

Alexandria	Lynchburg
Bedford	Manassas
Bristol	Manassas Park
Buena Vista	Martinsville
Charlottesville	Newport News
Chesapeake	Norfolk
Clifton Forge	Norton
Colonial Heights	Petersburg
Covington	Poquoson
Danville	Portsmouth
Emporia	Radford
Fairfax	Richmond
Falls Church	Roanoke
Franklin	Salem
Fredericksburg	Staunton
Galax	Suffolk
Hampton	Virginia Beach
Harrisonburg	Waynesboro
Hopewell	Williamsburg
Lexington	Winchester

APPENDIX B
METROPOLITAN STATISTICAL AREAS AND COMPONENTS

(MSA = metropolitan statistical area; CMSA = consolidated MSA; PMSA = primary MSA; and NECMA = New England county metropolitan area. For further information, see Appendix A.)

MSA/ CMSA/ PMSA/ NECMA	State and County	Tital and Geographic Components	2000 Population	MSA/ CMSA/ PMSA/ NECMA	State and County	Tital and Geographic Components	2000 Population
0040		Abilene, TX MSA	126 555		13 063	Clayton County, GA	236 517
	48 441	Taylor County, TX	126 555		13 067	Cobb County, GA	607 751
0080		Akron, OH PMSA	694 960		13 077	Coweta County, GA	89 215
		(See Cleveland-Akron, OH CMSA)			13 089	De Kalb County, GA	665 865
0120		Albany, GA MSA	120 822		13 097	Douglas County, GA	92 174
	13 095	Dougherty County, GA	96 065		13 113	Fayette County, GA	91 263
	13 177	Lee County, GA	24 757		13 117	Forsyth County, GA	98 407
0160		Albany-Schenectady-Troy, NY MSA	875 583		13 121	Fulton County, GA	816 006
	36 001	Albany County, NY	294 565		13 135	Gwinnett County, GA	588 448
	36 057	Montgomery County, NY	49 708		13 151	Henry County, GA	119 341
	36 083	Rensselaer County, NY	152 538		13 217	Newton County, GA	62 001
	36 091	Saratoga County, NY	200 635		13 223	Paulding County, GA	81 678
	36 093	Schenectady County, NY	146 555		13 227	Pickens County, GA	22 983
	36 095	Schoharie County, NY	31 582		13 247	Rockdale County, GA	70 111
0200		Albuquerque, NM MSA	712 738		13 255	Spalding County, GA	58 417
	35 001	Bernalillo County, NM	556 678		13 297	Walton County, GA	60 687
	35 043	Sandoval County, NM	89 908	0560		Atlantic-Cape May, NJ PMSA	354 878
	35 061	Valencia County, NM	66 152			(See Philadelphia-Wilmington-Atlantic City, PA-NJ-DE-MD CMSA)	
0220		Alexandria, LA MSA	126 337	0580		Auburn-Opelika, AL MSA	115 092
	22 079	Rapides Parish, LA	126 337		01 081	Lee County, AL	115 092
0240		Allentown-Bethlehem-Easton, PA MSA	637 958	0600		Augusta-Aiken, GA-SC MSA	477 441
	42 025	Carbon County, PA	58 802		13 073	Columbia County, GA	89 288
	42 077	Lehigh County, PA	312 090		13 189	McDuffie County, GA	21 231
	42 095	Northampton County, PA	267 066		13 245	Richmond County, GA	199 775
0280		Altoona, PA MSA	129 144		45 003	Aiken County, SC	142 552
	42 013	Blair County, PA	129 144		45 037	Edgefield County, SC	24 595
0320		Amarillo, TX MSA	217 858	0640		Austin-San Marcos, TX MSA	1 249 763
	48 375	Potter County, TX	113 546		48 021	Bastrop County, TX	57 733
	48 381	Randall County, TX	104 312		48 055	Caldwell County, TX	32 194
0380		Anchorage, AK MSA	260 283		48 209	Hays County, TX	97 589
	02 020	Anchorage Borough, AK	260 283		48 453	Travis County, TX	812 280
0440		Ann Arbor, MI PMSA	578 736		48 491	Williamson County, TX	249 967
		(See Detroit-Ann Arbor-Flint, MI CMSA)		0680		Bakersfield, CA MSA	661 645
0450		Anniston, AL MSA	112 249		06 029	Kern County, CA	661 645
	01 015	Calhoun County, AL	112 249	0720		Baltimore, MD PMSA	2 552 994
0460		Appleton-Oshkosh-Neenah, WI MSA	358 365		08 872	(See Washington-Baltimore, DC-MD-VA-WV CMSA)	
	55 015	Calumet County, WI	40 631	0733		Bangor, ME NECMA	144 919
	55 087	Outagamie County, WI	160 971		23 019	Penobscot County, ME	144 919
	55 139	Winnebago County, WI	156 763	0743		Barnstable-Yarmouth, MA NECMA	222 230
0480		Asheville, NC MSA	225 965		25 001	Barnstable County, MA	222 230
	37 021	Buncombe County, NC	206 330	0760		Baton Rouge, LA MSA	602 894
	37 115	Madison County, NC	19 635		22 005	Ascension Parish, LA	76 627
0500		Athens, GA MSA	153 444		22 033	East Baton Rouge Parish, LA	412 852
	13 059	Clarke County, GA	101 489		22 063	Livingston Parish, LA	91 814
	13 195	Madison County, GA	25 730		22 121	West Baton Rouge Parish, LA	21 601
	13 219	Oconee County, GA	26 225	0840		Beaumont-Port Arthur, TX MSA	385 090
0520		Atlanta, GA MSA	4 112 198		48 199	Hardin County, TX	48 073
	13 013	Barrow County, GA	46 144		48 245	Jefferson County, TX	252 051
	13 015	Bartow County, GA	76 019		48 361	Orange County, TX	84 966
	13 045	Carroll County, GA	87 268	0860		Bellingham, WA MSA	166 814
	13 057	Cherokee County, GA	141 903		53 073	Whatcom County, WA	166 814

(MSA = metropolitan statistical area; CMSA = consolidated MSA; PMSA = primary MSA; and NECMA = New England county metropolitan area. For further information, see Appendix A.)

MSA/ CMSA/ PMSA/ NECMA	State and County	Tital and Geographic Components	2000 Population	MSA/ CMSA/ PMSA/ NECMA	State and County	Tital and Geographic Components	2000 Population
0870		Benton Harbor, MI MSA..............	162 453	1260		Bryan-College Station, TX MSA............	152 415
	26 021	Berrien County, MI...................	162 453		48 041	Brazos County, TX	152 415
0875		Bergen-Passaic, NJ PMSA...............	1 373 167	1280		Buffalo-Niagara Falls, NY MSA..............	1 170 111
		(See New York-Northern New Jersey-Long Island, NY-NJ-CT-PA CMSA)			36 029	Erie County, NY.................	950 265
					36 063	Niagara County, NY..............	219 846
0880		Billings, MT MSA..................	129 352	1303		Burlington, VT NECMA..............	198 889
	30 111	Yellowstone County, MT................	129 352		50 077	Chittenden County, VT.............	146 571
0920		Biloxi-Gulfport-Pascagoula, MS MSA	363 988		50 011	Franklin County, VT..............	45 417
	28 045	Hancock County, MS.............	42 967		50 013	Grand Isle County, VT..............	6 901
	28 047	Harrison County, MS.............	189 601	1320		Canton-Massillon, OH MSA..............	406 934
	28 059	Jackson County, MS..............	131 420		39 019	Carroll County, OH..............	28 836
0960		Binghamton, NY MSA..............	252 320		39 151	Stark County, OH..............	378 098
	36 007	Broome County, NY................	200 536	1350		Casper, WY MSA..............	66 533
	36 107	Tioga County, NY..............	51 784		56 025	Natrona County, WY..............	66 533
1000		Birmingham, AL MSA..............	921 106	1360		Cedar Rapids, IA MSA..............	191 701
	01 009	Blount County, AL..............	51 024		19 113	Linn County, IA..............	191 701
	01 073	Jefferson County, AL..............	662 047	1400		Champaign-Urbana, IL MSA..............	179 669
	01 115	St. Clair County, AL..............	64 742		17 019	Champaign County, IL..............	179 669
	01 117	Shelby County, AL..............	143 293				
1010		Bismarck, ND MSA..............	94 719	1480		Charleston, WV MSA..............	251 662
1010	38 015	Burleigh County, ND..............	69 416		54 039	Kanawha County, WV..............	200 073
1010	38 059	Morton County, ND..............	25 303		54 079	Putnam County, WV..............	51 589
1020		Bloomington, IN MSA..............	120 563	1440		Charleston-North Charleston, SC MSA	549 033
1020	18 105	Monroe County, IN..............	120 563		45 015	Berkeley County, SC..............	142 651
1040		Bloomington-Normal, IL MSA..............	150 433		45 019	Charleston County, SC..............	309 969
1040	17 113	McLean County, IL..............	150 433		45 035	Dorchester County, SC..............	96 413
1080		Boise City, ID MSA..............	432 345	1520		Charlotte-Gastonia-Rock Hill, NC-SC MSA	1 499 293
1080	16 001	Ada County, ID..............	300 904		37 025	Cabarrus County, NC..............	131 063
1080	16 027	Canyon County, ID..............	131 441		37 071	Gaston County, NC..............	190 365
1123		Boston-Worcester-Lawrence-Lowell-Brockton, MA-NH NECMA	6 057 826		37 109	Lincoln County, NC..............	63 780
	25 005	Bristol County, MA..............	534 678		37 119	Mecklenburg County, NC..............	695 454
	25 009	Essex County, MA..............	723 419		37 159	Rowan County, NC..............	130 340
	25 017	Middlesex County, MA..............	1 465 396		37 179	Union County, NC..............	123 677
	25 021	Norfolk County, MA..............	650 308		45 091	York County, SC..............	164 614
	25 023	Plymouth County, MA..............	472 822	1540		Charlottesville, VA MSA..............	159 576
	25 025	Suffolk County, MA..............	689 807		51 003	Albemarle County, VA..............	79 236
	25 027	Worcester County, MA..............	750 963		51 065	Fluvanna County, VA..............	20 047
	33 011	Hillsborough County, NH..............	380 841		51 079	Greene County, VA..............	15 244
	33 015	Rockingham County, NH..............	277 359		51 540	Charlottesville City, VA..............	45 049
	33 017	Strafford County, NH..............	112 233	1560		Chattanooga, TN-GA MSA..............	465 161
1125		Boulder-Longmont, CO PMSA..............	291 288		13 047	Catoosa County, GA..............	53 282
		(See Denver-Boulder-Greeley, CO CMSA)			13 083	Dade County, GA..............	15 154
1145		Brazoria, TX PMSA..............	241 767		13 295	Walker County, GA..............	61 053
		(See Houston-Galveston-Brazoria, TX CMSA)			47 065	Hamilton County, TN..............	307 896
					47 115	Marion County, TN..............	27 776
1150		Bremerton, WA PMSA..............	231 969	1580		Cheyenne, WY MSA..............	81 607
		(See Seattle-Tacoma-Bremerton, WA CMSA)			56 021	Laramie County, WY..............	81 607
1240		Brownsville-Harlingen-San Benito, TX MSA	335 227	14		Chicago-Gary-Kenosha, IL-IN-WI CMSA...........	9 157 540
	48 061	Cameron County, TX..............	335 227	1600		Chicago, IL PMSA..............	8 272 768
					17 031	Cook County, IL..............	5 376 741
					17 037	De Kalb County, IL..............	88 969
					17 043	Du Page County, IL..............	904 161
					17 063	Grundy County, IL..............	37 535

(MSA = metropolitan statistical area; CMSA = consolidated MSA; PMSA = primary MSA; and NECMA = New England county metropolitan area. For further information, see Appendix A.)

Geographic Codes		Tital and Geographic Components	2000 Population	Geographic Codes		Title and Geographic Components	2000 Population
MSA/ CMSA/ PMSA/ NECMA	State and County			MSA/ CMSA/ PMSA/ NECMA	State and County		
	17 089	Kane County, IL	404 119	1800		Columbus, GA-AL MSA	274 624
	17 093	Kendall County, IL	54 544		01 113	Russell County, AL	49 756
	17 097	Lake County, IL	644 356		13 053	Chattahoochee County, GA	14 882
	17 111	McHenry County, IL	260 077		13 145	Harris County, GA	23 695
	17 197	Will County, IL	502 266		13 215	Muscogee County, GA	186 291
2960		Gary, IN PMSA	631 362	1840		Columbus, OH MSA	1 540 157
	18 089	Lake County, IN	484 564		39 041	Delaware County, OH	109 989
	18 127	Porter County, IN	146 798		39 045	Fairfield County, OH	122 759
					39 049	Franklin County, OH	1 068 978
3740		Kankakee, IL PMSA	103 833		39 089	Licking County, OH	145 491
	17 091	Kankakee County, IL	103 833		39 097	Madison County, OH	40 213
					39 129	Pickaway County, OH	52 727
3800		Kenosha, WI PMSA	149 577				
	55 059	Kenosha County, WI	149 577	1880		Corpus Christi, TX MSA	380 783
					48 355	Nueces County, TX	313 645
1620		Chico-Paradise, CA MSA	203 171		48 409	San Patricio County, TX	67 138
	06 007	Butte County, CA	203 171				
				1890		Corvallis, OR MSA	78 153
21		Cincinnati-Hamilton, OH-KY-IN CMSA	1 979 202		41 003	Benton County, OR	78 153
1640		Cincinnati, OH-KY-IN PMSA	1 646 395	1900		Cumberland, MD-WV MSA	102 008
	18 029	Dearborn County, IN	46 109		24 001	Allegany County, MD	74 930
	18 115	Ohio County, IN	5 623		54 057	Mineral County, WV	27 078
	21 015	Boone County, KY	85 991				
	21 037	Campbell County, KY	88 616	31		Dallas-Fort Worth, TX CMSA	5 221 801
	21 077	Gallatin County, KY	7 870				
	21 081	Grant County, KY	22 384	1920		Dallas, TX PMSA	3 519 176
	21 117	Kenton County, KY	151 464		48 085	Collin County, TX	491 675
	21 191	Pendleton County, KY	14 390		48 113	Dallas County, TX	2 218 899
	39 015	Brown County, OH	42 285		48 121	Denton County, TX	432 976
	39 025	Clermont County, OH	177 977		48 139	Ellis County, TX	111 360
	30 061	Hamilton County, OH	845 303		48 213	Henderson County, TX	73 277
	39 165	Warren County, OH	158 383		48 231	Hunt County, TX	76 596
					48 257	Kaufman County, TX	71 313
3200		Hamilton-Middletown, OH PMSA	332 807		48 397	Rockwall County, TX	43 080
	39 017	Butler County, OH	332 807				
				2800		Fort Worth-Arlington, TX PMSA	1 702 625
1660		Clarksville-Hopkinsville, TN-KY MSA	207 033		48 221	Hood County, TX	41 100
	21 047	Christian County, KY	72 265		48 251	Johnson County, TX	126 811
	47 125	Montgomery County, TN	134 768		48 367	Parker County, TX	88 495
					48 439	Tarrant County, TX	1 446 219
28		Cleveland-Akron, OH CMSA	2 945 831				
				1950		Danville, VA MSA	110 156
80		Akron, OH PMSA	694 960		51 143	Pittsylvania County, VA	61 745
	39 133	Portage County, OH	152 061		51 590	Danville City, VA	48 411
	39 153	Summit County, OH	542 899				
				1960		Davenport-Moline-Rock Island, IA-IL MSA	359 062
1680		Cleveland-Lorain-Elyria, OH PMSA	2 250 871		17 073	Henry County, IL	51 020
	39 007	Ashtabula County, OH	102 728		17 161	Rock Island County, IL	149 374
	39 035	Cuyahoga County, OH	1 393 978		19 163	Scott County, IA	158 668
	39 055	Geauga County, OH	90 895				
	39 085	Lake County, OH	227 511	2000		Dayton-Springfield, OH MSA	950 558
	39 093	Lorain County, OH	284 664		39 023	Clark County, OH	144 742
	39 103	Medina County, OH	151 095		39 057	Greene County, OH	147 886
					39 109	Miami County, OH	98 868
1720		Colorado Springs, CO MSA	516 929		39 113	Montgomery County, OH	559 062
	08 041	El Paso County, CO	516 929				
				2020		Daytona Beach, FL MSA	493 175
1740		Columbia, MO MSA	135 454		12 035	Flagler County, FL	49 832
	29 019	Boone County, MO	135 454		12 127	Volusia County, FL	443 343
1760		Columbia, SC MSA	536 691	2030		Decatur, AL MSA	145 867
	45 063	Lexington County, SC	216 014		01 079	Lawrence County, AL	34 803
	45 079	Richland County, SC	320 677		01 103	Morgan County, AL	111 064

(MSA = metropolitan statistical area; CMSA = consolidated MSA; PMSA = primary MSA; and
NECMA = New England county metropolitan area. For further information, see Appendix A.)

MSA/ CMSA/ PMSA/ NECMA	State and County	Tital and Geographic Components	2000 Population	MSA/ CMSA/ PMSA/ NECMA	State and County	Tital and Geographic Components	2000 Population
2040		Decatur, IL MSA...	114 706	2330		Elkhart-Goshen, IN MSA....................................	182 791
	17 115	Macon County, IL	114 706		18 039	Elkhart County, IN	182 791
34		Denver-Boulder-Greeley, CO CMSA	2 581 506	2335		Elmira, NY MSA...	91 070
1125		Boulder-Longmont, CO PMSA	291 288		36 015	Chemung County, NY	91 070
	08 013	Boulder County, CO	291 288	2340		Enid, OK MSA...	57 813
2080		Denver, CO PMSA	2 109 282		40 047	Garfield County, OK	57 813
	08 001	Adams County, CO.......................................	363 857	2360		Erie, PA MSA..	280 843
	08 005	Arapahoe County, CO	487 967		42 049	Erie County, PA..	280 843
	08 031	Denver County, CO	554 636	2400		Eugene-Springfield, OR MSA	322 959
	08 035	Douglas County, CO	175 766		41 039	Lane County, OR..	322 959
	08 059	Jefferson County, CO	527 056	2440		Evansville-Henderson, IN-KY MSA......................	296 195
3060		Greeley, CO PMSA	180 936		18 129	Posey County, IN..	27 061
	08 123	Weld County, CO..	180 936		18 163	Vanderburgh County, IN................................	171 922
2120		Des Moines, IA MSA	456 022		18 173	Warrick County, IN	52 383
	19 049	Dallas County, IA	40 750		21 101	Henderson County, KY..................................	44 829
	19 153	Polk County, IA	374 601	2520		Fargo-Moorhead, ND-MN MSA...........................	174 367
	19 181	Warren County, IA	40 671		27 027	Clay County, MN	51 229
2162		Detroit-Ann Arbor-Flint, MI CMSA......................	5 456 428		38 017	Cass County, ND..	123 138
0440		Ann Arbor, MI PMSA..	578 736	2560		Fayetteville, NC MSA..	302 963
	26 091	Lenawee County, MI	98 890		37 051	Cumberland County, NC	302 963
	26 093	Livingston County, MI	156 951	2580		Fayetteville-Springdale-Rogers, AR MSA	311 121
	26 161	Washtenaw County, MI	322 895		05 007	Benton County, AR..	153 406
2160		Detroit, MI PMSA	4 441 551		05 143	Washington County, AR	157 715
	26 087	Lapeer County, MI..	87 904	2620		Flagstaff, AZ-UT MSA.......................................	122 366
	26 099	Macomb County, MI	788 149		04 005	Coconino County, AZ	116 320
	26 115	Monroe County, MI	145 945		49 025	Kane County, UT	6 046
	26 125	Oakland County, MI	1 194 156	2640		Flint, MI PMSA	436 141
	26 147	St. Clair County, MI	164 235			(See Detroit-Ann Arbor-Flint, MI CMSA)	
	26 163	Wayne County, MI..	2 061 162	2650		Florence, AL MSA..	142 950
2640		Flint, MI PMSA	436 141		01 033	Colbert County, AL	54 984
	26 049	Genesee County, MI.....................................	436 141		01 077	Lauderdale County, AL..................................	87 966
2180		Dothan, AL MSA	137 916	2655		Florence, SC MSA	125 761
	01 045	Dale County, AL	49 129		45 041	Florence County, SC	125 761
	01 069	Houston County, AL	88 787	2670		Fort Collins-Loveland, CO MSA..........................	251 494
2190		Dover, DE MSA	126 697		08 069	Larimer County, CO.......................................	251 494
	10 001	Kent County, DE	126 697	2680		Fort Lauderdale, FL PMSA	1 623 018
2200		Dubuque, IA MSA	89 143			(See Miami-Fort Lauderdale, FL CMSA)	
	19 061	Dubuque County, IA	89 143	2700		Fort Myers-Cape Coral, FL MSA	440 888
2240		Duluth-Superior, MN-WI MSA	243 815		12 071	Lee County, FL	440 888
	27 137	St. Louis County, MN	200 528	2710		Fort Pierce-Port St. Lucie, FL MSA	319 426
	55 031	Douglas County, WI	43 287		12 085	Martin County, FL...	126 731
2281		Dutchess County, NY PMSA	280 150		12 111	St. Lucie County, FL......................................	192 695
		(See New York-Northern New Jersey-Long Island, NY-NJ-CT-PA CMSA)		2720		Fort Smith, AR-OK MSA	207 290
2290		Eau Claire, WI MSA	148 337		05 033	Crawford County, AR.....................................	53 247
	55 017	Chippewa County, WI....................................	55 195		05 131	Sebastian County, AR	115 071
	55 035	Eau Claire County, WI...................................	93 142		40 135	Sequoyah County, OK....................................	38 972
2320		El Paso, TX MSA	679 622	2750		Fort Walton Beach, FL MSA	170 498
	48 141	El Paso County, TX	679 622		12 091	Okaloosa County, FL.....................................	170 498

(MSA = metropolitan statistical area; CMSA = consolidated MSA; PMSA = primary MSA; and NECMA = New England county metropolitan area. For further information, see Appendix A.)

MSA/ CMSA/ PMSA/ NECMA	State and County	Title and Geographic Components	2000 Population	MSA/ CMSA/ PMSA/ NECMA	State and County	Title and Geographic Components	2000 Population
				3150		Greenville, NC MSA	133 798
2760		Fort Wayne, IN MSA	502 141		37 147	Pitt County, NC	133 798
	18 001	Adams County, IN	33 625				
	18 003	Allen County, IN...........................	331 849	3160		Greenville-Spartanburg-Anderson, SC MSA.......	962 441
	18 033	De Kalb County, IN	40 285		45 007	Anderson County, SC...........................	165 740
	18 069	Huntington County, IN	38 075		45 021	Cherokee County, SC.	52 537
	18 179	Wells County, IN	27 600		45 045	Greenville County, SC...........................	379 616
	18 183	Whitley County, IN	30 707		45 077	Pickens County, SC...........................	110 757
					45 083	Spartanburg County, SC...........................	253 791
2800		Fort Worth-Arlington, TX PMSA	1 702 625				
		(See Dallas-Fort Worth, TX CMSA)		3180		Hagerstown, MD PMSA	131 923
						(See Washington-Baltimore, DC-MD-VA-WV CMSA)	
2840		Fresno, CA MSA	922 516				
	06 019	Fresno County, CA...........................	799 407	3240		Harrisburg-Lebanon-Carlisle, PA MSA	629 401
	06 039	Madera County, CA...........................	123 109		42 041	Cumberland County, PA	213 674
					42 043	Dauphin County, PA	251 798
2880		Gadsden, AL MSA	103 459		42 075	Lebanon County, PA	120 327
	01 055	Etowah County, AL...........................	103 459		42 099	Perry County, PA	43 602
2900		Gainesville, FL MSA...........................	217 955				
	12 001	Alachua County, FL...........................	217 955	3280		Hartford, CT NECMA	1 148 618
					09 003	Hartford County, CT...........................	857 183
2920		Galveston-Texas City, TX PMSA	250 158		09 007	Middlesex County, CT	155 071
		(See Houston-Galveston-Brazoria, TX CMSA)			09 013	Tolland County, CT...........................	136 364
				3285		Hattiesburg, MS MSA...........................	111 674
2975		Glens Falls, NY MSA	124 345		28 035	Forrest County, MS	72 604
	36 113	Warren County, NY	63 303		28 073	Lamar County, MS	39 070
	36 115	Washington County, NY	61 042				
				3290		Hickory-Morganton-Lenoir, NC MSA...........................	341 851
2980		Goldsboro, NC MSA...........................	113 329		37 003	Alexander County, NC...........................	33 603
	37 191	Wayne County, NC	113 329		37 023	Burke County, NC...........................	89 148
					37 027	Caldwell County, NC...........................	77 415
2985		Grand Forks, ND-MN MSA	97 478		37 035	Catawba County, NC...........................	141 685
	27 119	Polk County, MN...........................	31 369				
	38 035	Grand Forks County, ND...........................	66 109	3320		Honolulu, HI MSA...........................	876 156
					15 003	Honolulu County, HI	876 156
2995		Grand Junction, CO MSA	116 255				
	08 077	Mesa County, CO...........................	116 255	3350		Houma, LA MSA...........................	194 477
					22 057	Lafourche Parish, LA	89 974
3000		Grand Rapids-Muskegon-Holland, MI MSA........	1 088 514		22 109	Terrebonne Parish, LA	104 503
	26 005	Allegan County, MI	105 665				
	26 081	Kent County, MI...........................	574 335	3362		Houston-Galveston-Brazoria, TX CMSA.............	4 669 571
	26 121	Muskegon County, MI...........................	170 200				
	26 139	Ottawa County, MI...........................	238 314	1145		Brazoria, TX PMSA...........................	241 767
					48 039	Brazoria County, TX	241 767
3040		Great Falls, MT MSA...........................	80 357				
	30 013	Cascade County, MT...........................	80 357	2920		Galveston-Texas City, TX PMSA	250 158
						Galveston County, TX	250 158
3060		Greeley, CO PMSA	180 936				
		(See Denver-Boulder-Greeley, CO CMSA)		3360		Houston, TX PMSA...........................	4 177 646
					48 071	Chambers County, TX	26 031
3080		Green Bay, WI MSA...........................	226 778		48 157	Fort Bend County, TX	354 452
	55 009	Brown County, WI...........................	226 778		48 201	Harris County, TX...........................	3 400 578
					48 291	Liberty County, TX...........................	70 154
3120		Greensboro-Winston-Salem-High Point, NC MSA	1 251 509		48 339	Montgomery County, TX...........................	293 768
	37 001	Alamance County, NC	130 800		48 473	Waller County, TX...........................	32 663
	37 057	Davidson County, NC...........................	147 246				
	37 059	Davie County, NC...........................	34 835	3400		Huntington-Ashland, WV-KY-OH MSA...........................	315 538
	37 067	Forsyth County, NC...........................	306 067		21 019	Boyd County, KY	49 752
	37 081	Guilford County, NC	421 048		21 043	Carter County, KY...........................	26 889
	37 151	Randolph County, NC...........................	130 454		21 089	Greenup County, KY...........................	36 891
	37 169	Stokes County, NC	44 711		39 087	Lawrence County, OH	62 319
	37 197	Yadkin County, NC	36 348		54 011	Cabell County, WV	96 784
					54 099	Wayne County, WV...........................	42 903

Metropolitan Statistical Areas and Components – Continued

(MSA = metropolitan statistical area; CMSA = consolidated MSA; PMSA = primary MSA; and NECMA = New England county metropolitan area. For further information, see Appendix A.)

MSA/CMSA/PMSA/NECMA	State and County	Tital and Geographic Components	2000 Population	MSA/CMSA/PMSA/NECMA	State and County	Tital and Geographic Components	2000 Population
3440		Huntsville, AL MSA	342 376	3710		Joplin, MO MSA	157 322
	01 083	Limestone County, AL	65 676		29 097	Jasper County, MO	104 686
	01 089	Madison County, AL	276 700		29 145	Newton County, MO	52 636
3480		Indianapolis, IN MSA	1 607 486	3720		Kalamazoo-Battle Creek, MI MSA	452 851
	18 011	Boone County, IN	46 107		26 025	Calhoun County, MI	137 985
	18 057	Hamilton County, IN	182 740		26 077	Kalamazoo County, MI	238 603
	18 059	Hancock County, IN	55 391		26 159	Van Buren County, MI	76 263
	18 063	Hendricks County, IN	104 093				
	18 081	Johnson County, IN	115 209	3740		Kankakee, IL PMSA	103 833
	18 095	Madison County, IN	133 358			(See Chicago-Gary-Kenosha, IL-IN-WI CMSA)	
	18 097	Marion County, IN	860 454				
	18 109	Morgan County, IN	66 689	3760		Kansas City, MO-KS MSA	1 776 062
	18 145	Shelby County, IN	43 445		20 091	Johnson County, KS	451 086
3500		Iowa City, IA MSA	111 006		20 103	Leavenworth County, KS	68 691
	19 103	Johnson County, IA	111 006		20 121	Miami County, KS	28 351
					20 209	Wyandotte County, KS	157 882
3520		Jackson, MI MSA	158 422		29 037	Cass County, MO	82 092
	26 075	Jackson County, MI	158 422		29 047	Clay County, MO	184 006
					29 049	Clinton County, MO	18 979
3560		Jackson, MS MSA	440 801		29 095	Jackson County, MO	654 880
	28 049	Hinds County, MS	250 800		29 107	Lafayette County, MO	32 960
	28 089	Madison County, MS	74 674		29 165	Platte County, MO	73 781
	28 121	Rankin County, MS	115 327		29 177	Ray County, MO	23 354
3580		Jackson, TN MSA	107 377	3800		Kenosha, WI PMSA	149 577
	47 023	Chester County, TN	15 540			(See Chicago-Gary-Kenosha, IL-IN-WI CMSA)	
	47 113	Madison County, TN	91 837				
3600		Jacksonville, FL MSA	1 100 491	3810		Killeen-Temple, TX MSA	312 952
	12 019	Clay County, FL	140 814		48 027	Bell County, TX	237 974
	12 031	Duval County, FL	778 879		48 099	Coryell County, TX	74 978
	12 089	Nassau County, FL	57 663	3840		Knoxville, TN MSA	687 249
	12 109	St. Johns County, FL	123 135		47 001	Anderson County, TN	71 330
3605		Jacksonville, NC MSA	150 355		47 009	Blount County, TN	105 823
	37 133	Onslow County, NC	150 355		47 093	Knox County, TN	382 032
					47 105	Loudon County, TN	39 086
3610		Jamestown, NY MSA	139 750		47 155	Sevier County, TN	71 170
	36 013	Chautauqua County, NY	139 750		47 173	Union County, TN	17 808
3620		Janesville-Beloit, WI MSA	152 307	3850		Kokomo, IN MSA	101 541
	55 105	Rock County, WI	152 307		18 067	Howard County, IN	84 964
					18 159	Tipton County, IN	16 577
3640		Jersey City, NJ PMSA	608 975				
		(See New York-Northern New Jersey-Long Island, NY-NJ-CT-PA CMSA)		3870		La Crosse, WI-MN MSA	126 838
					27 055	Houston County, MN	19 718
					55 063	La Crosse County, WI	107 120
3660		Johnson City-Kingsport-Bristol, TN-VA MSA	480 091	3920		Lafayette, IN MSA	182 821
	47 019	Carter County, TN	56 742		18 023	Clinton County, IN	33 866
	47 073	Hawkins County, TN	53 563		18 157	Tippecanoe County, IN	148 955
	47 163	Sullivan County, TN	153 048				
	47 171	Unicoi County, TN	17 667	3880		Lafayette, LA MSA	385 647
	47 179	Washington County, TN	107 198		22 001	Acadia Parish, LA	58 861
	51 169	Scott County, VA	23 403		22 055	Lafayette Parish, LA	190 503
	51 191	Washington County, VA	51 103		22 097	St. Landry Parish, LA	87 700
	51 520	Bristol City, VA	17 367		22 099	St. Martin Parish, LA	48 583
3680		Johnstown, PA MSA	232 621				
	42 021	Cambria County, PA	152 598	3960		Lake Charles, LA MSA	183 577
	42 111	Somerset County, PA	80 023		22 019	Calcasieu Parish, LA	183 577
3700		Jonesboro, AR MSA	82 148	3980		Lakeland-Winter Haven, FL MSA	483 924
	5 031	Craighead County, AR	82 148		12 105	Polk County, FL	483 924

(MSA = metropolitan statistical area; CMSA = consolidated MSA; PMSA = primary MSA; and NECMA = New England county metropolitan area. For further information, see Appendix A.)

MSA/ CMSA/ PMSA/ NECMA	State and County	Title and Geographic Components	2000 Population
4000		Lancaster, PA MSA	470 658
	42 071	Lancaster County, PA	470 658
4040		Lansing-East Lansing, MI MSA	447 728
	26 037	Clinton County, MI	64 753
	26 045	Eaton County, MI	103 655
	26 065	Ingham County, MI	279 320
4080		Laredo, TX MSA	193 117
	48 479	Webb County, TX	193 117
4100		Las Cruces, NM MSA	174 682
	35 013	Dona Ana County, NM	174 682
4120		Las Vegas, NV-AZ MSA	1 563 282
	04 015	Mohave County, AZ	155 032
	32 003	Clark County, NV	1 375 765
	32 023	Nye County, NV	32 485
4150		Lawrence, KS MSA	99 962
	20 045	Douglas County, KS	99 962
4200		Lawton, OK MSA	114 996
	40 031	Comanche County, OK	114 996
4240		Lewiston-Auburn, ME NECMA	103 793
	23 001	Androscoggin County, ME	103 793
4280		Lexington, KY MSA	479 198
	21 017	Bourbon County, KY	19 360
	21 049	Clark County, KY	33 144
	21 067	Fayette County, KY	260 512
	21 113	Jessamine County, KY	39 041
	21 151	Madison County, KY	70 872
	21 209	Scott County, KY	33 001
	21 239	Woodford County, KY	23 208
4320		Lima, OH MSA	155 084
	39 003	Allen County, OH	108 473
	39 011	Auglaize County, OH	46 611
4360		Lincoln, NE MSA	250 291
	31 109	Lancaster County, NE	250 291
4400		Little Rock-North Little Rock, AR MSA	583 845
	05 045	Faulkner County, AR	86 014
	05 085	Lonoke County, AR	52 828
	05 119	Pulaski County, AR	361 474
	05 125	Saline County, AR	83 529
4420		Longview-Marshall, TX MSA	208 780
	48 183	Gregg County, TX	111 379
	48 203	Harrison County, TX	62 110
	48 459	Upshur County, TX	35 291
4472		Los Angeles-Riverside-Orange County, CA CMSA	16 373 645
4480		Los Angeles-Long Beach, CA PMSA	9 519 338
	06 037	Los Angeles County, CA	9 519 338
5945		Orange County, CA PMSA	2 846 289
	06 059	Orange County, CA	2 846 289
4520		Louisville, KY-IN MSA	1 025 598
	18 019	Clark County, IN	96 472
	18 043	Floyd County, IN	70 823
	18 061	Harrison County, IN	34 325
	18 143	Scott County, IN	22 960
	21 029	Bullitt County, KY	61 236
	21 111	Jefferson County, KY	693 604
	21 185	Oldham County, KY	46 178
4600		Lubbock, TX MSA	242 628
	48 303	Lubbock County, TX	242 628
4640		Lynchburg, VA MSA	214 911
	51 009	Amherst County, VA	31 894
	51 019	Bedford County, VA	60 371
	51 031	Campbell County, VA	51 078
	51 515	Bedford City, VA	6 299
	51 680	Lynchburg City, VA	65 269
4680		Macon, GA MSA	322 549
	13 021	Bibb County, GA	153 887
	13 153	Houston County, GA	110 765
	13 169	Jones County, GA	23 639
	13 225	Peach County, GA	23 668
	13 289	Twiggs County, GA	10 590
4720		Madison, WI MSA	426 526
	55 025	Dane County, WI	426 526
4800		Mansfield, OH MSA	175 818
	39 033	Crawford County, OH	46 966
	39 139	Richland County, OH	128 852
4880		McAllen-Edinburg-Mission, TX MSA	569 463
	48 215	Hidalgo County, TX	569 463
4800		Medford-Ashland, OR MSA	181 269
	41 029	Jackson County, OR	181 269
4900		Melbourne-Titusville-Palm Bay, FL MSA	476 230
	12 009	Brevard County, FL	476 230
4920		Memphis, TN-AR-MS MSA	1 135 614
	05 035	Crittenden County, AR	50 866
	28 033	De Soto County, MS	107 199
	47 047	Fayette County, TN	28 806
	47 157	Shelby County, TN	897 472
	47 167	Tipton County, TN	51 271
4940		Merced, CA MSA	210 554
	06 047	Merced County, CA	210 554
4992		Miami-Fort Lauderdale, FL CMSA	3 876 380
2680		Fort Lauderdale, FL PMSA	1 623 018
	12 011	Broward County, FL	1 623 018
5000		Miami, FL PMSA	2 253 362
	12 086	Miami-Dade County, FL	2 253 362
5082		Milwaukee-Racine, WI CMSA	1 689 572
5080		Milwaukee-Waukesha, WI PMSA	1 500 741
	55 079	Milwaukee County, WI	940 164
	55 089	Ozaukee County, WI	82 317
	55 131	Washington County, WI	117 493
	55 133	Waukesha County, WI	360 767

(MSA = metropolitan statistical area; CMSA = consolidated MSA; PMSA = primary MSA; and
NECMA = New England county metropolitan area. For further information, see Appendix A.)

MSA/ CMSA/ PMSA/ NECMA	State and County	Tital and Geographic Components	2000 Population	MSA/ CMSA/ PMSA/ NECMA	State and County	Tital and Geographic Components	2000 Population
6600		Racine, WI PMSA	188 831	5560		New Orleans, LA MSA	1 337 726
	55 101	Racine County, WI	188 831		22 051	Jefferson Parish, LA	455 466
5120		Minneapolis-St. Paul, MN-WI MSA	2 968 806		22 071	Orleans Parish, LA	484 674
	27 003	Anoka County, MN	298 084		22 075	Plaquemines Parish, LA	26 757
	27 019	Carver County, MN	70 205		22 087	St. Bernard Parish, LA	67 229
	27 025	Chisago County, MN	41 101		22 089	St. Charles Parish, LA	48 072
	27 037	Dakota County, MN	355 904		22 093	St. James Parish, LA	21 216
	27 053	Hennepin County, MN	1 116 200		22 095	St. John the Baptist Parish, LA	43 044
	27 059	Isanti County, MN	31 287		22 103	St. Tammany Parish, LA	191 268
	27 123	Ramsey County, MN	511 035	5600		New York, NY PMSA	9 314 235
	27 139	Scott County, MN	89 498			(See New York-Northern New Jersey-Long	
	27 141	Sherburne County, MN	64 417			Island, NY-NJ-CT-PA CMSA)	
	27 163	Washington County, MN..........................	201 130				
	27 171	Wright County, MN	89 986	70		New York-Northern New Jersey-Long Island,	21 199 865
	55 093	Pierce County, WI	36 804			NY-NJ-CT-PA CMSA	
	55 109	St. Croix County, WI	63 155				
				875		Bergen-Passaic, NJ PMSA	1 373 167
5140		Missoula, MT MSA	95 802		34 003	Bergen County, NJ	884 118
	30 063	Missoula County, MT	95 802		34 031	Passaic County, NJ	489 049
5160		Mobile, AL MSA	540 258	2281		Dutchess County, NY PMSA	280 150
	01 003	Baldwin County, AL	140 415		36 027	Dutchess County, NY	280 150
	01 097	Mobile County, AL	399 843				
				3640		Jersey City, NJ PMSA..........................	608 975
5170		Modesto, CA MSA..........................	446 997		34 017	Hudson County, NJ	608 975
	06 099	Stanislaus County, CA..........................	446 997				
				5015		Middlesex-Somerset-Hunterdon, NJ PMSA........	1 169 641
5190		Monmouth-Ocean, NJ PMSA..........................	1 126 217		34 019	Hunterdon County, NJ..........................	121 989
		(See New York-Northern New Jersey-Long			34 023	Middlesex County, NJ..........................	750 162
		Island, NY-NJ-CT-PA CMSA)			34 035	Somerset County, NJ	297 490
5200		Monroe, LA MSA..........................	147 250	5190		Monmouth-Ocean, NJ PMSA..........................	1 126 217
	22 073	Ouachita Parish, LA..........................	147 250		34 025	Monmouth County, NJ..........................	615 301
5240		Montgomery, AL MSA..........................	333 055		34 029	Ocean County, NJ	510 916
	01 001	Autauga County, AL	43 671	5380		Nassau-Suffolk, NY PMSA..........................	2 753 913
	01 051	Elmore County, AL	65 874		36 059	Nassau County, NY	1 334 544
	01 101	Montgomery County, AL..........................	223 510		36 103	Suffolk County, NY	1 419 369
5280		Muncie, IN MSA	118 769	5483		New Haven-Bridgeport-Stamford-Danbury-	1 706 575
	18 035	Delaware County, IN	118 769			Waterbury, CT NECMA..........................	
					09 001	Fairfield County, CT..........................	882 567
5330		Myrtle Beach, SC MSA	196 629		09 009	New Haven County, CT..........................	824 008
	45 051	Horry County, SC	196 629				
				5600		New York, NY PMSA	9 314 235
5345		Naples, FL MSA	251 377		36 005	Bronx County, NY	1 332 650
	12 021	Collier County, FL..........................	251 377		36 047	Kings County, NY	2 465 326
5360		Nashville, TN MSA..........................	1 231 311		36 061	New York County, NY	1 537 195
	47 021	Cheatham County, TN	35 912		36 079	Putnam County, NY	95 745
	47 037	Davidson County, TN	569 891		36 081	Queens County, NY	2 229 379
	47 043	Dickson County, TN..........................	43 156		36 085	Richmond County, NY	443 728
	47 147	Robertson County, TN..........................	54 433		36 087	Rockland County, NY	286 753
	47 149	Rutherford County, TN	182 023		36 119	Westchester County, NY	923 459
	47 165	Sumner County, TN..........................	130 449	5640		Newark, NJ PMSA	2 032 989
	47 187	Williamson County, TN..........................	126 638		34 013	Essex County, NJ	793 633
	47 189	Wilson County, TN..........................	88 809		34 027	Morris County, NJ	470 212
5380		Nassau-Suffolk, NY PMSA..........................	2 753 913		34 037	Sussex County, NJ	144 166
		(See New York-Northern New Jersey-Long			34 039	Union County, NJ	522 541
		Island, NY-NJ-CT-PA CMSA)			34 041	Warren County, NJ	102 437
5520		New London-Norwich, CT NECMA....................	259 088	5660		Newburgh, NY-PA PMSA..........................	387 669
	09 011	New London County, CT..........................	259 088		36 071	Orange County, NY	341 367
					42 103	Pike County, PA	46 302

Metropolitan Statistical Areas and Components – Continued

(MSA = metropolitan statistical area; CMSA = consolidated MSA; PMSA = primary MSA; and
NECMA = New England county metropolitan area. For further information, see Appendix A.)

MSA/ CMSA/ PMSA/ NECMA	State and County	Tital and Geographic Components	2000 Population	MSA/ CMSA/ PMSA/ NECMA	State and County	Tital and Geographic Components	2000 Population
8480		Trenton, NJ PMSA	350 761	6020		Parkersburg-Marietta, WV-OH MSA	151 237
	34 021	Mercer County, NJ	350 761		39 167	Washington County, OH	63 251
5720		Norfolk-Virginia Beach-Newport News, VA-NC	1 569 541		54 107	Wood County, WV	87 986
		MSA		6080		Pensacola, FL MSA	412 153
	37 053	Currituck County, NC	18 190		12 033	Escambia County, FL	294 410
	51 073	Gloucester County, VA	34 780		12 113	Santa Rosa County, FL	117 743
	51 093	Isle of Wight County, VA	29 728				
	51 095	James City, VA	48 102	6120		Peoria-Pekin, IL MSA	347 387
	51 115	Mathews County, VA	9 207		17 143	Peoria County, IL	183 433
	51 199	York County, VA	56 297		17 179	Tazewell County, IL	128 485
	51 550	Chesapeake City, VA	199 184		17 203	Woodford County, IL	35 469
	51 650	Hampton City, VA	146 437				
	51 700	Newport News City, VA	180 150	0102		Philadelphia-Wilmington-Atlantic City, PA-NJ-	6 188 463
	51 710	Norfolk City, VA	234 403			DE-MD CMSA	
	51 735	Poquoson City, VA	11 566				
	51 740	Portsmouth City, VA	100 565	560		Atlantic-Cape May, NJ PMSA	354 878
	51 800	Suffolk City, VA	63 677		34 001	Atlantic County, NJ	252 552
	51 810	Virginia Beach City, VA	425 257		34 009	Cape May County, NJ	102 326
	51 830	Williamsburg City, VA	11 998				
				6160		Philadelphia, PA-NJ PMSA	5 100 931
5775		Oakland, CA PMSA	2 392 557		34 005	Burlington County, NJ	423 394
		(See San Francisco-Oakland-San Jose, CA			34 007	Camden County, NJ	508 932
		CMSA)			34 015	Gloucester County, NJ	254 673
					34 033	Salem County, NJ	64 285
5790		Ocala, FL MSA	258 916		42 017	Bucks County, PA	597 635
	12 000	Marion County, FL	258 916		42 029	Chester County, PA	433 501
					42 045	Delaware County, PA	550 004
5800		Odessa-Midland, TX MSA	237 132		42 091	Montgomery County, PA	750 097
	48 135	Ector County, TX	121 123		42 101	Philadelphia County, PA	1 517 550
	48 329	Midland County, TX	116 009				
				8760		Vineland-Millville-Bridgeton, NJ PMSA	146 438
5880		Oklahoma City, OK MSA	1 083 346		34 011	Cumberland County, NJ	146 438
	40 017	Canadian County, OK	87 697				
	40 027	Cleveland County, OK	208 016	9160		Wilmington-Newark, DE-MD PMSA	586 216
	40 083	Logan County, OK	33 924		10 003	New Castle County, DE	500 265
	40 087	McClain County, OK	27 740		24 015	Cecil County, MD	85 951
	40 109	Oklahoma County, OK	660 448				
	40 125	Pottawatomie County, OK	65 521	6200		Phoenix-Mesa, AZ MSA	3 251 876
					04 013	Maricopa County, AZ	3 072 149
5910		Olympia, WA PMSA	207 355		04 021	Pinal County, AZ	179 727
		(See Seattle-Tacoma-Bremerton, WA CMSA)					
				6240		Pine Bluff, AR MSA	84 278
5920		Omaha, NE-IA MSA	716 998		05 069	Jefferson County, AR	84 278
	19 155	Pottawattamie County, IA	87 704				
	31 025	Cass County, NE	24 334	6280		Pittsburgh, PA MSA	2 358 695
	31 055	Douglas County, NE	463 585		42 003	Allegheny County, PA	1 281 666
	31 153	Sarpy County, NE	122 595		42 007	Beaver County, PA	181 412
	31 177	Washington County, NE	18 780		42 019	Butler County, PA	174 083
					42 051	Fayette County, PA	148 644
5945		Orange County, CA PMSA	2 846 289		42 125	Washington County, PA	202 897
		(See Los Angeles-Long Beach, CA PMSA)			42 129	Westmoreland County, PA	369 993
5960		Orlando, FL MSA	1 644 561	6323		Pittsfield, MA NECMA	134 953
	12 069	Lake County, FL	210 528		25 003	Berkshire County, MA	134 953
	12 095	Orange County, FL	896 344				
	12 097	Osceola County, FL	172 493	6340		Pocatello, ID MSA	75 565
	12 117	Seminole County, FL	365 196		16 005	Bannock County, ID	75 565
5990		Owensboro, KY MSA	91 545	6403		Portland, ME NECMA	265 612
	21 059	Daviess County, KY	91 545		23 005	Cumberland County, ME	265 612
6015		Panama City, FL MSA	148 217	6442		Portland-Salem, OR-WA CMSA	2 265 223
	12 005	Bay County, FL	148 217				
				6440		Portland-Vancouver, OR-WA PMSA	1 918 009
					41 005	Clackamas County, OR	338 391

Metropolitan Statistical Areas and Components – Continued

(MSA = metropolitan statistical area; CMSA = consolidated MSA; PMSA = primary MSA; and
NECMA = New England county metropolitan area. For further information, see Appendix A.)

MSA/CMSA/PMSA/NECMA	State and County	Tital and Geographic Components	2000 Population	MSA/CMSA/PMSA/NECMA	State and County	Tital and Geographic Components	2000 Population
	41 009	Columbia County, OR	43 560				
	41 051	Multnomah County, OR	660 486	6780		Riverside-San Bernardino, CA PMSA	3 254 821
	41 067	Washington County, OR	445 342			(See Los Angeles-Riverside-Orange County,	
	41 071	Yamhill County, OR	84 992			CA CMSA)	
	53 011	Clark County, WA	345 238				
				6800		Roanoke, VA MSA	235 932
7080		Salem, OR PMSA	347 214		51 023	Botetourt County, VA	30 496
	41 047	Marion County, OR	284 834		51 161	Roanoke County, VA	85 778
	41 053	Polk County, OR	62 380		51 770	Roanoke City, VA	94 911
					51 775	Salem City, VA	24 747
6483		Providence-Warwick-Pawtucket, RI NECMA	962 886				
	44 001	Bristol County, RI	50 648	6820		Rochester, MN MSA	124 277
	44 003	Kent County, RI	167 090		27 109	Olmsted County, MN	124 277
	44 007	Providence County, RI	621 602	6840		Rochester, NY MSA	1 098 201
	44 009	Washington County, RI	123 546		36 037	Genesee County, NY	60 370
					36 051	Livingston County, NY	64 328
6520		Provo-Orem, UT MSA	368 536		36 055	Monroe County, NY	735 343
	49 049	Utah County, UT	368 536		36 069	Ontario County, NY	100 224
6560		Pueblo, CO MSA	141 472		36 073	Orleans County, NY	44 171
	08 101	Pueblo County, CO	141 472		36 117	Wayne County, NY	93 765
6580		Punta Gorda, FL MSA	141 627	6880		Rockford, IL MSA	371 236
	12 015	Charlotte County, FL	141 627		17 007	Boone County, IL	41 786
6600		Racine, WI PMSA	188 831		17 141	Ogle County, IL	51 032
		(See Milwaukee-Waukesha, WI PMSA)			17 201	Winnebago County, IL	278 418
				6895		Rocky Mount, NC MSA	143 026
6640		Raleigh-Durham-Chapel Hill, NC MSA	1 187 941		37 065	Edgecombe County, NC	55 606
	37 037	Chatham County, NC	49 329		37 127	Nash County, NC	87 420
	37 063	Durham County, NC	223 314				
	37 069	Franklin County, NC	47 260	6922		Sacramento-Yolo, CA CMSA	1 796 857
	37 101	Johnston County, NC	121 965				
	37 135	Orange County, NC	118 227	6920		Sacramento, CA PMSA	1 628 197
	37 183	Wake County, NC	627 846		06 017	El Dorado County, CA	156 299
					06 061	Placer County, CA	248 399
6660		Rapid City, SD MSA	88 565		06 067	Sacramento County, CA	1 223 499
	46 103	Pennington County, SD	88 565				
				9270		Yolo, CA PMSA	168 660
6680		Reading, PA MSA	373 638		06 113	Yolo County, CA	168 660
	42 011	Berks County, PA	373 638				
				6960		Saginaw-Bay City-Midland, MI MSA	403 070
6690		Redding, CA MSA	163 256		26 017	Bay County, MI	110 157
	06 089	Shasta County, CA	163 256		26 111	Midland County, MI	82 874
					26 145	Saginaw County, MI	210 039
6720		Reno, NV MSA	339 486				
	32 031	Washoe County, NV	339 486	6980		St. Cloud, MN MSA	167 392
					27 009	Benton County, MN	34 226
6740		Richland-Kennewick-Pasco, WA MSA	191 822		27 145	Stearns County, MN	133 166
	53 005	Benton County, WA	142 475	7000		St. Joseph, MO MSA	102 490
	53 021	Franklin County, WA	49 347		29 003	Andrew County, MO	16 492
					29 021	Buchanan County, MO	85 998
6760		Richmond-Petersburg, VA MSA	996 512				
	51 036	Charles City, VA	6 926	7040		St. Louis, MO-IL MSA	2 603 607
	51 041	Chesterfield County, VA	259 903		17 027	Clinton County, IL	35 535
	51 053	Dinwiddie County, VA	24 533		17 083	Jersey County, IL	21 668
	51 075	Goochland County, VA	16 863		17 119	Madison County, IL	258 941
	51 085	Hanover County, VA	86 320		17 133	Monroe County, IL	27 619
	51 087	Henrico County, VA	262 300		17 163	St. Clair County, IL	256 082
	51 127	New Kent County, VA	13 462		29 071	Franklin County, MO	93 807
	51 145	Powhatan County, VA	22 377		29 099	Jefferson County, MO	198 099
	51 149	Prince George County, VA	33 047		29 113	Lincoln County, MO	38 944
	51 570	Colonial Heights City, VA	16 897		29 183	St. Charles County, MO	283 883
	51 670	Hopewell City, VA	22 354		29 189	St. Louis County, MO	1 016 315
	51 730	Petersburg City, VA	33 740		29 219	Warren County, MO	24 525
	51 760	Richmond City, VA	197 790				

Metropolitan Statistical Areas and Components – Continued

(MSA = metropolitan statistical area; CMSA = consolidated MSA; PMSA = primary MSA; and NECMA = New England county metropolitan area. For further information, see Appendix A.)

Geographic Codes		Tital and Geographic Components	2000 Population	Geographic Codes		Tital and Geographic Components	2000 Population
MSA/ CMSA/ PMSA/ NECMA	State and County			MSA/ CMSA/ PMSA/ NECMA	State and County		
	29 510	St. Louis City, MO...................	348 189		13 051	Chatham County, GA.....................	232 048
7080		Salem, OR PMSA	347 214		13 103	Effingham County, GA.....................	37 535
		(See Portland-Vancouver, OR-WA PMSA)		7560		Scranton-Wilkes-Barre-Hazleton, PA MSA	624 776
7120		Salinas, CA MSA..........................	401 762		42 037	Columbia County, PA.....................	64 151
	06 053	Monterey County, CA...................	401 762		42 069	Lackawanna County, PA.....................	213 295
7160		Salt Lake City-Ogden, UT MSA	1 333 914		42 079	Luzerne County, PA.....................	319 250
	49 011	Davis County, UT...................	238 994		42 131	Wyoming County, PA.....................	28 080
	49 035	Salt Lake County, UT...................	898 387	7602		Seattle-Tacoma-Bremerton, WA CMSA............	3 554 760
	49 057	Weber County, UT...................	196 533				
7200		San Angelo, TX MSA..........................	104 010	1150		Bremerton, WA PMSA	231 969
	48 451	Tom Green County, TX	104 010		53 035	Kitsap County, WA	231 969
7240		San Antonio, TX MSA	1 592 383	5910		Olympia, WA PMSA..........................	207 355
	48 029	Bexar County, TX..........................	1 392 931		53 067	Thurston County, WA..........................	207 355
	48 091	Comal County, TX..........................	78 021	7600		Seattle-Bellevue-Everett, WA PMSA	2 414 616
	48 187	Guadalupe County, TX..........................	89 023		53 029	Island County, WA..........................	71 558
	48 493	Wilson County, TX..........................	32 408		53 033	King County, WA..........................	1 737 034
					53 061	Snohomish County, WA..........................	606 024
7320		San Diego, CA MSA	2 813 833	8200		Tacoma, WA PMSA..........................	700 820
	06 073	San Diego County, CA..........................	2 813 833		53 053	Pierce County, WA..........................	700 820
7362		San Francisco-Oakland-San Jose, CA CMSA....	7 039 362	7610		Sharon, PA MSA..........................	120 293
5775		Oakland, CA PMSA..........................	2 392 557		42 085	Mercer County, PA..........................	120 293
	06 001	Alameda County, CA..........................	1 443 741	7620		Sheboygan, WI MSA..........................	112 646
	06 013	Contra Costa County, CA..........................	948 816		55 117	Sheboygan County, WI..........................	112 646
7360		San Francisco, CA PMSA..........................	1 731 183	7640		Sherman-Denison, TX MSA..........................	110 595
	06 041	Marin County, CA..........................	247 289		48 181	Grayson County, TX..........................	110 595
	06 075	San Francisco County, CA..........................	776 733	7680		Shreveport-Bossier City, LA MSA..........................	392 302
	06 081	San Mateo County, CA..........................	707 161		22 015	Bossier Parish, LA..........................	98 310
7400		San Jose, CA PMSA..........................	1 682 585		22 017	Caddo Parish, LA..........................	252 161
	06 085	Santa Clara County, CA..........................	1 682 585		22 119	Webster Parish, LA..........................	41 831
7485		Santa Cruz-Watsonville, CA PMSA..........................	255 602	7720		Sioux City, IA-NE MSA..........................	124 130
	06 087	Santa Cruz County, CA..........................	255 602		19 193	Woodbury County, IA..........................	103 877
7500		Santa Rosa, CA PMSA..........................	458 614		31 043	Dakota County, NE..........................	20 253
	06 097	Sonoma County, CA..........................	458 614	7760		Sioux Falls, SD MSA..........................	172 412
8720		Vallejo-Fairfield-Napa, CA PMSA	518 821		46 083	Lincoln County, SD..........................	24 131
	06 055	Napa County, CA..........................	124 279		46 099	Minnehaha County, SD..........................	148 281
	06 095	Solano County, CA..........................	394 542	7800		South Bend, IN MSA..........................	265 559
7460		San Luis Obispo-Atascadero-Paso Robles, CA MSA	246 681		18 141	St. Joseph County, IN..........................	265 559
				7840		Spokane, WA MSA..........................	417 939
	06 079	San Luis Obispo County, CA..........................	246 681		53 063	Spokane County, WA..........................	417 939
7480		Santa Barbara-Santa Maria-Lompoc, CA MSA ..	399 347	7880		Springfield, IL MSA..........................	201 437
	06 083	Santa Barbara County, CA..........................	399 347		17 129	Menard County, IL..........................	12 486
7490		Santa Fe, NM MSA..........................	147 635		17 167	Sangamon County, IL..........................	188 951
	35 028	Los Alamos County, NM..........................	18 343	8003		Springfield, MA NECMA..........................	608 479
	35 049	Santa Fe County, NM..........................	129 292		25 013	Hampden County, MA..........................	456 228
					25 015	Hampshire County, MA..........................	152 251
7510		Sarasota-Bradenton, FL MSA..........................	589 959				
	12 081	Manatee County, FL..........................	264 002	7920		Springfield, MO MSA..........................	325 721
	12 115	Sarasota County, FL..........................	325 957		29 043	Christian County, MO..........................	54 285
					29 077	Greene County, MO..........................	240 391
7520		Savannah, GA MSA..........................	293 000		29 225	Webster County, MO..........................	31 045
	13 029	Bryan County, GA..........................	23 417				

(MSA = metropolitan statistical area; CMSA = consolidated MSA; PMSA = primary MSA; and
NECMA = New England county metropolitan area. For further information, see Appendix A.)

MSA/CMSA/PMSA/NECMA	State and County	Title and Geographic Components	2000 Population	MSA/CMSA/PMSA/NECMA	State and County	Title and Geographic Components	2000 Population
8050		State College, PA MSA	135 758			Tyler, TX MSA	174 706
	42 027	Centre County, PA	135 758	8640		Smith County, TX	174 706
8080		Steubenville-Weirton, OH-WV MSA	132 008		48 423		
	39 081	Jefferson County, OH	73 894	8680		Utica-Rome, NY MSA	299 896
	54 009	Brooke County, WV	25 447		36 043	Herkimer County, NY	64 427
	54 029	Hancock County, WV	32 667		36 065	Oneida County, NY	235 469
8120		Stockton-Lodi, CA MSA	563 598	8720		Vallejo-Fairfield-Napa, CA PMSA	518 821
	06 077	San Joaquin County, CA	563 598			(See San Francisco-Oakland-San Jose, CA CMSA)	
8140		Sumter, SC MSA	104 646				
	45 085	Sumter County, SC	104 646	8735		Ventura, CA PMSA	753 197
8160		Syracuse, NY MSA	732 117			(See Los Angeles-Riverside-Orange County, CA CMSA)	753 197
	36 011	Cayuga County, NY	81 963				
	36 053	Madison County, NY	69 441	8750		Victoria, TX MSA	84 088
	36 067	Onondaga County, NY	458 336		48 469	Victoria County, TX	84 088
	36 075	Oswego County, NY	122 377				
				8760		Vineland-Millville-Bridgeton, NJ PMSA	146 438
8200		Tacoma, WA PMSA	700 820			(See Philadelphia-Wilmington-Atlantic City, PA-NJ-DE-MD CMSA)	
		(See Seattle-Tacoma-Bremerton, WA CMSA)					
8240		Tallahassee, FL MSA	284 539	8780		Visalia-Tulare-Porterville, CA MSA	368 021
	12 039	Gadsden County, FL	45 087		06 107	Tulare County, CA	368 021
	12 073	Leon County, FL	239 452				
				8800		Waco, TX MSA	213 517
8280		Tampa-St. Petersburg-Clearwater, FL MSA	2 395 997		48 309	McLennan County, TX	213 517
	12 053	Hernando County, FL	130 802				
	12 057	Hillsborough County, FL	998 948	8872		Washington-Baltimore, DC-MD-VA-WV CMSA	7 608 070
	12 101	Pasco County, FL	344 765				
	12 103	Pinellas County, FL	921 482	720		Baltimore, MD PMSA	2 552 994
					24 003	Anne Arundel County, MD	489 656
8320		Terre Haute, IN MSA	149 192		24 005	Baltimore County, MD	754 292
	18 021	Clay County, IN	26 556		24 013	Carroll County, MD	150 897
	18 165	Vermillion County, IN	16 788		24 025	Harford County, MD	218 590
	18 167	Vigo County, IN	105 848		24 027	Howard County, MD	247 842
					24 035	Queen Anne's County, MD	40 563
8360		Texarkana, TX-Texarkana, AR MSA	129 749		24 510	Baltimore City, MD	651 154
	05 091	Miller County, AR	40 443				
	48 037	Bowie County, TX	89 306	3180		Hagerstown, MD PMSA	131 923
					24 043	Washington County, MD	131 923
8400		Toledo, OH MSA	618 203				
	39 051	Fulton County, OH	42 084	8840		Washington, DC-MD-VA-WV PMSA	4 923 153
	39 095	Lucas County, OH	455 054		11 001	District of Columbia	572 059
	39 173	Wood County, OH	121 065		24 009	Calvert County, MD	74 563
					24 017	Charles County, MD	120 546
8440		Topeka, KS MSA	169 871		24 021	Frederick County, MD	195 277
	20 177	Shawnee County, KS	169 871		24 031	Montgomery County, MD	873 341
					24 033	Prince George's County, MD	801 515
8480		Trenton, NJ PMSA	350 761		51 013	Arlington County, VA	189 453
		(See New York-Northern New Jersey-Long Island, NY-NJ-CT-PA CMSA)			51 043	Clarke County, VA	12 652
					51 047	Culpeper County, VA	34 262
					51 059	Fairfax County, VA	969 749
8520		Tucson, AZ MSA	843 746		51 061	Fauquier County, VA	55 139
	04 019	Pima County, AZ	843 746		51 099	King George County, VA	16 803
					51 107	Loudoun County, VA	169 599
8560		Tulsa, OK MSA	803 235		51 153	Prince William County, VA	280 813
	40 037	Creek County, OK	67 367		51 177	Spotsylvania County, VA	90 395
	40 113	Osage County, OK	44 437		51 179	Stafford County, VA	92 446
	40 131	Rogers County, OK	70 641		51 187	Warren County, VA	31 584
	40 143	Tulsa County, OK	563 299		51 510	Alexandria City, VA	128 283
	40 145	Wagoner County, OK	57 491		51 600	Fairfax City, VA	21 498
					51 610	Falls Church City, VA	10 377
8600		Tuscaloosa, AL MSA	164 875		51 630	Fredericksburg City, VA	19 279
	01 125	Tuscaloosa County, AL	164 875		51 683	Manassas City, VA	35 135

(MSA = metropolitan statistical area; CMSA = consolidated MSA; PMSA = primary MSA; and NECMA = New England county metropolitan area. For further information, see Appendix A.)

MSA/ CMSA/ PMSA/ NECMA	State and County	Tital and Geographic Components	2000 Population	MSA/ CMSA/ PMSA/ NECMA	State and County	Tital and Geographic Components	2000 Population
	51 685	Manassas Park City, VA	10 290	9200		Wilmington, NC MSA	233 450
	54 003	Berkeley County, WV	75 905		37 019	Brunswick County, NC	73 143
	54 037	Jefferson County, WV	42 190		37 129	New Hanover County, NC	160 307
8920		Waterloo-Cedar Falls, IA MSA	128 012	9160		Wilmington-Newark, DE-MD PMSA	586 216
	19 013	Black Hawk County, IA	128 012			(See Philadelphia-Wilmington-Atlantic City, PA-NJ-DE-MD CMSA)	
8940		Wausau, WI MSA	125 834				
	55 073	Marathon County, WI	125 834	9260		Yakima, WA MSA	222 581
					53 077	Yakima County, WA	222 581
8960		West Palm Beach-Boca Raton, FL MSA	1 131 184	9270		Yolo, CA PMSA	168 660
	12 099	Palm Beach County, FL	1 131 184			(See Sacramento-Yolo, CA CMSA)	
9000		Wheeling, WV-OH MSA	153 172				
	39 013	Belmont County, OH	70 226	9280		York, PA MSA	381 751
	54 051	Marshall County, WV	35 519	9280	42 133	York County, PA	381 751
	54 069	Ohio County, WV	47 427				
				9320		Youngstown-Warren, OH MSA	594 746
9080		Wichita Falls, TX MSA	140 518	9320	39 029	Columbiana County, OH	112 075
	48 009	Archer County, TX	8 854	9320	39 099	Mahoning County, OH	257 555
	48 485	Wichita County, TX	131 664	9320	39 155	Trumbull County, OH	225 116
9040		Wichita, KS MSA	545 220	9340		Yuba City, CA MSA	139 149
	20 015	Butler County, KS	59 482	9340	06 101	Sutter County, CA	78 930
	20 079	Harvey County, KS	32 869	9340	06 115	Yuba County, CA	60 219
	20 173	Sedgwick County, KS	452 869				
				9360		Yuma, AZ MSA	160 026
9140		Williamsport, PA MSA	120 044	9360	04 027	Yuma County, AZ	160 026
	42 081	Lycoming County, PA	120 044				

APPENDIX C
METROPOLITAN STATISTICAL AREAS AND COMPONENTS BY STATE

The following table is arranged alphabetically by state. Under each state heading, all of the metropolitan areas that lie wholly or partly within that state are listed alphabetically along with their component counties, which are also listed alphabetically. For metropolitan areas that cross state lines, only the counties within a particular state are included under that state. However, the metropolitan area names include the two letter abbreviation for each state involved, and the remaining counties can be located under their respective state headings.

For states containing Consolidated Metropolitan Statistical Areas (CMSAs), or parts of such areas, the CMSAs appear first, followed by the Primary Metropolitan Statistical Areas (PMSAs) that make up the CMSA, and their component counties.

(MSA = metropolitan statistical area; CMSA = consolidated MSA; PMSA = primary MSA; and NECMA = New England county metropolitan area. For further information, see Appendix A.)

Geographic Codes MSA/CMSA/ PMSA/ NECMA	State and County	Title and Geographic Components	Geographic Codes MSA/CMSA/ PMSA/ NECMA	State and County	Title and Geographic Components
		ALABAMA	9360		YUMA, AZ MSA
0450		ANNISTON, AL MSA	9360	04 027	Yuma
	01 015	Calhoun			
0580		AUBURN-OPELIKA, AL MSA			**ARKANSAS**
	01 081	Lee	2580		FAYETTEVILLE-SPRINGDALE-ROGERS, AR MSA
1000		BIRMINGHAM, AL MSA		05 007	Benton
	01 009	Blount		05 143	Washington
	01 073	Jefferson	2720		FORT SMITH, AR-OK MSA
	01 115	St. Clair		05 033	Crawford
	01 117	Shelby		05 131	Sebastian
1800		COLUMBUS, GA-AL MSA	3700		JONESBORO, AR MSA
	01 113	Russell		5 031	Craighead
2030		DECATUR, AL MSA	4400		LITTLE ROCK-NORTH LITTLE ROCK, AR MSA
	01 079	Lawrence		06 016	Faulkner
	01 103	Morgan		05 085	Lonoke
2180		DOTHAN, AL MSA		05 119	Pulaski
	01 045	Dale		05 125	Saline
	01 069	Houston	4920		MEMPHIS, TN-AR-MS MSA
2650		FLORENCE, AL MSA		05 035	Crittenden
	01 033	Colbert	6240		PINE BLUFF, AR MSA
	01 077	Lauderdale		05 069	Jefferson
2880		GADSDEN, AL MSA	8360		TEXARKANA, TX-TEXARKANA, AR MSA
	01 055	Etowah		05 091	Miller
3440		HUNTSVILLE, AL MSA			
	01 083	Limestone			**CALIFORNIA**
	01 089	Madison	4472		LOS ANGELES-RIVERSIDE-ORANGE COUNTY, CA CMSA
5160		MOBILE, AL MSA	4480		LOS ANGELES-LONG BEACH, CA PMSA
	01 003	Baldwin		06 037	Los Angeles
	01 097	Mobile	5945		ORANGE COUNTY, CA PMSA
5240		MONTGOMERY, AL MSA		06 059	Orange
	01 001	Autauga	6780		RIVERSIDE-SAN BERNARDINO, CA PMSA
	01 051	Elmore			SAN BERNARDINO, CA
	01 101	Montgomery			RIVERSIDE, CA
8600		TUSCALOOSA, AL MSA	6922		SACRAMENTO-YOLO, CA CMSA
	01 125	Tuscaloosa	6920		SACRAMENTO, CA PMSA
				06 017	El Dorado
		ALASKA		06 061	Placer
0380		ANCHORAGE, AK MSA		06 067	Sacramento
	02 020	Anchorage	9270		YOLO, CA PMSA
				06 113	Yolo
		ARIZONA			SAN FRANCISCO-OAKLAND-SAN JOSE, CA CMSA
2620		FLAGSTAFF, AZ-UT MSA	7362		
	04 005	Coconino	5775		OAKLAND, CA PMSA
4120		LAS VEGAS, NV-AZ MSA		06 001	Alameda
	04 015	Mohave		06 013	Contra Costa
6200		PHOENIX-MESA, AZ MSA	7360		SAN FRANCISCO, CA PMSA
	04 013	Maricopa		06 041	Marin
	04 021	Pinal		06 075	San Francisco
8520		TUCSON, AZ MSA		06 081	San Mateo
	04 019	Pima	7400		SAN JOSE, CA PMSA
				06 085	Santa Clara

Geographic Codes MSA/CMSA/ PMSA/ NECMA	State and County	Title and Geographic Components	Geographic Codes MSA/CMSA/ PMSA/ NECMA	State and County	Title and Geographic Components
7485		SANTA CRUZ-WATSONVILLE, CA PMSA		09 007	Middlesex
	06 087	Santa Cruz		09 013	Tolland
7500		SANTA ROSA, CA PMSA	5520		NEW LONDON-NORWICH, CT NECMA
	06 097	Sonoma		09 011	New London
8720		VALLEJO-FAIRFIELD-NAPA, CA PMSA			
	06 055	Napa			**DELAWARE**
	06 095	Solano	6162		PHILADELPHIA-WILMINGTON-ATLANTIC CITY, PA-NJ-DE-MD CMSA
0680		BAKERSFIELD, CA MSA	9160		WILMINGTON-NEWARK, DE-MD PMSA
	06 029	Kern		10 003	New Castle
1620		CHICO-PARADISE, CA MSA	2190		DOVER, DE MSA
	06 007	Butte		10 001	Kent
2840		FRESNO, CA MSA			
	06 019	Fresno			**FLORIDA**
	06 039	Madera	4992		MIAMI-FORT LAUDERDALE, FL CMSA
4940		MERCED, CA MSA	2680		FORT LAUDERDALE, FL PMSA
	06 047	Merced		12 011	Broward
5170		MODESTO, CA MSA	5000		MIAMI, FL PMSA
	06 099	Stanislaus		12 086	Miami-Dade
6690		REDDING, CA MSA	2020		DAYTONA BEACH, FL MSA
	06 089	Shasta		12 035	Flagler
7120		SALINAS, CA MSA		12 127	Volusia
	06 053	Monterey	2700		FORT MYERS-CAPE CORAL, FL MSA
7320		SAN DIEGO, CA MSA		12 071	Lee
	06 073	San Diego	2710		FORT PIERCE-PORT ST. LUCIE, FL MSA
7460		SAN LUIS OBISPO-ATASCADERO-PASO ROBLES, CA MSA		12 085	Martin
	06 079	San Luis Obispo		12 111	St. Lucie
7480		SANTA BARBARA-SANTA MARIA-LOMPOC, CA MSA	2750		FORT WALTON BEACH, FL MSA
	06 083	Santa Barbara		12 091	Okaloosa
8120		STOCKTON-LODI, CA MSA	2900		GAINESVILLE, FL MSA
	06 077	San Joaquin		12 001	Alachua
8780		VISALIA-TULARE-PORTERVILLE, CA MSA	3600		JACKSONVILLE, FL MSA
	06 107	Tulare		12 019	Clay
9340		YUBA CITY, CA MSA		12 031	Duval
	06 101	Sutter		12 089	Nassau
	06 115	Yuba		12 109	St. Johns
			3980		LAKELAND-WINTER HAVEN, FL MSA
		COLORADO		12 105	Polk
34		DENVER-BOULDER-GREELEY, CO CMSA	4900		MELBOURNE-TITUSVILLE-PALM BAY, FL MSA
1125		BOULDER-LONGMONT, CO PMSA		12 009	Brevard
	08 013	Boulder	5345		NAPLES, FL MSA
2080		DENVER, CO PMSA		12 021	Collier
	08 001	Adams	5790		OCALA, FL MSA
	08 005	Arapahoe		12 083	Marion
	08 031	Denver	5960		ORLANDO, FL MSA
	08 035	Douglas		12 069	Lake
	08 059	Jefferson		12 095	Orange
3060		GREELEY, CO PMSA		12 097	Osceola
	08 123	Weld		12 117	Seminole
1720		COLORADO SPRINGS, CO MSA	6015		PANAMA CITY, FL MSA
	08 041	El Paso		12 005	Bay
2670		FORT COLLINS-LOVELAND, CO MSA	6080		PENSACOLA, FL MSA
	08 069	Larimer		12 033	Escambia
2995		GRAND JUNCTION, CO MSA		12 113	Santa Rosa
	08 077	Mesa	6580		PUNTA GORDA, FL MSA
6560		PUEBLO, CO MSA		12 015	Charlotte
	08 101	Pueblo	7510		SARASOTA-BRADENTON, FL MSA
				12 081	Manatee
		CONNECTICUT		12 115	Sarasota
70		NEW YORK-NORTHERN NEW JERSEY-LONG ISLAND, NY-NJ-CT-PA CMSA	8240		TALLAHASSEE, FL MSA
5483		NEW HAVEN-BRIDGEPORT-STAMFORD-DANBURY-WATERBURY, CT NECMA		12 039	Gadsden
		FAIRFIELD COUNTY, CT		12 073	Leon
		NEW HAVEN COUNTY, CT	8280		TAMPA-ST. PETERSBURG-CLEARWATER, FL MSA
3280		HARTFORD, CT NECMA		12 053	Hernando
	09 003	Hartford		12 057	Hillsborough
				12 101	Pasco
				12 103	Pinellas

Metropolitan Statistical Areas and Components by State – Continued

(MSA = metropolitan statistical area; CMSA = consolidated MSA; PMSA = primary MSA; and
NECMA = New England county metropolitan area. For further information, see Appendix A.)

Geographic Codes MSA/CMSA/ PMSA/ NECMA	State and County	Title and Geographic Components	Geographic Codes MSA/CMSA/ PMSA/ NECMA	State and County	Title and Geographic Components
8960		WEST PALM BEACH-BOCA RATON, FL MSA			**ILLINOIS**
	12 099	Palm Beach	1040		BLOOMINGTON-NORMAL, IL MSA
			1040	17 113	McLean
		GEORGIA	1400		CHAMPAIGN-URBANA, IL MSA
0120		ALBANY, GA MSA		17 019	Champaign
	13 095	DOUGHERTY COUNTY, GA	14		CHICAGO-GARY-KENOSHA, IL-IN-WI CMSA
	13 177	LEE COUNTY, GA	1600		CHICAGO, IL PMSA
0500		ATHENS, GA MSA		17 031	Cook
	13 059	Clarke		17 037	De Kalb
	13 195	Madison		17 043	Du Page
	13 219	Oconee		17 063	Grundy
0520		ATLANTA, GA MSA		17 089	Kane
	13 013	Barrow		17 093	Kendall
	13 015	Bartow		17 097	Lake
	13 045	Carroll		17 111	McHenry
	13 057	Cherokee		17 197	Will
	13 063	Clayton	3740		KANKAKEE, IL PMSA
	13 067	Cobb		17 091	Kankakee
	13 077	Coweta	1960		DAVENPORT-MOLINE-ROCK ISLAND, IA-IL MSA
	13 089	De Kalb		17 073	Henry
	13 097	Douglas		17 161	Rock Island
	13 113	Fayette	2040		DECATUR, IL MSA
	13 117	Forsyth		17 115	Macon
	13 121	Fulton	6120		PEORIA-PEKIN, IL MSA
	13 135	Gwinnett		17 143	Peoria
	13 151	Henry		17 179	Tazewell
	13 217	Newton		17 203	Woodford
	13 223	Paulding	6880		ROCKFORD, IL MSA
	13 227	Pickens		17 007	Boone
	13 247	Rockdale		17 111	Ogle
	13 255	Spalding		17 201	Winnebago
	13 297	Walton	7040		ST. LOUIS, MO-IL MSA
0600		AUGUSTA-AIKEN, GA-SC MSA		17 027	Clinton
	13 073	Columbia		17 083	Jersey
	13 189	McDuffie		17 119	Madison
	13 245	Richmond		17 133	Monroe
1560		CHATTANOOGA, TN-GA MSA		17 163	St. Clair
	13 047	Catoosa	7880		SPRINGFIELD, IL MSA
	13 083	Dade		17 129	Menard
	13 295	Walker		17 167	Sangamon
1800		COLUMBUS, GA-AL MSA			
	13 053	Chattahoochee			**INDIANA**
	13 145	Harris	1020		BLOOMINGTON, IN MSA
	13 215	Muscogee	1020	18 105	Monroe
4680		MACON, GA MSA	14		CHICAGO-GARY-KENOSHA, IL-IN-WI CMSA
	13 021	Bibb	2960		GARY, IN PMSA
	13 153	Houston		18 089	Lake
	13 169	Jones		18 127	Porter
	13 225	Peach	21		CINCINNATI-HAMILTON, OH-KY-IN CMSA
	13 289	Twiggs	1640		CINCINNATI, OH-KY-IN PMSA
7520		SAVANNAH, GA MSA		18 029	Dearborn
	13 029	Bryan		18 115	Ohio
	13 051	Chatham	2330		ELKHART-GOSHEN, IN MSA
	13 103	Effingham		18 039	Elkhart
			2440		EVANSVILLE-HENDERSON, IN-KY MSA
		HAWAII		18 129	Posey
3320		HONOLULU, HI MSA		18 163	Vanderburgh
	15 003	Honolulu		18 173	Warrick
			2760		FORT WAYNE, IN MSA
		IDAHO		18 001	Adams
1080		BOISE CITY, ID MSA		18 003	Allen
1080	16 001	Ada		18 033	De Kalb
1080	16 027	Canyon		18 069	Huntington
6340		POCATELLO, ID MSA		18 179	Wells
	16 005	Bannock		18 183	Whitley
			3480		INDIANAPOLIS, IN MSA
				18 011	Boone

Metropolitan Statistical Areas and Components by State – Continued

(MSA = metropolitan statistical area; CMSA = consolidated MSA; PMSA = primary MSA; and NECMA = New England county metropolitan area. For further information, see Appendix A.)

Geographic Codes MSA/CMSA/ PMSA/ NECMA	State and County	Title and Geographic Components
	18 057	Hamilton
	18 059	Hancock
	18 063	Hendricks
	18 081	Johnson
	18 095	Madison
	18 097	Marion
	18 109	Morgan
	18 145	Shelby
3850		KOKOMO, IN MSA
	18 067	Howard
	18 159	Tipton
3920		LAFAYETTE, IN MSA
	18 023	Clinton
	18 157	Tippecanoe
4520		LOUISVILLE, KY-IN MSA
	18 019	Clark
	18 043	Floyd
	18 061	Harrison
	18 143	Scott
7800		SOUTH BEND, IN MSA
	18 141	St. Joseph
5280		MUNCIE, IN MSA
	18 035	Delaware
8320		TERRE HAUTE, IN MSA
	18 021	Clay
	18 165	Vermillion
	18 167	Vigo
		IOWA
1360		CEDAR RAPIDS, IA MSA
	19 113	Linn
1960		DAVENPORT-MOLINE-ROCK ISLAND, IA-IL MSA
	19 163	Scott
2120		DES MOINES, IA MSA
	19 049	Dallas
	19 153	Polk
	19 181	Warren
2200		DUBUQUE, IA MSA
	19 061	Dubuque
3500		IOWA CITY, IA MSA
	19 103	Johnson
5920		OMAHA, NE-IA MSA
	19 155	Pottawattamie
7720		SIOUX CITY, IA-NE MSA
	19 193	Woodbury
8920		WATERLOO-CEDAR FALLS, IA MSA
	19 013	Black Hawk
		KANSAS
3760		KANSAS CITY, MO-KS MSA
	20 091	Johnson
	20 103	Leavenworth
	20 121	Miami
	20 209	Wyandotte
4150		LAWRENCE, KS MSA
	20 045	Douglas
8440		TOPEKA, KS MSA
	20 177	Shawnee
9040		WICHITA, KS MSA
	20 015	Butler
	20 079	Harvey
	20 173	Sedgwick
		KENTUCKY
21		CINCINNATI-HAMILTON, OH-KY-IN CMSA
1640		CINCINNATI, OH-KY-IN PMSA
	21 015	Boone
	21 037	Campbell
	21 077	Gallatin
	21 081	Grant
	21 117	Kenton
	21 191	Pendleton
1660		CLARKSVILLE-HOPKINSVILLE, TN-KY MSA
	21 047	Christian
2440		EVANSVILLE-HENDERSON, IN-KY MSA
	21 101	Henderson
3400		HUNTINGTON-ASHLAND, WV-KY-OH MSA
	21 019	Boyd
	21 043	Carter
	21 089	Greenup
4280		LEXINGTON, KY MSA
	21 017	Bourbon
	21 049	Clark
	21 067	Fayette
	21 113	Jessamine
	21 151	Madison
	21 209	Scott
	21 239	Woodford
4520		LOUISVILLE, KY-IN MSA
	21 029	Bullitt
	21 111	Jefferson
	21 185	Oldham
5990		OWENSBORO, KY MSA
	21 059	Daviess
		LOUISIANA
0220		ALEXANDRIA, LA MSA
	22 079	Rapides
0760		BATON ROUGE, LA MSA
	22 005	Ascension
	22 033	East Baton Rouge
	22 063	Livingston
	22 121	West Baton Rouge
3350		HOUMA, LA MSA
	22 057	Lafourche
	22 109	Terrebonne
3880		LAFAYETTE, LA MSA
	22 001	Acadia
	22 055	Lafayette
	22 097	St. Landry
	22 099	St. Martin
3960		LAKE CHARLES, LA MSA
	22 019	Calcasieu
5200		MONROE, LA MSA
	22 073	Ouachita
5560		NEW ORLEANS, LA MSA
	22 051	Jefferson
	22 071	Orleans
	22 075	Plaquemines
	22 087	St. Bernard
	22 089	St. Charles
	22 093	St. James
	22 095	St. John the Baptist
	22 103	St. Tammany
7680		SHREVEPORT-BOSSIER CITY, LA MSA
	22 015	Bossier
	22 017	Caddo
	22 119	Webster
		MAINE
0733		BANGOR, ME NECMA
	23 019	Penobscot
4240		LEWISTON-AUBURN, ME NECMA
	23 001	Androscoggin

Metropolitan Statistical Areas and Components by State – Continued

(MSA = metropolitan statistical area; CMSA = consolidated MSA; PMSA = primary MSA; and
NECMA = New England county metropolitan area. For further information, see Appendix A.)

Geographic Codes MSA/CMSA/ PMSA/ NECMA	State and County	Title and Geographic Components	Geographic Codes MSA/CMSA/ PMSA/ NECMA	State and County	Title and Geographic Components
6403		PORTLAND, ME NECMA		26 139	Ottawa
	23 005	Cumberland	3520		JACKSON, MI MSA
				26 075	Jackson
		MARYLAND	3720		KALAMAZOO-BATTLE CREEK, MI MSA
6162		PHILADELPHIA-WILMINGTON-ATLANTIC CITY, PA-NJ-DE-MD CMSA		26 025	Calhoun
				26 077	Kalamazoo
9160		WILMINGTON-NEWARK, DE-MD PMSA		26 159	Van Buren
	24 015	Cecil	4040		LANSING-EAST LANSING, MI MSA
8872		WASHINGTON-BALTIMORE, DC-MD-VA-WV CMSA		26 037	Clinton
0720		BALTIMORE, MD PMSA		26 045	Eaton
	24 003	Anne Arundel		26 065	Ingham
	24 005	Baltimore	6960		SAGINAW-BAY CITY-MIDLAND, MI MSA
	24 013	Carroll		26 017	Bay
	24 025	Harford		26 111	Midland
	24 027	Howard		26 145	Saginaw
	24 035	Queen Anne's			
	24 510	BALTIMORE CITY, MD			**MINNESOTA**
3180		HAGERSTOWN, MD PMSA	2240		DULUTH-SUPERIOR, MN-WI MSA
	24 043	Washington		27 137	St. Louis
8840		WASHINGTON, DC-MD-VA-WV PMSA	2520		FARGO-MOORHEAD, ND-MN MSA
	24 009	Calvert		27 027	Clay
	24 017	Charles	2985		GRAND FORKS, ND-MN MSA
	24 021	Frederick		27 119	Polk
	24 031	Montgomery	3870		LA CROSSE, WI-MN MSA
	24 033	Prince George's		27 055	Houston
1900		CUMBERLAND, MD-WV MSA	5120		MINNEAPOLIS-ST. PAUL, MN-WI MSA
	24 001	Allegany		27 003	Anoka
				27 019	Carver
		MASSACHUSETTS		27 025	Chisago
0743		BARNSTABLE-YARMOUTH, MA NECMA		27 037	Dakota
	25 001	Barnstable		27 053	Hennepin
1123		BOSTON-WORCESTER-LAWRENCE-LOWELL-BROCKTON, MA-NH NECMA		27 059	Isanti
				27 123	Ramsey
	25 005	Bristol		27 139	Scott
	25 009	Essex		27 141	Sherburne
	25 017	Middlesex		27 163	Washington
	25 021	Norfolk		27 171	Wright
	25 023	Plymouth	6820		ROCHESTER, MN MSA
	25 025	Suffolk		27 109	Olmsted
	25 027	Worcester	6980		ST. CLOUD, MN MSA
6323		PITTSFIELD, MA NECMA		27 009	Benton
	25 003	Berkshire		27 145	Stearns
8003		SPRINGFIELD, MA NECMA			
	25 013	Hampden			**MISSISSIPPI**
	25 015	Hampshire	0920		BILOXI-GULFPORT-PASCAGOULA, MS MSA
				28 045	Hancock
		MICHIGAN		28 047	Harrison
2162		DETROIT-ANN ARBOR-FLINT, MI CMSA		28 059	Jackson
0440		ANN ARBOR, MI PMSA	3285		HATTIESBURG, MS MSA
	26 091	Lenawee		28 035	Forrest
	26 093	Livingston		28 073	Lamar
	26 161	Washtenaw	3560		JACKSON, MS MSA
2160		DETROIT, MI PMSA		28 049	Hinds
	26 087	Lapeer		28 089	Madison
	26 099	Macomb		28 121	Rankin
	26 115	Monroe	4920		MEMPHIS, TN-AR-MS MSA
	26 125	Oakland		28 033	De Soto
	26 147	St. Clair			
	26 163	Wayne			**MISSOURI**
2640		FLINT, MI PMSA	1740		COLUMBIA, MO MSA
	26 049	Genesee		29 019	Boone
0870		BENTON HARBOR, MI MSA	3710		JOPLIN, MO MSA
	26 021	Berrien		29 097	Jasper
3000		GRAND RAPIDS-MUSKEGON-HOLLAND, MI MSA		29 145	Newton
	26 005	Allegan	3760		KANSAS CITY, MO-KS MSA
	26 081	Kent		29 037	Cass
	26 121	Muskegon		29 047	Clay

Metropolitan Statistical Areas and Components by State – Continued

(MSA = metropolitan statistical area; CMSA = consolidated MSA; PMSA = primary MSA; and NECMA = New England county metropolitan area. For further information, see Appendix A.)

Geographic Codes MSA/CMSA/ PMSA/ NECMA	State and County	Title and Geographic Components	Geographic Codes MSA/CMSA/ PMSA/ NECMA	State and County	Title and Geographic Components
	29 049	Clinton	5190		MONMOUTH-OCEAN, NJ PMSA
	29 095	Jackson		34 025	Monmouth
	29 107	Lafayette		34 029	Ocean
	29 165	Platte	5640		NEWARK, NJ PMSA
	29 177	Ray		34 013	Essex
7000		ST. JOSEPH, MO MSA		34 027	Morris
	29 003	Andrew		34 037	Sussex
	29 021	Buchanan		34 039	Union
7040		ST. LOUIS, MO-IL MSA		34 041	Warren
	29 071	Franklin	8480		TRENTON, NJ PMSA
	29 099	Jefferson		34 021	Mercer
	29 113	Lincoln	560		ATLANTIC-CAPE MAY, NJ PMSA
	29 183	St. Charles		34 001	Atlantic
	29 189	St. Louis		34 009	Cape May
	29 219	Warren	6160		PHILADELPHIA, PA-NJ PMSA
	29 510	St. Louis City		34 005	Burlington
7920		SPRINGFIELD, MO MSA		34 007	Camden
	29 043	Christian		34 015	Gloucester
	29 077	Greene		34 033	Salem
	29 225	Webster	8760		VINELAND-MILLVILLE-BRIDGETON, NJ PMSA
				34 011	Cumberland
		MONTANA			
0880		BILLINGS, MT MSA			**NEW MEXICO**
	30 111	Yellowstone	0200		ALBUQUERQUE, NM MSA
3040		GREAT FALLS, MT MSA		35 001	Bernalillo
	30 013	Cascade		35 043	Sandoval
5140		MISSOULA, MT MSA		35 061	Valencia
	30 063	Missoula	4100		LAS CRUCES, NM MSA
				35 013	Dona Ana
		NEBRASKA	7490		SANTA FE, NM MSA
4360		LINCOLN, NE MSA		35 028	Los Alamos
	31 109	Lancaster		35 049	Santa Fe
5920		OMAHA, NE-IA MSA			
	31 025	Cass			**NEW YORK**
	31 055	Douglas	70		NEW YORK-NORTHERN NEW JERSEY-LONG
	31 153	Sarpy			ISLAND, NY-NJ-CT-PA CMSA
	31 177	Washington	2281		DUTCHESS COUNTY, NY PMSA
7720		SIOUX CITY, IA-NE MSA		36 027	Dutchess
	31 043	Dakota	5380		NASSAU-SUFFOLK, NY PMSA
				36 059	Nassau
		NEVADA		36 103	Suffolk
4120		LAS VEGAS, NV-AZ MSA	5600		NEW YORK, NY PMSA
	32 003	Clark		36 005	Bronx
	32 023	Nye		36 047	Kings
6720		RENO, NV MSA		36 061	New York
	32 031	Washoe		36 079	Putnam
				36 081	Queens
		NEW HAMPSHIRE		36 085	Richmond
1123		BOSTON-WORCESTER-LAWRENCE-LOWELL-		36 087	Rockland
		BROCKTON, MA-NH NECMA		36 119	Westchester
	33 011	Hillsborough	5660		NEWBURGH, NY-PA PMSA
	33 015	Rockingham		36 071	Orange
	33 017	Strafford	0160		ALBANY-SCHENECTADY-TROY, NY MSA
				36 001	ALBANY COUNTY, NY
		NEW JERSEY		36 057	MONTGOMERY COUNTY, NY
70		NEW YORK-NORTHERN NEW JERSEY-LONG		36 083	RENSSELAER COUNTY, NY
		ISLAND, NY-NJ-CT-PA CMSA		36 091	SARATOGA COUNTY, NY
0875		BERGEN-PASSAIC, NJ PMSA		36 093	SCHENECTADY COUNTY, NY
	34 003	Bergen		36 095	SCHOHARIE COUNTY, NY
	34 031	Passaic	0960		BINGHAMTON, NY MSA
3640		JERSEY CITY, NJ PMSA		36 007	Broome
	34 017	HUDSON COUNTY, NJ		36 107	Tioga
5015		MIDDLESEX-SOMERSET-HUNTERDON, NJ PMSA	1280		BUFFALO-NIAGARA FALLS, NY MSA
	34 019	Hunterdon		36 029	Erie
	34 023	Middlesex		36 063	Niagara
	34 035	Somerset	2335		ELMIRA, NY MSA
				36 015	Chemung

(MSA = metropolitan statistical area; CMSA = consolidated MSA; PMSA = primary MSA; and
NECMA = New England county metropolitan area. For further information, see Appendix A.)

Geographic Codes MSA/CMSA/ PMSA/ NECMA	State and County	Title and Geographic Components	Geographic Codes MSA/CMSA/ PMSA/ NECMA	State and County	Title and Geographic Components
2281		DUTCHESS COUNTY, NY PMSA	6895		ROCKY MOUNT, NC MSA
2975		GLENS FALLS, NY MSA		37 065	Edgecombe
	36 113	Warren		37 127	Nash
	36 115	Washington	9200		WILMINGTON, NC MSA
3610		JAMESTOWN, NY MSA		37 019	Brunswick
	36 013	Chautauqua		37 129	New Hanover
6840		ROCHESTER, NY MSA			
	36 037	Genesee			**NORTH DAKOTA**
	36 051	Livingston	1010		BISMARCK, ND MSA
	36 055	Monroe	1010	38 015	Burleigh
	36 069	Ontario	1010	38 059	Morton
	36 073	Orleans	2520		FARGO-MOORHEAD, ND-MN MSA
	36 117	Wayne		38 017	Cass
8160		SYRACUSE, NY MSA	2985		GRAND FORKS, ND-MN MSA
	36 011	Cayuga		38 035	Grand Forks
	36 053	Madison			
	36 067	Onondaga			**OHIO**
	36 075	Oswego	21		CINCINNATI-HAMILTON, OH-KY-IN CMSA
8680		UTICA-ROME, NY MSA	1640		CINCINNATI, OH-KY-IN PMSA
	36 043	Herkimer		39 015	Brown
	36 065	Oneida		39 025	Clermont
				39 061	Hamilton
		NORTH CAROLINA		39 165	Warren
0480		ASHEVILLE, NC MSA	3200		HAMILTON-MIDDLETOWN, OH PMSA
	37 021	Buncombe		39 017	Butler
	37 115	Madison	28		CLEVELAND-AKRON, OH CMSA
1520		CHARLOTTE-GASTONIA-ROCK HILL, NC-SC MSA	0080		AKRON, OH PMSA
	37 025	Cabarrus		39 133	PORTAGE COUNTY, OH
	37 071	Gaston		39 153	SUMMIT COUNTY, OH
	37 109	Lincoln	1000		CLEVELAND-LORAIN-ELYRIA, OH PMSA
	37 119	Mecklenburg		39 007	Ashtabula
	37 159	Rowan		39 035	Cuyahoga
	37 179	Union		39 055	Geauga
2560		FAYETTEVILLE, NC MSA		39 085	Lake
	37 051	Cumberland		39 093	Lorain
2980		GOLDSBORO, NC MSA		39 103	Medina
	37 101	Wayne	1320		CANTON-MASSILLON, OH MSA
3120		GREENSBORO-WINSTON-SALEM-HIGH POINT, NC MSA		39 019	Carroll
				39 151	Stark
	37 001	Alamance	1840		COLUMBUS, OH MSA
	37 057	Davidson		39 041	Delaware
	37 059	Davie		39 045	Fairfield
	37 067	Forsyth		39 049	Franklin
	37 081	Guilford		39 089	Licking
	37 151	Randolph		39 097	Madison
	37 169	Stokes		39 129	Pickaway
	37 197	Yadkin	2000		DAYTON-SPRINGFIELD, OH MSA
3150		GREENVILLE, NC MSA		39 023	Clark
	37 147	Pitt		39 057	Greene
3290		HICKORY-MORGANTON-LENOIR, NC MSA		39 109	Miami
	37 003	Alexander		39 113	Montgomery
	37 023	Burke	3400		HUNTINGTON-ASHLAND, WV-KY-OH MSA
	37 027	Caldwell		39 087	Lawrence
	37 035	Catawba	4320		LIMA, OH MSA
3605		JACKSONVILLE, NC MSA		39 003	Allen
	37 133	Onslow		39 011	Auglaize
5720		NORFOLK-VIRGINIA BEACH-NEWPORT NEWS, VA-NC MSA	4800		MANSFIELD, OH MSA
				39 033	Crawford
	37 053	Currituck		39 139	Richland
6640		RALEIGH-DURHAM-CHAPEL HILL, NC MSA	6020		PARKERSBURG-MARIETTA, WV-OH MSA
	37 037	Chatham		39 167	Washington
	37 063	Durham	8080		STEUBENVILLE-WEIRTON, OH-WV MSA
	37 069	Franklin		39 081	Jefferson
	37 101	Johnston	8400		TOLEDO, OH MSA
	37 135	Orange		39 051	Fulton
	37 183	Wake		39 095	Lucas
				39 173	Wood

Metropolitan Statistical Areas and Components by State – Continued

(MSA = metropolitan statistical area; CMSA = consolidated MSA; PMSA = primary MSA; and
NECMA = New England county metropolitan area. For further information, see Appendix A.)

Geographic Codes MSA/CMSA/ PMSA/ NECMA	State and County	Title and Geographic Components	Geographic Codes MSA/CMSA/ PMSA/ NECMA	State and County	Title and Geographic Components
9000		WHEELING, WV-OH MSA	3240		HARRISBURG-LEBANON-CARLISLE, PA MSA
	39 013	Belmont		42 041	Cumberland
9320		YOUNGSTOWN-WARREN, OH MSA		42 043	Dauphin
9320	39 029	Columbiana		42 075	Lebanon
9320	39 099	Mahoning		42 099	Perry
9320	39 155	Trumbull	3680		JOHNSTOWN, PA MSA
				42 021	Cambria
		OKLAHOMA		42 111	Somerset
2340		ENID, OK MSA	4000		LANCASTER, PA MSA
	40 047	Garfield		42 071	Lancaster
2720		FORT SMITH, AR-OK MSA	6280		PITTSBURGH, PA MSA
	40 135	Sequoyah		42 003	Allegheny
4200		LAWTON, OK MSA		42 007	Beaver
	40 031	Comanche		42 019	Butler
5880		OKLAHOMA CITY, OK MSA		42 051	Fayette
	40 017	Canadian		42 125	Washington
	40 027	Cleveland		42 129	Westmoreland
	40 083	Logan	6680		READING, PA MSA
	40 087	McClain		42 011	Berks
	40 109	Oklahoma	7560		SCRANTON-WILKES-BARRE-HAZLETON, PA MSA
	40 125	Pottawatomie		42 037	Columbia
8560		TULSA, OK MSA		42 069	Lackawanna
	40 037	Creek		42 079	Luzerne
	40 113	Osage		42 131	Wyoming
	40 131	Rogers	7610		SHARON, PA MSA
	40 143	Tulsa		42 085	Mercer
	40 145	Wagoner	8050		STATE COLLEGE, PA MSA
				42 027	Centre
		OREGON	9140		WILLIAMSPORT, PA MSA
1890		CORVALLIS, OR MSA		42 081	Lycoming
	41 003	Benton	9280		YORK, PA MSA
6442		PORTLAND-SALEM, OR-WA CMSA	9280	42 133	York
6440		PORTLAND-VANCOUVER, OR-WA PMSA			
	41 005	Clackamas			**RHODE ISLAND**
	41 009	Columbia	6483		PROVIDENCE-WARWICK-PAWTUCKET, RI NECMA
	41 051	Multnomah		44 001	Bristol
	41 067	Washington		44 003	Kent
	41 071	Yamhill		44 007	Providence
7080		SALEM, OR PMSA		44 009	Washington
	41 047	Marion			
	41 053	Polk			**SOUTH CAROLINA**
2400		EUGENE-SPRINGFIELD, OR MSA	0600		AUGUSTA-AIKEN, GA-SC MSA
	41 039	Lane		45 003	Aiken
4890		MEDFORD-ASHLAND, OR MSA		45 037	Edgefield
	41 029	Jackson	1440		CHARLESTON-NORTH CHARLESTON, SC MSA
				45 015	Berkeley
		PENNSYLVANIA		45 019	Charleston
70		NEW YORK-NORTHERN NEW JERSEY-LONG		45 035	Dorchester
		ISLAND, NY-NJ-CT-PA CMSA	1520		CHARLOTTE-GASTONIA-ROCK HILL, NC-SC MSA
5660		NEWBURGH, NY-PA PMSA		45 091	York
	42 103	Pike	1760		COLUMBIA, SC MSA
6162		PHILADELPHIA-WILMINGTON-ATLANTIC CITY, PA-NJ-		45 063	Lexington
		DE-MD CMSA		45 079	Richland
6160		PHILADELPHIA, PA-NJ PMSA	2655		FLORENCE, SC MSA
	42 017	Bucks		45 041	Florence
	42 029	Chester	3160		GREENVILLE-SPARTANBURG-ANDERSON, SC MSA
	42 045	Delaware		45 007	Anderson
	42 091	Montgomery		45 021	Cherokee
	42 101	Philadelphia		45 045	Greenville
0240		ALLENTOWN-BETHLEHEM-EASTON, PA MSA		45 077	Pickens
	42 025	CARBON COUNTY, PA		45 083	Spartanburg
	42 077	Lehigh	5330		MYRTLE BEACH, SC MSA
	42 095	Northampton		45 051	Horry
0280		ALTOONA, PA MSA	8140		SUMTER, SC MSA
	42 013	Blair		45 085	Sumter
2360		ERIE, PA MSA			
	42 049	Erie			

Metropolitan Statistical Areas and Components by State – Continued

(MSA = metropolitan statistical area; CMSA = consolidated MSA; PMSA = primary MSA; and
NECMA = New England county metropolitan area. For further information, see Appendix A.)

Geographic Codes MSA/CMSA/ PMSA/ NECMA	State and County	Title and Geographic Components	Geographic Codes MSA/CMSA/ PMSA/ NECMA	State and County	Title and Geographic Components
		SOUTH DAKOTA		48 201	Harris
6660		RAPID CITY, SD MSA		48 291	Liberty
	46 103	PENNINGTON COUNTY, SD		48 339	Montgomery
7760		SIOUX FALLS, SD MSA		48 473	Waller
	46 083	LINCOLN COUNTY, SD	0040		ABILENE, TX MSA
	46 099	MINNEHAHA COUNTY, SD		48 441	TAYLOR COUNTY, TX
			0320		AMARILLO, TX MSA
		TENNESSEE		48 375	Potter
1560		CHATTANOOGA, TN-GA MSA		48 381	Randall
	47 065	Hamilton	0640		AUSTIN-SAN MARCOS, TX MSA
	47 115	Marion		48 021	Bastrop
1660		CLARKSVILLE-HOPKINSVILLE, TN-KY MSA		48 055	Caldwell
	47 125	Montgomery		48 209	Hays
3580		JACKSON, TN MSA		48 453	Travis
	47 023	Chester		48 491	Williamson
	47 113	Madison	0840		BEAUMONT-PORT ARTHUR, TX MSA
3660		JOHNSON CITY-KINGSPORT-BRISTOL, TN-VA MSA		48 199	Hardin
	47 019	Carter		48 245	Jefferson
	47 073	Hawkins		48 361	Orange
	47 163	Sullivan	1240		BROWNSVILLE-HARLINGEN-SAN BENITO, TX MSA
	47 171	Unicoi		48 061	Cameron
	47 179	Washington	1260		BRYAN-COLLEGE STATION, TX MSA
3840		KNOXVILLE, TN MSA		48 041	Brazos
	47 001	Anderson	1880		CORPUS CHRISTI, TX MSA
	47 009	Blount		48 355	Nueces
	47 093	Knox		48 409	San Patricio
	47 105	Loudon	2320		EL PASO, TX MSA
	47 155	Sevier		48 141	El Paso
	47 173	Union	3810		KILLEEN-TEMPLE, TX MSA
4920		MEMPHIS, TN-AR-MS MSA		48 027	Bell
	47 047	Fayette		48 099	Coryell
	47 157	Shelby	4080		LAREDO, TX MSA
	47 167	Tipton		48 479	Webb
5360		NASHVILLE, TN MSA	4420		LONGVIEW-MARSHALL, TX MSA
	47 021	Cheatham		48 183	Gregg
	47 037	Davidson		48 203	Harrison
	47 043	Dickson		48 459	Upshur
	47 147	Robertson	4600		LUBBOCK, TX MSA
	47 149	Rutherford		48 303	Lubbock
	47 165	Sumner	4880		MCALLEN-EDINBURG-MISSION, TX MSA
	47 187	Williamson		48 215	Hidalgo
	47 189	Wilson	5800		ODESSA-MIDLAND, TX MSA
				48 135	Ector
		TEXAS		48 329	Midland
31		DALLAS-FORT WORTH, TX CMSA	7200		SAN ANGELO, TX MSA
1920		DALLAS, TX PMSA		48 451	Tom Green
	48 085	Collin	7240		SAN ANTONIO, TX MSA
	48 113	Dallas		48 029	Bexar
	48 121	Denton		48 091	Comal
	48 139	Ellis		48 187	Guadalupe
	48 213	Henderson		48 493	Wilson
	48 231	Hunt	7640		SHERMAN-DENISON, TX MSA
	48 257	Kaufman		48 181	Grayson
	48 397	Rockwall	8360		TEXARKANA, TX-TEXARKANA, AR MSA
2800		FORT WORTH-ARLINGTON, TX PMSA		48 037	Bowie
	48 221	Hood	8640		TYLER, TX MSA
	48 251	Johnson		48 423	Smith
	48 367	Parker	8750		VICTORIA, TX MSA
	48 439	Tarrant		48 469	Victoria
3362		HOUSTON-GALVESTON-BRAZORIA, TX CMSA	8800		WACO, TX MSA
1145		BRAZORIA, TX PMSA		48 309	McLennan
	48 039	Brazoria	9080		WICHITA FALLS, TX MSA
2920		GALVESTON-TEXAS CITY, TX PMSA		48 009	Archer
		GALVESTON COUNTY, TX		48 485	Wichita
3360		HOUSTON, TX PMSA			
	48 071	Chambers			
	48 157	Fort Bend			

(MSA = metropolitan statistical area; CMSA = consolidated MSA; PMSA = primary MSA; and
NECMA = New England county metropolitan area. For further information, see Appendix A.)

Geographic Codes MSA/CMSA/ PMSA/ NECMA	State and County	Title and Geographic Components	Geographic Codes MSA/CMSA/ PMSA/ NECMA	State and County	Title and Geographic Components
		UTAH		51 800	Suffolk City
2620		FLAGSTAFF, AZ-UT MSA		51 810	Virginia Beach City
	49 025	Kane		51 830	Williamsburg City
6520		PROVO-OREM, UT MSA	6760		RICHMOND-PETERSBURG, VA MSA
	49 049	Utah		51 036	Charles City
7160		SALT LAKE CITY-OGDEN, UT MSA		51 041	Chesterfield
	49 011	Davis		51 053	Dinwiddie
	49 035	Salt Lake		51 075	Goochland
	49 057	Weber		51 085	Hanover
				51 087	Henrico
		VERMONT		51 127	New Kent
1303		BURLINGTON, VT NECMA		51 145	Powhatan
	50 077	Chittenden		51 149	Prince George
	50 011	Franklin		51 570	Colonial Heights City
	50 013	Grand Isle		51 670	Hopewell City
				51 730	Petersburg City
		VIRGINIA		51 760	Richmond City
8872		WASHINGTON-BALTIMORE, DC-MD-VA-WV CMSA	6800		ROANOKE, VA MSA
8840		WASHINGTON, DC-MD-VA-WV PMSA		51 023	Botetourt
	51 013	Arlington		51 161	Roanoke
	51 043	Clarke		51 770	Roanoke City
	51 047	Culpeper		51 775	Salem City
	51 059	Fairfax			
	51 061	Fauquier			**WASHINGTON**
	51 099	King George	6442		PORTLAND-SALEM, OR-WA CMSA
	51 107	Loudoun	6440		PORTLAND-VANCOUVER, OR-WA PMSA
	51 153	Prince William		53 011	Clark
	51 177	Spotsylvania	7602		SEATTLE-TACOMA-BREMERTON, WA CMSA
	51 179	Stafford	1150		BREMERTON, WA PMSA
	51 187	Warren		53 035	Kitsap
	51 510	Alexandria City	5910		OLYMPIA, WA PMSA
	51 600	Fairfax City		53 067	Thurston
	51 610	Falls Church City	7600		SEATTLE-BELLEVUE-EVERETT, WA PMSA
	51 630	Fredericksburg City		53 029	Island
	51 683	Manassas City		53 033	King
	51 685	Manassas Park City		53 061	Snohomish
1540		CHARLOTTESVILLE, VA MSA	8200		TACOMA, WA PMSA
	51 003	Albemarle		53 053	Pierce
	51 065	Fluvanna	0860		BELLINGHAM, WA MSA
	51 079	Greene		53 073	Whatcom
	51 540	Charlottesville City	6740		RICHLAND-KENNEWICK-PASCO, WA MSA
1950		DANVILLE, VA MSA		53 005	Benton
	51 143	Pittsylvania		53 021	Franklin
	51 590	Danville City	7840		SPOKANE, WA MSA
3660		JOHNSON CITY-KINGSPORT-BRISTOL, TN-VA MSA		53 063	Spokane
	51 169	Scott	9260		YAKIMA, WA MSA
	51 191	Washington		53 077	Yakima
	51 520	Bristol City			
4640		LYNCHBURG, VA MSA			**WEST VIRGINIA**
	51 009	Amherst	97		WASHINGTON-BALTIMORE, DC-MD-VA-WV CMSA
	51 019	Bedford	8840		WASHINGTON, DC-MD-VA-WV PMSA
	51 031	Campbell		54 003	Jefferson
	51 515	Bedford City		54 037	Berkeley
	51 680	Lynchburg City	1480		CHARLESTON, WV MSA
5720		NORFOLK-VIRGINIA BEACH-NEWPORT NEWS, VA-NC MSA		54 039	Kanawha
				54 079	Putnam
	51 073	Gloucester	1900		CUMBERLAND, MD-WV MSA
	51 093	Isle of Wight		54 057	Mineral
	51 095	James City	3400		HUNTINGTON-ASHLAND, WV-KY-OH MSA
	51 115	Mathews		54 011	Cabell
	51 199	York		54 099	Wayne
	51 550	Chesapeake City	6020		PARKERSBURG-MARIETTA, WV-OH MSA
	51 650	Hampton City		54 107	Wood
	51 700	Newport News City	8080		STEUBENVILLE-WEIRTON, OH-WV MSA
	51 710	Norfolk City		54 009	Brooke
	51 735	Poquoson City		54 029	Hancock
	51 740	Portsmouth City			

Metropolitan Statistical Areas and Components by State – Continued

(MSA = metropolitan statistical area; CMSA = consolidated MSA; PMSA = primary MSA; and NECMA = New England county metropolitan area. For further information, see Appendix A.)

Geographic Codes MSA/CMSA/ PMSA/ NECMA	State and County	Title and Geographic Components	Geographic Codes MSA/CMSA/ PMSA/ NECMA	State and County	Title and Geographic Components
9000		WHEELING, WV-OH MSA	3080		GREEN BAY, WI MSA
	54 051	Marshall		55 009	Brown
	54 069	Ohio	3620		JANESVILLE-BELOIT, WI MSA
				55 105	Rock
		WISCONSIN	3870		LA CROSSE, WI-MN MSA
14		CHICAGO-GARY-KENOSHA, IL-IN-WI CMSA		55 063	La Crosse
3800		KENOSHA, WI PMSA	4720		MADISON, WI MSA
	55 059	Kenosha		55 025	Dane
5082		MILWAUKEE-RACINE, WI CMSA	5120		MINNEAPOLIS-ST. PAUL, MN-WI MSA
5080		MILWAUKEE-WAUKESHA, WI PMSA		55 093	Pierce
	55 079	Milwaukee		55 109	St. Croix
	55 089	Ozaukee	7620		SHEBOYGAN, WI MSA
	55 131	Washington		55 117	Sheboygan
	55 133	Waukesha	8940		WAUSAU, WI MSA
6600		RACINE, WI PMSA		55 073	Marathon
	55 101	Racine			
0460		APPLETON-OSHKOSH-NEENAH, WI MSA			**WYOMING**
	55 015	Calumet	1350		CASPER, WY MSA
	55 087	Outagamie		56 025	Natrona
	55 139	Winnebago	1580		CHEYENNE, WY MSA
2240		DULUTH-SUPERIOR, MN-WI MSA		56 021	Laramie
	55 031	Douglas			
2290		EAU CLAIRE, WI MSA			
	55 017	Chippewa			
	55 035	Eau Claire			

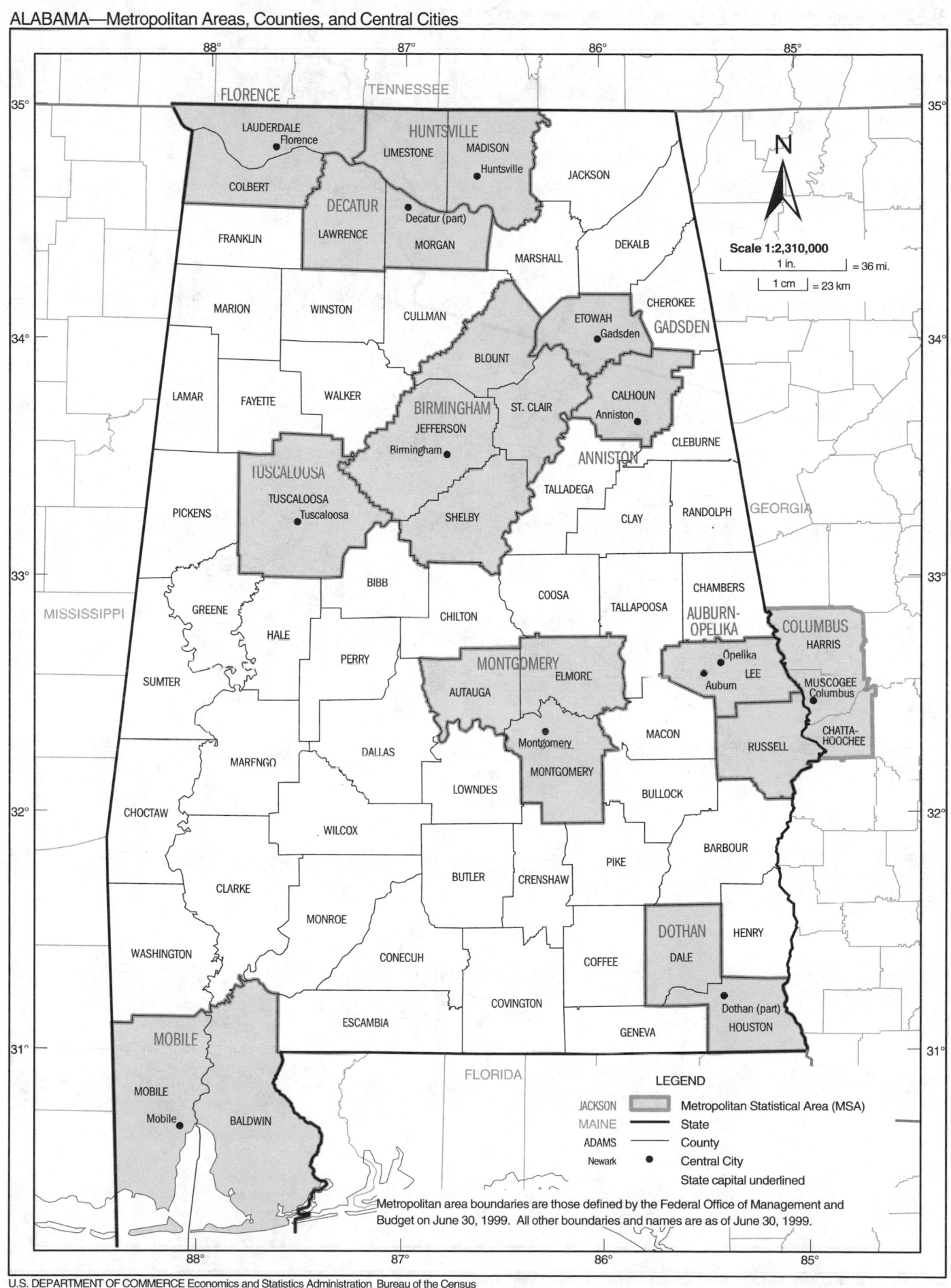

LEGEND

JACKSON	Metropolitan Statistical Area (MSA)
MAINE	State
ADAMS	County
Newark ●	Central City
	State capital underlined

Metropolitan area boundaries are those defined by the Federal Office of Management and Budget on June 30, 1999. All other boundaries and names are as of June 30, 1999.

Scale 1:2,310,000
1 in. = 36 mi.
1 cm = 23 km

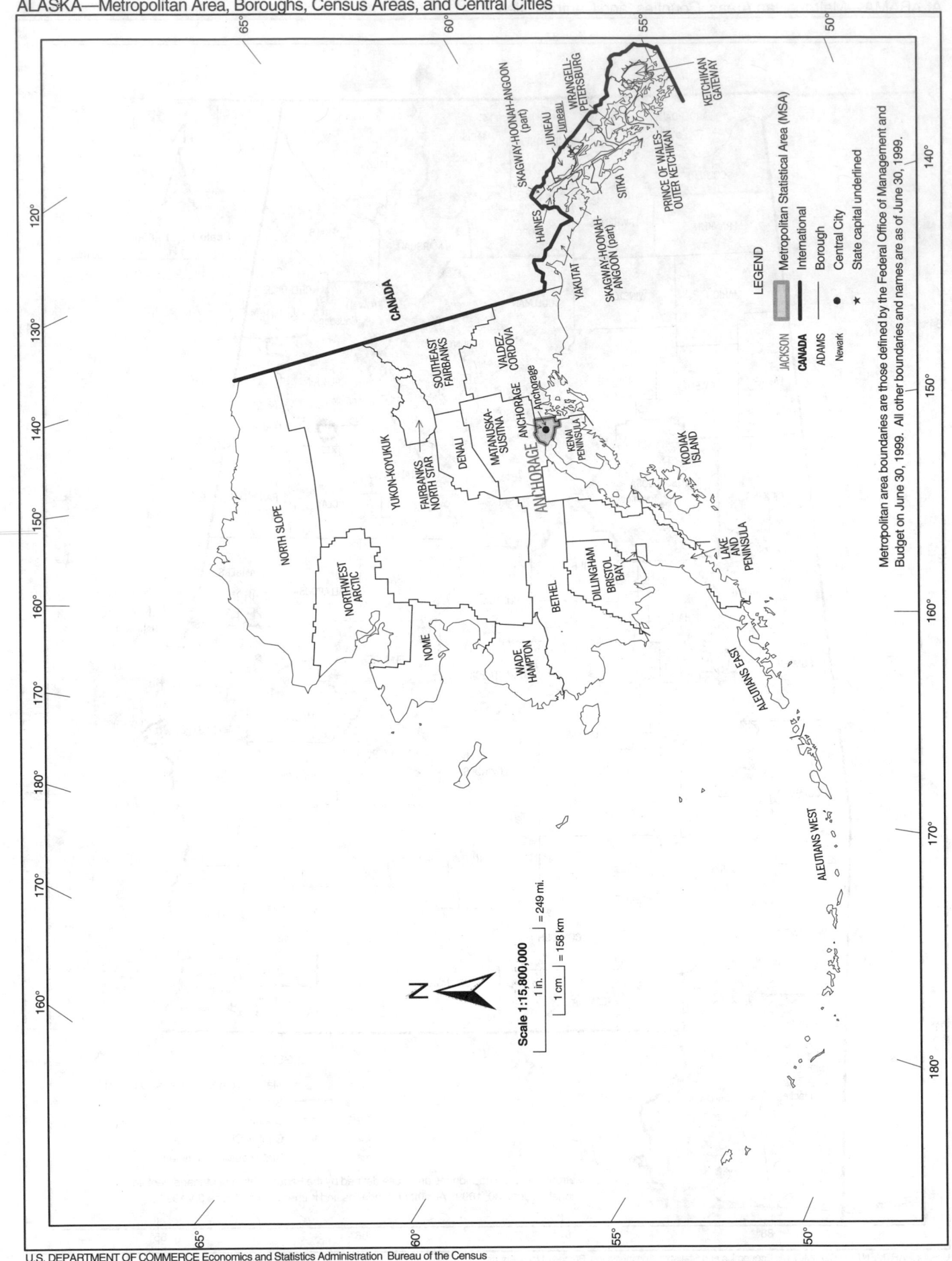

Scale 1:15,800,000

1 in. = 249 mi.

1 cm = 158 km

N

LEGEND

JACKSON — Metropolitan Statistical Area (MSA)

CANADA — International

ADAMS — Borough

Newark ● Central City

★ State capital underlined

Metropolitan area boundaries are those defined by the Federal Office of Management and Budget on June 30, 1999. All other boundaries and names are as of June 30, 1999.

CANADA

NORTH SLOPE

NORTHWEST ARCTIC

NOME

YUKON-KOYUKUK

FAIRBANKS NORTH STAR

DENALI

SOUTHEAST FAIRBANKS

MATANUSKA-SUSITNA

WADE HAMPTON

BETHEL

DILLINGHAM

BRISTOL BAY

LAKE AND PENINSULA

KODIAK ISLAND

ANCHORAGE

Anchorage

KENAI PENINSULA

VALDEZ-CORDOVA

YAKUTAT

SKAGWAY-HOONAH-ANGOON (part)

HAINES

SKAGWAY-HOONAH-ANGOON (part)

JUNEAU

Juneau

WRANGELL-PETERSBURG

SITKA

PRINCE OF WALES-OUTER KETCHIKAN

KETCHIKAN GATEWAY

ALEUTIANS EAST

ALEUTIANS WEST

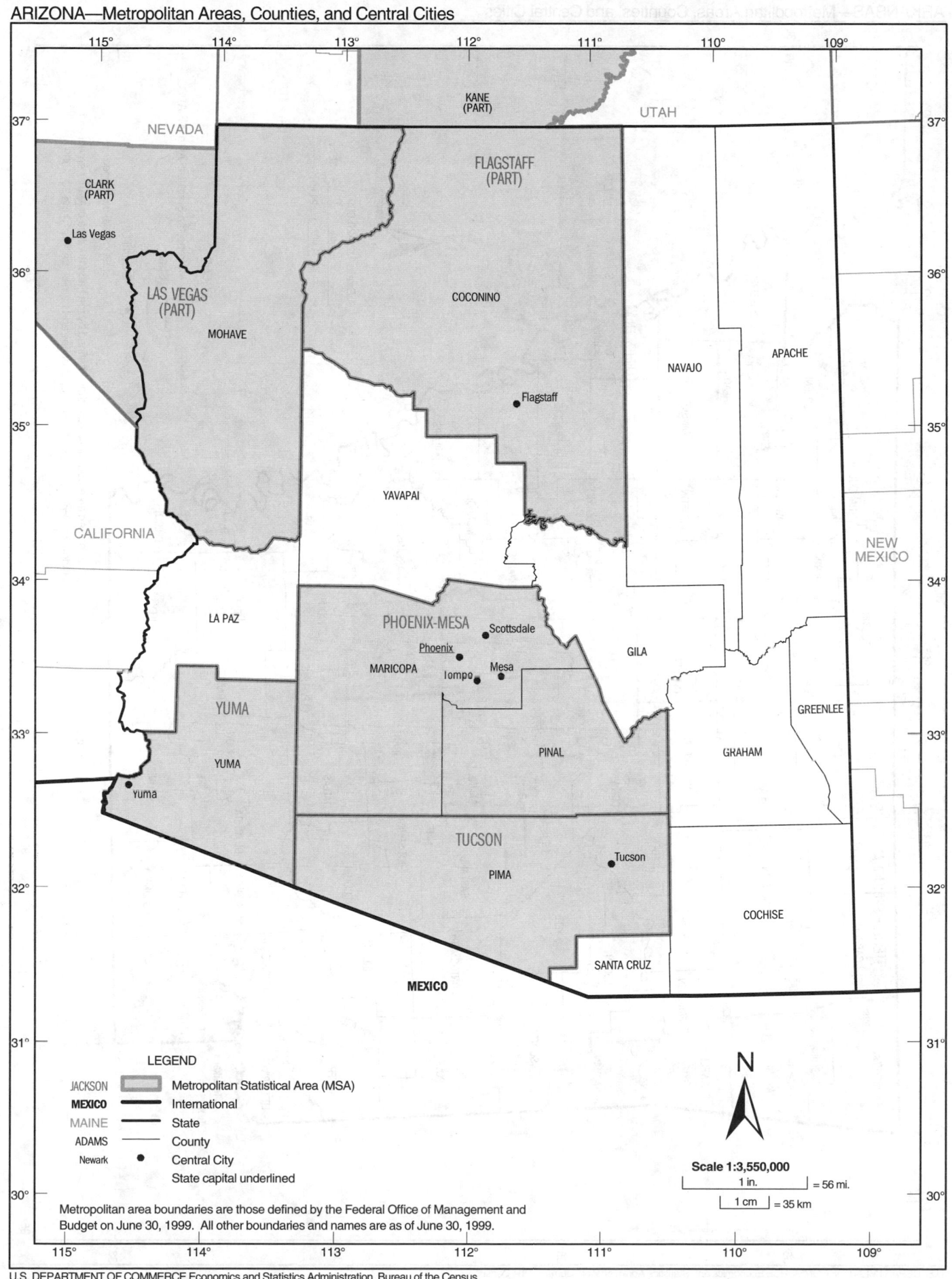

LEGEND

JACKSON	Metropolitan Statistical Area (MSA)
MEXICO	International
MAINE	State
ADAMS	County
Newark ●	Central City
	State capital underlined

Metropolitan area boundaries are those defined by the Federal Office of Management and Budget on June 30, 1999. All other boundaries and names are as of June 30, 1999.

N

Scale 1:3,550,000

| 1 in. | = 56 mi. |
| 1 cm | = 35 km |

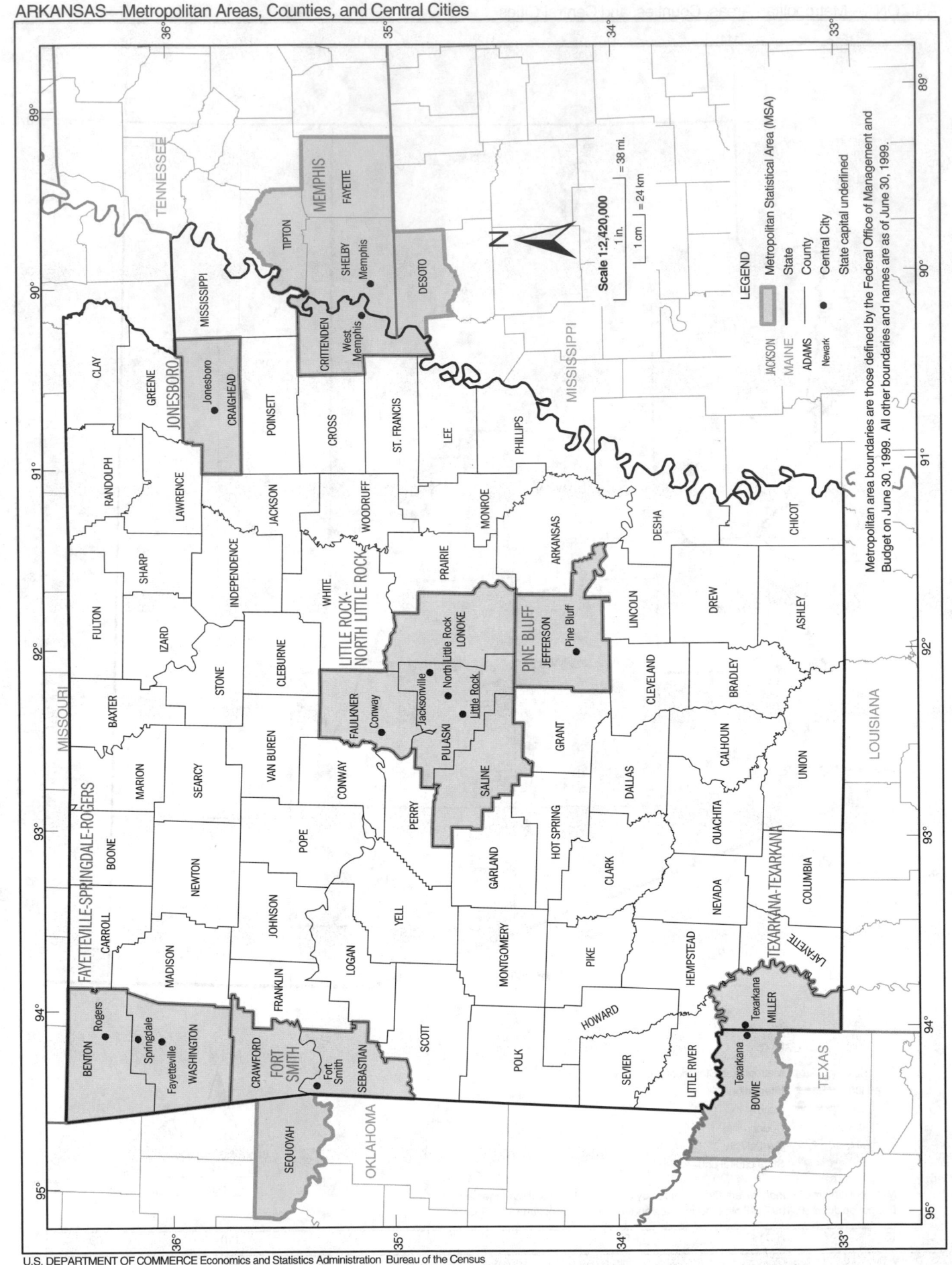

Scale 1:2,420,000

LEGEND

Metropolitan Statistical Area (MSA)
State
County
Central City
State capital underlined

JACKSON
MAINE
ADAMS
Newark

Metropolitan area boundaries are those defined by the Federal Office of Management and Budget on June 30, 1999. All other boundaries and names are as of June 30, 1999.

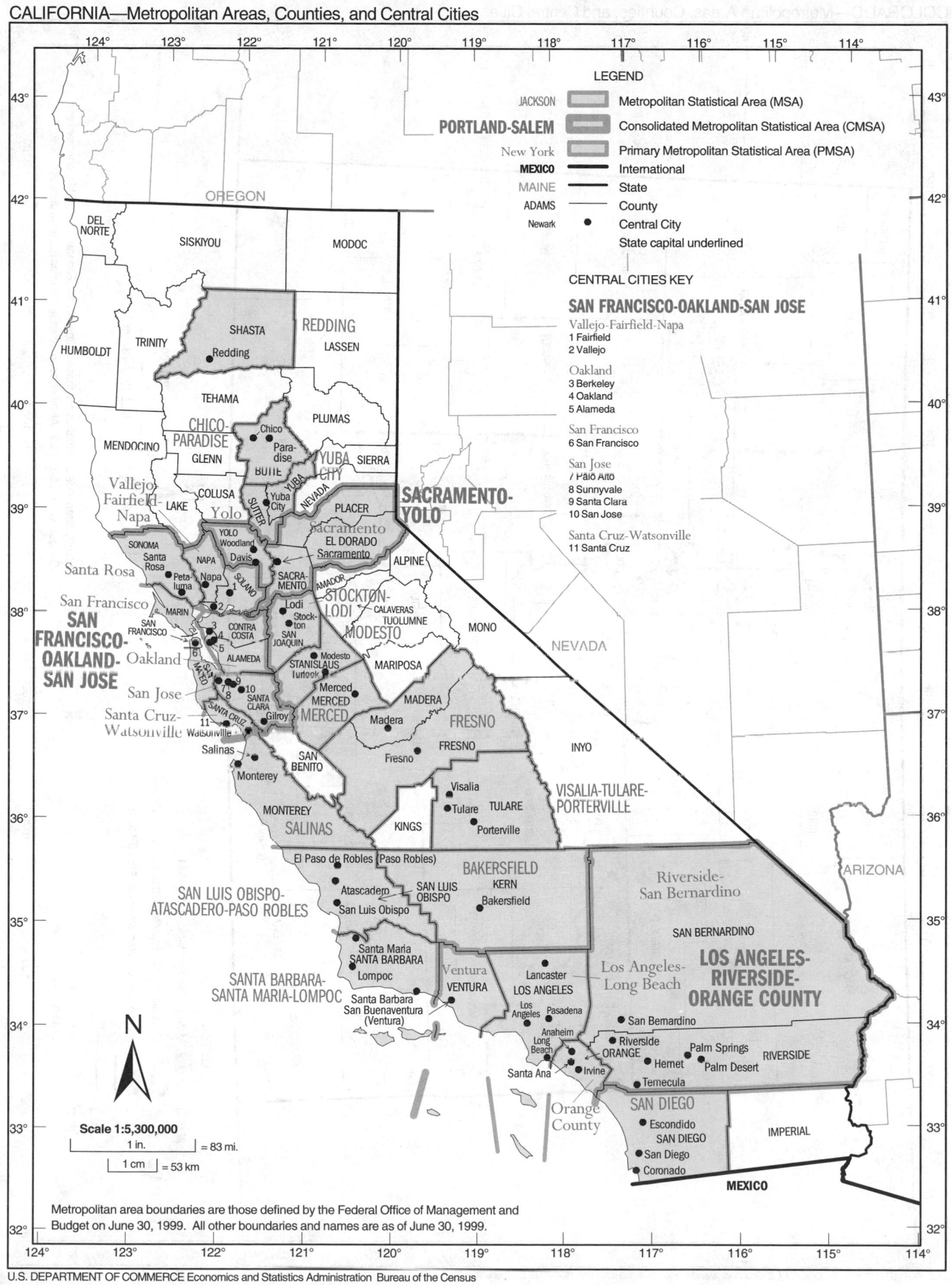

CALIFORNIA—Metropolitan Areas, Counties, and Central Cities

LEGEND

JACKSON — Metropolitan Statistical Area (MSA)

PORTLAND-SALEM — Consolidated Metropolitan Statistical Area (CMSA)

New York — Primary Metropolitan Statistical Area (PMSA)

MEXICO — International

MAINE — State

ADAMS — County

Newark ● — Central City

State capital underlined

CENTRAL CITIES KEY

SAN FRANCISCO-OAKLAND-SAN JOSE

Vallejo-Fairfield-Napa
1 Fairfield
2 Vallejo

Oakland
3 Berkeley
4 Oakland
5 Alameda

San Francisco
6 San Francisco

San Jose
7 Palo Alto
8 Sunnyvale
9 Santa Clara
10 San Jose

Santa Cruz-Watsonville
11 Santa Cruz

Scale 1:5,300,000
1 in. = 83 mi.
1 cm = 53 km

Metropolitan area boundaries are those defined by the Federal Office of Management and Budget on June 30, 1999. All other boundaries and names are as of June 30, 1999.

U.S. DEPARTMENT OF COMMERCE Economics and Statistics Administration Bureau of the Census

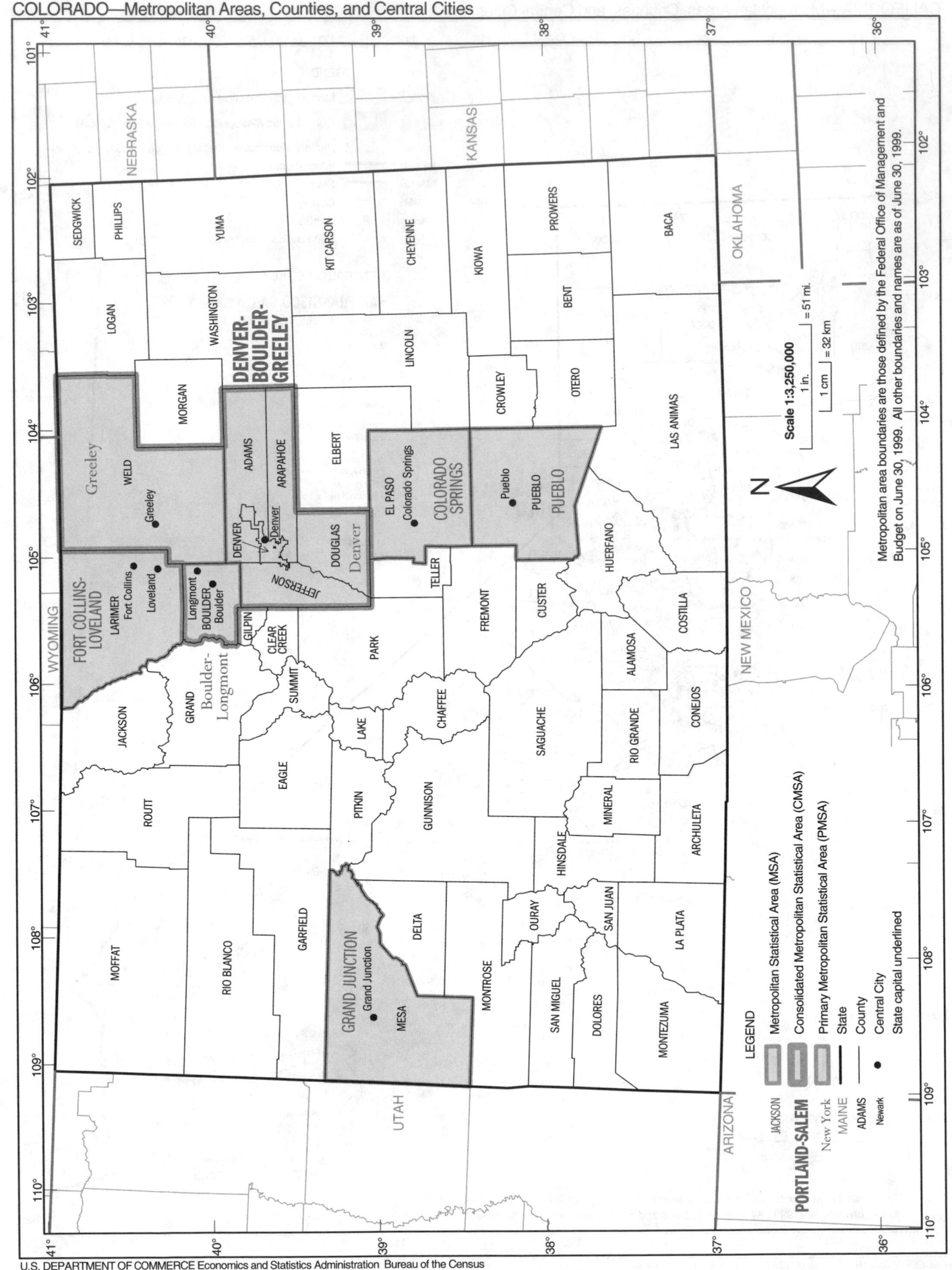

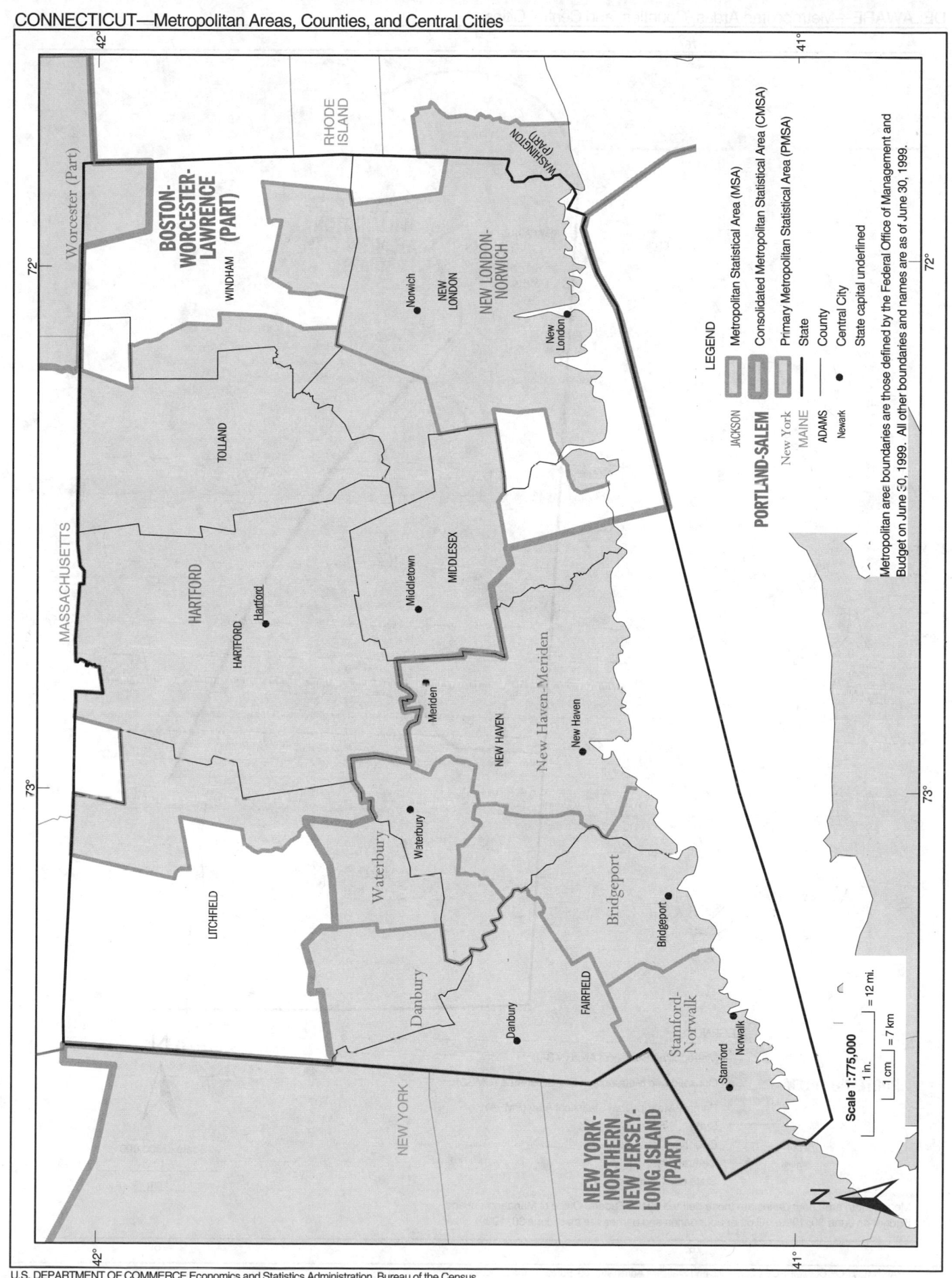

Scale 1:775,000

1 in. = 12 mi.

1 cm = 7 km

LEGEND

JACKSON	Metropolitan Statistical Area (MSA)
PORTLAND-SALEM	Consolidated Metropolitan Statistical Area (CMSA)
New York	Primary Metropolitan Statistical Area (PMSA)
MAINE	State
ADAMS	County
● Newark	Central City
	State capital underlined

Metropolitan area boundaries are those defined by the Federal Office of Management and Budget on June 30, 1999. All other boundaries and names are as of June 30, 1999.

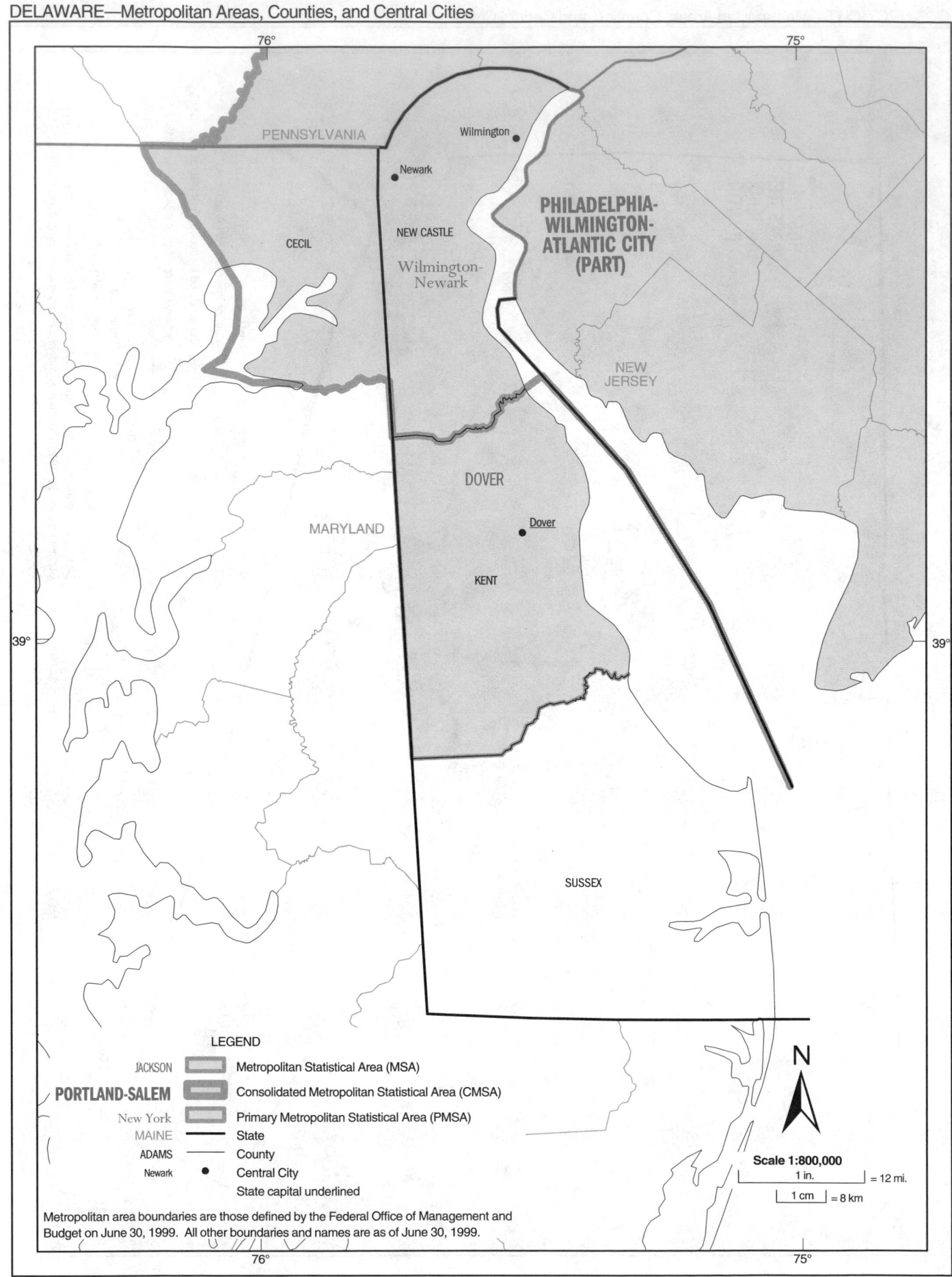

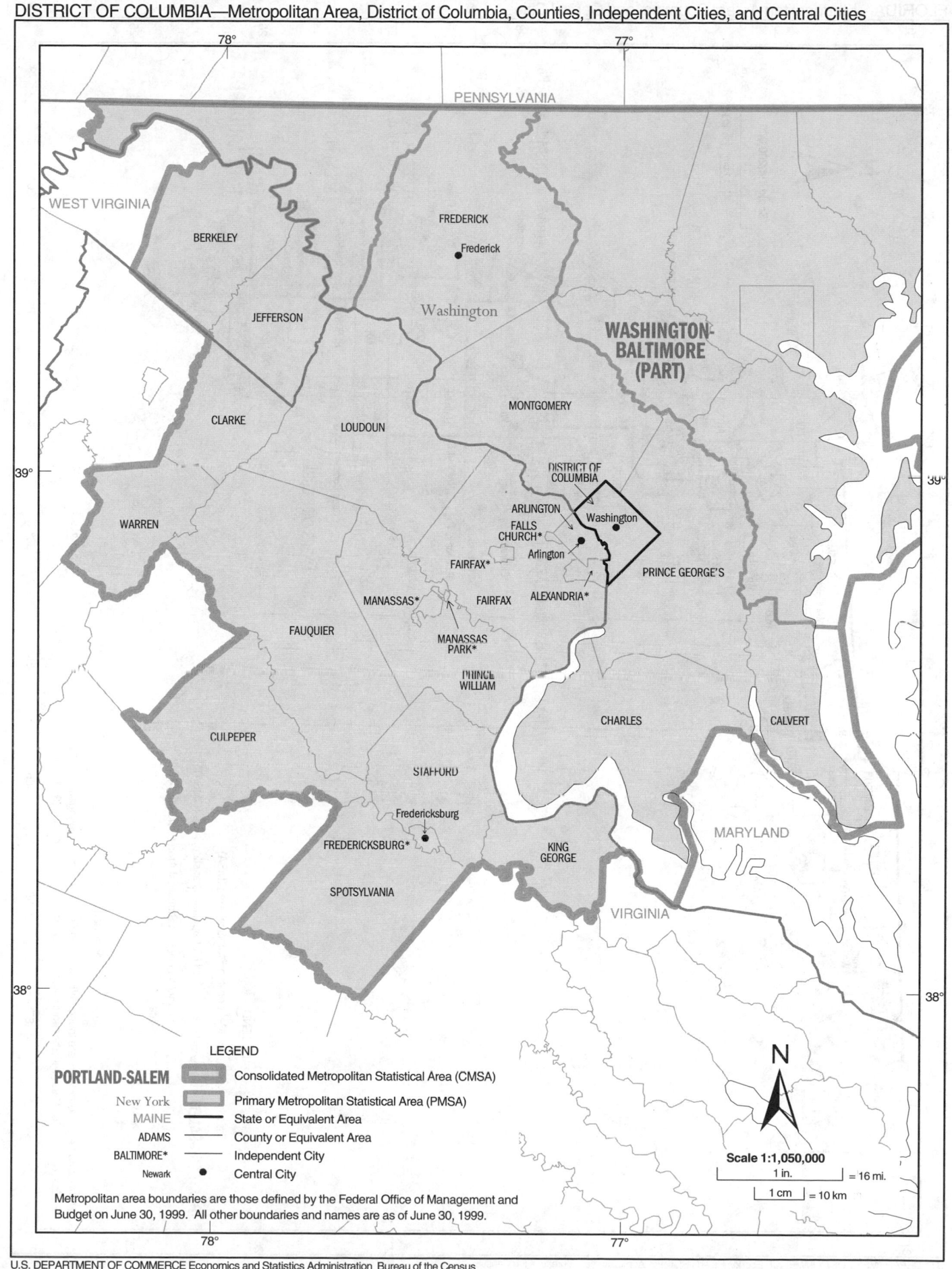

LEGEND

PORTLAND-SALEM ▢ Consolidated Metropolitan Statistical Area (CMSA)

New York ▢ Primary Metropolitan Statistical Area (PMSA)

MAINE ── State or Equivalent Area

ADAMS ── County or Equivalent Area

BALTIMORE* ── Independent City

Newark ● Central City

Metropolitan area boundaries are those defined by the Federal Office of Management and Budget on June 30, 1999. All other boundaries and names are as of June 30, 1999.

Scale 1:1,050,000

1 in. = 16 mi.

1 cm = 10 km

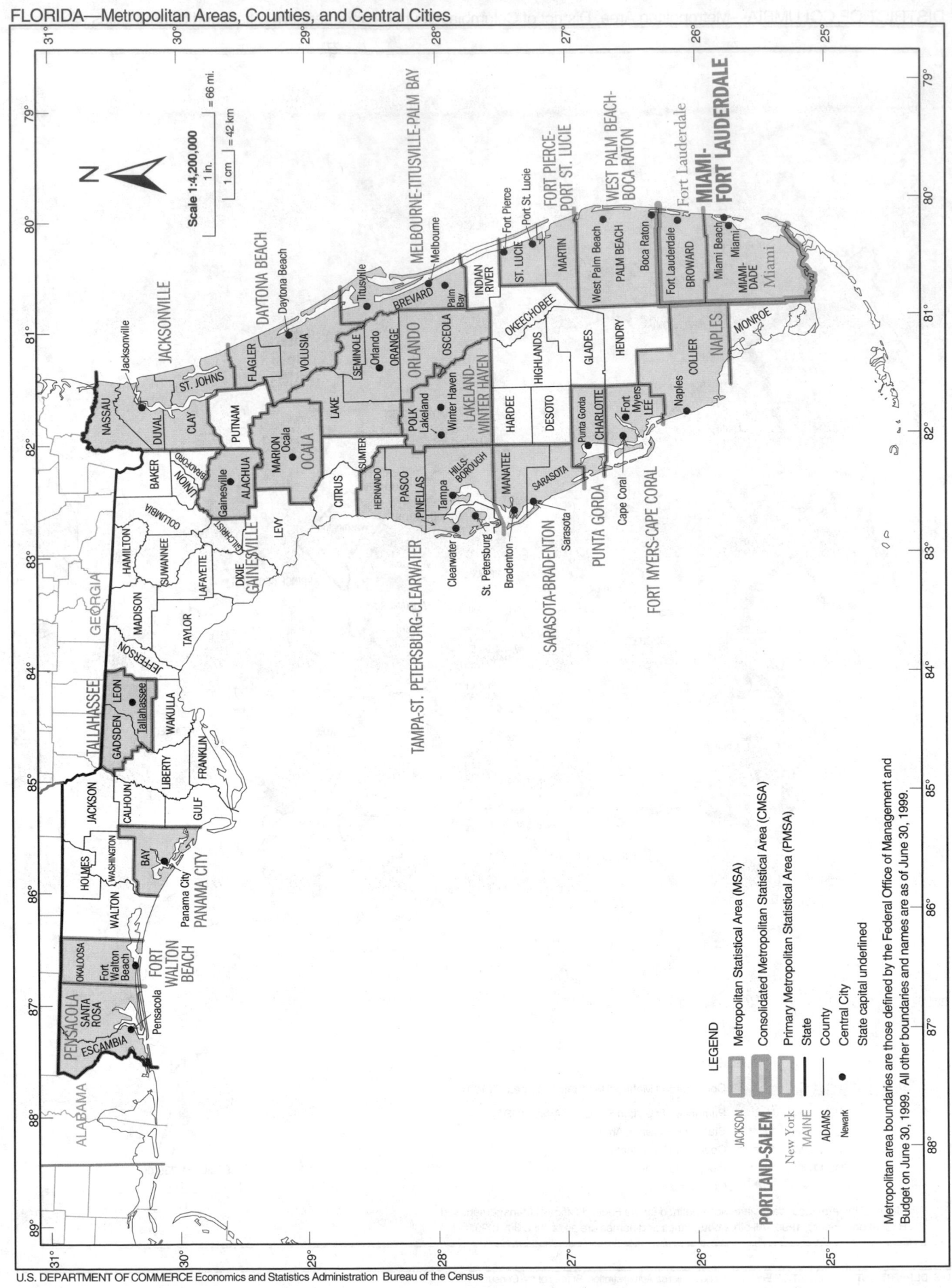

GEORGIA—Metropolitan Areas, Counties, and Central Cities

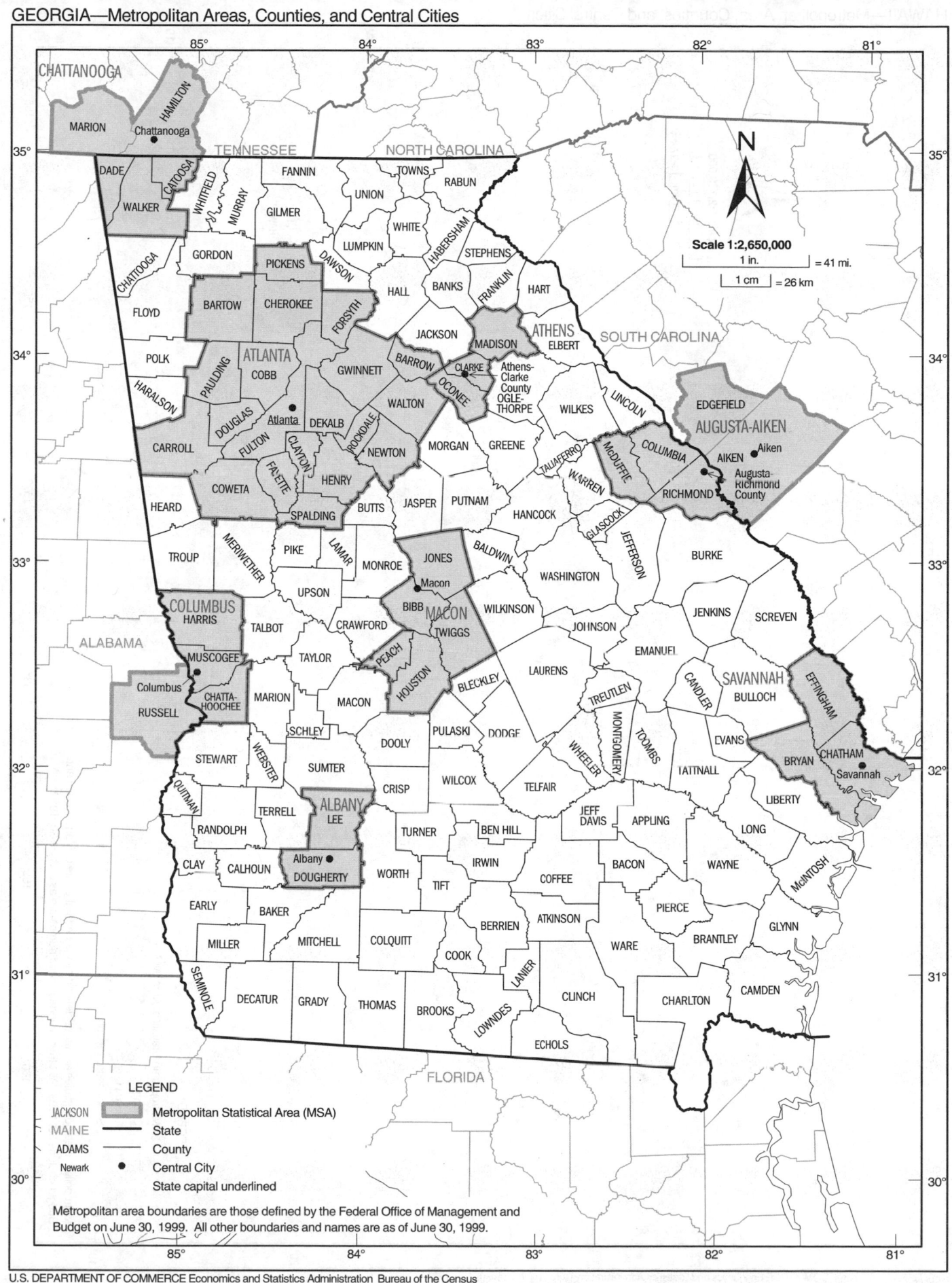

LEGEND

JACKSON	Metropolitan Statistical Area (MSA)
MAINE	State
ADAMS	County
Newark ●	Central City
	State capital underlined

Metropolitan area boundaries are those defined by the Federal Office of Management and Budget on June 30, 1999. All other boundaries and names are as of June 30, 1999.

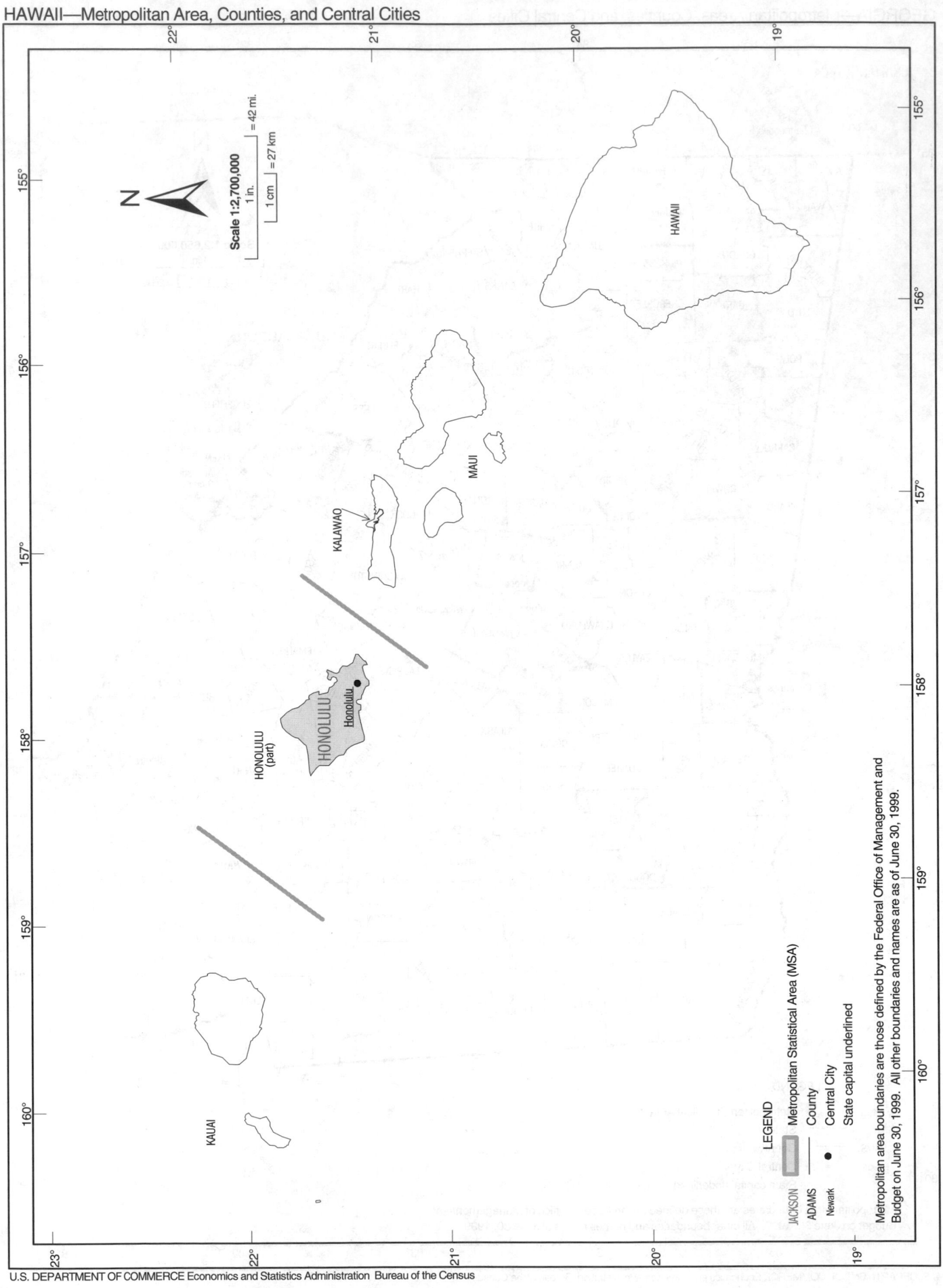

Scale 1:2,700,000

1 in. = 42 mi.

1 cm = 27 km

N

HAWAII

MAUI

KALAWAO

HONOLULU
(part)

HONOLULU

Honolulu

KAUAI

LEGEND

JACKSON

ADAMS

Newark

Metropolitan Statistical Area (MSA)

County

● Central City

State capital underlined

Metropolitan area boundaries are those defined by the Federal Office of Management and
Budget on June 30, 1999. All other boundaries and names are as of June 30, 1999.

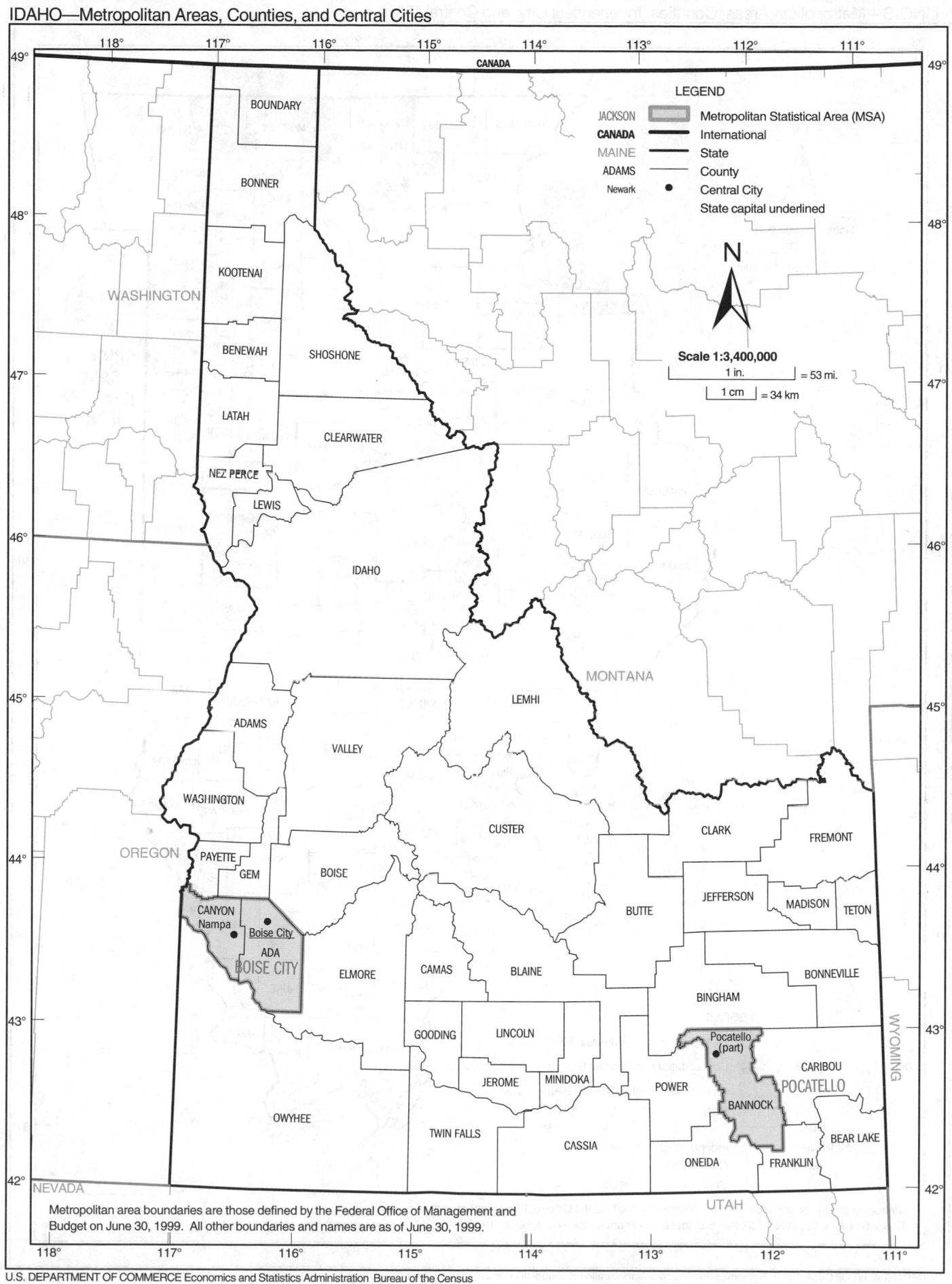

LEGEND

JACKSON	▨	Metropolitan Statistical Area (MSA)
CANADA	—	International
MAINE	—	State
ADAMS	—	County
Newark	●	Central City
		State capital underlined

N

Scale 1:3,400,000

1 in.	= 53 mi.
1 cm	= 34 km

Metropolitan area boundaries are those defined by the Federal Office of Management and Budget on June 30, 1999. All other boundaries and names are as of June 30, 1999.

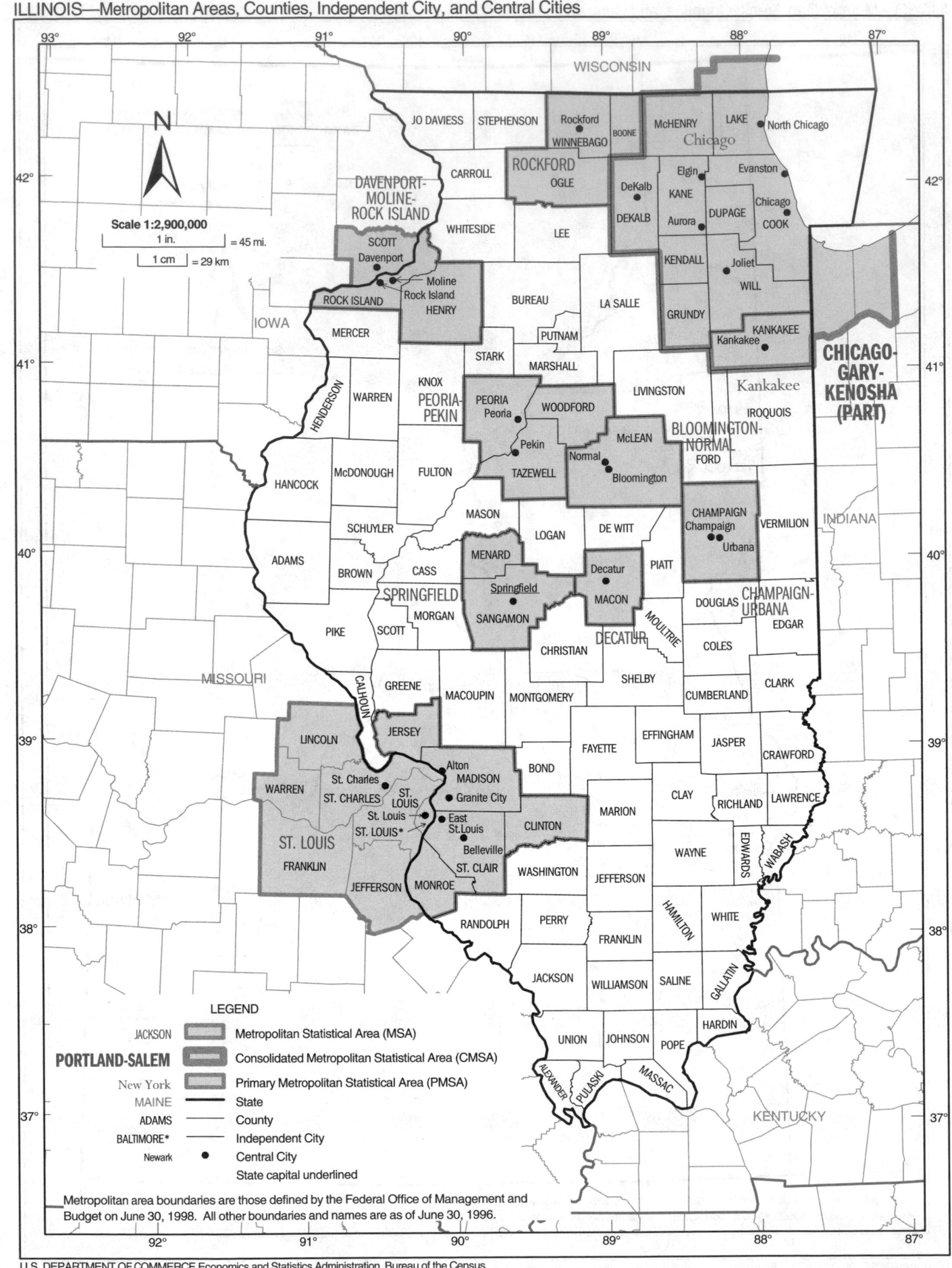

LEGEND

JACKSON	Metropolitan Statistical Area (MSA)
	Consolidated Metropolitan Statistical Area (CMSA)
PORTLAND-SALEM	
	Primary Metropolitan Statistical Area (PMSA)
New York	
MAINE	State
ADAMS	County
BALTIMORE*	Independent City
Newark	● Central City
	State capital underlined

Metropolitan area boundaries are those defined by the Federal Office of Management and Budget on June 30, 1998. All other boundaries and names are as of June 30, 1996.

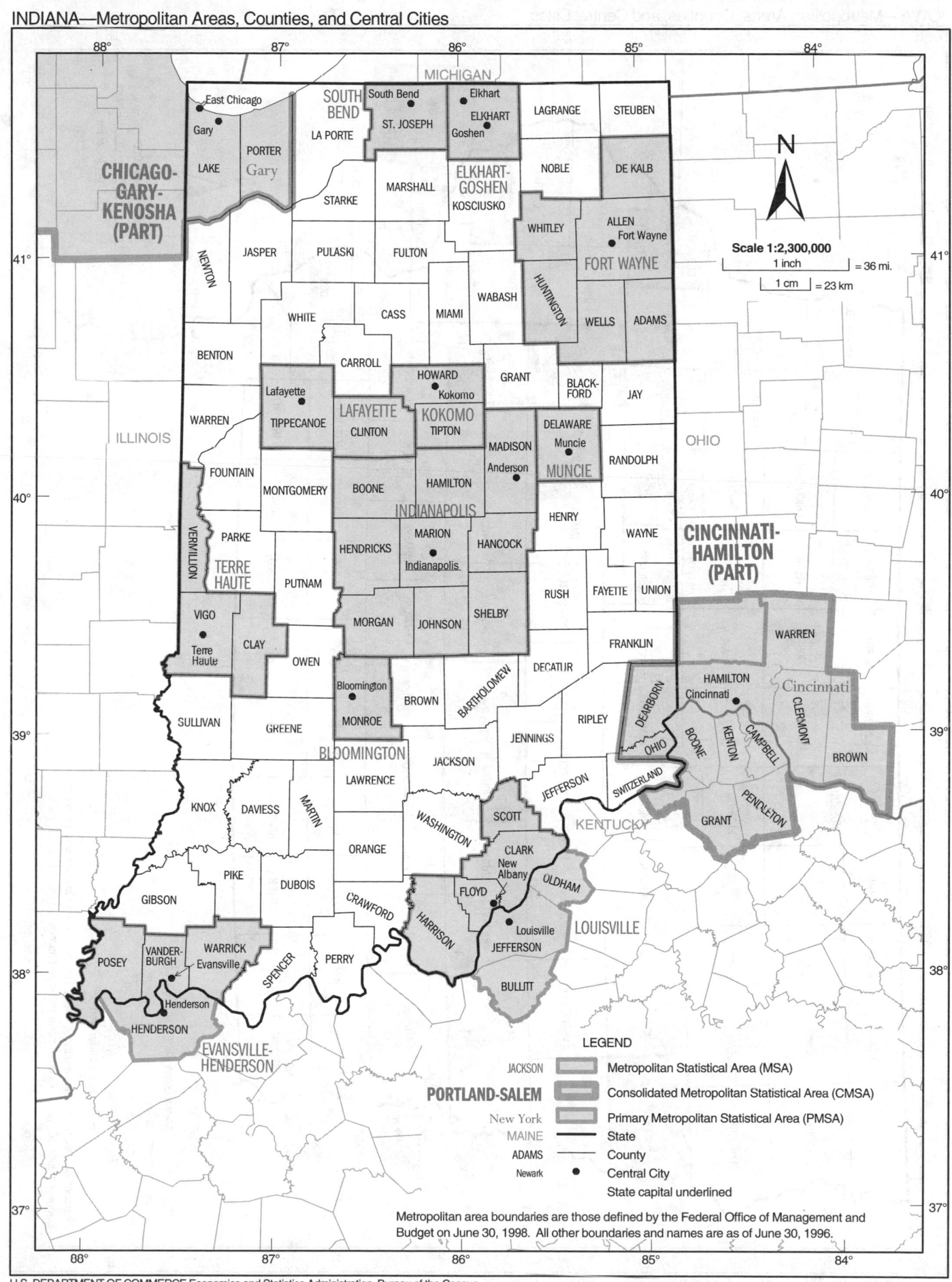

INDIANA—Metropolitan Areas, Counties, and Central Cities

MICHIGAN

East Chicago
Gary
CHICAGO-GARY-KENOSHA (PART)
LAKE
PORTER
Gary
NEWTON
JASPER
PULASKI
FULTON
WHITE
BENTON
WARREN
FOUNTAIN
PARKE
VERMILLION
TERRE HAUTE
VIGO
Terre Haute
CLAY
OWEN
PUTNAM
SULLIVAN
GREENE
KNOX
DAVIESS
MARTIN
GIBSON
PIKE
DUBOIS
POSEY
VANDER-BURGH
Evansville
WARRICK
SPENCER
PERRY
Henderson
HENDERSON
EVANSVILLE-HENDERSON

SOUTH BEND
South Bend
ST. JOSEPH
LA PORTE
STARKE
MARSHALL
CASS
MIAMI
CARROLL
Lafayette
LAFAYETTE
TIPPECANOE
CLINTON
MONTGOMERY
BOONE
HENDRICKS
MORGAN
MONROE
Bloomington
BLOOMINGTON
LAWRENCE
ORANGE
CRAWFORD
WASHINGTON
HARRISON

Elkhart
ELKHART
Goshen
ELKHART-GOSHEN
KOSCIUSKO
WABASH
HOWARD
Kokomo
KOKOMO
TIPTON
HAMILTON
INDIANAPOLIS
MARION
Indianapolis
JOHNSON
SHELBY
BROWN
BARTHOLOMEW
JACKSON
SCOTT
CLARK
New Albany
FLOYD

LAGRANGE
STEUBEN
NOBLE
DE KALB
WHITLEY
ALLEN
Fort Wayne
FORT WAYNE
HUNTINGTON
WELLS
ADAMS
GRANT
BLACK-FORD
JAY
DELAWARE
Muncie
MUNCIE
MADISON
Anderson
RANDOLPH
HANCOCK
HENRY
WAYNE
RUSH
FAYETTE
UNION
FRANKLIN
DECATUR
RIPLEY
JENNINGS
JEFFERSON
SWITZERLAND
OLDHAM
Louisville
JEFFERSON
LOUISVILLE
BULLITT

OHIO
CINCINNATI-HAMILTON (PART)
WARREN
DEARBORN
HAMILTON
Cincinnati
Cincinnati
CLERMONT
OHIO
BOONE
KENTON
CAMPBELL
BROWN
GRANT
PENDLETON
KENTUCKY

ILLINOIS

N

Scale 1:2,300,000
1 inch = 36 mi.
1 cm = 23 km

LEGEND

JACKSON — Metropolitan Statistical Area (MSA)
PORTLAND-SALEM — Consolidated Metropolitan Statistical Area (CMSA)
New York — Primary Metropolitan Statistical Area (PMSA)
MAINE — State
ADAMS — County
Newark ● Central City
State capital underlined

Metropolitan area boundaries are those defined by the Federal Office of Management and
Budget on June 30, 1998. All other boundaries and names are as of June 30, 1996.

U.S. DEPARTMENT OF COMMERCE Economics and Statistics Administration Bureau of the Census

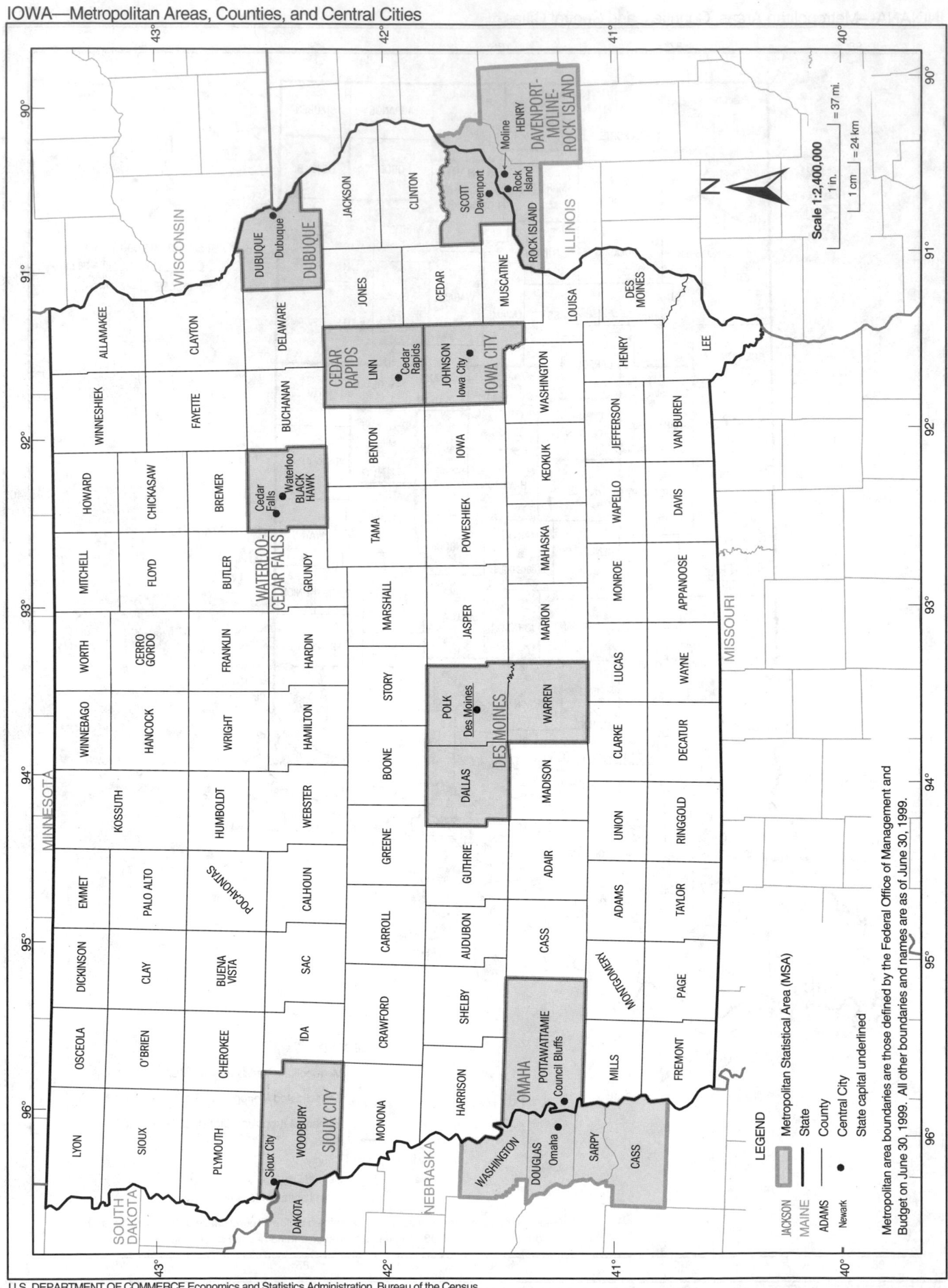

LEGEND

Metropolitan Statistical Area (MSA)

—— State

—— County

• Central City

State capital underlined

JACKSON

MAINE

ADAMS

Newark

Metropolitan area boundaries are those defined by the Federal Office of Management and Budget on June 30, 1999. All other boundaries and names are as of June 30, 1999.

Scale 1:2,400,000

1 in. = 37 mi.

1 cm = 24 km

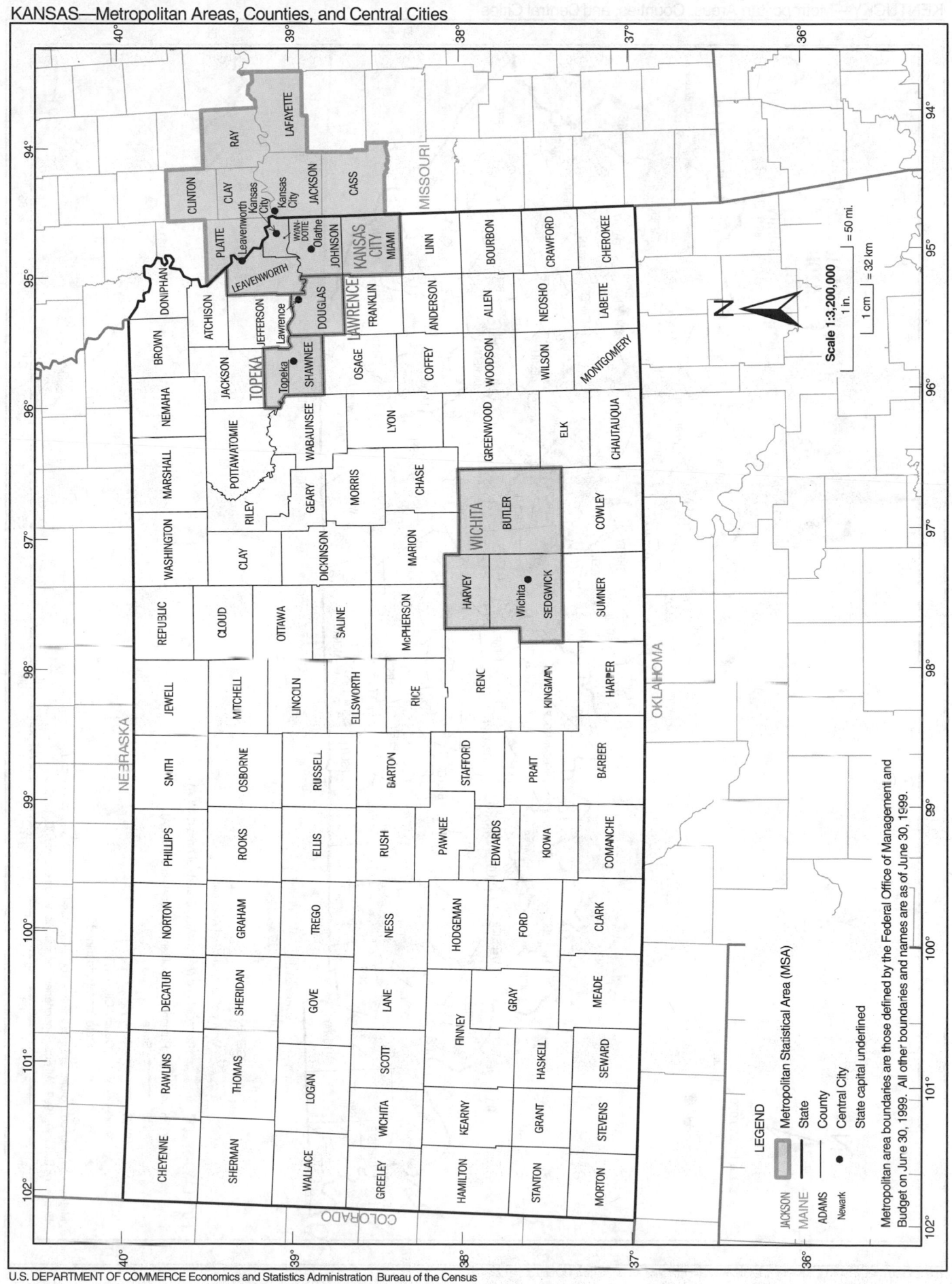

Scale 1:3,200,000

1 in. = 50 mi.

1 cm = 32 km

LEGEND

Metropolitan Statistical Area (MSA)

State

County

Central City

State capital underlined

JACKSON
MAINE
ADAMS
Newark

Metropolitan area boundaries are those defined by the Federal Office of Management and Budget on June 30, 1999. All other boundaries and names are as of June 30, 1999.

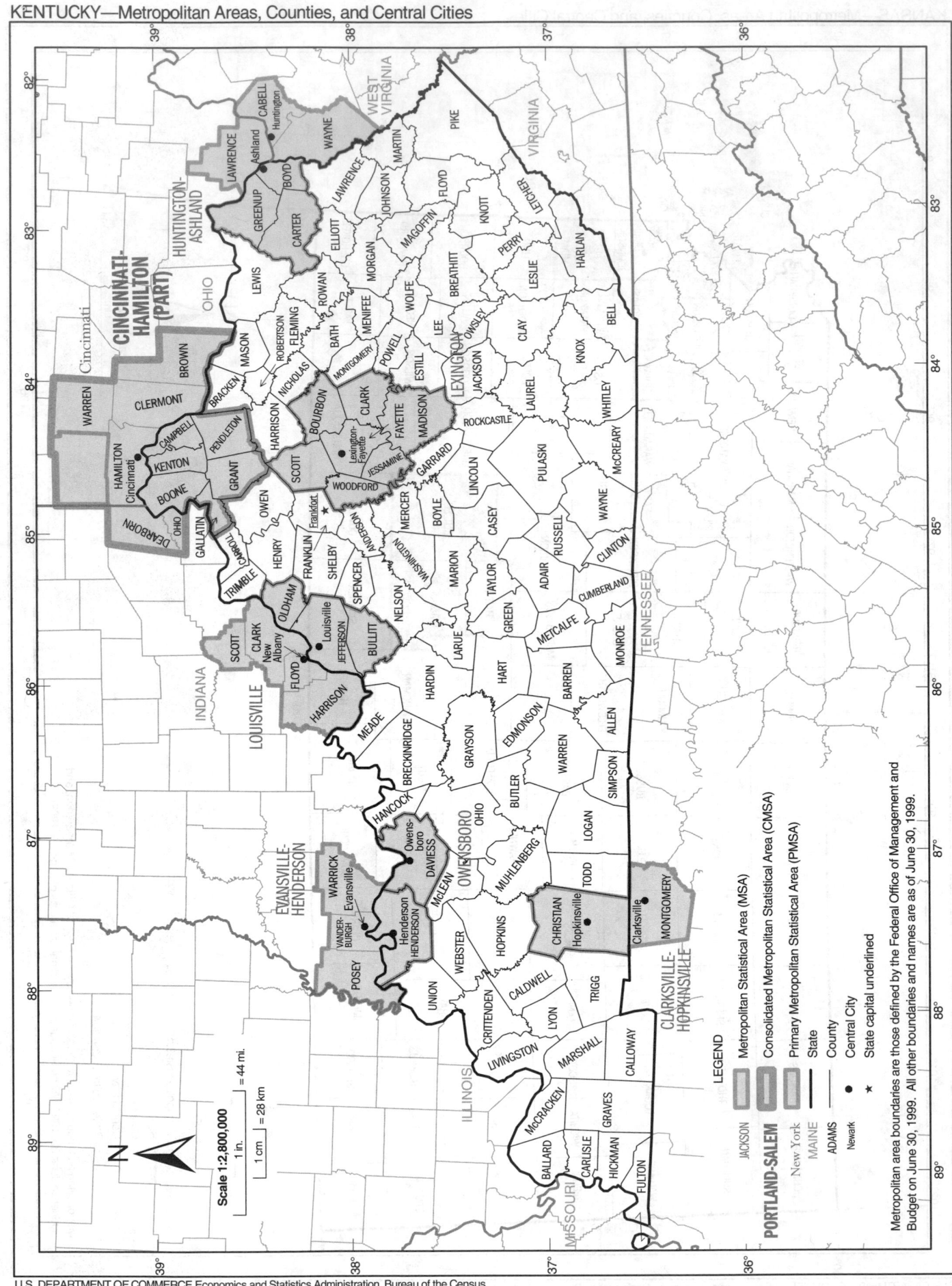

LEGEND

Metropolitan Statistical Area (MSA)

Consolidated Metropolitan Statistical Area (CMSA)

Primary Metropolitan Statistical Area (PMSA)

State

County

● Central City

★ State capital underlined

JACKSON

PORTLAND-SALEM

New York

MAINE

ADAMS

Newark

Metropolitan area boundaries are those defined by the Federal Office of Management and Budget on June 30, 1999. All other boundaries and names are as of June 30, 1999.

Scale 1:2,800,000

1 in. = 44 mi.

1 cm = 28 km

N

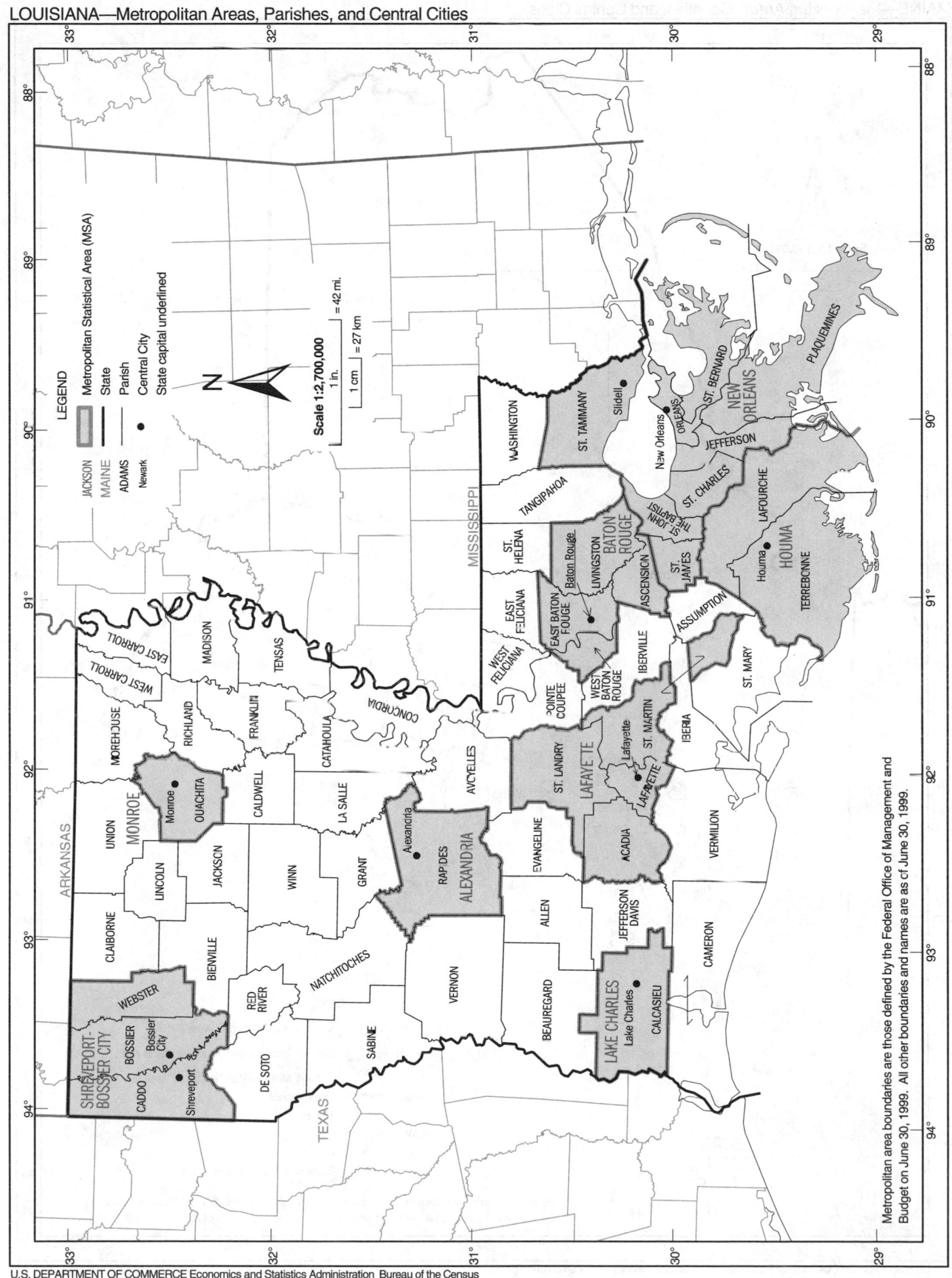

LEGEND

Metropolitan Statistical Area (MSA)
State
Parish
● Central City
State capital underlined

JACKSON
MAINE
ADAMS
Newark

N

Scale 1:2,700,000
1 in. = 42 mi.
1 cm = 27 km

MISSISSIPPI

ARKANSAS

TEXAS

WASHINGTON
ST. TAMMANY
Slidell
TANGIPAHOA
ST. HELENA
EAST FELICIANA
WEST FELICIANA
Baton Rouge
LIVINGSTON
BATON ROUGE
East Baton Rouge
ST. JOHN THE BAPTIST
ST. CHARLES
ORLEANS
New Orleans
JEFFERSON
ST. BERNARD
NEW ORLEANS
PLAQUEMINES
LAFOURCHE
HOUMA
Houma
TERREBONNE
ST. JAMES
ASCENSION
ASSUMPTION
IBERVILLE
WEST BATON ROUGE
POINTE COUPEE
ST. MARY
IBERIA
ST. MARTIN
Lafayette
LAFAYETTE
Lafayette
VERMILION
ST. LANDRY
AVOYELLES
EVANGELINE
ACADIA
JEFFERSON DAVIS
CAMERON
CALCASIEU
Lake Charles
LAKE CHARLES
BEAUREGARD
ALLEN
VERNON
Alexandria
RAPIDES
ALEXANDRIA
GRANT
LA SALLE
CATAHOULA
CONCORDIA
NATCHITOCHES
SABINE
DE SOTO
RED RIVER
WINN
CALDWELL
FRANKLIN
TENSAS
MADISON
RICHLAND
JACKSON
BIENVILLE
CLAIBORNE
LINCOLN
UNION
MOREHOUSE
OUACHITA
Monroe
MONROE
WEST CARROLL
EAST CARROLL
WEBSTER
BOSSIER
Bossier City
CADDO
Shreveport
SHREVEPORT-BOSSIER CITY

Metropolitan area boundaries are those defined by the Federal Office of Management and Budget on June 30, 1999. All other boundaries and names are as of June 30, 1999.

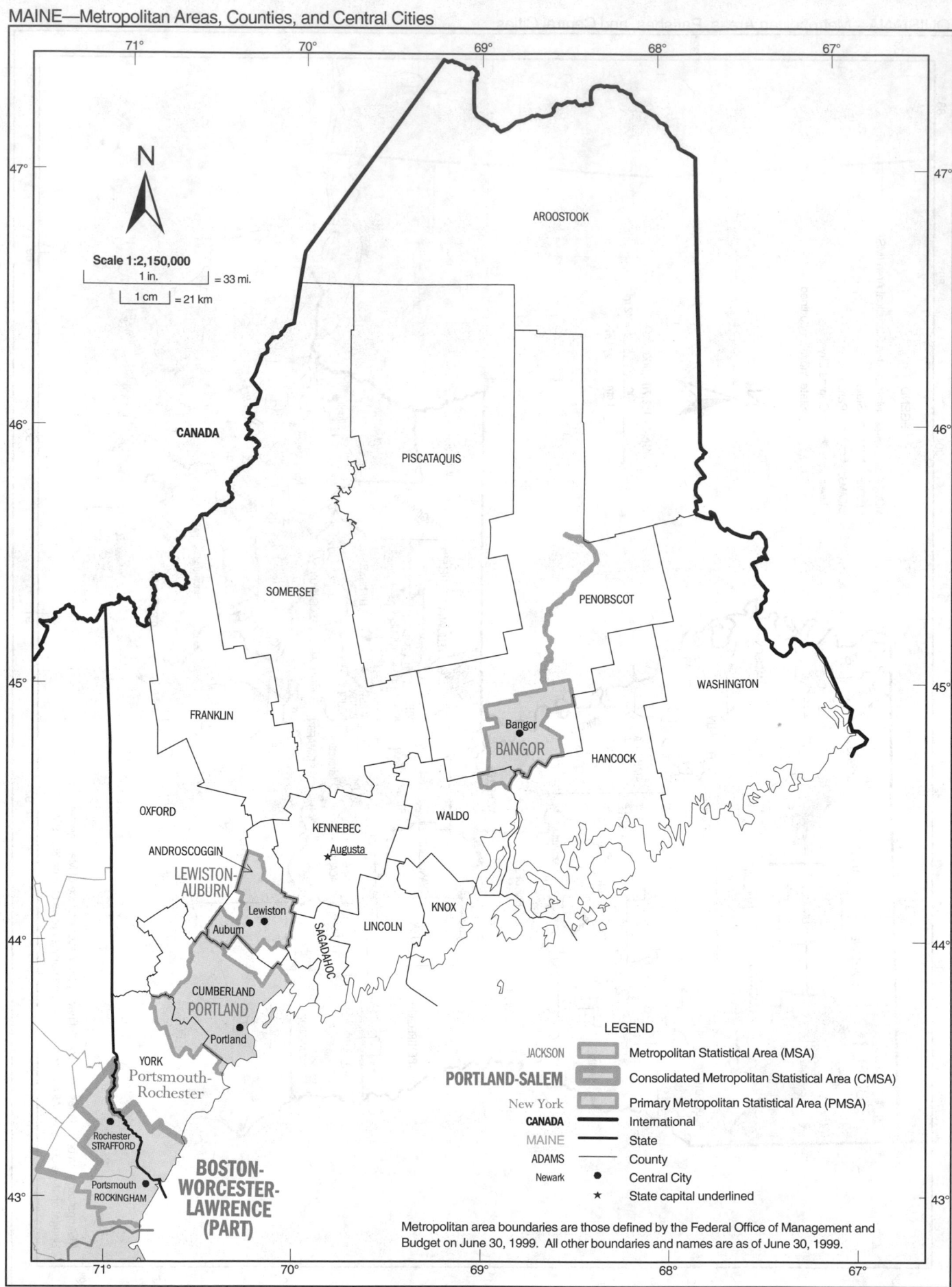

N

Scale 1:2,150,000

| 1 in. | = 33 mi. |

| 1 cm | = 21 km |

CANADA

AROOSTOOK

PISCATAQUIS

SOMERSET

PENOBSCOT

FRANKLIN

WASHINGTON

OXFORD

KENNEBEC

WALDO

ANDROSCOGGIN

Augusta

LEWISTON-AUBURN

HANCOCK

Bangor

BANGOR

Lewiston

Aubum

KNOX

SAGADAHOC

LINCOLN

CUMBERLAND

PORTLAND

Portland

YORK

Portsmouth-Rochester

Rochester
STRAFFORD

Portsmouth
ROCKINGHAM

BOSTON-WORCESTER-LAWRENCE (PART)

LEGEND

JACKSON		Metropolitan Statistical Area (MSA)
PORTLAND-SALEM		Consolidated Metropolitan Statistical Area (CMSA)
New York		Primary Metropolitan Statistical Area (PMSA)
CANADA		International
MAINE		State
ADAMS		County
Newark	●	Central City
	★	State capital underlined

Metropolitan area boundaries are those defined by the Federal Office of Management and Budget on June 30, 1999. All other boundaries and names are as of June 30, 1999.

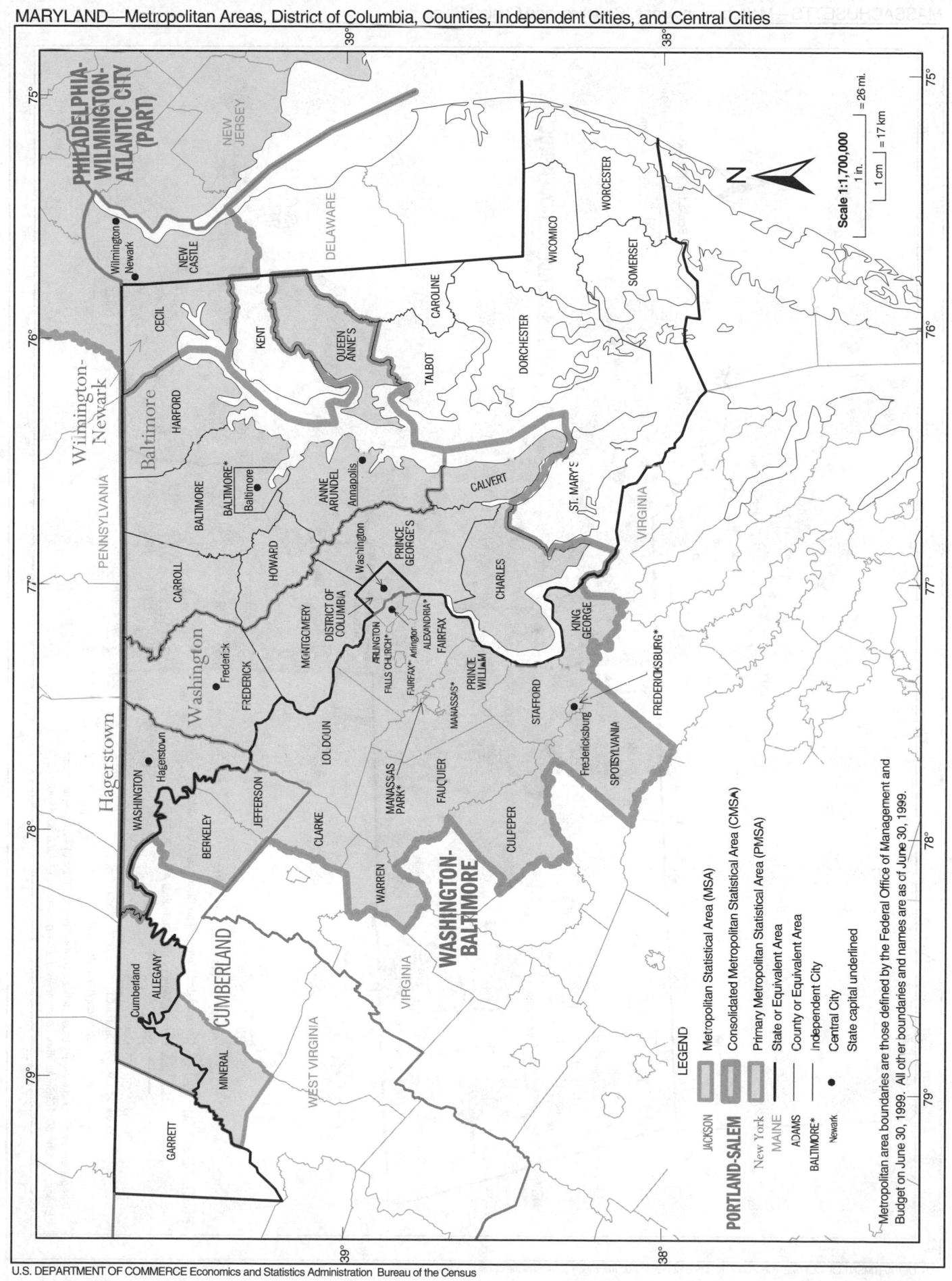

LEGEND

Metropolitan Statistical Area (MSA)

Consolidated Metropolitan Statistical Area (CMSA)

Primary Metropolitan Statistical Area (PMSA)

State or Equivalent Area

County or Equivalent Area

Independent City

● Central City

State capital underlined

JACKSON
PORTLAND-SALEM
New York
MAINE
ADAMS
BALTIMORE*
Newark

Metropolitan area boundaries are those defined by the Federal Office of Management and
Budget on June 30, 1999. All other boundaries and names are as of June 30, 1999.

Scale 1:1,700,000
1 in. = 26 mi.
1 cm = 17 km

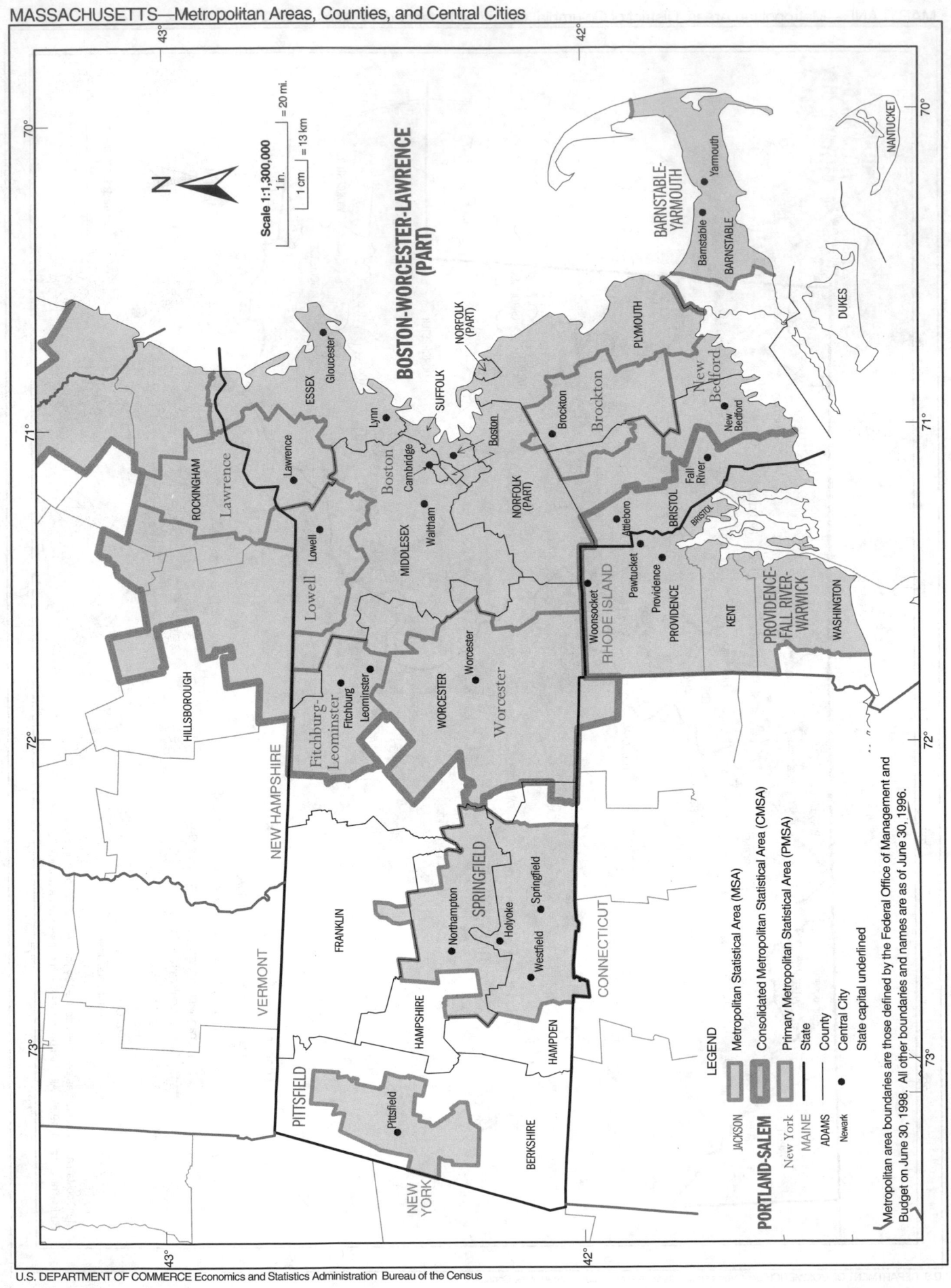

Scale 1:1,300,000

1 in. = 20 mi.

1 cm = 13 km

BOSTON-WORCESTER-LAWRENCE (PART)

BARNSTABLE-YARMOUTH

NANTUCKET

DUKES

NORFOLK (PART)

SUFFOLK

Yarmouth
Barnstable
BARNSTABLE

PLYMOUTH

New Bedford

Gloucester

ESSEX

Lynn

Boston

Brockton
Brockton

New Bedford

Lawrence
Lawrence

ROCKINGHAM

Cambridge

Fall River

Boston

Waltham
MIDDLESEX

NORFOLK (PART)

BRISTOL
BRISTOL

Lowell
Lowell

Attleboro

HILLSBOROUGH

Pawtucket

Woonsocket
RHODE ISLAND

Providence
Providence
PROVIDENCE

KENT

PROVIDENCE-FALL RIVER-WARWICK

WASHINGTON

Worcester

Fitchburg-Leominster
Leominster
Fitchburg

WORCESTER

Worcester

NEW HAMPSHIRE

FRANKLIN

SPRINGFIELD

Northampton

Holyoke
Springfield

Westfield

VERMONT

HAMPSHIRE

HAMPDEN

CONNECTICUT

PITTSFIELD

Pittsfield

BERKSHIRE

NEW YORK

LEGEND

Metropolitan Statistical Area (MSA)

Consolidated Metropolitan Statistical Area (CMSA)

Primary Metropolitan Statistical Area (PMSA)

State

County

Central City

State capital underlined

JACKSON

PORTLAND-SALEM

New York

MAINE

ADAMS

Newark

Metropolitan area boundaries are those defined by the Federal Office of Management and Budget on June 30, 1998. All other boundaries and names are as of June 30, 1996.

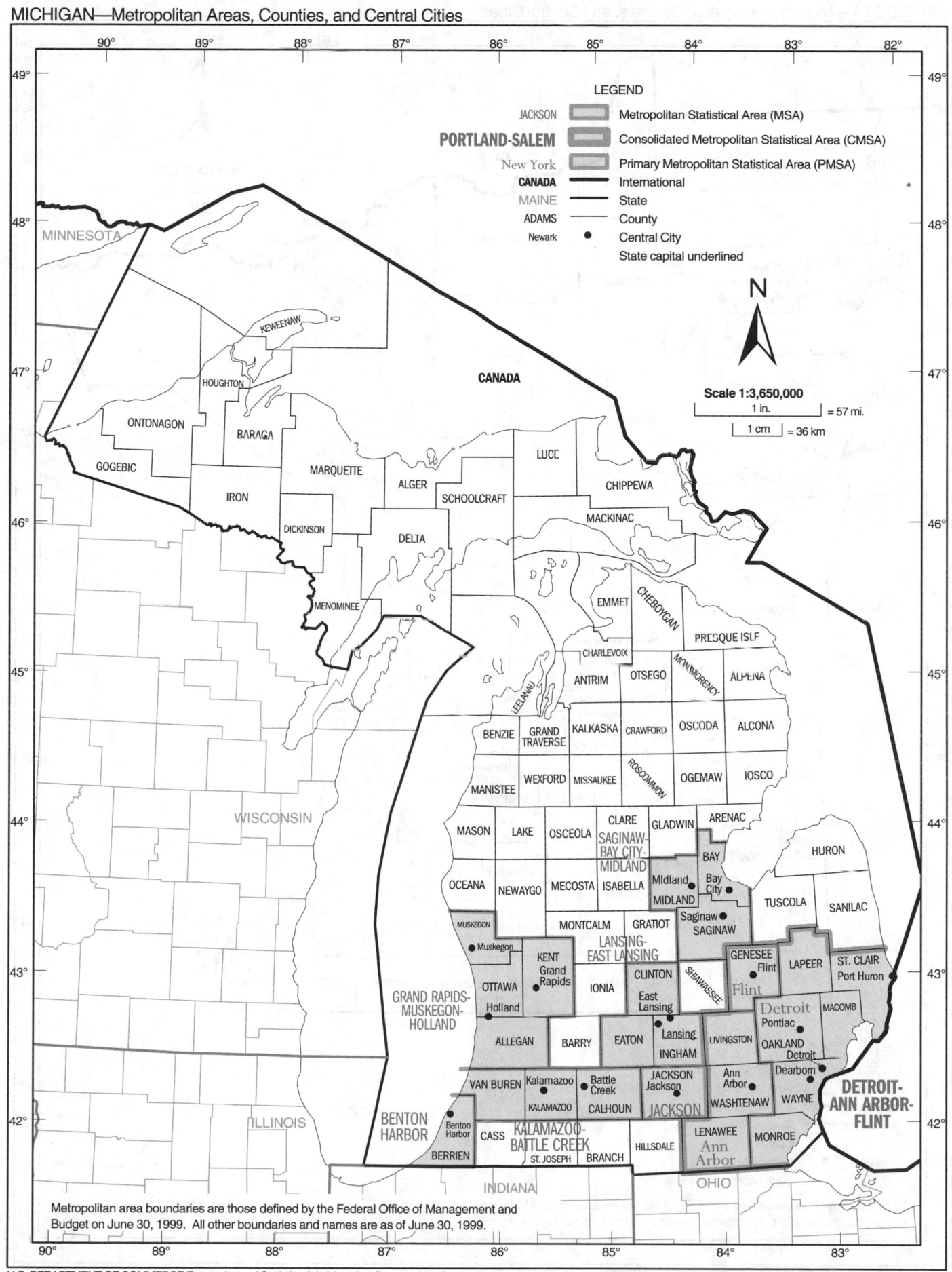

LEGEND

JACKSON	Metropolitan Statistical Area (MSA)
PORTLAND-SALEM	Consolidated Metropolitan Statistical Area (CMSA)
New York	Primary Metropolitan Statistical Area (PMSA)
CANADA	International
MAINE	State
ADAMS	County
Newark ●	Central City
	State capital underlined

Scale 1:3,650,000

1 in. = 57 mi.

1 cm = 36 km

Metropolitan area boundaries are those defined by the Federal Office of Management and Budget on June 30, 1999. All other boundaries and names are as of June 30, 1999.

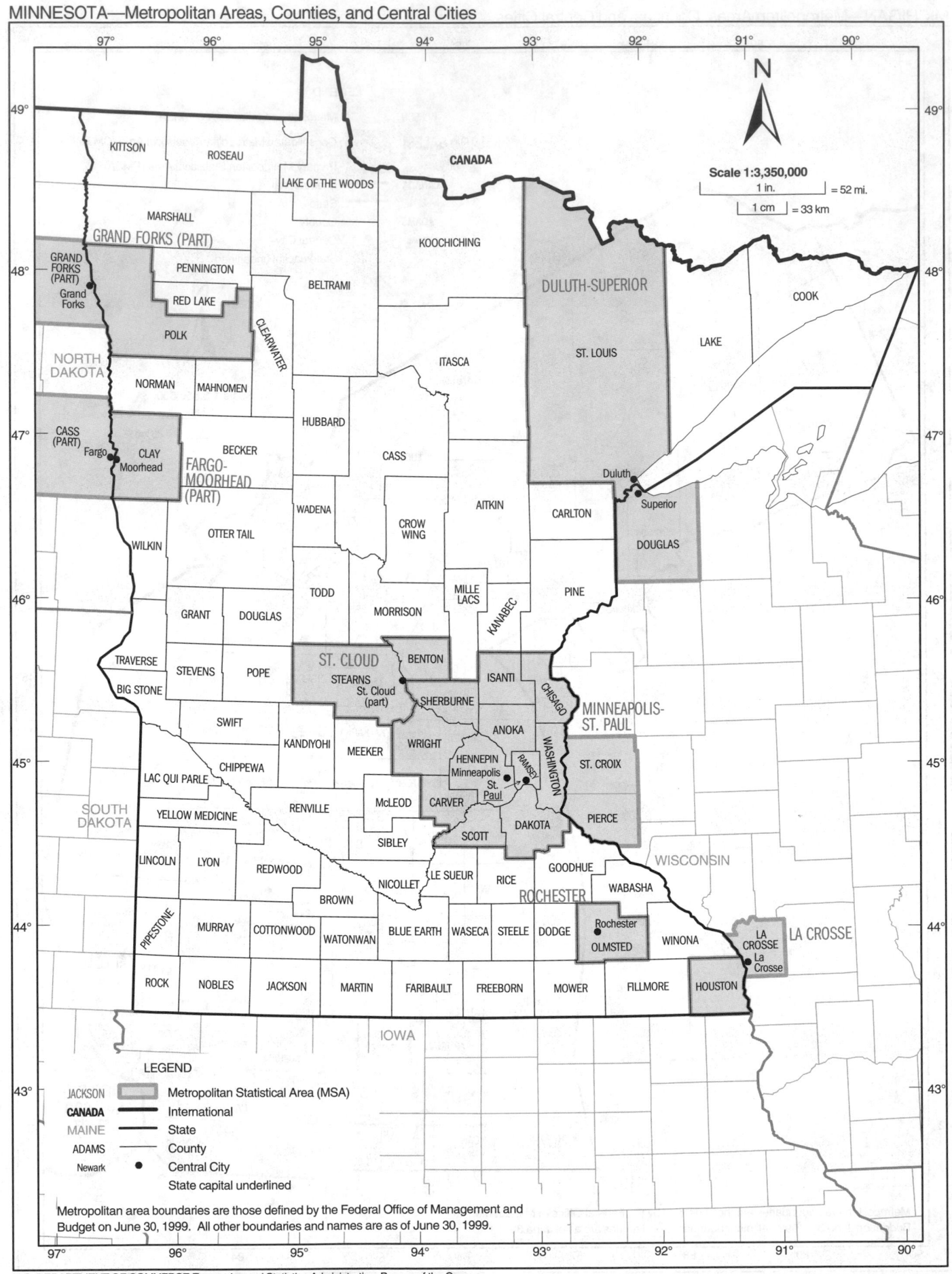

LEGEND

JACKSON	Metropolitan Statistical Area (MSA)
CANADA	International
MAINE	State
ADAMS	County
Newark ●	Central City
	State capital underlined

Metropolitan area boundaries are those defined by the Federal Office of Management and Budget on June 30, 1999. All other boundaries and names are as of June 30, 1999.

MISSISSIPPI—Metropolitan Areas, Counties, and Central Cities

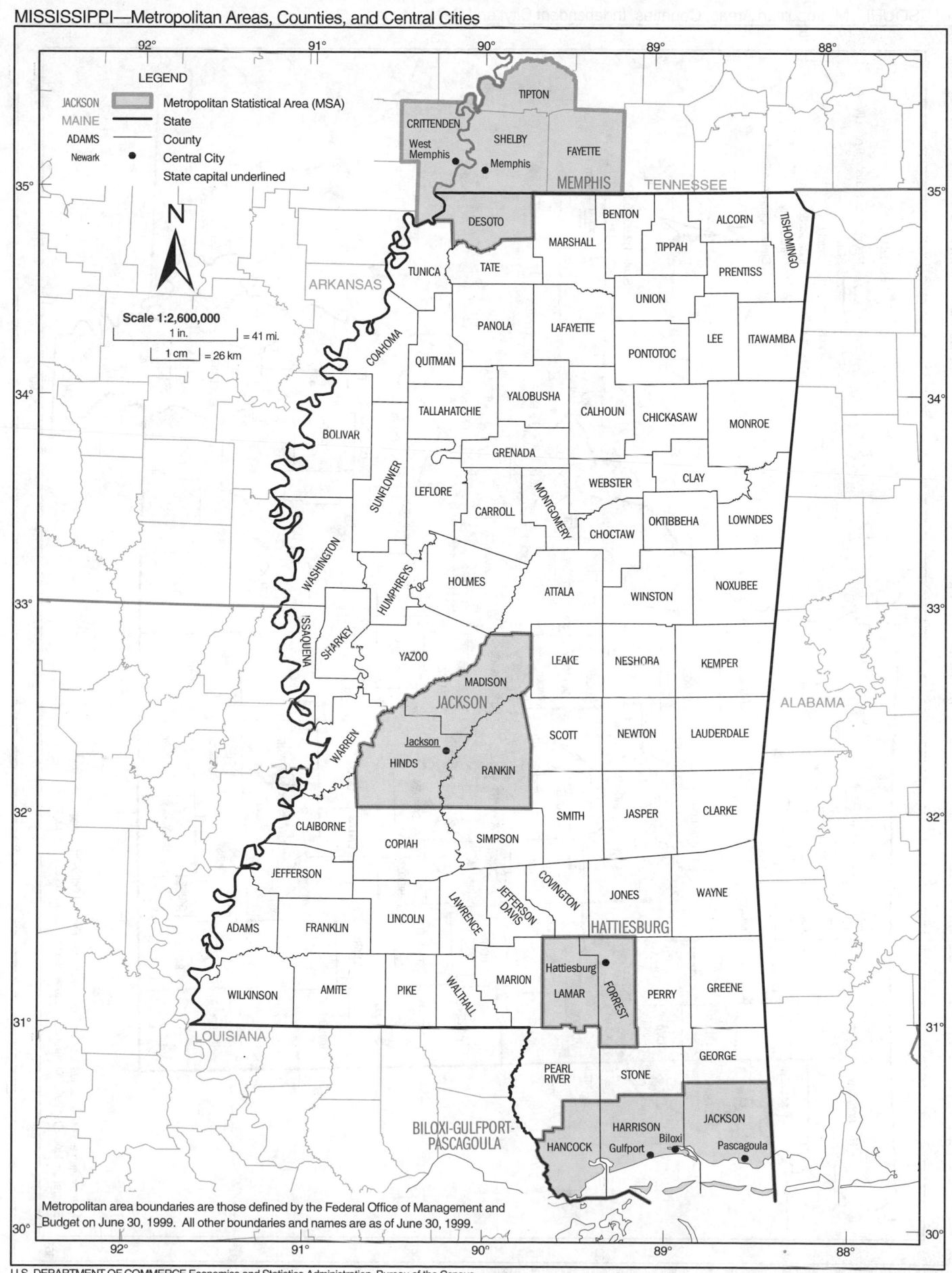

LEGEND

JACKSON	
MAINE	Metropolitan Statistical Area (MSA)
ADAMS	State
Newark ●	County
	Central City
	State capital underlined

Scale 1:2,600,000

1 in. = 41 mi.

1 cm = 26 km

Metropolitan area boundaries are those defined by the Federal Office of Management and Budget on June 30, 1999. All other boundaries and names are as of June 30, 1999.

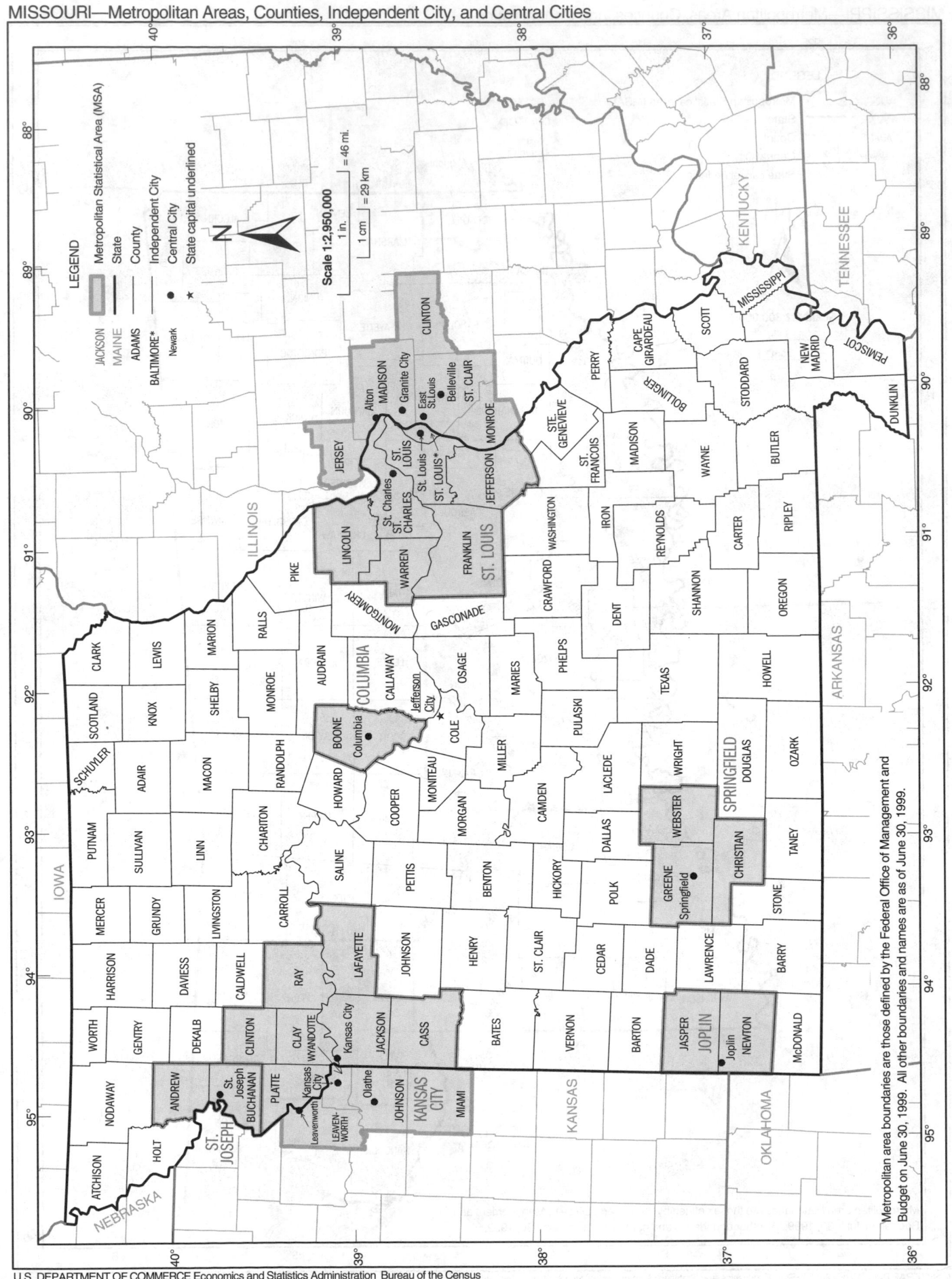

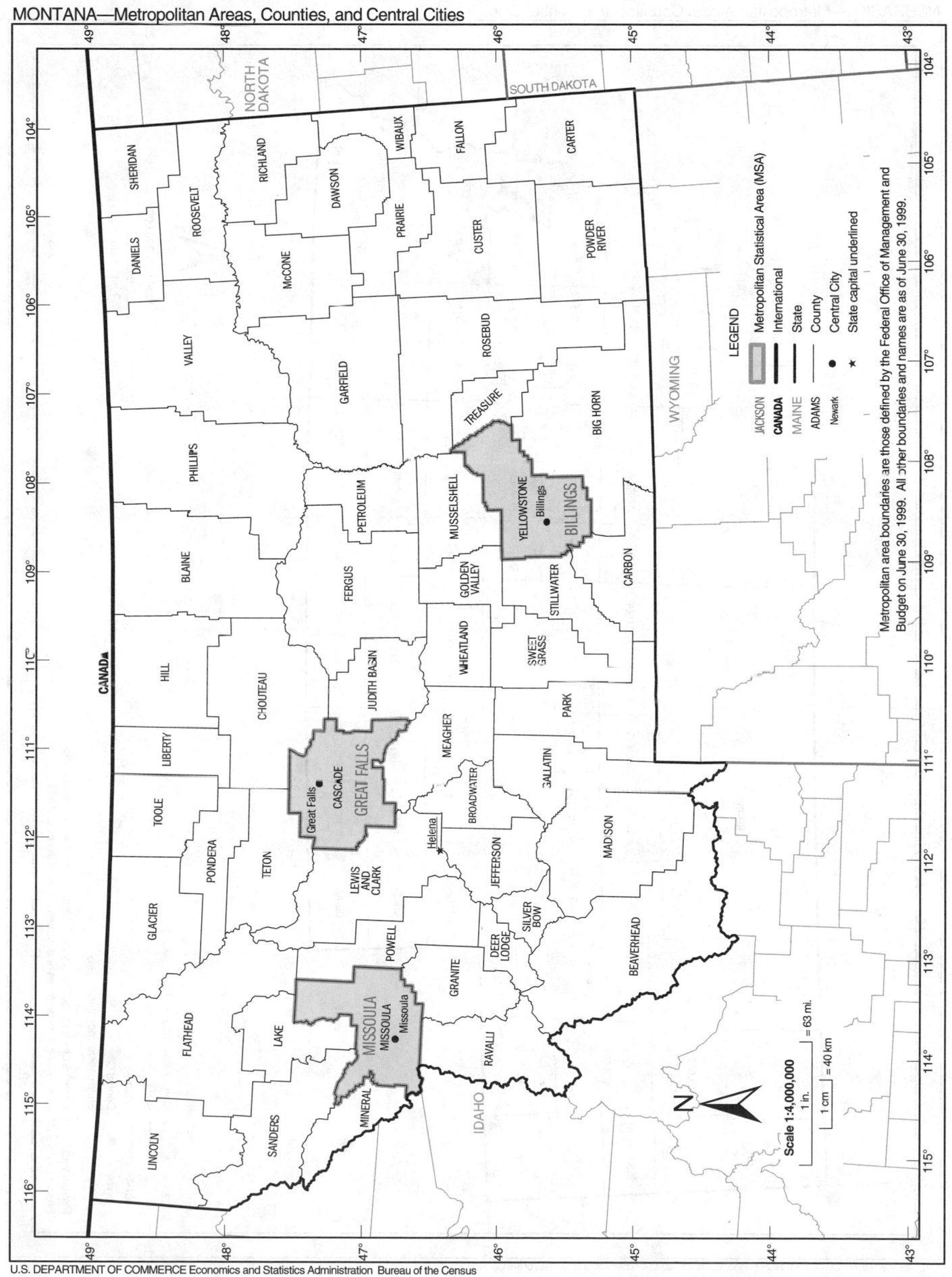

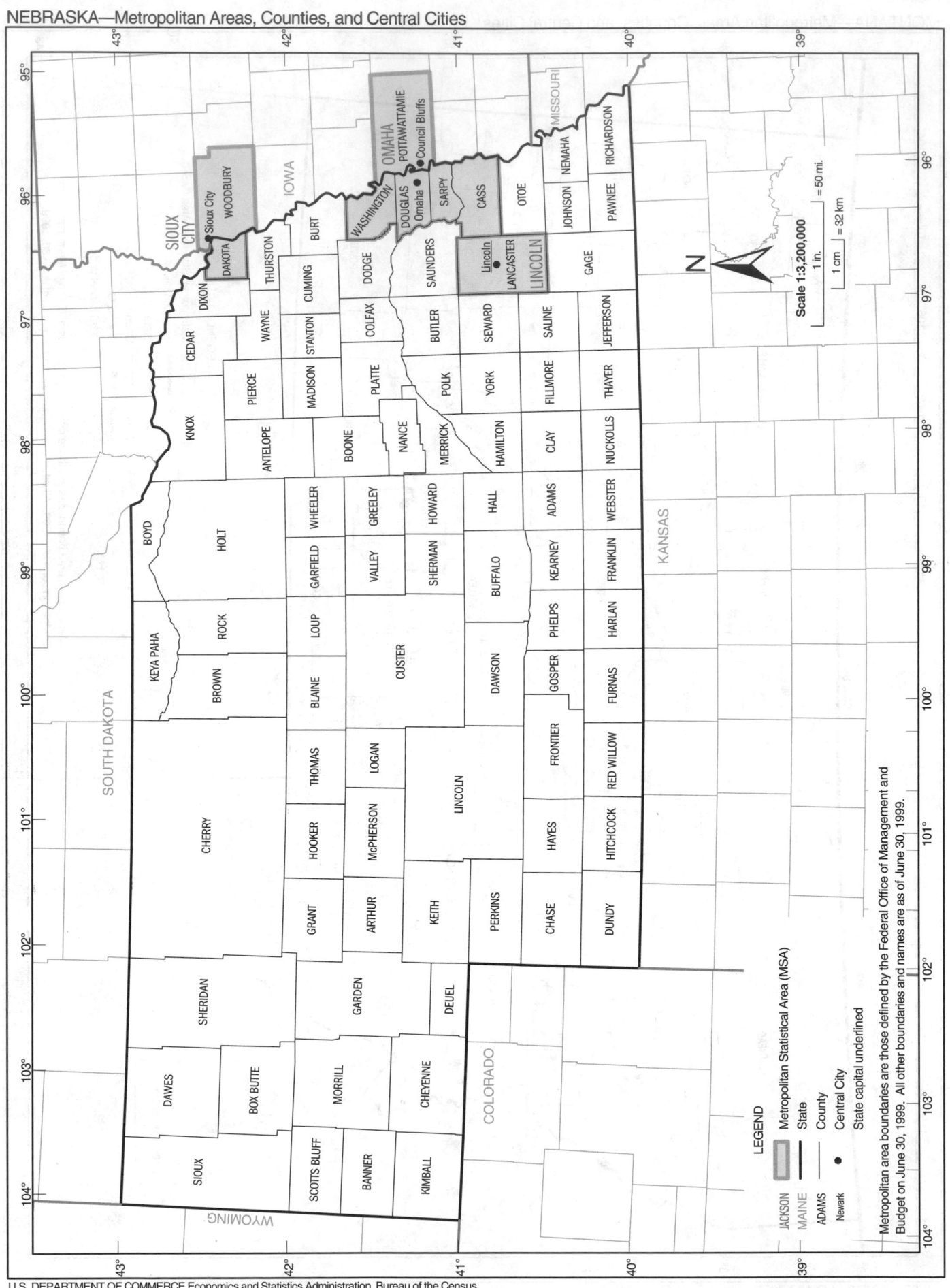

Scale 1:3,200,000

1 in. = 50 mi.

1 cm = 32 km

LEGEND

Metropolitan Statistical Area (MSA)

State

County

● Central City

State capital underlined

JACKSON
MAINE
ADAMS
Newark

Metropolitan area boundaries are those defined by the Federal Office of Management and Budget on June 30, 1999. All other boundaries and names are as of June 30, 1999.

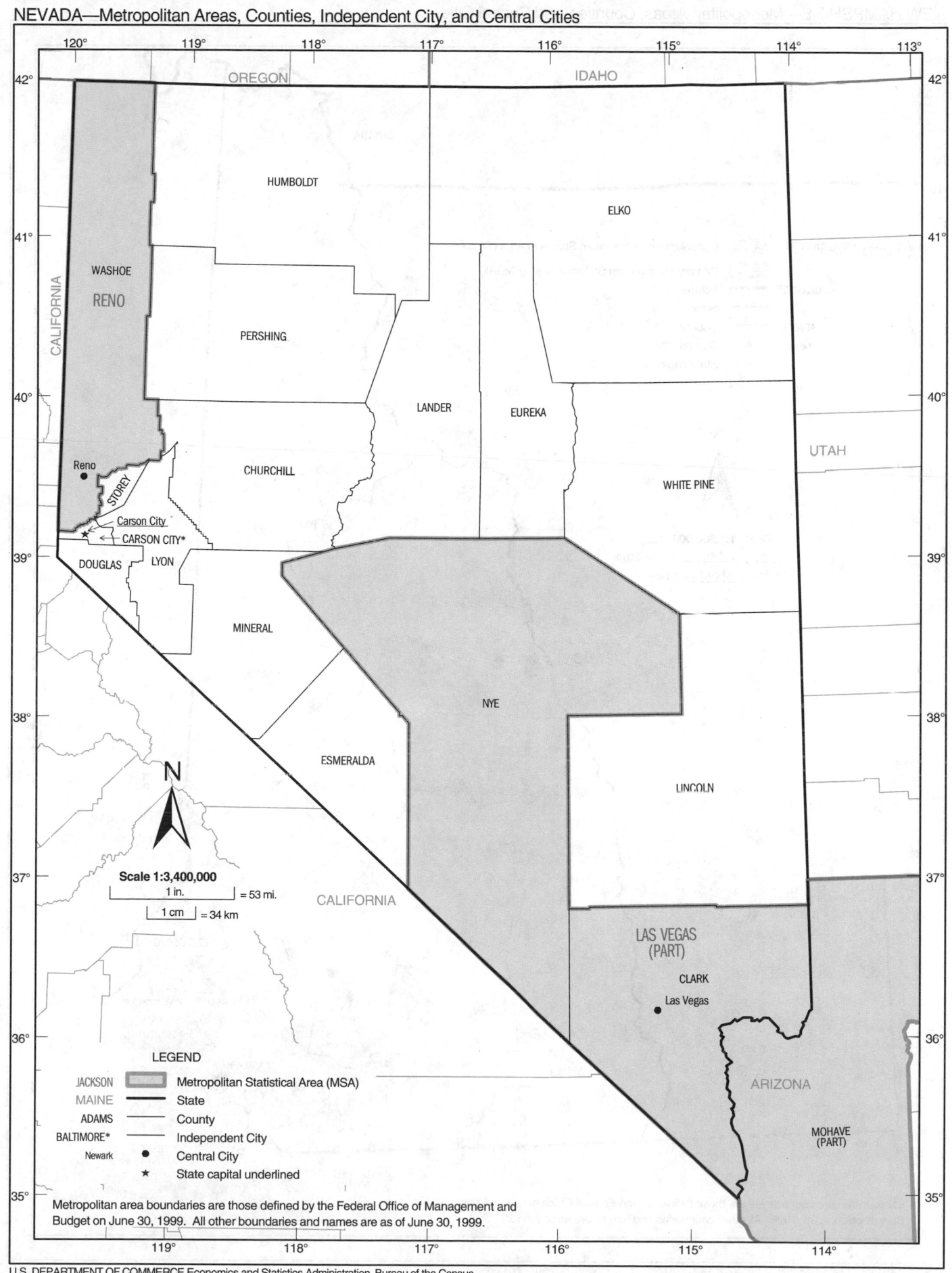

Scale 1:3,400,000

1 in. = 53 mi.

1 cm = 34 km

LEGEND

JACKSON		Metropolitan Statistical Area (MSA)
MAINE		State
ADAMS		County
BALTIMORE*		Independent City
Newark	●	Central City
	★	State capital underlined

Metropolitan area boundaries are those defined by the Federal Office of Management and Budget on June 30, 1999. All other boundaries and names are as of June 30, 1999.

U.S. DEPARTMENT OF COMMERCE Economics and Statistics Administration Bureau of the Census

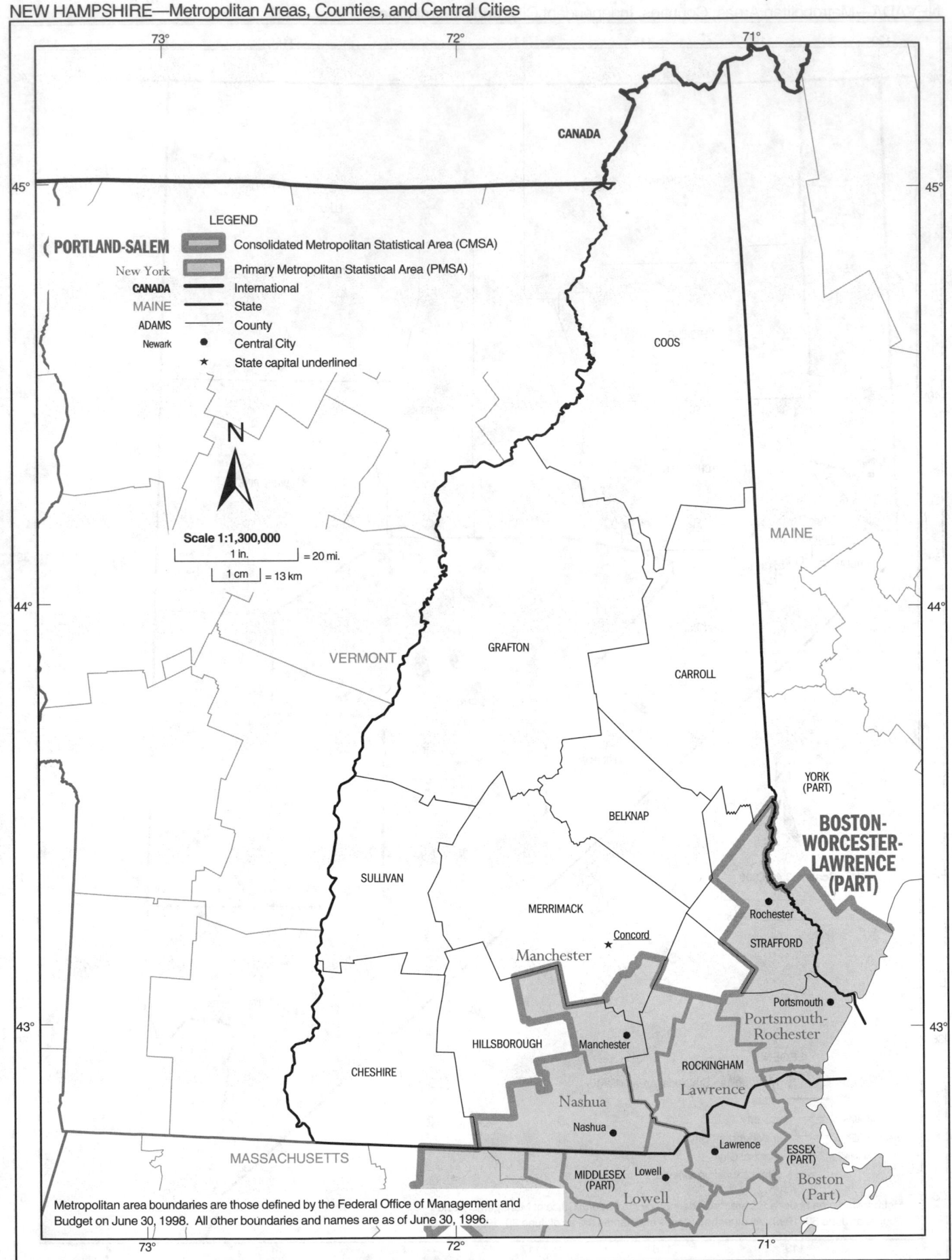

LEGEND

PORTLAND-SALEM — Consolidated Metropolitan Statistical Area (CMSA)

— Primary Metropolitan Statistical Area (PMSA)

New York

CANADA — International

MAINE — State

ADAMS — County

Newark ● Central City

★ State capital underlined

Scale 1:1,300,000

1 in. = 20 mi.

1 cm = 13 km

N

CANADA

COOS

MAINE

VERMONT

GRAFTON

CARROLL

BELKNAP

YORK (PART)

BOSTON-WORCESTER-LAWRENCE (PART)

SULLIVAN

MERRIMACK

★ Concord

Manchester

Rochester ●

STRAFFORD

HILLSBOROUGH

Manchester ●

Portsmouth ●

Portsmouth-Rochester

ROCKINGHAM

Lawrence

CHESHIRE

Nashua

Nashua ●

Lawrence ●

ESSEX (PART)

MASSACHUSETTS

MIDDLESEX (PART)

Lowell ●

Lowell

Boston (Part)

Metropolitan area boundaries are those defined by the Federal Office of Management and Budget on June 30, 1998. All other boundaries and names are as of June 30, 1996.

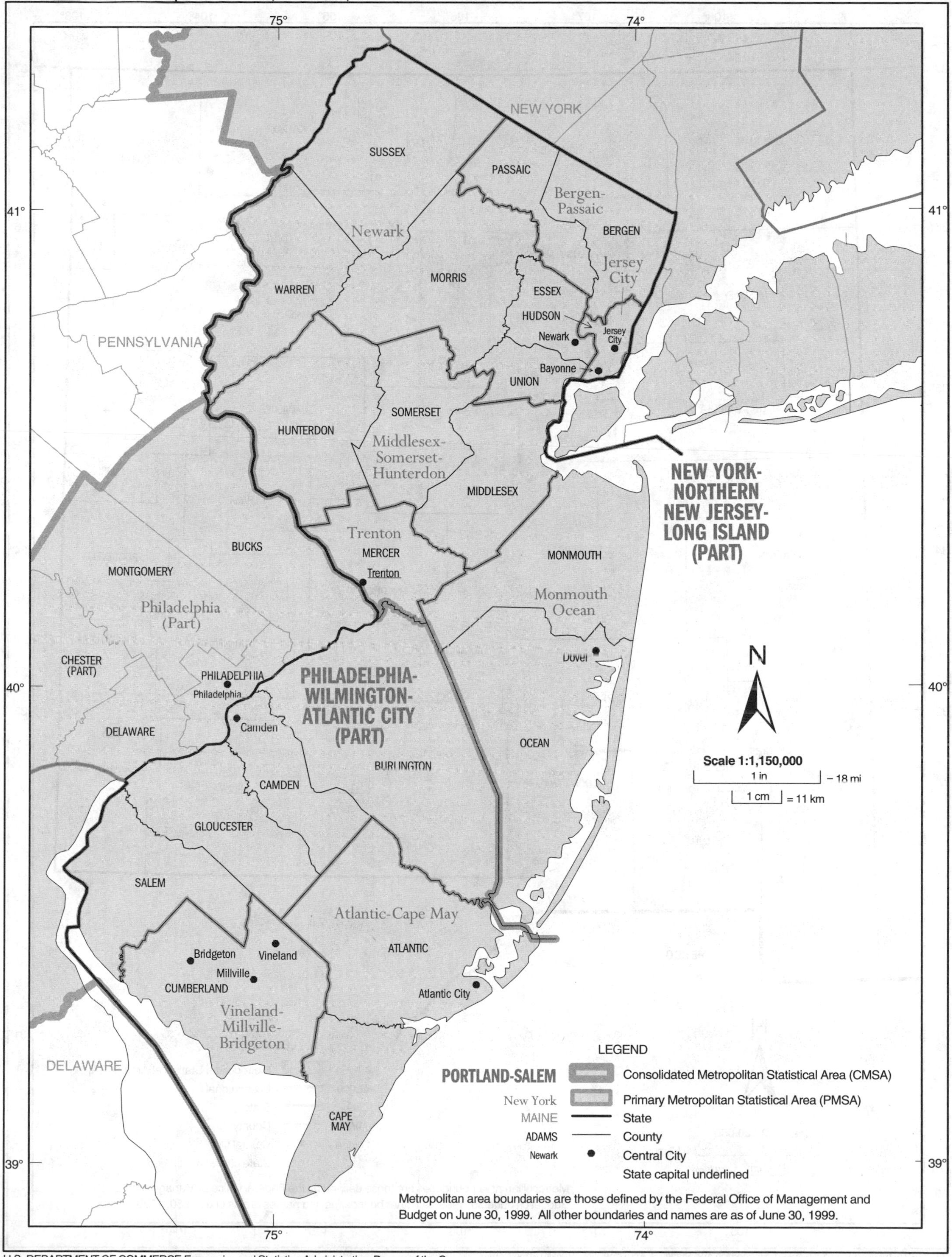

NEW YORK

75°   74°

41°   41°

SUSSEX

PASSAIC

Bergen-
Passaic

Newark   BERGEN

MORRIS   Jersey
WARREN   City

                        ESSEX

                HUDSON

            Newark   Jersey
                          City

            Bayonne

UNION

PENNSYLVANIA

HUNTERDON

SOMERSET

Middlesex-
Somerset-
Hunterdon

MIDDLESEX

NEW YORK-
NORTHERN
NEW JERSEY-
LONG ISLAND
(PART)

Trenton

BUCKS   MERCER

MONTGOMERY   Trenton

MONMOUTH

Philadelphia
(Part)   Monmouth
                                Ocean

CHESTER
(PART)   Dover

40°   40°

PHILADELPHIA   PHILADELPHIA-
Philadelphia   WILMINGTON-
                      ATLANTIC CITY   OCEAN
DELAWARE   (PART)
            Camden
                      BURLINGTON

                CAMDEN

        GLOUCESTER

    SALEM

                Atlantic-Cape May

            Bridgeton   Vineland   ATLANTIC

            Millville
    CUMBERLAND
                                    Atlantic City
        Vineland-
        Millville-
        Bridgeton

DELAWARE

                        CAPE
                        MAY

39°   39°

N

Scale 1:1,150,000
1 in   — 18 mi
1 cm   = 11 km

LEGEND

PORTLAND-SALEM ▨ Consolidated Metropolitan Statistical Area (CMSA)

New York   ▨ Primary Metropolitan Statistical Area (PMSA)

MAINE   —— State

ADAMS   —— County

Newark   •   Central City

            State capital underlined

Metropolitan area boundaries are those defined by the Federal Office of Management and
Budget on June 30, 1999. All other boundaries and names are as of June 30, 1999.

75°   74°

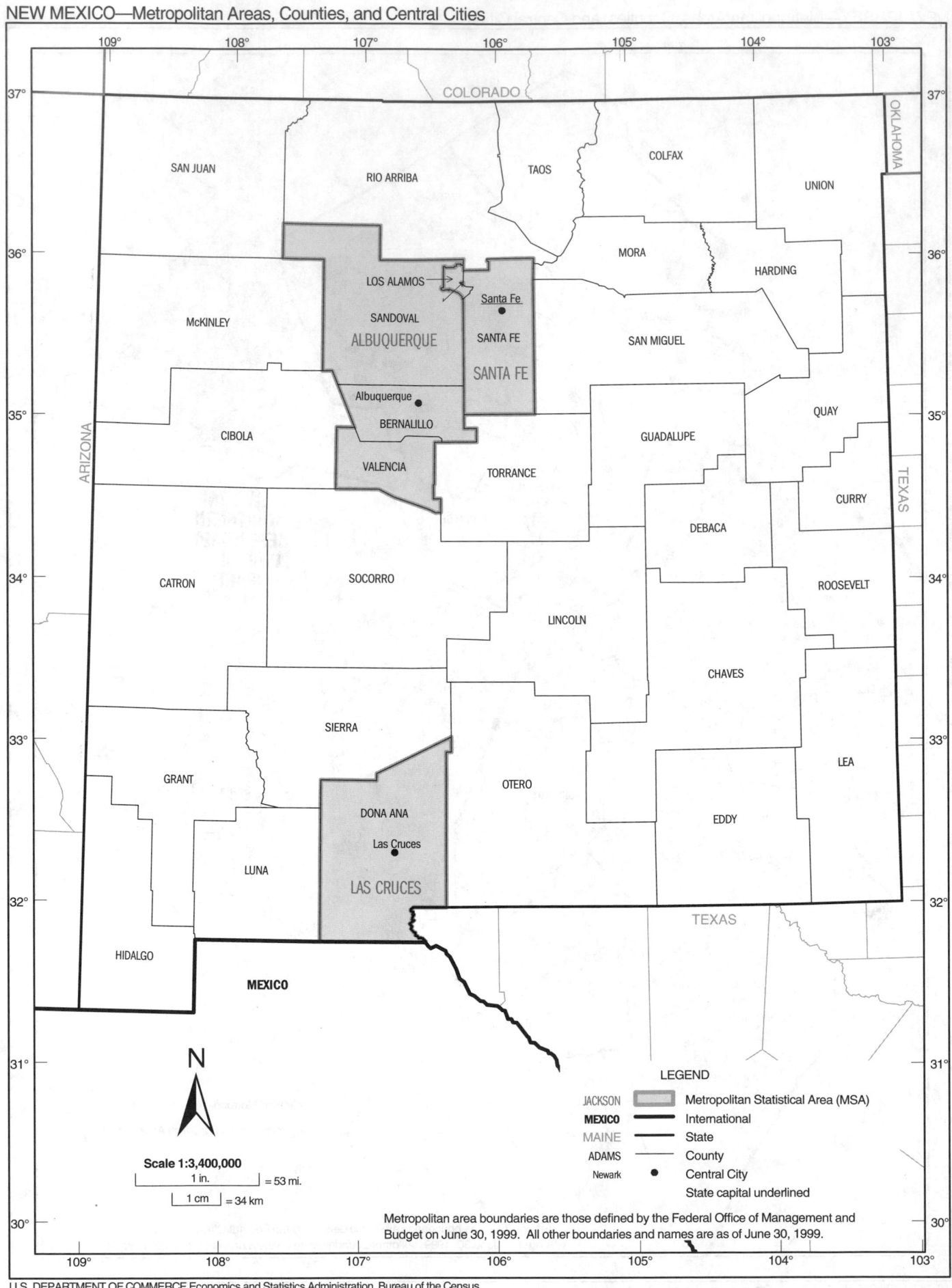

Scale 1:3,400,000

1 in. = 53 mi.

1 cm = 34 km

LEGEND

JACKSON   Metropolitan Statistical Area (MSA)

MEXICO   International

MAINE   State

ADAMS   County

Newark   ●   Central City

State capital underlined

Metropolitan area boundaries are those defined by the Federal Office of Management and Budget on June 30, 1999. All other boundaries and names are as of June 30, 1999.

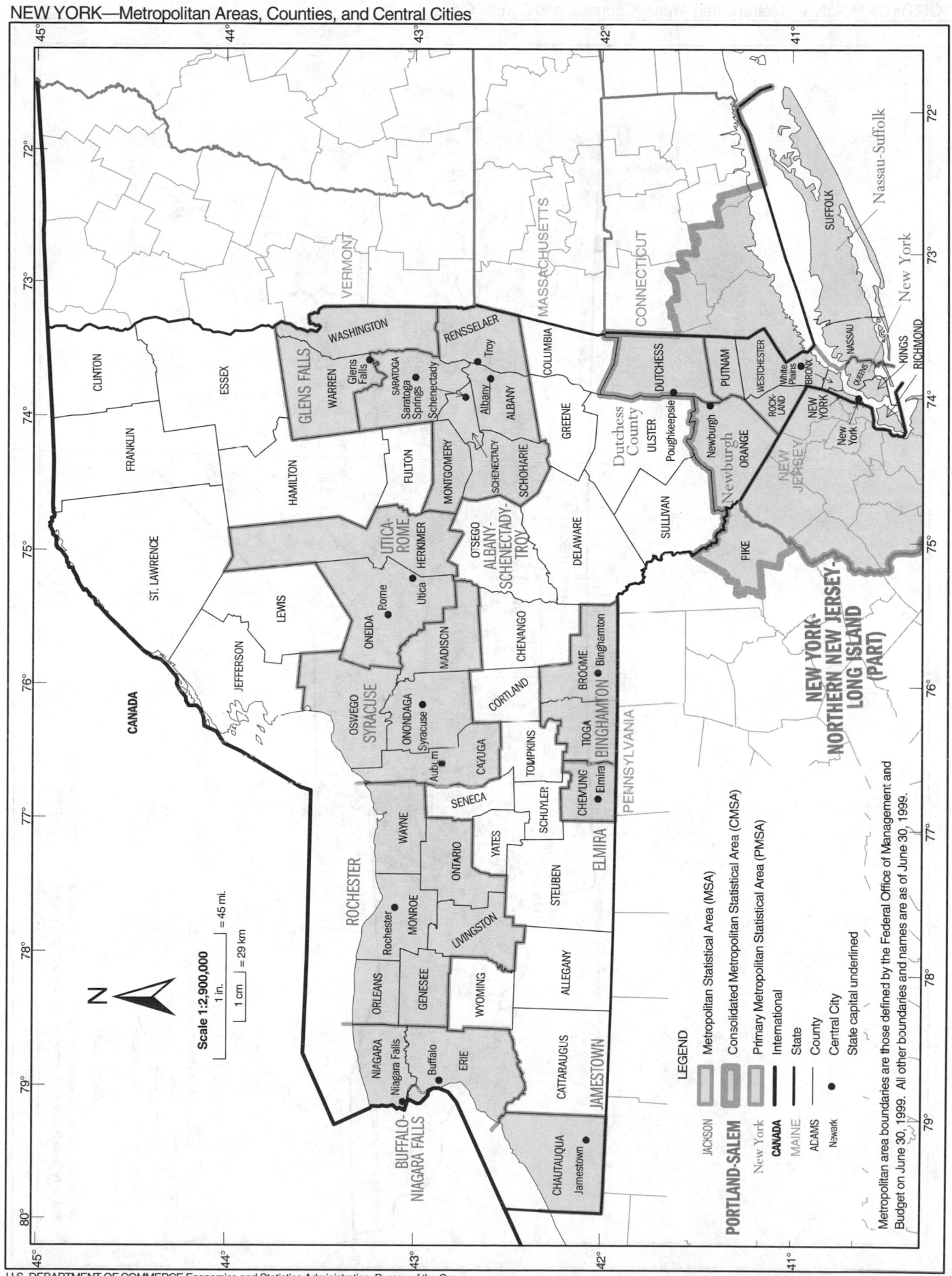

Scale 1:2,900,000

1 in. = 45 mi.

1 cm = 29 km

LEGEND

JACKSON	Metropolitan Statistical Area (MSA)
PORTLAND-SALEM	Consolidated Metropolitan Statistical Area (CMSA)
New York	Primary Metropolitan Statistical Area (PMSA)
CANADA	International
MAINE	State
ADAMS	County
Newark •	Central City
	State capital underlined

Metropolitan area boundaries are those defined by the Federal Office of Management and Budget on June 30, 1999. All other boundaries and names are as of June 30, 1999.

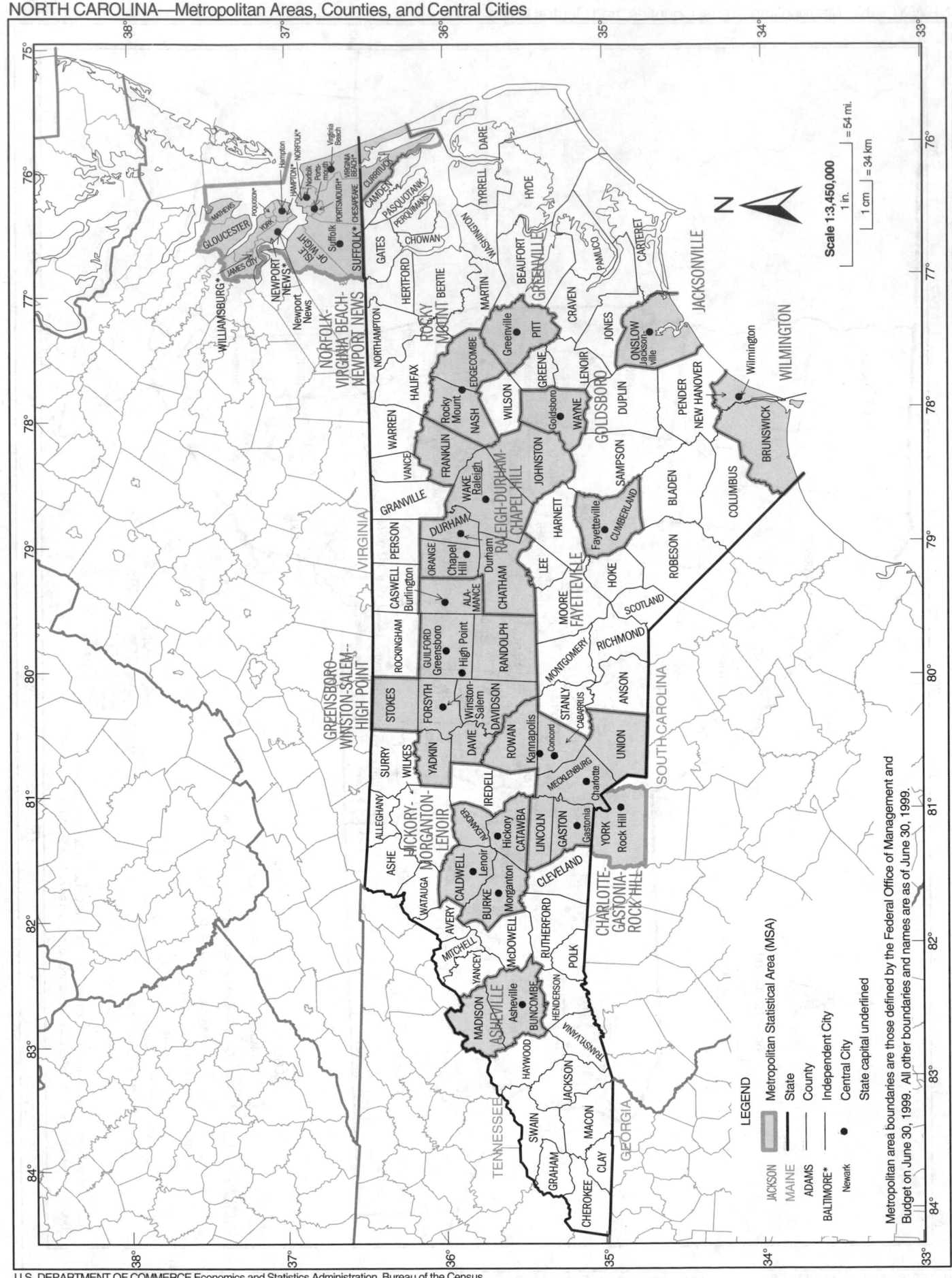

Scale 1:3,450,000

1 in. = 54 mi.

1 cm = 34 km

LEGEND

Metropolitan Statistical Area (MSA)

State

County

● Independent City

● Central City

State capital underlined

JACKSON
MAINE
ADAMS
BALTIMORE*
Newark

Metropolitan area boundaries are those defined by the Federal Office of Management and Budget on June 30, 1999. All other boundaries and names are as of June 30, 1999.

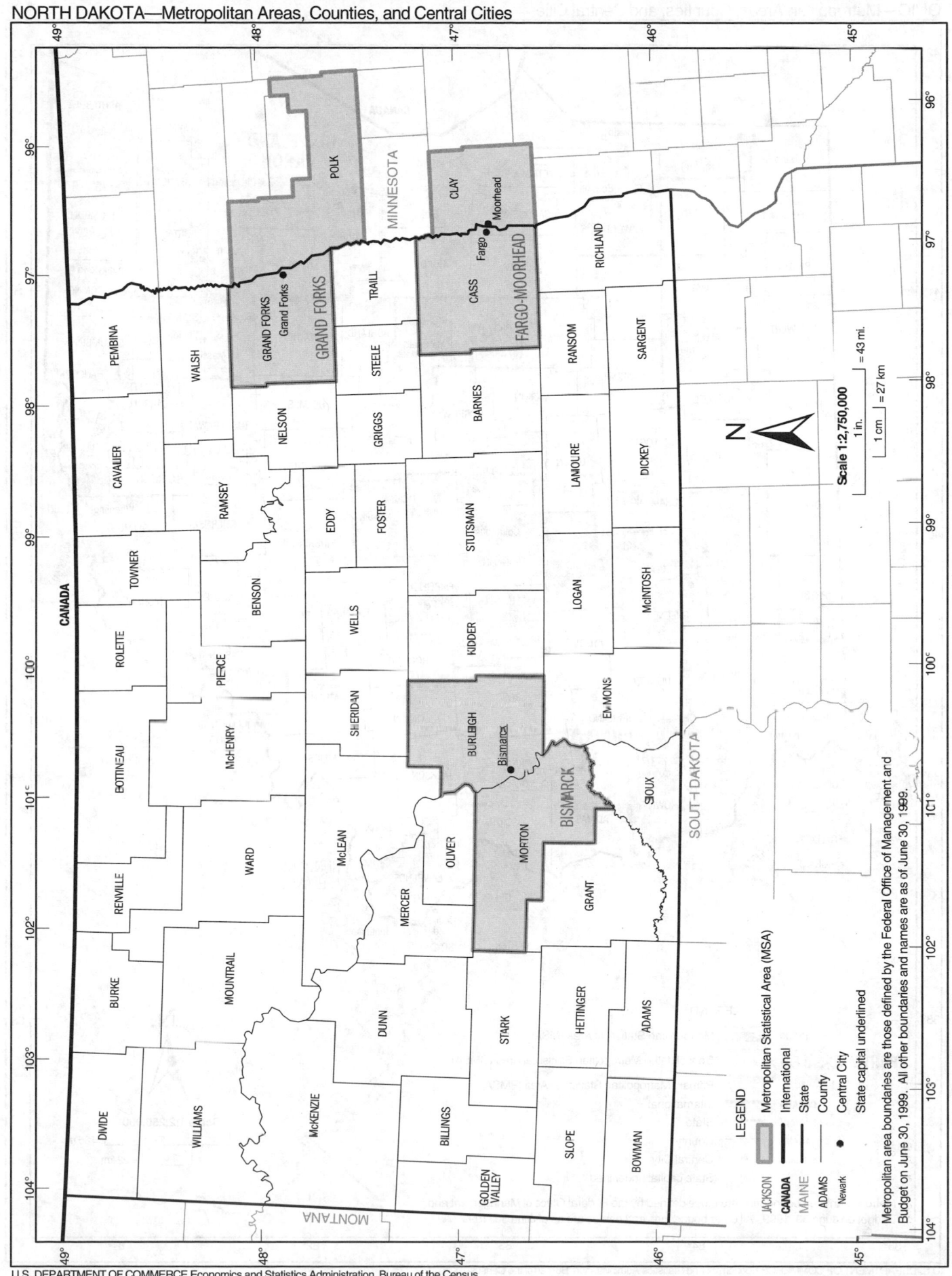

Scale 1:2,750,000

1 in. = 43 mi.

1 cm = 27 km

LEGEND

Metropolitan Statistical Area (MSA)

International

State

County

• Central City

JACKSON   State capital underlined

CANADA

MAINE

ADAMS

Newark

Metropolitan area boundaries are those defined by the Federal Office of Management and Budget on June 30, 1999. All other boundaries and names are as of June 30, 1999.

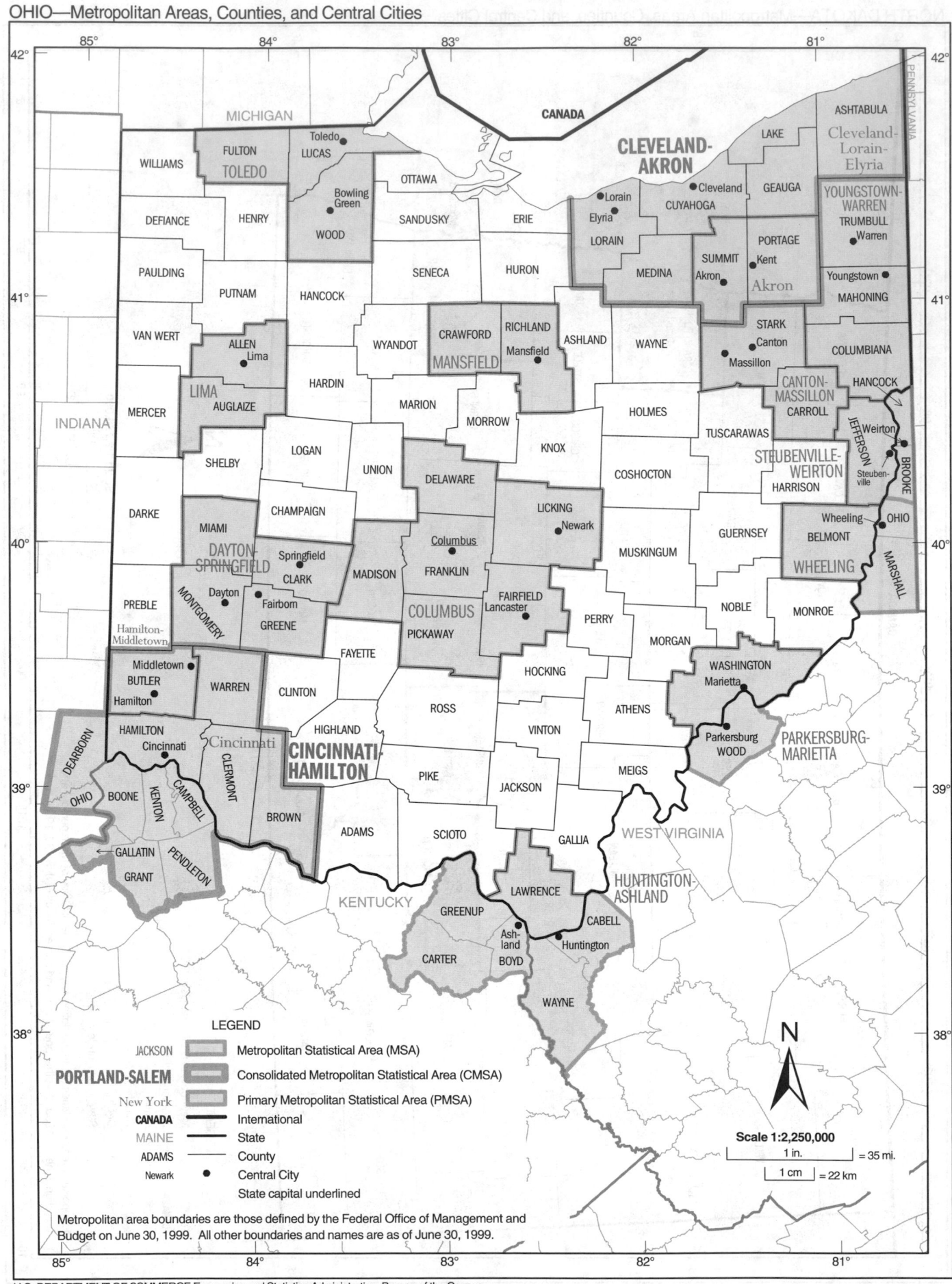

LEGEND

JACKSON — Metropolitan Statistical Area (MSA)

PORTLAND-SALEM — Consolidated Metropolitan Statistical Area (CMSA)

New York — Primary Metropolitan Statistical Area (PMSA)

CANADA — International

MAINE — State

ADAMS — County

Newark • Central City

State capital underlined

Scale 1:2,250,000

1 in. = 35 mi.

1 cm = 22 km

Metropolitan area boundaries are those defined by the Federal Office of Management and Budget on June 30, 1999. All other boundaries and names are as of June 30, 1999.

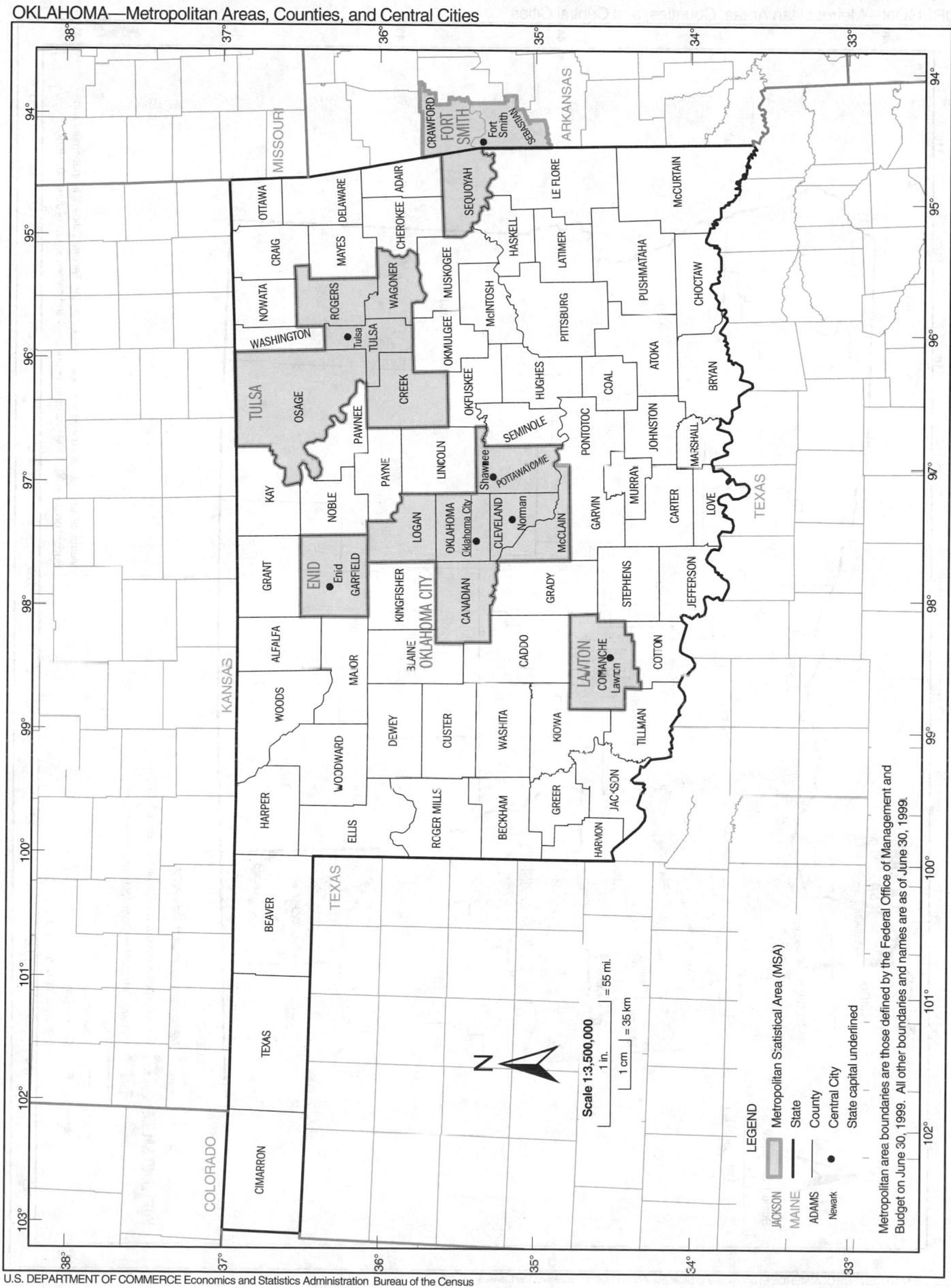

Scale 1:3,500,000

LEGEND

Metropolitan Statistical Area (MSA)

State

County

● Central City

State capital underlined

Metropolitan area boundaries are those defined by the Federal Office of Management and Budget on June 30, 1999. All other boundaries and names are as of June 30, 1999.

JACKSON
MAINE
ADAMS
● Newark

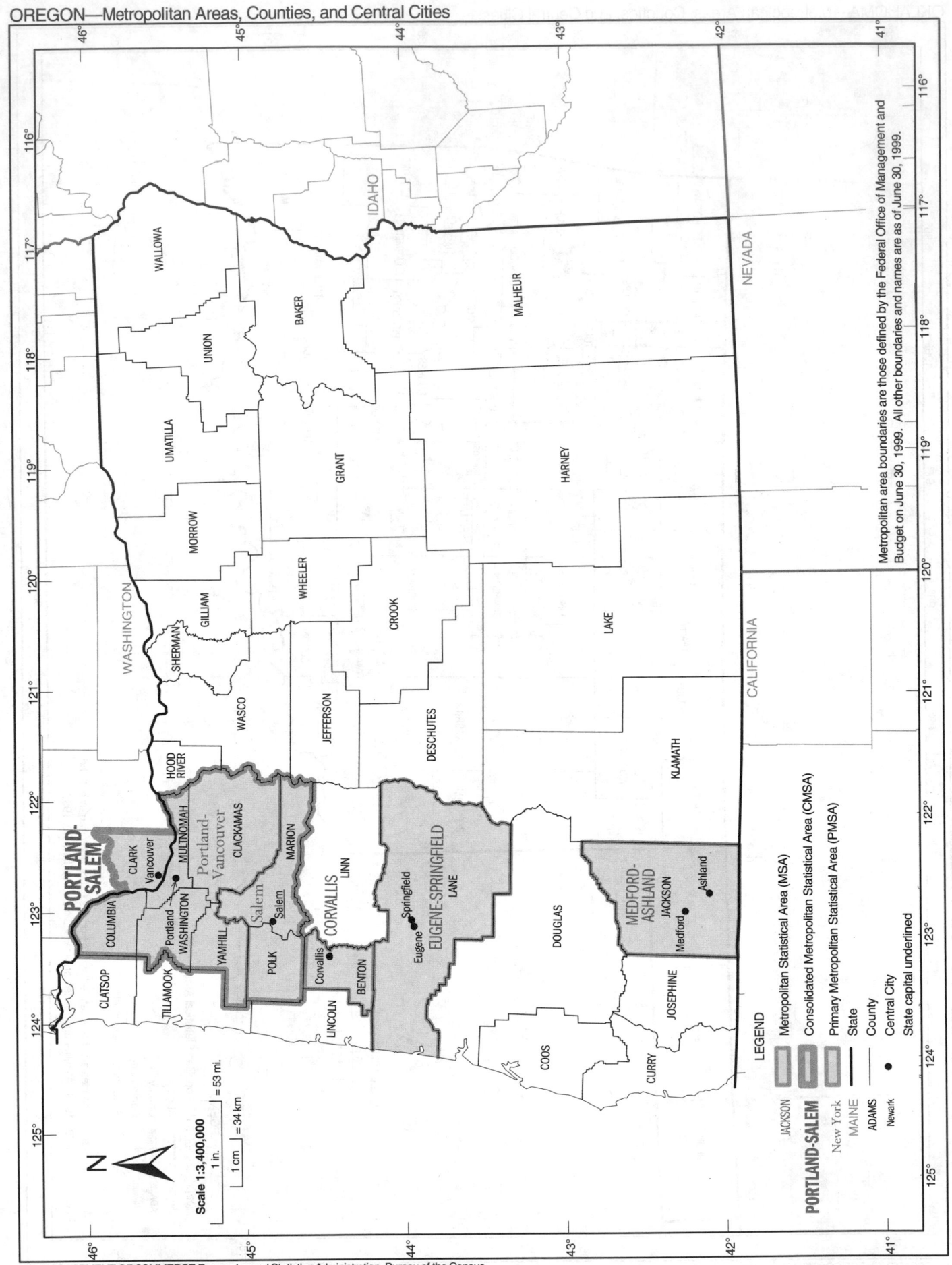

Metropolitan area boundaries are those defined by the Federal Office of Management and Budget on June 30, 1999. All other boundaries and names are as of June 30, 1999.

IDAHO

NEVADA

CALIFORNIA

WASHINGTON

WALLOWA

BAKER

UNION

MALHEUR

UMATILLA

GRANT

HARNEY

MORROW

WHEELER

GILLIAM

CROOK

LAKE

SHERMAN

WASCO

HOOD
RIVER

JEFFERSON

DESCHUTES

KLAMATH

PORTLAND-
SALEM

CLARK
Vancouver

MULTNOMAH

Portland-
Vancouver

CLACKAMAS

MARION

LINN

EUGENE-SPRINGFIELD

MEDFORD-
ASHLAND

Ashland

COLUMBIA

Portland

WASHINGTON

Salem

Salem

CORVALLIS

Springfield

LANE

JACKSON

CLATSOP

TILLAMOOK

YAMHILL

POLK

Corvallis

BENTON

Eugene

DOUGLAS

Medford

LINCOLN

COOS

JOSEPHINE

CURRY

LEGEND

Metropolitan Statistical Area (MSA)

Consolidated Metropolitan Statistical Area (CMSA)

Primary Metropolitan Statistical Area (PMSA)

State

County

● Central City

State capital underlined

JACKSON

PORTLAND-SALEM

New York
MAINE

ADAMS
Newark

Scale 1:3,400,000

1 in. = 53 mi.

1 cm = 34 km

N

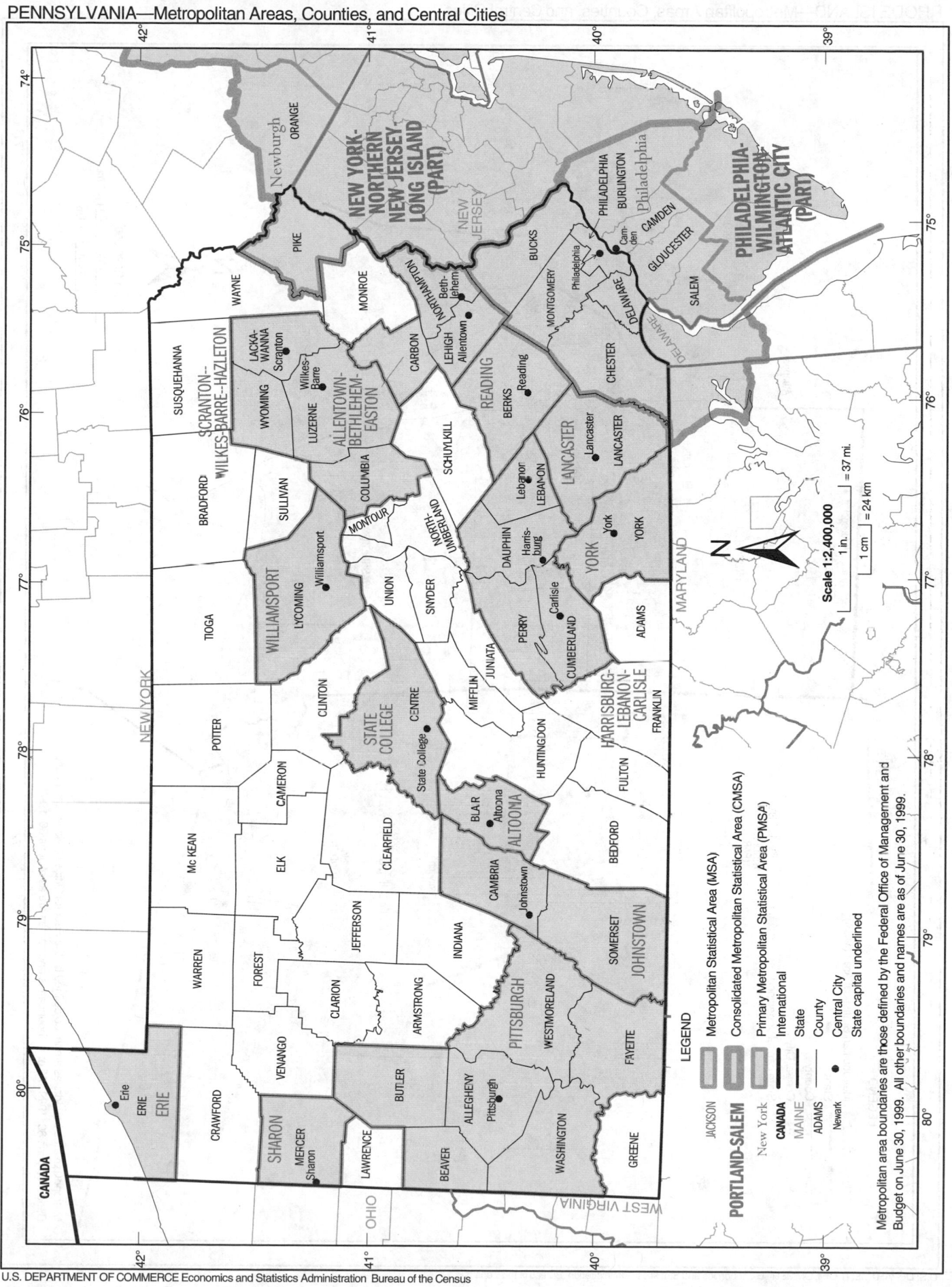

LEGEND

Metropolitan Statistical Area (MSA)

Consolidated Metropolitan Statistical Area (CMSA)

Primary Metropolitan Statistical Area (PMSA)

International

State

County

• Central City

State capital underlined

JACKSON

PORTLAND-SALEM

New York

CANADA

MAINE

ADAMS

• Newark

Metropolitan area boundaries are those defined by the Federal Office of Management and Budget on June 30, 1999. All other boundaries and names are as of June 30, 1999.

Scale 1:2,400,000

1 in. = 37 mi.

1 cm = 24 km

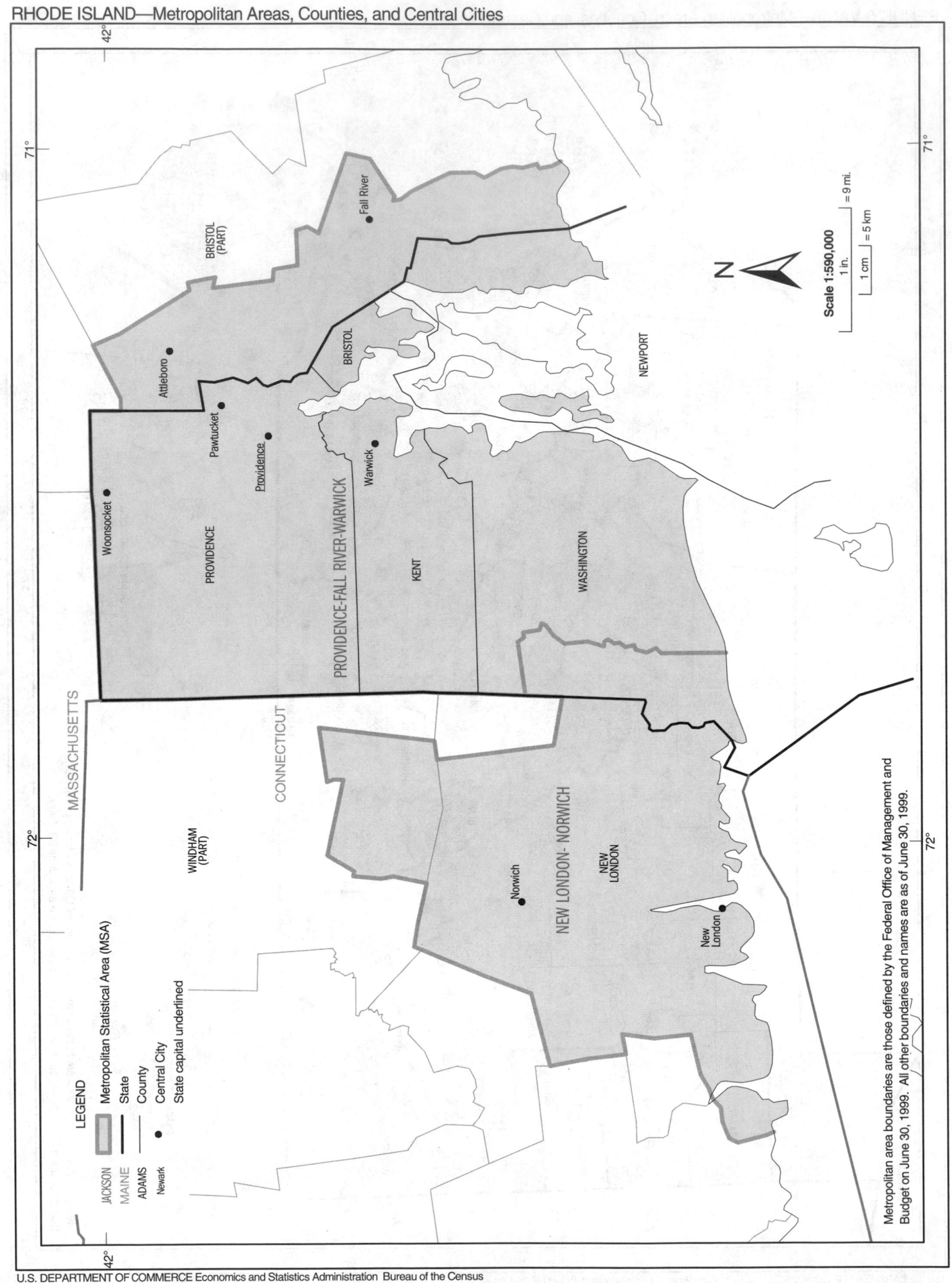

Scale 1:590,000

1 in. = 9 mi.

1 cm = 5 km

LEGEND

Metropolitan Statistical Area (MSA)
State
County
Central City
State capital underlined

JACKSON
MAINE
ADAMS
Newark

Metropolitan area boundaries are those defined by the Federal Office of Management and Budget on June 30, 1999. All other boundaries and names are as of June 30, 1999.

BRISTOL (PART)

Fall River

Attleboro

Pawtucket

Providence

Woonsocket

PROVIDENCE

PROVIDENCE-FALL RIVER-WARWICK

BRISTOL

Warwick

KENT

NEWPORT

WASHINGTON

MASSACHUSETTS

CONNECTICUT

WINDHAM (PART)

NEW LONDON- NORWICH

Norwich

NEW LONDON

New London

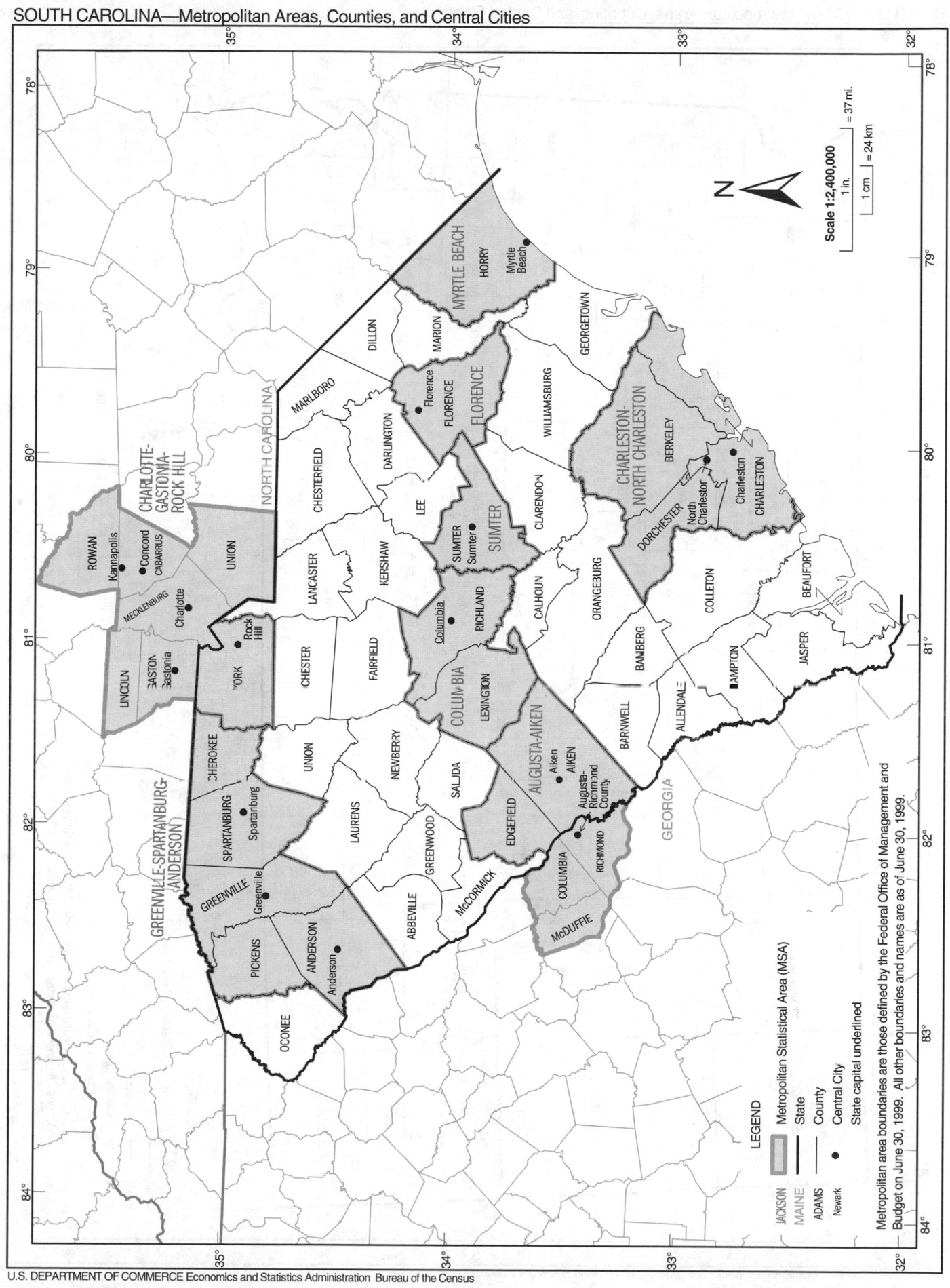

Scale 1:2,400,000

1 in. = 37 mi.

1 cm = 24 km

LEGEND

Metropolitan Statistical Area (MSA)

State

County

● Central City

State capital underlined

Metropolitan area boundaries are those defined by the Federal Office of Management and Budget on June 30, 1999. All other boundaries and names are as of June 30, 1999.

JACKSON
MAINE
ADAMS
Newark

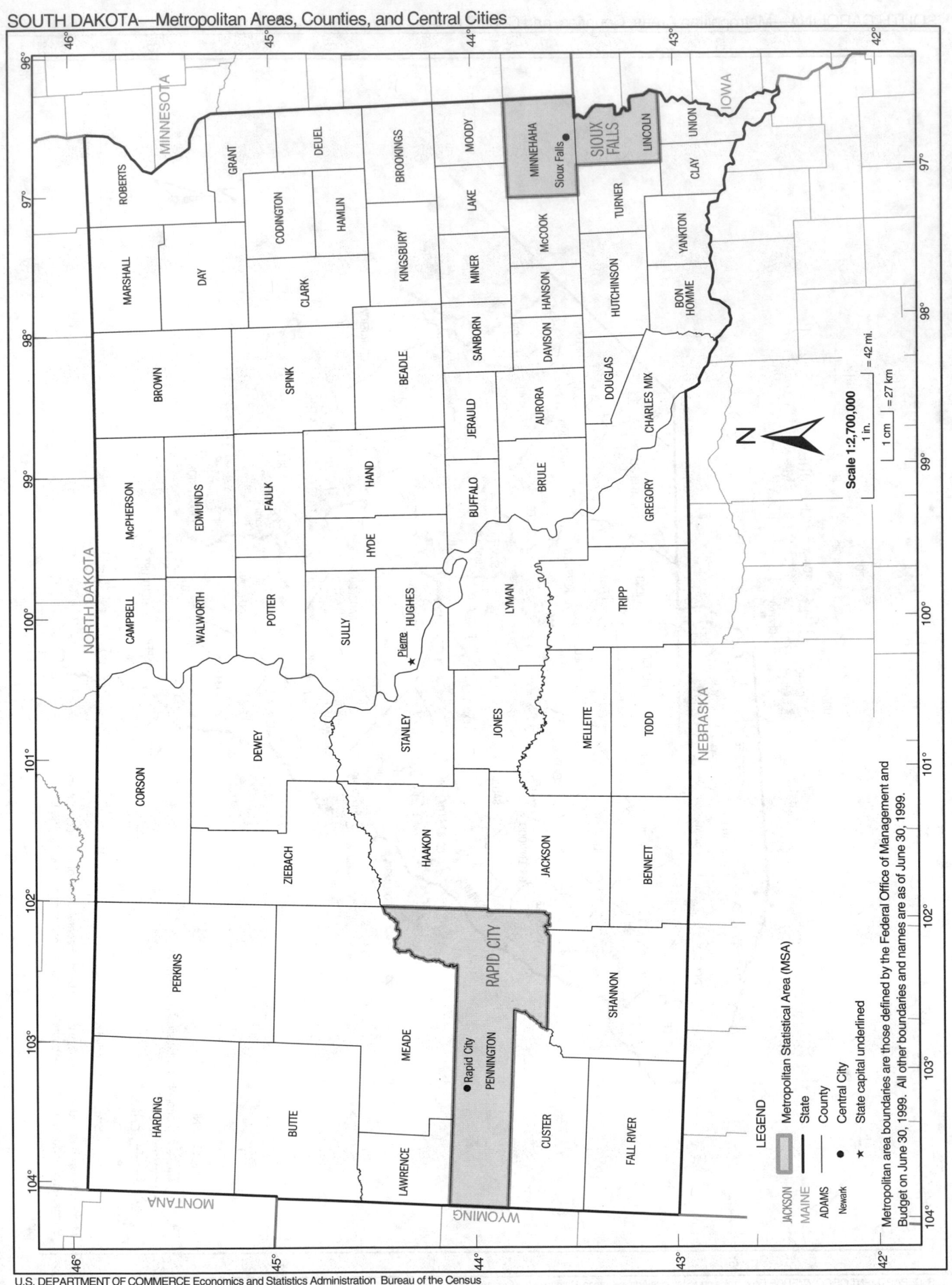

LEGEND

	Metropolitan Statistical Area (MSA)
	State
	County
●	Central City
★	State capital underlined

JACKSON	
MAINE	
ADAMS	
Newark	

Metropolitan area boundaries are those defined by the Federal Office of Management and Budget on June 30, 1999. All other boundaries and names are as of June 30, 1999.

Scale 1:2,700,000

1 in. = 42 mi.

1 cm = 27 km

N

TENNESSEE—Metropolitan Areas, Counties, Independent City, and Central Cities

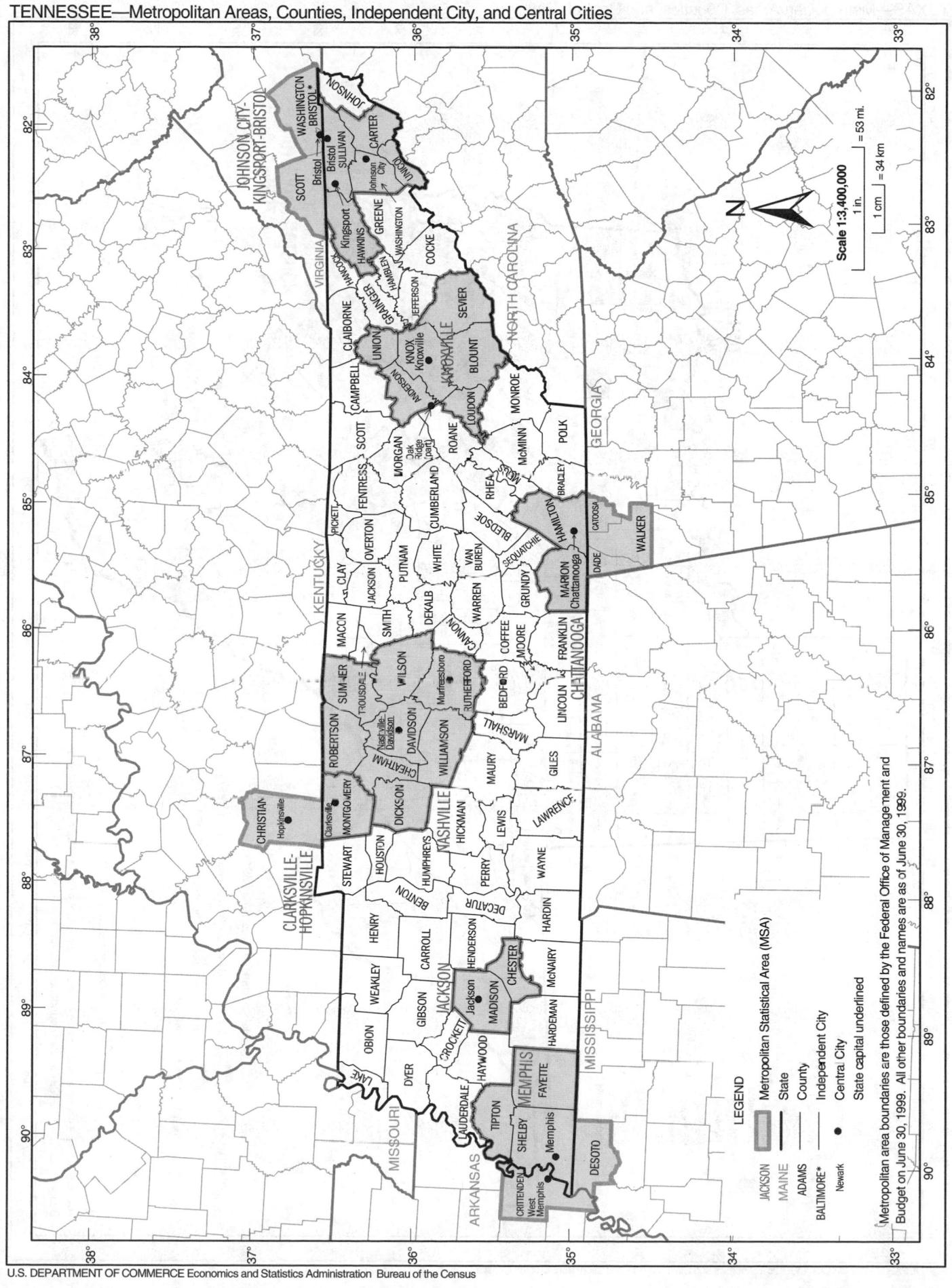

Scale 1:3,400,000

1 in. = 53 mi.
1 cm = 34 km

LEGEND

JACKSON	Metropolitan Statistical Area (MSA)
MAINE	State
ADAMS	County
BALTIMORE*	Independent City
● Newark	Central City
	State capital underlined

Metropolitan area boundaries are those defined by the Federal Office of Management and Budget on June 30, 1999. All other boundaries and names are as of June 30, 1999.

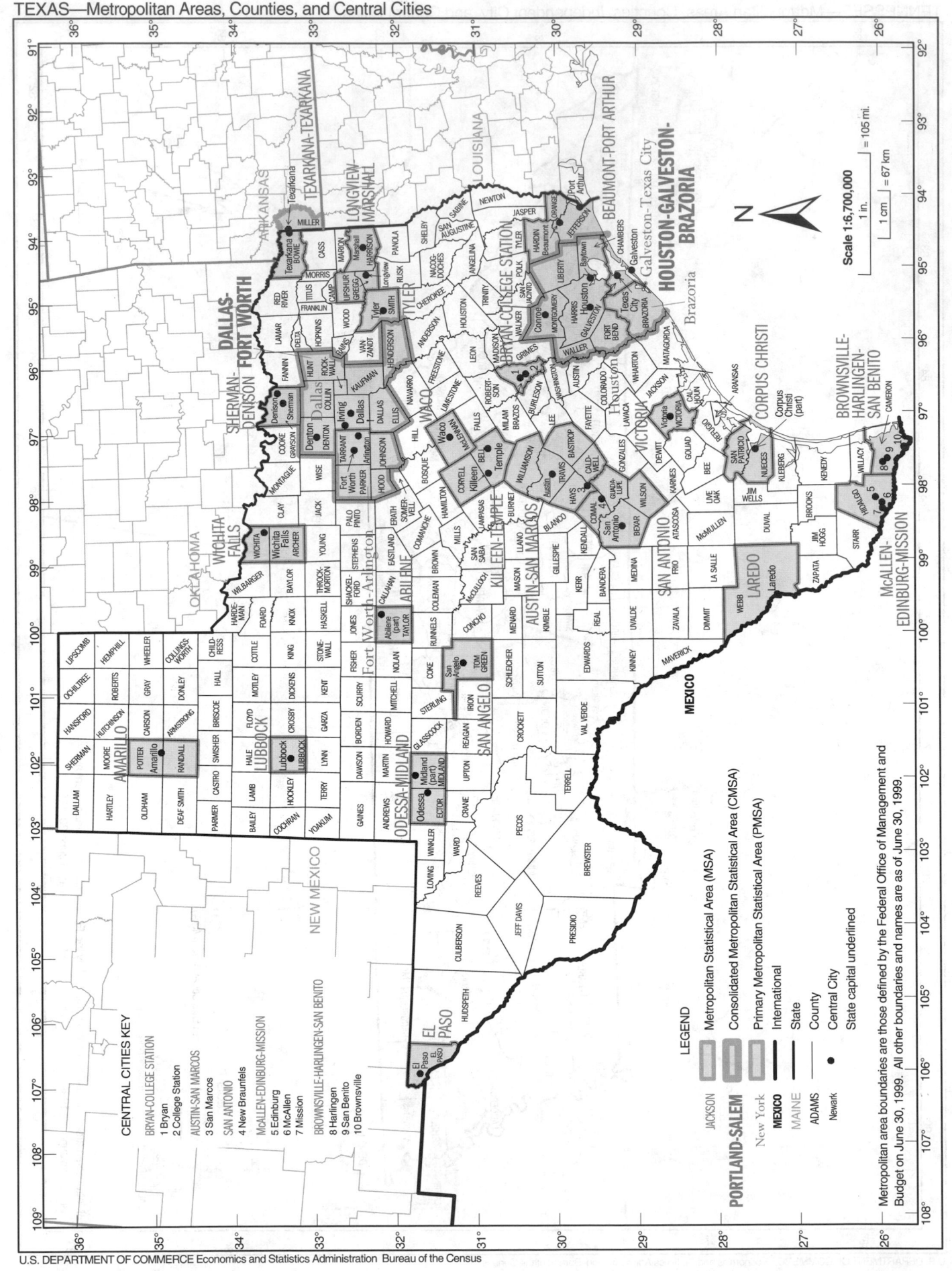

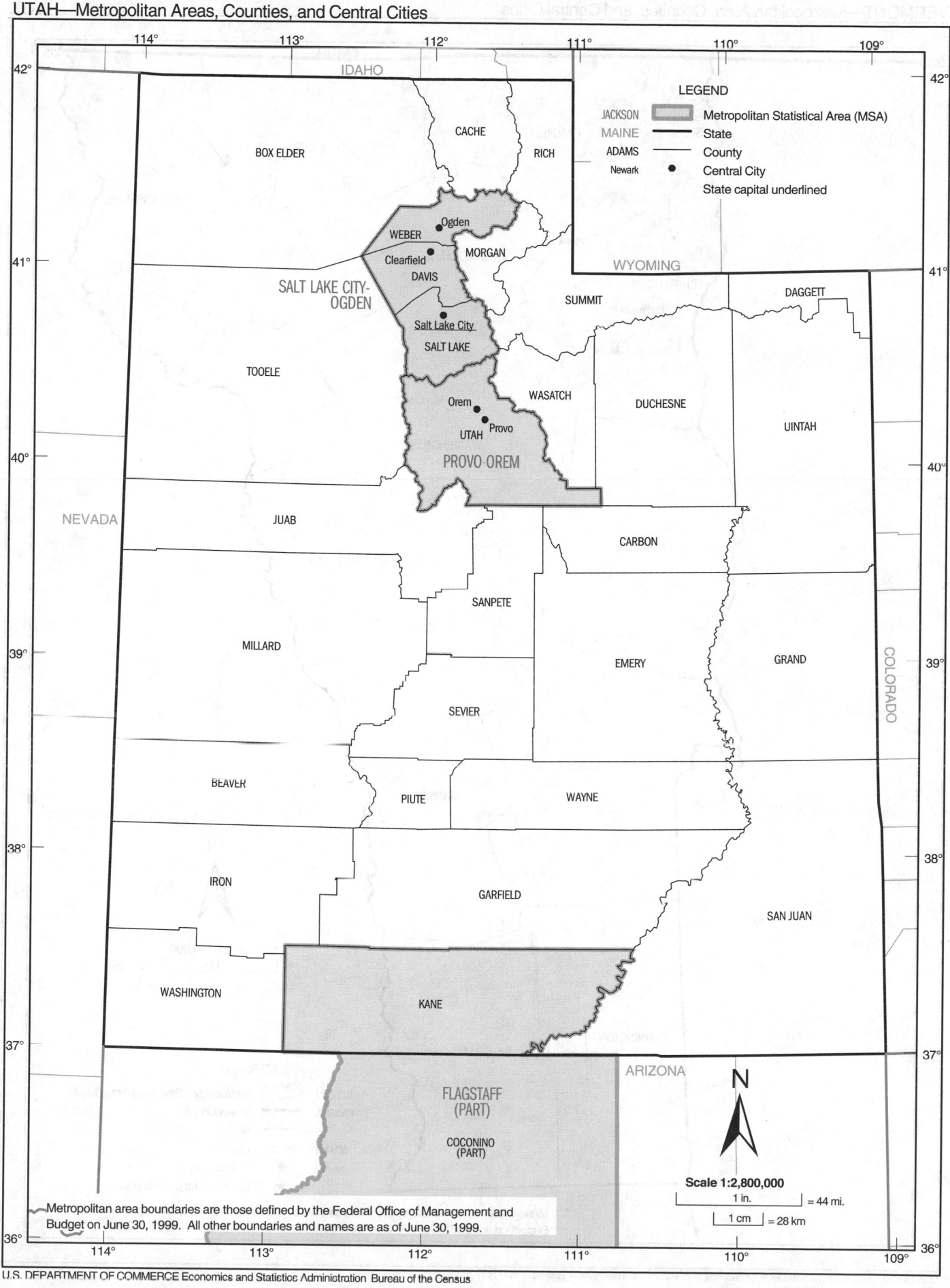

LEGEND

JACKSON — Metropolitan Statistical Area (MSA)
MAINE — State
ADAMS — County
Newark ● Central City
State capital underlined

IDAHO

BOX ELDER

CACHE

RICH

WEBER ● Ogden
MORGAN

Clearfield ●
DAVIS

SALT LAKE CITY-OGDEN

SUMMIT

DAGGETT

WYOMING

Salt Lake City
SALT LAKE

TOOELE

WASATCH

DUCHESNE

UINTAH

Orem ● ● Provo
UTAH
PROVO-OREM

NEVADA

JUAB

CARBON

SANPETE

MILLARD

EMERY

GRAND

COLORADO

SEVIER

BEAVER

PIUTE

WAYNE

IRON

GARFIELD

SAN JUAN

WASHINGTON

KANE

ARIZONA

FLAGSTAFF
(PART)

COCONINO
(PART)

N

Scale 1:2,800,000

1 in. = 44 mi.

1 cm = 28 km

Metropolitan area boundaries are those defined by the Federal Office of Management and Budget on June 30, 1999. All other boundaries and names are as of June 30, 1999.

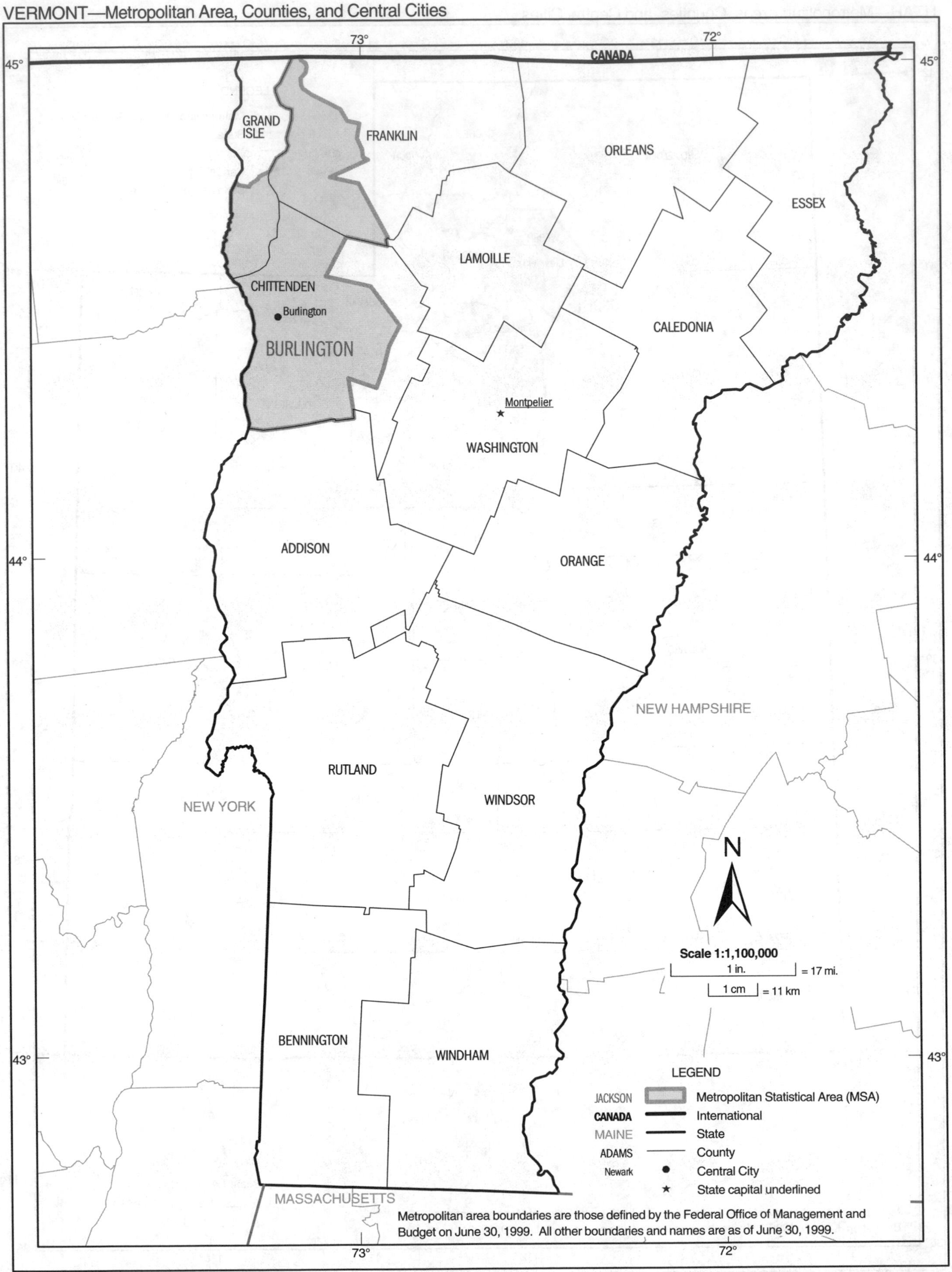

CANADA

45°

GRAND
ISLE

FRANKLIN

ORLEANS

ESSEX

LAMOILLE

CHITTENDEN

● Burlington

CALEDONIA

BURLINGTON

★ Montpelier

WASHINGTON

44°

ADDISON

ORANGE

NEW HAMPSHIRE

RUTLAND

NEW YORK

WINDSOR

N

Scale 1:1,100,000

| 1 in. | = 17 mi. |

| 1 cm | = 11 km |

BENNINGTON

43°

WINDHAM

LEGEND

JACKSON	Metropolitan Statistical Area (MSA)
CANADA	International
MAINE	State
ADAMS	County
Newark ●	Central City
★	State capital underlined

MASSACHUSETTS

Metropolitan area boundaries are those defined by the Federal Office of Management and
Budget on June 30, 1999. All other boundaries and names are as of June 30, 1999.

73°

72°

U.S. DEPARTMENT OF COMMERCE Economics and Statistics Administration Bureau of the Census

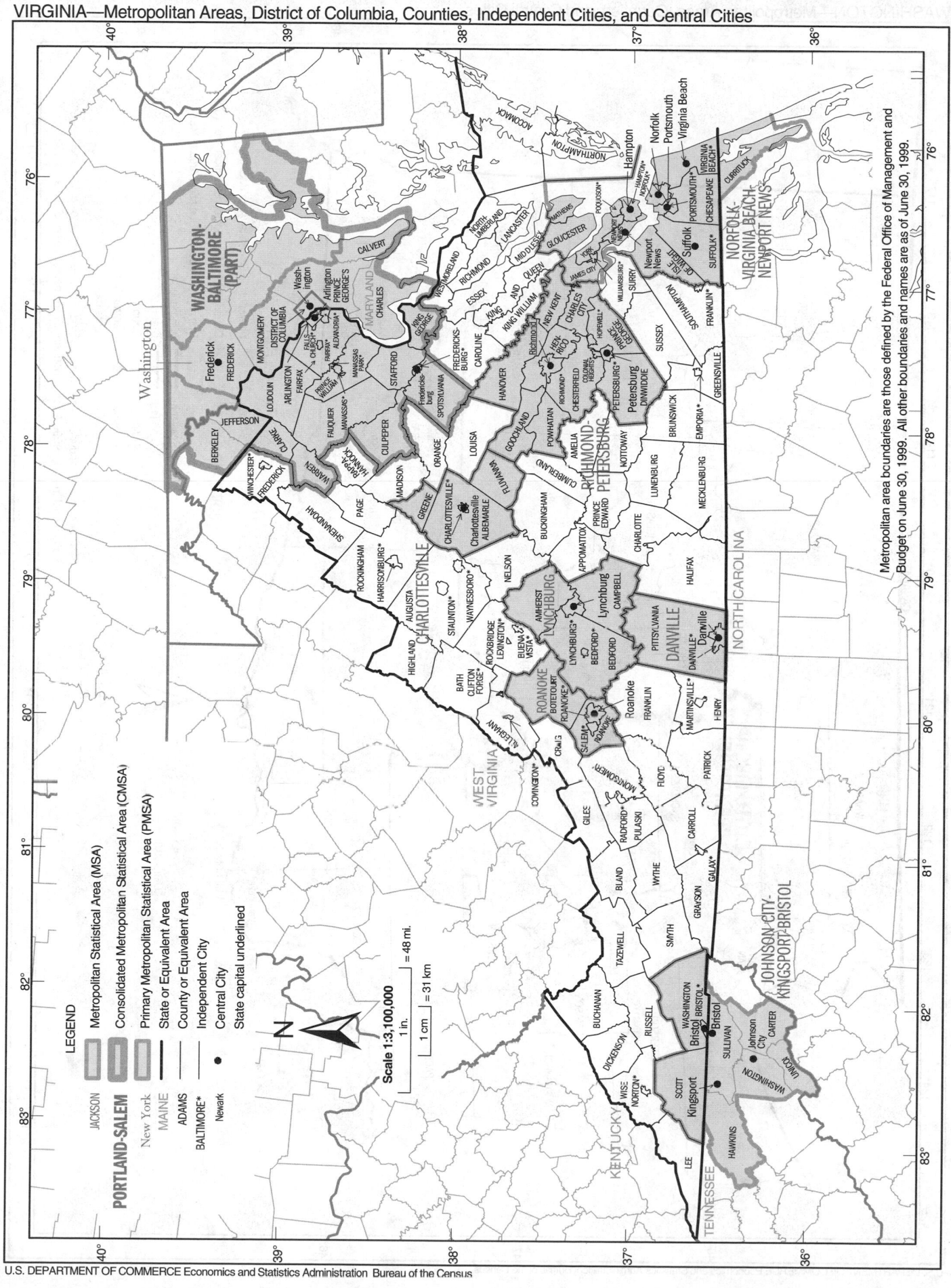

Metropolitan area boundaries are those defined by the Federal Office of Management and Budget on June 30, 1999. All other boundaries and names are as of June 30, 1999.

LEGEND

Metropolitan Statistical Area (MSA)

Consolidated Metropolitan Statistical Area (CMSA)

Primary Metropolitan Statistical Area (PMSA)

State or Equivalent Area

County or Equivalent Area

Independent City

● Central City

State capital underlined

JACKSON

PORTLAND-SALEM

New York

MAINE

ADAMS

BALTIMORE*

● Newark

N

Scale 1:3,100,000

1 in. = 48 mi.

1 cm = 31 km

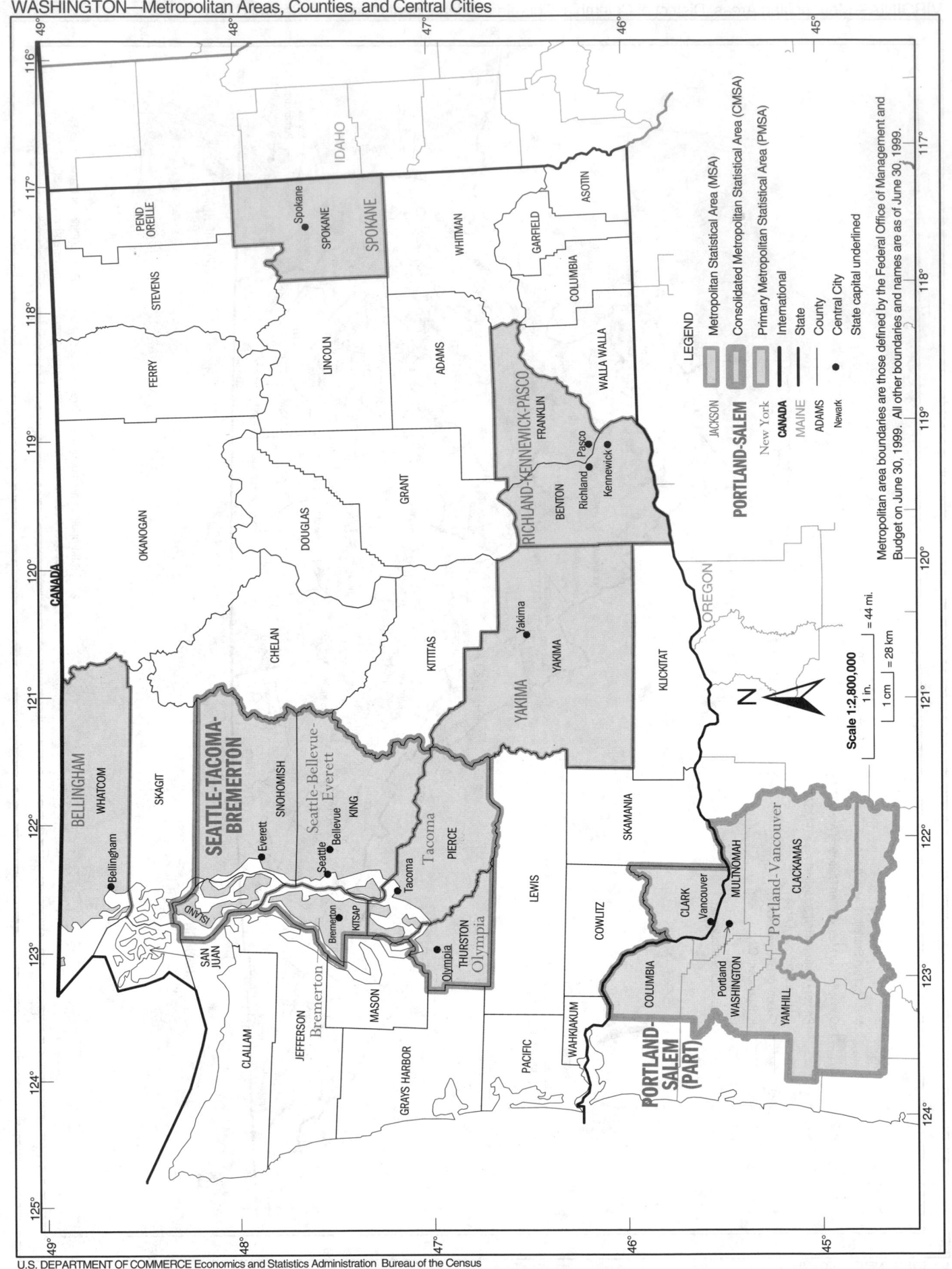

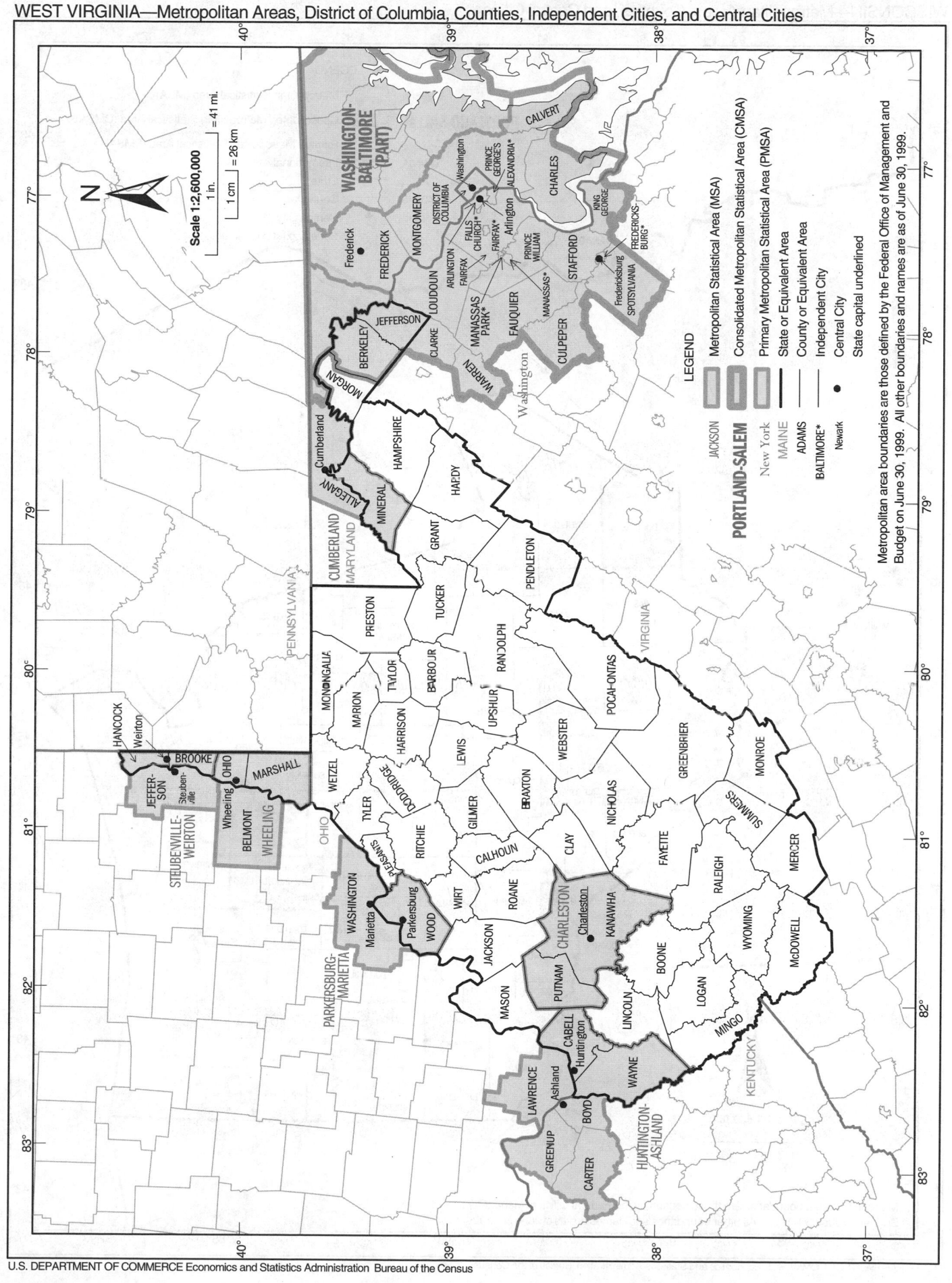

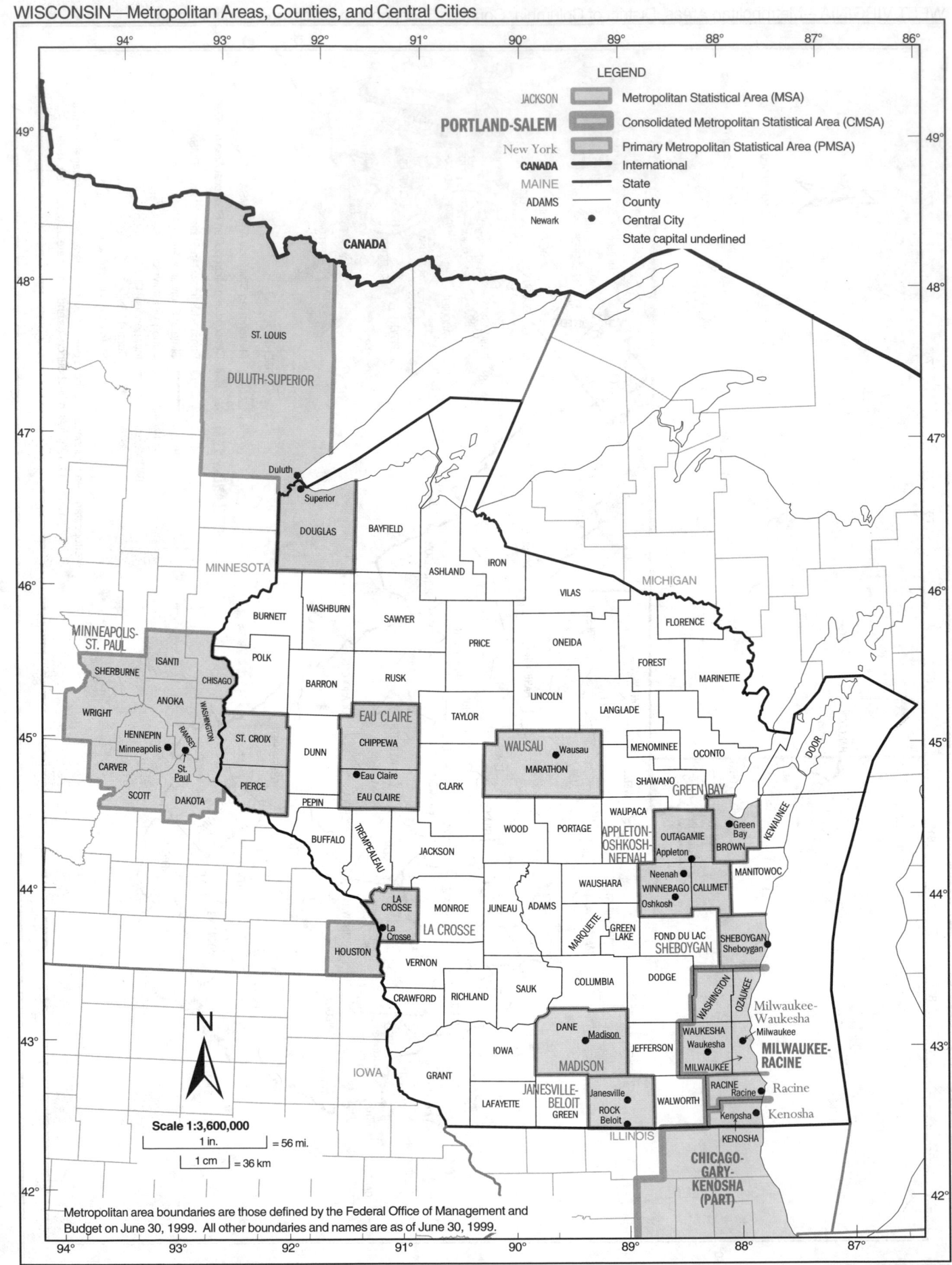

LEGEND

JACKSON — Metropolitan Statistical Area (MSA)

PORTLAND-SALEM — Consolidated Metropolitan Statistical Area (CMSA)

New York — Primary Metropolitan Statistical Area (PMSA)

CANADA — International

MAINE — State

ADAMS — County

Newark ● Central City

State capital underlined

Metropolitan area boundaries are those defined by the Federal Office of Management and Budget on June 30, 1999. All other boundaries and names are as of June 30, 1999.

Scale 1:3,600,000

1 in. = 56 mi.

1 cm = 36 km

N

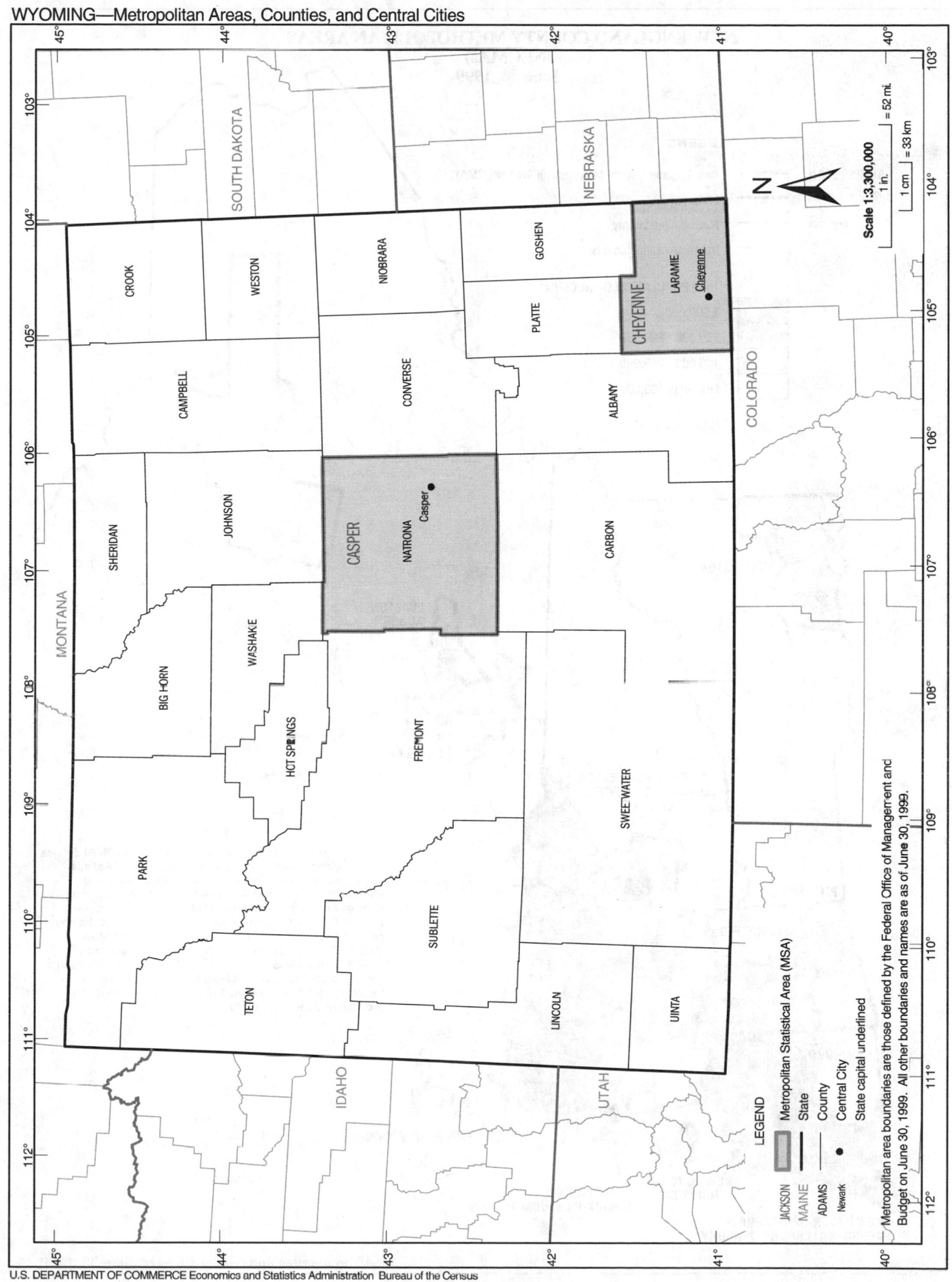

Scale 1:3,300,000

1 in. = 52 mi.

1 cm = 33 km

LEGEND

JACKSON — Metropolitan Statistical Area (MSA)

MAINE — State

ADAMS — County

Newark • Central City

State capital underlined

Metropolitan area boundaries are those defined by the Federal Office of Management and Budget on June 30, 1999. All other boundaries and names are as of June 30, 1999.

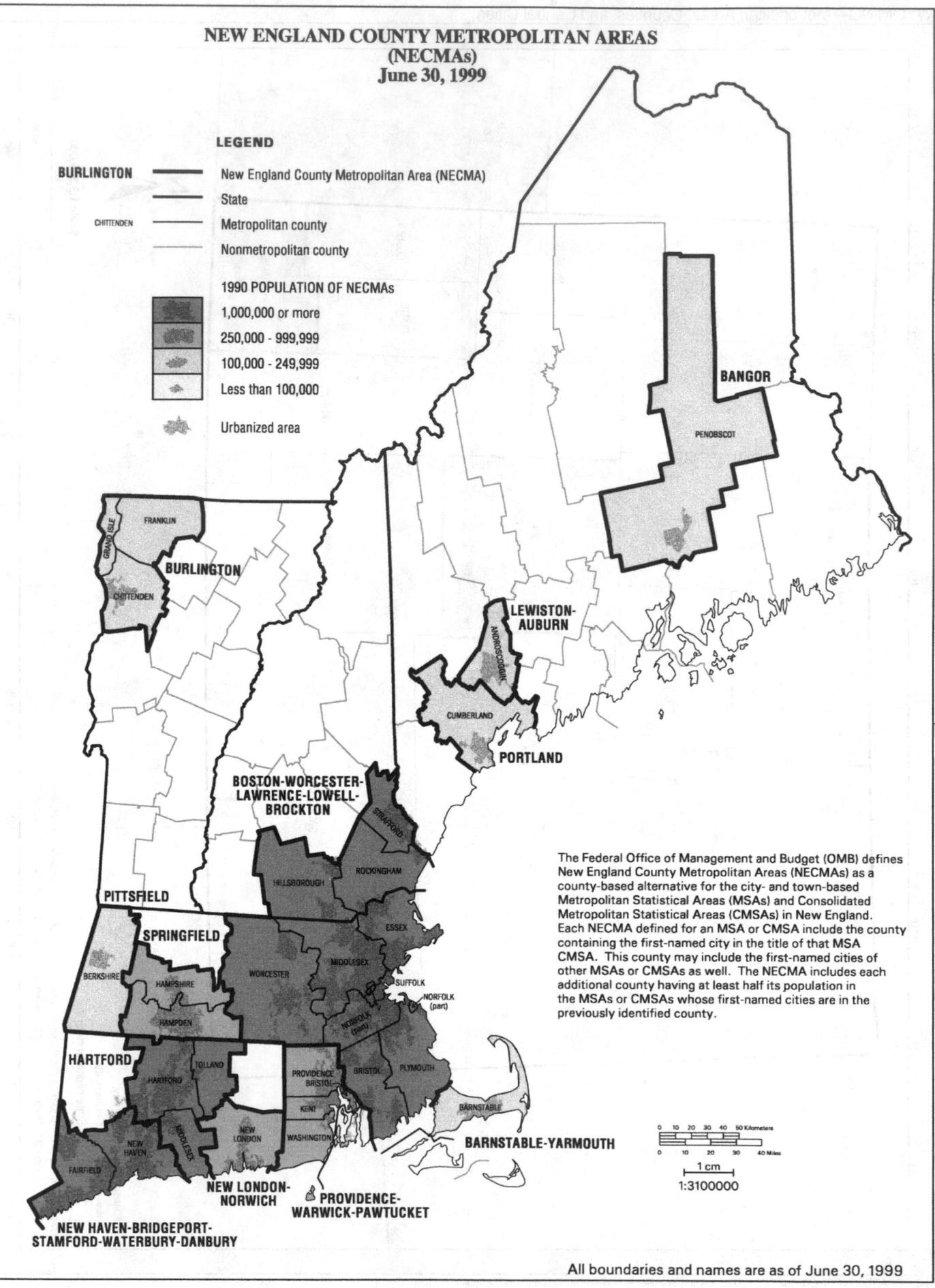

NEW ENGLAND COUNTY METROPOLITAN AREAS
(NECMAs)
June 30, 1999

LEGEND

BURLINGTON ——————— New England County Metropolitan Area (NECMA)

——————— State

CHITTENDEN ——————— Metropolitan county

——————— Nonmetropolitan county

1990 POPULATION OF NECMAs

1,000,000 or more

250,000 - 999,999

100,000 - 249,999

Less than 100,000

Urbanized area

BANGOR

PENOBSCOT

LEWISTON-AUBURN

ANDROSCOGGIN

CUMBERLAND

PORTLAND

GRAND ISLE

FRANKLIN

BURLINGTON

CHITTENDEN

BOSTON-WORCESTER-LAWRENCE-LOWELL-BROCKTON

STRAFFORD

ROCKINGHAM

HILLSBOROUGH

PITTSFIELD

SPRINGFIELD

BERKSHIRE

HAMPSHIRE

HAMPDEN

WORCESTER

MIDDLESEX

ESSEX

SUFFOLK

NORFOLK (part)

NORFOLK (main)

HARTFORD

HARTFORD

TOLLAND

PROVIDENCE BRISTOL

BRISTOL

PLYMOUTH

MIDDLESEX

NEW HAVEN

NEW LONDON

KENT

WASHINGTON

BARNSTABLE

FAIRFIELD

NEW LONDON-NORWICH

PROVIDENCE-WARWICK-PAWTUCKET

BARNSTABLE-YARMOUTH

NEW HAVEN-BRIDGEPORT-STAMFORD-WATERBURY-DANBURY

The Federal Office of Management and Budget (OMB) defines New England County Metropolitan Areas (NECMAs) as a county-based alternative for the city- and town-based Metropolitan Statistical Areas (MSAs) and Consolidated Metropolitan Statistical Areas (CMSAs) in New England. Each NECMA defined for an MSA or CMSA include the county containing the first-named city in the title of that MSA CMSA. This county may include the first-named cities of other MSAs or CMSAs as well. The NECMA includes each additional county having at least half its population in the MSAs or CMSAs whose first-named cities are in the previously identified county.

0 10 20 30 40 50 Kilometers

0 10 20 30 40 Miles

1 cm

1:3100000

All boundaries and names are as of June 30, 1999

APPENDIX E
CITIES BY COUNTY

The following table is arranged alphabetically by state. Under each state heading are listed all cities with a 2000 Census population over 25,000 along with their component counties and the population in each component.

State Code	Place Code	County Code	Geographic Area Name	2000 Population	State Code	Place Code	County Code	Geographic Area Name	2000 Population
01			**ALABAMA**..........	4 447 100	04			**ARIZONA**..........	5 130 632
01	03076		Auburn city..........	42 987	04	02830		Apache Junction city..........	31 814
01	03076	081	Lee County..........	42 987	04	02830	013	Maricopa County..........	273
					04	02830	021	Pinal County..........	31 541
01	05980		Bessemer city..........	29 672					
01	05980	073	Jefferson County..........	29 672	04	04720		Avondale city..........	35 883
					04	04720	013	Maricopa County..........	35 883
01	07000		Birmingham city..........	242 820					
01	07000	073	Jefferson County..........	242 307	04	08220		Bullhead City city..........	33 769
01	07000	117	Shelby County..........	513	04	08220	015	Mohave County..........	33 769
01	20104		Decatur city..........	53 929	04	10530		Casa Grande city..........	25 224
01	20104	083	Limestone County..........	83	04	10530	021	Pinal County..........	25 224
01	20104	103	Morgan County..........	53 846					
					04	12000		Chandler city..........	176 581
01	21184		Dothan city..........	57 737	04	12000	013	Maricopa County..........	176 581
01	21184	045	Dale County..........	650					
01	21184	067	Henry County..........	5	04	23620		Flagstaff city..........	52 894
01	21184	069	Houston County..........	57 082	04	23620	005	Coconino County..........	52 894
01	26896		Florence city..........	36 264	04	27400		Gilbert town..........	109 697
01	26896	077	Lauderdale County..........	36 264	04	27400	013	Maricopa County..........	109 697
01	28696		Gadsden city..........	38 978	04	27820		Glendale city..........	218 812
01	28696	055	Etowah County..........	38 978	04	27820	013	Maricopa County..........	218 812
01	35800		Homewood city..........	25 043	04	39370		Lake Havasu City city..........	41 938
01	35800	073	Jefferson County..........	25 043	04	39370	015	Mohave County..........	41 938
01	35896		Hoover city..........	62 742	04	46000		Mesa city..........	396 375
01	35896	073	Jefferson County..........	46 868	04	46000	013	Maricopa County..........	396 375
01	35896	117	Shelby County..........	15 874					
					04	51600		Oro Valley town..........	29 700
01	37000		Huntsville city..........	158 216	04	51600	019	Pima County..........	29 700
01	37000	083	Limestone County..........	264					
01	37000	089	Madison County..........	157 952	04	54050		Peoria city..........	108 364
					04	54050	013	Maricopa County..........	108 363
01	45784		Madison city..........	29 329	04	54050	025	Yavapai County..........	1
01	45784	083	Limestone County..........	139					
01	45784	089	Madison County..........	29 190	04	55000		Phoenix city..........	1321 045
					04	55000	013	Maricopa County..........	1321 045
01	50000		Mobile city..........	198 915					
01	50000	097	Mobile County..........	198 915	04	57380		Prescott city..........	33 938
					04	57380	025	Yavapai County..........	33 938
01	51000		Montgomery city..........	201 568					
01	51000	101	Montgomery County..........	201 568	04	65000		Scottsdale city..........	202 705
					04	65000	013	Maricopa County..........	202 705
01	59472		Phenix City city..........	28 265					
01	59472	081	Lee County..........	1 980	04	66820		Sierra Vista city..........	37 775
01	59472	113	Russell County..........	26 285	04	66820	003	Cochise County..........	37 775
01	62496		Prichard city..........	28 633	04	71510		Surprise city..........	30 848
01	62496	097	Mobile County..........	28 633	04	71510	013	Maricopa County..........	30 848
01	77256		Tuscaloosa city..........	77 906	04	73000		Tempe city..........	158 625
01	77256	125	Tuscaloosa County..........	77 906	04	73000	013	Maricopa County..........	158 625
02			**ALASKA**..........	626 932	04	77000		Tucson city..........	486 699
02	03000		Anchorage municipality..........	260 283	04	77000	019	Pima County..........	486 699
02	03000	020	Anchorage Municipality..........	260 283					
					04	85540		Yuma city..........	77 515
02	24230		Fairbanks city..........	30 224	04	85540	027	Yuma County..........	77 515
02	24230	090	Fairbanks North Star Borough....	30 224					
					05			**ARKANSAS**..........	2 673 400
02	36400		Juneau city and borough..........	30 711	05	15190		Conway city..........	43 167
02	36400	110	Juneau City and Borough..........	30 711	05	15190	045	Faulkner County..........	43 167

State Code	Place Code	County Code	Geographic Area Name	2000 Population	State Code	Place Code	County Code	Geographic Area Name	2000 Population
05	23290		Fayetteville city	58 047	06	04982		Bellflower city	72 878
05	23290	143	Washington County	58 047	06	04982	037	Los Angeles County	72 878
05	24550		Fort Smith city	80 268	06	04996		Bell Gardens city	44 054
05	24550	131	Sebastian County	80 268	06	04996	037	Los Angeles County	44 054
05	33400		Hot Springs city	35 750	06	05108		Belmont city	25 123
05	33400	051	Garland County	35 750	06	05108	081	San Mateo County	25 123
05	34750		Jacksonville city	29 916	06	05290		Benicia city	26 865
05	34750	119	Pulaski County	29 916	06	05290	095	Solano County	26 865
05	35710		Jonesboro city	55 515	06	06000		Berkeley city	102 743
05	35710	031	Craighead County	55 515	06	06000	001	Alameda County	102 743
05	41000		Little Rock city	183 133	06	06308		Beverly Hills city	33 784
05	41000	119	Pulaski County	183 133	06	06308	037	Los Angeles County	33 784
05	50450		North Little Rock city	60 433	06	08100		Brea city	35 410
05	50450	119	Pulaski County	60 433	06	08100	059	Orange County	35 410
05	55310		Pine Bluff city	55 085	06	08786		Buena Park city	78 282
05	55310	069	Jefferson County	55 085	06	08786	059	Orange County	78 282
05	60410		Rogers city	38 829	06	08954		Burbank city	100 316
05	60410	007	Benton County	38 829	06	08954	037	Los Angeles County	100 316
05	66080		Springdale city	45 798	06	09066		Burlingame city	28 158
05	66080	007	Benton County	2 011	06	09066	081	San Mateo County	28 158
05	66080	143	Washington County	43 787	06	09710		Calexico city	27 109
05	68810		Texarkana city	26 448	06	09710	025	Imperial County	27 109
05	68810	091	Miller County	26 448	06	10046		Camarillo city	57 077
05	74540		West Memphis city	27 666	06	10046	111	Ventura County	57 077
05	74540	035	Crittenden County	27 666	06	10345		Campbell city	38 138
06			**CALIFORNIA**	33 871 648	06	10345	085	Santa Clara County	38 138
06	00562		Alameda city	72 259					
06	00562	001	Alameda County	72 259	06	11194		Carlsbad city	78 247
					06	11194	073	San Diego County	78 247
06	00884		Alhambra city	85 804					
06	00884	037	Los Angeles County	85 804	06	11530		Carson city	89 730
					06	11530	037	Los Angeles County	89 730
06	02000		Anaheim city	328 014					
06	02000	059	Orange County	328 014	06	12048		Cathedral City city	42 647
					06	12048	065	Riverside County	42 647
06	02252		Antioch city	90 532					
06	02252	013	Contra Costa County	90 532	06	12524		Ceres city	34 609
					06	12524	099	Stanislaus County	34 609
06	02364		Apple Valley town	54 239					
06	02364	071	San Bernardino County	54 239	06	12552		Cerritos city	51 488
					06	12552	037	Los Angeles County	51 488
06	02462		Arcadia city	53 054					
06	02462	037	Los Angeles County	53 054	06	13014		Chico city	59 954
					06	13014	007	Butte County	59 954
06	03064		Atascadero city	26 411					
06	03064	079	San Luis Obispo County	26 411	06	13210		Chino city	67 168
					06	13210	071	San Bernardino County	67 168
06	03386		Azusa city	44 712					
06	03386	037	Los Angeles County	44 712	06	13392		Chula Vista city	173 556
					06	13392	073	San Diego County	173 556
06	03526		Bakersfield city	247 057					
06	03526	029	Kern County	247 057	06	13756		Claremont city	33 998
					06	13756	037	Los Angeles County	33 998
06	03666		Baldwin Park city	75 837					
06	03666	037	Los Angeles County	75 837	06	14218		Clovis city	68 468
					06	14218	019	Fresno County	68 468
06	04870		Bell city	36 664					
06	04870	037	Los Angeles County	36 664	06	14890		Colton city	47 662
					06	14890	071	San Bernardino County	47 662

Cities by County — Continued

State Code	Place Code	County Code	Geographic Area Name	2000 Population	State Code	Place Code	County Code	Geographic Area Name	2000 Population
06	15044		Compton city	93 493	06	24638		Folsom city	51 884
06	15044	037	Los Angeles County	93 493	06	24638	067	Sacramento County	51 884
06	16000		Concord city	121 780	06	24680		Fontana city	128 929
06	16000	013	Contra Costa County	121 780	06	24680	071	San Bernardino County	128 929
06	16350		Corona city	124 966	06	25338		Foster City city	28 803
06	16350	065	Riverside County	124 966	06	25338	081	San Mateo County	28 803
06	16532		Costa Mesa city	108 724	06	25380		Fountain Valley city	54 978
06	16532	059	Orange County	108 724	06	25380	059	Orange County	54 978
06	16742		Covina city	46 837	06	26000		Fremont city	203 413
06	16742	037	Los Angeles County	46 837	06	26000	001	Alameda County	203 413
06	17568		Culver City city	38 816	06	27000		Fresno city	427 652
06	17568	037	Los Angeles County	38 816	06	27000	019	Fresno County	427 652
06	17610		Cupertino city	50 546	06	28000		Fullerton city	126 003
06	17610	085	Santa Clara County	50 546	06	28000	059	Orange County	126 003
06	17750		Cypress city	46 229	06	28168		Gardena city	57 746
06	17750	059	Orange County	46 229	06	28168	037	Los Angeles County	57 746
06	17918		Daly City city	103 621	06	29000		Garden Grove city	165 196
06	17918	081	San Mateo County	103 621	06	29000	059	Orange County	165 196
06	17946		Dana Point city	35 110	06	29504		Gilroy city	41 464
06	17946	059	Orange County	35 110	06	29504	085	Santa Clara County	41 464
06	17988		Danville town	41 715	06	30000		Glendale city	194 973
06	17988	013	Contra Costa County	41 715	06	30000	037	Los Angeles County	194 973
06	18100		Davis city	60 308	06	30014		Glendora city	49 415
06	18100	113	Yolo County	60 308	06	30014	037	Los Angeles County	49 415
06	18394		Delano city	38 824	06	31960		Hanford city	41 686
06	18394	029	Kern County	38 824	06	31960	031	Kings County	41 686
06	19192		Diamond Bar city	56 287	06	32548		Hawthorne city	84 112
06	19192	037	Los Angeles County	56 287	06	32548	037	Los Angeles County	84 112
06	19766		Downey city	107 323	06	33000		Hayward city	140 030
06	19766	037	Los Angeles County	107 323	06	33000	001	Alameda County	140 030
06	20018		Dublin city	29 973	06	33182		Hemet city	58 812
06	20018	001	Alameda County	29 973	06	33182	065	Riverside County	58 812
06	20956		East Palo Alto city	29 506	06	33434		Hesperia city	62 582
06	20956	081	San Mateo County	29 506	06	33434	071	San Bernardino County	62 582
06	21712		El Cajon city	94 869	06	33588		Highland city	44 605
06	21712	073	San Diego County	94 869	06	33588	071	San Bernardino County	44 605
06	21782		El Centro city	37 835	06	34120		Hollister city	34 413
06	21782	025	Imperial County	37 835	06	34120	069	San Benito County	34 413
06	22230		El Monte city	115 965	06	36000		Huntington Beach city	189 594
06	22230	037	Los Angeles County	115 965	06	36000	059	Orange County	189 594
06	22678		Encinitas city	58 014	06	36056		Huntington Park city	61 348
06	22678	073	San Diego County	58 014	06	36056	037	Los Angeles County	61 348
06	22804		Escondido city	133 559	06	36294		Imperial Beach city	26 992
06	22804	073	San Diego County	133 559	06	36294	073	San Diego County	26 992
06	23042		Eureka city	26 128	06	36448		Indio city	49 116
06	23042	023	Humboldt County	26 128	06	36448	065	Riverside County	49 116
06	23182		Fairfield city	96 178	06	36546		Inglewood city	112 580
06	23182	095	Solano County	96 178	06	36546	037	Los Angeles County	112 580

State Code	Place Code	County Code	Geographic Area Name	2000 Population	State Code	Place Code	County Code	Geographic Area Name	2000 Population
06	36770		Irvine city	143 072	06	45778		Marina city	25 101
06	36770	059	Orange County	143 072	06	45778	053	Monterey County	25 101
06	39248		Laguna Niguel city	61 891	06	46114		Martinez city	35 866
06	39248	059	Orange County	61 891	06	46114	013	Contra Costa County	35 866
06	39290		La Habra city	58 974	06	46492		Maywood city	28 083
06	39290	059	Orange County	58 974	06	46492	037	Los Angeles County	28 083
06	39486		Lake Elsinore city	28 928	06	46870		Menlo Park city	30 785
06	39486	065	Riverside County	28 928	06	46870	081	San Mateo County	30 785
06	39496		Lake Forest city	58 707	06	46898		Merced city	63 893
06	39496	059	Orange County	58 707	06	46898	047	Merced County	63 893
06	39892		Lakewood city	79 345	06	47766		Milpitas city	62 698
06	39892	037	Los Angeles County	79 345	06	47766	085	Santa Clara County	62 698
06	40004		La Mesa city	54 749	06	48256		Mission Viejo city	93 102
06	40004	073	San Diego County	54 749	06	48256	059	Orange County	93 102
06	40032		La Mirada city	46 783	06	48354		Modesto city	188 856
06	40032	037	Los Angeles County	46 783	06	48354	099	Stanislaus County	188 856
06	40130		Lancaster city	118 718	06	48648		Monrovia city	36 929
06	40130	037	Los Angeles County	118 718	06	48648	037	Los Angeles County	36 929
06	40340		La Puente city	41 063	06	48788		Montclair city	33 049
06	40340	037	Los Angeles County	41 063	06	48788	071	San Bernardino County	33 049
06	40830		La Verne city	31 638	06	48816		Montebello city	62 150
06	40830	037	Los Angeles County	31 638	06	48816	037	Los Angeles County	62 150
06	40886		Lawndale city	31 711	06	48872		Monterey city	29 674
06	40886	037	Los Angeles County	31 711	06	48872	053	Monterey County	29 674
06	41992		Livermore city	73 345	06	48914		Monterey Park city	60 051
06	41992	001	Alameda County	73 345	06	48914	037	Los Angeles County	60 051
06	42202		Lodi city	56 999	06	49138		Moorpark city	31 415
06	42202	077	San Joaquin County	56 999	06	49138	111	Ventura County	31 415
06	42524		Lompoc city	41 103	06	49270		Moreno Valley city	142 381
06	42524	083	Santa Barbara County	41 103	06	49270	065	Riverside County	142 381
06	43000		Long Beach city	461 522	06	49278		Morgan Hill city	33 556
06	43000	037	Los Angeles County	461 522	06	49278	085	Santa Clara County	33 556
06	43280		Los Altos city	27 693	06	49670		Mountain View city	70 708
06	43280	085	Santa Clara County	27 693	06	49670	085	Santa Clara County	70 708
06	44000		Los Angeles city	3694 820	06	50076		Murrieta city	44 282
06	44000	037	Los Angeles County	3694 820	06	50076	065	Riverside County	44 282
06	44028		Los Banos city	25 869	06	50258		Napa city	72 585
06	44028	047	Merced County	25 869	06	50258	055	Napa County	72 585
06	44112		Los Gatos town	28 592	06	50398		National City city	54 260
06	44112	085	Santa Clara County	28 592	06	50398	073	San Diego County	54 260
06	44574		Lynwood city	69 845	06	50916		Newark city	42 471
06	44574	037	Los Angeles County	69 845	06	50916	001	Alameda County	42 471
06	45022		Madera city	43 207	06	51182		Newport Beach city	70 032
06	45022	039	Madera County	43 207	06	51182	059	Orange County	70 032
06	45400		Manhattan Beach city	33 852	06	52526		Norwalk city	103 298
06	45400	037	Los Angeles County	33 852	06	52526	037	Los Angeles County	103 298
06	45484		Manteca city	49 258	06	52582		Novato city	47 630
06	45484	077	San Joaquin County	49 258	06	52582	041	Marin County	47 630

State Code	Place Code	County Code	Geographic Area Name	2000 Population	State Code	Place Code	County Code	Geographic Area Name	2000 Population
06	53000		Oakland city	399 484	06	59514		Rancho Palos Verdes city	41 145
06	53000	001	Alameda County	399 484	06	59514	037	Los Angeles County	41 145
06	53322		Oceanside city	161 029	06	59920		Redding city	80 865
06	53322	073	San Diego County	161 029	06	59920	089	Shasta County	80 865
06	53896		Ontario city	158 007	06	59962		Redlands city	63 591
06	53896	071	San Bernardino County	158 007	06	59962	071	San Bernardino County	63 591
06	53980		Orange city	128 821	06	60018		Redondo Beach city	63 261
06	53980	059	Orange County	128 821	06	60018	037	Los Angeles County	63 261
06	54652		Oxnard city	170 358	06	60102		Redwood City city	75 402
06	54652	111	Ventura County	170 358	06	60102	081	San Mateo County	75 402
06	54806		Pacifica city	38 390	06	60466		Rialto city	91 873
06	54806	081	San Mateo County	38 390	06	60466	071	San Bernardino County	91 873
06	55156		Palmdale city	116 670	06	60620		Richmond city	99 216
06	55156	037	Los Angeles County	116 670	06	60620	013	Contra Costa County	99 216
06	55184		Palm Desert city	41 155	06	62000		Riverside city	255 166
06	55184	065	Riverside County	41 155	06	62000	065	Riverside County	255 166
06	55254		Palm Springs city	42 807	06	62364		Rocklin city	36 330
06	55254	065	Riverside County	42 807	06	62364	061	Placer County	36 330
06	55282		Palo Alto city	58 598	06	62546		Rohnert Park city	42 236
06	55282	085	Santa Clara County	58 598	06	62546	097	Sonoma County	42 236
06	55520		Paradise town	26 408	06	62896		Rosemead city	53 505
06	55520	007	Butte County	26 408	06	62896	037	Los Angeles County	53 505
06	55618		Paramount city	55 266	06	62938		Roseville city	79 921
06	55618	037	Los Angeles County	55 266	06	62938	061	Placer County	79 921
06	56000		Pasadena city	133 936	06	64000		Sacramento city	407 018
06	56000	037	Los Angeles County	133 936	06	64000	067	Sacramento County	407 018
06	56700		Perris city	36 189	06	64224		Salinas city	151 060
06	56700	065	Riverside County	36 189	06	64224	053	Monterey County	151 060
06	56784		Petaluma city	54 548	06	65000		San Bernardino city	185 401
06	56784	097	Sonoma County	54 548	06	65000	071	San Bernardino County	185 401
06	56924		Pico Rivera city	63 428	06	65028		San Bruno city	40 165
06	56924	037	Los Angeles County	63 428	06	65028	081	San Mateo County	40 165
06	57456		Pittsburg city	56 769	06	65042		San Buenaventura (Ventura) city	100 916
06	57456	013	Contra Costa County	56 769	06	65042	111	Ventura County	100 916
06	57526		Placentia city	46 488	06	65070		San Carlos city	27 718
06	57526	059	Orange County	46 488	06	65070	081	San Mateo County	27 718
06	57764		Pleasant Hill city	32 837	06	65084		San Clemente city	49 936
06	57764	013	Contra Costa County	32 837	06	65084	059	Orange County	49 936
06	57792		Pleasanton city	63 654	06	66000		San Diego city	1223 400
06	57792	001	Alameda County	63 654	06	66000	073	San Diego County	1223 400
06	58072		Pomona city	149 473	06	66070		San Dimas city	34 980
06	58072	037	Los Angeles County	149 473	06	66070	037	Los Angeles County	34 980
06	58240		Porterville city	39 615	06	67000		San Francisco city	776 733
06	58240	107	Tulare County	39 615	06	67000	075	San Francisco County	776 733
06	58520		Poway city	48 044	06	67042		San Gabriel city	39 804
06	58520	073	San Diego County	48 044	06	67042	037	Los Angeles County	39 804
06	59451		Rancho Cucamonga city	127 743	06	68000		San Jose city	894 943
06	59451	071	San Bernardino County	127 743	06	68000	085	Santa Clara County	894 943

State Code	Place Code	County Code	Geographic Area Name	2000 Population	State Code	Place Code	County Code	Geographic Area Name	2000 Population
06	68028		San Juan Capistrano city	33 826	06	75000		Stockton city	243 771
06	68028	059	Orange County	33 826	06	75000	077	San Joaquin County	243 771
06	68084		San Leandro city	79 452	06	75630		Suisun City city	26 118
06	68084	001	Alameda County	79 452	06	75630	095	Solano County	26 118
06	68154		San Luis Obispo city	44 174	06	77000		Sunnyvale city	131 760
06	68154	079	San Luis Obispo County	44 174	06	77000	085	Santa Clara County	131 760
06	68196		San Marcos city	54 977	06	78120		Temecula city	57 716
06	68196	073	San Diego County	54 977	06	78120	065	Riverside County	57 716
06	68252		San Mateo city	92 482	06	78148		Temple City city	33 377
06	68252	081	San Mateo County	92 482	06	78148	037	Los Angeles County	33 377
06	68294		San Pablo city	30 215	06	78582		Thousand Oaks city	117 005
06	68294	013	Contra Costa County	30 215	06	78582	111	Ventura County	117 005
06	68364		San Rafael city	56 063	06	80000		Torrance city	137 946
06	68364	041	Marin County	56 063	06	80000	037	Los Angeles County	137 946
06	68378		San Ramon city	44 722	06	80238		Tracy city	56 929
06	68378	013	Contra Costa County	44 722	06	80238	077	San Joaquin County	56 929
06	69000		Santa Ana city	337 977	06	80644		Tulare city	43 994
06	69000	059	Orange County	337 977	06	80644	107	Tulare County	43 994
06	69070		Santa Barbara city	92 325	06	80812		Turlock city	55 810
06	69070	083	Santa Barbara County	92 325	06	80812	099	Stanislaus County	55 810
06	69084		Santa Clara city	102 361	06	80854		Tustin city	67 504
06	69084	085	Santa Clara County	102 361	06	80854	059	Orange County	67 504
06	69088		Santa Clarita city	151 088	06	81204		Union City city	66 869
06	69088	037	Los Angeles County	151 088	06	81204	001	Alameda County	66 869
06	69112		Santa Cruz city	54 593	06	81344		Upland city	68 393
06	69112	087	Santa Cruz County	54 593	06	81344	071	San Bernardino County	68 393
06	69196		Santa Maria city	77 423	06	81554		Vacaville city	88 625
06	69196	083	Santa Barbara County	77 423	06	81554	095	Solano County	88 625
06	70000		Santa Monica city	84 084	06	81666		Vallejo city	116 760
06	70000	037	Los Angeles County	84 084	06	81666	095	Solano County	116 760
06	70042		Santa Paula city	28 598	06	82590		Victorville city	64 029
06	70042	111	Ventura County	28 598	06	82590	071	San Bernardino County	64 029
06	70098		Santa Rosa city	147 595	06	82954		Visalia city	91 565
06	70098	097	Sonoma County	147 595	06	82954	107	Tulare County	91 565
06	70224		Santee city	52 975	06	82996		Vista city	89 857
06	70224	073	San Diego County	52 975	06	82996	073	San Diego County	89 857
06	70280		Saratoga city	29 843	06	83332		Walnut city	30 004
06	70280	085	Santa Clara County	29 843	06	83332	037	Los Angeles County	30 004
06	70742		Seaside city	31 696	06	83346		Walnut Creek city	64 296
06	70742	053	Monterey County	31 696	06	83346	013	Contra Costa County	64 296
06	72016		Simi Valley city	111 351	06	83668		Watsonville city	44 265
06	72016	111	Ventura County	111 351	06	83668	087	Santa Cruz County	44 265
06	73080		South Gate city	96 375	06	84200		West Covina city	105 080
06	73080	037	Los Angeles County	96 375	06	84200	037	Los Angeles County	105 080
06	73262		South San Francisco city	60 552	06	84410		West Hollywood city	35 716
06	73262	081	San Mateo County	60 552	06	84410	037	Los Angeles County	35 716
06	73962		Stanton city	37 403	06	84550		Westminster city	88 207
06	73962	059	Orange County	37 403	06	84550	059	Orange County	88 207

State Code	Place Code	County Code	Geographic Area Name	2000 Population	State Code	Place Code	County Code	Geographic Area Name	2000 Population
06	84816		West Sacramento city	31 615	08	54330		Northglenn city	31 575
06	84816	113	Yolo County	31 615	08	54330	001	Adams County	31 563
					08	54330	123	Weld County	12
06	85292		Whittier city	83 680					
06	85292	037	Los Angeles County	83 680	08	62000		Pueblo city	102 121
					08	62000	101	Pueblo County	102 121
06	86328		Woodland city	49 151					
06	86328	113	Yolo County	49 151	08	77290		Thornton city	82 384
					08	77290	001	Adams County	82 384
06	86832		Yorba Linda city	58 918	08	77290	123	Weld County	0
06	86832	059	Orange County	58 918					
					08	83835		Westminster city	100 940
06	86972		Yuba City city	36 758	08	83835	001	Adams County	57 419
06	86972	101	Sutter County	36 758	08	83835	059	Jefferson County	43 521
06	87042		Yucaipa city	41 207	08	84440		Wheat Ridge city	32 913
06	87042	071	San Bernardino County	41 207	08	84440	059	Jefferson County	32 913
08			**COLORADO**	4 301 261	09			**CONNECTICUT**	3 405 565
08	03455		Arvada city	102 153	09	08000		Bridgeport city	139 529
08	03455	001	Adams County	2 847	09	08000	001	Fairfield County	139 529
08	03455	059	Jefferson County	99 306					
					09	08420		Bristol city	60 062
08	04000		Aurora city	276 393	09	08420	003	Hartford County	60 062
08	04000	001	Adams County	40 249					
08	04000	005	Arapahoe County	236 144	09	18430		Danbury city	74 848
08	04000	035	Douglas County	0	09	18430	001	Fairfield County	74 848
08	07850		Boulder city	94 673	09	37000		Hartford city	121 578
08	07850	013	Boulder County	94 673	09	37000	003	Hartford County	121 578
08	09280		Broomfield city	38 272	09	46450		Meriden city	58 244
08	09280	001	Adams County	15 239	09	46450	009	New Haven County	58 244
08	09280	013	Boulder County	21 474					
08	09280	059	Jefferson County	1 549	09	47290		Middletown city	43 167
08	09280	123	Weld County	10	09	47290	007	Middlesex County	43 167
08	16000		Colorado Springs city	360 890	09	47500		Milford city	52 305
08	16000	041	El Paso County	360 890					
					09	49880		Naugatuck borough	30 989
08	20000		Denver city	554 636	09	49880	009	New Haven County	30 989
08	20000	031	Denver County	554 636					
					09	50370		New Britain city	71 538
08	24785		Englewood city	31 727	09	50370	003	Hartford County	71 538
08	24785	005	Arapahoe County	31 727					
					09	52000		New Haven city	123 626
08	27425		Fort Collins city	118 652	09	52000	009	New Haven County	123 626
08	27425	069	Larimer County	118 652					
					09	52280		New London city	25 671
08	31660		Grand Junction city	41 986	09	52280	011	New London County	25 671
08	31660	077	Mesa County	41 986					
					09	55990		Norwalk city	82 951
08	32155		Greeley city	76 930	09	55990	001	Fairfield County	82 951
08	32155	123	Weld County	76 930					
					09	56200		Norwich city	36 117
08	43000		Lakewood city	144 126	09	56200	011	New London County	36 117
08	43000	059	Jefferson County	144 126					
					09	68100		Shelton city	38 101
08	45255		Littleton city	40 340	09	68100	001	Fairfield County	38 101
08	45255	005	Arapahoe County	40 168					
08	45255	035	Douglas County	63	09	73000		Stamford city	117 083
08	45255	059	Jefferson County	109	09	73000	001	Fairfield County	117 083
08	45970		Longmont city	71 093	09	76500		Torrington city	35 202
08	45970	013	Boulder County	71 069	09	76500	005	Litchfield County	35 202
08	45970	123	Weld County	24					
					09	80000		Waterbury city	107 271
08	46465		Loveland city	50 608	09	80000	009	New Haven County	107 271
08	46465	069	Larimer County	50 608					
					09	82800		West Haven city	52 360
					09	82800	009	New Haven County	52 360

Cities by County — Continued

State Code	Place Code	County Code	Geographic Area Name	2000 Population	State Code	Place Code	County Code	Geographic Area Name	2000 Population
10			**DELAWARE**	783 600	12	25175		Gainesville city	95 447
10	21200		Dover city	32 135	12	25175	001	Alachua County	95 447
10	21200	001	Kent County	32 135					
					12	27322		Greenacres city	27 569
10	50670		Newark city	28 547	12	27322	099	Palm Beach County	27 569
10	50670	003	New Castle County	28 547					
					12	28450		Hallandale city	34 282
10	77580		Wilmington city	72 664	12	28450	011	Broward County	34 282
10	77580	003	New Castle County	72 664					
					12	30000		Hialeah city	226 419
11			**DISTRICT OF COLUMBIA**	572 059	12	30000	086	Miami-Dade County	226 419
11	50000		Washington city	572 059					
11	50000	001	District of Columbia	572 059	12	32000		Hollywood city	139 357
					12	32000	011	Broward County	139 357
12			**FLORIDA**	15 982 378					
12	00950		Altamonte Springs city	41 200	12	32275		Homestead city	31 909
12	00950	117	Seminole County	41 200	12	32275	086	Miami-Dade County	31 909
12	01700		Apopka city	26 642	12	35000		Jacksonville city	735 617
12	01700	095	Orange County	26 642	12	35000	031	Duval County	735 617
12	07300		Boca Raton city	74 764	12	35875		Jupiter town	39 328
12	07300	099	Palm Beach County	74 764	12	35875	099	Palm Beach County	39 328
12	07875		Boynton Beach city	60 389	12	36550		Key West city	25 478
12	07875	099	Palm Beach County	60 389	12	36550	087	Monroe County	25 478
12	07950		Bradenton city	49 504	12	36950		Kissimmee city	47 814
12	07950	081	Manatee County	49 504	12	36950	097	Osceola County	47 814
12	10275		Cape Coral city	102 286	12	38250		Lakeland city	78 452
12	10275	071	Lee County	102 286	12	38250	105	Polk County	78 452
12	12875		Clearwater city	108 787	12	39075		Lake Worth city	35 133
12	12875	103	Pinellas County	108 787	12	39075	099	Palm Beach County	35 133
12	13275		Coconut Creek city	43 566	12	39425		Largo city	69 371
12	13275	011	Broward County	43 566	12	39425	103	Pinellas County	69 371
12	14125		Cooper City city	27 939	12	39525		Lauderdale Lakes city	31 705
12	14125	011	Broward County	27 939	12	39525	011	Broward County	31 705
12	14250		Coral Gables city	42 249	12	39550		Lauderhill city	57 585
12	14250	086	Miami-Dade County	42 249	12	39550	011	Broward County	57 585
12	14400		Coral Springs city	117 549	12	43125		Margate city	53 909
12	14400	011	Broward County	117 549	12	43125	011	Broward County	53 909
12	16475		Davie town	75 720	12	43975		Melbourne city	71 382
12	16475	011	Broward County	75 720	12	43975	009	Brevard County	71 382
12	16525		Daytona Beach city	64 112	12	45000		Miami city	362 470
12	16525	127	Volusia County	64 112	12	45000	086	Miami-Dade County	362 470
12	16725		Deerfield Beach city	64 583	12	45025		Miami Beach city	87 933
12	16725	011	Broward County	64 583	12	45025	086	Miami-Dade County	87 933
12	17100		Delray Beach city	60 020	12	45975		Miramar city	72 739
12	17100	099	Palm Beach County	60 020	12	45975	011	Broward County	72 739
12	18575		Dunedin city	35 691	12	49425		North Lauderdale city	32 264
12	18575	103	Pinellas County	35 691	12	49425	011	Broward County	32 264
12	24000		Fort Lauderdale city	152 397	12	49450		North Miami city	59 880
12	24000	011	Broward County	152 397	12	49450	086	Miami-Dade County	59 880
12	24125		Fort Myers city	48 208	12	49475		North Miami Beach city	40 786
12	24125	071	Lee County	48 208	12	49475	086	Miami-Dade County	40 786
12	24300		Fort Pierce city	37 516	12	50575		Oakland Park city	30 966
12	24300	111	St. Lucie County	37 516	12	50575	011	Broward County	30 966

State Code	Place Code	County Code	Geographic Area Name	2000 Population	State Code	Place Code	County Code	Geographic Area Name	2000 Population
12	50750		Ocala city...............	45 943	12	76582		Weston city...............	49 286
12	50750	083	Marion County	45 943	12	76582	011	Broward County	49 286
12	53000		Orlando city...............	185 951	12	76600		West Palm Beach city...............	82 103
12	53000	095	Orange County	185 951	12	76600	099	Palm Beach County...............	82 103
12	53150		Ormond Beach city...............	36 301	12	78275		Winter Haven city...............	26 487
12	53150	127	Volusia County	36 301	12	78275	105	Polk County	26 487
12	53575		Oviedo city...............	26 316	12	78325		Winter Springs city...............	31 666
12	53575	117	Seminole County	26 316	12	78325	117	Seminole County	31 666
12	54000		Palm Bay city...............	79 413	13			**GEORGIA**	8 186 453
12	54000	009	Brevard County	79 413	13	01052		Albany city...............	76 939
					13	01052	095	Dougherty County	76 939
12	54075		Palm Beach Gardens city	35 058	13	01696		Alpharetta city...............	34 854
12	54075	099	Palm Beach County...............	35 058	13	01696	121	Fulton County	34 854
12	54700		Panama City city	36 417	13	03436		Athens-Clarke County	101 489
12	54700	005	Bay County	36 417					
12	55775		Pembroke Pines city	137 427	13	04000		Atlanta city...............	416 474
12	55775	011	Broward County	137 427	13	04000	089	DeKalb County	29 775
					13	04000	121	Fulton County	386 699
12	55925		Pensacola city...............	56 255	13	04200		Augusta-Richmond County	199 775
12	55925	033	Escambia County...............	56 255					
12	56975		Pinellas Park city...............	45 658	13	19000		Columbus city...............	186 291
12	56975	103	Pinellas County...............	45 658					
12	57425		Plantation city...............	82 934	13	21380		Dalton city...............	27 912
12	57425	011	Broward County	82 934	13	21380	313	Whitfield County...............	27 912
12	57550		Plant City city...............	29 915	13	25720		East Point city	39 595
12	57550	057	Hillsborough County	29 915	13	25720	121	Fulton County	39 595
12	58050		Pompano Beach city	78 191	13	31908		Gainesville city...............	25 578
12	58050	011	Broward County	78 191	13	31908	139	Hall County	25 578
12	58575		Port Orange city...............	45 823	13	38964		Hinesville city...............	30 392
12	58575	127	Volusia County	45 823	13	38964	179	Liberty County...............	30 392
12	58715		Port St. Lucie city...............	88 769	13	44340		LaGrange city...............	25 998
12	58715	111	St. Lucie County	88 769	13	44340	285	Troup County	25 998
12	60975		Riviera Beach city...............	29 884	13	49000		Macon city...............	97 255
12	60975	099	Palm Beach County...............	29 884	13	49000	021	Bibb County...............	96 777
					13	49000	169	Jones County...............	478
12	63000		St. Petersburg city...............	248 232	13	49756		Marietta city...............	58 748
12	63000	103	Pinellas County...............	248 232	13	49756	067	Cobb County...............	58 748
12	63650		Sanford city...............	38 291	13	59724		Peachtree City city...............	31 580
12	63650	117	Seminole County	38 291	13	59724	113	Fayette County	31 580
12	64175		Sarasota city...............	52 715	13	66668		Rome city	34 980
12	64175	115	Sarasota County	52 715	13	66668	115	Floyd County	34 980
12	69700		Sunrise city...............	85 779	13	67284		Roswell city	79 334
12	69700	011	Broward County	85 779	13	67284	121	Fulton County	79 334
12	70600		Tallahassee city...............	150 624	13	69000		Savannah city...............	131 510
12	70600	073	Leon County...............	150 624	13	69000	051	Chatham County...............	131 510
12	70675		Tamarac city...............	55 588	13	71492		Smyrna city...............	40 999
12	70675	011	Broward County	55 588	13	71492	067	Cobb County...............	40 999
12	71000		Tampa city...............	303 447	13	78800		Valdosta city...............	43 724
12	71000	057	Hillsborough County	303 447	13	78800	185	Lowndes County...............	43 724
12	71900		Titusville city...............	40 670	13	80508		Warner Robins city...............	48 804
12	71900	009	Brevard County	40 670	13	80508	153	Houston County...............	48 787
					13	80508	225	Peach County...............	17

Cities by County — Continued

State Code	Place Code	County Code	Geographic Area Name	2000 Population	State Code	Place Code	County Code	Geographic Area Name	2000 Population
					17	04013		Bartlett village................................	36 706
15			**HAWAII**..	1 211 537	17	04013	031	Cook County...................................	12 196
15	14650		Hilo CDP...	40 759	17	04013	043	DuPage County..............................	24 508
15	14650	001	Hawaii County.............................	40 759	17	04013	089	Kane County...................................	2
15	17000		Honolulu CDP..................................	371 657	17	04845		Belleville city...................................	41 410
15	17000	003	Honolulu County............................	371 657	17	04845	163	St. Clair County............................	41 410
15	23150		Kailua CDP.......................................	36 513	17	05573		Berwyn city......................................	54 016
15	23150	003	Honolulu County............................	36 513	17	05573	031	Cook County...................................	54 016
15	28250		Kaneohe CDP...................................	34 970	17	06613		Bloomington city..............................	64 808
15	28250	003	Honolulu County............................	34 970	17	06613	113	McLean County..............................	64 808
15	51050		Mililani Town CDP...........................	28 608	17	07133		Bolingbrook village...........................	56 321
15	51050	003	Honolulu County............................	28 608	17	07133	043	DuPage County..............................	1 748
					17	07133	197	Will County....................................	54 573
15	62600		Pearl City CDP................................	30 976					
15	62600	003	Honolulu County............................	30 976	17	09447		Buffalo Grove village........................	42 909
					17	09447	031	Cook County...................................	14 418
15	77750		Waimalu CDP...................................	29 371	17	09447	097	Lake County...................................	28 491
15	77750	003	Honolulu County............................	29 371					
					17	09642		Burbank city....................................	27 902
15	79700		Waipahu CDP...................................	33 108	17	09642	031	Cook County...................................	27 902
15	79700	003	Honolulu County............................	33 108					
					17	10487		Calumet City city.............................	39 071
16			**IDAHO**..	1 293 953	17	10487	031	Cook County...................................	39 071
16	08830		Boise City city.................................	185 787					
16	08830	001	Ada County....................................	185 787	17	11332		Carol Stream village.........................	40 438
					17	11332	043	DuPage County..............................	40 438
16	12250		Caldwell city....................................	25 967					
16	12250	027	Canyon County..............................	25 967	17	11358		Carpentersville village.....................	30 586
					17	11358	089	Kane County...................................	30 586
16	16750		Coeur d'Alene city...........................	34 514					
16	16750	055	Kootenai County............................	34 514	17	12385		Champaign city................................	67 518
					17	12385	019	Champaign County........................	67 518
16	39700		Idaho Falls city................................	50 730					
16	39700	019	Bonneville County.........................	50 730	17	14000		Chicago city....................................	2 896 016
					17	14000	031	Cook County...................................	2 896 014
16	46540		Lewiston city...................................	30 904	17	14000	043	DuPage County..............................	2
16	46540	069	Nez Perce County........................	30 904					
					17	14026		Chicago Heights city.......................	32 776
16	52120		Meridian city...................................	34 919	17	14026	031	Cook County...................................	32 776
16	52120	001	Ada County....................................	34 919					
					17	14351		Cicero town....................................	85 616
16	56260		Nampa city......................................	51 867	17	14351	031	Cook County...................................	85 616
16	56260	027	Canyon County..............................	51 867					
					17	17887		Crystal Lake city.............................	38 000
16	64090		Pocatello city..................................	51 466	17	17887	111	McHenry County............................	38 000
16	64090	005	Bannock County...........................	51 442					
16	64090	077	Power County................................	24	17	18563		Danville city....................................	33 904
					17	18563	183	Vermilion County..........................	33 904
16	82810		Twin Falls city.................................	34 469					
16	82810	083	Twin Falls County.........................	34 469	17	18823		Decatur city....................................	81 860
					17	18823	115	Macon County...............................	81 860
17			**ILLINOIS**..	12 419 293					
17	00243		Addison village...............................	35 914	17	19161		DeKalb city.....................................	39 018
17	00243	043	DuPage County.............................	35 914	17	19161	037	DeKalb County..............................	39 018
17	01114		Alton city..	30 496	17	19642		Des Plaines city..............................	58 720
17	01114	119	Madison County...........................	30 496	17	19642	031	Cook County...................................	58 720
17	02154		Arlington Heights village.................	76 031	17	20292		Dolton village..................................	25 614
17	02154	031	Cook County...................................	76 031	17	20292	031	Cook County...................................	25 614
17	02154	097	Lake County...................................	0					
					17	20591		Downers Grove village.....................	48 724
17	03012		Aurora city......................................	142 990	17	20591	043	DuPage County..............................	48 724
17	03012	043	DuPage County.............................	38 905					
17	03012	089	Kane County...................................	100 290	17	22255		East St. Louis city...........................	31 542
17	03012	093	Kendall County.............................	840	17	22255	163	St. Clair County............................	31 542
17	03012	197	Will County....................................	2 955					

State Code	Place Code	County Code	Geographic Area Name	2000 Population	State Code	Place Code	County Code	Geographic Area Name	2000 Population
17	23074		Elgin city	94 487	17	51089		Mount Prospect village	56 265
17	23074	031	Cook County	20 474	17	51089	031	Cook County	56 265
17	23074	089	Kane County	74 013					
					17	51349		Mundelein village	30 935
17	23256		Elk Grove Village village	34 727	17	51349	097	Lake County	30 935
17	23256	031	Cook County	34 727					
17	23256	043	DuPage County	0	17	51622		Naperville city	128 358
					17	51622	043	DuPage County	90 984
17	23620		Elmhurst city	42 762	17	51622	197	Will County	37 374
17	23620	031	Cook County	0					
17	23620	043	DuPage County	42 762	17	53000		Niles village	30 068
					17	53000	031	Cook County	30 068
17	23724		Elmwood Park village	25 405					
17	23724	031	Cook County	25 405	17	53234		Normal town	45 386
					17	53234	113	McLean County	45 386
17	24582		Evanston city	74 239					
17	24582	031	Cook County	74 239	17	53481		Northbrook village	33 435
					17	53481	031	Cook County	33 435
17	27884		Freeport city	26 443					
17	27884	177	Stephenson County	26 443	17	53559		North Chicago city	35 918
					17	53559	097	Lake County	35 918
17	28326		Galesburg city	33 706					
17	28326	095	Knox County	33 706	17	54638		Oak Forest city	28 051
					17	54638	031	Cook County	28 051
17	29730		Glendale Heights village	31 765					
17	29730	043	DuPage County	31 765	17	54820		Oak Lawn village	55 245
					17	54820	031	Cook County	55 245
17	29756		Glen Ellyn village	26 999					
17	29756	043	DuPage County	26 999	17	54885		Oak Park village	52 524
					17	54885	031	Cook County	52 524
17	29938		Glenview village	41 847					
17	29938	031	Cook County	41 847	17	56640		Orland Park village	51 077
					17	56640	031	Cook County	51 071
17	30926		Granite City city	31 301	17	56640	197	Will County	6
17	30926	119	Madison County	31 301					
					17	57225		Palatine village	65 479
17	32018		Gurnee village	28 834	17	57225	031	Cook County	65 479
17	32018	097	Lake County	28 834					
					17	57875		Park Ridge city	37 775
17	32746		Hanover Park village	38 278	17	57875	031	Cook County	37 775
17	32746	031	Cook County	20 755					
17	32746	043	DuPage County	17 523	17	58447		Pekin city	33 857
					17	58447	143	Peoria County	0
17	33383		Harvey city	30 000	17	58447	179	Tazewell County	33 857
17	33383	031	Cook County	30 000					
					17	59000		Peoria city	112 936
17	34722		Highland Park city	31 365	17	59000	143	Peoria County	112 936
17	34722	097	Lake County	31 365					
					17	62367		Quincy city	40 366
17	35411		Hoffman Estates village	49 495	17	62367	001	Adams County	40 366
17	35411	031	Cook County	49 495					
17	35411	089	Kane County	0	17	65000		Rockford city	150 115
					17	65000	201	Winnebago County	150 115
17	38570		Joliet city	106 221					
17	38570	093	Kendall County	624	17	65078		Rock Island city	39 684
17	38570	197	Will County	105 597	17	65078	161	Rock Island County	39 684
17	38934		Kankakee city	27 491	17	66040		Round Lake Beach village	25 859
17	38934	091	Kankakee County	27 491	17	66040	097	Lake County	25 859
17	42028		Lansing village	28 332	17	66703		St. Charles city	27 896
17	42028	031	Cook County	28 332	17	66703	043	DuPage County	169
					17	66703	089	Kane County	27 727
17	44407		Lombard village	42 322					
17	44407	043	DuPage County	42 322	17	68003		Schaumburg village	75 386
					17	68003	031	Cook County	75 386
17	47774		Maywood village	26 987	17	68003	043	DuPage County	0
17	47774	031	Cook County	26 987					
					17	70122		Skokie village	63 348
17	49867		Moline city	43 768	17	70122	031	Cook County	63 348
17	49867	161	Rock Island County	43 768					

Cities by County — Continued

State Code	Place Code	County Code	Geographic Area Name	2000 Population	State Code	Place Code	County Code	Geographic Area Name	2000 Population
17	72000		Springfield city	111 454	18	34114		Hobart city	25 363
17	72000	167	Sangamon County	111 454	18	34114	089	Lake County	25 363
17	73157		Streamwood village	36 407	18	36000		Indianapolis city	791 926
17	73157	031	Cook County	36 407					
17	75484		Tinley Park village	48 401	18	38358		Jeffersonville city	27 362
17	75484	031	Cook County	45 887	18	38358	019	Clark County	27 362
17	75484	197	Will County	2 514	18	40392		Kokomo city	46 113
17	77005		Urbana city	36 395	18	40392	067	Howard County	46 113
17	77005	019	Champaign County	36 395	18	40788		Lafayette city	56 397
17	79293		Waukegan city	87 901	18	40788	157	Tippecanoe County	56 397
17	79293	097	Lake County	87 901	18	42426		Lawrence city	38 915
17	81048		Wheaton city	55 416	18	42426	097	Marion County	38 915
17	81048	043	DuPage County	55 416	18	46908		Marion city	31 320
17	81087		Wheeling village	34 496	18	46908	053	Grant County	31 320
17	81087	031	Cook County	34 496	18	48528		Merrillville town	30 560
17	81087	097	Lake County	0	18	48528	089	Lake County	30 560
17	82075		Wilmette village	27 651	18	48798		Michigan City city	32 900
17	82075	031	Cook County	27 651	18	48798	091	LaPorte County	32 900
17	83245		Woodridge village	30 934	18	49932		Mishawaka city	46 557
17	83245	031	Cook County	0	18	49932	141	St. Joseph County	46 557
17	83245	043	DuPage County	30 934	18	51876		Muncie city	67 430
17	83245	197	Will County	0	18	51876	035	Delaware County	67 430
18			**INDIANA**	6 080 485	18	52326		New Albany city	37 603
18	01468		Anderson city	59 734	18	52326	043	Floyd County	37 603
18	01468	095	Madison County	59 734	18	54180		Noblesville city	28 590
18	05860		Bloomington city	69 291	18	54180	057	Hamilton County	28 590
18	05860	105	Monroe County	69 291	18	61092		Portage city	33 496
18	10342		Carmel city	37 733	18	61092	127	Porter County	33 496
18	10342	057	Hamilton County	37 733	18	64260		Richmond city	39 124
18	14734		Columbus city	39 059	18	64260	177	Wayne County	39 124
18	14734	005	Bartholomew County	39 059	18	71000		South Bend city	107 789
18	19486		East Chicago city	32 414	18	71000	141	St. Joseph County	107 789
18	19486	089	Lake County	32 414	18	75428		Terre Haute city	59 614
18	20728		Elkhart city	51 874	18	75428	167	Vigo County	59 614
18	20728	039	Elkhart County	51 874	18	78326		Valparaiso city	27 428
18	22000		Evansville city	121 582	18	78326	127	Porter County	27 428
18	22000	163	Vanderburgh County	121 582	18	82862		West Lafayette city	28 778
18	23278		Fishers town	37 835	18	82862	157	Tippecanoe County	28 778
18	23278	057	Hamilton County	37 835	19			**IOWA**	2 926 324
18	25000		Fort Wayne city	205 727	19	01855		Ames city	50 731
18	25000	003	Allen County	205 727	19	01855	169	Story County	50 731
18	27000		Gary city	102 746	19	02305		Ankeny city	27 117
18	27000	089	Lake County	102 746	19	02305	153	Polk County	27 117
18	28386		Goshen city	29 383	19	06355		Bettendorf city	31 275
18	28386	039	Elkhart County	29 383	19	06355	163	Scott County	31 275
18	29898		Greenwood city	36 037	19	09550		Burlington city	26 839
18	29898	081	Johnson County	36 037	19	09550	057	Des Moines County	26 839
18	31000		Hammond city	83 048	19	11755		Cedar Falls city	36 145
18	31000	089	Lake County	83 048	19	11755	013	Black Hawk County	36 145

State Code	Place Code	County Code	Geographic Area Name	2000 Population	State Code	Place Code	County Code	Geographic Area Name	2000 Population
19	12000		Cedar Rapids city	120 758					
19	12000	113	Linn County	120 758	20	39350		Lenexa city	40 238
					20	39350	091	Johnson County	40 238
19	14430		Clinton city	27 772					
19	14430	045	Clinton County	27 772	20	44250		Manhattan city	44 831
					20	44250	149	Pottawatomie County	3
19	16860		Council Bluffs city	58 268	20	44250	161	Riley County	44 828
19	16860	155	Pottawattamie County	58 268					
					20	52575		Olathe city	92 962
19	19000		Davenport city	98 359	20	52575	091	Johnson County	92 962
19	19000	163	Scott County	98 359					
					20	53775		Overland Park city	149 080
19	21000		Des Moines city	198 682	20	53775	091	Johnson County	149 080
19	21000	153	Polk County	198 682					
					20	62700		Salina city	45 679
19	22395		Dubuque city	57 686	20	62700	169	Saline County	45 679
19	22395	061	Dubuque County	57 686					
					20	64500		Shawnee city	47 996
19	28515		Fort Dodge city	25 136	20	64500	091	Johnson County	47 996
19	28515	187	Webster County	25 136					
					20	71000		Topeka city	122 377
19	38595		Iowa City city	62 220	20	71000	177	Shawnee County	122 377
19	38595	103	Johnson County	62 220					
					20	79000		Wichita city	344 284
19	49485		Marion city	26 294	20	79000	173	Sedgwick County	344 284
19	49485	113	Linn County	26 294					
					21			**KENTUCKY**	4 041 769
19	49755		Marshalltown city	26 009	21	08902		Bowling Green city	49 296
19	49755	127	Marshall County	26 009	21	08902	227	Warren County	49 296
19	50160		Mason City city	29 172	21	17848		Covington city	43 370
19	50160	033	Cerro Gordo County	29 172	21	17848	117	Kenton County	43 370
19	73335		Sioux City city	85 013	21	28900		Frankfort city	27 741
19	73335	149	Plymouth County	0	21	28900	073	Franklin County	27 741
19	73335	193	Woodbury County	85 013					
					21	35866		Henderson city	27 373
19	79950		Urbandale city	29 072	21	35866	101	Henderson County	27 373
19	79950	049	Dallas County	327					
19	79950	153	Polk County	28 745	21	37918		Hopkinsville city	30 089
					21	37918	047	Christian County	30 089
19	82425		Waterloo city	68 747					
19	82425	013	Black Hawk County	68 747	21	40222		Jeffersontown city	26 633
					21	40222	111	Jefferson County	26 633
19	83910		West Des Moines city	46 403					
19	83910	049	Dallas County	3 878	21	46027		Lexington-Fayette	260 512
19	83910	153	Polk County	42 525	21	46027	067	Fayette County	260 512
20			**KANSAS**	2 688 418	21	48000		Louisville city	256 231
20	18250		Dodge City city	25 176	21	48000	111	Jefferson County	256 231
20	18250	057	Ford County	25 176					
					21	58620		Owensboro city	54 067
20	21275		Emporia city	26 760	21	58620	059	Daviess County	54 067
20	21275	111	Lyon County	26 760					
					21	58836		Paducah city	26 307
20	25325		Garden City city	28 451	21	58836	145	McCracken County	26 307
20	25325	055	Finney County	28 451					
					21	65226		Richmond city	27 152
20	33625		Hutchinson city	40 787	21	65226	151	Madison County	27 152
20	33625	155	Reno County	40 787					
					22			**LOUISIANA**	4 468 976
20	36000		Kansas City city	146 866	22	00975		Alexandria city	46 342
20	36000	209	Wyandotte County	146 866	22	00975	079	Rapides Parish	46 342
20	38900		Lawrence city	80 098	22	05000		Baton Rouge city	227 818
20	38900	045	Douglas County	80 098	22	05000	033	East Baton Rouge Parish	227 818
20	39000		Leavenworth city	35 420	22	08920		Bossier City city	56 461
20	39000	103	Leavenworth County	35 420	22	08920	015	Bossier Parish	56 461
20	39075		Leawood city	27 656	22	36255		Houma city	32 393
20	39075	091	Johnson County	27 656	22	36255	109	Terrebonne Parish	32 393

State Code	Place Code	County Code	Geographic Area Name	2000 Population	State Code	Place Code	County Code	Geographic Area Name	2000 Population
					25	07000		Boston city	589 141
22	39475		Kenner city	70 517	25	07000	025	Suffolk County	589 141
22	39475	051	Jefferson Parish	70 517					
					25	09000		Brockton city	94 304
22	40735		Lafayette city	110 257	25	09000	023	Plymouth County	94 304
22	40735	055	Lafayette Parish	110 257					
					25	11000		Cambridge city	101 355
22	41155		Lake Charles city	71 757	25	11000	017	Middlesex County	101 355
22	41155	019	Calcasieu Parish	71 757					
					25	13205		Chelsea city	35 080
22	51410		Monroe city	53 107	25	13205	025	Suffolk County	35 080
22	51410	073	Ouachita Parish	53 107					
					25	13660		Chicopee city	54 653
22	54035		New Iberia city	32 623	25	13660	013	Hampden County	54 653
22	54035	045	Iberia Parish	32 623					
					25	21990		Everett city	38 037
22	55000		New Orleans city	484 674	25	21990	017	Middlesex County	38 037
22	55000	071	Orleans Parish	484 674					
					25	23000		Fall River city	91 938
22	70000		Shreveport city	200 145	25	23000	005	Bristol County	91 938
22	70000	015	Bossier Parish	734					
22	70000	017	Caddo Parish	199 411	25	23875		Fitchburg city	39 102
					25	23875	027	Worcester County	39 102
22	70805		Slidell city	25 695					
22	70805	103	St. Tammany Parish	25 695	25	25100		Franklin city	29 560
					25	25100	021	Norfolk County	29 560
23			**MAINE**	1 274 923					
23	02795		Bangor city	31 473	25	26150		Gloucester city	30 273
23	02795	019	Penobscot County	31 473	25	26150	009	Essex County	30 273
					25	29405		Haverhill city	58 969
23	38740		Lewiston city	35 690	25	29405	009	Essex County	58 969
23	38740	001	Androscoggin County	35 690					
					25	30840		Holyoke city	39 838
23	60545		Portland city	64 249	25	30840	013	Hampden County	39 838
23	60545	005	Cumberland County	64 249					
					25	34550		Lawrence city	72 043
24			**MARYLAND**	5 296 486	25	34550	009	Essex County	72 043
24	01600		Annapolis city	35 838					
24	01600	003	Anne Arundel County	35 838	25	35075		Leominster city	41 303
					25	35075	027	Worcester County	41 303
24	04000		Baltimore city	651 154					
24	04000	510	Baltimore city	651 154	25	37000		Lowell city	105 167
					25	37000	017	Middlesex County	105 167
24	08775		Bowie city	50 269					
24	08775	033	Prince George's County	50 269	25	37490		Lynn city	89 050
					25	37490	009	Essex County	89 050
24	30325		Frederick city	52 767					
24	30325	021	Frederick County	52 767	25	37875		Malden city	56 340
					25	37875	017	Middlesex County	56 340
24	31175		Gaithersburg city	52 613					
24	31175	031	Montgomery County	52 613	25	38715		Marlborough city	36 255
					25	38715	017	Middlesex County	36 255
24	36075		Hagerstown city	36 687					
24	36075	043	Washington County	36 687	25	39835		Medford city	55 765
					25	39835	017	Middlesex County	55 765
24	67675		Rockville city	47 388					
24	67675	031	Montgomery County	47 388	25	40115		Melrose city	27 134
					25	40115	017	Middlesex County	27 134
25			**MASSACHUSETTS**	6 349 097					
25	00765		Agawam city	28 144	25	40710		Methuen city	43 789
25	00765	013	Hampden County	28 144	25	40710	009	Essex County	43 789
25	02690		Attleboro city	42 068	25	45000		New Bedford city	93 768
25	02690	005	Bristol County	42 068	25	45000	005	Bristol County	93 768
25	03600		Barnstable Town city	47 821	25	45560		Newton city	83 829
25	03600	001	Barnstable County	47 821	25	45560	017	Middlesex County	83 829
25	05595		Beverly city	39 862	25	46330		Northampton city	28 978
25	05595	009	Essex County	39 862	25	46330	015	Hampshire County	28 978

State Code	Place Code	County Code	Geographic Area Name	2000 Population	State Code	Place Code	County Code	Geographic Area Name	2000 Population
25	52490		Peabody city	48 129	26	29000		Flint city	124 943
25	52490	009	Essex County	48 129	26	29000	049	Genesee County	124 943
25	53960		Pittsfield city	45 793	26	31420		Garden City city	30 047
25	53960	003	Berkshire County	45 793	26	31420	163	Wayne County	30 047
25	55745		Quincy city	88 025	26	34000		Grand Rapids city	197 800
25	55745	021	Norfolk County	88 025	26	34000	081	Kent County	197 800
25	56585		Revere city	47 283	26	38640		Holland city	35 048
25	56585	025	Suffolk County	47 283	26	38640	005	Allegan County	7 202
					26	38640	139	Ottawa County	27 846
25	59105		Salem city	40 407					
25	59105	009	Essex County	40 407	26	40680		Inkster city	30 115
					26	40680	163	Wayne County	30 115
25	62535		Somerville city	77 478					
25	62535	017	Middlesex County	77 478	26	41420		Jackson city	36 316
					26	41420	075	Jackson County	36 316
25	67000		Springfield city	152 082					
25	67000	013	Hampden County	152 082	26	42160		Kalamazoo city	77 145
					26	42160	077	Kalamazoo County	77 145
25	69170		Taunton city	55 976					
25	69170	005	Bristol County	55 976	26	42820		Kentwood city	45 255
					26	42820	081	Kent County	45 255
25	72600		Waltham city	59 226					
25	72600	017	Middlesex County	59 226	26	46000		Lansing city	119 128
					26	46000	045	Eaton County	4 807
25	76030		Westfield city	40 072	26	46000	065	Ingham County	114 321
25	76030	013	Hampden County	40 072					
					26	47800		Lincoln Park city	40 008
25	81035		Woburn city	37 258	26	47800	163	Wayne County	40 008
25	81035	017	Middlesex County	37 258					
					26	49000		Livonia city	100 545
25	82000		Worcester city	172 648	26	49000	163	Wayne County	100 545
25	82000	027	Worcester County	172 648					
					26	50560		Madison Heights city	31 101
26			**MICHIGAN**	9 938 444	26	50560	125	Oakland County	31 101
26	01380		Allen Park city	29 376					
26	01380	163	Wayne County	29 376	26	53780		Midland city	41 685
					26	53780	017	Bay County	222
26	03000		Ann Arbor city	114 024	26	53780	111	Midland County	41 463
26	03000	161	Washtenaw County	114 024					
					26	56020		Mount Pleasant city	25 946
26	05920		Battle Creek city	53 364	26	56020	073	Isabella County	25 946
26	05920	025	Calhoun County	53 364					
					26	56320		Muskegon city	40 105
26	06020		Bay City city	36 817	26	56320	121	Muskegon County	40 105
26	06020	017	Bay County	36 817					
					26	59440		Novi city	47 386
26	12060		Burton city	30 308	26	59440	125	Oakland County	47 386
26	12060	049	Genesee County	30 308					
					26	59920		Oak Park city	29 793
26	21000		Dearborn city	97 775	26	59920	125	Oakland County	29 793
26	21000	163	Wayne County	97 775					
					26	65440		Pontiac city	66 337
26	21020		Dearborn Heights city	58 264	26	65440	125	Oakland County	66 337
26	21020	163	Wayne County	58 264					
					26	65560		Portage city	44 897
26	22000		Detroit city	951 270	26	65560	077	Kalamazoo County	44 897
26	22000	163	Wayne County	951 270					
					26	65820		Port Huron city	32 338
26	24120		East Lansing city	46 525	26	65820	147	St. Clair County	32 338
26	24120	037	Clinton County	34					
26	24120	065	Ingham County	46 491	26	69035		Rochester Hills city	68 825
					26	69035	125	Oakland County	68 825
26	24290		Eastpointe city	34 077					
26	24290	099	Macomb County	34 077	26	69800		Roseville city	48 129
					26	69800	099	Macomb County	48 129
26	27440		Farmington Hills city	82 111					
26	27440	125	Oakland County	82 111	26	70040		Royal Oak city	60 062
					26	70040	125	Oakland County	60 062

State Code	Place Code	County Code	Geographic Area Name	2000 Population	State Code	Place Code	County Code	Geographic Area Name	2000 Population
26	70520		Saginaw city	61 799	27	18188		Edina city	47 425
26	70520	145	Saginaw County	61 799	27	18188	053	Hennepin County	47 425
26	70760		St. Clair Shores city	63 096	27	22814		Fridley city	27 449
26	70760	099	Macomb County	63 096	27	22814	003	Anoka County	27 449
26	74900		Southfield city	78 296	27	31076		Inver Grove Heights city	29 751
26	74900	125	Oakland County	78 296	27	31076	037	Dakota County	29 751
26	74960		Southgate city	30 136	27	35180		Lakeville city	43 128
26	74960	163	Wayne County	30 136	27	35180	037	Dakota County	43 128
26	76460		Sterling Heights city	124 471	27	39878		Mankato city	32 427
26	76460	099	Macomb County	124 471	27	39878	013	Blue Earth County	32 427
					27	39878	079	Le Sueur County	0
26	79000		Taylor city	65 868	27	39878	103	Nicollet County	0
26	79000	163	Wayne County	65 868					
					27	40166		Maple Grove city	50 365
26	80700		Troy city	80 959	27	40166	053	Hennepin County	50 365
26	80700	125	Oakland County	80 959					
					27	40382		Maplewood city	34 947
26	84000		Warren city	138 247	27	40382	123	Ramsey County	34 947
26	84000	099	Macomb County	138 247					
					27	43000		Minneapolis city	382 618
26	86000		Westland city	86 602	27	43000	053	Hennepin County	382 618
26	86000	163	Wayne County	86 602					
					27	43252		Minnetonka city	51 301
26	88900		Wyandotte city	28 006	27	43252	053	Hennepin County	51 301
26	88900	163	Wayne County	28 006					
					27	43864		Moorhead city	32 177
26	88940		Wyoming city	69 368	27	43864	027	Clay County	32 177
26	88940	081	Kent County	69 368					
					27	47680		Oakdale city	26 653
27			**MINNESOTA**	4 919 479	27	47680	163	Washington County	26 653
27	01486		Andover city	26 588					
27	01486	003	Anoka County	26 588	27	51730		Plymouth city	65 894
					27	51730	053	Hennepin County	65 894
27	01900		Apple Valley city	45 527					
27	01900	037	Dakota County	45 527	27	54214		Richfield city	34 439
					27	54214	053	Hennepin County	34 439
27	06382		Blaine city	44 942					
27	06382	003	Anoka County	44 942	27	54880		Rochester city	85 806
27	06382	123	Ramsey County	0	27	54880	109	Olmsted County	85 806
27	06616		Bloomington city	85 172	27	55852		Roseville city	33 690
27	06616	053	Hennepin County	85 172	27	55852	123	Ramsey County	33 690
27	07948		Brooklyn Center city	29 172	27	56896		St. Cloud city	59 107
27	07948	053	Hennepin County	29 172	27	56896	009	Benton County	6 391
					27	56896	141	Sherburne County	5 982
27	07966		Brooklyn Park city	67 388	27	56896	145	Stearns County	46 734
27	07966	053	Hennepin County	67 388					
					27	57220		St. Louis Park city	44 126
27	08794		Burnsville city	60 220	27	57220	053	Hennepin County	44 126
27	08794	037	Dakota County	60 220					
					27	58000		St. Paul city	287 151
27	13114		Coon Rapids city	61 607	27	58000	123	Ramsey County	287 151
27	13114	003	Anoka County	61 607					
					27	59998		Shoreview city	25 924
27	13456		Cottage Grove city	30 582	27	59998	123	Ramsey County	25 924
27	13456	163	Washington County	30 582					
					27	71032		Winona city	27 069
27	17000		Duluth city	86 918	27	71032	169	Winona County	27 069
27	17000	137	St. Louis County	86 918					
					27	71428		Woodbury city	46 463
27	17288		Eagan city	63 557	27	71428	163	Washington County	46 463
27	17288	037	Dakota County	63 557					
					28			**MISSISSIPPI**	2 844 658
27	18116		Eden Prairie city	54 901	28	06220		Biloxi city	50 644
27	18116	053	Hennepin County	54 901	28	06220	047	Harrison County	50 644

State Code	Place Code	County Code	Geographic Area Name	2000 Population	State Code	Place Code	County Code	Geographic Area Name	2000 Population
28	15380		Columbus city	25 944	29	38000		Kansas City city	441 545
28	15380	087	Lowndes County	25 944	29	38000	037	Cass County	104
					29	38000	047	Clay County	84 009
28	29180		Greenville city	41 633	29	38000	095	Jackson County	322 806
28	29180	151	Washington County	41 633	29	38000	165	Platte County	34 626
28	29700		Gulfport city	71 127	29	39044		Kirkwood city	27 324
28	29700	047	Harrison County	71 127	29	39044	189	St. Louis County	27 324
28	31020		Hattiesburg city	44 779	29	41348		Lee's Summit city	70 700
28	31020	035	Forrest County	42 475	29	41348	037	Cass County	1 180
28	31020	073	Lamar County	2 304	29	41348	095	Jackson County	69 520
28	36000		Jackson city	184 256	29	42032		Liberty city	26 232
28	36000	049	Hinds County	183 723	29	42032	047	Clay County	26 232
28	36000	089	Madison County	533					
28	36000	121	Rankin County	0	29	46586		Maryland Heights city	25 756
					29	46586	189	St. Louis County	25 756
28	46640		Meridian city	39 968					
28	46640	075	Lauderdale County	39 968	29	54074		O'Fallon city	46 169
					29	54074	183	St. Charles County	46 169
28	55360		Pascagoula city	26 200					
28	55360	059	Jackson County	26 200	29	60788		Raytown city	30 388
					29	60788	095	Jackson County	30 388
28	69280		Southaven city	28 977					
28	69280	033	DeSoto County	28 977	29	64082		St. Charles city	60 321
					29	64082	183	St. Charles County	60 321
28	74840		Tupelo city	34 211					
28	74840	081	Lee County	34 211	29	64550		St. Joseph city	73 990
					29	64550	021	Buchanan County	73 990
28	76720		Vicksburg city	26 407					
28	76720	149	Warren County	26 407	29	65000		St. Louis city	348 189
					29	65000	510	St. Louis city	348 189
29			**MISSOURI**	5 595 211					
29	03160		Ballwin city	31 283	29	65126		St. Peters city	51 381
29	03160	189	St. Louis County	31 283	29	65126	183	St. Charles County	51 381
29	06652		Blue Springs city	48 080	29	70000		Springfield city	151 580
29	06652	095	Jackson County	48 080	29	70000	043	Christian County	4
					29	70000	077	Greene County	151 576
29	11242		Cape Girardeau city	35 349					
29	11242	031	Cape Girardeau County	35 349	29	75220		University City city	37 428
29	11242	201	Scott County	0	29	75220	189	St. Louis County	37 428
29	13600		Chesterfield city	46 802	29	79820		Wildwood city	32 884
29	13600	189	St. Louis County	46 802	29	79820	189	St. Louis County	32 884
29	15670		Columbia city	84 531	30			**MONTANA**	902 195
29	15670	019	Boone County	84 531	30	06550		Billings city	89 847
					30	06550	111	Yellowstone County	89 847
29	24778		Florissant city	50 497					
29	24778	189	St. Louis County	50 497	30	08950		Bozeman city	27 509
					30	08950	031	Gallatin County	27 509
29	27190		Gladstone city	26 365					
29	27190	047	Clay County	26 365	30	11390		Butte-Silver Bow	34 606
29	31276		Hazelwood city	26 206	30	32800		Great Falls city	56 690
29	31276	189	St. Louis County	26 206	30	32800	013	Cascade County	56 690
29	35000		Independence city	113 288	30	35600		Helena city	25 780
29	35000	047	Clay County	0	30	35600	049	Lewis and Clark County	25 780
29	35000	095	Jackson County	113 288					
					30	50200		Missoula city	57 053
29	37000		Jefferson City city	39 636	30	50200	063	Missoula County	57 053
29	37000	027	Callaway County	25					
29	37000	051	Cole County	39 611	31			**NEBRASKA**	1 711 263
					31	03950		Bellevue city	44 382
29	37592		Joplin city	45 504	31	03950	153	Sarpy County	44 382
29	37592	097	Jasper County	40 433					
29	37592	145	Newton County	5 071	31	17670		Fremont city	25 174
					31	17670	053	Dodge County	25 174

State Code	Place Code	County Code	Geographic Area Name	2000 Population	State Code	Place Code	County Code	Geographic Area Name	2000 Population
31	19595		Grand Island city	42 940	34	22470		Fair Lawn borough	31 637
31	19595	079	Hall County	42 940	34	22470	003	Bergen County	31 637
31	25055		Kearney city	27 431	34	24420		Fort Lee borough	35 461
31	25055	019	Buffalo County	27 431	34	24420	003	Bergen County	35 461
31	28000		Lincoln city	225 581	34	25770		Garfield city	29 786
31	28000	109	Lancaster County	225 581	34	25770	003	Bergen County	29 786
31	37000		Omaha city	390 007	34	28680		Hackensack city	42 677
31	37000	055	Douglas County	390 007	34	28680	003	Bergen County	42 677
32			**NEVADA**	1 998 257	34	32250		Hoboken city	38 577
32	09700		Carson City	52 457	34	32250	017	Hudson County	38 577
32	09700	510	Carson City	52 457					
					34	36000		Jersey City city	240 055
32	31900		Henderson city	175 381	34	36000	017	Hudson County	240 055
32	31900	003	Clark County	175 381					
					34	36510		Kearny town	40 513
32	40000		Las Vegas city	478 434	34	36510	017	Hudson County	40 513
32	40000	003	Clark County	478 434					
					34	40350		Linden city	39 394
32	51800		North Las Vegas city	115 488	34	40350	039	Union County	39 394
32	51800	003	Clark County	115 488					
					34	41310		Long Branch city	31 340
32	60600		Reno city	180 480	34	41310	025	Monmouth County	31 340
32	60600	031	Washoe County	180 480					
					34	46680		Millville city	26 847
32	68400		Sparks city	66 346	34	46680	011	Cumberland County	26 847
32	68400	031	Washoe County	66 346					
					34	51000		Newark city	273 546
33			**NEW HAMPSHIRE**	1 235 786	34	51000	013	Essex County	273 546
33	14200		Concord city	40 687					
33	14200	013	Merrimack County	40 687	34	51210		New Brunswick city	48 573
					34	51210	023	Middlesex County	48 573
33	18820		Dover city	26 884					
33	18820	017	Strafford County	26 884	34	55950		Paramus borough	25 737
					34	55950	003	Bergen County	25 737
33	45140		Manchester city	107 006					
33	45140	011	Hillsborough County	107 006	34	56550		Passaic city	67 861
					34	56550	031	Passaic County	67 861
33	50260		Nashua city	86 605					
33	50260	011	Hillsborough County	86 605	34	57000		Paterson city	149 222
					34	57000	031	Passaic County	149 222
33	65140		Rochester city	28 461					
33	65140	017	Strafford County	28 461	34	58200		Perth Amboy city	47 303
					34	58200	023	Middlesex County	47 303
34			**NEW JERSEY**	8 414 350					
34	02080		Atlantic City city	40 517	34	59190		Plainfield city	47 829
34	02080	001	Atlantic County	40 517	34	59190	039	Union County	47 829
34	03580		Bayonne city	61 842	34	61530		Rahway city	26 500
34	03580	017	Hudson County	61 842	34	61530	039	Union County	26 500
34	05170		Bergenfield borough	26 247	34	65790		Sayreville borough	40 377
34	05170	003	Bergen County	26 247	34	65790	023	Middlesex County	40 377
34	10000		Camden city	79 904	34	74000		Trenton city	85 403
34	10000	007	Camden County	79 904	34	74000	021	Mercer County	85 403
34	13690		Clifton city	78 672	34	74630		Union City city	67 088
34	13690	031	Passaic County	78 672	34	74630	017	Hudson County	67 088
34	19390		East Orange city	69 824	34	76070		Vineland city	56 271
34	19390	013	Essex County	69 824	34	76070	011	Cumberland County	56 271
34	21000		Elizabeth city	120 568	34	79040		Westfield town	29 644
34	21000	039	Union County	120 568	34	79040	039	Union County	29 644
34	21480		Englewood city	26 203	34	79610		West New York town	45 768
34	21480	003	Bergen County	26 203	34	79610	017	Hudson County	45 768

State Code	Place Code	County Code	Geographic Area Name	2000 Population
35			**NEW MEXICO**	1 819 046
35	01780		Alamogordo city	35 582
35	01780	035	Otero County	35 582
35	02000		Albuquerque city	448 607
35	02000	001	Bernalillo County	448 607
35	12150		Carlsbad city	25 625
35	12150	015	Eddy County	25 625
35	16420		Clovis city	32 667
35	16420	009	Curry County	32 667
35	25800		Farmington city	37 844
35	25800	045	San Juan County	37 844
35	32520		Hobbs city	28 657
35	32520	025	Lea County	28 657
35	39380		Las Cruces city	74 267
35	39380	013	Dona Ana County	74 267
35	63460		Rio Rancho city	51 765
35	63460	001	Bernalillo County	0
35	63460	043	Sandoval County	51 765
35	64930		Roswell city	45 293
35	64930	005	Chaves County	45 293
35	70500		Santa Fe city	62 203
35	70500	049	Santa Fe County	62 203
36			**NEW YORK**	18 976 457
36	01000		Albany city	95 658
36	01000	001	Albany County	95 658
36	03078		Auburn city	28 574
36	03078	011	Cayuga County	28 574
36	06607		Binghamton city	47 380
36	06607	007	Broome County	47 380
36	11000		Buffalo city	292 648
36	11000	029	Erie County	292 648
36	24229		Elmira city	30 940
36	24229	015	Chemung County	30 940
36	27485		Freeport village	43 783
36	27485	059	Nassau County	43 783
36	29113		Glen Cove city	26 622
36	29113	059	Nassau County	26 622
36	33139		Hempstead village	56 554
36	33139	059	Nassau County	56 554
36	38077		Ithaca city	29 287
36	38077	109	Tompkins County	29 287
36	38264		Jamestown city	31 730
36	38264	013	Chautauqua County	31 730
36	42554		Lindenhurst village	27 819
36	42554	103	Suffolk County	27 819
36	43335		Long Beach city	35 462
36	43335	059	Nassau County	35 462
36	47042		Middletown city	25 388
36	47042	071	Orange County	25 388
36	49121		Mount Vernon city	68 381
36	49121	119	Westchester County	68 381
36	50034		Newburgh city	28 259
36	50034	071	Orange County	28 259
36	50617		New Rochelle city	72 182
36	50617	119	Westchester County	72 182
36	51000		New York city	8008 278
36	51000	005	Bronx County	1332 650
36	51000	047	Kings County	2465 326
36	51000	061	New York County	1537 195
36	51000	081	Queens County	2229 379
36	51000	085	Richmond County	443 728
36	51055		Niagara Falls city	55 593
36	51055	063	Niagara County	55 593
36	53682		North Tonawanda city	33 262
36	53682	063	Niagara County	33 262
36	59223		Port Chester village	27 867
36	59223	119	Westchester County	27 867
36	59641		Poughkeepsie city	29 871
36	59641	027	Dutchess County	29 871
36	63000		Rochester city	219 773
36	63000	055	Monroe County	219 773
36	63418		Rome city	34 950
36	63418	065	Oneida County	34 950
36	65255		Saratoga Springs city	26 186
36	65255	091	Saratoga County	26 186
36	65508		Schenectady city	61 821
36	65508	093	Schenectady County	61 821
36	70420		Spring Valley village	25 464
36	70420	087	Rockland County	25 464
36	73000		Syracuse city	147 306
36	73000	067	Onondaga County	147 306
36	75484		Troy city	49 170
36	75484	083	Rensselaer County	49 170
36	76540		Utica city	60 651
36	76540	065	Oneida County	60 651
36	76705		Valley Stream village	36 368
36	76705	059	Nassau County	36 368
36	78608		Watertown city	26 705
36	78608	045	Jefferson County	26 705
36	81677		White Plains city	53 077
36	81677	119	Westchester County	53 077
36	84000		Yonkers city	196 086
36	84000	119	Westchester County	196 086
37			**NORTH CAROLINA**	8 049 313
37	02140		Asheville city	68 889
37	02140	021	Buncombe County	68 889
37	09060		Burlington city	44 917
37	09060	001	Alamance County	44 917

State Code	Place Code	County Code	Geographic Area Name	2000 Population	State Code	Place Code	County Code	Geographic Area Name	2000 Population
37	10740		Cary town	94 536	37	75000		Winston-Salem city	185 776
37	10740	037	Chatham County	19	37	75000	067	Forsyth County	185 776
37	10740	183	Wake County	94 517					
					38			**NORTH DAKOTA**	642 200
37	11800		Chapel Hill town	48 715	38	07200		Bismarck city	55 532
37	11800	063	Durham County	1 917	38	07200	015	Burleigh County	55 532
37	11800	135	Orange County	46 798					
					38	25700		Fargo city	90 599
37	12000		Charlotte city	540 828	38	25700	017	Cass County	90 599
37	12000	119	Mecklenburg County	540 828					
					38	32060		Grand Forks city	49 321
37	14100		Concord city	55 977	38	32060	035	Grand Forks County	49 321
37	14100	025	Cabarrus County	55 977					
					38	53380		Minot city	36 567
37	19000		Durham city	187 035	38	53380	101	Ward County	36 567
37	19000	063	Durham County	186 996					
37	19000	135	Orange County	39	39			**OHIO**	11 353 140
37	19000	183	Wake County	0	39	01000		Akron city	217 074
					39	01000	153	Summit County	217 074
37	22920		Fayetteville city	121 015					
37	22920	051	Cumberland County	121 015	39	03828		Barberton city	27 899
					39	03828	153	Summit County	27 899
37	25580		Gastonia city	66 277					
37	25580	071	Gaston County	66 277	39	04720		Beavercreek city	37 984
					39	04720	057	Greene County	37 984
37	26880		Goldsboro city	39 043					
37	26880	191	Wayne County	39 043	39	07972		Bowling Green city	29 636
					39	07972	173	Wood County	29 636
37	28000		Greensboro city	223 891					
37	28000	081	Guilford County	223 891	39	09680		Brunswick city	33 388
					39	09680	103	Medina County	33 388
37	28080		Greenville city	60 476					
37	28080	147	Pitt County	60 476	39	12000		Canton city	80 806
					39	12000	151	Stark County	80 806
37	31060		Hickory city	37 222					
37	31060	023	Burke County	63	39	15000		Cincinnati city	331 285
37	31060	027	Caldwell County	14	39	15000	061	Hamilton County	331 285
37	31060	035	Catawba County	37 145					
					39	16000		Cleveland city	478 403
37	31400		High Point city	85 839	39	16000	035	Cuyahoga County	478 403
37	31400	057	Davidson County	1 163					
37	31400	067	Forsyth County	6	39	16014		Cleveland Heights city	49 958
37	31400	081	Guilford County	84 656	39	16014	035	Cuyahoga County	49 958
37	31400	151	Randolph County	14					
					39	18000		Columbus city	711 470
37	34200		Jacksonville city	66 715	39	18000	041	Delaware County	1 891
37	34200	133	Onslow County	66 715	39	18000	045	Fairfield County	7 447
					39	18000	049	Franklin County	702 132
37	35200		Kannapolis city	36 910					
37	35200	025	Cabarrus County	27 890	39	19778		Cuyahoga Falls city	49 374
37	35200	159	Rowan County	9 020	39	19778	153	Summit County	49 374
37	43920		Monroe city	26 228	39	21000		Dayton city	166 179
37	43920	179	Union County	26 228	39	21000	113	Montgomery County	166 179
37	55000		Raleigh city	276 093	39	21434		Delaware city	25 243
37	55000	063	Durham County	0	39	21434	041	Delaware County	25 243
37	55000	183	Wake County	276 093					
					39	22694		Dublin city	31 392
37	57500		Rocky Mount city	55 893	39	22694	041	Delaware County	4 283
37	57500	065	Edgecombe County	17 297	39	22694	049	Franklin County	27 087
37	57500	127	Nash County	38 596	39	22694	159	Union County	22
37	58860		Salisbury city	26 462	39	23380		East Cleveland city	27 217
37	58860	159	Rowan County	26 462	39	23380	035	Cuyahoga County	27 217
37	74440		Wilmington city	75 838	39	25256		Elyria city	55 953
37	74440	129	New Hanover County	75 838	39	25256	093	Lorain County	55 953
37	74540		Wilson city	44 405	39	25704		Euclid city	52 717
37	74540	195	Wilson County	44 405	39	25704	035	Cuyahoga County	52 717

State Code	Place Code	County Code	Geographic Area Name	2000 Population	State Code	Place Code	County Code	Geographic Area Name	2000 Population
39	25914		Fairborn city	32 052					
39	25914	057	Greene County	32 052	39	57008		North Royalton city	28 648
					39	57008	035	Cuyahoga County	28 648
39	25970		Fairfield city	42 097					
39	25970	017	Butler County	42 097	39	61000		Parma city	85 655
39	25970	061	Hamilton County	0	39	61000	035	Cuyahoga County	85 655
39	27048		Findlay city	38 967	39	66390		Reynoldsburg city	32 069
39	27048	063	Hancock County	38 967	39	66390	045	Fairfield County	0
					39	66390	049	Franklin County	26 388
39	29106		Gahanna city	32 636	39	66390	089	Licking County	5 681
39	29106	049	Franklin County	32 636					
					39	70380		Sandusky city	27 844
39	29428		Garfield Heights city	30 734	39	70380	043	Erie County	27 844
39	29428	035	Cuyahoga County	30 734					
					39	71682		Shaker Heights city	29 405
39	32592		Grove City city	27 075	39	71682	035	Cuyahoga County	29 405
39	32592	049	Franklin County	27 075					
					39	74118		Springfield city	65 358
39	33012		Hamilton city	60 690	39	74118	023	Clark County	65 358
39	33012	017	Butler County	60 690					
					39	74944		Stow city	32 139
39	36610		Huber Heights city	38 212	39	74944	153	Summit County	32 139
39	36610	109	Miami County	35					
39	36610	113	Montgomery County	38 177	39	75098		Strongsville city	43 858
					39	75098	035	Cuyahoga County	43 858
39	39872		Kent city	27 906					
39	39872	133	Portage County	27 906	39	77000		Toledo city	313 619
					39	77000	095	Lucas County	313 619
39	40040		Kettering city	57 502					
39	40040	057	Greene County	0	39	77504		Trotwood city	27 420
39	40040	113	Montgomery County	57 502	39	77504	113	Montgomery County	27 420
39	41664		Lakewood city	56 646	39	79002		Upper Arlington city	33 686
39	41664	035	Cuyahoga County	56 646	39	79002	049	Franklin County	33 686
39	41720		Lancaster city	35 335	39	80892		Warren city	46 832
39	41720	045	Fairfield County	35 335	39	80892	155	Trumbull County	46 832
39	43554		Lima city	40 081	39	83342		Westerville city	35 318
39	43554	003	Allen County	40 081	39	83342	041	Delaware County	5 900
					39	83342	049	Franklin County	29 418
39	44856		Lorain city	68 652					
39	44856	093	Lorain County	68 652	39	83622		Westlake city	31 719
					39	83622	035	Cuyahoga County	31 719
39	47138		Mansfield city	49 346					
39	47138	139	Richland County	49 346	39	88000		Youngstown city	82 026
					39	88000	099	Mahoning County	82 026
39	47306		Maple Heights city	26 156	39	88000	155	Trumbull County	0
39	47306	035	Cuyahoga County	26 156					
					39	88084		Zanesville city	25 586
39	47754		Marion city	35 318	39	88084	119	Muskingum County	25 586
39	47754	101	Marion County	35 318					
					40			**OKLAHOMA**	3 450 654
39	48244		Massillon city	31 325	40	04450		Bartlesville city	34 748
39	48244	151	Stark County	31 325	40	04450	113	Osage County	2
					40	04450	147	Washington County	34 746
39	48790		Medina city	25 139					
39	48790	103	Medina County	25 139	40	09050		Broken Arrow city	74 859
					40	09050	143	Tulsa County	67 791
39	49056		Mentor city	50 278	40	09050	145	Wagoner County	7 068
39	49056	085	Lake County	50 278					
					40	23200		Edmond city	68 315
39	49840		Middletown city	51 605	40	23200	109	Oklahoma County	68 315
39	49840	017	Butler County	49 574					
39	49840	165	Warren County	2 031	40	23950		Enid city	47 045
					40	23950	047	Garfield County	47 045
39	54040		Newark city	46 279					
39	54040	089	Licking County	46 279	40	41850		Lawton city	92 757
					40	41850	031	Comanche County	92 757
39	56882		North Olmsted city	34 113					
39	56882	035	Cuyahoga County	34 113					

Cities by County — Continued

State Code	Place Code	County Code	Geographic Area Name	2000 Population	State Code	Place Code	County Code	Geographic Area Name	2000 Population
40	48350		Midwest City city	54 088	41	59000		Portland city	529 121
40	48350	109	Oklahoma County	54 088	41	59000	005	Clackamas County	747
					41	59000	051	Multnomah County	526 986
40	49200		Moore city	41 138	41	59000	067	Washington County	1 388
40	49200	027	Cleveland County	41 138					
					41	64900		Salem city	136 924
40	50050		Muskogee city	38 310	41	64900	047	Marion County	119 040
40	50050	101	Muskogee County	38 310	41	64900	053	Polk County	17 884
40	52500		Norman city	95 694					
40	52500	027	Cleveland County	95 694	41	69600		Springfield city	52 864
					41	69600	039	Lane County	52 864
40	55000		Oklahoma City city	506 132					
40	55000	017	Canadian County	26 311	41	73650		Tigard city	41 223
40	55000	027	Cleveland County	47 271	41	73650	067	Washington County	41 223
40	55000	109	Oklahoma County	432 498					
40	55000	125	Pottawatomie County	52	42			**PENNSYLVANIA**	12 281 054
					42	02000		Allentown city	106 632
40	59850		Ponca City city	25 919	42	02000	077	Lehigh County	106 632
40	59850	071	Kay County	25 919					
40	59850	113	Osage County	0	42	02184		Altoona city	49 523
					42	02184	013	Blair County	49 523
40	66800		Shawnee city	28 692					
40	66800	125	Pottawatomie County	28 692	42	06064		Bethel Park borough	33 556
					42	06064	003	Allegheny County	33 556
40	70300		Stillwater city	39 065					
40	70300	119	Payne County	39 065	42	06088		Bethlehem city	71 329
					42	06088	077	Lehigh County	19 029
40	75000		Tulsa city	393 049	42	06088	095	Northampton County	52 300
40	75000	113	Osage County	5 630					
40	75000	131	Rogers County	0	42	13208		Chester city	36 854
40	75000	143	Tulsa County	387 419	42	13208	045	Delaware County	36 854
41			**OREGON**	3 421 399	42	21648		Easton city	26 263
41	01000		Albany city	40 852	42	21648	095	Northampton County	26 263
41	01000	003	Benton County	5 104					
41	01000	043	Linn County	35 748	42	24000		Erie city	103 717
					42	24000	049	Erie County	103 717
41	05350		Beaverton city	76 129					
41	05350	067	Washington County	76 129	42	32800		Harrisburg city	48 950
					42	32800	043	Dauphin County	48 950
41	05800		Bend city	52 029					
41	05800	017	Deschutes County	52 029	42	41216		Lancaster city	56 348
					42	41216	071	Lancaster County	56 348
41	15800		Corvallis city	49 322					
41	15800	003	Benton County	49 322	42	52330		Municipality of Monroeville borough	29 349
41	23850		Eugene city	137 893	42	52330	003	Allegheny County	29 349
41	23850	039	Lane County	137 893					
					42	53368		New Castle city	26 309
41	31250		Gresham city	90 205	42	53368	073	Lawrence County	26 309
41	31250	051	Multnomah County	90 205					
					42	54656		Norristown borough	31 282
41	34100		Hillsboro city	70 186	42	54656	091	Montgomery County	31 282
41	34100	067	Washington County	70 186					
					42	60000		Philadelphia city	1 517 550
41	38500		Keizer city	32 203	42	60000	101	Philadelphia County	1 517 550
41	38500	047	Marion County	32 203					
					42	61000		Pittsburgh city	334 563
41	40550		Lake Oswego city	35 278	42	61000	003	Allegheny County	334 563
41	40550	005	Clackamas County	32 989					
41	40550	051	Multnomah County	2 274	42	61536		Plum borough	26 940
41	40550	067	Washington County	15	42	61536	003	Allegheny County	26 940
41	45000		McMinnville city	26 499	42	63624		Reading city	81 207
41	45000	071	Yamhill County	26 499	42	63624	011	Berks County	81 207
41	47000		Medford city	63 154	42	69000		Scranton city	76 415
41	47000	029	Jackson County	63 154	42	69000	069	Lackawanna County	76 415
41	55200		Oregon City city	25 754	42	73808		State College borough	38 420
41	55200	005	Clackamas County	25 754	42	73808	027	Centre County	38 420

E-22

Appendix E

State Code	Place Code	County Code	Geographic Area Name	2000 Population	State Code	Place Code	County Code	Geographic Area Name	2000 Population
42	85152		Wilkes-Barre city	43 123	45	70270		Summerville town	27 752
42	85152	079	Luzerne County	43 123	45	70270	015	Berkeley County	945
					45	70270	019	Charleston County	20
42	85312		Williamsport city	30 706	45	70270	035	Dorchester County	26 787
42	85312	081	Lycoming County	30 706					
					45	70405		Sumter city	39 643
42	87048		York city............................	40 862	45	70405	085	Sumter County........................	39 643
42	87048	133	York County	40 862					
					46			**SOUTH DAKOTA**	754 844
44			**RHODE ISLAND**........................	1 048 319	46	52980		Rapid City city	59 607
44	19180		Cranston city	79 269	46	52980	103	Pennington County	59 607
44	19180	007	Providence County	79 269					
					46	59020		Sioux Falls city	123 975
44	22960		East Providence city.................	48 688	46	59020	083	Lincoln County	6 620
44	22960	007	Providence County	48 688	46	59020	099	Minnehaha County.....................	117 355
44	49960		Newport city.........................	26 475	47			**TENNESSEE**	5 689 283
44	49960	005	Newport County	26 475	47	03440		Bartlett city........................	40 543
					47	03440	157	Shelby County	40 543
44	54640		Pawtucket city	72 958					
44	54640	007	Providence County	72 958	47	14000		Chattanooga city	155 554
					47	14000	065	Hamilton County	155 554
44	59000		Providence city	173 618	47	14000	115	Marion County	0
44	59000	007	Providence County	173 618					
					47	15160		Clarksville city.....................	103 455
44	74300		Warwick city	85 808	47	15160	125	Montgomery County	103 455
44	74300	003	Kent County	85 808					
					47	15400		Cleveland city.......................	37 192
44	80780		Woonsocket city	43 224	47	15400	011	Bradley County	37 192
44	80780	007	Providence County	43 224					
					47	16420		Collierville town	31 872
45			**SOUTH CAROLINA**	4 012 012	47	16420	157	Shelby County	31 872
45	00550		Aiken city...........................	25 337					
45	00550	003	Aiken County	25 337	47	16540		Columbia city........................	33 055
					47	16540	119	Maury County	33 055
45	01360		Anderson city........................	25 514					
45	01360	007	Anderson County......................	25 514	47	27740		Franklin city	41 842
					47	27740	187	Williamson County	41 842
45	13330		Charleston city......................	96 650					
45	13330	015	Berkeley County	1 122	47	28960		Germantown city	37 348
45	13330	019	Charleston County	95 528	47	28960	157	Shelby County	37 348
45	16000		Columbia city........................	116 278	47	33280		Hendersonville city	40 620
45	16000	063	Lexington County	402	47	33280	165	Sumner County........................	40 620
45	16000	079	Richland County	115 876					
					47	37640		Jackson city.........................	59 643
45	25810		Florence city........................	30 248	47	37640	113	Madison County.......................	59 643
45	25810	041	Florence County	30 248					
					47	38320		Johnson City city	55 469
45	29815		Goose Creek city.....................	29 208	47	38320	019	Carter County	1 138
45	29815	015	Berkeley County	29 208	47	38320	163	Sullivan County	240
45	29815	019	Charleston County	0	47	38320	179	Washington County	54 091
45	30850		Greenville city......................	56 002	47	39560		Kingsport city	44 905
45	30850	045	Greenville County	56 002	47	39560	073	Hawkins County.......................	2 907
					47	39560	163	Sullivan County	41 998
45	34045		Hilton Head Island town	33 862					
45	34045	013	Beaufort County......................	33 862	47	40000		Knoxville city.......................	173 890
					47	40000	093	Knox County	173 890
45	48535		Mount Pleasant town..................	47 609					
45	48535	019	Charleston County	47 609	47	48000		Memphis city	650 100
					47	48000	157	Shelby County	650 100
45	50875		North Charleston city................	79 641					
45	50875	019	Charleston County	76 244	47	51560		Murfreesboro city....................	68 816
45	50875	035	Dorchester County	3 397	47	51560	149	Rutherford County	68 816
45	61405		Rock Hill city.......................	49 765	47	52004		Nashville-Davidson...................	569 891
45	61405	091	York County	49 765					
					47	55120		Oak Ridge city.......................	27 387
45	68290		Spartanburg city	39 673	47	55120	001	Anderson County......................	24 610
45	68290	083	Spartanburg County..................	39 673	47	55120	145	Roane County.........................	2 777

State Code	Place Code	County Code	Geographic Area Name	2000 Population	State Code	Place Code	County Code	Geographic Area Name	2000 Population
47	69420		Smyrna town	25 569	48	17000		Corpus Christi city	277 454
47	69420	149	Rutherford County	25 569	48	17000	273	Kleberg County	0
					48	17000	355	Nueces County	277 450
48			**TEXAS**	20 851 820	48	17000	409	San Patricio County	4
48	01000		Abilene city	115 930					
48	01000	253	Jones County	5 488	48	19000		Dallas city	1188 580
48	01000	441	Taylor County	110 442	48	19000	085	Collin County	45 155
					48	19000	113	Dallas County	1121 131
48	01924		Allen city	43 554	48	19000	121	Denton County	22 273
48	01924	085	Collin County	43 554	48	19000	257	Kaufman County	0
					48	19000	397	Rockwall County	21
48	03000		Amarillo city	173 627					
48	03000	375	Potter County	99 833	48	19624		Deer Park city	28 520
48	03000	381	Randall County	73 794	48	19624	201	Harris County	28 520
48	04000		Arlington city	332 969	48	19792		Del Rio city	33 867
48	04000	439	Tarrant County	332 969	48	19792	465	Val Verde County	33 867
48	05000		Austin city	656 562	48	19972		Denton city	80 537
48	05000	453	Travis County	644 752	48	19972	121	Denton County	80 537
48	05000	491	Williamson County	11 810					
					48	20092		DeSoto city	37 646
48	06128		Baytown city	66 430	48	20092	113	Dallas County	37 646
48	06128	071	Chambers County	3 081					
48	06128	201	Harris County	63 349	48	21628		Duncanville city	36 081
					48	21628	113	Dallas County	36 081
48	07000		Beaumont city	113 866					
48	07000	245	Jefferson County	113 866	48	22660		Edinburg city	48 465
					48	22660	215	Hidalgo County	48 465
48	07132		Bedford city	47 152					
48	07132	439	Tarrant County	47 152	48	24000		El Paso city	563 662
					48	24000	141	El Paso County	563 662
48	08236		Big Spring city	25 233					
48	08236	227	Howard County	25 233	48	24768		Euless city	46 005
					48	24768	439	Tarrant County	46 005
48	10768		Brownsville city	139 722					
48	10768	061	Cameron County	139 722	48	25452		Farmers Branch city	27 508
					48	25452	113	Dallas County	27 508
48	10912		Bryan city	65 660					
48	10912	041	Brazos County	65 660	48	26232		Flower Mound town	50 702
					48	26232	121	Denton County	50 702
48	13024		Carrollton city	109 576	48	26232	439	Tarrant County	0
48	13024	085	Collin County	0					
48	13024	113	Dallas County	49 822	48	27000		Fort Worth city	534 694
48	13024	121	Denton County	59 754	48	27000	121	Denton County	44
					48	27000	439	Tarrant County	534 650
48	13492		Cedar Hill city	32 093					
48	13492	113	Dallas County	32 044	48	27648		Friendswood city	29 037
48	13492	139	Ellis County	49	48	27648	167	Galveston County	21 237
					48	27648	201	Harris County	7 800
48	13552		Cedar Park city	26 049					
48	13552	453	Travis County	541	48	27684		Frisco city	33 714
48	13552	491	Williamson County	25 508	48	27684	085	Collin County	30 312
					48	27684	121	Denton County	3 402
48	15364		Cleburne city	26 005					
48	15364	251	Johnson County	26 005	48	28068		Galveston city	57 247
					48	28068	167	Galveston County	57 247
48	15976		College Station city	67 890					
48	15976	041	Brazos County	67 890	48	29000		Garland city	215 768
					48	29000	085	Collin County	0
48	16432		Conroe city	36 811	48	29000	113	Dallas County	215 768
48	16432	339	Montgomery County	36 811	48	29000	397	Rockwall County	0
48	16612		Coppell city	35 958	48	29336		Georgetown city	28 339
48	16612	113	Dallas County	35 734	48	29336	491	Williamson County	28 339
48	16612	121	Denton County	224					
					48	30464		Grand Prairie city	127 427
48	16624		Copperas Cove city	29 592	48	30464	113	Dallas County	99 760
48	16624	027	Bell County	0	48	30464	139	Ellis County	46
48	16624	099	Coryell County	29 455	48	30464	439	Tarrant County	27 621
48	16624	281	Lampasas County	137					

State Code	Place Code	County Code	Geographic Area Name	2000 Population	State Code	Place Code	County Code	Geographic Area Name	2000 Population
48	30644		Grapevine city	42 059	48	46452	251	Johnson County	622
48	30644	113	Dallas County	0	48	46452	439	Tarrant County	27 280
48	30644	121	Denton County	2					
48	30644	439	Tarrant County	42 057	48	47892		Mesquite city	124 523
					48	47892	113	Dallas County	124 522
48	31928		Haltom City city	39 018	48	47892	257	Kaufman County	1
48	31928	439	Tarrant County	39 018					
					48	48072		Midland city	94 996
48	32372		Harlingen city	57 564	48	48072	317	Martin County	0
48	32372	061	Cameron County	57 564	48	48072	329	Midland County	94 996
48	35000		Houston city	1953 631	48	48768		Mission city	45 408
48	35000	157	Fort Bend County	33 384	48	48768	215	Hidalgo County	45 408
48	35000	201	Harris County	1919 789					
48	35000	339	Montgomery County	458	48	48804		Missouri City city	52 913
					48	48804	157	Fort Bend County	47 419
48	35528		Huntsville city	35 078	48	48804	201	Harris County	5 494
48	35528	471	Walker County	35 078					
					48	50256		Nacogdoches city	29 914
48	35576		Hurst city	36 273	48	50256	347	Nacogdoches County	29 914
48	35576	439	Tarrant County	36 273					
					48	50820		New Braunfels city	36 494
48	37000		Irving city	191 615	48	50820	091	Comal County	35 328
48	37000	113	Dallas County	191 615	48	50820	187	Guadalupe County	1 166
48	38632		Keller city	27 345	48	52356		North Richland Hills city	55 635
48	38632	439	Tarrant County	27 345	48	52356	439	Tarrant County	55 635
48	39148		Killeen city	86 911	48	53388		Odessa city	90 943
48	39148	027	Bell County	86 911	48	53388	135	Ector County	89 901
					48	53388	329	Midland County	1 042
48	39352		Kingsville city	25 575					
48	39352	273	Kleberg County	25 575	48	55080		Paris city	25 898
					48	55080	277	Lamar County	25 898
48	40588		Lake Jackson city	26 386					
48	40588	039	Brazoria County	26 386	48	56000		Pasadena city	141 674
					48	56000	201	Harris County	141 674
48	41212		Lancaster city	25 894					
48	41212	113	Dallas County	25 894	48	56348		Pearland city	37 640
					48	56348	039	Brazoria County	35 696
48	41440		La Porte city	31 880	48	56348	157	Fort Bend County	0
48	41440	201	Harris County	31 880	48	56348	201	Harris County	1 944
48	41464		Laredo city	176 576	48	57200		Pharr city	46 660
48	41464	479	Webb County	176 576	48	57200	215	Hidalgo County	46 660
48	41980		League City city	45 444	48	58016		Plano city	222 030
48	41980	167	Galveston County	45 306	48	58016	085	Collin County	219 890
48	41980	201	Harris County	138	48	58016	121	Denton County	2 140
48	42508		Lewisville city	77 737	48	58820		Port Arthur city	57 755
48	42508	113	Dallas County	2	48	58820	245	Jefferson County	57 755
48	42508	121	Denton County	77 735	48	58820	361	Orange County	0
48	43888		Longview city	73 344	48	61796		Richardson city	91 802
48	43888	183	Gregg County	71 746	48	61796	085	Collin County	20 873
48	43888	203	Harrison County	1 598	48	61796	113	Dallas County	70 929
48	45000		Lubbock city	199 564	48	63500		Round Rock city	61 136
48	45000	303	Lubbock County	199 564	48	63500	453	Travis County	1 076
					48	63500	491	Williamson County	60 060
48	45072		Lufkin city	32 709					
48	45072	005	Angelina County	32 709	48	63572		Rowlett city	44 503
					48	63572	113	Dallas County	37 462
48	45384		McAllen city	106 414	48	63572	397	Rockwall County	7 041
48	45384	215	Hidalgo County	106 414					
					48	64472		San Angelo city	88 439
48	45744		McKinney city	54 369	48	64472	451	Tom Green County	88 439
48	45744	085	Collin County	54 369					
					48	65000		San Antonio city	1144 646
48	46452		Mansfield city	28 031	48	65000	029	Bexar County	1144 646
48	46452	139	Ellis County	129	48	65000	091	Comal County	0

State Code	Place Code	County Code	Geographic Area Name	2000 Population	State Code	Place Code	County Code	Geographic Area Name	2000 Population
					49	57300		Orem city	84 324
48	65516		San Juan city	26 229	49	57300	049	Utah County	84 324
48	65516	215	Hidalgo County	26 229					
					49	62470		Provo city	105 166
48	65600		San Marcos city	34 733	49	62470	049	Utah County	105 166
48	65600	055	Caldwell County	0					
48	65600	209	Hays County	34 733	49	64340		Riverton city	25 011
					49	64340	035	Salt Lake County	25 011
48	67496		Sherman city	35 082					
48	67496	181	Grayson County	35 082	49	65110		Roy city	32 885
					49	65110	057	Weber County	32 885
48	68636		Socorro city	27 152					
48	68636	141	El Paso County	27 152	49	65330		St. George city	49 663
					49	65330	053	Washington County	49 663
48	70808		Sugar Land city	63 328					
48	70808	157	Fort Bend County	63 328	49	67000		Salt Lake City city	181 743
					49	67000	035	Salt Lake County	181 743
48	72176		Temple city	54 514					
48	72176	027	Bell County	54 514	49	67440		Sandy city	88 418
					49	67440	035	Salt Lake County	88 418
48	72368		Texarkana city	34 782					
48	72368	037	Bowie County	34 782	49	70850		South Jordan city	29 437
					49	70850	035	Salt Lake County	29 437
48	72392		Texas City city	41 521					
48	72392	071	Chambers County	0	49	75360		Taylorsville city	57 439
48	72392	167	Galveston County	41 521	49	75360	035	Salt Lake County	57 439
48	72530		The Colony city	26 531	49	82950		West Jordan city	68 336
48	72530	121	Denton County	26 531	49	82950	035	Salt Lake County	68 336
48	74144		Tyler city	83 650	49	83470		West Valley City city	108 896
48	74144	423	Smith County	83 650	49	83470	035	Salt Lake County	108 896
48	75428		Victoria city	60 603	50			**VERMONT**	608 827
48	75428	469	Victoria County	60 603	50	10675		Burlington city	38 889
					50	10675	007	Chittenden County	38 889
48	76000		Waco city	113 726					
48	76000	309	McLennan County	113 726	51			**VIRGINIA**	7 078 515
					51	01000		Alexandria city	128 283
48	77272		Weslaco city	26 935	51	01000	510	Alexandria city	128 283
48	77272	215	Hidalgo County	26 935					
					51	07784		Blacksburg town	39 573
48	79000		Wichita Falls city	104 197	51	07784	121	Montgomery County	39 573
48	79000	485	Wichita County	104 197					
					51	14968		Charlottesville city	45 049
49			**UTAH**	2 233 169	51	14968	540	Charlottesville city	45 049
49	07690		Bountiful city	41 301					
49	07690	011	Davis County	41 301	51	16000		Chesapeake city	199 184
					51	16000	550	Chesapeake city	199 184
49	13850		Clearfield city	25 974					
49	13850	011	Davis County	25 974	51	21344		Danville city	48 411
					51	21344	590	Danville city	48 411
49	20120		Draper city	25 220					
49	20120	035	Salt Lake County	25 220	51	35000		Hampton city	146 437
49	20120	049	Utah County	0	51	35000	650	Hampton city	146 437
49	43660		Layton city	58 474	51	35624		Harrisonburg city	40 468
49	43660	011	Davis County	58 474	51	35624	660	Harrisonburg city	40 468
49	45860		Logan city	42 670	51	44984		Leesburg town	28 311
49	45860	005	Cache County	42 670	51	44984	107	Loudoun County	28 311
49	49710		Midvale city	27 029	51	47672		Lynchburg city	65 269
49	49710	035	Salt Lake County	27 029	51	47672	680	Lynchburg city	65 269
49	53230		Murray city	34 024	51	48952		Manassas city	35 135
49	53230	035	Salt Lake County	34 024	51	48952	683	Manassas city	35 135
49	55980		Ogden city	77 226	51	56000		Newport News city	180 150
49	55980	057	Weber County	77 226	51	56000	700	Newport News city	180 150

State Code	Place Code	County Code	Geographic Area Name	2000 Population	State Code	Place Code	County Code	Geographic Area Name	2000 Population
51	57000		Norfolk city.............................	234 403	53	51300		Olympia city.................................	42 514
51	57000	710	Norfolk city...........................	234 403	53	51300	067	Thurston County........................	42 514
51	61832		Petersburg city.......................	33 740	53	53545		Pasco city......................................	32 066
51	61832	730	Petersburg city......................	33 740	53	53545	021	Franklin County............................	32 066
51	64000		Portsmouth city......................	100 565	53	56695		Puyallup city..................................	33 011
51	64000	740	Portsmouth city......................	100 565	53	56695	053	Pierce County...............................	33 011
51	67000		Richmond city........................	197 790	53	57535		Redmond city................................	45 256
51	67000	760	Richmond city........................	197 790	53	57535	033	King County..................................	45 256
51	68000		Roanoke city..........................	94 911	53	57745		Renton city....................................	50 052
51	68000	770	Roanoke city..........................	94 911	53	57745	033	King County..................................	50 052
51	76432		Suffolk city.............................	63 677	53	58235		Richland city..................................	38 708
51	76432	800	Suffolk city.............................	63 677	53	58235	005	Benton County..............................	38 708
51	82000		Virginia Beach city.................	425 257	53	61115		Sammamish city............................	34 104
51	82000	810	Virginia Beach city.................	425 257	53	61115	033	King County..................................	34 104
53			**WASHINGTON**.............................	5 894 121	53	63000		Seattle city....................................	563 374
53	03180		Auburn city................	40 314	53	63000	033	King County..................................	563 374
53	03180	033	King County	40 168					
53	03180	053	Pierce County	146	53	63960		Shoreline city................................	53 025
					53	63960	033	King County..................................	53 025
53	05210		Bellevue city	109 569					
53	05210	033	King County	109 569	53	67000		Spokane city..................................	195 629
					53	67000	063	Spokane County..........................	195 629
53	05280		Bellingham city	67 171					
53	05280	073	Whatcom County	67 171	53	70000		Tacoma city...................................	193 556
					53	70000	053	Pierce County...............................	193 556
53	07380		Bothell city	30 150					
53	07380	033	King County	16 185	53	74060		Vancouver city..............................	143 560
53	07380	061	Snohomish County	13 965	53	74060	011	Clark County.................................	143 560
53	07695		Bremerton city	37 259	53	75775		Walla Walla city.............................	29 686
53	07695	035	Kitsap County	37 259	53	75775	071	Walla Walla County.....................	29 686
53	17635		Des Moines city	29 267	53	77105		Wenatchee city..............................	27 856
53	17635	033	King County	29 267	53	77105	007	Chelan County.............................	27 856
53	20750		Edmonds city	39 515	53	80010		Yakima city....................................	71 845
53	20750	061	Snohomish County	39 515	53	80010	077	Yakima County.............................	71 845
53	22640		Everett city.............................	91 488	54			**WEST VIRGINIA**............................	1 808 344
53	22640	061	Snohomish County	91 488	54	14600		Charleston city.............................	53 421
					54	14600	039	Kanawha County........................	53 421
53	35275		Kennewick city........................	54 693					
53	35275	005	Benton County	54 693	54	39460		Huntington city..............................	51 475
					54	39460	011	Cabell County...............................	47 341
53	35415		Kent city..................................	79 524	54	39460	099	Wayne County..............................	4 134
53	35415	033	King County	79 524					
					54	55756		Morgantown city...........................	26 809
53	35940		Kirkland city............................	45 054	54	55756	061	Monongalia County....................	26 809
53	35940	033	King County	45 054					
					54	62140		Parkersburg city	33 099
53	36745		Lacey city	31 226	54	62140	107	Wood County................................	33 099
53	36745	067	Thurston County	31 226					
					54	86452		Wheeling city................................	31 419
53	40245		Longview city	34 660	54	86452	051	Marshall County...........................	360
53	40245	015	Cowlitz County	34 660	54	86452	069	Ohio County..................................	31 059
53	40840		Lynnwood city.........................	33 847	55			**WISCONSIN**...............................	5 363 675
53	40840	061	Snohomish County	33 847	55	02375		Appleton city.................................	70 087
					55	02375	015	Calumet County...........................	10 974
53	43955		Marysville city.........................	25 315	55	02375	087	Outagamie County......................	58 301
53	43955	061	Snohomish County	25 315	55	02375	139	Winnebago County......................	812
53	47560		Mount Vernon city	26 232	55	06500		Beloit city......................................	35 775
53	47560	057	Skagit County	26 232	55	06500	105	Rock County.................................	35 775

Cities by County — Continued

State Code	Place Code	County Code	Geographic Area Name	2000 Population	State Code	Place Code	County Code	Geographic Area Name	2000 Population
55	10025		Brookfield city	38 649	55	56375		New Berlin city	38 220
55	10025	133	Waukesha County	38 649	55	56375	133	Waukesha County	38 220
55	22300		Eau Claire city	61 704	55	58800		Oak Creek city	28 456
55	22300	017	Chippewa County	1 910	55	58800	079	Milwaukee County	28 456
55	22300	035	Eau Claire County	59 794					
					55	60500		Oshkosh city	62 916
55	26275		Fond du Lac city	42 203	55	60500	139	Winnebago County	62 916
55	26275	039	Fond du Lac County	42 203					
					55	66000		Racine city	81 855
55	27300		Franklin city	29 494	55	66000	101	Racine County	81 855
55	27300	079	Milwaukee County	29 494					
					55	72975		Sheboygan city	50 792
55	31000		Green Bay city	102 313	55	72975	117	Sheboygan County	50 792
55	31000	009	Brown County	102 313					
					55	78650		Superior city	27 368
55	31175		Greenfield city	35 476	55	78650	031	Douglas County	27 368
55	31175	079	Milwaukee County	35 476					
					55	84250		Waukesha city	64 825
55	37825		Janesville city	59 498	55	84250	133	Waukesha County	64 825
55	37825	105	Rock County	59 498					
					55	84475		Wausau city	38 426
55	39225		Kenosha city	90 352	55	84475	073	Marathon County	38 426
55	39225	059	Kenosha County	90 352					
					55	84675		Wauwatosa city	47 271
55	40775		La Crosse city	51 818	55	84675	079	Milwaukee County	47 271
55	40775	063	La Crosse County	51 818					
					55	85300		West Allis city	61 254
55	48000		Madison city	208 054	55	85300	079	Milwaukee County	61 254
55	48000	025	Dane County	208 054					
					55	85350		West Bend city	28 152
55	48500		Manitowoc city	34 053	55	85350	131	Washington County	28 152
55	48500	071	Manitowoc County	34 053					
					56			**WYOMING**	493 782
55	51000		Menomonee Falls village	32 647	56	13150		Casper city	49 644
55	51000	133	Waukesha County	32 647	56	13150	025	Natrona County	49 644
55	53000		Milwaukee city	596 974	56	13900		Cheyenne city	53 011
55	53000	079	Milwaukee County	596 974	56	13900	021	Laramie County	53 011
55	53000	131	Washington County	0					
55	53000	133	Waukesha County	0	56	45050		Laramie city	27 204
					56	45050	001	Albany County	27 204

APPENDIX F
SOURCE NOTES AND DEFINITIONS

All data in this volume are from the 2000 Census of Population and Housing. Most items are from 2000 Census Summary File 3 (SF3), with a few from Summary File 1 (SF1). Data are presented for the United States as a whole, all states and the District of Columbia, all counties and county equivalents, all metropolitan areas as defined at the time of the census, and all cities with a population of 25,000 or more at the time of the census. Detailed descriptions and further information about the geographic concepts can be found in Appendix A.

Part A includes basic characteristics such as age, race, Hispanic origin, household and family structures, foreign-born populations, and ancestry. Part B provides details on education, labor force characteristics, and income. Part C includes information on migration, housing, and transportation.

This volume includes key information in tables and text designed to help readers understand the concepts of the census, and how their local areas compare with the nation as a whole. Though a great deal of information is included here, much more is available from the Census Bureau. This section specifies the SF3 or SF1 table numbers where additional information can be found through the Census Bureau's American FactFinder at www.census.gov. Following the table specifications is a glossary of definitions adapted from the Census Bureau's Technical Documentation of SF3. Readers should refer to the Census Bureau's Technical Documentation for additional details, especially extensive information on standard distributions, derived measures (means, medians), detailed lists (for example, countries of birth, ancestries, languages, and occupations), limitations, and comparability with prior census years. The Technical Documentation also includes a copy of the Census Questionnaire. The full Technical Documentation is available on the web at (http://www.census.gov/prod/cen2000/doc/sf3.pdf).

PART A. AGE, ETHNICITY, AND HOUSEHOLD STRUCTURE

Table A-1.1. Race and Hispanic Origin
Source: SF3 Tables P145A through P145I
Definitions: Race, Hispanic Origin

Table A-1.2. Age
Source: SF3 Table P8
Definitions: Age, Sex

Table A-1.3. Median Age
Source: SF1 Table P13
Definitions: Age

Table A-1.4. Age by Race, Hispanic Origin, and Metropolitan/Central City Residence
Source: SF3 Tables P8 and P145A through P145I
Definitions: Age, Race, Hispanic Origin, Metropolitan/Central City Residence

Table A-1.5. Household Type by Age of Householder and Metropolitan/Central City Residence
Source: SF3 Tables P12, P13, PCT2, and PCT3
Definitions: Age, Household Type, Metropolitan/Central City Status

Table A-1.6. Race and Hispanic Origin of Householder by Household Type
Source: SF3 Tables P12 and P146A through P146I
Definitions: Race, Hispanic Origin, Household Type and Relationship

Table A-1.7. Married-Couple Families with Children Under 18 Years
Source: SF3 Table P12
Definitions: Household Type and Relationship

Table A-1.8. Grandparents' Responsibility for Care of Grandchildren
Source: SF3 Tables PCT8 and PCT9
Definitions: Household Type and Relationship, Grandparents as Caregivers

Table A-1.9. Single-Parent Family Households
Source: SF3 Table P12
Definitions: Household Type and Relationship

Table A-1.10. Unmarried Partner Households
Source: SF3 Table PCT1
Definitions: Household Type and Relationship

Table A-1.11. Foreign-Born Populations
Source: SF3 Table P21
Definitions: Place of Birth

Table A-1.12. Place of Birth and Citizenship Status of the Foreign-Born Population
Source: SF3 Table PCT20
Definitions: Citizenship, Place of Birth

Table A-1.13. States with Large Linguistically Isolated Populations
Source: SF3 Table PCT14
Definitions: Language Spoken at Home and Ability to Speak English

Table A-1.14. Language Spoken at Home
Source: SF3 Tables PCT12, PCT13, PCT14
Definitions: Language Spoken at Home and Ability to Speak English

Table A-1.15. Ancestry
Source: SF1 Tables PCT7 and PCT11; SF3 Table PCT18
Definitions: Ancestry, Race, Hispanic Origin

Table A-2. States
Items 1 through 42. Age by Sex
Source: SF3 Table P8, SF1 Table P13
Definitions: Age, Sex

Items 43 through 141. Age by Sex, Race and Hispanic Origin
Source: SF3 Tables P145A through P145I; SF1 Tables P13A through P13I
Definitions: Age, Sex, Race, Hispanic Origin

Items 142 through 164. Household Type
Source: SF3 Tables P10, P12, and PCT1
Definitions: Household Type and Relationship

Items 165 through 167. Population 30 Years and Over by Care of Grandchildren
Source: SF3 Table PCT8
Definitions: Grandparents as Caregivers

Items 168 through 229. Household Type by Age of Householder
Source: SF3 Tables P13 and PCT3
Definitions: Age, Household Type and Relationship

Items 230 through 294. Household Type by Race and Hispanic Origin of Householder
Source: SF3 Tables P146A through P146I
Definitions: Household Type and Relationship, Race, Hispanic Origin

Items 295 through 309. Place of Birth for the Foreign-Born Population
Source: SF3 Table PCT19
Definitions: Place of Birth

Items 310 through 321. Languages Spoken at Home
Source: SF3 Tables PCT12 and PCT14
Definitions: Language Spoken at Home and Ability to Speak English

Tables A-3, A-4, and A-5. Counties, Metropolitan Areas, and Cities
Items 1 through 10. Age
Source: SF3 Table P8, SF1 Table P13
Definitions: Age

Items 11 through 28. Age by Race and Hispanic Origin
Source: SF3 Tables P145A through P145I
Definitions: Age, Race, Hispanic Origin

Items 29 through 42. Household Type
Source: SF3 Tables P10, P12, P14, and PCT2
Definitions: Household Type and Relationship, Age

Item 43. Grandparents Who are Responsible for the Care of Their Grandchildren
Source: SF3 Table PCT8
Definitions: Grandparents as Caregivers

Items 44 through 53. Household Type by Race and Hispanic Origin of Householder
Source: SF3 Tables P146A through P146I
Definitions: Household Type and Relationship, Race, Hispanic Origin

Items 54 through 57. Place of Birth for the Foreign-Born Population
Source: SF3 Table PCT19
Definitions: Place of Birth

Items 58 and 59. Percent in Non-English Speaking Households
Source: SF3 Table PCT14
Definitions: Language Spoken at Home and Ability to Speak English

PART B. EDUCATION, LABOR FORCE, AND INCOME

Table B-1.1. Educational Attainment by Age
Source: SF3 Table PCT25
Definitions: Educational Attainment, Age, Metropolitan/Central City Status

Table B-1.2. Population with a High School Diploma or Higher
Source: SF3 Table P37
Definitions: Educational Attainment

Table B-1.3. Population with a Bachelor's Degree or Higher
Source: SF3 Table P37
Definitions: Educational Attainment

Table B-1.4. Educational Attainment by Race and Hispanic Origin
Source: SF3 Tables P148A through P148I
Definitions: Educational Attainment, Race, Hispanic Origin

Table B-1.5. School Enrollment and Labor Force Status for the Population 16 to 19 Years
Source: SF3 Tables P38 and P149A through P149I
Definitions: School Enrollment, Employment Status, Age, Race, Hispanic Origin

Table B-1.6. Population 16 to 19 Years Who are not Enrolled in School and not High School Graduates
Source: SF3 Table P38
Definitions: School Enrollment, Age

Table B-1.7. Population 25 Years and Over Enrolled in School
Source: SF3 Tables PCT23 and PCT24
Definitions: School Enrollment, Age

Table B-1.8. Enrollment in School, College, or Graduate School by Age
Source: SF3 Tables PCT23 and PCT24
Definitions: School Enrollment, Age

Table B-1-9. School Enrollment
Source: SF3 Tables P36 and P147A through P147I
Definitions: School Enrollment, Race, Hispanic Origin

Table B-1.10. Work Experience in 1999 by Sex, Race, and Hispanic Origin
Source: SF3 Tables P47 and P171A through P171I
Definitions: Work Status in 1999, Sex, Race, Hispanic Origin

Table B-1.11. Population 16 Years and Over Who Worked Full-Time in 1999
Source: SF3 Table P47
Definitions: Work Status in 1999

Table B-1.12. Employment Status by Age, Sex, Race, and Hispanic Origin
Source: SF3 Tables P43, PCT35, and P150A through P150I
Definitions: Employment Status, Age, Sex, Race, Hispanic Origin

Table B-1.13. Unemployment Rates for Persons 16 to 24 Years
Source: SF3 Table PCT35
Definitions: Employment Status

Table B-1.14. Employment Status of Parents by Age of Children
Source: SF3 Tables P46 and PCT70A through PCT70I
Definitions: Employment Status, Household Type and Relationship, Race, Hispanic Origin

Table B-1.15. Family Structure and Employment Status of Parents
Source: SF3 Table P46
Definitions: Employment Status, Household Type and Relationship

Table B-1.16. Employment Status of Mothers by Age of Children
Source: SF3 Table P45
Definitions: Employment Status, Household Type and Relationship

Table B-1.17. Employment Status by Family Type
Source: SF3 Table P44
Definitions: Employment Status, Household Type and Relationship

Table B-1.18. Self-Employed Persons
Source: SF3 Table P51
Definitions: Industry, Occupation, and Class of Worker

Table B-1.19. Selected Industries
Source: SF3 Table P51
Definitions: Industry, Occupation, and Class of Worker

Table B-1.20. Class of Worker, Occupation, and Industry, by Sex
Source: SF3 Tables P30, P49, P50, and P51
Definitions: Industry, Occupation, and Class of Worker

Table B-1.21. Median Incomes in 1999
Source: SF3 Tables P53, P56, PCT39, PCT40, PCT42, and PCT45
Definitions: Income in 1999, Age, Household Type and Relationship, Metropolitan/Central City Status

Table B-1.22. Median Household Income
Source: SF3 Table P53
Definitions: Income in 1999

Table B-1.23. High and Low Income Households by Age of Householder and Family Type
Source: SF3 Tables P55 and P92
Definitions: Income and Poverty Status in 1999, Age, Household Type and Relationship

Table B-1.24. Households with Income Exceeding $100,000
Source: SF3 Table P55
Definitions: Income in 1999

Table B-1.25. High and Low Income Families by Race, Hispanic Origin, and Family Type
Source: SF3 Tables P76, P90, P154A through P154I, and P160A through P160I

Definitions: Income and Poverty Status in 1999, Household Type and Relationship, Race, Hispanic Origin

Table B-1.26. Households by Sources of Income
Source: SF3 Tables P58, P59, P60, P61, P62, P63, P64, P65, P66
Definitions: Income in 1999

Table B-1.27. Veteran Status
Source: SF3 Table P39
Definitions: Veteran Status

Table B-1.28. Disability Status
Source: SF3 Table PCT26
Definitions: Disability Status

Table B-2. States
Items 1 through 36. Educational Attainment
Source: SF3 Tables P37, PCT25, P148A through P148I
Definitions: Educational Attainment, Age, Sex, Race, Hispanic Origin

Items 37 through 60. School Enrollment
Source: SF3 Tables P36, P147A through P147I, PCT23 and PCT24
Definitions: School Enrollment, Age, Sex, Race, Hispanic Origin

Items 61 through 73. School Enrollment and High School Completion for Persons 16 to 19 Years
Source: SF3 Tables P38 and P149A through P149I
Definitions: School Enrollment, Race, Hispanic Origin, Employment Status

Items 74 through 121. Work Status in 1999 by Sex, Race, and Hispanic Origin
Source: SF3 Tables P47, and PCT71A through PCT71I
Definitions: Work Status in 1999, Sex, Race, Hispanic Origin

Items 122 through 142. Employment Status by Sex and Age
Source: SF3 Tables P43 and PCT35
Definitions: Employment Status, Sex, Age

Items 143 through 163. Family Status and Employment Status of Parents and Householders
Source: SF3 Tables P44, P45, and P46
Definitions: Household Type and Relationship, Employment Status

Items 164 through 170. Class of Worker and Percent Who Worked at Home
Source: SF3 Tables P30 and P51
Definitions: Industry, Occupation, and Class of Worker; Journey to Work

Items 171 through 177. Occupation
Source: SF3 Table P50
Definitions: Industry, Occupation, and Class of Worker

Items 178 through 191. Industry
Source: SF3 Table P49
Definitions: Industry, Occupation, and Class of Worker

Item 192. Disability Status
Source: SF3 Table P42
Definitions: Disability Status

Items 193 through 196. Veteran Status
Source: SF3 Table P39
Definitions: Veteran Status

Items 197 through 224. Median and Per Capita Incomes
Source: SF3 Tables P53, P56, P77, P80, P82, PCT40, PCT42, and PCT45
Definitions: Income in 1999

Items 225 through 234. Sources of Income
Source: SF3 Tables P58, P59, P60, P61, P62, P63, P64, P65, P66
Definitions: Income in 1999

Items 235 through 241. Households with Income over $100,000
Source: SF3 Tables P52 and P55
Definitions: Income in 1999, Age

Items 242 through 258. Households and Families with Income Below Poverty
Source: SF3 Tables P90, P92, and P160A through P160I
Definitions: Income in 1999, Poverty Status, Household Type and Relationship, Age, Race, Hispanic Origin

Table B-3, B-4, and B-5. Counties, Metropolitan Areas, and Cities
Items 1 through 10. Educational Attainment
Source: SF3 Tables PCT25 and P148A through P148I
Definitions. Educational Attainment, Race, Hispanic Origin

Items 11 through 13. School Enrollment
Source: SF3 Table P36
Definitions: School Enrollment

Items 14 through 17. Population 16 to 19 Years by School Enrollment and Employment Status
Source: SF3 Table P38
Definitions: School Enrollment, Employment Status

Items 18 through 20. Employment Status
Source: SF3 Table P43
Definitions: Employment Status

Items 21 through 31. Work Status in 1999
Source: SF3 Tables P47 and PCT71A through PCT71I
Definitions: Work Status in 1999, Sex, Race, Hispanic Origin

Items 32 through 37. Employment Status of Parents and Couples
Source: SF3 Tables P44 and P46
Definitions: Employment Status, Household Type and Relationship

Items 38 through 41. Class of Worker
Source: SF3 Table P51
Definitions: Industry, Occupation, and Class of Worker

Item 42. Percent Who Worked at Home
Source: SF3 Table P34
Definitions: Journey to Work

Item 43. Percent with a Disability
Source: SF3 Table PCT26
Definitions: Disability Status

Item 44. Veterans
Source: SF3 Table P39
Definitions: Veteran Status

Items 45 through 50. Occupation
Source: SF3 Table P50
Definitions: Industry, Occupation, and Class of Worker

Items 51 through 56. Industry
Source: SF3 Table P51
Definitions: Industry, Occupation, and Class of Worker

Items 57 through 74. Income and Poverty
Source: SF3 Tables P52, P53, P58, P61, P62, P64, P65, P77, P80, P82, P90, P92, PCT40, PCT45
Definitions: Income in 1999, Poverty Status, Household Type and Relationship, Work Status in 1999.

PART C. MIGRATION, HOUSING, AND TRANSPORTATION

Table C-1.1. Migration
Source: SF3 Table P24 and PCT64A through PCT64I
Definitions: Residence 5 Years Ago, Race, Hispanic Origin

Table C-1.2. Population Who Lived in the Same House in 1995
Source: SF3 Table P24
Definitions: Residence 5 Years Ago

Table C-1.3. Housing Tenure and Household Type by Age of Householder
Source: SF3 Table H19
Definitions: Tenure, Household Type and Relationship, Age

Table C-1.4. Homeownership
Source: SF3 Table H7
Definitions: Tenure

Table C-1.5. Homeownership by Race and Hispanic Origin
Source: SF3 Tables H11, H12, and H13
Definitions: Tenure

Table C-1.6. Mean and Median Household Income by Age and Tenure
Source: SF3 Tables H14, HCT12, and HCT14
Definitions: Income in 1999, Age, Tenure

Table C-1.7. Median Owner-Estimated Housing Value
Source: SF3 Table H85
Definitions: Value

Table C-1.8. Owner and Renter Costs as a Percentage of Income
Source: SF3 Tables H70, H71, H95, and H96
Definitions: Selected Monthly Owner Costs; Selected Monthly Owner Costs as a Percentage of Income; Gross Rent, Gross Rent as a Percentage of Household Income in 1999, Age, Mortgage Status

Table C-1.9. Households with No Car or with 3 or More Cars
Source: SF3 Table H44
Definitions: Vehicles Available

Table C-1.10. Means of Transportation to Work
Source: SF3 Tables P30, P32, and P33
Definitions: Journey to Work

Table C-1.11. Vehicles Available
Source: SF3 Tables H44 and H45
Definitions: Vehicles Available, Tenure, Age

Table C-2. States
Items 1 through 54. Residence in 1995
Source: SF3 Tables P24, PCT64A through PCT64I
Definitions: Residence 5 Years Ago, Race, Hispanic Origin

Items 55 through 102. Homeownership
Source: SF3 Tables H7, H11, H12, H13, H14, H17, and H19
Definitions: Tenure, Age, Race, Hispanic Origin, Household Type and Relationship, Household Size

Items 103 and 104. Average Household Size
Source: SF3 Table H18
Definitions: Household Size, Tenure

Items 105 through 116. Household Income
Source: SF3 Tables HCT1, HCT12, and HCT14
Definitions: Income in 1999, Tenure, Age

Item 117. Median Housing Value
Source: SF3 Table H85
Definitions: Value

Items 118 and 119. Median Monthly Owner Costs as a Percentage of Income
Source: SF3 Table H95
Definitions: Selected Monthly Owner Costs; Mortgage Status

Items 120 and 121. Gross Rent
Source: SF3 Table H63
Definitions: Gross Rent

Items 122 through 135. Households Who Pay 35 Percent or More of Income for Housing Expenses
Source: SF3 Tables H71, H73, H96, and H97
Definitions: Gross Rent as a Percentage of Household Income in 1999; Selected Monthly Owner Costs as a Percentage of Household Income in 1999; Age, Tenure; Income in 1999

Items 136 through 143. Means of Transportation to Work
Source: SF3 Table P30
Definitions: Journey to Work

Items 144 through 146. Mean Travel Time to Work
Source: SF3 Tables P32 and P33
Definitions: Journey to Work

Items 147 through 152. Vehicles Available
Source: SF3 Tables H45 and H46
Definitions: Vehicles Available

Table C-3. Counties, Metropolitan Areas, and Cities
Items 1 through 6. Residence in 1995
Source: SF3 Table P24
Definitions: Residence 5 Years Ago

Items 7 through 18. Homeownership
Source: SF3 Tables H7, H14, and HCT1
Definitions: Tenure, Age, Household Type and Relationship

Items 19 through 21. Median Household Income
Source: SF3 Table HCT12
Definitions: Income in 1999, Tenure

Item 22. Median Housing Value
Source: SF3 Table H85
Definitions: Value

Items 23 and 24. Median Monthly Owner Costs as a Percentage of Income
Source: SF3 Table H95
Definitions: Selected Monthly Owner Costs, Mortgage Status

Item 25. Median Gross Rent
Source: SF3 Table H63
Definitions: Gross Rent

Items 26 and 27. Percentage Who Pay 35 Percent or More for Housing Expenses
Source: SF3 Tables H71 and H96
Definitions: Selected Monthly Owner Costs, Gross Rent, Tenure

Items 28 through 33. Means of Transportation to Work
Source: SF3 Table P30
Definitions: Journey to Work

Items 34 through 36. Vehicles Available
Source: SF3 Table H44
Definitions: Vehicles Available

DEFINITIONS

AGE

The data on age were derived from answers to the long-form questionnaire Item 4 and short form questionnaire Item 6. The age classification is based on the age of the person in complete years as of April 1, 2000, and usually was derived from the date of birth they provided. Their reported age was used only when date of birth was unavailable.

Data on age are used to determine the applicability of some of the sample questions for a person and to classify other characteristics in census tabulations. Age data are needed to interpret most social and economic characteristics used to plan and examine many programs and policies. Therefore, age is tabulated by single years of age and by many different groupings, such as 5-year age groups.

Median age. Median age divides the age distribution into two equal parts: half the population falls below the median age and half above it. Median age is computed on the basis of a single year of age standard distribution, and is rounded to the nearest tenth.

ANCESTRY

The data on ancestry were derived from answers to long-form questionnaire Item 10. The data represent self-classification by the ancestry group or groups with which they most closely identify. Ancestry refers to a person's ethnic origin or descent, "roots," heritage, or the place of birth of the person, the person's parents, or their ancestors before their arrival in the United States. Some ethnic identities, such as Egyptian or Polish, can be traced to geographic areas outside the United States, while other ethnicities, such as Pennsylvania German or Cajun, evolved in the United States.

The intent of the ancestry question was not to measure the degree of attachment the respondent had to a particular ethnicity. For example, a response of "Irish" might reflect total involvement in an Irish community or only a memory of ancestors several generations removed from the individual. Also, the question was intended to provide data for groups that were not included in the Hispanic origin and race questions. Official Hispanic origin data come from long-form questionnaire Item 5, and official race data come from long-form questionnaire Item 6. Therefore, although data on all groups are collected, the ancestry data shown in SF3 tabulations are for non-Hispanic and nonrace groups. Hispanic and race groups are included in the ancestry table in this book, however, based on the Hispanic origin and Race detail in tabulations from SF1.

The ancestry question allowed respondents to report one or more ancestry groups, although only the first two were coded. If a response was in terms of a dual ancestry, for example, "Irish English," the person was assigned two codes, in this case one for Irish and another for English. However, in certain cases, multiple responses such as "French Canadian," "Greek Cypriote," and "Scotch Irish" were assigned a single code reflecting their status as unique groups. If a person reported one of these unique groups in addition to another group, for example, "Scotch Irish English," resulting in three terms, that person received one code for the unique group (Scotch-Irish) and another one for the remaining group (English). If a person reported "English Irish French," only English and Irish were coded. Certain combinations of ancestries where the ancestry group is a part of another, such as "German-Bavarian," were coded as a single ancestry using the more specific group (Bavarian). Also, responses such as "Polish-American" or "Italian-American" were coded and tabulated as a single entry (Polish or Italian).

The Census Bureau accepted "American" as a unique ethnicity if it was given alone, with an ambiguous response, or with state names. If the respondent listed any other ethnic identity such as "Italian-American," generally the "American" portion of the response was not coded. However, distinct groups such as "American Indian," "Mexican American," and "African American" were coded and identified separately because they represented groups who considered themselves different from those who reported as "Indian," "Mexican," or "African," respectively.

In all tabulations, when respondents provided an unclassifiable ethnic identity (for example, "multinational," "adopted," or "I have no idea"), the answer was included in tabulation category "Unclassified or not reported."

In SF3, the tabulations on ancestry are presented using two types of data presentations — one using total people as the base, and the other using total responses as the base. In this volume, the table shows total responses as a percent of the total population. If all ancestry responses had been included in this table, the total would have been more than 100 percent of the population. Thus, this represents the percentage of people who mentioned a particular ancestry, whether it was alone, or in combination with others.

Unlike other census questions, there was no imputation for nonresponse to the ancestry question.

CITIZENSHIP

The data on citizenship were derived from answers to long-form questionnaire Item 13. Respondents were asked to select one of five categories: (1) born in the United States, (2) born in Puerto Rico or a U.S. Island Area (such as Guam), (3) born abroad of American parent(s), (4) naturalized citizen, (5) not a citizen. People not reporting citizenship were assigned citizenship based on a set of criteria including the citizenship status of other household members and place of birth.

Citizen. This category includes respondents who indicated that they were born in the United States, Puerto Rico, a U.S. Island Area, or abroad of American parent or parents. People who indicated that they were U.S. citizens through naturalization are also citizens.

Not a citizen. This category includes respondents who indicated that they were not U.S. citizens.

Native. The native population includes people born in the United States, Puerto Rico, or the U.S. Island Areas (such as Guam). People who were born in a foreign country but have at least one American (U.S. citizen) parent also are included in this category. The native population includes anyone who was a U.S. citizen at birth.

Foreign born. The foreign-born population includes all people who were not U.S. citizens at birth. Foreign-born people are those who indicated they were either a U.S. citizen by naturalization or they were not a citizen of the United States. Census 2000 does not ask about immigration status. The population surveyed includes all people who indicated that the United States was their usual place of residence on the census date. The foreign-born population includes: immigrants (legal permanent residents), temporary migrants (students), humanitarian migrants (refugees), and unauthorized migrants (people illegally residing in the United States).

The foreign-born population is shown by selected area, country, or region of birth. The places of birth shown in data products were chosen based on the number of respondents who reported that area or country of birth.

DISABILITY STATUS

The data on disability status were derived from answers to long-form questionnaire Items 16 and 17. Item 16 was a two-part question that asked about the existence of the following long-lasting conditions: (a) blindness, deafness, or a severe vision or hearing impairment (sensory disability) and (b) a condition that substantially limits one or more basic physical activities, such as walking, climbing stairs, reaching, lifting, or carrying (physical disability). Item 16 was asked of a sample of the population 5 years old and over. Item 17 was a four-part question that asked if the individual had a physical, mental, or emotional condition lasting 6 months or more that made it difficult to perform certain activities. The four activity categories were: (a) learning, remembering, or concentrating (mental disability); (b) dressing, bathing, or getting around inside the home (self-care disability); (c) going outside the home alone to shop or visit a doctor's office (going outside the home disability); and (d) working at a job or business (employment disability). Categories 17a and 17b were asked of a sample of the population 5 years old and over; 17c and 17d were asked of a sample of the population 16 years old and over.

Individuals were classified as having a disability if any of the following three conditions were true: (1) they were 5 years old and over and had a response of "yes" to a sensory, physical, mental or self-care disability; (2) they were 16 years old and over and had a response of "yes" to going outside the home disability; or (3) they were 16 to 64 years old and had a response of "yes" to employment disability.

DIVERSITY INDEX

The Diversity Index shown in the color map was developed by the Census Bureau and published in *Mapping Census 2000: The Geography of U.S. Diversity* (http://www.census.gov/population/www/cen2000/atlas.html). The map in this book used the Census Bureau's data file (based on the Census 2000 Redistricting data file) but the groupings used in our map differ slightly from those used in the Census Bureau's publication.

The diversity index reports the percentage of times two randomly selected people would differ by race/ethnicity. Working with percents expressed as ratios (e.g., 63 percent = 0.63), the index is calculated in three steps: A. Square the percent for each group, B. Sum the squares, and C. Subtract the sum from 1.00. Eight groups were used for the index: 1. White, not Hispanic; 2. Black or African American; 3. American Indian and Alaska Native (AIAN); 4. Asian; 5. Native Hawaiian and Other Pacific Islander (NHOPI); 6. Two or more races, not Hispanic; 7. Some other race, not Hispanic; and 8. Hispanic or Latino. People indicating Hispanic origin who also indicated Black, AIAN, Asian, or NHOPI were counted only in their race group (0.5 percent of the population). They were not included in the Hispanic group.

EDUCATIONAL ATTAINMENT

Data on educational attainment were derived from answers to long-form questionnaire Item 9. Data on attainment are tabulated for the population 25 years old and over. However, when educational attainment is cross-tabulated by other variables, the universe may change. (For example, in the tables dealing with at-risk youth, persons age 16 to 19 are tallied.) People are classified according to the highest degree or level of school completed. The order in which degrees were listed on the questionnaire suggested that doctorate degrees were "higher" than professional school degrees, which were "higher" than master's degrees. In this book, all of the aforementioned levels are combined into "Bachelor's Degree or Higher". The question included instructions for people currently enrolled in school to report the level of the previous grade attended or the highest degree received. Respondents who did not report educational attainment or enrollment level were assigned the attainment of a person of the same age, race, Hispanic or Latino origin, occupation and sex, where possible, who resided in the same or a nearby area. Respondents who filled more than one box were edited to the highest level or degree reported.

The question included a response category that allowed respondents to report completing the 12th grade without receiving a high school diploma. It allowed people who received either a high school diploma or the equivalent, for example, passed the Test of General Educational Development (G.E.D.) and did not attend college, to be reported as "high school graduate(s)."

Vocational and technical training, such as barber school training; business, trade, technical, and vocational schools; or other training for a specific trade, are specifically excluded.

High school graduate or higher. This category includes people whose highest degree was a high school diploma or its equivalent, people who attended college but did not receive a degree, and people who received a college, university, or professional degree. People who reported completing the 12th grade but not receiving a diploma are not high school graduates.

Not enrolled, not high school graduate. This category includes people of compulsory school attendance age or above who were not enrolled in school and were not high school graduates. These people may be referred to as "high school dropouts." However, there is no criterion regarding when they "dropped out" of school, so they may have never attended high school.

EMPLOYMENT STATUS

NOTE: *The Census Bureau has announced that there may be a problem or problems in the employment-status data of Census 2000 Summary File 3. The labor force data for some places where colleges are located appear to overstate the number in the labor force, the number unemployed, and the percent unemployed, probably because of reporting or processing error. The exact cause is unknown, but the Census Bureau will continue to research the problem.*

The following discussion refers to work during the "reference week" (see below) immediately preceding the census. For items concerning employment in the full year preceding the census see "Work Status in 1999."

The data on employment status (referred to as labor force status in previous censuses), were derived from answers to long-form questionnaire Items 21 and 25, which were asked of a sample of the population 15 years old and over. The series of questions on employment status was designed to identify, in this sequence: (1) people who worked at any time during the reference week; (2) people who did not work during the reference week, but who had jobs or businesses from which they were temporarily absent (excluding people on layoff); (3) people on temporary layoff who expected to be recalled to work within the next 6 months or who had been given a date to return to work, and who were available for work during the reference week; and (4) people who did not work during the reference week, who had looked for work during the reference week or the three previous weeks, and who were available for work during the reference week.

The employment status data shown in Census 2000 tabulations relate to people 16 years old and over.

Employed. All civilians 16 years old and over who were either (1) "at work" — those who did any work at all during the reference week as paid employees, worked in their own business or profession, worked on their own farm, or worked 15 hours or more as unpaid workers on a family farm or in a family business; or (2) were "with a job but not at work" — those who did not work during the reference week, but who had jobs or businesses from which they were temporarily absent because of illness, bad weather, industrial dispute, vacation, or other personal reasons.

Excluded from the employed are people whose only activity consisted of work around their own house (e.g., painting, repairing, or housework) or unpaid volunteer work for religious, charitable, and similar organizations. Also excluded are all institutionalized people and people on active duty in the United States Armed Forces.

Civilian employed. This term is defined exactly the same as the term "employed" above.

Unemployed. All civilians 16 years old and over were classified as unemployed if they were neither "at work" nor "with a job but not at work" during the reference week, were looking for work during the last 4 weeks, and were available to start a job. Also included as unemployed were civilians 16 years old and over who: did not work at all during the reference week, were on temporary layoff from a job, had been informed that they would be recalled to work within the next 6 months or had been given a date to return to work, and were available to return to work during the reference week, except for temporary illness. Examples of job seeking activities were:

- Registering at a public or private employment office
- Meeting with prospective employers
- Investigating possibilities for starting a professional practice or opening a business
- Placing or answering advertisements
- Writing letters of application
- Being on a union or professional register

Civilian labor force. Consists of people classified as employed or unemployed in accordance with the criteria described above.

Labor force. All people classified in the civilian labor force (that is, "employed" and "unemployed" people), plus members of the U.S. Armed Forces (people on active duty with the United States Army, Air Force, Navy, Marine Corps, or Coast Guard).

Not in labor force. All people 16 years old and over who are not classified as members of the labor force. This category consists mainly of students, individuals taking care of home or family, retired workers, seasonal workers enumerated in an off-season who were not looking for work, institutionalized people (all institutionalized people are placed in this category regardless of any work activities they may have done in the reference week), and people doing only incidental unpaid family work (fewer than 15 hours during the reference week).

Worker. The terms "worker" and "work" appear in connection with several subjects: employment status, journey-to-work, class of worker, and work status in 1999. Their meaning varies and, therefore, should be determined by referring to the definition of the subject in which they appear. When used in the concepts "Workers in Family," "Workers in Family in 1999," and "Full-Time, Year-Round Workers," the term "worker" relates to the meaning of work defined for the "Work Status in 1999" subject.

Full-time, year-round workers. See "Work status in 1999."

GRANDPARENTS AS CAREGIVERS

The data on grandparents as caregivers were derived from answers to long-form questionnaire Item 19, which was asked of a sample of the population 15 years old and over. Data were collected on whether a grandchild lives in the household, whether the grandparent has responsibility for the basic needs of the grandchild, and the duration of that responsibility. Because of the very low number of people under 30 years old who are grandparents, data are only shown for people 30 years old and over.

Existence of a grandchild in the household. This was determined by a "Yes" answer to the sample question, "Does this person have any of his/her own grandchildren under the age of 18 living in this house or apartment?"

Responsibility for basic needs. This question determines if the grandparent is financially responsible for food, shelter, clothing, day care, and so forth, for any or all grandchildren living in the household.

Duration of responsibility. The answer refers to the grandchild for whom the grandparent has been responsible for the longest period of time. Duration categories ranged from less than 6 months to 5 years or more.

GROSS RENT

The data on gross rent were obtained from answers to long-form questionnaire Items 45a–45d. Gross rent is the contract rent plus the estimated average monthly cost of utilities (electricity, gas, water and sewer) and fuels (oil, coal, kerosene, wood) if these are paid by the renter (or paid for the renter by someone else). Gross rent is intended to eliminate differentials that result from varying practices with respect to the inclusion of utilities and fuels as part of the rental payment. The estimated costs of utilities and fuels are reported on an annual basis but are converted to monthly figures for the tabulations. Renter units occupied without payment of cash rent are shown separately as "No cash rent" in the tabulations.

Median gross rent. Median gross rent divides the gross rent distribution into two equal parts: one-half of the cases falling below the median gross rent and one-half above the median. Median gross rent is computed on the basis of a standard distribution with the minimum value less than $100 and the maximum value $2000 or more. Median gross rent is rounded to the nearest whole dollar.

GROSS RENT AS A PERCENTAGE OF HOUSEHOLD INCOME IN 1999

Gross rent as a percentage of household income in 1999 is a computed ratio of monthly gross rent to monthly household income (total household income in 1999 divided by 12). The ratio is computed separately for each unit and is rounded to the nearest tenth. Units for which no cash rent is paid and units occupied by households that reported no income or a net loss in 1999 comprise the category "Not computed."

Median gross rent as a percentage of household income in 1999. This measure divides the gross rent as a percentage of household income distribution into two equal parts, one-half of the cases falling below the median gross rent as a percentage of household income and one-half above the median. Median gross rent as a percentage of household income is computed on the basis of a standard distribution with the minimum value less than 10 percent, and the maximum value 50 percent or more. Median gross rent as a percentage of household income is rounded to the nearest tenth.

HISPANIC ORIGIN

The data on the Hispanic or Latino population were derived from answers to long-form questionnaire Item 5, and short-form questionnaire Item 7. The terms ''Spanish,'' ''Hispanic origin,'' and ''Latino'' are used interchangeably. Some respondents identify with all three terms, while others may identify with only one of these three specific terms. Hispanics or Latinos who identify with the terms ''Spanish,'' ''Hispanic,'' or ''Latino'' are those who classify themselves in one of the specific Hispanic or Latino categories listed on the questionnaire — ''Mexican,'' ''Puerto Rican,'' or ''Cuban'' — as well as those who indicate that they are ''other Spanish, Hispanic, or Latino.'' People who do not identify with one of the specific origins listed on the questionnaire but indicate that they are ''other Spanish, Hispanic, or Latino'' are those whose origins are from Spain, the Spanish-speaking countries of Central or South America, the Dominican Republic, or people identifying themselves generally as Spanish, Spanish-American, Hispanic, Hispano, Latino, and so on. All write-in responses to the ''other Spanish/Hispanic/Latino'' category were coded.

Origin can be viewed as the heritage, nationality group, lineage, or country of birth of the person or the person's parents or ancestors before their arrival in the United States. People who identify their origin as Spanish, Hispanic, or Latino may be of any race.

Some tabulations are shown by the origin of the householder. In all cases where the origin of households, families, or occupied housing units is classified as Spanish, Hispanic, or Latino, the origin of the householder is used. If individuals could not provide a Hispanic origin response, their origin was assigned using specific rules of precedence of household relationship. For example, if origin was missing for a natural-born daughter in the household, then either the origin of the householder, another natural-born child, or the spouse of the householder was assigned. If Hispanic origin was not reported for anyone in the household, the origin of a householder in a previously processed household with the same race was assigned. For Census 2000, race and Spanish surnames were used to assist in assigning an origin.

HOUSEHOLD SIZE

This item is based on the count of people in occupied housing units. All people occupying the housing unit are counted, including the householder, occupants related to the householder, and lodgers, roomers, boarders, and so forth. For tabulations based on population data, ''household size'' is the number of people in households. The sample count of ''occupied housing units'' may not match the sample count of ''households.'' Consequently, the household size measures derived from housing and population-based data also may differ.

Average household size of occupied unit. A measure obtained by dividing the number of people living in occupied housing units by the number of occupied housing units. This measure is rounded to the nearest hundredth.

Average household size of owner-occupied unit. A measure obtained by dividing the number of people living in owner-occupied housing units by the total number of owner-occupied housing units. This measure is rounded to the nearest hundredth.

Average household size of renter-occupied unit. A measure obtained by dividing the number of people living in renter-occupied housing units by the total number of renter-occupied housing units. This measure is rounded to the nearest hundredth.

HOUSEHOLD TYPE AND RELATIONSHIP

Household

A household includes all of the people who occupy a housing unit. (People not living in households are classified as living in group quarters.) A housing unit is a house, an apartment, a mobile home, a group of rooms, or a single room occupied (or if vacant, intended for occupancy) as separate living quarters. Separate living quarters are those in which the occupants live separately from any other people in the building and that have direct access from the outside of the building or through a common hall. The occupants may be a single family, one person living alone, two or more families living together, or any other group of related or unrelated people who share living quarters.

In 100-percent tabulations, the count of households or householders always equals the count of occupied housing units. In sample tabulations, the numbers may differ as a result of the weighting process.

Average household size. A measure obtained by dividing the number of people in households by the total number of households (or householders). In cases where household members are tabulated by race or Hispanic origin, household members are classified by the race or Hispanic origin of the householder rather than the race or Hispanic origin of each individual. Average household size is rounded to the nearest hundredth.

Relationship to Householder

Householder. The data on relationship to householder were derived from the question, ''How is this person related to Person 1,'' which was asked of Persons 2 and higher in housing units. One person in each household is designated as the householder (Person 1). In most cases, the householder is the person, or one of the people, in whose name the home is owned, being bought, or rented. If there is no such person in the household, any adult household member 15 years old and over could be designated as the householder (i.e., Person 1).

Households are classified by type according to the sex of the householder and the presence of relatives. Two types of householders are distinguished: family householders and nonfamily householders. A family householder is a householder living with one or more individuals related to him or her by birth, marriage, or adoption. The householder and all of the people in the household related to him or her are family members. A nonfamily householder is a householder living alone or with nonrelatives only.

Spouse (husband/wife). A spouse (husband/wife) is a person married to and living with a householder. People in formal marriages, as well as people in common-law marriages, are included.

The number of spouses is equal to the number of "married-couple families" or "married-couple households" in 100-percent tabulations. Marital status categories cannot be inferred from the 100-percent tabulations since the marital status question was not included on the 100-percent form. In sample tabulations, the number of spouses may not be equal to the number of married-couple households due to the differences in the weighting procedures for sample data.

Child. A child is a son or daughter by birth, a stepchild, or an adopted child of the householder, regardless of the child's age or marital status. The category excludes sons-in-law, daughters-in-law, and foster children.

Own child. Own child is a never-married child under 18 years who is a son or daughter of the householder by birth, marriage (a stepchild), or adoption. For sample data, own children consists of sons/daughters of householders who are under 18 years old and who have never been married. In certain tabulations, own children are further classified as living with two parents or with one parent only. Own children living with two parents are by definition found only in married-couple families (Note: In the tabulation under "EMPLOYMENT STATUS" of own children under 6 years by employment status of parents, the number of "own children" includes any child under 6 years old in a family or a subfamily who is a son or daughter, by birth, marriage, or adoption, of a member of the householder's family, but not necessarily of the householder.)

Related children. Related children include the sons and daughters of the householder (including natural-born, adopted, or stepchildren) and all other people under 18 years old, regardless of marital status, in the household, who are related to the householder, except the spouse of the householder. Foster children are not included since they are not related to the householder.

Family Type

A family includes a householder and one or more other people living in the same household who are related to the householder by birth, marriage, or adoption. All people in a household who are related to the householder are regarded as members of his or her family. A family household may contain people not related to the householder, but those people are not included as part of the householder's family in census tabulations. Thus, the number of family households is equal to the number of families, but family households may include more members than do families. A household can contain only one family for purposes of census tabulations. Not all households contain families since a household may comprise a group of unrelated people or one person living alone. Families are classified by type as either a "married-couple family" or "other family" according to the presence of a spouse. "Other family" is further broken out according to the sex of the householder. The data on family type are based on answers to questions on sex and relationship that were asked on a 100-percent basis.

Married-couple family. This category includes a family in which the householder and his or her spouse are enumerated as members of the same household.

Other family:

Male householder, no wife present. This category includes a family with a male maintaining a household with no wife of the householder present.

Female householder, no husband present. This category includes a family with a female maintaining a household with no husband of the householder present.

Nonfamily household. This category includes a householder living alone or with nonrelatives only.

Unmarried-Partner Household

An unmarried-partner household is a household that includes a householder and an "unmarried partner." An "unmarried partner" can be of the same or of the opposite sex of the householder. An "unmarried partner" in an "unmarried-partner household" is an adult who is unrelated to the householder, but shares living quarters and has a close personal relationship with the householder. An unmarried-partner household may also be a family household or a nonfamily household, depending on the presence or absence of another person in the household who is related to the householder. There may be only one unmarried-partner per household, and an unmarried partner may not be included in a married-couple household as the householder cannot have both a spouse and an unmarried partner. In this book, unmarried-partner households are referred to as cohabiting couples.

"Traditional" Households, "Traditional" Families, and "Stay-at-Home" Parents.

Some of the maps and tables in this book refer to "traditional" households and families, and "stay-at-home parents", which are not Census Bureau definitions.

A *"Traditional" Household* consists of a married couple with children under 18.

"Children in Traditional Families" live with two married-couple parents, with only the father employed.

"Children with no Stay-at-Home Parent" are children who live with married-couple parents, both of whom are employed, or children who live with a single parent, and that parent is employed. This definition does not account for part-time work, parents who work at home, parents who work alternating shifts, or other circumstances which may result in one or both parents usually or always being at home. Under this definition, a "stay-at-home" parent is not employed.

INCOME IN 1999

The data on income in 1999 were derived from answers to long-form questionnaire Items 31 and 32, which were asked of a sample of the population 15 years old and over. "Total income" is the sum of the amounts reported separately for wage or salary income; net self-employment income; interest, dividends, or net rental or royalty income or income from estates and trusts; Social Security or railroad retirement income; Supplemental Security Income (SSI); public assistance or welfare payments; retirement, survivor, or disability pensions; and all other income. "Earnings" are defined as the sum of wage or salary income and net income from self-employment. "Earnings" represent the amount of income received regularly for people 16 years old and over before deductions for personal income taxes, Social Security, bond purchases, union dues, and Medicare deductions.

Receipts from the following sources are not included as income: capital gains, money received from the sale of property (unless the recipient was engaged in the business of selling such property); the value of income "in kind" from food stamps, public housing subsidies, medical care, employer contributions for individuals; withdrawal of bank deposits; money borrowed; tax refunds; exchange of money between relatives living in the same household; and gifts and lump-sum inheritances, insurance payments, and other types of lump-sum receipts.

Income Type in 1999

The eight types of income reported in the census are defined as follows:

1. **Wage or salary income.** Wage or salary income includes total money earnings received for work performed as an employee during the calendar year 1999. It includes wages, salary, armed forces pay, commissions, tips, piece-rate payments, and cash bonuses earned before deductions were made for taxes, bonds, pensions, union dues.

2. **Self-employment income.** Self-employment income includes both farm and nonfarm self-employment income.

Nonfarm self-employment income includes net money income (gross receipts minus expenses) from one's own business, professional enterprise, or partnership. Gross receipts include the value of all goods sold and services rendered. Expenses include costs of goods purchased, rent, heat, light, power, depreciation charges, wages and salaries paid, business taxes (not personal income taxes).

Farm self-employment income includes net money income (gross receipts minus operating expenses) from the operation of a farm by a person on his or her own account, as an owner, renter, or sharecropper. Gross receipts include the value of all products sold, government farm programs, money received from the rental of farm equipment to others, and incidental receipts from the sale of wood, sand, gravel. Operating expenses include cost of feed, fertilizer, seed, and other farming supplies, cash wages paid to farmhands, depreciation charges, cash rent, interest on farm mortgages, farm building repairs, farm taxes (not state and federal personal income taxes). The value of fuel, food, or other farm products used for family living is not included as part of net income.

3. **Interest, dividends, or net rental income.** Interest, dividends, or net rental income includes interest on savings or bonds, dividends from stockholdings or membership in associations, net income from rental of property to others and receipts from boarders or lodgers, net royalties, and periodic payments from an estate or trust fund.

4. **Social Security income.** Social Security income includes Social Security pensions and survivors' benefits, permanent disability insurance payments made by the Social Security Administration prior to deductions for medical insurance, and railroad retirement insurance checks from the U.S. government. Medicare reimbursements are not included.

5. **Supplemental Security Income (SSI).** Supplemental Security Income (SSI) is a nationwide U.S. assistance program administered by the Social Security Administration that guarantees a minimum level of income for needy aged, blind, or disabled individuals.

6. **Public assistance income.** Public assistance income includes general assistance and Temporary Assistance to Needy Families (TANF). Separate payments received for hospital or other medical care (vendor payments) are excluded. This does not include Supplemental Security Income (SSI).

7. **Retirement income.** Retirement income includes: (1) retirement pensions and survivor benefits from a former employer; labor union; or federal, state, or local government; and the U.S. military; (2) income from workers' compensation; disability income from companies or unions; federal, state, or local government; and the U.S. military; (3) periodic receipts from annuities and insurance; and (4) regular income from IRA and KEOGH plans. This does not include Social Security income.

8. **All other income.** All other income includes unemployment compensation, Veterans' Administration (VA) payments, alimony and child support, contributions received periodically from people not living in the household, military family allotments, and other kinds of periodic income other than earnings.

Income of households. This includes the income of the householder and all other individuals 15 years old and over in the household, whether they are related to the householder or not. Because many households consist of only one person, average household income is usually less than average family income. Although the household income statistics cover calendar year 1999, the characteristics of individuals and the composition of households refer to the time of enumeration (April 1, 2000). Thus, the income of the household does not include amounts received by individuals who were members of the household during all or part of calendar year 1999 if these individuals no longer resided in the household at the time of enumeration. Similarly, income amounts reported by individuals who did not reside in the household during 1999 but who were members of the household at the time of enumeration are included. However, the composition of most households was the same during 1999 as at the time of enumeration.

Income of families. In compiling statistics on family income, the incomes of all members 15 years old and over related to the householder are summed and treated as a single amount. Although the family income statistics cover calendar year 1999, the characteristics of individuals and the composition of families refer to the time of enumeration (April 1, 2000). Thus, the income of the family does not include amounts received by individuals who were members of the family during all or part of calendar year 1999 if these individuals no longer resided with the family at the time of enumeration. Similarly, income amounts reported by individuals who did not reside with the family during 1999 but who were members of the family at the time of enumeration are included. However, the composition of most families was the same during 1999 as at the time of enumeration.

Income of individuals. Income for individuals is obtained by summing the eight types of income for each person 15 years old and over. The characteristics of individuals are based on the time of enumeration (April 1, 2000), even though the amounts are for calendar year 1999.

Median income. The median divides the income distribution into two equal parts: half of the cases falls below the median income and half above the median. For households and families, the median income is based on the distribution of the total number of households and families including those with no income. The median income for individuals is based on individuals 15 years old and over with income. Median income for households, families, and individuals is computed on the basis of a standard distribution with the minimum value less than $2500 and the maximum value $200,000 or more. Median income is rounded to the nearest whole dollar. Median income figures are calculated using linear interpolation if the width of the interval containing the estimate is $2,500 or less. If the width of the interval containing the estimate is greater than $2,500, Pareto interpolation is used.

Mean income. Mean income is the amount obtained by dividing the aggregate income of a particular statistical universe by the number of units in that universe. Thus, mean household income is obtained by dividing total household income by the total number of households. For the various types of income, the means are based on households having those types of income. For households and families, the mean income is based on the distribution of the total number of households and families including those with no income. The mean income for individuals is based on individuals 15 years old and over with income. Mean income is rounded to the nearest whole dollar. Care should be exercised in using and interpreting mean income values for small subgroups of the population. Because the mean is influenced strongly by extreme values in the distribution, it is especially susceptible to the effects of sampling variability, misreporting, and processing errors. The median, which is not affected by extreme values, is, therefore, a better measure than the mean when the population base is small. The mean, nevertheless, is shown in some data products for most small subgroups because, when weighted according to the number of cases, the means can be added to obtained summary measures for areas and groups other than those shown in census tabulations.

Earnings. Earnings are defined as the sum of wage or salary income and net income from self-employment. ''Earnings'' represent the amount of income received regularly for people 16 years old and over before deductions for personal income taxes, social security, bond purchases, union dues, Medicare deductions, and so forth.

Per capita income. Per capita income is the mean income computed for every man, woman, and child in a particular group. It is derived by dividing the total income of a particular group by the total population in that group. The aggregate used to calculate per capita income is rounded. Per capita income is rounded to the nearest whole dollar.

INDUSTRY, OCCUPATION, AND CLASS OF WORKER

The data on industry, occupation, and class of worker were derived from answers to long-form questionnaire Items 27, 28, and 29 respectively, which were asked of a sample of the population 15 years old and over. Information on industry relates to the kind of business conducted by a person's employing organization; occupation describes the kind of work a person does on the job. For employed people, the data refer to the person's job during the reference week. For those who worked at two or more jobs, the data refer to the job at which the person worked the greatest number of hours during the reference week. For unemployed people, the data refer to their last job. The industry and occupation statistics are derived from the detailed classification systems developed for Census 2000 as described below.

Respondents provided the data for the tabulations by writing on the questionnaires descriptions of their industry and occupation. These descriptions were data captured and sent to an' automated coder (computer software), which assigned a portion of the written entries to categories in the classification system. The automated system assigned codes to 59 percent of the industry entries and 56 percent of the occupation entries. Those cases not coded by the computer were referred to clerical staff in the Census Bureau's National Processing Center in Jeffersonville, Indiana, for coding. The clerical staff converted the written questionnaire responses to codes by comparing these responses to entries in the *Alphabetical Index of Industries and Occupations*. For the industry code, these coders also referred to an Employer Name List. This list, prepared from the American Business Index (ABI), contained the names of business establishments and their North American Industrial Classification System (NAICS) codes converted to population census equivalents. This list facilitated coding and maintained industrial classification comparability.

Industry

The industry classification system used during Census 2000 was developed for the census and consists of 265 categories for employed people, classified into 14 major industry groups. From 1940 through 1990, the industrial classification was based on the *Standard Industrial Classification (SIC) Manual*. The Census 2000 classification was developed from the 1997 North American Industry Classification System (NAICS) published by the Office of Management and Budget, Executive Office of the President. NAICS is an industry description system that groups establishments into industries based on the activities in which they are primarily engaged. The NAICS differs from most industry classifications because it is a supply-based, or production-oriented economic concept. Census data, which were collected from households, differ in detail and nature from those obtained from establishment surveys. Therefore, the census classification system, while defined in NAICS terms, cannot reflect the full detail in all categories. NAICS shows a more detailed hierarchical structure than that used for Census 2000. The expansion from 11 divisions in the SIC to 20 sectors in the NAICS provides groupings that are meaningful and useful for economic analysis. Various statistical programs that previously sampled or published at the SIC levels face problems with the coverage for 20 sectors instead of 11 divisions. These programs requested an alternative aggregation structure for production purposes which was approved and issued by the Office of Management and Budget on May 15, 2001, in the clarification Memorandum No. 2, ''NAICS Alternate Aggregation Structure for Use by U.S. Statistical Agencies.'' Several census data products will use the alternative aggregation, while others, such as Summary File 3 and Summary File 4, will use more detail. In the tables in this book, Tables B-1.18, B-1.20, and B-2 include all 13 broad industry categories from SF3. In Tables B-3, B-4, and B-5, the groups have been further combined: Construction and Manufacturing are presented as a single industry group; Wholesale and Retail Trade are presented as a single industry group; and the category "Service Industries" combines "Professional , Scientific, Management, Administrative, and Waste Management Services", "Educational, Health, and Social Services", "Arts, Entertainment, Recreation, Accommodation, and Food Services", and "Other Services."

Occupation

The occupational classification system used during Census 2000 consists of 509 specific occupational categories for employed people arranged into 23 major occupational groups. This classification was developed based on the *Standard Occupational Classification (SOC) Manual: 2000,* which includes a hierarchical structure showing 23 major occupational groups divided into 96 minor groups, 449 broad groups, and 821 detailed occupations. For Census 2000, tabulations with occupation as the primary characteristic present several levels of occupational detail. Some occupation groups are related closely to certain industries. Operators of transportation equipment, farm operators and workers, and healthcare providers account for major portions of their respective industries of transportation, agriculture, and health care. However, the industry categories include people in other occupations. For example, people employed in agriculture include truck drivers and bookkeepers; people employed in the transportation industry include mechanics, freight handlers, and payroll clerks; and people employed in the health care industry include occupations such as security guard and secretary.

Class of Worker

The data on class of worker were derived from answers to long-form questionnaire Item 29. The information on class of worker refers to the same job as a respondent's industry and occupation, categorizing people according to the type of ownership of the employing organization. The class of worker categories are defined as follows:

Private wage and salary workers. Private wage and salary workers include people who worked for wages, salary, commission, tips, pay-in-kind, or piece rates for a private for-profit employer or a private not-for-profit, tax-exempt, or charitable organization.

In this book, self-employed people whose business was incorporated are categorized as self-employed, although many Census Bureau tabulations include them with private wage and salary workers because they are paid employees of their own companies.

Government workers. Government workers includes people who were employees of any federal, tribal, state, or local governmental unit, regardless of the activity of the particular agency. Employees of foreign governments, the United Nations, or other formal international organizations were classified as "federal government," unlike the 1990 census when they were classified as "private not-for-profit."

Self-employed. Self-employed includes people who worked for profit or fees in their own unincorporated business, professional practice, or trade, or who operated a farm, and persons who were self-employed in their own incorporated businesses.

Unpaid family workers. Unpaid family workers includes people who worked 15 hours or more without pay in a business or on a farm operated by a relative.

The industry category, "Public administration," is limited to regular government functions, such as legislative, judicial, administrative, and regulatory activities of governments. Other government organizations, such as schools, hospitals, liquor stores, and bus lines, are classified by industry according to the activity in which they are engaged. On the other hand, the class of worker government categories include all government workers.

In some cases, respondents supplied industry, occupation, or class of worker descriptions that were not sufficiently specific for a precise classification or did not report on these items at all. In the coding operation, certain types of incomplete entries were corrected using the *Alphabetical Index of Industries and Occupations.* For example, it was possible in certain situations to assign an industry code based on the occupation reported, or vice versa.

Following the coding operations, there was a computer edit and an allocation process. The edit first determined whether a respondent was in the universe that required an industry and occupation code. The codes for the three items (industry, occupation, and class of worker) were checked to ensure they were valid and were edited for their relation to each other. Invalid and inconsistent codes were either blanked or changed to a consistent code.

If one or more of the three codes was blank after the edit, a code was assigned from a "similar" person based on other items, such as age, sex, education, farm or nonfarm residence, and weeks worked. If all of the labor force and income data were blank, all of these economic items were assigned from one other person or one other household who provided all the necessary data.

JOURNEY TO WORK

Means of Transportation to Work

The data on means of transportation to work were derived from answers to long-form questionnaire Item 23a, which was asked of a sample of the population 15 years old and over. This question was asked of people who indicated in Question 21 that they worked at some time during the reference week. Means of transportation to work refers to the principal mode of travel or type of conveyance that the worker usually used to get from home to work during the reference week. Data were tabulated for workers 16 years old and over; that is, members of the armed forces and civilians who were at work during the reference week.

People who used different means of transportation on different days of the week were asked to specify the one they used most often, that is, the greatest number of days. People who used more than one means of transportation to get to work each day were asked to report the one used for the longest distance during the work trip. The category "Car, truck, or van — drove alone" includes people who usually drove alone to work, as well as people who were driven to work by someone who then drove back home or to a nonwork destination during the reference week. The category ''Car, truck, or van — carpooled'' includes workers who reported that two or more people usually rode to work in the vehicle during the reference week. The category ''Public transportation'' includes workers who usually used a bus or trolley bus, streetcar or trolley car, subway or elevated, railroad, ferryboat, or taxicab during the reference week. The category ''Other means'' includes workers who used a mode of travel that is not identified separately. The category ''Other means'' may vary from table to table, depending on the amount of detail shown in a particular distribution.

The means of transportation data for some areas may show workers using modes of public transportation that are not available in those areas (for example, subway or elevated riders in a metropolitan area where there actually is no subway or elevated service). This result is largely due to people who worked during the reference week at a location that was different from their usual place of work (such as people away from home on business in an area where subway service was available) and people who used more than one means of transportation each day but whose principal means was unavailable where they lived (for example, residents of nonmetropolitan areas who drove to the fringe of a metropolitan area and took the commuter railroad most of the distance to work).

Travel Time to Work

The data on travel time to work were derived from answers to long-form questionnaire Item 24b, which was asked of a sample of the population 15 years old and over. This question was asked of people who indicated in Question 21 that they worked at some time during the reference week and who reported in Question 23a that they worked outside their home. Travel time to work refers to the total number of minutes that it usually took the person to get from home to work each day during the reference week. The elapsed time includes time spent waiting for public transportation, picking up passengers in carpools, and time spent in other activities related to getting to work. Data were tabulated for workers 16 years old and over; that is, members of the armed forces and civilians who were at work during the reference week.

Mean travel time to work (minutes). Mean travel time to work is the average travel time in minutes that workers usually took to get from home to work (one way) during the reference week. This measure is obtained by dividing the total number of minutes taken to get from home to work by the number of workers 16 years old and over who did not work at home. The travel time includes time spent waiting for public transportation, picking up passengers in carpools, and time spent in other activities related to getting to work. Mean travel times of workers having specific characteristics also are computed. For example, the mean travel time of workers traveling 45 or more minutes is computed by dividing the aggregate travel time of workers whose travel time was 45 or more minutes by the number of workers whose travel time was 45 or more minutes. Mean travel time to work is rounded to the nearest tenth.

LANGUAGE SPOKEN AT HOME AND ABILITY TO SPEAK ENGLISH

Language Spoken at Home

Data on language spoken at home were derived from answers to long-form questionnaire Items 11a and 11b. Data were edited to include in tabulations only the population 5 years old and over. Questions 11a and 11b referred to languages spoken at home in an effort to measure the current use of languages other than English. People who knew languages other than English but did not use them at home or who only used them elsewhere were excluded. Most people who reported speaking a language other than English at home also speak English. The questions did not permit determination of the primary or dominant language of people who spoke both English and another language.

Instructions to enumerators and questionnaire assistance center staff stated that a respondent should mark ''Yes'' in Question 11a if the person sometimes or always spoke a language other than English at home. Also, respondents were instructed not to mark ''Yes'' if a language other than English was spoken only at school or work, or if speaking another language was limited to a few expressions or slang of the other language. For Question 11b, respondents were instructed to print the name of the non-English language spoken at home. If the person spoke more than one language other than English, the person was to report the language spoken more often or the language learned first.

For people who indicated that they spoke a language other than English at home in Question 11a, but failed to specify the name of the language in Question 11b, the language was assigned based on the language of other speakers in the household, on the language of a person of the same Spanish origin or detailed race group living in the same or a nearby area, or of a person of the same place of birth or ancestry. In all cases where a person was assigned a non-English language, it was assumed that the language was spoken at home. People for whom a language other than English was entered in Question 11b, and for whom Question 11a was blank were assumed to speak that other language at home.

The write-in responses listed in Question 11b (specific language spoken) were optically scanned or keyed onto computer files, then coded into more than 380 detailed language categories using an automated coding system. The automated procedure compared write-in responses reported by respondents with entries in a master code list, which initially contained approximately 2,000 language names, and added variants and misspellings found in the 1990 census. Each write-in response was given a numeric code that was associated with one of the detailed categories in the dictionary. If the respondent listed more than one non-English language, only the first was coded. The write-in responses represented the names people used for languages they speak. They may not match the names or categories used by linguists. The sets of categories used are sometimes geographic and sometimes linguistic.

Household language. In households where one or more people (5 years old and over) speak a language other than English, the household language assigned to all household members is the non-English language spoken by the first person with a non-English language in the following order: householder, spouse, parent, sibling, child, grandchild, in-laws, other relatives, step-child, unmarried partner, housemate or roommate, and other non-relatives. Thus, a person who speaks only English may have a non-English household language assigned to him/her in tabulations of individuals by household language.

Ability to Speak English

Data on ability to speak English were derived from the answers to long-form questionnaire Item 11c. Respondents who reported that they spoke a language other than English in long-form questionnaire Item 11a were asked to indicate their ability to speak English in one of the following categories: "Very well," "Well," "Not well," or "Not at all." The data on ability to speak English represent the person's own perception about his or her own ability or, because census questionnaires are usually completed by one household member, the responses may represent the perception of another household member. Respondents were not instructed on how to interpret the response categories in Question 11c. People who reported that they spoke a language other than English at home, but whose ability to speak English was not reported, were assigned the English-language ability of a randomly selected person of the same age, Hispanic origin, nativity and year of entry, and language group.

Linguistic isolation. A household in which no person 14 years old and over speaks only English and no person 14 years old and over who speaks a language other than English speaks English "Very well" is classified as "linguistically isolated." In other words, a household in which all members 14 years old and over speak a non-English language and also speak English less than "Very well" (have difficulty with English) is "linguistically isolated." All the members of a linguistically isolated household are tabulated as linguistically isolated, including members under 14 years old who may speak only English.

METROPOLITAN/CENTRAL CITY STATUS

The general concept of a metropolitan area (MA) is one of a large population nucleus, together with adjacent communities that have a high degree of economic and social integration with that nucleus. (See Appendix A for more information about Metropolitan Areas.) The territory, population, and housing units in MAs are referred to as "metropolitan." The metropolitan category is subdivided into "inside central city" and "outside central city." The territory, population, and housing units located outside territory designated "metropolitan" are referred to as "nonmetropolitan."

Central City

In each metropolitan statistical area and consolidated metropolitan statistical area, the largest place and, in some cases, one or more additional places are designated as "central cities" under the official standards. A few primary metropolitan statistical areas do not have central cities.

MORTGAGE STATUS

The data on mortgage status were obtained from answers to long-form questionnaire Items 47a and 48a, which were asked on a sample basis at owner-occupied housing units. "Mortgage" refers to all forms of debt where the property is pledged as security for repayment of the debt, including deeds of trust; trust deeds; contracts to purchase; land contracts; junior mortgages; and home equity loans. A mortgage is considered a first mortgage if it has prior claim over any other mortgage or if it is the only mortgage on the property. All other mortgages, (second, third, and so on) are considered junior mortgages. A home equity loan is generally a junior mortgage. If no first mortgage is reported, but a junior mortgage or home equity loan is reported, then the loan is considered a first mortgage. In most census data products, the tabulations for "Selected Monthly Owner Costs" and "Selected Monthly Owner Costs as a Percentage of Household Income in 1999" usually are shown separately for units "with a mortgage" and for units "not mortgaged." The category "not mortgaged" comprises housing units owned free and clear of debt.

PLACE OF BIRTH

The data on place of birth were derived from answers to long-form questionnaire Item 12. Respondents were asked to report the U.S. state, Puerto Rico, U.S. Island Area, or foreign country where they were born. People not reporting a place of birth were assigned the state or country of birth of another family member or their residence 5 years earlier, or were imputed the response of another person with similar characteristics. People born outside the United States were asked to report their place of birth according to current international boundaries. Since numerous changes in boundaries of foreign countries have occurred in the last century, some people may have reported their place of birth in terms of boundaries that existed at the time of their birth or emigration, or in accordance with their own national preference.

POVERTY STATUS IN 1999

The poverty data were derived from answers to long-form questionnaire Items 31 and 32, the same questions used to derive income data. (For more information, see "Income in 1999.") The Census Bureau uses the federal government's official poverty definition. The Social Security Administration (SSA) developed the original poverty definition in 1964, which federal interagency committees subsequently revised in 1969 and 1980. The Office of Management and Budget's (OMB's) *Directive 14* prescribes this definition as the official poverty measure for federal agencies to use in their statistical work.

Derivation of the Current Poverty Measure

When the Social Security Administration (SSA) created the poverty definition in 1964, it focused on family food consumption. The U.S. Department of Agriculture (USDA) used its data about the nutritional needs of children and adults to construct food plans for families. Within each food plan, dollar amounts varied according to the total number of people in the family and the family's composition, such as the number of children within each family. The cheapest of these plans, the Economy Food Plan, was designed to address the dietary needs of families on an austere budget. Since the USDA's 1955 Food Consumption Survey showed that families of three or more people across all income levels spent roughly one-third of their income on food, the SSA multiplied the cost of the Economy Food Plan by three to obtain dollar figures for the poverty thresholds. Since the Economy Food Plan budgets varied by family size and composition, so too did the poverty thresholds. For 2-person families, the thresholds were adjusted by slightly higher factors because those households had higher fixed costs. Thresholds for unrelated individuals were calculated as a fixed proportion of the corresponding thresholds for 2-person families. The poverty thresholds are revised annually to allow for changes in the cost of living as reflected in the Consumer Price Index (CPI-U). The poverty thresholds are the same for all parts of the country — they are not adjusted for regional, state or local variations in the cost of living. For a detailed discussion of the poverty definition, see U.S. Census Bureau, Current Population Reports, *"Poverty in the United States: 1999,"* P-60-210.

How Poverty Status is Determined

The poverty status of families and unrelated individuals in 1999 was determined using 48 thresholds (income cutoffs) arranged in a two dimensional matrix. The matrix consists of family size (from 1 person to 9 or more people) cross-classified by presence and number of family members under 18 years old (from no children present to 8 or more children present). Unrelated individuals and 2-person families were further differentiated by the age of the reference person (RP) (under 65 years old and 65 years old and over). To determine a person's poverty status, one compares the person's total family income with the poverty threshold appropriate for that person's family size and composition (see table below). If the total income of that person's family is less than the threshold appropriate for that family, then the person is considered poor, together with every member of his or her family. If a person is not living with anyone related by birth, marriage, or adoption, then the person's own income is compared with his or her poverty threshold.

Weighted average thresholds. Even though the official poverty data are based on the 48 thresholds arranged by family size and number of children within the family, data users often want to get an idea of the "average" threshold for a given family size. The weighted average thresholds provide that summary. They are weighted averages because for any given family size, families with a certain number of children may be more or less common than families with a different number of children. In other words, among 3-person families, there are more families with two adults and one child than families with three adults. To get the weighted average threshold for families of a particular size, multiply each threshold by the number of families for whom that threshold applies; then add up those products, and divide by the total number of families who are of that family size. For example, for 3-person families, 1999 weighted thresholds were calculated in the following way using information from the 2000 Current Population Survey:

Family type	Number of families		Threshold	
No children (three adults)	5,213	*	$13,032	= $67,935,816
One child (two adults)	8,208	*	$13,410	= $110,069,280
Two children (one adult)	2,656	*	$13,423	= $35,651,488
Totals	16,077		$213,656,584	

Source: Current Population Survey, March 2000.

Dividing $213,656,584 by 16,077 (the total number of 3-person families) yields $13,290, the weighted average threshold for 3-person families. Please note that the thresholds are weighted not just by the number of poor families, but by all families for which the thresholds apply: the thresholds are used to determine which families are *at* or *above* poverty, as well as below poverty.

Individuals for whom poverty status is determined. Poverty status was determined for all people except institutionalized people, people in military group quarters, people in college dormitories, and unrelated individuals under 15 years old. These groups also were excluded from the numerator and denominator when calculating poverty rates. They are considered neither "poor" nor "nonpoor."

Specified poverty levels. For various reasons, the official poverty definition does not satisfy all the needs of data users. Therefore, some of the data reflect the number of people below different percentages of the poverty level. These specified poverty levels are obtained by multiplying the official thresholds by the appropriate factor. For example, the average income cutoff at 125 percent of the poverty level was $21,286 ($17,029 x 1.25) in 1999 for family of four people.

POVERTY STATUS OF HOUSEHOLDS IN 1999

The data on poverty status of households were derived from answers to the income questions. The income items were asked on a sample basis. Since poverty is defined at the family level and not the household level, the poverty status of the household is determined by the poverty status of the householder. Households are classified as poor when the total 1999 income of the householder's family is below the appropriate poverty threshold. (For nonfamily householders, their own income is compared with the appropriate threshold.) The income of people living in the household who are unrelated to the householder is not considered when determining the poverty status of a household, nor does their presence affect the family size in determining the appropriate threshold. The poverty thresholds vary depending upon three criteria: size of family, number of children, and, for 1- and 2-person families, age of the householder.

Poverty Threshold in 1999, by Size of Family and Number of Related Children Under 18 Years Old (dollars)

Size of family unit	Weighed average threshold	None	One	Two	Three	Four	Five	Six	Seven	Eight or More
One person (unrelated individual)	8501									
Under 65 years old	8667	8667								
65 years and over old and over	7990	7990								
Two people	10869									
Householder under 65 years old	11214	11156	11483							
Householder 65 years old and over	10075	10070	11440							
Three people	13290	13032	13410	13423						
Four people	17029	17184	17465	16895	16954					
Five people	20127	20723	21024	20380	19882	19578				
Six people	22727	23835	23930	23436	22964	22261	21845			
Seven people	25912	27425	27596	27006	26595	25828	24934	23953		
Eight people	28967	30673	30944	30387	29899	29206	28327	27412	27180	
Nine people or more	34417	36897	37076	36583	36169	35489	34554	33708	33499	32208

Related children under 18 years old

RACE

The data on race were derived from answers to long-form questionnaire Item 6 and short-form questionnaire Item 8. The concept of race, as used by the Census Bureau, reflects self-identification by people according to the race or races with which they most closely identify. These categories are socio-political constructs and should not be interpreted as being scientific or anthropological in nature. Furthermore, the race categories include both racial and national-origin groups.

The racial classifications used by the Census Bureau adhere to the October 30, 1997, Federal Register Notice entitled, *"Revisions to the Standards for the Classification of Federal Data on Race and Ethnicity,"* issued by the Office of Management and Budget (OMB). These standards govern the categories used to collect and present federal data on race and ethnicity. The OMB requires five minimum categories (White, Black or African American, American Indian or Alaska Native, Asian, and Native Hawaiian or Other Pacific Islander) for race. The race categories are described below with a sixth category, "Some other race," added with OMB approval. In addition to the five race groups, the OMB also states that respondents should be offered the option of selecting one or more races. If an individual did not provide a race response, the race or races of the householder or other household members were assigned using specific rules of precedence of household relationship. For example, if race was missing for a natural-born child in the household, then either the race or races of the householder, another natural-born child, or the spouse of the householder were assigned. If race was not reported for anyone in the household, the race or races of a householder in a previously processed household were assigned.

White. A person having origins in any of the original peoples of Europe, the Middle East, or North Africa. It includes people who indicate their race as "White" or report entries such as Irish, German, Italian, Lebanese, Near Easterner, Arab, or Polish.

Black or African American. A person having origins in any of the Black racial groups of Africa. It includes people who indicate their race as "Black, African Am., or Negro," or provide written entries such as African American, Afro-American, Kenyan, Nigerian, or Haitian.

American Indian and Alaska Native. A person having origins in any of the original peoples of North and South America (including Central America) and who maintain tribal affiliation or community attachment. It includes people who classified themselves as described below.

American Indian. This category includes people who indicated their race as "American Indian," entered the name of an Indian tribe, or reported such entries as Canadian Indian, French American Indian, or Spanish American Indian.

Alaska Native. This category includes written responses of Eskimos, Aleuts, and Alaska Indians as well as entries such as Arctic Slope, Inupiat, Yupik, Alutiiq, Egegik, and Pribilovian. The Alaska tribes are the Alaskan Athabascan, Tlingit, and Haida. The information for Census 2000 is based on the American Indian Tribal Classification List for the 1990 census, which was expanded to list the individual Alaska Native Villages when provided as a written response for race.

Asian. A person having origins in any of the original peoples of the Far East, Southeast Asia, or the Indian subcontinent including, for example, Cambodia, China, India, Japan, Korea, Malaysia, Pakistan, the Philippine Islands, Thailand, and Vietnam. It includes "Asian Indian," "Chinese," "Filipino," "Korean," "Japanese," "Vietnamese," and "Other Asian." In this volume, many tables combine **Asian** with **Native Hawaiian and Other Pacific Islander**.

Native Hawaiian and Other Pacific Islander. A person having origins in any of the original peoples of Hawaii, Guam, Samoa, or other Pacific Islands. It includes people who indicate their race as "Native Hawaiian," "Guamanian or Chamorro," "Samoan," and "Other Pacific Islander."

Native Hawaiian. This category includes people who indicate their race as "Native Hawaiian" or who identify themselves as "Part Hawaiian" or "Hawaiian." In this volume, many tables combine **Asian** with **Native Hawaiian and Other Pacific Islander**.

Some other race. This category includes all other responses not included in the "White," "Black or African American," "American Indian or Alaska Native," "Asian," and "Native Hawaiian or Other Pacific Islander" race categories described above. Respondents providing write-in entries such as multiracial, mixed, interracial, or a Hispanic/Latino group (for example, Mexican, Puerto Rican, or Cuban) in the "Some other race" write-in space are included in this category.

Two or more races. People may have chosen to provide two or more races either by checking two or more race response check boxes, by providing multiple write-in responses, or by some combination of check boxes and write-in responses. The race response categories shown on the questionnaire are collapsed into the five minimum races identified by the OMB, and the Census Bureau "Some other race" category. For data product purposes, "Two or more races" refers to combinations of two or more of the following race categories:

1. White
2. Black or African American
3. American Indian and Alaska Native
4. Asian
5. Native Hawaiian and Other Pacific Islander
6. Some other race

There are 57 possible combinations involving the race categories shown above. Thus, according to this approach, a response of "White" and "Asian" was tallied as two or more races, while a response of "Japanese" and "Chinese" was not because "Japanese" and "Chinese" are both Asian responses.

REFERENCE WEEK

The data on employment status and commuting to work are related to a 1-week time period, known as the reference week. For each person, this week is the full calendar week, Sunday through Saturday, preceding the date the questionnaire was completed. This calendar week is not the same for all people since the enumeration was not completed in 1 week. The occurrence of holidays during the enumeration period probably had no effect on the overall measurement of employment status.

RESIDENCE 5 YEARS AGO

The data on residence 5 years earlier were derived from answers to long-form questionnaire Item 15, which was asked of a sample of the population 5 years old and over. This question asked for the state (or foreign country), U.S. county, city or town, and ZIP Code of residence on April 1, 1995, for those people who reported that on that date they lived in a different house than their current residence. Residence 5 years earlier is used in conjunction with location of current residence to determine the extent of residential mobility of the population and the resulting redistribution of the population across the various states, metropolitan areas, and regions of the country. People living in the

United States in 1995 were asked to report the name of the city, county, state, and ZIP Code where they lived. People living outside the United States were asked to report the name of the foreign country or U.S. Island Area where they were living in 1995. In this book, Puerto Rico is combined with "outside the United States."

When no information on previous residence was reported for a person, information for other family members, if available, was used to assign a location of residence in 1995. All cases of nonresponse or incomplete response that were not assigned a previous residence based on information from other family members were imputed the previous residence of another person with similar characteristics who provided complete information on residence 5 years earlier.

The tabulation category, "Same house," includes all people 5 years old and over who did not move during the 5 years as well as those who had moved but by Census Day had returned to their 1995 residence. The category, "Different house in the United States," includes people who lived in the United States 5 years earlier but lived in a different house or apartment from the one they occupied on Census Day. These movers are then further subdivided according to the type of move. In most tabulations, movers within the U.S. are divided into three groups according to their previous residence: "Different house, same county," "Different county, same state," and "Different state." The last group may be further subdivided into region of residence in 1995. The tables in this book include regions: Northeast (ME, NH, VT, MA, RI, CT, NY, PA); Midwest (ND, SD, NE, KS, MN, IA, MO, IL, WI, MI, IN, OH); South (TX, OK, AK, IA, MS, AL, GA, FL, NC, SC, TN, KY, WV, VA, DC, DE, MD) and West (WA, OR, CA, MT, ID, WY, NV, UT, CO, AZ, NM). An additional category, "Abroad," includes those whose previous residence was in a foreign country, Puerto Rico, American Samoa, Guam, the Commonwealth of the Northern Mariana Islands, or the U.S. Virgin Islands, including members of the armed forces and their dependents. The number of people who were living in a different house 5 years earlier is somewhat less than the total number of moves during the 5-year period. Some people in the same house at the two dates had moved during the 5-year period but by the time of the census had returned to their 1995 residence. Other people who were living in a different house had made one or more intermediate moves. For similar reasons, the number of people living in a different county, metropolitan area, or state, or the number moving between nonmetropolitan areas, may be understated.

SCHOOL ENROLLMENT

Data on school enrollment were derived from answers to long-form questionnaire Items 8a and 8b. People were classified as enrolled in school if they reported attending a "regular" public or private school or college at any time between February 1, 2000, and the time of enumeration. The question included instructions to "include only nursery school or preschool, kindergarten, elementary school, and schooling which leads to a high school diploma or a college degree" as regular school or college. Respondents who did not answer the enrollment question were assigned the enrollment status and type of school of a person with the same age, sex, and race/Hispanic or Latino origin whose residence was in the same or a nearby area.

Grade in Which Enrolled

The data on grade or level in which enrolled were derived from long-form questionnaire Item 8b. People who were enrolled in school were classified as enrolled in "Nursery school, preschool," "Kindergarten," "Grade 1 to 4" or "Grade 5 to 8," "Grade 9 to 12," "College undergraduate years (freshman to senior)" or "Graduate and professional school (for example: medical, dental, or law school)."

Public and private school. Public and private school includes people who attended school in the reference period and indicated they were enrolled by marking one of the questionnaire categories for either "public school, public college" or "private school, private college." Schools supported and controlled primarily by a federal, state, or local government are defined as public (including tribal schools). Those supported and controlled primarily by religious organizations or other private groups are private.

School Enrollment and Employment Status

Tabulation of data on school enrollment, educational attainment, and employment status for the population 16 to 19 years old allows for calculating the proportion of people 16 to 19 years old who are not enrolled in school and not high school graduates ("dropouts") and an unemployment rate for the "dropout" population.

SELECTED MONTHLY OWNER COSTS

The data on selected monthly owner costs were obtained from answers to long-form questionnaire Items 45a-d, 47b, 48b, 49, 50, 52, and 53b, which were asked on a sample basis at owner-occupied housing units. Selected monthly owner costs are the sum of payments for mortgages, deeds of trust, contracts to purchase, or similar debts on the property (including payments for the first mortgage, second mortgage, home equity loans, and other junior mortgages); real estate taxes; fire, hazard, and flood insurance on the property; utilities (electricity, gas, water and sewer); and fuels (oil, coal, kerosene, wood). It also includes, where appropriate, the monthly condominium fees or mobile home costs (installment loan payments, personal property taxes, site rent, registration fees, and license fees). Selected monthly owner costs were tabulated separately for all owner-occupied units, specified owner-occupied units, and owner-occupied mobile homes and, usually, are shown separately for units "with a mortgage" and for units "not mortgaged." In this volume, the tables include "specified owner-occupied housing units."

Specified owner-occupied housing units. Specified owner-occupied units include only 1-family houses on less than 10 acres without a business or medical office on the property. The data for "specified units" exclude mobile homes, houses with a business or medical office, houses on 10 or more acres, and housing units in multiunit buildings.

Median selected monthly owner costs. This measure divides the selected monthly owner costs distribution into two equal parts: half of the costs falls below the median selected monthly owner costs and half above it. Medians are shown separately for units "with a mortgage" and for units "not mortgaged." Median selected monthly owner costs are computed on the basis of a standard distribution. The minimum value for all owners is less than $100, with a maximum of $1000 or more for those without a mortgage, and $4000 or more for those with a mortgage. Median selected monthly owner costs are rounded to the nearest whole dollar.

SELECTED MONTHLY OWNER COSTS AS A PERCENTAGE OF HOUSEHOLD INCOME IN 1999

The information on selected monthly owner costs as a percentage of household income in 1999 is the computed ratio of selected monthly owner costs to monthly household income in 1999. The ratio was computed separately for each unit and rounded to the nearest whole percentage. It is based on questions asked of a sample of households. The data are tabulated separately for all owner-occupied housing units and specified owner-occupied housing units. In this volume, data are shown for "specified owner-occupied housing units." Separate distributions are shown for units "with a mortgage" and for units "not mortgaged." Units occupied by households reporting no income or a net loss in 1999 are included in the "not computed" category.

Median selected monthly owner costs as a percentage of household income. This measure divides the selected monthly owner costs as a percentage of household income distribution into two equal parts, one-half of the cases falling below the median selected monthly owner costs as a percentage of household income and one-half above the median. Median selected monthly owner costs as a percentage of household income is computed on the basis of a standard distribution, with a minimum of less than 10 percent and a maximum or 50 percent or more. (Note that the median monthly owner costs for those without a mortgage is often in the minimum category which is indicated as 9.9 percent.) Median selected monthly owner costs as a percentage of household income is rounded to the nearest tenth.

SEX

The data on sex were derived from answers to long-form questionnaire Item 3 and short-form questionnaire Item 5. Individuals were asked to mark either "male" or "female" to indicate their sex. For most cases in which sex was not reported, it was determined from the person's first name and household relationship. Otherwise, sex was imputed according to the relationship to the householder and the age of the person.

TENURE

The data on tenure, which was asked at all occupied housing units, were obtained from answers to long-form questionnaire Item 33 and short-form questionnaire Item 2. All occupied housing units are classified as either owner occupied or renter occupied.

Owner occupied. A housing unit is owner occupied if the owner or co-owner lives in the unit even if it is mortgaged or not fully paid for. The owner or co-owner must live in the unit and usually is Person 1 on the questionnaire. The unit is "Owned by you or someone in this household with a mortgage or loan" if it is being purchased with a mortgage or some other debt arrangement, such as a deed of trust, trust deed, contract to purchase, land contract, or purchase agreement. The unit is also considered owned with a mortgage if it is built on leased land and there is a mortgage on the unit. Mobile homes occupied by owners with installment loans balances are also included in this category. A housing unit is "Owned by you or someone in this household free and clear (without a mortgage or loan)" if there is no mortgage or other similar debt on the house, apartment, or mobile home including units built on leased land if the unit is owned outright without a mortgage.

The tenure item on the Census 2000 questionnaire distinguishes between units owned with a mortgage or loan and those owned free and clear. In the sample data products, as in the 100-percent products, the tenure item provides data for total owner-occupied units. Detailed information that identifies mortgaged and nonmortgaged units are provided in other sample housing matrices. (For more information, see discussion under "Mortgage Status," "Selected Monthly Owner Costs," and "Selected Monthly Owner Costs as a Percentage of Household Income in 1999.")

Renter occupied. All occupied housing units that are not owner occupied, whether they are rented for cash rent or occupied without payment of cash rent, are classified as renter occupied. "No cash rent" units are separately identified in the rent tabulations. Such units are generally provided free by friends or relatives or in exchange for services, such as resident manager, caretaker, minister, or tenant farmer. Housing units on military bases also are classified in the "No cash rent" category. "Rented for cash rent" includes units in continuing care, sometimes called life care arrangements. These arrangements usually involve a contract between one or more individuals and a service provider guaranteeing the individual shelter, usually a house or apartment, and services, such as meals or transportation to shopping or recreation.

VALUE

The data on value (also referred to as "price asked" for vacant units) were obtained from answers to long-form questionnaire Item 51, which was asked on a sample basis at owner-occupied housing units and units that were being bought, or vacant for sale at the time of enumeration. Value is the respondent's estimate of how much the property (house and lot, mobile home and lot, or condominium unit) would sell for if it were for sale. If the house or mobile home was owned or being bought, but the land on which it sits was not, the respondent was asked to estimate the combined value of the house or mobile home and the land. For vacant units, value was the price asked for the property. Value was tabulated separately for all owner-occupied and vacant-for-sale housing units, owner-occupied and vacant-for-sale mobile homes, and specified owner-occupied and specified vacant-for-sale housing units. The number used in this book refers to all owner-occupied units.

Median value. The median divides the value distribution into two equal parts: half of the cases fall below the median value of the property (house and lot, mobile home and lot, or condominium unit) and half above the median. Median value is computed on the basis of a standard distribution with a minimum value of less than $10,000 and a maximum value of $1,000,000 or more. Median value calculations are rounded to the nearest hundred dollars.

VEHICLES AVAILABLE

The data on vehicles available were obtained from answers to long-form questionnaire Item 43, which was asked on a sample basis at occupied housing units. These data show the number of passenger cars, vans, and pickup or panel trucks of 1-ton capacity or less kept at home and available for the use of household members. Vehicles rented or leased for 1 month or more, company vehicles, and police and government vehicles are included if kept at home and used for nonbusiness purposes. Dismantled or immobile vehicles are excluded. Vehicles kept at home but used only for business purposes also are excluded.

Aggregate vehicles available. To calculate aggregate vehicles available, a value of "7" is assigned to vehicles available for occupied units falling within the terminal category, "6 or more." ·

Vehicles per household (Mean vehicles available). Vehicles per household is computed by dividing aggregate vehicles available by the number of occupied housing units. Vehicles per household is rounded to the nearest tenth.

VETERAN STATUS

Data on veteran status, period of military service, and years of military service were derived from answers to long-form questionnaire Item 20, which was asked of a sample of the population 15 years old and over.

Veteran status. The data on veteran status were derived from answers to long-form questionnaire Item 20a. For census data products, a "civilian veteran" is a person 18 years old and over who, at the time of the enumeration, had served on active duty in the U.S. Army, Navy, Air Force, Marine Corps, or Coast Guard in the past (even for a short time), but was not then on active duty, or who had served in the Merchant Marine during World War II. People who had served in the National Guard or Military Reserves were classified as veterans only if they had ever been called or ordered to active duty, not counting the 4 to 6 months for initial training or yearly summer camps. All other civilians 18 years old and over were classified as nonveterans.

WORK STATUS IN 1999

The following discussion refers to employment during the full year preceding the census, 1999. For items relating to current employment at the time of the census, see "Employment Status"

The data on work status in 1999 were derived from answers to long-form questionnaire Item 30a, which was asked of a sample of the population 15 years old and over. People 16 years old and over who worked 1 or more weeks according to the criteria described below are classified as ''Worked in 1999.'' All other people 16 years old and over are classified as ''Did not work in 1999.'' Some earnings tabulations showing work status in 1999 include 15 year olds; these people, by definition, are classified as ''Did not work in 1999.''

Weeks worked in 1999. The data on weeks worked in 1999 were derived from answers to long-form questionnaire Item 30b, which was asked of people 15 years old and over who indicated in long-form questionnaire Item 30a that they worked in 1999. The data were tabulated for people 16 years old and over and pertain to the number of weeks during 1999 in which a person did any work for pay or profit (or took paid vacation or paid sick leave) or worked without pay on a family farm or in a family business. Weeks on active duty in the armed forces also are included as weeks worked.

Usual hours worked per week in 1999. The data on usual hours worked in 1999 were derived from answers to long-form questionnaire Item 30c. This question was asked of people 15 years old and over who indicated that they worked in 1999 in Question 30a, and the data are tabulated for people 16 years old and over. The respondent was asked to report the number of hours usually worked during the weeks worked in 1999. If their hours varied considerably from week to week during 1999, the respondent was asked to report an approximate average of the hours worked each week. People 16 years old and over who reported that they usually worked 35 or more hours each week are classified as ''Usually worked full time''; people who reported that they usually worked 1 to 34 hours each week are classified as ''Usually worked part time.''

Full-time, year-round workers. Full-time, year-round workers consists of people 16 years old and over who usually worked 35 hours or more per week for 50 to 52 weeks in 1999. The term ''worker'' in these concepts refers to people classified as ''Worked in 1999'' as defined above. The term ''worked'' in these concepts means ''worked one or more weeks in 1999'' as defined above under ''Weeks Worked in 1999.''